THE ESPN BASEBALL ENCYCLOPEDIA

FOURTH EDITION

2007 BASEBALL SCHEDULE ON ESPN/ESPN2

Spring Training

DAY	DATE	TIME (EST)	NETWORK	GAME
Fri	Mar 2	1 p.m.	ESPN	PIT vs. ATL
Mon	Mar 5	1 p.m.	ESPN	DET at NYY
Wed	Mar 21	1 p.m.	ESPN	BOS at PIT
Thu	Mar 22	1 p.m.	ESPN	BOS at PHI
Fri	Mar 23	1 p.m.	ESPN	ATL at PHI
Mon	Mar 26	1 p.m.	ESPN	BOS at CIN
Tue	Mar 27	1 p.m.	ESPN	NYY at MIN
Wed	Mar 28	1 p.m.	ESPN	ATL at NYM
Fri	Mar 30	1 p.m.	ESPN	NYY at DET
Sat	Mar 31	5 p.m.	ESPN	CLE vs. STL

Regular Season

DAY	DATE	TIME (EST)	NETWORK	GAME
Sun	Apr 1	8 p.m.	ESPN2	NYM at STL
Mon	Apr 2	1 p.m.	ESPN	TB at NYY
Mon	Apr 2	2 p.m.	ESPN2	CHC at CIN
Mon	Apr 2	4 p.m.	ESPN	BOS at KC
Mon	Apr 2	7 p.m.	ESPN2	TBD
Mon	Apr 2	10 p.m.	ESPN2	TEX at LAA
Wed	Apr 4	7 p.m.	ESPN2	TBD
Sun	Apr 8	8 p.m.	ESPN	BOS at TEX
Mon	Apr 9	7 p.m.	ESPN	**NYY** at **MIN**
Wed	Apr 11	7 p.m.	ESPN2	TBD
Sun	Apr 15	8 p.m.	ESPN	SD at LAD
Mon	Apr 16	7 p.m.	ESPN	**NYM** at **PHI**
Wed	Apr 18	7 p.m.	ESPN2	TBD
Sun	Apr 22	8 p.m.	ESPN	NYY as BOS
Mon	Apr 23	7 p.m.	ESPN	NYY at **TB**
Wed	Apr 25	8 p.m.	ESPN	TBD
Sun	Apr 29	8 p.m.	ESPN	CHC at STL
Mon	Apr 30	7 p.m.	ESPN	**STL** at **MIL**
Wed	May 2	8 p.m.	ESPN	TBD
Sun	May 6	8 p.m.	ESPN	PHI at SF
Mon	May 7	7 p.m.	ESPN	**SEA** at NYY
Wed	May 9	7 p.m.	ESPN	TBD
Sun	May 13	8 p.m.	ESPN	DET at MIN
Mon	May 14	7 p.m.	ESPN	**CHC** at **NYM**
Wed	May 16	8 p.m.	ESPN	TBD
Sun	May 20	8 p.m.	ESPN	NYY at NYM
Mon	May 21	7 p.m.	ESPN	**BOS** at **NYY**
Wed	May 23	7 p.m.	ESPN	TBD
Sun	May 27	8 p.m.	ESPN	CLE at DET
Tue	May 29	7 p.m.	ESPN	**SF** at **NYM**
Wed	May 30	7 p.m.	ESPN2	TBD
Sun	June 3	8 p.m.	ESPN	TBD
Mon	June 4	7 p.m.	ESPN	NYY at **CWS**
Wed	June 6	8 p.m.	ESPN	TBD
Sun	June 10	8 p.m.	ESPN	TBD
Mon	June 11	7 p.m.	ESPN	**CWS** at **PHI**
Wed	June 13	7 p.m.	ESPN	TBD
Sun	June 17	8 p.m.	ESPN	TBD
Mon	June 18	7 p.m.	ESPN	**BOS** at **ATL**
Wed	June 20	7:30 p.m.	ESPN	TBD
Sun	June 24	8 p.m.	ESPN	TBD
Mon	June 25	7 p.m.	ESPN2	TBD
Wed	June 27	7 p.m.	ESPN	TBD
Sun	July 1	8 p.m.	ESPN	TBD
Mon	July 2	7 p.m.	ESPN	**MIN** at NYY
Wed	July 4	7 p.m.	ESPN	TBD
Sun	July 8	8 p.m.	ESPN	ATL at SD
Mon	July 9		All-Star Break	
Sun	July 15	6 p.m.	ESPN	STL at PHI
Mon	July 16	TBD	ESPN	**SF** at **CHC**
Sun	July 22	8 p.m.	ESPN	TBD
Mon	July 23	TBD	ESPN2	TBD
Sun	July 29	8 p.m.	ESPN	TBD
Mon	July 30	TBD	ESPN	**PHI** at **CHC**
Sun	Aug 5	8 p.m.	ESPN	TBD
Mon	Aug 6	TBD	ESPN	**SD** at **STL**
Sun	Aug 12	8 p.m.	ESPN	TBD
Mon	Aug 13	TBD	ESPN2	TBD
Sun	Aug 19	8 p.m.	ESPN	TBD
Mon	Aug 20	TBD	ESPN2	TBD
Sun	Aug 26	8 p.m.	ESPN	TBD
Mon	Aug 27	TBD	ESPN2	TBD
Sun	Sept 2	8 p.m.	ESPN2	TBD
Fri	Sept 7	TBD	ESPN	LAD at SF
Sun	Sept 9	8 p.m.	ESPN	TBD
Fri	Sept 14	TBD	ESPN	**NYY** at **BOS**
Sun	Sept 16	8 p.m.	ESPN	TBD
Fri	Sept 21	TBD	ESPN	**HOU** at **STL**
Sun	Sept 23	8 p.m.	ESPN	TBD
Fri	Sept 28	TBD	ESPN	**DET** at **CWS**

Sunday games are exclusive, full national
Co-exist games (games that also air with teams' local carriers) in bold
All games, except Sundays, are subject to blackout
Every game is in HD

THE ESPN BASEBALL ENCYCLOPEDIA

FOURTH EDITION

EDITED BY GARY GILLETTE AND PETE PALMER

FOREWORD BY PETER GAMMONS

ASSOCIATE EDITORS STUART SHEA, MATTHEW SILVERMAN, GREG SPIRA, DOUG WHITE

CONTRIBUTORS RICK BENNER, BILL DEANE, SEAN LAHMAN, JAMES A. RILEY, MARSHALL D. WRIGHT

STERLING PUBLISHING CO., INC.
NEW YORK

Published by Sterling Publishing Co., Inc.
387 Park Avenue South, New York, NY 10016

Distributed in Canada by Sterling Publishing
℅ Canadian Manda Group, 165 Dufferin Street,
Toronto, Ontario, Canada M6K 3H6

Distributed in the United Kingdom by GMC Distribution Services,
Castle Place, 166 High Street, Lewes, East Sussex, England BN7 1XU

Distributed in Australia by Capricorn Link (Australia) Pty. Ltd.
P.O. Box 704, Windsor, NSW 2756, Australia

ISBN-13: 978-1-4027-4771-7
ISBN-10: 1-4027-4771-3

Typesetting by Scribe, Inc. (www.scribenet.com)

Printed in the U.S.A.

2 4 6 8 10 9 7 5 3 1

For information about custom editions, special sales, premium and
corporate purchases, please contact Sterling Special Sales
Department at 800-805-5489 or specialsales@sterlingpub.com.

CONTENTS

DEDICATION

Dedicated to Lenny Yochim and Deacon Jones, two veteran scouts and ex-major leaguers whose company I have had the pleasure of sharing. Lenny is a former pitcher for the Pirates and the epitome of a gracious Southern gentleman. Deacon is a former first baseman for the White Sox and was the 1950 American Legion Player of the Year. Both are incredibly knowledgeable men who have generously shared their experiences as well as their wisdom, for which I am very grateful.

—Gary Gillette

Dedicated to two friends, now gone, who showed me when I was young that there was nothing wrong with maintaining my fascination with baseball as an adult—my English teacher from Mount Hermon, Jack Baldwin, and my fellow engineer at Raytheon, Mason Huse.

—Pete Palmer

ACKNOWLEDGMENTS

No baseball encyclopedia could be prepared without the assistance of many others in the field. The editors hereby extend their appreciation for many different favors—some small, some large—to the honor roll of kind people listed below:

Jim Albright, Jamie Alexander, William Anderson Jr., Stephen Bannen, Carlos Bauer, Evelyn Begley, Alex Belth, Greg Beston, Cliff Blau, Arnie Braunstein, Douglas Brei, Ed Brown, Jeffrey Burk, J.P. Callault, Jim Callis, Bill Carle, Keith Carlson, James Catron, Ryan Chamberlain, Mike Cinoman, Andy Clarke, Glen Cobb, Clem Comly, Bob Curto, Clay Davenport, Donald M. Davis, Kevin Davis, Merl DeMoll, Dan Dischley, Beth Dowd, Mike Dugan, Steve Elsberry, Alan Fisher, F.X. Flinn, John Foley, Sean Forman, Marcus Fredericks, Marty Friedrich, Jim Furtado, Steve Geitscher, Ray Gonzalez, John Green, Joe Haardt, Paul Hagen, Gary Hailey, Layton Hall, Hank Hammer, Chris Hand, Paul Hartnett, Ed Hartig, Bill Hickman, Howard Hilton, Bob Hoie, Dan Holmes, Shane Holmes, Sean Holtz, David Horwich, Frederick Ivor-Campbell, Jonathan Jacobs, Jay Jaffe, Bill James, Kevin Johnson, Richard Johnson, Christina Kahrl, Chris Kaminiski, Margaret Kane, Bill Kearns, Jim Keller, Dave Kirsch, Paul Kisko, Herm Krabbenhoft, David Kronheim, Gary LaFollett, Joseph La Freniere, Craig Lammers, Leonte Landino, Matt Lemoine, Fred Lenger, Daniel Levine, Michael Lewis, Don Luce, Paul Lynch, Mike Mackay, Rich Malatzky, Steve Mann, Lou Marinaro, Bruce Markusen, Josh Mathes, Kenneth Matinale, John McCann, Corey McCart, Bob McConnell, Trent McCotter, Wayne McElreavy, Fred McKie, Bill McNeil, Andrew Milner, Jim Moore, Bill Moose, Kevin Morgan, Cyril Morong, Peter Morris, Rod Nelson, Rob Neyer, David Nemec, Ray Nemec, Bill Nowlin, John O'Malley, Marc Okkonen, Rob Olds, Mat Olkin, Phyllis Otto, Doug Pappas, Marvin Peixoto, Fred Percival, Jim Quinlan, John Racano, John Ratzlaff, Bob Richardson, Chuck Rosciam, Ken Rosenthal, Bob Rosiek, Bruce Roth, Tom Ruane, Andy Samet, Mike Sandler, William Schade, Bob Schatzle, Michael Schell, Richard Schrader, John Schwartz, Alan Schwarz, Ron Selter, Ron Shandler, Tom Shieber, Nate Silver, Joe Simenic, Bill Slayback, Dave Smith, Lyle Spatz, Ted Spencer, Dave Statz, Mike Statz, Paul Statz, Marc Stephenson, Chuck Stevens, John Thorn, Bob Tiemann, Tom Tippett, Stephen Tomlinson, Wayne Townsend, Neal Traven, Jules Tygiel, Dixie Tourangeau, David Urban, Frank Vaccaro, John Vaughan, David Vincent, Bill Way, Joe Wayman, Royce Webb, Jim Weigand, Dave Weiner, Paul Wendt, Harold Wexler, Jim Wheeler, Frank Williams, Vic Wilson, Walt Wilson, Keith Woolner, John Zajc, Andy Zimbalist, and Larry Zuckerman. Special thanks go to David Pietrusza, Peter Bird, Kevin Saldana, and Bill Weiss for their assistance and advice.

Every baseball encyclopedia involves a huge amount of complicated design, typesetting, and editorial work. In our case, we are truly blessed to have collaborated with Jeremy C. Ellis, Andy Brown, Heath Missimer, David Rech, and Brandon Smith of Scribe in Philadelphia. We are indebted to Nathaniel Marunas, our editor at Barnes & Noble and to Jen Boudinot and Devorah Klein, his ace majordomos. We are also very grateful for the support of B&N President and CEO Steve Riggio, B&N Publishing President Alan Kahn, and to Bruce Lubin, B&N Publisher. Kudos to creative director Jeff Batzli; art director Kevin Ullrich; designer Kevin Baier; designer Christine Heun; photo researcher Lori Epstein; and production managers Michael Vagnetti and Charles Ryf. As Yogi might say, we look forward with even greater anticipation to working with everyone for many years to come.

Finally, the editors know damn well that they couldn't have gotten the job done without the love and support of their Hall of Fame spouses, namely Vicki Gillette, Beth Palmer, Cecilia Garibay, Debbie Silverman, and Anita White.

FOREWORD

Dave Powers was a special assistant to President John F. Kennedy and a major force in collecting many of the late president's artifacts for the JFK Museum in Boston. Whenever a visitor who had some relation to baseball stopped by Powers' office, he would pull out a bound copy of the 1961 *Baseball Register* and proudly show it off.

"This was the president's lucky book," Powers said. "It was his inaugural year, it has a picture of Ted Williams on the inside cover and it was that year's matter of record."

I know someone who keeps two copies of *The Baseball Encyclopedia* readily available in his house, one in his office, one in the bathroom. Which is not all that unusual, as I also know someone who keeps two copies of Bill James' handbook in his house, and someone else who keeps Lee Sinins's *Sabermetric Baseball Encyclopedia* on two laptop computers, just in case one gets infected with a virus and shuts off.

In baseball, statistics and numbers matter. They *really* matter.

Why else would a SABR scholar named Richard "Dixie" Tourangeau spend weeks in the archives of Cooperstown and uncover that a nineteenth-century no-hitter credited to Vic Willis was actually a one-hitter? The historic difference between a no-hitter and one-hitter matters; ask the Mets.

Why else, when the Special Records Committee in 1968 discovered that 37 times prior to 1920 game-ending "home runs" (*walk off pieces*, in twenty-first century jargon) had been credited as singles, doubles, or triples, and that one "triple" hit by Babe Ruth had actually pushed his total to 715, did the SRC make a gut-wrenching reversal of its previous ruling and allow 714 to stand because of its historic significance?

Why else have historians continued for many decades—now with the help of a godsend called Retrosheet—to plow through the numbers of great players, verifying and completing information as well as looking for mistakes? Pete Palmer and others have discovered four mistakes in the batting records of Ty Cobb since 1969, which have changed Cobb's career hits total from 4,191 to 4,189. The original edition of the Macmillan encyclopedia credited Cobb with 4,192 hits, then in subsequent editions listed him with the traditional figure of 4,191. *Total Baseball* later corrected that figure to 4,189. Why else would it be important to get Wee Willie Keeler's 1897 average right (.424, not .432)? As for Cap Anson's hit totals, suffice to say only Pete Palmer and Gary Gillette can explain why they change as much as the president's job approval ratings.

All these figures matter, because so much of baseball is judged by numbers. Everyone understood why 61* was the appropriate title for Billy Crystal's poignant film about Roger Maris. Pitchers are automatically bound for the Hall of Fame with 300 wins, batters with 3,000 hits. There are those Red Sox fans who revere Jim Rice and wonder why he's not in Cooperstown (after all, he finished in the top five in MVP balloting six times in a 12-year span), but look it up in *The ESPN Baseball Encyclopedia*: Rice batted .298 with 382 home runs, while Wade Boggs batted .328, had 3,010 hits and his career OPS was .858, Rice's .854.

They even changed the rules when numbers got askew. In *The Numbers Game*, Alan Schwarz points out how rules were altered in the nineteenth century by statisticians. Then came the aftermath of the 1968 season, which produced league-leading earned run averages of 1.12 by Bob Gibson and 1.60 by Luis Tiant, an American League batting race that nearly had no .300 hitter—Carl Yastrzemski won it at .301. In the offseason, Major League Baseball voted to lower the mound from 15 to 10 inches and restore the strike zone to its pre-1963 dimensions.

No one seems to care much that there are a number of pitchers in the Hall of Fame who either admitted or were known to have doctored baseballs. But corked bats and steroids raise heated, near-hysterical debates because the home run records are "pure" numbers.

Back when Macmillan first published *The Baseball Encyclopedia*, it was essential to the needs of the era. But this library disguised as a book has nearly 40 pages of annual, era, and career leaders in a number of statistics. To an entire generation that has grown up with Pete Palmer, Bill James, Steve Hirdt, and *Baseball Prospectus*, Palmer and Gillette not only provide the core stats—I am still trying to fathom Earl Webb's 67 doubles—but also stats that give a reader hours of pleasure simply turning pages: adjusted earned run average by era, pitchers' batting averages by all-time leaders and by eras, fielding wins, batter-fielder wins, pitcher wins . . . well, start turning, and find your own favorites.

For anyone who takes the Hall of Fame seriously, the rundown of the annual voting is another fascinating exercise. Just how difficult it is to reach Cooperstown is evidenced by the fact that Jeff Burroughs was an American League MVP, and yet got the same vote fraction—0.2 percent—as Jerry Remy on his one and only appearance on the ballot. One can appreciate that Matty Alou was a terrific slap hitter, but his percentage of the vote (1.3 percent) was higher than either of his brothers, Felipe (0.8 percent) or Jesus (0.3 percent). It should be noted that, while Joe Torre now seems a lock for the Hall because of his playing and managerial record, the highest vote that Torre got for his playing skills was only 22.2 percent, Billy Martin 0.3 percent. Torre now also has four World Series rings as a manager, Martin one.

Another fascinating section is the Ex Post Facto awards, where Palmer and Gillette pick who would have won awards before they became functions of the baseball writers. Cy Young would have won five Cy Young Awards, as well as the 1902 MVP in the American League. Babe Ruth would have won four MVPs, including the American League award he actually won in 1923, Ty Cobb five, Honus Wagner six. And Ruth would have won the 1915 Rookie of the Year and the 1916 Cy Young awards.

There is even the listing of retired uniform numbers, including Harold Baines' number 3 with the White Sox, retired while he was an active player for the Texas Rangers. (Is there anything lonelier than being a South Sider in a town of North Siders?) Otherwise, in keeping with the significance of numbers and baseball, there are few frivolous, irrational selections, and when one looks at the retired numbers of the Yankees, Dodgers, and Reds one appreciates how special that retirement ceremony remains.

For many, perusing the encyclopedia means finding gems that slipped through the cracks, like Frank (Moonlight) Graham, who in 1905 did make a defensive appearance for the New York Nationals. Then there is Tom and Jim Paciorek's older brother John, whose career line reads 1 game, 3 AB, 4 R, 3 H, 3 RBI, a 1.000 AVG, 1.000 OBP, 1.000 SLG. He played the final game of the 1963 season for the Houston Colt .45s, hurt his back in the off-season, and never made it back to the show. Or Hall of Famer Robin Yount's older brother Larry, who is listed for one appearance (in 1971) for Houston, but no stats other than playing in 1 game. He pulled a muscle warming up after coming out of the bullpen, never actually threw a pitch in the major leagues, but since he was announced, he is part of Major League Baseball history.

Sometimes we remember individuals too fondly. Bo Jackson is a good example. He was such an electrifying figure, such a decent man, and he not only made some of the greatest commercials and hit unforgettable home runs, but made a throw to nail Harold Reynolds at the plate in the old HO-scaled Seattle Kingdome that might be the single best throw of the era. Granted, Jackson's career was cut short by a hip injury before he fully developed as a baseball player, but the fact remains his career history sits in black and white as a Prince concert, while his career OPS of .783 is exactly the same as Al Martin's.

There are names each one of us bookmark for family reasons. Daff Gammons was a distant cousin from the Rhode Island Gammons who played 28 games for the 1901 Boston Nationals, hitting a rousing .194 with a .242 on-base percentage. (Hey, he almost matched Billy Beane's career OBP of .246.)

What was never quite explained was, Why "Daff?" Nicknames are such a great reason to have an *ESPN Baseball Encyclopedia* at hand. Calvin Coolidge Julius Caesar Tuskahoma "Buster" McLish. Hurricane Hazle, he of the .403 average for the 1957 Braves, only to be sold to the Tigers the next spring. Willie "Puddin' Head" Jones. "Piano Legs" Hickman. "Honest John" Anderson. Charles F. "Alderman" Briody, who also went by the nickname "Fatty." "Glass Arm Eddie" Brown. Three different Careys called "Scoops." Jake "Eagle Eye" Beckley and Max "Camera Eye" Bishop. "Bananas" Benes. Lots of Mooses, Docs, Dukes, Lefties, and Reds, but only one Tuffy (Rhodes).

Baseball encompasses so many of our lives because of its countless layers of fascination, a Mike Cameron catch in the seventh inning of a meaningless September game, a Pokey Reese slide across the outfield grass to snatch away a sure single, Brad Radke's delivery, or Randy Johnson's fiery power. But there is so much more, from debates on the Hall of Fame or the Johnson-Koufax-Carlton-Grove-Spahn argument to remembering a couple of former players—catcher Dave Schmidt of the 1981 Red Sox and pitcher Mark Ciardi of the 1987 Brewers—who are currently successful Hollywood producers of movies (Racing Stripes and Miracle, respectively).

That's where *The ESPN Baseball Encyclopedia* comes into play, time after time, day after day, the Library of Congress of a very simple game.

You can look it up.

—*Peter Gammons*

INTRODUCTION

The past is never dead. It's not even past. —William Faulkner

Faulkner penned that memorable line in 1951. Though the titan of American letters was not talking about the National Pastime, his apt turn of phrase would serve well as a requiem for thousands of big-league ballplayers. Most of them are long past playing, but their exploits live on in the pages of this book as well as in the hearts and memories of uncounted millions of baseball fans worldwide.

Baseball in 1951 was in the midst of a postwar boom, though troubling signs had already started to appear. Even then, the Grand Old Game had more than a century of history to brag about, including eighty years of professional play. Other professional team sports in the United States were still in their infancy, though pro football was soon to explode into a formidable rival to the National Game.

Now baseball boasts more than a century and a quarter of carefully documented history. A major part of that documentation is the voluminous amount of baseball statistics that have been compiled and calculated. These statistics record the successes and failures of the more than 16,000 big league players who have worn the uniforms of almost 150 different clubs in half a dozen major leagues.

The value of baseball statistics lies primarily in their completeness and accuracy. Because they are so well designed and so comprehensive, baseball statistics have a magical quality that most mere numbers lack. Because they are so accurate, baseball statistics can be relied upon to form opinions and to make judgments over many decades of play.

Nevertheless, there is a paradox inherent in the historical accuracy of baseball statistics. Too many people mistakenly believe that baseball stats are engraved in stone, like birth and death dates on a granite tombstone. If the Macmillan Baseball Encyclopedia showed that Babe Ruth hit 714 career home runs, or that Ty Cobb finished with 4,191 hits and a career batting average of .367, most people believe that these are immutable facts.

Not so. At least four mistakes have been found in the past twenty-five years in the official batting records for Cobb. The net result in correcting these errors in pre-computer record keeping is that "The Georgia Peach" has 4,189 hits and a career .366 average *to the best of our knowledge*. So, when the nation watched as Pete Rose broke the all-time hits record on September 11, 1985 with his 4,192nd base hit, few knew that Rose already had broken Cobb's record three days earlier. By the way, the first edition of the Macmillan encyclopedia showed Ty Cobb with 4,192 official career hits, though that was changed without explanation to 4,191 in subsequent editions.

As for "The Sultan of Swat," how many people are aware that he used to have 715 home runs? His current career total of 714 home runs is accurate to the best of our knowledge—provided that one accepts a curious decision of the Special Baseball Records Committee on May 5, 1969. As part of the massive effort to computerize and clean up the game's official statistics and records, this committee was formed and charged with deciding how best to handle certain anomalies and inconsistencies.

In 1968 the Special Records Committee had voted to change the thirty-seven instances prior to 1920 where game-ending home runs were counted only as singles, doubles, or triples (whatever was needed to drive home the winning run). These over-the-fence hits were not home runs according to the scoring practices of their day, but became so with the 1968 ruling. The Special Records Committee also made other changes in previous scoring practices, many of them quite significant: e.g., counting stats in all tie games of five or more innings; not counting walks, wild pitches, passed balls, balks, and hit batsmen as errors at any time; and neither counting walks as outs (as was done in 1876) nor as hits (as was done in 1887).

The committee was logically prepared to count those hits as home runs until a controversy arose because doing so changed Ruth's official career total to 715. Fear of changing one of the game's most important records caused the committee to retract its earlier—and more enlightened—decision. Thus, "The Bambino" lost a home run, and his career total remained at the apparently sacrosanct number of 714.

Regardless of such high-profile examples of historical mistakes or inconsistencies, the level of accuracy of baseball statistics is exceedingly high—so high that it exceeds the standards of accuracy in virtually every other field of endeavor. Twenty-first century Americans make life-changing decisions every day based on evidence supported by underlying statistics not nearly as accurate as baseball stats.

This superlative accuracy is the reason that fans, researchers, and historians can argue about the number of hits compiled by a Hall of Fame player who started his career in 1871 and finished in 1897, more than a century ago. Cap Anson has been dead since 1922, yet his career is still under the contemporary microscope. Good history depends on truly accurate research, not on false allegiance to previously published numbers.

History is process, not perfection. We trust that our effort has contributed to the process of recording and understanding the history of our National Pastime.

New in this edition. As always, we endeavor to add new features to each edition of *The ESPN Baseball Encyclopedia* while keeping the price of our tome as affordable as possible. The list of new material in this edition includes:

1. Annual leaders in seven new categories—Bases on Balls, Outfield Assists, Catcher Caught Stealing Percentage, Games Started, Wins Above Team, Fewest Hits/Game, and Strikeouts/Game—making a total of 42 categories of league leaders for each season;
2. All-Time World Series and Postseason leaders in 20 categories (in Postseason section);
3. The most complete register of big-league coaches ever published, showing the names, teams, and years for every coach in major league history;
4. A comprehensive Umpire Register that calls the roll for all the men in blue;
5. A brief history of the original National Association, from 1857-70 (at the end of the Historical Record);
6. Year-by-year stats for a typical game from 1871-2006 (at end of Glossary);
7. 2006 season statistics and summaries for the AL & NL (at front of Historical Record);
8. Updates to the Top 100 Black Baseball/Negro Leagues players after the 2006 special Hall of Fame election;
9. Biographical information for the pioneer/executives inducted into the Hall of Fame in 2006 (at the end of the Hall of Fame section);
10. Lists of the hitters and pitchers selected to the most All-Star Games (in All-Star section);
11. Histories and past champions of Babe Ruth, PONY, and Dixie youth baseball organizations (in the International & Amateur section)
12. Dick Howser Award winners;
13. Updated player weight ranges, showing the highest and lowest playing weights for almost every player for the past five decades; and
14. An updated, thought-provoking "*NO*Asterisks!" essay putting the so-called steroids era into perspective (at the top of the encyclopedia lineup).

There are now fifty years of play-by-play records available, completely covering the era of divisional play and the careers of almost 7,600 players: more than 46 percent of everyone who has played since 1901 and more than 51 percent of all players in major league history.

In addition to all of this new content, the whole encyclopedia has been redesigned to make it more readable—even though it's still jam-packed with history, stats, and information. The most visible elements of the new design can be found in the player registers, but a handy thumb index has also been added to the volume.

All for the same incredible retail price of $24.95! That makes *The ESPN Baseball Encyclopedia* the only complete baseball encyclopedia *since the 1970s* to be published for less than $25. And you can take that to the bank.

Baseball Encyclopedia on the Web

For the latest news and updates about *The Baseball Encyclopedia*, including extra statistical content that we couldn't squeeze into the book, information on upcoming author appearances, and new articles about baseball history, visit us on the web at http://www.247baseball.com.

To subscribe to our *Baseball Encyclopedia* newsletter, which will include updates, Q&As, and other features, send an e-mail with "Subscribe Newsletter" as the subject to subscribe@247baseball.com and you will be registered to receive the newsletter.

If you have any corrections or suggestions for future editions of *The Baseball Encyclopedia* please e-mail us at

feedback@247baseball.com

or send a letter to:

The Baseball Encyclopedia
c/o Barnes & Noble, Inc.
122 Fifth Avenue, 5th floor
New York, NY 10011

The Process

Like every reference work that is not created from whole cloth, this encyclopedia builds on the foundation of its predecessors, most importantly the groundbreaking work done by John Thorn and Pete Palmer in *Total Baseball*. When *Total Baseball* made its debut in 1989, all previous baseball encyclopedias were instantly obsolete, including the beloved official *Baseball Encyclopedia* that had been published by Macmillan since 1969.

All of the editors who worked on this book have worked previously on, or contributed to, one or more editions of *Total Baseball*. Furthermore, Palmer, the co-editor of the first seven editions of *Total Baseball*, has edited, co-edited, or contributed in one way or another to every complete baseball encyclopedia (i.e., encyclopedias that include year-by-year career registers) published since 1965.

Most of the data underlying the statistics in this encyclopedia comes from a new database compiled by Palmer in the past five years. Much of the remaining data comes from various databases compiled by Gary Gillette in the past six years. Other information has been generously provided by Retrosheet or by members of the Society for American Baseball Research (SABR).

In compiling his new database, Palmer—like everyone before him—has relied on the standard sources of official and unofficial statistics. He has also done new research into historical areas that have heretofore been neglected. After forty years of indefatigable work in the field, there are very few sources of information that Palmer has not examined carefully. Moreover, he has kept detailed records of the mistakes and omissions in each source, so that he can avoid repeating the mistakes of earlier reference books.

While these standard sources are generally accurate, Palmer has made tens of thousands of corrections to the original source material. Many mistakes were simply found by adding up the stats for all players on a team and comparing those totals to the reported team totals. Others were made from the input of various researchers who compared box scores or play-by-play records to the official data. Many of the hardest-to-find mistakes were corrected by comparing statistics in multiple reliable sources and looking for telltale differences. Thousands of hours have been spent compiling, checking, verifying, and correcting this new database.

National Association Statistics. One of the decisions made by the Special Records Committee was to exclude the National Association from major league status. The editors respectfully disagree with that decision and, therefore, have included complete NA records in this encyclopedia. The National Association certainly had its problems—as the Special Records Committee indicated—but it was indisputably the Major League Baseball of its day. To use current standards of reliability as a reason for excluding the NA doesn't make sense.

Despite this, however, we have *not* included NA stats in the totals of the many players who played in both the NA and the NL. Instead, a separate totals line is shown for the NA if a player also later played in the NL. The reason? If the NA and NL totals were combined, they would not match what is in the official records. For most players, that wouldn't be a problem. For some players—like Cap Anson—it would further confuse the picture.

Sources. The primary sources for most of the statistics contained herein are the official National and American League records, starting in 1903 for the NL and 1905 for the AL. The source data for most of the earlier years come from computer printouts at the Hall of Fame originally compiled by Information Concepts, Incorporated, (ICI) for the 1969 *Baseball Encyclopedia*. These ICI printouts were turned over to the Hall in return for access to Lee Allen's biographical data. The primary source for 1876–90 NL statistics are the records compiled by historian John Tattersall and held by SABR. For the National Association (1871–75), records compiled from box scores by Bob Tiemann and Bob Richardson are the primary sources.

Tattersall used the figures from the annual official guides for basic batting and pitching stats for most players, though it should be noted that official pitching stats in those days consisted simply of games, wins, and losses. Tattersall obtained extra-base hits, batter walks, and strikeouts from figures compiled in *The Boston Globe* by Clarence Dow for some years of the 1876–90 period. The unheralded Dow was one of the great early statisticians, though he unfortunately died at the age of 38 in 1893. Dow actually played one game for the Boston Unions in 1884.

Since runs batted in were not officially defined from 1876–90, Tattersall determined RBIs as best he could from newspaper accounts of games. He also retroactively compiled "official" stats from box scores for all players appearing in less than 15 games; those reserve players were not shown in the stats printed in the annual official guides. Tattersall was forced to use box scores for the years when the *Globe* did not publish statistics.

In addition to filling in these gaps in the record, Tattersall counted stats from tie games for 1878–84, which had been excluded at that time. He also counted stats from various other games that had previously been excluded from the official records—for example, for 1877 Cincinnati games, where the team dropped out of the league after 58 games (almost a complete season). Tattersall also wisely standardized the handling of walks, which were counted as outs in 1876 and as hits in 1887 in the NL; ICI had done this for the 1887 American Association.

For the most part, Tattersall did not make other changes in the official stats as found in the guides. One notable exception was in 1879, when Tattersall was sure that, due to a clerical error, Cap Anson really had only 72 hits (not 90) and batted .317 (not .407). To our knowledge, Tattersall never changed any other official stats from 1871–90 unless he found a clerical or arithmetical error. All of his decisions were endorsed by the Special Records Committee in 1968.

Filling the gaps. Certain other stats were found in box scores. For batters hit-by-pitch, the work was done by John Tattersall, Pete Palmer, John Schwartz, Alex Haas, and others through 1917 in the NL and 1920 in the AL (when the statistic was first kept officially). Likewise, box scores were used for pitcher hit-batsmen before 1903 in the NL and 1908 in the AL.

Runs batted in for years where the totals were not previously complete (1885–87 and 1890 AA) were obtained mostly from incomplete data on the ICI printouts and from newspaper game accounts. Approximately 10 percent of RBIs had to be estimated from other player batting stats, including data on some players for the 1882–84 AA. David Neft supplied some additional RBI data for 1880–84 NL.

Many corrections to home run totals were made by Tattersall and by SABR stalwart Bob McConnell. Over the years, other SABR members also took it upon themselves to research different areas. Frank Williams carefully went over the 1901–19 AL pitching stats and corrected many errors. Joe Wayman did the same for shutouts throughout major league history. Walt Wilson checked games started, which were not kept officially in the AL until 1926 and in the NL until 1938.

Biographical data came originally from research done by Hy Turkin and S.C. Thompson in the 1950s, with additional help later from Bill Haber. Biographical information for current players is collected by the editors and exchanged with the SABR Biographical Committee, which was founded by Cliff Kachline. Richard Topp and the current chairmen, Bill Carle and David Vincent, later made valuable contributions, with yeoman help from Rich Malatsky and Peter Morris.

Manager data was originally compiled by Richard Topp and Bob Tiemann, who made many changes in the previous listings for early managers. They determined that the captain was really what we call the manager today, and that the listed manager was really the club's business manager.

New in 2004 edition. Pitcher run support was obtained from Retrosheet game logs, which were compiled by Tom Ruane from various sources. This data originated with Bob Tiemann's notebook data, which was computerized by Arnie Braunstein. Play-by-plays compiled by Retrosheet, Project Scoresheet, The Baseball Workshop, and by the editors from 1969–2005 were used to calculate blown saves, defensive innings, range, opponents' stolen base and caught stealing stats for catchers, plus throwing for outfielders and DP rates for infielders. Extensive examination and testing of more than thirty years of play-by-plays provided the information needed to refine Palmer's previous estimates of defensive innings before 1969, as well as improve Palmer's defensive evaluations.

There are now more than thirty-five years of play-by-play records available, completely covering the era of divisional play and the careers of almost 6,000 players: more than 40 percent of everyone who has played since 1901 and more than 35 percent of all players in major league history.

Caught stealing for the 1913 NL came from newly discovered data compiled by Ernie Lanigan. Lanigan compiled caught stealing stats from 1912–19 and sold the data to different newspapers, though only about half of it has been found. Since Lanigan sold various features to papers across the country, it is certainly possible that there is more data out there that has not yet been found. We have checked The Sporting News and Sporting Life, but not individual city papers. If anyone knows of a newspaper that contains caught stealing stats for 1912–19 that are not shown in this book, please contact the editors.

New in 2005 edition. The most important addition to the 2005 edition was a Black Baseball/Negro Leagues section that includes: Top 100 Negro League player list with extensive biographical information, years and teams played for, and capsule biographies; Ex Post Facto MVP, Pitcher of the Year, and Rookie of the Year Awards for black baseball from 1910–1950; Year-by-year standings for all eight Negro major leagues; Details of every East-West All-Star Game; Game scores for Negro League postseason series; and Home ballparks for all Negro League teams.

Other new information included in the 2005 edition: Expanded biographical information for all major league players, including colleges and Negro League service; College World Series champions for NCAA Divisions I, II, and III plus NAIA Baseball champions and CWS Most Outstanding Player awards; Little League and American Legion champions; Spring training sites for all teams from 1901–2004; Complete games at position for every player for every season and for their career, including outfield games by LF-CF-RF; Expanded lists of All-Time Leaders; Expanded Hall of Fame voting data; Biographical information for Hall of Famers who were not players or managers; and home runs hit by pitchers.

Last—but certainly not least—this edition shows Days spent on the DL, year-by-year and career, for every player in major league history. (The Disabled List started in 1941 and was rarely used before the late 1940s.) The editors have compiled this groundbreaking DL data from a variety of historical sources—it has never been published because this is the first time it has ever been compiled.

New in 2006 edition. Continuing our commitment to compile and publish information that has never been included in any previous baseball encyclopedia, this new edition includes three important additions.

First, we have added complete draft information for all major league players selected in the history of the amateur and first-year player drafts (1965–2005). In addition to the drafting team and year, the round and ordinal pick number is also shown along with the type of draft (i.e., Regular or Secondary, January or June). While each year's draft information has been routinely published in many annual reference books, it has never before been compiled in an encyclopedia.

Second, for many players who played in 1950 or later, we have included detailed playing weight information instead of a single nominal weight—often taken from a player's debut season and therefore liable to be inaccurate for those who had long careers. For players whose weight varied by more than 10 pounds from the previously shown weight, we now show a weight range for their career. Given the outcry over the effects of the so-called steroid era, this information is certainly topical.

Finally, we have added more texture to the Black Baseball/Negro Leagues section of the encyclopedia. Jim Riley has written synopses for each year of black baseball from 1910–50, covering both the major Negro Leagues as well as independent black baseball.

SABR and Retrosheet. Any reader who pays careful attention to the explanations and introductions in this work will come across multiple references to both of these eminent non-profit organizations. For information on the Society for American Baseball Research, please see their page at the very end of the encyclopedia.

Some of the information in this encyclopedia came from the files of Retrosheet, an organization founded for the collection, computerization, and free public distribution of detailed play-by-play information of as many major league games as possible. Much of the information is currently available at www.Retrosheet.org and more is added regularly as additional data files are proofed and readied for release.

Retrosheet has become a standard source of information for many teams, writers, and announcers. It also provides box scores and play-by-play accounts for fans interested in specific games, such as the first one they ever attended. Dozens of ballplayers have received detailed analyses of their careers.

Jayson Stark of ESPN wrote, "Do we even remember life before Retrosheet? I am eternally grateful that Retrosheet pasted every one of them [box scores] into its notebook out there in cyberspace." Peter Gammons calls Retrosheet a "godsend."

Not all the box scores are there yet, but more are on the way all the time as this epic effort continues. The website also includes a "most wanted" list of games for which Retrosheet still needs a scoresheet. If you have scoresheets of any games from 1947–73, or if you think there might still be some scoresheets or an old scorebook in your attic or in your parent's attic, please check out this list!

Slip-Sliding Away: The Ever-Changing Hit Total of Cap Anson. Tattersall's painstaking research was invaluable in creating official records for many players and in supplementing the skimpy official records for those included in the annual guides. Everyone has heretofore accepted Tattersall's numbers without questioning them. However, Pete Palmer has discovered that in 1889, Tattersall—for unknown reasons—changed the official hits totals for most of the White Stockings regulars. In this case, Tattersall apparently believed that the Chicago club (now the Cubs) had erroneously been given an extra 67 hits by either a generous scorer or by a league error, since his box scores did not agree with the league figures published in the official guide.

After poring over the surviving records and after careful reflection, we have decided to undo the changes Tattersall made to the official NL stats for the 1889 Chicago batters. We believe that there is not nearly enough evidence to prove any error that justified those changes. In those days, the teams, not the leagues, employed the official scorers. As one might imagine, there was a lot of favoritism in the selection of official scorers, whose names were kept secret to prevent players or fans from assailing them for controversial decisions.

Since the official scorer's decisions were unknown, virtually every nineteenth century newspaper box score was different. As a consequence, there was no way during the season to tell what the official statistics would later say (i.e., what would be published in the postseason compilations for the annual guides). Even if the official scorer in Chicago in 1889 awarded a somewhat higher number of hits rather than errors for some players—which is pure speculation at this point—it was the duty of those scorers to make judgments based on what they saw.

In 1897 public accusations were made that Baltimore official scorers unfairly aided Orioles outfielder Willie Keeler, who finished the season with a .432 average. One of those casting aspersions on the integrity of the Baltimore scorers was John Heydler, who would later become NL president. (Keeler's average was later revised to .424, based on ICI research.) Corrections due to obvious clerical or arithmetic mistakes were frequently made in the ICI process and in the decades since. In no other case, however, has the judgment of an historian decades later been substituted for the judgment of the scorer of the day about whether a batted ball should have been scored a hit or an error. The White Stockings' anonymous official scorer in the 1890s was later found to have been a female friend of team owner Al Spalding, yet her presumably non-objective decisions have never been overturned.

Why did Tattersall decide to make these changes? We cannot know for sure, as no documentation of Tattersall's reasoning—if, indeed, he recorded any—has survived. It appears that his changes to the White Stockings hit totals in 1889 were an attempt to reconcile the new league pitching stats that Tattersall was compiling with the existing official league batting stats. While that is understandable, the fact remains that there are thousands of differences between the batting and pitching stats in those years, most of which will never be reconciled because the source material (i.e., the official scoresheets) have been lost and only the final totals survive. Attempts to match the official totals for seasons in the 1880s by compiling stats from newspaper box scores have produced large and irreconcilable discrepancies.

Aside from the changes in scoring practices endorsed by the Special Records Committee, no one has ever changed any other official statistic without clear evidence that it was wrong. In fact, in many cases, "official" statistics continue to be published by reputable sources even though it has been documented that they are wrong. For example, there is overwhelming evidence of skullduggery in the final two games played by the St. Louis Browns in 1910, when well-regarded Nap Lajoie was in a tight race for the AL batting title with unpopular Ty Cobb. That malfeasance almost certainly resulted in a number of extra hits for Lajoie—it's theoretically possible, though not very likely, that Lajoie would have gone 8-for-8 had the Browns not played deep at third base and allowed him to lay down seven uncontested bunt hits—yet no one has ever adjusted his hit totals.

If you're still reading at this point, you may enjoy this comparison of the differing career hit totals for Cap Anson in various reference sources. The first entry shows what The Sporting News (longtime publisher of the official annual guides and record books) and Elias Sports Bureau list for Anson. The other entries show the wandering totals for Anson in various encyclopedias—most of them official—in the past half-century.

Cap Anson's Hits, by the Books

***The Sporting News* and Elias Sports Bureau**
(official statisticians for MLB)

3,081 Matches official guide data for 1876–97, Anson's entire NL career.

***Barnes Official Encyclopedia of Baseball*, 1951–79**
(1st–10th editions)

3,516 Includes 435 hits in the National Association, 1871–75.

***Macmillan Baseball Encyclopedia*, 1969**
(1st edition, official)

2,995 Sources Tattersall 1876–90; 72 instead of 90 in 1879 (correcting league error); ICI printouts 1891–97; 86 not 67 in 1877 (includes games vs. Cincinnati that had been thrown out); includes 6 hits in tie games 1878–84 which originally were not counted in the official averages); does not include 60 walks that were counted as hits in 1887; has 161 instead of official 177 in 1889 due to Tattersall change in official stats; has 17 fewer hits from ICI printouts 1891–97.

***Macmillan Baseball Encyclopedia*, 1974–88**
(2nd–7th editions, official)

3,041 Restored the 18 hits in 1879 which everyone else had concluded was a league error or an intentional mistake to help his average; also restored the 16 in 1889 that Tattersall had changed; then used official guide figures in 1894 (+5) and 1897 (+7) for a total of +46. They used the ICI figures for 1891–93 and 1895–96 and also used Tattersall's tie games for 1878–84.

***Macmillan Baseball Encyclopedia*, 1990–96**
(8th–10th editions; 8th edition official)

3,000 Apparently reverted to 1st edition number, then arbitrarily added 5 hits in 1894 without explanation.

***Total Baseball*, 1989–99**
(1st–6th editions; 4th–6th editions official)

2,995 Same sources and corrections as Macmillan, 1st edition.

***Total Baseball*, 2001–04**
(7th edition, official; 8th edition, unofficial)

3,056 Per edict from Major League Baseball, reversing Special Records Committee decision to count bases on balls as walks for all seasons. Therefore, counts 60 walks in 1887 as hits; it also includes 1 hit in a protested game in 1894 that was not counted by ICI, though it should have been.

***Barnes & Noble Baseball Encyclopedia*, 2004**
(1st edition, unofficial)
ESPN Baseball Encyclopedia
(2005 and 2006 editions, unofficial)

3,012 ICI total with restoration of 16 hits subtracted without explanation by Tattersall in 1889; also counts 1 hit in 1894 protested game.

Historical Standards. Whenever any comprehensive reference work is published, questions arise as to why certain changes were made to previously published works, as well as why other changes *weren't* made. Fair enough.

Because of ongoing research into baseball records by many devoted fans—especially SABR and Retrosheet members—apparent errors in many of baseball's official statistics and records are surfacing. As work continues, even more discrepancies will arise.

In general, the farther back one delves into the past, the less accurate are the official statistics. That is understandable, and there is no shame in admitting that close scrutiny of the records of bygone eras will inevitably produce hundreds of differences.

In the past few years, a few of baseball's most prominent all-time records have been changed: Hack Wilson's major league single-season RBI record, Walter Johnson's AL

career strikeout record, and Babe Ruth's career walks record among them. Two decades ago, Ty Cobb's 1910 hits total and batting average were corrected as a result of Pete Palmer's research—and the resulting controversy reached all the way to the commissioner's office.

In most cases, the changes actually were quite small, and usually made when some player had a shot at tying or breaking the record. Yet, because of unrealistic public expectations that hold baseball records as infallible, these changes often provoked cries of outrage from pundits and fans.

As you read this, scores of researchers are poring over the records of baseball's distant past, uncovering valuable new information as well as potential corrections. As an example, SABR member Trent McCotter has checked the official daily logs for a handful of famous players from the American League in the 1920s (Ruth, Cobb, Gehrig, etc.). While doing this, he found a dozen errors just on games where someone hit a home run and was credited with no RBI, plus several entries in the wrong column and other items that don't add up. Based on Ron Liebman's study of Ruth's runs batted in and the Elias corrections to Ruth's walks, it's possible that figures in this period might be off by around one part in 300—a tiny percentage (.00333), really, but still a very meaningful number of hits, runs, or RBIs.

In the past, most of the really big errors in the official records have been found by comparing the sums of the players to their team totals, but many small errors are still uncorrected. Before 1935, the sum of the players usually did not equal the AL team total for at bats, runs or hits, although it was usually off by only a few. Extra base hits were better, but walks and strikeouts were worse. The National League has always been more accurate than the American League. For example, from 1921–30 there are only 75 cases of items not adding up in the NL and 652 in the AL. Most of the NL problems had to do with the batting totals not being equal to the pitching totals, as the NL was not as careful with pitching as they were with batting and fielding. As time went on, accuracy improved gradually, and today the official stats are virtually perfect.

Another example will suffice. In the 2005 edition of this encyclopedia, two new players were added who had fallen into the historical cracks: Bill Ford and Ed Carfrey. Ford started one game for the Boston Braves in 1936, getting no one out but allowing 3 runs in his only big-league appearance. Carfrey played one game at shortstop for Philadelphia in the American Association in 1890; his sole game was erroneously credited to another player when the official stats were computerized.

It is often said that baseball's most important records are sacred. That is thoughtless and silly: baseball records are mere numbers, after all, and should be no more venerated than census data. Baseball records should be respected for their comprehensiveness and accuracy. The players who accomplish great feats that are recorded by those numbers should be admired for their skill and honored for their endurance. The game itself should be celebrated, not mere numbers.

While we carefully monitor the progress of current research into past records, we have decided to not make any other changes to the statistics in this edition until we have a better grasp of the extent of the discrepancies that are being uncovered. We are also conferring with other experts in the field to establish a set of rigorous, professional, and yet common-sense standards that should be applied to this new research, as well as what level of documentation should be required before more changes are made. As the saga of Cap Anson's career hit totals shows, we aren't afraid to make changes when we are confident they are warranted. We don't believe that the voluminous records of the National Pastime are sacrosanct, and we will be carefully reviewing all future research with an eye toward incorporating it in future editions of our encyclopedia.

Twice-Told Tales: Tales told at the time and retold a century later by reconstructing their statistics. A perfect example of the kind of dedication to the National Pastime that money can't buy is the story of Joe Wayman, an amateur researcher who devoted himself to researching nineteenth-century scoring practices and their impact on pitching records. As with most other advances in documenting the history of the early game, there is little if any economic reward for such work, so it is done by fans who love the game—amateurs in the pure sense of the word.

Here is the saga of Joe Wayman and how he has restored a lost part of baseball's historical tapestry—individual pitching records from the late nineteenth century that had been lost for 100 years.

Nineteenth-century scoring practices regarding pitching decisions were well defined, even though they were not formulated in either the Official Playing Rules or the League Constitution. At the same time, because the practices were not expressed in writing, they varied, giving scorers more leeway in their individual interpretations.

Pitching records, inevitably, are influenced by the judgments of official scorers. In the nineteenth century, perforce, since they did not agree amongst themselves, these judgments had more impact than there has ever been since.

Essentially, there were four popular scoring conventions of the day:

- Leaving after pitching $4^2/_3$ innings with a lead that lasted thereafter (both reasonable and consistent under the rules of those days as well as today);
- Pitching the most or least effectively (a reasonable practice still in use today for relievers when the starting pitcher doesn't last at least five innings);
- Pitching the bulk of the game before being removed with his team trailing, then having his club rally to win the game (not very common and partly a function of luck);
- Favoritism in borderline situations.

How, then, can these practices be verified? Sadly, of all the official NL records from 1876 through 1902, only the summaries in the annual official guides remain.

One pitching statistic dominates the entire era: *GP* for "Games Played." It was the *sine qua non* of the period and was not at all the same as the modern "games pitched" or "appearances." Unfortunately, the exact meaning—and, therefore, the critical importance—of GP has either been misunderstood, or worse, overlooked, by almost all serious baseball researchers. Until Wayman embarked on his quest.

Here is the key: the Games Played for a club's pitchers, when totaled, equal the number of games that their club played. Ergo, nineteenth-century GP's represent what are today called pitching decisions. (Yes, it's true that Saves have now lumped together by writers and fans along with Wins and Losses as pitching decisions, but a Save by definition, cannot be a decision since it is dependent on a specific relationship to a particular kind of decision, the Win.)

When was the GP statistic compiled? With what other records did it share the stage? There were four periods during which the GP stat was used:

1. 1876–1889. A singular GP number was published. Deriving Won-Lost records for pitchers necessitated a day-by-day compilation from newspapers;
2. 1890–1892. The NL published both GPs and Wins for pitchers. With these, Wins, Losses, and Ties (Ties were also decisions) can reliably be determined;
3. 1893–1900. A new wrinkle, WLP (Won-Lost Percentage), was introduced. On the other hand, the NL dropped Wins! Even so, Wins, Losses, and Ties could still be deduced for pitchers;
4. 1901–1902. No pitching records were published at all! Fielding records, however, had always agreed with pitchers' GPs, so they could be used.

Where is the mother lode from which this precious treasure of nineteenth-century pitching records can be extracted? Since 1975, Joe Wayman has visited the Hall of Fame Library in Cooperstown, NY; the Library of Congress in Washington, DC; the Amateur Athletic Foundation Library in Los Angeles; and many other libraries to do research in various publications including *Sporting Life*, *The Sporting News*, the *New York Clipper*, the annual *Spalding Guide*, plus numerous local metropolitan daily newspapers from NL cities. He compiled day-by-day and year-by-year pitching statistics such as game appearances, games started, complete games, and games finished from scoring descriptions, for nearly 30,000 games, particularly noting the pitchers' workload.

In addition, Wayman also utilized the Information Concepts, Inc. (ICI) sheets at the Hall of Fame for the game counts from 1891–1902. John Tattersall's summary records from 1876–90, which are the foundation of most nineteenth-century stats included in the *ESPN Baseball Encyclopedia*, *Total Baseball*, and the defunct *Macmillan Baseball Encyclopedia* were compared with Wayman's conclusions and agreed to a whopping 99.9 percent! All three of these encyclopedias, of course, were not compiled until the late twentieth century.

The forebears of the nineteenth-century GP and scoring practices were two giants of the game:

- Henry Chadwick. One of early baseball's greatest minds, the originator of many innovative baseball statistics, and often called the father of baseball, Chadwick devised a newfangled Won-Lost system in 1884 that graced the pages of the 1885 Spalding Guide. The National League took notice after a number of minor leagues released W-L records for 1889 and 1890, and the Senior Circuit adopted the new convention by incorporating a Wins column in its official pitching averages in 1890;
- Al Spalding. His 1908 record book recognized the important GP statistic in its own day.

Why does GP matter? Because it was the Rosetta Stone needed to unlock wins, losses, and ties for pitchers in the nineteenth century, adding detailed day-by-day records to what had previously been only season totals.

There are a couple of minor problems, as with almost every historical statistic. Scorers would sometimes award two GPs in a game when a team used more than one pitcher. Sorting these out requires careful analysis, especially to evaluate if there was an offsetting adjustment in the club's season totals.

Another issue is that, to merit inclusion in the official averages published after each season in the nineteenth century, a pitcher had to have been credited with at least six decisions in 1876–78, with 10 decisions in 1879, and with 15 decisions from 1880–1900. In such cases, the missing pitchers' records can be determined from Complete Game statistics and from decisions in their team's multiple-pitcher games.

Joseph M. Wayman spent 30 years investigating nearly 30,000 mostly forgotten baseball games that maybe one fan in a thousand either knows or cares about. Some of these discoveries have been documented in Wayman's *Grandstand Baseball Annual*, which is still being published. He is a prototype of the kind of painstaking researcher who follows his passion to the ends of the earth—or, at least, to the ends of many dusty library shelves all over the country. Wayman welcomes input from others, and future revisions in light of new evidence are certainly possible.

This is just one story of many. There are many other devoted researchers that most baseball fans have never heard of, like Frank Williams, who spent an enormous amount of time and energy filling in missing information and cleaning up problems with early twentieth century statistics. They also walk quietly and humbly among the legions of baseball fans who unknowingly benefit from their devotion to our National Game.

There are many other delicious chestnuts of information buried in the annals of the 135-year history of major league baseball but, without any further ado . . . Let's go on to "The Show."

—*Gary Gillette*

NO ASTERISKS!

The Hall of Fame election in January 2007 was notable more for an absence than for the presence of Cal Ripken Jr. and Tony Gwynn. As the new members of the Hall basked in the inevitable glory of their elevation, a giant redwood cast a long shadow across the proceedings.

Less than 10 years ago, Mark McGwire was a giant in the world of sports, smashing tape-measure home runs and thrilling fans worldwide. Along with Sammy Sosa, McGwire and the great home run chase of 1998 put Major League Baseball back on the map. Cal Ripken may have pulled the ailing National Game off of its deathbed in 1995 when he broke Lou Gehrig's seemingly unassailable consecutive-games streak, but it was Sammy and Mark who put the Grand Old Game back on its feet.

Good Times. By all accounts, the last few years have been very good for Major League Baseball. Indeed, according to Commissioner Bud Selig and the growing chorus of pundits that echo him, baseball has never been more popular. The commissioner has been repeating this mantra for years, of course, but people finally started jumping over to his sunny side of the fence in the second half of 2004.

The commissioner has also converted much of the media into believing that competitive balance in baseball has been restored due to the synergistic effects the wild-card format, the revenue-sharing plan of 2002, and the unprecedented luxury tax instituted after that collective bargaining agreement. That historic agreement was renewed with only minor changes in 2006, so the sport is now guaranteed to enjoy labor peace through 2011.

Among other notable achievements of the past year was yet another all-time attendance record, shattering the record set only a year ago (which in turn broke the record set in 2004). Partly as a result, unbelievably large amounts of money have been flowing into the game from both old and new revenue streams. The wild spending on free agents, both foreign and domestic, in the 2006-07 offseason indicated just how profitable most franchises really are. More importantly, the plethora of long-term, guaranteed contracts—many of them back-loaded—shows how much money the owners believe will be flowing to them in the near future.

On the field, as if to underscore it all with a dramatic flourish, the past three seasons have featured exciting and unpredictable postseason play capped by underdog teams winning the last three World Championships. The 2004 Red Sox—the only team to come back from a 3-games-to-0 deficit in a postseason series—won the World Series for the first time in more than eight decades. As did the 2005 White Sox, finally exorcising the ghosts of the 1919 Black Sox.

The 2006 season provided more evidence for the optimists. Toronto appeared to have finally mounted a serious challenge to the stranglehold that New York and Boston have had on the AL East. The AL Central witnessed a barnburner of a race between the Twins and the Tigers. The Athletics reprised their patented second-half hot streak in the AL West and won their first postseason series of the Billy Beane era.

In the senior circuit, the NL Central saw a dogfight even though all the contenders had mediocre records. The West saw a Southern California duel between the Padres and Dodgers. And the Mets returned to the postseason after laying waste to the NL East.

Talk of another subway series filled the air as both Gotham teams broke ground on their billion-dollar new ballparks. St. Louis, one of the finest baseball cities in the land, opened the third incarnation of Busch Stadium. Oakland finally secured a site for its planned new high-tech ballpark, ending more than three decades of speculation about the team leaving the Bay Area. After 10 years of rancor and threats, Minnesota thankfully secured the financing for its new downtown park.

The 2006 postseason featured more than its share of upsets and stirring performances. And the Fall Classic featured two teams that no one expected to survive, both led by no-nonsense veteran managers with reputations as diamond geniuses. Most remarkably, the ongoing labor negotiations were concluded without public disputes or apparent acrimony, leading to the announcement of the new pact during the All-Star break. What more could a baseball fan ask for?

Dark Lining to the Silver Cloud. In the lead-up to those critical negotiations in 2002, many owners and analysts—including the commissioner's own Blue Ribbon Panel on the game's economics—were saying that baseball was in grave danger. According to who? According to the same group that now sees the world through rose-colored Oakleys. The truth was, of course, that the game was neither in as much danger then as the doomsayers declaimed, nor are the skies as blue as the bobbleheads believe now.

So, the $64,000,000 question—about half the going rate for a frontline free agent these days—is, Why isn't anyone watching? Television ratings for MLB's so-called jewel events—the All-Star Game, the League Championship Series, and the World Series—are so low that they seem to defy explanation in an era of record crowds. Not that this paradox stopped the spinmeisters at MLB and Fox Sports from trying out one explanation after another in their quest to put a happy face on the record-low Nielsen numbers.

One of the latest excuses trotted out is that the Fall Classic has started on Saturdays for the past 20 years, and Saturday is the lowest night of the week for primetime TV viewership. That might explain the 8.0 rating for Game 1 of the 2006 Series, but how does it explain the 10.1 overall rating? Oh, yes, *that* was explained away by the Detroit and St. Louis markets; adjusting for their size, the Series ratings were about the same as in 2005.

How does that explain the fact that World Series Games 3, 4, and 5 didn't even crack the top 10 most-watched TV shows of the week? More Americans managed to find the time to watch ABC's *Desperate Housewives,* to tune into *three* permutations of the hit *CSI* series on CBS, to remember to view a dinosaur like *60 Minutes*, to show up for a *regular-season* NFL game on NBC, and to gawk at several different reality shows.

Despite the weak ratings, MLB managed to secure new national TV contracts with Fox and TBS that, combined with the existing contract with ESPN, will produce a nice bump in revenue. As part of the new deal, the World Series will henceforth start on Tuesday. Whether that change can revive the Fall Classic's ratings, which have plumbed seven record-lows since the strike, is an open question. And even with the increased revenue, MLB's TV contracts are dwarfed by the mountain of money the NFL receives from the networks.

The Specter of Steroids. There's no denying, though, that the majority of baseball fans feel good about the game again. The malaise that had lingered over the National Pastime since the nuclear winter of 1994-95 finally dissipated in the mid-2000s, and the future looks brighter now than it has since the early 1990s.

With the sun shining brightly, Major League Baseball is busily making plans in 2007 to celebrate another record-breaking performance when the great Barry Bonds could well pass Hammerin' Hank Aaron with his 756th home run. Only 21 home runs away from tying Aaron's record—one of only two candidates for the most important record in professional sports, along with the single-season home run mark that Bonds already owns—Bonds will hold the baseball world in his thrall as he climbs ever closer to the great Aaron's magical lifetime total of 755. And with 26 notches on his comeback belt after a lost 2005 campaign, Bonds has shown that he's ready, willing, and able to surmount the intense scrutiny and unbelievable pressure, as
he did in 2006 when he passed the immortal Babe Ruth, to claim the grand prize.

Uno momento, por favor. No one outside of San Francisco appears to be planning any festivities, and an angry mob of politicians, writers, commentators, broadcasters, fans, and big-league pitchers have embarked on a crusade. With a self-appointed agenda of cleansing the game of the stain of steroids, this populist movement wants to suppress the scoring and home run records of the past 15 years, now dubbed the "steroids era" by the punditocracy.

In 2005, just when baseball fans thought it was safe to go back into the water and enjoy their favorite game again, a renewed and seemingly interminable focus on steroids ripped the scab off of the National Pastime's festering wound. Retired slugger Jose Canseco, who hit 462 home runs in his career and won a Most Valuable Player trophy, penned a tell-all book in which he admitted using steroids and accused many prominent ballplayers of the same. While Canseco's credibility was certainly in question, some of his charges had the ring of truth. Regardless, all of them made front-page news.

Televised Congressional hearings on steroids in March 2005 thoroughly embarrassed the ballplayers that were called to testify, as well as the game they once played so well. Acclaimed as worldwide as heroes in 1998, sluggers Mark McGwire and Sammy Sosa saw their reputations tarnished when they refused to forthrightly answer questions about possible steroid usage. Sosa was hoping to stage a comeback after sitting out 2006, while McGwire was a virtual hermit

Since the Major League Baseball Players Association bowed to public and Congressional pressure in spring 2005, accepting suspensions for players testing positive for banned substances for the first time, more than a dozen major leaguers and scores of minor leaguers have tested positive. Many of the malefactors suspended have been pitchers; about the same percentage as the number of roster slots devoted to pitching. Yet where is the outcry against unnaturally pumped-up hurlers trying to take advantage of hitters?

The announcement of every new suspension has stirred the controversy a bit more. But the volcanic event that reshaped baseball's landscape occurred in midseason 2005 when Rafael Palmeiro, who had slammed 566 home runs in his career and had stroked his 3000th hit only two weeks earlier, was suspended for steroid usage. Widely regarded as a future first-ballot Hall of Famer, the uproar couldn't have been greater unless Palmeiro had waved his finger in front of Congress, testifying that he had "never used steroids. Period." Which, of course, he had patronizingly done only a few months earlier.

Picking and Choosing Evidence. In the eyes of the crusaders, this was proof positive that the game had been corrupted by performance-enhancing drugs and that the offensive records of 1990s and 2000s were tainted. Bolstered by this new evidence, passionate calls were soon heard demanding that recent slugging records be accompanied by a shameful asterisk. Some unthinking zealots went so far as to demand that the career statistics for guilty players be expunged from the record books. The simple-minded simplicity of this notion, combined with the tsunami of public anger about steroids, created a perfect storm of righteous indignation about the supposed sullying of some the game's most important records.

If accomplishing things that no one has done previously is accepted as *prima facie* evidence of cheating, where is the sniggering suspicion about fortysomething marvels like the great Roger Clemens? Why is it that the Rocket's unreal 1.87 ERA at age 42 in 2005—more than a run-and-a-half better than the league average, posted in a hitters' park, and the best of his 22-year-career—is to be enthusiastically cheered while the greatest player of the past 50 years crushing home runs in his 40s is to be cynically jeered?

It's hard enough to find anything positive in the steroid scandal that plagues Major League Baseball, although the relentless grandstanding that the media and politicians have wallowed in has gotten completely out of hand. And it's probably going to stick with the game for quite a while as retired sluggers like McGwire from the so-called steroids era become eligible for the Hall of Fame. The tiny percentage of the vote that Big Mac received in the 2007 Hall election is just a taste of things to come.

All too often, however, simplicity leads to simplistic solutions, and adding a scarlet asterisk to selected records to shame players is a remedy that is neither right nor necessary. The simple truth is that *all* major league home run records have been controversial—both *when* they were set, *and* for decades afterward. Steroids may have added a different kind of controversial factor, but it is a distinction without a meaningful difference.

Déjà vu-doo. The story of the first important home run record imparts a lesson that should have been learned a century ago. The earliest home run record of consequence was set by Ed Williamson, third basemen for the Chicago White Stockings [now the Cubs]. Williamson hit 27 home runs in 107 games in 1884 in Chicago's Lake Front Park, which seems Ruthian given the playing conditions of that age. What was so controversial? Chicago's Lake Front Park had a left-field foul line 180-feet long—or short—that season, turning dozens of easy fly balls into tainted round-trippers. The wooden park, rebuilt in 1883, had power alleys of only 280 and 252 feet, measured only 300 feet to dead center, and was only 196 feet down the right field line. Its capacity was a mere 5,000 souls—cozy enough confines for a beer-league softball game.

Prior to 1884, balls hit on the fly over that tempting left field fence at Lake Front Park were, quite reasonably, adjudicated to be ground-rule doubles. The whole National League hit a total of 124 homers in 395 games in 1883, for a rate of 1 home run every 6 games, whereas the mighty Cubs "bashed" 142 home runs in 112 games in 1884, more than 8 times the league average a year earlier. In games *not* involving the Cubs, the league's home run rate was slightly less than the previous season.

When the White Stockings moved to West Side Park in 1885, where both foul lines were only 216 feet long, Williamson managed only 3 homers despite playing in 6 more games. Prior to 1884, Williamson had a career total of 8 home runs in 481 games, and he managed to hit only 29 more round-trippers in 615 games before retiring. *Despite the anomalous and controversial circumstances under which it was set, Williamson's mark stood in the record books for 35 years—with* no *asterisk.*

To be fair, Williamson was somewhat of a slugger before setting the home run record, and he led the league with 49 doubles in only 99 games in 1883. *Slugging* in days of yore, when the softer baseball was tattered, torn, and discolored for most of the game, was defined mostly by line drives to the gaps that fell in for doubles and triples. The over-the-fence power that is commonly meant by *slugging* since Babe Ruth stood the baseball world on its head in 1920 was unheard of back then, except for anomalies like Lakefront Park.

This nineteenth century story might seem quaintly irrelevant to today's circumstances, but a review of twentieth century home run records reinforces the lesson instead of contravening it. Babe Ruth set the baseball world agog by hitting a record 54 homers in 1920, then—just for those that didn't immediately understand the revolutionary impact of that event—the Bambino drove the point home by hitting 59 the following year. Finally, capping a decade of dominance with the 1927 Yankees, playing on perhaps the greatest team ever assembled, Ruth smashed his famous 60 home runs.

All of Ruth's records were extremely controversial, as dedicated defenders of the dying Deadball-era style of play maintained that Ruth was a mere basher who couldn't or wouldn't play what was then called "scientific baseball." Somehow, illogically, Ruth's critics thought that their disdain made The Sultan of Swat's titanic accomplishments less impressive. The deep-seated belief in the superiority of the sacrificial one-run, contact-and-baserunning game practiced by Ty Cobb and his colleagues persisted long after the game had irrevocably changed. Evidence can be seen in the vote totals for the first Hall of Fame election in 1936, when The Georgia Peach received more votes than any of the five immortals who were enshrined in the initial class—including Ruth, Honus Wagner, Christy Mathewson, and Walter Johnson.

Apocryphal Asterisks and Selective Memory. More than three decades later, Roger Maris' 1961 challenge to Ruth's single-season record was derided as being a product of expansion: both because of the weaker pitching and the new, longer 162-game schedule.

The fact that many baseball fans erroneously believe to this day that Maris' record was accompanied by an asterisk speaks to the enduring fallacies of so many of the National Pastime's legends. Its persistence explains the title of Billy Crystal's well-received 2001 HBO movie, *61**, a title that didn't need a word of explanation to anyone older than 50 nor to millions of baseball fans in their 20s, 30s, or 40s. Ford Frick's acute conflict of interest—the commissioner had been the ghostwriter of Ruth's autobiography in his previous vocation as a sportswriter—was seldom mentioned by those deifying Ruth and demeaning Maris.

A decade later, when indefatigable Hank Aaron was about to eclipse Ruth's career record of 714 homers, the words had changed even though the tune was the same. Defenders of The Sultan of Swat screamed out that Aaron had the benefit of facing expansion pitching for most of his career while getting almost 4,000 more at-bats than Ruth. The overtly racist death threats of many of Aaron's assailants was well publicized, but there was an implicit and subtle racism being practiced by the press and the electronic media by ignoring that Ruth had benefited from segregated baseball by never having to face talented black pitchers.

Fast forward to 1998, when much of the world was transfixed by the great home-run chase that forever entwined the memories of a personable Cubs' slugger and a brooding Cardinals' basher. McGwire launched his 70 moonshots and hammered his name into the record books, pursued closely for most of the season by the smiling Sosa and his 66 bombs. Smaller ballparks, pitching staffs diluted by two more expansion rounds, and supplements like androstendione were cited by the new wave of nattering nabobs that desperately wanted to set up straw sluggers as a way of dismissing their record-shattering seasons.

Baseball history has now progressed to Barry Bonds, whose intense batting eye, lightning-quick swing, tremendous power, and Prussian-like plate discipline have formed a combination that has laid waste to hordes of pitchers as well as hordes of batting records. As the holder of the single-season record with 73 home runs and the potential future career record holder with 755-plus, Bonds' refusal to kowtow to the media has generated almost as much controversy as his Olympian feats.

When Bonds set his record in 2001; in distinct contrast to the events of just three summers earlier, the national reaction was a giant yawn. Many baseball fans, led on by commentators attempting to foment outrage, refused to acknowledge Bonds as the legitimate owner of the single most important individual record in professional sports. In a poll conducted by ESPN in February 2005, more respondents voted for Roger Maris as the legitimate holder of the record than anyone else, with Bonds finishing a distant fourth after Ruth and McGwire. The idea that Maris' extremely controversial feat would four decades later be hailed as the gold standard surely must have set Ford Frick spinning in his grave.

All Records Are Products of Their Times. The long and carefully documented history of the National Pastime should teach thoughtful fans and scholars many lessons. One of the most important is that, whenever a player breaks an important baseball record, it is *always* controversial. Most often, the detractors advance the same timeworn or irrelevant arguments in an attempt to impugn the integrity of both the player and the new record he set. Sometimes, their points are well taken, but merely pointing out that the new record holder has enjoyed substantial—and possibly unique—advantages in no way destroys the validity of the new record.

All record-setting performances are the products of their times and are frequently accomplished in unique circumstances. All players that set important records both enjoyed and exploited whatever significant advantages time and fate gave them. None of that has been changed by Palmeiro's positive steroid test, nor anyone else's steroid usage, real or imagined.

Finally, none of this even scratches the issue of the monumental hypocrisy of the handwringers. Baseball history is replete with pitchers that used spitballs, scuffballs, greaseballs, and other assorted illegal tricks to give them an edge over the hitters. The hallowed Hall of Fame has memorialized in bronze several notorious cheaters who, because they were pitchers, have gotten a free pass. And that doesn't just refer to the notorious Gaylord Perry, who published his autobiography *Me and the Spitter* while *still pitching!* Until Pedro Martinez came along, the career record for winning percentage—one of the most important pitching records on the books—was held by Whitey Ford, stalwart of the championship Yankees' pitching staffs of the 1950s and early 1960s. Ford was well-known for his ingenuity in modifying pristine baseballs to his advantage, and he had plenty of help from his teammates.

Pitchers? Cheating? Say It Ain't So! The plain truth is that steroid usage is part and parcel of a long and dishonorable tradition in baseball. A refresher course in the history of pitcher cheating here will put things in perspective.

Since the very beginning of organized baseball, pitchers and hitters have waged a war for supremacy in their critical individual contest and, therefore, for control of the game itself. Most of that war is, of course, fought on the field, but the battle is also joined in how the rules are written and whether they are strictly enforced.

In 1874, batters were first required to stand in a box rather than run toward the pitch and swing. The number of balls needed for a walk was nine. Pitchers threw from just 45 feet from the plate, but were only allowed to release the ball sidearm or underhand. During the 1880s, pitchers were also, at various times, required to pitch without a windup and from a "pitcher's box." And because the game back then centered on putting the ball in play, hurlers in the first decade of professional ball were mandated to ask batters what kind of pitch they would like and where they wanted it located—high, low, or at the belt.

However, as players looked to gain advantage in what is now erroneously thought of as a gentleman's game, they began to cheat. Pitchers, for their part, were dismayed by the ever-decreasing number of balls needed for a walk as the rules changed from eight to seven to six to the current four wayward pitches in just 20 years. Many early moundsmen skirted the rules by putting a "break" on the ball by flicking their wrists in order to make their offerings harder to hit. Pitchers also began changing their arm angles, seeing how much they could get away with by flinging the ball at increasingly high angles. In 1883, the National League responded to this illegitimate practice by passing a rule prohibiting any pitches being thrown from above the shoulder.

Soon, those restrictive rules—which now seem hopelessly quaint—were overhauled or eliminated. Pitchers were finally allowed to legally throw breaking balls, deliver with a long windup, and even throw straight overhand if they wanted to. As pitchers gained more freedom, they gained corresponding tactical advantages that tended to stifle the offense. The official response was to lengthen the distance between the pitcher and the hitter, which was finally set at the contemporary 60 feet, six inches in 1893, which led to a brief boom in scoring.

A succession of rules changes after 1893 chipped away at the batters' superiority, culminating with the adoption of the crucial rules change by the NL in 1901 that counted foul balls as strikes, followed by the upstart AL in 1903. The foul-strike rule set the stage for what is now known as the low-scoring Deadball Era, which defined the game until the home run renaissance of the 1920s, partially a result of rules changes that outlawed the deliberate defacing of the baseball by enterprising pitchers.

Before 1920, pitchers were legally allowed to spit on the ball, rub it with dirt or other substances, and even cut its cover. Such was the ethos of the Deadball Era when pitching, defense, speed, and one-run tactics were judged morally superior to batting in general and slugging in particular. Allowing pitchers to coat baseballs with all kinds of wet, sticky substances was bad enough, but it was combined with a penurious attitude that kept battered and discolored balls in play for the whole game.

Then the roof caved in on the dirty (literally) practices of the first two decades of the century. In August 1920, star Cleveland shortstop Ray Chapman died when his skull was fractured by a high, inside pitch from pitcher Carl Mays. While it is not clear that Chapman's death was caused by a hard-to-see pitch, something had to be done in response to the tragedy since Chapman was as popular in his day as Nomar Garciaparra is today. The major leagues quickly adopted a policy where scuffed or dirty baseballs were removed from play and replaced with clean ones. This decision, combined with the end of the spitter, emery, and shine ball and the strategic revolution wrought by the power hitting of the great Babe Ruth, tremendously increased offense and changed the game forever.

When grandfathered Burleigh Grimes (what a perfect name for a spitballer!) pitched his last big-league game in 1934, the legal spitter breathed its last gasp. That's not to say, though, that the spitball or its outside-the-rules cousins disappeared from the game. Far from it. Furthermore, with the anti-steroid crusade in full swing today, we're sure to see even more of the "wink, wink; nudge, nudge" attitude about pitcher cheating while out-of-bounds sluggers are pilloried.

Ballplayers are, above all else, competitors, and many will do anything to win—including cheating, lying, and taking performance-enhancing drugs. Plenty of pitchers, especially those with fading stuff and those who made it to the majors mostly by their cunning and guile, have been willing to try anything legal or outlawed to help give their pitches an extra break.

In November 2005, Major League Baseball and the union agreed to a far more stringent policy on steroid testing, with more severe penalties and with provisions for amphetamine testing for the first time as well. Whether this new program will help restore the game's reputation or sully it further will be determined by how many violators are caught. And, because of the double standard, who the culprits are.

Reversal of Fortune. Without truly understanding the context, no one can make valid judgments about the integrity of any record-setting feat. It will take more time and a helluva lot of more research before we truly understand what effects steroids have had on the game. The fact is that scoring and home run rates started declining after the controversial 1999-2000 peak. In 2004-05, while the wits were saying that the beefed-up steroid testing program has deterred usage of illegal performance enhancers, offensive levels were essentially indistinguishable from the preceding two seasons when the program was regarded as ineffectual.

In 2006, though, a curious thing occurred: home run rates and scoring ticked upward again. With no easy explanation and no moral lesson to draw from this unexpected development since the vector should have pointed in the other direction, the wits seem to be half right.

The fact is that baseball is a complex game, subject to many competing forces. Some of those forces are well understood, others barely comprehended. Literally no one knows whether the drop in scoring and home runs that started after 2000 (not after 2001 as is commonly but erroneously believed) will continue, or whether 2006 presages the start of another climb in offense.

History is composed of facts. Facts should be accompanied with explanations. Explanations should engender insight. Insight should produce understanding. Well-intentioned but wrongheaded asterisks and ignorant statistical book-burnings add nothing to the historical record and demean the history of our beloved game.

Home Run Rates and Scoring Since 1901

This table shows home run rates and scoring on a per-game basis in the majors since 1901, both year-by-year and by decade. Also shown are strikeout and walk rates, both related to scoring. A casual perusal of the data shows random fluctuations as well as major historical trends. Even at the peak of the so-called steroids era, scoring was within historical norms and similar to other major offensive eras like the 1930s and 1950s when the players weren't juiced and the game was supposedly pure. True, home runs reached an all-time peak, but so did strikeouts—which ain't a coincidence. Careful perusal of the data should persuade even conspiracy theorists that there is no smoking gun, and that the knoll in the background isn't grassy—it's just the pitcher's mound.

YEAR	HR/G	CHG	R/G	CHG	SO/G	CHG	BB/G	CHG
1901	0.20		4.99		3.14		2.46	
1902	0.16	-20%	4.43	-11%	2.98	-5%	2.44	-1%
1903	0.15	-6%	4.44	0%	3.58	20%	2.41	-1%
1904	0.13	-13%	3.72	-16%	3.72	4%	2.23	-7%
1905	0.14	8%	3.90	5%	3.87	4%	2.50	12%
1906	0.11	-21%	3.62	-7%	3.70	-4%	2.51	0%
1907	0.10	-9%	3.53	-2%	3.53	-5%	2.47	-2%
1908	0.11	10%	3.39	-4%	3.66	4%	2.36	-4%
1909	0.10	-9%	3.55	5%	3.77	3%	2.62	11%
1910	0.14	40%	3.84	8%	3.92	4%	2.97	13%
1911	0.21	50%	4.51	17%	4.00	2%	3.17	7%
1912	0.18	-14%	4.53	0%	3.97	-1%	3.12	-2%
1913	0.19	6%	4.04	-11%	3.83	-4%	2.95	-5%
1914	0.17	-11%	3.75	-7%	3.92	2%	2.99	1%
1915	0.15	-12%	3.79	1%	3.85	-2%	3.01	1%
1916	0.15	0%	3.56	-6%	3.82	-1%	2.84	-6%
1917	0.13	-13%	3.59	1%	3.46	-9%	2.77	-2%
1918	0.12	-8%	3.63	1%	2.89	-16%	2.83	2%
1919	0.20	67%	3.87	7%	3.07	6%	2.68	-5%
1920	0.26	30%	4.36	13%	2.95	-4%	2.77	3%
1921	0.38	46%	4.86	11%	2.83	-4%	2.80	1%
1922	0.43	13%	4.87	0%	2.80	-1%	2.93	5%
1923	0.40	-7%	4.82	-1%	2.84	1%	3.08	5%
1924	0.36	-10%	4.76	-1%	2.69	-5%	2.99	-3%
1925	0.48	33%	5.13	8%	2.72	1%	3.16	6%
1926	0.35	-27%	4.64	-10%	2.76	1%	3.12	-1%
1927	0.37	6%	4.75	2%	2.79	1%	3.01	-4%
1928	0.44	19%	4.73	0%	2.88	3%	3.12	4%
1929	0.55	25%	5.19	10%	2.86	-1%	3.26	4%
1930	0.63	15%	5.55	7%	3.21	12%	3.11	-5%
1931	0.43	-32%	4.81	-13%	3.20	0%	3.10	0%
1932	0.55	28%	4.91	2%	3.19	0%	3.06	-1%
1933	0.44	-20%	4.48	-9%	3.03	-5%	3.00	-2%
1934	0.55	25%	4.91	10%	3.45	14%	3.21	7%
1935	0.54	-2%	4.90	0%	3.26	-6%	3.19	-1%
1936	0.55	2%	5.19	6%	3.33	2%	3.40	7%
1937	0.58	5%	4.87	-6%	3.63	9%	3.41	0%
1938	0.60	3%	4.89	0%	3.41	-6%	3.53	4%
1939	0.59	-2%	4.82	-1%	3.46	1%	3.44	-3%
1940	0.64	8%	4.68	-3%	3.66	6%	3.35	-3%
1941	0.53	-17%	4.49	-4%	3.55	-3%	3.57	7%
1942	0.44	-17%	4.08	-9%	3.40	-4%	3.43	-4%
1943	0.37	-16%	3.92	-4%	3.46	2%	3.38	-1%
1944	0.42	14%	4.17	6%	3.29	-5%	3.19	-6%
1945	0.41	-2%	4.18	0%	3.27	-1%	3.37	6%
1946	0.49	20%	4.01	-4%	3.91	20%	3.54	5%
1947	0.63	29%	4.36	9%	3.69	-6%	3.71	5%
1948	0.63	0%	4.58	5%	3.65	-1%	3.89	5%
1949	0.69	10%	4.61	1%	3.61	-1%	4.05	4%
1950	0.84	22%	4.85	5%	3.86	7%	4.02	-1%
1951	0.75	-11%	4.55	-6%	3.77	-2%	3.73	-7%
1952	0.69	-8%	4.18	-8%	4.19	11%	3.54	-5%
1953	0.84	22%	4.61	10%	4.12	-2%	3.50	-1%
1954	0.78	-7%	4.38	-5%	4.13	0%	3.65	4%
1955	0.90	15%	4.49	3%	4.39	6%	3.67	1%
1956	0.93	3%	4.45	-1%	4.64	6%	3.63	-1%
1957	0.89	-4%	4.31	-3%	4.84	4%	3.31	-9%
1958	0.91	2%	4.28	-1%	4.95	2%	3.29	-1%
1959	0.91	0%	4.38	2%	5.09	3%	3.31	1%
1960	0.86	-5%	4.31	-2%	5.18	2%	3.39	2%
1961	0.95	10%	4.53	5%	5.23	1%	3.46	2%
1962	0.93	-2%	4.46	-2%	5.42	4%	3.37	-3%
1963	0.84	-10%	3.95	-11%	5.80	7%	2.96	-12%
1964	0.85	1%	4.04	2%	5.91	2%	2.96	0%
1965	0.83	-2%	3.99	-1%	5.94	1%	3.09	4%
1966	0.85	2%	3.99	0%	5.82	-2%	2.89	-6%
1967	0.71	-16%	3.77	-6%	5.99	3%	2.98	3%
1968	0.61	-14%	3.42	-9%	5.89	-2%	2.82	-5%
1969	0.80	31%	4.07	19%	5.77	-2%	3.45	22%
1970	0.88	10%	4.34	7%	5.75	0%	3.53	2%
1971	0.74	-16%	3.89	-10%	5.41	-6%	3.23	-8%
1972	0.68	-8%	3.69	-5%	5.57	3%	3.15	-2%
1973	0.80	18%	4.21	14%	5.24	-6%	3.37	7%
1974	0.68	-15%	4.12	-2%	5.01	-4%	3.33	-1%
1975	0.70	3%	4.21	2%	4.98	-1%	3.46	4%
1976	0.58	-17%	3.99	-5%	4.83	-3%	3.20	-8%
1977	0.87	50%	4.47	12%	5.16	7%	3.27	2%
1978	0.70	-20%	4.10	-8%	4.77	-8%	3.23	-1%
1979	0.82	17%	4.46	9%	4.77	0%	3.24	0%
1980	0.73	-11%	4.29	-4%	4.80	1%	3.13	-3%
1981	0.64	-12%	4.00	-7%	4.75	-1%	3.18	2%
1982	0.80	25%	4.30	8%	5.04	6%	3.16	-1%
1983	0.78	-3%	4.31	0%	5.15	2%	3.20	1%
1984	0.77	-1%	4.26	-1%	5.34	4%	3.16	-1%
1985	0.86	12%	4.33	2%	5.34	0%	3.29	4%
1986	0.91	6%	4.41	2%	5.87	10%	3.38	3%
1987	1.06	16%	4.72	7%	5.96	2%	3.42	1%
1988	0.76	-28%	4.14	-12%	5.56	-7%	3.09	-10%
1989	0.73	-4%	4.13	0%	5.61	1%	3.21	4%
1990	0.79	8%	4.26	3%	5.67	1%	3.29	2%
1991	0.80	1%	4.31	1%	5.80	2%	3.32	1%
1992	0.72	-10%	4.12	-4%	5.59	-4%	3.25	-2%
1993	0.89	24%	4.60	12%	5.80	4%	3.33	2%
1994	1.03	16%	4.92	7%	6.18	7%	3.48	5%
1995	1.01	-2%	4.85	-1%	6.30	2%	3.53	1%
1996	1.09	8%	5.04	4%	6.46	3%	3.55	1%
1997	1.02	-6%	4.77	-5%	6.61	2%	3.46	-3%
1998	1.04	2%	4.79	0%	6.56	-1%	3.38	-2%
1999	1.14	10%	5.08	6%	6.41	-2%	3.68	9%
2000	1.17	3%	5.14	1%	6.45	1%	3.75	2%
2001	1.12	-4%	4.78	-7%	6.67	3%	3.25	-13%
2002	1.04	-7%	4.62	-3%	6.47	-3%	3.35	3%
2003	1.07	3%	4.73	2%	6.34	-2%	3.27	-2%
2004	1.12	5%	4.81	2%	6.55	3%	3.34	2%
2005	1.03	-8%	4.59	-5%	6.30	-4%	3.13	-6%
2006	1.11	8%	4.86	6%	6.52	3%	3.26	4%

YEARS	HR/G	CHG	R/G	CHG	SO/G	CHG	BB/G	CHG
1901-1910	0.13		3.92		3.60		2.50	
1911-1920	0.18	38%	3.97	1%	3.59	0%	2.91	16%
1921-1930	0.44	144%	4.93	24%	2.84	-21%	3.06	5%
1931-1940	0.55	25%	4.85	-2%	3.36	18%	3.27	7%
1941-1950	0.54	-2%	4.32	-11%	3.57	6%	3.62	11%
1951-1960	0.85	57%	4.39	2%	4.53	27%	3.50	-3%
1961-1970	0.82	-4%	4.06	-8%	5.76	27%	3.16	-10%
1971-1980	0.73	-11%	4.15	2%	5.05	-12%	3.26	3%
1981-1990	0.82	12%	4.30	4%	5.45	8%	3.24	-1%
1991-2000	1.00	22%	4.77	11%	6.23	14%	3.48	7%
2000-2006	1.08	8%	4.73	-1%	6.48	4%	3.27	-6%

THE LONG SEASON: THE HISTORICAL RECORD

Part of what makes baseball special is its long season. It's been said that baseball isn't a sprint, but a marathon, and the historical record bears this out. Having to play nearly every day for six months or more affects everything about the game. A manager's strategy can change completely between March and October, given injuries, trades, predictable and not-so-predictable changes in player performance, and the capricious nature of rookies. A season that, at times, seems endless works its charms and wreaks havoc concurrently in many different ways. The best teams of all time still lose series during the season, and even the worst teams fashion together some form of a winning streak.

The long season is a player's chance to make or break his career. It gives a manager the option of sticking with a declining veteran until he rebounds—or until his poor performance sinks the team. After more than 100 games and four months of play, a team can sometimes pull a pennant out of its cap by promoting an untested but promising rookie. The guy who hits .375 in April may hit .130 in May and end up back in the minors, or a Hurricane Hazle can hit .403 down the stretch to win a pennant—and never be seen again.

When pitcher Jim Brosnan penned his 1959 diary, *The Long Season*, one thing he communicated expertly was the way baseball's fortunes could turn 360 degrees within those six months: from despair to ecstasy, with a whole lot of excitement and some stultifying ennui in between. That's how baseball has been for every one of its long seasons dating back to the nineteenth century: a roller-coaster ride of great stories buried inside a simple yet puzzling game that seems, to outsiders and other unfortunates, almost impenetrable.

For those of us who don't get to play the game for half a year at a time, baseball's long season provides artistic, scientific, emotional, and even spiritual fulfillment, and its memories keep us warm through many a long winter. A distillation of more than a century of baseball seasons is presented in this section—to learn about, argue about, and to savor—from team records to top individual performances, using both traditional statistics and new methods of measurement.

Needless to say, condensing the events of a baseball season into a single page is a very difficult task. Nevertheless, the format of this Historical Record section attempts to do justice to each of the 254 pennant races since 1871 in a concise manner, from the erratic and incomplete campaigns of the National Association, the original professional league; to the ill-conceived single season of the ill-fated Union Association in 1884; to the 130-year span of the National League, now in its third century of competition.

The top part of each Historical Record page includes final standings for the league along with extensive team batting, baserunning, pitching, and fielding statistics. Alongside the standings are each team's home wins and losses, allowing an examination of how each club fared in its home park as well as on the road. Separate park factors are listed for both batters and pitchers, showing how much each team's home field helped or hurt offensively and defensively. Note that these park factors are not simply the inverse of each other, as the calculations for each are related but not exactly the same.

Most of the team stats categories are also represented in the Batter and Pitcher Registers, though a few different stats of relevance at a team level are also included (e.g., Games in Relief). Because the official records were not as extensive, some categories will be blank for part or all of the nineteenth century (e.g., Hit Batsmen and Sacrifice Hits); others will also be blank for part of the first half of the twentieth century (e.g., Caught Stealing).

Below the standings and team statistics are individual league-leaders in 35 categories of batting, pitching, and fielding stats. Each category lists the top five players (unless multiple tied players would lengthen the list past the top five). The first and last categories—Batter-Fielder Wins and Pitcher Wins—are in boldface to indicate their importance.

Among the batting and pitching leaders, the minimums for qualifying as a league leader for any average or rate statistics are normally the same as qualifying for the batting or ERA titles. However, the minimum for qualifying as a league leader in Base Runners per 9 Innings was deliberately set low enough to include relief pitchers (60 innings pitched). Relief pitchers are unlikely to qualify for the league-leaders in many other pitching categories, such as Opponents' Average and Opponents OBP, as a result of the higher innings pitched requirements. The relief pitching categories (starting with Games and ending with Relief Ranking) have been grouped together for ease of comparison.

One category of team pitching stats is completely new: WPB. This represents the sum of wild pitches and passed balls—at a team level, there is no difference between them.

At the bottom of each page is a 300–350 word essay that gives a snapshot of what it was like to be a baseball fan that season. Each page in the Historical Record includes a summary of the pennant race and the postseason, along with comments about the level of scoring and why it might have increased or decreased. If attendance went up or down substantially, it will also be noted. The effects of major off-field events like wars, strikes, and lockouts are also briefly summarized.

Each yearly essay notes the comings and goings of the greatest players in the game's history, as well as some of its lesser lights. The debut or rookie seasons for standout players who would influence the course of the game for a decade or more are also shown, along with the final years of those stalwarts headed into retirement. Untimely deaths are listed along with the passing of those ballplayers who defined their eras: When a man of the stature of Babe Ruth, Ty Cobb, Mickey Mantle, Joe DiMaggio, or Ted Williams passes from the scene, the game is changed in invisible—yet very real—ways.

The lists below show all abbreviations used in the Historical Record section. Those that have not been defined elsewhere are explained here. Further information about the formulas and computations used can also be found in the Glossary.

Team and League Batting and Basestealing

W: Wins

L: Losses

T: Ties. Ties only happen if the game has completed 5 or more full innings, the game was tied after the last completed inning, and no further runs have been scored unless the home team has gone ahead in the bottom of the current inning.

PCT: Winning Percentage. Calculated by dividing the number of wins by the number of wins and losses.

GB: Games Behind. The number of games behind first place. If the team in question finished 83-79 and the team in first place finished 95-66, the team in question finished 12.5 games behind.

HW: Home Wins.

HL: Home Losses.

R: Runs.

OR: Opponent Runs.

PA: Plate Appearances.

H: Hits.

2B: Doubles.

3B: Triples.

HR: Home Runs.

BB: Bases on Balls. Generally referred to today as walks.

SO: Strikeouts.

HB: Hit Batsmen.

SH: Sacrifice Hits. Sacrifice flies were counted as sacrifice hits from 1908–1930 and in 1939.

AVG: Batting Average. Hits divided by at bats.

OBP: On-Base Percentage. Hits plus walks plus hit-by-pitch divided by at-bats plus walks plus hit-by-pitch plus sacrifice flies: (H+BB+HBP)/(AB+BB+HBP+SF). Sacrifice flies (SF) were not used in the OBP calculation for 1908–30 and 1939 since they were combined with sacrifice bunts in the official stats.

SLG: Slugging Average. Total bases divided by at bats.

OPS: On-Base Percentage plus Slugging Average. The figure is multiplied by 1000, so .320 plus .500 would be 820.

AOPS: Adjusted On-Base plus Slugging. On-base percentage and slugging average are added and normalized for the context of the offensive level of the league and the team's home park(s) and then converted to a scale in which 100 is average.

BR: Batting Runs. The number of runs the team should have scored compared to the average team based on the team's offensive production.

ABR: Adjusted Batting Runs. Batting runs adjusted for the home park and the league average offensive level but ignoring the offensive contributions of pitchers. The entire league average batting stats are used for teams, since teams either have pitcher batting or they don't, depending on the league rules. For individual batters, BR, ABR, and AOPS are calculated using league figures with pitcher batting subtracted. Thus the team definition is slightly different from the player definition.

PF: Hitters' Park Factor. This measure of how the team's home park affects offense is used to adjust the team's raw offensive performance in a way that takes into account the context of the team's home park. This also includes a correction for not having to face your own pitchers, which ends up being used in AOPS and ABR.

SB: Stolen Bases. Totals are available for all seasons in all leagues from 1886 on, as well as for all the seasons of the National Association.

CS: Caught Stealing. These totals are available for all American League teams in 1914–15 and from 1920 on; caught stealing totals are available for all National League teams in 1913, 1915, from 1920–26, and from 1951 on.

BSA: Basestealing Average. Stolen bases divided by stolen bases plus caught stealing; not possible unless caught stealing totals are available.

BSR: Basestealing Runs. The number of runs added by a team's basestealing attempts.

Team and League Pitching and Fielding

CG: Complete Games.

SHO: Shutouts.

GR: Games in Relief. The total number of relief appearances made by the team's pitchers.

SV: Saves. Saves became an official statistic in 1969. Saves are calculated based on the official definition of saves at the time. Saves before 1969 are based on how many times a relief pitcher finished pitching a victory for his team without getting a win.

IP: Innings Pitched.

H: Hits Allowed.

HR: Home Runs Allowed.

BB: Bases on Balls Allowed.

SO: Strikeouts.

BR/9: Baserunners Allowed Per 9 Innings.

ERA: Earned Run Average. Calculated by dividing earned runs by innings pitched and multiplying by 9.

AERA: Adjusted Earned Run Average. Calculated by normalizing ERA for the context of the offensive level of the league and the team's home park(s) and converting to a scale in which 100 is average.

OAV: Opponents' Batting Average. Hits allowed divided by opponent at bats.

OOB: Opponents' On-Base Percentage.

PR: Pitching Runs. Indicates how many runs the team's pitcher allowed to score compared to the average pitcher.

APR: Adjusted Pitching Runs. Indicates how many runs the team's pitcher allowed to score compared to the average pitcher in the context of the team's home park(s) and the offensive level of the league.

PF: Pitchers' Park Factor. This measures how the team's home park affects pitching. It is used to adjust the team's raw pitching performance in a way that takes the context of the team's home park into account. Again, there is a correction for pitchers not having to face their own batters. Park factor is used in the APR and AERA calculation.

OSB: Opponents' Stolen Bases.

OCS: Opponents' Caught Stealing.

FA: Fielding Average. Assists plus putouts divided by assists plus putouts plus errors: (A+PO/A+PO+E).

E: Errors.

WPB: Wild Pitches plus Passed Balls.

DP: Double Plays.

FW: Fielding Wins. Total number of wins the team achieved through its fielding compared to the average team in the context of the offensive level of the league and the team's home park(s).

PW: Pitching Wins. Total number of wins the team achieved through its pitching compared to the average team in the context of the offensive level of the league and the team's home park(s).

BW: Batting Wins. The total number of wins the team achieved through its hitting compared to the average team in the context of the offensive level of the league and the team's home park(s).

BSW: Basestealing Wins. Total number of wins the team achieved through its basestealing compared to the average team in the context of the offensive level of the league and the team's home park(s).

DIF: Differential. This measures the difference between how many games the team was projected to win based on its hitting, pitching, fielding, and baserunning, and how many games the team actually won. It is measured in the same way as teams measure how many games in the standings they are behind another.

Leaderboards

Not shown among team statistics

BFW: Batter-Fielder Wins. The sum of a player's batting wins, basestealing wins, and fielding wins, this figure indicates how many games the player won or lost for his team compared to an average player.

Total Bases. Calculated by adding singles plus 2x doubles plus 3x triples plus 4x home runs.

RBI: Runs Batted In.

Fielding Runs Infield and Outfield. Fielding Runs measures how many runs the player saves or loses for his team in the field compared to an average fielder. The formula takes into account assists, putouts, errors, and double plays. All of these defensive statistics are adjusted for the context in several different ways. Defensive innings are based on play-by-play from 1969 forward; they are estimated for previous years.

Fewest Bases on Balls Per Game.

Games.

Adjusted Relief Runs. Adjusted Relief Runs indicates how many runs the pitcher allowed to score compared to the average pitcher in the context of the offensive level of the league and the pitcher's home park(s). Relief pitchers are identified as pitchers who averaged less than 3 innings per appearance.

Relief Ranking. Calculated by putting Adjusted Relief Runs into the context of the importance of the relief innings thrown by the relief pitcher while taking into account the number of saves and decisions assigned to the pitcher.

Adjusted Starter Runs. This indicates how many runs the pitcher allowed to score compared to the average pitcher in the context of the offensive level of the league and the pitcher's home park(s). Starting pitchers are identified as pitchers who average at least 3 innings per appearance.

Pitcher Wins. Individual pitcher wins are calculated by adding up pitching, batting, fielding, and basestealing wins for individual pitchers; different from team pitching wins.

2006 NATIONAL LEAGUE

TEAM	W	L	T	PCT	GB	HW	HL	R	OR	PA	H	2B	3B	HR	BB	SO	HB	SH	AVG	OBP	SLG	OPS	AOPS	BR	ABR	PF	SB	CS	BSA	BSR
East																														
NY	97	65	0	.599	—	**50**	31	834	731	6291	1469	323	41	200	547	1071	62	77	.264	.334	.445	779	105	33	**49**	98	**146**	35	**81**	**20**
Phi	85	77	0	.525	12	41	40	**865**	812	6509	1518	294	41	216	**626**	1203	**95**	57	.267	.347	.447	**794**	103	**74**	32	105	92	25	79	11
Atl	79	83	0	.488	18	40	41	849	805	6283	1510	312	26	**222**	526	1169	52	78	.270	.337	**.455**	792	**106**	55	44	101	52	35	60	-1
Fla	78	84	0	.481	19	42	39	758	772	6191	1454	309	42	182	497	1249	74	76	.264	.331	.435	766	105	4	41	95	110	58	65	4
Was	71	91	0	.438	26	41	40	746	872	6283	1437	322	22	164	594	1156	69	76	.262	.338	.418	756	103	1	37	96	123	62	66	5
Central																														
StL	83	78	0	.516	—	49	31	781	762	6225	1484	292	27	184	531	922	61	71	.269	.337	.431	768	100	15	7	101	59	32	65	2
Hou	82	80	0	.506	1.5	44	37	735	719	6325	1407	275	27	174	585	1076	73	100	.255	.332	.409	741	92	-37	-56	103	79	36	69	5
Cin	80	82	0	.494	3.5	42	39	749	801	6292	1419	291	12	217	614	1192	59	66	.257	.336	.432	768	95	16	-28	106	124	33	79	16
Mil	75	87	0	.463	8.5	48	33	730	833	6128	1400	301	20	180	502	1233	82	58	.258	.327	.420	747	94	-30	-37	101	71	37	66	3
Pit	67	95	0	.414	16.5	43	38	691	797	6217	1462	286	17	141	459	1200	89	62	.263	.327	.397	724	88	-74	-89	102	68	23	75	7
Chi	66	96	0	.407	17.5	36	45	716	834	6146	1496	271	46	166	395	928	43	84	.268	.319	.422	741	92	-60	-74	102	121	49	71	9
West																														
SD	88	74	0	.543	—	43	38	731	**679**	6286	1465	298	38	161	564	1104	40	59	.263	.332	.416	748	101	-24	16	95	123	31	80	16
LA	88	74	0	.543	—	49	32	820	751	6394	**1552**	307	**58**	153	601	959	51	66	**.276**	**.348**	.432	780	103	50	46	101	128	49	72	11
SF	76	85	0	.472	11.5	43	38	746	790	6136	1418	297	52	163	494	**891**	53	80	.259	.324	.422	746	94	-39	-43	101	58	25	70	4
Ari	76	86	0	.469	12	39	42	773	788	6330	1506	**331**	38	160	504	965	67	61	.267	.331	.424	755	92	-12	-55	106	76	30	72	6
Col	76	86	0	.469	12	44	37	813	812	6347	1504	325	54	157	561	1108	60	**119**	.270	.341	.433	774	94	30	-38	109	85	50	63	1
Total	1295	—	—	—	—	694	601	12337	—	100383	23501	4834	561	2840	8600	17426	1030	1190	.265	.334	.427	761	—	—	—	—	1515	610	71	120

TEAM	CG	SHO	GR	SV	IP	H	HR	BB	SO	BR/9	ERA	AERA	OAV	OOB	PR	APR	PF	OSB	OCS	FA	E	WPB	DP	FW	PW	BW	BSW	DIF
East																												
NY	5	**12**	474	43	1461.1	1402	180	527	1161	12.3	4.14	106	.253	.323	55	40	98	111	40	.983	104	47	131	.1	3.9	**4.7**	**1.2**	6.1
Phi	4	6	500	42	1460.1	1561	211	512	1138	13.2	4.60	102	.275	.339	-19	12	104	94	35	.983	104	69	153	.1	1.2	3.1	.3	-.7
Atl	6	6	522	38	1441.1	1529	183	572	1049	13.5	4.60	98	.273	.343	-17	-12	101	101	30	.984	99	47	146	.3	-1.2	4.3	-.8	-4.6
Fla	6	6	438	41	1433.1	1465	166	622	1088	13.6	4.37	98	.267	.347	19	-15	95	69	46	.979	126	61	166	-.9	-1.5	4.0	-.3	-4.3
Was	1	3	517	32	1436.1	1535	193	584	960	13.9	5.03	87	.274	.349	-87	-111	97	110	30	.978	131	58	123	-1.1	-10.7	3.6	-.2	-1.5
Central																												
StL	6	9	469	38	1429.2	1475	193	504	970	13.0	4.54	96	.268	.337	-8	-32	97	63	32	.984	98	**43**	170	.4	-3.1	.7	-.5	5.1
Hou	5	**12**	497	42	1468.2	1425	182	480	1160	12.0	4.08	**110**	.256	.319	66	**67**	100	78	28	**.987**	**80**	51	164	**1.2**	**6.5**	-5.4	-.2	-1.0
Cin	**9**	10	476	36	1445.2	1576	213	**464**	1053	13.1	4.51	104	.278	.337	-4	30	105	**50**	35	.979	128	49	139	-1.0	2.9	-2.7	.8	-1.0
Mil	7	8	427	43	1425.2	1454	177	514	1145	12.9	4.82	93	.265	.333	-52	-53	100	97	31	.980	117	60	126	-.5	-5.1	-3.6	-.4	3.6
Pit	2	10	505	39	1435.0	1545	156	620	1060	14.0	4.52	101	.281	.357	-5	9	102	102	**52**	.983	104	77	168	.1	.9	-8.6	-.0	-6.3
Chi	2	7	**542**	29	1439.0	1396	210	687	**1250**	13.4	4.74	97	.255	.342	-41	-25	102	118	39	.982	106	80	122	.0	-2.4	-7.2	.1	-5.6
West																												
SD	4	11	475	**50**	1463.2	**1385**	176	468	1097	**11.7**	**3.87**	107	**.249**	**.312**	**101**	48	92	150	26	.985	92	45	138	.7	4.6	1.5	.8	-.7
LA	1	10	454	40	1460.1	1524	**152**	492	1068	12.7	4.23	104	.269	.330	42	25	98	110	38	.982	115	61	174	-.4	2.4	4.5	.3	.2
SF	7	9	438	37	1429.2	1422	153	584	992	13.1	4.63	96	.261	.337	-22	-32	99	98	40	.985	91	55	132	.7	-3.1	-4.2	-.3	2.4
Ari	8	9	461	34	1459.2	1503	168	536	1115	12.9	4.48	104	.267	.335	1	29	104	90	45	.983	104	64	172	.1	2.8	-5.3	-.1	-2.4
Col	5	8	499	34	1447.1	1549	155	553	952	13.5	4.66	103	.277	.346	-27	20	107	99	42	.985	91	51	**190**	.7	1.9	-3.7	-.6	-3.3
Total	78	136	7694	618	23137.0	—	—	—	—	13.0	4.49	—	.265	.334	—	—	—	—	—	.983	1690	918	2414	—	—	—	—	—

BATTER-FIELDER WINS	BATTING AVERAGE	ON-BASE PERCENTAGE	SLUGGING AVERAGE	ON-BASE PLUS SLUGGING	ADJUSTED OPS	ADJUSTED BATTER RUNS
Pujols-StL 5.5	Sanchez-Pit .... .344	Bonds-SF .... .443	Pujols-StL .... .671	Pujols-StL 1102	Pujols-StL 175	Pujols-StL 63.4
Beltran-NY 5.4	Cabrera-Fla .... .339	Pujols-StL .... .431	Howard-Phi .... .659	Howard-Phi 1084	Howard-Phi 165	Howard-Phi 59.5
Furcal-LA 4.7	Pujols-StL .... .331	Cabrera-Fla .... .430	Berkman-Hou .... .621	Berkman-Hou 1041	Cabrera-Fla 161	Cabrera-Fla 58.4
Cabrera-Fla 4.7	Atkins-Col .... .329	Johnson-Was .... .428	Beltran-NY .... .594	Cabrera-Fla 998	Berkman-Hou 159	Berkman-Hou 51.0
Soriano-Was 4.3	Holliday-Col .... .326	Howard-Phi .... .425	Holliday-Col .... .586	Beltran-NY 982	Beltran-NY 151	Johnson-Was 45.1

RUNS	HITS	DOUBLES	TRIPLES	HOME RUNS	TOTAL BASES	RUNS BATTED IN
Utley-Phi 131	Pierre-Chi 204	Sanchez-Pit 53	Reyes-NY 17	Howard-Phi 58	Howard-Phi 383	Howard-Phi 149
Rollins-Phi 127	Utley-Phi 203	Gonzalez-Ari 52	Roberts-SD 13	Pujols-StL 49	Soriano-Was 362	Pujols-StL 137
Beltran-NY 127	Sanchez-Pit 200	Cabrera-Fla 50	Pierre-Chi 13	Soriano-Was 46	Pujols-StL 359	Berkman-Hou 136
Reyes-NY 122	Atkins-Col 198	Rolen-StL 48	Lofton-LA 12	Berkman-Hou 45	Holliday-Col 353	Jones-Atl 129
		Atkins-Col 48	Finley-SF 12		Utley-Phi 347	Atkins-Col 120

BASES ON BALLS	STOLEN BASES	BASE STEALING RUNS	FIELDING RUNS-INFIELD	FIELDING RUNS-OUTFIELD	OUTFIELD ASSISTS	CATCHER CS PCT.
Bonds-SF 115	Reyes-NY 64	Roberts-SD 8.7	Carroll-Col 40.6	Soriano-Was 16.2	Soriano-Was 22	Paulino-Pit 36.2
Dunn-Cin 112	Pierre-Chi 58	Reyes-NY 8.1	Everett-Hou 27.8	Kearns-Cin-Was .. 13.2	Hawpe-Col 16	Miller-Mil 32.1
Johnson-Was 110	Ramirez-Fla 51	Rollins-Phi 6.5	Furcal-LA 26.1	Winn-SF 11.2	Francoeur-Atl 13	Martin-LA 31.1
Howard-Phi 108	Roberts-SD 49	Ramirez-Fla 6.0	Rolen-StL 23.1	Beltran-NY 11.0	Beltran-NY 13	Estrada-Ari 29.0
Giles-SD 104	Lopez-Cin-Was 44	Pierre-Chi 5.8	Hudson-Ari 23.0	Victorino-Phi 9.4	Freel-Cin 12	Alfonzo-SF 25.7

WINS	WINNING PCT.	WINS ABOVE TEAM	GAMES STARTED	COMPLETE GAMES	FEWEST HITS/GAME	FEWEST BB/GAME
Zambrano-Chi 16	Zambrano-Chi .... .696	Zambrano-Chi 6.0	Smoltz-Atl 35	Harang-Cin 6	Young-SD 6.72	Lieber-Phi 1.29
Webb-Ari 16	Glavine-NY .... .682	Webb-Ari 4.9	Pettitte-Hou 35	Webb-Ari 5	Zambrano-Chi 6.81	Oswalt-Hou 1.55
Smoltz-Atl 16	Webb-Ari .... .667	Capps-Pit 4.2	Hudson-Atl 35	Carpenter-StL 5	Cain-SF 7.41	Maddux-Chi-LA 1.59
Penny-LA 16	Lowe-LA .... .667	Smoltz-Atl 4.2	Harang-Cin 35	Willis-Fla 4	Carpenter-StL 7.88	Bush-Mil 1.63
Lowe-LA 16		Villarreal-Atl 4.1	Arroyo-Cin 35		Olsen-Fla 7.97	Carpenter-StL 1.75
Harang-Cin 16						

STRIKEOUTS	STRIKEOUTS/GAME	GAMES	SAVES	BASE RUNNERS/9	ADJUSTED RELIEF RUNS	RELIEF RANKING
Harang-Cin 216	Peavy-SD 9.56	Torres-Pit 94	Hoffman-SD 46	Saito-LA 8.39	Saito-LA 21.0	Saito-LA 31.2
Peavy-SD 215	Hernandez-Ari-NY ... 9.09	Rauch-Was 85	Wagner-NY 40	Hoffman-SD 8.86	Wagner-NY 16.5	Gonzalez-Pit 29.4
Smoltz-Atl 211	Zambrano-Chi 8.83	Capps-Pit 85	Borowski-Fla 36	Clemens-Hou 9.69	Geary-Phi 16.2	Wagner-NY 27.2
Zambrano-Chi 210	Myers-Phi 8.59	Howry-Chi 84	Gordon-Phi 34	Sheets-Mil 10.02	Feliciano-NY 15.9	Hoffman-SD 25.0
Myers-Phi 189	Cain-SF 8.45	Stanton-Was-SF 82	Isringhausen-StL 33	Carpenter-StL 10.03	Wheeler-Hou 15.4	Feliciano-NY 21.3

INNINGS PITCHED	OPPONENTS' AVG.	OPPONENTS' OBP	EARNED RUN AVERAGE	ADJUSTED ERA	ADJUSTED STARTER RUNS	PITCHER WINS
Arroyo-Cin 240.2	Young-SD .... .206	Carpenter-StL .... .279	Oswalt-Hou 2.98	Oswalt-Hou 151	Oswalt-Hou 38.5	**Oswalt-Hou 3.8**
Webb-Ari 235.0	Zambrano-Chi .... .208	Young-SD .... .287	Carpenter-StL 3.09	Webb-Ari 151	Webb-Ari 38.0	**Webb-Ari 3.7**
Harang-Cin 234.1	Cain-SF .... .222	Webb-Ari .... .289	Webb-Ari 3.10	Arroyo-Cin 143	Arroyo-Cin 35.9	**Arroyo-Cin 3.5**
Smoltz-Atl 232.0	Carpenter-StL .... .235	Arroyo-Cin .... .296	Arroyo-Cin 3.29	Carpenter-StL 141	Carpenter-StL 31.9	**Zambrano-Chi 3.2**
Willis-Fla 223.1	Schmidt-SF .... .238	Smoltz-Atl .... .298	Zambrano-Chi 3.41	Zambrano-Chi 135	Smoltz-Atl 29.0	**Saito-LA 3.1**

It's In The Cards

Controversy continued to hound slugger Barry Bonds as two negative books were published about Bonds; one by San Francisco Chronicle reporters that detailed his alleged steroid and hGH usage. Reacting to the negative press, commissioner Bud Selig announced that former U.S. Senator George Mitchell would investigate past use of steroids in baseball. The owners and players union continued to cooperate by agreeing to ban amphetamines.

Bonds took it all in stride, however, resuming his chase of Hank Aaron's home run record. He passed Babe Ruth's 714 in late May, finishing with 26 homers and within 21 of Aaron. In September, San Diego's Trevor Hoffman became the all-time saves leader, passing Lee Smith's 478. A former NL closer whose career was marred by numerous drug suspensions, Steve Howe, died in April after using methamphetamine before his fatal car crash.

St. Louis basked in the limelight all year. Former Redbirds closer Bruce Sutter was inducted into the Hall of Fame in January, and new Busch Stadium opened in April. The Cards won the NL Central by a hair despite playing very poorly down the stretch. Finally, the underdog Redbirds won their first World Series since Sutter closed out their 1982 world championship.

New York won the NL East with a league-best 97 win as Atlanta missed out on the postseason for the first time since 1990. San Diego dueled LA in the West; both finished with 88 wins, but the Padres became division champs on their better head-to-head record.

Neither Division Series was competitive as the Mets swept the Dodgers and the Cardinals bested the Padres in four games. The NLCS was a different story, as St. Louis and New York seesawed back and forth for seven games. In the finale, Endy Chavez made a spectacular catch in the sixth inning, robbing Scott Rolen of what would have been a go-ahead home run, yet St. Louis won anyway when Yadier Molina belted a two-run bomb in the ninth. St. Louis took the World Series in five games, taking advantage of Detroit's very sloppy fielding to make their 83 wins the fewest in history for a world champion.

2006 AMERICAN LEAGUE

TEAM	W	L	T	PCT	GB	HW	HL	R	OR	PA	H	2B	3B	HR	BB	SO	HB	SH	AVG	OBP	SLG	OPS	AOPS	BR	ABR	PF	SB	CS	BSA	BSR
EAST																														
NY	97	65	0	.599	—	50	31	**930**	767	6455	**1608**	327	21	210	649	1053	72	34	.285	**.363**	.461	**824**	**112**	**117**	**118**	100	139	35	**80**	**18**
Tor	87	75	0	.537	10	50	31	809	754	6241	1591	348	27	199	514	906	63	16	.284	.348	.463	811	104	74	40	104	65	33	66	3
Bos	86	76	0	.531	11	48	33	820	825	6435	1510	327	16	192	**672**	1056	66	22	.269	.351	.435	786	100	37	19	102	51	23	69	3
Bal	70	92	0	.432	27	40	41	768	899	6238	1556	288	20	164	474	878	**73**	40	.277	.339	.424	763	99	-26	-1	97	121	32	79	15
TB	61	101	0	.377	36	41	40	689	856	6040	1395	267	33	190	441	1106	47	35	.255	.314	.420	734	89	-106	-98	99	134	52	72	11
CENTRAL																														
Min	96	66	0	.593	—	**54**	27	801	683	6228	**1608**	275	34	143	490	**872**	50	31	**.287**	.347	.425	772	99	-3	-2	100	101	42	71	8
Det	95	67	0	.586	1	46	35	822	**675**	6198	1548	294	40	203	430	1133	45	45	.274	.329	.449	778	101	-16	-1	98	60	40	60	-1
Chi	90	72	0	.556	6	49	32	868	794	6318	1586	291	20	**236**	502	1056	58	44	.280	.342	**.464**	806	104	55	35	102	93	48	66	4
Cle	78	84	0	.481	18	44	37	870	782	6302	1576	351	27	196	556	1204	54	30	.280	.349	.457	806	**112**	65	103	96	55	23	71	4
KC	62	100	0	.383	34	34	47	757	971	6227	1515	335	37	124	474	1040	64	**52**	.271	.332	.411	743	93	-65	-51	98	65	34	66	2
WEST																														
Oak	93	69	0	.574	—	49	32	771	727	6281	1429	266	22	175	650	976	50	25	.260	.340	.412	752	96	-38	-20	98	61	20	75	6
LA	89	73	0	.549	4	45	36	766	732	6221	1539	309	29	159	486	914	42	31	.274	.334	.425	759	99	-37	-9	96	**148**	57	72	13
Tex	80	82	0	.494	13	39	42	835	784	6272	1571	**357**	23	183	505	1061	40	18	.278	.338	.446	784	101	15	15	100	53	24	69	3
Sea	78	84	0	.481	15	44	37	756	792	6213	1540	266	**42**	172	404	974	63	38	.272	.325	.424	749	98	-72	-22	94	106	37	74	10
Total	1134	—	—	—	—	633	501	11262	—	87669	21572	4301	391	2546	7247	14229	787	461	.275	.339	.437	776	—	—	—	—	1252	500	71	100

TEAM	CG	SHO	GR	SV	IP	H	HR	BB	SO	BR/9	ERA	AERA	OAV	OOB	PR	APR	PF	OSB	OCS	FA	E	WPB	DP	FW	PW	BW	BSW	DIF
EAST																												
NY	5	8	**489**	43	1443.2	1463	170	496	1019	12.6	4.41	103	.262	.326	23	19	99	92	47	.983	104	63	145	-.4	1.8	**11.2**	**1.0**	2.4
Tor	6	6	482	42	1428.1	1447	185	504	1076	12.7	4.37	108	.262	.328	29	55	104	130	32	.984	99	68	157	-.0	5.2	3.8	-.4	-2.5
Bos	3	6	454	46	1441.1	1570	181	509	1070	13.4	4.83	97	.278	.343	-43	-25	102	108	23	**.989**	**66**	76	174	**2.4**	-2.4	1.8	-.4	3.6
Bal	5	9	472	35	1419.0	1579	216	613	1016	14.2	5.35	84	.284	.357	-125	-133	99	80	**50**	.983	102	74	156	-.3	-12.6	-.0	.7	1.2
TB	3	7	444	33	1420.1	1600	180	606	979	14.4	4.96	94	.286	.358	-63	-47	102	108	46	.981	116	78	156	-1.3	-4.4	-9.3	.4	-5.4
CENTRAL																												
Min	1	6	421	40	1439.1	1490	182	**356**	**1164**	**11.8**	3.95	115	.267	**.312**	97	97	100	54	31	.986	84	**44**	135	1.1	9.2	-.2	.0	4.9
Det	3	**16**	390	46	1448.0	1420	160	489	1003	12.2	**3.84**	**117**	.257	.321	**115**	**104**	98	**49**	35	.983	106	50	162	-.6	**9.8**	-.0	-.8	5.6
Chi	5	11	398	46	1449.0	1534	200	433	1012	12.6	4.61	101	.271	.326	-9	9	103	116	34	.985	90	64	145	.6	.9	3.3	-.3	4.5
Cle	**13**	13	377	24	1423.1	1583	166	429	948	13.0	4.41	98	.282	.335	23	-16	95	128	34	.981	118	53	165	-1.4	-1.5	9.7	-.3	-9.5
KC	3	5	473	35	1426.1	1648	213	637	904	14.8	5.65	83	.292	.367	-174	-150	103	58	30	.984	98	95	**189**	.0	-14.2	-4.8	-.5	.5
WEST																												
Oak	5	11	444	**54**	1451.2	1525	162	529	1003	13.1	4.21	108	.272	.338	56	52	99	88	41	.986	84	54	173	1.1	4.9	-1.9	-.1	8.0
LA	5	12	380	50	1452.2	**1410**	**158**	471	**1164**	12.0	4.04	110	**.254**	.316	84	67	98	77	40	.979	124	93	154	-1.9	6.3	-.9	.6	3.9
Tex	3	8	**489**	42	1431.1	1558	162	496	972	13.3	4.60	102	.278	.341	-6	12	103	67	40	.984	98	45	174	.0	1.1	1.4	-.4	-3.2
Sea	6	6	429	47	1446.2	1500	183	560	1067	13.1	4.60	96	.267	.337	-6	-33	97	72	38	.985	88	63	150	.8	-3.1	-2.1	.3	1.2
Total	66	124	6142	583	20121.0	—	—	—	—	13.1	4.56	—	.275	.339	—	—	—	—	—	.984	1377	920	2235	—	—	—	—	—

BATTER-FIELDER WINS	BATTING AVERAGE	ON-BASE PERCENTAGE	SLUGGING AVERAGE	ON-BASE PLUS SLUGGING	ADJUSTED OPS	ADJUSTED BATTER RUNS
Hafner-Cle 5.4	Mauer-Min .... .347	Ramirez-Bos .... .439	Hafner-Cle .... .659	Hafner-Cle 1097	Hafner-Cle 187	Hafner-Cle 64.2
Mauer-Min 5.0	Jeter-NY .... .343	Hafner-Cle .... .439	Ortiz-Bos .... .636	Ramirez-Bos 1058	Ramirez-Bos 168	Ortiz-Bos 55.9
Ortiz-Bos 4.5	Cano-NY .... .342	Mauer-Min .... .429	Dye-Chi .... .622	Ortiz-Bos 1049	Ortiz-Bos 163	Ramirez-Bos 50.4
Young-Tex 4.2	Tejada-Bal .... .330	Jeter-NY .... .417	Ramirez-Bos .... .619	Thome-Chi 1014	Thome-Chi 156	Thome-Chi 45.0
Tejada-Bal 4.1	Guerrero-LA .... .329	Thome-Chi .... .416	Thome-Chi .... .598	Dye-Chi 1006	Dye-Chi 152	Dye-Chi 40.8
RUNS	**HITS**	**DOUBLES**	**TRIPLES**	**HOME RUNS**	**TOTAL BASES**	**RUNS BATTED IN**
Sizemore-Cle 134	Suzuki-Sea 224	Sizemore-Cle 53	Crawford-TB 16	Ortiz-Bos 54	Ortiz-Bos 355	Ortiz-Bos 137
Jeter-NY 118	Young-Tex 217	Young-Tex 52	Sizemore-Cle 11	Dye-Chi 44	Sizemore-Cle 349	Morneau-Min 130
Ortiz-Bos 115	Tejada-Bal 214	Lowell-Bos 47	Suzuki-Sea 9	Thome-Chi 42	Guerrero-LA 335	Ibanez-Sea 123
Damon-NY 115	Jeter-NY 214	Overbay-Tor 46	Granderson-Det 9	Hafner-Cle 42	Dye-Chi 335	Rodriguez-NY 121
Rodriguez-NY 113	Guerrero-LA 200			Thomas-Oak 39		Dye-Chi 120
BASES ON BALLS	**STOLEN BASES**	**BASE STEALING RUNS**	**FIELDING RUNS-INFIELD**	**FIELDING RUNS-OUTFIELD**	**OUTFIELD ASSISTS**	**CATCHER CS PCT.**
Ortiz-Bos 119	Crawford-TB 58	Crawford-TB 9.6	Inge-Det 24.7	Markakis-Bal 8.3	Rivera-LA 13	Buck-KC 34.0
Giambi-NY 110	Figgins-LA 52	Suzuki-Sea 9.2	Young-Tex 22.7	DeJesus-KC 7.6	Monroe-Det 12	Johjima-Sea 33.7
Thome-Chi 107	Suzuki-Sea 45	Patterson-Bal 6.8	Crede-Chi 21.9	Patterson-Bal 7.4	Johnson-Tor 12	Napoli-LA 30.9
Ramirez-Bos 100	Patterson-Bal 45	Figgins-LA 5.8	Kinsler-Tex 21.7	Gathright-TB-KC 7.2	DeJesus-KC 12	Kendall-Oak 30.4
Hafner-Cle 100	Podsednik-Chi 40	Jeter-NY 5.7	Lowell-Bos 20.8	Crawford-TB 4.7	Cabrera-NY 12	Varitek-Bos 22.0
WINS	**WINNING PCT.**	**WINS ABOVE TEAM**	**GAMES STARTED**	**COMPLETE GAMES**	**FEWEST HITS/GAME**	**FEWEST BB/GAME**
Wang-NY 19	Halladay-Tor .... .762	Santana-Min 5.7	Zito-Oak 34	Sabathia-Cle 6	Santana-Min 7.16	Schilling-Bos 1.24
Santana-Min 19	Wang-NY .... .760	Wang-NY 5.5	Santana-Min 34	Halladay-Tor 4	Santana-LA 7.99	Halladay-Tor 1.39
Garland-Chi 18	Santana-Min .... .760	Halladay-Tor 5.5	Millwood-Tex 34	Westbrook-Cle 3	Mussina-NY 8.39	Mussina-NY 1.60
	Garland-Chi .... .720	Garland-Chi 5.1	Haren-Oak 34	Lackey-LA 3	Lackey-Ala 8.39	Silva-Min 1.60
		Weaver-LA 4.4	Bonderman-Det 34	Benson-Bal 3	Beckett-Bos 8.40	Garland-Chi 1.75
STRIKEOUTS	**STRIKEOUTS/GAME**	**GAMES**	**SAVES**	**BASE RUNNERS/9**	**ADJUSTED RELIEF RUNS**	**RELIEF RANKING**
Santana-Min 245	Santana-Min 9.44	Proctor-NY 83	Rodriguez-LA 47	Papelbon-Bos 7.11	Papelbon-Bos 27.6	Papelbon-Bos 47.1
Bonderman-Det 202	Bonderman-Det 8.50	Rincon-Min 75	Jenks-Chi 41	Nathan-Min 7.24	Ryan-Tor 26.1	Rivera-NY 46.1
Lackey-LA 190	Hernandez-Sea 8.29	Camp-TB 75	Ryan-Tor 38	Ryan-Tor 7.71	Zumaya-Det 23.8	Nathan-Min 43.1
Vazquez-Chi 184	Vazquez-Chi 8.17	Shields-LA 74	Street-Oak 37	Putz-Sea 8.50	Nathan-Min 23.1	Rodriguez-Ala 39.9
Schilling-Bos 183	Schilling-Bos 8.07		Jones-Det 37	Liriano-Min 9.07	Rivera-NY 23.0	Ryan-Tor 37.5
INNINGS PITCHED	**OPPONENTS' AVG.**	**OPPONENTS' OBP**	**EARNED RUN AVERAGE**	**ADJUSTED ERA**	**ADJUSTED STARTER RUNS**	**PITCHER WINS**
Santana-Min 233.2	Santana-Min .... .216	Santana-Min .... .258	Santana-Min 2.77	Santana-Min 165	Santana-Min 45.9	**Rivera-NY 4.6**
Haren-Oak 223.0	Santana-LA .... .241	Mussina-NY .... .279	Halladay-Tor 3.19	Halladay-Tor 148	Halladay-Tor 37.6	**Papelbon-Bos 4.6**
Zito-Oak 221.0	Mussina-NY .... .241	Halladay-Tor .... .283	Sabathia-Cle 3.22	Sabathia-Cle 134	Liriano-Min 32.5	**Santana-Min 4.6**
Halladay-Tor 220.0	Beckett-Bos .... .245	Sabathia-Cle .... .293	Mussina-NY 3.51	Mussina-NY 129	Weaver-LA 28.0	**Nathan-Min 4.2**
Wang-NY 218.0	Lackey-LA .... .245	Haren-Oak .... .301	Lackey-Ala 3.56	Lackey-Ala 125	Wang-NY 23.5	**Rodriguez-Ala 3.9**

HALL OF SHAME?

Hall of Fame voting produced an unexpected controversy in February the size of a Category 5 hurricane. A special election to bestow overdue honor on great Negro League and pre-Negro League ballplayers passed over in earlier elections elevated 12 players posthumously along with five pioneer/executives (including Effa Manley, the first woman elected to the Hall). Inexplicably, however, dignified baseball ambassador par excellence Buck O'Neil was passed over. O'Neil was a great first baseman and manager in the Negro Leagues as well as a pioneering scout and the first black coach in MLB. The tragedy was emphasized by O'Neil's subsequent death at age 94 in October.

March saw MLB's inaugural World Baseball Classic kick off with games in Japan, Puerto Rico, and the U.S. Many American superstars passed on the event and interest was tepid at best in the States as the U.S. was eliminated in the second round. Other countries took the new tournament more seriously, producing some riveting baseball before Japan beat Cuba for the WBC championship.

Popular Hall of Famer Kirby Puckett died of a stroke in early March, and Yankees pitcher Cory Lidle perished in October while piloting a private plane. Rod Dedeaux, legendary baseball coach at USC, died in December. Dedeaux led the Trojans to a record 11 NCAA titles while coaching 59 future big leaguers.

The surprising Tigers boasted the best record in the AL for most of the season before losing the Central crown to the Twins on the final day and limping into the postseason as the Wild Card. Frank Thomas capped a remarkable comeback by helping the Athletics claim the AL West. Oakland then won its first postseason series since 1990 by sweeping Minnesota in the Division Series. Detroit faced the mighty Yankees—AL East champs for the ninth straight year—as serious underdogs in the ALDS. But the Tigers upended New York in four games before sweeping Oakland in the ALCS. Now heavy favorites, things fell apart quickly for Detroit in the Fall Classic, with their one victory marred by controversy when Kenny Rogers was caught with a suspicious smudge on his pitching hand.

2005 NATIONAL LEAGUE

TEAM	W	L	T	PCT	GB	HW	HL	R	OR	PA	H	2B	3B	HR	BB	SO	HB	SH	AVG	OBP	SLG	OPS	AOPS	BR	ABR	PF	SB	CS	BSA	BSR
East																														
Atl	90	72	0	.556	—	**53**	28	769	674	6186	1453	308	37	184	534	1084	45	75	.265	.333	.435	768	104	42	35	101	92	32	74	9
Phi	88	74	0	.543	2	46	35	807	726	6345	1494	282	35	167	**639**	1083	56	62	.270	**.348**	.423	771	103	69	42	104	116	27	**81**	16
Fla	83	79	0	.512	7	45	36	717	732	6213	1499	306	32	128	512	918	67	82	**.272**	.339	.409	748	106	17	56	95	96	38	72	8
NY	83	79	0	.512	7	48	33	722	648	6146	1421	279	32	175	486	1075	48	69	.258	.322	.416	738	99	-24	-8	98	**153**	40	79	**20**
Was	81	81	0	.500	9	41	40	639	673	6142	1367	311	32	117	491	1090	**89**	**91**	.252	.322	.386	708	94	-69	-39	96	45	45	50	-6
Central																														
StL	100	62	0	.617	—	50	31	805	634	6246	1494	287	26	170	534	947	62	77	.270	.339	.423	762	102	37	21	102	83	36	70	6
Hou	89	73	1	.549	11	**53**	28	693	**609**	6139	1400	281	32	161	481	1037	72	82	.256	.322	.408	730	93	-34	-45	102	115	44	72	10
Mil	81	81	0	.500	19	46	35	726	697	6156	1413	327	19	175	531	1162	73	66	.259	.331	.423	754	101	20	16	101	79	34	70	5
Chi	79	83	0	.488	21	38	43	703	714	6159	**1506**	323	23	194	419	920	50	69	.270	.324	.440	764	101	25	1	103	65	39	63	1
Cin	73	89	1	.451	27	42	39	**820**	889	6320	1453	**335**	15	**222**	611	1303	62	43	.261	.339	**.446**	**785**	**109**	**84**	**80**	101	72	23	76	8
Pit	67	95	0	.414	33	34	47	680	769	6221	1445	292	38	139	471	1092	72	56	.259	.322	.400	722	93	-48	-49	100	73	30	71	6
West																														
SD	82	80	0	.506	—	46	35	684	726	6271	1416	269	**39**	130	600	977	49	72	.257	.333	.391	724	99	-31	2	96	99	44	69	6
Ari	77	85	0	.475	5	36	45	696	856	6327	1419	291	27	191	606	1094	55	71	.256	.332	.421	753	96	20	-17	105	67	26	72	6
SF	75	87	0	.463	7	37	44	649	745	6077	1427	299	26	128	431	**901**	49	**91**	.261	.319	.396	715	90	-65	-81	103	71	35	67	3
LA	71	91	0	.438	11	40	41	685	755	6131	1374	284	21	149	541	1094	67	57	.253	.326	.395	721	92	-43	-48	101	58	35	62	1
Col	67	95	0	.414	15	40	41	740	862	6237	1477	280	34	150	509	1103	64	88	.267	.333	.411	744	88	-1	-78	112	65	32	67	3
Total	1297	—	—	—	—	695	601	11535	—	99316	23058	4754	468	2580	8396	16880	980	1151	.262	.330	.414	744	—	—	—	—	1349	560	71	101

TEAM	CG	SHO	GR	SV	IP	H	HR	BB	SO	BR/9	ERA	AERA	OAV	OOB	PR	APR	PF	OSB	OCS	FA	E	WPB	DP	FW	PW	BW	BSW	DIF
East																												
Atl	8	12	484	38	1443.2	1487	145	520	929	12.7	3.98	106	.268	.333	38	37	100	89	36	**.986**	**86**	50	170	**.7**	3.7	3.5	.3	.8
Phi	4	6	442	40	1435.0	1379	189	487	1159	12.2	4.21	103	.253	.320	1	18	103	82	26	.985	90	48	132	.5	1.8	4.2	1.0	-.5
Fla	14	**15**	449	42	1442.1	1459	**116**	563	1125	13.0	4.16	96	.266	.339	10	-27	95	118	38	.983	103	54	177	-.0	-2.7	5.6	.2	-1.0
NY	8	11	392	38	1435.2	1390	135	491	1012	12.1	3.76	110	.255	.321	74	60	98	107	25	.983	106	**37**	146	-.2	6.0	-.8	**1.4**	-4.4
Was	4	9	470	**51**	1458.0	1456	140	539	997	12.8	3.87	106	.262	.333	57	38	97	76	41	.985	92	56	156	.4	3.8	-3.9	-1.2	.9
Central																												
StL	**15**	14	436	48	1445.2	1399	153	443	974	11.8	**3.49**	**120**	.257	.318	**118**	**113**	99	**32**	33	.984	100	53	**196**	.0	**11.3**	2.1	-.0	5.6
Hou	6	11	434	45	1443.0	**1336**	155	**440**	1164	**11.4**	3.51	**120**	**.246**	**.308**	113	112	100	53	31	.985	89	44	146	.6	11.2	-4.5	.4	.3
Mil	7	6	395	46	1438.0	1382	169	569	1173	12.5	3.97	107	.251	.324	39	42	101	86	34	.980	119	74	139	-.8	4.2	1.6	-.1	-4.9
Chi	8	10	457	39	1440.0	1357	186	576	**1256**	12.4	4.19	104	.250	.325	4	26	103	90	40	.983	101	63	136	.0	2.6	.0	-.5	-4.2
Cin	2	1	491	31	1433.0	1657	219	492	955	14.0	5.15	83	.290	.352	-148	-142	101	76	35	.983	104	62	133	-.0	-14.2	**8.0**	.2	-1.9
Pit	4	14	451	35	1436.0	1456	162	612	958	13.4	4.42	96	.267	.344	-33	-31	100	64	36	.981	117	69	193	-.7	-3.1	-4.9	-.0	-5.3
West																												
SD	4	8	456	45	1455.1	1452	146	503	1133	12.4	4.13	95	.259	.322	14	-38	93	94	25	.982	109	48	136	-.3	-3.8	.2	-.0	5.0
Ari	6	10	458	45	1456.1	1580	193	537	1038	13.5	4.84	91	.278	.345	-100	-65	105	78	28	.985	94	69	159	.3	-6.5	-1.7	-.0	3.9
SF	4	8	**511**	46	1444.1	1456	151	592	972	13.0	4.33	98	.263	.336	-18	-16	100	78	**54**	.985	90	43	146	.5	-1.6	-8.1	-.3	3.5
LA	6	9	458	40	1427.1	1434	182	471	1004	12.4	4.38	95	.263	.327	-26	-39	98	130	34	.983	106	45	141	-.2	-3.9	-4.8	-.5	-.6
Col	4	4	459	37	1418.2	1600	175	604	981	14.5	5.13	91	.287	.362	-143	-68	110	102	37	.981	118	79	158	-.7	-6.8	-7.8	-.3	1.7
Total	104	148	7243	666	23052.1	—	—	—	—	12.8	4.22	—	.262	.330	—	—	—	—	—	.983	1624	894	2464	—	—	—	—	—

BATTER-FIELDER WINS	BATTING AVERAGE	ON-BASE PERCENTAGE	SLUGGING AVERAGE	ON-BASE PLUS SLUGGING	ADJUSTED OPS	ADJUSTED BATTER RUNS
Lee-Chi................6.3	Lee-Chi.................335	Helton-Col............445	Lee-Chi.................662	Lee-Chi...............1080	Lee-Chi.................173	Lee-Chi................65.3
Furcal-Atl............5.0	Pujols-StL.............330	Pujols-StL.............430	Pujols-StL.............609	Pujols-StL...........1039	Pujols-StL.............166	Pujols-StL............60.6
Pujols-StL...........4.6	Cabrera-Fla...........323	Giles-SD...............423	Delgado-Fla..........582	Delgado-Fla..........981	Delgado-Fla..........162	Delgado-Fla.........49.9
Eckstein-StL......4.2	Helton-Col.............320	Lee-Chi.................418	Griffey-Cin............576	Helton-Col.............979	Cabrera-Fla...........153	Cabrera-Fla..........47.0
Bay-Pit................4.2	Casey-Cin.............312	Berkman-Hou.......411	A.Jones-Atl...........575	Bay-Pit...................961	Bay-Pit...................149	Bay-Pit..................46.3

RUNS	HITS	DOUBLES	TRIPLES	HOME RUNS	TOTAL BASES	RUNS BATTED IN
Pujols-StL............129	Lee-Chi.................199	Lee-Chi....................50	Reyes-NY..................17	A.Jones-Atl.............51	Lee-Chi.................393	A.Jones-Atl...........128
Lee-Chi.................120	Cabrera-Fla...........198	Helton-Col...............45	Pierre-Fla.................13	Lee-Chi....................46	Pujols-StL.............360	Pujols-StL............117
Rollins-Phi............115	Rollins-Phi.............196	Giles-Atl...................45	Rollins-Phi................11	Pujols-StL................41	Cabrera-Fla...........344	Burrell-Phi.............117
Bay-Pit...................110	Pujols-StL.............195	Bay-Pit.....................44	Furcal-Atl..................11	Dunn-Cin..................40	A.Jones-Atl...........337	Cabrera-Fla...........116
Dunn-Cin..............107	Reyes-NY.............190		Roberts-SD..............10	Glaus-Ari..................37	Bay-Pit...................335	Delgado-Fla..........115

BASES ON BALLS	STOLEN BASES	BASE STEALING RUNS	FIELDING RUNS-INFIELD	FIELDING RUNS-OUTFIELD	OUTFIELD ASSISTS	CATCHER CS PCT.
Giles-SD...............119	Reyes-NY................60	Reyes-NY.............7.9	Eckstein-StL........33.0	Jenkins-Mil...........11.2	Floyd-NY..................15	Schneider-Was....40.0
Abreu-Phi..............117	Pierre-Fla.................57	Rollins-Phi............6.9	Furcal-Atl.............31.3	Clark-Mil................10.9	Francoeur-Atl...........13	Matheny-SF.........38.2
Dunn-Cin..............114	Furcal-Atl.................46	Furcal-Atl..............6.6	J.Wilson-Pit.........26.6	Floyd-NY..................8.4	Cabrera-Fla..............12	Miller-Mil..............31.6
Helton-Col.............106	Rollins-Phi...............41	Pierre-Fla..............6.6	Perez-Chi.............25.0	Guillen-Was............6.5	A.Jones-Atl..............11	Castro-NY............31.4
Burrell-Phi...............99	Freel-Cin...................36	Freel-Cin................4.4	Counsell-Ari..........21.6	Ellison-SF................5.0		Estrada-Atl...........31.0

WINS	WINNING PCT.	WINS ABOVE TEAM	GAMES STARTED	COMPLETE GAMES	FEWEST HITS/GAME	FEWEST BB/GAME
Willis-Fla..................22	Carpenter-StL.......808	Carpenter-StL.......7.0	7 players tied..........35	Willis-Fla....................7	Clemens-Hou.......6.43	Maddux-Chi.........1.44
Carpenter-StL.........21	Willis-Fla...............688	Willis-Fla................6.6	35	Carpenter-StL...........7	Martinez-NY........6.59	Pettitte-Hou..........1.66
Oswalt-Hou.............20	Mulder-StL............667	Sosa-Atl..................4.8	35	Oswalt-Hou................4	Zambrano-Chi.......6.85	Lieber-Phi.............1.69
Capuano-Mil...........18	Pettitte-Hou...........654	Zambrano-Chi........4.5	35	Martinez-NY...............4	Peavy-SD..............7.18	Weaver-LA............1.73
			35	Burnett-Fla................4	Carpenter-StL......7.60	Morris-StL.............1.73

STRIKEOUTS	STRIKEOUTS/GAME	GAMES	SAVES	BASE RUNNERS/9	ADJUSTED RELIEF RUNS	RELIEF RANKING
Peavy-SD...............216	Prior-Chi.............10.15	Eyre-SF....................86	C.Cordero-Was.......47	Wagner-Phi.........7.88	Wagner-Phi..........22.5	Wagner-Phi..........37.4
Carpenter-StL........213	Peavy-SD...............9.58	Sanchez-LA.............79	Hoffman-SD.............43	Martinez-NY.........8.71	Carrasco-Was.......20.2	Turnbow-Mil..........36.7
Myers-Phi...............208	Myers-Phi...............8.69	Majewski-Was.........79	Lidge-Hou................42	C.Cordero-Was.....8.96	Turnbow-Mil..........18.4	Lidge-Hou.............28.9
Martinez-NY...........208	Schmidt-SF.............8.63		Jones-Fla.................40	A.Reyes-StL.........9.05	Linebrink-SD.........18.1	C.Cordero-Was....28.6
D.Davis-Mil.............208	Martinez-NY...........8.63			Wise-Mil...............9.09	Wheeler-Hou.........17.1	Jones-Fla..............27.3

INNINGS PITCHED	OPPONENTS' AVG.	OPPONENTS' OBP	EARNED RUN AVERAGE	ADJUSTED ERA	ADJUSTED STARTER RUNS	PITCHER WINS
Hernandez-Was.246.1	Clemens-Hou........198	Martinez-NY.........252	Clemens-Hou.......1.87	Clemens-Hou........225	Clemens-Hou.......53.6	**Willis-Fla.............5.8**
Oswalt-Hou........241.2	Martinez-NY.........204	Clemens-Hou........261	Pettitte-Hou..........2.39	Pettitte-Hou...........177	Pettitte-Hou..........44.3	**Clemens-Hou.....5.7**
Carpenter-StL....241.2	Zambrano-Chi.......212	Pettitte-Hou...........268	Willis-Fla..............2.63	Willis-Fla...............152	Carpenter-StL.......38.8	**Pettitte-Hou........4.8**
Willis-Fla...........236.1	Peavy-SD..............217	Peavy-SD..............271	Martinez-NY.........2.82	Carpenter-StL.......148	Willis-Fla..............36.4	**Oswalt-Hou.........4.4**
Smoltz-Atl..........229.2	Prior-Chi...............227	Carpenter-StL.......273	Carpenter-StL......2.83	Martinez-NY.........147	Oswalt-Hou..........34.5	**Wagner-Phi.........3.8**

Astros Blast Off in Second Half, Then Flame Out in World Series

The Washington Nationals began play after MLB finally moved the orphaned franchise from Montreal. The former Expos were glad to have a permanent home after many years of rumor and uncertainty and after two years of splitting home games between Canada and Puerto Rico. The good feelings in the nation's capital lasted all summer as the reborn Nats stayed in contention most of the season despite having one of the worst offenses in the league. The Cardinals closed out their 40-year history in Busch Stadium with a championship series loss to the Astros. The Gateway City's new park, also to be called Busch Stadium, opens in April 2006.

Seemingly ageless at 43, Roger Clemens continued to amaze and delight baseball fans with incredible performances on the mound. Clemens posted a league-best 1.87 ERA (more than half a run better than anybody else in baseball) and helped Houston rebound from a 21-35 start all the way to their first-ever World Series. Houston's strong rotation, which included Andy Pettitte and Roy Oswalt, helped make the Astros the hottest team in the league in the second half. While they couldn't catch the Cardinals in the NL Central, they claimed the NL Wild Card and then beat NL East winner Atlanta in the NLDS. The Astros clinched their first-ever postseason series win with Chris Burke's home run in the bottom of the 18th inning of the fourth game. Clemens, who threw the last three innings in relief when the Astros ran out of pitchers, wound up the winning pitcher in the longest postseason game (in both innings and time) in baseball history. St. Louis swept San Diego, winner of the NL West but barely above .500 at 82-80, in the other Division Series, but Houston prevailed in the LCS in six games. NLCS MVP Oswalt allowed only two runs in 14 innings, winning both of his starts. The magic ended in the World Series, however, as the Astros were swept by the even hotter White Sox.

Pete Rose remained on the suspended list for betting on baseball and, as a result, wasn't on the Hall of Fame ballot released in November, thus ending his chances of being elected to the Hall by the baseball writers.

2005 AMERICAN LEAGUE

TEAM	W	L	T	PCT	GB	HW	HL	R	OR	PA	H	2B	3B	HR	BB	SO	HB	SH	AVG	OBP	SLG	OPS	AOPS	BR	ABR	PF	SB	CS	BSA	BSR
EAST																														
NY	95	67	0	.586	—	53	28	886	789	6405	1552	259	16	229	637	989	73	28	.276	.355	.450	805	**114**	117	**123**	99	84	27	76	9
Bos	95	67	0	.586	—	**54**	27	**910**	805	6403	**1579**	**339**	21	199	**653**	1044	47	14	**.281**	**.357**	.454	**811**	109	**139**	101	104	45	12	79	6
Tor	80	82	0	.494	15	43	38	775	705	6233	1480	307	39	136	486	955	**89**	21	.265	.331	.407	738	90	-25	-61	105	72	35	67	4
Bal	74	88	0	.457	21	36	45	729	800	6134	1492	296	27	189	447	902	54	40	.269	.327	.434	761	101	7	9	100	83	37	69	5
TB	67	95	0	.414	28	40	41	750	936	6118	1519	289	40	157	412	990	69	34	.274	.329	.425	754	101	-5	9	98	151	49	76	**16**
CENTRAL																														
Chi	99	63	0	.611	—	47	34	741	645	6145	1450	253	23	200	435	1002	79	**53**	.262	.322	.425	747	93	-23	-50	104	137	67	67	7
Cle	93	69	0	.574	6	43	38	790	**642**	6255	1522	337	30	207	503	1093	54	39	.271	.334	.453	787	111	65	95	97	62	36	63	1
Min	83	79	0	.512	16	45	36	688	662	6192	1441	269	32	134	485	978	59	42	.259	.323	.391	714	88	-80	-92	102	102	44	70	7
Det	71	91	0	.438	28	39	42	723	787	6135	1521	283	**45**	168	384	1038	53	44	.272	.321	.428	749	99	-22	-8	98	66	28	70	5
KC	56	106	0	.346	43	34	47	701	935	6086	1445	289	34	126	424	1008	63	46	.263	.320	.396	716	92	-77	-54	97	53	33	62	0
WEST																														
LA	95	67	0	.586	—	49	32	761	643	6182	1520	278	30	147	447	848	29	43	.270	.325	.409	734	97	-46	-26	97	**161**	57	74	15
Oak	88	74	0	.543	7	45	36	772	658	6275	1476	310	20	155	537	**819**	52	19	.262	.330	.407	737	96	-28	-22	99	31	22	58	-1
Tex	79	83	0	.488	16	44	37	865	858	6300	1528	311	29	**260**	495	1112	48	9	.267	.329	**.468**	797	106	73	51	103	67	15	**82**	9
Sea	69	93	0	.426	26	39	42	699	751	6095	1408	289	34	130	466	986	48	37	.256	.317	.391	708	94	-94	-43	93	102	47	68	6
Total	1134	—	—	—	—	611	523	10790	—	86958	20933	4109	420	2437	6811	13764	817	469	.268	.330	.424	755	—	—	—	—	1216	509	70	89

TEAM	CG	SHO	GR	SV	IP	H	HR	BB	SO	BR/9	ERA	AERA	OAV	OOB	PR	APR	PF	OSB	OCS	FA	E	WPB	DP	FW	PW	BW	BSW	DIF
EAST																												
NY	8	**14**	418	46	1430.2	1495	164	463	985	12.8	4.52	95	.269	.332	-26	-37	99	125	**50**	.984	95	48	151	.5	-3.6	**11.9**	.3	4.9
Bos	6	8	442	38	1429.0	1550	164	440	959	13.1	4.74	96	.276	.335	-61	-32	104	87	29	.982	109	69	135	-.4	-3.1	9.8	-.0	7.8
Tor	**9**	8	432	35	1447.0	1475	185	444	958	12.4	4.06	113	.264	.324	46	79	105	100	35	.985	95	45	154	.5	7.6	-5.9	-.2	-3.0
Bal	2	9	**474**	38	1427.2	1458	180	580	1052	13.2	4.56	96	.263	.336	-34	-27	101	115	34	.982	107	83	154	-.3	-2.6	.9	-.1	-4.8
TB	1	4	401	43	1421.2	1570	194	615	949	14.2	5.39	81	.280	.355	-164	-156	101	68	45	.979	124	66	139	-1.5	-15.1	.9	**.9**	.8
CENTRAL																												
Chi	**9**	10	412	**54**	1475.2	1392	167	459	1040	11.6	**3.61**	**125**	.249	.310	**121**	**142**	104	103	25	.985	94	74	166	.6	**13.7**	-4.8	.0	8.4
Cle	6	10	409	51	1452.2	1363	157	413	1050	**11.3**	**3.61**	115	.247	**.302**	120	92	95	103	33	.983	106	**32**	156	-.2	8.9	9.2	-.5	-5.3
Min	**9**	8	396	44	1464.1	1458	169	**348**	965	11.4	3.71	118	.261	.307	104	107	101	**44**	36	.984	102	44	**171**	.0	10.3	-8.9	.0	.5
Det	7	2	425	37	1435.2	1504	193	461	907	12.6	4.51	95	.272	.330	-25	-39	98	60	49	.982	110	57	**171**	-.5	-3.8	-.8	-.1	-4.8
KC	4	4	443	25	1413.1	1640	178	580	924	14.6	5.49	80	.291	.362	-179	-175	100	70	44	.979	125	74	163	-1.6	-16.9	-5.2	-.6	-.7
WEST																												
LA	7	11	378	**54**	1464.1	1419	158	443	**1126**	11.7	3.68	116	.254	.312	110	98	98	68	42	**.986**	87	83	139	1.1	9.5	-2.5	.8	5.1
Oak	**9**	12	410	38	1450.1	**1315**	**154**	504	1075	11.7	3.69	119	**.241**	.311	107	109	100	109	25	**.986**	88	46	166	1.0	10.5	-2.1	-.7	-1.7
Tex	2	6	454	46	1440.0	1589	159	522	932	13.6	4.96	92	.279	.343	-98	-64	104	69	26	.982	108	55	149	-.4	-6.2	4.9	.3	-.6
Sea	6	7	433	39	1427.2	1483	179	496	892	12.8	4.49	93	.268	.332	-22	-54	96	89	43	**.986**	**86**	50	144	**1.2**	-5.2	-4.2	-.0	-3.7
Total	85	113	5927	588	20180.0	—	—	—	—	12.6	4.35	—	.268	.330	—	—	—	—	—	.983	1436	826	2158	—	—	—	—	—

BATTER-FIELDER WINS	BATTING AVERAGE	ON-BASE PERCENTAGE	SLUGGING AVERAGE	ON-BASE PLUS SLUGGING	ADJUSTED OPS	ADJUSTED BATTER RUNS
A.Rodriguez-NY 6.0	M.Young-Tex .331	Giambi-NY .440	A.Rodriguez-NY .610	A.Rodriguez-NY 1031	A.Rodriguez-NY 171	A.Rodriguez-NY 65.5
Tejada-Bal 4.9	A.Rodriguez-NY .321	A.Rodriguez-NY .421	Ortiz-Bos .604	Hafner-Cle 1003	Hafner-Cle 169	Hafner-Cle 52.3
Roberts-Bal 4.9	Guerrero-LA .317	Hafner-Cle .408	Hafner-Cle .595	Ortiz-Bos 1001	Giambi-NY 159	Ortiz-Bos 51.1
Jeter-NY 4.5	Damon-Bos .316	Ortiz-Bos .397	M.Ramirez-Bos .594	M.Ramirez-Bos 982	Guerrero-LA 156	Giambi-NY 43.4
Hafner-Cle 4.4	Roberts-Bal .314	Guerrero-LA .394	Teixeira-Tex .575	Giambi-NY 975	Ortiz-Bos 156	Guerrero-Ala 43.3

RUNS	HITS	DOUBLES	TRIPLES	HOME RUNS	TOTAL BASES	RUNS BATTED IN
A.Rodriguez-NY 124	M.Young-Tex 221	Tejada-Bal 50	Crawford-TB 15	A.Rodriguez-NY 48	Teixeira-Tex 370	Ortiz-Bos 148
Jeter-NY 122	Suzuki-Sea 206	Roberts-Bal 45	Suzuki-Sea 12	Ortiz-Bos 47	A.Rodriguez-NY 369	Teixeira-Tex 144
Ortiz-Bos 119	Jeter-NY 202	Matsui-NY 45	Sizemore-Cle 11	M.Ramirez-Bos 45	Ortiz-Bos 363	M.Ramirez-Bos 144
Damon-Bos 117	Tejada-Bal 199	Soriano-Tex 43	Figgins-LA 10	Teixeira-Tex 43	M.Young-Tex 343	A.Rodriguez-NY 130
M.Young-Tex 114	Damon-Bos 197		Inge-Det 9	Konerko-Chi 40	Tejada-Bal 337	Sheffield-NY 123

BASES ON BALLS	STOLEN BASES	BASE STEALING RUNS	FIELDING RUNS-INFIELD	FIELDING RUNS-OUTFIELD	OUTFIELD ASSISTS	CATCHER CS PCT.
Giambi-NY 108	Figgins-LA 62	Figgins-Ala 7.7	Hudson-Tor 28.3	Suzuki-Sea 12.8	M.Ramirez-Bos 17	Rodriguez-Det 51.5
Ortiz-Bos 102	Podsednik-Chi 59	Crawford-TB 7.3	Inge-Det 23.7	Crawford-TB 8.7	Wells-Tor 12	Buck-KC 34.1
A.Rodriguez-NY 91	Crawford-TB 46	Soriano-Tex 5.9	Tejada-Bal 14.2	Hollins-TB 8.4	Long-KC 12	Posada-NY 30.2
Sexson-Sea 89	Lugo-TB 39	Podsednik-Chi 4.9	Infante-Det 12.0	Reed-Sea 7.9		Varitek-Bos 24.4
Konerko-Chi 81	Suzuki-Sea 33	Lugo-TB 4.7	Millar-Bos 10.1	Nixon-Bos 7.6		Martinez-Cle 23.2

WINS	WINNING PCT.	WINS ABOVE TEAM	GAMES STARTED	COMPLETE GAMES	FEWEST HITS/GAME	FEWEST BB/GAME
Colon-LA 21	Lee-Cle .783	Lee-Cle 6.1	Zito-Oak 35	Halladay-Tor 5	Santana-Min 6.99	Silva-Min .43
Lee-Cle 18	Colon-LA .724	Colon-Ala 5.5	R.Lopez-Bal 35	R.Johnson-NY 4	Zito-Oak 7.29	Wells-Bos 1.03
Garland-Chi 18	Santana-Min .696	Small-NY 5.0		Bonderman-Det 4	Contreras-Chi 7.78	Radke-Min 1.03
R.Johnson-NY 17	Wells-Bos .682	Santana-Min 4.7			Blanton-Oak 7.96	Byrd-LA 1.23
	Contreras-Chi .682	Halladay-Tor 4.3			R.Johnson-NY 8.26	Towers-Tor 1.25

STRIKEOUTS	STRIKEOUTS/GAME	GAMES	SAVES	BASE RUNNERS/9	ADJUSTED RELIEF RUNS	RELIEF RANKING
Santana-Min 238	Santana-Min 9.25	Timlin-Bos 81	Wickman-Cle 45	Howry-Cle 8.01	Rivera-NY 23.5	Rivera-NY 47.1
R.Johnson-NY 211	Lackey-LA 8.57	Schoeneweis-Tor 80	Rodriguez-Ala 45	Rivera-NY 8.27	Street-Oak 22.8	Shields-Ala 29.0
Lackey-LA 199	Kazmir-TB 8.42	Howry-Cle 79	Rivera-NY 43	Nathan-Min 8.74	Duchscherer-Oak 19.8	Hermanson-Chi 27.7
Kazmir-TB 174	R.Johnson-NY 8.42	Gordon-NY 79	Nathan-Min 43	Santana-Min 8.78	Timlin-Bos 19.0	Street-Oak 27.5
Zito-Oak 171	C.Young-Tex 7.49	Shields-LA 78	Baez-TB 41	Politte-Chi 8.82	Politte-Chi 18.7	Crain-Min 27.0

INNINGS PITCHED	OPPONENTS' AVG.	OPPONENTS' OBP	EARNED RUN AVERAGE	ADJUSTED ERA	ADJUSTED STARTER RUNS	PITCHER WINS
Buehrle-Chi 236.2	Santana-Min .210	Santana-Min .250	Millwood-Cle 2.86	Santana-Min 152	Santana-Min 40.4	**Rivera-NY 4.9**
Santana-Min 231.2	Zito-Oak .221	R.Johnson-NY .291	Santana-Min 2.87	Millwood-Cle 146	Halladay-Tor 33.5	**Santana-Min 3.7**
Zito-Oak 228.1	Contreras-Chi .232	Colon-LA .291	Buehrle-Chi 3.12	Buehrle-Chi 145	Buehrle-Chi 31.3	**Halladay-Tor 3.7**
Garcia-Chi 228.0	Blanton-Oak .236	Buehrle-Chi .295	Washburn-LA 3.20	Washburn-Ala 134	Millwood-Cle 26.9	**Buehrle-Chi 3.0**
R.Johnson-NY 225.2	R.Johnson-NY .243	Radke-Min .295	Silva-Min 3.44	Rogers-Tex 132	Harden-Oak 25.2	**Shields-LA 2.9**

BY ANY OTHER NAME

Prior to the season, the Angels announced that they would henceforth be known as the Los Angeles Angels of Anaheim in an effort to market the franchise better in Los Angeles. That decision brought a lawsuit by the Anaheim city government, claiming the club's lease called for them to be known as the Anaheim Angels. It also brought a scornful response from SoCal's other ballclub, who sold merchandise saying they were the "Los Angeles Dodgers of Los Angeles." Manny Ramirez, one of the heroes of Boston's 2004 World Series championship squad, alternated saying he wanted a trade and then saying he was happy playing for the Red Sox. This led one teammate to opine that it was just "Manny being Manny."

Cleveland, operating on a thrifty budget of $41 million, rallied from 15 games back in the AL Central in the last two months to come within 1 1/2 games of the Central Division-leading White Sox, but the surprising Sox trounced the Indians in the last week of the season to sew up their postseason berth. At the other hand of the financial spectrum, a record $208 million payroll barely got the Yankees into October, as the Bronx Bombers spent much of the first half in third place before rallying past the Orioles and Red Sox to win their eighth straight AL East title. New York was then eliminated in five games by the Angels, who had beaten the pesky Athletics in the AL West in one ALDS. Chicago swept the Wild Card winner Boston in the other.

After losing the first game of what turned out to be an extremely controversial ALCS, Chicago rallied in the ninth inning to win the second game with the help of a disputed dropped third strike. The stunned Angels never recovered, losing the next three games. Chicago's starting pitching ultimately was the difference in the series, as the Sox hurlers threw four consecutive complete games, a first in LCS play. Chicago then claimed its first World Championship since 1917 with a four-game sweep of Houston. The Sox lost only one game in three postseason series, equaling the best postseason mark since the Wild Card and Division Series format was instituted in 1995.

2004 NATIONAL LEAGUE

TEAM	W	L	T	PCT	GB	HW	HL	R	OR	PA	H	2B	3B	HR	BB	SO	HB	SH	AVG	OBP	SLG	OPS	AOPS	BR	ABR	PF	SB	CS	BSA	BSR
EAST																														
Atl	96	66	0	.593	—	49	32	803	668	6339	1503	304	37	178	587	1158	59	75	.270	.343	.434	777	104	49	43	101	86	32	73	8
Phi	86	76	0	.531	10	42	39	840	781	6456	1505	303	23	215	645	1133	58	64	.267	.345	.443	788	105	75	49	103	100	27	79	13
Fla	83	79	0	.512	13	42	38	718	700	6160	1447	275	32	148	499	968	58	77	.264	.329	.406	735	99	-40	-4	95	96	43	69	6
NY	71	91	0	.438	25	38	43	684	731	6208	1376	289	20	185	512	1159	61	69	.249	.317	.409	726	93	-69	-53	98	107	23	**82**	15
Mon	67	95	0	.414	29	35	45	635	769	6138	1361	276	27	151	496	925	35	**100**	.249	.313	.392	705	83	-110	-135	104	109	38	74	11
CENTRAL																														
StL	105	57	0	.648	—	**53**	28	**855**	**659**	6297	**1544**	319	24	214	548	1085	51	73	**.278**	.344	**.460**	**804**	**110**	101	**91**	101	111	47	70	8
Hou	92	70	0	.568	13	48	33	803	698	6269	1458	294	36	187	590	999	61	98	.267	.342	.436	778	102	50	24	103	89	30	75	9
Chi	89	73	0	.549	16	45	37	789	665	6281	1508	308	29	**235**	489	1080	38	78	.268	.328	.458	786	103	47	23	103	66	28	70	5
Cin	76	86	0	.469	29	40	41	750	907	6278	1380	287	28	194	599	1335	81	55	.250	.331	.418	749	100	-15	1	98	77	25	75	8
Pit	72	89	0	.447	32.5	39	41	680	744	6114	1428	267	**39**	142	415	1066	**95**	79	.260	.321	.401	722	91	-74	-74	100	63	40	61	0
Mil	67	94	0	.416	37.5	36	45	634	757	6187	1358	295	32	135	540	1312	68	56	.248	.321	.387	708	86	-94	-100	101	**138**	40	78	**16**
WEST																														
LA	93	69	0	.574	—	49	32	761	684	6244	1450	226	30	203	536	1092	62	69	.262	.332	.423	755	100	-9	1	99	102	41	71	8
SF	91	71	0	.562	2	47	35	850	770	6466	1500	314	33	183	**705**	**874**	72	92	.270	**.357**	.438	795	106	**103**	73	104	43	23	65	1
SD	87	75	0	.537	6	42	39	768	705	6313	1521	304	32	139	566	910	56	52	.273	.342	.414	756	105	15	55	95	52	25	68	3
Col	68	94	0	.420	25	38	43	833	923	6333	1531	**331**	34	202	568	1181	54	97	.275	.345	.455	800	98	91	-4	113	44	33	57	-2
Ari	51	111	0	.315	42	29	52	615	899	6113	1401	295	38	135	441	1022	35	56	.253	.310	.393	703	80	-120	-159	107	53	32	62	0
Total	1295	—	—	—	—	672	623	12018	—	100196	23271	4687	494	2846	8736	17299	944	1190	.263	.333	.423	756	—	—	—	—	1336	527	72	109

TEAM	CG	SHO	GR	SV	IP	H	HR	BB	SO	BR/9	ERA	AERA	OAV	OOB	PR	APR	PF	OSB	OCS	FA	E	WPB	DP	FW	PW	BW	BSW	DIF
EAST																												
Atl	4	13	483	48	1450.0	1475	154	523	1025	12.6	**3.74**	115	.265	.329	**90**	90	100	91	29	.981	116	46	171	-.7	8.8	4.2	.1	2.5
Phi	4	5	476	43	1462.2	1488	214	502	1070	12.7	4.45	99	.264	.330	-25	-6	103	103	26	.987	81	47	142	1.3	-.6	4.8	.6	-1.1
Fla	6	**14**	404	53	1439.0	1395	166	513	1116	12.3	4.10	100	.256	.324	33	1	95	118	38	.986	86	46	153	1.0	.0	-.4	-.0	1.4
NY	2	6	474	31	1449.0	1452	156	592	977	13.0	4.09	105	.261	.335	35	32	100	100	39	.978	137	42	144	-1.9	3.1	-5.2	.8	-6.8
Mon	**11**	11	462	31	1447.0	1477	191	582	1032	13.3	4.33	106	.266	.342	-4	38	107	58	41	.984	99	50	172	.3	3.7	-13.2	.4	-5.1
CENTRAL																												
StL	4	12	469	**57**	1453.2	1378	169	440	1041	**11.7**	3.75	114	.251	**.313**	**90**	83	99	**53**	29	.985	97	51	154	.4	8.1	**8.9**	.1	6.4
Hou	2	13	493	47	1443.0	1416	174	525	1282	12.5	4.05	108	.258	.328	40	49	101	101	39	.983	101	49	136	.1	4.8	2.4	.2	3.5
Chi	3	6	460	42	1465.1	**1363**	169	545	**1346**	12.2	3.81	**116**	**.247**	.321	80	**97**	103	108	39	.986	86	59	126	1.0	**9.5**	2.3	-.2	-4.6
Cin	5	8	497	47	1443.2	1595	236	572	992	13.8	5.19	83	.280	.348	-142	-144	100	67	29	.981	113	91	123	-.5	-14.1	.0	.1	9.5
Pit	3	8	464	46	1428.0	1451	**149**	576	1079	13.2	4.29	101	.267	.342	3	5	100	72	38	.983	103	47	**189**	.0	.5	-7.3	-.7	-1.1
Mil	6	10	423	42	1442.0	1440	164	476	1098	12.3	4.24	103	.259	.320	10	22	102	89	29	.981	117	66	132	-.8	2.2	-9.8	**.9**	-5.9
WEST																												
LA	2	6	459	51	1453.1	1386	178	521	1066	12.1	4.01	103	.254	.323	48	21	96	96	40	**.988**	**73**	58	145	**1.7**	2.1	.0	.1	8.0
SF	8	8	**521**	46	1457.0	1481	161	548	1020	12.8	4.29	101	.265	.332	2	5	101	72	24	.984	101	63	153	.1	.5	7.2	-.6	2.8
SD	3	8	437	44	1441.0	1460	184	**422**	1079	12.1	4.03	98	.263	.318	44	-17	91	69	25	.982	108	**36**	146	-.3	-1.7	5.4	-.4	2.9
Col	3	2	473	36	1435.1	1634	198	697	947	15.1	5.54	86	.290	.372	-197	-114	110	111	32	.986	89	81	161	.8	-11.2	-.4	-.9	-1.4
Ari	5	6	471	33	1436.0	1480	197	668	1153	13.9	4.98	91	.266	.350	-107	-65	106	97	**50**	.977	139	89	144	-2.0	-6.4	-15.6	-.7	-5.3
Total	71	136	7466	697	23146.0	—	—	—	—	12.8	4.30	—	.263	.333	—	—	—	—	—	.983	1646	921	2391	—	—	—	—	—

BATTER-FIELDER WINS	BATTING AVERAGE	ON-BASE PERCENTAGE	SLUGGING AVERAGE	ON-BASE PLUS SLUGGING	ADJUSTED OPS	ADJUSTED BATTER RUNS
Bonds-SF 10.7	Bonds-SF............362	Bonds-SF............609	Bonds-SF............812	Bonds-SF...........1422	Bonds-SF............255	Bonds-SF..........118.5
Rolen-StL........... 6.4	Helton-Col...........347	Helton-Col...........469	Pujols-StL 657	Helton-Col..........1088	Pujols-StL 171	Pujols-StL 64.7
Helton-Col 6.2	Loretta-SD 335	Berkman-Hou 450	Edmonds-StL........643	Pujols-StL 1072	Edmonds-StL........168	Helton-Col............57.1
Beltre-LA 5.8	Beltre-LA.............334	J.Drew-Atl 436	Beltre-LA.............629	Edmonds-StL......1061	Beltre-LA..............160	Edmonds-StL.......54.6
Edmonds-StL..... 5.1	Pujols-StL 331	Abreu-Phi.............428	Helton-Col............620	Beltre-LA............1017	Helton-Col............159	Berkman-Hou 54.6

RUNS	HITS	DOUBLES	TRIPLES	HOME RUNS	TOTAL BASES	RUNS BATTED IN
Pujols-StL 133	Pierre-Fla.............221	Overbay-Mil 53	J.Wilson-Pit............12	Beltre-LA................48	Pujols-StL 389	Castilla-Col 131
Bonds-SF.............129	Loretta-SD 208	Pujols-StL 51	Rollins-Phi 12	Pujols-StL 46	Beltre-LA..............376	Rolen-StL.............124
Rollins-Phi 119	J.Wilson-Pit..........201	Helton-Col..............49	Pierre-Fla................12	Dunn-Cin 46	Helton-Col............339	Pujols-StL 123
J.Drew-Atl 118	Beltre-LA..............200		Izturis-LA 9	Bonds-SF................45	Alou-Chi...............335	Beltre-LA..............121
Abreu-Phi.............118	Pujols-StL 196				Dunn-Cin 323	Cabrera-Fla 112

BASES ON BALLS	STOLEN BASES	BASE STEALING RUNS	FIELDING RUNS-INFIELD	FIELDING RUNS-OUTFIELD	OUTFIELD ASSISTS	CATCHER CS PCT.
Bonds-SF.............232	Podsednik-Mil 70	Podsednik-Mil 10.9	J.Wilson-Pit..........27.4	Payton-SD 14.2	Hidalgo-Hou-NY 14	Schneider-Mon 50.0
Helton-Col............127	Pierre-Fla...............45	Abreu-Phi...............7.1	Rolen-StL.............22.3	Clark-Mil 10.2	Rivera-Mon 14	Kendall-Pit 36.3
Berkman-Hou 127	Abreu-Phi...............40	Roberts-LA 6.9	Helton-Col............20.2	J.Drew-Atl 5.0	Cabrera-Fla 13	Hernandez-SD.....28.4
Abreu-Phi.............127	Freel-Cin 37	Beltran-Hou 6.2	Perez-SF-Chi 14.8	Hidalgo-Hou-NY 4.9	Abreu-Phi.................13	LoDuca-LA-Fla 27.9
J.Drew-Atl 118	Roberts-LA 33	Freel-Cin 4.6	Furcal-Atl 14.5	Bradley-LA.............4.8	J.Drew-Atl 12	Ausmus-Hou 26.4

WINS	WINNING PCT.	WINS ABOVE TEAM	GAMES STARTED	COMPLETE GAMES	FEWEST HITS/GAME	FEWEST BB/GAME
Oswalt-Hou.............20	Clemens-Hou........818	Clemens-Hou.........6.8	Webb-Ari.................35	Hernandez-Mon........9	Johnson-Ari 6.48	Wells-SD.................92
Schmidt-SF.............18	Carpenter-StL.......750	Johnson-Ari 5.5	Oswalt-Hou 35	Lidle-Cin-Phi 5	Schmidt-SF 6.60	Sheets-Mil............1.22
Pavano-Fla 18	Schmidt-SF...........720	Pavano-Fla 5.3	Johnson-Ari 35	Sheets-Mil.................5	Perez-Pit..............6.66	Maddux-Chi 1.40
Clemens-Hou..........18	Peavy-SD..............714	Estes-Col 5.0	Hernandez-Mon......35	Schmidt-SF 4	Clemens-Hou.......7.10	Johnson-Ari 1.61
	Pavano-Fla 692	Schmidt-SF 5.0		Johnson-Ari 4	Leiter-NY 7.15	Lima-LA 1.80

STRIKEOUTS	STRIKEOUTS/GAME	GAMES	SAVES	BASE RUNNERS/9	ADJUSTED RELIEF RUNS	RELIEF RANKING
Johnson-Ari 290	Perez-Pit............10.97	Brower-SF 89	Isringhausen-StL 47	Benitez-Fla 7.36	Lidge-Hou............25.9	Lidge-Hou............40.3
Sheets-Mil.............264	Johnson-Ari 10.62	King-StL..................86	Benitez-Fla 47	Johnson-Ari 8.46	Benitez-Fla 22.7	Benitez-Fla 37.4
Schmidt-SF...........251	Schmidt-SF........10.04	Torres-Pit 84	Gagne-LA 45	Gagne-LA 8.74	Otsuka-SD 20.9	Gagne-LA 34.5
Perez-Pit...............239	Sheets-Mil..........10.03	Reitsma-Atl 84	Smoltz-Atl 44	Lidge-Hou............8.84	Linebrink-SD........18.3	Ayala-Mon............32.7
Clemens-Hou........218	Clement-Chi.........9.45	Cormier-Phi 84	Mesa-Pit 43	Sheets-Mil...........9.00	Ayala-Mon............17.9	Madson-Phi 23.9

INNINGS PITCHED	OPPONENTS' AVG.	OPPONENTS' OBP	EARNED RUN AVERAGE	ADJUSTED ERA	ADJUSTED STARTER RUNS	PITCHER WINS
Hernandez-Mon.255.0	Johnson-Ari 197	Johnson-Ari 241	Peavy-SD............2.27	Johnson-Ari 175	Johnson-Ari 47.4	**Johnson-Ari........ 5.3**
Johnson-Ari 245.2	Schmidt-SF...........202	Sheets-Mil............255	Johnson-Ari 2.60	Peavy-SD.............174	Sheets-Mil............41.1	**Zambrano-Chi.... 4.3**
Sheets-Mil..........237.0	Perez-Pit...............207	Schmidt-SF..........272	Sheets-Mil............2.70	Sheets-Mil.............163	Zambrano-Chi......36.1	**Sheets-Mil 4.1**
Oswalt-Hou........237.0	Clemens-Hou........217	Wells-SD..............285	Zambrano-Chi......2.75	Zambrano-Chi.......161	Clemens-Hou.......32.8	**Peavy-SD 4.1**
Schmidt-SF........225.0	Leiter-NY 218	Carpenter-StL.......291	Clemens-Hou.......2.98	Clemens-Hou........147	Peavy-SD.............32.2	**Lidge-Hou........... 4.0**

Say It Ain't, Sosa

Two new parks opened on the opposite ends of the country as well as of the baseball spectrum. Citizens Bank Park in Philadelphia quickly became one of the best venues for hitters outside of Colorado, while many sluggers complained it was easier to hit one out of the Grand Canyon than San Diego's Petco Park.

Two 40-year-old pitchers dominated the league. Roger Clemens, after ending a brief retirement, signed with Houston and beat out Arizona's Randy Johnson to become the oldest Cy Young Award winner. Ray Boone, father of Bob and grandfather of Bret and Aaron, passed during the year, as did Ken Caminiti, the 1996 NL MVP, who died of a drug overdose.

The Braves surprised many by winning the East yet again, their 10th straight division title and 13th in 14 years. The Cardinals claimed the Central division, winning a major league best 105 games, while Los Angeles won the West despite trading popular catcher Paul Lo Duca late in the year. Houston overtook Chicago for the Wild Card berth as the Cubs collapsed in the final days of September after fighting with each other (and the team's television broadcasters) all season. Sammy Sosa didn't dress for the season's final game and left Wrigley Field in the early innings, earning himself an $87,400 fine.

The Cardinals quickly eliminated the Dodgers in four games in their Division Series, while the Astros outslugged the Braves in five games for the club's first postseason series win in the team's 43-year history. The Cardinals won the first two NLCS games at home before the Astros rallied to take the next three games to come tantalizingly close to their first World Series berth. But Jim Edmonds' 12th inning blast in Game 6 kept the Cardinals alive, and St. Louis then beat up on Roger Clemens in Game 7, with Scott Rolen providing the key blow with a two-run bomb. St. Louis offered little resistance to Boston in the World Series, quickly and quietly losing all four games.

2004 AMERICAN LEAGUE

TEAM	W	L	T	PCT	GB	HW	HL	R	OR	PA	H	2B	3B	HR	BB	SO	HB	SH	AVG	OBP	SLG	OPS	AOPS	BR	ABR	PF	SB	CS	BSA	BSR
EAST																														
NY	101	61	0	.623	—	**57**	24	897	808	6364	1483	281	20	**242**	**670**	982	**80**	37	.268	.353	.458	811	109	91	93	100	84	33	72	7
Bos	98	64	0	.605	3	55	26	**949**	768	6515	1613	**373**	25	222	659	1189	69	12	**.282**	**.360**	**.472**	**832**	109	**145**	90	106	68	30	69	4
Bal	78	84	0	.481	23	38	43	842	830	6429	**1614**	319	18	169	528	949	57	46	.281	.345	.432	777	102	20	30	99	101	41	71	8
TB	70	91	0	.435	30.5	41	39	714	842	6098	1416	278	46	145	469	944	55	35	.258	.320	.405	725	90	-99	-82	98	132	42	**76**	14
Tor	67	94	0	.416	33.5	40	41	719	823	6177	1438	290	34	145	513	1083	71	20	.260	.328	.403	731	84	-79	-117	106	58	31	65	2
CENTRAL																														
Min	92	70	0	.568	—	49	32	780	**715**	6286	1494	310	24	191	513	982	64	46	.266	.332	.431	763	95	-21	-41	103	116	46	72	9
Chi	83	79	0	.512	9	46	35	865	831	6196	1481	284	19	**242**	499	1030	63	**58**	.268	.333	.457	790	100	26	1	103	78	51	60	-1
Cle	80	82	0	.494	12	44	37	858	857	6449	1565	345	29	184	606	1009	78	47	.276	.351	.444	795	**110**	63	**98**	96	94	55	63	1
Det	72	90	0	.444	20	38	43	827	844	6284	1531	284	**54**	201	518	1144	50	50	.272	.337	.449	786	107	21	55	96	86	50	63	1
KC	58	104	0	.358	34	33	47	720	905	6153	1432	261	29	150	461	1057	76	40	.259	.322	.397	719	86	-110	-108	100	67	48	58	-2
WEST																														
Ana	92	70	0	.568	—	45	36	836	734	6295	1603	272	37	162	450	**942**	73	56	**.282**	.341	.429	770	103	-5	31	96	**143**	46	**76**	**15**
Oak	91	71	0	.562	1	52	29	793	742	6459	1545	336	15	189	608	1061	55	25	.270	.343	.433	776	102	19	27	99	47	22	68	3
Tex	89	73	0	.549	3	51	30	860	794	6256	1492	323	34	227	500	1099	61	23	.266	.329	.457	786	98	19	-11	104	69	36	66	3
Sea	63	99	0	.389	29	38	44	698	823	6362	1544	276	20	136	492	1058	54	46	.270	.331	.396	727	94	-88	-50	95	110	42	72	10
Total	1133	—	—	—	—	627	506	11358	—	88323	21251	4232	404	2605	7486	14529	906	541	.270	.338	.433	771	—	—	—	—	1253	573	69	75

TEAM	CG	SHO	GR	SV	IP	H	HR	BB	SO	BR/9	ERA	AERA	OAV	OOB	PR	APR	PF	OSB	OCS	FA	E	WPB	DP	FW	PW	BW	BSW	DIF
EAST																												
NY	1	5	436	**59**	1443.2	1532	182	445	1058	12.7	4.69	98	.271	.328	-9	-16	99	90	32	.984	99	70	148	.6	-1.5	8.8	.2	12.0
Bos	4	**12**	437	36	1451.1	**1430**	**159**	447	1132	**12.2**	4.18	**117**	**.255**	**.318**	73	**107**	105	123	31	.981	118	60	129	-.5	**10.1**	8.5	-.1	-1.0
Bal	8	10	452	27	1455.1	1488	**159**	687	1090	13.8	4.70	99	.264	.348	-11	-7	101	82	39	.982	110	83	161	-.0	-.7	2.8	.2	-5.4
TB	3	5	401	35	1417.0	1459	192	580	923	13.5	4.81	97	.265	.342	-28	-23	101	67	32	.980	119	63	139	-.6	-2.2	-7.7	.8	-.8
Tor	6	11	431	37	1421.0	1505	181	608	956	13.8	4.91	100	.273	.348	-44	-3	106	91	41	.985	91	71	150	1.0	-.3	-11.0	-.3	-2.9
CENTRAL																												
Min	4	9	435	48	1476.0	1523	167	**431**	1123	**12.2**	**4.03**	115	.267	.323	**98**	97	100	73	44	.984	101	51	158	.5	9.2	-3.9	.3	4.9
Chi	8	8	399	34	1432.1	1505	224	527	1013	13.1	4.91	96	.272	.338	-45	-34	101	90	48	.984	100	57	167	.5	-3.2	.0	-.6	5.2
Cle	8	8	**479**	32	1466.2	1553	201	579	1115	13.5	4.81	90	.271	.342	-30	-82	94	117	40	.983	106	58	152	.2	-7.7	**9.3**	-.4	-2.3
Det	7	9	432	35	1439.2	1542	190	530	995	13.3	4.93	91	.275	.340	-47	-75	97	71	41	.977	144	81	160	-2.0	-7.1	5.2	-.4	-4.7
KC	6	3	409	25	1420.1	1638	208	518	887	14.0	5.15	90	.290	.352	-82	-78	101	84	35	.978	131	77	169	-1.3	-7.4	-10.2	-.7	-3.5
WEST																												
Ana	2	11	343	50	1454.1	1476	170	502	**1164**	12.5	4.28	104	.263	.326	56	30	96	87	44	.985	**90**	72	126	**1.1**	2.8	2.9	**.9**	3.2
Oak	**10**	8	414	35	1471.1	1466	164	544	1034	12.7	4.17	111	.262	.332	75	73	100	74	**49**	**.986**	91	53	**172**	**1.1**	6.9	2.5	-.2	-.3
Tex	5	9	468	52	1439.2	1536	182	547	979	13.5	4.53	109	.273	.344	17	60	106	71	39	.981	117	**50**	152	-.5	5.7	-1.0	-.2	4.1
Sea	7	7	414	28	1459.1	1498	212	575	1036	13.2	4.76	94	.265	.338	-21	-50	96	**64**	38	.983	103	56	140	.4	-4.7	-4.7	.4	-9.4
Total	79	115	5950	533	20248.0	—	—	—	—	13.1	4.63	—	.270	.338	—	—	—	—	—	.982	1520	902	2123	—	—	—	—	—

BATTER-FIELDER WINS	BATTING AVERAGE	ON-BASE PERCENTAGE	SLUGGING AVERAGE	ON-BASE PLUS SLUGGING	ADJUSTED OPS	ADJUSTED BATTER RUNS
Tejada-Bal 6.6	Suzuki-Sea 372	Mora-Bal 419	Ramirez-Bos.........613	Ramirez-Bos.......1009	Hafner-Cle 162	Guerrero-Ana.......54.3
Guillen-Det 5.6	Mora-Bal 340	Suzuki-Sea 414	Ortiz-Bos 603	Hafner-Cle 993	Guerrero-Ana........161	Hafner-Cle 47.9
Guerrero-Ana..... 5.2	Guerrero-Ana........337	Hafner-Cle 410	Guerrero-Ana........598	Guerrero-Ana........989	Mora-Bal 155	Mora-Bal 47.8
Mora-Bal 5.1	Rodriguez-Det 334	Posada-NY 400	Hafner-Cle 583	Ortiz-Bos 983	Ramirez-Bos.........150	Ramirez-Bos........43.7
Chavez-Oak........ 3.9	Durazo-Oak 321	Chavez-Oak..........397	Mora-Bal 562	Mora-Bal 981	Ortiz-Bos 143	Ortiz-Bos 37.8
RUNS	**HITS**	**DOUBLES**	**TRIPLES**	**HOME RUNS**	**TOTAL BASES**	**RUNS BATTED IN**
Guerrero-Ana........124	Suzuki-Sea 262	Roberts-Bal 50	Crawford-TB 19	Ramirez-Bos..........43	Guerrero-Ana........366	Tejada-Bal.............150
Damon-Bos...........123	M.Young-Tex.........216	Belliard-Cle 48	Figgins-Ana 17	Ortiz-Bos 41	Ortiz-Bos 351	Ortiz-Bos 139
Sheffield-NY 117	Guerrero-Ana........206	Ortiz-Bos 47	Guillen-Det.............10	Konerko-Chi...........41	Tejada-Bal.............349	Ramirez-Bos.........130
M.Young-Tex.........114	Tejada-Bal.............203	Ramirez-Bos...........44	M.Young-Tex.............9	Guerrero-Ana..........39	Ramirez-Bos.........348	Guerrero-Ana........126
Rodriguez-NY.......112	Kotsay-Oak...........190	Jeter-NY 44	Infante-Det...............9	Teixeira-Tex............38	M.Young-Tex 333	Sheffield-NY 121
BASES ON BALLS	**STOLEN BASES**	**BASE STEALING RUNS**	**FIELDING RUNS-INFIELD**	**FIELDING RUNS-OUTFIELD**	**OUTFIELD ASSISTS**	**CATCHER CS PCT.**
Chavez-Oak............95	Crawford-TB 59	Crawford-TB 7.7	Hudson-Tor 33.2	Baldelli-TB 10.0	Higginson-Det.........13	Blanco-Min...........49.2
Sheffield-NY 92	Suzuki-Sea 36	Rodriguez-NY........4.8	Tejada-Bal............28.4	Crawford-TB 9.4	Guerrero-Ana..........13	Miller-Oak 43.2
Posada-NY 88	Figgins-Ana 34	Suzuki-Sea 4.1	Uribe-Chi 19.6	Suzuki-Sea 8.9	Suzuki-Sea 12	Olivo-Chi-Sea 34.7
Matsui-NY...............88	Roberts-Bal 29	Ford-Min 3.7	Guillen-Det...........17.0	Guerrero-Ana.........7.7		Hall-TB.................34.3
Bellhorn-Bos...........88	Rodriguez-NY.........28	Jeter-NY 3.7	Valentin-Chi 17.0	Ibanez-Sea 5.7		Wilson-Sea 33.3
WINS	**WINNING PCT.**	**WINS ABOVE TEAM**	**GAMES STARTED**	**COMPLETE GAMES**	**FEWEST HITS/GAME**	**FEWEST BB/GAME**
Schilling-Bos...........21	Schilling-Bos.........778	Santana-Min 6.6	Rogers-Tex 35	Westbrook-Cle..........5	Santana-Min 6.16	Lieber-NY 92
Santana-Min 20	Santana-Min 769	Schilling-Bos..........6.5	Buehrle-Chi.............35	Ponson-Bal 5	Lilly-Tor 7.80	Radke-Min 1.07
Rogers-Tex 18	Mulder-Oak...........680	Rogers-Tex 4.0		Mulder-Oak..............5	P.Martinez-Bos 8.00	Schilling-Bos........1.39
Colon-Ana...............18	Rogers-Tex 667	Mulder-Oak............3.8		Buehrle-Chi..............4	Harden-Oak 8.11	Silva-Min..............1.55
Mulder-Oak.............17	P.Martinez-Bos 640	C.Lee-Cle 3.4			Schilling-Bos........8.18	Buehrle-Chi..........1.87
STRIKEOUTS	**STRIKEOUTS/GAME**	**GAMES**	**SAVES**	**BASE RUNNERS/9**	**ADJUSTED RELIEF RUNS**	**RELIEF RANKING**
Santana-Min 265	Santana-Min 10.46	Quantrill-NY............86	Rivera-NY 53	Gordon-NY 8.03	Gordon-NY 24.3	Rivera-NY 47.4
P.Martinez-Bos 227	P.Martinez-Bos 9.41	Gordon-NY 80	Cordero-Tex............49	Santana-Min 8.64	Nathan-Min..........24.3	Cordero-Tex.........41.5
Schilling-Bos.........203	Escobar-Ana........8.25	Rincon-Min 77	Nathan-Min.............44	Nathan-Min..........9.08	Rodriguez-Ana.....24.2	Foulke-Bos...........38.7
Escobar-Ana.........191	Bonderman-Det...8.22	Timlin-Bos...............76	Percival-Ana 33	Takatsu-Chi..........9.10	Foulke-Bos...........24.1	Nathan-Min 37.3
Garcia-Sea-Chi.....184	C.Lee-Cle 8.09	Ryan-Bal.................76	Foulke-Bos..............32	Rodriguez-Ana.....9.11	Rivera-NY 24.0	Rincon-Min 33.8
INNINGS PITCHED	**OPPONENTS' AVG.**	**OPPONENTS' OBP**	**EARNED RUN AVERAGE**	**ADJUSTED ERA**	**ADJUSTED STARTER RUNS**	**PITCHER WINS**
Buehrle-Chi........245.1	Santana-Min 192	Santana-Min 249	Santana-Min 2.61	Santana-Min 178	Santana-Min 51.9	**Santana-Min....... 5.6**
Santana-Min 228.0	Lilly-Tor 230	Schilling-Bos.........271	Schilling-Bos........3.26	Schilling-Bos..........150	Schilling-Bos........42.7	**Rivera-NY 4.9**
Schilling-Bos.......226.2	P.Martinez-Bos 238	Radke-Min 291	Westbrook-Cle.....3.38	Radke-Min 133	Radke-Min 27.8	**Schilling-Bos 4.5**
Mulder-Oak.......225.2	Schilling-Bos.........239	P.Martinez-Bos 301	Radke-Min 3.48	Hudson-Oak 131	P.Martinez-Bos 25.8	**Cordero-Tex 4.1**
Radke-Min 219.2	Garcia-Sea-Chi.....241	Garcia-Sea-Chi.....302	Hudson-Oak 3.53	R.Lopez-Bal.........130	Hudson-Oak 22.3	**Foulke-Bos 3.8**

"The Idiots" Finally Beat the "Evil Empire"

Not everything that happened in the world of baseball in 2004 involved the Red Sox or Yankees, though it often seemed that way. Seattle's Ichiro Suzuki quietly totaled 262 hits, breaking George Sisler's single-season record. Equally as impressive was Minnesota pitcher Johan Santana, who won 13 straight decisions in the second half and was AL's unanimous Cy Young Award winner.

Despite these feats, most observers were focused on the simmering feud between the Red Sox and Yankees from the start of spring training. The Yankees intensified the rivalry by trading in February for All-Star shortstop Alex Rodriguez, who had nearly been traded to Boston two months earlier. That deal helped the Yankees win the AL East title again, though Boston made it close and easily claimed the league's Wild Card berth. Neither team had any problems in the Division Series as the Red Sox swept Anaheim (who had survived a tough AL West race over the Athletics and the surprising Rangers) and the Yankees beat Minnesota in four.

The result was another epic ALCS clash. New York won the first three games and led by a run entering the bottom of the ninth of Game 4. Down to their last outs, the Sox rallied for a run in the ninth off Mariano Rivera, the premier postseason closer in history. Boston then won that game, as well as Game 5, on extra inning hits by David Ortiz. Curt Schilling won Game 6 for Boston despite needing innovative temporary surgery on his right ankle before the game. Boston then scored six runs in the first two innings of an easy Game 7 win, making the Sox the first team in baseball history to win a postseason series after losing the first three games.

The Red Sox, who dubbed themselves "The Idiots" during the season, had no trouble sweeping the Cardinals in the World Series for the franchise's first World Championship since 1918. Manny Ramirez, who ironically would have been dealt had the Sox acquired A-Rod before the season, was the Series MVP.

2003 NATIONAL LEAGUE

TEAM	W	L	T	PCT	GB	HW	HL	R	OR	PA	H	2B	3B	HR	BB	SO	HB	SH	AVG	OBP	SLG	OPS	AOPS	BR	ABR	PF	SB	CS	BSA	BSR
EAST																														
Atl	101	61	0	.623	—	55	26	**907**	740	6378	**1608**	321	31	**235**	545	**933**	49	65	**.284**	.349	**.475**	**824**	**119**	**152**	**158**	99	68	22	**76**	7
Fla	91	71	0	.562	10	53	28	751	692	6185	1459	292	44	157	515	978	57	82	.266	.333	.421	754	105	7	39	96	**150**	74	67	7
Phi	86	76	0	.531	15	49	32	791	697	6333	1448	325	27	166	**651**	1155	55	46	.261	.343	.419	762	111	39	104	93	72	29	71	6
Mon	83	79	0	.512	18	52	29	711	716	6116	1404	294	25	144	522	990	45	72	.258	.326	.401	727	92	-43	-58	102	100	39	72	**8**
NY	66	95	0	.410	34.5	34	46	642	754	6007	1317	262	24	124	489	1035	54	78	.247	.314	.374	688	88	-120	-94	96	70	31	69	5
CENTRAL																														
Chi	88	74	0	.543	—	44	37	724	683	6187	1431	302	24	172	492	1158	50	80	.259	.323	.416	739	94	-25	-40	102	73	31	70	5
Hou	87	75	0	.537	1	48	33	805	677	6320	1466	308	30	191	557	1021	81	61	.263	.336	.431	767	99	38	-2	105	66	30	69	4
StL	85	77	0	.525	3	48	33	876	796	6466	1580	**342**	32	196	580	952	73	**87**	.279	**.350**	.454	804	115	122	133	99	82	32	72	7
Pit	75	87	0	.463	13	39	42	753	801	6314	1492	275	45	163	529	1049	**87**	79	.267	.338	.420	758	101	20	12	101	86	37	70	6
Cin	69	93	0	.426	19	35	46	694	886	6210	1349	239	21	182	524	1326	79	66	.245	.318	.395	713	95	-81	-47	95	80	34	70	6
Mil	68	94	0	.420	20	31	50	714	873	6268	1423	266	24	196	547	1221	71	62	.256	.329	.419	748	100	-6	-1	99	99	39	72	**8**
WEST																														
SF	100	61	0	.621	—	**57**	24	755	638	6204	1440	281	29	180	593	980	40	76	.264	.338	.425	763	102	32	22	101	53	37	59	-1
LA	85	77	0	.525	15.5	46	35	574	**556**	6036	1328	260	25	124	407	985	72	71	.243	.303	.368	671	81	-167	-151	97	80	36	69	5
Ari	84	78	0	.519	16.5	45	36	717	685	6261	1467	303	**47**	152	531	1006	45	63	.263	.330	.417	747	91	-7	-63	108	76	38	67	3
Col	74	88	0	.457	26.5	49	32	853	892	6282	1472	330	31	198	619	1134	52	55	.267	.344	.445	789	97	87	-13	114	63	37	63	1
SD	64	98	0	.395	36.5	35	46	678	831	6245	1442	257	32	128	565	1073	57	50	.261	.333	.388	721	102	-48	21	91	76	39	66	3
Total	1295	—	—	—	—	720	575	11945	—	99812	23126	4657	491	2708	8666	16996	967	1093	.262	.332	.417	749	—	—	—	—	1294	585	69	80

TEAM	CG	SHO	GR	SV	IP	H	HR	BB	SO	BR/9	ERA	AERA	OAV	OOB	PR	APR	PF	OSB	OCS	FA	E	WPB	DP	FW	PW	BW	BSW	DIF
EAST																												
Atl	4	7	489	51	1456.1	1425	147	555	992	12.5	4.10	102	.257	.327	29	16	98	91	34	.981	121	60	**166**	-.8	1.6	**15.5**	.2	3.5
Fla	7	11	395	36	1445.1	1415	128	530	1132	12.4	4.04	101	.258	.325	39	10	96	70	25	**.987**	78	62	162	**1.6**	1.0	3.8	.2	3.4
Phi	9	13	437	33	1443.2	1386	142	536	1060	12.5	4.04	98	.253	.327	38	-13	93	112	24	.984	97	69	146	.5	-1.3	10.2	.0	-4.6
Mon	**15**	10	437	42	1437.2	1467	181	**463**	1028	12.5	4.01	111	.264	.327	43	65	104	**40**	38	.983	102	82	152	.3	6.4	-5.7	**.3**	.8
NY	3	10	412	38	1413.1	1497	168	576	907	13.5	4.48	93	.273	.345	-32	-48	98	98	52	.980	118	50	158	-.7	-4.7	-9.2	.0	.1
CENTRAL																												
Chi	13	14	420	36	1456.1	1304	143	617	**1404**	12.3	3.83	113	.241	.324	73	81	101	70	42	.983	106	75	157	.0	8.0	-3.9	.0	2.9
Hou	1	5	**502**	50	1450.0	1350	161	565	1139	12.3	3.86	114	.248	.326	67	86	103	86	48	.985	95	**44**	149	.6	8.5	-.2	-.0	-2.8
StL	9	10	460	41	1463.2	1544	210	508	969	13.0	4.60	89	.271	.336	-52	-82	96	55	24	**.987**	**77**	60	138	**1.6**	-8.1	13.1	.2	-2.9
Pit	7	10	457	44	1444.1	1527	178	502	926	13.0	4.64	93	.272	.336	-57	-51	101	69	26	.980	123	60	159	-.9	-5.0	1.2	.0	-1.4
Cin	4	5	475	38	1446.1	1578	209	590	932	13.8	5.09	82	.278	.349	-130	-154	97	77	28	.977	141	55	152	-1.9	-15.1	-4.6	.0	9.6
Mil	5	3	460	44	1452.0	1590	219	575	1034	13.8	5.02	86	.279	.348	-120	-114	101	100	37	.981	114	71	142	-.4	-11.2	-.0	**.3**	-1.6
WEST																												
SF	7	10	461	43	1437.1	1349	136	546	1006	12.1	3.73	114	.250	.321	88	83	99	67	29	**.987**	80	76	163	1.4	8.2	2.2	-.6	8.3
LA	3	**17**	438	**58**	1457.2	**1254**	**127**	526	1289	**11.2**	**3.16**	**130**	**.234**	**.306**	**182**	**162**	96	117	**75**	.981	119	58	164	-.7	**15.9**	-14.9	.0	3.6
Ari	7	11	452	42	1455.0	1379	150	526	1291	12.2	3.84	120	.250	.322	71	116	108	84	38	.983	107	67	132	-.0	11.4	-6.2	-.2	-2.0
Col	3	4	500	34	1420.0	1629	200	552	866	14.4	5.20	94	.290	.359	-146	-44	114	73	42	.981	116	59	165	-.5	-4.3	-1.3	-.4	-.5
SD	2	10	473	31	1431.1	1458	208	611	1091	13.4	4.87	82	.264	.341	-94	-147	94	95	25	.983	102	79	141	.3	-14.5	2.1	-.2	-4.7
Total	99	150	7268	661	23110.1	—	—	—	—	12.8	4.28	—	.262	.332	—	—	—	—	—	.983	1696	1027	2446	—	—	—	—	—

BATTER-FIELDER WINS	BATTING AVERAGE	ON-BASE PERCENTAGE	SLUGGING AVERAGE	ON-BASE PLUS SLUGGING	ADJUSTED OPS	ADJUSTED BATTER RUNS
Bonds-SF 8.2	Pujols-StL 359	Bonds-SF.............529	Bonds-SF.............749	Bonds-SF...........1278	Bonds-SF.............226	Bonds-SF.............87.1
Pujols-StL........... 7.1	Helton-Col............358	Helton-Col............458	Pujols-StL 667	Pujols-StL 1106	Pujols-StL 186	Pujols-StL 78.3
Helton-Col 5.9	Bonds-SF.............341	Pujols-StL 439	Helton-Col.............630	Helton-Col...........1088	Sheffield-Atl 165	Sheffield-Atl 58.1
Giles-Atl.............. 5.7	Renteria-StL 330	Giles-Pit-SD..........427	Edmonds-StL..........617	Sheffield-Atl 1023	Helton-Col.............159	Helton-Col.............57.3
Lopez-Atl 5.4	Sheffield-Atl 330	Walker-Col 422	Sheffield-Atl 604	Edmonds-StL.......1002	Thome-Phi.............158	Thome-Phi.............51.2
RUNS	**HITS**	**DOUBLES**	**TRIPLES**	**HOME RUNS**	**TOTAL BASES**	**RUNS BATTED IN**
Pujols-StL 137	Pujols-StL 212	Pujols-StL 51	Furcal-Atl 10	Thome-Phi..............47	Pujols-StL 394	Wilson-Col 141
Helton-Col.............135	Helton-Col.............209	Rolen-StL.................49	Finley-Ari 10	Sexson-Mil..............45	Helton-Col.............367	Sheffield-Atl 132
Furcal-Atl 130	Pierre-Fla..............204	Helton-Col...............49	Lofton-Pit-Chi............8	Bonds-SF.................45	Sheffield-Atl 348	Thome-Phi.............131
Sheffield-Atl 126	Renteria-StL 194	Green-LA.................49	Podsednik-Mil 8	Pujols-StL 43	Sexson-Mil.............332	Sexson-Mil.............124
	Furcal-Atl 194	Giles-Atl..................49		Lopez-Atl 43	Thome-Phi.............331	Pujols-StL 124
BASES ON BALLS	**STOLEN BASES**	**BASE STEALING RUNS**	**FIELDING RUNS-INFIELD**	**FIELDING RUNS-OUTFIELD**	**OUTFIELD ASSISTS**	**CATCHER CS PCT.**
Bonds-SF..............148	Pierre-Fla...............65	Pierre-Fla...............7.3	Cora-LA 30.8	Cruz-SF 14.7	Hidalgo-Hou............22	Schneider-Mon 52.9
Thome-Phi............111	Podsednik-Mil 43	Podsednik-Mil 6.0	Gonzalez-Chi.......25.6	Hidalgo-Hou.........14.3	Cruz-SF 18	Wilson-NY............44.6
Helton-Col.............111	Roberts-LA 40	Renteria-StL 5.0	Helton-Col............19.8	Kotsay-SD............13.7	Kotsay-SD...............13	Johnson-Col 41.9
Abreu-Phi..............109	Renteria-StL 34	Furcal-Atl 4.8	Giles-Atl...............18.3	Edmonds-StL.......12.8	Nady-SD 12	Miller-Chi 39.1
Berkman-Hou 107	Lofton-Pit-Chi..........30	Cabrera-Mon 4.6	Izturis-LA 17.5	Encarnacion-Fla 5.6	Edmonds-StL..........12	Ausmus-Hou.........35.2
WINS	**WINNING PCT.**	**WINS ABOVE TEAM**	**GAMES STARTED**	**COMPLETE GAMES**	**FEWEST HITS/GAME**	**FEWEST BB/GAME**
Ortiz-Atl 21	Schmidt-SF..........773	Prior-Chi 5.9	Maddux-Atl 36	Hernandez-Mon........8	Wood-Chi...............6.48	Maddux-Atl 1.36
Williams-StL............18	Prior-Chi 750	Ortiz-Atl 5.3	Millwood-Phi 35	Schmidt-SF...............5	Schmidt-SF..........6.59	Schilling-Ari..........1.71
Prior-Chi 18	Ortiz-Atl 750	Trachsel-NY 5.1		Morris-StL.................5	Webb-Ari...............6.97	Sheets-Mil............1.75
Schmidt-SF.............17	Williams-StL..........667	Leiter-NY 4.8		Millwood-Phi 5	Nomo-LA 7.21	Schmidt-SF...........1.99
		Schmidt-SF............4.8			Ortiz-Atl 7.50	Ohka-Mon............2.04
STRIKEOUTS	**STRIKEOUTS/GAME**	**GAMES**	**SAVES**	**BASE RUNNERS/9**	**ADJUSTED RELIEF RUNS**	**RELIEF RANKING**
Wood-Chi.............266	Wood-Chi..........11.35	Quantrill-LA............89	Gagne-LA 55	Gagne-LA 6.56	Gagne-LA 27.8	Gagne-LA 48.1
Prior-Chi 245	Prior-Chi 10.43	Villarreal-Ari 86	Smoltz-Atl 45	Smoltz-Atl 7.83	Mota-LA...............27.1	Wagner-Hou 35.4
Vazquez-Mon........241	Schilling-Ari.......10.39	Martin-LA................80	Wagner-Hou 44	Wagner-Hou 8.16	Wagner-Hou 24.7	Smoltz-Atl 34.2
Schmidt-SF...........208	Vazquez-Mon.......9.40	King-Atl 80	Worrell-SF 38	Cormier-Phi 8.50	Cormier-Phi 22.6	Villarreal-Ari.........26.3
Schilling-Ari...........194	Schmidt-SF...........9.01		Biddle-Mon 34	Schmidt-SF..........8.80	Smoltz-Atl 22.4	Mantei-Ari.............23.2
INNINGS PITCHED	**OPPONENTS' AVG.**	**OPPONENTS' OBP**	**EARNED RUN AVERAGE**	**ADJUSTED ERA**	**ADJUSTED STARTER RUNS**	**PITCHER WINS**
Hernandez-Mon.233.1	Schmidt-SF..........200	Schmidt-SF...........250	Schmidt-SF..........2.34	Schmidt-SF...........182	Schmidt-SF.........45.4	**Prior-Chi 5.1**
Vazquez-Mon.....230.2	Wood-Chi.............203	Schilling-Ari...........270	Brown-LA.............2.39	Prior-Chi 179	Prior-Chi 42.5	**Gagne-LA........... 4.9**
Millwood-Phi 222.0	Webb-Ari..............212	Vazquez-Mon........278	Prior-Chi 2.43	Brown-LA..............173	Brown-LA.............39.4	**Brown-LA........... 4.2**
Williams-StL.......220.2	Ortiz-Atl 223	Prior-Chi 283	Webb-Ari..............2.84	Webb-Ari...............163	Webb-Ari.............32.3	**Schmidt-SF 4.0**
Sheets-Mil.........220.2	Nomo-LA 223	Brown-LA...............290	Schilling-Ari.........2.95	Schilling-Ari...........157	Hernandez-Mon...31.2	**Wagner-Hou 3.6**

Reeling in the Prize Fish

The Hall of Fame canceled an anniversary retrospective on *Bull Durham,* one of the most popular baseball movies ever, because lead actors Susan Sarandon and Tim Robbins, both political activists, were critical of the U.S.-led war in Iraq. Sammy Sosa clubbed his 500th career homer during the season's first week, though his hitting prowess came under scrutiny in June when he was caught using a corked bat.

Cincinnati opened Great American Ball Park, which instantly became one of the homer-happiest parks, while the Expos played 22 "home" games in San Juan, Puerto Rico. Bobby Bonds, Barry's father, and Hall of Famer Warren Spahn died.

Florida was 16-22 when skipper Jeff Torborg was fired and replaced with 72-year-old Jack McKeon. That move, and the help of rookie midseason call-ups Dontrelle Willis and Miguel Cabrera, made Florida the best team after the All-Star break. Ivan Rodriguez drove in 6 runs and withstood a series-ending collision to lead the Marlins over the Giants in a four-game NLDS. Chicago eliminated Atlanta in a five-game Division Series.

The Cubs were just five outs away from their first World Series appearance since 1945 when disaster struck in Game 6 of the NLCS. A fan prevented left fielder Moises Alou from reaching into the stands for a foul ball, which, compounded by an error, opened the door for 8 runs. Chicago led 5-3 early in Game 7, but Florida came back again. The Marlins bested the Yankees in six games in the World Series, with Brad Penny winning twice and brash Josh Beckett tossing a complete-game shutout in the clincher.

2003 AMERICAN LEAGUE

TEAM	W	L	T	PCT	GB	HW	HL	R	OR	PA	H	2B	3B	HR	BB	SO	HB	SH	AVG	OBP	SLG	OPS	AOPS	BR	ABR	PF	SB	CS	BSA	BSR
EAST																														
NY	101	61	1	.623	—	50	32	877	716	6430	1518	304	14	230	**684**	1042	81	25	.271	.356	.453	809	113	116	128	99	98	33	75	10
Bos	95	67	0	.586	6	53	28	**961**	809	6530	**1667**	**371**	40	238	620	943	53	24	**.289**	**.360**	**.491**	**851**	**117**	**199**	**158**	104	88	35	72	7
Tor	86	76	0	.531	15	41	40	894	826	6364	1580	357	33	190	546	1081	**90**	11	.279	.349	.455	804	106	98	64	104	37	25	60	-1
Bal	71	91	1	.438	30	40	40	743	820	6241	1516	277	24	152	431	902	54	51	.268	.323	.405	728	92	-73	-69	99	89	36	71	7
TB	63	99	0	.389	38	36	45	715	852	6212	1501	298	38	137	420	1030	56	32	.265	.320	.404	724	92	-82	-67	98	**142**	42	**77**	**17**
CENTRAL																														
Min	90	72	0	.556	—	48	33	801	758	6324	1567	318	**45**	155	512	1027	63	42	.277	.341	.431	772	98	29	0	104	94	44	68	5
Chi	86	76	0	.531	4	51	30	791	715	6148	1445	303	19	220	519	916	58	43	.263	.331	.446	777	99	26	-6	104	77	29	73	7
KC	83	79	0	.512	7	40	40	836	867	6239	1526	288	39	162	476	926	75	63	.274	.336	.427	763	94	7	-44	107	120	42	74	12
Cle	68	94	0	.420	22	38	43	699	778	6187	1413	296	26	158	466	1062	62	46	.254	.316	.401	717	88	-96	-94	100	86	61	59	-2
Det	43	119	0	.265	47	23	58	591	928	6070	1312	201	39	153	443	1099	47	**65**	.240	.300	.375	675	81	-188	-161	96	98	63	61	0
WEST																														
Oak	96	66	0	.593	—	**57**	24	768	643	6187	1398	317	24	176	556	898	59	22	.254	.327	.417	744	95	-33	-37	101	48	14	**77**	6
Sea	93	69	0	.574	3	50	31	795	**637**	6281	1509	290	33	139	586	989	53	35	.271	.344	.410	754	103	1	44	95	108	37	74	11
Ana	77	85	0	.475	19	45	37	736	743	6119	1473	276	33	150	476	**838**	56	50	.268	.330	.413	743	99	-35	-6	96	129	61	68	7
Tex	71	91	0	.438	25	43	38	826	969	6293	1506	274	36	**239**	488	1052	75	24	.266	.330	.454	784	97	32	-20	107	65	25	72	6
Total	1135	—	—	—	—	615	519	11033	—	87625	20931	4170	443	2499	7223	13805	882	533	.267	.333	.428	761	—	—	—	—	1279	547	70	90

TEAM	CG	SHO	GR	SV	IP	H	HR	BB	SO	BR/9	ERA	AERA	OAV	OOB	PR	APR	PF	OSB	OCS	FA	E	WPB	DP	FW	PW	BW	BSW	DIF
EAST																												
NY	8	12	367	**49**	1462.0	1512	145	**375**	1119	11.9	4.02	109	.265	.314	82	62	97	92	37	.981	114	**46**	126	-.4	5.9	12.3	.3	1.9
Bos	5	6	437	36	1464.2	1503	153	488	**1141**	12.7	4.48	104	.263	.327	7	28	103	101	35	.982	113	64	130	-.4	2.7	**15.1**	.0	-3.4
Tor	14	6	443	36	1435.0	1560	184	485	984	13.2	4.69	101	.276	.337	-27	8	105	126	32	.981	117	66	161	-.7	.8	6.1	-.7	-.5
Bal	9	3	425	41	1449.2	1579	198	526	981	13.6	4.76	97	.278	.346	-38	-26	102	121	37	.983	105	54	164	.0	-2.5	-6.6	.0	-1.0
TB	7	7	372	30	1436.2	1454	196	639	877	13.7	4.93	93	.264	.347	-65	-55	101	65	41	.983	103	74	158	.1	-5.3	-6.4	**1.0**	-7.5
CENTRAL																												
Min	7	8	399	45	1462.0	1526	187	402	997	12.2	4.41	102	.268	.319	19	14	99	70	27	.985	87	72	114	1.0	1.3	.0	-.1	6.8
Chi	12	4	361	36	1431.0	1364	162	518	1056	12.2	4.17	110	.253	.321	56	66	101	**58**	29	.984	93	52	154	.7	6.3	-.6	.0	-1.5
KC	7	10	407	36	1438.2	1569	190	566	865	13.8	5.05	95	.279	.348	-85	-36	106	95	42	.982	108	68	143	-.1	-3.4	-4.2	.5	9.3
Cle	5	7	428	34	1459.1	1477	179	501	943	12.6	4.21	105	.264	.329	52	36	98	84	43	.980	126	60	178	-1.2	3.4	-9.0	-.8	-5.5
Det	3	5	451	27	1438.2	1616	195	557	764	13.9	5.30	83	.286	.352	-124	-153	97	128	**54**	.978	138	63	**194**	-1.8	-14.6	-15.4	-.6	-5.5
WEST																												
Oak	**16**	14	364	48	1441.2	**1336**	**140**	499	1018	11.8	**3.63**	**126**	**.246**	.314	**143**	**150**	101	91	43	.983	107	50	145	-.0	**14.4**	-3.5	-.0	4.3
Sea	8	**15**	366	38	1441.0	1340	173	466	1001	**11.6**	3.76	115	.247	**.311**	122	95	96	62	32	**.989**	**65**	47	159	**2.3**	9.1	4.2	.4	-4.0
Ana	5	9	375	39	1431.1	1444	190	486	980	12.6	4.28	102	.261	.327	40	16	97	80	48	.982	105	64	138	.0	1.5	-.6	.0	-5.0
Tex	4	3	**494**	43	1433.1	1625	208	603	1009	14.4	5.67	88	.288	.360	-182	-103	110	96	45	.985	94	62	168	.6	-9.9	-1.9	-.0	1.2
Total	110	109	5689	538	20225.0	—	—	—	—	12.9	4.52	—	.267	.333	—	—	—	—	—	.983	1475	842	2132	—	—	—	—	—

BATTER-FIELDER WINS	BATTING AVERAGE	ON-BASE PERCENTAGE	SLUGGING AVERAGE	ON-BASE PLUS SLUGGING	ADJUSTED OPS	ADJUSTED BATTER RUNS
Rodriguez-Tex....6.7	Mueller-Bos..........326	Ramirez-Bos.........427	Rodriguez-Tex......600	Delgado-Tor.........1019	Delgado-Tor..........160	Delgado-Tor.........55.6
Posada-NY..........5.1	Ramirez-Bos.........325	Delgado-Tor..........426	Delgado-Tor..........593	Ramirez-Bos.......1014	Ramirez-Bos.........158	Ramirez-Bos........52.6
Chavez-Oak........4.2	Jeter-NY...............324	Giambi-NY............412	Ortiz-Bos.............592	Rodriguez-Tex......995	Rodriguez-Tex......148	Giambi-NY...........45.0
Ramirez-Bos......4.1	Wells-Tor..............317	Martinez-Sea........406	Ramirez-Bos.........587	Nixon-Bos.............975	Giambi-NY............148	Rodriguez-Tex.....44.0
Delgado-Tor.......4.1	Ordonez-Chi.........317	Posada-NY...........405	Nixon-Bos.............578	Ortiz-Bos..............961	Nixon-Bos.............147	Huff-TB................39.5
RUNS	**HITS**	**DOUBLES**	**TRIPLES**	**HOME RUNS**	**TOTAL BASES**	**RUNS BATTED IN**
Rodriguez-Tex......124	Wells-Tor...............215	Wells-Tor................49	Guzman-Min...........14	Rodriguez-Tex........47	Wells-Tor..............373	Delgado-Tor..........145
Garciaparra-Bos...120	Suzuki-Sea...........212	Anderson-Ana.........49	Garciaparra-Bos.....13	Thomas-Chi............42	Rodriguez-Tex......364	Rodriguez-Tex......118
Wells-Tor..............118	Young-Tex.............204	Huff-TB...................47	Beltran-KC.............10	Delgado-Tor...........42	Soriano-NY...........358	Wells-Tor..............117
Ramirez-Bos.........117	Anderson-Ana.......201	Ordonez-Chi...........46		Giambi-NY..............41	Huff-TB................353	Boone-Sea............117
Delgado-Tor..........117						Anderson-Ana.......116
BASES ON BALLS	**STOLEN BASES**	**BASE STEALING RUNS**	**FIELDING RUNS-INFIELD**	**FIELDING RUNS-OUTFIELD**	**OUTFIELD ASSISTS**	**CATCHER CS PCT.**
Giambi-NY............129	Crawford-TB...........55	Crawford-TB..........8.6	Hudson-Tor..........44.6	Cameron-Sea......16.2	Baldelli-TB..............14	B.Molina-Ana.......44.4
Delgado-Tor..........109	Sanchez-Det..........44	Beltran-KC............7.6	Ellis-Oak..............30.0	Anderson-Ana.......13.3	Matsui-NY...............13	Hall-TB..................43.6
Thomas-Chi..........100	Beltran-KC..............41	Soriano-NY...........4.9	Chavez-Oak...........23.1	Crawford-TB........10.6	Anderson-Ana.........13	Inge-Det...............36.4
Durazo-Oak..........100	Soriano-NY.............35	Suzuki-Sea...........4.7	B.Phillips-Cle.......15.7	Baldelli-TB...........10.3	Suzuki-Sea.............12	Bard-Cle...............35.9
Ramirez-Bos...........97	Suzuki-Sea.............34	Damon-Bos............4.5	Valentin-Chi.........13.7	Suzuki-Sea............9.2	Ramirez-Bos...........11	Olivo-Chi..............35.8
WINS	**WINNING PCT.**	**WINS ABOVE TEAM**	**GAMES STARTED**	**COMPLETE GAMES**	**FEWEST HITS/GAME**	**FEWEST BB/GAME**
Halladay-Tor............22	Halladay-Tor..........759	Halladay-Tor...........7.8	Halladay-Tor............36	Mulder-Oak...............9	Martinez-Bos.......7.09	Wells-NY.................85
Pettitte-NY..............21	Moyer-Sea............750	Moyer-Sea.............6.4	Zito-Oak..................35	Halladay-Tor.............9	Zito-Oak..............7.23	Halladay-Tor.........1.08
Moyer-Sea...............21	Pettitte-NY............724	Loaiza-Chi.............6.1	Thomson-Tex...........35	Colon-Chi..................9	Hudson-Oak.........7.39	Radke-Min............1.19
Loaiza-Chi...............21	Lowe-Bos...............708	Ponson-Bal............5.0	Buehrle-Chi..............35		Loaiza-Chi...........7.79	Mussina-NY.........1.68
	Loaiza-Chi.............700	Pettitte-NY.............4.5			Zambrano-TB......7.88	Mulder-Oak..........1.93
STRIKEOUTS	**STRIKEOUTS/GAME**	**GAMES**	**SAVES**	**BASE RUNNERS/9**	**ADJUSTED RELIEF RUNS**	**RELIEF RANKING**
Loaiza-Chi............207	Martinez-Bos.......9.93	Miller-Tor................79	Foulke-Oak.............43	Foulke-Oak..........8.72	Marte-Chi.............25.9	Foulke-Oak..........48.0
Martinez-Bos........206	Loaiza-Chi...........8.23	Walker-Det..............78	Guardado-Min..........41	Guardado-Min.......8.82	Hasegawa-Sea....24.5	M.Rivera-NY........42.6
Halladay-Tor.........204	Mussina-NY.........8.18	Ryan-Bal..................76	M.Rivera-NY............40	Riske-Cle.............9.04	Foulke-Oak..........24.4	Hawkins-Min........30.9
Mussina-NY..........195	Clemens-NY.........8.08	Grimsley-KC............76	Julio-Bal..................36	F.Rodriguez-Ana..9.10	Donnelly-Ana.......23.9	Hasegawa-Sea....28.2
Clemens-NY.........190	Escobar-Tor.........7.94	Hawkins-Min............74	Percival-Ana............33	Mateo-Sea............9.14	M.Rivera-NY........21.8	Cordero-Tex........26.8
INNINGS PITCHED	**OPPONENTS' AVG.**	**OPPONENTS' OBP**	**EARNED RUN AVERAGE**	**ADJUSTED ERA**	**ADJUSTED STARTER RUNS**	**PITCHER WINS**
Halladay-Tor.......266.0	Martinez-Bos........215	Martinez-Bos........272	Martinez-Bos.......2.22	Martinez-Bos........210	Martinez-Bos.......48.8	**Loaiza-Chi..........5.5**
Colon-Chi...........242.0	Zito-Oak................219	Mussina-NY..........275	Hudson-Oak.........2.70	Hudson-Oak..........170	Hudson-Oak.........47.7	**Foulke-Oak.........4.8**
Hudson-Oak.........240.0	Hudson-Oak.........223	Halladay-Tor.........275	Loaiza-Chi...........2.90	Loaiza-Chi............158	Loaiza-Chi...........43.6	**Hudson-Oak........4.5**
Zito-Oak.............231.2	Loaiza-Chi............233	Hudson-Oak.........280	Mulder-Oak..........3.13	Mulder-Oak..........146	Halladay-Tor.........40.1	**Martinez-Bos......4.4**
Buehrle-Chi........230.1	Zambrano-TB.......237	Loaiza-Chi............286	Halladay-Tor.........3.25	Halladay-Tor..........146	Mulder-Oak..........32.4	**M.Rivera-NY.......4.3**

WHEN PUSH CAME TO SHOVE

Boston surprised traditionalists by adding 278 seats atop the Green Monster. They quickly became the hottest ticket in baseball. Baltimore pitcher Steve Bechler died in spring training after collapsing during a workout. An over-the-counter diet supplement containing ephedra was linked to his death. Larry Doby, the AL's first black player, also died.

The season-opening series in Tokyo between Seattle and Oakland was canceled because of security concerns related to the U.S.-led war in Iraq. Yankees hurler Roger Clemens won his 300th game and recorded his 4,000th strikeout on the same night against the Cardinals. Toronto's Roy Halladay won 15 straight decisions, a victory shy of the league record for one season. Rafael Palmeiro smacked career homer number 500 for Texas, which led the league in long balls hit as well as allowed.

The small-market Twins won the Central for the second straight year, but they were dispatched in four games in the ALDS by the Yankees. The Red Sox rallied to win Games 3, 4, and 5 to beat Oakland in the other Division Series. The ALCS was marred by a bench-clearing brawl in Game 3; New York bench coach Don Zimmer charged Pedro Martinez, Boston's starting pitcher, who casually moved aside and pushed Zimmer to the ground. Two Yankees later were involved in a bullpen brawl between innings with a partisan groundskeeper. Aaron Boone's leadoff homer in the bottom of the 11th of Game 7 sent the Yankees to the World Series again. New York was shocked in the Fall Classic for the second time in three years as the Marlins won in six games.

2002 NATIONAL LEAGUE

TEAM	W	L	T	PCT	GB	HW	HL	R	OR	PA	H	2B	3B	HR	BB	SO	HB	SH	AVG	OBP	SLG	OPS	AOPS	BR	ABR	PF	SB	CS	BSA	BSR
EAST																														
Atl	101	59	1	.631	—	52	28	708	**565**	6223	1428	280	25	164	558	1028	54	67	.260	.331	.409	740	99	0	1	100	76	39	66	3
Mon	83	79	0	.512	19	49	32	735	718	6250	1432	300	36	162	575	1104	46	**108**	.261	.334	.418	752	97	23	-15	105	118	64	65	4
Phi	80	81	0	.497	21.5	40	40	710	724	6322	1428	**325**	**41**	165	640	1095	53	67	.259	.339	.422	761	112	46	99	94	104	43	71	8
Fla	79	83	0	.488	23	46	35	699	763	6260	1433	280	32	146	595	1130	61	59	.261	.337	.403	740	103	5	34	96	**177**	73	71	**13**
NY	75	86	0	.466	26.5	38	43	690	703	6150	1409	238	22	160	486	1044	63	75	.256	.322	.395	717	99	-56	-17	94	87	42	67	4
CENTRAL																														
StL	97	65	0	.599	—	52	29	787	648	6246	1475	285	26	175	542	**927**	67	83	.268	.338	.425	763	104	45	40	101	86	42	67	4
Hou	84	78	0	.519	13	47	34	749	695	6252	1441	291	32	167	589	1120	59	64	.262	.338	.417	755	95	31	-24	108	71	27	72	6
Cin	78	84	0	.481	19	38	43	709	774	6254	1386	297	21	169	583	1188	66	95	.253	.330	.408	738	95	-3	-27	104	116	52	69	7
Pit	72	89	0	.447	24.5	38	42	641	730	6049	1300	263	20	142	537	1109	**73**	68	.244	.319	.381	700	87	-80	-92	102	86	49	64	2
Chi	67	95	0	.414	30	36	45	706	759	6242	1351	259	29	**200**	585	1269	44	78	.246	.321	.413	734	97	-24	-23	100	63	21	75	7
Mil	56	106	0	.346	41	31	50	627	821	6083	1369	269	29	139	500	1125	55	79	.253	.320	.390	710	92	-65	-60	99	94	50	65	3
WEST																														
Ari	98	64	0	.605	—	**55**	26	**819**	674	6316	1471	283	**41**	165	**643**	1016	50	62	.267	**.346**	.423	769	97	67	-6	110	92	46	67	4
SF	95	66	1	.590	2.5	50	31	783	616	6298	1465	300	35	198	616	961	65	68	.267	.344	**.442**	**786**	**115**	**95**	**124**	97	74	21	**78**	9
LA	92	70	0	.568	6	46	35	713	643	6146	1464	286	29	155	428	940	53	67	.264	.320	.409	729	102	-36	4	94	96	37	72	8
Col	73	89	0	.451	25	47	34	778	898	6164	**1508**	283	**41**	152	497	1043	56	49	**.274**	.337	.423	760	92	35	-54	114	103	53	66	4
SD	66	96	0	.407	32	41	40	662	815	6178	1393	243	29	136	547	1062	30	45	.253	.321	.381	702	97	-81	-21	91	71	44	62	0
Total	1294	—	—	—	—	706	587	11516	—	99433	22753	4482	488	2595	8921	17161	895	1134	.259	.331	.410	741	—	—	—	—	1514	703	68	87

TEAM	CG	SHO	GR	SV	IP	H	HR	BB	SO	BR/9	ERA	AERA	OAV	OOB	PR	APR	PF	OSB	OCS	FA	E	WPB	DP	FW	PW	BW	BSW	DIF
EAST																												
Atl	3	**15**	469	**57**	1467.1	**1302**	123	554	1058	11.6	**3.13**	**129**	**.240**	.313	**158**	**149**	98	96	55	.982	114	52	170	-.3	**14.9**	.1	-.2	6.5
Mon	9	3	437	39	1453.0	1475	165	508	1088	12.6	3.97	110	.265	.329	22	60	106	85	44	.978	139	63	160	-1.7	6.0	-1.5	-.1	-.7
Phi	5	9	450	47	1449.2	1381	153	570	1075	12.5	4.17	92	.252	.328	-10	-59	93	74	34	**.986**	88	80	156	1.2	-5.9	9.9	.3	-5.9
Fla	11	12	461	36	1456.1	1449	151	631	1104	13.2	4.36	90	.262	.341	-42	-75	96	93	**61**	.983	106	61	163	.2	-7.5	3.4	**.8**	1.2
NY	9	10	451	36	1442.2	1408	163	543	1107	12.5	3.89	101	.256	.327	34	9	96	151	53	.976	144	**33**	138	-2.0	.9	-1.7	-.1	-2.6
CENTRAL																												
StL	4	9	472	42	1446.1	1355	141	547	1009	12.2	3.70	109	.251	.323	65	53	98	86	34	.983	103	49	168	.4	5.3	4.0	-.1	6.5
Hou	2	11	480	43	1445.0	1423	151	546	1219	12.6	4.00	108	.260	.330	17	48	105	104	36	**.986**	**83**	43	149	**1.5**	4.8	-2.4	.0	-.9
Cin	2	8	462	42	1453.2	1502	173	550	980	13.1	4.27	100	.269	.338	-27	-2	104	**67**	42	.981	120	80	169	-.6	-.2	-2.7	.2	.4
Pit	2	7	458	47	1412.2	1447	163	572	920	13.2	4.23	99	.268	.342	-20	-7	102	94	44	.982	115	46	**177**	-.4	-.7	-9.2	-.3	2.1
Chi	11	9	390	23	1441.1	1373	167	606	**1333**	12.7	4.29	94	.253	.331	-30	-40	99	112	54	.981	114	59	144	-.3	-4.0	-2.3	.2	-7.6
Mil	7	4	446	32	1432.1	1468	199	666	1026	13.8	4.73	87	.268	.352	-99	-99	100	109	49	.983	103	76	154	.4	-9.9	-6.0	-.2	-9.2
WEST																												
Ari	**14**	10	422	40	1446.2	1361	170	**421**	1303	**11.4**	3.92	114	.247	**.305**	30	82	109	77	43	.985	89	61	116	1.1	8.2	-.6	-.1	8.4
SF	10	13	417	43	1437.1	1349	**116**	523	992	11.9	3.54	111	.251	.319	90	66	96	87	36	.985	90	43	166	1.1	6.6	**12.4**	.4	-6.0
LA	4	**15**	423	56	1457.2	1311	165	555	1132	11.8	3.69	105	.241	.315	67	33	95	110	53	.985	90	45	134	1.1	3.3	.4	.3	6.0
Col	1	8	**506**	43	1426.2	1554	225	582	920	13.9	5.20	91	.277	.349	-174	-67	115	87	23	.982	112	54	158	-.2	-6.7	-5.4	-.1	4.4
SD	5	10	459	40	1436.1	1522	177	582	1108	13.6	4.62	84	.274	.346	-82	-126	94	76	40	.979	128	65	162	-1.1	-12.6	-2.1	-.5	1.3
Total	99	153	7203	666	23105.0	—	—	—	—	12.7	4.11	—	.259	.331	—	—	—	—	—	.982	1738	910	2484	—	—	—	—	—

BATTER-FIELDER WINS	BATTING AVERAGE	ON-BASE PERCENTAGE	SLUGGING AVERAGE	ON-BASE PLUS SLUGGING	ADJUSTED OPS	ADJUSTED BATTER RUNS
Bonds-SF 11.5	Bonds-SF .370	Bonds-SF .582	Bonds-SF .799	Bonds-SF 1381	Bonds-SF 269	Bonds-SF 126.2
Giles-Pit 5.5	Walker-Col .338	Giles-Pit .450	Giles-Pit .622	Giles-Pit 1072	Giles-Pit 176	Giles-Pit 63.5
Edmonds-StL 4.9	V.Guerrero-Mon .336	C.Jones-Atl .435	Walker-Col .602	Walker-Col 1023	Sosa-Chi 158	V.Guerrero-Mon 51.3
Kent-SF 4.8	Helton-Col .329	Helton-Col .429	Sosa-Chi .594	V.Guerrero-Mon 1010	Edmonds-StL 156	Abreu-Phi 51.2
Rolen-Phi-StL 4.4	C.Jones-Atl .327	Walker-Col .421	V.Guerrero-Mon .593	Helton-Col 1006	C.Jones-Atl 155	C.Jones-Atl 50.2
RUNS	**HITS**	**DOUBLES**	**TRIPLES**	**HOME RUNS**	**TOTAL BASES**	**RUNS BATTED IN**
Sosa-Chi 122	V.Guerrero-Mon 206	Abreu-Phi 50	Rollins-Phi 10	Sosa-Chi 49	V.Guerrero-Mon 364	Berkman-Hou 128
Pujols-StL 118	Kent-SF 195	Lowell-Fla 44	Rolen-Phi-StL 8	Bonds-SF 46	Kent-SF 352	Pujols-StL 127
Bonds-SF 117	Vidro-Mon 190	Vidro-Mon 43	Wilkerson-Mon 8	Green-LA 42	Berkman-Hou 334	Burrell-Phi 116
Green-LA 110	Pujols-StL 185	Cabrera-Mon 43	McCracken-Ari 8	Berkman-Hou 42	Pujols-StL 331	Green-LA 114
Helton-Col 107	Castillo-Fla 185		Furcal-Atl 8	V.Guerrero-Mon 39	Sosa-Chi 330	V.Guerrero-Mon 111
BASES ON BALLS	**STOLEN BASES**	**BASE STEALING RUNS**	**FIELDING RUNS-INFIELD**	**FIELDING RUNS-OUTFIELD**	**OUTFIELD ASSISTS**	**CATCHER CS PCT.**
Bonds-SF 198	Castillo-Fla 48	Roberts-LA 6.4	Reese-Pit 27.8	Shinjo-SF 12.1	Walker-Col 14	LaRue-Cin 45.2
Giles-Pit 135	Pierre-Col 47	Pierre-Col 6.1	Uribe-Col 26.5	Sanders-SF 8.7	V.Guerrero-Mon 14	Johnson-Fla 40.3
Dunn-Cin 128	Roberts-LA 45	Castillo-Fla 5.3	Cabrera-Mon 21.2	Owens-Fla 8.6	Wilkerson-Mon 13	J.Lopez-Atl 37.9
C.Jones-Atl 107	V.Guerrero-Mon 40	Fox-Fla 4.4	Rolen-Phi-StL 20.2	Perez-NY 6.8	Giles-Pit 13	Miller-Ari 37.9
Berkman-Hou 107	Sanchez-Mil 37	Boone-Cin 4.2	J.Wilson-Pit 19.9	Edmonds-StL 5.5	Sanders-SF 12	Lieberthal-Phi 35.4
WINS	**WINNING PCT.**	**WINS ABOVE TEAM**	**GAMES STARTED**	**COMPLETE GAMES**	**FEWEST HITS/GAME**	**FEWEST BB/GAME**
Johnson-Ari 24	Johnson-Ari .828	Johnson-Ari 8.9	Glavine-Atl 36	Johnson-Ari 8	Burnett-Fla 6.74	Schilling-Ari 1.15
Schilling-Ari 23	Miller-Hou .789	Schilling-Ari 6.9	Schilling-Ari 35	Burnett-Fla 7	Johnson-Ari 6.82	Perez-LA 1.54
Oswalt-Hou 19	Schilling-Ari .767	Miller-Hou 5.6	Johnson-Ari 35	Schilling-Ari 5	Moss-Atl 7.04	Vazquez-Mon 1.91
Millwood-Atl 18	Nomo-LA .727	Oswalt-Hou 5.3		Hernandez-SF 5	Clement-Chi 7.11	Maddux-Atl 2.03
Glavine-Atl 18	Maddux-Atl .727	Jennings-Col 5.2			Wood-Chi 7.12	Ohka-Mon 2.10
STRIKEOUTS	**STRIKEOUTS/GAME**	**GAMES**	**SAVES**	**BASE RUNNERS/9**	**ADJUSTED RELIEF RUNS**	**RELIEF RANKING**
Johnson-Ari 334	Johnson-Ari 11.56	Quantrill-LA 86	Smoltz-Atl 55	Gagne-LA 7.98	Dotel-Hou 25.7	Kim-Ari 40.7
Schilling-Ari 316	Schilling-Ari 10.97	Dotel-Hou 83	Gagne-LA 52	Dotel-Hou 8.23	Hammond-Atl 23.8	Gagne-LA 31.9
Wood-Chi 217	Schmidt-SF 9.52	Worrell-SF 80	M.Williams-Pit 46	Timlin-StL-Phi 8.75	Kim-Ari 21.1	Nen-SF 30.4
Clement-Chi 215	Clement-Chi 9.44	Jones-Col 79	Mesa-Phi 45	Schilling-Ari 8.81	Gagne-LA 19.3	Dotel-Hou 26.6
Oswalt-Hou 208	Duckworth-Phi 9.22		Nen-SF 43	Isringhausen-StL 8.95	Eischen-Mon 16.2	Hammond-Atl 25.3
INNINGS PITCHED	**OPPONENTS' AVG.**	**OPPONENTS' OBP**	**EARNED RUN AVERAGE**	**ADJUSTED ERA**	**ADJUSTED STARTER RUNS**	**PITCHER WINS**
Johnson-Ari 260.0	Johnson-Ari .208	Schilling-Ari .251	Johnson-Ari 2.32	Johnson-Ari 193	Johnson-Ari 54.6	**Johnson-Ari 5.7**
Schilling-Ari 259.1	Burnett-Fla .209	Perez-LA .262	Maddux-Atl 2.62	Maddux-Atl 154	Schilling-Ari 35.1	**Kim-Ari 4.3**
Oswalt-Hou 233.0	Clement-Chi .215	Johnson-Ari .273	Glavine-Atl 2.96	Oswalt-Hou 144	Oswalt-Hou 31.6	**Schilling-Ari 3.6**
Vazquez-Mon 230.1	Schmidt-SF .218	Wolf-Phi .285	Perez-LA 3.00	Dessens-Cin 141	Maddux-Atl 30.8	**Maddux-Atl 3.6**
Glavine-Atl 224.2	Moss-Atl .221	Millwood-Atl .292	Oswalt-Hou 3.01	Schilling-Ari 139	Glavine-Atl 26.0	**Oswalt-Hou 3.5**

MONTY HALL WOULD HAVE BEEN PROUD

In a transaction worthy of *Let's Make a Deal*, Florida owner John Henry bought the Red Sox and sold the Marlins to Montreal owner Jeffrey Loria. What was behind door number three? The Expos. The other 29 clubs took ownership of Montreal, rather than sell to an owner who would oppose contraction. Several Latin players were found to be older than previously thought. The discrepancies were discovered during increased background checks following the 2001 terrorist attacks.

The Rockies began treating baseballs in a Coors Field "humidor" in an attempt to decrease scoring. It seemed to work and helped league scoring drop to its lowest level since 1992, the last season BC: Before Colorado. Even so, Barry Bonds became only the fourth player to hit 600 home runs. Tragedy claimed the life of two active players: San Diego outfielder Mike Darr was killed in a car wreck during spring training, and St. Louis pitcher Darryl Kile died of heart problems in midseason. Hall of Famer Enos Slaughter and legendary Cardinals broadcaster Jack Buck also passed.

St. Louis overpowered Randy Johnson in Game 1 of the NLDS and wound up sweeping their series with Arizona. Three Bonds homers helped San Francisco beat Atlanta in a five-game Division Series. Bonds homered only once in the NLCS, as he was walked 10 times, but the Giants beat St. Louis in five with clutch hitting by the rest of the lineup. San Francisco was a win away from a World Series title, but the Giants dropped two heartbreakers and lost to Anaheim in seven.

2002 AMERICAN LEAGUE

TEAM	W	L	T	PCT	GB	HW	HL	R	OR	PA	H	2B	3B	HR	BB	SO	HB	SH	AVG	OBP	SLG	OPS	AOPS	BR	ABR	PF	SB	CS	BSA	BSR
East																														
NY	103	58	0	.640	—	52	28	**897**	697	6377	1540	314	12	223	**640**	1171	72	23	.275	**.354**	**.455**	**809**	**114**	**124**	**132**	99	100	38	72	9
Bos	93	69	0	.574	10.5	42	39	859	665	6332	1560	**348**	33	177	545	944	72	22	.277	.345	.444	789	106	78	63	102	80	28	74	8
Tor	78	84	0	.481	25.5	42	39	813	828	6230	1457	305	38	187	522	1142	53	17	.261	.327	.430	757	95	-1	-29	104	71	18	**80**	9
Bal	67	95	0	.414	36.5	34	47	667	773	6096	1353	311	27	165	452	993	64	40	.246	.309	.403	712	93	-98	-61	95	110	48	70	7
TB	55	106	0	.342	48	30	51	673	918	6198	1418	297	35	133	456	1115	58	44	.253	.314	.390	704	88	-112	-98	98	102	45	69	7
Central																														
Min	94	67	0	.584	—	**54**	27	768	712	6196	1518	**348**	36	167	472	1089	56	34	.272	.332	.437	769	99	26	0	103	79	62	56	-4
Chi	81	81	0	.500	13.5	47	34	856	798	6207	1475	289	29	217	555	952	49	48	.268	.338	.449	787	103	62	31	104	75	31	71	6
Cle	74	88	0	.457	20.5	39	42	739	837	6099	1349	255	26	192	542	1000	56	39	.249	.321	.412	733	91	-51	-64	102	52	37	58	-2
KC	62	100	0	.383	32.5	37	44	737	891	6206	1415	285	**42**	140	524	921	52	44	.256	.323	.398	721	81	-68	-147	113	**140**	65	68	8
Det	55	106	0	.342	39	33	47	575	864	5920	1340	265	37	124	363	1035	64	30	.248	.300	.379	679	82	-163	-141	96	65	44	60	-1
West																														
Oak	103	59	0	.636	—	**54**	27	800	654	6291	1450	279	28	205	609	1008	68	20	.261	.339	.432	771	104	35	41	99	46	20	70	3
Ana	99	63	0	.611	4	**54**	27	851	**644**	6327	**1603**	333	32	152	462	**805**	**74**	**49**	**.282**	.341	.433	774	106	44	58	98	117	51	70	8
Sea	93	69	0	.574	10	48	33	814	699	6362	1531	285	31	152	629	1003	51	41	.275	.350	.419	769	108	49	78	97	137	58	70	**10**
Tex	72	90	0	.444	31	42	39	843	882	6332	1510	304	27	**230**	554	1055	62	48	.269	.338	**.455**	793	106	76	53	103	62	34	65	2
Total	1132	—	—	—	—	608	524	10892	—	87173	20519	4218	433	2464	7325	14233	851	499	.264	.331	.424	755	—	—	—	—	1236	579	68	69

TEAM	CG	SHO	GR	SV	IP	H	HR	BB	SO	BR/9	ERA	AERA	OAV	OOB	PR	APR	PF	OSB	OCS	FA	E	WPB	DP	FW	PW	BW	BSW	DIF
East																												
NY	9	11	334	53	1452.0	1441	144	**403**	1135	11.7	3.87	112	.256	.309	94	75	97	92	39	.979	127	69	117	-1.2	7.2	**12.7**	.4	3.4
Bos	5	17	338	51	1446.0	**1339**	146	430	**1157**	**11.5**	3.75	119	**.246**	**.308**	113	114	100	118	50	.983	104	51	140	.2	11.0	6.1	.3	-5.5
Tor	6	6	461	41	1438.1	1504	177	590	991	13.5	4.80	96	.269	.344	-55	-29	104	107	41	.982	107	75	159	.0	-2.8	-2.8	.4	2.2
Bal	8	3	407	31	1450.2	1491	208	549	967	13.0	4.46	97	.266	.336	0	-21	97	103	44	.985	91	76	**173**	.9	-2.0	-5.9	.2	-7.2
TB	**12**	3	306	25	1440.1	1567	215	620	925	14.3	5.29	85	.279	.357	-133	-123	101	92	53	.979	126	75	168	-1.2	-11.8	-9.4	.2	-3.3
Central																												
Min	8	9	435	47	1444.2	1454	184	439	1026	12.1	4.12	108	.261	.318	54	54	100	**57**	27	**.987**	**74**	67	124	**1.9**	5.2	.0	-.9	7.3
Chi	7	7	423	35	1423.0	1422	190	528	945	12.7	4.53	99	.260	.330	-11	-5	101	99	38	.984	97	63	157	.6	-.5	3.0	.1	-3.2
Cle	9	4	421	34	1424.2	1508	142	603	1058	13.7	4.91	90	.274	.348	-71	-76	99	126	**59**	.981	113	67	161	-.4	-7.3	-6.2	-.7	7.5
KC	**12**	6	421	30	1441.0	1587	212	572	909	13.8	5.21	96	.281	.349	-120	-33	112	90	36	.979	130	76	153	-1.4	-3.2	-14.1	.3	-.6
Det	11	7	372	33	1414.0	1593	163	463	794	13.5	4.92	89	.285	.343	-73	-88	98	72	34	.977	142	82	148	-2.1	-8.5	-13.6	-.6	-.8
West																												
Oak	9	**19**	408	48	1452.0	1391	**135**	474	1021	11.9	**3.68**	**122**	.252	.315	**126**	**128**	100	68	46	.984	102	**49**	144	.3	**12.3**	3.9	-.2	5.6
Ana	7	14	400	**54**	1452.1	1345	169	509	999	11.8	3.69	121	.247	.314	124	127	100	78	51	.986	87	59	151	1.2	12.2	5.6	.3	-1.3
Sea	8	12	343	43	1445.1	1422	178	441	1063	11.9	4.07	106	.257	.315	62	38	96	66	35	.985	88	**49**	134	1.1	3.7	7.5	**.5**	-.8
Tex	4	4	**487**	33	1439.2	1528	194	669	1030	14.2	5.15	93	.272	.355	-111	-56	107	74	28	.984	99	95	152	.5	-5.4	5.1	-.3	-8.9
Total	115	122	5556	558	20164.0	—	—	—	—	12.8	4.46	—	.264	.331	—	—	—	—	—	.982	1487	953	2081	—	—	—	—	—

BATTER-FIELDER WINS	BATTING AVERAGE	ON-BASE PERCENTAGE	SLUGGING AVERAGE	ON-BASE PLUS SLUGGING	ADJUSTED OPS	ADJUSTED BATTER RUNS
A.Rodriguez-Tex 7.4	Ramirez-Bos.........349	Ramirez-Bos.........450	Thome-Cle............677	Thome-Cle..........1122	Thome-Cle............190	Thome-Cle...........68.3
Garciaparra-Bos 5.4	Sweeney-KC.........340	Thome-Cle............445	Ramirez-Bos..........647	Ramirez-Bos.......1097	Ramirez-Bos..........184	Giambi-NY...........65.8
Thome-Cle.......... 5.1	B.Williams-NY.......333	Giambi-NY............435	A.Rodriguez-Tex...623	Giambi-NY..........1034	Giambi-NY............173	Ramirez-Bos........56.6
Ramirez-Bos 4.6	Suzuki-Sea...........321	Sweeney-KC.........417	Giambi-NY............598	A.Rodriguez-Tex.1015	A.Rodriguez-Tex...160	A.Rodriguez-Tex..54.3
Giambi-NY.......... 4.5	Ordonez-Chi.........320	B.Williams-NY.......415	Ordonez-Chi.........597	Sweeney-KC.........979	Ordonez-Chi.........149	Ordonez-Chi........42.0
RUNS	**HITS**	**DOUBLES**	**TRIPLES**	**HOME RUNS**	**TOTAL BASES**	**RUNS BATTED IN**
Soriano-NY...........128	Soriano-NY...........209	Garciaparra-Bos.....56	Damon-Bos.............11	A.Rodriguez-Tex.....57	A.Rodriguez-Tex...389	A.Rodriguez-Tex...142
A.Rodriguez-Tex...125	Suzuki-Sea...........208	Anderson-Ana.........56	Winn-TB....................9	Thome-Cle..............52	Soriano-NY...........381	Ordonez-Chi.........135
Jeter-NY...............124	B.Williams-NY.......204	Soriano-NY.............51	Young-Tex.................8	Palmeiro-Tex...........43	Ordonez-Chi.........352	Tejada-Oak...........131
Giambi-NY............120	Tejada-Oak...........204	Ordonez-Chi...........47	Suzuki-Sea...............8	Giambi-NY..............41	Anderson-Ana.......344	Anderson-Ana.......123
Damon-Bos...........118	Garciaparra-Bos...197	Beltran-KC..............44	Beltran-KC................7	Soriano-NY.............39	Tejada-Oak...........336	Giambi-NY............122
BASES ON BALLS	**STOLEN BASES**	**BASE STEALING RUNS**	**FIELDING RUNS-INFIELD**	**FIELDING RUNS-OUTFIELD**	**OUTFIELD ASSISTS**	**CATCHER CS PCT.**
Thome-Cle............122	Soriano-NY.............41	Jeter-NY................6.0	Bordick-Bal...........26.2	Erstad-Ana...........19.4	Fick-Det..................21	B.Molina-Ana.......44.9
Giambi-NY............109	Beltran-KC..............35	Beltran-KC.............5.3	Garciaparra-Bos..18.8	Jones-Min............13.3	Higginson-Det.........15	Hernandez-Oak...40.0
Palmeiro-Tex.........104	Jeter-NY.................32	Damon-Bos............4.7	Young-Tex............13.9	Fick-Det.................9.3	Winn-TB..................13	Hall-TB.................37.5
Delgado-Tor..........102		Soriano-NY............4.5	Vizquel-Cle...........12.7	Suzuki-Sea............6.7	Beltran-KC..............12	I.Rodriguez-Tex...36.6
Olerud-Sea............98		Cameron-Sea........4.0	Chavez-Oak.........12.2	Rowand-Chi...........5.8		Gil-Bal.................36.5
WINS	**WINNING PCT.**	**WINS ABOVE TEAM**	**GAMES STARTED**	**COMPLETE GAMES**	**FEWEST HITS/GAME**	**FEWEST BB/GAME**
Zito-Oak..................23	Martinez-Bos........833	Zito-Oak................7.8	Zito-Oak..................35	Byrd-KC....................7	Martinez-Bos.......6.50	Reed-Min............1.24
Lowe-Bos................21	Zito-Oak................821	Martinez-Bos.........7.8		Kennedy-TB.............5	Wakefield-Bos......6.67	Byrd-KC...............1.50
Martinez-Bos..........20	Washburn-Ana......750	Halladay-Tor..........6.8		Buehrle-Chi..............5	Lowe-Bos............6.80	Milton-Min............1.58
		Lowe-Bos...............5.8			Zito-Oak..............7.14	Martinez-Bos.......1.81
		Byrd-KC.................5.7			Moyer-Sea...........7.73	Lidle-Oak.............1.83
STRIKEOUTS	**STRIKEOUTS/GAME**	**GAMES**	**SAVES**	**BASE RUNNERS/9**	**ADJUSTED RELIEF RUNS**	**RELIEF RANKING**
Martinez-Bos........239	Martinez-Bos.....10.79	Koch-Oak................84	Guardado-Min.........45	Rhodes-Sea.........7.49	Romero-Min.........23.8	Percival-Ana........32.9
Clemens-NY.........192	Clemens-NY........9.60	Romero-Min............81	Koch-Oak................44	Groom-Bal...........8.42	Groom-Bal...........19.8	Julio-Bal...............31.0
Zito-Oak................182	Mussina-NY.........7.60	Stanton-NY.............79	Urbina-Bos..............40	Hawkins-Min........8.74	Hawkins-Min........19.7	Rhodes-Sea.........30.7
Mussina-NY..........182	Wakefield-Bos......7.38	Karsay-NY...............78	Percival-Ana...........40	Martinez-Bos.......8.98	Rhodes-Sea.........16.5	Romero-Min.........29.6
Garcia-Sea...........181	Garcia-Sea...........7.28	Escobar-Tor............76	Escobar-Tor............38	Lowe-Bos............9.26	Percival-Ana.......16.5	Koch-Oak.............24.6
INNINGS PITCHED	**OPPONENTS' AVG.**	**OPPONENTS' OBP**	**EARNED RUN AVERAGE**	**ADJUSTED ERA**	**ADJUSTED STARTER RUNS**	**PITCHER WINS**
Halladay-Tor.......239.1	Martinez-Bos........198	Martinez-Bos........254	Martinez-Bos.......2.26	Martinez-Bos........198	Lowe-Bos............48.2	**Lowe-Bos............6.2**
Buehrle-Chi.........239.0	Wakefield-Bos.......204	Lowe-Bos..............266	Lowe-Bos............2.58	Lowe-Bos..............173	Martinez-Bos.......45.9	**Martinez-Bos.....5.2**
Hudson-Oak.........238.1	Lowe-Bos..............211	Wakefield-Bos.......276	Zito-Oak..............2.75	Zito-Oak................163	Zito-Oak...............43.1	**Zito-Oak.............4.9**
Moyer-Sea...........230.2	Zito-Oak................218	Moyer-Sea............278	Wakefield-Bos......2.81	Wakefield-Bos.......159	Hudson-Oak.........39.4	**Halladay-Tor......4.0**
Zito-Oak..............229.1	Moyer-Sea............230	Reed-Min..............288	Halladay-Tor.........2.93	Halladay-Tor.........158	Halladay-Tor.........39.4	**Hudson-Oak.......3.8**

(Labor) Peace of Mind

Major League Baseball endured a rocky season as the plan to contract two teams failed because of Minnesota state court rulings. Then, in the Midsummer Classic in Milwaukee's new Miller Park, the commissioner had to declare the All-Star Game a tie when both leagues ran out of pitchers after the 11th inning. After the rough start, however, things improved dramatically when a deadline deal averted a strike by the players.

Texas superstar Alex Rodriguez became the first shortstop with back-to-back 50 home runs seasons. Ted Williams, called by many—including himself—the greatest hitter ever, died.

The Twins, who would have been contracted if Selig had his way, won the Central. Many expected a quick exit, but the Twins survived a five-game ALDS against Oakland, which rode a league-record 20-game winning streak to the West title. The A's had the tying run on base with two outs in the ninth, but Twins closer "Everyday" Eddie Guardado finally shut the door. Wild Card Anaheim pounded the Yankees in the other ALDS, batting .376 and scoring 31 runs in four games. The Angels' hitting continued in a five-game win over the Twins in the ALCS.

The Angels capped a magical season with a seven-game triumph over San Francisco in the World Series. Facing elimination, Anaheim rallied from a 5-0 deficit in Game 6, and then won the next night behind rookie starter John Lackey. Francisco Rodriguez, aka K-Rod, didn't make his big league debut until September 18, but he had 5 wins during Anaheim's unlikely October run and led an outstanding bullpen.

2001 NATIONAL LEAGUE

TEAM	W	L	T	PCT	GB	HW	HL	R	OR	PA	H	2B	3B	HR	BB	SO	HB	SH	AVG	OBP	SLG	OPS	AOPS	BR	ABR	PF	SB	CS	BSA	BSR
EAST																														
Atl	88	74	0	.543	—	40	41	729	**643**	6152	1432	263	24	174	493	1039	45	64	.260	.324	.412	736	93	-45	-51	101	85	46	65	3
Phi	86	76	0	.531	2	47	34	746	719	6219	1431	295	29	164	551	1125	43	67	.260	.329	.414	743	101	-22	15	95	**153**	47	**77**	**17**
NY	82	80	0	.506	6	44	37	642	713	6156	1361	273	18	147	545	1062	65	52	.249	.323	.387	710	95	-89	-38	93	66	48	58	-2
Fla	76	86	0	.469	12	46	34	742	744	6184	1461	**325**	30	166	470	1145	67	60	.264	.326	.423	749	100	-17	9	97	89	40	69	6
Mon	68	94	0	.420	20	34	47	670	812	6026	1361	320	28	131	478	1071	60	64	.253	.319	.396	715	90	-81	-75	99	101	51	66	4
CENTRAL																														
Hou	93	69	0	.574	—	44	37	847	769	6325	1500	313	29	208	581	1119	**89**	71	.271	.347	.451	798	103	95	37	107	64	49	57	-3
StL	93	69	0	.574	—	**54**	28	814	684	6177	1469	274	32	199	529	1089	65	83	.270	.339	.441	780	103	47	31	102	91	35	72	8
Chi	88	74	0	.543	5	48	33	777	701	6219	1409	268	32	194	577	1077	66	**117**	.261	.336	.430	766	105	23	50	97	67	36	65	2
Mil	68	94	0	.420	25	36	45	740	806	6148	1378	273	30	209	488	1399	72	65	.251	.319	.426	745	98	-36	-19	98	66	36	65	2
Cin	66	96	0	.407	27	27	54	735	850	6222	1464	304	22	176	468	1172	65	66	.262	.324	.419	743	91	-31	-68	105	103	54	66	4
Pit	62	100	0	.383	31	38	43	657	858	6027	1333	256	25	161	467	1106	67	60	.247	.313	.393	706	84	-107	-122	103	93	73	56	-5
WEST																														
Ari	92	70	0	.568	—	48	33	818	677	6346	1494	284	35	208	587	1052	57	71	.267	.341	.442	783	99	55	3	107	71	38	65	2
SF	90	72	0	.556	2	49	32	799	748	6408	1493	304	40	**235**	625	1090	50	67	.266	.342	.460	802	**118**	95	**152**	94	57	42	58	-2
LA	86	76	0	.531	6	44	37	758	744	6169	1399	264	27	206	519	1062	56	57	.255	.323	.425	748	104	-25	24	94	89	42	68	5
SD	79	83	0	.488	13	35	46	789	812	6278	1379	273	26	161	**678**	**1273**	41	29	.252	.336	.399	735	103	-28	34	92	129	44	75	13
Col	73	89	0	.451	19	41	40	**923**	906	6393	**1663**	324	**61**	213	511	1027	61	81	**.292**	**.354**	**.483**	**837**	100	**166**	8	120	132	54	71	10
Total	1296	—	—	—	—	675	621	12186	—	99449	23027	4613	488	2952	8567	17908	969	1074	.261	.331	.425	756	—	—	—	—	1456	735	66	63

TEAM	CG	SHO	GR	SV	IP	H	HR	BB	SO	BR/9	ERA	AERA	OAV	OOB	PR	APR	PF	OSB	OCS	FA	E	WPB	DP	FW	PW	BW	BSW	DIF
EAST																												
Atl	5	13	411	41	1447.1	1363	153	499	1133	11.8	**3.59**	**120**	.250	.314	**123**	115	99	102	50	.983	103	50	133	.4	11.2	-5.0	-.0	.4
Phi	8	7	473	47	1445.1	1417	170	527	1086	12.5	4.15	99	.259	.329	33	-8	94	57	32	.985	91	49	145	1.1	-.8	1.5	**1.3**	2.0
NY	6	**14**	397	**48**	1445.2	1418	186	**438**	1191	11.8	4.07	99	.257	.314	46	-6	93	131	40	.983	101	64	132	.5	-.6	-3.7	-.6	5.3
Fla	5	11	430	32	1438.0	1397	151	617	1119	13.0	4.32	96	.257	.338	5	-28	96	75	51	.983	103	50	**174**	.4	-2.7	.9	.2	-3.8
Mon	5	11	**491**	28	1431.1	1509	190	525	1103	13.2	4.68	92	.272	.339	-52	-60	99	128	33	.982	108	67	139	.1	-5.8	-7.3	.0	-.0
CENTRAL																												
Hou	7	6	405	**48**	1454.2	1453	221	486	1228	12.4	4.37	105	.261	.325	-3	33	105	66	49	.982	110	**46**	138	.0	3.2	3.6	-.7	5.8
StL	8	11	484	38	1435.1	1389	196	526	1083	12.5	3.93	110	.256	.328	68	63	99	**51**	37	.982	110	52	156	.0	6.1	3.0	.4	2.4
Chi	8	6	452	41	1437.0	1357	164	550	**1344**	12.3	4.03	104	.249	.321	53	26	96	106	46	.982	109	61	113	.0	2.5	4.9	-.2	-.3
Mil	3	8	489	28	1436.1	1452	197	667	1057	13.7	4.64	92	.265	.350	-45	-57	98	93	47	.983	103	69	156	.4	-5.5	-1.8	-.2	-5.8
Cin	2	2	461	35	1442.2	1572	198	515	943	13.3	4.77	96	.279	.341	-67	-29	105	75	**62**	.978	138	74	136	-1.5	-2.8	-6.6	.0	-4.0
Pit	8	9	410	36	1416.1	1493	167	549	908	13.5	5.05	88	.272	.344	-108	-89	103	97	37	.978	133	58	168	-1.3	-8.7	-11.9	-.9	3.7
WEST																												
Ari	**12**	13	421	34	1459.2	**1352**	195	461	1297	**11.5**	3.87	**120**	**.247**	**.311**	79	**117**	106	107	55	**.986**	**84**	57	148	**1.5**	**11.4**	.3	-.2	-2.0
SF	3	8	439	47	1463.1	1437	**145**	579	1080	12.6	4.18	98	.258	.329	28	-17	94	86	45	.981	118	58	170	-.4	-1.7	**14.8**	-.6	-3.1
LA	3	5	408	46	1450.2	1387	184	524	1212	12.3	4.25	97	.252	.323	17	-23	95	82	51	.981	116	53	138	-.3	-2.2	2.3	.1	5.1
SD	5	6	422	46	1440.2	1519	219	476	1088	12.8	4.52	92	.269	.330	-27	-64	95	94	52	.976	145	61	127	-1.9	-6.2	3.3	.9	2.0
Col	8	8	476	26	1430.0	1522	239	598	1058	13.7	5.29	101	.275	.350	-149	4	122	100	36	.984	96	52	167	.8	.4	.8	.6	-10.6
Total	96	138	7069	621	23074.1	—	—	—	—	12.7	4.36	—	.261	.331	—	—	—	—	—	.982	1768	921	2340	—	—	—	—	—

BATTER-FIELDER WINS	BATTING AVERAGE	ON-BASE PERCENTAGE	SLUGGING AVERAGE	ON-BASE PLUS SLUGGING	ADJUSTED OPS	ADJUSTED BATTER RUNS
Bonds-SF 11.7	L.Walker-Col .350	Bonds-SF .515	Bonds-SF .863	Bonds-SF 1379	Bonds-SF 263	Bonds-SF 132.8
Sosa-Chi 8.6	Helton-Col .336	L.Walker-Col .449	Sosa-Chi .737	Sosa-Chi 1174	Sosa-Chi 204	Sosa-Chi 93.7
Gonzalez-Ari 5.8	Alou-Hou .331	Sosa-Chi .437	Gonzalez-Ari .688	Gonzalez-Ari 1117	Gonzalez-Ari 171	Gonzalez-Ari 67.4
Nevin-SD 5.2	Berkman-Hou .331	Helton-Col .432	Helton-Col .685	Helton-Col 1116	Sheffield-LA 166	C.Jones-Atl 56.3
Pujols-StL 5.0	C.Jones-Atl .330	Berkman-Hou .430	L.Walker-Col .662	L.Walker-Col 1111	C.Jones-Atl 162	Sheffield-LA 54.3

RUNS	HITS	DOUBLES	TRIPLES	HOME RUNS	TOTAL BASES	RUNS BATTED IN
Sosa-Chi 146	Aurilia-SF 206	Berkman-Hou 55	Rollins-Phi 12	Bonds-SF 73	Sosa-Chi 425	Sosa-Chi 160
Helton-Col 132	Pierre-Col 202	Helton-Col 54	Uribe-Col 11	Sosa-Chi 64	Gonzalez-Ari 419	Helton-Col 146
Bonds-SF 129	Gonzalez-Ari 198	Kent-SF 49	Pierre-Col 11	Gonzalez-Ari 57	Bonds-SF 411	Gonzalez-Ari 142
Gonzalez-Ari 128	Helton-Col 197	Abreu-Phi 48	Castillo-Fla 10	Helton-Col 49	Helton-Col 402	Bonds-SF 137
Bagwell-Hou 126	Pujols-StL 194	Pujols-StL 47		Green-LA 49	Green-LA 370	

BASES ON BALLS	STOLEN BASES	BASE STEALING RUNS	FIELDING RUNS-INFIELD	FIELDING RUNS-OUTFIELD	OUTFIELD ASSISTS	CATCHER CS PCT.
Bonds-SF 177	Rollins-Phi 46	Rollins-Phi 7.3	Cabrera-Mon 29.0	Shinjo-NY 12.7	Burrell-Phi 18	Ausmus-Hou 47.7
Sosa-Chi 116	Pierre-Col 46	Pierre-Col 4.2	Polanco-StL 24.3	A.Jones-Atl 11.1	Sheffield-LA 17	Blanco-Mil 42.3
Bagwell-Hou 106	Guerrero-Mon 37	Reese-Cin 4.1	Cirillo-Col 17.9	Jordan-Atl 10.2	Guerrero-Mon 14	Johnson-Fla 41.6
Abreu-Phi 106	Abreu-Phi 36	Glanville-Phi 4.1	Lugo-Hou 15.6	Glanville-Phi 6.3	Burnitz-Mil 13	Miller-Ari 36.4
Gonzalez-Ari 100	Castillo-Fla 33	Womack-Ari 3.7	Bagwell-Hou 15.0	Sosa-Chi 5.9		Estrada-Phi 35.4

WINS	WINNING PCT.	WINS ABOVE TEAM	GAMES STARTED	COMPLETE GAMES	FEWEST HITS/GAME	FEWEST BB/GAME
Schilling-Ari 22	Schilling-Ari .786	Schilling-Ari 7.7	Schilling-Ari 35	Schilling-Ari 6	Johnson-Ari 6.52	Maddux-Atl 1.04
Morris-StL 22	Johnson-Ari .778	Johnson-Ari 7.2	Park-LA 35	Vazquez-Mon 5	Wood-Chi 6.56	Schilling-Ari 1.37
Johnson-Ari 21	Lieber-Chi .769	Lieber-Chi 7.0	Glavine-Atl 35	Lieber-Chi 5	Park-LA 7.04	Lieber-Chi 1.59
Lieber-Chi 20	Morris-StL .733	Morris-StL 6.3			Burnett-Fla 7.53	Jones-SD 1.75
	Glavine-Atl .696	Oswalt-Hou 5.2			Burkett-Atl 7.67	Vazquez-Mon 1.77

STRIKEOUTS	STRIKEOUTS/GAME	GAMES	SAVES	BASE RUNNERS/9	ADJUSTED RELIEF RUNS	RELIEF RANKING
Johnson-Ari 372	Johnson-Ari 13.41	Kline-StL 89	Nen-SF 45	Rodriguez-SF 9.07	Rodriguez-SF 23.2	Wagner-Hou 26.1
Schilling-Ari 293	Wood-Chi 11.20	Lloyd-Mon 84	Shaw-LA 43	Reed-NY 9.16	Kline-StL 21.4	Rodriguez-SF 26.0
Park-LA 218	Schilling-Ari 10.27	King-Mil 82	Hoffman-SD 43	Nen-SF 9.39	Dotel-Hou 20.9	Kim-Ari 25.3
Wood-Chi 217	Wolf-Phi 8.39	Fassero-Chi 82	Benitez-NY 43	Schilling-Ari 9.71	Weathers-Mil-Chi 18.6	Batista-Ari 22.3
Vazquez-Mon 208	Park-LA 8.38		Mesa-Phi 42	Johnson-Ari 9.73	Kim-Ari 18.5	Dotel-Hou 22.2

INNINGS PITCHED	OPPONENTS' AVG.	OPPONENTS' OBP	EARNED RUN AVERAGE	ADJUSTED ERA	ADJUSTED STARTER RUNS	PITCHER WINS
Schilling-Ari 256.2	Wood-Chi .202	Schilling-Ari .273	Johnson-Ari 2.49	Johnson-Ari 186	Johnson-Ari 56.2	**Johnson-Ari 5.4**
Johnson-Ari 249.2	Johnson-Ari .203	Johnson-Ari .274	Schilling-Ari 2.98	Schilling-Ari 156	Schilling-Ari 46.8	**Schilling-Ari 4.4**
Park-LA 234.0	Park-LA .216	Vazquez-Mon .274	Burkett-Atl 3.04	Burkett-Atl 142	Maddux-Atl 33.8	**Maddux-Atl 4.2**
Maddux-Atl 233.0	Burkett-Atl .230	Maddux-Atl .278	Maddux-Atl 3.05	Maddux-Atl 141	Kile-StL 32.3	**Kile-StL 3.6**
Lieber-Chi 232.1	Burnett-Fla .231	Lieber-Chi .290	Kile-StL 3.09	Kile-StL 140	Burkett-Atl 31.1	**Morris-StL 3.3**

BONDS IS BEST

New ballparks opened in Pittsburgh and Milwaukee. Compared to recent openings, attendance was good the first season, but the numbers for both also-rans dropped by one-quarter the following season—a new stadium was no longer a cure-all. Umpire Al Clark was fired following allegations he broke MLB rules: exchanging first-class plane tickets for economy class (and pocketing the difference) and soliciting players' autographs to sell as memorabilia.

Barry Bonds had one of the most impressive seasons ever, breaking Mark McGwire's record with 73 home runs, and setting single-season marks for walks (177) and slugging percentage (.863). Sammy Sosa became the first player with 60 or more homers in three seasons. McGwire retired after the season, fifth on the all-time home run list; Tony Gwynn also hung up the spikes. Hall of Famers Eddie Mathews and Willie Stargell died.

Arizona won the West for the second time in four years, behind the pitching duo of Randy Johnson and Curt Schilling. Johnson fanned 20 Reds in May, equaling the nine-inning record, but he was removed when the game went into extra innings. Schilling, who won 22 during the season, tossed a complete-game in Game 5 of the Division Series as the Diamondbacks beat St. Louis in the bottom of the ninth. Atlanta swept Houston in the other Division Series. Johnson won both his starts in the D-backs' five-game NLCS victory over the Braves. Arizona and the Yankees played a seven-game World Series thriller, with Johnson winning three times, including Game 7 in relief. It took a ninth-inning rally, capped by a broken-bat hit by Luis Gonzalez, to give Arizona the title.

2001 AMERICAN LEAGUE

TEAM	W	L	T	PCT	GB	HW	HL	R	OR	PA	H	2B	3B	HR	BB	SO	HB	SH	AVG	OBP	SLG	OPS	AOPS	BR	ABR	PF	SB	CS	BSA	BSR
EAST																														
NY	95	65	1	.594	—	51	28	804	713	6233	1488	289	20	203	519	1035	64	30	.267	.334	.435	769	100	12	4	101	161	53	75	17
Bos	82	79	0	.509	13.5	41	40	772	745	6264	1493	316	29	198	520	1131	70	28	.266	.334	.439	773	102	21	19	100	46	35	57	-2
Tor	80	82	0	.494	16	40	42	767	753	6284	1489	287	36	195	470	1094	74	34	.263	.325	.430	755	95	-25	-42	102	156	55	74	15
Bal	63	98	1	.391	32.5	30	50	687	829	6150	1359	262	24	136	514	989	77	38	.248	.319	.380	699	89	-123	-87	95	133	53	72	11
TB	62	100	0	.383	34	37	44	672	887	6104	1426	311	21	121	456	1116	54	45	.258	.320	.388	708	87	-111	-100	98	115	52	69	7
CENTRAL																														
Cle	91	71	0	.562	—	44	36	897	821	6357	1559	294	37	212	577	1076	69	49	.278	.350	.458	808	107	100	65	104	79	41	66	3
Min	85	77	0	.525	6	47	34	771	766	6182	1514	328	38	164	495	1083	64	25	.272	.337	.433	770	96	17	-25	106	146	67	69	9
Chi	83	79	0	.512	8	46	35	798	795	6150	1463	300	29	214	520	998	52	**63**	.268	.334	.451	785	99	42	-6	106	123	59	68	6
Det	66	96	0	.407	25	37	44	724	876	6144	1439	291	**60**	139	466	972	51	41	.260	.320	.409	729	93	-72	-55	98	133	61	69	8
KC	65	97	0	.401	26	35	46	729	858	6176	1503	277	37	152	406	**898**	44	36	.266	.318	.409	727	82	-82	-147	110	100	42	70	7
WEST																														
Sea	116	46	0	.716	—	**57**	24	**927**	**627**	6474	**1637**	310	38	169	614	989	62	48	**.288**	**.360**	.445	805	**117**	**112**	**164**	95	**174**	42	**81**	**24**
Oak	102	60	0	.630	14	53	28	884	645	6385	1469	**334**	22	199	**640**	1021	**88**	25	.264	.345	.439	784	104	61	57	101	68	29	70	5
Ana	75	87	0	.463	41	39	42	691	730	6221	1447	275	26	158	494	1001	77	46	.261	.327	.405	732	90	-59	-73	102	116	52	69	7
Tex	73	89	0	.451	43	41	41	890	968	6388	1566	326	23	**246**	548	1093	75	25	.275	.344	**.471**	**815**	109	109	82	103	97	32	75	10
Total	1133	—	—	—	—	598	534	11013	—	87512	20852	4200	440	2506	7239	14496	921	533	.267	.334	.428	762	—	—	—	—	1647	673	71	127

TEAM	CG	SHO	GR	SV	IP	H	HR	BB	SO	BR/9	ERA	AERA	OAV	OOB	PR	APR	PF	OSB	OCS	FA	E	WPB	DP	FW	PW	BW	BSW	DIF
EAST																												
NY	7	9	362	**57**	1451.1	1429	158	465	**1266**	12.1	4.02	110	.257	.318	72	67	99	146	45	.982	109	75	132	.3	6.4	.4	.8	7.2
Bos	3	9	424	48	1448.0	1412	**146**	544	1259	12.7	4.15	107	.254	.329	53	46	99	223	51	.981	113	77	129	.0	4.4	1.8	-1.1	-3.7
Tor	7	10	471	41	1462.2	1553	165	490	1041	13.0	4.28	107	.275	.339	31	47	102	112	47	.985	97	**43**	184	1.0	4.5	-4.0	.6	-3.1
Bal	10	6	392	31	1432.1	1504	194	528	938	13.2	4.67	92	.269	.337	-32	-61	96	157	51	.979	125	52	137	-.6	-5.8	-8.3	.2	-2.9
TB	1	6	370	30	1423.2	1513	207	569	1030	13.6	4.94	91	.273	.345	-73	-69	101	113	44	.977	139	83	144	-1.4	-6.6	-9.6	-.2	-1.2
CENTRAL																												
Cle	3	4	**483**	42	1446.2	1512	148	573	1218	13.3	4.64	99	.270	.341	-27	-9	102	128	60	.982	107	70	137	.4	-.9	6.2	-.6	4.8
Min	12	8	402	45	1441.1	1494	192	445	965	12.5	4.51	103	.268	.325	-6	24	104	**73**	43	.982	108	62	118	.4	2.3	-2.4	.0	3.7
Chi	8	9	406	51	1433.1	1465	181	500	921	12.9	4.55	102	.266	.334	-13	15	104	107	40	.981	118	70	149	-.2	1.4	-.6	-.3	1.7
Det	**16**	2	391	34	1429.1	1624	180	553	859	14.2	5.01	88	.288	.357	-85	-95	99	104	50	.979	131	70	164	-1.0	-9.1	-5.3	-.1	.4
KC	5	1	396	30	1440.0	1537	209	576	911	13.6	4.87	102	.276	.348	-63	12	111	105	45	.981	117	83	**204**	-.2	1.1	-14.1	-.2	-2.7
WEST																												
Sea	8	**14**	391	56	1465.0	**1293**	160	465	1051	**11.2**	**3.54**	120	**.236**	**.301**	**152**	122	95	**73**	29	**.986**	**83**	46	137	**1.8**	11.7	**15.7**	**1.4**	4.4
Oak	13	9	416	44	1463.1	1384	153	**440**	1117	11.5	3.59	**127**	.249	.308	144	**154**	102	124	55	.980	125	46	151	-.6	**14.8**	5.5	-.4	1.8
Ana	6	1	384	43	1437.2	1452	168	525	947	12.8	4.20	111	.263	.331	44	68	104	109	59	.983	103	62	142	.7	6.5	-7.0	-.2	-6.0
Tex	4	3	410	37	1438.1	1670	222	596	951	14.6	5.71	83	.293	.362	-198	-142	107	79	**66**	.981	114	72	167	.0	-13.6	7.9	.0	-2.4
Total	103	91	5698	589	20213.0	—	—	—	—	12.9	4.47	—	.267	.334	—	—	—	—	—	.981	1589	911	2095	—	—	—	—	—

BATTER-FIELDER WINS	BATTING AVERAGE	ON-BASE PERCENTAGE	SLUGGING AVERAGE	ON-BASE PLUS SLUGGING	ADJUSTED OPS	ADJUSTED BATTER RUNS
A.Rodriguez-Tex 6.9	Suzuki-Sea .350	J.Giambi-Oak .477	J.Giambi-Oak .660	J.Giambi-Oak 1137	J.Giambi-Oak 196	J.Giambi-Oak 84.2
J.Giambi-Oak 6.3	J.Giambi-Oak .342	Martinez-Sea .423	Thome-Cle .624	Thome-Cle 1040	Thome-Cle 163	A.Rodriguez-Tex 56.2
Alomar-Cle 5.6	Alomar-Cle .336	Thome-Cle .416	A.Rodriguez-Tex .622	A.Rodriguez-Tex 1021	Martinez-Sea 163	Thome-Cle 51.7
Martinez-Sea 4.1	Boone-Sea .331	Alomar-Cle .415	Ramirez-Bos .609	Ramirez-Bos 1014	Ramirez-Bos 162	Ramirez-Bos 50.0
Ramirez-Bos 3.8	Catalanotto-Tex .330	Delgado-Tor .408	Gonzalez-Cle .590	Martinez-Sea 966	A.Rodriguez-Tex 160	Martinez-Sea 49.9
RUNS	**HITS**	**DOUBLES**	**TRIPLES**	**HOME RUNS**	**TOTAL BASES**	**RUNS BATTED IN**
A.Rodriguez-Tex 133	Suzuki-Sea 242	J.Giambi-Oak 47	Guzman-Min 14	A.Rodriguez-Tex 52	A.Rodriguez-Tex 393	Boone-Sea 141
Suzuki-Sea 127	Boone-Sea 206	Sweeney-KC 46	Beltran-KC 12	Thome-Cle 49	Boone-Sea 360	Gonzalez-Cle 140
Boone-Sea 118	Stewart-Tor 202	Stewart-Tor 44	Alomar-Cle 12	Palmeiro-Tex 47	J.Giambi-Oak 343	A.Rodriguez-Tex 135
Alomar-Cle 113	A.Rodriguez-Tex 201	Chavez-Oak 43	Cedeno-Det 11	Ramirez-Bos 41	Palmeiro-Tex 338	Ramirez-Bos 125
Jeter-NY 110	Anderson-Ana 194	Durham-Chi 42	Durham-Chi 10	Glaus-Ana 41	Thome-Cle 328	Thome-Cle 124
BASES ON BALLS	**STOLEN BASES**	**BASE STEALING RUNS**	**FIELDING RUNS-INFIELD**	**FIELDING RUNS-OUTFIELD**	**OUTFIELD ASSISTS**	**CATCHER CS PCT.**
J.Giambi-Oak 129	Suzuki-Sea 56	Suzuki-Sea 7.4	Gonzalez-Tor 33.3	Hunter-Min 18.6	Mondesi-Tor 18	I.Rodriguez-Tex 60.3
Thome-Cle 111	Cedeno-Det 55	Cedeno-Det 6.8	Menechino-Oak 17.6	Singleton-Chi 7.3	Hunter-Min 14	Pierzynski-Min 32.3
Delgado-Tor 111	Soriano-NY 43	Beltran-KC 6.5	Halter-Det 14.4	Suzuki-Sea 7.0	Beltran-KC 14	B.Molina-Ana 31.8
Glaus-Ana 107	McLemore-Sea 39	McLemore-Sea 6.1	Easley-Det 12.7	Higginson-Det 6.7	Salmon-Ana 13	Fletcher-Tor 29.2
Palmeiro-Tex 101	Knoblauch-NY 38	Cameron-Sea 5.7	Chavez-Oak 12.3	Salmon-Ana 6.2		Fordyce-Bal 19.8
WINS	**WINNING PCT.**	**WINS ABOVE TEAM**	**GAMES STARTED**	**COMPLETE GAMES**	**FEWEST HITS/GAME**	**FEWEST BB/GAME**
Mulder-Oak 21	Clemens-NY .870	Clemens-NY 8.2	Zito-Oak 35	Sparks-Det 8	Sabathia-Cle 7.44	Radke-Min 1.04
Moyer-Sea 20	Abbott-Sea .810	Sabathia-Cle 5.7	Hudson-Oak 35	Radke-Min 6	Garcia-Sea 7.50	Mussina-NY 1.65
Clemens-NY 20	Sabathia-Cle .773	Quantrill-Tor 4.6		Mulder-Oak 6	Buehrle-Chi 7.64	Pettitte-NY 1.84
Hudson-Oak 18	Moyer-Sea .769	Sparks-Det 4.3		Weaver-Det 5	Zito-Oak 7.73	Moyer-Sea 1.89
Garcia-Sea 18		Mulder-Oak 4.3			Nomo-Bos 7.77	Loaiza-Tor 1.89
STRIKEOUTS	**STRIKEOUTS/GAME**	**GAMES**	**SAVES**	**BASE RUNNERS/9**	**ADJUSTED RELIEF RUNS**	**RELIEF RANKING**
Nomo-Bos 220	Nomo-Bos 10.00	Quantrill-Tor 80	M.Rivera-NY 50	Rhodes-Sea 7.81	Foulke-Chi 21.0	Foulke-Chi 42.0
Mussina-NY 214	Clemens-NY 8.70	Stanton-NY 76	Sasaki-Sea 45	M.Rivera-NY 8.26	Rhodes-Sea 20.2	M.Rivera-NY 37.0
Clemens-NY 213	Zito-Oak 8.61	Grimsley-KC 73	Foulke-Chi 42	Sasaki-Sea 8.51	M.Rivera-NY 18.5	Levine-Ana 33.9
Zito-Oak 205	Sabathia-Cle 8.53	Foulke-Chi 72	Percival-Ana 39	Zimmerman-Tex 8.58	Zimmerman-Tex 18.2	Zimmerman-Tex 30.8
Colon-Cle 201	Mussina-NY 8.42		Koch-Tor 36	Pineiro-Sea 8.84	Levine-Ana 17.0	Wickman-Cle 25.1
INNINGS PITCHED	**OPPONENTS' AVG.**	**OPPONENTS' OBP**	**EARNED RUN AVERAGE**	**ADJUSTED ERA**	**ADJUSTED STARTER RUNS**	**PITCHER WINS**
Garcia-Sea 238.2	Garcia-Sea .225	Mussina-NY .274	Garcia-Sea 3.05	Mays-Min 148	Mays-Min 37.6	**Mays-Min 4.4**
Hudson-Oak 235.0	Sabathia-Cle .228	Buehrle-Chi .279	Mussina-NY 3.15	Buehrle-Chi 141	Garcia-Sea 33.6	**Foulke-Chi 4.2**
Mays-Min 233.2	Zito-Oak .230	Garcia-Sea .283	Mays-Min 3.16	Mussina-NY 141	Mussina-NY 33.4	**M.Rivera-NY 3.8**
Sparks-Det 232.0	Buehrle-Chi .230	Moyer-Sea .285	Buehrle-Chi 3.29	Garcia-Sea 139	Buehrle-Chi 32.2	**Mussina-NY 3.7**
	Nomo-Bos .231	Mays-Min .289	Hudson-Oak 3.37	Hudson-Oak 135	Mulder-Oak 29.9	**Mulder-Oak 3.6**

TRAGEDY AFFECTS ALL

Baseball, like the rest of the world, was affected by the September 11 terrorist attacks in New York, Washington, D.C., and Pennsylvania. Games were postponed for six days while the nation evaluated its new travel procedures. No contests were lost, however, as the season was extended by a week. That meant a first-ever November finish for the World Series.

Texas and Toronto began the season in Puerto Rico, the third consecutive season opener outside the U.S. or Canada. Cal Ripken, Harold Baines, and Paul O'Neill retired; Lou Boudreau died.

Seattle's Ichiro Suzuki, a former Japanese superstar, finished the year with 242 hits, the highest total since 1930. The right fielder, known simply as Ichiro on two continents, helped the Mariners to a league-record 116 wins. Oakland, a distant second, won 102 games to take the Wild Card.

The Yankees, East champs again, looked in trouble against the A's in the Division Series. Oakland won the first two games, but New York came back, thanks to one of the most replayed defensive gems in postseason history. With the Yankees leading Game 3, 1-0, shortstop Derek Jeter ranged across the diamond to corral a throw from right field, and threw off balance to catcher Jorge Posada to nail Jeremy Giambi. Like New York, Seattle survived a five-game ALDS. Jamie Moyer and three relievers held Cleveland to 4 hits and 1 run in the deciding game. New York became the first club to win an LCS four straight times—spoiling a guarantee by Mariners manager Lou Piniella—but the Yankees were finally beaten in the World Series by Arizona.

2000 NATIONAL LEAGUE

TEAM	W	L	T	PCT	GB	HW	HL	R	OR	PA	H	2B	3B	HR	BB	SO	HB	SH	AVG	OBP	SLG	OPS	AOPS	BR	ABR	PF	SB	CS	BSA	BSR
East																														
Atl	95	67	0	.586	—	51	30	810	**714**	6275	1490	274	26	179	595	1010	59	87	.271	.346	.429	775	101	7	17	99	148	56	73	13
NY	94	68	0	.580	1	**55**	26	807	738	6327	1445	281	20	198	675	1037	45	70	.263	.346	.430	776	106	13	63	94	66	46	59	-2
Fla	79	82	0	.491	15.5	43	38	731	797	6202	1441	274	29	160	540	1184	60	42	.262	.331	.409	740	96	-70	-29	95	**168**	55	75	**18**
Mon	67	95	0	.414	28	37	44	738	902	6152	1475	310	35	178	476	1048	29	78	.266	.326	.432	758	95	-49	-51	100	58	48	55	-4
Phi	65	97	0	.401	30	34	47	708	830	6273	1386	304	40	144	611	1117	44	70	.251	.329	.400	729	89	-92	-86	99	102	30	**77**	12
Central																														
StL	95	67	0	.586	—	50	31	887	771	6369	1481	259	25	235	675	1253	**84**	79	.270	.356	.455	811	107	84	68	102	87	51	63	1
Cin	85	77	1	.525	10	43	38	825	765	6372	1545	302	36	200	559	995	64	56	.274	.343	.447	790	100	32	10	103	100	38	72	9
Mil	73	89	1	.451	22	42	39	740	826	6354	1366	297	25	177	620	1245	61	61	.246	.325	.403	728	89	-95	-87	99	72	44	62	0
Hou	72	90	0	.444	23	39	42	938	944	6444	1547	289	36	**249**	673	1129	83	57	.278	.361	**.477**	**838**	107	**137**	70	108	114	52	69	7
Pit	69	93	0	.426	26	37	44	793	888	6369	1506	**320**	31	168	564	1032	66	59	.267	.339	.424	763	97	-24	-23	100	86	40	68	5
Chi	65	97	0	.401	30	38	43	764	904	6397	1426	272	23	183	632	1120	54	**89**	.256	.335	.411	746	93	-56	-44	98	93	37	72	8
West																														
SF	97	65	0	.599	—	**55**	26	925	747	6418	1535	304	44	226	**709**	1032	51	73	.278	**.362**	.472	834	**122**	133	**202**	93	79	39	67	4
LA	86	76	0	.531	11	44	37	798	729	6312	1408	265	28	211	668	1083	51	66	.257	.341	.431	772	104	-4	39	95	95	42	69	6
Ari	85	77	0	.525	12	47	34	792	754	6240	1466	282	44	179	535	975	59	61	.265	.333	.429	762	93	-29	-54	103	97	44	69	6
Col	82	80	0	.506	15	48	33	**968**	897	6453	**1664**	**320**	**53**	161	601	**907**	42	75	**.294**	**.362**	.455	817	90	102	-72	123	131	61	68	7
SD	76	86	0	.469	21	41	40	752	815	6290	1413	279	37	157	602	1177	46	39	.254	.330	.402	732	95	-87	-37	94	131	53	71	10
Total	1296	—	—	—	—	704	592	12976	—	101247	23594	4632	532	3005	9735	17344	898	1062	.266	.342	.432	773	—	—	—	—	1627	736	69	100

TEAM	CG	SHO	GR	SV	IP	H	HR	BB	SO	BR/9	ERA	AERA	OAV	OOB	PR	APR	PF	OSB	OCS	FA	E	WPB	DP	FW	PW	BW	BSW	DIF
East																												
Atl	13	9	376	**53**	1440.1	1428	165	**484**	1093	**12.2**	**4.05**	**111**	.258	**.319**	**93**	**75**	97	99	33	.979	129	**32**	138	-.6	**7.1**	1.6	.6	5.3
NY	8	10	411	49	1450.0	1398	164	574	1164	12.6	4.16	105	**.252**	.327	76	34	94	133	46	.980	118	42	121	-.0	3.2	5.9	-.8	4.7
Fla	5	4	429	48	1429.2	1477	169	650	1051	13.7	4.59	95	.269	.348	6	-36	95	104	55	.980	125	61	144	-.5	-3.4	-2.7	**1.1**	4.0
Mon	4	7	452	39	1424.2	1575	181	579	1011	14.0	5.13	92	.282	.353	-79	-66	102	123	38	.978	132	74	151	-.8	-6.2	-4.8	-1.0	-1.2
Phi	8	6	414	34	1438.2	1458	201	640	1123	13.4	4.77	96	.265	.343	-23	-31	99	77	44	.983	100	58	136	1.0	-2.9	-8.1	.5	-6.5
Central																												
StL	10	7	386	37	1433.2	1403	196	606	1100	13.0	4.38	106	.259	.338	39	41	100	**70**	**66**	.981	111	57	148	.4	3.9	6.4	-.5	3.9
Cin	8	7	387	42	1456.1	1446	190	659	1015	13.3	4.33	110	.261	.341	49	68	103	81	33	.982	111	108	156	.4	6.4	.9	.3	-4.0
Mil	2	7	433	29	1466.1	1501	174	728	967	14.1	4.63	100	.269	.357	-1	-4	100	86	58	.981	118	72	**187**	.0	-.4	-8.2	-.6	1.2
Hou	8	2	410	30	1437.2	1596	234	598	1064	14.1	5.42	90	.281	.352	-125	-78	106	111	32	.978	133	61	149	-.9	-7.4	6.6	.0	-7.5
Pit	5	7	466	27	1449.0	1554	163	711	1070	14.4	4.94	94	.277	.361	-50	-49	100	101	42	.979	132	79	169	-.8	-4.6	-2.2	-.1	-4.3
Chi	10	5	421	39	1454.2	1505	231	658	1143	13.8	5.25	87	.268	.348	-101	-112	99	94	54	.983	100	51	139	1.0	-10.6	-4.2	.2	-2.4
West																												
SF	9	**15**	384	47	1444.1	1452	**151**	623	1076	13.2	4.21	103	.266	.342	68	23	94	97	48	**.985**	**93**	58	173	**1.3**	2.2	**19.1**	-.2	-6.4
LA	9	11	371	36	1445.0	**1379**	176	600	1154	12.8	4.10	108	**.252**	.332	84	55	96	106	52	.978	135	75	151	-1.0	5.2	3.7	-.0	-2.9
Ari	**16**	8	390	38	1443.2	1441	190	500	**1220**	12.4	4.35	110	.262	.326	45	68	103	102	56	.982	107	34	138	.6	6.4	-5.1	-.0	2.1
Col	7	2	**479**	33	1430.0	1568	221	588	1001	14.0	5.26	110	.281	.354	-99	68	125	102	35	**.985**	94	55	176	**1.3**	6.4	-6.8	.0	.0
SD	5	5	443	46	1459.1	1443	191	649	1071	13.3	4.52	98	.258	.340	18	-13	96	106	50	.977	141	79	155	-1.3	-1.2	-3.5	.4	.7
Total	127	112	6652	627	23103.1	—	—	—	—	13.4	4.63	—	.266	.342	—	—	—	—	—	.981	1879	996	2431	—	—	—	—	—

BATTER-FIELDER WINS	BATTING AVERAGE	ON-BASE PERCENTAGE	SLUGGING AVERAGE	ON-BASE PLUS SLUGGING	ADJUSTED OPS	ADJUSTED BATTER RUNS
Bonds-SF 6.8	Helton-Col .372	Helton-Col .463	Helton-Col .698	Helton-Col 1162	Bonds-SF 193	Bonds-SF 73.5
Kent-SF 6.4	Alou-Hou .355	Bonds-SF .440	Bonds-SF .688	Bonds-SF 1127	Sheffield-LA 178	Sheffield-LA 63.9
Alfonzo-NY 5.6	V.Guerrero-Mon .345	Sheffield-LA .438	V.Guerrero-Mon .664	Sheffield-LA 1081	Kent-SF 166	Kent-SF 63.3
Helton-Col 5.4	Hammonds-Col .335	Giles-Pit .432	Sheffield-LA .643	V.Guerrero-Mon 1074	V.Guerrero-Mon 165	Sosa-Chi 57.2
Hidalgo-Hou 4.8	Castillo-Fla .334	Alfonzo-NY .425	Hidalgo-Hou .636	Sosa-Chi 1040	Sosa-Chi 161	V.Guerrero-Mon 55.0

RUNS	HITS	DOUBLES	TRIPLES	HOME RUNS	TOTAL BASES	RUNS BATTED IN
Bagwell-Hou 152	Helton-Col 216	Helton-Col 59	Womack-Ari 14	Sosa-Chi 50	Helton-Col 405	Helton-Col 147
Helton-Col 138	Vidro-Mon 200	Cirillo-Col 53	Perez-Col 11	Bonds-SF 49	Sosa-Chi 383	Sosa-Chi 138
Edmonds-StL 129	A.Jones-Atl 199	Vidro-Mon 51	V.Guerrero-Mon 11	Bagwell-Hou 47	V.Guerrero-Mon 379	Bagwell-Hou 132
Bonds-SF 129	V.Guerrero-Mon 197	Gonzalez-Ari 47	Abreu-Phi 10	Hidalgo-Hou 44	Bagwell-Hou 363	Kent-SF 125
A.Jones-Atl 122	Kent-SF 196	Green-LA 44		V.Guerrero-Mon 44		

BASES ON BALLS	STOLEN BASES	BASE STEALING RUNS	FIELDING RUNS-INFIELD	FIELDING RUNS-OUTFIELD	OUTFIELD ASSISTS	CATCHER CS PCT.
Bonds-SF 117	Castillo-Fla 62	E.Young-Chi 9.4	Perez-Col 36.5	Hidalgo-Hou 14.3	Bergeron-Mon 16	Blanco-Mil 58.2
Giles-Pit 114	Goodwin-Col-LA 55	Goodwin-Col-LA 8.6	Meares-Pit 21.7	Kotsay-Fla 11.2	Kotsay-Fla 14	Santiago-Cin 42.4
Bagwell-Hou 107	E.Young-Chi 54	Womack-Ari 6.1	Morris-Pit 19.3	Abreu-Phi 10.6	Giles-Pit 14	Lieberthal-Phi 39.7
Helton-Col 103	Womack-Ari 45	Castillo-Fla 5.9	Helton-Col 18.7	Jenkins-Mil 7.1	Abreu-Phi 13	Girardi-Chi 37.6
Edmonds-StL 103	Furcal-Atl 40	Reese-Cin 5.3	Beltre-LA 16.9	Jordan-Atl 6.2		Gonzalez-SD 35.7

WINS	WINNING PCT.	WINS ABOVE TEAM	GAMES STARTED	COMPLETE GAMES	FEWEST HITS/GAME	FEWEST BB/GAME
Glavine-Atl 21	Johnson-Ari .731	Johnson-Ari 6.2	Millwood-Atl 35	Schilling-Phi-Ari 8	Park-LA 6.89	Maddux-Atl 1.52
Kile-StL 20	Estes-SF .714	Elarton-Hou 6.2	Maddux-Atl 35	Johnson-Ari 8	Ankiel-StL 7.05	Anderson-Ari 1.65
Maddux-Atl 19	Elarton-Hou .708	Glavine-Atl 4.8	Lieber-Chi 35	Maddux-Atl 6	Brown-LA 7.08	Reed-NY 1.66
Johnson-Ari 19	Glavine-Atl .700	White-Cin-Col 4.6	Johnson-Ari 35	Lieber-Chi 6	Johnson-Ari 7.31	Brown-LA 1.84
Park-LA 18	Kile-StL .690	Kile-StL 4.2	Glavine-Atl 35		Person-Phi 7.48	Schilling-Phi-Ari 1.93

STRIKEOUTS	STRIKEOUTS/GAME	GAMES	SAVES	BASE RUNNERS/9	ADJUSTED RELIEF RUNS	RELIEF RANKING
Johnson-Ari 347	Johnson-Ari 12.56	Kline-Mon 83	Alfonseca-Fla 45	Nen-SF 7.91	White-Cin-Col 25.8	Nen-SF 41.8
Park-LA 217	Ankiel-StL 9.98	Sullivan-Cin 79	Hoffman-SD 43	White-Cin-Col 8.79	Nen-SF 20.9	Graves-Cin 41.2
Brown-LA 216	Astacio-Col 8.85	Myers-Col 78	Nen-SF 41	Hoffman-SD 8.96	Graves-Cin 20.6	White-Cin-Col 38.8
Dempster-Fla 209	Leiter-NY 8.65	Wendell-NY 77	Benitez-NY 41	Benitez-NY 9.12	Leskanic-Mil 18.2	Benitez-NY 30.8
Leiter-NY 200	Park-LA 8.64		Graves-Cin 30	Brown-LA 9.27	Williamson-Cin 17.7	Leskanic-Mil 30.7

INNINGS PITCHED	OPPONENTS' AVG.	OPPONENTS' OBP	EARNED RUN AVERAGE	ADJUSTED ERA	ADJUSTED STARTER RUNS	PITCHER WINS
Lieber-Chi 251.0	Brown-LA .213	Brown-LA .261	Brown-LA 2.58	Johnson-Ari 181	Johnson-Ari 52.9	**Maddux-Atl 5.0**
Maddux-Atl 249.1	Park-LA .214	Maddux-Atl .276	Johnson-Ari 2.64	D'Amico-Mil 174	Brown-LA 48.2	**Johnson-Ari 5.0**
Johnson-Ari 248.2	Ankiel-StL .219	Johnson-Ari .288	D'Amico-Mil 2.66	Brown-LA 172	Maddux-Atl 43.3	**Graves-Cin 4.3**
Glavine-Atl 241.0	Johnson-Ari .224	Schilling-Phi-Ari .294	Maddux-Atl 3.00	Maddux-Atl 151	D'Amico-Mil 34.3	**Park-LA 4.1**
Hernandez-SF 240.0	Leiter-NY .228	Glavine-Atl .296	Hampton-NY 3.14	Hampton-NY 139	Park-LA 30.2	**Nen-SF 4.1**

Rocking the Boat

Atlanta reliever John Rocker, who saved 38 games the previous season, was suspended for two weeks after making incendiary and racist comments in an interview with *Sports Illustrated.* Rocker instantly became the most hated player in baseball, and was booed vociferously in every road ballpark—especially in his least favorite city, New York.

The Reds pulled off the last "Deal of the Century," acquiring hometown legend Ken Griffey Jr., and sending Seattle four relatively unknown players. Griffey signed a long-term deal with Cincinnati at a below-market rate, and later became the youngest player to hit 400 homers. The Cubs and Mets opened the year in Tokyo, the first regular-season games played outside North America. Chicago's Sammy Sosa hit 50 homers for the third straight year and Todd Helton of the Rockies hit the most doubles since 1936. Will Clark, Dwight Gooden, and Orel Hershiser retired.

Atlanta's vaunted pitching fell apart in the Division Series against the Cardinals, giving up 24 runs in the St. Louis sweep. The Cards won Game 1 despite starter Rick Ankiel's postseason-record 5 wild pitches in the third inning. The Wild Card Mets scraped by San Francisco in four games, clinching the NLDS with a complete-game, 1-hit shutout by unheralded Bobby Jones. Ankiel's control problems played a part in the Cardinals' five-game NLCS loss. He walked 3, threw 2 wild pitches, and allowed 2 runs in the first inning of Game 2, ultimately a 6-5 New York victory. Mets fans were ecstatic over their first pennant since 1986, but the club was dismissed in five games by the hated Yankees in the World Series.

2000 AMERICAN LEAGUE

TEAM	W	L	T	PCT	GB	HW	HL	R	OR	PA	H	2B	3B	HR	BB	SO	HB	SH	AVG	OBP	SLG	OPS	AOPS	BR	ABR	PF	SB	CS	BSA	BSR
EAST																														
NY	87	74	0	.540	—	44	36	871	814	6310	1541	294	25	205	631	1007	57	16	.277	.354	.450	804	103	28	40	99	99	48	67	5
Bos	85	77	0	.525	2.5	42	39	792	**745**	6371	1503	316	32	167	611	1019	42	40	.267	.341	.423	764	89	-59	-82	103	43	30	59	-1
Tor	83	79	0	.512	4.5	45	36	861	908	6326	1562	328	21	**244**	526	1026	**60**	29	.275	.341	.469	810	100	21	-8	103	89	34	72	8
Bal	74	88	0	.457	13.5	44	37	794	913	6237	1508	310	22	184	558	900	49	27	.272	.341	.435	776	100	-37	4	95	**126**	65	66	5
TB	69	92	0	.429	18	36	44	733	842	6206	1414	253	22	162	558	1022	51	52	.257	.329	.399	728	85	-138	-130	99	90	46	66	4
CENTRAL																														
Chi	95	67	0	.586	—	46	35	**978**	839	6406	1615	325	33	216	591	960	53	55	.286	.356	.470	826	103	70	37	104	119	42	74	11
Cle	90	72	0	.556	5	**48**	33	950	816	6512	1639	310	30	221	685	1057	51	41	**.288**	**.367**	.470	**837**	106	**105**	**72**	104	113	34	77	13
Det	79	83	0	.488	16	43	38	823	827	6340	1553	307	41	177	562	982	43	42	.275	.343	.438	781	97	-29	-22	99	83	38	69	5
KC	77	85	0	.475	18	42	39	879	930	6394	**1644**	281	27	150	511	**840**	48	56	**.288**	.348	.425	773	90	-36	-81	106	121	35	**78**	**14**
Min	69	93	0	.426	26	36	45	748	880	6281	1516	325	**49**	116	556	1021	35	24	.270	.337	.407	744	82	-99	-147	107	90	45	67	4
WEST																														
Oak	91	70	0	.565	—	47	34	947	813	6432	1501	281	23	239	750	1159	52	26	.270	.360	.458	818	**107**	59	71	99	40	15	73	4
Sea	91	71	0	.562	0.5	47	34	907	780	6444	1481	300	26	198	**775**	1073	48	**63**	.269	.361	.442	803	104	41	56	98	122	56	69	7
Ana	82	80	0	.506	9.5	46	35	864	869	6373	1574	309	34	236	608	1024	47	47	.280	.352	**.472**	824	104	60	34	103	93	52	64	2
Tex	71	91	0	.438	20.5	42	39	848	974	6363	1601	**330**	35	173	580	922	39	48	.283	.352	.446	798	100	13	1	101	69	47	59	-1
Total	1132	—	—	—	—	608	524	11995	—	88995	21652	4269	420	2688	8502	14012	675	566	.276	.349	.443	792	—	—	—	—	1297	587	69	80

TEAM	CG	SHO	GR	SV	IP	H	HR	BB	SO	BR/9	ERA	AERA	OAV	OOB	PR	APR	PF	OSB	OCS	FA	E	WPB	DP	FW	PW	BW	BSW	DIF
EAST																												
NY	9	6	382	40	1424.1	1458	177	577	1040	13.2	4.76	100	.263	.336	24	1	97	91	37	.981	109	62	132	.2	.0	3.7	-.0	2.6
Bos	7	**12**	425	**46**	1452.2	**1433**	173	498	1121	**12.3**	**4.23**	**118**	**.257**	**.322**	**110**	**123**	102	159	47	.982	109	59	120	.2	**11.3**	-7.5	-.6	.6
Tor	**15**	4	388	37	1437.1	1615	195	560	978	14.0	5.14	98	.285	.354	-37	-18	102	99	38	.984	100	**48**	176	.7	-1.6	-.7	.2	3.4
Bal	14	6	396	33	1433.1	1547	202	665	1017	14.1	5.37	87	.275	.352	-73	-113	96	104	31	.981	116	57	151	-.2	-10.4	.4	-.0	3.2
TB	10	8	401	38	1431.1	1553	198	533	955	13.5	4.86	101	.277	.345	8	4	100	114	46	.981	118	71	169	-.4	.4	-11.9	-.2	.6
CENTRAL																												
Chi	5	7	**466**	43	1450.1	1509	195	614	1037	13.5	4.66	108	.270	.346	41	61	103	79	**58**	.978	133	56	**190**	-1.2	5.6	3.4	.5	5.7
Cle	6	5	462	34	1442.1	1511	173	666	**1213**	13.8	4.84	103	.270	.350	12	26	102	109	42	**.988**	**72**	60	147	**2.4**	2.4	**6.6**	.7	-3.0
Det	6	6	429	44	1443.1	1583	177	**496**	978	13.3	4.71	104	.280	.340	33	30	100	**55**	42	.983	105	58	171	.5	2.7	-2.0	-.0	-3.1
KC	10	6	329	29	1439.1	1585	239	693	927	14.5	5.48	95	.282	.362	-90	-40	106	118	38	.983	102	84	185	.6	-3.7	-7.4	**.8**	5.7
Min	6	4	412	35	1432.2	1634	212	516	1042	13.7	5.14	102	.287	.347	-37	16	107	64	33	.983	102	81	155	.6	1.5	-13.5	-.2	-.5
WEST																												
Oak	7	11	381	43	1435.1	1535	**158**	615	963	13.8	4.58	106	.274	.348	53	43	99	92	39	.978	134	54	164	-1.3	3.9	6.5	-.2	1.5
Sea	4	10	383	44	1441.2	1442	167	634	998	13.2	4.49	107	.262	.339	67	51	98	82	38	.984	99	51	176	.8	4.7	5.1	.1	-.7
Ana	5	3	441	**46**	1448.0	1534	228	662	846	13.9	5.00	103	.273	.351	-15	23	105	101	56	.978	134	53	182	-1.2	2.1	3.1	-.3	-2.6
Tex	3	4	415	39	1429.0	1683	202	661	918	15.2	5.52	92	.294	.369	-96	-67	103	65	37	.978	135	**48**	162	-1.3	-6.1	.0	-.6	-2.0
Total	107	92	5710	551	20141.0	—	—	—	—	13.7	4.91	—	.276	.349	—	—	—	—	—	.982	1568	842	2280	—	—	—	—	—

BATTER-FIELDER WINS	BATTING AVERAGE	ON-BASE PERCENTAGE	SLUGGING AVERAGE	ON-BASE PLUS SLUGGING	ADJUSTED OPS	ADJUSTED BATTER RUNS
A.Rodriguez-Sea 6.6	Garciaparra-Bos ...372	J.Giambi-Oak........476	M.Ramirez-Cle......697	M.Ramirez-Cle....1154	J.Giambi-Oak........185	Delgado-Tor.........76.7
J.Giambi-Oak..... 5.1	Erstad-Ana...........355	Delgado-Tor..........470	Delgado-Tor..........664	Delgado-Tor.......1134	M.Ramirez-Cle......181	J.Giambi-Oak.........76.6
Garciaparra-Bos 5.0	M.Ramirez-Cle.......351	M.Ramirez-Cle......457	J.Giambi-Oak.........647	J.Giambi-Oak.......1123	Delgado-Tor..........178	Thomas-Chi.........58.4
Glaus-Ana........... 4.9	Delgado-Tor..........344	Thomas-Chi..........436	Thomas-Chi..........625	Thomas-Chi........1061	A.Rodriguez-Sea ..160	M.Ramirez-Cle.....58.3
Delgado-Tor 4.7	Jeter-NY...............339	Garciaparra-Bos ...434	A.Rodriguez-Sea ..606	Garciaparra-Bos .1033	Thomas-Chi..........160	A.Rodriguez-Sea .54.7
RUNS	**HITS**	**DOUBLES**	**TRIPLES**	**HOME RUNS**	**TOTAL BASES**	**RUNS BATTED IN**
Damon-KC...........136	Erstad-Ana............240	Delgado-Tor...........57	Guzman-Min...........20	Glaus-Ana..............47	Delgado-Tor..........378	Martinez-Sea........145
A.Rodriguez-Sea ..134	Damon-KC............214	Garciaparra-Bos 51	Kennedy-Ana..........11	Thomas-Chi............43	Erstad-Ana............366	Sweeney-KC.........144
Erstad-Ana...........121	Sweeney-KC.........206	D.Cruz-Det.............46	Damon-KC..............10	J.Giambi-Oak..........43	Thomas-Chi..........364	Thomas-Chi..........143
Durham-Chi...........121	Jeter-NY...............201	Olerud-Sea.............45	Durham-Chi..............9		Glaus-Ana.............340	J.Giambi-Oak.........137
Glaus-Ana.............120	Garciaparra-Bos ...197				Dye-KC.................337	Delgado-Tor..........137
BASES ON BALLS	**STOLEN BASES**	**BASE STEALING RUNS**	**FIELDING RUNS-INFIELD**	**FIELDING RUNS-OUTFIELD**	**OUTFIELD ASSISTS**	**CATCHER CS PCT.**
J.Giambi-Oak........137	Damon-KC.............46	R.Alomar-Cle 7.2	Velarde-Oak.........22.0	Martinez-TB-Tx-Tor .11.5	Higginson-Det.........19	Rodriguez-Tex 48.7
Delgado-Tor..........123	R.Alomar-Cle..........39	Damon-KC..............7.0	Sanchez-KC 19.1	Higginson-Det..........9.7	Martinez-TB-Tx-Tor....15	Molina-Ana 36.7
Thome-Cle.............118	DeShields-Bal..........37	DeShields-Bal.........4.6	Valentin-Chi 17.9	Erstad-Ana.............8.6	Salmon-Ana............12	C.Johnson-Bal-Chi ..30.8
Thomas-Chi...........112	Henderson-Sea 31	Lofton-Cle..............4.2	Olerud-Sea 14.5	Jones-Min...............7.1	Ordonez-Chi............12	Hernandez-Oak ...28.4
Glaus-Ana.............112		Cairo-TB.................3.7	R.Alomar-Cle........14.3	Salmon-Ana.............5.8	Hunter-Min..............12	Flaherty-TB............26.9
WINS	**WINNING PCT.**	**WINS ABOVE TEAM**	**GAMES STARTED**	**COMPLETE GAMES**	**FEWEST HITS/GAME**	**FEWEST BB/GAME**
D.Wells-Tor 20	Hudson-Oak 769	Hudson-Oak 6.7	D.Wells-Tor 35	D.Wells-Tor 9	P.Martinez-Bos 5.31	D.Wells-Tor 1.21
Hudson-Oak 20	P.Martinez-Bos 750	D.Wells-Tor 6.5	Helling-Tex..............35	P.Martinez-Bos 7	Hudson-Oak 7.52	P.Martinez-Bos 1.33
Pettitte-NY 19	Burba-Cle 727	P.Martinez-Bos 6.2		Ponson-Bal 6	Colon-Cle...............7.80	Mussina-Bal..........1.74
P.Martinez-Bos 18	D.Wells-Tor 714	Pettitte-NY 4.8		Mussina-Bal...............6	Clemens-NY 8.10	Milton-Min.............1.98
Sele-Sea..................17	Pettitte-NY 679	Burba-Cle 4.6			Abbott-Sea............8.25	Moehler-Det..........2.02
STRIKEOUTS	**STRIKEOUTS/GAME**	**GAMES**	**SAVES**	**BASE RUNNERS/9**	**ADJUSTED RELIEF RUNS**	**RELIEF RANKING**
P.Martinez-Bos 284	P.Martinez-Bos ..11.78	Wunsch-Chi.............83	Lowe-Bos................42	P.Martinez-Bos 7.22	Lowe-Bos.............25.0	Lowe-Bos..............41.3
Colon-Cle..............212	Colon-Cle...........10.15	Venafro-Tex.............77	Jones-Det 42	Foulke-Chi 9.20	Tam-Oak...............20.5	Koch-Tor 38.7
Mussina-Bal..........210	Nomo-Det 8.57	Wells-Min.................76	Sasaki-Sea 37	Rivera-NY 9.87	Foulke-Chi 20.5	Rivera-NY 33.2
Finley-Cle 189	Burba-Cle 8.47	Trombley-Bal...........75	Rivera-NY 36	Wells-Min............10.32	Koch-Tor 19.3	Mecir-TB-Oak 27.2
Clemens-NY 188	Clemens-NY 8.28	Lowe-Bos..................74		Rhodes-Sea..........10.38	Mecir-TB-Oak 18.3	Nelson-NY 26.1
INNINGS PITCHED	**OPPONENTS' AVG.**	**OPPONENTS' OBP**	**EARNED RUN AVERAGE**	**ADJUSTED ERA**	**ADJUSTED STARTER RUNS**	**PITCHER WINS**
Mussina-Bal.......237.2	P.Martinez-Bos 167	P.Martinez-Bos 213	P.Martinez-Bos 1.74	P.Martinez-Bos 288	P.Martinez-Bos 78.3	**P.Martinez-Bos .. 8.4**
D.Wells-Tor 229.2	Hudson-Oak 227	Mussina-Bal..........291	Clemens-NY 3.70	Sirotka-Chi............133	Mussina-Bal.........26.1	**Lowe-Bos............ 3.9**
Rogers-Tex 227.1	Colon-Cle..............233	Hernandez-NY.......298	Mussina-Bal.........3.79	Colon-Cle..............129	Sirotka-Chi...........23.3	**Koch-Tor 3.6**
Radke-Min 226.2	Clemens-NY 236	Milton-Min.............303	Sirotka-Chi...........3.79	Clemens-NY 129	D.Wells-Tor 23.1	**Rivera-NY 3.2**
Ponson-Bal 222.0	Abbott-Sea............243	Hudson-Oak 306	Colon-Cle.............3.88	Mussina-Bal..........124	Colon-Cle.............22.9	**Mecir-TB-Oak..... 2.5**

THREE TIMES FOR YANKEES

Umpires formed a new union to replace the one broken a year earlier in their botched mass resignation. One of its first duties was to agree to merge the league staffs, so arbiters could work games in both leagues. New parks opened in Detroit, San Francisco, and Houston, lifting average attendance to near pre-strike levels. Slugger Albert Belle had to retire because of a degenerative hip condition. Pitching sensations Mark Mulder and Barry Zito debuted with Oakland; Hall of Famer Bob Lemon died.

The Yankees had the worst record of any team in the postseason, but their veteran-laden squad held off upstart Oakland in the Division Series. While the A's defeated Roger Clemens twice, they did not win at home after the opener. Following an overnight trip to Oakland for Game 5, the Yankees scored 6 runs in the top of the first and then held on. Seattle, which didn't clinch the Wild Card until the season's final day, swept the White Sox in the other ALDS. The Yankees dispatched the Mariners in six games, including the first complete-game ALCS shutout in fifteen years—a 15-strikeout, 1-hit masterpiece by Clemens.

New York's first Subway Series since 1956 was big on talk, low on ratings, and just five games start to finish—although three games were decided in the eigth inning or later. The Mets broke the Yankees' 14-game World Series winning streak but little else as the Yanks claimed baseball's first "three-peat" since the 1972–74 A's. After the season Alex Rodriguez signed a 10-year, $252 million contract with Texas, the richest deal in American pro sports history.

1999 NATIONAL LEAGUE

TEAM	W	L	T	PCT	GB	HW	HL	R	OR	PA	H	2B	3B	HR	BB	SO	HB	SH	AVG	OBP	SLG	OPS	AOPS	BR	ABR	PF	SB	CS	BSA	BSR
EAST																														
Atl	103	59	0	.636	—	**56**	25	840	**661**	6351	1481	309	23	197	608	962	53	74	.266	.341	.436	777	101	11	18	99	148	66	69	9
NY	97	66	0	.595	6.5	49	32	853	711	6454	1553	297	14	181	717	994	48	63	.279	**.363**	.434	797	**111**	75	**118**	95	150	61	71	12
Phi	77	85	0	.475	26	41	40	841	846	6386	1539	302	44	161	631	1081	46	70	.275	.351	.431	782	101	27	17	101	125	35	**78**	15
Mon	68	94	0	.420	35	35	46	718	853	6149	1473	**320**	**47**	163	438	939	53	71	.265	.323	.427	750	97	-63	-33	96	70	51	58	-2
Fla	64	98	0	.395	39	35	45	691	852	6216	1465	266	44	128	479	1145	59	44	.263	.325	.395	720	91	-114	-73	94	92	46	67	4
CENTRAL																														
Hou	97	65	0	.599	—	50	32	823	675	6402	1463	293	23	168	**728**	1138	52	79	.267	.355	.420	775	102	28	40	99	166	75	69	10
Cin	96	67	0	.589	1.5	45	37	865	711	6377	1536	312	37	209	569	1125	45	70	.272	.341	.451	792	101	34	9	103	164	54	75	**17**
Pit	78	83	0	.484	18.5	45	36	775	782	6233	1417	282	40	171	573	1197	**60**	**87**	.259	.334	.419	753	94	-43	-46	100	112	44	72	9
StL	75	86	0	.466	21.5	38	42	809	838	6353	1461	274	27	194	613	1202	51	75	.262	.338	.426	764	96	-18	-30	102	134	48	74	13
Mil	74	87	0	.460	22.5	32	48	815	886	6433	1524	299	30	165	658	1065	55	**87**	.273	.353	.426	779	102	27	24	100	81	33	71	6
Chi	67	95	0	.414	30	34	47	747	920	6201	1411	255	35	189	571	1170	39	65	.257	.329	.420	749	93	-55	-51	100	60	44	58	-2
WEST																														
Ari	100	62	0	.617	—	52	29	**908**	676	6415	1566	289	46	216	588	1045	48	61	.277	.347	.459	806	107	64	59	101	137	39	**78**	16
SF	86	76	0	.531	14	49	32	872	831	6448	1507	307	18	188	696	1028	**60**	**87**	.271	.356	.434	790	**111**	52	114	93	109	56	66	4
LA	77	85	0	.475	23	37	44	793	787	6338	1480	253	23	187	594	1030	52	74	.266	.339	.420	759	101	-25	16	95	167	68	71	13
SD	74	88	0	.457	26	46	35	710	781	6136	1360	256	22	153	631	1169	35	36	.252	.332	.393	725	95	-90	-34	93	**174**	67	72	15
Col	72	90	0	.444	28	39	42	906	1028	6368	**1644**	305	39	**223**	508	**863**	43	54	**.288**	.348	**.472**	**820**	88	**87**	-96	126	70	43	62	0
Total	1295	—	—	—	—	683	612	12966	—	101260	23880	4619	512	2893	9602	17153	799	1097	.268	.342	.429	771	—	—	—	—	1959	830	70	140

TEAM	CG	SHO	GR	SV	IP	H	HR	BB	SO	BR/9	ERA	AERA	OAV	OOB	PR	APR	PF	OSB	OCS	FA	E	WPB	DP	FW	PW	BW	BSW	DIF
EAST																												
Atl	9	9	394	45	1471.0	1398	142	507	1197	**11.8**	**3.63**	**123**	.251	**.314**	**152**	**140**	98	108	45	.982	111	**44**	127	.6	**13.2**	1.7	.0	6.5
NY	5	7	439	49	1456.2	1372	167	617	1172	12.6	4.27	102	.252	.331	47	12	95	134	44	**.989**	**68**	48	147	**3.3**	1.1	**11.1**	.3	-.3
Phi	11	6	441	32	1438.1	1494	212	627	1030	13.6	4.92	95	.269	.347	-58	-41	102	94	35	.983	100	80	144	1.3	-3.9	1.6	.6	-3.6
Mon	6	4	432	44	1434.1	1505	152	572	1043	13.4	4.69	95	.270	.342	-21	-40	98	157	47	.974	160	62	125	-2.4	-3.8	-3.1	-1.0	-2.7
Fla	6	5	453	33	1435.2	1560	171	655	943	14.2	4.90	89	.281	.359	-54	-87	96	94	67	.979	127	56	150	-.4	-8.2	-6.9	-.5	-1.0
CENTRAL																												
Hou	12	8	339	48	1458.2	1485	**128**	**478**	**1204**	12.4	3.83	116	.267	.326	119	99	97	94	43	.983	106	63	175	.9	9.4	3.8	.1	1.9
Cin	6	**11**	381	**55**	1462.0	**1309**	190	636	1081	12.3	3.98	118	**.241**	.324	94	111	103	124	34	.983	105	76	139	1.0	10.5	.9	**.8**	1.4
Pit	8	3	425	34	1433.1	1444	160	633	1083	13.4	4.33	106	.263	.343	37	42	101	99	50	.976	147	63	179	-1.7	4.0	-4.3	.0	-.5
StL	5	3	**454**	38	1445.1	1519	161	667	1025	14.0	4.74	97	.273	.355	-29	-22	101	**80**	**69**	.978	132	68	163	-.8	-2.1	-2.8	.4	-.2
Mil	2	5	453	40	1442.2	1618	213	616	987	14.3	5.07	91	.284	.356	-82	-76	101	177	44	.979	127	77	146	-.4	-7.2	2.3	-.3	-.9
Chi	11	6	441	32	1430.2	1619	221	529	980	13.7	5.27	87	.286	.346	-112	-111	100	100	43	.977	139	73	135	-1.1	-10.5	-4.8	-1.0	3.5
WEST																												
Ari	**16**	9	382	42	1467.1	1387	176	543	1198	12.1	3.77	122	.249	.320	128	135	101	138	66	.983	104	56	132	1.0	12.8	5.6	.7	-1.0
SF	6	3	450	42	1456.1	1486	194	655	1076	13.5	4.71	91	.265	.345	-24	-76	94	129	53	.983	105	70	155	.9	-7.2	10.8	-.5	.9
LA	8	6	399	37	1453.0	1438	192	594	1077	13.0	4.45	98	.258	.334	18	-16	95	156	56	.978	137	66	137	-1.0	-1.5	1.5	.4	-3.4
SD	5	6	403	43	1420.1	1454	193	529	1078	12.8	4.47	95	.266	.332	15	-34	94	114	45	.979	129	88	151	-.5	-3.2	-3.2	.6	-.6
Col	12	2	420	33	1429.0	1700	237	737	1032	15.7	6.01	96	.301	.384	-231	-29	127	163	63	.981	118	79	**189**	.1	-2.7	-9.1	-.8	3.5
Total	128	93	6706	647	23134.2	—	—	—	—	13.3	4.56	—	.268	.342	—	—	—	—	—	.980	1915	1069	2394	—	—	—	—	—

BATTER-FIELDER WINS	BATTING AVERAGE	ON-BASE PERCENTAGE	SLUGGING AVERAGE	ON-BASE PLUS SLUGGING	ADJUSTED OPS	ADJUSTED BATTER RUNS
Bagwell-Hou 5.3	Walker-Col .379	Walker-Col .458	Walker-Col .710	Walker-Col 1168	McGwire-StL 175	C.Jones-Atl 66.8
Ventura-NY 4.6	Gonzalez-Ari .336	Bagwell-Hou .454	McGwire-StL .697	McGwire-StL 1120	C.Jones-Atl 170	Bagwell-Hou 66.3
Biggio-Hou 4.3	Abreu-Phi .335	Abreu-Phi .446	Sosa-Chi .635	C.Jones-Atl 1074	Bagwell-Hou 165	McGwire-StL 62.7
McGwire-StL 4.1	Casey-Cin .332	C.Jones-Atl .441	C.Jones-Atl .633	Bagwell-Hou 1045	Giles-Pit 157	Giles-Pit 48.5
Sosa-Chi 4.1	Cirillo-Mil .326	Olerud-NY .427	Giles-Pit .614	Giles-Pit 1032	Walker-Col 152	Abreu-Phi 46.6

RUNS	HITS	DOUBLES	TRIPLES	HOME RUNS	TOTAL BASES	RUNS BATTED IN
Bagwell-Hou 143	Gonzalez-Ari 206	Biggio-Hou 56	Perez-Col 11	McGwire-StL 65	Sosa-Chi 397	McGwire-StL 147
Bell-Ari 132	Glanville-Phi 204	Vidro-Mon 45	Abreu-Phi 11	Sosa-Chi 63	V.Guerrero-Mon 366	Williams-Ari 142
Biggio-Hou 123	Cirillo-Mil 198	Gonzalez-Ari 45	Womack-Ari 10	Vaughn-Cin 45	McGwire-StL 363	Sosa-Chi 141
Alfonzo-NY 123	Casey-Cin 197	Grace-Chi 44	Finley-Ari 10	C.Jones-Atl 45	C.Jones-Atl 359	Bichette-Col 133
		Jenkins-Mil 43			Helton-Col 339	V.Guerrero-Mon 131

BASES ON BALLS	STOLEN BASES	BASE STEALING RUNS	FIELDING RUNS-INFIELD	FIELDING RUNS-OUTFIELD	OUTFIELD ASSISTS	CATCHER CS PCT.
Bagwell-Hou 149	Womack-Ari 72	Womack-Ari 11.3	Benjamin-Pit 34.8	A.Jones-Atl 17.3	Kotsay-Fla 19	Castillo-StL 50.7
McGwire-StL 133	Cedeno-NY 66	Cedeno-NY 8.6	Perez-Col 26.7	Kotsay-Fla 12.4	Bichette-Col 17	Redmond-Fla 37.8
C.Jones-Atl 126	Young-LA 51	Glanville-Phi 6.8	Ventura-NY 18.5	Jenkins-Mil 10.6	Hidalgo-Hou 15	Miller-Ari 35.0
Olerud-NY 125	Castillo-Fla 50	Reese-Cin 5.9	Biggio-Hou 17.7	Sosa-Chi 9.3	V.Guerrero-Mon 15	Eusebio-Hou 33.9
Abreu-Phi 109		Renteria-StL 5.3	Reese-Cin 16.9	Hidalgo-Hou 8.5	Jenkins-Mil 14	Lieberthal-Phi 32.0

WINS	WINNING PCT.	WINS ABOVE TEAM	GAMES STARTED	COMPLETE GAMES	FEWEST HITS/GAME	FEWEST BB/GAME
Hampton-Hou 22	Hampton-Hou .846	Hampton-Hou 8.5	Reynolds-Hou 35	Johnson-Ari 12	Millwood-Atl 6.63	Reynolds-Hou 1.44
Lima-Hou 21	Millwood-Atl .720	Bottenfield-StL 6.5	Lima-Hou 35	Schilling-Phi 8	Johnson-Ari 6.86	Maddux-Atl 1.52
Maddux-Atl 19	Bottenfield-StL .720	Brown-LA 5.5	Johnson-Ari 35	Astacio-Col 7	Brown-LA 7.49	Lima-Hou 1.61
	Schilling-Phi .714	Schilling-Phi 5.1	Glavine-Atl 35	Brown-LA 5	Hampton-Hou 7.76	Woodard-Mil 1.75
	Maddux-Atl .679	Astacio-Col 4.7	Brown-LA 35		Daal-Ari 7.88	Smoltz-Atl 1.93

STRIKEOUTS	STRIKEOUTS/GAME	GAMES	SAVES	BASE RUNNERS/9	ADJUSTED RELIEF RUNS	RELIEF RANKING
Johnson-Ari 364	Johnson-Ari 12.06	Kline-Mon 82	Urbina-Mon 41	Wagner-Hou 7.11	Wagner-Hou 24.5	Williamson-Cin 44.7
Brown-LA 221	Hitchcock-SD 8.49	Wendell-NY 80	Hoffman-SD 40	Hoffman-SD 8.42	Benitez-NY 22.5	Wagner-Hou 38.0
Astacio-Col 210	Lieber-Chi 8.23	Telford-Mon 79	Wagner-Hou 39	Millwood-Atl 9.12	Williamson-Cin 22.3	Graves-Cin 31.9
Millwood-Atl 205	Nomo-Mil 8.22	Sullivan-Cin 79	Rocker-Atl 38	Benitez-NY 9.35	Sullivan-Cin 21.0	Rocker-Atl 30.9
Reynolds-Hou 197	Astacio-Col 8.15	Benitez-NY 77		Williamson-Cin 9.45	Remlinger-Atl 20.2	Benitez-NY 29.7

INNINGS PITCHED	OPPONENTS' AVG.	OPPONENTS' OBP	EARNED RUN AVERAGE	ADJUSTED ERA	ADJUSTED STARTER RUNS	PITCHER WINS
Johnson-Ari 271.2	Millwood-Atl .202	Millwood-Atl .258	Johnson-Ari 2.48	Johnson-Ari 186	Johnson-Ari 62.1	**Hampton-Hou 5.3**
Brown-LA 252.1	Johnson-Ari .208	Johnson-Ari .266	Millwood-Atl 2.68	Millwood-Atl 167	Millwood-Atl 44.1	**Johnson-Ari 5.1**
Lima-Hou 246.1	Brown-LA .222	Brown-LA .273	Hampton-Hou 2.90	Hampton-Hou 153	Hampton-Hou 40.7	**Millwood-Atl 4.3**
Hampton-Hou 239.0	Daal-Ari .236	Schilling-Phi .287	Brown-LA 3.00	Brown-LA 145	Brown-LA 36.7	**Williamson-Cin 4.3**
Glavine-Atl 234.0	Schilling-Phi .237	Smoltz-Atl .288	Smoltz-Atl 3.19	Smoltz-Atl 140	Smoltz-Atl 28.6	**Wagner-Hou 3.7**

An All-Century Re-Pete

Under pressure from its corporate sponsor, Commissioner Bud Selig agreed to let Pete Rose participate in on-field ceremonies during the World Series for baseball's All-Century Team. Rose, in the 10th year of lifetime ban for "conduct relating to gambling," was overwhelmingly voted to the team by fans. Marge Schott, Cincinnati's twice-suspended owner, was forced to sell controlling interest to Carl Lindner, one of the team's limited partners.

Mark McGwire hit 65 homers and Sammy Sosa slammed 63 as they became the first players in history to belt 60 or more in two different seasons. Three workers were killed at the Miller Park construction site in Milwaukee when a crane collapsed. The accident ultimately delayed opening of the new park by a year. Dodgers star Pee Wee Reese died.

Arizona won 100 games and became the first team to make the postseason in its second year. Yet the Diamondbacks were surprised in four games by the Mets, who reached the NLDS by winning a one-game playoff with the Reds for the Wild Card. The Braves advanced to the NLCS for the fifth straight year with a four-game Division Series win against Houston. Atlanta defeated New York in six games, but the Braves had to work for it. After dropping the first three games, the Mets rallied for two wins; 15-inning, rain-drenched Game 5 ended on Robin Ventura's grand slam that changed to an RBI-single when one of the celebrating runners passed Ventura during his trot. The Braves won Game 6, and the series, in 11 innings, but Atlanta was swept by the Yankees in the World Series.

1999 AMERICAN LEAGUE

TEAM	W	L	T	PCT	GB	HW	HL	R	OR	PA	H	2B	3B	HR	BB	SO	HB	SH	AVG	OBP	SLG	OPS	AOPS	BR	ABR	PF	SB	CS	BSA	BSR
EAST																														
NY	98	64	0	.605	—	48	33	900	731	6416	1568	302	36	193	718	978	55	22	.282	.366	.453	819	**110**	84	**98**	99	104	57	65	3
Bos	94	68	0	.580	4	49	32	836	**718**	6321	1551	334	42	176	597	928	55	34	.278	.350	.448	798	99	27	0	103	67	39	63	1
Tor	84	78	0	.519	14	40	41	883	862	6369	1580	**337**	14	212	578	1077	76	28	.280	.352	.457	809	103	50	35	102	119	48	71	9
Bal	78	84	0	.481	20	41	40	851	815	6409	1572	299	21	203	615	890	61	41	.279	.353	.447	800	107	34	65	97	107	46	70	7
TB	69	93	0	.426	29	33	48	772	913	6272	1531	272	29	145	544	1042	64	30	.274	.343	.411	754	91	-65	-77	102	73	49	60	-1
CENTRAL																														
Cle	97	65	0	.599	—	47	34	**1009**	860	6553	1629	309	32	209	743	1099	55	**54**	.289	**.373**	.467	**840**	107	**135**	85	105	**147**	50	75	**15**
Chi	75	86	1	.466	21.5	38	42	777	870	6262	1563	298	37	162	499	**810**	34	40	.277	.337	.429	766	92	-52	-65	102	110	50	69	7
Det	69	92	0	.429	27.5	38	43	747	882	6095	1433	289	34	212	458	1049	**82**	35	.261	.326	.443	769	93	-60	-71	102	108	70	61	-1
KC	64	97	0	.398	32.5	33	47	856	921	6325	1584	294	**52**	151	535	932	64	46	.282	.348	.433	781	94	-12	-43	104	127	39	**77**	14
Min	63	97	1	.394	33	31	50	686	845	6124	1450	285	30	105	500	978	49	24	.264	.328	.384	712	77	-151	-185	105	118	60	66	5
WEST																														
Tex	95	67	0	.586	—	51	30	945	859	6388	**1653**	304	29	230	611	937	29	35	**.293**	.361	**.479**	**840**	106	112	58	106	111	54	67	6
Oak	87	75	0	.537	8	**52**	29	893	846	6440	1430	287	20	235	**770**	1129	71	39	.259	.355	.446	801	106	39	65	97	70	37	65	2
Sea	79	83	0	.488	16	43	38	859	905	6310	1499	263	21	**244**	610	1095	42	38	.269	.343	.455	798	103	13	22	99	130	45	74	13
Ana	70	92	0	.432	25	37	44	711	826	6131	1404	248	22	158	511	1022	43	41	.256	.322	.395	717	82	-154	-153	100	71	45	61	0
Total	1132	—	—	—	—	581	551	11725	—	88415	21447	4121	419	2635	8289	13966	780	507	.275	.347	.439	786	—	—	—	—	1462	689	68	80

TEAM	CG	SHO	GR	SV	IP	H	HR	BB	SO	BR/9	ERA	AERA	OAV	OOB	PR	APR	PF	OSB	OCS	FA	E	WPB	DP	FW	PW	BW	BSW	DIF
EAST																												
NY	6	10	359	**50**	1439.2	1402	**158**	581	1111	12.8	4.13	114	.255	.330	116	95	97	131	48	.982	111	67	132	.2	8.8	**9.1**	-.3	-.8
Bos	6	**12**	412	**50**	1436.2	**1396**	160	**469**	**1131**	**12.0**	**4.00**	**124**	**.253**	**.315**	**137**	**151**	102	159	58	.979	127	59	132	-.6	**14.0**	.0	-.4	.1
Tor	14	9	377	39	1439.0	1582	191	575	1009	13.8	4.92	100	.280	.349	-11	-2	101	124	53	.983	106	68	165	.4	-.2	3.2	.3	-.8
Bal	**17**	11	393	33	1435.0	1468	198	647	982	13.6	4.77	98	.269	.348	14	-13	97	93	50	**.986**	**89**	60	191	**1.3**	-1.2	6.0	.1	-9.2
TB	6	5	453	45	1433.0	1606	172	695	1055	14.9	5.06	98	.286	.370	-32	-16	102	101	**69**	.978	135	64	**198**	-1.1	-1.5	-7.1	-.6	-1.7
CENTRAL																												
Cle	3	6	**466**	46	1450.1	1503	197	634	1120	13.6	4.89	104	.268	.346	-5	28	104	118	46	.983	106	62	154	.4	2.6	7.9	**.9**	4.2
Chi	6	3	409	39	1438.1	1608	210	596	968	14.2	4.92	100	.282	.353	-10	1	101	102	46	.977	136	74	149	-1.1	.0	-6.0	.1	1.4
Det	4	6	421	33	1421.0	1528	209	583	976	13.8	5.17	96	.276	.349	-50	-30	103	81	44	.982	106	55	156	.4	-2.8	-6.6	-.6	-1.9
KC	11	3	416	29	1420.2	1607	202	643	831	14.7	5.35	95	.288	.365	-78	-42	104	111	49	.980	125	70	188	-.6	-3.9	-4.0	.8	-8.8
Min	13	8	417	34	1423.1	1591	208	487	927	13.3	5.00	103	.283	.341	-23	24	106	73	37	.985	92	69	150	1.1	2.2	-17.1	-.0	-3.2
WEST																												
Tex	6	9	439	47	1436.1	1626	186	509	979	13.6	5.07	102	.286	.346	-34	13	106	**47**	52	.981	119	**52**	169	-.2	1.2	5.4	.0	7.6
Oak	6	5	406	48	1438.1	1537	160	569	967	13.5	4.69	101	.274	.344	26	4	97	110	51	.980	122	75	166	-.4	.4	6.0	-.3	.4
Sea	7	6	346	40	1433.2	1613	191	684	980	14.9	5.24	91	.287	.368	-60	-75	98	107	50	.981	113	71	182	.0	-6.9	2.0	.7	2.2
Ana	4	7	400	37	1431.1	1472	177	624	877	13.5	4.79	102	.269	.346	10	13	100	103	62	.983	106	85	156	.4	1.2	-14.2	-.5	2.0
Total	109	100	5714	570	20076.2	—	—	—	—	13.7	4.86	—	.275	.347	—	—	—	—	—	.981	1593	931	2288	—	—	—	—	—

BATTER-FIELDER WINS	BATTING AVERAGE	ON-BASE PERCENTAGE	SLUGGING AVERAGE	ON-BASE PLUS SLUGGING	ADJUSTED OPS	ADJUSTED BATTER RUNS
R.Alomar-Cle 5.1	Garciaparra-Bos ...357	Martinez-Sea 447	M.Ramirez-Cle......663	M.Ramirez-Cle....1105	M.Ramirez-Cle......170	M.Ramirez-Cle.....59.1
Garciaparra-Bos 4.7	Jeter-NY 349	M.Ramirez-Cle......442	Palmeiro-Tex.........630	Palmeiro-Tex.......1050	Martinez-Sea........156	Jeter-NY 55.5
M.Ramirez-Cle ... 4.4	Williams-NY..........342	Jeter-NY 438	Garciaparra-Bos ...603	Garciaparra-Bos .1022	Palmeiro-Tex.........155	Giambi-Oak 50.2
Williams-NY 4.3	Martinez-Sea........337	Williams-NY..........435	Gonzalez-Tex........601	Martinez-Sea 1001	Jeter-NY 154	Palmeiro-Tex........49.3
Rodriguez-Tex.... 4.2	M.Ramirez-Cle......333	Fernandez-Tor 427	Green-Tor 588	Jeter-NY 989	Garciaparra-Bos ...152	Martinez-Sea 48.8
RUNS	**HITS**	**DOUBLES**	**TRIPLES**	**HOME RUNS**	**TOTAL BASES**	**RUNS BATTED IN**
R.Alomar-Cle.........138	Jeter-NY 219	Green-Tor 45	Offerman-Bos 11	Griffey-Sea 48	Green-Tor 361	M.Ramirez-Cle......165
Jeter-NY 134	Surhoff-Bal............207	Sweeney-KC...........44	Jeter-NY 9	Palmeiro-Tex...........47	Palmeiro-Tex.........356	Palmeiro-Tex.........148
Green-Tor 134	Williams-NY..........202	Dye-KC 44	Febles-KC.................9	M.Ramirez-Cle........44	Griffey-Sea 349	Griffey-Sea 134
M.Ramirez-Cle......131	Velarde-Ana-Oak ..200	Garciaparra-Bos 42	Damon-KC................9	Delgado-Tor 44	M.Ramirez-Cle......346	Delgado-Tor 134
Griffey-Sea 123	Rodriguez-Tex 199				Jeter-NY 346	Gonzalez-Tex........128
BASES ON BALLS	**STOLEN BASES**	**BASE STEALING RUNS**	**FIELDING RUNS-INFIELD**	**FIELDING RUNS-OUTFIELD**	**OUTFIELD ASSISTS**	**CATCHER CS PCT.**
Thome-Cle............127	Hunter-Det-Sea 44	Hunter-Det-Sea 6.9	Bordick-Bal 35.1	Dye-KC 14.3	Dye-KC 17	Rodriguez-Tex 54.7
Giambi-Oak 105	Vizquel-Cle 42	Vizquel-Cle 6.1	Sanchez-KC 29.4	Singleton-Chi 11.9	Belle-Bal 17	Flaherty-TB..........40.0
Jaha-Oak 101	Goodwin-Tex...........39	R.Alomar-Cle 6.0	Cairo-TB 27.4	Hunter-Det-Sea 9.9	Surhoff-Bal.............16	C.Johnson-Bal 38.0
Belle-Bal 101	Stewart-Tor 37	Damon-KC.............5.8	Valentin-Bos 12.4	Ordonez-Chi 7.4	Beltran-KC.............16	Ausmus-Det.........37.2
Williams-NY 100	R.Alomar-Cle 37	Anderson-Bal.........5.5	Bush-Tor 10.1	Surhoff-Bal............5.7	Hunter-Det-Sea 15	Diaz-Cle...............35.1
WINS	**WINNING PCT.**	**WINS ABOVE TEAM**	**GAMES STARTED**	**COMPLETE GAMES**	**FEWEST HITS/GAME**	**FEWEST BB/GAME**
P.Martinez-Bos 23	P.Martinez-Bos 852	P.Martinez-Bos 9.3	Helling-Tex.............35	D.Wells-Tor 7	P.Martinez-Bos 6.75	Heredia-Oak 1.53
Sele-Tex..................18	Colon-Cle..............783	Mussina-Bal...........6.3		Ponson-Bal 6	Cone-NY.............7.63	P.Martinez-Bos 1.56
Mussina-Bal............18	Mussina-Bal...........720	Colon-Cle...............5.7		Erickson-Bal 6	Hernandez-NY.....7.85	Radke-Min 1.81
Colon-Cle................18	Garcia-Sea 680	Garcia-Sea 5.2			Colon-Cle............8.12	Moyer-Sea 1.89
	Sele-Tex................667	Hudson-Oak 4.5			Milton-Min............8.29	Mussina-Bal.........2.30
STRIKEOUTS	**STRIKEOUTS/GAME**	**GAMES**	**SAVES**	**BASE RUNNERS/9**	**ADJUSTED RELIEF RUNS**	**RELIEF RANKING**
P.Martinez-Bos 313	P.Martinez-Bos ..13.20	Wells-Min................76	Rivera-NY 45	Zimmerman-Tex...7.70	Foulke-Chi 31.7	Rivera-NY 46.2
Finley-Ana 200	Finley-Ana 8.44	Groom-Oak.............76	Wetteland-Tex.........43	Foulke-Chi 8.20	Lowe-Bos.............28.3	Zimmerman-Tex...33.6
Sele-Tex.................186	Cone-NY...............8.24	Trombley-Min 75	Hernandez-TB 43	Rivera-NY 8.35	Zimmerman-Tex...26.0	Lowe-Bos.............27.9
Cone-NY................177	Sele-Tex...............8.17	Lowe-Bos................74	Jackson-Cle 39	P.Martinez-Bos 8.69	Rivera-NY 23.1	Hernandez-TB 26.1
Burba-Cle 174	Clemens-NY 7.82	Lloyd-Tor.................74	Mesa-Sea 33	Lowe-Bos.............9.30	Brocail-Det...........22.7	Karsay-Cle...........24.2
INNINGS PITCHED	**OPPONENTS' AVG.**	**OPPONENTS' OBP**	**EARNED RUN AVERAGE**	**ADJUSTED ERA**	**ADJUSTED STARTER RUNS**	**PITCHER WINS**
D.Wells-Tor 231.2	P.Martinez-Bos 205	P.Martinez-Bos 248	P.Martinez-Bos 2.07	P.Martinez-Bos 241	P.Martinez-Bos 67.2	**P.Martinez-Bos .. 8.1**
Erickson-Bal 230.1	Cone-NY...............229	Milton-Min..............299	Cone-NY...............3.44	Radke-Min 138	Radke-Min 32.6	**Rivera-NY 4.5**
Moyer-Sea 228.0	Hernandez-NY......233	Hernandez-NY......311	Mussina-Bal.........3.50	Cone-NY...............137	Cone-NY..............27.1	**Radke-Min 3.5**
Burba-Cle 220.0	Colon-Cle..............242	Moyer-Sea 311	Radke-Min 3.75	Mussina-Bal..........134	Saberhagen-Bos..26.7	**Saberhagen-Bos 3.2**
Helling-Tex.........219.1	Milton-Min.............243	Mussina-Bal..........312	Rosado-KC..........3.85	Rosado-KC...........132	Mussina-Bal.........26.6	**Mussina-Bal 3.2**

THE UMPS DEFINITELY BLEW THAT CALL

The Orioles traveled to Cuba for a spring exhibition game against the Cuban national team, the first game involving American pros there in forty years. The Mariners gleefully moved into Safeco Field in mid-July, while teary-eyed fans in Detroit said farewell to beloved Tiger Stadium. Yankees legend Joe DiMaggio died in March, while an awe-struck Ted Williams was lauded at the All-Star Game at Fenway Park.

In what was perhaps the game's worst negotiating tactic ever, most of baseball's umpires resigned en masse in July, attempting to get around a no-strike clause in their contract. Many resignations were accepted and twenty-two umps wound up losing their jobs.

Pedro Martinez averaged a record 13.2 strikeouts per game. Tampa Bay's 35-year-old reliever Jim Morris became the oldest rookie in nearly thirty years.

The Yankees were postseason juggernauts again. For the second straight year, they permitted Texas 1 run in a three-game Division Series sweep. After losing the first two games in the other ALDS, the Red Sox pummeled Cleveland pitchers in the final three games, including the greatest scoring display in postseason history: a 23-7 rout in Game 4. Aside from a lopsided Boston win in Game 3, it was all New York in the ALCS. In the other games the Yanks outscored the Red Sox, 22-8, in the first meeting between the long-time rivals in the postseason. The Yankees crushed Atlanta for their 25th world championship, and eighth by sweep. The Braves held eighth-inning leads in Games 1 and 3, but New York rallied to win both times.

1998 NATIONAL LEAGUE

TEAM	W	L	T	PCT	GB	HW	HL	R	OR	PA	H	2B	3B	HR	BB	SO	HB	SH	AVG	OBP	SLG	OPS	AOPS	BR	ABR	PF	SB	CS	BSA	BSR
East																														
Atl	106	56	0	.654	—	**56**	25	826	**581**	6215	1489	297	26	215	548	1062	61	76	.272	.342	.453	795	114	104	111	99	98	43	70	7
NY	88	74	0	.543	18	47	34	706	645	6255	1425	289	24	136	572	1049	37	88	.259	.330	.394	724	98	-29	-6	97	62	46	57	-2
Phi	75	87	0	.463	31	40	41	713	808	6300	1482	286	36	126	508	1080	45	65	.264	.326	.395	721	94	-38	-39	100	97	45	68	6
Mon	65	97	0	.401	41	39	42	644	783	6041	1348	280	32	147	439	1058	60	87	.249	.310	.394	704	92	-86	-68	97	91	46	66	4
Fla	54	108	0	.333	52	31	50	667	923	6227	1381	277	36	114	525	1120	45	70	.248	.317	.373	690	92	-107	-66	94	115	57	67	5
Central																														
Hou	102	60	0	.630	—	55	26	**874**	620	6441	1578	326	28	166	621	1122	72	58	.280	**.356**	.436	792	**116**	121	**146**	97	155	51	75	16
Chi	90	73	0	.552	12.5	51	31	831	792	6393	1494	250	34	212	601	1223	39	67	.264	.337	.433	770	103	56	28	104	65	44	60	-1
StL	83	79	1	.512	19	48	34	810	782	6413	1444	292	30	**223**	676	1179	42	68	.258	.341	.441	782	111	84	89	99	133	41	**76**	15
Cin	77	85	0	.475	25	39	42	750	760	6268	1441	298	28	138	608	1107	37	78	.262	.337	.402	739	98	7	0	101	95	42	69	6
Mil	74	88	0	.457	28	38	43	707	812	6232	1439	266	17	152	532	1039	66	61	.260	.330	.396	726	94	-28	-40	102	81	59	58	-3
Pit	69	93	1	.426	33	40	40	650	718	6111	1395	271	35	107	393	1060	**91**	78	.254	.311	.374	685	83	-116	-120	101	**159**	51	**76**	**17**
West																														
SD	98	64	0	.605	—	54	27	749	635	6243	1390	292	30	167	604	1072	48	56	.253	.330	.409	739	106	-2	54	93	79	37	68	4
SF	89	74	0	.546	9.5	49	32	845	739	6484	1540	292	26	161	**678**	1040	44	81	.274	.353	.421	774	115	87	132	95	102	51	67	5
LA	83	79	0	.512	15	48	33	669	678	6076	1374	209	27	159	447	1056	36	91	.252	.310	.387	697	91	-102	-70	95	137	53	72	12
Col	77	85	0	.475	21	42	39	826	855	6277	**1640**	**333**	36	183	469	**949**	37	**98**	**.291**	.347	**.461**	**808**	96	**132**	-21	121	67	47	59	-2
Ari	65	97	0	.401	33	34	47	665	812	6116	1353	235	**46**	159	489	1239	64	45	.246	.314	.393	707	90	-83	-84	100	73	38	66	3
Total	1298	—	—	—	—	711	586	11932	—	100092	23213	4493	491	2565	8710	17455	824	1167	.262	.331	.410	741	—	—	—	—	1609	751	68	91

TEAM	CG	SHO	GR	SV	IP	H	HR	BB	SO	BR/9	ERA	AERA	OAV	OOB	PR	APR	PF	OSB	OCS	FA	E	WPB	DP	FW	PW	BW	BSW	DIF
East																												
Atl	**24**	**23**	354	45	1438.2	**1291**	**117**	467	**1232**	**11.2**	**3.25**	**128**	**.240**	**.303**	**156**	**147**	98	85	40	**.985**	**91**	64	139	**1.3**	**14.5**	11.0	.1	-1.9
NY	9	16	399	46	1458.0	1381	152	532	1129	12.2	3.76	109	.253	.325	76	59	97	117	**64**	.984	101	51	151	.8	5.8	-.6	-.8	1.7
Phi	21	10	385	32	1463.0	1476	188	544	1176	12.8	4.64	93	.262	.331	-66	-52	102	87	33	.982	110	88	131	.3	-5.1	-3.8	.0	2.6
Mon	4	5	443	39	1427.0	1448	156	533	1017	12.9	4.38	96	.264	.332	-24	-29	99	132	**64**	.975	155	68	127	-2.1	-2.9	-6.7	-.2	-4.1
Fla	11	3	420	24	1449.2	1617	182	715	1016	14.8	5.18	78	.287	.370	-153	-189	96	109	54	.979	129	80	177	-.7	-18.7	-6.5	-.0	-1.0
Central																												
Hou	12	11	340	44	1471.1	1435	147	**465**	1187	11.9	3.50	116	.256	.315	119	94	96	**75**	42	.983	108	59	144	.4	9.3	**14.4**	1.0	-4.1
Chi	7	7	**449**	56	1477.1	1528	180	575	1207	13.1	4.47	99	.266	.336	-39	-11	104	120	43	.984	101	55	107	.8	-1.1	2.8	-.7	6.7
StL	6	10	428	44	1469.2	1513	151	558	972	13.0	4.31	98	.268	.337	-12	-17	99	92	44	.978	142	**48**	160	-1.4	-1.7	8.8	.9	-4.6
Cin	6	8	366	42	1441.1	1400	170	573	1098	12.6	4.44	97	.256	.330	-34	-24	101	117	46	.980	122	70	142	-.3	-2.4	.0	.0	-1.3
Mil	2	2	416	39	1451.0	1538	188	550	1063	13.3	4.63	94	.275	.344	-64	-47	102	125	34	.982	110	62	192	.3	-4.6	-3.9	-.9	2.1
Pit	7	10	395	41	1449.0	1433	147	530	1112	12.4	3.91	109	.259	.324	52	58	101	95	39	.977	140	59	161	-1.3	5.7	-11.8	**1.1**	-5.7
West																												
SD	14	11	369	**59**	1454.2	1384	139	501	1217	12.0	3.63	109	.252	.318	97	57	94	94	40	.983	104	80	155	.6	5.6	5.3	-.2	5.6
SF	6	6	433	44	1477.0	1457	171	562	1089	12.6	4.18	96	.259	.330	8	-27	95	97	39	.984	101	71	157	.8	-2.7	13.0	-.0	-3.6
LA	16	10	342	47	1447.1	1332	135	587	1178	12.3	3.81	106	.246	.324	68	37	95	93	57	.978	134	54	154	-1.0	3.7	-6.9	.6	5.6
Col	9	5	406	36	1432.2	1583	174	562	951	13.9	4.99	104	.285	.355	-121	24	122	108	52	.984	102	56	**193**	.7	2.4	-2.1	-.8	-4.3
Ari	7	6	368	37	1432.1	1463	188	489	908	12.5	4.63	92	.266	.328	-64	-57	101	93	63	.984	100	58	125	.8	-5.6	-8.3	-.3	-2.7
Total	161	143	6313	675	23240.0	—	—	—	—	12.7	4.23	—	.262	.331	—	—	—	—	—	.981	1850	1023	2415	—	—	—	—	—

BATTER-FIELDER WINS	BATTING AVERAGE	ON-BASE PERCENTAGE	SLUGGING AVERAGE	ON-BASE PLUS SLUGGING	ADJUSTED OPS	ADJUSTED BATTER RUNS
McGwire-StL......7.1	Walker-Col............363	McGwire-StL.........470	McGwire-StL.........752	McGwire-StL.......1222	McGwire-StL.........217	McGwire-StL........96.3
Bonds-SF............6.7	Olerud-NY.............354	Olerud-NY.............447	Sosa-Chi...............647	Walker-Col..........1075	Bonds-SF..............182	Bonds-SF..............73.9
Piazza-LA-Fla-NY ... 6.0	Bichette-Col..........331	Walker-Col............445	Walker-Col............630	Bonds-SF............1047	Olerud-NY.............167	Olerud-NY.............60.7
Biggio-Hou.........5.6	Piazza-LA-Fla-NY.328	Bonds-SF..............438	Bonds-SF..............609	Sosa-Chi.............1024	Bagwell-Hou.........161	Bagwell-Hou........53.3
Rolen-Phi............5.1	Kendall-Pit............327	Sheffield-Fla-LA....428	Vaughn-SD...........597	Olerud-NY.............998	Alou-Hou..............159	Alou-Hou..............51.6

RUNS	HITS	DOUBLES	TRIPLES	HOME RUNS	TOTAL BASES	RUNS BATTED IN
Sosa-Chi..............134	Bichette-Col..........219	Biggio-Hou..............51	Dellucci-Ari.............12	McGwire-StL...........70	Sosa-Chi...............416	Sosa-Chi...............158
McGwire-StL.........130	Biggio-Hou............210	Young-Cin...............48	B.Larkin-Cin............10	Sosa-Chi................66	McGwire-StL.........383	McGwire-StL.........147
Bagwell-Hou.........124	Castilla-Col...........206	Bichette-Col............48	W.Guerrero-LA-Mon.....9	Vaughn-SD.............50	Castilla-Col...........380	Castilla-Col...........144
C.Jones-Atl...........123	V.Guerrero-Mon....202	Walker-Col..............46	Perez-Col..................9	Castilla-Col.............46	V.Guerrero-Mon....367	Kent-SF.................128
Biggio-Hou............123				Galarraga-Atl..........44	Vaughn-SD...........342	Burnitz-Mil............125

BASES ON BALLS	STOLEN BASES	BASE STEALING RUNS	FIELDING RUNS-INFIELD	FIELDING RUNS-OUTFIELD	OUTFIELD ASSISTS	CATCHER CS PCT.
McGwire-StL.........162	Womack-Pit............58	Womack-Pit.........10.0	Perez-Col............29.4	A.Jones-Atl..........20.0	Kotsay-Fla...............20	Johnson-Fla-LA...39.8
Bonds-SF..............130	Biggio-Hou..............50	Biggio-Hou............8.2	Vina-Mil................28.4	Kotsay-Fla............18.5	A.Jones-Atl.............20	Stinnett-Ari...........37.2
Bagwell-Hou.........109	Young-LA................42	Young-LA...............4.7	Cirillo-Mil..............21.7	Rodriguez-Chi........9.4	Abreu-Phi................17	Widger-Mon.........36.4
Olerud-NY...............96	Renteria-Fla............41	B.Larkin-Cin...........4.7	Veras-SD..............20.3	Dunwoody-Fla.......7.4	Guillen-Pit...............16	Ausmus-Hou.........35.6
C.Jones-Atl.............96	Bonds-SF................28	A.Jones-Atl............4.5	Andrews-Mon......18.2	Sosa-Chi................7.4		Lieberthal-Phi......35.3

WINS	WINNING PCT.	WINS ABOVE TEAM	GAMES STARTED	COMPLETE GAMES	FEWEST HITS/GAME	FEWEST BB/GAME
Glavine-Atl..............20	Smoltz-Atl............850	Smoltz-Atl..............6.0	Schilling-Phi...........35	Schilling-Phi...........15	Wood-Chi.............6.32	Anderson-Ari........1.04
Tapani-Chi..............19	Glavine-Atl............769	Leiter-NY...............5.4	Reynolds-Hou.........35	Maddux-Atl...............9	Leiter-NY.............7.04	Reed-NY..............1.23
Reynolds-Hou.........19	Leiter-NY.............739	Glavine-Atl.............4.8	Kile-Col..................35	Hernandez-Fla..........9	Maddux-Atl..........7.21	Lima-Hou.............1.23
Maddux-Atl..............18	Brown-SD.............720	Tapani-Chi.............4.5	Brown-SD...............35	C.Perez-Mon-LA.......7	Harnisch-Cin.........7.58	Maddux-Atl..........1.61
Brown-SD...............18	Reynolds-Hou.......704	R.Johnson-Hou......4.2		Brown-SD.................7	Smoltz-Atl............7.78	Brown-SD............1.72

STRIKEOUTS	STRIKEOUTS/GAME	GAMES	SAVES	BASE RUNNERS/9	ADJUSTED RELIEF RUNS	RELIEF RANKING
Schilling-Phi..........300	Wood-Chi...........12.58	Beck-Chi.................81	Hoffman-SD............53	Hoffman-SD.........7.77	Nen-SF.................23.6	Nen-SF.................47.2
Brown-SD.............257	Schilling-Phi.......10.05	Nen-SF...................78	Beck-Chi.................51	Nen-SF................8.63	Urbina-Mon..........22.7	Urbina-Mon..........45.4
Wood-Chi..............233	Smoltz-Atl...........9.29	McElroy-Col............78	Shaw-Cin-LA..........48	Maddux-Atl..........9.07	Hoffman-SD.........22.0	Hoffman-SD.........43.9
Reynolds-Hou.......209	Brown-SD...........9.00	Kline-Mon...............78	Nen-SF...................40	Urbina-Mon..........9.09	Shaw-Cin-LA.......19.5	Shaw-Cin-LA.......39.0
Maddux-Atl...........204	Millwood-Atl.........8.41	Telford-Mon.............77	J.Franco-NY............38	R.Johnson-Hou....9.18	Acevedo-StL........18.6	Acevedo-StL........23.6

INNINGS PITCHED	OPPONENTS' AVG.	OPPONENTS' OBP	EARNED RUN AVERAGE	ADJUSTED ERA	ADJUSTED STARTER RUNS	PITCHER WINS
Schilling-Phi.......268.2	Wood-Chi..............196	Maddux-Atl...........260	Maddux-Atl..........2.22	Maddux-Atl...........187	Maddux-Atl..........52.5	**Maddux-Atl.........6.4**
Brown-SD...........257.0	Leiter-NY.............216	Brown-SD.............279	Brown-SD............2.38	Glavine-Atl............168	Brown-SD............46.7	**Glavine-Atl.........5.6**
Maddux-Atl.........251.0	Maddux-Atl...........220	Schilling-Phi..........282	Leiter-NY.............2.47	Leiter-NY..............167	Glavine-Atl...........45.4	**Brown-SD...........4.9**
C.Perez-Mon-LA 241.0	Harnisch-Cin.........228	Smoltz-Atl.............285	Glavine-Atl...........2.47	Brown-SD.............167	Leiter-NY.............36.9	**Nen-SF................4.8**
Hernandez-Fla...234.1	Smoltz-Atl............231	Lima-Hou..............285	Daal-Ari................2.88	Daal-Ari.................149	Schilling-Phi.........32.7	**Urbina-Mon........4.5**

The Year They'll All Remember

Sluggers Mark McGwire and Sammy Sosa put on a season-long show. McGwire broke Roger Maris' record first, smashing his 62nd homer on September 8 against the Cubs. Sosa briefly took the league lead on the third-to-last day of the season when he smacked his 66th homer. Not to be outdone, McGwire tied Sosa that night and clubbed four more in the final two games to finish with 70. The "Mark & Sammy Power Tour" captivated the attention of hundreds of millions of fans and non-fans around the world, though McGwire's usage of the legal, over-the-counter supplement androstenedione generated some controversy.

The addition of two teams, the Diamondbacks and (surprise!) the Brewers, brought a record 2,565 homers to the sixteen-team NL, but scoring per game remained essentially unchanged. Chicago rookie Kerry Wood fanned 20 Astros in only his fifth start, tying the single-game record. Rupert Murdoch, head of the FOX media empire, bought the Dodgers from Peter O'Malley, whose family had controlled the franchise since 1950. Chicago lost two legendary broadcasters: Harry Caray died in February, while Jack Brickhouse passed in August.

Sosa's power helped the Cubs win the Wild Card after a one-game playoff with the Giants, who overtook the Mets in a furious final week. The Division Series saw Atlanta sweep Chicago, while San Diego, allowing 1 run in each of its victories, beat Houston in four. The Padres won the first three games of the NLCS and closed it out with a 5-0 shutout over the Braves in Game 6, only to be swept by the powerful Yankees in the Series.

1998 AMERICAN LEAGUE

TEAM	W	L	T	PCT	GB	HW	HL	R	OR	PA	H	2B	3B	HR	BB	SO	HB	SH	AVG	OBP	SLG	OPS	AOPS	BR	ABR	PF	SB	CS	BSA	BSR
EAST																														
NY	114	48	0	.704	—	**62**	19	**965**	**656**	6444	1625	290	31	207	**653**	1025	57	32	.288	**.364**	.460	**824**	**118**	**125**	**167**	96	153	63	71	**12**
Bos	92	70	0	.568	22	51	30	876	729	6299	1568	**338**	35	205	541	1049	70	35	.280	.348	.463	811	107	79	60	102	72	39	65	2
Tor	88	74	1	.543	26	51	30	816	768	6323	1482	316	19	221	564	1132	**87**	43	.266	.340	.448	788	103	31	28	100	**184**	81	69	**12**
Bal	79	83	0	.488	35	42	39	817	785	6304	1520	303	11	214	593	**903**	58	44	.273	.347	.447	794	107	48	63	98	86	48	64	2
TB	63	99	0	.389	51	33	48	620	751	6156	1450	267	**43**	111	473	1107	37	53	.261	.321	.385	706	81	-141	-157	103	120	73	62	1
CENTRAL																														
Cle	89	73	0	.549	—	46	35	850	779	6376	1530	334	30	198	630	1061	41	30	.272	.347	.448	795	101	55	24	104	143	60	70	10
Chi	80	82	1	.494	9	44	37	861	931	6280	1516	291	38	198	551	916	47	38	.271	.339	.444	783	104	17	31	98	127	46	73	**12**
KC	72	89	0	.447	16.5	29	51	714	899	6191	1459	274	40	134	475	984	60	45	.263	.324	.399	723	84	-101	-128	104	135	50	73	**12**
Min	70	92	0	.432	19	35	46	734	818	6262	1499	285	32	115	506	915	45	18	.266	.328	.389	717	84	-111	-129	103	112	54	67	6
Det	65	97	0	.401	24	32	49	722	863	6242	1494	306	29	165	455	1070	62	16	.264	.323	.415	738	89	-80	-89	101	122	62	66	5
WEST																														
Tex	88	74	0	.543	—	48	33	940	871	6401	**1637**	314	32	201	595	1045	39	41	**.289**	.357	.462	819	105	104	56	106	82	47	64	2
Ana	85	77	0	.525	3	42	39	787	783	6278	1530	314	27	147	510	1028	48	49	.272	.335	.415	750	92	-43	-57	102	93	45	67	5
Sea	76	85	0	.472	11.5	42	39	859	855	6327	1553	321	28	**234**	558	1081	57	36	.276	.345	**.468**	813	108	78	71	101	115	39	**75**	**12**
Oak	74	88	0	.457	14	39	42	804	866	6282	1413	295	13	149	633	1122	55	**58**	.257	.338	.397	735	92	-62	-54	99	131	47	74	**12**
Total	1134	—	—	—	—	596	537	11365	—	88165	21276	4248	408	2499	7737	14438	763	538	.271	.340	.432	771	—	—	—	—	1675	754	69	105

TEAM	CG	SHO	GR	SV	IP	H	HR	BB	SO	BR/9	ERA	AERA	OAV	OOB	PR	APR	PF	OSB	OCS	FA	E	WPB	DP	FW	PW	BW	BSW	DIF
EAST																												
NY	**22**	**16**	334	48	1456.2	**1357**	**156**	466	1080	**11.7**	**3.82**	**114**	**.247**	**.312**	**133**	**95**	94	102	51	.984	98	49	146	.9	**9.0**	**15.7**	**.4**	7.0
Bos	5	8	432	**53**	1436.0	1406	168	504	1025	12.3	4.18	113	.255	.321	75	85	102	132	58	.983	105	97	128	.5	8.0	5.7	-.5	-2.6
Tor	10	11	384	47	1465.0	1443	169	587	1154	12.7	4.28	109	.256	.329	60	60	100	149	47	.979	125	**43**	131	-.6	5.7	2.6	**.4**	-1.1
Bal	16	10	402	37	1431.1	1505	169	535	1065	13.1	4.74	96	.272	.338	-15	-32	98	182	53	**.987**	**81**	63	144	**1.8**	-3.0	5.9	-.5	-6.2
TB	7	7	410	28	1443.0	1425	171	643	1008	13.4	4.35	110	.261	.345	47	68	103	97	61	.985	94	62	**178**	1.1	6.4	-14.8	-.6	-10.1
CENTRAL																												
Cle	9	4	423	47	1460.0	1552	171	563	1037	13.5	4.44	107	.274	.344	33	52	103	110	47	.982	110	**43**	146	.2	4.9	2.3	.2	.4
Chi	8	4	405	42	1438.2	1569	211	580	911	13.8	5.22	88	.278	.348	-92	-106	98	122	59	.977	140	67	161	-1.4	-10.0	2.9	**.4**	7.0
KC	6	5	388	46	1436.1	1590	196	568	999	13.9	5.15	94	.281	.350	-80	-46	104	80	43	.980	125	83	172	-.7	-4.3	-12.1	**.4**	8.1
Min	7	8	432	42	1447.2	1622	180	**457**	952	13.2	4.75	101	.284	.338	-16	6	103	101	45	.982	108	66	135	.3	.6	-12.2	-.1	.4
Det	9	4	**446**	32	1446.1	1551	185	595	947	13.6	4.93	96	.277	.348	-45	-29	102	120	**69**	.982	115	74	164	-.0	-2.7	-8.4	-.2	-4.6
WEST																												
Tex	10	8	402	46	1431.1	1624	164	519	994	13.8	4.99	98	.285	.346	-55	-16	105	**64**	55	.980	121	72	140	-.4	-1.5	5.3	-.5	4.1
Ana	3	5	415	52	1444.0	1481	164	630	1091	13.5	4.49	106	.267	.344	26	39	102	156	65	.983	106	98	146	.4	3.7	-5.4	-.2	5.5
Sea	17	7	368	31	1424.1	1530	196	528	**1156**	13.4	4.93	95	.273	.340	-45	-41	101	127	49	.979	125	72	139	-.7	-3.9	6.7	**.4**	-7.1
Oak	12	4	408	39	1434.0	1555	179	529	922	13.4	4.81	96	.276	.342	-25	-30	99	103	48	.977	141	81	155	-1.5	-2.8	-5.1	**.4**	2.0
Total	141	101	5649	590	20194.2	—	—	—	—	13.2	4.65	—	.271	.340	—	—	—	—	—	.981	1594	970	2085	—	—	—	—	—

BATTER-FIELDER WINS	BATTING AVERAGE	ON-BASE PERCENTAGE	SLUGGING AVERAGE	ON-BASE PLUS SLUGGING	ADJUSTED OPS	ADJUSTED BATTER RUNS
Belle-Chi 5.8	Williams-NY .... .339	Martinez-Sea .... .429	Belle-Chi .... .655	Belle-Chi 1055	Belle-Chi 173	Belle-Chi 66.9
Griffey-Sea 5.0	Vaughn-Bos .... .337	Williams-NY .... .422	Gonzalez-Tex .... .630	Thome-Cle 997	Williams-NY 164	Martinez-Sea 51.7
Rodriguez-Sea ... 4.4	Belle-Chi .... .328	Thome-Cle .... .413	Griffey-Sea .... .611	Williams-NY 997	Martinez-Sea 156	Williams-NY 49.5
Martinez-Sea 4.2	Davis-Bal .... .327	Salmon-Ana .... .410	M.Ramirez-Cle ...... .599	Gonzalez-Tex 997	Davis-Bal 152	Vaughn-Bos 46.0
Williams-NY 4.0	Jeter-NY .... .324	Offerman-KC .... .403	Delgado-Tor .... .592	Vaughn-Bos 993	Vaughn-Bos 151	Griffey-Sea 42.3
RUNS	**HITS**	**DOUBLES**	**TRIPLES**	**HOME RUNS**	**TOTAL BASES**	**RUNS BATTED IN**
Jeter-NY 127	Rodriguez-Sea 213	Gonzalez-Tex 50	Offerman-KC 13	Griffey-Sea 56	Belle-Chi 399	Gonzalez-Tex 157
Durham-Chi 126	Vaughn-Bos 205	Belle-Chi 48	Damon-KC 10	Belle-Chi 49	Griffey-Sea 387	Belle-Chi 152
Rodriguez-Sea 123	Jeter-NY 203	Martinez-Sea 46	Winn-TB 9	Canseco-Tor 46	Rodriguez-Sea 384	Griffey-Sea 146
Griffey-Sea 120	Belle-Chi 200	Valentin-Bos 44		M.Ramirez-Cle 45	Gonzalez-Tex 382	M.Ramirez-Cle 145
Knoblauch-NY 117	Garciaparra-Bos ... 195	Delgado-Tor 43		Gonzalez-Tex 45	Vaughn-Bos 360	Rodriguez-Sea 124
BASES ON BALLS	**STOLEN BASES**	**BASE STEALING RUNS**	**FIELDING RUNS-INFIELD**	**FIELDING RUNS-OUTFIELD**	**OUTFIELD ASSISTS**	**CATCHER CS PCT.**
Henderson-Oak 118	Henderson-Oak 66	Henderson-Oak ... 10.0	Easley-Det 25.7	Lawton-Min 14.3	Lofton-Cle 19	Rodriguez-Tex 56.3
Thomas-Chi 110	Lofton-Cle 54	Lofton-Cle 8.4	Alomar-Bal 21.0	Griffey-Sea 7.6	McCracken-TB 18	Difelice-TB 39.5
Martinez-Sea 106	Stewart-Tor 51	Offerman-KC 5.7	Bordick-Bal 20.9	Anderson-Ana 5.3	Higginson-Det 18	Flaherty-TB 37.7
Salmon-Ana 90	Rodriguez-Sea 46	Nixon-Min 5.7	Valentin-Bos 18.2	Ordonez-Chi 4.6	Green-Tor 14	Steinbach-Min 35.1
	Offerman-KC 45	Rodriguez-Sea 5.6	Segui-Sea 17.6	McCracken-TB 4.6		Hinch-Oak 34.0
WINS	**WINNING PCT.**	**WINS ABOVE TEAM**	**GAMES STARTED**	**COMPLETE GAMES**	**FEWEST HITS/GAME**	**FEWEST BB/GAME**
Helling-Tex 20	Wells-NY .... .818	Clemens-Tor 7.0	Erickson-Bal 36	Erickson-Bal 11	Clemens-Tor 6.48	Wells-NY 1.22
Cone-NY 20	Clemens-Tor .... .769	Helling-Tex 6.4		Wells-NY 8	Martinez-Bos 7.24	Saberhagen-Bos.. 1.49
Clemens-Tor 20	Helling-Tex .... .741	Martinez-Bos 5.4		Rogers-Oak 7	Irabu-NY 7.70	Moyer-Sea 1.61
Sele-Tex 19	Cone-NY .... .741	Rogers-Oak 5.1		Fassero-Sea 7	Cone-NY 8.06	Mussina-Bal 1.79
Martinez-Bos 19	Martinez-Bos .... .731	Wells-NY 4.6			Rogers-Oak 8.11	Radke-Min 1.81
STRIKEOUTS	**STRIKEOUTS/GAME**	**GAMES**	**SAVES**	**BASE RUNNERS/9**	**ADJUSTED RELIEF RUNS**	**RELIEF RANKING**
Clemens-Tor 271	Clemens-Tor 10.39	Runyan-Det 88	Gordon-Bos 46	Jackson-Cle 8.44	Jackson-Cle 22.8	Gordon-Bos 36.8
Martinez-Bos 251	Martinez-Bos 9.67	Quantrill-Tor 82	Wetteland-Tex 42	Wetteland-Tex 8.85	Gordon-Bos 18.4	Wetteland-Tex 31.6
Johnson-Sea 213	Cone-NY 9.06	Swindell-Min-Bos 81	Percival-Ana 42	Gordon-Bos 9.08	Rivera-NY 18.3	Jackson-Cle 31.1
Finley-Ana 212	Finley-Ana 8.54	Guardado-Min 79	Jackson-Cle 40	Wells-NY 9.45	Quantrill-Tor 18.1	Rivera-NY 26.7
Cone-NY 209	Saunders-TB 8.05	Plesac-Tor 78	Aguilera-Min 38	Brocail-Det 9.48	Wetteland-Tex 18.0	Lopez-TB 20.3
INNINGS PITCHED	**OPPONENTS' AVG.**	**OPPONENTS' OBP**	**EARNED RUN AVERAGE**	**ADJUSTED ERA**	**ADJUSTED STARTER RUNS**	**PITCHER WINS**
Erickson-Bal 251.1	Clemens-Tor .... .197	Wells-NY .... .265	Clemens-Tor 2.65	Clemens-Tor 176	Clemens-Tor 51.5	**Clemens-Tor 5.2**
Rogers-Oak 238.2	Martinez-Bos .... .217	Clemens-Tor .... .277	Martinez-Bos 2.89	Martinez-Bos 164	Martinez-Bos 46.9	**Martinez-Bos 4.6**
Clemens-Tor 234.2	Irabu-NY .... .233	Martinez-Bos .... .278	Rogers-Oak 3.17	Rogers-Oak 146	Rogers-Oak 38.5	**Rogers-Oak 3.8**
Moyer-Sea 234.1	Cone-NY .... .237	Mussina-Bal .... .282	Finley-Ana 3.39	Finley-Ana 140	Finley-Ana 30.5	**Gordon-Bos 3.5**
Belcher-KC 234.0	Wells-NY .... .239	Moyer-Sea .... .295	Wells-NY 3.49	Arrojo-TB 135	Moyer-Sea 30.4	**Arrojo-TB 3.3**

Selig Not Acting Anymore

Expansion took place for the second time in five years with the addition of Tampa Bay and Arizona. Milwaukee agreed to move to the National League so the Devil Rays and Diamondbacks could be placed in different leagues, marking the first time an AL team had joined the NL. Brewers owner Bud Selig, acting commissioner since 1992, finally was given the title full time.

Chicago's Albert Belle smacked 99 extra-base hits (49 homers, 48 doubles and 2 triples), the second highest number of extra-base hits since 1949, behind Belle's own 103 in 1995. Baltimore's Cal Ripken voluntarily ended his consecutive games played streak at 2,632 when he took himself out of the starting lineup just before Baltimore's final home game of the season. Paul Molitor and Dennis Eckersley retired; Dan Quisenberry and Mark Belanger died a week apart.

The Yankees won 114 games, an AL record, and breezed through the postseason. Texas led the league in hitting and placed second in runs, but scored just once in a three-game Division Series sweep by the Yankees. Cleveland rallied for three straight wins over Boston to win the other ALDS in four. The Tribe won two of the first three against the Yankees, but New York blanked Cleveland, 4-0, in Game 4, and then won the next two games to take the ALCS in six. New York cruised through San Diego in the World Series. Although the Padres took three-run leads into the seventh in Games 1 and 3, the Yankees won both times. The Series ended with a 3-0 shutout of the Padres in Game 4.

1997 NATIONAL LEAGUE

TEAM	W	L	T	PCT	GB	HW	HL	R	OR	PA	H	2B	3B	HR	BB	SO	HB	SH	AVG	OBP	SLG	OPS	AOPS	BR	ABR	PF	SB	CS	BSA	BSR
East																														
Atl	101	61	0	.623	—	50	31	791	**581**	6312	1490	268	37	174	597	1160	52	83	.270	.343	.426	769	105	56	46	101	108	58	65	3
Fla	92	70	0	.568	9	**52**	29	740	669	6299	1410	272	28	136	**686**	**1074**	61	71	.259	.346	.395	741	104	14	50	96	115	58	66	5
NY	88	74	0	.543	13	50	31	777	709	6248	1448	274	28	153	550	1029	57	58	.262	.332	.405	737	103	-11	27	95	97	74	57	-5
Mon	78	84	0	.481	23	45	36	691	740	6131	1423	**339**	34	172	420	1084	73	72	.258	.316	.425	741	99	-22	-13	99	75	46	62	0
Phi	68	94	0	.420	33	38	43	668	840	6126	1390	290	35	116	519	1032	40	74	.255	.322	.385	707	91	-72	-62	99	92	56	62	1
Central																														
Hou	84	78	0	.519	—	46	35	777	660	6362	1427	314	40	133	633	1085	**100**	74	.259	.344	.403	747	104	25	52	97	171	74	70	12
Pit	79	83	0	.488	5	43	38	725	760	6200	1440	291	**52**	129	481	1161	92	77	.262	.329	.404	733	94	-25	-37	102	160	50	**76**	**18**
Cin	76	86	0	.469	8	40	41	651	764	6152	1386	269	27	142	518	1113	45	75	.253	.321	.389	710	88	-73	-84	102	**190**	67	74	**18**
StL	73	89	0	.451	11	41	40	689	708	6211	1409	269	39	144	543	1191	42	58	.255	.324	.396	720	93	-52	-53	100	164	60	73	15
Chi	68	94	0	.420	16	42	39	687	759	6095	1444	269	39	127	451	1003	34	83	.263	.321	.396	717	89	-64	-85	103	116	60	66	5
West																														
SF	90	72	0	.556	—	48	33	784	793	6296	1415	266	37	172	642	1120	46	64	.258	.337	.414	751	103	22	39	98	121	49	71	9
LA	88	74	0	.543	2	47	34	742	645	6216	1488	242	33	174	498	1079	33	**105**	.268	.330	.418	748	107	-1	51	94	131	64	67	6
Col	83	79	0	.512	7	47	34	**923**	908	6336	**1611**	269	40	**239**	562	1060	63	73	**.288**	**.357**	**.478**	**835**	100	**180**	8	123	137	65	68	7
SD	76	86	0	.469	14	39	42	795	891	6369	1519	275	16	152	604	1129	35	63	.271	.342	.407	749	**108**	22	**74**	94	140	60	70	10
Total	1134	—	—	—	—	628	506	10440	—	87353	20300	3907	485	2163	7704	15320	773	1030	.263	.333	.410	744	—	—	—	—	1817	841	68	105

TEAM	CG	SHO	GR	SV	IP	H	HR	BB	SO	BR/9	ERA	AERA	OAV	OOB	PR	APR	PF	OSB	OCS	FA	E	WPB	DP	FW	PW	BW	BSW	DIF
East																												
Atl	21	**17**	374	37	1465.2	**1319**	**111**	**450**	1196	**11.1**	**3.18**	**132**	**.241**	**.301**	**166**	**165**	100	124	54	.982	114	49	136	.3	**16.3**	4.5	-.4	-.7
Fla	12	10	404	39	1446.2	1353	131	639	1188	12.8	3.83	106	.250	.334	60	37	96	95	70	.981	116	48	167	.2	3.6	4.9	-.2	2.5
NY	7	8	376	**49**	1459.1	1452	160	504	982	12.4	3.95	101	.262	.326	41	9	95	106	44	.981	120	57	165	-.0	.9	2.7	-1.2	4.7
Mon	**27**	14	390	37	1447.0	1365	149	557	1138	12.3	4.14	101	.250	.325	10	6	99	192	42	.979	132	65	150	-.7	.6	-1.3	-.7	-.9
Phi	13	7	409	35	1420.1	1441	171	616	1209	13.4	4.85	87	.265	.342	-102	-101	100	107	57	.982	108	89	134	.7	-9.9	-6.1	-.6	3.0
Central																												
Hou	16	12	354	37	1459.0	1379	134	511	1138	12.0	3.66	109	.251	.319	87	57	95	**92**	57	.979	131	52	169	-.7	5.6	5.1	.4	-7.5
Pit	6	8	451	41	1436.0	1503	143	560	1080	13.3	4.28	100	.271	.342	-13	-1	102	109	66	.979	131	72	149	-.7	-.0	-3.6	**1.0**	1.4
Cin	5	8	423	**49**	1449.0	1408	173	558	1159	12.7	4.41	97	.255	.330	-34	-21	102	139	48	.982	**106**	77	129	**.8**	-2.1	-8.3	**1.0**	3.5
StL	5	3	399	39	1455.2	1422	124	536	1130	12.5	3.88	108	.259	.328	52	50	100	134	66	.980	123	66	156	-.2	4.9	-5.2	.7	-8.3
Chi	6	4	441	37	1429.0	1451	185	590	1072	13.1	4.44	97	.266	.339	-38	-19	103	146	59	.981	112	51	117	.5	-1.9	-8.4	-.2	-3.0
West																												
SF	5	9	**481**	45	1446.0	1494	160	578	1044	13.1	4.39	94	.270	.340	-31	-46	98	108	73	.980	125	57	157	-.3	-4.5	3.8	.1	9.8
LA	6	6	412	45	1459.1	1325	163	546	**1232**	11.8	3.62	108	**.241**	.313	94	49	93	118	58	.981	116	**47**	104	.2	4.8	5.0	-.2	-2.9
Col	9	5	426	38	1432.2	1697	196	566	870	14.6	5.25	98	.300	.367	-167	-12	123	130	54	**.983**	111	55	**202**	.5	-1.2	.8	-.0	1.9
SD	5	2	426	43	1450.0	1581	172	596	1059	13.9	4.98	79	.280	.352	-125	-182	93	171	**75**	.979	132	66	132	-.7	-17.9	**7.3**	.2	6.1
Total	143	113	5766	571	20255.2	—	—	—	—	12.8	4.20	—	.263	.333	—	—	—	—	—	.981	1677	851	2067	—	—	—	—	—

BATTER-FIELDER WINS	BATTING AVERAGE	ON-BASE PERCENTAGE	SLUGGING AVERAGE	ON-BASE PLUS SLUGGING	ADJUSTED OPS	ADJUSTED BATTER RUNS
Biggio-Hou 8.2	Gwynn-SD .372	Walker-Col .452	Walker-Col .720	Walker-Col 1172	Piazza-LA 189	Piazza-LA 72.9
Piazza-LA 7.7	Walker-Col .366	Bonds-SF .446	Piazza-LA .638	Piazza-LA 1070	Bonds-SF 172	Bagwell-Hou 65.2
Bonds-SF 6.2	Piazza-LA .362	Piazza-LA .431	Bagwell-Hou .592	Bonds-SF 1031	Bagwell-Hou 170	Bonds-SF 64.8
Bagwell-Hou 6.0	Lofton-Atl .333	Bagwell-Hou .425	Galarraga-Col .585	Bagwell-Hou 1017	Walker-Col 164	Walker-Col 56.4
Caminiti-SD 5.0	Joyner-SD .327	Sheffield-Fla .424	Lankford-StL .585	Lankford-StL 996	Gwynn-SD 160	Gwynn-SD 52.2
RUNS	**HITS**	**DOUBLES**	**TRIPLES**	**HOME RUNS**	**TOTAL BASES**	**RUNS BATTED IN**
Biggio-Hou 146	Gwynn-SD 220	Grudzielanek-Mon 54	DeShields-StL 14	Walker-Col 49	Walker-Col 409	Galarraga-Col 140
Walker-Col 143	Walker-Col 208	Gwynn-SD 49	Perez-Col 10	Bagwell-Hou 43	Piazza-LA 355	Bagwell-Hou 135
Bonds-SF 123	Piazza-LA 201	Walker-Col 46	Womack-Pit 9	Galarraga-Col 41	Galarraga-Col 351	Walker-Col 130
Galarraga-Col 120		Lansing-Mon 45	Randa-Pit 9		Castilla-Col 335	Piazza-LA 124
Bagwell-Hou 109		Mondesi-LA 42	Guerrero-LA 9		Bagwell-Hou 335	Kent-SF 121
BASES ON BALLS	**STOLEN BASES**	**BASE STEALING RUNS**	**FIELDING RUNS-INFIELD**	**FIELDING RUNS-OUTFIELD**	**OUTFIELD ASSISTS**	**CATCHER CS PCT.**
Bonds-SF 145	Womack-Pit 60	Womack-Pit 10.8	Young-Col 25.5	A.Jones-Atl 17.3	Gilkey-NY 17	Ausmus-Hou 49.5
Bagwell-Hou 127	D.Sanders-Cin 56	D.Sanders-Cin 7.8	Biggio-Hou 25.4	Glanville-Chi 9.2	Sosa-Chi 16	Johnson-Fla 47.5
Sheffield-Fla 121	DeShields-StL 55	DeShields-StL 7.2	Weiss-Col 19.0	Mondesi-LA 8.6	Sheffield-Fla 14	Kendall-Pit 37.1
Snow-SF 96	Biggio-Hou 47	Biggio-Hou 6.8	Randa-Pit 18.6	Sosa-Chi 7.4	A.Jones-Atl 14	Lieberthal-Phi 34.8
Lankford-StL 95	Young-Col-LA 45	Bonds-SF 5.3	Rolen-Phi 18.5	Finley-SD 5.8		Lopez-Atl 31.4
WINS	**WINNING PCT.**	**WINS ABOVE TEAM**	**GAMES STARTED**	**COMPLETE GAMES**	**FEWEST HITS/GAME**	**FEWEST BB/GAME**
Neagle-Atl 20	Maddux-Atl .826	Estes-SF 6.9	Smoltz-Atl 35	Martinez-Mon 13	Martinez-Mon 5.89	Maddux-Atl .77
Maddux-Atl 19	Neagle-Atl .800	Maddux-Atl 6.6	Schilling-Phi 35	Perez-Mon 8	Park-LA 6.98	Reed-NY 1.34
Kile-Hou 19	Estes-SF .792	Neagle-Atl 6.4		Smoltz-Atl 7	Estes-SF 7.25	Neagle-Atl 1.89
Estes-SF 19	Kile-Hou .731	Kile-Hou 6.3		Schilling-Phi 7	Kile-Hou 7.32	Schilling-Phi 2.05
	Martinez-Mon .680	Martinez-Mon 5.3		Hampton-Hou 7	Schilling-Phi 7.36	Perez-Mon 2.09
STRIKEOUTS	**STRIKEOUTS/GAME**	**GAMES**	**SAVES**	**BASE RUNNERS/9**	**ADJUSTED RELIEF RUNS**	**RELIEF RANKING**
Schilling-Phi 319	Martinez-Mon 11.37	Tavarez-SF 89	Shaw-Cin 42	Martinez-Mon 8.73	Shaw-Cin 20.1	Shaw-Cin 27.5
Martinez-Mon 305	Schilling-Phi 11.29	Belinda-Cin 84	Hoffman-SD 37	Maddux-Atl 8.74	Frascatore-StL 15.2	Hoffman-SD 25.3
Smoltz-Atl 241	Nomo-LA 10.11	Shaw-Cin 78	Beck-SF 37	Shaw-Cin 8.75	Osuna-LA 13.4	J.Franco-NY 21.1
Nomo-LA 233	A.Benes-StL 8.90	Rojas-Chi-NY 77	J.Franco-NY 36	Hoffman-SD 9.18	Martin-Hou 13.2	Wagner-Hou 18.2
	Smoltz-Atl 8.47		Eckersley-StL 36	Schilling-Phi 9.59	Hoffman-SD 13.1	McMichael-NY 18.1
INNINGS PITCHED	**OPPONENTS' AVG.**	**OPPONENTS' OBP**	**EARNED RUN AVERAGE**	**ADJUSTED ERA**	**ADJUSTED STARTER RUNS**	**PITCHER WINS**
Smoltz-Atl 256.0	Martinez-Mon .184	Martinez-Mon .249	Martinez-Mon 1.90	Martinez-Mon 220	Martinez-Mon 57.8	**Martinez-Mon 5.8**
Kile-Hou 255.2	Park-LA .213	Maddux-Atl .256	Maddux-Atl 2.20	Maddux-Atl 191	Maddux-Atl 54.3	**Maddux-Atl 5.3**
Schilling-Phi 254.1	Estes-SF .223	Schilling-Phi .271	Kile-Hou 2.57	Kile-Hou 156	Kile-Hou 40.0	**Kile-Hou 4.0**
Martinez-Mon 241.1	Schilling-Phi .224	Reed-NY .272	Valdez-LA 2.65	Brown-Fla 151	Brown-Fla 37.4	**Smoltz-Atl 3.9**
Glavine-Atl 240.0	Kile-Hou .225	Neagle-Atl .277	Brown-Fla 2.69	Valdez-LA 147	Glavine-Atl 34.3	**Brown-Fla 3.8**

Wild Things

On April 15, the 50th anniversary of Jackie Robinson's momentous debut, baseball permanently retired Robinson's uniform number 42 during a Dodgers-Mets game at Shea Stadium. Bud Selig's surprise announcement upstaged President Bill Clinton, who spoke during a break in the fifth inning.

The Braves opened Turner Field, the rebuilt former outdoor track stadium used in the 1996 Olympics. Outfielders Brett Butler and Eric Davis returned to action after cancer treatments, while pitcher Pete Harnisch recovered from clinical depression. Butler, Ryne Sandberg, and Fernando Valenzuela retired. Former Phillies star Richie Ashburn and Curt Flood, whose holdout ultimately led to players gaining free agent rights, died.

Atlanta had the best record in baseball and was expecting another trip to the Fall Classic following a dominating NLDS sweep of Houston. But the Marlins, who swept San Francisco in the other Division Series, pounded Greg Maddux for 5 runs early in NLCS opener and the Braves never really recovered. Livian Hernandez won once in relief and fanned 15 as a starter—aided by a liberal strike zone—as Florida, in just its fifth season of existence, headed to the World Series.

Six lackluster Series games were outshone by Game 7. Cleveland led by a run heading into the ninth, but Craig Counsell's sacrifice fly tied the game. Edgar Renteria singled with the bases loaded in the bottom of the 11th to make the Marlins the first Wild Card world champion. Victory celebrations would be short and sweet, however, as the Marlins quickly dismantled their expensive team simply to cut payroll.

1997 AMERICAN LEAGUE

TEAM	W	L	T	PCT	GB	HW	HL	R	OR	PA	H	2B	3B	HR	BB	SO	HB	SH	AVG	OBP	SLG	OPS	AOPS	BR	ABR	PF	SB	CS	BSA	BSR
EAST																														
Bal	98	64	0	.605	—	46	35	812	**681**	6340	1498	264	22	196	586	952	**65**	46	.268	.341	.429	770	103	5	30	97	63	26	71	5
NY	96	66	0	.593	2	**47**	33	891	688	6527	1636	325	23	161	**676**	954	37	34	.287	**.362**	.436	798	108	85	94	99	99	58	63	1
Det	79	83	0	.488	19	42	39	784	790	6189	1415	268	32	176	578	1164	49	34	.258	.332	.415	747	94	-48	-44	100	**161**	72	69	10
Bos	78	84	0	.481	20	39	42	851	857	6430	**1684**	**373**	32	185	514	1044	59	21	**.291**	.352	.463	815	109	100	81	102	68	48	59	-2
Tor	76	86	0	.469	22	42	39	654	694	6109	1333	275	**41**	147	487	1138	59	38	.244	.310	.389	699	81	-154	-156	100	134	50	73	12
CENTRAL																														
Cle	86	75	0	.534	—	44	37	868	815	6304	1589	301	22	220	617	955	37	45	.286	.358	.467	825	109	120	86	104	118	59	67	5
Chi	80	81	0	.497	6	45	36	779	833	6200	1498	260	28	158	569	**901**	33	47	.273	.341	.417	758	100	-17	10	97	106	52	67	5
Mil	78	83	0	.484	8	**47**	33	681	742	6096	1415	294	27	135	494	967	58	48	.260	.325	.398	723	87	-93	-101	101	103	55	65	3
Min	68	94	0	.420	18.5	35	46	772	861	6265	1522	305	40	132	495	1121	60	20	.270	.333	.409	742	91	-57	-69	102	151	52	**74**	**15**
KC	67	94	0	.416	19	33	47	747	820	6295	1478	256	35	158	561	1061	42	**51**	.264	.333	.407	740	89	-62	-84	103	130	66	66	6
WEST																														
Sea	90	72	0	.556	—	45	36	**925**	833	6384	1574	312	21	**264**	626	1110	49	46	.280	.355	**.485**	**840**	**117**	**143**	**146**	100	89	40	69	6
Ana	84	78	0	.519	6	46	36	829	794	6387	1531	279	25	161	617	953	45	40	.272	.346	.416	762	98	-4	-6	100	126	72	64	3
Tex	77	85	0	.475	13	39	42	807	823	6265	1547	311	27	187	500	1116	34	28	.274	.334	.438	772	94	-4	-54	107	72	37	66	3
Oak	65	97	0	.401	25	35	46	764	946	6369	1451	274	23	197	642	1181	49	49	.260	.339	.423	762	98	-14	-12	100	71	36	66	3
Total	1132	——		—	—	585	547	11164	—	88160	21171	4097	398	2477	7962	14617	676	547	.271	.340	.428	768	—	—	—	—	1491	723	67	75

TEAM	CG	SHO	GR	SV	IP	H	HR	BB	SO	BR/9	ERA	AERA	OAV	OOB	PR	APR	PF	OSB	OCS	FA	E	WPB	DP	FW	PW	BW	BSW	DIF
EAST																												
Bal	8	10	400	**59**	1461.0	**1404**	164	563	1139	**12.3**	3.91	113	**.253**	**.323**	106	83	97	149	50	.984	97	**50**	148	.8	7.9	2.9	-.0	5.4
NY	11	10	368	51	1467.2	1463	**144**	532	1165	12.5	**3.84**	116	.260	.327	**118**	102	97	111	47	.983	104	81	156	.5	9.7	8.9	-.4	-3.7
Det	13	8	417	42	1445.2	1476	178	552	982	12.9	4.56	101	.266	.334	1	8	101	130	48	**.985**	92	62	146	**1.1**	.8	-4.2	.4	-.1
Bos	7	4	417	40	1451.2	1569	149	611	987	13.9	4.85	96	.277	.351	-46	-32	102	171	53	.978	135	87	**179**	-1.3	-3.0	7.7	-.7	-5.7
Tor	**19**	**16**	336	34	1442.2	1453	167	497	1150	12.4	3.92	**117**	.263	.326	104	**106**	100	77	64	.984	94	65	150	1.0	**10.1**	-14.8	.6	-1.9
CENTRAL																												
Cle	4	3	428	39	1425.2	1528	181	575	1036	13.6	4.73	99	.276	.347	-26	-5	103	126	54	.983	106	67	159	.3	-.5	8.2	-.0	-2.5
Chi	6	7	389	52	1422.1	1505	175	575	961	13.4	4.73	93	.271	.340	-27	-54	97	119	52	.978	127	87	131	-.9	-5.1	1.0	-.0	4.6
Mil	6	8	367	44	1427.1	1419	177	542	1016	12.7	4.22	110	.261	.333	55	63	101	106	52	.980	121	57	171	-.5	6.0	-9.6	-.2	1.9
Min	10	4	390	30	1434.0	1596	187	**495**	908	13.3	5.00	93	.283	.342	-69	-52	102	85	46	.983	101	80	170	.6	-4.9	-6.6	**.9**	-3.0
KC	11	5	393	29	1443.0	1530	186	531	961	13.2	4.70	101	.274	.340	-21	6	104	72	42	**.985**	**91**	76	168	**1.1**	.6	-8.0	.0	-7.3
WEST																												
Sea	9	8	392	38	1447.2	1500	192	598	**1207**	13.5	4.78	95	.267	.342	-35	-41	99	99	**66**	.979	126	60	143	-.8	-3.9	**13.9**	.0	-.3
Ana	9	5	400	39	1454.2	1506	202	605	1050	13.4	4.52	102	.269	.343	8	14	101	101	63	.980	123	76	140	-.6	1.3	-.6	-.2	3.1
Tex	8	9	382	33	1429.2	1598	169	541	925	13.7	4.69	103	.283	.347	-20	24	106	**60**	56	.980	121	61	155	-.5	2.3	-5.1	-.2	-.4
Oak	2	1	**480**	38	1445.1	1734	197	642	953	15.2	5.48	84	.301	.372	-147	-142	101	131	48	.980	122	56	170	-.6	-13.5	-1.1	-.2	-.6
Total	123	98	5559	568	20198.1	—	—	—	—	13.3	4.56	—	.271	.340	—	—	—	—	—	.982	1560	965	2186	—	—	—	—	—

BATTER-FIELDER WINS	BATTING AVERAGE	ON-BASE PERCENTAGE	SLUGGING AVERAGE	ON-BASE PLUS SLUGGING	ADJUSTED OPS	ADJUSTED BATTER RUNS
Griffey-Sea......... 6.0	F.Thomas-Chi 347	F.Thomas-Chi 456	Griffey-Sea 646	F.Thomas-Chi 1067	F.Thomas-Chi 183	F.Thomas-Chi 71.9
F.Thomas-Chi..... 5.1	E.Martinez-Sea.....330	E.Martinez-Sea.....456	F.Thomas-Chi 611	Griffey-Sea 1028	Griffey-Sea 164	E.Martinez-Sea....59.7
E.Martinez-Sea.. 4.7	Justice-Cle...........329	Thome-Cle...........423	Justice-Cle...........596	Justice-Cle..........1013	E.Martinez-Sea.....163	Griffey-Sea 56.3
Valentin-Bos 4.0	Williams-NY..........328	Vaughn-Bos..........420	Gonzalez-Tex........589	E.Martinez-Sea...1009	Justice-Cle...........156	Thome-Cle...........44.4
Rodriguez-Tex.... 4.0	Ramirez-Cle..........328	Justice-Cle...........418	Thome-Cle...........579	Thome-Cle..........1001	Thome-Cle............154	Justice-Cle...........43.1

RUNS	HITS	DOUBLES	TRIPLES	HOME RUNS	TOTAL BASES	RUNS BATTED IN
Griffey-Sea 125	Garciaparra-Bos ...209	Valentin-Bos 47	Garciaparra-Bos 11	Griffey-Sea 56	Griffey-Sea 393	Griffey-Sea 147
Garciaparra-Bos ...122	Greer-Tex..............193	Cirillo-Mil................46	Knoblauch-Min.........10	Martinez-NY 44	Garciaparra-Bos ...365	Martinez-NY 141
Knoblauch-Min......117	Jeter-NY 190	Belle-Chi.................45	Damon-KC................8	Gonzalez-Tex..........42	Martinez-NY 343	Gonzalez-Tex........131
Jeter-NY 116	Anderson-Ana.......189	Garciaparra-Bos 44	Burnitz-Mil 8	Thome-Cle..............40	F.Thomas-Chi 324	Salmon-Ana..........129
	Rodriguez-Tex 187			Buhner-Sea 40	Greer-Tex..............319	F.Thomas-Chi 125

BASES ON BALLS	STOLEN BASES	BASE STEALING RUNS	FIELDING RUNS-INFIELD	FIELDING RUNS-OUTFIELD	OUTFIELD ASSISTS	CATCHER CS PCT.
Thome-Cle............120	Hunter-Det..............74	Knoblauch-Min.....10.1	Cirillo-Mil..............24.0	Cameron-Chi 13.0	Higginson-Det.........20	Rodriguez-Tex 57.0
E.Martinez-Sea.....119	Knoblauch-Min........62	Hunter-Det...........10.0	King-KC 21.2	Salmon-Ana.........10.1	Salmon-Ana............15	Wilson-Sea 43.1
Buhner-Sea 119	Goodwin-KC-Tex.....50	Nixon-Tor 6.8	Brosius-Oak.........18.8	Anderson-Ana........9.9	Anderson-Ana.........14	Santiago-Tor 39.2
F.Thomas-Chi 109	Nixon-Tor 47	Goodwin-KC-Tex....5.4	Valentin-Bos 17.7	Higginson-Det........8.6	Burnitz-Mil 13	Girardi-NY............34.3
Phillips-Chi-Ana....102	Vizquel-Cle 43	Vizquel-Cle 5.3	Meares-Min.........14.7	Edmonds-Ana........7.4	Cordova-Min 12	Alomar-Cle...........31.1

WINS	WINNING PCT.	WINS ABOVE TEAM	GAMES STARTED	COMPLETE GAMES	FEWEST HITS/GAME	FEWEST BB/GAME
Clemens-Tor 21	Johnson-Sea 833	Clemens-Tor 8.1	Radke-Min 35	Hentgen-Tor..............9	Johnson-Sea 6.21	Burkett-Tex...........1.43
Radke-Min 20	Moyer-Sea............773	Johnson-Sea 7.9	Pettitte-NY 35	Clemens-Tor 9	Clemens-Tor 6.95	Tewksbury-Min.....1.65
Johnson-Sea 20	Clemens-Tor 750	Radke-Min 7.1	Hentgen-Tor............35	Wells-NY...................5	Cone-NY..............7.15	Radke-Min 1.80
Pettitte-NY 18	Pettitte-NY 720	Moyer-Sea 5.8	Fassero-Sea 35	Tewksbury-Min..........5	Thompson-Det.....7.58	Wells-NY..............1.86
Moyer-Sea 17	Erickson-Bal 696	Blair-Det.................4.6		Johnson-Sea 5	Gordon-Bos 7.64	Moyer-Sea 2.05

STRIKEOUTS	STRIKEOUTS/GAME	GAMES	SAVES	BASE RUNNERS/9	ADJUSTED RELIEF RUNS	RELIEF RANKING
Clemens-Tor 292	Johnson-Sea 12.30	Myers-Det...............88	Myers-Bal 45	Jones-Mil 8.29	Quantrill-Tor.........23.9	Jones-Mil 46.0
Johnson-Sea 291	Cone-NY............10.25	Groom-Oak.............78	Rivera-NY 43	Wetteland-Tex......8.86	Jones-Mil 23.0	Rivera-NY 41.5
Cone-NY...............222	Clemens-Tor 9.95	Quantrill-Tor............77	Jones-Mil 36	Clemens-Tor 9.68	Rivera-NY 20.8	Myers-Bal 38.7
Mussina-Bal..........218	Mussina-Bal.........8.73	Nelson-NY 77	Wetteland-Tex.........31	Johnson-Sea 9.89	Wickman-Mil 20.0	Wetteland-Tex.......37.5
Appier-KC.............196	Finley-Ana 8.51	Slocumb-Bos-Sea...76	Jones-Det 31	Rhodes-Bal..........9.91	Myers-Bal 19.3	Quantrill-Tor.........34.2

INNINGS PITCHED	OPPONENTS' AVG.	OPPONENTS' OBP	EARNED RUN AVERAGE	ADJUSTED ERA	ADJUSTED STARTER RUNS	PITCHER WINS
Hentgen-Tor.......264.0	Johnson-Sea 194	Clemens-Tor 273	Clemens-Tor 2.05	Clemens-Tor 224	Clemens-Tor........74.8	**Clemens-Tor....... 7.9**
Clemens-Tor.......264.0	Clemens-Tor 213	Johnson-Sea 277	Johnson-Sea 2.28	Johnson-Sea 199	Johnson-Sea 53.0	**Johnson-Sea....... 5.6**
Pettitte-NY 240.1	Cone-NY.................218	Mussina-Bal..........282	Cone-NY...............2.82	Cone-NY...............158	Pettitte-NY 42.3	**Jones-Mil 4.5**
Radke-Min 239.2	Gordon-Bos 226	Thompson-Det......289	Pettitte-NY 2.88	Pettitte-NY 154	Thompson-Det.....38.7	**Thompson-Det... 4.1**
Appier-KC...........235.2	Thompson-Det......233	Radke-Min 293	Thompson-Det.....3.02	Thompson-Det......153	Cone-NY..............36.4	**Pettitte-NY.......... 4.1**

INTERLEAGUE AFFAIR

Interleague play began during the regular season for the first time in history. Pushed for by acting commissioner Bud Selig, it was decried by purists and led to some dramatic differences in the schedules of competing teams. New York and Chicago enthusiasts have sold out every Mets-Yankees and Cubs-White Sox game since. Acting Commissioner Bud Selig failed to pass his radical realignment plan. Several clubs were adamantly against the idea, which would have created divisions based solely on geographic location.

Before the season Cleveland outfielder Albert Belle jumped to a division rival and became the first eight-figure player. He signed as a free agent with the White Sox for $11 million per year (plus an escape clause if he did not remain among the top three MLB players in salary). A midseason trade sent Oakland slugger Mark McGwire to St. Louis. McGwire hit a combined 58 home runs, making him the second player to slug at least 50 in consecutive seasons after Babe Ruth in 1927–28; ironically, McGwire did not lead either league in homers. Bartolo Colon, Magglio Ordonez, and Miguel Tejada all debuted.

Cleveland, Central champs for the third straight season, had a fierce battle with the Wild Card Yankees in the ALDS. Facing elimination in Game 4, Cleveland rallied for a run in the eighth and another in the ninth to survive. The Indians nearly blew an early four-run lead in Game 5, but held on to advance. Baltimore shut down Seattle's potent offense to win the other ALDS in four games. Though the O's blanked Cleveland in the ALCS opener, Cleveland scored the winning run in the eighth inning or later four times to take the series in six. The Indians came within two outs of winning their first World Series title since 1948, but dropped a heartbreaker to Florida in Game 7.

1996 NATIONAL LEAGUE

TEAM	W	L	T	PCT	GB	HW	HL	R	OR	PA	H	2B	3B	HR	BB	SO	HB	SH	AVG	OBP	SLG	OPS	AOPS	BR	ABR	PF	SB	CS	BSA	BSR
East																														
Atl	96	66	0	.593	—	**56**	25	773	**648**	6290	1514	264	28	197	530	1032	27	69	.270	.333	.432	765	100	48	1	106	83	43	66	3
Mon	88	74	0	.543	8	50	31	741	668	6170	1441	297	27	148	492	1077	58	79	.262	.327	.406	733	96	-12	-28	102	108	34	**76**	12
Fla	80	82	0	.494	16	52	29	688	703	6192	1413	240	30	150	553	1122	55	41	.257	.329	.393	722	98	-30	-10	97	99	46	68	6
NY	71	91	0	.438	25	42	39	746	779	6220	1515	267	**47**	147	445	1069	33	75	.270	.324	.412	736	103	-14	25	95	97	48	67	5
Phi	67	95	0	.414	29	35	46	650	790	6171	1405	249	39	132	536	1092	45	54	.256	.325	.387	712	93	-54	-57	101	117	41	74	11
Central																														
StL	88	74	0	.543	—	48	33	759	706	6177	1468	281	31	142	495	1089	44	**88**	.267	.330	.407	737	99	-4	-6	100	149	58	72	12
Hou	82	80	0	.506	6	48	33	753	792	6269	1445	297	29	129	554	1057	**84**	68	.262	.336	.397	733	**106**	2	**64**	93	180	63	74	18
Cin	81	81	0	.500	7	46	35	778	773	6213	1398	259	36	191	604	1134	34	71	.256	.331	.422	753	101	29	17	102	171	63	73	16
Chi	76	86	0	.469	12	43	38	772	771	6229	1388	267	19	175	523	1090	61	66	.251	.320	.401	721	91	-39	-64	104	108	50	68	6
Pit	73	89	0	.451	15	36	44	776	833	6336	1509	**319**	33	138	510	**989**	40	72	.266	.329	.407	736	96	-4	-31	104	126	49	72	11
West																														
SD	91	71	0	.562	—	45	36	771	682	6417	1499	285	24	147	601	1014	50	59	.265	.338	.402	740	104	15	51	96	109	55	66	5
LA	90	72	0	.556	1	47	34	703	652	6185	1396	215	33	150	516	1190	22	74	.252	.316	.384	700	95	-85	-42	94	124	40	**76**	13
Col	83	79	0	.512	8	55	26	**961**	964	6332	**1607**	297	37	**221**	527	1108	82	81	**.287**	**.355**	**.472**	**827**	99	**181**	0	124	**201**	66	75	**21**
SF	68	94	0	.420	23	38	44	752	862	6316	1400	245	21	153	**615**	1189	48	77	.253	.331	.388	719	97	-32	-15	98	113	53	68	6
Total	1134	—	—	—	—	641	493	10623	—	87517	20398	3782	434	2220	7501	15252	683	974	.262	.330	.408	738	—	—	—	—	1785	709	72	145

TEAM	CG	SHO	GR	SV	IP	H	HR	BB	SO	BR/9	ERA	AERA	OAV	OOB	PR	APR	PF	OSB	OCS	FA	E	WPB	DP	FW	PW	BW	BSW	DIF
East																												
Atl	**14**	9	408	46	1469.0	1372	120	**451**	**1245**	**11.3**	3.52	**126**	**.247**	**.304**	113	**142**	105	116	44	.980	130	60	143	-.1	**13.9**	.0	-.7	1.9
Mon	11	7	433	43	1441.1	**1353**	152	482	1206	11.8	3.78	114	**.247**	.312	70	85	103	156	48	.980	126	56	121	.0	8.3	-2.7	.2	1.2
Fla	8	**13**	417	41	1443.0	1386	**113**	598	1050	12.7	3.95	104	.256	.334	42	26	98	**84**	57	.982	111	61	**187**	1.0	2.5	-1.0	-.4	-3.2
NY	10	10	335	41	1440.0	1517	159	532	999	13.1	4.22	95	.272	.337	-1	-34	95	125	33	.974	159	70	163	-1.9	-3.3	2.4	-.5	-6.7
Phi	12	6	387	42	1423.1	1463	160	510	1044	12.7	4.48	96	.267	.331	-42	-27	102	88	44	.981	116	81	145	.7	-2.6	-5.6	.0	-6.6
Central																												
StL	13	11	413	43	1452.1	1380	173	539	1050	12.1	3.97	107	.251	.319	39	42	100	104	54	.980	125	**51**	139	.2	4.1	-.6	.2	3.2
Hou	13	4	371	35	1447.0	1541	154	539	1163	13.4	4.37	89	.274	.342	-24	-87	92	115	55	.978	138	79	130	-.6	-8.5	**6.3**	.8	3.1
Cin	6	8	425	**52**	1443.0	1447	167	591	1089	13.0	4.32	99	.263	.336	-16	-7	101	146	50	.980	121	73	145	.4	-.7	1.7	.6	-1.9
Chi	10	10	439	34	1456.1	1447	184	546	1027	12.7	4.36	100	.260	.330	-23	1	104	129	50	**.983**	**104**	61	147	**1.4**	.0	-6.3	-.4	.1
Pit	5	7	422	37	1453.1	1602	183	479	1044	13.2	4.61	95	.281	.339	-63	-36	104	185	57	.980	128	72	144	-.0	-3.5	-3.0	.0	-1.5
West																												
SD	5	11	411	47	1489.0	1395	138	506	1194	11.8	3.72	108	.248	.313	81	51	95	136	54	.981	118	73	136	.6	5.0	5.0	-.5	-.0
LA	6	9	383	50	1466.1	1378	125	534	1212	12.0	**3.46**	113	.249	.317	**123**	78	93	171	39	.980	125	54	143	.2	7.6	-4.1	.3	5.1
Col	5	4	**447**	34	1422.2	1597	198	624	932	14.5	5.59	93	.285	.361	-218	-50	124	122	55	.976	149	85	167	-1.3	-4.9	.0	**1.0**	7.2
SF	9	8	425	35	1442.1	1520	194	570	997	13.5	4.71	88	.273	.345	-80	-94	98	108	**69**	.978	136	71	165	-.5	-9.2	-1.5	-.4	-1.4
Total	127	117	5716	580	20289.0	—	—	—	—	12.7	4.21	—	.262	.330	—	—	—	—	—	.979	1786	947	2075	—	—	—	—	—

BATTER-FIELDER WINS	BATTING AVERAGE	ON-BASE PERCENTAGE	SLUGGING AVERAGE	ON-BASE PLUS SLUGGING	ADJUSTED OPS	ADJUSTED BATTER RUNS
Bonds-SF 7.6	Gwynn-SD 353	Sheffield-Fla 465	Burks-Col.............639	Sheffield-Fla 1090	Sheffield-Fla 190	Sheffield-Fla 79.3
Caminiti-SD 7.4	Burks-Col.............344	Bonds-SF.............461	Sheffield-Fla 624	Bonds-SF............1076	Bonds-SF..............186	Bagwell-Hou 79.1
Bagwell-Hou 7.1	Piazza-LA............336	Bagwell-Hou 451	Caminiti-SD 621	Burks-Col............1047	Bagwell-Hou 182	Bonds-SF.............75.0
Larkin-Cin........... 6.0	Johnson-NY..........333	Piazza-LA.............422	Bonds-SF..............615	Caminiti-SD 1028	Caminiti-SD 176	Caminiti-SD 61.6
Gilkey-NY........... 5.9	Grace-Chi 331	Henderson-SD......410	Galarraga-Col.......601	Bagwell-Hou 1021	Piazza-LA.............167	Piazza-LA.............55.2

RUNS	HITS	DOUBLES	TRIPLES	HOME RUNS	TOTAL BASES	RUNS BATTED IN
Burks-Col.............142	Johnson-NY..........227	Bagwell-Hou 48	Johnson-NY............21	Galarraga-Col.........47	Burks-Col..............392	Galarraga-Col.......150
Finley-SD.............126	Burks-Col.............211	Finley-SD...............45	Howard-Cin............10	Sheffield-Fla 42	Galarraga-Col.......376	Bichette-Col..........141
Bonds-SF..............122	Grissom-Atl...........207	Burks-Col...............45	Grissom-Atl............10	Bonds-SF................42	Finley-SD..............348	Caminiti-SD 130
Galarraga-Col 119	Grudzielanek-Mon 201	Gilkey-NY...............44	Finley-SD..................9	Hundley-NY 41	Castilla-Col 345	Bonds-SF..............129
Sheffield-Fla 118	Bichette-Col..........198	Rodriguez-Mon.......42			Caminiti-SD 339	Burks-Col..............128

BASES ON BALLS	STOLEN BASES	BASE STEALING RUNS	FIELDING RUNS-INFIELD	FIELDING RUNS-OUTFIELD	OUTFIELD ASSISTS	CATCHER CS PCT.
Bonds-SF..............151	Young-Col 53	Johnson-NY...........6.8	Castilla-Col 33.8	Gilkey-NY.............17.5	Gilkey-NY................18	Johnson-Fla.........47.6
Sheffield-Fla 142	Johnson-NY............50	DeShields-LA.........6.7	Young-Col 27.4	Jordan-StL 10.8	Bell-Hou..................16	Manwaring-SF-Hou.44.6
Bagwell-Hou 135	DeShields-LA.........48	Bonds-SF...............6.3	Andrews-Mon 16.2	Merced-Pit 10.0	Sosa-Chi.................15	J.Reed-Col...........29.2
Henderson-SD......125	Bonds-SF................40	Bell-Hou.................5.3	Caminiti-SD 14.8	Santangelo-Mon 7.3	Merced-Pit 14	Lopez-Atl 27.1
Larkin-Cin 96	Martin-Pit................38	Lankford-StL 5.3	Gagne-LA 13.8	Mondesi-LA 6.9		Hundley-NY 24.6

WINS	WINNING PCT.	WINS ABOVE TEAM	GAMES STARTED	COMPLETE GAMES	FEWEST HITS/GAME	FEWEST BB/GAME
Smoltz-Atl 24	Smoltz-Atl 750	Smoltz-Atl 7.0	Glavine-Atl 36	Schilling-Phi.............8	Leiter-Fla 6.39	Maddux-Atl 1.03
A.Benes-StL 18	Martinez-LA..........714	Petkovsek-StL........4.4		Smoltz-Atl 6	Smoltz-Atl 7.06	Brown-Fla 1.27
Ritz-Col...................17	Valdez-LA 682	Neagle-Pit-Atl 4.1			Nomo-LA 7.09	Darwin-Pit-Hou 1.48
Brown-Fla 17	A.Benes-StL 643	Martinez-LA...........4.1			Brown-Fla 7.22	Reynolds-Hou......1.66
	Neagle-Pit-Atl 640	Gardner-SF............3.7			Schilling-Phi.........7.31	Tewksbury-SD 1.87

STRIKEOUTS	STRIKEOUTS/GAME	GAMES	SAVES	BASE RUNNERS/9	ADJUSTED RELIEF RUNS	RELIEF RANKING
Smoltz-Atl 276	Smoltz-Atl 9.79	Clontz-Atl................81	Worrell-LA...............44	Hoffman-SD.........8.49	Nen-Fla................20.0	Hoffman-SD.........37.7
Nomo-LA 234	Nomo-LA 9.22	Patterson-Chi.........79	Brantley-Cin............44	Smoltz-Atl 9.08	Shaw-Cin 19.7	Nen-Fla................27.9
Martinez-Mon 222	Martinez-Mon 9.22	Shaw-Cin 78	Hoffman-SD............42	Brown-Fla 9.12	Hoffman-SD.........18.8	J.Franco-NY.........25.5
Fassero-Mon.........222	Kile-Hou...............9.00	Dewey-SF 78	Wohlers-Atl 39	Maddux-Atl 9.40	Ryan-Phi..............15.9	Shaw-Cin 25.1
Kile-Hou.................219	Schilling-Phi.........8.93	Wohlers-Atl 77	Rojas-Mon 36	Rojas-Mon 9.56	Adams-Chi...........15.5	Brantley-Cin.........21.5

INNINGS PITCHED	OPPONENTS' AVG.	OPPONENTS' OBP	EARNED RUN AVERAGE	ADJUSTED ERA	ADJUSTED STARTER RUNS	PITCHER WINS
Smoltz-Atl 253.2	Leiter-Fla 202	Smoltz-Atl 260	Brown-Fla 1.89	Brown-Fla 218	Brown-Fla 56.5	**Brown-Fla 6.9**
Maddux-Atl 245.0	Smoltz-Atl 216	Brown-Fla 262	Maddux-Atl 2.72	Maddux-Atl 164	Maddux-Atl 43.9	**Smoltz-Atl........... 5.2**
Reynolds-Hou....239.0	Nomo-LA 218	Maddux-Atl 264	Leiter-Fla 2.93	Smoltz-Atl 151	Smoltz-Atl 40.4	**Maddux-Atl......... 4.8**
Navarro-Chi 236.2	Brown-Fla 220	Schilling-Phi..........278	Smoltz-Atl 2.94	Glavine-Atl 149	Glavine-Atl 35.0	**Glavine-Atl 4.4**
Glavine-Atl 235.1	Schilling-Phi..........223	Reynolds-Hou.......288	Glavine-Atl 2.98	Trachsel-Chi..........144	Leiter-Fla 31.0	**Hoffman-SD 3.7**

Schott Herself in the Foot

Cincinnati owner Marge Schott was removed from day-to-day operations of the Reds for a second time after telling a reporter that Adolf Hitler was good at first, but then "went too far." Schott also looked petty after the tragic death of umpire John McSherry on Opening Day. McSherry, working the plate for Cincy's game against Montreal, collapsed behind home plate and died from a massive heart attack only minutes into the contest. Schott protested the cancellation of the game, saying, "I feel cheated."

In August the Mets and Padres played a regular-season series in Monterey, Mexico. They were the first big league games played outside the U.S. or Canada. It was the final season for Ozzie Smith, Andre Dawson, and longtime Dodgers skipper Tommy Lasorda. Scott Rolen, Vladimir Guerrero, and Andruw Jones debuted. San Diego third baseman Ken Caminiti, who later admitted he took steroids regularly during the 1996 season, was the overwhelming choice for MVP.

Both Division Series ended quickly. The Braves easily swept the Dodgers, who won the Wild Card despite losing their final three regular-season games to the division-winning Padres. San Diego lost three straight to St. Louis to set up a classic NLCS. Atlanta won the first game, but allowed 5 runs in the seventh inning the next night and squandered leads in Games 3 and 4 to fall behind three games to one. However, Atlanta's bats and arms came alive at the same time as the Braves outscored St. Louis, 32-1, in the final three games. The Braves were denied a second straight World Series title, falling in six games to the Yankees.

1996 AMERICAN LEAGUE

TEAM	W	L	T	PCT	GB	HW	HL	R	OR	PA	H	2B	3B	HR	BB	SO	HB	SH	AVG	OBP	SLG	OPS	AOPS	BR	ABR	PF	SB	CS	BSA	BSR
EAST																														
NY	92	70	0	.568	—	49	31	871	787	6414	1621	293	28	162	632	909	41	41	.288	.360	.436	796	100	17	19	100	96	46	68	5
Bal	88	74	1	.543	4	43	38	949	903	6493	1557	299	29	**257**	645	915	61	31	.274	.350	.472	822	106	50	57	99	76	40	66	3
Bos	85	77	0	.525	7	47	34	928	921	6545	1631	308	31	209	642	1020	67	33	.283	.359	.457	816	102	48	32	102	91	44	67	5
Tor	74	88	0	.457	18	35	46	766	809	6295	1451	302	35	177	529	1105	**92**	38	.259	.331	.420	751	89	-103	-97	99	116	38	75	12
Det	53	109	0	.327	39	27	54	783	1103	6202	1413	257	21	204	546	1268	29	48	.256	.323	.420	743	86	-126	-127	100	87	50	64	2
CENTRAL																														
Cle	99	62	0	.615	—	**51**	29	952	**769**	6486	**1665**	335	23	218	671	**844**	43	34	**.293**	**.369**	.475	844	111	114	116	100	160	50	**76**	**18**
Chi	85	77	0	.525	14.5	44	37	898	794	6497	1586	284	33	195	**701**	927	34	56	.281	.360	.447	807	107	35	76	96	105	41	72	9
Mil	80	82	0	.494	19.5	38	43	894	899	6434	1578	304	40	178	624	986	53	45	.279	.353	.441	794	95	0	-34	104	101	48	68	5
Min	78	84	0	.481	21.5	39	43	877	900	6397	1633	332	**47**	118	576	958	65	20	.288	.357	.425	782	95	-14	-27	102	143	53	73	13
KC	75	86	0	.466	24	37	43	746	786	6229	1477	286	38	123	529	943	43	**66**	.267	.332	.398	730	83	-136	-138	100	**195**	85	70	13
WEST																														
Tex	90	72	1	.556	—	50	31	928	799	6494	1622	323	32	221	660	1041	31	32	.284	.358	.469	827	101	69	13	106	83	26	**76**	9
Sea	85	76	0	.528	4.5	43	38	**993**	895	6517	1625	**343**	19	245	670	1052	75	46	.287	.366	**.484**	**850**	**112**	**123**	**120**	100	90	39	70	6
Oak	78	84	0	.481	12	40	41	861	900	6402	1492	283	21	243	640	1114	58	35	.265	.344	.452	796	100	-9	2	99	58	35	62	1
Cal	70	91	0	.435	19.5	43	38	762	943	6320	1571	256	24	192	527	974	29	45	.276	.339	.431	770	92	-67	-76	101	53	39	58	-2
Total	1133	—	—	—	—	586	546	12208	—	89725	21922	4205	421	2742	8592	14056	721	570	.277	.350	.445	795	—	—	—	—	1454	634	70	98

TEAM	CG	SHO	GR	SV	IP	H	HR	BB	SO	BR/9	ERA	AERA	OAV	OOB	PR	APR	PF	OSB	OCS	FA	E	WPB	DP	FW	PW	BW	BSW	DIF
EAST																												
NY	6	**9**	411	**52**	1440.0	**1469**	**143**	610	1139	13.3	4.65	106	**.265**	.341	55	48	99	120	42	.985	91	72	146	1.2	4.4	1.7	-.2	3.9
Bal	13	1	378	44	1468.2	1604	209	597	1047	13.7	5.14	96	.280	.349	-25	-33	99	135	37	.984	97	52	173	.9	-3.0	5.2	-.4	4.2
Bos	17	5	409	37	1458.0	1606	185	722	**1165**	14.7	4.98	102	.279	.360	1	17	102	147	36	.978	135	74	152	-1.2	1.5	2.9	-.2	1.0
Tor	**19**	7	303	35	1445.2	1476	187	610	1033	13.2	4.57	110	.266	.340	68	70	100	74	41	.982	110	77	187	.2	6.4	-8.8	.5	-5.2
Det	10	4	**426**	22	1432.2	1699	241	784	957	16.1	6.38	80	.296	.384	-221	-202	102	117	54	.978	137	89	157	-1.4	-18.4	-11.6	-.5	3.8
CENTRAL																												
Cle	13	**9**	382	46	1452.1	1530	173	484	1033	**12.7**	**4.34**	**113**	.271	**.331**	**105**	90	98	104	52	.980	124	60	156	-.7	8.2	10.6	**1.0**	-.6
Chi	7	4	391	43	1461.0	1529	174	616	1039	13.4	4.52	105	.270	.343	77	40	95	105	55	.982	109	67	145	.2	3.6	6.9	.2	-7.0
Mil	6	4	384	42	1447.1	1570	213	635	846	14.1	5.14	101	.278	.354	-23	8	104	96	40	.978	134	65	180	-1.2	.7	-3.1	-.2	2.7
Min	13	5	387	31	1439.2	1561	233	581	959	13.6	5.28	97	.277	.346	-46	-23	103	84	42	.984	94	60	142	1.1	-2.1	-2.5	.5	-.0
KC	17	8	322	35	1450.0	1563	176	**460**	926	12.9	4.55	110	.277	.335	71	75	101	69	42	.982	111	67	184	.0	6.8	-12.6	.5	-.4
WEST																												
Tex	**19**	6	347	43	1449.1	1569	168	582	976	13.6	4.65	**113**	.278	.347	55	**92**	105	**62**	**56**	**.986**	**87**	48	150	**1.5**	**8.4**	1.2	.2	-2.2
Sea	4	4	403	34	1431.2	1562	216	605	1000	14.0	5.21	95	.279	.353	-35	-39	100	78	42	.982	110	**45**	155	.1	-3.6	**10.9**	-.0	-2.9
Oak	7	5	418	34	1456.1	1638	205	644	884	14.4	5.20	96	.287	.362	-33	-38	100	117	41	.984	103	71	**195**	.6	-3.5	.2	-.5	.3
Cal	12	8	383	38	1439.0	1546	219	662	1052	14.3	5.30	95	.275	.357	-49	-40	101	146	54	.979	128	92	156	-.9	-3.6	-6.9	-.8	1.8
Total	163	79	5344	536	20271.2	—	—	—	—	13.9	4.99	—	.277	.350	—	—	—	—	—	.982	1570	939	2278	—	—	—	—	—

BATTER-FIELDER WINS
- **Alomar-Bal......... 6.1**
- **Rodriguez-Sea... 5.6**
- **Thome-Cle.......... 5.3**
- **McGwire-Oak..... 5.0**
- **F.Thomas-Chi..... 4.9**

BATTING AVERAGE
- Rodriguez-Sea......358
- F.Thomas-Chi 349
- Molitor-Min...........341
- Knoblauch-Min......341
- Greer-Tex.............332

ON-BASE PERCENTAGE
- McGwire-Oak........467
- E.Martinez-Sea.....464
- F.Thomas-Chi 459
- Thome-Cle............450
- Knoblauch-Min......448

SLUGGING AVERAGE
- McGwire-Oak........730
- Gonzalez-Tex........643
- Anderson-Bal........637
- Rodriguez-Sea......631
- Griffey-Sea 628

ON-BASE PLUS SLUGGING
- McGwire-Oak......1198
- F.Thomas-Chi 1085
- Thome-Cle..........1062
- E.Martinez-Sea...1059
- Rodriguez-Sea....1045

ADJUSTED OPS
- McGwire-Oak........199
- F.Thomas-Chi 180
- Thome-Cle............166
- E.Martinez-Sea.....165
- Rodriguez-Sea......160

ADJUSTED BATTER RUNS
- F.Thomas-Chi 71.5
- McGwire-Oak.......70.8
- E.Martinez-Sea....60.1
- Thome-Cle...........57.3
- Rodriguez-Sea.....56.1

RUNS
- Rodriguez-Sea......141
- Knoblauch-Min......140
- Lofton-Cle.............132
- Alomar-Bal............132
- Griffey-Sea 125

HITS
- Molitor-Min............225
- Rodriguez-Sea.......215
- Lofton-Cle..............210
- Vaughn-Bos...........207
- Knoblauch-Min......197

DOUBLES
- Rodriguez-Sea........54
- E.Martinez-Sea.......52
- Rodriguez-Tex 47
- Cordova-Min 46
- Cirillo-Mil................46

TRIPLES
- Knoblauch-Min........14
- Vina-Mil...................10

HOME RUNS
- McGwire-Oak..........52
- Anderson-Bal..........50
- Griffey-Sea 49
- Belle-Cle.................48
- Gonzalez-Tex..........47

TOTAL BASES
- Rodriguez-Sea......379
- Belle-Cle...............375
- Vaughn-Bos..........370
- Anderson-Bal........369
- Gonzalez-Tex........348

RUNS BATTED IN
- Belle-Cle 148
- Gonzalez-Tex........144
- Vaughn-Bos..........143
- Palmeiro-Bal.........142
- Griffey-Sea 140

BASES ON BALLS
- Phillips-Chi............125
- Thome-Cle............123
- E.Martinez-Sea.....123
- McGwire-Oak........116
- F.Thomas-Chi 109

STOLEN BASES
- Lofton-Cle...............75
- Goodwin-KC 66
- Nixon-Tor 54
- Knoblauch-Min........45
- Vizquel-Cle 35

BASE STEALING RUNS
- Lofton-Cle 10.6
- Nixon-Tor 7.3
- Goodwin-KC 6.8
- Durham-Chi 5.2
- Knoblauch-Min.......5.0

FIELDING RUNS-INFIELD
- Gonzalez-Tor 28.4
- McLemore-Tex......23.7
- Fryman-Det..........22.6
- Alomar-Bal...........22.0
- Vina-Mil................18.2

FIELDING RUNS-OUTFIELD
- Becker-Min...........17.2
- Phillips-Chi.............9.4
- Green-Tor 7.8
- Mieske-Mil 7.0
- Bragg-Sea-Bos 6.1

OUTFIELD ASSISTS
- Ramirez-Cle...........19
- Becker-Min.............18
- Salmon-Cal.............13
- Phillips-Chi.............13
- Lofton-Cle..............13

CATCHER CS PCT.
- Rodriguez-Tex 51.1
- Karkovice-Chi 40.7
- Wilson-Sea 39.0
- Macfarlane-KC.....38.7
- O'Brien-Tor 37.5

WINS
- Pettitte-NY 21
- Hentgen-Tor............20
- Mussina-Bal............19
- Nagy-Cle.................17

WINNING PCT.
- Nagy-Cle..............773
- Pettitte-NY 724
- Hentgen-Tor.........667
- Pavlik-Tex.............652
- Mussina-Bal.........633

WINS ABOVE TEAM
- Hentgen-Tor..........6.5
- Pettitte-NY 5.9
- Nagy-Cle................4.9
- Moyer-Bos-Sea......4.9
- Rhodes-Bal............4.0

GAMES STARTED
- Mussina-Bal...........36

COMPLETE GAMES
- Hentgen-Tor...........10
- Pavlik-Tex.................7
- Hill-Tex.....................7

FEWEST HITS/GAME
- Guzman-Tor.........7.58
- Clemens-Bos.......8.01
- Hentgen-Tor........8.06
- Appier-KC 8.18
- Fernandez-Chi.....8.65

FEWEST BB/GAME
- Haney-KC 2.01
- Wells-Bal 2.05
- Radke-Min 2.21
- Nagy-Cle..............2.47
- Fernandez-Chi.....2.51

STRIKEOUTS
- Clemens-Bos........257
- Finley-Cal 215
- Appier-KC.............207
- Mussina-Bal..........204
- Fernandez-Chi......200

STRIKEOUTS/GAME
- Clemens-Bos.......9.53
- Appier-KC 8.82
- Finley-Cal 8.13
- Guzman-Tor.........7.91
- Mussina-Bal.........7.55

GAMES
- Myers-Det..............83
- Guardado-Min.........83
- Stanton-Bos-Tex.....81
- Slocumb-Bos 75

SAVES
- Wetteland-NY 43
- Mesa-Cle 39
- Hernandez-Chi 38
- Percival-Cal 36
- Fetters-Mil..............32

BASE RUNNERS/9
- Percival-Cal 8.64
- M.Rivera-NY 9.11
- Guzman-Tor.......10.45
- Wetteland-NY 10.60
- Cone-NY...........10.75

ADJUSTED RELIEF RUNS
- M.Rivera-NY 35.3
- Hernandez-Chi 27.4
- Percival-Cal 22.8
- Plunk-Cle.............22.6
- James-Cal 21.1

RELIEF RANKING
- Hernandez-Chi 54.7
- M.Rivera-NY 35.5
- Slocumb-Bos 34.3
- Wetteland-NY 28.5
- Percival-Cal 26.6

INNINGS PITCHED
- Hentgen-Tor.......265.2
- Fernandez-Chi...258.0
- Hill-Tex.............250.2
- Mussina-Bal.......243.1
- Clemens-Bos.....242.2

OPPONENTS' AVG.
- Guzman-Tor..........228
- Clemens-Bos........237
- Hentgen-Tor..........241
- Appier-KC.............245
- Fernandez-Chi......253

OPPONENTS' OBP
- Guzman-Tor..........289
- Radke-Min 302
- Nagy-Cle..............306
- Fernandez-Chi......307
- Hentgen-Tor..........308

EARNED RUN AVERAGE
- Guzman-Tor.........2.93
- Hentgen-Tor.........3.22
- Nagy-Cle..............3.41
- Fernandez-Chi.....3.45
- Appier-KC............3.62

ADJUSTED ERA
- Guzman-Tor..........171
- Hentgen-Tor..........156
- Hill-Tex.................145
- Nagy-Cle..............144
- Clemens-Bos........140

ADJUSTED STARTER RUNS
- Hentgen-Tor.........52.7
- Guzman-Tor.........43.0
- Hill-Tex...............42.3
- Clemens-Bos.......41.1
- Nagy-Cle.............38.9

PITCHER WINS
- **Hentgen-Tor....... 5.2**
- **Hernandez-Chi... 5.1**
- **Hill-Tex.............. 3.9**
- **Guzman-Tor 3.8**
- **Appier-KC.......... 3.5**

The Yankees Ride Again

Home runs were hit at a record pace; the 2,742 long balls at the rate of 1.21 per team per game remain AL marks. Oakland's Mark McGwire and Baltimore's Brady Anderson, who never before or after surpassed 24 homers, each surpassed 50. It was the first season since 1961 that two players had reached that plateau.

Baltimore's Roberto Alomar spat in the face of umpire John Hirschbeck during a heated argument in the final series of the year. Although Alomar was suspended, umps were incensed that Alomar was allowed to play in the postseason. Mel Allen, the longtime radio voice of the Yankees, and narrator of *This Week in Baseball*, died, as did former A's owner Charlie Finley. Nomar Garciaparra made his debut.

Both Division Series were decided in four games. Despite owning the league's best record, Cleveland was thwarted by Orioles second baseman Roberto Alomar, who tied Game 4 in the ninth and won it with a homer in the 12th. Texas, playing in the postseason for the first time, won Game 1 of the other Division Series and got 5 home runs from Juan Gonzalez, but the Yankees took three close games. New York then cruised past Baltimore in five games in the ALCS.

The Yankees appeared dead after scoring only once against Atlanta in two World Series losses at Yankee Stadium. New York won Game 3, but fell behind 6-0 to the Braves in Game 4, and many conceded Atlanta its second straight world championship. The Yankees, however, mounted a fierce comeback, tying the game on a Jim Leyritz homer and winning in 10 innings. Momentum shifted, and the Yankees captured their first Series title since 1978.

1995 NATIONAL LEAGUE

TEAM	W	L	T	PCT	GB	HW	HL	R	OR	PA	H	2B	3B	HR	BB	SO	HB	SH	AVG	OBP	SLG	OPS	AOPS	BR	ABR	PF	SB	CS	BSA	BSR
EAST																														
Atl	90	54	0	.625	—	**44**	28	645	**540**	5464	1202	210	27	168	520	933	40	56	.250	.326	.409	735	94	-11	-40	105	73	43	63	1
NY	69	75	0	.479	21	40	32	657	618	5581	1323	218	34	125	446	994	42	**92**	.267	.330	.400	730	100	-17	6	97	58	39	60	-1
Phi	69	75	0	.479	21	35	37	615	658	5611	1296	263	30	94	497	884	46	77	.262	.332	.384	716	94	-31	-33	100	72	25	74	7
Fla	67	76	0	.469	22.5	37	34	673	673	5569	1278	214	29	144	517	916	49	69	.262	.335	.406	741	98	8	-3	102	131	53	71	10
Mon	66	78	0	.458	24	31	41	621	638	5451	1268	265	24	118	400	901	56	58	.259	.320	.394	714	90	-48	-70	104	120	49	71	9
CENTRAL																														
Cin	85	59	0	.590	—	**44**	28	747	623	5574	1326	**277**	35	161	519	946	40	62	.270	.342	.440	782	109	80	72	101	**190**	68	74	**18**
Hou	76	68	0	.528	9	36	36	747	674	5857	1403	260	22	109	**566**	992	**69**	78	.275	**.353**	.399	752	**111**	47	**99**	94	176	60	**75**	**18**
Chi	73	71	0	.507	12	34	38	693	671	5543	1315	267	39	158	440	953	34	71	.265	.327	.430	757	104	23	24	100	105	37	74	10
StL	62	81	0	.434	22.5	39	33	563	658	5349	1182	238	24	107	436	920	46	48	.247	.314	.374	688	84	-90	-100	102	79	46	63	1
Pit	58	86	0	.403	27	31	41	629	736	5501	1281	245	27	125	456	972	24	51	.259	.323	.396	719	92	-39	-53	102	84	55	60	-1
WEST																														
LA	78	66	0	.542	—	39	33	634	609	5543	1303	191	31	140	468	1023	30	68	.264	.329	.400	729	104	-23	26	93	127	45	74	12
Col	77	67	0	.535	1	**44**	28	**785**	783	5647	**1406**	259	**43**	**200**	484	943	56	82	**.282**	.350	**.471**	**821**	94	**142**	-39	128	125	59	68	7
SD	70	74	0	.486	8	40	32	668	672	5526	1345	231	20	116	447	**872**	35	56	.272	.334	.397	731	101	-12	7	97	124	46	73	11
SF	67	77	0	.465	11	37	35	652	776	5603	1256	229	33	152	472	1060	57	79	.253	.323	.404	727	98	-29	-14	98	138	46	**75**	14
Total	1007	—	—	—	—	531	476	9329	—	77819	18184	3367	418	1917	6668	13309	624	947	.263	.331	.408	739	—	—	—	—	1602	671	70	118

TEAM	CG	SHO	GR	SV	IP	H	HR	BB	SO	BR/9	ERA	AERA	OAV	OOB	PR	APR	PF	OSB	OCS	FA	E	WPB	DP	FW	PW	BW	BSW	DIF
EAST																												
Atl	**18**	11	339	34	1291.2	**1184**	**107**	436	**1087**	**11.5**	**3.44**	**126**	.244	**.309**	**106**	**122**	103	132	37	.982	100	46	113	.6	**12.0**	-3.9	-.7	10.0
NY	9	9	298	36	1291.0	1296	133	**401**	901	12.1	3.88	104	.262	.319	44	24	97	127	40	.979	115	53	125	-.3	2.4	.6	-.9	-4.8
Phi	8	8	341	41	1290.1	1241	134	538	980	12.8	4.21	100	.254	.333	-4	1	101	137	38	.982	97	76	139	.8	.0	-3.2	-.1	-.5
Fla	12	7	400	29	1286.0	1299	139	562	994	13.3	4.27	100	.264	.343	-13	3	103	**82**	53	.979	115	**44**	143	-.3	.3	-.3	.2	-4.4
Mon	7	9	396	42	1283.2	1286	128	416	950	12.3	4.11	105	.262	.325	10	26	103	145	56	.980	109	51	119	.1	2.6	-6.9	.0	-1.8
CENTRAL																												
Cin	8	10	330	38	1289.1	1270	131	424	903	12.0	4.03	103	.260	.320	21	20	100	92	30	**.986**	**79**	69	140	**1.9**	2.0	7.1	**.9**	1.1
Hou	6	8	394	32	1320.1	1357	118	460	1056	12.7	4.06	95	.266	.331	17	-32	92	120	49	.979	121	67	120	-.6	-3.1	**9.7**	**.9**	-2.9
Chi	6	**12**	414	**45**	1301.0	1313	162	518	926	12.9	4.13	101	.262	.333	7	6	100	123	56	.979	115	57	115	-.3	.6	2.4	.2	-1.8
StL	4	6	377	38	1265.2	1290	135	445	842	12.6	4.09	105	.268	.333	13	26	102	132	**64**	.980	113	60	**156**	-.2	2.6	-9.8	-.7	-1.3
Pit	11	7	391	29	1275.1	1407	130	477	871	13.7	4.70	93	.283	.350	-74	-48	104	125	61	.978	122	77	138	-.7	-4.7	-5.2	-.9	-2.5
WEST																												
LA	16	11	355	37	1295.0	1188	125	462	1060	11.7	3.66	106	**.243**	.311	76	32	92	108	45	.976	130	68	120	-1.2	3.1	2.6	.4	1.1
Col	1	1	**456**	43	1288.1	1443	160	512	891	13.9	4.97	108	.286	.355	-113	44	128	100	43	.981	107	72	146	.2	4.3	-3.8	-.1	4.4
SD	6	10	337	35	1284.2	1242	142	512	1047	12.6	4.13	98	.255	.331	7	-10	97	91	54	.980	108	68	130	.2	-1.0	.7	.3	-2.1
SF	12	5	381	34	1293.2	1368	173	505	801	13.4	4.86	85	.275	.345	-98	-108	99	88	45	.980	108	50	142	.2	-10.6	-1.4	.6	6.3
Total	124	114	5209	513	18056.0	—	—	—	—	12.7	4.18	—	.263	.331	—	—	—	—	—	.980	1539	858	1846	—	—	—	—	—

BATTER-FIELDER WINS	BATTING AVERAGE	ON-BASE PERCENTAGE	SLUGGING AVERAGE	ON-BASE PLUS SLUGGING	ADJUSTED OPS	ADJUSTED BATTER RUNS
Bonds-SF 5.6	Gwynn-SD .368	Bonds-SF .431	Bichette-Col .620	Bonds-SF 1009	Piazza-LA 173	Bonds-SF 56.0
Piazza-LA 4.9	Piazza-LA .346	Biggio-Hou .406	Walker-Col .607	Piazza-LA 1006	Bonds-SF 168	Piazza-LA 44.2
Caminiti-SD 4.4	Bichette-Col .340	Gwynn-SD .404	Piazza-LA .606	Walker-Col 988	R.Sanders-Cin 153	Biggio-Hou 40.2
Biggio-Hou 4.4	Bell-Hou .334	Weiss-Col .403	R.Sanders-Cin .579	Bichette-Col 984	Karros-LA 146	R.Sanders-Cin 38.7
R.Sanders-Cin 4.0	Grace-Chi .326	Piazza-LA .400	Bonds-SF .577	R.Sanders-Cin 975	Bagwell-Hou 145	Karros-LA 35.8
RUNS	**HITS**	**DOUBLES**	**TRIPLES**	**HOME RUNS**	**TOTAL BASES**	**RUNS BATTED IN**
Biggio-Hou 123	Gwynn-SD 197	Grace-Chi 51	Butler-NY-LA 9	Bichette-Col 40	Bichette-Col 359	Bichette-Col 128
Bonds-SF 109	Bichette-Col 197	McRae-Chi 38	Young-Col 9	Walker-Col 36	Walker-Col 300	Sosa-Chi 119
Finley-SD 104	Grace-Chi 180	Bichette-Col 38	D.Sanders-Cin-SF 8	Sosa-Chi 36	Castilla-Col 297	Galarraga-Col 106
Bichette-Col 102		R.Sanders-Cin 36	Gonzalez-Hou-Chi 8	Bonds-SF 33	Karros-LA 295	Karros-LA 105
Larkin-Cin 98			Finley-SD 8		Bonds-SF 292	Conine-Fla 105
BASES ON BALLS	**STOLEN BASES**	**BASE STEALING RUNS**	**FIELDING RUNS-INFIELD**	**FIELDING RUNS-OUTFIELD**	**OUTFIELD ASSISTS**	**CATCHER CS PCT.**
Bonds-SF 120	Veras-Fla 56	Larkin-Cin 9.5	Bagwell-Hou 17.7	Mondesi-LA 8.9	Mondesi-LA 16	Johnson-Fla 42.7
Weiss-Col 98	Larkin-Cin 51	Sosa-Chi 5.0	Reed-SD 17.7	Sosa-Chi 8.3	Walker-Col 13	Parent-Pit-Chi 39.3
Veras-Fla 80	DeShields-LA 39	Veras-Fla 5.0	Vizcaino-NY 15.4	Gonzalez-Hou-Chi 7.0	Sosa-Chi 13	Eusebio-Hou 30.5
Biggio-Hou 80	R.Sanders-Cin 36	Mondesi-LA 4.5	Lansing-Mon 15.1	Carr-Fla 6.4	R.Sanders-Cin 12	Fletcher-Mon 30.3
Bagwell-Hou 79	Finley-SD 36	Lansing-Mon 4.5	Weiss-Col 13.9	D.Lewis-SF-Cin 5.1	Bonds-SF 12	Manwaring-SF 28.6
WINS	**WINNING PCT.**	**WINS ABOVE TEAM**	**GAMES STARTED**	**COMPLETE GAMES**	**FEWEST HITS/GAME**	**FEWEST BB/GAME**
Maddux-Atl 19	Maddux-Atl .905	Maddux-Atl 8.1	Portugal-SF-Cin 31	Maddux-Atl 10	Nomo-LA 5.83	Maddux-Atl .99
Schourek-Cin 18	Schourek-Cin .720	Martinez-LA 4.9	Neagle-Pit 31	Leiter-SF 7	Maddux-Atl 6.31	Reynolds-Hou 1.76
Martinez-LA 17	Martinez-LA .708	Schourek-Cin 4.5	Loaiza-Pit 31	Valdez-LA 6	Martinez-Mon 7.30	Neagle-Pit 1.93
Glavine-Atl 16	Glavine-Atl .696	Rapp-Fla 4.3	Drabek-Hou 31	Neagle-Pit 5	Schourek-Cin 7.47	Saberhagen-NY-Col 1.94
		Navarro-Chi 4.3	Ashby-SD 31		Valdez-LA 7.65	Smiley-Cin 1.99
STRIKEOUTS	**STRIKEOUTS/GAME**	**GAMES**	**SAVES**	**BASE RUNNERS/9**	**ADJUSTED RELIEF RUNS**	**RELIEF RANKING**
Nomo-LA 236	Nomo-LA 11.10	Leskanic-Col 76	Myers-Chi 38	Maddux-Atl 7.47	Reed-Col 22.8	Wohlers-Atl 31.5
Smoltz-Atl 193	Smoltz-Atl 9.02	Veres-Hou 72	Henke-StL 36	Reed-Col 8.89	Veres-Hou 20.1	Worrell-LA 23.4
Maddux-Atl 181	Reynolds-Hou 8.32	Reed-Col 71	Beck-SF 33	Brantley-Cin 9.47	Leskanic-Col 17.7	Henke-StL 22.8
Reynolds-Hou 175	Martinez-Mon 8.04	Perez-Fla 69	Worrell-LA 32	Schilling-Phi 9.70	Bottalico-Phi 17.5	Reed-Col 18.5
Martinez-Mon 174	Foster-Chi 7.84		Slocumb-Phi 32	Nomo-LA 9.74	Wohlers-Atl 15.7	Leskanic-Col 17.8
INNINGS PITCHED	**OPPONENTS' AVG.**	**OPPONENTS' OBP**	**EARNED RUN AVERAGE**	**ADJUSTED ERA**	**ADJUSTED STARTER RUNS**	**PITCHER WINS**
Neagle-Pit 209.2	Nomo-LA .182	Maddux-Atl .224	Maddux-Atl 1.63	Maddux-Atl 265	Maddux-Atl 61.8	**Maddux-Atl 6.5**
Maddux-Atl 209.2	Maddux-Atl .197	Nomo-LA .269	Nomo-LA 2.54	Nomo-LA 152	Nomo-LA 30.2	**Glavine-Atl 3.3**
Martinez-LA 206.1	Martinez-Mon .227	Valdez-LA .277	Ashby-SD 2.94	Glavine-Atl 140	Glavine-Atl 25.9	**Wohlers-Atl 3.1**
Hamilton-SD 204.1	Valdez-LA .228	Schourek-Cin .281	Valdez-LA 3.05	Ashby-SD 138	Smoltz-Atl 23.1	**Schourek-Cin 2.7**
Navarro-Chi 200.1	Schourek-Cin .228	Reynolds-Hou .300	Glavine-Atl 3.08	Smoltz-Atl 136	Ashby-SD 21.4	**Worrell-LA 2.4**

BRAVE NEW WORLD

Players' union head Donald Fehr claimed all 835 players without signed contracts were free agents because baseball imposed new work rules, including a salary cap. Owners, of course, said no. Baseball officials must have figured that with no players, they needed no umpires, and with players still on strike, locked out its arbiters. Replacements—umpires, that is—were used for a week once the players came to terms.

Suspended for sixty days for violating MLB's drug policy, Darryl Strawberry was released by the Giants, then pleaded guilty to tax evasion. The Dodgers had to forfeit a game to St. Louis in August after Los Angeles fans flung giveaway baseballs onto the field following a controversial call. Hideo Nomo, 13-6 and leading the league in strikeouts for those Dodgers, became the first Japanese player in thirty-one years to debut in the big leagues.

Former Reds outfielders Vada Pinson and Gus Bell died, but Cincinnati, sparked by MVP Barry Larkin, won the Central and swept Los Angeles in the Division Series. Colorado, in only its third season, had four 30-homer men at new Coors Field and claimed the Wild Card despite a league-worst 4.97 ERA. Atlanta, with 19-2 Greg Maddux, had the best record in the league and lost only once in reaching the World Series, besting the Rockies in the Division Series and sweeping the Reds in the NLCS.

Atlanta pitchers dominated the World Series, holding Cleveland's potent offense to a collective .179 average. Tom Glavine and Mark Wohlers combined on a 1-0, 1-hit shutout in Game 6, with Dave Justice's home run providing the difference. The win gave the Braves their first Series crown since 1957 and made them the first franchise to win world championships in three different cities.

1995 AMERICAN LEAGUE

TEAM	W	L	T	PCT	GB	HW	HL	R	OR	PA	H	2B	3B	HR	BB	SO	HB	SH	AVG	OBP	SLG	OPS	AOPS	BR	ABR	PF	SB	CS	BSA	BSR
East																														
Bos	86	58	0	.597	—	42	30	791	698	5716	1399	**286**	31	175	560	923	**65**	45	.280	.357	.455	812	106	79	55	103	99	44	69	6
NY	79	65	1	.549	7	46	26	749	688	5699	1365	280	34	122	**625**	851	39	20	.276	.357	.420	777	102	31	38	99	50	30	63	1
Bal	71	73	0	.493	15	36	36	704	640	5531	1267	229	27	173	574	803	39	40	.262	.342	.428	770	97	-4	-17	102	92	45	67	4
Det	60	84	0	.417	26	35	37	654	844	5535	1204	228	29	159	551	987	41	35	.247	.327	.404	731	89	-80	-80	100	73	36	67	3
Tor	56	88	0	.389	30	29	43	642	777	5650	1309	275	27	140	492	906	44	33	.260	.328	.409	737	90	-70	-71	100	75	16	**82**	**11**
Central																														
Cle	100	44	0	.694	—	**54**	18	**840**	**607**	5684	**1461**	279	23	**207**	542	**766**	35	31	**.291**	**.361**	**.479**	**840**	**114**	**125**	**108**	102	**132**	53	71	10
KC	70	74	0	.486	30	35	37	629	691	5526	1275	240	35	119	475	849	43	**66**	.260	.328	.396	724	85	-91	-104	102	120	53	69	8
Chi	68	76	1	.472	32	38	34	755	758	5770	1417	252	37	146	576	767	32	46	.280	.354	.431	785	107	32	65	96	110	39	74	**11**
Mil	65	79	0	.451	35	33	39	740	747	5631	1329	249	**42**	128	502	800	46	41	.266	.336	.409	745	88	-52	-90	106	105	40	72	9
Min	56	88	0	.389	44	29	43	703	889	5588	1398	270	34	120	471	916	58	18	.279	.346	.419	765	97	-11	-15	101	105	57	65	3
West																														
Sea	79	66	0	.545	—	46	27	796	708	5670	1377	276	20	182	549	871	39	52	.276	.350	.448	798	105	47	38	101	110	41	73	10
Cal	78	67	0	.538	1	39	33	801	697	5690	1390	252	25	186	564	889	36	33	.277	.352	.448	800	107	52	59	99	58	39	60	-1
Tex	74	70	0	.514	4.5	41	31	691	720	5566	1304	247	24	138	526	877	33	49	.265	.338	.410	748	90	-43	-65	103	90	47	66	3
Oak	67	77	0	.465	11.5	38	34	730	761	5616	1296	228	18	169	565	911	45	32	.264	.341	.420	761	102	-15	21	95	112	46	71	9
Total	1010	——		—	—	541	468	10225	—	78872	18791	3591	406	2164	7572	12116	595	541	.270	.344	.427	771	—	—	—	—	1331	586	69	88

TEAM	CG	SHO	GR	SV	IP	H	HR	BB	SO	BR/9	ERA	AERA	OAV	OOB	PR	APR	PF	OSB	OCS	FA	E	WPB	DP	FW	PW	BW	BSW	DIF
East																												
Bos	7	9	370	39	1292.2	1338	**127**	476	888	12.9	4.39	110	.268	.334	46	64	103	80	41	.978	120	86	151	-1.2	6.0	5.2	-.0	4.1
NY	18	5	302	35	1284.2	1286	159	535	908	13.0	4.56	101	.261	.334	22	9	98	117	40	**.986**	74	70	121	**1.4**	.8	3.6	-.5	1.7
Bal	**19**	**10**	336	29	1267.0	**1165**	149	523	930	12.3	4.31	111	**.245**	.322	56	64	101	98	43	**.986**	**72**	**38**	141	**1.4**	6.0	-1.6	-.2	-6.6
Det	5	3	366	38	1275.0	1509	170	536	729	14.8	5.49	88	.296	.365	-110	-95	102	102	38	.981	106	70	143	-.4	-8.9	-7.5	-.3	5.2
Tor	16	8	265	22	1292.2	1336	145	654	894	14.2	4.88	97	.267	.356	-24	-19	101	98	50	.982	97	104	131	.0	-1.8	-6.7	**.4**	-8.1
Central																												
Cle	10	**10**	335	**50**	1301.0	1261	135	**445**	926	**12.1**	**3.83**	**123**	.255	**.320**	**127**	**128**	100	117	38	.982	101	59	142	-.2	**12.0**	**10.1**	**.4**	5.7
KC	11	**10**	308	37	1288.0	1323	142	503	763	13.0	4.49	107	.268	.338	32	43	102	78	29	.984	90	56	168	.4	4.0	-9.8	.2	3.1
Chi	12	4	**373**	36	1284.2	1374	164	617	892	14.2	4.85	92	.275	.356	-20	-58	95	106	**59**	.980	108	57	131	-.5	-5.4	6.1	**.4**	-4.6
Mil	7	4	321	31	1286.0	1391	146	603	699	14.3	4.82	104	.280	.360	-16	25	106	110	36	.981	105	79	**186**	-.4	2.3	-8.4	.3	-.8
Min	7	2	336	27	1272.2	1450	210	533	790	14.3	5.76	83	.287	.356	-149	-132	102	102	25	.981	100	63	141	-.1	-12.4	-1.4	-.3	-1.8
West																												
Sea	9	8	324	39	1289.1	1343	149	591	**1068**	13.8	4.50	106	.268	.347	31	38	101	88	46	.980	104	63	108	-.3	3.6	3.6	**.4**	-.7
Cal	8	9	368	42	1284.1	1310	163	486	901	12.9	4.52	104	.265	.333	28	27	100	88	46	.982	95	55	120	.2	2.5	5.5	-.7	-2.1
Tex	14	4	310	34	1285.0	1385	152	514	838	13.6	4.66	104	.278	.346	8	25	103	**55**	44	.982	98	70	156	.0	2.3	-6.1	-.3	6.1
Oak	8	4	358	34	1273.0	1320	153	556	890	13.6	4.93	92	.269	.347	-31	-60	96	92	51	.981	102	60	151	-.2	-5.6	2.0	.3	-1.4
Total	151	90	4672	493	17976.0	—	—	—	—	13.5	4.71	—	.270	.344	—	—	—	—	—	.982	1372	930	1990	—	—	—	—	—

BATTER-FIELDER WINS	BATTING AVERAGE	ON-BASE PERCENTAGE	SLUGGING AVERAGE	ON-BASE PLUS SLUGGING	ADJUSTED OPS	ADJUSTED BATTER RUNS
E.Martinez-Sea..5.8	E.Martinez-Sea.....356	E.Martinez-Sea.....479	Belle-Cle..............690	E.Martinez-Sea...1107	E.Martinez-Sea.....184	E.Martinez-Sea....73.4
Salmon-Cal.........5.0	Knoblauch-Min......333	F.Thomas-Chi 454	E.Martinez-Sea.....628	Belle-Cle............1091	F.Thomas-Chi 183	F.Thomas-Chi 70.2
Belle-Cle.............5.0	Salmon-Cal..........330	Thome-Cle............438	F.Thomas-Chi 606	F.Thomas-Chi 1061	Belle-Cle..............174	Belle-Cle..............60.1
Valentin-Bos 4.6	Boggs-NY 324	Salmon-Cal...........429	Salmon-Cal...........594	Salmon-Cal.........1024	Salmon-Cal...........165	Salmon-Cal...........55.3
F.Thomas-Chi.....4.5	Murray-Cle............323	Davis-Cal..............429	Palmeiro-Bal 583	Thome-Cle............996	Thome-Cle............154	McGwire-Oak.......51.3

RUNS	HITS	DOUBLES	TRIPLES	HOME RUNS	TOTAL BASES	RUNS BATTED IN
E.Martinez-Sea.....121	Johnson-Chi 186	E.Martinez-Sea.......52	Lofton-Cle..............13	Belle-Cle................50	Belle-Cle..............377	Vaughn-Bos..........126
Belle-Cle..............121	E.Martinez-Sea.....182	Belle-Cle.................52	Johnson-Chi 12	F.Thomas-Chi 40	Palmeiro-Bal 323	Belle-Cle...............126
Edmonds-Cal........120	Knoblauch-Min......179	Puckett-Min.............39	Anderson-Bal..........10	Buhner-Sea 40	E.Martinez-Sea.....321	Buhner-Sea 121
Phillips-Cal...........119	Salmon-Cal...........177	Valentin-Bos 37	B.Williams-NY...........9		Salmon-Cal...........319	E.Martinez-Sea.....113
Salmon-Cal...........111	Baerga-Cle 175	T.Martinez-Sea 35	Knoblauch-Min..........8		Vaughn-Bos...........316	

BASES ON BALLS	STOLEN BASES	BASE STEALING RUNS	FIELDING RUNS-INFIELD	FIELDING RUNS-OUTFIELD	OUTFIELD ASSISTS	CATCHER CS PCT.
F.Thomas-Chi 136	Lofton-Cle..............54	Johnson-Chi 6.7	Fryman-Det..........27.3	Cordova-Min 13.8	Higginson-Det.........13	Rodriguez-Tex 48.1
E.Martinez-Sea.....116	Nixon-Tex................50	Lofton-Cle..............6.6	Gil-Tex..................18.3	Edmonds-Cal.......11.7	Cordova-Min 12	Fabregas-Cal.......38.6
Phillips-Cal...........113	Goodwin-KC 50	Javier-Oak 6.2	Alicea-Bos 14.9	Javier-Oak 8.6	Becker-Min..............12	Wilson-Sea 36.8
Tettleton-Tex 107	Knoblauch-Min........46	Alomar-Tor.............5.6	Gagne-KC............12.4	Becker-Min.............7.4	Lofton-Cle...............11	Macfarlane-Bos ...35.4
Thome-Cle..............97	Coleman-KC-Sea ...42	Goodwin-KC 4.7	Vina-Mil................12.2	Salmon-Cal............6.8	Greenwell-Bos 11	Karkovice-Chi 34.3

WINS	WINNING PCT.	WINS ABOVE TEAM	GAMES STARTED	COMPLETE GAMES	FEWEST HITS/GAME	FEWEST BB/GAME
Mussina-Bal............19	Johnson-Sea 900	Johnson-Sea 8.0	Gubicza-KC 33	McDowell-NY............8	Johnson-Sea 6.68	Mussina-Bal.........2.03
Cone-Tor-NY...........18	Hanson-Bos..........750	Cone-Tor-NY..........6.2	Mussina-Bal............32	Erickson-Min-Bal 7	Appier-KC............7.29	Martinez-Cle........2.21
Johnson-Sea 18	Nagy-Cle...............727	Mussina-Bal...........5.8	Finley-Cal 32	Mussina-Bal..............7	Wakefield-Bos......7.51	Radke-Min 2.34
Rogers-Tex 17	Hershiser-Cle........727	Rogers-Tex 5.3			Mussina-Bal.........7.59	K.Brown-Bal.........2.51
	Rogers-Tex 708	Stottlemyre-Oak.....4.4			Cone-Tor-NY.........7.65	Gubicza-KC 2.62

STRIKEOUTS	STRIKEOUTS/GAME	GAMES	SAVES	BASE RUNNERS/9	ADJUSTED RELIEF RUNS	RELIEF RANKING
Johnson-Sea 294	Johnson-Sea 12.35	Orosco-Bal.............65	Mesa-Cle 46	Percival-Cal 7.78	Mesa-Cle.............25.5	Mesa-Cle.............44.5
Stottlemyre-Oak....205	Stottlemyre-Oak...8.80	McDowell-Tex 64	Smith-Cal................37	Wetteland-NY 7.92	Nelson-Sea..........22.4	Aguilera-Min-Bos .27.7
Finley-Cal 195	Finley-Cal 8.65	Wickman-NY...........63	Aguilera-Min-Bos 32	Mesa-Cle 9.28	Percival-Cal 22.0	Nelson-Sea..........26.6
Cone-Tor-NY.........191	Appier-KC............8.27	Belinda-Bos 63	Hernandez-Chi 32	Johnson-Sea 9.66	Tavarez-Cle.........16.7	Tavarez-Cle..........21.2
Appier-KC.............185	Leiter-Tor 7.52	Ayala-Sea 63		Mussina-Bal.........9.66	Plunk-Cle.............15.4	Wetteland-NY 20.6

INNINGS PITCHED	OPPONENTS' AVG.	OPPONENTS' OBP	EARNED RUN AVERAGE	ADJUSTED ERA	ADJUSTED STARTER RUNS	PITCHER WINS
Cone-Tor-NY......229.1	Johnson-Sea 201	Johnson-Sea 266	Johnson-Sea 2.48	Johnson-Sea 193	Johnson-Sea 53.9	**Johnson-Sea......4.6**
Mussina-Bal.......221.2	Appier-KC.............221	Mussina-Bal..........270	Wakefield-Bos......2.95	Wakefield-Bos.......165	Wakefield-Bos.....37.9	**Mesa-Cle............4.3**
McDowell-NY.....217.2	Mussina-Bal..........226	Wakefield-Bos.......300	Martinez-Cle........3.08	Martinez-Cle 153	Mussina-Bal.........36.0	**Wakefield-Bos....4.2**
Johnson-Sea 214.1	Wakefield-Bos.......227	K.Brown-Bal..........302	Mussina-Bal.........3.29	Mussina-Bal..........145	Martinez-Cle........33.7	**Mussina-Bal 4.1**
Gubicza-KC 213.1	Cone-Tor-NY.........228	Martinez-Cle 302	Rogers-Tex 3.38	Rogers-Tex 143	Rogers-Tex 31.9	**Rogers-Tex 3.4**

Ripken and "The Streak" Pull Baseball Off the DL

Owners announced plans to use replacement players if a labor deal wasn't reached by Opening Day. Baltimore owner Peter Angelos refused to sign replacements players, thus the O's played no exhibition contests. His stated motive: preserving Cal Ripken's consecutive games streak. Angelos' stand led to his being virtually ostracized by other owners.

A March 31 injunction against MLB by U.S. District Court judge Sonia Sotomayor ended the strike. Fans were understandably bitter and jaded all summer, but the harsh feeling seemed to relent for one magical night at Camden Yards. On September 6, on national television, Ripken broke Lou Gehrig's record by playing in his 2,131st consecutive game.

Yankees great Mickey Mantle died in August, two months after receiving a liver transplant, while colorful umpire Ron Luciano committed suicide. Two Yankees greats retired—Dave Winfield and Don Mattingly—as Derek Jeter and Jason Giambi debuted. Eddie Murray collected his 3,000th hit.

Sparked by Albert Belle, the first player to hit 50 homers and 50 doubles in a season, Cleveland won the Central by an amazing 30 games and swept Boston to reach the ALCS. Seattle climaxed a furious comeback by winning a one-game playoff against California to reach the postseason for the first time. The Mariners then outlasted the Wild Card Yankees in the other inaugural AL Division Series. Game 5 ended with starters Randy Johnson and Jack McDowell pitching in relief. Edgar Martinez drove home the tying and winning runs in the home 11th, sending the Kingdome into a frenzy. Despite Jay Buhner's 3 homers for Seattle, Cleveland's outstanding starting pitching prevailed in a six-game ALCS. The Tribe, however, ran out of steam in the World Series, losing to Atlanta in six.

1994 NATIONAL LEAGUE

TEAM	W	L	T	PCT	GB	HW	HL	R	OR	PA	H	2B	3B	HR	BB	SO	HB	SH	AVG	OBP	SLG	OPS	AOPS	BR	ABR	PF	SB	CS	BSA	BSR
EAST																														
Mon	74	40	0	.649	—	32	20	585	454	4514	1111	246	30	108	379	669	40	53	.278	.343	.435	778	106	51	46	101	**137**	36	**79**	**18**
Atl	68	46	0	.596	6	31	24	542	**448**	4349	1031	198	18	**137**	377	**668**	22	60	.267	.333	.434	767	100	26	6	104	48	31	61	0
NY	55	58	0	.487	18.5	23	30	506	526	4347	966	164	21	117	336	807	**52**	59	.250	.316	.394	710	90	-59	-53	99	25	26	49	-4
Phi	54	61	0	.470	20.5	34	26	521	497	4436	1028	208	28	80	396	711	31	51	.262	.332	.390	722	91	-30	-38	102	67	24	74	6
Fla	51	64	0	.443	23.5	25	34	468	576	4387	1043	180	24	94	349	746	40	42	.266	.330	.396	726	90	-31	-50	104	65	26	71	5
CENTRAL																														
Cin	66	48	1	.579	—	**37**	22	**609**	490	4511	**1142**	211	36	124	388	738	29	53	**.286**	**.350**	**.449**	**799**	113	**79**	80	100	119	51	70	8
Hou	66	49	0	.574	0.5	**37**	22	602	503	4500	1099	**252**	25	120	394	718	43	**73**	.278	.347	.445	792	**117**	71	**103**	95	124	44	74	12
StL	53	61	1	.465	13	23	33	535	621	4450	1026	213	27	108	**434**	686	33	44	.263	.339	.414	753	101	16	17	100	76	46	62	1
Pit	53	61	0	.465	13	32	29	466	580	4299	1001	198	23	80	349	725	22	36	.259	.322	.384	706	88	-57	-65	102	53	25	68	3
Chi	49	64	0	.434	16.5	20	39	500	549	4386	1015	189	26	109	364	750	27	54	.259	.325	.404	729	94	-30	-30	100	69	53	57	-3
WEST																														
LA	58	56	0	.509	—	33	22	532	509	4371	1055	160	29	115	366	687	19	51	.270	.333	.414	747	105	-2	28	95	74	37	67	3
SF	55	60	0	.478	3.5	29	31	504	500	4364	963	159	32	123	364	719	39	65	.249	.318	.402	720	96	-47	-28	96	114	40	74	11
Col	53	64	0	.453	6.5	25	32	573	638	4493	1098	206	**39**	125	378	761	23	50	.274	.337	.439	776	91	39	-43	117	91	53	63	1
SD	47	70	0	.402	12.5	26	31	479	531	4518	1117	200	19	92	319	762	31	67	.275	.330	.401	731	98	-25	-8	97	79	37	68	4
Total	803	—	—	—	—	407	395	7422	—	61925	14695	2784	377	1532	5193	10147	451	758	.267	.333	.415	747	—	—	—	—	1141	529	68	66

TEAM	CG	SHO	GR	SV	IP	H	HR	BB	SO	BR/9	ERA	AERA	OAV	OOB	PR	APR	PF	OSB	OCS	FA	E	WPB	DP	FW	PW	BW	BSW	DIF
EAST																												
Mon	4	**8**	259	**46**	1036.2	970	100	**288**	805	**11.3**	**3.56**	119	.247	**.302**	**75**	76	100	99	32	.979	94	**35**	90	-.5	7.5	4.5	**1.3**	4.2
Atl	**16**	**8**	244	26	1026.1	**929**	**76**	378	**865**	11.7	3.57	**121**	**.242**	.311	73	**82**	102	90	32	.982	81	46	85	.3	**8.1**	.6	-.5	2.5
NY	7	3	238	35	1023.0	1069	117	332	640	12.5	4.13	101	.271	.328	9	4	99	68	34	.980	89	36	112	-.2	.4	-5.2	-.9	4.4
Phi	7	6	243	30	1024.1	1028	98	377	699	12.6	3.85	111	.261	.328	41	48	102	87	30	.978	94	56	96	-.4	4.7	-3.7	.1	-4.2
Fla	5	7	300	30	1015.0	1069	120	428	649	13.6	4.50	99	.274	.349	-32	-6	106	**59**	**52**	.978	95	75	111	-.5	-.6	-4.9	.0	-.6
CENTRAL																												
Cin	6	6	261	27	1038.1	1037	117	339	799	12.2	3.78	110	.262	.322	50	46	99	78	39	.983	73	58	91	.8	4.5	7.9	.3	-4.5
Hou	9	6	268	29	1029.2	1043	102	367	739	12.6	3.97	100	.265	.331	28	-2	94	85	36	.983	76	51	110	.6	-.2	**10.1**	.7	-2.8
StL	7	7	**330**	29	1018.0	1154	134	355	632	13.7	5.14	83	.289	.351	-105	-101	101	70	40	.982	80	46	119	.4	-9.9	1.7	-.4	4.2
Pit	8	2	285	24	1005.2	1094	117	370	650	13.5	4.64	94	.281	.347	-47	-29	104	78	31	.980	91	**35**	**131**	-.3	-2.9	-6.4	-.2	5.7
Chi	5	5	286	27	1023.2	1054	120	392	717	12.9	4.47	94	.268	.335	-29	-29	100	75	46	.982	81	51	110	.2	-2.9	-3.0	-.8	-1.2
WEST																												
LA	14	5	239	20	1014.0	1041	90	354	732	12.7	4.17	95	.267	.331	4	-23	95	90	33	.980	88	54	104	-.1	-2.3	2.8	-.2	.8
SF	2	4	288	33	1025.1	1014	122	372	655	12.5	3.99	102	.262	.330	26	8	96	76	35	**.985**	**68**	38	113	**1.1**	.8	-2.8	.6	-2.2
Col	4	5	329	28	1031.0	1185	120	448	703	14.7	5.15	97	.292	.366	-108	-17	118	87	44	.981	84	55	117	.2	-1.7	-4.2	-.4	.5
SD	8	6	273	27	1045.2	1008	99	393	862	12.3	4.08	101	.252	.321	15	6	98	99	45	.975	111	59	82	-1.3	.6	-.8	-.0	-9.9
Total	102	78	3843	411	14356.2	—	—	—	—	12.8	4.21	—	.267	.333	—	—	—	—	—	.980	1205	695	1471	—	—	—	—	—

BATTER-FIELDER WINS	BATTING AVERAGE	ON-BASE PERCENTAGE	SLUGGING AVERAGE	ON-BASE PLUS SLUGGING	ADJUSTED OPS	ADJUSTED BATTER RUNS
Bagwell-Hou 7.7	Gwynn-SD .394	Gwynn-SD .454	Bagwell-Hou .750	Bagwell-Hou 1201	Bagwell-Hou 219	Bagwell-Hou 72.8
Bonds-SF 4.8	Bagwell-Hou .368	Bagwell-Hou .451	Mitchell-Cin .681	Mitchell-Cin 1110	Mitchell-Cin 186	Bonds-SF 49.9
Gwynn-SD 4.0	Alou-Mon .339	Mitchell-Cin .429	Bonds-SF .647	Bonds-SF 1073	Bonds-SF 182	Gwynn-SD 47.0
Mitchell-Cin 3.8	Morris-Cin .335	Justice-Atl .427	McGriff-Atl .623	Gwynn-SD 1022	Gwynn-SD 171	Mitchell-Cin 41.4
Biggio-Hou 3.7	Mitchell-Cin .326	Bonds-SF .426	Williams-SF .607	McGriff-Atl 1012	Alou-Mon 153	Alou-Mon 33.1
RUNS	**HITS**	**DOUBLES**	**TRIPLES**	**HOME RUNS**	**TOTAL BASES**	**RUNS BATTED IN**
Bagwell-Hou 104	Gwynn-SD 165	Walker-Mon 44	Lewis-SF 9	Williams-SF 43	Bagwell-Hou 300	Bagwell-Hou 116
Grissom-Mon 96	Bichette-Col 147	Biggio-Hou 44	Butler-LA 9	Bagwell-Hou 39	Williams-SF 270	Williams-SF 96
Lankford-StL 89	Bagwell-Hou 147	Gwynn-SD 35	R.Sanders-Cin 8	Bonds-SF 37	Bichette-Col 265	Bichette-Col 95
Bonds-SF 89	Morris-Cin 146	Bell-Pit 35	Mondesi-LA 8	McGriff-Atl 34	McGriff-Atl 264	McGriff-Atl 94
Biggio-Hou 88	Conine-Fla 144	Bichette-Col 33	Kingery-Col 8	Galarraga-Col 31	Bonds-SF 253	Piazza-LA 92
BASES ON BALLS	**STOLEN BASES**	**BASE STEALING RUNS**	**FIELDING RUNS-INFIELD**	**FIELDING RUNS-OUTFIELD**	**OUTFIELD ASSISTS**	**CATCHER CS PCT.**
Bonds-SF 74	Biggio-Hou 39	Biggio-Hou 7.2	Sanchez-Chi 20.4	Whiten-StL 11.2	Mondesi-LA 16	Santiago-Fla 47.1
Justice-Atl 69	D.Sanders-Atl-Cin 38	Grissom-Mon 5.8	Garcia-Pit 18.0	Grissom-Mon 9.0	R.Sanders-Cin 12	Manwaring-SF 34.4
Dykstra-Phi 68	Grissom-Mon 36	Larkin-Cin 5.0	Bell-Pit 17.7	R.Sanders-Cin 6.4	Bonds-SF 10	Girardi-Col 34.4
Butler-LA 68	Carr-Fla 32	Carr-Fla 4.2	Bagwell-Hou 15.4	Carr-Fla 6.1	Bichette-Col 10	Hundley-NY 33.8
Bagwell-Hou 65	Lewis-SF 30	Clayton-SF 4.0	Karros-LA 13.3	Gonzalez-Hou 5.7		Taubensee-Hou-Cin 28.3
WINS	**WINNING PCT.**	**WINS ABOVE TEAM**	**GAMES STARTED**	**COMPLETE GAMES**	**FEWEST HITS/GAME**	**FEWEST BB/GAME**
Maddux-Atl 16	Saberhagen-NY .778	Saberhagen-NY 5.5	Rijo-Cin 26	Maddux-Atl 10	Maddux-Atl 6.68	Saberhagen-NY .66
Hill-Mon 16	Hill-Mon .762	Jackson-Phi 4.8		Drabek-Hou 6	Martinez-Mon 7.15	Tewksbury-StL 1.27
Saberhagen-NY 14	Maddux-Atl .727	Freeman-Col 4.3		Candiotti-LA 5	Drabek-Hou 7.21	Maddux-Atl 1.38
Jackson-Phi 14	Jackson-Phi .700	Maddux-Atl 4.1			Avery-Atl 7.54	Reynolds-Hou 1.52
Glavine-Atl 13	Martinez-Mon .688	Hill-Mon 3.9			Fassero-Mon 7.72	Swindell-Hou 1.58
STRIKEOUTS	**STRIKEOUTS/GAME**	**GAMES**	**SAVES**	**BASE RUNNERS/9**	**ADJUSTED RELIEF RUNS**	**RELIEF RANKING**
Benes-SD 189	Benes-SD 9.87	Reed-Col 61	Franco-NY 30	Maddux-Atl 8.33	Jones-Phi 12.8	Brantley-Cin 25.1
Rijo-Cin 171	Rijo-Cin 8.93	Rojas-Mon 58	Beck-SF 28	Saberhagen-NY 9.44	McElroy-Cin 12.7	Jones-Phi 24.1
Maddux-Atl 156	Martinez-Mon 8.83	Bautista-Chi 58	Jones-Phi 27	Drabek-Hou 9.78	Brantley-Cin 12.6	Carrasco-Cin 22.8
Saberhagen-NY 143	Neagle-Pit 8.01	Munoz-Col 57	Wetteland-Mon 25	Jones-Hou 9.78	Jackson-SF 12.4	Hoffman-SD 20.7
Martinez-Mon 142	Reynolds-Hou 7.98	Burba-SF 57		Wetteland-Mon 9.90	Carrasco-Cin 11.7	Wetteland-Mon 19.9
INNINGS PITCHED	**OPPONENTS' AVG.**	**OPPONENTS' OBP**	**EARNED RUN AVERAGE**	**ADJUSTED ERA**	**ADJUSTED STARTER RUNS**	**PITCHER WINS**
Maddux-Atl 202.0	Maddux-Atl .207	Maddux-Atl .243	Maddux-Atl 1.56	Maddux-Atl 277	Maddux-Atl 58.0	**Maddux-Atl 6.8**
Jackson-Phi 179.1	Martinez-Mon .220	Saberhagen-NY .271	Saberhagen-NY 2.74	Saberhagen-NY 152	Saberhagen-NY 29.6	**Saberhagen-NY 3.1**
Saberhagen-NY 177.1	Drabek-Hou .220	Drabek-Hou .275	Drabek-Hou 2.84	Fassero-Mon 142	Freeman-Col 22.7	**Drabek-Hou 2.7**
Rijo-Cin 172.1	Avery-Atl .227	Ashby-SD .285	Fassero-Mon 2.99	Drabek-Hou 139	Henry-Mon 22.3	**Brantley-Cin 2.6**
Benes-SD 172.1	Fassero-Mon .229	Fassero-Mon .285	Reynolds-Hou 3.05	Rijo-Cin 136	Drabek-Hou 21.6	**Henry-Mon 2.5**

Summertime Strikeout

The 1994 season was like a wonderful outdoor party held under a black sky. Major league per-game attendance was even higher than 1993's record rate, San Diego's Tony Gwynn flirted with .400, San Francisco third baseman Matt Williams was on pace to possibly break Roger Maris' single-season home run record, Greg Maddux of Atlanta was enjoying his best season to that point, and Jeff Bagwell, hitting in the pitcher-dominant Astrodome, had 116 RBIs in 110 games. A broken hand ended Bagwell's season early; everyone else waited helplessly for the storm. It hit on August 12.

The strike ended Montreal's dream season, as les Expos owned the best record in baseball and had a 6-game lead in the East over the Braves, who held a slight advantage over the Astros in the new Wild Card standings. The star-crossed Expos seemed a lock to make the postseason for the first time since 1981. Felipe Alou's club, with All-Stars Moises Alou, Wil Cordero, Marquis Grissom, Darrin Fletcher, and 16-game winner Ken Hill, plus dominant seasons from Larry Walker and John Wetteland, would never look the same again.

Central leader Cincinnati and West frontrunner Los Angeles led tight races as of the strike, though Major League Baseball declined to officially name any division winners. The decision by owners to cancel the remainder of the season meant the first year with no World Series since 1904. In December owners declared an impasse in negotiations and implemented new rules, including a salary cap. Players appealed to the National Labor Relations Board, which also heard unfair labor practice claims by owners against players.

1994 AMERICAN LEAGUE

TEAM	W	L	T	PCT	GB	HW	HL	R	OR	PA	H	2B	3B	HR	BB	SO	HB	SH	AVG	OBP	SLG	OPS	AOPS	BR	ABR	PF	SB	CS	BSA	BSR
EAST																														
NY	70	43	0	.619	—	33	24	670	534	4611	1155	238	16	139	**530**	660	31	27	**.290**	**.374**	.462	**836**	**118**	**102**	**128**	97	55	40	58	-2
Bal	63	49	0	.563	6.5	28	27	589	**497**	4384	1047	185	20	139	438	655	39	16	.272	.349	.438	787	96	12	-20	106	69	13	**84**	11
Tor	55	60	0	.478	16	33	26	566	579	4461	1064	210	30	115	387	691	38	30	.269	.336	.424	760	93	-31	-38	101	79	26	75	8
Bos	54	61	0	.470	17	31	33	552	621	4446	1038	222	19	120	404	723	31	38	.263	.334	.421	755	89	-38	-63	105	81	38	68	5
Det	53	62	0	.461	18	34	24	652	671	4574	1048	216	25	161	520	897	34	17	.265	.352	.454	806	105	44	35	101	46	33	58	-1
CENTRAL																														
Chi	67	46	0	.593	—	34	19	633	498	4556	1133	175	**39**	121	497	**568**	20	**51**	.287	.366	.444	810	109	56	63	99	77	27	74	7
Cle	66	47	0	.584	1	**35**	16	**679**	562	4493	**1165**	**240**	20	**167**	382	629	18	33	**.290**	.351	**.484**	835	111	75	68	101	131	48	73	**12**
KC	64	51	0	.557	4	**35**	24	574	532	4390	1051	211	38	100	376	698	33	32	.269	.335	.419	754	89	-40	-66	105	**140**	62	69	9
Min	53	60	0	.469	14	32	27	594	688	4408	1092	239	23	103	359	635	**41**	22	.276	.340	.427	767	95	-19	-23	101	94	30	76	10
Mil	53	62	0	.461	15	24	32	547	586	4494	1045	238	21	99	417	680	33	28	.263	.335	.408	743	86	-52	-79	105	59	37	61	0
WEST																														
Tex	52	62	0	.456	—	31	32	613	697	4531	1114	198	27	124	437	730	36	41	.280	.353	.436	789	101	19	12	101	82	35	70	6
Oak	51	63	0	.447	1	24	32	549	589	4395	1009	178	13	113	417	686	18	24	.260	.330	.399	729	94	-70	-27	92	91	39	70	6
Sea	49	63	0	.438	2	22	22	569	616	4361	1045	211	18	153	372	652	26	48	.269	.335	.451	786	98	-2	-15	102	48	21	70	3
Cal	47	68	0	.409	5.5	23	40	543	660	4443	1042	178	16	120	402	715	27	42	.264	.334	.409	743	88	-56	-65	102	65	54	55	-5
Total	797	—	—	—	—	419	378	8330	—	62547	15048	2939	325	1774	5938	9619	425	449	.273	.345	.434	779	—	—	—	—	1117	503	69	70

TEAM	CG	SHO	GR	SV	IP	H	HR	BB	SO	BR/9	ERA	AERA	OAV	OOB	PR	APR	PF	OSB	OCS	FA	E	WPB	DP	FW	PW	BW	BSW	DIF
EAST																												
NY	8	2	241	31	1019.2	1045	120	398	656	12.9	4.34	106	.267	.335	52	30	96	55	29	.982	80	56	122	.1	2.8	**11.8**	-.6	-.6
Bal	13	4	234	37	997.2	1005	131	**351**	666	12.5	4.31	117	.263	.327	54	78	105	61	28	**.986**	**57**	**23**	103	**1.5**	7.2	-1.8	**.6**	-.4
Tor	13	4	221	26	1025.0	1053	127	482	**832**	13.8	4.70	104	.266	.348	12	19	102	101	43	.981	81	68	105	.2	1.8	-3.5	.3	-1.2
Bos	6	3	**308**	30	1029.1	1104	120	450	729	13.9	4.93	102	.276	.351	-15	11	105	98	38	.981	81	62	124	.2	1.0	-5.8	.0	1.1
Det	15	1	246	20	1018.0	1139	148	449	560	14.3	5.38	91	.282	.356	-66	-51	103	94	36	.981	82	67	90	.1	-4.7	3.2	-.6	-2.6
CENTRAL																												
Chi	13	**9**	239	20	1011.1	**964**	115	377	754	**12.1**	**3.96**	118	**.250**	**.317**	**94**	84	98	81	30	.981	79	31	91	.2	7.8	5.8	.2	-3.5
Cle	**17**	5	222	21	1018.2	1097	**94**	404	666	13.6	4.36	109	.275	.346	49	44	99	75	33	.980	90	65	119	-.4	4.1	6.3	**.6**	-1.1
KC	5	6	247	**38**	1031.2	1018	95	392	717	12.6	4.23	**119**	.260	.328	65	**86**	105	91	30	.982	80	65	102	.2	**7.9**	-6.1	.4	4.0
Min	6	4	272	29	1005.0	1197	153	388	602	14.5	5.68	87	.299	.361	-98	-82	103	85	**53**	.982	75	48	99	.4	-7.6	-2.1	.5	5.3
Mil	11	3	252	23	1036.0	1071	127	421	577	13.2	4.62	110	.269	.340	20	49	106	117	28	.981	85	41	**130**	-.0	4.5	-7.3	-.5	-1.2
WEST																												
Tex	10	4	301	26	1023.0	1176	157	394	683	14.1	5.45	89	.288	.351	-75	-70	101	**47**	33	.976	106	59	106	-1.4	-6.5	1.1	.0	1.6
Oak	12	**9**	**308**	23	1003.1	979	128	510	732	13.7	4.80	93	.257	.347	0	-38	93	60	45	.979	88	47	105	-.3	-3.5	-2.5	.0	.2
Sea	13	7	252	21	984.0	1051	109	486	763	14.3	4.99	99	.274	.357	-21	-8	103	69	39	.977	95	49	102	-.8	-.7	-1.4	-.2	-3.9
Cal	11	4	257	21	1027.0	1149	150	436	682	14.3	5.42	91	.287	.360	-70	-57	102	83	38	.983	76	59	110	.5	-5.3	-6.0	-.9	1.2
Total	153	65	3600	366	14229.2	—	—	—	—	13.5	4.80	—	.273	.345	—	—	—	—	—	.981	1155	740	1508	—	—	—	—	—

BATTER-FIELDER WINS	BATTING AVERAGE	ON-BASE PERCENTAGE	SLUGGING AVERAGE	ON-BASE PLUS SLUGGING	ADJUSTED OPS	ADJUSTED BATTER RUNS
Thomas-Chi........5.2	O'Neill-NY.............359	Thomas-Chi..........487	Thomas-Chi..........729	Thomas-Chi........1217	Thomas-Chi..........212	Thomas-Chi.........75.4
Belle-Cle.............4.5	Belle-Cle...............357	O'Neill-NY.............460	Belle-Cle...............714	Belle-Cle.............1152	Belle-Cle...............190	Belle-Cle..............56.6
Griffey-Sea.........4.2	Thomas-Chi..........353	Belle-Cle..............438	Griffey-Sea 674	Griffey-Sea 1076	O'Neill-NY.............179	O'Neill-NY............47.9
O'Neill-NY...........4.0	Lofton-Cle.............349	Boggs-NY 433	O'Neill-NY.............603	O'Neill-NY...........1064	Griffey-Sea 167	Griffey-Sea 42.5
Lofton-Cle...........3.8	Boggs-NY 342	Clark-Tex 431	Hamelin-KC 599	Hamelin-KC 987	Davis-Cal 146	Lofton-Cle............30.0
RUNS	**HITS**	**DOUBLES**	**TRIPLES**	**HOME RUNS**	**TOTAL BASES**	**RUNS BATTED IN**
Thomas-Chi..........106	Lofton-Cle.............160	Knoblauch-Min........45	L.Johnson-Chi 14	Griffey-Sea 40	Belle-Cle...............294	Puckett-Min...........112
Lofton-Cle.............105	Molitor-Tor.............155	Belle-Cle.................35	Coleman-KC...........12	Thomas-Chi............38	Griffey-Sea 292	Carter-Tor 103
Griffey-Sea 94	Belle-Cle...............147	Thomas-Chi............34	Lofton-Cle.................9	Belle-Cle.................36	Thomas-Chi..........291	Thomas-Chi...........101
Phillips-Det 91	Thomas-Chi..........141	Fryman-Det............34	Diaz-Mil.....................7	Canseco-Tex...........31	Lofton-Cle.............246	Belle-Cle...............101
Belle-Cle.................90				Fielder-Det.............28	Palmeiro-Bal.........240	Franco-Chi..............98
BASES ON BALLS	**STOLEN BASES**	**BASE STEALING RUNS**	**FIELDING RUNS-INFIELD**	**FIELDING RUNS-OUTFIELD**	**OUTFIELD ASSISTS**	**CATCHER CS PCT.**
Thomas-Chi..........109	Lofton-Cle...............60	Lofton-Cle..............9.0	Valentin-Mil..........21.3	Edmonds-Cal.........8.3	Puckett-Min.............13	Walbeck-Min........39.3
Tettleton-Det...........97	Coleman-KC...........50	Coleman-KC..........8.2	Espinoza-Cle 15.8	Curtis-Cal 7.3	Lofton-Cle...............13	Rodriguez-Tex 38.3
Phillips-Det 95	Nixon-Bos...............42	Anderson-Bal.........6.5	Gallego-NY..........15.7	L.Johnson-Chi 7.3	Griffey-Sea 12	Wilson-Sea 38.2
O'Neill-NY...............72	Knoblauch-Min........35	Nixon-Bos...............5.7	Fielder-Det...........15.5	Ward-Mil 6.1	Coleman-KC...........11	Alomar-Cle...........33.8
Henderson-Oak 72	Anderson-Bal..........31	Knoblauch-Min.......5.6	Gagne-KC............13.4	Puckett-Min............5.9	Buhner-Sea 11	Borders-Tor..........33.0
WINS	**WINNING PCT.**	**WINS ABOVE TEAM**	**GAMES STARTED**	**COMPLETE GAMES**	**FEWEST HITS/GAME**	**FEWEST BB/GAME**
Key-NY 17	Bere-Chi 857	Key-NY 5.8	8 players tied 25	Johnson-Sea 9	Clemens-Bos.......6.54	Gubicza-KC 1.80
Mussina-Bal............16	Key-NY 810	Cone-KC.................5.4	25	Martinez-Cle.............7	Cone-KC..............6.82	Gullickson-Det 1.95
Cone-KC.................16	Clark-Cle..............786	Mussina-Bal...........5.3	25	Finley-Cal 7	Johnson-Sea 6.91	Wegman-Mil 2.02
McDonald-Bal.........14	Mussina-Bal..........762	Bere-Chi 4.8	25		Ontiveros-Oak 7.26	Ontiveros-Oak 2.03
	Cone-KC..............762	Johnson-Sea 4.6	25		Bere-Chi 7.56	McDowell-Chi 2.09
STRIKEOUTS	**STRIKEOUTS/GAME**	**GAMES**	**SAVES**	**BASE RUNNERS/9**	**ADJUSTED RELIEF RUNS**	**RELIEF RANKING**
Johnson-Sea 204	Johnson-Sea 10.67	Wickman-NY...........53	L.Smith-Bal.............33	Ontiveros-Oak 9.75	Eichhorn-Bal........21.2	Eichhorn-Bal........30.1
Clemens-Bos........168	Clemens-Bos.......8.86	Mesa-Cle 51	Montgomery-KC 27	Cone-KC............10.01	Castillo-Tor...........16.9	Plunk-Cle 20.4
Finley-Cal 148	Appier-KC 8.42	Guthrie-Min.............50	Aguilera-Min 23	Clemens-Bos.....10.49	Plunk-Cle 16.7	Fetters-Mil............19.6
Hentgen-Tor..........147	Langston-Cal 8.22	Brewer-KC 50	Eckersley-Oak 19	Mussina-Bal.......10.51	Ryan-Bos...............13.4	Ryan-Bos...............19.6
Appier-KC.............145	Bere-Chi 8.07	Willis-Min 49	Ayala-Sea 18	Wickman-NY......10.54	Howe-NY 13.3	Risley-Sea 19.1
INNINGS PITCHED	**OPPONENTS' AVG.**	**OPPONENTS' OBP**	**EARNED RUN AVERAGE**	**ADJUSTED ERA**	**ADJUSTED STARTER RUNS**	**PITCHER WINS**
Finley-Cal 183.1	Clemens-Bos........203	Ontiveros-Oak 271	Ontiveros-Oak 2.65	Clemens-Bos........177	Cone-KC..............38.7	**Cone-KC.............4.3**
McDowell-Chi 181.0	Cone-KC...............209	Cone-KC...............277	Clemens-Bos.......2.85	Cone-KC...............171	Clemens-Bos........38.5	**Mussina-Bal........4.0**
Eldred-Mil 179.0	Johnson-Sea 216	Clemens-Bos.........288	Cone-KC...............2.94	Ontiveros-Oak 169	Mussina-Bal.........36.9	**Johnson-Sea......3.5**
Martinez-Cle......176.2	Ontiveros-Oak 217	Mussina-Bal..........291	Mussina-Bal.........3.06	Mussina-Bal..........165	Johnson-Sea 34.0	**Clemens-Bos 3.2**
Mussina-Bal.......176.1	Bere-Chi 229	Martinez-Cle.........298	Johnson-Sea 3.19	Johnson-Sea 155	Bones-Mil.............27.7	**Eichhorn-Bal......3.0**

CROSSING THE RUBICON

The high-velocity rhetoric started flying early in the year as owners tried to link revenue sharing to a salary cap in labor negotiations. Players steadfastly refused a cap, however. Milwaukee owner Bud Selig, now interim commissioner, was given total control over negotiations. Talks were fruitless, and the players went on strike on August 12. The season, including the postseason, was officially pronounced kaput on September 14.

Before the catastrophe, two new ballparks opened: Jacobs Field in Cleveland and the Ballpark in Arlington in Texas. Also new was baseball's revamped postseason format, which included three divisions in each league for the first time and a Wild Card postseason berth for the second place team with the best record.

Cleveland slugger Albert Belle was caught using a corked bat. Basketball superstar Michael Jordan, in what proved to be a temporary retirement from basketball, signed a minor league contract with White Sox. The glory of the NBA spent the summer struggling at Double-A, hitting only .202 and slugging .266 in his lone season in baseball. Goose Gossage, Kent Hrbek, Bo Jackson, and Jack Morris retired. Eighteen-year-old shortstop Alex Rodriguez debuted for Seattle.

Seattle's Ken Griffey Jr. led the league with 40 home runs, and was close to a pace needed to break Roger Maris' revered record. Chicago's Frank Thomas (38) and Belle (36) were right behind Griffey. For all the immense damage it wrought, the strike saved baseball the embarrassment of a division champion 10 games under .500: the Rangers, who led the four-team West. Baseball's decision not to officially declare division champions robbed deserving AL leaders Chicago (Central) and New York (East) of titles. Cleveland, which had not reached the postseason since 1954, was the leading Wild Card team.

1993 NATIONAL LEAGUE

TEAM	W	L	T	PCT	GB	HW	HL	R	OR	PA	H	2B	3B	HR	BB	SO	HB	SH	AVG	OBP	SLG	OPS	AOPS	BR	ABR	PF	SB	CS	BSA	BSR
East																														
Phi	97	65	0	.599	—	52	29	**877**	740	6527	**1555**	**297**	51	156	**665**	1049	42	84	.274	**.351**	.426	**777**	**115**	**121**	**135**	98	91	32	74	9
Mon	94	68	1	.580	3	**55**	26	732	682	6233	1410	270	36	122	542	**860**	48	100	.257	.326	.386	712	92	-23	-53	104	**228**	56	**80**	**31**
StL	87	75	0	.537	10	49	32	758	744	6279	1508	262	34	118	588	882	27	59	.272	.341	.395	736	103	35	40	99	153	72	68	8
Chi	84	78	1	.519	13	43	38	738	739	6216	1521	259	32	161	446	923	34	67	.270	.325	.414	739	103	17	23	99	100	43	70	7
Pit	75	87	0	.463	22	40	41	707	806	6268	1482	267	50	110	536	972	55	76	.267	.335	.393	728	100	11	14	100	92	55	63	1
Fla	64	98	0	.395	33	35	46	581	724	6125	1356	197	31	94	498	1054	51	58	.248	.314	.346	660	77	-128	-161	106	117	56	68	6
NY	59	103	0	.364	38	28	53	672	744	6056	1350	228	37	158	448	879	24	89	.248	.305	.390	695	91	-76	-67	99	79	50	61	0
West																														
Atl	104	58	0	.642	—	51	30	767	**559**	6234	1444	239	29	**169**	560	946	36	73	.262	.331	.408	739	101	27	10	102	125	48	72	11
SF	103	59	0	.636	1	50	31	808	636	6271	1534	269	33	168	516	930	46	102	**.276**	.340	**.427**	767	114	83	110	97	120	65	65	4
Hou	85	77	0	.525	19	44	37	716	630	6130	1459	288	37	138	497	911	40	82	.267	.330	.409	739	107	26	51	97	103	60	63	2
LA	81	81	0	.500	23	41	40	675	662	6261	1458	234	28	130	492	937	27	**107**	.261	.321	.383	704	98	-47	-8	95	126	61	67	6
Cin	73	89	0	.451	31	41	40	722	785	6163	1457	261	28	137	485	1025	32	63	.264	.324	.396	720	97	-12	-16	101	142	59	71	11
Col	67	95	0	.414	37	39	42	758	967	6073	1507	278	**59**	142	388	944	46	70	.273	.323	.422	745	89	26	-79	117	146	90	62	1
SD	61	101	0	.377	43	34	47	679	772	6135	1386	239	28	153	443	1046	**59**	80	.252	.312	.389	701	91	-60	-65	101	92	41	69	6
Total	1135	—	—	—	—	602	532	10190	—	86971	20427	3588	513	1956	7104	13358	567	1110	.264	.327	.399	726	—	—	—	—	1714	788	69	101

TEAM	CG	SHO	GR	SV	IP	H	HR	BB	SO	BR/9	ERA	AERA	OAV	OOB	PR	APR	PF	OSB	OCS	FA	E	WPB	DP	FW	PW	BW	BSW	DIF
East																												
Phi	**24**	11	350	46	1472.2	1419	129	573	**1117**	12.4	3.95	100	.251	.322	14	1	98	101	49	.977	141	86	123	-.4	.0	**13.5**	.2	2.7
Mon	8	7	385	**61**	1456.2	1369	119	521	934	12.0	3.55	118	.249	.317	80	98	103	172	51	.975	159	60	144	-1.4	9.8	-5.3	**2.4**	7.5
StL	5	7	423	54	1453.0	1553	152	**383**	775	12.3	4.09	98	.276	.324	-8	-10	100	112	54	.975	159	54	157	-1.4	-1.0	4.0	.0	4.4
Chi	8	5	422	56	1449.2	1514	153	470	905	12.6	4.18	96	.273	.332	-22	-24	100	84	**69**	.982	115	57	162	1.1	-2.4	2.3	-.0	2.0
Pit	12	5	384	34	1445.2	1557	153	485	832	13.0	4.77	86	.280	.339	-117	-110	101	148	51	.983	105	74	161	1.7	-11.0	1.4	-.6	2.5
Fla	4	5	409	48	1440.1	1437	135	598	945	12.9	4.13	106	.261	.334	-14	34	108	118	51	.980	125	114	130	.5	3.4	-16.1	-.1	-4.7
NY	16	8	297	22	1438.0	1483	139	434	867	12.3	4.05	99	.269	.324	-2	-7	99	143	56	.975	156	**36**	143	-1.3	-.7	-6.7	-.7	-12.6
West																												
Atl	18	**16**	353	46	1455.0	**1297**	**101**	480	1036	**11.1**	**3.14**	**129**	**.240**	**.303**	**146**	**147**	100	121	53	.983	108	59	146	1.5	**14.7**	1.0	.4	5.5
SF	4	9	414	50	1456.2	1385	168	442	982	11.6	3.61	109	.253	.313	69	52	97	**81**	66	**.984**	**101**	48	**169**	**1.9**	5.2	11.0	-.3	4.3
Hou	18	14	324	42	1441.1	1363	117	476	1056	11.7	3.49	111	.251	.313	88	63	96	110	42	.979	126	67	141	.5	6.3	5.1	-.5	-7.3
LA	17	9	346	36	1472.2	1406	103	567	1043	12.3	3.50	110	.254	.324	88	61	96	129	66	.979	133	62	141	.0	6.1	-.8	-.1	-5.2
Cin	11	8	375	37	1434.0	1510	158	508	996	12.9	4.51	89	.272	.336	-74	-77	100	134	56	.980	121	59	133	.8	-7.7	-1.6	.4	.2
Col	9	0	**453**	35	1431.1	1664	181	609	913	14.6	5.41	88	.294	.362	-218	-85	118	119	56	.973	167	93	149	-1.9	-8.5	-7.9	-.6	4.9
SD	8	6	397	32	1437.2	1470	148	558	957	12.9	4.23	98	.266	.334	-30	-15	102	142	68	.974	160	77	129	-1.5	-1.5	-6.5	-.1	-10.4
Total	162	110	5332	599	20284.2	—	—	—	—	12.5	4.04	—	.264	.327	—	—	—	—	—	.978	1876	946	2028	—	—	—	—	—

BATTER-FIELDER WINS	BATTING AVERAGE	ON-BASE PERCENTAGE	SLUGGING AVERAGE	ON-BASE PLUS SLUGGING	ADJUSTED OPS	ADJUSTED BATTER RUNS
Bonds-SF 8.0	Galarraga-Col 370	Bonds-SF 458	Bonds-SF 677	Bonds-SF 1136	Bonds-SF 207	Bonds-SF 89.9
Dykstra-Phi 5.6	Gwynn-SD 358	Kruk-Phi 430	Galarraga-Col 602	Galarraga-Col 1005	Piazza-LA 155	Dykstra-Phi 47.8
Bell-Pit 5.4	Jefferies-StL 342	Dykstra-Phi 420	Williams-SF 561	Piazza-LA 932	Bagwell-Hou 146	Kruk-Phi 41.7
Wilkins-Chi 5.4	Bonds-SF 336	Merced-Pit 414	Piazza-LA 561	McGriff-SD-Atl 924	Kruk-Phi 145	Piazza-LA 40.2
Piazza-LA 5.3	Grace-Chi 325	Jefferies-StL 408	McGriff-SD-Atl 549	Kruk-Phi 905	Dykstra-Phi 144	Bagwell-Hou 36.3
RUNS	**HITS**	**DOUBLES**	**TRIPLES**	**HOME RUNS**	**TOTAL BASES**	**RUNS BATTED IN**
Dykstra-Phi 143	Dykstra-Phi 194	Hayes-Col 45	Finley-Hou 13	Bonds-SF 46	Bonds-SF 365	Bonds-SF 123
Bonds-SF 129	Grace-Chi 193	Dykstra-Phi 44	Butler-LA 10	Justice-Atl 40	Williams-SF 325	Justice-Atl 120
Gant-Atl 113	Grissom-Mon 188	Bichette-Col 43	Morandini-Phi 9	Williams-SF 38	Gant-Atl 309	Gant-Atl 117
McGriff-SD-Atl 111	Bell-Pit 187	Gwynn-SD 41	Bell-Pit 9	McGriff-SD-Atl 37	Piazza-LA 307	Piazza-LA 112
Blauser-Atl 110	Jefferies-StL 186	Biggio-Hou 41		Gant-Atl 36	Dykstra-Phi 307	Williams-SF 110
BASES ON BALLS	**STOLEN BASES**	**BASE STEALING RUNS**	**FIELDING RUNS-INFIELD**	**FIELDING RUNS-OUTFIELD**	**OUTFIELD ASSISTS**	**CATCHER CS PCT.**
Dykstra-Phi 129	Carr-Fla 58	Grissom-Mon 8.2	O.Smith-StL 23.4	Gonzalez-Hou......14.9	Gilkey-StL 19	Manwaring-SF 45.9
Bonds-SF 126	Grissom-Mon 53	Jefferies-StL 7.0	Bell-Pit 21.5	Plantier-SD 9.9	Sosa-Chi 17	Wilkins-Chi 45.9
Daulton-Phi 117	Nixon-Atl 47	DeShields-Mon 6.0	Lemke-Atl 18.4	Bichette-Col 9.1	Snyder-LA 14	Pagnozzi-StL 34.1
Kruk-Phi 111	Lewis-SF 46	Nixon-Atl 5.8	Thompson-SF 16.8	Merced-Pit 8.8	Plantier-SD 14	Daulton-Phi 33.6
Butler-LA 86	Jefferies-StL 46	Davis-LA 5.5	Vizcaino-Chi 15.2	Carr-Fla 7.1	Bichette-Col 14	Girardi-Col 31.2
WINS	**WINNING PCT.**	**WINS ABOVE TEAM**	**GAMES STARTED**	**COMPLETE GAMES**	**FEWEST HITS/GAME**	**FEWEST BB/GAME**
Glavine-Atl 22	Portugal-Hou 818	Portugal-Hou 7.2	Rijo-Cin 36	Maddux-Atl 8	Harnisch-Hou 7.07	Tewksbury-StL 84
Burkett-SF 22	Greene-Phi 800	Glavine-Atl 6.3	Maddux-Atl 36		Swift-SF 7.54	Arocha-StL 1.48
Swift-SF 21	Glavine-Atl 786	Burkett-SF 5.5	Glavine-Atl 36		Rijo-Cin 7.62	Burkett-SF 1.55
Maddux-Atl 20	Burkett-SF 759	Greene-Phi 5.3			Smoltz-Atl 7.68	Avery-Atl 1.73
	Avery-Atl 750	Swift-SF 4.1			Maddux-Atl 7.69	Maddux-Atl 1.75
STRIKEOUTS	**STRIKEOUTS/GAME**	**GAMES**	**SAVES**	**BASE RUNNERS/9**	**ADJUSTED RELIEF RUNS**	**RELIEF RANKING**
Rijo-Cin 227	Rijo-Cin 7.94	Jackson-SF 81	Myers-Chi 53	Harvey-Fla 7.57	Fassero-Mon........28.5	Wetteland-Mon 50.3
Smoltz-Atl 208	Smoltz-Atl 7.68	West-Phi 76	Beck-SF 48	Beck-SF 8.28	Wetteland-Mon 25.1	Harvey-Fla 36.1
Maddux-Atl 197	Guzman-Chi 7.68	Beck-SF 76	Harvey-Fla 45	S.Fernandez-NY ..9.10	McMichael-Atl 20.8	Fassero-Mon.........29.4
Schilling-Phi 186	Harnisch-Hou 7.65	McMichael-Atl 74		Wetteland-Mon 9.28	Harvey-Fla 19.0	Gott-LA 27.2
Harnisch-Hou 185	Greene-Phi 7.52			McMichael-Atl 9.52	P.Martinez-LA 16.5	Beck-SF 24.3
INNINGS PITCHED	**OPPONENTS' AVG.**	**OPPONENTS' OBP**	**EARNED RUN AVERAGE**	**ADJUSTED ERA**	**ADJUSTED STARTER RUNS**	**PITCHER WINS**
Maddux-Atl 267.0	Harnisch-Hou 214	Maddux-Atl 273	Maddux-Atl 2.36	Maddux-Atl 172	Maddux-Atl 46.6	**Maddux-Atl 5.3**
Rijo-Cin 257.1	Swift-SF 226	Swift-SF 277	Rijo-Cin 2.48	Rijo-Cin 162	Rijo-Cin 45.1	**Wetteland-Mon .. 5.1**
Smoltz-Atl 243.2	Rijo-Cin 230	Rijo-Cin 278	Portugal-Hou 2.77	Portugal-Hou 140	Swift-SF 28.1	**Rijo-Cin 4.8**
Glavine-Atl 239.1	Smoltz-Atl 230	Mulholland-Phi 282	Swift-SF 2.82	Swift-SF 139	Avery-Atl 27.3	**Swift-SF 4.1**
Drabek-Hou 237.2	Maddux-Atl 232	Harnisch-Hou 289	Avery-Atl 2.94	Avery-Atl 138	Portugal-Hou 25.4	**Harvey-Fla 3.7**

A Race for the Ages

The NL expanded for the first time since 1969, adding the Colorado Rockies and Florida Marlins. More than 80,000 watched Colorado's opener in Denver's Mile High Stadium as the Rockies went on to draw more than 4.4 million fans, shattering the individual club record. The Marlins also surpassed three million, propelling MLB to a new all-time record. Aided substantially by Denver's thin air, NL offense increased tremendously. Runs per game jumped 16 percent, and home runs per game were up 33 percent. Conspiracy theorists blamed their favorite chimera, a "juiced ball."

Cincinnati's problems continued as owner Marge Schott was suspended from daily activities for a year because of racist comments, and new Reds skipper Tony Perez was fired after only 44 games. Houston hired Bob Watson as baseball's second African-American general manager. Mets hurler Anthony Young lost 16 straight decisions and a record 27 straight over two years. Dodgers stars Roy Campanella and Don Drysdale died, as did Johnny Mize. Dale Murphy retired in Colorado; Trevor Hoffman debuted in Florida.

In the last year before the Wild Card, the NL West experienced one of the greatest races ever. The Braves and Giants battled all season, both winning more than 100 games, and the clubs were tied going into the final day. The Braves beat the Rockies, meaning that the Giants knew as their game with the Dodgers began they had to beat their bitter rivals to force a one-game playoff. But Los Angeles overpowered San Francisco, 12-1, spoiling what had been a magical season for the Bay Area. Philadelphia edged out Montreal in the East, then upset the mighty Braves in six games in the NLCS. However, the fightin' Phils' mojo evaporated ten days later, north of the border, in the World Series against Toronto.

1993 AMERICAN LEAGUE

TEAM	W	L	T	PCT	GB	HW	HL	R	OR	PA	H	2B	3B	HR	BB	SO	HB	SH	AVG	OBP	SLG	OPS	AOPS	BR	ABR	PF	SB	CS	BSA	BSR
EAST																														
Tor	95	67	0	.586	—	48	33	847	742	6319	1556	317	42	159	588	861	52	46	**.279**	.350	**.436**	786	108	88	73	102	**170**	49	**78**	**20**
NY	88	74	0	.543	7	**50**	31	821	761	6359	**1568**	294	24	178	629	910	43	22	**.279**	.353	.435	788	**113**	96	120	97	39	35	53	-4
Bal	85	77	0	.525	10	48	33	786	745	6309	1470	287	24	157	655	930	41	49	.267	.346	.413	759	98	39	2	105	73	54	57	-3
Det	85	77	0	.525	10	44	37	**899**	837	6505	1546	282	38	178	**765**	1122	35	33	.275	**.362**	.434	**796**	**113**	**124**	**123**	100	104	63	62	1
Bos	80	82	0	.494	15	43	38	686	698	6195	1451	**319**	29	114	508	871	**62**	**80**	.264	.330	.395	725	88	-39	-82	106	73	38	66	3
Cle	76	86	0	.469	19	46	35	790	813	6267	1547	264	31	141	488	843	49	39	.275	.335	.409	744	99	-7	-9	100	159	55	74	16
Mil	69	93	0	.426	26	38	43	733	792	6222	1426	240	25	125	555	932	40	57	.258	.328	.378	706	90	-80	-73	99	138	93	60	-2
WEST																														
Chi	94	68	0	.580	—	45	36	776	**664**	6253	1454	228	**44**	162	604	**834**	33	72	.265	.338	.411	749	102	7	20	98	106	57	65	3
Tex	86	76	0	.531	8	**50**	31	835	751	6166	1472	284	39	**181**	483	984	48	69	.267	.329	.431	760	105	15	40	97	113	67	63	1
KC	84	78	0	.519	10	43	38	675	694	6101	1455	294	35	125	428	936	52	48	.263	.320	.397	717	85	-69	-112	107	100	75	57	-4
Sea	82	80	0	.506	12	46	35	734	731	6288	1429	272	24	161	624	901	56	63	.260	.339	.406	745	97	4	-12	102	91	68	57	-4
Cal	71	91	0	.438	23	44	37	684	770	6089	1399	259	24	114	564	930	38	50	.260	.331	.380	711	88	-63	-85	103	169	100	63	2
Min	71	91	0	.438	23	36	45	693	830	6209	1480	261	27	121	493	850	51	27	.264	.327	.385	712	90	-72	-79	101	83	59	58	-2
Oak	68	94	0	.420	26	38	43	715	846	6293	1408	260	21	158	622	1048	33	46	.254	.330	.394	724	99	-43	-3	95	131	59	69	8
Total	1134	—	—	—	—	619	515	10674	—	87575	20661	3861	427	2074	8006	12952	633	701	.267	.337	.408	745	—	—	—	—	1549	872	64	36

TEAM	CG	SHO	GR	SV	IP	H	HR	BB	SO	BR/9	ERA	AERA	OAV	OOB	PR	APR	PF	OSB	OCS	FA	E	WPB	DP	FW	PW	BW	BSW	DIF
EAST																												
Tor	11	11	344	**50**	1441.1	1441	134	620	1023	13.1	4.21	104	.261	.336	18	25	101	136	64	.982	107	89	144	.5	2.4	7.1	**1.7**	2.3
NY	11	**13**	332	38	1438.1	1467	170	552	899	12.8	4.35	96	.266	.333	-5	-29	97	115	47	.983	105	**40**	166	.6	-2.8	11.7	-.6	-1.8
Bal	21	10	329	42	1442.2	1427	153	579	900	12.8	4.31	105	.261	.333	2	30	104	96	64	.984	100	47	171	.9	2.9	.2	-.5	.6
Det	11	7	375	36	1436.2	1547	188	542	828	13.4	4.65	93	.276	.342	-52	-49	101	102	57	.979	132	76	148	-1.0	-4.8	**12.0**	-.2	-2.0
Bos	9	11	389	44	1452.1	**1379**	127	552	997	**12.3**	3.77	**122**	**.252**	**.322**	88	**128**	107	92	44	.980	122	53	155	-.4	**12.5**	-8.0	.0	-5.1
Cle	7	8	410	45	1445.2	1591	182	591	888	13.8	4.58	95	.281	.351	-41	-33	101	113	68	.976	148	50	**174**	-1.9	-3.2	-.9	1.3	-.3
Mil	**26**	6	353	29	1447.0	1511	153	522	810	13.0	4.45	97	.271	.336	-21	-24	100	115	51	.979	131	57	148	-.9	-2.3	-7.1	-.4	-1.2
WEST																												
Chi	16	11	322	48	1454.0	1398	125	566	974	12.4	**3.70**	114	.255	.328	**100**	83	97	**82**	**82**	.982	112	66	153	.2	8.1	1.9	.0	2.8
Tex	20	6	359	45	1438.1	1476	144	562	957	13.0	4.28	98	.267	.337	6	-16	97	95	67	.979	132	70	145	-1.0	-1.6	3.9	-.2	3.8
KC	16	6	303	48	1445.1	**1379**	**105**	571	985	12.4	4.04	114	.254	.327	45	84	107	119	71	.984	97	91	150	1.0	8.2	-10.9	-.6	5.3
Sea	22	10	353	41	1453.2	1421	135	605	**1083**	13.0	4.20	106	.259	.337	20	40	103	105	68	**.985**	**90**	70	173	**1.5**	3.9	-1.2	-.6	-2.5
Cal	**26**	6	320	41	1430.1	1482	153	550	843	13.1	4.34	104	.270	.339	-3	28	105	122	52	.980	120	65	161	-.3	2.7	-8.3	-.0	-4.1
Min	5	3	356	44	1444.1	1591	148	**514**	901	13.4	4.71	93	.283	.344	-63	-49	102	137	66	.984	100	64	160	.9	-4.8	-7.7	-.4	2.0
Oak	8	2	**424**	42	1452.1	1551	157	680	864	14.1	4.90	84	.276	.356	-94	-131	96	120	71	.982	111	54	161	.2	-12.7	-.3	.5	-.7
Total	209	110	4969	593	20222.1	—	—	—	—	13.0	4.32	—	.267	.337	—	—	—	—	—	.981	1607	892	2209	—	—	—	—	—

BATTER-FIELDER WINS	BATTING AVERAGE	ON-BASE PERCENTAGE	SLUGGING AVERAGE	ON-BASE PLUS SLUGGING	ADJUSTED OPS	ADJUSTED BATTER RUNS
Olerud-Tor.......... 5.7	Olerud-Tor............363	Olerud-Tor.............473	Gonzalez-Tex........632	Olerud-Tor..........1072	Olerud-Tor............184	Olerud-Tor............75.0
Hoiles-Bal.......... 5.3	Molitor-Tor............332	Phillips-Det...........443	Griffey-Sea...........617	Thomas-Chi........1033	Thomas-Chi..........179	Thomas-Chi.........66.8
Griffey-Sea......... 5.1	Alomar-Tor............326	Henderson-Oak-Tor..432	Thomas-Chi..........607	Griffey-Sea........1025	Griffey-Sea...........169	Griffey-Sea.........58.7
Palmeiro-Tex...... 4.9	Lofton-Cle.............325	Thomas-Chi..........426	Olerud-Tor.............599	Hoiles-Bal...........1001	Gonzalez-Tex........169	Gonzalez-Tex........48.8
Henderson-Oak-Tor...4.5	Baerga-Cle...........321	Hoiles-Bal.............416	Hoiles-Bal.............585	Gonzalez-Tex......1000	Hoiles-Bal.............159	Palmeiro-Tex........43.3

RUNS	HITS	DOUBLES	TRIPLES	HOME RUNS	TOTAL BASES	RUNS BATTED IN
Palmeiro-Tex.........124	Molitor-Tor.............211	Olerud-Tor..............54	Johnson-Chi...........14	Gonzalez-Tex..........46	Griffey-Sea..........359	Belle-Cle...............129
Molitor-Tor.............121	Olerud-Tor.............200	White-Tor...............42	Cora-Chi................13	Griffey-Sea...........45	Gonzalez-Tex.........339	Thomas-Chi.............128
White-Tor..............116	Baerga-Cle...........200	Valentin-Bos...........40	Hulse-Tex................10	Thomas-Chi............41	Thomas-Chi...........333	Carter-Tor............121
Lofton-Cle.............116	Alomar-Tor............192	Palmeiro-Tex...........40	McRae-KC...............9	Belle-Cle.................38	Palmeiro-Tex.........331	Gonzalez-Tex.........118
Henderson-Oak-Tor..114	Lofton-Cle............185	Puckett-Min.............39	Fernandez-Tor..........9	Palmeiro-Tex...........37	Olerud-Tor............330	Fielder-Det............117

BASES ON BALLS	STOLEN BASES	BASE STEALING RUNS	FIELDING RUNS-INFIELD	FIELDING RUNS-OUTFIELD	OUTFIELD ASSISTS	CATCHER CS PCT.
Phillips-Det..........132	Lofton-Cle..............70	Lofton-Cle...........10.5	Gallego-NY.........26.2	Kirby-Cle.............14.1	Kirby-Cle................19	Karkovice-Chi......53.8
Henderson-Oak-Tor..120	Polonia-Cal............55	Henderson-Oak-Tor...8.9	Boggs-NY............21.3	Hamilton-Mil.........10.7	Belle-Cle.................16	Valle-Sea.............45.6
Olerud-Tor.............114	Alomar-Tor..............55	Alomar-Tor.............6.8	Vizquel-Sea........19.7	Belle-Cle..............10.6	Puckett-Min............13	Ortiz-Cle..............45.3
Thomas-Chi............112	Henderson-Oak-Tor....53	White-Tor...............6.1	Joyner-KC............19.2	McLemore-Bal........9.0	McLemore-Bal........13	Rodriguez-Tex.......44.3
Tettleton-Det.........109	Curtis-Cal..............48	Johnson-Chi...........5.3	Whitaker-Det........18.3	Mack-Min...............8.9	Curtis-Cal..............13	Macfarlane-KC.......43.1

WINS	WINNING PCT.	WINS ABOVE TEAM	GAMES STARTED	COMPLETE GAMES	FEWEST HITS/GAME	FEWEST BB/GAME
McDowell-Chi.........22	Key-NY.................750	Johnson-Sea.........6.0	Moore-Det..............36	Finley-Cal..............13	Johnson-Sea.......6.52	Key-NY...............1.64
Johnson-Sea..........19	Johnson-Sea..........704	Key-NY..................5.9	Eldred-Mil...............36	Brown-Tex...............12	Appier-KC.............6.90	Darwin-Bos...........1.92
Hentgen-Tor............19	Appier-KC...............692	Appier-KC..............5.2	Tapani-Min.............35	McDowell-Chi.........10	Cone-KC...............7.26	Wells-Det..............2.02
	McDowell-Chi........688	Guzman-Tor............5.1	Langston-Cal..........35	Johnson-Sea..........10	Alvarez-Chi..........7.28	Tapani-Min...........2.27
	Hentgen-Tor............679	Wickman-NY...........4.9	Finley-Cal...............35	Eldred-Mil.................8	McDonald-Bal......7.56	Doherty-Det..........2.34

STRIKEOUTS	STRIKEOUTS/GAME	GAMES	SAVES	BASE RUNNERS/9	ADJUSTED RELIEF RUNS	RELIEF RANKING
Johnson-Sea........308	Johnson-Sea.....10.86	Harris-Bos..............80	D.Ward-Tor.............45	Montgomery-KC..9.27	Montgomery-KC..22.1	Montgomery-KC..44.2
Langston-Cal........196	Perez-NY.............8.17	Radinsky-Chi..........73	Montgomery-KC.....45	Aguilera-Min........9.33	D.Ward-Tor...........18.5	D.Ward-Tor............31.5
Guzman-Tor..........194	Guzman-Tor.........7.90	D.Ward-Tor..............71	Henke-Tex...............40	D.Ward-Tor............9.42	Hernandez-Chi....17.8	Hernandez-Chi.....29.1
Cone-KC...............191	Clemens-Bos.......7.51	Nelson-Sea..............71	Hernandez-Chi........38	Darwin-Bos..........9.73	Lilliquist-Cle.........14.0	Henke-Tex............23.3
Finley-Cal............187	Banks-Min...........7.25	Fossas-Bos.............71	Eckersley-Oak........36	Hernandez-Chi....9.84	Mills-Bal..............13.7	Lilliquist-Cle.........19.5

INNINGS PITCHED	OPPONENTS' AVG.	OPPONENTS' OBP	EARNED RUN AVERAGE	ADJUSTED ERA	ADJUSTED STARTER RUNS	PITCHER WINS
Eldred-Mil..........258.0	Johnson-Sea........203	Darwin-Bos...........272	Appier-KC............2.56	Appier-KC............180	Appier-KC............50.6	**Appier-KC........ 5.1**
McDowell-Chi......256.2	Appier-KC.............212	Appier-KC.............279	Alvarez-Chi..........2.95	Viola-Bos............148	Langston-Cal.......37.0	**Montgomery-KC 4.5**
Langston-Cal.....256.1	Cone-KC...............223	Key-NY.................279	Key-NY...............3.00	Finley-Cal............144	Johnson-Sea.......34.7	**Langston-Cal..... 3.8**
Johnson-Sea.....255.1	McDonald-Bal.......228	Johnson-Sea........290	Fernandez-Chi.....3.13	Alvarez-Chi...........143	Cone-KC..............33.4	**Finley-Cal.......... 3.5**
Cone-KC...........254.0	Bosio-Sea............229	Langston-Cal........295	Viola-Bos............3.14	Darwin-Bos...........142	Darwin-Bos..........33.4	**Darwin-Bos........ 3.5**

WALK-OFF TO THE NORTH

Tragedy struck in spring training as Cleveland pitchers Tim Crews and Steve Olin were killed in a boating accident. Indians hurler Bob Ojeda also was badly hurt in the crash. Cliff Young, another Cleveland pitcher, died in a truck accident in November. Also passing were second baseman Charlie Gehringer and catcher Bill Dickey, both Hall of Famers, and Royals owner Ewing Kauffman. It was the last season for George Brett, Robin Yount, Carlton Fisk and Nolan Ryan, all future Hall of Famers.

On the bright side, Bo Jackson made a remarkable comeback from hip replacement surgery, hitting 16 homers for the White Sox. Minnesota's Dave Winfield collected his 3,000th hit. Toronto first baseman John Olerud carried a .400 batting average into August; Olerud, Paul Molitor, and Roberto Alomar finished 1-2-3 in the batting race, a first for teammates. Outfielders Shawn Green (Blue Jays) and Jim Edmonds (Angels) began their careers.

Toronto in the East and Chicago in the West were runaway division winners. The visiting team won the first four games of the ALCS before Toronto finally won at home in Game 5. The Jays then won their second straight AL pennant by scoring 3 runs in the top of the ninth inning of Game 6. Alomar and Molitor were the hitting stars in an offensively-charged World Series against the Phillies, but it was Joe Carter's dramatic walk-off home run against "Wild Thing" Mitch Williams in the bottom of the ninth inning in Game 6 that gave the Jays their second consecutive world championship.

Ominously, Congress considered legislation that would take away baseball's exemption from antitrust laws as dark storm clouds gathered on the labor front. The silver lining was that the exciting 1993 season was played to completion in front of a record number of fans.

1992 NATIONAL LEAGUE

TEAM	W	L	T	PCT	GB	HW	HL	R	OR	PA	H	2B	3B	HR	BB	SO	HB	SH	AVG	OBP	SLG	OPS	AOPS	BR	ABR	PF	SB	CS	BSA	BSR
EAST																														
Pit	96	66	0	.593	—	**53**	28	**693**	595	6266	1409	272	**54**	106	569	872	25	89	.255	.324	.381	705	105	50	**53**	100	110	53	67	6
Mon	87	75	0	.537	9	43	38	648	581	6120	1381	263	37	102	463	976	43	82	.252	.313	.370	683	100	-3	1	99	196	63	76	**21**
StL	83	79	0	.512	13	45	36	631	604	6230	**1464**	262	44	94	495	996	32	68	**.262**	.323	.375	698	**107**	30	46	98	**208**	118	64	4
Chi	78	84	0	.481	18	43	38	593	624	6156	1420	221	41	104	417	**816**	31	78	.254	.307	.364	671	92	-35	-52	103	77	51	60	-1
NY	72	90	0	.444	24	41	40	599	653	6059	1254	259	17	93	**572**	956	28	74	.235	.310	.342	652	91	-50	-45	99	129	52	71	10
Phi	70	92	0	.432	26	41	40	686	717	6171	1392	255	36	118	509	1059	**52**	64	.253	.320	.377	697	103	28	28	100	127	31	**80**	17
WEST																														
Atl	98	64	0	.605	—	51	30	682	**569**	6142	1391	223	48	**138**	493	924	26	93	.254	.316	**.388**	704	99	32	-7	106	126	60	68	7
Cin	90	72	0	.556	8	**53**	28	660	609	6162	1418	**281**	44	99	563	888	21	66	.260	**.328**	.382	**710**	104	**61**	43	103	125	65	66	5
SD	82	80	0	.506	16	45	36	617	636	6074	1396	255	30	135	453	864	26	78	.255	.313	.386	699	101	23	12	102	69	52	57	-3
Hou	81	81	0	.500	17	47	34	608	668	6162	1350	255	38	96	506	1025	48	88	.246	.313	.359	672	100	-19	6	96	139	54	72	12
SF	72	90	0	.444	26	42	39	574	647	6070	1330	220	36	105	435	1067	39	101	.244	.302	.355	657	96	-60	-30	95	112	64	64	2
LA	63	99	0	.389	35	37	44	548	636	6037	1333	201	34	72	503	899	24	**102**	.248	.313	.339	652	92	-57	-51	99	142	78	65	4
Total	972	—	—	—	—	541	431	7539	—	73649	16538	2967	459	1262	5978	11342	395	983	.252	.315	.368	684	—	—	—	—	1560	741	68	84

TEAM	CG	SHO	GR	SV	IP	H	HR	BB	SO	BR/9	ERA	AERA	OAV	OOB	PR	APR	PF	OSB	OCS	FA	E	WPB	DP	FW	PW	BW	BSW	DIF
EAST																												
Pit	20	20	354	43	1479.2	1410	101	455	844	11.5	3.35	103	.254	.312	25	19	99	124	**73**	.984	101	63	144	.9	2.0	**5.7**	-.1	6.5
Mon	11	14	349	49	1468.0	**1296**	92	525	1014	11.5	3.25	107	**.238**	.309	41	38	99	199	68	.980	124	57	113	-.4	4.1	.1	**1.5**	.7
StL	10	9	**424**	47	1480.0	1405	118	**400**	842	**11.2**	3.38	101	.252	**.303**	20	6	98	124	39	**.985**	**94**	49	146	**1.3**	.6	5.0	-.3	-4.6
Chi	16	11	372	37	1469.0	1337	107	575	901	12.0	3.39	107	.246	.320	18	36	103	116	72	.982	114	82	142	.2	3.9	-5.6	-.9	-.6
NY	17	13	333	34	1446.2	1404	98	482	1025	12.0	3.66	96	.256	.318	-25	-26	100	148	67	.981	116	44	134	.0	-2.8	-4.8	.3	-1.7
Phi	**27**	7	323	34	1428.0	1387	113	549	851	12.4	4.11	85	.257	.325	-96	-96	100	111	53	.978	131	56	128	-.8	-10.3	3.0	1.1	-4.0
WEST																												
Atl	26	**24**	338	41	1460.0	1321	89	489	948	11.3	**3.14**	**116**	.242	.305	**58**	**80**	104	149	66	.982	109	71	121	.4	**8.6**	-.8	.0	8.7
Cin	9	11	357	**55**	1449.2	1362	109	470	**1060**	11.5	3.46	104	.251	.312	6	21	103	104	54	.984	96	62	128	1.2	2.3	4.6	-.2	1.2
SD	9	11	363	46	1461.1	1444	111	439	971	11.7	3.56	101	.261	.315	-9	4	102	141	69	.982	115	**27**	127	.0	.4	1.3	-1.1	.3
Hou	5	12	422	45	1459.1	1386	114	539	978	12.1	3.72	91	.252	.320	-35	-56	97	129	54	.981	114	58	125	.2	-6.0	.6	.5	4.7
SF	9	12	386	30	1461.0	1385	128	502	927	11.8	3.61	92	.253	.318	-17	-48	95	**74**	64	.982	113	50	**174**	.2	-5.2	-3.2	-.5	-.3
LA	18	13	353	29	1438.0	1401	**82**	553	981	12.4	3.41	102	.257	.326	15	9	99	141	62	.972	174	84	136	-3.2	1.0	-5.5	-.3	-9.9
Total	177	157	4374	490	17500.2	—	—	—	—	11.8	3.50	—	.252	.315	—	—	—	—	—	.981	1401	703	1618	—	—	—	—	—

BATTER-FIELDER WINS	BATTING AVERAGE	ON-BASE PERCENTAGE	SLUGGING AVERAGE	ON-BASE PLUS SLUGGING	ADJUSTED OPS	ADJUSTED BATTER RUNS
Bonds-Pit............7.9	Sheffield-SD 330	Bonds-Pit..............456	Bonds-Pit..............624	Bonds-Pit............1080	Bonds-Pit..............205	Bonds-Pit.............75.1
Sheffield-SD.......6.0	VanSlyke-Pit 324	Kruk-Phi.................423	Sheffield-SD 580	Sheffield-SD 965	Sheffield-SD 168	Sheffield-SD 49.0
Sandberg-Chi.....5.6	Kruk-Phi.................323	Butler-LA...............413	McGriff-SD............556	McGriff-SD............950	McGriff-SD............164	McGriff-SD...........47.4
Larkin-Cin...........5.5	Roberts-Cin 323	McGriff-SD............394	Daulton-Phi...........524	Daulton-Phi...........908	Daulton-Phi...........156	VanSlyke-Pit 41.5
Daulton-Phi 4.9	Gwynn-SD 317	Roberts-Cin 393	Sandberg-Chi 510	VanSlyke-Pit 886	Clark-SF 152	Kruk-Phi...............40.0

RUNS	HITS	DOUBLES	TRIPLES	HOME RUNS	TOTAL BASES	RUNS BATTED IN
Bonds-Pit.............109	VanSlyke-Pit 199	VanSlyke-Pit 45	Sanders-Atl.............14	McGriff-SD..............35	Sheffield-SD 323	Daulton-Phi...........109
Hollins-Phi 104	Pendleton-Atl 199	Lankford-StL 40	Finley-Hou 13	Bonds-Pit................34	Sandberg-Chi 312	Pendleton-Atl 105
VanSlyke-Pit 103	Sandberg-Chi 186	Duncan-Phi.............40	VanSlyke-Pit 12	Sheffield-SD 33	VanSlyke-Pit 310	McGriff-SD............104
Sandberg-Chi 100	Grace-Chi 185	Clark-SF 40	Butler-LA.................11	Hollins-Phi 27	Pendleton-Atl 303	Bonds-Pit..............103
Grissom-Mon..........99	Sheffield-SD 184		Alicea-StL 11	Daulton-Phi.............27		Sheffield-SD 100

BASES ON BALLS	STOLEN BASES	BASE STEALING RUNS	FIELDING RUNS-INFIELD	FIELDING RUNS-OUTFIELD	OUTFIELD ASSISTS	CATCHER CS PCT.
Bonds-Pit.............127	Grissom-Mon..........78	Grissom-Mon.......12.6	Thompson-SF......25.5	Jackson-SD 14.4	Jackson-SD 18	Manwaring-SF 50.5
McGriff-SD..............96	DeShields-Mon.......46	Finley-Hou 6.5	Wallach-Mon........18.7	Gonzalez-Hou......13.5	Walker-Mon 16	Girardi-Chi 41.0
Butler-LA.................95	Roberts-Cin 44	O.Smith-StL 6.3	Sharperson-LA 18.2	Sanders-Cin.........10.7	O'Neill-Cin 12	Olson-Atl..............39.1
Biggio-Hou..............94	Finley-Hou 44	Bonds-Pit...............5.8	Harris-LA 15.8	Nixon-Atl.................9.5		Santiago-SD 36.5
Kruk-Phi..................92	O.Smith-StL 43	DeShields-Mon......4.9	O.Smith-StL 15.8	O'Neill-Cin 9.2		Daulton-Phi..........35.8

WINS	WINNING PCT.	WINS ABOVE TEAM	GAMES STARTED	COMPLETE GAMES	FEWEST HITS/GAME	FEWEST BB/GAME
Maddux-Chi 20	Tewksbury-StL 762	Tewksbury-StL 5.7	Smoltz-Atl 35	Mulholland-Phi........12	Schilling-Phi.........6.56	Tewksbury-StL 77
Glavine-Atl 20	Glavine-Atl 714	Maddux-Chi 5.6	Maddux-Chi 35	Schilling-Phi............10	Maddux-Chi 6.75	Cormier-StL 1.60
	Leibrandt-Atl 682	Morgan-Chi............4.7	Avery-Atl 35	Drabek-Pit...............10	Fernandez-NY 6.79	Swindell-Cin.........1.73
	Morgan-Chi...........667	Glavine-Atl 4.4		Smoltz-Atl 9	Martinez-Mon 6.84	Mulholland-Phi.....1.81
	Maddux-Chi 645	Hernandez-Hou 4.0		Maddux-Chi 9	Cone-NY.............7.41	Tomlin-Pit............1.81

STRIKEOUTS	STRIKEOUTS/GAME	GAMES	SAVES	BASE RUNNERS/9	ADJUSTED RELIEF RUNS	RELIEF RANKING
Smoltz-Atl 215	Cone-NY..............9.79	Boever-Hou.............81	L.Smith-StL.............43	Beck-SF 7.73	Rojas-Mon 23.4	D.Jones-Hou........36.1
Cone-NY................214	Fernandez-NY 8.09	D.Jones-Hou...........80	Myers-SD................38	Schilling-Phi.........8.95	D.Jones-Hou........18.0	Rojas-Mon 20.9
Maddux-Chi 199	Smoltz-Atl 7.84	Perez-StL................77	Wetteland-Mon 37	Tewksbury-StL 9.27	Beck-SF 16.9	Perez-StL.............18.2
Fernandez-NY 193	Rijo-Cin................7.29	Hernandez-Hou 77	D.Jones-Hou............36	D.Jones-Hou........9.51	Perez-StL.............15.7	Beck-SF 15.5
Drabek-Pit.............177	Harnisch-Hou 7.14	Innis-NY..................76	M.Williams-Phi........29	Rojas-Mon 9.57	Hernandez-Hou ...15.3	Hernandez-Hou ...14.1

INNINGS PITCHED	OPPONENTS' AVG.	OPPONENTS' OBP	EARNED RUN AVERAGE	ADJUSTED ERA	ADJUSTED STARTER RUNS	PITCHER WINS
Maddux-Chi 268.0	Schilling-Phi..........201	Schilling-Phi..........253	Swift-SF 2.08	Maddux-Chi 166	Maddux-Chi 43.9	**Maddux-Chi........6.0**
Drabek-Pit..........256.2	Maddux-Chi 210	Tewksbury-StL 265	Tewksbury-StL 2.16	Swift-SF 160	Tewksbury-StL 32.4	**D.Jones-Hou 3.9**
Smoltz-Atl 246.2	Fernandez-NY 210	Martinez-Mon 271	Maddux-Chi 2.18	Tewksbury-StL 158	Schilling-Phi.........28.2	**Schilling-Phi.......3.0**
Morgan-Chi........240.0	Martinez-Mon 211	Maddux-Chi 272	Schilling-Phi.........2.35	Schilling-Phi..........150	Morgan-Chi..........26.3	**Glavine-Atl 3.0**
Avery-Atl 233.2	Cone-NY...............223	Fernandez-NY 273	Martinez-Mon 2.47	Morgan-Chi...........142	Swift-SF 24.7	**Rijo-Cin 3.0**

PIRATES LEAVE THEIR HEART WITH FRANCISCO

Commissioner Fay Vincent announced his plan to realign the divisions, which would have put Atlanta and Cincinnati in the East and St. Louis and Chicago in the West, making the layout geographical. The Reds and Cubs vehemently opposed the move, which was later blocked by a U.S. District Court judge. That debacle, combined with an inability to break the union, sealed the commish's fate as owners voted 18-9 to fire Vincent, who finally resigned in September. One of Vincent's most outspoken critics was Milwaukee owner Bud Selig, who effectively became commissioner as chair of the owners' Executive Council. Owners also prevented the Giants from moving to Tampa-St. Petersburg.

The Reds were in turmoil again, with skipper Lou Piniella and reliever Rob Dibble fighting in the clubhouse, and owner Marge Schott accused of making anti-Semitic remarks. Pedro Martinez and Mike Piazza, debuted for the Dodgers in September, while Gary Carter, Jack Clark and Pedro Guerrero called it a career. Hall of Fame second baseman Billy Herman passed away. Philadelphia's Mickey Morandini turned the league's first unassisted triple play since 1927.

Barry Bonds won his second MVP award and led the Pirates and an unheralded mound staff to a third consecutive East title. Atlanta, with strong starters and a mix-and-match bullpen, took its second straight West crown. The Braves again eliminated Pittsburgh in a thrilling seven-game NLCS. The Braves were down 2-0 in the last of the ninth of Game 7. But the Pirates fell apart on the hill and in the field, and Sid Bream slid in with the winning run with two outs on pinch hitter Francisco Cabrera's two-run single. After this emotional peak, however, Atlanta lost the World Series again, this time to Toronto in six games.

1992 AMERICAN LEAGUE

TEAM	W	L	T	PCT	GB	HW	HL	R	OR	PA	H	2B	3B	HR	BB	SO	HB	SH	AVG	OBP	SLG	OPS	AOPS	BR	ABR	PF	SB	CS	BSA	BSR
EAST																														
Tor	96	66	0	.593	—	**53**	28	780	682	6224	1458	265	40	163	561	933	47	26	.263	.333	**.414**	**747**	103	63	27	105	129	39	**77**	15
Mil	92	70	0	.568	4	**53**	28	740	**604**	6181	1477	272	35	82	511	779	33	61	.268	.330	.375	705	98	-11	-1	99	**256**	115	69	**16**
Bal	89	73	0	.549	7	43	38	705	656	6292	1423	243	36	148	647	827	51	50	.259	.340	.398	738	103	56	32	103	89	48	65	3
NY	76	86	0	.469	20	41	40	733	746	6252	1462	281	18	163	536	903	42	26	.261	.328	.406	734	104	35	36	100	78	37	68	4
Cle	76	86	0	.469	20	41	40	674	746	6199	1495	227	24	127	448	885	45	42	.266	.323	.383	706	98	-27	-19	99	144	67	68	8
Det	75	87	0	.463	21	38	42	**791**	794	6310	1411	256	16	**182**	675	1055	24	43	.256	.337	.407	744	106	**65**	54	101	66	45	59	-1
Bos	73	89	0	.451	23	44	37	599	669	6186	1343	259	21	84	591	865	31	60	.246	.321	.347	668	81	-83	-125	107	44	48	48	-7
WEST																														
Oak	96	66	0	.593	—	51	30	745	672	6274	1389	219	24	142	**707**	831	49	**72**	.258	**.346**	.386	732	**110**	55	**93**	95	143	59	71	11
Min	90	72	0	.556	6	48	33	747	653	6267	**1544**	275	27	104	527	834	**53**	46	**.277**	.341	.391	732	101	47	19	104	123	74	62	1
Chi	86	76	0	.531	10	50	32	738	690	6267	1434	269	36	110	622	784	31	47	.261	.336	.383	719	102	21	26	99	160	57	74	15
Tex	77	85	0	.475	19	36	45	682	753	6238	1387	266	23	159	550	1036	50	56	.250	.321	.393	714	102	-5	17	97	81	44	65	2
KC	72	90	0	.444	24	44	37	610	667	6082	1411	**284**	**42**	75	439	**741**	51	45	.256	.315	.364	679	87	-74	-94	103	131	71	65	4
Cal	72	90	0	.444	24	41	40	579	671	5916	1306	202	20	88	416	882	40	56	.243	.301	.338	639	78	-158	-164	101	160	101	61	0
Sea	64	98	0	.395	32	38	43	679	799	6179	1466	278	24	149	474	841	38	52	.263	.323	.402	725	101	13	5	101	100	55	65	3
Total	1134	—	—	—	—	621	513	9802	—	86867	20006	3596	386	1776	7704	12196	585	682	.259	.328	.385	713	—	—	—	—	1704	860	66	74

TEAM	CG	SHO	GR	SV	IP	H	HR	BB	SO	BR/9	ERA	AERA	OAV	OOB	PR	APR	PF	OSB	OCS	FA	E	WPB	DP	FW	PW	BW	BSW	DIF
EAST																												
Tor	18	14	284	49	1440.2	1346	124	541	954	12.1	3.91	105	.248	.318	5	29	104	144	63	.985	93	81	109	1.4	3.0	2.7	1.0	6.9
Mil	19	14	338	39	1457.0	**1344**	127	**435**	793	**11.3**	**3.43**	113	**.246**	**.305**	**82**	71	98	96	53	**.986**	**89**	**42**	146	**1.6**	7.2	-.1	**1.1**	1.2
Bal	20	**16**	290	48	1464.0	1419	124	518	846	12.1	3.79	107	.256	.322	25	43	103	131	44	.985	93	60	168	1.4	4.4	3.3	-.2	-.8
NY	20	9	308	44	1452.2	1453	129	612	851	13.0	4.21	94	.263	.338	-43	-42	100	164	62	.982	114	68	165	.2	-4.3	3.7	-.1	-4.5
Cle	13	7	379	46	1470.0	1507	159	566	890	12.9	4.11	96	.268	.336	-28	-29	100	109	64	.978	141	62	**176**	-1.3	-3.0	-1.9	.3	.9
Det	10	4	355	36	1435.2	1534	155	564	693	13.3	4.60	87	.277	.343	-105	-96	101	102	62	.981	116	65	164	.1	-9.8	5.5	-.6	-1.2
Bos	22	13	328	39	1448.2	1403	107	535	943	12.3	3.58	**118**	.255	.323	57	**98**	108	114	51	.978	139	58	170	-1.2	**10.0**	-12.7	-1.3	-2.9
WEST																												
Oak	8	9	**400**	**58**	1447.0	1396	129	601	843	12.7	3.73	101	.256	.331	34	7	96	118	76	.979	125	75	158	-.4	.7	**9.5**	.6	4.6
Min	16	13	323	50	1453.0	1391	121	479	923	11.8	3.70	110	.254	.316	38	58	104	152	60	.985	95	66	155	1.3	5.9	1.9	-.4	.3
Chi	21	5	292	52	1461.2	1400	123	550	810	12.3	3.82	101	.252	.323	19	9	98	120	57	.979	129	48	134	-.6	.9	2.6	1.0	1.0
Tex	19	3	359	42	1460.1	1471	113	598	**1034**	13.0	4.09	93	.264	.337	-24	-45	97	**87**	**84**	.975	154	91	153	-2.0	-4.6	1.7	-.3	1.2
KC	9	12	340	44	1447.1	1426	**106**	512	834	12.3	3.81	107	.259	.323	21	41	104	107	52	.980	122	56	164	-.2	4.2	-9.6	-.1	-3.3
Cal	**26**	13	297	42	1446.0	1449	130	532	888	12.6	3.84	104	.264	.331	16	27	102	120	70	.979	134	47	172	-.9	2.7	-16.7	-.5	6.4
Sea	21	9	372	30	1445.0	1467	129	661	894	13.6	4.55	88	.266	.348	-97	-87	102	140	62	.982	112	70	170	.3	-8.9	.5	-.2	-8.8
Total	242	141	4665	619	20329.0	—	—	—	—	12.5	3.94	—	.259	.328	—	—	—	—	—	.981	1656	889	2204	—	—	—	—	—

BATTER-FIELDER WINS	BATTING AVERAGE	ON-BASE PERCENTAGE	SLUGGING AVERAGE	ON-BASE PLUS SLUGGING	ADJUSTED OPS	ADJUSTED BATTER RUNS
Ventura-Chi........5.1	E.Martinez-Sea.....343	Thomas-Chi..........439	McGwire-Oak........585	Thomas-Chi..........975	McGwire-Oak........178	Thomas-Chi.........66.4
E.Martinez-Sea..4.9	Puckett-Min...........329	Tartabull-NY..........409	E.Martinez-Sea.....544	McGwire-Oak........970	Thomas-Chi..........175	McGwire-Oak.......51.0
R.Henderson-Oak...4.5	Thomas-Chi...........323	Alomar-Tor............405	Thomas-Chi..........536	E.Martinez-Sea.....948	E.Martinez-Sea.....162	E.Martinez-Sea.....45.4
Thomas-Chi........4.4	Molitor-Mil.............320	E.Martinez-Sea.....404	Griffey-Sea...........535	Tartabull-NY..........898	Tartabull-NY..........151	R.Henderson-Oak36.4
Baerga-Cle.........3.7	Mack-Min..............315	Mack-Min..............394	Gonzalez-Tex........529	Griffey-Sea...........896	Griffey-Sea...........147	Molitor-Mil............35.7
RUNS	**HITS**	**DOUBLES**	**TRIPLES**	**HOME RUNS**	**TOTAL BASES**	**RUNS BATTED IN**
Phillips-Det...........114	Puckett-Min...........210	Thomas-Chi............46	Johnson-Chi...........12	Gonzalez-Tex..........43	Puckett-Min..........313	Fielder-Det............124
Thomas-Chi..........108	Baerga-Cle...........205	E.Martinez-Sea.......46	Devereaux-Bal........11	McGwire-Oak..........42	Carter-Tor............310	Carter-Tor.............119
Alomar-Tor............105	Molitor-Mil.............195	Yount-Mil...............40	Anderson-Bal..........10	Fielder-Det.............35	Gonzalez-Tex........309	Thomas-Chi............115
Puckett-Min...........104	Mack-Min..............189	Mattingly-NY...........40	Raines-Chi...............9	Carter-Tor..............34	Thomas-Chi..........307	Belle-Cle...............112
Knoblauch-Min......104	Thomas-Chi...........185	Griffey-Sea.............39		Belle-Cle.................34	Devereaux-Bal......303	Bell-Chi..................112
BASES ON BALLS	**STOLEN BASES**	**BASE STEALING RUNS**	**FIELDING RUNS-INFIELD**	**FIELDING RUNS-OUTFIELD**	**OUTFIELD ASSISTS**	**CATCHER CS PCT.**
Thomas-Chi...........122	Lofton-Cle...............66	Lofton-Cle............10.3	Reed-Bos..............30.4	Raines-Chi...............9.6	Curtis-Cal...............16	Rodriguez-Tex.....51.8
Tettleton-Det.........122	Listach-Mil..............54	Raines-Chi.............7.8	Ventura-Chi..........26.1	Wilson-Oak.............8.1	Whiten-Cle..............14	Alomar-Cle...........44.9
Phillips-Det...........114	Anderson-Bal..........53	Alomar-Tor..............7.6	Gagne-Min............19.3	White-Tor................7.3	Lofton-Cle...............14	Pena-Bos..............33.1
Milligan-Bal...........106	Polonia-Cal.............51	White-Tor................6.7	Sojo-Cal................14.4	Lofton-Cle...............7.0	Buhner-Sea.............14	Valle-Sea..............32.3
Tartabull-NY..........103	Alomar-Tor..............49	R.Henderson-Oak..6.7	Gaetti-Cal.............13.7	Anderson-Bal..........5.4		Ortiz-Cle...............31.4
WINS	**WINNING PCT.**	**WINS ABOVE TEAM**	**GAMES STARTED**	**COMPLETE GAMES**	**FEWEST HITS/GAME**	**FEWEST BB/GAME**
Morris-Tor..............21	Mussina-Bal..........783	Morris-Tor..............6.8	Sutcliffe-Bal...........36	McDowell-Chi.........13	Johnson-Sea.......6.59	Bosio-Mil..............1.71
Brown-Tex...............21	Morris-Tor.............778	Mussina-Bal............6.4	Moore-Oak..............36	Clemens-Bos...........11	Guzman-Tor.........6.73	Mussina-Bal..........1.79
McDowell-Chi..........20	Guzman-Tor...........762	Brown-Tex...............6.3		Brown-Tex...............11	Appier-KC............7.21	Wegman-Mil.........1.89
Mussina-Bal............18	Bosio-Mil...............727	Fleming-Sea...........5.8		Perez-NY.................10	Clemens-Bos.......7.41	Tapani-Min............1.96
Clemens-Bos..........18	McDowell-Chi.......667	Clemens-Bos.........5.1		Nagy-Cle..................10	Smiley-Min...........7.66	Gullickson-Det.....2.03
STRIKEOUTS	**STRIKEOUTS/GAME**	**GAMES**	**SAVES**	**BASE RUNNERS/9**	**ADJUSTED RELIEF RUNS**	**RELIEF RANKING**
Johnson-Sea........241	Johnson-Sea.....10.31	Rogers-Tex.............81	Eckersley-Oak........51	Eckersley-Oak.....8.32	D.Ward-Tor...........22.0	Eckersley-Oak.....35.7
Perez-NY...............218	Guzman-Tor.........8.22	D.Ward-Tor.............79	Aguilera-Min...........41	Lilliquist-Cle.........8.61	Eckersley-Oak.....18.3	Olin-Cle................29.8
Clemens-Bos.........208	Perez-NY..............7.92	Olin-Cle..................72	Montgomery-KC.....39	Hernandez-Chi....8.75	Harris-Bos............17.9	J.Russell-Tex-Oak....28.1
Guzman-Tex.........179	Clemens-Bos........7.59	Lilliquist-Cle..........71	Olson-Bal...............36	Eldred-Mil.............9.06	Hernandez-Chi.....17.7	Hernandez-Chi....27.3
McDowell-Chi........178	Guzman-Tex.........7.19	Harris-Bos..............70	Henke-Tor..............34	Willis-Min.............9.53	Frohwirth-Bal.......17.4	D.Ward-Tor...........25.8
INNINGS PITCHED	**OPPONENTS' AVG.**	**OPPONENTS' OBP**	**EARNED RUN AVERAGE**	**ADJUSTED ERA**	**ADJUSTED STARTER RUNS**	**PITCHER WINS**
Brown-Tex.........265.2	Johnson-Sea........206	Mussina-Bal..........278	Clemens-Bos.......2.41	Clemens-Bos........177	Clemens-Bos.......45.1	**Clemens-Bos.....5.3**
Wegman-Mil.......261.2	Guzman-Tor..........207	Clemens-Bos.........278	Appier-KC...........2.46	Appier-KC.............166	Mussina-Bal.........40.9	**Appier-KC.........4.1**
McDowell-Chi....260.2	Appier-KC.............217	Appier-KC.............281	Mussina-Bal.........2.54	Mussina-Bal..........160	Appier-KC...........37.7	**Mussina-Bal.......3.8**
Nagy-Cle............252.0	Clemens-Bos........224	Smiley-Min............286	Guzman-Tor.........2.64	Guzman-Tor..........156	Guzman-Tor.........29.1	**Eckersley-Oak...3.8**
Perez-NY............247.2	Smiley-Min............231	Guzman-Tor...........286	Abbott-Cal...........2.77	Abbott-Cal............145	Nagy-Cle..............27.9	**Guzman-Tor.......3.2**

A Special on Canadian Club

Oriole Park at Camden Yards opened in April, making several other parks instantly obsolete. It started a craze for ballparks designed with idiosyncrasies, asymmetrical dimensions, and memorable features, like the Baltimore & Ohio Warehouse beyond right field. Camden Yards drew three million people for every non-strike season through 2001.

In August Bret Boone debuted with Seattle. Following grandfather Ray and dad Bob, Bret became the first third-generation player in big league history. Rookie Jeff Kent was part of the year's biggest trading deadline deal, going from Toronto to the Mets for David Cone. It was the final season for Bert Blyleven, Brian Downing, and Willie Randolph. Jean Yawkey, Red Sox owner since 1976, died without an heir, leaving the club out of family control for the first time since 1933.

Milwaukee's Robin Yount and Kansas City's George Brett each surpassed 3,000 career hits. Texas' Juan Gonzalez hammered 43 long balls to become, at 22, the youngest home run champ ever. Oakland reliever Dennis Eckersley won both the MVP and Cy Young awards.

Bolstered by Mark McGwire's 42 homers, Oakland, which traded Jose Canseco to Texas at midseason, again won the West. The A's were denied a fourth straight World Series appearance by Toronto, winners in the East by just 4 games over surprising Milwaukee.

The Blue Jays were sparked by a great season from second sacker Roberto Alomar and won four of the last five ALCS contests, slugging 10 home runs and hitting Eckersley hard. Toronto capped its magic season by beating the Braves in six games in the World Series. Pat Borders' timely hitting and some excellent bullpen work helped the Jays win a low-scoring series, bringing the World Series trophy north of the border for the first time.

1991 NATIONAL LEAGUE

TEAM	W	L	T	PCT	GB	HW	HL	R	OR	PA	H	2B	3B	HR	BB	SO	HB	SH	AVG	OBP	SLG	OPS	AOPS	BR	ABR	PF	SB	CS	BSA	BSR
East																														
Pit	98	64	0	.605	—	52	32	**768**	632	6269	**1433**	**259**	50	126	**620**	901	35	**99**	**.263**	**.338**	.398	**736**	**114**	**107**	**115**	99	124	46	73	11
StL	84	78	0	.519	14	52	32	651	648	6020	1366	239	**53**	68	532	857	21	58	.255	.322	.357	679	96	-13	-20	101	202	110	65	6
Phi	78	84	0	.481	20	47	36	629	680	6133	1332	248	33	111	490	1026	21	52	.241	.303	.358	661	92	-60	-54	99	92	30	**75**	10
Chi	77	83	0	.481	20	46	37	695	734	6130	1395	232	26	159	442	879	36	75	.253	.309	.390	699	97	9	-21	105	123	64	66	5
NY	77	84	0	.478	20.5	40	42	640	646	6076	1305	250	24	117	578	**789**	27	60	.244	.317	.365	682	97	-6	-3	100	153	70	69	9
Mon	71	90	0	.441	26.5	33	35	579	655	6035	1329	236	42	95	484	1056	28	64	.246	.308	.357	665	93	-48	-41	99	**221**	100	69	**14**
West																														
Atl	94	68	0	.580	—	48	33	749	644	6182	1407	255	30	141	563	906	32	86	.258	.328	.393	721	102	68	28	106	165	76	68	10
LA	93	69	0	.574	1	**54**	27	665	**565**	6159	1366	191	29	108	583	957	28	94	.253	.326	.359	685	100	0	12	98	126	68	65	4
SD	84	78	0	.519	10	42	39	636	646	6057	1321	204	36	121	501	1069	32	78	.244	.310	.362	672	91	-38	-57	103	101	64	61	0
SF	75	87	0	.463	19	43	38	649	697	6097	1345	215	48	141	471	973	**40**	90	.246	.309	.381	690	102	-12	7	97	95	57	63	1
Cin	74	88	0	.457	20	39	42	689	691	6134	1419	250	27	**164**	488	1006	32	72	.258	.320	**.403**	723	104	58	30	104	124	56	69	8
Hou	65	97	0	.401	29	37	44	605	717	6147	1345	240	43	79	502	1027	35	63	.244	.309	.347	656	95	-65	-31	95	125	68	65	4
Total	970	—	—	—	—	533	437	7955	—	73439	16363	2819	441	1430	6254	11446	367	891	.250	.317	.373	689	—	—	—	—	1651	809	67	80

TEAM	CG	SHO	GR	SV	IP	H	HR	BB	SO	BR/9	ERA	AERA	OAV	OOB	PR	APR	PF	OSB	OCS	FA	E	WPB	DP	FW	PW	BW	BSW	DIF
East																												
Pit	**18**	11	353	**51**	1456.2	1411	117	**401**	919	11.4	3.44	104	.256	.308	39	26	98	142	73	.981	120	49	134	.4	2.7	**12.0**	.5	1.5
StL	9	5	**369**	**51**	1435.1	1367	114	454	822	11.7	3.69	102	.255	.315	0	10	102	121	81	**.982**	**107**	**41**	133	**1.1**	1.0	-2.1	-.0	3.0
Phi	16	11	321	35	1463.0	1346	111	670	988	12.7	3.86	96	.246	.329	-29	-27	100	151	47	.981	119	90	111	.4	-2.8	-5.6	.3	4.7
Chi	12	4	360	40	1456.2	1415	117	542	927	12.3	4.03	97	.257	.324	-57	-21	106	139	64	**.982**	113	67	120	.7	-2.2	-2.2	-.2	.9
NY	12	11	314	39	1437.1	1403	108	410	1028	11.5	3.56	103	.257	.309	20	18	100	134	75	.977	143	71	112	-1.0	1.9	-.3	.2	-4.3
Mon	12	**14**	367	39	1440.1	**1304**	111	584	909	12.0	3.64	100	.244	.320	7	0	99	149	81	.979	133	73	128	-.4	.0	-4.3	**.8**	-5.5
West																												
Atl	**18**	7	345	48	1452.2	**1304**	118	481	969	**11.2**	3.49	111	**.240**	**.303**	32	60	105	149	59	.978	138	80	122	-.7	6.3	2.9	.3	4.1
LA	15	**14**	367	40	1458.0	1312	**96**	500	1028	11.4	**3.06**	**118**	.241	.306	**101**	**90**	98	145	60	.980	123	56	126	.2	**9.4**	1.3	-.3	1.4
SD	14	11	334	47	1452.2	1385	139	457	921	11.5	3.57	106	.252	.308	18	36	103	**109**	65	**.982**	113	58	130	.8	3.8	-6.0	-.7	5.1
SF	10	10	334	45	1442.0	1397	143	544	905	12.3	4.03	89	.257	.326	-56	-72	98	129	**83**	**.982**	109	53	**151**	1.0	-7.5	.7	-.6	.4
Cin	7	11	354	43	1440.0	1372	127	560	997	12.3	3.83	99	.253	.323	-24	-4	103	140	60	.979	125	80	131	.0	-.4	3.1	.1	-9.9
Hou	7	13	365	36	1453.0	1347	129	651	**1033**	12.6	4.00	88	.247	.328	-51	-80	96	143	61	.974	161	62	129	-2.0	-8.4	-3.2	-.3	-2.1
Total	150	122	4183	514	17387.2	—	—	—	—	11.9	3.68	—	.250	.317	—	—	—	—	—	.980	1504	780	1527	—	—	—	—	—

BATTER-FIELDER WINS	BATTING AVERAGE	ON-BASE PERCENTAGE	SLUGGING AVERAGE	ON-BASE PLUS SLUGGING	ADJUSTED OPS	ADJUSTED BATTER RUNS
Larkin-Cin 6.2	Pendleton-Atl .319	Bonds-Pit .410	Clark-SF .536	Bonds-Pit .924	Bonds-Pit 162	Bonds-Pit 48.2
Bonds-Pit 5.6	Morris-Cin .318	Butler-LA .401	Johnson-NY .535	Clark-SF .895	Clark-SF 153	Bonilla-Pit 42.6
Pendleton-Atl 5.1	Gwynn-SD .317	McGriff-SD .396	Pendleton-Atl .517	McGriff-SD .890	Bonilla-Pit 150	Clark-SF 38.1
Bonilla-Pit 4.3	McGee-SF .312	Bonilla-Pit .391	Bonds-Pit .514	Larkin-Cin .884	Johnson-NY 146	McGriff-SD 36.0
Thompson-SF 3.6	Jose-StL .305	Bagwell-Hou .387	Larkin-Cin .506	Bonilla-Pit .883	McGriff-SD 145	Johnson-NY 34.1
RUNS	**HITS**	**DOUBLES**	**TRIPLES**	**HOME RUNS**	**TOTAL BASES**	**RUNS BATTED IN**
Butler-LA 112	Pendleton-Atl 187	Bonilla-Pit 44	Lankford-StL 15	Johnson-NY 38	Pendleton-Atl 303	Johnson-NY 117
Johnson-NY 108	Butler-LA 182	Jose-StL 40	Gwynn-SD 11	Williams-SF 34	Clark-SF 303	Clark-SF 116
Sandberg-Chi 104	Sabo-Cin 175	Zeile-StL 36	Finley-Hou 10	Gant-Atl 32	Johnson-NY 302	Bonds-Pit 116
Bonilla-Pit 102	Bonilla-Pit 174	O'Neill-Cin 36	Grissom-Mon 9	McGriff-SD 31	Williams-SF 294	McGriff-SD 106
Gant-Atl 101	Jose-StL 173		Gonzalez-Hou 9	Dawson-Chi 31	Sabo-Cin 294	Gant-Atl 105
BASES ON BALLS	**STOLEN BASES**	**BASE STEALING RUNS**	**FIELDING RUNS-INFIELD**	**FIELDING RUNS-OUTFIELD**	**OUTFIELD ASSISTS**	**CATCHER CS PCT.**
Butler-LA 108	Grissom-Mon 76	Grissom-Mon 10.8	Lind-Pit 25.8	Gonzalez-Hou 8.9	Jose-StL 15	Cerone-NY 45.1
Bonds-Pit 107	Nixon-Atl 72	Nixon-Atl 8.5	Larkin-Cin 22.9	O'Neill-Cin 8.8	Grissom-Mon 15	Wilkins-Chi 39.5
McGriff-SD 105	DeShields-Mon 56	Bonds-Pit 4.9	Griffin-LA 20.8	Grissom-Mon 8.2	O'Neill-Cin 13	Reed-Cin 32.9
DeShields-Mon 95	Lankford-StL 44	O.Smith-StL 4.6	Pendleton-Atl 19.6	Bonds-Pit 6.4	Finley-Hou 13	LaValliere-Pit 30.2
Bonilla-Pit 90	Bonds-Pit 43	DeShields-Mon 4.3	Grace-Chi 16.8	Gwynn-SD 4.7	Bonds-Pit 13	Oliver-Cin 28.6
WINS	**WINNING PCT.**	**WINS ABOVE TEAM**	**GAMES STARTED**	**COMPLETE GAMES**	**FEWEST HITS/GAME**	**FEWEST BB/GAME**
Smiley-Pit 20	Smiley-Pit .714	Rijo-Cin 5.3	Maddux-Chi 37	D.Martinez-Mon 9	Harnisch-Hou 7.02	Smith-Pit 1.14
Glavine-Atl 20	Rijo-Cin .714	Smiley-Pit 4.4	Smoltz-Atl 36	Glavine-Atl 9	Rijo-Cin 7.27	Tewksbury-StL 1.79
Avery-Atl 18	Avery-Atl .692	Avery-Atl 3.9	Leibrandt-Atl 36	Mulholland-Phi 8	DeJesus-Phi 7.28	Mulholland-Phi 1.90
Martinez-LA 17	Hurst-SD .652	Williams-Phi 3.9	Browning-Cin 36	Maddux-Chi 7	Hill-StL 7.30	Smiley-Pit 1.91
	Glavine-Atl .645	Pena-NY-Atl 3.6			Glavine-Atl 7.33	B.Smith-StL 2.04
STRIKEOUTS	**STRIKEOUTS/GAME**	**GAMES**	**SAVES**	**BASE RUNNERS/9**	**ADJUSTED RELIEF RUNS**	**RELIEF RANKING**
Cone-NY 241	Cone-NY 9.32	Jones-Mon 77	L.Smith-StL 47	Berenguer-Atl 9.23	McElroy-Chi 17.2	Williams-Phi 27.4
Maddux-Chi 198	Rijo-Cin 7.58	Assenmacher-Chi 75	Dibble-Cin 31	Innis-NY 9.46	Maddux-SD 14.4	L.Smith-StL 24.2
Glavine-Atl 192	Harnisch-Hou 7.14	Stanton-Atl 74	Williams-Phi 30	Maddux-SD 9.67	Williams-Phi 13.7	Pena-NY-Atl 16.1
Rijo-Cin 172	Gooden-NY 7.11	Burke-Mon-NY 72	Franco-NY 30	Stanton-Atl 9.69	Brantley-SF 12.9	McElroy-Chi 13.1
Harnisch-Hou 172	Glavine-Atl 7.01	Agosto-StL 72	Righetti-SF 24	Harris-SD 9.74	Pena-NY-Atl 12.5	Maddux-SD 13.0
INNINGS PITCHED	**OPPONENTS' AVG.**	**OPPONENTS' OBP**	**EARNED RUN AVERAGE**	**ADJUSTED ERA**	**ADJUSTED STARTER RUNS**	**PITCHER WINS**
Maddux-Chi 263.0	Harnisch-Hou .212	Rijo-Cin .272	D.Martinez-Mon 2.39	D.Martinez-Mon 152	Glavine-Atl 33.2	**Glavine-Atl 4.9**
Glavine-Atl 246.2	Rijo-Cin .219	Glavine-Atl .277	Rijo-Cin 2.51	Glavine-Atl 152	D.Martinez-Mon 29.6	**D.Martinez-Mon 3.6**
Morgan-LA 236.1	Glavine-Atl .222	Morgan-LA .278	Glavine-Atl 2.55	Rijo-Cin 152	Rijo-Cin 26.4	**Williams-Phi 2.9**
Drabek-Pit 234.2	Hill-StL .224	D.Martinez-Mon .282	Belcher-LA 2.62	DeLeon-StL 138	Benes-SD 22.2	**Rijo-Cin 2.8**
Cone-NY 232.2	DeJesus-Phi .224	Benes-SD .285	Harnisch-Hou 2.70	Belcher-LA 138	Harnisch-Hou 21.5	**L.Smith-StL 2.5**

Pete Rose Just Won't Go Away

On New Year's Day Pete Rose was released from federal prison after serving five months for income tax evasion. The Hall of Fame caused much controversy less than two weeks later by announcing a change in eligibility rules. No player on the permanently ineligible list, as Rose had been for eighteen months, could now be listed on the annual ballot. In more pleasant news, especially for fans in Denver and Miami, the NL announced that those cities would receive expansion franchises for the 1993 season.

Baseball lost one of its most colorful characters when Leo Durocher passed away the day before the postseason began. Durocher, who won more than 2,000 games as a big league skipper, titled his autobiography, *Nice Guys Finish Last.* Meanwhile, Houston rookie Jeff Bagwell began his journey to 400-plus home runs. Mark Wohlers also made his debut later in the year. It was the last season for Dave Parker, Rick Reuschel, and Ken Griffey Sr., the first major leaguer to play alongside his son.

The Pirates, with Barry Bonds, Andy Van Slyke, and Bobby Bonilla spearheading the league's best offense, had no trouble repeating as NL champs, finishing 14 games ahead of St. Louis. Atlanta, which finished last in the West in 1990, battled Los Angeles all season and didn't eliminate the Dodgers until the next to last game. The Braves had great seasons from outfielder Ron Gant, MVP Terry Pendleton, and a devastating young pitching trio of Tom Glavine, Steve Avery, and John Smoltz.

Those hurlers, especially Avery, made the difference in a thrilling NLCS, hurling 3 shutouts, including back-to-back blankings in Games 6 and 7 in Pittsburgh. The Braves lost a heartbreaking World Series to Minnesota, dropping the final two games in extra innings.

1991 AMERICAN LEAGUE

TEAM	W	L	T	PCT	GB	HW	HL	R	OR	PA	H	2B	3B	HR	BB	SO	HB	SH	AVG	OBP	SLG	OPS	AOPS	BR	ABR	PF	SB	CS	BSA	BSR
East																														
Tor	91	71	0	.562	—	46	35	684	**622**	6167	1412	295	45	133	499	1043	**58**	56	.257	.322	.400	722	94	-6	-33	104	148	53	74	**14**
Det	84	78	0	.519	7	49	32	817	794	6359	1372	259	26	**209**	**699**	1185	31	38	.247	.333	.416	749	104	52	37	102	109	47	70	8
Bos	84	78	0	.519	7	43	38	731	712	6256	1486	**305**	25	126	593	820	32	50	.269	.340	.401	741	99	47	7	106	59	39	60	-1
Mil	83	79	0	.512	8	43	37	799	744	6308	1523	247	**53**	116	556	802	23	52	.271	.336	.396	732	104	21	36	98	106	68	61	0
NY	71	91	0	.438	20	39	42	674	777	6140	1418	249	19	147	473	861	39	37	.256	.316	.387	703	92	-49	-54	101	109	36	**75**	11
Bal	67	95	0	.414	24	33	48	686	796	6257	1421	256	29	170	528	974	33	47	.254	.319	.401	720	102	-18	9	96	50	33	60	-1
Cle	57	105	0	.352	34	30	52	576	759	6070	1390	236	26	79	449	888	43	62	.254	.313	.350	663	82	-122	-127	101	84	58	59	-2
West																														
Min	95	67	0	.586	—	**51**	30	776	652	6215	**1557**	270	42	140	526	**747**	40	44	**.280**	**.344**	.420	764	105	82	45	105	107	68	61	0
Chi	87	75	0	.537	8	46	35	758	681	6358	1464	226	39	139	610	896	37	**76**	.262	.336	.391	727	102	10	25	98	134	74	64	4
Tex	85	77	0	.525	10	46	35	**829**	814	6441	1539	288	31	177	596	1039	42	59	.270	.341	**.424**	**765**	**112**	**87**	**101**	98	102	50	67	5
Oak	84	78	0	.519	11	47	34	760	776	6192	1342	246	19	159	642	981	50	41	.248	.331	.389	720	103	0	40	95	**151**	64	70	11
Sea	83	79	0	.512	12	45	36	702	674	6236	1400	268	29	126	588	811	37	55	.255	.328	.383	711	96	-19	-22	100	97	44	69	6
KC	82	80	0	.506	13	40	41	727	722	6242	1475	290	41	117	523	969	35	53	.264	.328	.394	722	98	-4	-10	101	119	68	64	2
Cal	81	81	0	.500	14	40	41	653	649	6050	1396	245	29	115	448	928	38	63	.255	.314	.374	688	89	-81	-82	100	94	56	63	1
Total	1134	—	—	—	—	598	536	10172	—	87291	20195	3680	453	1953	7730	12944	538	733	.260	.329	.395	724	—	—	—	—	1469	758	66	58

TEAM	CG	SHO	GR	SV	IP	H	HR	BB	SO	BR/9	ERA	AERA	OAV	OOB	PR	APR	PF	OSB	OCS	FA	E	WPB	DP	FW	PW	BW	BSW	DIF
East																												
Tor	10	**16**	347	**60**	1462.2	**1301**	121	523	971	**11.5**	**3.50**	**120**	**.238**	**.307**	**96**	**113**	103	118	53	.980	127	76	115	-.6	**11.3**	-3.3	**1.0**	1.6
Det	18	8	326	38	1450.1	1570	148	593	739	13.6	4.51	93	.280	.348	-66	-53	102	88	56	.983	104	62	171	.7	-5.3	3.7	.4	3.5
Bos	15	13	328	45	1439.2	1405	147	530	999	12.3	4.01	108	.257	.323	13	47	106	97	53	.981	116	**53**	165	.0	4.7	.7	-.5	-1.9
Mil	23	11	341	41	1463.2	1498	147	527	859	12.7	4.14	96	.266	.332	-8	-26	97	115	47	.981	118	69	176	-.0	-2.6	3.6	-.4	1.5
NY	3	11	377	37	1444.0	1510	152	506	936	12.8	4.42	94	.271	.334	-52	-41	102	134	51	.979	133	66	181	-.9	-4.1	-5.4	.7	-.2
Bal	8	8	372	42	1457.2	1534	147	504	868	12.8	4.59	86	.273	.333	-80	-104	97	111	51	**.985**	**91**	57	172	**1.4**	-10.4	.9	-.5	-5.4
Cle	22	8	289	33	1441.1	1551	110	**441**	862	12.7	4.23	98	.276	.329	-22	-10	102	102	47	.976	149	67	150	-1.8	-1.0	-12.7	-.6	-7.9
West																												
Min	21	12	291	53	1449.1	1402	139	488	876	11.9	3.69	116	.255	.317	64	89	104	118	43	**.985**	95	69	161	1.2	8.9	4.5	-.4	-.2
Chi	**28**	8	338	40	1478.0	1302	154	601	923	11.8	3.79	105	.239	.315	50	34	97	96	67	.982	116	64	151	.0	3.4	2.5	-.0	.0
Tex	9	10	386	41	1479.0	1486	151	662	**1022**	13.3	4.47	91	.262	.341	-61	-70	99	107	58	.979	134	92	138	-1.0	-7.0	**10.1**	.0	1.8
Oak	14	10	**397**	49	1444.1	1425	155	655	892	13.3	4.57	84	.260	.342	-77	-124	94	116	60	.982	107	68	150	.5	-12.4	4.0	.7	10.2
Sea	10	13	383	48	1464.1	1387	136	628	1003	12.7	3.79	109	.253	.332	50	56	101	**84**	44	.983	110	106	**187**	.3	5.6	-2.2	.2	-1.9
KC	17	12	295	41	1466.0	1473	**105**	529	1004	12.6	3.92	106	.261	.327	28	35	101	94	56	.980	125	58	141	-.5	3.5	-1.0	-.2	-.8
Cal	18	10	310	50	1441.2	1351	141	543	990	12.1	3.69	112	.250	.321	65	68	101	89	**72**	.984	102	72	156	.8	6.8	-8.2	-.3	.9
Total	216	150	4780	618	20382.0	—	—	—	—	12.6	4.09	—	.260	.329	—	—	—	—	—	.981	1627	979	2214	—	—	—	—	—

BATTER-FIELDER WINS	BATTING AVERAGE	ON-BASE PERCENTAGE	SLUGGING AVERAGE	ON-BASE PLUS SLUGGING	ADJUSTED OPS	ADJUSTED BATTER RUNS
C.Ripken-Bal...... 8.5	Franco-Tex............341	Thomas-Chi..........453	Tartabull-KC..........593	Thomas-Chi........1006	Thomas-Chi..........181	Thomas-Chi.........71.1
Thomas-Chi........ 5.8	Boggs-Bos............332	Randolph-Mil 424	C.Ripken-Bal.........566	Tartabull-KC..........990	Tartabull-KC..........170	C.Ripken-Bal........54.5
K.Griffey-Sea 4.6	Randolph-Mil 327	Boggs-Bos............421	Canseco-Oak........556	C.Ripken-Bal.........940	C.Ripken-Bal.........163	Palmeiro-Tex........49.5
Phillips-Det......... 4.1	K.Griffey-Sea 327	Franco-Tex............408	Thomas-Chi...........553	K.Griffey-Sea 926	Canseco-Oak........159	Tartabull-KC.........46.8
Boggs-Bos.......... 3.8	Molitor-Mil............325	E.Martinez-Sea.....405	Palmeiro-Tex.........532	Palmeiro-Tex.........922	Palmeiro-Tex.........156	Canseco-Oak.......45.6

RUNS	HITS	DOUBLES	TRIPLES	HOME RUNS	TOTAL BASES	RUNS BATTED IN
Molitor-Mil.............133	Molitor-Mil.............216	Palmeiro-Tex...........49	Molitor-Mil...............13	Fielder-Det..............44	C.Ripken-Bal.........368	Fielder-Det............133
Palmeiro-Tex.........115	C.Ripken-Bal.........210	C.Ripken-Bal..........46	Johnson-Chi 13	Canseco-Oak..........44	Palmeiro-Tex.........336	Canseco-Oak.........122
Canseco-Oak........115	Sierra-Tex 203	Sierra-Tex 44	Alomar-Tor 11	C.Ripken-Bal..........34	Sierra-Tex 332	Sierra-Tex 116
White-Tor 110	Palmeiro-Tex.........203		White-Tor 10	Carter-Tor 33	Molitor-Mil............325	C.Ripken-Bal.........114
Sierra-Tex 110	Franco-Tex...........201		Devereaux-Bal 10	Thomas-Chi.............32	Carter-Tor 321	Thomas-Chi...........109

BASES ON BALLS	STOLEN BASES	BASE STEALING RUNS	FIELDING RUNS-INFIELD	FIELDING RUNS-OUTFIELD	OUTFIELD ASSISTS	CATCHER CS PCT.
Thomas-Chi..........138	R.Henderson-Oak...58	Alomar-Tor............7.8	Sojo-Cal..............26.6	Orsulak-Bal..........17.2	Orsulak-Bal............22	Rodriguez-Tex 48.6
Tettleton-Det 101	Alomar-Tor 53	R.Henderson-Oak..6.5	Vizquel-Sea 26.1	Whiten-Tor-Cle.....10.4	Sierra-Tex 15	Borders-Tor..........35.9
R.Henderson-Oak...98	Raines-Chi.............51	Raines-Chi............6.0	Espinoza-NY........21.0	Bichette-Mil...........8.9	K.Griffey-Sea 15	Skinner-Cle..........34.1
Clark-Bos...............96	Polonia-Cal 48	Cuyler-Det 5.5	C.Ripken-Bal........19.5	Buhner-Sea 7.2	Buhner-Sea 15	Pena-Bos.............33.1
Davis-Min...............95	Cuyler-Det 41	Franco-Tex............4.8	Baerga-Cle 16.5	R.Henderson-Oak..6.5	Bichette-Mil............14	Nokes-NY 27.2

WINS	WINNING PCT.	WINS ABOVE TEAM	GAMES STARTED	COMPLETE GAMES	FEWEST HITS/GAME	FEWEST BB/GAME
Gullickson-Det 20	Erickson-Min.........714	Langston-Cal 6.1	Welch-Oak....................35	McDowell-Chi 15	Ryan-Tex.............5.31	Swindell-Cle.........1.17
Erickson-Min...........20	Langston-Cal 704	Gullickson-Det 5.8	Stewart-Oak..................35	Clemens-Bos 13	Johnson-Sea 6.75	Sanderson-NY.....1.25
Langston-Cal 19	Gullickson-Det 690	Finley-Cal 5.1	Morris-Min.....................35	Navarro-Mil 10	Langston-Cal 6.94	Tapani-Min 1.48
	Wegman-Mil 682	Erickson-Min..........4.9	McDowell-Chi 35	Morris-Min..............10	Clemens-Bos 7.26	Gullickson-Det 1.75
	Moore-Oak...........680	Moore-Oak............4.7	Gullickson-Det 35	Terrell-Det 8	McDowell-Chi 7.52	Wegman-Mil 1.86
			Clemens-Bos 35			

STRIKEOUTS	STRIKEOUTS/GAME	GAMES	SAVES	BASE RUNNERS/9	ADJUSTED RELIEF RUNS	RELIEF RANKING
Clemens-Bos 241	Ryan-Tex...........10.56	D.Ward-Tor.............81	Harvey-Cal.............46	Gray-Bos.............7.30	Frohwirth-Bal 22.0	Harvey-Cal..........32.8
Johnson-Sea 228	Johnson-Sea 10.19	Olson-Bal................72	Eckersley-Oak 43	Harvey-Cal...........7.89	Swift-Sea 21.3	Aguilera-Min 28.2
Ryan-Tex...............203	Clemens-Bos 7.99	Jackson-Sea 72	Aguilera-Min 42	Eckersley-Oak 8.29	Harvey-Cal...........19.8	Farr-NY 27.4
McDowell-Chi 191	Hanson-Sea.........7.37	Swift-Sea 71	Reardon-Bos 40	Eichhorn-Cal........8.60	Eichhorn-Cal........18.8	D.Ward-Tor...........24.4
Langston-Cal 183	Appier-KC 6.85		Montgomery-KC 33	Frohwirth-Bal 8.78	Flanagan-Bal 18.4	Radinsky-Chi 22.9

INNINGS PITCHED	OPPONENTS' AVG.	OPPONENTS' OBP	EARNED RUN AVERAGE	ADJUSTED ERA	ADJUSTED STARTER RUNS	PITCHER WINS
Clemens-Bos 271.1	Ryan-Tex..............172	Ryan-Tex..............263	Clemens-Bos 2.62	Clemens-Bos........165	Clemens-Bos.......46.5	**Clemens-Bos 4.7**
McDowell-Chi 253.2	Johnson-Sea 213	Clemens-Bos........270	Candiotti-Cle-Tor.....2.65	Candiotti-Cle-Tor......159	Candiotti-Cle-Tor.....38.9	Candiotti-Cle-Tor.......4.1
Morris-Min.........246.2	Langston-Cal 215	Tapani-Min 277	Wegman-Mil 2.84	Tapani-Min 143	Tapani-Min...........35.7	**J.Abbott-Cal....... 4.0**
Langston-Cal 246.1	Clemens-Bos 221	Sanderson-NY 279	J.Abbott-Cal 2.89	J.Abbott-Cal..........143	J.Abbott-Cal.........33.4	**Tapani-Min.......... 3.5**
Tapani-Min 244.0	Candiotti-Cle-Tor......228	Saberhagen-KC....280	Ryan-Tex.............2.91	Wegman-Mil 141	Langston-Cal 31.2	**Harvey-Cal.......... 3.4**

Morris Dance

The year began sadly as Hall of Fame shortstop Luke Appling passed away two days after New Year's Day at age 83, then three days later, 32-year-old Alan Wiggins died of AIDS complications. Also passing was Hall of Fame outfielder James "Cool Papa" Bell, a Negro Leagues superstar. The terrible run of bad luck off the field continued in July when respected umpire Steve Palermo, was partially paralyzed when shot in the back during a restaurant robbery.

Baltimore hurler Jim Palmer, already elected to the Hall of Fame, attempted a brief and unsuccessful comeback during spring training. Chicago's "New" Comiskey Park opened to trumpet fanfare, though the stadium would be horribly outdated within a few years as more fashionable "retro" ballparks opened.

May 1 was a historic night. In Texas Nolan Ryan extended his own record by throwing a seventh no-hitter, and in Oakland Rickey Henderson copped Lou Brock's all-time stolen base record. As Dwight Evans was concluding his memorable twenty-year career, future postseason heroes Mike Mussina, Ivan Rodriguez, and Bernie Williams were making their first appearances.

Minnesota, last-place finishers the year before, and Toronto had easy times winning their respective division titles. The Twins, buffed up by free agent Jack Morris and rookie Chuck Knoblauch, had three strong starters and a solid all-around club, while the Blue Jays sported a spectacular three-man bullpen in Tom Henke, Duane Ward, and Mike Timlin.

Behind Kirby Puckett's bat and Jack Morris' arm, Minnesota cruised past the Blue Jays in five games in the ALCS, then beat Atlanta in one of the game's most memorable World Series. Both the Twins and Braves had heroes galore, but Morris' 10-inning, complete-game shutout in Game 7 took the cake.

1990 NATIONAL LEAGUE

TEAM	W	L	T	PCT	GB	HW	HL	R	OR	PA	H	2B	3B	HR	BB	SO	HB	SH	AVG	OBP	SLG	OPS	AOPS	BR	ABR	PF	SB	CS	BSA	BSR
East																														
Pit	95	67	0	.586	—	49	32	733	619	6156	1395	**288**	42	138	**582**	914	24	**96**	.259	**.330**	.405	**735**	**112**	**68**	**93**	97	137	52	72	12
NY	91	71	0	.562	4	**52**	29	**775**	613	6182	1410	278	21	**172**	536	851	32	54	.256	.323	**.408**	731	106	52	51	100	110	33	**77**	13
Mon	85	77	0	.525	10	47	34	662	598	6189	1363	227	**43**	114	576	1024	26	87	.250	.322	.370	692	99	-19	5	97	**235**	99	70	17
Phi	77	85	0	.475	18	41	40	646	729	6245	1410	237	27	103	**582**	915	30	59	.255	.327	.363	690	96	-18	-17	100	108	35	76	12
Chi	77	85	0	.475	18	39	42	690	774	6148	**1474**	240	36	136	406	869	30	61	.263	.314	.392	706	93	-10	-54	107	151	50	75	16
StL	70	92	0	.432	25	34	47	599	698	6127	1398	255	41	73	517	**844**	21	77	.256	.320	.358	678	91	-46	-50	101	221	74	75	**23**
West																														
Cin	91	71	0	.562	—	46	35	693	**597**	6163	1466	284	40	125	466	913	**42**	88	**.265**	.325	.399	724	101	37	9	104	166	66	72	13
LA	86	76	0	.531	5	47	34	728	685	6179	1436	222	27	129	538	952	31	71	.262	.328	.382	710	103	17	33	98	141	65	68	8
SF	85	77	0	.525	6	49	32	719	710	6215	1459	221	35	152	488	973	33	76	.262	.323	.396	719	107	22	46	97	109	56	66	4
SD	75	87	0	.463	16	37	44	673	673	6218	1429	243	35	123	509	902	28	79	.257	.320	.380	700	97	-9	-16	101	138	59	70	10
Hou	75	87	0	.463	16	49	32	573	656	6075	1301	209	32	94	548	997	28	79	.242	.313	.345	658	89	-85	-69	97	179	83	68	10
Atl	65	97	0	.401	26	37	44	682	821	6084	1376	263	26	162	473	1010	27	49	.250	.311	.396	707	94	-8	-43	106	92	55	63	1
Total	972	—	—	—	—	527	445	8173	—	73981	16917	2967	405	1521	6221	11164	352	876	.256	.321	.383	704	—	—	—	—	1787	727	71	139

TEAM	CG	SHO	GR	SV	IP	H	HR	BB	SO	BR/9	ERA	AERA	OAV	OOB	PR	APR	PF	OSB	OCS	FA	E	WPB	DP	FW	PW	BW	BSW	DIF
East																												
Pit	18	8	364	43	1447.0	1367	135	**413**	848	**11.3**	3.40	107	.251	.305	63	41	96	135	68	.979	134	51	125	-.4	4.2	**9.6**	.0	.6
NY	18	**14**	268	41	1440.0	1339	119	444	**1217**	**11.3**	3.42	110	.246	**.304**	59	54	99	201	71	.978	132	71	107	-.3	5.6	5.3	.1	-.6
Mon	18	11	341	**50**	1473.1	1349	127	510	991	11.6	**3.37**	109	**.245**	.311	**70**	51	97	194	45	.982	110	**48**	134	.9	5.3	.5	.6	-3.3
Phi	18	7	**374**	35	1449.0	1381	124	651	840	12.8	4.07	95	.253	.333	-45	-35	102	104	56	.981	117	77	**150**	.5	-3.6	-1.8	.0	.8
Chi	13	7	346	42	1442.2	1510	121	572	877	13.2	4.34	94	.271	.340	-87	-38	108	**98**	56	.980	124	86	136	.1	-3.9	-5.6	.5	4.9
StL	8	13	364	39	1443.1	1432	**98**	475	833	12.1	3.87	99	.261	.320	-13	-4	101	144	**76**	.979	130	56	114	-.2	-.4	-5.2	**1.2**	-6.4
West																												
Cin	14	12	316	**50**	1456.1	**1338**	124	543	1029	11.8	3.39	**116**	.246	.316	64	**86**	104	135	60	**.983**	**102**	67	126	**1.4**	**8.9**	.9	.1	-1.4
LA	**29**	12	339	29	1442.0	1364	137	478	1021	11.7	3.72	99	.249	.310	11	-7	97	134	59	.979	130	73	123	-.2	-.7	3.4	-.4	2.9
SF	14	6	335	45	1446.1	1477	131	553	788	12.8	4.08	90	.267	.333	-46	-71	96	147	53	**.983**	107	**48**	148	1.1	-7.3	4.7	-.8	6.2
SD	21	12	288	35	1461.2	1437	147	507	928	12.1	3.68	104	.258	.320	19	25	101	132	60	.977	141	**48**	141	-.8	2.6	-1.6	-.2	-5.9
Hou	12	6	348	37	1450.0	1396	130	496	854	12.0	3.61	103	.255	.318	30	20	98	182	61	.978	131	54	124	-.3	2.1	-7.1	-.2	-.5
Atl	17	8	346	30	1429.2	1527	128	579	938	13.4	4.58	88	.275	.343	-125	-82	106	181	62	.974	158	76	133	-1.8	-8.5	-4.4	-1.1	-.2
Total	200	116	4029	476	17381.1	—	—	—	—	12.2	3.79	—	.256	.321	—	—	—	—	—	.980	1516	755	1561	—	—	—	—	—

BATTER-FIELDER WINS	BATTING AVERAGE	ON-BASE PERCENTAGE	SLUGGING AVERAGE	ON-BASE PLUS SLUGGING	ADJUSTED OPS	ADJUSTED BATTER RUNS
Bonds-Pit 6.4	McGee-StL .335	Dykstra-Phi .418	Bonds-Pit .565	Bonds-Pit .970	Bonds-Pit 171	Bonds-Pit 53.6
Dykstra-Phi 4.8	Murray-LA .330	Magadan-NY .417	Sandberg-Chi .559	Murray-LA .934	Murray-LA 160	Murray-LA 47.9
Sandberg-Chi 4.3	Magadan-NY .328	Murray-LA .414	Mitchell-SF .544	Daniels-LA .920	Daniels-LA 155	J.Clark-SD 36.9
Larkin-Cin 4.2	Dykstra-Phi .325	Bonds-Pit .406	Gant-Atl .539	Sandberg-Chi .913	Mitchell-SF 151	Dykstra-Phi 35.9
Murray-LA 3.9	Dawson-Chi .310	Butler-SF .397	Justice-Atl .535	Justice-Atl .908	Magadan-NY 142	Daniels-LA 35.3

RUNS	HITS	DOUBLES	TRIPLES	HOME RUNS	TOTAL BASES	RUNS BATTED IN
Sandberg-Chi 116	Dykstra-Phi 192	Jefferies-NY 40	Duncan-Cin 11	Sandberg-Chi 40	Sandberg-Chi 344	Williams-SF 122
Bonilla-Pit 112	Butler-SF 192	Bonilla-Pit 39	Gwynn-SD 10	Strawberry-NY 37	Bonilla-Pit 324	Bonilla-Pit 120
Butler-SF 108	Sandberg-Chi 188	Sabo-Cin 38	L.Smith-Atl 9	Mitchell-SF 35	Gant-Atl 310	Carter-SD 115
Gant-Atl 107	Wallach-Mon 185	Wallach-Mon 37	Coleman-StL 9	Williams-SF 33	Williams-SF 301	Bonds-Pit 114
Dykstra-Phi 106	Larkin-Cin 185	Johnson-NY 37	Butler-SF 9	Bonds-Pit 33	Wallach-Mon 295	Strawberry-NY 108

BASES ON BALLS	STOLEN BASES	BASE STEALING RUNS	FIELDING RUNS-INFIELD	FIELDING RUNS-OUTFIELD	OUTFIELD ASSISTS	CATCHER CS PCT.
J.Clark-SD 104	Coleman-StL 77	Coleman-StL 11.0	Grace-Chi 25.3	Wilson-Hou 10.0	McReynolds-NY 14	Oliver-Cin 40.2
Bonds-Pit 93	Yelding-Hou 64	Bonds-Pit 6.9	Treadway-Atl 23.9	Bonds-Pit 7.8	Bonds-Pit 14	Girardi-Chi 37.0
Butler-SF 90	Bonds-Pit 52	Nixon-Mon 6.4	Larkin-Cin 21.0	Hatcher-Cin 7.4	McGee-StL 13	Daulton-Phi 35.0
Dykstra-Phi 89	Butler-SF 51	Roberts-SD 5.9	Thompson-SF 20.1	Dykstra-Phi 6.8	Daniels-LA 13	LaValliere-Pit 34.6
V.Hayes-Phi 87	Nixon-Mon 50	Dykstra-Phi 5.5	Lind-Pit 19.8	Walker-Mon 6.4	Carter-SD 13	Santiago-SD 34.1

WINS	WINNING PCT.	WINS ABOVE TEAM	GAMES STARTED	COMPLETE GAMES	FEWEST HITS/GAME	FEWEST BB/GAME
Drabek-Pit 22	Drabek-Pit .786	Drabek-Pit 7.4	Viola-NY 35	Martinez-LA 12	Fernandez-NY 6.52	Darwin-Hou 1.72
Viola-NY 20	Martinez-LA .769	Martinez-LA 7.2	Maddux-Chi 35	Hurst-SD 9	Rijo-Cin 6.90	Whitson-SD 1.85
Martinez-LA 20	Gooden-NY .731	Gooden-NY 5.6	Browning-Cin 35	Drabek-Pit 9	Martinez-LA 7.34	Leibrandt-Atl 1.94
Gooden-NY 19	Viola-NY .625	Tudor-StL 4.7		Maddux-Chi 8	Drabek-Pit 7.39	D.Martinez-Mon 1.95
	Browning-Cin .625	Darwin-Hou 4.0			Darwin-Hou 7.52	Browning-Cin 2.06

STRIKEOUTS	STRIKEOUTS/GAME	GAMES	SAVES	BASE RUNNERS/9	ADJUSTED RELIEF RUNS	RELIEF RANKING
Cone-NY 233	Cone-NY 9.91	Agosto-Hou 82	Franco-NY 33	Tomlin-Pit 8.69	Dibble-Cin 22.5	Myers-Cin 27.7
Martinez-LA 223	Fernandez-NY 9.08	Assenmacher-Chi 74	Myers-Cin 31	Dibble-Cin 8.91	Brantley-SF 20.2	Dibble-Cin 27.4
Gooden-NY 223	Gooden-NY 8.63	Harris-SD 73	L.Smith-StL 27	Tudor-StL 9.35	Harris-SD 19.3	Harris-SD 26.4
Viola-NY 182	Martinez-LA 8.56	McDowell-Phi 72	Smith-Hou 23	Darwin-Hou 9.46	Charlton-Cin 19.1	Brantley-SF 24.9
Fernandez-NY 181	DeLeon-StL 8.08	Akerfelds-Phi 71	Lefferts-SD 23	Drabek-Pit 9.69	Myers-Cin 16.3	Charlton-Cin 23.8

INNINGS PITCHED	OPPONENTS' AVG.	OPPONENTS' OBP	EARNED RUN AVERAGE	ADJUSTED ERA	ADJUSTED STARTER RUNS	PITCHER WINS
Viola-NY 249.2	Fernandez-NY .200	Darwin-Hou .266	Darwin-Hou 2.21	Darwin-Hou 169	Whitson-SD 31.8	**Viola-NY 3.7**
Maddux-Chi 237.0	Rijo-Cin .212	Drabek-Pit .274	Smith-Mon-Pit 2.55	Whitson-SD 148	Viola-NY 30.6	**Drabek-Pit 3.6**
Martinez-LA 234.1	Martinez-LA .220	D.Martinez-Mon .274	Whitson-SD 2.60	Rijo-Cin 147	Darwin-Hou 29.3	**Whitson-SD 3.3**
Gooden-NY 232.2	Drabek-Pit .225	Fernandez-NY .277	Viola-NY 2.67	Smith-Mon-Pit 144	Rijo-Cin 26.0	**Myers-Cin 3.0**
	Darwin-Hou .225	Martinez-LA .278	Rijo-Cin 2.70	Viola-NY 141	Drabek-Pit 24.9	**Rijo-Cin 2.9**

Hunt for a Reds October

The season began a week late as players scrambled to get in condition after the owners ended their lockout of spring training camps. By adding doubleheaders and extending the season three days, all teams played a full 162-game schedule. The NL announced in June that it would expand to fourteen teams, the same number as the AL, for 1993. The finalist cities were Buffalo, Denver, Miami, Orlando, Tampa-St. Petersburg, and Washington, D.C.

The decline and fall of Pete Rose continued, as the former superstar pled guilty to filing false income tax returns and was sentenced to five months in federal prison. Moises Alou, Felipe's son, debuted in June, while Luis Gonzalez made his first appearance in September. Keith Hernandez hung up the spikes after seventeen seasons. Bo Diaz, former catcher for the Phillies and Reds, died one year after retiring when he was crushed by a satellite dish he was installing.

Cincinnati led the West wire-to-wire, sparked by the Nasty Boys bullpen trio of Randy Myers, Rob Dibble and Norm Charlton. Pittsburgh, behind Barry Bonds' MVP performance (his first of a record six), won 10 of 11 games late in the season to hold off the Mets in the East. Doug Drabek, enjoying a career year with 22 wins and the Cy Young Award, led a pedestrian Pirates staff.

While the Reds dropped the first game of the NLCS to Pittsburgh, they rallied to take four of the next five. Cincinnati then brought back memories of the Big Red Machine by sweeping heavily favored Oakland in the World Series. Series MVP Jose Rijo dominated Oakland hitters, winning Games 1 and 4, while Billy Hatcher set offensive records by getting hits in seven consecutive at bats and batting .750 (9-for-12).

1990 AMERICAN LEAGUE

TEAM	W	L	T	PCT	GB	HW	HL	R	OR	PA	H	2B	3B	HR	BB	SO	HB	SH	AVG	OBP	SLG	OPS	AOPS	BR	ABR	PF	SB	CS	BSA	BSR
EAST																														
Bos	88	74	0	.543	—	**51**	30	699	664	6234	**1502**	298	31	106	598	795	28	48	**.272**	**.344**	.395	739	101	61	24	105	53	52	50	-7
Tor	86	76	0	.531	2	44	37	**767**	661	6223	1479	263	**50**	167	526	970	28	18	.265	.328	**.419**	**747**	105	54	38	102	111	52	68	6
Det	79	83	0	.488	9	39	42	750	754	6224	1418	241	32	**172**	634	952	34	36	.259	.337	.409	746	**107**	**63**	54	101	82	57	59	-2
Cle	77	85	0	.475	11	41	40	732	737	6087	1465	266	41	110	458	836	29	54	.267	.324	.391	715	99	-7	-6	100	107	52	67	5
Bal	76	85	0	.472	11.5	40	40	669	698	6223	1328	234	22	132	**660**	962	40	72	.245	.330	.370	700	98	-20	-2	97	94	52	64	2
Mil	74	88	0	.457	14	39	42	732	760	6185	1408	247	36	128	519	821	33	59	.256	.320	.384	704	96	-26	-23	100	**164**	72	69	11
NY	67	95	0	.414	21	37	44	603	749	6036	1322	208	19	147	427	1027	**53**	37	.241	.300	.366	666	84	-114	-119	101	119	45	**73**	10
WEST																														
Oak	103	59	0	.636	—	**51**	30	733	**570**	6238	1379	209	22	164	651	992	46	60	.254	.336	.391	727	**107**	31	**58**	96	141	54	72	**12**
Chi	94	68	0	.580	9	49	31	682	633	6038	1393	251	44	106	478	903	36	**75**	.258	.320	.379	699	97	-37	-24	98	140	90	61	-1
Tex	83	79	0	.512	20	47	35	676	696	6176	1416	257	27	110	575	1054	34	54	.259	.331	.376	707	97	-10	-13	100	115	48	71	9
Cal	80	82	0	.494	23	42	39	690	706	6267	1448	237	27	147	566	1000	28	58	.260	.329	.391	720	103	9	21	98	69	43	62	0
Sea	77	85	0	.475	26	38	43	640	680	6205	1419	251	26	107	596	**749**	40	41	.259	.333	.373	706	96	-5	-14	101	105	51	67	5
KC	75	86	0	.466	27.5	45	36	707	709	6098	1465	**316**	44	100	498	879	27	31	.267	.328	.395	723	102	16	25	99	107	62	63	2
Min	74	88	0	.457	29	41	40	666	729	6086	1458	281	39	100	445	**749**	**53**	40	.265	.324	.385	709	91	-17	-57	106	96	53	64	3
Total	1133	—	—	—	—	604	529	9746	—	86320	19900	3559	460	1796	7631	12689	509	683	.259	.327	.388	715	—	—	—	—	1503	783	66	57

TEAM	CG	SHO	GR	SV	IP	H	HR	BB	SO	BR/9	ERA	AERA	OAV	OOB	PR	APR	PF	OSB	OCS	FA	E	WPB	DP	FW	PW	BW	BSW	DIF
EAST																												
Bos	15	13	323	44	1442.0	1439	**92**	519	997	12.5	3.72	110	.261	.327	30	56	105	127	58	.980	123	70	154	-.2	5.7	2.4	-1.1	.2
Tor	6	9	317	48	1454.0	1434	143	**445**	892	11.9	3.84	103	.260	.317	11	18	101	95	67	**.986**	**86**	57	144	**2.0**	1.8	3.9	.2	-2.9
Det	15	12	300	45	1430.1	1401	154	661	856	13.3	4.39	90	.259	.341	-76	-65	102	136	59	.979	131	91	178	-.7	-6.6	5.5	-.6	.4
Cle	12	10	301	47	1427.1	1491	163	518	860	12.9	4.26	92	.270	.334	-57	-53	101	97	53	.981	117	64	146	.2	-5.4	-.6	.0	1.7
Bal	10	5	357	43	1435.1	1445	161	537	776	12.5	4.04	94	.264	.328	-21	-38	98	103	44	.985	93	**39**	151	1.6	-3.9	-.2	-.2	-1.8
Mil	23	13	340	42	1445.0	1558	121	469	771	12.9	4.08	95	.275	.331	-28	-33	99	111	45	.976	149	58	152	-1.8	-3.4	-2.3	.7	-.2
NY	15	6	342	41	1444.2	1430	144	618	909	12.9	4.21	95	.261	.336	-49	-36	102	106	**83**	.980	126	110	164	-.4	-3.7	-12.1	.6	1.6
WEST																												
Oak	18	**16**	303	64	1456.0	**1287**	123	494	831	**11.2**	**3.18**	**117**	**.238**	**.302**	**118**	**93**	95	**73**	44	**.986**	87	64	152	**2.0**	**9.5**	**5.9**	**.8**	3.9
Chi	17	10	**367**	**68**	1449.1	1313	106	548	914	11.8	3.61	106	.244	.316	48	37	98	89	60	.980	124	48	169	-.3	3.8	-2.4	-.5	12.5
Tex	**25**	9	302	36	1444.2	1343	113	623	997	12.5	3.83	102	.248	.327	12	15	101	131	52	.979	133	96	161	-.8	1.5	-1.3	.5	2.1
Cal	21	13	269	42	1454.0	1482	106	544	944	12.8	3.79	101	.267	.334	18	6	98	91	69	.978	142	65	**186**	-1.4	.6	2.1	-.4	-2.0
Sea	21	7	312	41	1443.1	1319	120	606	**1064**	12.3	3.69	107	.243	.321	34	44	102	120	56	.979	130	87	152	-.6	4.5	-1.4	.0	-6.5
KC	18	8	312	33	1420.2	1449	116	560	1006	13.0	3.93	98	.264	.334	-5	-13	99	115	28	.980	122	72	161	-.2	-1.3	2.5	-.2	-6.3
Min	13	13	310	43	1435.2	1509	134	489	872	12.7	4.12	101	.273	.332	-35	4	106	109	65	.983	101	66	161	1.1	.4	-5.8	-.1	-2.6
Total	229	144	4455	637	20182.1	—	—	—	—	12.5	3.91	—	.259	.327	—	—	—	—	—	.981	1664	987	2231	—	—	—	—	—

BATTER-FIELDER WINS	BATTING AVERAGE	ON-BASE PERCENTAGE	SLUGGING AVERAGE	ON-BASE PLUS SLUGGING	ADJUSTED OPS	ADJUSTED BATTER RUNS
R.Henderson-Oak... 7.7	Brett-KC................329	R.Henderson-Oak.439	Fielder-Det............592	R.Henderson-Oak...1016	R.Henderson-Oak.189	R.Henderson-Oak64.2
Fielder-Det 4.4	R.Henderson-Oak.325	McGriff-Tor............400	R.Henderson-Oak.577	Fielder-Det............969	Fielder-Det............166	Fielder-Det...........50.6
McGriff-Tor......... 4.3	Palmeiro-Tex.........319	E.Martinez-Sea.....397	J.Canseco-Oak.....543	McGriff-Tor............930	J.Canseco-Oak.....159	McGriff-Tor...........43.7
Fisk-Chi.............. 4.1	Trammell-Det 304	Brett-KC................387	McGriff-Tor............530	J.Canseco-Oak.....914	McGriff-Tor............155	Brett-KC...............39.7
Parrish-Cal 3.8	Boggs-Bos............302	Davis-Sea.............387	Brett-KC...............515	Brett-KC...............902	Brett-KC...............153	J.Canseco-Oak....38.0

RUNS	HITS	DOUBLES	TRIPLES	HOME RUNS	TOTAL BASES	RUNS BATTED IN
R.Henderson-Oak.119	Palmeiro-Tex.........191	J.Reed-Bos............45	Fernandez-Tor 17	Fielder-Det..............51	Fielder-Det............339	Fielder-Det............132
Fielder-Det............104	Boggs-Bos............187	Brett-KC..................45	Sosa-Chi.................10	McGwire-Oak..........39	Gruber-Tor............303	Gruber-Tor 118
Reynolds-Sea 100	Kelly-NY...............183	Calderon-Chi 44	Polonia-NY-Cal 9	J.Canseco-Oak.......37	McGriff-Tor............295	McGwire-Oak.........108
Yount-Mil.................98	Greenwell-Bos 181	Boggs-Bos.............44	Liriano-Tor-Min..........9	McGriff-Tor.............35	K.Griffey-Sea 287	J.Canseco-Oak.....101
Phillips-Det 97		Harper-Min 42	Johnson-Chi 9	Gruber-Tor 31	Burks-Bos.............286	Sierra-Tex 96

BASES ON BALLS	STOLEN BASES	BASE STEALING RUNS	FIELDING RUNS-INFIELD	FIELDING RUNS-OUTFIELD	OUTFIELD ASSISTS	CATCHER CS PCT.
McGwire-Oak........110	R.Henderson-Oak...65	R.Henderson-Oak10.8	Espinoza-NY........22.9	Orsulak-Bal............8.9	Barfield-NY 16	Geren-NY 43.3
Tettleton-Bal..........106	Sax-NY 43	Sax-NY 6.3	Reynolds-Sea 20.1	Deer-Mil 8.5	Sosa-Chi.................14	Borders-Tor..........42.6
Phillips-Det 99	Kelly-NY..................42	Cole-Cle.................5.7	Whitaker-Det........17.7	Gladden-Min 8.5	Deer-Mil..................14	Myers-Tor.............39.4
R.Henderson-Oak...97	Cole-Cle...................40	Wilson-Tor.............3.7	Phillips-Det 15.4	Webster-Cle...........8.0	Greenwell-Bos 13	Alomar-Cle...........34.2
McGriff-Tor.............94	Pettis-Tex 38	Cotto-Sea 3.6	Quintana-Bos.......13.2	Mack-Min 8.0		Macfarlane-KC.....17.1

WINS	WINNING PCT.	WINS ABOVE TEAM	GAMES STARTED	COMPLETE GAMES	FEWEST HITS/GAME	FEWEST BB/GAME
Welch-Oak.............27	Welch-Oak............818	Welch-Oak.............9.2	Stewart-Oak...........36	Stewart-Oak...........11	Ryan-Tex.............6.04	Anderson-Min 1.86
Stewart-Oak...........22	Clemens-Bos 778	Clemens-Bos 7.5	Morris-Det..............36	Morris-Det..............11	Johnson-Sea 7.13	Swindell-Cle.........1.97
Clemens-Bos..........21	Stieb-Tor 750	Stieb-Tor 6.1	Welch-Oak.............35		Clemens-Bos.......7.61	Clemens-Bos 2.13
	Boddicker-Bos 680	Hanson-Sea...........5.5	Perez-Chi...............35		Stewart-Oak.........7.62	Knudson-Mil.........2.14
		Finley-Cal 5.2			Stieb-Tor 7.72	Wells-Tor..............2.14

STRIKEOUTS	STRIKEOUTS/GAME	GAMES	SAVES	BASE RUNNERS/9	ADJUSTED RELIEF RUNS	RELIEF RANKING
Ryan-Tex...............232	Ryan-Tex...........10.24	Thigpen-Chi...........77	Thigpen-Chi...........57	Eckersley-Oak 5.52	Farr-KC................26.9	Eckersley-Oak 44.7
Witt-Tex.................221	Witt-Tex...............8.96	Ward-Tor 73	Eckersley-Oak 48	Nelson-Oak..........9.04	Eckersley-Oak 25.0	Thigpen-Chi.........40.1
Hanson-Sea..........211	Clemens-Bos.......8.24	Montgomery-KC 73	Jones-Cle 43	McDonald-Bal......9.33	Thigpen-Chi.........20.1	Farr-KC 38.4
Clemens-Bos........209	Gordon-KC 8.06	Rogers-Tex 69	Olson-Bal...............37	Henke-Tor 9.40	Swift-Sea 19.1	Olson-Bal.............25.1
Langston-Cal 195	Hanson-Sea..........8.05	Henneman-Det.......69	Righetti-NY 36	Thigpen-Chi.........9.44	Nelson-Oak..........19.1	Jones-Chi 24.3

INNINGS PITCHED	OPPONENTS' AVG.	OPPONENTS' OBP	EARNED RUN AVERAGE	ADJUSTED ERA	ADJUSTED STARTER RUNS	PITCHER WINS
Stewart-Oak.......267.0	Ryan-Tex..............188	Ryan-Tex...............267	Clemens-Bos.......1.93	Clemens-Bos........212	Clemens-Bos.......50.6	**Clemens-Bos 6.2**
Morris-Det..........249.2	Johnson-Sea 216	Clemens-Bos........278	Finley-Cal 2.40	Finley-Cal 160	Stewart-Oak.........36.7	**Eckersley-Oak ... 4.7**
Welch-Oak.........238.0	Clemens-Bos........228	Wells-Tor...............283	Stewart-Oak.........2.56	Stewart-Oak.........146	Finley-Cal 36.4	**Stewart-Oak....... 4.3**
Hanson-Sea.......236.0	Stieb-Tor 230	Hanson-Sea..........287	Appier-KC............2.76	Appier-KC............140	Stieb-Tor 23.3	**Thigpen-Chi........ 4.2**
Finley-Cal 236.0	Stewart-Oak..........231	Black-Cle-Tor........290	Stieb-Tor 2.93	Stieb-Tor 135	Hanson-Sea.........22.9	**Farr-KC................ 4.1**

March Comes In Like a Lion; A's Go Out Like Lambs

Although a spring lockout by the owners delayed the start of the regular season by a week, a full 162-game schedule was played after Commissioner Fay Vincent ordered the opening of the training camps. This angered many owners who believed that the formerly solid Players Association was about to crack, with several star players reportedly on the verge of crossing the "picket lines."

Toronto led the East by 1 game in late September, but lost six of its last eight and fell to Boston. Roger Clemens was again outstanding for the Red Sox, leading the league in ERA while pitching in Fenway Park. The Jays had a more impressive club than Boston but suffered from a lack of lefty relief and inconsistent starting pitching (David Wells shuttled between both roles and won 11 games). Behemoth first baseman Cecil Fielder of Detroit, signed after playing in Japan, hit 51 homers.

Oakland's Rickey Henderson shattered Ty Cobb's career AL steals record. Teammate Bob Welch won the Cy Young with 27 victories, the AL's most since 1968, although Clemens probably deserved the award. With Mark McGwire and Jose Canseco combining for 76 homers, the A's had little trouble in the West. Texas' 43-year-old Nolan Ryan won his 300th game and pitched his sixth no-hitter. The second-place White Sox, in their final season at venerable Comiskey Park, won 90 games for the first time since 1983. Chicago was led by Bobby Thigpen's record 57-save season plus rookie slugger Frank Thomas.

The AL West's top clubs of the 1980s, California and Kansas City, lost two players each to retirement: Bob Boone, Fred Lynn, Dan Quisenberry, and Frank White all sat down. The A's swept Boston in the ALCS, allowing just 4 runs, but they were in turn broomed out by the Reds in the World Series.

1989 NATIONAL LEAGUE

TEAM	W	L	T	PCT	GB	HW	HL	R	OR	PA	H	2B	3B	HR	BB	SO	HB	SH	AVG	OBP	SLG	OPS	AOPS	BR	ABR	PF	SB	CS	BSA	BSR
EAST																														
Chi	93	69	0	.574	—	48	33	**702**	623	6141	**1438**	235	45	124	472	921	26	80	**.261**	.319	.387	**706**	100	**52**	7	107	136	57	70	10
NY	87	75	0	.537	6	51	30	683	595	6130	1351	**280**	21	**147**	504	934	33	56	.246	.311	.385	696	108	33	62	96	158	53	**75**	**16**
StL	86	76	2	.531	7	46	35	632	608	6141	1418	263	47	73	507	**848**	21	78	.258	**.321**	.363	684	98	17	-5	103	155	54	74	15
Mon	81	81	0	.500	12	44	37	632	630	6206	1353	267	30	100	**572**	958	35	71	.247	.319	.361	680	98	16	4	102	**160**	70	70	11
Pit	74	88	2	.457	19	39	42	637	680	6260	1334	263	**53**	95	563	914	24	83	.241	.311	.359	670	100	-12	9	97	155	69	69	10
Phi	67	95	1	.414	26	38	42	629	735	6126	1324	215	36	123	558	926	22	57	.243	.314	.364	678	99	0	0	100	106	50	68	6
WEST																														
SF	92	70	0	.568	—	**53**	28	699	600	6138	1365	241	52	141	508	1071	**40**	82	.250	.316	**.390**	**706**	**110**	49	**68**	97	87	54	62	0
SD	89	73	0	.549	3	46	35	642	626	6119	1360	215	32	120	552	1013	9	**95**	.251	.319	.369	688	102	21	20	100	136	67	67	6
Hou	86	76	0	.531	6	47	35	647	669	6200	1316	239	28	97	530	860	27	83	.239	.306	.345	651	95	-50	-29	97	144	62	70	10
LA	77	83	0	.481	14	44	37	554	**536**	6123	1313	241	17	89	507	885	27	83	.240	.306	.339	645	91	-60	-52	99	81	54	60	-1
Cin	75	87	0	.463	17	38	43	632	691	6158	1362	243	28	128	493	1028	30	66	.247	.309	.370	679	96	1	-19	103	128	71	64	3
Atl	63	97	1	.394	28	33	46	584	680	6079	1281	201	22	128	485	996	24	65	.234	.298	.350	648	89	-67	-79	102	83	54	61	-1
Total	973	—	—	—	—	527	443	7673	—	73821	16215	2903	411	1365	6251	11354	318	899	.246	.312	.365	678	—	—	—	—	1529	715	68	86

TEAM	CG	SHO	GR	SV	IP	H	HR	BB	SO	BR/9	ERA	AERA	OAV	OOB	PR	APR	PF	OSB	OCS	FA	E	WPB	DP	FW	PW	BW	BSW	DIF
EAST																												
Chi	18	10	338	**55**	1460.1	1369	106	532	918	11.9	3.43	110	.250	.316	11	52	108	87	56	.980	124	56	130	.6	5.6	.7	.3	4.8
NY	24	12	274	38	1454.1	**1260**	115	532	**1108**	11.3	3.29	100	**.231**	**.301**	33	0	94	158	57	.976	144	61	110	-.6	.0	6.6	**.9**	-1.0
StL	18	18	**358**	43	1461.0	1330	**84**	482	844	11.3	3.36	109	.243	.306	21	46	105	133	55	**.982**	**112**	52	134	**1.4**	4.9	-.5	.8	-1.6
Mon	20	13	287	35	1468.1	1344	120	519	1059	11.6	3.48	102	.245	.312	3	14	102	166	70	.979	136	51	126	-.1	1.5	.4	.4	-2.2
Pit	20	9	325	40	1487.2	1394	121	539	827	11.9	3.64	93	.248	.314	-24	-43	97	190	56	.975	160	74	130	-1.4	-4.6	1.0	.3	-2.3
Phi	10	10	348	33	1433.1	1408	127	613	899	12.9	4.04	89	.259	.335	-87	-72	103	113	66	.979	133	97	136	.1	-7.7	.0	-.1	-6.3
WEST																												
SF	12	16	318	47	1457.0	1320	120	471	802	11.2	3.30	102	.243	.304	31	12	97	96	56	**.982**	114	48	135	1.2	1.3	**7.3**	-.8	2.1
SD	21	11	245	52	1457.1	1359	133	481	933	11.5	3.38	104	.249	.310	19	20	100	**68**	44	.976	154	56	147	-1.1	2.1	2.1	-.1	5.0
Hou	19	12	346	38	1479.1	1379	105	551	965	11.9	3.64	93	.247	.315	-25	-41	97	170	40	.977	142	64	121	-.4	-4.4	-3.1	.3	12.6
LA	**25**	**19**	285	36	1463.1	1278	95	504	1052	**11.1**	**2.95**	**116**	.237	.304	**89**	**80**	98	99	72	.981	118	63	**153**	.8	**8.6**	-5.6	-.9	-6.0
Cin	16	9	339	37	1464.1	1404	125	559	981	12.3	3.73	96	.253	.323	-38	-21	103	141	65	.980	121	**47**	108	.8	-2.2	-2.0	-.4	-2.0
Atl	15	8	340	33	1447.2	1370	114	**468**	966	11.5	3.70	99	.250	.309	-33	-7	105	108	**78**	.976	152	62	124	-1.1	-.7	-8.4	-.9	-5.9
Total	218	147	3803	487	17534.0	—	—	—	—	11.7	3.49	—	.246	.312	—	—	—	—	—	.978	1610	731	1554	—	—	—	—	—

BATTER-FIELDER WINS	BATTING AVERAGE	ON-BASE PERCENTAGE	SLUGGING AVERAGE	ON-BASE PLUS SLUGGING	ADJUSTED OPS	ADJUSTED BATTER RUNS
Mitchell-SF 6.2	Gwynn-SD .336	L.Smith-Atl .415	Mitchell-SF .635	Mitchell-SF 1023	Mitchell-SF 194	Mitchell-SF 67.0
Clark-SF 5.1	Clark-SF .333	J.Clark-SD .410	Johnson-NY .559	Clark-SF .953	Clark-SF 176	Clark-SF 60.2
L.Smith-Atl 4.8	L.Smith-Atl .315	Clark-SF .407	Clark-SF .546	L.Smith-Atl .948	Johnson-NY 170	Johnson-NY 52.3
Oquendo-StL 4.3	Grace-Chi .314	Grace-Chi .405	Davis-Cin .541	Johnson-NY .928	L.Smith-Atl 167	L.Smith-Atl 46.4
Bonilla-Pit 4.2	Guerrero-StL .311	Raines-Mon .395	L.Smith-Atl .533	Davis-Cin .908	Davis-Cin 154	J.Clark-SD 37.4
RUNS	**HITS**	**DOUBLES**	**TRIPLES**	**HOME RUNS**	**TOTAL BASES**	**RUNS BATTED IN**
Sandberg-Chi 104	Gwynn-SD 203	Wallach-Mon 42	Thompson-SF 11	Mitchell-SF 47	Mitchell-SF 345	Mitchell-SF 125
Johnson-NY 104	Clark-SF 196	Guerrero-StL 42	Bonilla-Pit 10	Johnson-NY 36	Clark-SF 321	Guerrero-StL 117
Clark-SF 104	R.Alomar-SD 184	Johnson-NY 41	VanSlyke-Pit 9	Davis-Hou 34	Johnson-NY 319	Clark-SF 111
Mitchell-SF 100	Guerrero-StL 177	Clark-SF 38	Coleman-StL 9	Davis-Cin 34	Bonilla-Pit 302	Johnson-NY 101
Butler-SF 100	Sandberg-Chi 176	Bonilla-Pit 37	Clark-SF 9	Sandberg-Chi 30	Sandberg-Chi 301	Davis-Cin 101
BASES ON BALLS	**STOLEN BASES**	**BASE STEALING RUNS**	**FIELDING RUNS-INFIELD**	**FIELDING RUNS-OUTFIELD**	**OUTFIELD ASSISTS**	**CATCHER CS PCT.**
J.Clark-SD 132	Coleman-StL 65	Coleman-StL 10.8	Pendleton-StL 34.9	Young-Hou 14.2	Young-Hou 15	Berryhill-Chi 43.1
V.Hayes-Phi 101	Samuel-Phi-NY 42	Johnson-NY 6.2	Oquendo-StL 24.9	Bonds-Pit 12.2	Bonds-Pit 14	Santiago-SD 41.0
Raines-Mon 93	R.Alomar-SD 42	Raines-Mon 5.9	Thon-Phi 19.6	McReynolds-NY 7.6	Gwynn-SD 13	Scioscia-LA 39.2
Bonds-Pit 93	Raines-Mon 41	Samuel-Phi-NY 5.0	Uribe-SF 17.3	Strawberry-NY 4.9	Butler-SF 11	Manwaring-SF 36.7
	Johnson-NY 41	Nixon-Mon 3.9	Foley-Mon 15.5	Dykstra-NY-Phi 4.3		Reed-Cin 35.7
WINS	**WINNING PCT.**	**WINS ABOVE TEAM**	**GAMES STARTED**	**COMPLETE GAMES**	**FEWEST HITS/GAME**	**FEWEST BB/GAME**
Scott-Hou 20	Bielecki-Chi .720	Scott-Hou 5.0	Browning-Cin 37	Hurst-SD 10	DeLeon-StL 6.36	Robinson-SF 1.69
Maddux-Chi 19	D.Martinez-Mon .696	D.Martinez-Mon 4.9	DeLeon-StL 36	Belcher-LA 10	Fernandez-NY 6.44	Lilliquist-Atl 1.85
Magrane-StL 18	Reuschel-SF .680	Glavine-Atl 4.8	Maddux-Chi 35	Scott-Hou 9	Howell-Phi 6.84	D.Martinez-Mon 1.90
Bielecki-Chi 18	Scott-Hou .667	Bielecki-Chi 4.8		Magrane-StL 9	Smoltz-Atl 6.92	Whitson-SD 1.90
Reuschel-SF 17	Magrane-StL .667	DiPino-StL 4.5		Browning-Cin 9	Garrelts-SF 6.94	Glavine-Atl 1.94
STRIKEOUTS	**STRIKEOUTS/GAME**	**GAMES**	**SAVES**	**BASE RUNNERS/9**	**ADJUSTED RELIEF RUNS**	**RELIEF RANKING**
DeLeon-StL 201	Langston-Mon 8.92	Williams-Chi 76	Davis-SD 44	Andersen-Hou 8.93	Lancaster-Chi 18.2	Davis-SD 26.6
Belcher-LA 200	Fernandez-NY 8.12	Dibble-Cin 74	Williams-Chi 36	Garrelts-SF 9.08	Andersen-Hou 17.6	Howell-LA 26.1
Fernandez-NY 198	Belcher-LA 7.83	Parrett-Phi 72	Franco-Cin 32	Howell-LA 9.26	Dibble-Cin 17.5	Dibble-Cin 24.5
Cone-NY 190	Cone-NY 7.78	Dayley-StL 71	Howell-LA 28	Lancaster-Chi 9.29	Davis-SD 17.4	Burke-Mon 19.7
Hurst-SD 179	DeLeon-StL 7.39	Agosto-Hou 71	Burke-Mon 28	Darwin-Hou 9.37	Howell-LA 17.0	Darwin-Hou 18.5
INNINGS PITCHED	**OPPONENTS' AVG.**	**OPPONENTS' OBP**	**EARNED RUN AVERAGE**	**ADJUSTED ERA**	**ADJUSTED STARTER RUNS**	**PITCHER WINS**
Hershiser-LA 256.2	DeLeon-StL .197	Garrelts-SF .258	Garrelts-SF 2.28	Langston-Mon 149	Hershiser-LA 32.1	**Hershiser-LA 4.4**
Browning-Cin 249.2	Fernandez-NY .198	Scott-Hou .267	Hershiser-LA 2.31	Hershiser-LA 148	Garrelts-SF 23.1	**Maddux-Chi 2.9**
Hurst-SD 244.2	Smoltz-Atl .212	DeLeon-StL .268	Langston-Mon 2.39	Garrelts-SF 148	Hurst-SD 22.1	**Howell-LA 2.8**
DeLeon-StL 244.2	Garrelts-SF .212	Fernandez-NY .271	Whitson-SD 2.66	Whitson-SD 132	Whitson-SD 21.3	**Davis-SD 2.7**
Drabek-Pit 244.1	Scott-Hou .212	Smiley-Pit .273	Hurst-SD 2.69	Hurst-SD 131	Langston-Mon 20.5	**Whitson-SD 2.5**

Shaken to the Core

Just before Opening Day, NL President Bart Giamatti was appointed commissioner, and Bill White became the first African American league president. Giamatti immediately was presented with serious allegations against Pete Rose, accused of gambling on baseball games in which he was involved. Despite being Cincinnati's manager since 1984, Rose's shady dealings made him appear guilty to many.

In late August Rose—with no other option—signed an agreement banning him for life from the game, even though he denied gambling on baseball. Nine days later, Giamatti died of a heart attack, and Fay Vincent became the new commissioner.

Horror also visited the playing field. Giants pitcher Dave Dravecky suffered a broken arm while pitching, ending his career. He eventually lost the arm. Darrell Evans, Mike Schmidt, and Kent Tekulve also called it quits. Late in the season, Montreal debuted Larry Walker and Marquis Grissom, but the Expos goofed by trading Randy Johnson for Mark Langston, who soon departed via free agency.

San Francisco won again, with a veteran pitching staff and Kevin Mitchell's MVP season; Will Clark finished second in the voting. Despite Tony Gwynn's fourth batting title and reliever Mark Davis' Cy Young, the Padres fell just short.

Chicago, in another potentially earth-shaking event, captured the East despite a string of injuries. Outfielders Jerome Walton was Rookie of the Year, but Ryne Sandberg and Greg Maddux did most of the heavy lifting.

The Giants beat Chicago in a five-game NLCS. First basemen Clark and Mark Grace put on hitting shows, but San Francisco won three straight squeakers at home to wrap things up. The Bay Area was struck by an earthquake in the middle of a four-game A's World Series sweep of the Giants. Baseball's core had been shaken, and it would get worse.

1989 AMERICAN LEAGUE

TEAM	W	L	T	PCT	GB	HW	HL	R	OR	PA	H	2B	3B	HR	BB	SO	HB	SH	AVG	OBP	SLG	OPS	AOPS	BR	ABR	PF	SB	CS	BSA	BSR
East																														
Tor	89	73	0	.549	—	46	35	731	651	6216	1449	265	40	142	521	923	31	30	.260	.323	.398	721	103	19	29	99	144	58	71	11
Bal	87	75	0	.537	2	47	34	708	686	6173	1369	238	33	129	593	957	30	63	.252	.326	.379	705	101	-5	13	97	118	55	68	7
Bos	83	79	0	.512	6	46	35	**774**	735	6455	**1571**	**326**	30	108	**643**	755	36	52	**.277**	**.351**	**.403**	**754**	**105**	**114**	**63**	106	56	35	62	0
Mil	81	81	0	.500	8	45	36	707	679	6083	1415	235	32	126	455	791	**50**	51	.259	.318	.382	700	97	-23	-19	99	**165**	62	73	15
NY	74	87	0	.460	14.5	41	40	698	792	6094	1470	229	23	130	502	831	27	58	.269	.331	.391	722	104	25	30	99	137	60	70	9
Cle	73	89	0	.451	16	41	40	604	654	6110	1340	221	26	127	499	934	35	72	.245	.310	.365	675	88	-74	-86	102	74	51	59	-2
Det	59	103	0	.364	30	38	43	617	816	6132	1315	198	24	116	585	899	37	35	.242	.318	.351	669	90	-75	-62	98	103	50	67	5
West																														
Oak	99	63	0	.611	—	54	27	712	**576**	6110	1414	220	25	127	562	855	34	36	.261	.331	.381	712	103	12	35	97	157	55	74	15
KC	92	70	0	.568	7	**55**	26	690	635	6150	1428	227	41	101	554	897	29	42	.261	.329	.373	702	97	-10	-9	100	154	51	**75**	**16**
Cal	91	71	0	.562	8	52	29	669	578	6102	1422	208	37	**145**	429	1011	28	54	.256	.311	.386	697	97	-43	-32	98	89	40	69	6
Tex	83	79	0	.512	16	45	36	695	714	6098	1433	260	**46**	122	503	989	34	63	.263	.326	.394	720	100	18	5	102	101	49	67	5
Min	80	82	0	.494	19	45	36	740	738	6207	1542	278	35	117	478	**743**	39	51	.276	.334	.402	736	99	55	8	107	111	53	68	6
Sea	73	89	0	.451	26	40	41	694	728	6133	1417	237	29	134	489	838	45	35	.257	.320	.384	704	95	-16	-37	103	81	55	60	-1
Chi	69	92	0	.429	29.5	35	45	693	750	6132	1493	262	36	94	464	873	28	**85**	.271	.328	.383	711	102	4	17	98	97	52	65	3
Total	1133	—	—	—	—	630	503	9732	—	86195	20078	3404	457	1718	7277	12296	483	727	.261	.326	.384	709	—	—	—	—	1587	726	69	95

TEAM	CG	SHO	GR	SV	IP	H	HR	BB	SO	BR/9	ERA	AERA	OAV	OOB	PR	APR	PF	OSB	OCS	FA	E	WPB	DP	FW	PW	BW	BSW	DIF
East																												
Tor	12	12	277	38	1467.0	1408	99	478	849	11.8	3.58	106	.255	.317	49	34	98	115	54	.980	127	74	164	-.1	3.5	3.0	.4	1.3
Bal	16	7	312	44	1448.1	1518	134	486	676	12.6	4.00	95	.272	.331	-19	-31	98	114	51	**.986**	**87**	**46**	163	**2.3**	-3.2	1.3	.0	5.5
Bos	14	9	297	42	1460.1	1448	131	548	1054	12.5	4.01	102	.261	.328	-20	15	106	161	58	.980	127	51	162	-.1	1.5	**6.4**	-.7	-5.1
Mil	16	8	291	45	1432.1	1463	129	457	812	12.2	3.80	101	.265	.321	14	8	99	113	46	.975	155	**46**	164	-1.8	.8	-1.9	.8	2.1
NY	15	9	278	44	1414.2	1550	150	521	787	13.4	4.50	86	.281	.344	-98	-98	100	81	51	.980	122	49	**183**	.1	-10.0	3.1	.2	.0
Cle	23	13	287	38	1453.0	1423	107	**452**	844	11.8	3.65	109	.257	.313	38	51	102	126	50	.981	118	60	126	.4	5.2	-8.8	-.9	-4.0
Det	24	4	252	26	1427.1	1514	150	652	831	13.9	4.53	84	.274	.352	-103	-114	99	126	**65**	.979	130	60	153	-.3	-11.6	-6.3	-.2	-3.6
West																												
Oak	17	**20**	317	**57**	1448.1	1287	103	510	930	**11.3**	**3.09**	**120**	**.238**	**.305**	**128**	**102**	95	89	48	.979	129	84	159	-.2	**10.4**	3.6	.8	3.4
KC	27	13	264	38	1451.2	1415	**86**	455	978	11.7	3.55	109	.257	.314	54	52	100	**79**	56	.982	114	68	139	.7	5.3	-.9	**.9**	5.0
Cal	**32**	**20**	252	38	1454.1	1384	113	465	897	11.6	3.28	116	.253	.312	97	89	98	111	42	.985	96	65	173	1.7	9.1	-3.3	-.0	2.5
Tex	26	7	321	44	1434.1	**1279**	119	654	**1112**	12.4	3.91	102	.239	.324	-4	11	103	140	51	.978	136	107	137	-.6	1.1	.5	-.2	1.2
Min	19	8	297	38	1429.1	1495	139	500	851	12.8	4.28	97	.269	.332	-63	-21	107	115	49	.982	107	54	141	1.1	-2.1	.8	-.0	-.7
Sea	15	10	**330**	44	1438.0	1422	114	560	897	12.7	4.00	101	.259	.330	-19	5	104	115	52	.977	143	57	168	-1.1	.5	-3.8	-.8	-2.9
Chi	9	5	321	46	1422.0	1472	144	539	778	12.9	4.23	91	.269	.335	-54	-63	99	102	53	.975	151	71	176	-1.6	-6.4	1.7	-.4	-4.8
Total	265	145	4096	582	20181.0	—	—	—	—	12.4	3.88	—	.261	.326	—	—	—	—	—	.980	1742	892	2208	—	—	—	—	—

BATTER-FIELDER WINS	BATTING AVERAGE	ON-BASE PERCENTAGE	SLUGGING AVERAGE	ON-BASE PLUS SLUGGING	ADJUSTED OPS	ADJUSTED BATTER RUNS
R.Henderson-NY-Oak 4.6	Puckett-Min..........339	Boggs-Bos............430	Sierra-Tex............543	McGriff-Tor...........924	McGriff-Tor...........161	McGriff-Tor..........50.1
Boggs-Bos.........4.3	Lansford-Oak........336	Davis-Sea............424	McGriff-Tor...........525	Davis-Sea............920	Davis-Sea............155	Davis-Sea...........42.6
Molitor-Mil.........4.1	Boggs-Bos............330	R.Henderson-NY-Oak.411	Yount-Mil.............511	Yount-Mil.............896	Yount-Mil.............152	Yount-Mil............42.6
McGriff-Tor.........4.0	Yount-Mil.............318	McGriff-Tor...........399	Esasky-Bos..........500	Sierra-Tex............889	Sierra-Tex............146	Boggs-Bos...........41.3
Yount-Mil...........4.0	Franco-Tex...........316	Lansford-Oak........398	Davis-Sea............496	Boggs-Bos...........879	Baines-Chi-Tex.....143	Sierra-Tex...........34.8
RUNS	**HITS**	**DOUBLES**	**TRIPLES**	**HOME RUNS**	**TOTAL BASES**	**RUNS BATTED IN**
R.Henderson-NY-Oak113	Puckett-Min..........215	Boggs-Bos.............51	Sierra-Tex.............14	McGriff-Tor.............36	Sierra-Tex............344	Sierra-Tex............119
Boggs-Bos...........113	Sax-NY................205	Puckett-Min............45	White-Cal...............13	Carter-Cle..............35	Yount-Mil.............314	Mattingly-NY.........113
Yount-Mil.............101	Boggs-Bos...........205	Reed-Bos...............42	Bradley-Bal............10	McGwire-Oak.........33	Carter-Cle............303	Esasky-Bos..........108
Sierra-Tex............101	Yount-Mil.............195	Bell-Tor..................41		Jackson-KC............32	Mattingly-NY.........301	Jackson-KC..........105
McGriff-Tor.............98		Yount-Mil................38		Esasky-Bos............30	Puckett-Min..........295	Carter-Cle............105
BASES ON BALLS	**STOLEN BASES**	**BASE STEALING RUNS**	**FIELDING RUNS-INFIELD**	**FIELDING RUNS-OUTFIELD**	**OUTFIELD ASSISTS**	**CATCHER CS PCT.**
R.Henderson-NY-Oak126	R.Henderson-NY-Oak .77	R.Henderson-NY-Oak 12.0	Reynolds-Sea.....24.6	Snyder-Cle..........12.9	Barfield-Tor-NY.......20	Valle-Sea............42.2
McGriff-Tor...........119	Espy-Tex...............45	Pettis-Det..............4.2	Howell-Cal..........24.1	Puckett-Min.........10.7	Snyder-Cle.............18	Boone-KC...........41.7
Boggs-Bos...........107	White-Cal...............44	White-Cal..............4.1	Buechele-Tex.......18.8	Barfield-Tor-NY......9.9	Sierra-Tex..............13	Slaught-NY.........38.8
Seitzer-KC...........102	Sax-NY..................43	Felder-Mil..............4.0	Espinoza-NY........18.5	Polonia-Oak-NY.....8.8	Puckett-Min............13	Whitt-Tor.............31.1
Davis-Sea............101	Pettis-Det...............43	Franco-Tex............3.6	Gantner-Mil.........17.8	Orsulak-Bal...........6.0	Griffey-Sea............12	Allanson-Cle.......28.3
WINS	**WINNING PCT.**	**WINS ABOVE TEAM**	**GAMES STARTED**	**COMPLETE GAMES**	**FEWEST HITS/GAME**	**FEWEST BB/GAME**
Saberhagen-KC......23	Saberhagen-KC....793	Saberhagen-KC.....8.3	Stewart-Oak...........36	Saberhagen-KC......12	Ryan-Tex.............6.09	Key-Tor...............1.13
Stewart-Oak...........21	Blyleven-Cal.........773	Blyleven-Cal..........5.7	Milacki-Bal.............36	Morris-Det..............10	Gordon-KC..........6.74	Saberhagen-KC...1.48
Moore-Oak.............19	Davis-Oak............731	Ballard-Bal............4.9	Gubicza-KC...........36	Finley-Cal.................9	Stieb-Tor.............7.14	Blyleven-Cal........1.64
Davis-Oak..............19	Stewart-Oak.........700	Bankhead-Sea.......4.9			Saberhagen-KC...7.17	Bosio-Mil.............1.84
Ballard-Bal.............18	Ballard-Bal...........692	Henneman-Det......4.5			Moore-Oak..........7.19	Witt-Cal...............1.96
STRIKEOUTS	**STRIKEOUTS/GAME**	**GAMES**	**SAVES**	**BASE RUNNERS/9**	**ADJUSTED RELIEF RUNS**	**RELIEF RANKING**
Ryan-Tex..............301	Ryan-Tex...........11.32	Crim-Mil.................76	Russell-Tex............38	Saberhagen-KC...8.71	Montgomery-KC..25.5	Montgomery-KC..33.7
Clemens-Bos........230	Gordon-KC..........8.45	Murphy-Bos............74	Thigpen-Chi............34	Burns-Oak...........8.88	Olson-Bal............20.5	Henke-Tor...........29.4
Saberhagen-KC....193	Clemens-Bos.......8.17	Rogers-Tex............73	Schooler-Sea.........33	Russell-Tex..........8.92	Henke-Tor...........19.5	Russell-Tex.........29.3
Gubicza-KC..........173	Witt-Tex...............7.69	Russell-Tex............71	Plesac-Mil..............33	Montgomery-KC..9.10	Lamp-Bos............19.4	Jones-Cle...........27.2
Bosio-Mil..............173	Viola-Min.............7.07	Guetterman-NY......70	Eckersley-Oak........33	Plesac-Mil...........9.39	Minton-Cal..........17.5	Olson-Bal............26.6
INNINGS PITCHED	**OPPONENTS' AVG.**	**OPPONENTS' OBP**	**EARNED RUN AVERAGE**	**ADJUSTED ERA**	**ADJUSTED STARTER RUNS**	**PITCHER WINS**
Saberhagen-KC.262.1	Ryan-Tex...............187	Saberhagen-KC....251	Saberhagen-KC...2.16	Saberhagen-KC....179	Saberhagen-KC...48.4	**Saberhagen-KC. 5.3**
Stewart-Oak.......257.2	Gordon-KC...........210	Ryan-Tex..............275	Finley-Cal...........2.57	Finley-Cal............149	Blyleven-Cal.........31.7	**Moore-Oak.........3.7**
Gubicza-KC.......255.0	Saberhagen-KC....217	Moore-Oak...........286	Moore-Oak..........2.61	Moore-Oak...........142	Moore-Oak..........30.0	**Montgomery-KC 3.5**
Clemens-Bos.....253.1	Stieb-Tor.............219	Blyleven-Cal.........287	Blyleven-Cal........2.73	Blyleven-Cal.........140	Finley-Cal...........27.6	**Finley-Cal..........3.2**
Milacki-Bal........243.0	Moore-Oak...........219	Bosio-Mil..............289	McCaskill-Cal......2.93	Clemens-Bos........132	Clemens-Bos.......25.7	**Russell-Tex.........3.1**

Get Outta My Nest, It's Starting to Rumble

Baltimore, last-place finishers the year before, led the East for most of the summer on Jeff Ballard's 18-8 surprise season and a balanced lineup. Toronto, after a 12-24 start, hired Cito Gaston as manager. While the Orioles came to earth, the Blue Jays stayed hot and pulled into a first-place tie on August 31. Through the final month, both teams played well, and Toronto won the title by taking two thrilling contests from Baltimore at SkyDome on the season's last weekend.

In their new domed stadium, Toronto—featuring sluggers Fred McGriff and George Bell—topped three million fans, an AL first. Robin Yount won his second MVP for Milwaukee. Tommy John retired at 46, and Jim Rice quit with elbow problems. Former Angels hurler Donnie Moore was a suicide, and on Christmas, Billy Martin perished in a car crash.

Despite another Cy Young for Kansas City's Bret Saberhagen, Tony LaRussa's A's easily won the West. Dave Stewart enjoyed his third straight 20-win season, and Dennis Eckersley was dominating in relief. A thrill for third-place California was the rookie season of lefty Jim Abbott, born without a right hand. Seattle debuted two rookies, Omar Vizquel and Ken Griffey Jr., on Opening Day. Texas gave cups of coffee to kid outfielders Juan Gonzalez and Sammy Sosa.

Rickey Henderson, back in the A's fold after a midseason deal, went to town in the ALCS: Henderson reached base 15 times, stole 8 bases, scored 8 runs, and even hit 2 homers. While Oakland beat Toronto in five, the final two were nail-biters.

The A's-Giants World Series was longer and more earth-shaking than anyone would have guessed. Prior to Game 3, with Oakland up two games to none, a deadly earthquake hit the Bay Area. After a ten-day hiatus, the series resumed. The Athletics twice more wiped the floor with the Giants to sweep the Series, outscoring the NL champs, 32-14.

1988 NATIONAL LEAGUE

TEAM	W	L	T	PCT	GB	HW	HL	R	OR	PA	H	2B	3B	HR	BB	SO	HB	SH	AVG	OBP	SLG	OPS	AOPS	BR	ABR	PF	SB	CS	BSA	BSR
EAST																														
NY	100	60	0	.625	—	**56**	24	**703**	**532**	6105	1387	251	24	**152**	544	842	32	65	.256	**.325**	**.396**	**721**	**118**	**99**	**129**	96	140	51	73	13
Pit	85	75	0	.531	15	43	38	651	616	6090	1327	240	45	110	**553**	947	32	66	.247	.317	.369	686	104	34	40	99	119	60	66	5
Mon	81	81	1	.500	20	43	38	628	592	6169	1400	260	**48**	107	454	1053	32	66	.251	.309	.373	682	97	12	-19	105	189	89	68	10
Chi	77	85	1	.475	24	39	42	660	694	6202	**1481**	**262**	46	113	403	910	21	57	**.261**	.310	.383	693	100	30	0	105	120	46	72	10
StL	76	86	0	.469	25	41	40	578	633	6177	1373	207	33	71	484	**827**	22	105	.249	.309	.337	646	90	-49	-59	102	**234**	64	**79**	**29**
Phi	65	96	1	.404	35.5	38	42	597	734	6054	1294	246	31	106	489	981	**47**	67	.239	.306	.355	661	94	-21	-35	102	112	49	70	7
WEST																														
LA	94	67	1	.584	—	45	36	628	544	6045	1346	217	25	99	437	947	32	95	.248	.305	.352	657	98	-33	-16	97	131	46	74	13
Cin	87	74	0	.540	7	45	35	641	596	6062	1334	246	25	122	479	922	37	69	.246	.309	.368	677	97	7	-14	104	207	56	**79**	26
SD	83	78	0	.516	11	47	34	594	583	6032	1325	205	35	94	494	892	21	**106**	.247	.310	.351	661	98	-21	-9	98	123	50	71	10
SF	83	79	0	.512	11.5	45	36	670	626	6175	1353	227	44	113	550	1023	33	91	.248	.318	.368	686	108	32	61	96	121	78	61	-1
Hou	82	80	0	.506	12.5	44	37	617	631	6127	1338	239	31	96	474	840	38	77	.244	.306	.351	657	99	-32	-8	96	198	71	74	19
Atl	54	106	0	.338	39.5	28	51	555	741	6013	1319	228	28	96	432	848	21	74	.242	.298	.348	646	87	-57	-79	104	95	69	58	-3
Total	969	—	—	—	—	514	453	7522	—	73251	16277	2828	415	1279	5793	11032	368	938	.248	.310	.363	673	—	—	—	—	1789	729	71	138

TEAM	CG	SHO	GR	SV	IP	H	HR	BB	SO	BR/9	ERA	AERA	OAV	OOB	PR	APR	PF	OSB	OCS	FA	E	WPB	DP	FW	PW	BW	BSW	DIF
EAST																												
NY	31	22	241	46	1439.0	**1253**	**78**	**404**	**1100**	**10.6**	**2.91**	112	**.235**	**.291**	**86**	59	95	204	52	**.981**	**115**	56	127	**.9**	6.4	**13.9**	.2	-1.3
Pit	12	11	313	46	1440.2	1349	108	469	790	11.6	3.47	99	.250	.311	-3	-4	100	142	58	.980	125	74	128	.3	-.4	4.3	-.7	1.5
Mon	18	12	307	43	1482.2	1310	122	476	923	11.1	3.08	**118**	.238	.301	60	**86**	105	194	58	.978	142	53	145	-.5	**9.3**	-2.0	-.2	-6.6
Chi	30	10	290	29	1464.1	1494	115	490	897	12.4	3.84	95	.265	.325	-64	-32	106	139	**77**	.980	125	71	128	.5	-3.4	.0	-.2	-.8
StL	17	14	333	42	1470.2	1387	91	486	881	11.6	3.47	101	.252	.312	-4	7	102	118	62	**.981**	121	69	131	.6	.8	-6.4	**1.9**	-1.9
Phi	16	6	336	36	1433.0	1447	118	628	859	13.3	4.14	87	.265	.341	-110	-82	105	185	66	.976	145	70	139	-.7	-8.8	-3.8	-.5	-1.7
WEST																												
LA	**32**	**24**	295	**49**	1463.1	1291	84	473	1029	11.0	2.96	113	.237	.299	78	63	97	126	74	.977	142	50	126	-.5	6.8	-1.7	.2	8.8
Cin	24	13	**343**	43	1455.0	1271	121	504	934	11.1	3.35	107	.237	.303	16	34	103	129	72	.980	125	46	131	.4	3.7	-1.5	1.6	2.4
SD	30	9	238	39	1449.0	1332	112	439	885	11.1	3.28	104	.247	.304	27	19	99	**74**	56	**.981**	120	52	**147**	.6	2.0	-1.0	-.2	.9
SF	25	13	290	42	1462.1	1323	99	422	875	10.9	3.39	96	.242	.298	10	-22	95	119	44	.980	129	63	145	.2	-2.4	6.6	-1.4	-1.0
Hou	21	15	284	40	1474.2	1339	123	478	1049	11.3	3.41	98	.242	.304	7	-14	96	211	47	.978	138	**39**	124	-.3	-1.5	-.9	.8	2.9
Atl	14	4	318	25	1446.0	1481	108	524	810	12.7	4.09	89	.268	.334	-103	-65	106	148	62	.976	151	57	138	-1.1	-7.0	-8.5	-1.6	-7.8
Total	270	153	3588	480	17480.2	—	—	—	—	11.6	3.45	—	.248	.310	—	—	—	—	—	.979	1578	700	1609	—	—	—	—	—

BATTER-FIELDER WINS	BATTING AVERAGE	ON-BASE PERCENTAGE	SLUGGING AVERAGE	ON-BASE PLUS SLUGGING	ADJUSTED OPS	ADJUSTED BATTER RUNS
Strawberry-NY 4.9	Gwynn-SD .313	Daniels-Cin .397	Strawberry-NY .545	Strawberry-NY .911	Strawberry-NY 166	Clark-SF 50.6
Smith-StL 4.6	Palmeiro-Chi .307	Butler-SF .393	Galarraga-Mon .540	Clark-SF .894	Clark-SF 163	Strawberry-NY 47.5
Gibson-LA 4.4	Dawson-Chi .303	Clark-SF .386	Clark-SF .508	Galarraga-Mon .893	Gibson-LA 151	Gibson-LA 37.8
Larkin-Cin 4.3	Galarraga-Mon .302	Gibson-LA .377	VanSlyke-Pit .506	Gibson-LA .860	Bonds-Pit 146	Galarraga-Mon 34.7
VanSlyke-Pit 4.1	Perry-Atl .300	Gwynn-SD .373	Dawson-Chi .504	Daniels-Cin .860	Galarraga-Mon 146	Bonilla-Pit 34.0
RUNS	**HITS**	**DOUBLES**	**TRIPLES**	**HOME RUNS**	**TOTAL BASES**	**RUNS BATTED IN**
Butler-SF 109	Galarraga-Mon 184	Galarraga-Mon 42	VanSlyke-Pit 15	Strawberry-NY 39	Galarraga-Mon 329	Clark-SF 109
Gibson-LA 106	Dawson-Chi 179	Palmeiro-Chi 41	Coleman-StL 10	Davis-Hou 30	Dawson-Chi 298	Strawberry-NY 101
Clark-SF 102	Palmeiro-Chi 178	Sabo-Cin 40	Young-Hou 9	Galarraga-Mon 29	VanSlyke-Pit 297	VanSlyke-Pit 100
VanSlyke-Pit 101	Sax-LA 175	Bream-Pit 37	Samuel-Phi 9	Clark-SF 29	Strawberry-NY 296	Bonilla-Pit 100
Strawberry-NY 101	Larkin-Cin 174		Butler-SF 9	McReynolds-NY 27	Clark-SF 292	
BASES ON BALLS	**STOLEN BASES**	**BASE STEALING RUNS**	**FIELDING RUNS-INFIELD**	**FIELDING RUNS-OUTFIELD**	**OUTFIELD ASSISTS**	**CATCHER CS PCT.**
Clark-SF 100	Coleman-StL 81	Smith-StL 9.4	Smith-StL 21.0	Murphy-Atl 10.6	McReynolds-NY 18	Santiago-SD 44.7
Butler-SF 97	Young-Hou 65	Coleman-StL 8.4	Wallach-Mon 19.3	Thompson-Phi 6.9	Murphy-Atl 15	Scioscia-LA 41.4
Daniels-Cin 87	Smith-StL 57	McGee-StL 6.9	Bream-Pit 19.0	James-Phi 5.8	Coleman-StL 14	Berryhill-Chi 40.7
Johnson-NY 86	Sabo-Cin 46	Davis-Cin 6.7	R.Alomar-SD 15.5	McReynolds-NY 5.5	Bradley-Phi 14	Diaz-Cin 40.4
	Nixon-Mon 46	Larkin-Cin 6.3	Dunston-Chi 13.6	Bradley-Phi 5.3	VanSlyke-Pit 12	LaValliere-Pit 35.3
WINS	**WINNING PCT.**	**WINS ABOVE TEAM**	**GAMES STARTED**	**COMPLETE GAMES**	**FEWEST HITS/GAME**	**FEWEST BB/GAME**
Jackson-Cin 23	Cone-NY .870	Cone-NY 7.9	Reuschel-SF 36	Jackson-Cin 15	Fernandez-NY 6.11	B.Smith-Mon 1.45
Hershiser-LA 23	Browning-Cin .783	Jackson-Cin 7.6	Browning-Cin 36	Hershiser-LA 15	Perez-Mon 6.37	Mahler-Atl 1.52
Cone-NY 20	Jackson-Cin .742	Hershiser-LA 6.7	Jackson-Cin 35	Show-SD 13	Rijo-Cin 6.67	Reuschel-SF 1.54
Reuschel-SF 19	Hershiser-LA .742	Browning-Cin 6.5		Sutcliffe-Chi 12	Scott-Hou 6.67	Ojeda-NY 1.56
	Maddux-Chi .692	Maddux-Chi 5.9		Gooden-NY 10	Cone-NY 6.93	Tudor-StL-LA 1.87
STRIKEOUTS	**STRIKEOUTS/GAME**	**GAMES**	**SAVES**	**BASE RUNNERS/9**	**ADJUSTED RELIEF RUNS**	**RELIEF RANKING**
Ryan-Hou 228	Ryan-Hou 9.33	Murphy-Cin 76	Franco-Cin 39	Myers-NY 8.47	Franco-Cin 17.9	Franco-Cin 35.7
Cone-NY 213	Fernandez-NY 9.10	Robinson-Pit 75	Gott-Pit 34	Perez-Mon 8.81	Holton-LA 15.6	Davis-SD 29.4
DeLeon-StL 208	Rijo-Cin 8.89	Agosto-Hou 75	Worrell-StL 32	Franco-Cin 9.10	Davis-SD 15.5	Myers-NY 24.6
Scott-Hou 190	DeLeon-StL 8.31	Tekulve-Phi 70	Davis-SD 28	J.Howell-LA 9.14	Harris-Phi 13.0	Pena-LA 18.6
Fernandez-NY 189	Cone-NY 8.29	Franco-Cin 70	Bedrosian-Phi 28	Scott-Hou 9.18	Pena-LA 12.6	Parrett-Mon 17.8
INNINGS PITCHED	**OPPONENTS' AVG.**	**OPPONENTS' OBP**	**EARNED RUN AVERAGE**	**ADJUSTED ERA**	**ADJUSTED STARTER RUNS**	**PITCHER WINS**
Hershiser-LA 267.0	Fernandez-NY .191	Perez-Mon .252	Magrane-StL 2.18	Magrane-StL 162	Hershiser-LA 34.5	**Hershiser-LA 4.5**
Jackson-Cin 260.2	Perez-Mon .196	Scott-Hou .260	Cone-NY 2.22	Tudor-StL-LA 150	Cone-NY 27.6	**Franco-Cin 4.0**
Browning-Cin 250.2	Scott-Hou .204	Ojeda-NY .261	Hershiser-LA 2.26	Rijo-Cin 150	Tudor-StL-LA 24.2	**Davis-SD 3.6**
Mahler-Atl 249.0	Rijo-Cin .209	Hershiser-LA .269	Tudor-StL-LA 2.32	Perez-Mon 149	Jackson-Cin 24.1	**Jackson-Cin 3.0**
Maddux-Chi 249.0	Cone-NY .213	Fernandez-NY .271	Rijo-Cin 2.39	Hershiser-LA 148	Perez-Mon 23.8	**Cone-NY 2.8**

"I Don't Believe What I Just Saw"

Despite an undermanned offense and several pitching injuries, Los Angeles clung to the West Division lead. Free agent signing Kirk Gibson was MVP, while Orel Hershiser's record 59 scoreless innings won him a unanimous Cy Young. John Tudor's late-season acquisition buffed up the rotation.

The Mets, meanwhile, easily wrapped up the East. Darryl Strawberry enjoyed another spectacular season, as did Kevin McReynolds. Five Mets starters won in double figures. Manager Davey Johnson effectively platooned Mookie Wilson and Lenny Dykstra and found a position for late-season sensation Gregg Jefferies.

New York led in attendance, while second-place Pittsburgh's gate increased 61 percent. Wrigley Field saw its first night game on August 9; lights were difficult for many fans to accept. Cincinnati's Chris Sabo was Rookie of the Year, but several players not as impressive as freshmen had longer careers: Mark Grace, Roberto Alomar, Tom Glavine, Craig Biggio, and John Smoltz.

Owners were found guilty of collusion against 1987 free agents. This greased the path for Peter Ueberroth's resignation. Several "new-look" free agents were also granted their freedom and the owners paid hundreds of millions in damages.

Scoring dropped 14 percent to 3.88 runs per game, the lowest since 1968, and homers fell 30 percent. Both Los Angeles and New York played in great pitchers' parks. Injuries ended Bruce Sutter's career, while Steve Carlton, Dave Concepcion, Ted Simmons, and Don Sutton retired. Giants 1930s ace Carl Hubbell passed away at 85.

Nobody expected the Dodgers to win the NLCS, but Tommy Lasorda's boys hung in, winning a 12-inning Game 4 to knot the series. In Game 7 Hershiser threw yet another complete-game shutout—he had eight during the season and added a final one in the World Series. Los Angeles then shocked prohibitive favorite Oakland in the World Series. An injured Gibson limped off the bench and ripped Dennis Eckersley for a magical game-winning homer in the opener, sparking the five-game upset. Most games were close, and Los Angeles pitchers held the A's to just 11 runs.

1988 AMERICAN LEAGUE

TEAM	W	L	T	PCT	GB	HW	HL	R	OR	PA	H	2B	3B	HR	BB	SO	HB	SH	AVG	OBP	SLG	OPS	AOPS	BR	ABR	PF	SB	CS	BSA	BSR
EAST																														
Bos	89	73	0	.549	—	53	28	**813**	689	6334	**1569**	**310**	39	124	**623**	**728**	45	66	**.283**	**.357**	.420	**777**	**112**	**146**	**108**	105	65	36	64	2
Det	88	74	0	.543	1	50	31	703	658	6153	1358	213	28	143	588	841	29	66	.250	.324	.378	702	99	-21	3	97	87	42	67	4
Tor	87	75	0	.537	2	45	36	763	680	6193	1491	271	**47**	**158**	521	935	31	34	.268	.332	.419	751	108	69	62	101	107	36	75	11
Mil	87	75	0	.537	2	47	34	682	**616**	6064	1409	258	26	113	439	911	37	59	.257	.314	.375	689	91	-57	-65	101	**159**	55	74	16
NY	85	76	0	.528	3.5	46	34	772	748	6297	1469	272	12	148	588	935	30	36	.263	.333	.395	728	103	37	40	100	146	39	**79**	**18**
Cle	78	84	0	.481	11	44	37	666	731	6045	1435	235	28	134	416	866	37	36	.261	.314	.387	701	92	-38	-57	103	97	50	66	4
Bal	54	107	0	.335	34.5	34	46	550	789	5979	1275	199	20	137	504	869	32	40	.238	.305	.359	664	87	-105	-91	98	69	44	61	0
WEST																														
Oak	104	58	0	.642	—	**54**	27	800	620	6356	1474	251	22	156	580	926	**65**	54	.263	.336	.399	735	108	51	76	97	129	54	70	9
Min	91	71	0	.562	13	47	34	759	672	6180	1508	294	31	151	528	832	55	37	.274	.340	**.421**	761	109	97	73	103	107	63	63	1
KC	84	77	0	.522	19.5	44	36	704	648	6085	1419	275	40	121	486	944	33	46	.259	.321	.391	712	97	-9	-18	101	137	54	72	11
Cal	75	87	0	.463	29	35	46	714	771	6215	1458	258	31	124	469	819	49	63	.261	.321	.385	706	99	-19	-2	98	86	52	62	1
Chi	71	90	0	.441	32.5	40	41	631	757	6039	1327	224	35	132	446	908	34	**67**	.244	.303	.370	673	87	-96	-95	100	98	46	68	5
Tex	70	91	0	.435	33.5	38	43	637	735	6157	1378	227	39	112	542	1022	35	48	.252	.320	.368	688	90	-50	-67	103	130	57	70	9
Sea	68	93	0	.422	35.5	37	44	664	744	6017	1397	271	27	148	461	787	38	40	.257	.317	.398	715	95	-6	-37	105	95	61	61	0
Total	1131	——		—	—	614	517	9858	—	86114	19967	3558	425	1901	7191	12323	550	692	.259	.324	.391	715	—	—	—	—	1512	689	69	91

TEAM	CG	SHO	GR	SV	IP	H	HR	BB	SO	BR/9	ERA	AERA	OAV	OOB	PR	APR	PF	OSB	OCS	FA	E	WPB	DP	FW	PW	BW	BSW	DIF
EAST																												
Bos	26	14	250	37	1426.1	1415	143	493	**1085**	12.3	3.97	104	.259	.322	-1	23	104	107	48	.984	93	59	123	1.6	2.3	**10.9**	-.5	-6.4
Det	34	8	220	36	1445.2	1361	150	497	890	11.8	3.71	103	.248	.312	41	21	97	**80**	43	.982	109	65	129	.6	2.1	.3	-.3	4.2
Tor	16	**17**	294	47	1449.0	1404	143	528	904	12.4	3.80	104	.256	.326	27	26	100	120	55	.982	110	60	170	.6	2.6	6.3	.5	-3.9
Mil	30	8	252	51	1449.1	1355	125	**437**	832	**11.2**	3.45	**116**	.248	**.303**	84	**88**	101	95	45	.981	120	46	146	-.0	**8.9**	-6.6	1.0	2.7
NY	16	5	**304**	43	1456.0	1512	157	487	861	12.7	4.26	93	.267	.328	-48	-48	100	85	29	.978	134	**41**	161	-.9	-4.9	4.0	**1.2**	5.0
Cle	35	10	230	46	1434.0	1501	120	442	812	12.4	4.16	99	.270	.326	-31	-5	104	99	53	.980	124	46	131	-.3	-.5	-5.8	-.3	3.8
Bal	20	7	287	26	1416.0	1506	153	523	709	13.2	4.54	87	.274	.340	-90	-97	99	136	56	.980	119	60	172	.0	-9.8	-9.2	-.7	-6.8
WEST																												
Oak	22	9	290	**64**	1489.1	1376	116	553	983	11.8	**3.44**	110	.247	.316	**87**	62	96	93	56	.983	105	75	151	.9	6.3	7.7	.2	7.9
Min	18	9	265	52	1431.2	1457	146	453	897	12.3	3.93	104	.266	.325	6	23	103	112	41	**.986**	**84**	56	155	**2.1**	2.3	7.4	-.6	-1.2
KC	29	12	253	32	1428.1	1415	**102**	465	886	12.1	3.65	109	.258	.318	49	54	101	117	42	.980	124	67	147	-.3	5.5	-1.8	.5	-.3
Cal	26	9	262	33	1455.2	1503	135	568	817	13.1	4.32	90	.270	.338	-57	-73	98	98	**64**	.979	135	81	175	-.9	-7.4	-.2	-.6	3.0
Chi	11	9	293	43	1439.0	1467	138	533	754	12.7	4.12	97	.266	.331	-25	-20	101	108	53	.976	154	71	**177**	-2.1	-2.0	-9.6	-.2	4.3
Tex	**41**	11	251	31	1438.2	**1310**	129	654	912	12.6	4.05	101	**.244**	.329	-13	7	103	145	52	.979	131	108	145	-.7	.7	-6.8	.2	-4.0
Sea	28	11	292	28	1428.0	1385	144	558	981	12.5	4.15	101	.256	.327	-30	3	105	117	52	.980	123	66	168	-.2	.3	-3.7	-.7	-8.2
Total	352	139	3743	569	20187.0	—	—	—	—	12.4	3.97	—	.259	.324	—	—	—	—	—	.981	1665	901	2150	—	—	—	—	—

BATTER-FIELDER WINS	BATTING AVERAGE	ON-BASE PERCENTAGE	SLUGGING AVERAGE	ON-BASE PLUS SLUGGING	ADJUSTED OPS	ADJUSTED BATTER RUNS
Boggs-Bos..........6.4	Boggs-Bos............366	Boggs-Bos............476	Canseco-Oak........569	Boggs-Bos............965	Canseco-Oak........171	Boggs-Bos...........62.2
Canseco-Oak.....5.9	Puckett-Min...........356	Greenwell-Bos......416	McGriff-Tor............552	Canseco-Oak........959	Boggs-Bos............165	Canseco-Oak.......59.9
Puckett-Min........4.9	Greenwell-Bos......325	Davis-Sea.............412	Gaetti-Min.............551	Greenwell-Bos......946	Winfield-NY...........158	Greenwell-Bos.....49.1
Greenwell-Bos...4.7	Winfield-NY...........322	Winfield-NY...........398	Puckett-Min...........545	McGriff-Tor............928	Greenwell-Bos......157	Winfield-NY..........45.3
C.Ripken-Bal......4.2	Molitor-Mil.............312	Henderson-NY......394	Greenwell-Bos......531	Winfield-NY...........927	McGriff-Tor............156	Puckett-Min..........42.1

RUNS	HITS	DOUBLES	TRIPLES	HOME RUNS	TOTAL BASES	RUNS BATTED IN
Boggs-Bos............128	Puckett-Min...........234	Boggs-Bos..............45	Yount-Mil.................11	Canseco-Oak..........42	Puckett-Min...........358	Canseco-Oak........124
Canseco-Oak........120	Boggs-Bos............214	Ray-Cal...................42	Wilson-KC..............11	McGriff-Tor.............34	Canseco-Oak........347	Puckett-Min...........121
Henderson-NY......118	Greenwell-Bos......192	Puckett-Min............42	Reynolds-Sea.........11	McGwire-Oak..........32	Greenwell-Bos......313	Greenwell-Bos......119
Molitor-Mil.............115	Yount-Mil...............190	Brett-KC..................42	Greenwell-Bos..........8	Murray-Bal..............28	Brett-KC...............300	Evans-Bos............111
Puckett-Min...........109	Molitor-Mil.............190	Fernandez-Tor........41		Gaetti-Min...............28	Carter-Cle.............297	Winfield-NY...........107

BASES ON BALLS	STOLEN BASES	BASE STEALING RUNS	FIELDING RUNS-INFIELD	FIELDING RUNS-OUTFIELD	OUTFIELD ASSISTS	CATCHER CS PCT.
Boggs-Bos............125	Henderson-NY........93	Henderson-NY.....15.9	Guillen-Chi..........40.8	Barfield-Tor..........13.1	Snyder-Cle.............16	Boone-Cal...........40.0
Clark-NY...............113	Pettis-Det...............44	Pettis-Det..............6.2	Gruber-Tor...........26.4	Gladden-Min........12.1		Gedman-Bos.......38.5
C.Ripken-Bal.........102	Molitor-Mil..............41	Molitor-Mil.............5.5	Schofield-Cal.......21.7	Snyder-Cle............9.6		Nokes-Det...........38.3
Davis-Sea...............95	Canseco-Oak..........40	Wilson-KC..............5.3	White-KC.............20.9	Puckett-Min............9.3		Allanson-Cle........35.0
Greenwell-Bos........87		Redus-Chi...............5.0	Randolph-NY.......13.9	White-Cal...............8.5		Hassey-Oak.........31.6

WINS	WINNING PCT.	WINS ABOVE TEAM	GAMES STARTED	COMPLETE GAMES	FEWEST HITS/GAME	FEWEST BB/GAME
Viola-Min.................24	Viola-Min..............774	Viola-Min................8.3	Stewart-Oak............37	Stewart-Oak............14	Robinson-Det.......6.33	Anderson-Min......1.65
Stewart-Oak............21	Hurst-Bos..............750	Gubicza-KC...........6.3	Welch-Oak.............36	Clemens-Bos..........14	Higuera-Mil..........6.65	Swindell-Cle.........1.67
Gubicza-KC............20	Gubicza-KC.........714	Hurst-Bos...............5.8		Witt-Tex..................13	Stieb-Tor.............6.82	Alexander-Det......1.81
	Davis-Oak.............696	Langston-Sea........3.9		Witt-Cal..................12	Witt-Tex...............6.92	Bosio-Mil.............1.88
	Stieb-Tor..............667	Stieb-Tor...............3.8		Swindell-Cle...........12	Hough-Tex...........7.21	Viola-Min.............1.90

STRIKEOUTS	STRIKEOUTS/GAME	GAMES	SAVES	BASE RUNNERS/9	ADJUSTED RELIEF RUNS	RELIEF RANKING
Clemens-Bos........291	Clemens-Bos.......9.92	Crim-Mil..................70	Eckersley-Oak........45	Eckersley-Oak.....7.93	Henneman-Det....19.7	Henneman-Det....37.7
Langston-Sea.......235	Langston-Sea......8.09	Thigpen-Chi............68	Reardon-Min..........42	Higuera-Mil..........9.22	Mirabella-Mil........15.7	Harvey-Cal...........25.8
Viola-Min..............193	Witt-Tex...............7.64	Williams-Tex...........67	Jones-Cle...............37	McMurtry-Tex.......9.30	Jones-Cle............15.3	Jones-Cle............23.8
Stewart-Oak..........192	Higuera-Mil..........7.60	Henneman-Det.......65	Thigpen-Chi...........34	Jones-Cle............9.40	Jackson-Sea........14.4	Eckersley-Oak.....23.3
Higuera-Mil...........192	Moore-Sea..........7.16		Plesac-Mil.............30	Harvey-Cal...........9.47	Harvey-Cal...........14.2	Reardon-Min........23.0

INNINGS PITCHED	OPPONENTS' AVG.	OPPONENTS' OBP	EARNED RUN AVERAGE	ADJUSTED ERA	ADJUSTED STARTER RUNS	PITCHER WINS
Stewart-Oak.......275.2	Robinson-Det........197	Higuera-Mil...........263	Anderson-Min......2.45	Anderson-Min.......167	Higuera-Mil..........40.2	**Viola-Min.............4.7**
Gubicza-KC.......269.2	Higuera-Mil...........207	Clemens-Bos........270	Higuera-Mil..........2.45	Higuera-Mil...........163	Viola-Min.............40.1	**Higuera-Mil.........4.4**
Clemens-Bos.....264.0	Stieb-Tor...............210	Robinson-Det........282	Viola-Min.............2.64	Viola-Min...............155	Gubicza-KC.........37.3	**Gubicza-KC........3.9**
Langston-Sea....261.1	Witt-Tex.................216	Viola-Min..............286	Gubicza-KC.........2.70	Gubicza-KC..........148	Clemens-Bos.......34.3	**Henneman-Det..3.9**
Saberhagen-KC.260.2	Clemens-Bos........220	Swindell-Cle..........286	Clemens-Bos.......2.93	Clemens-Bos........141	Anderson-Min......31.0	**Anderson-Min....3.8**

OAKLAND SURPRISE

Some years, it's better just to stay home. The Baltimore Orioles lost their first 21 games of the season and finished a deep last. As scoring dropped 11 percent to its lowest full-season total since 1978, several big names from that time retired: Don Baylor, Chris Chambliss, Ron Guidry, Graig Nettles, and Joe Niekro.

The balance of power in the AL switched from East to West in the late 1980s; the league's best teams were now Oakland and Minnesota. The A's had a veteran staff led by 21-game winner Dave Stewart, who survived a record 16 balks called by umpires trying to enforce a short-lived edict from the commissioner's office. "Bash Brothers" Mark McGwire and MVP Jose Canseco (the first player with 40 homers and 40 steals in the same year), plowed up enough runs for 104 wins, the franchise's highest total since Connie Mack's Philadelphia juggernaut of 1931. The Twins actually won six more games than their world championship team of '87, but Oakland kept them at arm's length. Cy Young winner Frank Viola couldn't make up for lineup gaps and a lack of quality pitching.

Early in the schedule, the Yankees and Tigers paced the East. Slumping Boston fired manager John McNamara, and got hot under new skipper Joe Morgan. With Wade Boggs claiming his fifth batting title in six years, and Dwight Evans, Ellis Burks, and Mike Greenwell fashioning the league's top outfield, Boston won even though the team didn't have a dependable *third* starter until Mike Boddicker's arrival in July. Detroit, Milwaukee, Toronto, and New York all finished within 5 games. A second-place finish was the end of the road for the Tigers, the oldest team in the league and about to collapse.

Oakland took care of business in the ALCS, sweeping Boston in four with excellent pitching and Canseco's 3 homers. The World Series against the Dodgers, however, was anything but businesslike. After Kirk Gibson's pinch-homer sunk the A's in Game 1, Oakland fell in five.

1987 NATIONAL LEAGUE

TEAM	W	L	T	PCT	GB	HW	HL	R	OR	PA	H	2B	3B	HR	BB	SO	HB	SH	AVG	OBP	SLG	OPS	AOPS	BR	ABR	PF	SB	CS	BSA	BSR
EAST																														
StL	95	67	0	.586	—	**49**	32	798	693	6297	1449	252	49	94	**644**	933	18	84	.263	**.340**	.378	718	95	-9	-28	103	**248**	72	78	**29**
NY	92	70	0	.568	3	**49**	32	**823**	698	6333	**1499**	287	34	192	592	1012	31	70	**.268**	.339	**.434**	**773**	**115**	**84**	**119**	96	159	49	76	18
Mon	91	71	0	.562	4	48	33	741	720	6162	1467	**310**	39	120	501	918	35	57	.265	.328	.401	729	95	-4	-30	104	166	74	69	11
Pit	80	82	0	.494	15	47	34	723	744	6222	1464	282	45	131	535	914	29	71	.264	.330	.403	733	99	4	-5	101	140	58	71	11
Phi	80	82	0	.494	15	43	38	702	749	6190	1390	248	**51**	169	587	1109	25	63	.254	.327	.410	737	98	7	-18	104	111	49	69	7
Chi	76	85	0	.472	18.5	40	40	720	801	6197	1475	244	33	**209**	504	1064	21	59	.264	.326	.432	758	102	38	8	104	109	48	69	7
WEST																														
SF	90	72	0	.556	—	46	35	783	**669**	6248	1458	274	32	205	511	1094	**39**	55	.260	.324	.430	754	110	33	71	95	126	97	57	-6
Cin	84	78	0	.519	6	42	39	783	752	6196	1478	262	29	192	514	928	31	57	.266	.330	.427	757	102	42	14	104	169	46	**79**	21
Hou	76	86	0	.469	14	47	34	648	678	6143	1386	238	28	122	526	936	24	58	.253	.318	.373	691	92	-79	-54	96	162	46	78	20
LA	73	89	0	.451	17	40	41	635	675	6114	1389	236	23	125	445	923	31	82	.252	.309	.371	680	87	-111	-95	98	128	59	68	8
Atl	69	92	0	.429	20.5	42	39	747	829	6227	1401	284	24	152	641	**834**	38	**86**	.258	.339	.403	742	98	33	4	104	135	68	67	6
SD	65	97	0	.401	25	37	44	668	763	6177	1419	209	48	113	577	992	27	81	.260	.332	.378	710	98	-37	-10	96	198	91	69	12
Total	971	—	—	—	—	530	441	8771	—	74506	17275	3126	435	1824	6577	11657	349	823	.261	.328	.404	732	—	—	—	—	1851	757	71	142

TEAM	CG	SHO	GR	SV	IP	H	HR	BB	SO	BR/9	ERA	AERA	OAV	OOB	PR	APR	PF	OSB	OCS	FA	E	WPB	DP	FW	PW	BW	BSW	DIF
EAST																												
StL	10	7	362	48	1466.0	1484	**129**	533	873	12.5	3.91	107	.265	.331	28	46	103	**100**	49	**.982**	**116**	62	172	**.9**	4.6	-2.8	**1.7**	9.6
NY	16	7	308	**51**	1454.0	1407	135	510	1032	12.1	3.84	100	.254	.319	38	-3	94	161	57	.978	137	51	137	-.3	-.3	**11.8**	.6	-.8
Mon	16	8	335	50	1450.1	1428	145	**446**	1012	**11.8**	3.92	**109**	.257	**.312**	26	**52**	104	202	46	.976	147	55	122	-.9	**5.2**	-3.0	-.0	8.8
Pit	25	**13**	313	39	1445.0	1377	164	562	914	12.2	4.20	99	.253	.323	-19	-6	102	134	84	.980	123	70	147	.5	-.6	-.5	-.0	-.3
Phi	13	7	389	48	1448.1	1453	167	587	877	12.9	4.18	102	.263	.335	-16	16	105	184	63	.980	121	52	137	.6	1.6	-1.8	-.5	-.9
Chi	11	5	327	48	1434.2	1524	159	628	1024	13.7	4.55	95	.275	.349	-76	-36	106	169	69	.979	130	71	154	.0	-3.6	.8	-.5	-1.3
WEST																												
SF	19	10	348	38	1471.0	1407	146	547	1038	12.1	**3.68**	105	.255	.323	**66**	29	94	132	**87**	.980	129	74	**183**	.1	2.9	7.1	-1.8	.7
Cin	7	6	**392**	44	1452.1	1486	170	485	919	12.4	4.24	99	.267	.326	-27	-4	103	139	75	.979	130	**46**	137	.0	-.4	1.4	.9	1.0
Hou	13	**13**	316	33	1441.1	**1363**	141	525	**1137**	12.0	3.84	102	**.250**	.317	38	14	96	199	54	.981	**116**	50	113	**.9**	1.4	-5.4	.8	-2.7
LA	**29**	8	281	32	1455.0	1415	130	565	1097	12.4	3.72	107	.255	.325	59	43	98	120	65	.975	155	62	144	-1.3	4.3	-9.5	-.4	-1.1
Atl	16	4	324	32	1427.2	1529	163	587	837	13.6	4.63	93	.276	.347	-87	-45	106	185	57	**.982**	**116**	53	170	.8	-4.5	.4	-.6	-7.7
SD	14	10	335	33	1433.1	1402	175	602	897	12.8	4.27	93	.256	.332	-30	-51	97	126	51	.976	147	77	135	-.9	-5.1	-1.0	.0	-9.1
Total	189	98	4030	496	17379.0	—	—	—	—	12.5	4.08	—	.261	.328	—	—	—	—	—	.979	1567	723	1751	—	—	—	—	—

BATTER-FIELDER WINS	BATTING AVERAGE	ON-BASE PERCENTAGE	SLUGGING AVERAGE	ON-BASE PLUS SLUGGING	ADJUSTED OPS	ADJUSTED BATTER RUNS
Davis-Cin 5.9	Gwynn-SD 370	Clark-StL..............459	Clark-StL..............597	Clark-StL............1055	Clark-StL..............173	Gwynn-SD 55.3
Gwynn-SD 5.8	Guerrero-LA.........338	Gwynn-SD 447	Davis-Cin 593	Murphy-Atl 997	Strawberry-NY......163	Clark-StL..............53.3
Raines-Mon 4.9	Raines-Mon 330	Raines-Mon 429	Strawberry-NY......583	Davis-Cin 991	Gwynn-SD 160	Strawberry-NY.....51.2
Murphy-Atl 4.6	Kruk-SD...............313	Murphy-Atl 417	Clark-SF 580	Strawberry-NY......981	Guerrero-LA..........156	Murphy-Atl 49.7
Smith-StL........... 4.3	James-Atl.............312	Guerrero-LA.........416	Murphy-Atl 580	Gwynn-SD 958	Murphy-Atl 155	Guerrero-LA.........46.3
RUNS	**HITS**	**DOUBLES**	**TRIPLES**	**HOME RUNS**	**TOTAL BASES**	**RUNS BATTED IN**
Raines-Mon 123	Gwynn-SD 218	Wallach-Mon..........42	Samuel-Phi 15	Dawson-Chi 49	Dawson-Chi 353	Dawson-Chi 137
Coleman-StL.........121	Guerrero-LA.........184	Smith-StL...............40	Gwynn-SD 13	Murphy-Atl 44	Samuel-Phi 329	Wallach-Mon.........123
Davis-Cin 120	Smith-StL..............182	Galarraga-Mon 40	VanSlyke-Pit 11	Strawberry-NY 39	Murphy-Atl 328	Schmidt-Phi 113
Gwynn-SD 119	Coleman-StL.........180		McGee-StL 11	Davis-Cin 37	Strawberry-NY 310	Clark-StL...............106
Murphy-Atl 115			Coleman-StL...........10	Johnson-NY............36	Clark-SF 307	
BASES ON BALLS	**STOLEN BASES**	**BASE STEALING RUNS**	**FIELDING RUNS-INFIELD**	**FIELDING RUNS-OUTFIELD**	**OUTFIELD ASSISTS**	**CATCHER CS PCT.**
Clark-StL..............136	Coleman-StL.........109	Coleman-StL........16.3	Hubbard-Atl 28.3	Bonds-Pit.............16.4	Wilson-Phi 18	LaValliere-Pit 45.2
Hayes-Phi 121	Gwynn-SD 56	Raines-Mon 9.3	Hernandez-NY.....16.3	Davis-Cin 15.5	Hatcher-Hou 16	Diaz-Cin...............36.4
Murphy-Atl 115	Hatcher-Hou 53	Davis-Cin 8.9	Templeton-SD......13.4	Wilson-Phi 9.9	Coleman-StL...........16	Scioscia-LA..........35.6
Strawberry-NY........97	Raines-Mon 50	Hatcher-Hou 8.5	Santana-NY 12.6	Raines-Mon 6.9	Bonds-Pit................15	Santiago-SD 32.5
Raines-Mon 90	Davis-Cin 50	Gwynn-SD 8.1	Smith-StL............11.8	Hatcher-Hou 5.1	Murphy-Atl 14	J.Davis-Chi 30.4
WINS	**WINNING PCT.**	**WINS ABOVE TEAM**	**GAMES STARTED**	**COMPLETE GAMES**	**FEWEST HITS/GAME**	**FEWEST BB/GAME**
Sutcliffe-Chi 18	Gooden-NY...........682	Sutcliffe-Chi 5.1	Z.Smith-Atl.............36	Reuschel-Pit-SF 12	Ryan-Hou 6.55	Reuschel-Pit-SF ..1.67
Rawley-Phi..............17	Sutcliffe-Chi 643	Leach-NY...............4.9	Scott-Hou................36	Valenzuela-LA 12	Scott-Hou.............7.23	Heaton-Mon.........1.72
Scott-Hou................16	Welch-LA 625	Welch-LA 4.2	Rawley-Phi..............36	Hershiser-LA..........10	Welch-LA 7.30	Gullickson-Cin 2.13
Hershiser-LA...........16	Rawley-Phi...........607	Z.Smith-Atl.............4.2		Z.Smith-Atl...............9	Dunne-Pit.............7.88	Forsch-StL 2.26
	Z.Smith-Atl..........600	Dunne-Pit...............3.9		Scott-Hou..................8	Darling-NY 7.93	Drabek-Pit............2.35
STRIKEOUTS	**STRIKEOUTS/GAME**	**GAMES**	**SAVES**	**BASE RUNNERS/9**	**ADJUSTED RELIEF RUNS**	**RELIEF RANKING**
Ryan-Hou 270	Ryan-Hou 11.48	Tekulve-Phi 90	Bedrosian-Phi.........40	Burke-Mon...........8.01	Burke-Mon 28.0	Worrell-StL...........31.8
Scott-Hou..............233	Scott-Hou.............8.47	Murphy-Cin.............87	Smith-Chi................36	Perez-Mon 8.83	McGaffigan-Mon..23.3	Franco-Cin...........29.3
Welch-LA...............196	Sebra-Mon...........7.92	Williams-Cin............85	Worrell-StL..............33	Smith-Hou............9.15	Williams-Cin.........18.6	Burke-Mon 29.1
Valenzuela-LA 190	Gooden-NY..........7.41	J.Robinson-SF-Pit.....81	Franco-Cin 32	Perry-StL-Cin.......9.78	Worrell-StL...........16.4	Smith-Chi..............22.8
Hershiser-LA.........190	Darling-NY 7.24	McCullers-SD 78	McDowell-NY..........25	Reuschel-Pit-SF 10.19	J.Robinson-SF-Pit ...15.8	J.Robinson-SF-Pit ...22.7
INNINGS PITCHED	**OPPONENTS' AVG.**	**OPPONENTS' OBP**	**EARNED RUN AVERAGE**	**ADJUSTED ERA**	**ADJUSTED STARTER RUNS**	**PITCHER WINS**
Hershiser-LA......264.2	Ryan-Hou 199	Scott-Hou..............281	Ryan-Hou 2.76	Ryan-Hou 142	Ryan-Hou 26.9	**Hershiser-LA...... 3.5**
Welch-LA 251.2	Scott-Hou..............217	Reuschel-Pit-SF ...282	Dunne-Pit.............3.03	Dunne-Pit..............138	Hershiser-LA........26.1	**Worrell-StL 3.2**
Valenzuela-LA ...251.0	Welch-LA 221	Ryan-Hou 284	Hershiser-LA........3.06	Reuschel-Pit-SF ...132	Welch-LA 25.2	**Franco-Cin.......... 2.9**
Scott-Hou..........247.2	Darling-NY 233	Welch-LA 289	Reuschel-Pit-SF ..3.09	Hershiser-LA.........130	Reuschel-Pit-SF ..23.9	**Burke-Mon.......... 2.9**
Z.Smith-Atl.........242.0	Dunne-Pit.............240	Drabek-Pit.............294	Gooden-NY.........3.21	Welch-LA 124	Scott-Hou............21.8	**Ryan-Hou............ 2.5**

Hum-Birds

Prior to the season, some very attractive free agents found surprisingly little interest. "Unwanted" Andre Dawson gave the Cubs a blank contract, then for a relatively small salary hit 49 homers and captured MVP honors. He couldn't carry Chicago out of last place, however. St. Louis jumped to an early lead, and then held off the Mets to win Whitey Herzog's last title.

Vince Coleman cleared 100 steals for the third time, Jack Clark led the NL in slugging and on-base percentage, and Ozzie Smith finished second in MVP voting. No St. Louis pitcher won more than 11, but eight won at least eight. The Cardinals—along with the Mets—became the first besides Los Angeles to draw three million; league attendance increased 10 percent.

Mets sluggers Darryl Strawberry and Howard Johnson did their best, but Dwight Gooden was suspended for drug possession and several hurlers suffered injuries. Philadelphia's Steve Bedrosian won an extraordinarily close Cy Young vote over Ricks Sutcliffe and Reuschel.

Last in 1985, Roger Craig's "Hum Baby" Giants acquired Reuschel, Kevin Mitchell, Dave Dravecky, and Don Robinson in midseason deals and won the West Division. Will Clark led the attack. The remarkable Eric Davis couldn't quite carry Cincinnati to the division crown; the Reds lacked pitching. Padres receiver Benito Santiago took Rookie of the Year. Houston's Nolan Ryan was 8-16 but fanned a record 11.48 hitters per game.

The .261 league average was the decade's highest, as was the scoring rate. Homers also increased 19 percent. Former Dodgers infielders Ron Cey, Steve Garvey, and Davey Lopes all retired, as did 48-year-old Phil Niekro.

San Francisco went up three games to two in the NLCS on timely hitting and veteran pitching, but John Tudor and Danny Cox shut out the Giants in Games 6 and 7 at Busch Stadium. St. Louis couldn't win the World Series, however, falling in seven to Minnesota.

1987 AMERICAN LEAGUE

TEAM	W	L	T	PCT	GB	HW	HL	R	OR	PA	H	2B	3B	HR	BB	SO	HB	SH	AVG	OBP	SLG	OPS	AOPS	BR	ABR	PF	SB	CS	BSA	BSR
EAST																														
Det	98	64	0	.605	—	54	27	**896**	735	6443	1535	274	32	**225**	**653**	913	46	39	.272	.349	**.451**	**800**	**114**	**94**	**131**	96	106	50	68	6
Tor	96	66	0	.593	2	52	29	845	**655**	6293	1514	277	38	215	555	970	38	30	.269	.336	.446	782	103	43	23	102	126	50	72	10
Mil	91	71	0	.562	7	48	33	862	817	6368	1552	272	46	163	598	1040	32	63	.276	.346	.428	774	101	41	15	103	**176**	74	70	**13**
NY	89	73	0	.549	9	51	30	788	758	6219	1445	239	16	196	604	949	28	38	.262	.336	.418	754	99	-5	1	99	105	43	71	8
Bos	78	84	0	.481	20	50	30	842	825	6359	**1554**	273	26	174	606	**825**	**57**	52	**.278**	**.352**	.430	782	103	64	40	103	77	45	63	1
Bal	67	95	0	.414	31	31	51	729	880	6185	1437	219	20	211	524	939	22	31	.258	.322	.418	740	96	-50	-32	98	69	45	61	-1
Cle	61	101	0	.377	37	35	46	742	957	6212	1476	267	30	187	489	977	31	44	.263	.324	.422	746	95	-36	-43	101	140	54	72	12
WEST																														
Min	85	77	0	.525	—	**56**	25	786	806	6088	1422	258	35	196	523	898	38	47	.261	.328	.430	758	95	-8	-36	104	113	65	63	2
KC	83	79	0	.512	2	46	35	715	691	6128	1443	239	40	168	523	1034	30	34	.262	.328	.412	740	91	-42	-62	103	125	43	**74**	12
Oak	81	81	0	.500	4	42	39	806	789	6238	1432	263	33	199	593	1056	36	50	.260	.333	.428	761	107	5	60	94	140	63	69	9
Sea	78	84	0	.481	7	40	41	760	801	6139	1499	282	**48**	161	500	863	43	38	.272	.335	.428	763	95	9	-30	105	174	73	70	**13**
Chi	77	85	0	.475	8	38	43	748	746	6164	1427	**283**	36	173	487	971	33	54	.258	.319	.415	734	90	-57	-77	103	138	52	73	12
Tex	75	87	0	.463	10	43	38	823	849	6248	1478	264	35	194	567	1081	24	42	.266	.333	.430	763	99	9	4	101	120	71	63	2
Cal	75	87	0	.463	10	38	43	770	803	6301	1406	257	26	172	590	926	35	**70**	.252	.326	.401	727	94	-64	-40	97	125	44	**74**	12
Total	1134	—	—	—	—	624	510	11112	—	87385	20620	3667	461	2634	7812	13442	493	632	.265	.333	.425	759	—	—	—	—	1734	772	69	111

TEAM	CG	SHO	GR	SV	IP	H	HR	BB	SO	BR/9	ERA	AERA	OAV	OOB	PR	APR	PF	OSB	OCS	FA	E	WPB	DP	FW	PW	BW	BSW	DIF
EAST																												
Det	33	10	247	31	1456.0	1430	180	563	976	12.5	4.02	106	.256	.325	70	38	95	118	43	.980	122	85	147	.1	3.6	**12.5**	-.2	1.0
Tor	18	8	**336**	43	1454.0	**1323**	158	567	1064	**11.8**	**3.74**	**121**	**.244**	**.316**	**115**	**123**	101	123	59	.982	111	69	148	.8	**11.7**	2.2	.2	.1
Mil	28	6	282	45	1464.0	1548	169	529	1039	12.9	4.62	99	.271	.333	-27	-5	103	119	58	.976	145	58	155	-1.3	-.5	1.4	**.5**	9.9
NY	19	10	278	**47**	1446.1	1475	179	542	900	12.8	4.36	101	.266	.332	16	10	99	114	63	.983	102	83	155	1.3	1.0	.0	.0	5.6
Bos	**47**	**13**	236	16	1436.0	1584	190	517	1034	13.4	4.77	95	.282	.344	-50	-34	102	109	60	.982	110	67	158	.8	-3.2	3.8	-.7	-3.7
Bal	17	6	294	30	1439.2	1555	226	547	870	13.3	5.01	88	.276	.341	-88	-94	99	145	57	.982	111	57	**174**	.8	-9.0	-3.1	-.9	-1.9
Cle	24	8	308	25	1422.2	1566	219	606	849	14.1	5.28	86	.278	.351	-131	-113	102	111	51	.975	153	90	128	-1.8	-10.8	-4.1	.4	-3.7
WEST																												
Min	16	4	289	39	1427.1	1465	210	564	990	13.1	4.63	100	.266	.337	-27	0	104	168	46	**.984**	**98**	83	147	**1.6**	.0	-3.4	-.6	6.4
KC	44	11	225	26	1424.0	1424	**128**	548	923	12.7	3.86	119	.261	.330	95	111	103	124	**66**	.979	131	71	151	-.5	10.6	-5.9	.4	-2.6
Oak	18	6	328	40	1445.2	1442	176	531	1042	12.5	4.32	96	.258	.324	22	-30	93	117	54	.977	142	70	122	-1.1	-2.9	5.7	.1	-1.8
Sea	39	10	251	33	1430.2	1503	199	**497**	919	12.8	4.49	105	.272	.332	-5	36	106	111	50	.980	122	51	150	.1	3.4	-2.9	**.5**	-4.2
Chi	29	12	270	37	1447.2	1436	189	537	792	12.5	4.30	107	.259	.327	26	49	104	98	51	.981	116	**46**	**174**	.5	4.7	-7.3	.4	-2.2
Tex	20	3	329	27	1444.1	1388	199	760	**1103**	13.7	4.63	97	.253	.347	-28	-21	101	205	56	.976	151	134	148	-1.7	-2.0	.4	-.6	-2.1
Cal	20	7	244	36	1457.1	1481	212	504	941	12.5	4.38	99	.264	.327	13	-11	97	**72**	58	.981	117	65	162	.4	-1.0	-3.8	.4	-1.9
Total	372	114	3917	475	20195.2	—	—	—	—	12.9	4.46	—	.265	.333	—	—	—	—	—	.980	1731	1029	2119	—	—	—	—	—

BATTER-FIELDER WINS	BATTING AVERAGE	ON-BASE PERCENTAGE	SLUGGING AVERAGE	ON-BASE PLUS SLUGGING	ADJUSTED OPS	ADJUSTED BATTER RUNS
Boggs-Bos.........6.5	Boggs-Bos...........363	Boggs-Bos...........461	McGwire-Oak........618	Boggs-Bos.........1049	Boggs-Bos...........172	Boggs-Bos...........64.5
Trammell-Det.....6.1	Molitor-Mil............353	Molitor-Mil............438	Bell-Tor................605	Molitor-Mil...........1003	McGwire-Oak........167	McGwire-Oak.......53.5
Fernandez-Tor ...4.1	Trammell-Det........343	Evans-Bos............417	Boggs-Bos............588	McGwire-Oak........987	Molitor-Mil...........159	Trammell-Det.......49.7
Molitor-Mil..........3.9	Puckett-Min...........332	Randolph-NY........411	Evans-Bos............569	Evans-Bos............986	Trammell-Det........157	Evans-Bos..........48.0
McGwire-Oak.....3.5	Mattingly-NY.........327	Trammell-Det........402	Molitor-Mil............566	Bell-Tor................957	Evans-Bos............155	Molitor-Mil...........43.3

RUNS	HITS	DOUBLES	TRIPLES	HOME RUNS	TOTAL BASES	RUNS BATTED IN
Molitor-Mil.............114	Seitzer-KC............207	Molitor-Mil..............41	Wilson-KC...............15	McGwire-Oak..........49	Bell-Tor................369	Bell-Tor.................134
Bell-Tor.................111	Puckett-Min...........207	Boggs-Bos..............40	Polonia-Oak............10	Bell-Tor..................47	McGwire-Oak........344	Evans-Bos............123
Whitaker-Det.........110	Trammell-Det.........205		P.Bradley-Sea.........10		Puckett-Min...........333	McGwire-Oak.........118
Downing-Cal.........110	Boggs-Bos.............200		Yount-Mil...................9		Trammell-Det.........329	Joyner-Cal............117
	Yount-Mil...............198				Boggs-Bos............324	Mattingly-NY..........115

BASES ON BALLS	STOLEN BASES	BASE STEALING RUNS	FIELDING RUNS-INFIELD	FIELDING RUNS-OUTFIELD	OUTFIELD ASSISTS	CATCHER CS PCT.
Evans-Bos............106	Reynolds-Sea.........60	Wilson-KC...............9.1	Barrett-Bos...........32.6	White-Cal.............17.6	Sierra-Tex...............17	Boone-Cal............46.3
Downing-Cal.........106	Wilson-KC...............59	Redus-Chi...............7.6	Reynolds-Sea.......24.0	Kingery-Sea.........13.6	Barfield-Tor.............17	Whitt-Tor...............35.7
Boggs-Bos............105	Redus-Chi...............52	Molitor-Mil...............6.4	White-KC...............22.1	Barfield-Tor..........13.4	White-Cal................16	Bando-Cle.............33.3
Evans-Det.............100	Molitor-Mil..............45	Henderson-NY.......6.2	Salazar-KC...........20.3	Braggs-Mil............10.2	Snyder-Cle..............16	Kennedy-Bal.........30.6
Butler-Cle................91	Henderson-NY.........41	Reynolds-Sea........6.2	Gagne-Min.............19.3	Gladden-Min............7.1		Slaught-Tex..........25.6

WINS	WINNING PCT.	WINS ABOVE TEAM	GAMES STARTED	COMPLETE GAMES	FEWEST HITS/GAME	FEWEST BB/GAME
Stewart-Oak............20	Clemens-Bos........690	Clemens-Bos.........6.5	Hough-Tex..............40	Clemens-Bos..........18	Key-Tor................7.24	Long-Chi..............1.49
Clemens-Bos..........20	Key-Tor.................680	Alexander-Det.........4.5	Stewart-Oak............37	Saberhagen-KC......15	Hough-Tex............7.51	Saberhagen-KC...1.86
Langston-Sea.........19	Saberhagen-KC....643	Saberhagen-KC......4.3	Clancy-Tor..............37	Hurst-Bos...............15	Morris-Det.............7.68	Sutton-Cal............1.93
	Higuera-Mil...........643	Stewart-Oak...........4.2	Blyleven-Min...........37	Langston-Sea.........14	Stewart-Oak..........7.71	Bannister-Chi.........1.93
		Langston-Sea.........4.1		Higuera-Mil.............14	DeLeon-Chi..........7.73	Young-Oak............1.95

STRIKEOUTS	STRIKEOUTS/GAME	GAMES	SAVES	BASE RUNNERS/9	ADJUSTED RELIEF RUNS	RELIEF RANKING
Langston-Sea.......262	Langston-Sea......8.67	Eichhorn-Tor...........89	Henke-Tor...............34	Henke-Tor.............8.33	Henke-Tor............21.6	Henke-Tor............29.2
Clemens-Bos.........256	Higuera-Mil...........8.25	Williams-Tex............85	Righetti-NY.............31	Alexander-Det......9.07	Eichhorn-Tor.........19.8	Thigpen-Chi..........28.4
Higuera-Mil...........240	Clemens-Bos.........8.18	Mohorcic-Tex..........74	Reardon-Min...........31	Eckersley-Oak.....9.26	Mohorcic-Tex........18.3	Mohorcic-Tex........27.9
Hough-Tex.............223	Bosio-Mil...............7.94	Henke-Tor...............72	Plesac-Mil...............23	Key-Tor..................9.59	Thigpen-Chi..........17.8	Plesac-Mil.............27.8
Morris-Det.............208	Nieves-Mil.............7.50	Musselman-Tor........68	Buice-Cal................17	Wilkinson-Sea.......9.67	Eckersley-Oak......16.8	Eichhorn-Tor.........23.7

INNINGS PITCHED	OPPONENTS' AVG.	OPPONENTS' OBP	EARNED RUN AVERAGE	ADJUSTED ERA	ADJUSTED STARTER RUNS	PITCHER WINS
Hough-Tex.........285.1	Key-Tor.................221	Key-Tor.................272	Key-Tor.................2.76	Key-Tor.................164	Clemens-Bos.......49.2	**Clemens-Bos.....4.5**
Clemens-Bos.....281.2	Hough-Tex............223	Bannister-Chi........285	Viola-Min...............2.90	Viola-Min...............160	Key-Tor.................47.9	**Viola-Min.............4.5**
Langston-Sea.....272.0	Morris-Det.............228	Morris-Det.............293	Clemens-Bos.........2.97	Clemens-Bos........154	Viola-Min...............45.9	**Key-Tor...............4.3**
Blyleven-Min......267.0	Stewart-Oak..........229	Young-Oak............293	Saberhagen-KC...3.36	Saberhagen-KC....137	Saberhagen-KC...38.3	**Saberhagen-KC.3.8**
Morris-Det.........266.0	DeLeon-Chi...........230	Viola-Min...............293	Morris-Det............3.38	Leibrandt-KC........135	Leibrandt-KC.......30.3	**Leibrandt-KC......3.3**

Twinkies in a Box

Milwaukee won 13 straight to start the season, but the Brewers fell off the pace despite Paul Molitor's 39-game hitting streak. Boston didn't win despite Roger Clemens' second consecutive Cy Young. The real race was at the border.

The Tigers and Blue Jays hung close into September. Toronto's George Bell was MVP, while Doyle Alexander went 9-0 for Detroit when acquired from Atlanta in August (for farmhand John Smoltz). Detroit was old; only one regular and one starter were under 29. Toronto, meanwhile, struggled to find starting pitching. From September 24-26, the Jays swept the Tigers to build a lead of $3^1/_2$; from that point, Toronto lost four straight while Detroit perked up. In a thrilling Jays-Tigers set on the final weekend at Detroit, the Tigers won to move into a tie on Friday, moved ahead with a comeback victory Saturday, and clinched on Frank Tanana's 1-0 shutout on Sunday.

Hitters bashed a record 2,634 homers; Rookie of the Year Mark McGwire led the league with 49. Strikeouts also rose to their highest levels since 1968; Nolan Ryan established a big league mark for whiffs per game. Reggie Jackson retired from Oakland. Hal McRae hung it up for Kansas City, which also lost manager Dick Howser to cancer.

The A's and Royals struck around in the race until the end, but the title went to Minnesota, 29-52 on the road but great in the Metrodome. Minnesota was carried by four position players—Kirby Puckett, Tom Brunansky, Kent Hrbek, and Gary Gaetti—and starting pitchers Bert Blyleven and Frank Viola. Others helped in limited roles, and the Twins ground out a title.

Then Minnesota surprised Detroit in five for the league title as Brunansky hit .412 with 9 RBIs. Few expected the "Twinkies" to beat the Cardinals in the World Series, but—true to form—the Twins lost all three on the road but won their four in the dome. Viola, Blyleven, and reliever Jeff Reardon were magnificent.

1986 NATIONAL LEAGUE

TEAM	W	L	T	PCT	GB	HW	HL	R	OR	PA	H	2B	3B	HR	BB	SO	HB	SH	AVG	OBP	SLG	OPS	AOPS	BR	ABR	PF	SB	CS	BSA	BSR
EAST																														
NY	108	54	0	.667	—	**55**	26	**783**	578	6348	**1462**	261	31	148	**631**	968	31	75	**.263**	**.339**	**.401**	**740**	**112**	**87**	**103**	98	118	48	71	9
Phi	86	75	0	.534	21.5	49	31	739	713	6229	1386	266	39	154	589	1154	**40**	66	.253	.327	.400	727	102	52	26	104	153	59	72	13
StL	79	82	0	.491	28.5	42	39	601	611	6120	1270	216	48	58	568	905	20	**108**	.236	.309	.327	636	81	-123	-122	100	**262**	78	**77**	**30**
Mon	78	83	0	.484	29.5	36	44	637	688	6173	1401	255	**50**	110	537	1016	33	53	.254	.322	.379	701	99	-2	1	100	193	95	67	9
Chi	70	90	0	.438	37	42	38	680	781	6127	1409	258	27	**155**	508	966	15	54	.256	.318	.398	716	96	21	-27	108	132	62	68	7
Pit	64	98	0	.395	44	31	50	663	700	6157	1366	**273**	33	111	569	929	20	68	.250	.321	.374	695	96	-10	-27	103	152	84	64	4
WEST																														
Hou	96	66	0	.593	—	52	29	654	**569**	6095	1388	244	32	125	536	916	24	53	.255	.322	.381	703	103	2	21	97	163	75	68	10
Cin	86	76	0	.531	10	43	38	732	717	6246	1404	237	35	144	586	920	18	65	.254	.325	.387	712	98	20	-6	104	177	53	**77**	20
SF	83	79	0	.512	13	46	35	698	618	6209	1394	269	29	114	536	1087	37	101	.253	.322	.375	697	103	-7	27	95	148	93	61	0
SD	74	88	0	.457	22	43	38	656	723	6118	1442	239	25	136	484	917	18	66	.261	.321	.388	709	103	8	23	98	96	68	59	-3
LA	73	89	0	.451	23	46	35	638	679	6101	1373	232	14	130	478	966	32	81	.251	.313	.370	683	101	-43	2	93	155	67	70	11
Atl	72	89	0	.447	23.5	41	40	615	719	6067	1348	241	24	138	538	**904**	24	79	.250	.319	.381	700	95	-5	-34	105	93	76	55	-6
Total	969	—	—	—	—	526	443	8096	—	73990	16643	2991	387	1523	6560	11648	312	869	.253	.322	.380	702	—	—	—	—	1842	858	68	105

TEAM	CG	SHO	GR	SV	IP	H	HR	BB	SO	BR/9	ERA	AERA	OAV	OOB	PR	APR	PF	OSB	OCS	FA	E	WPB	DP	FW	PW	BW	BSW	DIF
EAST																												
NY	27	11	252	46	1484.0	1304	**103**	509	1083	11.2	**3.11**	**115**	.236	.302	**100**	**80**	96	159	55	.978	138	48	145	.1	**8.3**	**10.7**	.0	7.9
Phi	22	11	321	39	1451.2	1473	130	553	874	12.7	3.85	101	.265	.331	-22	6	105	216	70	.978	137	68	157	.1	.6	2.7	.4	1.6
StL	17	4	287	46	1466.1	1364	135	**485**	761	11.5	3.37	109	.250	.311	56	51	99	**91**	60	**.981**	**123**	**47**	178	**.9**	5.3	-12.7	**2.2**	2.8
Mon	15	9	326	50	1466.1	1350	119	566	1051	12.0	3.78	99	.246	.318	-11	-7	101	200	54	.979	133	70	132	.3	-.7	.1	.0	-2.2
Chi	11	6	346	42	1445.0	1546	143	557	962	13.2	4.49	91	.279	.344	-124	-62	109	132	**102**	.980	124	72	147	.8	-6.4	-2.8	-.2	-1.4
Pit	17	9	**356**	30	1450.2	1397	138	570	924	12.4	3.90	99	.255	.327	-30	-3	104	137	80	.978	143	68	134	-.2	-.3	-2.8	-.5	-13.2
WEST																												
Hou	18	**19**	299	**51**	1456.1	**1203**	116	523	**1160**	**10.8**	3.15	114	**.225**	**.295**	92	76	97	176	62	.979	130	59	108	.6	7.9	2.2	.1	4.2
Cin	14	8	313	45	1468.0	1465	136	524	924	12.3	3.91	98	.264	.326	-32	-11	103	135	69	.978	140	52	160	.0	-1.1	-.6	1.2	5.6
SF	18	10	346	35	1460.1	1264	121	591	992	11.6	3.33	106	.236	.313	62	32	95	137	88	.977	143	70	149	-.2	3.3	2.8	-.9	-3.1
SD	13	7	350	32	1443.1	1406	150	607	934	12.7	3.99	92	.258	.333	-44	-55	98	159	65	.978	137	52	135	.2	-5.7	2.4	-1.2	-2.6
LA	**35**	14	280	25	1454.1	1428	115	499	1051	12.1	3.76	92	.256	.319	-7	-53	93	123	73	.971	181	62	118	-2.2	-5.5	.2	.2	-.7
Atl	17	5	309	39	1424.2	1443	117	576	932	12.9	3.97	99	.266	.338	-41	-3	106	177	80	.978	141	55	**181**	-.1	-.3	-3.5	-1.5	-3.0
Total	224	113	3785	480	17471.0	—	—	—	—	12.1	3.72	—	.253	.322	—	—	—	—	—	.978	1670	723	1744	—	—	—	—	—

BATTER-FIELDER WINS	BATTING AVERAGE	ON-BASE PERCENTAGE	SLUGGING AVERAGE	ON-BASE PLUS SLUGGING	ADJUSTED OPS	ADJUSTED BATTER RUNS
Sax-LA 4.9	Raines-Mon .334	Raines-Mon .413	Schmidt-Phi .547	Schmidt-Phi .937	Schmidt-Phi 151	Schmidt-Phi 41.0
Raines-Mon 4.8	Sax-LA .332	Hernandez-NY .413	Strawberry-NY .507	Raines-Mon .889	Raines-Mon 146	Raines-Mon 39.2
Hernandez-NY 4.6	Gwynn-SD .329	Sax-LA .390	McReynolds-SD .504	Strawberry-NY .865	Strawberry-NY 140	Hernandez-NY 36.1
Gwynn-SD 4.2	Bass-Hou .311	Schmidt-Phi .390	Davis-Hou .493	McReynolds-SD .862	Hernandez-NY 140	Sax-LA 34.6
Hubbard-Atl 3.7	Hernandez-NY .310	Gwynn-SD .381	Bass-Hou .486	Hayes-Phi .859	McReynolds-SD 140	Gwynn-SD 30.7
RUNS	**HITS**	**DOUBLES**	**TRIPLES**	**HOME RUNS**	**TOTAL BASES**	**RUNS BATTED IN**
Hayes-Phi 107	Gwynn-SD 211	Hayes-Phi 46	Webster-Mon 13	Schmidt-Phi 37	Parker-Cin 304	Schmidt-Phi 119
Gwynn-SD 107	Sax-LA 210	Sax-LA 43	Samuel-Phi 12	Parker-Cin 31	Schmidt-Phi 302	Parker-Cin 116
Schmidt-Phi 97	Raines-Mon 194	Dunston-Chi 37	Raines-Mon 10	Davis-Hou 31	Gwynn-SD 300	Carter-NY 105
Davis-Cin 97	Hayes-Phi 186	Bream-Pit 37	Coleman-StL 8	Murphy-Atl 29	Murphy-Atl 293	Davis-Hou 101
	Bass-Hou 184	Samuel-Phi 36			Hayes-Phi 293	Hayes-Phi 98
BASES ON BALLS	**STOLEN BASES**	**BASE STEALING RUNS**	**FIELDING RUNS-INFIELD**	**FIELDING RUNS-OUTFIELD**	**OUTFIELD ASSISTS**	**CATCHER CS PCT.**
Hernandez-NY 94	Coleman-StL 107	Coleman-StL 18.6	Hubbard-Atl 39.6	Wilson-Phi 14.8	Wilson-Phi 20	LaValliere-StL 41.0
Schmidt-Phi 89	Davis-Cin 80	Davis-Cin 13.8	Ramirez-Atl 22.9	Gwynn-SD 14.3	Gwynn-SD 19	Diaz-Cin 35.3
C.Davis-SF 84	Raines-Mon 70	Raines-Mon 12.3	Bream-Pit 21.4	Wilson-NY 9.0	Raines-Mon 13	Scioscia-LA 33.1
Oberkfell-Atl 83	Duncan-LA 48	Duncan-LA 6.0	Dunston-Chi 21.2	VanSlyke-StL 5.5	Moreland-Chi 13	Kennedy-SD 30.9
Doran-Hou 81		Bonds-Pit 5.5	Pendleton-StL 19.0	Dykstra-NY 4.0		Virgil-Atl 30.6
WINS	**WINNING PCT.**	**WINS ABOVE TEAM**	**GAMES STARTED**	**COMPLETE GAMES**	**FEWEST HITS/GAME**	**FEWEST BB/GAME**
Valenzuela-LA 21	Ojeda-NY .783	Valenzuela-LA 6.8	Mahler-Atl 39	Valenzuela-LA 20	Scott-Hou 5.95	Eckersley-Chi 1.93
Krukow-SF 20	Gooden-NY .739	Krukow-SF 6.0	Browning-Cin 39	Rhoden-Pit 12	Youmans-Mon 5.96	Sanderson-Chi 1.96
Scott-Hou 18	Fernandez-NY .727	Ojeda-NY 4.4	Knepper-Hou 38	Gooden-NY 12	Ryan-Hou 6.02	Krukow-SF 2.02
Ojeda-NY 18	Darling-NY .714	Kerfeld-Hou 4.2	Scott-Hou 37	Krukow-SF 10	Fernandez-NY 7.09	Welch-LA 2.10
	Krukow-SF .690	Rhoden-Pit 4.1	Gullickson-Cin 37		Gooden-NY 7.09	Ojeda-NY 2.15
STRIKEOUTS	**STRIKEOUTS/GAME**	**GAMES**	**SAVES**	**BASE RUNNERS/9**	**ADJUSTED RELIEF RUNS**	**RELIEF RANKING**
Scott-Hou 306	Scott-Hou 10.00	Lefferts-SD 83	Worrell-StL 36	Scott-Hou 8.37	Worrell-StL 17.6	Worrell-StL 35.2
Valenzuela-LA 242	Ryan-Hou 9.81	McDowell-NY 75	Reardon-Mon 35	Horton-StL 9.33	Horton-StL 17.5	Orosco-NY 24.1
Youmans-Mon 202	Fernandez-NY 8.81	Worrell-StL 74	Smith-Hou 33	Krukow-SF 9.66	McGaffigan-Mon 16.4	Tekulve-Phi 22.1
Gooden-NY 200	Youmans-Mon 8.30	Franco-Cin 74	Smith-Chi 31	Ojeda-NY 9.90	Tekulve-Phi 16.1	Garber-Atl 21.3
Fernandez-NY 200	Valenzuela-LA 8.09	Tekulve-Phi 73		Gooden-NY 10.12	McCullers-SD 14.2	McCullers-SD 19.7
INNINGS PITCHED	**OPPONENTS' AVG.**	**OPPONENTS' OBP**	**EARNED RUN AVERAGE**	**ADJUSTED ERA**	**ADJUSTED STARTER RUNS**	**PITCHER WINS**
Scott-Hou 275.1	Scott-Hou .186	Scott-Hou .242	Scott-Hou 2.22	Scott-Hou 162	Scott-Hou 45.1	**Scott-Hou 4.5**
Valenzuela-LA 269.1	Ryan-Hou .188	Krukow-SF .269	Ojeda-NY 2.57	Ojeda-NY 140	Rhoden-Pit 31.4	**Rhoden-Pit 4.4**
Knepper-Hou 258.0	Youmans-Mon .188	Ojeda-NY .278	Darling-NY 2.81	Rhoden-Pit 137	Ojeda-NY 24.6	**Worrell-StL 3.7**
Rhoden-Pit 253.2	Gooden-NY .215	Gooden-NY .278	Rhoden-Pit 2.84	Darling-NY 128	Darling-NY 21.0	**Orosco-NY 2.6**
Gooden-NY 250.0	Fernandez-NY .216	Ryan-Hou .283	Gooden-NY 2.84	Cox-StL 127	Gooden-NY 20.1	**Tekulve-Phi 2.3**

Fast Forward to October

Mike Schmidt won his third MVP, eighth homer crown, and 10th Gold Glove. The Giants debuted rookies Will Clark and Robby Thompson on the same day, while Pittsburgh welcomed Barry Bonds. Other future stars taking bows included Rookie of the Year Todd Worrell, Reds shortstop Barry Larkin, and Chicago's Greg Maddux and Rafael Palmeiro. Veterans Pete Rose, Tony Perez, and Cesar Cedeno all retired. But the whole season seemed like window dressing for the titanic clashes of October.

New York, which captured the East by 21 1/2 games, the league's biggest margin since 1902, faced Houston in the NLCS. The Astros also won the West going away, as Cy Young winner Mike Scott no-hit the Giants to clinch the division title.

Despite Scott's two victories, the Mets took the NLCS, winning three times in their last at bat. Houston blew a 4-0 lead and lost Game 3 on Lenny Dykstra's two-run homer in the home ninth. The Mets won Game 5 in the 12th, 2-1. In Game 6—perhaps the best LCS game ever—Houston led 3-0 in the ninth when New York tied the score. Both teams tallied in the 14th. The Mets scored three in the top of the 16th; Houston rebounded with two. Finally, Jesse Orosco fanned Kevin Bass with two on, sending the Mets to the World Series.

After Boston won the first two World Series games in New York, the Mets snagged a pair at Fenway Park. Boston won a tight Game 5, and led 2-0, 3-2, and 5-3 (with two out in the 10th) in quest of the Series-clinching victory, but the Mets kept coming back, and won miraculously to force Game 7. The Red Sox leapt in front 3-0, but the Mets battered five Red Sox pitchers over the last three innings to win the clincher, 8-5.

1986 AMERICAN LEAGUE

TEAM	W	L	T	PCT	GB	HW	HL	R	OR	PA	H	2B	3B	HR	BB	SO	HB	SH	AVG	OBP	SLG	OPS	AOPS	BR	ABR	PF	SB	CS	BSA	BSR
EAST																														
Bos	95	66	0	.590	—	**51**	30	794	696	6255	1488	**320**	21	144	595	**707**	**66**	44	.271	.346	.415	761	105	67	62	101	41	34	55	-3
NY	90	72	0	.556	5.5	41	39	797	738	6325	1512	275	23	188	645	911	28	36	.271	**.347**	**.430**	**777**	**111**	**93**	**98**	99	139	48	**74**	**14**
Det	87	75	0	.537	8.5	49	32	798	714	6269	1447	234	30	**198**	613	885	43	52	.263	.338	.424	762	106	53	51	100	138	58	70	10
Tor	86	76	1	.531	9.5	42	39	809	733	6318	1540	285	35	181	496	848	33	24	.269	.329	.427	756	101	30	9	103	110	59	65	4
Cle	84	78	1	.519	11.5	45	35	**831**	841	6287	**1620**	270	**45**	157	456	944	24	56	**.284**	.337	**.430**	767	109	55	67	99	**141**	54	72	12
Mil	77	84	0	.478	18	41	39	667	734	6124	1393	255	38	127	530	986	27	53	.255	.321	.385	706	88	-60	-82	103	100	50	67	5
Bal	73	89	0	.451	22.5	37	42	708	760	6202	1425	223	13	169	563	862	31	33	.258	.327	.395	722	96	-28	-20	99	64	34	65	2
WEST																														
Cal	92	70	0	.568	—	50	32	786	684	6296	1387	236	36	167	**671**	860	40	**91**	.255	.338	.404	742	102	23	31	99	109	42	72	9
Tex	87	75	0	.537	5	**51**	30	771	743	6148	1479	248	43	184	511	1088	35	31	.267	.331	.428	759	102	35	14	103	103	85	55	-7
KC	76	86	0	.469	16	45	36	654	**673**	6128	1403	264	**45**	137	474	919	36	24	.252	.313	.390	703	88	-79	-93	102	97	46	68	5
Oak	76	86	0	.469	16	47	36	731	760	6127	1370	213	25	163	553	983	32	56	.252	.322	.390	712	100	-50	3	93	139	61	70	9
Chi	72	90	0	.444	20	41	40	644	699	6030	1335	197	34	121	487	940	34	50	.247	.310	.363	673	79	-130	-151	104	115	54	68	6
Min	71	91	0	.438	21	43	38	741	839	6151	1446	257	39	196	501	977	37	44	.261	.325	.428	753	100	20	-2	103	81	61	57	-4
Sea	67	95	0	.414	25	41	41	718	835	6185	1392	243	41	158	572	1148	34	52	.253	.326	.399	725	95	-29	-37	101	93	76	55	-6
Total	1134	—	—	—	—	624	509	10449	—	86845	20237	3520	468	2290	7667	13058	500	646	.262	.330	.408	737	—	—	—	—	1470	762	66	57

TEAM	CG	SHO	GR	SV	IP	H	HR	BB	SO	BR/9	ERA	AERA	OAV	OOB	PR	APR	PF	OSB	OCS	FA	E	WPB	DP	FW	PW	BW	BSW	DIF
EAST																												
Bos	36	6	254	41	1429.2	1469	167	**474**	1033	12.4	3.93	107	.266	.325	38	41	100	79	62	.979	129	71	146	-.2	4.0	6.1	-.7	5.2
NY	13	8	289	**58**	1443.1	1461	175	492	878	12.3	4.11	100	.263	.323	11	3	99	95	45	.979	127	57	153	.0	.3	**9.6**	**1.0**	-1.9
Det	33	12	239	38	1443.2	1374	183	571	880	12.3	4.02	103	.251	.323	25	22	100	87	49	.982	108	62	163	1.1	2.2	5.0	.6	-2.9
Tor	16	12	290	44	1476.0	1467	164	487	1002	12.2	4.08	104	.261	.322	16	26	102	95	46	**.984**	**100**	**47**	150	**1.7**	2.6	.9	.0	-.0
Cle	31	7	290	34	1447.2	1548	167	605	744	13.7	4.58	91	.273	.346	-64	-64	100	113	41	.975	157	83	148	-1.7	-6.3	6.6	.8	3.7
Mil	29	12	237	32	1431.2	1478	158	494	952	12.6	4.01	108	.267	.328	26	52	104	95	**75**	.976	146	72	146	-1.2	5.1	-8.1	.0	.5
Bal	17	6	262	39	1436.2	1451	177	535	954	12.6	4.30	97	.263	.328	-20	-23	100	123	56	.978	135	59	163	-.5	-2.3	-2.0	-.2	-3.1
WEST																												
Cal	29	12	246	40	1456.0	1356	153	478	955	**11.5**	3.84	107	.248	**.309**	54	47	99	**61**	56	.983	107	56	156	1.2	4.6	3.0	.5	1.6
Tex	15	8	**328**	41	1450.1	1356	145	736	**1059**	13.2	4.11	105	.249	.340	11	33	103	165	51	.980	122	119	160	.3	3.2	1.4	-1.1	2.2
KC	24	**13**	230	31	1440.2	1413	**121**	479	888	12.1	**3.82**	**112**	.258	.319	**56**	**69**	102	85	66	.980	123	59	153	.2	**6.8**	-9.1	.0	-3.0
Oak	22	8	286	37	1433.0	**1334**	166	667	937	12.8	4.31	90	**.247**	.330	-21	-72	93	139	53	.978	135	78	120	-.5	-7.1	.3	.5	1.8
Chi	18	8	297	38	1442.1	1361	143	561	895	12.2	3.93	110	.251	.323	39	62	104	116	56	.981	117	69	142	.6	6.1	-14.8	.2	-1.0
Min	**39**	6	240	24	1432.2	1579	200	503	937	13.4	4.77	91	.281	.342	-94	-67	104	111	44	.980	118	70	168	.5	-6.6	-.2	-.8	-3.0
Sea	33	5	281	27	1439.2	1590	171	585	944	13.9	4.65	92	.283	.353	-76	-62	102	106	62	.975	156	63	**191**	-1.7	-6.1	-3.6	-1.0	-1.6
Total	355	123	3769	524	20203.1	—	—	—	—	12.7	4.18	—	.262	.330	—	—	—	—	—	.979	1780	965	2159	—	—	—	—	—

BATTER-FIELDER WINS	BATTING AVERAGE	ON-BASE PERCENTAGE	SLUGGING AVERAGE	ON-BASE PLUS SLUGGING	ADJUSTED OPS	ADJUSTED BATTER RUNS
Boggs-Bos..........5.4	Boggs-Bos............357	Boggs-Bos............453	Mattingly-NY.........573	Mattingly-NY.........967	Mattingly-NY.........162	Mattingly-NY........58.2
Ripken-Bal..........4.6	Mattingly-NY.........352	P.Bradley-Sea.......405	Barfield-Tor...........559	Boggs-Bos............939	Boggs-Bos............155	Boggs-Bos...........53.5
Trammell-Det.....4.5	Puckett-Min...........328	Brett-KC................401	Puckett-Min...........537	Barfield-Tor...........927	Barfield-Tor...........145	Barfield-Tor..........36.9
Mattingly-NY......4.5	Tabler-Cle.............326	Murray-Bal............396	Bell-Tor.................532	Puckett-Min...........903	Puckett-Min...........138	Puckett-Min..........33.5
Barfield-Tor........4.3	Rice-Bos...............324	Mattingly-NY.........394	Gaetti-Min.............518	Brett-KC................881	Rice-Bos...............136	Rice-Bos..............33.1
RUNS	**HITS**	**DOUBLES**	**TRIPLES**	**HOME RUNS**	**TOTAL BASES**	**RUNS BATTED IN**
Henderson-NY......130	Mattingly-NY.........238	Mattingly-NY..........53	Butler-Cle...............14	Barfield-Tor.............40	Mattingly-NY.........388	Carter-Cle.............121
Puckett-Min...........119	Puckett-Min...........223	Boggs-Bos..............47	Sierra-Tex...............10	Kingman-Oak..........35	Puckett-Min...........365	Canseco-Oak........117
Mattingly-NY.........117	Fernandez-Tor......213	Rice-Bos.................39	Fernandez-Tor..........9	Gaetti-Min...............34	Carter-Cle.............341	Mattingly-NY.........113
Carter-Cle.............108	Boggs-Bos............207	Buckner-Bos...........39	Carter-Cle.................9	Deer-Mil..................33	Bell-Tor.................341	Rice-Bos...............110
		Barrett-Bos.............39		Canseco-Oak..........33	Barfield-Tor...........329	
BASES ON BALLS	**STOLEN BASES**	**BASE STEALING RUNS**	**FIELDING RUNS-INFIELD**	**FIELDING RUNS-OUTFIELD**	**OUTFIELD ASSISTS**	**CATCHER CS PCT.**
Boggs-Bos............105	Henderson-NY........87	Henderson-NY.....12.8	Owen-Sea-Bos....35.8	Barfield-Tor..........16.0	Barfield-Tor.............20	Boone-Cal............51.2
Evans-Bos..............97	Pettis-Cal...............50	Pettis-Cal...............6.4	Reynolds-Sea......30.2	Pettis-Cal.............10.5	Bell-Tor..................17	Gedman-Bos.......49.5
Randolph-NY..........94	Cangelosi-Chi.........50	Gibson-Det.............5.4	Buckner-Bos........19.5	Rice-Bos.................8.4	Rice-Bos.................16	Parrish-Det..........44.3
Jackson-Cal............92	Wilson-KC...............34	Cangelosi-Chi........5.1	Guillen-Chi...........18.3	Henderson-Sea-Bos..7.8	Baines-Chi..............15	Sundberg-KC.......38.7
Evans-Det...............91	Gibson-Det.............34	Wilson-KC..............4.7	Gaetti-Min............17.0	Baines-Chi.............7.5	McDowell-Tex.........13	Skinner-Chi-NY....36.0
WINS	**WINNING PCT.**	**WINS ABOVE TEAM**	**GAMES STARTED**	**COMPLETE GAMES**	**FEWEST HITS/GAME**	**FEWEST BB/GAME**
Clemens-Bos..........24	Clemens-Bos........857	Clemens-Bos.........9.7	Viola-Min.................37	Candiotti-Cle...........17	Clemens-Bos.......6.34	Guidry-NY............1.78
Morris-Det...............21	Rasmussen-NY....750	Morris-Det.............6.6	Moore-Sea..............37	Blyleven-Min...........16	Rasmussen-NY...7.13	Boyd-Bos.............1.89
Higuera-Mil.............20	Morris-Det............724	Rasmussen-NY.....5.7	Langston-Sea.........36	Morris-Det...............15	Witt-Cal................7.29	Blyleven-Min........1.92
Witt-Cal...................18	Higuera-Mil...........645	Higuera-Mil............5.7	Blyleven-Min...........36	Higuera-Mil.............15	Hough-Tex...........7.35	Wegman-Mil........1.95
Rasmussen-NY......18	Witt-Cal................643	Eichhorn-Tor..........3.9		Witt-Cal...................14	Cowley-Chi..........7.37	Sutton-Cal...........2.13
STRIKEOUTS	**STRIKEOUTS/GAME**	**GAMES**	**SAVES**	**BASE RUNNERS/9**	**ADJUSTED RELIEF RUNS**	**RELIEF RANKING**
Langston-Sea.......245	Langston-Sea......9.21	Williams-Tex............80	Righetti-NY.............46	Clemens-Bos.......8.86	Eichhorn-Tor........43.9	Eichhorn-Tor........55.7
Clemens-Bos........238	Hurst-Bos............8.62	Righetti-NY.............74	Aase-Bal.................34	Eichhorn-Tor........9.00	Righetti-NY..........20.9	Righetti-NY..........41.9
Morris-Det............223	Clemens-Bos.......8.43	Harris-Tex...............73	Henke-Tor...............27	Henke-Tor............9.46	Harris-Tex............17.6	Harris-Tex............31.8
Blyleven-Min.........215	Correa-Tex...........8.41	Eichhorn-Tor...........69	Hernandez-Det.......24	Candelaria-Cal.....9.52	Clear-Mil..............16.0	Plesac-Mil............27.1
Witt-Cal................208	Rijo-Oak...............8.18		Moore-Cal...............21	Haas-Oak............9.71	Mohorcic-Tex.......15.3	Clear-Mil..............26.3
INNINGS PITCHED	**OPPONENTS' AVG.**	**OPPONENTS' OBP**	**EARNED RUN AVERAGE**	**ADJUSTED ERA**	**ADJUSTED STARTER RUNS**	**PITCHER WINS**
Blyleven-Min......271.2	Clemens-Bos........195	Clemens-Bos........252	Clemens-Bos.......2.48	Clemens-Bos........169	Clemens-Bos.......48.8	**Eichhorn-Tor......5.8**
Witt-Cal.............269.0	Rasmussen-NY....217	Witt-Cal................275	Higuera-Mil.........2.79	Higuera-Mil...........156	Higuera-Mil..........43.3	**Higuera-Mil.........5.1**
Morris-Det..........267.0	Witt-Cal................221	Morris-Det............287	Witt-Cal...............2.84	Witt-Cal.................145	Witt-Cal...............38.4	**Clemens-Bos.....5.1**
Moore-Sea.........266.0	Hough-Tex............221	Sutton-Cal............287	Hurst-Bos............2.99	Hurst-Bos.............140	Morris-Det...........27.8	**Righetti-NY.........4.2**
Clemens-Bos.....254.0	Correa-Tex...........223	Rasmussen-NY....289	D.Jackson-KC......3.20	D.Jackson-KC.......134	Hurst-Bos.............24.0	**Witt-Cal...............3.8**

Sorrow in Beantown

Despite Dave Righetti's record 46 saves and amazing seasons from Don Mattingly and Rickey Henderson, it wasn't the Yankees' year. The AL East went to Boston. Roger Clemens, who primed Hub hysteria in April with the major leagues' first 20-K nine-inning game, was both MVP and Cy Young. Wade Boggs led the league in both batting and on-base percentage for the third time; four Red Sox drove in 90 or more runs. Boston wrapped it up with an 11-game win streak starting August 30.

Kansas City collapsed in the West, and the Angels easily stepped into the breach. Rookie first baseman Wally Joyner was a surprise, leavening an old team with a young bat. Four California regulars were 35 or older, and the bench and bullpen were stocked with graybeards as well. Rookies also sparked second-place Texas; Ruben Sierra impressed with power and speed, while Pete Incaviglia slugged 30 homers but fanned an AL-record 185 times. The Rookie of the Year, however, was Jose Canseco of third-place Oakland. Others making their first major league appearances included Mark McGwire, Jamie Moyer, Kevin Brown, Fred McGriff, and Chuck Finley. Minnesota's Bert Blyleven allowed 50 home runs, a new record, but ended 17-14; his team finished 20 games under .500.

Each LCS again went seven games. Each team blew out the other, and then the Angels took the next two in Anaheim with dramatic late-inning rallies. California couldn't pull the trigger. Boston, trailing 5-2 in the ninth in Game 5, took the lead on Dave Henderson's home run; the Angels tied it, but the Red Sox won in the 11th. Back at Fenway, the Red Sox twice blasted the Angels to reach the World Series. The Fall Classic, however, was painful for Boston fans. Just one strike away from winning, the Red Sox found a way to lose Game 6 to the Mets; another lead slipped away in Game 7.

Two Tigers first basemen, Hank Greenberg and Norm Cash, passed on. Following the season, Bobby Grich and Tom Seaver retired.

1985 NATIONAL LEAGUE

TEAM	W	L	T	PCT	GB	HW	HL	R	OR	PA	H	2B	3B	HR	BB	SO	HB	SH	AVG	OBP	SLG	OPS	AOPS	BR	ABR	PF	SB	CS	BSA	BSR
EAST																														
StL	101	61	0	.623	—	**54**	27	**747**	572	6182	1446	245	**59**	87	**586**	853	18	70	**.264**	**.335**	.379	**714**	**107**	**52**	**56**	99	**314**	96	77	**35**
NY	98	64	0	.605	3	51	30	695	**568**	6248	1425	239	35	134	546	872	20	89	.257	.323	.385	708	106	32	46	98	117	53	69	7
Mon	84	77	0	.522	16.5	44	37	633	636	6053	1342	242	49	118	492	880	26	61	.247	.310	.375	685	103	-20	16	95	169	77	69	10
Chi	77	84	1	.478	23.5	41	39	686	729	6177	1397	239	28	**150**	562	937	18	66	.254	.324	**.390**	**714**	95	42	-22	110	182	49	**79**	23
Phi	75	87	0	.463	26	41	40	667	673	6122	1343	238	47	141	527	1095	25	49	.245	.312	.383	695	98	-1	-17	103	122	51	71	9
Pit	57	104	0	.354	43.5	35	45	568	708	6099	1340	251	28	80	514	842	14	91	.247	.311	.347	658	91	-63	-58	99	110	60	65	3
WEST																														
LA	95	67	0	.586	—	48	33	682	579	6222	1434	226	28	129	539	846	31	**104**	.261	.328	.382	710	106	38	54	98	136	58	70	10
Cin	89	72	1	.553	5.5	47	34	677	666	6143	1385	249	34	114	576	856	23	72	.255	.327	.376	703	98	28	-5	105	159	70	69	10
SD	83	79	0	.512	12	44	37	650	622	6150	1405	241	28	109	513	**809**	23	75	.255	.320	.368	688	99	-8	-2	99	60	39	61	0
Hou	83	79	0	.512	12	44	37	706	691	6192	**1457**	**261**	42	121	477	873	23	66	.261	.319	.388	707	105	25	41	98	96	56	63	2
Atl	66	96	0	.407	29	32	49	632	781	6207	1359	213	28	126	553	849	22	65	.246	.315	.363	678	90	-29	-64	106	72	52	58	-2
SF	62	100	0	.383	33	38	43	556	674	6063	1263	217	31	115	488	962	**37**	93	.233	.299	.348	647	90	-95	-70	96	99	55	64	3
Total	971	—	—	—	—	519	451	7899	—	73858	16596	2861	437	1424	6373	10674	280	901	.252	.319	.374	692	—	—	—	—	1636	716	70	109

TEAM	CG	SHO	GR	SV	IP	H	HR	BB	SO	BR/9	ERA	AERA	OAV	OOB	PR	APR	PF	OSB	OCS	FA	E	WPB	DP	FW	PW	BW	BSW	DIF
EAST																												
StL	**37**	20	296	44	1464.0	1343	**98**	453	798	11.2	3.10	115	.246	.305	79	75	99	104	37	**.983**	**108**	48	166	**1.7**	7.9	**5.9**	**2.7**	1.8
NY	32	19	243	37	1488.0	1306	111	515	**1039**	11.1	3.11	112	.237	.302	80	65	97	122	65	.982	115	50	138	1.3	6.8	4.8	-.2	4.3
Mon	13	13	323	**53**	1457.0	1346	99	509	870	11.6	3.55	97	.247	.312	7	-19	96	189	45	.981	121	62	152	.8	-2.0	1.7	.0	2.9
Chi	20	8	313	42	1442.1	1492	156	519	820	12.7	4.16	96	.271	.333	-91	-24	111	137	**82**	.979	134	48	150	.1	-2.5	-2.3	1.5	-.2
Phi	24	9	315	30	1447.0	1424	115	596	899	12.7	3.68	101	.259	.331	-15	4	103	164	55	.978	139	49	142	-.2	.4	-1.8	-.0	-4.4
Pit	15	6	297	29	1445.1	1406	107	584	962	12.6	3.97	91	.255	.329	-61	-56	101	105	72	.979	133	54	127	.1	-5.9	-6.1	-.6	-11.0
WEST																												
LA	**37**	**21**	250	36	1465.0	**1280**	102	462	979	**10.8**	**2.96**	**118**	**.234**	**.295**	**102**	**89**	97	**99**	67	.974	166	49	131	-1.8	**9.4**	5.7	.0	.7
Cin	24	11	287	45	1451.1	1347	131	535	910	11.8	3.71	102	.248	.315	-19	11	105	133	57	.980	122	52	142	.8	1.2	-.5	.0	6.9
SD	26	19	283	44	1451.1	1399	127	**443**	727	11.6	3.40	104	.257	.313	30	23	99	138	65	.980	124	**29**	158	.7	2.4	-.2	-1.0	.0
Hou	17	9	282	42	1458.0	1393	119	543	909	12.1	3.66	95	.254	.321	-11	-31	97	144	59	.976	152	105	159	-1.0	-3.3	4.3	-.7	2.7
Atl	9	9	**351**	29	1457.1	1512	134	642	776	13.5	4.19	92	.271	.347	-98	-53	107	158	59	.976	159	43	**197**	-1.4	-5.6	-6.7	-1.2	-.1
SF	13	5	321	24	1448.0	1348	125	572	985	12.1	3.61	96	.247	.319	-3	-26	96	143	53	.976	148	77	134	-.7	-2.7	-7.4	-.6	-7.5
Total	267	149	3561	455	17474.2	—	—	—	—	12.0	3.59	—	.252	.319	—	—	—	—	—	.979	1621	666	1796	—	—	—	—	—

BATTER-FIELDER WINS	BATTING AVERAGE	ON-BASE PERCENTAGE	SLUGGING AVERAGE	ON-BASE PLUS SLUGGING	ADJUSTED OPS	ADJUSTED BATTER RUNS
Guerrero-LA 5.8	McGee-StL .353	Guerrero-LA .422	Guerrero-LA .577	Guerrero-LA .999	Guerrero-LA 182	Guerrero-LA 56.4
Hubbard-Atl 5.6	Guerrero-LA .320	Scioscia-LA .407	Parker-Cin .551	Murphy-Atl .927	Raines-Mon 154	Raines-Mon 44.1
Sandberg-Chi 5.4	Raines-Mon .320	Raines-Mon .405	Murphy-Atl .539	Parker-Cin .916	Clark-StL 151	Murphy-Atl 41.8
Raines-Mon 5.3	Gwynn-SD .317	Rose-Cin .395	Schmidt-Phi .532	Schmidt-Phi .907	Murphy-Atl 149	Parker-Cin 37.8
Carter-NY 4.6	Parker-Cin .312	Clark-StL .393	Marshall-LA .515	Clark-StL .895	Schmidt-Phi 148	Schmidt-Phi 37.0
RUNS	**HITS**	**DOUBLES**	**TRIPLES**	**HOME RUNS**	**TOTAL BASES**	**RUNS BATTED IN**
Murphy-Atl 118	McGee-StL 216	Parker-Cin 42	McGee-StL 18	Murphy-Atl 37	Parker-Cin 350	Parker-Cin 125
Raines-Mon 115	Parker-Cin 198	Wilson-Phi 39	Samuel-Phi 13	Parker-Cin 34	Murphy-Atl 332	Murphy-Atl 111
McGee-StL 114	Gwynn-SD 197	Herr-StL 38	Raines-Mon 13	Schmidt-Phi 33	McGee-StL 308	Herr-StL 110
Sandberg-Chi 113	Sandberg-Chi 186	Wallach-Mon 36	Garner-Hou 10	Guerrero-LA 33	Sandberg-Chi 307	Moreland-Chi 106
Coleman-StL 107	Murphy-Atl 185		Coleman-StL 10	Carter-NY 32	Schmidt-Phi 292	Wilson-Phi 102
BASES ON BALLS	**STOLEN BASES**	**BASE STEALING RUNS**	**FIELDING RUNS-INFIELD**	**FIELDING RUNS-OUTFIELD**	**OUTFIELD ASSISTS**	**CATCHER CS PCT.**
Murphy-Atl 90	Coleman-StL 110	Coleman-StL 15.4	Hubbard-Atl 59.9	Wilson-Phi 15.8	Wilson-Phi 18	Scioscia-LA 35.5
Schmidt-Phi 87	Raines-Mon 70	Raines-Mon 12.3	Wallach-Mon 35.8	Milner-Cin 14.3	Coleman-StL 16	Davis-Chi 34.3
Martinez-SD 87	McGee-StL 56	Lopes-Chi 8.9	Pendleton-StL 25.9	Gwynn-SD 10.6	Gwynn-SD 14	Porter-StL 33.3
Rose-Cin 86	Sandberg-Chi 54	Sandberg-Chi 8.0	O.Smith-StL 18.1	McReynolds-SD 8.8	VanSlyke-StL 13	Cerone-Atl 29.6
Law-Mon 86	Samuel-Phi 53	McGee-StL 6.7	Ramirez-Atl 15.0	Hayes-Phi 7.8	Martinez-SD 13	Virgil-Phi 23.1
WINS	**WINNING PCT.**	**WINS ABOVE TEAM**	**GAMES STARTED**	**COMPLETE GAMES**	**FEWEST HITS/GAME**	**FEWEST BB/GAME**
Gooden-NY 24	Hershiser-LA .864	Gooden-NY 9.5	Mahler-Atl 39	Gooden-NY 16	Fernandez-NY 5.71	Hoyt-SD .86
Tudor-StL 21	Gooden-NY .857	Hershiser-LA 7.7	Browning-Cin 38	Valenzuela-LA 14	Gooden-NY 6.44	Eckersley-Chi 1.01
Andujar-StL 21	Smith-Mon .783	Smith-Mon 6.7	Andujar-StL 38	Tudor-StL 14	Hershiser-LA 6.72	Lynch-NY 1.27
Browning-Cin 20	Darling-NY .727	Scott-Hou 5.3	Knepper-Hou 37	Cox-StL 10	Tudor-StL 6.84	Tudor-StL 1.60
Hershiser-LA 19	Tudor-StL .724	Hawkins-SD 5.3	Bedrosian-Atl 37	Andujar-StL 10	Soto-Cin 6.87	Smith-Mon 1.66
STRIKEOUTS	**STRIKEOUTS/GAME**	**GAMES**	**SAVES**	**BASE RUNNERS/9**	**ADJUSTED RELIEF RUNS**	**RELIEF RANKING**
Gooden-NY 268	Fernandez-NY 9.51	Burke-Mon 78	Reardon-Mon 41	Tudor-StL 8.61	Franco-Cin 16.7	Franco-Cin 26.6
Soto-Cin 214	Gooden-NY 8.72	M.Davis-SF 77	Smith-Chi 33	Gooden-NY 8.75	Burke-Mon 16.3	Gossage-SD 21.7
Ryan-Hou 209	DeLeon-Pit 8.24	Garrelts-SF 74	Smith-Hou 27	Eckersley-Chi 8.88	Carman-Phi 14.2	Carman-Phi 21.4
Valenzuela-LA 208	Ryan-Hou 8.11	Carman-Phi 71	Power-Cin 27	Gossage-SD 9.34	Gossage-SD 14.1	Niedenfuer-LA 20.7
Fernandez-NY 180	Soto-Cin 7.50	Minton-SF 68	Gossage-SD 26	Niedenfuer-LA 9.39	Lahti-StL 13.6	Lahti-StL 19.8
INNINGS PITCHED	**OPPONENTS' AVG.**	**OPPONENTS' OBP**	**EARNED RUN AVERAGE**	**ADJUSTED ERA**	**ADJUSTED STARTER RUNS**	**PITCHER WINS**
Gooden-NY 276.2	Fernandez-NY .181	Tudor-StL .249	Gooden-NY 1.53	Gooden-NY 229	Gooden-NY 62.7	**Gooden-NY 7.6**
Tudor-StL 275.0	Gooden-NY .201	Eckersley-Chi .254	Tudor-StL 1.93	Tudor-StL 185	Tudor-StL 50.0	**Tudor-StL 5.6**
Valenzuela-LA 272.1	Hershiser-LA .206	Gooden-NY .254	Hershiser-LA 2.03	Hershiser-LA 173	Hershiser-LA 36.8	**Hershiser-LA 3.8**
Andujar-StL 269.2	Tudor-StL .209	Hershiser-LA .267	Reuschel-Pit 2.27	Reuschel-Pit 160	Valenzuela-LA 30.9	**Reuschel-Pit 3.6**
Mahler-Atl 266.2	Soto-Cin .211	Smith-Mon .268	Welch-LA 2.31	Welch-LA 151	Reuschel-Pit 27.3	**Valenzuela-LA 3.6**

CARDINAL NUMBERS

After sliding in 1983–84, did the Cardinals have anything left? Yes. The NL East was a two-horse race after early August, and the Redbirds outran the Mets. The pundits said it was all about speed, but Cardinals baseball was multi-faceted. While Rookie of the Year Vince Coleman swiped 110 bases, and the team combined for 314 (most in the NL since 1912), MVP Willie McGee's .353 average, Jack Clark's power, and Tommy Herr and Ozzie Smith's on-base skills proved just as important. John Tudor and Joaquin Andujar each won 20 games with a good bullpen in reserve.

Again the Mets were bridesmaids, and New York waved goodbye to 23-year vet Rusty Staub, but attendance rose another 50 percent. Dwight Gooden, 24-4 with a 1.53 ERA, was a unanimous Cy Young. Chicago's pitching crumbled, and the club released Larry Bowa in favor of rookie Shawon Dunston. Montreal began building a roof over Olympic Stadium in September.

Los Angeles, with an excellent offense despite a big ballpark, had few problems after July as the Padres fell apart. Four excellent Dodgers starters benefited from Pedro Guerrero's bat. Cincinnati improved to second on Dave Parker's comeback season. The club's most emotional moment came September 11, when Pete Rose became "hit king," collecting safety No. 4,192 against the Padres.

The Dodgers won the first two NLCS games at home on fine pitching; however, the Cardinals bats evened the series. Smith won Game 5 with a ninth-inning blast off Tom Niedenfuer (the Wizard's first career home run batting left-handed). In Game 6 Los Angeles lost a 4-1 lead, moved ahead in the eighth, but lost in the ninth. Clark's three-run homer (also off Niedenfuer) gave St. Louis a 7-5 win and the pennant. The Cardinals blew a three-to-one lead in games to the Royals and lost the World Series, but the franchise had reasserted itself.

1985 AMERICAN LEAGUE

TEAM	W	L	T	PCT	GB	HW	HL	R	OR	PA	H	2B	3B	HR	BB	SO	HB	SH	AVG	OBP	SLG	OPS	AOPS	BR	ABR	PF	SB	CS	BSA	BSR
East																														
Tor	99	62	0	.615	—	54	26	759	**588**	6106	1482	281	**53**	158	503	807	30	21	.269	.331	.425	756	102	44	22	103	144	77	65	5
NY	97	64	0	.602	2	**58**	22	**839**	660	6236	1458	272	31	176	620	771	**50**	48	.267	.344	.425	769	**111**	86	**100**	98	**155**	53	**75**	**16**
Det	84	77	0	.522	15	44	37	729	688	6221	1413	254	45	202	526	926	27	40	.253	.318	.424	742	101	7	9	100	75	41	65	2
Bal	83	78	0	.516	16	45	36	818	764	6211	1451	234	22	**214**	604	908	19	31	.263	.336	**.430**	766	110	65	82	98	69	43	62	0
Bos	81	81	1	.500	18.5	43	37	800	720	6419	**1615**	**292**	31	162	562	816	30	50	**.282**	**.347**	.429	**776**	106	**100**	63	104	66	27	71	5
Mil	71	90	0	.441	28	40	40	690	802	6158	1467	250	44	101	462	**746**	19	54	.263	.319	.379	698	90	-71	-70	100	69	34	67	3
Cle	60	102	0	.370	39.5	38	43	729	861	6120	1465	254	31	116	492	817	15	38	.265	.324	.385	709	93	-44	-41	100	132	72	65	4
West																														
KC	91	71	0	.562	—	50	32	687	639	6094	1384	261	49	154	473	840	36	44	.252	.313	.401	714	93	-49	-54	101	128	48	73	11
Cal	90	72	0	.556	1	49	30	732	703	6263	1364	215	31	153	**648**	902	39	**99**	.251	.333	.386	719	96	-17	-16	100	106	51	68	5
Chi	85	77	1	.525	6	45	36	736	720	6088	1386	247	37	146	471	843	43	59	.253	.315	.392	707	88	-56	-85	105	108	56	66	4
Min	77	85	0	.475	14	49	35	705	782	6128	1453	282	41	141	502	779	31	39	.264	.326	.407	733	93	0	-43	106	68	44	61	0
Oak	77	85	0	.475	14	43	36	757	787	6215	1475	230	34	155	508	861	16	63	.264	.325	.401	726	104	-17	36	93	117	58	67	5
Sea	74	88	0	.457	17	42	41	719	818	6185	1410	277	38	171	564	942	31	28	.255	.326	.412	738	99	9	2	101	94	35	73	8
Tex	62	99	0	.385	28.5	37	43	617	785	6003	1359	213	41	129	530	819	33	34	.253	.322	.381	703	90	-57	-70	102	130	76	63	2
Total	1132	—	—	—	—	637	494	10317	—	86447	20182	3562	528	2178	7465	11777	419	648	.261	.327	.406	733	—	—	—	—	1461	715	67	71

TEAM	CG	SHO	GR	SV	IP	H	HR	BB	SO	BR/9	ERA	AERA	OAV	OOB	PR	APR	PF	OSB	OCS	FA	E	WPB	DP	FW	PW	BW	BSW	DIF
East																												
Tor	18	9	316	47	1448.0	**1312**	147	484	823	**11.3**	**3.31**	**128**	.243	**.306**	**135**	**147**	102	83	44	.980	125	39	164	.2	**14.5**	2.2	.0	1.6
NY	25	9	271	**49**	1440.1	1373	157	518	907	11.9	3.69	110	.251	.316	74	59	98	107	46	.979	126	52	172	.2	5.8	**9.9**	**1.1**	-.5
Det	31	**11**	250	40	1456.0	1313	141	556	943	11.7	3.78	109	**.240**	.311	59	53	99	93	53	.977	143	72	152	-.8	5.2	.9	-.3	-1.5
Bal	32	6	238	33	1427.1	1480	160	568	793	13.1	4.38	93	.270	.338	-36	-51	98	130	37	.979	129	**36**	168	-.0	-5.0	8.1	-.5	-.0
Bos	35	8	202	29	1461.1	1487	130	540	913	12.7	4.06	106	.265	.331	14	40	104	94	**62**	.977	145	48	161	-.8	4.0	6.2	.0	-9.4
Mil	34	5	248	37	1437.0	1510	175	499	777	12.8	4.39	96	.271	.331	-39	-31	101	109	56	.977	142	63	153	-.7	-3.1	-6.9	-.2	1.4
Cle	24	7	306	28	1421.0	1556	170	547	702	13.6	4.91	85	.281	.346	-121	-118	100	134	53	.977	141	59	161	-.6	-11.7	-4.1	-.1	-4.5
West																												
KC	27	**11**	216	41	1461.0	1433	**103**	463	846	11.9	3.49	120	.257	.315	107	111	101	92	50	.980	127	52	160	.1	11.0	-5.3	.6	3.6
Cal	22	8	250	41	1457.1	1453	171	514	767	12.3	3.91	105	.263	.326	38	35	99	**79**	56	**.982**	112	53	**202**	1.0	3.5	-1.6	.0	6.1
Chi	20	8	305	39	1451.2	1411	161	569	**1023**	12.5	4.07	107	.256	.327	13	43	105	112	55	**.982**	**111**	65	152	**1.1**	4.3	-8.4	-.1	7.2
Min	**41**	7	237	34	1426.1	1468	164	**462**	767	12.4	4.48	99	.268	.326	-53	-8	107	100	54	.980	120	64	139	.5	-.8	-4.3	-.5	1.0
Oak	10	6	299	41	1453.0	1451	172	607	785	12.9	4.41	88	.259	.331	-43	-92	94	104	51	.977	140	67	137	-.6	-9.1	3.6	.0	2.1
Sea	23	8	**335**	30	1432.0	1456	154	637	868	13.4	4.68	90	.265	.343	-84	-70	102	105	57	.980	122	83	156	.4	-6.9	.2	.3	-1.0
Tex	18	5	264	33	1411.2	1479	173	501	863	12.9	4.56	93	.269	.331	-65	-46	103	119	41	.980	120	66	145	.5	-4.5	-6.9	-.3	-7.2
Total	360	108	3737	522	20184.0	—	—	—	—	12.5	4.15	—	.261	.327	—	—	—	—	—	.979	1803	819	2222	—	—	—	—	—

BATTER-FIELDER WINS	BATTING AVERAGE	ON-BASE PERCENTAGE	SLUGGING AVERAGE	ON-BASE PLUS SLUGGING	ADJUSTED OPS	ADJUSTED BATTER RUNS
Henderson-NY ... 6.9	Boggs-Bos ... .368	Boggs-Bos ... .450	Brett-KC ... .585	Brett-KC ... 1022	Brett-KC ... 177	Brett-KC ... 64.4
Brett-KC ... 6.6	Brett-KC ... .335	Brett-KC ... .436	Mattingly-NY ... .567	Mattingly-NY ... .939	Henderson-NY ... 158	Mattingly-NY ... 51.3
Boggs-Bos ... 5.6	Mattingly-NY ... .324	Harrah-Tex ... .432	Barfield-Tor ... .536	Henderson-NY ... .934	Mattingly-NY ... 158	Boggs-Bos ... 50.6
Ripken-Bal ... 4.5	Henderson-NY ... .314	Henderson-NY ... .419	Murray-Bal ... .523	Boggs-Bos ... .928	Murray-Bal ... 150	Henderson-NY ... 48.8
Murray-Bal ... 4.4	Butler-Cle ... .311	Murray-Bal ... .383	Evans-Det ... .519	Murray-Bal ... .906	Boggs-Bos ... 148	Murray-Bal ... 42.5
RUNS	**HITS**	**DOUBLES**	**TRIPLES**	**HOME RUNS**	**TOTAL BASES**	**RUNS BATTED IN**
Henderson-NY ... 146	Boggs-Bos ... 240	Mattingly-NY ... 48	Wilson-KC ... 21	Evans-Det ... 40	Mattingly-NY ... 370	Mattingly-NY ... 145
Ripken-Bal ... 116	Mattingly-NY ... 211	Buckner-Bos ... 46	Butler-Cle ... 14	Fisk-Chi ... 37	Brett-KC ... 322	Murray-Bal ... 124
Murray-Bal ... 111	Buckner-Bos ... 201	Boggs-Bos ... 42	Puckett-Min ... 13	Balboni-KC ... 36	Bradley-Sea ... 319	Winfield-NY ... 114
Evans-Bos ... 110	Puckett-Min ... 199	Cooper-Mil ... 39	Fernandez-Tor ... 10	Mattingly-NY ... 35	Boggs-Bos ... 312	Baines-Chi ... 113
Brett-KC ... 108	Baines-Chi ... 198			G.Thomas-Sea ... 32	Murray-Bal ... 305	Brett-KC ... 112
BASES ON BALLS	**STOLEN BASES**	**BASE STEALING RUNS**	**FIELDING RUNS-INFIELD**	**FIELDING RUNS-OUTFIELD**	**OUTFIELD ASSISTS**	**CATCHER CS PCT.**
Evans-Bos ... 114	Henderson-NY ... 80	Henderson-NY ... 14.1	Buckner-Bos ... 25.4	Barfield-Tor ... 15.1	Barfield-Tor ... 22	Boone-Cal ... 44.1
Harrah-Tex ... 113	Pettis-Cal ... 56	Pettis-Cal ... 9.2	Owen-Sea ... 24.6	Butler-Cle ... 13.9	Puckett-Min ... 19	Gedman-Bos ... 43.4
Brett-KC ... 103	Butler-Cle ... 47	Smith-KC ... 6.3	White-KC ... 22.5	Henderson-NY ... 10.0	Butler-Cle ... 19	Kearney-Sea ... 40.2
Henderson-NY ... 99	Wilson-KC ... 43	Perconte-Sea ... 6.1	Gaetti-Min ... 17.5	Puckett-Min ... 9.8	Brunansky-Min ... 14	Wynegar-NY ... 38.1
Boggs-Bos ... 96	Smith-KC ... 40	Wilson-KC ... 5.6	Barrett-Bos ... 16.3	Pettis-Cal ... 8.8		Salas-Min ... 36.6
WINS	**WINNING PCT.**	**WINS ABOVE TEAM**	**GAMES STARTED**	**COMPLETE GAMES**	**FEWEST HITS/GAME**	**FEWEST BB/GAME**
Guidry-NY ... 22	Guidry-NY ... .786	Guidry-NY ... 7.1	Blyleven-Cle-Min ... 37	Blyleven-Cle-Min ... 24	Stieb-Tor ... 7.00	Haas-Mil ... 1.39
Saberhagen-KC ... 20	Saberhagen-KC ... .769	Saberhagen-KC ... 6.7	Smithson-Min ... 37	Moore-Sea ... 14	Hough-Tex ... 7.12	Saberhagen-KC ... 1.45
Viola-Min ... 18	Leibrandt-KC ... .654	Lamp-Tor ... 5.5	Codiroli-Oak ... 37	Hough-Tex ... 14	Petry-Det ... 7.16	Guidry-NY ... 1.46
Burns-Chi ... 18	Higuera-Mil ... .652	Moore-Sea ... 4.8		Morris-Det ... 13	Morris-Det ... 7.42	Butcher-Min ... 1.86
		Higuera-Mil ... 4.8		Boyd-Bos ... 13	Higuera-Mil ... 7.88	Key-Tor ... 2.12
STRIKEOUTS	**STRIKEOUTS/GAME**	**GAMES**	**SAVES**	**BASE RUNNERS/9**	**ADJUSTED RELIEF RUNS**	**RELIEF RANKING**
Blyleven-Cle-Min ... 206	Bannister-Chi ... 8.46	Quisenberry-KC ... 84	Quisenberry-KC ... 37	Ontiveros-Oak ... 7.96	James-Chi ... 24.8	Moore-Cal ... 47.1
Bannister-Chi ... 198	Hurst-Bos ... 7.42	VandeBerg-Sea ... 76	James-Chi ... 32	Hernandez-Det ... 8.18	Quisenberry-KC ... 24.6	James-Chi ... 44.6
Morris-Det ... 191	Burns-Chi ... 6.82	Righetti-NY ... 74	Moore-Cal ... 31	James-Chi ... 9.41	Moore-Cal ... 23.7	Quisenberry-KC ... 42.9
Hurst-Bos ... 189	Morris-Det ... 6.69	Hernandez-Det ... 74	Hernandez-Det ... 31	Saberhagen-KC ... 9.56	Cliburn-Cal ... 22.7	Righetti-NY ... 31.8
Witt-Cal ... 180	Tanana-Tex-Det ... 6.66	Nunez-Sea ... 70		Fisher-NY ... 9.70	Harris-Tex ... 21.5	Hernandez-Det ... 31.8
INNINGS PITCHED	**OPPONENTS' AVG.**	**OPPONENTS' OBP**	**EARNED RUN AVERAGE**	**ADJUSTED ERA**	**ADJUSTED STARTER RUNS**	**PITCHER WINS**
Blyleven-Cle-Min 293.2	Stieb-Tor ... .213	Saberhagen-KC ... .271	Stieb-Tor ... 2.48	Stieb-Tor ... 171	Stieb-Tor ... 47.1	**Stieb-Tor ... 4.9**
Boyd-Bos ... 272.1	Hough-Tex ... .215	Guidry-NY ... .277	Leibrandt-KC ... 2.69	Leibrandt-KC ... 155	Saberhagen-KC ... 36.5	**Moore-Cal ... 4.8**
Stieb-Tor ... 265.0	Petry-Det ... .217	Key-Tor ... .282	Saberhagen-KC ... 2.87	Saberhagen-KC ... 146	Leibrandt-KC ... 36.5	**James-Chi ... 4.5**
Alexander-Tor ... 260.2	Morris-Det ... .225	Hough-Tex ... .283	Key-Tor ... 3.00	Key-Tor ... 141	Blyleven-Cle-Min ... 32.4	**Quisenberry-KC 4.4**
Guidry-NY ... 259.0	Higuera-Mil ... .235	Petry-Det ... .285	Blyleven-Cle-Min ... 3.16	Seaver-Chi ... 137	Key-Tor ... 29.2	**Leibrandt-KC ... 4.0**

Cards Get Royal Flush

California, with Rod Carew collecting his 3,000th hit in his final season, led the West in early September, but Kansas City took 12 of 13 to forge ahead, then three of four from the Angels in the final week to clinch. The Royals essentially won with a six-man staff: five starters (including 21-year-old Cy Young winner Bret Saberhagen) and Dan Quisenberry. George Brett had another great year, while Steve Balboni provided unexpected power.

Toronto used three big streaks to motor ahead of the Yankees, clinching on the penultimate day with a home win over New York. (The following day, Yankees hurler Phil Niekro won his 300th game.) Yankee Don Mattingly was MVP, but the Blue Jays' outfield of Jesse Barfield, Lloyd Moseby, and George Bell defeated all comers. Despite cold weather and a bad ballpark, Toronto boasted the league's second-best attendance.

Tom Seaver won his 300th game in New York—at Yankee Stadium as a member of the White Sox. A rotator cuff tear ended Rollie Fingers' career, while declining production finished Al Oliver's. Smokey Joe Wood passed on at 95 and cancer-stricken Roger Maris died at just 51.

In the first year of a best-of-seven League Championship Series, the Jays and Royals went the limit. Big rallies gave Toronto three wins in the first four games, which would have ended the series a year earlier. The opportunistic Royals took full advantage, winning Games 5 and 6 with good pitching. Kansas City blew out the home Jays with a four-run sixth in the decisive game. Brett hit .348 with 3 homers.

In the "I-70" World Series Kansas City again fell behind three games to one as St. Louis won three close contests. Unfazed, Danny Jackson won 6-1 in Game 5 to send the Series back to Kansas City. Trailing 1-0 in the ninth of Game 6, the Royals rallied—with the help of a controversial call—and Dane Iorg's two-run single sent the Series to a seventh game. Kansas City, with momentum, big bats, and Saberhagen, captured its first championship, 11-0.

1984 NATIONAL LEAGUE

TEAM	W	L	T	PCT	GB	HW	HL	R	OR	PA	H	2B	3B	HR	BB	SO	HB	SH	AVG	OBP	SLG	OPS	AOPS	BR	ABR	PF	SB	CS	BSA	BSR
East																														
Chi	96	65	0	.596	—	**51**	29	**762**	658	6143	1415	240	47	136	**567**	967	**29**	59	.260	.331	.397	728	102	80	23	108	154	66	70	11
NY	90	72	0	.556	6.5	48	33	652	676	6066	1400	235	25	107	500	1001	20	59	.257	.320	.369	689	100	2	10	99	149	54	73	14
StL	84	78	0	.519	12.5	44	37	652	645	6086	1369	225	44	75	516	924	23	68	.252	.317	.351	668	96	-36	-22	98	**220**	71	76	**24**
Phi	81	81	0	.500	15.5	39	42	720	690	6283	1494	**248**	51	**147**	555	1084	**29**	39	**.266**	**.333**	**.407**	**740**	**112**	**103**	**91**	102	186	60	76	20
Mon	78	83	0	.484	18	39	42	593	585	6042	1367	242	36	96	470	**782**	25	74	.251	.312	.362	674	99	-32	-6	96	131	38	**78**	16
Pit	75	87	0	.463	21.5	41	40	615	**567**	6119	1412	237	33	98	438	841	19	81	.255	.310	.363	673	95	-38	-39	100	96	62	61	-1
West																														
SD	92	70	0	.568	—	48	33	686	634	6119	1425	207	42	109	472	810	24	64	.259	.317	.371	688	99	-4	-7	101	152	68	69	10
Hou	80	82	0	.494	12	43	38	693	630	6201	1465	222	**67**	79	494	837	17	87	.264	.323	.371	694	108	11	56	94	105	61	63	2
Atl	80	82	0	.494	12	38	43	632	655	6106	1338	234	27	111	555	896	20	64	.247	.317	.361	678	90	-16	-59	107	140	85	62	1
LA	79	83	0	.488	13	40	41	580	600	6041	1316	213	23	102	488	829	14	**92**	.244	.306	.348	654	89	-69	-68	100	109	69	61	0
Cin	70	92	0	.432	22	39	42	627	747	6200	1342	238	30	106	566	978	12	71	.244	.313	.356	669	90	-33	-61	105	160	63	72	13
SF	66	96	0	.407	26	35	46	682	807	6290	**1499**	229	26	112	528	980	17	51	.265	.328	.375	703	107	31	51	97	126	76	62	1
Total	971	—	—	—	—	505	466	7894	—	73696	16842	2770	451	1278	6149	10929	249	809	.255	.319	.369	688	—	—	—	—	1728	773	69	110

TEAM	CG	SHO	GR	SV	IP	H	HR	BB	SO	BR/9	ERA	AERA	OAV	OOB	PR	APR	PF	OSB	OCS	FA	E	WPB	DP	FW	PW	BW	BSW	DIF
East																												
Chi	19	8	271	50	1434.0	1458	99	**442**	879	12.1	3.75	104	.267	.321	-26	22	109	134	69	.981	121	50	137	1.1	2.3	2.4	.2	9.5
NY	12	15	278	50	1442.2	1371	104	573	1028	12.3	3.60	99	.252	.324	-2	-5	99	150	64	.979	129	55	154	.7	-.5	1.1	.5	7.3
StL	19	12	313	**51**	1449.0	1427	94	494	808	12.1	3.58	98	.262	.324	1	-14	98	125	65	**.982**	**118**	64	**184**	**1.3**	-1.5	-2.3	**1.6**	3.9
Phi	11	6	287	35	1458.1	1416	101	448	904	11.6	3.62	101	.253	**.308**	-5	6	102	145	50	.975	161	51	112	-1.2	.6	**9.6**	1.1	-10.1
Mon	19	10	272	48	1431.0	1333	114	474	861	11.5	3.31	104	.249	.310	45	24	96	138	67	.978	132	48	147	.4	2.5	-.6	.7	-5.6
Pit	27	13	246	34	1470.0	1344	102	502	995	**11.4**	**3.11**	**117**	.246	**.308**	**78**	**84**	101	**115**	71	.980	128	49	142	.7	**8.8**	-4.1	-1.1	-10.4
West																												
SD	13	**17**	285	44	1460.1	**1327**	122	563	812	11.8	3.48	103	**.244**	.315	17	17	100	125	46	.978	138	56	144	.1	1.8	-.7	.0	9.7
Hou	24	13	312	29	1449.1	1350	91	502	950	11.6	3.32	101	.248	.311	44	4	93	188	68	.979	133	83	160	.4	.4	5.9	-.7	-7.0
Atl	17	7	278	49	1447.0	1401	122	525	859	12.1	3.57	108	.257	.322	3	42	107	155	63	.978	139	**44**	153	.0	4.4	-6.2	-.9	1.6
LA	**39**	16	259	27	1460.2	1381	**76**	499	**1033**	11.7	3.17	112	.250	.313	68	63	99	132	**74**	.975	163	52	146	-1.3	6.6	-7.1	-1.0	.8
Cin	25	6	327	25	1461.1	1445	128	578	946	12.6	4.16	91	.259	.328	-92	-57	106	149	70	.977	139	51	116	.0	-6.0	-6.4	.4	.9
SF	9	7	**359**	38	1461.0	1589	125	549	854	13.4	4.39	80	.278	.342	-131	-142	98	172	66	.973	173	76	134	-1.9	-14.9	5.4	-.9	-2.6
Total	234	130	3487	480	17424.2	—	—	—	—	12.0	3.59	—	.255	.319	—	—	—	—	—	.978	1674	679	1729	—	—	—	—	—

BATTER-FIELDER WINS	BATTING AVERAGE	ON-BASE PERCENTAGE	SLUGGING AVERAGE	ON-BASE PLUS SLUGGING	ADJUSTED OPS	ADJUSTED BATTER RUNS
Sandberg-Chi 6.6	Gwynn-SD .351	Matthews-Chi .410	Murphy-Atl .547	Schmidt-Phi .919	Schmidt-Phi 155	Schmidt-Phi 40.4
O.Smith-StL 5.0	Lacy-Pit .321	Gwynn-SD .410	Schmidt-Phi .536	Murphy-Atl .919	C.Davis-SF 148	Hernandez-NY 38.5
Raines-Mon 4.8	C.Davis-SF .315	Hernandez-NY .409	Sandberg-Chi .520	Sandberg-Chi .887	Cruz-Hou 147	Cruz-Hou 37.6
Schmidt-Phi 4.7	Sandberg-Chi .314	Raines-Mon .393	C.Davis-SF .507	C.Davis-SF .875	Murphy-Atl 145	Murphy-Atl 36.4
Hernandez-NY 4.6	Ray-Pit .312	Schmidt-Phi .383	Durham-Chi .505	Durham-Chi .874	Hernandez-NY 144	Raines-Mon 36.2

RUNS	HITS	DOUBLES	TRIPLES	HOME RUNS	TOTAL BASES	RUNS BATTED IN
Sandberg-Chi 114	Gwynn-SD 213	Ray-Pit 38	Sandberg-Chi 19	Schmidt-Phi 36	Murphy-Atl 332	Schmidt-Phi 106
Wiggins-SD 106	Sandberg-Chi 200	Raines-Mon 38	Samuel-Phi 19	Murphy-Atl 36	Sandberg-Chi 331	Carter-Mon 106
Raines-Mon 106	Raines-Mon 192	Sandberg-Chi 36	Cruz-Hou 13	Carter-Mon 27	Samuel-Phi 310	Murphy-Atl 100
Samuel-Phi 105	Samuel-Phi 191	Samuel-Phi 36		Strawberry-NY 26	Carter-Mon 290	Strawberry-NY 97
Matthews-Chi 101	Cruz-Hou 187			Cey-Chi 25	Schmidt-Phi 283	Cey-Chi 97

BASES ON BALLS	STOLEN BASES	BASE STEALING RUNS	FIELDING RUNS-INFIELD	FIELDING RUNS-OUTFIELD	OUTFIELD ASSISTS	CATCHER CS PCT.
Matthews-Chi 103	Raines-Mon 75	Raines-Mon 13.0	O.Smith-StL 31.5	Milner-Cin 13.8	L.Smith-StL 18	Pena-Pit 39.9
Hernandez-NY 97	Samuel-Phi 72	Samuel-Phi 10.6	Reynolds-Hou 24.1	Lacy-Pit 13.7	Martinez-SD 15	Scioscia-LA 39.5
Schmidt-Phi 92	Wiggins-SD 70	Wiggins-SD 8.1	Sax-LA 22.9	Martinez-SD 11.0	Lacy-Pit 15	Trevino-Cin-Atl 35.5
Thompson-Pit 87	L.Smith-StL 50	Wilson-NY 7.0	Wallach-Mon 22.4	McReynolds-SD 9.9	Leonard-SF 14	Porter-StL 33.1
Raines-Mon 87		Redus-Cin 6.7	Sandberg-Chi 22.3	Wilson-NY 9.5		Davis-Chi 32.4

WINS	WINNING PCT.	WINS ABOVE TEAM	GAMES STARTED	COMPLETE GAMES	FEWEST HITS/GAME	FEWEST BB/GAME
Andujar-StL 20	Sutcliffe-Chi .941	Sutcliffe-Chi 7.4	Niekro-Hou 38	Soto-Cin 13	Gooden-NY 6.65	Gullickson-Mon 1.47
Soto-Cin 18	Soto-Cin .720	Soto-Cin 6.9	Andujar-StL 36	Valenzuela-LA 12	Soto-Cin 6.86	Candelaria-Pit 1.65
Gooden-NY 17	Gooden-NY .654	Dawley-Hou 3.7		Andujar-StL 12	DeLeon-Pit 6.88	Whitson-SD 2.00
Sutcliffe-Chi 16	Show-SD .625	Rhoden-Pit 3.5		Knepper-Hou 11	Ryan-Hou 7.01	Pena-LA 2.08
Niekro-Hou 16		Perez-Atl 3.4		Mahler-Atl 9	Andujar-StL 7.51	Knepper-Hou 2.12

STRIKEOUTS	STRIKEOUTS/GAME	GAMES	SAVES	BASE RUNNERS/9	ADJUSTED RELIEF RUNS	RELIEF RANKING
Gooden-NY 276	Gooden-NY 11.39	Power-Cin 78	Sutter-StL 45	Denny-Phi 9.04	Sutter-StL 26.3	Sutter-StL 40.7
Valenzuela-LA 240	Ryan-Hou 9.65	Lavelle-SF 77	Smith-Chi 33	Smith-Hou 9.43	Dawley-Hou 16.9	Bedrosian-Atl 25.5
Ryan-Hou 197	Valenzuela-LA 8.28	Minton-SF 74	Orosco-NY 31	Lefferts-SD 9.62	Lefferts-SD 16.7	Dawley-Hou 24.8
Soto-Cin 185	Berenyi-Cin-NY 7.27	Tekulve-Pit 72	Holland-Phi 29	Orosco-NY 9.72	Bedrosian-Atl 13.8	Orosco-NY 19.2
Carlton-Phi 163	DeLeon-Pit 7.16	Sutter-StL 71	Gossage-SD 25	Gooden-NY 9.74	Sisk-NY 11.6	Power-Cin 17.2

INNINGS PITCHED	OPPONENTS' AVG.	OPPONENTS' OBP	EARNED RUN AVERAGE	ADJUSTED ERA	ADJUSTED STARTER RUNS	PITCHER WINS
Andujar-StL 261.1	Gooden-NY .202	Gooden-NY .269	Pena-LA 2.48	Pena-LA 143	Gooden-NY 24.2	**Sutter-StL 4.4**
Valenzuela-LA 261.0	Soto-Cin .209	Hershiser-LA .278	Gooden-NY 2.60	Gooden-NY 137	Rhoden-Pit 23.7	**Rhoden-Pit 3.5**
Niekro-Hou 248.1	Ryan-Hou .211	Andujar-StL .284	Hershiser-LA 2.66	Hershiser-LA 134	Pena-LA 22.8	**Gooden-NY 3.0**
Rhoden-Pit 238.1	DeLeon-Pit .214	Soto-Cin .284	Rhoden-Pit 2.72	Rhoden-Pit 134	Hershiser-LA 19.3	**Dawley-Hou 2.8**
Soto-Cin 237.1	Hershiser-LA .225	Ryan-Hou .286	Candelaria-Pit 2.72	Candelaria-Pit 134	Denny-Phi 18.9	**Bedrosian-Atl 2.6**

Padres Castigate Cubs

In the thirty-nine years since the Cubs had won, television, rock music, computers, and black voting rights had come along. It was about time for Chicago, and they pulled away from the surprising Mets in August. MVP second baseman Ryne Sandberg starred in all facets and was ably supported by a veteran Cubs lineup. Midseason trades brought in Dennis Eckersley, still a dependable starter, and Rick Sutcliffe, who went 16-1 for the Cubs and took home the Cy Young.

Mets hurler Dwight Gooden, just 19, was Rookie of the Year and finished second in Cy Young balloting. First baseman Keith Hernandez was outstanding, and rookie manager Davey Johnson eagerly inserted talented youngsters into New York's lineup and rotation.

Cubs attendance rose 42 percent, while Mets crowds increased 66 percent. League attendance, however, decreased in eight cities and fell 3.6 percent. Peter Ueberroth was tabbed as the new commissioner to bring financial sensibility to the game, and he *did* help baseball garner more television money. Terry Pendleton debuted for St. Louis, while the Reds welcomed Jose Rijo and Eric Davis. It was the end, though, for Joe Morgan and Tug McGraw.

San Diego, strong defensively and deep in decent pitchers, won the West by July. Tony Gwynn nailed down his first batting crown. Manager Dick Williams moved outfielder Alan Wiggins to second base, creating an instant leadoff man.

Chicago easily won the first two NLCS games at Wrigley Field, winning by a combined score of 17-2. Back in San Diego, the Padres walloped the Cubs in Game 3, and then won a seesaw Game 4 on Steve Garvey's ninth-inning homer. Chicago led the deciding game, 3-2, until Cubs errors and big hits gave San Diego a four-run seventh and their first pennant. It almost didn't matter that the Padres lost to the Tigers in the World Series. San Diego fans had no expectations of glory.

1984 AMERICAN LEAGUE

TEAM	W	L	T	PCT	GB	HW	HL	R	OR	PA	H	2B	3B	HR	BB	SO	HB	SH	AVG	OBP	SLG	OPS	AOPS	BR	ABR	PF	SB	CS	BSA	BSR
EAST																														
Det	104	58	0	.642	—	**53**	29	**829**	**643**	6373	1529	254	46	**187**	602	941	34	48	.271	**.342**	.432	774	**113**	105	**106**	100	106	68	61	0
Tor	89	73	1	.549	15	49	32	750	696	6283	1555	**275**	**68**	143	460	816	**52**	35	.273	.331	.421	752	102	51	21	104	**193**	67	**74**	**19**
NY	87	75	0	.537	17	51	30	758	679	6356	1560	**275**	32	130	534	**673**	38	64	.276	.339	.404	743	109	50	77	97	62	38	62	0
Bos	86	76	0	.531	18	41	40	810	764	6250	**1598**	259	45	181	500	842	20	36	**.283**	.341	**.441**	**782**	110	**113**	73	105	38	25	60	0
Bal	85	77	0	.525	19	44	37	681	667	6186	1374	234	23	160	**620**	884	22	45	.252	.328	.391	719	100	-2	10	98	51	36	59	-1
Cle	75	87	1	.463	29	41	39	761	766	6374	1498	222	39	123	600	815	27	37	.265	.335	.384	719	96	4	-11	102	126	77	62	1
Mil	67	94	0	.416	36.5	38	43	641	734	6057	1446	232	36	96	432	**673**	26	42	.262	.317	.370	687	92	-77	-54	97	52	57	48	-9
WEST																														
KC	84	78	0	.519	—	44	37	673	686	6063	1487	269	52	117	400	832	24	41	.268	.317	.399	716	96	-25	-33	101	106	64	62	1
Cal	81	81	0	.500	3	37	44	696	697	6166	1363	211	30	150	556	928	29	65	.249	.319	.381	700	93	-47	-46	100	80	51	61	0
Min	81	81	0	.500	3	47	34	673	675	6107	1473	259	33	114	437	735	24	26	.265	.318	.385	703	88	-45	-78	105	39	30	57	-2
Oak	77	85	0	.475	7	44	37	738	796	6161	1415	257	29	158	568	871	22	37	.259	.327	.404	731	107	21	68	94	145	64	69	10
Sea	74	88	0	.457	10	42	39	682	774	6211	1429	244	34	129	519	871	42	**66**	.258	.324	.384	708	96	-31	-27	99	116	62	65	4
Chi	74	88	0	.457	10	43	38	679	736	6156	1360	225	38	172	523	883	39	37	.247	.314	.395	709	90	-38	-71	105	109	49	69	7
Tex	69	92	0	.429	14.5	34	46	656	714	6099	1452	227	29	120	420	807	20	47	.261	.313	.377	690	87	-78	-101	104	81	50	62	0
Total	1134	—	—	—	—	608	525	10027	—	86842	20539	3443	534	1980	7171	11571	419	626	.264	.326	.398	724	—	—	—	—	1304	738	64	29

TEAM	CG	SHO	GR	SV	IP	H	HR	BB	SO	BR/9	ERA	AERA	OAV	OOB	PR	APR	PF	OSB	OCS	FA	E	WPB	DP	FW	PW	BW	BSW	DIF
EAST																												
Det	19	8	268	**51**	1464.0	**1358**	130	489	914	**11.5**	**3.49**	**113**	**.246**	**.308**	**81**	**76**	99	**68**	52	.979	127	63	162	.3	**7.6**	**10.7**	-.2	4.6
Tor	34	10	257	33	1464.0	1433	140	528	875	12.3	3.86	107	.257	.323	21	42	103	75	40	.980	123	51	166	.6	4.2	2.1	**1.7**	-.6
NY	15	12	287	43	1465.1	1485	**120**	518	**992**	12.4	3.78	101	.264	.325	35	9	96	88	60	.977	142	41	**177**	-.5	.9	7.7	-.2	-1.9
Bos	40	12	201	32	1442.0	1524	141	517	927	12.9	4.18	100	.270	.332	-29	3	105	111	**67**	.977	143	47	128	-.6	.3	7.3	-.2	-1.8
Bal	**48**	**13**	208	32	1439.1	1393	137	512	714	12.1	3.71	105	.256	.320	44	32	98	99	48	**.981**	123	67	166	.5	3.2	1.0	-.3	-.4
Cle	21	7	**308**	35	1467.2	1523	141	545	803	12.8	4.26	97	.269	.332	-43	-22	103	100	47	.977	146	60	163	-.7	-2.2	-1.1	-.1	-1.9
Mil	13	7	283	41	1433.0	1532	137	480	785	12.8	4.06	96	.274	.331	-10	-28	97	96	59	.978	136	53	156	-.3	-2.8	-5.4	-1.1	-3.9
WEST																												
KC	18	9	214	50	1444.0	1426	136	**433**	724	11.8	3.92	103	.258	.312	11	19	101	94	51	.979	131	**34**	157	.0	1.9	-3.3	-.1	4.4
Cal	36	12	203	26	1458.0	1526	143	474	754	12.5	3.96	101	.271	.328	6	5	100	71	49	.980	128	48	170	.2	.5	-4.6	-.2	4.1
Min	32	9	249	38	1437.2	1429	159	463	713	12.1	3.85	110	.260	.319	23	57	106	92	58	.980	**120**	42	134	**.7**	5.7	-7.8	-.4	1.8
Oak	15	6	282	44	1430.0	1554	155	592	695	13.7	4.48	84	.278	.348	-78	-120	94	94	**67**	.975	146	56	159	-.8	-12.1	6.8	.8	1.2
Sea	26	4	292	35	1442.0	1497	138	619	972	13.5	4.31	93	.270	.345	-50	-47	101	88	58	.979	128	64	143	.2	-4.7	-2.7	.2	.0
Chi	43	9	238	32	1454.1	1416	155	483	840	12.0	4.13	101	.256	.317	-23	6	105	100	41	**.981**	122	43	160	.6	.6	-7.1	.5	-1.5
Tex	38	6	190	21	1438.2	1443	148	518	863	12.5	3.91	107	.260	.325	13	39	104	128	41	.977	138	95	138	-.4	3.9	-10.2	-.2	-4.7
Total	398	124	3480	513	20280.0	—	—	—	—	12.5	3.99	—	.264	.326	—	—	—	—	—	.979	1853	764	2179	—	—	—	—	—

BATTER-FIELDER WINS	BATTING AVERAGE	ON-BASE PERCENTAGE	SLUGGING AVERAGE	ON-BASE PLUS SLUGGING	ADJUSTED OPS	ADJUSTED BATTER RUNS
Ripken-Bal 9.4	Mattingly-NY .343	Murray-Bal .410	Baines-Chi .541	Evans-Bos .920	Mattingly-NY 158	Murray-Bal 50.3
Mattingly-NY 5.3	Winfield-NY .340	Boggs-Bos .407	Mattingly-NY .537	Murray-Bal .918	Murray-Bal 157	Mattingly-NY 46.7
Yount-Mil 5.2	Boggs-Bos .325	Henderson-Oak .399	Evans-Bos .532	Mattingly-NY .918	Winfield-NY 155	Winfield-NY 43.1
Murray-Bal 5.1	Bell-Tex .315	Winfield-NY .393	Armas-Bos .531	Winfield-NY .908	Davis-Sea 146	Evans-Bos 41.5
Henderson-Oak 4.6	Trammell-Det .314	Davis-Sea .391	Hrbek-Min .522	Hrbek-Min .906	Henderson-Oak 146	Davis-Sea 40.0

RUNS	HITS	DOUBLES	TRIPLES	HOME RUNS	TOTAL BASES	RUNS BATTED IN
Evans-Bos 121	Mattingly-NY 207	Mattingly-NY 44	Moseby-Tor 15	Armas-Bos 43	Armas-Bos 339	Armas-Bos 123
Henderson-Oak 113	Boggs-Bos 203	Parrish-Tex 42	Collins-Tor 15	Kingman-Oak 35	Evans-Bos 335	Rice-Bos 122
Boggs-Bos 109	Ripken-Bal 195	Bell-Tor 39	Gibson-Det 10	Thornton-Cle 33	Ripken-Bal 327	Kingman-Oak 118
Butler-Cle 108	Winfield-NY 193	Ripken-Bal 37	Baines-Chi 10	Parrish-Det 33	Mattingly-NY 324	Davis-Sea 116
Armas-Bos 107		Evans-Bos 37		Murphy-Oak 33	Easler-Bos 310	

BASES ON BALLS	STOLEN BASES	BASE STEALING RUNS	FIELDING RUNS-INFIELD	FIELDING RUNS-OUTFIELD	OUTFIELD ASSISTS	CATCHER CS PCT.
Murray-Bal 107	Henderson-Oak 66	Wilson-KC 8.6	Ripken-Bal 39.3	Vukovich-Cle 18.8	Puckett-Min 16	Sundberg-Mil 50.0
Davis-Sea 97	Collins-Tor 60	Collins-Tor 8.3	White-KC 29.0	Puckett-Min 17.8	Murphy-Oak 14	Laudner-Min 49.2
Evans-Bos 96	Butler-Cle 52	Henderson-Oak 8.2	Bell-Tex 23.8	Murphy-Oak 11.0	Kittle-Chi 14	Boone-Cal 43.5
Thornton-Cle 91	Pettis-Cal 48	Garcia-Tor 5.9	Cruz-Chi 23.6	Henderson-Oak 7.7		Kearney-Sea 41.6
Boggs-Bos 89	Wilson-KC 47	Moseby-Tor 5.4	Boggs-Bos 22.3	Davis-Oak 6.7		Gedman-Bos 41.1

WINS	WINNING PCT.	WINS ABOVE TEAM	GAMES STARTED	COMPLETE GAMES	FEWEST HITS/GAME	FEWEST BB/GAME
Boddicker-Bal 20	Alexander-Tor .739	Blyleven-Cle 7.0	Smithson-Min 36	Hough-Tex 17	Stieb-Tor 7.25	Hoyt-Chi 1.64
Morris-Det 19	Blyleven-Cle .731	Alexander-Tor 5.3	Hough-Tex 36	Boddicker-Bal 16	Blyleven-Cle 7.49	Smithson-Min 1.93
Blyleven-Cle 19	Petry-Det .692	Langston-Sea 4.8	Clancy-Tor 36	Dotson-Chi 14	Boddicker-Bal 7.51	Guidry-NY 2.02
Viola-Min 18	Wilcox-Det .680	Boddicker-Bal 4.6		Blyleven-Cle 12	Langston-Sea 7.52	Alexander-Tor 2.03
Petry-Det 18		Lopez-Det 4.2		Beattie-Sea 12	Mason-Tex 7.76	Haas-Mil 2.04

STRIKEOUTS	STRIKEOUTS/GAME	GAMES	SAVES	BASE RUNNERS/9	ADJUSTED RELIEF RUNS	RELIEF RANKING
Langston-Sea 204	Langston-Sea 8.16	Hernandez-Det 80	Quisenberry-KC 44	Hernandez-Det 8.72	Hernandez-Det 33.8	Hernandez-Det 41.3
Stieb-Tor 198	Witt-Cal 7.15	Quisenberry-KC 72	Caudill-Oak 36	Quisenberry-KC 9.26	Quisenberry-KC 21.0	Camacho-Cle 30.4
Witt-Cal 196	Moore-Sea 6.71	Lopez-Det 71	Hernandez-Det 32	Waddell-Cle 9.84	Camacho-Cle 17.7	Quisenberry-KC 27.4
Blyleven-Cle 170	Stieb-Tor 6.67	Camacho-Cle 69	Righetti-NY 31	Saberhagen-KC 10.05	Corbett-Cal 17.6	Righetti-NY 26.7
Hough-Tex 164	Berenguer-Det 6.31	Caudill-Oak 68	Davis-Min 29	Caudill-Oak 10.09	Righetti-NY 16.0	Caudill-Oak 26.4

INNINGS PITCHED	OPPONENTS' AVG.	OPPONENTS' OBP	EARNED RUN AVERAGE	ADJUSTED ERA	ADJUSTED STARTER RUNS	PITCHER WINS
Stieb-Tor 267.0	Stieb-Tor .221	Black-KC .283	Boddicker-Bal 2.79	Stieb-Tor 146	Stieb-Tor 39.9	**Hernandez-Det 4.3**
Hough-Tex 266.0	Blyleven-Cle .224	Alexander-Tor .284	Stieb-Tor 2.83	Blyleven-Cle 144	Blyleven-Cle 33.2	**Boddicker-Bal 3.9**
Alexander-Tor 261.2	Boddicker-Bal .228	Blyleven-Cle .285	Blyleven-Cle 2.87	Boddicker-Bal 140	Boddicker-Bal 31.5	**Stieb-Tor 3.5**
Boddicker-Bal 261.1	Langston-Sea .230	Mason-Tex .285	Niekro-NY 3.09	Alexander-Tor 132	Alexander-Tor 28.9	**Blyleven-Cle 3.4**
Viola-Min 257.2	Berenguer-Det .232	Seaver-Chi .288	Zahn-Cal 3.12	Viola-Min 132	Viola-Min 27.5	**Camacho-Cle 3.1**

Runaway Tigers

Riding a 35-5 start, the Detroit Tigers dominated the league. Drawing league-leading crowds to the corner of Michigan and Trumbull, the Tigers led the league in scoring and ERA. Under Sparky Anderson, Detroit won 104 games with a great middle infield of Lou Whitaker and Alan Trammell, star right fielder Kirk Gibson, and slugging catcher Lance Parrish. Three strong starters were supplemented by reliever Willie Hernandez, who won the Cy Young and MVP trophies. Lefty Hernandez and righty Aurelio Lopez appeared in a combined 151 games.

On-base percentage became an official statistic, and the AL's first declared leader was Eddie Murray of the Orioles. While stolen bases dipped to their lowest level since 1973, strikeouts were their highest since the inception of the DH. Seattle rookie Mark Langston paced the league in whiffs and walks. Toronto rose to second in the East, using speed and power while debuting southpaw Jimmy Key as a co-closer. Shoulder miseries forced Jim Palmer to retire from the Orioles, but AL hitters found an equally annoying successor in Boston's 21-year-old rookie Roger Clemens.

The Angels contended with four 20-homer hitters, but again lacked a solid bullpen. The Twins, showing improvement in their third year in the Metrodome, welcomed rookie center fielder Kirby Puckett. Chicago crumbled to fifth. Kansas City was the West's only team over .500. The Royals, riding a hot September, made their sixth postseason appearance since 1976 despite losing Willie Wilson to a drug suspension; George Brett playing just 104 games due to injury; using rookie starters Bret Saberhagen, Mark Gubicza, and Danny Jackson; and allowing more runs than they scored. Dan Quisenberry was again a late-inning savior.

Detroit swept the Royals easily in the ALCS. In the World Series Jack Morris twice went the distance in victories, and Trammell and Gibson were the hitting stars. The five-game win against the Padres sparked celebrations and rioting all over the Motor City.

1983 NATIONAL LEAGUE

TEAM	W	L	T	PCT	GB	HW	HL	R	OR	PA	H	2B	3B	HR	BB	SO	HB	SH	AVG	OBP	SLG	OPS	AOPS	BR	ABR	PF	SB	CS	BSA	BSR
East																														
Phi	90	72	1	.556	—	**50**	31	696	635	6218	1352	209	45	125	**640**	906	26	80	.249	.329	.373	702	102	17	23	99	143	75	66	5
Pit	84	78	0	.519	6	41	40	659	648	6169	1460	238	29	121	497	873	19	84	.264	.325	.383	708	99	18	-2	103	124	77	62	0
Mon	82	80	1	.506	8	46	35	677	646	6293	1482	**297**	41	102	509	**733**	**38**	78	.264	.326	.386	712	103	34	34	100	138	44	**76**	15
StL	79	83	0	.488	11	44	37	679	710	6238	**1496**	262	**63**	83	543	879	24	72	.270	.335	.384	719	**104**	48	**44**	101	**207**	89	70	14
Chi	71	91	0	.438	19	43	38	701	719	6132	1436	272	42	140	470	868	29	71	.261	.319	**.401**	720	100	37	5	105	84	40	68	4
NY	68	94	0	.420	22	41	41	575	680	6009	1314	172	26	112	436	1031	31	66	.241	.300	.344	644	85	-118	-115	99	141	64	69	9
West																														
LA	91	71	1	.562	—	48	32	654	**609**	6129	1358	197	34	**146**	541	925	22	86	.250	.318	.379	697	99	-7	-7	100	166	76	69	10
Atl	88	74	0	.543	3	46	34	**746**	640	6195	1489	218	45	130	582	847	17	78	**.272**	**.341**	.400	**741**	**104**	**91**	40	107	146	88	62	1
Hou	85	77	0	.525	6	46	36	643	646	6173	1412	239	60	97	517	869	19	81	.257	.320	.375	695	**104**	-8	30	95	164	95	63	3
SD	81	81	1	.500	10	47	34	653	653	6163	1384	207	34	93	482	822	20	**89**	.250	.311	.351	662	92	-77	-59	97	179	67	73	**16**
SF	79	83	0	.488	12	43	38	687	697	6126	1324	206	30	142	619	990	28	64	.247	.325	.375	700	103	12	32	97	140	78	64	4
Cin	74	88	0	.457	17	36	45	623	710	6057	1274	236	35	107	588	1006	19	72	.239	.314	.356	670	89	-47	-68	104	154	77	67	7
Total	974	—	—	—	—	531	441	7993	—	73902	16781	2753	484	1398	6424	10749	292	921	.255	.322	.376	698	—	—	—	—	1786	870	67	88

TEAM	CG	SHO	GR	SV	IP	H	HR	BB	SO	BR/9	ERA	AERA	OAV	OOB	PR	APR	PF	OSB	OCS	FA	E	WPB	DP	FW	PW	BW	BSW	DIF
East																												
Phi	20	10	300	41	1461.2	1429	111	**464**	**1092**	11.8	3.34	108	.256	.314	47	42	99	167	79	.976	152	57	117	-.7	4.4	2.4	-.2	3.2
Pit	25	14	290	41	1462.1	1378	109	563	1061	12.1	3.55	105	.252	.321	12	29	103	126	64	**.982**	115	61	165	1.4	3.0	-.2	-.8	-.5
Mon	**38**	**15**	252	34	1471.0	1406	120	479	899	11.7	3.58	101	.254	.315	8	6	100	115	86	.981	116	46	130	1.4	.6	3.6	.8	-5.4
StL	22	10	327	27	1460.2	1479	115	525	709	12.5	3.79	96	.266	.330	-26	-23	101	**110**	64	.976	152	74	173	-.8	-2.4	**4.6**	.7	-4.1
Chi	9	10	**369**	42	1428.2	1496	117	498	807	12.7	4.08	93	.274	.335	-71	-41	105	152	66	**.982**	115	67	164	1.4	-4.3	.5	-.4	-7.3
NY	18	7	274	33	1451.0	1384	97	615	717	12.5	3.68	100	.256	.331	-8	-2	101	194	73	.976	151	58	171	-.7	-.2	-12.0	.2	-.2
West																												
LA	27	12	278	40	1464.0	1336	97	495	1000	**11.4**	**3.10**	**116**	.244	**.307**	**85**	**81**	99	114	**88**	.974	168	58	132	-1.7	**8.5**	-.7	.3	3.7
Atl	18	4	305	**48**	1440.2	1412	132	540	895	12.3	3.67	105	.260	.327	-7	28	106	172	68	.978	137	**40**	**176**	.1	2.9	4.2	-.7	.4
Hou	22	14	261	**48**	1466.1	**1276**	**94**	570	904	11.5	3.45	99	**.236**	.309	29	-5	94	182	54	.977	147	84	165	-.5	-.5	3.1	-.5	2.3
SD	23	5	294	44	1467.2	1389	144	528	850	11.9	3.62	97	.253	.320	1	-20	97	152	74	.979	129	42	135	.6	-2.1	-6.2	**.9**	6.7
SF	20	9	276	47	1445.2	1431	127	520	881	12.3	3.70	96	.259	.323	-11	-26	98	167	73	.973	171	64	109	-1.9	-2.7	3.3	-.4	-.4
Cin	34	5	271	29	1441.1	1365	135	627	934	12.6	3.98	96	.253	.330	-57	-26	105	135	81	.981	**114**	43	121	**1.5**	-2.7	-7.1	-.0	1.4
Total	276	115	3497	474	17461.0	—	—	—	—	12.1	3.63	—	.255	.322	—	—	—	—	—	.978	1667	694	1758	—	—	—	—	—

BATTER-FIELDER WINS	BATTING AVERAGE	ON-BASE PERCENTAGE	SLUGGING AVERAGE	ON-BASE PLUS SLUGGING	ADJUSTED OPS	ADJUSTED BATTER RUNS
Schmidt-Phi 6.4	Madlock-Pit .323	Schmidt-Phi .399	Murphy-Atl .540	Murphy-Atl .933	Schmidt-Phi 156	Schmidt-Phi 45.1
Thon-Hou 6.2	L.Smith-StL .321	Hernandez-StL-NY .396	Dawson-Mon .539	Schmidt-Phi .923	Evans-SF 150	Murphy-Atl 38.7
Raines-Mon 4.6	Cruz-Hou .318	Murphy-Atl .393	Guerrero-LA .531	Guerrero-LA .904	Guerrero-LA 149	Guerrero-LA 38.2
Carter-Mon 4.4	Hendrick-StL .318	Raines-Mon .393	Schmidt-Phi .524	Evans-SF .894	Murphy-Atl 147	Evans-SF 37.1
Sandberg-Chi 4.2	Knight-Hou .304	Madlock-Pit .386	Evans-SF .516	Dawson-Mon .877	Cruz-Hou 142	Cruz-Hou 34.2
RUNS	**HITS**	**DOUBLES**	**TRIPLES**	**HOME RUNS**	**TOTAL BASES**	**RUNS BATTED IN**
Raines-Mon 133	Dawson-Mon 189	Ray-Pit 38	Butler-Atl 13	Schmidt-Phi 40	Dawson-Mon 341	Murphy-Atl 121
Murphy-Atl 131	Cruz-Hou 189	Oliver-Mon 38	Moreno-Hou 11	Murphy-Atl 36	Murphy-Atl 318	Dawson-Mon 113
Schmidt-Phi 104	Ramirez-Atl 185	Buckner-Chi 38	Green-StL 10	Guerrero-LA 32	Guerrero-LA 310	Schmidt-Phi 109
Dawson-Mon 104	Oliver-Mon 184	Carter-Mon 37	Dawson-Mon 10	Dawson-Mon 32	Thon-Hou 283	Guerrero-LA 103
	Raines-Mon 183			Evans-SF 30	Schmidt-Phi 280	Kennedy-SD 98
BASES ON BALLS	**STOLEN BASES**	**BASE STEALING RUNS**	**FIELDING RUNS-INFIELD**	**FIELDING RUNS-OUTFIELD**	**OUTFIELD ASSISTS**	**CATCHER CS PCT.**
Schmidt-Phi 128	Raines-Mon 90	Raines-Mon 14.9	Sandberg-Chi 44.3	Milner-Cin 12.8	Raines-Mon 21	Yeager-LA 43.8
Thompson-Pit 99	Wiggins-SD 66	Wiggins-SD 10.0	Bowa-Chi 25.6	Raines-Mon 9.4	Leonard-SF 17	Porter-StL 43.2
Raines-Mon 97	S.Sax-LA 56	Wilson-NY 6.3	Hubbard-Atl 24.9	Butler-Atl 5.7	Clark-SF 17	Bilardello-Cin 37.9
Murphy-Atl 90	Wilson-NY 54	McGee-StL 5.8	Buckner-Chi 21.8	Clark-SF 5.5	L.Smith-StL 14	Diaz-Phi 36.8
Morgan-Phi 89	L.Smith-StL 43	Dernier-Phi 5.3	Schmidt-Phi 21.7	Leonard-SF 4.2	Butler-Atl 13	Pena-Pit 35.6
WINS	**WINNING PCT.**	**WINS ABOVE TEAM**	**GAMES STARTED**	**COMPLETE GAMES**	**FEWEST HITS/GAME**	**FEWEST BB/GAME**
Denny-Phi 19	Denny-Phi .760	Denny-Phi 6.3	Niekro-Hou 38	Soto-Cin 18	Ryan-Hou 6.14	Hammaker-SF 1.67
Soto-Cin 17	Perez-Atl .652	Orosco-NY 4.3	Carlton-Phi 37	Rogers-Mon 13	Soto-Cin 6.81	Ruthven-Phi-Chi 1.87
Rogers-Mon 17	McWilliams-Pit .652	Reed-Phi 3.9	Rogers-Mon 36	Gullickson-Mon 10	Welch-LA 7.24	Denny-Phi 1.97
Gullickson-Mon 17	Candelaria-Pit .652	Monge-Phi-SD 3.6	Denny-Phi 36		Hammaker-SF 7.68	Reuss-LA 2.01
Lea-Mon 16	McMurtry-Atl .625	Soto-Cin 3.6			Pena-LA 7.73	Candelaria-Pit 2.05
STRIKEOUTS	**STRIKEOUTS/GAME**	**GAMES**	**SAVES**	**BASE RUNNERS/9**	**ADJUSTED RELIEF RUNS**	**RELIEF RANKING**
Carlton-Phi 275	Carlton-Phi 8.73	Campbell-Chi 82	Smith-Chi 29	Niedenfuer-LA 8.08	Orosco-NY 23.9	Orosco-NY 45.9
Soto-Cin 242	Ryan-Hou 8.39	Tekulve-Pit 76	Holland-Phi 25	Dawley-Hou 8.36	Smith-Chi 22.8	Smith-Chi 39.7
McWilliams-Pit 199	Soto-Cin 7.96	Hernandez-Chi-Phi 74	Minton-SF 22	Howe-LA 8.91	Tekulve-Pit 19.6	Howe-LA 30.7
Valenzuela-LA 189	McWilliams-Pit 7.53	Scherrer-Cin 73	Sutter-StL 21	Holland-Phi 9.13	Niedenfuer-LA 19.0	Tekulve-Pit 27.9
Ryan-Hou 183	Berenyi-Cin 7.29	Minton-SF 73	Reardon-Mon 21	DiPino-Hou 9.21	Howe-LA 15.9	Niedenfuer-LA 23.9
INNINGS PITCHED	**OPPONENTS' AVG.**	**OPPONENTS' OBP**	**EARNED RUN AVERAGE**	**ADJUSTED ERA**	**ADJUSTED STARTER RUNS**	**PITCHER WINS**
Carlton-Phi 283.2	Ryan-Hou .195	Hammaker-SF .266	Hammaker-SF 2.25	Hammaker-SF 158	Denny-Phi 32.5	**Orosco-NY 5.2**
Soto-Cin 273.2	Soto-Cin .208	Soto-Cin .278	Denny-Phi 2.37	Denny-Phi 152	Soto-Cin 30.3	**Smith-Chi 4.3**
Rogers-Mon 273.0	Welch-LA .222	Pena-LA .283	Welch-LA 2.65	Soto-Cin 142	Hammaker-SF 22.5	**Denny-Phi 3.4**
Niekro-Hou 263.2	Hammaker-SF .228	Welch-LA .291	Soto-Cin 2.70	Welch-LA 136	Welch-LA 21.7	**Howe-LA 3.4**
Valenzuela-LA 257.0	Pena-LA .229	Denny-Phi .293	Pena-LA 2.75	Pena-LA 132	Smith-Mon 18.0	**Soto-Cin 3.0**

One More for Cincinnati East

With the departure of Joe Morgan, Tony Perez, Pete Rose, and others, the Reds had declined. In 1982 they had crashed into the basement. Following the 1983 season, Johnny Bench, shifted uncomfortably to third base, retired at 35. The Big Red Machine was dead.

But it lived, one last time, in Philadelphia. With a hot September under new manager Paul Owens, the Phillies squeezed out one last division title as Cincinnati East. Morgan, Rose, and Perez all played key roles for the Phillies. Von Hayes was the only young regular, and the pitching depended heavily on graybeards and reliever Al Holland.

For the first time (excluding 1981) since 1931, the NL had no 20-game winner. As a result, Phillies right-hander John Denny was voted the Cy Young winner. His career was effectively destroyed by elbow problems the next season. Thirty-nine-year-old Fergie Jenkins had the second-best ERA among Cubs starters, but chose to retire. Mets right field prospect Darryl Strawberry lived up to the hype, winning Rookie of the Year honors.

The Dodgers edged Atlanta in the West, getting hot in August just as the Braves cooled. Dale Murphy won his second straight MVP for the Braves, but the late-season acquisition of Len Barker backfired in Atlanta; the club was demoralized when news leaked that Brett Butler was the player to be named going to Cleveland.

Pedro Guerrero was the main cog in Los Angeles' offense. Fernando Valenzuela was not as sharp as he was in his first two seasons, although he remained among the leaders in strikeouts and innings; Bob Welch and Alejandro Pena provided solid rotation support. In the postseason, though, the Dodgers didn't get much hitting or pitching—Valenzuela won their lone game against Philadelphia. Los Angeles dropped the last two games by 7-2 tallies. Steve Carlton was excellent in two starts, and he also pitched well in the World Series. Unfortunately for the Phillies, the offense was out to lunch, and they lost to the Orioles in five games.

1983 AMERICAN LEAGUE

TEAM	W	L	T	PCT	GB	HW	HL	R	OR	PA	H	2B	3B	HR	BB	SO	HB	SH	AVG	OBP	SLG	OPS	AOPS	BR	ABR	PF	SB	CS	BSA	BSR
EAST																														
Bal	98	64	0	.605	—	50	31	799	652	6272	1492	283	27	**168**	601	800	23	46	.269	**.340**	.421	761	109	74	85	99	61	33	65	2
Det	92	70	0	.568	6	48	33	789	679	6246	1530	283	53	156	508	831	39	48	.274	.335	.427	762	110	68	86	98	93	53	64	2
NY	91	71	0	.562	7	51	30	770	703	6279	1535	269	40	153	533	686	37	37	.273	.337	.416	753	109	53	77	97	84	42	67	4
Tor	89	73	0	.549	9	48	33	795	726	6213	1546	268	**58**	167	510	810	32	36	**.277**	.338	**.436**	**774**	104	**88**	37	107	131	72	65	4
Mil	87	75	0	.537	11	52	29	764	708	6240	**1556**	281	57	132	475	**665**	27	61	**.277**	.333	.418	751	**113**	43	**100**	93	101	49	67	5
Bos	78	84	0	.481	20	38	43	724	775	6251	1512	**287**	32	142	536	758	28	49	.270	.335	.409	744	97	37	-17	108	30	26	54	-2
Cle	70	92	0	.432	28	36	45	704	785	6222	1451	249	31	86	**605**	691	29	48	.265	.338	.369	707	90	-21	-48	104	109	71	61	-1
WEST																														
Chi	99	63	0	.611	—	**55**	26	**800**	650	6163	1439	270	42	157	527	888	**43**	53	.262	.329	.413	742	99	27	-4	104	165	50	77	19
KC	79	83	1	.488	20	45	36	696	767	6083	1515	273	54	109	397	722	23	32	.271	.320	.397	717	95	-34	-39	101	182	47	**79**	**24**
Tex	77	85	1	.475	22	44	37	639	**609**	6161	1429	242	33	106	442	767	29	38	.255	.310	.366	676	86	-111	-104	99	119	60	66	5
Oak	74	88	0	.457	25	42	39	708	782	6188	1447	237	28	121	524	872	31	55	.262	.326	.381	707	99	-35	4	95	**235**	98	71	17
Cal	70	92	0	.432	29	35	46	722	779	6294	1467	241	22	154	509	835	31	**68**	.260	.322	.393	715	96	-30	-28	100	41	39	51	-5
Min	70	92	0	.432	29	37	44	709	822	6171	1463	280	41	141	467	802	29	29	.261	.319	.401	720	93	-23	-51	104	44	29	60	0
Sea	60	102	0	.370	39	30	51	558	740	5905	1280	247	31	111	460	840	24	40	.240	.301	.360	661	78	-137	-159	104	144	80	64	4
Total	1135	——		—	—	611	523	10177	—	86688	20662	3710	549	1903	7094	10967	425	640	.266	.328	.401	728	—	—	—	—	1539	749	67	76

TEAM	CG	SHO	GR	SV	IP	H	HR	BB	SO	BR/9	ERA	AERA	OAV	OOB	PR	APR	PF	OSB	OCS	FA	E	WPB	DP	FW	PW	BW	BSW	DIF
EAST																												
Bal	36	**15**	225	38	1452.1	1451	130	452	774	11.9	3.63	110	.261	.316	70	60	98	98	47	.981	121	41	159	.5	6.0	8.5	-.3	2.3
Det	42	9	205	28	1451.0	**1318**	170	522	875	11.6	3.80	103	**.242**	.309	42	22	97	**80**	**63**	.980	125	71	142	.3	2.2	8.6	-.3	.2
NY	**47**	12	202	32	1456.2	1449	116	455	892	11.9	3.86	102	.260	.315	33	13	97	110	52	.978	139	42	157	-.5	1.3	7.7	-.1	1.6
Tor	43	8	257	32	1445.1	1434	145	517	835	12.4	4.12	105	.259	.325	-10	32	107	83	47	.981	115	**32**	148	.9	3.2	3.7	-.1	.4
Mil	35	10	211	43	1454.0	1513	133	491	689	12.6	4.02	94	.270	.329	6	-43	93	157	47	**.982**	**113**	37	162	**1.0**	-4.3	**10.0**	-.0	-.6
Bos	29	7	201	42	1446.1	1572	158	493	767	13.0	4.34	101	.279	.337	-44	6	108	155	53	.979	130	36	168	.0	.6	-1.7	-.7	-1.2
Cle	34	8	226	25	1441.2	1531	120	529	794	13.1	4.43	96	.275	.339	-60	-26	105	101	56	.980	122	70	174	.5	-2.6	-4.8	-.6	-3.5
WEST																												
Chi	35	12	243	48	1445.1	1355	128	**447**	877	**11.4**	3.67	115	.248	**.307**	63	84	104	99	45	.981	120	50	158	.6	8.4	-.4	1.4	8.1
KC	19	8	229	**49**	1437.2	1535	133	471	593	12.7	4.25	96	.274	.330	-30	-25	101	109	53	.974	165	44	178	-1.9	-2.5	-3.9	**1.9**	4.4
Tex	43	11	190	32	1466.2	1392	**97**	471	826	11.7	**3.31**	**122**	.252	.313	**122**	**119**	99	101	**63**	**.982**	**113**	50	151	**1.0**	**11.9**	-10.4	-.0	-6.5
Oak	22	12	**287**	33	1454.1	1462	135	626	719	13.1	4.34	89	.263	.337	-46	-80	95	95	50	.974	157	57	157	-1.5	-8.0	.4	1.2	.9
Cal	39	7	237	23	1474.0	1636	130	496	668	13.2	4.31	94	.284	.341	-41	-46	99	83	61	.977	154	57	**190**	-1.3	-4.6	-2.8	-1.0	-1.3
Min	20	5	268	39	1437.1	1559	163	580	748	13.6	4.66	91	.280	.348	-96	-60	105	136	57	.980	121	52	170	.5	-6.0	-5.1	-.5	.0
Sea	25	9	282	39	1418.1	1455	145	544	**910**	12.9	4.12	104	.268	.337	-9	23	105	132	55	.978	136	64	159	-.3	2.3	-15.9	-.1	-7.0
Total	469	133	3263	503	20281.0	—	—	—	—	12.5	4.06	—	.266	.328	—	—	—	—	—	.979	1831	703	2273	—	—	—	—	—

BATTER-FIELDER WINS	BATTING AVERAGE	ON-BASE PERCENTAGE	SLUGGING AVERAGE	ON-BASE PLUS SLUGGING	ADJUSTED OPS	ADJUSTED BATTER RUNS
Ripken-Bal..........7.0	Boggs-Bos............361	Boggs-Bos............444	Brett-KC................563	Brett-KC................947	Murray-Bal............157	Murray-Bal...........47.6
Yount-Mil.............5.6	Carew-Cal............339	Henderson-Oak....414	Rice-Bos...............550	Boggs-Bos............931	Brett-KC................156	Yount-Mil..............44.3
Henderson-Oak.5.1	Whitaker-Det.........320	Carew-Cal............409	Murray-Bal............538	Murray-Bal............930	Yount-Mil...............153	Boggs-Bos...........43.2
Grich-Cal 4.9	Trammell-Det........319	Singleton-Bal........393	Fisk-Chi................518	Rice-Bos...............911	Boggs-Bos............146	Ripken-Bal...........40.1
Boggs-Bos..........4.4	Ripken-Bal............318	Murray-Bal............393	Ripken-Bal............517	Ripken-Bal............888	Ripken-Bal............144	Brett-KC...............37.1
RUNS	**HITS**	**DOUBLES**	**TRIPLES**	**HOME RUNS**	**TOTAL BASES**	**RUNS BATTED IN**
Ripken-Bal............121	Ripken-Bal............211	Ripken-Bal..............47	Yount-Mil.................10	Rice-Bos..................39	Rice-Bos...............344	Rice-Bos...............126
Murray-Bal............115	Boggs-Bos............210	Boggs-Bos..............44	Herndon-Det.............9	Armas-Bos..............36	Ripken-Bal............343	Cooper-Mil............126
Cooper-Mil............106	Whitaker-Det.........206	Yount-Mil.................42	Griffin-Tor.................9	Kittle-Chi.................35	Cooper-Mil............336	Winfield-NY...........116
Henderson-Oak....105	Cooper-Mil............203	Parrish-Det 42	Gibson-Det 9	Murray-Bal..............33	Murray-Bal............313	Parrish-Det 114
Moseby-Tor..........104	Rice-Bos...............191				Winfield-NY...........307	Murray-Bal............111
BASES ON BALLS	**STOLEN BASES**	**BASE STEALING RUNS**	**FIELDING RUNS-INFIELD**	**FIELDING RUNS-OUTFIELD**	**OUTFIELD ASSISTS**	**CATCHER CS PCT.**
Henderson-Oak....103	Henderson-Oak....108	Henderson-Oak...17.1	T.Cruz-Sea-Bal....24.2	Ward-Min.............18.5	Ward-Min.................24	Boone-Cal............44.0
Singleton-Bal..........99	R.Law-Chi...............77	R.Law-Chi...........12.7	Fletcher-Chi.........22.9	Brunansky-Min.....13.4	Rice-Bos.................21	Sundberg-Tex 39.2
Boggs-Bos..............92	Wilson-KC...............59	Wilson-KC............10.2	White-KC 22.2	Davis-Oak............10.8	D.Henderson-Sea...17	Wynegar-NY 38.9
Thornton-Cle 87	J.Cruz-Sea-Chi.......57	J.Cruz-Sea-Chi......8.3	J.Cruz-Sea-Chi....18.5	Collins-Tor.............9.9		Whitt-Tor 37.9
Murray-Bal..............86	Sample-Tex............44	Sample-Tex............6.9	Grich-Cal 17.8	Rice-Bos................9.7		Kearney-Oak 37.8
WINS	**WINNING PCT.**	**WINS ABOVE TEAM**	**GAMES STARTED**	**COMPLETE GAMES**	**FEWEST HITS/GAME**	**FEWEST BB/GAME**
Hoyt-Chi..................24	Dotson-Chi............759	Dotson-Chi.............6.2	Petry-Det 38	Guidry-NY...............21	Boddicker-Bal 7.09	Hoyt-Chi...............1.07
Dotson-Chi..............22	McGregor-Bal 720	Guidry-NY..............5.4	Morris-Det...............37	Morris-Det...............20	Stieb-Tor 7.22	McGregor-Bal 1.56
Guidry-NY...............21	Hoyt-Chi................706	Haas-Mil 5.0	Stieb-Tor 36	Stieb-Tor 14	Conroy-Oak 7.82	John-Cal 1.88
Morris-Det...............20	Guidry-NY.............700	Hoyt-Chi.................4.9	McGregor-Bal 36	Rawley-NY..............13	Hough-Tex 7.82	Honeycutt-Tex......1.91
Petry-Det 19	Boddicker-Bal 667	Sutcliffe-Cle 4.9	Hoyt-Chi..................36	McGregor-Bal 12	Dotson-Chi...........7.84	Eckersley-Bos......1.99
STRIKEOUTS	**STRIKEOUTS/GAME**	**GAMES**	**SAVES**	**BASE RUNNERS/9**	**ADJUSTED RELIEF RUNS**	**RELIEF RANKING**
Morris-Det.............232	Bannister-Chi.......7.99	Quisenberry-KC......69	Quisenberry-KC......45	Quisenberry-KC...8.35	Quisenberry-KC...32.7	Quisenberry-KC...38.4
Bannister-Chi........193	Morris-Det............7.11	VandeBerg-Sea 68	Stanley-Bos 33	Hoyt-Chi...............9.25	Stanley-Bos 21.1	Stanley-Bos 33.2
Stieb-Tor 187	Righetti-NY 7.01	Davis-Min................66	Davis-Min................30	Warren-Oak 9.59	T.Martinez-Bal 19.3	Gossage-NY 31.4
Righetti-NY 169	Conroy-Oak 6.21	T.Martinez-Bal 65	Caudill-Sea 26	Boddicker-Bal 9.70	Barojas-Chi..........17.4	T.Martinez-Bal 28.1
Sutcliffe-Cle 160	Gott-Tor................6.16	Stanley-Bos 64	Ladd-Mil..................25	T.Martinez-Bal 9.84	Lopez-Det............16.8	Lopez-Det............27.6
INNINGS PITCHED	**OPPONENTS' AVG.**	**OPPONENTS' OBP**	**EARNED RUN AVERAGE**	**ADJUSTED ERA**	**ADJUSTED STARTER RUNS**	**PITCHER WINS**
Morris-Det..........293.2	Boddicker-Bal 216	Hoyt-Chi................260	Honeycutt-Tex......2.42	Honeycutt-Tex.......167	Stieb-Tor 37.1	**Quisenberry-KC 4.0**
Stieb-Tor 278.0	Stieb-Tor 219	Boddicker-Bal 273	Boddicker-Bal 2.77	Boddicker-Bal 145	Honeycutt-Tex......29.1	**Honeycutt-Tex ... 3.8**
Petry-Det 266.1	Conroy-Oak 232	Morris-Det.............287	Stieb-Tor 3.04	Stieb-Tor 143	Dotson-Chi...........26.7	**Stieb-Tor 3.7**
Hoyt-Chi.............260.2	Bannister-Chi........233	Guidry-NY.............288	Hough-Tex 3.18	Young-Sea 131	Hough-Tex 26.5	**Stanley-Bos........ 3.4**
McGregor-Bal 260.0	Morris-Det.............233	Stieb-Tor 291	McGregor-Bal 3.18	Dotson-Chi............131	McGregor-Bal 24.5	**Dotson-Chi 3.3**

Ripken the Best Bird

This was the year of the great shortstop parade. Greg Gagne, Tony Fernandez, Spike Owen, and Dick Schofield all made their major league debuts. For the first time, five AL clubs drew more than two million fans—and two other clubs barely missed the mark.

Five teams clustered atop the AL East in August. While the Blue Jays and Brewers slid from contention, the Orioles turned it on and had no competition in September. Joe Altobelli struck it rich in his first season as Orioles manager. Cal Ripken, setting a new standard for shortstops, was a deserving MVP, and Eddie Murray could have been. When Jim Palmer came up lame, 21-year-old Storm Davis stepped into the rotation.

The White Sox routed the West; their 20-game winning margin was the largest in league history. But it was a war of attrition; Texas and California had shots at the top in June, but tanked as Chicago began winning. The White Sox, who reached the postseason for the first time since 1959, were the only division club to clear .500. Dan Quisenberry saved 45 games for the second-place Royals, establishing a new record and voiding the preconception that relief aces were sideburned, fire-tossing behemoths.

In his final season, Boston's Carl Yastrzemski set the all-time games played record—he still holds the AL mark. Gaylord Perry retired after winning his 300th game; Jim Kaat called it quits at 44; and Bert Campaneris and Bobby Murcer closed it out with the Yankees.

Baltimore beat Chicago in the ALCS, holding the White Sox to 4 runs and taking the deciding Game 4 in 10 innings on a Tito Landrum homer. The Orioles took that momentum into the World Series. After losing the opener, 2-1, Baltimore roared back to take three close games before blowing out the Phillies, 5-0, clinching its first title since 1970. Scott McGregor and Mike Boddicker combined to allow just 2 runs in 26 innings for the Orioles.

1982 NATIONAL LEAGUE

TEAM	W	L	T	PCT	GB	HW	HL	R	OR	PA	H	2B	3B	HR	BB	SO	HB	SH	AVG	OBP	SLG	OPS	AOPS	BR	ABR	PF	SB	CS	BSA	BSR
East																														
StL	92	70	0	.568	—	46	35	685	**609**	6196	1439	239	**52**	67	569	805	30	87	.264	**.334**	.364	698	98	25	6	103	**200**	91	69	12
Phi	89	73	0	.549	3	**51**	30	664	654	6107	1417	245	25	112	506	831	24	85	.260	.323	.376	699	98	16	-5	103	128	76	63	2
Mon	86	76	0	.531	6	40	41	697	616	6221	1454	270	38	133	503	816	**35**	85	.262	.325	.396	721	103	55	30	104	156	56	**74**	**15**
Pit	84	78	0	.519	8	42	39	724	696	6234	**1535**	**272**	40	134	447	862	28	78	**.273**	.327	**.408**	**735**	106	**81**	48	105	161	75	68	9
Chi	73	89	0	.451	19	38	43	676	709	6141	1436	239	46	102	460	869	25	76	.260	.317	.375	692	95	-5	-29	104	132	70	65	5
NY	65	97	0	.401	27	33	48	609	723	6108	1361	227	26	97	456	1005	25	64	.247	.305	.350	655	89	-76	-78	100	137	58	70	10
West																														
Atl	89	73	0	.549	—	42	39	**739**	702	6229	1411	215	22	**146**	554	869	29	96	.256	.325	.383	708	102	34	20	102	151	77	66	6
LA	88	74	0	.543	1	43	38	691	612	6361	1487	222	32	138	528	**804**	30	**106**	.264	.327	.388	715	**109**	47	**69**	97	151	56	73	14
SF	87	75	0	.537	2	45	36	673	687	6227	1393	213	30	133	**607**	915	17	59	.253	.327	.376	703	103	28	35	99	130	56	70	9
SD	81	81	0	.500	8	43	38	675	658	6159	1435	217	**52**	81	429	877	22	86	.257	.311	.359	670	99	-53	-14	94	165	77	68	9
Hou	77	85	0	.475	12	43	38	569	620	6008	1342	236	48	74	435	830	19	68	.247	.302	.349	651	94	-87	-40	92	140	61	70	9
Cin	61	101	0	.377	28	33	48	545	661	6099	1375	228	34	82	470	817	21	88	.251	.310	.350	660	90	-64	-66	100	131	69	66	5
Total	972	—	—	—	—	499	473	7947	—	74090	17085	2823	445	1299	5964	10300	305	978	.258	.319	.373	692	—	—	—	—	1782	822	68	104

TEAM	CG	SHO	GR	SV	IP	H	HR	BB	SO	BR/9	ERA	AERA	OAV	OOB	PR	APR	PF	OSB	OCS	FA	E	WPB	DP	FW	PW	BW	BSW	DIF
East																												
StL	25	10	318	47	1465.1	1420	94	502	689	11.9	3.37	109	.258	.320	37	48	102	149	64	**.981**	124	60	169	.9	5.0	.6	.3	4.0
Phi	**38**	13	287	33	1456.1	1395	86	472	**1002**	11.7	3.61	102	.255	.314	-1	12	102	154	64	**.981**	**121**	60	138	**1.1**	1.3	-.5	-.7	6.8
Mon	34	10	250	43	1460.2	1371	110	**448**	936	11.3	3.31	**111**	.250	.306	46	**60**	103	121	75	.980	122	55	117	**1.1**	**6.3**	3.2	**.7**	-6.2
Pit	19	7	280	39	1466.2	1434	118	521	933	12.2	3.81	98	.257	.321	-34	-11	104	**108**	72	.977	145	71	133	-.3	-1.2	5.0	.0	-.6
Chi	9	7	**354**	43	1447.1	1510	125	452	764	12.4	3.92	96	.272	.327	-51	-22	105	156	76	.979	132	45	110	.5	-2.3	-3.0	-.4	-2.7
NY	15	5	278	37	1447.1	1508	119	582	759	13.1	3.88	94	.273	.341	-45	-34	102	153	86	.972	175	**38**	134	-2.0	-3.6	-8.2	.1	-2.4
West																												
Atl	15	11	314	**51**	1463.0	1484	126	502	813	12.4	3.82	96	.267	.328	-36	-22	102	167	67	.979	137	50	**186**	.2	-2.3	2.1	-.3	8.3
LA	37	**16**	295	28	1488.1	1356	**81**	468	932	**11.2**	**3.26**	106	**.244**	**.303**	**56**	35	96	127	69	.979	139	51	131	.0	3.7	**7.2**	.6	-4.6
SF	18	4	323	45	1465.1	1507	109	466	810	12.3	3.64	98	.270	.326	-6	-10	99	185	**96**	.973	173	40	125	-1.9	-1.1	3.7	.0	5.2
SD	20	11	277	41	1476.0	1348	139	502	765	11.4	3.52	97	**.244**	.307	13	-18	95	136	43	.976	152	39	142	-.7	-1.9	-1.5	.0	4.0
Hou	37	**16**	244	31	1446.2	**1338**	87	479	899	11.5	3.42	97	.247	.310	30	-17	92	177	57	.978	136	93	154	.3	-1.8	-4.2	.0	1.7
Cin	22	7	293	31	1460.1	1414	105	570	998	12.4	3.66	100	.258	.328	-10	1	102	149	53	.980	128	62	158	.7	.1	-6.9	-.4	-13.5
Total	289	117	3513	469	17543.1	—	—	—	—	12.0	3.60	—	.258	.319	—	—	—	—	—	.978	1684	664	1697	—	—	—	—	—

BATTER-FIELDER WINS	BATTING AVERAGE	ON-BASE PERCENTAGE	SLUGGING AVERAGE	ON-BASE PLUS SLUGGING	ADJUSTED OPS	ADJUSTED BATTER RUNS
Carter-Mon 6.8	Oliver-Mon .331	Schmidt-Phi .403	Schmidt-Phi .547	Schmidt-Phi .949	Schmidt-Phi 159	Schmidt-Phi 45.1
Schmidt-Phi 6.3	Madlock-Pit .319	Morgan-SF .400	Guerrero-LA .536	Guerrero-LA .914	Guerrero-LA 158	Guerrero-LA 44.0
O.Smith-StL 4.7	Durham-Chi .312	Hernandez-StL .397	Durham-Chi .521	Durham-Chi .909	Lezcano-SD 150	Oliver-Mon 40.2
Guerrero-LA 4.3	L.Smith-StL .307	Oliver-Mon .392	Oliver-Mon .514	Oliver-Mon .906	Oliver-Mon 147	Thompson-Pit 37.5
Thon-Hou 4.3	Buckner-Chi .306	Thompson-Pit .391	Thompson-Pit .511	Thompson-Pit .902	Durham-Chi 147	Murphy-Atl 36.2
RUNS	**HITS**	**DOUBLES**	**TRIPLES**	**HOME RUNS**	**TOTAL BASES**	**RUNS BATTED IN**
L.Smith-StL 120	Oliver-Mon 204	Oliver-Mon 43	Thon-Hou 10	Kingman-NY 37	Oliver-Mon 317	Oliver-Mon 109
Murphy-Atl 113	Buckner-Chi 201	Kennedy-SD 42	Wilson-NY 9	Murphy-Atl 36	Guerrero-LA 308	Murphy-Atl 109
Schmidt-Phi 108	Dawson-Mon 183	Dawson-Mon 37	Puhl-Hou 9	Schmidt-Phi 35	Murphy-Atl 303	Buckner-Chi 105
Dawson-Mon 107	L.Smith-StL 182	Knight-Hou 36	Moreno-Pit 9	Horner-Atl 32	Dawson-Mon 303	Hendrick-StL 104
Sandberg-Chi 103	Ray-Pit 182			Guerrero-LA 32	Buckner-Chi 290	Clark-SF 103
BASES ON BALLS	**STOLEN BASES**	**BASE STEALING RUNS**	**FIELDING RUNS-INFIELD**	**FIELDING RUNS-OUTFIELD**	**OUTFIELD ASSISTS**	**CATCHER CS PCT.**
Schmidt-Phi 107	Raines-Mon 78	Raines-Mon 11.6	O.Smith-StL 35.5	Lezcano-SD 9.4	L.Smith-StL 16	Pena-Pit 41.6
Thompson-Pit 101	L.Smith-StL 68	Wilson-NY 7.2	Concepcion-Cin 18.8	Dawson-Mon 8.2	Lezcano-SD 16	Carter-Mon 40.5
Hernandez-StL 100	Moreno-Pit 60	L.Smith-StL 5.9	Hubbard-Atl 18.5	Dernier-Phi 7.9	Davis-SF 16	Davis-Chi 37.5
Murphy-Atl 93	Wilson-NY 58	Thon-Hou 5.3	Schmidt-Phi 18.5	Householder-Cin 7.9	Matthews-Phi 14	May-SF 34.6
Clark-SF 90	S.Sax-LA 49	Wiggins-SD 5.2	Thon-Hou 18.4	Wilson-NY 7.7	Householder-Cin 14	Porter-StL 32.6
WINS	**WINNING PCT.**	**WINS ABOVE TEAM**	**GAMES STARTED**	**COMPLETE GAMES**	**FEWEST HITS/GAME**	**FEWEST BB/GAME**
Carlton-Phi 23	Niekro-Atl .810	Niekro-Atl 6.4	Carlton-Phi 38	Carlton-Phi 19	Ryan-Hou 7.05	Bird-Chi 1.41
Valenzuela-LA 19	Rogers-Mon .704	Carlton-Phi 5.6	Valenzuela-LA 37	Valenzuela-LA 18	Soto-Cin 7.06	Hammaker-SF 1.44
Rogers-Mon 19	Carlton-Phi .676	Rogers-Mon 5.6	Reuss-LA 37	Niekro-Hou 16	Lea-Mon 7.35	Andujar-StL 1.69
Reuss-LA 18	Lollar-SD .640	Lollar-SD 3.9	Andujar-StL 37	Rogers-Mon 14	Lollar-SD 7.43	Reuss-LA 1.77
	Forsch-StL .625	Niekro-Hou 3.6	Welch-LA 36	Soto-Cin 13	Niekro-Hou 7.47	Candelaria-Pit 1.91
STRIKEOUTS	**STRIKEOUTS/GAME**	**GAMES**	**SAVES**	**BASE RUNNERS/9**	**ADJUSTED RELIEF RUNS**	**RELIEF RANKING**
Carlton-Phi 286	Soto-Cin 9.57	Tekulve-Pit 85	Sutter-StL 36	DeLeon-SD 8.29	Minton-SF 24.0	Minton-SF 35.6
Soto-Cin 274	Ryan-Hou 8.81	Minton-SF 78	Minton-SF 30	Howe-LA 9.42	Scurry-Pit 20.7	Garber-Atl 28.1
Ryan-Hou 245	Carlton-Phi 8.71	Scurry-Pit 76	Garber-Atl 30	Soto-Cin 9.68	Bedrosian-Atl 20.2	Reardon-Mon 26.4
Valenzuela-LA 199	Candelaria-Pit 6.85	Reardon-Mon 75	Reardon-Mon 26	Niekro-Hou 9.77	Reardon-Mon 19.5	DeLeon-SD 26.0
Rogers-Mon 179	Welch-LA 6.72	Hernandez-Chi 75	Tekulve-Pit 20	Andujar-StL 9.96	DeLeon-SD 17.2	Bedrosian-Atl 21.5
INNINGS PITCHED	**OPPONENTS' AVG.**	**OPPONENTS' OBP**	**EARNED RUN AVERAGE**	**ADJUSTED ERA**	**ADJUSTED STARTER RUNS**	**PITCHER WINS**
Carlton-Phi 295.2	Ryan-Hou .213	Soto-Cin .271	Rogers-Mon 2.40	Rogers-Mon 154	Rogers-Mon 39.0	**Minton-SF 3.9**
Valenzuela-LA 285.0	Soto-Cin .215	Sutton-Hou .277	Niekro-Hou 2.47	Andujar-StL 149	Andujar-StL 33.2	**Rogers-Mon 3.8**
Rogers-Mon 277.0	Lea-Mon .222	Reuss-LA .277	Andujar-StL 2.47	Niekro-Hou 135	Niekro-Hou 30.1	**Garber-Atl 3.2**
Niekro-Hou 270.0	Lollar-SD .224	Niekro-Hou .278	Soto-Cin 2.79	Soto-Cin 131	Soto-Cin 25.1	**Andujar-StL 3.0**
Andujar-StL 265.2	Niekro-Hou .229	Andujar-StL .281	Valenzuela-LA 2.87	Candelaria-Pit 128	Carlton-Phi 19.0	**DeLeon-SD 2.9**

My Beer's Better Than Yours

The NL West was nothing if not streaky. Atlanta, featuring Bob Horner and MVP Dale Murphy, won its first 13 games of the season under new manager Joe Torre. The Braves then fell apart in late July, losing 19 of 21 to sag below the streaking Dodgers. Meanwhile, San Francisco, featuring veterans Reggie Smith (in his last season), Joe Morgan, and Jack Clark plus rookie Chili Davis, won 10 straight in August, and then 18 of 21 in September.

With the title in sight, Los Angeles lost eight straight; on September 26, one game separated the Braves, Giants, and Dodgers. Atlanta won five of their final seven to capture the division as Los Angeles and San Francisco knocked each other out.

Steve Sax was the fourth successive Dodger to be Rookie of the Year. A superior crew of freshmen became regulars in '82, including Davis, Ryne Sandberg, Willie McGee, and Tony Gwynn. Willie Stargell ended his career as a pinch hitter for Pittsburgh, a team ready for collapse amid shady characters and an aging lineup. The Mets, hoping for a quick fix, traded for George Foster and then made him the first $2 million player. He didn't help.

Whitey Herzog's Cardinals battled the Phillies starting in July, and then pulled away in September. Lonnie Smith sparked the offense, and Bruce Sutter led the NL in saves for the fourth consecutive time. Steve Carlton won his fourth Cy Young for the Phillies, but Mike Schmidt aside, Philadelphia's lineup couldn't deliver.

St. Louis easily swept Atlanta in the NLCS. The Cardinals then played a rollicking, entertaining seven-game World Series against Milwaukee. The final contest between beer towns was a seesaw affair; St. Louis came back in the late innings to win. This was the NL's fourth straight Series victory.

NL owners worked to bounce Bowie Kuhn from the commissioner's chair, feeling that he was too weak in negotiations and had no long-term vision. The game had no full-time commissioner until 1984.

1982 AMERICAN LEAGUE

TEAM	W	L	T	PCT	GB	HW	HL	R	OR	PA	H	2B	3B	HR	BB	SO	HB	SH	AVG	OBP	SLG	OPS	AOPS	BR	ABR	PF	SB	CS	BSA	BSR
EAST																														
Mil	95	67	1	.586	—	48	34	**891**	717	6337	1599	277	41	**216**	484	714	18	56	.279	.335	**.455**	**790**	**120**	109	**154**	95	84	52	62	0
Bal	94	68	1	.580	1	53	28	774	687	6325	1478	259	27	179	634	796	25	57	.266	.341	.419	760	108	71	77	99	49	38	56	-3
Bos	89	73	0	.549	6	49	32	753	713	6262	1536	271	31	136	547	736	28	53	.274	.340	.407	747	98	42	-2	106	42	39	52	-4
Det	83	79	0	.512	12	47	34	729	685	6166	1489	237	40	177	470	807	26	41	.266	.324	.418	742	101	13	9	101	93	66	58	-3
NY	79	83	0	.488	16	42	39	709	716	6244	1417	225	37	161	590	719	24	55	.256	.328	.398	726	99	-5	5	99	69	45	61	-1
Tor	78	84	0	.481	17	44	37	651	701	6067	1447	262	45	106	415	749	28	48	.262	.314	.383	697	83	-72	-124	109	118	81	59	-2
Cle	78	84	0	.481	17	41	40	683	748	6359	1458	225	32	109	**651**	**625**	**35**	74	.262	.341	.373	714	96	-11	-15	101	151	68	69	9
WEST																														
Cal	93	69	0	.574	—	52	29	814	**670**	6350	1518	268	26	186	613	760	**35**	**114**	.274	**.347**	.433	780	112	**113**	104	101	55	53	51	-6
KC	90	72	0	.556	3	**56**	25	784	717	6177	**1603**	**295**	**58**	132	442	758	25	32	**.285**	.337	.428	765	107	68	62	101	133	48	**73**	12
Chi	87	75	0	.537	6	49	31	786	710	6242	1523	266	52	136	533	866	30	54	.273	.337	.413	750	104	44	40	101	136	58	70	10
Sea	76	86	0	.469	17	42	39	651	712	6181	1431	259	33	130	456	806	22	42	.254	.311	.381	692	86	-85	-107	104	131	82	62	0
Oak	68	94	0	.420	25	36	45	691	819	6154	1286	211	27	149	582	948	20	50	.236	.309	.367	676	88	-107	-87	97	**232**	87	**73**	**21**
Tex	64	98	0	.395	29	38	43	590	749	6020	1354	204	26	115	447	750	32	64	.249	.308	.359	667	86	-131	-105	96	63	45	58	-2
Min	60	102	0	.370	33	37	44	657	819	6115	1427	234	44	148	474	887	24	22	.257	.316	.396	712	91	-46	-67	103	38	33	54	-3
Total	1135	—	—	—	—	634	500	10163	—	86999	20566	3493	519	2080	7338	10921	372	762	.264	.328	.402	730	—	—	—	—	1394	795	64	28

TEAM	CG	SHO	GR	SV	IP	H	HR	BB	SO	BR/9	ERA	AERA	OAV	OOB	PR	APR	PF	OSB	OCS	FA	E	WPB	DP	FW	PW	BW	BSW	DIF
EAST																												
Mil	34	6	213	**47**	1467.1	1514	152	511	717	12.5	3.98	96	.270	.330	15	-26	94	121	62	.980	125	56	**185**	.1	-2.6	**15.4**	-.2	1.3
Bal	38	8	231	34	1462.1	1436	147	488	719	**12.0**	3.99	102	.257	**.317**	14	11	100	98	51	**.984**	**101**	42	140	**1.4**	1.1	7.7	-.5	3.3
Bos	23	11	214	33	1453.0	1557	155	478	816	12.8	4.03	108	.276	.334	7	47	107	101	55	.981	121	**40**	172	.3	4.7	-.2	-.6	3.8
Det	**45**	5	228	27	1451.0	**1371**	172	554	740	12.1	**3.80**	107	**.251**	.321	**44**	45	100	84	63	.981	117	68	165	.5	4.5	.9	-.5	-3.4
NY	24	8	251	39	1459.0	1471	113	491	939	12.2	3.99	101	.264	.323	13	5	99	98	44	.979	128	56	158	-.0	.5	.5	-.3	-2.6
Tor	41	**13**	220	25	1443.2	1428	147	493	776	12.1	3.95	**114**	.257	.319	20	**80**	110	78	46	.978	136	45	146	-.5	**8.0**	-12.4	-.4	2.3
Cle	31	9	221	30	1468.1	1433	122	589	882	12.5	4.11	101	.257	.327	-5	6	102	125	60	.980	123	62	129	.2	.6	-1.5	.7	-3.0
WEST																												
Cal	40	10	248	27	1464.0	1436	124	482	728	**12.0**	3.82	107	.259	.321	42	43	100	**66**	**77**	.983	108	**40**	171	1.0	4.3	10.4	-.8	-2.9
KC	16	12	228	45	1431.0	1443	163	471	650	12.2	4.08	100	.262	.320	-1	-1	100	85	53	.979	127	49	140	-.0	-.1	6.2	1.0	1.9
Chi	30	10	258	41	1439.0	1502	**99**	**460**	753	12.4	3.87	105	.270	.326	33	32	100	102	60	.976	154	41	173	-1.5	3.2	4.0	.8	-.5
Sea	23	11	**303**	39	1476.1	1431	173	547	**1002**	12.2	3.88	110	.256	.324	32	62	105	118	51	.978	139	57	158	-.7	6.2	-10.7	-.2	.4
Oak	42	6	239	22	1456.0	1506	177	648	697	13.5	4.54	87	.268	.343	-76	-100	97	97	58	.974	160	66	140	-1.8	-10.0	-8.7	**1.9**	5.6
Tex	32	5	214	24	1431.0	1554	128	483	690	13.1	4.28	91	.280	.339	-33	-68	95	93	59	.981	121	53	169	.3	-6.8	-10.5	-.4	.4
Min	26	7	244	30	1433.0	1484	208	643	812	13.4	4.72	90	.269	.344	-103	-70	105	128	57	.982	108	51	162	1.0	-7.0	-6.7	-.5	-7.8
Total	445	121	3312	463	20335.0	—	—	—	—	12.5	4.07	—	.264	.328	—	—	—	—	—	.980	1768	726	2208	—	—	—	—	—

BATTER-FIELDER WINS	BATTING AVERAGE	ON-BASE PERCENTAGE	SLUGGING AVERAGE	ON-BASE PLUS SLUGGING	ADJUSTED OPS	ADJUSTED BATTER RUNS
Yount-Mil 7.1	Wilson-KC .332	Evans-Bos .402	Yount-Mil .578	Yount-Mil .957	Yount-Mil 168	Yount-Mil 58.1
DeCinces-Cal 5.7	Yount-Mil .331	Harrah-Cle .398	Winfield-NY .560	Murray-Bal .940	Murray-Bal 157	Murray-Bal 44.4
Bell-Tex 5.6	Carew-Cal .319	Henderson-Oak .398	Murray-Bal .549	Evans-Bos .936	DeCinces-Cal 148	Evans-Bos 42.4
Grich-Cal 4.2	Murray-Bal .316	Carew-Cal .396	DeCinces-Cal .548	DeCinces-Cal .916	Evans-Bos 146	Harrah-Cle 38.4
Bernazard-Chi 4.2	Cooper-Mil .313	Murray-Bal .391	McRae-KC .542	McRae-KC .910	McRae-KC 145	DeCinces-Cal 38.3
RUNS	**HITS**	**DOUBLES**	**TRIPLES**	**HOME RUNS**	**TOTAL BASES**	**RUNS BATTED IN**
Molitor-Mil 136	Yount-Mil 210	Yount-Mil 46	Wilson-KC 15	Thomas-Mil 39	Yount-Mil 367	McRae-KC 133
Yount-Mil 129	Cooper-Mil 205	McRae-KC 46	Herndon-Det 13	R.Jackson-Cal 39	Cooper-Mil 345	Cooper-Mil 121
Evans-Bos 122	Molitor-Mil 201	White-KC 45	Yount-Mil 12	Winfield-NY 37	McRae-KC 332	Thornton-Cle 116
Henderson-Oak 119	Wilson-KC 194	DeCinces-Cal 42	Mumphrey-NY 10	Oglivie-Mil 34	Evans-Bos 325	Yount-Mil 114
Downing-Cal 109	McRae-KC 189	Cowens-Sea 39			DeCinces-Cal 315	Thomas-Mil 112
BASES ON BALLS	**STOLEN BASES**	**BASE STEALING RUNS**	**FIELDING RUNS-INFIELD**	**FIELDING RUNS-OUTFIELD**	**OUTFIELD ASSISTS**	**CATCHER CS PCT.**
Henderson-Oak 116	Henderson-Oak 130	Henderson-Oak 13.9	Bell-Tex 37.7	Brunansky-Min 11.3	Winfield-NY 17	Boone-Cal 58.2
Evans-Bos 112	Garcia-Tor 54	Molitor-Mil 5.9	Bernazard-Chi 31.1	Wilson-KC 11.0	Oglivie-Mil 15	Martinez-Tor 46.0
Thornton-Cle 109	J.Cruz-Sea 46	J.Cruz-Sea 5.6	DeCinces-Cal 22.8	Mitchell-Min 10.6	Barfield-Tor 15	Allenson-Bos 43.8
Hargrove-Cle 101	Molitor-Mil 41	Dilone-Cle 5.5	Almon-Chi 19.7	Ward-Min 10.6		Sweet-Sea 37.5
Murphy-Oak 94	Wilson-KC 37	Garcia-Tor 4.9	Grich-Cal 16.6	Murphy-Oak 9.9		Dempsey-Bal 36.5
WINS	**WINNING PCT.**	**WINS ABOVE TEAM**	**GAMES STARTED**	**COMPLETE GAMES**	**FEWEST HITS/GAME**	**FEWEST BB/GAME**
Hoyt-Chi 19	Vuckovich-Mil .750	Vuckovich-Mil 5.2	Clancy-Tor 40	Stieb-Tor 19	Sutcliffe-Cle 7.25	John-NY-Cal 1.58
Zahn-Cal 18	Palmer-Bal .750	Palmer-Bal 4.4	D.Martinez-Bal 39	Morris-Det 17	Ujdur-Det 7.58	Eckersley-Bos 1.73
Vuckovich-Mil 18	Zahn-Cal .692	Hough-Tex 4.3	Stieb-Tor 38	Langford-Oak 15	Righetti-NY 7.62	Hoyt-Chi 1.80
Gura-KC 18	Petry-Det .625	Zahn-Cal 4.1	Leal-Tor 38	Hoyt-Chi 14	Palmer-Bal 7.73	Haas-Mil 1.82
	Gura-KC .600	Burns-Chi 3.9			Barker-Cle 7.76	Langford-Oak 1.86
STRIKEOUTS	**STRIKEOUTS/GAME**	**GAMES**	**SAVES**	**BASE RUNNERS/9**	**ADJUSTED RELIEF RUNS**	**RELIEF RANKING**
Bannister-Sea 209	Righetti-NY 8.02	VandeBerg-Sea 78	Quisenberry-KC 35	Gossage-NY 8.81	Stanley-Bos 23.5	Spillner-Cle 42.0
Barker-Cle 187	Bannister-Sea 7.62	T.Martinez-Bal 76	Gossage-NY 30	Quisenberry-KC 9.09	Quisenberry-KC 23.1	Caudill-Sea 41.5
Righetti-NY 163	Beattie-Sea 7.31	Quisenberry-KC 72	Fingers-Mil 29	Stoddard-Sea 9.22	Spillner-Cle 23.0	Quisenberry-KC 37.3
Guidry-NY 162	Barker-Cle 6.88	Caudill-Sea 70	Caudill-Sea 26	Fingers-Mil 9.49	Burgmeier-Bos 21.4	Gossage-NY 31.7
Tudor-Bos 146	Tudor-Bos 6.72	Spillner-Cle 65	Davis-Min 22	Caudill-Sea 9.50	Caudill-Sea 20.8	Clear-Bos 29.0
INNINGS PITCHED	**OPPONENTS' AVG.**	**OPPONENTS' OBP**	**EARNED RUN AVERAGE**	**ADJUSTED ERA**	**ADJUSTED STARTER RUNS**	**PITCHER WINS**
Stieb-Tor 288.1	Sutcliffe-Cle .226	Palmer-Bal .286	Sutcliffe-Cle 2.96	Stanley-Bos 140	Stieb-Tor 36.2	**Caudill-Sea 4.2**
Clancy-Tor 266.2	Righetti-NY .229	Eckersley-Bos .296	Stanley-Bos 3.10	Sutcliffe-Cle 140	Sutcliffe-Cle 27.3	**Spillner-Cle 4.2**
Morris-Det 266.1	Ujdur-Det .230	Stieb-Tor .298	Palmer-Bal 3.13	Stieb-Tor 139	Petry-Det 23.8	**Quisenberry-KC 4.2**
Caldwell-Mil 258.0	Palmer-Bal .231	Barker-Cle .299	Petry-Det 3.22	Palmer-Bal 130	Palmer-Bal 23.0	**Stieb-Tor 3.9**
D.Martinez-Bal 252.0	Barker-Cle .232	Hoyt-Chi .301	Stieb-Tor 3.25	Beattie-Sea 128	Clancy-Tor 21.2	**Gossage-NY 3.2**

Harvey's Wallbangers

With Rotisserie® baseball gaining popularity, and *The Bill James Baseball Abstrac* first printed by a major publisher, interest in the analytical side of the game began to grow. But there was no accounting for streaks.

In early September, the white-hot Royals seemed poised to win, but they cooled while the Angels caught fire. California, featuring a veteran lineup acquired through trades and free agency, led the league in attendance, almost doubling their 1981 total, and setting a new league mark. Newest Angel Reggie Jackson led the league in homers, and set the career record for strikeouts, which he still holds. Manager Gene Mauch seemed to keep together his shaky pitching staff with duct tape and bailing wire.

Oakland began to crumble, falling to fifth despite Rickey Henderson's record 130 steals. In their last season at Metropolitan Stadium, the Twins were terrible, but rookies Gary Gaetti, Tom Brunansky, and Kent Hrbek developed camaraderie amidst the rebuilding. In Boston, Wade Boggs debuted at .349; Don Mattingly got in his first swings for the Yankees.

MVP Robin Yount headed the Brewers' bruising offense, and the pitching was barely good enough. Milwaukee got hot in June shortly after Harvey Kuenn was named manager; the Brewers took over the East in mid-July. Baltimore, riding Eddie Murray and top rookie Cal Ripken, took three from the Brewers on the last weekend to tie the race. On the season's last day, Milwaukee stretch pickup Don Sutton defeated Jim Palmer.

California took the first two ALCS contests with complete games from Tommy John and Bruce Kison. Their pitching collapsed in Milwaukee as the Brewers won the next two games with big innings. In the deciding tilt, California took a 3-1 lead, but Cecil Cooper's seventh-inning, bases-loaded single gave Milwaukee a 4-3 win. The Brewers went to their first—and to date, only—World Series and played valiantly, but they lost to the Cardinals in seven.

1981 NATIONAL LEAGUE

TEAM	W	L	T	PCT	GB	HW	HL	R	OR	PA	H	2B	3B	HR	BB	SO	HB	SH	AVG	OBP	SLG	OPS	AOPS	BR	ABR	PF	SB	CS	BSA	BSR
EastSplit Season: First-half Winner PHI (34-21); Second-half Winner MON (30-23)																														
StL	59	43	1	.578	—	32	21	464	417	4013	936	158	**45**	50	379	495	16	46	.265	.336	.377	713	103	43	23	105	88	45	66	4
Mon	60	48	0	.556	2	**38**	18	443	394	4068	883	146	28	81	368	498	16	63	.246	.316	.370	686	97	2	-11	103	**138**	40	**78**	**16**
Phi	59	48	0	.551	2.5	36	19	**491**	472	4141	**1002**	165	25	69	372	**432**	**23**	44	**.273**	**.341**	**.389**	**730**	107	**68**	42	106	103	46	69	7
Pit	46	56	1	.451	13	22	28	407	425	3959	920	176	30	55	278	494	15	54	.257	.311	.369	680	93	-9	-28	105	122	52	70	9
NY	41	62	2	.398	18.5	24	27	348	432	3885	868	136	35	57	304	603	13	41	.248	.308	.356	664	94	-28	-27	100	103	42	71	8
Chi	38	65	3	.369	21.5	27	30	370	483	3984	838	138	29	57	342	611	13	53	.236	.303	.340	643	83	-53	-73	106	72	41	64	1
WestSplit Season: First-half Winner LA (36-21); Second-half Winner HOU (33-20)																														
Cin	66	42	0	.611	—	32	22	464	440	4123	972	**190**	24	64	375	553	18	53	.267	.335	.385	720	**111**	57	**59**	100	58	37	61	0
LA	63	47	0	.573	4	33	23	450	356	4188	984	133	20	**82**	331	550	17	62	.262	.323	.374	697	108	15	35	96	73	46	61	0
Hou	61	49	0	.555	6	31	20	394	**331**	4155	948	160	35	45	340	488	8	**79**	.257	.318	.356	674	103	-13	12	94	81	43	65	3
SF	56	55	0	.505	11.5	29	24	427	414	4258	941	161	26	63	**386**	543	14	65	.250	.320	.357	677	101	-7	7	97	89	50	64	2
Atl	50	56	1	.472	15	22	27	395	416	4055	886	148	22	64	321	540	18	56	.243	.306	.349	655	91	-42	-43	100	98	39	72	8
SD	41	69	0	.373	26	20	35	382	455	4184	963	170	35	32	311	525	14	72	.256	.313	.346	659	100	-34	2	92	83	62	57	-3
Total	644	—	—	—	—	346	294	5035	—	49013	11141	1881	354	719	4107	6332	185	688	.255	.319	.364	683	—	—	—	—	1108	543	67	54

TEAM	CG	SHO	GR	SV	IP	H	HR	BB	SO	BR/9	ERA	AERA	OAV	OOB	PR	APR	PF	OSB	OCS	FA	E	WPB	DP	FW	PW	BW	BSW	DIF
StL	11	5	219	**33**	943.0	902	52	290	388	11.5	3.63	100	.255	.312	-14	-1	104	94	40	**.981**	82	**27**	108	.6	-.1	2.5	-.0	5.1
Mon	20	12	183	23	975.0	902	58	**268**	520	11.0	3.30	108	.247	.300	21	28	102	**65**	48	.980	81	33	88	.9	3.0	-1.2	**1.2**	2.0
Phi	19	5	184	23	960.1	967	72	347	580	12.4	4.05	90	.267	.329	-60	-40	105	124	41	.980	86	34	90	.6	-4.3	4.5	.3	4.4
Pit	11	5	201	29	942.0	953	60	346	492	12.6	3.56	102	.266	.331	-8	8	104	**65**	34	.979	86	39	106	.4	.9	-3.0	.5	-3.8
NY	7	3	234	24	926.1	906	74	336	490	12.2	3.55	100	.259	.323	-6	-1	101	68	39	.968	130	31	89	-1.6	-.1	-2.9	.4	-6.2
Chi	6	2	**263**	20	956.2	983	59	388	532	13.1	4.01	93	.270	.340	-55	-26	107	109	55	.974	113	48	103	-.8	-2.8	-7.8	-.4	-1.7
West																												
Cin	25	14	182	20	965.2	863	67	393	593	11.8	3.73	94	.241	.315	-26	-24	100	107	35	**.981**	**80**	30	99	**1.0**	-2.6	**6.3**	-.5	7.8
LA	**26**	**19**	187	24	997.0	904	54	302	603	11.0	3.01	110	.245	.302	54	34	95	80	45	.980	87	32	101	.7	3.7	3.8	-.5	.4
Hou	23	**19**	164	25	990.0	**842**	**40**	300	**610**	**10.5**	**2.66**	**123**	**.231**	**.289**	**91**	**72**	94	86	52	.980	87	44	81	.7	**7.7**	1.3	-.2	-3.6
SF	8	9	211	**33**	1009.1	970	57	393	561	12.4	3.28	104	.256	.327	23	14	98	117	43	.977	102	43	102	.0	1.5	.8	-.3	-1.5
Atl	11	4	215	24	968.0	936	62	330	471	11.9	3.45	102	.257	.318	4	8	101	98	**58**	.976	102	35	93	-.2	.9	-4.6	.4	.6
SD	9	6	239	23	1002.0	1013	64	414	492	13.0	3.72	87	.268	.341	-25	-57	93	95	53	.977	102	35	**117**	-.0	-6.1	.2	-.8	-7.2
Total	176	103	2482	301	11635.1	—	—	—	—	11.9	3.49	—	.255	.319	—	—	—	—	—	.978	1138	431	1177	—	—	—	—	—

BATTER-FIELDER WINS	BATTING AVERAGE	ON-BASE PERCENTAGE	SLUGGING AVERAGE	ON-BASE PLUS SLUGGING	ADJUSTED OPS	ADJUSTED BATTER RUNS
Schmidt-Phi 7.1	Madlock-Pit .341	Schmidt-Phi .435	Schmidt-Phi .644	Schmidt-Phi 1080	Schmidt-Phi 193	Schmidt-Phi 46.3
Dawson-Mon 4.4	Rose-Phi .325	Madlock-Pit .412	Dawson-Mon .553	Dawson-Mon .918	Dawson-Mon 154	Foster-Cin 28.8
Concepcion-Cin 3.2	Baker-LA .320	Hernandez-StL .401	Foster-Cin .519	Madlock-Pit .907	Foster-Cin 153	Dawson-Mon 26.9
Foster-Cin 2.9	Schmidt-Phi .316	Matthews-Phi .398	Madlock-Pit .495	Foster-Cin .892	Madlock-Pit 150	Hernandez-StL 22.7
Trillo-Phi 2.6	Buckner-Chi .311	Rose-Phi .391	Hendrick-StL .485	Hernandez-StL .864	Cey-LA 146	Madlock-Pit 20.5

RUNS	HITS	DOUBLES	TRIPLES	HOME RUNS	TOTAL BASES	RUNS BATTED IN
Schmidt-Phi 78	Rose-Phi 140	Buckner-Chi 35	Richards-SD 12	Schmidt-Phi 31	Schmidt-Phi 228	Schmidt-Phi 91
Rose-Phi 73	Buckner-Chi 131	Jones-SD 34	Reynolds-Hou 12	Dawson-Mon 24	Dawson-Mon 218	Foster-Cin 90
Dawson-Mon 71	Concepcion-Cin 129	Concepcion-Cin 28	Herr-StL 9	Kingman-NY 22	Foster-Cin 215	Buckner-Chi 75
Hendrick-StL 67	Baker-LA 128	Hernandez-StL 27		Foster-Cin 22	Buckner-Chi 202	Carter-Mon 68
	Griffey-Cin 123	Chambliss-Atl 25		Hendrick-StL 18	Hendrick-StL 191	

BASES ON BALLS	STOLEN BASES	BASE STEALING RUNS	FIELDING RUNS-INFIELD	FIELDING RUNS-OUTFIELD	OUTFIELD ASSISTS	CATCHER CS PCT.
Schmidt-Phi 73	Raines-Mon 71	Raines-Mon 11.8	Schmidt-Phi 22.8	Dawson-Mon 12.0	Richards-SD 14	Davis-Chi 42.6
Morgan-SF 66	Moreno-Pit 39	Dawson-Mon 4.3	Smith-SD 22.2	Maddox-Phi 7.6	Clark-SF 14	Pena-Pit 42.6
Hernandez-StL 61	Scott-Mon 30	Lacy-Pit 4.2	Trillo-Phi 18.1	Easler-Pit 6.4	Easler-Pit 13	Ashby-Hou 39.8
Thompson-Pit 59		Scott-Mon 4.2	Flynn-NY 14.0	Wilson-NY 5.0	Murphy-Atl 11	O'Berry-Cin 38.8
Matthews-Phi 59		Lopes-LA 3.7	Templeton-StL 10.6	Griffey-Cin 5.0	Matthews-Phi 11	Benedict-Atl 36.6

WINS	WINNING PCT.	WINS ABOVE TEAM	GAMES STARTED	COMPLETE GAMES	FEWEST HITS/GAME	FEWEST BB/GAME
Seaver-Cin 14	Seaver-Cin .875	Seaver-Cin 5.7	Valenzuela-LA 25	Valenzuela-LA 11	Ryan-Hou 5.98	Perry-Atl 1.43
Valenzuela-LA 13	Carlton-Phi .765	Carlton-Phi 4.4	Soto-Cin 25	Soto-Cin 10	Seaver-Cin 6.49	Reuss-LA 1.59
Carlton-Phi 13	Ryan-Hou .688	Camp-Atl 3.3	Krukow-Chi 25	Carlton-Phi 10	Valenzuela-LA 6.55	Sutton-Hou 1.64
	Valenzuela-LA .650	Rhoden-Pit 3.1		Reuss-LA 8	Berenyi-Cin 6.93	Sorensen-StL 1.67
	Hooton-LA .647	Ryan-Hou 2.7		Rogers-Mon 7	Blue-SF 7.00	Solomon-Pit 1.91

STRIKEOUTS	STRIKEOUTS/GAME	GAMES	SAVES	BASE RUNNERS/9	ADJUSTED RELIEF RUNS	RELIEF RANKING
Valenzuela-LA 180	Carlton-Phi 8.48	Lucas-SD 57	Sutter-StL 25	Reardon-NY-Mon 9.09	Camp-Atl 14.6	Camp-Atl 26.9
Carlton-Phi 179	Ryan-Hou 8.46	Minton-SF 55	Minton-SF 21	Sutton-Hou 9.19	Reardon-NY-Mon 11.9	Lucas-SD 19.1
Soto-Cin 151	Valenzuela-LA 8.42	Tidrow-Chi 51	Allen-NY 18	Valenzuela-LA 9.45	Lucas-SD 11.4	Sambito-Hou 16.7
Ryan-Hou 140	Soto-Cin 7.77	Hume-Cin 51	Camp-Atl 17	Sambito-Hou 9.47	Holland-SF 11.1	Sutter-StL 14.3
Gullickson-Mon 115	Berenyi-Cin 7.57	Sambito-Hou 49		D.Smith-Hou 9.48	Falcone-NY 10.3	Holland-SF 13.4

INNINGS PITCHED	OPPONENTS' AVG.	OPPONENTS' OBP	EARNED RUN AVERAGE	ADJUSTED ERA	ADJUSTED STARTER RUNS	PITCHER WINS
Valenzuela-LA 192.1	Ryan-Hou .188	Sutton-Hou .265	Ryan-Hou 1.69	Ryan-Hou 194	Ryan-Hou 26.9	**Ryan-Hou 3.4**
Carlton-Phi 190.0	Valenzuela-LA .205	Valenzuela-LA .270	Knepper-Hou 2.18	Carlton-Phi 151	Carlton-Phi 23.6	**Camp-Atl 2.9**
Soto-Cin 175.0	Seaver-Cin .205	Knepper-Hou .278	Hooton-LA 2.28	Knepper-Hou 150	Knepper-Hou 21.2	**Valenzuela-LA 2.5**
Seaver-Cin 166.1	Berenyi-Cin .211	Sanderson-Mon .278	Reuss-LA 2.30	Hooton-LA 145	Valenzuela-LA 19.4	**Seaver-Cin 2.2**
Niekro-Hou 166.0	Blue-SF .217	Ryan-Hou .280	Carlton-Phi 2.42	Reuss-LA 144	Seaver-Cin 18.0	**Hooton-LA 2.1**

One Strike Away

Pushed by the owners on the free-agent compensation issue, the players went on strike in June and the game didn't resume until August. As a result, the owners instituted a "split season" with the winners in each half declared division co-champs, with a five-game Division Series to decide who advanced to the LCS. Unfortunately, the worst came to pass: Cincinnati and St. Louis posted the best overall division records but didn't "win" either half. The flawed system did, however, provide Montreal with its only postseason appearance to date.

Portly rookie southpaw Fernando Valenzuela of the Dodgers went a long way toward erasing the game's black eye. "Fernandomania" struck parks all over the league, giving fans a new idol—and the Dodgers a great pitcher who won Cy Young and Rookie of the Year honors. Philadelphia's 40-year-old Pete Rose shattered Stan Musial's NL hit record, but this time Charlie Hustle broke a record as a first baseman with little power rather than as a second baseman, third baseman, left fielder, or right fielder.

Los Angeles, first-half winners by a smidgen, scraped by Houston, sparked by Nolan Ryan and Don Sutton, in five games in the West. The Expos, with Andre Dawson and rookie Tim Raines providing the stickwork, defeated Philadelphia in the East. Mike Schmidt won another MVP; Carlton was great during the season, but 0-2 in the postseason.

The Montreal-Los Angeles NLCS went the full five. In the deciding contest, Ray Burris—a shutout winner in Game 2—went eight innings for Montreal against Valenzuela. With the game tied in the ninth, 1-1, Expos manager Jim Fanning brought in starter Steve Rogers on two days' rest, even though he had a rested bullpen. Rogers promptly allowed Rick Monday's pinch-homer that won the series.

The Yankees took the first two World Series games in New York, but the Dodgers roared back with three consecutive one-run victories. In Game 6 they walloped Tommy John and five relievers, 9-2, earning the Dodgers their first title since 1965.

1981 AMERICAN LEAGUE

TEAM	W	L	T	PCT	GB	HW	HL	R	OR	PA	H	2B	3B	HR	BB	SO	HB	SH	AVG	OBP	SLG	OPS	AOPS	BR	ABR	PF	SB	CS	BSA	BSR
EastSplit Season: First-half Winner NY (34-22); Second-half Winner MIL (31-22)																														
Mil	62	47	0	.569	—	28	21	493	459	4152	961	173	20	96	300	461	29	35	.257	.313	.391	704	106	9	29	96	39	36	52	-4
Bal	59	46	0	.562	1	33	22	429	437	3985	883	165	11	88	**404**	454	15	26	.251	.329	.379	708	104	25	27	100	41	34	55	-3
NY	59	48	0	.551	2	32	19	421	**343**	3994	889	148	22	100	391	434	7	40	.252	.325	.391	716	106	30	35	99	47	30	61	0
Det	60	49	0	.550	2	32	23	427	404	4109	922	148	29	65	**404**	500	18	50	.256	.331	.368	699	97	15	-2	104	61	37	62	0
Bos	59	49	0	.546	2.5	30	23	**519**	481	4281	**1052**	168	17	90	378	520	13	37	**.275**	**.340**	**.399**	**739**	105	**67**	35	107	32	31	51	-4
Cle	52	51	0	.505	7	25	29	431	442	3952	922	150	21	39	343	**379**	13	46	.263	.327	.351	678	96	-11	-9	99	**119**	37	**76**	**13**
Tor	37	69	0	.349	23.5	17	36	329	466	3887	797	137	23	61	284	556	20	44	.226	.286	.330	616	73	-106	-124	106	66	57	54	-5
WestSplit Season: First-half Winner OAK (37-23); Second-half Winner KC (30-23)																														
Oak	64	45	0	.587	—	**35**	21	458	403	4113	910	119	26	**104**	342	647	16	46	.247	.312	.379	691	102	-11	5	96	98	47	68	5
Tex	57	48	0	.543	5	32	24	452	389	3972	968	**178**	15	49	295	396	21	36	.270	.326	.369	695	105	7	28	95	46	41	53	-4
Chi	54	52	0	.509	8.5	25	24	476	423	4064	982	135	27	76	322	518	**43**	48	.272	.335	.387	722	**110**	40	**47**	99	86	44	66	4
KC	50	53	0	.485	11	19	28	397	405	3941	952	169	29	61	301	419	17	28	.267	.325	.383	708	103	17	17	100	100	53	65	3
Cal	51	59	0	.464	13.5	26	28	476	453	4191	944	134	16	97	393	571	29	**51**	.256	.330	.380	710	103	26	22	101	44	33	57	-2
Sea	44	65	1	.404	20	20	37	426	521	4201	950	148	13	89	329	553	27	41	.251	.314	.368	682	92	-19	-38	105	100	50	67	5
Min	41	68	1	.376	23	24	36	378	486	4025	884	147	**36**	47	275	497	11	36	.240	.293	.338	631	76	-90	-110	106	34	27	56	-2
Total	750	—	—	—	—	378	371	6112	—	56867	13016	2119	305	1062	4761	6905	279	564	.256	.321	.373	693	—	—	—	—	913	557	62	6

TEAM	CG	SHO	GR	SV	IP	H	HR	BB	SO	BR/9	ERA	AERA	OAV	OOB	PR	APR	PF	OSB	OCS	FA	E	WPB	DP	FW	PW	BW	BSW	DIF
Mil	11	4	**199**	**35**	986.0	994	72	352	448	12.4	3.91	89	.266	.328	-27	-51	95	70	40	.982	79	40	**135**	.3	-5.4	3.0	-.5	9.9
Bal	25	10	133	23	940.0	923	83	347	489	12.3	3.70	99	.260	.326	-4	-6	100	50	41	.983	68	40	114	.8	-.6	2.8	-.4	3.9
NY	16	**13**	161	30	948.0	**827**	**64**	287	**606**	**10.7**	**2.90**	**125**	**.235**	**.293**	**80**	**76**	99	70	35	.982	72	30	100	.7	**8.0**	3.7	-.0	-6.8
Det	33	**13**	146	22	969.1	840	83	373	476	11.5	3.53	107	.236	.310	14	26	103	58	40	**.984**	**67**	32	109	**1.0**	2.7	-.2	-.0	2.0
Bos	19	4	157	24	987.1	983	90	354	536	12.4	3.81	103	.262	.328	-17	11	107	93	35	.979	91	27	108	-.4	1.2	3.7	-.5	1.0
Cle	33	10	111	13	931.0	989	67	311	569	12.7	3.88	95	.274	.330	-23	-20	101	**48**	46	.978	87	38	91	-.4	-2.1	-.9	**1.3**	2.6
Tor	20	4	189	18	953.1	908	72	377	451	12.5	3.81	104	.252	.326	-17	14	108	55	36	.975	105	45	102	-1.3	1.5	-13.0	-.6	-2.6
West																												
Oak	**60**	11	112	10	993.0	883	80	370	505	11.6	3.30	107	.240	.311	40	25	96	50	45	.980	81	32	74	.2	2.6	.5	.5	5.6
Tex	23	**13**	142	18	940.1	851	67	322	488	11.4	3.40	102	.243	.308	27	8	95	50	38	**.984**	69	28	102	.7	.8	2.9	-.5	.5
Chi	20	8	173	23	940.2	891	73	336	529	12.0	3.47	104	.252	.319	19	15	99	74	37	.979	87	26	113	-.3	1.6	**4.9**	.4	-5.6
KC	24	8	127	24	922.1	909	75	**273**	404	11.7	3.56	101	.260	.313	10	5	99	72	26	.982	72	**20**	94	.5	.5	1.8	.3	-4.6
Cal	27	8	155	19	971.1	958	81	323	426	12.1	3.70	99	.261	.321	-4	-3	100	73	49	.977	101	24	120	-.9	-.3	2.3	-.3	-4.9
Sea	10	5	**199**	23	997.1	1039	76	360	478	12.8	4.23	92	.271	.334	-64	-37	106	85	35	.979	91	49	122	-.3	-3.9	-4.0	.5	-2.8
Min	13	6	165	22	979.2	1021	79	376	500	13.0	3.98	99	.272	.338	-35	-3	108	65	**53**	.978	96	22	103	-.6	-.3	-11.5	-.3	-.8
Total	334	117	2169	304	13459.2	—	—	—	—	12.1	3.66	—	.256	.321	—	—	—	—	—	.980	1166	453	1487	—	—	—	—	—

BATTER-FIELDER WINS	BATTING AVERAGE	ON-BASE PERCENTAGE	SLUGGING AVERAGE	ON-BASE PLUS SLUGGING	ADJUSTED OPS	ADJUSTED BATTER RUNS
Grich-Cal 5.2	Lansford-Bos .336	Hargrove-Cle .424	Grich-Cal .543	Evans-Bos .937	Grich-Cal 162	Evans-Bos 35.1
Bell-Tex 5.1	Paciorek-Sea .326	Evans-Bos .415	Murray-Bal .534	Grich-Cal .921	Evans-Bos 159	Henderson-Oak 30.3
Yount-Mil 4.7	Cooper-Mil .320	Henderson-Oak .408	Evans-Bos .522	Murray-Bal .895	Murray-Bal 156	Cooper-Mil 28.0
Henderson-Oak 4.6	Henderson-Oak .319	Kemp-Det .389	Paciorek-Sea .509	Paciorek-Sea .888	Lemon-Chi 154	Grich-Cal 27.9
Burleson-Cal 4.5	Hargrove-Cle .317	Lansford-Bos .389	Cooper-Mil .495	Lemon-Chi .874	Cooper-Mil 153	Murray-Bal 26.8
RUNS	**HITS**	**DOUBLES**	**TRIPLES**	**HOME RUNS**	**TOTAL BASES**	**RUNS BATTED IN**
Henderson-Oak 89	Henderson-Oak 135	Cooper-Mil 35	Castino-Min 9	Murray-Bal 22	Evans-Bos 215	Murray-Bal 78
Evans-Bos 84	Lansford-Bos 134	Oliver-Tex 29	Wilson-KC 7	Grich-Cal 22	Armas-Oak 211	Armas-Oak 76
Cooper-Mil 70	Wilson-KC 133	Paciorek-Sea 28	Henderson-Oak 7	Evans-Bos 22	Paciorek-Sea 206	Oglivie-Mil 72
Harrah-Cle 64	Cooper-Mil 133	Dauer-Bal 27	G.Brett-KC 7	Armas-Oak 22	Cooper-Mil 206	Evans-Bos 71
Rivers-Tex 62	Paciorek-Sea 132	G.Brett-KC 27	Baines-Chi 7		Murray-Bal 202	Winfield-NY 68
BASES ON BALLS	**STOLEN BASES**	**BASE STEALING RUNS**	**FIELDING RUNS-INFIELD**	**FIELDING RUNS-OUTFIELD**	**OUTFIELD ASSISTS**	**CATCHER CS PCT.**
Evans-Bos 85	Henderson-Oak 56	Cruz-Sea 6.7	Bell-Tex 34.3	Wilson-KC 17.6	Wilson-KC 14	Dempsey-Bal 44.4
Murphy-Oak 73	Cruz-Sea 43	Wilson-KC 4.7	Yount-Mil 30.0	Henderson-Oak 14.8	Rivers-Tex 12	Whitt-Tor 44.2
Kemp-Det 70	LeFlore-Chi 36	Henderson-Oak 4.6	Burleson-Cal 27.4	Manning-Cle 7.8	Orta-Cle 11	Parrish-Det 44.0
Henderson-Oak 64	Wilson-KC 34	Manning-Cle 4.4	Grich-Cal 18.3	Evans-Bos 6.1	Paciorek-Sea 10	Ott-Cal 40.8
Aikens-KC 62	Dilone-Cle 29	LeFlore-Chi 4.1	Castino-Min 17.3	Roenicke-Bal 4.6	Baines-Chi 10	Cerone-NY 35.8
WINS	**WINNING PCT.**	**WINS ABOVE TEAM**	**GAMES STARTED**	**COMPLETE GAMES**	**FEWEST HITS/GAME**	**FEWEST BB/GAME**
Vuckovich-Mil 14	Vuckovich-Mil .778	Vuckovich-Mil 4.8	Leonard-KC 26	Langford-Oak 18	McCatty-Oak 6.79	Honeycutt-Tex 1.20
Morris-Det 14	D.Martinez-Bal .737	D.Martinez-Bal 4.3	Zahn-Cal 25	McCatty-Oak 16	Morris-Det 6.95	Forsch-Cal 1.59
McCatty-Oak 14	McGregor-Bal .722	McGregor-Bal 3.7	Stieb-Tor 25	Morris-Det 15	Guidry-NY 7.09	Gura-KC 1.83
D.Martinez-Bal 14	Guidry-NY .688	Torrez-Bos 3.4	Morris-Det 25	Norris-Oak 12	Darwin-Tex 7.09	Leonard-KC 1.83
		Stieb-Tor 3.3		Gura-KC 12	Stewart-Bal 7.13	Guidry-NY 1.84
STRIKEOUTS	**STRIKEOUTS/GAME**	**GAMES**	**SAVES**	**BASE RUNNERS/9**	**ADJUSTED RELIEF RUNS**	**RELIEF RANKING**
Barker-Cle 127	Barker-Cle 7.41	Corbett-Min 54	Fingers-Mil 28	Fingers-Mil 7.96	Fingers-Mil 22.6	Fingers-Mil 41.4
Burns-Chi 108	Guidry-NY 7.37	Fingers-Mil 47	Gossage-NY 20	Davis-NY 8.88	Gossage-NY 14.3	Gossage-NY 27.3
Leonard-KC 107	Bannister-Sea 6.30	Rawley-Sea 46	Quisenberry-KC 18	Guidry-NY 9.00	Corbett-Min 12.1	Saucier-Det 17.9
Blyleven-Cle 107	Burns-Chi 6.20	Easterly-Mil 44	Corbett-Min 17	Gura-KC 9.30	Quisenberry-KC 12.0	Quisenberry-KC 16.3
Guidry-NY 104	Blyleven-Cle 6.04		Saucier-Det 13	Righetti-NY 9.66	Aase-Cal 10.6	Aase-Cal 15.7
INNINGS PITCHED	**OPPONENTS' AVG.**	**OPPONENTS' OBP**	**EARNED RUN AVERAGE**	**ADJUSTED ERA**	**ADJUSTED STARTER RUNS**	**PITCHER WINS**
Leonard-KC 201.2	McCatty-Oak .211	Guidry-NY .256	McCatty-Oak 2.33	Stewart-Bal 157	McCatty-Oak 27.1	**Fingers-Mil 4.6**
Morris-Det 198.0	Guidry-NY .214	Gura-KC .265	Stewart-Bal 2.32	McCatty-Oak 151	Righetti-NY 19.5	**McCatty-Oak 3.1**
Langford-Oak 195.1	Darwin-Tex .218	Honeycutt-Tex .272	Lamp-Chi 2.41	Lamp-Chi 150	Burns-Chi 17.7	**Gossage-NY 3.0**
McCatty-Oak 185.2	Morris-Det .218	McCatty-Oak .277	John-NY 2.63	John-NY 137	Morris-Det 16.7	**Righetti-NY 2.2**
Stieb-Tor 183.2	Lamp-Chi .222	Forsch-Cal .286	Burns-Chi 2.64	Burns-Chi 137	Stieb-Tor 16.7	**Stieb-Tor 2.0**

Shattered Season

On June 12 players called the first in-season strike in baseball history. Owners provoked the action by trying to force free-agent compensation onto the bargaining table through the courts. Once the owners' strike insurance ran out, they compromised, and the season resumed August 10. To revive interest in the destroyed season, the owners instituted a "split" format—the standings before the strike would stand, with the leading clubs declared first-half winners. The rest of the schedule would produce its own "winners."

The folly of the "split season" was palpable—why expect a team to push if it had *already clinched* a postseason berth? All four divisions had "split" championships. The ad hoc 1981 Division Series—a format institutionalized in the mid-1990s—helped the owners and NBC turn the strike into extra profits. Attendance was down almost everywhere, of course. Oakland's attendance had been so bad that their gate went up 55 percent *despite* the strike.

The league's biggest surprise was Toronto, which played at a .276 pre-strike clip. In the second half, playing sophomore Lloyd Moseby and rookies George Bell and Jesse Barfield, the Jays went 21-27; they would no longer be patsies.

Oakland, the West's first-half winner, had homer and steal leaders in Tony Armas and Rickey Henderson. They swept the Royals in three games in the West Division Series.

The Brewers and Yankees won the East, with Milwaukee's Rollie Fingers winning Cy Young and MVP honors. New York, however, won the East playoff, in five hotly-contested games. The Yankees defeated Oakland in four for the AL title before falling to the Dodgers in the World Series.

Postseason excitement aside, this was a disaster of historic proportions for baseball. With football and college sports taking over media and public consciousness, the last thing the major leagues needed was a crippling strike when it should have been the only game in town. Forgiveness came hard, and some people never returned to baseball.

1980 NATIONAL LEAGUE

TEAM	W	L	T	PCT	GB	HW	HL	R	OR	PA	H	2B	3B	HR	BB	SO	HB	SH	AVG	OBP	SLG	OPS	AOPS	BR	ABR	PF	SB	CS	BSA	BSR
EAST																														
Phi	91	71	0	.562	—	49	32	728	639	6265	1517	272	54	117	472	**708**	**33**	77	.270	.327	**.400**	727	101	62	17	107	140	62	69	9
Mon	90	72	0	.556	1	51	29	694	629	6164	1407	250	61	114	547	865	20	76	.257	.324	.388	712	102	36	22	102	237	82	74	23
Pit	83	79	0	.512	8	47	34	666	646	6125	1469	249	38	116	452	760	25	75	.266	.322	.388	710	100	27	4	104	209	102	67	10
StL	74	88	0	.457	17	41	40	**738**	710	6202	**1541**	**300**	49	101	451	781	21	73	**.275**	**.328**	**.400**	**728**	103	**66**	33	105	117	54	68	7
NY	67	95	0	.414	24	38	44	611	702	6130	1407	218	41	61	501	840	25	73	.257	.319	.345	664	92	-53	-45	99	158	99	61	0
Chi	64	98	0	.395	27	37	44	614	728	6217	1411	251	35	107	471	912	18	69	.251	.309	.365	674	86	-47	-94	108	93	64	59	-2
WEST																														
Hou	93	70	0	.571	—	**55**	26	637	**589**	6253	1455	231	**67**	75	540	755	13	89	.261	.326	.367	693	**108**	0	**59**	92	194	74	72	17
LA	92	71	0	.564	1	**55**	27	663	591	6221	1462	209	24	**148**	492	846	24	96	.263	.323	.388	711	107	29	48	97	123	72	63	2
Cin	89	73	1	.549	3.5	44	37	707	670	6208	1445	256	45	113	537	852	23	78	.262	.327	.386	713	106	41	55	98	156	43	**78**	19
Atl	81	80	0	.503	11	50	30	630	660	5958	1352	226	22	144	434	899	20	69	.250	.307	.380	687	96	-27	-33	101	73	52	58	-2
SF	75	86	0	.466	17	44	37	573	634	6045	1310	199	44	80	509	840	14	**100**	.244	.308	.342	650	90	-84	-64	97	100	58	63	2
SD	73	89	1	.451	19.5	45	36	591	654	6254	1410	195	43	67	**563**	791	21	92	.255	.324	.342	666	99	-50	-6	93	**239**	73	77	**27**
Total	973	—	—	—	—	556	416	7852	—	74042	17186	2856	523	1243	5969	9849	257	967	.259	.320	.374	695	—	—	—	—	1839	835	69	112

TEAM	CG	SHO	GR	SV	IP	H	HR	BB	SO	BR/9	ERA	AERA	OAV	OOB	PR	APR	PF	OSB	OCS	FA	E	WPB	DP	FW	PW	BW	BSW	DIF
EAST																												
Phi	25	8	277	40	1480.0	1419	87	530	889	12.0	3.43	**111**	.255	.319	28	**60**	106	166	79	.979	136	59	136	.2	**6.3**	1.8	-.0	1.7
Mon	33	15	280	36	1456.2	1447	100	460	823	11.9	3.48	104	.261	.317	20	23	101	**116**	71	.977	144	44	126	-.2	2.4	2.3	1.4	3.0
Pit	25	8	271	**43**	1458.1	1422	110	**451**	832	11.7	3.58	103	.259	.316	4	17	102	125	64	.978	137	**34**	154	.2	1.8	.4	.0	-.5
StL	**34**	9	297	27	1447.0	1454	90	495	664	12.3	8.93	95	.265	.326	-53	-29	104	169	68	.981	122	51	**174**	1.0	-3.1	3.5	-.2	-8.2
NY	17	9	324	33	1451.1	1473	140	510	886	12.4	3.85	94	.267	.328	-40	-40	100	132	80	.975	154	40	132	-.7	-4.2	-4.8	-1.0	-3.3
Chi	13	6	**344**	35	1479.0	1525	109	589	923	13.0	3.89	102	.272	.340	-47	10	110	154	**105**	.974	174	51	149	-1.7	1.1	-9.9	-1.2	-5.2
WEST																												
Hou	31	18	246	41	1482.2	1367	**69**	466	**929**	**11.3**	**3.10**	106	**.246**	**.305**	**82**	31	91	157	47	.978	140	62	145	.0	3.3	**6.2**	.8	1.1
LA	24	**19**	266	42	1472.2	**1358**	105	480	835	**11.3**	3.25	107	.247	.306	58	38	96	168	51	.981	123	44	149	1.0	4.0	5.1	-.8	1.2
Cin	30	12	262	37	1459.1	1404	113	506	833	11.9	3.85	91	.255	.317	-40	-55	98	187	57	**.983**	**106**	47	144	**1.9**	-5.8	5.8	1.0	5.1
Atl	29	9	289	37	1428.0	1397	131	454	696	11.8	3.77	98	.258	.316	-27	-14	102	144	64	.975	162	50	156	-1.2	-1.5	-3.5	-1.2	7.8
SF	27	10	288	35	1448.1	1446	92	492	811	12.2	3.46	101	.261	.323	24	8	97	156	74	.975	159	38	124	-1.0	.8	-6.8	-.8	2.2
SD	19	9	296	39	1466.1	1474	97	536	728	12.4	3.65	93	.267	.331	-8	-41	95	165	75	.980	132	45	157	.5	-4.3	-.6	**1.9**	-5.4
Total	307	132	3440	445	17529.2	—	—	—	—	12.0	3.60	—	.259	.320	—	—	—	—	—	.978	1689	565	1746	—	—	—	—	—

BATTER-FIELDER WINS	BATTING AVERAGE	ON-BASE PERCENTAGE	SLUGGING AVERAGE	ON-BASE PLUS SLUGGING	ADJUSTED OPS	ADJUSTED BATTER RUNS
Schmidt-Phi 6.8	Buckner-Chi..........324	Hernandez-StL 408	Schmidt-Phi 624	Schmidt-Phi 1004	Schmidt-Phi 167	Schmidt-Phi 49.3
Templeton-StL ... 5.3	Hernandez-StL 321	Cedeno-Hou 389	Clark-SF 517	Hernandez-StL 902	Clark-SF 156	Hernandez-StL 39.4
Carter-Mon 5.1	Templeton-StL 319	Clark-SF 382	Murphy-Atl 510	Clark-SF 900	Cedeno-Hou 150	Cedeno-Hou 35.3
Smith-SD 4.2	McBride-Phi..........309	Schmidt-Phi 380	Simmons-StL........505	Simmons-StL........880	Hernandez-StL 144	Easler-Pit..............35.3
Dawson-Mon 3.8	Cedeno-Hou 309	Driessen-Cin.........377	Baker-LA...............503	Murphy-Atl 858	Simmons-StL........138	Clark-SF 34.6
RUNS	**HITS**	**DOUBLES**	**TRIPLES**	**HOME RUNS**	**TOTAL BASES**	**RUNS BATTED IN**
Hernandez-StL 111	Garvey-LA 200	Rose-Phi.................42	Scott-Mon 13	Schmidt-Phi 48	Schmidt-Phi 342	Schmidt-Phi 121
Schmidt-Phi 104	Richards-SD 193	Dawson-Mon 41	Moreno-Pit...............13	Horner-Atl 35	Garvey-LA 307	Hendrick-StL.........109
Murphy-Atl 98	Hernandez-StL 191	Buckner-Chi............41	LeFlore-Mon 11	Murphy-Atl 33	Hernandez-StL 294	Garvey-LA 106
Dawson-Mon 96	Buckner-Chi..........187	Knight-Cin...............39	Herndon-SF 11	Carter-Mon 29	Baker-LA...............291	Carter-Mon 101
		Hernandez-StL 39		Baker-LA.................29	Murphy-Atl 290	Hernandez-StL 99
BASES ON BALLS	**STOLEN BASES**	**BASE STEALING RUNS**	**FIELDING RUNS-INFIELD**	**FIELDING RUNS-OUTFIELD**	**OUTFIELD ASSISTS**	**CATCHER CS PCT.**
Morgan-Hou............93	LeFlore-Mon 97	LeFlore-Mon 14.7	Smith-SD 38.5	Youngblood-NY....19.4	Richards-SD 21	Blackwell-Chi 40.9
Driessen-Cin...........93	Moreno-Pit..............96	Collins-Cin 10.0	Templeton-StL 35.5	Moreno-Pit...........11.3	Winfield-SD.............20	Carter-Mon 40.1
Tenace-SD..............92	Collins-Cin 79	Mumphrey-SD 9.7	Trillo-Phi...............24.3	Puhl-Hou................9.5	Youngblood-NY.......18	Benedict-Atl 36.7
Schmidt-Phi 89	Scott-Mon 63	Moreno-Pit.............9.6	Hubbard-Atl 21.2	Dawson-Mon 7.3	Cruz-Hou 16	Boone-Phi.............33.3
Hernandez-StL 86	Richards-SD 61	Scott-Mon 9.3	Schmidt-Phi 18.5	Richards-SD 6.9		May-SF 32.1
WINS	**WINNING PCT.**	**WINS ABOVE TEAM**	**GAMES STARTED**	**COMPLETE GAMES**	**FEWEST HITS/GAME**	**FEWEST BB/GAME**
Carlton-Phi..............24	Bibby-Pit 760	Carlton-Phi.............7.1	Reuschel-Chi..........38	Rogers-Mon............14	Soto-Cin...............5.96	Forsch-StL 1.38
Niekro-Hou 20	Reuss-LA..............750	Bibby-Pit 6.9	Niekro-Atl................38	Carlton-Phi..............13	Sutton-LA.............6.91	Reuss-LA.............1.57
Bibby-Pit 19	Carlton-Phi............727	Reuss-LA...............5.6	Carlton-Phi..............38	Niekro-Atl................11	Carlton-Phi...........7.19	Forsch-Hou...........1.66
Reuss-LA................18	Ruthven-Phi..........630	Ruhle-Hou 3.5	Rogers-Mon............37	Niekro-Hou 11	Seaver-Cin...........7.50	Candelaria-Pit......1.93
Ruthven-Phi............17	Niekro-Hou 625	Sutton-LA...............3.5	Lamp-Chi 37		Reuss-LA.............7.57	Sutton-LA.............1.99
STRIKEOUTS	**STRIKEOUTS/GAME**	**GAMES**	**SAVES**	**BASE RUNNERS/9**	**ADJUSTED RELIEF RUNS**	**RELIEF RANKING**
Carlton-Phi............286	Soto-Cin...............8.61	Tidrow-Chi 84	Sutter-Chi 28	Richard-Hou 8.31	McGraw-Phi.........23.2	McGraw-Phi.........30.3
Ryan-Hou 200	Carlton-Phi...........8.47	Tekulve-Pit..............78	Hume-Cin 25	McGraw-Phi.........8.48	Caudill-Chi 22.3	Camp-Atl..............25.4
Soto-Cin................182	Ryan-Hou 7.70	Hume-Cin 78	Fingers-SD 23	Sambito-Hou........8.87	Camp-Atl..............20.6	Sutter-Chi 22.5
Niekro-Atl..............176	Blyleven-Pit..........6.98	Camp-Atl.................77	Camp-Atl.................22	Sutton-LA.............8.99	Smith-Hou............17.6	Hume-Cin 22.5
Blyleven-Pit...........168	Welch-LA.............5.94	Romo-Pit.................74	Allen-NY 22	Reuss-LA.............9.14	Holland-SF...........15.3	Smith-Hou............21.9
INNINGS PITCHED	**OPPONENTS' AVG.**	**OPPONENTS' OBP**	**EARNED RUN AVERAGE**	**ADJUSTED ERA**	**ADJUSTED STARTER RUNS**	**PITCHER WINS**
Carlton-Phi.........304.0	Soto-Cin................187	Sutton-LA..............257	Sutton-LA.............2.20	Carlton-Phi............163	Carlton-Phi...........48.0	**Carlton-Phi 5.2**
Rogers-Mon.......281.0	Sutton-LA..............211	Reuss-LA..............260	Carlton-Phi...........2.34	Sutton-LA.............158	Sutton-LA.............31.9	**McGraw-Phi 3.3**
Niekro-Atl...........275.0	Carlton-Phi............218	Pastore-Cin...........275	Reuss-LA.............2.51	Reuss-LA..............138	Reuss-LA.............24.0	**Camp-Atl............ 2.9**
Reuschel-Chi.....257.0	Seaver-Cin............225	Carlton-Phi............276	Blue-SF................2.97	Rogers-Mon...........122	Rogers-Mon.........21.5	**Hume-Cin............ 2.6**
Niekro-Hou 256.0	Reuss-LA..............227	Soto-Cin................276	Rogers-Mon.........2.98	Zachry-NY 120	Richard-Hou 17.6	**Reuss-LA 2.5**

FINALLY, PHILLY

Defending world champion Pittsburgh, leading the East in late August, suddenly dropped 13 of 15 to fall from contention. The Phillies and Expos took the mantle, and the season went down to the last three games of the year—in Montreal. Philly captured the first two to clinch. Mike Schmidt, whose homer won the division-clinching game, was MVP, while Steve Carlton won his third Cy Young. Montreal's Gary Carter finished second in MVP voting.

Houston gave free agent Nolan Ryan the first $1 million annual salary. As it turned out, they really needed Ryan; fireballer J.R. Richard suffered a career-ending stroke on July 30. The Astros and Dodgers traded the West lead from June onward, spending six straight days tied in mid-September. Los Angeles lost five straight late in the month, but then swept a season-ending home series (with three one-run games) against Houston to force a playoff, also at Dodger Stadium. The Astros won, 7-1, behind Joe Niekro, for their first title.

The Dodgers, who led the NL league in attendance each year until 1986, had the Rookie of the Year in Steve Howe. Giants mainstay Willie McCovey retired. Game-winning RBI became an official statistic and would remain so through 1988.

Houston and Philadelphia hooked up in a wild five-game NLCS, with the last four contests decided in extra innings. After the Phillies' Game 1 win, the Astros won the next two. Philadelphia staved off elimination in Game 4 with three in the eighth and two in the 10th. In Game 5 Houston scored three in the seventh to go up, 5-2, but Philadelphia plated five in the eighth, and the Astros scored twice to tie it. The Phillies won in the 10th when Garry Maddox doubled home Del Unser.

The Phillies finally won their first World Series ever with a six-game triumph over Kansas City. Every game was close, with late-inning magic on both sides, but Carlton's two wins and great relief from Tug McGraw cinched it for the Phils.

1980 AMERICAN LEAGUE

TEAM	W	L	T	PCT	GB	HW	HL	R	OR	PA	H	2B	3B	HR	BB	SO	HB	SH	AVG	OBP	SLG	OPS	AOPS	BR	ABR	PF	SB	CS	BSA	BSR
East																														
NY	103	59	0	.636	—	**53**	28	820	662	6329	1484	239	34	189	643	739	28	51	.267	.343	.425	768	111	81	94	99	86	36	70	6
Bal	100	62	0	.617	3	50	31	805	**640**	6281	1523	258	29	156	587	766	21	42	.273	.342	.413	755	108	55	67	99	111	38	74	11
Mil	86	76	0	.531	17	40	42	811	682	6242	1555	**298**	36	**203**	455	745	25	58	.275	.329	**.448**	**777**	**114**	80	**100**	98	131	56	70	9
Bos	83	77	0	.519	19	36	45	757	767	6200	1588	297	36	162	475	720	32	40	.283	.340	.436	776	105	**89**	47	105	79	48	62	1
Det	84	78	1	.519	19	43	38	**830**	757	6444	1543	232	53	143	**645**	844	33	63	.273	.348	.409	757	104	66	46	103	75	68	52	-7
Cle	79	81	0	.494	23	44	35	738	807	6258	1517	221	40	89	617	625	37	60	.277	**.350**	.381	731	99	27	19	101	118	58	67	6
Tor	67	95	0	.414	36	35	46	624	762	6149	1398	249	53	126	448	813	33	63	.251	.309	.383	692	85	-95	-120	104	67	72	48	-10
West																														
KC	97	65	0	.599	—	49	32	809	694	6357	**1633**	266	**59**	115	508	709	38	34	**.286**	.345	.413	758	105	62	50	102	**185**	43	**81**	**26**
Oak	83	79	0	.512	14	46	35	686	642	6160	1424	212	35	137	506	824	19	99	.259	.322	.385	707	99	-54	-12	94	175	82	68	10
Min	77	84	0	.478	19.5	44	36	670	724	6130	1468	252	46	99	436	703	21	92	.265	.319	.381	700	85	-67	-111	107	62	46	57	-2
Tex	76	85	2	.472	20.5	39	41	756	752	6319	1616	263	27	124	480	**589**	23	70	.284	.339	.405	744	106	31	52	97	91	49	65	3
Chi	70	90	2	.438	26	37	42	587	722	6000	1408	255	38	91	399	670	**39**	67	.259	.311	.370	681	86	-105	-104	100	68	54	56	-4
Cal	65	95	0	.406	31	30	51	698	797	6134	1442	236	32	106	539	889	32	71	.265	.332	.378	710	95	-32	-22	99	91	63	59	-2
Sea	59	103	1	.364	38	36	45	610	793	6141	1359	211	35	104	483	727	19	**106**	.248	.308	.356	664	80	-139	-148	102	116	62	65	4
Total	1132	—	—	—	—	582	547	10201	—	87144	20958	3489	553	1844	7221	10363	400	916	.269	.331	.399	731	—	—	—	—	1455	775	65	49

TEAM	CG	SHO	GR	SV	IP	H	HR	BB	SO	BR/9	ERA	AERA	OAV	OOB	PR	APR	PF	OSB	OCS	FA	E	WPB	DP	FW	PW	BW	BSW	DIF
East																												
NY	29	**15**	210	**50**	1464.1	1433	**102**	463	845	11.8	3.58	110	.259	.316	73	61	98	**64**	**69**	.978	138	61	160	.0	6.1	9.4	.3	6.3
Bal	42	10	190	41	1460.0	1438	134	507	789	12.1	3.64	109	.261	.323	63	52	98	93	67	**.985**	**95**	54	178	**2.4**	5.2	6.7	.7	3.9
Mil	48	14	231	30	1450.0	1530	137	**420**	575	12.3	3.71	105	.273	.323	53	33	97	81	46	.977	147	39	189	-.5	3.3	**10.0**	.6	-8.3
Bos	30	8	238	43	1441.1	1557	129	481	696	12.9	4.38	97	.279	.337	-55	-18	106	107	45	.977	149	**34**	**206**	-.7	-1.8	4.7	-.2	1.1
Det	40	9	210	30	1467.1	1505	152	558	741	12.8	4.25	97	.267	.334	-35	-21	102	102	45	.979	133	78	165	.3	-2.1	4.6	-1.0	1.2
Cle	35	8	225	32	1428.0	1519	137	552	843	13.3	4.68	88	.275	.341	-103	-86	102	124	56	.983	105	69	143	1.8	-8.6	1.9	.3	3.7
Tor	39	9	**286**	23	1466.0	1523	135	635	705	13.4	4.19	103	.274	.348	-26	18	107	115	53	.979	133	49	**206**	.3	1.8	-12.0	-1.3	-2.8
West																												
KC	37	10	201	42	1459.1	1496	129	465	614	12.2	3.83	106	.267	.323	33	34	100	109	56	.978	141	50	150	-.2	3.4	5.0	**2.2**	5.5
Oak	**94**	9	146	13	1471.2	**1347**	142	521	769	**11.6**	**3.46**	110	**.244**	**.310**	**94**	59	94	87	66	.979	130	60	115	.5	5.9	-1.2	.6	-3.8
Min	35	9	213	30	1451.0	1502	120	468	744	12.4	3.93	**111**	.272	.328	16	**64**	108	76	59	.977	148	40	192	-.6	**6.4**	-11.1	-.5	2.4
Tex	35	6	256	25	1451.2	1561	119	519	**890**	13.1	4.02	96	.277	.339	2	-24	96	112	60	.977	147	79	169	-.5	-2.4	5.2	-.0	-6.8
Chi	32	12	236	42	1435.1	1434	108	563	724	12.8	3.92	103	.263	.333	18	21	100	124	58	.973	171	61	162	-1.9	2.1	-10.4	-.7	.9
Cal	22	6	268	30	1428.1	1548	141	529	725	13.3	4.52	87	.278	.342	-77	-92	98	147	41	.978	134	42	144	.1	-9.2	-2.2	-.5	-3.2
Sea	31	7	236	26	1457.1	1565	159	540	703	13.2	4.38	95	.278	.341	-56	-35	103	114	54	.977	149	44	189	-.6	-3.5	-14.8	.0	-3.2
Total	549	132	3146	457	20331.2	—	—	—	—	12.7	4.03	—	.269	.331	—	—	—	—	—	.978	1920	760	2368	—	—	—	—	—

BATTER-FIELDER WINS	BATTING AVERAGE	ON-BASE PERCENTAGE	SLUGGING AVERAGE	ON-BASE PLUS SLUGGING	ADJUSTED OPS	ADJUSTED BATTER RUNS
G.Brett-KC 6.5	G.Brett-KC............390	G.Brett-KC............454	G.Brett-KC............664	G.Brett-KC..........1118	G.Brett-KC............201	G.Brett-KC..........64.0
Henderson-Oak . 5.5	Cooper-Mil............352	Randolph-NY........427	Jackson-NY..........597	Jackson-NY..........995	Jackson-NY..........172	Jackson-NY.........51.6
Bell-Tex............... 5.1	Dilone-Cle.............341	Henderson-Oak....420	Oglivie-Mil............563	Cooper-Mil............926	Cooper-Mil............156	Cooper-Mil..........46.2
Randolph-NY...... 5.0	Rivers-Tex............333	Hargrove-Cle........415	Cooper-Mil............539	Oglivie-Mil............925	Oglivie-Mil............154	Oglivie-Mil..........42.3
Oglivie-Mil.......... 4.7	Carew-Cal.............331	Thompson-Det-Cal...398	Yount-Mil..............519	Singleton-Bal........882	Singleton-Bal........143	Singleton-Bal.......38.2
RUNS	**HITS**	**DOUBLES**	**TRIPLES**	**HOME RUNS**	**TOTAL BASES**	**RUNS BATTED IN**
Wilson-KC............133	Wilson-KC.............230	Yount-Mil...............49	Wilson-KC..............15	Oglivie-Mil..............41	Cooper-Mil............335	Cooper-Mil............122
Yount-Mil..............121	Cooper-Mil............219	Oliver-Tex...............43	Griffin-Tor..............15	Jackson-NY.............41	Oglivie-Mil............333	Oglivie-Mil............118
Bumbry-Bal...........118	Rivers-Tex.............210	Morrison-Chi...........40	Washington-KC........11	Thomas-Mil.............38	Murray-Bal............322	G.Brett-KC............118
Henderson-Oak.....111	Oliver-Tex.............209	McRae-KC...............39	Landreaux-Min........11	Armas-Oak.............35	Yount-Mil..............317	Oliver-Tex.............117
Trammell-Det........107	Bumbry-Bal...........205	Evans-Bos...............37	Yount-Mil................10	Murray-Bal..............32	Oliver-Tex.............315	Murray-Bal............116
BASES ON BALLS	**STOLEN BASES**	**BASE STEALING RUNS**	**FIELDING RUNS-INFIELD**	**FIELDING RUNS-OUTFIELD**	**OUTFIELD ASSISTS**	**CATCHER CS PCT.**
Randolph-NY........119	Henderson-Oak....100	Wilson-KC...........13.9	Burleson-Bos.......31.2	Wilson-KC...........13.9	Rivers-Tex..............19	Cerone-NY...........51.8
Henderson-Oak....117	Wilson-KC...............79	Henderson-Oak...12.9	Bell-Tex................26.6	Henderson-Oak...13.9	Oglivie-Mil..............18	Wynegar-Min.......44.5
Hargrove-Cle........111	Dilone-Cle...............61	Cruz-Sea...............7.4	Smalley-Min.........26.2	Oglivie-Mil...........12.9	Armas-Oak.............17	L.Cox-Sea............37.0
Murphy-Oak..........102	Cruz-Sea.................45	Dilone-Cle.............7.1	DeCinces-Bal.......26.1	Murphy-Oak.........11.9	Bailor-Tor...............16	Moore-Mil.............33.9
Harrah-Cle..............98	Bumbry-Bal.............44	Bumbry-Bal............5.8	Castino-Min.........21.4	Armas-Oak...........10.6		Sundberg-Tex......33.8
WINS	**WINNING PCT.**	**WINS ABOVE TEAM**	**GAMES STARTED**	**COMPLETE GAMES**	**FEWEST HITS/GAME**	**FEWEST BB/GAME**
Stone-Bal...............25	Stone-Bal.............781	Stone-Bal...............7.7	Leonard-KC............38	Langford-Oak..........28	Norris-Oak..........6.81	Matlack-Tex..........1.84
Norris-Oak.............22	May-NY.................750	Norris-Oak.............7.1	Stone-Bal...............37	Norris-Oak..............24	May-NY...............7.39	Splittorff-KC.........1.90
John-NY..................22	McGregor-Bal.......714	Darwin-Tex.............4.9	Flanagan-Bal..........37	Keough-Oak............20	Clancy-Tor...........7.79	John-NY................1.90
McGregor-Bal.........20	Norris-Oak............710	Barker-Cle.............4.3		John-NY..................16	Underwood-NY....7.84	Tanana-Cal..........1.99
Leonard-KC............20	John-NY................710	McGregor-Bal........4.1		Gura-KC..................16	Keough-Oak.........7.85	Langford-Oak.......1.99
STRIKEOUTS	**STRIKEOUTS/GAME**	**GAMES**	**SAVES**	**BASE RUNNERS/9**	**ADJUSTED RELIEF RUNS**	**RELIEF RANKING**
Barker-Cle............187	Barker-Cle...........6.83	Quisenberry-KC......75	Quisenberry-KC......33	May-NY.................9.39	Corbett-Min.........34.8	Corbett-Min..........45.2
Norris-Oak............180	May-NY................6.83	Corbett-Min............73	Gossage-NY...........33	Corbett-Min..........9.57	Burgmeier-Bos.....21.0	Burgmeier-Bos.....28.5
Guidry-NY.............166	Guidry-NY............6.80	Monge-Cle..............67	Farmer-Chi.............30	Norris-Oak............9.62	Gossage-NY........18.7	Quisenberry-KC...27.9
Leonard-KC...........155	Bannister-Sea......6.41	Lopez-Det...............67	Stoddard-Bal..........26	Burgmeier-Bos.....9.91	Garvin-Tor...........17.6	Gossage-NY.........27.4
Bannister-Sea.......155	Perry-Tex-NY.......5.91		Burgmeier-Bos........24	Lacey-Oak.........10.17	Darwin-Tex...........16.0	Garvin-Tor............24.9
INNINGS PITCHED	**OPPONENTS' AVG.**	**OPPONENTS' OBP**	**EARNED RUN AVERAGE**	**ADJUSTED ERA**	**ADJUSTED STARTER RUNS**	**PITCHER WINS**
Langford-Oak.....290.0	Norris-Oak...........209	May-NY.................268	May-NY.................2.46	May-NY.................161	Norris-Oak..........43.8	**Corbett-Min........ 4.8**
Norris-Oak.........284.1	May-NY.................224	Norris-Oak............270	Norris-Oak............2.53	Norris-Oak............151	Burns-Chi............33.8	**Norris-Oak.......... 4.8**
Gura-KC............283.1	Clancy-Tor...........233	Eckersley-Bos.......289	Burns-Chi.............2.84	Burns-Chi.............143	Gura-KC..............32.9	**Burns-Chi........... 3.8**
Leonard-KC.......280.1	Keough-Oak.........236	Burns-Chi.............293	Keough-Oak.........2.92	Gura-KC...............137	May-NY................29.1	**May-NY.............. 3.2**
John-NY.............265.1	Underwood-NY.....237	Langford-Oak........294	Gura-KC...............2.95	Erickson-Min.........135	Keough-Oak.........25.0	**Gura-KC............. 3.1**

.390

Kansas City's George Brett *looked* like a .400 hitter, with quick wrists, strong power, and in a good ballpark for his stroke. And despite various injuries, he was over .400 in early September, though a late slump brought him to .390—still the highest mark in the majors over a full season since 1941. An easy MVP, Brett helped the Royals destroy the West Division.

Prior to the season, Charlie Finley sold the A's. The new owners hired Billy Martin to pump up the team and the gate. With Rickey Henderson stealing 100 bases, the A's improved 29 games to second, and their attendance skyrocketed. Part of Martin's "win now" regimen involved his best pitchers doing all the work; his staff completed 94 games, most of any AL team since 1946. Most of the team's top pitchers soon came up lame.

The White Sox brought up rookie Harold Baines, and used 57-year-old Minnie Minoso for 2 at bats. While Reggie Jackson got the acclaim for the Yankees' division title, Willie Randolph, Tommy John, and Rich Gossage were also key performers. New York lost a member of its family as Elston Howard succumbed to cancer.

The Orioles were the league's first second-place 100-game winner since 1961. Steve Stone won 14 in a row and captured the Cy Young. The next year, he was finished by arm problems. Three big-name Tigers retired: Mark Fidrych with shoulder trouble and John Hiller and Willie Horton due to age.

Kansas City avenged their three ALCS defeats at New York's hands by sweeping the Yankees in three. The Royals supplemented their booming bats with excellent starting pitching and help from submarining reliever Dan Quisenberry. The World Series, however, went Philadelphia's way as they defeated Kansas City in six.

1979 NATIONAL LEAGUE

TEAM	W	L	T	PCT	GB	HW	HL	R	OR	PA	H	2B	3B	HR	BB	SO	HB	SH	AVG	OBP	SLG	OPS	AOPS	BR	ABR	PF	SB	CS	BSA	BSR
East																														
Pit	98	64	1	.605	—	48	33	**775**	643	6330	1541	264	52	148	483	855	32	98	.272	.330	**.416**	**746**	103	**68**	27	106	180	66	**73**	**17**
Mon	95	65	0	.594	2	**56**	25	701	**581**	6029	1445	273	42	143	432	890	27	67	.264	.319	.408	727	104	24	22	100	121	56	68	7
StL	86	76	1	.531	12	42	39	731	693	6347	**1594**	**279**	**63**	100	460	838	27	63	**.278**	.331	.401	732	103	46	32	102	116	69	63	1
Phi	84	78	1	.519	14	43	38	683	718	6219	1453	250	53	119	602	764	**37**	60	.266	**.340**	.396	736	102	65	33	104	128	76	63	2
Chi	80	82	0	.494	18	45	36	706	707	6182	1494	250	43	135	478	762	35	77	.269	.329	.403	732	96	40	-25	110	73	52	58	-2
NY	63	99	1	.389	35	28	53	593	706	6230	1399	255	41	74	498	817	35	66	.250	.313	.350	663	89	-90	-75	98	135	79	63	2
West																														
Cin	90	71	0	.559	—	48	32	731	644	6218	1445	266	31	132	**614**	902	19	62	.264	.338	.396	734	106	60	61	100	99	47	68	5
Hou	89	73	0	.549	1.5	52	29	583	582	6029	1382	224	52	49	461	**745**	22	109	.256	.315	.344	659	91	-96	-61	94	**190**	95	67	9
LA	79	83	0	.488	11.5	46	35	739	717	6188	1443	220	24	**183**	556	834	23	83	.263	.331	.412	743	**110**	63	**77**	98	106	46	70	7
SF	71	91	0	.438	19.5	38	43	672	751	6131	1328	192	36	125	580	925	20	89	.246	.319	.365	684	99	-47	0	93	140	73	66	5
SD	68	93	0	.422	22	39	42	603	681	6168	1316	193	53	93	534	770	32	**113**	.242	.311	.348	659	92	-101	-63	94	100	58	63	2
Atl	66	94	0	.413	23.5	34	45	669	763	6035	1389	220	28	126	490	818	23	62	.256	.318	.377	695	90	-31	-67	106	98	50	66	4
Total	971	—	—	—	—	519	450	8186	—	74106	17229	2886	518	1427	6188	9920	332	949	.261	.325	.385	709	—	—	—	—	1486	767	66	58

TEAM	CG	SHO	GR	SV	IP	H	HR	BB	SO	BR/9	ERA	AERA	OAV	OOB	PR	APR	PF	OSB	OCS	FA	E	WPB	DP	FW	PW	BW	BSW	DIF
East																												
Pit	24	7	326	**52**	1493.1	1424	125	504	904	11.8	3.41	115	.254	.316	53	79	105	108	52	.979	134	62	163	.4	8.2	2.8	**1.3**	4.4
Mon	33	18	260	39	1447.1	1379	116	**450**	813	11.5	**3.14**	**118**	.253	.310	**95**	**92**	99	103	77	.979	131	**32**	123	.4	**9.5**	2.3	.2	2.6
StL	38	10	275	25	1486.2	1449	127	501	788	11.9	3.72	102	.258	.318	1	13	102	134	52	.980	132	61	166	.5	1.3	3.3	-.4	.2
Phi	33	14	261	29	1441.1	1455	135	477	787	12.2	4.16	93	.266	.325	-69	-45	104	**95**	68	**.983**	**106**	41	148	**2.1**	-4.6	3.4	-.3	2.5
Chi	20	11	287	44	1446.2	1500	127	521	**933**	12.8	3.88	107	.270	.335	-24	38	111	123	67	.975	159	48	163	-1.1	3.9	-2.6	-.7	-.5
NY	16	10	**328**	36	1482.2	1486	120	607	819	12.9	3.84	96	.266	.338	-18	-23	99	136	**82**	.978	140	60	**168**	.0	-2.4	-7.7	-.3	-7.6
West																												
Cin	27	10	281	40	1440.1	1415	103	485	773	12.0	3.58	103	.260	.319	24	19	99	110	55	.980	124	39	152	.9	2.0	6.3	.0	.3
Hou	**55**	**19**	237	31	1447.2	**1278**	**90**	504	854	**11.2**	3.20	110	**.237**	**.304**	86	53	94	127	50	.978	138	73	146	.1	5.5	-6.3	.4	8.3
LA	30	6	240	34	1444.0	1425	101	555	811	12.5	3.83	94	.260	.329	-15	-36	97	118	63	.981	118	65	123	1.3	-3.7	**7.9**	.2	-7.8
SF	25	6	302	34	1436.0	1484	143	577	880	13.1	4.16	84	.269	.338	-69	-116	93	144	76	.974	163	67	138	-1.4	-12.0	.0	.0	3.3
SD	29	7	279	25	1453.0	1438	108	513	779	12.2	3.69	95	.263	.326	6	-29	94	107	76	.978	141	35	154	-.1	-3.0	-6.5	-.3	-2.6
Atl	32	3	283	34	1407.2	1496	132	494	779	13.0	4.18	96	.272	.335	-70	-25	107	181	48	.970	183	70	139	-2.7	-2.6	-6.9	-.0	-1.8
Total	362	121	3359	423	17426.2	—	—	—	—	12.3	3.73	—	.261	.325	—	—	—	—	—	.978	1669	653	1783	—	—	—	—	—

BATTER-FIELDER WINS	BATTING AVERAGE	ON-BASE PERCENTAGE	SLUGGING AVERAGE	ON-BASE PLUS SLUGGING	ADJUSTED OPS	ADJUSTED BATTER RUNS
Schmidt-Phi....... 5.6	Hernandez-StL 344	Rose-Phi..............418	Kingman-Chi.........613	Kingman-Chi.........956	Winfield-SD...........168	Winfield-SD...........55.8
Hernandez-StL .. 5.3	Rose-Phi..............331	Hernandez-StL 417	Schmidt-Phi 564	Winfield-SD...........953	Foster-Cin.............156	Hernandez-StL 46.4
Winfield-SD 5.2	Knight-Cin............318	Tenace-SD............403	Foster-Cin.............561	Schmidt-Phi 950	Schmidt-Phi 151	Schmidt-Phi 41.1
Templeton-StL... 4.9	Garvey-LA 315	Mazzilli-NY...........395	Winfield-SD...........558	Foster-Cin.............948	Hernandez-StL 151	Parker-Pit.............34.3
Concepcion-Cin 4.5	Horner-Atl 314	Winfield-SD...........395	Horner-Atl 552	Hernandez-StL 930	Parrish-Mon 144	Foster-Cin.............34.1
RUNS	**HITS**	**DOUBLES**	**TRIPLES**	**HOME RUNS**	**TOTAL BASES**	**RUNS BATTED IN**
Hernandez-StL 116	Templeton-StL 211	Hernandez-StL 48	Templeton-StL 19	Kingman-Chi...........48	Winfield-SD...........333	Winfield-SD...........118
Moreno-Pit...........110	Hernandez-StL 210	Cromartie-Mon 46	Moreno-Pit..............12	Schmidt-Phi 45	Parker-Pit.............327	Kingman-Chi.........115
Schmidt-Phi 109	Rose-Phi..............208	Parker-Pit...............45	McBride-Phi............12	Winfield-SD.............34	Kingman-Chi.........326	Schmidt-Phi 114
Parker-Pit.............109	Garvey-LA 204	Reitz-StL.................41	Dawson-Mon 12	Horner-Atl 33	Garvey-LA 322	Garvey-LA 110
Lopes-LA 109	Moreno-Pit............196	Rose-Phi..................40		Stargell-Pit..............32	Matthews-Atl.........317	Hernandez-StL 105
BASES ON BALLS	**STOLEN BASES**	**BASE STEALING RUNS**	**FIELDING RUNS-INFIELD**	**FIELDING RUNS-OUTFIELD**	**OUTFIELD ASSISTS**	**CATCHER CS PCT.**
Schmidt-Phi 120	Moreno-Pit..............77	Moreno-Pit.............9.6	Royster-Atl...........29.3	Maddox-Phi 17.2	Hendrick-StL...........20	Carter-Mon 46.8
Tenace-SD............105	North-SF.................58	Lopes-LA 8.3	Templeton-StL 24.2	McBride-Phi.........13.1	Youngblood-NY.......18	Yeager-LA............40.9
Lopes-LA 97	Taveras-Pit-NY.......44	Royster-Atl.............4.9	Concepcion-Cin...20.1	Youngblood-NY....10.3	Cromartie-Mon 16	Foote-Chi.............37.8
North-SF.................96	Lopes-LA 44	Scott-Mon 4.4	Smith-SD 19.5	Cromartie-Mon 9.8	Parker-Pit................15	Ott-Pit 31.4
Rose-Phi.................95	Scott-Mon 39	North-SF 4.4	Trillo-Phi..............18.3	Geronimo-Cin 6.3		Ashby-Hou...........30.4
WINS	**WINNING PCT.**	**WINS ABOVE TEAM**	**GAMES STARTED**	**COMPLETE GAMES**	**FEWEST HITS/GAME**	**FEWEST BB/GAME**
Niekro-Atl...............21	Seaver-Cin............727	Seaver-Cin.............4.6	Niekro-Atl...............44	Niekro-Atl...............23	Richard-Hou 6.77	Forsch-Hou..........1.77
Niekro-Hou 21	Niekro-Hou 656	Niekro-Hou 4.5	Jones-SD................39	Richard-Hou 19	Carlton-Phi...........7.24	Candelaria-Pit......1.78
Richard-Hou 18	Martinez-StL 652	Niekro-Atl..............4.4	Richard-Hou 38	Rogers-Mon............13	Niekro-Hou 7.54	Hume-Cin 1.82
Reuschel-Chi..........18	Sutcliffe-LA 630	Sutcliffe-LA 4.3	Niekro-Hou 38	Carlton-Phi.............13	Schatzeder-Mon ..7.56	Lee-Mon 1.86
Carlton-Phi..............18	Carlton-Phi............621	Reuschel-Chi 3.7		Hooton-LA 12	Andujar-Hou 7.79	Swan-NY 2.04
STRIKEOUTS	**STRIKEOUTS/GAME**	**GAMES**	**SAVES**	**BASE RUNNERS/9**	**ADJUSTED RELIEF RUNS**	**RELIEF RANKING**
Richard-Hou 313	Richard-Hou 9.64	Tekulve-Pit 94	Sutter-Chi 37	Sutter-Chi 8.79	Sutter-Chi 19.3	Sambito-Hou........37.5
Carlton-Phi............213	Carlton-Phi...........7.64	Romo-Pit.................84	Tekulve-Pit 31	Fulgham-StL 9.37	Sosa-Mon 19.1	Sutter-Chi 35.1
Niekro-Atl.............208	Sanderson-Mon ...7.39	Jackson-Pit 72	Garber-Atl...............25	Forsch-Hou..........9.62	Sambito-Hou........19.0	Sosa-Mon 34.0
Blyleven-Pit..........172	Blyleven-Pit..........6.52	Lavelle-SF...............70	Sambito-Hou...........22	Richard-Hou 9.88	Hume-Cin 18.2	Tekulve-Pit...........28.4
McGlothen-Chi......147	Krukow-Chi 6.50	Garber-Atl 68	Lavelle-SF...............20	Minton-SF 9.94	Tekulve-Pit 16.9	Littell-StL.............25.8
INNINGS PITCHED	**OPPONENTS' AVG.**	**OPPONENTS' OBP**	**EARNED RUN AVERAGE**	**ADJUSTED ERA**	**ADJUSTED STARTER RUNS**	**PITCHER WINS**
Niekro-Atl..........342.0	Richard-Hou 209	Forsch-Hou..........273	Richard-Hou 2.71	Hume-Cin 134	Richard-Hou 28.6	**Sambito-Hou...... 4.3**
Richard-Hou 292.1	Carlton-Phi...........219	Richard-Hou 276	Hume-Cin 2.76	Schatzeder-Mon ...131	Fulgham-StL 20.0	**Sutter-Chi 3.9**
Niekro-Hou 263.2	Schatzeder-Mon ...225	Sutton-LA.............288	Schatzeder-Mon ..2.83	Richard-Hou 130	Rogers-Mon.........19.2	**Sosa-Mon........... 3.5**
Jones-SD...........263.0	Niekro-Hou 228	Seaver-Cin...........289	Hooton-LA 2.97	Rogers-Mon..........124	Niekro-Atl.............18.2	**Tekulve-Pit 3.0**
Swan-NY 251.1	Andujar-Hou 233	Candelaria-Pit.......290	Niekro-Hou 3.00	Kison-Pit 123	Schatzeder-Mon ..16.8	**Richard-Hou....... 2.8**

Family Affair

After ten years, Montreal began to grow up. Under Dick Williams, the young Expos featured catcher Gary Carter and one of baseball's best outfields: Warren Cromartie, Andrew Dawson, and Ellis Valentine. The Pirates—adopting Sister Sledge's dance anthem "We Are Family"—led the division most of the season. In a crazy two-week stretch, the Bucs defeated the Expos five of six and took the NL East by two games.

Aging Cincinnati squeezed out one last title, with George Foster and Tom Seaver the stars. Relievers Doug Bair and Tom Hume did yeoman work as the Reds surged ahead of the Astros in September. Houston contended by playing 'little ball'; their 49 homers were the NL's fewest since 1946. Outfielders Jeffrey Leonard, Jose Cruz, and Terry Puhl provided line drives, steals, and on-base ability. Poor second-line pitching was Houston's downfall.

There were just two 20-game winners—ironically, brothers Phil (at 40!) and Joe Niekro. Dominating Cubs reliever Bruce Sutter won Cy Young honors. Houston's J.R. Richard led in ERA and strikeouts.

Cardinals left fielder Lou Brock sprinted into the sunset, ending his career shortly after collecting his 3,000th hit. The NL's superior leadoff man of the 1980s, Montreal's Tim Raines, debuted. Another rookie was skinny 22-year-old Mets reliever Jesse Orosco.

The Pirates eliminated the Reds in three straight, but the Orioles appeared to have the World Series in hand, winning three of the first four. However, Pittsburgh pitchers suddenly became stingy, permitting Baltimore to score but twice over the final three games. The Pirates got the key hits, including Willie Stargell's Series winner, a two-run homer in Game 7 at Baltimore. Kent Tekulve, who pitched 94 times during the season, racked up 3 saves for the "Fam-i-lee."

Stargell was elected league co-MVP with Cardinals first baseman and batting champion Keith Hernandez. Voting "Pops" as the league's best player in '79 was a sentimental selection; few would argue, though, about his choice as NLCS and World Series MVP. He batted .455 against Cincinnati and hit .400 with all 3 Pirates home runs against Baltimore.

1979 AMERICAN LEAGUE

TEAM	W	L	T	PCT	GB	HW	HL	R	OR	PA	H	2B	3B	HR	BB	SO	HB	SH	AVG	OBP	SLG	OPS	AOPS	BR	ABR	PF	SB	CS	BSA	BSR
EAST																														
Bal	102	57	0	.642	—	**55**	24	757	**582**	6106	1401	258	24	181	608	847	31	42	.261	.336	.419	755	106	28	56	97	99	49	67	5
Mil	95	66	0	.590	8	52	29	807	722	6227	1552	291	41	185	549	745	20	72	.280	.345	.448	793	**112**	98	96	100	100	53	65	3
Bos	91	69	0	.569	11.5	51	29	841	711	6184	1567	**310**	34	**194**	512	708	33	42	**.283**	.344	**.456**	**800**	108	**112**	67	106	60	43	58	-2
NY	89	71	0	.556	13.5	51	30	734	672	6061	1443	226	40	150	509	**590**	18	50	.266	.328	.406	734	99	-23	-11	98	65	46	59	-2
Det	85	76	0	.528	18	46	34	770	738	6080	1446	221	35	164	575	814	22	56	.269	.339	.415	754	99	23	-1	103	176	86	67	9
Cle	81	80	0	.503	22	47	34	760	805	6205	1388	206	29	138	**657**	786	**42**	70	.258	.340	.384	724	95	-20	-22	100	143	90	61	0
Tor	53	109	0	.327	50.5	32	49	613	862	6010	1362	253	34	95	448	663	36	65	.251	.311	.363	674	80	-143	-150	101	75	56	57	-3
WEST																														
Cal	88	74	0	.543	—	49	32	**866**	768	6311	1563	242	43	164	589	843	37	79	.282	**.351**	.429	780	**112**	84	**110**	97	100	53	65	3
KC	85	77	0	.525	3	46	35	851	816	6349	**1596**	286	**79**	116	528	675	35	57	.282	.343	.422	765	103	51	32	102	**207**	76	**73**	**19**
Tex	83	79	0	.512	5	44	37	750	698	6193	1549	252	26	140	461	607	33	78	.278	.334	.409	743	100	-1	5	99	79	51	61	0
Min	82	80	0	.506	6	39	42	764	725	6296	1544	256	46	112	526	693	31	**142**	.278	.341	.402	743	96	7	-25	104	66	45	59	-1
Chi	73	87	0	.456	14	33	46	730	748	6056	1505	290	33	127	454	668	36	58	.275	.333	.410	743	99	-2	-5	100	97	62	61	0
Sea	67	95	0	.414	21	36	45	711	820	6202	1490	250	52	132	515	725	28	61	.269	.331	.404	735	95	-19	-34	102	126	52	71	10
Oak	54	108	0	.333	34	31	50	573	860	5971	1276	188	32	108	482	751	20	75	.239	.302	.346	648	78	-195	-167	95	104	69	60	-1
Total	1128	—	—	—	—	612	516	10527	—	86251	20682	3529	548	2006	7413	10115	422	947	.270	.334	.408	743	—	—	—	—	1497	831	64	38

TEAM	CG	SHO	GR	SV	IP	H	HR	BB	SO	BR/9	ERA	AERA	OAV	OOB	PR	APR	PF	OSB	OCS	FA	E	WPB	DP	FW	PW	BW	BSW	DIF
EAST																												
Bal	52	**12**	167	30	1434.1	**1279**	133	467	786	**11.0**	**3.26**	**124**	**.241**	**.301**	**152**	**129**	96	88	58	.980	125	46	161	.8	**12.6**	5.5	.2	3.5
Mil	**61**	**12**	204	23	1439.2	1563	162	**381**	580	12.3	4.03	104	.279	.324	29	25	99	97	60	.980	127	58	153	.7	2.4	9.4	.0	1.9
Bos	47	11	198	29	1431.1	1487	133	463	731	12.5	4.03	110	.270	.328	29	62	105	116	41	.977	142	51	166	-.2	6.1	6.5	-.5	-1.0
NY	43	10	217	37	1432.1	1446	123	455	731	12.0	3.83	107	.268	.323	61	45	97	83	55	**.981**	122	60	183	1.0	4.4	-1.1	-.5	5.2
Det	25	5	221	37	1423.1	1429	167	547	802	12.8	4.27	102	.265	.335	-9	10	103	97	65	**.981**	**120**	75	184	**1.1**	1.0	-.0	.6	1.9
Cle	28	7	241	32	1431.2	1502	138	570	781	13.2	4.57	94	.272	.339	-56	-45	102	146	47	.978	134	60	149	.3	-4.4	-2.1	-.3	7.0
Tor	44	7	195	11	1417.0	1537	165	594	613	13.8	4.82	91	.281	.353	-95	-67	104	85	56	.975	159	72	187	-1.0	-6.5	-14.6	-.6	-5.2
WEST																												
Cal	46	9	209	33	1436.0	1463	131	573	**820**	13.0	4.34	94	.267	.336	-19	-44	97	138	51	.978	135	65	172	.3	-4.3	**10.7**	.0	.2
KC	42	7	239	27	1448.1	1477	165	536	640	12.7	4.45	96	.267	.331	-38	-31	101	**75**	59	.977	146	55	160	-.3	-3.0	3.1	**1.6**	2.6
Tex	26	10	217	**42**	1437.0	1371	135	532	773	12.1	3.86	107	.253	.321	56	44	98	90	58	.979	130	45	151	.6	4.3	.5	-.3	-3.1
Min	31	6	214	33	1444.1	1590	128	452	721	12.8	4.13	106	.285	.338	14	39	104	77	71	.979	134	**44**	**203**	.4	3.8	-2.4	-.4	-.4
Chi	28	9	236	37	1409.0	1365	**114**	618	675	12.9	4.10	104	.256	.334	18	22	101	135	66	.972	173	67	142	-1.9	2.1	-.5	-.3	-6.5
Sea	37	7	217	26	1438.0	1567	165	571	736	13.6	4.58	95	.281	.348	-57	-33	104	152	58	.978	141	50	170	.0	-3.2	-3.3	.7	-8.2
Oak	41	4	**243**	20	1429.1	1606	147	654	726	14.5	4.75	85	.288	.363	-84	-117	96	117	**86**	.972	174	87	137	-1.9	-11.4	-16.3	-.4	2.9
Total	551	116	3018	417	20051.2	—	—	—	—	12.8	4.22	—	.270	.334	—	—	—	—	—	.978	1962	835	2318	—	—	—	—	—

BATTER-FIELDER WINS	BATTING AVERAGE	ON-BASE PERCENTAGE	SLUGGING AVERAGE	ON-BASE PLUS SLUGGING	ADJUSTED OPS	ADJUSTED BATTER RUNS
Smalley-Min 5.6	Lynn-Bos 333	Lynn-Bos 423	Lynn-Bos 637	Lynn-Bos 1059	Lynn-Bos 173	Lynn-Bos 57.1
Lynn-Bos............5.3	Brett-KC...............329	Porter-KC.............421	Rice-Bos...............596	Lezcano-Mil 987	Lezcano-Mil 164	Singleton-Bal 50.6
Porter-KC...........5.0	Downing-Cal 326	Downing-Cal 418	Lezcano-Mil 573	Rice-Bos...............977	Singleton-Bal 157	Lezcano-Mil 45.7
Brett-KC.............4.9	Rice-Bos...............325	Lezcano-Mil 414	Brett-KC...............563	Kemp-Det.............941	Rice-Bos...............152	Rice-Bos..............44.0
Grich-Cal 3.9	Oliver-Tex.............323	Singleton-Bal 405	Jackson-NY 544	Brett-KC...............939	Jackson-NY 150	Baylor-Cal............41.1
RUNS	**HITS**	**DOUBLES**	**TRIPLES**	**HOME RUNS**	**TOTAL BASES**	**RUNS BATTED IN**
Baylor-Cal............120	Brett-KC...............212	Lemon-Chi.............44	Brett-KC.................20	Thomas-Mil............45	Rice-Bos...............369	Baylor-Cal............139
Brett-KC...............119	Rice-Bos...............201	Cooper-Mil.............44	Molitor-Mil..............16	Rice-Bos.................39	Brett-KC...............363	Rice-Bos...............130
Rice-Bos...............117	Bell-Tex................200	Lynn-Bos 42	Wilson-KC..............13	Lynn-Bos 39	Lynn-Bos 338	Thomas-Mil...........123
Lynn-Bos 116	Molitor-Mil............188	Brett-KC.................42	Randolph-NY..........13	Baylor-Cal..............36	Baylor-Cal............333	Lynn-Bos 122
Lansford-Cal 114	Lansford-Cal 188	Bell-Tex..................42		Singleton-Bal 35	Singleton-Bal 304	Porter-KC.............112
BASES ON BALLS	**STOLEN BASES**	**BASE STEALING RUNS**	**FIELDING RUNS-INFIELD**	**FIELDING RUNS-OUTFIELD**	**OUTFIELD ASSISTS**	**CATCHER CS PCT.**
Porter-KC.............121	Wilson-KC..............83	Wilson-KC............14.1	Smalley-Min.........32.6	Wilson-KC............13.1	Bosetti-Tor 18	Wynegar-Min 52.9
Singleton-Bal 109	LeFlore-Det............78	LeFlore-Det..........12.3	Dent-NY...............31.8	Bosetti-Tor 9.2	Bailor-Tor 16	Dempsey-Bal 48.4
Thomas-Mil............98	Cruz-Sea 49	Cruz-Sea 7.6	Burleson-Bos.......30.2	R.Miller-Cal............8.0	Evans-Bos 15	Parrish-Det 45.2
Randolph-NY 95	Bumbry-Bal............37	Otis-KC 4.8	Bell-Tex................28.4	Bonds-Cle..............7.0	Piniella-NY.............13	Sundberg-Tex 41.1
Thornton-Cle 90	Wills-Tex 35	Bumbry-Bal...........3.9	Cruz-Sea 19.9	Manning-Cle 6.9	R.Jones-Sea...........13	Cerone-Tor...........40.5
WINS	**WINNING PCT.**	**WINS ABOVE TEAM**	**GAMES STARTED**	**COMPLETE GAMES**	**FEWEST HITS/GAME**	**FEWEST BB/GAME**
Flanagan-Bal 23	Caldwell-Mil 727	Davis-NY 5.9	D.Martinez-Bal........39	D.Martinez-Bal........18	Ryan-Cal.............6.83	McGregor-Bal 1.19
John-NY..................21	Flanagan-Bal 719	John-NY.................5.6	Flanagan-Bal 38	Ryan-Cal.................17	Kravec-Chi 7.49	Caldwell-Mil 1.49
Koosman-Min..........20	Morris-Det............708	Morris-Det.............5.1	Jenkins-Tex............37	John-NY..................17	Guidry-NY............7.73	Sorensen-Mil 1.61
Guidry-NY...............18	John-NY................700	Guidry-NY.............4.5		Eckersley-Bos.........17	Morris-Det............8.15	Stanley-Bos 1.83
	Guidry-NY............692	Kern-Tex 4.1			Baumgarten-Chi ..8.26	John-NY...............2.12
STRIKEOUTS	**STRIKEOUTS/GAME**	**GAMES**	**SAVES**	**BASE RUNNERS/9**	**ADJUSTED RELIEF RUNS**	**RELIEF RANKING**
Ryan-Cal...............223	Ryan-Cal.............9.01	Marshall-Min...........90	Marshall-Min...........32	McGregor-Bal 9.79	Kern-Tex 38.7	Kern-Tex 61.5
Guidry-NY.............201	Guidry-NY............7.65	Monge-Cle..............76	Kern-Tex 29	Darwin-Tex...........9.81	Monge-Cle...........27.9	Marshall-Min........52.2
Flanagan-Bal 190	Flanagan-Bal 6.44	Kern-Tex 71	Stanhouse-Bal........21	Lyle-Tex 10.04	Lopez-Det............26.7	Monge-Cle...........51.2
Jenkins-Tex...........164	Jenkins-Tex..........5.70	Lyle-Tex 67	Lopez-Det...............21	Kern-Tex 10.26	Marshall-Min........26.1	Lopez-Det............38.3
Koosman-Min........157	Bannister-Sea......5.68	Heaverlo-Oak 62	Monge-Cle..............19	Guidry-NY..........10.43	Stoddard-Bal........15.9	Drago-Bos 26.2
INNINGS PITCHED	**OPPONENTS' AVG.**	**OPPONENTS' OBP**	**EARNED RUN AVERAGE**	**ADJUSTED ERA**	**ADJUSTED STARTER RUNS**	**PITCHER WINS**
D.Martinez-Bal...292.1	Ryan-Cal...............212	McGregor-Bal 273	Guidry-NY...........2.78	Eckersley-Bos.......149	Eckersley-Bos......38.9	**Kern-Tex 6.3**
John-NY.............276.1	Kravec-Chi 233	Guidry-NY............292	John-NY..............2.96	Guidry-NY.............148	Guidry-NY............34.8	**Marshall-Min 5.4**
Flanagan-Bal 265.2	Guidry-NY............236	Flanagan-Bal 296	Eckersley-Bos......2.99	John-NY................139	John-NY...............32.1	**Monge-Cle 5.2**
Koosman-Min.....263.2	Baumgarten-Chi ...243	Eckersley-Bos.......297	Flanagan-Bal 3.08	Morris-Det.............133	Koosman-Min.......28.6	**Eckersley-Bos ...4.0**
Jenkins-Tex........259.0	Morris-Det............244	Leonard-KC 297	Morris-Det...........3.28	Flanagan-Bal 131	Flanagan-Bal 27.2	**Lopez-Det...........3.9**

GIMME AN "O"

As scoring reached its highest level since 1950, four teams—Boston, New York, Kansas City, and California—attracted two million fans. Last-place Oakland, on the other hand, drew just over 300,000 fans. No team had drawn that few fans since, well, the A's—in 1954, their last year in Philadelphia. There was only one reason to watch these A's: rookie outfielder Rickey Henderson.

Although six clubs in the AL East finished over .500, the Orioles had no serious challenge after July. Underrated Ken Singleton had a superb season at bat and was ably supported by a mix of youngsters and veterans. Lefty Mike Flanagan took Cy Young honors; he came up big when Jim Palmer went down with elbow problems. The Brewers, led by home run champ Gorman Thomas, won 95 games, but finished 8 games back.

Toronto, miserable in its first two seasons, was even worse in year three. The Blue Jays ended 50½ out, the deepest last-place finish since 1954; rookie Dave Stieb was an impressive 8-8. Ron Guidry led the AL in ERA for the second straight time, but the Yankees' season ended when Thurman Munson was killed in an airplane crash on August 2. Catfish Hunter retired after the season.

California won a poor AL West; their record would have placed them fifth in the East. The Angels, fortified by trades that brought Rod Carew and Dan Ford, led the league in runs: MVP Don Baylor, Carney Lansford, and Ford each scored more than 100 times. California pitching was very thin, but it was good enough. The pitching-poor Royals couldn't turn it on early enough, the Rangers didn't hit, and the Twins just didn't have the horses, although reliever Mike Marshall pitched an AL-record 90 times.

Baltimore defeated the Angels in four games, three of them close, to win the ALCS. The Orioles lost the World Series in seven despite being up three games to one; just like 1971, the O's dropped Game 7 to the Pirates at home. It was Earl Weaver's last trip to the Fall Classic.

1978 NATIONAL LEAGUE

TEAM	W	L	T	PCT	GB	HW	HL	R	OR	PA	H	2B	3B	HR	BB	SO	HB	SH	AVG	OBP	SLG	OPS	AOPS	BR	ABR	PF	SB	CS	BSA	BSR
East																														
Phi	90	72	0	.556	—	54	28	708	586	6152	1404	248	32	133	552	866	**42**	61	.258	.328	.388	716	104	51	39	102	152	58	72	13
Pit	88	73	0	.547	1.5	**55**	26	684	637	6038	1390	239	**54**	115	480	874	**42**	64	.257	.320	.385	705	98	20	-12	105	**213**	90	70	15
Chi	79	83	0	.488	11	44	38	664	724	6258	**1461**	224	48	72	562	746	21	84	**.264**	.331	.361	692	89	10	-62	112	110	58	65	4
Mon	76	86	0	.469	14	41	39	633	611	6063	1404	269	31	121	396	881	35	62	.254	.306	.379	685	97	-27	-25	100	80	42	66	3
StL	69	93	0	.426	21	37	44	600	657	5965	1351	263	44	79	420	**713**	22	55	.249	.303	.358	661	90	-67	-64	100	97	42	70	7
NY	66	96	0	.407	24	33	47	607	690	6132	1332	227	47	86	549	829	24	71	.245	.314	.352	666	95	-48	-31	97	100	77	56	-5
West																														
LA	95	67	0	.586	—	54	27	**727**	**573**	6225	1435	251	27	**149**	610	818	20	111	**.264**	**.338**	**.402**	**740**	**113**	**102**	**100**	100	137	52	72	12
Cin	92	69	0	.571	2.5	49	31	710	688	6192	1378	**270**	32	136	**636**	899	26	84	.256	.334	.393	727	109	80	77	100	137	58	70	10
SF	89	73	0	.549	6	50	31	613	594	6102	1331	240	41	117	554	814	17	**127**	.248	.318	.374	692	102	-1	21	97	87	54	62	0
SD	84	78	0	.519	11	50	31	591	598	6081	1349	208	42	75	536	848	32	114	.252	.321	.348	669	100	-38	9	93	152	70	68	9
Hou	74	88	0	.457	21	50	31	605	634	6034	1408	231	45	70	434	743	22	76	.258	.313	.355	668	99	-52	-11	94	178	59	**75**	**19**
Atl	69	93	0	.426	26	39	42	600	750	6066	1313	191	39	123	550	874	27	61	.244	.315	.363	678	86	-30	-88	111	90	65	58	-3
Total	971	—	—	—	—	556	415	7742	—	73308	16556	2861	482	1276	6279	9905	330	970	.254	.320	.372	692	—	—	—	—	1533	725	68	84

TEAM	CG	SHO	GR	SV	IP	H	HR	BB	SO	BR/9	ERA	AERA	OAV	OOB	PR	APR	PF	OSB	OCS	FA	E	WPB	DP	FW	PW	BW	BSW	DIF
East																												
Phi	38	9	234	29	1436.1	1343	118	**393**	813	**11.0**	3.33	108	.251	**.303**	39	43	101	**91**	56	**.983**	**104**	**35**	156	**2.0**	4.5	4.1	.6	-2.3
Pit	30	13	272	44	1444.2	1366	103	499	880	11.8	3.41	109	.249	.313	26	48	104	138	47	.973	167	53	133	-1.4	5.1	-1.3	.9	4.3
Chi	24	7	**327**	38	1455.1	1475	125	539	768	12.7	4.05	100	.265	.331	-77	-2	113	118	62	.978	144	62	154	-.2	-.2	-6.6	-.3	5.2
Mon	42	13	267	32	1446.0	1332	117	572	740	12.0	3.42	104	.249	.323	24	22	100	108	61	.979	134	43	150	.4	2.3	-2.6	-.4	-4.6
StL	32	13	258	22	1437.2	**1300**	94	600	859	12.1	3.58	99	**.245**	.323	-1	-3	100	162	**78**	.978	136	72	155	.3	-.3	-6.8	.0	-5.2
NY	21	7	270	26	1455.1	1447	114	531	775	12.4	3.87	91	.265	.330	-48	-54	99	111	69	.979	132	49	160	.5	-5.7	-3.3	-1.3	-5.2
West																												
LA	46	16	198	38	1440.1	1362	107	440	800	11.4	**3.12**	**112**	.250	.307	**73**	**63**	98	105	56	.978	140	45	138	.0	**6.7**	**10.6**	.5	-3.8
Cin	16	10	299	46	1448.1	1437	122	567	908	12.6	3.81	93	.261	.329	-38	-43	99	106	60	.978	134	53	120	.3	-4.5	8.1	.3	7.2
SF	42	**17**	239	29	1455.0	1377	84	453	840	11.5	3.30	105	.252	.309	44	26	97	159	54	.977	146	38	118	-.3	2.8	2.2	-.7	4.0
SD	21	10	265	**55**	1433.2	1385	**74**	483	744	11.8	3.28	102	.257	.317	47	12	94	102	65	.975	160	44	**171**	-1.0	1.3	1.0	.2	1.6
Hou	**48**	**17**	218	23	1440.1	1328	86	578	**930**	12.1	3.63	92	.247	.320	-9	-52	93	167	59	.978	133	69	109	.4	-5.5	-1.2	**1.3**	-2.0
Atl	29	12	293	32	1440.1	1404	132	624	848	12.9	4.08	99	.257	.335	-81	-8	113	166	57	.975	153	99	126	-.6	-.8	-9.3	-1.1	-.1
Total	389	144	3140	414	17333.1	—	—	—	—	12.0	3.57	—	.254	.320	—	—	—	—	—	.978	1683	662	1690	—	—	—	—	—

BATTER-FIELDER WINS	BATTING AVERAGE	ON-BASE PERCENTAGE	SLUGGING AVERAGE	ON-BASE PLUS SLUGGING	ADJUSTED OPS	ADJUSTED BATTER RUNS
Parker-Pit 4.4	Parker-Pit............334	Burroughs-Atl.......432	Parker-Pit.............585	Parker-Pit.............979	Smith-LA..............163	Parker-Pit............47.1
Lopes-LA 4.3	Garvey-LA 316	Parker-Pit.............394	Smith-LA..............559	Burroughs-Atl........961	Parker-Pit.............162	Burroughs-Atl........40.8
Templeton-StL ... 4.2	Cruz-Hou 315	Tenace-SD............392	Foster-Cin............546	Smith-LA..............942	Clark-SF 154	Luzinski-Phi 40.7
Clark-SF 4.1	Madlock-SF 309	Luzinski-Phi 388	Clark-SF 537	Luzinski-Phi 914	Burroughs-Atl........152	Clark-SF 40.5
Simmons-StL 4.1	Winfield-SD...........308	Smith-LA..............382	Burroughs-Atl........529	Foster-Cin............906	Winfield-SD...........152	Foster-Cin............38.8
RUNS	**HITS**	**DOUBLES**	**TRIPLES**	**HOME RUNS**	**TOTAL BASES**	**RUNS BATTED IN**
DeJesus-Chi.........104	Garvey-LA 202	Rose-Cin................51	Templeton-StL 13	Foster-Cin..............40	Parker-Pit.............340	Foster-Cin............120
Rose-Cin..............103	Rose-Cin..............198	Clark-SF 46	Richards-SD 12	Luzinski-Phi 35	Foster-Cin............330	Parker-Pit.............117
Parker-Pit.............102	Cabell-Hou............195	Simmons-StL 40	Parker-Pit...............12	Parker-Pit...............30	Garvey-LA 319	Garvey-LA 113
Foster-Cin..............97	Parker-Pit.............194	Parrish-Mon 39		Smith-LA.................29	Clark-SF 318	Luzinski-Phi 101
Moreno-Pit..............95	Bowa-Phi 192	Perez-Mon..............38			Winfield-SD...........293	Clark-SF 98
BASES ON BALLS	**STOLEN BASES**	**BASE STEALING RUNS**	**FIELDING RUNS-INFIELD**	**FIELDING RUNS-OUTFIELD**	**OUTFIELD ASSISTS**	**CATCHER CS PCT.**
Burroughs-Atl........117	Moreno-Pit..............71	Lopes-LA 8.5	Templeton-StL 32.6	Cromartie-Mon 17.6	Valentine-Mon.........24	Yeager-LA...........46.7
Evans-SF 105	Taveras-Pit.............46	Moreno-Pit 7.9	Smith-SD 29.7	Valentine-Mon......10.6	Cromartie-Mon 24	Rader-Chi 40.6
Tenace-SD............101	Lopes-LA 45	McBride-Phi 5.1	Trillo-Chi..............29.4	S.Henderson-NY ...7.9	S.Henderson-NY 18	
Luzinski-Phi 100	DeJesus-Chi 41	Cruz-Hou...............5.0	Russell-LA 21.4	Clark-SF 7.7	Dawson-Mon 17	
Cey-LA....................96	Smith-SD 40	DeJesus-Chi 4.8	DeJesus-Chi 15.3	Puhl-Hou................6.6	Clark-SF 16	
WINS	**WINNING PCT.**	**WINS ABOVE TEAM**	**GAMES STARTED**	**COMPLETE GAMES**	**FEWEST HITS/GAME**	**FEWEST BB/GAME**
Perry-SD.................21	Perry-SD..............778	Perry-SD...............7.9	Niekro-Atl...............42	Niekro-Atl................22	Richard-Hou 6.28	Christenson-Phi...1.86
Grimsley-Mon 20	Hooton-LA 655	Grimsley-Mon 5.9	Perry-SD.................37	Grimsley-Mon 19	Swan-NY 7.12	Barr-SF 1.93
Niekro-Atl................19	Grimsley-Mon 645	Richard-Hou 5.0		Richard-Hou 16	Hooton-LA 7.47	R.Reuschel-Chi ...2.00
Hooton-LA 19	Blue-SF.................643	Tomlin-Cin.............3.9		Knepper-SF 16	Halicki-SF 7.51	Halicki-SF 2.04
	John-LA 630	D.Robinson-Pit.......3.7			Knepper-SF 7.55	Sutton-LA.............2.04
STRIKEOUTS	**STRIKEOUTS/GAME**	**GAMES**	**SAVES**	**BASE RUNNERS/9**	**ADJUSTED RELIEF RUNS**	**RELIEF RANKING**
Richard-Hou 303	Richard-Hou 9.90	Tekulve-Pit.............91	Fingers-SD 37	Garber-Phi-Atl......8.69	Garber-Phi-Atl......20.2	Bair-Cin...............32.4
Niekro-Atl.............248	Seaver-Cin...........7.83	Littell-StL...............72	Tekulve-Pit 31	Reed-Phi.............9.52	Tekulve-Pit...........18.9	Tekulve-Pit 27.9
Seaver-Cin............226	Vuckovich-StL 6.76	Moore-Chi...............71	Bair-Cin..................28	Fingers-SD 9.56	Bair-Cin...............18.5	Garber-Phi-Atl......26.1
Blyleven-Pit...........182	Blyleven-Pit..........6.72	Moffitt-SF 70	Sutter-Chi 27	Welch-LA 9.62	Reed-Phi..............15.4	Fingers-SD 22.5
Montefusco-SF 177	Niekro-Atl.............6.68	Bair-Cin..................70	Garber-Phi-Atl.........25	Swan-NY 9.72	D'Acquisto-SD 14.0	Forster-LA............20.3
INNINGS PITCHED	**OPPONENTS' AVG.**	**OPPONENTS' OBP**	**EARNED RUN AVERAGE**	**ADJUSTED ERA**	**ADJUSTED STARTER RUNS**	**PITCHER WINS**
Niekro-Atl...........334.1	Richard-Hou 196	Halicki-SF 270	Swan-NY 2.43	Swan-NY 146	Niekro-Atl............35.3	**Niekro-Atl 4.5**
Richard-Hou 275.1	Swan-NY 219	Swan-NY 275	Rogers-Mon.........2.47	Rogers-Mon..........145	Rogers-Mon.........28.1	**Bair-Cin.............. 3.4**
Grimsley-Mon 263.0	Halicki-SF 221	Hooton-LA 275	Vuckovich-StL 2.54	Vuckovich-StL 140	Swan-NY 25.8	**Hooton-LA 3.1**
Perry-SD............260.2	Hooton-LA 226	Christenson-Phi....282	Knepper-SF 2.63	Niekro-Atl.............140	Hooton-LA 24.8	**Tekulve-Pit 3.1**
Knepper-SF 260.0	Seaver-Cin...........227	D.Robinson-Pit......283	Hooton-LA 2.71	Knepper-SF 132	Knepper-SF 24.7	**Carlton-Phi......... 3.1**

Coming into Los Angeles

The Dodgers, who lost coach Jim Gilliam to cancer, became the first team in history to draw more than three million fans. While the AL surpassed the NL in overall attendance, thanks to the addition of two extra teams in 1977, the average Senior Circuit team drew approximately 200,000 more than their counterparts in the other league in '78.

The NL East compressed to a 24-game first-to-last gap, with the Phillies barely holding off the Pirates, who rose from fourth place with a torrid August stretch. Pittsburgh's Dave Parker was MVP, but the Bucs lacked the starting pitching or power to win. Amazingly, the Cubs had just one player—Dave Kingman—to hit more than 9 homers, ranking 11th in the league in long balls despite playing 81 games in the cozy confines of Wrigley Field.

Deep pitching and big power won the Dodgers another crown. Los Angeles didn't take the division lead until late August, but the Reds had just one top starter (Tom Seaver) and suffered poor performances from key regulars. Pete Rose did make the news, however, collecting his 3,000th hit and fashioning a 44-game hitting streak.

Last-place Atlanta showcased Rookie of the Year Bob Horner and catcher Dale Murphy, playing his first full season. Phil Niekro, at 39, was 19-18 for a team that won just 69 games. Another 39-year-old, San Diego's Gaylord Perry, became the first pitcher to win a Cy Young in each league, and teammate Rollie Fingers paced the NL in saves for the second straight season. The surprising Padres also broke in rookie Ozzie Smith at shortstop.

The NLCS was another breeze for the Dodgers, who hit Phillies starters very hard; only the fourth and final NLCS game was close. Once again, though, Los Angeles couldn't solve the Yankees in the World Series. After winning the first two, the Dodgers were outscored 28-8 as they dropped the last four.

1978 AMERICAN LEAGUE

TEAM	W	L	T	PCT	GB	HW	HL	R	OR	PA	H	2B	3B	HR	BB	SO	HB	SH	AVG	OBP	SLG	OPS	AOPS	BR	ABR	PF	SB	CS	BSA	BSR
East																														
NY	100	63	0	.613	—	55	26	735	**582**	6219	1489	228	38	125	505	695	42	37	.267	.329	.388	717	103	13	26	98	98	42	70	7
Bos	99	64	0	.607	1	**59**	23	796	657	6316	1493	270	46	172	582	835	24	65	.267	.336	.424	760	101	98	23	110	74	51	59	-2
Mil	93	69	0	.574	6.5	54	27	**804**	650	6227	**1530**	265	38	**173**	520	805	32	89	**.276**	**.339**	**.432**	**771**	**114**	**116**	**111**	101	95	53	64	2
Bal	90	71	0	.559	9	51	30	659	633	6079	1397	248	19	154	552	864	22	41	.258	.326	.396	722	108	21	63	94	75	61	55	-5
Det	86	76	0	.531	13.5	47	34	714	653	6299	1520	218	34	129	563	695	31	57	.271	**.339**	.392	731	102	44	22	103	90	38	70	7
Cle	69	90	0	.434	29	42	36	639	694	6011	1400	223	45	106	488	698	26	92	.261	.323	.379	702	98	-21	-15	99	64	63	50	-8
Tor	59	102	0	.366	40	37	44	590	775	6015	1358	217	39	98	448	645	23	77	.250	.308	.359	667	85	-97	-108	102	28	52	35	-12
West																														
KC	92	70	0	.568	—	56	25	743	634	6129	1469	**305**	**59**	98	498	644	30	55	.268	.329	.399	728	101	37	16	103	**216**	84	**72**	**18**
Tex	87	75	0	.537	5	52	30	692	632	6141	1353	216	36	132	**624**	779	32	83	.253	.332	.381	713	99	12	8	101	196	91	68	11
Cal	87	75	0	.537	5	50	31	691	666	6206	1417	226	28	108	539	682	**67**	72	.259	.330	.370	700	99	-13	9	97	86	69	55	-5
Min	73	89	0	.451	19	38	43	666	678	6323	1472	259	47	82	604	684	33	**109**	.267	**.339**	.375	714	99	23	5	103	99	56	64	2
Chi	71	90	0	.441	20.5	38	42	634	731	5955	1423	221	41	106	409	**625**	33	63	.264	.317	.379	696	94	-38	-45	101	83	68	55	-6
Oak	69	93	0	.426	23	38	42	532	690	5914	1304	200	31	100	433	800	25	108	.245	.303	.351	654	87	-121	-94	95	144	117	55	-9
Sea	56	104	0	.350	35	32	49	614	834	6023	1327	229	37	97	522	702	22	68	.248	.314	.359	673	89	-74	-73	100	123	47	**72**	11
Total	1131	—	—	—	—	649	482	9509	—	85857	19952	3325	538	1680	7287	10153	442	1016	.261	.326	.385	711	—	—	—	—	1471	892	62	11

TEAM	CG	SHO	GR	SV	IP	H	HR	BB	SO	BR/9	ERA	AERA	OAV	OOB	PR	APR	PF	OSB	OCS	FA	E	WPB	DP	FW	PW	BW	BSW	DIF
East																												
NY	39	16	188	**36**	1460.2	**1321**	111	478	817	**11.3**	**3.18**	115	**.243**	**.306**	**95**	78	97	83	61	**.982**	113	54	134	1.5	8.0	2.7	.6	5.6
Bos	57	15	178	26	1472.2	1530	137	464	706	12.4	3.54	**116**	.270	.327	37	**85**	109	114	55	.977	146	**24**	171	-.3	**8.8**	2.4	-.3	7.0
Mil	62	**19**	173	24	1436.0	1442	109	**398**	577	11.8	3.65	104	.262	.313	17	20	101	**80**	46	.977	150	38	144	-.6	2.1	**11.4**	.1	-1.0
Bal	**65**	16	161	33	1429.0	1340	107	509	754	11.7	3.56	99	.251	.316	32	-8	94	81	68	**.982**	**110**	51	166	**1.6**	-.8	6.5	-.6	2.8
Det	60	12	157	21	1455.2	1441	135	503	684	12.2	3.64	107	.263	.325	20	38	103	85	59	.981	118	58	**177**	1.2	3.9	2.3	.6	-3.0
Cle	36	6	214	28	1407.1	1397	**100**	568	739	12.7	3.97	95	.261	.332	-33	-31	100	129	59	.980	123	71	142	.8	-3.2	-1.5	-.9	-5.6
Tor	35	5	213	23	1429.1	1529	149	614	758	13.6	4.54	87	.279	.351	-123	-90	105	101	66	.979	131	63	163	.4	-9.3	-11.1	-1.3	-.2
West																												
KC	53	14	208	33	1439.0	1350	108	478	657	11.6	3.44	111	.251	.313	52	59	101	90	52	.976	150	48	153	-.6	6.1	1.6	**1.8**	2.1
Tex	54	12	170	25	1456.1	1431	108	421	776	11.6	3.36	111	.259	.312	66	62	99	84	75	.976	153	47	140	-.8	6.4	.8	1.0	-1.5
Cal	44	13	193	33	1455.2	1382	125	599	**892**	12.4	3.65	99	.253	.327	19	-5	96	154	**80**	.978	136	41	136	.2	-.5	.9	-.6	6.0
Min	48	9	176	26	1459.2	1468	102	520	703	12.5	3.69	104	.266	.330	11	21	102	91	76	.977	146	58	171	-.4	2.2	.5	.1	-10.4
Chi	38	9	200	33	1409.1	1380	128	586	710	12.8	4.21	90	.259	.334	-71	-66	101	129	60	.977	139	51	130	-.0	-6.8	-4.6	-.7	2.7
Oak	26	11	**271**	29	1433.1	1401	106	582	750	12.6	3.62	101	.259	.330	22	4	97	110	**80**	.971	179	47	145	-2.3	.4	-9.7	-1.0	.6
Sea	28	4	249	20	1419.1	1540	155	567	630	13.6	4.67	82	.280	.348	-144	-130	102	140	55	.978	141	37	174	-.2	-13.4	-7.5	1.0	-3.9
Total	645	161	2751	390	20163.1	—	—	—	—	12.4	3.76	—	.261	.326	—	—	—	—	—	.978	1935	688	2146	—	—	—	—	—

BATTER-FIELDER WINS	BATTING AVERAGE	ON-BASE PERCENTAGE	SLUGGING AVERAGE	ON-BASE PLUS SLUGGING	ADJUSTED OPS	ADJUSTED BATTER RUNS
Smalley-Min 5.1	Carew-Min .333	Carew-Min .411	Rice-Bos .600	Rice-Bos .970	Singleton-Bal 154	Rice-Bos 44.5
DeCinces-Bal 4.2	Oliver-Tex .324	Singleton-Bal .409	Hisle-Mil .533	Hisle-Mil .906	Rice-Bos 153	Singleton-Bal 41.3
Rice-Bos 4.2	Rice-Bos .315	Hargrove-Tex .388	DeCinces-Bal .526	Otis-KC .905	Hisle-Mil 152	Thornton-Cle 37.4
Yount-Mil 4.0	Piniella-NY .314	Randolph-NY .381	Otis-KC .525	Thornton-Cle .893	Thornton-Cle 152	Hisle-Mil 36.5
Fisk-Bos 3.9	Oglivie-Mil .303	Lynn-Bos .380	Thornton-Cle .516	Roberts-Sea .879	DeCinces-Bal 151	Murray-Bal 34.2
RUNS	**HITS**	**DOUBLES**	**TRIPLES**	**HOME RUNS**	**TOTAL BASES**	**RUNS BATTED IN**
LeFlore-Det 126	Rice-Bos 213	Brett-KC 45	Rice-Bos 15	Rice-Bos 46	Rice-Bos 406	Rice-Bos 139
Rice-Bos 121	LeFlore-Det 198	McRae-KC 39	Ford-Min 10	Hisle-Mil 34	Murray-Bal 293	Staub-Det 121
Baylor-Cal 103	Carew-Min 188	Fisk-Bos 39	Carew-Min 10	Baylor-Cal 34	Staub-Det 279	Hisle-Mil 115
Thornton-Cle 97	Munson-NY 183	DeCinces-Bal 37	Yount-Mil 9	Thornton-Cle 33	Baylor-Cal 279	Thornton-Cle 105
Hisle-Mil 96	Staub-Det 175	Ford-Min 36	Garr-Chi 9	Thomas-Mil 32	Thompson-Det 278	
BASES ON BALLS	**STOLEN BASES**	**BASE STEALING RUNS**	**FIELDING RUNS-INFIELD**	**FIELDING RUNS-OUTFIELD**	**OUTFIELD ASSISTS**	**CATCHER CS PCT.**
Hargrove-Tex 107	LeFlore-Det 68	Cruz-Sea 9.5	Belanger-Bal 30.3	Bosetti-Tor 14.4	Lezcano-Mil 18	Sundberg-Tex 48.3
Singleton-Bal 98	Cruz-Sea 59	LeFlore-Det 9.4	Bell-Cle 26.5	Bailor-Tor 9.7	Bosetti-Tor 17	Dempsey-Bal 47.0
Kemp-Det 97	Wills-Tex 52	Wills-Tex 6.5	Wills-Tex 21.7	R.Miller-Cal 8.0	Grubb-Cle-Tex 16	Cerone-Tor 40.2
Thornton-Cle 93	Dilone-Oak 50	Wilson-KC 5.9	Yount-Mil 20.6	Wilson-KC 7.1	Bonds-Chi-Tex 16	Ashby-Tor 39.0
Smalley-Min 85	Wilson-KC 46	Randolph-NY 5.5	Whitaker-Det 20.0	Roberts-Sea 6.1	Bailor-Tor 15	May-Det 38.9
WINS	**WINNING PCT.**	**WINS ABOVE TEAM**	**GAMES STARTED**	**COMPLETE GAMES**	**FEWEST HITS/GAME**	**FEWEST BB/GAME**
Guidry-NY 25	Guidry-NY .893	Guidry-NY 10.6	Leonard-KC 40	Caldwell-Mil 23	Guidry-NY 6.15	Jenkins-Tex 1.48
Caldwell-Mil 22	Stanley-Bos .882	Stanley-Bos 6.1	Flanagan-Bal 40	Leonard-KC 20	Ryan-Cal 7.02	Sorensen-Mil 1.60
Palmer-Bal 21	Gura-KC .800	Gura-KC 5.7	Splittorff-KC 38	Palmer-Bal 19	Gura-KC 7.43	Caldwell-Mil 1.66
Leonard-KC 21	Eckersley-Bos .714	Caldwell-Mil 5.7	Palmer-Bal 38	Matlack-Tex 18	Palmer-Bal 7.48	Matlack-Tex 1.70
	Caldwell-Mil .710	Jenkins-Tex 4.9	D.Martinez-Bal 38		Tiant-Bos 7.84	Rozema-Det 1.76
STRIKEOUTS	**STRIKEOUTS/GAME**	**GAMES**	**SAVES**	**BASE RUNNERS/9**	**ADJUSTED RELIEF RUNS**	**RELIEF RANKING**
Ryan-Cal 260	Ryan-Cal 9.97	Lacey-Oak 74	Gossage-NY 27	Guidry-NY 8.55	Gossage-NY 22.1	Gossage-NY 41.1
Guidry-NY 248	Guidry-NY 8.16	Heaverlo-Oak 69	LaRoche-Cal 25	Hiller-Det 9.65	Stanley-Bos 20.5	Marshall-Min 29.6
Leonard-KC 183	Kravec-Chi 6.83	Sosa-Oak 68	Stanhouse-Bal 24	Caldwell-Mil 9.79	Hiller-Det 15.2	Stanley-Bos 25.4
Flanagan-Bal 167	Underwood-Tor 6.33	Gossage-NY 63	Marshall-Min 21	Jenkins-Tex 9.83	Marshall-Min 14.8	Hiller-Det 24.9
Eckersley-Bos 162	Knapp-Cal 6.02		Hrabosky-KC 20	Gossage-NY 9.92	Sosa-Oak 13.3	Hrabosky-KC 18.7
INNINGS PITCHED	**OPPONENTS' AVG.**	**OPPONENTS' OBP**	**EARNED RUN AVERAGE**	**ADJUSTED ERA**	**ADJUSTED STARTER RUNS**	**PITCHER WINS**
Palmer-Bal 296.0	Guidry-NY .193	Guidry-NY .249	Guidry-NY 1.74	Guidry-NY 210	Guidry-NY 59.6	**Guidry-NY 6.4**
Leonard-KC 294.2	Ryan-Cal .220	Caldwell-Mil .273	Matlack-Tex 2.27	Matlack-Tex 165	Caldwell-Mil 44.7	**Caldwell-Mil 4.8**
Caldwell-Mil 293.1	Palmer-Bal .227	Jenkins-Tex .278	Caldwell-Mil 2.36	Caldwell-Mil 161	Matlack-Tex 38.0	**Gossage-NY 4.3**
Flanagan-Bal 281.1	Gura-KC .229	Matlack-Tex .283	Palmer-Bal 2.46	Goltz-Min 154	Palmer-Bal 36.0	**Palmer-Bal 4.0**
Sorensen-Mil 280.2	Tiant-Bos .234	Gura-KC .283	Goltz-Min 2.49	Palmer-Bal 143	Eckersley-Bos 31.9	**Matlack-Tex 4.0**

The Boston Massacre

Hoping to wipe out the past once and for all, Boston surged to a 14½-game lead by July 19. But when Bob Lemon replaced Billy Martin as New York's manager on July 24, the Yankees began winning. In just 12 days, they cut Boston's lead to 6½, where it remained until early September. With a four-game sweep of the Red Sox at Fenway (dubbed "The Boston Massacre"; no game was close), New York eventually plowed to a 3½-game advantage over the demoralized Sox.

Boston turned it on during the last week, though, winning their final eight to force a tie on the season's last day. In a classic one-game playoff, the Yankees overcame a 2-0 seventh-inning deficit on homers by Bucky Dent and Reggie Jackson to win, 5-4.

Ron Guidry—a remarkable 25-3 with a 1.74 ERA—won the Cy Young for the mostly veteran Yankees. Jim Rice took MVP honors for Boston. Lou Whitaker of Detroit was Rookie of the Year over impressive Milwaukee freshman Paul Molitor. Lost in all the Yankees-Red Sox hysteria was a 93-win season by the Brewers.

The slumping Royals and overachieving Angels were close heading into September, but Kansas City was great in the last month while California went 7-11 in a critical stretch. The Angels were devastated on September 24 when outfielder Lyman Bostock was murdered near Chicago. California finished tied with Texas for second. Jim Fregosi, the last original active Angel, retired as a player on June 1 to take California's managing job, and guided the club to a 62-54 mark.

The ALCS was tight; the last two games were one-run affairs, with the Yankees beating the Royals in four. The second straight Yankees-Dodgers World Series featured another New York comeback. After Los Angeles took the first two at home, New York took the next four. The clincher was a blowout of Don Sutton at Dodger Stadium. Dent and fill-in second baseman Brian Doyle both batted over .400; Reggie Jackson tormented the Dodgers with 2 more homers and drove in 8 runs.

1977 NATIONAL LEAGUE

TEAM	W	L	T	PCT	GB	HW	HL	R	OR	PA	H	2B	3B	HR	BB	SO	HB	SH	AVG	OBP	SLG	OPS	AOPS	BR	ABR	PF	SB	CS	BSA	BSR
EAST																														
Phi	101	61	0	.623	—	**60**	21	**847**	668	6290	1548	266	56	186	573	806	38	59	**.279**	**.346**	**.448**	**794**	**112**	**145**	**102**	105	135	68	67	6
Pit	96	66	0	.593	5	58	23	734	665	6262	**1550**	278	57	133	474	878	34	49	.274	.331	.413	744	100	36	11	104	**260**	120	68	15
StL	83	79	0	.512	18	52	31	737	688	6136	1490	252	56	96	489	823	25	66	.270	.330	.388	718	99	-14	-9	99	134	112	54	-10
Chi	81	81	0	.500	20	46	35	692	739	6286	1489	271	37	111	534	**796**	27	69	.266	.330	.387	717	88	-10	-81	111	64	45	59	-2
Mon	75	87	0	.463	26	38	43	665	736	6282	1474	**294**	50	138	478	877	21	69	.260	.318	.402	720	100	-20	-6	98	88	50	64	2
NY	64	98	0	.395	37	35	44	587	663	6069	1319	227	30	88	529	887	30	63	.244	.313	.346	659	85	-126	-105	97	98	81	55	-7
WEST																														
LA	98	64	0	.605	—	51	30	769	**582**	6327	1484	223	28	**191**	588	896	23	83	.266	.336	.418	754	106	58	54	101	114	62	65	3
Cin	88	74	0	.543	10	48	33	802	725	6261	1513	269	42	181	600	911	25	62	.274	.345	.436	781	**112**	118	100	102	170	64	**73**	15
Hou	81	81	0	.500	17	46	35	680	650	6200	1405	263	**60**	114	515	839	**40**	76	.254	.320	.385	705	102	-42	14	92	187	72	72	**16**
SF	75	87	0	.463	23	38	43	673	711	6215	1392	227	41	134	568	842	21	78	.253	.323	.383	706	94	-37	-38	100	90	59	60	-1
SD	69	93	0	.426	29	35	46	692	834	6353	1397	245	49	120	**602**	1057	29	**90**	.249	.324	.375	699	103	-49	25	90	133	57	70	9
Atl	61	101	0	.377	37	40	41	678	895	6205	1404	218	20	139	537	876	17	83	.254	.320	.376	696	83	-60	-125	111	82	53	61	-1
Total	972	—	—	—	—	547	425	8556	—	74886	17465	3033	526	1631	6487	10488	330	847	.262	.328	.396	724	—	—	—	—	1555	843	65	47

TEAM	CG	SHO	GR	SV	IP	H	HR	BB	SO	BR/9	ERA	AERA	OAV	OOB	PR	APR	PF	OSB	OCS	FA	E	WPB	DP	FW	PW	BW	BSW	DIF
EAST																												
Phi	31	7	246	**47**	1455.2	1451	134	482	856	12.1	3.71	108	.263	.323	32	49	103	119	62	.981	120	48	168	1.3	5.0	**10.3**	.2	3.2
Pit	25	**15**	278	39	1481.2	1406	149	485	890	11.6	3.61	111	.252	.311	50	66	103	102	63	.977	145	57	137	-.0	6.7	1.1	1.1	6.2
StL	26	10	305	31	1446.0	1420	139	532	768	12.3	3.81	102	.260	.326	16	14	100	117	62	.978	139	53	**174**	.3	1.4	-.9	-1.4	2.6
Chi	16	10	319	44	1468.0	1500	128	489	**942**	12.3	4.01	110	.266	.325	-16	57	113	134	85	.977	153	63	147	-.5	5.8	-8.2	-.6	3.5
Mon	31	11	307	33	1481.0	1426	135	579	856	12.3	4.01	96	.255	.325	-17	-26	99	135	63	.980	129	62	128	.8	-2.6	-.6	-.2	-3.4
NY	27	12	248	28	1433.2	**1378**	118	490	911	11.9	3.77	100	.254	.317	22	3	97	127	70	.978	134	**36**	132	.5	.3	-10.6	-1.1	-6.1
WEST																												
LA	34	13	238	39	1475.1	1393	119	**438**	930	**11.3**	**3.22**	**120**	**.251**	**.308**	**113**	**105**	99	108	59	.981	124	48	160	1.1	**10.6**	5.5	-.0	-.0
Cin	33	12	261	32	1437.1	1469	156	544	868	12.8	4.21	93	.267	.334	-49	-45	101	**87**	54	**.984**	**95**	61	154	**2.7**	-4.6	10.1	1.1	-2.4
Hou	**37**	11	234	28	1465.2	1384	**110**	545	871	12.0	3.54	102	**.251**	.319	61	13	92	143	80	.978	142	70	136	.0	1.3	1.4	**1.2**	-4.0
SF	27	10	312	33	1459.0	1501	114	529	854	12.7	3.75	105	.267	.331	26	30	101	158	75	.972	179	43	136	-2.0	3.0	-3.8	-.5	-2.7
SD	6	5	**382**	44	1466.1	1556	160	673	827	13.8	4.43	81	.276	.353	-85	-153	91	120	**87**	.971	189	67	142	-2.5	-15.5	2.5	.5	3.0
Atl	28	5	327	31	1445.1	1581	169	701	915	14.5	4.85	92	.279	.360	-151	-58	114	205	83	.972	175	98	127	-1.7	-5.9	-12.6	-.5	.8
Total	321	121	3457	429	17515.0	—	—	—	—	12.5	3.91	—	.262	.328	—	—	—	—	—	.977	1724	706	1741	—	—	—	—	—

BATTER-FIELDER WINS	BATTING AVERAGE	ON-BASE PERCENTAGE	SLUGGING AVERAGE	ON-BASE PLUS SLUGGING	ADJUSTED OPS	ADJUSTED BATTER RUNS
Schmidt-Phi....... 6.4	Parker-Pit............338	Smith-LA..............427	Foster-Cin............631	Foster-Cin..........1013	Smith-LA..............167	Foster-Cin...........53.7
Foster-Cin........... 5.8	Templeton-StL......322	Morgan-Cin...........417	Luzinski-Phi..........594	Smith-LA............1003	Foster-Cin............164	Smith-LA.............51.2
Parker-Pit........... 5.0	Foster-Cin............320	Tenace-SD............415	Smith-LA..............576	Luzinski-Phi..........988	Luzinski-Phi..........154	Luzinski-Phi.........43.7
Morgan-Cin......... 4.6	Griffey-Cin...........318	Simmons-StL........408	Schmidt-Phi..........574	Schmidt-Phi..........967	Schmidt-Phi..........149	Schmidt-Phi.........40.3
DeJesus-Chi....... 4.2	Simmons-StL........318	Parker-Pit............397	Bench-Cin............540	Parker-Pit............927	Hendrick-SD.........147	Parker-Pit............38.8

RUNS	HITS	DOUBLES	TRIPLES	HOME RUNS	TOTAL BASES	RUNS BATTED IN
Foster-Cin............124	Parker-Pit............215	Parker-Pit...............44	Templeton-StL........18	Foster-Cin..............52	Foster-Cin............388	Foster-Cin............149
Griffey-Cin...........117	Rose-Cin...............204	Cash-Mon...............42	Schmidt-Phi............11	Burroughs-Atl.........41	Parker-Pit............338	Luzinski-Phi..........130
Schmidt-Phi..........114	Templeton-StL......200	Hernandez-StL.......41	Richards-SD...........11	Luzinski-Phi...........39	Luzinski-Phi..........329	Garvey-LA............115
Morgan-Cin...........113	Foster-Cin............197	Cromartie-Mon.......41	Almon-SD..............11	Schmidt-Phi............38	Garvey-LA............322	Burroughs-Atl........114
Parker-Pit............107	Garvey-LA............192			Garvey-LA..............33	Schmidt-Phi..........312	

BASES ON BALLS	STOLEN BASES	BASE STEALING RUNS	FIELDING RUNS-INFIELD	FIELDING RUNS-OUTFIELD	OUTFIELD ASSISTS	CATCHER CS PCT.
Tenace-SD............125	Taveras-Pit.............70	Taveras-Pit............9.1	DeJesus-Chi........45.5	Parker-Pit............23.2	Parker-Pit...............26	Ott-Pit..................42.0
Morgan-Cin...........117	Cedeno-Hou...........61	Cedeno-Hou..........8.5	Trillo-Chi..............30.1	Winfield-SD..........11.6	Winfield-SD.............15	Yeager-LA............39.1
Smith-LA..............104	Richards-SD...........56	Richards-SD..........8.1	Schmidt-Phi.........26.6	Foster-Cin............10.9	Cedeno-Hou...........14	Dyer-Pit................35.4
Schmidt-Phi..........104	Moreno-Pit.............53	Morgan-Cin............7.3	Tyson-StL.............23.9	Hendrick-SD..........7.9	Richards-SD...........13	Hill-SF..................33.9
Cey-LA....................93	Morgan-Cin............49	Lopes-LA...............6.1	Russell-LA...........16.7	Geronimo-Cin........6.6	Foster-Cin..............12	Pocoroba-Atl.........33.5

WINS	WINNING PCT.	WINS ABOVE TEAM	GAMES STARTED	COMPLETE GAMES	FEWEST HITS/GAME	FEWEST BB/GAME
Carlton-Phi..............23	Candelaria-Pit.......800	Seaver-NY-Cin.......8.0	Niekro-Atl...............43	Niekro-Atl...............20	Seaver-NY-Cin.....6.85	Candelaria-Pit......1.95
Seaver-NY-Cin........21	Seaver-NY-Cin......778	Forsch-StL.............6.9	Rogers-Mon...........40	Seaver-NY-Cin........19	Richard-Hou........7.15	John-LA...............2.04
	Christenson-Phi....760	Candelaria-Pit........6.9	Burris-Chi...............39	Rogers-Mon...........17	Carlton-Phi..........7.28	Rau-LA................2.08
	John-LA................741	R.Reuschel-Chi.....5.7	Barr-SF..................38	Carlton-Phi.............17	Hooton-LA...........7.41	Barr-SF...............2.15
	Forsch-StL............741	John-LA.................5.2		Richard-Hou...........13	Candelaria-Pit......7.69	Lemongello-Hou..2.18

STRIKEOUTS	STRIKEOUTS/GAME	GAMES	SAVES	BASE RUNNERS/9	ADJUSTED RELIEF RUNS	RELIEF RANKING
Niekro-Atl.............:262	Koosman-NY.......7.62	Fingers-SD.............78	Fingers-SD.............35	Sosa-LA...............7.77	Gossage-Pit.........34.4	Gossage-Pit.........60.3
Richard-Hou.........:214	Richard-Hou........7.21	Tomlin-SD..............76	Sutter-Chi..............31	Sutter-Chi............7.80	Sutter-Chi............31.3	Sutter-Chi............44.7
Rogers-Mon..........206	Niekro-Atl............7.14	Spillner-SD............76	Gossage-Pit...........26	Gossage-Pit.........8.73	Lavelle-SF...........23.2	Lavelle-SF...........32.7
Carlton-Phi............198	Seaver-NY-Cin.....6.75	Metzger-SD-StL......75	Hough-LA...............22	Seaver-NY-Cin.....9.13	Garber-Phi...........18.7	Garber-Phi...........29.9
Seaver-NY-Cin......196	Matlack-NY..........6.55			Garber-Phi...........9.32	Reed-Phi..............17.7	Reed-Phi..............19.7

INNINGS PITCHED	OPPONENTS' AVG.	OPPONENTS' OBP	EARNED RUN AVERAGE	ADJUSTED ERA	ADJUSTED STARTER RUNS	PITCHER WINS
Niekro-Atl..........330.1	Seaver-NY-Cin......209	Seaver-NY-Cin......258	Candelaria-Pit.....2.34	Candelaria-Pit.......172	Candelaria-Pit......43.3	**Gossage-Pit....... 6.4**
Rogers-Mon.......301.2	Richard-Hou.........218	Candelaria-Pit.......274	Seaver-NY-Cin.....2.58	R.Reuschel-Chi....158	R.Reuschel-Chi...41.9	**Carlton-Phi......... 5.5**
Carlton-Phi.........283.0	Carlton-Phi............223	Hooton-LA............279	Hooton-LA...........2.62	Carlton-Phi............153	Seaver-NY-Cin.....40.2	**R.Reuschel-Chi.. 5.3**
Richard-Hou......267.0	Hooton-LA............225	Carlton-Phi............286	Carlton-Phi...........2.64	Seaver-NY-Cin......150	Carlton-Phi...........39.5	**Candelaria-Pit.... 5.0**
Seaver-NY-Cin...261.1	Koosman-NY........232	Sutton-LA.............289	John-LA...............2.78	Hooton-LA............147	Hooton-LA...........30.1	**Sutter-Chi........... 4.7**

RUNS, RUNS, RUNS

Scoring leapt to its highest since 1970, and although the Astros and Cardinals both pushed their outfield fences out, homers rose 27 percent. More homers were hit in every NL park except Wrigley Field. Stolen bases also rose again, reaching their highest per-game total since 1919.

Larry Dierker, Al Downing, Doug Rader, Ray Sadecki, Joe Torre, and Jimmy Wynn hung 'em up. All had been reduced to part-time status. And with great teams came terrible ones: the last-place Mets, managed by Torre, and Braves, managed for one night by maverick owner Ted Turner, both finished 37 games out of first.

The Expos moved from cozy Jarry Park to Olympic Stadium, a smaller field but with far more seats; attendance more than doubled for Montreal, which showed signs of life under Dick Williams. Outfielder Andre Dawson was Rookie of the Year.

Lou Brock shattered Ty Cobb's career steals mark, but the champ speed demons were the second-place Pirates, whose 260 swipes were the highest NL total since 1913. Despite the thievery, the Bucs scored 113 runs fewer than the division champion Phillies, who boasted seven players with double-figure home runs; Mike Schmidt (who became the first $500,000-a-year player) and Greg Luzinski combined for 77. Steve Carlton won his second Cy Young. Chicago led until August, but crumbled when Bruce Sutter went down with a shoulder injury and Philadelphia won 19 of 20.

While MVP George Foster of Cincinnati was spectacular, the Dodgers were better. Under rookie manager Tommy Lasorda, Los Angeles led by $11\frac{1}{2}$ on May 15, and the Reds never got much closer. Steve Garvey, Ron Cey, Reggie Smith, and Dusty Baker each hit 30 homers, and the superb infield of Garvey, Davey Lopes, Bill Russell, and Cey could not be matched.

While the Dodgers convincingly beat the Phillies in a four-game NLCS, the World Series went to the Yankees in six despite Smith's 3 homers. A different Reggie hit 3 homers in Game 6.

1977 AMERICAN LEAGUE

TEAM	W	L	T	PCT	GB	HW	HL	R	OR	PA	H	2B	3B	HR	BB	SO	HB	SH	AVG	OBP	SLG	OPS	AOPS	BR	ABR	PF	SB	CS	BSA	BSR
EAST																														
NY	100	62	0	.617	—	**55**	26	831	**651**	6260	1576	267	47	184	533	681	28	46	.281	.344	.444	788	**114**	106	**111**	99	93	57	62	-1
Bal	97	64	0	.602	2.5	54	27	719	653	6173	1433	231	25	148	560	945	24	48	.261	.329	.393	722	102	-22	20	94	90	51	64	2
Bos	97	64	0	.602	2.5	51	29	859	712	6184	1551	258	56	**213**	528	905	42	45	.281	.345	**.465**	**810**	106	**145**	56	111	66	47	58	-2
Det	74	88	0	.457	26	39	42	714	751	6177	1480	228	45	166	452	764	20	45	.264	.318	.410	728	92	-28	-63	105	60	46	57	-3
Cle	71	90	0	.441	28.5	37	44	676	739	6204	1476	221	46	100	531	688	34	94	.269	.334	.380	714	97	-32	-12	97	87	87	50	-11
Mil	67	95	0	.414	33	37	44	639	765	6087	1425	255	46	125	443	862	22	60	.258	.314	.389	703	90	-74	-75	100	85	67	56	-5
Tor	54	107	0	.335	45.5	25	55	605	822	6055	1367	230	41	100	499	819	23	81	.252	.316	.365	681	84	-107	-115	101	65	55	54	-5
WEST																														
KC	102	60	0	.630	—	**55**	26	822	**651**	6268	1549	**299**	**77**	146	522	687	**45**	49	.277	.340	.436	776	109	84	75	101	170	87	**66**	7
Tex	94	68	0	.580	8	44	37	767	657	6342	1497	265	39	135	**596**	904	39	**116**	.270	.342	.405	747	102	38	28	101	154	85	64	4
Chi	90	72	0	.556	12	48	33	844	771	6322	1568	254	52	192	559	**666**	34	33	.278	.344	.444	788	113	108	108	100	42	44	49	-6
Min	84	77	0	.522	17.5	48	32	**867**	776	6382	**1588**	273	60	123	563	754	43	81	**.282**	**.348**	.417	765	108	73	82	99	105	65	62	0
Cal	74	88	0	.457	28	39	42	675	695	6113	1380	233	40	131	542	880	36	74	.255	.324	.386	710	96	-47	-22	97	159	89	64	4
Sea	64	98	0	.395	38	29	52	624	855	6044	1398	218	33	133	426	769	35	81	.256	.312	.381	693	88	-94	-91	100	110	67	62	1
Oak	63	98	0	.391	38.5	35	46	605	749	6020	1284	176	37	117	516	910	36	64	.240	.308	.352	660	80	-149	-142	99	**176**	89	**66**	**8**
Total	1131	—	—	—	—	596	535	10247	—	86631	20572	3408	644	2013	7270	11234	461	917	.266	.330	.405	735	—	—	—	—	1462	936	61	-6

TEAM	CG	SHO	GR	SV	IP	H	HR	BB	SO	BR/9	ERA	AERA	OAV	OOB	PR	APR	PF	OSB	OCS	FA	E	WPB	DP	FW	PW	BW	BSW	DIF
EAST																												
NY	52	16	154	34	1449.1	1395	139	486	758	11.8	3.61	110	.254	**.315**	73	57	97	89	60	.979	132	52	151	.6	5.7	**11.0**	.1	1.6
Bal	**65**	11	169	23	1451.0	1414	124	494	737	12.0	3.74	102	.260	.322	51	14	94	77	72	**.983**	**106**	37	**189**	**2.0**	1.4	2.0	.2	10.9
Bos	40	13	209	40	1428.0	1555	158	**378**	758	12.3	4.11	109	.278	.325	-8	52	110	**69**	54	.978	133	**19**	162	.5	5.2	5.6	-.2	5.4
Det	44	3	198	23	1457.0	1526	162	470	784	12.5	4.13	104	.271	.327	-11	26	106	90	69	.978	142	43	153	.0	2.6	-6.3	-.3	-3.1
Cle	45	8	230	30	1452.1	1441	136	550	876	12.5	4.10	97	.261	.329	-6	-19	98	158	64	.979	130	55	145	.7	-1.9	-1.2	-1.1	-6.0
Mil	38	6	215	25	1431.0	1461	136	566	719	13.0	4.32	95	.268	.337	-42	-36	101	105	59	.978	139	61	165	.2	-3.6	-7.5	-.5	-2.7
Tor	40	3	187	20	1428.1	1538	152	623	771	13.7	4.57	93	.278	.350	-81	-51	104	85	75	.974	164	69	133	-1.2	-5.1	-11.4	-.5	-8.3
WEST																												
KC	41	15	219	**42**	1460.2	**1377**	**110**	499	850	11.8	**3.52**	**114**	**.251**	**.315**	**88**	**82**	99	84	51	.978	137	69	145	.3	**8.1**	7.5	.7	4.3
Tex	49	**17**	200	31	1472.1	1412	134	471	864	**11.7**	3.56	**114**	.255	**.315**	81	81	100	**69**	60	.982	117	49	156	1.5	8.0	2.8	.4	.3
Chi	34	3	221	40	1444.2	1557	136	516	842	13.2	4.25	96	.277	.339	-31	-29	100	130	77	.974	159	50	125	-.9	-2.9	10.7	-.6	2.6
Min	35	4	242	25	1442.0	1546	151	507	737	13.0	4.36	91	.278	.340	-48	-63	98	107	67	.978	143	58	184	-.0	-6.3	8.1	.0	1.6
Cal	53	13	185	26	1437.2	1383	136	572	**965**	12.5	3.72	105	.256	.330	54	33	97	129	78	.976	147	61	137	-.2	3.3	-2.2	.4	-8.3
Sea	18	1	**280**	31	1433.0	1508	194	578	785	13.5	4.83	86	.272	.344	-123	-109	102	146	60	.976	147	64	162	-.2	-10.8	-9.0	.1	3.0
Oak	32	4	249	26	1436.2	1459	145	560	788	12.8	4.04	100	.265	.333	3	-3	99	123	**91**	.970	190	67	136	-2.7	-.3	-14.1	**.8**	-1.2
Total	586	117	2958	416	20224.0	—	—	—	—	12.6	4.06	—	.266	.330	—	—	—	—	—	.977	1986	754	2143	—	—	—	—	—

BATTER-FIELDER WINS	BATTING AVERAGE	ON-BASE PERCENTAGE	SLUGGING AVERAGE	ON-BASE PLUS SLUGGING	ADJUSTED OPS	ADJUSTED BATTER RUNS
Carew-Min ... 6.5	Carew-Min ... 388	Carew-Min ... 449	Rice-Bos ... 593	Carew-Min ... 1019	Carew-Min ... 178	Carew-Min ... 69.3
Fisk-Bos ... 4.6	Bostock-Min ... 336	Singleton-Bal ... 438	Carew-Min ... 570	Rice-Bos ... 969	Singleton-Bal ... 167	Singleton-Bal ... 57.7
Brett-KC ... 4.6	Singleton-Bal ... 328	Hargrove-Tex ... 420	Jackson-NY ... 550	Singleton-Bal ... 945	Page-Oak ... 153	Page-Oak ... 39.8
Singleton-Bal ... 4.6	Rivers-NY ... 326	Page-Oak ... 405	Hisle-Min ... 533	Page-Oak ... 926	Jackson-NY ... 150	Jackson-NY ... 38.1
Page-Oak ... 4.5	LeFlore-Det ... 325	Fisk-Bos ... 402	Brett-KC ... 532	Jackson-NY ... 925	Thornton-Cle ... 148	Hargrove-Tex ... 37.9

RUNS	HITS	DOUBLES	TRIPLES	HOME RUNS	TOTAL BASES	RUNS BATTED IN
Carew-Min ... 128	Carew-Min ... 239	McRae-KC ... 54	Carew-Min ... 16	Rice-Bos ... 39	Rice-Bos ... 382	Hisle-Min ... 119
Fisk-Bos ... 106	LeFlore-Det ... 212	Jackson-NY ... 39	Rice-Bos ... 15	Nettles-NY ... 37	Carew-Min ... 351	Bonds-Cal ... 115
Brett-KC ... 105	Rice-Bos ... 206	Lemon-Chi ... 38	Cowens-KC ... 14	Bonds-Cal ... 37	McRae-KC ... 330	Rice-Bos ... 114
	Bostock-Min ... 199	Carew-Min ... 38	Brett-KC ... 13	Scott-Bos ... 33	Cowens-KC ... 318	Hobson-Bos ... 112
	Burleson-Bos ... 194		Bostock-Min ... 12	Jackson-NY ... 32	LeFlore-Det ... 310	Cowens-KC ... 112

BASES ON BALLS	STOLEN BASES	BASE STEALING RUNS	FIELDING RUNS-INFIELD	FIELDING RUNS-OUTFIELD	OUTFIELD ASSISTS	CATCHER CS PCT.
Harrah-Tex ... 109	Patek-KC ... 53	Page-Oak ... 7.5	Campaneris-Tex ... 26.1	Lemon-Chi ... 23.1	Yastrzemski-Bos ... 16	Dempsey-Bal ... 57.7
Singleton-Bal ... 107	Page-Oak ... 42	Patek-KC ... 7.1	Burleson-Bos ... 20.1	Yastrzemski-Bos ... 9.7	Cowens-KC ... 14	Sundberg-Tex ... 56.1
Hargrove-Tex ... 103	Remy-Cal ... 41	Harrah-Tex ... 4.2	Smalley-Min ... 19.7	R.Jones-Sea ... 9.4	Bowling-Tor ... 14	Ashby-Tor ... 48.0
Gross-Oak ... 86	Bonds-Cal ... 41	White-KC ... 3.3	Belanger-Bal ... 18.9	Armas-Oak ... 8.8		Fisk-Bos ... 45.5
Mayberry-KC ... 83	LeFlore-Det ... 39	Remy-Cal ... 3.1	Brett-KC ... 18.0	Lezcano-Mil ... 8.6		May-Det ... 44.1

WINS	WINNING PCT.	WINS ABOVE TEAM	GAMES STARTED	COMPLETE GAMES	FEWEST HITS/GAME	FEWEST BB/GAME
Palmer-Bal ... 20	Splittorff-KC ... 727	Rozema-Det ... 5.0	Palmer-Bal ... 39	Ryan-Cal ... 22	Ryan-Cal ... 5.96	Rozema-Det ... 1.40
Leonard-KC ... 20	T.Johnson-Min ... 696	Goltz-Min ... 4.7	Goltz-Min ... 39	Palmer-Bal ... 22	Blyleven-Tex ... 6.94	Jenkins-Bos ... 1.68
Goltz-Min ... 20	Guidry-NY ... 696	T.Johnson-Min ... 4.6	Garland-Cle ... 38	Leonard-KC ... 21	Palmer-Bal ... 7.42	Hartzell-Cal ... 1.81
Ryan-Cal ... 19	Rozema-Det ... 682	Medich-Oak-Sea ... 4.3	Blue-Oak ... 38	Garland-Cle ... 21	Guidry-NY ... 7.43	Eckersley-Cle ... 1.96
		Tanana-Cal ... 4.1		Tanana-Cal ... 20	Tanana-Cal ... 7.50	Cleveland-Bos ... 2.03

STRIKEOUTS	STRIKEOUTS/GAME	GAMES	SAVES	BASE RUNNERS/9	ADJUSTED RELIEF RUNS	RELIEF RANKING
Ryan-Cal ... 341	Ryan-Cal ... 10.26	Lyle-NY ... 72	Campbell-Bos ... 31	Foucault-Det ... 9.81	Lyle-NY ... 26.2	Campbell-Bos ... 42.7
Leonard-KC ... 244	Tanana-Cal ... 7.65	T.Johnson-Min ... 71	Lyle-NY ... 26	Blyleven-Tex ... 9.86	Campbell-Bos ... 22.3	Lyle-NY ... 42.1
Tanana-Cal ... 205	Guidry-NY ... 7.52	Campbell-Bos ... 69	LaGrow-Chi ... 25	Eckersley-Cle ... 10.01	LaGrow-Chi ... 17.1	Romo-Sea ... 28.3
Palmer-Bal ... 193	Leonard-KC ... 7.50	McClure-Mil ... 68	Kern-Cle ... 18	Guidry-NY ... 10.21	Romo-Sea ... 16.3	LaGrow-Chi ... 25.3
Eckersley-Cle ... 191	Blyleven-Tex ... 6.98	LaGrow-Chi ... 66	LaRoche-Cle-Cal ... 17	Tanana-Cal ... 10.22	Torrealba-Oak ... 16.0	T.Johnson-Min ... 23.0

INNINGS PITCHED	OPPONENTS' AVG.	OPPONENTS' OBP	EARNED RUN AVERAGE	ADJUSTED ERA	ADJUSTED STARTER RUNS	PITCHER WINS
Palmer-Bal ... 319.0	Ryan-Cal ... 193	Eckersley-Cle ... 276	Tanana-Cal ... 2.54	Tanana-Cal ... 155	Tanana-Cal ... 41.8	**Campbell-Bos ... 4.5**
Goltz-Min ... 303.0	Blyleven-Tex ... 214	Blyleven-Tex ... 278	Blyleven-Tex ... 2.72	Blyleven-Tex ... 150	Ryan-Cal ... 38.4	**Lyle-NY ... 4.3**
Ryan-Cal ... 299.0	Guidry-NY ... 224	Leonard-KC ... 283	Ryan-Cal ... 2.77	Ryan-Cal ... 142	Palmer-Bal ... 37.7	**Ryan-Cal ... 4.3**
Leonard-KC ... 292.2	Tanana-Cal ... 227	Guidry-NY ... 283	Guidry-NY ... 2.82	Guidry-NY ... 141	Blyleven-Tex ... 34.8	**Tanana-Cal ... 4.1**
Garland-Cle ... 282.2	Leonard-KC ... 227	Tanana-Cal ... 284	Palmer-Bal ... 2.91	Rozema-Det ... 140	Leonard-KC ... 30.3	**Blyleven-Tex ... 3.7**

Room for Two More

The AL expanded to 14 teams, adding Seattle and Toronto. Runs per team per game rose 13 percent to its highest rate since 1961—not so coincidentally, another expansion year. League attendance was up five million, and two AL teams—the Yankees and Red Sox—drew two million fans in the same year for the first time since 1949.

With free agents Reggie Jackson and Don Gullett, plus holdovers Graig Nettles, Thurman Munson, and Sparky Lyle (the first AL reliever to win a Cy Young), the Yankees leapt from third place in August to win the division. As Boog Powell and Brooks Robinson retired, Baltimore finished second. First baseman Eddie Murray was the league's top rookie, but the Birds' lineup was mediocre. Third-place Boston had an ordinary offense away from Fenway Park. Meanwhile, the awful Tigers debuted Alan Trammell, Lou Whitaker, Lance Parrish, and Jack Morris.

Bill Veeck's ramshackle White Sox led the West for much of the year, but slumped just as the other contenders turned hot. Texas won 14 straight, but Kansas City captured 17 in a row to take the division. The Royals had six players with double-digit homers, excellent defense, and a very deep bullpen. Rod Carew's .388 was the highest batting average since 1941. Nolan Ryan fanned 341 but walked 204, the most since Bob Feller in 1938. With their key players gone, Oakland finished last, below the expansion Mariners, and their attendance was the league's lowest since 1970.

The Yanks and Royals traded booming hits, and wins, in the first four ALCS games. The Royals led the decisive fifth contest at Kansas City, 3-1, after seven. A Yankees run in the eighth tightened the game, and in the ninth, New York scored three times off three pitchers (handing Sparky Lyle his second victory) to move to the World Series.

New York then took it to the Dodgers, winning in six games. Jackson hit 3 home runs in the deciding game, but just as important to the Yankees were pitchers Lyle, Mike Torrez, and Ron Guidry.

1976 NATIONAL LEAGUE

TEAM	W	L	T	PCT	GB	HW	HL	R	OR	PA	H	2B	3B	HR	BB	SO	HB	SH	AVG	OBP	SLG	OPS	AOPS	BR	ABR	PF	SB	CS	BSA	BSR
East																														
Phi	101	61	0	.623	—	53	28	770	557	6236	1505	259	45	110	542	793	40	59	.272	.338	.395	733	110	110	81	104	127	70	64	3
Pit	92	70	0	.568	9	47	34	708	630	6177	1499	249	56	110	433	807	29	61	.267	.321	.391	712	106	49	37	102	130	45	74	13
NY	86	76	0	.531	15	45	37	615	538	6129	1334	198	34	102	561	797	28	92	.246	.319	.352	671	101	-20	9	96	66	58	53	-6
Chi	75	87	0	.463	26	42	39	611	728	6155	1386	216	24	105	490	834	30	75	.251	.313	.356	669	88	-27	-78	109	74	74	50	-10
StL	72	90	0	.444	29	37	44	629	671	6181	1432	243	57	63	512	860	22	86	.260	.323	.359	682	98	1	-11	102	123	55	69	8
Mon	55	107	0	.340	46	27	53	531	734	5992	1275	224	32	94	433	841	16	75	.235	.291	.340	631	80	-110	-134	105	86	44	66	4
West																														
Cin	102	60	0	.630	—	49	32	857	633	6538	1599	271	63	141	681	902	28	67	.280	.357	.424	781	125	219	195	103	210	57	79	26
LA	92	70	0	.568	10	49	32	608	543	6125	1371	200	34	91	486	744	29	91	.251	.313	.349	662	95	-41	-35	99	144	55	72	12
Hou	80	82	0	.494	22	46	36	625	657	6111	1401	195	50	66	530	719	21	57	.256	.322	.347	669	104	-22	32	92	150	57	72	13
SF	74	88	0	.457	28	40	41	595	686	6123	1340	211	37	85	518	778	25	80	.246	.312	.345	657	89	-49	-67	103	88	55	62	0
SD	73	89	0	.451	29	42	38	570	662	6047	1327	216	37	64	488	716	23	125	.247	.310	.337	647	97	-66	-18	92	92	46	67	4
Atl	70	92	0	.432	32	34	47	620	700	6107	1309	170	30	82	589	811	19	107	.245	.320	.334	654	87	-45	-78	106	74	61	55	-5
Total	972	—	—	—	—	511	461	7739	—	73921	16778	2652	499	1113	6263	9602	310	975	.255	.320	.361	681	—	—	—	—	1364	677	67	63

TEAM	CG	SHO	GR	SV	IP	H	HR	BB	SO	BR/9	ERA	AERA	OAV	OOB	PR	APR	PF	OSB	OCS	FA	E	WPB	DP	FW	PW	BW	BSW	DIF
East																												
Phi	34	9	247	44	1459.0	1377	98	397	918	11.1	3.08	116	.250	.301	69	78	102	103	38	.981	115	44	148	1.7	8.3	8.6	-.2	1.6
Pit	45	12	237	35	1466.1	1402	95	460	762	11.5	3.36	105	.253	.310	22	25	101	94	66	.975	163	39	142	-1.0	2.7	3.9	.8	4.6
NY	53	18	183	25	1449.0	1248	97	419	1025	10.5	2.94	114	.233	.290	91	68	96	103	58	.979	131	51	116	.8	7.2	1.0	-1.2	-2.8
Chi	27	12	329	33	1471.1	1511	123	490	850	12.4	3.93	99	.268	.327	-71	-8	111	112	59	.978	140	49	145	.3	-.8	-8.3	-1.6	4.5
StL	35	15	298	26	1453.2	1416	91	581	731	12.5	3.60	99	.258	.329	-16	-4	102	87	72	.973	174	77	163	-1.7	-.4	-1.2	.3	-6.0
Mon	26	10	309	21	1440.0	1442	89	659	783	13.4	3.99	94	.266	.347	-79	-36	107	113	69	.976	155	74	179	-.6	-3.8	-14.2	-.1	-7.2
West																												
Cin	33	12	274	45	1471.0	1436	100	491	790	11.9	3.51	100	.258	.318	-1	-2	100	94	51	.984	102	49	157	2.5	-.2	20.7	2.2	-4.2
LA	47	17	182	28	1470.2	1330	97	479	747	11.2	3.02	113	.243	.305	79	64	97	114	55	.980	128	46	154	1.0	6.8	-3.7	.7	6.2
Hou	42	17	235	29	1444.1	1349	82	662	780	12.7	3.56	91	.250	.332	-9	-59	92	166	59	.978	140	89	155	.3	-6.3	3.4	.8	.7
SF	27	18	304	31	1461.2	1464	68	518	746	12.3	3.53	103	.263	.325	-4	17	104	136	46	.971	186	62	153	-2.4	1.8	-7.1	-.6	1.2
SD	47	11	258	18	1432.1	1368	87	543	652	12.1	3.65	90	.253	.321	-24	-61	94	104	53	.978	141	57	148	.2	-6.5	-1.9	-.1	.3
Atl	33	13	264	27	1438.0	1435	86	564	818	12.8	3.86	98	.261	.332	-58	-11	108	138	51	.973	167	98	151	-1.3	-1.2	-8.3	-1.1	.8
Total	449	164	3120	362	17457.1	—	—	—	—	12.0	3.50	—	.255	.320	—	—	—	—	—	.977	1742	735	1811	—	—	—	—	—

BATTER-FIELDER WINS	BATTING AVERAGE	ON-BASE PERCENTAGE	SLUGGING AVERAGE	ON-BASE PLUS SLUGGING	ADJUSTED OPS	ADJUSTED BATTER RUNS
Morgan-Cin......... 6.7	Madlock-Chi..........339	Morgan-Cin...........444	Morgan-Cin...........576	Morgan-Cin.........1020	Morgan-Cin...........186	Morgan-Cin..........60.2
Schmidt-Phi 5.9	Griffey-Cin 336	Madlock-Chi..........412	Foster-Cin.............530	Madlock-Chi..........912	Watson-Hou..........150	Schmidt-Phi 39.7
Concepcion-Cin 4.2	Maddox-Phi 330	Rose-Cin...............404	Schmidt-Phi 524	Schmidt-Phi 900	Foster-Cin.............149	Watson-Hou.........38.8
Cey-LA................ 3.9	Rose-Cin...............323	Griffey-Cin 401	Monday-Chi 507	Foster-Cin............894	Schmidt-Phi 149	Rose-Cin..............38.1
Maddox-Phi 3.7	Morgan-Cin...........320	Cey-LA..................386	Kingman-NY 506	Rose-Cin..............854	Madlock-Chi..........146	Madlock-Chi.........33.8

RUNS	HITS	DOUBLES	TRIPLES	HOME RUNS	TOTAL BASES	RUNS BATTED IN
Rose-Cin..............130	Rose-Cin..............215	Rose-Cin.................42	Cash-Phi.................12	Schmidt-Phi 38	Schmidt-Phi 306	Foster-Cin.............121
Morgan-Cin...........113	Montanez-SF-Atl...206	Johnstone-Phi.........38	Geronimo-Cin 11	Kingman-NY 37	Rose-Cin...............299	Morgan-Cin...........111
Schmidt-Phi 112	Garvey-LA 200	Maddox-Phi 37	Parker-Pit................10	Monday-Chi 32	Foster-Cin.............298	Schmidt-Phi 107
Griffey-Cin 111	Buckner-LA...........193	Garvey-LA 37	W.Davis-SD 10	Foster-Cin...............29	Garvey-LA 284	Watson-Hou..........102
Monday-Chi 107				Morgan-Cin.............27		Luzinski-Phi 95

BASES ON BALLS	STOLEN BASES	BASE STEALING RUNS	FIELDING RUNS-INFIELD	FIELDING RUNS-OUTFIELD	OUTFIELD ASSISTS	CATCHER CS PCT.
Wynn-Atl...............127	Lopes-LA 63	Lopes-LA 10.4	Royster-Atl...........25.0	Maddox-Phi 14.1	Wynn-Atl 17	Yeager-LA............40.4
Morgan-Cin...........114	Morgan-Cin.............60	Morgan-Cin..........10.1	Stennett-Pit..........23.8	Johnstone-Phi........8.9	Winfield-SD.............15	Sanguillen-Pit 38.8
Schmidt-Phi 100	Taveras-Pit..............58	Taveras-Pit.............8.9	Schmidt-Phi 18.1	Winfield-SD...........7.6	Gross-Hou 13	Swisher-Chi 36.7
Cey-LA...................89	Cedeno-Hou 58	Cedeno-Hou 7.5	Foli-Mon...............16.9	Cruz-Hou 7.1		Kendall-SD...........33.9
Rose-Cin.................86	Brock-StL...............56	Brock-StL 5.7	Concepcion-Cin ...16.8	Wynn-Atl 7.1		Rader-SF 24.3

WINS	WINNING PCT.	WINS ABOVE TEAM	GAMES STARTED	COMPLETE GAMES	FEWEST HITS/GAME	FEWEST BB/GAME
Jones-SD................22	Carlton-Phi...........741	Jones-SD...............6.2	Jones-SD................40	Jones-SD................25	Richard-Hou 6.84	Nolan-Cin............1.02
Sutton-LA................21	Candelaria-Pit.......696	Koosman-NY 5.6	Richard-Hou 39	Koosman-NY 17	Seaver-NY 7.01	Kaat-Phi...............1.27
Koosman-NY 21	Sutton-LA..............677	Niekro-Atl..............4.9	R.Reuschel-Chi 37	Matlack-NY 16	Candelaria-Pit......7.08	Jones-SD.............1.43
Richard-Hou 20	Koosman-NY 677	Carlton-Phi.............4.7	Niekro-Atl................37	Sutton-LA................15	Messersmith-Atl...7.21	Matlack-NY 1.96
Carlton-Phi..............20	Rooker-Pit............652	Sutton-LA...............4.6	Barr-SF 37	Richard-Hou 14	Falcone-StL 7.34	Lonborg-Phi 2.03

STRIKEOUTS	STRIKEOUTS/GAME	GAMES	SAVES	BASE RUNNERS/9	ADJUSTED RELIEF RUNS	RELIEF RANKING
Seaver-NY 235	Seaver-NY 7.80	Murray-Mon 81	Eastwick-Cin...........26	Reed-Phi..............8.58	Hough-LA 17.4	Eastwick-Cin........29.7
Richard-Hou 214	Koosman-NY 7.28	Metzger-SD 77	Lockwood-NY 19	Lockwood-NY 9.35	Eastwick-Cin........15.8	Hough-LA 27.0
Koosman-NY 200	Carlton-Phi...........6.95	Hough-LA 77	Forsch-Hou.............19	Jones-SD.............9.36	Reed-Phi..............15.4	Reed-Phi..............20.1
Carlton-Phi............195	Richard-Hou 6.62	Eastwick-Cin...........71	Hough-LA 18	Sutter-Chi 9.61	Moffitt-SF 13.1	Lavelle-SF............18.9
Niekro-Atl.............173	Zachry-Cin...........6.31	Borbon-Cin 69	Metzger-SD 16	Candelaria-Pit......9.61	Tekulve-Pit 13.1	Moffitt-SF 17.8

INNINGS PITCHED	OPPONENTS' AVG.	OPPONENTS' OBP	EARNED RUN AVERAGE	ADJUSTED ERA	ADJUSTED STARTER RUNS	PITCHER WINS
Jones-SD...........315.1	Richard-Hou 212	Jones-SD.............265	Denny-StL............2.52	Denny-StL.............142	Seaver-NY 26.4	**Hough-LA 3.1**
Richard-Hou 291.0	Seaver-NY 213	Candelaria-Pit.......271	Rau-LA 2.57	Rau-LA 132	Montefusco-SF 24.0	**Eastwick-Cin...... 2.9**
Seaver-NY 271.0	Candelaria-Pit.......216	Seaver-NY 272	Seaver-NY 2.59	Seaver-NY 129	Rau-LA 22.8	**Koosman-NY 2.9**
Niekro-Atl...........270.2	Messersmith-Atl....219	Nolan-Cin.............275	Koosman-NY 2.69	Montefusco-SF 128	Denny-StL............22.1	**Rau-LA 2.9**
Sutton-LA...........267.2	Falcone-StL 222	Koosman-NY 278	Zachry-Cin...........2.74	Zachry-Cin............128	Jones-SD.............20.9	**Denny-StL........... 2.4**

Red Moon Rising

There were no pennant races in the NL's centennial season; the Phillies and Reds ran away with their respective divisions. This was the Phillies' first title of any kind in more than a quarter-century, and they did it convincingly. An extraordinary bullpen supported a lefty-loaded rotation, while Mike Schmidt won his third straight homer crown and a .300-hitting outfield (Jay Johnstone, Garry Maddox, and Greg Luzinski) chipped in. Philadelphia was also defensively strong where it counted.

Cincinnati easily outclassed the Dodgers again in the West as Joe Morgan was a repeat MVP. Pete Rose enjoyed another terrific season, and George Foster began to blossom into a fine power hitter. Walter Alston retired from second-place Los Angeles in September following twenty-three seasons as the franchise's manager.

At midseason of otherwise bad campaigns, the Cubs and Cardinals brought up rookies Bruce Sutter and Garry Templeton. Stolen bases continued to rise as homers fell to their lowest level since 1968. The Cardinals hit just 63 homers, fewest for an NL club since 1963. It was especially tough to homer in Busch Stadium, the Astrodome, or San Diego Stadium.

San Diego's finesse lefty Randy Jones won Cy Young honors, and Houston's hard-throwing starter J.R. Richard blossomed at age 26. Former Cub Billy Williams ended his career in Oakland as the A's dynasty ground to a halt.

The postseason was all Reds. Cincy swept the NLCS in three, and then blew out the Yankees in four to win back-to-back World Series crowns. Foster hit 2 homers in the NLCS, while Johnny Bench homered twice in Game 4 to clinch the World Series sweep.

The Pirates were hit hard after the season. Hurler Bob Moose was killed in an auto crash on October 9, while manager Danny Murtaugh, who had just retired after fifteen seasons, died less than two months later.

1976 AMERICAN LEAGUE

TEAM	W	L	T	PCT	GB	HW	HL	R	OR	PA	H	2B	3B	HR	BB	SO	HB	SH	AVG	OBP	SLG	OPS	AOPS	BR	ABR	PF	SB	CS	BSA	BSR
East																														
NY	97	62	0	.610	—	45	35	730	**575**	6156	1496	231	36	120	470	**616**	35	50	.269	.328	.389	717	**110**	65	**69**	100	163	65	71	13
Bal	88	74	0	.543	10.5	42	39	619	598	6091	1326	213	28	119	519	883	23	57	.243	.310	.358	668	101	-33	2	95	150	61	71	12
Bos	83	79	0	.512	15.5	46	35	716	660	6154	1448	257	53	**134**	500	832	29	55	.263	.324	**.402**	**726**	100	**81**	5	112	95	70	58	-4
Cle	81	78	0	.509	16	44	35	615	615	6029	1423	189	38	85	479	631	11	67	.263	.321	.359	680	100	-4	0	99	75	69	52	-8
Det	74	87	0	.460	24	36	44	609	709	6018	1401	207	38	101	450	730	31	46	.257	.315	.365	680	95	-9	-34	104	107	59	64	3
Mil	66	95	0	.410	32	36	45	570	655	6056	1326	170	38	88	511	909	23	78	.246	.311	.340	651	93	-60	-49	98	62	61	50	-8
West																														
KC	90	72	0	.556	—	49	32	713	611	6197	1490	**259**	**57**	65	484	650	31	71	.269	.327	.371	698	103	39	34	101	218	106	67	11
Oak	87	74	0	.540	2.5	**51**	30	686	598	6106	1319	208	33	113	**592**	818	**45**	58	.246	.323	.361	684	104	15	42	96	**341**	123	**73**	**32**
Min	85	77	0	.525	5	44	37	**743**	704	6307	**1526**	222	51	81	550	714	41	**93**	**.274**	**.341**	.375	716	108	79	66	102	146	75	66	6
Tex	76	86	0	.469	14	39	42	616	652	6269	1390	213	26	80	568	809	29	72	.250	.321	.341	662	92	-31	-43	102	87	45	66	3
Cal	76	86	0	.469	14	38	43	550	631	6101	1265	210	23	63	534	812	42	92	.235	.306	.318	624	88	-104	-69	94	126	80	61	0
Chi	64	97	0	.398	25.5	35	45	586	745	6171	1410	209	46	73	471	739	34	79	.255	.314	.349	663	93	-38	-42	101	120	53	69	8
Total	967	—	—	—	—	505	462	7753	—	73655	16820	2588	467	1122	6128	9143	374	818	.256	.320	.361	681	—	—	—	—	1690	867	66	68

TEAM	CG	SHO	GR	SV	IP	H	HR	BB	SO	BR/9	ERA	AERA	OAV	OOB	PR	APR	PF	OSB	OCS	FA	E	WPB	DP	FW	PW	BW	BSW	DIF
East																												
NY	62	15	156	37	1455.0	**1300**	97	448	674	**10.9**	**3.19**	107	**.241**	**.298**	**53**	37	97	**110**	67	.980	126	55	141	.9	3.9	**7.3**	.8	4.6
Bal	59	16	171	23	1468.2	1396	**80**	489	678	11.7	3.32	99	.255	.315	33	-4	94	127	65	**.982**	**118**	44	157	**1.5**	-.4	.2	.7	5.1
Bos	49	13	195	27	1458.0	1495	109	**409**	673	12.0	3.52	**110**	.267	.318	-1	**52**	110	115	60	.978	141	41	148	.2	**5.5**	.5	-1.0	-3.2
Cle	30	**17**	237	**46**	1432.0	1361	**80**	533	928	12.1	3.47	101	.255	.324	8	7	100	163	72	.980	121	51	159	1.2	.7	.0	-1.5	1.0
Det	55	12	164	20	1431.1	1426	101	550	738	12.6	3.87	96	.263	.331	-56	-22	106	140	71	.974	168	52	161	-1.4	-2.3	-3.6	-.3	1.2
Mil	45	10	202	27	1435.1	1406	99	567	677	12.6	3.64	96	.260	.331	-20	-21	100	144	69	.975	152	70	160	-.5	-2.2	-5.2	-1.5	-5.1
West																												
KC	41	12	**248**	35	1472.1	1356	83	493	735	11.5	3.21	109	.247	.309	51	48	100	146	66	.978	139	**38**	147	.3	5.1	3.6	.6	-.6
Oak	39	15	233	29	1459.1	1412	96	415	711	11.5	3.26	103	.255	.308	42	18	96	126	63	.977	144	51	130	-.0	1.9	4.5	**2.8**	-2.6
Min	29	11	221	23	1459.0	1421	89	610	762	12.8	3.69	97	.259	.335	-29	-20	101	157	81	.973	172	72	**182**	-1.6	-2.1	7.0	.0	.7
Tex	63	15	196	15	1472.0	1464	106	461	773	12.0	3.45	104	.262	.320	10	21	102	120	82	.976	156	57	142	-.7	2.2	-4.6	-.3	-1.7
Cal	**64**	15	177	17	1477.1	1323	95	553	**992**	11.7	3.36	100	**.241**	.313	26	-2	95	191	**88**	.977	150	42	139	-.3	-.2	-7.3	-.6	3.5
Chi	54	10	166	22	1448.0	1460	87	600	802	13.0	4.25	84	.266	.338	-118	-109	101	151	82	.979	130	45	155	.7	-11.6	-4.5	.2	-1.5
Total	590	161	2366	321	17468.1	—	—	—	—	12.0	3.52	—	.256	.320	—	—	—	—	—	.977	1717	618	1821	—	—	—	—	—

BATTER-FIELDER WINS
- **Grich-Bal** 4.8
- **Nettles-NY** 4.2
- **Brett-KC** 4.1
- **Belanger-Bal** 3.7
- **McRae-KC** 3.7

BATTING AVERAGE
- Brett-KC .333
- McRae-KC .332
- Carew-Min .331
- Bostock-Min .323
- LeFlore-Det .316

ON-BASE PERCENTAGE
- McRae-KC .407
- Hargrove-Tex .397
- Carew-Min .395
- Staub-Det .386
- Carty-Cle .379

SLUGGING AVERAGE
- R.Jackson-Bal .502
- Rice-Bos .482
- Nettles-NY .475
- Lynn-Bos .467
- Carew-Min .463

ON-BASE PLUS SLUGGING
- McRae-KC .868
- Carew-Min .858
- R.Jackson-Bal .853
- Brett-KC .839
- Lynn-Bos .835

ADJUSTED OPS
- R.Jackson-Bal 157
- McRae-KC 154
- Tenace-Oak 149
- Carew-Min 149
- Brett-KC 145

ADJUSTED BATTER RUNS
- McRae-KC 39.5
- Carew-Min 38.2
- Brett-KC 35.3
- R.Jackson-Bal 34.8
- Carty-Cle 31.9

RUNS
- White-NY 104
- Carew-Min 97
- Rivers-NY 95
- Brett-KC 94

HITS
- Brett-KC 215
- Carew-Min 200
- Chambliss-NY 188
- Munson-NY 186
- Rivers-NY 184

DOUBLES
- Otis-KC 40
- McRae-KC 34
- Evans-Bos 34
- Carty-Cle 34
- Brett-KC 34

TRIPLES
- Brett-KC 14
- Garner-Oak 12
- Carew-Min 12
- Poquette-KC 10
- Bostock-Min 9

HOME RUNS
- Nettles-NY 32
- R.Jackson-Bal 27
- Bando-Oak 27

TOTAL BASES
- Brett-KC 298
- Chambliss-NY 283
- Rice-Bos 280
- Carew-Min 280
- Nettles-NY 277

RUNS BATTED IN
- L.May-Bal 109
- Munson-NY 105
- Yastrzemski-Bos 102

BASES ON BALLS
- Hargrove-Tex 97
- Harrah-Tex 91
- Grich-Bal 86
- White-NY 83
- Staub-Det 83

STOLEN BASES
- North-Oak 75
- LeFlore-Det 58
- Campaneris-Oak 54
- Baylor-Oak 52
- Patek-KC 51

BASE STEALING RUNS
- Campaneris-Oak 7.7
- Baylor-Oak 7.2
- Rivers-NY 7.0
- North-Oak 6.3
- Patek-KC 6.0

FIELDING RUNS-INFIELD
- Remy-Cal 19.2
- White-KC 18.2
- Nettles-NY 16.9
- Kuiper-Cle 16.8
- Belanger-Bal 16.3

FIELDING RUNS-OUTFIELD
- Beniquez-Tex 12.9
- Hisle-Min 10.9
- Lemon-Chi 7.5
- Evans-Bos 7.2
- Lezcano-Mil 5.8

OUTFIELD ASSISTS
- Beniquez-Tex 18
- Hisle-Min 16
- Evans-Bos 15
- LeFlore-Det 14

CATCHER CS PCT.
- Sundberg-Tex 42.1
- Fisk-Bos 35.7
- Etchebarren-Cal 34.6
- Martinez-KC 33.3
- Haney-Oak 32.5

WINS
- Palmer-Bal 22
- Tiant-Bos 21
- Garland-Bal 20

WINNING PCT.
- Campbell-Min .773
- Garland-Bal .741
- Ellis-NY .680
- Fidrych-Det .679

WINS ABOVE TEAM
- Garland-Bal 6.4
- Fidrych-Det 6.3
- Campbell-Min 6.1
- Tanana-Cal 5.7
- Tiant-Bos 4.9

GAMES STARTED
- Palmer-Bal 40
- Torrez-Oak 39
- Ryan-Cal 39
- Tiant-Bos 38
- Slaton-Mil 38

COMPLETE GAMES
- Fidrych-Det 24
- Tanana-Cal 23
- Palmer-Bal 23

FEWEST HITS/GAME
- Ryan-Cal 6.11
- Tanana-Cal 6.62
- Eckersley-Cle 7.00
- Palmer-Bal 7.29
- Brett-NY-Chi 7.67

FEWEST BB/GAME
- Bird-KC 1.41
- Jenkins-Bos 1.85
- Perry-Tex 1.87
- Blue-Oak 1.90
- Fidrych-Det 1.91

STRIKEOUTS
- Ryan-Cal 327
- Tanana-Cal 261
- Blyleven-Min-Tex 219
- Eckersley-Cle 200
- Hunter-NY 173

STRIKEOUTS/GAME
- Ryan-Cal 10.35
- Eckersley-Cle 9.03
- Tanana-Cal 8.15
- Blyleven-Min-Tex 6.62
- Campbell-Min 6.17

GAMES
- Campbell-Min 78
- Fingers-Oak 70
- Lindblad-Oak 65
- Lyle-NY 64
- LaRoche-Cle 61

SAVES
- Lyle-NY 23
- LaRoche-Cle 21
- Fingers-Oak 20
- Campbell-Min 20
- Littell-KC 16

BASE RUNNERS/9
- Tanana-Cal 9.18
- Gura-KC 9.77
- G.Jackson-Bal-NY 9.81
- Fidrych-Det 9.81
- Burgmeier-Min 9.83

ADJUSTED RELIEF RUNS
- Littell-KC 17.4
- Hiller-Det 17.0
- Fingers-Oak 14.9
- LaRoche-Cle 14.4
- Burgmeier-Min 14.2

RELIEF RANKING
- Hiller-Det 29.5
- Fingers-Oak 28.8
- Littell-KC 24.1
- Lyle-NY 21.5
- Kern-Cle 21.2

INNINGS PITCHED
- Palmer-Bal 315.0
- Hunter-NY 298.2
- Blue-Oak 298.1
- Blyleven-Min-Tex 297.2
- Slaton-Mil 292.2

OPPONENTS' AVG.
- Ryan-Cal .195
- Tanana-Cal .203
- Eckersley-Cle .214
- Palmer-Bal .224
- Brett-NY-Chi .233

OPPONENTS' OBP
- Tanana-Cal .261
- Fidrych-Det .277
- Palmer-Bal .278
- Blue-Oak .279
- Bird-KC .279

EARNED RUN AVERAGE
- Fidrych-Det 2.34
- Blue-Oak 2.35
- Tanana-Cal 2.43
- Torrez-Oak 2.50
- Palmer-Bal 2.51

ADJUSTED ERA
- Fidrych-Det 159
- Blue-Oak 143
- Tanana-Cal 138
- Torrez-Oak 135
- Palmer-Bal 131

ADJUSTED STARTER RUNS
- Fidrych-Det 36.1
- Blue-Oak 34.4
- Tanana-Cal 31.4
- Palmer-Bal 27.5
- Tiant-Bos 24.2

PITCHER WINS
- **Fidrych-Det** 4.5
- **Blue-Oak** 3.5
- **Tanana-Cal** 3.3
- **Fingers-Oak** 3.2
- **Hiller-Det** 3.2

New York State of Mind

Prior to the season, Oakland owner Charlie Finley traded Reggie Jackson and Ken Holtzman to Baltimore. During the year, he tried to sell Vida Blue, Rollie Fingers, and Joe Rudi, but Bowie Kuhn blocked the sales—thus forcing the stubborn Finley, unwilling to pay high salaries, to watch his players test free agency.

Free agency came at a time when the AL set a new attendance record, which invalidated the poormouth cries of many successful owners. Detroit's fortunes were temporarily improved by Mark "The Bird" Fidrych, whose baffling deliveries made him Rookie of the Year and one of the league's best attractions. Tigers attendance increased 38 percent and tickets for his starts were hard to find. But as the economics changed, more stars of the 1960s retired, including Hank Aaron, Bill Freehan, Tony Oliva, and Frank Robinson.

In renovated Yankee Stadium, East champ New York led the league in attendance for the first time since 1964, and did so the remainder of the decade. Thurman Munson was MVP and in-season acquisitions Holtzman, Grant Jackson, and Doyle Alexander bolstered the staff.

The three-time bridesmaid Royals won the West. George Brett won his first batting title, and Whitey Herzog's Royals used a line-drive and speed-based attack. But the real runners were the A's, who swiped an all-time record 341 bases, with eight players in double figures. Bill North, Bert Campaneris, and Don Baylor all topped 50. For all that, the team didn't score much and had just three solid pitchers.

Come-from-behind victories and seesawing leads defined the ALCS. In Game 5 at Yankee Stadium, John Mayberry's two-run homer put Kansas City in front, but New York rallied for a 6-3 lead. Brett's dramatic three-run homer tied the score in the eighth. Yankees first baseman Chris Chambliss ended the series with a homer in the last of the ninth. The momentum didn't carry, as the Yankees lost in four to the overpowering Reds, but the swagger was back.

Texas infielder Danny Thompson died of leukemia after the season.

1975 NATIONAL LEAGUE

TEAM	W	L	T	PCT	GB	HW	HL	R	OR	PA	H	2B	3B	HR	BB	SO	HB	SH	AVG	OBP	SLG	OPS	AOPS	BR	ABR	PF	SB	CS	BSA	BSR
EAST																														
Pit	92	69	0	.571	—	52	28	712	565	6111	1444	255	47	**138**	468	832	**38**	76	.263	.323	**.402**	725	106	43	40	101	49	28	64	1
Phi	86	76	0	.531	6.5	51	30	735	694	6363	1506	**283**	42	125	610	960	31	88	.269	.342	**.402**	744	108	102	65	105	126	57	69	8
NY	82	80	0	.506	10.5	42	39	646	625	6237	1430	217	34	101	501	805	37	75	.256	.319	.361	680	98	-38	-18	97	32	26	55	-2
StL	82	80	1	.506	10.5	45	36	662	689	6207	**1527**	239	46	81	444	**649**	29	92	**.273**	.327	.375	702	97	5	-24	105	116	49	70	8
Mon	75	87	0	.463	17.5	39	42	601	690	6272	1346	216	31	98	579	954	27	110	.244	.317	.348	665	87	-64	-93	105	108	58	65	3
Chi	75	87	0	.463	17.5	42	39	712	827	6323	1419	229	41	95	650	802	30	107	.259	.338	.368	706	97	34	1	105	67	55	55	-5
WEST																														
Cin	108	54	0	.667	—	**64**	17	**840**	586	6418	1515	278	37	124	**691**	916	35	66	.271	**.353**	.401	**754**	**114**	**134**	**123**	101	**168**	36	**82**	**24**
LA	88	74	0	.543	20	49	32	648	**534**	6246	1355	217	31	118	611	825	31	104	.248	.325	.365	690	102	-9	19	96	138	52	73	12
SF	80	81	0	.497	27.5	46	35	659	671	6186	1412	235	45	84	604	775	22	62	.259	.333	.365	698	97	11	-11	103	99	47	68	5
SD	71	91	0	.438	37	38	43	552	683	6151	1324	215	22	78	506	754	37	**133**	.244	.310	.335	645	91	-101	-62	93	85	50	63	1
Atl	67	94	0	.416	40.5	37	43	583	739	6092	1323	179	28	107	543	759	18	72	.244	.313	.346	659	86	-78	-95	103	55	38	59	-1
Hou	64	97	1	.398	43.5	37	44	664	711	6211	1401	218	**54**	84	523	762	32	97	.254	.320	.359	679	101	-39	9	93	133	62	68	8
Total	971	—	—	—	—	542	428	8014	—	74817	17002	2781	458	1233	6730	9793	367	1082	.257	.327	.369	696	—	—	—	—	1176	558	68	63

TEAM	CG	SHO	GR	SV	IP	H	HR	BB	SO	BR/9	ERA	AERA	OAV	OOB	PR	APR	PF	OSB	OCS	FA	E	WPB	DP	FW	PW	BW	BSW	DIF
EAST																												
Pit	43	14	226	31	1437.1	1302	**79**	551	768	11.7	3.01	**119**	.243	.313	98	**92**	99	81	35	.976	151	56	147	.2	**9.6**	4.2	-.4	-2.0
Phi	33	11	283	30	1455.0	1353	111	546	897	11.9	3.82	98	.249	.317	-33	-11	104	69	52	.976	152	60	156	.2	-1.1	6.8	.3	-1.1
NY	40	14	229	31	1466.0	1344	99	580	**989**	12.0	3.39	103	.246	.319	38	19	97	116	63	.976	151	56	144	.3	2.0	-1.9	-.8	1.4
StL	33	13	272	36	1454.2	1452	98	571	824	12.7	3.57	106	.260	.328	8	34	105	110	39	.973	171	86	140	-.8	3.5	-2.5	.3	.5
Mon	30	12	271	25	1480.0	1448	102	665	831	13.1	3.72	104	.259	.339	-17	21	107	78	46	.973	180	85	**179**	-1.3	2.2	-9.7	-.2	3.1
Chi	27	8	**298**	33	1444.1	1587	130	551	850	13.6	4.49	86	.281	.347	-140	-94	107	93	54	.972	179	**50**	152	-1.3	-9.8	.1	-1.1	6.1
WEST																												
Cin	22	8	277	**50**	1459.0	1422	112	487	663	12.0	3.37	106	.257	.319	41	33	99	**61**	29	**.984**	**102**	52	173	**3.0**	3.4	**12.8**	**2.0**	5.8
LA	**51**	**18**	169	21	1469.2	**1215**	104	**448**	894	**10.4**	**2.92**	117	**.225**	**.285**	**114**	85	94	68	33	.979	127	51	106	1.6	8.9	2.0	.7	-6.2
SF	37	9	259	24	1432.2	1406	92	612	856	12.9	3.74	102	.259	.336	-19	9	105	114	47	.976	146	64	164	.5	.9	-1.1	-.0	-.8
SD	40	12	290	20	1463.1	1494	99	521	713	12.5	3.48	100	.266	.329	23	1	96	118	51	.971	188	51	163	-1.8	.1	-6.5	-.4	-1.4
Atl	32	4	267	24	1430.0	1543	101	519	669	13.3	3.91	96	.278	.341	-47	-22	104	147	44	.972	175	90	147	-1.1	-2.3	-9.9	-.7	.5
Hou	39	6	265	25	1458.1	1436	106	679	839	13.3	4.04	84	.262	.343	-67	-113	94	125	**65**	.979	137	113	166	1.1	-11.8	.9	.3	-7.0
Total	427	129	3106	350	17450.1	—	—	—	—	12.4	3.62	—	.257	.327	—	—	—	—	—	.976	1859	814	1837	—	—	—	—	—

BATTER-FIELDER WINS	BATTING AVERAGE	ON-BASE PERCENTAGE	SLUGGING AVERAGE	ON-BASE PLUS SLUGGING	ADJUSTED OPS	ADJUSTED BATTER RUNS
Morgan-Cin.........8.1	Madlock-Chi..........354	Morgan-Cin..........466	Parker-Pit..............541	Morgan-Cin...........974	Morgan-Cin...........169	Morgan-Cin..........57.4
Bench-Cin...........5.4	Simmons-StL.........332	Rose-Cin..............406	Luzinski-Phi..........540	Luzinski-Phi..........934	Watson-Hou..........152	Luzinski-Phi.........43.0
Schmidt-Phi.......5.2	Sanguillen-Pit.......328	Wynn-LA...............403	Schmidt-Phi..........523	Parker-Pit.............898	Luzinski-Phi..........151	Rose-Cin..............33.3
Evans-Atl............4.4	Morgan-Cin...........327	Madlock-Chi..........402	Bench-Cin.............519	Stargell-Pit............891	Parker-Pit.............146	Thornton-Chi.......32.7
Simmons-StL.....3.5	Watson-Hou..........324	Cardenal-Chi........397	Foster-Cin.............518	Schmidt-Phi..........890	Stargell-Pit............145	Watson-Hou.........32.4

RUNS	HITS	DOUBLES	TRIPLES	HOME RUNS	TOTAL BASES	RUNS BATTED IN
Rose-Cin..............112	Cash-Phi..............213	Rose-Cin.................47	Garr-Atl....................11	Schmidt-Phi............38	Luzinski-Phi..........322	Luzinski-Phi..........120
Cash-Phi...............111	Rose-Cin..............210	Cash-Phi.................40	Parker-Pit................10	Kingman-NY...........36	Garvey-LA............314	Bench-Cin.............110
Lopes-LA..............108	Garvey-LA............210	Oliver-Pit.................39	Kessinger-Chi.........10	Luzinski-Phi............34	Parker-Pit.............302	Perez-Cin.............109
Morgan-Cin...........107	Simmons-StL........193	Bench-Cin...............39	Joshua-SF..............10	Bench-Cin...............28	Schmidt-Phi..........294	Staub-NY.............105
Thomas-SF.............99	Millan-NY.............191	Garvey-LA..............38	Gross-Hou..............10		Rose-Cin..............286	

BASES ON BALLS	STOLEN BASES	BASE STEALING RUNS	FIELDING RUNS-INFIELD	FIELDING RUNS-OUTFIELD	OUTFIELD ASSISTS	CATCHER CS PCT.
Morgan-Cin...........132	Lopes-LA................77	Lopes-LA.............12.7	Evans-Atl..............31.3	Maddox-SF-Phi....14.5	Staub-NY................15	Oates-Atl-Phi.......44.2
Wynn-LA...............110	Morgan-Cin............67	Morgan-Cin..........11.2	Stennett-Pit..........25.7	Geronimo-Cin......11.4	Gross-Hou..............14	May-Hou..............42.0
Evans-Atl..............105	Brock-StL................56	Brock-StL...............6.7	Schmidt-Phi.........18.7	Foster-Cin.............9.6	Cardenal-Chi..........14	Grote-NY.............34.3
Schmidt-Phi..........101	Cedeno-Hou...........50	Concepcion-Cin.....5.2	Trillo-Chi...............18.0	Cardenal-Chi.........9.3	Maddox-SF-Phi.......13	Foote-Mon...........32.0
	Cardenal-Chi..........34	Cedeno-Hou..........5.1	Cash-Phi...............17.6	Unser-NY..............8.6	Unser-NY................13	Swisher-Chi.........30.9

WINS	WINNING PCT.	WINS ABOVE TEAM	GAMES STARTED	COMPLETE GAMES	FEWEST HITS/GAME	FEWEST BB/GAME
Seaver-NY..............22	Gullett-Cin.............789	Seaver-NY.............7.2	Messersmith-LA......40	Messersmith-LA......19	Messersmith-LA...6.83	Nolan-Cin.............1.24
Jones-SD................20	Seaver-NY............710	Jones-SD...............6.1	Morton-Atl...............39	Jones-SD................18	Seaver-NY...........6.97	Jones-SD.............1.77
Messersmith-LA......19	Hooton-Chi-LA......667	Hrabosky-StL.........5.2	Rau-LA...................38	Seaver-NY.............15	Warthen-Mon.......6.98	Reed-Atl-StL........1.91
Hooton-Chi-LA........18	Murray-Mon..........652	Murray-Mon...........4.5		Reuss-Pit................15	Sutton-LA.............7.15	Rau-LA.................2.13
Reuss-Pit................18		Hooton-Chi-LA.......4.3			Hooton-Chi-LA.....7.29	Barr-SF.................2.14

STRIKEOUTS	STRIKEOUTS/GAME	GAMES	SAVES	BASE RUNNERS/9	ADJUSTED RELIEF RUNS	RELIEF RANKING
Seaver-NY............243	Montefusco-SF....7.94	Garber-Phi.............71	Hrabosky-StL..........22	Jones-SD.............9.41	Hrabosky-StL.......19.9	Hrabosky-StL.......39.5
Montefusco-SF.....215	Richard-Hou........7.80	McEnaney-Cin........70	Eastwick-Cin...........22	Sutton-LA.............9.45	Apodaca-NY........18.7	Apodaca-NY........20.4
Messersmith-LA....213	Seaver-NY...........7.80	Tomlin-SD...............67	Giusti-Pit.................17	Messersmith-LA...9.65	Hilgendorf-Phi......14.2	Eastwick-Cin........14.7
Carlton-Phi............192	Warthen-Mon.......6.87	Borbon-Cin.............67	McEnaney-Cin........15	Hrabosky-StL.......9.80	Eastwick-Cin........10.9	Garman-StL.........14.5
Richard-Hou.........176	Carlton-Phi..........6.77	Garman-StL............66	Knowles-Chi............15	Hooton-Chi-LA.....9.89	C.Carroll-Cin........10.5	McGraw-Phi.........14.2

INNINGS PITCHED	OPPONENTS' AVG.	OPPONENTS' OBP	EARNED RUN AVERAGE	ADJUSTED ERA	ADJUSTED STARTER RUNS	PITCHER WINS
Messersmith-LA.321.2	Messersmith-LA....213	Sutton-LA.............263	Jones-SD.............2.24	Jones-SD.............156	Messersmith-LA...42.7	**Seaver-NY.........4.6**
Jones-SD...........285.0	Sutton-LA.............213	Jones-SD..............269	Messersmith-LA...2.29	Messersmith-LA....149	Seaver-NY...........37.9	**Messersmith-LA 4.5**
Seaver-NY.........280.1	Seaver-NY............214	Hooton-Chi-LA.....274	Seaver-NY...........2.38	Seaver-NY............148	Jones-SD.............37.4	**Jones-SD............4.5**
Morton-Atl..........277.2	Warthen-Mon........217	Messersmith-LA....275	Reuss-Pit.............2.54	Reuss-Pit..............141	Reuss-Pit.............30.3	**Hrabosky-StL.....4.2**
Niekro-Atl...........275.2	Hooton-Chi-LA......219	Nolan-Cin.............275	Forsch-StL...........2.86	Forsch-StL............133	Montefusco-SF....25.3	**Reuss-Pit...........4.1**

Free and Clear

The Reds cruised in a lopsided pennant "race." Joe Morgan was an easy MVP, enjoying one of the greatest seasons ever for a second baseman. Everyone in Cincinnati's lineup contributed offensively and defensively, and the deep pitching featured left-right relief combo Will McEnaney and Rawly Eastwick.

The NL East was again tightly packed, with just $17^{1}/_{2}$ games separating first from last. Pittsburgh used six strong starting pitchers, including rookie John Candelaria, to withstand Philadelphia's challenge to win its fourth crown in five years. The Pirates favored power and boasted little speed. Philadelphia stole 126 bases, but could hit the long ball, too; third baseman Mike Schmidt won the second of his eight NL home run crowns.

The Cardinals lost 1930s star Joe Medwick, who passed away, and Bob Gibson, who hung up the spikes. Claude Osteen and Vada Pinson also retired. Astros pitcher Don Wilson died in his car of carbon monoxide poisoning.

Pirates second baseman Rennie Stennett had one of the great afternoons of all time, going 7-for-7 in a 22-0 massacre at Wrigley Field to tie Wilbert Robinson's 1892 mark. Giants mainstay Juan Marichal retired, while the club welcomed Jack Clark and Rookie of the Year John Montefusco.

The Pirates were no match for the Reds, who took the NLCS in three games. But the 1975 World Series was different; packed with drama, controversy, great plays, and unexpected heroes, five of the seven games were one-run affairs. The Reds won Games 2, 3, and 7 with dramatic rallies in their last at bats; the Red Sox won two games with big innings and took a nail-biting, 12-inning, Game 6 on Carlton Fisk's barely-fair homer. The next night Morgan's ninth-inning single plated Pete Rose with the Series-winning run.

The biggest change of the year came December 23, when federal arbitrator Peter Seitz ruled baseball's reserve clause invalid, opening the door for free agency, distribution of talent, and increased salaries. Litigant Andy Messersmith (and the newly retired Dave McNally) first benefited from the ruling, but the doors soon blew out and nearly every club entered the market.

1975 AMERICAN LEAGUE

TEAM	W	L	T	PCT	GB	HW	HL	R	OR	PA	H	2B	3B	HR	BB	SO	HB	SH	AVG	OBP	SLG	OPS	AOPS	BR	ABR	PF	SB	CS	BSA	BSR
EAST																														
Bos	95	65	0	.594	—	47	34	**796**	709	6175	**1500**	**284**	44	134	565	741	34	75	**.275**	**.344**	**.417**	**761**	105	**112**	**50**	108	66	58	53	-6
Bal	90	69	0	.566	4.5	44	33	682	**553**	6211	1382	224	33	124	580	834	38	73	.252	.326	.373	699	103	-13	28	94	104	55	65	4
NY	83	77	0	.519	12	43	35	681	588	6038	1430	230	39	110	486	710	30	54	.264	.325	.382	707	100	-3	4	99	102	59	63	2
Cle	79	80	0	.497	15.5	41	39	688	703	6057	1409	201	25	**153**	525	**667**	24	64	.261	.327	.392	719	102	16	14	100	106	89	54	-8
Mil	68	94	0	.420	28	36	45	675	792	6081	1343	242	34	146	553	922	28	73	.250	.320	.389	709	99	-1	-5	101	65	64	50	-8
Det	57	102	0	.358	37.5	31	49	570	786	5852	1338	171	39	125	383	872	28	37	.249	.301	.366	667	84	-101	-124	104	63	57	53	-6
WEST																														
Oak	98	64	0	.605	—	**54**	27	758	606	6184	1376	220	33	151	609	846	**51**	74	.254	.333	.391	724	**106**	35	**50**	98	183	82	**69**	**12**
KC	91	71	0	.562	7	51	30	710	649	6230	1431	263	**58**	118	591	675	29	68	.261	.333	.394	727	102	42	24	103	155	75	67	8
Tex	79	83	0	.488	19	39	41	714	733	6342	1431	208	17	134	**613**	863	25	64	.256	.330	.371	701	99	-9	-2	99	102	62	62	1
Min	76	83	0	.478	20.5	39	43	724	736	6225	1497	215	28	121	563	746	40	62	.271	.341	.386	727	104	47	40	101	81	48	63	1
Chi	75	86	0	.466	22.5	42	39	655	703	6243	1400	209	38	94	611	800	40	50	.255	.331	.358	689	94	-24	-32	101	101	54	65	3
Cal	72	89	0	.447	25.5	35	46	628	723	6141	1324	195	41	55	593	811	27	**97**	.246	.322	.328	650	90	-100	-57	93	**220**	108	67	11
Total	963	—	—	—	—	502	461	8281	—	73779	16861	2662	429	1465	6672	9487	394	791	.258	.328	.379	707	—	—	—	—	1348	811	62	13

TEAM	CG	SHO	GR	SV	IP	H	HR	BB	SO	BR/9	ERA	AERA	OAV	OOB	PR	APR	PF	OSB	OCS	FA	E	WPB	DP	FW	PW	BW	BSW	DIF
EAST																												
Bos	62	11	167	31	1436.2	1463	145	**490**	720	12.4	3.98	102	.265	.325	-33	11	107	111	60	.977	139	**37**	142	.9	1.1	**5.1**	-.7	8.6
Bal	**70**	**19**	149	21	1451.0	1285	110	500	717	**11.1**	**3.17**	112	.242	**.306**	**98**	63	94	93	62	**.983**	**107**	47	**175**	**2.6**	6.4	2.9	.3	-1.7
NY	**70**	11	147	20	1424.0	1325	104	502	809	11.7	3.29	**113**	.249	.314	78	**67**	98	**80**	71	.978	135	48	148	1.1	**6.8**	.4	.0	-5.4
Cle	37	6	218	33	1435.1	1395	136	599	800	12.7	3.84	99	.258	.333	-10	-7	101	121	74	.978	134	66	156	1.1	-.7	1.4	-.9	-1.4
Mil	36	10	223	34	1431.2	1496	133	624	643	13.7	4.34	89	.271	.348	-89	-77	102	118	73	.971	180	85	162	-1.4	-7.9	-.5	-.9	-2.3
Det	52	10	155	17	1396.0	1496	137	533	787	13.3	4.27	94	.275	.340	-77	-36	107	123	68	.972	173	59	141	-1.1	-3.7	-12.7	-.7	-4.3
WEST																												
Oak	36	10	**245**	**44**	1448.0	**1267**	**102**	523	784	11.4	3.27	111	**.236**	**.306**	82	62	96	110	50	.977	143	60	140	.7	6.3	**5.1**	**1.1**	3.7
KC	52	11	204	25	1456.2	1422	108	498	815	12.0	3.47	111	.258	.320	50	61	102	119	64	.976	155	53	151	.0	6.2	2.5	.7	.5
Tex	60	16	224	17	1465.2	1456	123	518	792	12.4	3.86	97	.261	.327	-14	-16	100	96	71	.971	191	60	173	-2.0	-1.6	-.2	.0	1.8
Min	57	7	163	22	1423.0	1381	137	617	846	12.9	4.05	94	.257	.335	-43	-36	101	119	79	.973	170	58	147	-.9	-3.7	4.1	.0	-3.0
Chi	34	7	209	39	1452.1	1489	107	655	799	13.5	3.93	99	.268	.347	-24	-8	103	109	**80**	.978	140	38	155	.9	-.8	-3.3	.2	-2.5
Cal	59	**19**	192	16	1453.1	1386	123	613	**975**	12.6	3.89	92	.253	.330	-18	-54	95	150	65	.971	184	74	164	-1.6	-5.5	-5.8	1.0	3.5
Total	625	137	2296	319	17273.2	—	—	—	—	12.5	3.78	—	.258	.328	—	—	—	—	—	.975	1851	685	1854	—	—	—	—	—

BATTER-FIELDER WINS	BATTING AVERAGE	ON-BASE PERCENTAGE	SLUGGING AVERAGE	ON-BASE PLUS SLUGGING	ADJUSTED OPS	ADJUSTED BATTER RUNS
Harrah-Tex.........6.9	Carew-Min............359	Carew-Min............421	Lynn-Bos..............566	Lynn-Bos..............967	Mayberry-KC........167	Mayberry-KC.......55.3
Carew-Min..........6.7	Lynn-Bos..............331	Mayberry-KC........416	Mayberry-KC........547	Mayberry-KC........963	Carew-Min............159	Singleton-Bal.......50.8
Grich-Bal............6.4	Munson-NY...........318	Singleton-Bal........415	Powell-Cle............524	Carew-Min............919	Lynn-Bos..............159	Carew-Min...........43.9
Mayberry-KC......4.5	Rice-Bos...............309	Harrah-Tex............403	Scott-Mil...............515	Powell-Cle............901	Singleton-Bal.........155	Lynn-Bos.............42.2
Munson-NY.........4.5	C.Washington-Oak...308	Lynn-Bos..............401	Bonds-NY.............512	Bonds-NY.............888	Powell-Cle............153	Bonds-NY............37.5
RUNS	**HITS**	**DOUBLES**	**TRIPLES**	**HOME RUNS**	**TOTAL BASES**	**RUNS BATTED IN**
Lynn-Bos..............103	Brett-KC................195	Lynn-Bos................47	Rivers-Cal..............13	Scott-Mil..................36	Scott-Mil................318	Scott-Mil................109
Mayberry-KC..........95	Carew-Min............192	Jackson-Oak...........39	Brett-KC..................13	Jackson-Oak...........36	Mayberry-KC.........303	Mayberry-KC.........106
Bonds-NY...............93	Munson-NY...........190	McRae-KC..............38	Orta-Chi..................10	Mayberry-KC..........34	Jackson-Oak.........303	Lynn-Bos..............105
Rice-Bos.................92	C.Washington-Oak182	Mayberry-KC..........38	Cowens-KC..............8	Bonds-NY...............32	Lynn-Bos..............299	Jackson-Oak.........104
		Chambliss-NY.........38			Brett-KC................289	
BASES ON BALLS	**STOLEN BASES**	**BASE STEALING RUNS**	**FIELDING RUNS-INFIELD**	**FIELDING RUNS-OUTFIELD**	**OUTFIELD ASSISTS**	**CATCHER CS PCT.**
Mayberry-KC........119	Rivers-Cal...............70	Rivers-Cal............10.5	Belanger-Bal........29.5	Evans-Bos...........18.7	Stanton-Cal.............16	Sundberg-Tex......45.8
Singleton-Bal........118	C.Washington-Oak .40	Otis-KC..................4.7	Rodriguez-Det......26.5	North-Oak............11.4	Evans-Bos..............15	Downing-Chi........42.6
Grich-Bal..............107	Otis-KC...................39	Patek-KC...............4.6	Grich-Bal.............26.2	Sharp-Chi-Mil......11.1		Borgmann-Min.....42.5
Tenace-Oak..........106	Carew-Min..............35	Carew-Min.............4.6	Dent-Chi..............18.2	Manning-Cle........10.2		Duncan-Bal..........42.0
Harrah-Tex.............98	Remy-Cal................34	Alomar-NY.............4.1	Harrah-Tex...........16.5	White-NY...............8.1		Hendricks-Bal......39.7
WINS	**WINNING PCT.**	**WINS ABOVE TEAM**	**GAMES STARTED**	**COMPLETE GAMES**	**FEWEST HITS/GAME**	**FEWEST BB/GAME**
Palmer-Bal..............23	Torrez-Bal............690	Palmer-Bal.............5.1	Wood-Chi................43	Hunter-NY...............30	Hunter-NY...........6.80	Jenkins-Tex..........1.87
Hunter-NY...............23	Leonard-KC..........682	Moret-Bos..............5.0	Kaat-Chi..................41	G.Perry-Cle-Tex......25	Ryan-Cal..............6.91	G.Perry-Cle-Tex...2.06
Blue-Oak.................22	Palmer-Bal...........676	Tanana-Cal............4.8	Hunter-NY...............39	Palmer-Bal..............25	Palmer-Bal...........7.05	Grimsley-Bal........2.15
Torrez-Bal...............20	Blue-Oak..............667	Hunter-NY..............4.8		Jenkins-Tex.............22	Eckersley-Cle.......7.09	Palmer-Bal...........2.23
Kaat-Chi..................20	Lee-Bos................654	Torrez-Bal..............4.8		Blyleven-Min...........20	Blyleven-Min........7.15	Hunter-NY............2.28
STRIKEOUTS	**STRIKEOUTS/GAME**	**GAMES**	**SAVES**	**BASE RUNNERS/9**	**ADJUSTED RELIEF RUNS**	**RELIEF RANKING**
Tanana-Cal............269	Tanana-Cal..........9.41	Fingers-Oak............75	Gossage-Chi...........26	Hunter-NY...........9.22	Gossage-Chi........31.4	Gossage-Chi........46.9
G.Perry-Cle-Tex....233	Ryan-Cal..............8.45	Lindblad-Oak..........68	Fingers-Oak............24	Palmer-Bal...........9.33	Todd-Oak.............17.1	Fingers-Oak.........18.7
Blyleven-Min.........233	Blyleven-Min........7.61	Gossage-Chi...........62	Murphy-Mil..............20	Fingers-Oak.........9.52	Hiller-Det..............13.8	LaRoche-Cle........18.0
Palmer-Bal............193	Eckersley-Cle.......7.33	LaRoche-Cle...........61	LaRoche-Cle...........17	Blyleven-Min......10.02	LaRoche-Cle.........13.5	Todd-Oak.............17.7
Blue-Oak...............189	G.Perry-Cle-Tex...6.86	Foucault-Tex..........59	Drago-Bos...............15	Tanana-Cal........10.18	Lindblad-Oak.......12.3	Hiller-Det.............15.0
INNINGS PITCHED	**OPPONENTS' AVG.**	**OPPONENTS' OBP**	**EARNED RUN AVERAGE**	**ADJUSTED ERA**	**ADJUSTED STARTER RUNS**	**PITCHER WINS**
Hunter-NY..........328.0	Hunter-NY............208	Hunter-NY.............261	Palmer-Bal...........2.09	Palmer-Bal............170	Palmer-Bal...........53.0	**Palmer-Bal..........5.7**
Palmer-Bal.........323.0	Ryan-Cal...............213	Palmer-Bal............266	Hunter-NY............2.58	Eckersley-Cle........146	Hunter-NY............41.7	**Gossage-Chi.......5.1**
G.Perry-Cle-Tex.305.2	Eckersley-Cle........215	Blyleven-Min.........281	Eckersley-Cle.......2.60	Hunter-NY.............144	Tanana-Cal...........31.9	**Hunter-NY..........4.4**
Kaat-Chi............303.2	Palmer-Bal............216	G.Perry-Cle-Tex....284	Tanana-Cal..........2.62	Tanana-Cal...........137	Blyleven-Min........25.6	**Tanana-Cal.........3.2**
Wood-Chi...........291.1	Blyleven-Min.........219	Tanana-Cal...........286	Figueroa-Cal........2.91	Blyleven-Min.........128	Eckersley-Cle.......25.3	**Busby-KC............2.9**

The Red and the Black

Boston had no trouble after June, pulling away while the Brewers and Yankees sagged, and the Orioles didn't get going until it was too late. Red Sox center fielder Fred Lynn was an immediate sensation, winning Rookie of the Year as well as MVP honors. Fellow freshman Jim Rice was nearly as good.

It was a fine season all around for rookies. Dennis Eckersley, Jerry Remy, and Lyman Bostock all played well, and Butch Hobson and Willie Randolph also made their first appearances. It was the end, however, for Harmon Killebrew, who hit .199 in Kansas City.

New York owner George Steinbrenner came out with a huge contract for free agent Catfish Hunter, but his 23 wins couldn't carry a mediocre staff. Cleveland made Frank Robinson the game's first African American manager; Robby also served as a part-time DH and homered in his first at bat Opening Day.

Kansas City's John Mayberry, Hal McRae, and George Brett blossomed, but the Royals, couldn't deter the A's from their fifth straight division title. A 13-of-14 stretch in June put Oakland well ahead. Despite playing in a pitcher's park, the offense was superb, boasting power, speed, and on-base ability. Alvin Dark used seven starters 10 or more times, and Vida Blue won 20 games for the third time. Nolan Ryan went down with elbow problems, allowing his Angels teammate, 21-year-old Frank Tanana, to lead the AL in strikeouts.

Boston easily crushed the A's to win the league pennant, but the World Series was another Hub disappointment. Indelible moments—Luis Tiant's twisting, Bernie Carbo's swinging, Dwight Evans' leaping, Carlton Fisk's gesturing—made the seven-game loss to Cincinnati even tougher to swallow.

Lefty Grove and Casey Stengel died, and the Oakland dynasty also came to an end. A's owner Charlie Finley—not unlike franchise predecessor Connie Mack—would be forced to trade or sell his stars. Many of Finley's "mustache gang" eventually walked away as free agents, happily moving to greener, calmer, but less storied pastures.

1974 NATIONAL LEAGUE

TEAM	W	L	T	PCT	GB	HW	HL	R	OR	PA	H	2B	3B	HR	BB	SO	HB	SH	AVG	OBP	SLG	OPS	AOPS	BR	ABR	PF	SB	CS	BSA	BSR
EAST																														
Pit	88	74	0	.543	—	**52**	29	751	657	6361	**1560**	238	46	114	514	828	38	54	**.274**	.335	.391	726	112	65	85	97	55	31	64	1
StL	86	75	0	.534	1.5	44	37	677	643	6318	1492	216	46	83	531	752	**44**	68	.265	.331	.365	696	100	7	7	100	**172**	62	74	**16**
Phi	80	82	0	.494	8	46	35	676	701	6117	1434	233	**50**	95	469	822	26	84	.261	.320	.373	693	95	-9	-38	105	115	58	66	5
Mon	79	82	0	.491	8.5	42	38	662	657	6190	1355	201	29	86	652	812	33	106	.254	.335	.350	685	92	3	-33	106	124	49	72	10
NY	71	91	0	.438	17	36	45	572	646	6226	1286	183	22	96	597	**735**	29	87	.235	.311	.329	640	85	-100	-97	99	43	23	65	1
Chi	66	96	0	.407	22	32	49	669	826	6344	1397	221	42	110	621	857	29	80	.251	.327	.365	692	95	0	-28	104	78	73	52	-8
WEST																														
LA	102	60	0	.630	—	**52**	29	**798**	**561**	6332	1511	231	34	**139**	597	820	28	86	.272	.342	**.401**	**743**	**118**	**105**	**134**	96	149	75	67	7
Cin	98	64	1	.605	4	50	31	776	631	6372	1437	**271**	35	135	**693**	940	30	68	.260	**.343**	.394	737	114	101	113	99	146	49	**75**	15
Atl	88	74	1	.543	14	46	35	661	563	6279	1375	202	37	120	571	772	24	**109**	.249	.319	.363	682	93	-25	-48	104	72	44	62	0
Hou	81	81	0	.500	21	46	35	653	632	6120	1441	222	41	110	471	864	29	83	.263	.322	.378	700	106	4	35	96	108	65	62	1
SF	72	90	0	.444	30	37	44	634	723	6159	1380	228	38	93	548	869	30	75	.252	.322	.358	680	92	-28	-54	104	107	51	68	6
SD	60	102	0	.370	42	36	45	541	830	6117	1239	196	27	99	564	900	20	83	.229	.302	.330	632	86	-124	-97	95	85	45	65	3
Total	972	—	—	—	—	519	452	8070	—	74935	16907	2642	447	1280	6828	9971	360	983	.255	.326	.367	693	—	—	—	—	1254	625	67	57

TEAM	CG	SHO	GR	SV	IP	H	HR	BB	SO	BR/9	ERA	AERA	OAV	OOB	PR	APR	PF	OSB	OCS	FA	E	WPB	DP	FW	PW	BW	BSW	DIF
EAST																												
Pit	**51**	9	229	17	1466.0	1428	93	543	721	12.3	3.49	99	.256	.323	21	-3	96	85	54	.975	162	58	154	-.5	-.3	8.8	-.4	-.7
StL	37	13	293	20	1473.1	1399	97	616	794	12.5	3.48	103	.254	.329	22	19	100	119	57	.977	147	57	**192**	.4	2.0	.7	**1.2**	1.3
Phi	46	4	283	19	1447.1	1394	111	682	892	13.1	3.91	97	.257	.341	-47	-18	105	122	52	.976	148	75	168	.4	-1.9	-4.0	.0	4.5
Mon	35	8	223	**27**	1429.0	1340	99	544	822	12.0	3.60	107	.249	.319	3	36	106	89	64	.976	153	74	157	.0	3.7	-3.4	.5	-2.4
NY	46	15	212	14	1470.1	1433	99	504	908	12.0	3.42	105	.257	.320	33	30	99	113	48	.975	158	52	150	-.2	3.1	-10.1	-.4	-2.4
Chi	23	6	347	26	1466.1	1593	122	576	895	13.6	4.28	89	.277	.344	-108	-70	106	126	54	.969	199	81	141	-2.6	-7.3	-2.9	-1.3	-.8
WEST																												
LA	33	19	209	23	1465.1	**1272**	112	**464**	**943**	**10.8**	**2.97**	115	**.233**	**.294**	**105**	77	95	76	47	.975	157	55	122	-.2	8.0	**14.0**	.2	-1.0
Cin	34	11	256	**27**	1466.1	1364	126	536	875	11.8	3.41	102	.247	.314	33	13	96	**56**	41	.979	134	59	151	1.2	1.4	11.8	1.1	1.6
Atl	46	**21**	215	22	1474.1	1343	97	488	772	11.3	3.05	**124**	.244	.307	93	**115**	105	107	50	.979	132	64	161	1.3	**12.0**	-5.0	-.5	-.8
Hou	36	18	272	18	1450.2	1396	**84**	601	738	12.6	3.46	100	.255	.331	25	2	96	123	56	**.982**	**113**	65	161	**2.4**	.2	3.6	-.4	-5.9
SF	27	11	292	25	1439.0	1409	116	559	756	12.5	3.78	101	.257	.325	-26	4	105	107	36	.972	175	**51**	153	-1.2	.4	-5.6	.1	-2.7
SD	25	7	**352**	19	1445.2	1536	124	715	855	14.3	4.58	78	.275	.359	-155	-163	99	131	**65**	.973	170	71	126	-.9	-17.0	-10.1	-.2	7.2
Total	439	142	3183	257	17493.2	—	—	—	—	12.4	3.62	—	.255	.326	—	—	—	—	—	.976	1848	762	1836	—	—	—	—	—

BATTER-FIELDER WINS	**BATTING AVERAGE**	**ON-BASE PERCENTAGE**	**SLUGGING AVERAGE**	**ON-BASE PLUS SLUGGING**	**ADJUSTED OPS**	**ADJUSTED BATTER RUNS**
Schmidt-Phi 7.3	Garr-Atl .353	Morgan-Cin .427	Schmidt-Phi .546	Stargell-Pit .944	Stargell-Pit 168	Stargell-Pit 49.3
Morgan-Cin 7.0	Oliver-Pit .321	Stargell-Pit .407	Stargell-Pit .537	Schmidt-Phi .941	Morgan-Cin 160	Morgan-Cin 49.1
Bench-Cin 5.7	Gross-Hou .314	Bailey-Mon .396	Smith-StL .528	Morgan-Cin .921	Smith-StL 156	Schmidt-Phi 44.0
Evans-Atl 4.7	Buckner-LA .314	Schmidt-Phi .395	Bench-Cin .507	Smith-StL .917	Schmidt-Phi 155	Wynn-LA 41.0
Cash-Phi 4.4	Madlock-Chi .313	Gross-Hou .393	Garr-Atl .503	Garr-Atl .886	Wynn-LA 153	Smith-StL 38.9
RUNS	**HITS**	**DOUBLES**	**TRIPLES**	**HOME RUNS**	**TOTAL BASES**	**RUNS BATTED IN**
Rose-Cin 110	Garr-Atl 214	Rose-Cin 45	Garr-Atl 17	Schmidt-Phi 36	Bench-Cin 315	Bench-Cin 129
Schmidt-Phi 108	Cash-Phi 206	Oliver-Pit 38	Oliver-Pit 12	Bench-Cin 33	Schmidt-Phi 310	Schmidt-Phi 116
Bench-Cin 108	Garvey-LA 200	Bench-Cin 38	Cash-Phi 11	Wynn-LA 32	Garr-Atl 305	Garvey-LA 111
Morgan-Cin 107	Oliver-Pit 198	Stargell-Pit 37	Metzger-Hou 10	Perez-Cin 28	Garvey-LA 301	Wynn-LA 108
Brock-StL 105	Stennett-Pit 196		Bowa-Phi 10	Cedeno-Hou 26	Oliver-Pit 293	Simmons-StL 103
BASES ON BALLS	**STOLEN BASES**	**BASE STEALING RUNS**	**FIELDING RUNS-INFIELD**	**FIELDING RUNS-OUTFIELD**	**OUTFIELD ASSISTS**	**CATCHER CS PCT.**
Evans-Atl 126	Brock-StL 118	Brock-StL 14.4	Foli-Mon 34.8	Geronimo-Cin 10.5	Staub-NY 19	Sanguillen-Pit 39.8
Morgan-Cin 120	Lopes-LA 59	Morgan-Cin 8.6	Cash-Phi 30.7	Anderson-Phi 9.8	Gross-Hou 15	Foote-Mon 38.5
Wynn-LA 108	Morgan-Cin 58	Lintz-Mon 8.6	Schmidt-Phi 28.3	Rose-Cin 9.3	Cardenal-Chi 15	Yeager-LA 37.5
Schmidt-Phi 106	Cedeno-Hou 57	Concepcion-Cin 6.9	Evans-Atl 26.6	Zisk-Pit 6.9	Unser-Phi 13	M.May-Hou 36.9
Rose-Cin 106	Lintz-Mon 50	Lopes-LA 6.7	Stennett-Pit 20.9	Cedeno-Hou 6.4	Geronimo-Cin 13	Grote-NY 35.4
WINS	**WINNING PCT.**	**WINS ABOVE TEAM**	**GAMES STARTED**	**COMPLETE GAMES**	**FEWEST HITS/GAME**	**FEWEST BB/GAME**
P.Niekro-Atl 20	Messersmith-LA .769	Messersmith-LA 5.4	Sutton-LA 40	P.Niekro-Atl 18	Capra-Atl 6.76	Barr-SF 1.76
Messersmith-LA 20	Sutton-LA .679	Caldwell-SF 5.3	P.Niekro-Atl 39	Carlton-Phi 17	Messersmith-LA 6.99	Reed-Atl 1.98
Sutton-LA 19	Capra-Atl .667	John-LA 4.2	Messersmith-LA 39	Lonborg-Phi 16	P.Niekro-Atl 7.41	Ellis-Pit 2.09
Billingham-Cin 19	Torrez-Mon .652	Torrez-Mon 4.0	Lonborg-Phi 39	Rooker-Pit 15	Gullett-Cin 7.44	Lonborg-Phi 2.23
	Billingham-Cin .633	Koosman-NY 3.7	Carlton-Phi 39		Wilson-Hou 7.48	Marshall-LA 2.42
STRIKEOUTS	**STRIKEOUTS/GAME**	**GAMES**	**SAVES**	**BASE RUNNERS/9**	**ADJUSTED RELIEF RUNS**	**RELIEF RANKING**
Carlton-Phi 240	Seaver-NY 7.67	Marshall-LA 106	Marshall-LA 21	Murray-Mon 8.91	Marshall-LA 24.2	Marshall-LA 33.7
Messersmith-LA 221	Carlton-Phi 7.42	Hardy-SD 76	Moffitt-SF 15	House-Atl 9.12	Taylor-Mon 20.1	C.Carroll-Cin 26.1
Seaver-NY 201	Bonham-Chi 7.08	Borbon-Cin 73	Borbon-Cin 14	Leon-Atl 9.96	House-Atl 19.8	House-Atl 18.7
P.Niekro-Atl 195	D'Acquisto-SF 6.99	Forsch-Hou 70	Giusti-Pit 12	Messersmith-LA 9.97	Murray-Mon 19.4	Taylor-Mon 18.1
Matlack-NY 195	Norman-Cin 6.81	Sosa-SF 68		P.Niekro-Atl 10.21	C.Carroll-Cin 15.8	Leon-Atl 14.6
INNINGS PITCHED	**OPPONENTS' AVG.**	**OPPONENTS' OBP**	**EARNED RUN AVERAGE**	**ADJUSTED ERA**	**ADJUSTED STARTER RUNS**	**PITCHER WINS**
P.Niekro-Atl 302.1	Capra-Atl .208	Messersmith-LA .277	Capra-Atl 2.28	Capra-Atl 166	P.Niekro-Atl 45.0	**P.Niekro-Atl 5.0**
Messersmith-LA 292.1	Messersmith-LA .212	Matlack-NY .283	P.Niekro-Atl 2.38	P.Niekro-Atl 159	Matlack-NY 35.7	**Messersmith-LA 3.8**
Carlton-Phi 291.0	Gullett-Cin .222	P.Niekro-Atl .284	Matlack-NY 2.41	Matlack-NY 150	Capra-Atl 32.7	**Marshall-LA 3.7**
Lonborg-Phi 283.0	P.Niekro-Atl .225	Reed-Atl .285	Marshall-LA 2.42	Marshall-LA 142	Messersmith-LA 30.9	**Capra-Atl 3.5**
Sutton-LA 276.0	Matlack-NY .226	Capra-Atl .286	Messersmith-LA 2.59	Barr-SF 139	Barr-SF 29.5	**Rooker-Pit 3.3**

Records, Records, Records

Henry Aaron, boosted by a mid-career move to hitter-friendly Fulton County Stadium, had slowly closed in on Babe Ruth's all-time home run record. Despite the media pressure, the hate mail, and the nagging injuries, the 40-year-old Aaron tied the record on Opening Day in Cincinnati and then broke it in Atlanta against Los Angeles on April 8.

The Braves finished third with surprising pitching, but Atlanta never contended. Cincinnati was excellent, but the Dodgers were even better. Los Angeles, led from start to finish. The Dodgers shored up a mediocre bullpen by acquiring Mike Marshall from Montreal, and the muttonchopped screwballer set a big-league mark with 106 appearances and became the first reliever to win the Cy Young. The Dodgers also got big production from center fielder Jimmy Wynn and first baseman Steve Garvey, an All-Star write-in starter and eventual MVP.

With Willies Mays and McCovey departed, the Giants sank to fifth. Their attendance, just 50 percent of their 1971 total, was the league's lowest figure of the decade. Both Felipe and Matty Alou ended their major league careers. Catastrophic control problems forced Pirates hurler Steve Blass from the game, while Orlando Cepeda and Ron Santo's careers ground to disappointing halts in the AL. Former Cardinals pitching great—and beloved TV announcer—Dizzy Dean passed away, and Kent Tekulve, Keith Hernandez, and Gary Carter made their major league bows.

Lou Brock of St. Louis used his 35-year-old legs to steal 118 bases, shattering Maury Wills's record, and his club almost took the NL East crown. But the Cardinals didn't hit enough, and Willie Stargell's Pirates, sometimes known as the Pittsburgh Lumber Company, led the league in batting average and took a see-saw race.

A four-game NLCS went easily to the Dodgers; Pirates reliever Dave Giusti allowed 13 hits in 3.1 innings of "relief." The World Series, however, was no celebration as the Oakland A's beat Los Angeles in five. Four of the games were decided by 3-2 scores.

1974 AMERICAN LEAGUE

TEAM	W	L	T	PCT	GB	HW	HL	R	OR	PA	H	2B	3B	HR	BB	SO	HB	SH	AVG	OBP	SLG	OPS	AOPS	BR	ABR	PF	SB	CS	BSA	BSR
East																														
Bal	91	71	0	.562	—	46	35	659	612	6230	1418	226	27	116	509	770	**58**	72	.256	.322	.370	692	101	-1	16	98	145	58	**71**	**12**
NY	89	73	0	.549	2	47	34	671	623	6181	1451	220	30	101	515	**690**	21	49	.263	.324	.368	692	100	1	8	99	53	35	60	-1
Bos	84	78	0	.519	7	46	35	**696**	661	6214	1449	**236**	31	109	**569**	811	33	64	.264	.333	.377	710	97	42	-5	107	104	58	64	3
Cle	77	85	0	.475	14	40	41	662	694	6019	1395	201	19	131	432	756	26	56	.255	.311	.370	681	96	-38	-34	99	79	68	54	-6
Mil	76	86	0	.469	15	40	41	647	660	6090	1335	228	**49**	120	500	909	27	56	.244	.309	.369	678	94	-42	-40	100	106	75	59	-3
Det	72	90	0	.444	19	36	45	620	768	6106	1375	200	35	131	436	784	24	41	.247	.303	.366	669	89	-68	-89	104	67	38	64	1
West																														
Oak	90	72	0	.556	—	**49**	32	689	**551**	6048	1315	205	37	132	568	876	38	60	.247	.321	.373	694	105	2	42	94	**164**	93	64	4
Tex	84	76	1	.525	5	42	38	690	698	6123	1482	198	39	99	508	710	38	81	**.272**	**.336**	.377	713	**108**	41	**58**	98	113	80	59	-3
Min	82	80	1	.506	8	48	33	673	669	6302	**1530**	190	37	111	520	791	46	64	**.272**	**.336**	.378	714	102	42	20	103	74	45	62	1
Chi	80	80	3	.500	9	46	34	684	721	6235	1492	225	23	**135**	519	858	26	70	.268	.330	**.389**	**719**	103	**50**	32	103	64	53	55	-4
KC	77	85	0	.475	13	40	41	667	662	6263	1448	232	42	89	550	768	32	56	.259	.327	.364	691	94	-1	-37	106	146	76	66	6
Cal	68	94	1	.420	22	36	45	618	657	6085	1372	203	31	95	509	801	45	**82**	.254	.321	.356	677	100	-30	4	95	119	79	60	-1
Total	973	—	—	—	—	516	454	7976	—	73896	17062	2564	400	1369	6135	9524	414	751	.258	.323	.371	694	—	—	—	—	1234	758	62	6

TEAM	CG	SHO	GR	SV	IP	H	HR	BB	SO	BR/9	ERA	AERA	OAV	OOB	PR	APR	PF	OSB	OCS	FA	E	WPB	DP	FW	PW	BW	BSW	DIF
East																												
Bal	57	**16**	185	25	1474.0	1393	101	480	701	11.6	3.27	106	.253	.314	56	35	96	91	58	**.980**	128	50	174	1.0	3.7	1.7	**1.2**	2.5
NY	53	13	182	24	1455.1	1402	104	528	829	12.1	3.31	107	.256	.323	50	38	98	**80**	55	.977	142	54	158	.2	4.0	.8	-.2	3.1
Bos	**71**	12	139	18	1455.1	1462	126	463	751	12.1	3.72	103	.262	.320	-16	18	106	108	60	.977	145	51	156	.0	1.9	-.5	.3	1.3
Cle	45	9	214	27	1445.2	1419	138	479	650	12.0	3.80	96	.260	.320	-30	-27	101	92	48	.977	146	**30**	157	-.0	-2.8	-3.6	-.7	3.1
Mil	43	11	189	24	1457.2	1476	126	493	621	12.3	3.76	97	.266	.326	-23	-20	101	103	56	**.980**	**127**	62	168	**1.1**	-2.1	-4.2	-.4	.6
Det	54	7	154	15	1455.2	1443	148	621	869	13.0	4.16	92	.262	.338	-88	-52	106	134	79	.975	158	75	155	-.7	-5.4	-9.3	.0	6.4
West																												
Oak	49	12	**216**	28	1439.2	**1322**	**90**	**430**	755	**11.1**	**2.95**	**113**	**.246**	**.302**	**107**	**67**	92	83	59	.977	141	37	154	.3	**7.0**	4.4	.4	-3.0
Tex	62	**16**	189	12	1433.2	1423	126	449	871	12.0	3.82	94	.260	.318	-33	-39	99	99	60	.974	163	59	164	-1.1	-4.1	**6.1**	-.4	3.4
Min	43	11	189	**29**	1455.1	1436	115	513	934	12.3	3.64	102	.260	.325	-4	14	103	119	**86**	.976	151	43	164	-.3	1.5	2.1	.0	-2.3
Chi	55	11	201	**29**	1465.2	1470	103	548	826	12.7	3.94	95	.263	.332	-52	-30	104	111	69	.977	147	60	**188**	-.0	-3.1	3.3	-.5	.3
KC	54	13	209	17	1471.2	1477	91	482	731	12.2	3.51	109	.263	.322	17	47	106	115	55	.976	152	71	166	-.4	4.9	-3.9	.6	-5.2
Cal	64	13	190	12	1439.0	1339	101	649	**986**	12.7	3.52	98	.248	.332	15	-9	96	98	72	.976	147	73	150	-.0	-.9	.4	-.2	-12.3
Total	650	144	2257	260	17448.2	—	—	—	—	12.2	3.62	—	.258	.323	—	—	—	—	—	.977	1747	665	1954	—	—	—	—	—

BATTER-FIELDER WINS	BATTING AVERAGE	ON-BASE PERCENTAGE	SLUGGING AVERAGE	ON-BASE PLUS SLUGGING	ADJUSTED OPS	ADJUSTED BATTER RUNS
Carew-Min 6.9	Carew-Min .364	Carew-Min .433	D.Allen-Chi .563	D.Allen-Chi .938	Jackson-Oak 170	Burroughs-Tex 50.0
Grich-Bal 6.0	Orta-Chi .316	Yastrzemski-Bos .414	Jackson-Oak .514	Jackson-Oak .905	Burroughs-Tex 164	Jackson-Oak 48.9
Jackson-Oak 5.3	McRae-KC .310	Burroughs-Tex .397	Burroughs-Tex .504	Burroughs-Tex .901	D.Allen-Chi 164	Carew-Min 42.0
Harrah-Tex 3.3	Piniella-NY .305	Maddox-NY .395	Rudi-Oak .484	Carew-Min .879	Carew-Min 149	D.Allen-Chi 37.7
Burroughs-Tex 3.0	Maddox-NY .303	Jackson-Oak .391	Freehan-Det .479	Yastrzemski-Bos .859	Robinson-Cal-Cle 143	Yastrzemski-Bos 32.7

RUNS	HITS	DOUBLES	TRIPLES	HOME RUNS	TOTAL BASES	RUNS BATTED IN
Yastrzemski-Bos 93	Carew-Min 218	Rudi-Oak 39	Rivers-Cal 11	D.Allen-Chi 32	Rudi-Oak 287	Burroughs-Tex 118
Grich-Bal 92	Davis-Bal 181	Scott-Mil 36	Otis-KC 9	Jackson-Oak 29	K.Henderson-Chi 281	Bando-Oak 103
Jackson-Oak 90	Money-Mil 178	McRae-KC 36		Tenace-Oak 26	Burroughs-Tex 279	Rudi-Oak 99
Otis-KC 87	K.Henderson-Chi 176	K.Henderson-Chi 35		Darwin-Min 25	Carew-Min 267	K.Henderson-Chi 95
Carew-Min 86	Rudi-Oak 174	Burroughs-Tex 33		Burroughs-Tex 25		Darwin-Min 94

BASES ON BALLS	STOLEN BASES	BASE STEALING RUNS	FIELDING RUNS-INFIELD	FIELDING RUNS-OUTFIELD	OUTFIELD ASSISTS	CATCHER CS PCT.
Tenace-Oak 110	North-Oak 54	Jackson-Oak 3.8	Nettles-NY 20.3	Evans-Bos 11.6	Murcer-NY 21	Rodriguez-Cal 47.9
Yastrzemski-Bos 104	Carew-Min 38	Coggins-Bal 3.6	Doyle-Cal 17.8	North-Oak 11.4	Maddox-NY 18	Porter-Mil 41.5
Burroughs-Tex 91	Lowenstein-Cle 36	Pinson-KC 2.9	Grich-Bal 15.6	Maddox-NY 10.0	Spikes-Cle 16	Herrmann-Chi 40.0
Grich-Bal 90	Campaneris-Oak 34	Blair-Bal 2.8	Rodriguez-Det 15.0	Piniella-NY 9.3	Piniella-NY 16	Sundberg-Tex 39.1
	Patek-KC 33	North-Oak 2.8	Bell-Cle 14.5	Jackson-Oak 6.2		Borgmann-Min 37.1

WINS	WINNING PCT.	WINS ABOVE TEAM	GAMES STARTED	COMPLETE GAMES	FEWEST HITS/GAME	FEWEST BB/GAME
Jenkins-Tex 25	Cuellar-Bal .688	Jenkins-Tex 7.0	Wood-Chi 42	Jenkins-Tex 29	Ryan-Cal 5.98	Jenkins-Tex 1.23
Hunter-Oak 25	Jenkins-Tex .676	Ryan-Cal 6.3		G.Perry-Cle 28	G.Perry-Cle 6.42	Hunter-Oak 1.30
	Hunter-Oak .676	Hunter-Oak 6.0		Lolich-Det 27	DalCanton-KC 6.93	Holtzman-Oak 1.80
	Tiant-Bos .629	Busby-KC 5.6		Ryan-Cal 26	Hassler-Cal 7.33	Kaat-Chi 2.04
		G.Perry-Cle 5.4		Tiant-Bos 25	Hunter-Oak 7.58	Wright-Mil 2.09

STRIKEOUTS	STRIKEOUTS/GAME	GAMES	SAVES	BASE RUNNERS/9	ADJUSTED RELIEF RUNS	RELIEF RANKING
Ryan-Cal 367	Ryan-Cal 9.93	Fingers-Oak 76	Forster-Chi 24	Hunter-Oak 8.99	Murphy-Mil 24.2	Murphy-Mil 44.3
Blyleven-Min 249	Blyleven-Min 7.98	Murphy-Mil 70	Murphy-Mil 20	Jenkins-Tex 9.29	Lyle-NY 22.0	Hiller-Det 36.8
Jenkins-Tex 225	Jenkins-Tex 6.17	Foucault-Tex 69	Campbell-Min 19	G.Perry-Cle 9.35	Hiller-Det 18.4	Lyle-NY 27.3
G.Perry-Cle 216	Busby-KC 6.10	Lyle-NY 66	Buskey-NY-Cle 18	Jackson-Bal 9.59	Foucault-Tex 17.4	Campbell-Min 23.2
Lolich-Det 202	G.Perry-Cle 6.03	Campbell-Min 63	Fingers-Oak 18	Garland-Bal 9.59	Campbell-Min 15.7	Foucault-Tex 21.7

INNINGS PITCHED	OPPONENTS' AVG.	OPPONENTS' OBP	EARNED RUN AVERAGE	ADJUSTED ERA	ADJUSTED STARTER RUNS	PITCHER WINS
Ryan-Cal 332.2	Ryan-Cal .190	Hunter-Oak .258	Hunter-Oak 2.49	G.Perry-Cle 145	G.Perry-Cle 41.9	**Murphy-Mil 5.0**
Jenkins-Tex 328.1	G.Perry-Cle .204	Jenkins-Tex .262	G.Perry-Cle 2.51	Blyleven-Min 141	Hunter-Oak 35.4	**G.Perry-Cle 4.5**
G.Perry-Cle 322.1	DalCanton-KC .211	G.Perry-Cle .270	Hassler-Cal 2.61	Fitzmorris-KC 137	Tiant-Bos 32.4	**Hiller-Det 3.9**
Wood-Chi 320.1	Hassler-Cal .225	Blyleven-Min .290	Blyleven-Min 2.66	Hunter-Oak 134	Blyleven-Min 30.7	**Hunter-Oak 3.9**
Hunter-Oak 318.1	Hunter-Oak .229	Tiant-Bos .291	Fitzmorris-KC 2.79	Hassler-Cal 133	Jenkins-Tex 28.4	**Blyleven-Min 3.7**

Sprinting to a Dynasty

Following the 1973 World Series, A's manager Dick Williams quit, unable to stomach capricious owner Charlie Finley. Under Alvin Dark, who'd worked for Finley back in the 1960s, the A's won their fourth consecutive AL West title. Catfish Hunter led an extraordinary staff and earned Cy Young honors. Four Oakland batters hit 20 or more homers. Oakland also brought Finley's long-standing speed obsession to fruition, using former Olympic sprinter Herb Washington 92 times as a pinch runner—he never batted or took the field.

Under new skipper Billy Martin, the Rangers leapt from last to second as Fergie Jenkins won 25 games and Jeff Burroughs was MVP. Nolan Ryan fanned 367 hitters for the last-place Angels, but he walked 202.

The Red Sox, leading by 8 games near the end of August, crumbled. Cozy Fenway Park disguised a mediocre offense, and Luis Tiant's heroics weren't enough. Meanwhile, Baltimore caught fire the last two weeks, rising from fourth at the beginning of September to win; the Birds captured 16 of their final 18. Mike Cuellar and Dave McNally were a combined 10-0 with a sub-2.00 ERA in September.

New York finished second on strong pitching, although shoulder troubles ended Mel Stottlemyre's career. Due to stadium renovations, the Yankees played at Shea Stadium in 1974–75; the Yankees drew more people than they had in a decade. Milwaukee gave a job to 18-year-old rookie shortstop Robin Yount, who stayed in the lineup until 1993. Detroit's great era ended as Norm Cash and Al Kaline, who garnered his 3,000th hit, retired.

Oakland wrapped up the ALCS in four, then edged Los Angeles in a competitive five-game World Series. Four of the A's-Dodgers contests were decided by one run. It was Oakland's third straight Series crown, a feat unmatched since the 1951–53 Yankees. Over the winter, though, Finley "forgot" a payment on Hunter's contract, and the pitcher was ruled a free agent.

1973 NATIONAL LEAGUE

TEAM	W	L	T	PCT	GB	HW	HL	R	OR	PA	H	2B	3B	HR	BB	SO	HB	SH	AVG	OBP	SLG	OPS	AOPS	BR	ABR	PF	SB	CS	BSA	BSR
EAST																														
NY	82	79	0	.509	—	43	38	608	588	6164	1345	198	24	85	540	805	23	108	.246	.315	.338	653	88	-82	-78	99	27	22	55	-2
StL	81	81	0	.500	1.5	43	38	643	603	6177	1418	240	35	75	531	796	29	89	.259	.325	.357	682	95	-23	-26	101	100	46	68	6
Pit	80	82	0	.494	2.5	41	40	704	693	6167	1465	**257**	44	154	432	842	27	60	.261	.315	.405	720	107	29	43	98	23	30	43	-5
Mon	79	83	0	.488	3.5	43	38	668	702	6251	1345	190	23	125	**695**	**777**	**44**	**115**	.251	**.340**	.364	704	98	32	7	104	77	68	53	-7
Chi	77	84	0	.478	5	41	39	614	655	6070	1322	201	21	117	575	855	20	75	.247	.320	.357	677	87	-35	-79	108	65	58	53	-6
Phi	71	91	0	.438	11.5	38	43	642	717	6156	1381	218	29	134	476	979	33	56	.249	.310	.371	681	91	-41	-58	103	51	47	52	-5
WEST																														
Cin	99	63	0	.611	—	**50**	31	741	621	6304	1398	232	34	137	639	947	31	78	.254	.332	.383	715	109	46	**78**	96	**148**	55	**73**	**13**
LA	95	66	1	.590	3.5	**50**	31	675	**565**	6267	1473	219	29	110	497	795	28	81	.263	.323	.371	694	101	-6	17	97	109	50	69	6
SF	88	74	0	.543	11	47	34	739	702	6274	1452	212	**52**	161	590	913	35	75	.262	.335	.407	742	107	87	55	104	112	52	68	6
Hou	82	80	0	.506	17	41	40	681	672	6153	1391	216	35	134	469	962	33	83	.251	.312	.376	688	97	-30	-25	99	92	48	66	3
Atl	76	85	1	.472	22.5	40	40	**799**	774	6384	**1497**	219	34	**206**	608	870	34	65	**.266**	.339	**.427**	**766**	**110**	**136**	**78**	108	84	40	68	4
SD	60	102	0	.370	39	31	50	548	770	5985	1330	198	26	112	401	966	21	73	.244	.296	.351	647	92	-114	-67	92	88	36	71	7
Total	971	—	—	—	—	508	462	8062	—	74352	16817	2600	386	1550	6453	10507	358	958	.254	.322	.376	698	—	—	—	—	976	552	64	22

TEAM	CG	SHO	GR	SV	IP	H	HR	BB	SO	BR/9	ERA	AERA	OAV	OOB	PR	APR	PF	OSB	OCS	FA	E	WPB	DP	FW	PW	BW	BSW	DIF
EAST																												
NY	47	15	194	40	1465.0	1345	127	490	**1027**	11.4	3.26	112	.245	.307	65	62	99	67	43	.980	126	**46**	140	1.1	6.5	-8.1	-.4	2.5
StL	42	14	264	36	1460.2	1366	**105**	486	867	11.6	3.25	113	.248	.310	66	67	100	74	53	.975	159	72	149	-.7	7.0	-2.7	.4	-4.0
Pit	26	11	284	**44**	1450.2	1426	110	564	839	12.6	3.73	94	.258	.329	-12	-37	96	84	39	.976	151	51	156	-.3	-3.9	4.5	-.7	-.7
Mon	26	6	272	38	1451.2	1356	128	681	866	12.8	3.71	103	.250	.334	-9	15	104	76	50	.974	163	83	156	-.9	1.6	.7	-.9	-2.4
Chi	27	13	249	40	1437.2	1471	128	**438**	885	12.1	3.66	108	.267	.322	1	42	108	78	53	.975	157	54	155	-.7	4.4	-8.2	-.8	1.8
Phi	**49**	11	257	22	1447.1	1435	131	632	919	13.1	3.99	95	.263	.341	-53	-30	104	65	**60**	.979	134	80	**179**	.7	-3.1	-6.0	-.7	-.8
WEST																												
Cin	39	**17**	267	43	1473.0	1389	135	518	801	11.8	3.40	101	.252	.318	42	7	94	**43**	33	**.982**	**115**	49	162	**1.8**	.7	**8.1**	**1.2**	6.2
LA	45	15	212	38	1491.0	**1270**	129	461	961	**10.6**	**3.00**	**116**	**.231**	**.292**	**109**	**83**	95	74	36	.981	125	71	166	1.2	**8.6**	1.8	.4	2.4
SF	33	8	252	**44**	1452.1	1442	145	485	787	12.1	3.79	101	.257	.318	-21	8	105	103	34	.974	163	73	138	-.9	.8	5.7	.4	.9
Hou	45	14	268	26	1460.2	1389	111	575	907	12.3	3.75	97	.252	.323	-14	-18	99	102	43	.981	116	67	140	1.7	-1.9	-2.6	.1	3.6
Atl	34	9	**287**	35	1462.0	1467	144	575	803	12.7	4.25	93	.263	.332	-95	-44	108	119	**60**	.974	166	75	142	-1.1	-4.6	**8.1**	.2	-7.2
SD	34	10	269	23	1430.0	1461	157	548	845	12.8	4.16	84	.267	.334	-79	-108	96	84	44	.973	170	67	152	-1.3	-11.2	-7.0	.5	-2.0
Total	447	143	3075	429	17482.0	—	—	—	—	12.2	3.66	—	.254	.322	—	—	—	—	—	.977	1745	788	1835	—	—	—	—	—

BATTER-FIELDER WINS	BATTING AVERAGE	ON-BASE PERCENTAGE	SLUGGING AVERAGE	ON-BASE PLUS SLUGGING	ADJUSTED OPS	ADJUSTED BATTER RUNS
Morgan-Cin......... 7.4	Rose-Cin..............338	Singleton-Mon 425	Stargell-Pit...........646	Stargell-Pit..........1038	Stargell-Pit...........187	Stargell-Pit..........62.5
Evans-Atl 6.3	Cedeno-Hou 320	Fairly-Mon............422	Evans-Atl 556	Evans-Atl 959	Perez-Cin.............160	Morgan-Cin..........48.9
Stargell-Pit......... 5.7	Maddox-SF 319	Morgan-Cin...........406	Johnson-Atl...........546	Perez-Cin..............919	Morgan-Cin...........155	Perez-Cin.............47.5
Cedeno-Hou....... 4.6	Perez-Cin..............314	Watson-Hou..........403	Cedeno-Hou 537	Johnson-Atl...........916	Evans-Atl 153	Evans-Atl 46.4
Simmons-StL..... 4.1	Watson-Hou..........312	Evans-Atl 403	Bonds-SF.............530	Cedeno-Hou 913	Cedeno-Hou 152	Singleton-Mon 42.2

RUNS	HITS	DOUBLES	TRIPLES	HOME RUNS	TOTAL BASES	RUNS BATTED IN
Bonds-SF.............131	Rose-Cin..............230	Stargell-Pit.............43	Metzger-Hou...........14	Stargell-Pit.............44	Bonds-SF.............341	Stargell-Pit............119
Morgan-Cin...........116	Garr-Atl.................200	Oliver-Pit................38	Matthews-SF 10	Johnson-Atl............43	Stargell-Pit...........337	May-Hou 105
Rose-Cin...............115	Brock-StL.............193	Staub-NY................36	Maddox-SF 10	Evans-Atl 41	Evans-Atl 331	Evans-Atl 104
Evans-Atl 114	Simmons-StL........192	Simmons-StL...........36	Davis-LA...................9	Aaron-Atl.................40	Johnson-Atl...........305	Bench-Cin.............104
Brock-StL.............110	Oliver-Pit..............191	Rose-Cin.................36		Bonds-SF................39	Oliver-Pit..............303	Singleton-Mon 103

BASES ON BALLS	STOLEN BASES	BASE STEALING RUNS	FIELDING RUNS-INFIELD	FIELDING RUNS-OUTFIELD	OUTFIELD ASSISTS	CATCHER CS PCT.
Evans-Atl 124	Brock-StL................70	Morgan-Cin...........9.5	Kessinger-Chi 26.7	Unser-Phi.............14.3	Singleton-Mon 20	Boone-Phi............47.4
Singleton-Mon 123	Morgan-Cin.............67	Brock-StL..............8.4	Foli-Mon...............18.3	Rose-Cin.................7.6	Staub-NY................17	Hundley-Chi..........40.5
Morgan-Cin...........111	Cedeno-Hou 56	Cedeno-Hou 7.1	Schmidt-Phi 18.1	Williams-Chi...........6.3	Gaston-SD..............16	Oates-Atl..............40.3
McCovey-SF 105	Bonds-SF................43	Baker-Atl...............4.2	Evans-Atl 17.2	Bonds-SF...............5.9	Rose-Cin.................15	Kendall-SD...........36.9
Monday-Chi 92	Lopes-LA 36	Garr-Atl 3.8	Stennett-Pit.........16.5	Cedeno-Hou 5.5		Jutze-Hou 32.8

WINS	WINNING PCT.	WINS ABOVE TEAM	GAMES STARTED	COMPLETE GAMES	FEWEST HITS/GAME	FEWEST BB/GAME
Bryant-SF 24	John-LA 696	Bryant-SF 5.8	Reuss-Hou.............40	Seaver-NY 18	Seaver-NY 6.80	Marichal-SF 1.61
Seaver-NY 19	Gullett-Cin............692	Seaver-NY 4.9	Carlton-Phi.............40	Carlton-Phi..............18	Sutton-LA............6.88	Jenkins-Chi..........1.89
Billingham-Cin 19	Bryant-SF 667	Stone-NY 4.6	Billingham-Cin 40	Billingham-Cin 16	Twitchell-Phi.........6.93	Barr-SF 1.91
Sutton-LA................18	Seaver-NY 655	Giusti-Pit...............3.6	Bryant-SF 39		Wilson-Hou 7.03	Sutton-LA.............1.97
Gullett-Cin..............18	Billingham-Cin 655	Morton-Atl.............3.4	Jenkins-Chi............38		Messersmith-LA...7.07	Seaver-NY 1.99

STRIKEOUTS	STRIKEOUTS/GAME	GAMES	SAVES	BASE RUNNERS/9	ADJUSTED RELIEF RUNS	RELIEF RANKING
Seaver-NY 251	Seaver-NY 7.79	Marshall-Mon.........92	Marshall-Mon..........31	Seaver-NY 8.91	Marshall-Mon.......22.0	Marshall-Mon.......35.4
Carlton-Phi...........223	Moore-Mon 7.71	Borbon-Cin 80	McGraw-NY 25	Sutton-LA............9.02	Borbon-Cin 18.0	Borbon-Cin 24.4
Matlack-NY 205	Matlack-NY 7.62	Sosa-SF.................71	Giusti-Pit.................20	Rogers-Mon.........9.60	Moffitt-SF 15.6	Locker-Chi 21.8
Sutton-LA.............200	Sutton-LA............7.02	Giusti-Pit 67	Brewer-LA...............20	R.Hernandez-Pit10.04	Locker-Chi 12.8	Giusti-Pit..............17.9
	Carlton-Phi...........6.84	Segui-StL...............65		Messersmith-LA.10.06	Giusti-Pit..............12.6	Moffitt-SF 15.6

INNINGS PITCHED	OPPONENTS' AVG.	OPPONENTS' OBP	EARNED RUN AVERAGE	ADJUSTED ERA	ADJUSTED STARTER RUNS	PITCHER WINS
Carlton-Phi.........293.1	Seaver-NY 206	Seaver-NY 252	Seaver-NY 2.08	Seaver-NY 175	Seaver-NY 50.8	**Seaver-NY 5.5**
Billingham-Cin ...293.1	Sutton-LA.............209	Sutton-LA.............257	Sutton-LA.............2.42	Twitchell-Phi..........152	Rogers-Mon.........32.1	**Marshall-Mon..... 4.1**
Seaver-NY 290.0	Wilson-Hou 213	Messersmith-LA....278	Twitchell-Phi.........2.50	Sutton-LA..............144	Sutton-LA............32.0	**Rogers-Mon........ 3.8**
Reuss-Hou.........279.1	Messersmith-LA....214	Gibson-StL...........281	Marshall-Mon.......2.66	Marshall-Mon........143	Twitchell-Phi.........30.5	**Renko-Mon......... 3.5**
Jenkins-Chi........271.0	Renko-Mon 218	Briles-Pit 287	Messersmith-LA...2.70	Renko-Mon 136	Renko-Mon 25.6	**Sutton-LA 3.2**

Power of Belief

The Dodgers cruised along atop the NL West through August, but they picked the wrong time to slump. Cincinnati, barely over .500 through June, had two separate seven-game September win streaks as Los Angeles' pitching rusted down the stretch. The Reds scraped out the division title with just four good hitters; MVP Pete Rose and Joe Morgan again did the heavy lifting.

Dave Winfield joined the Padres without visiting the minors, while Dave Parker debuted in Pittsburgh and Ken Griffey with Cincinnati. The Expos' Mike Marshall was the league's most discussed pitcher, setting a new record with 92 appearances, winning 14, and saving 31. But the biggest number of the year was 713—Henry Aaron's end-of-season career home run total.

The NL East had a nutty race. As no team seemed to be able to clear .500, everyone but Philadelphia had a chance to win in the last week. The Cubs blew a big lead in July; the Cardinals surged ahead in August but fell back. New York sputtered until late August when they won 19 of 26, moving from last to first in 27 days. On September 23 just 2½ separated the front-running Mets from the fifth-place Cubs.

Despite challenges from St. Louis and Pittsburgh, the Mets clinched the day after the season's scheduled ending—thanks to a rainout—as Tom Seaver won in Chicago. New York finished with the lowest winning percentage ever for a champion (.509). Seaver took his second Cy Young in a close vote, while Rusty Staub headed a mediocre offense.

The underdog Mets (slogan: "Ya Gotta Believe!") then took out the favored Reds in a five-game NLCS. Cincinnati won 2-1 twice, but New York won three blowouts, two behind Seaver—shortstop Bud Harrelson did lose a one-sided brawl with Rose. In the World Series, New York fell in seven, with Willie Mays, now a Mets reserve, playing for the last time in the major leagues.

1973 AMERICAN LEAGUE

TEAM	W	L	T	PCT	GB	HW	HL	R	OR	PA	H	2B	3B	HR	BB	SO	HB	SH	AVG	OBP	SLG	OPS	AOPS	BR	ABR	PF	SB	CS	BSA	BSR
East																														
Bal	97	65	0	.599	—	**50**	31	754	**561**	6335	1474	229	**48**	119	**648**	752	**43**	58	.266	**.345**	.389	734	105	**63**	59	101	**146**	64	70	**10**
Bos	89	73	0	.549	8	48	33	738	647	6223	1472	235	30	147	581	799	31	54	.267	.338	**.401**	**739**	101	60	17	106	114	45	**72**	9
Det	85	77	0	.525	12	47	34	642	674	6135	1400	213	32	157	509	722	39	48	.254	.320	.390	710	93	-10	-51	107	28	30	48	-4
NY	80	82	0	.494	17	**50**	31	641	610	6064	1435	212	17	131	489	**680**	22	27	.261	.322	.378	700	99	-25	-10	98	47	43	52	-5
Mil	74	88	0	.457	23	40	41	708	731	6227	1399	229	40	145	563	977	42	61	.253	.325	.388	713	101	2	11	99	110	66	63	1
Cle	71	91	0	.438	26	34	47	680	826	6178	1429	205	29	**158**	471	793	32	40	.256	.315	.387	702	95	-30	-44	102	60	68	47	-11
West																														
Oak	94	68	0	.580	—	**50**	31	**758**	615	6257	1431	216	28	147	595	919	35	**67**	.260	.333	.389	722	**108**	29	**63**	96	128	57	69	8
KC	88	74	0	.543	6	48	33	755	752	6274	1440	239	40	114	644	696	26	49	.261	.339	.381	720	95	34	-18	108	105	69	60	-1
Min	81	81	0	.500	13	37	44	738	692	6331	**1521**	**240**	44	120	598	954	34	34	**.270**	.342	.393	735	102	58	26	104	87	46	65	3
Cal	79	83	0	.488	15	43	38	629	657	6153	1395	183	29	93	509	816	34	60	.253	.318	.348	666	93	-87	-43	93	59	47	56	-3
Chi	77	85	0	.475	17	40	41	652	705	6135	1400	228	38	111	537	952	32	49	.256	.324	.372	696	93	-28	-51	104	83	73	53	-7
Tex	57	105	0	.352	37	35	46	619	844	6113	1397	195	29	110	503	791	27	45	.255	.318	.361	679	94	-65	-42	96	91	53	63	1
Total	972	—	—	—	—	522	450	8314	—	74425	17193	2624	404	1552	6647	9851	397	592	.259	.328	.381	710	—	—	—	—	1058	661	62	1

TEAM	CG	SHO	GR	SV	IP	H	HR	BB	SO	BR/9	ERA	AERA	OAV	OOB	PR	APR	PF	OSB	OCS	FA	E	WPB	DP	FW	PW	BW	BSW	DIF
East																												
Bal	67	14	140	26	1461.2	**1297**	124	475	715	**11.0**	**3.07**	**123**	**.240**	**.302**	**122**	**116**	99	70	54	.981	119	43	184	1.3	**11.9**	6.0	**1.0**	-4.2
Bos	67	10	144	33	1440.1	1417	158	499	808	12.2	3.65	110	.259	.323	27	57	105	72	45	.979	127	**30**	162	.8	5.8	1.7	.9	-1.3
Det	39	11	211	**46**	1447.2	1468	154	493	911	12.4	3.90	105	.265	.326	-13	29	107	107	71	**.982**	**112**	58	144	**1.7**	3.0	-5.2	-.4	5.0
NY	47	16	143	39	1427.2	1379	109	**457**	708	11.7	3.34	111	.254	.313	75	59	97	61	52	.976	156	54	172	-.8	6.0	-1.0	-.5	-4.7
Mil	50	11	217	28	1454.0	1476	119	623	671	13.2	3.98	95	.265	.340	-27	-29	100	81	**73**	.977	145	66	167	-.2	-3.0	1.1	.0	-5.1
Cle	55	9	206	21	1464.2	1532	172	602	883	13.4	4.58	86	.271	.343	-125	-100	104	109	47	.978	139	114	174	.2	-10.2	-4.5	-1.1	5.7
West																												
Oak	46	16	203	41	1457.1	1311	143	494	797	11.3	3.29	108	.241	.305	86	47	93	**54**	60	.978	137	61	170	.3	4.8	**6.4**	.8	.7
KC	40	7	213	41	1449.1	1521	114	617	790	13.5	4.19	98	.273	.346	-60	-13	108	86	49	.974	167	51	**192**	-1.4	-1.3	-1.8	-.1	11.7
Min	48	**18**	190	34	1451.2	1443	115	519	879	12.4	3.77	105	.259	.324	7	30	104	93	54	.978	139	80	147	.2	3.1	2.7	.3	-6.2
Cal	**72**	13	164	19	1456.1	1351	**104**	614	**1010**	12.4	3.53	101	.246	.324	46	8	94	105	40	.975	156	72	153	-.8	.8	-4.4	-.3	2.7
Chi	48	15	176	35	1456.0	1484	110	574	848	13.0	3.86	102	.266	.336	-8	13	104	110	57	.977	144	71	165	-.1	1.3	-5.2	-.7	.7
Tex	35	10	**241**	27	1430.0	1514	130	680	831	14.1	4.64	81	.273	.353	-131	-143	98	109	58	.974	161	70	164	-1.1	-14.6	-4.3	.0	-4.1
Total	614	150	2248	390	17396.2	—	—	—	—	12.5	3.82	—	.259	.328	—	—	—	—	—	.977	1702	770	1994	—	—	—	—	—

BATTER-FIELDER WINS	BATTING AVERAGE	ON-BASE PERCENTAGE	SLUGGING AVERAGE	ON-BASE PLUS SLUGGING	ADJUSTED OPS	ADJUSTED BATTER RUNS
Carew-Min..........5.8	Carew-Min............350	Mayberry-KC........417	Jackson-Oak.........531	Jackson-Oak.........914	Jackson-Oak.........164	Jackson-Oak........46.9
Grich-Bal............5.4	Scott-Mil...............306	Carew-Min............411	Bando-Oak...........498	Mayberry-KC........895	Robinson-Cal........152	Bando-Oak...........41.9
Munson-NY.........4.9	Davis-Bal..............306	Yastrzemski-Bos...407	Robinson-Cal........489	Carew-Min............881	Bando-Oak...........152	Robinson-Cal.......39.2
Jackson-Oak......4.1	Murcer-NY............304	Tenace-Oak..........387	Scott-Mil...............488	Bando-Oak...........873	Carew-Min............143	Mayberry-KC.......34.5
Patek-KC............4.1	May-Mil.................303	Jackson-Oak.........383	Munson-NY...........487	Yastrzemski-Bos...870	Scott-Mil...............142	Carew-Min...........34.4
RUNS	**HITS**	**DOUBLES**	**TRIPLES**	**HOME RUNS**	**TOTAL BASES**	**RUNS BATTED IN**
Jackson-Oak...........99	Carew-Min............203	Garcia-Mil..............32	Carew-Min..............11	Jackson-Oak..........32	Scott-Mil...............295	Jackson-Oak.........117
Scott-Mil.................98	May-Mil.................189	Bando-Oak.............32	Bumbry-Bal.............11	Robinson-Cal..........30	May-Mil.................295	Scott-Mil................107
North-Oak...............98	Murcer-NY............187	Scott-Mil.................30	Orta-Chi..................10	Burroughs-Tex........30	Bando-Oak...........295	Mayberry-KC........100
Carew-Min..............98	Scott-Mil...............185	Chambliss-Cle........30	Coggins-Bal..............9	Bando-Oak.............29	Murcer-NY............286	Bando-Oak.............98
Bando-Oak.............97	Johnson-Tex.........179	Carew-Min..............30	Coluccio-Mil.............8		Jackson-Oak.........286	Robinson-Cal..........97
BASES ON BALLS	**STOLEN BASES**	**BASE STEALING RUNS**	**FIELDING RUNS-INFIELD**	**FIELDING RUNS-OUTFIELD**	**OUTFIELD ASSISTS**	**CATCHER CS PCT.**
Mayberry-KC........122	Harper-Bos............54	Harper-Bos............7.0	Patek-KC..............39.8	North-Oak...........15.4	North-Oak..............14	Fosse-Oak...........55.9
Grich-Bal..............107	North-Oak..............53	North-Oak..............4.7	Nettles-NY...........32.7	Burroughs-Tex.......9.7	Murcer-NY.............14	Munson-NY.........48.5
Yastrzemski-Bos...105	Nelson-Tex.............43	Campaneris-Oak...4.0	Bell-Cle................27.2	Coluccio-Mil..........8.4	Blair-Bal.................14	Healy-KC.............44.9
Tenace-Oak..........101	Carew-Min..............41	Baylor-Bal.............3.9	Grich-Bal..............26.8	Blair-Bal.................5.6		Suarez-Tex..........39.0
Briggs-Mil................87	Patek-KC...............36	Nelson-Tex............3.9	Clarke-NY............16.2	Stanley-Det...........4.9		Fisk-Bos..............38.6
WINS	**WINNING PCT.**	**WINS ABOVE TEAM**	**GAMES STARTED**	**COMPLETE GAMES**	**FEWEST HITS/GAME**	**FEWEST BB/GAME**
Wood-Chi................24	Hunter-Oak...........808	Hunter-Oak............7.6	Wood-Chi...............48	Perry-Cle................29	Bibby-Tex............6.04	Kaat-Min-Chi........1.73
Coleman-Det..........23	Palmer-Bal............710	Colborn-Mil............5.7	Lolich-Det...............42	Ryan-Cal.................26	Ryan-Cal.............6.57	Blyleven-Min........1.86
Palmer-Bal..............22	Blue-Oak...............690	Moret-Bos..............5.4	Bahnsen-Chi...........42	Blyleven-Min..........25	Palmer-Bal...........6.83	Holtzman-Oak......2.00
	Splittorff-KC..........645	Palmer-Bal.............5.0	Perry-Cle................41	Tiant-Bos................23	Tiant-Bos.............7.18	Wood-Chi.............2.28
	Colborn-Mil...........625	Blue-Oak...............4.4		Colborn-Mil............22	Blue-Oak.............7.30	Lolich-Det............2.30
STRIKEOUTS	**STRIKEOUTS/GAME**	**GAMES**	**SAVES**	**BASE RUNNERS/9**	**ADJUSTED RELIEF RUNS**	**RELIEF RANKING**
Ryan-Cal..............383	Ryan-Cal............10.57	Hiller-Det................65	Hiller-Det.................38	Jackson-Bal.........8.74	Hiller-Det.............34.8	Hiller-Det.............61.1
Blyleven-Min.........258	Bibby-Tex.............7.74	Fingers-Oak...........62	Lyle-NY...................27	Lyle-NY.................9.18	Reynolds-Bal.......22.8	Acosta-Chi...........31.9
Singer-Cal............241	Blyleven-Min........7.14	Bird-KC...................54	Fingers-Oak............22	Hiller-Det.............9.19	Fingers-Oak.........20.3	Fingers-Oak.........29.5
Perry-Cle.............238	Stone-Chi.............7.04	Knowles-Oak..........52	Bird-KC...................20	Beene-NY.............9.40	Jackson-Bal.........17.4	Reynolds-Bal.......26.3
Lolich-Det............214	Singer-Cal............6.87		Acosta-Chi..............18	Reynolds-Bal.......9.65	Acosta-Chi...........16.8	Jackson-Bal.........19.9
INNINGS PITCHED	**OPPONENTS' AVG.**	**OPPONENTS' OBP**	**EARNED RUN AVERAGE**	**ADJUSTED ERA**	**ADJUSTED STARTER RUNS**	**PITCHER WINS**
Wood-Chi.........359.1	Bibby-Tex.............192	Tiant-Bos.............278	Palmer-Bal...........2.40	Blyleven-Min.........158	Blyleven-Min........48.2	**Hiller-Det............6.7**
Perry-Cle..........344.0	Ryan-Cal...............203	Hunter-Oak...........282	Blyleven-Min........2.52	Palmer-Bal............157	Palmer-Bal...........47.0	**Blyleven-Min......5.3**
Ryan-Cal...........326.0	Palmer-Bal............211	Blyleven-Min.........284	Lee-Bos...............2.75	Lee-Bos.................146	Lee-Bos...............36.7	**Palmer-Bal..........4.8**
Blyleven-Min......325.0	Tiant-Bos..............219	Holtzman-Oak.......286	Ryan-Cal..............2.87	Medich-NY............126	Ryan-Cal..............30.0	**Lee-Bos...............3.6**
Singer-Cal.........315.2	Blue-Oak...............224	Palmer-Bal............288	Medich-NY...........2.95	Ryan-Cal...............125	Holtzman-Oak......23.1	**Acosta-Chi.........3.3**

All A's Again

With the AL adopting the designated hitter, scoring increased 23 percent, the biggest rise since 1911. Perhaps not coincidentally, attendance leapt to a new all-time high. Oakland took the AL West lead in July. When the Royals made a run in August, the A's responded, winning 13 of 14. Reggie Jackson won his only MVP, and four teammates scored 89 or more runs while three starters won 20.

Kansas City's new stadium sported artificial turf and a much smaller outfield, which helped center fielder Amos Otis develop. In addition, the Royals debuted George Brett and Frank White. California's Nolan Ryan, an overpowering pitcher in a great pitcher's park, threw his first two no-hitters and set an all-time mark with 383 strikeouts.

With an offense that appeared unprepossessing but was quite effective, Baltimore won 14 straight in August to break open a tough AL East race with Boston and Detroit. Jim Palmer was the Cy Young winner, as again Earl Weaver let his starters finish their business. Detroit's John Hiller saved 38, setting a record that lasted until 1983, but the aging Tigers were slowing up. Boston and Luis Aparicio parted ways in a postseason salary dispute, ending the 39-year-old's career.

Four of the five ALCS games were close, but Catfish Hunter came through with a Game 5 shutout (his second win of the series) to send Oakland to the World Series. Despite being outhit, outscored, and outpitched by the Mets, Oakland won the Series in seven. Two games went extra innings and there was much human drama. New York's Rusty Staub played right field with a dead arm, Oakland owner Charlie Finley forced Mike Andrews off the roster after 2 errors, and Willie Mays ended his career. Darold Knowles, the only pitcher to appear in seven games, and Rollie Fingers pitched 20 innings of relief between them, allowing the Mets 1 run.

1972 NATIONAL LEAGUE

TEAM	W	L	T	PCT	GB	HW	HL	R	OR	PA	H	2B	3B	HR	BB	SO	HB	SH	AVG	OBP	SLG	OPS	AOPS	BR	ABR	PF	SB	CS	BSA	BSR
East																														
Pit	96	59	0	.619	—	**49**	29	691	**512**	6021	**1505**	**251**	**47**	110	404	871	25	52	**.274**	.324	**.397**	**721**	113	75	85	99	49	30	62	0
Chi	85	70	1	.548	11	46	31	685	567	5950	1346	206	40	133	565	815	28	67	.257	**.330**	.387	717	99	76	9	111	69	47	59	-1
NY	83	73	0	.532	13.5	41	37	528	578	5883	1154	175	31	105	589	990	34	86	.225	.307	.332	639	89	-67	-58	98	41	41	50	-5
StL	75	81	0	.481	21.5	40	37	568	600	5884	1383	214	42	70	437	793	27	58	.260	.317	.355	672	98	-14	-10	99	104	48	68	6
Mon	70	86	0	.449	26.5	35	43	513	609	5817	1205	156	22	91	474	828	**49**	**108**	.234	.303	.325	628	83	-94	-103	102	68	66	51	-8
Phi	59	97	0	.378	37.5	28	51	503	635	5862	1240	200	36	98	487	930	22	69	.236	.302	.344	646	88	-66	-80	103	42	50	46	-8
West																														
Cin	95	59	0	.617	—	42	34	707	557	6003	1317	214	44	124	**606**	914	37	65	.251	**.330**	.380	710	113	70	**105**	95	**140**	63	69	9
Hou	84	69	0	.549	10.5	41	36	**708**	636	5936	1359	233	38	134	524	907	32	62	.258	.326	.393	719	**114**	**78**	99	97	111	56	66	5
LA	85	70	0	.548	10.5	41	34	584	527	5903	1349	178	39	98	480	786	24	89	.256	.319	.360	679	101	-1	8	99	82	39	68	4
Atl	70	84	1	.455	25	36	41	628	730	5938	1363	186	17	144	532	**770**	35	55	.258	.328	.382	710	99	62	8	109	47	35	57	-2
SF	69	86	0	.445	26.5	34	43	662	649	5858	1281	211	36	**150**	480	964	30	64	.244	.309	.384	693	101	18	8	102	123	45	**73**	**11**
SD	58	95	0	.379	36.5	26	54	488	665	5750	1181	168	38	102	407	976	15	90	.227	.283	.332	615	86	-135	-100	93	78	46	63	1
Total	930	—	—	—	—	459	470	7265	—	70805	15683	2392	430	1359	5985	10544	358	865	.248	.315	.365	680	—	—	—	—	954	566	63	12

TEAM	CG	SHO	GR	SV	IP	H	HR	BB	SO	BR/9	ERA	AERA	OAV	OOB	PR	APR	PF	OSB	OCS	FA	E	WPB	DP	FW	PW	BW	BSW	DIF
East																												
Pit	39	15	205	48	1414.1	1282	90	433	838	11.1	2.81	118	.243	.302	102	84	96	54	41	.978	136	**40**	**171**	-.0	9.0	9.1	-.1	.5
Chi	54	19	197	32	1398.2	1329	112	**421**	824	11.5	3.22	118	.251	.309	37	83	110	95	46	.979	132	44	148	.2	8.9	1.0	-.2	-2.4
NY	32	12	207	41	1414.2	1263	118	486	**1059**	11.3	3.26	104	.240	.306	30	19	98	60	61	.980	116	60	122	1.1	2.0	-6.2	-.6	8.8
StL	**64**	13	216	13	1399.2	1290	87	531	912	11.8	3.42	100	.247	.317	5	1	99	91	55	.977	141	71	146	-.3	.1	-1.1	.5	-2.3
Mon	39	11	217	23	1401.1	1281	103	579	888	12.1	3.59	99	.245	.321	-21	-5	103	73	**67**	.978	134	58	141	.0	-.5	-11.1	-1.0	4.5
Phi	43	13	263	15	1400.0	1318	117	536	927	12.1	3.66	98	.251	.321	-33	-9	104	87	45	.981	116	66	142	1.1	-1.0	-8.6	-1.0	-9.5
West																												
Cin	25	15	239	**60**	1412.2	1313	129	435	806	11.3	3.21	101	.247	.305	38	5	94	**31**	40	**.982**	**110**	47	143	**1.3**	.5	**11.3**	.9	4.0
Hou	38	14	245	31	1385.1	1340	114	498	971	12.2	3.77	89	.256	.323	-48	-65	97	99	37	.980	116	75	151	.9	-7.0	10.6	.4	2.5
LA	50	**23**	176	29	1403.0	**1196**	**83**	429	856	**10.6**	**2.78**	**120**	**.230**	**.291**	**104**	**91**	97	79	37	.974	162	55	145	-1.5	**9.8**	.9	.3	-2.0
Atl	40	4	220	27	1377.0	1412	155	512	732	12.7	4.27	89	.266	.331	-126	-66	110	96	37	.974	156	105	130	-1.1	-7.1	.9	-.3	.7
SF	44	8	219	23	1386.1	1309	130	507	771	12.0	3.69	95	.250	.318	-37	-30	101	87	53	.974	156	63	121	-1.1	-3.2	.9	**1.1**	-6.1
SD	39	17	**270**	19	1403.2	1350	121	618	960	12.9	3.78	88	.255	.334	-50	-76	96	98	46	.976	144	75	146	-.6	-8.2	-10.8	.0	1.0
Total	507	164	2674	361	16796.2	—	—	—	—	11.8	3.45	—	.248	.315	—	—	—	—	—	.978	1619	759	1706	—	—	—	—	—

BATTER-FIELDER WINS	BATTING AVERAGE	ON-BASE PERCENTAGE	SLUGGING AVERAGE	ON-BASE PLUS SLUGGING	ADJUSTED OPS	ADJUSTED BATTER RUNS
Bench-Cin 6.5	Williams-Chi 333	Morgan-Cin 417	Williams-Chi 606	Williams-Chi 1005	Bench-Cin 169	Bench-Cin 50.8
Morgan-Cin 5.8	Garr-Atl 325	Williams-Chi 398	Stargell-Pit 558	Stargell-Pit 930	Williams-Chi 165	Williams-Chi 49.6
Cedeno-Hou 5.3	Baker-Atl 321	Santo-Chi 391	Bench-Cin 541	Cedeno-Hou 921	Stargell-Pit 165	Cedeno-Hou 47.3
Santo-Chi 3.9	Cedeno-Hou 320	Aaron-Atl 390	Cedeno-Hou 537	Bench-Cin 920	Cedeno-Hou 165	Morgan-Cin 44.1
Williams-Chi 3.8	Watson-Hou 312	Wynn-Hou 389	Aaron-Atl 514	Aaron-Atl 904	Hebner-Pit 153	Stargell-Pit 42.1

RUNS	HITS	DOUBLES	TRIPLES	HOME RUNS	TOTAL BASES	RUNS BATTED IN
Morgan-Cin 122	Rose-Cin 198	Montanez-Phi 39	Bowa-Phi 13	Bench-Cin 40	Williams-Chi 348	Bench-Cin 125
Bonds-SF 118	Brock-StL 193	Cedeno-Hou 39	Rose-Cin 11	Colbert-SD 38	Cedeno-Hou 300	Williams-Chi 122
Wynn-Hou 117	Williams-Chi 191	Simmons-StL 36	Sanguillen-Pit 8	Williams-Chi 37	Bench-Cin 291	Stargell-Pit 112
Rose-Cin 107	Simmons-StL 180	Williams-Chi 34	Cedeno-Hou 8	Aaron-Atl 34	May-Hou 290	Colbert-SD 111
Cedeno-Hou 103	Garr-Atl 180		Brock-StL 8	Stargell-Pit 33	Colbert-SD 286	May-Hou 98

BASES ON BALLS	STOLEN BASES	BASE STEALING RUNS	FIELDING RUNS-INFIELD	FIELDING RUNS-OUTFIELD	OUTFIELD ASSISTS	CATCHER CS PCT.
Morgan-Cin 115	Brock-StL 63	Bonds-SF 7.6	Helms-Hou 28.8	Baker-Atl 12.3	Carbo-Cin-StL 15	Rader-SF 34.6
Wynn-Hou 103	Morgan-Cin 58	Brock-StL 7.6	Foli-Mon 18.4	Rose-Cin 9.9	Rose-Cin 15	Bateman-Mon-Phi34.3
Bench-Cin 100	Cedeno-Hou 55	Morgan-Cin 6.8	Rader-Hou 17.6	Henderson-SF 8.5	Montanez-Phi 15	Hundley-Chi 30.6
Aaron-Atl 92	Bonds-SF 44	Cedeno-Hou 4.8	Kessinger-Chi 16.7	Montanez-Phi 8.1	Henderson-SF 14	Edwards-Hou 28.6
Evans-Atl 90	Tolan-Cin 42	Hernandez-SD 4.2	Santo-Chi 14.6	Lum-Atl 5.6	Cardenal-Chi 11	

WINS	WINNING PCT.	WINS ABOVE TEAM	GAMES STARTED	COMPLETE GAMES	FEWEST HITS/GAME	FEWEST BB/GAME
Carlton-Phi 27	Nolan-Cin 750	Carlton-Phi 11.7	Carlton-Phi 41	Carlton-Phi 30	Sutton-LA 6.14	Pappas-Chi 1.34
Seaver-NY 21	Carlton-Phi 730	Gibson-StL 5.1	Arlin-SD 37	Jenkins-Chi 23	Carlton-Phi 6.68	Nolan-Cin 1.53
Osteen-LA 20	Pappas-Chi 708	Pappas-Chi 4.7	Niekro-Atl 36	Gibson-StL 23	Gibson-StL 7.32	Niekro-Atl 1.69
Jenkins-Chi 20	Blass-Pit 704	Sutton-LA 4.6	Jenkins-Chi 36	Wise-StL 20	Seaver-NY 7.39	Ellis-Pit 1.82
	Ellis-Pit 682	Bryant-SF 4.6		Sutton-LA 18	Bryant-SF 7.40	Moose-Pit 1.87

STRIKEOUTS	STRIKEOUTS/GAME	GAMES	SAVES	BASE RUNNERS/9	ADJUSTED RELIEF RUNS	RELIEF RANKING
Carlton-Phi 310	Seaver-NY 8.55	Marshall-Mon 65	Carroll-Cin 37	Brewer-LA 7.81	Marshall-Mon 21.8	Marshall-Mon 43.6
Seaver-NY 249	Reuss-Hou 8.16	Carroll-Cin 65	McGraw-NY 27	Sutton-LA 8.35	McGraw-NY 18.7	Brewer-LA 35.3
Gibson-StL 208	Koosman-NY 8.12	Borbon-Cin 62	Giusti-Pit 22	Carlton-Phi 8.97	Brewer-LA 17.6	McGraw-NY 33.0
Sutton-LA 207	Carlton-Phi 8.06	Ross-SD 60	Marshall-Mon 18	Willoughby-SF 9.03	R.Hernandez-Pit..13.8	Giusti-Pit 24.4
Jenkins-Chi 184	Norman-SD 7.10			Nolan-Cin 9.10	Giusti-Pit 12.3	Carroll-Cin 19.9

INNINGS PITCHED	OPPONENTS' AVG.	OPPONENTS' OBP	EARNED RUN AVERAGE	ADJUSTED ERA	ADJUSTED STARTER RUNS	PITCHER WINS
Carlton-Phi 346.1	Sutton-LA 189	Sutton-LA 240	Carlton-Phi 1.97	Carlton-Phi 183	Carlton-Phi 60.4	**Carlton-Phi 7.4**
Jenkins-Chi 289.1	Carlton-Phi 206	Carlton-Phi 257	Nolan-Cin 1.99	Nolan-Cin 163	Sutton-LA 39.2	**Marshall-Mon 4.9**
Niekro-Atl 282.1	Gibson-StL 224	Nolan-Cin 259	Sutton-LA 2.08	Sutton-LA 161	Gibson-StL 31.3	**Gibson-StL 4.4**
Gibson-StL 278.0	Seaver-NY 224	Niekro-Atl 274	Matlack-NY 2.32	Matlack-NY 146	Matlack-NY 25.7	**Osteen-LA 4.2**
Sutton-LA 272.2	Bryant-SF 224	McAndrew-NY 276	Gibson-StL 2.46	Gibson-StL 139	Blass-Pit 24.1	**Brewer-LA 4.0**

Best Pitcher on the Worst Team

Prior to the season, the penny-pinching Cardinals sent Steve Carlton to the Phillies for Rick Wise. In addition to completing St. Louis' post-1968 destruction, the deal also helped Philadelphia build a powerhouse. Carlton was 27-10 for a horrible Phillies club in 1972, earning Cy Young honors and finishing fifth in MVP voting. Future Phils debuting around Lefty included Bob Boone and Mike Schmidt; Greg Luzinski hit 18 homers in his first year as a regular.

There was doubt, however, that the season would begin. For the first time, players went on strike, wiping out the first 12 days of the season. Mets manager Gil Hodges died of a heart attack during spring training; Yogi Berra took charge of the club. Chicago's Billy Williams finished second in MVP voting in both 1970 and 1972, but the Cubs couldn't catch the Pirates either year. The '72 Bucs boasted deep pitching and seven regulars who hit at least .280.

The Reds pulled away from surprising Houston in July and coasted to a division crown. Johnny Bench again was MVP, with Clay Carroll saving an all-time record 37. Pete Rose and new acquisition Joe Morgan set the table like perhaps no other combination in history.

Pittsburgh and Cincinnati traded wins through the first four NLCS contests. In Game 5, with Cincinnati down 3-2 in the last of the ninth, Bench led off with a game-tying homer; two outs and two singles later, Bob Moose's wild pitch gave the game—and pennant—to the Reds. Cincinnati was denied again in the World Series, however, as Oakland won a tight Series in seven.

Following the season, Bill Mazeroski, Hoyt Wilhelm, and Maury Wills retired. Pie Traynor, Jackie Robinson, and Gabby Hartnett passed away. The most shocking death of the year, however, was that of Roberto Clemente, lost in a December 31 air crash en route to earthquake-torn Nicaragua. Clemente had collected his 3,000th and final hit on September 30.

1972 AMERICAN LEAGUE

TEAM	W	L	T	PCT	GB	HW	HL	R	OR	PA	H	2B	3B	HR	BB	SO	HB	SH	AVG	OBP	SLG	OPS	AOPS	BR	ABR	PF	SB	CS	BSA	BSR
EAST																														
Det	86	70	0	.551	—	44	34	558	514	5721	1206	179	32	122	483	793	31	74	.237	.305	.356	661	99	17	-2	104	17	21	45	-4
Bos	85	70	0	.548	0.5	52	26	**640**	620	5871	1289	**229**	**34**	124	522	858	37	56	.248	.318	**.376**	**694**	107	**86**	51	106	66	30	**69**	**4**
Bal	80	74	0	.519	5	38	39	519	**430**	5676	1153	193	29	100	507	935	36	65	.229	.302	.339	641	93	-11	-31	104	78	41	66	3
NY	79	76	0	.510	6.5	46	31	557	527	5793	1288	201	24	103	491	**689**	29	74	.249	.316	.357	673	109	47	60	98	71	42	63	1
Cle	72	84	0	.462	14	43	34	472	519	5769	1220	187	18	91	420	762	26	83	.234	.293	.330	623	88	-55	-72	104	49	53	48	-8
Mil	65	91	0	.417	21	37	42	493	595	5733	1204	167	22	88	472	868	29	78	.235	.302	.328	630	96	-36	-27	98	64	57	53	-6
WEST																														
Oak	93	62	0	.600	—	48	29	604	457	5846	1248	195	29	**134**	463	886	**47**	**100**	.240	.306	.366	.672	**111**	37	66	95	87	48	64	2
Chi	87	67	0	.565	5.5	**55**	23	566	538	5721	1208	170	28	108	511	991	34	68	.238	.310	.346	656	100	14	3	102	100	52	66	**4**
Min	77	77	0	.500	15.5	42	32	537	535	5848	1277	182	31	93	478	905	35	73	.244	.310	.344	654	96	8	-18	105	53	41	56	-3
KC	76	78	0	.494	16.5	44	33	580	545	5845	**1317**	220	26	78	**534**	711	34	72	**.255**	**.327**	.353	680	110	68	**71**	100	85	44	66	3
Cal	75	80	0	.484	18	44	36	454	533	5639	1249	171	26	78	358	850	25	66	.242	.293	.330	623	96	-59	-33	95	57	37	61	0
Tex	54	100	0	.351	38.5	31	46	461	628	5680	1092	166	17	56	503	926	30	84	.217	.290	.290	580	82	-115	-101	97	**126**	73	63	2
Total	929	—	—	—	—	524	405	6441	—	69142	14751	2260	316	1175	5742	10174	393	893	.239	.306	.343	649	—	—	—	—	853	539	61	-1

TEAM	CG	SHO	GR	SV	IP	H	HR	BB	SO	BR/9	ERA	AERA	OAV	OOB	PR	APR	PF	OSB	OCS	FA	E	WPB	DP	FW	PW	BW	BSW	DIF
EAST																												
Det	46	11	248	33	1388.1	1212	101	465	952	11.2	2.96	107	.236	.304	15	30	103	87	46	**.984**	**96**	55	137	**1.9**	3.4	-.2	-.4	3.3
Bos	48	20	216	25	1382.2	1309	101	512	918	12.1	3.47	93	.251	.321	-63	-35	106	66	40	.978	130	42	141	-.0	-4.0	5.8	**.5**	5.3
Bal	**62**	20	167	21	1371.2	1116	**85**	**395**	788	**10.0**	**2.53**	**123**	.224	**.282**	**81**	**86**	102	44	44	.983	100	41	150	1.6	**9.8**	-3.5	.4	-5.2
NY	35	19	188	39	1373.1	1306	87	419	625	11.5	3.05	98	.252	.310	2	-10	97	**42**	34	.978	134	57	**179**	-.3	-1.1	6.8	.1	-4.0
Cle	47	13	255	25	1410.0	1232	123	534	846	11.5	2.92	111	.237	.311	23	49	106	66	43	.981	116	59	157	.8	5.6	-8.2	-.9	-3.3
Mil	37	14	216	32	1391.2	1289	116	486	740	11.7	3.45	88	.247	.312	-61	-62	100	65	43	.977	139	51	145	-.5	-7.0	-3.1	-.7	-1.7
WEST																												
Oak	42	**23**	236	**43**	1417.2	1170	96	418	862	10.2	2.58	110	.226	.284	76	45	93	72	38	.979	130	42	146	-.0	5.1	7.5	.2	2.7
Chi	36	14	248	42	1385.1	1269	94	431	936	11.2	3.12	100	.245	.305	-9	-1	102	75	**60**	.977	135	70	136	-.4	-.1	.3	**.5**	9.7
Min	37	17	203	34	1399.1	1188	105	444	838	10.7	2.84	113	.230	.294	35	54	105	69	48	.974	159	**33**	133	-1.8	6.1	-2.0	-.3	-2.0
KC	44	16	242	28	1381.1	1293	**85**	405	801	11.3	3.24	94	.251	.307	-27	-32	99	86	42	.981	116	54	164	.7	-3.6	**8.1**	.4	-6.5
Cal	57	18	192	16	1377.2	**1109**	90	620	**1000**	11.5	3.06	96	**.222**	.310	0	-22	96	102	44	.981	114	70	135	.8	-2.5	-3.8	.0	2.9
Tex	11	8	**324**	34	1374.2	1258	92	613	868	12.6	3.53	86	.246	.329	-71	-75	99	77	56	.972	166	58	147	-2.2	-8.5	-11.5	.2	-1.0
Total	502	193	2735	372	16653.2	—	—	—	—	11.3	3.06	—	.239	.306	—	—	—	—	—	.979	1535	632	1770	—	—	—	—	—

BATTER-FIELDER WINS	BATTING AVERAGE	ON-BASE PERCENTAGE	SLUGGING AVERAGE	ON-BASE PLUS SLUGGING	ADJUSTED OPS	ADJUSTED BATTER RUNS
D.Allen-Chi 5.8	Carew-Min .318	D.Allen-Chi .420	D.Allen-Chi .603	D.Allen-Chi 1023	D.Allen-Chi 198	D.Allen-Chi 65.1
Fisk-Bos 5.1	Piniella-KC .312	May-Chi .405	Fisk-Bos .538	Fisk-Bos .909	Murcer-NY 169	Murcer-NY 47.7
Murcer-NY 4.3	D.Allen-Chi .308	Mayberry-KC .394	Murcer-NY .537	Mayberry-KC .900	Mayberry-KC 168	Mayberry-KC 44.5
Patek-KC 4.2	May-Chi .308	White-NY .384	Mayberry-KC .507	Murcer-NY .898	Epstein-Oak 165	Epstein-Oak 38.1
Mayberry-KC 3.5	Rudi-Oak .305	Scheinblum-KC .383	Epstein-Oak .490	Epstein-Oak .866	Fisk-Bos 159	May-Chi 36.0

RUNS	HITS	DOUBLES	TRIPLES	HOME RUNS	TOTAL BASES	RUNS BATTED IN
Murcer-NY 102	Rudi-Oak 181	Piniella-KC 33	Rudi-Oak 9	D.Allen-Chi 37	Murcer-NY 314	D.Allen-Chi 113
Rudi-Oak 94	Piniella-KC 179	Rudi-Oak 32	Fisk-Bos 9	Murcer-NY 33	D.Allen-Chi 305	Mayberry-KC 100
Harper-Bos 92	Murcer-NY 171	Murcer-NY 30	Blair-Bal 8	Killebrew-Min 26	Rudi-Oak 288	Murcer-NY 96
D.Allen-Chi 90	Carew-Min 170	White-NY 29	Murcer-NY 7	Epstein-Oak 26	Mayberry-KC 255	Scott-Mil 88
Tovar-Min 86	May-Chi 161	Harper-Bos 29	Kelly-Chi 7		Piniella-KC 253	Powell-Bal 81

BASES ON BALLS	STOLEN BASES	BASE STEALING RUNS	FIELDING RUNS-INFIELD	FIELDING RUNS-OUTFIELD	OUTFIELD ASSISTS	CATCHER CS PCT.
White-NY 99	Campaneris-Oak 52	Campaneris-Oak 6.5	Patek-KC 37.7	Berry-Cal 8.0	May-Chi 13	Herrmann-Chi 50.0
D.Allen-Chi 99	Nelson-Tex 51	Nelson-Tex 5.3	Michael-NY 24.0	Ford-Tex 7.4	Berry-Cal 13	Munson-NY 47.5
Killebrew-Min 94	Patek-KC 33	Patek-KC 4.8	Rodriguez-Det 20.2	Blair-Bal 5.3	Pinson-Cal 11	Oates-Bal 42.9
May-Chi 79	Kelly-Chi 32	Baylor-Bal 4.6	Clarke-NY 15.3	May-Mil 5.2	Murcer-NY 11	Rodriguez-Mil 40.8
	Otis-KC 28	Kelly-Chi 3.9	Killebrew-Min 10.9	Unser-Cle 4.4	Ford-Tex 11	Fisk-Bos 39.1

WINS	WINNING PCT.	WINS ABOVE TEAM	GAMES STARTED	COMPLETE GAMES	FEWEST HITS/GAME	FEWEST BB/GAME
Wood-Chi 24	Hunter-Oak .750	Perry-Cle 6.4	Wood-Chi 49	Perry-Cle 29	Ryan-Cal 5.26	Peterson-NY 1.58
Perry-Cle 24	Tiant-Bos .714	Hunter-Oak 5.9	Lolich-Det 41	Lolich-Det 23	Hunter-Oak 6.09	Nelson-KC 1.61
Lolich-Det 22	Odom-Oak .714	Palmer-Bal 5.9	Bahnsen-Chi 41	Wood-Chi 20	Nelson-KC 6.23	Kline-NY 1.68
	Palmer-Bal .677	Wright-Cal 4.5	Perry-Cle 40	Ryan-Cal 20	Tiant-Bos 6.44	Holtzman-Oak 1.76
	Kline-NY .640	Tiant-Bos 4.2	Bradley-Chi 40	Palmer-Bal 18	Messersmith-Cal 6.63	Wood-Chi 1.77

STRIKEOUTS	STRIKEOUTS/GAME	GAMES	SAVES	BASE RUNNERS/9	ADJUSTED RELIEF RUNS	RELIEF RANKING
Ryan-Cal 329	Ryan-Cal 10.43	Lindblad-Tex 66	Lyle-NY 35	Nelson-KC 7.89	Lyle-NY 13.6	Lyle-NY 25.9
Lolich-Det 250	Messersmith-Cal 7.53	Fingers-Oak 65	Forster-Chi 29	Hunter-Oak 8.32	Knowles-Oak 11.3	Knowles-Oak 13.5
Perry-Cle 234	May-Cal 7.41	Granger-Min 63	Fingers-Oak 21	Kaat-Min 9.05	Bell-Mil 10.8	Forster-Chi 13.5
Blyleven-Min 228	Bradley-Chi 7.23		Granger-Min 19	Perry-Cle 9.11	Harrison-Bal 9.6	Abernathy-KC 9.5
Coleman-Det 222	Blyleven-Min 7.14		Sanders-Mil 17	Alexander-Bal 9.23	Forster-Chi 8.2	Fingers-Oak 9.1

INNINGS PITCHED	OPPONENTS' AVG.	OPPONENTS' OBP	EARNED RUN AVERAGE	ADJUSTED ERA	ADJUSTED STARTER RUNS	PITCHER WINS
Wood-Chi 376.2	Ryan-Cal .171	Nelson-KC .234	Tiant-Bos 1.91	Perry-Cle 170	Perry-Cle 49.2	**Perry-Cle 6.8**
Perry-Cle 342.2	Hunter-Oak .189	Hunter-Oak .241	Perry-Cle 1.92	Tiant-Bos 170	Palmer-Bal 30.2	**Palmer-Bal 4.1**
Lolich-Det 327.1	Nelson-KC .196	Perry-Cle .261	Hunter-Oak 2.04	Palmer-Bal 151	Hunter-Oak 29.2	**Hunter-Oak 3.1**
Hunter-Oak 295.1	Tiant-Bos .202	Palmer-Bal .268	Palmer-Bal 2.07	Nelson-KC 147	Wood-Chi 24.7	**Lyle-NY 3.1**
Blyleven-Min 287.1	Perry-Cle .205	Tiant-Bos .275	Nelson-KC 2.08	Paul-Tex 140	Lolich-Det 24.6	**Ryan-Cal 2.9**

FIRST STRIKE

Players went on strike in spring training, canceling the first 13 days of action. Once the strike ended, the AL East saw its first close race. New York, Baltimore, Boston, and Detroit bunched together in August, with the division lead switching seemingly every hour through Labor Day. The Yankees and Orioles faded while the Red Sox and Tigers split four in mid-September at Fenway and met three times to close the schedule at Detroit. The Tigers took the first two to win by a mere half-game.

The West again went to Oakland, although the resurgent White Sox—with knuckleballer Wilbur Wood, who made 49 starts, and MVP Dick Allen—made a run in August. Nolan Ryan, in his first year as an Angel, set a new record for fewest hits allowed per game; he also recorded his first of six 300-strikeout seasons. Minnesota's Rod Carew won his first of six batting titles in the decade. Moving from Washington to Texas, the Rangers had an attendance bump…of just 6,000.

With labor strife taking games off the schedule as well as a continued scoring reduction—only Bobby Murcer cleared 100 runs—attendance dipped for the third straight year. The Yankees failed to draw one million for the first time since 1945. Boston, second to Detroit in attendance and the standings, boasted Rookie of the Year Carlton Fisk plus Sparky Lyle, whose 35 saves set a league record.

In a thrilling ALCS, each team came back once in the bottom of the 10th to win. Oakland prevailed, winning the first two on the coast, then losing two and taking the deciding game in Detroit as Blue Moon Odom and Vida Blue held off the Tigers, 2-1. However, Reggie Jackson injured his knee and missed the World Series.

Six of the seven games in the see-saw Reds-A's Series were one-run affairs. Each team had dramatic come-from-behind wins and good pitching; the unlikely hero was Oakland's Gene Tenace, who hit 4 homers, including long balls in his first 2 at bats. Catfish Hunter won Game 7 in relief, holding off the Reds, 3-2.

1971 NATIONAL LEAGUE

TEAM	W	L	T	PCT	GB	HW	HL	R	OR	PA	H	2B	3B	HR	BB	SO	HB	SH	AVG	OBP	SLG	OPS	AOPS	BR	ABR	PF	SB	CS	BSA	BSR
EAST																														
Pit	97	65	0	.599	—	**52**	28	**788**	599	6283	**1555**	223	**61**	**154**	469	919	29	62	.274	.330	**.416**	**746**	**116**	**120**	**115**	101	65	31	68	3
StL	90	72	1	.556	7	45	36	739	699	6300	1542	225	54	95	543	757	25	63	**.275**	**.338**	.385	723	106	92	58	105	**124**	53	70	9
NY	83	79	0	.512	14	44	37	588	**550**	6178	1365	203	29	98	547	958	28	91	.249	.319	.351	670	96	-20	-19	100	89	43	67	5
Chi	83	79	0	.512	14	44	37	637	648	6131	1401	202	34	128	527	772	34	92	.258	.325	.378	703	91	42	-45	115	44	32	58	-2
Mon	71	90	1	.441	25.5	36	44	622	729	6098	1312	197	29	88	543	800	**78**	**102**	.246	.322	.343	665	94	-18	-26	101	51	43	54	-4
Phi	67	95	0	.414	30	34	47	558	688	6171	1289	209	35	123	499	1031	34	55	.233	.298	.350	648	89	-75	-77	100	63	39	62	0
WEST																														
SF	90	72	0	.556	—	51	30	706	644	6258	1348	224	36	140	**654**	1042	37	69	.247	.329	.378	707	107	61	70	99	101	36	**74**	**10**
LA	89	73	0	.549	1	42	39	663	587	6155	1469	213	38	95	489	755	21	72	.266	.325	.370	695	108	28	63	95	76	40	66	3
Atl	82	80	0	.506	8	43	39	643	699	6172	1434	192	30	153	434	**747**	28	91	.257	.312	.385	697	97	16	-24	107	57	46	55	-4
Hou	79	83	0	.488	11	39	42	585	567	6105	1319	**230**	52	71	478	888	29	65	.240	.302	.340	642	91	-81	-64	97	101	51	66	4
Cin	79	83	0	.488	11	46	35	586	581	5973	1306	203	28	138	438	907	27	69	.241	.300	.366	666	95	-46	-40	99	59	33	64	1
SD	61	100	0	.379	28.5	33	48	486	610	5935	1250	184	31	96	438	966	25	87	.233	.293	.332	625	89	-120	-86	94	70	45	61	0
Total	972	—	—	—	—	509	462	7601	—	73759	16590	2505	457	1379	6059	10542	395	918	.252	.316	.366	683	—	—	—	—	900	492	65	26

TEAM	CG	SHO	GR	SV	IP	H	HR	BB	SO	BR/9	ERA	AERA	OAV	OOB	PR	APR	PF	OSB	OCS	FA	E	WPB	DP	FW	PW	BW	BSW	DIF
EAST																												
Pit	43	15	229	**48**	1461.0	1426	108	470	813	11.9	3.31	103	.257	.316	26	15	98	**42**	45	.979	133	54	164	.0	1.6	**12.3**	.0	1.9
StL	56	14	**274**	22	1467.0	1482	104	576	911	12.9	3.85	94	.263	.333	-63	-35	105	54	36	.978	142	80	155	-.4	-3.8	6.2	.7	6.2
NY	42	13	211	22	1466.1	**1227**	100	529	**1157**	**11.0**	**2.99**	**115**	**.227**	**.299**	**78**	**73**	99	78	28	.981	114	54	135	1.2	**7.8**	-2.0	.3	-5.3
Chi	**75**	17	202	13	1444.0	1458	132	411	900	11.8	3.61	109	.262	.314	-23	46	113	81	52	.980	126	56	150	.5	4.9	-4.8	-.4	1.9
Mon	49	8	215	25	1434.1	1418	133	658	829	13.2	4.12	87	.260	.341	-104	-85	103	87	43	.976	150	74	164	-.9	-9.1	-2.8	-.7	4.0
Phi	31	10	253	25	1470.2	1396	132	525	838	12.0	3.71	96	.254	.320	-41	-26	102	110	**60**	.981	122	80	158	.7	-2.8	-8.3	-.2	-3.4
WEST																												
SF	45	14	252	30	1454.2	1324	128	471	831	11.3	3.32	103	.242	.303	24	15	98	74	23	.972	179	65	153	-2.6	1.6	7.5	**.8**	1.6
LA	48	**18**	187	33	1449.2	1363	110	**399**	853	11.1	3.23	100	.250	.301	37	2	94	77	42	.979	131	56	159	.2	.2	6.8	.0	.7
Atl	40	11	224	31	1474.2	1529	152	485	823	12.5	3.75	99	.269	.328	-46	-4	107	84	33	.977	146	89	**180**	-.7	-.4	-2.6	-.7	5.3
Hou	43	10	245	25	1471.1	1318	**75**	475	914	11.3	3.13	107	.241	.307	55	39	97	68	44	.983	106	82	152	1.6	4.2	-6.9	.2	-1.2
Cin	27	11	255	38	1444.0	1298	112	501	750	11.4	3.35	101	.243	.310	18	3	97	50	32	**.984**	**103**	**44**	174	**1.8**	.3	-4.3	-.1	.3
SD	47	10	237	17	1438.0	1351	93	559	923	12.1	3.22	103	.249	.321	39	16	96	95	54	.974	161	70	144	-1.6	1.7	-9.2	-.2	-10.2
Total	546	151	2784	329	17475.2	—	—	—	—	11.9	3.47	—	.252	.316	—	—	—	—	—	.979	1613	804	1888	—	—	—	—	—

BATTER-FIELDER WINS	BATTING AVERAGE	ON-BASE PERCENTAGE	SLUGGING AVERAGE	ON-BASE PLUS SLUGGING	ADJUSTED OPS	ADJUSTED BATTER RUNS
Stargell-Pit 4.9	Torre-StL .363	Mays-SF .425	H.Aaron-Atl .669	H.Aaron-Atl 1079	H.Aaron-Atl 190	Stargell-Pit 59.4
H.Aaron-Atl 4.2	Garr-Atl .343	Torre-StL .421	Stargell-Pit .628	Stargell-Pit 1026	Stargell-Pit 186	H.Aaron-Atl 58.5
Mays-SF 3.7	Beckert-Chi .342	H.Aaron-Atl .410	Torre-StL .555	Torre-StL 976	Torre-StL 167	Torre-StL 57.0
Torre-StL 3.7	Clemente-Pit .341	Hunt-Mon .402	May-Cin .532	Mays-SF 907	Mays-SF 159	Allen-LA 41.5
Bonds-SF 3.5	H.Aaron-Atl .327	Stargell-Pit .398	Bonds-SF .512	Williams-Chi 888	Allen-LA 152	Mays-SF 40.6
RUNS	**HITS**	**DOUBLES**	**TRIPLES**	**HOME RUNS**	**TOTAL BASES**	**RUNS BATTED IN**
Brock-StL 126	Torre-StL 230	Cedeno-Hou 40	Morgan-Hou 11	Stargell-Pit 48	Torre-StL 352	Torre-StL 137
Bonds-SF 110	Garr-Atl 219	Brock-StL 37	Metzger-Hou 11	H.Aaron-Atl 47	H.Aaron-Atl 331	Stargell-Pit 125
Stargell-Pit 104	Brock-StL 200	Torre-StL 34	Davis-LA 10	May-Cin 39	Stargell-Pit 321	H.Aaron-Atl 118
Garr-Atl 101	Davis-LA 198	Staub-Mon 34	Gaston-SD 9	Johnson-Phi 34	Bonds-SF 317	Bonds-SF 102
Torre-StL 97		Davis-LA 33			Williams-Chi 300	Montanez-Phi 99
BASES ON BALLS	**STOLEN BASES**	**BASE STEALING RUNS**	**FIELDING RUNS-INFIELD**	**FIELDING RUNS-OUTFIELD**	**OUTFIELD ASSISTS**	**CATCHER CS PCT.**
Mays-SF 112	Brock-StL 64	Brock-StL 7.4	Helms-Cin 26.1	Lum-Atl 8.7	Staub-Mon 20	Sanguillen-Pit 51.4
Dietz-SF 97	Morgan-Hou 40	Morgan-Hou 6.0	Sizemore-StL 17.6	Garr-Atl 8.5	Garr-Atl 15	Edwards-Hou 42.1
Bailey-Mon 97	Garr-Atl 30	Agee-NY 4.1	Harrelson-NY 14.7	Alou-Hou 7.7	Rose-Cin 13	Simmons-StL 42.0
Allen-LA 93		Mays-SF 4.0	Robertson-Pit 13.7	Clemente-Pit 7.3		Barton-SD 41.1
Morgan-Hou 88		Harrelson-NY 3.7	Kessinger-Chi 11.3	Day-Mon 7.2		Bateman-Mon 32.4
WINS	**WINNING PCT.**	**WINS ABOVE TEAM**	**GAMES STARTED**	**COMPLETE GAMES**	**FEWEST HITS/GAME**	**FEWEST BB/GAME**
Jenkins-Chi 24	Gullett-Cin .727	Jenkins-Chi 6.2	Stoneman-Mon 39	Jenkins-Chi 30	Wilson-Hou 6.55	Jenkins-Chi 1.02
Seaver-NY 20	Downing-LA .690	Gullett-Cin 5.5	Jenkins-Chi 39	Seaver-NY 21	Seaver-NY 6.60	Marichal-SF 1.81
Downing-LA 20	Carlton-StL .690	Seaver-NY 5.4	Osteen-LA 38	Stoneman-Mon 20	Kirby-SD 7.17	Stone-Atl 1.82
Carlton-StL 20	Ellis-Pit .679	Downing-LA 5.1		Gibson-StL 20	Gentry-NY 7.39	Hands-Chi 1.86
Ellis-Pit 19	Seaver-NY .667	Carlton-StL 5.0			Stoneman-Mon 7.42	Sutton-LA 1.87
STRIKEOUTS	**STRIKEOUTS/GAME**	**GAMES**	**SAVES**	**BASE RUNNERS/9**	**ADJUSTED RELIEF RUNS**	**RELIEF RANKING**
Seaver-NY 289	Seaver-NY 9.08	Granger-Cin 70	Giusti-Pit 30	Seaver-NY 8.64	McGraw-NY 22.4	McGraw-NY 30.8
Jenkins-Chi 263	Kirby-SD 7.78	J.Johnson-SF 67	Marshall-Mon 23	Brewer-LA 8.74	Miller-Chi-SD-Pit 17.8	Brewer-LA 26.0
Stoneman-Mon 251	Stoneman-Mon 7.67	Marshall-Mon 66	Brewer-LA 22	Wilson-Hou 9.44	Brewer-LA 14.2	Miller-Chi-SD-Pit 25.2
Kirby-SD 231	Jenkins-Chi 7.28	McMahon-SF 61	J.Johnson-SF 18	McGraw-NY 9.49	Ray-Hou 13.2	Frisella-NY 19.6
Sutton-LA 194	Gentry-NY 6.86	Carroll-Cin 61	Upshaw-Atl 17	Jenkins-Chi 9.58	Frisella-NY 12.3	Ray-Hou 18.0
INNINGS PITCHED	**OPPONENTS' AVG.**	**OPPONENTS' OBP**	**EARNED RUN AVERAGE**	**ADJUSTED ERA**	**ADJUSTED STARTER RUNS**	**PITCHER WINS**
Jenkins-Chi 325.0	Wilson-Hou .202	Seaver-NY .252	Seaver-NY 1.76	Seaver-NY 195	Seaver-NY 54.8	**Seaver-NY 6.7**
Stoneman-Mon 294.2	Seaver-NY .206	Wilson-Hou .266	Roberts-SD 2.10	Roberts-SD 158	Jenkins-Chi 36.3	**Jenkins-Chi 5.6**
Seaver-NY 286.1	Kirby-SD .216	Jenkins-Chi .269	Wilson-Hou 2.45	Jenkins-Chi 142	Roberts-SD 36.2	**Roberts-SD 4.7**
Perry-SF 280.0	Cumberland-SF .223	Marichal-SF .273	Forsch-Hou 2.53	Wilson-Hou 137	Wilson-Hou 28.5	**McGraw-NY 3.6**
Marichal-SF 279.0	Gentry-NY .224	Nolan-Cin .275	Sutton-LA 2.54	Forsch-Hou 133	Sutton-LA 22.0	**Brewer-LA 3.0**

Pittsburgh's Glory

San Francisco looked like a shoo-in for NL West honors, leading by $8^1/_2$ in early September, but a late slide and a furious Los Angeles rally closed the gap. But the Dodgers could get no closer as the Giants held a 1-game lead over the final five days. Willie Mays and Willie McCovey were declining and injured, respectively, but Bobby Bonds, Ken Henderson, and Dick Dietz provided the hitting; Juan Marichal headed a very thin rotation.

An 11-game July winning streak put the Bucs over the top in the East. Seven Pittsburgh pitchers made at least 13 starts, and Willie Stargell was the league's dominant power hitter. On the other side of the state, and the standings, the Phillies opened Veterans Stadium, another bowl-shaped artificial turf stadium; their attendance more than doubled. The league reached a new all-time attendance high, with everyone but San Diego clearing a million.

MVP Joe Torre of the Cardinals hit .363, the NL's highest since 1948. Atlanta's Earl Williams was Rookie of the Year. Fergie Jenkins captured the Cy Young, but the Cubs lacked the offense to win. Ernie Banks and Jim Bunning retired, neither ever appearing in a World Series.

The Pirates disposed of the Giants in four games—the first League Championship Series in six tries that did not end in a sweep. Bucs first baseman Bob Robertson hit 4 homers in the NLCS, including 3 long balls at Candlestick in Game 2. Pittsburgh lost the first two World Series games at Baltimore as the Orioles tallied 16 runs. The Pirates, however, won the next three with pitching and big rallies (Game 4 was the first World Series game played at night).

The Orioles came back from a 2-0 deficit to win a 10-inning thriller in Game 6. Roberto Clemente, who hit .414 in the Series and played astounding defense, clubbed a homer the next day in the deciding 2-1 victory. Steve Blass, who allowed just 7 hits—and 4 walks—in 18 innings, racked up his second complete-game victory of the Series.

1971 AMERICAN LEAGUE

TEAM	W	L	T	PCT	GB	HW	HL	R	OR	PA	H	2B	3B	HR	BB	SO	HB	SH	AVG	OBP	SLG	OPS	AOPS	BR	ABR	PF	SB	CS	BSA	BSR
EAST																														
Bal	101	57	0	.639	—	53	24	**742**	**530**	6143	1382	207	25	158	**672**	844	46	85	**.261**	**.347**	.398	**745**	**117**	**137**	**132**	101	66	38	63	1
Det	91	71	0	.562	12	**54**	27	701	645	6196	1399	214	38	**179**	540	854	**55**	62	.254	.325	**.405**	730	108	88	58	104	35	43	45	-7
Bos	85	77	0	.525	18	47	33	691	667	6107	1360	**246**	28	161	552	871	32	75	.252	.322	.397	719	102	72	24	107	51	34	60	-1
NY	82	80	0	.506	21	44	37	648	641	6164	1377	195	**43**	97	581	**717**	37	77	.254	.328	.360	688	107	22	54	95	75	55	58	-3
Was	63	96	0	.396	38.5	35	46	537	660	5986	1219	189	30	86	575	956	28	58	.230	.307	.326	633	90	-86	-61	95	68	45	60	-1
Cle	60	102	0	.370	43	29	52	543	747	6061	1303	200	20	109	467	868	31	67	.238	.300	.342	642	80	-85	-131	110	57	37	61	0
WEST																														
Oak	101	60	0	.627	—	46	35	691	564	6191	1383	195	25	160	542	1018	37	80	.252	.321	.384	705	108	41	54	98	80	53	60	-1
KC	85	76	0	.528	16	44	37	603	566	5914	1323	225	40	80	490	819	25	45	.250	.313	.353	666	96	-28	-23	99	**130**	46	**74**	**13**
Chi	79	83	0	.488	22.5	39	42	617	597	6114	1346	185	30	138	562	870	51	81	.250	.325	.373	698	101	33	16	103	83	65	56	-4
Cal	76	86	0	.469	25.5	35	46	511	576	6079	1271	213	18	96	441	827	29	83	.231	.290	.329	619	87	-132	-95	93	72	34	68	4
Min	74	86	0	.463	26.5	37	42	654	670	6072	**1406**	197	31	116	512	846	25	64	.260	.323	.372	695	100	27	9	103	66	44	60	-1
Mil	69	92	0	.429	32	34	48	534	609	5904	1188	160	23	104	543	924	30	**107**	.229	.304	.329	633	86	-90	-85	99	82	53	61	-1
Total	966	—	—	—	—	497	469	7472	—	72931	15957	2426	351	1484	6477	10414	426	884	.247	.317	.364	681	—	—	—	—	865	547	61	-1

TEAM	CG	SHO	GR	SV	IP	H	HR	BB	SO	BR/9	ERA	AERA	OAV	OOB	PR	APR	PF	OSB	OCS	FA	E	WPB	DP	FW	PW	BW	BSW	DIF
EAST																												
Bal	**71**	15	177	22	1415.1	1257	125	**416**	793	**10.8**	**2.99**	**114**	.239	**.295**	**74**	66	98	56	51	.981	112	53	148	.7	7.1	**14.2**	.1	-.0
Det	53	11	265	32	1468.1	1355	126	609	**1000**	12.3	3.63	100	.247	.325	-28	-3	105	81	41	**.983**	**106**	52	156	**1.2**	-.3	6.2	-.7	3.6
Bos	44	11	247	35	1443.0	1424	136	535	871	12.5	3.80	98	.259	.327	-55	-13	107	78	31	.981	116	55	149	.6	-1.4	2.6	-.0	2.3
NY	67	15	189	12	1452.0	1382	126	423	707	11.3	3.43	96	.252	.306	4	-26	95	**38**	40	.981	125	58	159	.1	-2.8	5.8	-.3	-1.8
Was	30	10	315	26	1418.2	1376	132	554	762	12.5	3.70	91	.258	.331	-37	-53	97	84	45	.977	141	66	170	-1.0	-5.7	-6.6	-.0	-3.2
Cle	21	7	**325**	32	1440.0	1352	154	770	937	13.6	4.28	90	.252	.348	-130	-59	112	73	52	.981	116	84	159	.6	-6.3	-14.1	.0	-1.2
WEST																												
Oak	57	18	227	36	1469.1	**1229**	131	501	999	**10.8**	3.05	109	**.228**	.296	67	46	96	72	33	.981	117	54	157	.5	4.9	5.8	-.0	9.3
KC	34	15	264	**44**	1420.1	1301	**84**	496	775	11.6	3.25	106	.247	.314	33	30	99	68	43	.979	132	52	**178**	-.4	3.2	-2.5	**1.4**	2.7
Chi	46	19	259	32	1450.1	1348	100	468	976	11.4	3.12	**114**	.247	.307	55	**68**	103	102	48	.975	160	75	128	-1.9	**7.3**	1.7	-.4	-8.7
Cal	39	11	243	32	1481.0	1246	101	607	904	11.5	3.10	105	.230	.310	60	25	94	85	49	.980	131	85	159	-.2	2.7	-10.2	.4	2.3
Min	43	9	252	25	1416.2	1384	139	529	895	12.4	3.81	93	.257	.326	-55	-43	102	73	44	.980	118	54	134	.4	-4.6	1.0	-.0	-2.7
Mil	32	**23**	238	32	1416.1	1303	130	569	795	12.1	3.38	103	.247	.321	13	16	101	55	**70**	.977	138	**41**	152	-.7	1.7	-9.1	-.0	-3.3
Total	537	164	3001	360	17291.1	—	—	—	—	11.9	3.46	—	.247	.317	—	—	—	—	—	.980	1512	729	1849	—	—	—	—	—

BATTER-FIELDER WINS	BATTING AVERAGE	ON-BASE PERCENTAGE	SLUGGING AVERAGE	ON-BASE PLUS SLUGGING	ADJUSTED OPS	ADJUSTED BATTER RUNS
Nettles-Cle 5.9	Oliva-Min 337	Murcer-NY 427	Oliva-Min 546	Murcer-NY 969	Murcer-NY 182	Murcer-NY 60.5
Melton-Chi..........4.9	Murcer-NY...........331	Rettenmund-Bal.....422	Murcer-NY 543	Oliva-Min 915	Oliva-Min 153	White-NY 39.2
Murcer-NY..........4.5	Rettenmund-Bal....318	Kaline-Det............416	Cash-Det 531	Cash-Det 903	White-NY 152	Rettenmund-Bal...35.2
Patek-KC............4.3	Tovar-Min.............311	Buford-Bal............413	F.Robinson-Bal 510	F.Robinson-Bal 894	F.Robinson-Bal 152	Buford-Bal............34.8
White-NY............3.8	Carew-Min 307	White-NY 388	Jackson-Oak.........508	Buford-Bal............890	Buford-Bal.............151	F.Robinson-Bal 33.0
RUNS	**HITS**	**DOUBLES**	**TRIPLES**	**HOME RUNS**	**TOTAL BASES**	**RUNS BATTED IN**
Buford-Bal..............99	Tovar-Min.............204	Smith-Bos..............33	Patek-KC 11	Melton-Chi 33	Smith-Bos............302	Killebrew-Min 119
Tovar-Min...............94	Alomar-Cal............179	Schaal-KC 31	Carew-Min 10	Jackson-Oak..........32	Jackson-Oak.........288	F.Robinson-Bal 99
Murcer-NY 94	Carew-Min 177	Rodriguez-Det 30	Blair-Bal 8	Cash-Det 32	Murcer-NY............287	Smith-Bos...............96
Carew-Min 88	Smith-Bos 175	Oliva-Min 30		Smith-Bos..............30	Melton-Chi 267	Murcer-NY 94
Jackson-Oak...........87	Murcer-NY 175				Oliva-Min 266	Bando-Oak 94
BASES ON BALLS	**STOLEN BASES**	**BASE STEALING RUNS**	**FIELDING RUNS-INFIELD**	**FIELDING RUNS-OUTFIELD**	**OUTFIELD ASSISTS**	**CATCHER CS PCT.**
Killebrew-Min 114	Otis-KC...................52	Otis-KC..................8.6	Nettles-Cle..........46.1	Tovar-Min.............14.1	Yastrzemski-Bos 16	Rodriguez-Mil 57.7
Yastrzemski-Bos ...106	Patek-KC 49	Patek-KC 5.9	Michael-NY...........24.6	Yastrzemski-Bos ..10.7	Smith-Bos...............15	Herrmann-Chi........40.6
Schaal-KC 103	Alomar-Cal..............39	Alomar-Cal.............5.1	Melton-Chi 23.7	Unser-Was.............9.6	Jackson-Oak...........15	Mitterwald-Min 38.5
Petrocelli-Bos..........91	Campaneris-Oak 34	Campaneris-Oak ...5.0	Alomar-Cal...........22.8	Stanley-Det............9.3	Tovar-Min...............14	Casanova-Was 34.7
Murcer-NY 91		Harper-Mil..............4.4	Patek-KC 21.6	Otis-KC..................8.2	Pinson-Cle..............11	Stephenson-Cal...29.5
WINS	**WINNING PCT.**	**WINS ABOVE TEAM**	**GAMES STARTED**	**COMPLETE GAMES**	**FEWEST HITS/GAME**	**FEWEST BB/GAME**
Lolich-Det 25	McNally-Bal 808	McNally-Bal 6.7	Lolich-Det 45	Lolich-Det 29	Blue-Oak..............6.03	Peterson-NY 1.38
Blue-Oak.................24	Dobson-Oak 750	Blue-Oak................6.1	Wood-Chi...............42	Blue-Oak.................24	McDowell-Cle 6.71	Kline-NY 1.50
Wood-Chi................22	Blue-Oak...............750	Wood-Chi...............5.7	Perry-Min...............39	Wood-Chi................22	May-Cal 6.91	Kaat-Min 1.62
McNally-Bal 21	Dobson-Bal...........714	Messersmith-Cal....5.0	Bradley-Chi............39	Cuellar-Bal..............21	Messersmith-Cal..7.29	Wood-Chi.............1.67
Hunter-Oak.............21		Coleman-Det 4.8	Blue-Oak.................39	Palmer-Bal..............20	Wright-Cal............7.32	Drago-KC..............1.72
STRIKEOUTS	**STRIKEOUTS/GAME**	**GAMES**	**SAVES**	**BASE RUNNERS/9**	**ADJUSTED RELIEF RUNS**	**RELIEF RANKING**
Lolich-Det 308	Blue-Oak..............8.68	Sanders-Mil 83	Sanders-Mil 31	Blue-Oak..............8.68	Sanders-Mil 22.9	Sanders-Mil 40.5
Blue-Oak...............301	McDowell-Cle 8.05	Scherman-Det........69	Abernathy-KC 23	Fingers-Oak..........9.19	Burgmeier-KC.......15.0	Burgmeier-KC......30.0
Coleman-Det 236	Johnson-Chi 7.74	Burgmeier-KC.........67	Scherman-Det 20	Wood-Chi.............9.19	Mingori-Cle 13.7	Scherman-Det 18.5
Blyleven-Min 224	Coleman-Det 7.43	Abernathy-KC.........63	Fingers-Oak............17	Grzenda-Was.......9.21	Grzenda-Was.......10.8	Abernathy-KC.......12.0
Wood-Chi...............210	Lolich-Det 7.37		Burgmeier-KC.........17	Sanders-Mil 9.84	Scherman-Det.....10.6	Grzenda-Was........11.4
INNINGS PITCHED	**OPPONENTS' AVG.**	**OPPONENTS' OBP**	**EARNED RUN AVERAGE**	**ADJUSTED ERA**	**ADJUSTED STARTER RUNS**	**PITCHER WINS**
Lolich-Det 376.0	Blue-Oak..............189	Blue-Oak..............251	Blue-Oak.............1.82	Wood-Chi..............186	Wood-Chi............55.1	**Wood-Chi 5.7**
Wood-Chi.............334.0	McDowell-Cle 207	Wood-Chi..............263	Wood-Chi.............1.91	Blue-Oak...............183	Blue-Oak.............53.6	**Blue-Oak..............5.3**
Blue-Oak.............312.0	May-Cal 213	Kline-NY 275	Palmer-Bal 2.68	Siebert-Bos...........128	Lolich-Det 28.0	**Sanders-Mil.........4.5**
Cuellar-Bal.........292.1	Messersmith-Cal...218	Dobson-Bal...........278	Hedlund-KC 2.71	Palmer-Bal............127	Palmer-Bal...........23.3	**Burgmeier-KC....3.7**
Coleman-Det 286.0	Palmer-Bal............221	Hunter-Oak...........281	Blyleven-Min 2.81	Hedlund-KC..........127	Blyleven-Min 22.9	**Siebert-Bos.........3.3**

The Beltway Bandit

After missing the 1970 season as his case against baseball's reserve clause went to Federal Court, Curt Flood joined Washington but retired after 13 games. Those Senators were a sad bunch. As manager Ted Williams fumed, owner Bob Short hauled in problems and rejects like Denny McLain, Don Wert, Jerry Janeski, and Joe Foy; things worked out as well as could be expected. The Senators lost 96 games, but Cleveland kept them out of the basement.

Boston made an early run at the AL East title, but the Orioles again improved as the weather got hotter, clearing 100 wins for the third consecutive season. Earl Weaver's club again paced in runs and fewest allowed, with four 20-game winners in his rotation and Don Buford and Merv Rettenmund ranking among the league's top four in on-base percentage.

With Aurelio Rodriguez, Ed Brinkman, and Joe Coleman heisted from Washington, the Tigers improved under Billy Martin. Yankees center fielder Bobby Murcer enjoyed a breakout season.

Oakland won the franchise's first crown since 1931 on the left arm of MVP and Cy Young winner Vida Blue, who led the AL in ERA and shutouts. Only Reggie Jackson starred on offense, but everyone in Dick Williams' lineup made a solid contribution. Defending champion Minnesota collapsed to fifth, declining 23 games amidst poor pitching; Tony Oliva won the batting title but tore up his knee. Kansas City finished second but never contended.

Baltimore swept the A's in the ALCS, then lost a painful seven-game World Series to the Pirates.

Following the season, the carpetbagging Short—refusing to pay his rent bills and citing poor attendance—moved the Senators to Dallas for 1972 and renamed them the Texas Rangers. As Short left the nation's capital without a major league team for the first time since 1900, it was fitting, then, that two great Senators of years past, Goose Goslin and Heinie Manush, died.

1970 NATIONAL LEAGUE

TEAM	W	L	T	PCT	GB	HW	HL	R	OR	PA	H	2B	3B	HR	BB	SO	HB	SH	AVG	OBP	SLG	OPS	AOPS	BR	ABR	PF	SB	CS	BSA	BSR
EAST																														
Pit	89	73	0	.549	—	50	32	729	664	6231	**1522**	235	**70**	130	444	871	44	53	**.270**	.325	.406	731	102	8	10	100	66	34	66	3
Chi	84	78	0	.519	5	46	34	806	679	6229	1424	228	44	179	607	844	20	75	.259	.333	.415	748	94	50	-35	112	39	16	71	3
NY	83	79	0	.512	6	44	38	695	**630**	6275	1358	211	42	120	684	1062	26	74	.249	.333	.370	703	94	-21	-29	101	118	54	69	7
StL	76	86	0	.469	13	34	47	744	747	6376	1497	218	51	113	569	961	26	52	.263	.331	.379	710	94	-22	-42	103	117	47	71	9
Phi	73	88	0	.453	15.5	40	40	594	730	6099	1299	224	58	101	519	1066	25	62	.238	.305	.356	661	85	-127	-113	98	72	64	53	-7
Mon	73	89	0	.451	16	39	41	687	807	6251	1284	211	35	136	659	972	39	**107**	.237	.323	.365	688	91	-61	-62	100	65	45	59	-1
WEST																														
Cin	102	60	0	.630	—	**57**	24	775	681	6222	1498	253	45	**191**	547	984	29	58	**.270**	.336	**.436**	**772**	**112**	95	90	101	115	52	69	7
LA	87	74	0	.540	14.5	39	42	749	684	6293	1515	233	67	87	541	841	24	72	**.270**	.334	.382	716	102	-6	22	96	**138**	57	71	10
SF	86	76	0	.531	16	48	33	**831**	826	6469	1460	**257**	35	165	**729**	1005	**56**	66	.262	**.351**	.409	760	111	**98**	**107**	99	83	27	**75**	9
Hou	79	83	0	.488	23	44	37	744	763	6305	1446	250	47	129	598	911	27	63	.259	.332	.391	723	104	6	36	96	114	41	74	**11**
Atl	76	86	0	.469	26	42	39	736	772	6202	1495	215	24	160	522	**736**	38	54	**.270**	.334	.404	738	98	32	-9	106	58	34	63	1
SD	63	99	0	.389	39	31	50	681	788	6145	1353	208	36	172	500	1164	39	83	.246	.312	.391	703	98	-51	-26	96	60	45	57	-3
Total	971	—	—	—	—	514	457	8771	—	75097	17151	2743	554	1683	6919	11417	393	819	.258	.329	.392	721	—	—	—	—	1045	516	67	49

TEAM	CG	SHO	GR	SV	IP	H	HR	BB	SO	BR/9	ERA	AERA	OAV	OOB	PR	APR	PF	OSB	OCS	FA	E	WPB	DP	FW	PW	BW	BSW	DIF
EAST																												
Pit	36	13	288	43	1453.2	1386	106	625	990	12.7	3.70	107	.255	.334	56	42	98	64	56	.979	137	55	**195**	.3	4.2	1.0	-.1	2.6
Chi	**59**	9	205	25	1435.0	1402	143	**475**	1000	11.9	3.76	**120**	.256	.316	46	**106**	111	71	48	.978	137	59	146	.3	**10.6**	-3.5	-.1	-4.3
NY	47	10	228	32	1459.2	**1260**	135	575	**1064**	**11.5**	**3.45**	118	**.233**	**.307**	**97**	98	100	64	42	.979	124	54	136	1.0	9.8	-2.9	.3	-6.2
StL	51	11	278	20	1475.2	1483	**102**	632	960	13.0	4.06	102	.263	.337	-2	13	102	86	45	.977	150	86	159	-.4	1.3	-4.2	.5	-2.2
Phi	24	8	277	36	1461.0	1483	132	538	1047	12.7	4.17	96	.265	.330	-20	-25	99	122	47	**.981**	**114**	71	134	**1.5**	-2.5	-11.3	-1.1	5.8
Mon	29	10	285	32	1438.2	1434	162	716	914	13.8	4.50	92	.261	.349	-73	-56	103	78	45	.977	141	61	193	.0	-5.6	-6.2	-.5	4.2
WEST																												
Cin	32	15	252	**60**	1444.2	1370	118	592	843	12.4	3.69	109	.251	.325	57	56	100	**46**	38	.976	151	53	173	-.5	5.6	9.0	.3	6.6
LA	37	**17**	227	42	1458.2	1394	164	496	880	11.9	3.82	101	.250	.314	37	4	95	106	28	.978	135	66	135	.4	.4	2.2	.6	3.0
SF	50	7	253	30	1457.2	1514	156	604	931	13.3	4.50	88	.267	.339	-74	-88	98	114	31	.973	170	106	153	-1.5	-8.8	**10.7**	.5	4.1
Hou	36	6	**302**	35	1456.0	1491	131	577	942	13.0	4.23	92	.265	.336	-30	-58	96	78	**58**	.978	140	103	144	.1	-5.8	3.6	**.7**	-.6
Atl	45	9	204	24	1430.2	1451	185	478	960	12.3	4.33	99	.261	.320	-45	-7	106	123	32	.977	141	74	118	.0	-.7	-.9	-.3	-3.2
SD	24	9	279	32	1440.1	1483	149	611	886	13.3	4.36	92	.267	.341	-50	-57	99	93	46	.975	158	**42**	159	-.9	-5.7	-2.6	-.7	-8.2
Total	470	124	3078	411	17411.2	—	—	—	—	12.6	4.05	—	.258	.329	—	—	—	—	—	.977	1698	830	1845	—	—	—	—	—

BATTER-FIELDER WINS	BATTING AVERAGE	ON-BASE PERCENTAGE	SLUGGING AVERAGE	ON-BASE PLUS SLUGGING	ADJUSTED OPS	ADJUSTED BATTER RUNS
McCovey-SF 6.5	Carty-Atl 366	Carty-Atl 454	McCovey-SF 612	McCovey-SF 1056	McCovey-SF 182	McCovey-SF 66.5
Bench-Cin.......... 5.9	Torre-StL..............325	McCovey-SF 444	Perez-Cin.............589	Carty-Atl 1037	Carty-Atl 167	Perez-Cin............52.0
Perez-Cin........... 4.6	Sanguillen-Pit 325	Dietz-SF...............426	Bench-Cin.............587	Hickman-Chi.......1001	Perez-Cin.............162	Carty-Atl 48.8
Carty-Atl 4.0	Williams-Chi.........322	Hickman-Chi 419	Williams-Chi..........586	Perez-Cin.............990	Dietz-SF...............153	Dietz-SF...............44.4
Morgan-Hou 3.9	Parker-LA.............319	Perez-Cin.............401	Carty-Atl 584	Williams-Chi..........977	Hickman-Chi 148	Carbo-Cin 41.3

RUNS	HITS	DOUBLES	TRIPLES	HOME RUNS	TOTAL BASES	RUNS BATTED IN
Williams-Chi.........137	Williams-Chi.........205	Parker-LA..............47	Davis-LA 16	Bench-Cin..............45	Williams-Chi.........373	Bench-Cin............148
Bonds-SF.............134	Rose-Cin..............205	McCovey-SF 39	Kessinger-Chi 14	Williams-Chi...........42	Bench-Cin............355	Williams-Chi.........129
Rose-Cin..............120	Torre-StL..............203	Rose-Cin................37	Clemente-Pit...........10	Perez-Cin...............40	Perez-Cin.............346	Perez-Cin.............129
Brock-StL.............114	Brock-StL.............202	Dietz-SF.................36	Bonds-SF................10	McCovey-SF 39	Bonds-SF.............334	McCovey-SF 126
Tolan-Cin 112	Alou-Pit................201	Bonds-SF...............36			Gaston-SD............317	H.Aaron-Atl...........118

BASES ON BALLS	STOLEN BASES	BASE STEALING RUNS	FIELDING RUNS-INFIELD	FIELDING RUNS-OUTFIELD	OUTFIELD ASSISTS	CATCHER CS PCT.
McCovey-SF 137	Tolan-Cin 57	Bonds-SF...............7.1	Alley-Pit 31.4	Staub-Mon.............6.3	Stargell-Pit..............16	Edwards-Hou.......45.4
Staub-Mon............112	Brock-StL................51	Brock-StL..............6.0	Maxvill-StL 27.6	Bonds-SF...............5.8	Henderson-SF 15	Bateman-Mon......44.0
Dietz-SF...............109	Bonds-SF................48	Tolan-Cin 5.5	Rader-Hou 25.3	Jones-NY...............5.8	Alou-Pit...................15	Sanguillen-Pit 43.4
Wynn-Hou.............106	Morgan-Hou............42	Morgan-Hou...........4.7	Wine-Mon 18.7	Davis-LA 5.7		Grote-NY 39.4
Morgan-Hou..........102	Davis-LA 38	Harrelson-NY.........3.7	Santo-Chi.............18.3	Henderson-SF 3.9		Cannizzaro-SD 32.9

WINS	WINNING PCT.	WINS ABOVE TEAM	GAMES STARTED	COMPLETE GAMES	FEWEST HITS/GAME	FEWEST BB/GAME
Perry-SF 23	Gibson-StL............767	Gibson-StL............9.2	Perry-SF 41	Jenkins-Chi............24	Simpson-Cin........6.39	Jenkins-Chi..........1.73
Gibson-StL.............23	Nolan-Cin.............720	Morton-Mon 5.1	Jenkins-Chi............39	Perry-SF 23	Seaver-NY 7.12	Marichal-SF 1.78
Jenkins-Chi............22	Walker-Pit 714	Perry-SF 5.0	Sutton-LA................38	Gibson-StL.............23	Walker-Pit 7.12	Osteen-LA 1.81
Merritt-Cin..............20	Perry-SF 639	Simpson-Cin 4.7	Holtzman-Chi..........38	Seaver-NY 19	Gentry-NY 7.41	McAndrew-NY 1.86
	Merritt-Cin............625	Walker-Pit 4.2	Hands-Chi...............38	Dierker-Hou 17	Jenkins-Chi..........7.62	Merritt-Cin...........2.04

STRIKEOUTS	STRIKEOUTS/GAME	GAMES	SAVES	BASE RUNNERS/9	ADJUSTED RELIEF RUNS	RELIEF RANKING
Seaver-NY 283	Seaver-NY 8.76	Herbel-SD-NY.........76	Granger-Cin...........35	Jenkins-Chi..........9.55	Selma-Phi...........20.3	Selma-Phi 30.1
Jenkins-Chi..........274	Gibson-StL..........8.39	Selma-Phi 73	Giusti-Pit.................26	Singer-LA.............9.56	Carroll-Cin 15.3	Granger-Cin.........22.3
Gibson-StL...........274	Veale-Pit 7.93	Linzy-SF-StL...........67	Brewer-LA...............24	Seaver-NY 9.82	C.Taylor-StL 14.5	Carroll-Cin 22.2
Perry-SF 214	Jenkins-Chi..........7.88	Granger-Cin...........67	Raymond-Mon 23	Brewer-LA.........10.01	Gullett-Cin...........14.4	McMahon-SF 21.7
Holtzman-Chi........202	Stoneman-Mon....7.63	Giusti-Pit 66	Selma-Phi 22	McAndrew-NY ...10.06	McMahon-SF 12.3	Giusti-Pit.............17.3

INNINGS PITCHED	OPPONENTS' AVG.	OPPONENTS' OBP	EARNED RUN AVERAGE	ADJUSTED ERA	ADJUSTED STARTER RUNS	PITCHER WINS
Perry-SF 328.2	Simpson-Cin 198	Jenkins-Chi...........264	Seaver-NY 2.82	Seaver-NY 144	Seaver-NY 39.8	**Gibson-StL 4.5**
Jenkins-Chi........313.0	Seaver-NY 214	Seaver-NY 272	Simpson-Cin........3.02	Simpson-Cin.........134	Jenkins-Chi..........37.1	**Seaver-NY 4.4**
Gibson-StL.........294.0	Walker-Pit 219	McAndrew-NY 279	Walker-Pit 3.04	Pappas-Atl-Chi......134	Gibson-StL...........34.3	**Jenkins-Chi 3.9**
Seaver-NY 290.2	Jenkins-Chi...........224	Perry-SF 289	Gibson-StL...........3.12	Holtzman-Chi........133	Holtzman-Chi.......31.4	**Selma-Phi 3.2**
Holtzman-Chi.....287.2	Gentry-NY 224	Gibson-StL...........293	Koosman-NY 3.14	Jenkins-Chi...........133	Perry-SF 26.3	**Holtzman-Chi..... 3.0**

The Times They Are A-Changin'

Veteran outfielder Curt Flood sat out the season, refusing a trade from St. Louis to Philadelphia. Instead he filed suit to challenge baseball's reserve clause, which bound him to the team that first signed him. Flood lost, but he laid the groundwork for free agency.

Two rust-belt clubs built new "cereal bowl" artificial turf parks in midseason: the Reds opened Riverfront Stadium and the Pirates debuting Three Rivers Stadium. In April 1970 only one NL team used turf; by 1979 half did. Great crowds in New York and the new parks helped spike NL attendance. Scoring rose nearly a half-run per game, with homers an all-time high until 1987. But it wasn't just slugging; speed was also back, with steals per game the highest since 1929.

The top NL shortstops of the decade debuted on consecutive days: Dave Concepcion and Larry Bowa. Twenty-year-old Houston outfielder Cesar Cedeno was an immediate sensation.

In a closely bunched NL East, the Pirates pulled away from the Cubs and Mets in September. Last-place Montreal improved 21 games and finished just 16 out. Willie Stargell and Roberto Clemente's bats, and deep pitching, won for Pittsburgh.

Cincinnati, finally showing its tremendous talent, led from opening day and was never challenged. Johnny Bench was the MVP for his awesome power and fine defense, and Tony Perez and Lee May also dented the fences. Wayne Granger's 35 saves established a new mark. The Reds won the NLCS in three nail-biters, allowing just 3 runs to the vaunted Pirates.

During the postseason, umpires in both leagues briefly went on strike—the first-ever arbiter walkout. A few days later, the Reds hosted the first World Series game on plastic, but the Baltimore Orioles won the Fall Classic in five games, including three one-run affairs.

1970 AMERICAN LEAGUE

TEAM	W	L	T	PCT	GB	HW	HL	R	OR	PA	H	2B	3B	HR	BB	SO	HB	SH	AVG	OBP	SLG	OPS	AOPS	BR	ABR	PF	SB	CS	BSA	BSR
East																														
Bal	108	54	0	.667	—	**59**	22	**792**	**574**	6416	1424	213	25	179	**717**	952	44	64	.257	**.344**	.401	745	**110**	105	**92**	102	84	39	68	5
NY	93	69	1	.574	15	53	28	680	612	6211	1381	208	**41**	111	588	**808**	25	60	.251	.324	.365	689	100	-18	12	96	105	61	63	2
Bos	87	75	0	.537	21	52	29	786	722	6250	**1450**	**252**	28	**203**	594	855	40	34	**.262**	.335	**.428**	**763**	109	**123**	72	107	50	48	51	-6
Det	79	83	0	.488	29	42	39	666	731	6199	1282	207	38	148	656	825	34	83	.238	.322	.374	696	97	-3	-9	101	29	30	49	-4
Cle	76	86	0	.469	32	43	38	649	675	6124	1358	197	23	183	503	909	37	76	.249	.314	.394	708	96	1	-30	105	25	36	41	-7
Was	70	92	0	.432	38	40	41	626	689	6223	1302	184	28	138	635	989	**46**	44	.238	.321	.358	679	97	-36	-6	96	72	42	63	1
West																														
Min	98	64	0	.605	—	51	30	744	605	6143	1438	230	**41**	153	501	905	42	79	**.262**	.327	.403	730	105	50	39	102	57	52	52	-6
Oak	89	73	0	.549	9	49	32	678	593	6105	1338	208	24	171	584	977	36	73	.249	.325	.392	717	107	30	52	97	**131**	68	66	5
Cal	86	76	0	.531	12	43	38	631	630	6114	1391	197	40	114	447	922	29	69	.251	.309	.363	672	94	-68	-49	97	69	27	**72**	**6**
Mil	65	97	1	.401	33	38	42	613	751	6170	1305	202	24	126	592	985	36	**115**	.242	.319	.358	677	93	-41	-41	100	91	73	55	-6
KC	65	97	0	.401	33	35	44	611	705	6128	1341	202	**41**	97	514	958	21	63	.244	.309	.348	657	87	-91	-93	100	97	53	65	3
Chi	56	106	0	.346	42	31	53	633	822	6132	1394	192	20	123	477	872	42	51	.253	.315	.362	677	90	-52	-73	104	53	33	62	0
Total	973	—	—	—	—	536	436	8109	—	74215	16404	2492	373	1746	6808	10957	432	811	.250	.322	.379	701	—	—	—	—	863	562	61	-7

TEAM	CG	SHO	GR	SV	IP	H	HR	BB	SO	BR/9	ERA	AERA	OAV	OOB	PR	APR	PF	OSB	OCS	FA	E	WPB	DP	FW	PW	BW	BSW	DIF
East																												
Bal	**60**	12	228	31	1478.2	1317	139	469	941	**11.0**	**3.15**	**117**	.240	**.300**	**93**	**88**	99	55	43	.981	117	56	148	**1.1**	**9.1**	**9.5**	.6	6.7
NY	36	6	239	49	1471.2	1386	**130**	**451**	777	11.4	3.24	110	.249	.306	77	56	96	**40**	41	.980	130	**44**	146	.4	5.8	1.2	.3	4.3
Bos	38	8	284	44	1446.1	1391	156	594	1003	12.6	3.87	103	.251	.327	-25	17	107	73	34	.974	156	83	131	-1.2	1.8	7.5	-.6	-1.5
Det	33	9	288	39	1447.1	1443	153	623	1045	13.1	4.09	92	.260	.336	-61	-52	101	68	54	.978	133	71	142	.2	-5.4	-.9	-.4	4.5
Cle	34	8	312	35	1451.1	1333	163	689	**1076**	12.8	3.91	102	.247	.335	-31	15	108	57	54	.979	133	76	168	.2	1.6	-3.1	-.7	-2.9
Was	20	11	**316**	40	1457.2	1375	139	611	823	12.4	3.80	95	.252	.328	-13	-32	97	56	49	**.982**	**116**	63	173	**1.1**	-3.3	-.6	.2	-8.4
West																												
Min	26	12	269	**58**	1448.1	1329	**130**	486	940	11.5	3.23	114	.244	.308	78	76	100	55	49	.980	123	49	130	.7	7.9	4.0	-.6	4.9
Oak	33	**15**	309	40	1442.2	**1253**	134	542	858	11.4	3.30	107	**.234**	.307	66	38	95	70	39	.977	141	68	152	-.3	3.9	5.4	.6	-1.6
Cal	21	10	314	49	1462.1	1280	154	559	922	11.6	3.48	104	.237	.312	37	23	98	77	41	.980	127	79	169	.5	2.4	-5.1	**.7**	6.5
Mil	31	2	283	27	1446.2	1397	146	587	895	12.6	4.21	90	.255	.330	-79	-68	102	106	51	.978	136	55	142	.0	-7.1	-4.3	-.6	-4.2
KC	30	11	268	25	1463.2	1346	138	641	915	12.4	3.78	99	.247	.328	-11	-8	101	100	**62**	.976	152	72	162	-.9	-.8	-9.6	.4	-5.0
Chi	20	6	280	30	1430.1	1554	164	556	762	13.6	4.54	85	.280	.347	-132	-101	104	106	45	.975	165	90	**187**	-1.7	-10.5	-7.6	.0	-5.3
Total	382	110	3390	467	17447.0	—	—	—	—	12.2	3.71	—	.250	.322	—	—	—	—	—	.978	1629	806	1850	—	—	—	—	—

BATTER-FIELDER WINS	BATTING AVERAGE	ON-BASE PERCENTAGE	SLUGGING AVERAGE	ON-BASE PLUS SLUGGING	ADJUSTED OPS	ADJUSTED BATTER RUNS
Harper-Mil 5.6	Johnson-Cal 329	Yastrzemski-Bos ...452	Yastrzemski-Bos ...592	Yastrzemski-Bos .1044	Yastrzemski-Bos ...174	Yastrzemski-Bos ..64.5
Yastrzemski-Bos5.5	Yastrzemski-Bos ...329	Howard-Was 416	Powell-Bal 549	Howard-Was 962	Howard-Was 172	Howard-Was 61.3
Aparicio-Chi....... 5.3	Oliva-Min 325	Powell-Bal 412	Killebrew-Min 546	Powell-Bal 962	Powell-Bal 162	Killebrew-Min 49.2
Fregosi-Cal......... 4.6	Aparicio-Chi..........313	Killebrew-Min 411	Howard-Was 546	Killebrew-Min 957	Killebrew-Min 161	Powell-Bal...........49.0
Howard-Was....... 4.3	F.Robinson-Bal 306	Bando-Oak 407	Harper-Mil............522	F.Robinson-Bal 918	F.Robinson-Bal 150	Harper-Mil............38.6
RUNS	**HITS**	**DOUBLES**	**TRIPLES**	**HOME RUNS**	**TOTAL BASES**	**RUNS BATTED IN**
Yastrzemski-Bos ...125	Oliva-Min 204	Tovar-Min...............36	Tovar-Min................13	Howard-Was...........44	Yastrzemski-Bos ...335	Howard-Was 126
Tovar-Min..............120	Johnson-Cal 202	Otis-KC....................36	Stanley-Det.............11	Killebrew-Min..........41	Oliva-Min 323	T.Conigliaro-Bos ...116
White-NY 109	Tovar-Min..............195	Oliva-Min 36	Otis-KC.....................9	Yastrzemski-Bos 40	Harper-Mil..............315	Powell-Bal..............114
Smith-Bos..............109	Yastrzemski-Bos ...186	Harper-Mil................35		T.Conigliaro-Bos 36	Howard-Was.........309	Killebrew-Min 113
Harper-Mil.............104	White-NY 180	Cardenas-Min 34		Powell-Bal...............35	Powell-Bal..............289	Oliva-Min 107
BASES ON BALLS	**STOLEN BASES**	**BASE STEALING RUNS**	**FIELDING RUNS-INFIELD**	**FIELDING RUNS-OUTFIELD**	**OUTFIELD ASSISTS**	**CATCHER CS PCT.**
Howard-Was.........132	Campaneris-Oak 42	Otis-KC....................6.6	Brinkman-Was.......31.4	Oliva-Min 13.3	Smith-Bos...............15	Fosse-Cle 54.5
Yastrzemski-Bos ...128	Harper-Mil..............38	Campaneris-Oak ...5.7	Knoop-Chi.............27.3	Blair-Bal................12.1	Otis-KC....................15	Mitterwald-Min 53.4
Killebrew-Min 128	Alomar-Cal.............35	Stroud-Was.............3.6	Nettles-Cle............26.0	Alou-Oak..................7.8	Murcer-NY 15	Munson-NY...........51.6
Bando-Oak 118	Kelly-KC..................34	Alomar-Cal..............3.5	Aparicio-Chi..........25.3	Tovar-Min.................7.5	Buford-Bal...............13	Casanova-Was 51.1
Buford-Bal.............109	Otis-KC....................33	Johnson-Cal 3.0	Leon-Cle................16.8	Smith-Bos.................6.8		Hendricks-Bal.........48.0
WINS	**WINNING PCT.**	**WINS ABOVE TEAM**	**GAMES STARTED**	**COMPLETE GAMES**	**FEWEST HITS/GAME**	**FEWEST BB/GAME**
Perry-Min...............24	Cuellar-Bal............750	McDowell-Cle 5.5	Perry-Min 40	Cuellar-Bal..............21	Messersmith-Cal..6.66	Peterson-NY 1.38
McNally-Bal 24	McNally-Bal 727	Wright-Cal...............5.0	McNally-Bal 40	McDowell-Cle 19	McDowell-Cle 6.96	Perry-Min 1.84
Cuellar-Bal..............24	Perry-Min 667	Cuellar-Bal..............4.7	Hunter-Oak...............40	Palmer-Bal...............17	Segui-Oak............7.22	Cox-Was................2.06
Wright-Cal...............22	Palmer-Bal.............667	Hargan-Cle 4.3	Dobson-Oak 40	McNally-Bal 16	Johnson-KC..........7.49	Cuellar-Bal............2.09
	Siebert-Bos...........652	Williams-Min 4.3	Cuellar-Bal..............40	Culp-Bos..................15	Culp-Bos..............7.56	Horlen-Chi 2.14
STRIKEOUTS	**STRIKEOUTS/GAME**	**GAMES**	**SAVES**	**BASE RUNNERS/9**	**ADJUSTED RELIEF RUNS**	**RELIEF RANKING**
McDowell-Cle 304	McDowell-Cle 8.97	Wood-Chi...............77	Perranoski-Min........34	Hall-Bal...................8.36	Grant-Oak............25.6	McDaniel-NY 32.4
Lolich-Det 230	Johnson-KC.........8.66	Grant-Oak...............72	McDaniel-NY 29	McDaniel-NY 8.95	Hall-Min 22.2	Knowles-Was.......30.7
Johnson-KC...........206	Cain-Det 7.77	Knowles-Was..........71	Timmermann-Det ...27	Sanders-Mil 9.06	Sanders-Mil 20.9	Perranoski-Min......25.8
Palmer-Bal............199	Lolich-Det 7.59	Williams-Min 68	Knowles-Was...........27	Hall-Min 9.39	McDaniel-NY 20.0	Grant-Oak.............24.2
Culp-Bos...............197	Messersmith-Cal..7.49		Grant-Oak................24	Williams-Min 9.69	Williams-Min.........19.6	Hall-Min 23.0
INNINGS PITCHED	**OPPONENTS' AVG.**	**OPPONENTS' OBP**	**EARNED RUN AVERAGE**	**ADJUSTED ERA**	**ADJUSTED STARTER RUNS**	**PITCHER WINS**
Palmer-Bal.........305.0	Messersmith-Cal...205	Peterson-NY 279	Segui-Oak............2.56	Segui-Oak.............138	Palmer-Bal...........35.0	**McDaniel-NY...... 3.5**
McDowell-Cle 305.0	McDowell-Cle 213	Cuellar-Bal............284	Palmer-Bal...........2.71	McDowell-Cle 137	McDowell-Cle 33.3	**Knowles-Was 3.2**
Cuellar-Bal.........297.2	Segui-Oak.............222	Perry-Min 286	Wright-Cal............2.83	Palmer-Bal.............136	Culp-Bos..............22.1	**Palmer-Bal.......... 3.1**
McNally-Bal 296.0	Culp-Bos...............224	Blyleven-Min 288	Peterson-NY 2.90	Culp-Bos...............131	Wright-Cal............20.9	**Perry-Min........... 3.1**
Perry-Min...........278.2	Johnson-KC..........228	Messersmith-Cal...289	McDowell-Cle 2.92	Wright-Cal.............128	Perry-Min.............19.6	**McDowell-Cle..... 2.9**

This One's for the Birds

As spring training adjourned, the expansion Seattle Pilots—the subject of pitcher Jim Bouton's controversial book *Ball Four*—were sold to car salesman Bud Selig, moved to Milwaukee, and rechristened the Brewers.

Once again, Baltimore was the class of the league, pacing the East from May on. The Yankees had a brief flurry in June, but the Orioles pulled away as the Senators and Tigers declined 16 and 17 games apiece. Baltimore boasted no league leaders in the hitting categories, but with MVP Boog Powell and Frank Robinson, they topped the loop in scoring. The Birds had a deep rotation and a solid bullpen that garnered few saves; the starters completed 60 games, the AL's most in a decade. The rich got richer as the Orioles also welcomed rookies Bobby Grich and Don Baylor. The league's top freshman, however, was Yankees catcher Thurman Munson.

Sparked by the arms of Cy Young winner Jim Perry and 19-year-old Bert Blyleven, Minnesota won its second straight West title. California made a brief run in July but fell back, and the Athletics came on too late. Chicago fell into the basement for the first time since 1948.

Baltimore swept the Twins in the ALCS, then stomped the Reds in a five-game World Series. Brooks Robinson grabbed the headlines with several great defensive plays, but the key was that the Orioles battered Cincinnati pitching and came back from deficits of three or more runs in three of their victories.

Neither division champ escaped tragedy, however. The Twins lost two outfielders, veteran Bob Allison to retirement and rookie Herm Hill to a drowning in Venezuela during winter ball. Former Orioles catcher Dick Brown, forced from the game in 1966 with a brain tumor, also died.

1969 NATIONAL LEAGUE

TEAM	W	L	T	PCT	GB	HW	HL	R	OR	PA	H	2B	3B	HR	BB	SO	HB	SH	AVG	OBP	SLG	OPS	AOPS	BR	ABR	PF	SB	CS	BSA	BSR
EAST																														
NY	100	62	0	.617	—	**52**	30	632	541	6102	1311	184	41	109	527	1089	33	82	.242	.311	.351	662	90	-53	-68	103	66	43	61	-1
Chi	92	70	1	.568	8	49	32	720	611	6243	1400	215	40	142	559	928	36	72	.253	.323	.384	707	93	38	-42	113	30	32	48	-5
Pit	88	74	0	.543	12	47	34	725	652	6235	1557	220	**52**	119	454	944	46	73	**.277**	.334	.398	732	**115**	83	**100**	98	74	34	**69**	**4**
StL	87	75	0	.537	13	42	38	595	**540**	6152	1403	**228**	44	90	503	876	23	57	.253	.316	.359	675	95	-25	-30	101	87	49	64	2
Phi	63	99	0	.389	37	30	51	645	745	6080	1304	227	35	137	549	1130	26	61	.241	.312	.372	684	100	-10	6	98	73	49	60	-1
Mon	52	110	0	.321	48	24	57	582	791	6073	1300	202	33	125	529	962	38	57	.240	.310	.359	669	94	-40	-43	101	52	52	50	-7
WEST																														
Atl	93	69	0	.574	—	50	31	691	631	6098	1411	195	22	141	485	**665**	32	87	.258	.321	.380	701	102	20	15	101	59	48	55	-4
SF	90	72	0	.556	3	**52**	29	713	636	6375	1325	187	28	136	**711**	1054	**66**	82	.242	.334	.361	695	103	35	44	99	71	32	**69**	**4**
Cin	89	73	1	.549	4	50	31	**798**	768	6301	**1558**	224	42	**171**	474	1042	46	**100**	**.277**	**.335**	**.422**	**757**	113	**133**	93	105	79	56	59	-2
LA	85	77	0	.525	8	50	31	645	561	6166	1405	185	**52**	97	484	823	21	96	.254	.315	.359	674	101	-35	6	94	80	51	61	0
Hou	81	81	0	.500	12	**52**	29	676	668	6196	1284	208	40	104	699	972	41	68	.240	.330	.352	682	99	10	20	99	**101**	58	64	2
SD	52	110	0	.321	41	28	53	468	746	5891	1203	180	42	99	423	1143	35	56	.225	.285	.329	614	81	-158	-142	97	45	44	51	-5
Total	973	—	—	—	—	526	446	7890	—	73912	16461	2455	471	1470	6397	11628	443	891	.250	.319	.369	688	—	—	—	—	817	548	60	-12

TEAM	CG	SHO	GR	SV	IP	H	HR	BB	SO	BR/9	ERA	AERA	OAV	OOB	PR	APR	PF	OSB	OCS	FA	E	WPB	DP	FW	PW	BW	BSW	DIF
EAST																												
NY	51	**28**	203	35	1468.1	**1217**	119	517	1012	**10.8**	2.99	**123**	**.227**	**.296**	99	**108**	102	55	48	.980	122	63	146	1.4	**11.3**	-7.1	.0	13.4
Chi	58	22	245	27	1454.1	1366	118	475	1017	11.6	3.34	120	.248	.310	41	97	112	59	54	.979	136	**50**	149	.6	10.2	-4.4	-.4	5.0
Pit	39	9	267	33	1445.2	1348	**96**	553	1124	12.1	3.61	96	.248	.320	-3	-22	97	62	50	.975	155	**50**	169	-.5	-2.3	**10.5**	**.5**	-1.2
StL	63	12	183	26	1460.1	1289	99	511	1004	11.3	**2.94**	122	.237	.305	**106**	105	100	77	40	.978	138	60	144	.5	11.0	-3.1	.3	-2.7
Phi	47	14	236	21	1434.0	1494	134	570	921	13.2	4.14	86	.270	.340	-88	-94	99	68	47	.978	137	76	157	.5	-9.9	.6	.0	-9.3
Mon	26	8	299	21	1426.0	1429	145	702	973	13.8	4.33	85	.263	.350	-117	-99	103	92	49	.971	184	87	**179**	-2.1	-10.4	-4.5	-.6	-11.3
WEST																												
Atl	38	7	221	42	1445.0	1334	144	438	893	11.2	3.53	103	.245	.302	11	14	101	78	27	**.981**	**115**	71	114	**1.8**	1.5	1.6	-.3	7.5
SF	**71**	15	174	17	1473.2	1381	120	461	906	11.5	3.26	108	.248	.307	55	43	98	64	43	.974	169	73	155	-1.3	4.5	4.6	**.5**	.6
Cin	23	11	307	**44**	1465.0	1478	149	611	818	13.2	4.11	91	.262	.338	-84	-55	105	**42**	43	.974	167	93	158	-1.1	-5.8	9.8	-.1	5.2
LA	47	20	190	31	1457.0	1324	122	**420**	975	11.0	3.08	109	.242	.299	83	46	93	80	43	.980	126	68	130	1.2	4.8	.6	.1	-2.7
Hou	52	11	256	34	1435.2	1347	111	547	**1221**	12.1	3.60	99	.247	.318	-1	-7	99	66	**55**	.975	153	88	136	-.4	-.7	2.1	.3	-1.3
SD	16	9	**322**	25	1422.1	1454	113	592	764	13.2	4.24	84	.267	.341	-102	-106	100	74	49	.975	156	86	140	-.5	-11.1	-14.9	-.4	-2.0
Total	531	166	2903	356	17387.1	—	—	—	—	12.1	3.59	—	.250	.319	—	—	—	—	—	.977	1758	865	1777	—	—	—	—	—

BATTER-FIELDER WINS	BATTING AVERAGE	ON-BASE PERCENTAGE	SLUGGING AVERAGE	ON-BASE PLUS SLUGGING	ADJUSTED OPS	ADJUSTED BATTER RUNS
McCovey-SF....... 6.5	Rose-Cin..............348	McCovey-SF.........453	McCovey-SF.........656	McCovey-SF.......1108	McCovey-SF.........211	McCovey-SF........80.2
Wynn-Hou.......... 5.8	Clemente-Pit.........345	Wynn-Hou.............436	H.Aaron-Atl...........607	H.Aaron-Atl.........1003	H.Aaron-Atl...........176	H.Aaron-Atl..........56.7
H.Aaron-Atl 5.1	Jones-NY..............340	Rose-Cin...............428	Allen-Phi...............573	Clemente-Pit..........955	Clemente-Pit..........170	Wynn-Hou.............54.7
Staub-Mon.......... 4.8	Alou-Pit.................331	Staub-Mon............426	Stargell-Pit............556	Staub-Mon............952	Allen-Phi...............167	Staub-Mon............53.6
Clemente-Pit...... 4.8	McCovey-SF.........320	Jones-NY..............422	Clemente-Pit.........544	Allen-Phi...............949	Wynn-Hou.............167	Rose-Cin...............50.3
RUNS	**HITS**	**DOUBLES**	**TRIPLES**	**HOME RUNS**	**TOTAL BASES**	**RUNS BATTED IN**
Rose-Cin..............120	Alou-Pit.................231	Alou-Pit..................41	Clemente-Pit...........12	McCovey-SF...........45	H.Aaron-Atl...........332	McCovey-SF.........126
Bonds-SF..............120	Rose-Cin...............218	Kessinger-Chi.........38	Rose-Cin.................11	H.Aaron-Atl............44	Perez-Cin.............331	Santo-Chi..............123
Wynn-Hou.............113	Brock-StL..............195	Williams-Chi............33	Williams-Chi............10	May-Cin..................38	McCovey-SF.........322	Perez-Cin..............122
Kessinger-Chi.......109	Tolan-Cin..............194	Rose-Cin.................33	Tolan-Cin................10	Perez-Cin................37	Rose-Cin...............321	May-Cin.................110
Alou-Pit.................105	Williams-Chi..........188	Brock-StL................33	Brock-StL................10	Wynn-Hou...............33	May-Cin................321	Banks-Chi.............106
BASES ON BALLS	**STOLEN BASES**	**BASE STEALING RUNS**	**FIELDING RUNS-INFIELD**	**FIELDING RUNS-OUTFIELD**	**OUTFIELD ASSISTS**	**CATCHER CS PCT.**
Wynn-Hou.............148	Brock-StL................53	Bonds-SF...............8.5	Kessinger-Chi......24.8	Callison-Phi.........11.9	Staub-Mon.............16	Bench-Cin............57.1
McCovey-SF.........121	Morgan-Hou...........49	Brock-StL...............6.8	Lanier-SF.............23.6	Flood-StL...............7.0	Williams-Chi............15	Grote-NY..............56.3
Staub-Mon............110	Bonds-SF................45	Morgan-Hou...........5.9	Wine-Mon............19.6	Hisle-Phi................6.9	Flood-StL................14	Hundley-Chi..........50.0
Morgan-Hou..........110	Wills-Mon-LA..........40	Wynn-Hou..............2.6	Money-Phi...........17.6	Clemente-Pit..........5.7	Clemente-Pit...........14	Edwards-Hou.......48.0
Santo-Chi................96	Tolan-Cin................26	Alou-Pit..................2.0	Maxvill-StL...........14.3	Jones-NY................4.6	Brown-SD...............14	Sanguillen-Pit......43.9
WINS	**WINNING PCT.**	**WINS ABOVE TEAM**	**GAMES STARTED**	**COMPLETE GAMES**	**FEWEST HITS/GAME**	**FEWEST BB/GAME**
Seaver-NY..............25	Seaver-NY...........781	Seaver-NY.............7.7	Jenkins-Chi.............42	Gibson-StL..............28	Seaver-NY...........6.65	Marichal-SF.........1.62
Niekro-Atl................23	Marichal-SF..........656	Moose-Pit..............5.4	Sutton-LA................41	Marichal-SF.............27	Maloney-Cin........6.80	Niekro-Atl.............1.80
Marichal-SF............21	Merritt-Cin.............654	Marichal-SF...........4.3	Osteen-LA...............41	Perry-SF..................26	Singer-LA..............6.96	Jenkins-Chi..........2.05
Jenkins-Chi..............21	Koosman-NY.........654	Dierker-Hou...........4.2	Hands-Chi...............41	Jenkins-Chi..............23	Koosman-NY.......6.98	Niekro-Chi-SD......2.07
	Reed-Atl................643	Singer-LA...............4.0	Singer-LA................40	Niekro-Atl................21	Carlton-StL..........7.05	Osteen-LA............2.07
STRIKEOUTS	**STRIKEOUTS/GAME**	**GAMES**	**SAVES**	**BASE RUNNERS/9**	**ADJUSTED RELIEF RUNS**	**RELIEF RANKING**
Jenkins-Chi...........273	Griffin-Hou...........9.56	Granger-Cin...........90	Gladding-Hou.........29	Marichal-SF.........9.13	McGraw-NY.........14.1	McGraw-NY.........19.0
Gibson-StL............269	Wilson-Hou...........9.40	McGinn-Mon...........74	Upshaw-Atl.............27	Dierker-Hou..........9.23	Granger-Cin............9.5	Taylor-NY..............17.2
Singer-LA..............247	Moose-Pit..............8.74	Regan-Chi...............71	Granger-Cin............27	Singer-LA..............9.35	Upshaw-Atl.............9.1	Brewer-LA..............13.9
Wilson-Hou............235	Selma-SD-Chi......8.54	Carroll-Cin...............71	Brewer-LA...............20	Niekro-Atl.............9.40	Taylor-NY...............8.9	Upshaw-Atl...........13.1
Perry-SF.................233	Veale-Pit...............8.49	Reberger-SD...........67	Regan-Chi...............17	Seaver-NY............9.58	DiLauro-NY.............8.7	Granger-Cin..........12.9
INNINGS PITCHED	**OPPONENTS' AVG.**	**OPPONENTS' OBP**	**EARNED RUN AVERAGE**	**ADJUSTED ERA**	**ADJUSTED STARTER RUNS**	**PITCHER WINS**
Perry-SF............325.1	Seaver-NY............207	Dierker-Hou..........261	Marichal-SF.........2.10	Marichal-SF...........167	Gibson-StL............50.2	**Gibson-StL..........6.3**
Osteen-LA..........321.0	Maloney-Cin.........208	Marichal-SF..........261	Carlton-StL..........2.17	Seaver-NY............166	Marichal-SF..........45.3	**Seaver-NY..........5.3**
Singer-LA............315.2	Singer-LA..............210	Singer-LA..............261	Gibson-StL...........2.18	Carlton-StL...........165	Seaver-NY............43.2	**Marichal-SF.........5.0**
Gibson-StL..........314.0	Dierker-Hou..........214	Niekro-Atl..............264	Seaver-NY............2.21	Gibson-StL............165	Hands-Chi.............42.4	**Carlton-StL..........5.0**
Jenkins-Chi.........311.1	Carlton-StL...........216	Seaver-NY............272	Koosman-NY.......2.28	Hands-Chi.............161	Dierker-Hou..........40.0	**Niekro-Atl...........4.6**

MAGICAL MYSTERY METS

The wackiest decade in American history reached an appropriate end as the New York Mets, of all teams, rallied in September to win the NL East, the NLCS, and the World Series. The Mets made a run at the Cubs in July, but sagged as Chicago—with four fine starters and strong hitters in Ron Santo and Billy Williams—built a 9½ game lead in late August. But the Cubs lost 10 of 11 down the stretch as the Mets rallied furiously. With Tom Seaver winning nine times in the last five weeks, the pitching-rich Mets won going away.

Five teams in the NL West, meanwhile, stood poised to win. In fact, on September 10, first-place San Francisco and fifth-place Houston were separated by just 2 games. By September 22, though, only the Giants and Braves remained, but San Francisco lost four to the brutal Padres as Atlanta won 10 straight to clinch. This was the Giants' fifth consecutive second-place finish.

Seaver was a near-unanimous Cy Young and finished a close second in MVP voting behind the Giants' Willie McCovey. Bobby Bonds fanned a new record 187 times, and Jimmy Wynn walked 148 times, also setting an NL mark. Pitcher Wayne Granger made history with his 90 appearances. For the first time, saves were an official statistic. Macmillan published the first edition of its ground-breaking *Baseball Encyclopedia*, setting the standard for sports reference for 20 years.

A sore arm forced Don Drysdale to retire, and Ken Boyer was released. It was also goodbye to former top relievers Roy Face, Dick Radatz, and John Wyatt. Gene Mauch reappeared in a new country with a new team: the Montreal Expos. Almost eight years of experience in Philly prepared him for the 110 losses.

The first National League Championship Series packed surprising power as New York swept the Braves. The World Series was another shock; after Baltimore took Game 1, the Mets roared back to win the next four. Great catches by Tommie Agee and Ron Swoboda, clutch homers from Donn Clendenon and Al Weis, and excellent pitching buried the Orioles.

1969 AMERICAN LEAGUE

TEAM	W	L	T	PCT	GB	HW	HL	R	OR	PA	H	2B	3B	HR	BB	SO	HB	SH	AVG	OBP	SLG	OPS	AOPS	BR	ABR	PF	SB	CS	BSA	BSR
EAST																														
Bal	109	53	0	.673	—	**60**	21	779	**517**	6328	1465	234	29	175	634	**806**	43	74	.265	**.343**	.414	**757**	**117**	**139**	**131**	101	82	45	65	2
Det	90	72	0	.556	19	46	35	701	601	6155	1316	188	29	182	578	922	30	63	.242	.316	.387	703	99	17	-10	104	35	28	56	-2
Bos	87	75	0	.537	22	46	35	743	736	6294	1381	234	37	**197**	**658**	923	32	67	.251	.333	**.415**	748	110	113	78	105	41	47	47	-7
Was	86	76	0	.531	23	47	34	694	644	6196	1365	171	40	148	630	900	32	51	.251	.330	.378	708	110	36	74	95	52	40	57	-3
NY	80	81	1	.497	28.5	48	32	562	587	5990	1247	210	**44**	94	565	840	14	63	.235	.308	.344	652	91	-74	-53	97	119	74	62	0
Cle	62	99	0	.385	46.5	33	48	573	717	6014	1272	173	24	119	535	906	24	47	.237	.307	.345	652	85	-79	-95	103	85	37	70	6
WEST																														
Min	97	65	0	.599	—	57	24	**790**	618	6424	**1520**	**246**	32	163	599	906	43	65	**.268**	.340	.408	748	113	121	100	103	115	70	62	1
Oak	88	74	0	.543	9	49	32	740	678	6403	1400	210	28	148	617	953	**63**	74	.249	.329	.376	705	108	33	61	96	100	39	72	8
Cal	71	91	1	.438	26	43	38	528	652	5980	1221	151	29	88	516	929	32	**75**	.230	.300	.319	619	83	-142	-119	96	54	39	58	-2
KC	69	93	1	.426	28	36	45	586	688	6122	1311	179	32	98	522	901	43	57	.240	.309	.338	647	86	-87	-94	101	129	70	65	4
Chi	68	94	0	.420	29	41	40	625	723	6158	1346	210	27	112	552	844	49	70	.247	.320	.357	677	92	-24	-53	105	54	22	71	4
Sea	64	98	1	.395	33	34	47	639	799	6205	1276	179	27	125	626	1015	34	72	.234	.316	.346	662	92	-54	-49	99	**167**	59	**74**	**16**
Total	973	——		—	—	540	431	7960	—	74269	16120	2385	378	1649	7032	10845	439	778	.246	.321	.369	690	—	—	—	—	1033	570	64	28

TEAM	CG	SHO	GR	SV	IP	H	HR	BB	SO	BR/9	ERA	AERA	OAV	OOB	PR	APR	PF	OSB	OCS	FA	E	WPB	DP	FW	PW	BW	BSW	DIF
EAST																												
Bal	50	**20**	235	36	1473.2	**1194**	**117**	**498**	897	**10.5**	**2.83**	**127**	**.223**	**.290**	**130**	**125**	99	**48**	51	**.984**	**101**	**48**	145	**2.2**	**13.1**	**13.7**	-.0	-1.0
Det	**55**	**20**	251	28	1455.1	1250	128	586	**1032**	11.6	3.31	113	.232	.310	50	69	104	109	44	.979	130	60	130	.5	7.2	-1.0	-.5	2.7
Bos	30	7	298	41	1466.2	1423	155	685	935	13.2	3.92	97	.256	.341	-49	-16	105	84	51	.975	157	82	**178**	-1.0	-1.7	8.2	-1.0	1.5
Was	28	10	311	41	1447.1	1310	135	656	835	12.4	3.49	100	.244	.328	22	2	97	84	**58**	.978	140	70	159	-.0	.2	7.8	-.6	-2.4
NY	53	13	199	20	1440.2	1258	118	522	801	11.2	3.23	109	.236	.304	63	47	97	76	43	.979	131	65	158	.5	4.9	-5.6	-.2	-.1
Cle	35	7	294	22	1437.0	1330	134	681	1000	12.9	3.94	96	.248	.335	-51	-22	105	87	53	.976	145	71	153	-.4	-2.3	-10.0	.4	-6.2
WEST																												
Min	41	8	302	**43**	1497.2	1388	119	524	906	11.7	3.24	112	.246	.313	64	66	100	70	35	.977	150	66	177	-.6	6.9	10.5	-.1	-.7
Oak	42	14	276	36	1480.2	1356	163	586	887	12.0	3.71	93	.245	.320	-15	-48	95	84	48	.979	136	81	162	.2	-5.0	6.4	.6	4.8
Cal	25	9	285	39	1438.1	1294	126	517	885	11.7	3.54	99	.242	.313	13	-8	96	89	56	.978	136	94	164	.2	-.8	-12.5	-.5	3.5
KC	42	10	249	25	1464.2	1357	136	560	894	11.9	3.72	99	.246	.316	-15	-4	102	75	43	.975	157	69	114	-1.0	-.4	-9.9	.2	-.9
Chi	29	10	265	25	1437.2	1470	146	564	810	12.9	4.21	91	.267	.337	-93	-55	106	109	47	.981	122	95	163	1.0	-5.8	-5.6	.2	-2.8
Sea	21	6	**357**	33	1463.2	1490	172	653	963	13.5	4.35	84	.264	.343	-118	-115	100	117	46	.974	167	82	149	-1.5	-12.1	-5.1	**1.4**	.3
Total	451	134	3322	389	17503.1	—	—	—	—	12.1	3.62	—	.246	.321	—	—	—	—	—	.978	1672	883	1852	—	—	—	—	—

BATTER-FIELDER WINS	BATTING AVERAGE	ON-BASE PERCENTAGE	SLUGGING AVERAGE	ON-BASE PLUS SLUGGING	ADJUSTED OPS	ADJUSTED BATTER RUNS
Petrocelli-Bos....7.6	Carew-Min............332	Killebrew-Min........427	Jackson-Oak.........608	Jackson-Oak.......1018	Jackson-Oak.........189	Jackson-Oak........69.6
Jackson-Oak......6.3	Smith-Bos.............309	F.Robinson-Bal 415	Petrocelli-Bos........589	Killebrew-Min......1011	Howard-Was.........180	Howard-Was........64.5
Aparicio-Chi.......5.4	Oliva-Min 309	Jackson-Oak.........410	Killebrew-Min 584	Petrocelli-Bos........992	Killebrew-Min........176	Killebrew-Min.......63.6
Cardenas-Min 4.9	F.Robinson-Bal 308	Petrocelli-Bos........403	Howard-Was 574	Howard-Was.........976	Petrocelli-Bos........168	Petrocelli-Bos.......50.9
Killebrew-Min.....4.6	Powell-Bal.............304	Howard-Was.........402	Powell-Bal.............559	F.Robinson-Bal 955	F.Robinson-Bal 164	F.Robinson-Bal 49.4

RUNS	HITS	DOUBLES	TRIPLES	HOME RUNS	TOTAL BASES	RUNS BATTED IN
Jackson-Oak.........123	Oliva-Min 197	Oliva-Min 39	Unser-Was................8	Killebrew-Min..........49	Howard-Was.........340	Killebrew-Min........140
F.Robinson-Bal 111	Clarke-NY.............183	Jackson-Oak...........36	Smith-Bos.................7	Howard-Was...........48	Jackson-Oak.........334	Powell-Bal.............121
Howard-Was.........111	Blair-Bal................178	Johnson-Bal............34	Clarke-NY.................7	Jackson-Oak...........47	Killebrew-Min........324	Jackson-Oak.........118
Killebrew-Min.........106	Howard-Was..........175	Petrocelli-Bos..........32		Yastrzemski-Bos 40	Oliva-Min 316	Bando-Oak 113
Bando-Oak 106	Horton-Cle............174	Blair-Bal..................32		Petrocelli-Bos..........40	Petrocelli-Bos........315	

BASES ON BALLS	STOLEN BASES	BASE STEALING RUNS	FIELDING RUNS-INFIELD	FIELDING RUNS-OUTFIELD	OUTFIELD ASSISTS	CATCHER CS PCT.
Killebrew-Min.........145	Harper-Sea.............73	Campaneris-Oak .10.8	Knoop-Cal-Chi.....32.5	Blair-Bal...............11.7	Yastrzemski-Bos 17	Rodriguez-KC......45.3
Jackson-Oak.........114	Campaneris-Oak 62	Harper-Sea............9.8	Aparicio-Chi.........32.5	Piniella-KC...........10.1	Oliva-Min 14	Azcue-Cle-Bos-Cal ..44.9
Bando-Oak 111	Tovar-Min................45	Cardenal-Cle 5.8	Cardenas-Min......23.2	Tovar-Min..............9.4	Jackson-Oak...........14	Gibson-Bos..........41.2
Howard-Was.........102	Kelly-KC..................40	Tovar-Min..............5.7	McMullen-Was.....21.4	Comer-Sea 7.3	Comer-Sea 14	Roof-Oak 37.7
Yastrzemski-Bos ...101	Foy-KC....................37	Kelly-KC.................4.3	Brinkman-Was 19.7	Voss-Cal 7.1	Blair-Bal..................14	McNertney-Sea....35.4

WINS	WINNING PCT.	WINS ABOVE TEAM	GAMES STARTED	COMPLETE GAMES	FEWEST HITS/GAME	FEWEST BB/GAME
McLain-Det.............24	Palmer-Bal............800	McLain-Det 7.3	McLain-Det 41	Stottlemyre-NY 24	Messersmith-Cal..6.08	Peterson-NY 1.42
Cuellar-Bal.............23	Perry-Min 769	Perry-Min 6.1	McNally-Bal 40	McLain-Det.............23	Palmer-Bal...........6.51	Bosman-Was.......1.82
	McNally-Bal 741	McDowell-Cle 5.4	Stottlemyre-NY 39	McDowell-Cle 18	Cuellar-Bal...........6.60	McLain-Det..........1.86
	McLain-Det...........727	Nagy-Bos...............5.0	Cuellar-Bal.............39	Cuellar-Bal.............18	Lolich-Det 6.86	Perry-Min 2.27
	Odom-Oak............714	Bosman-Was 4.5		Peterson-NY 16	Odom-Oak...........6.96	Cuellar-Bal...........2.45

STRIKEOUTS	STRIKEOUTS/GAME	GAMES	SAVES	BASE RUNNERS/9	ADJUSTED RELIEF RUNS	RELIEF RANKING
McDowell-Cle 279	McDowell-Cle 8.81	Wood-Chi................76	Perranoski-Min........31	Hall-Bal................8.09	K.Tatum-Cal.........22.2	Perranoski-Min.....40.7
Lolich-Det 271	Lolich-Det 8.69	Perranoski-Min........75	K.Tatum-Cal............22	Wilhelm-Cal 9.05	Perranoski-Min.....20.3	K.Tatum-Cal.........33.5
Messersmith-Cal...211	Messersmith-Cal..7.60	Lyle-Bos..................71	Lyle-Bos..................17	Peterson-NY 9.07	Lyle-Bos..............14.0	Watt-Bal...............19.4
Boswell-Min 190	Butler-KC.............7.25	Locker-Chi-Sea.......68	Watt-Bal..................16	Cuellar-Bal...........9.07	Watt-Bal..............13.9	Drabowsky-KC.....19.1
	Williams-Cle.........7.01	Segui-Sea..............66	Higgins-Was 16	Drabowsky-KC.....9.18	Hall-Bal...............13.1	Lyle-Bos..............18.7

INNINGS PITCHED	OPPONENTS' AVG.	OPPONENTS' OBP	EARNED RUN AVERAGE	ADJUSTED ERA	ADJUSTED STARTER RUNS	PITCHER WINS
McLain-Det........325.0	Messersmith-Cal...190	Cuellar-Bal...........260	Bosman-Was.......2.19	Bosman-Was........160	McLain-Det..........37.2	**Perranoski-Min..4.3**
Stottlemyre-NY ..303.0	Palmer-Bal............200	Bosman-Was........260	Palmer-Bal..........2.34	Palmer-Bal............154	Cuellar-Bal..........35.7	**K.Tatum-Cal.......4.1**
Cuellar-Bal.........290.2	Cuellar-Bal............204	Peterson-NY 261	Cuellar-Bal..........2.38	Cuellar-Bal............151	Messersmith-Cal..27.9	**Stottlemyre-NY..3.8**
McDowell-Cle 285.0	Lolich-Det 210	Palmer-Bal...........272	Messersmith-Cal..2.52	Messersmith-Cal...139	Palmer-Bal...........27.5	**Cuellar-Bal 3.8**
Lolich-Det 280.2	McDowell-Cle 213	Messersmith-Cal...274	Peterson-NY 2.55	Peterson-NY 138	Peterson-NY 26.9	**Peterson-NY.......3.4**

A Whole New Game

In less than a decade, the league had expanded by a third, added divisions, and instituted a new set of league championship series. It was a shock to the system. Responding to pressure from fans, hitters, and the media, the leagues shrunk the strike zone, which now ranged from the armpits to the top of the knees. AL scoring per game increased 20 percent.

Reggie Jackson of Oakland was on a record home run pace, but settled for "just" 47, third best in the AL. For the first time, five men hit 40 or more homers. Sam McDowell of Cleveland took his fourth strikeout crown, and Lou Piniella was Rookie of the Year for expansion Kansas City, which finished ahead of Chicago and fellow expansion team Seattle in the West.

Three future catching mainstays debuted: Thurman Munson, Carlton Fisk, and Rick Dempsey. Meanwhile, pitcher Paul Edmondson of Chicago perished in an accident traveling to 1970 spring training.

Minnesota's Rod Carew won the first of his seven batting titles, and under the tutelage of rookie manager Billy Martin, Carew stole home seven times. Tony Oliva led the AL in hits, Harmon Killebrew was MVP, and the Twins won the West. They were no match, however, for the Orioles, who took the inaugural American League Championship Series in three straight. Neither division race was close.

Feisty Earl Weaver, in his first full season as manager in Baltimore, knew how to structure a lineup. His club led the East in runs and its pitching was the league's best. Mike Cuellar (co-Cy Young winner with Denny McLain) and Dave McNally each earned 20 wins. However, the Orioles were a surprise World Series loser as the Cinderella New York Mets won in five. The Orioles tallied just 9 runs.

With two new clubs added, AL attendance again reached an all-time high. But most clubs' attendance fell, with seven clubs drawing fewer than a million, as football—busily merging the AFL and NFL—made further inroads on the American psyche.

1968 NATIONAL LEAGUE

TEAM	W	L	T	PCT	GB	HW	HL	R	OR	PA	H	2B	3B	HR	BB	SO	HB	SH	AVG	OBP	SLG	OPS	AOPS	BR	ABR	PF	SB	CS	BSA	BSR
StL	97	65	0	.599	—	**47**	34	583	**472**	6080	1383	227	**48**	73	378	897	32	67	.249	.298	.346	644	101	2	9	99	110	45	**71**	**8**
SF	88	74	1	.543	9	42	39	599	529	6132	1301	162	33	108	**508**	904	47	92	.239	.307	.341	648	102	20	20	100	50	37	57	-2
Chi	84	78	1	.519	13	**47**	34	612	611	6020	1319	203	43	**130**	415	854	36	74	.242	.298	.366	664	99	36	0	107	41	30	58	-1
Cin	83	79	1	.512	14	40	41	**690**	673	6286	**1573**	**281**	36	106	379	938	37	64	**.273**	**.320**	**.389**	**709**	**113**	**134**	**91**	106	59	55	52	-6
Atl	81	81	1	.500	16	41	40	514	549	6118	1399	179	31	80	414	**782**	36	86	.252	.307	.339	646	101	8	6	100	83	44	65	3
Pit	80	82	1	.494	17	40	41	583	532	6163	1404	180	44	80	422	953	33	96	.252	.306	.343	649	104	16	25	99	**130**	59	69	**8**
Phi	76	86	0	.469	21	38	43	543	615	5966	1253	178	30	100	462	1003	22	64	.233	.294	.333	627	95	-24	-23	100	58	51	53	-5
LA	76	86	0	.469	21	41	40	470	509	5935	1234	202	36	67	439	980	18	79	.230	.289	.319	608	96	-61	-23	93	57	43	57	-3
NY	73	89	1	.451	24	32	49	473	499	6027	1252	178	30	81	379	1203	43	75	.228	.281	.315	596	84	-93	-96	101	72	45	62	0
Hou	72	90	0	.444	25	42	39	510	588	5994	1233	205	28	66	479	988	**48**	**97**	.231	.298	.317	615	94	-38	-28	98	44	51	46	-8
Total	813	—	—	—	—	410	400	5577	—	60721	13351	1995	359	891	4275	9502	352	794	.243	.300	.341	641	—	—	—	—	704	460	60	-6

TEAM	CG	SHO	GR	SV	IP	H	HR	BB	SO	BR/9	ERA	AERA	OAV	OOB	PR	APR	PF	OSB	OCS	FA	E	WPB	DP	FW	PW	BW	BSW	DIF
StL	63	**30**	196	32	1479.1	1282	82	375	971	10.3	**2.49**	**116**	.234	.285	**82**	**69**	97	**50**	36	.978	140	**40**	135	-.0	**7.9**	1.0	**1.0**	6.1
SF	**77**	20	167	16	1469.0	1302	86	**344**	942	**10.2**	2.71	109	.236	**.282**	45	39	99	93	47	.975	162	79	125	-1.3	4.5	2.3	-.2	1.7
Chi	46	12	221	32	1453.2	1399	138	392	894	11.3	3.41	93	.254	.304	-69	-39	106	**50**	49	**.981**	**119**	50	149	**1.2**	-4.5	.0	-.0	6.3
Cin	24	16	**321**	**38**	1490.1	1399	114	573	963	12.2	3.56	89	.250	.321	-96	-63	106	62	49	.978	144	79	144	-.2	-7.2	**10.4**	-.6	-.3
Atl	44	16	199	29	1474.2	1326	87	362	871	10.5	2.92	103	.241	.290	11	12	100	88	34	.980	125	68	139	.9	1.4	.7	.4	-3.3
Pit	42	19	244	30	1487.0	1322	73	485	897	11.2	2.74	107	.240	.304	40	31	98	61	50	.979	139	62	162	.0	3.6	2.9	**1.0**	-8.5
Phi	42	12	227	27	1448.1	1416	91	421	935	11.7	3.36	89	.257	.313	-61	-57	101	56	56	.980	127	49	**163**	.7	-6.5	-2.6	-.5	4.0
LA	38	23	218	31	1448.2	1293	**65**	414	994	10.8	2.69	103	.241	.297	48	14	93	65	**62**	.977	144	60	144	-.3	1.6	-2.6	-.3	-3.4
NY	45	25	212	32	1483.1	**1250**	87	430	1014	10.5	2.72	111	**.230**	.290	43	48	101	71	49	.979	133	70	142	.4	5.5	-11.0	.0	-3.0
Hou	50	12	243	23	1446.2	1362	68	479	**1021**	11.7	3.26	91	.249	.311	-44	-49	99	108	28	.975	156	89	129	-1.0	-5.6	-3.2	-.8	1.7
Total	471	185	2248	290	14681.0	—	—	—	—	11.0	2.99	—	.243	.300	—	—	—	—	—	.978	1389	646	1432	—	—	—	—	—

BATTER-FIELDER WINS	BATTING AVERAGE	ON-BASE PERCENTAGE	SLUGGING AVERAGE	ON-BASE PLUS SLUGGING	ADJUSTED OPS	ADJUSTED BATTER RUNS
H.Aaron-Atl 5.0	Rose-Cin .335	Rose-Cin .391	McCovey-SF .545	McCovey-SF .923	McCovey-SF 176	McCovey-SF 49.3
McCovey-SF 4.9	Alou-Pit .332	McCovey-SF .378	Allen-Phi .520	Allen-Phi .872	Allen-Phi 161	Wynn-Hou 41.4
Wynn-Hou 4.7	Alou-Atl .317	Wynn-Hou .376	Williams-Chi .500	Rose-Cin .861	Mays-SF 158	H.Aaron-Atl 39.7
Santo-Chi 4.4	A.Johnson-Cin .312	Staub-Hou .373	H.Aaron-Atl .498	Mays-SF .860	Wynn-Hou 158	Rose-Cin 39.5
Haller-LA 4.1	Flood-StL .301	Mays-SF .372	Mays-SF .488	H.Aaron-Atl .852	H.Aaron-Atl 154	Allen-Phi 38.2

RUNS	HITS	DOUBLES	TRIPLES	HOME RUNS	TOTAL BASES	RUNS BATTED IN
Beckert-Chi 98	Rose-Cin 210	Brock-StL 46	Brock-StL 14	McCovey-SF 36	Williams-Chi 321	McCovey-SF 105
Rose-Cin 94	Alou-Atl 210	Rose-Cin 42	Clemente-Pit 12	Allen-Phi 33	H.Aaron-Atl 302	Williams-Chi 98
Perez-Cin 93	Beckert-Chi 189	Bench-Cin 40	Davis-LA 10	Banks-Chi 32	Rose-Cin 294	Santo-Chi 98
Brock-StL 92	A.Johnson-Cin 188	Staub-Hou 37	Allen-Phi 9	Williams-Chi 30	Alou-Atl 290	Perez-Cin 92
Williams-Chi 91	Flood-StL 186	Alou-Atl 37	Williams-Chi 8	H.Aaron-Atl 29	McCovey-SF 285	Allen-Phi 90

BASES ON BALLS	STOLEN BASES	BASE STEALING RUNS	FIELDING RUNS-INFIELD	FIELDING RUNS-OUTFIELD	OUTFIELD ASSISTS	CATCHER CS PCT.
Santo-Chi 96	Brock-StL 62	Brock-StL 9.4	Kessinger-Chi 26.6	H.Aaron-Atl 11.9	Wynn-Hou 20	Ryan-Phi 57.6
Wynn-Hou 90	Wills-Pit 52	Davis-LA 4.4	Alley-Pit 25.8	Wynn-Hou 10.6	Rose-Cin 20	Hundley-Chi 50.0
Hunt-SF 78	Davis-LA 36	H.Aaron-Atl 4.4	Mazeroski-Pit 20.4	Flood-StL 9.1	Swoboda-NY 14	Haller-LA 49.0
Allen-Phi 74	H.Aaron-Atl 28	Wills-Pit 4.1	Santo-Chi 20.1	Clemente-Pit 7.4	Fairly-LA 13	May-Pit 47.4
Staub-Hou 73	Jones-NY 23	Taylor-Phi 3.1	Lanier-SF 16.7	Phillips-Chi 4.1	H.Aaron-Atl 13	Bench-Cin 47.3

WINS	WINNING PCT.	WINS ABOVE TEAM	GAMES STARTED	COMPLETE GAMES	FEWEST HITS/GAME	FEWEST BB/GAME
Marichal-SF 26	Blass-Pit .750	Marichal-SF 8.7	Jenkins-Chi 40	Marichal-SF 30	Gibson-StL 5.85	Hands-Chi 1.25
Gibson-StL 22	Marichal-SF .743	Blass-Pit 6.6	Perry-SF 38	Gibson-StL 28	Bolin-SF 6.52	Marichal-SF 1.27
Jenkins-Chi 20	Gibson-StL .710	Koosman-NY 5.3	Marichal-SF 38	Jenkins-Chi 20	Veale-Pit 6.86	Seaver-NY 1.55
	Briles-StL .633	Gibson-StL 5.0		Perry-SF 19	Jarvis-Atl 7.10	Pappas-Cin-Atl 1.57
		Short-Phi 4.4		Koosman-NY 17	Moose-Pit 7.17	Niekro-Atl 1.58

STRIKEOUTS	STRIKEOUTS/GAME	GAMES	SAVES	BASE RUNNERS/9	ADJUSTED RELIEF RUNS	RELIEF RANKING
Gibson-StL 268	Singer-LA 7.97	Abernathy-Cin 78	Regan-LA-Chi 25	Gibson-StL 7.89	Kline-Pit 15.3	Kline-Pit 23.0
Jenkins-Chi 260	Gibson-StL 7.92	Regan-LA-Chi 73	Carroll-Atl-Cin 17	Jarvis-Atl 8.93	Regan-LA-Chi 11.9	Regan-LA-Chi 18.5
Singer-LA 227	Maloney-Cin 7.87	Carroll-Atl-Cin 68	Hoerner-StL 17	Seaver-NY 9.06	Abernathy-Cin 9.6	Linzy-SF 14.6
Marichal-SF 218	Jenkins-Chi 7.60	Taylor-NY 58	Brewer-LA 14	Bolin-SF 9.07	Linzy-SF 7.8	Abernathy-Cin 13.0
Sadecki-SF 206	Wilson-Hou 7.55	Linzy-SF 57		Hands-Chi 9.15	Koonce-NY 7.2	Koonce-NY 8.6

INNINGS PITCHED	OPPONENTS' AVG.	OPPONENTS' OBP	EARNED RUN AVERAGE	ADJUSTED ERA	ADJUSTED STARTER RUNS	PITCHER WINS
Marichal-SF 325.2	Gibson-StL .184	Gibson-StL .233	Gibson-StL 1.12	Gibson-StL 258	Gibson-StL 59.6	**Gibson-StL 7.6**
Jenkins-Chi 308.0	Bolin-SF .200	Jarvis-Atl .252	Bolin-SF 1.99	Bolin-SF 148	Seaver-NY 26.2	**Seaver-NY 3.1**
Gibson-StL 304.2	Veale-Pit .211	Bolin-SF .258	Veale-Pit 2.05	Koosman-NY 145	Koosman-NY 25.3	**Koosman-NY 2.8**
Perry-SF 290.2	Jarvis-Atl .214	Seaver-NY .261	Koosman-NY 2.08	Veale-Pit 142	Veale-Pit 23.6	**Marichal-SF 2.5**
Seaver-NY 278.0	Moose-Pit .218	Hands-Chi .262	Blass-Pit 2.12	Blass-Pit 138	Bolin-SF 20.2	**Jenkins-Chi 2.5**

No Hitting, Please

They called '68 the "Year of the Pitcher." And for good reason. Batting average fell to an all-time low, and slugging percentage was the lowest since 1919. Runs per game were just 3.43, the fewest in sixty years. It was really the Year of Bob Gibson. His 1.12 ERA is the best since 1914, and hasn't been matched. Only two pitchers have ever topped his 13 shutouts. Gibson was a unanimous Cy Young pick and won a close MVP vote.

Juan Marichal won 26 and threw 30 complete games, the most since 1952. Don Drysdale didn't allow an earned run for a record 58.2 consecutive innings. The Cubs didn't score in 48 innings; Fergie Jenkins lost 1-0 five times. Willie McCovey's 105 RBIs were the fewest for a league leader since 1920.

With the Cardinals dominating, the race was never close. The Giants were again bridesmaids, and the Cubs scraped into third. Cincinnati catcher Johnny Bench was Rookie of the Year, and New York improved 12 games due to an excellent young mound staff under new manager Gil Hodges. The difference from first to last was just 25 games, the fewest in a decade.

St. Louis magic ran out in the World Series as the Tigers, down three games to one, won it all. St. Louis scored just twice in the final two games at Busch Stadium. Cardinals owner Augie Busch, incensed, began disassembling his club.

The NL announced that new franchises in San Diego and Montreal would join the league in 1969. Not all went smoothly; veteran pitcher Larry Jackson retired after being selected by Montreal in the expansion draft. Bowie Kuhn was the new commissioner, combining a willingness to do the owners' bidding with the baseball knowledge lacking in predecessor William "Spike" Eckert. Kuhn inherited a troubled game. Attendance had dropped again in 1968, and the newly galvanized Players Association was making noises.

1968 AMERICAN LEAGUE

TEAM	W	L	T	PCT	GB	HW	HL	R	OR	PA	H	2B	3B	HR	BB	SO	HB	SH	AVG	OBP	SLG	OPS	AOPS	BR	ABR	PF	SB	CS	BSA	BSR
Det	103	59	2	.636	—	**56**	25	**671**	**492**	6179	1292	190	39	**185**	521	964	**61**	73	.235	.307	**.385**	**692**	**113**	**102**	**84**	103	26	32	45	-5
Bal	91	71	0	.562	12	47	33	579	497	6022	1187	**215**	28	133	570	1019	48	80	.225	.304	.352	656	105	45	46	100	78	32	**71**	6
Cle	86	75	1	.534	16.5	43	37	516	504	5988	1266	210	36	75	427	858	39	69	.234	.293	.327	620	96	-34	-25	98	115	61	65	4
Bos	86	76	0	.531	17	46	35	614	611	6036	1253	207	17	125	**582**	974	33	77	.236	**.313**	.352	665	102	67	31	106	76	62	55	-5
NY	83	79	2	.512	20	39	42	536	531	5992	1137	154	34	109	566	958	30	56	.214	.292	.318	610	94	-48	-31	97	90	50	64	2
Oak	82	80	1	.506	21	44	38	569	544	6026	**1300**	192	40	94	472	1022	35	78	**.240**	.304	.343	647	107	19	44	96	**147**	61	**71**	**11**
Min	79	83	0	.488	24	41	40	562	546	5974	1274	207	**41**	105	445	966	49	69	.237	.299	.350	649	98	20	-10	106	98	54	64	3
Cal	67	95	0	.414	36	32	49	498	615	5942	1209	170	33	83	447	1080	52	75	.227	.291	.318	609	94	-53	-37	97	62	50	55	-4
Chi	67	95	0	.414	36	36	45	463	527	5965	1233	169	33	71	397	**840**	40	**90**	.228	.284	.311	595	86	-85	-91	101	90	50	64	2
Was	65	96	0	.404	37.5	34	47	524	665	5971	1208	160	37	124	454	960	39	46	.224	.287	.336	623	98	-35	-17	97	29	19	60	0
Total	812	—	—	—	—	418	391	5532	—	60095	12359	1874	338	1104	4881	9641	426	713	.230	.297	.339	637	—	—	—	—	811	471	63	14

TEAM	CG	SHO	GR	SV	IP	H	HR	BB	SO	BR/9	ERA	AERA	OAV	OOB	PR	APR	PF	OSB	OCS	FA	E	WPB	DP	FW	PW	BW	BSW	DIF
Det	**59**	19	238	29	1489.2	1180	129	486	1115	**10.3**	2.71	111	.217	**.284**	44	49	101	80	40	**.983**	**105**	50	133	**2.0**	5.6	**9.6**	-.7	5.4
Bal	53	16	234	31	1451.0	1111	101	502	1044	**10.3**	**2.66**	110	.212	.285	51	43	98	80	**59**	.981	120	77	131	1.0	4.9	5.3	.5	-1.8
Cle	48	**23**	222	32	1464.1	**1087**	98	540	**1157**	**10.3**	**2.66**	**112**	**.206**	.285	**53**	**51**	100	61	44	.979	127	64	130	.6	**5.8**	-2.9	.3	1.6
Bos	55	17	225	31	1447.0	1303	115	523	972	11.7	3.33	95	.241	.312	-57	-27	106	104	42	.979	128	92	147	.6	-3.1	3.6	-.7	4.7
NY	45	14	204	27	1467.1	1308	99	424	831	10.8	2.79	104	.240	.297	31	20	98	**57**	48	.979	139	**34**	142	.0	2.3	-3.6	.0	3.2
Oak	45	18	252	29	1455.2	1220	124	505	997	10.9	2.94	96	.227	.295	6	-21	95	92	38	.977	145	75	136	-.4	-2.4	5.0	**1.1**	-2.3
Min	46	14	229	29	1433.1	1224	**92**	**414**	996	10.5	2.89	107	.229	.288	13	29	104	78	36	.973	170	61	117	-2.0	3.3	-1.1	.2	-2.4
Cal	29	11	320	31	1437.0	1234	131	519	869	11.2	3.43	85	.233	.303	-72	-84	98	84	56	.977	140	86	**156**	-.2	-9.6	-4.2	-.6	.7
Chi	20	11	**322**	**40**	1468.0	1290	97	451	834	11.1	2.75	110	.236	.301	38	45	102	88	55	.977	151	56	152	-.8	5.2	-10.4	.0	-8.0
Was	26	11	296	28	1439.2	1402	118	517	826	12.3	3.64	80	.258	.325	-106	-118	98	86	54	.976	148	82	144	-.7	-13.5	-1.9	-.2	.8
Total	426	154	2542	307	14553.0	—	—	—	—	10.9	2.98	—	.230	.297	—	—	—	—	—	.978	1373	677	1388	—	—	—	—	—

BATTER-FIELDER WINS	**BATTING AVERAGE**	**ON-BASE PERCENTAGE**	**SLUGGING AVERAGE**	**ON-BASE PLUS SLUGGING**	**ADJUSTED OPS**	**ADJUSTED BATTER RUNS**
Yastrzemski-Bos6.3	Yastrzemski-Bos ...301	Yastrzemski-Bos ...426	F.Howard-Was 552	Yastrzemski-Bos ...922	F.Howard-Was 173	Yastrzemski-Bos ..53.1
Freehan-Det 5.2	Cater-Oak............290	F.Robinson-Bal 390	Horton-Det............543	Horton-Det............895	Yastrzemski-Bos ...169	F.Howard-Was 49.4
F.Howard-Was 4.5	Oliva-Min 289	Mantle-NY.............385	Harrelson-Bos.......518	F.Howard-Was 890	Horton-Det............165	Horton-Det...........39.1
Campaneris-Oak4.2	Horton-Det............285	Monday-Oak 371	Yastrzemski-Bos ...495	Harrelson-Bos.......874	Harrelson-Bos.......154	Harrelson-Bos......34.8
B.Robinson-Bal.. 3.3	Uhlaender-Min 283	Andrews-Bos 368	Oliva-Min 477	F.Robinson-Bal 834	F.Robinson-Bal 153	F.Robinson-Bal 31.9
RUNS	**HITS**	**DOUBLES**	**TRIPLES**	**HOME RUNS**	**TOTAL BASES**	**RUNS BATTED IN**
McAuliffe-Det 95	Campaneris-Oak ..177	Smith-Bos 37	Fregosi-Cal 13	F.Howard-Was 44	F.Howard-Was 330	Harrelson-Bos.......109
Yastrzemski-Bos 90	Tovar-Min 167	B.Robinson-Bal.......36	McCraw-Chi 12	Horton-Det..............36	Horton-Det............278	F.Howard-Was 106
White-NY 89	F.Howard-Was 164	Yastrzemski-Bos 32	Stroud-Was............10	Harrelson-Bos.........35	Harrelson-Bos.......277	Northrup-Det...........90
Tovar-Min................89	Aparicio-Chi..........164	Tovar-Min...............31	McAuliffe-Det 10	Jackson-Oak...........29	Yastrzemski-Bos ...267	Powell-Bal...............85
Stanley-Det............88	Yastrzemski-Bos ...162		Campaneris-Oak 9		Northrup-Det.........259	Horton-Det..............85
BASES ON BALLS	**STOLEN BASES**	**BASE STEALING RUNS**	**FIELDING RUNS-INFIELD**	**FIELDING RUNS-OUTFIELD**	**OUTFIELD ASSISTS**	**CATCHER CS PCT.**
Yastrzemski-Bos ...119	Campaneris-Oak 62	Campaneris-Oak ...5.9	Clarke-NY 29.0	Yastrzemski-Bos ..11.2	Unser-Was.............22	Azcue-Cle 48.9
Mantle-NY.............106	Cardenal-Cle 40	Tovar-Min...............3.2	Aparicio-Chi 20.1	Unser-Was...........10.0	White-NY 14	Gibbs-NY 46.9
Foy-Bos 84	Tovar-Min................35	Foy-Bos 2.9	Belanger-Bal........19.3	Davalillo-Cle-Cal........6.6	Jackson-Oak...........14	Rodgers-Cal 42.9
McAuliffe-Det 82	Buford-Bal...............27	McCraw-Chi...........2.7	Knoop-Cal............19.1	Cardenal-Cle 6.5	Yastrzemski-Bos 12	Josephson-Chi.....39.6
Andrews-Bos 81	Foy-Bos 26	Nelson-Cle.............2.6	B.Robinson-Bal....18.6	Jackson-Oak..........6.3	Cardenal-Cle 12	Casanova-Was 37.7
WINS	**WINNING PCT.**	**WINS ABOVE TEAM**	**GAMES STARTED**	**COMPLETE GAMES**	**FEWEST HITS/GAME**	**FEWEST BB/GAME**
McLain-Det 31	McLain-Det 838	McLain-Det 11.4	McLain-Det 41	McLain-Det 28	Tiant-Cle 5.30	Peterson-NY 1.23
McNally-Bal 22	Culp-Bos...............727	Tiant-Cle 6.1	Chance-Min 39	Tiant-Cle.................19	McNally-Bal 5.77	McLain-Det 1.69
Tiant-Cle.................21	Tiant-Cle...............700	McNally-Bal 5.3	McDowell-Cle 37	Stottlemyre-NY 19	McDowell-Cle 6.06	Ellsworth-Bos.......1.70
Stottlemyre-NY 21	Ellsworth-Bos........696	Culp-Bos................5.0		McNally-Bal 18	Siebert-Cle 6.33	Kaat-Min 1.73
Hardin-Bal...............18	McNally-Bal 688	Stottlemyre-NY 4.9		Hardin-Bal...............16	McLain-Det 6.46	McNally-Bal 1.81
STRIKEOUTS	**STRIKEOUTS/GAME**	**GAMES**	**SAVES**	**BASE RUNNERS/9**	**ADJUSTED RELIEF RUNS**	**RELIEF RANKING**
McDowell-Cle 283	McDowell-Cle 9.47	Wood-Chi................88	Worthington-Min 18	McNally-Bal 7.91	Wood-Chi.............20.0	Wood-Chi.............32.9
McLain-Det 280	Tiant-Cle 9.20	Wilhelm-Chi 72	Wood-Chi................16	Tiant-Cle 7.98	Wilhelm-Chi 13.8	Romo-Cle 16.2
Tiant-Cle...............264	Lolich-Det 8.06	Locker-Chi 70	Higgins-Was 13	McLain-Det 8.30	Romo-Cle 13.6	Wilhelm-Chi 14.5
Chance-Min 234	Culp-Bos..............7.90	Perranoski-Min........66		Romo-Cle 8.32	McMahon-Chi-Det10.6	Drabowsky-Bal 8.9
McNally-Bal 202	McLain-Det 7.50			Messersmith-Cal..8.85	Locker-Chi 7.3	McMahon-Chi-Det .8.5
INNINGS PITCHED	**OPPONENTS' AVG.**	**OPPONENTS' OBP**	**EARNED RUN AVERAGE**	**ADJUSTED ERA**	**ADJUSTED STARTER RUNS**	**PITCHER WINS**
McLain-Det 336.0	Tiant-Cle 168	McNally-Bal 232	Tiant-Cle 1.60	Tiant-Cle 185	Tiant-Cle 39.7	**Tiant-Cle 4.4**
Chance-Min 292.0	McNally-Bal 182	Tiant-Cle 233	McDowell-Cle 1.81	McDowell-Cle 164	McLain-Det 36.3	**McLain-Det......... 4.4**
Stottlemyre-NY ..278.2	McDowell-Cle 189	McLain-Det 243	McNally-Bal 1.95	McLain-Det 154	McNally-Bal 30.9	**McNally-Bal........ 4.3**
McNally-Bal 273.0	Siebert-Cle 198	Chance-Min 260	McLain-Det 1.96	John-Chi 153	McDowell-Cle 28.4	**Wood-Chi 3.8**
McDowell-Cle 269.0	McLain-Det 200	Nash-Oak 269	John-Chi 1.98	McNally-Bal 150	Bahnsen-NY 25.8	**McDowell-Cle..... 3.3**

Burning Bright

The pennant-winning Tigers helped unite a riot-torn city, becoming the only AL team in the decade to draw more than two million fans. Denny McLain won 31 games, capturing the Cy Young and MVP trophies, and Detroit had the league's top attack—but that wasn't saying much.

The league batting average of .230 is the lowest ever recorded, and the 3.41 runs scored per game per team remains the fewest in AL history. As clubs tried to create runs by any means possible, stolen bases rose again by 19 percent. Cleveland's Luis Tiant allowed just 5.30 hits a game, a new record.

Chicago's Wilbur Wood pitched 88 games, another record, as his White Sox fell 22 games into eighth place. Gigantic Frank Howard won the home run title, but the Senators still finished last. Oakland improved $19^1/_2$ games with a very young (and cheap) club. Catfish Hunter pitched the AL's first perfect game in the regular season since 1922.

For the World Series, Detroit manager Mayo Smith wanted shortstop Ray Oyler and his weak bat out of the lineup, so he shifted outfielder Mickey Stanley to short. The move allowed the Tigers to get Al Kaline into the lineup; the veteran hit .379 with 2 homers.

The Tigers trailed three games to one before capturing Game 5, behind Mickey Lolich; McLain won Game 6 in St. Louis, 13-1. Jim Northrup's three-run triple broke open a scoreless tie in the deciding contest, and Lolich won his third game of the Series, defeating Bob Gibson, 4-1.

Prior to the 1969 season, Mickey Mantle announced his retirement. Elston Howard and Roger Maris, already with other clubs, also hung up the spikes. The AL and NL announced expansion to 12 clubs each for 1969, with each loop split into East and West divisions and new League Championship Series to determine the pennant winners. And baseball felt obliged to correct the obvious pitching domination prior to the next season.

1967 NATIONAL LEAGUE

TEAM	W	L	T	PCT	GB	HW	HL	R	OR	PA	H	2B	3B	HR	BB	SO	HB	SH	AVG	OBP	SLG	OPS	AOPS	BR	ABR	PF	SB	CS	BSA	BSR
StL	101	60	0	.627	—	49	32	695	557	6152	1462	225	40	115	443	919	**45**	54	.263	.320	.379	699	**108**	53	**62**	99	**102**	54	65	4
SF	91	71	0	.562	10.5	**51**	31	652	**551**	6205	1354	201	39	140	520	978	42	92	.245	.313	.372	685	104	24	33	99	22	30	42	-6
Chi	87	74	1	.540	14	49	34	**702**	624	6148	1373	211	49	128	509	912	34	**93**	.251	.316	.378	694	100	45	16	105	63	50	56	-4
Cin	87	75	0	.537	14.5	49	32	604	563	6012	1366	251	54	109	372	969	31	56	.248	.297	.372	669	88	-20	-80	111	92	63	59	-2
Phi	82	80	0	.506	19.5	45	35	612	581	6096	1306	221	47	103	**545**	1033	27	90	.242	.313	.357	670	98	1	-5	101	79	62	56	-4
Pit	81	81	1	.500	20.5	49	32	679	693	6255	**1585**	193	**62**	91	387	914	36	63	**.277**	**.324**	**.380**	**704**	**108**	**58**	55	101	79	37	68	4
Atl	77	85	0	.475	24.5	48	33	631	640	6088	1307	191	29	**158**	512	947	33	57	.240	.307	.372	679	102	10	19	99	55	45	55	-4
LA	73	89	0	.451	28.5	42	39	519	595	6110	1285	203	38	82	485	**881**	43	91	.236	.301	.332	633	96	-74	-25	92	56	47	54	-4
Hou	69	93	0	.426	32.5	46	35	626	742	6177	1372	**259**	46	93	537	934	26	65	.249	.317	.364	681	106	24	47	97	88	38	**70**	**6**
NY	61	101	0	.377	40.5	36	42	498	672	5928	1288	178	23	83	362	981	37	68	.238	.288	.325	613	83	-121	-113	98	58	44	57	-3
Total	810	—	—	—	—	464	345	6218	—	61171	13698	2133	427	1102	4672	9468	354	729	.249	.310	.363	673	—	—	—	—	694	470	60	-12

TEAM	CG	SHO	GR	SV	IP	H	HR	BB	SO	BR/9	ERA	AERA	OAV	OOB	PR	APR	PF	OSB	OCS	FA	E	WPB	DP	FW	PW	BW	BSW	DIF
StL	44	17	272	**45**	1465.0	1313	97	431	956	10.9	3.05	108	.239	.297	54	40	97	**45**	48	.978	140	48	127	.0	4.3	**6.7**	.6	8.9
SF	**64**	17	215	25	1474.1	**1283**	113	453	990	**10.8**	**2.92**	113	**.234**	**.294**	**75**	62	97	75	47	.979	134	66	149	.4	6.7	3.6	-.5	-.2
Chi	47	7	244	28	1457.0	1352	142	463	888	11.4	3.48	102	.246	.306	-17	9	105	57	38	**.981**	**121**	**39**	143	**1.1**	1.0	1.7	-.3	3.0
Cin	34	**18**	235	39	1468.0	1328	101	498	**1065**	11.5	3.05	**123**	.241	.306	54	**103**	111	81	44	.980	**121**	71	124	**1.1**	**11.2**	-8.7	-.0	2.5
Phi	46	17	214	23	1453.2	1372	**86**	403	967	11.2	3.10	110	.250	.304	44	49	101	63	41	.978	137	53	174	.2	5.3	-.5	-.3	-3.7
Pit	35	5	283	35	1458.1	1439	108	561	820	12.5	3.74	90	.261	.330	-59	-61	100	60	44	.978	141	55	**186**	.0	-6.6	6.0	.6	.0
Atl	35	5	276	32	1454.0	1377	118	449	862	11.6	3.47	96	.251	.310	-16	-25	98	86	54	.978	138	101	148	.2	-2.7	2.1	-.3	-3.2
LA	41	17	229	24	1473.0	1421	93	**393**	967	11.3	3.21	96	.254	.306	27	-20	92	58	48	.975	160	52	144	-1.1	-2.2	-2.7	-.3	-1.7
Hou	35	8	**294**	21	1445.2	1444	120	485	1060	12.3	4.03	82	.260	.322	-105	-117	98	82	48	.974	159	92	120	-1.0	-12.7	5.1	**.8**	-4.2
NY	36	10	277	19	1433.2	1369	124	536	893	12.1	3.73	91	.253	.321	-56	-54	100	87	**58**	.975	157	76	147	-.9	-5.8	-12.2	-.2	-.8
Total	417	121	2539	291	14582.2	—	—	—	—	11.6	3.38	—	.249	.310	—	—	—	—	—	.978	1408	653	1462	—	—	—	—	—

BATTER-FIELDER WINS	BATTING AVERAGE	ON-BASE PERCENTAGE	SLUGGING AVERAGE	ON-BASE PLUS SLUGGING	ADJUSTED OPS	ADJUSTED BATTER RUNS
Santo-Chi............7.7	Clemente-Pit.........357	Allen-Phi..............404	Aaron-Atl..............573	Allen-Phi..............970	Allen-Phi..............173	Aaron-Atl.............53.1
Aaron-Atl............5.4	Gonzalez-Phi........339	Clemente-Pit.........400	Allen-Phi..............566	Clemente-Pit.........954	Clemente-Pit.........170	Clemente-Pit........51.5
Clemente-Pit......5.1	Alou-Pit................338	Cepeda-StL..........399	Clemente-Pit.........554	Aaron-Atl..............943	Aaron-Atl..............169	Cepeda-StL.........50.7
Allen-Phi............4.7	Flood-StL.............335	Staub-Hou............398	McCovey-SF.........535	Cepeda-StL..........923	Cepeda-StL..........166	Allen-Phi.............46.3
Cepeda-StL........4.6	Staub-Hou...........333	Gonzalez-Phi........396	Cepeda-StL..........524	McCovey-SF.........913	McCovey-SF.........162	Santo-Chi............43.6
RUNS	**HITS**	**DOUBLES**	**TRIPLES**	**HOME RUNS**	**TOTAL BASES**	**RUNS BATTED IN**
Brock-StL.............113	Clemente-Pit.........209	Staub-Hou.............44	Pinson-Cin.............13	Aaron-Atl................39	Aaron-Atl..............344	Cepeda-StL..........111
Aaron-Atl..............113	Brock-StL.............206	Cepeda-StL............37	Williams-Chi...........12	Wynn-Hou..............37	Brock-StL.............325	Clemente-Pit.........110
Santo-Chi.............107	Pinson-Cin...........187	Aaron-Atl................37	Brock-StL...............12	Santo-Chi...............31	Clemente-Pit.........324	Aaron-Atl..............109
Clemente-Pit.........103	Wills-Pit................186		Morgan-Hou............11	McCovey-SF...........31	Williams-Chi..........305	Wynn-Hou............107
Wynn-Hou............102	Alou-Pit................186			Hart-SF..................29	Santo-Chi.............300	Perez-Cin.............102
BASES ON BALLS	**STOLEN BASES**	**BASE STEALING RUNS**	**FIELDING RUNS-INFIELD**	**FIELDING RUNS-OUTFIELD**	**OUTFIELD ASSISTS**	**CATCHER CS PCT.**
Santo-Chi...............96	Brock-StL...............52	Brock-StL..............5.1	Santo-Chi.............31.4	Gonzalez-Phi.........8.0	Clemente-Pit..........17	Dalrymple-Phi......57.7
Morgan-Hou............81	Wills-Pit..................29	Morgan-Hou..........4.6	Mazeroski-Pit.......21.1	Phillips-Chi............7.4	Phillips-Chi.............13	McCarver-StL......55.2
Phillips-Chi.............80	Morgan-Hou............29	Pinson-Cin............2.9	Lanier-SF.............20.2	Aaron-Atl................6.1		Grote-NY.............49.3
Hart-SF...................77	Pinson-Cin.............26	Wills-Pit.................2.9	Wine-Phi.............18.1	Flood-StL...............4.8		May-Pit...............46.2
Allen-Phi.................75	Phillips-Chi.............24	Allen-Phi...............2.7	Fuentes-SF..........17.2	Clemente-Pit.........4.7		Roseboro-LA.......45.8
WINS	**WINNING PCT.**	**WINS ABOVE TEAM**	**GAMES STARTED**	**COMPLETE GAMES**	**FEWEST HITS/GAME**	**FEWEST BB/GAME**
McCormick-SF........22	Hughes-StL...........727	McCormick-SF.......5.3	Bunning-Phi...........40	Jenkins-Chi............20	Hughes-StL.........6.64	Pappas-Cin..........1.57
Jenkins-Chi............20	McCormick-SF......688	Seaver-NY............4.7	Osteen-LA.............39	Seaver-NY.............18	Wilson-Hou..........6.90	Osteen-LA...........1.62
Osteen-LA.............17	Veale-Pit..............667	Holtzman-Chi.........4.5	Jenkins-Chi...........38	Perry-SF.................18	Perry-SF.............7.10	Johnson-Atl.........1.63
Bunning-Phi...........17	Jenkins-Chi...........606	Cuellar-Hou...........4.4	Drysdale-LA...........38	Marichal-SF...........18	Queen-Cin...........7.13	Niekro-Chi...........1.70
	Jarvis-Atl..............600	Veale-Pit...............4.4			Niekro-Atl............7.13	L.Jackson-Phi......1.86
STRIKEOUTS	**STRIKEOUTS/GAME**	**GAMES**	**SAVES**	**BASE RUNNERS/9**	**ADJUSTED RELIEF RUNS**	**RELIEF RANKING**
Bunning-Phi..........253	Nolan-Cin.............8.18	Perranoski-LA.........70	Abernathy-Cin.........28	Hughes-StL..........8.78	Abernathy-Cin......25.6	Abernathy-Cin......34.7
Jenkins-Chi...........236	Veale-Pit.............7.94	Abernathy-Cin.........70	Linzy-SF.................17	Abernathy-Cin......9.23	Linzy-SF.............18.3	Linzy-SF.............31.5
Perry-SF...............230	Carlton-StL..........7.83	Willis-StL................65	Face-Pit.................17	Linzy-SF.............9.50	McBean-Pit..........12.6	Hall-Phi...............19.8
Nolan-Cin.............206	Wilson-Hou..........7.78	Face-Pit.................61	Perranoski-LA.........16	Farrell-Hou-Phi....9.64	Nottebart-Cin.......12.2	Farrell-Hou-Phi....18.4
Cuellar-Hou..........203	Gibson-StL...........7.55		Hoerner-StL............15	Lamabe-NY-StL...9.64	Farrell-Hou-Phi....11.2	Face-Pit..............15.3
INNINGS PITCHED	**OPPONENTS' AVG.**	**OPPONENTS' OBP**	**EARNED RUN AVERAGE**	**ADJUSTED ERA**	**ADJUSTED STARTER RUNS**	**PITCHER WINS**
Bunning-Phi.......302.1	Hughes-StL...........203	Hughes-StL...........251	Niekro-Atl............1.87	Niekro-Atl.............178	Bunning-Phi.........35.2	**Bunning-Phi.......3.9**
Perry-SF............293.0	Wilson-Hou...........209	Bunning-Phi.........271	Bunning-Phi.........2.29	Bunning-Phi..........149	Niekro-Atl............27.3	**Abernathy-Cin...3.8**
Jenkins-Chi........289.1	Perry-SF...............214	Queen-Cin...........271	Short-Phi.............2.39	Nolan-Cin.............145	Nolan-Cin............26.8	**Linzy-SF.............3.5**
Osteen-LA.........288.1	Queen-Cin............215	Perry-SF...............273	Nolan-Cin............2.58	Short-Phi..............142	Short-Phi.............25.1	**Niekro-Atl..........3.0**
Drysdale-LA.......282.0	Bunning-Phi..........217	Niekro-Atl.............275	Perry-SF..............2.61	Queen-Cin............136	Perry-SF.............22.6	**Jenkins-Chi........2.8**

Gibson the Head Bird

St. Louis improved 18 games to win another flag despite losing ace Bob Gibson for much of the season to a broken leg. First sacker Orlando "El Toro" Cepeda, liberated from the Giants the previous year, was the league's unanimous MVP both for his hitting and his infectious charm. Tim McCarver, perhaps the game's top all-around receiver, finished second. The Cardinals were fast, strong defensively, deep in pitching, and blessed with racial harmony; they also benefited from an excellent outfield of Lou Brock, Curt Flood, and Roger Maris.

Cincinnati led the league through May and much of June, but injuries destroyed their chances. The Giants only began to hit late in the season. San Francisco was the NL's hottest club in the last month and finished second.

As pitcher Ferguson Jenkins enjoyed his first of six straight 20-win seasons, the Cubs—sparked by veterans Billy Williams and Ron Santo—improved 28½ games and leapt from last to third. Despite pitching in a good hitting park, Atlanta's Phil Niekro won the ERA crown.

The last-place Mets showed impressive arms, debuting Rookie of the Year Tom Seaver as well as 1968's runner-up, Jerry Koosman. Nolan Ryan, Tug McGraw, and Dick Selma quickly followed.

The 1967 season was first time that the leagues had separate Cy Young awards. The award had resided in southern California since 1962, thanks to Don Drysdale, Sandy Koufax, and Dean Chance; in 1967 it moved north up the freeway. San Francisco lefty Mike McCormick, the runaway winner, may be the least remembered Cy Young recipient ever. This was the last go-round for several key veterans of earlier seasons, including Lew Burdette, Dick Groat, Vern Law, and Curt Simmons.

The World Series was Bob Gibson's stage. Tossing complete-game victories in Games 1, 4, and 7, he allowed only 2 runs in 27 innings. Brock hit .414 and scored 8 runs. The dogged Red Sox came back to win Games 5 and 6, but Gibson himself homered in the 7-2 deciding game.

1967 AMERICAN LEAGUE

TEAM	W	L	T	PCT	GB	HW	HL	R	OR	PA	H	2B	3B	HR	BB	SO	HB	SH	AVG	OBP	SLG	OPS	AOPS	BR	ABR	PF	SB	CS	BSA	BSR
Bos	92	70	0	.568	—	49	32	**722**	614	6149	**1394**	**216**	39	**158**	522	1020	31	85	**.255**	.321	**.395**	**716**	109	**120**	66	108	68	59	54	-6
Min	91	71	2	.562	1	52	29	671	590	6116	1309	**216**	48	131	512	976	46	66	.240	.309	.369	678	98	45	-4	108	55	37	60	-1
Det	91	71	1	.562	1	52	29	683	587	6200	1315	192	36	152	**626**	994	**51**	78	.243	**.325**	.376	701	**111**	103	**84**	103	37	21	64	1
Chi	89	73	0	.549	3	49	33	531	**491**	6000	1209	181	34	89	480	**849**	38	67	.225	.291	.320	611	90	-82	-62	96	124	82	60	-1
Cal	84	77	0	.522	7.5	**53**	30	567	587	5902	1265	170	37	114	453	1021	31	**88**	.238	.301	.349	650	102	-15	7	96	40	36	53	-4
Was	76	85	0	.472	15.5	40	40	550	637	6044	1211	168	25	115	472	1037	37	63	.223	.288	.326	614	91	-83	-62	96	53	37	59	-1
Bal	76	85	0	.472	15.5	35	42	654	592	6164	1312	215	44	138	531	1002	41	82	.240	.310	.372	682	109	56	61	99	54	37	59	-1
Cle	75	87	0	.463	17	36	45	559	613	6037	1282	213	35	131	413	984	50	85	.235	.293	.359	652	97	-15	-20	101	53	65	45	-11
NY	72	90	1	.444	20	43	38	522	621	6118	1225	166	17	100	532	1043	30	78	.225	.296	.317	613	90	-75	-55	96	63	37	63	1
KC	62	99	0	.385	29.5	37	44	533	660	5938	1244	212	**50**	69	452	1019	42	59	.233	.296	.330	626	94	-55	-37	97	**132**	59	**69**	**8**
Total	810	—	—	—	—	446	362	5992	—	60668	12766	1949	365	1197	4993	9945	397	751	.236	.303	.351	654	—	—	—	—	679	470	59	-15

TEAM	CG	SHO	GR	SV	IP	H	HR	BB	SO	BR/9	ERA	AERA	OAV	OOB	PR	APR	PF	OSB	OCS	FA	E	WPB	DP	FW	PW	BW	BSW	DIF
Bos	41	9	254	44	1459.1	1307	142	477	1010	11.3	3.36	104	.239	.304	-21	19	108	63	38	.977	142	64	142	-.6	2.1	7.3	-.5	2.7
Min	**58**	18	219	24	1461.0	1336	115	**396**	1089	10.9	3.14	110	.243	.296	15	49	107	70	48	.978	132	63	123	.1	5.4	-.4	.0	4.8
Det	46	17	254	40	1443.2	1230	151	472	1038	10.8	3.32	98	.230	.295	-14	-9	101	79	38	.978	132	63	126	.0	-1.0	**9.3**	.3	1.4
Chi	36	**24**	292	39	1490.1	**1197**	**87**	465	927	**10.4**	**2.45**	**127**	**.219**	**.287**	**129**	**112**	96	70	53	.979	138	84	149	-.3	**12.4**	-6.8	.0	2.8
Cal	19	14	301	**46**	1430.1	1246	118	525	892	11.4	3.19	98	.237	.308	6	-8	97	**49**	**63**	**.982**	**111**	74	135	**1.3**	-.9	.8	-.3	2.6
Was	24	14	**330**	39	1473.1	1334	113	495	878	11.4	3.38	93	.242	.307	-25	-37	98	57	46	.978	144	60	**167**	-.8	-4.1	-6.8	.0	7.1
Bal	29	17	248	36	1457.1	1218	116	566	1034	11.2	3.32	95	.228	.304	-15	-28	98	79	48	.980	124	76	144	.5	-3.1	6.7	.0	-8.7
Cle	49	14	236	27	1477.2	1258	120	559	**1189**	11.3	3.25	101	.231	.305	-3	3	101	65	47	.981	116	93	138	1.0	.3	-2.2	-1.0	-4.1
NY	37	16	251	27	1480.2	1375	110	480	898	11.5	3.24	97	.249	.310	-2	-19	97	71	54	.976	154	**40**	144	-1.3	-2.1	-6.1	.3	.2
KC	26	10	265	34	1428.0	1265	125	558	990	11.7	3.68	87	.238	.313	-71	-80	99	76	36	.978	132	61	120	-.0	-8.8	-4.1	**1.0**	-6.6
Total	365	153	2650	356	14601.2	—	—	—	—	11.2	3.23	—	.236	.303	—	—	—	—	—	.979	1325	678	1388	—	—	—	—	—

BATTER-FIELDER WINS	BATTING AVERAGE	ON-BASE PERCENTAGE	SLUGGING AVERAGE	ON-BASE PLUS SLUGGING	ADJUSTED OPS	ADJUSTED BATTER RUNS
Yastrzemski-Bos 6.9	Yastrzemski-Bos .326	Yastrzemski-Bos .418	Yastrzemski-Bos .622	Yastrzemski-Bos 1040	Yastrzemski-Bos 189	Yastrzemski-Bos 67.2
B.Robinson-Bal 5.3	F.Robinson-Bal .311	Kaline-Det .411	F.Robinson-Bal .576	F.Robinson-Bal .979	F.Robinson-Bal 189	F.Robinson-Bal 55.1
Kaline-Det 5.1	Kaline-Det .308	Killebrew-Min .408	Killebrew-Min .558	Killebrew-Min .965	Kaline-Det 176	Killebrew-Min 54.5
F.Robinson-Bal 4.3	Scott-Bos .303	F.Robinson-Bal .403	Kaline-Det .541	Kaline-Det .952	Killebrew-Min 170	Kaline-Det 47.4
Killebrew-Min 4.2	Blair-Bal .293	Mantle-NY .391	Howard-Was .511	Mincher-Cal .854	Mincher-Cal 156	Mincher-Cal 35.6
RUNS	**HITS**	**DOUBLES**	**TRIPLES**	**HOME RUNS**	**TOTAL BASES**	**RUNS BATTED IN**
Yastrzemski-Bos 112	Yastrzemski-Bos 189	Oliva-Min 34	Blair-Bal 12	Yastrzemski-Bos 44	Yastrzemski-Bos 360	Yastrzemski-Bos 121
Killebrew-Min 105	Tovar-Min 173	Tovar-Min 32	Buford-Chi 9	Killebrew-Min 44	Killebrew-Min 305	Killebrew-Min 113
Tovar-Min 98	Scott-Bos 171	Yastrzemski-Bos 31		Howard-Was 36	F.Robinson-Bal 276	F.Robinson-Bal 94
Kaline-Det 94	Fregosi-Cal 171	D.Johnson-Bal 30		F.Robinson-Bal 30	B.Robinson-Bal 265	Howard-Was 89
McAuliffe-Det 92	B.Robinson-Bal 164	Campaneris-KC 29			Howard-Was 265	Oliva-Min 83
BASES ON BALLS	**STOLEN BASES**	**BASE STEALING RUNS**	**FIELDING RUNS-INFIELD**	**FIELDING RUNS-OUTFIELD**	**OUTFIELD ASSISTS**	**CATCHER CS PCT.**
Killebrew-Min 131	Campaneris-KC 55	Campaneris-KC 6.5	B.Robinson-Bal 32.1	Blair-Bal 9.1	Hershberger-KC 17	Azcue-Cle 52.5
Mantle-NY 107	Buford-Chi 34	Clarke-NY 3.2	Clarke-NY 16.3	Monday-KC 8.4	Monday-KC 14	Casanova-Was 49.3
McAuliffe-Det 105	Agee-Chi 28	Valentine-Was 2.7	Cullen-Was 14.6	Oliva-Min 7.6	Kaline-Det 14	Zimmerman-Min 47.3
Yastrzemski-Bos 91	McCraw-Chi 24	Agee-Chi 2.7	Oyler-Det 13.6	Hershberger-KC 7.5		Gibbs-NY 46.8
Kaline-Det 83	Clarke-NY 21	Aparicio-Bal 2.2	McCraw-Chi 11.0	Kaline-Det 7.1		Howard-NY-Bos 36.0
WINS	**WINNING PCT.**	**WINS ABOVE TEAM**	**GAMES STARTED**	**COMPLETE GAMES**	**FEWEST HITS/GAME**	**FEWEST BB/GAME**
Wilson-Det 22	Horlen-Chi .731	Lonborg-Bos 5.8	Lonborg-Bos 39	Chance-Min 18	Peters-Chi 6.47	Merritt-Min 1.19
Lonborg-Bos 22	Lonborg-Bos .710	Horlen-Chi 5.8	Chance-Min 39	Lonborg-Bos 15	Boswell-Min 6.55	Kaat-Min 1.44
Chance-Min 20	Wilson-Det .667	Wilson-Det 4.7	Wilson-Det 38	Hargan-Cle 15	Horlen-Chi 6.56	Stange-Bos 1.59
Horlen-Chi 19	Sparma-Det .640	Santiago-Bos 3.6	Kaat-Min 38		Siebert-Cle 6.60	Horlen-Chi 2.02
McLain-Det 17	Peters-Chi .593	Downing-NY 3.4			Downing-NY 7.05	Peterson-NY 2.13
STRIKEOUTS	**STRIKEOUTS/GAME**	**GAMES**	**SAVES**	**BASE RUNNERS/9**	**ADJUSTED RELIEF RUNS**	**RELIEF RANKING**
Lonborg-Bos 246	Tiant-Cle 9.22	Locker-Chi 77	Rojas-Cal 27	Horlen-Chi 8.72	Wilhelm-Chi 16.1	Wilhelm-Chi 22.4
McDowell-Cle 236	McDowell-Cle 8.99	Rojas-Cal 72	Wyatt-Bos 20	Drabowsky-Bal 8.78	Drabowsky-Bal 15.7	Drabowsky-Bal 21.9
Chance-Min 220	Boswell-Min 8.25	Kelso-Cal 69	Locker-Chi 20	Hiller-Det 9.14	Locker-Chi 15.0	Locker-Chi 17.9
Tiant-Cle 219	Lonborg-Bos 8.10	Womack-NY 65	Womack-NY 18	Merritt-Min 9.21	McMahon-Bos-Chi 14.2	Wyatt-Bos 17.3
Peters-Chi 215	Phoebus-Bal 7.75	McMahon-Bos-Chi 63	Worthington-Min 16	Watt-Bal 9.29	Watt-Bal 11.8	Gladding-Det 15.2
INNINGS PITCHED	**OPPONENTS' AVG.**	**OPPONENTS' OBP**	**EARNED RUN AVERAGE**	**ADJUSTED ERA**	**ADJUSTED STARTER RUNS**	**PITCHER WINS**
Chance-Min 283.2	Peters-Chi .199	Horlen-Chi .253	Horlen-Chi 2.06	Horlen-Chi 151	Horlen-Chi 33.5	**Horlen-Chi 3.8**
Lonborg-Bos 273.1	Boswell-Min .202	Merritt-Min .260	Peters-Chi 2.28	Siebert-Cle 137	Peters-Chi 24.1	**Peters-Chi 3.6**
Wilson-Det 264.0	Siebert-Cle .202	Siebert-Cle .266	Siebert-Cle 2.38	Merritt-Min 137	Merritt-Min 22.8	**Drabowsky-Bal 2.8**
Kaat-Min 263.1	Horlen-Chi .203	John-Chi .275	John-Chi 2.47	Peters-Chi 136	Chance-Min 17.8	**Wilhelm-Chi 2.4**
Peters-Chi 260.0	Downing-NY .217	Peters-Chi .276	Merritt-Min 2.53	Chance-Min 127	Siebert-Cle 16.9	**Siebert-Cle 2.2**

Boston's Summer of Love

In possibly the greatest and nuttiest pennant race of all time, four clubs converged in late July and bunched closer as the year went on. Chicago had excellent pitching and terrible hitting, even outside of cavernous Comiskey Park, but lacked a fourth starter. Boston featured a passel of young talent, led by Cy Young winner Jim Lonborg and slugger Carl Yastrzemski. Minnesota had Harmon Killebrew and Rookie of the Year Rod Carew, while Detroit's lineup sported four players with 20 or more homers. The Orioles slid to sixth as their young pitchers came up lame.

From early August until late September, the closely packed teams changed positions nearly hourly. The ongoing dramas and great performances added to the character of the race.

Chicago, in a position to win, dropped five straight to Kansas City and Washington in the last week to fall from contention. Minnesota came into the last two days of the season leading Boston and Detroit by 1 game. As the Tigers split two home doubleheaders with California, the Red Sox won their last two games at Fenway—over Minnesota. MVP Yastrzemski's hitting carried the day; rarely had one player so impacted a close pennant race. Yaz is the last player to date to collect a Triple Crown. Fittingly, AL attendance rose to an all-time high.

As the dissension-ridden A's sank to last, Charlie Finley finally swung a deal to move the franchise to Oakland, which gave the Angels a West Coast partner. Finley gave rookies Joe Rudi and Reggie Jackson a taste of major league baseball—Kansas City style; they hit .186 and .178 in their respective debuts.

The Red Sox magic faded in the World Series, as the Cardinals won in seven. It was the Junior Circuit's fifth Series defeat of the decade. Bob Gibson threw 3 complete-game wins for St. Louis, while Lonborg tossed a one-hitter in Game 2.

1966 NATIONAL LEAGUE

TEAM	W	L	T	PCT	GB	HW	HL	R	OR	PA	H	2B	3B	HR	BB	SO	HB	SH	AVG	OBP	SLG	OPS	AOPS	BR	ABR	PF	SB	CS	BSA	BSR
LA	95	67	0	.586	—	**53**	28	606	**490**	6066	1399	201	27	108	430	**830**	**49**	84	.256	.314	.362	676	102	-36	17	92	94	64	59	-2
SF	93	68	0	.578	1.5	47	34	675	626	6083	1373	195	31	181	414	860	32	70	.248	.303	.392	695	95	-16	-34	103	29	30	49	-4
Pit	92	70	0	.568	3	46	35	759	641	6229	**1586**	**238**	**66**	158	405	1011	35	73	**.279**	**.329**	**.428**	**757**	**116**	**116**	**115**	100	64	60	52	-7
Phi	87	75	0	.537	8	48	33	696	640	6256	1448	224	49	117	510	969	29	78	.258	.322	.378	700	101	13	12	100	56	42	57	-2
Atl	85	77	1	.525	10	43	38	**782**	683	6286	1476	220	32	**207**	**512**	913	40	72	.263	.326	.424	750	112	108	96	102	59	47	56	-3
StL	83	79	0	.512	12	43	38	571	577	5963	1377	196	61	108	345	977	35	59	.251	.298	.368	666	90	-70	-73	101	**144**	61	**70**	**10**
Cin	76	84	0	.475	18	46	33	692	702	6043	1434	232	33	149	394	877	20	69	.260	.309	.395	704	93	8	-45	109	70	50	58	-2
Hou	72	90	1	.444	23	45	36	612	695	6170	1405	203	35	112	491	885	34	**97**	.255	.318	.365	683	103	-18	29	93	90	47	66	3
NY	66	95	0	.410	28.5	32	49	587	761	5951	1286	187	35	98	446	992	42	63	.239	.301	.342	643	87	-100	-87	98	55	46	54	-4
Chi	59	103	0	.364	36	32	49	644	809	6213	1418	203	43	140	457	998	47	80	.254	.313	.380	693	97	-6	-14	101	76	47	62	0
Total	809	—	—	—	—	435	373	6624	—	61260	14202	2099	412	1378	4404	9312	363	745	.256	.313	.384	697	—	—	—	—	737	494	60	-11

TEAM	CG	SHO	GR	SV	IP	H	HR	BB	SO	BR/9	ERA	AERA	OAV	OOB	PR	APR	PF	OSB	OCS	FA	E	WPB	DP	FW	PW	BW	BSW	DIF
LA	**52**	**20**	214	35	1458.0	**1287**	**84**	**356**	**1084**	**10.3**	**2.62**	**126**	**.237**	**.286**	**159**	**119**	91	**54**	42	.979	133	**53**	128	.9	**12.5**	1.8	-.0	-1.0
SF	**52**	14	250	27	1476.2	1370	140	359	973	10.7	3.24	113	.244	.292	61	69	102	84	43	.974	168	67	131	-1.2	7.2	-3.6	-.3	10.3
Pit	35	12	285	**43**	1463.1	1445	125	463	898	12.0	3.52	101	.261	.321	13	8	99	71	35	.978	141	58	**215**	.4	.8	**12.1**	-.6	-1.7
Phi	**52**	15	245	23	1459.2	1439	137	412	928	11.8	3.57	101	.258	.315	6	4	100	69	51	**.982**	**113**	60	147	**2.0**	.4	1.3	-.0	2.4
Atl	37	10	**290**	36	1469.1	1430	129	485	884	11.9	3.68	99	.257	.317	-12	-7	101	69	**64**	.976	154	110	139	-.3	-.7	10.1	-.2	-4.9
StL	47	19	261	32	1459.2	1345	130	448	892	11.3	3.11	115	.246	.306	80	77	100	55	49	.977	145	**53**	166	.2	8.1	-7.7	**1.2**	.2
Cin	28	10	270	35	1436.0	1408	153	490	1043	12.2	4.08	96	.258	.322	-76	-26	108	102	57	.980	122	65	133	1.4	-2.7	-4.7	-.0	2.2
Hou	34	13	261	26	1443.2	1468	130	391	929	11.8	3.76	91	.262	.313	-24	-57	95	70	44	.972	174	85	126	-1.4	-6.0	3.0	.4	-5.1
NY	37	9	288	22	1427.0	1497	166	521	773	12.9	4.17	87	.272	.337	-89	-84	101	85	51	.975	159	92	171	-.6	-8.8	-9.1	-.3	4.4
Chi	28	6	285	24	1458.0	1513	184	479	908	12.5	4.33	85	.268	.326	-118	-104	102	78	58	.974	166	58	132	-1.0	-10.9	-1.5	.1	-8.8
Total	402	128	2649	303	14551.1	—	—	—	—	11.7	3.61	—	.256	.313	—	—	—	—	—	.977	1475	701	1488	—	—	—	—	—

BATTER-FIELDER WINS	BATTING AVERAGE	ON-BASE PERCENTAGE	SLUGGING AVERAGE	ON-BASE PLUS SLUGGING	ADJUSTED OPS	ADJUSTED BATTER RUNS
Santo-Chi....7.6	Alou-Pit....342	Santo-Chi....412	Allen-Phi....632	Allen-Phi....1027	Allen-Phi....181	Allen-Phi....57.2
Allen-Phi....5.0	Alou-Atl....327	Morgan-Hou....410	McCovey-SF....586	McCovey-SF....977	Stargell-Pit....164	Santo-Chi....50.5
Mazeroski-Pit....4.8	Carty-Atl....326	Allen-Phi....396	Stargell-Pit....581	Stargell-Pit....962	McCovey-SF....163	McCovey-SF....44.9
Torre-Atl....4.5	Allen-Phi....317	McCovey-SF....391	Torre-Atl....560	Santo-Chi....950	Santo-Chi....161	Stargell-Pit....42.4
Mays-SF....3.9	Clemente-Pit....317	Carty-Atl....391	Mays-SF....556	Torre-Atl....943	Torre-Atl....157	Torre-Atl....41.8
RUNS	**HITS**	**DOUBLES**	**TRIPLES**	**HOME RUNS**	**TOTAL BASES**	**RUNS BATTED IN**
Alou-Atl....122	Alou-Atl....218	Callison-Phi....40	McCarver-StL....13	Aaron-Atl....44	Alou-Atl....355	Aaron-Atl....127
Aaron-Atl....117	Rose-Cin....205	Rose-Cin....38	Brock-StL....12	Allen-Phi....40	Clemente-Pit....342	Clemente-Pit....119
Allen-Phi....112	Clemente-Pit....202	Pinson-Cin....35	Clemente-Pit....11	Mays-SF....37	Allen-Phi....331	Allen-Phi....110
Clemente-Pit....105	Beckert-Chi....188	Alou-Atl....32		Torre-Atl....36	Aaron-Atl....325	White-Phi....103
Williams-Chi....100				McCovey-SF....36	Mays-SF....307	Mays-SF....103
BASES ON BALLS	**STOLEN BASES**	**BASE STEALING RUNS**	**FIELDING RUNS-INFIELD**	**FIELDING RUNS-OUTFIELD**	**OUTFIELD ASSISTS**	**CATCHER CS PCT.**
Santo-Chi....95	Brock-StL....74	Brock-StL....10.0	Mazeroski-Pit....41.3	Clemente-Pit....9.7	Clemente-Pit....17	Dalrymple-Phi....46.8
Morgan-Hou....89	Jackson-Hou....49	Jackson-Hou....5.9	Santo-Chi....24.9	Aaron-Atl....8.2	Phillips-Phi-Chi....14	Hundley-Chi....43.1
McCovey-SF....76	Wills-LA....38	Aaron-Atl....3.6	Groat-Phi....21.1	Staub-Hou....7.7	Staub-Hou....13	Roseboro-LA....42.5
Aaron-Atl....76	Phillips-Phi-Chi....32	Harper-Cin....2.9	Maxvill-StL....17.8	Phillips-Phi-Chi....7.1		McCarver-StL....40.7
Menke-Atl....71	Harper-Cin....29	Phillips-Phi-Chi....1.8	Alley-Pit....14.9	Shannon-StL....5.3		Bateman-Hou....34.7
WINS	**WINNING PCT.**	**WINS ABOVE TEAM**	**GAMES STARTED**	**COMPLETE GAMES**	**FEWEST HITS/GAME**	**FEWEST BB/GAME**
Koufax-LA....27	Marichal-SF....806	Marichal-SF....9.2	Koufax-LA....41	Koufax-LA....27	Marichal-SF....6.68	Marichal-SF....1.05
Marichal-SF....25	Koufax-LA....750	Koufax-LA....8.2	Bunning-Phi....41	Marichal-SF....25	Koufax-LA....6.72	Law-Pit....1.22
Perry-SF....21	Perry-SF....724	Regan-LA....6.4	Drysdale-LA....40	Gibson-StL....20	Gibson-StL....6.74	Perry-SF....1.41
Gibson-StL....21	Short-Phi....667	Perry-SF....5.7	Short-Phi....39	Short-Phi....19	Maloney-Cin....6.97	Drysdale-LA....1.48
Short-Phi....20	Maloney-Cin....667	Gibson-StL....4.9		Bunning-Phi....16	Bolin-SF....6.98	Bunning-Phi....1.58
STRIKEOUTS	**STRIKEOUTS/GAME**	**GAMES**	**SAVES**	**BASE RUNNERS/9**	**ADJUSTED RELIEF RUNS**	**RELIEF RANKING**
Koufax-LA....317	Koufax-LA....8.83	Carroll-Atl....73	Regan-LA....21	Marichal-SF....7.88	Regan-LA....23.9	Regan-LA....37.3
Bunning-Phi....252	Maloney-Cin....8.65	Mikkelsen-Pit....71	McCool-Cin....18	Regan-LA....8.41	Carroll-Atl....19.4	McCool-Cin....26.4
Veale-Pit....229	Sutton-LA....8.34	Knowles-Phi....69	Face-Pit....18	Jarvis-Atl....8.52	Hoerner-StL....16.9	Carroll-Atl....21.5
Gibson-StL....225	Veale-Pit....7.68	Regan-LA....65	Raymond-Hou....16	Koufax-LA....8.86	McCool-Cin....15.1	Hoerner-StL....18.5
Marichal-SF....222	Jenkins-Phi-Chi....7.32	McDaniel-SF....64	Linzy-SF....16	Gibson-StL....9.41	Woodeshick-StL....13.2	Linzy-SF....14.4
INNINGS PITCHED	**OPPONENTS' AVG.**	**OPPONENTS' OBP**	**EARNED RUN AVERAGE**	**ADJUSTED ERA**	**ADJUSTED STARTER RUNS**	**PITCHER WINS**
Koufax-LA....323.0	Marichal-SF....202	Marichal-SF....230	Koufax-LA....1.73	Koufax-LA....191	Koufax-LA....60.4	**Koufax-LA....6.1**
Bunning-Phi....314.0	Koufax-LA....205	Koufax-LA....252	Cuellar-Hou....2.22	Marichal-SF....165	Marichal-SF....49.1	**Marichal-SF....5.8**
Marichal-SF....307.1	Gibson-StL....207	Gibson-StL....265	Marichal-SF....2.23	Cuellar-Hou....154	Bunning-Phi....42.4	**Gibson-StL....4.4**
Gibson-StL....280.1	Bolin-SF....211	Bunning-Phi....268	Bunning-Phi....2.41	Bunning-Phi....149	Gibson-StL....34.6	**Bunning-Phi....4.4**
Drysdale-LA....273.2	Maloney-Cin....214	Cuellar-Hou....273	Gibson-StL....2.44	Gibson-StL....147	Maloney-Cin....25.5	**Regan-LA....4.1**

The Last Roundup

Prior to the season, Don Drysdale and Sandy Koufax staged a joint holdout. The Dodgers eventually paid each more than $100,000. Koufax won his third Cy Young and finished just behind Roberto Clemente in MVP voting. As Drysdale struggled, rookie Don Sutton provided a solid fourth starter.

Since winning the 1960 World Series, Pittsburgh had rebuilt with blacks and Latinos, becoming the game's colorblind franchise. The '66 Pirates took the league lead in August, with Los Angeles and San Francisco close behind. Matty Alou, Willie Stargell, and Clemente provided the firepower for the Bucs.

The Dodgers reeled off seven straight wins in mid-September to grab first place. Though the Giants, keyed by 20-game winners Juan Marichal and Gaylord Perry, surged in the final week, the Dodgers again took the flag on closing day. The Giants swept three from Pittsburgh to finish second. Any of the three teams could have won going into the last weekend.

Nolan Ryan made his major league debut with the Mets in 1966; he would later eclipse Koufax for most strikeouts in a season and Walter Johnson for most strikeouts ever. Veterans Robin Roberts, Frank Thomas, Del Crandall, and Joe Adcock ended their careers in '66. Rebuilding St. Louis opened up new Busch Stadium. The Cubs fell to last, but acquired Fergie Jenkins, Bill Hands, and Randy Hundley.

The league posted its highest average attendance until 1977. Eight NL teams surpassed one million. Interest in baseball history was galvanized by *The Glory of Their Times*, an essential book of interviews with players from the early twentieth century.

Los Angeles fell apart in the World Series, fielding poorly and scoring nothing in the final three games to suffer an unceremonious sweep at the hands of the Orioles. Following the season, Koufax retired due to chronic damage in his pitching elbow. Jim Gilliam also called it quits and Maury Wills and Tommy Davis were traded, bringing the golden era of Dodgers baseball—which began twenty years earlier in Brooklyn—to a climactic end.

1966 AMERICAN LEAGUE

TEAM	W	L	T	PCT	GB	HW	HL	R	OR	PA	H	2B	3B	HR	BB	SO	HB	SH	AVG	OBP	SLG	OPS	AOPS	BR	ABR	PF	SB	CS	BSA	BSR
Bal	97	63	0	.606	—	48	31	**755**	601	6199	**1426**	**243**	35	175	514	926	39	82	**.258**	**.324**	**.409**	**733**	**118**	**118**	**130**	98	55	43	56	-3
Min	89	73	0	.549	9	**49**	32	663	581	6035	1341	219	33	144	513	844	39	49	.249	.316	.382	698	100	52	11	106	67	42	61	0
Det	88	74	0	.543	10	42	39	719	698	6195	1383	224	45	**179**	**551**	987	33	67	.251	.321	.406	727	111	105	88	102	41	34	55	-3
Chi	83	79	1	.512	15	45	36	574	**517**	6021	1235	193	40	87	476	872	**44**	**109**	.231	.297	.331	628	92	-84	-45	93	**153**	78	66	6
Cle	81	81	0	.500	17	41	40	574	586	6040	1300	156	25	155	450	914	27	56	.237	.297	.360	657	94	-41	-41	100	53	41	56	-3
Cal	80	82	0	.494	18	42	39	604	643	6038	1244	179	54	122	525	1062	38	69	.232	.303	.354	657	98	-31	-14	97	80	54	60	-1
KC	74	86	0	.463	23	42	39	564	648	5873	1259	212	**56**	70	421	982	26	71	.236	.294	.337	631	90	-85	-68	97	132	50	**73**	**12**
Was	71	88	0	.447	25.5	42	36	557	659	5905	1245	185	40	126	450	1069	20	84	.234	.295	.355	650	93	-52	-46	99	53	37	59	-1
Bos	72	90	0	.444	26	40	41	655	731	6175	1318	228	44	145	542	1020	32	65	.240	.310	.376	686	93	26	-36	110	35	24	59	-1
NY	70	89	1	.440	26.5	35	46	611	612	5936	1254	182	36	162	485	**817**	21	58	.235	.299	.374	673	103	-7	16	96	49	29	63	1
Total	806	—	—	—	—	426	379	6276	—	60417	13005	2021	408	1365	4927	9493	319	710	.240	.306	.369	674	—	—	—	—	718	432	62	7

TEAM	CG	SHO	GR	SV	IP	H	HR	BB	SO	BR/9	ERA	AERA	OAV	OOB	PR	APR	PF	OSB	OCS	FA	E	WPB	DP	FW	PW	BW	BSW	DIF
Bal	23	13	253	**51**	1466.1	1267	127	514	1070	11.1	3.32	100	.233	.301	19	2	97	82	**49**	**.981**	**115**	76	142	**1.3**	.2	**14.0**	-.4	1.9
Min	**52**	11	202	28	1438.2	1246	139	**392**	1015	10.4	3.13	115	.232	.286	48	71	105	72	42	.977	139	57	118	.0	7.6	1.2	-.0	-.8
Det	36	11	271	38	1454.1	1356	185	520	1026	11.9	3.85	90	.247	.315	-67	-59	101	57	33	.980	120	63	142	1.1	-6.3	9.5	-.4	3.2
Chi	38	**22**	239	34	1475.1	**1229**	**101**	403	896	**10.2**	**2.68**	**118**	**.226**	**.282**	**123**	**86**	92	81	41	.976	159	92	149	-1.1	**9.2**	-4.8	.6	-1.9
Cle	49	15	226	28	1467.1	1260	129	489	**1111**	10.9	3.23	107	.232	.297	34	35	100	**49**	44	.978	138	67	132	.0	3.8	-4.4	-.4	1.0
Cal	31	12	296	40	1457.1	1364	136	511	836	11.8	3.56	94	.251	.317	-21	-34	98	72	46	.979	136	65	**186**	.2	-3.7	-1.5	-.2	4.1
KC	19	11	306	47	1435.0	1281	106	630	854	12.2	3.56	96	.241	.323	-19	-25	99	82	43	.977	139	72	154	-.0	-2.7	-7.3	**1.2**	2.9
Was	25	6	295	35	1419.0	1282	154	448	866	11.1	3.70	93	.242	.302	-42	-38	101	56	47	.977	142	57	139	-.3	-4.1	-4.9	-.2	1.0
Bos	32	10	**311**	31	1463.2	1402	164	577	977	12.4	3.92	97	.253	.325	-78	-16	111	114	**49**	.975	155	66	153	-.9	-1.7	-3.9	-.2	-2.3
NY	29	7	227	32	1415.2	1318	124	443	842	11.3	3.41	97	.248	.306	3	-15	97	53	38	.977	142	**45**	142	-.3	-1.6	1.7	.0	-9.4
Total	334	118	2626	364	14492.2	—	—	—	—	11.3	3.44	—	.240	.306	—	—	—	—	—	.978	1385	660	1457	—	—	—	—	—

BATTER-FIELDER WINS	BATTING AVERAGE	ON-BASE PERCENTAGE	SLUGGING AVERAGE	ON-BASE PLUS SLUGGING	ADJUSTED OPS	ADJUSTED BATTER RUNS
F.Robinson-Bal .. 6.3	F.Robinson-Bal 316	F.Robinson-Bal 410	F.Robinson-Bal 637	F.Robinson-Bal ...1047	F.Robinson-Bal 200	F.Robinson-Bal 78.0
Fregosi-Cal......... 4.4	Oliva-Min 307	Kaline-Det.............392	Killebrew-Min 538	Killebrew-Min 929	Kaline-Det.............161	Killebrew-Min 44.2
Tresh-NY............ 4.2	Kaline-Det.............288	Killebrew-Min 391	Kaline-Det.............534	Kaline-Det.............927	Powell-Bal.............159	Kaline-Det............41.6
McAuliffe-Det..... 3.8	Powell-Bal.............287	McAuliffe-Det 373	Powell-Bal.............532	Powell-Bal.............903	Killebrew-Min 155	Powell-Bal............38.5
Kaline-Det 3.8	Killebrew-Min 281	Powell-Bal.............372	McAuliffe-Det 509	McAuliffe-Det 882	McAuliffe-Det 148	Mantle-NY............32.0
RUNS	**HITS**	**DOUBLES**	**TRIPLES**	**HOME RUNS**	**TOTAL BASES**	**RUNS BATTED IN**
F.Robinson-Bal 122	Oliva-Min 191	Yastrzemski-Bos 39	Knoop-Cal...............11	F.Robinson-Bal 49	F.Robinson-Bal 367	F.Robinson-Bal 122
Oliva-Min 99	F.Robinson-Bal 182	B.Robinson-Bal.......35	Campaneris-KC......10	Killebrew-Min 39	Oliva-Min 312	Killebrew-Min 110
Cash-Det 98	Aparicio-Bal 182	F.Robinson-Bal 34	Brinkman-Was 9	Powell-Bal...............34	Killebrew-Min 306	Powell-Bal.............109
Agee-Chi..................98	Agee-Chi...............172	Oliva-Min 32		Cash-Det 32	Cash-Det 288	B.Robinson-Bal.....100
	Cash-Det 168	Fregosi-Cal 32		Pepitone-NY 31	Agee-Chi...............281	Horton-Det............100
BASES ON BALLS	**STOLEN BASES**	**BASE STEALING RUNS**	**FIELDING RUNS-INFIELD**	**FIELDING RUNS-OUTFIELD**	**OUTFIELD ASSISTS**	**CATCHER CS PCT.**
Killebrew-Min 103	Campaneris-KC......52	Campaneris-KC......7.9	Knoop-Cal............21.8	Northrup-Det........10.1	Yastrzemski-Bos 15	Azcue-Cle 62.2
Foy-Bos 91	Buford-Chi 51	Buford-Chi 3.5	Boyer-NY 20.0	Yastrzemski-Bos 9.7	Hershberger-KC 14	Casanova-Was 46.4
F.Robinson-Bal 87	Agee-Chi.................44	Agee-Chi................3.4	Fregosi-Cal 19.4	Hershberger-KC 9.4	Tresh-NY.................12	Rodgers-Cal 42.0
Tresh-NY..................86	Aparicio-Bal 25	Tartabull-KC-Bos ...2.8	Weis-Chi 12.8	Oliva-Min 8.8	Agee-Chi.................12	Etchebarren-Bal...39.4
Yastrzemski-Bos 84	Cardenal-Cal 24	Salmon-Cle.............1.9	Buford-Chi 10.6	Lock-Was.................4.8		Battey-Min 37.9
WINS	**WINNING PCT.**	**WINS ABOVE TEAM**	**GAMES STARTED**	**COMPLETE GAMES**	**FEWEST HITS/GAME**	**FEWEST BB/GAME**
Kaat-Min 25	Siebert-Cle 667	Nash-KC.................5.6	Kaat-Min 41	Kaat-Min 19	McDowell-Cle 6.02	Kaat-Min 1.62
McLain-Det 20	Kaat-Min 658	Kaat-Min 5.6	McLain-Det 38	McLain-Det 14	Boswell-Min 6.38	Peterson-NY 1.67
Wilson-Bos-Det.......18	Wilson-Bos-Det.....621	Siebert-Cle 4.4	Wilson-Bos-Det.......37	Wilson-Bos-Det.......13	Peters-Chi............6.86	Grant-Min.............1.77
Siebert-Cle 16	Palmer-Bal............600	Wilson-Bos-Det......3.7	Chance-Cal.............37	Bell-Cle...................12	McLain-Det 6.98	Peters-Chi............1.98
Palmer-Bal...............15	McLain-Det 588	Krausse-KC 3.5	Bell-Cle 37		Chance-Cal..........7.14	Hargan-Cle 2.11
STRIKEOUTS	**STRIKEOUTS/GAME**	**GAMES**	**SAVES**	**BASE RUNNERS/9**	**ADJUSTED RELIEF RUNS**	**RELIEF RANKING**
McDowell-Cle 225	McDowell-Cle 10.42	Fisher-Chi-Bal.........67	Aker-KC 32	Wilhelm-Chi 7.52	Aker-KC 18.6	Aker-KC 28.2
Kaat-Min 205	Boswell-Min 9.19	Cox-Was 66	Kline-Was 23	Drabowsky-Bal 8.63	Wilhelm-Chi 13.2	S.Miller-Bal 20.1
Wilson-Bos-Det.....200	Lolich-Det 7.64	Aker-KC 66	Sherry-Det 20	S.Miller-Bal 8.90	Worthington-Min ..12.2	McMahon-Cle-Bos ..17.5
Richert-Was..........195	Richert-Was.........7.14	Worthington-Min 65	Fisher-Chi-Bal.........19	Aker-KC 8.92	S.Miller-Bal 12.1	Worthington-Min ..15.1
Bell-Cle 194	Bell-Cle 6.87	Kline-Was 63	S.Miller-Bal 18	Peters-Chi............8.97	Lines-Was.............11.1	Locker-Chi 13.8
INNINGS PITCHED	**OPPONENTS' AVG.**	**OPPONENTS' OBP**	**EARNED RUN AVERAGE**	**ADJUSTED ERA**	**ADJUSTED STARTER RUNS**	**PITCHER WINS**
Kaat-Min 304.2	McDowell-Cle 188	Peters-Chi.............260	Peters-Chi............1.98	Peters-Chi.............160	Peters-Chi............28.9	**Peters-Chi........... 4.0**
McLain-Det 264.1	Boswell-Min 197	Richert-Was..........270	Horlen-Chi 2.43	Perry-Min 142	Kaat-Min 24.9	**Kaat-Min 3.6**
Wilson-Bos-Det..264.0	Peters-Chi.............212	Kaat-Min 270	Hargan-Cle 2.48	Hargan-Cle 138	Perry-Min 20.4	**Wilson-Bos-Det.. 3.6**
Chance-Cal........259.2	McLain-Det 214	Ortega-Was 274	Perry-Min 2.54	Kaat-Min 131	Horlen-Chi 20.2	**Aker-KC 3.2**
Bell-Cle 254.1	Richert-Was..........215	Siebert-Cle 276	John-Chi 2.62	Horlen-Chi 130	Hargan-Cle 19.9	**Perry-Min............ 2.4**

Rare Birds

Cleveland reeled off 10 wins to open the season, and led the league through May, but a poor attack proved their undoing. The Orioles, meanwhile, used a 21-6 run to zoom ahead and never looked back. MVP Frank Robinson, acquired the past winter from the Reds, collected the Triple Crown, and the Orioles got good performances from a young rotation; former "Baby Bird" Steve Barber was the old hand at 27. This was a team built for the long term; four position regulars were 24 or younger.

Minnesota, Detroit, and Chicago scrambled for the crumbs. The Twins came up second, with Oliva and Killebrew the big hitters. Detroit moved up with starters Denny McLain and Mickey Lolich, but saw managers Chuck Dressen and Bob Swift die during the same year; impressively, the Tigers still finished third with 88 wins. Fourth-place Chicago, playing in the league's worst run environment, had pitching but predictably feeble hitting.

Seventh-place Kansas City premiered Sal Bando and Rick Monday; Jack Aker saved 32 games to set a new mark. The ninth-place Red Sox decided to promote minor league skipper Dick Williams; they had already made George Scott and Joe Foy regulars with Mike Andrews and Reggie Smith en route. The Angels moved to a new park in Anaheim.

The American League was wide open; the Yankees had collapsed into the cellar. New York lost Bobby Richardson to retirement, with Roger Maris, Mickey Mantle, Whitey Ford, and Jim Bouton pulling up lame.

Emmett Ashford was the game's first black umpire, giving the AL a much-overdue chance to show some vision. By this time, Robinson, Oliva, Willie Horton, and Rookie of the Year Tommie Agee were among the game's biggest stars, and the AL's best teams had gotten the message on integration.

The Birds swept the Dodgers to collect their first-ever world title. Los Angeles didn't score after the third inning of Game 1. Frank Robinson smacked 2 homers, including a blast in the clincher that provided the margin of victory in Dave McNally's 1-0 shutout.

1965 NATIONAL LEAGUE

TEAM	W	L	T	PCT	GB	HW	HL	R	OR	PA	H	2B	3B	HR	BB	SO	HB	SH	AVG	OBP	SLG	OPS	AOPS	BR	ABR	PF	SB	CS	BSA	BSR
SF	95	67	1	.586	2	**51**	30	682	593	6119	1384	169	43	159	476	**844**	31	80	.252	.313	.385	698	100	21	3	103	47	27	64	1
Pit	90	72	1	.556	7	49	32	675	580	6249	1506	217	57	111	419	1008	35	67	.265	.317	.382	699	102	25	22	101	51	38	57	-2
Cin	89	73	0	.549	8	49	32	**825**	704	6355	**1544**	**268**	**61**	183	**538**	1003	50	73	**.273**	**.339**	**.439**	**778**	**118**	**192**	**136**	107	82	40	67	4
Mil	86	76	0	.531	11	44	37	708	633	6077	1419	243	28	**196**	408	976	37	58	.256	.310	.416	726	109	69	65	101	64	37	63	1
Phi	85	76	1	.528	11.5	45	35	654	667	6172	1380	205	53	144	494	1091	36	75	.250	.313	.384	697	105	23	35	98	46	32	59	-1
StL	80	81	1	.497	16.5	42	39	707	674	6204	1415	234	46	109	477	882	35	72	.254	.314	.371	685	91	4	-53	109	100	52	66	4
Chi	72	90	2	.444	25	40	41	635	723	6205	1316	202	33	134	532	948	43	48	.238	.307	.358	665	92	-33	-48	102	65	47	58	-2
Hou	65	97	0	.401	32	36	45	569	711	6122	1299	188	42	97	502	877	46	57	.237	.305	.340	645	95	-74	-31	93	90	37	**71**	7
NY	50	112	2	.309	47	29	52	495	752	5976	1202	203	27	107	392	1129	39	76	.221	.277	.327	604	79	-166	-148	96	28	42	40	-9
Total	813	—	—	—	—	435	374	6558	—	61586	13794	2122	422	1318	4730	9649	404	709	.249	.311	.374	685	—	—	—	—	745	429	63	14

TEAM	CG	SHO	GR	SV	IP	H	HR	BB	SO	BR/9	ERA	AERA	OAV	OOB	PR	APR	PF	OSB	OCS	FA	E	WPB	DP	FW	PW	BW	BSW	DIF
LA	**58**	**23**	202	34	1476.0	**1223**	127	425	1079	**10.3**	**2.81**	116	**.224**	**.283**	**119**	80	92	**53**	33	.979	134	**60**	135	.8	8.5	-2.0	**1.0**	7.7
SF	42	17	262	**42**	1465.1	1325	137	408	1060	10.9	3.20	112	.238	.293	55	64	102	65	30	.976	148	75	124	.0	6.8	.3	-.0	6.9
Pit	49	17	246	27	1479.0	1324	**89**	469	882	11.2	3.01	**117**	.241	.304	87	**83**	99	54	33	.977	152	65	**189**	-.1	**8.8**	2.3	-.4	-1.6
Cin	43	9	244	34	1457.1	1355	136	587	**1113**	12.3	3.88	96	.247	.322	-56	-21	106	91	46	**.981**	**117**	98	142	**1.8**	-2.2	**14.4**	.3	-6.2
Mil	43	4	266	38	1447.2	1336	123	541	966	11.8	3.52	100	.246	.316	3	1	100	84	**58**	.978	140	96	145	.5	.1	6.9	-.0	-2.4
Phi	50	18	246	21	1468.2	1426	116	466	1071	12.0	3.53	98	.256	.318	2	-12	98	74	54	.975	157	63	153	-.5	-1.3	3.7	-.3	2.8
StL	40	11	261	35	1461.1	1414	166	467	916	11.8	3.77	102	.255	.315	-37	11	109	80	35	.979	130	70	152	1.1	1.2	-5.6	.3	2.6
Chi	33	9	292	35	1472.0	1470	154	481	855	12.1	3.78	98	.260	.320	-39	-15	104	82	49	.974	171	65	166	-1.2	-1.6	-5.1	-.4	-.8
Hou	29	7	256	26	1461.0	1459	123	**388**	931	11.6	3.84	87	.260	.310	-49	-84	95	70	42	.974	166	78	130	-1.0	-8.9	-3.3	.6	-3.5
NY	29	11	**301**	14	1454.2	1462	147	498	776	12.4	4.06	87	.262	.326	-84	-86	100	92	49	.974	171	72	153	-1.2	-9.1	-15.6	-1.1	-4.0
Total	416	126	2576	306	14643.0	—	—	—	—	11.6	3.54	—	.249	.311	—	—	—	—	—	.977	1486	742	1489	—	—	—	—	—

BATTER-FIELDER WINS	BATTING AVERAGE	ON-BASE PERCENTAGE	SLUGGING AVERAGE	ON-BASE PLUS SLUGGING	ADJUSTED OPS	ADJUSTED BATTER RUNS
Mays-SF 6.9	Clemente-Pit .329	Mays-SF .398	Mays-SF .645	Mays-SF 1043	Mays-SF 184	Mays-SF 61.8
Santo-Chi 6.2	H.Aaron-Mil .318	Robinson-Cin .386	H.Aaron-Mil .560	H.Aaron-Mil 938	H.Aaron-Mil 161	Williams-Chi 47.5
Wynn-Hou 5.1	Mays-SF .317	Rose-Cin .382	Williams-Chi .552	Williams-Chi 929	Williams-Chi 155	H,Aaron-Mil 47.1
H.Aaron-Mil 4.8	Williams-Chi .315	McCovey-SF .381	Robinson-Cin .540	Robinson-Cin 925	McCovey-SF 152	Robinson-Cin 39.6
Allen-Phi 4.2	Rose-Cin .312	H.Aaron-Mil .379	McCovey-SF .539	McCovey-SF 920	Robinson-Cin 148	McCovey-SF 39.5
RUNS	**HITS**	**DOUBLES**	**TRIPLES**	**HOME RUNS**	**TOTAL BASES**	**RUNS BATTED IN**
Harper-Cin 126	Rose-Cin 209	H.Aaron-Mil 40	Callison-Phi 16	Mays-SF 52	Mays-SF 360	Johnson-Cin 130
Mays-SF 118	Pinson-Cin 204	Williams-Chi 39	Clendenon-Pit 14	McCovey-SF 39	Williams-Chi 356	Robinson-Cin 113
Rose-Cin 117	Williams-Chi 203	Rose-Cin 35	Clemente-Pit 14	Williams-Chi 34	Pinson-Cin 324	Mays-SF 112
Williams-Chi 115	Clemente-Pit 194	Brock-StL 35	Allen-Phi 14	Santo-Chi 33	H.Aaron-Mil 319	Williams-Chi 108
	Flood-StL 191	Pinson-Cin 34	Morgan-Hou 12	Robinson-Cin 33	Johnson-Cin 317	Stargell-Pit 107
BASES ON BALLS	**STOLEN BASES**	**BASE STEALING RUNS**	**FIELDING RUNS-INFIELD**	**FIELDING RUNS-OUTFIELD**	**OUTFIELD ASSISTS**	**CATCHER CS PCT.**
Morgan-Hou 97	Wills-LA 94	Wills-LA 9.8	Mazeroski-Pit 25.9	Callison-Phi 15.3	Callison-Phi 21	Cannizzaro-NY 52.5
Santo-Chi 88	Brock-StL 63	Wynn-Hou 8.1	Alley-Pit 23.8	Mays-SF 9.6	Clemente-Pit 16	Dalrymple-Phi 51.4
McCovey-SF 88	Wynn-Hou 43	Harper-Cin 5.6	Santo-Chi 22.0	Wynn-Hou 9.0	Lewis-NY 14	Edwards-Cin 42.5
Wynn-Hou 84	Harper-Cin 35	Brock-StL 4.4	Wills-LA 17.7	Clemente-Pit 6.8	Wynn-Hou 13	Pagliaroni-Pit 31.1
Harper-Cin 78	W.Davis-LA 25	H.Aaron-Mil 3.9	Wine-Phi 16.5	H.Aaron-Mil 5.7	Mays-SF 13	Haller-SF 31.1
WINS	**WINNING PCT.**	**WINS ABOVE TEAM**	**GAMES STARTED**	**COMPLETE GAMES**	**FEWEST HITS/GAME**	**FEWEST BB/GAME**
Koufax-LA 26	Koufax-LA .765	Koufax-LA 8.0	Drysdale-LA 42	Koufax-LA 27	Koufax-LA 5.79	Marichal-SF 1.40
Cloninger-Mil 24	Maloney-Cin .690	Cloninger-Mil 6.8	Koufax-LA 41	Marichal-SF 24	Maloney-Cin 6.66	Law-Pit 1.45
Drysdale-LA 23	Ellis-Cin .688	Ellis-Cin 5.7	Short-Phi 40	Gibson-StL 20	Marichal-SF 6.83	Bruce-Hou 1.49
Marichal-SF 22	Cloninger-Mil .686	Maloney-Cin 5.1	Osteen-LA 40	Drysdale-LA 20	Bolin-SF 6.90	Farrell-Hou 1.51
Ellis-Cin 22	Bunning-Phi .679	Bunning-Phi 5.1		Cloninger-Mil 16	Gibson-StL 7.31	Johnson-Hou-Mil 1.87
STRIKEOUTS	**STRIKEOUTS/GAME**	**GAMES**	**SAVES**	**BASE RUNNERS/9**	**ADJUSTED RELIEF RUNS**	**RELIEF RANKING**
Koufax-LA 382	Koufax-LA 10.24	Abernathy-Chi 84	Abernathy-Chi 31	Koufax-LA 7.83	Linzy-SF 17.5	Linzy-SF 33.3
Veale-Pit 276	Veale-Pit 9.34	Woodeshick-Hou-StL .78	McCool-Cin 21	Marichal-SF 8.35	McBean-Pit 16.0	O'Dell-Mil 24.0
Gibson-StL 270	Maloney-Cin 8.60	McDaniel-Chi 71	Linzy-SF 21	Roberts-Hou 8.41	Abernathy-Chi 14.8	Woodeshick-Hou-StL 21.8
Bunning-Phi 268	Bunning-Phi 8.29	Baldschun-Phi 65		Law-Pit 9.11	O'Dell-Mil 14.5	McBean-Pit 20.9
Maloney-Cin 244	Gibson-StL 8.13			O'Dell-Mil 9.62	McDaniel-Chi 14.3	Perranoski-LA 19.0
INNINGS PITCHED	**OPPONENTS' AVG.**	**OPPONENTS' OBP**	**EARNED RUN AVERAGE**	**ADJUSTED ERA**	**ADJUSTED STARTER RUNS**	**PITCHER WINS**
Koufax-LA 335.2	Koufax-LA .179	Koufax-LA .227	Koufax-LA 2.04	Marichal-SF 169	Marichal-SF 48.0	**Marichal-SF 6.0**
Drysdale-LA 308.1	Marichal-SF .205	Marichal-SF .239	Marichal-SF 2.13	Law-Pit 163	Koufax-LA 47.6	**Koufax-LA 5.5**
Gibson-StL 299.0	Maloney-Cin .206	Law-Pit .261	Law-Pit 2.15	Koufax-LA 160	Maloney-Cin 33.9	**Maloney-Cin 4.6**
Short-Phi 297.1	Bolin-SF .214	Drysdale-LA .279	Maloney-Cin 2.54	Maloney-Cin 148	Law-Pit 30.9	**Law-Pit 4.3**
Marichal-SF 295.1	Gibson-StL .222	Bunning-Phi .279	Bunning-Phi 2.60	Shaw-SF 136	Bunning-Phi 30.8	**Drysdale-LA 4.2**

Batting Around

The pennant race got ugly on August 22, when Giants pitcher Juan Marichal smashed Dodgers catcher John Roseboro in the head with a bat. The incident resulted in a fine and suspension for Marichal, and cemented tensions between the clubs.

San Francisco appeared to have the race in control, reeling off 14 straight wins in mid-September as Los Angeles foundered, but the Dodgers came back with 13 victories in a row, tying things up on September 26. While the Giants struggled over the last weekend, the Dodgers took the crown by winning three of four from Milwaukee, allowing only 3 runs in the series.

Cy Young winner Sandy Koufax outdid himself, fanning a record 382; he also pitched his fourth no-hitter—a perfect game—on September 9. When Tommy Davis broke an ankle, Rookie of the Year Jim Lefebvre and veteran outfielder Lou Johnson picked up the slack. Mays powered the Giants, winning his second MVP; he was the league's first 50-homer man since 1949, aside from Mays' own 1955 season. When Orlando Cepeda went down with knee troubles, Willie McCovey stepped in and hit 39 homers.

Chicago's Ted Abernanthy pitched 85 times and notched 31 saves to set records. Cincinnati's hard-throwing Jim Maloney threw two extra-inning no-hitters, one of which he won. Warren Spahn, 44, retired with totals—notably 363 wins and 382 complete games—that would have been extraordinary even in the Dead Ball Era.

The Mets opened Shea Stadium in 1964, and this season Houston moved into the Astrodome. The first domed ballpark drew two million fans—and spawned millions of complaints about AstroTurf. Disappointed Phillies fans, meanwhile, began staying away; the club's attendance fell each year through 1969. The fifth-place Braves announced they would move to Atlanta for 1966.

A seven-game World Series against Minnesota should have been called The Sandy Koufax Show. After losing Game 2—he did not pitch in the opener in observance of Yom Kippur—Koufax shut out the Twins in Games 5 and 7. The final contest, a dominating 3-hitter pitched on just two days' rest, gave the Dodgers their third title in seven years.

1965 AMERICAN LEAGUE

TEAM	W	L	T	PCT	GB	HW	HL	R	OR	PA	H	2B	3B	HR	BB	SO	HB	SH	AVG	OBP	SLG	OPS	AOPS	BR	ABR	PF	SB	CS	BSA	BSR
Min	102	60	0	.630	—	51	30	**774**	600	6213	**1396**	**257**	42	150	554	969	35	77	**.254**	.324	.399	723	**107**	87	56	104	92	33	**74**	**9**
Chi	95	67	0	.586	7	48	33	647	**555**	6217	1354	200	38	125	533	916	**43**	89	.246	.315	.364	679	105	1	43	94	50	33	60	-1
Bal	94	68	0	.580	8	46	33	641	578	6138	1299	227	38	125	529	907	28	**95**	.238	.307	.363	670	94	-20	-32	102	67	31	68	4
Det	89	73	0	.549	13	47	34	680	602	6064	1278	190	27	162	554	952	37	69	.238	.312	.374	686	100	11	4	101	57	41	58	-2
Cle	87	75	0	.537	15	**52**	30	663	613	6138	1367	198	21	156	506	**857**	33	90	.250	.315	.379	694	102	26	21	101	109	46	70	8
NY	77	85	0	.475	25	40	43	611	604	6081	1286	196	31	149	489	951	19	72	.235	.299	.364	663	95	-44	-40	99	35	20	64	1
Cal	75	87	0	.463	27	46	34	527	569	5956	1279	200	36	92	443	973	22	93	.239	.297	.341	638	89	-83	-70	98	107	57	65	4
Was	70	92	0	.432	32	36	45	591	721	6078	1227	179	33	136	570	1125	34	63	.228	.304	.350	654	93	-48	-39	99	30	19	61	0
Bos	62	100	0	.383	40	34	47	669	791	6220	1378	244	40	**165**	**607**	964	30	57	.251	**.327**	**.400**	**727**	**107**	**99**	**57**	106	47	24	66	2
KC	59	103	0	.364	43	33	48	585	755	6058	1294	186	**59**	110	521	1020	35	74	.240	.309	.358	667	97	-28	-19	99	**110**	51	68	6
Total	810	—	—	—	—	433	377	6388	—	61163	13158	2077	365	1370	5306	9634	316	779	.242	.311	.369	680	—	—	—	—	704	355	66	31

TEAM	CG	SHO	GR	SV	IP	H	HR	BB	SO	BR/9	ERA	AERA	OAV	OOB	PR	APR	PF	OSB	OCS	FA	E	WPB	DP	FW	PW	BW	BSW	DIF
Min	32	12	299	45	1457.1	1278	166	503	934	11.2	3.14	113	.235	.301	52	66	103	53	34	.973	172	60	158	-2.3	7.0	6.0	**.6**	9.6
Chi	21	14	267	**53**	1481.2	1261	122	**460**	946	**10.6**	2.99	107	**.231**	**.292**	76	35	92	80	38	.980	127	108	156	.6	3.7	4.6	-.4	5.6
Bal	32	**15**	228	41	1477.2	1268	120	510	939	11.0	**2.98**	**116**	.233	.300	**78**	**79**	100	71	41	.980	126	**48**	152	.6	**8.4**	-3.4	.0	7.3
Det	**45**	14	240	31	1455.0	1283	137	509	1069	11.4	3.35	104	.237	.306	17	20	101	**51**	33	**.981**	116	71	126	1.3	2.1	.4	-.5	4.7
Cle	41	13	282	41	1458.1	**1254**	129	500	**1156**	11.0	3.30	106	.232	.298	26	30	101	**51**	40	**.981**	**114**	74	127	**1.4**	3.2	2.2	.5	-1.3
NY	41	11	252	31	1459.2	1337	126	511	1001	11.6	3.28	104	.245	.311	29	20	98	69	34	.978	137	59	**166**	-.0	2.1	-4.3	-.2	-1.6
Cal	39	14	236	33	1441.2	1259	**91**	563	847	11.5	3.17	107	.237	.312	46	37	98	57	29	**.981**	123	72	149	.8	3.9	-7.5	.0	-3.4
Was	21	8	327	40	1435.2	1376	160	633	867	12.8	3.93	88	.254	.334	-75	-72	101	74	**43**	.977	143	70	148	-.4	-7.7	-4.2	-.3	1.6
Bos	33	9	268	25	1439.1	1443	158	543	993	12.6	4.24	88	.260	.327	-125	-76	108	101	36	.974	162	58	129	-1.6	-8.1	**6.1**	-.1	-15.2
KC	18	7	**378**	32	1433.0	1399	161	574	882	12.6	4.24	82	.256	.329	-124	-118	101	97	27	.977	139	87	142	-.2	-12.6	-2.0	.3	-7.5
Total	323	117	2777	372	14539.1	—	—	—	—	11.6	3.46	—	.242	.311	—	—	—	—	—	.978	1359	707	1453	—	—	—	—	—

BATTER-FIELDER WINS
Buford-Chi.......... 5.3
Fregosi-Cal.......... 3.7
Yastrzemski-Bos3.5
Knoop-Cal 3.5
Versalles-Min..... 3.3

BATTING AVERAGE
Oliva-Min 321
Yastrzemski-Bos ...312
Davalillo-Cle..........301
Robinson-Bal........297
Wagner-Cle...........294

ON-BASE PERCENTAGE
Yastrzemski-Bos...395
Colavito-Cle..........383
Blefary-Bal............381
Oliva-Min 378
Mantilla-Bos..........374

SLUGGING AVERAGE
Yastrzemski-Bos...536
Conigliaro-Bos.......512
Cash-Det 512
Wagner-Cle...........495
Oliva-Min 491

ON-BASE PLUS SLUGGING
Yastrzemski-Bos...932
Cash-Det 883
Oliva-Min 870
Wagner-Cle...........864
Colavito-Cle...........851

ADJUSTED OPS
Yastrzemski-Bos...154
Cash-Det 147
Wagner-Cle...........143
Oliva-Min 141
Colavito-Cle...........140

ADJUSTED BATTER RUNS
Yastrzemski-Bos ..38.1
Colavito-Cle 34.7
Oliva-Min 32.2
Cash-Det 31.2
Wagner-Cle..........29.1

RUNS
Versalles-Min........126
Oliva-Min 107
Tresh-NY.................94
Buford-Chi 93
Colavito-Cle 92

HITS
Oliva-Min 185
Versalles-Min........182
Colavito-Cle 170
Tresh-NY...............168
Fregosi-Cal 167

DOUBLES
Yastrzemski-Bos 45
Versalles-Min 45
Oliva-Min 40
Tresh-NY.................29
Richardson-NY 28

TRIPLES
Versalles-Min 12
Campaneris-KC......12
Aparicio-Bal 10
W.Smith-Cal.............9

HOME RUNS
Conigliaro-Bos........32
Cash-Det 30
Horton-Det..............29
Wagner-Cle............28

TOTAL BASES
Versalles-Min 308
Tresh-NY...............287
Oliva-Min 283
Colavito-Cle 277
Conigliaro-Bos......267

RUNS BATTED IN
Colavito-Cle 108
Horton-Det............104
Oliva-Min 98
Mantilla-Bos............92
Whitfield-Cle 90

BASES ON BALLS
Colavito-Cle 93
Blefary-Bal..............88
Mantilla-Bos............79
Cash-Det 77
Robinson-Chi..........76

STOLEN BASES
Campaneris-KC......51
Cardenal-Cal 37
Versalles-Min 27
Davalillo-Cle............26
Aparicio-Bal 26

BASE STEALING RUNS
Campaneris-KC.....4.6
Versalles-Min.........4.2
Davalillo-Cle..........3.3
Aparicio-Bal 3.3
Cardenal-Cal 2.9

FIELDING RUNS-INFIELD
Knoop-Cal............22.9
Buford-Chi 21.5
Boyer-NY 21.4
Hansen-Chi..........13.2
Fregosi-Cal 9.6

FIELDING RUNS-OUTFIELD
Conigliaro-Bos.......9.0
Allison-Min.............8.4
Davalillo-Cle...........7.5
Hershberger-KC 5.3
Oliva-Min 3.0

OUTFIELD ASSISTS
Hershberger-KC 14
Cardenal-Cal 12

CATCHER CS PCT.
Battey-Min 48.1
Brown-Bal 44.6
Azcue-Cle............39.6
Freehan-Det.........36.1
Rodgers-Cal 33.3

WINS
Grant-Min.................21
Stottlemyre-NY 20
Kaat-Min 18
McDowell-Cle 17

WINNING PCT.
Grant-Min.............750
McLain-Det...........727
Stottlemyre-NY 690
Fisher-Chi.............682
Siebert-Cle 667

WINS ABOVE TEAM
Stottlemyre-NY 6.6
Grant-Min...............5.2
McLain-Det 4.7
Siebert-Cle 3.8
Chance-Cal............3.6

GAMES STARTED
Kaat-Min 42
Grant-Min.................39
Stottlemyre-NY 37
Lolich-Det 37

COMPLETE GAMES
Stottlemyre-NY 18
McDowell-Cle 14
Grant-Min.................14
McLain-Det 13

FEWEST HITS/GAME
McDowell-Cle 5.87
Fisher-Chi............6.42
Siebert-Cle 6.63
Richert-Was.........6.77
Brunet-Cal 6.81

FEWEST BB/GAME
Terry-Cle..............1.25
Monbouquette-Bos . 1.57
Horlen-Chi 1.60
Ford-NY 1.84
Grant-Min.............2.03

STRIKEOUTS
McDowell-Cle 325
Lolich-Det 226
McLain-Det 192
Siebert-Cle 191
Downing-NY 179

STRIKEOUTS/GAME
McDowell-Cle 10.71
Siebert-Cle 9.11
Lolich-Det 8.35
McLain-Det..........7.84
Morehead-Bos.......7.61

GAMES
Fisher-Chi...............82
Kline-Was 74
B.Lee-Cal................69
Dickson-KC..............68
S.Miller-Bal 67

SAVES
Kline-Was 29
S.Miller-Bal 24
Fisher-Chi 24
B.Lee-Cal................23
Radatz-Bos.............22

BASE RUNNERS/9
Wilhelm-Chi 7.63
Fisher-Chi............8.87
S.Miller-Bal 9.05
Siebert-Cle 9.06
Hall-Bal................9.13

ADJUSTED RELIEF RUNS
Wilhelm-Chi 23.3
S.Miller-Bal 22.4
B.Lee-Cal.............20.3
Fisher-Chi............15.2
Hamilton-NY 12.5

RELIEF RANKING
S.Miller-Bal 44.3
B.Lee-Cal.............29.3
Wilhelm-Chi 26.7
Worthington-Min ..22.7
Fisher-Chi.............22.5

INNINGS PITCHED
Stottlemyre-NY ..291.0
McDowell-Cle 273.0
Grant-Min...........270.1
Kaat-Min 264.1
Newman-Cal......260.2

OPPONENTS' AVG.
McDowell-Cle 185
Fisher-Chi.............205
Siebert-Cle 206
Brunet-Cal 209
Richert-Was..........210

OPPONENTS' OBP
Siebert-Cle 259
Fisher-Chi.............259
Terry-Cle...............268
McLain-Det...........273
Horlen-Chi 279

EARNED RUN AVERAGE
McDowell-Cle 2.18
Fisher-Chi............2.40
Siebert-Cle 2.43
Brunet-Cal 2.56
Richert-Was.........2.60

ADJUSTED ERA
McDowell-Cle 160
Siebert-Cle 143
Perry-Min 135
Richert-Was..........134
Pappas-Bal 133

ADJUSTED STARTER RUNS
McDowell-Cle 37.5
Stottlemyre-NY 24.3
Siebert-Cle 22.0
McLain-Det..........20.1
Richert-Was.........19.0

PITCHER WINS
S.Miller-Bal......... 4.9
McDowell-Cle..... 3.8
B.Lee-Cal 3.2
Stottlemyre-NY.. 2.8
Wilhelm-Chi........ 2.7

New Favorites

As scoring decreased, teams brought back "small-ball" strategy. Stolen bases increased 30 percent. Tellingly, however, the powerful Twins won the AL by 7 games, pulling away from Chicago and Baltimore in September. Minnesota had surprise MVP Zoilo Versalles, and four teammates connected for at least 20 home runs. In addition, the Twins posted the league's third-best ERA despite allowing the most homers in the majors.

The Yankees stumbled out of the gate and couldn't recover, finishing sixth—their worst placing since 1925—even as Mel Stottlemyre and Whitey Ford racked up 36 wins. Certainly the Yankees were unlucky. Tony Kubek was forced to retire due to a back problem, and injuries shelved Mickey Mantle, Roger Maris, and Elston Howard. But the team's reticence (some called it racism) to develop blacks and Latins had caught up.

Chicago's Eddie Fisher broke the mark for appearances with 82. Cleveland lefty "Sudden Sam" McDowell fanned 10.71 men per nine innings, a record that stood until 1984. Baltimore's Mark Belanger, Davey Johnson, and Jim Palmer made their major league debuts, as did Catfish Hunter of Kansas City and Roy White and Bobby Murcer of New York.

In the first amateur draft—designed to filter unsigned players through a system that would check ever-escalating bonuses—the Athletics made outfielder Rick Monday the initial pick. For an execrable last-place club, the A's made plenty of news. Satchel Paige, activated at age 58 to qualify for a pension, pitched 3 scoreless innings. Kansas City's 1965 attendance was the lowest of any franchise during the decade, and blowhard owner Charley Finley endlessly threatened to move the team.

A thrilling World Series went to the Dodgers, who shut out the Twins three times. Sandy Koufax allowed just 3 hits in winning the clincher at Metropolitan Stadium, the only game won by the visiting team.

1964 NATIONAL LEAGUE

TEAM	W	L	T	PCT	GB	HW	HL	R	OR	PA	H	2B	3B	HR	BB	SO	HB	SH	AVG	OBP	SLG	OPS	AOPS	BR	ABR	PF	SB	CS	BSA	BSR
StL	93	69	0	.574	—	**48**	33	715	652	6196	**1531**	240	53	109	427	925	18	94	**.272**	.324	.392	716	99	62	4	109	73	51	59	-2
Phi	92	70	0	.568	1	46	35	693	632	6116	1415	241	51	130	440	924	40	97	.258	.315	.391	706	106	42	51	99	30	35	46	-6
Cin	92	70	1	.568	1	47	34	660	**566**	6153	1383	220	38	130	457	974	33	65	.249	.308	.372	680	95	-10	-32	104	90	36	**71**	7
SF	90	72	0	.556	3	44	37	656	587	6194	1360	185	38	**165**	**505**	900	33	78	.246	.310	.382	692	99	15	1	102	64	35	65	2
Mil	88	74	0	.543	5	45	36	**803**	744	6206	1522	**274**	32	159	486	**825**	38	54	**.272**	**.333**	**.418**	**751**	**117**	**138**	**133**	101	53	41	56	-3
Pit	80	82	0	.494	13	42	39	663	636	6119	1469	225	**54**	121	408	970	24	87	.264	.315	.389	704	105	34	35	100	39	33	54	-3
LA	80	82	2	.494	13	41	40	614	572	6120	1375	180	39	79	438	893	19	**120**	.250	.305	.340	645	95	-73	-28	93	**141**	60	70	**10**
Chi	76	86	0	.469	17	40	41	649	724	6157	1391	239	50	145	499	1041	25	55	.251	.314	.390	704	101	39	12	104	70	49	59	-2
Hou	66	96	0	.407	27	41	40	495	628	5859	1214	162	41	70	381	872	**49**	87	.229	.285	.315	600	80	-163	-135	94	40	48	45	-8
NY	53	109	1	.327	40	33	48	569	776	6045	1372	195	31	103	353	932	48	52	.246	.296	.348	644	90	-87	-73	98	36	31	54	-3
Total	812	—	—	—	—	427	383	6517	—	61165	14032	2161	427	1211	4394	9256	327	789	.254	.311	.374	685	—	—	—	—	636	419	60	-7

TEAM	CG	SHO	GR	SV	IP	H	HR	BB	SO	BR/9	ERA	AERA	OAV	OOB	PR	APR	PF	OSB	OCS	FA	E	WPB	DP	FW	PW	BW	BSW	DIF
StL	47	10	232	38	1445.1	1405	133	410	877	11.5	3.43	111	.255	.308	17	56	108	57	27	.973	172	49	147	-.7	5.9	.4	-.1	6.5
Phi	37	17	273	**41**	1461.0	1402	129	440	1009	11.7	3.36	103	.252	.312	28	17	98	58	45	.975	157	72	150	.0	1.8	5.4	-.6	4.3
Cin	54	14	203	35	1467.0	1306	112	436	**1122**	10.9	3.07	**118**	.238	.296	75	**86**	102	70	43	**.979**	**130**	69	137	**1.6**	**9.1**	-3.4	.8	2.9
SF	48	17	251	30	1476.1	1348	118	480	1023	11.4	3.19	112	.241	.304	57	61	101	70	36	.975	159	**45**	136	-.0	6.4	.1	.3	2.2
Mil	45	14	268	39	1434.2	1411	160	452	906	11.8	4.12	86	.257	.314	-92	-95	100	49	33	.977	143	87	139	.8	-10.0	**14.0**	-.2	2.4
Pit	42	14	**274**	29	1443.2	1429	92	476	951	12.1	3.52	100	.260	.320	2	-2	99	67	36	.972	177	74	**179**	-1.0	-.2	3.7	-.2	-3.2
LA	47	**19**	213	27	1483.2	**1289**	**88**	458	1062	**10.8**	**2.95**	110	**.232**	**.292**	**96**	51	92	**39**	44	.973	170	65	126	-.5	5.4	-3.0	**1.1**	-4.0
Chi	**58**	11	255	19	1445.0	1510	144	423	737	12.1	4.08	91	.270	.321	-87	-56	105	52	51	.975	162	65	147	-.2	-5.9	1.3	-.1	-.0
Hou	30	9	248	31	1428.0	1421	105	**353**	852	11.4	3.41	100	.260	.306	20	1	97	95	38	.976	149	62	124	.5	.1	-14.3	-.8	-.6
NY	40	10	266	15	1438.2	1511	130	466	717	12.7	4.25	84	.272	.332	-115	-107	101	79	**66**	.974	167	85	154	-.4	-11.3	-7.7	-.2	-8.4
Total	448	135	2483	304	14523.1	—	—	—	—	11.6	3.54	—	.254	.311	—	—	—	—	—	.975	1586	673	1439	—	—	—	—	—

BATTER-FIELDER WINS	BATTING AVERAGE	ON-BASE PERCENTAGE	SLUGGING AVERAGE	ON-BASE PLUS SLUGGING	ADJUSTED OPS	ADJUSTED BATTER RUNS
Santo-Chi........... 7.1	Clemente-Pit.........339	Santo-Chi.............398	Mays-SF 607	Mays-SF 990	Mays-SF 171	Mays-SF 54.2
Allen-Phi 5.9	Carty-Mil 330	Robinson-Cin........396	Santo-Chi.............564	Santo-Chi.............962	Allen-Phi 163	Allen-Phi 52.9
Mays-SF 5.8	Aaron-Mil 328	Aaron-Mil 393	Allen-Phi 557	Robinson-Cin........943	Santo-Chi..............162	Santo-Chi.............50.9
Menke-Mil........... 5.3	Torre-Mil...............321	Clemente-Pit.........388	Carty-Mil 554	Carty-Mil 942	Carty-Mil 162	Robinson-Cin.......47.1
Robinson-Cin 4.5	Allen-Phi 318	Carty-Mil 388	Robinson-Cin........548	Allen-Phi 939	Robinson-Cin........158	Aaron-Mil 41.3

RUNS	HITS	DOUBLES	TRIPLES	HOME RUNS	TOTAL BASES	RUNS BATTED IN
Allen-Phi 125	Flood-StL..............211	Maye-Mil 44	Santo-Chi................13	Mays-SF 47	Allen-Phi 352	Boyer-StL..............119
Mays-SF 121	Clemente-Pit.........211	Clemente-Pit...........40	Allen-Phi 13	Williams-Chi............33	Mays-SF 351	Santo-Chi..............114
Brock-Chi-StL 111	Williams-Chi..........201	Williams-Chi...........39	Brock-Chi-StL 11	Hart-SF....................31	Williams-Chi..........343	Mays-SF 111
Robinson-Cin........103	Allen-Phi 201	Robinson-Cin..........38	Pinson-Cin..............11	Cepeda-SF 31	Santo-Chi..............334	Torre-Mil................109
Aaron-Mil 103	Brock-Chi-StL 200	Allen-Phi 38		Callison-Phi 31	Callison-Phi 322	Callison-Phi 104

BASES ON BALLS	STOLEN BASES	BASE STEALING RUNS	FIELDING RUNS-INFIELD	FIELDING RUNS-OUTFIELD	OUTFIELD ASSISTS	CATCHER CS PCT.
Santo-Chi................86	Wills-LA 53	Wills-LA 5.7	Mazeroski-Pit.......34.7	W.Davis-LA..........14.6	Callison-Phi 19	Roseboro-LA 60.4
Mathews-Mil 85	Brock-Chi-StL 43	W.Davis-LA............4.7	Santo-Chi.............19.6	Callison-Phi 13.7	W.Davis-LA.............16	Bertell-Chi............54.0
Mays-SF 82	W.Davis-LA.............42	Harper-Cin.............4.2	Kasko-Hou...........12.6	Aaron-Mil 9.9	Brock-Chi-StL 15	Dalrymple-Phi......49.2
Robinson-Cin..........79	Harper-Cin..............24	Aaron-Mil 3.4	Schofield-Pit 12.4	Altman-NY 9.7	Williams-Chi............14	Gonder-NY 42.9
Boyer-StL................70	Robinson-Cin..........23	Robinson-Cin.........3.3	Menke-Mil 11.8	T.Davis-LA 7.2	Pinson-Cin..............14	Edwards-Cin 39.7

WINS	WINNING PCT.	WINS ABOVE TEAM	GAMES STARTED	COMPLETE GAMES	FEWEST HITS/GAME	FEWEST BB/GAME
Jackson-Chi............24	Koufax-LA.............792	Jackson-Chi...........8.2	Drysdale-LA............40	Marichal-SF 22	Koufax-LA............6.22	Bunning-Phi.........1.46
Marichal-SF 21	Marichal-SF 724	Koufax-LA..............7.5	Bunning-Phi............39	Drysdale-LA............21	Drysdale-LA.........6.78	Bruce-Hou 1.47
Sadecki-StL 20	O'Toole-Cin...........708	Marichal-SF 6.2	Veale-Pit 38	Jackson-Chi............19	Short-Phi 7.10	Law-Pit.................1.50
	Bunning-Phi..........704	Bruce-Hou 4.9	Jackson-Chi............38	Gibson-StL..............17	Veale-Pit 7.14	Marichal-SF 1.74
	Jackson-Chi..........686	Bunning-Phi...........4.8		Ellsworth-Chi 16	Maloney-Cin 7.29	Jackson-Chi.........1.75

STRIKEOUTS	STRIKEOUTS/GAME	GAMES	SAVES	BASE RUNNERS/9	ADJUSTED RELIEF RUNS	RELIEF RANKING
Veale-Pit 250	Koufax-LA............9.00	B.Miller-LA..............74	Woodeshick-Hou 23	Koufax-LA............8.35	McBean-Pit..........15.4	McBean-Pit..........25.5
Gibson-StL............245	Maloney-Cin 8.92	Perranoski-LA.........72	McBean-Pit.............22	Drysdale-LA.........8.96	Ellis-Cin 14.5	Ellis-Cin 17.6
Drysdale-LA..........237	Veale-Pit 8.05	Baldschun-Phi 71	Baldschun-Phi 21	Short-Phi 9.34	McCool-Cin..........11.7	McCool-Cin..........15.0
Koufax-LA.............223	Gibson-StL...........7.67	Taylor-StL................63	McDaniel-Chi..........15	Ellis-Cin 9.56	Roebuck-Phi 11.4	Roebuck-Phi 14.7
Bunning-Phi..........219	Lemaster-Mil........7.53	McDaniel-Chi..........63		McCool-Cin..........9.67	B.Miller-LA............9.5	B.Miller-LA..........10.1

INNINGS PITCHED	OPPONENTS' AVG.	OPPONENTS' OBP	EARNED RUN AVERAGE	ADJUSTED ERA	ADJUSTED STARTER RUNS	PITCHER WINS
Drysdale-LA.......321.1	Koufax-LA.............191	Koufax-LA.............240	Koufax-LA............1.74	Koufax-LA.............187	Drysdale-LA.........41.4	**Drysdale-LA 5.0**
Jackson-Chi.......297.2	Drysdale-LA..........207	Drysdale-LA..........255	Drysdale-LA.........2.18	Short-Phi 157	Koufax-LA............41.4	**Koufax-LA 4.3**
Gibson-StL.........287.1	Veale-Pit 217	Short-Phi 266	Short-Phi 2.20	Drysdale-LA..........148	Short-Phi 31.4	**Short-Phi 3.6**
Bunning-Phi.......284.1	Short-Phi 217	Jackson-Chi..........272	Marichal-SF 2.48	Marichal-SF 144	Marichal-SF 29.6	**Marichal-SF 3.1**
Veale-Pit 279.2	Bolin-SF................220	Marichal-SF 272	Bunning-Phi.........2.63	O'Toole-Cin...........136	Gibson-StL...........26.6	**McBean-Pit......... 2.9**

A Philly Disappointment

The 1964 season has gone into legend as one of the NL's great races, but all the excitement came in the last two weeks. Boasting top rookie Richie Allen, outfielder Johnny Callison, and pitchers Jim Bunning and Chris Short, Philadelphia broke away from San Francisco in midsummer and led by $6^1/_2$ on September 20. But with World Series tickets printed, Philadelphia dropped 10 straight, including three to hard-charging Cincinnati, winners of nine straight, and three to St. Louis, which had risen from the depths in August.

With the Giants awakening from their doldrums on the strength of Willie Mays, Juan Marichal, and rookie Japanese reliever Masanori Murakami, a four-way tie loomed in the last weekend. The Mets, of all teams, beat the Cardinals in the first two games of the season-ending series before St. Louis held on to take the finale. The Reds—aware that manager Fred Hutchinson was dying of cancer—lost to the Phillies. Philadelphia and Cincinnati both finished 1 game out.

Lou Brock, acquired midseason from the Cubs, ignited the Redbirds' attack. Ken Boyer was MVP, and Ray Sadecki and Bob Gibson combined for 39 wins. Veteran reliever Barney Schultz, like Pedro Ramos in the AL, was vital down the stretch. The Phillies seized up at the finish line as manager Gene Mauch relied almost solely on Bunning and Short.

Several longtime NL stars began their careers in 1964, including Phil Niekro, Tony Perez, and Larry Dierker. Duke Snider retired. Prior to the season, Cubs infielder Ken Hubbs was killed in a plane crash, and Colts reliever Jim Umbricht died of cancer

The World Series went seven games. Both the Cardinals and Yankees blew leads, had exciting late-inning rallies, hit crucial home runs, and boasted great pitching performances. However, St. Louis' two wins at New York helped withstand Jim Bouton's two victories for the Yankees. Tim McCarver hit .478 and slugged a 10th inning homer to win Game 5. Gibson went all the way in Game 7 for a 7-5 win.

1964 AMERICAN LEAGUE

TEAM	W	L	T	PCT	GB	HW	HL	R	OR	PA	H	2B	3B	HR	BB	SO	HB	SH	AVG	OBP	SLG	OPS	AOPS	BR	ABR	PF	SB	CS	BSA	BSR
NY	99	63	2	.611	—	50	31	730	577	6358	**1442**	208	35	162	520	976	31	68	.253	.317	.387	704	100	12	1	102	54	18	**75**	**6**
Chi	98	64	0	.605	1	**52**	29	642	**501**	6246	1356	184	40	106	**562**	**902**	**52**	**96**	.247	.320	.353	673	97	-33	-15	97	75	39	66	3
Bal	97	65	1	.599	2	49	32	679	567	6143	1357	229	20	162	537	1019	27	69	.248	.316	.387	703	101	17	20	100	78	38	67	4
Det	85	77	1	.525	14	46	35	699	678	6183	1394	199	**57**	157	517	912	40	71	.253	.319	.395	714	102	33	23	102	60	27	69	4
LA	82	80	0	.506	17	45	36	544	551	5975	1297	186	27	102	472	920	26	78	.242	.304	.344	648	95	-91	-31	90	49	39	56	-3
Min	79	83	1	.488	20	40	41	**737**	678	6318	1413	227	46	**221**	553	1019	44	74	.252	**.322**	**.427**	**749**	**113**	**99**	**94**	101	46	22	68	2
Cle	79	83	2	.488	20	41	40	689	693	6257	1386	208	22	164	500	1063	49	63	.247	.312	.380	692	99	-8	-3	99	**79**	51	61	0
Bos	72	90	0	.444	27	45	36	688	793	6106	1425	**253**	29	186	504	917	28	35	**.258**	**.322**	.416	738	106	79	45	105	18	16	53	-2
Was	62	100	0	.383	37	31	50	578	733	6037	1246	199	28	125	514	1124	28	66	.231	.299	.348	647	86	-95	-92	100	47	30	61	0
KC	57	105	1	.352	42	26	55	621	836	6192	1321	216	29	166	548	1104	42	53	.239	.311	.379	690	95	-13	-32	103	34	20	63	0
Total	814	—	—	—	—	425	385	6607	—	61815	13637	2109	333	1551	5227	9956	367	673	.247	.315	.382	696	—	—	—	—	540	300	64	14

TEAM	CG	SHO	GR	SV	IP	H	HR	BB	SO	BR/9	ERA	AERA	OAV	OOB	PR	APR	PF	OSB	OCS	FA	E	WPB	DP	FW	PW	BW	BSW	DIF
NY	46	18	215	**45**	1506.2	1312	129	504	989	11.0	3.15	115	.234	.299	79	78	100	33	25	.983	109	55	158	1.1	8.2	.1	**.5**	8.1
Chi	44	20	219	**45**	1467.2	**1216**	124	**401**	955	**10.1**	**2.72**	**127**	**.226**	**.282**	**147**	**125**	95	31	27	.981	122	84	164	.2	**13.1**	-1.6	.2	5.0
Bal	44	17	238	41	1458.2	1292	129	456	939	11.0	3.16	113	.239	.300	76	68	99	62	26	**.985**	**95**	51	159	**1.9**	7.2	2.1	.3	4.6
Det	35	11	248	35	1453.0	1343	164	536	993	12.0	3.84	95	.244	.316	-35	-29	101	**25**	31	.982	111	59	137	1.0	-3.0	2.4	.3	3.4
LA	30	**28**	285	41	1450.2	1273	**100**	530	965	11.5	2.91	113	.236	.309	115	67	91	52	**37**	.978	138	**50**	**168**	-.7	7.0	-3.3	-.5	-1.6
Min	**47**	4	277	29	1477.2	1361	181	545	1099	11.8	3.58	100	.243	.312	8	1	99	51	35	.977	145	91	131	-1.1	.1	**9.9**	.0	-11.0
Cle	37	16	277	37	1487.2	1443	154	565	**1162**	12.3	3.75	96	.255	.324	-21	-25	99	61	31	.981	118	83	149	.6	-2.6	-.3	-.1	.5
Bos	21	9	252	38	1422.0	1464	178	571	1094	13.1	4.50	86	.266	.336	-138	-95	106	75	26	.977	138	61	123	-.7	-10.0	4.7	-.4	-2.7
Was	27	5	291	26	1435.1	1417	172	505	794	12.2	3.98	93	.259	.322	-57	-44	102	54	36	.979	127	63	145	-.0	-4.6	-9.7	-.1	-4.5
KC	18	6	**344**	27	1455.2	1516	220	614	966	13.5	4.71	81	.269	.344	-175	-136	105	96	26	.975	158	73	152	-1.9	-14.3	-3.4	-.1	-4.3
Total	349	134	2646	364	14615.0	—	—	—	—	11.8	3.63	—	.247	.315	—	—	—	—	—	.980	1261	670	1486	—	—	—	—	—

BATTER-FIELDER WINS	BATTING AVERAGE	ON-BASE PERCENTAGE	SLUGGING AVERAGE	ON-BASE PLUS SLUGGING	ADJUSTED OPS	ADJUSTED BATTER RUNS
Fregosi-LA 5.6	Oliva-Min 323	Mantle-NY.............423	Powell-Bal.............606	Mantle-NY...........1015	Mantle-NY.............177	Mantle-NY.............52.9
Hansen-Chi 4.7	B.Robinson-Bal.....317	Allison-Min............404	Mantle-NY.............591	Powell-Bal...........1005	Powell-Bal.............176	Allison-Min...........45.7
Powell-Bal 4.6	Howard-NY...........313	Powell-Bal.............399	Oliva-Min 557	Allison-Min............957	Allison-Min............163	Powell-Bal.............45.5
Allison-Min 4.5	Mantle-NY.............303	Robinson-Chi........388	Allison-Min............553	Killebrew-Min........924	Killebrew-Min........153	Oliva-Min 42.6
Howard-NY 4.2	Robinson-Chi........301	Kaline-Det.............383	Killebrew-Min........548	Oliva-Min 916	Oliva-Min 150	Killebrew-Min........42.6

RUNS	HITS	DOUBLES	TRIPLES	HOME RUNS	TOTAL BASES	RUNS BATTED IN
Oliva-Min 109	Oliva-Min 217	Oliva-Min 43	Versalles-Min..........10	Killebrew-Min..........49	Oliva-Min 374	B.Robinson-Bal.....118
Howser-Cle...........101	B.Robinson-Bal.....194	Bressoud-Bos.........41	Rollins-Min..............10	Powell-Bal...............39	B.Robinson-Bal.....319	Stuart-Bos 114
Killebrew-Min..........95	Richardson-NY 181	B.Robinson-Bal.......35	Yastrzemski-Bos 9	Mantle-NY...............35	Killebrew-Min........316	Mantle-NY.............111
Wagner-Cle.............94	Howard-NY 172	Versalles-Min 33	Oliva-Min 9	Colavito-KC 34	Colavito-KC 298	Killebrew-Min........111
Versalles-Min 94	Versalles-Min 171		Fregosi-LA 9	Stuart-Bos 33	Stuart-Bos 296	Colavito-KC 102

BASES ON BALLS	STOLEN BASES	BASE STEALING RUNS	FIELDING RUNS-INFIELD	FIELDING RUNS-OUTFIELD	OUTFIELD ASSISTS	CATCHER CS PCT.
Siebern-Bal...........106	Aparicio-Bal 57	Aparicio-Bal 6.6	Knoop-LA.............37.9	Yastrzemski-Bos ..19.5	Yastrzemski-Bos 19	Martin-Chi.............53.1
Mantle-NY...............99	Weis-Chi 22	Tresh-NY.................2.9	Hansen-Chi..........17.9	Brandt-Bal............12.5	Lock-Was................19	Howard-NY 49.1
Killebrew-Min 93	Davalillo-Cle............21	Weis-Chi 2.4	Green-KC 13.3	King-Was 9.8	Clinton-Bos-LA 18	Rodgers-LA 47.8
Allison-Min..............92	Howser-Cle.............20	Wagner-Cle............2.4	Adair-Bal..............13.1	Lock-Was...............9.1	Brandt-Bal...............14	Brown-Bal 40.6
Causey-KC 88	Hinton-Was.............17	Howser-Cle............2.0	Fregosi-LA 9.8	Hinton-Was............6.9		Brumley-Was 40.4

WINS	WINNING PCT.	WINS ABOVE TEAM	GAMES STARTED	COMPLETE GAMES	FEWEST HITS/GAME	FEWEST BB/GAME
Peters-Chi...............20	Bunker-Bal............792	Bunker-Bal............6.3	Bouton-NY 37	Chance-LA..............15	Horlen-Chi 6.07	Monbouquette-Bos .1.54
Chance-LA..............20	Ford-NY 739	Chance-LA.............6.1		Pascual-Min............14	Chance-LA...........6.27	Pappas-Bal 1.72
Wickersham-Det 19	Peters-Chi.............714	Radatz-Bos............4.9		Pappas-Bal 13	Bunker-Bal...........6.77	Newman-LA..........1.85
Pizarro-Chi..............19	Pappas-Bal 696	Lolich-Det 4.6		Osteen-Was............13	Peters-Chi............7.14	Bouton-NY 1.99
Bunker-Bal..............19	Chance-LA............690	Peters-Chi.............4.4		Kaat-Min 13	Pizarro-Chi...........7.27	Pizarro-Chi...........2.07

STRIKEOUTS	STRIKEOUTS/GAME	GAMES	SAVES	BASE RUNNERS/9	ADJUSTED RELIEF RUNS	RELIEF RANKING
Downing-NY 217	McDowell-Cle 9.19	Wyatt-KC 81	Radatz-Bos.............29	Hall-Bal................7.60	B.Lee-LA..............27.9	Radatz-Bos..........46.7
Pascual-Min..........213	Downing-NY 8.00	Radatz-Bos.............79	Wilhelm-Chi 27	Horlen-Chi 8.59	Radatz-Bos..........25.9	Wilhelm-Chi 39.6
Chance-LA............207	Pena-KC 7.55	Wilhelm-Chi 73	Miller-Bal.................23	Wilhelm-Chi 8.63	Wilhelm-Chi 21.4	B.Lee-LA..............27.9
Peters-Chi.............205	Stigman-Min 7.53	McMahon-Cle 70	Wyatt-KC 20	Fisher-Chi 8.71	Stock-Bal-KC 19.4	Worthington-Min ..27.5
Lolich-Det 192	Morehead-Bos.....7.51	Miller-Bal.................66	B.Lee-LA..................19	Chance-LA...........9.12	Hall-Bal 17.5	Hall-Bal 20.7

INNINGS PITCHED	OPPONENTS' AVG.	OPPONENTS' OBP	EARNED RUN AVERAGE	ADJUSTED ERA	ADJUSTED STARTER RUNS	PITCHER WINS
Chance-LA.........278.1	Horlen-Chi 190	Horlen-Chi 248	Chance-LA...........1.65	Chance-LA............199	Chance-LA...........57.7	**Chance-LA 5.6**
Peters-Chi..........273.2	Chance-LA............195	Chance-LA............260	Horlen-Chi 1.88	Horlen-Chi 184	Ford-NY 38.8	**Radatz-Bos......... 4.9**
Bouton-NY 271.1	Bunker-Bal............207	Pizarro-Chi............267	Ford-NY 2.13	Ford-NY 170	Horlen-Chi 36.7	**Wilhelm-Chi........ 4.2**
Pascual-Min.......267.1	Peters-Chi.............219	Bunker-Bal............267	Peters-Chi............2.50	Peters-Chi.............138	Peters-Chi............29.0	**Horlen-Chi 4.0**
Osteen-Was.......257.0	Pizarro-Chi............219	Bouton-NY 272	Pizarro-Chi...........2.56	Pizarro-Chi............135	Pizarro-Chi...........24.3	**Peters-Chi........... 3.9**

RAGGED END OF THE STRING

The Yankees struggled most of the way under new skipper Yogi Berra. Dissension racked the ranks in New York as the Orioles and White Sox ran the roost. On August 28 the Yankees were in third, $4^1/_2$ games out. But a great September, which included 11 straight wins, propelled New York to the top. Baltimore and Chicago suffered key losses to second-division teams down the stretch.

Mickey Mantle and Roger Maris were great again for New York, and despite just three regular starters, the pitching was good enough. Veteran reliever Pedro Ramos was sterling in September.

The White Sox nearly pulled it out with a strong rotation and spectacular 40-year-old reliever Hoyt Wilhelm. Orioles third baseman Brooks Robinson dazzled with bat and glove to garner MVP honors. Baltimore also had Boog Powell, Luis Aparicio, and moundsmen Robin Roberts and Harvey Haddix.

The Twins fell to sixth, but Rookie of the Year Tony Oliva hit 32 homers, led the AL in runs, hits, and doubles, and won the batting title. Another rookie, 19-year-old Tony Conigliaro, hit 24 homers in only 111 games. Luis Tiant, Bert Campaneris, Mickey Lolich, Denny McLain, and Mel Stottlemyre also made impressive debuts.

Los Angeles' Dean Chance, pitching in spacious Chavez Ravine, won the Cy Young, leading the league in several key categories. In the bullpen, John Wyatt established a new major league best with 81 appearances for last-place Kansas City, and Boston's hard-throwing Dick Radatz had 29 saves. Six clubs had relief aces, the most to that point, and save totals were rising.

Once again, the Yankees looked human in the World Series, losing a seven-game tilt to the Cardinals. Nobody knew it at the time, but New York's long dynasty was over. Berra was canned after the Series—replaced by St. Louis manager Johnny Keane—Mantle's injuries had taken their toll, and several young players' careers quickly fell apart.

1963 NATIONAL LEAGUE

TEAM	W	L	T	PCT	GB	HW	HL	R	OR	PA	H	2B	3B	HR	BB	SO	HB	SH	AVG	OBP	SLG	OPS	AOPS	BR	ABR	PF	SB	CS	BSA	BSR
LA	99	63	1	.611	—	**53**	28	640	**550**	6045	1361	178	34	110	453	**867**	26	85	.251	.309	.357	666	106	-3	42	93	**124**	70	64	**3**
StL	93	69	0	.574	6	**53**	28	**747**	628	6283	**1540**	**231**	**66**	128	458	915	25	85	**.271**	**.326**	.403	729	107	**119**	55	109	77	42	**65**	2
SF	88	74	0	.543	11	50	31	725	641	6176	1442	206	35	**197**	441	889	45	72	.258	.316	**.414**	**730**	**118**	112	**120**	99	55	49	53	-5
Phi	87	75	0	.537	12	45	36	642	578	6092	1390	228	54	126	403	955	44	**87**	.252	.306	.381	687	105	28	36	99	56	39	59	-1
Cin	86	76	0	.531	13	46	35	648	594	6040	1333	225	44	122	474	960	**47**	62	.246	.310	.371	681	100	28	9	103	92	58	61	0
Mil	84	78	1	.519	15	45	36	677	603	6211	1345	204	39	139	**525**	954	43	82	.244	.312	.370	682	104	32	39	99	75	52	59	-2
Chi	82	80	0	.506	17	43	38	570	578	5987	1286	205	44	127	439	1049	36	64	.238	.297	.363	660	91	-21	-51	105	68	60	53	-6
Pit	74	88	0	.457	25	42	39	567	595	6110	1385	181	49	108	454	940	29	63	.250	.309	.359	668	98	-4	-8	101	57	41	58	-2
Hou	66	96	0	.407	33	44	37	464	640	5983	1184	170	39	62	456	938	30	86	.220	.283	.301	584	80	-161	-131	94	39	30	57	-2
NY	51	111	0	.315	48	34	47	501	774	5921	1168	156	35	96	457	1078	**47**	46	.219	.285	.315	600	78	-131	-138	102	41	52	44	-9
Total	811	—	—	—	—	455	355	6181	—	60848	13434	1984	439	1215	4560	9545	372	732	.245	.306	.364	669	—	—	—	—	684	493	58	-22

TEAM	CG	SHO	GR	SV	IP	H	HR	BB	SO	BR/9	ERA	AERA	OAV	OOB	PR	APR	PF	OSB	OCS	FA	E	WPB	DP	FW	PW	BW	BSW	DIF
LA	51	**24**	209	29	1469.2	1329	111	402	**1095**	**10.8**	**2.85**	106	.239	**.293**	**71**	30	92	**48**	31	.975	159	60	129	-.0	3.3	4.6	**.6**	9.6
StL	49	17	243	32	1463.0	1329	124	463	978	11.3	3.32	107	.241	.303	-5	34	108	84	44	.976	147	69	136	.6	3.7	6.0	.5	1.3
SF	46	9	247	30	1469.0	1380	126	464	954	11.5	3.35	96	.246	.306	-9	-24	97	69	39	.975	156	**53**	113	.1	-2.6	**13.0**	-.3	-3.2
Phi	45	12	242	31	1457.1	**1262**	113	553	1052	11.4	3.09	105	**.235**	.309	32	24	98	79	61	.978	142	62	147	.9	2.6	3.9	.1	-1.6
Cin	55	22	182	**36**	1439.2	1307	117	425	1048	11.1	3.29	102	.242	.300	-1	8	102	69	46	.978	135	81	127	1.3	.9	1.0	.2	1.6
Mil	**56**	18	262	25	1471.2	1327	149	489	924	11.3	3.27	99	.241	.304	4	-8	98	62	45	**.980**	**129**	69	161	**1.8**	-.9	4.2	.0	-2.1
Chi	45	15	217	28	1457.0	1357	119	400	851	11.0	3.08	**114**	.249	.301	34	**66**	107	**48**	**65**	.976	155	62	172	.2	**7.2**	-5.5	-.4	-.4
Pit	34	16	**292**	33	1448.0	1350	99	457	900	11.5	3.10	107	.249	.311	31	33	100	82	53	.972	182	57	**195**	-1.4	3.6	-.9	.0	-8.3
Hou	36	16	232	20	1450.1	1341	**95**	**378**	937	10.9	3.44	92	.245	.295	-24	-48	96	82	49	.974	162	65	100	-.3	-5.2	-14.2	.0	4.7
NY	42	5	233	12	1427.2	1452	162	529	806	12.8	4.12	85	.263	.330	-132	-95	106	61	60	.967	210	81	151	-3.1	-10.3	-15.0	-.7	-.9
Total	459	154	2359	276	14553.1	—	—	—	—	11.4	3.29	—	.245	.306	—	—	—	—	—	.975	1577	659	1431	—	—	—	—	—

BATTER-FIELDER WINS	BATTING AVERAGE	ON-BASE PERCENTAGE	SLUGGING AVERAGE	ON-BASE PLUS SLUGGING	ADJUSTED OPS	ADJUSTED BATTER RUNS
Mays-SF 6.0	T.Davis-LA 326	Mathews-Mil 399	H.Aaron-Mil 586	H.Aaron-Mil 977	H.Aaron-Mil 180	H.Aaron-Mil 65.6
Mazeroski-Pit 5.7	Clemente-Pit 320	H.Aaron-Mil 391	Mays-SF 582	Mays-SF 962	Mays-SF 176	Mays-SF 58.1
H.Aaron-Mil 5.4	Groat-StL 319	Mays-SF 380	McCovey-SF 566	Cepeda-SF 929	Cepeda-SF 166	Cepeda-SF 47.5
Mathews-Mil 5.3	H.Aaron-Mil 319	Robinson-Cin 379	Cepeda-SF 563	McCovey-SF 915	McCovey-SF 161	McCovey-SF 42.3
Callison-Phi 4.2	Cepeda-SF 316	Groat-StL 377	Pinson-Cin 514	Pinson-Cin 861	Mathews-Mil 147	Mathews-Mil 40.6
RUNS	**HITS**	**DOUBLES**	**TRIPLES**	**HOME RUNS**	**TOTAL BASES**	**RUNS BATTED IN**
H.Aaron-Mil 121	Pinson-Cin 204	Groat-StL 43	Pinson-Cin 14	McCovey-SF 44	H.Aaron-Mil 370	H.Aaron-Mil 130
Mays-SF 115	Groat-StL 201	Pinson-Cin 37	Gonzalez-Phi 12	H.Aaron-Mil 44	Mays-SF 347	Boyer-StL 111
Flood-StL 112	H.Aaron-Mil 201	Williams-Chi 36	Groat-StL 11	Mays-SF 38	Pinson-Cin 335	White-StL 109
White-StL 106	White-StL 200	Gonzalez-Phi 36	Callison-Phi 11	Cepeda-SF 34	Cepeda-SF 326	Pinson-Cin 106
McCovey-SF 103	Flood-StL 200	Callison-Phi 36	Brock-Chi 11	Howard-LA 28	White-StL 323	Mays-SF 103
BASES ON BALLS	**STOLEN BASES**	**BASE STEALING RUNS**	**FIELDING RUNS-INFIELD**	**FIELDING RUNS-OUTFIELD**	**OUTFIELD ASSISTS**	**CATCHER CS PCT.**
Mathews-Mil 124	Wills-LA 40	H.Aaron-Mil 5.1	Mazeroski-Pit 55.5	Callison-Phi 19.0	Callison-Phi 26	Bertell-Chi 60.8
Robinson-Cin 81	H.Aaron-Mil 31	Pinson-Cin 3.1	Hubbs-Chi 19.3	Brock-Chi 10.4	Brock-Chi 17	Dalrymple-Phi 47.2
H.Aaron-Mil 78	Pinson-Cin 27	Gilliam-LA 2.4	Schofield-Pit 16.7	W.Davis-LA 10.1	W.Davis-LA 16	Edwards-Cin 46.3
Boyer-StL 70	Robinson-Cin 26	Maye-Mil 2.4	Mathews-Mil 14.1	Flood-StL 8.1	Williams-Chi 13	Roseboro-LA 42.9
Schofield-Pit 69	W.Davis-LA 25	Harper-Cin 2.3	Wine-Phi 14.0	Robinson-Cin 7.1	Robinson-Cin 13	Pagliaroni-Pit 41.3
WINS	**WINNING PCT.**	**WINS ABOVE TEAM**	**GAMES STARTED**	**COMPLETE GAMES**	**FEWEST HITS/GAME**	**FEWEST BB/GAME**
Marichal-SF 25	Perranoski-LA 842	Koufax-LA 9.3	Sanford-SF 42	Spahn-Mil 22	Koufax-LA 6.19	Friend-Pit 1.47
Koufax-LA 25	Koufax-LA 833	Marichal-SF 8.7	Drysdale-LA 42	Koufax-LA 20	Culp-Phi 6.55	Farrell-Hou 1.56
Spahn-Mil 23	Spahn-Mil 767	Spahn-Mil 8.5	Marichal-SF 40	Ellsworth-Chi 19	Maloney-Cin 6.58	Nuxhall-Cin 1.62
Maloney-Cin 23	Maloney-Cin 767	Maloney-Cin 8.3	Koufax-LA 40	Marichal-SF 18	Ellsworth-Chi 6.90	Drysdale-LA 1.63
Ellsworth-Chi 22	Marichal-SF 758	Ellsworth-Chi 6.7	Friend-Pit 38	Drysdale-LA 17	Farrell-Hou 7.16	Koufax-LA 1.68
STRIKEOUTS	**STRIKEOUTS/GAME**	**GAMES**	**SAVES**	**BASE RUNNERS/9**	**ADJUSTED RELIEF RUNS**	**RELIEF RANKING**
Koufax-LA 306	Maloney-Cin 9.53	Perranoski-LA 69	McDaniel-Chi 22	Koufax-LA 7.96	Perranoski-LA 20.2	Perranoski-LA 34.2
Maloney-Cin 265	Koufax-LA 8.86	Baldschun-Phi 65	Perranoski-LA 21	Shantz-StL 8.39	Veale-Pit 17.6	Woodeshick-Hou .27.6
Drysdale-LA 251	Culp-Phi 7.79	Bearnarth-NY 58	Face-Pit 16	Umbricht-Hou 8.76	Klippstein-Phi 16.4	Baldschun-Phi 18.3
Marichal-SF 248	Short-Phi 7.27	Sisk-Pit 57	Baldschun-Phi 16	Farrell-Hou 8.81	Woodeshick-Hou .15.5	Klippstein-Phi 17.1
Gibson-StL 204	Lemaster-Mil 7.22	McDaniel-Chi 57	Henry-Cin 14	Marichal-SF 9.02	Taylor-StL 11.7	Veale-Pit 15.8
INNINGS PITCHED	**OPPONENTS' AVG.**	**OPPONENTS' OBP**	**EARNED RUN AVERAGE**	**ADJUSTED ERA**	**ADJUSTED STARTER RUNS**	**PITCHER WINS**
Marichal-SF 321.1	Koufax-LA 189	Koufax-LA 230	Koufax-LA 1.88	Ellsworth-Chi 167	Koufax-LA 46.9	**Ellsworth-Chi 5.0**
Drysdale-LA 315.1	Maloney-Cin 202	Farrell-Hou 255	Ellsworth-Chi 2.11	Koufax-LA 161	Ellsworth-Chi 44.0	**Koufax-LA 4.1**
Koufax-LA 311.0	Culp-Phi 206	Marichal-SF 255	Friend-Pit 2.34	Simmons-StL 143	Marichal-SF 28.6	**Perranoski-LA 3.9**
Ellsworth-Chi 290.2	Ellsworth-Chi 210	Ellsworth-Chi 262	Marichal-SF 2.41	Friend-Pit 141	Friend-Pit 27.0	**Woodeshick-Hou 3.2**
Sanford-SF 284.1	Broglio-StL 216	Friend-Pit 267	Simmons-StL 2.48	Jackson-Chi 137	Jackson-Chi 22.7	**Jackson-Chi 3.1**

ROGER, DODGERS!

For the first several months, the Giants, Reds, Cardinals, and Dodgers jousted. Eventually, Los Angeles won 17 of 20 and made some space. But in late August, the Cardinals started their own streak, winning 19 of 20. This set up a crucial three-game set at St. Louis, which the Dodgers swept to end the race. St. Louis fans then had to deal with another disappointment as Stan Musial retired.

A healthy Sandy Koufax took the Cy Young and MVP, capitalizing on the newly enlarged strike zone and the comfortable dimensions of Chavez Ravine. The Dodgers, sixth in runs, were the NL's second-best offense on the road—better even than St. Louis, which led the league in scoring due to small Busch Stadium. While sore-legged Maury Wills' steals dropped to 40, Tommy Davis' batting title and Frank Howard's homers carried the day for the Dodgers.

The league batting average of .245 was the worst in fifty-four years, and the new hitting conditions sorted the haves from the have-nots. The last-place Mets' .219 average was the lowest of any team since 1908.

On September 10 Felipe, Matty, and Jesus Alou all played in the Giants' outfield. On September 27 Houston fielded an all-rookie lineup including Joe Morgan, Jimmy Wynn, and Jerry Grote. They sat another frosh, Rusty Staub, already the Colts' regular first baseman.

Milwaukee's Henry Aaron won his second of four home run titles. Cincinnati's scrappy second baseman Pete Rose was Rookie of the Year, and Gil Hodges retired to go into managing. Prior to the season, Rogers Hornsby, one of the game's greatest hitters, died.

Fittingly, the World Series was all pitching. Holding New York to a .171 average, the Dodgers pinned the Yankees with their first-ever four-game sweep. (The 1922 Giants also kept the Yankees from the win column, but that Series featured a tie). Koufax fanned 15 in Game 1 and captured the decisive fourth game as well.

1963 AMERICAN LEAGUE

TEAM	W	L	T	PCT	GB	HW	HL	R	OR	PA	H	2B	3B	HR	BB	SO	HB	SH	AVG	OBP	SLG	OPS	AOPS	BR	ABR	PF	SB	CS	BSA	BSR
NY	104	57	0	.646	—	**58**	22	714	547	6067	1387	197	35	188	434	**808**	31	66	.252	.309	.403	712	105	25	31	99	42	26	62	0
Chi	94	68	0	.580	10.5	49	33	683	**544**	6242	1379	208	**40**	114	571	896	40	79	.250	.323	.365	688	101	5	17	98	64	28	70	4
Min	91	70	0	.565	13	48	33	**767**	602	6233	**1408**	223	35	**225**	547	912	41	84	**.255**	.325	**.430**	**755**	**115**	**118**	**103**	102	32	14	70	2
Bal	86	76	0	.531	18.5	48	33	644	621	6055	1359	207	32	146	469	940	28	73	.249	.310	.380	690	103	-7	18	96	**97**	34	**74**	**9**
Det	79	83	0	.488	25.5	47	34	700	703	6242	1388	195	36	148	**592**	908	38	64	.252	**.327**	.382	709	102	44	21	103	73	32	70	5
Cle	79	83	0	.488	25.5	41	40	635	702	6136	1314	214	29	169	469	1102	40	**88**	.239	.301	.381	682	97	-26	-20	99	59	36	62	0
Bos	76	85	0	.472	28	44	36	666	704	6145	1403	**247**	34	171	475	954	26	44	.252	.312	.400	712	102	33	12	103	27	16	63	0
KC	73	89	0	.451	31.5	36	45	615	704	6172	1356	225	38	95	529	829	25	77	.247	.313	.353	666	88	-40	-73	106	47	26	64	1
LA	70	91	0	.435	34	39	42	597	660	6127	1378	208	38	95	448	916	**43**	84	.250	.309	.354	663	97	-54	-16	94	43	30	59	-1
Was	56	106	0	.346	48.5	31	49	578	812	6069	1237	190	35	138	497	963	30	57	.227	.293	.351	644	86	-98	-96	100	68	28	71	5
Total	808	—	—	—	—	441	367	6599	—	61488	13609	2114	352	1489	5031	9228	342	716	.247	.312	.380	692	—	—	—	—	552	270	67	27

TEAM	CG	SHO	GR	SV	IP	H	HR	BB	SO	BR/9	ERA	AERA	OAV	OOB	PR	APR	PF	OSB	OCS	FA	E	WPB	DP	FW	PW	BW	BSW	DIF
NY	**59**	19	180	31	1449.0	**1239**	115	476	965	**10.8**	3.07	114	**.232**	**.295**	89	73	97	**36**	18	.982	110	**42**	162	1.4	7.7	3.3	-.3	11.5
Chi	49	**21**	211	39	1469.0	1311	**100**	**440**	932	10.9	**2.97**	**118**	.239	.297	**107**	**90**	97	51	32	.979	131	60	163	.3	**9.5**	1.8	.1	1.4
Min	58	13	234	30	1446.1	1322	162	459	941	11.2	3.28	111	.242	.302	56	58	100	43	23	.976	144	70	140	-.5	6.1	**10.8**	-.0	-5.8
Bal	35	8	248	**43**	1452.0	1353	137	507	913	11.7	3.45	101	.248	.314	29	4	96	47	24	**.984**	**99**	**42**	157	**2.1**	.4	1.9	**.7**	-.0
Det	42	7	240	28	1456.1	1407	195	477	930	11.9	3.90	96	.253	.315	-44	-25	103	38	25	.982	113	63	124	1.3	-2.6	2.2	.2	-3.1
Cle	40	14	257	25	1469.0	1390	176	478	**1018**	11.6	3.79	95	.249	.309	-27	-28	100	51	34	.977	143	50	129	-.4	-2.9	-2.1	-.3	3.7
Bos	29	7	241	32	1449.2	1367	152	539	1009	12.0	3.97	95	.248	.316	-55	-29	104	62	17	.978	135	62	119	-.0	-3.0	1.3	-.3	-2.4
KC	35	11	247	29	1458.0	1417	156	540	887	12.4	3.92	100	.256	.324	-47	-3	108	96	26	.980	127	54	131	.5	-.3	-7.7	-.2	-.3
LA	30	13	**315**	31	1455.1	1317	120	578	889	12.0	3.52	97	.242	.318	17	-17	94	56	**41**	.974	163	66	155	-1.6	-1.8	-1.7	-.4	-5.0
Was	29	8	276	25	1447.0	1486	176	537	744	12.8	4.42	84	.266	.331	-126	-111	102	73	28	.971	182	66	**165**	-2.6	-11.7	-10.1	.2	-.9
Total	406	121	2449	313	14551.2	—	—	—	—	11.7	3.63	—	.247	.312	—	—	—	—	—	.978	1347	575	1445	—	—	—	—	—

BATTER-FIELDER WINS	BATTING AVERAGE	ON-BASE PERCENTAGE	SLUGGING AVERAGE	ON-BASE PLUS SLUGGING	ADJUSTED OPS	ADJUSTED BATTER RUNS
Yastrzemski-Bos4.2	Yastrzemski-Bos...321	Yastrzemski-Bos...418	Killebrew-Min........555	Allison-Min............911	Allison-Min............150	Yastrzemski-Bos..40.7
Battey-Min.........4.0	Kaline-Det............312	Pearson-LA...........402	Allison-Min............533	Killebrew-Min........904	Killebrew-Min........147	Allison-Min...........37.7
Hansen-Chi........3.9	Rollins-Min............307	Cash-Det..............386	Howard-NY...........528	Yastrzemski-Bos...894	Yastrzemski-Bos...145	Killebrew-Min.......32.2
Allison-Min.........3.8	Pearson-LA...........304	Allison-Min............378	Stuart-Bos............521	Kaline-Det............889	Kaline-Det............142	Kaline-Det...........31.4
Howard-NY.........3.4	Ward-Chi..............295	Kaline-Det............375	Hall-Min...............521	Howard-NY...........869	Howard-NY...........141	Pearson-LA..........31.2

RUNS	HITS	DOUBLES	TRIPLES	HOME RUNS	TOTAL BASES	RUNS BATTED IN
Allison-Min.............99	Yastrzemski-Bos...183	Yastrzemski-Bos.....40	Versalles-Min..........13	Killebrew-Min..........45	Stuart-Bos............319	Stuart-Bos............118
Pearson-LA.............92	Ward-Chi..............177	Ward-Chi................34	Hinton-Was............12	Stuart-Bos..............42	Ward-Chi..............289	Kaline-Det............101
Yastrzemski-Bos.....91	Pearson-LA...........176	Torres-LA...............32	Fregosi-LA.............12	Allison-Min.............35	Killebrew-Min........286	Killebrew-Min..........96
Tresh-NY.................91	Kaline-Det............172	Causey-KC.............32	Cimoli-KC..............11	Hall-Min..................33	Kaline-Det............283	Colavito-Det............91
Colavito-Det............91	Fregosi-LA...........170	Alvis-Cle.................32		Howard-NY............28	Allison-Min...........281	Allison-Min.............91

BASES ON BALLS	STOLEN BASES	BASE STEALING RUNS	FIELDING RUNS-INFIELD	FIELDING RUNS-OUTFIELD	OUTFIELD ASSISTS	CATCHER CS PCT.
Yastrzemski-Bos.....95	Aparicio-Bal............40	Aparicio-Bal...........6.7	Hansen-Chi.........27.5	Hall-Min...............10.5	Yastrzemski-Bos.....18	Azcue-KC-Cle......41.9
Pearson-LA.............92	Hinton-Was.............25	Tartabull-KC..........3.2	Boyer-NY............21.9	Yastrzemski-Bos....8.8	Lock-Was...............14	Rodgers-LA.........41.0
Allison-Min.............90	Wood-Det...............18	Weis-Chi................3.0	Richardson-NY....12.9	Allison-Min.............8.5	Cimoli-KC..............14	Howard-NY.........40.5
Cash-Det.................89	Snyder-Bal..............18	Richardson-NY......3.0	Causey-KC.........11.6	Hinton-Was............6.9		Triandos-Det........37.5
Colavito-Det............84	Pearson-LA.............17	Hinton-Was...........2.3	Moran-LA..............8.8	Clinton-Bos............6.7		Battey-Min...........33.9

WINS	WINNING PCT.	WINS ABOVE TEAM	GAMES STARTED	COMPLETE GAMES	FEWEST HITS/GAME	FEWEST BB/GAME
Ford-NY..................24	Ford-NY................774	Ford-NY.................6.4	Terry-NY.................37	Terry-NY.................18	Downing-NY........5.84	Donovan-Cle........1.22
Pascual-Min............21	Bouton-NY...........750	Monbouquette-Bos 6.3	Ford-NY.................37	Pascual-Min............18	Bouton-NY...........6.89	Terry-NY..............1.31
Bouton-NY..............21	Radatz-Bos..........714	Pascual-Min...........5.3	Monbouquette-Bos .36	Stigman-Min...........15	Drabowsky-KC.....6.97	Herbert-Chi..........1.40
Monbouquette-Bos .20	Peters-Chi............704	Radatz-Bos............5.2	McBride-LA............36	Herbert-Chi.............14	Morehead-Bos.....7.06	Monbouquette-Bos .1.42
Barber-Bal..............20	Pascual-Min.........700	Bouton-NY.............4.7	Barber-Bal.............36	Aguirre-Det.............14	McBride-LA.........7.10	Roberts-Bal.........1.43

STRIKEOUTS	STRIKEOUTS/GAME	GAMES	SAVES	BASE RUNNERS/9	ADJUSTED RELIEF RUNS	RELIEF RANKING
Pascual-Min..........202	Downing-NY........8.76	S.Miller-Bal.............71	S.Miller-Bal.............27	Dailey-Min............8.20	Radatz-Bos..........26.0	Radatz-Bos..........48.1
Bunning-Det..........196	Ramos-Cle...........8.24	Radatz-Bos.............66	Radatz-Bos.............25	Hall-Bal.................8.95	Dailey-Min............20.5	Dailey-Min............24.2
Stigman-Min.........193	Pascual-Min.........7.32	Dailey-Min..............66	Wyatt-KC................21	Fowler-LA............8.97	S.Miller-Bal..........13.8	S.Miller-Bal..........21.8
Peters-Chi.............189	Stigman-Min........7.21	Lamabe-Bos...........65	Wilhelm-Chi............21	Wilhelm-Chi.........9.24	Wilhelm-Chi.........12.6	Wilhelm-Chi.........15.2
Ford-NY................189	Bunning-Det.........7.10	Wyatt-KC................63	Dailey-Min..............21	Cheney-Was........9.24	Fowler-LA...........11.4	Fowler-LA...........12.1

INNINGS PITCHED	OPPONENTS' AVG.	OPPONENTS' OBP	EARNED RUN AVERAGE	ADJUSTED ERA	ADJUSTED STARTER RUNS	PITCHER WINS
Ford-NY............269.1	Downing-NY.........184	Terry-NY...............271	Peters-Chi...........2.33	Peters-Chi............150	Peters-Chi...........33.6	**Radatz-Bos.........5.0**
Terry-NY...........268.0	Morehead-Bos......211	Ramos-Cle...........272	Pizarro-Chi..........2.39	Pascual-Min..........148	Pascual-Min.........33.2	**Peters-Chi...........4.8**
Monbouquette-Bos266.2	Bouton-NY...........212	Roberts-Bal..........272	Pascual-Min.........2.46	Pizarro-Chi............147	Bouton-NY...........27.5	**Pascual-Min.......4.7**
Barber-Bal.........258.2	Drabowsky-KC......214	Downing-NY.........277	Bouton-NY...........2.53	Bouton-NY............139	Pizarro-Chi..........25.2	**Pizarro-Chi.........3.0**
Roberts-Bal.......251.1	Peters-Chi............216	Peters-Chi............277	Downing-NY........2.56	Stange-Min...........139	Ford-NY..............22.3	**Dailey-Min...........2.9**

Brother, Can You Spare a Bat?

Baseball authorities decided that the game had become too dependent on home runs. Therefore, to balance the game in favor of the pitcher, the strike zone was enlarged before the season and would now range from the top of the shoulders to the top of the knees. The result was an offensive disaster. Scoring fell to its lowest since 1946, and would continue to decline through 1968.

The odd thing? Home runs didn't decrease much. Strikeouts, however, shot up; the Indians set an all-time high for whiffs, and for the third straight year, a wild swinger broke the individual record. Chicago slugger Dave Nicholson's 175 strikeouts shattered the mark by 33.

Despite Nicholson's whiffs, the White Sox finished second on big seasons from rookies Gary Peters and Pete Ward. Minnesota, with a fearsome attack that topped the AL in homers both at home and on the road, led in scoring, but had very poor second-line pitching.

Early Wynn won his 300th career game, and then was immediately released by Cleveland, who also gave lefty Tommy John his first exposure to the majors. And in a year in which Harmon Killebrew won his third home run crown, Frank "Home Run" Baker, who had captured four such titles, died at 77.

Once again, the Yankees won, and easily. Excellent pitching and Elston Howard's MVP performance sprung the club from a tangle in June. They never looked back despite losing Mickey Mantle to injury. For the first time since 1951, the Yankees had two 20-game winners—Whitey Ford and Jim Bouton. But neither pitcher won in the World Series; in fact, no Yankee won. The Yankees, with six World Series sweeps to their credit, were themselves swept by the Dodgers. New York scored just 4 runs. Mantle batted just .133; Clete Boyer hit .077.

1962 NATIONAL LEAGUE

TEAM	W	L	T	PCT	GB	HW	HL	R	OR	PA	H	2B	3B	HR	BB	SO	HB	SH	AVG	OBP	SLG	OPS	AOPS	BR	ABR	PF	SB	CS	BSA	BSR
SF	103	62	0	.624	—	**61**	21	**878**	690	6277	**1552**	235	32	**204**	523	822	42	76	**.278**	**.341**	**.441**	**782**	**118**	**126**	**141**	98	73	50	59	-1
LA	102	63	0	.618	1	54	29	842	697	6362	1510	192	**65**	140	572	886	32	**83**	.268	.337	.400	737	111	39	90	94	**198**	43	**82**	**29**
Cin	98	64	0	.605	3.5	58	23	802	685	6273	1523	**252**	40	167	498	903	41	57	.270	.332	.417	749	104	57	32	103	66	39	63	1
Pit	93	68	0	.578	8	51	30	706	**626**	6035	1468	240	**65**	108	432	836	17	54	.268	.321	.394	715	98	-16	-17	100	50	39	56	-3
Mil	86	76	0	.531	15.5	49	32	730	665	6155	1376	204	38	181	581	975	34	47	.252	.326	.403	729	105	17	37	97	57	27	68	3
StL	84	78	1	.519	17.5	44	37	774	664	6307	1528	221	31	137	515	846	45	69	.271	.335	.394	729	93	23	-44	110	86	41	68	5
Phi	81	80	0	.503	20	46	34	705	759	6131	1410	199	39	142	531	923	**53**	**83**	.260	.330	.390	720	103	5	27	97	79	42	65	3
Hou	64	96	2	.400	36.5	32	48	592	717	6198	1370	170	47	105	493	**806**	38	75	.246	.310	.351	661	91	-120	-71	93	42	30	58	-1
Chi	59	103	0	.364	42.5	32	49	632	827	6173	1398	196	56	126	504	1044	39	54	.253	.317	.377	694	89	-55	-78	104	78	50	61	0
NY	40	120	1	.250	60.5	22	58	617	948	6242	1318	166	40	139	**616**	991	32	58	.240	.318	.361	679	88	-76	-86	102	59	48	55	-4
Total	812	—	—	—	—	449	361	7278	—	62153	14453	2075	453	1449	5265	9032	373	656	.261	.327	.393	720	—	—	—	—	788	409	66	30

TEAM	CG	SHO	GR	SV	IP	H	HR	BB	SO	BR/9	ERA	AERA	OAV	OOB	PR	APR	PF	OSB	OCS	FA	E	WPB	DP	FW	PW	BW	BSW	DIF
SF	**62**	10	216	39	1461.2	1399	148	503	886	11.9	3.79	100	.251	**.314**	24	0	96	65	26	.977	142	**47**	153	1.0	.0	**14.1**	-.4	5.9
LA	44	8	249	**46**	1488.2	**1386**	115	588	**1104**	12.1	3.62	100	**.245**	.317	54	-3	92	59	34	.970	193	71	144	-2.1	.3	9.0	**2.6**	9.7
Cin	51	13	222	35	1460.2	1397	149	567	964	12.4	3.75	107	.254	.327	31	43	102	75	36	.977	145	67	144	.6	4.3	3.2	-.2	9.1
Pit	40	13	263	41	1432.1	1433	118	466	897	12.1	**3.37**	117	.262	.320	**90**	89	100	86	31	.976	152	66	**177**	.2	8.9	-1.7	-.6	5.8
Mil	59	10	206	24	1434.2	1443	151	**407**	802	**11.8**	3.68	103	.262	.315	42	20	96	**49**	44	**.980**	**124**	50	154	**1.9**	2.0	3.7	.0	-2.6
StL	53	**17**	208	25	1463.1	1394	149	517	914	11.9	3.55	**120**	.252	.318	64	**108**	108	73	40	.979	132	76	170	1.5	**10.8**	-4.4	.2	-5.0
Phi	43	7	247	24	1426.2	1469	155	574	863	13.2	4.28	90	.268	.341	-53	-66	98	67	47	.977	138	89	167	1.0	-6.6	2.7	.0	3.4
Hou	34	9	264	19	1453.2	1446	**113**	471	1047	12.1	3.83	98	.259	.319	19	-15	95	119	43	.973	173	99	149	-1.0	-1.5	-7.1	-.4	-6.0
Chi	29	4	**309**	26	1438.1	1509	159	601	783	13.5	4.54	91	.272	.346	-95	-59	105	101	**58**	.977	146	99	171	.6	-5.9	-7.8	-.3	-8.6
NY	43	4	254	10	1430.0	1577	192	571	772	13.8	5.04	83	.281	.349	-175	-129	106	94	50	.967	210	97	167	-3.3	-12.9	-8.6	-.7	-14.5
Total	458	95	2438	289	14490.0	—	—	—	—	12.5	3.94	—	.261	.327	—	—	—	—	—	.975	1555	761	1596	—	—	—	—	—

BATTER-FIELDER WINS	BATTING AVERAGE	ON-BASE PERCENTAGE	SLUGGING AVERAGE	ON-BASE PLUS SLUGGING	ADJUSTED OPS	ADJUSTED BATTER RUNS
Mays-SF 6.1	T.Davis-LA 346	Robinson-Cin 421	Robinson-Cin 624	Robinson-Cin 1045	Robinson-Cin 172	Robinson-Cin 64.8
Robinson-Cin 5.7	Robinson-Cin 342	Musial-StL 416	H.Aaron-Mil 618	H.Aaron-Mil 1008	H.Aaron-Mil 171	H.Aaron-Mil 58.3
H.Aaron-Mil 5.2	Musial-StL 330	Skinner-Pit 395	Mays-SF 615	Mays-SF 999	Mays-SF 167	Mays-SF 57.7
Mazeroski-Pit 4.7	White-StL 324	Altman-Chi 393	Howard-LA 560	Musial-StL 924	T.Davis-LA 151	T.Davis-LA 44.4
T.Davis-LA 3.8	H.Aaron-Mil 323	H.Aaron-Mil 390	T.Davis-LA 535	T.Davis-LA 910	Howard-LA 149	Mathews-Mil 31.6

RUNS	HITS	DOUBLES	TRIPLES	HOME RUNS	TOTAL BASES	RUNS BATTED IN
Robinson-Cin 134	T.Davis-LA 230	Robinson-Cin 51	Wills-LA 10	Mays-SF 49	Mays-SF 382	T.Davis-LA 153
Wills-LA 130	Wills-LA 208	Mays-SF 36	Virdon-Pit 10	H.Aaron-Mil 45	Robinson-Cin 380	Mays-SF 141
Mays-SF 130	Robinson-Cin 208	Groat-Pit 34	W.Davis-LA 10	Robinson-Cin 39	H.Aaron-Mil 366	Robinson-Cin 136
H.Aaron-Mil 127	White-StL 199		Callison-Phi 10	Banks-Chi 37	T.Davis-LA 356	H.Aaron-Mil 128
T.Davis-LA 120	Groat-Pit 199			Cepeda-SF 35	Cepeda-SF 324	Howard-LA 119

BASES ON BALLS	STOLEN BASES	BASE STEALING RUNS	FIELDING RUNS-INFIELD	FIELDING RUNS-OUTFIELD	OUTFIELD ASSISTS	CATCHER CS PCT.
Mathews-Mil 101	Wills-LA 104	Wills-LA 18.3	Mazeroski-Pit 41.2	Callison-Phi 22.0	Callison-Phi 24	Dalrymple-Phi 42.4
Gilliam-LA 93	W.Davis-LA 32	W.Davis-LA 4.6	Lillis-Hou 16.2	Clemente-Pit 9.7	Howard-LA 19	Roseboro-LA 38.7
Ashburn-NY 81	Pinson-Cin 26	Mays-SF 3.3	Groat-Pit 15.6	Mays-SF 6.5	Clemente-Pit 19	Edwards-Cin 37.8
Mays-SF 78	Javier-StL 26	Pinson-Cin 2.9	McMillan-Mil 13.2	Flood-StL 6.2	Williams-Chi 18	Haller-SF 35.7
	Taylor-Phi 20	Javier-StL 2.6	Santo-Chi 12.9	W.Davis-LA 5.2	Thomas-NY 14	Burgess-Pit 28.6

WINS	WINNING PCT.	WINS ABOVE TEAM	GAMES STARTED	COMPLETE GAMES	FEWEST HITS/GAME	FEWEST BB/GAME
Drysdale-LA 25	Purkey-Cin 821	Purkey-Cin 8.3	Drysdale-LA 41	Spahn-Mil 22	Koufax-LA 6.54	Shaw-Mil 1.76
Sanford-SF 24	Sanford-SF 774	Sanford-SF 7.0	Podres-LA 40	O'Dell-SF 20	Gibson-StL 6.70	Friend-Pit 1.82
Purkey-Cin 23	Drysdale-LA 735	Drysdale-LA 6.1	O'Dell-SF 39	Mahaffey-Phi 20	Bennett-Phi 7.42	Spahn-Mil 1.84
Jay-Cin 21	Pierce-SF 727	Roebuck-LA 3.5	Mahaffey-Phi 39	Drysdale-LA 19	Drysdale-LA 7.79	Pierce-SF 1.94
	Shaw-Mil 625	Pierce-SF 3.3	Sanford-SF 38		Broglio-StL 7.81	Purkey-Cin 2.00

STRIKEOUTS	STRIKEOUTS/GAME	GAMES	SAVES	BASE RUNNERS/9	ADJUSTED RELIEF RUNS	RELIEF RANKING
Drysdale-LA 232	Koufax-LA 10.55	Perranoski-LA 70	Face-Pit 28	Face-Pit 9.20	Face-Pit 20.4	Face-Pit 40.9
Koufax-LA 216	Johnson-Hou 8.13	Baldschun-Phi 67	Perranoski-LA 20	Umbricht-Hou 9.40	McMahon-Mil-Hou 19.5	McMahon-Mil-Hou 28.6
Gibson-StL 208	Gibson-StL 8.01	Roebuck-LA 64	Miller-SF 19	Koufax-LA 9.42	Shantz-Hou-StL 15.1	Baldschun-Phi 21.1
Farrell-Hou 203	Bennett-Phi 7.68	Face-Pit 63	McDaniel-StL 14	Shantz-Hou-StL 9.88	Umbricht-Hou 12.8	Shantz-Hou-StL 19.1
O'Dell-SF 195	Farrell-Hou 7.56	Olivo-Pit 62		Farrell-Hou 10.06	Baldschun-Phi 11.8	Elston-Chi 19.1

INNINGS PITCHED	OPPONENTS' AVG.	OPPONENTS' OBP	EARNED RUN AVERAGE	ADJUSTED ERA	ADJUSTED STARTER RUNS	PITCHER WINS
Drysdale-LA 314.1	Koufax-LA 197	Koufax-LA 261	Koufax-LA 2.54	Gibson-StL 150	Purkey-Cin 34.7	**Gibson-StL 4.7**
Purkey-Cin 288.1	Gibson-StL 204	Farrell-Hou 279	Shaw-Mil 2.80	Purkey-Cin 143	Gibson-StL 34.5	**Face-Pit 4.1**
O'Dell-SF 280.2	Bennett-Phi 224	Drysdale-LA 282	Purkey-Cin 2.81	Koufax-LA 143	Broglio-StL 31.1	**Spahn-Mil 3.5**
Mahaffey-Phi 274.0	Drysdale-LA 230	Pierce-SF 283	Drysdale-LA 2.83	Broglio-StL 142	Friend-Pit 27.4	**Drysdale-LA 3.3**
Jay-Cin 273.0	Farrell-Hou 233	Spahn-Mil 284	Gibson-StL 2.85	Shaw-Mil 136	Drysdale-LA 27.1	**Purkey-Cin 3.0**

SHADES OF '51

The new ten-team National League had great teams, mediocre teams, and the Mets, perhaps the worst ever. Between first and last lay 60½ games, the largest gap in 27 years.

The Giants, Reds, and Dodgers battled at the top. Cincinnati hung close, but down the stretch the New York transplants provided the thrills.

Los Angeles, playing in new Chavez Ravine, saw attendance increase by 56 percent; solid pitching and expansive surroundings translated into the club's first 100-win season since 1953. Despite Maury Wills' record 104 steals and MVP award, Tommy Davis was the Dodgers' key. Don Drysdale took the Cy Young, while Sandy Koufax led in ERA. The two were 1-2 in strikeouts although Koufax missed two months with circulatory problems.

The Giants scored more runs than any team since 1953. Willie Mays, second in MVP voting, and Orlando Cepeda each drove in and scored more than 100. Meanwhile, 20-homer man Willie McCovey sat on the bench.

The Phillies improved nearly 30 games, and Pittsburgh debuted Willie Stargell and Bob Veale. Chicago's Ken Hubbs was Rookie of the Year—teammate Billy Williams had won the award the previous year. Richie Ashburn, the first batter in Mets history, retired rather than risk another 120-loss season.

While home runs rose to a record high, they decreased per game due to large new parks. Sparked by Wills, the stolen base made a comeback. Steals per game reached their highest level since the 1920s. League attendance rose annually through 1966; the Dodgers drew two million each year. In yet another honor, Jackie Robinson became the first African American Hall of Famer.

LA led by 4 games in mid-September. At that point, the Dodgers began losing, and despite playing .500 ball over the last two weeks, the Giants forced a tie. With their three-game playoff tied one game each, the Dodgers took a 4-2 lead to the top of the ninth in the third game. The Giants capitalized on walks and bobbles to win the game, and the pennant, 6-4. The World Series went to the Yankees in seven tight games.

1962 AMERICAN LEAGUE

TEAM	W	L	T	PCT	GB	HW	HL	R	OR	PA	H	2B	3B	HR	BB	SO	HB	SH	AVG	OBP	SLG	OPS	AOPS	BR	ABR	PF	SB	CS	BSA	BSR
NY	96	66	0	.593	—	**50**	30	**817**	680	6393	**1509**	240	29	199	584	842	32	79	**.267**	.337	**.426**	**763**	**115**	**89**	**116**	97	42	29	59	-1
Min	91	71	1	.562	5	45	36	798	713	6362	1445	215	39	185	649	823	31	71	.260	**.338**	.412	750	104	68	39	104	33	20	62	0
LA	86	76	0	.531	10	40	41	718	706	6255	1377	232	35	137	602	917	29	**82**	.250	.325	.380	705	99	-22	1	97	46	27	63	1
Det	85	76	0	.528	10.5	49	33	758	692	6234	1352	191	36	**209**	**651**	894	33	56	.248	.330	.411	741	101	41	15	104	69	21	77	8
Chi	85	77	0	.525	11	43	38	707	**658**	6297	1415	250	56	92	620	**674**	41	**82**	.257	.334	.372	706	96	-11	-7	100	76	40	66	3
Cle	80	82	0	.494	16	43	38	682	745	6137	1341	202	22	180	502	939	**54**	52	.245	.312	.388	700	97	-48	-27	97	35	16	69	2
Bal	77	85	0	.475	19	44	38	652	680	6158	1363	225	34	156	516	931	32	75	.248	.314	.387	701	100	-43	2	94	45	32	58	-1
Bos	76	84	0	.475	19	39	40	707	756	6177	1429	**257**	53	146	525	923	27	59	.258	.324	.403	727	98	10	-12	103	39	33	54	-3
KC	72	90	0	.444	24	39	42	745	837	6302	1467	220	**58**	116	556	803	42	78	.263	.332	.386	718	95	2	-31	105	76	21	**78**	**9**
Was	60	101	1	.373	35.5	27	53	599	716	6072	1370	206	38	132	466	789	15	71	.250	.308	.373	681	90	-85	-80	99	**99**	53	65	3
Total	809	—	—	—	—	419	389	7183	—	62387	14068	2238	400	1552	5671	8535	336	705	.255	.325	.394	719	—	—	—	—	560	292	66	21

TEAM	CG	SHO	GR	SV	IP	H	HR	BB	SO	BR/9	ERA	AERA	OAV	OOB	PR	APR	PF	OSB	OCS	FA	E	WPB	DP	FW	PW	BW	BSW	DIF
NY	33	10	248	42	1470.1	1375	146	499	838	**11.6**	3.70	101	**.247**	**.310**	44	8	94	**34**	26	.979	131	**34**	151	.4	.8	**11.7**	-.3	2.5
Min	**53**	11	241	27	1463.1	1400	166	**493**	**948**	11.9	3.89	105	.253	.317	13	30	103	41	31	.980	129	68	**173**	.5	3.0	3.9	-.2	2.8
LA	23	**15**	**345**	**47**	1466.0	1412	**118**	616	858	12.8	3.70	104	.253	.330	**45**	27	97	52	35	.973	175	55	153	-2.2	2.7	.1	-.1	4.5
Det	46	8	245	35	1443.2	1452	169	503	873	12.4	3.81	**107**	.259	.321	26	**41**	103	47	26	.974	156	45	114	-1.1	**4.1**	1.5	.6	-.6
Chi	50	13	265	28	1451.2	1380	123	537	821	12.0	3.73	105	.251	.317	38	29	98	72	24	**.982**	**110**	46	153	**1.6**	2.9	-.7	.0	.1
Cle	45	12	242	31	1441.0	1410	174	594	780	12.7	4.14	94	.258	.331	-27	-44	98	54	**37**	.978	139	43	168	-.1	-4.4	-2.7	-.0	6.2
Bal	32	8	253	33	1462.1	**1373**	147	549	898	12.0	**3.69**	100	.249	.318	**45**	1	93	80	**37**	.980	122	78	152	.9	.1	.2	-.3	-4.9
Bos	34	12	222	40	1437.2	1416	159	632	923	13.1	4.22	98	.258	.337	-40	-14	104	70	19	.979	131	60	152	.3	-1.4	-1.2	-.5	-1.1
KC	32	4	274	33	1434.0	1450	199	655	825	13.5	4.79	88	.263	.343	-131	-85	106	65	25	.979	132	88	131	.3	-8.5	-3.1	**.7**	1.7
Was	38	11	266	13	1445.0	1400	151	593	771	12.5	4.04	100	.256	.328	-12	-1	102	45	32	.978	139	46	160	-.1	-.1	-8.0	.0	-12.3
Total	386	104	2601	329	14515.0	—	—	—	—	12.4	3.97	—	.255	.325	—	—	—	—	—	.978	1364	563	1507	—	—	—	—	—

BATTER-FIELDER WINS	BATTING AVERAGE	ON-BASE PERCENTAGE	SLUGGING AVERAGE	ON-BASE PLUS SLUGGING	ADJUSTED OPS	ADJUSTED BATTER RUNS
Mantle-NY 5.0	Runnels-Bos 326	Mantle-NY............486	Mantle-NY............605	Mantle-NY...........1091	Mantle-NY............198	Mantle-NY............62.9
Bressoud-Bos 3.7	Mantle-NY............321	Siebern-KC...........412	Killebrew-Min........545	Killebrew-Min.........912	Siebern-KC...........138	Siebern-KC...........36.5
Boyer-NY 3.6	Robinson-Chi........312	Cunningham-Chi...410	Colavito-Det..........514	Siebern-KC...........907	Killebrew-Min........137	Killebrew-Min.......30.1
Colavito-Det....... 3.2	Hinton-Was...........310	Runnels-Bos.........408	Cash-Det..............513	Cash-Det..............894	Cash-Det..............134	Colavito-Det.........28.7
B.Robinson-Bal.. 3.1	Siebern-KC...........308	Robinson-Chi........384	Allison-Min...........511	Colavito-Det..........885	Colavito-Det..........132	Robinson-Chi.......28.7

RUNS	HITS	DOUBLES	TRIPLES	HOME RUNS	TOTAL BASES	RUNS BATTED IN
Pearson-LA...........115	Richardson-NY 209	Robinson-Chi..........45	Cimoli-KC 15	Killebrew-Min..........48	Colavito-Det..........309	Killebrew-Min........126
Siebern-KC...........114	Lumpe-KC 193	Yastrzemski-Bos 43	Robinson-Chi..........10	Cash-Det 39	B.Robinson-Bal.....308	Siebern-KC...........117
Allison-Min............102	B.Robinson-Bal.....192	Bressoud-Bos.........40	Lumpe-KC 10	Wagner-LA.............37	Wagner-LA............306	Colavito-Det..........112
Yastrzemski-Bos 99	Yastrzemski-Bos ...191	Richardson-NY 38	Clinton-Bos.............10	Colavito-Det............37	Yastrzemski-Bos ...303	Robinson-Chi........109
Richardson-NY 99	Robinson-Chi........187				Killebrew-Min........301	Wagner-LA............107

BASES ON BALLS	STOLEN BASES	BASE STEALING RUNS	FIELDING RUNS-INFIELD	FIELDING RUNS-OUTFIELD	OUTFIELD ASSISTS	CATCHER CS PCT.
Mantle-NY............122	Aparicio-Chi............31	Wood-Det 4.2	Versalles-Min 34.9	Colavito-Det.........12.4	Yastrzemski-Bos 15	Howard-NY 54.8
Siebern-KC...........110	Hinton-Was............28	Howser-KC 3.5	Boyer-NY 34.3	DelGreco-KC 9.0	Robinson-Chi..........13	Schmidt-Was 53.3
Killebrew-Min 106	Wood-Det 24	Charles-KC...........3.0	Cottier-Was..........23.7	Yastrzemski-Bos 8.4	Kirkland-Cle............11	Rodgers-LA 45.9
Cash-Det 104	Charles-KC............20	Hinton-Was...........2.7	Bressoud-Bos......22.7	Bruton-Det 8.0	Colavito-Det............10	Battey-Min 44.3
Cunningham-Chi...101		Aparicio-Chi...........2.6	Kindall-Cle 22.7	Green-Min.............6.0	Allison-Min 10	Retzer-Was..........39.6

WINS	WINNING PCT.	WINS ABOVE TEAM	GAMES STARTED	COMPLETE GAMES	FEWEST HITS/GAME	FEWEST BB/GAME
Terry-NY 23	Herbert-Chi..........690	Donovan-Cle..........5.8	Terry-NY 39	Pascual-Min............18	Aguirre-Det 6.75	Donovan-Cle........1.69
Pascual-Min............20	Ford-NY 680	Herbert-Chi...........5.7	Kralick-Min.............37	Kaat-Min 16	Cheney-Was........6.96	Terry-NY 1.72
Herbert-Chi............20	Donovan-Cle.........667	Bunning-Det..........4.5	Ford-NY 37	Donovan-Cle...........16	Belinsky-LA..........7.16	Mossi-Det 1.80
Donovan-Cle...........20	Aguirre-Det 667	Wickersham-KC.....4.1		Terry-NY 14	Wilson-Bos 7.67	Roberts-Bal 1.93
Bunning-Det...........19	Terry-NY 657	Aguirre-Det 3.9			Stenhouse-Was ...7.72	Pascual-Min.........2.06

STRIKEOUTS	STRIKEOUTS/GAME	GAMES	SAVES	BASE RUNNERS/9	ADJUSTED RELIEF RUNS	RELIEF RANKING
Pascual-Min..........206	Pizarro-Chi..........7.66	Radatz-Bos............62	Radatz-Bos............24	Hall-Bal................9.20	Radatz-Bos..........26.4	Radatz-Bos..........39.8
Bunning-Det..........184	Cheney-Was........7.63	Wyatt-KC 59	Bridges-NY 18	Terry-NY 9.55	Hall-Bal................21.4	Wilhelm-Bal 34.1
Terry-NY 176	Pascual-Min.........7.20		Fox-Det..................16	Aguirre-Det 9.67	Wilhelm-Bal 17.0	Hall-Bal................22.0
Pizarro-Chi............173	Belinsky-LA.........6.97		Wilhelm-Bal 15	Wilhelm-Bal 9.77	Fox-Det................14.6	Fox-Det................18.0
Kaat-Min 173	Estrada-Bal.........6.65		Bell-Cle..................12	Pena-KC 9.94	Fowler-LA 10.7	Fowler-LA 10.2

INNINGS PITCHED	OPPONENTS' AVG.	OPPONENTS' OBP	EARNED RUN AVERAGE	ADJUSTED ERA	ADJUSTED STARTER RUNS	PITCHER WINS
Terry-NY 298.2	Aguirre-Det 205	Aguirre-Det 267	Aguirre-Det 2.21	Aguirre-Det 184	Aguirre-Det 40.6	**Radatz-Bos......... 3.9**
Kaat-Min 269.0	Cheney-Was.........213	Terry-NY 268	Roberts-Bal 2.78	Roberts-Bal 133	Ford-NY 27.3	**Kaat-Min 3.8**
Bunning-Det.......258.0	Belinsky-LA..........216	Pascual-Min.........285	Ford-NY 2.90	Chance-LA...........130	Kaat-Min 27.3	**Pascual-Min 3.7**
Pascual-Min.......257.2	Terry-NY 231	Roberts-Bal 288	Chance-LA...........2.96	Kaat-Min 130	Pascual-Min.........24.4	**Wilhelm-Bal........ 3.5**
Ford-NY 257.2	Wilson-Bos 231	Fisher-Chi............291	Fisher-Chi 3.10	Ford-NY 129	Roberts-Bal 22.9	**Aguirre-Det 3.4**

CARRYING THE MANTLE

The Indians led the AL at the start of July, but Cleveland soon dropped into the second division as the Yankees took over. Minnesota and Los Angeles hung around until September, although neither got close enough to scare New York. Mickey Mantle took home his third MVP trophy, even though he missed nearly 40 games with knee problems. The team's balanced attack led the AL in scoring. But New Yorkers again seemed blasé about success; with National League baseball back in the city, the Yankees' attendance dropped every year from 1962 through 1966.

The Twins finished second as Harmon Killebrew captured his first home run title (and set a new strikeout mark). All eight Minnesota regulars hit homers in double figures, and Camilo Pascual paced the AL in strikeouts, shutouts, and complete games. Outfielder Tony Oliva went 4-for-9 in his first big league action.

The surprising Angels ended up third. Moving from tiny Wrigley Field to huge Chavez Ravine, the Angels saw attendance increase 90 percent to break the million mark. Rookie pitcher Bo Belinsky took Tinseltown by storm, throwing a no-hitter and dating starlet Mamie Van Doren, though the nightlife led to a quick loss of effectiveness for the pitcher.

Boston's Pete Runnells won his second batting crown, but the Red Sox, beginning a fallow period, ended to eighth. The Orioles dropped to seventh as their young pitchers began to crumble under heavy workloads.

All seven games in the Yankees-Giants World Series were close. The big stars—Mantle, Maris, Mays, and McCovey—were non-factors. Unlikely heroes like Chuck Hiller, Bill Stafford, and Clete Boyer dominated the entertaining Series. With the Yankees up three games to two, California rain delayed the proceedings by three days. The Giants won Game 6, but Raph Terry shut out the Giants on 4 hits to win the decider, 1-0. The Series ended when second baseman Bobby Richardson caught McCovey's hard liner with the tying and winning runs in scoring position.

1961 NATIONAL LEAGUE

TEAM	W	L	T	PCT	GB	HW	HL	R	OR	PA	H	2B	3B	HR	BB	SO	HB	SH	AVG	OBP	SLG	OPS	AOPS	BR	ABR	PF	SB	CS	BSA	BSR
Cin	93	61	0	.604	—	47	30	710	**653**	5796	1414	**247**	35	158	423	761	29	50	.270	.325	.421	746	102	20	11	101	70	33	**68**	**4**
LA	89	65	0	.578	4	45	32	735	697	5940	1358	193	40	157	**596**	796	23	96	.262	**.338**	.405	743	95	30	-29	109	**86**	45	66	3
SF	85	69	1	.552	8	45	32	**773**	655	5887	1379	219	32	183	506	764	30	70	.264	.329	**.423**	**752**	108	**36**	64	96	79	54	59	-2
Mil	83	71	1	.539	10	45	32	712	656	5958	1365	199	34	**188**	534	880	34	62	.258	.328	.415	743	**109**	19	**66**	94	70	43	62	0
StL	80	74	1	.519	13	**48**	29	703	668	5944	1436	236	51	103	494	745	33	70	.271	.334	.393	727	89	-3	-66	110	46	28	62	0
Pit	75	79	0	.487	18	38	39	694	675	5867	**1448**	232	**57**	128	428	**721**	27	64	**.273**	.328	.410	738	101	7	5	100	26	30	46	-5
Chi	64	90	2	.416	29	40	37	689	800	6000	1364	238	51	176	539	1027	32	52	.255	.325	.418	743	101	17	8	101	35	25	58	-1
Phi	47	107	1	.305	46	22	55	584	796	5870	1265	185	50	103	475	928	**46**	**108**	.243	.310	.357	667	83	-126	-118	99	56	30	65	2
Total	619	—	—	—	—	330	286	5600	—	47262	11029	1749	350	1196	3995	6622	254	572	.262	.327	.405	732	—	—	—	—	468	288	62	2

TEAM	CG	SHO	GR	SV	IP	H	HR	BB	SO	BR/9	ERA	AERA	OAV	OOB	PR	APR	PF	OSB	OCS	FA	E	WPB	DP	FW	PW	BW	BSW	DIF
Cin	46	**12**	210	**40**	1370.0	**1300**	147	500	829	12.0	3.78	107	.250	.318	38	42	101	68	34	.977	134	63	124	.7	4.2	1.1	**.4**	9.7
LA	40	10	239	35	1378.1	1346	167	544	**1105**	12.7	4.04	107	.256	.329	-2	43	108	53	32	.975	144	80	162	.1	4.3	-2.9	.3	10.2
SF	39	9	235	30	1388.0	1306	152	502	924	**11.9**	3.77	101	**.249**	**.316**	40	6	95	63	30	.977	133	43	126	.8	.6	6.4	-.2	.5
Mil	**57**	8	194	16	1391.1	1357	153	493	652	12.1	3.89	96	.258	.322	21	-26	93	**42**	33	**.982**	**111**	**41**	152	**2.0**	-2.6	**6.5**	-.0	.0
StL	49	10	184	24	1368.2	1334	136	570	823	12.7	**3.74**	**118**	.256	.330	**44**	**92**	109	68	41	.972	166	61	165	-1.1	**9.1**	-6.5	-.0	1.5
Pit	34	9	236	29	1362.0	1442	**121**	**400**	759	12.3	3.92	102	.274	.326	17	10	99	44	25	.975	150	58	**187**	-.2	1.0	.5	-.5	-2.7
Chi	34	6	248	25	1385.0	1492	165	465	755	12.9	4.48	93	.277	.336	-70	-45	104	61	34	.970	183	85	175	-2.0	-4.5	.8	-.1	-7.2
Phi	29	9	**257**	13	1383.1	1452	155	521	775	13.1	4.61	88	.273	.340	-88	-81	101	69	**59**	.976	146	80	179	.0	-8.0	-11.7	.2	-10.5
Total	328	73	1803	212	11026.2	—	—	—	—	12.5	4.03	—	.262	.327	—	—	—	—	—	.976	1167	511	1270	—	—	—	—	—

BATTER-FIELDER WINS	BATTING AVERAGE	ON-BASE PERCENTAGE	SLUGGING AVERAGE	ON-BASE PLUS SLUGGING	ADJUSTED OPS	ADJUSTED BATTER RUNS
Aaron-Mil 5.1	Clemente-Pit .351	Moon-LA .434	Robinson-Cin .611	Robinson-Cin 1015	Aaron-Mil 165	Aaron-Mil 54.9
Robinson-Cin 5.1	Pinson-Cin .343	Robinson-Cin .404	Cepeda-SF .609	Mays-SF .977	Robinson-Cin 164	Robinson-Cin 51.9
Mays-SF 4.5	Boyer-StL .329	Mathews-Mil .402	Aaron-Mil .594	Aaron-Mil .974	Mays-SF 162	Mays-SF 51.8
Boyer-StL 4.1	Moon-LA .328	Boyer-StL .397	Mays-SF .584	Cepeda-SF .970	Cepeda-SF 158	Mathews-Mil 48.9
Mathews-Mil 4.1	Aaron-Mil .327	Mays-SF .393	Stuart-Pit .581	Clemente-Pit .949	Mathews-Mil 156	Cepeda-SF 45.4

RUNS	HITS	DOUBLES	TRIPLES	HOME RUNS	TOTAL BASES	RUNS BATTED IN
Mays-SF 129	Pinson-Cin 208	Aaron-Mil 39	Altman-Chi 12	Cepeda-SF 46	Aaron-Mil 358	Cepeda-SF 142
Robinson-Cin 117	Clemente-Pit 201	Pinson-Cin 34	White-StL 11	Mays-SF 40	Cepeda-SF 356	Robinson-Cin 124
Aaron-Mil 115	Aaron-Mil 197	Santo-Chi 32	Callison-Phi 11	Robinson-Cin 37	Mays-SF 334	Mays-SF 123
Boyer-StL 109	Boyer-StL 194	Robinson-Cin 32	Boyer-StL 11	Stuart-Pit 35	Robinson-Cin 333	Aaron-Mil 120
	Cepeda-SF 182	Mays-SF 32		Adcock-Mil 35	Clemente-Pit 320	Stuart-Pit 117

BASES ON BALLS	STOLEN BASES	BASE STEALING RUNS	FIELDING RUNS-INFIELD	FIELDING RUNS-OUTFIELD	OUTFIELD ASSISTS	CATCHER CS PCT.
Mathews-Mil 93	Wills-LA 35	Robinson-Cin 3.8	Mazeroski-Pit 37.1	Clemente-Pit 9.4	Clemente-Pit 27	Dalrymple-Phi 55.6
Moon-LA 89	Pinson-Cin 23	Wills-LA 2.5	Malkmus-Phi 24.2	Flood-StL 8.4	Pinson-Cin 19	Torre-Mil 49.1
Mays-SF 81	Robinson-Cin 22	Maye-Mil 1.9	Banks-Chi 17.9	Pinson-Cin 7.5	Robinson-Cin 15	Roseboro-LA 46.6
Gilliam-LA 79	Aaron-Mil 21	Pinson-Cin 1.6	Boyer-StL 14.2	Robinson-Cin 5.8	Flood-StL 13	Bertell-Chi 43.5
	Mays-SF 18	Gonzalez-Phi 1.5	Gilliam-LA 13.7	Aaron-Mil 4.0	Aaron-Mil 13	Burgess-Pit 37.5

WINS	WINNING PCT.	WINS ABOVE TEAM	GAMES STARTED	COMPLETE GAMES	FEWEST HITS/GAME	FEWEST BB/GAME
Spahn-Mil 21	Podres-LA .783	Podres-LA 6.0	Cardwell-Chi 38	Spahn-Mil 21	Koufax-LA 7.46	Burdette-Mil 1.09
Jay-Cin 21	O'Toole-Cin .679	Miller-SF 4.2	Drysdale-LA 37	Koufax-LA 15	Jay-Cin 7.90	Friend-Pit 1.72
O'Toole-Cin 19	Jay-Cin .677	Spahn-Mil 3.6	Burdette-Mil 36	Jay-Cin 14	Gibson-StL 7.92	Purkey-Cin 1.86
	Burdette-Mil .621	Jay-Cin 3.4		Burdette-Mil 14	Sadecki-StL 7.92	Spahn-Mil 2.19
	Spahn-Mil .618	O'Toole-Cin 3.1			Spahn-Mil 8.09	Ellsworth-Chi 2.31

STRIKEOUTS	STRIKEOUTS/GAME	GAMES	SAVES	BASE RUNNERS/9	ADJUSTED RELIEF RUNS	RELIEF RANKING
Koufax-LA 269	Koufax-LA 9.47	Baldschun-Phi 65	Miller-SF 17	Miller-SF 9.81	Miller-SF 16.3	Miller-SF 28.0
Williams-LA 205	Williams-LA 7.84	Miller-SF 63	Face-Pit 17	Face-Pit 10.27	Perranoski-LA 15.7	Perranoski-LA 20.9
Drysdale-LA 182	Gibson-StL 7.07	Face-Pit 62	Henry-Cin 16	K.Johnson-Cin 10.30	Henry-Cin 9.6	Brosnan-Cin 15.1
O'Toole-Cin 178	Drysdale-LA 6.71	Elston-Chi 58	Brosnan-Cin 16	Sturdivant-Pit 10.40	McMahon-Mil 8.3	Schultz-Chi 13.8
Gibson-StL 166	Gibbon-Pit 6.68	Anderson-Chi 57	L.Sherry-LA 15	Spahn-Mil 10.42	Brosnan-Cin 7.6	Henry-Cin 11.3

INNINGS PITCHED	OPPONENTS' AVG.	OPPONENTS' OBP	EARNED RUN AVERAGE	ADJUSTED ERA	ADJUSTED STARTER RUNS	PITCHER WINS
Burdette-Mil 272.1	Koufax-LA .222	Spahn-Mil .291	Spahn-Mil 3.02	Simmons-StL 141	O'Toole-Cin 25.8	**Spahn-Mil 4.1**
Spahn-Mil 262.2	Jay-Cin .236	Koufax-LA .295	O'Toole-Cin 3.10	Gibson-StL 136	Gibson-StL 24.3	**Miller-SF 3.1**
Cardwell-Chi 259.1	Sadecki-StL .238	Burdette-Mil .295	Simmons-StL 3.13	O'Toole-Cin 131	Spahn-Mil 22.8	**Gibson-StL 2.9**
Koufax-LA 255.2	Gibson-StL .239	Purkey-Cin .296	McCormick-SF 3.20	Spahn-Mil 124	Simmons-StL 21.0	**O'Toole-Cin 2.6**
O'Toole-Cin 252.2	O'Toole-Cin .240	Jackson-StL .301	Gibson-StL 3.24	Koufax-LA 123	Koufax-LA 19.9	**Simmons-StL 2.5**

Cincinnati Surprise

Cincinnati took the flag in one of the oddest seasons ever. The Reds were 17 games over .500 at home despite being outscored at Crosley Field. Cincinnati had the league's best pitching—as well as a more efficient offense—on the road. The club had Vada Pinson, the major league leader in hits, and MVP Frank Robinson, plus a few other decent regulars. Jerry Lynch enjoyed one of the all-time great seasons for a bench player, and five pitchers—three starters and two relievers—carried the load.

Second-place Los Angeles, mixing the unproven and the elderly, never capitalized despite the Reds' early-season sputtering. For the third straight year, however, Dodgers hurlers paced the NL in strikeouts.

The aging Pirates fell to eighth, although Roberto Clemente won his first of four batting titles. Chicago debuted Lou Brock and Kenny Hubbs on September 10. Neither would be around when the Cubs finally turned it around years later.

Meanwhile, the Phillies lost 23 straight, falling far into the basement with the NL's worst record in a decade.

As runs per game rose to 4.52, the highest of the 1960s, complete games dropped to a new low; only Warren Spahn finished more than 15. Despite excellent seasons by Spahn and Hank Aaron, Milwaukee's classic era was over. Fans deserted the Braves; attendance plunged 26 percent, then 30 more in 1962. Attendance fell in every NL city except Cincinnati, so the league decided to pre-empt a proposed rival, the Continental League, by expanding to New York and Houston for 1962.

The Yankees blew apart the Reds, taking the World Series in five games. "Embarrassing, wasn't it?" wrote Cincy reliever Jim Brosnan the next year in a *Sports Illustrated* article. Just a few months after throwing out the first pitch at Game 3, former Reds outfielder Dummy Hoy died at age 99.

1961 AMERICAN LEAGUE

TEAM	W	L	T	PCT	GB	HW	HL	R	OR	PA	H	2B	3B	HR	BB	SO	HB	SH	AVG	OBP	SLG	OPS	AOPS	BR	ABR	PF	SB	CS	BSA	BSR
NY	109	53	1	.673	—	**65**	16	827	612	6239	1461	194	40	**240**	543	785	35	57	.263	.330	**.442**	**772**	**118**	79	**124**	95	28	18	61	0
Det	101	61	1	.623	8	50	31	**841**	671	6378	1481	215	**53**	180	673	867	38	64	**.266**	**.347**	.421	768	108	**96**	73	103	98	36	73	**9**
Bal	95	67	1	.586	14	48	33	691	**588**	6211	1393	227	36	149	581	902	23	78	.254	.326	.390	716	101	-16	10	97	39	30	57	-2
Chi	86	76	1	.531	23	53	28	765	726	6285	1475	216	46	138	550	**612**	**57**	71	.265	.335	.395	730	103	16	28	98	**100**	40	71	8
Cle	78	83	0	.484	30.5	40	41	737	752	6252	**1493**	**257**	39	150	492	720	28	73	**.266**	.326	.406	732	104	9	30	97	34	11	**76**	4
Bos	76	86	1	.469	33	50	31	729	792	6307	1401	251	37	112	647	847	29	81	.254	.334	.374	708	94	-19	-36	102	56	36	61	0
Min	70	90	1	.438	38	36	44	707	778	6156	1353	215	40	167	597	840	33	67	.250	.326	.397	723	94	-5	-43	106	47	43	52	-5
LA	70	91	1	.435	38.5	46	36	744	784	6252	1331	218	22	189	**681**	1068	30	80	.245	.331	.398	729	91	15	-61	111	37	28	57	-2
Was	61	100	0	.379	47.5	33	46	618	776	6062	1307	217	44	119	558	917	21	73	.244	.315	.367	682	89	-84	-74	99	81	47	63	1
KC	61	100	1	.379	47.5	33	47	683	863	6164	1342	216	47	90	580	772	25	**89**	.247	.320	.354	674	84	-91	-102	102	58	22	73	5
Total	811	—	—	—	—	454	353	7342	—	62306	14037	2226	404	1534	5902	8330	319	733	.256	.329	.395	724	—	—	—	—	578	311	65	18

TEAM	CG	SHO	GR	SV	IP	H	HR	BB	SO	BR/9	ERA	AERA	OAV	OOB	PR	APR	PF	OSB	OCS	FA	E	WPB	DP	FW	PW	BW	BSW	DIF
NY	47	14	201	**39**	1451.0	1288	137	542	866	**11.5**	3.46	107	.239	.311	91	45	92	**43**	31	**.980**	**124**	46	**180**	**1.6**	4.5	**12.3**	-.2	9.8
Det	**62**	12	220	30	1459.1	1404	170	**469**	836	11.7	3.55	116	.252	.311	78	88	102	45	**39**	.976	146	42	147	.3	8.7	7.2	**.7**	3.0
Bal	54	**21**	168	33	1471.1	**1226**	**109**	617	926	**11.5**	**3.22**	**120**	**.227**	**.308**	**132**	**108**	96	52	31	**.980**	128	75	173	1.4	**10.7**	1.0	-.4	1.3
Chi	39	3	260	33	1448.2	1491	158	498	814	12.4	4.06	97	.268	.326	-5	-23	97	48	32	**.980**	128	**35**	138	1.4	-2.3	2.8	.6	2.5
Cle	35	12	228	23	1443.1	1426	178	599	801	12.8	4.15	95	.258	.331	-20	-34	98	53	38	.977	139	58	142	.6	-3.4	3.0	.2	-2.9
Bos	35	6	231	30	1442.2	1472	167	679	831	13.5	4.29	97	.266	.345	-43	-19	104	68	24	.977	144	55	170	.4	-1.9	-3.6	-.2	.2
Min	49	14	217	23	1432.1	1415	163	570	914	12.8	4.28	99	.256	.329	-41	-6	105	56	24	.972	174	58	150	-1.4	-.6	-4.3	-.7	-3.0
LA	25	5	**311**	34	1438.0	1391	180	713	**973**	13.4	4.31	105	.254	.341	-46	28	112	78	32	.969	192	77	154	-2.4	2.8	-6.0	-.4	-4.4
Was	39	8	220	21	1425.0	1405	131	586	666	12.8	4.23	95	.260	.333	-33	-34	100	83	34	.975	156	78	171	-.4	-3.4	-7.3	-.0	-8.3
KC	32	5	268	23	1415.0	1519	141	629	703	14.0	4.74	88	.275	.351	-113	-85	104	52	26	.972	175	75	160	-1.4	-8.4	-10.1	.3	.2
Total	417	100	2324	289	14426.2	—	—	—	—	12.6	4.02	—	.256	.329	—	—	—	—	—	.976	1506	599	1585	—	—	—	—	—

BATTER-FIELDER WINS	BATTING AVERAGE	ON-BASE PERCENTAGE	SLUGGING AVERAGE	ON-BASE PLUS SLUGGING	ADJUSTED OPS	ADJUSTED BATTER RUNS
Cash-Det....7.6	Cash-Det....361	Cash-Det....487	Mantle-NY....687	Cash-Det....1148	Mantle-NY....210	Mantle-NY....85.6
Mantle-NY....7.5	Kaline-Det....324	Mantle-NY....448	Cash-Det....662	Mantle-NY....1135	Cash-Det....198	Cash-Det....83.0
Gentile-Bal....5.5	Piersall-Cle....322	Gentile-Bal....423	Gentile-Bal....646	Gentile-Bal....1069	Gentile-Bal....189	Gentile-Bal....65.4
Colavito-Det....4.6	Mantle-NY....317	Pearson-LA....420	Maris-NY....620	Killebrew-Min....1012	Maris-NY....170	Maris-NY....56.8
Howard-NY....4.5	Gentile-Bal....302	Killebrew-Min....405	Killebrew-Min....606	Maris-NY....993	Killebrew-Min....159	Colavito-Det....49.4
RUNS	**HITS**	**DOUBLES**	**TRIPLES**	**HOME RUNS**	**TOTAL BASES**	**RUNS BATTED IN**
Maris-NY....132	Cash-Det....193	Kaline-Det....41	Wood-Det....14	Maris-NY....61	Maris-NY....366	Maris-NY....142
Mantle-NY....132	B.Robinson-Bal....192	B.Robinson-Bal....38	Lumpe-KC....9	Mantle-NY....54	Cash-Det....354	Gentile-Bal....141
Colavito-Det....129	Kaline-Det....190	Kubek-NY....38	Keough-Was....9	Killebrew-Min....46	Mantle-NY....353	Colavito-Det....140
Cash-Det....119	Francona-Cle....178	Siebern-KC....36		Gentile-Bal....46	Colavito-Det....338	Cash-Det....132
Kaline-Det....116	Richardson-NY....173	Power-Cle....34		Colavito-Det....45	Killebrew-Min....328	Mantle-NY....128
BASES ON BALLS	**STOLEN BASES**	**BASE STEALING RUNS**	**FIELDING RUNS-INFIELD**	**FIELDING RUNS-OUTFIELD**	**OUTFIELD ASSISTS**	**CATCHER CS PCT.**
Mantle-NY....126	Aparicio-Chi....53	Aparicio-Chi....7.1	Boyer-NY....28.5	Kaline-Det....13.5	Colavito-Det....16	Brown-Det....55.8
Cash-Det....124	Howser-KC....37	Howser-KC....5.0	Lumpe-KC....21.2	Landis-Chi....7.8	Jensen-Bos....14	Triandos-Bal....47.6
Colavito-Det....113	Wood-Det....30	Wood-Det....3.5	Kubek-NY....17.9	Piersall-Cle....7.6	Allison-Min....14	Roarke-Det....45.2
Killebrew-Min....107	Hinton-Was....22	Hinton-Was....3.1	Causey-KC....17.3	Colavito-Det....7.2		Lollar-Chi....44.9
Allison-Min....103	Bruton-Det....22	Bruton-Det....2.7	Power-Cle....16.5	Jensen-Bos....6.7		Romano-Cle....39.2
WINS	**WINNING PCT.**	**WINS ABOVE TEAM**	**GAMES STARTED**	**COMPLETE GAMES**	**FEWEST HITS/GAME**	**FEWEST BB/GAME**
Ford-NY....25	Ford-NY....862	Ford-NY....9.1	Ford-NY....39	Lary-Det....22	Estrada-Bal....6.75	Mossi-Det....1.76
Lary-Det....23	Terry-NY....842	Terry-NY....5.2	Bunning-Det....37	Pascual-Min....15	Pappas-Bal....6.79	Brown-Bal....1.78
Barber-Bal....18	Arroyo-NY....750	Schwall-Bos....4.8	McBride-LA....36	Barber-Bal....14	Barber-Bal....7.03	Donovan-Was....1.87
Bunning-Det....17	Lary-Det....719	Lary-Det....4.7	Lary-Det....36		Pascual-Min....7.31	Terry-NY....2.01
Terry-NY....16		Latman-Cle....4.4			Donovan-Was....7.36	McClain-Was....2.04
STRIKEOUTS	**STRIKEOUTS/GAME**	**GAMES**	**SAVES**	**BASE RUNNERS/9**	**ADJUSTED RELIEF RUNS**	**RELIEF RANKING**
Pascual-Min....221	Pizarro-Chi....8.69	Arroyo-NY....65	Arroyo-NY....29	Donovan-Was....9.39	Arroyo-NY....20.7	Arroyo-NY....41.5
Ford-NY....209	Pascual-Min....7.88	Morgan-LA....59	Wilhelm-Bal....18	Morgan-LA....9.43	Morgan-LA....18.1	Wilhelm-Bal....30.3
Bunning-Det....194	Estrada-Bal....6.79	Lown-Chi....59	Fornieles-Bos....15	Hall-Bal....9.71	Wilhelm-Bal....18.0	Fox-Det....25.4
Pizarro-Chi....188	McBride-LA....6.70	Kunkel-KC....58	Moore-Min....14	Terry-NY....9.80	Fox-Det....16.2	Morgan-LA....22.3
McBride-LA....180	Ford-NY....6.65	Fornieles-Bos....57	Fox-Det....12	Fowler-LA....9.81	Hillman-Bos....12.4	Funk-Cle....16.2
INNINGS PITCHED	**OPPONENTS' AVG.**	**OPPONENTS' OBP**	**EARNED RUN AVERAGE**	**ADJUSTED ERA**	**ADJUSTED STARTER RUNS**	**PITCHER WINS**
Ford-NY....283.0	Estrada-Bal....207	Donovan-Was....267	Donovan-Was....2.40	Donovan-Was....167	Hoeft-Bal....28.2	**Arroyo-NY....4.4**
Lary-Det....275.1	Pappas-Bal....208	Terry-NY....275	Stafford-NY....2.68	Stafford-NY....139	Mossi-Det....27.9	**Lary-Det....3.3**
Bunning-Det....268.0	Pascual-Min....217	Bunning-Det....284	Mossi-Det....2.96	Mossi-Det....139	Donovan-Was....26.9	**Donovan-Was....3.3**
Ramos-Min....264.1	Barber-Bal....218	Brown-Bal....284	Pappas-Bal....3.04	Archer-KC....131	Bunning-Det....25.7	**Wilhelm-Bal....3.0**
Pascual-Min....252.1	Donovan-Was....224	Lary-Det....290	Pizarro-Chi....3.05	Schwall-Bos....129	Lary-Det....25.3	**Stafford-NY....2.8**

As the Records Fall

Expansion to ten teams and 162 games meant more games, more traveling, and many new faces. Debuts included Carl Yastrzemski, who replaced Ted Williams in Boston; new Yankees Al Downing and Tom Tresh; Angels Dean Chance and Jim Fregosi; Cleveland's Sam McDowell; Detroit's Bill Freehan; and Baltimore's Boog Powell. By the mid-1960s, all had made significant contributions.

Playing more games, hitters clubbed 41 percent more homers—but home runs per contest also rose 8 percent, due largely to Los Angeles' tiny Wrigley Field, home to more than 3 homers *per game*. Expansion raised total attendance, but most teams' admissions declined; Chicago, Boston, Cleveland, and Baltimore experienced frightening decreases. One team that didn't draw, in 1961 or later, was the "new" Washington Senators, arguably the least successful franchise in league history.

Roger Maris and Mickey Mantle spent the summer chasing Babe Ruth's single-season homer record. Mantle dropped out due to injury, but Maris took it to the wire, clubbing No. 61 on closing day. Maris won his second straight MVP, but he lost a lot of hair in the grueling chase. The Yankees' 240 homers set an all-time record.

Detroit's rookie infielder Jake Wood broke the strikeout record; whiffs rose to 5.14 per game, a new high, and would keep rising. Yankee Luis Arroyo's 29 (unofficial) saves also established a new mark. The changes in baseball reflected strongly against the death of Dead Ball Era denizen Ty Cobb.

Detroit, flush with offense from Norm Cash, Al Kaline, and newly acquired Rocky Colavito, hung neck-and-neck with New York until early September. The Yankees simply out-clubbed them.

Under new manager Ralph Houk, the Bronx Bombers won a fairly easy five-game World Series from Cincinnati, blowing apart the Reds in the final two contests, 7-0, and 13-5. Whitey Ford broke Babe Ruth's mark for consecutive scoreless innings in Series play.

1960 NATIONAL LEAGUE

TEAM	W	L	T	PCT	GB	HW	HL	R	OR	PA	H	2B	3B	HR	BB	SO	HB	SH	AVG	OBP	SLG	OPS	AOPS	BR	ABR	PF	SB	CS	BSA	BSR
Pit	95	59	1	.617	—	**52**	25	**734**	**593**	6029	**1493**	**236**	56	120	486	**747**	20	69	**.276**	**.335**	.407	**742**	108	**73**	69	101	34	24	59	-1
Mil	88	66	0	.571	7	51	26	724	658	5868	1393	198	48	**170**	463	793	23	59	.265	.323	**.417**	740	**117**	58	**116**	93	69	37	65	2
StL	86	68	1	.558	9	51	26	639	616	5806	1317	213	48	138	501	792	31	52	.254	.321	.393	714	93	14	-38	109	48	35	58	-2
LA	82	72	0	.532	13	42	35	662	**593**	5935	1333	216	38	126	529	837	27	**102**	.255	.324	.383	707	93	7	-33	106	**95**	53	64	2
SF	79	75	2	.513	16	45	32	671	631	5923	1357	220	**62**	130	467	846	33	60	.255	.317	.393	710	106	-1	41	94	86	45	**66**	**3**
Cin	67	87	0	.435	28	37	40	640	692	5940	1324	230	40	140	512	858	**34**	60	.250	.318	.388	706	97	0	-11	102	73	37	**66**	**3**
Chi	60	94	2	.390	35	33	44	634	776	5960	1293	213	48	119	**531**	897	19	64	.243	.313	.369	682	93	-48	-41	99	51	34	60	-1
Phi	59	95	0	.383	36	31	46	546	691	5748	1235	196	44	99	448	1054	33	66	.239	.302	.351	653	84	-103	-104	100	45	48	48	-7
Total	619	—	—	—	—	342	274	5250	—	47209	10745	1722	384	1042	3937	6824	220	532	.255	.319	.388	707	—	—	—	—	501	313	62	1

TEAM	CG	SHO	GR	SV	IP	H	HR	BB	SO	BR/9	ERA	AERA	OAV	OOB	PR	APR	PF	OSB	OCS	FA	E	WPB	DP	FW	PW	BW	BSW	DIF
Pit	47	11	205	33	1399.2	1363	**105**	**386**	811	**11.3**	3.49	107	.257	**.307**	42	41	100	44	32	**.979**	128	**35**	**163**	.7	4.2	7.1	-.1	6.1
Mil	**55**	13	182	28	1387.1	1327	130	518	807	12.2	3.76	91	.251	.320	0	-57	91	**38**	33	.976	141	57	137	-.0	-5.9	**11.9**	.2	4.8
StL	37	11	217	30	1371.0	1316	127	511	906	12.1	3.64	112	.253	.319	18	64	109	50	37	.976	141	48	152	.0	6.6	-3.9	-.2	6.5
LA	46	13	204	20	1398.0	**1218**	154	564	**1122**	11.7	**3.40**	**117**	**.234**	.311	**56**	**84**	106	42	34	**.979**	**125**	63	142	**.9**	**8.6**	-3.4	.2	-1.3
SF	**55**	**16**	214	26	1396.0	1288	107	512	897	11.8	3.44	101	.245	.313	50	6	93	77	20	.972	166	55	117	-1.3	.6	4.2	**.3**	-1.8
Cin	33	8	253	**35**	1390.1	1417	134	442	740	12.3	4.00	96	.267	.326	-37	-27	102	56	43	**.979**	**125**	43	155	**.9**	-2.8	-1.1	**.3**	-7.2
Chi	36	6	**260**	25	1402.2	1393	152	565	805	12.8	4.35	87	.260	.333	-92	-89	100	91	**59**	.977	143	54	133	-.0	-9.2	-4.2	-.1	-3.5
Phi	45	6	199	16	1375.1	1423	133	439	736	12.3	4.01	97	.270	.325	-38	-19	103	103	55	.974	155	53	129	-.8	-2.0	-10.7	-.7	-3.8
Total	354	84	1734	213	11120.1	—	—	—	—	12.1	3.76	—	.255	.319	—	—	—	—	—	.977	1124	408	1128	—	—	—	—	—

BATTER-FIELDER WINS	BATTING AVERAGE	ON-BASE PERCENTAGE	SLUGGING AVERAGE	ON-BASE PLUS SLUGGING	ADJUSTED OPS	ADJUSTED BATTER RUNS
Banks-Chi 6.0	Groat-Pit .325	Ashburn-Chi .415	Robinson-Cin .595	Robinson-Cin 1002	Mathews-Mil 170	Mathews-Mil 56.6
Mays-SF 5.0	Larker-LA .323	Robinson-Cin .407	Aaron-Mil .566	Mathews-Mil .948	Robinson-Cin 169	Mays-SF 51.1
Robinson-Cin 4.6	Mays-SF .319	Mathews-Mil .397	Boyer-StL .562	Mays-SF .936	Mays-SF 164	Robinson-Cin 47.7
Aaron-Mil 4.5	Clemente-Pit .314	Moon-LA .383	Mays-SF .555	Boyer-StL .932	Aaron-Mil 161	Aaron-Mil 45.8
Boyer-StL 4.5	Boyer-StL .304	Mays-SF .381	Banks-Chi .554	Aaron-Mil .919	Banks-Chi 145	Banks-Chi 36.3

RUNS	HITS	DOUBLES	TRIPLES	HOME RUNS	TOTAL BASES	RUNS BATTED IN
Bruton-Mil 112	Mays-SF 190	Pinson-Cin 37	Bruton-Mil 13	Banks-Chi 41	Aaron-Mil 334	Aaron-Mil 126
Mathews-Mil 108	Pinson-Cin 187	Cepeda-SF 36	Pinson-Cin 12	Aaron-Mil 40	Banks-Chi 331	Mathews-Mil 124
Pinson-Cin 107	Groat-Pit 186	Skinner-Pit 33	Mays-SF 12	Mathews-Mil 39	Mays-SF 330	Banks-Chi 117
Mays-SF 107	Bruton-Mil 180	Robinson-Cin 33	Aaron-Mil 11	Boyer-StL 32	Boyer-StL 310	Mays-SF 103
Aaron-Mil 102	Clemente-Pit 179	Banks-Chi 32		Robinson-Cin 31	Pinson-Cin 308	Boyer-StL 97

BASES ON BALLS	STOLEN BASES	BASE STEALING RUNS	FIELDING RUNS-INFIELD	FIELDING RUNS-OUTFIELD	OUTFIELD ASSISTS	CATCHER CS PCT.
Ashburn-Chi 116	Wills-LA 50	Wills-LA 6.8	Mazeroski-Pit 30.1	Walters-Phi 9.0	Clemente-Pit 19	Smith-StL 51.5
Mathews-Mil 111	Pinson-Cin 32	Pinson-Cin 2.8	Wills-LA 25.5	Virdon-Pit 4.8	Walters-Phi 17	Burgess-Pit 50.0
Gilliam-LA 96	T.Taylor-Chi-Phi 26	Javier-StL 2.8	Javier-StL 16.9	Aaron-Mil 4.0	Kirkland-SF 16	Bailey-Cin 47.1
Robinson-Cin 82	Mays-SF 25	Blasingame-SF 2.4	Boyer-StL 15.8	Mays-SF 3.9	Moon-LA 15	Crandall-Mil 44.1
Spencer-StL 81	Bruton-Mil 22	Ashburn-Chi 2.1	Gilliam-LA 15.3	Kirkland-SF 2.4		Schmidt-SF 22.4

WINS	WINNING PCT.	WINS ABOVE TEAM	GAMES STARTED	COMPLETE GAMES	FEWEST HITS/GAME	FEWEST BB/GAME
Spahn-Mil 21	Broglio-StL .700	Broglio-StL 5.5	Jackson-StL 38	Spahn-Mil 18	Broglio-StL 6.84	Burdette-Mil 1.14
Broglio-StL 21	Law-Pit .690	Purkey-Cin 4.9	Friend-Pit 37	Law-Pit 18	Koufax-LA 6.84	Roberts-Phi 1.29
Law-Pit 20	Spahn-Mil .677	Spahn-Mil 4.5	Hobbie-Chi 36	Burdette-Mil 18	Williams-LA 7.03	Law-Pit 1.33
Burdette-Mil 19	Buhl-Mil .640	McDaniel-StL 3.7	Drysdale-LA 36	Hobbie-Chi 16	Drysdale-LA 7.16	Friend-Pit 1.47
	Purkey-Cin .607	Farrell-Phi 3.3		Friend-Pit 16	Buhl-Mil 7.62	Haddix-Pit 1.98

STRIKEOUTS	STRIKEOUTS/GAME	GAMES	SAVES	BASE RUNNERS/9	ADJUSTED RELIEF RUNS	RELIEF RANKING
Drysdale-LA 246	Koufax-LA 10.13	Face-Pit 68	McDaniel-StL 26	McDaniel-StL 8.51	McDaniel-StL 24.7	McDaniel-StL 42.9
Koufax-LA 197	Drysdale-LA 8.23	McDaniel-StL 65	Face-Pit 24	Brosnan-Cin 9.18	Brosnan-Cin 15.0	Face-Pit 21.6
S.Jones-SF 190	Williams-LA 7.60	Elston-Chi 60	Henry-Cin 17	Face-Pit 9.58	Roebuck-LA 14.0	Farrell-Phi 20.8
Broglio-StL 188	Broglio-StL 7.48	Farrell-Phi 59	Brosnan-Cin 12	Marichal-SF 9.63	Farrell-Phi 12.7	Brosnan-Cin 16.3
Friend-Pit 183	S.Jones-SF 7.31	Roebuck-LA 58		Drysdale-LA 9.90	Face-Pit 11.5	Roebuck-LA 14.0

INNINGS PITCHED	OPPONENTS' AVG.	OPPONENTS' OBP	EARNED RUN AVERAGE	ADJUSTED ERA	ADJUSTED STARTER RUNS	PITCHER WINS
Jackson-StL 282.0	Koufax-LA .207	Drysdale-LA .274	McCormick-SF 2.70	Broglio-StL 149	Drysdale-LA 32.9	**McDaniel-StL 4.7**
Friend-Pit 275.2	Williams-LA .210	Friend-Pit .280	Broglio-StL 2.74	Drysdale-LA 140	Broglio-StL 31.5	**Broglio-StL 4.4**
Burdette-Mil 275.2	Broglio-StL .213	Williams-LA .280	Drysdale-LA 2.84	Simmons-Phi-StL 134	McCormick-SF 24.9	**Drysdale-LA 4.0**
Law-Pit 271.2	Drysdale-LA .215	Law-Pit .286	Williams-LA 3.00	Williams-LA 133	Friend-Pit 24.6	**McCormick-SF 3.0**
Drysdale-LA 269.0	Buhl-Mil .229	Burdette-Mil .287	Friend-Pit 3.00	Podres-LA 129	Podres-LA 21.1	**Face-Pit 2.6**

The Wait Is Over

Pittsburgh took an early lead in the NL race, trying to win for the first time in 35 seasons. Milwaukee caught Pittsburgh in July, but then dropped 11 of 15. Victory was sweet for Pirates fans, not far removed from the horror of the early 1950s. Pittsburgh had it all: four quality starters, a bullpen ace, a solid everyday lineup, and a strong bench. Vernon Law won the Cy Young, while scrappy shortstop Dick Groat took MVP honors with equally fiery teammate Don Hoak second.

Milwaukee wasted Henry Aaron, Eddie Mathews, and Warren Spahn's great years; lousy middle-infield production doomed the Braves to second. The third-place Cardinals got nothing from their entire outfield, including 39-year-old Stan Musial. Fifth-place San Francisco moved into windy Candlestick Park, where Juan Marichal debuted July 19 with a one-hitter. Ron Santo joined the Cubs, but the Dodgers' Frank Howard was Rookie of the Year.

Gotham's NL glory days were quickly turning to memory; Alvin Dark, Carl Furillo, and Don Newcombe played their last games. Meanwhile, Dodgers hurler Sandy Koufax set a mark for strikeouts per game, then broke it in 1962. Bespectacled Reds reliever Jim Brosnan penned *The Long Season*, a diary of the 1959 campaign. Some dubbed Brosnan a "traitor" for discussing the goings-on of a major league clubhouse.

The Pirates certainly didn't *look* like a league champion in the three World Series games they lost to the Yankees: 16-3, 10-0, and 12-0. Pittsburgh captured three close ones, however. After taking a 4-0 lead in Game 7, the Pirates fell behind. Down 7-4 in the eighth, Hal Smith's homer put Pittsburgh ahead, 9-7. But the Yankees tied things in the ninth. The baseball season ended suddenly when Bill Mazeroski led off the home ninth with a home run. The last time the Pirates had won the World Series, in 1925, they counted two world championships to the Yankees' one; by the time Mazeroski touched home plate in the bedlam of Forbes Field, the tally was 19-3 in favor of New York—but the Bucs enjoyed their day.

1960 AMERICAN LEAGUE

TEAM	W	L	T	PCT	GB	HW	HL	R	OR	PA	H	2B	3B	HR	BB	SO	HB	SH	AVG	OBP	SLG	OPS	AOPS	BR	ABR	PF	SB	CS	BSA	BSR
NY	97	57	1	.630	—	**55**	22	**746**	627	5981	1377	215	40	**193**	537	818	28	81	.260	.329	**.426**	**755**	**115**	**62**	**106**	94	37	23	62	0
Bal	89	65	0	.578	8	44	33	682	**606**	5911	1307	206	33	123	596	801	36	72	.253	.332	.377	709	99	-7	2	99	37	24	61	0
Chi	87	67	0	.565	10	51	26	741	617	5966	1402	**242**	38	112	567	648	**54**	95	**.270**	**.345**	.396	741	107	60	67	99	**122**	48	**72**	**10**
Cle	76	78	0	.494	21	39	38	667	693	5921	**1415**	218	20	127	444	**573**	32	**97**	.267	.325	.388	713	101	-12	9	97	58	25	70	4
Was	73	81	0	.474	24	32	45	672	696	6004	1283	205	**43**	147	584	883	48	86	.244	.324	.384	708	98	-19	-12	99	52	43	55	-4
Det	71	83	0	.461	26	40	37	633	644	5990	1243	188	34	150	**636**	728	33	85	.239	.324	.375	699	93	-32	-49	103	66	32	67	3
Bos	65	89	0	.422	32	36	41	658	775	5931	1359	234	32	124	570	798	25	70	.261	.333	.389	722	98	18	-5	104	34	28	55	-2
KC	58	96	1	.377	39	34	43	615	756	5858	1303	212	34	110	513	744	12	75	.249	.316	.366	682	89	-70	-74	101	16	11	59	0
Total	617	—	—	—	—	331	285	5414	—	47562	10689	1720	274	1086	4447	5993	268	661	.255	.328	.388	716	—	—	—	—	422	234	64	11

TEAM	CG	SHO	GR	SV	IP	H	HR	BB	SO	BR/9	ERA	AERA	OAV	OOB	PR	APR	PF	OSB	OCS	FA	E	WPB	DP	FW	PW	BW	BSW	DIF
NY	38	**16**	**263**	**42**	1398.0	1225	123	609	712	12.0	**3.52**	102	**.238**	.320	**55**	11	93	43	30	.979	129	52	162	.2	1.1	**10.7**	-.1	8.1
Bal	**48**	11	177	22	1375.2	**1222**	**117**	552	785	**11.8**	**3.52**	108	.241	.317	54	45	98	54	23	**.982**	**108**	58	172	**1.4**	4.6	.2	-.1	6.0
Chi	42	11	254	26	1381.0	1338	127	533	695	12.3	3.60	105	.258	.326	41	28	98	41	31	**.982**	109	**28**	**175**	**1.4**	2.8	6.8	**.9**	-1.8
Cle	32	10	219	30	1382.1	1308	161	636	771	12.8	3.95	95	.252	.334	-12	-34	97	59	32	.978	128	51	165	.2	-3.4	.9	.3	1.1
Was	34	10	258	35	1405.1	1392	130	538	775	12.6	3.77	103	.260	.329	16	18	100	**40**	**40**	.973	165	54	159	-2.1	1.8	-1.2	-.5	-1.9
Det	40	7	209	25	1405.2	1336	141	**474**	**824**	11.9	3.64	**109**	.251	**.316**	37	**49**	102	53	32	.977	138	50	138	-.5	**5.0**	-5.0	.2	-5.7
Bos	34	6	252	23	1361.0	1440	127	580	767	13.6	4.62	87	.273	.346	-113	-84	104	49	25	.976	141	67	156	-.6	-8.5	-.5	-.3	-2.0
KC	44	4	227	14	1374.0	1428	160	525	664	13.1	4.38	91	.271	.339	-77	-59	103	83	21	.979	127	54	149	.3	-6.0	-7.5	-.1	-5.7
Total	312	75	1859	217	11083.0	—	—	—	—	12.5	3.87	—	.255	.328	—	—	—	—	—	.978	1045	414	1276	—	—	—	—	—

BATTER-FIELDER WINS	BATTING AVERAGE	ON-BASE PERCENTAGE	SLUGGING AVERAGE	ON-BASE PLUS SLUGGING	ADJUSTED OPS	ADJUSTED BATTER RUNS
Aparicio-Chi....... 3.9	Runnels-Bos.........320	Yost-Det................414	Maris-NY...............581	Mantle-NY.............957	Mantle-NY.............166	Mantle-NY............51.4
Maris-NY............. 3.7	Smith-Chi..............315	Woodling-Bal 401	Mantle-NY.............558	Maris-NY...............952	Maris-NY...............164	Maris-NY..............42.4
Mantle-NY........... 3.6	Minoso-Chi 311	Runnels-Bos 401	Killebrew-Was.......534	Sievers-Chi 930	Sievers-Chi 152	Williams-Bos........41.7
Runnels-Bos....... 3.5	Skowron-NY 309	Mantle-NY............399	Sievers-Chi 534	Killebrew-Was.......909	Killebrew-Was.......145	Sievers-Chi 34.1
Williams-Bos...... 3.4	Kuenn-Cle.............308	Sievers-Chi 396	Skowron-NY 528	Skowron-NY 881	Skowron-NY 144	Skowron-NY 30.5

RUNS	HITS	DOUBLES	TRIPLES	HOME RUNS	TOTAL BASES	RUNS BATTED IN
Mantle-NY.............119	Minoso-Chi 184	Francona-Cle..........36	Fox-Chi 10	Mantle-NY...............40	Mantle-NY.............294	Maris-NY...............112
Maris-NY.................98	Robinson-Bal.......175	Skowron-NY 34	Robinson-Bal...........9	Maris-NY.................39	Maris-NY...............290	Minoso-Chi 105
Minoso-Chi 89	Fox-Chi 175	Minoso-Chi 32		Lemon-Was 38	Skowron-NY 284	Wertz-Bos.............103
Landis-Chi 89	Smith-Chi..............169	Freese-Chi..............32		Colavito-Det............35	Minoso-Chi 284	Lemon-Was 100
Sievers-Chi 87	Runnels-Bos.........169			Killebrew-Was.........31	Lemon-Was 268	Gentile-Bal..............98

BASES ON BALLS	STOLEN BASES	BASE STEALING RUNS	FIELDING RUNS-INFIELD	FIELDING RUNS-OUTFIELD	OUTFIELD ASSISTS	CATCHER CS PCT.
Yost-Det................125	Aparicio-Chi............51	Aparicio-Chi...........8.4	Aparicio-Chi.........33.5	Piersall-Cle 8.6	Tuttle-KC.................16	Battey-Was 58.6
Mantle-NY.............111	Landis-Chi 23	Landis-Chi 3.0	Boyer-NY 24.0	Tuttle-KC................8.4	Minoso-Chi 14	Lollar-Chi 54.4
Allison-Was.............92	Green-Was 21	Kaline-Det..............2.8	Power-Cle 21.1	Allison-Was............4.8	Landis-Chi 13	Berberet-Det........47.5
Woodling-Bal 84	Kaline-Det...............19	Piersall-Cle 2.2	Fox-Chi 19.4	Stephens-Bos-Bal..4.5	Lemon-Was 11	Triandos-Bal.........41.5
Landis-Chi 80	Piersall-Cle 18	Mantle-NY..............2.0	Robinson-Bal.......16.8	Lopez-NY...............3.5	Colavito-Det............11	Romano-Cle 35.7

WINS	WINNING PCT.	WINS ABOVE TEAM	GAMES STARTED	COMPLETE GAMES	FEWEST HITS/GAME	FEWEST BB/GAME
Perry-Cle 18	Perry-Cle 643	Perry-Cle 4.7	Ramos-Was...........36	Lary-Det..................15	Estrada-Bal..........6.99	Brown-Bal 1.25
Estrada-Bal.............18	Ditmar-NY............625	Coates-NY 4.2	Perry-Cle 36	Ramos-Was............14	Turley-NY.............7.17	Mossi-Det 1.82
B.Daley-KC.............16	Estrada-Bal..........621	B.Daley-KC...........3.8	Lary-Det.................36	Herbert-KC 14	Barber-Bal 7.33	Hall-KC 1.88
	Pappas-Bal 577	Monbouquette-Bos 3.4	Wynn-Chi 35	Wynn-Chi................13	Bunning-Det.........7.75	Lary-Det...............2.03
		Fornieles-Bos 3.4	B.Daley-KC 35	B.Daley-KC 13	Ford-NY 7.85	Pierce-Chi............2.11

STRIKEOUTS	STRIKEOUTS/GAME	GAMES	SAVES	BASE RUNNERS/9	ADJUSTED RELIEF RUNS	RELIEF RANKING
Bunning-Det..........201	Bunning-Det.........7.18	Fornieles-Bos 70	Klippstein-Cle 14	Staley-Chi 9.52	Staley-Chi 15.4	Staley-Chi 28.2
Ramos-Was..........160	Bell-Cle 6.34	Staley-Chi 64	Fornieles-Bos 14	Brown-Bal 10.08	Fornieles-Bos 15.2	Fornieles-Bos 23.1
Wynn-Chi..............158	Estrada-Bal..........6.21	Clevenger-Was 53	Moore-Chi-Was.......13	Wilhelm-Bal 10.10	Sisler-Det.............13.7	Sisler-Det.............20.9
Lary-Det................149	Wynn-Chi.............5.99	Moore-Chi-Was.......51	B.Shantz-NY...........11	Aguirre-Det 10.27	Aguirre-Det 12.7	Aguirre-Det 12.7
Estrada-Bal...........144	Monbouquette-Bos .5.61	Kutyna-KC 51		Stafford-NY 10.35	Stobbs-Was 6.7	B.Shantz-NY 10.1

INNINGS PITCHED	OPPONENTS' AVG.	OPPONENTS' OBP	EARNED RUN AVERAGE	ADJUSTED ERA	ADJUSTED STARTER RUNS	PITCHER WINS
Lary-Det............274.1	Estrada-Bal..........218	Brown-Bal 283	Baumann-Chi.......2.67	Bunning-Det..........142	Bunning-Det.........30.6	**Staley-Chi 3.2**
Ramos-Was.......274.0	Turley-NY.............222	Bunning-Det..........292	Bunning-Det........2.79	Baumann-Chi........141	Baumann-Chi.......20.8	**Fornieles-Bos..... 2.6**
Perry-Cle 261.1	Barber-Bal 226	Mossi-Det 293	Brown-Bal 3.06	Brown-Bal 125	Herbert-KC 18.4	**Bunning-Det....... 2.5**
Herbert-KC 252.2	Ford-NY 235	Ford-NY 297	Ditmar-NY...........3.06	Herbert-KC 121	Kralick-Was..........16.8	**Herbert-KC 2.3**
Bunning-Det.......252.0	Bunning-Det..........236	Hall-KC 299	Ford-NY 3.08	Barber-Bal 118	Brown-Bal 13.4	**Sisler-Det........... 2.2**

Casey's Last Flag

The Yankees, eerily resembling the 1959 model, sleepwalked through much of the season, but eventually woke up; they overtook surprising Baltimore in September and brought it home by winning their final 15 contests. Right fielder Roger Maris won the MVP award for the Yankees, who set a league record with 193 homers. New York was the only AL club to draw more than one million fans each year of the decade. Once again, Casey Stengel manipulated a staff of largely undistinguished pitchers into a cohesive unit, and the starting lineup was successfully rebuilt.

Baltimore's "Baby Birds" staff, including four starting pitchers aged 21 or 22, propelled the Orioles from seventh place to second. Third-place Chicago reacquired Minnie Minoso, but had a poorly constructed offense and thin starting pitching. Washington, with young talent beginning to jell, rose from last to fifth, and announced plans to move to the Twin Cities for 1961. The AL scheduled a new expansion club for the capital, with another slated for Los Angeles; the move from eight to ten teams proved a seismic shift.

Owner Arnold Johnson of last-place Kansas City had, for years, been feeding talent to the Yankees—including Roger Maris—for very little in return. Johnson's death in 1960 ended that. Charlie Finley bought the club in 1961.

Boston's Ted Williams homered in his last at bat at Fenway to close out a spectacular career. The Yankees also lost Gil McDougald to the rocking chair, while two-time batting titlist Mickey Vernon hung 'em up to manage the new Senators.

Following the Yankees' disappointing World Series loss to the Pirates, New York management pulled what would later be called a "Steinbrenner" and sacked Stengel, the most successful manager in history. It was arguable that the game had passed The Old Professor by, but still. . . .

1959 NATIONAL LEAGUE

TEAM	W	L	T	PCT	GB	HW	HL	R	OR	PA	H	2B	3B	HR	BB	SO	HB	SH	AVG	OBP	SLG	OPS	AOPS	BR	ABR	PF	SB	CS	BSA	BSR
LA	88	68	0	.564	—	46	32	705	670	6033	1360	196	46	148	**591**	891	28	**100**	.257	.334	.396	730	94	16	-32	107	**84**	51	62	1
Mil	86	70	1	.551	2	**49**	29	724	623	6010	1426	216	36	**177**	488	765	27	64	.265	.326	.417	743	**114**	31	**97**	92	41	14	**75**	4
SF	83	71	0	.539	4	42	35	705	**613**	5890	1377	239	35	167	473	875	25	73	.261	.322	.414	736	104	17	33	98	81	34	70	**6**
Pit	78	76	1	.506	9	47	30	651	680	5952	1414	230	42	112	442	**715**	24	77	.263	.320	.384	704	95	-41	-35	99	32	26	55	-2
Cin	74	80	0	.481	13	43	34	**764**	738	5922	**1448**	**258**	34	161	499	763	32	53	**.274**	**.337**	**.427**	**764**	107	**80**	59	103	65	28	70	5
Chi	74	80	1	.481	13	38	39	673	688	5939	1321	209	44	163	498	911	**43**	62	.249	.317	.398	715	97	-24	-17	99	32	19	63	0
StL	71	83	0	.461	16	42	35	641	725	5907	1432	244	**49**	118	485	747	19	60	.269	.331	.400	731	95	14	-28	106	65	53	55	-4
Phi	64	90	1	.416	23	37	40	599	725	5735	1237	196	38	113	498	858	34	59	.242	.312	.362	674	85	-94	-103	102	39	46	46	-8
Total	620	—	—	—	—	344	274	5462	—	47388	11015	1788	324	1159	3974	6525	232	548	.260	.325	.400	725	—	—	—	—	439	271	62	2

TEAM	CG	SHO	GR	SV	IP	H	HR	BB	SO	BR/9	ERA	AERA	OAV	OOB	PR	APR	PF	OSB	OCS	FA	E	WPB	DP	FW	PW	BW	BSW	DIF
LA	43	14	241	**26**	1411.2	1317	157	614	**1077**	12.6	3.79	**111**	.247	.329	24	**64**	107	**24**	32	**.981**	**114**	59	154	**1.5**	**6.4**	-3.2	.0	5.3
Mil	**69**	**18**	167	18	1400.2	1406	**128**	429	775	11.9	3.51	101	.260	.315	68	6	90	36	30	.979	127	**30**	138	.8	.6	**9.8**	.4	-3.5
SF	52	12	205	23	1376.1	**1279**	139	500	873	**11.8**	**3.47**	110	**.246**	**.314**	**74**	54	97	50	35	.974	152	36	118	-.8	5.4	3.3	**.6**	-2.6
Pit	48	7	225	17	1393.1	1432	134	**418**	730	12.1	3.90	99	.267	.320	7	-5	98	56	32	.975	154	53	**165**	-.8	-.5	-3.5	-.2	6.1
Cin	44	7	232	**26**	1357.1	1460	162	456	690	12.9	4.31	94	.275	.335	-55	-38	103	40	**39**	.978	126	35	157	.7	-3.8	5.9	.5	-6.3
Chi	30	11	**250**	25	1391.0	1337	152	519	765	12.2	4.01	98	.254	.321	-10	-10	100	107	28	.977	140	46	142	-.0	-1.0	-1.7	-.0	-.2
StL	36	8	231	21	1363.0	1427	137	564	846	13.3	4.34	98	.271	.341	-59	-14	107	53	38	.975	146	61	158	-.4	-1.4	-2.8	-.4	-.9
Phi	54	8	190	15	1354.0	1357	150	474	769	12.4	4.27	96	.261	.324	-49	-24	104	73	38	.973	154	53	132	-.8	-2.4	-10.4	-.8	1.4
Total	376	85	1741	171	11047.1	—	—	—	—	12.4	3.95	—	.260	.325	—	—	—	—	—	.977	1113	373	1164	—	—	—	—	—

BATTER-FIELDER WINS	BATTING AVERAGE	ON-BASE PERCENTAGE	SLUGGING AVERAGE	ON-BASE PLUS SLUGGING	ADJUSTED OPS	ADJUSTED BATTER RUNS
Aaron-Mil 6.6	Aaron-Mil .355	Cunningham-StL .453	Aaron-Mil .636	Aaron-Mil 1037	Aaron-Mil 188	Aaron-Mil 77.3
Banks-Chi 6.4	Cunningham-StL .345	Aaron-Mil .401	Banks-Chi .596	Mathews-Mil 983	Mathews-Mil 172	Mathews-Mil 59.6
Mathews-Mil 6.0	Cepeda-SF .317	Moon-LA .394	Mathews-Mil .593	Robinson-Cin 975	Mays-SF 157	Mays-SF 46.9
Mays-SF 4.0	Pinson-Cin .316	Robinson-Cin .391	Robinson-Cin .583	Banks-Chi 970	Banks-Chi 156	Banks-Chi 45.9
Boyer-StL 3.5	Mays-SF .313	Mathews-Mil .390	Mays-SF .583	Mays-SF 964	Robinson-Cin 152	Robinson-Cin 41.8

RUNS	HITS	DOUBLES	TRIPLES	HOME RUNS	TOTAL BASES	RUNS BATTED IN
Pinson-Cin 131	Aaron-Mil 223	Pinson-Cin 47	Neal-LA 11	Mathews-Mil 46	Aaron-Mil 400	Banks-Chi 143
Mays-SF 125	Pinson-Cin 205	Aaron-Mil 46	Moon-LA 11	Banks-Chi 45	Mathews-Mil 352	Robinson-Cin 125
Mathews-Mil 118	Cepeda-SF 192	Mays-SF 43	White-StL 9	Aaron-Mil 39	Banks-Chi 351	Aaron-Mil 123
Aaron-Mil 116	Temple-Cin 186	Cimoli-StL 40	Pinson-Cin 9	Robinson-Cin 36	Mays-SF 335	Bell-Cin 115
Robinson-Cin 106	Mathews-Mil 182		Dark-Chi 9	Mays-SF 34	Pinson-Cin 330	Mathews-Mil 114

BASES ON BALLS	STOLEN BASES	BASE STEALING RUNS	FIELDING RUNS-INFIELD	FIELDING RUNS-OUTFIELD	OUTFIELD ASSISTS	CATCHER CS PCT.
Gilliam-LA 96	Mays-SF 27	Mays-SF 4.5	Blasingame-StL 20.3	Virdon-Pit 12.1	H.Anderson-Phi 17	Roseboro-LA 59.5
Cunningham-StL 88	T.Taylor-Chi 23	Pinson-Cin 2.5	Neal-LA 19.8	H.Anderson-Phi 11.7	Virdon-Pit 16	E.Bailey-Cin 57.4
Moon-LA 81	Gilliam-LA 23	Temple-Cin 2.0	Koppe-Phi 12.7	Pinson-Cin 6.4	Bell-Cin 15	Crandall-Mil 52.5
Mathews-Mil 80	Cepeda-SF 23	T.Taylor-Chi 1.9	Boyer-StL 11.9	Clemente-Pit 6.1	Moon-LA 13	Landrith-SF 51.1
Ashburn-Phi 79	Pinson-Cin 21	Cepeda-SF 1.9	Grammas-StL 11.2	Post-Phi 5.9		H.Smith-StL 42.1

WINS	WINNING PCT.	WINS ABOVE TEAM	GAMES STARTED	COMPLETE GAMES	FEWEST HITS/GAME	FEWEST BB/GAME
Spahn-Mil 21	Face-Pit .947	Face-Pit 8.6	Burdette-Mil 39	Spahn-Mil 21	Haddix-Pit 7.58	Newcombe-Cin 1.09
S.Jones-SF 21	Law-Pit .667	Law-Pit 5.0	Antonelli-SF 38	Law-Pit 20	S.Jones-SF 7.71	Burdette-Mil 1.18
Burdette-Mil 21	Antonelli-SF .655	Antonelli-SF 4.3	Jackson-StL 37	Burdette-Mil 20	Hobbie-Chi 7.85	Roberts-Phi 1.22
Antonelli-SF 19	Buhl-Mil .625	Conley-Phi 3.8		Roberts-Phi 19	Drysdale-LA 7.88	Purkey-Cin 1.78
		Newcombe-Cin 3.1			Antonelli-SF 7.88	Law-Pit 1.79

STRIKEOUTS	STRIKEOUTS/GAME	GAMES	SAVES	BASE RUNNERS/9	ADJUSTED RELIEF RUNS	RELIEF RANKING
Drysdale-LA 242	Drysdale-LA 8.05	Henry-Chi 65	McMahon-Mil 15	Henry-Chi 9.25	Henry-Chi 20.0	Face-Pit 27.0
S.Jones-SF 209	S.Jones-SF 6.95	Elston-Chi 65	McDaniel-StL 15	Haddix-Pit 9.63	Miller-SF 16.5	Henry-Chi 26.8
Koufax-LA 173	Podres-LA 6.69	McDaniel-StL 62	Elston-Chi 13	Craig-LA 9.90	Face-Pit 13.5	Miller-SF 15.1
Antonelli-SF 165	Broglio-StL 6.60	McMahon-Mil 60	Henry-Chi 12	Newcombe-Cin 10.05	McMahon-Mil 9.9	Elston-Chi 13.3
McCormick-SF 151	McCormick-SF 6.02	Miller-SF 59		Conley-Phi 10.15	Elston-Chi 6.8	McMahon-Mil 12.9

INNINGS PITCHED	OPPONENTS' AVG.	OPPONENTS' OBP	EARNED RUN AVERAGE	ADJUSTED ERA	ADJUSTED STARTER RUNS	PITCHER WINS
Spahn-Mil 292.0	S.Jones-SF .228	Haddix-Pit .271	S.Jones-SF 2.83	Conley-Phi 137	Law-Pit 30.5	**S.Jones-SF 3.6**
Burdette-Mil 289.2	Haddix-Pit .228	Newcombe-Cin .279	Miller-SF 2.84	S.Jones-SF 135	S.Jones-SF 30.3	**Newcombe-Cin 3.6**
Antonelli-SF 282.0	Antonelli-SF .233	Conley-Phi .280	Buhl-Mil 2.86	Miller-SF 134	Craig-LA 30.3	**Spahn-Mil 3.4**
S.Jones-SF 270.2	Drysdale-LA .233	Law-Pit .281	Spahn-Mil 2.96	Law-Pit 130	Antonelli-SF 25.5	**Law-Pit 3.1**
Drysdale-LA 270.2	Conley-Phi .235	Antonelli-SF .285	Law-Pit 2.98	Jackson-StL 128	Jackson-StL 25.1	**Drysdale-LA 2.9**

THE SUN-KISSED DODGERS

San Francisco, enjoying great years from Willie Mays and Orlando Cepeda, looked to have the race wrapped up in mid-August, but Los Angeles and underachieving Milwaukee caught fire around Labor Day. In mid-September the Dodgers came into San Francisco and swept three, and the Giants dropped like a stone. Milwaukee stayed hot, the Dodgers kept winning, and the season ended in a deadlock.

The resulting playoff was just as close. Underdog Los Angeles won two one-run games, the second in 12 innings, to take the pennant, effectively ending Milwaukee's run of success.

Don Drysdale, winning his first strikeout title, led Los Angeles' patchwork mound staff, and 26-year-old midseason call-up Maury Wills anchored an unspectacular infield. Milwaukee's Warren Spahn led the NL in wins for the sixth time, but Red Schoendienst's illness, and manager Fred Haney's use of weak-hitting first baseman Frank Torre, hamstrung a great attack.

An amazing rookie class sowed the seeds of success for many 1960s clubs. St. Louis debuted Bob Gibson and Tim McCarver, while the Phillies welcomed Chris Short. The Cubs brought up Billy Williams, while the Dodgers summoned Wills and Tommy Davis. San Francisco's Willie McCovey, the most impressive of all, won Rookie of the Year honors.

The Los Angeles Coliseum's ridiculous 252-foot left field fence led baseball to enact a rule that new ballparks must reach 325 feet at all fences and 400 to center. Still, the Dodgers were only fifth in home runs. Chicago's Ernie Banks won MVP honors again. Pittsburgh's Roy Face set an all-time winning percentage mark, while Cincinnati's Vada Pinson blossomed into a star.

Larry Sherry pitched just 14 times in relief (with 9 starts) during the regular season, but he was a bullpen wizard in the World Series. Sherry had 2 wins and 2 saves as Los Angeles wiped out the favored White Sox in six games. Second baseman Charlie Neal hit .370 with 2 homers and Gil Hodges batted .391.

1959 AMERICAN LEAGUE

TEAM	W	L	T	PCT	GB	HW	HL	R	OR	PA	H	2B	3B	HR	BB	SO	HB	SH	AVG	OBP	SLG	OPS	AOPS	BR	ABR	PF	SB	CS	BSA	BSR
Chi	94	60	2	.610	—	**47**	30	669	**588**	6054	1325	220	**46**	97	580	**634**	**49**	84	.250	.327	.364	691	96	-19	-10	99	**113**	53	68	**6**
Cle	89	65	0	.578	5	43	34	**745**	646	5860	1390	216	25	**167**	433	721	39	60	**.263**	.321	**.408**	729	**109**	31	**59**	96	33	36	48	-5
NY	79	75	1	.513	15	40	37	687	647	5980	**1397**	224	40	153	457	828	30	76	.260	.319	.402	721	107	16	41	97	45	22	67	2
Det	76	78	0	.494	18	41	36	713	732	5948	1346	196	30	160	580	737	44	73	.258	**.335**	.400	**735**	102	**58**	20	105	34	17	67	2
Bos	75	79	0	.487	19	43	34	726	696	5985	1335	**248**	28	125	**626**	810	23	65	.256	**.335**	.385	720	98	41	9	105	68	25	**73**	**6**
Bal	74	80	1	.481	20	38	39	551	621	5883	1240	182	23	109	536	690	20	**88**	.238	.310	.345	655	87	-98	-85	98	36	24	60	0
KC	66	88	0	.429	28	37	40	681	760	5885	1383	231	43	117	481	780	33	69	**.263**	.326	.390	716	100	16	4	102	34	24	59	-1
Was	63	91	0	.409	31	34	43	619	701	5734	1205	173	32	163	517	881	26	64	.237	.308	.379	687	93	-45	-42	100	51	34	60	-1
Total	618	—	—	—	—	323	293	5391	—	47329	10621	1690	267	1091	4210	6081	264	579	.253	.323	.384	707	—	—	—	—	414	235	64	9

TEAM	CG	SHO	GR	SV	IP	H	HR	BB	SO	BR/9	ERA	AERA	OAV	OOB	PR	APR	PF	OSB	OCS	FA	E	WPB	DP	FW	PW	BW	BSW	DIF
Chi	44	13	**242**	**36**	1425.1	1297	129	525	761	11.7	**3.29**	**114**	.242	**.311**	**91**	**76**	97	56	28	**.979**	130	**31**	141	.6	**7.7**	-1.0	**.5**	9.2
Cle	**58**	7	190	23	1383.2	**1230**	148	635	799	12.3	3.75	98	**.239**	.323	18	-10	95	60	30	.978	127	51	138	.7	-1.0	**6.0**	-.6	7.0
NY	38	**15**	222	28	1399.0	1281	120	594	**836**	12.2	3.60	101	.244	.322	40	7	94	42	32	.978	131	41	160	.5	.7	4.2	.0	-3.5
Det	53	9	197	24	1360.0	1327	177	**432**	829	11.9	4.20	97	.254	.315	-52	-20	105	45	32	.978	**124**	38	131	**.9**	-2.0	2.0	.0	-2.0
Bos	38	9	222	25	1364.0	1386	135	589	724	13.2	4.17	97	.266	.341	-47	-16	105	**37**	28	.978	131	51	**167**	.5	-1.6	.9	**.5**	-2.3
Bal	45	**15**	180	30	1400.1	1290	**111**	476	735	**11.5**	3.56	106	.246	**.311**	47	35	98	40	**43**	.976	146	85	163	-.4	3.5	-8.6	-.1	2.5
KC	44	8	241	21	1360.2	1452	148	492	703	13.2	4.35	92	.274	.338	-74	-51	104	49	20	.973	160	56	156	-1.2	-5.2	.4	-.2	-4.8
Was	46	10	214	21	1360.0	1358	123	467	694	12.3	4.01	98	.259	.321	-23	-14	101	85	22	.973	162	56	140	-1.4	-1.4	-4.3	-.2	-6.7
Total	366	86	1708	208	11053.0	—	—	—	—	12.3	3.86	—	.253	.323	—	—	—	—	—	.977	1111	409	1196	—	—	—	—	—

BATTER-FIELDER WINS	BATTING AVERAGE	ON-BASE PERCENTAGE	SLUGGING AVERAGE	ON-BASE PLUS SLUGGING	ADJUSTED OPS	ADJUSTED BATTER RUNS
Runnels-Bos....... 3.9	Kuenn-Det 353	Yost-Det..................435	Kaline-Det.............530	Kaline-Det.............940	Mantle-NY.............152	Mantle-NY...........40.7
Mantle-NY........... 3.6	Kaline-Det.............327	Runnels-Bos.........415	Killebrew-Was.......516	Mantle-NY.............904	Kaline-Det.............149	Francona-Cle........40.3
Kaline-Det 3.6	Runnels-Bos.........314	Kaline-Det.............410	Mantle-NY.............514	Kuenn-Det 903	Kuenn-Det 140	Kaline-Det............36.5
Jensen-Bos 3.3	Fox-Chi 306	Kuenn-Det 402	Colavito-Cle 512	Yost-Det................871	Woodling-Bal 139	Yost-Det 33.8
Berra-NY............ 3.3	Minoso-Cle 302	Woodling-Bal 402	Lemon-Was 510	Killebrew-Was.......870	Killebrew-Was.......137	Kuenn-Det 31.8
RUNS	**HITS**	**DOUBLES**	**TRIPLES**	**HOME RUNS**	**TOTAL BASES**	**RUNS BATTED IN**
Yost-Det................115	Kuenn-Det 198	Kuenn-Det 42	Allison-Was..............9	Killebrew-Was.........42	Colavito-Cle 301	Jensen-Bos...........112
Mantle-NY.............104	Fox-Chi 191	Malzone-Bos...........34	McDougald-NY 8	Colavito-Cle 42	Killebrew-Was.......282	Colavito-Cle 111
Power-Cle 102	Runnels-Bos.........176	Fox-Chi 34		Lemon-Was 33	Kuenn-Det 281	Killebrew-Was.......105
Jensen-Bos...........101	Power-Cle 172	Williams-KC 33		Maxwell-Det............31	Mantle-NY.............278	Lemon-Was 100
Kuenn-Det 99	Minoso-Cle 172	Runnels-Bos............33		Mantle-NY...............31	Allison-Was..........275	Maxwell-Det............95
BASES ON BALLS	**STOLEN BASES**	**BASE STEALING RUNS**	**FIELDING RUNS-INFIELD**	**FIELDING RUNS-OUTFIELD**	**OUTFIELD ASSISTS**	**CATCHER CS PCT.**
Yost-Det................135	Aparicio-Chi............56	Aparicio-Chi...........7.8	Gardner-Bal.........21.8	Jensen-Bos..........10.5	Tuttle-KC.................17	Berberet-Det........55.8
Runnels-Bos...........95	Mantle-NY...............21	Mantle-NY..............3.6	Kubek-NY 13.3	Minoso-Cle 9.7	Minoso-Cle 14	Triandos-Bal.........45.0
Mantle-NY...............93	Landis-Chi 20	Jensen-Bos............2.7	Power-Cle 11.9	Tuttle-KC................7.6	Tasby-Bal................13	White-Bos 44.4
Buddin-Bos 92	Jensen-Bos.............20	Malzone-Bos..........1.3	Malzone-Bos..........9.7	Landis-Chi 5.8	Jensen-Bos.............12	House-KC 32.7
Killebrew-Was.........90	Allison-Was.............13	Yost-Det 1.3	Runnels-Bos 9.0	Maxwell-Det...........5.6	Stephens-Bos 11	
WINS	**WINNING PCT.**	**WINS ABOVE TEAM**	**GAMES STARTED**	**COMPLETE GAMES**	**FEWEST HITS/GAME**	**FEWEST BB/GAME**
Wynn-Chi................22	Shaw-Chi 750	Pascual-Was..........5.7	Wynn-Chi................37	Pascual-Was...........17	Score-Cle.............6.89	Brown-Bal 1.76
McLish-Cle.............19	McLish-Cle............704	Shaw-Chi 4.8	Foytack-Det 37	Pappas-Bal 15	Ditmar-NY 6.95	Lary-Det................1.86
Shaw-Chi 18	Wynn-Chi..............688	Mossi-Det 4.7	Ramos-Was.............35	Mossi-Det 15	Wilhelm-Bal 7.09	Garver-KC 1.88
	Mossi-Det 654	McLish-Cle.............4.6	Bunning-Det............35	Wynn-Chi.................14	Wynn-Chi.............7.11	Mossi-Det 1.93
		Lary-Det.................4.2	Pierce-Chi...............33	Bunning-Det............14	O'Dell-Bal 7.36	Ramos-Was 2.00
STRIKEOUTS	**STRIKEOUTS/GAME**	**GAMES**	**SAVES**	**BASE RUNNERS/9**	**ADJUSTED RELIEF RUNS**	**RELIEF RANKING**
Bunning-Det..........201	Score-Cle.............8.23	Staley-Chi 67	Lown-Chi 15	Shantz-NY 9.22	Staley-Chi 17.2	Duren-NY.............23.7
Pascual-Was.........185	Bunning-Det.........7.25	Lown-Chi 60	Staley-Chi 14	Ditmar-NY............9.62	Duren-NY.............16.2	Staley-Chi 22.0
Wynn-Chi..............179	Pascual-Was........6.98	Clevenger-Was 50	Loes-Bal 14	Pascual-Was......10.33	Shantz-NY 12.2	Lown-Chi 14.3
Score-Cle..............147	Turley-NY 6.47	Shaw-Chi 47	Duren-NY.................14	Mossi-Det 10.34	Lown-Chi 10.1	Shantz-NY 12.5
Wilhelm-Bal 139	Wynn-Chi.............6.30		Fornieles-Bos 11	O'Dell-Bal 10.43	Fornieles-Bos 9.3	Fornieles-Bos 11.0
INNINGS PITCHED	**OPPONENTS' AVG.**	**OPPONENTS' OBP**	**EARNED RUN AVERAGE**	**ADJUSTED ERA**	**ADJUSTED STARTER RUNS**	**PITCHER WINS**
Wynn-Chi...........255.2	Score-Cle..............210	Ditmar-NY 268	Wilhelm-Bal 2.19	Wilhelm-Bal 173	Wilhelm-Bal 39.8	**Pascual-Was 4.7**
Bunning-Det.......249.2	Ditmar-NY.............211	Pascual-Was.........282	Pascual-Was........2.64	Pascual-Was.........148	Pascual-Was........33.8	**Wilhelm-Bal........ 3.7**
Foytack-Det 240.1	Wynn-Chi..............216	O'Dell-Bal 284	Shaw-Chi 2.69	Shaw-Chi 140	Shaw-Chi 30.7	**Shaw-Chi 2.9**
Pascual-Was......238.2	O'Dell-Bal 220	Mossi-Det 284	Ditmar-NY............2.90	Walker-Bal 130	Mossi-Det 19.5	**Daley-KC 2.9**
McLish-Cle.........235.1	Wilhelm-Bal 224	Brown-Bal.............289	Walker-Bal 2.92	O'Dell-Bal 129	O'Dell-Bal 18.7	**Perry-Cle............. 2.7**

GOING TO A GO-GO

All eight teams were bunched together until late June, when the White Sox and Indians forged ahead. Up by 1½ games on August 26, Chicago invaded Cleveland and took four straight, effectively ending the race. The "Go-Go" White Sox were called hitless, but outside cavernous Comiskey Park, Chicago had the league's third-best offense. Sherm Lollar's power, Luis Aparicio's defense and speed, and MVP Nellie Fox and Jim Landis' on-base ability supported a short pitching staff. Early Wynn won 22.

Despite Rocky Colavito's 42 homers, the Indians fell again. Cleveland hero Nap Lajoie died at 84, and former Indian Larry Doby ended his career as a part-timer in Chicago.

A slow start put the Yankees in seventh, and Casey Stengel's club never really came together. The pitching was mediocre; what worked with Tom Sturdivant and Bob Turley didn't with Duke Maas and Eli Grba. Mickey Mantle's slump and the aging of Hank Bauer and Yogi Berra contributed to New York's distant third-place finish. Perhaps as a result of New York's sputtering, AL attendance was its highest since 1949. Crowds increased in seven cities, doubling in Cleveland and nearly doing so in Chicago (now owned by Bill Veeck).

Even as steals rose to their highest level since the war, home runs increased as well; strikeouts rose for the sixth straight year to 4.92, a new high. Two pitchers who won 498 games between them—Jim Perry and Jim Kaat—debuted. The Red Sox became the last club to integrate, two years after Detroit had done so. The AL remained far behind the NL in employment of African Americans and dark-skinned Latinos, but would soon shorten the gap.

While the White Sox won Game 1 of the World Series, 11-0, they were outscored by the Dodgers the rest of the way, 21-12. Both teams batted .261, but Los Angeles won in six games. Chicago hasn't reached the Series since.

1958 NATIONAL LEAGUE

TEAM	W	L	T	PCT	GB	HW	HL	R	OR	PA	H	2B	3B	HR	BB	SO	HB	SH	AVG	OBP	SLG	OPS	AOPS	BR	ABR	PF	SB	CS	BSA	BSR
Mil	92	62	0	.597	—	48	29	675	**541**	5859	1388	221	21	167	478	646	36	**79**	**.266**	.329	.412	741	**110**	15	**79**	92	26	8	**76**	3
Pit	84	70	0	.545	8	**49**	28	662	607	5779	1386	229	**68**	134	396	753	28	68	.264	.317	.410	727	100	-24	-6	97	30	15	67	1
SF	80	74	0	.519	12	44	33	**727**	698	5996	1399	**250**	42	170	531	817	34	68	.263	.331	.422	753	106	**40**	57	98	64	29	69	**4**
Cin	76	78	0	.494	16	40	37	695	621	5980	1359	242	40	123	572	765	21	76	.258	.331	.389	720	91	-16	-50	105	61	38	62	0
StL	72	82	0	.468	20	39	38	619	704	5891	1371	216	39	111	533	**637**	20	44	.261	.329	.380	709	90	-37	-61	104	44	43	51	-5
Chi	72	82	0	.468	20	35	42	709	725	5902	1402	207	49	**182**	487	853	**45**	42	.265	.330	**.426**	**756**	107	38	50	98	39	23	63	1
LA	71	83	0	.461	21	39	38	668	761	5804	1297	166	50	172	495	850	25	68	.251	.317	.402	719	92	-37	-56	103	**73**	47	61	0
Phi	69	85	0	.448	23	35	42	664	762	6081	**1424**	238	56	124	**573**	871	38	70	**.266**	**.339**	.400	739	102	22	32	99	51	33	61	0
Total	616	—	—	—	—	329	287	5419	—	47292	11026	1769	365	1183	4065	6192	247	515	.262	.328	.405	733	—	—	—	—	388	236	62	3

TEAM	CG	SHO	GR	SV	IP	H	HR	BB	SO	BR/9	ERA	AERA	OAV	OOB	PR	APR	PF	OSB	OCS	FA	E	WPB	DP	FW	PW	BW	BSW	DIF
Mil	**72**	**16**	149	17	1376.0	**1261**	125	426	773	**11.2**	**3.21**	110	**.244**	**.303**	**113**	53	89	41	34	.980	120	27	152	.8	5.3	**8.0**	.3	.6
Pit	43	10	222	**41**	1367.0	1344	**123**	470	679	12.1	3.56	109	.261	.323	59	47	98	45	36	.978	133	45	173	.1	4.7	-.6	.0	2.7
SF	38	7	255	25	1389.1	1400	166	512	775	12.6	3.98	96	.263	.330	-4	-26	97	41	**37**	.975	152	41	156	-.9	-2.6	5.7	**.4**	.4
Cin	50	7	219	20	1385.1	1422	148	**419**	705	12.1	3.73	**111**	.267	.322	34	**61**	105	37	28	**.983**	**100**	**25**	148	**1.9**	**6.2**	-5.0	-.0	-4.0
StL	45	6	240	25	1381.2	1398	158	567	822	13.1	4.12	100	.264	.338	-25	2	105	74	23	.974	153	48	163	-.9	.2	-6.2	-.5	2.4
Chi	27	5	**293**	24	1361.0	1322	142	619	805	13.1	4.22	93	.254	.336	-40	-46	99	61	25	.975	150	48	161	-.8	-4.6	5.0	.0	-4.7
LA	30	7	284	31	1368.1	1399	173	606	**855**	13.4	4.47	92	.267	.344	-79	-55	104	**33**	31	.975	146	76	**198**	-.6	-5.5	-5.6	-.0	5.8
Phi	51	6	221	15	1397.0	1480	148	446	778	12.5	4.32	92	.272	.326	-58	-56	100	56	22	.978	129	58	136	.3	-5.6	3.2	-.0	-5.9
Total	356	64	1883	198	11025.2	—	—	—	—	12.5	3.95	—	.262	.328	—	—	—	—	—	.977	1083	368	1287	—	—	—	—	—

BATTER-FIELDER WINS	BATTING AVERAGE	ON-BASE PERCENTAGE	SLUGGING AVERAGE	ON-BASE PLUS SLUGGING	ADJUSTED OPS	ADJUSTED BATTER RUNS
Mays-SF 6.2	Ashburn-Phi .350	Ashburn-Phi .440	Banks-Chi .614	Mays-SF 1002	Mays-SF 167	Mays-SF 59.2
Banks-Chi 5.9	Mays-SF .347	Musial-StL .423	Mays-SF .583	Banks-Chi 980	Banks-Chi 157	Aaron-Mil 48.4
Ashburn-Phi 4.4	Musial-StL .337	Mays-SF .419	Aaron-Mil .546	Musial-StL 950	Aaron-Mil 157	Banks-Chi 47.0
Boyer-StL 4.0	Aaron-Mil .326	Temple-Cin .405	Thomas-Pit .528	Aaron-Mil 931	Musial-StL 145	Ashburn-Phi 38.5
Aaron-Mil 3.9	Skinner-Pit .321	Skinner-Pit .387	Musial-StL .528	H.Anderson-Phi 897	H.Anderson-Phi 137	Musial-StL 34.7

RUNS	HITS	DOUBLES	TRIPLES	HOME RUNS	TOTAL BASES	RUNS BATTED IN
Mays-SF 121	Ashburn-Phi 215	Cepeda-SF 38	Ashburn-Phi 13	Banks-Chi 47	Banks-Chi 379	Banks-Chi 129
Banks-Chi 119	Mays-SF 208	Groat-Pit 36	Virdon-Pit 11	Thomas-Pit 35	Mays-SF 350	Thomas-Pit 109
Aaron-Mil 109	Aaron-Mil 196	Musial-StL 35	Mays-SF 11	Robinson-Cin 31	Aaron-Mil 328	H.Anderson-Phi 97
Boyer-StL 101	Banks-Chi 193	H.Anderson-Phi 34	Banks-Chi 11	Mathews-Mil 31	Cepeda-SF 309	Mays-SF 96
Ashburn-Phi 98	Cepeda-SF 188	Aaron-Mil 34		Aaron-Mil 30	Thomas-Pit 297	Cepeda-SF 96

BASES ON BALLS	STOLEN BASES	BASE STEALING RUNS	FIELDING RUNS-INFIELD	FIELDING RUNS-OUTFIELD	OUTFIELD ASSISTS	CATCHER CS PCT.
Ashburn-Phi 97	Mays-SF 31	Mays-SF 4.7	Zimmer-LA 30.1	Clemente-Pit 21.4	Clemente-Pit 22	Foiles-Pit 50.0
Temple-Cin 91	Ashburn-Phi 30	Blasingame-StL 2.7	Boyer-StL 25.2	Flood-StL 15.9	Skinner-Pit 19	Bailey-Cin 48.5
Mathews-Mil 85	T.Taylor-Chi 21	T.Taylor-Chi 2.5	Logan-Mil 17.6	Ashburn-Phi 11.1	Flood-StL 18	Crandall-Mil 48.3
Cunningham-StL 82	Blasingame-StL 20	Ashburn-Phi 2.4	Mazeroski-Pit 16.5	Mays-SF 6.7	Mays-SF 17	Schmidt-SF 45.8
	Gilliam-LA 18	Zimmer-LA 2.4	T.Taylor-Chi 14.6	Green-StL 6.0	Thomson-Chi 13	Lopata-Phi 28.6

WINS	WINNING PCT.	WINS ABOVE TEAM	GAMES STARTED	COMPLETE GAMES	FEWEST HITS/GAME	FEWEST BB/GAME
Spahn-Mil 22	Spahn-Mil .667	Purkey-Cin 3.7	Friend-Pit 38	Spahn-Mil 23	Jones-StL 7.34	Burdette-Mil 1.63
Friend-Pit 22	Burdette-Mil .667	Spahn-Mil 3.5	Spahn-Mil 36	Roberts-Phi 21	Koufax-LA 7.49	Roberts-Phi 1.70
Burdette-Mil 20	Friend-Pit .611	Witt-Pit 3.4	Burdette-Mil 36	Burdette-Mil 19	Miller-SF 7.91	Law-Pit 1.73
Roberts-Phi 17	Purkey-Cin .607	Roberts-Phi 3.4	Jones-StL 35	Purkey-Cin 17	Spahn-Mil 7.98	Purkey-Cin 1.76
Purkey-Cin 17	Antonelli-SF .552	Friend-Pit 3.3		Friend-Pit 16	Brosnan-Chi-StL 7.99	Newcombe-LA-Cin 1.93

STRIKEOUTS	STRIKEOUTS/GAME	GAMES	SAVES	BASE RUNNERS/9	ADJUSTED RELIEF RUNS	RELIEF RANKING
Jones-StL 225	Jones-StL 8.10	Elston-Chi 69	Face-Pit 20	Henry-Chi 8.96	Elston-Chi 11.4	Elston-Chi 20.6
Spahn-Mil 150	Koufax-LA 7.43	Klippstein-Cin-LA 57	Labine-LA 14	Jay-Mil 9.68	Henry-Chi 10.6	Henry-Chi 12.3
Podres-LA 143	Drott-Chi 6.83	Face-Pit 57	Farrell-Phi 11	Porterfield-Pit 10.06	Face-Pit 9.4	Face-Pit 12.1
Antonelli-SF 143	Podres-LA 6.12	Hobbie-Chi 55		Spahn-Mil 10.40	Schmidt-Cin 7.2	Farrell-Phi 11.0
Friend-Pit 135	Miller-SF 5.88			Miller-SF 10.43	Porterfield-Pit 7.1	Porterfield-Pit 8.2

INNINGS PITCHED	OPPONENTS' AVG.	OPPONENTS' OBP	EARNED RUN AVERAGE	ADJUSTED ERA	ADJUSTED STARTER RUNS	PITCHER WINS
Spahn-Mil 290.0	Koufax-LA .220	Miller-SF .286	Miller-SF 2.47	Miller-SF 154	Jones-StL 30.7	**Spahn-Mil 4.1**
Burdette-Mil 275.1	Jones-StL .223	Spahn-Mil .287	Jones-StL 2.88	Jones-StL 143	Witt-Pit 26.8	**Burdette-Mil 2.9**
Friend-Pit 274.0	Miller-SF .233	Roberts-Phi .292	Burdette-Mil 2.91	Roberts-Phi 122	Miller-SF 26.7	**Roberts-Phi 2.6**
Roberts-Phi 269.2	Spahn-Mil .237	Burdette-Mil .300	Spahn-Mil 3.07	Brosnan-Chi-StL 121	Roberts-Phi 20.8	**Witt-Pit 2.5**
	Antonelli-SF .239	Purkey-Cin .304	Roberts-Phi 3.24	Burdette-Mil 121	Burdette-Mil 19.0	**Jones-StL 2.5**

Last of the Braves

Milwaukee spent the first half of the season underachieving, but turned on the burners in August and strolled to another relatively easy NL crown. Both Warren Spahn and Lew Burdette won 20 for the Braves, but most of the lineup slumped. The Giants and Dodgers, in their new California surroundings, had fallen into rebuilding mode. East Coast stalwarts Pee Wee Reese and Sal Maglie retired. San Francisco finished a surprising third despite playing youngsters, including Orlando Cepeda (a unanimous Rookie of the Year) and Felipe Alou.

Pittsburgh leapt from seventh to second, improving 22 games under manager Danny Murtaugh. While the team, featuring a cadre of players in their mid-20s, still had a few holes to fill, the Pirates had served notice that their days as a joke were through.

St. Louis' Sam Jones won his third strikeout crown, while Ernie Banks of the fifth-place Cubs took MVP honors. The Phillies, sparked by batting titlist Richie Ashburn, became the first last-place team to lead the NL in batting average; they also paced in hits, walks, and on-base percentage. Philadelphia pitchers, on the other hand, allowed the most runs and the highest opponent batting average in the league.

Unfortunately, the bloom was coming off the rose in Milwaukee, as attendance began to fall even as the Braves won their second straight league title. In fact, fans dropped the team like a hot potato; attendance fell by 11 percent or more every year until 1963. Once again, however, franchise shifting pumped league coffers as the Dodgers' and Giants' moves to the West Coast—and the surprising rise of the Pirates—lifted NL attendance 15 percent.

In retrospect, the World Series was the beginning of the end for the Braves in Milwaukee; up three games to one, and with the final two contests at County Stadium, the Braves lost three straight to the Yankees. This time, Burdette was racked. It was the franchise's last World Series appearance until 1991.

1958 AMERICAN LEAGUE

TEAM	W	L	T	PCT	GB	HW	HL	R	OR	PA	H	2B	3B	HR	BB	SO	HB	SH	AVG	OBP	SLG	OPS	AOPS	BR	ABR	PF	SB	CS	BSA	BSR
NY	92	62	1	.597	—	44	33	**759**	577	5971	**1418**	212	39	**164**	537	822	26	72	**.268**	.336	**.416**	**752**	**116**	**89**	**117**	96	48	32	60	-1
Chi	82	72	1	.532	10	47	30	634	615	5935	1348	191	42	101	518	**669**	**49**	72	.257	.327	.367	694	99	-14	-1	98	**101**	33	**75**	**11**
Bos	79	75	1	.513	13	**49**	28	697	691	5972	1335	**229**	30	155	**638**	820	27	60	.256	**.338**	.400	738	102	75	28	107	29	22	57	-1
Cle	77	76	0	.503	14.5	42	34	694	635	5840	1340	210	31	161	494	819	40	69	.258	.325	.403	728	108	39	56	98	50	49	51	-6
Det	77	77	0	.500	15	43	34	659	606	5805	1384	**229**	41	109	463	678	22	**75**	.266	.326	.389	715	95	21	-24	107	48	32	60	-1
Bal	74	79	1	.484	17.5	46	31	521	**575**	5720	1233	195	19	108	483	731	28	62	.241	.308	.350	658	91	-85	-55	95	33	35	49	-5
KC	73	81	2	.474	19	43	34	642	713	5845	1297	196	**50**	138	452	747	25	64	.247	.307	.381	688	92	-43	-54	102	22	36	38	-8
Was	61	93	2	.396	31	33	44	553	747	5763	1240	161	38	121	477	751	35	57	.240	.307	.357	664	90	-82	-71	98	22	41	35	-10
Total	619	——		—	—	347	268	5159	—	46851	10595	1623	290	1057	4062	6037	252	531	.254	.322	.383	705	—	—	—	—	353	280	56	-20

TEAM	CG	SHO	GR	SV	IP	H	HR	BB	SO	BR/9	ERA	AERA	OAV	OOB	PR	APR	PF	OSB	OCS	FA	E	WPB	DP	FW	PW	BW	BSW	DIF
NY	53	**21**	184	**33**	1379.0	**1201**	116	557	796	11.8	**3.22**	110	**.235**	.313	**85**	51	94	43	**45**	.978	128	**33**	**182**	-.1	5.3	**12.1**	.2	-2.4
Chi	55	15	204	25	1389.2	1296	152	515	751	11.8	3.61	101	.250	.317	25	5	97	37	34	.981	114	39	160	.7	.5	-.1	**1.4**	2.5
Bos	44	5	201	28	1380.0	1396	121	521	695	12.7	3.92	102	.264	.332	-23	13	106	36	38	.976	145	37	172	-1.1	1.3	2.9	.2	-1.3
Cle	51	2	221	20	1373.1	1283	123	604	766	12.5	3.73	98	.249	.328	6	-13	97	50	33	.974	152	68	171	-1.5	-1.3	5.8	-.4	-2.0
Det	**59**	8	220	19	1357.1	1294	133	437	**797**	11.8	3.59	**112**	.252	.314	26	**62**	107	40	32	**.982**	**106**	43	140	**1.1**	**6.4**	-2.5	.2	-5.2
Bal	55	15	183	28	1369.2	1277	**106**	**403**	749	**11.3**	3.40	106	.249	**.306**	57	32	95	**28**	25	.980	114	46	159	.6	3.3	-5.7	-.3	-.5
KC	42	9	**237**	25	1398.1	1405	150	467	721	12.2	4.15	94	.262	.323	-59	-36	104	39	34	.979	125	66	166	.1	-3.7	-5.6	-.6	5.8
Was	28	6	222	28	1376.2	1443	156	558	762	13.3	4.53	84	.272	.341	-116	-108	101	80	39	.980	118	58	163	.5	-11.2	-7.3	-.8	2.8
Total	387	81	1672	206	11024.0	—	—	—	—	12.2	3.77	—	.254	.322	—	—	—	—	—	.979	1002	390	1313	—	—	—	—	—

BATTER-FIELDER WINS	BATTING AVERAGE	ON-BASE PERCENTAGE	SLUGGING AVERAGE	ON-BASE PLUS SLUGGING	ADJUSTED OPS	ADJUSTED BATTER RUNS
Mantle-NY.......... 5.5	Williams-Bos.........328	Williams-Bos.........458	Colavito-Cle..........620	Williams-Bos.......1042	Mantle-NY............189	Mantle-NY............71.2
Colavito-Cle....... 5.0	Runnels-Bos.........322	Mantle-NY.............443	Cerv-KC.................592	Mantle-NY...........1035	Colavito-Cle...........183	Colavito-Cle..........57.1
Cerv-KC.............. 4.4	Kuenn-Det............319	Runnels-Bos..........416	Mantle-NY.............592	Colavito-Cle.........1024	Williams-Bos..........174	Williams-Bos.........48.3
Runnels-Bos....... 4.1	Kaline-Det.............313	Colavito-Cle..........405	Williams-Bos.........584	Cerv-KC.................963	Cerv-KC.................158	Cerv-KC................38.7
Kaline-Det.......... 3.7	Power-KC-Cle.......312	Jensen-Bos............396	Sievers-Was..........544	Jensen-Bos............931	Sievers-Was...........148	Jensen-Bos............37.1
RUNS	**HITS**	**DOUBLES**	**TRIPLES**	**HOME RUNS**	**TOTAL BASES**	**RUNS BATTED IN**
Mantle-NY............127	Fox-Chi..................187	Kuenn-Det..............39	Power-KC-Cle.........10	Mantle-NY................42	Mantle-NY.............307	Jensen-Bos............122
Runnels-Bos..........103	Malzone-Bos..........185	Power-KC-Cle..........37	Tuttle-KC....................9	Colavito-Cle............41	Cerv-KC.................305	Colavito-Cle...........113
Power-KC-Cle..........98	Power-KC-Cle.........184	Kaline-Det...............34	Lemon-Was..............9	Sievers-Was............39	Colavito-Cle..........303	Sievers-Was...........108
Minoso-Cle..............94	Runnels-Bos...........183	Runnels-Bos............32	Aparicio-Chi..............9	Cerv-KC...................38	Sievers-Was..........299	Cerv-KC..................104
Cerv-KC...................93	Kuenn-Det.............179	Jensen-Bos..............31	Harris-Det..................8	Jensen-Bos..............35	Jensen-Bos...........293	Mantle-NY................97
BASES ON BALLS	**STOLEN BASES**	**BASE STEALING RUNS**	**FIELDING RUNS-INFIELD**	**FIELDING RUNS-OUTFIELD**	**OUTFIELD ASSISTS**	**CATCHER CS PCT.**
Mantle-NY.............129	Aparicio-Chi.............29	Aparicio-Chi...........4.3	Kubek-NY.............21.2	Kaline-Det............20.4	Kaline-Det...............23	White-Bos............56.8
Jensen-Bos..............99	Rivera-Chi.................21	Rivera-Chi...............3.6	Buddin-Bos..........18.5	Cerv-KC................13.4	Maris-Cle-KC...........15	Triandos-Bal..........51.0
Williams-Bos............98	Landis-Chi...............19	Mantle-NY...............2.9	Malzone-Bos.........16.5	Williams-Bal............7.6	Jensen-Bos..............14	Lollar-Chi.............47.3
Runnels-Bos............87	Mantle-NY................18	Wilson-Det...............2.2	Aparicio-Chi..........14.9	Minoso-Cle..............5.1	Colavito-Cle.............14	Chiti-KC................44.1
Colavito-Cle.............84	Minoso-Cle..............14		Bridges-Was..........12.3	Busby-Bal................4.1		Wilson-Det............41.9
WINS	**WINNING PCT.**	**WINS ABOVE TEAM**	**GAMES STARTED**	**COMPLETE GAMES**	**FEWEST HITS/GAME**	**FEWEST BB/GAME**
Turley-NY.................21	Turley-NY..............750	Turley-NY...............6.0	Ramos-Was............37	Turley-NY.................19	Turley-NY.............6.53	Donovan-Chi.........1.92
Pierce-Chi................17	McLish-Cle............667	McLish-Cle..............4.4	Wynn-Chi................34	Pierce-Chi................19	Bell-Cle.................6.97	O'Dell-Bal.............2.07
McLish-Cle...............16	Pierce-Chi...............607	Hyde-Was................4.2	Lary-Det..................34	Lary-Det...................19	Ford-NY................7.14	Sullivan-Bos..........2.21
Lary-Det...................16	Portocarrero-Bal...577	Delock-Bos..............3.1	Donovan-Chi...........34	Harshman-Bal..........17	Pierce-Chi.............7.49	Lary-Det.................2.35
	Foytack-Det...........536	Portocarrero-Bal....2.7	Bunning-Det............34		Portocarrero-Bal..7.61	Pierce-Chi..............2.42
STRIKEOUTS	**STRIKEOUTS/GAME**	**GAMES**	**SAVES**	**BASE RUNNERS/9**	**ADJUSTED RELIEF RUNS**	**RELIEF RANKING**
Wynn-Chi...............179	Pascual-Was........7.41	Clevenger-Was.......55	Duren-NY.................20	Wilhelm-Cle-Bal...9.76	Hyde-Was............21.3	Hyde-Was.............32.6
Bunning-Det...........177	Bunning-Det..........7.25	Tomanek-Cle-KC....54	Hyde-Was.................18	Ford-NY................9.81	Duren-NY.............13.5	Duren-NY..............24.1
Turley-NY..............168	Wynn-Chi..............6.72	Hyde-Was................53	Kiely-Bos..................12	Pierce-Chi.............9.96	Kiely-Bos................8.5	Kiely-Bos.................9.5
Harshman-Bal.........161	Turley-NY..............6.16	Wall-Bos..................52	Wall-Bos...................10	Portocarrero-Bal 10.25	Wall-Bos.................5.4	Wall-Bos..................8.3
Pascual-Was...........146	Harshman-Bal......6.13			Hyde-Was..........10.40	Daley-KC.................4.4	Morgan-Det.............4.5
INNINGS PITCHED	**OPPONENTS' AVG.**	**OPPONENTS' OBP**	**EARNED RUN AVERAGE**	**ADJUSTED ERA**	**ADJUSTED STARTER RUNS**	**PITCHER WINS**
Lary-Det.............260.1	Turley-NY..............206	Ford-NY.................276	Ford-NY................2.01	Ford-NY.................176	Ford-NY...............37.4	**Ford-NY................3.9**
Ramos-Was.......259.1	Bell-Cle..................213	Pierce-Chi..............279	Pierce-Chi..............2.68	Lary-Det.................139	Lary-Det................31.8	**Lary-Det...............3.5**
Donovan-Chi......248.0	Ford-NY..................217	O'Dell-Bal...............284	Harshman-Bal......2.89	Pierce-Chi...............136	Pierce-Chi.............25.8	**Hyde-Was............3.4**
Turley-NY...........245.1	Pierce-Chi..............227	Portocarrero-Bal...284	Lary-Det.................2.90	Harshman-Bal.......124	Turley-NY..............22.1	**Harshman-Bal....3.3**
Pierce-Chi..........245.0	Grant-Cle...............228	Harshman-Bal.......292	O'Dell-Bal.............2.97	McLish-Cle............122	Wilhelm-Cle-Bal...18.1	**Pierce-Chi............3.0**

Yankees Take Rematch

The New York Yankees were again AL champs, this time with no challenges. As the Yankees started ferociously, the rest of the league was so bad that the Kansas City Athletics held second for nearly a month. New York drew well—with no National League competition for the first time—but few other teams boasted strong gates.

Those who went to games didn't see an overabundance of offense. Teams scored an average of just 4.17 times per game, the lowest total in a decade. Mickey Mantle led the AL in walks and runs and finished fourth in steals (the top three thieves were Chicagoans—only the White Sox used stolen bases as a weapon). Ted Williams hit .328 and won his final batting title at age 40.

Yankees righty Bob Turley won 21 games despite leading the AL with 128 walks, but Whitey Ford, just 14-7, was New York's top twirler, towering over the league with a 2.01 ERA. The second-place White Sox, just 82-72, rate as one of the worst-ever pre-expansion runners-up. The Yankees' poor late-season performance—they were barely .500 the last two months, and Hoyt Wilhelm no-hit them on September 20—foreshadowed New York's 1959 collapse.

Hall of Famer Tris Speaker and star outfielder Harry Heilmann died in 1958. Meanwhile, Norm Cash and Johnny Callison debuted with the White Sox. They soon departed for other teams, one reason why Chicago didn't win in the 1960s.

Down three games to one in the World Series, the Yankees appeared headed for a second straight Series loss to the Braves. But Turley shut out Milwaukee, 7-0 in Game 5; then, back in Wisconsin, the Yankees—using Turley in relief twice—took the final two contests. The inability to win just one more Series game was, in essence, the end of the Milwaukee Braves.

1957 NATIONAL LEAGUE

TEAM	W	L	T	PCT	GB	HW	HL	R	OR	PA	H	2B	3B	HR	BB	SO	HB	SH	AVG	OBP	SLG	OPS	AOPS	BR	ABR	PF	SB	CS	BSA	BSR
Mil	95	59	1	.617	—	**45**	32	**772**	613	6050	1469	221	**62**	**199**	461	729	30	64	.269	.327	**.442**	769	**120**	81	**140**	93	35	16	**69**	2
StL	87	67	0	.565	8	42	35	737	666	6082	**1497**	235	43	132	493	672	18	45	**.274**	.333	.405	738	102	37	23	102	58	44	57	-3
Bro	84	70	0	.545	11	43	34	690	**591**	5944	1325	188	38	147	**550**	848	33	78	.253	.325	.387	712	89	-11	-69	110	60	34	64	1
Cin	80	74	0	.519	15	**45**	32	747	781	6104	1452	**251**	33	187	546	752	37	84	.269	**.338**	.432	**770**	105	**102**	50	107	51	36	59	-1
Phi	77	77	2	.500	18	38	39	623	656	5921	1311	213	44	117	534	758	**45**	52	.250	.322	.375	697	96	-38	-18	97	57	26	**69**	**3**
NY	69	85	0	.448	26	37	40	643	701	5892	1349	171	54	157	447	**669**	25	32	.252	.311	.393	704	94	-46	-44	100	**64**	38	63	1
Pit	62	92	1	.403	33	36	41	586	696	5942	1447	231	60	92	374	733	23	**97**	.268	.315	.384	699	96	-48	-29	97	46	35	57	-2
Chi	62	92	2	.403	33	31	46	628	722	5947	1312	223	31	147	461	989	26	58	.244	.305	.380	685	90	-77	-67	98	28	25	53	-3
Total	619	—	—	—	—	317	299	5426	—	47882	11162	1733	365	1178	3866	6150	237	510	.260	.322	.400	722	—	—	—	—	399	254	61	-1

TEAM	CG	SHO	GR	SV	IP	H	HR	BB	SO	BR/9	ERA	AERA	OAV	OOB	PR	APR	PF	OSB	OCS	FA	E	WPB	DP	FW	PW	BW	BSW	DIF
Mil	**60**	9	183	24	1411.0	1347	**124**	570	693	12.3	3.47	101	.253	.325	64	5	90	57	37	.981	120	**31**	173	1.0	.5	**14.2**	.2	2.0
StL	46	11	229	**29**	1413.1	1385	140	506	778	12.2	3.78	105	.257	.322	16	29	102	45	29	.979	131	62	168	.4	2.9	2.3	-.3	4.6
Bro	44	**18**	204	**29**	1399.0	**1285**	144	456	**891**	**11.4**	**3.35**	**124**	**.244**	**.305**	**82**	**118**	107	**37**	31	.979	127	38	136	.6	**12.0**	-7.0	.1	1.3
Cin	40	5	**279**	**29**	1395.2	1486	179	429	707	12.7	4.62	89	.275	.331	-116	-75	106	44	26	**.982**	**107**	36	139	**1.7**	-7.6	5.1	-.0	4.0
Phi	54	9	209	23	1401.2	1363	139	**412**	858	11.5	3.79	100	.254	.307	13	1	98	71	24	.976	136	37	117	.2	.1	-1.8	**.3**	1.2
NY	35	9	270	20	1398.2	1436	150	471	701	12.5	4.01	98	.267	.327	-20	-12	101	**37**	30	.974	161	40	**180**	-1.3	-1.2	-4.5	.1	-1.1
Pit	47	9	264	15	1395.0	1463	158	421	663	12.3	3.88	98	.270	.323	0	-14	98	45	27	.972	170	40	143	-1.7	-1.4	-2.9	-.2	-8.7
Chi	30	5	263	26	1403.1	1397	144	601	859	13.0	4.13	94	.261	.336	-39	-41	100	63	**50**	.975	149	53	140	-.5	-4.2	-6.8	-.3	-3.2
Total	356	75	1901	195	11217.2	—	—	—	—	12.2	3.88	—	.260	.322	—	—	—	—	—	.977	1101	337	1196	—	—	—	—	—

BATTER-FIELDER WINS	BATTING AVERAGE	ON-BASE PERCENTAGE	SLUGGING AVERAGE	ON-BASE PLUS SLUGGING	ADJUSTED OPS	ADJUSTED BATTER RUNS
Mays-NY 5.7	Musial-StL 351	Musial-StL 422	Mays-NY 626	Musial-StL 1034	Mays-NY 174	Mays-NY 60.6
Musial-StL 4.7	Mays-NY 333	Mays-NY 407	Musial-StL 612	Mays-NY 1033	Musial-StL 172	Aaron-Mil 58.1
Aaron-Mil 4.7	Robinson-Cin 322	Bouchee-Phi 394	Aaron-Mil 600	Aaron-Mil 978	Aaron-Mil 170	Musial-StL 53.7
Mathews-Mil 4.3	Aaron-Mil 322	Ashburn-Phi 390	Snider-Bro 587	Snider-Bro 955	Mathews-Mil 157	Mathews-Mil 47.9
Banks-Chi 3.9	Groat-Pit 315	Temple-Cin 387	Banks-Chi 579	Banks-Chi 939	Banks-Chi 150	Banks-Chi 41.4
RUNS	**HITS**	**DOUBLES**	**TRIPLES**	**HOME RUNS**	**TOTAL BASES**	**RUNS BATTED IN**
Aaron-Mil 118	Schoendienst-NY-Ml 200	Hoak-Cin 39	Mays-NY 20	Aaron-Mil 44	Aaron-Mil 369	Aaron-Mil 132
Banks-Chi 113	Aaron-Mil 198	Musial-StL 38	Virdon-Pit 11	Banks-Chi 43	Mays-NY 366	Ennis-StL 105
Mays-NY 112	Robinson-Cin 197	Bouchee-Phi 35	Mathews-Mil 9	Snider-Bro 40	Banks-Chi 344	Musial-StL 102
Mathews-Mil 109	Mays-NY 195	Banks-Chi 34	Bruton-Mil 9	Mays-NY 35	Robinson-Cin 323	Banks-Chi 102
Blasingame-StL 108	Ashburn-Phi 186	Moryn-Chi 33		Mathews-Mil 32	Mathews-Mil 309	Hodges-Bro 98
BASES ON BALLS	**STOLEN BASES**	**BASE STEALING RUNS**	**FIELDING RUNS-INFIELD**	**FIELDING RUNS-OUTFIELD**	**OUTFIELD ASSISTS**	**CATCHER CS PCT.**
Temple-Cin 94	Mays-NY 38	Temple-Cin 2.4	Logan-Mil 24.7	Ashburn-Phi 24.2	Ashburn-Phi 18	Bailey-Cin 46.2
Ashburn-Phi 94	Gilliam-Bro 26	Gilliam-Bro 2.2	Blasingame-StL 20.2	Robinson-Cin 12.6	Thomas-Pit 14	Neeman-Chi 43.9
Mathews-Mil 90	Blasingame-StL 21	Fernandez-Phi 2.2	O'Connell-Mil-NY 18.0	Clemente-Pit 11.1	Mays-NY 14	Thomas-NY 42.9
Bouchee-Phi 84	Temple-Cin 19	Mays-NY 1.7	Spencer-NY 18.0	Post-Cin 9.6		Campanella-Bro 41.7
Snider-Bro 77	Fernandez-Phi 18	Robinson-Cin 1.5	Dark-StL 17.1	Thomas-Pit 6.6		Foiles-Pit 37.5
WINS	**WINNING PCT.**	**WINS ABOVE TEAM**	**GAMES STARTED**	**COMPLETE GAMES**	**FEWEST HITS/GAME**	**FEWEST BB/GAME**
Spahn-Mil 21	Buhl-Mil 720	Sanford-Phi 6.1	Friend-Pit 38	Spahn-Mil 18	Sanford-Phi 7.38	Newcombe-Bro 1.49
Sanford-Phi 19	Sanford-Phi 704	Drott-Chi 4.3	Gomez-NY 36	Friend-Pit 17	Podres-Bro 7.71	Roberts-Phi 1.55
Buhl-Mil 18	Spahn-Mil 656	Farrell-Phi 4.1	Spahn-Mil 35	Gomez-NY 16	Drott-Chi 7.86	Law-Pit 1.67
Drysdale-Bro 17	Drysdale-Bro 654	Buhl-Mil 3.8		Sanford-Phi 15	Buhl-Mil 7.93	Purkey-Pit 1.90
Burdette-Mil 17	Burdette-Mil 654	Drysdale-Bro 3.6			Worthington-NY 7.99	Jeffcoat-Cin 2.00
STRIKEOUTS	**STRIKEOUTS/GAME**	**GAMES**	**SAVES**	**BASE RUNNERS/9**	**ADJUSTED RELIEF RUNS**	**RELIEF RANKING**
Sanford-Phi 188	Jones-StL 7.59	Lown-Chi 67	Labine-Bro 17	Podres-Bro 9.78	Roebuck-Bro 12.8	Farrell-Phi 17.8
Drott-Chi 170	Haddix-Phi 7.17	Face-Pit 59	Grissom-NY 14	Roberts-Phi 10.45	Farrell-Phi 11.4	Roebuck-Bro 14.4
Drabowsky-Chi 170	Sanford-Phi 7.15	Labine-Bro 58	Lown-Chi 12	Newcombe-Bro 10.56	Miller-Phi 8.6	Miller-Phi 10.9
Jones-StL 154	Drott-Chi 6.68	Worthington-NY 55	Wilhelm-StL 11	Spahn-Mil 10.66	Grissom-NY 8.0	Grissom-NY 10.0
Drysdale-Bro 148	Drabowsky-Chi 6.38	Grissom-NY 55		V.McDaniel-StL 10.70	Brosnan-Chi 7.0	Labine-Bro 8.3
INNINGS PITCHED	**OPPONENTS' AVG.**	**OPPONENTS' OBP**	**EARNED RUN AVERAGE**	**ADJUSTED ERA**	**ADJUSTED STARTER RUNS**	**PITCHER WINS**
Friend-Pit 277.0	Sanford-Phi 221	Podres-Bro 273	Podres-Bro 2.66	Podres-Bro 156	Drysdale-Bro 33.3	**Drysdale-Bro 4.1**
Spahn-Mil 271.0	Podres-Bro 230	Roberts-Phi 283	Drysdale-Bro 2.69	Drysdale-Bro 155	Podres-Bro 31.2	**Podres-Bro 3.4**
Burdette-Mil 256.2	Drott-Chi 234	Newcombe-Bro 288	Spahn-Mil 2.69	Law-Pit 132	Spahn-Mil 25.6	**Spahn-Mil 3.1**
Lawrence-Cin 250.1	Drysdale-Bro 236	Law-Pit 290	Buhl-Mil 2.74	Spahn-Mil 130	Buhl-Mil 18.9	**Newcombe-Bro 2.1**
Roberts-Phi 249.2	Spahn-Mil 237	Spahn-Mil 291	Law-Pit 2.87	Buhl-Mil 128	Sanford-Phi 17.5	**Farrell-Phi 1.9**

On, Wisconsin!

All-Star ballot stuffing led Commissioner Ford Frick to override the election of eight Cincinnati players in the All-Star Game. He inserted Hank Aaron, Willie Mays, and Stan Musial into the lineup—the NL only had 4 hits and lost in Baltimore. Players, coaches, and managers were subsequently awarded the voting. Fans lost the franchise until 1970. Cincy All-Star shortstop Roy McMillan was a recipient of the inaugural Gold Glove, an award for fielders; Gil Hodges and Mays were the other NL choices. After just one player was honored at each position, the leagues awarded individual sets of winners in 1958.

The pennant chase was a quagmire, involving the Braves, Dodgers, Cardinals, Redlegs (it was the Communist-scared '50s), and Phillies. However, a 17-2 August spurt lifted the Braves up to stay. When the Cardinals threatened in September, Milwaukee won eight in a row to wrap things up. Unheralded rookie Bob "Hurricane" Hazle hit .403 in 41 games down the stretch, but a midseason deal to acquire second baseman Red Schoendienst really put the Braves over the top. Despite playing in a pitcher's park, Milwaukee led the NL in runs.

For just the second time since 1946, an NL team outside New York played in the World Series, and Milwaukee was fit for battle. Down two games to one, the Braves came back from a 5-4 deficit in the bottom of the 10th to win, 7-5, on a home run by Eddie Mathews. Milwaukee then took Game 5 behind Lew Burdette, 1-0. The Yanks won at home in Game 6, but Burdette, who had a 0.67 ERA in 27 innings, won for the third time to clinch. Aaron hit .393 with 3 homers.

Both the Dodgers and Giants departed for the West Coast following the 1957 season. Willie Mays said goodbye to New York by hitting 20 triples, a feat unmatched in the NL until 1996. Dodgers catcher Roy Campanella would never play in Los Angeles, however; in January 1958, he was paralyzed in a car accident.

1957 AMERICAN LEAGUE

TEAM	W	L	T	PCT	GB	HW	HL	R	OR	PA	H	2B	3B	HR	BB	SO	HB	SH	AVG	OBP	SLG	OPS	AOPS	BR	ABR	PF	SB	CS	BSA	BSR
NY	98	56	0	.636	—	**48**	29	**723**	**534**	5993	**1412**	200	**54**	145	562	709	24	93	**.268**	.339	**.409**	**748**	**112**	75	**87**	98	49	38	56	-3
Chi	90	64	1	.584	8	45	32	707	566	6083	1369	208	41	106	**633**	745	**68**	75	.260	**.345**	.375	720	102	42	38	101	**109**	51	**68**	**6**
Bos	82	72	0	.532	16	44	33	721	668	5995	1380	**231**	32	153	624	739	25	41	.262	.341	.405	746	104	**80**	40	106	29	21	58	-1
Det	78	76	0	.506	20	45	32	614	614	6005	1376	224	37	116	504	**643**	27	96	.257	.323	.378	701	95	-18	-34	103	36	47	43	-9
Bal	76	76	2	.500	21	42	33	597	588	5966	1326	191	39	87	504	699	34	**110**	.252	.318	.353	671	95	-68	-29	94	57	35	62	0
Cle	76	77	0	.497	21.5	40	37	682	722	5919	1304	199	26	140	591	786	26	78	.252	.329	.382	711	101	11	18	99	40	47	46	-8
KC	59	94	1	.386	38.5	37	40	563	710	5656	1262	195	40	**166**	364	760	24	62	.244	.295	.394	689	91	-64	-73	102	35	27	56	-2
Was	55	99	0	.357	43	28	49	603	808	5895	1274	215	38	111	527	733	46	50	.244	.316	.363	679	92	-55	-48	99	13	38	25	-10
Total	616	—	—	—	—	329	285	5210	—	47512	10703	1663	307	1024	4309	5814	274	605	.255	.326	.382	708	—	—	—	—	368	304	55	-25

TEAM	CG	SHO	GR	SV	IP	H	HR	BB	SO	BR/9	ERA	AERA	OAV	OOB	PR	APR	PF	OSB	OCS	FA	E	WPB	DP	FW	PW	BW	BSW	DIF
NY	41	13	179	**42**	1395.1	**1198**	110	580	**810**	11.7	**3.00**	**120**	**.234**	.315	**122**	**96**	95	40	**51**	.980	123	39	**183**	.2	**9.9**	**9.0**	.0	1.8
Chi	**59**	**16**	200	27	1401.2	1305	124	**470**	665	11.6	3.35	112	.248	.311	69	62	99	38	31	**.982**	**107**	42	169	**1.1**	6.4	3.9	**.9**	.6
Bos	55	9	171	23	1376.2	1391	116	498	692	12.6	3.88	103	.264	.329	-14	16	105	34	31	.976	149	34	179	-1.2	1.7	4.1	.2	.2
Det	52	9	209	21	1417.2	1330	147	505	756	11.9	3.56	108	.250	.318	37	46	102	**33**	31	.980	121	**31**	151	.3	4.8	-3.5	-.6	.0
Bal	44	13	195	25	1408.0	1272	**95**	493	767	**11.5**	3.46	104	.243	**.310**	51	21	95	41	49	.981	112	43	159	.8	2.2	-3.0	.3	-.3
Cle	46	7	204	23	1380.2	1381	130	618	807	13.3	4.06	92	.261	.340	-42	-54	98	61	34	.974	153	60	154	-1.4	-5.6	1.9	-.5	5.1
KC	26	6	**250**	19	1369.2	1344	153	565	626	12.7	4.19	94	.260	.333	-61	-34	104	53	28	.979	125	67	162	.1	-3.5	-7.5	.1	-6.7
Was	31	5	234	16	1377.0	1482	149	580	691	13.7	4.85	80	.278	.349	-162	-142	103	68	49	.979	128	44	159	-.0	-14.7	-5.0	-.7	-1.6
Total	354	78	1642	196	11126.2	—	—	—	—	12.4	3.79	—	.255	.326	—	—	—	—	—	.979	1018	360	1316	—	—	—	—	—

BATTER-FIELDER WINS	BATTING AVERAGE	ON-BASE PERCENTAGE	SLUGGING AVERAGE	ON-BASE PLUS SLUGGING	ADJUSTED OPS	ADJUSTED BATTER RUNS
Mantle-NY..........8.0	Williams-Bos.........388	Williams-Bos.........526	Williams-Bos.........731	Williams-Bos.......1257	Williams-Bos.........227	Mantle-NY............94.0
Williams-Bos......7.3	Mantle-NY.............365	Mantle-NY.............512	Mantle-NY.............665	Mantle-NY...........1177	Mantle-NY.............223	Williams-Bos.........84.3
Fox-Chi..............6.0	Woodling-Cle........321	Woodling-Cle........408	Sievers-Was..........579	Sievers-Was..........967	Sievers-Was..........163	Sievers-Was.........49.1
McDougald-NY..5.3	Boyd-Bal...............318	Minoso-Chi...........408	Woodling-Cle........521	Woodling-Cle........929	Woodling-Cle........155	Woodling-Cle.......35.0
Sievers-Was.......4.0	Fox-Chi.................317	Fox-Chi.................403	Wertz-Cle..............485	Minoso-Chi...........862	Minoso-Chi...........136	Minoso-Chi..........33.9
RUNS	**HITS**	**DOUBLES**	**TRIPLES**	**HOME RUNS**	**TOTAL BASES**	**RUNS BATTED IN**
Mantle-NY.............121	Fox-Chi.................196	Minoso-Chi.............36	Simpson-KC-NY.......9	Sievers-Was............42	Sievers-Was..........331	Sievers-Was..........114
Fox-Chi..................110	Malzone-Bos.........185	Gardner-Bal............36	McDougald-NY.........9	Williams-Bos...........38	Mantle-NY.............315	Wertz-Cle..............105
Piersall-Bos..........103	Minoso-Chi...........176	Malzone-Bos...........31	Bauer-NY..................9	Mantle-NY...............34	Williams-Bos.........307	Minoso-Chi...........103
Sievers-Was............99	Mantle-NY.............173	Kuenn-Det..............30	Fox-Chi......................8	Wertz-Cle................28	Kaline-Det.............276	Malzone-Bos.........103
	Kuenn-Det............173		Boyd-Bal...................8	Zernial-KC..............27	Malzone-Bos.........271	Jensen-Bos...........103
BASES ON BALLS	**STOLEN BASES**	**BASE STEALING RUNS**	**FIELDING RUNS-INFIELD**	**FIELDING RUNS-OUTFIELD**	**OUTFIELD ASSISTS**	**CATCHER CS PCT.**
Mantle-NY.............146	Aparicio-Chi............28	Aparicio-Chi...........3.4	Bridges-Was........27.7	Maxwell-Det...........10.1	Jensen-Bos..............16	Triandos-Bal.........66.7
Williams-Bos.........119	Rivera-Chi................18	Rivera-Chi..............3.3	McDougald-NY....26.4	Woodling-Cle..........8.9	Pilarcik-Bal..............15	Daley-Bos..............50.0
Smith-Cle.................79	Minoso-Chi...............18	Mantle-NY...............2.5	Fox-Chi..................24.6	Colavito-Cle............8.6	Kaline-Det................13	House-Det.............48.8
Minoso-Chi..............79	Mantle-NY................16	Landis-Chi...............1.7	Malzone-Bos........21.0	Kaline-Det...............6.8		White-Bos.............47.7
Wertz-Cle.................78		Martin-NY-KC..........1.3	Klaus-Bos..............21.0	Maris-Cle.................6.8		Lollar-Chi..............47.7
WINS	**WINNING PCT.**	**WINS ABOVE TEAM**	**GAMES STARTED**	**COMPLETE GAMES**	**FEWEST HITS/GAME**	**FEWEST BB/GAME**
Pierce-Chi................20	Sturdivant-NY.......727	Bunning-Det...........6.6	Wynn-Cle..................37	Pierce-Chi................16	Turley-NY.............6.12	F.Sullivan-Bos......1.80
Bunning-Det.............20	Donovan-Chi.........727	Donovan-Chi..........4.2	Lary-Det....................35	Donovan-Chi............16	Bunning-Det.........7.20	Donovan-Chi.........1.84
Sturdivant-NY.........16	Bunning-Det..........714	Narleski-Cle............3.2	Pierce-Chi.................34	Brewer-Bos...............15	Foytack-Det..........7.43	Shantz-NY............2.08
Donovan-Chi.............16	Wilson-Chi.............652	Sturdivant-NY.........3.1	Moore-Bal..................32		Sturdivant-NY.......7.59	Loes-Bal.................2.14
Brewer-Bos...............16	Pierce-Chi.............625	Loes-Bal..................2.8	Brewer-Bos...............32		F.Sullivan-Bos......7.70	Bunning-Det..........2.42
STRIKEOUTS	**STRIKEOUTS/GAME**	**GAMES**	**SAVES**	**BASE RUNNERS/9**	**ADJUSTED RELIEF RUNS**	**RELIEF RANKING**
Wynn-Cle.................184	Turley-NY.............7.76	Zuverink-Bal............56	Grim-NY.....................19	O'Dell-Bal..............9.68	Staley-Chi.............19.4	Zuverink-Bal.........19.1
Bunning-Det............182	Johnson-Bal..........6.58	Hyde-Was.................52	Narleski-Cle..............16	F.Sullivan-Bos......9.76	Zuverink-Bal..........13.1	Grim-NY..................18.2
Johnson-Bal............177	Wynn-Cle..............6.30	Clevenger-Was.........52	Delock-Bos................11	Bunning-Det.......10.00	Trucks-KC.............10.8	Trucks-KC..............14.9
Pierce-Chi...............171	Bunning-Det..........6.13	Delock-Bos...............49	Zuverink-Bal...............9	Brown-Bal...........10.26	Grim-NY...................9.1	Staley-Chi..............12.9
Turley-NY................152	Pierce-Chi.............5.99	Trucks-KC................48	Clevenger-Was...........8	Donovan-Chi.......10.44	Lehman-Bal.............7.3	Lehman-Bal............12.1
INNINGS PITCHED	**OPPONENTS' AVG.**	**OPPONENTS' OBP**	**EARNED RUN AVERAGE**	**ADJUSTED ERA**	**ADJUSTED STARTER RUNS**	**PITCHER WINS**
Bunning-Det.......267.1	Turley-NY...............194	F.Sullivan-Bos.......273	Shantz-NY............2.45	Shantz-NY.............147	F.Sullivan-Bos......34.5	**F.Sullivan-Bos....3.5**
Wynn-Cle...........263.0	Bunning-Det...........218	Bunning-Det...........277	Sturdivant-NY.......2.54	F.Sullivan-Bos.......146	Bunning-Det.........32.5	**Bunning-Det.......3.4**
Pierce-Chi..........257.0	Foytack-Det............226	Pierce-Chi...............287	Bunning-Det...........2.69	Bunning-Det...........143	Sturdivant-NY.......24.9	**Shantz-NY...........2.7**
Johnson-Bal.......242.0	F.Sullivan-Bos.......230	Johnson-Bal............287	Turley-NY..............2.71	Sturdivant-NY.......141	Donovan-Chi.........22.9	**Sturdivant-NY....2.6**
F.Sullivan-Bos....240.2	Sturdivant-NY.......232	Donovan-Chi...........291	F.Sullivan-Bos......2.73	Donovan-Chi.........135	Shantz-NY............21.3	**Donovan-Chi.......2.4**

The Battle of Mickey and Teddy

The Yankees were again the class of the league. New York had 21-year-old Bobby Richardson at second and 20-year-old utility infielder Tony Kubek meshing with 41-year-old outfielder Enos Slaughter, the usual veterans like Yogi Berra and Hank Bauer, and a staff of reasonably talented arms. Mickey Mantle again was voted Most Valuable Player, hitting .365 with 146 walks, and three New York hurlers finished among the league's top five in ERA.

Al Lopez left Cleveland, where he had managed for six years, to take over the White Sox, who finished second after leading the league through June. Chicago became the first club since 1945 to steal more than 100 bases, more than doubling the number of steals of the runner-up (Orioles). Chicago's middle infield duo of Luis Aparicio (the league steals leader) and Nellie Fox (AL-high 196 hits) were turning heads. Meanwhile, the last-place Senators stole just 13 bases in 154 games, the fewest ever.

Ted Williams, 39, became the oldest player ever to win a batting crown; his .388 mark was the highest average in the game since his own .406 in '41. Just to make things a little sweeter, he kicked in 119 walks and 38 homers, but lost to Mantle in a much-disputed MVP vote. Boston finished a surprise third despite a mediocre—at best—pitching corps.

The Indians sank to sixth as their pitching fell apart, but the Tribe did install 22-year-old rookie Roger Maris in the outfield. The tragedy of the season involved Cleveland's Herb Score, who took a Gil McDougald line drive to his right eye on May 7. After a layoff, he returned, hurt his arm, and was never again effective.

A disappointing World Series loss to Milwaukee again showed that the Yankees were, indeed, human. Oddly, they outscored and outhit the Braves in the Series and had a better ERA, but the Braves came up in the clinches.

1956 NATIONAL LEAGUE

TEAM	W	L	T	PCT	GB	HW	HL	R	OR	PA	H	2B	3B	HR	BB	SO	HB	SH	AVG	OBP	SLG	OPS	AOPS	BR	ABR	PF	SB	CS	BSA	BSR
Bro	93	61	0	.604	—	**52**	25	720	601	5884	1315	212	36	179	**649**	738	17	86	.258	**.342**	.419	761	102	86	32	108	65	37	64	1
Mil	92	62	1	.597	1	47	29	709	**569**	5897	1350	212	54	177	486	714	20	**142**	.259	.323	.423	746	**112**	38	**83**	94	29	20	59	-1
Cin	91	63	1	.591	2	51	26	**775**	658	6003	1406	201	32	**221**	528	760	**51**	90	.266	.336	**.441**	**777**	107	**105**	58	106	45	22	**67**	2
StL	76	78	2	.494	17	43	34	678	698	5986	**1443**	**234**	49	124	503	**622**	33	41	**.268**	.333	.399	732	102	26	26	100	41	35	54	-3
Phi	71	83	0	.461	22	40	37	668	738	5910	1313	207	49	121	585	673	27	52	.252	.329	.381	710	99	-11	2	98	45	23	66	2
NY	67	87	0	.435	26	37	40	540	650	5709	1268	192	45	145	402	659	21	59	.244	.299	.382	681	89	-88	-84	99	**67**	34	66	**3**
Pit	66	88	3	.429	27	35	43	588	653	5757	1340	199	**57**	110	383	752	18	95	.257	.307	.380	687	92	-74	-61	98	24	33	42	-6
Chi	60	94	3	.390	33	39	38	597	708	5852	1281	202	50	142	446	776	13	87	.244	.302	.382	684	91	-82	-71	98	55	38	59	-1
Total	621	—	—	—	—	344	272	5275	—	46998	10716	1659	372	1219	3982	5694	200	652	.256	.321	.401	722	—	—	—	—	371	242	61	-3

TEAM	CG	SHO	GR	SV	IP	H	HR	BB	SO	BR/9	ERA	AERA	OAV	OOB	PR	APR	PF	OSB	OCS	FA	E	WPB	DP	FW	PW	BW	BSW	DIF
Bro	46	**12**	201	**30**	1368.2	**1251**	171	441	**772**	**11.3**	3.57	**111**	**.244**	**.305**	31	57	105	**32**	27	**.981**	**111**	51	149	**1.4**	5.8	3.3	.1	5.3
Mil	**64**	**12**	177	27	1393.1	1295	**133**	467	639	11.5	**3.11**	**111**	.247	.309	**102**	**59**	92	33	30	.979	130	29	159	.3	**6.0**	**8.5**	-.0	.2
Cin	47	4	231	29	1389.0	1406	141	458	653	12.3	3.85	103	.265	.325	-12	19	106	50	31	**.981**	113	26	147	1.3	1.9	5.9	.2	4.5
StL	41	**12**	234	**30**	1388.2	1339	155	546	709	12.3	3.97	95	.257	.327	-30	-28	100	52	26	.978	134	53	**172**	.1	-2.9	2.7	-.3	-.7
Phi	57	4	212	15	1377.1	1407	172	**437**	750	12.2	4.20	89	.266	.323	-66	-74	99	63	23	.975	144	**23**	140	-.6	-7.6	.2	.2	1.7
NY	31	9	263	28	1378.0	1287	144	551	765	12.2	3.78	100	.250	.324	-1	1	100	35	30	.976	144	48	143	-.6	.1	-8.6	**.3**	-1.3
Pit	37	8	**266**	24	1376.1	1406	142	469	662	12.4	3.74	101	.267	.327	5	5	100	47	35	.973	162	54	140	-1.5	.5	-6.2	-.6	-3.2
Chi	37	6	220	17	1392.0	1325	161	613	744	12.7	3.96	95	.252	.332	-29	-29	100	59	**40**	.976	144	41	141	-.4	-3.0	-7.3	-.0	-6.3
Total	360	67	1804	200	11063.1	—	—	—	—	12.1	3.77	—	.256	.321	—	—	—	—	—	.977	1082	325	1191	—	—	—	—	—

BATTER-FIELDER WINS	BATTING AVERAGE	ON-BASE PERCENTAGE	SLUGGING AVERAGE	ON-BASE PLUS SLUGGING	ADJUSTED OPS	ADJUSTED BATTER RUNS
Aaron-Mil 4.1	Aaron-Mil .328	Snider-Bro .399	Snider-Bro .598	Snider-Bro .997	Adcock-Mil 154	Snider-Bro 43.3
Mays-NY 4.1	Virdon-StL-Pit .319	Gilliam-Bro .399	Adcock-Mil .597	Robinson-Cin .936	Aaron-Mil 154	Aaron-Mil 43.1
McMillan-Cin 3.7	Clemente-Pit .311	Moon-StL .390	Aaron-Mil .558	Adcock-Mil .934	Snider-Bro 152	Mathews-Mil 37.4
Musial-StL 3.6	Musial-StL .310	Musial-StL .386	Robinson-Cin .558	Mays-NY .926	Mays-NY 146	Musial-StL 37.3
Snider-Bro 3.2	Boyer-StL .306	Ashburn-Phi .384	Mays-NY .557	Aaron-Mil .923	Mathews-Mil 146	Mays-NY 37.0

RUNS	HITS	DOUBLES	TRIPLES	HOME RUNS	TOTAL BASES	RUNS BATTED IN
Robinson-Cin 122	Aaron-Mil 200	Aaron-Mil 34	Bruton-Mil 15	Snider-Bro 43	Aaron-Mil 340	Musial-StL 109
Snider-Bro 112	Ashburn-Phi 190	Snider-Bro 33	Aaron-Mil 14	Robinson-Cin 38	Snider-Bro 324	Adcock-Mil 103
Aaron-Mil 106	Virdon-StL-Pit 185	Musial-StL 33	Walls-Pit 11	Adcock-Mil 38	Mays-NY 322	Kluszewski-Cin 102
Mathews-Mil 103	Musial-StL 184	Lopata-Phi 33	Moon-StL 11	Mathews-Mil 37	Robinson-Cin 319	Snider-Bro 101
Gilliam-Bro 102	Boyer-StL 182	Bell-Cin 31	Virdon-StL-Pit 10		Musial-StL 310	Boyer-StL 98

BASES ON BALLS	STOLEN BASES	BASE STEALING RUNS	FIELDING RUNS-INFIELD	FIELDING RUNS-OUTFIELD	OUTFIELD ASSISTS	CATCHER CS PCT.
Snider-Bro 99	Mays-NY 40	Mays-NY 5.3	McMillan-Cin 28.5	Ashburn-Phi 18.7	Moryn-Chi 18	Crandall-Mil 48.7
Gilliam-Bro 95	Gilliam-Bro 21	Ashburn-Phi 1.9	Robinson-Bro 19.0	King-Chi 11.9	Clemente-Pit 17	Campanella-Bro 44.2
Jones-Phi 92	White-NY 15	Temple-Cin 1.7	Blasingame-StL 16.5	Irvin-Chi 10.0	Aaron-Mil 17	Sarni-StL-NY 42.0
Mathews-Mil 91	Temple-Cin 14	Gilliam-Bro 1.5	Baker-Chi 13.4	Moryn-Chi 6.4	Post-Cin 16	Bailey-Cin 41.1
Moon-StL 80	Reese-Bro 13	Reese-Bro 1.5	Gilliam-Bro 11.3	Post-Cin 6.3	Mays-NY 14	Landrith-Chi 39.7

WINS	WINNING PCT.	WINS ABOVE TEAM	GAMES STARTED	COMPLETE GAMES	FEWEST HITS/GAME	FEWEST BB/GAME
Newcombe-Bro 27	Newcombe-Bro .794	Newcombe-Bro 9.2	Friend-Pit 42	Roberts-Phi 22	Maglie-Bro 7.26	Roberts-Phi 1.21
Spahn-Mil 20	Buhl-Mil .692	Antonelli-NY 5.9	Kline-Pit 39	Spahn-Mil 20	Newcombe-Bro 7.35	Newcombe-Bro 1.54
Antonelli-NY 20	Lawrence-Cin .655	Rush-Chi 3.7	Roberts-Phi 37	Friend-Pit 19	Jones-Chi 7.39	Spahn-Mil 1.66
	Burdette-Mil .655	Freeman-Cin 3.7	Newcombe-Bro 36	Newcombe-Bro 18	Mizell-StL 7.42	Fowler-Cin 1.77
	Spahn-Mil .645	Simmons-Phi 3.7	Antonelli-NY 36	Burdette-Mil 16	Craig-Bro 7.64	Burdette-Mil 1.83

STRIKEOUTS	STRIKEOUTS/GAME	GAMES	SAVES	BASE RUNNERS/9	ADJUSTED RELIEF RUNS	RELIEF RANKING
Jones-Chi 176	Jones-Chi 8.40	Face-Pit 68	Labine-Bro 19	Newcombe-Bro 9.00	Grissom-NY 20.2	Freeman-Cin 14.2
Haddix-StL-Phi 170	Haddix-StL-Phi 6.64	Wilhelm-NY 64	Freeman-Cin 18	Spahn-Mil 9.73	Acker-Cin 14.8	Bessent-Bro 13.5
Friend-Pit 166	Mizell-StL 6.60	Freeman-Cin 64	Lown-Chi 13	Acker-Cin 9.79	Bessent-Bro 12.9	Labine-Bro 12.0
Roberts-Phi 157	Nuxhall-Cin 5.38	Labine-Bro 62	Jackson-StL 9	Grissom-NY 9.82	Labine-Bro 7.4	Acker-Cin 11.5
Mizell-StL 153	Worthington-NY 5.16	Lown-Chi 61	Bessent-Bro 9	Maglie-Bro 9.94	Freeman-Cin 7.3	Grissom-NY 10.1

INNINGS PITCHED	OPPONENTS' AVG.	OPPONENTS' OBP	EARNED RUN AVERAGE	ADJUSTED ERA	ADJUSTED STARTER RUNS	PITCHER WINS
Friend-Pit 314.1	Newcombe-Bro .221	Newcombe-Bro .257	Burdette-Mil 2.70	Maglie-Bro 138	Spahn-Mil 28.1	**Newcombe-Bro 4.1**
Roberts-Phi 297.1	Jones-Chi .221	Spahn-Mil .275	Spahn-Mil 2.78	Antonelli-NY 132	Antonelli-NY 26.1	**Spahn-Mil 3.7**
Spahn-Mil 281.1	Mizell-StL .222	Rush-Chi .280	Antonelli-NY 2.86	Newcombe-Bro 130	Newcombe-Bro 25.7	**Antonelli-NY 3.5**
Newcombe-Bro 268.0	Maglie-Bro .222	Maglie-Bro .281	Maglie-Bro 2.87	Burdette-Mil 128	Maglie-Bro 23.1	**Burdette-Mil 2.6**
Kline-Pit 264.0	Craig-Bro .231	Burdette-Mil .281	Newcombe-Bro 3.06	Spahn-Mil 124	Burdette-Mil 23.0	**Dickson-Phi-StL 1.9**

The Last of Flatbush

The Braves streaked to a big lead by Labor Day, but lost five straight to give hope to Brooklyn and Cincinnati (sparked by Rookie of the Year Frank Robinson). While Cincy dropped five straight, and couldn't recover, Brooklyn and Milwaukee juggled the lead until the last weekend. Brooklyn swept three from Pittsburgh at Ebbets Field while the Braves dropped two of three at St. Louis. Don Newcombe of the Dodgers was voted Most Valuable Player as well as winner of the first Cy Young Award, which was only given to one pitcher in the major leagues until 1967.

The Braves had blossoming star Hank Aaron as well as the league's best pitching. The Dodgers countered with Clem Labine, the NL's best reliever, and 19-year-old rookie Don Drysdale, who pitched well. Cincinnati's 3.85 ERA was middle of the pack, but the lineup's 221 homers tied the all-time record.

Nineteen-year-old Bill Mazeroski took over at second base for the Pirates, who improved to seventh after four straight years in the basement. The Phillies moved in their center field fence, and Robin Roberts promptly served up 46 homers, setting a mark that lasted three decades.

After winning the first two World Series games, Brooklyn looked to rack up another championship. But it was not to be. Don Larsen's Game 5 perfecto, and a 9-0 Game 7 embarrassment at Ebbets, gave the Yankees yet another title.

The golden era for both New York teams was over. Ralph Branca and Monte Irvin played their final games, and when Walter O'Malley traded Jackie Robinson to the Giants following the Series, Robinson chose to retire. Brooklyn had the league's second-highest attendance in both 1955 and 1956, but the Giants' gate was dropping. The success of the Braves in Milwaukee, and problems getting new facilities built in New York, led O'Malley and Horace Stoneham to consider relocating.

En route to winter ball, Cardinals outfielder Charlie Peete—expected to contend for a starting job in 1957—was killed in an airplane crash.

1956 AMERICAN LEAGUE

TEAM	W	L	T	PCT	GB	HW	HL	R	OR	PA	H	2B	3B	HR	BB	SO	HB	SH	AVG	OBP	SLG	OPS	AOPS	BR	ABR	PF	SB	CS	BSA	BSR
NY	97	57	0	.630	—	**49**	28	**857**	631	6075	1433	193	55	**190**	615	755	30	82	.270	.347	**.434**	**781**	**115**	78	**105**	97	51	37	58	-2
Cle	88	66	1	.571	9	46	31	712	**581**	5988	1256	199	23	153	681	764	40	81	.244	.335	.381	716	92	-34	-49	102	40	32	56	-2
Chi	85	69	0	.552	12	46	31	776	634	6122	1412	218	43	128	619	660	**75**	**86**	.267	.349	.397	746	101	31	20	101	**70**	33	**68**	**4**
Bos	84	70	1	.545	13	43	34	780	751	6215	1473	**261**	45	139	**727**	687	25	68	.275	**.362**	.419	**781**	100	**106**	14	112	28	19	60	0
Det	82	72	1	.532	15	37	40	789	699	6144	**1494**	209	50	150	644	**618**	28	58	**.279**	.356	.420	776	110	84	82	100	43	26	62	0
Bal	69	85	0	.448	28	41	36	571	705	5790	1242	198	34	91	563	725	22	84	.244	.320	.350	670	89	-125	-78	92	39	42	48	-6
Was	59	95	1	.383	38	32	45	652	924	6043	1302	198	**62**	112	690	877	41	75	.250	.341	.377	718	95	-28	-27	100	37	34	52	-4
KC	52	102	0	.338	45	22	55	619	831	5860	1325	204	41	112	480	727	20	67	.252	.315	.370	685	86	-111	-113	100	40	30	57	-2
Total	618	—	—	—	—	316	300	5756	—	48237	10937	1680	353	1075	5019	5813	281	601	.260	.341	.394	735	—	—	—	—	348	253	58	-12

TEAM	CG	SHO	GR	SV	IP	H	HR	BB	SO	BR/9	ERA	AERA	OAV	OOB	PR	APR	PF	OSB	OCS	FA	E	WPB	DP	FW	PW	BW	BSW	DIF
NY	50	10	181	**35**	1382.0	1285	114	652	732	12.9	3.63	107	.249	.335	82	40	93	34	32	.977	136	**31**	**214**	.6	3.9	**10.3**	-.0	5.3
Cle	**67**	**17**	182	24	1384.0	**1233**	116	564	**845**	**11.9**	**3.32**	**127**	**.238**	**.314**	**129**	**134**	101	51	23	.978	129	41	130	1.0	**13.1**	-4.8	-.0	1.7
Chi	65	11	196	13	1389.0	1351	118	**524**	722	12.3	3.73	110	.255	.324	67	59	99	**28**	21	**.979**	**122**	42	160	**1.3**	5.8	2.0	**.5**	-1.6
Bos	50	8	178	20	1398.0	1354	130	668	712	13.3	4.17	111	.254	.340	-1	64	111	39	29	.972	169	41	168	-1.2	6.3	1.4	.1	.4
Det	62	10	187	15	1379.0	1389	140	655	788	13.6	4.06	101	.264	.348	15	9	99	32	35	.976	140	40	151	.4	.9	8.0	.1	-4.5
Bal	38	10	231	24	1360.2	1362	**99**	547	715	12.8	4.20	93	.263	.334	-6	-45	94	58	33	.977	137	40	142	.5	-4.4	-7.6	-.4	4.0
Was	36	1	244	18	1368.2	1539	171	730	663	15.1	5.33	81	.287	.373	-179	-147	104	55	**40**	.972	171	50	173	-1.3	-14.4	-2.6	-.2	.6
KC	30	3	**251**	18	1370.1	1424	187	679	636	14.1	4.86	89	.271	.357	-107	-78	104	51	**40**	.973	166	57	187	-1.1	-7.6	-11.1	-.0	-5.2
Total	398	70	1650	167	11031.2	—	—	—	—	13.2	4.16	—	.260	.341	—	—	—	—	—	.975	1170	342	1325	—	—	—	—	—

BATTER-FIELDER WINS	BATTING AVERAGE	ON-BASE PERCENTAGE	SLUGGING AVERAGE	ON-BASE PLUS SLUGGING	ADJUSTED OPS	ADJUSTED BATTER RUNS
Mantle-NY 8.1	Mantle-NY .353	Williams-Bos .479	Mantle-NY .705	Mantle-NY 1169	Mantle-NY 213	Mantle-NY 90.0
Berra-NY 4.3	Williams-Bos .345	Mantle-NY .464	Williams-Bos .605	Williams-Bos 1084	Williams-Bos 164	Williams-Bos 43.6
Kaline-Det 3.9	Kuenn-Det .332	Nieman-Chi-Bal .436	Maxwell-Det .534	Minoso-Chi 950	Nieman-Chi-Bal 156	Minoso-Chi 42.5
McDougald-NY 3.5	Maxwell-Det .326	Minoso-Chi .425	Berra-NY .534	Maxwell-Det 948	Maxwell-Det 150	Nieman-Chi-Bal 40.0
Maxwell-Det 3.4	Nieman-Chi-Bal .320	Maxwell-Det .414	Kaline-Det .530	Nieman-Chi-Bal 931	Minoso-Chi 149	Maxwell-Det 37.5

RUNS	HITS	DOUBLES	TRIPLES	HOME RUNS	TOTAL BASES	RUNS BATTED IN
Mantle-NY 132	Kuenn-Det 196	Piersall-Bos 40	Simpson-KC 11	Mantle-NY 52	Mantle-NY 376	Mantle-NY 130
Fox-Chi 109	Kaline-Det 194	Kuenn-Det 32	Minoso-Chi 11	Wertz-Cle 32	Kaline-Det 327	Kaline-Det 128
Minoso-Chi 106	Fox-Chi 192	Kaline-Det 32	Lemon-Was 11	Berra-NY 30	Jensen-Bos 287	Wertz-Cle 106
	Mantle-NY 188		Jensen-Bos 11	Sievers-Was 29	Minoso-Chi 286	Simpson-KC 105
	Jensen-Bos 182			Maxwell-Det 28		Berra-NY 105

BASES ON BALLS	STOLEN BASES	BASE STEALING RUNS	FIELDING RUNS-INFIELD	FIELDING RUNS-OUTFIELD	OUTFIELD ASSISTS	CATCHER CS PCT.
Yost-Was 151	Aparicio-Chi 21	Aparicio-Chi 3.2	McDougald-NY 8.8	Kaline-Det 12.2	Kaline-Det 18	Wilson-Det 56.3
Mantle-NY 112	Rivera-Chi 20	Avila-Cle 2.3	DeMaestri-KC 8.8	Piersall-Bos 7.3	Tuttle-Det 13	House-Det 50.0
Williams-Bos 102	Avila-Cle 17	Mantle-NY 1.9	Yost-Was 8.3	Maxwell-Det 6.4	Jensen-Bos 13	White-Bos 48.0
Doby-Chi 102	Minoso-Chi 12	Jensen-Bos 1.4	Power-KC 7.8	Lemon-Was 4.2	Maxwell-Det 12	Lollar-Chi 43.6
Sievers-Was 100		Pilarcik-KC 1.3	Buddin-Bos 6.9	Stephens-Bos 3.5	Lemon-Was 11	Smith-Bal-KC 38.2

WINS	WINNING PCT.	WINS ABOVE TEAM	GAMES STARTED	COMPLETE GAMES	FEWEST HITS/GAME	FEWEST BB/GAME
Lary-Det 21	Ford-NY .760	Pierce-Chi 5.1	Lary-Det 38	Pierce-Chi 21	Score-Cle 5.85	Stobbs-Was 2.03
	Wynn-Cle .690	Ford-NY 4.9	Wynn-Cle 35	Lemon-Cle 21	Larsen-NY 6.66	Donovan-Chi 2.26
	Score-Cle .690	Brewer-Bos 4.7	Lemon-Cle 35	Lary-Det 20	Harshman-Chi 7.27	Kucks-NY 2.89
	Pierce-Chi .690	Wynn-Cle 4.6	Hoeft-Det 34		Brewer-Bos 7.37	Wynn-Cle 2.95
	Brewer-Bos .679	Score-Cle 4.6	Ditmar-KC 34		Foytack-Det 7.42	Sturdivant-NY 2.96

STRIKEOUTS	STRIKEOUTS/GAME	GAMES	SAVES	BASE RUNNERS/9	ADJUSTED RELIEF RUNS	RELIEF RANKING
Score-Cle 263	Score-Cle 9.49	Zuverink-Bal 62	Zuverink-Bal 16	Score-Cle 10.58	Narleski-Cle 17.7	Narleski-Cle 16.1
Pierce-Chi 192	Pascual-Was 7.73	Crimian-KC 54	Mossi-Cle 11	Donovan-Chi 10.62	Grim-NY 9.3	Delock-Bos 11.1
Foytack-Det 184	Foytack-Det 6.47	Gorman-KC 52	Morgan-NY 11	Wynn-Cle 10.66	Byerly-Was 7.7	Mossi-Cle 9.4
Hoeft-Det 172	Pierce-Chi 6.25	Mossi-Cle 48	Shantz-KC 9	Brown-Bal 10.68	Delock-Bos 7.1	Byerly-Was 9.4
Lary-Det 165	Sturdivant-NY 6.25	Delock-Bos 48	Delock-Bos 9	Sturdivant-NY 10.80	Mossi-Cle 6.7	Grim-NY 9.3

INNINGS PITCHED	OPPONENTS' AVG.	OPPONENTS' OBP	EARNED RUN AVERAGE	ADJUSTED ERA	ADJUSTED STARTER RUNS	PITCHER WINS
Lary-Det 294.0	Score-Cle .186	Donovan-Chi .290	Ford-NY 2.47	Score-Cle 166	Wynn-Cle 46.3	**Wynn-Cle 5.1**
Wynn-Cle 277.2	Larsen-NY .204	Score-Cle .290	Score-Cle 2.53	Ford-NY 156	Score-Cle 44.9	**Score-Cle 4.9**
Pierce-Chi 276.1	Brewer-Bos .220	Wynn-Cle .291	Wynn-Cle 2.72	Wynn-Cle 154	Ford-NY 37.7	**Lemon-Cle 4.6**
Foytack-Det 256.0	Harshman-Chi .221	Sturdivant-NY .291	Lemon-Cle 3.03	Lemon-Cle 139	Lary-Det 31.7	**Ford-NY 4.6**
Lemon-Cle 255.1	Sturdivant-NY .224	Ford-NY .301	Harshman-Chi 3.10	Sullivan-Bos 135	Lemon-Cle 30.7	**Brewer-Bos 3.9**

His Favorite Year

Mickey Mantle had perhaps his greatest season, winning the Triple Crown and MVP honors, as the Yankees won another flag. Yogi Berra, Moose Skowron, and Gil McDougald contributed significantly on offense, and Whitey Ford captured the ERA title. These are the Yankees that people remember, with Mantle doing it all, Elston Howard and Joe Collins platooning, hard-nosed Hank Bauer in right field, Billy Martin at second, and otherwise undistinguished pitchers like Johnny Kucks, Don Larsen, and Tom Sturdivant enjoying their greatest moments.

The second-place Indians again had a trio of 20-game winners, but their offense had declined sharply. The race was never close. Third-place Chicago added shortstop Luis Aparicio, whose speed and defense garnered him Rookie of the Year honors.

For the first time, AL homers rose over 1,000; every team had a slow-footed slugger or two. Jim Lemon of the Senators whiffed 138 times to set a new record, while his teammate, Eddie Yost, collected 151 walks.

Orioles catcher Tom Gastall died September 20 in a private plane crash. Beloved A's owner-manager Connie Mack passed away at age 93; Mack's longtime lieutenant, Al Simmons, died three months later of a heart attack. Injured Al Rosen and aging Bob Feller retired from the Indians, and down the pennant stretch, the Yankees released Phil Rizzuto. The Scooter would start a forty-season run in the broadcast booth the following spring.

It didn't look like a great World Series for the Yankees, however, as they lost the first two at Ebbets Field. However, after New York tied things up with Ford and Sturdivant tossing complete-game victories, Don Larsen threw a perfect game at Brooklyn in Game 5, fanning Dale Mitchell for the last out. Clem Labine blanked the Yankees in Game 6, but Kucks breezed to a 9-0 win to give the Bronx its sixth championship in eight years. And after 13 "Subway Series" between New York's three teams since 1921—the Yankees winning 10 times—this would be the last of its kind until 2000.

1955 NATIONAL LEAGUE

TEAM	W	L	T	PCT	GB	HW	HL	R	OR	PA	H	2B	3B	HR	BB	SO	HB	SH	AVG	OBP	SLG	OPS	AOPS	BR	ABR	PF	SB	CS	BSA	BSR
Bro	98	55	1	.641	—	**56**	21	**857**	**650**	6037	1406	**230**	44	**201**	**674**	718	**41**	75	**.271**	**.356**	**.448**	**804**	**115**	**147**	**124**	103	**79**	56	59	-2
Mil	85	69	0	.552	13.5	46	31	743	668	5920	1377	219	55	182	504	735	28	72	.261	.326	.427	753	109	26	64	95	42	27	61	0
NY	80	74	0	.519	18.5	44	35	702	673	5940	1377	173	34	169	497	**581**	36	69	.260	.325	.402	727	97	-17	-18	100	38	22	**63**	**1**
Phi	77	77	0	.500	21.5	46	31	675	666	5864	1300	214	50	132	652	673	24	53	.255	.340	.395	735	102	16	29	98	44	32	58	-2
Cin	75	79	0	.487	23.5	46	31	761	684	5978	**1424**	216	28	181	556	657	33	76	.270	.341	.425	766	102	65	23	106	51	36	59	-1
Chi	72	81	1	.471	26	43	33	626	713	5766	1287	187	55	164	428	806	22	69	.247	.305	.398	703	90	-79	-77	100	37	35	51	-4
StL	68	86	0	.442	30.5	41	36	654	757	5855	1375	228	36	143	458	597	31	56	.261	.321	.400	721	95	-30	-29	100	64	59	52	-7
Pit	60	94	0	.390	38.5	36	39	560	767	5790	1262	210	**60**	91	471	652	21	**93**	.244	.308	.361	669	83	-129	-121	99	22	22	50	-3
Total	616	—	—	—	—	358	257	5578	—	47150	10808	1677	362	1263	4240	5419	236	563	.259	.328	.407	735	—	—	—	—	377	289	57	-18

TEAM	CG	SHO	GR	SV	IP	H	HR	BB	SO	BR/9	ERA	AERA	OAV	OOB	PR	APR	PF	OSB	OCS	FA	E	WPB	DP	FW	PW	BW	BSW	DIF
Bro	46	11	209	**37**	1378.0	1296	168	483	**773**	**11.7**	**3.68**	**110**	**.248**	**.313**	**54**	**58**	101	**36**	24	.978	133	40	156	.5	**5.8**	**12.3**	.0	2.9
Mil	**61**	5	203	12	1383.0	1339	**138**	591	654	12.7	3.85	98	.256	.331	29	-15	93	38	45	.975	152	40	155	-.6	-1.5	6.4	.2	3.5
NY	52	6	246	14	1386.2	1347	155	560	721	12.7	3.77	107	.257	.332	41	39	100	42	37	.976	142	42	165	.0	3.9	-1.8	**.3**	.6
Phi	58	11	193	21	1356.2	**1291**	161	477	657	11.9	3.93	101	.251	.315	17	6	98	43	29	**.981**	**110**	46	117	**1.8**	.6	2.9	.0	-5.3
Cin	38	**12**	245	22	1363.0	1373	161	**443**	576	12.1	3.95	107	.264	.322	13	41	105	37	28	.977	139	**38**	169	.2	4.1	2.3	.1	-8.6
Chi	47	10	209	23	1378.1	1306	153	601	686	12.6	4.17	98	.251	.330	-21	-13	101	73	42	.975	147	52	147	-.3	-1.3	-7.6	-.2	4.9
StL	42	10	**274**	15	1376.2	1376	185	549	730	12.9	4.56	89	.262	.334	-80	-76	101	42	35	.975	146	45	152	-.2	-7.5	-2.9	-.5	2.1
Pit	41	5	199	16	1362.0	1480	142	536	622	13.5	4.39	94	.281	.347	-54	-41	102	66	**49**	.972	166	49	**175**	-1.4	-4.1	-12.0	-.0	.5
Total	385	70	1778	160	10984.1	—	—	—	—	12.5	4.04	—	.259	.328	—	—	—	—	—	.976	1135	352	1236	—	—	—	—	—

BATTER-FIELDER WINS	BATTING AVERAGE	ON-BASE PERCENTAGE	SLUGGING AVERAGE	ON-BASE PLUS SLUGGING	ADJUSTED OPS	ADJUSTED BATTER RUNS
Mays-NY 6.8	Ashburn-Phi .338	Ashburn-Phi .449	Mays-NY .659	Mays-NY 1059	Mays-NY 176	Mays-NY 61.6
Banks-Chi 5.1	Mays-NY .319	Snider-Bro .418	Snider-Bro .628	Snider-Bro 1046	Mathews-Mil 175	Mathews-Mil 57.8
Mathews-Mil 4.9	Musial-StL .319	Mathews-Mil .413	Mathews-Mil .601	Mathews-Mil 1014	Snider-Bro 169	Snider-Bro 57.0
Snider-Bro 4.5	Campanella-Bro .318	Musial-StL .408	Banks-Chi .596	Campanella-Bro 978	Musial-StL 156	Musial-StL 47.7
Musial-StL 4.5	Aaron-Mil .314	Mays-NY .400	Kluszewski-Cin .585	Musial-StL 974	Campanella-Bro 153	Ashburn-Phi 40.5

RUNS	HITS	DOUBLES	TRIPLES	HOME RUNS	TOTAL BASES	RUNS BATTED IN
Snider-Bro 126	Kluszewski-Cin 192	Logan-Mil 37	Mays-NY 13	Mays-NY 51	Mays-NY 382	Snider-Bro 136
Mays-NY 123	Aaron-Mil 189	Aaron-Mil 37	Long-Pit 13	Kluszewski-Cin 47	Kluszewski-Cin 358	Mays-NY 127
Post-Cin 116	Bell-Cin 188	Snider-Bro 34	Bruton-Mil 12	Banks-Chi 44	Banks-Chi 355	Ennis-Phi 120
Kluszewski-Cin 116	Post-Cin 186	Post-Cin 33	Clemente-Pit 11	Snider-Bro 42	Post-Cin 345	Banks-Chi 117
Gilliam-Bro 110		Ashburn-Phi 32		Mathews-Mil 41	Snider-Bro 338	Kluszewski-Cin 113

BASES ON BALLS	STOLEN BASES	BASE STEALING RUNS	FIELDING RUNS-INFIELD	FIELDING RUNS-OUTFIELD	OUTFIELD ASSISTS	CATCHER CS PCT.
Mathews-Mil 109	Bruton-Mil 25	Mays-NY 3.9	McMillan-Cin 17.9	Mays-NY 11.7	Mays-NY 23	Crandall-Mil 53.7
Ashburn-Phi 105	Mays-NY 24	Temple-Cin 2.8	Groat-Pit 16.7	Clemente-Pit 10.8	Clemente-Pit 18	Sarni-StL 45.5
Snider-Bro 104	Boyer-StL 22	Bruton-Mil 1.7	O'Connell-Mil 14.3	Bruton-Mil 8.7	Bruton-Mil 17	Katt-NY 44.7
Thompson-NY 84	Temple-Cin 19	Robinson-Bro 1.6	Robinson-Bro 11.0	King-Chi 6.5	Post-Cin 13	Shepard-Pit 40.8
	Gilliam-Bro 15	Blaylock-Phi 1.0	Musial-StL 8.3	Greengrass-Cin-Phi 5.8		Campanella-Bro 40.4

WINS	WINNING PCT.	WINS ABOVE TEAM	GAMES STARTED	COMPLETE GAMES	FEWEST HITS/GAME	FEWEST BB/GAME
Roberts-Phi 23	Newcombe-Bro .800	Newcombe-Bro 6.1	Roberts-Phi 38	Roberts-Phi 26	Jones-Chi 6.52	Newcombe-Bro 1.46
Newcombe-Bro 20	Roberts-Phi .622	Roberts-Phi 5.5	Jones-Chi 34	Newcombe-Bro 17	Buhl-Mil 7.50	Roberts-Phi 1.56
Spahn-Mil 17	Nuxhall-Cin .586	Friend-Pit 4.6	Antonelli-NY 34	Spahn-Mil 16	Rush-Chi 7.85	Hacker-Chi 1.82
Nuxhall-Cin 17	Spahn-Mil .548	Nuxhall-Cin 3.3			Antonelli-NY 7.88	Friend-Pit 2.34
		Bessent-Bro 3.2			Dickson-Phi 7.92	Spahn-Mil 2.38

STRIKEOUTS	STRIKEOUTS/GAME	GAMES	SAVES	BASE RUNNERS/9	ADJUSTED RELIEF RUNS	RELIEF RANKING
Jones-Chi 198	Jones-Chi 7.37	Labine-Bro 60	Meyer-Phi 16	Rogovin-Phi 9.49	Freeman-Cin 17.7	Freeman-Cin 23.9
Roberts-Phi 160	Haddix-StL 6.49	Wilhelm-NY 59	Roebuck-Bro 12	Newcombe-Bro 10.05	Miller-Phi 16.3	Miller-Phi 20.0
Haddix-StL 150	Podres-Bro 6.44	LaPalme-StL 56	Labine-Bro 11	Crone-Mil 10.20	Labine-Bro 12.6	Labine-Bro 16.3
Newcombe-Bro 143	Conley-Mil 6.09	Grissom-NY 55	Freeman-Cin 11	Bessent-Bro 10.23	Bessent-Bro 10.8	Bessent-Bro 14.9
Antonelli-NY 143	Newcombe-Bro 5.51	Freeman-Cin 52	Grissom-NY 8	Roberts-Phi 10.24	LaPalme-StL 10.7	Jeffcoat-Chi 11.8

INNINGS PITCHED	OPPONENTS' AVG.	OPPONENTS' OBP	EARNED RUN AVERAGE	ADJUSTED ERA	ADJUSTED STARTER RUNS	PITCHER WINS
Roberts-Phi 305.0	Jones-Chi .206	Newcombe-Bro .279	Friend-Pit 2.83	Friend-Pit 145	Friend-Pit 24.9	**Newcombe-Bro 4.0**
Nuxhall-Cin 257.0	Buhl-Mil .227	Roberts-Phi .279	Newcombe-Bro 3.20	Newcombe-Bro 127	Nuxhall-Cin 23.1	**Roberts-Phi 3.4**
Spahn-Mil 245.2	Rush-Chi .234	Hacker-Chi .282	Buhl-Mil 3.21	Nuxhall-Cin 122	Schmidt-StL 20.0	**Nuxhall-Cin 2.8**
Jones-Chi 241.2	Antonelli-NY .234	Friend-Pit .291	Spahn-Mil 3.26	Roberts-Phi 121	Newcombe-Bro 19.2	**Friend-Pit 2.7**
Antonelli-NY 235.1	Dickson-Phi .238	Rush-Chi .293	Roberts-Phi 3.28	Antonelli-NY 121	Roberts-Phi 18.4	**Freeman-Cin 2.5**

Is It Next Year Already?

There was no pennant race in 1955 as the Dodgers, 22-2 on May 10, cruised to an easy title over Milwaukee and New York. For the victorious Dodgers, Roy Campanella won his third MVP trophy, while 19-year-old lefty Sandy Koufax made his major league debut for his hometown team. Brooklyn's pitching was superb, especially considering the bandbox that was Ebbets Field.

The league saw another all-time high in homers in 1955; this was the only season until 1999 in which teams hit more than one per game. The uppercut era was in full "swing"—strikeouts rose and did so until 1960. Philadelphia's Robin Roberts illustrated the era: for the fourth straight year he led the NL in wins and also allowed a major league record 41 homers.

The Cardinals finished seventh but showcased promising youngsters Ken Boyer and Lindy McDaniel. Phil Cavaretta and Ralph Kiner ended their storied careers. Attendance fell for the seventh straight year in Pittsburgh, but the Pirates added rookie outfielder Roberto Clemente. And as a new icon came to Steeltown, a past one left: the beloved Honus Wagner died at age 81.

The 1955 World Series offered a surprise ending for people who had become accustomed to the Yankees-Dodgers plots of 1941, '47, '49, '52, and '53. It started familiarly with the Yankees winning the first two games at home, just as they had done when the teams last met. Brooklyn, though, came back to take the next three at home, blowing apart New York pitching. For Game 6 Dodgers manager Walter Alston used his sixth starting pitcher of the series, but Karl Spooner didn't finish the first as the Yankees won, 5-1.

The Dodgers, who had twice lost seventh games to the Yanks in the past, sent Johnny Podres against Whitey Ford in the finale. Gil Hodges drove in runs in the fourth and sixth, and Sandy Amoros' great running catch snuffed out a sixth-inning Yankees rally. Podres went all the way for the 2-0 win that finally brought "next year" to Flatbush.

1955 AMERICAN LEAGUE

TEAM	W	L	T	PCT	GB	HW	HL	R	OR	PA	H	2B	3B	HR	BB	SO	HB	SH	AVG	OBP	SLG	OPS	AOPS	BR	ABR	PF	SB	CS	BSA	BSR
NY	96	58	0	.623	—	**52**	25	762	569	5944	1342	179	**55**	**175**	609	658	46	79	.260	.340	**.418**	**758**	**112**	70	**82**	98	55	25	69	3
Cle	93	61	0	.604	3	49	28	698	601	6050	1325	195	31	148	**723**	715	35	87	.257	.349	.394	743	102	63	36	104	28	24	54	-2
Chi	91	63	1	.591	5	49	28	725	**557**	5999	1401	204	36	116	567	595	**58**	**111**	**.268**	.344	.388	732	100	32	12	103	**69**	45	61	-1
Bos	84	70	0	.545	12	47	31	755	652	6131	1392	**241**	39	137	707	733	29	69	.264	**.351**	.402	753	100	**83**	18	109	43	17	**72**	**4**
Det	79	75	0	.513	17	46	31	**775**	658	6073	**1407**	211	38	130	641	**583**	21	71	.266	.345	.394	739	107	48	66	98	41	22	65	1
KC	63	91	1	.409	33	33	43	638	911	5916	1395	189	46	121	463	725	26	58	.261	.322	.382	704	94	-44	-51	101	22	36	38	-8
Bal	57	97	2	.370	39	30	47	540	754	5933	1263	177	39	54	560	742	19	70	.240	.314	.320	634	83	-162	-123	93	34	46	43	-9
Was	53	101	0	.344	43	28	49	598	789	5833	1277	178	54	80	538	654	36	79	.248	.322	.351	673	92	-89	-56	95	25	32	44	-6
Total	618	—	—	—	—	334	282	5491	—	47879	10802	1574	338	961	4808	5405	270	624	.258	.336	.381	717	—	—	—	—	317	247	56	-17

TEAM	CG	SHO	GR	SV	IP	H	HR	BB	SO	BR/9	ERA	AERA	OAV	OOB	PR	APR	PF	OSB	OCS	FA	E	WPB	DP	FW	PW	BW	BSW	DIF
NY	52	19	190	33	1372.1	**1163**	108	688	731	12.3	**3.23**	116	**.232**	.326	**111**	82	95	**27**	25	.978	128	31	**180**	.5	8.2	**8.2**	.5	1.6
Cle	45	15	215	**36**	1386.1	1285	111	558	**877**	12.1	3.39	**118**	.245	.319	88	**92**	101	36	28	**.981**	**108**	48	152	**1.7**	**9.2**	3.6	.0	1.5
Chi	55	**20**	202	23	1378.0	1301	111	**497**	720	**11.9**	3.37	117	.251	**.317**	90	89	100	30	23	**.981**	111	**25**	147	1.5	8.9	1.2	.1	2.2
Bos	44	9	187	34	1384.1	1333	128	582	674	12.7	3.72	115	.253	.329	37	81	108	47	34	.977	136	34	140	.0	8.1	1.8	**.6**	-3.5
Det	**66**	16	185	12	1380.1	1381	126	517	629	12.6	3.79	101	.261	.328	26	8	97	40	36	.976	139	38	159	-.2	.8	6.6	.3	-5.6
KC	29	9	**255**	23	1382.0	1486	175	707	572	14.6	5.35	78	.278	.363	-214	-172	105	36	23	.976	146	50	174	-.5	-17.2	-5.1	-.6	9.5
Bal	35	10	235	22	1388.2	1403	103	625	595	13.4	4.21	91	.266	.344	-39	-64	96	53	38	.972	167	64	159	-1.7	-6.4	-12.3	-.7	1.1
Was	37	10	229	16	1354.2	1450	**99**	634	607	14.2	4.62	83	.279	.359	-100	-124	97	48	**40**	.974	154	45	170	-1.0	-12.4	-5.6	-.4	-4.5
Total	363	108	1698	199	11026.2	—	—	—	—	13.0	3.96	—	.258	.336	—	—	—	—	—	.977	1089	335	1281	—	—	—	—	—

BATTER-FIELDER WINS	BATTING AVERAGE	ON-BASE PERCENTAGE	SLUGGING AVERAGE	ON-BASE PLUS SLUGGING	ADJUSTED OPS	ADJUSTED BATTER RUNS
Mantle-NY 5.5	Kaline-Det .340	Mantle-NY .431	Mantle-NY .611	Mantle-NY 1042	Mantle-NY 181	Mantle-NY 62.2
Kaline-Det 4.9	Power-KC .319	Kaline-Det .421	Kaline-Det .546	Kaline-Det .967	Kaline-Det 163	Kaline-Det 53.6
Fox-Chi 4.4	Kell-Chi .312	Smith-Cle .407	Zernial-KC .508	Smith-Cle .880	Sievers-Was 136	Williams-Bos 52.2
Williams-Bos 4.3	Fox-Chi .311	Yost-Was .407	Doby-Cle .505	Doby-Cle .874	Vernon-Was 133	Smith-Cle 31.6
McDougald-NY 3.7	Kuenn-Det .306	Goodman-Bos .394	Power-KC .505	Power-KC .859	Smith-Cle 132	Vernon-Was 25.7
RUNS	**HITS**	**DOUBLES**	**TRIPLES**	**HOME RUNS**	**TOTAL BASES**	**RUNS BATTED IN**
Smith-Cle 123	Kaline-Det 200	Kuenn-Det 38	Mantle-NY 11	Mantle-NY 37	Kaline-Det 321	Jensen-Bos 116
Mantle-NY 121	Fox-Chi 198	Power-KC 34	Carey-NY 11	Zernial-KC 30	Mantle-NY 316	Boone-Det 116
Kaline-Det 121	Power-KC 190	Goodman-Bos 31	Power-KC 10	Williams-Bos 28	Power-KC 301	Berra-NY 108
Tuttle-Det 102	Kuenn-Det 190	White-Bos 30			Smith-Cle 287	Sievers-Was 106
Kuenn-Det 101	Smith-Cle 186	Finigan-KC 30			Jensen-Bos 275	Kaline-Det 102
BASES ON BALLS	**STOLEN BASES**	**BASE STEALING RUNS**	**FIELDING RUNS-INFIELD**	**FIELDING RUNS-OUTFIELD**	**OUTFIELD ASSISTS**	**CATCHER CS PCT.**
Mantle-NY 113	Rivera-Chi 25	Torgeson-Det 2.0	Fox-Chi 31.1	Rivera-Chi 11.4	Rivera-Chi 22	House-Det 48.8
Goodman-Bos 99	Minoso-Chi 19	Busby-Was-Chi 1.6	McDougald-NY 22.3	Minoso-Chi 5.6	Minoso-Chi 19	Berra-NY 46.8
Yost-Was 95	Jensen-Bos 16	Mantle-NY 1.4	Miranda-Bal 20.3	Zernial-KC 5.1	Kaline-Det 14	Lollar-Chi 45.5
Fain-Det-Cle 94	Busby-Was-Chi 12	Minoso-Chi 1.4	Power-KC 14.2	Bauer-NY 5.1	Bauer-NY 13	Smith-Bal 43.9
Smith-Cle 93	Smith-Cle 11	Klaus-Bos 1.3	Carey-NY 10.2	Tuttle-Det 4.8	Tuttle-Det 12	White-Bos 42.7
WINS	**WINNING PCT.**	**WINS ABOVE TEAM**	**GAMES STARTED**	**COMPLETE GAMES**	**FEWEST HITS/GAME**	**FEWEST BB/GAME**
F.Sullivan-Bos 18	Byrne-NY .762	Hoeft-Det 4.8	F.Sullivan-Bos 35	Ford-NY 18	Turley-NY 6.13	Gromek-Det 1.84
Lemon-Cle 18	Ford-NY .720	Byrne-NY 4.2	Turley-NY 34	Hoeft-Det 17	Score-Cle 6.26	Donovan-Chi 2.31
Ford-NY 18	Hoeft-Det .696	Narleski-Cle 3.8	Ford-NY 33		Ford-NY 6.67	Garcia-Cle 2.39
Wynn-Cle 17	Lemon-Cle .643	Ford-NY 3.6	Score-Cle 32		Pierce-Chi 7.09	Garver-Det 2.61
Turley-NY 17	Donovan-Chi .625	Kellner-KC 3.0	Garver-Det 32		Harshman-Chi 7.23	Porterfield-Was 2.73
STRIKEOUTS	**STRIKEOUTS/GAME**	**GAMES**	**SAVES**	**BASE RUNNERS/9**	**ADJUSTED RELIEF RUNS**	**RELIEF RANKING**
Score-Cle 245	Score-Cle 9.70	Narleski-Cle 60	Narleski-Cle 19	Kinder-Bos 9.85	Consuegra-Chi 17.5	Kinder-Bos 21.0
Turley-NY 210	Turley-NY 7.66	Mossi-Cle 57	Kinder-Bos 18	Consuegra-Chi 9.97	Kiely-Bos 14.1	Hurd-Bos 17.1
Pierce-Chi 157	Pierce-Chi 6.87	Gorman-KC 57	Gorman-KC 18	Pierce-Chi 10.02	Mossi-Cle 12.9	Consuegra-Chi 15.9
Ford-NY 137	Harshman-Chi 5.82	Dorish-Chi-Bal 48	Konstanty-NY 11	Ford-NY 10.71	Kinder-Bos 10.7	Konstanty-NY 13.7
Hoeft-Det 133	Hoeft-Det 5.44	Moore-Bal 46	Morgan-NY 10	Hoeft-Det 10.96	Dorish-Chi-Bal 10.1	Mossi-Cle 13.2
INNINGS PITCHED	**OPPONENTS' AVG.**	**OPPONENTS' OBP**	**EARNED RUN AVERAGE**	**ADJUSTED ERA**	**ADJUSTED STARTER RUNS**	**PITCHER WINS**
F.Sullivan-Bos 260.0	Turley-NY .193	Pierce-Chi .277	Pierce-Chi 1.97	Pierce-Chi 201	Pierce-Chi 44.7	**Pierce-Chi 5.3**
Ford-NY 253.2	Score-Cle .194	Ford-NY .296	Ford-NY 2.63	F.Sullivan-Bos 148	Ford-NY 34.4	**Ford-NY 3.4**
Turley-NY 246.2	Ford-NY .208	Hoeft-Det .296	Wynn-Cle 2.82	Ford-NY 143	F.Sullivan-Bos 33.9	**F.Sullivan-Bos 3.4**
Wilson-Bal 235.1	Pierce-Chi .213	Wilson-Bal .297	Score-Cle 2.85	Wynn-Cle 142	Wynn-Cle 28.4	**Wynn-Cle 3.3**
Lary-Det 235.0	Harshman-Chi .224	Wynn-Cle .304	F.Sullivan-Bos 2.91	Score-Cle 140	Score-Cle 27.6	**Hoeft-Det 2.7**

Pinstripe Changes

Cleveland, the Yankees, the White Sox, and the Red Sox were bunched together by late August. The standings changed almost hourly from August 25 to September 5. Boston and Chicago dropped out after Labor Day, but the Indians got hot and the Yankees hung tough. With the race in hand, Cleveland promptly lost five straight, including three to fifth-place Detroit while the New York swept Boston, starting a nine-game winning streak. The Yankees clinched on September 23.

The Yankees again had spectacular pitching, with seven men making 10 or more starts. Mickey Mantle was the league's top hitter. Injuries and age began to erode Cleveland's lineup and pitching staff, and the club didn't recover. As Yogi Berra won his third MVP, his eventual successor, Elston Howard, was the Yankees' first African American player. Other rookies on the scene included Jim Bunning, Rocky Colavito, and 18-year-old Brooks Robinson. The most impressive freshman, Cleveland's fireballing Herb Score, set a record, fanning 9.70 hitters per game.

Boston first baseman Harry Agganis passed away on June 27 of a heart problem, sending the Hub into mourning. The great Cy Young, who threw the first pitch in the modern World Series as well as seemingly every other pitch from 1890–1911, died at 88. Three outstanding pitchers appeared in their final games: Hal Newhouser, Vic Raschi, and Johnny Sain.

Al Kaline of the Tigers became the youngest batting champion in history, while the sixth-place Athletics, in their first season in Kansas City, ranked second in attendance. Complete games fell by 100 to an all-time low, while saves rose to a new high; for the first time, the complete games leader, Whitey Ford, had fewer than 20.

Ford won Game 6 of the World Series with a nine-inning performance, but for the first time since 1942, the Yankees lost a Series. The Brooklyn Dodgers won their first title with a 2-0 Game 7 victory at Yankee Stadium.

1954 NATIONAL LEAGUE

TEAM	W	L	T	PCT	GB	HW	HL	R	OR	PA	H	2B	3B	HR	BB	SO	HB	SH	AVG	OBP	SLG	OPS	AOPS	BR	ABR	PF	SB	CS	BSA	BSR
NY	97	57	0	.630	—	**53**	23	732	**550**	5936	1386	194	42	**186**	522	**561**	33	84	.264	.332	.424	756	101	15	11	101	30	23	57	-1
Bro	92	62	0	.597	5	45	32	778	740	6058	1418	246	56	**186**	**634**	625	**35**	79	.270	.349	**.444**	**793**	**109**	**103**	**78**	103	46	39	54	-4
Mil	89	65	0	.578	8	43	34	670	556	5921	1395	217	41	139	471	619	**35**	**110**	.265	.327	.401	728	102	-34	12	94	54	31	**64**	**1**
Phi	75	79	0	.487	22	39	39	659	614	5937	1384	243	**58**	102	604	620	10	84	.267	.341	.395	736	98	0	1	100	30	27	53	-3
Cin	74	80	0	.481	23	41	36	729	763	5972	1369	221	46	147	557	645	29	101	.262	.333	.406	739	95	-8	-27	103	47	30	61	0
StL	72	82	0	.468	25	33	44	**799**	790	6127	**1518**	**285**	**58**	119	582	586	30	44	**.281**	**.350**	.421	771	106	69	63	101	**63**	46	58	-2
Chi	64	90	0	.416	33	40	37	700	766	5965	1412	229	45	159	478	693	32	56	.263	.325	.412	737	96	-22	-29	101	46	31	60	-1
Pit	53	101	0	.344	44	31	46	557	845	5836	1260	181	57	76	566	737	25	99	.248	.323	.350	673	82	-122	-113	99	21	13	62	0
Total	616	—	—	—	—	325	291	5624	—	47752	11142	1816	403	1114	4414	5086	229	657	.265	.335	.407	742	—	—	—	—	337	240	58	-10

TEAM	CG	SHO	GR	SV	IP	H	HR	BB	SO	BR/9	ERA	AERA	OAV	OOB	PR	APR	PF	OSB	OCS	FA	E	WPB	DP	FW	PW	BW	BSW	DIF
NY	45	**19**	235	33	1390.0	**1258**	113	613	692	12.3	**3.09**	**130**	**.243**	.326	**151**	**147**	99	29	31	.975	154	38	172	-.5	**14.6**	1.1	.0	4.9
Bro	39	8	231	**36**	1393.2	1399	164	533	**762**	12.6	4.31	95	.261	.328	-36	-34	100	28	29	.978	129	32	138	.8	-3.4	**7.7**	-.3	10.1
Mil	63	13	193	21	1394.2	1296	**106**	553	698	12.1	3.19	117	.250	.323	137	91	92	42	32	**.981**	**116**	33	171	**1.5**	9.0	1.2	**.2**	.0
Phi	**78**	14	139	12	1365.1	1329	133	**450**	570	**11.8**	3.59	112	.256	**.315**	73	68	99	37	21	.975	145	**29**	133	-.0	6.7	.0	-.2	-8.6
Cin	34	8	235	27	1367.1	1491	169	547	537	13.6	4.50	93	.282	.351	-65	-45	103	**24**	31	.977	137	33	**194**	.4	-4.5	-2.7	.1	3.6
StL	40	11	**262**	18	1390.1	1484	170	535	680	13.4	4.50	91	.275	.343	-66	-59	101	27	24	.976	146	43	178	-.0	-5.8	6.2	-.0	-5.2
Chi	41	6	210	19	1374.1	1375	131	619	622	13.2	4.51	93	.264	.340	-66	-45	103	71	31	.974	154	49	164	-.5	-4.5	-2.9	.0	-5.2
Pit	37	4	195	15	1346.0	1510	128	564	525	14.0	4.92	85	.287	.354	-127	-106	103	79	**41**	.971	173	46	136	-1.6	-10.5	-11.2	.1	-.9
Total	377	83	1700	181	11021.2	—	—	—	—	12.9	4.07	—	.265	.335	—	—	—	—	—	.976	1154	303	1286	—	—	—	—	—

BATTER-FIELDER WINS	BATTING AVERAGE	ON-BASE PERCENTAGE	SLUGGING AVERAGE	ON-BASE PLUS SLUGGING	ADJUSTED OPS	ADJUSTED BATTER RUNS
Mays-NY 6.2	Mays-NY..............345	Ashburn-Phi.........441	Mays-NY..............667	Mays-NY............1078	Mathews-Mil 177	Snider-Bro 61.5
Mathews-Mil....... 5.4	Mueller-NY...........342	Musial-StL............428	Snider-Bro 647	Snider-Bro 1071	Mays-NY...............176	Mays-NY.............61.4
Musial-StL 4.7	Snider-Bro 341	Snider-Bro 423	Kluszewski-Cin 642	Kluszewski-Cin ...1049	Snider-Bro 170	Musial-StL...........61.4
Schoendienst-StL ... 4.5	Musial-StL............330	Mathews-Mil 423	Musial-StL............607	Musial-StL..........1036	Musial-StL............166	Mathews-Mil 58.3
Snider-Bro 4.3	Kluszewski-Cin 326	Mays-NY..............411	Mathews-Mil 603	Mathews-Mil 1026	Kluszewski-Cin 165	Kluszewski-Cin 54.3
RUNS	**HITS**	**DOUBLES**	**TRIPLES**	**HOME RUNS**	**TOTAL BASES**	**RUNS BATTED IN**
Snider-Bro 120	Mueller-NY...........212	Musial-StL.............41	Mays-NY.................13	Kluszewski-Cin 49	Snider-Bro 378	Kluszewski-Cin 141
Musial-StL............120	Snider-Bro 199	Snider-Bro 39	Hamner-Phi 11	Hodges-Bro 42	Mays-NY..............377	Snider-Bro 130
Mays-NY..............119	Musial-StL............195	Repulski-StL 39	Snider-Bro 10	Sauer-Chi 41	Kluszewski-Cin 368	Hodges-Bro 130
Ashburn-Phi..........111	Mays-NY..............195	Hamner-Phi 39		Mays-NY................41	Musial-StL............359	Musial-StL............126
Gilliam-Bro...........107	Moon-StL 193				Hodges-Bro 335	Ennis-Phi 119
BASES ON BALLS	**STOLEN BASES**	**BASE STEALING RUNS**	**FIELDING RUNS-INFIELD**	**FIELDING RUNS-OUTFIELD**	**OUTFIELD ASSISTS**	**CATCHER CS PCT.**
Ashburn-Phi.........125	Bruton-Mil 34	Bruton-Mil 2.9	Schoendienst-StL 27.7	Ashburn-Phi.........13.2	Thomas-Pit.............14	Seminick-Cin 58.6
Mathews-Mil 113	Temple-Cin 21	Fondy-Chi 2.7	Grammas-StL 22.2	Mays-NY.................9.5	Mueller-NY.............14	Westrum-NY 55.9
Musial-StL............103	Fondy-Chi 20	Temple-Cin 2.2	Logan-Mil............12.6	Thomas-Pit 7.2	Bruton-Mil 14	Campanella-Bro...52.4
Thompson-NY 90	Moon-StL 18	Torgeson-Phi 1.2	Fondy-Chi 8.4	Furillo-Bro..............4.0		Katt-NY 47.6
Reese-Bro 90	Ashburn-Phi............11	Mathews-Mil 1.1	Hodges-Bro 6.8	Gordon-Pit 3.1		Crandall-Mil 45.3
WINS	**WINNING PCT.**	**WINS ABOVE TEAM**	**GAMES STARTED**	**COMPLETE GAMES**	**FEWEST HITS/GAME**	**FEWEST BB/GAME**
Roberts-Phi 23	Antonelli-NY..........750	Roberts-Phi 5.4	Roberts-Phi 38	Roberts-Phi 29	Antonelli-NY.........7.27	Roberts-Phi 1.50
Spahn-Mil 21	Lawrence-StL 714	Lawrence-StL 5.3	Erskine-Bro.............37	Spahn-Mil 23	Roberts-Phi 7.73	Minner-Chi...........2.06
Antonelli-NY............21	Gomez-NY............654	Antonelli-NY...........5.2	Antonelli-NY............37	Simmons-Phi 21	Conley-Mil............7.92	Hacker-Chi............2.10
Haddix-StL..............18	Spahn-Mil 636	Nuxhall-Cin 3.9	Haddix-StL..............35	Antonelli-NY............18	Lawrence-StL 8.00	Burdette-Mil 2.34
Erskine-Bro.............18	Roberts-Phi 605	Haddix-StL.............3.9	Spahn-Mil 34		Wehmeier-Cin-Phi...8.02	Meyer-Bro............2.45
STRIKEOUTS	**STRIKEOUTS/GAME**	**GAMES**	**SAVES**	**BASE RUNNERS/9**	**ADJUSTED RELIEF RUNS**	**RELIEF RANKING**
Roberts-Phi 185	Haddix-StL..........6.38	Hughes-Bro 60	Hughes-Bro 24	Roberts-Phi 9.36	Wilhelm-NY..........23.2	Grissom-NY.........36.8
Haddix-StL............184	Erskine-Bro.........5.74	Hetki-Pit.................58	Smith-Cin................20	Johnson-Mil 10.15	Grissom-NY 23.0	Wilhelm-NY..........33.3
Erskine-Bro...........166	Littlefield-Pit.........5.34	Brazle-StL...............58	Grissom-NY............19	Smith-Cin...........10.22	Jolly-Mil...............16.5	Jolly-Mil...............26.0
Antonelli-NY..........152	Antonelli-NY.........5.29	Wilhelm-NY.............57	Jolly-Mil..................10	Poholsky-StL......10.61	Smith-Cin.............12.4	Smith-Cin.............24.8
Spahn-Mil 136	Conley-Mil...........5.23	Grissom-NY............56	Hetki-Pit....................9	Antonelli-NY.......10.72	Johnson-Mil 11.5	Hughes-Bro 14.2
INNINGS PITCHED	**OPPONENTS' AVG.**	**OPPONENTS' OBP**	**EARNED RUN AVERAGE**	**ADJUSTED ERA**	**ADJUSTED STARTER RUNS**	**PITCHER WINS**
Roberts-Phi 336.2	Antonelli-NY..........219	Roberts-Phi 266	Antonelli-NY.........2.30	Antonelli-NY..........176	Antonelli-NY.........49.5	**Antonelli-NY....... 5.3**
Spahn-Mil 283.1	Roberts-Phi 231	Antonelli-NY..........292	Burdette-Mil 2.76	Simmons-Phi 144	Roberts-Phi 44.5	**Roberts-Phi....... 4.3**
Erskine-Bro........260.1	Simmons-Phi 239	Hacker-Chi............299	Simmons-Phi 2.81	Gomez-NY............140	Simmons-Phi 29.5	**Grissom-NY....... 3.7**
Haddix-StL..........259.2	Littlefield-Pit..........239	Spahn-Mil 300	Gomez-NY............2.88	Roberts-Phi 136	Gomez-NY............27.2	**Wilhelm-NY 3.2**
Antonelli-NY.......258.2	Wehmeier-Cin-Phi....239	Burdette-Mil 300	Conley-Mil............2.96	Burdette-Mil 135	Burdette-Mil 25.6	**Spahn-Mil 3.2**

New York Life

Prior to the season, the Braves traded young hurler Johnny Antonelli to the Giants for outfielder Bobby Thomson. While Thomson broke his leg in spring training and played just 43 games, Antonelli broke out for New York, winning 21 and pacing the NL in ERA. With Willie Mays back from the army and winning MVP honors with his first great season, the Giants didn't miss Thomson. Pulling away from Brooklyn with superb pitching and the league's best home run offense, the Giants won their last pennant in New York. Thomson's injury did help Milwaukee, however. When the veteran went down, manager Charlie Grimm filled the gap with rookie Hank Aaron.

Attendance rose another 8 percent as the third-place Braves were the first NL team ever to draw two million. The game became a little less homespun in 1954, as players were no longer allowed to leave their gloves on the field. In addition, the use of relief pitching continued to gain steam as complete games fell sharply to an all-time low of 377.

After trading slugger Ralph Kiner, the Pirates removed the temporary fencing in left field, restoring Forbes Field to its larger dimensions. It didn't help the team, which again finished last, but Pittsburgh was beginning to rebuild.

In the World Series, the Giants blew away favored Cleveland in a four-game sweep. Three huge pinch hits by New York's Dusty Rhodes—one a three-run homer that won Game 1—provided the offensive difference. Willie Mays' catch of Vic Wertz' tremendous drive to center field in the opening game remains one of the great plays ever made in the postseason. The Giants effectively shut down the Indians' offense, allowing just 9 runs—and 4 of those runs came after New York had built a 7-0 lead in Game 4. The surprise win triggered a short period of NL dominance, as the Senior Circuit won five world titles in seven seasons.

1954 AMERICAN LEAGUE

TEAM	W	L	T	PCT	GB	HW	HL	R	OR	PA	H	2B	3B	HR	BB	SO	HB	SH	AVG	OBP	SLG	OPS	AOPS	BR	ABR	PF	SB	CS	BSA	BSR
Cle	111	43	2	.721	—	**59**	18	746	**504**	6048	1368	188	39	**156**	637	668	23	**107**	.262	.341	.403	744	108	77	65	102	30	33	48	-5
NY	103	51	1	.669	8	54	23	**805**	563	6027	1400	215	59	133	650	632	20	84	**.268**	**.348**	**.408**	**756**	**118**	**103**	**131**	97	34	41	45	-7
Chi	94	60	1	.610	17	45	32	711	521	5972	1382	203	47	94	604	**536**	**51**	96	.267	.347	.379	726	103	53	30	103	**98**	58	63	**1**
Bos	69	85	2	.448	42	38	39	700	728	6207	**1436**	**244**	41	123	**654**	660	23	78	.266	.345	.395	740	98	78	3	111	51	30	63	**1**
Det	68	86	1	.442	43	35	42	584	664	5865	1351	215	41	90	492	603	19	80	.258	.322	.367	689	97	-37	-25	98	48	44	52	-5
Was	66	88	1	.429	45	37	41	632	680	6005	1292	188	**69**	81	610	719	27	77	.246	.325	.355	680	97	-47	-12	95	37	21	**64**	**1**
Bal	54	100	0	.351	57	32	45	483	668	5838	1309	195	49	52	468	634	21	99	.251	.313	.338	651	91	-107	-64	93	30	31	49	-4
Phi	51	103	2	.331	60	29	47	542	875	5823	1228	191	41	94	504	677	28	54	.236	.305	.342	647	83	-119	-121	100	30	29	51	-4
Total	621	—	—	—	—	329	287	5203	—	47785	10766	1639	386	823	4619	5129	212	675	.257	.331	.373	704	—	—	—	—	358	287	56	-22

TEAM	CG	SHO	GR	SV	IP	H	HR	BB	SO	BR/9	ERA	AERA	OAV	OOB	PR	APR	PF	OSB	OCS	FA	E	WPB	DP	FW	PW	BW	BSW	DIF
Cle	**77**	12	160	36	1419.1	**1220**	89	**486**	678	**10.9**	**2.78**	**132**	**.232**	**.297**	**148**	**142**	99	43	35	.979	128	**19**	148	.7	**14.7**	6.7	-.2	12.1
NY	51	16	182	**37**	1379.1	1284	86	552	655	12.2	3.26	105	.251	.325	71	29	92	34	33	.979	126	27	**198**	.8	3.0	**13.5**	-.4	9.1
Chi	60	**23**	176	33	1383.0	1255	94	517	701	11.6	3.05	122	.244	.312	103	105	100	**32**	35	**.982**	**108**	27	149	**1.8**	10.8	3.1	**.4**	.9
Bos	41	10	**224**	22	1412.1	1434	118	612	**707**	13.3	4.01	102	.265	.341	-46	14	110	57	36	.972	176	37	163	-2.0	1.4	.3	**.4**	-8.2
Det	58	13	179	13	1383.0	1375	138	506	603	12.5	3.81	97	.261	.328	-13	-18	99	34	40	.978	129	**19**	131	.6	-1.9	-2.6	-.2	-4.9
Was	69	10	158	7	1383.1	1396	79	573	562	13.0	3.84	93	.265	.338	-18	-46	96	51	29	.977	137	33	172	.2	-4.8	-1.2	**.4**	-5.6
Bal	58	6	156	8	1373.1	1279	**78**	688	668	13.0	3.88	92	.250	.338	-24	-47	96	56	**46**	.975	147	32	152	-.4	-4.9	-6.6	-.1	-11.0
Phi	49	3	182	13	1371.1	1523	141	685	555	14.7	5.18	75	.285	.366	-222	-185	105	51	33	.972	169	52	163	-1.6	-19.1	-12.5	-.1	7.3
Total	463	93	1417	169	11105.0	—	—	—	—	12.6	3.72	—	.257	.331	—	—	—	—	—	.977	1120	246	1276	—	—	—	—	—

BATTER-FIELDER WINS	BATTING AVERAGE	ON-BASE PERCENTAGE	SLUGGING AVERAGE	ON-BASE PLUS SLUGGING	ADJUSTED OPS	ADJUSTED BATTER RUNS
Williams-Bos......5.1	Avila-Cle..............341	Williams-Bos.........513	Minoso-Chi...........535	Williams-Bos.......1148	Williams-Bos.........193	Williams-Bos........60.7
Avila-Cle............4.8	Minoso-Chi............320	Minoso-Chi............411	Mantle-NY.............525	Minoso-Chi............946	Mantle-NY.............160	Mantle-NY..........46.9
Berra-NY............4.4	Noren-NY.............319	Mantle-NY.............408	Rosen-Cle...............506	Mantle-NY.............933	Minoso-Chi...........154	Minoso-Chi..........43.5
Minoso-Chi.........4.1	Fox-Chi..................319	Yost-Was...............405	Vernon-Was...........492	Rosen-Cle..............910	Rosen-Cle.............148	Rosen-Cle............33.6
Mantle-NY...........3.8	Berra-NY...............307	Rosen-Cle..............404	Berra-NY................488	Avila-Cle................880	Noren-NY..............140	Avila-Cle.............30.5

RUNS	HITS	DOUBLES	TRIPLES	HOME RUNS	TOTAL BASES	RUNS BATTED IN
Mantle-NY............129	Kuenn-Det............201	Vernon-Was............33	Minoso-Chi.............18	Doby-Cle..................32	Minoso-Chi...........304	Doby-Cle...............126
Minoso-Chi...........119	Fox-Chi..................201	Smith-Cle................29	Runnels-Was...........15	Williams-Bos...........29	Vernon-Was...........294	Berra-NY...............125
Avila-Cle...............112	Avila-Cle...............189	Minoso-Chi..............29	Vernon-Was.............14	Mantle-NY................27	Mantle-NY.............285	Jensen-Bos.............117
Fox-Chi..................111	Busby-Was............187		Mantle-NY...............12	Jensen-Bos..............25	Berra-NY...............285	Minoso-Chi...........116
Carrasquel-Chi.....106	Minoso-Chi...........182		Tuttle-Det................11		Doby-Cle...............279	

BASES ON BALLS	STOLEN BASES	BASE STEALING RUNS	FIELDING RUNS-INFIELD	FIELDING RUNS-OUTFIELD	OUTFIELD ASSISTS	CATCHER CS PCT.
Williams-Bos.........136	Jensen-Bos.............22	Busby-Was............3.0	Coleman-NY.........14.6	Diering-Bal.............9.8	Mantle-NY...............20	House-Det...........55.3
Yost-Was...............131	Rivera-Chi...............18	Jacobs-Phi.............2.7	Carrasquel-Chi.....13.2	Power-Phi...............8.0	Tuttle-Det...............18	Lollar-Chi.............51.4
Mantle-NY.............102	Minoso-Chi..............18	Jensen-Bos............2.4	Carey-NY.............12.5	Kaline-Det..............7.3	Diering-Bal.............17	Courtney-Bal.......44.3
Smith-Cle................88	Jacobs-Phi...............17	Cavarretta-Chi..........9	McDougald-NY......10.2	Sievers-Was...........7.2	Kaline-Det...............16	Hegan-Cle............44.3
	Busby-Was..............17	Michaels-Chi.............8	Terwilliger-Was.....10.0	Renna-Phi...............6.1		White-Bos............40.0

WINS	WINNING PCT.	WINS ABOVE TEAM	GAMES STARTED	COMPLETE GAMES	FEWEST HITS/GAME	FEWEST BB/GAME
Wynn-Cle................23	Consuegra-Chi.....842	Consuegra-Chi......5.9	Wynn-Cle................36	Porterfield-Was.......21	Turley-Bal.............6.48	Lopat-NY...............1.75
Lemon-Cle..............23	Grim-NY.................769	Grim-NY..................4.5	Turley-Bal................35	Lemon-Cle..............21	Ford-NY...............7.26	Gromek-Det.........2.03
Grim-NY..................20	Lemon-Cle.............767	Turley-Bal...............3.5	Garcia-Cle..............34	Wynn-Cle................20	Wynn-Cle.............7.48	Garver-Det...........2.27
Trucks-Chi..............19	Garcia-Cle............704	Gromek-Det............3.3		Gromek-Det............17	Coleman-Bal.........7.48	Garcia-Cle............2.47
Garcia-Cle..............19	Houtteman-Cle.....682	Sullivan-Bos...........3.1			Reynolds-NY........7.61	Zuverink-Det........2.75

STRIKEOUTS	STRIKEOUTS/GAME	GAMES	SAVES	BASE RUNNERS/9	ADJUSTED RELIEF RUNS	RELIEF RANKING
Turley-Bal.............185	Pierce-Chi............7.06	Dixon-Was-Phi........54	Sain-NY...................22	Mossi-Cle..............9.29	Mossi-Cle..............18.6	Mossi-Cle.............15.8
Wynn-Cle...............155	Harshman-Chi.....6.81	Martin-Phi-Chi.........48	Kinder-Bos..............15	Sain-NY.................9.47	Narleski-Cle.........14.6	Narleski-Cle..........13.7
Trucks-Chi.............152	Turley-Bal............6.73	Pascual-Was...........48	Narleski-Cle............13	Dorish-Chi.............9.74	Dorish-Chi.............12.9	Dorish-Chi............12.3
Pierce-Chi..............148	Hoeft-Det..............5.86	Kinder-Bos..............48		Garcia-Cle..........10.19	Miller-Det...............8.1	Kinder-Bos............10.6
Harshman-Chi......134	Reynolds-NY.......5.72			Wynn-Cle............10.24	Kinder-Bos..............6.4	Sain-NY..................8.5

INNINGS PITCHED	OPPONENTS' AVG.	OPPONENTS' OBP	EARNED RUN AVERAGE	ADJUSTED ERA	ADJUSTED STARTER RUNS	PITCHER WINS
Wynn-Cle...........270.2	Turley-Bal.............203	Garcia-Cle............282	Garcia-Cle...........2.64	Garcia-Cle............139	Garcia-Cle...........31.0	**Gromek-Det.........3.7**
Trucks-Chi.........264.2	Wynn-Cle..............225	Wynn-Cle..............283	Lemon-Cle...........2.72	Lemon-Cle............135	Trucks-Chi............29.6	**Lemon-Cle...........3.7**
Garcia-Cle.........258.2	Ford-NY................227	Garver-Det............286	Wynn-Cle.............2.73	Wynn-Cle..............135	Wynn-Cle..............29.4	**Wynn-Cle............3.6**
Lemon-Cle.........258.1	Trucks-Chi............228	Gromek-Det..........294	Gromek-Det.........2.74	Gromek-Det..........135	Gromek-Det.........28.0	**Trucks-Chi...........3.3**
Gromek-Det.......252.2	Garcia-Cle............229	Trucks-Chi.............296	Trucks-Chi...........2.79	Trucks-Chi............134	Lemon-Cle...........25.4	**Garcia-Cle...........3.0**

Tribal Gathering

The Indians, bridesmaids three straight times, stormed the altar in 1954. By July Cleveland, New York, and Chicago were the only three contenders. The Tribe would not be denied, pulling away in August and leaving two very good clubs in the dust. Cleveland allowed fewer runs than any full-season AL team since 1917. Featuring five top-flight right-handed starters, a lefty-righty relief duo, and a veteran southpaw middleman, the Indians had one of the greatest staffs ever. And the offense wasn't shoddy, featuring Al Rosen, Larry Doby, and batting champ Bobby Avila.

And Cleveland handily beat Casey Stengel's best team. The Yankees won 103 games and were the only major league team to score 800 runs, but they still lost by 8 games. Despite the Indians' victory, Yogi Berra won his second MVP award, and Mickey Mantle consolidated his position as the league's top center fielder.

The poor got poorer in 1954: there had not been a 60-game spread from first to last since 1939. Even in New York, winning was tired, as Yankees attendance declined each of the last six years. The league champion Indians' attendance was just half of the club's 1948 total.

White Sox third baseman Cass Michaels' career was ended by a beanball that fractured his skull, while Johnny Pesky played out the string in Washington. Thirty-nine-year-old Allie Reynolds retired after another excellent season in New York. The sixth-place Senators called on two rookies who make considerable impact in the coming years: pitcher Camilo Pascual and infielder Harmon Killebrew. In their first season in Baltimore, the Orioles finished seventh. Following the season, the Mack family sold the last-place A's to Arnold Johnson, who moved the club to Kansas City.

While Cleveland set league records for victories and winning percentage, they crumbled in the World Series. The New York Giants ripped apart Tribe pitching and snuffed out their powerful offense, winning in four straight. It was the most shocking sweep since the 1914 "Miracle" Braves.

1953 NATIONAL LEAGUE

TEAM	W	L	T	PCT	GB	HW	HL	R	OR	PA	H	2B	3B	HR	BB	SO	HB	SH	AVG	OBP	SLG	OPS	AOPS	BR	ABR	PF	SB	CS	BSA	BSR
Bro	105	49	1	.682	—	**60**	17	**955**	689	6138	**1529**	274	59	**208**	**655**	686	35	75	**.285**	**.366**	**.474**	**840**	**121**	**194**	**173**	102	**90**	47	66	**3**
Mil	92	62	3	.597	13	45	31	738	**589**	5895	1422	227	52	156	439	637	27	80	.266	.325	.415	740	104	-24	23	94	46	27	63	1
StL	83	71	3	.539	22	48	30	768	713	6065	1474	**281**	56	140	574	617	**39**	55	.273	.347	.424	771	107	58	59	100	18	22	45	-4
Phi	83	71	2	.539	22	48	29	716	666	5916	1400	228	**62**	115	530	**597**	29	67	.265	.335	.396	731	97	-25	-21	99	42	21	67	2
NY	70	84	1	.455	35	38	39	768	747	5956	1452	195	45	176	499	608	28	67	.271	.336	.422	758	101	18	5	102	31	21	60	-1
Cin	68	86	1	.442	37	38	39	714	788	5912	1396	190	34	166	485	701	16	68	.261	.325	.403	728	94	-45	-50	101	25	20	56	-1
Chi	65	89	1	.422	40	43	34	633	835	5873	1372	204	57	137	514	746	14	73	.260	.328	.399	727	93	-43	-58	102	49	21	**70**	**3**
Pit	50	104	0	.325	55	26	51	622	887	5902	1297	178	49	99	524	715	36	**89**	.247	.319	.356	675	82	-133	-129	99	41	39	51	-5
Total	622	—	—	—	—	346	270	5914	—	47657	11342	1777	414	1197	4220	5307	224	574	.266	.335	.411	747	—	—	—	—	342	218	61	-1

TEAM	CG	SHO	GR	SV	IP	H	HR	BB	SO	BR/9	ERA	AERA	OAV	OOB	PR	APR	PF	OSB	OCS	FA	E	WPB	DP	FW	PW	BW	BSW	DIF
Bro	51	11	212	29	1380.2	1337	169	509	**817**	12.1	4.10	104	.253	.320	29	25	99	**22**	25	**.980**	**118**	28	161	**1.7**	2.4	**16.7**	**.3**	7.0
Mil	72	**14**	159	15	1387.0	**1282**	**107**	539	738	**12.0**	**3.30**	**119**	**.245**	**.318**	**153**	**105**	92	48	33	.976	143	31	169	.4	**10.1**	2.2	.1	2.2
StL	51	11	234	**36**	1386.2	1406	139	533	732	12.9	4.23	101	.262	.333	9	5	99	53	29	.977	138	40	161	.7	.5	5.7	-.4	-.4
Phi	**76**	13	165	15	1369.2	1410	138	**410**	637	12.1	3.80	111	.265	.320	74	63	98	40	16	.975	147	33	161	.0	6.1	-2.0	.2	1.7
NY	46	10	217	20	1365.2	1403	146	610	647	13.4	4.25	101	.264	.343	5	6	100	33	30	.975	151	51	151	-.2	.6	.5	-.0	-7.8
Cin	47	7	202	15	1365.0	1484	179	488	506	13.2	4.64	94	.279	.343	-53	-42	102	35	18	.978	129	**24**	**176**	1.1	-4.0	-4.8	-.0	-1.1
Chi	38	3	**238**	22	1359.0	1491	151	554	623	13.8	4.79	93	.276	.347	-76	-49	104	47	**34**	.967	193	35	141	-2.5	-4.7	-5.6	**.3**	.5
Pit	49	4	211	10	1358.0	1529	168	577	607	14.1	5.22	86	.285	.356	-141	-108	104	64	33	.973	163	76	139	-.9	-10.4	-12.4	-.5	-2.8
Total	430	73	1638	162	10971.2	—	—	—	—	12.9	4.29	—	.266	.335	—	—	—	—	—	.975	1182	318	1259	—	—	—	—	—

BATTER-FIELDER WINS	BATTING AVERAGE	ON-BASE PERCENTAGE	SLUGGING AVERAGE	ON-BASE PLUS SLUGGING	ADJUSTED OPS	ADJUSTED BATTER RUNS
Schoendienst-StL ... 6.5	Furillo-Bro 344	Musial-StL 437	Snider-Bro 627	Snider-Bro 1046	Mathews-Mil 175	Musial-StL 65.6
Mathews-Mil ... 6.1	Schoendienst-StL .342	Robinson-Bro 425	Mathews-Mil 627	Musial-StL 1046	Musial-StL 169	Mathews-Mil 65.3
Campanella-Bro 5.0	Musial-StL 337	Snider-Bro 419	Campanella-Bro....611	Mathews-Mil 1033	Snider-Bro 165	Snider-Bro 57.8
Musial-StL ... 4.4	Snider-Bro 336	Irvin-NY 406	Musial-StL 609	Campanella-Bro..1006	Campanella-Bro....154	Campanella-Bro...41.2
Snider-Bro ... 3.9	Mueller-NY 333	Mathews-Mil 406	Furillo-Bro 580	Furillo-Bro 973	Furillo-Bro 146	Kluszewski-Cin 34.7
RUNS	**HITS**	**DOUBLES**	**TRIPLES**	**HOME RUNS**	**TOTAL BASES**	**RUNS BATTED IN**
Snider-Bro 132	Ashburn-Phi 205	Musial-StL 53	Gilliam-Bro 17	Mathews-Mil 47	Snider-Bro 370	Campanella-Bro....142
Musial-StL 127	Musial-StL 200	Dark-NY 41	Bruton-Mil 14	Snider-Bro 42	Mathews-Mil 363	Mathews-Mil 135
Dark-NY 126	Snider-Bro 198	Snider-Bro 38	Hemus-StL 11	Campanella-Bro....41	Musial-StL 361	Snider-Bro 126
Gilliam-Bro 125	Dark-NY 194	Furillo-Bro 38	Fondy-Chi 11	Kluszewski-Cin 40	Kluszewski-Cin 325	Ennis-Phi 125
	Schoendienst-StL .193	Bell-Cin 37		Kiner-Pit-Chi 35	Bell-Cin 320	Hodges-Bro 122
BASES ON BALLS	**STOLEN BASES**	**BASE STEALING RUNS**	**FIELDING RUNS-INFIELD**	**FIELDING RUNS-OUTFIELD**	**OUTFIELD ASSISTS**	**CATCHER CS PCT.**
Musial-StL 105	Bruton-Mil 26	Reese-Bro 2.7	Schoendienst-StL 28.6	Ashburn-Phi 17.7	Ashburn-Phi 18	Campanella-Bro...52.5
Kiner-Pit-Chi 100	Reese-Bro 22	Robinson-Bro 2.3	Logan-Mil 20.8	Thomas-Pit 6.4	Thomas-Pit 17	Crandall-Mil 44.8
Gilliam-Bro 100	Gilliam-Bro 21	Bruton-Mil 1.9	Bridges-Cin 13.8	Marshall-Cin 4.9	Thomson-NY 16	Garagiola-Pit-Chi 37.2
Mathews-Mil 99	Robinson-Bro 17	Miksis-Chi 1.5	McMillan-Cin 10.0	Jeffcoat-Chi 4.7	Bell-Cin 16	Seminick-Cin 35.1
Hemus-StL 86	Snider-Bro 16	Torgeson-Phi 1.2	Bilko-StL 9.2	Bell-Cin 4.6	Bruton-Mil 15	Lopata-Phi 34.6
WINS	**WINNING PCT.**	**WINS ABOVE TEAM**	**GAMES STARTED**	**COMPLETE GAMES**	**FEWEST HITS/GAME**	**FEWEST BB/GAME**
Spahn-Mil 23	Erskine-Bro 769	Spahn-Mil 7.1	Roberts-Phi 41	Roberts-Phi 33	Spahn-Mil 7.15	Roberts-Phi 1.58
Roberts-Phi 23	Spahn-Mil 767	Haddix-StL 5.4	Mizell-StL 33	Spahn-Mil 24	Gomez-NY 7.32	Raffensberger-Cin ...1.71
Haddix-StL 20	Meyer-Bro 750	Staley-StL 4.3	Haddix-StL 33	Simmons-Phi 19	Mizell-StL 7.74	Minner-Chi 1.79
Erskine-Bro 20	Burdette-Mil 750	Burdette-Mil 4.1	Erskine-Bro 33	Haddix-StL 19	Erskine-Bro 7.77	Staley-StL 2.11
Staley-StL 18	Haddix-StL 690	Baczewski-Chi-Cin.....4.1		Erskine-Bro 16	Haddix-StL 7.83	Hacker-Chi 2.19
STRIKEOUTS	**STRIKEOUTS/GAME**	**GAMES**	**SAVES**	**BASE RUNNERS/9**	**ADJUSTED RELIEF RUNS**	**RELIEF RANKING**
Roberts-Phi 198	Mizell-StL 6.94	Wilhelm-NY 68	Brazle-StL 18	Spahn-Mil 9.55	Wilhelm-NY 18.3	Labine-Bro 26.8
Erskine-Bro 187	Erskine-Bro 6.82	Brazle-StL 60	Wilhelm-NY 15	Labine-Bro 9.95	Labine-Bro 17.5	Wilhelm-NY 21.3
Mizell-StL 173	Antonelli-Mil 6.72	Hetki-Pit 54	Hughes-Bro 9	Roberts-Phi 10.05	White-StL 11.5	White-StL 15.6
Haddix-StL 163	Klippstein-Chi 6.07	Smith-Cin 50	Leonard-Chi 8	Milliken-Bro 10.40	Johnson-Mil 9.4	Hughes-Bro 8.8
Spahn-Mil 148	Haddix-StL 5.80		Burdette-Mil 8	Haddix-StL 10.42	Hughes-Bro 9.0	Johnson-Mil 7.3
INNINGS PITCHED	**OPPONENTS' AVG.**	**OPPONENTS' OBP**	**EARNED RUN AVERAGE**	**ADJUSTED ERA**	**ADJUSTED STARTER RUNS**	**PITCHER WINS**
Roberts-Phi 346.2	Spahn-Mil 217	Spahn-Mil 270	Spahn-Mil 2.10	Spahn-Mil 187	Roberts-Phi 58.5	**Spahn-Mil 7.0**
Spahn-Mil 265.2	Gomez-NY 218	Roberts-Phi 276	Roberts-Phi 2.75	Roberts-Phi 153	Spahn-Mil 57.3	**Roberts-Phi 6.4**
Haddix-StL 253.0	Mizell-StL 227	Haddix-StL 287	Haddix-StL 3.06	Haddix-StL 139	Haddix-StL 32.6	**Haddix-StL 4.5**
Erskine-Bro 246.2	Erskine-Bro 230	Hacker-Chi 299	Antonelli-Mil 3.18	Simmons-Phi 131	Simmons-Phi 25.0	**Labine-Bro 2.5**
Simmons-Phi 238.0	Haddix-StL 232	Simmons-Phi 302	Simmons-Phi 3.21	Gomez-NY 126	Gomez-NY 20.3	**Simmons-Phi 2.3**

Brooklyn Blast

The Dodgers became the NL's first repeat champions since 1944, winning a race that wasn't close after mid-July. With MVP winner Roy Campanella and yet another African American Rookie of the Year in Jim Gilliam, Brooklyn easily outclassed the surprising Braves. The Dodgers were the league's last 100-game winner until 1962. Brooklyn again led the world in runs, in both home and road games, while Milwaukee sported the league's best pitching. The Dodgers dominated at Ebbets Field with a .779 winning percentage. No NL team had compiled a better home record since 1902.

Boston's move to Milwaukee, and the team's sudden rise to contention, juiced up NL attendance; the Braves drew league record crowds, causing tickets sales to increase 17 percent although attendance fell in five other cities. Turnout in Milwaukee, when compared to Boston in '52, was up an absurd 549 percent.

The Braves added two more impressive rookies to the mix, outfielder Bill Bruton and pitcher Bob Buhl, while the Cubs debuted Ernie Banks and last-place Pittsburgh introduced Elroy Face. The Cardinals began a dry spell, due to poor pitching, as several of their great 1940s stars—Harry Brecheen, Marty Marion, and Johnny Mize—played their last games, all for other clubs. The Pirates lost youngsters Vern Law and Dick Groat to military service, while the Giants did without Willie Mays and the Dodgers lost Don Newcombe, as the Korean conflict took its toll.

Runs per game rose to 4.75, the highest of the 1950s, as league batters yet again set an all-time record for home runs. The league ERA leapt more than a half a run, with only Warren Spahn and Robin Roberts finishing under the 3.00 mark, and bullpen use continued to increase.

The World Series was a high-scoring affair, with New York and Brooklyn combining for 17 homers in six games. Predictably, the Yankees came out on top.

1953 AMERICAN LEAGUE

TEAM	W	L	T	PCT	GB	HW	HL	R	OR	PA	H	2B	3B	HR	BB	SO	HB	SH	AVG	OBP	SLG	OPS	AOPS	BR	ABR	PF	SB	CS	BSA	BSR
NY	99	52	0	.656	—	50	27	**801**	**547**	5961	1420	226	52	139	**656**	644	34	77	**.273**	**.359**	**.417**	**776**	**120**	**115**	**144**	97	34	44	44	-8
Cle	92	62	1	.597	8.5	**53**	24	770	627	6019	1426	201	29	**160**	609	683	35	90	.270	.349	.410	759	114	77	98	97	33	29	53	-3
Chi	89	65	2	.578	11.5	41	36	716	592	5987	1345	226	**53**	74	601	**530**	**54**	**120**	.258	.341	.364	705	93	-17	-37	103	**73**	55	57	-3
Bos	84	69	0	.549	16	38	38	656	632	5879	1385	255	37	101	496	601	38	99	.264	.332	.384	716	94	-9	-43	105	33	45	42	-8
Was	76	76	0	.500	23.5	39	36	687	614	5858	1354	230	**53**	69	596	604	31	82	.263	.343	.368	711	100	-5	12	98	65	36	**64**	**2**
Det	60	94	4	.390	40.5	30	47	695	923	6152	**1479**	**259**	44	108	506	603	30	63	.266	.331	.387	718	100	-10	-1	99	30	35	46	-6
Phi	59	95	3	.383	41.5	27	50	632	799	6028	1398	205	38	116	498	602	24	51	.256	.321	.372	693	89	-64	-87	104	41	24	63	1
StL	54	100	0	.351	46.5	23	54	555	778	5877	1310	214	25	112	507	644	17	89	.249	.317	.363	680	87	-85	-96	102	17	34	33	-8
Total	618	——		—	—	301	312	5512	—	47761	11117	1816	331	879	4469	4911	263	671	.262	.337	.383	720	—	—	—	—	326	302	52	-34

TEAM	CG	SHO	GR	SV	IP	H	HR	BB	SO	BR/9	ERA	AERA	OAV	OOB	PR	APR	PF	OSB	OCS	FA	E	WPB	DP	FW	PW	BW	BSW	DIF
NY	50	**18**	176	**39**	1358.1	**1286**	94	500	604	**12.1**	**3.20**	115	.251	**.321**	**120**	80	92	33	31	.979	126	**25**	182	.3	8.0	**14.4**	-.4	1.1
Cle	**81**	11	135	15	1373.0	1311	**92**	519	586	12.2	3.64	103	.253	.325	53	17	94	46	30	.979	127	37	**197**	.4	1.7	9.8	.1	2.9
Chi	57	17	184	33	1403.2	1299	113	583	**714**	12.2	3.41	**118**	**.246**	.324	91	**95**	101	41	35	**.980**	125	41	144	.6	**9.5**	-3.7	.1	5.5
Bos	41	15	214	37	1373.0	1333	**92**	584	642	12.7	3.58	**118**	.254	.331	63	91	105	39	32	.975	148	36	173	-.9	9.1	-4.3	-.4	3.9
Was	76	16	132	10	1344.2	1313	112	**478**	515	12.2	3.66	106	.258	.324	50	36	98	35	32	.979	**120**	28	173	**.7**	3.6	1.2	**.6**	-6.1
Det	50	2	218	16	1415.0	1633	154	585	645	14.4	5.25	77	.291	.363	-198	-183	102	55	47	.978	135	63	149	.1	-18.3	-.1	-.2	1.5
Phi	51	7	165	11	1409.0	1475	121	594	566	13.6	4.67	92	.271	.349	-106	-56	107	**28**	**53**	.977	137	66	161	-.0	-5.6	-8.7	.5	-4.2
StL	28	10	**250**	24	1383.2	1467	101	626	639	13.8	4.48	94	.273	.351	-74	-40	105	49	42	.974	152	41	165	-1.0	-4.0	-9.6	-.4	-8.0
Total	434	96	1474	185	11060.1	—	—	—	—	12.9	3.99	—	.262	.337	—	—	—	—	—	.978	1070	337	1344	—	—	—	—	—

BATTER-FIELDER WINS	BATTING AVERAGE	ON-BASE PERCENTAGE	SLUGGING AVERAGE	ON-BASE PLUS SLUGGING	ADJUSTED OPS	ADJUSTED BATTER RUNS
Rosen-Cle 7.4	Vernon-Was .337	Woodling-NY .429	Rosen-Cle .613	Rosen-Cle 1034	Rosen-Cle 181	Rosen-Cle 68.0
Berra-NY 3.8	Rosen-Cle .336	Rosen-Cle .422	Zernial-Phi .559	Vernon-Was .921	Vernon-Was 151	Vernon-Was 43.5
Boone-Cle-Det 3.6	Goodman-Bos .313	Minoso-Chi .410	Berra-NY .523	Zernial-Phi .914	Woodling-NY 147	Boone-Cle-Det 31.9
Strickland-Cle 3.3	Minoso-Chi .313	Fain-Chi .405	Boone-Cle-Det .519	Boone-Cle-Det .909	Boone-Cle-Det 146	Woodling-NY 31.7
Vernon-Was 3.0	Busby-Was .312	Yost-Was .403	Vernon-Was .518	Woodling-NY .898	Mantle-NY 145	Mantle-NY 31.4

RUNS	HITS	DOUBLES	TRIPLES	HOME RUNS	TOTAL BASES	RUNS BATTED IN
Rosen-Cle 115	Kuenn-Det 209	Vernon-Was 43	Rivera-Chi 16	Rosen-Cle 43	Rosen-Cle 367	Rosen-Cle 145
Yost-Was 107	Vernon-Was 205	Kell-Bos 41	Vernon-Was 11	Zernial-Phi 42	Vernon-Was 315	Vernon-Was 115
Mantle-NY 105	Rosen-Cle 201	White-Bos 34	Piersall-Bos 9	Doby-Cle 29	Zernial-Phi 311	Boone-Cle-Det 114
Minoso-Chi 104	Philley-Phi 188	Kuenn-Det 33	Philley-Phi 9	Berra-NY 27	Philley-Phi 263	Zernial-Phi 108
Vernon-Was 101	Busby-Was 183	Goodman-Bos 33		Boone-Cle-Det 26	Berra-NY 263	Berra-NY 108

BASES ON BALLS	STOLEN BASES	BASE STEALING RUNS	FIELDING RUNS-INFIELD	FIELDING RUNS-OUTFIELD	OUTFIELD ASSISTS	CATCHER CS PCT.
Yost-Was 123	Minoso-Chi 25	Michaels-Phi 1.5	Strickland-Cle 21.0	Busby-Was 12.9	Philley-Phi 18	Astroth-Phi 65.8
Fain-Chi 108	Rivera-Chi 22	Coan-Was 1.5	Hunter-StL 13.9	Groth-StL 12.2	Groth-StL 18	Murray-Phi 64.9
Doby-Cle 96	Jensen-Was 18	Jensen-Was 1.2	Dropo-Det 12.5	Piersall-Bos 10.9	Zernial-Phi 17	Courtney-StL 50.0
Gernert-Bos 88	Philley-Phi 13	Philley-Phi 1.1	Avila-Cle 12.5	Zernial-Phi 5.3		Berra-NY 48.1
Rosen-Cle 85	Busby-Was 13	Zernial-Phi .9	Rosen-Cle 9.4	Lund-Det 5.1		White-Bos 46.6

WINS	WINNING PCT.	WINS ABOVE TEAM	GAMES STARTED	COMPLETE GAMES	FEWEST HITS/GAME	FEWEST BB/GAME
Porterfield-Was 22	Lopat-NY .800	Porterfield-Was 6.9	Byrd-Phi 37	Porterfield-Was 24	Pierce-Chi 7.16	Lopat-NY 1.61
Parnell-Bos 21	Ford-NY .750	Parnell-Bos 6.4	B.Lemon-Cle 36	B.Lemon-Cle 23	McDermott-Bos 7.37	Sain-NY 2.14
B.Lemon-Cle 21	Parnell-Bos .724	Trucks-StL-Chi 5.2	Garcia-Cle 35	Garcia-Cle 21	Raschi-NY 7.46	A.Kellner-Phi 2.28
Trucks-StL-Chi 20	Porterfield-Was .688	Lopat-NY 4.5	Wynn-Cle 34	Pierce-Chi 19	Masterson-Was 7.85	Porterfield-Was 2.58
		Ford-NY 3.7	Parnell-Bos 34	Trucks-StL-Chi 17	Trucks-StL-Chi 7.97	Hoeft-Det 2.64

STRIKEOUTS	STRIKEOUTS/GAME	GAMES	SAVES	BASE RUNNERS/9	ADJUSTED RELIEF RUNS	RELIEF RANKING
Pierce-Chi 186	Pierce-Chi 6.17	Kinder-Bos 69	Kinder-Bos 27	Raschi-NY 10.24	Kinder-Bos 24.7	Kinder-Bos 47.3
Trucks-StL-Chi 149	Gray-Det 5.88	Stuart-StL 60	Dorish-Chi 18	Lopat-NY 10.35	Dorish-Chi 11.0	Dorish-Chi 14.0
Wynn-Cle 138	Masterson-Was 5.14	Martin-Phi 58	Reynolds-NY 13	Kinder-Bos 10.43	Paige-StL 8.7	Paige-StL 9.9
Parnell-Bos 136	Parnell-Bos 5.08	Paige-StL 57	Paige-StL 11	Keegan-Chi 10.49	Kuzava-NY 5.9	Kuzava-NY 6.9
Garcia-Cle 134	Trucks-StL-Chi 5.07	Dorish-Chi 55	Sain-NY 9	Pierce-Chi 10.65	Bearden-Chi 4.4	Bearden-Chi 4.1

INNINGS PITCHED	OPPONENTS' AVG.	OPPONENTS' OBP	EARNED RUN AVERAGE	ADJUSTED ERA	ADJUSTED STARTER RUNS	PITCHER WINS
B.Lemon-Cle 286.2	Pierce-Chi .218	Raschi-NY .283	Lopat-NY 2.42	Lopat-NY 152	Pierce-Chi 37.8	**Kinder-Bos 5.2**
Garcia-Cle 271.2	McDermott-Bos .224	Lopat-NY .288	Pierce-Chi 2.72	Pierce-Chi 148	Trucks-StL-Chi 31.8	**McDermott-Bos 4.1**
Pierce-Chi 271.1	Raschi-NY .224	Pierce-Chi .292	Trucks-StL-Chi 2.93	McDermott-Bos 140	Parnell-Bos 27.8	**Trucks-StL-Chi 3.6**
Trucks-StL-Chi 264.1	Masterson-Was .232	Masterson-Was .304	Sain-NY 3.00	Trucks-StL-Chi 139	Lopat-NY 25.5	**Pierce-Chi 3.5**
Porterfield-Was 255.0	Trucks-StL-Chi .238	Garcia-Cle .307	Ford-NY 3.00	Parnell-Bos 137	McDermott-Bos 25.2	**Porterfield-Was 3.3**

Ho-Hum

The pennant race wasn't close in 1953, with the Yankees easily shaking off the Indians and White Sox to capture their 20th AL crown in 33 seasons. More than in previous years, the Yankees had a stable lineup, although per usual, manager Casey Stengel had six pitchers make at least 15 starts—one of whom was also his relief ace, Allie Reynolds. New York led the AL in runs and ERA by healthy margins.

Cleveland third baseman Al Rosen nearly won the Triple Crown, leading in the power categories and losing the batting championship to Washington's Mickey Vernon by less than a point. Rosen's MVP trophy didn't make up for another second-place finish, however.

Boston's Ellis Kinder racked up 27 saves (figured retroactively), tying Joe Page's record, helping his team finish fourth even with Ted Williams spending most of the season in the marines—Teddy Ballgame even survived his plane being shot down in Korea.

Eighteen-year-old outfielder Al Kaline of sixth-place Detroit made his debut, and to honor the Athletics' retired owner-manager, Shibe Park was renamed Connie Mack Stadium. The A's, however, tumbled to seventh and attendance fell by half. Overall, league attendance dropped for the fifth straight year as New York's victory routine proved tiresome. Football was already making huge inroads into the American postwar consciousness.

The St. Louis Browns' final season didn't pass without more weirdness. Alva "Bobo" Holloman pitched a no-hitter in his first major league start, May 6, but was subsequently shelled back to the minors. The AL forced Bill Veeck to sell the club, and the Browns moved to Baltimore.

The World Series went six games, with Stengel calling on five different starters. In an even more power-dominated Series than in 1952, the Yankees used big innings to win Games 1 and 5, then captured the deciding contest in the last of the ninth on Billy Martin's record-setting 12th hit. For the Yankees, it was their fifth straight world title.

1952 NATIONAL LEAGUE

TEAM	W	L	T	PCT	GB	HW	HL	R	OR	PA	H	2B	3B	HR	BB	SO	HB	SH	AVG	OBP	SLG	OPS	AOPS	BR	ABR	PF	SB	CS	BSA	BSR
Bro	96	57	2	.627	—	45	33	**775**	603	6068	1380	199	32	**153**	**663**	699	35	104	.262	**.348**	**.399**	**747**	**113**	**111**	**103**	101	**90**	49	**65**	**3**
NY	92	62	0	.597	4.5	**50**	27	722	639	5891	1337	186	**56**	151	536	672	38	88	.256	.329	**.399**	728	107	54	49	101	30	31	49	-4
StL	88	66	0	.571	8.5	48	29	677	630	5845	1386	**247**	54	97	537	**479**	**43**	65	**.267**	.340	.391	731	110	71	70	100	33	32	51	-4
Phi	87	67	0	.565	9.5	47	29	657	**552**	5875	1353	237	45	93	540	534	23	**107**	.260	.332	.376	708	104	28	35	99	60	41	59	-1
Chi	77	77	1	.500	19.5	42	35	628	631	5836	**1408**	223	45	107	422	712	21	63	.264	.321	.383	704	101	4	-4	101	50	40	56	-3
Cin	69	85	0	.448	27.5	38	39	615	659	5785	1303	212	45	104	480	709	18	53	.249	.314	.366	680	95	-37	-35	100	32	42	43	-8
Bos	64	89	2	.418	32	31	45	569	651	5828	1214	187	31	110	483	711	32	92	.233	.301	.343	644	88	-104	-85	97	58	34	63	1
Pit	42	112	1	.273	54.5	23	54	515	793	5775	1201	181	30	92	486	724	26	70	.231	.300	.331	631	79	-127	-140	103	43	41	51	-5
Total	618	—	—	—	—	324	291	5158	—	46903	10582	1672	338	907	4147	5240	236	642	.253	.323	.374	697	—	—	—	—	396	310	56	-21

TEAM	CG	SHO	GR	SV	IP	H	HR	BB	SO	BR/9	ERA	AERA	OAV	OOB	PR	APR	PF	OSB	OCS	FA	E	WPB	DP	FW	PW	BW	BSW	DIF
Bro	45	11	196	24	1399.1	1295	121	544	**773**	12.0	3.53	103	.247	.321	31	17	98	29	38	**.982**	**106**	37	169	**2.0**	1.8	**10.6**	**.6**	4.5
NY	49	12	**226**	**31**	1371.0	1282	121	538	655	12.2	3.59	103	.248	.323	22	17	99	**28**	40	.974	158	37	**175**	-.8	1.8	5.1	-.1	9.1
StL	49	12	208	27	1361.1	1274	119	501	712	11.9	3.66	101	.247	.317	11	8	100	36	36	.977	141	31	159	.1	.8	7.2	-.1	3.0
Phi	**80**	**17**	142	16	1386.2	1306	**96**	**373**	609	**11.0**	**3.07**	**119**	.249	**.301**	**102**	**92**	98	50	34	.975	150	**17**	145	-.4	**9.5**	3.6	.2	-2.9
Chi	59	15	168	15	1386.1	**1265**	101	534	661	11.9	3.58	107	**.240**	.314	23	40	103	83	30	.976	146	65	123	-.1	4.1	-.4	-.0	-3.6
Cin	56	11	173	12	1363.1	1377	111	517	579	12.8	4.01	94	.267	.338	-43	-36	101	56	41	**.982**	107	24	145	1.9	-3.7	-3.6	-.6	-2.0
Bos	63	11	175	13	1396.0	1388	106	525	687	12.5	3.78	96	.259	.329	-7	-27	97	51	42	.975	154	45	143	-.5	-2.8	-8.8	.4	-.8
Pit	43	5	204	8	1363.2	1395	132	615	564	13.4	4.65	86	.265	.345	-139	-92	107	63	**49**	.970	182	34	167	-2.0	-9.5	-14.5	-.2	-8.8
Total	444	94	1492	146	11027.2	—	—	—	—	12.2	3.73	—	.253	.323	—	—	—	—	—	.976	1144	290	1226	—	—	—	—	—

BATTER-FIELDER WINS	BATTING AVERAGE	ON-BASE PERCENTAGE	SLUGGING AVERAGE	ON-BASE PLUS SLUGGING	ADJUSTED OPS	ADJUSTED BATTER RUNS
Robinson-Bro..... 5.7	Musial-StL............336	Robinson-Bro........440	Musial-StL.............538	Musial-StL.............970	Musial-StL.............167	Musial-StL.............57.7
Schoendienst-StL ... 5.4	Baumholtz-Chi 325	Musial-StL............432	Sauer-Chi 531	Robinson-Bro........904	Robinson-Bro........149	Robinson-Bro.......41.9
Musial-StL 4.2	Kluszewski-Cin 320	Hemus-StL............392	Kluszewski-Cin 509	Kluszewski-Cin 892	Kluszewski-Cin 146	Hodges-Bro 32.9
Hemus-StL 3.9	Robinson-Bro........308	Hodges-Bro 386	Kiner-Pit................500	Sauer-Chi 892	Gordon-Bos 144	Gordon-Bos 32.6
Sauer-Chi............ 3.1	Snider-Bro 303	Slaughter-StL........386	Hodges-Bro 500	Hodges-Bro 886	Sauer-Chi 143	Sauer-Chi 32.6

RUNS	HITS	DOUBLES	TRIPLES	HOME RUNS	TOTAL BASES	RUNS BATTED IN
Musial-StL............105	Musial-StL............194	Musial-StL..............42	Thomson-NY 14	Sauer-Chi 37	Musial-StL.............311	Sauer-Chi 121
Hemus-StL............105	Schoendienst-StL .188	Schoendienst-StL ...40	Slaughter-StL..........12	Kiner-Pit..................37	Sauer-Chi 301	Thomson-NY 108
Robinson-Bro........104	Adams-Cin............180	McMillan-Cin...........32	Kluszewski-Cin 11	Hodges-Bro 32	Thomson-NY 293	Ennis-Phi 107
Lockman-NY...........99	Dark-NY.................177	Sauer-Chi 31	Ennis-Phi 10	Mathews-Bos..........25	Ennis-Phi 281	Hodges-Bro 102
Reese-Bro 94	Lockman-NY.........176	Ashburn-Phi............31		Gordon-Bos 25	Snider-Bro 264	Slaughter-StL........101

BASES ON BALLS	STOLEN BASES	BASE STEALING RUNS	FIELDING RUNS-INFIELD	FIELDING RUNS-OUTFIELD	OUTFIELD ASSISTS	CATCHER CS PCT.
Kiner-Pit................110	Reese-Bro 30	Reese-Bro 4.8	Schoendienst-StL 35.6	Sauer-Chi 10.3	Ashburn-Phi............23	Campanella-Bro...55.8
Hodges-Bro 107	Jethroe-Bos 28	Jethroe-Bos 3.0	Logan-Bos 12.5	Jeffcoat-Chi 10.0	Pafko-Bro................18	Westrum-NY 54.8
Robinson-Bro........106	Robinson-Bro..........24	Robinson-Bro.........2.8	McMillan-Cin........10.3	Ashburn-Phi...........7.9	Sauer-Chi 17	D.Rice-StL 50.0
Musial-StL...............96	Ashburn-Phi............16	Davis-Pit 1.3	Adams-Cin.............7.0	Adcock-Cin 6.8		Cooper-Bos 46.3
Hemus-StL..............96		Ryan-Phi................1.1	Hemus-StL.............5.0	Wyrostek-Cin-Phi...6.8		Garagiola-Pit........42.6

WINS	WINNING PCT.	WINS ABOVE TEAM	GAMES STARTED	COMPLETE GAMES	FEWEST HITS/GAME	FEWEST BB/GAME
Roberts-Phi 28	Wilhelm-NY...........833	Roberts-Phi 10.6	Roberts-Phi 37	Roberts-Phi 30	Hacker-Chi...........7.01	Roberts-Phi 1.23
Maglie-NY...............18	Roberts-Phi 800	Wilhelm-NY............5.5	Spahn-Bos..............35	Dickson-Pit 21	Wilhelm-NY..........7.17	Hacker-Chi...........1.51
Staley-StL 17	Black-Bro 789	Yuhas-StL 4.8	Hearn-NY 34	Spahn-Bos...............19	Erskine-Bro..........7.27	Raffensberger-Cin ...1.64
Rush-Chi..................17	Maglie-NY.............692	Black-Bro 4.4	Dickson-Pit 34	Raffensberger-Cin 18	Rush-Chi..............7.37	Staley-StL 1.95
Raffensberger-Cin 17	Hacker-Chi............625	Roe-Bro 4.0		Rush-Chi..................17	Loes-Bro 7.40	Drews-Phi 2.05

STRIKEOUTS	STRIKEOUTS/GAME	GAMES	SAVES	BASE RUNNERS/9	ADJUSTED RELIEF RUNS	RELIEF RANKING
Spahn-Bos............183	Mizell-StL.............6.92	Wilhelm-NY.............71	Brazle-StL...............16	Hacker-Chi...........8.56	Black-Bro 22.9	Black-Bro 33.0
Rush-Chi...............157	Simmons-Phi 6.30	Black-Bro 56	Black-Bro 15	Black-Bro 9.11	Wilhelm-NY..........18.5	Wilhelm-NY..........21.7
Roberts-Phi 148	Wilhelm-NY..........6.10	Yuhas-StL 54	Wilhelm-NY.............11	Miller-StL 9.31	Leonard-Chi.........12.3	Brazle-StL............20.7
Mizell-StL..............146	Wade-Bro.............5.90	Smith-Cin................53	Leonard-Chi............11	Roberts-Phi 9.33	Brazle-StL............12.0	Yuhas-StL 15.0
Simmons-Phi 141	Erskine-Bro..........5.70	Main-Pit 48		Ramsdell-Chi 9.40	Yuhas-StL 10.7	Leonard-Chi.........11.2

INNINGS PITCHED	OPPONENTS' AVG.	OPPONENTS' OBP	EARNED RUN AVERAGE	ADJUSTED ERA	ADJUSTED STARTER RUNS	PITCHER WINS
Roberts-Phi 330.0	Hacker-Chi............212	Hacker-Chi............247	Wilhelm-NY..........2.43	Wilhelm-NY...........152	Roberts-Phi 42.8	**Roberts-Phi........ 4.6**
Spahn-Bos.........290.0	Rush-Chi...............216	Roberts-Phi 263	Hacker-Chi...........2.58	Hacker-Chi............149	Hacker-Chi...........27.3	**Rush-Chi 4.0**
Dickson-Pit 277.2	Wilhelm-NY...........220	Rush-Chi...............282	Roberts-Phi 2.59	Rush-Chi...............143	Raffensberger-Cin ...25.6	**Black-Bro 3.3**
Rush-Chi............250.1	Erskine-Bro...........220	Erskine-Bro...........289	Loes-Bro 2.69	Roberts-Phi 141	Rush-Chi..............25.5	**Hacker-Chi 3.1**
Raffensberger-Cin .247.0	Loes-Bro 224	Spahn-Bos............291	Rush-Chi..............2.70	Loes-Bro 135	Drews-Phi 25.0	**Drews-Phi 2.9**

Dodgers Blue Again

The Dodgers were again the class of the league early on, but this time didn't crumble down the stretch. Only for a short time in mid-September, when the Dodgers slumped and the Giants turned on the heat, was the race close.

League batting average was just .253, the lowest between 1942 and 1963, and runs per game fell to 4.17, the fewest of the decade. NL home runs dipped below 1,000 for the first time since 1950, and for the last time to date. Strikeouts rose once more. Despite this, complete games dropped to a new low, and two 28-year-old freshman relievers were the league's sensations. Despite leading the NL in appearances, ERA, and winning percentage, the Giants' Hoyt Wilhelm lost Rookie of the Year balloting to Brooklyn's Joe Black.

Philadelphia's Robin Roberts won 28, the most by a Senior Circuit hurler since 1935, while Stan Musial took his third straight batting title for the third-place Cardinals. Pittsburgh did a full swan dive into the basement, posting the league's worst record since 1935 despite Ralph Kiner's seventh straight home run crown.

League attendance fell another 12.5 percent. Boston's gate dropped another 42 percent as the club announced its move to Milwaukee—the first major league franchise relocation since 1903. The Braves added to their growing arsenal with the debut of third baseman Eddie Mathews, who tied for fourth in the league in homers.

Recently retired Arky Vaughan, one of the greatest shortstops in baseball history, drowned in a fishing accident. And outfielder Pete Reiser, robbed of a potentially great career by catastrophic injuries, played his last game.

In the fourth all-New York World Series in five years, the Dodgers led the Yankees three games to two and had the final two games in Ebbets Field, but they couldn't close the deal despite Duke Snider's .345 average, 4 homers, and 8 RBIs. Brooklyn fans were starting to wonder if next year would ever come.

1952 AMERICAN LEAGUE

TEAM	W	L	T	PCT	GB	HW	HL	R	OR	PA	H	2B	3B	HR	BB	SO	HB	SH	AVG	OBP	SLG	OPS	AOPS	BR	ABR	PF	SB	CS	BSA	BSR
NY	95	59	0	.617	—	49	28	727	**557**	5990	**1411**	221	**56**	129	566	652	36	94	**.267**	.341	.403	744	121	89	136	94	52	42	55	-3
Cle	93	61	1	.604	2	49	28	**763**	606	6060	1399	211	49	**148**	626	749	20	84	.262	.342	**.404**	**746**	**122**	**95**	**147**	94	46	39	54	-4
Chi	81	73	2	.526	14	44	33	610	568	6036	1337	199	38	80	541	**521**	**58**	**121**	.252	.327	.348	675	93	-36	-41	101	**61**	38	**62**	0
Phi	79	75	1	.513	16	45	32	664	723	5975	1305	212	35	89	**683**	561	27	102	.253	**.343**	.359	702	96	29	-11	106	52	43	55	-4
Was	78	76	3	.506	17	42	35	598	608	6046	1282	225	44	50	580	607	30	79	.239	.317	.326	643	88	-98	-78	97	48	37	56	-2
Bos	76	78	0	.494	19	**50**	27	668	658	5885	1338	**233**	34	113	542	739	31	66	.255	.328	.377	705	96	16	-31	108	59	47	56	-3
StL	64	90	1	.416	31	42	35	604	733	6001	1340	225	46	82	540	720	22	86	.250	.322	.356	678	92	-39	-56	103	30	34	47	-5
Det	50	104	2	.325	45	32	45	557	738	5914	1278	190	37	103	553	605	23	80	.243	.318	.352	670	92	-54	-59	101	27	38	42	-7
Total	621	—	—	—	—	353	263	5191	—	47907	10690	1716	339	794	4631	5154	247	712	.253	.330	.365	695	—	—	—	—	375	318	54	-29

TEAM	CG	SHO	GR	SV	IP	H	HR	BB	SO	BR/9	ERA	AERA	OAV	OOB	PR	APR	PF	OSB	OCS	FA	E	WPB	DP	FW	PW	BW	BSW	DIF
NY	72	**21**	143	27	1381.0	**1240**	94	581	666	12.1	**3.14**	106	.243	.324	**82**	31	90	49	40	.979	127	**21**	**199**	.8	3.2	14.1	.0	-.2
Cle	**80**	19	143	18	1407.0	1278	94	556	671	11.9	3.32	101	.241	**.316**	55	4	91	50	40	.975	155	34	141	-.8	.4	**15.3**	-.0	1.2
Chi	53	15	**190**	**28**	1416.2	1251	86	578	**774**	**11.7**	3.25	**112**	**.238**	**.316**	66	**63**	99	63	34	**.980**	**123**	37	158	**1.1**	**6.5**	-4.3	**.4**	.2
Phi	73	11	137	15	1384.1	1402	113	**526**	562	12.8	4.15	95	.263	.333	-74	-28	108	37	**48**	.977	140	32	148	.0	-2.9	-1.1	-.0	6.0
Was	75	10	137	15	1429.2	1405	**78**	577	574	12.7	3.37	105	.258	.332	48	30	97	42	31	.978	132	34	152	.6	3.1	-8.1	.2	5.2
Bos	53	7	176	24	1372.1	1332	107	623	624	13.1	3.80	104	.256	.340	-20	19	107	**35**	37	.976	145	37	181	-.3	2.0	-3.2	.0	.5
StL	48	6	181	18	1399.0	1388	111	598	581	13.0	4.12	95	.260	.339	-69	-30	107	51	47	.974	155	38	176	-.8	-3.1	-5.8	-.1	-3.1
Det	51	10	182	14	1388.1	1394	111	591	702	13.0	4.25	90	.262	.338	-89	-66	104	48	41	.975	152	50	145	-.6	-6.8	-6.1	-.4	-13.1
Total	505	99	1289	159	11178.1	—	—	—	—	12.5	3.67	—	.253	.330	—	—	—	—	—	.977	1129	283	1300	—	—	—	—	—

BATTER-FIELDER WINS	BATTING AVERAGE	ON-BASE PERCENTAGE	SLUGGING AVERAGE	ON-BASE PLUS SLUGGING	ADJUSTED OPS	ADJUSTED BATTER RUNS
Fain-Phi....4.5	Fain-Phi....327	Fain-Phi....438	Doby-Cle....541	Mantle-NY....924	Doby-Cle....166	Mantle-NY....48.4
Doby-Cle....4.4	Mitchell-Cle....323	Valo-Phi....432	Mantle-NY....530	Doby-Cle....924	Mantle-NY....166	Rosen-Cle....47.1
Mantle-NY....3.9	Mantle-NY....311	Mantle-NY....394	Rosen-Cle....524	Rosen-Cle....911	Rosen-Cle....162	Doby-Cle....45.8
Berra-NY....3.5	Kell-Det-Bos....311	Joost-Phi....388	Easter-Cle....513	Wertz-Det-StL....887	Easter-Cle....144	Fain-Phi....32.5
Goodman-Bos....3.4	Woodling-NY....309	Rosen-Cle....387	Wertz-Det-StL....506	Fain-Phi....867	Wertz-Det-StL....143	Woodling-NY....28.7

RUNS	HITS	DOUBLES	TRIPLES	HOME RUNS	TOTAL BASES	RUNS BATTED IN
Doby-Cle....104	Fox-Chi....192	Fain-Phi....43	Avila-Cle....11	Doby-Cle....32	Rosen-Cle....297	Rosen-Cle....105
Avila-Cle....102	Avila-Cle....179	Mantle-NY....37	Simpson-Cle....10	Easter-Cle....31	Mantle-NY....291	Robinson-Chi....104
Rosen-Cle....101	Robinson-Chi....176	Vernon-Was....33	Rizzuto-NY....10	Berra-NY....30	Dropo-Bos-Det....282	Doby-Cle....104
Berra-NY....97	Fain-Phi....176	Robinson-Chi....33	Fox-Chi....10	Dropo-Bos-Det....29	Doby-Cle....281	Zernial-Phi....100
Minoso-Chi....96				Zernial-Phi....29	Robinson-Chi....277	Berra-NY....98

BASES ON BALLS	STOLEN BASES	BASE STEALING RUNS	FIELDING RUNS-INFIELD	FIELDING RUNS-OUTFIELD	OUTFIELD ASSISTS	CATCHER CS PCT.
Yost-Was....129	Minoso-Chi....22	Jensen-NY-Was....1.9	Goodman-Bos....23.0	Philley-Phi....6.9	Jensen-NY-Was....17	White-Bos....50.0
Joost-Phi....122	Rivera-StL-Chi....21	Rizzuto-NY....1.6	Rizzuto-NY....21.4	Busby-Chi-Was....6.7	Bauer-NY....16	Courtney-StL....47.8
Fain-Phi....105	Jensen-NY-Was....18	Rivera-StL-Chi....1.5	Martin-NY....18.3	Woodling-NY....5.9	Mantle-NY....15	Astroth-Phi....46.5
Valo-Phi....101	Rizzuto-NY....17	Throneberry-Bos....1.1	Fain-Phi....17.9	Rivera-StL-Chi....4.6	Groth-Det....14	Berra-NY....45.0
Doby-Cle....90	Throneberry-Bos....16	Goodman-Bos....1.1	McDougald-NY....16.2	Jensen-NY-Was....2.3	Philley-Phi....13	Hegan-Cle....44.4

WINS	WINNING PCT.	WINS ABOVE TEAM	GAMES STARTED	COMPLETE GAMES	FEWEST HITS/GAME	FEWEST BB/GAME
Shantz-Phi....24	Shantz-Phi....774	Shantz-Phi....9.2	Lemon-Cle....36	Lemon-Cle....28	Lemon-Cle....6.86	Shantz-Phi....2.03
Wynn-Cle....23	Raschi-NY....727	Reynolds-NY....4.1	Garcia-Cle....36	Shantz-Phi....27	Raschi-NY....7.02	Pillette-StL....2.41
Lemon-Cle....22	Reynolds-NY....714	Raschi-NY....3.5	Wynn-Cle....33	Reynolds-NY....24	Reynolds-NY....7.15	Marrero-Was....2.59
Garcia-Cle....22	Lemon-Cle....667	Lemon-Cle....3.2	Shantz-Phi....33	Wynn-Cle....19	Dobson-Chi....7.36	Houtteman-Det....2.65
Reynolds-NY....20	Garcia-Cle....667	Garcia-Cle....3.2	A.Kellner-Phi....33	Garcia-Cle....19	Shantz-Phi....7.40	Garcia-Cle....2.68

STRIKEOUTS	STRIKEOUTS/GAME	GAMES	SAVES	BASE RUNNERS/9	ADJUSTED RELIEF RUNS	RELIEF RANKING
Reynolds-NY....160	McDermott-Bos....6.50	Kennedy-Chi....47	Dorish-Chi....11	Shantz-Phi....9.56	Dorish-Chi....11.9	Dorish-Chi....17.3
Wynn-Cle....153	Reynolds-NY....5.89	Paige-StL....46	Paige-StL....10	Dobson-Chi....10.05	Kennedy-Chi....5.5	Kennedy-Chi....3.7
Shantz-Phi....152	Trucks-Det....5.89	Garcia-Cle....46	Sain-NY....7	Lemon-Cle....10.09	Littlefield-Det-StL....3.6	Consuegra-Was....3.1
Pierce-Chi....144	Gray-Det....5.54	Hooper-Phi....43		Gromek-Cle....10.20	Consuegra-Was....3.5	Littlefield-Det-StL....2.9
Garcia-Cle....143	Grissom-Chi....5.26			Pierce-Chi....10.43	Newsom-Was-Phi....1.7	Newsom-Was-Phi....2.3

INNINGS PITCHED	OPPONENTS' AVG.	OPPONENTS' OBP	EARNED RUN AVERAGE	ADJUSTED ERA	ADJUSTED STARTER RUNS	PITCHER WINS
Lemon-Cle....309.2	Lemon-Cle....208	Shantz-Phi....272	Reynolds-NY....2.06	Reynolds-NY....161	Shantz-Phi....42.7	**Shantz-Phi....5.1**
Garcia-Cle....292.1	Raschi-NY....216	Lemon-Cle....279	Garcia-Cle....2.37	Shantz-Phi....160	Reynolds-NY....35.3	**Lemon-Cle....4.4**
Wynn-Cle....285.2	Reynolds-NY....218	Dobson-Chi....280	Shantz-Phi....2.48	Dobson-Chi....145	Garcia-Cle....33.3	**Reynolds-NY....4.1**
Shantz-Phi....279.2	Dobson-Chi....222	Pierce-Chi....289	Lemon-Cle....2.50	Pierce-Chi....142	Pierce-Chi....33.0	**Garcia-Cle....3.7**
Pierce-Chi....255.1	Shantz-Phi....225	Reynolds-NY....300	Dobson-Chi....2.51	Garcia-Cle....141	Lemon-Cle....30.2	**Pierce-Chi....3.5**

By the Skin of Their Teeth

The Indians spent August and September shadowing the Yankees, and both clubs were 19-5 in the final month, with the Yankees only clinching in the final weekend. However, the Tribe's mediocre play in August had already doomed them. Once again, the Indians had a trio of 20-game winners, but Bob Feller began to show signs of wear. The Yankees had the better pitching despite the military-related absence of Whitey Ford and Tom Morgan; Allie Reynolds led the AL in ERA and strikeouts. Twenty-year-old Mickey Mantle became the club's offensive lynchpin.

Cleveland again had power to spare, with Larry Doby and Luke Easter finishing 1-2 in homers. The third-place White Sox didn't hit, but had speed and a fine bullpen. Ferris Fain won his second straight batting title, and his Athletics ended a surprising fourth.

For the third straight year, the Yankees lost an outfielder as Charlie Keller retired due to back problems. Boston player-manager Lou Boudreau also hung up his glove. Runs fell for the second year in a row, decreasing to just 4.18 per game, and the top five ERA qualifiers all had better averages than 1951's ERA champ.

Bob Neighbors, who had played for the 1939 Browns, went missing in action in Korea on August 8. Neighbors was the only major league player lost to the Korean War.

In a seesaw World Series dominated by home runs, the Dodgers had a three-games-to-two lead, but the Yankees worked their magic again, taking the final two games at Ebbets Field. Vic Raschi started and won Game 6 with relief help from Reynolds, and both came in to relieve the next day. Bob Kuzava saved the deciding game for the second straight season. The Yankees hit 10 homers in the Series: Johnny Mize slugged 3, Yogi Berra and Mantle added 2 apiece. Once again, Stengel's boys had scraped by.

1951 NATIONAL LEAGUE

TEAM	W	L	T	PCT	GB	HW	HL	R	OR	PA	H	2B	3B	HR	BB	SO	HB	SH	AVG	OBP	SLG	OPS	AOPS	BR	ABR	PF	SB	CS	BSA	BSR
NY	98	59	0	.624	—	**50**	28	781	**641**	6153	1396	201	53	179	**671**	624	40	82	.260	.347	.418	765	111	92	86	101	55	34	62	0
Bro	97	60	1	.618	1	49	29	**855**	672	6214	**1511**	**249**	37	**184**	603	649	**44**	75	**.275**	**.352**	**.434**	**786**	**116**	**134**	**117**	102	**89**	70	56	-5
StL	81	73	1	.526	15.5	44	34	683	671	6003	1404	230	**57**	95	569	**492**	31	86	.264	.339	.382	721	99	8	4	101	30	30	50	-4
Bos	76	78	1	.494	20.5	42	35	723	662	5968	1385	234	37	130	565	617	31	79	.262	.336	.394	730	111	22	76	93	80	34	**70**	**6**
Phi	73	81	0	.474	23.5	38	39	648	644	5961	1384	199	47	108	505	525	21	**103**	.260	.326	.375	701	96	-41	-31	99	63	28	69	4
Cin	68	86	1	.442	28.5	35	42	559	667	5775	1309	215	33	88	415	577	11	64	.248	.304	.351	655	81	-137	-145	102	44	40	52	-4
Pit	64	90	1	.416	32.5	32	45	689	845	5973	1372	218	56	137	557	615	22	76	.258	.331	.397	728	99	11	-9	103	29	27	52	-3
Chi	62	92	1	.403	34.5	32	45	614	750	5862	1327	200	47	103	477	647	22	56	.250	.315	.364	679	86	-89	-99	102	63	30	68	3
Total	622	—	—	—	—	322	297	5552	—	47909	11088	1746	367	1024	4362	4746	222	621	.260	.331	.390	721	—	—	—	—	453	293	61	-3

TEAM	CG	SHO	GR	SV	IP	H	HR	BB	SO	BR/9	ERA	AERA	OAV	OOB	PR	APR	PF	OSB	OCS	FA	E	WPB	DP	FW	PW	BW	BSW	DIF
NY	64	9	189	18	1412.2	**1334**	148	**482**	625	**11.7**	**3.48**	**113**	**.248**	**.313**	**75**	**69**	99	41	40	.972	171	35	175	-1.0	**6.9**	8.6	.0	5.0
Bro	64	10	179	13	1423.1	1360	150	549	**693**	12.2	3.88	101	.253	.326	13	8	99	**21**	36	.979	129	39	**192**	**1.3**	.8	**11.7**	-.5	5.2
StL	58	9	183	**23**	1387.2	1391	119	568	546	12.8	3.95	100	.264	.338	1	2	100	49	30	**.980**	**125**	**26**	187	**1.3**	.2	.4	-.4	2.4
Bos	**73**	16	164	12	1389.0	1378	**96**	595	604	13.0	3.75	98	.259	.337	33	-12	93	67	**47**	.976	145	44	157	.3	-1.2	7.6	**.6**	-8.3
Phi	57	**19**	179	15	1384.2	1373	110	497	570	12.3	3.81	101	.258	.324	23	6	97	50	30	.977	138	46	146	.6	.6	-3.1	.4	-2.5
Cin	55	14	204	**23**	1390.2	1357	119	490	584	12.2	3.70	110	.255	.323	40	56	103	75	29	.977	140	48	141	.5	5.6	-14.5	-.4	-.2
Pit	40	9	**226**	22	1380.1	1479	157	609	580	13.8	4.79	88	.274	.350	-128	-82	107	58	36	.972	170	36	178	-1.1	-8.2	-.9	-.3	-2.5
Chi	48	10	185	10	1385.2	1416	125	572	544	13.1	4.34	94	.265	.340	-58	-36	103	92	45	.971	181	60	161	-1.7	-3.6	-9.9	.3	-.1
Total	459	96	1509	136	11154.0	—	—	—	—	12.6	3.96	—	.260	.331	—	—	—	—	—	.975	1199	334	1337	—	—	—	—	—

BATTER-FIELDER WINS	BATTING AVERAGE	ON-BASE PERCENTAGE	SLUGGING AVERAGE	ON-BASE PLUS SLUGGING	ADJUSTED OPS	ADJUSTED BATTER RUNS
Robinson-Bro 7.3	Musial-StL .355	Kiner-Pit .452	Kiner-Pit .627	Kiner-Pit 1079	Musial-StL 182	Musial-StL 70.1
Musial-StL 6.1	Ashburn-Phi .344	Musial-StL .449	Musial-StL .614	Musial-StL 1063	Kiner-Pit 182	Kiner-Pit 68.7
Campanella-Bro 5.9	Robinson-Bro .338	Robinson-Bro .429	Campanella-Bro .590	Campanella-Bro 983	Campanella-Bro 158	Robinson-Bro 44.7
Kiner-Pit 5.0	Campanella-Bro .325	Irvin-NY .415	Thomson-NY .562	Robinson-Bro 957	Robinson-Bro 153	Campanella-Bro 40.8
Ashburn-Phi 4.2	Irvin-NY .312	Stanky-NY .401	Hodges-Bro .527	Thomson-NY 947	Thomson-NY 150	Irvin-NY 39.9
RUNS	**HITS**	**DOUBLES**	**TRIPLES**	**HOME RUNS**	**TOTAL BASES**	**RUNS BATTED IN**
Musial-StL 124	Ashburn-Phi 221	Dark-NY 41	Musial-StL 12	Kiner-Pit 42	Musial-StL 355	Irvin-NY 121
Kiner-Pit 124	Musial-StL 205	Kluszewski-Cin 35	Bell-Pit 12	Hodges-Bro 40	Kiner-Pit 333	Kiner-Pit 109
Hodges-Bro 118	Furillo-Bro 197	Robinson-Bro 33	Irvin-NY 11	Campanella-Bro 33	Hodges-Bro 307	Gordon-Bos 109
Dark-NY 114	Dark-NY 196	Campanella-Bro 33	Jethroe-Bos 10	Thomson-NY 32	Campanella-Bro 298	Musial-StL 108
Robinson-Bro 106	Robinson-Bro 185		Baumholtz-Chi 10	Musial-StL 32		Campanella-Bro 108
BASES ON BALLS	**STOLEN BASES**	**BASE STEALING RUNS**	**FIELDING RUNS-INFIELD**	**FIELDING RUNS-OUTFIELD**	**OUTFIELD ASSISTS**	**CATCHER CS PCT.**
Kiner-Pit 137	Jethroe-Bos 35	Jethroe-Bos 5.9	Robinson-Bro 19.1	Ashburn-Phi 21.4	Furillo-Bro 24	Campanella-Bro 62.5
Stanky-NY 127	Ashburn-Phi 29	Ashburn-Phi 4.3	Schoendienst-StL 16.8	Furillo-Bro 12.4	Sauer-Chi 19	Westrum-NY 53.1
Westrum-NY 104	Robinson-Bro 25	Robinson-Bro 2.7	Hemus-StL 12.1	Sauer-Chi 8.4	Jethroe-Bos 18	Cooper-Bos 42.9
Torgeson-Bos 102	Torgeson-Bos 20	Jackson-Chi 2.0	Johnson-StL 9.6	Merriman-Cin 6.0	Bell-Pit 18	McCullough-Pit 42.6
Musial-StL 98	Reese-Bro 20	Irvin-NY 1.9	Strickland-Pit 8.6	Musial-StL 5.2	Ashburn-Phi 15	D.Rice-StL 41.1
WINS	**WINNING PCT.**	**WINS ABOVE TEAM**	**GAMES STARTED**	**COMPLETE GAMES**	**FEWEST HITS/GAME**	**FEWEST BB/GAME**
Maglie-NY 23	Roe-Bro .880	Roe-Bro 9.0	Roberts-Phi 39	Spahn-Bos 26	Maglie-NY 7.67	Raffensberger-Cin 1.38
Jansen-NY 23	Maglie-NY .793	Maglie-NY 7.3	Maglie-NY 37	Roberts-Phi 22	Newcombe-Bro 7.78	Jansen-NY 1.81
Spahn-Bos 22	Newcombe-Bro .690	Dickson-Pit 5.2	Spahn-Bos 36	Maglie-NY 22	Blackwell-Cin 7.89	Roberts-Phi 1.83
Roe-Bro 22	Jansen-NY .676	Spahn-Bos 5.1	Newcombe-Bro 36	Roe-Bro 19	Branca-Bro 7.94	Roe-Bro 2.24
Roberts-Phi 21	Hearn-NY .654	Roberts-Phi 4.6	Dickson-Pit 35	Dickson-Pit 19	Queen-Pit 7.97	Sain-Bos 2.53
STRIKEOUTS	**STRIKEOUTS/GAME**	**GAMES**	**SAVES**	**BASE RUNNERS/9**	**ADJUSTED RELIEF RUNS**	**RELIEF RANKING**
Spahn-Bos 164	Queen-Pit 6.58	Wilks-StL-Pit 65	Wilks-StL-Pit 13	Labine-Bro 9.92	Wilks-StL-Pit 13.8	Leonard-Chi 21.0
Newcombe-Bro 164	Rush-Chi 5.49	Werle-Pit 59	Smith-Cin 11	Raffensberger-Cin 9.99	Brazle-StL 13.8	Wilks-StL-Pit 13.9
Maglie-NY 146	Newcombe-Bro 5.43	Konstanty-Phi 58	Konstanty-Phi 9	Roberts-Phi 10.03	Perkowski-Cin 11.9	Brazle-StL 10.2
Jansen-NY 145	Branca-Bro 5.21	Spencer-NY 57	Brazle-StL 7	Jansen-NY 10.11	Leonard-Chi 11.4	Smith-Cin 10.0
Rush-Chi 129	Spahn-Bos 4.75	Brazle-StL 56		Maglie-NY 10.45	Kennedy-NY 10.6	Perkowski-Cin 9.7
INNINGS PITCHED	**OPPONENTS' AVG.**	**OPPONENTS' OBP**	**EARNED RUN AVERAGE**	**ADJUSTED ERA**	**ADJUSTED STARTER RUNS**	**PITCHER WINS**
Roberts-Phi 315.0	Maglie-NY .230	Roberts-Phi .278	Nichols-Bos 2.88	Maglie-NY 134	Maglie-NY 34.7	**Roberts-Phi 3.8**
Spahn-Bos 310.2	Newcombe-Bro .230	Jansen-NY .279	Maglie-NY 2.93	Roe-Bro 129	Jansen-NY 31.1	**Spahn-Bos 3.6**
Maglie-NY 298.0	Blackwell-Cin .233	Raffensberger-Cin .279	Spahn-Bos 2.98	Jansen-NY 129	Roberts-Phi 30.2	**Jansen-NY 3.2**
Dickson-Pit 288.2	Queen-Pit .233	Maglie-NY .289	Roberts-Phi 3.03	Nichols-Bos 127	Spahn-Bos 29.0	**Maglie-NY 3.0**
Jansen-NY 278.2	Branca-Bro .237	Newcombe-Bro .297	Jansen-NY 3.04	Roberts-Phi 127	Roe-Bro 27.6	**Blackwell-Cin 2.5**

Thomson's Blast Caps the Greatest Rally

The 1951 race looked like a cakewalk for Brooklyn; on August 12 the Dodgers led the slumping Giants by 13½ as Roy Campanella, Don Newcombe, Gil Hodges, Jackie Robinson, and Duke Snider were enjoying great seasons. At that point, however, the Giants, sparked by eventual Rookie of the Year Willie Mays and RBI champ Monte Irvin, won 16 straight to cut the lead to 5 games by Labor Day. Giants pitchers Larry Jansen and Sal Maglie were nearly unbeatable down the stretch.

On closing day, with both teams tied, New York won and Brooklyn managed a dramatic 14-inning victory at Philadelphia to force a best-of-three playoff. The teams split the first two, but the Dodgers jumped out in the third game and led, 4-1, in the last of the ninth. The Giants, though, rallied off Newcombe; with two on, two out, and the Dodgers up by two, Ralph Branca came in to face Bobby Thomson, who unloaded a three-run blast into the left field seats.

This, the first baseball game televised coast-to-coast, acquired a mythical quality over the years. Even in defeat, the Dodgers were honored; Campanella was voted MVP. What 1950s chauvinists don't admit is that fan interest sagged even during this great race; NL attendance dropped 13 percent. Boston's attendance fell by nearly half as rumors had the club moving to Milwaukee.

Commissioner Happy Chandler was forced out after trying to keep owners from signing high school players; Ford Frick, NL president, took the job and promised to keep out of the way. Warren Giles was voted the NL's new prexy.

Even though the charging Giants won two of the first three, the Yankees won the World Series in six. Bronx bats hammered Jansen and Maglie mercilessly. Irvin and Alvin Dark both batted over .400, but no other Giants regular even surpassed .240.

1951 AMERICAN LEAGUE

TEAM	W	L	T	PCT	GB	HW	HL	R	OR	PA	H	2B	3B	HR	BB	SO	HB	SH	AVG	OBP	SLG	OPS	AOPS	BR	ABR	PF	SB	CS	BSA	BSR
NY	98	56	0	.636	—	**56**	22	798	621	5927	1395	208	48	**140**	605	547	37	91	.269	.349	**.408**	**757**	**113**	61	**90**	96	78	39	**67**	**4**
Cle	93	61	1	.604	5	53	24	696	**594**	5946	1346	208	35	**140**	606	632	27	63	.256	.336	.389	725	106	-1	41	94	52	35	60	-1
Bos	87	67	0	.565	11	50	25	**804**	725	6211	1428	233	32	127	**756**	594	18	59	.266	**.358**	.392	750	98	**67**	-4	110	20	21	49	-3
Chi	81	73	1	.526	17	39	38	714	644	6128	**1453**	229	**64**	86	596	524	**51**	**103**	**.270**	.349	.385	734	105	22	38	98	**99**	70	59	-3
Det	73	81	0	.474	25	36	41	685	741	6008	1413	231	35	104	568	525	18	86	.265	.338	.380	718	99	-15	-18	100	37	34	52	-4
Phi	70	84	0	.455	28	38	41	736	745	6049	1381	**262**	43	102	677	565	34	61	.262	.349	.386	735	101	33	18	102	47	36	57	-2
Was	62	92	0	.403	36	32	44	672	764	5979	1399	242	45	54	560	**515**	26	64	.263	.336	.355	691	93	-60	-48	98	45	38	54	-3
StL	52	102	0	.338	46	24	53	611	882	5848	1288	223	47	86	521	693	16	92	.247	.317	.357	674	84	-105	-122	103	35	38	48	-6
Total	617	—	—	—	—	328	288	5716	—	48096	11103	1836	349	839	4889	4595	227	619	.262	.342	.381	723	—	—	—	—	413	311	57	-18

TEAM	CG	SHO	GR	SV	IP	H	HR	BB	SO	BR/9	ERA	AERA	OAV	OOB	PR	APR	PF	OSB	OCS	FA	E	WPB	DP	FW	PW	BW	BSW	DIF
NY	66	**24**	158	22	1367.0	1290	92	562	**664**	12.4	3.56	107	.250	.328	85	44	93	41	47	.975	144	28	190	.3	4.3	**8.9**	**.6**	6.9
Cle	**76**	10	135	19	1391.1	**1287**	**85**	577	642	**12.2**	**3.38**	112	**.245**	**.323**	**114**	68	92	54	36	**.978**	**134**	29	151	**.9**	6.7	4.0	.1	4.2
Bos	46	7	**210**	**24**	1399.0	1413	99	599	658	13.2	4.14	108	.264	.342	-2	46	108	47	27	.977	141	37	184	.5	4.5	-.4	-.0	5.5
Chi	74	11	150	14	1418.1	1353	109	**549**	572	**12.2**	3.50	**115**	.252	**.323**	97	**86**	98	57	25	.975	151	25	176	.0	**8.5**	3.7	-.0	-8.1
Det	51	8	195	17	1384.0	1385	103	602	597	13.2	4.29	97	.262	.342	-26	-18	101	71	43	.973	163	53	166	-.7	-1.8	-1.8	-.2	.4
Phi	52	7	157	22	1358.0	1421	109	569	437	13.4	4.47	96	.272	.347	-52	-27	104	**34**	46	**.978**	136	42	**204**	.8	-2.7	1.8	.0	-6.9
Was	58	6	160	13	1366.1	1429	110	630	475	13.7	4.49	91	.269	.348	-55	-59	99	52	36	.973	160	**23**	148	-.5	-5.8	-4.7	-.0	-3.9
StL	56	5	180	9	1370.1	1525	132	801	550	15.5	5.18	85	.282	.379	-160	-112	107	58	**51**	.971	172	41	179	-1.2	-11.0	-12.0	-.4	-.4
Total	479	78	1345	140	11054.1	—	—	—	—	13.2	4.12	—	.262	.342	—	—	—	—	—	.975	1201	278	1398	—	—	—	—	—

BATTER-FIELDER WINS	BATTING AVERAGE	ON-BASE PERCENTAGE	SLUGGING AVERAGE	ON-BASE PLUS SLUGGING	ADJUSTED OPS	ADJUSTED BATTER RUNS
Fain-Phi 4.3	Fain-Phi .344	Williams-Bos .464	Williams-Bos .556	Williams-Bos 1019	Doby-Cle 163	Williams-Bos 52.1
Joost-Phi 4.3	Minoso-Cle-Chi .326	Fain-Phi .451	Doby-Cle .512	Doby-Cle 941	Williams-Bos 159	Doby-Cle 44.7
Williams-Bos 4.1	Kell-Det .319	Doby-Cle .428	Zernial-Chi-Phi .511	Minoso-Cle-Chi 922	Minoso-Cle-Chi 152	Minoso-Cle-Chi 41.5
Doby-Cle 3.8	Williams-Bos .318	Yost-Was .423	Wertz-Det .511	Fain-Phi 921	Fain-Phi 146	Yost-Was 34.5
Berra-NY 3.5	Fox-Chi .313	Minoso-Cle-Chi .422	Minoso-Cle-Chi .500	Wertz-Det 894	Wertz-Det 140	Fain-Phi 33.4

RUNS	HITS	DOUBLES	TRIPLES	HOME RUNS	TOTAL BASES	RUNS BATTED IN
DiMaggio-Bos 113	Kell-Det 191	Yost-Was 36	Minoso-Cle-Chi 14	Zernial-Chi-Phi 33	Williams-Bos 295	Zernial-Chi-Phi 129
Minoso-Cle-Chi 112	Fox-Chi 189	Mele-Was 36	Coleman-StL-Chi 12	Williams-Bos 30	Zernial-Chi-Phi 292	Williams-Bos 126
Yost-Was 109	DiMaggio-Bos 189	Kell-Det 36	Fox-Chi 12	Robinson-Chi 29	Robinson-Chi 279	Robinson-Chi 117
Williams-Bos 109	Minoso-Cle-Chi 173		Young-StL 9		Berra-NY 269	Easter-Cle 103
Joost-Phi 107	Williams-Bos 169				DiMaggio-Bos 267	Rosen-Cle 102

BASES ON BALLS	STOLEN BASES	BASE STEALING RUNS	FIELDING RUNS-INFIELD	FIELDING RUNS-OUTFIELD	OUTFIELD ASSISTS	CATCHER CS PCT.
Williams-Bos 144	Minoso-Cle-Chi 31	Minoso-Cle-Chi 3.3	Fain-Phi 16.2	Coan-Was 18.4	Zernial-Chi-Phi 18	Berra-NY 53.8
Yost-Was 126	Busby-Chi 26	Rizzuto-NY 2.9	Stephens-Bos 11.8	Noren-Was 12.3	Coan-Was 17	Moss-StL-Bos 40.5
Joost-Phi 106	Rizzuto-NY 18	Busby-Chi 1.9	Carrasquel-Chi 11.6	Zernial-Chi-Phi 8.5	Busby-Chi 16	Hegan-Cle 37.9
Doby-Cle 101		Carrasquel-Chi 1.7	Priddy-Det 11.3	Delsing-StL 7.7		Ginsberg-Det 37.5
Rosen-Cle 85		McDougald-NY 1.3	Rizzuto-NY 11.2	Busby-Chi 6.7		Masi-Chi 25.0

WINS	WINNING PCT.	WINS ABOVE TEAM	GAMES STARTED	COMPLETE GAMES	FEWEST HITS/GAME	FEWEST BB/GAME
Feller-Cle 22	Feller-Cle .733	Garver-StL 7.9	Wynn-Cle 34	Garver-StL 24	Reynolds-NY 6.96	Hutchinson-Det 1.29
Raschi-NY 21	Lopat-NY .700	Feller-Cle 5.6	Raschi-NY 34	Wynn-Cle 21	McDermott-Bos 7.38	Lopat-NY 2.72
Lopat-NY 21	Reynolds-NY .680	Shantz-Phi 5.5	Lemon-Cle 34	Lopat-NY 20	Wynn-Cle 7.45	Pierce-Chi 2.73
	Raschi-NY .677	Kinder-Bos 4.3	Feller-Cle 32	Pierce-Chi 18	Rogovin-Det-Chi 7.85	Hooper-Phi 2.90
	Shantz-Phi .643	Martin-Phi 4.0	Lopat-NY 31		Lopat-NY 8.02	Garcia-Cle 2.91

STRIKEOUTS	STRIKEOUTS/GAME	GAMES	SAVES	BASE RUNNERS/9	ADJUSTED RELIEF RUNS	RELIEF RANKING
Raschi-NY 164	McDermott-Bos 6.65	Kinder-Bos 63	Kinder-Bos 14	Aloma-Chi 10.13	Kinder-Bos 24.3	Kinder-Bos 28.4
Wynn-Cle 133	Gray-Det 5.97	Brissie-Phi-Cle 56	Scheib-Phi 10	Zoldak-Phi 10.62	Aloma-Chi 18.5	Aloma-Chi 16.2
Lemon-Cle 132	Raschi-NY 5.71	Garcia-Cle 47	Brissie-Phi-Cle 9	Lopat-NY 10.85	Masterson-Bos 7.2	Brissie-Phi-Cle 4.2
Gray-Det 131	Reynolds-NY 5.13	Scheib-Phi 46	Reynolds-NY 7	Kinder-Bos 10.91	Brissie-Phi-Cle 5.2	Masterson-Bos 3.8
McDermott-Bos 127	Lemon-Cle 4.51		Garcia-Cle 6	Rogovin-Det-Chi 10.97	Ostrowski-NY 3.1	Ostrowski-NY 3.3

INNINGS PITCHED	OPPONENTS' AVG.	OPPONENTS' OBP	EARNED RUN AVERAGE	ADJUSTED ERA	ADJUSTED STARTER RUNS	PITCHER WINS
Wynn-Cle 274.1	Reynolds-NY .213	Lopat-NY .298	Rogovin-Det-Chi 2.78	Rogovin-Det-Chi 146	Rogovin-Det-Chi 29.7	**Parnell-Bos 3.3**
Lemon-Cle 263.1	Wynn-Cle .225	Rogovin-Det-Chi .301	Lopat-NY 2.91	Parnell-Bos 137	Pierce-Chi 28.0	**Lopat-NY 3.3**
Raschi-NY 258.1	McDermott-Bos .226	Wynn-Cle .301	Wynn-Cle 3.02	McDermott-Bos 133	Wynn-Cle 26.7	**Pierce-Chi 3.1**
Garcia-Cle 254.0	Rogovin-Det-Chi .235	Hutchinson-Det .302	Pierce-Chi 3.03	Pierce-Chi 133	Lopat-NY 26.2	**Wynn-Cle 3.1**
Feller-Cle 249.2	Lopat-NY .239	Reynolds-NY .304	Reynolds-NY 3.05	Lopat-NY 131	Parnell-Bos 23.7	**Garver-StL 2.9**

A Nation Turns Its Eyes From Joltin' Joe to The Mick

Perennial doormat Chicago jumped out in front and led the league during June. Outfielder Minnie Minoso helped manager Paul Richards turn the White Sox around. Chicago faded while the Yankees, Red Sox, and Indians took over. Cleveland and New York stayed neck-and-neck, with Boston close behind. On September 15-16, with the Indians up one game, New York took two from the Tribe at Yankee Stadium, starting Cleveland on a fatal slide.

Despite losing Whitey Ford to military service, New York pitchers led in shutouts and strikeouts, and catcher Yogi Berra was MVP. Casey Stengel continued his successful platoon system, supplementing what appeared to be an unprepossessing lineup. Bob Feller, Mike Garcia, and Early Wynn each won 20 for Cleveland, but three offensive dead spots negated Larry Doby and Al Rosen's hitting. Despite their big bats—Vern Stephens, Ted Williams, and Bobby Doerr (whose career was ended by knee problems)—the Red Sox didn't hit enough.

Bill Veeck, now owner of the St. Louis Browns, had to get creative to draw fans to his poor team. On August 19 he sent three-foot, seven-inch Eddie Gaedel to the plate as a pinch hitter. Five days later fans voted on in-game decisions with placards. The Browns drew 16 percent more fans than in 1950, but the club finished last both on the field and in attendance.

The Yankees took six games to win a defensive-oriented World Series from the Giants. The heroes were Eddie Lopat, who allowed 1 run in 18 innings, and four relievers who tossed 7.2 scoreless innings. Bob Kuzava saved decisive Game 6 for Vic Raschi.

After hitting .261 in the Series, 36-year-old Joe DiMaggio retired; injuries rendered him unable to play to his own standards. The Yankees had already broken in his successor, Mickey Mantle.

Hy Turkin and S.C. Thompson's *Official Encyclopedia of Baseball*, the first modern baseball reference, was published. In December "Shoeless" Joe Jackson, 62, became the first of the Black Sox to die.

1950 NATIONAL LEAGUE

TEAM	W	L	T	PCT	GB	HW	HL	R	OR	PA	H	2B	3B	HR	BB	SO	HB	SH	AVG	OBP	SLG	OPS	AOPS	BR	ABR	PF	SB	CS	BSA	BSR
Phi	91	63	3	.591	—	47	30	722	**624**	6051	1440	225	55	125	535	569	24	66	.265	.334	.396	730	100	-16	-4	98	33			
Bro	89	65	1	.578	2	**48**	30	**847**	724	6086	**1461**	247	46	**194**	607	632	27	**88**	**.272**	**.349**	**.444**	**793**	**113**	**109**	**92**	102	**77**			
NY	86	68	0	.558	5	44	32	735	643	5981	1352	204	50	133	**627**	629	**41**	75	.258	.342	.392	734	100	3	-1	101	42			
Bos	83	71	2	.539	8	46	31	785	736	6079	1411	246	36	148	615	616	27	74	.263	.342	.405	747	110	26	78	94	71			
StL	78	75	0	.510	12.5	47	29	693	670	5917	1353	255	50	102	606	604	23	73	.259	.339	.386	725	93	-12	-44	105	23			
Cin	66	87	0	.431	24.5	38	38	654	734	5845	1366	**257**	27	99	504	**497**	16	72	.260	.327	.376	703	91	-64	-66	100	37			
Chi	64	89	1	.418	26.5	35	42	643	772	5794	1298	224	47	161	479	767	31	54	.248	.315	.401	716	95	-56	-48	99	46			
Pit	57	96	1	.373	33.5	33	44	681	857	5976	1404	227	**59**	138	564	693	31	54	.264	.338	.406	744	99	11	-12	103	43			
Total	618	—	—	—	—	338	276	5760	—	47729	11085	1885	370	1100	4537	5007	220	556	.261	.336	.401	737	—	—	—	—	372	—	—	—

TEAM	CG	SHO	GR	SV	IP	H	HR	BB	SO	BR/9	ERA	AERA	OAV	OOB	PR	APR	PF	OSB	OCS	FA	E	WPB	DP	FW	PW	BW	BSW	DIF
Phi	57	13	167	**27**	1406.0	1324	122	**530**	620	**12.0**	**3.50**	**116**	.250	**.320**	**101**	**88**	98	47	*29*	.975	151	34	155	.1	**8.6**	-.4	—	5.7
Bro	62	10	195	21	1389.2	1397	163	591	**772**	13.0	4.28	96	.263	.339	-22	-29	99	33	*38*	**.979**	**127**	35	**183**	**1.4**	-2.8	**9.0**	—	4.5
NY	70	**19**	179	15	1375.0	**1268**	140	536	596	**12.0**	3.71	110	**.246**	**.320**	66	59	99	**31**	*38*	.977	137	37	181	.8	5.8	-.0	—	2.6
Bos	**88**	7	135	10	1385.1	1411	129	554	615	13.0	4.14	93	.263	.336	0	-48	93	53	***44***	.970	182	35	146	-1.7	-4.7	7.6	—	4.7
StL	57	10	185	14	1356.0	1398	**119**	535	603	13.0	3.97	108	.268	.339	26	47	104	37	*30*	.978	130	**31**	172	1.1	4.6	-4.3	—	.1
Cin	67	7	157	13	1357.2	1363	145	582	686	13.2	4.32	98	.259	.338	-26	-13	102	64	*31*	.976	140	49	132	.5	-1.3	-6.5	—	-3.3
Chi	55	9	199	19	1371.1	1452	130	593	559	13.6	4.28	98	.271	.347	-21	-11	101	70	*42*	.968	201	43	169	-2.8	-1.1	-4.7	—	-3.9
Pit	42	6	**213**	16	1368.2	1472	152	616	556	13.9	4.96	88	.275	.353	-124	-83	106	37	*38*	.977	136	39	165	.8	-8.1	-1.2	—	-11.0
Total	498	81	1430	135	11009.2	—	—	—	—	13.0	4.14	—	.261	.336	—	—	—	—	—	.975	1204	303	1303	—	—	—	—	—

BATTER-FIELDER WINS	BATTING AVERAGE	ON-BASE PERCENTAGE	SLUGGING AVERAGE	ON-BASE PLUS SLUGGING	ADJUSTED OPS	ADJUSTED BATTER RUNS
Robinson-Bro..... 5.0	Musial-StL............346	Stanky-NY 460	Musial-StL.............596	Musial-StL...........1034	Musial-StL..............161	Musial-StL............52.7
Stanky-NY 4.6	Robinson-Bro........328	Musial-StL.............437	Pafko-Chi 591	Kiner-Pit.................998	Gordon-Bos 160	Kiner-Pit...............45.4
Musial-StL 3.8	Snider-Bro 321	Robinson-Bro........423	Kiner-Pit.................590	Pafko-Chi................989	Pafko-Chi...............158	Gordon-Bos 43.8
Gordon-Bos........ 3.6	Ennis-Phi 311	Glaviano-StL.........421	Gordon-Bos 557	Gordon-Bos 960	Kiner-Pit.................154	Pafko-Chi 43.1
Seminick-Phi 3.6	Kluszewski-Cin 307	Torgeson-Bos 412	Snider-Bro 553	Snider-Bro 932	Elliott-Bos 143	Torgeson-Bos 40.7

RUNS	HITS	DOUBLES	TRIPLES	HOME RUNS	TOTAL BASES	RUNS BATTED IN
Torgeson-Bos 120	Snider-Bro 199	Schoendienst-StL ...43	Ashburn-Phi............14	Kiner-Pit..................47	Snider-Bro 343	Ennis-Phi 126
Stanky-NY 115	Musial-StL.............192	Musial-StL...............41	Bell-Pit 11	Pafko-Chi 36	Musial-StL.............331	Kiner-Pit.................118
Kiner-Pit................112	Furillo-Bro.............189	Robinson-Bro..........39	Snider-Bro 10	Sauer-Chi 32	Ennis-Phi 328	Hodges-Bro 113
Snider-Bro 109	Ennis-Phi 185	Kluszewski-Cin 37	Smalley-Chi 9	Hodges-Bro 32	Kiner-Pit.................323	Kluszewski-Cin 111
Musial-StL.............105	Waitkus-Phi............182	Dark-NY...................36	Schoendienst-StL 9		Pafko-Chi 304	Musial-StL.............109

BASES ON BALLS	STOLEN BASES	BASE STEALING RUNS	FIELDING RUNS-INFIELD	FIELDING RUNS-OUTFIELD	OUTFIELD ASSISTS	CATCHER CS PCT.
Stanky-NY 144	Jethroe-Bos 35		Smalley-Chi 19.6	Bell-Pit 4.5	Furillo-Bro...............18	Westrum-NY 54.4
Kiner-Pit................122	Reese-Bro 17		Cox-Bro 12.1	Lockman-NY..........4.1	Jethroe-Bos 17	D.Rice-StL 49.1
Torgeson-Bos 119	Snider-Bro 16		Schoendienst-StL 11.8	Marshall-Bos..........3.6	Thomson-NY 15	McCullough-Pit 48.7
Westrum-NY..........92	Torgeson-Bos 15		Robinson-Bro.......10.9	Gordon-Bos 3.5	Snider-Bro 15	Campanella-Bro...48.0
Reese-Bro 91	Ashburn-Phi............14		Thompson-NY 8.2	Adcock-Cin 3.5	Kiner-Pit..................13	Cooper-Cin-Bos...42.1

WINS	WINNING PCT.	WINS ABOVE TEAM	GAMES STARTED	COMPLETE GAMES	FEWEST HITS/GAME	FEWEST BB/GAME
Spahn-Bos..............21	Maglie-NY.............818	Maglie-NY..............6.9	Spahn-Bos..............39	Bickford-Bos 27	Blackwell-Cin 7.00	Raffensberger-Cin ...1.51
Sain-Bos.................20	Konstanty-Phi 696	Hiller-Chi.................4.5	Roberts-Phi 39	Spahn-Bos..............25	Maglie-NY............7.38	Jansen-NY...........1.80
Roberts-Phi 20	Simmons-Phi 680	Blackwell-Cin 3.4	Bickford-Bos 39	Sain-Bos..................25	Simmons-Phi 7.46	Sain-Bos 2.26
	Roberts-Phi 645	Konstanty-Phi 3.3	Sain-Bos 37	Roberts-Phi 21	Spahn-Bos...........7.62	Roberts-Phi 2.28
		Hearn-StL-NY........3.3		Jansen-NY..............21	Jansen-NY............7.79	Roe-Bro 2.37

STRIKEOUTS	STRIKEOUTS/GAME	GAMES	SAVES	BASE RUNNERS/9	ADJUSTED RELIEF RUNS	RELIEF RANKING
Spahn-Bos............191	Blackwell-Cin 6.48	Konstanty-Phi 74	Konstanty-Phi 22	Hearn-StL-NY......8.60	Konstanty-Phi 24.1	Konstanty-Phi 40.6
Blackwell-Cin 188	Simmons-Phi 6.12	Dickson-Pit 51	Werle-Pit....................8	Konstanty-Phi 9.36	Smith-Cin...............4.0	Smith-Cin................3.9
Jansen-NY............161	Spahn-Bos..........5.87	Werle-Pit..................48	Hogue-Bos.................7	Jansen-NY...........9.62	Kramer-NY.............2.2	Kramer-NY.............2.1
Simmons-Phi 146	Palica-Bro 5.86	Maglie-NY................47	Branca-Bro 7	Roberts-Phi 10.68	Leonard-Chi...........1.7	Leonard-Chi...........1.5
Roberts-Phi 146	Jansen-NY...........5.27	Brazle-StL...............46		Church-Phi.........10.71		

INNINGS PITCHED	OPPONENTS' AVG.	OPPONENTS' OBP	EARNED RUN AVERAGE	ADJUSTED ERA	ADJUSTED STARTER RUNS	PITCHER WINS
Bickford-Bos 311.2	Blackwell-Cin 210	Jansen-NY............271	Hearn-StL-NY......2.49	Maglie-NY.............151	Roberts-Phi 37.7	**Konstanty-Phi.... 3.8**
Roberts-Phi 304.1	Simmons-Phi 223	Roberts-Phi 297	Maglie-NY............2.71	Blackwell-Cin 143	Jansen-NY...........32.8	**Blackwell-Cin..... 3.6**
Spahn-Bos.........293.0	Maglie-NY.............226	Brecheen-StL.........298	Blackwell-Cin 2.97	Lanier-StL 137	Blackwell-Cin 32.5	**Jansen-NY.......... 3.6**
Sain-Bos............278.1	Spahn-Bos............227	Spahn-Bos............299	Jansen-NY...........3.01	Jansen-NY............136	Maglie-NY............31.8	**Roberts-Phi........ 3.2**
Jansen-NY.........275.0	Jansen-NY............232	Blackwell-Cin 301	Roberts-Phi 3.02	Roberts-Phi 134	Roe-Bro 24.5	**Maglie-NY........... 3.1**

Whizzing Into a Title

Prior to the season, the strike zone was shrunk to a range from the armpits to the top of knees. While league scoring rose 2.6 percent, which was predictable, strikeouts also increased by 10 percent—to an all-time NL high of 4.05 per game—which was not. Homers skyrocketed another 18 percent to 1,100, marking the first time either league had cracked four digits. Seven NL clubs cleared 100 long balls; the Reds hit 99.

Boston's farm system was producing players; Joe Adcock and Sam Jethroe made their debuts, and in 1951, Johnny Logan made his first appearance. Grover Cleveland Alexander, perhaps the NL's greatest right-hander ever, died destitute in a Nebraska rooming house at age 63. Meanwhile, two fine pitchers of the 1940s, Kirby Higbe and Bucky Walters, were finished.

The Phillies, nicknamed the "Whiz Kids" because of youngsters Robin Roberts, Curt Simmons, Granny Hamner, Willie Jones, and Richie Ashburn, emerged from the pack in July. However, a veteran—33-year-old reliever Jim Konstanty—was league MVP, appearing in relief a record 74 times and saving 22, an NL mark.

Philly was well in front until the fence-busting Dodgers, led by Duke Snider and Gil Hodges, made their move. Nine games down on September 18, the Dodgers won 13 of 15 while the Phils slumped. The lead was just one game with only one left to play—a showdown at Ebbets Field. But the Whiz Kids came through, defeating Brooklyn 4-1 on a Dick Sisler homer in the 10th. The heroics were through for the Phillies, however. The Yankees took them out in four straight in a competitive, but short, World Series.

For baseball, the postwar boom was over; for the third straight season, NL attendance dropped sharply. Owners in the minors and majors began worrying about television and the exodus to the suburbs.

1950 AMERICAN LEAGUE

TEAM	W	L	T	PCT	GB	HW	HL	R	OR	PA	H	2B	3B	HR	BB	SO	HB	SH	AVG	OBP	SLG	OPS	AOPS	BR	ABR	PF	SB	CS	BSA	BSR
NY	98	56	1	.636	—	53	24	914	691	6164	1511	234	**70**	159	687	**463**	31	85	.282	.367	.441	808	**116**	92	**118**	97	41	28	59	-1
Det	95	59	3	.617	3	50	30	837	713	6232	1518	285	50	114	**722**	480	19	**110**	.282	.369	.417	786	104	65	38	103	23	40	37	-9
Bos	94	60	0	.610	4	**55**	22	**1027**	804	6322	**1665**	**287**	61	161	719	582	25	62	**.302**	**.385**	**.464**	**849**	112	**189**	101	110	32	17	**65**	**1**
Cle	92	62	1	.597	6	49	28	806	**654**	6080	1417	222	46	**164**	693	624	**38**	86	.269	.358	.422	780	109	40	68	97	40	34	54	-3
Was	67	87	1	.435	31	35	42	690	813	6028	1365	190	53	76	671	606	32	74	.260	.347	.360	707	91	-96	-62	95	**42**	25	63	0
Chi	60	94	2	.390	38	35	42	625	749	5945	1368	172	47	93	551	566	28	106	.260	.333	.364	697	86	-131	-113	97	19	22	46	-4
StL	58	96	0	.377	40	27	47	684	916	5970	1269	235	43	106	690	744	20	97	.246	.337	.370	707	84	-101	-125	104	39	40	49	-5
Phi	52	102	0	.338	46	29	48	670	913	5993	1361	204	53	100	685	493	23	73	.261	.349	.378	727	94	-58	-44	98	**42**	25	63	0
Total	620	—	—	—	—	333	283	6253	—	48734	11474	1829	423	973	5418	4558	216	693	.271	.356	.402	759	—	—	—	—	278	231	55	-20

TEAM	CG	SHO	GR	SV	IP	H	HR	BB	SO	BR/9	ERA	AERA	OAV	OOB	PR	APR	PF	OSB	OCS	FA	E	WPB	DP	FW	PW	BW	BSW	DIF
NY	66	**12**	141	**31**	1372.2	1322	118	708	**712**	13.5	4.15	103	.255	.348	65	23	94	26	29	.980	119	**27**	188	1.3	2.2	**11.0**	.1	6.4
Det	**72**	9	153	20	1407.1	1444	141	**553**	576	13.0	4.12	114	.267	.339	71	86	102	26	26	**.981**	120	33	194	1.3	8.1	3.6	-.6	5.7
Bos	66	6	183	28	1362.1	1413	121	748	630	14.4	4.88	100	.270	.364	-46	2	107	31	22	**.981**	**111**	38	181	**1.7**	.2	9.5	**.3**	5.4
Cle	69	11	184	16	1378.2	**1289**	120	647	674	**12.8**	**3.75**	**115**	**.248**	**.333**	**126**	**94**	95	**24**	36	.978	129	29	160	.7	**8.8**	6.4	-.0	-.8
Was	59	7	156	18	1364.2	1479	**99**	648	486	14.2	4.66	96	.278	.359	-12	-25	98	49	29	.972	167	37	181	-1.4	-2.3	-5.8	.2	-.7
Chi	62	7	182	9	1365.2	1370	107	734	566	14.0	4.41	102	.263	.356	26	12	98	49	32	.977	140	36	181	.2	1.1	-10.6	-.1	-7.6
StL	56	7	**188**	14	1365.1	1629	129	651	448	15.2	5.20	95	.295	.372	-94	-35	108	36	**38**	.967	196	37	155	-3.1	-3.3	-11.7	-.2	-.7
Phi	50	3	153	18	1346.1	1528	138	729	466	15.3	5.49	83	.287	.376	-136	-141	99	37	19	.974	155	49	**208**	-.8	-13.2	-4.1	.2	-7.1
Total	500	62	1340	154	10963.0	—	—	—	—	14.0	4.58	—	.271	.356	—	—	—	—	—	.976	1137	286	1448	—	—	—	—	—

BATTER-FIELDER WINS	BATTING AVERAGE	ON-BASE PERCENTAGE	SLUGGING AVERAGE	ON-BASE PLUS SLUGGING	ADJUSTED OPS	ADJUSTED BATTER RUNS
Rizzuto-NY 4.0	Goodman-Bos 354	Doby-Cle..............442	DiMaggio-NY 585	Doby-Cle..............986	Doby-Cle..............156	Doby-Cle.............46.9
Rosen-Cle 4.0	Kell-Det................340	Yost-Was..............440	Dropo-Bos 583	DiMaggio-NY 979	DiMaggio-NY 152	DiMaggio-NY 39.5
Berra-NY............. 3.8	DiMaggio-Bos.......328	Pesky-Bos.............437	Evers-Det.............551	Dropo-Bos 961	Rosen-Cle.............146	Rosen-Cle............39.2
Doby-Cle 3.2	Doby-Cle..............326	Fain-Phi 430	Doby-Cle..............545	Evers-Det.............959	Evers-Det.............139	Williams-Bos........34.1
Priddy-Det 3.0	Zarilla-Bos 325	Goodman-Bos 427	Rosen-Cle.............543	Rosen-Cle.............948	Berra-NY..............136	Yost-Was.............31.7
RUNS	**HITS**	**DOUBLES**	**TRIPLES**	**HOME RUNS**	**TOTAL BASES**	**RUNS BATTED IN**
DiMaggio-Bos.......131	Kell-Det................218	Kell-Det..................56	Evers-Det................11	Rosen-Cle..............37	Dropo-Bos 326	Stephens-Bos.......144
Stephens-Bos.......125	Rizzuto-NY 200	Wertz-Det 37	Doerr-Bos 11	Dropo-Bos 34	Stephens-Bos.......321	Dropo-Bos 144
Rizzuto-NY 125	DiMaggio-Bos.......193	Rizzuto-NY 36	DiMaggio-Bos.........11	DiMaggio-NY 32	Berra-NY..............318	Berra-NY..............124
Berra-NY..............116	Berra-NY..............192	Evers-Det...............35		Stephens-Bos.........30	Kell-Det................310	Wertz-Det 123
	Stephens-Bos.......185	Stephens-Bos.........34		Zernial-Chi.............29	DiMaggio-NY 307	DiMaggio-NY 122
BASES ON BALLS	**STOLEN BASES**	**BASE STEALING RUNS**	**FIELDING RUNS-INFIELD**	**FIELDING RUNS-OUTFIELD**	**OUTFIELD ASSISTS**	**CATCHER CS PCT.**
Yost-Was...............141	DiMaggio-Bos.........15	DiMaggio-Bos........1.9	Priddy-Det...........27.9	Woodling-NY 12.4	Noren-Was.............20	Hegan-Cle 61.7
Fain-Phi 133	Valo-Phi 12	Vernon-Cle-Was 1.4	Pesky-Bos...........16.4	Noren-Was............9.2	Philley-Chi 19	Lollar-StL 52.9
Pesky-Bos............104	Rizzuto-NY 12	Collins-NY.............1.1	Carrasquel-Chi 10.7	Sievers-StL 7.3	Woodling-NY 16	Berra-NY.............52.8
Joost-Phi..............103	Coan-Was..............10	Avila-Cle 1.1	Fain-Phi 10.7	Chapman-Phi.........5.2	Wood-StL................16	Robinson-Det.......50.0
Rosen-Cle............100	Lipon-Det..................9	Jensen-NY................9	Doerr-Bos 9.4	Philley-Chi 4.6		Masi-Chi 38.9
WINS	**WINNING PCT.**	**WINS ABOVE TEAM**	**GAMES STARTED**	**COMPLETE GAMES**	**FEWEST HITS/GAME**	**FEWEST BB/GAME**
B.Lemon-Cle...........23	Raschi-NY 724	Hooper-Phi 5.5	B.Lemon-Cle...........37	B.Lemon-Cle...........22	Wynn-Cle.............6.99	Hutchinson-Det....1.86
Raschi-NY 21	Wynn-Cle..............692	Raschi-NY 4.1	Houtteman-Det.......34	Garver-StL 22	Pierce-Chi...........7.76	Lopat-NY 2.48
Houtteman-Det.......19	Lopat-NY 692	B.Lemon-Cle..........4.1	Feller-Cle 34	Parnell-Bos 21	Cain-Chi...............8.02	Overmire-StL 2.52
	Hutchinson-Det.....680	Ford-NY 3.7	Raschi-NY 32	Houtteman-Det 21	Reynolds-NY 8.04	Trout-Det.............3.12
	B.Lemon-Cle.........676	Wynn-Cle...............3.5	Lopat-NY 32		Raschi-NY 8.14	Houtteman-Det....3.24
STRIKEOUTS	**STRIKEOUTS/GAME**	**GAMES**	**SAVES**	**BASE RUNNERS/9**	**ADJUSTED RELIEF RUNS**	**RELIEF RANKING**
B.Lemon-Cle.........170	Wynn-Cle.............6.02	Harris-Was.............53	Harris-Was..............15	Gromek-Cle 10.56	Judson-Chi 7.8	Ferrick-StL-NY.....10.6
Reynolds-NY 160	Reynolds-NY 5.98	Kinder-Bos..............48	Page-NY 13	Ford-NY 11.33	Aloma-Chi.............5.7	Aloma-Chi..............5.8
Raschi-NY 155	Raschi-NY 5.44	Ferrick-StL-NY........46	Ferrick-StL-NY........11	Ferrick-StL-NY...11.38	Ferrick-StL-NY.......5.3	Flores-Cle 5.0
Wynn-Cle..............143	B.Lemon-Cle........5.31	Judson-Chi 46	Kinder-Bos................9	Wynn-Cle...........11.41	Flores-Cle 4.2	Benton-Cle.............4.0
Feller-Cle 119	Byrne-NY 5.22	Brissie-Phi 46	Brissie-Phi 8	Ostrowski-StL-NY .11.50	Benton-Cle.............4.0	Judson-Chi 3.9
INNINGS PITCHED	**OPPONENTS' AVG.**	**OPPONENTS' OBP**	**EARNED RUN AVERAGE**	**ADJUSTED ERA**	**ADJUSTED STARTER RUNS**	**PITCHER WINS**
B.Lemon-Cle......288.0	Wynn-Cle.............212	Wynn-Cle.............305	Wynn-Cle............3.20	Garver-StL 146	Garver-StL 39.1	**Garver-StL.......... 4.9**
Houtteman-Det ..274.2	Pierce-Chi.............228	Lopat-NY 317	Garver-StL 3.39	Parnell-Bos 136	Houtteman-Det 37.5	**Wynn-Cle 3.7**
Garver-StL.........260.0	Reynolds-NY 242	Houtteman-Det 322	Feller-Cle 3.43	Wynn-Cle.............135	Parnell-Bos 30.1	**Houtteman-Det.. 3.7**
Raschi-NY 256.2	Raschi-NY 243	Feller-Cle 325	Lopat-NY 3.47	Houtteman-Det 132	Wynn-Cle.............27.6	**B.Lemon-Cle 3.4**
Parnell-Bos........249.0	Cain-Chi...............244	Raschi-NY 327	Houtteman-Det 3.54	Feller-Cle 126	Feller-Cle 27.2	**Parnell-Bos......... 3.1**

Casey, Part II

A four-way race rolled into September with the clubs holding the exact positions in which they finished: New York, Detroit, Boston, and Cleveland. First, the seventh-place Browns knocked out the Indians, who then damaged the Red Sox and Tigers as the Yankees turned on the juice in the last week. While Yogi Berra and Joe DiMaggio enjoyed spectacular seasons for New York, shortstop Phil Rizzuto's surprise performance garnered him the MVP trophy.

Detroit used control pitching and on-base ability to finish just 3 games back. Cleveland led the league in ERA and homers, but Joe Gordon and Jim Hegan hit .235 and .219 in a league that batted .271.

The third-place Red Sox trampled their opponents at home, but were barely .500 on the road. Their offense scored a staggering 1,027 runs overall, by far highest in the AL, but ranked just fourth in scoring away from home. Mostly because Boston scored a ridiculous 8.16 runs per game at Fenway, league runs per contest jumped to 5.04, the most between 1939 and 1994. Homers also increased 27 percent to 973, another new record.

Whitey Ford successfully debuted for the Yankees while Tommy Henrich retired. Veteran middle infielders Gordon and Luke Appling also called it quits, and Philadelphia manager Connie Mack stepped down at age 87; he had managed the Athletics for half a century.

Many AL teams were slow to sign blacks, and for several years the Junior Circuit developed few impressive youngsters. The top rookie of 1950 was 27-year-old first baseman Walt Dropo.

The Yankees got a tougher bargain than they counted on in the World Series against the Phillies, but swept anyway. The first three games were one-run affairs, and in Game 4 Ford led, 5-0, in the ninth until Philly scored twice. Allie Reynolds, the Game 2 winner, came in to save the day. New York held Philadelphia to just 5 runs overall.

1949 NATIONAL LEAGUE

TEAM	W	L	T	PCT	GB	HW	HL	R	OR	PA	H	2B	3B	HR	BB	SO	HB	SH	AVG	OBP	SLG	OPS	AOPS	BR	ABR	PF	SB	CS	BSA	BSR
Bro	97	57	2	.630	—	48	29	**879**	651	6173	1477	236	47	**152**	638	570	**33**	**102**	.274	**.354**	**.419**	**773**	**110**	**106**	**73**	104	**117**			
StL	96	58	3	.623	1	**51**	26	766	**616**	6151	**1513**	**281**	54	102	569	**482**	25	94	**.277**	.348	.404	752	103	64	29	105	17			
Phi	81	73	0	.526	16	40	37	662	668	5935	1349	232	**55**	122	528	670	26	74	.254	.325	.388	713	100	-28	-9	97	27			
Bos	75	79	3	.487	22	43	34	706	719	6139	1376	246	33	103	**684**	656	23	96	.258	.345	.374	719	105	10	51	95	28			
NY	73	81	2	.474	24	43	34	736	693	6009	1383	203	52	147	613	523	24	64	.261	.340	.401	741	105	35	36	100	43			
Pit	71	83	0	.461	26	36	41	681	760	5870	1350	191	41	126	548	554	22	86	.259	.332	.384	716	96	-16	-33	103	48			
Cin	62	92	2	.403	35	35	42	627	770	5994	1423	264	35	86	429	559	20	76	.260	.316	.368	684	88	-84	-91	101	31			
Chi	61	93	0	.396	36	33	44	593	773	5723	1336	212	53	97	396	573	26	87	.256	.312	.373	685	91	-88	-72	97	53			
Total	622	—	—	—	—	329	287	5650	—	47994	11207	1865	370	935	4405	4587	199	679	.262	.334	.389	723	—	—	—	—	364	—	—	—

TEAM	CG	SHO	GR	SV	IP	H	HR	BB	SO	BR/9	ERA	AERA	OAV	OOB	PR	APR	PF	OSB	OCS	FA	E	WPB	DP	FW	PW	BW	BSW	DIF
Bro	62	**15**	193	17	1408.2	**1306**	132	582	**743**	12.2	3.80	108	**.246**	.324	37	46	102	**25**	*31*	**.980**	**122**	31	162	**1.5**	4.6	**7.2**	—	6.7
StL	64	13	187	**19**	1407.2	1356	**87**	507	606	**12.1**	**3.44**	**121**	.252	**.319**	**94**	**110**	103	40	*25*	.976	146	**29**	149	.3	**10.9**	2.9	—	5.0
Phi	58	12	190	15	1391.2	1389	104	**502**	495	12.4	3.89	101	.268	.335	23	9	98	56	*39*	.974	156	35	141	-.5	.9	-.9	—	4.5
Bos	**68**	12	159	11	1400.0	1466	110	520	589	12.9	3.99	95	.268	.334	8	-35	94	49	*32*	.976	148	30	144	.1	-3.5	5.1	—	-3.7
NY	**68**	10	186	9	1374.1	1328	132	544	516	12.4	3.82	104	.249	.321	33	25	99	50	*26*	.973	161	43	134	-.6	2.5	3.6	—	-9.4
Pit	53	9	179	15	1356.0	1452	142	535	556	13.4	4.57	92	.274	.344	-79	-53	104	35	*38*	.978	132	34	**173**	.9	-5.3	-3.3	—	1.7
Cin	55	10	**210**	6	1401.2	1423	124	640	538	13.4	4.34	96	.264	.345	-47	-24	104	41	*39*	.977	138	48	150	.6	-2.4	-9.0	—	-4.2
Chi	44	8	200	17	1357.2	1487	104	575	544	13.8	4.50	90	.279	.351	-70	-71	100	68	***43***	.970	186	56	160	-2.1	-7.0	-7.1	—	.3
Total	472	89	1504	109	11097.2	—	—	—	—	12.8	4.04	—	.262	.334	—	—	—	—	—	.975	1189	306	1213	—	—	—	—	—

BATTER-FIELDER WINS	BATTING AVERAGE	ON-BASE PERCENTAGE	SLUGGING AVERAGE	ON-BASE PLUS SLUGGING	ADJUSTED OPS	ADJUSTED BATTER RUNS
Kiner-Pit 5.1	Robinson-Bro........342	Musial-StL............438	Kiner-Pit..............658	Kiner-Pit.............1089	Kiner-Pit...............183	Kiner-Pit..............67.0
Musial-StL 5.1	Musial-StL............338	Robinson-Bro........432	Musial-StL............624	Musial-StL...........1062	Musial-StL............174	Musial-StL............66.9
Robinson-Bro..... 5.0	Slaughter-StL........336	Kiner-Pit...............432	Robinson-Bro........528	Robinson-Bro........960	Robinson-Bro........150	Robinson-Bro.......45.7
B.Elliott-Bos....... 4.0	Furillo-Bro............322	Slaughter-StL........418	Ennis-Phi..............525	Slaughter-StL........929	Gordon-NY...........142	Slaughter-StL.......35.5
Campanella-Bro 3.1	Kiner-Pit...............310	Stanky-Bos...........417	Thomson-NY........518	Gordon-NY...........909	Slaughter-StL........141	Gordon-NY..........33.1
RUNS	**HITS**	**DOUBLES**	**TRIPLES**	**HOME RUNS**	**TOTAL BASES**	**RUNS BATTED IN**
Reese-Bro............132	Musial-StL............207	Musial-StL..............41	Slaughter-StL..........13	Kiner-Pit..................54	Musial-StL............382	Kiner-Pit...............127
Musial-StL............128	Robinson-Bro........203	Ennis-Phi................39	Musial-StL...............13	Musial-StL...............36	Kiner-Pit...............361	Robinson-Bro........124
Robinson-Bro........122	Thomson-NY........198	Robinson-Bro..........38	Robinson-Bro..........12	Sauer-Cin-Chi.........31	Thomson-NY........332	Musial-StL............123
Kiner-Pit...............116	Slaughter-StL........191	Hatton-Cin..............38	Ennis-Phi................11	Thomson-NY..........27	Ennis-Phi..............320	Hodges-Bro..........115
Schoendienst-StL.102	Schoendienst-StL.190		Ashburn-Phi............11	Gordon-NY.............26	Robinson-Bro........313	Ennis-Phi..............110
BASES ON BALLS	**STOLEN BASES**	**BASE STEALING RUNS**	**FIELDING RUNS-INFIELD**	**FIELDING RUNS-OUTFIELD**	**OUTFIELD ASSISTS**	**CATCHER CS PCT.**
Kiner-Pit...............117	Robinson-Bro..........37		Schoendienst-StL 27.5	Ashburn-Phi.........10.4	Sauer-Cin-Chi.........16	Campanella-Bro...54.5
Reese-Bro............116	Reese-Bro..............26		Smalley-Chi.........17.6	Thomson-NY.........7.6	Ennis-Phi................16	McCullough-Pit....48.6
Stanky-Bos...........113			Marion-StL...........12.4	Holmes-Bos...........6.2	Marshall-NY............13	Garagiola-StL......45.5
Musial-StL............107			Reich-Chi.............12.2	Diering-StL............6.2	Furillo-Bro..............13	Cooper-NY-Cin....44.8
Gordon-NY.............95			B.Elliott-Bos.........11.4	Sauer-Cin-Chi........4.5	Ashburn-Phi............13	Seminick-Phi........44.4
WINS	**WINNING PCT.**	**WINS ABOVE TEAM**	**GAMES STARTED**	**COMPLETE GAMES**	**FEWEST HITS/GAME**	**FEWEST BB/GAME**
Spahn-Bos..............21	Roe-Bro................714	Spahn-Bos.............4.7	Spahn-Bos..............38	Spahn-Bos..............25	Staley-StL............8.09	Koslo-NY.............1.83
Pollet-StL................20	Pollet-StL.............690	Meyer-Phi..............4.6	Raffensberger-Cin......38	Raffensberger-Cin......20	Koslo-NY..............8.19	Roe-Bro...............1.86
Raffensberger-Cin......18	Newcombe-Bro.....680	Raffensberger-Cin.....4.0	Sain-Bos.................36	Newcombe-Bro.......19	Newcombe-Bro....8.21	Werle-Pit..............2.08
	Meyer-Phi.............680	Chambers-Pit.........3.8	Bickford-Bos...........36	Pollet-StL................17	Kennedy-NY........8.38	Jansen-NY...........2.15
	Munger-StL...........652	Heintzelman-Phi....3.4	Jansen-NY..............35	Jansen-NY..............17	Meyer-Phi............8.41	Leonard-Chi.........2.15
STRIKEOUTS	**STRIKEOUTS/GAME**	**GAMES**	**SAVES**	**BASE RUNNERS/9**	**ADJUSTED RELIEF RUNS**	**RELIEF RANKING**
Spahn-Bos............151	Newcombe-Bro....5.49	Wilks-StL................59	Wilks-StL..................9	Koslo-NY...........10.02	Konstanty-Phi........8.1	Konstanty-Phi......11.8
Newcombe-Bro.....149	Branca-Bro..........5.26	Konstanty-Phi.........53	Potter-Bos.................7	Staley-StL..........10.40	Erautt-Cin..............7.8	Erautt-Cin..............9.5
Jansen-NY............113	Chambers-Pit.......4.72	Palica-Bro...............49	Konstanty-Phi............7	Roe-Bro.............10,45	Wilks-StL................7.3	Palica-Bro..............8.5
Roe-Bro................109	Roe-Bro...............4.61	Banta-Bro...............48	Staley-StL.................6	Bonham-Pit........10.52	Hogue-Bos.............5.1	Wilks-StL...............8.5
Branca-Bro...........109	Spahn-Bos...........4.50	Muncrief-Pit-Chi......47	Palica-Bro.................6	Wilks-StL...........10.88	Palica-Bro..............5.0	Hogue-Bos.............3.0
INNINGS PITCHED	**OPPONENTS' AVG.**	**OPPONENTS' OBP**	**EARNED RUN AVERAGE**	**ADJUSTED ERA**	**ADJUSTED STARTER RUNS**	**PITCHER WINS**
Spahn-Bos.........302.1	Staley-StL............238	Koslo-NY..............278	Koslo-NY.............2.50	Koslo-NY..............159	Pollet-StL............35.2	**Pollet-StL........... 4.2**
Raffensberger-Cin .284.0	Koslo-NY..............239	Staley-StL............286	Staley-StL...........2.73	Staley-StL............152	Koslo-NY.............34.5	**Koslo-NY............ 4.1**
Jansen-NY.........259.2	Kennedy-NY.........242	Roe-Bro................293	Pollet-StL............2.77	Pollet-StL.............150	Roe-Bro...............31.9	**Newcombe-Bro.. 2.9**
Heintzelman-Phi 250.0	Newcombe-Bro.....243	Spahn-Bos............299	Roe-Bro...............2.79	Roe-Bro................147	Newcombe-Bro....27.3	**Staley-StL.......... 2.9**
Newcombe-Bro..244.1	Spahn-Bos............245	Newcombe-Bro.....301	Heintzelman-Phi..3.02	Brazle-StL.............131	Heintzelman-Phi..24.9	**Roe-Bro.............. 2.6**

Jackie's Back

Some had labeled Jackie Robinson a one-year wonder after he slumped in 1948. But he had not yet begun to fight; his comeback season netted MVP honors and sparked the Dodgers in their thrilling pennant drive against the Cardinals.

Both contenders played in extreme hitters' parks. Brooklyn won with an overwhelming offense and mediocre hurling, while St. Louis had a spectacularly good staff and several weak hitters. The Cardinals were in the driver's seat, up $1^1/_2$ games with one week left, but four straight losses doomed them to second place as the Dodgers capitalized. Once again, outfielders Stan Musial and Enos Slaughter had to carry the Cardinals attack. In a sign of what was to come, the Phillies improved by 15 games and leapt into to third place.

For the third straight season, the Dodgers debuted an impressive African American player as pitcher Don Newcombe won Rookie of the Year. Del Crandall and former Negro Leaguer Monte Irvin also made their first appearances in the majors, while it was the last year of service for Mort Cooper and Dixie Walker.

Ralph Kiner's 54 homers were the most in the majors since 1930, and NL home runs rose to 935, a new mark. For the first time, six clubs hit over 100 homers each. There was tragedy off the field. Pirates hurler Tiny Bonham died September 15 after an emergency appendectomy, and Phillies first baseman Eddie Waitkus was shot by a crazed admirer in a Chicago hotel room—he recovered to play six more years in the majors. In the face of a lawsuit that threatened baseball's reserve clause, Happy Chandler rescinded the ban on players who jumped to the Mexican League in 1946.

For the third time in the decade, the Yankees beat the Dodgers in the World Series, this time in five games. All were tight contests but the last, when the Brooklyn pitching collapsed.

1949 AMERICAN LEAGUE

TEAM	W	L	T	PCT	GB	HW	HL	R	OR	PA	H	2B	3B	HR	BB	SO	HB	SH	AVG	OBP	SLG	OPS	AOPS	BR	ABR	PF	SB	CS	BSA	BSR
NY	97	57	1	.630	—	54	23	829	637	6043	1396	215	60	115	731	539	**32**	84	.269	.362	.400	762	108	59	59	100	58	30	**66**	**2**
Bos	96	58	1	.623	1	**61**	16	**896**	667	6250	**1500**	**272**	36	**131**	**835**	510	17	78	**.282**	**.381**	**.420**	**801**	**111**	**154**	**93**	107	43	25	63	1
Cle	89	65	0	.578	8	49	28	675	**574**	5958	1358	194	58	112	601	534	23	113	.260	.339	.384	723	99	-35	-21	98	44	40	52	-4
Det	87	67	1	.565	10	50	27	751	655	6140	1405	215	51	88	751	502	23	107	.267	.361	.378	739	102	21	19	100	39	52	43	-10
Phi	81	73	0	.526	16	52	25	726	725	6048	1331	214	49	82	783	**493**	25	**117**	.260	.361	.369	730	104	8	34	97	36	25	59	-1
Chi	63	91	0	.409	34	32	45	648	737	6003	1340	207	**66**	43	702	596	13	84	.257	.347	.347	694	93	-68	-46	97	**62**	55	53	-6
StL	53	101	1	.344	44	36	41	667	913	5847	1301	213	30	117	631	700	21	83	.254	.339	.377	716	92	-41	-68	104	38	39	49	-5
Was	50	104	0	.325	47	26	51	584	868	5912	1330	207	41	81	593	495	22	63	.254	.333	.356	689	90	-96	-82	98	46	33	58	-1
Total	618	—	—	—	—	360	256	5776	—	48201	10961	1737	391	769	5627	4369	176	729	.263	.353	.379	732	—	—	—	—	366	299	55	-24

TEAM	CG	SHO	GR	SV	IP	H	HR	BB	SO	BR/9	ERA	AERA	OAV	OOB	PR	APR	PF	OSB	OCS	FA	E	WPB	DP	FW	PW	BW	BSW	DIF
NY	59	12	159	**36**	1371.1	**1231**	98	812	**671**	13.6	3.69	110	**.242**	.351	77	56	96	54	**42**	.977	138	40	195	.0	5.4	5.7	**.5**	8.3
Bos	84	16	120	16	1377.0	1375	82	661	598	13.5	3.97	110	.262	.347	34	57	104	35	28	.980	120	31	207	1.1	5.5	**9.1**	.4	2.9
Cle	65	10	168	19	1383.2	1275	82	**611**	594	**12.4**	**3.36**	**119**	.247	**.329**	**129**	**103**	95	**32**	37	**.983**	**103**	**27**	192	**2.1**	**10.0**	-2.0	-.0	2.1
Det	70	**19**	152	12	1393.2	1338	102	628	631	12.8	3.77	110	.254	.335	66	61	99	45	37	.978	131	40	174	.4	5.9	1.8	-.7	2.5
Phi	**85**	9	107	11	1365.0	1359	105	758	490	14.1	4.23	97	.263	.360	-5	-19	98	46	40	.976	140	43	**217**	-.1	-1.8	3.3	.2	2.5
Chi	57	10	174	17	1363.1	1362	108	693	502	13.7	4.30	97	.264	.353	-15	-19	99	51	38	.977	141	34	180	-.2	-1.8	-4.5	-.3	-7.2
StL	43	3	**231**	16	1341.1	1583	113	685	432	15.4	5.21	87	.294	.377	-151	-94	108	47	38	.971	166	41	154	-1.6	-9.1	-6.6	-.2	-6.4
Was	44	9	206	9	1345.2	1438	**79**	779	451	15.0	5.10	84	.276	.373	-134	-124	101	56	39	.973	161	47	168	-1.4	-12.1	-8.0	.2	-5.7
Total	507	88	1317	136	10941.0	—	—	—	—	13.8	4.20	—	.263	.353	—	—	—	—	—	.977	1100	303	1487	—	—	—	—	—

BATTER-FIELDER WINS	BATTING AVERAGE	ON-BASE PERCENTAGE	SLUGGING AVERAGE	ON-BASE PLUS SLUGGING	ADJUSTED OPS	ADJUSTED BATTER RUNS
Williams-Bos...... 6.4	Kell-Det................343	Williams-Bos.........490	Williams-Bos.........650	Williams-Bos.......1141	Williams-Bos.........187	Williams-Bos........79.9
Doerr-Bos 5.1	Williams-Bos.........343	Appling-Chi...........439	Stephens-Bos.......539	Henrich-NY...........942	Henrich-NY...........148	Joost-Phi..............37.8
Joost-Phi 5.1	Dillinger-StL..........324	Joost-Phi...............429	Henrich-NY...........526	Stephens-Bos.......930	Joost-Phi...............138	DiMaggio-NY.........32.1
Michaels-Chi...... 4.5	Mitchell-Cle...........317	Kell-Det.................424	Doerr-Bos 497	Kell-Det.................892	Kell-Det.................136	Henrich-NY............30.6
Stephens-Bos 3.9	Doerr-Bos 309	Michaels-Chi.........417	Berra-NY...............480	Doerr-Bos 890	Stephens-Bos.......135	Stephens-Bos......29.6

RUNS	HITS	DOUBLES	TRIPLES	HOME RUNS	TOTAL BASES	RUNS BATTED IN
Williams-Bos.........150	Mitchell-Cle...........203	Williams-Bos..........39	Mitchell-Cle............23	Williams-Bos..........43	Williams-Bos.........368	Williams-Bos.........159
Joost-Phi..............128	Williams-Bos.........194	Kell-Det..................38	Dillinger-StL 13	Stephens-Bos.........39	Stephens-Bos.......329	Stephens-Bos.......159
DiMaggio-Bos.......126	DiMaggio-Bos.......186	DiMaggio-Bos.........34	Valo-Phi 12		Wertz-Det 283	Wertz-Det 133
Stephens-Bos.......113	Wertz-Det 185	Zarilla-StL-Bos........33			Mitchell-Cle...........274	Doerr-Bos 109
Pesky-Bos.............111	Pesky-Bos.............185	Stephens-Bos 31			Doerr-Bos 269	Chapman-Phi.........108

BASES ON BALLS	STOLEN BASES	BASE STEALING RUNS	FIELDING RUNS-INFIELD	FIELDING RUNS-OUTFIELD	OUTFIELD ASSISTS	CATCHER CS PCT.
Williams-Bos.........162	Dillinger-StL............20	Rizzuto-NY 1.9	Doerr-Bos 27.1	Valo-Phi 9.4	Philley-Chi 16	Hegan-Cle 52.4
Joost-Phi..............149	Rizzuto-NY 18	Philley-Chi 1.5	Pesky-Bos............18.9	Evers-Det...............8.0	Kokos-StL 16	Guerra-Phi...........48.0
Fain-Phi 136	Valo-Phi 14	Tebbetts-Bos..........1.4	Vernon-Cle...........16.1	Kokos-StL 7.4	Wertz-Det 14	Lollar-StL 45.2
Appling-Chi...........121	Philley-Chi 13	Fain-Phi 1.4	Michaels-Chi........15.0	Mapes-NY...............6.4	Sievers-StL 14	Moss-StL 44.2
Valo-Phi 119		Mapes-NY..............1.3	Baker-Chi.............11.0	DiMaggio-Bos........5.8	Mapes-NY...............14	Robinson-Det.......43.1

WINS	WINNING PCT.	WINS ABOVE TEAM	GAMES STARTED	COMPLETE GAMES	FEWEST HITS/GAME	FEWEST BB/GAME
Parnell-Bos.............25	Kinder-Bos............793	Parnell-Bos 7.6	Raschi-NY 37	Parnell-Bos 27	Byrne-NY.............5.74	Hutchinson-Det....2.48
Kinder-Bos..............23	Parnell-Bos 781	Kinder-Bos.............7.3	Newhouser-Det.......35	Newhouser-Det.......22	Lemon-Cle...........6.79	Houtteman-Det 2.61
Lemon-Cle..............22	Reynolds-NY 739	Lemon-Cle 4.9	Wight-Chi................33	Lemon-Cle 22	Trucks-Det 6.84	Lopat-NY 2.88
Raschi-NY 21	Lemon-Cle 688	Scarborough-Was..4.3	Parnell-Bos 33	Raschi-NY 21	Gray-Det..............7.52	Garcia-Cle 3.07
Kellner-Phi 20		Kellner-Phi 4.0	Lemon-Cle 33		Pierce-Chi............7.60	Wynn-Cle..............3.12

STRIKEOUTS	STRIKEOUTS/GAME	GAMES	SAVES	BASE RUNNERS/9	ADJUSTED RELIEF RUNS	RELIEF RANKING
Trucks-Det 153	Byrne-NY.............5.92	Page-NY 60	Page-NY 27	Hutchinson-Det..10.49	Page-NY 22.7	Page-NY...............41.9
Newhouser-Det.....144	Trucks-Det 5.01	Welteroth-Was 52	Benton-Cle..............10	Trucks-Det 11.03	Paige-Cle............10.3	Paige-Cle 13.7
Lemon-Cle............138	Pierce-Chi............4.98	Ferrick-StL 50	Ferrick-StL 6	Garcia-Cle 11.07	Ferrick-StL 7.7	Ferrick-StL 7.6
Kinder-Bos............138	Kinder-Bos...........4.93	Kennedy-StL...........48	Paige-Cle 5	Benton-Cle.........11.14	Papish-Cle 6.0	Papish-Cle 3.0
Byrne-NY 129	Garcia-Cle 4.82	Surkont-Chi.............44		Paige-Cle...........11.28	Starr-StL 2.2	Starr-StL 1.9

INNINGS PITCHED	OPPONENTS' AVG.	OPPONENTS' OBP	EARNED RUN AVERAGE	ADJUSTED ERA	ADJUSTED STARTER RUNS	PITCHER WINS
Parnell-Bos 295.1	Byrne-NY..............183	Hutchinson-Det.....290	Garcia-Cle 2.36	Garcia-Cle 169	Parnell-Bos..........49.2	**Lemon-Cle......... 5.6**
Newhouser-Det..292.0	Lemon-Cle............211	Trucks-Det 301	Parnell-Bos 2.77	Parnell-Bos 157	Trucks-Det 42.1	**Parnell-Bos......... 5.2**
Lemon-Cle.........279.2	Trucks-Det 211	Garcia-Cle 308	Trucks-Det 2.81	Trucks-Det 148	Lemon-Cle...........33.8	**Page-NY.............. 4.0**
Trucks-Det 275.0	Gray-Det...............227	Lemon-Cle............309	Hutchinson-Det....2.96	Hutchinson-Det.....141	Garcia-Cle 33.6	**Garcia-Cle 3.7**
Raschi-NY 274.2	Pierce-Chi.............228	Gumpert-Chi.........318	Lemon-Cle...........2.99	Lemon-Cle............133	Benton-Cle...........30.9	**Trucks-Det 3.5**

The First of Casey

While Cleveland stumbled early, Boston and New York put on a show. The oft-injured Yankees, with skipper Casey Stengel taking the helm, held a steady lead from July into late August, when the consistently improving Red Sox cut sagging New York's lead from 8 games to $1^1/_2$ in a month.

New York hung on through September, then lost three straight at Boston with a week left. In the season's final series at New York, the Yankees, one game behind, won two pressure-packed games from the Red Sox to steal the crown from Boston skipper Joe McCarthy, who had enjoyed his share of New York glory.

Boston led the league in runs, thanks to Ted Williams, and got fine pitching from Mel Parnell and Ellis Kinder. Despite using a patchwork lineup, New York's offense was just fine; Joe DiMaggio was great when healthy and Yogi Berra developed into a terrific two-way player. Yankees pitching was deep and Joe Page's 27 saves set a new mark.

The White Sox brought in Comiskey Park's fences by 20 feet, and then returned them in early May. They finished sixth anyway. Third-place Cleveland debuted two more black players: Cuban outfielder Minnie Minoso and first baseman Luke Easter.

Baseball was now ruled by the slugging strategy of waiting for a good pitch and uppercutting it. In 1949, seven AL pitching staffs walked more hitters than they struck out. Behemoths Walt Dropo, Gus Zernial, and Roy Sievers debuted in '49, and similar lead-footed boppers ruled the game for much of the coming decade.

A strong Dodgers club was favored in the World Series, but Yankees pitching carried the day in a five-game victory. Joe Page again worked his magic in the late innings, and Allie Reynolds tossed 12.1 scoreless innings. This improbable season thus kicked off the next phase of Bronx Bombers' greatness.

1948 NATIONAL LEAGUE

TEAM	W	L	T	PCT	GB	HW	HL	R	OR	PA	H	2B	3B	HR	BB	SO	HB	SH	AVG	OBP	SLG	OPS	AOPS	BR	ABR	PF	SB	CS	BSA	BSR
Bos	91	62	1	.595	—	45	31	739	**584**	6125	**1458**	**272**	49	95	**671**	536	17	**140**	**.275**	**.359**	.399	**758**	**114**	**101**	**115**	98	43			
StL	85	69	1	.552	6.5	44	33	742	646	5994	1396	238	**58**	105	594	**521**	22	76	.263	.340	.389	729	98	31	-8	106	24			
Bro	84	70	1	.545	7.5	36	41	744	669	6047	1393	256	54	91	601	684	18	100	.261	.338	.381	719	98	15	-8	103	**114**			
Pit	83	71	2	.539	8.5	**47**	31	706	701	5943	1388	191	54	108	580	578	21	56	.263	.338	.380	718	99	7	-7	102	68			
NY	78	76	1	.506	13.5	37	40	**780**	703	5960	1352	210	49	**164**	599	648	19	65	.256	.334	**.408**	742	106	45	41	101	51			
Phi	66	88	1	.429	25.5	32	44	591	728	5830	1367	227	39	91	440	598	21	82	.259	.318	.368	686	94	-65	-54	98	68			
Cin	64	89	0	.418	27	32	45	588	751	5700	1266	221	37	104	478	586	16	79	.247	.313	.365	678	92	-77	-57	97	42			
Chi	64	90	1	.416	27.5	35	42	597	705	5894	1402	225	44	87	443	578	**29**	70	.262	.322	.369	691	97	-55	-29	96	39			
Total	619	—	—	—	—	308	307	5487	—	47493	11022	1840	384	845	4406	4729	163	668	.261	.333	.383	716	—	—	—	—	449	—	—	—

TEAM	CG	SHO	GR	SV	IP	H	HR	BB	SO	BR/9	ERA	AERA	OAV	OOB	PR	APR	PF	OSB	OCS	FA	E	WPB	DP	FW	PW	BW	BSW	DIF
Bos	**70**	10	167	17	1389.1	1354	93	**430**	579	**11.6**	**3.37**	**114**	**.249**	**.306**	**89**	**73**	97	63	*35*	.976	143	**19**	132	.7	**7.3**	**11.5**	—	-5.0
StL	60	13	205	18	1368.0	1392	103	476	625	12.4	3.91	105	.262	.324	7	27	103	**20**	*33*	**.980**	**119**	30	138	**2.1**	2.7	-.8	—	4.0
Bro	52	9	211	**22**	1392.2	**1328**	119	633	**670**	12.9	3.75	106	.253	.337	31	36	101	37	*43*	.973	161	49	151	-.2	3.6	-.8	—	4.4
Pit	65	5	166	19	1371.2	1373	120	564	543	12.9	4.15	98	.261	.335	-29	-12	103	53	***49***	.977	137	56	150	1.2	-1.2	-.7	—	6.7
NY	54	**15**	**230**	21	1373.0	1425	122	556	527	13.2	3.93	100	.269	.342	4	0	100	49	*25*	.974	156	30	134	.1	.0	4.1	—	-3.2
Phi	61	6	162	15	1362.1	1385	95	556	550	13.0	4.08	97	.262	.335	-18	-20	100	86	*46*	.964	210	45	126	-2.8	-2.0	-5.4	—	-.8
Cin	40	8	211	20	1343.1	1410	104	572	599	13.4	4.47	87	.270	.344	-77	-86	99	80	*26*	.973	158	30	135	-.1	-8.6	-5.7	—	1.9
Chi	51	7	220	10	1355.1	1355	**89**	619	636	13.2	4.00	97	.261	.342	-7	-15	99	61	*41*	.972	172	38	**152**	-.7	-1.5	-2.9	—	-7.9
Total	453	73	1572	142	10955.2	—	—	—	—	12.8	3.95	—	.261	.333	—	—	—	—	—	.974	1256	297	1118	—	—	—	—	—

BATTER-FIELDER WINS	BATTING AVERAGE	ON-BASE PERCENTAGE	SLUGGING AVERAGE	ON-BASE PLUS SLUGGING	ADJUSTED OPS	ADJUSTED BATTER RUNS
Musial-StL 7.2	Musial-StL............376	Musial-StL...............450	Musial-StL.............702	Musial-StL...........1152	Musial-StL.............196	Musial-StL............82.1
Pafko-Chi........... 4.2	Ashburn-Phi..........333	B.Elliott-Bos..........423	Mize-NY...............564	Mize-NY...............959	Mize-NY...............156	Mize-NY...............44.8
Mize-NY.............. 4.2	Holmes-Bos...........325	Ashburn-Phi..........410	Gordon-NY 537	Gordon-NY 927	Gordon-NY 148	B.Elliott-Bos.........41.3
Gordon-NY 3.0	Dark-Bos...............322	Slaughter-StL........409	Kiner-Pit...............533	Kiner-Pit...............924	Kiner-Pit...............145	Kiner-Pit...............36.8
B.Elliott-Bos....... 2.9	Slaughter-StL........321	Mize-NY...............395	Ennis-Phi 525	B.Elliott-Bos..........897	B.Elliott-Bos..........145	Gordon-NY 35.1

RUNS	HITS	DOUBLES	TRIPLES	HOME RUNS	TOTAL BASES	RUNS BATTED IN
Musial-StL.............135	Musial-StL.............230	Musial-StL..............46	Musial-StL...............18	Mize-NY..................40	Musial-StL.............429	Musial-StL.............131
Lockman-NY.........117	Holmes-Bos..........190	Ennis-Phi 40	Hopp-Pit.................12	Kiner-Pit..................40	Mize-NY...............316	Mize-NY................125
Mize-NY................110	Rojek-Pit...............186	Dark-Bos..................39	Slaughter-StL...........11	Musial-StL...............39	Ennis-Phi 309	Kiner-Pit................123
Robinson-Bro........108	Slaughter-StL.........176	Robinson-Bro..........38	Waitkus-Chi 10	Sauer-Cin 35	Kiner-Pit................296	Gordon-NY 107
Kiner-Pit................104	Dark-Bos...............175	Holmes-Bos............35	Lockman-NY............10		Pafko-Chi..............283	Pafko-Chi..............101

BASES ON BALLS	STOLEN BASES	BASE STEALING RUNS	FIELDING RUNS-INFIELD	FIELDING RUNS-OUTFIELD	OUTFIELD ASSISTS	CATCHER CS PCT.
B.Elliott-Bos..........131	Ashburn-Phi............32		Gustine-Pit............12.6	Ashburn-Phi............9.1	Marshall-NY............16	D.Rice-StL 58.6
Kiner-Pit................112	Reese-Bro 25		Smalley-Chi 10.7	Furillo-Bro..............7.2	Ennis-Phi 15	Campanella-Bro...55.8
Mize-NY..................94	Rojek-Pit.................24		Pafko-Chi.............10.3	Hermanski-Bro 5.8	Sauer-Cin 14	Kluttz-Pit 51.9
	Robinson-Bro...........22		Marion-StL............10.3	Sauer-Cin 4.4	Ashburn-Phi.............14	Scheffing-Chi.........41.7
	Torgeson-Bos 19		Waitkus-Chi 8.0	Jeffcoat-Chi 3.4		FitzGerald-Pit.......40.9

WINS	WINNING PCT.	WINS ABOVE TEAM	GAMES STARTED	COMPLETE GAMES	FEWEST HITS/GAME	FEWEST BB/GAME
Sain-Bos.................24	Brecheen-StL........741	Brecheen-StL.........6.3	Sain-Bos.................39	Sain-Bos.................28	Schmitz-Chi 6.92	Roe-Bro 1.67
Brecheen-StL.........20	Jones-NY..............667	Schmitz-Chi 5.1	Jansen-NY..............36	Brecheen-StL..........21	Barney-Bro 7.04	Jansen-NY...........1.75
Schmitz-Chi 18	Sain-Bos...............615	Sewell-Pit..............5.0	Spahn-Bos..............35	Schmitz-Chi 18	Brecheen-StL........7.44	Raffensberger-Cin...1.85
Jansen-NY..............18	Jansen-NY............600	Jones-NY...............4.4	Barney-Bro 34	Spahn-Bos..............16	Branca-Bro 7.89	Brecheen-StL........1.89
VanderMeer-Cin 17	Schmitz-Chi 581	VanderMeer-Cin 4.1	VanderMeer-Cin 33	Leonard-Phi............16	Roe-Bro 7.90	Leonard-Phi.........2.15

STRIKEOUTS	STRIKEOUTS/GAME	GAMES	SAVES	BASE RUNNERS/9	ADJUSTED RELIEF RUNS	RELIEF RANKING
Brecheen-StL........149	Brecheen-StL........5.75	Gumbert-Cin...........61	Gumbert-Cin...........17	Potter-Bos............9.00	Wilks-StL 21.3	Wilks-StL 22.3
Barney-Bro 138	Branca-Bro 5.09	Wilks-StL 57	Wilks-StL 13	Brecheen-StL.......9.41	Hansen-NY..........10.2	Minner-Bro.............9.6
Sain-Bos...............137	Barney-Bro 5.04	Higbe-Pit.................56	Higbe-Pit.................10	Roe-Bro 9.68	Minner-Bro.............9.2	Trinkle-NY..............8.9
Jansen-NY.............126	Higbe-Pit..............4.90	Jones-NY.................55	Trinkle-NY.................7	Wilks-StL 10.47	Dobernic-Chi 8.1	Dobernic-Chi 7.9
Branca-Bro 122	Meyer-Chi 4.86	Dobernic-Chi 54	Behrman-Bro 7	Schmitz-Chi 10.60	Higbe-Pit................7.9	Higbe-Pit.................7.9

INNINGS PITCHED	OPPONENTS' AVG.	OPPONENTS' OBP	EARNED RUN AVERAGE	ADJUSTED ERA	ADJUSTED STARTER RUNS	PITCHER WINS
Sain-Bos............314.2	Schmitz-Chi 215	Brecheen-StL........265	Brecheen-StL.......2.24	Brecheen-StL.........183	Brecheen-StL.......46.9	**Sain-Bos 5.3**
Jansen-NY.........277.0	Barney-Bro 217	Roe-Bro 271	Leonard-Phi.........2.51	Leonard-Phi...........157	Sain-Bos..............43.0	**Brecheen-StL...... 5.3**
Spahn-Bos.........257.0	Brecheen-StL........222	Schmitz-Chi 295	Sain-Bos..............2.60	Roe-Bro 152	Leonard-Phi...........31.4	**Schmitz-Chi 3.8**
Dickson-StL 252.1	Branca-Bro 232	Sain-Bos...............296	Roe-Bro 2.63	Schmitz-Chi 148	Schmitz-Chi 30.5	**Leonard-Phi 3.7**
Barney-Bro 246.2	Roe-Bro 233	Raffensberger-Cin....296	Schmitz-Chi 2.64	Sain-Bos...............147	Roe-Bro 26.5	**Roe-Bro.............. 2.6**

Triumph of the Brave

Brooklyn general manager Branch Rickey was glad that things worked out with Jackie Robinson. For 1948 he imported catcher Roy Campanella from the Negro Leagues. But despite bringing in their left and center field fences, Dodgers hitters slumped, and the team fell to third. Manager Leo Durocher quit at midseason and took the helm of the hated Giants.

Stan Musial won his third batting title in six years, and led the NL in hits, runs, doubles, triples, and RBIs, while Harry Brecheen was arguably the league's top pitcher. However, teammate Murry Dickson gave up 39 homers, a new major league record, and the rest of the staff didn't give Brecheen much support; the Cardinals finished second.

The NL's class club was in Boston, which hadn't had a Senior Circuit champ since 1914. MVP Bob Elliott and a supporting cast including Alvin Dark, Tommy Holmes, and Jeff Heath, provided the hitting. Even with Johnny Sain and Warren Spahn combining to complete 44 games, the pitching was thin; the staff completed just 70, the lowest league-leading total to date.

And the Braves were no sure thing; on September 1, they were tied with Dodgers for the lead, with the Cardinals and surprising Pirates close behind. But a 14-of-15 streak, nine of them won by Spahn or Sain, put Boston ahead to stay.

Former stars Arky Vaughan and Joe Medwick retired, while Philadelphia's Richie Ashburn and Brooklyn's Carl Erskine made impressive major league debuts. And the Chicago Cubs fell into the cellar for first time since 1925, beginning a 20-year period of intense frustration.

Despite good pitching, the Braves couldn't do much in the World Series; five of the games were close, but aside from an 11-5 Game 5 blowout, Boston had no offense. Within just a few years, the Braves fell out of contention and attendance sagged, forcing a move to Milwaukee.

1948 AMERICAN LEAGUE

TEAM	W	L	T	PCT	GB	HW	HL	R	OR	PA	H	2B	3B	HR	BB	SO	HB	SH	AVG	OBP	SLG	OPS	AOPS	BR	ABR	PF	SB	CS	BSA	BSR
Cle	97	58	1	.626	—	48	30	840	**568**	6201	**1534**	242	54	**155**	646	575	24	85	**.282**	.360	.431	**791**	**119**	113	**136**	97	54	44	55	-4
Bos	96	59	0	.619	1	**55**	23	**907**	720	6284	1471	**277**	40	121	**823**	552	**32**	66	.274	**.374**	.409	783	109	**124**	82	105	38	17	**69**	**2**
NY	94	60	0	.610	2.5	50	27	857	633	6048	1480	251	**75**	139	623	**478**	23	78	.278	.356	**.432**	788	116	99	107	99	24	24	50	-3
Phi	84	70	0	.545	12.5	36	41	729	735	6049	1345	231	47	68	726	523	22	120	.260	.353	.362	715	96	-18	-19	100	40	32	56	-2
Det	78	76	0	.506	18.5	39	38	700	726	6063	1396	219	58	78	671	504	27	**130**	.267	.353	.375	728	96	-1	-20	103	22	32	41	-6
StL	59	94	2	.386	37	34	42	671	849	6013	1438	251	62	63	578	572	19	113	.271	.345	.378	723	96	-21	-39	103	63	44	59	-2
Was	56	97	1	.366	40	29	48	578	796	5783	1245	203	**75**	31	568	572	20	84	.244	.322	.331	653	81	-156	-140	97	**76**	48	61	0
Chi	51	101	2	.336	44.5	27	48	559	814	5872	1303	172	39	55	595	528	12	73	.251	.329	.331	660	84	-138	-118	97	46	47	49	-6
Total	618	—	—	—	—	318	297	5841	—	48313	11212	1846	450	710	5230	4304	179	749	.266	.349	.382	731	—	—	—	—	363	288	56	-21

TEAM	CG	SHO	GR	SV	IP	H	HR	BB	SO	BR/9	ERA	AERA	OAV	OOB	PR	APR	PF	OSB	OCS	FA	E	WPB	DP	FW	PW	BW	BSW	DIF
Cle	66	**26**	196	**30**	1409.1	**1246**	82	625	593	**12.1**	**3.22**	**126**	**.239**	**.323**	**167**	**138**	95	**31**	31	**.982**	114	**24**	183	**1.4**	**13.4**	**13.2**	-.1	-8.3
Bos	70	11	141	13	1379.1	1445	83	592	513	13.4	4.26	103	.270	.345	4	20	102	40	28	.981	116	31	174	1.2	1.9	7.9	**.4**	7.0
NY	62	16	162	24	1365.2	1289	94	641	654	12.9	3.75	109	.250	.336	82	53	95	49	40	.979	120	40	161	.9	5.1	10.4	-.0	.6
Phi	**74**	7	137	18	1368.2	1456	86	638	486	13.9	4.43	97	.275	.355	-21	-20	100	39	34	.981	**113**	42	180	1.3	-1.9	-1.8	.0	9.4
Det	60	5	187	22	1377.0	1367	92	**589**	**678**	12.9	4.15	105	.259	.335	21	33	102	49	28	.974	155	44	143	-.9	3.2	-1.9	-.3	1.0
StL	35	4	**243**	20	1373.1	1513	103	737	531	14.9	5.01	91	.281	.371	-109	-65	106	67	30	.972	168	54	**190**	-1.6	-6.3	-3.8	.0	-5.9
Was	42	4	201	22	1357.1	1439	**81**	734	446	14.6	4.65	93	.273	.364	-55	-46	101	35	**59**	.974	154	31	144	-.9	-4.5	-13.6	.3	-1.8
Chi	35	2	210	23	1345.2	1454	89	673	403	14.4	4.89	87	.280	.365	-90	-95	99	53	38	.974	160	47	176	-1.2	-9.2	-11.4	-.3	-2.8
Total	444	75	1477	172	10976.1	—	—	—	—	13.6	4.29	—	.266	.349	—	—	—	—	—	.977	1100	313	1351	—	—	—	—	—

BATTER-FIELDER WINS	BATTING AVERAGE	ON-BASE PERCENTAGE	SLUGGING AVERAGE	ON-BASE PLUS SLUGGING	ADJUSTED OPS	ADJUSTED BATTER RUNS
Boudreau-Cle.....7.1	Williams-Bos.........369	Williams-Bos.........497	Williams-Bos.........615	Williams-Bos.......1112	Williams-Bos.........185	Williams-Bos........71.5
Williams-Bos......5.9	Boudreau-Cle 355	Boudreau-Cle 453	DiMaggio-NY 598	DiMaggio-NY 994	Boudreau-Cle 166	Boudreau-Cle 57.8
DiMaggio-NY......4.5	Mitchell-Cle...........336	Appling-Chi...........423	Henrich-NY...........554	Boudreau-Cle 987	DiMaggio-NY 164	DiMaggio-NY 49.7
Priddy-StL 4.5	Zarilla-StL 329	Goodman-Bos 414	Boudreau-Cle 534	Henrich-NY...........945	Henrich-NY...........151	Henrich-NY..........40.8
Doerr-Bos 3.7	McCosky-Phi 326	Fain-Phi 412	Keltner-Cle............522	Keltner-Cle............917	Keltner-Cle............146	Keltner-Cle...........36.5
RUNS	**HITS**	**DOUBLES**	**TRIPLES**	**HOME RUNS**	**TOTAL BASES**	**RUNS BATTED IN**
Henrich-NY...........138	Dillinger-StL..........207	Williams-Bos...........44	Henrich-NY.............14	DiMaggio-NY 39	DiMaggio-NY 355	DiMaggio-NY 155
DiMaggio-Bos.......127	Mitchell-Cle...........204	Henrich-NY 42	Stewart-NY-Was 13	Gordon-Cle.............32	Henrich-NY...........326	Stephens-Bos.......137
Williams-Bos.........124	Boudreau-Cle 199	Majeski-Phi.............41	Yost-Was.................11	Keltner-Cle.............31	Williams-Bos.........313	Williams-Bos.........127
Pesky-Bos.............124	DiMaggio-NY 190	Priddy-StL...............40	Mullin-Det 11	Stephens-Bos.........29	Stephens-Bos.......299	Gordon-Cle...........124
Boudreau-Cle 116	Williams-Bos.........188	DiMaggio-Bos 40	DiMaggio-NY 11	Doerr-Bos 27	Boudreau-Cle 299	Majeski-Phi...........120
BASES ON BALLS	**STOLEN BASES**	**BASE STEALING RUNS**	**FIELDING RUNS-INFIELD**	**FIELDING RUNS-OUTFIELD**	**OUTFIELD ASSISTS**	**CATCHER CS PCT.**
Williams-Bos.........126	Dillinger-StL............28	Dillinger-StL...........2.3	Priddy-StL............22.5	Coan-Was............11.9	Philley-Chi 22	Early-Was 63.8
Joost-Phi...............119	Coan-Was...............23	Coan-Was..............1.9	Pellagrini-StL 17.9	Philley-Chi 9.6	DiMaggio-Bos.........13	Evans-Was 59.0
Fain-Phi 113	Vernon-Was............15	Robertson-Was......1.8	Michaels-Chi........16.3	DiMaggio-Bos........8.7	Mitchell-Cle.............12	Hegan-Cle 49.0
DiMaggio-Bos.......101	Mitchell-Cle.............13	Tucker-Cle..............1.7	Baker-Chi.............15.8	Hodgin-Chi.............2.5	Doby-Cle.................12	Niarhos-NY 44.7
Pesky-Bos..............99		DiMaggio-Bos 1.5	Appling-Chi 13.4	Henrich-NY 1.8		Rosar-Phi.............43.6
WINS	**WINNING PCT.**	**WINS ABOVE TEAM**	**GAMES STARTED**	**COMPLETE GAMES**	**FEWEST HITS/GAME**	**FEWEST BB/GAME**
Newhouser-Det.......21	Kramer-Bos 783	Scarborough-Was..5.7	Feller-Cle 38	Lemon-Cle..............20	Shea-NY 6.76	Hutchinson-Det....1.95
Lemon-Cle..............20	Bearden-Cle 741	Kramer-Bos 5.4	Lemon-Cle..............37	Newhouser-Det.......19	Lemon-Cle 7.08	Zoldak-StL-Cle.....2.42
Bearden-Cle 20	Raschi-NY 704	Newhouser-Det......5.2	Newhouser-Det.......35	Raschi-NY 18	Bearden-Cle 7.33	Lopat-NY 2.62
Raschi-NY 19	Reynolds-NY 696	Bearden-Cle 4.7	Sanford-StL 33	Feller-Cle 18	Scarborough-Was8.06	Kramer-Bos 2.81
Feller-Cle 19		Raschi-NY 3.7			Trucks-Det 8.08	Houtteman-Det 2.85
STRIKEOUTS	**STRIKEOUTS/GAME**	**GAMES**	**SAVES**	**BASE RUNNERS/9**	**ADJUSTED RELIEF RUNS**	**RELIEF RANKING**
Feller-Cle..............164	Brissie-Phi 5.89	Page-NY 55	Christopher-Cle 17	Paige-Cle...........10.40	Klieman-Cle.........13.6	Christopher-Cle ...11.6
Lemon-Cle............147	Feller-Cle 5.27	Widmar-StL.............49	Page-NY 16	Hutchinson-Det..11.08	Christopher-Cle 8.2	Klieman-Cle...........9.2
Newhouser-Det.....143	Trucks-Det 5.23	Biscan-StL 47	Houtteman-Det.......10	Lemon-Cle 11.12	Thompson-Was 4.1	Thompson-Was 4.7
Brissie-Phi 127	Raschi-NY 5.01	Thompson-Was 46	Ferrick-Was 10	Gumpert-NY-Chi 11.18	Widmar-StL............2.3	Ferrick-Was 2.6
Raschi-NY 124	Newhouser-Det....4.73		Judson-Chi 8	Gromek-Cle 11.49	Ferrick-Was 2.2	Widmar-StL............2.1
INNINGS PITCHED	**OPPONENTS' AVG.**	**OPPONENTS' OBP**	**EARNED RUN AVERAGE**	**ADJUSTED ERA**	**ADJUSTED STARTER RUNS**	**PITCHER WINS**
Lemon-Cle.........293.2	Shea-NY...............208	Hutchinson-Det.....297	Bearden-Cle 2.43	Bearden-Cle.........167	Bearden-Cle 42.9	**Lemon-Cle.......... 6.6**
Feller-Cle...........280.1	Lemon-Cle 216	Lemon-Cle 302	Scarborough-Was2.82	Scarborough-Was.154	Lemon-Cle...........42.5	**Bearden-Cle....... 5.5**
Newhouser-Det..272.1	Bearden-Cle 229	Scarborough-Was.307	Lemon-Cle 2.82	Newhouser-Det.....145	Newhouser-Det....38.3	**Newhouser-Det . 4.5**
Dobson-Bos.......245.1	Scarborough-Was.233	Newhouser-Det.....309	Newhouser-Det....3.01	Lemon-Cle............144	Scarborough-Was28.8	**Scarborough-Was... 3.4**
Reynolds-NY 236.1	Trucks-Det 240	Raschi-NY 310	Parnell-Bos..........3.14	Parnell-Bos...........140	Parnell-Bos..........26.4	**Parnell-Bos......... 2.2**

A Real Tribe

Bill Veeck was baseball's master showman, but he brought the crowds back to Cleveland not with stunts, but by building an integrated club that would contend for the next decade.

In early August the Indians, Red Sox, Yankees, and the surprising Athletics sat atop the AL in a virtual knot. While Philadelphia dropped out in early September, the other three teams kept winning, landing in a three-way tie September 23.

Cleveland attempted to pull away, but Boston knocked out New York October 2 and moved into a tie with the Indians, losers of two of three to Detroit, on the season's final day. In the league's first-ever playoff, the Indians invaded Fenway Park and whipped the Red Sox, 8-3, with rookie Gene Bearden winning his 20th.

The Indians, who had the league's best pitching and a strong offense, debuted two great pitchers: Negro Leagues legend Satchel Paige and Mike Garcia, the "Big Bear." Cleveland shortstop Lou Boudreau, nearing the end of his great playing career, was league MVP. Cleveland also set a new record by drawing 2,620,627 fans. Boston's excellent attack couldn't quite negate a mediocre pitching staff, while the Yankees didn't hit enough and had a poor season from Joe Page. Both clubs set new attendance marks for their parks as league attendance rose another 17 percent to the highest total yet.

Babe Ruth's death from cancer on August 16 set America into mourning. The Bambino was still a beloved hero and his body was visited by more than 100,000 at Yankee Stadium.

The World Series pitted faux Native Americans from Cleveland and Boston. Despite Bob Feller's two losses, the Indians won with fine pitching from Bob Lemon and Bearden. While the Braves took Game 5, 11-5, they scored but six times in the other five contests. Larry Doby, at .318, was the hottest Cleveland hitter.

1947 NATIONAL LEAGUE

TEAM	W	L	T	PCT	GB	HW	HL	R	OR	PA	H	2B	3B	HR	BB	SO	HB	SH	AVG	OBP	SLG	OPS	AOPS	BR	ABR	PF	SB	CS	BSA	BSR
Bro	94	60	1	.610	—	**52**	25	774	667	6125	1428	241	50	83	**732**	561	**29**	115	.272	**.364**	.384	748	102	67	38	104	**88**			
StL	89	65	2	.578	5	46	31	780	634	6131	**1462**	235	**65**	115	612	511	**29**	68	.270	.347	.401	748	101	41	9	104	28			
Bos	86	68	0	.558	8	50	27	701	**626**	5954	1444	**265**	42	85	558	**500**	14	**129**	**.275**	.346	.390	736	105	22	40	98	58			
NY	81	73	1	.526	13	45	31	**830**	761	5924	1446	220	48	**221**	494	568	23	64	.271	.335	**.454**	**789**	**114**	**93**	**88**	101	29			
Cin	73	81	0	.474	21	42	35	681	755	5954	1372	242	43	95	539	530	21	95	.259	.330	.375	705	95	-47	-42	99	46			
Chi	69	85	1	.448	25	36	43	569	722	5859	1373	231	48	71	471	578	19	64	.259	.321	.361	682	91	-95	-70	96	22			
Pit	62	92	2	.403	32	32	45	745	817	6008	1385	216	44	156	607	687	24	70	.261	.340	.406	746	102	31	11	103	30			
Phi	62	92	1	.403	32	38	38	589	687	5828	1354	210	52	60	464	594	26	82	.258	.321	.352	673	88	-112	-90	96	60			
Total	620	—	—	—	—	341	275	5669	—	47783	11264	1860	392	886	4477	4529	185	687	.265	.338	.390	729	—	—	—	—	361	—	—	—

TEAM	CG	SHO	GR	SV	IP	H	HR	BB	SO	BR/9	ERA	AERA	OAV	OOB	PR	APR	PF	OSB	OCS	FA	E	WPB	DP	FW	PW	BW	BSW	DIF
Bro	47	**14**	**223**	**34**	1375.0	**1299**	104	626	592	12.8	3.82	108	**.251**	.336	37	48	102	42	*38*	.978	129	47	**169**	.9	4.7	3.7	—	7.6
StL	65	12	187	20	1397.2	1417	106	495	**642**	12.4	**3.53**	**117**	.266	.330	**83**	**92**	102	39	*27*	**.979**	**128**	33	**169**	**1.1**	**9.0**	.9	—	1.0
Bos	**74**	**14**	167	13	1362.2	1342	**93**	**453**	494	**11.9**	3.62	108	.255	**.316**	67	43	96	52	*37*	.974	153	**22**	124	-.6	4.2	3.9	—	1.4
NY	58	6	212	14	1363.2	1428	122	590	553	13.4	4.44	92	.267	.342	-58	-56	100	**29**	*27*	.974	155	40	136	-.7	-5.5	**8.7**	—	1.5
Cin	54	13	190	13	1365.1	1442	102	589	633	13.5	4.41	93	.274	.349	-53	-46	101	45	***41***	.977	138	**22**	134	.3	-4.5	-4.1	—	4.3
Chi	46	8	216	15	1367.0	1449	106	618	571	13.7	4.04	98	.274	.353	4	-13	97	43	*34*	.975	150	40	159	-.4	-1.3	-6.9	—	.5
Pit	44	9	211	13	1374.0	1488	155	592	530	13.9	4.68	90	.278	.354	-95	-68	104	52	*39*	.975	149	47	131	-.2	-6.7	1.1	—	-9.2
Phi	70	8	161	14	1362.0	1399	98	513	514	12.8	3.96	101	.276	.346	15	8	99	59	*38*	.974	152	52	140	-.5	.8	-8.9	—	-6.5
Total	458	84	1567	136	10967.1	—	—	—	—	13.1	4.06	—	.265	.338	—	—	—	—	—	.976	1154	303	1162	—	—	—	—	—

BATTER-FIELDER WINS	BATTING AVERAGE	ON-BASE PERCENTAGE	SLUGGING AVERAGE	ON-BASE PLUS SLUGGING	ADJUSTED OPS	ADJUSTED BATTER RUNS
Kiner-Pit 5.3	Walker-StL-Phi......363	Galan-Cin 449	Kiner-Pit......639	Kiner-Pit......1055	Kiner-Pit......172	Kiner-Pit......58.3
Mize-NY......5.0	B.Elliott-Bos 317	Walker-StL-Phi......436	Mize-NY......614	Mize-NY......998	Mize-NY......160	Mize-NY......48.0
B.Elliott-Bos......3.8	Cavarretta-Chi 314	Kurowski-StL......420	W.Cooper-NY 586	Kurowski-StL......964	Walker-StL-Phi......150	B.Elliott-Bos......40.9
Walker-StL-Phi...3.8	Kiner-Pit......313	Kiner-Pit......417	Kurowski-StL......544	B.Elliott-Bos......927	B.Elliott-Bos......148	Walker-StL-Phi.....38.9
Marshall-NY 3.0	Musial-StL......312	Walker-Bro......415	Marshall-NY......528	W.Cooper-NY 926	Kurowski-StL......148	Kurowski-StL......37.9
RUNS	**HITS**	**DOUBLES**	**TRIPLES**	**HOME RUNS**	**TOTAL BASES**	**RUNS BATTED IN**
Mize-NY......137	Holmes-Bos......191	Miller-Cin 38	Walker-StL-Phi......16	Mize-NY......51	Kiner-Pit......361	Mize-NY......138
Robinson-Bro......125	Walker-StL-Phi......186	B.Elliott-Bos......35	Slaughter-StL......13	Kiner-Pit......51	Mize-NY......360	Kiner-Pit......127
Kiner-Pit......118	Musial-StL......183	Ryan-Bos......33	Musial-StL......13	Marshall-NY......36	Marshall-NY......310	W.Cooper-NY 122
Musial-StL......113	Gustine-Pit......183	Holmes-Bos......33	Schoendienst-StL 9	W.Cooper-NY 35	W.Cooper-NY 302	B.Elliott-Bos......113
Kurowski-StL......108	Baumholtz-Cin......182	Baumholtz-Cin......32	Baumholtz-Cin......9	Thomson-NY 29	Musial-StL......296	Marshall-NY......107
BASES ON BALLS	**STOLEN BASES**	**BASE STEALING RUNS**	**FIELDING RUNS-INFIELD**	**FIELDING RUNS-OUTFIELD**	**OUTFIELD ASSISTS**	**CATCHER CS PCT.**
Reese-Bro 104	Robinson-Bro......29		Verban-Phi......17.5	Marshall-NY......9.4	Marshall-NY......19	Scheffing-Chi......47.9
Greenberg-Pit......104	Reiser-Bro 14		Gustine-Pit......16.4	Kiner-Pit......8.4	Baumholtz-Cin......18	Lamanno-Cin......47.5
Stanky-Bro......103	Walker-StL-Phi......13		Marion-StL......15.6	Holmes-Bos......5.5	Walker-StL-Phi......15	W.Cooper-NY 46.7
Kiner-Pit......98	Hopp-Bos......13		Kerr-NY......11.9	Ennis-Phi 4.2	Slaughter-StL......15	Edwards-Bro......44.3
Walker-Bro......97	Torgeson-Bos 11		Lowrey-Chi 10.2	Walker-StL-Phi......4.2		Rice-StL......42.4
WINS	**WINNING PCT.**	**WINS ABOVE TEAM**	**GAMES STARTED**	**COMPLETE GAMES**	**FEWEST HITS/GAME**	**FEWEST BB/GAME**
Blackwell-Cin......22	Jansen-NY......808	Jansen-NY......8.3	Branca-Bro 36	Blackwell-Cin......23	Taylor-Bro 7.22	Jansen-NY......2.07
Spahn-Bos......21	Munger-StL......762	Blackwell-Cin......8.2	Spahn-Bos......35	Spahn-Bos......22	Blackwell-Cin......7.48	Rowe-Phi 2.07
Sain-Bos......21	Blackwell-Cin......733	Leonard-Phi......5.1	Sain-Bos......35	Sain-Bos......22	Spahn-Bos......7.61	Leonard-Phi......2.18
Jansen-NY......21	Hatten-Bro 680	Munger-StL......5.0	Higbe-Bro-Pit......33	Jansen-NY......20	Lombardi-Bro......8.04	Barrett-Bos 2.26
Branca-Bro 21	Spahn-Bos......677	Spahn-Bos......4.9	Blackwell-Cin......33	Leonard-Phi......19	Branca-Bro 8.07	Brazle-StL......2.57
STRIKEOUTS	**STRIKEOUTS/GAME**	**GAMES**	**SAVES**	**BASE RUNNERS/9**	**ADJUSTED RELIEF RUNS**	**RELIEF RANKING**
Blackwell-Cin......193	Blackwell-Cin......6.36	Trinkle-NY......62	Casey-Bro......18	Poat-NY 9.90	Lanfranconi-Bos 7.4	Lanfranconi-Bos 8.6
Branca-Bro 148	Munger-StL......4.93	Higbe-Bro-Pit......50	Trinkle-NY......10	Spahn-Bos......10.25	Kush-Chi......7.0	Kush-Chi......8.5
Sain-Bos......132	Branca-Bro 4.76	Behrman-Bro-Pt-Bro ..50	Gumbert-Cin......10	Blackwell-Cin 10.75	Gumbert-Cin......3.1	Gumbert-Cin......6.1
Spahn-Bos......123	Brazle-StL......4.55	Kush-Chi......47	Behrman-Bro-Pt-Bro 8	Leonard-Phi......10.84	Casey-Bro......2.4	Casey-Bro......4.9
Munger-StL......123	Sain-Bos......4.47	Dickson-StL 47		Jansen-NY......10.85	Trinkle-NY 2.1	Trinkle-NY 2.9
INNINGS PITCHED	**OPPONENTS' AVG.**	**OPPONENTS' OBP**	**EARNED RUN AVERAGE**	**ADJUSTED ERA**	**ADJUSTED STARTER RUNS**	**PITCHER WINS**
Spahn-Bos......289.2	Taylor-Bro 225	Spahn-Bos......283	Spahn-Bos......2.33	Spahn-Bos......167	Spahn-Bos......51.9	**Spahn-Bos......5.3**
Branca-Bro 280.0	Spahn-Bos......226	Barrett-Bos 292	Blackwell-Cin......2.47	Blackwell-Cin......166	Blackwell-Cin......46.2	**Blackwell-Cin.....4.5**
Blackwell-Cin.....273.0	Blackwell-Cin......234	Blackwell-Cin......304	Branca-Bro 2.67	Branca-Bro 155	Branca-Bro 42.6	**Branca-Bro......4.2**
Sain-Bos......266.0	Branca-Bro 240	Leonard-Phi......306	Leonard-Phi......2.68	Leonard-Phi......149	Leonard-Phi......32.6	**Leonard-Phi 3.9**
Jansen-NY......248.0	Lombardi-Bro......241	Jansen-NY......306	Brazle-StL......2.84	Brazle-StL......146	Jansen-NY......23.5	**Brazle-StL......3.0**

Hello to the Modern Era

Money, race, and television—they were the biggest issues of 1947, perhaps baseball's first true modern season. The Pirates, flush with money from new investor Bing Crosby, opened their wallets to lure Hank Greenberg east with an unprecedented $100,000 deal. The club shortened the left field fences to aid him (and Ralph Kiner), but Pittsburgh tied for last anyway.

On the other side of the pennant race were the Dodgers, who overtook the surprising Braves in midsummer and held off the Cardinals. Blessed with excellent pitching from 21-year old Ralph Branca and reliever Hugh Casey, Brooklyn had a lineup full of on-base machines and a 28-year-old rookie first baseman named Jackie Robinson.

Robinson, the majors' first twentieth-century African American, withstood heckling and threats to lead the Dodgers' efforts. His performance was spectacular enough to make him the first official Rookie of the Year. Several other future stars debuted, including Duke Snider, Ted Kluzewski, and Curt Simmons.

Former favorites Billy Herman, Ernie Lombardi, and Mel Ott ended their careers, and two stars from the first part of the century, Johnny Evers and Hal Chase, passed away. (Evers' double-play partner Joe Tinker died the next year.)

From 1947–49, six NL teams drew more than a million fans every year—everyone but Cincinnati and Philadelphia. Scoring rose 15% in 1947, with homers up 58 percent. Johnny Mize and Kiner became the first NLers with 50 homers since 1930. Cincinnati's Ewell "The Whip" Blackwell won 16 straight and nearly threw back-to-back no-hitters.

In the first televised World Series, and one of the most entertaining ever, the Yankees defeated the Dodgers in seven. Six of the games were nail-biters, and for the first time, any American with access to a TV could look in. And for that, and many other, reasons, the game was never the same.

1947 AMERICAN LEAGUE

TEAM	W	L	T	PCT	GB	HW	HL	R	OR	PA	H	2B	3B	HR	BB	SO	HB	SH	AVG	OBP	SLG	OPS	AOPS	BR	ABR	PF	SB	CS	BSA	BSR
NY	97	57	1	.630	—	**55**	22	**794**	**568**	6031	**1439**	230	**72**	**115**	610	581	**27**	86	**.271**	.349	**.407**	**756**	**117**	**110**	**118**	99	27	23	54	-2
Det	85	69	4	.552	12	46	31	714	642	6148	1363	**234**	42	103	**762**	565	13	97	.258	**.353**	.377	730	106	82	61	103	52	60	46	-10
Bos	83	71	3	.539	14	49	30	720	669	6099	1412	206	54	103	666	590	16	95	.265	.349	.382	731	102	72	21	107	41	35	54	-3
Cle	80	74	3	.519	17	38	39	687	588	5976	1392	**234**	51	112	502	609	14	93	.259	.324	.385	709	106	8	26	97	29	25	54	-2
Phi	78	76	2	.506	19	39	38	633	614	5971	1311	218	52	61	605	563	24	**144**	.252	.333	.349	682	94	-23	-35	102	37	33	53	-3
Chi	70	84	1	.455	27	32	43	553	661	5837	1350	211	41	53	492	**527**	15	56	.256	.321	.342	663	93	-71	-49	96	**91**	57	**61**	0
Was	64	90	0	.416	33	36	41	496	675	5717	1234	186	48	42	525	534	8	72	.241	.313	.321	634	84	-121	-107	97	53	51	51	-6
StL	59	95	0	.383	38	29	48	564	744	5819	1238	189	52	90	583	664	15	76	.241	.320	.350	670	90	-57	-68	102	69	49	58	-2
Total	623	—	—	—	—	324	292	5161	—	47598	10739	1708	412	679	4745	4633	132	719	.256	.333	.364	698	—	—	—	—	399	333	55	-29

TEAM	CG	SHO	GR	SV	IP	H	HR	BB	SO	BR/9	ERA	AERA	OAV	OOB	PR	APR	PF	OSB	OCS	FA	E	WPB	DP	FW	PW	BW	BSW	DIF
NY	73	14	140	21	1374.1	**1221**	95	628	**691**	**12.2**	**3.39**	104	**.238**	**.323**	**48**	23	95	61	32	.981	109	27	151	1.5	2.4	**12.2**	.2	3.7
Det	**77**	**15**	137	18	1398.2	1382	79	**531**	648	12.4	3.57	106	.258	.326	21	30	102	41	36	.975	155	35	142	-1.0	3.1	6.3	-.7	.2
Bos	64	13	**184**	19	1391.1	1383	84	575	586	12.8	3.81	102	.261	.335	-16	11	105	57	29	.977	137	47	172	-.0	1.1	2.2	.0	2.6
Cle	55	13	182	**29**	1402.1	1244	94	628	590	**12.2**	3.44	101	.240	.325	41	7	94	**31**	48	**.983**	**104**	36	178	**1.9**	.7	2.7	.2	-2.5
Phi	70	12	125	15	1391.1	1291	85	597	493	12.3	3.51	**109**	.247	.326	30	**45**	103	37	**55**	.976	143	**19**	161	-.4	**4.7**	-3.6	.0	.3
Chi	47	11	**184**	27	1391.0	1384	76	603	522	13.0	3.64	100	.261	.339	11	3	99	58	40	.975	155	48	**180**	-1.2	.3	-5.1	**.4**	-1.5
Was	67	**15**	143	12	1362.0	1408	**63**	579	551	13.2	3.97	94	.267	.342	-40	-37	101	51	48	.976	143	23	151	-.5	-3.8	-11.1	-.2	2.7
StL	50	7	141	13	1365.0	1426	103	604	552	13.4	4.33	90	.272	.348	-94	-65	105	63	45	.977	134	28	169	.0	-6.7	-7.0	.2	-4.4
Total	503	100	1236	154	11076.0	—	—	—	—	12.7	3.71	—	.256	.333	—	—	—	—	—	.977	1080	263	1304	—	—	—	—	—

BATTER-FIELDER WINS	BATTING AVERAGE	ON-BASE PERCENTAGE	SLUGGING AVERAGE	ON-BASE PLUS SLUGGING	ADJUSTED OPS	ADJUSTED BATTER RUNS
Williams-Bos......7.2	Williams-Bos.........343	Williams-Bos.........499	Williams-Bos.........634	Williams-Bos.......1133	Williams-Bos.........199	Williams-Bos........82.7
Boudreau-Cle.....5.3	McCosky-Phi 328	Fain-Phi 414	DiMaggio-NY 522	DiMaggio-NY 913	DiMaggio-NY 154	DiMaggio-NY 38.0
Cullenbine-Det...3.6	Pesky-Bos............324	Cullenbine-Det......401	Gordon-Cle 496	Henrich-NY...........857	Henrich-NY...........139	Henrich-NY..........27.9
Doerr-Bos 3.3	Wright-Chi............324	McCosky-Phi 395	Henrich-NY...........485	Heath-StL 850	Gordon-Cle...........136	McQuinn-NY........25.0
Stephens-StL.....3.1	Kell-Det................320	McQuinn-NY.........395	Heath-StL 485	Gordon-Cle...........842	Heath-StL 133	Fain-Phi 24.4

RUNS	HITS	DOUBLES	TRIPLES	HOME RUNS	TOTAL BASES	RUNS BATTED IN
Williams-Bos.........125	Pesky-Bos............207	Boudreau-Cle 45	Henrich-NY.............13	Williams-Bos...........32	Williams-Bos.........335	Williams-Bos.........114
Henrich-NY...........109	Kell-Det................188	Williams-Bos..........40	Vernon-Was............12	Gordon-Cle.............29	Gordon-Cle...........279	Henrich-NY.............98
Pesky-Bos.............106	Williams-Bos.........181	Henrich-NY.............35	Philley-Chi 11	Heath-StL 27	DiMaggio-NY 279	DiMaggio-NY 97
Stirnweiss-NY.......102	McCosky-Phi 179	DiMaggio-NY 31		Cullenbine-Det.........24	Henrich-NY...........267	Jones-Chi-Bos........96
DiMaggio-NY 97				York-Bos-Chi...........21	Pesky-Bos............250	

BASES ON BALLS	STOLEN BASES	BASE STEALING RUNS	FIELDING RUNS-INFIELD	FIELDING RUNS-OUTFIELD	OUTFIELD ASSISTS	CATCHER CS PCT.
Williams-Bos.........162	Dillinger-StL 34	Dillinger-StL 2.9	Doerr-Bos 25.2	DiMaggio-Bos 15.0	DiMaggio-Bos 19	Rosar-Phi.............60.0
Cullenbine-Det......137	Philley-Chi 21	Valo-Phi 1.4	Boudreau-Cle 18.8	Chapman-Phi.........8.2	Chapman-Phi..........16	Hegan-Cle 55.8
Lake-Det..............120	Vernon-Was............12	Binks-Phi 1.1	Rizzuto-NY 17.7	Spence-Was 6.2	Henrich-NY 13	Swift-Det.............47.6
Joost-Phi..............114	Pesky-Bos...............12	Kolloway-Chi..........1.0	Cullenbine-Det.....17.5	Lindell-NY 5.6	Spence-Was 12	Evans-Was 47.4
Fain-Phi 95		Tucker-Chi.................8	Kell-Det...............16.2	Henrich-NY 4.6	Lewis-Was 11	Early-StL.............44.2

WINS	WINNING PCT.	WINS ABOVE TEAM	GAMES STARTED	COMPLETE GAMES	FEWEST HITS/GAME	FEWEST BB/GAME
Feller-Cle 20	Reynolds-NY 704	Marchildon-Phi.......5.5	Feller-Cle 37	Newhouser-Det.......24	Shea-NY 6.40	Galehouse-StL-Bos .2.48
Reynolds-NY 19	Dobson-Bos..........692	Dobson-Bos...........4.9	Newhouser-Det.......36	Wynn-Was 22	Feller-Cle 6.92	Hutchinson-Det....2.50
Marchildon-Phi........19	Marchildon-Phi......679	Haynes-Chi............4.8	Marchildon-Phi........35	Lopat-Chi................22	Marchildon-Phi.....7.42	Lopat-Chi 2.60
Hutchinson-Det.......18	Feller-Cle 645	Feller-Cle 4.8		Marchildon-Phi........21	Embree-Cle 7.58	Muncrief-StL 2.60
Dobson-Bos............18	Hutchinson-Det.....643	Wynn-Was 3.8		Feller-Cle 20	Masterson-Was....7.65	Dobson-Bos.........2.87

STRIKEOUTS	STRIKEOUTS/GAME	GAMES	SAVES	BASE RUNNERS/9	ADJUSTED RELIEF RUNS	RELIEF RANKING
Feller-Cle 196	Feller-Cle 5.90	Klieman-Cle............58	Page-NY 17	Chandler-NY........9.91	Page-NY 18.1	Page-NY 30.3
Newhouser-Det.....176	Hughson-Bos.......5.66	Page-NY 56	Klieman-Cle............17	Feller-Cle...........10.87	Christopher-Phi......7.7	Christopher-Phi....15.4
Masterson-Was.....135	Newhouser-Det....5.56	Johnson-Bos...........45	Christopher-Phi.......12	Dobson-Bos.......10.90	Murphy-Bos 7.3	Klieman-Cle 7.6
Reynolds-NY 129	Trucks-Det 5.38	Savage-Phi 44	Ferrick-Was 9	Raschi-NY 11.01	Klieman-Cle...........5.9	Ferrick-Was 5.6
Marchildon-Phi......128	Kinder-StL............5.09	Christopher-Phi.......44		Shea-NY............11.08	Ferrick-Was 3.6	Murphy-Bos 3.6

INNINGS PITCHED	OPPONENTS' AVG.	OPPONENTS' OBP	EARNED RUN AVERAGE	ADJUSTED ERA	ADJUSTED STARTER RUNS	PITCHER WINS
Feller-Cle 299.0	Shea-NY 200	Dobson-Bos..........299	Haynes-Chi..........2.42	Haynes-Chi...........151	Feller-Cle 28.7	**Newhouser-Det . 3.7**
Newhouser-Det..285.0	Feller-Cle 215	Feller-Cle 300	Chandler-NY........2.46	Fowler-Phi.............136	Newhouser-Det....28.0	**Hutchinson-Det . 3.7**
Marchildon-Phi...276.2	Marchildon-Phi......224	Shea-NY 303	Feller-Cle 2.68	Dobson-Bos..........132	Lopat-Chi.............26.0	**Page-NY 3.3**
Masterson-Was..253.0	Reynolds-NY 227	Hutchinson-Det.....304	Fowler-Phi............2.81	Newhouser-Det.....131	Fowler-Phi............26.0	**Feller-Cle 3.2**
Lopat-Chi...........252.2	Embree-Cle 233	Lopat-Chi 307	Lopat-Chi 2.81	Feller-Cle 130	Dobson-Bos.........23.1	**Lopat-Chi............ 2.9**

It's . . . the Yankees

In April the Indians brought the power alleys at Municipal Stadium in by 70 feet, then a few weeks later shortened center field by 58. While this significantly increased home run production, the team made a much more important alteration July 5, when owner Bill Veeck made Larry Doby the league's first African American player. Cleveland also broke in rookie pitcher Bob Lemon, while infielder Nellie Fox began his career in Philadelphia. Red Ruffing, 43, retired with 273 wins, while catcher Al Lopez hung it up at 39.

The pennant race held few thrills. In late June New York emerged from a crowded field and pulled away. Under new manager Bucky Harris the Yankees led the league in runs and in fewest allowed. While few players had statistically impressive seasons, there were no weak spots. Joe Page, 29, became the league's dominant reliever. The second-place Tigers felt the loss of Hank Greenberg. Boston, with several offensive black holes, fell to third despite Ted Williams' Triple Crown. The Philadelphia A's improved by 29 games and had their first winning record since 1933.

The advance in glove technology, improvements in groundskeeping, and better defensive skill helped AL fielders, for the first time ever, complete more double plays than they made errors. Stolen bases, which had increased during World War II, dropped to the lowest level in league history—only to drop again in 1948.

Three of the seven games in an exciting Dodgers-Yankees World Series were one-run affairs. New York took the first two, then Brooklyn captured the following pair at Ebbets Field, including a thrilling Game 4 in which Yankees pitcher Bill Bevens lost his no-hitter, and the game, on Cookie Lavagetto's ninth-inning two-run pinch-double. After the well-matched clubs split the next two, the final contest took place at Yankee Stadium. Brooklyn's weary pitching staff couldn't hold off the Yankees, and Page saved the 5-2 win with five scoreless relief innings.

1946 NATIONAL LEAGUE

TEAM	W	L	T	PCT	GB	HW	HL	R	OR	PA	H	2B	3B	HR	BB	SO	HB	SH	AVG	OBP	SLG	OPS	AOPS	BR	ABR	PF	SB	CS	BSA	BSR
StL	98	58	0	.628	—	49	29	**712**	**545**	6020	**1426**	**265**	56	81	530	537	21	97	**.265**	.334	**.381**	**715**	105	56	28	104	58			
Bro	96	60	1	.615	2	**56**	22	701	570	6134	1376	233	**66**	55	**691**	575	17	**141**	.260	**.348**	.361	709	**106**	**63**	**56**	101	**100**			
Chi	82	71	2	.536	14.5	44	33	626	581	6024	1344	223	50	56	586	599	24	116	.254	.331	.346	677	100	-8	5	98	43			
Bos	81	72	1	.529	15.5	45	31	630	592	5940	1377	238	48	44	558	**468**	22	135	.264	.337	.353	690	101	18	11	101	60			
Phi	69	85	1	.448	28	41	36	560	705	5772	1351	209	40	80	417	590	19	103	.258	.315	.359	674	100	-32	-15	97	41			
Cin	67	87	2	.435	30	35	42	523	570	5934	1262	206	33	65	493	604	**28**	122	.239	.307	.327	634	88	-102	-82	96	82			
Pit	63	91	1	.409	34	37	40	552	668	5907	1300	202	52	60	592	555	15	101	.250	.328	.344	672	95	-19	-33	103	48			
NY	61	93	0	.396	36	38	39	612	685	5836	1326	176	37	**121**	532	546	27	86	.255	.328	.374	702	104	25	21	101	46			
Total	621	—	—	—	—	345	272	4916	—	47567	10762	1752	382	562	4399	4474	173	901	.256	.329	.355	684	—	—	—	—	478	—	—	—

TEAM	CG	SHO	GR	SV	IP	H	HR	BB	SO	BR/9	ERA	AERA	OAV	OOB	PR	APR	PF	OSB	OCS	FA	E	WPB	DP	FW	PW	BW	BSW	DIF
StL	**75**	**18**	180	15	1397.0	1326	63	493	607	11.9	**3.01**	**115**	.254	.322	**63**	**69**	101	41	*36*	**.980**	**124**	29	167	**2.1**	**7.3**	3.0	—	7.6
Bro	52	14	**223**	**28**	1418.0	**1280**	58	671	**647**	12.5	3.05	111	**.243**	.331	58	53	99	**37**	***60***	.972	174	44	154	-.9	5.6	**5.9**	—	7.3
Chi	59	15	187	11	1393.0	1370	58	527	619	12.4	3.24	102	.256	.325	26	15	97	56	*37*	.976	146	28	119	.7	1.6	.5	—	2.7
Bos	74	10	167	12	1371.0	1291	76	478	566	11.7	3.35	102	.249	**.314**	10	13	101	74	*39*	.972	169	32	129	-.8	1.4	1.2	—	2.7
Phi	55	11	185	23	1369.0	1442	73	542	490	13.3	3.99	86	.273	.344	-88	-85	101	66	*49*	.975	148	44	144	.6	-9.0	-1.6	—	2.1
Cin	69	17	146	11	1413.1	1334	70	**467**	506	**11.6**	3.08	109	.252	**.314**	53	43	98	47	*58*	.975	155	**17**	**192**	.2	4.6	-8.7	—	-6.1
Pit	61	10	181	6	1370.0	1406	**50**	561	458	13.1	3.72	95	.269	.342	-46	-28	103	88	*48*	.970	184	28	127	-1.6	-3.0	-3.5	—	-5.9
NY	47	8	216	13	1353.1	1313	114	660	581	13.2	3.92	88	.256	.343	-76	-71	101	69	*43*	.973	159	38	121	-.2	-7.5	2.2	—	-10.5
Total	492	103	1485	119	11084.2	—	—	—	—	12.5	3.41	—	.256	.329	—	—	—	—	—	.974	1259	260	1153	—	—	—	—	—

BATTER-FIELDER WINS	BATTING AVERAGE	ON-BASE PERCENTAGE	SLUGGING AVERAGE	ON-BASE PLUS SLUGGING	ADJUSTED OPS	ADJUSTED BATTER RUNS
Musial-StL 5.8	Musial-StL .365	Stanky-Bro .436	Musial-StL .587	Musial-StL 1021	Musial-StL 180	Musial-StL 66.0
Mize-NY 4.8	Hopp-Bos .333	Musial-StL .434	Ennis-Phi .485	Kurowski-StL 853	Ennis-Phi 144	Mize-NY 43.8
Cavarretta-Chi 3.0	Walker-Bro .319	Cavarretta-Chi .401	Slaughter-StL .465	Ennis-Phi 849	Cavarretta-Chi 140	Cavarretta-Chi 30.4
Stanky-Bro 2.9	Ennis-Phi .313	Herman-Bro-Bos .395	Kurowski-StL .462	Walker-Bro 839	Walker-Bro 136	Walker-Bro 28.2
Ennis-Phi 2.9	Holmes-Bos .310	Walker-Bro .391	Walker-Bro .448	Slaughter-StL 838	Kurowski-StL 136	Ennis-Phi 28.2
RUNS	**HITS**	**DOUBLES**	**TRIPLES**	**HOME RUNS**	**TOTAL BASES**	**RUNS BATTED IN**
Musial-StL 124	Musial-StL 228	Musial-StL 50	Musial-StL 20	Kiner-Pit 23	Musial-StL 366	Slaughter-StL 130
Slaughter-StL 100	Walker-Bro 184	Holmes-Bos 35	Reese-Bro 10	Mize-NY 22	Slaughter-StL 283	Walker-Bro 116
Stanky-Bro 98	Slaughter-StL 183	Kurowski-StL 32	Cavarretta-Chi 10	Slaughter-StL 18	Ennis-Phi 262	Musial-StL 103
Schoendienst-StL 94	Holmes-Bos 176	Herman-Bro-Bos 31	Walker-Bro 9	Ennis-Phi 17	Walker-Bro 258	Kurowski-StL 89
Cavarretta-Chi 89	Schoendienst-StL 170				Holmes-Bos 241	Kiner-Pit 81
BASES ON BALLS	**STOLEN BASES**	**BASE STEALING RUNS**	**FIELDING RUNS-INFIELD**	**FIELDING RUNS-OUTFIELD**	**OUTFIELD ASSISTS**	**CATCHER CS PCT.**
Stanky-Bro 137	Reiser-Bro 34		Marion-StL 18.1	Ennis-Phi 10.1	Slaughter-StL 23	Edwards-Bro 55.6
Fletcher-Pit 111	Haas-Cin 22		Handley-Pit 12.0	Furillo-Bro 8.7	Wyrostek-Phi 18	Mueller-Cin 52.5
Cavarretta-Chi 88	Hopp-Bos 21		Gustine-Pit 7.8	Gilbert-Chi-Phi 6.0	Holmes-Bos 17	Seminick-Phi 39.7
Reese-Bro 87	Adams-Cin 16		Kerr-NY 7.6	Holmes-Bos 5.4	Ennis-Phi 16	McCullough-Chi 38.8
Hack-Chi 83	Walker-Bro 14		McCormick-Phi 4.8	Wyrostek-Phi 4.7		Masi-Bos 35.0
WINS	**WINNING PCT.**	**WINS ABOVE TEAM**	**GAMES STARTED**	**COMPLETE GAMES**	**FEWEST HITS/GAME**	**FEWEST BB/GAME**
Pollet-StL 21	Dickson-StL .714	Rowe-Phi 4.1	Koslo-NY 35	Sain-Bos 24	Kennedy-NY 7.38	Cooper-Bos 1.76
Sain-Bos 20	Higbe-Bro .680	Wilks-StL 4.0	Sain-Bos 34	Pollet-StL 22	Schmitz-Chi 7.38	Raffensberger-Phi 1.79
Higbe-Bro 17	Pollet-StL .677	Kush-Chi 3.4	Pollet-StL 32	Koslo-NY 17	Blackwell-Cin 7.41	Beggs-Cin 1.85
Dickson-StL 15	Sain-Bos .588	Ostermueller-Pit 3.4	Schmitz-Chi 31	Ostermueller-Pit 16	Higbe-Bro 7.60	Heusser-Cin 2.09
Brecheen-StL 15	Brecheen-StL .500	Lanier-StL 3.0		Cooper-Bos 15	Sain-Bos 7.64	Strincevich-Pit 2.25
STRIKEOUTS	**STRIKEOUTS/GAME**	**GAMES**	**SAVES**	**BASE RUNNERS/9**	**ADJUSTED RELIEF RUNS**	**RELIEF RANKING**
Schmitz-Chi 135	Higbe-Bro 5.72	Trinkle-NY 48	Raffensberger-Phi 6	Rowe-Phi 9.20	Casey-Bro 13.5	Casey-Bro 21.1
Higbe-Bro 134	Schmitz-Chi 5.42	Dickson-StL 47	Pollet-StL 5	Cooper-Bos 9.95	Thompson-NY 11.6	Thompson-NY 18.4
Sain-Bos 129	Blackwell-Cin 4.63	Behrman-Bro 47	Karl-Phi 5	Beggs-Cin 10.18	Malloy-Cin 3.5	Malloy-Cin 3.3
Koslo-NY 121	Brecheen-StL 4.55	Casey-Bro 46	Herring-Bro 5	Spahn-Bos 10.31	Budnick-NY 1.1	Wilks-StL .7
Brecheen-StL 117	Voiselle-NY 4.50		Casey-Bro 5	Sain-Bos 10.66	Wilks-StL .9	Budnick-NY .6
INNINGS PITCHED	**OPPONENTS' AVG.**	**OPPONENTS' OBP**	**EARNED RUN AVERAGE**	**ADJUSTED ERA**	**ADJUSTED STARTER RUNS**	**PITCHER WINS**
Pollet-StL 266.0	Schmitz-Chi .221	Cooper-Bos .276	Pollet-StL 2.10	Pollet-StL 165	Pollet-StL 34.7	**Sain-Bos 5.4**
Koslo-NY 265.1	Kennedy-NY .224	Beggs-Cin .287	Sain-Bos 2.21	Sain-Bos 155	Sain-Bos 33.9	**Pollet-StL 4.3**
Sain-Bos 265.0	Blackwell-Cin .226	Sain-Bos .294	Beggs-Cin 2.32	Beggs-Cin 144	Brecheen-StL 25.2	**Brecheen-StL 3.1**
Brecheen-StL 231.1	Higbe-Bro .229	Dickson-StL .295	Blackwell-Cin 2.45	Brecheen-StL 139	Blackwell-Cin 19.9	**Beggs-Cin 2.6**
Schmitz-Chi 224.1	Sain-Bos .230	Pollet-StL .300	Brecheen-StL 2.49	Blackwell-Cin 136	Beggs-Cin 19.8	**Ostermueller-Pit 2.5**

Contract Jumping, Integration, and More!

The Dodgers and Cardinals, rejuvenated by players returning from the service, hung together at the top of the NL for the entire 1946 season, working in lockstep from July to the end. The teams matched win for win and ended the year in a tie—the first in major league history. Both teams blew chances to win outright in the final regular-season weekend. In a best-of-three playoff, the Cardinals got fine pitching from Howie Pollet, Murry Dickson, and Harry Brecheen to win the series in two.

Once again attendance reached an all-time NL record, increasing 69 percent. Five teams drew a million, an unprecedented total; the Dodgers set an all-time league record. Even with many veterans returning, several impressive youngsters debuted, including Carl Furillo, Ralph Kiner, Alvin Dark, and Bobby Thomson.

One of the year's odder stories involved the Mexican League, headed by entrepreneur Jorge Pasquel. Determined to make his league a serious player, he and his cohorts spent many thousands to lure away key players from the Cardinals, Dodgers, and Giants. New Commissioner Happy Chandler banned all jumpers from returning for five years, although this edict was softened when the Mexican League began to have problems paying its contracts.

The World Series was one of the best in history, with the Cardinals and Red Sox trading victories in the first six contests. In Game 7 Boston tied the score with 2 runs in the visiting eighth, but the Cardinals won in the bottom of the frame when Harry Walker's single scored the hustling Enos Slaughter from first. Brecheen had 3 wins, allowing just 1 earned run in 20 innings.

For all the exciting baseball played during the season, the most significant event of the year occurred out of the country. In Montreal, Dodgers farmhand Jackie Robinson became the first African American in professional ball in more than sixty years.

1946 AMERICAN LEAGUE

TEAM	W	L	T	PCT	GB	HW	HL	R	OR	PA	H	2B	3B	HR	BB	SO	HB	SH	AVG	OBP	SLG	OPS	AOPS	BR	ABR	PF	SB	CS	BSA	BSR
Bos	104	50	2	.675	—	**61**	16	**792**	594	6126	**1441**	**268**	50	109	**687**	661	15	**106**	**.271**	**.356**	**.402**	**758**	**113**	**142**	**100**	106	45	36	56	-3
Det	92	62	1	.597	12	48	30	704	567	6057	1373	212	41	108	622	616	13	104	.258	.337	.374	711	100	43	4	106	65	41	**61**	0
NY	87	67	0	.565	17	47	30	684	**547**	5879	1275	208	50	**136**	627	706	**33**	80	.248	.334	.387	721	107	56	47	101	48	35	58	-2
Was	76	78	1	.494	28	38	38	608	706	5958	1388	260	**63**	60	511	641	24	86	.260	.327	.366	693	106	2	42	94	51	50	50	-6
Chi	74	80	1	.481	30	40	38	562	595	5911	1364	206	44	37	501	600	20	78	.257	.323	.333	656	94	-66	-44	96	**78**	64	55	-5
Cle	68	86	2	.442	36	36	41	537	638	5857	1285	233	56	79	506	697	13	96	.245	.313	.356	669	99	-50	-10	94	57	49	54	-5
StL	66	88	2	.429	38	35	41	621	710	5921	1350	220	46	84	465	713	16	67	.251	.313	.356	669	89	-55	-82	105	23	35	40	-7
Phi	49	105	1	.318	55	31	46	529	680	5796	1317	220	51	40	482	**594**	9	105	.253	.318	.338	656	91	-70	-67	99	39	30	57	-2
Total	621	—	—	—	—	336	280	5037	—	47505	10793	1827	401	653	4401	5228	143	722	.256	.328	.364	692	—	—	—	—	406	340	54	-30

TEAM	CG	SHO	GR	SV	IP	H	HR	BB	SO	BR/9	ERA	AERA	OAV	OOB	PR	APR	PF	OSB	OCS	FA	E	WPB	DP	FW	PW	BW	BSW	DIF
Bos	79	15	151	**20**	1396.2	1359	89	501	667	12.1	3.38	108	.254	.319	19	42	105	**39**	28	**.977**	**139**	24	163	**1.5**	4.4	**10.5**	.0	10.6
Det	**94**	**18**	101	15	1402.0	1277	97	**497**	**896**	**11.5**	3.22	**114**	**.241**	**.307**	45	**65**	104	47	37	.974	155	35	138	.5	**6.8**	.4	**.4**	6.9
NY	68	17	152	17	1361.0	**1232**	**66**	552	653	11.9	3.13	110	.243	.319	56	49	99	42	49	.975	150	23	**174**	.7	5.1	4.9	.2	-.9
Was	71	8	157	10	1396.1	1459	81	547	537	13.1	3.74	89	.269	.339	-36	-64	96	55	46	.966	211	64	162	-2.8	-6.7	4.4	-.2	4.4
Chi	62	9	142	16	1392.1	1348	80	508	550	12.1	**3.10**	110	.255	.323	**63**	50	97	55	43	.972	175	49	170	-.7	5.2	-4.6	-.1	-2.8
Cle	63	16	170	13	1388.2	1282	84	649	789	12.6	3.62	91	.245	.331	-17	-51	94	42	42	.975	147	36	147	1.0	-5.3	-1.0	-.1	-3.5
StL	63	13	**193**	12	1382.1	1465	73	573	574	13.3	3.95	94	.272	.343	-69	-32	107	84	41	.974	159	46	157	.3	-3.4	-8.6	-.3	1.0
Phi	61	10	145	5	1342.2	1371	83	577	562	13.2	3.90	91	.264	.340	-59	-52	101	42	**54**	.971	167	**20**	141	-.2	-5.4	-7.0	.2	-15.5
Total	561	106	1211	108	11062.0	—	—	—	—	12.5	3.50	—	.256	.328	—	—	—	—	—	.973	1303	297	1252	—	—	—	—	—

BATTER-FIELDER WINS	BATTING AVERAGE	ON-BASE PERCENTAGE	SLUGGING AVERAGE	ON-BASE PLUS SLUGGING	ADJUSTED OPS	ADJUSTED BATTER RUNS
Williams-Bos......8.1	Vernon-Was..........353	Williams-Bos.........497	Williams-Bos.........667	Williams-Bos.......1164	Williams-Bos.........211	Williams-Bos........88.3
Doerr-Bos...........4.8	Williams-Bos.........342	Keller-NY..............405	Greenberg-Det......604	Greenberg-Det......977	Vernon-Was..........163	Vernon-Was.........48.9
Pesky-Bos...........4.6	Pesky-Bos............335	Vernon-Was..........403	Keller-NY..............533	Keller-NY..............938	Greenberg-Det......160	Keller-NY.............45.6
Vernon-Was........4.3	Kell-Phi-Det..........322	Pesky-Bos............401	DiMaggio-NY........511	Vernon-Was..........910	Keller-NY..............158	Greenberg-Det.....40.6
Greenberg-Det...3.9	DiMaggio-Bos.......316	DiMaggio-Bos.......393	Edwards-Cle.........509	DiMaggio-NY........878	Edwards-Cle.........151	Cullenbine-Det.....38.9
RUNS	**HITS**	**DOUBLES**	**TRIPLES**	**HOME RUNS**	**TOTAL BASES**	**RUNS BATTED IN**
Williams-Bos.........142	Pesky-Bos.............208	Vernon-Was...........51	Edwards-Cle...........16	Greenberg-Det........44	Williams-Bos.........343	Greenberg-Det......127
Pesky-Bos.............115	Vernon-Was..........207	Spence-Was...........50	Lewis-Was..............13	Williams-Bos..........38	Greenberg-Det......316	Williams-Bos.........123
Lake-Det...............105	Appling-Chi...........180	Pesky-Bos..............43	Kell-Phi-Det............10	Keller-NY................30	Vernon-Was..........298	York-Bos...............119
Keller-NY................98	Williams-Bos.........176	Williams-Bos...........37	Spence-Was...........10	Seerey-Cle..............26	Spence-Was.........287	Doerr-Bos.............116
Doerr-Bos...............95	Lewis-Was............170	Doerr-Bos..............34	Keller-NY................10	DiMaggio-NY..........25	Keller-NY.............287	Keller-NY.............101
BASES ON BALLS	**STOLEN BASES**	**BASE STEALING RUNS**	**FIELDING RUNS-INFIELD**	**FIELDING RUNS-OUTFIELD**	**OUTFIELD ASSISTS**	**CATCHER CS PCT.**
Williams-Bos.........156	Case-Cle.................28	Case-Cle................2.3	Doerr-Bos............27.3	Zarilla-StL..............9.6	Lewis-Was..............16	Hegan-Cle...........55.3
Keller-NY..............113	Stirnweiss-NY.........18	Stirnweiss-NY........1.9	Gordon-NY...........18.1	Chapman-Phi.........8.1	Spence-Was...........15	Rosar-Phi.............54.4
Lake-Det...............103	Lake-Det.................15	Dillinger-StL...........1.4	Boudreau-Cle......17.2	Judnich-StL............5.2	DiMaggio-NY..........15	Robinson-NY.......49.0
Cullenbine-Det........88		Evers-Det...............1.2	Rizzuto-NY..........16.7	Lewis-Was.............2.4		Tresh-Chi.............45.5
Henrich-NY.............87		Wright-Chi..............1.1	Pesky-Bos............12.3	Williams-Bos..........2.4		Tebbetts-Det........44.2
WINS	**WINNING PCT.**	**WINS ABOVE TEAM**	**GAMES STARTED**	**COMPLETE GAMES**	**FEWEST HITS/GAME**	**FEWEST BB/GAME**
Newhouser-Det.......26	Ferriss-Bos...........806	Feller-Cle...............8.6	Feller-Cle................42	Feller-Cle................36	Newhouser-Det....6.61	Hughson-Bos.......1.65
Feller-Cle................26	Newhouser-Det.....743	Newhouser-Det......7.4	Hughson-Bos..........35	Newhouser-Det.......29	Feller-Cle.............6.71	Lopat-Chi.............1.87
Ferriss-Bos.............25	Chandler-NY.........714	Ferriss-Bos............7.1	Ferriss-Bos.............35	Ferriss-Bos.............26	Chandler-NY........6.99	Leonard-Was.......2.00
Hughson-Bos..........20	Harris-Bos.............654	Chandler-NY..........5.5	Newhouser-Det.......34	Trout-Det.................23	Embree-Cle.........7.65	Flores-Phi............2.21
Chandler-NY..........20	Hughson-Bos........645	Caldwell-Chi..........4.9		Hughson-Bos..........21	Bevens-NY...........7.68	Ferriss-Bos..........2.33
STRIKEOUTS	**STRIKEOUTS/GAME**	**GAMES**	**SAVES**	**BASE RUNNERS/9**	**ADJUSTED RELIEF RUNS**	**RELIEF RANKING**
Feller-Cle..............348	Newhouser-Det....8.46	Feller-Cle................48	Klinger-Bos..............9	Ruffing-NY...........8.85	Caldwell-Chi........12.9	Caldwell-Chi........24.4
Newhouser-Det.....275	Feller-Cle............8.43	Savage-Phi.............40	Caldwell-Chi.............8	Caldwell-Chi........8.93	Klinger-Bos............8.3	Klinger-Bos............9.5
Hughson-Bos........172	Trucks-Det...........6.12	Ferriss-Bos.............40	Murphy-NY...............7	Newhouser-Det....9.66	Kinder-StL..............4.7	Lemon-Cle.............3.8
Trucks-Det............161	Hutchinson-Det....6.00	Hughson-Bos..........39	Ferrick-Cle-StL..........6	Gumpert-NY........9.84	Lemon-Cle.............4.3	Kinder-StL..............3.0
Trout-Det...............151	Hughson-Bos.......5.57	Caldwell-Chi...........39		Hughson-Bos.......9.87		
INNINGS PITCHED	**OPPONENTS' AVG.**	**OPPONENTS' OBP**	**EARNED RUN AVERAGE**	**ADJUSTED ERA**	**ADJUSTED STARTER RUNS**	**PITCHER WINS**
Feller-Cle...........371.1	Newhouser-Det.....201	Newhouser-Det.....269	Newhouser-Det....1.94	Newhouser-Det.....189	Newhouser-Det....51.1	**Newhouser-Det . 6.4**
Newhouser-Det..292.2	Feller-Cle..............208	Hughson-Bos........274	Chandler-NY........2.10	Chandler-NY.........164	Feller-Cle.............50.1	**Feller-Cle............ 5.4**
Hughson-Bos.....278.0	Chandler-NY.........218	Chandler-NY.........288	Feller-Cle.............2.18	Trout-Det...............156	Chandler-NY........38.5	**Trout-Det............ 4.7**
Trout-Det...........276.1	Embree-Cle..........227	Lopat-Chi..............288	Bevens-NY...........2.23	Bevens-NY............154	Trout-Det..............37.0	**Chandler-NY...... 4.5**
Ferriss-Bos........274.0	Bevens-NY............232	Feller-Cle..............291	Flores-Phi............2.32	Flores-Phi.............153	Bevens-NY..........33.6	**Bevens-NY.......... 3.2**

Goodbye and Hello

Boston improved by 33 games, leaping from seventh to first. The core of the club—Ted Williams, Bobby Doerr, Johnny Pesky, Tex Hughson, Mickey Harris, and Dom DiMaggio—came home and made up for lost time. Despite two offensive dead spots, the Red Sox led the AL in runs by nearly 100, leaving second-place Detroit in the dust. Former contenders Washington, St. Louis, and Chicago all finished below .500.

With the boys back home, attendance shot up 72 percent to establish a new league record. This was the first time that the *average* AL team drew more than a million fans. In 1946 five clubs topped a million, and even St. Louis had its second-best attendance ever. The Yankees became the first club ever to draw two million customers. (New York's 1946 attendance was higher than the totals for the previous three seasons combined.)

Home runs increased by more than half, and continued to rise until 1950. Not coincidentally, strikeouts also reached a new high. Hal Newhouser, dispelling criticism that he was just a wartime star, set an AL mark with 8.46 whiffs per game. Two top catchers debuted in 1946, Sherm Lollar with the Indians and Yogi Berra, arguably the best in league history, with the Yankees. With Berra on the way, Bill Dickey retired. Ted Lyons, Chicago's 46-year-old "Sunday pitcher," retired following three years in the army—he went 1-4 but still had a 2.32 ERA.

Former Yankees star Tony Lazzeri died after falling down a flight of stairs, while Walter Johnson succumbed from a brain tumor. Manager Joe McCarthy departed the Yankees in midseason amid clashes with owner Larry MacPhail. And in another shocking departure, the Tigers waived Hank Greenberg, who wanted a $20,000 raise. Pittsburgh convinced Greenberg to play in 1947 by making him the game's first $100,000 player.

The World Series was a classic, with the St. Louis Cardinals winning in seven games. The final contest was a nail-biter all the way as the lead changed hands three times.

1945 NATIONAL LEAGUE

TEAM	W	L	T	PCT	GB	HW	HL	R	OR	PA	H	2B	3B	HR	BB	SO	HB	SH	AVG	OBP	SLG	OPS	AOPS	BR	ABR	PF	SB	CS	BSA	BSR
Chi	98	56	1	.636	—	**49**	26	735	**532**	6034	1465	229	52	57	554	462	32	**150**	**.277**	**.349**	.372	721	**109**	54	70	98	69			
StL	95	59	1	.617	3	48	29	756	582	6166	**1498**	256	44	64	515	488	26	138	.273	.338	.371	709	102	27	10	102	55			
Bro	87	67	1	.565	11	48	30	**795**	724	6183	1468	257	**71**	57	**629**	**434**	25	111	.271	**.349**	.376	**725**	**109**	**69**	**75**	99	77			
Pit	82	72	1	.532	16	45	34	753	686	6038	1425	**259**	56	72	590	480	17	88	.267	.342	.377	719	102	48	20	104	81			
NY	78	74	2	.513	19	47	30	668	701	5991	1439	175	35	**114**	501	457	**40**	100	.269	.336	**.379**	715	103	30	19	102	38			
Bos	67	85	2	.441	30	36	38	721	728	6078	1453	229	25	101	520	510	26	91	.267	.334	.374	708	102	21	17	101	**82**			
Cin	61	93	0	.396	37	36	41	536	694	5796	1317	221	26	56	392	532	26	95	.249	.304	.333	637	85	-124	-112	98	71			
Phi	46	108	0	.299	52	22	55	548	865	5738	1278	197	27	56	449	501	15	71	.246	.307	.326	633	84	-125	-110	97	54			
Total	618	—	—	—	—	331	283	5512	—	48024	11343	1823	336	577	4150	3864	207	844	.265	.333	.364	696	—	—	—	—	527	—	—	—

TEAM	CG	SHO	GR	SV	IP	H	HR	BB	SO	BR/9	ERA	AERA	OAV	OOB	PR	APR	PF	OSB	OCS	FA	E	WPB	DP	FW	PW	BW	BSW	DIF
Chi	**86**	15	135	14	1366.1	**1301**	**57**	**385**	541	**11.3**	**2.98**	**123**	**.249**	**.304**	**125**	**106**	96	**43**	*33*	**.980**	**121**	**24**	124	**3.4**	**10.6**	7.0	—	.0
StL	77	**18**	156	9	1408.2	1351	70	497	510	12.0	3.24	116	.253	.320	88	80	99	70	*53*	.977	137	**24**	150	2.4	8.0	1.0	—	6.6
Bro	61	7	163	18	1392.1	1357	74	586	**557**	12.8	3.70	101	.253	.331	15	7	99	60	*36*	.962	230	41	144	-3.2	.7	**7.5**	—	5.0
Pit	73	8	142	16	1387.1	1477	61	455	518	12.7	3.76	105	.272	.331	6	26	104	77	*42*	.971	178	**24**	141	-.0	2.6	2.0	—	.5
NY	53	13	179	21	1374.2	1401	85	528	529	12.8	4.06	96	.263	.332	-40	-22	103	**43**	*42*	.973	166	33	112	.6	-2.2	1.9	—	1.7
Bos	57	7	166	13	1391.2	1474	99	557	404	13.3	4.04	95	.272	.342	-37	-32	101	64	***54***	.969	193	25	**160**	-1.1	-3.2	1.7	—	-6.4
Cin	77	11	132	6	1365.2	1438	70	534	372	13.2	4.00	94	.271	.340	-31	-37	99	76	*36*	.976	146	31	138	1.8	-3.7	-11.2	—	-2.9
Phi	31	4	**212**	**26**	1352.2	1544	61	608	432	14.5	4.64	83	.285	.360	-126	-122	101	94	*45*	.962	234	50	150	-3.5	-12.2	-11.0	—	-4.2
Total	515	83	1285	123	11039.1	—	—	—	—	12.8	3.80	—	.265	.333	—	—	—	—	—	.971	1405	252	1119	—	—	—	—	—

BATTER-FIELDER WINS	BATTING AVERAGE	ON-BASE PERCENTAGE	SLUGGING AVERAGE	ON-BASE PLUS SLUGGING	ADJUSTED OPS	ADJUSTED BATTER RUNS
Hack-Chi 5.3	Cavarretta-Chi .355	Cavarretta-Chi .449	Holmes-Bos .577	Holmes-Bos .997	Holmes-Bos 175	Holmes-Bos 63.9
Holmes-Bos 5.1	Holmes-Bos .352	Galan-Bro .423	Kurowski-StL .511	Cavarretta-Chi .949	Cavarretta-Chi 167	Cavarretta-Chi 50.2
Cavarretta-Chi 4.1	Rosen-Bro .325	Hack-Chi .420	Cavarretta-Chi .500	Ott-NY .910	Ott-NY 150	Galan-Bro 39.6
Stanky-Bro 3.7	Hack-Chi .323	Holmes-Bos .420	Ott-NY .499	Kurowski-StL .894	Kurowski-StL 144	Ott-NY 33.2
Lombardi-NY 2.8	Kurowski-StL .323	Stanky-Bro .417	Olmo-Bro .462	Galan-Bro .864	Galan-Bro 142	Hack-Chi 32.7

RUNS	HITS	DOUBLES	TRIPLES	HOME RUNS	TOTAL BASES	RUNS BATTED IN
Stanky-Bro 128	Holmes-Bos 224	Holmes-Bos 47	Olmo-Bro 13	Holmes-Bos 28	Holmes-Bos 367	Walker-Bro 124
Rosen-Bro 126	Rosen-Bro 197	Walker-Bro 42	Pafko-Chi 12	Workman-Bos 25	Adams-Phi-StL 279	Holmes-Bos 117
Holmes-Bos 125	Hack-Chi 193	Galan-Bro 36	Rucker-NY 11	Adams-Phi-StL 22	Rosen-Bro 279	Pafko-Chi 110
Galan-Bro 114	Clay-Cin 184	Elliott-Pit 36	Rosen-Bro 11	Ott-NY 21	Walker-Bro 266	Olmo-Bro 110
Hack-Chi 110		Cavarretta-Chi 34	Cavarretta-Chi 10	Kurowski-StL 21	Kurowski-StL 261	Adams-Phi-StL 109

BASES ON BALLS	STOLEN BASES	BASE STEALING RUNS	FIELDING RUNS-INFIELD	FIELDING RUNS-OUTFIELD	OUTFIELD ASSISTS	CATCHER CS PCT.
Stanky-Bro 148	Schoendienst-StL 26		Kerr-NY 30.2	Gillenwater-Bos 17.0	Gillenwater-Bos 24	Lombardi-NY 48.1
Galan-Bro 114	Barrett-Pit 25		Coscarart-Pit 21.2	Walker-Bro 9.6	Walker-Bro 18	O'Dea-StL 45.5
Hack-Chi 99	Clay-Cin 19		Hack-Chi 19.6	DiMaggio-Phi 9.0	Lowrey-Chi 17	Rice-StL 43.4
Nicholson-Chi 92			Johnson-Chi 15.4	Russell-Pit 5.0	DiMaggio-Phi 16	Salkeld-Pit 35.7
Sanders-StL 83			Mesner-Cin 15.0	Schoendienst-StL 4.7		Lopez-Pit 33.9

WINS	WINNING PCT.	WINS ABOVE TEAM	GAMES STARTED	COMPLETE GAMES	FEWEST HITS/GAME	FEWEST BB/GAME
Barrett-Bos-StL 23	Brecheen-StL .789	Brecheen-StL 4.6	Voiselle-NY 35	Barrett-Bos-StL 24	Prim-Chi 7.73	Prim-Chi 1.25
Wyse-Chi 22	Burkhart-StL .692	Borowy-Chi 3.9	Barrett-Bos-StL 34	Wyse-Chi 23	Brecheen-StL 7.78	Barrett-Bos-StL 1.71
Gregg-Bro 18	Wyse-Chi .688	Mungo-NY 3.7	Wyse-Chi 34	Passeau-Chi 19	Gregg-Bro 7.82	Roe-Pit 1.76
Burkhart-StL 18	Barrett-Bos-StL .657	Barrett-Bos-StL 3.6	Gregg-Bro 34	Strincevich-Pit 18	Mungo-NY 7.92	Wyse-Chi 1.78
Passeau-Chi 17	Passeau-Chi .654	M.Cooper-StL-Bos 3.0	Roe-Pit 31	Heusser-Cin 18	Passeau-Chi 8.13	Strincevich-Pit 1.93

STRIKEOUTS	STRIKEOUTS/GAME	GAMES	SAVES	BASE RUNNERS/9	ADJUSTED RELIEF RUNS	RELIEF RANKING
Roe-Pit 148	Roe-Pit 5.67	Karl-Phi 67	Karl-Phi 15	Prim-Chi 9.04	Karl-Phi 14.5	Karl-Phi 14.3
Gregg-Bro 139	Mungo-NY 4.97	Adams-NY 65	Adams-NY 15	Beck-Cin-Pit 10.00	Buker-Bro 4.2	Adams-NY 6.0
Voiselle-NY 115	Gregg-Bro 4.92	Hutchings-Bos 57	Rescigno-Pit 9	Maglie-NY 10.25	Adams-NY 3.2	Buker-Bro 4.5
Mungo-NY 101	Hutchings-Bos 4.82	Barrett-Bos-StL 45		Roe-Pit 10.53		
Hutchings-Bos 99	Prim-Chi 4.79	Fox-Cin 45		Passeau-Chi 10.55		

INNINGS PITCHED	OPPONENTS' AVG.	OPPONENTS' OBP	EARNED RUN AVERAGE	ADJUSTED ERA	ADJUSTED STARTER RUNS	PITCHER WINS
Barrett-Bos-StL 284.2	Prim-Chi .228	Prim-Chi .256	Borowy-Chi 2.13	Prim-Chi 152	Passeau-Chi 32.6	**Passeau-Chi 3.9**
Wyse-Chi 278.1	Gregg-Bro .232	Passeau-Chi .289	Prim-Chi 2.40	Brecheen-StL 149	Wyse-Chi 32.3	**Wyse-Chi 3.3**
Gregg-Bro 254.1	Brecheen-StL .238	Barrett-Bos-StL .295	Passeau-Chi 2.46	Passeau-Chi 149	Roe-Pit 31.7	**Roe-Pit 3.2**
Roe-Pit 235.0	Mungo-NY .238	Wyse-Chi .296	Brecheen-StL 2.52	Walters-Cin 140	Barrett-Bos-StL 24.6	**Prim-Chi 2.9**
Voiselle-NY 232.1	Passeau-Chi .238	Roe-Pit .296	Walters-Cin 2.68	Roe-Pit 137	Brecheen-StL 22.9	**Walters-Cin 2.6**

Chicago's Last Stand

With the war drawing to a merciful close, NL attendance rose 32 percent to its highest total since 1930. Many veterans, such as Paul Derringer, Leo Durocher, Lloyd Waner, and Lon Warneke, played their last innings in 1945, as did Dick Sipek, a deaf outfielder employed by the Reds.

The surprise team of the season was Chicago, which improved by 23 games. In early July the Cubs were stalled in fourth place, but Chicago then won 16 of 17 to pass the Dodgers for the league lead. Holding off a late St. Louis challenge, the Cubs won their last NL pennant of the century. Phil Cavaretta won the batting title and was named league MVP. Stan Hack, Andy Pafko and Bill Nicholson provided punch, but the team's real strength was pitching. Graybeards Ray Prim, Claude Passeau, and Paul Derringer combined for 46 wins, Hank Wyse was 22-10, and Hank Borowy—who came over from New York in an odd midseason waiver deal—went 11-2 with Chicago while leading the NL in ERA. Chicago's favorite patsies were the seventh-place Reds, who dropped 21 of 22 to the Cubs. Chicago was also very good at doubling up opponents, winning 20 doubleheaders.

While the Cardinals remained strong, they too were hit hard by the war; outfielders Danny Litwhiler and Stan Musial were finally inducted after several deferrals. Rookie Red Schoendienst filled in ably, pacing the NL in steals, but the missing big bats, and several pitching injuries, proved too much. Ace Adams of the Giants was again the league's top reliever. Boston's Tommy Holmes, whose 37-game hitting streak was the NL's longest since 1897, led the league in doubles, hits, and homers. The Phillies finished last for the eighth time in ten years, but their stock would soon rise.

A sloppy but entertaining World Series saw the Tigers walk away with the victory. Borowy, 2-2 in the Series, got the decision in each of the last three games; he won Game 6 for the Cubs in relief but was hit hard in Games 5 and 7.

1945 AMERICAN LEAGUE

TEAM	W	L	T	PCT	GB	HW	HL	R	OR	PA	H	2B	3B	HR	BB	SO	HB	SH	AVG	OBP	SLG	OPS	AOPS	BR	ABR	PF	SB	CS	BSA	BSR
Det	88	65	2	.575	—	**50**	26	633	565	5885	1345	**227**	47	77	517	533	9	102	.256	.324	.361	685	98	21	-16	106	60	54	53	-6
Was	87	67	2	.565	1.5	46	31	622	562	6008	1375	197	**63**	27	545	489	23	114	.258	.330	.334	664	107	-9	47	92	**110**	65	**63**	**1**
StL	81	70	3	.536	6	47	27	597	**548**	5866	1302	215	37	63	500	555	15	**124**	.249	.316	.341	657	91	-29	-56	105	25	31	45	-5
NY	81	71	0	.533	6.5	48	28	**676**	606	5925	1343	189	61	**93**	**618**	567	**36**	95	.259	**.343**	**.373**	**716**	108	**90**	**59**	105	64	43	60	-1
Cle	73	72	2	.503	11	44	33	557	**548**	5536	1249	216	48	65	505	578	14	119	.255	.326	.359	685	**109**	24	50	96	19	31	38	-7
Chi	71	78	1	.477	15	44	29	596	633	5661	1330	204	55	22	470	467	14	100	**.262**	.326	.337	663	101	-14	2	97	78	54	59	-2
Bos	71	83	3	.461	17.5	42	35	599	674	6018	**1393**	225	44	50	541	534	23	87	.260	.330	.346	676	100	14	0	102	72	50	59	-2
Phi	52	98	3	.347	34.5	39	35	494	638	5861	1297	201	37	33	449	**463**	20	96	.245	.306	.316	622	86	-98	-96	100	25	45	36	-10
Total	612	—	—	—	—	360	244	4774	—	46760	10634	1674	392	430	4145	4186	154	837	.255	.325	.346	671	—	—	—	—	453	373	55	-31

TEAM	CG	SHO	GR	SV	IP	H	HR	BB	SO	BR/9	ERA	AERA	OAV	OOB	PR	APR	PF	OSB	OCS	FA	E	WPB	DP	FW	PW	BW	BSW	DIF
Det	78	**19**	131	**16**	1393.2	1305	48	538	**588**	12.1	2.99	**118**	.250	.322	58	**78**	105	49	52	.975	158	40	173	.4	**8.4**	-1.7	-.2	4.7
Was	82	**19**	110	11	1412.1	1307	42	**440**	550	**11.2**	**2.92**	106	**.242**	**.301**	**69**	30	92	45	33	.970	183	58	124	-1.0	3.2	5.0	**.5**	2.2
StL	**91**	10	110	8	1382.2	1307	59	506	570	11.8	3.14	112	.249	.316	34	55	105	60	36	.976	143	**23**	123	1.2	5.9	-6.0	-.1	4.6
NY	78	9	102	14	1355.0	1277	66	485	474	11.8	3.45	100	.250	.316	-13	1	103	74	53	.971	175	35	170	-.7	.1	**6.3**	.3	-1.0
Cle	76	14	116	12	1302.1	**1269**	**39**	501	497	12.4	3.31	98	.257	.328	8	-9	97	68	45	**.977**	**126**	41	149	**1.7**	-1.0	5.4	-.3	-5.3
Chi	84	13	86	13	1330.2	1400	63	448	486	12.7	3.69	90	.270	.332	-49	-56	99	**35**	50	.970	180	26	139	-1.1	-6.0	.2	.2	3.2
Bos	71	15	**135**	13	1390.2	1389	58	656	490	13.4	3.80	90	.264	.348	-67	-60	101	52	**56**	.973	169	48	**198**	-.1	-6.4	.0	.2	.3
Phi	65	11	120	8	1381.0	1380	55	571	531	12.9	3.62	95	.262	.337	-40	-29	102	70	48	.973	168	27	160	-.3	-3.1	-10.3	-.7	-8.7
Total	625	110	910	95	10948.1	—	—	—	—	12.3	3.36	—	.255	.325	—	—	—	—	—	.973	1302	298	1236	—	—	—	—	—

BATTER-FIELDER WINS	BATTING AVERAGE	ON-BASE PERCENTAGE	SLUGGING AVERAGE	ON-BASE PLUS SLUGGING	ADJUSTED OPS	ADJUSTED BATTER RUNS
Stirnweiss-NY....7.2	Stirnweiss-NY.......309	Lake-Bos..............412	Stirnweiss-NY.......476	Stirnweiss-NY.......862	Stirnweiss-NY.......143	Stirnweiss-NY......33.9
Lake-Bos............6.5	Cuccinello-Chi......308	Cullenbine-Cle-Det...402	Stephens-StL........473	Cullenbine-Cle-Det...846	Estalella-Phi..........142	Heath-Cle............33.0
Mayo-Det............3.5	Dickshot-Chi.........302	Estalella-Phi..........399	Cullenbine-Cle-Det...444	Estalella-Phi..........834	Kuhel-Was............137	Cullenbine-Cle-Det..30.9
Cullenbine-Cle-Det....3.1	Estalella-Phi..........299	Grimes-NY............395	Etten-NY...............437	Stephens-StL........825	Cullenbine-Cle-Det...137	Lake-Bos.............28.6
Boudreau-Cle.....2.7	Myatt-Was.............296	Etten-NY...............387	Estalella-Phi..........435	Etten-NY...............824	Lake-Bos..............136	Kuhel-Was...........27.5

RUNS	HITS	DOUBLES	TRIPLES	HOME RUNS	TOTAL BASES	RUNS BATTED IN
Stirnweiss-NY.......107	Stirnweiss-NY.......195	Moses-Chi..............35	Stirnweiss-NY.........22	Stephens-StL..........24	Stirnweiss-NY.......301	Etten-NY...............111
Stephens-StL..........90	Moses-Chi.............168	Stirnweiss-NY.........32	Moses-Chi..............15	Cullenbine-Cle-Det.....18	Stephens-StL........270	Cullenbine-Cle-Det.....93
Cullenbine-Cle-Det.....83	Stephens-StL........165	Binks-Was..............32	Kuhel-Was..............13	York-Det.................18	Etten-NY...............247	Stephens-StL..........89
	Hall-Phi.................161	McQuinn-StL...........31	Dickshot-Chi...........10	Etten-NY.................18	York-Det...............246	York-Det.................87
	Etten-NY...............161		Peck-Phi...................9	Heath-Cle...............15	Moses-Chi............239	Binks-Was..............81

BASES ON BALLS	STOLEN BASES	BASE STEALING RUNS	FIELDING RUNS-INFIELD	FIELDING RUNS-OUTFIELD	OUTFIELD ASSISTS	CATCHER CS PCT.
Cullenbine-Cle-Det...113	Stirnweiss-NY.........33	Dickshot-Chi..........2.9	Stirnweiss-NY......25.2	Cullenbine-Cle-Det....9.1	Cullenbine-Cle-Det.....23	Tresh-Chi.............58.8
Lake-Bos..............106	Myatt-Was..............30	Myatt-Was.............2.8	Lake-Bos.............23.7	Case-Was..............8.6	Case-Was...............17	Swift-Det.............52.7
Grimes-NY...............97	Case-Was...............30	Metkovich-Bos.......2.1	Kell-Phi...............21.8	Mackiewicz-Cle......7.3	B.Johnson-Bos.......15	Richards-Det........50.0
Etten-NY.................90	Metkovich-Bos........19	Stirnweiss-NY........1.3	Mayo-Det.............20.3	Byrnes-StL............6.5	Culberson-Bos........14	Ferrell-Was..........44.2
Kuhel-Was..............79	Dickshot-Chi...........18	Crosetti-NY............1.2	Hall-Phi...............20.1	Moses-Chi.............6.2		Rosar-Phi.............41.9

WINS	WINNING PCT.	WINS ABOVE TEAM	GAMES STARTED	COMPLETE GAMES	FEWEST HITS/GAME	FEWEST BB/GAME
Newhouser-Det.......25	Newhouser-Det.....735	Newhouser-Det......7.4	Newhouser-Det.......36	Newhouser-Det.......29	Newhouser-Det....6.86	Bonham-NY.........1.10
Ferriss-Bos.............21	Leonard-Was.........708	Ferriss-Bos............7.1	Newsom-Phi...........34	Ferriss-Bos.............26	Wolff-Was............7.20	Leonard-Was.......1.46
Wolff-Was...............20	Gromek-Cle..........679	Gromek-Cle...........5.6	Potter-StL..............32	Wolff-Was...............21	Potter-StL.............7.47	Wolff-Was............1.91
Gromek-Cle............19	Ferriss-Bos...........677	Muncrief-StL..........4.4	Trout-Det...............31	Potter-StL...............21	Lee-Chi.................8.20	Overmire-Det.......2.33
	Wolff-Was.............667	Leonard-Was.........4.4	Ferriss-Bos.............31	Gromek-Cle............21	Niggeling-Was.....8.20	Gromek-Cle.........2.37

STRIKEOUTS	STRIKEOUTS/GAME	GAMES	SAVES	BASE RUNNERS/9	ADJUSTED RELIEF RUNS	RELIEF RANKING
Newhouser-Det.....212	Newhouser-Det....6.09	Berry-Phi................52	Turner-NY...............10	Wolff-Was............9.14	Berry-Phi.............15.0	Berry-Phi.............16.8
Potter-StL.............129	Kramer-StL..........4.62	Reynolds-Cle..........44	Berry-Phi..................5	Potter-StL.............9.90	Holcombe-NY.........7.4	Holcombe-NY.........7.2
Newsom-Phi.........127	Niggeling-Was.....4.58	Pieretti-Was...........44		Newhouser-Det..10.02	Barrett-Bos............6.9	Barrett-Bos............5.6
Reynolds-Cle........112	Potter-StL............4.55	Trout-Det...............41		Leonard-Was.....10.21	Zoldak-StL................1	Zoldak-StL................0
	Newsom-Phi........4.44	Newhouser-Det.......40		Bonham-NY.......10.41		

INNINGS PITCHED	OPPONENTS' AVG.	OPPONENTS' OBP	EARNED RUN AVERAGE	ADJUSTED ERA	ADJUSTED STARTER RUNS	PITCHER WINS
Newhouser-Det..313.1	Newhouser-Det.....211	Wolff-Was.............258	Newhouser-Det....1.81	Newhouser-Det.....194	Newhouser-Det....58.4	**Newhouser-Det.7.6**
Ferriss-Bos........264.2	Wolff-Was.............215	Potter-StL..............279	Benton-Det..........2.02	Benton-Det...........174	Wolff-Was............31.3	**Potter-StL...........3.6**
Newsom-Phi......257.1	Potter-StL.............226	Leonard-Was........279	Wolff-Was............2.12	Wolff-Was.............146	Potter-StL............30.4	**Wolff-Was...........3.3**
Potter-StL..........255.1	Niggeling-Was......240	Newhouser-Det.....281	Leonard-Was.......2.13	Leonard-Was........146	Benton-Det..........24.4	**Ferriss-Bos.........3.0**
Gromek-Cle.......251.0	Benton-Det...........241	Bonham-NY..........288	Lee-Chi................2.44	Potter-StL.............143	Leonard-Was.......21.2	**Gromek-Cle........2.6**

End of the Patchwork Era

During the last and most depleted baseball season of the war years, the AL debuted a one-armed player (outfielder Pete Gray of St. Louis) and a one-legged player (pitcher Bert Shepard of Washington). And both their usually mediocre clubs were, again, in the pennant race. For the fifth straight season, home runs dropped. Only one player, Vern Stephens of the Browns, even hit 20, while the entire White Sox squad hit just 22—Chicago had slugged 25 in 1919.

The fourth-place Yankees again topped the AL in runs, with second baseman George "Snuffy" Stirnweiss beating up on substandard pitching. St. Louis had excellent hurling, but an even poorer attack than in 1944, and finished third. Second-place Washington boasted a speed-based offense and Roger Wolff, one of the most obscure 20-game winners of modern times.

Detroit's Hal Newhouser won his second straight MVP, this time with a 25-9 season that helped carry the Tigers over the top with the lowest winning percentage ever for an AL champ. Hank Greenberg, who returned at midseason from the military, hit a grand slam against St. Louis on September 30 to clinch the flag.

The World Series, an entertaining, sloppy, uneven affair, featured the Tigers and the equally-not-great Cubs. (Asked for his pre-Series prediction, Chicago sportswriter Warren Brown opined, "I don't think either team can win it.") The clubs went to the brink, although the quality of play was far from solid. Game 6, a sloppy, 8-7, error-filled 12-inning affair won by Chicago on the brink of elimination, sapped their pitching; the Tigers won the final contest 9-3, behind Newhouser.

Harry O'Neill of the 1939 Athletics perished at Iwo Jima on March 6. He was the second and final big leaguer to die in World War II, but more than 50 American professional ballplayers were killed in the conflict.

1944 NATIONAL LEAGUE

TEAM	W	L	T	PCT	GB	HW	HL	R	OR	PA	H	2B	3B	HR	BB	SO	HB	SH	AVG	OBP	SLG	OPS	AOPS	BR	ABR	PF	SB	CS	BSA	BSR
StL	105	49	3	.682	—	**54**	22	**772**	**490**	6170	**1507**	**274**	59	**100**	544	473	27	**124**	**.275**	**.344**	**.402**	**746**	**114**	**113**	**99**	102	37			
Pit	90	63	5	.588	14.5	49	28	744	662	6099	1441	248	**80**	70	**573**	616	18	80	.265	.338	.379	717	104	58	29	104	**87**			
Cin	89	65	1	.578	16	45	33	573	537	5821	1340	229	31	51	423	**391**	27	100	.254	.313	.338	651	92	-74	-52	96	51			
Chi	75	79	3	.487	30	35	42	702	669	6108	1425	236	46	71	520	521	21	105	.261	.328	.360	688	101	-1	3	99	53			
NY	67	87	1	.435	38	39	36	682	773	5953	1398	191	47	93	512	480	20	115	.263	.331	.370	701	103	20	22	100	39			
Bos	65	89	1	.422	40	38	40	593	674	5868	1299	250	39	79	456	509	18	112	.246	.308	.353	661	88	-60	-83	104	37			
Bro	63	91	1	.409	42	37	39	690	832	6011	1450	255	51	56	486	451	14	118	.269	.331	.366	697	104	17	29	98	45			
Phi	61	92	1	.399	43.5	29	49	539	658	5911	1331	199	42	55	470	500	**31**	109	.251	.316	.336	652	92	-73	-53	97	32			
Total	623	—	—	—	—	326	289	5295	—	47941	11191	1882	395	575	3984	3941	176	863	.261	.326	.363	689	—	—	—	—	381	—	—	—

TEAM	CG	SHO	GR	SV	IP	H	HR	BB	SO	BR/9	ERA	AERA	OAV	OOB	PR	APR	PF	OSB	OCS	FA	E	WPB	DP	FW	PW	BW	BSW	DIF
StL	89	**26**	113	12	1427.0	**1228**	55	468	**637**	**10.8**	**2.67**	**132**	**.233**	**.298**	**148**	**138**	98	35	*30*	**.982**	**112**	22	**162**	**3.7**	**14.2**	**10.2**	—	-.0
Pit	77	10	140	19	1414.1	1466	65	435	452	12.2	3.44	108	.265	.321	27	43	103	43	*35*	.970	191	23	122	-1.1	4.4	3.0	—	7.2
Cin	**93**	17	96	12	1398.1	1292	60	**390**	369	10.9	2.97	117	.246	.300	99	83	97	**31**	*19*	.978	137	**14**	153	2.0	8.5	-5.3	—	6.8
Chi	70	11	156	13	1400.2	1484	75	458	545	12.5	3.59	98	.274	.331	4	-9	98	49	***44***	.970	186	35	151	-.8	-.9	.3	—	-.5
NY	47	4	**200**	**21**	1363.2	1413	116	587	499	13.4	4.29	85	.265	.342	-103	-93	102	45	*35*	.971	179	49	128	-.5	-9.5	2.3	—	-2.2
Bos	70	13	132	12	1388.1	1430	80	527	454	12.8	3.67	104	.267	.335	-9	21	106	76	*41*	.971	182	23	160	-.7	2.2	-8.5	—	-4.9
Bro	50	4	187	13	1367.2	1471	75	660	487	14.3	4.68	76	.274	.357	-162	-175	98	54	*35*	.966	197	48	112	-1.7	-18.0	3.0	—	2.6
Phi	66	11	155	6	1395.1	1407	**49**	459	496	12.2	3.64	99	.261	.321	-4	-4	100	48	*33*	.972	177	41	138	-.5	-.4	-5.4	—	-9.2
Total	562	96	1179	108	11155.1	—	—	—	—	12.4	3.61	—	.261	.326	—	—	—	—	—	.972	1361	255	1126	—	—	—	—	—

BATTER-FIELDER WINS	BATTING AVERAGE	ON-BASE PERCENTAGE	SLUGGING AVERAGE	ON-BASE PLUS SLUGGING	ADJUSTED OPS	ADJUSTED BATTER RUNS
Musial-StL 5.5	Walker-Bro .357	Musial-StL .440	Musial-StL .549	Musial-StL .990	Musial-StL 174	Musial-StL 60.7
Walker-Bro 4.9	Musial-StL .347	Walker-Bro .434	Nicholson-Chi .545	Ott-NY .967	Walker-Bro 173	Walker-Bro 54.8
Galan-Bro 4.5	Medwick-NY .337	Galan-Bro .426	Ott-NY .544	Walker-Bro .963	Ott-NY 171	Galan-Bro 50.8
McCormick-Cin 3.8	Hopp-StL .336	Ott-NY .423	Walker-Bro .529	Nicholson-Chi .935	Nicholson-Chi 162	Nicholson-Chi 49.5
Nicholson-Chi 3.8	Cavarretta-Chi .321	Hopp-StL .404	Weintraub-NY .524	Galan-Bro .922	Galan-Bro 162	Ott-NY 41.7
RUNS	**HITS**	**DOUBLES**	**TRIPLES**	**HOME RUNS**	**TOTAL BASES**	**RUNS BATTED IN**
Nicholson-Chi 116	Musial-StL 197	Musial-StL 51	Barrett-Pit 19	Nicholson-Chi 33	Nicholson-Chi 317	Nicholson-Chi 122
Musial-StL 112	Cavarretta-Chi 197	Galan-Bro 43	Elliott-Pit 16	Ott-NY 26	Musial-StL 312	Elliott-Pit 108
Russell-Pit 109	Holmes-Bos 195	Holmes-Bos 42	Cavarretta-Chi 15	Northey-Phi 22	Holmes-Bos 288	Northey-Phi 104
Hopp-StL 106	Walker-Bro 191		Russell-Pit 14	McCormick-Cin 20	Walker-Bro 283	Sanders-StL 102
Cavarretta-Chi 106	Russell-Pit 181		Musial-StL 14	Kurowski-StL 20	Northey-Phi 283	McCormick-Cin 102
BASES ON BALLS	**STOLEN BASES**	**BASE STEALING RUNS**	**FIELDING RUNS-INFIELD**	**FIELDING RUNS-OUTFIELD**	**OUTFIELD ASSISTS**	**CATCHER CS PCT.**
Galan-Bro 101	Barrett-Pit 28		Kerr-NY 19.3	Pafko-Chi 10.2	Pafko-Chi 24	Lopez-Pit 46.9
Nicholson-Chi 93	Lupien-Phi 18		Williams-Cin 15.6	Russell-Pit 9.1	Northey-Phi 24	W.Cooper-StL 44.4
Ott-NY 90	Hughes-Chi 16		Hughes-Chi 13.4	Medwick-NY 7.1	Russell-Pit 20	Lombardi-NY 41.3
Musial-StL 90	Hopp-StL 15		Luby-NY 12.5	Olmo-Bro 5.2	Nicholson-Chi 18	Mueller-Cin 38.8
Barrett-Pit 86	Kerr-NY 14		McCormick-Cin 12.3	Musial-StL 3.3	Walker-Bro 17	
WINS	**WINNING PCT.**	**WINS ABOVE TEAM**	**GAMES STARTED**	**COMPLETE GAMES**	**FEWEST HITS/GAME**	**FEWEST BB/GAME**
Walters-Cin 23	Wilks-StL .810	Walters-Cin 6.9	Voiselle-NY 41	Tobin-Bos 28	Walters-Cin 7.36	Raffensberger-Phi 1.57
M.Cooper-StL 22	Brecheen-StL .762	Voiselle-NY 5.3	Tobin-Bos 36	Walters-Cin 27	Wilks-StL 7.50	Strincevich-Pit 1.75
Voiselle-NY 21	M.Cooper-StL .759	Wilks-StL 4.6	Wyse-Chi 34	Voiselle-NY 25	Lanier-StL 7.70	Davis-Bro 1.81
Sewell-Pit 21	Walters-Cin .742	M.Cooper-StL 4.1	Andrews-Bos 34	Sewell-Pit 24	Heusser-Cin 7.71	Shoun-Cin 1.87
Tobin-Bos 18	Sewell-Pit .636	Passeau-Chi 3.6		M.Cooper-StL 22	Voiselle-NY 7.94	Derringer-Chi 1.95
STRIKEOUTS	**STRIKEOUTS/GAME**	**GAMES**	**SAVES**	**BASE RUNNERS/9**	**ADJUSTED RELIEF RUNS**	**RELIEF RANKING**
Voiselle-NY 161	Lanier-StL 5.66	Adams-NY 65	Adams-NY 13	Wilks-StL 9.66	Karl-Phi 10.5	Karl-Phi 5.8
Lanier-StL 141	Javery-Bos 4.85	Webber-Bro 48	Schmidt-StL 5	Heusser-Cin 9.72	Donnelly-StL 9.9	Donnelly-StL 4.9
Javery-Bos 137	Raffensberger-Phi 4.73	Rescigno-Pit 48	Rescigno-Pit 5	Karl-Phi 9.91		
Raffensberger-Phi 136	Voiselle-NY 4.63	Voiselle-NY 43	Davis-Bro 4	Munger-StL 10.04		
	Melton-Bro 4.37	Tobin-Bos 43	Cuccurullo-Pit 4	DeLaCruz-Cin 10.16		
INNINGS PITCHED	**OPPONENTS' AVG.**	**OPPONENTS' OBP**	**EARNED RUN AVERAGE**	**ADJUSTED ERA**	**ADJUSTED STARTER RUNS**	**PITCHER WINS**
Voiselle-NY 312.2	Walters-Cin .219	Wilks-StL .275	Heusser-Cin 2.38	Heusser-Cin 146	Walters-Cin 34.0	**Walters-Cin 4.7**
Tobin-Bos 299.1	Wilks-StL .227	Heusser-Cin .275	Walters-Cin 2.40	Walters-Cin 145	M.Cooper-StL 33.1	**Tobin-Bos 3.8**
Sewell-Pit 286.0	Heusser-Cin .231	Walters-Cin .281	M.Cooper-StL 2.46	M.Cooper-StL 143	Munger-StL 29.1	**M.Cooper-StL 3.7**
Walters-Cin 285.0	Voiselle-NY .232	DeLaCruz-Cin .284	Wilks-StL 2.64	Wilks-StL 133	Wilks-StL 25.0	**Munger-StL 3.4**
Raffensberger-Phi 258.2	Lanier-StL .234	Raffensberger-Phi .285	Lanier-StL 2.65	Lanier-StL 133	Heusser-Cin 24.6	**Heusser-Cin 3.1**

Baby Face

The use of young players, by now a cliché of wartime baseball, reached a crest on June 10 when 15-year-old Joe Nuxhall pitched for the Cincinnati Reds. He remains the youngest big leaguer in history. Sixteen-year-old Tommy Brown played shortstop for the Dodgers, with 17-year-old Eddie Miksis filling in at both short and third. Eighteen-year-olds Cal McLish and Ralph Branca pitched for Brooklyn, who fell to seventh, crushed by wartime losses. The Phillies showcased infielders Putsy Caballero, 16, and Granny Hamner, 17, as well as hurler Rogers McKee, also 17. New York had two 19-year-old pitchers, and the Braves used two 17-year-olds.

Tellingly, the Cardinals, who became the first NL team to win 100 games three straight seasons, had no teenagers on their team. St. Louis was in control by May and coasted to another pennant. Outfielder Stan Musial and Johnny Hopp fattened up on wartime pitching, but the MVP went to their teammate, slick-fielding shortstop Marty Marion. Pittsburgh finished a surprising second; a patchwork pitching staff and a line-drive attack helped them finish just above Cincinnati, for whom hurler Bucky Walters had another dominating season.

In the game's only all-St. Louis World Series, the Cardinals snuffed out their crosstown rivals' attack, and the Browns committed 10 errors. The Cardinals came back from a two-games-to-one deficit to take the next three, allowing the Browns but 2 runs in the process. Four of the six games were decided by 1 or 2 runs, and excellent pitching—allowing the Browns just a .183 average—carried the day.

Judge Kenesaw Mountain Landis died on November 25 at age 78. The autocratic Commissioner served baseball for nearly a quarter-century, but with declining power; he could not stop the subjugation of the minors to the majors. But never again would the game be commanded by a strong, independent voice.

1944 AMERICAN LEAGUE

TEAM	W	L	T	PCT	GB	HW	HL	R	OR	PA	H	2B	3B	HR	BB	SO	HB	SH	AVG	OBP	SLG	OPS	AOPS	BR	ABR	PF	SB	CS	BSA	BSR
StL	89	65	0	.578	—	**54**	23	684	587	5928	1328	223	45	72	531	604	21	107	.252	.323	.352	675	94	-3	-37	106	44	33	57	-2
Det	88	66	2	.571	1	43	34	658	**581**	6011	1405	220	44	60	**532**	500	24	111	.263	.332	.354	686	97	22	-12	106	61	55	53	-6
NY	83	71	0	.539	6	47	31	674	617	5978	1410	216	**74**	**96**	523	627	22	102	.264	.333	**.387**	**720**	108	74	51	103	91	31	**75**	**9**
Bos	77	77	2	.500	12	47	30	**739**	676	6052	1456	**277**	56	69	522	505	20	110	**.270**	**.336**	.380	716	**112**	**77**	**86**	99	60	40	60	-1
Phi	72	82	1	.468	17	39	37	525	594	5873	1364	169	47	36	422	490	17	**122**	.257	.314	.327	641	90	-78	-70	99	42	32	57	-2
Cle	72	82	1	.468	17	39	38	643	677	6119	**1458**	270	50	70	512	593	19	107	.266	.331	.372	703	111	50	78	96	48	42	53	-4
Chi	71	83	0	.461	18	41	36	543	662	5819	1307	210	55	23	439	**448**	21	67	.247	.307	.320	627	86	-99	-92	99	66	47	58	-2
Was	64	90	0	.416	25	40	37	592	664	5926	1386	186	42	33	470	477	**29**	108	.261	.324	.330	654	97	-43	-15	96	**127**	59	68	7
Total	619	——		—	—	350	266	5058	—	47706	11114	1771	413	459	3951	4244	173	834	.260	.325	.353	678	—	—	—	—	539	339	61	0

TEAM	CG	SHO	GR	SV	IP	H	HR	BB	SO	BR/9	ERA	AERA	OAV	OOB	PR	APR	PF	OSB	OCS	FA	E	WPB	DP	FW	PW	BW	BSW	DIF
StL	71	16	127	17	1397.1	1392	58	469	**581**	12.1	3.17	114	.259	.320	41	63	105	76	31	.972	171	**30**	142	.5	6.6	-3.9	-.2	9.0
Det	**87**	**20**	119	8	1400.0	1373	**39**	452	568	11.9	**3.09**	**116**	.257	.318	**54**	**72**	104	**37**	**60**	.970	190	32	184	-.5	**7.6**	-1.3	-.6	5.8
NY	78	9	111	13	1390.1	1351	82	532	529	12.3	3.39	103	.257	.326	7	15	102	57	40	**.974**	**156**	38	170	**1.3**	1.6	5.4	**.9**	-3.2
Bos	58	7	150	17	1394.1	1404	66	592	524	13.0	3.82	89	.263	.339	-60	-66	99	69	38	.972	171	40	154	.6	-6.9	**9.0**	-.1	-2.6
Phi	72	10	107	14	1397.1	**1345**	58	**390**	534	**11.4**	3.26	107	**.252**	**.307**	27	35	102	98	50	.971	176	42	127	.2	3.7	-7.4	-.2	-1.3
Cle	48	7	**200**	**18**	1419.1	1428	40	621	524	13.2	3.65	90	.265	.344	-35	-58	96	78	45	**.974**	165	40	**192**	.9	-6.1	8.2	-.4	-7.6
Chi	64	5	112	17	1390.2	1411	68	420	481	12.0	3.58	96	.264	.320	-23	-23	100	56	40	.970	183	44	154	-.2	-2.4	-9.7	-.2	6.5
Was	83	13	110	11	1381.0	1410	48	475	503	12.4	3.49	93	.264	.327	-10	-38	95	68	35	.964	218	62	156	-2.3	-4.0	-1.6	.7	-5.9
Total	561	87	1036	115	11170.1	—	—	—	—	12.3	3.43	—	.260	.325	—	—	—	—	—	.971	1430	328	1279	—	—	—	—	—

BATTER-FIELDER WINS	BATTING AVERAGE	ON-BASE PERCENTAGE	SLUGGING AVERAGE	ON-BASE PLUS SLUGGING	ADJUSTED OPS	ADJUSTED BATTER RUNS
Boudreau-Cle..... 7.5	Boudreau-Cle 327	B.Johnson-Bos 431	Doerr-Bos 528	B.Johnson-Bos 959	B.Johnson-Bos 175	B.Johnson-Bos 56.6
Stirnweiss-NY.... 6.8	Doerr-Bos 325	Boudreau-Cle 406	B.Johnson-Bos 528	Doerr-Bos 927	Doerr-Bos 166	Spence-Was 44.0
Spence-Was 5.4	B.Johnson-Bos 324	Doerr-Bos 399	Lindell-NY 500	Spence-Was 877	Spence-Was 157	Doerr-Bos 39.9
B.Johnson-Bos .. 5.3	Stirnweiss-NY 319	Etten-NY 399	Spence-Was 486	Etten-NY 865	Boudreau-Cle 146	Boudreau-Cle 39.4
Doerr-Bos 5.1	Spence-Was 316	Byrnes-StL............396		Lindell-NY 851	Etten-NY 142	Etten-NY 34.8
RUNS	**HITS**	**DOUBLES**	**TRIPLES**	**HOME RUNS**	**TOTAL BASES**	**RUNS BATTED IN**
Stirnweiss-NY.......125	Stirnweiss-NY.......205	Boudreau-Cle 45	Stirnweiss-NY 16	Etten-NY 22	Lindell-NY.............297	Stephens-StL.........109
B.Johnson-Bos 106	Boudreau-Cle 191	Keltner-Cle.............41	Lindell-NY...............16	Stephens-StL..........20	Stirnweiss-NY.......296	B.Johnson-Bos 106
Cullenbine-Cle........98	Spence-Was 187	B.Johnson-Bos 40	Gutteridge-StL 11	York-Det..................18	Spence-Was 288	Lindell-NY.............103
Doerr-Bos 95	Lindell-NY.............178	Fox-Bos 37	Doerr-Bos 10	Spence-Was 18	B.Johnson-Bos 277	Spence-Was 100
Metkovich-Bos 94	Rocco-Cle.............174	Stirnweiss-NY 35		Lindell-NY 18		York-Det..................98
BASES ON BALLS	**STOLEN BASES**	**BASE STEALING RUNS**	**FIELDING RUNS-INFIELD**	**FIELDING RUNS-OUTFIELD**	**OUTFIELD ASSISTS**	**CATCHER CS PCT.**
Etten-NY 97	Stirnweiss-NY 55	Stirnweiss-NY 8.3	Mayo-Det 33.5	Spence-Was 15.4	Spence-Was 29	Richards-Det........62.3
B.Johnson-Bos 95	Case-Was...............49	Case-Was 4.5	Boudreau-Cle 20.2	Tucker-Chi............10.8	B.Johnson-Bos 23	Garbark-NY 42.0
Cullenbine-Cle........87	Myatt-Was..............26	Myatt-Was..............2.2	Stirnweiss-NY......18.0	B.Johnson-Bos 5.2	Cullenbine-Cle........15	Tresh-Chi 40.0
McQuinn-StL...........85	Moses-Chi 21	Moses-Chi 2.2	Rocco-Cle............16.6	Garrison-Bos-Phi...4.9	Outlaw-Det.............14	Rosar-Cle 38.7
Higgins-Det.............81	Gutteridge-StL 20	Gutteridge-StL 1.6	Hoover-Det 14.8	Lindell-NY 4.0	Cramer-Det.............13	Ferrell-Was 35.4
WINS	**WINNING PCT.**	**WINS ABOVE TEAM**	**GAMES STARTED**	**COMPLETE GAMES**	**FEWEST HITS/GAME**	**FEWEST BB/GAME**
Newhouser-Det.......29	Hughson-Bos........783	Newhouser-Det......9.8	Trout-Det.................40	Trout-Det.................33	Gromek-Cle 7.07	Harris-Phi.............1.34
Trout-Det.................27	Newhouser-Det.....763	Hughson-Bos.........7.0	Dietrich-Chi.............36	Newhouser-Det.......25	Niggeling-Was 7.17	Leonard-Was 1.45
Potter-StL...............19	Potter-StL.............731	Trout-Det................5.3	Newhouser-Det.......34		Newhouser-Det....7.61	Bonham-NY 1.73
Hughson-Bos..........18	Trout-Det..............659	Potter-StL...............5.3	Newsom-Phi 33		Hughson-Bos.......7.61	Gorsica-Det 1.78
	Borowy-NY 586	Maltzberger-Chi.....3.0	Grove-Chi 33		Borowy-NY 7.98	Hamlin-Phi............1.80
STRIKEOUTS	**STRIKEOUTS/GAME**	**GAMES**	**SAVES**	**BASE RUNNERS/9**	**ADJUSTED RELIEF RUNS**	**RELIEF RANKING**
Newhouser-Det.....187	Newhouser-Det....5.39	Heving-Cle.............63	Maltzberger-Chi......12	Berry-Phi 8.33	Berry-Phi 17.2	Berry-Phi 29.2
Trout-Det...............144	Niggeling-Was 5.29	Berry-Phi 53	Caster-StL 12	Hughson-Bos.......9.52	Heving-Cle...........13.5	Heving-Cle...........13.7
Newsom-Phi 142	Gromek-Cle 5.08	Trout-Det.................49	Berry-Phi 12	Maltzberger-Chi...9.95	Maltzberger-Chi.....6.8	Maltzberger-Chi...12.1
Kramer-StL...........124	Hughson-Bos.......4.96	Newhouser-Det.......47	Heving-Cle..............10	Trout-Det...........10.24	Caster-StL 5.6	Caster-StL 9.3
Niggeling-Was 121	Newsom-Phi 4.82	Klieman-Cle............47	Barrett-Bos 8	Leonard-Was 10.28		
INNINGS PITCHED	**OPPONENTS' AVG.**	**OPPONENTS' OBP**	**EARNED RUN AVERAGE**	**ADJUSTED ERA**	**ADJUSTED STARTER RUNS**	**PITCHER WINS**
Trout-Det...........352.1	Gromek-Cle 219	Hughson-Bos........267	Trout-Det.............2.12	Trout-Det..............168	Trout-Det.............53.1	**Trout-Det 8.2**
Newhouser-Det..312.1	Niggeling-Was 221	Leonard-Was 284	Newhouser-Det....2.22	Newhouser-Det.....161	Newhouser-Det....44.7	**Newhouser-Det . 6.1**
Newsom-Phi 265.0	Hughson-Bos........225	Trout-Det...............284	Hughson-Bos.......2.26	Hughson-Bos........151	Hughson-Bos.......26.6	**Kramer-StL.......... 3.4**
Kramer-StL 257.0	Newhouser-Det.....230	Gromek-Cle 290	Niggeling-Was 2.32	Kramer-StL 145	Kramer-StL 26.6	**Berry-Phi 3.2**
Borowy-NY 252.2	Borowy-NY 236	Newhouser-Det.....293	Kramer-StL 2.49	Niggeling-Was 141	Niggeling-Was 23.0	**Hughson-Bos 3.1**

Brownout

In a year that stretched baseball's ability to take itself seriously, a squad of especially unlikely heroes won the flag. The perpetually bad St. Louis Browns took advantage of a war-decimated league and climbed atop a four-team tangle by mid-August. Shortstop Vern Stephens was the club's only real threat at bat, but a veteran pitching staff, quality infield defense, and other teams' shortcomings kept the Brownies in the hunt.

At that point, the Red Sox dropped out. The Yankees got hot, but cooled off again, leaving the race to the Browns and Tigers. Detroit was fueled by Hal Newhouser and Dizzy Trout's pitching and outfielder Dick Wakefield's activation from the military rolls.

Both teams were on fire the last two weeks, but the Brownies came out on top, taking four straight from New York while the Tigers fell to Washington on the season's last day. This would be St. Louis' only AL crown, and the fact that it was accomplished by a collection of military-deferred 4-Fs, alcoholics, and graybeards is almost irrelevant.

The first big league player to die in World War II was 27-year-old Elmer Gedeon. A captain in the Army Air Corps, Gedeon's plane was shot down over France on April 20. He had played the outfield for the 1939 Senators.

During the 1940s, few teams altered their ballparks; due to the war, most construction was out. But this year, Detroit reconfigured its grounds, giving Tiger Stadium the dimensions it retained until closing in 1999. Total tickets sold skyrocketed 30 percent for the AL in 1944, and for the first time since 1925, the Browns didn't finish last in attendance. They came in fifth.

As if adhering to the demands of the war on travel, Sportsman's Park was the site for all six World Series games. The first all-St. Louis World Series was a much closer affair than anyone expected. The Browns actually went up two games to one before the deeper Cardinals took the next three.

1943 NATIONAL LEAGUE

TEAM	W	L	T	PCT	GB	HW	HL	R	OR	PA	H	2B	3B	HR	BB	SO	HB	SH	AVG	OBP	SLG	OPS	AOPS	BR	ABR	PF	SB	CS	BSA	BSR
StL	105	49	3	.682	—	**58**	21	679	**475**	6057	**1515**	259	72	70	428	438	19	**172**	**.279**	.333	**.391**	**724**	**110**	**92**	62	104	40			
Cin	87	67	1	.565	18	48	29	608	543	5910	1362	229	47	43	445	476	17	119	.256	.315	.340	655	96	-36	-28	99	49			
Bro	81	72	0	.529	23.5	46	31	**716**	675	6009	1444	**263**	35	39	**580**	**422**	21	99	.272	**.346**	.357	703	**110**	76	**75**	100	58			
Pit	80	74	3	.519	25	47	30	669	605	6030	1401	240	**73**	42	573	566	18	86	.262	.335	.357	692	103	46	24	103	**64**			
Chi	74	79	1	.484	30.5	36	38	632	599	5970	1380	207	56	52	574	522	21	96	.261	.336	.351	687	107	38	48	99	53			
Bos	68	85	0	.444	36.5	38	39	465	612	5780	1213	202	36	39	469	609	17	98	.233	.299	.309	608	82	-122	-115	99	56			
Phi	64	90	3	.416	41	33	43	571	676	5918	1321	186	36	66	499	556	21	101	.249	.316	.335	651	98	-39	-15	96	29			
NY	55	98	3	.359	49.5	34	43	558	713	5900	1309	153	33	**81**	480	470	**23**	107	.247	.313	.335	648	92	-52	-56	101	35			
Total	621	—	—	—	—	340	274	4898	—	47574	10945	1739	388	432	4048	4059	157	878	.258	.324	.347	672	—	—	—	—	384	—	—	—

TEAM	CG	SHO	GR	SV	IP	H	HR	BB	SO	BR/9	ERA	AERA	OAV	OOB	PR	APR	PF	OSB	OCS	FA	E	WPB	DP	FW	PW	BW	BSW	DIF
StL	**94**	**21**	104	15	1427.0	**1246**	**33**	477	**639**	**11.0**	**2.57**	**131**	**.237**	**.303**	**129**	**127**	99	**30**	*34*	.976	151	33	183	.9	**13.6**	6.6	—	6.9
Cin	78	18	119	17	1404.0	1299	38	579	498	12.1	3.13	106	.251	.328	39	28	98	41	***50***	**.980**	**125**	21	**193**	**2.2**	3.0	-3.0	—	7.8
Bro	50	13	182	**22**	1369.2	1326	59	637	588	13.1	3.88	86	.254	.338	-76	-80	99	46	*39*	.972	168	35	137	-.3	-8.5	**8.0**	—	5.4
Pit	74	11	157	12	1404.0	1424	44	422	396	11.9	3.08	113	.264	.319	47	58	103	33	*44*	.973	170	24	159	-.2	6.2	2.6	—	-5.5
Chi	67	13	160	14	1386.0	1379	53	**394**	513	11.6	3.31	101	.258	.311	11	4	99	37	*19*	.973	168	34	138	-.3	.4	5.1	—	-7.8
Bos	87	13	99	4	1397.2	1361	66	441	409	11.8	3.25	105	.255	.314	20	25	101	81	*40*	.972	176	**18**	139	-.8	2.7	-12.3	—	1.9
Phi	66	10	140	14	1392.2	1436	59	451	431	12.3	3.79	89	.267	.326	-62	-64	100	55	*38*	.969	189	39	143	-1.3	-6.8	-1.6	—	-3.3
NY	35	6	**208**	19	1394.2	1474	80	626	588	13.7	4.08	84	.272	.350	-108	-97	102	61	*35*	.973	166	43	140	-.0	-10.4	-6.0	—	-5.1
Total	551	105	1169	117	11175.2	—	—	—	—	12.2	3.38	—	.258	.324	—	—	—	—	—	.974	1313	247	1232	—	—	—	—	—

BATTER-FIELDER WINS	BATTING AVERAGE	ON-BASE PERCENTAGE	SLUGGING AVERAGE	ON-BASE PLUS SLUGGING	ADJUSTED OPS	ADJUSTED BATTER RUNS
Musial-StL 5.7	Musial-StL .357	Musial-StL .425	Musial-StL .562	Musial-StL .988	Musial-StL 176	Musial-StL 60.7
Nicholson-Chi 4.5	Herman-Bro .330	Galan-Bro .412	Nicholson-Chi .531	Nicholson-Chi .917	Nicholson-Chi 166	Nicholson-Chi 50.1
Mueller-Cin 3.8	W.Cooper-StL .318	Herman-Bro .398	W.Cooper-StL .463	Elliott-Pit .820	Tipton-Cin 138	Galan-Bro 29.9
Galan-Bro 3.6	Elliott-Pit .315	Fletcher-Pit .395	Elliott-Pit .444	Tipton-Cin .819	Galan-Bro 136	Herman-Bro 29.6
Witek-NY 3.2	Witek-NY .314	Tipton-Cin .395	Triplett-StL-Phi .439	Galan-Bro .818	Herman-Bro 135	Tipton-Cin 28.1
RUNS	**HITS**	**DOUBLES**	**TRIPLES**	**HOME RUNS**	**TOTAL BASES**	**RUNS BATTED IN**
Vaughan-Bro 112	Musial-StL 220	Musial-StL 48	Musial-StL 20	Nicholson-Chi 29	Musial-StL 347	Nicholson-Chi 128
Musial-StL 108	Witek-NY 195	Herman-Bro 41	Klein-StL 14	Ott-NY 18	Nicholson-Chi 323	Elliott-Pit 101
Nicholson-Chi 95	Herman-Bro 193	DiMaggio-Pit 41	Lowrey-Chi 12	Northey-Phi 16	Elliott-Pit 258	Herman-Bro 100
Cavarretta-Chi 93	Nicholson-Chi 188	Vaughan-Bro 39	Elliott-Pit 12	Triplett-StL-Phi 15	Klein-StL 257	DiMaggio-Pit 88
Stanky-Chi 92	Vaughan-Bro 186	Holmes-Bos 33		DiMaggio-Pit 15		
BASES ON BALLS	**STOLEN BASES**	**BASE STEALING RUNS**	**FIELDING RUNS-INFIELD**	**FIELDING RUNS-OUTFIELD**	**OUTFIELD ASSISTS**	**CATCHER CS PCT.**
Galan-Bro 103	Vaughan-Bro 20		Miller-Cin 23.8	DiMaggio-Pit 11.9	Workman-Bos 22	Mueller-Cin 54.5
Ott-NY 95	Lowrey-Chi 13		Wietelmann-Bos 18.2	Litwhiler-Phi-StL 6.9	Walker-Bro 20	W.Cooper-StL 50.0
Fletcher-Pit 95	Workman-Bos 12		Marion-StL 16.2	Galan-Bro 6.4	Northey-Phi 19	McCullough-Chi 29.2
Stanky-Chi 92	Russell-Pit 12		Witek-NY 15.3	Lowrey-Chi 5.7	Holmes-Bos 18	
Tipton-Cin 85	Gustine-Pit 12		Frey-Cin 12.9	Musial-StL 4.5		
WINS	**WINNING PCT.**	**WINS ABOVE TEAM**	**GAMES STARTED**	**COMPLETE GAMES**	**FEWEST HITS/GAME**	**FEWEST BB/GAME**
Sewell-Pit 21	M.Cooper-StL .724	Sewell-Pit 6.4	VanderMeer-Cin 36	Sewell-Pit 25	Wyatt-Bro 6.92	Rowe-Phi 1.31
Riddle-Cin 21	Sewell-Pit .700	Rowe-Phi 4.6	Javery-Bos 35	Tobin-Bos 24	VanderMeer-Cin 7.10	Wyse-Chi 1.96
M.Cooper-StL 21	Lanier-StL .682	Wyatt-Bro 4.5	Walters-Cin 34	M.Cooper-StL 24	M.Cooper-StL 7.49	Derringer-Chi 2.02
Bithorn-Chi 18	Riddle-Cin .656	Shoun-Cin 4.1	Andrews-Bos 34	Andrews-Bos 23	Krist-StL 7.72	Davis-Bro 2.14
Javery-Bos 17	Bithorn-Chi .600	Riddle-Cin 4.0			Barrett-Chi-Phi 7.94	Wyatt-Bro 2.14
STRIKEOUTS	**STRIKEOUTS/GAME**	**GAMES**	**SAVES**	**BASE RUNNERS/9**	**ADJUSTED RELIEF RUNS**	**RELIEF RANKING**
VanderMeer-Cin 174	VanderMeer-Cin 5.42	Adams-NY 70	Webber-Bro 10	Pollet-StL 8.90	Beggs-Cin 10.6	Adams-NY 12.2
M.Cooper-StL 141	Higbe-Bro 5.25	Webber-Bro 54	Adams-NY 9	Wyatt-Bro 9.07	Adams-NY 9.4	Beggs-Cin 12.0
Javery-Bos 134	Lanier-StL 5.19	Head-Bro 47	Shoun-Cin 7	Brecheen-StL 9.31	Prim-Chi 3.6	Prim-Chi 3.9
Lanier-StL 123	M.Cooper-StL 4.63	Shoun-Cin 45	Head-Bro 6	Gumbert-StL 9.95	Brandt-Pit 2.2	Brandt-Pit 1.7
Higbe-Bro 108	Head-Bro 4.40	Mungo-NY 45	Beggs-Cin 6	Warneke-Chi 10.19		
INNINGS PITCHED	**OPPONENTS' AVG.**	**OPPONENTS' OBP**	**EARNED RUN AVERAGE**	**ADJUSTED ERA**	**ADJUSTED STARTER RUNS**	**PITCHER WINS**
Javery-Bos 303.0	Wyatt-Bro .207	Wyatt-Bro .255	Pollet-StL 1.75	Lanier-StL 177	M.Cooper-StL 32.9	**Sewell-Pit 3.9**
VanderMeer-Cin 289.0	VanderMeer-Cin .224	Rowe-Phi .279	Lanier-StL 1.90	M.Cooper-StL 146	Lanier-StL 30.8	**M.Cooper-StL 3.3**
Andrews-Bos 283.2	M.Cooper-StL .226	M.Cooper-StL .286	M.Cooper-StL 2.30	Sewell-Pit 137	Sewell-Pit 26.9	**Rowe-Phi 3.3**
M.Cooper-StL 274.0	Krist-StL .233	Andrews-Bos .291	Wyatt-Bro 2.49	Wyatt-Bro 135	Andrews-Bos 25.6	**Andrews-Bos 3.2**
Sewell-Pit 265.1	Barrett-Chi-Phi .237	Bithorn-Chi .294	Sewell-Pit 2.54	Butcher-Pit 134	Bithorn-Chi 23.2	**Tobin-Bos 3.1**

Life During Wartime

World War II was taking a bite out of baseball's economy. Attendance fell 13 percent further after dropping 9 percent in 1942. And it took a bite out of the ball, too—with cork and rubber unavailable to Spalding, the 1943 baseballs were made from a cork substitute called balata. The ball was deader than vaudeville, and public outcry soon forced the manufacture of a livelier spheroid.

Talent was draining from baseball as well. The Dodgers, losing Hugh Casey, Larry French, Pee Wee Reese, and Pete Reiser to military service, dropped to a distant third. The Reds sacrificed Ewell Blackwell to the war for three years; the Cubs lost Eddie Waitkus for four. Johnny Sain and Warren Spahn departed Boston from 1943–45, and the Giants lived without Johnny Mize for the same span.

St. Louis' excellent farm system produced Harry Brecheen, Lou Klein, and Al Brazle to supplement a club that lost Johnny Beazley, Frank Crespi, Terry Moore, and Enos Slaughter for three seasons. Buoyed by big years from Stan Musial and Mort Cooper, the Cardinals ran away with the pennant. Only a late flurry by second-place Cincinnati cut St. Louis' winning margin under 20; this was the league's least competitive race in nearly forty years.

Breaking his own record for relief appearances, Ace Adams of the Giants became the first pitcher to appear in 70 games since 1883. The Phillies changed their name to the Blue Jays, but didn't get any better. In Brooklyn, 19-year-old first baseman Gil Hodges got his first major league at bats, while across town at the Polo Grounds, Carl Hubbell retired at 40 with arm problems. The Giants finished last.

Despite their great regular season, the Cardinals—perhaps challenged for competition—lost to the Yankees in a five-game World Series. The Cards, who batted just .224, actually outhit New York—only not when it counted. They scored 2 runs or less in all four losses.

1943 AMERICAN LEAGUE

TEAM	W	L	T	PCT	GB	HW	HL	R	OR	PA	H	2B	3B	HR	BB	SO	HB	SH	AVG	OBP	SLG	OPS	AOPS	BR	ABR	PF	SB	CS	BSA	BSR
NY	98	56	1	.636	—	**54**	23	**669**	**542**	6024	1350	218	**59**	**100**	**624**	562	25	93	.256	**.337**	**.376**	**713**	**114**	**98**	**93**	101	46	60	43	-11
Was	84	69	0	.549	13.5	44	32	666	595	5965	1328	245	50	47	605	579	**39**	88	.254	.336	.347	683	110	49	74	96	142	55	**72**	**12**
Cle	82	71	0	.536	15.5	44	33	600	577	5968	1344	**246**	45	55	567	521	11	121	.255	.329	.350	679	112	35	76	94	47	58	45	-10
Chi	82	72	1	.532	16	40	36	573	594	5909	1297	193	46	33	561	581	22	72	.247	.322	.320	642	94	-34	-33	100	**173**	87	67	8
Det	78	76	1	.506	20	45	32	632	560	5983	**1401**	200	47	77	483	553	13	**123**	**.261**	.324	.359	683	98	29	-16	108	40	43	48	-6
StL	72	80	1	.474	25	44	33	596	604	5865	1269	229	36	78	569	646	15	106	.245	.322	.349	671	100	16	3	102	37	43	46	-7
Bos	68	84	3	.447	29	39	36	563	607	6010	1314	223	42	57	486	591	19	113	.244	.308	.332	640	92	-49	-58	102	86	61	59	-2
Phi	49	105	1	.318	49	27	51	497	717	5798	1219	174	44	26	430	**465**	29	95	.232	.294	.297	591	78	-143	-141	100	55	42	57	-3
Total	617	—	—	—	—	337	276	4796	—	47522	10522	1728	369	473	4325	4498	173	811	.249	.322	.341	663	—	—	—	—	626	449	58	-19

TEAM	CG	SHO	GR	SV	IP	H	HR	BB	SO	BR/9	ERA	AERA	OAV	OOB	PR	APR	PF	OSB	OCS	FA	E	WPB	DP	FW	PW	BW	BSW	DIF
NY	**83**	14	98	13	1415.1	1229	60	489	653	**11.0**	**2.93**	110	**.234**	**.301**	**58**	47	98	**48**	50	.974	160	31	166	.2	5.1	**10.1**	-.9	6.5
Was	61	16	134	**21**	1388.0	1293	**48**	540	495	12.0	3.18	101	.246	.318	17	3	97	59	51	.971	179	49	145	-1.0	.3	8.0	**1.6**	-1.4
Cle	64	14	**158**	20	1406.1	1234	52	606	585	11.9	3.15	99	.239	.322	23	-7	94	57	61	.975	157	**13**	**183**	.3	-.8	8.2	-.8	-1.4
Chi	70	12	109	19	1400.1	1352	54	501	476	12.1	3.20	104	.255	.324	15	21	101	66	43	.973	166	35	167	-.0	2.3	-3.6	1.1	5.3
Det	67	**18**	130	20	1411.2	**1226**	51	549	**706**	11.4	3.00	**117**	**.234**	.308	46	**76**	107	84	**80**	.971	177	32	130	-.7	**8.2**	-1.7	-.4	-4.4
StL	64	10	130	14	1385.0	1397	74	**488**	572	12.4	3.41	97	.263	.327	-18	-13	101	124	54	.975	**152**	32	127	**.6**	-1.4	.3	-.5	-3.0
Bos	62	13	140	16	1426.1	1369	61	615	513	12.6	3.45	96	.257	.335	-25	-22	101	80	55	**.976**	153	45	179	**.6**	-2.4	-6.3	.0	-.0
Phi	73	5	107	13	1394.0	1421	73	536	503	12.9	4.05	84	.265	.336	-117	-98	103	108	55	.973	162	43	148	.1	-10.6	-15.3	-.0	-2.2
Total	544	102	1006	136	11227.0	—	—	—	—	12.0	3.30	—	.249	.322	—	—	—	—	—	.973	1306	280	1245	—	—	—	—	—

BATTER-FIELDER WINS	BATTING AVERAGE	ON-BASE PERCENTAGE	SLUGGING AVERAGE	ON-BASE PLUS SLUGGING	ADJUSTED OPS	ADJUSTED BATTER RUNS
Boudreau-Cle 6.8	Appling-Chi .328	Appling-Chi .419	York-Det .527	Keller-NY .922	Keller-NY 167	Keller-NY 45.1
Appling-Chi 6.3	Wakefield-Det .316	Cullenbine-Cle .407	Keller-NY .525	York-Det .893	Heath-Cle 157	Appling-Chi 36.7
Gordon-NY 5.6	Hodgin-Chi .314	Keller-NY .396	Stephens-StL .482	Heath-Cle .850	York-Det 148	Cullenbine-Cle 34.4
York-Det 4.6	Cramer-Det .300	Boudreau-Cle .388	Heath-Cle .481	Stephens-StL .839	Cullenbine-Cle 146	York-Det 33.3
Keller-NY 4.0	Case-Was .294	Curtright-Chi .382	Wakefield-Det .434	Appling-Chi .825	Appling-Chi 142	Heath-Cle 30.4
RUNS	**HITS**	**DOUBLES**	**TRIPLES**	**HOME RUNS**	**TOTAL BASES**	**RUNS BATTED IN**
Case-Was 102	Wakefield-Det 200	Wakefield-Det 38	Moses-Chi 12	York-Det 34	York-Det 301	York-Det 118
Keller-NY 97	Appling-Chi 192	Case-Was 36	Lindell-NY 12	Keller-NY 31	Wakefield-Det 275	Etten-NY 107
Wakefield-Det 91	Cramer-Det 182	Gutteridge-StL 35	York-Det 11	Stephens-StL 22	Keller-NY 269	Johnson-NY 94
York-Det 90	Case-Was 180	Etten-NY 35	Keller-NY 11	Heath-Cle 18	Doerr-Bos 249	Stephens-StL 91
Vernon-Was 89			Spence-Was 10		Stephens-StL 247	Spence-Was 88
BASES ON BALLS	**STOLEN BASES**	**BASE STEALING RUNS**	**FIELDING RUNS-INFIELD**	**FIELDING RUNS-OUTFIELD**	**OUTFIELD ASSISTS**	**CATCHER CS PCT.**
Keller-NY 106	Case-Was 61	Case-Was 8.5	Boudreau-Cle 25.1	Tucker-Chi 9.2	Laabs-StL 16	Rosar-Cle 54.8
Gordon-NY 98	Moses-Chi 56	Moses-Chi 7.4	Gordon-NY 24.7	Byrnes-StL 6.9	Tucker-Chi 14	Richards-Det 49.5
Cullenbine-Cle 96	Tucker-Chi 29	Appling-Chi 3.1	York-Det 18.6	Moses-Chi 6.6	Cullenbine-Cle 14	Early-Was 46.4
Boudreau-Cle 90	Appling-Chi 27	Culberson-Bos 3.1	Clift-StL-Was 15.4	Johnson-Was 6.5	Hockett-Cle 13	Tresh-Chi 41.7
Appling-Chi 90	Vernon-Was 24	Vernon-Was 2.5	Bloodworth-Det 15.4	Laabs-StL 4.6	Byrnes-StL 13	Partee-Bos 40.8
WINS	**WINNING PCT.**	**WINS ABOVE TEAM**	**GAMES STARTED**	**COMPLETE GAMES**	**FEWEST HITS/GAME**	**FEWEST BB/GAME**
Trout-Det 20	Chandler-NY .833	Chandler-NY 7.0	Wynn-Was 33	Hughson-Bos 20	Reynolds-Cle 6.34	Leonard-Was 1.88
Chandler-NY 20	Smith-Cle .708	Smith-Cle 4.9	Bagby-Cle 33	Chandler-NY 20	Niggeling-StL-Was 6.66	Chandler-NY 1.92
Wynn-Was 18	Bonham-NY .652	Trout-Det 4.6	Hughson-Bos 32	Wensloff-NY 18	Haefner-Was 6.86	Bonham-NY 2.07
Smith-Cle 17	Trout-Det .625	Judd-Bos 3.3		Trout-Det 18	Chandler-NY 7.01	Muncrief-StL 2.11
Bagby-Cle 17	Grove-Chi .625	Trucks-Det 3.3		Grove-Chi 18	Wensloff-NY 7.21	Trucks-Det 2.31
STRIKEOUTS	**STRIKEOUTS/GAME**	**GAMES**	**SAVES**	**BASE RUNNERS/9**	**ADJUSTED RELIEF RUNS**	**RELIEF RANKING**
Reynolds-Cle 151	Reynolds-Cle 6.84	Brown-Bos 49	Maltzberger-Chi 14	Chandler-NY 9.07	Brown-Bos 11.6	Caster-StL 18.0
Newhouser-Det 144	Newhouser-Det 6.62	Trout-Det 44	Heving-Cle 9	Murphy-NY 9.79	Maltzberger-Chi 10.8	Brown-Bos 15.9
Chandler-NY 134	Bridges-Det 5.82	Wolff-Phi 41	Brown-Bos 9	Trucks-Det 9.90	Caster-StL 9.6	Maltzberger-Chi 14.3
Bridges-Det 124	Trucks-Det 5.24	Ryba-Bos 40	Murphy-NY 8	Bonham-NY 9.97	Murphy-NY 5.6	Murphy-NY 11.2
Trucks-Det 118	Chandler-NY 4.77	Carrasquel-Was 39	Caster-StL 8	Wensloff-NY 10.07	Heving-Cle 4.3	Naymick-Cle 5.0
INNINGS PITCHED	**OPPONENTS' AVG.**	**OPPONENTS' OBP**	**EARNED RUN AVERAGE**	**ADJUSTED ERA**	**ADJUSTED STARTER RUNS**	**PITCHER WINS**
Bagby-Cle 273.0	Reynolds-Cle .202	Chandler-NY .261	Chandler-NY 1.64	Chandler-NY 197	Chandler-NY 42.1	**Chandler-NY 5.3**
Hughson-Bos 266.0	Niggeling-StL-Was .204	Trucks-Det .276	Bonham-NY 2.27	Bridges-Det 147	Bonham-NY 26.0	**Trout-Det 4.1**
Wynn-Was 256.2	Haefner-Was .208	Wensloff-NY .282	Haefner-Was 2.29	Trout-Det 142	Trout-Det 25.8	**Bridges-Det 2.6**
Chandler-NY 253.0	Chandler-NY .215	Bonham-NY .282	Bridges-Det 2.39	Bonham-NY 141	Bridges-Det 23.9	**Bonham-NY 2.5**
Trout-Det 246.2	Wensloff-NY .219	Niggeling-StL-Was .282	Trout-Det 2.48	Haefner-Was 140	Hughson-Bos 19.6	**Caster-StL 2.0**

Fathers Playing Catch with Sons

On September 6, 16-year-old Carl Scheib debuted as a pitcher for the Philadelphia A's. He became the youngest player in AL history, and joined others, like 20-year-olds Gene Woodling and George Kell, 18-year-old Vern Benson, and 17-year-old Cass Michaels in 1943's force-feeding derby.

In addition, several graybeards profited from the lack of available bodies. Forty-year-old Mike Ryba pitched 40 times for the Red Sox, who also used 41-year-old Al Simmons in the outfield. Joe Kuhel, Chicago's 37-year-old first baseman, batted .213 in 153 games. Johnny Niggeling, at 39, made 26 starts.

The Yankees won the pennant once more—but with Nick Etten at first base, outfielders Bud Matheny and Johnny Lindell replacing Joe DiMaggio and Tommy Henrich, and, again, a deep veteran pitching staff. Boston dropped into seventh and the Browns to sixth, leaving the Senators, Indians, and White Sox as the Yankees' closest pursuers.

For the third straight year, attendance declined, and average scoring fell for the fifth straight season to 3.89 runs per team—the fewest until 1966. As a result, speed became a factor. The Senators and White Sox both stole more bases than any AL club since 1923. Washington outfielder George Case's 61 steals were the highest individual total in more than a decade. The Yankees were the exception, with a major league-high 100 home runs.

Spud Chandler was a very good pitcher—but his 20-4 record and 1.64 ERA for the Yankees are reflective of the talent he was facing during the war years. Only three AL players hit 20 home runs in 1943. Yankees pitching was the World Series secret. St. Louis scored just 9 runs as New York won easily in five games. Chandler notched 2 complete-game victories, allowing just 1 earned run. Bill Dickey played in his last of eight Fall Classics and collected 4 RBIs.

1942 NATIONAL LEAGUE

TEAM	W	L	T	PCT	GB	HW	HL	R	OR	PA	H	2B	3B	HR	BB	SO	HB	SH	AVG	OBP	SLG	OPS	AOPS	BR	ABR	PF	SB	CS	BSA	BSR
StL	106	48	2	.688	—	**60**	17	**755**	**480**	6124	**1454**	**282**	**69**	60	551	507	22	**130**	**.268**	**.338**	**.379**	**717**	109	**112**	61	108	71			
Bro	104	50	1	.675	2	57	22	742	512	5990	1398	263	34	62	**572**	**484**	14	119	.265	**.338**	.362	700	**110**	85	**74**	102	**81**			
NY	85	67	2	.559	20	47	31	675	600	5879	1323	162	35	**109**	558	511	**34**	77	.254	.330	.361	691	108	58	55	101	39			
Cin	76	76	2	.500	29	38	39	527	545	5860	1216	198	39	66	483	549	23	94	.231	.299	.321	620	88	-83	-82	100	42			
Pit	66	81	4	.449	36.5	41	34	585	631	5754	1250	173	49	54	537	536	26	87	.245	.320	.330	650	95	-17	-31	103	41			
Chi	68	86	1	.442	38	36	41	591	665	5984	1360	224	41	75	509	607	19	104	.254	.321	.353	674	108	24	49	96	63			
Bos	59	89	2	.399	44	33	36	515	645	5661	1216	210	19	68	474	507	20	90	.240	.307	.329	636	94	-47	-36	98	49			
Phi	42	109	0	.278	62.5	23	51	394	706	5567	1174	168	37	44	392	488	16	99	.232	.289	.306	595	84	-130	-107	95	37			
Total	613	—	—	—	—	335	271	4784	—	46819	10391	1680	323	538	4076	4189	174	800	.249	.318	.343	661	—	—	—	—	423	—	—	—

TEAM	CG	SHO	GR	SV	IP	H	HR	BB	SO	BR/9	ERA	AERA	OAV	OOB	PR	APR	PF	OSB	OCS	FA	E	WPB	DP	FW	PW	BW	BSW	DIF
StL	70	**18**	149	15	1410.1	**1192**	49	473	**651**	**10.7**	**2.55**	**134**	**.228**	**.294**	**120**	**133**	103	**33**	***56***	.972	169	43	137	-.1	**14.3**	6.5	—	8.3
Bro	67	16	165	**24**	1398.2	1205	73	493	612	11.1	2.84	115	.231	.302	73	65	98	35	*39*	**.977**	**138**	**19**	150	**1.7**	7.0	**7.9**	—	10.4
NY	70	12	153	13	1370.0	1299	94	493	497	11.9	3.31	101	.250	.316	0	7	101	43	*34*	**.977**	**138**	29	128	1.6	.8	5.9	—	.7
Cin	**80**	12	115	8	1411.2	1213	**47**	526	616	11.2	2.82	117	.230	.302	78	74	99	57	*45*	.971	177	28	**158**	-.7	7.9	-8.8	—	1.6
Pit	64	13	156	11	1351.1	1376	62	**435**	426	12.1	3.58	94	.262	.320	-41	-30	102	61	*42*	.969	184	29	128	-1.3	-3.2	-3.3	—	.4
Chi	71	10	150	14	1400.2	1447	70	525	507	12.8	3.60	89	.267	.334	-44	-65	97	48	*48*	.973	170	37	136	-.2	-7.0	5.3	—	-7.1
Bos	68	9	162	8	1334.0	1326	82	518	414	12.6	3.76	89	.260	.331	-66	-62	101	67	*41*	.976	142	40	138	1.1	-6.7	-3.9	—	-5.6
Phi	51	2	**184**	6	1341.0	1328	61	605	472	13.1	4.12	80	.260	.342	-120	-122	100	79	*45*	.968	194	36	147	-1.9	-13.1	-11.5	—	-7.0
Total	541	92	1234	99	11017.2	—	—	—	—	11.9	3.31	—	.249	.318	—	—	—	—	—	.973	1312	261	1122	—	—	—	—	—

BATTER-FIELDER WINS	BATTING AVERAGE	ON-BASE PERCENTAGE	SLUGGING AVERAGE	ON-BASE PLUS SLUGGING	ADJUSTED OPS	ADJUSTED BATTER RUNS
Nicholson-Chi.... 4.1	Lombardi-Bos 330	Fletcher-Pit 417	Mize-NY................521	Ott-NY...................912	Ott-NY...................165	Ott-NY..................50.1
Ott-NY 3.9	Slaughter-StL........318	Ott-NY...................415	Ott-NY...................497	Slaughter-StL........906	Mize-NY................161	Slaughter-StL.......41.8
Slaughter-StL 3.5	Musial-StL.............315	Slaughter-StL........412	Slaughter-StL........494	Mize-NY................901	Nicholson-Chi 156	Nicholson-Chi 41.8
Reese-Bro........... 3.3	Reiser-Bro 310	Hack-Chi...............402	Musial-StL.............490	Musial-StL.............888	Slaughter-StL........153	Mize-NY...............40.5
Musial-StL 3.2	Mize-NY.................305	Musial-StL.............397	Lombardi-Bos 482	Nicholson-Chi 859	Musial-StL.............148	Hack-Chi..............35.6

RUNS	HITS	DOUBLES	TRIPLES	HOME RUNS	TOTAL BASES	RUNS BATTED IN
Ott-NY...................118	Slaughter-StL........188	Marion-StL.............38	Slaughter-StL..........17	Ott-NY.....................30	Slaughter-StL........292	Mize-NY................110
Slaughter-StL.........100	Nicholson-Chi 173	Medwick-Bro...........37	Nicholson-Chi 11	Mize-NY..................26	Mize-NY................282	Camilli-Bro............109
Mize-NY..................97	Medwick-Bro.........166	Hack-Chi.................36	Musial-StL...............10	Camilli-Bro..............26	Nicholson-Chi 280	Slaughter-StL..........98
Hack-Chi.................91	Hack-Chi...............166	Herman-Bro............34	Litwhiler-Phi..............9	Nicholson-Chi 21	Ott-NY...................273	Medwick-Bro...........96
	Elliott-Pit 166	Reiser-Bro 33		West-Bos 16	Camilli-Bro............247	Ott-NY.....................93

BASES ON BALLS	STOLEN BASES	BASE STEALING RUNS	FIELDING RUNS-INFIELD	FIELDING RUNS-OUTFIELD	OUTFIELD ASSISTS	CATCHER CS PCT.
Ott-NY...................109	Reiser-Bro 20		May-Phi 19.1	DiMaggio-Pit........12.0	DiMaggio-Pit...........20	W.Cooper-StL......57.7
Fletcher-Pit...........105	Reese-Bro 15		Reese-Bro 18.2	Musial-StL.............7.4	Nicholson-Chi 18	Owen-Bro 53.4
Camilli-Bro..............97	Fernandez-Bos.......15		Fletcher-Pit..........11.1	Nicholson-Chi 6.9	Holmes-Bos............16	McCullough-Chi...50.0
Hack-Chi.................94	Merullo-Chi.............14		Glossop-Phi.........10.4	Barrett-Pit 5.5	Slaughter-StL..........15	Lamanno-Cin.......46.2
Slaughter-StL..........88	Hopp-StL 14		Bragan-Phi............8.9	Holmes-Bos...........5.2	Ott-NY.....................15	Danning-NY.........43.6

WINS	WINNING PCT.	WINS ABOVE TEAM	GAMES STARTED	COMPLETE GAMES	FEWEST HITS/GAME	FEWEST BB/GAME
M.Cooper-StL 22	French-Bro............789	Passeau-Chi 4.7	Javery-Bos..............37	Tobin-Bos................28	M.Cooper-StL 6.69	Warneke-StL-Chi .1.79
Beazley-StL 21	Beazley-StL 778	Beazley-StL 4.4	M.Cooper-StL 35	Passeau-Chi 24	VanderMeer-Cin ..6.93	Lohrman-StL-NY .1.85
Wyatt-Bro................19	M.Cooper-StL 759	Lohrman-StL-NY ...3.9	Passeau-Chi 34	M.Cooper-StL 22	Higbe-Bro 7.31	Hubbell-NY 1.94
Passeau-Chi 19	Wyatt-Bro..............731	M.Cooper-StL 3.8		Walters-Cin.............21	Starr-Cin 7.42	Derringer-Cin.......2.11
VanderMeer-Cin 18	Davis-Bro..............714	French-Bro.............3.6		VanderMeer-Cin 21	Beazley-StL 7.57	M.Cooper-StL 2.20

STRIKEOUTS	STRIKEOUTS/GAME	GAMES	SAVES	BASE RUNNERS/9	ADJUSTED RELIEF RUNS	RELIEF RANKING
VanderMeer-Cin ...186	VanderMeer-Cin ..6.86	Adams-NY 61	Casey-Bro...............13	M.Cooper-StL 9.04	Adams-NY 14.0	Adams-NY 19.7
M.Cooper-StL 152	Lanier-StL 5.20	Casey-Bro...............50	Adams-NY 11	Shoun-StL-Cin.....9.69	Casey-Bro............13.0	Beggs-Cin............14.0
Higbe-Bro 115	M.Cooper-StL 4.91	Podgajny-Phi 43	Beggs-Cin.................8	Melton-NY............9.84	Beggs-Cin............10.6	Casey-Bro............12.8
Walters-Cin...........109	Higbe-Bro 4.67	Beazley-StL 43	Sain-Bos...................6	Beggs-Cin..........10.05	Shoun-StL-Cin.......8.6	Shoun-StL-Cin.......4.3
Melton-Phi 107	Melton-Phi 4.60		Gumbert-StL.............5	Lohrman-StL-NY10.07	Webber-Bro 2.9	Webber-Bro 2.7

INNINGS PITCHED	OPPONENTS' AVG.	OPPONENTS' OBP	EARNED RUN AVERAGE	ADJUSTED ERA	ADJUSTED STARTER RUNS	PITCHER WINS
Tobin-Bos...........287.2	M.Cooper-StL 204	M.Cooper-StL 258	M.Cooper-StL 1.78	M.Cooper-StL 193	M.Cooper-StL 46.6	**M.Cooper-StL..... 4.7**
M.Cooper-StL 278.2	VanderMeer-Cin ...208	Lohrman-StL-NY ..281	Beazley-StL 2.13	Beazley-StL 161	Beazley-StL 27.6	**Beazley-StL........ 3.5**
Passeau-Chi 278.1	Higbe-Bro 223	Wyatt-Bro..............286	Davis-Bro.............2.36	Davis-Bro..............138	VanderMeer-Cin ..24.6	**French-Bro 3.3**
Starr-Cin 276.2	Wyatt-Bro..............225	Warneke-StL-Chi ..286	VanderMeer-Cin ..2.43	Lohrman-StL-NY ..136	Starr-Cin 24.5	**VanderMeer-Cin 3.1**
Javery-Bos.........261.0	Starr-Cin 226	Davis-Bro..............287	Lohrman-StL-NY .2.48	VanderMeer-Cin ...135	French-Bro...........22.0	**Walters-Cin......... 2.5**

WHERE DID *YOU* COME FROM?

It looked like a cinch. On August 15 Brooklyn, starring 23-year-olds Pee Wee Reese and Pete Reiser, held a $9^1/_2$ game lead over second-place St. Louis, which had played well all season but recently stumbled. But from that point, the Bums never knew what hit them. The Cardinals went 43-8 down the stretch, overtaking Brooklyn in mid-September. In winning 12 of their final 13, they held off the late-charging Dodgers. St. Louis pulled it off despite a starting infield with just 9 homers and only two pitchers with more than 13 wins. But they still led the league in runs and ERA.

For the third consecutive season, scoring dropped, this time to 3.90 runs per game. For the only time between 1918 and 1963, the league average sank below .250. As a result, the performances of Cardinals outfielders Enos Slaughter and Stan Musial look especially good. MVP Mort Cooper led the league in wins, shutouts, and ERA, and rookie Johnny Beazley won 21.

Relief pitching gained some definition in 1942 as Giants right-hander Ace Adams set a record with 61 bullpen appearances (he broke it the next year). While some teams continued to shuttle their best starters in and out of late-inning jobs, many clubs were already using a particular reliever in clutch situations.

Seeing their first action were two Braves pitchers who blossomed after the war: Warren Spahn and Johnny Sain. But 21-year-old Al Montgomery, Boston's backup catcher in 1941, was killed April 26 in a car wreck.

The World Series was highly anticipated; both the Cardinals and Yankees cleared 100 wins. But the classic went just five games; after losing the first contest, St. Louis took the next four to stun the New Yorkers. All five games were entertaining and close. Beazley twice fired complete-game victories, including the clincher.

1942 AMERICAN LEAGUE

TEAM	W	L	T	PCT	GB	HW	HL	R	OR	PA	H	2B	3B	HR	BB	SO	HB	SH	AVG	OBP	SLG	OPS	AOPS	BR	ABR	PF	SB	CS	BSA	BSR
NY	103	51	0	.669	—	**58**	19	**801**	**507**	6009	1429	223	57	**108**	591	556	**29**	84	.269	.346	.394	740	**118**	105	**122**	98	69	33	68	4
Bos	93	59	0	.612	9	53	24	761	594	5984	**1451**	**244**	55	103	591	508	22	**123**	**.276**	**.352**	**.403**	**755**	116	**135**	109	103	68	61	53	-6
StL	82	69	0	.543	19.5	40	37	730	637	5947	1354	239	**62**	98	**609**	607	13	96	.259	.338	.385	723	109	70	59	102	37	38	49	-5
Cle	75	79	2	.487	28	39	39	590	659	5931	1344	223	58	50	500	544	24	90	.253	.320	.345	665	100	-45	-7	94	69	74	48	-11
Det	73	81	2	.474	30	43	34	589	587	5928	1313	217	37	76	509	476	19	73	.246	.314	.344	658	85	-58	-103	108	39	40	49	-5
Chi	66	82	0	.446	34	35	35	538	609	5552	1215	214	36	25	497	**427**	16	90	.246	.316	.318	634	87	-87	-75	98	**114**	70	62	1
Was	62	89	0	.411	39.5	35	42	653	817	5949	1364	224	49	40	581	536	19	54	.258	.333	.341	674	98	-14	-7	99	98	29	**77**	**11**
Phi	55	99	0	.357	48	25	51	549	801	5822	1315	213	46	33	440	490	23	74	.249	.309	.325	634	86	-104	-101	99	44	45	49	-6
Total	611	—	—	—	—	328	281	5211	—	47122	10785	1797	400	533	4318	4144	165	684	.257	.329	.357	686	—	—	—	—	538	390	58	-18

TEAM	CG	SHO	GR	SV	IP	H	HR	BB	SO	BR/9	ERA	AERA	OAV	OOB	PR	APR	PF	OSB	OCS	FA	E	WPB	DP	FW	PW	BW	BSW	DIF
NY	**88**	**18**	89	**17**	1375.0	**1259**	71	**431**	558	**11.2**	**2.91**	118	**.244**	**.304**	**115**	87	94	**37**	50	**.976**	**142**	**21**	**190**	**2.0**	8.9	**12.5**	.6	1.9
Bos	84	11	108	**17**	1358.2	1260	65	553	500	12.1	3.44	108	.247	.322	32	42	102	62	48	.974	157	34	156	1.0	4.3	11.2	-.4	.9
StL	68	12	140	13	1363.0	1387	63	505	488	12.7	3.59	103	.262	.330	10	17	101	86	43	.972	167	51	143	.4	1.7	6.0	-.3	-1.4
Cle	61	12	**162**	11	1402.2	1353	61	560	448	12.4	3.59	96	.254	.327	10	-24	94	63	36	.974	163	24	175	1.0	-2.5	-.7	-.9	1.1
Det	65	12	126	14	1399.1	1321	60	598	**671**	12.5	3.13	**126**	.248	.326	82	**118**	108	71	56	.969	194	42	142	-.8	**12.1**	-10.6	-.3	-4.5
Chi	86	8	75	8	1314.1	1304	74	473	432	12.3	3.58	100	.258	.325	11	3	98	58	31	.970	173	43	144	-.1	.3	-7.7	.3	-.9
Was	68	12	125	11	1346.2	1496	**50**	558	496	13.8	4.58	80	.279	.349	-139	-139	100	65	**66**	.962	222	41	133	-2.7	-14.2	-.7	**1.4**	2.7
Phi	67	5	114	9	1374.2	1404	89	639	546	13.5	4.45	85	.263	.344	-120	-99	103	96	60	.969	188	58	124	-.6	-10.1	-10.3	-.4	-.6
Total	587	90	939	100	10934.1	—	—	—	—	12.6	3.66	—	.257	.329	—	—	—	—	—	.971	1406	314	1207	—	—	—	—	—

BATTER-FIELDER WINS	BATTING AVERAGE	ON-BASE PERCENTAGE	SLUGGING AVERAGE	ON-BASE PLUS SLUGGING	ADJUSTED OPS	ADJUSTED BATTER RUNS
Williams-Bos...... 8.5	Williams-Bos.........356	Williams-Bos........499	Williams-Bos.........648	Williams-Bos.......1147	Williams-Bos.........214	Williams-Bos........89.9
Gordon-NY 5.8	Pesky-Bos............331	Keller-NY 417	Keller-NY 513	Keller-NY 930	Keller-NY 164	Keller-NY.............50.4
Rizzuto-NY 4.6	Spence-Was 323	Judnich-StL...........413	Judnich-StL...........499	Judnich-StL...........912	Gordon-NY 156	Gordon-NY 41.9
Pesky-Bos 4.5	Gordon-NY 322	Fleming-Cle 412	DiMaggio-NY 498	Gordon-NY 900	Judnich-StL...........153	Fleming-Cle 40.1
Keller-NY............ 4.2	Case-Was.............320	Gordon-NY 409	Laabs-StL 498	Laabs-StL 878	DiMaggio-NY 148	DiMaggio-NY 36.6

RUNS	HITS	DOUBLES	TRIPLES	HOME RUNS	TOTAL BASES	RUNS BATTED IN
Williams-Bos.........141	Pesky-Bos.............205	Kolloway-Chi...........40	Spence-Was 15	Williams-Bos...........36	Williams-Bos.........338	Williams-Bos.........137
DiMaggio-NY 123	Spence-Was 203	Clift-StL...................39	Heath-Cle 13	Laabs-StL 27	DiMaggio-NY 304	DiMaggio-NY 114
DiMaggio-Bos.......110	Williams-Bos.........186	Heath-Cle 37	DiMaggio-NY 13	Keller-NY 26	Keller-NY 279	Keller-NY 108
Clift-StL.................108	DiMaggio-NY 186	DiMaggio-Bos.........36	McQuillen-StL 12	York-Det..................21	Spence-Was 272	Gordon-NY 103
Keller-NY 106	Keltner-Cle...........179			DiMaggio-NY 21	DiMaggio-Bos.......272	Doerr-Bos 102

BASES ON BALLS	STOLEN BASES	BASE STEALING RUNS	FIELDING RUNS-INFIELD	FIELDING RUNS-OUTFIELD	OUTFIELD ASSISTS	CATCHER CS PCT.
Williams-Bos.........145	Case-Was...............44	Case-Was...............7.6	Rizzuto-NY 30.0	DiMaggio-Bos......13.1	DiMaggio-Bos.........19	Dickey-NY............59.5
Keller-NY 114	Vernon-Was............25	Vernon-Was...........3.4	Pesky-Bos............19.6	Moses-Chi 6.1	Johnson-Phi............18	Early-Was 50.6
Fleming-Cle 106	Rizzuto-NY 22	Rizzuto-NY 2.7	York-Det...............15.3	Johnson-Phi...........5.4	Williams-Bos...........15	Peacock-Bos........44.6
Clift-StL.................106	Kuhel-Chi................22	Keller-NY 2.4	Doerr-Bos 12.0	Chartak-NY-Was-StL .5.4	Cramer-Det.............15	Tebbetts-Det 43.2
Cullenbine-SL-W-NY ..92		Appling-Chi 2.0	Keltner-Cle...........11.3	Cullenbine-SL-W-NY .4.7	Moses-Chi 14	Conroy-Bos...........42.3

WINS	WINNING PCT.	WINS ABOVE TEAM	GAMES STARTED	COMPLETE GAMES	FEWEST HITS/GAME	FEWEST BB/GAME
Hughson-Bos..........22	Bonham-NY 808	Hughson-Bos.........7.0	Bagby-Cle...............35	Hughson-Bos..........22	Newhouser-Det....6.71	Bonham-NY............96
Bonham-NY 21	Borowy-NY 789	Bonham-NY 6.0	Auker-StL................34	Bonham-NY 22	Niggeling-StL.......7.55	Lyons-Chi.............1.30
Marchildon-Phi........17	Hughson-Bos........786	Marchildon-Phi.......5.4	Marchildon-Phi........31	Lyons-Chi................20	Dobson-Bos.........7.64	Ruffing-NY 1.91
Bagby-Cle...............17	Chandler-NY.........762	Lyons-Chi..............4.9	Hudson-Was...........31	Hudson-Was...........19	Trucks-Det 7.89	Breuer-NY.............2.03
Chandler-NY...........16	Bagby-Cle.............654	Bagby-Cle..............4.8			Chandler-NY........7.89	Bagby-Cle............2.13

STRIKEOUTS	STRIKEOUTS/GAME	GAMES	SAVES	BASE RUNNERS/9	ADJUSTED RELIEF RUNS	RELIEF RANKING
Newsom-Was 113	Newhouser-Det....5.05	Haynes-Chi............40	Murphy-NY 11	Bonham-NY 8.92	Ferrick-Cle 14.5	Haynes-Chi..........13.3
Hughson-Bos.........113	Bridges-Det..........5.02	Caster-StL 39	Haynes-Chi...............6	Lyons-Chi.............9.73	Haynes-Chi...........10.5	Caster-StL 9.5
Marchildon-Phi......110	Trucks-Det 4.88		Brown-Bos................6	Ferrick-Cle 9.74	Caster-StL 7.5	Ferrick-Cle 9.2
Benton-Det 110	Newsom-Was 4.76		Newhouser-Det.........5	Butland-Bos.........9.78	Brown-Bos.............1.7	Brown-Bos..............3.3
Niggeling-StL........107	Niggeling-StL.......4.67		Caster-StL 5	Ruffing-NY........10.55		

INNINGS PITCHED	OPPONENTS' AVG.	OPPONENTS' OBP	EARNED RUN AVERAGE	ADJUSTED ERA	ADJUSTED STARTER RUNS	PITCHER WINS
Hughson-Bos.....281.0	Newhouser-Det.....207	Bonham-NY..........259	Lyons-Chi.............2.10	Lyons-Chi..............172	Hughson-Bos.......35.0	**Lyons-Chi............3.8**
Bagby-Cle..........270.2	Niggeling-StL........226	Lyons-Chi..............275	Bonham-NY 2.27	Newhouser-Det.....161	Bonham-NY.........31.3	**Hughson-Bos..... 3.7**
Auker-StL...........249.0	Dobson-Bos..........231	Ruffing-NY 292	Chandler-NY.........2.38	Bonham-NY 152	Lyons-Chi.............29.2	**Bonham-NY........ 3.0**
Marchildon-Phi...244.0	Trucks-Det 231	Breuer-NY.............295	Newhouser-Det....2.45	Chandler-NY.........145	White-Det.............24.9	**Chandler-NY 3.0**
Hudson-Was......239.1	Borowy-NY 233	Hughson-Bos........296	Borowy-NY 2.52	Trucks-Det 144	Benton-Det 24.9	**Newhouser-Det . 2.9**

You're in the Army Now

At no point after mid-May was the pennant race close, as the Yankees buzzed their way to an even better record than in 1941. Joe McCarthy wielded deep pitching, with seven men starting 13 or more games, and a peerless outfield of Tommy Henrich, Joe DiMaggio, and Charlie Keller to lead in runs by 40 and ERA by 22 points.

The Red Sox, again a strong second, added another piece by promoting rookie shortstop Johnny Pesky, who hit .331. Ted Williams had another spectacular year, taking the Triple Crown, but the Bosox were weak at key positions, and their pitching wasn't up to standard. While the race featured little drama, the third-place team caused a buzz. The St. Louis Browns, 43-111 in 1939 and sixth the next two years, improved by $12^1/_2$ games with a strong second half. Rookie shortstop Vern Stephens was a keeper. What the Browns showed most, though, was how World War II was affecting baseball.

When the war hit home in December 1941, the country needed healthy bodies. Therefore, many great players got the call; between 1943–45 Cleveland lost Bob Feller, Boston sacrificed Williams, Pesky, and Dom DiMaggio, and the Yankees lost Joe DiMaggio and Henrich. Detroit's Hank Greenberg, who joined the military before the U.S. was even in the war, played less than 100 games between 1941–45. Teammate Charlie Gehringer's career ended when he was called into service. Browns pitcher Elden Auker retired to devote time to a war job. Washington infielder Cecil Travis never recovered from his service. Johnny Sturm, the Yankees' first baseman in 1941, spent the next four years in the military and never returned to the majors. Two men who appeared briefly in the major leagues, Elmer Gedeon (Senators) and Harry O'Neill (Athletics), were killed in action.

Previously "good" teams were no longer a lock. Until the war was over, it was every club for itself. The Yankees' surprise five-game loss in the World Series to St. Louis showed that teams with good farm systems were in the best shape.

1941 NATIONAL LEAGUE

TEAM	W	L	T	PCT	GB	HW	HL	R	OR	PA	H	2B	3B	HR	BB	SO	HB	SH	AVG	OBP	SLG	OPS	AOPS	BR	ABR	PF	SB	CS	BSA	BSR
Bro	100	54	3	.649	—	52	25	**800**	581	6218	**1494**	**286**	**69**	**101**	**600**	535	27	106	**.272**	**.347**	**.405**	**752**	**113**	**132**	**98**	104	36			
StL	97	56	2	.634	2.5	**53**	24	734	589	6151	1482	254	56	70	540	543	**28**	**126**	**.272**	.340	.377	717	102	63	17	107	47			
Cin	88	66	0	.571	12	45	34	616	**564**	5819	1288	213	33	64	477	**428**	22	102	.247	.313	.337	650	89	-74	-76	100	**68**			
Pit	81	73	2	.526	19	45	32	690	643	5954	1417	233	65	56	547	516	15	95	.268	.338	.368	706	105	38	41	100	59			
NY	74	79	3	.484	25.5	38	39	667	706	6018	1401	248	35	95	504	518	23	96	.260	.326	.371	697	101	16	3	102	36			
Chi	70	84	1	.455	30	38	39	666	670	5902	1323	239	25	99	559	670	14	99	.253	.327	.365	692	105	11	36	96	39			
Bos	62	92	2	.403	38	32	44	592	720	5968	1357	231	38	48	471	608	13	70	.251	.312	.334	646	92	-84	-59	96	61			
Phi	43	111	1	.279	57	23	52	501	793	5796	1277	188	38	64	451	596	22	90	.244	.307	.331	638	89	-101	-80	96	65			
Total	622	—	—	—	—	326	289	5266	—	47826	11039	1892	359	597	4149	4414	164	784	.258	.326	.361	688	—	—	—	—	411	—	—	—

TEAM	CG	SHO	GR	SV	IP	H	HR	BB	SO	BR/9	ERA	AERA	OAV	OOB	PR	APR	PF	OSB	OCS	FA	E	WPB	DP	FW	PW	BW	BSW	DIF
Bro	66	17	157	**22**	1421.0	**1236**	81	495	603	**11.1**	**3.14**	117	**.233**	**.300**	**78**	82	101	**34**	*40*	.974	162	**29**	125	.9	8.4	**10.1**	—	3.6
StL	64	15	171	20	1416.1	1289	85	502	**659**	11.5	3.19	**118**	.242	.310	70	**87**	104	42	*48*	.973	172	32	146	.2	**8.9**	1.7	—	9.6
Cin	**89**	**19**	112	10	1386.2	1300	61	510	627	11.9	3.17	114	.250	.319	72	67	99	64	*46*	**.975**	**152**	39	147	**1.3**	6.9	-7.8	—	10.7
Pit	71	8	150	12	1374.1	1392	66	492	410	12.4	3.48	104	.260	.323	23	19	99	47	*42*	.968	196	33	130	-1.1	2.0	4.2	—	-1.0
NY	55	12	175	18	1391.2	1455	90	539	566	13.0	3.94	94	.269	.337	-48	-38	102	46	*41*	.974	160	37	144	.9	-3.9	.3	—	.2
Chi	74	8	145	9	1364.2	1431	**60**	**449**	548	12.5	3.72	94	.267	.327	-13	-34	97	59	*39*	.970	180	30	139	-.3	-3.5	3.7	—	-6.9
Bos	62	10	176	9	1385.2	1440	75	554	446	13.2	3.95	90	.269	.341	-49	-59	98	53	*47*	.969	191	36	**174**	-.9	-6.1	-6.1	—	-2.0
Phi	35	4	**201**	9	1372.1	1499	79	606	552	14.0	4.50	82	.279	.355	-132	-119	102	66	***52***	.969	187	46	147	-.7	-12.2	-8.2	—	-12.9
Total	516	93	1287	109	11112.2	—	—	—	—	12.4	3.63	—	.258	.326	—	—	—	—	—	.972	1400	282	1152	—	—	—	—	—

BATTER-FIELDER WINS	BATTING AVERAGE	ON-BASE PERCENTAGE	SLUGGING AVERAGE	ON-BASE PLUS SLUGGING	ADJUSTED OPS	ADJUSTED BATTER RUNS
Reiser-Bro 4.5	Reiser-Bro .343	Fletcher-Pit .421	Reiser-Bro .558	Reiser-Bro .964	Reiser-Bro 163	Camilli-Bro 46.5
Fletcher-Pit 3.6	Cooney-Bos .319	Hack-Chi .417	Camilli-Bro .556	Camilli-Bro .962	Camilli-Bro 162	Reiser-Bro 43.7
Camilli-Bro 3.3	Medwick-Bro .318	Camilli-Bro .407	Mize-StL .535	Mize-StL .941	Mize-StL 153	Fletcher-Pit 39.8
Hack-Chi 3.1	Hack-Chi .317	Reiser-Bro .406	Medwick-Bro .517	Ott-NY .898	Ott-NY 149	Hack-Chi 39.5
Ott-NY 3.0	Mize-StL .317	Mize-StL .406	Slaughter-StL .496	Slaughter-StL .886	Fletcher-Pit 148	Ott-NY 38.2

RUNS	HITS	DOUBLES	TRIPLES	HOME RUNS	TOTAL BASES	RUNS BATTED IN
Reiser-Bro 117	Hack-Chi 186	Reiser-Bro 39	Reiser-Bro 17	Camilli-Bro 34	Reiser-Bro 299	Camilli-Bro 120
Hack-Chi 111	Reiser-Bro 184	Mize-StL 39	Fletcher-Pit 13	Ott-NY 27	Camilli-Bro 294	Young-NY 104
Medwick-Bro 100	Litwhiler-Phi 180	Rucker-NY 38	Hopp-StL 11	Nicholson-Chi 26	Medwick-Bro 278	Mize-StL 100
Rucker-NY 95	Rucker-NY 179	Dallessandro-Chi 36	Medwick-Bro 10	Young-NY 25	Litwhiler-Phi 275	DiMaggio-Pit 100
Fletcher-Pit 95	Medwick-Bro 171		Elliott-Pit 10	Dahlgren-Bos-Chi 23	Young-NY 265	Nicholson-Chi 98

BASES ON BALLS	STOLEN BASES	BASE STEALING RUNS	FIELDING RUNS-INFIELD	FIELDING RUNS-OUTFIELD	OUTFIELD ASSISTS	CATCHER CS PCT.
Fletcher-Pit 118	Murtaugh-Phi 18		May-Phi 23.9	Litwhiler-Phi 13.3	Walker-Bro 19	Owen-Bro 54.7
Camilli-Bro 104	Benjamin-Phi 17		Stringer-Chi 23.8	Walker-Bro 9.9	Ott-NY 19	Mancuso-StL 51.9
Ott-NY 100	Handley-Pit 16		Miller-Bos 13.3	VanRobays-Pit 6.1	Reiser-Bro 14	Berres-Bos 48.3
Hack-Chi 99	Frey-Cin 16		Werber-Cin 10.1	West-Bos 5.4	Moore-StL 14	Warren-Phi 46.8
	Hopp-StL 15		Fletcher-Pit 9.9	Moore-Bos 5.2		Lopez-Pit 45.3

WINS	WINNING PCT.	WINS ABOVE TEAM	GAMES STARTED	COMPLETE GAMES	FEWEST HITS/GAME	FEWEST BB/GAME
Wyatt-Bro 22	E.Riddle-Cin .826	E.Riddle-Cin 7.3	Higbe-Bro 39	Walters-Cin 27	VanderMeer-Cin 6.84	Passeau-Chi 2.03
Higbe-Bro 22	Higbe-Bro .710	Krist-StL 5.0	Wyatt-Bro 35	Wyatt-Bro 23	Wyatt-Bro 6.96	Derringer-Cin 2.13
Walters-Cin 19	White-StL .708	Higbe-Bro 3.2	Walters-Cin 35	Tobin-Bos 20	White-StL 7.24	Lohrman-NY 2.26
E.Riddle-Cin 19	Wyatt-Bro .688	Carpenter-NY 2.9		Passeau-Chi 20	Higbe-Bro 7.37	Tobin-Bos 2.27
	Warneke-StL .654	White-StL 2.8			E.Riddle-Cin 7.48	Lee-Chi 2.31

STRIKEOUTS	STRIKEOUTS/GAME	GAMES	SAVES	BASE RUNNERS/9	ADJUSTED RELIEF RUNS	RELIEF RANKING
VanderMeer-Cin 202	VanderMeer-Cin 8.03	Higbe-Bro 48	Brown-NY 8	Wyatt-Bro 9.58	Pressnell-Chi 4.5	Pressnell-Chi 4.8
Wyatt-Bro 176	M.Cooper-StL 5.69	Pearson-Phi 46	Crouch-Phi-StL 7	Davis-Bro 9.91	Brown-NY 2.9	Brown-NY 3.7
Walters-Cin 129	Wyatt-Bro 5.49	Casey-Bro 45	Casey-Bro 7	E.Riddle-Cin 10.14	Crouch-Phi-StL .7	Crouch-Phi-StL .6
Higbe-Bro 121	White-StL 5.01	Hutchings-Cin-Bos 44	Pearson-Phi 6	White-StL 10.50		
M.Cooper-StL 118	Melton-NY 4.63	Johnson-Bos 43		Pollet-StL 10.67		

INNINGS PITCHED	OPPONENTS' AVG.	OPPONENTS' OBP	EARNED RUN AVERAGE	ADJUSTED ERA	ADJUSTED STARTER RUNS	PITCHER WINS
Walters-Cin 302.0	Wyatt-Bro .212	Wyatt-Bro .270	E.Riddle-Cin 2.24	E.Riddle-Cin 160	Wyatt-Bro 41.6	**Wyatt-Bro 5.3**
Higbe-Bro 298.0	VanderMeer-Cin .214	E.Riddle-Cin .282	Wyatt-Bro 2.34	White-StL 157	E.Riddle-Cin 30.5	**E.Riddle-Cin 3.5**
Wyatt-Bro 288.1	White-StL .217	White-StL .287	White-StL 2.40	Wyatt-Bro 157	White-StL 28.1	**Walters-Cin 3.3**
Sewell-Pit 249.0	Higbe-Bro .220	Sewell-Pit .299	VanderMeer-Cin 2.82	VanderMeer-Cin 127	Walters-Cin 26.7	**White-StL 3.0**
Warneke-StL 246.0	E.Riddle-Cin .224	Tobin-Bos .300	Walters-Cin 2.83	Walters-Cin 127	VanderMeer-Cin 19.2	**VanderMeer-Cin 2.1**

Brooklyn Celebrates

The first thrilling Cardinals-Dodgers confrontation of the decade took place in 1941. From Opening Day, the two clubs clung to one another, soaring high above the rest of the league; defending champ Cincinnati never quite got it together, finishing third only with a late surge.

Joe Medwick's midseason trade from St. Louis to Brooklyn sparked controversy, and Ducky went on to finish third in the league in runs. As August rolled into September, the Redbirds and Bums stood in a flat-footed tie. A September 4 doubleheader loss at Chicago, however, started the Cardinals on a downswing from which they could not recover. Leo Durocher's Dodgers kept the pressure on down the stretch and on September 25 clinched Brooklyn's first flag since 1920.

Dodger hurlers Kirby Higbe and Whitlow Wyatt tied for the league lead in victories, and Pete Reiser played like the game's next big star. Meanwhile, the Dodgers became the first NL team since 1931 to draw a million fans, and, thanks to a series of beanball scares, they also were the first to don batting helmets.

St. Louis, weak offensively except for first sacker Johnny Mize, hung in the race on the wings of their deep pitching staff. Despite the pennant loss, a late-season .426 showing from 20-year-old rookie Stan Musial showed that the Cardinals had much to anticipate.

Catcher Gabby Hartnett ended his career for fifth-place New York. The floundering Braves, showing indecision typical of a loser, again fiddled with their field dimensions—as they would continue to do throughout the decade.

The World Series was painful for Dodgers fans. Just one strike away from a Series-tying win in Game 4, a wild pitch by Hugh Casey set off a Yankees rally that won that game and carried into the next. New York's 3-1 win the next day clinched the Series.

1941 AMERICAN LEAGUE

TEAM	W	L	T	PCT	GB	HW	HL	R	OR	PA	H	2B	3B	HR	BB	SO	HB	SH	AVG	OBP	SLG	OPS	AOPS	BR	ABR	PF	SB	CS	BSA	BSR
NY	101	53	2	.656	—	**51**	26	830	**631**	6137	1464	243	60	**151**	616	565	**28**	49	.269	.346	.419	765	111	64	75	99	51	33	61	0
Bos	84	70	1	.545	17	47	30	**865**	750	6177	**1517**	**304**	55	124	683	567	20	**115**	**.283**	**.366**	**.430**	**796**	**115**	**142**	**121**	102	67	51	57	-3
Chi	77	77	2	.500	24	38	39	638	649	6012	1376	245	47	47	510	**476**	24	74	.255	.322	.343	665	84	-130	-122	99	**91**	53	63	1
Det	75	79	1	.487	26	43	34	686	743	6077	1412	247	55	81	602	584	23	82	.263	.340	.375	715	87	-27	-92	110	43	28	61	0
Cle	75	79	1	.487	26	42	35	677	668	5914	1350	249	**84**	103	512	605	18	101	.256	.323	.393	716	101	-43	-8	95	63	47	57	-3
Was	70	84	2	.455	31	40	37	728	798	6067	1502	257	80	52	470	488	14	62	.272	.331	.376	707	99	-58	-25	95	79	36	**69**	**5**
StL	70	84	3	.455	31	40	37	765	823	6285	1440	281	58	91	**775**	552	13	89	.266	.360	.390	750	103	61	35	103	50	39	56	-3
Phi	64	90	0	.416	37	36	41	713	840	5994	1431	240	69	85	574	588	8	76	.268	.340	.387	727	102	-9	9	98	27	36	43	-7
Total	622	—	—	—	—	337	279	5902	—	48663	11492	2066	508	734	4742	4425	148	648	.266	.341	.389	730	—	—	—	—	471	323	59	-9

TEAM	CG	SHO	GR	SV	IP	H	HR	BB	SO	BR/9	ERA	AERA	OAV	OOB	PR	APR	PF	OSB	OCS	FA	E	WPB	DP	FW	PW	BW	BSW	DIF
NY	75	13	119	**26**	1396.1	**1309**	81	598	589	12.4	3.53	112	**.248**	.325	96	66	95	**44**	36	.973	165	35	**196**	.5	6.4	7.3	.1	9.7
Bos	70	8	137	11	1372.0	1453	88	611	574	13.7	4.19	100	.270	.347	-6	-3	101	54	34	.972	172	42	139	.0	-.3	**11.7**	-.2	-4.3
Chi	**106**	**14**	63	4	1416.0	1362	89	**521**	564	**12.1**	**3.52**	**116**	.252	**.320**	**99**	**92**	99	54	46	.971	180	50	145	-.3	**8.9**	-11.8	.2	3.0
Det	52	8	157	16	1381.2	1399	80	645	**697**	13.4	4.18	109	.260	.341	-4	52	110	69	46	.969	186	39	129	-.7	5.0	-8.9	.1	2.5
Cle	68	10	133	19	1377.0	1366	71	660	617	13.4	3.90	101	.259	.344	39	7	95	50	37	**.976**	**142**	**34**	158	**1.7**	.7	-.8	-.2	-3.4
Was	69	8	140	7	1389.1	1524	**69**	603	544	13.9	4.35	93	.279	.353	-32	-49	98	59	**48**	.969	187	68	169	-.7	-4.7	-2.4	**.6**	.3
StL	65	7	**158**	10	1389.0	1563	120	549	454	13.8	4.72	91	.283	.350	-88	-62	104	64	38	.975	151	41	156	1.3	-6.0	3.4	-.2	-5.5
Phi	64	3	125	18	1365.1	1516	136	557	386	13.8	4.83	87	.279	.348	-104	-97	101	77	38	.967	200	69	150	-1.6	-9.4	.9	-.6	-2.3
Total	569	71	1032	111	11086.2	—	—	—	—	13.3	4.15	—	.266	.341	—	—	—	—	—	.972	1383	378	1242	—	—	—	—	—

BATTER-FIELDER WINS	BATTING AVERAGE	ON-BASE PERCENTAGE	SLUGGING AVERAGE	ON-BASE PLUS SLUGGING	ADJUSTED OPS	ADJUSTED BATTER RUNS
Williams-Bos......8.5	Williams-Bos.........406	Williams-Bos.........553	Williams-Bos.........735	Williams-Bos.......1287	Williams-Bos.........232	Williams-Bos......101.7
DiMaggio-NY......6.6	Travis-Was............359	Cullenbine-StL......452	DiMaggio-NY........643	DiMaggio-NY......1083	DiMaggio-NY........186	DiMaggio-NY.......67.7
Travis-Was..........5.1	DiMaggio-NY........357	DiMaggio-NY........440	Heath-Cle.............586	Keller-NY.............996	Heath-Cle.............165	Heath-Cle............50.4
Keller-NY............4.0	Heath-Cle.............340	Keller-NY.............416	Keller-NY.............580	Heath-Cle.............982	Keller-NY.............163	Keller-NY............48.0
S.Chapman-Phi..3.7	Siebert-Phi...........334	Foxx-Bos..............412	S.Chapman-Phi....543	Travis-Was...........930	Travis-Was...........152	Travis-Was...........43.6
RUNS	**HITS**	**DOUBLES**	**TRIPLES**	**HOME RUNS**	**TOTAL BASES**	**RUNS BATTED IN**
Williams-Bos.........135	Travis-Was............218	Boudreau-Cle.........45	Heath-Cle...............20	Williams-Bos..........37	DiMaggio-NY........348	DiMaggio-NY........125
DiMaggio-NY........122	Heath-Cle.............199	DiMaggio-NY..........43	Travis-Was.............19	Keller-NY...............33	Heath-Cle.............343	Heath-Cle.............123
DiMaggio-Bos.......117	DiMaggio-NY........193	Judnich-StL............40	Keltner-Cle.............13	Henrich-NY............31	Williams-Bos.........335	Keller-NY.............122
Clift-StL................108	Appling-Chi...........186	Travis-Was.............39		DiMaggio-NY..........30	Travis-Was...........316	Williams-Bos.........120
	Williams-Bos.........185	Kuhel-Chi...............39		York-Det.................27	S.Chapman-Phi....300	York-Det...............111
BASES ON BALLS	**STOLEN BASES**	**BASE STEALING RUNS**	**FIELDING RUNS-INFIELD**	**FIELDING RUNS-OUTFIELD**	**OUTFIELD ASSISTS**	**CATCHER CS PCT.**
Williams-Bos.........147	Case-Was...............33	Case-Was.............4.1	Bloodworth-Was..27.2	Case-Was............11.7	S.Chapman-Phi......21	Tresh-Chi............47.9
Cullenbine-StL......121	Kuhel-Chi...............20	Kuhel-Chi..............2.7	Keltner-Cle..........20.3	S.Chapman-Phi...11.7	Case-Was...............21	Dickey-NY............45.8
Clift-StL................113	Heath-Cle...............18	Kreevich-Chi..........2.0	Rizzuto-NY..........19.0	Lewis-Was...........11.4	Heath-Cle...............20	Tebbetts-Det........44.0
Keller-NY.............102	Tabor-Bos...............17	Rizzuto-NY............1.3	Boudreau-Cle......13.4	B.Johnson-Phi.......8.7	B.Johnson-Phi........17	Early-Was............43.8
	Kreevich-Chi...........17	Fox-Bos.................1.3	Gordon-NY............8.6	Moses-Phi.............7.8		Hemsley-Cle........41.3
WINS	**WINNING PCT.**	**WINS ABOVE TEAM**	**GAMES STARTED**	**COMPLETE GAMES**	**FEWEST HITS/GAME**	**FEWEST BB/GAME**
Feller-Cle...............25	Gomez-NY...........750	Feller-Cle...............7.6	Feller-Cle...............40	Lee-Chi..................30	Benton-Det..........7.42	Lyons-Chi............1.78
Lee-Chi..................22	Ruffing-NY...........714	Lee-Chi..................6.4	Newsom-Det..........36	Feller-Cle...............28	Feller-Cle............7.45	Leonard-Was.......1.90
D.Newsome-Bos.....19	Benton-Det..........714	Benton-Det............5.0	Lee-Chi..................34	Smith-Chi...............21	Lee-Chi...............7.73	Muncrief-StL........2.23
Leonard-Was.........18	Lee-Chi.................667	Leonard-Was.........4.2		Lyons-Chi...............19	Donald-NY...........7.98	Ruffing-NY...........2.62
	Feller-Cle.............658	D.Newsome-Bos....4.1		Leonard-Was.........19	Chandler-NY........8.03	Lee-Chi...............2.76
STRIKEOUTS	**STRIKEOUTS/GAME**	**GAMES**	**SAVES**	**BASE RUNNERS/9**	**ADJUSTED RELIEF RUNS**	**RELIEF RANKING**
Feller-Cle.............260	Feller-Cle............6.82	Feller-Cle...............44	Murphy-NY............15	Humphries-Chi...10.55	Murphy-NY.........17.5	Murphy-NY.........30.1
Newsom-Det.........175	Newsom-Det........6.29	Newsom-Det..........43	Ferrick-Phi...............7	Lee-Chi.............10.61	Heving-Cle..........13.2	Heving-Cle..........13.9
Lee-Chi.................130	Newhouser-Det....5.51	Brown-Cle..............41	Benton-Det..............7	Bonham-NY.......10.66	Carrasquel-Was.....6.6	Brown-Cle.............5.2
Rigney-Chi............119	Harris-Bos............5.15	Ryba-Bos................40	Ryba-Bos.................6	Ruffing-NY.........11.25	Brown-Cle.............6.0	Carrasquel-Was.....5.2
	Rigney-Chi...........4.52	Benton-Det.............38		Benton-Det........11.30	Thomas-Det.............3	Thomas-Det.............1
INNINGS PITCHED	**OPPONENTS' AVG.**	**OPPONENTS' OBP**	**EARNED RUN AVERAGE**	**ADJUSTED ERA**	**ADJUSTED STARTER RUNS**	**PITCHER WINS**
Feller-Cle...........343.0	Benton-Det...........221	Lee-Chi.................293	Lee-Chi...............2.37	Lee-Chi.................173	Lee-Chi...............56.1	**Lee-Chi...............6.5**
Lee-Chi.............300.1	Feller-Cle..............226	Benton-Det...........302	Benton-Det..........2.97	Benton-Det...........153	Feller-Cle............34.3	**Feller-Cle...........3.6**
Smith-Chi...........263.1	Lee-Chi..................232	Ruffing-NY...........306	Wagner-Bos.........3.07	Wagner-Bos..........136	Smith-Chi............28.1	**Smith-Chi...........3.4**
Leonard-Was.....256.0	Donald-NY............237	Chandler-NY.........307	Russo-NY............3.09	Smith-Chi.............129	Benton-Det..........24.1	**Murphy-NY.........2.9**
Newsom-Det......250.1	Chandler-NY.........239	Lyons-Chi.............308	Feller-Cle............3.15	Harris-Bos............128	Wagner-Bos.........22.3	**Benton-Det.........2.6**

Joltin' Joe and Teddy Ballgame

The final year of normal baseball before America entered World War II was the stuff of legend, as immortals like Joe DiMaggio and Ted Williams grabbed the headlines and Mickey Owen grabbed the goat's horns. The Yankees returned to the top after a season in third place. Emerging from a five-team scramble in July, New York left everyone in the dust as they took league honors by 17 games.

The old Yankees were gone; in their place were a passel of new stars, including DiMaggio, Phil Rizzuto, Charlie Keller, Joe Gordon, and Tommy Henrich. DiMaggio hit .357 and enthralled the nation with his 56-game hitting streak. Keller batted .298 with 33 homers and 122 RBIs, and Johnny "Grandma" Murphy—one of the first true relief aces—saved 15 games.

Lacking a staff anchor, Joe McCarthy used seven starting pitchers at least 14 times, getting excellent performance from most of them. Both 32-year-old Lefty Gomez and Red Ruffing, 37, won 15. Finishing in second place were the Red Sox, who couldn't turn Williams' season (.406 average, 37 homers, 145 walks, and 135 runs—all of which led the AL) into a pennant because of mediocre pitching.

A few players left for the military during the season, most notably three-time home run champ Hank Greenberg. Fans were also busy in other matters. It was the first of three consecutive seasons of decreasing league attendance; NL attendance actually increased by 8 percent in 1941 before falling the next two years.

The Yankees won the World Series from the Dodgers in five games, four of which were decided by only one run. The one that wasn't (Game 4) featured a ninth-inning, four-run rally that began when Dodgers catcher Owen dropped a third strike that would have ended the game in favor of Brooklyn and tied the Series.

1940 NATIONAL LEAGUE

TEAM	W	L	T	PCT	GB	HW	HL	R	OR	PA	H	2B	3B	HR	BB	SO	HB	SH	AVG	OBP	SLG	OPS	AOPS	BR	ABR	PF	SB	CS	BSA	BSR
Cin	100	53	2	.654	—	**55**	21	707	**528**	5986	1427	264	38	89	453	503	36	**125**	.266	.327	.379	706	100	9	2	101	72			
Bro	88	65	3	.575	12	41	37	697	621	6089	1421	256	**70**	93	522	570	20	77	.260	.327	.383	710	96	15	-26	106	56			
StL	84	69	3	.549	16	41	36	747	699	6087	**1514**	266	61	**119**	479	610	21	88	.275	.336	**.411**	**747**	106	84	42	106	**97**			
Pit	78	76	2	.506	22.5	40	34	**809**	783	6115	1511	**276**	68	76	**553**	494	33	63	**.276**	**.346**	.394	740	**112**	**87**	**93**	99	69			
Chi	75	79	0	.487	25.5	40	37	681	636	5970	1441	272	48	86	482	566	29	70	.267	.331	.384	715	106	28	42	98	63			
NY	72	80	0	.474	27.5	33	43	663	659	5900	1423	201	46	91	453	**478**	**37**	86	.267	.329	.374	703	99	1	-4	101	45			
Bos	65	87	0	.428	34.5	35	40	623	745	5810	1366	219	50	59	402	581	17	62	.256	.311	.349	660	93	-86	-53	95	48			
Phi	50	103	0	.327	50	24	55	494	750	5673	1225	180	35	75	435	527	14	87	.238	.300	.331	631	83	-137	-116	96	25			
Total	617	—	—	—	—	309	303	5421	—	47630	11328	1934	416	688	3779	4329	207	658	.264	.326	.376	702	—	—	—	—	475	—	—	—

TEAM	CG	SHO	GR	SV	IP	H	HR	BB	SO	BR/9	ERA	AERA	OAV	OOB	PR	APR	PF	OSB	OCS	FA	E	WPB	DP	FW	PW	BW	BSW	DIF
Cin	**91**	10	106	11	1407.2	**1263**	73	445	557	**11.0**	**3.05**	**124**	**.240**	**.302**	**125**	**117**	98	51	*29*	**.981**	**117**	22	158	**2.9**	**11.8**	.2	—	8.6
Bro	65	**17**	169	14	1433.0	1366	101	**393**	**639**	11.2	3.50	114	.248	**.302**	56	76	104	52	*35*	.970	183	22	110	-.3	7.7	-2.6	—	6.8
StL	71	10	168	14	1396.0	1457	83	488	550	12.7	3.83	104	.266	.329	3	23	104	63	*51*	.971	174	45	134	.1	2.3	4.2	—	.8
Pit	49	8	**215**	**24**	1388.2	1569	**72**	492	491	13.6	4.36	87	.283	.345	-79	-86	99	80	*55*	.966	217	32	161	-2.0	-8.7	**9.4**	—	2.3
Chi	69	12	151	14	1392.0	1418	74	430	564	12.1	3.54	106	.262	.319	47	33	97	58	*48*	.968	199	**21**	143	-1.2	3.3	4.2	—	-8.4
NY	57	11	166	18	1360.1	1383	110	473	606	12.4	3.79	102	.262	.325	9	14	101	**44**	*49*	.977	139	36	132	1.6	1.4	-.4	—	-6.6
Bos	76	9	148	12	1359.0	1444	83	573	435	13.6	4.36	85	.274	.349	-77	-100	97	58	***61***	.970	184	31	**169**	-.6	-10.1	-5.4	—	5.1
Phi	66	5	133	8	1357.0	1429	92	475	485	12.8	4.40	89	.270	.333	-83	-74	101	69	*43*	.970	181	48	136	-.4	-7.5	-11.7	—	-6.9
Total	544	82	1256	115	11093.2	—	—	—	—	12.4	3.85	—	.264	.326	—	—	—	—	—	.972	1394	257	1143	—	—	—	—	—

BATTER-FIELDER WINS	BATTING AVERAGE	ON-BASE PERCENTAGE	SLUGGING AVERAGE	ON-BASE PLUS SLUGGING	ADJUSTED OPS	ADJUSTED BATTER RUNS
Vaughan-Pit 5.1	Garms-Pit .355	Fletcher-Pit .418	Mize-StL .636	Mize-StL 1039	Mize-StL 173	Mize-StL 56.9
Hack-Chi 4.5	Davis-Pit .326	Ott-NY .407	Nicholson-Chi .534	Camilli-Bro .926	Nicholson-Chi 148	Fletcher-Pit 33.9
Mize-StL 3.6	Lombardi-Cin .319	Mize-StL .404	Camilli-Bro .529	Nicholson-Chi .899	Camilli-Bro 144	Camilli-Bro 33.2
Miller-Bos 3.4	Cooney-Bos .318	Camilli-Bro .397	DiMaggio-Cin-Pit .519	Slaughter-StL .874	Gleeson-Chi 139	Ott-NY 32.2
Danning-NY 3.1	Hack-Chi .317	Hack-Chi .395	Slaughter-StL .504	Ott-NY .864	Fletcher-Pit 137	Nicholson-Chi 30.9

RUNS	HITS	DOUBLES	TRIPLES	HOME RUNS	TOTAL BASES	RUNS BATTED IN
Vaughan-Pit 113	F.McCormick-Cin 191	F.McCormick-Cin 44	Vaughan-Pit 15	Mize-StL 43	Mize-StL 368	Mize-StL 137
Mize-StL 111	Hack-Chi 191	Vaughan-Pit 40	Ross-Bos 14	Nicholson-Chi 25	F.McCormick-Cin 298	F.McCormick-Cin 127
Werber-Cin 105	Mize-StL 182	Gleeson-Chi 39	Slaughter-StL 13	Rizzo-Pit-Cin-Phi 24	Medwick-StL-Bro 280	VanRobays-Pit 116
Frey-Cin 102	Vaughan-Pit 178	Hack-Chi 38	Mize-StL 13	Camilli-Bro 23	Camilli-Bro 271	Fletcher-Pit 104
Hack-Chi 101	Medwick-StL-Bro 175	Walker-Bro 37	Camilli-Bro 13		Vaughan-Pit 269	Young-NY 101

BASES ON BALLS	STOLEN BASES	BASE STEALING RUNS	FIELDING RUNS-INFIELD	FIELDING RUNS-OUTFIELD	OUTFIELD ASSISTS	CATCHER CS PCT.
Fletcher-Pit 119	Frey-Cin 22		Herman-Chi 20.3	Moore-StL 13.0	West-Bos 16	Berres-Pit-Bos 50.0
Ott-NY 100	Hack-Chi 21		Witek-NY 16.2	Moore-Bro-Bos 5.4	Gleeson-Chi 14	Danning-NY 49.3
Camilli-Bro 89	Moore-StL 18		May-Phi 15.8	Ross-Bos 5.4	DiMaggio-Cin-Pit 13	Owen-StL 45.3
Vaughan-Pit 88	Werber-Cin 16		Frey-Cin 15.0	West-Bos 4.8		Davis-Pit 45.1
Mize-StL 82	Reese-Bro 15		Miller-Bos 14.8	Slaughter-StL 4.5		Lopez-Bos-Pit 44.3

WINS	WINNING PCT.	WINS ABOVE TEAM	GAMES STARTED	COMPLETE GAMES	FEWEST HITS/GAME	FEWEST BB/GAME
Walters-Cin 22	Fitzsimmons-Bro .889	Fitzsimmons-Bro 6.9	Derringer-Cin 37	Walters-Cin 29	Walters-Cin 7.11	Derringer-Cin 1.46
Passeau-Chi 20	Sewell-Pit .762	Sewell-Pit 5.8	Walters-Cin 36	Derringer-Cin 26	Higbe-Phi 7.70	Turner-Cin 1.54
Derringer-Cin 20	Walters-Cin .688	Passeau-Chi 4.6	Mulcahy-Phi 36	Mulcahy-Phi 21	Thompson-Cin 7.87	Hamlin-Bro 1.68
	Thompson-Cin .640	Beggs-Cin 3.4	Higbe-Phi 36	Passeau-Chi 20	Casey-Bro 7.95	Davis-StL-Bro 1.79
	Derringer-Cin .625	Higbe-Phi 2.9	Wyatt-Bro 34	Higbe-Phi 20	Sullivan-Bos 7.97	Warneke-StL 1.82

STRIKEOUTS	STRIKEOUTS/GAME	GAMES	SAVES	BASE RUNNERS/9	ADJUSTED RELIEF RUNS	RELIEF RANKING
Higbe-Phi 137	Melton-NY 4.91	Shoun-StL 54	Brown-NY 7	Fitzsimmons-Bro 9.78	Beggs-Cin 15.4	Beggs-Cin 30.3
Wyatt-Bro 124	Schumacher-NY 4.88	Brown-Pit 48	Brown-Pit 7	Derringer-Cin 9.95	Russell-StL 6.8	Russell-StL 8.2
Passeau-Chi 124	Wyatt-Bro 4.66	Passeau-Chi 46	Beggs-Cin 7	Walters-Cin 9.97	Raffensberger-Chi 3.1	Raffensberger-Chi 4.0
Schumacher-NY 123	Hamlin-Bro 4.49	Casey-Bro 44	Shoun-StL 5	Pressnell-Bro 10.14	Hutchings-Cin 2.8	Pressnell-Bro 3.6
	Higbe-Phi 4.36	Raffensberger-Chi 43	Passeau-Chi 5	Passeau-Chi 10.33	Brown-NY 2.5	Brown-NY 3.1

INNINGS PITCHED	OPPONENTS' AVG.	OPPONENTS' OBP	EARNED RUN AVERAGE	ADJUSTED ERA	ADJUSTED STARTER RUNS	PITCHER WINS
Walters-Cin 305.0	Walters-Cin .220	Derringer-Cin .276	Walters-Cin 2.48	Walters-Cin 153	Walters-Cin 44.1	**Passeau-Chi 5.1**
Derringer-Cin 296.2	Higbe-Phi .232	Passeau-Chi .278	Passeau-Chi 2.50	Passeau-Chi 150	Passeau-Chi 37.1	**Walters-Cin 4.7**
Higbe-Phi 283.0	Thompson-Cin .233	Walters-Cin .283	Sewell-Pit 2.80	Sewell-Pit 136	Derringer-Cin 25.0	**Beggs-Cin 3.2**
Passeau-Chi 280.2	Passeau-Chi .237	Tamulis-Bro .288	Fitzsimmons-Bro 2.81	Turner-Cin 131	Sewell-Pit 20.5	**Olsen-Chi 2.5**
Mulcahy-Phi 280.0	Casey-Bro .237	Hamlin-Bro .292	Turner-Cin 2.89	Hamlin-Bro 131	Fitzsimmons-Bro 18.7	**Sewell-Pit 2.5**

Reds Take It All

The dominant NL teams of the 1940s were St. Louis and Brooklyn. Listing the top debut players for the teams in 1940 tells why: The Cardinals brought up shortstop Marty Marion and pitchers Harry Brecheen and Walker Cooper, while the Dodgers summoned shortstop Pee Wee Reese and outfielder Pete Reiser.

While AL attendance rose, the NL's fell nearly 7 percent. To increase ticket sales, the Giants, Cardinals, and Pirates added lights to their parks, while the Braves changed their park's dimensions, moving in the foul lines and the center-field fences.

The Reds and Dodgers were the early leaders in the '40 race. In mid-July, once the surprising Giants fell from the race, Brooklyn began to slump. The Reds, meanwhile, took 19 of 21 to surge ahead. Brooklyn continued to stumble, and Cincinnati kept winning. The pitching-and-defense Reds set a new NL record with a .981 fielding percentage. Bucky Walters led the NL in wins, ERA, and innings, and was ably supported by Paul Derringer. Frank McCormick sparked a mediocre attack by topping the loop in hits and doubles.

There was one casualty. On August 2, following a tough loss, backup catcher Willard Hershberger took his life. By World Series time, everyday receiver Ernie Lombardi was too banged-up to play. Therefore, with Hershberger out of the picture, 40-year-old coach Jimmie Wilson was forced into action for six of the seven games. He hit .353.

The Tigers won their three games by an aggregate of 22-6, and led 1-0, 2-1, and 3-2 in games, but the Reds won the last two contests at home, clinching their first world championship since 1919. Derringer and Walters won all four games for Cincinnati. Detroit's Bobo Newsom won Game 5 three days after his father died, then fell 2-1 in a tension-filled finale.

1940 AMERICAN LEAGUE

TEAM	W	L	T	PCT	GB	HW	HL	R	OR	PA	H	2B	3B	HR	BB	SO	HB	SH	AVG	OBP	SLG	OPS	AOPS	BR	ABR	PF	SB	CS	BSA	BSR
Det	90	64	1	.584	—	50	29	**888**	717	6183	1549	**312**	65	134	**664**	556	24	77	**.286**	**.366**	.442	**808**	105	**130**	50	110	66	39	63	1
Cle	89	65	1	.578	1	51	30	710	**637**	5957	1422	287	61	101	519	597	16	61	.265	.332	.398	730	98	-43	-22	97	53	36	60	-1
NY	88	66	1	.571	2	**52**	24	817	671	6046	1371	243	66	**155**	648	606	**36**	76	.259	.344	.418	762	107	25	58	96	59	36	62	0
Chi	82	72	1	.532	8	41	36	735	672	6002	1499	238	63	73	496	569	10	**110**	.278	.340	.387	727	93	-45	-54	101	52	60	46	-10
Bos	82	72	0	.532	8	45	34	872	825	6174	**1566**	301	**80**	145	590	597	12	91	**.286**	.356	**.449**	805	**110**	110	**76**	104	55	49	53	-5
StL	67	87	2	.435	23	37	39	757	882	6051	1423	278	58	118	556	642	16	63	.263	.333	.401	734	94	-35	-50	102	51	40	56	-3
Was	64	90	0	.416	26	36	41	665	811	5912	1453	266	67	52	468	**504**	18	61	.271	.331	.374	705	95	-87	-41	94	**94**	40	**70**	**7**
Phi	54	100	0	.351	36	29	42	703	932	5948	1391	242	53	105	556	656	19	69	.262	.334	.387	721	95	-55	-40	98	48	33	59	-1
Total	619	—	—	—	—	341	275	6147	—	48273	11674	2167	513	883	4497	4727	151	608	.271	.342	.407	750	—	—	—	—	478	333	59	-11

TEAM	CG	SHO	GR	SV	IP	H	HR	BB	SO	BR/9	ERA	AERA	OAV	OOB	PR	APR	PF	OSB	OCS	FA	E	WPB	DP	FW	PW	BW	BSW	DIF
Det	59	10	171	**23**	1375.1	1425	102	570	**752**	13.2	4.01	**119**	.266	.338	57	**105**	109	54	**56**	.968	194	33	116	-.7	**9.9**	4.7	.2	-1.2
Cle	72	**13**	151	22	1375.0	**1328**	**86**	512	686	12.2	**3.63**	116	.254	.324	**115**	93	96	**42**	47	**.975**	**149**	33	164	**1.7**	8.8	-2.1	.0	3.5
NY	76	10	125	14	1373.0	1389	119	511	559	12.6	3.89	104	.261	.328	76	24	92	43	43	**.975**	152	**28**	158	1.6	2.3	5.5	.1	1.6
Chi	**83**	10	91	18	1386.2	1335	111	**480**	574	**11.9**	3.74	118	**.250**	**.313**	99	**105**	101	55	32	.969	185	46	125	-.2	**9.9**	-5.1	-.8	1.2
Bos	51	4	178	16	1379.2	1568	124	625	613	14.5	4.89	92	.284	.359	-77	-58	103	64	32	.972	173	48	156	.4	-5.5	**7.2**	-.3	3.2
StL	64	4	**180**	9	1373.1	1592	113	646	439	14.8	5.12	89	.290	.367	-113	-79	105	63	33	.974	158	60	**179**	1.3	-7.5	-4.7	-.1	1.0
Was	74	6	122	7	1350.0	1494	93	618	618	14.2	4.59	91	.281	.359	-31	-67	95	65	54	.968	194	70	166	-.7	-6.3	-3.9	**.8**	-2.9
Phi	72	4	117	12	1345.0	1543	135	534	488	14.0	5.22	85	.283	.348	-125	-114	101	92	36	.960	238	55	131	-3.1	-10.8	-3.8	.0	-5.4
Total	551	61	1135	121	10958.0	—	—	—	—	13.4	4.38	—	.271	.342	—	—	—	—	—	.970	1443	373	1195	—	—	—	—	—

BATTER-FIELDER WINS	BATTING AVERAGE	ON-BASE PERCENTAGE	SLUGGING AVERAGE	ON-BASE PLUS SLUGGING	ADJUSTED OPS	ADJUSTED BATTER RUNS
DiMaggio-NY......4.5	DiMaggio-NY........352	Williams-Bos.........442	Greenberg-Det......670	Greenberg-Det....1103	DiMaggio-NY........176	Greenberg-Det.....57.4
Greenberg-Det...4.5	Appling-Chi...........348	Greenberg-Det......433	DiMaggio-NY........626	DiMaggio-NY......1051	Greenberg-Det......166	DiMaggio-NY.......56.3
Williams-Bos......4.0	Williams-Bos.........344	Gehringer-Det.......428	Williams-Bos.........594	Williams-Bos.......1036	Williams-Bos.........159	Williams-Bos........53.1
Gordon-NY.........3.8	Radcliff-StL...........342	DiMaggio-NY........425	York-Det...............583	York-Det...............993	Foxx-Bos..............148	Foxx-Bos..............39.2
Boudreau-Cle.....3.5	Greenberg-Det......340	Appling-Chi...........420	Foxx-Bos..............581	Foxx-Bos..............993	Keller-NY.............142	York-Det..............37.3
RUNS	**HITS**	**DOUBLES**	**TRIPLES**	**HOME RUNS**	**TOTAL BASES**	**RUNS BATTED IN**
Williams-Bos.........134	Radcliff-StL...........200	Greenberg-Det.......50	McCosky-Det..........19	Greenberg-Det........41	Greenberg-Det......384	Greenberg-Det......150
Greenberg-Det......129	McCosky-Det........200	York-Det.................46	Keller-NY................15	Foxx-Bos................36	York-Det...............343	York-Det...............134
McCosky-Det........123	Cramer-Bos..........200	Boudreau-Cle.........46	Finney-Bos.............15	York-Det.................33	Williams-Bos.........333	DiMaggio-NY........133
Gordon-NY...........112	Appling-Chi...........197	Williams-Bos..........43	Williams-Bos...........14	Johnson-Phi...........31	DiMaggio-NY........318	Foxx-Bos..............119
Kuhel-Chi..............111	Wright-Chi.............196	Moses-Phi...............41	Appling-Chi.............13	DiMaggio-NY...........31	Gordon-NY...........315	Williams-Bos.........113
BASES ON BALLS	**STOLEN BASES**	**BASE STEALING RUNS**	**FIELDING RUNS-INFIELD**	**FIELDING RUNS-OUTFIELD**	**OUTFIELD ASSISTS**	**CATCHER CS PCT.**
Keller-NY.............106	Case-Was...............35	Case-Was.............4.2	Heffner-StL..........15.7	Kreevich-Chi..........6.9	DiMaggio-Bos.........16	Tebbetts-Det........54.5
Clift-StL.................104	Walker-Was............21	Walker-Was...........3.2	Gordon-NY..........13.8	Solters-Chi.............6.2	Johnson-Phi............15	Hemsley-Cle........51.6
Gehringer-Det.......101	Gordon-NY.............18	Gehringer-Det.......2.2	Bloodworth-Was..13.7	Johnson-Phi............5.6	Greenberg-Det.........14	Dickey-NY............50.9
Foxx-Bos...............101	Lewis-Was..............15	Bartell-Det............1.9	Doerr-Bos............13.4	DiMaggio-Bos........5.6	Williams-Bos...........13	Ferrell-Was.........44.4
Williams-Bos..........96	Kreevich-Chi...........15	Rosar-NY...............1.2	Bartell-Det...........13.4	Moses-Phi.............4.7	S.Chapman-Phi......13	Tresh-Chi............36.5
WINS	**WINNING PCT.**	**WINS ABOVE TEAM**	**GAMES STARTED**	**COMPLETE GAMES**	**FEWEST HITS/GAME**	**FEWEST BB/GAME**
Feller-Cle................27	Rowe-Det.............842	Newsom-Det..........7.6	Feller-Cle...............37	Feller-Cle...............31	Feller-Cle............6.88	Lyons-Chi............1.79
Newsom-Det...........21	Newsom-Det.........808	Feller-Cle..............7.2	Leonard-Was.........35	Lee-Chi...................24	Rigney-Chi............7.70	Lee-Chi................2.21
Milnar-Cle...............18	Feller-Cle.............711	Rowe-Det..............6.2	Auker-StL...............35	Leonard-Was..........23	Smith-Chi.............7.77	Rowe-Det............2.29
Hudson-Was...........17	Smith-Cle.............682	Auker-StL..............4.3	Newsom-Det..........34		Bridges-Det..........7.79	Leonard-Was.......2.43
	Milnar-Cle............643	Babich-Phi.............4.0	Chase-Was............34		Newsom-Det.........8.01	Russo-NY............2.61
STRIKEOUTS	**STRIKEOUTS/GAME**	**GAMES**	**SAVES**	**BASE RUNNERS/9**	**ADJUSTED RELIEF RUNS**	**RELIEF RANKING**
Feller-Cle..............261	Feller-Cle............7.33	Feller-Cle...............43	Benton-Det.............17	Bonham-NY.........8.70	Eisenstat-Cle.......10.6	Brown-Chi...........10.3
Newsom-Det.........164	Bridges-Det..........6.06	Benton-Det............42	Brown-Chi...............10	Feller-Cle..........10.34	Brown-Chi.............6.0	Eisenstat-Cle.........8.0
Rigney-Chi.........141	Wilson-Bos..........5.82	Wilson-Bos.............41	Murphy-NY...............9	Murphy-NY........10.37	Trotter-StL.............4.4	Murphy-NY............7.5
Bridges-Det...........133	Newsom-Det........5.59	Heusser-Phi...........41		Rigney-Chi..........10.65	Murphy-NY............3.7	Benton-Det............6.7
Chase-Was...........129	Smith-Chi.............5.17	Dobson-Cle............40		Lyons-Chi...........10.87	Benton-Det............3.3	Trotter-StL..............5.5
INNINGS PITCHED	**OPPONENTS' AVG.**	**OPPONENTS' OBP**	**EARNED RUN AVERAGE**	**ADJUSTED ERA**	**ADJUSTED STARTER RUNS**	**PITCHER WINS**
Feller-Cle...........320.1	Feller-Cle.............210	Feller-Cle.............285	Feller-Cle............2.61	Newsom-Det.........168	Feller-Cle............61.5	**Feller-Cle...........6.8**
Leonard-Was.....289.0	Smith-Chi.............228	Lyons-Chi.............287	Newsom-Det.........2.83	Feller-Cle.............161	Newsom-Det........47.0	**Rigney-Chi...........4.1**
Rigney-Chi.........280.2	Bridges-Det..........229	Rigney-Chi............292	Rigney-Chi...........3.11	Rigney-Chi............142	Rigney-Chi...........38.9	**Newsom-Det......3.9**
Newsom-Det......264.0	Rigney-Chi............230	Lee-Chi.................300	Smith-Chi.............3.21	Bridges-Det..........141	Bridges-Det.........27.1	**Rowe-Det............3.1**
Auker-StL..........263.2	Newsom-Det.........238	Russo-NY.............303	Chase-Was..........3.23	Smith-Chi.............138	Rowe-Det.............25.6	**Bonham-NY........2.8**

Tigers Fill Their Tank

The AL race of 1940 was made possible by a poor start from the usually dominant Yankees. Detroit and Cleveland made hay while New York struggled, and the Indians led into September. The Tribe—a league laughingstock due to a much-publicized player rebellion against autocratic manager Ossie Vitt—dropped five straight (three to the Tigers) while the Yankees won 19 of 23 to create a three-way tie on September 9. New York dropped out, but the Tigers and Indians clustered until Detroit took three of four from Cleveland in late September. In the clincher, unknown Floyd Giebell shut out Bob Feller and the Indians for his third (and last) major league victory.

Hank Greenberg led the AL in doubles, homers, and RBIs for overpowering Detroit, while 21-year-old Feller took the pitching Triple Crown. New York had deep pitching and power, but several regulars slumped. Fourth-place Boston made rookie Dom, the youngest DiMaggio, their center fielder.

Each AL team had an attendance bump, sending league sales to their highest total to date. The Tigers, the only AL team to top the million mark in the 1930s, became the only AL team to do so in the new decade until 1945, when they did it again. While homers rose to 883, a new league high that would last until 1950, runs per team fell to 4.97 per game—the top rate in what would be a pitching-friendly decade.

White Sox second baseman Jackie Hayes began to lose his sight, and was forced to retire midseason at age 33. Another veteran infielder, Billy Rogell, 35, finished his fourteen-season career but would live another 63 years.

The World Series was one of the best in years. The teams traded wins until the Reds pulled out Game 7. Detroit's Bobo Newsom, whose father died midway through the Series, was 2-1 with a 1.38 ERA.

1939 NATIONAL LEAGUE

TEAM	W	L	T	PCT	GB	HW	HL	R	OR	PA	H	2B	3B	HR	BB	SO	HB	SH	AVG	OBP	SLG	OPS	AOPS	BR	ABR	PF	SB	CS	BSA	BSR
Cin	97	57	2	.630	—	**55**	25	767	**595**	6106	1493	269	60	98	500	538	**35**	**193**	.278	.343	.405	748	106	52	48	101	46			
StL	92	61	2	.601	4.5	51	27	**779**	633	6116	**1601**	**332**	**62**	98	475	566	27	167	**.294**	**.354**	**.432**	**786**	**110**	**127**	**79**	106	44			
Bro	84	69	4	.549	12.5	51	27	708	645	6047	1420	265	57	78	**564**	639	26	107	.265	.338	.380	718	96	2	-22	104	59			
Chi	84	70	2	.545	13	44	34	724	678	5990	1407	263	**62**	91	523	553	34	140	.266	.336	.391	727	99	11	-1	102	**61**			
NY	77	74	0	.510	18.5	41	33	703	685	5767	1395	211	38	**116**	498	499	32	108	.272	.340	.396	736	103	27	22	101	26			
Pit	68	85	0	.444	28.5	35	42	666	721	5923	1453	261	60	63	477	**420**	21	156	.276	.338	.384	722	102	4	15	98	44			
Bos	63	88	1	.417	32.5	37	35	572	659	5795	1395	199	39	56	366	494	21	122	.264	.314	.348	662	91	-122	-80	93	41			
Phi	45	106	1	.298	50.5	29	44	553	856	5707	1341	232	40	49	421	486	9	144	.261	.318	.351	669	89	-100	-83	97	47			
Total	616	—	—	—	—	343	267	5472	—	47451	11505	2032	418	649	3824	4195	205	1137	.272	.335	.386	721	—	—	—	—	368	—	—	—

TEAM	CG	SHO	GR	SV	IP	H	HR	BB	SO	BR/9	ERA	AERA	OAV	OOB	PR	APR	PF	OSB	OCS	FA	E	WPB	DP	FW	PW	BW	BSW	DIF
Cin	**86**	13	143	9	1403.2	**1340**	81	499	**637**	12.0	**3.27**	**117**	**.255**	.322	**101**	**89**	98	42	*43*	.974	162	45	170	.6	**8.9**	4.8	—	5.7
StL	45	**18**	**210**	**32**	1384.2	1377	76	498	603	12.3	3.59	115	.260	.326	50	76	105	39	*31*	.971	177	43	140	-.2	7.6	**7.9**	—	.2
Bro	69	9	138	13	1410.1	1431	93	**399**	528	**11.9**	3.64	110	.263	**.317**	43	58	103	42	*39*	.972	176	30	157	-.0	5.8	-2.2	—	3.9
Chi	72	8	136	13	1392.1	1504	74	430	584	12.6	3.80	104	.276	.331	18	20	101	34	***44***	.970	186	33	126	-.6	2.0	-.1	—	5.7
NY	55	6	163	20	1319.0	1412	86	477	505	13.1	4.07	96	.275	.340	-22	-20	100	57	*36*	**.975**	**153**	40	151	**.8**	-2.0	2.2	—	.5
Pit	53	10	157	15	1354.0	1537	70	423	464	13.2	4.15	92	.287	.342	-36	-51	98	41	*35*	.972	168	**26**	153	.1	-5.1	1.5	—	-5.0
Bos	68	11	144	15	1358.1	1400	**63**	513	430	12.8	3.71	100	.271	.339	31	-3	94	**32**	*41*	.971	181	30	**178**	-.6	-.3	-8.0	—	-3.6
Phi	67	3	133	12	1326.2	1502	106	579	447	14.4	5.17	77	.289	.365	-185	-167	102	81	*38*	.970	171	47	136	-.0	-16.7	-8.3	—	-5.4
Total	515	78	1224	129	10949.0	—	—	—	—	12.8	3.92	—	.272	.335	—	—	—	—	—	.972	1374	294	1211	—	—	—	—	—

BATTER-FIELDER WINS	BATTING AVERAGE	ON-BASE PERCENTAGE	SLUGGING AVERAGE	ON-BASE PLUS SLUGGING	ADJUSTED OPS	ADJUSTED BATTER RUNS
Mize-StL 4.3	Mize-StL .349	Ott-NY .449	Mize-StL .626	Mize-StL 1070	Mize-StL 174	Mize-StL 61.8
Frey-Cin 4.0	McCormick-Cin .332	Mize-StL .444	Ott-NY .581	Ott-NY 1030	Ott-NY 173	Ott-NY 46.8
Vaughan-Pit 4.0	Medwick-StL .332	Camilli-Bro .409	Leiber-Chi .556	Camilli-Bro 933	Camilli-Bro 144	Camilli-Bro 38.5
Ott-NY 3.4	P.Waner-Pit .328	Goodman-Cin .401	Camilli-Bro .524	Goodman-Cin 916	Goodman-Cin 144	Goodman-Cin 29.9
Camilli-Bro 3.2	Arnovich-Phi .324	Arnovich-Phi .397	Goodman-Cin .515	Medwick-StL 886	West-Bos 139	Leiber-Chi 29.8

RUNS	HITS	DOUBLES	TRIPLES	HOME RUNS	TOTAL BASES	RUNS BATTED IN
Werber-Cin 115	McCormick-Cin 209	Slaughter-StL 52	Herman-Chi 18	Mize-StL 28	Mize-StL 353	McCormick-Cin 128
Hack-Chi 112	Medwick-StL 201	Medwick-StL 48	Goodman-Cin 16	Ott-NY 27	McCormick-Cin 312	Medwick-StL 117
Herman-Chi 111	Mize-StL 197	Mize-StL 44	Mize-StL 14	Camilli-Bro 26	Medwick-StL 307	Mize-StL 108
Camilli-Bro 105	Slaughter-StL 193	McCormick-Cin 41	Camilli-Bro 12	Leiber-Chi 24	Camilli-Bro 296	Camilli-Bro 104
	Brown-StL 192			Lombardi-Cin 20	Slaughter-StL 291	Leiber-Chi 88

BASES ON BALLS	STOLEN BASES	BASE STEALING RUNS	FIELDING RUNS-INFIELD	FIELDING RUNS-OUTFIELD	OUTFIELD ASSISTS	CATCHER CS PCT.
Camilli-Bro 110	Handley-Pit 17		Jurges-NY 19.5	Arnovich-Phi 14.3	Slaughter-StL 18	Lopez-Bos 57.1
Ott-NY 100	Hack-Chi 17		Frey-Cin 14.1	Slaughter-StL 13.2	Moore-StL 16	Hartnett-Chi 55.3
Mize-StL 92	Werber-Cin 15		Vaughan-Pit 11.3	Moore-StL 7.6	Goodman-Cin 16	Lombardi-Cin 51.6
Werber-Cin 91	Lavagetto-Bro 14		Hassett-Bos 10.6	Goodman-Cin 6.6		Mueller-Pit 48.1
Lavagetto-Bro 78	Hassett-Bos 13		May-Phi 9.9	Medwick-StL 4.8		Owen-StL 47.8

WINS	WINNING PCT.	WINS ABOVE TEAM	GAMES STARTED	COMPLETE GAMES	FEWEST HITS/GAME	FEWEST BB/GAME
Walters-Cin 27	Derringer-Cin .781	Derringer-Cin 7.5	Walters-Cin 36	Walters-Cin 31	Walters-Cin 7.05	Derringer-Cin 1.05
Derringer-Cin 25	Walters-Cin .711	Walters-Cin 5.1	Lee-Chi 36	Derringer-Cin 28	Bowman-StL 7.49	Hubbell-NY 1.40
Davis-StL 22	French-Chi .652	Gumbert-NY 3.8	Hamlin-Bro 36	Lee-Chi 20	Moore-Cin 8.49	Davis-StL 1.74
Hamlin-Bro 20	Gumbert-NY .621	Posedel-Bos 3.3	Passeau-Phi-Chi 35	Hamlin-Bro 19	Hamlin-Bro 8.51	Hamlin-Bro 1.80
Lee-Chi 19	Hamlin-Bro .606	French-Chi 3.0	Derringer-Cin 35	Posedel-Bos 18	Hubbell-NY 8.77	Root-Chi 1.83

STRIKEOUTS	STRIKEOUTS/GAME	GAMES	SAVES	BASE RUNNERS/9	ADJUSTED RELIEF RUNS	RELIEF RANKING
Passeau-Phi-Chi 137	Cooper-StL 5.55	Shoun-StL 53	Shoun-StL 9	Hubbell-NY 10.29	Shoun-StL 3.2	J.Russell-Chi 2.2
Walters-Cin 137	Tamulis-Bro 4.71	Sewell-Pit 52	Bowman-StL 9	Walters-Cin 10.30	J.Russell-Chi 2.1	Shoun-StL 1.7
Cooper-StL 130	French-Chi 4.55	Bowman-StL 51	Davis-StL 7	Hamlin-Bro 10.31		
Derringer-Cin 128	Passeau-Phi-Chi 4.49	Davis-StL 49	Brown-NY 7	Johnson-Phi 10.38		
Lee-Chi 105	Bowman-StL 4.15	Brown-Pit 47	Brown-Pit 7	Wyatt-Bro 10.65		

INNINGS PITCHED	OPPONENTS' AVG.	OPPONENTS' OBP	EARNED RUN AVERAGE	ADJUSTED ERA	ADJUSTED STARTER RUNS	PITCHER WINS
Walters-Cin 319.0	Walters-Cin .220	Hubbell-NY .280	Walters-Cin 2.29	Walters-Cin 168	Walters-Cin 54.4	**Walters-Cin 8.2**
Derringer-Cin 301.0	Bowman-StL .232	Hamlin-Bro .285	Bowman-StL 2.60	Bowman-StL 158	Derringer-Cin 30.5	**Derringer-Cin 2.9**
Lee-Chi 282.1	Hamlin-Bro .248	Walters-Cin .291	Hubbell-NY 2.75	Hubbell-NY 143	Bowman-StL 27.9	**Davis-StL 2.8**
Passeau-Phi-Chi 274.1	Hubbell-NY .249	Derringer-Cin .295	Casey-Bro 2.93	Casey-Bro 137	Casey-Bro 25.0	**Bowman-StL 2.7**
Hamlin-Bro 269.2	Moore-Cin .254	Bowman-StL .302	Derringer-Cin 2.93	Derringer-Cin 131	Thompson-Cin 21.9	**Casey-Bro 2.7**

QUEEN CITY RENAISSANCE

Just 3½ games separated the eight teams in mid-May. From this point, however, the Cincinnati Reds asserted their dominance under second-year manager Bill McKechnie by winning 12 straight to leap to the top of the league. The Reds continued to lead the league, but slowed down, playing just .500 ball in August while the St. Louis Cardinals caught fire, taking 19 of 21 games. Responding to the challenge, Cincinnati recovered in September and clinched the pennant.

For the Reds, who captured their first flag since 1919, Bucky Walters (the league's MVP) and Paul Derringer combined for 52 victories; their progress made up for Johnny Vander Meer's slump. Bill Werber, purchased from the Athletics, proved an outstanding leadoff man, while first baseman Frank McCormick developed into a star. Cincinnati also enjoyed good defense. The pitching was efficient, and whenever runners got on, infielders Lonny Frey, Billy Myers, and Werber erased them; the Reds' 170 double plays were the third-highest total ever for an NL pennant winner.

Second-place St. Louis, playing in small Sportsman's Park, again had good offensive numbers. Their real strength, however, was the pitching of Curt Davis, Lon Warneke, and Mort Cooper. Slugger Johnny Mize didn't hurt; he won the first of his four home run crowns and his lone batting title in 1939.

Leo Durocher was hired to get the Brooklyn Dodgers out of the doldrums; this he did, moving the club from seventh to third and goosing the gate by 44 percent. Ebbets Field was also the site, on August 26, of the first-ever baseball telecast. The Dodgers had a decent enough offense, but a patchwork pitching staff provided the strength.

The Hall of Fame was dedicated in Cooperstown, New York. The opening lineup of inductees (alive and dead) elected since 1936 included National Leaguers Honus Wagner, Christy Mathewson, Grover Cleveland Alexander, Cy Young, John McGraw, Wee Willie Keeler, Buck Ewing, Al Spalding, Charley Radbourn, and Cap Anson. The World Series downstate was ho hum. The Yankees swept the Reds, who scored but 8 runs and only led for four innings of the entire series.

1939 AMERICAN LEAGUE

TEAM	W	L	T	PCT	GB	HW	HL	R	OR	PA	H	2B	3B	HR	BB	SO	HB	SH	AVG	OBP	SLG	OPS	AOPS	BR	ABR	PF	SB	CS	BSA	BSR
NY	106	45	1	.702	—	**52**	25	**967**	**556**	6129	1521	259	55	**166**	**701**	543	**36**	92	.287	**.374**	**.451**	**825**	**119**	**137**	**152**	98	72	37	66	3
Bos	89	62	1	.589	17	42	32	890	795	6054	**1543**	287	57	124	591	505	15	140	**.291**	.363	.436	799	106	81	49	104	42	44	49	-6
Cle	87	67	0	.565	20.5	44	33	797	700	6007	1490	**291**	**79**	85	557	574	14	120	.280	.350	.413	763	105	4	33	97	72	46	61	0
Chi	85	69	1	.552	22.5	50	27	755	737	6033	1451	220	56	64	579	502	21	**154**	.275	.349	.374	723	89	-64	-83	103	**113**	61	65	4
Det	81	73	1	.526	26.5	42	35	849	762	6108	1487	277	67	124	620	592	16	146	.279	.356	.426	782	99	45	-14	108	88	38	**70**	**6**
Was	65	87	1	.428	41.5	37	39	702	797	6026	1483	249	**79**	44	547	**460**	11	134	.278	.346	.379	725	98	-65	-7	93	94	47	67	4
Phi	55	97	1	.362	51.5	28	48	711	1022	5965	1438	282	55	98	503	532	15	138	.271	.336	.400	736	96	-55	-39	98	60	34	64	1
StL	43	111	2	.279	64.5	18	59	733	1035	6133	1453	242	50	91	559	606	20	132	.268	.339	.381	720	88	-81	-96	102	48	38	56	-3
Total	615	—	—	—	—	313	298	6404	—	48455	11866	2107	498	796	4657	4314	148	1056	.279	.352	.407	759	—	—	—	—	589	345	63	9

TEAM	CG	SHO	GR	SV	IP	H	HR	BB	SO	BR/9	ERA	AERA	OAV	OOB	PR	APR	PF	OSB	OCS	FA	E	WPB	DP	FW	PW	BW	BSW	DIF
NY	**87**	**15**	93	**26**	1348.2	**1208**	85	567	565	**11.9**	**3.31**	**132**	**.241**	**.319**	**196**	**166**	94	49	32	**.978**	**126**	**29**	159	**2.9**	**15.3**	**14.0**	.2	-1.9
Bos	52	4	**187**	20	1350.2	1533	77	543	539	14.0	4.56	104	.287	.355	9	25	102	85	43	.970	180	31	147	.0	2.3	4.5	-.7	7.2
Cle	69	10	142	13	1364.2	1394	**75**	602	614	13.3	4.08	108	.267	.344	81	51	95	67	43	.970	180	37	148	.2	4.7	3.0	-.1	2.1
Chi	62	5	125	21	1377.0	1470	99	**454**	535	12.7	4.31	110	.275	.333	48	63	102	73	41	.972	167	35	140	1.0	5.8	-7.6	.3	8.6
Det	64	8	150	16	1367.1	1430	104	574	**633**	13.3	4.29	114	.268	.341	50	86	106	65	53	.967	198	47	147	-.6	7.9	-1.3	**.5**	-2.4
Was	72	4	122	10	1354.2	1420	**75**	602	521	13.6	4.60	94	.271	.348	2	-41	94	**47**	34	.966	205	70	**167**	-1.1	-3.8	-.6	.3	-5.7
Phi	50	6	155	12	1342.2	1687	148	579	397	15.3	5.79	81	.307	.375	-175	-159	102	103	43	.964	210	49	131	-1.4	-14.7	-3.6	.0	-1.4
StL	56	3	181	3	1371.1	1724	133	739	516	16.4	6.01	81	.310	.393	-212	-166	105	100	**56**	.968	199	49	144	-.6	-15.3	-8.8	-.4	-8.8
Total	512	55	1155	121	10877.0	—	—	—	—	13.8	4.62	—	.279	.352	—	—	—	—	—	.969	1465	347	1183	—	—	—	—	—

BATTER-FIELDER WINS	BATTING AVERAGE	ON-BASE PERCENTAGE	SLUGGING AVERAGE	ON-BASE PLUS SLUGGING	ADJUSTED OPS	ADJUSTED BATTER RUNS
DiMaggio-NY 5.5	DiMaggio-NY .381	Foxx-Bos .464	Foxx-Bos .694	Foxx-Bos 1158	DiMaggio-NY 185	Foxx-Bos 62.0
Foxx-Bos 5.2	Foxx-Bos .360	Selkirk-NY .452	DiMaggio-NY .671	DiMaggio-NY 1119	Foxx-Bos 185	DiMaggio-NY 59.0
Johnson-Phi 4.8	Johnson-Phi .338	DiMaggio-NY .448	Greenberg-Det .622	Williams-Bos 1045	Williams-Bos 158	Williams-Bos 52.7
Dickey-NY 4.5	Trosky-Cle .335	Keller-NY .447	Williams-Bos .609	Greenberg-Det 1042	Trosky-Cle 157	Johnson-Phi 49.4
Williams-Bos 4.1	Rolfe-NY .329	Johnson-Phi .440	Trosky-Cle .589	Trosky-Cle 994	Johnson-Phi 156	Greenberg-Det 40.1

RUNS	HITS	DOUBLES	TRIPLES	HOME RUNS	TOTAL BASES	RUNS BATTED IN
Rolfe-NY 139	Rolfe-NY 213	Rolfe-NY 46	Lewis-Was 16	Foxx-Bos 35	Williams-Bos 344	Williams-Bos 145
Williams-Bos 131	McQuinn-StL 195	Williams-Bos 44	McCosky-Det 14	Greenberg-Det 33	Foxx-Bos 324	DiMaggio-NY 126
Foxx-Bos 130	Keltner-Cle 191	Greenberg-Det 42	McQuinn-StL 13	Williams-Bos 31	Rolfe-NY 321	Johnson-Phi 114
McCosky-Det 120	McCosky-Det 190	McQuinn-StL 37	Campbell-Cle 13	DiMaggio-NY 30	McQuinn-StL 318	Greenberg-Det 112
Johnson-Phi 115	Williams-Bos 185	Keltner-Cle 35		Gordon-NY 28	Greenberg-Det 311	

BASES ON BALLS	STOLEN BASES	BASE STEALING RUNS	FIELDING RUNS-INFIELD	FIELDING RUNS-OUTFIELD	OUTFIELD ASSISTS	CATCHER CS PCT.
Clift-StL 111	Case-Was 51	Case-Was 5.3	Doerr-Bos 26.5	Johnson-Phi 9.7	Kreevich-Chi 18	Tebbetts-Det 47.1
Williams-Bos 107	Kreevich-Chi 23	McCosky-Det 3.0	Clift-StL 12.9	Kreevich-Chi 9.5	Johnson-Phi 15	Ferrell-Was 41.9
Appling-Chi 105	Fox-Det 23	Kuhel-Chi 2.2	Trosky-Cle 11.5	Fox-Det 8.4	Hoag-StL 13	Hemsley-Cle 39.7
Selkirk-NY 103	McCosky-Det 20	Welaj-Was 2.2	Lewis-Was 10.9	Walker-Chi 7.6	DiMaggio-NY 13	Dickey-NY 39.7
Johnson-Phi 99		Chapman-Cle 1.9	Crosetti-NY 9.8	DiMaggio-NY 4.5		Glenn-StL 37.7

WINS	WINNING PCT.	WINS ABOVE TEAM	GAMES STARTED	COMPLETE GAMES	FEWEST HITS/GAME	FEWEST BB/GAME
Feller-Cle 24	Grove-Bos .789	Leonard-Was 7.7	Newsom-StL-Det 37	Newsom-StL-Det 24	Feller-Cle 6.89	Lyons-Chi 1.36
Ruffing-NY 21	Ruffing-NY .750	Feller-Cle 7.1	Feller-Cle 35	Feller-Cle 24	Hadley-NY 7.71	Leonard-Was 1.97
Newsom-StL-Det 20	Feller-Cle .727	Bridges-Det 5.1	Leonard-Was 34	Ruffing-NY 22	Gomez-NY 7.86	Beckmann-Phi 2.38
Leonard-Was 20	Leonard-Was .714	Grove-Bos 4.9		Leonard-Was 21	Ruffing-NY 8.14	Lee-Chi 2.68
Bridges-Det 17	Bridges-Det .708	Newsom-StL-Det 4.7		Grove-Bos 17	Chase-Was 8.34	Grove-Bos 2.73

STRIKEOUTS	STRIKEOUTS/GAME	GAMES	SAVES	BASE RUNNERS/9	ADJUSTED RELIEF RUNS	RELIEF RANKING
Feller-Cle 246	Feller-Cle 7.46	Brown-Chi 61	Murphy-NY 19	Lyons-Chi 9.85	Brown-Chi 10.5	Brown-Chi 20.4
Newsom-StL-Det 192	Newsom-StL-Det 5.92	Dean-Phi 54	Brown-Chi 18	Russo-NY 9.93	Heving-Bos 6.1	Heving-Bos 8.1
Bridges-Det 129	Bridges-Det 5.86	Dickman-Bos 48	Heving-Bos 7	Hildebrand-NY 10.23	Dickman-Bos 1.5	Dickman-Bos 1.5
Rigney-Chi 119	Rigney-Chi 4.90	Heving-Bos 46	Dean-Phi 7	Ruffing-NY 11.11		
Chase-Was 118	Gomez-NY 4.64		Appleton-Was 6	Leonard-Was 11.26		

INNINGS PITCHED	OPPONENTS' AVG.	OPPONENTS' OBP	EARNED RUN AVERAGE	ADJUSTED ERA	ADJUSTED STARTER RUNS	PITCHER WINS
Feller-Cle 296.2	Feller-Cle .210	Lyons-Chi .276	Grove-Bos 2.54	Grove-Bos 186	Feller-Cle 54.2	**Feller-Cle 6.0**
Newsom-StL-Det 291.2	Gomez-NY .235	Ruffing-NY .301	Lyons-Chi 2.76	Lyons-Chi 171	Grove-Bos 45.2	**Ruffing-NY 4.8**
Leonard-Was 269.1	Hadley-NY .237	Feller-Cle .303	Feller-Cle 2.85	Feller-Cle 154	Newsom-StL-Det 42.2	**Grove-Bos 3.7**
Lee-Chi 235.0	Ruffing-NY .240	Bridges-Det .304	Ruffing-NY 2.93	Ruffing-NY 149	Ruffing-NY 37.8	**Lyons-Chi 3.7**
Ruffing-NY 233.1	Bridges-Det .243	Leonard-Was .305	Hadley-NY 2.98	Hadley-NY 146	Lyons-Chi 31.7	**Newsom-StL-Det 3.5**

Williams Can't Unseat Yankees

An unparalleled rookie class graced the American League in 1939. Say hello to Ted Williams, Charlie Keller, Dizzy Trout, Mickey Vernon, Early Wynn, and Hal Newhouser, all of whom affected baseball in the 1940s and beyond. Let's focus on Williams, a lithe 20-year-old from San Diego. He was second in the league in doubles and walks, fifth in hits, and third in homers. The Red Sox ended up second, their best finish in two decades, on his hitting, that of Jimmie Foxx, and the ninth and final ERA crown won by ageless Lefty Grove.

But New York again rolled over the competition, leaving the Red Sox 17 games behind. It is a tribute to the Yankees that they kept winning even when Lou Gehrig was forced to retire due to a condition eventually defined as Amyotrophic Lateral Sclerosis. The disease would kill him in 1941, shortly before he would have turned 38. (Three other greats also left the active ranks in '39: Jimmy Dykes, Tony Lazzeri, and Heinie Manush.)

How did the Yanks do it? Balance, again, was the secret. All eight regulars hit at least 10 homers, and the Yankees led the league in runs, ERA, and saves. Keller, Joe DiMaggio, and George Selkirk comprised a top outfield, while manager Joe McCarthy gave seven pitchers at least 10 starts—and each won at least 10 games.

Another four-game World Series sweep, this one over Cincinnati, established the Yankees as perhaps the AL's greatest team to date. Bill Dickey, DiMaggio, and Keller did the damage as New York outscored the Reds 20-8. It was New York's eighth world championship since 1923, and even more dominating, it was their fifth sweep.

But even perfection becomes boring; attendance at Yankee Stadium dropped 11 percent. The Athletics, hoping to increase their gate, hosted the league's first night game on May 16. And while scoring dropped, the league's 512 complete games still ranked as the lowest total ever.

1938 NATIONAL LEAGUE

TEAM	W	L	T	PCT	GB	HW	HL	R	OR	PA	H	2B	3B	HR	BB	SO	HB	SH	AVG	OBP	SLG	OPS	AOPS	BR	ABR	PF	SB	CS	BSA	BSR
Chi	89	63	2	.586	—	44	33	713	**597**	5972	1435	242	70	65	522	476	29	88	.269	.338	.377	715	100	26	7	103	49			
Pit	86	64	2	.573	2	44	33	707	630	6007	1511	265	66	65	485	**409**	19	81	**.279**	**.340**	.388	728	106	49	44	101	47			
NY	83	67	2	.553	5	43	30	705	637	5841	1424	210	36	**125**	465	528	**33**	88	.271	.334	.396	730	106	45	39	101	31			
Cin	82	68	1	.547	6	43	34	723	634	5878	1495	251	57	110	366	518	32	**89**	.277	.327	.406	733	**110**	42	**62**	97	19			
Bos	77	75	1	.507	12	**45**	30	561	618	5775	1311	199	39	54	424	548	23	78	.250	.309	.333	642	91	-121	-61	90	49			
StL	71	80	5	.470	17.5	36	41	**725**	722	6039	**1542**	**288**	74	91	412	492	16	83	**.279**	.331	**.407**	**738**	103	**56**	16	106	55			
Bro	69	80	2	.463	18.5	31	41	704	710	5853	1322	225	**79**	61	**611**	615	20	80	.257	.338	.367	705	98	14	-1	102	**66**			
Phi	45	105	1	.300	43	26	48	550	840	5713	1318	233	29	40	423	507	12	86	.254	.312	.333	645	85	-111	-95	97	38			
Total	610	—	—	—	—	312	290	5388	—	47078	11358	1913	450	611	3708	4093	184	673	.267	.329	.376	705	—	—	—	—	354	—	—	—

TEAM	CG	SHO	GR	SV	IP	H	HR	BB	SO	BR/9	ERA	AERA	OAV	OOB	PR	APR	PF	OSB	OCS	FA	E	WPB	DP	FW	PW	BW	BSW	DIF
Chi	67	**16**	148	**18**	1396.2	1414	71	454	**583**	12.1	**3.37**	**113**	.262	.322	**64**	**66**	101	40	*30*	**.978**	**135**	42	151	**2.3**	**6.6**	.7	—	3.4
Pit	57	8	144	15	1379.2	1406	71	432	557	12.2	3.46	109	.266	.324	49	50	100	44	***45***	.974	163	24	**168**	.5	5.0	4.4	—	1.1
NY	59	8	142	**18**	1349.0	1370	87	**389**	497	**11.9**	3.62	104	.261	**.314**	24	20	99	37	*24*	.973	168	**20**	147	.2	2.0	3.9	—	1.9
Cin	72	11	130	16	1362.0	**1329**	75	463	542	**11.9**	3.62	101	**.254**	.316	25	3	96	37	*33*	.971	172	39	133	-.1	.3	**6.2**	—	.6
Bos	**83**	15	109	12	1380.0	1375	**66**	465	413	12.2	3.40	101	.258	.322	58	3	91	**27**	*42*	.972	173	23	136	-.0	.3	-6.1	—	6.9
StL	58	10	**179**	16	1384.2	1482	77	474	534	12.8	3.84	103	.272	.333	-9	16	104	48	*43*	.967	199	36	145	-1.4	1.6	1.6	—	-6.3
Bro	56	12	155	14	1332.0	1464	88	446	469	13.1	4.07	96	.278	.338	-42	-25	103	47	*31*	.973	157	52	148	.8	-2.5	-.1	—	-3.6
Phi	68	3	140	6	1329.1	1516	76	582	492	14.4	4.93	79	.285	.358	-169	-151	103	74	*35*	.966	201	40	135	-1.8	-15.2	-9.6	—	-3.4
Total	520	83	1147	115	10913.1	—	—	—	—	12.6	3.78	—	.267	.329	—	—	—	—	—	.972	1368	276	1163	—	—	—	—	—

BATTER-FIELDER WINS	BATTING AVERAGE	ON-BASE PERCENTAGE	SLUGGING AVERAGE	ON-BASE PLUS SLUGGING	ADJUSTED OPS	ADJUSTED BATTER RUNS
Ott-NY 6.4	Lombardi-Cin .342	Ott-NY .442	Mize-StL .614	Mize-StL 1036	Ott-NY 178	Ott-NY 62.3
Vaughan-Pit 6.4	Mize-StL .337	Vaughan-Pit .433	Ott-NY .583	Ott-NY 1024	Mize-StL 172	Mize-StL 53.0
Lombardi-Cin 4.1	McCormick-Cin .327	Mize-StL .422	Medwick-StL .536	Lombardi-Cin 915	Lombardi-Cin 154	Vaughan-Pit 37.6
Hack-Chi 4.0	Medwick-StL .322	Hack-Chi .411	Goodman-Cin .533	Medwick-StL 905	Goodman-Cin 149	Goodman-Cin 36.5
Mize-StL 3.9	Vaughan-Pit .322	Suhr-Pit .394	Lombardi-Cin .524	Goodman-Cin 901	Vaughan-Pit 140	Lombardi-Cin 35.3
RUNS	**HITS**	**DOUBLES**	**TRIPLES**	**HOME RUNS**	**TOTAL BASES**	**RUNS BATTED IN**
Ott-NY 116	McCormick-Cin 209	Medwick-StL 47	Mize-StL 16	Ott-NY 36	Mize-StL 326	Medwick-StL 122
Hack-Chi 109	Hack-Chi 195	McCormick-Cin 40	Gutteridge-StL 15	Goodman-Cin 30	Medwick-StL 316	Ott-NY 116
Camilli-Bro 106	L.Waner-Pit 194	Young-Pit 36	Suhr-Pit 14	Mize-StL 27	Ott-NY 307	Rizzo-Pit 111
Goodman-Cin 103	Medwick-StL 190	Martin-Phi 36	Riggs-Cin 13	Camilli-Bro 24	Goodman-Cin 303	McCormick-Cin 106
Medwick-StL 100	Mize-StL 179		Koy-Bro 13	Rizzo-Pit 23	Rizzo-Pit 285	Mize-StL 102
BASES ON BALLS	**STOLEN BASES**	**BASE STEALING RUNS**	**FIELDING RUNS-INFIELD**	**FIELDING RUNS-OUTFIELD**	**OUTFIELD ASSISTS**	**CATCHER CS PCT.**
Camilli-Bro 119	Hack-Chi 16		Bartell-NY 25.9	Arnovich-Phi 17.4	Rosen-Bro 19	Lombardi-Cin 51.7
Ott-NY 118	Lavagetto-Bro 15		Young-Pit 25.1	DiMaggio-Bos 10.5	DiMaggio-Bos 19	Todd-Pit 50.0
Vaughan-Pit 104	Koy-Bro 15		Herman-Chi 21.5	Rosen-Bro 9.1	Arnovich-Phi 18	Owen-StL 45.9
Hack-Chi 94	Vaughan-Pit 14		Vaughan-Pit 16.7	Medwick-StL 8.0	L.Waner-Pit 15	Hartnett-Chi 41.7
Suhr-Pit 87	Gutteridge-StL 14		Kampouris-Cin-NY 13.2	Craft-Cin 7.1	Craft-Cin 15	Atwood-Phi 37.5
WINS	**WINNING PCT.**	**WINS ABOVE TEAM**	**GAMES STARTED**	**COMPLETE GAMES**	**FEWEST HITS/GAME**	**FEWEST BB/GAME**
Lee-Chi 22	Lee-Chi .710	Lee-Chi 5.4	Lee-Chi 37	Derringer-Cin 26	VanderMeer-Cin 7.07	Davis-StL 1.40
Derringer-Cin 21	Bryant-Chi .633	Tamulis-Bro 3.7	Derringer-Cin 37	Turner-Bos 22	Bauers-Pit 7.67	Derringer-Cin 1.44
Bryant-Chi 19	Brown-Pit .625	Weiland-StL 3.6		Walters-Phi-Cin 20	Bryant-Chi 7.82	Hubbell-NY 1.66
Weiland-StL 16	VanderMeer-Cin .600	Warneke-StL 3.3		MacFayden-Bos 19	MacFayden-Bos 8.52	Root-Chi 1.68
	Derringer-Cin .600	Klinger-Pit 2.9		Lee-Chi 19	Klinger-Pit 8.59	Turner-Bos 1.81
STRIKEOUTS	**STRIKEOUTS/GAME**	**GAMES**	**SAVES**	**BASE RUNNERS/9**	**ADJUSTED RELIEF RUNS**	**RELIEF RANKING**
Bryant-Chi 135	Hubbell-NY 5.23	Coffman-NY 51	Coffman-NY 12	Dean-Chi 8.68	Brown-NY 17.6	Brown-NY 16.3
Derringer-Cin 132	VanderMeer-Cin 4.99	Brown-Pit 51	Root-Chi 8	Brown-NY 9.40	Russell-Chi 5.6	Coffman-NY 4.5
VanderMeer-Cin 125	Weiland-StL 4.61	McGee-StL 47	Hamlin-Bro 6	Hubbell-NY 10.36	Coffman-NY 3.7	Russell-Chi 3.8
Lee-Chi 121	Bryant-Chi 4.49	Mulcahy-Phi 46	Errickson-Bos 6	Johnson-Phi 10.63	Shoun-StL 7	Shoun-StL 7
				Derringer-Cin 10.67		
INNINGS PITCHED	**OPPONENTS' AVG.**	**OPPONENTS' OBP**	**EARNED RUN AVERAGE**	**ADJUSTED ERA**	**ADJUSTED STARTER RUNS**	**PITCHER WINS**
Derringer-Cin 307.0	VanderMeer-Cin .213	Hubbell-NY .285	Lee-Chi 2.66	Lee-Chi 144	Lee-Chi 38.6	**Lee-Chi 4.1**
Lee-Chi 291.0	Bauers-Pit .233	Derringer-Cin .291	Root-Chi 2.86	Root-Chi 134	Derringer-Cin 27.8	**Derringer-Cin 2.9**
Bryant-Chi 270.1	Bryant-Chi .235	Root-Chi .294	Derringer-Cin 2.93	Fitzsimmons-Bro 129	Bryant-Chi 22.1	**Bryant-Chi 2.6**
Turner-Bos 268.0	MacFayden-Bos .247	Lohrman-NY .294	MacFayden-Bos 2.95	Klinger-Pit 127	Fitzsimmons-Bro 18.0	**Bauers-Pit 2.1**
Mulcahy-Phi 267.1	Schumacher-NY .248	Schumacher-NY .299	Klinger-Pit 2.99	Derringer-Cin 124	Bauers-Pit 17.8	

Cubs Glow One Last Time

For all intents and purposes, 1938 looked like Pittsburgh's year. A 24-7 record in July allowed them to overtake the sliding Giants, and the Pirates led for all of August and most of September. Then the elements took over. A mid-September hurricane stopped play for four days and gave tired Chicago time to recover; the team the reeled off seven straight wins to catch the stumbling Pirates, who had led by seven on Labor Day.

Chicago knocked Pittsburgh out with a three-game sweep September 27-29 at Wrigley Field. Player-manager Gabby Hartnett's dramatic "homer in the gloamin'," hit just before the umpires were set to call the game by darkness, provided the key hit in the second game. Pittsburgh had great relief pitching from Mace Brown, and a solid line-drive offense, but didn't have Chicago's rotation: Bill Lee of the Cubs led the NL in wins and ERA, while 19-game winner Clay Bryant had a superior season in an otherwise nondescript career.

Cincinnati leapt to fourth, raising attendance by 72 percent. Overpowering Johnny Vander Meer threw no-hitters in consecutive starts, while catcher Ernie Lombardi was MVP. Rebuilding St. Louis debuted future stars Mort Cooper and Enos Slaughter.

Stolen bases fell to just .29 per contest, the lowest total to that point in history. Vince DiMaggio again paced the league with 138 strikeouts, setting a record that lasted until 1956. Several teams altered their ballparks in 1938. The Cubs redesigned Wrigley Field, adding the bleachers still in use, while the Giants chopped 50 feet from center field with a temporary fence. The Phillies moved into Shibe Park, the Athletics' headquarters, on July 4; Shibe was much larger than the tiny Baker Bowl.

The Cubs had no more luck in the World Series than other NL teams of the period, losing to the Yankees in four. While 1938 was the Cubs' eleventh straight year among the NL's top three, it was also the *end* of the franchise as a consistent winner; Chicago did not contend again until 1945.

1938 AMERICAN LEAGUE

TEAM	W	L	T	PCT	GB	HW	HL	R	OR	PA	H	2B	3B	HR	BB	SO	HB	SH	AVG	OBP	SLG	OPS	AOPS	BR	ABR	PF	SB	CS	BSA	BSR
NY	99	53	5	.651	—	**55**	22	**966**	**710**	6259	1480	283	63	**174**	**749**	616	**39**	61	.274	.366	**.446**	**812**	**111**	81	**86**	100	**91**	28	**76**	**10**
Bos	88	61	1	.591	9.5	52	23	902	751	6004	1566	298	56	98	650	463	13	**112**	**.299**	**.378**	.434	**812**	105	**91**	51	105	55	51	52	-6
Cle	86	66	1	.566	13	46	30	847	782	6000	1506	**300**	**89**	113	550	605	16	78	.281	.350	.434	784	104	8	25	98	83	36	70	6
Det	84	70	1	.545	16	48	31	862	795	6060	1434	219	52	137	693	581	22	75	.272	.359	.411	770	94	-2	-46	106	76	41	65	2
Was	75	76	1	.497	23.5	44	33	814	873	6158	**1602**	278	72	85	573	**379**	18	93	.293	.362	.416	778	108	11	74	93	65	37	64	1
Chi	65	83	1	.439	32	33	39	709	752	5805	1439	239	55	67	514	489	14	78	.277	.343	.383	726	86	-94	-110	102	56	39	59	-1
StL	55	97	4	.362	44	31	43	755	962	6049	1498	273	36	92	590	528	20	106	.281	.355	.397	752	95	-36	-34	100	51	40	56	-3
Phi	53	99	2	.349	46	28	47	726	956	5934	1410	243	62	98	605	590	22	78	.270	.348	.396	744	95	-58	-38	97	65	53	55	-4
Total	613	—	—	—	—	337	268	6581	—	48269	11935	2133	485	864	4924	4251	164	681	.281	.358	.415	773	—	—	—	—	542	325	63	5

TEAM	CG	SHO	GR	SV	IP	H	HR	BB	SO	BR/9	ERA	AERA	OAV	OOB	PR	APR	PF	OSB	OCS	FA	E	WPB	DP	FW	PW	BW	BSW	DIF
NY	**91**	**11**	91	13	1382.0	1436	**85**	566	567	**13.1**	**3.91**	**116**	**.268**	**.339**	**134**	**101**	95	52	37	.973	169	39	177	.5	**9.1**	**7.8**	**.8**	4.8
Bos	67	10	147	15	1316.1	1472	102	**528**	484	13.8	4.46	111	.281	.349	48	67	103	63	35	.968	190	**27**	172	-1.1	6.1	4.6	-.6	4.6
Cle	68	5	145	**17**	1353.0	**1416**	100	681	**717**	14.1	4.60	101	**.268**	.355	29	7	97	82	**49**	.974	151	39	145	1.2	.6	2.3	.5	5.4
Det	75	3	134	11	1348.1	1532	110	608	435	14.4	4.79	104	.287	.361	1	31	104	**48**	35	**.976**	147	37	172	1.6	2.8	-4.2	.1	6.6
Was	59	6	**156**	11	1360.1	1472	92	655	515	14.3	4.94	91	.276	.358	-22	-68	94	64	39	.970	180	60	**179**	-.5	-6.1	6.7	.0	-.6
Chi	83	5	84	9	1316.1	1449	101	550	432	13.8	4.36	112	.279	.350	62	76	102	57	42	.967	196	33	155	-1.6	6.9	-9.9	-.2	-4.2
StL	71	3	134	7	1344.2	1584	132	737	632	15.7	5.80	86	.295	.382	-151	-120	104	89	**49**	.975	**145**	37	163	**1.8**	-10.8	-3.1	-.3	-8.5
Phi	56	4	143	12	1324.0	1573	142	599	473	14.9	5.48	88	.292	.365	-101	-94	101	87	39	.965	206	43	119	-1.8	-8.5	-3.4	-.4	-8.9
Total	570	47	1034	95	10745.0	—	—	—	—	14.3	4.79	—	.281	.358	—	—	—	—	—	.971	1384	315	1282	—	—	—	—	—

BATTER-FIELDER WINS	BATTING AVERAGE	ON-BASE PERCENTAGE	SLUGGING AVERAGE	ON-BASE PLUS SLUGGING	ADJUSTED OPS	ADJUSTED BATTER RUNS
Foxx-Bos.....5.8	Foxx-Bos.....349	Foxx-Bos.....462	Foxx-Bos.....704	Foxx-Bos.....1166	Foxx-Bos.....180	Foxx-Bos.....71.9
Clift-StL.....5.3	Heath-Cle.....343	Myer-Was.....454	Greenberg-Det.....683	Greenberg-Det.....1122	Greenberg-Det.....167	Greenberg-Det.....58.3
Greenberg-Det.....4.5	Chapman-Bos.....340	Greenberg-Det.....438	Heath-Cle.....602	York-Det.....995	Heath-Cle.....146	Clift-StL.....38.9
Cronin-Bos.....4.4	Myer-Was.....336	Averill-Cle.....429	DiMaggio-NY.....581	Heath-Cle.....985	Dickey-NY.....144	Johnson-Phi.....36.0
Dickey-NY.....4.1	Travis-Was.....335	Cronin-Bos.....428	York-Det.....579	Dickey-NY.....981	Clift-StL.....143	Myer-Was.....34.1
RUNS	**HITS**	**DOUBLES**	**TRIPLES**	**HOME RUNS**	**TOTAL BASES**	**RUNS BATTED IN**
Greenberg-Det.....144	Vosmik-Bos.....201	Cronin-Bos.....51	Heath-Cle.....18	Greenberg-Det.....58	Foxx-Bos.....398	Foxx-Bos.....175
Foxx-Bos.....139	Cramer-Bos.....198	McQuinn-StL.....42	Averill-Cle.....15	Foxx-Bos.....50	Greenberg-Det.....380	Greenberg-Det.....146
Gehringer-Det.....133	Almada-Was-StL.....197	Trosky-Cle.....40	DiMaggio-NY.....13	Clift-StL.....34	DiMaggio-NY.....348	DiMaggio-NY.....140
Rolfe-NY.....132	Foxx-Bos.....197	Chapman-Bos.....40		York-Det.....33	Johnson-Phi.....311	York-Det.....127
DiMaggio-NY.....129	Rolfe-NY.....196	Vosmik-Bos.....37		DiMaggio-NY.....32	Heath-Cle.....302	Clift-StL.....118
BASES ON BALLS	**STOLEN BASES**	**BASE STEALING RUNS**	**FIELDING RUNS-INFIELD**	**FIELDING RUNS-OUTFIELD**	**OUTFIELD ASSISTS**	**CATCHER CS PCT.**
Greenberg-Det.....119	Crosetti-NY.....27	Lary-Cle.....3.0	Gordon-NY.....20.5	Johnson-Phi.....9.6	Johnson-Phi.....21	Dickey-NY.....42.0
Foxx-Bos.....119	Lary-Cle.....23	Gehringer-Det.....2.7	Crosetti-NY.....18.4	Cramer-Bos.....5.5	DiMaggio-NY.....20	Desautels-Bos.....40.0
Clift-StL.....118	Werber-Phi.....19	Rolfe-NY.....2.5	Clift-StL.....15.2	Chapman-Bos.....5.4	Cramer-Bos.....15	R.Ferrell-Was.....38.3
Gehringer-Det.....113	Lewis-Was.....17	Crosetti-NY.....1.7	Rogell-Det.....9.8	Moses-Phi.....4.3	Chapman-Bos.....15	Pytlak-Cle.....35.4
Gehrig-NY.....107	Fox-Det.....16	Moses-Phi.....1.5	Doerr-Bos.....9.0	Vosmik-Bos.....3.5		Hayes-Phi.....29.0
WINS	**WINNING PCT.**	**WINS ABOVE TEAM**	**GAMES STARTED**	**COMPLETE GAMES**	**FEWEST HITS/GAME**	**FEWEST BB/GAME**
Ruffing-NY.....21	Ruffing-NY.....750	Newsom-StL.....6.5	Newsom-StL.....40	Newsom-StL.....31	Feller-Cle.....7.29	Leonard-Was.....2.14
Newsom-StL.....20	Pearson-NY.....696	Ruffing-NY.....4.6	Caster-Phi.....40	Ruffing-NY.....22	Allen-Cle.....8.51	Harder-Cle.....2.33
Gomez-NY.....18	Harder-Cle.....630	Stratton-Chi.....4.5	Feller-Cle.....36	Gomez-NY.....20	Pearson-NY.....8.82	Lyons-Chi.....2.40
Harder-Cle.....17	Stratton-Chi.....625	Grove-Bos.....4.4	Gomez-NY.....32	Feller-Cle.....20	Rigney-Chi.....8.84	Chandler-NY.....2.46
Feller-Cle.....17	Feller-Cle.....607	Caster-Phi.....3.3		Caster-Phi.....20	Hadley-NY.....8.87	Thomas-Phi.....2.63
STRIKEOUTS	**STRIKEOUTS/GAME**	**GAMES**	**SAVES**	**BASE RUNNERS/9**	**ADJUSTED RELIEF RUNS**	**RELIEF RANKING**
Feller-Cle.....240	Feller-Cle.....7.78	Humphries-Cle.....45	Murphy-NY.....11	Leonard-Was.....11.32	Murphy-NY.....4.9	Murphy-NY.....6.1
Newsom-StL.....226	Newsom-StL.....6.17	Newsom-StL.....44	McKain-Bos.....6	Eisenstat-Det.....11.56	McKain-Bos.....3.5	McKain-Bos.....3.3
L.Mills-StL.....134	L.Mills-StL.....5.73	E.Smith-Phi.....43	Humphries-Cle.....6	Harris-Bos.....11.76		
Gomez-NY.....129	Grove-Bos.....5.44	Bagby-Bos.....43	Potter-Phi.....5	Ruffing-NY.....11.94		
Ruffing-NY.....127	Allen-Cle.....5.04	Appleton-Was.....43	Appleton-Was.....5	Stratton-Chi.....12.03		
INNINGS PITCHED	**OPPONENTS' AVG.**	**OPPONENTS' OBP**	**EARNED RUN AVERAGE**	**ADJUSTED ERA**	**ADJUSTED STARTER RUNS**	**PITCHER WINS**
Newsom-StL.....329.2	Feller-Cle.....220	Leonard-Was.....305	Grove-Bos.....3.08	Grove-Bos.....160	Ruffing-NY.....37.1	**Ruffing-NY.....4.5**
Caster-Phi.....281.1	Allen-Cle.....246	Stratton-Chi.....315	Ruffing-NY.....3.31	Lee-Chi.....140	Lee-Chi.....33.0	**Lee-Chi.....3.4**
Feller-Cle.....277.2	Hadley-NY.....254	Ruffing-NY.....317	Gomez-NY.....3.35	Rigney-Chi.....138	Grove-Bos.....32.5	**Gomez-NY.....3.2**
Ruffing-NY.....247.1	Stratton-Chi.....255	Harder-Cle.....319	Leonard-Was.....3.43	Ruffing-NY.....137	Gomez-NY.....31.0	**Grove-Bos.....3.0**
Lee-Chi.....245.1	Rigney-Chi.....256	Grove-Bos.....319	Lee-Chi.....3.49	Gomez-NY.....135	Rigney-Chi.....25.9	**Leonard-Was.....2.8**

Crushing the Competition

While it was again a Yankees year, fans in Boston and Cleveland had plenty to cheer about. Both teams hung in with New York through late July, but couldn't compete with the Yankees' 48-13 record from July 1 through August 30. With the great all-around play of Joe DiMaggio, catcher Bill Dickey contributing another fine year at bat, and rookie Joe Gordon at second base, the Yankees were able to withstand the sudden decline of Lou Gehrig. Joe McCarthy began using Johnny Murphy in tough relief situations, which made the aging starting staff look even better.

Boston got great seasons from Jimmie Foxx and Joe Cronin, but a punchless outfield and thin pitching doomed the club. Cleveland's Bob Feller, a 19-year-old fireballer with a great fastball and a large ego, led the league in both walks and strikeouts. The Indians also gave 20-year-old infielder Lou Boudreau his first taste of the big leagues. St. Louis had one spectacular pitcher—30-year-old Bobo Newsom, who was 20-16 for the 55-97 Browns and led the league in starts and complete games. Two former star outfielders, Goose Goslin and Mule Haas, saw their careers grind to a halt with the clubs of their youth, Washington and Philadelphia, respectively.

While hitters set yet another new home run record, stolen bases continued to plummet; just two players swiped more than 20 sacks. However, the Yankees cornered the market in this field, as well, leading the loop in stolen bases as well as runs, home runs, and bases on balls.

When the New York met up with the Cubs in the World Series, nobody gave Chicago a chance. They were right. The Bombers' sweep was still impressive—the Yankees outscored the Cubs, 22-9, and put together late-inning rallies to break open close contests in Games 2 and 4.

1937 NATIONAL LEAGUE

TEAM	W	L	T	PCT	GB	HW	HL	R	OR	PA	H	2B	3B	HR	BB	SO	HB	SH	AVG	OBP	SLG	OPS	AOPS	BR	ABR	PF	SB	CS	BSA	BSR
NY	95	57	0	.625	—	**50**	25	732	602	5862	1484	251	41	**111**	412	492	**31**	90	.278	.334	.403	737	105	41	32	101	45			
Chi	93	61	0	.604	3	46	32	**811**	682	6028	1537	253	74	96	**538**	496	22	**119**	**.287**	**.355**	**.416**	**771**	**111**	**118**	**85**	104	71			
Pit	86	68	0	.558	10	46	32	704	647	5996	**1550**	223	**86**	47	463	**480**	11	89	.285	.343	.384	727	104	27	27	100	32			
StL	81	73	3	.526	15	45	33	789	733	5966	1543	**264**	67	94	385	569	16	89	.282	.331	.406	737	104	35	21	102	**78**			
Bos	79	73	0	.520	16	43	33	579	**556**	5740	1265	200	41	63	485	707	18	113	.247	.314	.339	653	91	-110	-54	91	45			
Bro	62	91	2	.405	33.5	36	39	616	772	5893	1401	258	53	37	469	583	20	109	.265	.327	.354	681	90	-55	-65	102	69			
Phi	61	92	2	.399	34.5	29	45	724	869	5993	1482	258	37	103	478	640	16	75	.273	.334	.391	725	95	24	-31	108	66			
Cin	56	98	1	.364	40	28	51	612	706	5763	1329	215	59	73	437	586	24	72	.254	.315	.360	675	94	-80	-49	95	53			
Total	617	—	—	—	—	323	290	5567	—	47241	11591	1922	458	624	3667	4553	158	756	.272	.332	.382	714	—	—	—	—	459	—	—	—

TEAM	CG	SHO	GR	SV	IP	H	HR	BB	SO	BR/9	ERA	AERA	OAV	OOB	PR	APR	PF	OSB	OCS	FA	E	WPB	DP	FW	PW	BW	BSW	DIF
NY	67	11	142	17	1361.0	**1341**	86	404	**653**	11.7	3.43	**113**	**.258**	.314	73	**70**	99	36	***55***	.974	159	35	143	.9	**6.9**	3.2	—	8.0
Chi	73	11	148	13	1381.1	1434	91	502	596	12.8	3.97	100	.267	.332	-10	0	102	47	*50*	**.975**	**151**	44	141	**1.5**	.0	**8.4**	—	6.1
Pit	67	12	149	17	1366.1	1398	71	428	643	12.2	3.56	108	.264	.321	53	46	99	99	*47*	.970	181	29	135	-.2	4.6	2.7	—	1.9
StL	81	10	141	4	1392.0	1546	95	448	571	13.0	3.98	100	.281	.337	-10	-1	102	62	*51*	.973	164	43	127	1.0	-.0	2.1	—	1.1
Bos	**85**	**16**	103	10	1359.1	1344	60	**372**	387	**11.4**	**3.22**	111	.259	**.310**	**105**	60	92	**30**	*52*	**.975**	157	**14**	128	1.0	6.0	-5.4	—	1.4
Bro	63	5	160	8	1362.2	1470	68	476	592	13.0	4.13	98	.274	.336	-33	-14	103	65	*51*	.964	217	42	127	-2.2	-1.4	-6.4	—	-4.5
Phi	59	6	**178**	15	1373.2	1629	115	501	529	14.2	5.05	86	.297	.359	-174	-103	111	42	*41*	.970	184	27	**157**	-.3	-10.2	-3.1	—	-1.9
Cin	64	10	162	**18**	1358.1	1428	**38**	533	581	13.1	3.94	95	.270	.339	-4	-33	95	78	*48*	.966	208	47	139	-1.6	-3.3	-4.9	—	-11.2
Total	559	81	1183	102	10954.2	—	—	—	—	12.7	3.91	—	.272	.332	—	—	—	—	—	.971	1421	281	1097	—	—	—	—	—

BATTER-FIELDER WINS	BATTING AVERAGE	ON-BASE PERCENTAGE	SLUGGING AVERAGE	ON-BASE PLUS SLUGGING	ADJUSTED OPS	ADJUSTED BATTER RUNS
Bartell-NY 6.1	Medwick-StL 374	Camilli-Phi 446	Medwick-StL 641	Medwick-StL 1056	Medwick-StL 179	Medwick-StL 67.6
Medwick-StL 6.0	Mize-StL 364	Mize-StL 427	Mize-StL 595	Camilli-Phi 1034	Mize-StL 171	Mize-StL 56.2
Herman-Chi 4.9	Hartnett-Chi 354	Medwick-StL 414	Camilli-Phi 587	Mize-StL 1021	Camilli-Phi 165	Camilli-Phi 46.7
Camilli-Phi 3.8	P.Waner-Pit 354	P.Waner-Pit 413	Hartnett-Chi 548	Ott-NY 931	Ott-NY 149	Ott-NY 41.4
Ott-NY 3.5	Whitney-Phi 341	Ott-NY 408	Ott-NY 523	Herman-Chi 875	P.Waner-Pit 132	P.Waner-Pit 30.1
RUNS	**HITS**	**DOUBLES**	**TRIPLES**	**HOME RUNS**	**TOTAL BASES**	**RUNS BATTED IN**
Medwick-StL 111	Medwick-StL 237	Medwick-StL 56	Vaughan-Pit 17	Ott-NY 31	Medwick-StL 406	Medwick-StL 154
Herman-Chi 106	P.Waner-Pit 219	Mize-StL 40	Suhr-Pit 14	Medwick-StL 31	Mize-StL 333	Demaree-Chi 115
Hack-Chi 106	Mize-StL 204	Bartell-NY 38	Handley-Pit 12	Camilli-Phi 27	Demaree-Chi 298	Mize-StL 113
Galan-Chi 104	Demaree-Chi 199	Phelps-Bro 37	Goodman-Cin 12	Mize-StL 25	Ott-NY 285	Suhr-Pit 97
Demaree-Chi 104	Herman-Chi 189	Moore-NY 37	Herman-Chi 11	Galan-Chi 18	Camilli-Phi 279	Ott-NY 95
BASES ON BALLS	**STOLEN BASES**	**BASE STEALING RUNS**	**FIELDING RUNS-INFIELD**	**FIELDING RUNS-OUTFIELD**	**OUTFIELD ASSISTS**	**CATCHER CS PCT.**
Ott-NY 102	Galan-Chi 23		Bartell-NY 35.5	Moore-Bos 11.2	Moore-Bos 21	Lopez-Bos 60.8
Camilli-Phi 90	Hack-Chi 16		Whitehead-NY 28.4	T.Moore-StL 7.7	DiMaggio-Bos 21	Mancuso-NY 60.4
Suhr-Pit 83			Riggs-Cin 18.1	DiMaggio-Bos 7.5	Demaree-Chi 17	Danning-NY 58.5
Hack-Chi 83			Herman-Chi 15.4	Arnovich-Phi 6.8	P.Waner-Pit 16	Atwood-Phi 52.5
Galan-Chi 79			Young-Pit 13.0	Galan-Chi 5.4		Hartnett-Chi 51.7
WINS	**WINNING PCT.**	**WINS ABOVE TEAM**	**GAMES STARTED**	**COMPLETE GAMES**	**FEWEST HITS/GAME**	**FEWEST BB/GAME**
Hubbell-NY 22	Hubbell-NY 733	Fette-Bos 5.3	Weiland-StL 34	Turner-Bos 24	Mungo-Bro 7.60	D.Dean-StL 1.51
Turner-Bos 20	Melton-NY 690	Hubbell-NY 5.0	Walters-Phi 34	Fette-Bos 23	Grissom-Cin 7.77	Root-Chi 1.61
Melton-NY 20	Fette-Bos 667	Turner-Bos 4.8	Passeau-Phi 34	Weiland-StL 21	Melton-NY 7.84	Hoyt-Pit-Bro 1.66
Fette-Bos 20	Carleton-Chi 667	Warneke-StL 3.4	Lee-Chi 34		Carleton-Chi 7.91	Turner-Bos 1.82
Warneke-StL 18	Turner-Bos 645	Melton-NY 3.0	Blanton-Pit 34		Turner-Bos 7.99	Castleman-NY 1.85
STRIKEOUTS	**STRIKEOUTS/GAME**	**GAMES**	**SAVES**	**BASE RUNNERS/9**	**ADJUSTED RELIEF RUNS**	**RELIEF RANKING**
Hubbell-NY 159	Mungo-Bro 6.82	Mulcahy-Phi 56	Melton-NY 7	Turner-Bos 9.82	Coffman-NY 5.6	Coffman-NY 7.4
Grissom-Cin 149	Grissom-Cin 6.00	Jorgens-Phi 52	Brown-Pit 7	Melton-NY 10.05		
Blanton-Pit 143	Bauers-Pit 5.66		Grissom-Cin 6	Castleman-NY ...10.16		
Melton-NY 142	Henshaw-Bro 5.64		Root-Chi 5	Root-Chi 10.53		
	LaMaster-Phi 5.51		Hollingsworth-Cin 5	Tobin-Pit 10.66		
INNINGS PITCHED	**OPPONENTS' AVG.**	**OPPONENTS' OBP**	**EARNED RUN AVERAGE**	**ADJUSTED ERA**	**ADJUSTED STARTER RUNS**	**PITCHER WINS**
Passeau-Phi 292.1	Mungo-Bro 229	Turner-Bos 274	Turner-Bos 2.38	Turner-Bos 150	Turner-Bos 36.2	**Turner-Bos 4.8**
Lee-Chi 272.1	Grissom-Cin 232	Melton-NY 280	Melton-NY 2.61	Melton-NY 149	Melton-NY 32.5	**Melton-NY 3.4**
Weiland-StL 264.1	Melton-NY 233	Castleman-NY 287	D.Dean-StL 2.69	D.Dean-StL 148	D.Dean-StL 25.4	**D.Dean-StL 2.8**
Hubbell-NY 261.2	Turner-Bos 235	Root-Chi 290	Bauers-Pit 2.88	Mungo-Bro 139	Fette-Bos 22.9	**Fette-Bos 2.8**
Fette-Bos 259.0	Carleton-Chi 236	D.Dean-StL 291	Fette-Bos 2.88	Bauers-Pit 134	Bauers-Pit 21.5	**Mungo-Bro 2.8**

Cardinals Sing Bye-Bye as Giants Tread

As the rest of the league floundered, the Cubs and Giants emerged in July. Chicago was up by $6^1/_2$ as late as August 13, but the Cubs fell apart for the second straight year as the Giants shot to the top. New York won 37 of its final 51. Carl Hubbell was spectacular again, and unheralded Cliff Melton—who won 20 and saved 7—was even better, giving the Giants a devastating 1-2 lefty combo. Mel Ott led the league in homers and walks, while Chicago lacked anyone up to the level of New York's stars.

The already popular All-Star Game claimed its first serious casualty. Earl Averill's liner broke Dizzy Dean's big toe, causing the popular Cardinals hurler to alter his delivery, which in turn ruined his arm. With Dean's effectiveness curtailed, the Cardinals fell to fourth despite Joe Medwick's Triple Crown. Dean's injury marked the end of the first great St. Louis era. Five classic Cardinals ended their careers in 1937: Jim Bottomley, Frankie Frisch, Chick Hafey, Jesse Haines, and Rogers Hornsby. In addition, Pittsburgh's Pie Traynor, considered the league's finest third baseman until the 1960s, retired.

The Boston Braves, who had improved 41 games in two years, ended fifth as two 30-year old rookies, Lou Fette and Jim Turner, won 20 each (Turner also led the league in ERA). The Reds finished in the cellar for the last time until 1982. Strikeouts per game rose to 3.69, the highest level between 1916 and 1948. Oddly enough, league leader Hubbell whiffed just 159—the 1936 leader, Van Mungo, struck out 238—and Boston rookie Vince DiMaggio was the sole player to fan more than 100 times.

Once again, however, the Giants did nothing with the Yankees in the World Series, falling in five games, only one of which was close. The Giants did not hit a home run until the final game of the Series when Ott hit a two-run homer.

1937 AMERICAN LEAGUE

TEAM	W	L	T	PCT	GB	HW	HL	R	OR	PA	H	2B	3B	HR	BB	SO	HB	SH	AVG	OBP	SLG	OPS	AOPS	BR	ABR	PF	SB	CS	BSA	BSR
NY	102	52	3	.662	—	**57**	20	**979**	**671**	6291	1554	282	73	**174**	**709**	607	**34**	61	.283	.369	**.456**	**825**	**113**	**113**	**107**	101	60	36	63	1
Det	89	65	1	.578	13	49	28	935	841	6264	**1611**	309	62	150	656	711	22	70	**.292**	**.370**	.452	822	111	109	89	102	89	45	66	**4**
Chi	86	68	0	.558	16	47	30	780	730	5956	1478	280	76	67	549	**447**	19	**111**	.280	.350	.400	750	95	-39	-38	100	70	34	**67**	**4**
Cle	83	71	2	.539	19	50	28	817	768	6040	1499	304	76	103	570	551	21	96	.280	.352	.423	775	100	5	0	101	78	51	60	-1
Bos	80	72	2	.526	21	44	29	821	775	6084	1506	269	64	100	601	557	26	103	.281	.357	.411	768	96	-1	-31	104	79	61	56	-4
Was	73	80	5	.477	28.5	43	35	757	841	6259	1559	245	**84**	47	591	503	23	67	.279	.351	.379	730	94	-79	-44	96	61	35	64	1
Phi	54	97	3	.358	46.5	27	50	699	854	5886	1398	278	60	94	583	557	5	70	.267	.341	.397	738	93	-64	-52	98	**95**	48	66	**4**
StL	46	108	2	.299	56	25	51	715	1023	6123	1573	**327**	44	71	514	510	14	85	.285	.348	.399	747	93	-45	-50	101	30	27	53	-3
Total	622	—	—	—	—	342	271	6503	—	48903	12178	2294	539	806	4773	4443	164	663	.281	.355	.415	770	—	—	—	—	562	337	63	6

TEAM	CG	SHO	GR	SV	IP	H	HR	BB	SO	BR/9	ERA	AERA	OAV	OOB	PR	APR	PF	OSB	OCS	FA	E	WPB	DP	FW	PW	BW	BSW	DIF
NY	**82**	**15**	100	**21**	1396.0	**1417**	92	**506**	652	**12.5**	**3.65**	**122**	**.261**	**.325**	**151**	**128**	96	**52**	39	.972	170	**23**	134	.2	**11.7**	**9.8**	.0	3.2
Det	70	6	132	11	1378.0	1521	102	635	485	14.2	4.87	96	.279	.357	-38	-30	101	75	35	**.976**	**147**	43	149	**1.4**	-2.8	8.2	**.3**	4.9
Chi	70	**15**	108	**21**	1351.1	1435	115	532	533	13.2	4.17	110	.273	.341	68	65	100	59	43	.971	174	34	173	-.2	6.0	-3.5	**.3**	6.5
Cle	64	4	**160**	15	1364.2	1529	**61**	566	630	14.0	4.39	105	.285	.356	35	33	100	81	**54**	.974	159	26	153	.8	3.0	.0	-.2	2.4
Bos	74	6	132	14	1366.0	1518	92	597	**682**	14.0	4.48	106	.279	.352	21	39	103	62	32	.970	177	31	139	-.4	3.6	-2.8	-.4	4.1
Was	75	5	122	14	1398.2	1498	96	671	524	14.1	4.58	97	.275	.357	7	-24	96	74	51	.972	170	36	**181**	.3	-2.2	-4.0	.0	2.5
Phi	65	6	143	9	1335.0	1490	105	613	469	14.3	4.85	97	.281	.358	-35	-20	102	75	38	.967	198	55	150	-1.7	-1.8	-4.8	**.3**	-13.5
StL	55	2	157	8	1363.0	1768	143	653	468	16.2	6.00	80	.315	.390	-209	-170	105	84	45	.972	173	42	166	-.0	-15.6	-4.6	-.3	-10.4
Total	555	59	1054	113	10952.2	—	—	—	—	14.1	4.62	—	.281	.355	—	—	—	—	—	.972	1368	290	1245	—	—	—	—	—

BATTER-FIELDER WINS	BATTING AVERAGE	ON-BASE PERCENTAGE	SLUGGING AVERAGE	ON-BASE PLUS SLUGGING	ADJUSTED OPS	ADJUSTED BATTER RUNS
Clift-StL........7.4	Gehringer-Det.......371	Gehrig-NY............473	DiMaggio-NY 673	Gehrig-NY...........1116	Gehrig-NY.............177	Gehrig-NY............74.1
DiMaggio-NY......5.7	Gehrig-NY.............351	Gehringer-Det.......458	Greenberg-Det......668	Greenberg-Det....1105	Greenberg-Det......171	Greenberg-Det.....65.3
Dickey-NY..........5.6	DiMaggio-NY 346	Greenberg-Det......436	York-Det................651	DiMaggio-NY 1085	DiMaggio-NY 168	DiMaggio-NY 60.1
Greenberg-Det...5.1	Bonura-Chi 345	Johnson-Phi..........425	Gehrig-NY.............643	Dickey-NY.............987	Johnson-Phi..........147	Gehringer-Det......43.0
Gehrig-NY..........4.8	Travis-Was 344	Dickey-NY.............417	Bonura-Chi 573	Bonura-Chi 984	Bonura-Chi 146	Johnson-Phi.........38.2
RUNS	**HITS**	**DOUBLES**	**TRIPLES**	**HOME RUNS**	**TOTAL BASES**	**RUNS BATTED IN**
DiMaggio-NY 151	Bell-StL.................218	Bell-StL...................51	Walker-Chi..............16	DiMaggio-NY 46	DiMaggio-NY 418	Greenberg-Det......183
Rolfe-NY 143	DiMaggio-NY 215	Greenberg-Det........49	Kreevich-Chi 16	Greenberg-Det........40	Greenberg-Det......397	DiMaggio-NY 167
Gehrig-NY.............138	Walker-Det...........213	Moses-Phi..............48	Stone-Was..............15	Gehrig-NY...............37	Gehrig-NY.............366	Gehrig-NY.............159
Greenberg-Det......137	Lewis-Was 210	Vosmik-StL 47	DiMaggio-NY 15	Foxx-Bos.................36	Moses-Phi.............357	Dickey-NY.............133
Gehringer-Det.......133	Gehringer-Det.......209	Lary-Cle..................46	Greenberg-Det........14	York-Det..................35	Trosky-Cle............329	Trosky-Cle............128
BASES ON BALLS	**STOLEN BASES**	**BASE STEALING RUNS**	**FIELDING RUNS-INFIELD**	**FIELDING RUNS-OUTFIELD**	**OUTFIELD ASSISTS**	**CATCHER CS PCT.**
Gehrig-NY.............127	Chapman-Was-Bos 35	Chapman-Was-Bos3.5	Clift-StL...............41.3	Johnson-Phi...........9.6	Bell-StL...................22	Dickey-NY............41.8
Greenberg-Det......102	Werber-Phi 35	Werber-Phi 3.2	Hayes-Chi............23.4	West-StL................9.2	DiMaggio-NY 21	Sewell-Chi 40.5
Foxx-Bos.................99	Walker-Det.............23	Walker-Det............2.6	Hale-Cle...............22.4	Almada-Bos-Was...7.5	Solters-Cle.............19	Pytlak-Cle 40.4
Johnson-Phi............98		Hill-Was-Phi...........2.6	Appling-Chi..........16.7	Stone-Was.............7.2	Almada-Bos-Was....17	Brucker-Phi..........36.4
Clift-StL..................98		Kreevich-Chi 1.9	Foxx-Bos.............11.4	Vosmik-StL 7.0	West-StL.................17	R.Ferrell-Bos-Was ...36.1
WINS	**WINNING PCT.**	**WINS ABOVE TEAM**	**GAMES STARTED**	**COMPLETE GAMES**	**FEWEST HITS/GAME**	**FEWEST BB/GAME**
Gomez-NY..............21	Allen-Cle...............938	Allen-Cle................7.0	Newsom-Was-Bos..37	W.Ferrell-Bos-Was......26	Gomez-NY...........7.53	Stratton-Chi 2.02
Ruffing-NY..............20	Stratton-Chi 750	Lawson-Det 4.7	W.Ferrell-Bos-Was......35	Gomez-NY..............25	Stratton-Chi 7.76	Hudlin-Cle............2.20
Lawson-Det 18	Ruffing-NY............741	Stratton-Chi 4.7	Gomez-NY..............34	Ruffing-NY..............22	Smith-Phi.............8.15	Marcum-Bos 2.30
Grove-Bos...............17	Lawson-Det 720	Grove-Bos..............4.0	DeShong-Was 34	Grove-Bos...............21	Allen-Cle..............8.17	Ruffing-NY...........2.39
Auker-Det...............17	Gomez-NY............656	Ruffing-NY 3.6	Caster-Phi...............33	DeShong-Was 20	Ruffing-NY...........8.50	Lyons-Chi.............2.39
STRIKEOUTS	**STRIKEOUTS/GAME**	**GAMES**	**SAVES**	**BASE RUNNERS/9**	**ADJUSTED RELIEF RUNS**	**RELIEF RANKING**
Gomez-NY............194	Gomez-NY...........6.27	Brown-Chi...............53	Brown-Chi...............18	Stratton-Chi 9.89	Brown-Chi............12.0	Brown-Chi............20.0
Newsom-Was-Bos 166	Wilson-Bos 5.57	Wilson-Bos 51	Murphy-NY 10	Gomez-NY.........10.57	Fink-Phi 5.7	Murphy-NY 6.6
Grove-Bos.............153	Newsom-Was-Bos...5.43	Newsom-Was-Bos..41	Wilson-Bos 7	Ruffing-NY.........10.92	Cohen-Was............5.1	Cohen-Was............5.8
Feller-Cle 150	Grove-Bos............5.26	Kelley-Phi...............41	Malone-NY...............6	Chandler-NY......10.93	Murphy-NY 4.1	Fink-Phi 2.8
Bridges-Det...........138	Bridges-Det..........5.06	Heving-Cle.............40		Allen-Cle...........11.55	Wyatt-Cle..............2.9	Wyatt-Cle...............1.8
INNINGS PITCHED	**OPPONENTS' AVG.**	**OPPONENTS' OBP**	**EARNED RUN AVERAGE**	**ADJUSTED ERA**	**ADJUSTED STARTER RUNS**	**PITCHER WINS**
W.Ferrell-Bos-Was.281.0	Gomez-NY............223	Stratton-Chi 280	Gomez-NY...........2.33	Stratton-Chi 191	Gomez-NY...........66.9	**Gomez-NY 6.8**
Gomez-NY.........278.1	Stratton-Chi 234	Gomez-NY...........287	Stratton-Chi 2.40	Gomez-NY............191	Grove-Bos............48.5	**Stratton-Chi 4.3**
Newsom-Was-Bos 275.1	Smith-Phi 242	Ruffing-NY 296	Allen-Cle.............2.55	Allen-Cle...............181	Ruffing-NY 43.2	**Ruffing-NY..........4.0**
DeShong-Was ...264.1	Allen-Cle...............244	Lee-Chi.................312	Ruffing-NY...........2.98	Grove-Bos............157	Allen-Cle.............40.3	**Grove-Bos...........3.9**
Grove-Bos.........262.0	Ruffing-NY 247	Allen-Cle..............313	Grove-Bos............3.02	Ruffing-NY............149	Stratton-Chi 38.8	**Allen-Cle............2.7**

Goofy, Joe D., and Another Title

New York broke from the pack in June and coasted to another easy pennant. Despite excellent defense and the bats of Charlie Gehringer and Hank Greenberg, Detroit didn't have the firepower to contend with the Yankees. New York had the three top run scorers, three of the top four RBI men, and the league's best pitchers in Lefty Gomez and Red Ruffing. The multi-dimensional Joe DiMaggio had become the league's gem, and Lou Gehrig enjoyed his last great season. The Yankees also added two rookies, pitcher Spud Chandler and outfielder Tommy Henrich.

Attendance rose in every AL city but Boston; ironically, the Red Sox had their best year since 1918. Finishing 80-72, they added their first real homegrown star, second baseman Bobby Doerr. Detroit once again drew a million fans, and the league's overall turnstile clicks were the most in over a decade.

While overall runs fell by 500, AL hitters established another new record for homers. Hitters were both walking and striking out more than ever as the uppercut swing became better established. Cleveland's Johnny Allen set an all-time single-season record for winning percentage at .938, while the last-place Browns had a staff ERA over 6.00 for the second straight year. They'd once again reach that low in 1939.

The White Sox enlarged Comiskey Park, which significantly cut scoring, but Detroit shrunk its left field, which increased run production. Yankee Stadium's formerly cavernous center field was cut from 26 feet to a still huge 461 feet, and scoring there *increased* slightly.

The Yankees again wiped the floor with the Giants in the World Series. After three easy wins by the Yankees, the Giants staved off elimination in Game 4 behind Carl Hubbell, 7-2. Goofy Gomez shut down the Giants in Game 5 and also drove in the winning run.

1936 NATIONAL LEAGUE

TEAM	W	L	T	PCT	GB	HW	HL	R	OR	PA	H	2B	3B	HR	BB	SO	HB	SH	AVG	OBP	SLG	OPS	AOPS	BR	ABR	PF	SB	CS	BSA	BSR
NY	92	62	0	.597	—	**52**	26	742	621	6038	1529	237	48	97	431	**452**	**35**	123	.281	.337	.395	732	104	18	26	99	31			
StL	87	67	1	.565	5	43	33	795	794	6065	1554	**332**	60	88	442	577	15	71	.281	.336	**.410**	**746**	**106**	44	**47**	100	**69**			
Chi	87	67	0	.565	5	50	27	755	**603**	6069	1545	275	36	76	491	462	32	**137**	**.286**	**.349**	.392	741	104	48	31	102	68			
Pit	84	70	2	.545	8	46	30	**804**	718	6211	**1596**	283	**80**	60	**517**	502	26	82	**.286**	**.349**	.397	**746**	105	**57**	39	102	37			
Cin	74	80	0	.481	18	42	34	722	760	5904	1476	224	73	82	410	584	34	67	.274	.329	.388	717	**106**	-18	29	94	68			
Bos	71	83	3	.461	21	35	43	631	715	6041	1450	207	45	67	433	582	31	99	.265	.322	.356	678	94	-90	-46	94	23			
Bro	67	87	2	.435	25	37	40	662	752	6068	1518	263	43	33	390	458	25	79	.272	.323	.353	676	87	-93	-99	101	55			
Phi	54	100	0	.351	38	30	48	726	874	6040	1538	250	46	**103**	451	586	21	103	.281	.339	.401	740	95	32	-37	110	50			
Total	620	—	—	—	—	335	281	5837	—	48436	12206	2071	431	606	3565	4203	219	761	.278	.335	.386	722	—	—	—	—	401	—	—	—

TEAM	CG	SHO	GR	SV	IP	H	HR	BB	SO	BR/9	ERA	AERA	OAV	OOB	PR	APR	PF	OSB	OCS	FA	E	WPB	DP	FW	PW	BW	BSW	DIF
NY	60	12	148	22	1385.2	1458	75	401	500	12.2	**3.46**	**113**	.273	.327	**86**	**69**	97	40	***48***	.974	168	34	164	1.1	**6.7**	2.5	—	4.6
StL	65	5	166	**24**	1398.0	1610	89	434	559	13.4	4.47	88	.289	.344	-71	-85	98	41	*39*	.974	156	50	134	1.9	-8.3	**4.6**	—	11.9
Chi	**77**	**18**	139	10	1382.1	**1413**	77	434	597	12.2	3.54	**113**	**.265**	.324	74	**69**	99	39	*46*	**.976**	**146**	34	156	**2.4**	**6.7**	3.0	—	-2.1
Pit	67	5	137	12	1395.1	1475	74	**379**	559	**12.1**	3.89	104	.269	**.319**	20	25	101	68	*44*	.967	199	31	113	-.5	2.4	3.8	—	1.3
Cin	50	6	161	23	1367.1	1576	**51**	418	459	13.3	4.22	91	.287	.341	-31	-64	95	48	*46*	.969	191	46	150	-.2	-6.2	2.8	—	.6
Bos	61	7	134	13	1413.1	1566	69	451	421	13.0	3.94	97	.281	.337	12	-18	95	**38**	*43*	.971	189	**26**	**175**	.1	-1.8	-4.5	—	.1
Bro	59	7	**169**	18	1403.0	1466	84	528	**651**	13.0	3.98	104	.266	.333	5	21	103	76	*47*	.966	208	43	107	-1.0	2.0	-9.7	—	-1.4
Phi	51	7	**169**	14	1365.1	1630	87	515	454	14.4	4.64	98	.292	.356	-95	-15	113	51	*33*	.959	252	33	144	-3.7	-1.5	-3.6	—	-14.3
Total	490	67	1223	136	11110.1	—	—	—	—	12.9	4.02	—	.278	.335	—	—	—	—	—	.969	1509	297	1143	—	—	—	—	—

BATTER-FIELDER WINS	BATTING AVERAGE	ON-BASE PERCENTAGE	SLUGGING AVERAGE	ON-BASE PLUS SLUGGING	ADJUSTED OPS	ADJUSTED BATTER RUNS
Bartell-NY 5.7	P.Waner-Pit .373	Vaughan-Pit .453	Ott-NY .588	Ott-NY 1036	Ott-NY 179	Ott-NY 65.1
Medwick-StL 5.2	Phelps-Bro .367	Ott-NY .448	Camilli-Phi .577	Camilli-Phi 1018	Medwick-StL 157	P.Waner-Pit 50.7
Herman-Chi 5.2	Medwick-StL .351	P.Waner-Pit .446	Mize-StL .577	P.Waner-Pit 965	Camilli-Phi 156	Medwick-StL 49.1
Ott-NY 4.8	Demaree-Chi .350	Camilli-Phi .441	Medwick-StL .577	Medwick-StL 964	P.Waner-Pit 156	Camilli-Phi 46.7
P.Waner-Pit 4.7	Vaughan-Pit .335	Suhr-Pit .410	P.Waner-Pit .520	Vaughan-Pit 927	Vaughan-Pit 146	Vaughan-Pit 45.7

RUNS	HITS	DOUBLES	TRIPLES	HOME RUNS	TOTAL BASES	RUNS BATTED IN
Vaughan-Pit 122	Medwick-StL 223	Medwick-StL 64	Goodman-Cin 14	Ott-NY 33	Medwick-StL 367	Medwick-StL 138
P.Martin-StL 121	P.Waner-Pit 218	Herman-Chi 57	Medwick-StL 13	Camilli-Phi 28	Ott-NY 314	Ott-NY 135
Ott-NY 120	Demaree-Chi 212	P.Waner-Pit 53	Camilli-Phi 13	Klein-Chi-Phi 25	Klein-Chi-Phi 308	Suhr-Pit 118
Medwick-StL 115	Herman-Chi 211	Moore-StL 39		Berger-Bos 25	Camilli-Phi 306	Klein-Chi-Phi 104
Suhr-Pit 111	Moore-NY 205	Moore-Bos 38		Mize-StL 19	P.Waner-Pit 304	

BASES ON BALLS	STOLEN BASES	BASE STEALING RUNS	FIELDING RUNS-INFIELD	FIELDING RUNS-OUTFIELD	OUTFIELD ASSISTS	CATCHER CS PCT.
Vaughan-Pit 118	P.Martin-StL 23		Bartell-NY 42.6	Medwick-StL 14.0	Moore-Bos 32	Mancuso-NY 56.4
Camilli-Phi 116	S.Martin-StL 17		Whitehead-NY 32.1	Moore-Bos 13.1	Moore-NY 25	Hartnett-Chi 52.6
Ott-NY 111	Hack-Chi 17		Kampouris-Cin 22.4	Moore-StL 13.0	Ott-NY 20	Padden-Pit 46.0
Suhr-Pit 95	Chiozza-Phi 17		Cuccinello-Bos 17.6	Cooney-Bro 8.5		Ogrodowski-StL 44.8
Hack-Chi 89			Herman-Chi 17.0	Moore-NY 8.3		Lombardi-Cin 44.0

WINS	WINNING PCT.	WINS ABOVE TEAM	GAMES STARTED	COMPLETE GAMES	FEWEST HITS/GAME	FEWEST BB/GAME
Hubbell-NY 26	Hubbell-NY .813	Hubbell-NY 9.5	Mungo-Bro 37	D.Dean-StL 28	Hubbell-NY 7.85	Lucas-Pit 1.33
D.Dean-StL 24	Lucas-Pit .789	Lucas-Pit 5.4	Derringer-Cin 37	Hubbell-NY 25	Mungo-Bro 7.94	Derringer-Cin 1.34
Derringer-Cin 19	French-Chi .667	D.Dean-StL 4.4	Hubbell-NY 34	Mungo-Bro 22	Lee-Chi 8.28	D.Dean-StL 1.51
	D.Dean-StL .649	French-Chi 3.6	D.Dean-StL 34	MacFayden-Bos 21	D.Dean-StL 8.86	Hubbell-NY 1.69
	Lee-Chi .621	MacFayden-Bos 3.5		Lee-Chi 20	Blanton-Pit 8.97	Gabler-NY 1.89

STRIKEOUTS	STRIKEOUTS/GAME	GAMES	SAVES	BASE RUNNERS/9	ADJUSTED RELIEF RUNS	RELIEF RANKING
Mungo-Bro 238	Mungo-Bro 6.87	Derringer-Cin 51	D.Dean-StL 11	Hubbell-NY 9.68	Johnson-Phi 4.6	Johnson-Phi 5.1
D.Dean-StL 195	D.Dean-StL 5.57	D.Dean-StL 51	Brennan-Cin 9	D.Dean-StL 10.46	Bryant-Chi 3.6	Bryant-Chi 1.8
Blanton-Pit 127	Blanton-Pit 4.85	Passeau-Phi 49	Smith-Bos 8	Lucas-Pit 10.61	Root-Chi 3	Root-Chi 3
Hubbell-NY 123	Weaver-Pit 4.31	Brown-Pit 47	Johnson-Phi 7	Hoyt-Pit 10.65		
Derringer-Cin 121	Warneke-Chi 4.23		Coffman-NY 7	Blanton-Pit 11.19		

INNINGS PITCHED	OPPONENTS' AVG.	OPPONENTS' OBP	EARNED RUN AVERAGE	ADJUSTED ERA	ADJUSTED STARTER RUNS	PITCHER WINS
D.Dean-StL 315.0	Mungo-Bro .234	Hubbell-NY .276	Hubbell-NY 2.31	Hubbell-NY 169	Hubbell-NY 59.6	**Hubbell-NY 6.2**
Mungo-Bro 311.2	Hubbell-NY .236	D.Dean-StL .285	MacFayden-Bos 2.87	MacFayden-Bos 134	MacFayden-Bos 30.4	**D.Dean-StL 3.0**
Hubbell-NY 304.0	Lee-Chi .246	Lucas-Pit .287	Gabler-NY 3.12	Passeau-Phi 130	Mungo-Bro 27.6	**MacFayden-Bos 2.8**
Derringer-Cin 282.1	D.Dean-StL .253	Blanton-Pit .301	D.Dean-StL 3.17	Lucas-Pit 128	D.Dean-StL 26.9	**Mungo-Bro 2.7**
MacFayden-Bos 266.2	Blanton-Pit .257	Mungo-Bro .305	Lucas-Pit 3.18	Gabler-NY 125	Lee-Chi 19.3	**Passeau-Phi 2.4**

King Carl Reigns

After two years of late-season collapses, it was the Giants' turn to make a big run down the stretch. Tied for fourth place with a .500 record in mid-July, the Giants went on a 34-5 tear, moving from 10½ down to 3 up by the end of August. New York held on for dear life in September to claim the pennant.

The Giants rode to the flag on the left arm of King Carl Hubbell, who won his last 15 decisions, paced the league in ERA by more than half a run, and garnered league MVP honors. Seven Giants pitchers made 10 or more starts as manager Bill Terry searched for rotation depth. Shortstop Dick Bartell had a big year in the field and at bat, while Mel Ott led the league in homers for third of his six times. Three Giants of classic vintage—Travis Jackson, Freddie Lindstrom, and Terry—played in their last big league games.

While the second-place Cubs had excellent and very deep starting pitching, their attack was poor. Charlie Grimm ended his 20-year playing career as a player, but Jolly Cholly, the 1935 pennant still under his belt, remained as manager in his first of three stints at the helm of the Cubbies. Joe Medwick of the third-place Cardinals led the league in hits, RBIs, and doubles (64, a league record). St. Louis also benefited from the efforts of rookie first baseman Johnny Mize, who hit .329 with 19 homers.

While the Pirates had two great offensive players in Paul Waner, who won his third batting title, and shortstop Arky Vaughan, who paced the NL in on-base percentage for the third straight season. Mediocre pitching doomed the Bucs to fourth.

In the World Series, the thin Giants staff was battered around by the Yankees, who won in six games. Only Hubbell, 1-1 with a 2.25 ERA, escaped relatively unscathed.

1936 AMERICAN LEAGUE

TEAM	W	L	T	PCT	GB	HW	HL	R	OR	PA	H	2B	3B	HR	BB	SO	HB	SH	AVG	OBP	SLG	OPS	AOPS	BR	ABR	PF	SB	CS	BSA	BSR
NY	102	51	2	.667	—	**56**	21	**1065**	**731**	6391	1676	315	83	**182**	**700**	594	33	67	.300	**.381**	**.483**	**864**	**124**	**164**	**203**	97	77	40	66	3
Det	83	71	0	.539	19.5	44	33	921	871	6226	1638	326	55	94	640	462	**34**	88	.300	.377	.431	808	106	61	58	100	73	49	60	-1
Chi	81	70	2	.536	20	43	32	920	873	6283	1597	282	56	60	684	417	26	107	.292	.374	.397	771	94	-8	-39	104	66	29	69	4
Was	82	71	0	.536	20	42	35	889	799	6094	1601	293	**84**	62	576	**398**	24	61	.295	.365	.414	779	105	-9	42	94	**104**	42	71	**8**
Cle	80	74	3	.519	22.5	49	30	921	862	6253	**1715**	**357**	82	123	514	470	16	77	**.304**	.364	.461	825	109	71	63	101	66	53	55	-4
Bos	74	80	1	.481	28.5	47	29	775	764	6098	1485	288	62	86	584	465	23	**108**	.276	.349	.400	749	86	-73	-116	106	55	44	56	-3
StL	57	95	3	.375	44.5	31	43	804	1064	6107	1502	299	66	79	625	627	19	72	.279	.356	.403	759	91	-51	-73	103	62	20	**76**	7
Phi	53	100	1	.346	49	31	46	714	1045	5990	1443	240	60	72	524	590	19	74	.269	.336	.376	712	84	-156	-142	98	59	43	58	-2
Total	618	—	—	—	—	343	269	7009	—	49442	12657	2400	548	758	4847	4023	194	654	.289	.363	.421	784	—	—	—	—	562	320	64	12

TEAM	CG	SHO	GR	SV	IP	H	HR	BB	SO	BR/9	ERA	AERA	OAV	OOB	PR	APR	PF	OSB	OCS	FA	E	WPB	DP	FW	PW	BW	BSW	DIF
NY	77	6	119	**21**	1400.1	**1474**	84	663	**624**	13.8	**4.17**	112	**.271**	.351	**135**	81	92	**47**	43	.973	163	41	148	.8	7.2	**17.9**	.1	-.5
Det	76	**13**	127	13	1360.0	1568	100	562	526	14.2	5.00	99	.289	.358	6	-7	98	58	30	**.975**	**153**	49	159	**1.3**	-.6	5.1	-.2	.4
Chi	**80**	5	104	8	1365.0	1603	104	578	414	14.5	5.06	103	.293	.363	-4	20	103	58	46	.973	168	43	**174**	.4	1.8	-3.4	.2	6.6
Was	78	8	112	14	1345.2	1484	**73**	588	462	14.0	4.58	104	.279	.353	68	31	95	73	**47**	.970	182	47	163	-.4	2.7	3.7	**.6**	-1.1
Cle	74	6	155	12	1389.1	1604	**73**	607	619	14.5	4.83	104	.289	.362	32	32	100	75	46	.971	178	59	154	.0	2.8	5.6	-.5	-5.0
Bos	78	11	143	9	1372.1	1501	78	**552**	584	**13.6**	4.39	**121**	.277	**.346**	99	**134**	106	81	44	.972	165	**37**	139	.7	**11.8**	-10.2	-.4	-4.9
StL	54	3	**193**	13	1348.1	1776	115	609	399	16.2	6.24	86	.314	.385	-180	-122	107	69	25	.969	188	53	143	-.6	-10.8	-6.4	.5	-1.6
Phi	68	3	130	12	1352.1	1645	131	696	405	15.7	6.08	84	.300	.381	-156	-144	101	101	39	.965	209	91	152	-1.9	-12.7	-12.5	-.3	3.9
Total	585	55	1083	102	10933.1	—	—	—	—	14.6	5.04	—	.289	.363	—	—	—	—	—	.971	1406	420	1232	—	—	—	—	—

BATTER-FIELDER WINS	BATTING AVERAGE	ON-BASE PERCENTAGE	SLUGGING AVERAGE	ON-BASE PLUS SLUGGING	ADJUSTED OPS	ADJUSTED BATTER RUNS
Gehrig-NY...........6.6	Appling-Chi...........388	Gehrig-NY.............478	Gehrig-NY.............696	Gehrig-NY...........1174	Gehrig-NY.............193	Gehrig-NY............90.9
Gehringer-Det....6.1	Averill-Cle.............378	Appling-Chi...........474	Trosky-Cle.............644	Foxx-Bos.............1071	Averill-Cle.............159	Averill-Cle............55.2
Appling-Chi........5.4	Dickey-NY.............362	Foxx-Bos...............440	Foxx-Bos...............631	Averill-Cle...........1065	Foxx-Bos...............153	Foxx-Bos..............49.2
Dickey-NY...........4.2	Gehringer-Det.......354	Averill-Cle.............438	Averill-Cle.............627	Trosky-Cle...........1026	Trosky-Cle.............148	Gehringer-Det......44.4
Averill-Cle..........3.8	Gehrig-NY.............354	Gehringer-Det.......431	Dickey-NY.............617	Gehringer-Det.......987	Stone-Was.............145	Trosky-Cle............40.9

RUNS	HITS	DOUBLES	TRIPLES	HOME RUNS	TOTAL BASES	RUNS BATTED IN
Gehrig-NY.............167	Averill-Cle.............232	Gehringer-Det.........60	Rolfe-NY.................15	Gehrig-NY...............49	Trosky-Cle.............405	Trosky-Cle.............162
Clift-StL.................145	Gehringer-Det.......227	Walker-Det..............55	DiMaggio-NY..........15	Trosky-Cle...............42	Gehrig-NY.............403	Gehrig-NY.............152
Gehringer-Det.......144	Trosky-Cle.............216	Chapman-NY-Was..50	Averill-Cle..............15	Foxx-Bos.................41	Averill-Cle.............385	Foxx-Bos...............143
Crosetti-NY...........137	Bell-StL.................212	Hale-Cle..................50	B.Johnson-Phi........14	DiMaggio-NY..........29	Foxx-Bos...............369	Bonura-Chi............138
Averill-Cle.............136	Radcliff-Chi...........207			Averill-Cle..............28	DiMaggio-NY........367	Solters-StL............134

BASES ON BALLS	STOLEN BASES	BASE STEALING RUNS	FIELDING RUNS-INFIELD	FIELDING RUNS-OUTFIELD	OUTFIELD ASSISTS	CATCHER CS PCT.
Gehrig-NY.............130	Lary-StL..................37	Lary-StL..................5.0	Hale-Cle...............16.7	Solters-StL...........12.5	DiMaggio-NY..........22	Dickey-NY............46.7
Lary-StL.................117	Powell-Was-NY.......26	Hill-Was.................2.4	Gehringer-Det......15.6	Cramer-Bos.........11.4	Cramer-Bos............20	Sewell-Chi............44.6
Clift-StL.................115	Werber-Bos............23	Powell-Was-NY......1.9	Appling-Chi..........14.8	DiMaggio-NY.........8.1	Kreevich-Chi...........17	Bolton-Was...........37.3
Foxx-Bos...............105	Chapman-NY-Was..20	Stone-Was.............1.8	Hayes-Chi............13.4	West-StL................6.4	Solters-StL.............16	Hayworth-Det.......33.3
Lazzeri-NY..............97	Hughes-Cle.............20	Sewell-Chi.............1.7	Bonura-Chi..........11.0	Stone-Was.............5.8	Weatherly-Cle.........15	R.Ferrell-Bos.......30.7

WINS	WINNING PCT.	WINS ABOVE TEAM	GAMES STARTED	COMPLETE GAMES	FEWEST HITS/GAME	FEWEST BB/GAME
Bridges-Det.............23	Pearson-NY..........731	Kennedy-Chi..........6.1	Newsom-Was.........38	W.Ferrell-Bos..........28	Pearson-NY.........7.71	Lyons-Chi.............2.23
Kennedy-Chi...........21	Kennedy-Chi.........700	Bridges-Det............6.0	W.Ferrell-Bos..........38	Bridges-Det.............26	Grove-Bos............8.42	Grove-Bos.............2.31
Ruffing-NY..............20	Bridges-Det...........676	Allen-Cle................5.3	Bridges-Det.............38	Ruffing-NY..............25	Allen-Cle..............8.67	Rowe-Det..............2.35
W.Ferrell-Bos..........20	Allen-Cle...............667	Kelley-Phi...............4.9	Rowe-Det................35	Newsom-Was.........24	Gomez-NY...........8.78	Andrews-StL.........2.35
Allen-Cle.................20	Rowe-Det..............655	Rowe-Det...............4.3	Kennedy-Chi...........34	Grove-Bos...............22	Bridges-Det...........8.83	Marcum-Bos.........2.69

STRIKEOUTS	STRIKEOUTS/GAME	GAMES	SAVES	BASE RUNNERS/9	ADJUSTED RELIEF RUNS	RELIEF RANKING
Bridges-Det............175	Allen-Cle..............6.11	VanAtta-StL............52	Malone-NY.................9	Grove-Bos..........10.87	Brown-Chi..............2.9	Brown-Chi..............2.9
Allen-Cle................165	Bridges-Det..........5.35	Knott-StL.................47	Knott-StL...................6	Walberg-Bos......12.11	Gumpert-Phi.............5	Gumpert-Phi.............2
Newsom-Was.......156	Gomez-NY............5.01		Murphy-NY...............5	Rowe-Det.............12.18		
Grove-Bos.............130	Newsom-Was......4.91		Brown-Chi.................5	Ruffing-NY.........12.19		
Pearson-NY..........118	Pearson-NY.........4.76		Hildebrand-Cle..........4	Allen-Cle............12.30		

INNINGS PITCHED	OPPONENTS' AVG.	OPPONENTS' OBP	EARNED RUN AVERAGE	ADJUSTED ERA	ADJUSTED STARTER RUNS	PITCHER WINS
W.Ferrell-Bos.....301.0	Pearson-NY..........233	Grove-Bos.............297	Grove-Bos............2.81	Grove-Bos.............189	Grove-Bos............67.0	**Grove-Bos...........6.6**
Bridges-Det........294.2	Grove-Bos.............246	Rowe-Det..............321	Allen-Cle..............3.44	Allen-Cle..............146	Allen-Cle.............42.8	**W.Ferrell-Bos.....4.4**
Newsom-Was....285.2	Gomez-NY............254	Ruffing-NY............323	Appleton-Was......3.53	Bridges-Det...........137	Bridges-Det..........42.8	**Allen-Cle.............4.3**
Kennedy-Chi......274.1	Appleton-Was.......254	Appleton-Was.......324	Bridges-Det..........3.60	Appleton-Was.......135	W.Ferrell-Bos.......35.7	**Bridges-Det........4.2**
Ruffing-NY.........271.0	Bridges-Det...........255	Bridges-Det...........326	Pearson-NY.........3.71	Kelley-Phi..............132	Kelley-Phi............33.6	**Ruffing-NY..........3.9**

The Dominators

The defending world champion Tigers stumbled out of the gate when first baseman Hank Greenberg broke his wrist in April and was lost for the year. The loss a few weeks later of catcher Mickey Cochrane to an emotional breakdown shot the club's chances.

That was enough to clear the way for the Yankees, who led the league in runs by 140 and fewest runs allowed by 33. Seven New Yorkers reached double figures in homers, while six hurlers won in double figures. After a brief challenge from Boston, which had imported stars like Jimmie Foxx and Joe Cronin, New York widened the gap and eventually won by $19^1/_2$ games. The Red Sox were sixth.

League hitters continued their feast, setting new records for home runs and scoring. The 5.67 runs tallied by the average AL team has never been equaled, much less surpassed. For the first time, no club had an ERA under 4.00, and Lefty Grove—working in the unfriendly atmosphere of Fenway Park—was the only pitcher to record an ERA under 3.44. St. Louis and Philadelphia each posted ERAs over 6.00.

Fans saw the future of baseball as two of the greats in history, Joe DiMaggio and Bob Feller, debuted in 1936. DiMaggio, already famous for his exploits in the Pacific Coast League, hit .323 with 88 extra-base hits, tying for the lead in triples with Yankees teammate Red Rolfe. Feller, just 17, fanned 76 men in just 62 innings with Cleveland. Baseball began to officially celebrate its history in 1936, electing five players to the newly created Hall of Fame in Cooperstown, New York. Three of the five were AL stalwarts: Ty Cobb, Babe Ruth, and Walter Johnson.

The World Series went six games, with the Yankees defeating the Giants. Five of the games were close, but in the late innings, the Bronx Bombers and their unstoppable attack were able to salt things away.

1935 NATIONAL LEAGUE

TEAM	W	L	T	PCT	GB	HW	HL	R	OR	PA	H	2B	3B	HR	BB	SO	HB	SH	AVG	OBP	SLG	OPS	AOPS	BR	ABR	PF	SB	CS	BSA	BSR
Chi	100	54	0	.649	—	**56**	21	**847**	**597**	6133	1581	**303**	62	88	**464**	471	**33**	**150**	**.288**	**.347**	.414	**761**	**110**	**86**	**81**	101	66			
StL	96	58	0	.623	4	53	24	829	625	5977	1548	286	59	86	404	521	19	97	.284	.335	.405	740	101	35	6	104	71			
NY	91	62	3	.595	8.5	50	27	770	675	6163	**1608**	248	56	**123**	392	479	32	116	.286	.336	**.416**	752	**110**	53	68	98	32			
Pit	86	67	0	.562	13.5	46	31	743	647	5973	1543	255	**90**	66	457	437	24	77	.285	.343	.402	745	103	48	24	103	30			
Bro	70	83	1	.458	29.5	38	38	711	767	5937	1496	235	62	59	430	520	27	70	.277	.333	.376	709	99	-23	-7	98	60			
Cin	68	85	1	.444	31.5	41	35	646	772	5798	1403	244	68	73	392	547	30	80	.265	.319	.378	697	96	-53	-32	97	**72**			
Phi	64	89	3	.418	35.5	35	43	685	871	5944	1466	249	32	92	392	661	26	84	.269	.322	.378	700	85	-47	-109	110	52			
Bos	38	115	0	.248	61.5	25	50	575	852	5761	1396	233	33	75	353	**436**	19	80	.263	.311	.362	673	93	-99	-47	92	20			
Total	617	—	—	—	—	344	269	5806	—	47686	12041	2053	462	662	3284	4072	210	754	.277	.331	.391	722	—	—	—	—	403	—	—	—

TEAM	CG	SHO	GR	SV	IP	H	HR	BB	SO	BR/9	ERA	AERA	OAV	OOB	PR	APR	PF	OSB	OCS	FA	E	WPB	DP	FW	PW	BW	BSW	DIF
Chi	**81**	12	118	14	1394.1	**1417**	85	400	589	11.9	**3.26**	**121**	.263	.317	**118**	**106**	98	45	***54***	.970	186	45	**163**	.3	**10.3**	**7.9**	—	4.5
StL	73	10	139	18	1384.2	1445	68	377	**602**	12.0	3.52	116	.267	.318	76	87	102	43	*12*	**.972**	**164**	34	133	**1.6**	8.5	.6	—	8.4
NY	76	10	134	11	1403.2	1433	106	411	524	12.0	3.78	102	**.262**	.318	37	12	96	46	*40*	**.972**	174	46	129	1.1	1.2	6.6	—	5.6
Pit	76	**15**	118	11	1365.2	1428	**63**	**312**	549	**11.6**	3.42	120	.265	**.307**	91	101	102	64	*41*	.968	190	34	94	.0	9.8	2.3	—	-2.7
Bro	62	11	145	**20**	1358.0	1519	88	436	480	13.1	4.22	94	.281	.337	-31	-37	99	**42**	*44*	.969	188	49	146	.2	-3.6	-.7	—	-2.4
Cin	59	9	161	12	1356.0	1490	65	438	500	13.0	4.30	93	.278	.336	-43	-50	99	52	*50*	.966	204	40	139	-.7	-4.9	-3.1	—	.2
Phi	53	8	**202**	15	1374.2	1652	106	505	475	14.4	4.76	95	.295	.358	-113	-31	113	50	*34*	.963	228	28	145	-2.0	-3.0	-10.6	—	3.1
Bos	54	6	136	5	1330.0	1645	81	404	355	14.0	4.93	77	.303	.354	-135	-180	94	61	*33*	.967	197	**21**	101	-.4	-17.5	-4.6	—	-16.0
Total	534	81	1153	106	10967.0	—	—	—	—	12.7	4.02	—	.277	.331	—	—	—	—	—	.968	1531	297	1050	—	—	—	—	—

BATTER-FIELDER WINS	BATTING AVERAGE	ON-BASE PERCENTAGE	SLUGGING AVERAGE	ON-BASE PLUS SLUGGING	ADJUSTED OPS	ADJUSTED BATTER RUNS
Vaughan-Pit 6.6	Vaughan-Pit..........385	Vaughan-Pit..........491	Vaughan-Pit..........607	Vaughan-Pit........1098	Vaughan-Pit..........187	Vaughan-Pit.........69.2
Herman-Chi........ 5.2	Medwick-StL.........353	Ott-NY..................407	Medwick-StL.........576	Medwick-StL.........962	Ott-NY...................159	Ott-NY..................51.1
Hartnett-Chi....... 4.7	Hartnett-Chi.........344	Hack-Chi..............406	Ott-NY..................555	Ott-NY...................962	Berger-Bos...........151	Medwick-StL........41.6
Berger-Bos......... 4.4	Lombardi-Cin........343	Galan-Chi.............399	Berger-Bos...........548	R.Collins-StL.........915	Medwick-StL.........149	Berger-Bos..........40.3
Ott-NY................ 4.2	Herman-Chi.........341	P.Waner-Pit..........392	Hartnett-Chi..........545	Berger-Bos...........903	Leiber-NY............143	Leiber-NY............37.4

RUNS	HITS	DOUBLES	TRIPLES	HOME RUNS	TOTAL BASES	RUNS BATTED IN
Galan-Chi............133	Herman-Chi..........227	Herman-Chi...........57	Goodman-Cin.........18	Berger-Bos............34	Medwick-StL.........365	Berger-Bos...........130
Medwick-StL.........132	Medwick-StL.........224	Medwick-StL...........46	L.Waner-Pit............14	Ott-NY....................31	Ott-NY..................329	Medwick-StL.........126
Martin-StL............121		Allen-Phi................46	Medwick-StL...........13	Camilli-Phi.............25	Berger-Bos...........323	R.Collins-StL.........122
Ott-NY..................113		Martin-StL..............41		Medwick-StL...........23	Herman-Chi..........317	Ott-NY..................114
Herman-Chi.........113		Galan-Chi...............41		R.Collins-StL...........23	Leiber-NY............314	Leiber-NY............107

BASES ON BALLS	STOLEN BASES	BASE STEALING RUNS	FIELDING RUNS-INFIELD	FIELDING RUNS-OUTFIELD	OUTFIELD ASSISTS	CATCHER CS PCT.
Vaughan-Pit...........97	Galan-Chi..............22		Jurges-Chi..........24.9	Allen-Phi.............12.7	Allen-Phi................26	Hartnett-Chi.........53.8
Galan-Chi..............87	Martin-StL..............20		Herman-Chi.........16.0	Berger-Bos............9.2	Watkins-Phi............18	Mancuso-NY........47.8
Ott-NY...................82	Bordagaray-Bro......18		Cuccinello-Bro.......8.1	T.Moore-StL...........6.8	J.Moore-Phi............18	Lopez-Bro............47.4
Suhr-Pit.................70	Hack-Chi................14		Riggs-Cin...............8.1	Lee-Bos..................6.1	Boyle-Bro...............18	Lombardi-Cin.......45.8
Frey-Bro.................66	Goodman-Cin.........14		Stripp-Bro..............7.1	Goodman-Cin........5.1		Padden-Pit...........44.9

WINS	WINNING PCT.	WINS ABOVE TEAM	GAMES STARTED	COMPLETE GAMES	FEWEST HITS/GAME	FEWEST BB/GAME
D.Dean-StL............28	Lee-Chi.................769	Derringer-Cin.........6.8	D.Dean-StL............36	D.Dean-StL............29	Blanton-Pit..........7.79	Clark-Bro.............1.22
Hubbell-NY............23	Castleman-NY......714	D.Dean-StL............5.1	Hubbell-NY............35	Hubbell-NY............24	Schumacher-NY..8.08	Hubbell-NY..........1.46
Derringer-Cin.........22	D.Dean-StL...........700	Lee-Chi..................5.0	Schumacher-NY.....33	Blanton-Pit............23	Parmelee-NY.......8.52	Hoyt-Pit................1.48
Warneke-Chi..........20	Schumacher-NY...679	Mungo-Bro............4.3	Derringer-Cin.........33	Warneke-Chi..........20	Swift-Pit..............8.53	Derringer-Cin.......1.59
Lee-Chi..................20	Hubbell-NY..........657	Davis-Phi..............3.5	P.Dean-StL.............33	Derringer-Cin.........20	Hollingsworth-Cin...8.57	Johnson-Phi.........1.60

STRIKEOUTS	STRIKEOUTS/GAME	GAMES	SAVES	BASE RUNNERS/9	ADJUSTED RELIEF RUNS	RELIEF RANKING
D.Dean-StL...........190	Mungo-Bro..........6.00	Jorgens-Phi...........53	Leonard-Bro.............8	Blanton-Pit..........9.80		
Hubbell-NY...........150	D.Dean-StL..........5.26	D.Dean-StL............50	Johnson-Phi.............6	Swift-Pit............10.21		
Mungo-Bro...........143	Blanton-Pit...........5.02	Bivin-Phi................47	Hoyt-Pit...................6	Clark-Bro...........10.61		
P.Dean-StL...........143	P.Dean-StL..........4.77	Smith-Bos..............46		Warneke-Chi......10.66		
Blanton-Pit...........142	Hollingsworth-Cin...4.62	P.Dean-StL.............46		Schumacher-NY 10.66		

INNINGS PITCHED	OPPONENTS' AVG.	OPPONENTS' OBP	EARNED RUN AVERAGE	ADJUSTED ERA	ADJUSTED STARTER RUNS	PITCHER WINS
D.Dean-StL........325.1	Blanton-Pit...........229	Blanton-Pit...........272	Blanton-Pit..........2.58	Blanton-Pit...........159	Blanton-Pit..........41.3	**D.Dean-StL......... 4.5**
Hubbell-NY........302.2	Schumacher-NY...238	Swift-Pit...............282	Swift-Pit..............2.70	Swift-Pit...............152	D.Dean-StL..........37.8	**Blanton-Pit......... 4.4**
Derringer-Cin.....276.2	Hollingsworth-Cin....243	Clark-Bro..............289	Schumacher-NY..2.89	D.Dean-StL...........135	Swift-Pit..............31.2	**Swift-Pit.............. 3.3**
P.Dean-StL.........269.2	Swift-Pit...............247	Schumacher-NY...292	French-Chi...........2.96	Schumacher-NY...133	French-Chi...........27.9	**Warneke-Chi...... 3.3**
	P.Dean-StL...........249	P.Dean-StL...........292	Lee-Chi................2.96	French-Chi...........133	Schumacher-NY..27.5	**Schumacher-NY 3.2**

And There Was Light

Once again, the Giants started fast but flattened; by August, the dangerous Cardinals took over the league lead. But the Cubs had a surprise in store. In third place on Labor Day, Chicago captured 21 straight and won the pennant by besting Dizzy and Paul Dean in St. Louis September 25-26. Lon Warneke and Bill Lee won 20 apiece for Chicago, which led the league in both runs and ERA.

Other than Joe Medwick and Ripper Collins, St. Louis lacked offense, despite playing in a hitter's park. Chicago had a great defensive infield and topped the loop in walks and doubles. Third-place New York had Carl Hubbell and Mel Ott, but lacked depth. On the other side of the world, the Boston Braves were the NL's worst team ever, declining 40 games from their previous year's performance. Even a cameo by Babe Ruth couldn't save a team that posted just one good position player, outfielder Wally Berger.

The majors' first night game took place at Cincinnati on May 24. The Reds played 8 night games in 1935, and the excitement helped to raise team attendance 117 percent. Other clubs with poor gates noted Cincinnati's success and planned accordingly. League attendance rose 14 percent and would continue to increase throughout the decade.

Dodgers outfielder Len Koenecke, fifth in the NL in on-base percentage in 1934, had a mediocre season. On September 17 he became violent on a plane after being sent to the minors. When he assaulted a pilot, he was beaten to death with a fire extinguisher. Three longtime stars played their final games. Complications from a broken leg shut down shortstop Rabbit Maranville, while pitchers Dolf Luque and Dazzy Vance made their last appearances.

The Cubs outhomered the Tigers in the World Series, 5-1, but the 25 walks issued by Chicago made the difference in a tight six-game affair. Although Warneke won twice, the Cubs were left standing on the field—as they had been in 1929—to watch a foe celebrate a bottom-of-the-ninth clincher.

1935 AMERICAN LEAGUE

TEAM	W	L	T	PCT	GB	HW	HL	R	OR	PA	H	2B	3B	HR	BB	SO	HB	SH	AVG	OBP	SLG	OPS	AOPS	BR	ABR	PF	SB	CS	BSA	BSR
Det	93	58	1	.616	—	**53**	25	**919**	665	6179	1573	301	83	106	**627**	456	19	110	**.290**	**.366**	**.435**	**801**	**116**	**97**	**129**	97	70	45	61	0
NY	89	60	0	.597	3	41	33	818	**632**	5917	1462	255	70	104	604	469	28	71	.280	.358	.416	774	111	42	89	94	68	46	60	-1
Cle	82	71	3	.536	12	48	29	776	739	6099	1573	**324**	77	93	460	567	17	88	.284	.341	.421	762	100	3	-11	102	63	54	54	-5
Bos	78	75	1	.510	16	41	37	718	732	6055	1458	281	63	69	609	470	21	**137**	.276	.353	.392	745	92	-9	-57	107	**91**	59	61	-1
Chi	74	78	1	.487	19.5	42	34	738	750	6025	1460	262	42	74	580	**405**	19	112	.275	.348	.382	730	92	-40	-58	103	46	28	62	0
Was	67	86	1	.438	27	37	39	823	903	6299	**1591**	255	**95**	32	596	406	**37**	74	.285	.357	.381	738	99	-22	5	97	54	37	59	-1
StL	65	87	3	.428	28.5	31	44	718	930	6088	1446	291	51	73	593	561	14	116	.270	.344	.384	728	90	-47	-79	105	45	25	**64**	**1**
Phi	58	91	0	.389	34	30	42	710	869	5847	1470	243	44	**112**	475	602	17	86	.279	.341	.406	747	99	-25	-19	99	43	35	55	-3
Total	611	—	—	—	—	323	283	6220	—	48509	12033	2212	525	663	4544	3936	172	794	.280	.351	.402	753	—	—	—	—	480	329	59	-10

TEAM	CG	SHO	GR	SV	IP	H	HR	BB	SO	BR/9	ERA	AERA	OAV	OOB	PR	APR	PF	OSB	OCS	FA	E	WPB	DP	FW	PW	BW	BSW	DIF
Det	**87**	**16**	95	11	1364.0	1440	78	522	584	13.1	3.82	109	.271	.339	96	57	94	**44**	41	**.978**	**128**	26	154	**2.3**	5.3	**12.1**	.1	-2.3
NY	76	12	120	13	1331.0	**1276**	91	516	**594**	**12.2**	**3.60**	112	**.251**	**.321**	**126**	72	91	**44**	35	.974	151	30	114	.8	6.7	8.3	.0	-1.4
Cle	67	12	138	**21**	1396.0	1527	68	**457**	498	12.9	4.15	108	.278	.335	47	54	101	54	37	.972	177	**24**	147	-.3	5.1	-1.0	-.4	2.1
Bos	82	6	138	11	1376.0	1520	**67**	520	470	13.5	4.05	**117**	.280	.346	62	**100**	107	49	**55**	.969	194	33	136	-1.4	**9.4**	-5.3	.0	-1.2
Chi	80	8	102	8	1360.2	1443	105	574	436	13.5	4.38	106	.272	.346	12	35	104	71	43	.976	146	44	133	1.3	3.3	-5.4	.1	-1.3
Was	67	5	143	12	1378.2	1672	89	613	456	15.1	5.25	82	.302	.374	-122	-146	97	80	34	.972	171	44	**186**	-.0	-13.7	.5	.0	3.7
StL	42	4	**219**	15	1380.1	1667	92	641	435	15.2	5.26	91	.297	.371	-124	-67	108	54	35	.970	187	38	138	-.9	-6.3	-7.4	**.2**	3.4
Phi	58	7	148	10	1326.1	1486	73	704	469	15.0	5.12	89	.285	.372	-97	-83	102	84	49	.968	190	46	150	-1.4	-7.8	-1.8	-.2	-5.3
Total	559	70	1103	101	10913.0	—	—	—	—	13.8	4.46	—	.280	.351	—	—	—	—	—	.972	1344	285	1158	—	—	—	—	—

BATTER-FIELDER WINS	BATTING AVERAGE	ON-BASE PERCENTAGE	SLUGGING AVERAGE	ON-BASE PLUS SLUGGING	ADJUSTED OPS	ADJUSTED BATTER RUNS
Foxx-Phi............5.9	Myer-Was............349	Gehrig-NY............466	Foxx-Phi...............636	Foxx-Phi...............1096	Foxx-Phi...............182	Gehrig-NY............71.7
Myer-Was...........5.3	Vosmik-Cle...........348	Foxx-Phi...............461	Greenberg-Det......628	Gehrig-NY...........1049	Gehrig-NY............180	Foxx-Phi...............70.0
Gehrig-NY..........5.3	Foxx-Phi...............346	Cochrane-Det.......452	Gehrig-NY.............583	Greenberg-Det....1039	Greenberg-Det......171	Greenberg-Det.....63.7
Appling-Chi.......5.1	Cramer-Phi...........332	Myer-Was............440	Vosmik-Cle...........537	Vosmik-Cle...........946	Vosmik-Cle...........140	Myer-Was............41.8
Greenberg-Det...5.0	Gehringer-Det.......330	Appling-Chi..........437	Fox-Det.................513	Gehringer-Det.......911	Myer-Was.............139	Gehringer-Det.....36.8
RUNS	**HITS**	**DOUBLES**	**TRIPLES**	**HOME RUNS**	**TOTAL BASES**	**RUNS BATTED IN**
Gehrig-NY.............125	Vosmik-Cle...........216	Vosmik-Cle.............47	Vosmik-Cle.............20	Greenberg-Det........36	Greenberg-Det......389	Greenberg-Det.......170
Gehringer-Det.......123	Myer-Was.............215	Greenberg-Det........46	Stone-Was..............18	Foxx-Phi..................36	Foxx-Phi...............340	Gehrig-NY.............119
Greenberg-Det......121	Cramer-Phi...........214	Solters-Bos-StL......45	Greenberg-Det........16	Gehrig-NY...............30	Vosmik-Cle...........333	Foxx-Phi.................115
Foxx-Phi.................118	Greenberg-Det......203	Fox-Det...................38	Cronin-Bos..............14	Johnson-Phi............28	Solters-Bos-StL....314	Trosky-Cle.............113
Chapman-NY........118		Chapman-NY..........38	Averill-Cle...............13	Trosky-Cle...............26	Gehrig-NY.............312	Solters-Bos-StL....112
BASES ON BALLS	**STOLEN BASES**	**BASE STEALING RUNS**	**FIELDING RUNS-INFIELD**	**FIELDING RUNS-OUTFIELD**	**OUTFIELD ASSISTS**	**CATCHER CS PCT.**
Gehrig-NY............132	Werber-Bos............29	Lary-Was-StL..........4.8	Appling-Chi...........24.9	Solters-Bos-StL...13.5	Chapman-NY.........25	R.Ferrell-Bos.......53.5
Appling-Chi...........122	Lary-Was-StL.........28	Werber-Bos............3.9	Travis-Was...........19.2	Chapman-NY.......13.4	Almada-Bos...........22	Dickey-NY............44.3
Foxx-Phi.................114	Almada-Bos...........20	Hughes-Cle............1.8	Melillo-StL-Bos....17.0	West-StL.............11.4	R.Johnson-Bos.......21	Cochrane-Det......42.9
Myer-Was.................96	White-Det...............19	Solters-Bos-StL......1.7	Werber-Bos..........13.6	Selkirk-NY.............5.0	Solters-Bos-StL......20	Hemsley-StL.........41.6
Cochrane-Det..........96	Chapman-NY...........17		Berger-Cle...........12.1	Johnson-Phi...........4.1	Johnson-Phi............13	Sewell-Chi...........37.0
WINS	**WINNING PCT.**	**WINS ABOVE TEAM**	**GAMES STARTED**	**COMPLETE GAMES**	**FEWEST HITS/GAME**	**FEWEST BB/GAME**
W.Ferrell-Bos..........25	Auker-Det.............720	W.Ferrell-Bos.........6.4	W.Ferrell-Bos..........38	W.Ferrell-Bos..........31	Allen-NY...............8.03	Harder-Cle...........1.66
Harder-Cle..............22	Broaca-NY............682	Harder-Cle.............5.5	Harder-Cle..............35	Grove-Bos...............23	Ruffing-NY............8.15	Grove-Bos.............2.14
Bridges-Det.............21	Bridges-Det..........677	Marcum-Phi...........5.4	Whitehill-Was..........34	Bridges-Det.............23	Gomez-NY............8.16	Rowe-Det..............2.22
Grove-Bos...............20	Harder-Cle............667	Grove-Bos..............4.5	Rowe-Det.................34	Rowe-Det.................21	Whitehead-Chi.....8.46	Andrews-StL.........2.24
Rowe-Det.................19	Lyons-Chi..............652	Andrews-StL..........4.2	Bridges-Det.............34		Grove-Bos.............8.87	Hudlin-Cle.............2.37
STRIKEOUTS	**STRIKEOUTS/GAME**	**GAMES**	**SAVES**	**BASE RUNNERS/9**	**ADJUSTED RELIEF RUNS**	**RELIEF RANKING**
Bridges-Det...........163	Allen-NY...............6.09	VanAtta-NY-StL.......58	Knott-StL...................7	Grove-Bos...........11.11	L.Brown-Cle.........13.7	L.Brown-Cle.........16.2
Rowe-Det...............140	Bridges-Det..........5.35	Walkup-StL.............55		Rowe-Det............11.17	Hogsett-Det...........6.6	Hogsett-Det...........8.2
Gomez-NY.............138	Gomez-NY............5.05	Andrews-StL...........50		Ruffing-NY..........11.27	DeShong-NY.........6.5	DeShong-NY.........4.9
Grove-Bos..............121	VanAtta-NY-StL....4.63	Thomas-StL............49		Allen-NY.............11.37	Wilson-Bos............3.7	Wilson-Bos............3.8
Allen-NY.................113	Rowe-Det..............4.57	Knott-StL................48		Gomez-NY..........11.38		
INNINGS PITCHED	**OPPONENTS' AVG.**	**OPPONENTS' OBP**	**EARNED RUN AVERAGE**	**ADJUSTED ERA**	**ADJUSTED STARTER RUNS**	**PITCHER WINS**
W.Ferrell-Bos.....322.1	Allen-NY...............238	Rowe-Det..............301	Grove-Bos............2.70	Grove-Bos.............176	Grove-Bos............55.0	**W.Ferrell-Bos.....6.8**
Harder-Cle.........287.1	Ruffing-NY............239	Grove-Bos.............302	Lyons-Chi.............3.02	Lyons-Chi..............153	W.Ferrell-Bos.......41.2	**Grove-Bos...........5.5**
Whitehill-Was.....279.1	Gomez-NY............242	Ruffing-NY............303	Ruffing-NY...........3.12	Harder-Cle............137	Harder-Cle...........38.6	**Ruffing-NY..........4.2**
Rowe-Det...........275.2	Whitehead-Chi......250	Allen-NY...............307	Gomez-NY...........3.18	Andrews-StL.........135	Lyons-Chi.............29.9	**Harder-Cle...........4.1**
Bridges-Det........274.1	Broaca-NY............254	Harder-Cle............307	Harder-Cle...........3.29	W.Ferrell-Bos........135	Andrews-StL.........28.3	**Rowe-Det............3.2**

Tigers Finally Destroy Prey

After a quick start by the White Sox, the AL race became a five-team mess in June. The Yankees tried to pull away, but a hot July propelled the Detroit Tigers into the lead. Detroit kept winning, and despite a late slump held off New York to win its second straight pennant. The Yankees had an excellent strikeout-oriented pitching staff, but couldn't score runs like the Tigers, who had offense from seven lineup spots and boasted four quality starting pitchers. The Tigers' success led to a financial windfall as they became the first AL club to draw one million fans since 1930.

Meanwhile, in St. Louis, the Browns drew just 80,000 fans. This horrible total is partially due to club's playing 19 home doubleheaders. Three times during the 1930s, however, the Brownies pulled in fewer than 100,000 fans for the season. The last team before the Browns to draw less than six figures was the 1917 Senators; when St. Louis drew 93,000 a year later, it marked the last time anyone has gone below six figures. Connie Mack's Athletics, all their talent now distributed through the league, predictably drew 62 percent fewer fans than had come to witness the A's last pennant four years earlier. They would finish either last or seventh every year until 1943.

It was the end of an era as three glory-days Yankees retired. Babe Ruth played his last game not in the Bronx, but for the Boston Braves; center fielder Earle Combs' career was ended by a broken collarbone; and pitcher Sad Sam Jones was done at 43.

The six-game World Series featured three games decided by one-run, with Detroit winning two in its final turn. Game 6, played to 48,420 screaming fans in Detroit, climaxed with Goose Goslin's ninth-inning single scoring Mickey Cochrane for the Series-winning run. It was the Tigers' first world championship in their thirty-five-year history. Tommy Bridges won twice for Detroit, while unheralded outfielder Pete Fox batted .385.

1934 NATIONAL LEAGUE

TEAM	W	L	T	PCT	GB	HW	HL	R	OR	PA	H	2B	3B	HR	BB	SO	HB	SH	AVG	OBP	SLG	OPS	AOPS	BR	ABR	PF	SB	CS	BSA	BSR
StL	95	58	1	.621	—	48	29	**799**	656	5988	**1582**	**294**	75	104	392	535	18	76	**.288**	.337	**.425**	**762**	102	**63**	15	107	**69**			
NY	93	60	0	.608	2	**49**	26	760	**583**	5934	1485	240	41	**126**	406	526	24	**108**	.275	.329	.405	734	105	7	25	98	19			
Chi	86	65	1	.570	8	47	30	705	639	5841	1494	263	44	101	375	630	26	93	.279	.330	.402	732	103	5	20	98	59			
Bos	78	73	1	.517	16	40	35	683	714	5854	1460	233	44	83	375	440	28	81	.272	.323	.378	701	101	-54	-1	93	30			
Pit	74	76	1	.493	19.5	45	32	735	713	5878	1541	281	**77**	52	440	**398**	18	59	.287	.344	.398	742	102	34	17	102	44			
Bro	71	81	1	.467	23.5	43	33	748	795	6074	1526	284	52	79	**548**	555	22	77	.281	**.350**	.396	746	**112**	55	**97**	95	55			
Phi	56	93	0	.376	37	35	36	675	794	5724	1480	286	35	56	398	534	29	79	.284	.338	.384	722	87	0	-81	113	52			
Cin	52	99	1	.344	42	30	47	590	801	5785	1428	227	65	55	313	532	**33**	78	.266	.311	.364	675	88	-111	-97	98	34			
Total	608	—	—	—	—	337	268	5695	—	47078	11996	2108	433	656	3247	4150	198	651	.279	.333	.394	727	—	—	—	—	362	—	—	—

TEAM	CG	SHO	GR	SV	IP	H	HR	BB	SO	BR/9	ERA	AERA	OAV	OOB	PR	APR	PF	OSB	OCS	FA	E	WPB	DP	FW	PW	BW	BSW	DIF
StL	**78**	**15**	146	16	1386.2	1463	77	411	**689**	12.4	3.69	115	.268	.323	58	79	104	41	*32*	.972	166	31	**141**	.3	7.7	1.5	—	9.0
NY	68	13	129	**30**	1370.0	**1384**	75	**351**	499	**11.5**	**3.19**	**121**	**.260**	**.308**	**132**	**107**	95	45	*37*	.972	179	46	**141**	-.5	**10.4**	2.4	—	4.2
Chi	73	11	129	9	1361.1	1432	80	417	633	12.3	3.76	103	.269	.325	46	19	95	37	***48***	**.977**	**137**	45	135	**1.9**	1.9	1.9	—	4.8
Bos	62	12	138	20	1359.2	1512	78	405	462	12.8	4.11	93	.279	.331	-7	-47	94	43	*38*	.972	169	**19**	120	.0	-4.6	-.0	—	7.2
Pit	63	8	159	8	1329.2	1523	78	354	487	12.9	4.20	98	.284	.332	-20	-13	101	66	*-4*	.975	145	22	118	1.4	-1.3	1.7	—	-2.8
Bro	66	6	166	12	1354.1	1540	81	475	520	13.6	4.48	87	.285	.346	-63	-91	96	47	*36*	.970	180	53	**141**	-.6	-8.9	**9.4**	—	-5.0
Phi	52	8	175	15	1297.0	1501	126	437	416	13.6	4.76	99	.288	.347	-101	-3	116	**36**	*32*	.966	197	28	140	-1.8	-.3	-7.9	—	-8.5
Cin	51	3	**182**	19	1347.2	1645	**61**	389	438	13.8	4.37	93	.299	.348	-46	-43	101	47	*37*	.970	181	35	136	-.7	-4.2	-9.4	—	-9.2
Total	513	76	1224	129	10806.1	—	—	—	—	12.9	4.06	—	.279	.333	—	—	—	—	—	.972	1354	279	1072	—	—	—	—	—

BATTER-FIELDER WINS	BATTING AVERAGE	ON-BASE PERCENTAGE	SLUGGING AVERAGE	ON-BASE PLUS SLUGGING	ADJUSTED OPS	ADJUSTED BATTER RUNS
Vaughan-Pit 5.5	P.Waner-Pit...........362	Vaughan-Pit..........431	Collins-StL 615	Collins-StL 1008	Ott-NY...................170	Ott-NY...................59.1
P.Waner-Pit......... 4.3	Terry-NY 354	P.Waner-Pit..........429	Ott-NY...................591	Ott-NY.................1006	Collins-StL 155	P.Waner-Pit..........47.3
Collins-StL.......... 3.7	Cuyler-Chi.............338	Ott-NY...................415	DeLancey-StL.......565	P.Waner-Pit...........968	P.Waner-Pit...........154	Collins-StL 45.7
Ott-NY 3.6	Vaughan-Pit..........333	Terry-NY 414	Berger-Bos 546	Vaughan-Pit..........942	Koenecke-Bro.......152	Vaughan-Pit.........43.1
Hartnett-Chi 3.6	Collins-StL 333	Koenecke-Bro 411	P.Waner-Pit...........539	Koenecke-Bro.......919	Berger-Bos 148	Berger-Bos 38.4

RUNS	HITS	DOUBLES	TRIPLES	HOME RUNS	TOTAL BASES	RUNS BATTED IN
P.Waner-Pit...........122	P.Waner-Pit...........217	Cuyler-Chi..............42	Medwick-StL...........18	Ott-NY.....................35	Collins-StL 369	Ott-NY...................135
Ott-NY...................119	Terry-NY 213	Allen-Phi 42	P.Waner-Pit.............16	Collins-StL 35	Ott-NY...................344	Collins-StL 128
Collins-StL 116	Collins-StL 200	Vaughan-Pit............41	Suhr-Pit...................13	Berger-Bos 34	Berger-Bos 336	Berger-Bos 121
Vaughan-Pit..........115	Medwick-StL.........198	Medwick-StL 40	Collins-StL 12	Hartnett-Chi 22	Medwick-StL.........328	Medwick-StL.........106
Medwick-StL.........110		Collins-StL 40		Klein-Chi.................20	P.Waner-Pit...........323	Suhr-Pit.................103

BASES ON BALLS	STOLEN BASES	BASE STEALING RUNS	FIELDING RUNS-INFIELD	FIELDING RUNS-OUTFIELD	OUTFIELD ASSISTS	CATCHER CS PCT.
Vaughan-Pit............94	Martin-StL...............23		Critz-NY 27.3	K.Davis-StL-Phi ...13.7	Boyle-Bro................20	Hartnett-Chi 55.4
Ott-NY.....................85	Cuyler-Chi...............15		Bartell-Phi............18.4	Allen-Phi 10.6	Allen-Phi 19	Hogan-Bos...........50.0
Koenecke-Bro.........70	Bartell-Phi...............13		Ryan-NY 10.3	Boyle-Bro...............8.6	J.Moore-Cin-Phi......18	Mancuso-NY........48.4
Leslie-Bro 69	Taylor-Bro 12		Jackson-NY 9.6	J.Moore-Cin-Phi.....7.8	P.Waner-Pit.............15	Spohrer-Bos 46.2
P.Waner-Pit.............68			Frey-Bro.................9.5	Thompson-Bos 7.7	Cuyler-Chi...............15	DeLancey-StL......43.8

WINS	WINNING PCT.	WINS ABOVE TEAM	GAMES STARTED	COMPLETE GAMES	FEWEST HITS/GAME	FEWEST BB/GAME
D.Dean-StL.............30	D.Dean-StL 811	D.Dean-StL 10.5	Mungo-Bro..............38	Hubbell-NY 25	Parmelee-NY 7.90	Hubbell-NY 1.06
Schumacher-NY 23	Hoyt-Pit..................714	C.Davis-Phi............5.4	Fitzsimmons-NY 37	D.Dean-StL 24	Hubbell-NY 8.22	Freitas-Cin 1.47
Warneke-Chi...........22	Schumacher-NY ...697	Warneke-Chi..........5.2	Schumacher-NY 36	Warneke-Chi...........23	D.Dean-StL 8.32	Frey-Cin 1.54
Hubbell-NY 21	Warneke-Chi.........688	Hoyt-Pit...................5.0	Warneke-Chi...........35	Mungo-Bro..............22	Warneke-Chi........8.43	Leonard-Bro.........1.62
	Frankhouse-Bos ...654	Schumacher-NY 4.5	Hubbell-NY 35	Brandt-Bos..............20	Mungo-Bro...........8.56	Fitzsimmons-NY ..1.74

STRIKEOUTS	STRIKEOUTS/GAME	GAMES	SAVES	BASE RUNNERS/9	ADJUSTED RELIEF RUNS	RELIEF RANKING
D.Dean-StL 195	P.Dean-StL...........5.79	C.Davis-Phi.............51	Hubbell-NY 8	Hubbell-NY 9.35	Haines-StL.............6.3	Haines-StL.............5.2
Mungo-Bro............184	D.Dean-StL 5.63	Hansen-Phi.............50	Luque-NY 7	S.Johnson-Cin-Phi 10.00	Bell-NY 1.9	Bell-NY 2.6
P.Dean-StL............150	Weaver-Chi..........5.55	D.Dean-StL 50	D.Dean-StL 7	Warneke-Chi......10.53		
Warneke-Chi.........143	Mungo-Bro...........5.25	Hubbell-NY 49	Bell-NY 6	D.Dean-StL 10.66		
Derringer-Cin........122	Malone-Chi 5.23	French-Pit 49		Hoyt-Pit.............10.81		

INNINGS PITCHED	OPPONENTS' AVG.	OPPONENTS' OBP	EARNED RUN AVERAGE	ADJUSTED ERA	ADJUSTED STARTER RUNS	PITCHER WINS
Mungo-Bro.........315.1	Parmelee-NY 238	Hubbell-NY 263	Hubbell-NY 2.30	Hubbell-NY 168	Hubbell-NY 55.5	**D.Dean-StL 6.1**
Hubbell-NY 313.0	Hubbell-NY 239	Warneke-Chi.........287	D.Dean-StL 2.66	C.Davis-Phi...........160	D.Dean-StL 50.6	**Hubbell-NY 5.9**
D.Dean-StL 311.2	D.Dean-StL 241	D.Dean-StL 289	Hoyt-Pit................2.93	D.Dean-StL 159	C.Davis-Phi..........42.8	**C.Davis-Phi......... 5.7**
Schumacher-NY 297.0	Warneke-Chi.........244	P.Dean-StL...........292	C.Davis-Phi..........2.95	Hoyt-Pit.................141	Hoyt-Pit................23.3	**Schumacher-NY 3.3**
Warneke-Chi......291.1	P.Dean-StL...........248	Hoyt-Pit.................296	Fitzsimmons-NY ..3.04	Walker-StL 135	Warneke-Chi........22.9	**Fitzsimmons-NY 3.2**

Dizzy, My Head Is Spinning

Dizzy Dean served notice of his greatness in 1934, becoming the last pitcher to win 30 games until 1968. With Dizzy and rookie brother Paul "Daffy" leading the mound staff, and an attack boasting Joe Medwick and Ripper Collins, St. Louis mounted a thrilling late-season comeback.

The Giants—sparked by Mel Ott and Carl Hubbell, who won 21 and saved 8—took the lead in June, but St. Louis won 33 of its last 45 while New York played .500 ball down the stretch. Dizzy clinched the pennant by shutting out Cincinnati on September 30.

It was a disappointing season for the Giants, who led by seven on September 5, but a great triumph for the "Gashouse Gang" Cardinals and their all-out style of play.

Third-place Chicago debuted Augie Galan, Bill Lee, and Phil Cavaretta, all of whom would contribute in 1935. The Reds finished last for the fourth straight year, but new owner Powel Crosley served notice that he would pay for quality players. Two great New York managers died in 1933. John McGraw succumbed two years after leaving the Giants, while Little Napoleon's one-time pal and longtime adversary Wilbert Robinson passed on three years after departing Brooklyn.

Perhaps the top pitcher of 1934 was Philadelphia rookie Curt Davis, who led the league in appearances and went 19-17 with a seventh-place team playing in the tiny Baker Bowl. Scoring increased by 18 percent, making performances like Davis' less common; only four pitchers had sub-3.00 ERAs.

The World Series was wild and woolly, with a few routs and a few nail biters. In the seventh game, St. Louis blew out Elden Auker en route to an 11-0 shellacking of the Tigers. Pepper Martin, Collins, and Medwick each had 11 hits in the Series, while the Deans—as promised by Dizzy—earned all the wins. The Cardinals' victory was the Senior Circuit's final world title of the decade.

1934 AMERICAN LEAGUE

TEAM	W	L	T	PCT	GB	HW	HL	R	OR	PA	H	2B	3B	HR	BB	SO	HB	SH	AVG	OBP	SLG	OPS	AOPS	BR	ABR	PF	SB	CS	BSA	BSR
Det	101	53	0	.656	—	**54**	26	**958**	708	6239	**1644**	**349**	53	74	639	528	**24**	101	**.300**	**.376**	.424	**800**	113	**119**	117	100	**125**	55	69	8
NY	94	60	0	.610	7	53	24	842	**669**	6177	1494	226	61	135	**700**	597	20	89	.278	.364	.419	783	**117**	69	**133**	93	71	46	61	0
Cle	85	69	0	.552	16	47	31	814	763	6028	1550	340	46	100	526	**433**	19	87	.287	.353	.423	776	105	48	36	102	52	32	62	0
Bos	76	76	1	.500	24	42	35	820	775	6045	1465	287	**70**	51	610	535	11	85	.274	.350	.383	733	90	-27	-77	107	116	47	**71**	**9**
Phi	68	82	3	.453	31	34	40	764	838	5920	1491	236	50	**144**	491	584	13	99	.280	.343	**.425**	768	108	16	46	96	57	35	62	0
StL	67	85	2	.441	33	36	39	674	800	5922	1417	252	59	62	514	631	19	101	.268	.335	.373	708	82	-87	-140	108	43	31	58	-1
Was	66	86	3	.434	34	34	40	729	806	6170	1512	278	**70**	51	570	447	21	**131**	.278	.348	.382	730	99	-36	-6	96	47	42	53	-4
Chi	53	99	1	.349	47	29	46	704	946	5994	1395	237	40	71	565	524	17	111	.263	.336	.363	699	84	-99	-119	103	36	27	57	-2
Total	615	——		—	—	329	281	6305	—	48495	11968	2205	449	688	4615	4279	144	804	.279	.351	.399	750	—	—	—	—	547	315	63	10

TEAM	CG	SHO	GR	SV	IP	H	HR	BB	SO	BR/9	ERA	AERA	OAV	OOB	PR	APR	PF	OSB	OCS	FA	E	WPB	DP	FW	PW	BW	BSW	DIF
Det	74	**13**	128	14	1370.2	1467	86	**488**	640	12.9	4.06	108	.273	.335	67	52	98	**43**	44	**.974**	159	25	150	1.2	4.8	10.9	.6	6.5
NY	**83**	**13**	111	10	1382.2	**1349**	71	542	**656**	**12.4**	**3.76**	108	**.254**	**.324**	**114**	53	90	68	32	.973	**157**	**22**	151	**1.3**	4.9	**12.4**	-.1	-1.4
Cle	72	8	143	19	1367.0	1476	**70**	582	554	13.7	4.28	106	.275	.349	·33	40	101	64	30	.972	172	49	164	.4	3.7	3.3	-.1	.6
Bos	68	9	138	9	1361.0	1527	**70**	543	538	13.8	4.32	**111**	.283	.351	27	**68**	107	61	30	.969	188	36	141	-.5	**6.3**	-7.2	**.7**	.6
Phi	68	8	144	8	1337.0	1429	84	693	480	14.4	5.01	87	.275	.363	-77	-97	97	80	41	.967	196	45	166	-1.0	-9.0	4.3	-.1	-1.2
StL	50	6	**172**	**20**	1350.0	1499	94	632	499	14.3	4.49	**111**	.283	.361	1	**68**	111	68	**48**	.969	187	37	160	-.4	**6.3**	-13.0	-.2	-1.7
Was	61	4	163	12	1381.1	1622	74	503	412	13.9	4.68	92	.295	.355	-28	-57	96	49	42	**.974**	162	36	**167**	1.0	-5.3	-.6	-.5	-4.7
Chi	72	5	118	8	1355.0	1599	139	628	506	14.9	5.41	88	.292	.367	-137	-96	105	114	**48**	.966	207	60	126	-1.6	-8.9	-11.1	-.3	-1.1
Total	548	66	1117	100	10904.2	—	—	—	—	13.8	4.50	—	.279	.351	—	—	—	—	—	.970	1428	310	1225	—	—	—	—	—

BATTER-FIELDER WINS	BATTING AVERAGE	ON-BASE PERCENTAGE	SLUGGING AVERAGE	ON-BASE PLUS SLUGGING	ADJUSTED OPS	ADJUSTED BATTER RUNS
Gehrig-NY..........7.9	Gehrig-NY............363	Gehrig-NY............465	Gehrig-NY............706	Gehrig-NY..........1172	Gehrig-NY............213	Gehrig-NY..........100.4
Foxx-Phi.............6.1	Gehringer-Det.......356	Gehringer-Det.......450	Foxx-Phi...............653	Foxx-Phi.............1102	Foxx-Phi...............188	Foxx-Phi..............73.4
Gehringer-Det....6.0	Manush-Was.........349	Foxx-Phi...............449	Greenberg-Det......600	Greenberg-Det....1005	Greenberg-Det......156	Gehringer-Det......49.6
Averill-Cle..........4.1	Simmons-Chi........344	Cochrane-Det.......428	Trosky-Cle............598	Trosky-Cle............987	Trosky-Cle............149	Greenberg-Det......48.7
Werber-Bos........3.9	Vosmik-Cle...........341	Myer-Was.............419	Averill-Cle............569	Averill-Cle............982	Averill-Cle............149	Averill-Cle............45.5
RUNS	**HITS**	**DOUBLES**	**TRIPLES**	**HOME RUNS**	**TOTAL BASES**	**RUNS BATTED IN**
Gehringer-Det.......134	Gehringer-Det.......214	Greenberg-Det........63	Chapman-NY..........13	Gehrig-NY..............49	Gehrig-NY............409	Gehrig-NY............165
Werber-Bos..........129	Gehrig-NY............210	Gehringer-Det.........50	Manush-Was...........11	Foxx-Phi.................44	Trosky-Cle............374	Trosky-Cle............142
Gehrig-NY............128	Trosky-Cle............206	Averill-Cle..............48		Trosky-Cle..............35	Greenberg-Det......356	Greenberg-Det......139
Averill-Cle............128	Cramer-Phi...........202	Trosky-Cle..............45		Johnson-Phi............34	Foxx-Phi...............352	Foxx-Phi...............130
Foxx-Phi...............120	Greenberg-Det......201	Hale-Cle.................44		Averill-Cle..............31	Averill-Cle............340	Gehringer-Det.......127
BASES ON BALLS	**STOLEN BASES**	**BASE STEALING RUNS**	**FIELDING RUNS-INFIELD**	**FIELDING RUNS-OUTFIELD**	**OUTFIELD ASSISTS**	**CATCHER CS PCT.**
Foxx-Phi...............111	Werber-Bos............40	White-Det..............4.1	Hale-Cle..............25.9	Johnson-Phi..........8.6	Johnson-Phi............17	Cochrane-Det......50.0
Gehrig-NY............109	White-Det...............28	Werber-Bos...........3.5	Werber-Bos.........17.1	Byrd-NY.................6.1	Pepper-StL..............15	Berry-Phi.............35.4
Ruth-NY...............104	Chapman-NY..........26	Lazzeri-NY.............2.1	Melillo-StL...........16.6	Stone-Was.............4.7	Goslin-Det..............15	R.Ferrell-Bos.......32.9
Myer-Was.............102	Fox-Det..................25	Fox-Det..................2.0	Warstler-Phi.........15.8	West-StL................4.6		Dickey-NY............32.4
	Walker-Det.............20	Rogell-Det.............1.8	Cronin-Was..........13.4	Chapman-NY.........4.1		Hayes-Phi............31.5
WINS	**WINNING PCT.**	**WINS ABOVE TEAM**	**GAMES STARTED**	**COMPLETE GAMES**	**FEWEST HITS/GAME**	**FEWEST BB/GAME**
Gomez-NY.............26	Gomez-NY...........839	Gomez-NY.............9.9	Bridges-Det............35	Gomez-NY.............25	Gomez-NY..........7.13	W.Ferrell-Bos.......2.44
Rowe-Det...............24	Rowe-Det.............750	Rowe-Det...............5.2	Pearson-Cle...........33	Bridges-Det............23	Ruffing-NY..........8.15	Auker-Det.............2.46
Bridges-Det............22	Marberry-Det........750	W.Ferrell-Bos.........4.8	Gomez-NY..............33	Lyons-Chi...............21	Bridges-Det.........8.15	Blaeholder-StL.....2.61
Harder-Cle.............20	Auker-Det.............682	Earnshaw-Chi........4.6	Blaeholder-StL........33	Rowe-Det...............20	Burke-Was..........8.30	Rowe-Det.............2.74
Ruffing-NY.............19	Bridges-Det..........667	Knott-StL................4.0			Murphy-NY..........8.36	Weaver-Was.........2.77
STRIKEOUTS	**STRIKEOUTS/GAME**	**GAMES**	**SAVES**	**BASE RUNNERS/9**	**ADJUSTED RELIEF RUNS**	**RELIEF RANKING**
Gomez-NY...........158	Ruffing-NY..........5.23	Russell-Was...........54	Russell-Was.............7	Gomez-NY.........10.19	Pennock-Bos.........8.9	Pennock-Bos.........4.5
Bridges-Det..........151	Gomez-NY...........5.05	Newsom-StL...........47	L.Brown-Cle.............6	Rowe-Det...........11.54	McColl-Was...........5.0	Bean-Cle...............4.5
Ruffing-NY...........149	Rowe-Det.............5.04	Rowe-Det...............45	Newsom-StL.............5	Bridges-Det........11.65	Bean-Cle...............4.2	McColl-Was...........2.9
Rowe-Det.............149	Pearson-Cle.........4.95	Knott-StL................45		Murphy-NY.........11.66	Wells-StL..............1.2	Wells-StL.................9
Pearson-Cle..........140	Bridges-Det.........4.94			Harder-Cle.........11.77	Russell-Was.............9	Russell-Was.............8
INNINGS PITCHED	**OPPONENTS' AVG.**	**OPPONENTS' OBP**	**EARNED RUN AVERAGE**	**ADJUSTED ERA**	**ADJUSTED STARTER RUNS**	**PITCHER WINS**
Gomez-NY.........281.2	Gomez-NY............215	Gomez-NY............282	Gomez-NY..........2.33	Harder-Cle...........174	Gomez-NY...........59.3	**Harder-Cle..........5.7**
Bridges-Det........275.0	Ruffing-NY...........236	Ruffing-NY...........310	Harder-Cle..........2.61	Gomez-NY...........174	Harder-Cle...........50.1	**Gomez-NY..........5.5**
Rowe-Det...........266.0	Bridges-Det..........241	Rowe-Det.............312	Murphy-NY..........3.12	Ostermueller-Bos..138	Rowe-Det.............31.5	**Rowe-Det...........4.5**
Newsom-StL......262.1	Burke-Was...........245	Bridges-Det..........312	Burke-Was..........3.21	Burke-Was...........134	Bridges-Det..........27.7	**Newsom-StL......2.9**
Ruffing-NY.........256.1	Benton-Phi...........249	Harder-Cle...........316	Auker-Det............3.42	W.Ferrell-Bos........132	Ostermueller-Bos 26.5	**W.Ferrell-Bos.....2.8**

Tigers Have AL by the Tail

For the first six weeks of the season, the Detroit Tigers, pennant-less since 1909, looked like nothing special. Then they began to win and shot up in the AL standings. By July, only the Yankees were a threat, and Detroit's 23-6 August put away the New Yorkers.

While the acquisitions of player-manager Mickey Cochrane and left fielder Goose Goslin helped push the Tigers over the hump, second baseman Charlie Gehringer and first baseman Hank Greenberg did most of the damage. Tommy Bridges won 16 straight games, and the pitching was deep if not spectacular. Second-place New York relied, uncharacteristically, on pitching rather than offense to contend. Lefty Gomez was now the league's top hurler and, aside from Triple Crown winner Lou Gehrig, the Yanks lacked big thumpers.

As the A's and Senators fell back into the second division, the Red Sox—last place finishers for most of the previous decade—bounded into fourth as new owner Tom Yawkey spent money on players like Billy Werber and Wes Ferrell. The pennant fever surrounding the Tigers and the increased interest in the Red Sox brought huge attendance gains as the overall league gate rose 29 percent.

Three ballparks were made smaller for the 1934 season. The Red Sox, who also replaced the wooden grandstands with concrete and steel, brought in the right-field fences at Fenway by 24 feet (after the fence had been pushed back a year earlier); the White Sox shrunk left and right field at Comiskey by 20 feet; and Detroit decreased left field at Briggs by 28 feet as AL ERA increased from 4.29 to 4.50.

The boisterous Cardinals bested the Tigers in a seven-game World Series, with the denouement an 11-0 debacle in Detroit. Angry fans threw so much debris at St. Louis left fielder Joe "Ducky" Medwick that he was removed from the game by Commissioner Landis for his own safety. The hometown crowd was mostly frustrated with their club, though, which couldn't win either of the final two games at home.

1933 NATIONAL LEAGUE

TEAM	W	L	T	PCT	GB	HW	HL	R	OR	PA	H	2B	3B	HR	BB	SO	HB	SH	AVG	OBP	SLG	OPS	AOPS	BR	ABR	PF	SB	CS	BSA	BSR
NY	91	61	4	.599	—	48	27	636	**515**	5939	1437	204	41	**82**	377	477	15	86	.263	.312	.361	673	100	-16	-6	98	31			
Pit	87	67	0	.565	5	50	27	667	619	5962	**1548**	249	**84**	39	366	**334**	20	**147**	**.285**	**.333**	**.383**	**716**	**111**	**70**	**71**	100	34			
Chi	86	68	0	.558	6	**56**	23	646	536	5785	1422	**256**	51	72	392	475	30	108	.271	.325	.380	705	107	50	52	100	52			
Bos	83	71	2	.539	9	45	31	552	531	5728	1320	217	56	54	326	428	25	134	.252	.299	.345	644	98	-73	-26	92	25			
StL	82	71	1	.536	9.5	47	30	**687**	609	5911	1486	**256**	61	57	391	528	32	101	.276	.329	.378	707	103	55	22	105	**99**			
Bro	65	88	4	.425	26.5	36	41	617	695	5872	1413	224	51	62	**397**	453	18	90	.263	.316	.359	675	103	-8	19	96	82			
Phi	60	92	0	.395	31	32	40	607	760	5796	1439	240	41	60	381	479	29	125	.274	.326	.369	695	93	34	-39	113	55			
Cin	58	94	1	.382	33	37	42	496	643	5653	1267	208	37	34	349	354	**33**	115	.246	.298	.320	618	83	-111	-104	99	30			
Total	618	—	—	—	—	351	261	4908	—	46646	11332	1854	422	460	2979	3528	202	906	.266	.317	.362	679	—	—	—	—	408	—	—	—

TEAM	CG	SHO	GR	SV	IP	H	HR	BB	SO	BR/9	ERA	AERA	OAV	OOB	PR	APR	PF	OSB	OCS	FA	E	WPB	DP	FW	PW	BW	BSW	DIF
NY	75	**23**	126	15	1408.2	**1280**	61	400	555	**10.9**	**2.71**	**118**	**.242**	**.299**	**98**	**81**	96	53	*45*	.973	178	42	156	-.5	**8.6**	-.6	—	7.5
Pit	70	16	144	12	1373.1	1417	54	313	401	11.5	3.27	101	.264	.308	10	7	99	69	*36*	.972	166	24	133	.2	.7	**7.5**	—	1.6
Chi	**95**	16	97	9	1362.0	1316	51	413	488	11.6	2.93	112	.254	.312	62	53	98	35	*43*	.973	168	37	**163**	.0	5.6	5.5	—	-2.2
Bos	85	15	102	**16**	1403.0	1391	54	355	383	11.3	2.96	103	.261	.309	58	15	92	**29**	*37*	**.978**	**138**	**20**	148	**2.1**	1.6	-2.8	—	5.0
StL	73	11	128	**16**	1382.2	1391	55	452	**635**	12.1	3.37	103	.261	.321	-5	15	104	51	*42*	.973	162	37	119	.4	1.6	2.3	—	1.2
Bro	71	9	133	10	1386.1	1502	51	374	415	12.4	3.73	86	.275	.326	-60	-82	96	49	***52***	.971	177	38	120	-.3	-8.7	2.0	—	-4.5
Phi	52	10	**170**	13	1336.2	1563	87	410	341	13.6	4.34	88	.293	.348	-150	-69	114	66	*45*	.970	183	41	156	-1.1	-7.3	-4.1	—	-3.5
Cin	74	13	113	8	1352.0	1470	**47**	**257**	310	11.6	3.42	99	.279	.314	-13	-5	102	56	*39*	.971	177	37	139	-.6	-.5	-11.0	—	-5.8
Total	595	113	1013	99	11004.2	—	—	—	—	11.9	3.34	—	.266	.317	—	—	—	—	—	.973	1349	276	1134	—	—	—	—	—

BATTER-FIELDER WINS	BATTING AVERAGE	ON-BASE PERCENTAGE	SLUGGING AVERAGE	ON-BASE PLUS SLUGGING	ADJUSTED OPS	ADJUSTED BATTER RUNS
Klein-Phi 5.6	Klein-Phi .368	Klein-Phi .422	Klein-Phi .602	Klein-Phi 1025	Berger-Bos 177	Klein-Phi 54.9
Berger-Bos 4.7	Davis-Phi .349	Davis-Phi .395	Berger-Bos .566	Berger-Bos .932	Klein-Phi 168	Berger-Bos 50.4
Vaughan-Pit 3.8	Stephenson-Chi .329	Vaughan-Pit .388	B.Herman-Chi .502	Davis-Phi .867	Vaughan-Pit 146	Vaughan-Pit 35.3
B.Herman-Chi 3.7	Piet-Pit .323	Martin-StL .387	Medwick-StL .497	Vaughan-Pit .866	B.Herman-Chi 142	Ott-NY 31.7
Critz-NY 3.1	Terry-NY .322	Terry-NY .375	Vaughan-Pit .478	B.Herman-Chi .855	Ott-NY 139	P.Waner-Pit 29.3
RUNS	**HITS**	**DOUBLES**	**TRIPLES**	**HOME RUNS**	**TOTAL BASES**	**RUNS BATTED IN**
Martin-StL 122	Klein-Phi 223	Klein-Phi 44	Vaughan-Pit 19	Klein-Phi 28	Klein-Phi 365	Klein-Phi 120
P.Waner-Pit 101	Fullis-Phi 200	Medwick-StL 40	P.Waner-Pit 16	Berger-Bos 27	Berger-Bos 299	Berger-Bos 106
Klein-Phi 101	P.Waner-Pit 191	Lindstrom-Pit 39	Martin-StL 12	Ott-NY 23	Medwick-StL 296	Ott-NY 103
Ott-NY 98	Traynor-Pit 190	P.Waner-Pit 38	B.Herman-Chi 12	Medwick-StL 18	P.Waner-Pit 282	Medwick-StL 98
Medwick-StL 92	Martin-StL 189	Berger-Bos 37			Vaughan-Pit 274	Vaughan-Pit 97
BASES ON BALLS	**STOLEN BASES**	**BASE STEALING RUNS**	**FIELDING RUNS-INFIELD**	**FIELDING RUNS-OUTFIELD**	**OUTFIELD ASSISTS**	**CATCHER CS PCT.**
Ott-NY 75	Martin-StL 26		Critz-NY 45.0	Klein-Phi 8.1	Klein-Phi 21	Hogan-Bos 58.5
Suhr-Pit 72	Fullis-Phi 18		B.Herman-Chi 29.0	Medwick-StL 7.3	Moore-NY 19	Hartnett-Chi 53.8
Martin-StL 67	Frisch-StL 18		Jurges-Chi 22.8	Lindstrom-Pit 6.3	Medwick-StL 17	Mancuso-NY 47.7
Vaughan-Pit 64	Klein-Phi 15		Ryan-NY 16.5	Hafey-Cin 6.2	P.Waner-Pit 16	J.Wilson-StL 47.6
P.Waner-Pit 60	Orsatti-StL 14		Bartell-Phi 8.8	Rice-Cin 4.1	Hafey-Cin 16	Lombardi-Cin 42.9
WINS	**WINNING PCT.**	**WINS ABOVE TEAM**	**GAMES STARTED**	**COMPLETE GAMES**	**FEWEST HITS/GAME**	**FEWEST BB/GAME**
Hubbell-NY 23	Cantwell-Bos .667	Cantwell-Bos 4.8	French-Pit 35	Warneke-Chi 26	Schumacher-NY 6.92	Lucas-Cin .74
Dean-StL 20	Hubbell-NY .657	Hubbell-NY 3.2	Fitzsimmons-NY 35	Dean-StL 26	Hubbell-NY 7.46	Hubbell-NY 1.37
Cantwell-Bos 20	Meine-Pit .652	Tinning-Chi 3.0	Beck-Bro 35	Brandt-Bos 23	Parmelee-NY 7.87	Swift-Pit 1.48
Bush-Chi 20	Bush-Chi .625	Mungo-Bro 3.0	Warneke-Chi 34	Hubbell-NY 22	Brandt-Bos 8.01	Hansen-Phi 1.60
Schumacher-NY 19	Schumacher-NY .613	Bush-Chi 2.9	Dean-StL 34		Mungo-Bro 8.09	French-Pit 1.70
STRIKEOUTS	**STRIKEOUTS/GAME**	**GAMES**	**SAVES**	**BASE RUNNERS/9**	**ADJUSTED RELIEF RUNS**	**RELIEF RANKING**
Dean-StL 199	Dean-StL 6.11	Dean-StL 48	Collins-Phi 6	Hubbell-NY 8.92	Bell-NY 13.3	Bell-NY 13.9
Hubbell-NY 156	Parmelee-NY 5.44	French-Pit 47	Hubbell-NY 5	Schumacher-NY 9.88	Luque-NY 5.7	Luque-NY 7.1
Carleton-StL 147	Carleton-StL 4.78	Liska-Phi 45	Harris-Pit 5	Betts-Bos 10.41		
Warneke-Chi 133	Hubbell-NY 4.55	Hubbell-NY 45	Bell-NY 5	Bell-NY 10.42		
Parmelee-NY 132	Warneke-Chi 4.17	Carleton-StL 44		Swift-Pit 10.47		
INNINGS PITCHED	**OPPONENTS' AVG.**	**OPPONENTS' OBP**	**EARNED RUN AVERAGE**	**ADJUSTED ERA**	**ADJUSTED STARTER RUNS**	**PITCHER WINS**
Hubbell-NY 308.2	Schumacher-NY .214	Hubbell-NY .260	Hubbell-NY 1.66	Hubbell-NY 193	Hubbell-NY 55.3	**Hubbell-NY 7.3**
Dean-StL 293.0	Hubbell-NY .227	Schumacher-NY .280	Warneke-Chi 2.00	Warneke-Chi 163	Warneke-Chi 38.9	**Warneke-Chi 5.8**
French-Pit 291.1	Parmelee-NY .232	Swift-Pit .285	Schumacher-NY 2.16	Schumacher-NY 149	Schumacher-NY 33.3	**Schumacher-NY 4.4**
Brandt-Bos 287.2	Mungo-Bro .236	Betts-Bos .290	Brandt-Bos 2.60	Root-Chi 126	Brandt-Bos 21.1	**Brandt-Bos 3.5**
Warneke-Chi 287.1	Warneke-Chi .244	Cantwell-Bos .291	Root-Chi 2.60	French-Pit 122	French-Pit 20.7	**Bush-Chi 2.0**

Pitching Royalty and a Guy Named Mel

Three members of the Giants made the job easier for player-manager Bill Terry. Slugger Mel Ott led the league in walks and finished top five in runs, homers, and RBIs, while "King Carl" Hubbell and "Prince Hal" Schumacher were the pitching top twosome in the league. New York surged ahead in mid-June and never looked back, improving from seventh to win the flag.

Pittsburgh, Chicago, Boston (which set a new NL mark with a .978 fielding percentage), and St. Louis bunched together fighting for second. The Pirates were the eventual runners-up, finishing 5 games back.

Despite Chuck Klein winning the Triple Crown, the Phillies ended seventh. Philadelphia sold Klein to the Cubs for $125,000 after the season; they finished seventh again in 1934 and lost one more game than the previous year. Last-place Cincinnati was the final stop for two great pitchers. Eppa Rixey went 6-3 at age 42, while 23-year-vet Jack Quinn pitched his last game at the age of 50.

Due to the depression, major league teams cut their rosters to 23, and even Commissioner Landis took a pay cut. The average yearly salary for a major league player was $6,000. NL attendance fell another 18 percent in 1933, bringing league totals to their lowest since 1919. During the 1930s, the Cubs and Giants were the loop's only consistent draws. Both Chicago and New York had good ballparks, large populations, charismatic players, and were competitive most of the decade. In 1933 Cubs President William L. Veeck proposed a midseason slate of interleague games and a split season to spark more interest; he died a few months later.

Defeating the Washington Senators in five games, the Giants captured their first World Series since 1922. Hubbell pitched 20 innings without allowing an earned run, capturing Games 1 and 4. Ott's homer in the 10th-inning was the deciding blow in the final contest.

1933 AMERICAN LEAGUE

TEAM	W	L	T	PCT	GB	HW	HL	R	OR	PA	H	2B	3B	HR	BB	SO	HB	SH	AVG	OBP	SLG	OPS	AOPS	BR	ABR	PF	SB	CS	BSA	BSR
Was	99	53	1	.651	—	46	30	850	**665**	6212	**1586**	281	**86**	60	539	**395**	21	**128**	**.287**	.353	.402	755	107	46	55	99	65	50	57	-3
NY	91	59	2	.607	7	**51**	23	**927**	768	6069	1495	241	75	**144**	**700**	506	17	78	.283	**.369**	**.440**	**809**	**129**	**156**	**215**	94	**76**	59	56	-4
Phi	79	72	1	.523	19.5	46	29	875	853	6051	1519	**297**	57	139	625	618	16	80	.285	.362	**.440**	802	118	140	131	101	34	34	50	-4
Cle	75	76	0	.497	23.5	45	32	654	669	5806	1366	218	77	50	448	426	17	101	.261	.321	.360	681	82	-109	-136	105	36	40	47	-6
Det	75	79	1	.487	25	43	35	722	733	6091	1479	283	78	57	475	523	21	93	.269	.329	.380	709	92	-55	-68	102	68	50	58	-3
Chi	67	83	1	.447	31	35	41	683	814	5991	1448	231	53	43	538	416	**27**	108	.272	.342	.360	702	96	-51	-20	96	43	46	48	-7
Bos	63	86	0	.423	34.5	32	40	700	758	5857	1407	294	56	50	525	464	15	116	.271	.339	.377	716	97	-25	-18	99	58	37	**61**	0
StL	55	96	2	.364	43.5	30	46	669	820	5907	1337	244	64	64	520	556	15	87	.253	.322	.360	682	81	-104	-142	106	72	60	55	-5
Total	608	—	—	—	—	328	276	6080	—	47984	11637	2089	546	607	4370	3904	149	791	.273	.342	.390	732	—	—	—	—	452	376	55	-32

TEAM	CG	SHO	GR	SV	IP	H	HR	BB	SO	BR/9	ERA	AERA	OAV	OOB	PR	APR	PF	OSB	OCS	FA	E	WPB	DP	FW	PW	BW	BSW	DIF
Was	68	5	150	**26**	1389.2	1415	64	**452**	447	**12.2**	3.82	109	**.263**	**.322**	71	57	98	**31**	30	**.979**	**131**	22	149	**2.6**	5.4	5.2	.0	9.7
NY	70	8	123	22	1354.2	1426	66	612	**711**	13.6	4.36	89	.267	.344	-13	-80	91	35	39	.972	165	45	122	.4	-7.6	**20.4**	.0	2.8
Phi	69	6	142	14	1343.2	1523	77	644	423	14.6	4.81	89	.283	.361	-79	-78	100	67	38	.966	203	42	121	-1.9	-7.4	12.4	.0	.4
Cle	**74**	**12**	124	7	1350.0	**1382**	**60**	465	437	12.4	**3.71**	**120**	.264	.325	**86**	**107**	104	43	**65**	.974	156	**18**	127	.9	**10.1**	-12.9	-.2	1.5
Det	69	6	129	17	1398.0	1415	84	561	575	12.9	3.95	109	**.263**	.335	52	56	101	93	55	.971	178	21	**167**	-.2	5.3	-6.4	.0	-.8
Chi	53	8	**167**	13	1371.1	1505	85	519	423	13.5	4.45	95	.277	.343	-26	-33	99	70	37	.970	186	41	143	-1.0	-3.1	-1.9	-.3	-1.7
Bos	60	4	146	14	1327.2	1396	75	591	467	13.6	4.35	101	.271	.348	-10	4	102	68	60	.966	204	22	133	-2.2	.4	-1.7	**.4**	-8.3
StL	55	7	147	10	1360.2	1574	96	531	426	14.0	4.82	97	.289	.354	-82	-23	109	45	52	.976	149	30	162	1.5	-2.2	-13.4	-.0	-6.3
Total	518	56	1128	123	10895.2	—	—	—	—	13.3	4.28	—	.273	.342	—	—	—	—	—	.972	1372	241	1124	—	—	—	—	—

BATTER-FIELDER WINS
- **Foxx-Phi.............6.9**
- **Ruth-NY.............4.7**
- **Gehrig-NY...........4.7**
- **Cochrane-Phi.....4.1**
- **Cronin-Was.........3.9**

BATTING AVERAGE
- Foxx-Phi...............356
- Manush-Was............336
- Gehrig-NY.............334
- Simmons-Chi.........331
- Gehringer-Det.......325

ON-BASE PERCENTAGE
- Cochrane-Phi........459
- Foxx-Phi...............449
- Bishop-Phi 446
- Ruth-NY................442
- Gehrig-NY.............424

SLUGGING AVERAGE
- Foxx-Phi................703
- Gehrig-NY.............605
- Ruth-NY.................582
- Cochrane-Phi.........515
- Johnson-Phi..........505

ON-BASE PLUS SLUGGING
- Foxx-Phi..............1153
- Gehrig-NY............1030
- Ruth-NY...............1023
- Cochrane-Phi.........974
- Johnson-Phi..........892

ADJUSTED OPS
- Foxx-Phi................199
- Gehrig-NY.............181
- Ruth-NY.................180
- Cochrane-Phi.........156
- Dickey-NY..............138

ADJUSTED BATTER RUNS
- Foxx-Phi...............82.4
- Gehrig-NY............70.1
- Ruth-NY................58.8
- Cochrane-Phi.......42.6
- Johnson-Phi.........27.7

RUNS
- Gehrig-NY............138
- Foxx-Phi...............125
- Manush-Was.........115
- Chapman-NY........112
- Cramer-Phi...........109

HITS
- Manush-Was.........221
- Gehringer-Det.......204
- Foxx-Phi...............204
- Simmons-Chi........200
- Gehrig-NY.............198

DOUBLES
- Cronin-Was............45
- Johnson-Phi...........44
- Burns-StL...............43
- Rogell-Det..............42
- Gehringer-Det.........42

TRIPLES
- Manush-Was...........17
- Combs-NY..............16
- Averill-Cle..............16
- Myer-Was...............15
- Reynolds-StL..........14

HOME RUNS
- Foxx-Phi.................48
- Ruth-NY..................34
- Gehrig-NY...............32
- Johnson-Phi............21
- Lazzeri-NY..............18

TOTAL BASES
- Foxx-Phi...............403
- Gehrig-NY............359
- Manush-Was.........302
- Gehringer-Det.......294
- Simmons-Chi........291

RUNS BATTED IN
- Foxx-Phi...............163
- Gehrig-NY............139
- Simmons-Chi........119
- Cronin-Was...........118
- Kuhel-Was............107

BASES ON BALLS
- Ruth-NY...............114
- Cochrane-Phi........106
- Bishop-Phi............106
- Foxx-Phi.................96
- Swanson-Chi..........93

STOLEN BASES
- Chapman-NY..........27
- Walker-Det.............26
- Swanson-Chi..........19
- Kuhel-Was..............17

BASE STEALING RUNS
- Walker-Det............2.6
- Werber-NY-Bos......1.5
- Kuhel-Was................9
- Stumpf-Bos...............9
- Lazzeri-NY................9

FIELDING RUNS-INFIELD
- Melillo-StL...........22.3
- Rogell-Det............18.9
- Scharein-StL.........16.1
- Appling-Chi.............8.5
- Foxx-Phi..................6.8

FIELDING RUNS-OUTFIELD
- Chapman-NY.......14.1
- Simmons-Chi.........9.4
- Schulte-Was..........7.6
- West-StL..................5.2
- Goslin-Was.............4.6

OUTFIELD ASSISTS
- Chapman-NY..........24
- Campbell-StL..........18
- Goslin-Was.............17
- Johnson-Phi............16

CATCHER CS PCT.
- Dickey-NY............55.4
- Shea-Bos-StL......51.6
- Sewell-Was..........48.1
- Ferrell-StL-Bos....45.9
- Hayworth-Det.......38.1

WINS
- Grove-Phi..............24
- Crowder-Was..........24
- Whitehill-Was..........22

WINNING PCT.
- Grove-Phi.............750
- Whitehill-Was........733
- Stewart-Was.........714
- Allen-NY..............682

WINS ABOVE TEAM
- Grove-Phi...............8.6
- Whitehill-Was.........4.2
- Marberry-Det.........3.2
- VanAtta-NY.............3.1
- Hildebrand-Cle.......3.0

GAMES STARTED
- Whitehill-Was..........37
- Hadley-StL..............36
- Blaeholder-StL........36
- Crowder-Was..........35

COMPLETE GAMES
- Grove-Phi................21
- Whitehill-Was..........19
- Hadley-StL..............19
- Ruffing-NY..............18

FEWEST HITS/GAME
- Bridges-Det..........7.42
- Weiland-Bos 8.20
- Allen-NY................8.33
- Gomez-NY...........8.36
- Hildebrand-Cle.....8.37

FEWEST BB/GAME
- Brown-Cle............1.65
- Marberry-Det........2.30
- Stewart-Was.........2.34
- Harder-Cle...........2.38
- Blaeholder-StL.....2.43

STRIKEOUTS
- Gomez-NY............163
- Hadley-StL............149
- Ruffing-NY............122
- Bridges-Det...........120
- Allen-NY...............119

STRIKEOUTS/GAME
- Gomez-NY...........6.25
- Allen-NY..............5.80
- Ruffing-NY...........4.67
- Bridges-Det.........4.64
- Fischer-Det..........4.58

GAMES
- Crowder-Was..........52
- Russell-Was............50
- Welch-Bos..............47
- Kline-Bos................46

SAVES
- Russell-Was............13
- Hogsett-Det..............9
- Moore-NY..................8
- Heving-Chi.................6
- Grove-Phi..................6

BASE RUNNERS/9
- Heving-Chi.........10.83
- Russell-Was.......11.03
- Pearson-Cle.......11.04
- Marberry-Det.....11.10
- Stewart-Was......11.24

ADJUSTED RELIEF RUNS
- Russell-Was.........19.6
- Heving-Chi...........17.4
- Gray-StL..................7.3
- Faber-Chi.................7.2
- Burke-Was...............5.5

RELIEF RANKING
- Russell-Was.........30.3
- Heving-Chi...........17.9
- Gray-StL..................7.1
- Faber-Chi.................6.2
- Burke-Was...............5.4

INNINGS PITCHED
- Hadley-StL.........316.2
- Crowder-Was.....299.1
- Grove-Phi...........275.1
- Whitehill-Was.....270.0
- Blaeholder-StL...255.2

OPPONENTS' AVG.
- Bridges-Det...........226
- Gomez-NY.............240
- Allen-NY...............242
- Weiland-Bos.........244
- Hildebrand-Cle......245

OPPONENTS' OBP
- Marberry-Det........302
- Stewart-Was.........304
- Harder-Cle............309
- Brown-Cle.............310
- Grove-Phi.............316

EARNED RUN AVERAGE
- Pearson-Cle.........2.33
- Harder-Cle...........2.95
- Bridges-Det..........3.09
- Gomez-NY...........3.18
- Grove-Phi.............3.20

ADJUSTED ERA
- Harder-Cle............151
- Bridges-Det...........140
- Grove-Phi..............134
- Marberry-Det........131
- Brown-Cle.............130

ADJUSTED STARTER RUNS
- Harder-Cle...........35.1
- Grove-Phi.............34.5
- Pearson-Cle.........29.5
- Marberry-Det.......29.5
- Bridges-Det..........28.8

PITCHER WINS
- **Harder-Cle..........4.4**
- **Bridges-Det........3.2**
- **Pearson-Cle........3.1**
- **Grove-Phi............3.1**
- **Russell-Was.......3.1**

LAST GASP FOR THE SENATORS AND A'S

Following up on a strong finish in 1932, the Washington Senators moved ahead of the Yankees in June, withstood a challenge in late July, and then pulled away at the end. Player-manager Joe Cronin, just 26, keyed a line-drive power offense, three 30-something starters combined for 59 wins, and Jack Russell carried on the relief tradition of Firpo Marberry (departed to Detroit), winning 12 and being credited retroactively with 13 saves.

Prior to the season, Connie Mack looked at the finances and decided to tear apart his A's. After trading Al Simmons, Jimmy Dykes, and Mule Haas, the Athletics only finished third because of Jimmie Foxx (the Triple Crown winner), Lefty Grove, and Mickey Cochrane. After another attendance dip in '33, Mack finished the destruction by dealing Grove to Boston and Cochrane to Detroit. It was the finish of the Athletics as a competitive team in Philadelphia.

The Tigers spent 1933 in fifth place, breaking in two rookie pitchers who would soon be very important: Schoolboy Rowe and Elden Auker. Though the White Sox were a sixth-place crew, they remained in the news. Comiskey Park was the site of the first midsummer All-Star game. The AL won the game before a packed house, 4-2; Ruth christened the event with the first All-Star homer.

Red Faber, 44, the last active player from the 1919 White Sox and still a mainstay of the club, pitched in his last game. The same year, "Black Sox" manager Kid Gleason died, his heart still broken from the betrayal carried out by "his boys."

Although Lou Gehrig was outstanding, and Babe Ruth had his final big year, it was the Senators' grand finale. For 1920s holdovers Ossie Bluege, Sam Rice, and Goose Goslin (brought back for one year by owner Clark Griffith), it was their third flag in a decade—and the franchise's last in the capital. Washington's five-game World Series loss to the Giants was the end, rather than the beginning, of the excitement in D.C.

1932 NATIONAL LEAGUE

TEAM	W	L	T	PCT	GB	HW	HL	R	OR	PA	H	2B	3B	HR	BB	SO	HB	SH	AVG	OBP	SLG	OPS	AOPS	BR	ABR	PF	SB	CS	BSA	BSR
Chi	90	64	0	.584	—	**53**	24	720	**633**	6006	1519	296	60	69	398	514	28	118	.278	.330	.392	722	101	1	8	99	48			
Pit	86	68	0	.558	4	45	31	701	711	5906	1543	274	**90**	48	358	**385**	**31**	96	.285	.333	.395	728	103	7	20	98	71			
Bro	81	73	0	.526	.9	44	34	752	747	5944	1538	296	59	110	388	574	24	99	.283	.334	.420	754	**110**	56	**72**	98	61			
Phi	78	76	0	.506	12	45	32	**844**	796	6108	**1608**	**330**	67	**122**	**446**	547	27	**125**	**.292**	**.348**	**.442**	**790**	105	**136**	44	112	71			
Bos	77	77	1	.500	13	44	33	649	655	5977	1460	262	53	63	347	496	19	105	.265	.311	.366	677	90	-96	-72	96	36			
StL	72	82	2	.468	18	42	35	684	717	5972	1467	307	51	76	420	514	25	69	.269	.324	.385	709	93	-24	-43	103	**92**			
NY	72	82	0	.468	18	37	40	755	706	5950	1527	263	54	116	348	391	23	49	.276	.322	.406	728	103	-1	14	98	31			
Cin	60	94	1	.390	30	33	44	575	715	5999	1429	265	68	47	436	436	20	100	.263	.320	.362	682	92	-78	-56	97	35			
Total	618	——		—	—	343	273	5680	—	47862	12091	2293	502	651	3141	3857	197	761	.276	.328	.396	724	—	—	—	—	445	—	—	—

TEAM	CG	SHO	GR	SV	IP	H	HR	BB	SO	BR/9	ERA	AERA	OAV	OOB	PR	APR	PF	OSB	OCS	FA	E	WPB	DP	FW	PW	BW	BSW	DIF
Chi	79	9	132	7	1401.0	**1444**	68	409	527	12.1	**3.44**	**109**	**.264**	.319	**68**	**51**	97	**29**	*47*	.973	173	43	146	.4	**5.0**	.8	—	6.8
Pit	71	12	126	12	1377.0	1472	86	338	377	11.9	3.75	102	.270	.314	20	11	98	63	*30*	.969	185	33	124	-.4	1.1	2.0	—	6.3
Bro	61	7	153	16	1379.2	1538	72	403	497	12.8	4.27	89	.282	.334	-60	-69	98	57	*52*	.971	183	31	**169**	-.3	-6.8	**7.1**	—	4.0
Phi	59	4	**160**	**17**	1384.0	1589	107	450	459	13.5	4.47	99	.287	.344	-91	-8	114	60	*33*	.968	194	23	133	-.9	-.8	4.4	—	-1.6
Bos	72	8	124	8	1414.0	1483	**61**	420	440	12.3	3.53	107	.272	.328	55	37	97	43	*45*	**.976**	**152**	**22**	145	**1.7**	3.7	-7.1	—	1.7
StL	70	**13**	139	9	1396.0	1533	76	455	**681**	13.0	3.97	99	.282	.340	-14	-5	101	68	***63***	.971	175	43	155	.4	-.5	-4.3	—	-.6
NY	57	3	156	16	1375.1	1533	112	387	506	12.7	3.83	97	.280	.330	8	-19	96	60	*37*	.969	191	33	143	-.7	-1.9	1.4	—	-3.8
Cin	**83**	6	112	6	1394.2	1505	69	**276**	359	**11.6**	3.79	102	.274	**.311**	14	10	99	65	*43*	.971	178	35	129	.1	1.0	-5.5	—	-12.6
Total	552	62	1102	91	11121.2	—	—	—	—	12.5	3.88	—	.276	.328	—	—	—	—	—	.971	1431	263	1144	—	—	—	—	—

BATTER-FIELDER WINS	BATTING AVERAGE	ON-BASE PERCENTAGE	SLUGGING AVERAGE	ON-BASE PLUS SLUGGING	ADJUSTED OPS	ADJUSTED BATTER RUNS
Ott-NY 5.2	O'Doul-Bro .... .368	Ott-NY .... .424	Klein-Phi .... .646	Klein-Phi 1050	Ott-NY 175	Ott-NY 64.0
Klein-Phi 4.9	Terry-NY .... .350	O'Doul-Bro .... .423	Ott-NY .... .601	Ott-NY 1025	O'Doul-Bro 164	O'Doul-Bro 54.3
Terry-NY 4.8	Klein-Phi .... .348	Hurst-Phi .... .412	Terry-NY .... .580	O'Doul-Bro .... .978	Klein-Phi 158	Klein-Phi 52.8
Herman-Cin 4.5	P.Waner-Pit .... .341	Klein-Phi .... .404	O'Doul-Bro .... .555	Terry-NY .... .962	Terry-NY 158	Terry-NY 49.3
O'Doul-Bro 4.0	Hurst-Phi .... .339	P.Waner-Pit .... .397	Hurst-Phi .... .547	Hurst-Phi .... .959	Herman-Cin 152	Herman-Cin 41.9
RUNS	**HITS**	**DOUBLES**	**TRIPLES**	**HOME RUNS**	**TOTAL BASES**	**RUNS BATTED IN**
Klein-Phi 152	Klein-Phi 226	P.Waner-Pit 62	Herman-Cin 19	Ott-NY 38	Klein-Phi 420	Hurst-Phi 143
Terry-NY 124	Terry-NY 225	Klein-Phi 50	Suhr-Pit 16	Klein-Phi 38	Terry-NY 373	Klein-Phi 137
O'Doul-Bro 120	O'Doul-Bro 219	Stephenson-Chi 49	Klein-Phi 15	Terry-NY 28	Ott-NY 340	Whitney-Phi 124
Ott-NY 119	P.Waner-Pit 215	Bartell-Phi 48		Hurst-Phi 24	O'Doul-Bro 330	Wilson-Bro 123
Bartell-Phi 118	Herman-Chi 206			Wilson-Bro 23	P.Waner-Pit 321	Ott-NY 123
BASES ON BALLS	**STOLEN BASES**	**BASE STEALING RUNS**	**FIELDING RUNS-INFIELD**	**FIELDING RUNS-OUTFIELD**	**OUTFIELD ASSISTS**	**CATCHER CS PCT.**
Ott-NY 100	Klein-Phi 20		Jurges-Chi 30.0	Herman-Cin 13.2	Klein-Phi 29	Spohrer-Bos 52.7
Hurst-Phi 65	Piet-Pit 19		Cuccinello-Bro 20.8	Lee-Phi 9.2	Lindstrom-NY 18	Lopez-Bro 48.8
Bartell-Phi 64	Watkins-StL 18		Frisch-StL 15.8	L.Waner-Pit 9.0	Herman-Cin 18	Lombardi-Cin 45.6
Suhr-Pit 63	Frisch-StL 18		Stripp-Bro 15.6	K.Davis-Phi 8.1	K.Davis-Phi 15	Mancuso-StL 42.9
	K.Davis-Phi 16		Terry-NY 15.1	Klein-Phi 6.7	Wilson-Bro 14	Hogan-NY 42.4
WINS	**WINNING PCT.**	**WINS ABOVE TEAM**	**GAMES STARTED**	**COMPLETE GAMES**	**FEWEST HITS/GAME**	**FEWEST BB/GAME**
Warneke-Chi 22	Warneke-Chi .... .786	Warneke-Chi 7.5	Clark-Bro 36	Lucas-Cin 28	Swetonic-Pit 7.41	Swift-Pit 1.09
Clark-Bro 20	Bush-Chi .... .633	Hubbell-NY 4.8	Mungo-Bro 33	Warneke-Chi 25	Brown-Bos 7.90	Lucas-Cin 1.17
Bush-Chi 19	Rhem-StL-Phi .... .625	Clark-Bro 4.0	French-Pit 33	Hubbell-NY 22	Warneke-Chi 8.03	Hubbell-NY 1.27
	Clark-Bro .... .625	Brown-Bos 3.9	Dean-StL 33		Hubbell-NY 8.24	Benton-Cin 1.35
	Hubbell-NY .... .621	Rhem-StL-Phi 3.3			Malone-Chi 8.43	Betts-Bos 1.42
STRIKEOUTS	**STRIKEOUTS/GAME**	**GAMES**	**SAVES**	**BASE RUNNERS/9**	**ADJUSTED RELIEF RUNS**	**RELIEF RANKING**
Dean-StL 191	Dean-StL 6.01	French-Pit 47	Quinn-Bro 8	Hubbell-NY 9.63	Quinn-Bro 5.3	Quinn-Bro 6.6
Hubbell-NY 137	Hallahan-StL 5.51	Dean-StL 46	Benge-Phi 6	Swift-Pit 9.78	Frankhouse-Bos 2	Frankhouse-Bos 2
Malone-Chi 120	Vance-Bro 5.28	Carleton-StL 44	Luque-NY 5	Lucas-Cin 9.92		
Carleton-StL 113	Carleton-StL 5.18	Collins-Phi 43	Cantwell-Bos 5	Warneke-Chi 10.17		
Brown-Bos 110	Brown-Bos 4.65			Rixey-Cin 10.32		
INNINGS PITCHED	**OPPONENTS' AVG.**	**OPPONENTS' OBP**	**EARNED RUN AVERAGE**	**ADJUSTED ERA**	**ADJUSTED STARTER RUNS**	**PITCHER WINS**
Dean-StL 286.0	Swetonic-Pit .... .221	Hubbell-NY .... .268	Warneke-Chi 2.37	Warneke-Chi 159	Warneke-Chi 45.2	**Hubbell-NY 4.7**
Hubbell-NY 284.0	Warneke-Chi .... .237	Swift-Pit .... .272	Hubbell-NY 2.50	Hubbell-NY 148	Hubbell-NY 39.6	**Lucas-Cin 4.4**
Warneke-Chi 277.0	Hubbell-NY .... .238	Lucas-Cin .... .274	Betts-Bos 2.80	Swetonic-Pit 135	Lucas-Cin 26.4	**Warneke-Chi 4.3**
French-Pit 274.1	Brown-Bos .... .238	Warneke-Chi .... .283	Swetonic-Pit 2.82	Betts-Bos 134	Betts-Bos 23.3	**Cantwell-Bos 2.6**
Clark-Bro 273.0	Malone-Chi .... .244	Swetonic-Pit .... .286	Lucas-Cin 2.94	Lucas-Cin 131	Swetonic-Pit 20.8	**Dean-StL 2.5**

MANAGERIAL CH-CH-CH-CH-CHANGES

The Chicago Cubs led in the early going, but by August were in second and scuffling with brusque manager Rogers Hornsby. Charlie Grimm assumed the reins on August 7, and the Cubs reeled off a 14-game winning streak, rolling to the NL title. While the Cubs lacked a world-class offense, rookie Lon Warneke was arguably the league's top pitcher. Stan Hack began his long career as a part-time third baseman.

Home runs rose 30 percent, but overall scoring did not change significantly from 1931. Brooklyn's Ebbets Field was shrunk significantly in left and center fields, which increased runs, while the Pirates heightened Forbes Field's right-field wall, which had little effect.

The Pirates led the league for six weeks, but fell off the pace and finished second. Twenty-year-old rookie Arky Vaughan would become the team's best shortstop since Honus Wagner, while Paul Waner took advantage of spacious Forbes Field to hit 62 doubles. Led by slugger Chuck Klein, the Phillies led the NL in scoring, finishing .500 for first time since 1917. Cardinals rookie Joe Medwick batted .349 in a late-season trial.

New York saw the end of an era as manager John McGraw, in ill health and feuding with his players, quit with the Giants in last. Despite a sixth-place finish in 1932, the team improved quickly under Bill Terry.

Parity ruled the day; the Cubs' 90 wins were the fewest for an NL flag winner since 1915, and the distance from first to seventh in the standings was just 18 games. The lack of overwhelming skill from the NL champs showed in the World Series as the Yankees swept Chicago. Although the pennant race was interesting, NL attendance dropped another 16 percent as the true level of the economic depression sank in.

1932 AMERICAN LEAGUE

TEAM	W	L	T	PCT	GB	HW	HL	R	OR	PA	H	2B	3B	HR	BB	SO	HB	SH	AVG	OBP	SLG	OPS	AOPS	BR	ABR	PF	SB	CS	BSA	BSR
NY	107	47	2	.695	—	**62**	15	**1002**	724	6346	1564	279	82	160	**766**	527	27	76	.286	**.376**	.454	**830**	**128**	**176**	**232**	95	77	66	54	-6
Phi	94	60	0	.610	13	51	26	981	752	6299	**1606**	303	52	**172**	647	630	21	94	**.290**	.366	**.457**	823	115	153	119	104	38	23	62	0
Was	93	61	0	.604	14	51	26	840	**716**	6141	1565	303	**100**	61	505	442	26	95	.284	.347	.408	755	102	6	17	99	70	47	60	-1
Cle	87	65	1	.572	19	43	33	845	747	6121	1544	**310**	74	78	566	454	**33**	**110**	.285	.357	.413	770	99	46	-6	107	52	54	49	-7
Det	76	75	2	.503	29.5	42	34	799	787	5993	1479	291	80	80	486	523	13	85	.273	.335	.401	736	92	-37	-66	104	**103**	49	**68**	**6**
StL	63	91	0	.409	44	33	42	736	898	6065	1502	274	69	67	507	528	19	90	.276	.339	.388	727	89	-47	-88	106	69	62	53	-7
Chi	49	102	1	.325	56.5	28	49	667	897	5903	1426	274	56	36	459	**386**	19	89	.267	.327	.360	687	90	-124	-78	94	89	58	61	-1
Bos	43	111	0	.279	64	27	50	566	915	5856	1331	253	57	53	469	539	12	80	.251	.314	.351	665	80	-175	-158	97	46	46	50	-6
Total	615	—	—	—	—	337	275	6436	—	48724	12017	2287	570	707	4405	4029	170	719	.277	.346	.404	750	—	—	—	—	544	405	57	-22

TEAM	CG	SHO	GR	SV	IP	H	HR	BB	SO	BR/9	ERA	AERA	OAV	OOB	PR	APR	PF	OSB	OCS	FA	E	WPB	DP	FW	PW	BW	BSW	DIF
NY	**96**	**11**	93	15	1408.0	1425	93	561	**780**	**12.8**	**3.98**	102	**.260**	.331	**78**	17	91	65	38	.969	188	37	124	.2	1.6	**21.5**	-.3	7.1
Phi	95	10	92	10	1386.0	1477	112	511	595	13.0	4.45	102	.271	.336	4	11	101	68	49	**.979**	**124**	36	142	**3.8**	1.0	11.0	.3	.9
Was	66	10	139	**22**	1383.1	1463	73	526	437	13.0	4.16	104	.271	.337	49	25	96	**44**	48	**.979**	125	**23**	157	**3.8**	2.3	1.6	.2	8.2
Cle	94	6	92	8	1377.1	1506	**70**	**446**	439	**12.8**	4.12	**115**	.273	**.329**	55	**90**	106	57	41	.969	191	24	129	-.2	**8.3**	-.6	-.4	3.8
Det	67	9	120	17	1362.2	**1421**	89	592	521	13.5	4.30	109	.269	.346	27	58	105	67	51	.969	187	31	154	.0	5.4	-6.1	**.8**	.4
StL	63	8	150	11	1376.2	1592	103	574	496	14.3	5.01	97	.290	.359	-81	-22	108	61	53	.969	188	29	156	.0	-2.0	-8.1	-.4	-3.5
Chi	50	2	166	12	1348.2	1551	88	580	379	14.4	4.82	90	.287	.359	-52	-77	97	76	**67**	.958	264	37	**170**	-4.6	-7.1	-7.2	.2	-7.7
Bos	42	3	**188**	7	1362.0	1574	79	612	365	14.6	5.02	90	.289	.364	-81	-79	100	106	58	.963	233	33	165	-2.6	-7.3	-14.6	-.3	-9.2
Total	573	59	1040	102	11004.2	—	—	—	—	13.6	4.48	—	.277	.346	—	—	—	—	—	.969	1500	250	1197	—	—	—	—	—

BATTER-FIELDER WINS	BATTING AVERAGE	ON-BASE PERCENTAGE	SLUGGING AVERAGE	ON-BASE PLUS SLUGGING	ADJUSTED OPS	ADJUSTED BATTER RUNS
Foxx-Phi 6.7	Alexander-Det-Bos .367	Ruth-NY .489	Foxx-Phi .749	Foxx-Phi 1218	Ruth-NY 206	Foxx-Phi 91.5
Ruth-NY 6.5	Foxx-Phi .364	Foxx-Phi .469	Ruth-NY .661	Ruth-NY 1150	Foxx-Phi 203	Ruth-NY 80.5
Gehrig-NY 5.1	Gehrig-NY .349	Gehrig-NY .451	Gehrig-NY .621	Gehrig-NY 1072	Gehrig-NY 184	Gehrig-NY 79.4
Cochrane-Phi 4.2	Manush-Was .342	Bishop-Phi .412	Averill-Cle .569	Averill-Cle 961	Lazzeri-NY 140	Alexander-Det-Bos 34.5
Lazzeri-NY 3.9	Ruth-NY .341	Cochrane-Phi .412	Simmons-Phi .548	Cochrane-Phi 921	Averill-Cle 137	Averill-Cle 33.0
RUNS	**HITS**	**DOUBLES**	**TRIPLES**	**HOME RUNS**	**TOTAL BASES**	**RUNS BATTED IN**
Foxx-Phi 151	Simmons-Phi 216	McNair-Phi 47	Cronin-Was 18	Foxx-Phi 58	Foxx-Phi 438	Foxx-Phi 169
Simmons-Phi 144	Manush-Was 214	Gehringer-Det 44	Myer-Was 16	Ruth-NY 41	Gehrig-NY 370	Simmons-Phi 151
Combs-NY 143	Foxx-Phi 213	Cronin-Was 43	Lazzeri-NY 16	Simmons-Phi 35	Simmons-Phi 367	Gehrig-NY 151
Gehrig-NY 138	Gehrig-NY 208		Chapman-NY 15	Gehrig-NY 34	Averill-Cle 359	Ruth-NY 137
Manush-Was 121	Averill-Cle 198			Averill-Cle 32	Manush-Was 325	Averill-Cle 124
BASES ON BALLS	**STOLEN BASES**	**BASE STEALING RUNS**	**FIELDING RUNS-INFIELD**	**FIELDING RUNS-OUTFIELD**	**OUTFIELD ASSISTS**	**CATCHER CS PCT.**
Ruth-NY 130	Chapman-NY 38	Walker-Det 4.5	Warstler-Bos 22.8	Vosmik-Cle 18.9	Goslin-StL 16	Spencer-Was 50.0
Foxx-Phi 116	Walker-Det 30	Johnson-Det-Bos 2.3	Appling-Chi 14.8	West-Was 14.7	Webb-Bos-Det 15	Berry-Bos-Chi 47.2
Bishop-Phi 110	Johnson-Det-Bos 20	Chapman-NY 2.1	Rogell-Det 11.3	Funk-Chi 5.5	West-Was 15	Ferrell-StL 45.2
Gehrig-NY 108	Cissell-Chi-Cle 18	Blue-Chi 1.6	Melillo-StL 11.3	Goslin-StL 4.8	Funk-Chi 15	Grube-Chi 44.6
Cochrane-Phi 100		Schuble-Det 1.3	Kamm-Cle 9.3	Chapman-NY 4.1		Sewell-Cle 43.4
WINS	**WINNING PCT.**	**WINS ABOVE TEAM**	**GAMES STARTED**	**COMPLETE GAMES**	**FEWEST HITS/GAME**	**FEWEST BB/GAME**
Crowder-Was 26	Allen-NY .810	Grove-Phi 5.6	Crowder-Was 39	Grove-Phi 27	Allen-NY 7.59	Brown-Cle 1.71
Grove-Phi 25	Gomez-NY .774	Gomez-NY 4.7	Blaeholder-StL 36	Ferrell-Cle 26	Ruffing-NY 7.61	Crowder-Was 2.12
Gomez-NY 24	Ruffing-NY .720	Allen-NY 4.3	Hadley-Chi-StL 35	Ruffing-NY 22	Bridges-Det 7.79	Gray-StL 2.31
Ferrell-Cle 23	Grove-Phi .714	Weaver-Was 4.0	Walberg-Phi 34		Grove-Phi 8.30	Harder-Cle 2.40
Weaver-Was 22	Weaver-Was .688	Crowder-Was 3.9	Ferrell-Cle 34		Crowder-Was 8.78	Grove-Phi 2.44
STRIKEOUTS	**STRIKEOUTS/GAME**	**GAMES**	**SAVES**	**BASE RUNNERS/9**	**ADJUSTED RELIEF RUNS**	**RELIEF RANKING**
Ruffing-NY 190	Ruffing-NY 6.60	Marberry-Was 54	Marberry-Was 13	Grove-Phi 10.77	Kimsey-StL-Chi 7.7	Kimsey-StL-Chi 7.2
Grove-Phi 188	Gomez-NY 5.97	Gray-StL 52	Moore-Bos-NY 8	Crowder-Was 10.90	Faber-Chi 4.5	Faber-Chi 5.6
Gomez-NY 176	Grove-Phi 5.80	Crowder-Was 50	Hogsett-Det 7	Allen-NY 11.39	Krausse-Phi 0	Krausse-Phi 0
Hadley-Chi-StL 145	Hadley-Chi-StL 5.26		Grove-Phi 7	Ruffing-NY 11.71		
Pipgras-NY 111	Allen-NY 5.11		Faber-Chi 6	Sorrell-Det 12.06		
INNINGS PITCHED	**OPPONENTS' AVG.**	**OPPONENTS' OBP**	**EARNED RUN AVERAGE**	**ADJUSTED ERA**	**ADJUSTED STARTER RUNS**	**PITCHER WINS**
Crowder-Was 327.0	Ruffing-NY .226	Grove-Phi .292	Grove-Phi 2.84	Grove-Phi 159	Grove-Phi 54.0	**Grove-Phi 5.9**
Grove-Phi 291.2	Allen-NY .228	Crowder-Was .295	Ruffing-NY 3.09	Bridges-Det 140	Crowder-Was 36.9	**Ferrell-Cle 4.0**
Ferrell-Cle 287.2	Bridges-Det .233	Allen-NY .306	Lyons-Chi 3.28	Hogsett-Det 133	Ferrell-Cle 31.8	**Ruffing-NY 4.0**
Walberg-Phi 272.0	Grove-Phi .241	Ruffing-NY .311	Crowder-Was 3.33	Lyons-Chi 132	Ruffing-NY 31.8	**Crowder-Was 3.8**
Gomez-NY 265.1	Crowder-Was .252	Brown-Cle .314	Bridges-Det 3.36	Ruffing-NY 132	Lyons-Chi 27.9	**Lyons-Chi 3.1**

The Babe's Last Hurrah

While the AL's slugging torch passed from Babe Ruth to the younger Jimmie Foxx and Lou Gehrig, the Yankees were on the way up. Bill Dickey, Ben Chapman, and rookie shortstop Frankie Crosetti provided vital shots of youth, and New York no longer depended on one or two sluggers to carry the club.

The Athletics were strong hitters, but their pitching (besides Lefty Grove) was no longer the best in the league. As a result, the Yankees—with terrific mound work from Red Ruffing and Johnny Allen, as well as 24 wins from "Goofy" Gomez—won comfortably, giving skipper Joe McCarthy his first AL title.

A record 707 homers flew from AL parks in 1932, and for the first time since 1922, a non-Yankee (Foxx) captured the individual crown. The Red Sox scored the league's fewest runs, allowed the most, and absorbed 111 losses to finish last for the seventh time in eight years. Several canny trades soon lifted the club into the first division.

Attendance dropped another 19 percent, and the AL suffered its worst full season totals since 1915. Chicago's plight during the 1930s was especially strange. Attendance for the mostly moribund team ping-ponged each year: down 42 percent, up 71, down 41, up 98, down 6, up 33, down 42, and so on until 1939–40, when they had two straight years of growth. The Indians, finishing fourth for the third of four straight years, opened new Lakefront Stadium on July 31. The cavernous park, the first built with public money, was a failure from the start—it had been commissioned in the hopes of drawing the Olympics. Oddly shaped League Park housed the Tribe's weekday games until 1946.

Ruth's last, and greatest, October show resulted in New York's third World Series sweep since 1927. The 37-year-old star, ripped mercilessly by Cubs bench jockeys, hit .333 with 2 homers while Lou Gehrig batted .529 with 3 bombs. Ruth's "called shot" at Wrigley Field in Game 3 has passed into baseball lore.

1931 NATIONAL LEAGUE

TEAM	W	L	T	PCT	GB	HW	HL	R	OR	PA	H	2B	3B	HR	BB	SO	HB	SH	AVG	OBP	SLG	OPS	AOPS	BR	ABR	PF	SB	CS	BSA	BSR
StL	101	53	0	.656	—	**54**	24	815	614	5989	1554	**353**	74	60	432	475	**32**	90	.286	.342	.411	753	105	66	37	104	**114**			
NY	87	65	1	.572	13	50	27	768	**599**	5840	1554	251	64	**101**	383	**395**	26	59	**.289**	.340	.416	756	112	59	78	98	83			
Chi	84	70	2	.545	17	50	27	**828**	710	6178	**1578**	340	66	84	**577**	641	25	125	**.289**	**.360**	**.422**	**782**	**115**	**138**	**124**	102	49			
Bro	79	73	1	.520	21	46	29	681	673	5814	1464	240	**77**	71	409	512	27	69	.276	.331	.390	721	101	-7	-2	99	45			
Pit	75	79	1	.487	26	44	33	636	691	5999	1425	243	70	41	493	454	16	**130**	.266	.330	.360	690	93	-56	-49	99	59			
Phi	66	88	1	.429	35	40	36	684	828	5935	1502	299	52	81	437	492	23	100	.279	.336	.400	736	96	29	-24	108	42			
Bos	64	90	2	.416	37	36	41	533	680	5809	1367	221	59	34	368	430	22	123	.258	.309	.341	650	84	-142	-122	96	46			
Cin	58	96	0	.377	43	38	39	592	742	5861	1439	241	70	21	403	463	22	93	.269	.323	.352	675	94	-88	-50	94	24			
Total	618	—	—	—	—	358	256	5537	—	47425	11883	2188	532	493	3502	3862	193	789	.277	.334	.387	721	—	—	—	—	462	—	—	—

TEAM	CG	SHO	GR	SV	IP	H	HR	BB	SO	BR/9	ERA	AERA	OAV	OOB	PR	APR	PF	OSB	OCS	FA	E	WPB	DP	FW	PW	BW	BSW	DIF
StL	80	**17**	111	**20**	1384.2	1470	65	449	**626**	12.6	3.45	**114**	.273	.332	63	**72**	102	51	***67***	**.974**	160	41	169	**1.0**	**7.2**	3.7	—	12.2
NY	**90**	**17**	105	12	1360.2	**1341**	71	422	570	**11.8**	**3.30**	112	**.255**	**.313**	**85**	61	96	**37**	*40*	**.974**	**159**	28	126	**1.0**	6.1	7.8	—	-3.8
Chi	80	8	144	8	1385.2	1448	54	524	541	13.0	3.97	97	.268	.337	-17	-19	100	49	*52*	.973	169	38	141	.6	-1.9	**12.3**	—	-4.0
Bro	64	9	142	18	1356.0	1520	56	**351**	546	12.5	3.84	99	.283	.329	3	-5	99	57	*46*	.969	187	27	154	-.7	-.5	-.2	—	4.4
Pit	89	9	97	5	1390.0	1489	55	442	345	12.6	3.66	105	.274	.331	32	28	100	59	*38*	.968	194	30	167	-.9	2.8	-4.9	—	1.0
Phi	60	6	**163**	16	1360.1	1603	75	511	499	14.2	4.58	93	.293	.358	-108	-46	110	79	*53*	.966	210	38	149	-1.9	-4.6	-2.4	—	-2.2
Bos	78	12	122	9	1380.1	1465	66	406	419	12.3	3.90	97	.272	.325	-5	-18	98	57	*42*	.973	170	29	141	.5	-1.8	-12.1	—	.4
Cin	70	7	133	6	1345.0	1545	**51**	399	317	13.1	4.22	89	.294	.346	-53	-75	97	73	*40*	.973	165	**23**	**194**	.7	-7.5	-5.0	—	-7.3
Total	611	85	1017	94	10962.2	—	—	—	—	12.8	3.86	—	.277	.334	—	—	—	—	—	.971	1414	254	1241	—	—	—	—	—

BATTER-FIELDER WINS	BATTING AVERAGE	ON-BASE PERCENTAGE	SLUGGING AVERAGE	ON-BASE PLUS SLUGGING	ADJUSTED OPS	ADJUSTED BATTER RUNS
Terry-NY 3.7	Hafey-StL..............349	Hafey-StL..............404	Klein-Phi 584	Klein-Phi 982	Ott-NY...................153	Terry-NY 42.0
Berger-Bos 3.6	Terry-NY 349	Cuyler-Chi.............404	Hornsby-Chi...........574	Hafey-StL..............973	Hafey-StL..............153	Klein-Phi 40.0
Cuccinello-Cin ... 3.5	Bottomley-StL 348	P.Waner-Pit 404	Hafey-StL..............569	Ott-NY...................937	Terry-NY 150	Ott-NY...................38.1
Ott-NY 3.4	Klein-Phi 337	Grantham-Pit 400	Ott-NY...................545	Terry-NY 926	Klein-Phi 149	Berger-Bos 36.7
P.Waner-Pit......... 3.1	O'Doul-Bro............336	Klein-Phi 398	Arlett-Phi..............538	Berger-Bos 892	Berger-Bos 143	Hornsby-Chi.........34.2
RUNS	**HITS**	**DOUBLES**	**TRIPLES**	**HOME RUNS**	**TOTAL BASES**	**RUNS BATTED IN**
Terry-NY 121	L.Waner-Pit...........214	Adams-StL.............46	Terry-NY 20	Klein-Phi 31	Klein-Phi 347	Klein-Phi 121
Klein-Phi 121	Terry-NY 213	Berger-Bos 44	Herman-Bro............16	Ott-NY.....................29	Terry-NY 323	Ott-NY....................115
English-Chi 117	English-Chi 202	Terry-NY 43	Traynor-Pit 15	Berger-Bos 19	Herman-Bro..........320	Terry-NY 112
Cuyler-Chi.............110	Cuyler-Chi.............202	Herman-Bro...........43	Bissonette-Bro........14	Herman-Bro............18	Berger-Bos 316	Traynor-Pit 103
Ott-NY...................104	Klein-Phi 200	Bartell-Phi..............43		Arlett-Phi.................18	Cuyler-Chi.............290	Herman-Bro............97
BASES ON BALLS	**STOLEN BASES**	**BASE STEALING RUNS**	**FIELDING RUNS-INFIELD**	**FIELDING RUNS-OUTFIELD**	**OUTFIELD ASSISTS**	**CATCHER CS PCT.**
Ott-NY.....................80	Frisch-StL 28		Hurst-Phi.............11.4	P.Waner-Pit..........13.8	P.Waner-Pit.............28	Wilson-StL 52.2
P.Waner-Pit.............73	Herman-Bro............17		Frisch-StL 10.9	Crabtree-Cin 10.3	Herman-Bro............24	O'Farrell-NY.........52.0
Cuyler-Chi...............72	Martin-StL...............16		Terry-NY 10.3	L.Waner-Pit..........10.1	L.Waner-Pit.............20	Hogan-NY............51.9
Grantham-Pit 71	Adams-StL..............16		Maguire-Bos 10.1	Berger-Bos 4.1	Ott-NY.....................20	Hartnett-Chi 50.0
English-Chi 68	Watkins-StL 15		Jackson-NY 9.7	Ott-NY....................2.5	Crabtree-Cin 19	Lopez-Bro 49.3
WINS	**WINNING PCT.**	**WINS ABOVE TEAM**	**GAMES STARTED**	**COMPLETE GAMES**	**FEWEST HITS/GAME**	**FEWEST BB/GAME**
Meine-Pit 19	Derringer-StL 692	Brandt-Bos.............5.8	Meine-Pit 35	Lucas-Cin 24	Hubbell-NY 7.66	Johnson-StL 1.40
Hallahan-StL...........19	Hallahan-StL.........679	J.Elliott-Phi.............5.1	Johnson-Cin 33	Brandt-Bos..............23	Walker-NY 7.97	Lucas-Cin 1.47
J.Elliott-Phi.............19	Bush-Chi...............667	Meine-Pit 4.0	French-Pit...............33	Meine-Pit 22	Brandt-Bos...........8.21	Cantwell-Bos 1.96
	Grimes-StL 654	Bush-Chi.................3.6	Fitzsimmons-NY 33	Hubbell-NY 21	Fitzsimmons-NY ..8.59	Clark-Bro 2.01
		Lucas-Cin 3.6		French-Pit 20	Root-Chi 8.61	Zachary-Bos 2.08
STRIKEOUTS	**STRIKEOUTS/GAME**	**GAMES**	**SAVES**	**BASE RUNNERS/9**	**ADJUSTED RELIEF RUNS**	**RELIEF RANKING**
Hallahan-StL.........159	Vance-Bro............6.17	J.Elliott-Phi.............52	Quinn-Bro 15	Hubbell-NY 10.23	Lindsey-StL............7.2	Quinn-Bro 10.3
Hubbell-NY 155	Hallahan-StL........5.75	Johnson-Cin 42	Lindsey-StL...............7	Walker-NY 10.49	Quinn-Bro 5.8	Lindsey-StL.........10.1
Vance-Bro.............150	Derringer-StL 5.70	Collins-Phi 42	J.Elliott-Phi...............5	Johnson-StL 10.50	May-Chi 1.8	May-Chi 2.1
Derringer-StL 134	Hubbell-NY 5.63		Hallahan-StL.............4	Fitzsimmons-NY 10.79		
Root-Chi 131	Root-Chi 4.70		Collins-Phi 4	Mooney-NY........11.05		
INNINGS PITCHED	**OPPONENTS' AVG.**	**OPPONENTS' OBP**	**EARNED RUN AVERAGE**	**ADJUSTED ERA**	**ADJUSTED STARTER RUNS**	**PITCHER WINS**
Meine-Pit 284.0	Hubbell-NY 227	Hubbell-NY 282	Walker-NY 2.26	Walker-NY 164	Walker-NY 37.3	**Hubbell-NY......... 3.4**
French-Pit...........275.2	Walker-NY 231	Walker-NY 283	Hubbell-NY 2.65	Hubbell-NY 139	Hubbell-NY 29.9	**Brandt-Bos......... 3.4**
Johnson-Cin 262.1	Brandt-Bos............244	Johnson-StL 286	Brandt-Bos...........2.92	Benge-Phi.............134	Benge-Phi............25.7	**Fitzsimmons-NY 2.9**
Fitzsimmons-NY 253.2	Fitzsimmons-NY ...251	Fitzsimmons-NY ...296	Meine-Pit 2.98	Johnson-StL 131	Meine-Pit 25.0	**Walker-NY 2.9**
Root-Chi 251.0	Root-Chi 252	Cantwell-Bos 301	Johnson-StL 3.00	Brandt-Bos............130	Brandt-Bos...........23.8	**Benge-Phi.......... 2.9**

Wild Horses

Several Senior Circuit clubs altered their ballparks in 1931, but this alone could not have been responsible for the spectacular decrease in offense. NL teams plated just 4.48 runs a game, the smallest output in more than a decade, with homers dropping a stunning 45 percent. The league also adopted a rule abolishing home runs on fair balls bouncing into the stands; they'd be doubles instead, as was already the law in the AL.

Into this new environment stepped the Cardinals, who led wire to wire. A tough, gritty team with homespun, rural players who liked to raise a ruckus on and off the diamond, St. Louis hit only 60 homers—fourth in the loop—but led in steals and finished second in runs. Hard-nosed competitors like Frankie Frisch, Pepper Martin, Ripper Collins, and Burleigh Grimes defined the club, and rookie Paul Derringer was 18-8 to give the team a strong second starter behind Wild Bill Hallahan.

The second-place Giants ended 13 out. The lack of a pennant race, and the fifth through eight place clubs each finishing between 26 and 43 games behind, factored in a frightening attendance drop of 15.6 percent, the biggest fall since 1918.

Along with Derringer, several key players debuted in 1931. Boston third baseman Bucky Walters eventually washed out as a hitter, then became the dominant NL right-hander of the early 1940s. Ernie Lombardi, who would later catch Walters (as well as Derringer) in Cincinnati, hit .297 for Brooklyn. Dixie Walker, later a favorite in Brooklyn, collected the first of his 2,064 hits. Wilbert Robinson finally stepped down in Brooklyn, allowing the team to change names, from Robins back to Dodgers, as well as managers; with a 1,399-1,398 career record, "Uncle Robbie" quit while he was ahead, barely.

St. Louis took home the NL's first World Series title since the Cards' win in 1926. Martin ran wild in the Series, hitting .500 and scoring 5 runs. This seven-game loss was it for Mack's club; after 1932, the Athletics never again contended in Philadelphia.

1931 AMERICAN LEAGUE

TEAM	W	L	T	PCT	GB	HW	HL	R	OR	PA	H	2B	3B	HR	BB	SO	HB	SH	AVG	OBP	SLG	OPS	AOPS	BR	ABR	PF	SB	CS	BSA	BSR
Phi	107	45	1	.704	—	**60**	15	858	**626**	6019	1544	311	64	118	528	543	**35**	79	.287	.355	.435	790	107	96	45	106	25	23	52	-3
NY	94	59	2	.614	13.5	51	25	**1067**	760	6471	**1667**	277	78	**155**	**748**	554	28	87	**.297**	**.383**	**.457**	**840**	**135**	**222**	**285**	94	**138**	68	67	**7**
Was	92	62	2	.597	16	55	22	843	690	6183	1588	308	**93**	49	481	459	30	96	.285	.345	.400	745	100	6	2	101	72	64	53	-7
Cle	78	76	1	.506	30	45	31	885	833	6112	1612	**321**	69	71	555	**433**	21	91	.296	.363	.419	782	105	95	48	106	63	60	51	-7
StL	63	91	0	.409	45	39	38	721	870	5935	1455	287	62	76	488	580	12	61	.271	.333	.390	723	92	-41	-66	104	73	80	48	-12
Bos	62	90	1	.408	45	39	40	625	800	5864	1409	289	34	37	405	565	12	68	.262	.315	.349	664	85	-155	-119	95	42	43	49	-6
Det	61	93	0	.396	47	36	41	651	836	5993	1456	292	69	43	480	468	20	63	.268	.330	.371	701	87	-80	-103	103	117	75	61	-1
Chi	56	97	3	.366	51.5	31	45	704	939	6099	1423	238	69	27	483	445	30	**105**	.260	.323	.343	666	86	-151	-111	94	94	39	**71**	**7**
Total	618	—	—	—	—	356	257	6354	—	48676	12154	2323	538	576	4168	4047	188	650	.278	.344	.396	740	—	—	—	—	624	452	58	-21

TEAM	CG	SHO	GR	SV	IP	H	HR	BB	SO	BR/9	ERA	AERA	OAV	OOB	PR	APR	PF	OSB	OCS	FA	E	WPB	DP	FW	PW	BW	BSW	DIF
Phi	**97**	**12**	82	16	1365.1	**1342**	73	457	574	**11.9**	**3.47**	**130**	**.256**	**.316**	**138**	**152**	103	66	51	**.976**	**141**	30	151	3.2	**14.2**	4.2	-.0	9.5
NY	78	4	132	17	1410.1	1461	67	543	**686**	12.9	4.20	94	.263	.332	28	-41	91	71	54	.972	169	24	131	1.7	-3.8	**26.5**	**.9**	-7.8
Was	60	7	145	**24**	1394.1	1434	73	498	582	12.6	3.76	114	.264	.327	95	83	98	**65**	45	**.976**	142	28	148	**3.3**	7.7	.2	-.4	4.2
Cle	76	6	124	9	1354.2	1577	64	561	470	14.4	4.63	100	.286	.355	-38	-2	106	76	64	.963	232	30	143	-2.0	-.2	4.5	-.4	-.8
StL	65	4	129	10	1362.0	1623	84	**448**	436	13.8	4.76	97	.293	.348	-57	-17	106	69	51	.963	232	**20**	**160**	-2.1	-1.6	-6.1	-.9	-3.3
Bos	61	5	161	10	1366.2	1559	**54**	473	365	13.5	4.60	94	.285	.344	-33	-45	98	70	56	.970	188	28	127	.4	-4.2	-11.1	-.3	1.2
Det	86	5	92	6	1384.1	1549	79	597	511	14.1	4.59	100	.282	.355	-32	-1	105	95	**72**	.964	220	33	139	-1.4	-.0	-9.6	.2	-5.1
Chi	54	6	**170**	10	1390.1	1613	82	588	421	14.5	5.04	85	.287	.358	-101	-125	97	112	59	.961	245	29	131	-2.7	-11.6	-10.3	**.9**	3.3
Total	577	49	1035	102	11028.0	—	—	—	—	13.5	4.38	—	.278	.344	—	—	—	—	—	.968	1569	222	1130	—	—	—	—	—

BATTER-FIELDER WINS	BATTING AVERAGE	ON-BASE PERCENTAGE	SLUGGING AVERAGE	ON-BASE PLUS SLUGGING	ADJUSTED OPS	ADJUSTED BATTER RUNS
Ruth-NY 8.1	Simmons-Phi 390	Ruth-NY 495	Ruth-NY 700	Ruth-NY 1195	Ruth-NY 223	Ruth-NY 104.4
Gehrig-NY 6.0	Ruth-NY 373	Morgan-Cle 451	Gehrig-NY 662	Gehrig-NY 1108	Gehrig-NY 199	Gehrig-NY 91.0
Simmons-Phi 4.6	Morgan-Cle 351	Gehrig-NY 446	Simmons-Phi 641	Simmons-Phi 1085	Simmons-Phi 172	Simmons-Phi 52.4
Cochrane-Phi..... 4.5	Cochrane-Phi........349	Simmons-Phi 444	Averill-Cle 576	Averill-Cle 979	Webb-Bos 151	Webb-Bos 47.0
Cronin-Was......... 4.5	Gehrig-NY 341	Blue-Chi 430	Foxx-Phi 567	Cochrane-Phi........976	Goslin-StL 147	Goslin-StL 41.3

RUNS	HITS	DOUBLES	TRIPLES	HOME RUNS	TOTAL BASES	RUNS BATTED IN
Gehrig-NY 163	Gehrig-NY 211	Webb-Bos 67	Johnson-Det 19	Ruth-NY 46	Gehrig-NY 410	Gehrig-NY 184
Ruth-NY 149	Averill-Cle 209	Alexander-Det.........47	Gehrig-NY 15	Gehrig-NY 46	Ruth-NY 374	Ruth-NY 163
Averill-Cle 140	Simmons-Phi 200	Kress-StL 46	Blue-Chi 15	Averill-Cle 32	Averill-Cle 361	Averill-Cle 143
Combs-NY 120	Ruth-NY 199	Cronin-Was 44	Vosmik-Cle 14	Foxx-Phi..................30	Simmons-Phi 329	Simmons-Phi 128
Chapman-NY 120	Webb-Bos 196		Reynolds-Chi 14	Goslin-StL 24	Goslin-StL 328	Cronin-Was 126

BASES ON BALLS	STOLEN BASES	BASE STEALING RUNS	FIELDING RUNS-INFIELD	FIELDING RUNS-OUTFIELD	OUTFIELD ASSISTS	CATCHER CS PCT.
Ruth-NY 128	Chapman-NY 61	Chapman-NY 5.4	Melillo-StL 35.3	West-Was 13.6	Johnson-Det 25	Dickey-NY 46.6
Blue-Chi 127	Johnson-Det 33	Cissell-Chi 1.9	Burns-StL 18.8	Johnson-Det 11.4	Webb-Bos 21	Cochrane-Phi.......45.1
Gehrig-NY 117	Burns-StL 19	H.Walker-Det 1.9	Rhyne-Bos 18.0	Oliver-Bos 5.8	Oliver-Bos 15	Berry-Bos 44.4
Bishop-Phi 112	Lazzeri-NY 18	Blue-Chi 1.8	Hodapp-Cle 15.2	Simmons-Phi 5.5	Goslin-StL 14	Sewell-Cle 43.8
Lary-NY 88	Cissell-Chi 18	Reynolds-Chi 1.6	McManus-Det-Bos..13.1	Chapman-NY 5.3	Chapman-NY 14	Ferrell-StL 42.9

WINS	WINNING PCT.	WINS ABOVE TEAM	GAMES STARTED	COMPLETE GAMES	FEWEST HITS/GAME	FEWEST BB/GAME
Grove-Phi 31	Grove-Phi 886	Grove-Phi 11.8	Gray-StL 37	Grove-Phi 27	Hadley-Was 7.26	Pennock-NY 1.43
Ferrell-Cle 22	Marberry-Was 800	Ferrell-Cle 5.8	Thomas-Chi 36	Ferrell-Cle 27	Gomez-NY 7.63	Gray-StL 1.88
Gomez-NY 21	Mahaffey-Phi.........789	Marberry-Was 5.4	Walberg-Phi 35	Earnshaw-Phi 23	Grove-Phi 7.76	Grove-Phi 1.93
Earnshaw-Phi 21	Earnshaw-Phi 750	MacFayden-Bos.....4.5	Ferrell-Cle 35	Whitehill-Det 22	Johnson-NY 8.07	Brown-Cle 2.12
Walberg-Phi 20	Gomez-NY 700	Gomez-NY 3.9		Stewart-StL 20	Earnshaw-Phi 8.15	Blaeholder-StL.....2.23

STRIKEOUTS	STRIKEOUTS/GAME	GAMES	SAVES	BASE RUNNERS/9	ADJUSTED RELIEF RUNS	RELIEF RANKING
Grove-Phi..............175	Hadley-Was 6.21	Hadley-Was 55	Moore-Bos 10	Grove-Phi.............9.73	Kimsey-StL 7	Kimsey-StL 8
Earnshaw-Phi 152	Gomez-NY 5.56	Moore-Bos 53	Hadley-Was 8	Earnshaw-Phi 10.64		
Gomez-NY 150	Bridges-Det..........5.46	Caraway-Chi 51	Marberry-Was 7	Gomez-NY 10.93		
Ruffing-NY 132	Grove-Phi.............5.46	Frasier-Chi 46	Kimsey-StL 7	Coffman-StL 11.27		
Hadley-Was 124	Ruffing-NY 5.01	Fischer-Was............46	Earnshaw-Phi 6	Uhle-Det 11.33		

INNINGS PITCHED	OPPONENTS' AVG.	OPPONENTS' OBP	EARNED RUN AVERAGE	ADJUSTED ERA	ADJUSTED STARTER RUNS	PITCHER WINS
Walberg-Phi 291.0	Hadley-Was 218	Grove-Phi 271	Grove-Phi 2.06	Grove-Phi 218	Grove-Phi 73.9	**Grove-Phi 8.2**
Grove-Phi 288.2	Gomez-NY 226	Earnshaw-Phi 288	Gomez-NY 2.67	Gomez-NY 149	Gomez-NY 36.5	**Ferrell-Cle 5.0**
Earnshaw-Phi 281.2	Grove-Phi 229	Gomez-NY 295	Hadley-Was 3.06	Hadley-Was 140	Walberg-Phi 28.2	**Gomez-NY 3.6**
Ferrell-Cle 276.1	Johnson-NY 234	Coffman-StL 298	Brown-Was 3.20	Brown-Was 134	Earnshaw-Phi 27.8	**Earnshaw-Phi 3.1**
Whitehill-Det 271.1	Earnshaw-Phi 236	Uhle-Det 304	Marberry-Was......3.45	Uhle-Det 131	Brown-Was 27.2	**Brown-Was 3.0**

A Sticky End

There was little drama in the American League race, as Connie Mack's Athletics wiped up the competition. New York, with Joe McCarthy over to manage from the Cubs, finished 13½ games out despite a late charge. Led by Babe Ruth and Lou Gehrig again, the Yankees outscored their opponents at home and on the road. But New York's pitching wasn't nearly up to the Athletics' standards, and Mack's club had its own three-pronged attack of Jimmie Foxx, Al Simmons, and Mickey Cochrane. Philly also had 20-game winners Rube Walberg and George Earnshaw—and Lefty Grove, who set a major league mark for winning percentage and dominated other mound categories as well.

Homers fell 14 percent and overall scoring dropped 5 percent. Part of this change was due to park adjustments. The Tigers enlarged Navin Field's left field by 28 feet, and runs and homers fell dramatically. The Senators removed left-field seats at Griffith Stadium, relocating the wall to 407 feet, and scoring dropped slightly. On the other hand, Boston brought in Fenway's right-field fence by 33 feet, and runs in their home games increased slightly, though homers did not. (They moved the fence back in 1933.)

Reflecting the downfall of the running game, the 0.5 stolen bases per game was the *highest* rate of the decade. Boston's unheralded Earl Webb set an all-time mark with 67 doubles. And in a frightening development, AL attendance fell 17 percent in 1931, and the league had its lowest total since 1919.

White Sox owner Charles Comiskey died in October after his team pulled up last. The Old Roman had to be pleased to outlive AL founder and adversary Ban Johnson by eight months. In addition, October was the effective end of the Athletics dynasty, which began crumbling in a surprising seven-game World Series loss to St. Louis.

1930 NATIONAL LEAGUE

TEAM	W	L	T	PCT	GB	HW	HL	R	OR	PA	H	2B	3B	HR	BB	SO	HB	SH	AVG	OBP	SLG	OPS	AOPS	BR	ABR	PF	SB	CS	BSA	BSR
StL	92	62	0	.597	—	**53**	24	**1004**	784	6204	1732	**373**	89	104	479	496	28	185	.314	.372	.471	843	105	77	46	103	72			
Chi	90	64	2	.584	2	51	26	998	870	6354	1722	305	72	**171**	**588**	635	**37**	148	.309	**.378**	**.481**	**859**	**111**	**113**	**106**	101	70			
NY	87	67	0	.565	5	46	31	959	814	6161	1769	264	83	143	422	**382**	21	165	**.319**	.369	.473	842	110	63	83	98	59			
Bro	86	68	0	.558	6	49	28	871	**738**	6088	1654	303	73	122	481	541	27	147	.304	.364	.454	818	103	22	33	99	53			
Pit	80	74	0	.519	12	42	35	891	928	6058	1622	285	**119**	86	494	449	22	**196**	.303	.365	.449	814	101	12	9	100	**76**			
Bos	70	84	0	.455	22	39	38	693	835	5870	1503	246	78	66	332	397	28	154	.281	.326	.393	719	81	-192	-169	97	69			
Cin	59	95	0	.383	33	37	40	665	857	5880	1475	265	67	74	445	489	16	174	.281	.339	.400	739	87	-137	-100	95	48			
Phi	52	102	2	.338	40	35	42	944	1199	6288	**1783**	345	44	126	450	459	23	148	.315	.367	.458	825	97	42	-21	107	34			
Total	618	—	—	—	—	352	264	7025	—	48903	13260	2386	625	892	3691	3848	202	1317	.303	.360	.448	808	—	—	—	—	481	—	—	—

TEAM	CG	SHO	GR	SV	IP	H	HR	BB	SO	BR/9	ERA	AERA	OAV	OOB	PR	APR	PF	OSB	OCS	FA	E	WPB	DP	FW	PW	BW	BSW	DIF
StL	63	5	150	**21**	1380.2	1594	87	476	**639**	13.7	4.39	114	.293	.353	89	94	101	52	**57**	.970	183	53	**176**	.2	8.3	4.1	—	2.5
Chi	67	6	174	12	1403.2	1642	111	528	601	14.1	4.80	102	.294	.357	26	14	98	**47**	*49*	.973	170	41	167	1.0	1.2	**9.4**	—	1.4
NY	64	6	157	19	1363.1	1546	117	439	522	13.3	4.61	103	.290	.348	54	19	95	59	*44*	**.974**	164	**26**	144	1.3	1.7	7.3	—	-.3
Bro	74	**13**	138	15	1372.0	**1480**	115	**394**	526	**12.4**	**4.03**	**122**	**.278**	**.330**	**144**	**136**	99	59	*46*	.972	174	32	167	.7	**12.0**	2.9	—	-6.6
Pit	**80**	7	107	13	1361.1	1730	128	438	393	14.5	5.24	95	.313	.367	-41	-40	100	61	*55*	.965	216	33	164	-1.8	-3.5	.8	—	7.5
Bos	71	6	124	11	1361.0	1624	117	475	424	14.0	4.91	100	.302	.360	9	3	99	51	*33*	.971	178	**26**	167	.4	.3	-14.9	—	7.2
Cin	61	6	149	11	1335.0	1650	**75**	**394**	361	13.9	5.08	95	.310	.361	-15	-38	97	65	*46*	.973	**161**	42	164	**1.4**	-3.4	-8.8	—	-7.2
Phi	54	3	**201**	7	1372.2	1993	142	543	384	16.8	6.71	81	.346	.405	-266	-172	110	87	*42*	.962	239	34	169	-3.0	-15.2	-1.9	—	-5.0
Total	534	52	1200	109	10949.2	—	—	—	—	14.1	4.97	—	.303	.360	—	—	—	—	—	.970	1485	287	1318	—	—	—	—	—

BATTER-FIELDER WINS	BATTING AVERAGE	ON-BASE PERCENTAGE	SLUGGING AVERAGE	ON-BASE PLUS SLUGGING	ADJUSTED OPS	ADJUSTED BATTER RUNS
Klein-Phi 5.7	Terry-NY 401	Ott-NY...................458	Wilson-Chi 723	Wilson-Chi 1177	Wilson-Chi 177	Wilson-Chi 75.7
Terry-NY 5.6	Herman-Bro..........393	Herman-Bro..........455	Klein-Phi 687	Herman-Bro.........1132	Herman-Bro..........171	Herman-Bro.........72.1
Lindstrom-NY 4.7	Klein-Phi 386	Wilson-Chi 454	Herman-Bro..........678	Klein-Phi 1123	Terry-NY 159	Terry-NY 61.3
Wilson-Chi 4.7	O'Doul-Phi 383	O'Doul-Phi 453	Hafey-StL..............652	Terry-NY 1071	Klein-Phi 155	Klein-Phi 57.7
Hartnett-Chi....... 4.1	Lindstrom-NY........379	Terry-NY 452	Hartnett-Chi..........630	Hafey-StL............1059	Ott-NY...................152	Ott-NY..................50.2
RUNS	**HITS**	**DOUBLES**	**TRIPLES**	**HOME RUNS**	**TOTAL BASES**	**RUNS BATTED IN**
Klein-Phi 158	Terry-NY 254	Klein-Phi 59	Comorosky-Pit........23	Wilson-Chi 56	Klein-Phi 445	Wilson-Chi 191
Cuyler-Chi.............155	Klein-Phi 250	Cuyler-Chi...............50	P.Waner-Pit.............18	Klein-Phi 40	Wilson-Chi 423	Klein-Phi 170
English-Chi 152	Herman-Bro..........241	Herman-Bro............48	English-Chi 17	Berger-Bos 38	Herman-Bro..........416	Cuyler-Chi.............134
Wilson-Chi 146	Lindstrom-NY........231	Comorosky-Pit........47	Cuyler-Chi...............17	Hartnett-Chi 37	Terry-NY 392	Herman-Bro...........130
Herman-Bro..........143	Cuyler-Chi.............228	Frisch-StL 46	Terry-NY 15	Herman-Bro............35	Cuyler-Chi.............351	Terry-NY 129
BASES ON BALLS	**STOLEN BASES**	**BASE STEALING RUNS**	**FIELDING RUNS-INFIELD**	**FIELDING RUNS-OUTFIELD**	**OUTFIELD ASSISTS**	**CATCHER CS PCT.**
Wilson-Chi 105	Cuyler-Chi...............37		Frisch-StL 22.3	Klein-Phi 21.2	Klein-Phi 44	Wilson-StL 51.5
Ott-NY..................103	P.Waner-Pit.............18		Whitney-Phi 20.8	Heilmann-Cin.......11.3	Ott-NY....................23	Hartnett-Chi.........47.4
English-Chi 100	Herman-Bro............18		Terry-NY 13.9	Welsh-Bos 7.0	Cuyler-Chi...............21	Lopez-Bro.............44.9
Grantham-Pit 81			Durocher-Cin 11.3	Sothern-Phi-Pit 6.6	Heilmann-Cin..........16	Sukeforth-Cin.......43.9
Suhr-Pit...................80			Gilbert-Bro 9.3	Bressler-Bro...........6.1	Sothern-Phi-Pit 15	Hemsley-Pit 43.3
WINS	**WINNING PCT.**	**WINS ABOVE TEAM**	**GAMES STARTED**	**COMPLETE GAMES**	**FEWEST HITS/GAME**	**FEWEST BB/GAME**
Malone-Chi 20	Fitzsimmons-NY ...731	Collins-Phi 5.8	Kremer-Pit 38	Malone-Chi 22	Vance-Bro............8.39	Clark-Bro 1.71
Kremer-Pit 20	Malone-Chi 690	Fitzsimmons-NY 5.5	Malone-Chi 35	Brame-Pit................22	Hallahan-StL........8.84	Kolp-Cin 1.82
Fitzsimmons-NY 19	Brame-Pit..............680	Brame-Pit...............4.7	French-Pit 35	French-Pit 21	Fitzsimmons-NY ..9.23	Johnson-StL 1.82
	Kremer-Pit 625	Malone-Chi 4.3	Walker-NY 34	Vance-Bro...............20	Elliott-Bro 9.26	Lucas-Cin 1.88
	Hallahan-StL.........625	Kremer-Pit 4.2	Seibold-Bos 33	Seibold-Bos 20	Clark-Bro 9.41	Vance-Bro............1.91
STRIKEOUTS	**STRIKEOUTS/GAME**	**GAMES**	**SAVES**	**BASE RUNNERS/9**	**ADJUSTED RELIEF RUNS**	**RELIEF RANKING**
Hallahan-StL.........177	Hallahan-StL........6.71	Elliott-Phi 48	Bell-StL 8	Vance-Bro..........10.47	Bell-StL 11.2	Lindsey-StL............8.4
Vance-Bro.............173	Vance-Bro............6.02	Collins-Phi 47	Heving-NY 6	Thurston-Bro......10.78	Lindsey-StL............7.5	Bell-StL 7.9
Malone-Chi 142	Root-Chi 5.07	Bush-Chi..................46	Clark-Bro 6	Clark-Bro 11.11		
Root-Chi 124	Malone-Chi 4.70	Pruett-NY................45		Kolp-Cin.............11.44		
Hubbell-NY 117	Johnson-StL 4.41	Malone-Chi 45		Fitzsimmons-NY 11.63		
INNINGS PITCHED	**OPPONENTS' AVG.**	**OPPONENTS' OBP**	**EARNED RUN AVERAGE**	**ADJUSTED ERA**	**ADJUSTED STARTER RUNS**	**PITCHER WINS**
Kremer-Pit 276.0	Vance-Bro.............246	Vance-Bro.............289	Vance-Bro............2.61	Vance-Bro.............188	Vance-Bro............64.1	**Vance-Bro........... 6.4**
French-Pit 274.2	Hallahan-StL.........260	Clark-Bro 306	Hubbell-NY 3.87	Elliott-Bro.............124	Malone-Chi 26.1	**Malone-Chi......... 2.6**
Malone-Chi 271.2	Fitzsimmons-NY ...266	Fitzsimmons-NY ...314	Walker-NY 3.93	Malone-Chi 124	Hubbell-NY 24.8	**Seibold-Bos........ 2.0**
Vance-Bro..........258.2	Walker-NY 268	Kolp-Cin................314	Malone-Chi 3.94	Grimes-Bos-StL 123	Elliott-Bro............23.4	**Clark-Bro 2.0**
Seibold-Bos 251.0	Malone-Chi 271	Hubbell-NY 327	Elliott-Bro.............3.95	Hubbell-NY 122	Seibold-Bos 20.3	**Root-Chi.............. 1.9**

Truly Offensive

If 1929 was a bad dream for pitchers, 1930 was hell. The league changed the ball, winding it tighter and reducing the size of the stitches, which impaired the pitcher's grip. The resulting league average rose to .303, the OPS .808, and runs per team per game to 5.68. None of these numbers have ever been topped.

For the Phillies, Chuck Klein scored 158 runs and hit .386 with 40 homers, and Lefty O'Doul scored 122 runs. The team hit .315 but finished last—with a 6.71 team ERA. Philadephia's *average* game was a 7-6 loss. Even Grover Cleveland Alexander—back where he started—was finished after a short trial at age 43; his 9.14 ERA was almost equal to his ERAs added together with the Phils from 1913–17.

The true star of 1930 was Brooklyn's Dazzy Vance, whose 2.61 ERA led the league by more than a run; the league average was 4.98. Chicago's Hack Wilson was a slugging machine. His 56 homers survived as an NL record until 1998, and his RBI mark still stands—later research, in fact, resulted in his total *improving* to 191 almost seven decades after the fact.

St. Louis bounced back to top the league in runs, thanks to Jim Bottomley, Chick Hafey, Frankie Frisch, and an excellent bench. The Cardinals went 21-4 in September, passing the Cubs and the surprising Robins. Giants first baseman Bill Terry became the last NLer to hit over .400, but McGraw's men finished 5 games back.

Hall of Fame shortstop Dave Bancroft hung 'em up, as did Cy Williams, who hit 251 career homers. Cubs pitcher Hal Carlson died suddenly May 30 of a stomach hemorrhage, while rookie Lon Warneke of Chicago began his 192-win career. Dizzy Dean debuted with a 3-hitter for St. Louis on September 28.

Most believed that attendance would drop because of 1929's financial crash, but a 50 percent gain in Brooklyn helped overall attendance jump 10.6 percent. This unexpected leap was whistling in the dark—the bad times were about to begin.

1930 AMERICAN LEAGUE

TEAM	W	L	T	PCT	GB	HW	HL	R	OR	PA	H	2B	3B	HR	BB	SO	HB	SH	AVG	OBP	SLG	OPS	AOPS	BR	ABR	PF	SB	CS	BSA	BSR
Phi	102	52	0	.662	—	**58**	18	951	751	6158	1573	319	74	125	599	531	32	**182**	.294	.369	.452	821	108	106	66	104	48	33	59	-1
Was	94	60	0	.610	8	56	21	892	**689**	6116	1620	300	98	57	537	**438**	**38**	171	.302	.369	.426	795	106	59	55	100	**101**	67	60	-1
NY	86	68	0	.558	16	47	29	**1062**	898	6272	**1683**	298	**110**	**152**	**644**	569	19	161	**.309**	**.384**	**.488**	**872**	**131**	**208**	**259**	96	91	60	60	-1
Cle	81	73	0	.526	21	44	33	890	915	6130	1654	**358**	59	72	490	461	26	175	.304	.364	.431	795	102	60	27	104	51	47	52	-5
Det	75	79	0	.487	27	45	33	783	833	5927	1504	298	90	82	461	508	25	144	.284	.344	.421	765	96	-19	-34	102	98	70	58	-3
StL	64	90	0	.416	38	38	40	751	886	5941	1415	289	67	75	497	550	15	151	.268	.333	.391	724	85	-96	-120	103	93	71	57	-4
Chi	62	92	0	.403	40	34	44	729	884	5995	1496	256	90	63	389	479	32	155	.276	.328	.391	719	89	-117	-92	97	74	40	**65**	**2**
Bos	52	102	0	.338	50	30	46	612	814	5807	1393	257	68	47	358	552	19	144	.264	.313	.365	678	79	-197	-172	96	42	35	55	-3
Total	616	—	—	—	—	352	264	6670	—	48346	12338	2375	656	673	3975	4088	206	1283	.288	.351	.421	772	—	—	—	—	598	423	59	-16

TEAM	CG	SHO	GR	SV	IP	H	HR	BB	SO	BR/9	ERA	AERA	OAV	OOB	PR	APR	PF	OSB	OCS	FA	E	WPB	DP	FW	PW	BW	BSW	DIF
Phi	72	**8**	136	**21**	1371.0	1457	84	488	**672**	12.9	4.28	109	.274	.337	56	58	101	79	44	**.975**	**145**	36	121	**3.0**	5.2	6.0	.0	10.7
Was	**78**	6	111	14	1369.0	**1367**	**52**	504	524	**12.5**	**3.96**	**116**	**.264**	**.332**	**104**	**97**	99	57	53	.974	157	19	150	2.3	**8.8**	5.0	.0	.9
NY	65	7	**150**	15	1367.2	1566	93	524	572	13.9	4.88	88	.287	.352	-36	-98	93	82	48	.965	207	50	132	-.7	-8.9	**23.4**	.0	-4.9
Cle	68	5	139	14	1360.0	1663	85	528	442	14.6	4.88	99	.305	.368	-36	-9	104	92	51	.962	237	31	156	-2.5	-.8	2.4	-.3	5.2
Det	68	4	137	17	1351.2	1507	86	570	574	14.0	4.70	102	.286	.359	-8	13	103	105	47	.967	192	44	156	.2	1.2	-3.1	-.0	-.2
StL	68	5	122	10	1371.2	1639	124	449	470	13.9	5.07	96	.300	.356	-65	-29	105	59	**64**	.970	188	**14**	152	.4	-2.6	-10.9	-.2	.3
Chi	63	2	146	10	1361.0	1629	74	**407**	471	13.6	4.71	98	.300	.352	-10	-15	99	78	61	.962	235	31	136	-2.4	-1.4	-8.3	**.4**	-3.3
Bos	**78**	4	92	5	1360.1	1515	75	488	356	13.4	4.68	98	.286	.348	-6	-12	99	**50**	55	.968	196	30	**161**	-.0	-1.1	-15.6	-.0	-8.2
Total	560	41	1033	106	10912.1	—	—	—	—	13.6	4.65	—	.288	.351	—	—	—	—	—	.968	1557	255	1164	—	—	—	—	—

BATTER-FIELDER WINS	BATTING AVERAGE	ON-BASE PERCENTAGE	SLUGGING AVERAGE	ON-BASE PLUS SLUGGING	ADJUSTED OPS	ADJUSTED BATTER RUNS
Gehrig-NY 7.7	Simmons-Phi .381	Ruth-NY .493	Ruth-NY .732	Ruth-NY 1225	Ruth-NY 216	Ruth-NY 100.0
Ruth-NY 7.6	Gehrig-NY .379	Gehrig-NY .473	Gehrig-NY .721	Gehrig-NY 1194	Gehrig-NY 207	Gehrig-NY 98.5
Cronin-Was 6.9	Ruth-NY .359	Foxx-Phi .429	Simmons-Phi .708	Simmons-Phi 1130	Simmons-Phi 173	Simmons-Phi 58.1
Simmons-Phi 4.5	Reynolds-Chi .359	Bishop-Phi .426	Foxx-Phi .637	Foxx-Phi 1066	Foxx-Phi 159	Foxx-Phi 51.3
Cochrane-Phi 3.8	Cochrane-Phi .357	Combs-NY .424		Morgan-Cle 1014	Morgan-Cle 148	Morgan-Cle 42.3

RUNS	HITS	DOUBLES	TRIPLES	HOME RUNS	TOTAL BASES	RUNS BATTED IN
Simmons-Phi 152	Hodapp-Cle 225	Hodapp-Cle 51	Combs-NY 22	Ruth-NY 49	Gehrig-NY 419	Gehrig-NY 174
Ruth-NY 150	Gehrig-NY 220	Manush-StL-Was 49	Reynolds-Chi 18	Gehrig-NY 41	Simmons-Phi 392	Simmons-Phi 165
Gehringer-Det 144	Simmons-Phi 211	Morgan-Cle 47	Gehrig-NY 17	Goslin-Was-StL 37	Ruth-NY 379	Foxx-Phi 156
Gehrig-NY 143	Rice-Was 207	Gehringer-Det 47	Simmons-Phi 16	Foxx-Phi 37	Foxx-Phi 358	Ruth-NY 153
Combs-NY 129	Morgan-Cle 204			Simmons-Phi 36		Goslin-Was-StL 138

BASES ON BALLS	STOLEN BASES	BASE STEALING RUNS	FIELDING RUNS-INFIELD	FIELDING RUNS-OUTFIELD	OUTFIELD ASSISTS	CATCHER CS PCT.
Ruth-NY 136	McManus-Det 23	Lary-NY 2.4	Cronin-Was 26.5	Haas-Phi 7.4	Jolley-Chi 17	Berry-Bos 54.5
Bishop-Phi 128	Gehringer-Det 19	McManus-Det 2.3	Melillo-StL 24.7	Oliver-Bos 6.0	Goslin-Was-StL 15	Ferrell-StL 50.0
Gehrig-NY 101	Goslin-Was-StL 17	Reynolds-Chi 2.1	Goldman-Cle 15.3	Johnson-Det 4.9	Johnson-Det 15	Spencer-Was 46.7
Foxx-Phi 93	Johnson-Det 17	Simmons-Phi 1.3	Kamm-Chi 12.5	Goslin-Was-StL 4.5	Rice-Was 13	Tate-Was-Chi 38.2
Blue-StL 81	Cronin-Was 17	Dickey-NY 1.2	Hodapp-Cle 10.3	Harris-Chi-Was 4.1		Dickey-NY 35.9

WINS	WINNING PCT.	WINS ABOVE TEAM	GAMES STARTED	COMPLETE GAMES	FEWEST HITS/GAME	FEWEST BB/GAME
Grove-Phi 28	Grove-Phi .848	Grove-Phi 10.1	Earnshaw-Phi 39	Lyons-Chi 29	Hadley-Was 8.37	Pennock-NY 1.15
Ferrell-Cle 25	Marberry-Was .750	Lyons-Chi 7.1	Lyons-Chi 36	Crowder-StL-Was 25	Grove-Phi 8.44	Lyons-Chi 1.72
Lyons-Chi 22	Jones-Was .682	Stewart-StL 6.6	Crowder-StL-Was 35	Ferrell-Cle 25	Collins-StL 8.81	Grove-Phi 1.86
Earnshaw-Phi 22	Ferrell-Cle .658	Ferrell-Cle 6.4	Ferrell-Cle 35	Stewart-StL 23	Crowder-StL-Was 8.88	Russell-Bos 2.08
Stewart-StL 20	Ruffing-Bos-NY .652	Wells-NY 4.3		Grove-Phi 22	Gaston-Bos 8.97	Brown-Cle 2.15

STRIKEOUTS	STRIKEOUTS/GAME	GAMES	SAVES	BASE RUNNERS/9	ADJUSTED RELIEF RUNS	RELIEF RANKING
Grove-Phi 209	Grove-Phi 6.46	Grove-Phi 50	Grove-Phi 9	Grove-Phi 10.45	Quinn-Phi 2.4	Quinn-Phi 4.2
Earnshaw-Phi 193	Johnson-NY 5.90	Earnshaw-Phi 49	Braxton-Was-Chi 6	Burke-Was 11.38		
Hadley-Was 162	Earnshaw-Phi 5.87	Pipgras-NY 44	Quinn-Phi 6	Stewart-StL 11.69		
Ferrell-Cle 143	Hadley-Was 5.60	Johnson-NY 44	Sullivan-Det 5	Rommel-Phi 11.74		
Ruffing-Bos-NY 131	Ruffing-Bos-NY 5.32	Ferrell-Cle 43	McKain-Chi 5	Lyons-Chi 11.79		

INNINGS PITCHED	OPPONENTS' AVG.	OPPONENTS' OBP	EARNED RUN AVERAGE	ADJUSTED ERA	ADJUSTED STARTER RUNS	PITCHER WINS
Lyons-Chi 297.2	Grove-Phi .247	Grove-Phi .288	Grove-Phi 2.54	Grove-Phi 184	Grove-Phi 65.8	**Grove-Phi 6.9**
Ferrell-Cle 296.2	Hadley-Was .247	Stewart-StL .315	Ferrell-Cle 3.31	Ferrell-Cle 146	Ferrell-Cle 45.9	**Ferrell-Cle 5.9**
Earnshaw-Phi 296.0	Crowder-StL-Was .259	Lyons-Chi .319	Stewart-StL 3.45	Stewart-StL 141	Stewart-StL 40.8	**Stewart-StL 4.4**
Grove-Phi 291.0	Collins-StL .259	Marberry-Was .321	Uhle-Det 3.65	Uhle-Det 131	Uhle-Det 31.3	**Lyons-Chi 3.7**
Crowder-StL-Was 279.2	Gaston-Bos .259	Crowder-StL-Was .321	Hadley-Was 3.73	Sorrell-Det 124	Crowder-StL-Was 29.6	**Uhle-Det 3.4**

Hitters Explode, but Pitching Carries the A's

Manager Walter Johnson's Senators, fifth in 1929, improved by 22 games and kept the race close until mid-July. Despite playing in a huge park, the Senators had good hitters like young shortstop Joe Cronin. But once again, the Athletics won by plenty.

Philadelphia enlarged Shibe Park in left and right field before the season, which helps explain how Lefty Grove's ERA declined from 2.81 to 2.54. But those changes don't explain how he dominated a league where offense increased by 8 percent. The incredible Grove was supported ably by George Earnshaw. Jimmie Foxx and Al Simmons provided the power, but the entire lineup added value.

The AL's 673 long balls set a new mark, while runs per team per game increased to 5.41, also an all-time record. Washington's 3.97 ERA was the highest to that point to lead the league. Foxx topped batters with 66 strikeouts, the lowest league-leading total for which figures are available. Despite becoming the first team in the twentieth century to top 1,000 runs, the Yankees floundered due to substandard pitching. Rookie Lefty Gomez and new acquisition Red Ruffing soon helped sort things out.

It was a tough time, though, at the box office. The Yankees were the last AL club to draw one million fans until 1935. The depression cut attendance nearly everywhere; despite the quality of the club, crowds fell each year from 1930–32 in Philadelphia. Hoping that fans would embrace hitting, speed and defense went out the window. This was the age of Smead Jolley, Zeke Bonura, and Buzz Arlett—sluggers whose modest hitting gifts are overstated by the offensive inflation of the era.

Grove and Earnshaw each won twice in the six-game World Series, allowing St. Louis just 7 runs in 5 starts between them. Only in Game 3 did anyone besides Grove or Earnshaw throw a pitch for the Athletics.

1929 NATIONAL LEAGUE

TEAM	W	L	T	PCT	GB	HW	HL	R	OR	PA	H	2B	3B	HR	BB	SO	HB	SH	AVG	OBP	SLG	OPS	AOPS	BR	ABR	PF	SB	CS	BSA	BSR
Chi	98	54	4	.645	—	**52**	25	**982**	758	6252	1655	**310**	46	139	**589**	567	29	163	.303	.373	.452	825	**111**	98	**96**	100	103			
Pit	88	65	1	.575	10.5	45	31	904	780	6198	1663	285	**116**	60	503	**335**	29	176	.303	.364	.430	794	101	25	5	102	94			
NY	84	67	1	.556	13.5	39	37	897	**709**	6060	1594	251	47	136	482	405	**36**	154	.296	.358	.436	794	103	18	21	100	85			
StL	78	74	2	.513	20	43	32	831	806	6030	1569	**310**	84	100	490	455	22	154	.293	.354	.438	792	101	13	5	101	72			
Phi	71	82	1	.464	27.5	39	37	897	1032	6216	**1693**	305	51	**153**	573	470	24	135	**.309**	**.377**	**.467**	**844**	108	**130**	70	107	59			
Bro	70	83	0	.458	28.5	42	35	755	888	5954	1535	282	69	99	504	454	22	155	.291	.355	.427	782	102	-1	16	98	80			
Cin	66	88	1	.429	33	38	39	686	760	5882	1478	258	79	34	412	347	26	175	.281	.336	.379	715	87	-137	-104	95	**134**			
Bos	56	98	0	.364	43	34	43	657	876	5923	1481	252	77	33	408	432	27	**197**	.280	.335	.375	710	85	-146	-118	96	65			
Total	616	—	—	—	—	332	279	6609	—	48515	12668	2253	569	754	3961	3465	215	1309	.294	.357	.426	783	—	—	—	—	692	—	—	—

TEAM	CG	SHO	GR	SV	IP	H	HR	BB	SO	BR/9	ERA	AERA	OAV	OOB	PR	APR	PF	OSB	OCS	FA	E	WPB	DP	FW	PW	BW	BSW	DIF
Chi	79	**14**	139	21	1398.2	1542	77	537	548	13.5	4.16	111	**.284**	.350	86	71	98	67	*72*	**.975**	**154**	36	**169**	**1.4**	6.5	**8.7**	—	5.4
Pit	79	5	134	13	1379.0	**1530**	96	439	409	13.0	4.36	109	**.284**	.340	54	61	101	87	*67*	.970	181	31	136	-.2	5.5	.5	—	5.7
NY	68	9	131	13	1372.0	1536	102	**387**	431	**12.7**	**3.97**	**115**	.287	**.337**	**113**	**96**	97	**63**	*26*	**.975**	158	24	163	.9	**8.7**	1.9	—	-3.1
StL	**83**	6	115	8	1359.2	1604	101	474	453	13.9	4.66	100	.297	.357	8	-1	99	76	*63*	.971	174	26	149	.2	-.0	.5	—	1.5
Phi	45	5	**204**	**24**	1348.0	1743	122	616	369	16.0	6.13	85	.319	.391	-212	-129	110	96	*64*	.969	191	30	153	-.8	-11.7	6.4	—	.7
Bro	59	8	173	16	1358.0	1553	92	549	**549**	14.2	4.92	94	.290	.360	-32	-49	98	146	*65*	.968	192	45	113	-.9	-4.5	1.5	—	-2.6
Cin	75	5	121	8	1369.1	1558	**61**	413	347	13.1	4.41	103	.292	.345	46	23	97	73	***74***	.974	162	**19**	148	.9	2.1	-9.5	—	-4.5
Bos	78	4	108	12	1352.2	1604	103	530	366	14.4	5.12	91	.302	.367	-62	-69	99	84	*66*	.967	204	32	146	-1.5	-6.3	-10.7	—	-2.5
Total	566	56	1125	115	10937.1	—	—	—	—	13.8	4.71	—	.294	.357	—	—	—	—	—	.971	1416	243	1177	—	—	—	—	—

BATTER-FIELDER WINS
Hornsby-Chi **6.8**
Ott-NY **5.0**
O'Doul-Phi **4.5**
Whitney-Phi **3.7**
Wilson-Chi **3.6**

BATTING AVERAGE
O'Doul-Phi 398
Herman-Bro 381
Hornsby-Chi 380
Terry-NY 372
Stephenson-Chi....362

ON-BASE PERCENTAGE
O'Doul-Phi 465
Hornsby-Chi...........459
Ott-NY....................449
Stephenson-Chi....445
Cuyler-Chi..............438

SLUGGING AVERAGE
Hornsby-Chi...........679
Klein-Phi 657
Ott-NY....................635
Hafey-StL...............632
O'Doul-Phi 622

ON-BASE PLUS SLUGGING
Hornsby-Chi........1139
O'Doul-Phi 1087
Ott-NY.................1084
Klein-Phi 1065
Herman-Bro..........1047

ADJUSTED OPS
Hornsby-Chi..........178
Ott-NY...................166
Herman-Bro 160
O'Doul-Phi 157
Wilson-Chi.............155

ADJUSTED BATTER RUNS
Hornsby-Chi.........75.7
Ott-NY...................61.1
O'Doul-Phi 59.1
Herman-Bro 53.1
Wilson-Chi 49.4

RUNS
Hornsby-Chi..........156
O'Doul-Phi 152
Ott-NY...................138
Wilson-Chi 135
L.Waner-Pit...........134

HITS
O'Doul-Phi 254
L.Waner-Pit............234
Hornsby-Chi...........229
Terry-NY 226
Klein-Phi 219

DOUBLES
Frederick-Bro 52
Hornsby-Chi.............47
Hafey-StL................47
Klein-Phi 45
Kelly-Cin 45

TRIPLES
L.Waner-Pit.............20
P.Waner-Pit.............15
Walker-Cin...............15
Whitney-Phi 14

HOME RUNS
Klein-Phi 43
Ott-NY.....................42
Wilson-Chi 39
Hornsby-Chi.............39
O'Doul-Phi 32

TOTAL BASES
Hornsby-Chi..........409
Klein-Phi 405
O'Doul-Phi 397
Wilson-Chi 355
Herman-Bro..........348

RUNS BATTED IN
Wilson-Chi 159
Ott-NY...................151
Hornsby-Chi..........149
Klein-Phi 145
Bottomley-StL 137

BASES ON BALLS
Ott-NY...................113
Grantham-Pit 93
P.Waner-Pit 89
Hornsby-Chi.............87
Walker-Cin 85

STOLEN BASES
Cuyler-Chi...............43
Swanson-Cin 33
Frisch-StL 24
Herman-Bro.............21
Allen-Cin 21

BASE STEALING RUNS

FIELDING RUNS-INFIELD
Whitney-Phi 23.4
Maranville-Bos 21.4
Jackson-NY 15.2
English-Chi 14.0
Thompson-Phi 11.1

FIELDING RUNS-OUTFIELD
Ott-NY.....................7.8
L.Waner-Pit............7.2
Orsatti-StL 6.9
Allen-Cin 4.6
Richbourg-Bos......4.5

OUTFIELD ASSISTS
Ott-NY.....................26
L.Waner-Pit.............22
Roush-NY 18
Klein-Phi 18

CATCHER CS PCT.
Z.Taylor-Bos-Chi..50.0
Gooch-Bro-Cin.....48.0
Wilson-StL 47.1
Hemsley-Pit 44.8
Lerian-Phi.............44.2

WINS
Malone-Chi 22
Root-Chi 19
Lucas-Cin 19

WINNING PCT.
Root-Chi 760
Bush-Chi................720
Grimes-Pit.............708
Malone-Chi 688
Kremer-Pit 643

WINS ABOVE TEAM
Lucas-Cin 5.8
Root-Chi 4.6
Grimes-Pit..............4.2
Morrison-Bro..........3.9
Moss-Bro 3.2

GAMES STARTED
Clark-Bro 39
Willoughby-Phi........35
Hubbell-NY 35
Lucas-Cin 32

COMPLETE GAMES
Lucas-Cin 28

FEWEST HITS/GAME
Lucas-Cin 8.90
Hubbell-NY 9.17
Kremer-Pit 9.18
Johnson-StL 9.18
Bush-Chi..............9.21

FEWEST BB/GAME
Vance-Bro............1.83
Lucas-Cin 1.93
Petty-Pit 2.05
Hubbell-NY 2.25
Clark-Bro 2.29

STRIKEOUTS
Malone-Chi 166
Clark-Bro 140
Vance-Bro.............126
Root-Chi 124
Hubbell-NY 106

STRIKEOUTS/GAME
Malone-Chi 5.60
Vance-Bro............4.90
Clark-Bro 4.52
May-Cin 4.16
Root-Chi 4.10

GAMES
Bush-Chi..................50
Willoughby-Phi........49
Sweetland-Phi 43
Root-Chi 43
Collins-Phi 43

SAVES
Morrison-Bro.............8
Bush-Chi....................8
Koupal-Bro-Phi 6

BASE RUNNERS/9
Lucas-Cin 10.87
Scott-NY 11.39
Hubbell-NY 11.62
Kremer-Pit 11.65
Petty-Pit 11.67

ADJUSTED RELIEF RUNS
Hill-Pit-StL..................5

RELIEF RANKING
Hill-Pit-StL..................3

INNINGS PITCHED
Clark-Bro 279.0
Root-Chi 272.0
Bush-Chi.............270.2
Lucas-Cin 270.0
Hubbell-NY 268.0

OPPONENTS' AVG.
Lucas-Cin 257
Johnson-StL 265
Hubbell-NY 265
Bush-Chi................265
Grimes-Pit.............269

OPPONENTS' OBP
Lucas-Cin 297
Hubbell-NY 313
Clark-Bro 316
Vance-Bro.............316
Petty-Pit 317

EARNED RUN AVERAGE
Walker-NY 3.09
Grimes-Pit............3.13
Root-Chi 3.47
Malone-Chi 3.57
Lucas-Cin 3.60

ADJUSTED ERA
Grimes-Pit.............152
Walker-NY 148
Root-Chi 133
Johnson-StL 129
Malone-Chi 129

ADJUSTED STARTER RUNS
Root-Chi 36.5
Grimes-Pit............36.1
Malone-Chi 33.4
Lucas-Cin 31.3
Walker-NY 30.5

PITCHER WINS
Lucas-Cin **4.3**
Grimes-Pit **4.0**
Malone-Chi **3.5**
Root-Chi **2.7**
Clark-Bro **2.7**

Blowup

The big story was hitting, as teams scored an astounding 5.36 runs per game while league batters clubbed 754 home runs and hit .294—all historical highs. The Phillies' pitchers posted a ghastly 6.13 ERA, allowing more than 1,000 runs (the first time a team ever did this), but still finished fifth by clubbing 153 homers. Braves Field was shrunk 30 feet in center and 67 in right, but hitting increased just as much elsewhere. Raising the left-field wall at Baker Bowl to 12 feet didn't cut decrease extra-base hits.

The outmanned Reds tried the running game, swiping 134 bases, but still finished seventh. This year was the death knell for the steal; no NL club would steal even 100 sacks until 1941, and it would be 1962 before a team would best Cincinnati's total.

As the defending champion Cardinals slumped, and were forced to retool, the Cubs sailed into the breach, running away with the NL flag after overtaking the Pirates in July. In winning their first title since 1918, Chicago became the fourth team to take a chance on Rogers Hornsby in four years, and the star second sacker enjoyed his last great season.

Pitcher Bobo Newsom began his twenty-year, nine-team major league odyssey with the Robins/Dodgers. Pitching their last seasons were Carl Mays, 7-2 at 38 for the Giants, and Art Nehf, 8-5 for the Cubs at 37. It was also sayonara for Dead Ball Era standout Max Carey, 39, who led the NL in steals ten times.

Catcher Peck Lerian, following his second season as Phillies catcher, died October 22 after being hit by a car. George Stallings, superstitious skipper of the 1914 "Miracle Braves," died in Georgia. "Iron Man" Joe McGinnity, who had consecutive 30-wins seasons for the 1903–04 Giants, breathed his last in Brooklyn. Plenty of current pitchers wished they could do the same.

1929 AMERICAN LEAGUE

TEAM	W	L	T	PCT	GB	HW	HL	R	OR	PA	H	2B	3B	HR	BB	SO	HB	SH	AVG	OBP	SLG	OPS	AOPS	BR	ABR	PF	SB	CS	BSA	BSR
Phi	104	46	1	.693	—	**57**	16	901	**615**	5988	1539	288	76	122	543	440	**28**	**213**	.296	**.365**	.451	**816**	111	**115**	84	104	63	39	62	0
NY	88	66	0	.571	18	49	28	899	775	6103	1587	262	74	**142**	554	518	25	145	.295	.364	.450	814	**123**	111	**174**	93	52	50	51	-6
Cle	81	71	0	.533	24	44	32	717	736	5868	1525	294	79	62	453	**363**	26	202	.294	.354	.417	771	100	27	0	104	75	87	46	-14
StL	79	73	2	.520	26	41	36	733	713	5976	1426	277	64	46	**589**	431	22	191	.276	.352	.381	733	91	-31	-58	104	70	47	60	-1
Was	71	81	1	.467	34	37	40	730	776	5995	1445	244	66	48	556	400	17	185	.276	.347	.375	722	90	-56	-61	101	89	63	59	-2
Det	70	84	1	.455	36	38	39	**926**	928	6253	**1671**	**339**	**97**	110	521	496	18	122	**.299**	.360	**.453**	813	114	112	108	100	95	75	56	-5
Chi	59	93	0	.388	46	35	41	627	792	5849	1406	240	74	37	425	436	22	154	.268	.325	.363	688	83	-138	-131	99	**109**	65	**63**	**1**
Bos	58	96	1	.377	48	32	45	605	803	5778	1377	285	69	28	413	494	**28**	177	.267	.325	.365	690	85	-131	-116	98	86	82	51	-10
Total	613	—	—	—	—	333	277	6138	—	47810	11976	2229	599	595	4054	3578	186	1389	.284	.349	.407	757	—	—	—	—	639	508	56	-37

TEAM	CG	SHO	GR	SV	IP	H	HR	BB	SO	BR/9	ERA	AERA	OAV	OOB	PR	APR	PF	OSB	OCS	FA	E	WPB	DP	FW	PW	BW	BSW	DIF
Phi	70	9	126	**24**	1357.0	**1371**	73	487	**573**	**12.4**	**3.44**	**123**	**.264**	**.329**	**121**	**119**	100	89	44	**.975**	**146**	38	117	**2.6**	**11.2**	7.9	.4	6.8
NY	64	12	**144**	18	1366.2	1475	83	485	484	13.1	4.19	92	.278	.341	7	-57	91	78	54	.971	178	27	153	.8	-5.4	**16.4**	-.1	-.7
Cle	80	8	102	10	1352.0	1570	56	488	389	13.9	4.05	109	.295	.357	28	54	105	88	66	.968	198	24	**162**	-.6	5.1	.0	-.9	1.4
StL	83	**15**	117	10	1371.0	1469	100	**462**	415	12.8	4.08	108	.279	.340	25	49	104	**59**	61	**.975**	156	**22**	148	2.2	4.6	-5.5	.3	1.3
Was	62	3	138	17	1354.2	1429	**48**	496	494	12.9	4.34	98	.276	.342	-15	-16	100	66	74	.968	195	38	156	-.3	-1.5	-5.8	.3	2.3
Det	82	5	139	9	1390.1	1641	73	646	467	15.0	4.96	86	.301	.377	-111	-104	101	110	71	.961	242	44	149	-3.0	-9.8	10.2	-.0	-4.3
Chi	78	5	100	7	1357.2	1481	84	505	328	13.4	4.41	97	.284	.351	-26	-22	101	75	61	.970	188	33	153	.0	-2.1	-12.4	**.5**	-3.2
Bos	**84**	9	105	5	1366.2	1537	78	496	416	13.6	4.43	96	.291	.355	-28	-25	101	74	**77**	.965	218	44	159	-1.6	-2.4	-10.9	-.5	-3.6
Total	603	66	971	100	10916.0	—	—	—	—	13.4	4.24	—	.284	.349	—	—	—	—	—	.969	1521	270	1197	—	—	—	—	—

BATTER-FIELDER WINS	BATTING AVERAGE	ON-BASE PERCENTAGE	SLUGGING AVERAGE	ON-BASE PLUS SLUGGING	ADJUSTED OPS	ADJUSTED BATTER RUNS
Ruth-NY............5.4	Fonseca-Cle.........369	Foxx-Phi...............463	Ruth-NY...............697	Ruth-NY..............1128	Ruth-NY................199	Ruth-NY..............72.3
Lazzeri-NY..........5.2	Simmons-Phi........365	Gehrig-NY.............431	Simmons-Phi........642	Foxx-Phi..............1088	Foxx-Phi................171	Gehrig-NY...........63.0
Simmons-Phi.....5.1	Manush-StL..........355	Ruth-NY................430	Foxx-Phi...............625	Simmons-Phi......1040	Gehrig-NY............170	Foxx-Phi..............58.9
Gehrig-NY..........4.5	Lazzeri-NY...........354	Lazzeri-NY...........429	Gehrig-NY............584	Gehrig-NY...........1015	Lazzeri-NY...........164	Lazzeri-NY..........53.7
Foxx-Phi.............4.3	Foxx-Phi...............354	Fonseca-Cle.........427	Alexander-Det.......580	Lazzeri-NY............991	Simmons-Phi........158	Simmons-Phi.......46.1

RUNS	HITS	DOUBLES	TRIPLES	HOME RUNS	TOTAL BASES	RUNS BATTED IN
Gehringer-Det.......131	Gehringer-Det.......215	Manush-StL...........45	Gehringer-Det.........19	Ruth-NY..................46	Simmons-Phi........373	Simmons-Phi........157
Johnson-Det.........128	Alexander-Det.......215	Johnson-Det..........45	Scarritt-Bos............17	Gehrig-NY...............35	Alexander-Det.......363	Ruth-NY................154
Gehrig-NY.............127	Simmons-Phi........212	Gehringer-Det.........45	B.Miller-Phi............16	Simmons-Phi..........34	Ruth-NY................348	Alexander-Det.......137
Foxx-Phi................123	Fonseca-Cle.........209	Fonseca-Cle...........44		Foxx-Phi..................33	Gehringer-Det.......337	Gehrig-NY.............126
Ruth-NY................121	Manush-StL..........204			Alexander-Det.........25		Heilmann-Det........120

BASES ON BALLS	STOLEN BASES	BASE STEALING RUNS	FIELDING RUNS-INFIELD	FIELDING RUNS-OUTFIELD	OUTFIELD ASSISTS	CATCHER CS PCT.
Bishop-Phi............128	Gehringer-Det.........27	Gehringer-Det........2.4	Melillo-StL............20.4	Simmons-Phi.......19.6	West-Was..............25	Schang-StL..........49.2
Blue-StL................126	Cissell-Chi.............25	B.Miller-Phi............1.8	Durocher-NY........20.2	West-Was............13.2	Johnson-Det...........25	Berg-Chi..............45.6
Gehrig-NY.............122	Rothrock-Bos..........24	Myer-Was..............1.7	Kerr-Chi..............17.1	B.Barrett-Chi-Bos......6.9	Rice-Was................20	L.Sewell-Cle........43.2
Foxx-Phi................103	B.Miller-Phi............24	Goslin-Was............1.4	J.Sewell-Cle.........14.4	Johnson-Det..........6.3	Simmons-Phi..........19	Dickey-NY............42.0
Cronin-Was.............85	Johnson-Det...........20	Reynolds-Chi.........1.0	McManus-Det.......6.9	Schulte-StL............6.2	B.Barrett-Chi-Bos.......17	Cochrane-Phi.......31.9

WINS	WINNING PCT.	WINS ABOVE TEAM	GAMES STARTED	COMPLETE GAMES	FEWEST HITS/GAME	FEWEST BB/GAME
Earnshaw-Phi.........24	Grove-Phi.............769	Zachary-NY...........6.0	Grove-Phi................37	Thomas-Chi............24	Earnshaw-Phi......8.23	Russell-Bos.........1.58
Ferrell-Cle..............21	Earnshaw-Phi.......750	Ferrell-Cle.............5.6	Gray-StL.................37	Uhle-Det.................23	Wells-NY..............8.33	Pennock-NY.........1.60
Grove-Phi................20	Ferrell-Cle............677	Marberry-Was........5.0	Crowder-StL...........34	Gray-StL.................23	Marberry-Was......8.38	Thomas-Chi.........2.08
Marberry-Was.........19	Walberg-Phi..........621	Rommel-Phi...........3.9		Hudlin-Cle...............22	Walberg-Phi.........8.61	Uhle-Det..............2.10
	Marberry-Was.......613	Grove-Phi..............3.7		Lyons-Chi................21	McKain-Chi..........9.00	Quinn-Phi............2.18

STRIKEOUTS	STRIKEOUTS/GAME	GAMES	SAVES	BASE RUNNERS/9	ADJUSTED RELIEF RUNS	RELIEF RANKING
Grove-Phi..............170	Grove-Phi............5.56	Marberry-Was.........49	Marberry-Was.........11	Marberry-Was....11.07		
Earnshaw-Phi.......149	Earnshaw-Phi......5.27	Earnshaw-Phi.........44	Moore-NY.................8	Stewart-StL........11.43		
Pipgras-NY...........125	Pipgras-NY..........4.99	Gray-StL.................43	Shores-Phi................7	Thomas-Chi.......11.44		
Marberry-Was.......121	Hadley-Was.........4.52	Ferrell-Cle..............43	Ferrell-Cle................5	Heimach-NY......11.56		
	Marberry-Was......4.35			Grove-Phi..........11.83		

INNINGS PITCHED	OPPONENTS' AVG.	OPPONENTS' OBP	EARNED RUN AVERAGE	ADJUSTED ERA	ADJUSTED STARTER RUNS	PITCHER WINS
Gray-StL............305.0	Earnshaw-Phi.......241	Marberry-Was.......308	Grove-Phi............2.81	Grove-Phi..............150	Grove-Phi............42.6	**Marberry-Was....4.0**
Hudlin-Cle..........280.1	Wells-NY..............248	Thomas-Chi..........310	Marberry-Was......3.06	Marberry-Was.......139	Hudlin-Cle...........34.2	**Grove-Phi...........3.6**
Grove-Phi...........275.1	Marberry-Was.......252	Grove-Phi.............316	Thomas-Chi.........3.19	Thomas-Chi..........134	Marberry-Was......33.3	**Hudlin-Cle..........3.5**
Walberg-Phi.......267.2	Walberg-Phi.........254	Hudlin-Cle............318	Earnshaw-Phi......3.29	Hudlin-Cle............133	Earnshaw-Phi......26.9	**Ferrell-Cle..........3.3**
Crowder-StL......266.2	Grove-Phi.............262	Walberg-Phi..........320	Hudlin-Cle...........3.34	Earnshaw-Phi.......129	Gray-StL..............23.9	**Thomas-Chi........2.7**

Mack Is Back

Babe Ruth led the league in homers again; Lou Gehrig hit .300 with 126 RBIs. But it was the Yankees' turn to be blown away. The Athletics pulled away in June and the race was never in doubt. Philadelphia had five players score 100 runs or more, and they scored just 2 runs more than New York for the season. The pitching was the difference. Lefty Grove, George Earnshaw, and Rube Walberg were Philadelphia's leading starters, and Connie Mack used relief pitchers efficiently.

Meanwhile, the Yankees dealt with the sudden death, due to blood poisoning, of manager Miller Huggins in late September. His passing effectively ended the first phase of the club's dynasty. The Indians improved 20 games and leapt to third, largely due to batting titlist Lew Fonseca and the heroics of rookie outfielder Earl Averill. Fifth-place Detroit had the loop's best offense and worst pitching, with only some of this attributable to their home field.

The game was changing—again. AL hitters set a new record with 595 homers, but 1929 was also the last year that batter strikeouts were fewer than three per game. From now on, there would be more whiffs as well as long balls.

The Athletics were distinct underdogs to the Cubs in the World Series. But Mack's surprising Game 1 starter—35-year-old Howard Ehmke, who appeared just 11 times all year—shut down Chicago, 3-1. The A's also won the next day. The Cubs captured Game 3 at Philadelphia, and led 8-0 in the seventh the next afternoon. But the Athletics exploded for a 10-run rally, ignited when Hack Wilson lost a flyball in the sun that scored three runs. The comeback, never equaled in Series history, turned the tide. Philadelphia rallied in the ninth inning of Game 5; Mule Haas' two-run shot tied things up. Al Simmons and Bing Miller doubled to give the Athletics their first title since 1913.

1928 NATIONAL LEAGUE

TEAM	W	L	T	PCT	GB	HW	HL	R	OR	PA	H	2B	3B	HR	BB	SO	HB	SH	AVG	OBP	SLG	OPS	AOPS	BR	ABR	PF	SB	CS	BSA	BSR
StL	95	59	0	.617	—	42	35	807	636	6144	1505	**292**	70	113	**568**	438	**32**	187	.281	.353	.425	778	108	77	63	102	82			
NY	93	61	1	.604	2	51	26	807	653	6103	1600	276	59	**118**	444	376	27	173	.293	.349	**.430**	779	**110**	69	**66**	100	62			
Chi	91	63	0	.591	4	**52**	25	714	**615**	6009	1460	251	64	92	508	517	31	210	.278	.345	.402	747	103	12	22	99	**83**			
Pit	85	67	0	.559	9	47	30	**837**	704	6037	**1659**	246	**100**	52	435	352	29	202	**.309**	**.364**	.421	**785**	108	**86**	55	104	64			
Cin	78	74	1	.513	16	44	33	648	686	5808	1449	229	67	32	386	**330**	26	**212**	.280	.333	.368	701	91	-80	-70	98	**83**			
Bro	77	76	2	.503	17.5	41	35	665	640	5992	1393	229	70	66	557	510	**32**	160	.266	.340	.374	714	94	-47	-37	99	81			
Bos	50	103	0	.327	44.5	25	51	631	878	5893	1439	241	41	52	447	377	27	191	.275	.335	.367	702	95	-70	-35	95	60			
Phi	43	109	0	.283	51	26	49	660	957	5917	1396	257	47	85	503	510	21	159	.267	.333	.382	715	90	-48	-70	103	53			
Total	614	—	—	—	—	328	284	5769	—	47903	11901	2021	518	610	3848	3410	225	1494	.281	.344	.397	741	—	—	—	—	568	—	—	—

TEAM	CG	SHO	GR	SV	IP	H	HR	BB	SO	BR/9	ERA	AERA	OAV	OOB	PR	APR	PF	OSB	OCS	FA	E	WPB	DP	FW	PW	BW	BSW	DIF
StL	**83**	4	119	**21**	1415.1	1470	86	**399**	422	**12.1**	3.38	118	.270	**.323**	97	98	100	55	*53*	.974	160	25	134	1.3	9.6	6.2	—	.9
NY	79	7	126	16	1394.0	1454	77	405	399	**12.1**	3.67	107	.273	.327	50	38	98	53	*35*	.972	178	29	175	.3	3.7	**6.4**	—	5.5
Chi	75	12	122	14	1380.2	1383	**56**	508	531	12.5	3.40	113	.267	.336	91	72	96	**38**	***70***	**.975**	**156**	26	176	**1.6**	7.0	2.1	—	3.3
Pit	82	8	112	11	1354.0	1422	66	446	385	12.6	3.95	103	.274	.335	7	16	102	88	*55*	.967	201	33	123	-1.3	1.6	5.4	—	3.3
Cin	68	11	120	11	1371.2	1516	58	410	355	12.7	3.94	100	.289	.342	8	2	99	67	*61*	.974	162	21	**194**	1.1	.2	-6.8	—	7.5
Bro	75	**16**	141	15	1396.0	**1378**	59	468	**551**	**12.1**	**3.25**	**122**	**.261**	.324	**115**	**113**	100	93	*58*	.965	217	**18**	113	-2.0	**11.0**	-3.6	—	-4.9
Bos	54	1	168	6	1360.0	1596	100	524	343	14.2	4.83	81	.298	.363	-127	-142	98	79	*54*	.969	193	36	141	-.7	-13.9	-3.4	—	-8.5
Phi	42	4	**189**	11	1346.2	1664	108	675	402	15.9	5.61	76	.315	.397	-242	-188	107	95	***70***	.971	181	29	171	-.0	-18.4	-6.8	—	-7.7
Total	558	63	1097	105	11018.1	—	—	—	—	13.0	3.99	—	.281	.344	—	—	—	—	—	.971	1448	217	1227	—	—	—	—	—

BATTER-FIELDER WINS	BATTING AVERAGE	ON-BASE PERCENTAGE	SLUGGING AVERAGE	ON-BASE PLUS SLUGGING	ADJUSTED OPS	ADJUSTED BATTER RUNS
Hornsby-Bos...... 6.1	Hornsby-Bos.........387	Hornsby-Bos.........498	Hornsby-Bos.........632	Hornsby-Bos.......1130	Hornsby-Bos.........204	Hornsby-Bos........83.4
Lindstrom-NY 4.9	P.Waner-Pit...........370	P.Waner-Pit...........446	Bottomley-StL.......628	Bottomley-StL 1030	Bottomley-StL 163	Bottomley-StL 50.6
Hartnett-Chi....... 4.7	Lindstrom-NY........358	Grantham-Pit 408	Hafey-StL..............604	Wilson-Chi 992	Wilson-Chi 159	P.Waner-Pit..........49.4
Jackson-NY........ 4.2	Sisler-Bos 340	Stephenson-Chi....407	Wilson-Chi 588	P.Waner-Pit...........992	Hafey-StL..............152	Wilson-Chi 44.6
P.Waner-Pit......... 3.9	Herman-Bro..........340	Wilson-Chi 404	P.Waner-Pit...........547	Hafey-StL..............990	P.Waner-Pit...........152	Bissonette-Bro.....38.2

RUNS	HITS	DOUBLES	TRIPLES	HOME RUNS	TOTAL BASES	RUNS BATTED IN
P.Waner-Pit...........142	Lindstrom-NY........231	P.Waner-Pit.............50	Bottomley-StL 20	Wilson-Chi 31	Bottomley-StL 362	Bottomley-StL 136
Bottomley-StL 123	P.Waner-Pit...........223	Hafey-StL................46	P.Waner-Pit.............19	Bottomley-StL 31	Lindstrom-NY........330	Traynor-Pit 124
L.Waner-Pit...........121	L.Waner-Pit...........221	Hornsby-Bos...........42	L.Waner-Pit.............14	Hafey-StL................27	P.Waner-Pit...........329	Wilson-Chi 120
Douthit-StL............111	Richbourg-Bos......206	Bottomley-StL 42	Bressler-Bro............13	Bissonette-Bro 25	Bissonette-Bro 319	Hafey-StL...............111
Frisch-StL 107	Traynor-Pit 192	Lindstrom-NY..........39	Bissonette-Bro 13	Hornsby-Bos...........21	Hafey-StL..............314	Lindstrom-NY........107

BASES ON BALLS	STOLEN BASES	BASE STEALING RUNS	FIELDING RUNS-INFIELD	FIELDING RUNS-OUTFIELD	OUTFIELD ASSISTS	CATCHER CS PCT.
Hornsby-Bos.........107	Cuyler-Chi...............37		Maguire-Chi.........49.1	Douthit-StL..........13.3	Sothern-Phi 19	Hartnett-Chi 62.5
Douthit-StL.............84	Frisch-StL 29		Jackson-NY 28.0	Leach-Phi 5.6	Cuyler-Chi...............18	Wilson-Phi-StL.....50.5
Bressler-Bro............80	Walker-Cin 19		Lindstrom-NY.......14.6	P.Waner-Pit 5.4	Harper-NY-StL 17	Picinich-Cin..........47.2
Wilson-Chi 77	Thompson-Phi 19		Ford-Cin...............14.5	Sothern-Phi 5.3	L.Waner-Pit.............15	Taylor-Bos............41.7
P.Waner-Pit.............77			Kelly-Cin 7.9	Richbourg-Bos.......3.8		DeBerry-Bro 41.0

WINS	WINNING PCT.	WINS ABOVE TEAM	GAMES STARTED	COMPLETE GAMES	FEWEST HITS/GAME	FEWEST BB/GAME
Grimes-Pit...............25	Benton-NY 735	Vance-Bro..............6.8	Rixey-Cin 37	Grimes-Pit..............28	Vance-Bro............7.26	Alexander-StL 1.37
Benton-NY 25	Haines-StL............714	Benton-NY 6.6	Grimes-Pit...............37	Benton-NY 28	Blake-Chi 7.82	Sherdel-StL..........2.03
Vance-Bro...............22	Bush-Chi...............714	Grimes-Pit..............4.6	Benton-NY 36	Vance-Bro...............24	Malone-Chi 7.83	Benton-NY 2.06
Sherdel-StL.............21	Fitzsimmons-NY ...690	Haines-StL.............4.1		Sherdel-StL.............20	McWeeny-Bro......8.04	Rixey-Cin 2.07
	Vance-Bro............688	Fitzsimmons-NY 3.7		Haines-StL..............20	Root-Chi 8.13	Grimes-Pit............2.10

STRIKEOUTS	STRIKEOUTS/GAME	GAMES	SAVES	BASE RUNNERS/9	ADJUSTED RELIEF RUNS	RELIEF RANKING
Vance-Bro.............200	Vance-Bro............6.42	Grimes-Pit...............48	Sherdel-StL...............5	Vance-Bro............9.79		
Malone-Chi 155	Malone-Chi 5.57	Kolp-Cin..................44	Haid-StL....................5	Hubbell-NY 10.23		
Root-Chi 122	Root-Chi 4.63	Rixey-Cin 43	Carlson-Chi...............4	Benton-NY 10.73		
Grimes-Pit...............97	Clark-Bro 3.93		Benton-NY 4	Grimes-Pit..........10.81		
Benton-NY 90	Ring-Phi..............3.58			Lucas-Cin 11.08		

INNINGS PITCHED	OPPONENTS' AVG.	OPPONENTS' OBP	EARNED RUN AVERAGE	ADJUSTED ERA	ADJUSTED STARTER RUNS	PITCHER WINS
Grimes-Pit.........330.2	Vance-Bro.............221	Vance-Bro.............277	Vance-Bro............2.09	Vance-Bro.............191	Vance-Bro............60.5	**Vance-Bro........... 7.2**
Benton-NY 310.1	McWeeny-Bro.......235	Grimes-Pit.............297	Blake-Chi 2.47	Blake-Chi..............156	Benton-NY 42.6	**Grimes-Pit 4.9**
Rixey-Cin 291.1	Malone-Chi 236	Benton-NY 300	Nehf-Chi 2.65	Clark-Bro 148	Blake-Chi 37.4	**Benton-NY.......... 4.1**
Vance-Bro..........280.1	Blake-Chi 240	Sherdel-StL...........303	Clark-Bro 2.68	Nehf-Chi 145	Grimes-Pit............32.0	**Blake-Chi............ 4.0**
Fitzsimmons-NY 261.1	Root-Chi 242	Lucas-Cin 304	Benton-NY 2.73	Benton-NY 144	Sherdel-StL..........30.9	**Sherdel-StL 3.9**

Holding Off the Giants

St. Louis, featuring an aging pitching staff and a veteran lineup, didn't lead the league in batting average, home runs, or ERA, but drew more walks than any other team and allowed fewer walks as well. First sacker Jim Bottomley was the club's best hitter, and 41-year-old Grover Cleveland Alexander finished 16-9. Moving ahead for good in early June, the Cardinals won the flag despite the dogged efforts of the Giants, who went 25-8 in September. John McGraw had found he could not get along with irascible Rogers Hornsby and dealt the him to seventh-place Boston in the off-season. As a result, New York's offense suffered. Hornsby, meanwhile, won his seventh (and last) batting title in near-obscurity for the pathetic Bees.

The Cubs continued to rise into contention, finishing just four games out as Hack Wilson hit 31 homers to tie Bottomley for the lead. The hard-drinking Wilson also fanned 94 times, a modern NL record. On the mound, Brooklyn's Dazzy Vance led the NL in strikeouts for the seventh (and last) time, but another outstanding pitcher debuted on July 26 when lefty Carl Hubbell pitched his first game for the Giants. Four days later, the Phillies gave slugging outfielder Chuck Klein his first major league action.

Six teams in the NL finished over .500, while Philadelphia and Boston—who desperately named Hornsby player-manager in midseason—ended a combined 95 games back. Large ticket sale drops in Boston, Philadelphia, and Pittsburgh, who dropped to fourth, led attendance to dip 8 percent.

Hitting was on the rise again as runs increased by 2.6 percent. Although league average fell a point, home runs skyrocketed by more than 25 percent and strikeouts decreased. Another indication of increased hitting? NL pitchers tossed just 558 complete games, by far the lowest total to date.

1928 AMERICAN LEAGUE

TEAM	W	L	T	PCT	GB	HW	HL	R	OR	PA	H	2B	3B	HR	BB	SO	HB	SH	AVG	OBP	SLG	OPS	AOPS	BR	ABR	PF	SB	CS	BSA	BSR
NY	101	53	0	.656	—	**52**	25	**894**	685	6070	**1578**	269	79	**133**	**562**	544	25	146	**.296**	**.365**	**.450**	**815**	**124**	**147**	**177**	97	51	52	50	-7
Phi	98	55	0	.641	2.5	**52**	25	829	**615**	5990	1540	**323**	75	89	533	442	**31**	200	.295	.363	.436	799	112	120	97	103	59	55	52	-6
StL	82	72	0	.532	19	44	33	772	742	6007	1431	276	76	63	548	479	28	**214**	.274	.346	.393	739	97	3	-19	103	78	43	**64**	**2**
Was	75	79	1	.487	26	37	43	718	705	6009	1510	277	93	40	481	**390**	28	180	.284	.346	.393	739	101	0	5	99	108	63	63	**2**
Chi	72	82	1	.468	29	37	40	656	725	5907	1405	231	77	24	469	488	**31**	200	.270	.334	.358	692	88	-92	-83	99	**144**	88	62	1
Det	68	86	0	.442	33	36	41	744	804	5949	1476	265	**97**	62	469	438	25	163	.279	.340	.401	741	99	-5	-16	102	113	79	59	-3
Cle	62	92	1	.403	39	29	48	674	830	5984	1535	299	61	34	377	426	30	191	.285	.335	.382	717	93	-49	-56	101	50	52	49	-7
Bos	57	96	1	.373	43.5	26	47	589	770	5754	1356	260	62	38	395	512	21	206	.264	.319	.361	680	86	-119	-108	98	97	68	59	-2
Total	617	—	—	—	—	313	302	5876	—	47670	11831	2200	620	483	3834	3719	219	1500	.281	.344	.397	741	—	—	—	—	700	500	58	-21

TEAM	CG	SHO	GR	SV	IP	H	HR	BB	SO	BR/9	ERA	AERA	OAV	OOB	PR	APR	PF	OSB	OCS	FA	E	WPB	DP	FW	PW	BW	BSW	DIF
NY	82	13	112	**21**	1375.1	1466	59	452	487	12.7	3.74	101	.276	.335	46	3	93	102	64	.968	194	28	136	-.0	.3	**17.1**	-.4	7.1
Phi	81	**15**	103	16	1367.2	**1349**	66	**424**	**607**	**11.8**	**3.36**	**119**	**.259**	**.318**	**103**	**98**	99	83	45	.970	181	29	124	.6	**9.5**	9.4	-.3	2.3
StL	80	6	128	15	1374.1	1487	93	454	456	12.8	4.17	101	.282	.340	-20	3	104	98	51	.969	189	19	146	.2	.3	-1.8	**.4**	5.9
Was	77	**15**	118	10	1384.0	1420	**40**	466	462	12.5	3.88	103	.272	.335	25	19	99	72	62	**.972**	**178**	30	146	**1.0**	1.8	.5	**.4**	-5.7
Chi	**88**	6	93	11	1378.0	1518	66	501	418	13.4	3.98	102	.287	.352	8	8	100	**59**	60	.970	186	27	149	.5	.8	-8.0	**.4**	1.4
Det	65	5	130	16	1372.0	1481	58	567	451	13.7	4.32	95	.281	.355	-42	-33	102	86	71	.965	218	31	140	-1.5	-3.2	-1.5	-.0	-2.8
Cle	71	4	122	15	1378.0	1615	52	511	416	14.2	4.47	93	.303	.369	-66	-51	103	90	72	.965	221	41	**187**	-1.6	-4.9	-5.4	-.4	-2.7
Bos	70	5	**131**	9	1352.0	1492	49	452	407	13.2	4.39	93	.288	.349	-53	-44	102	110	**77**	.971	**178**	**18**	139	.9	-4.3	-10.4	.0	-5.8
Total	614	69	937	113	10981.1	—	—	—	—	13.0	4.04	—	.281	.344	—	—	—	—	—	.969	1545	223	1167	—	—	—	—	—

BATTER-FIELDER WINS	BATTING AVERAGE	ON-BASE PERCENTAGE	SLUGGING AVERAGE	ON-BASE PLUS SLUGGING	ADJUSTED OPS	ADJUSTED BATTER RUNS
Ruth-NY 7.1	Goslin-Was .379	Gehrig-NY .467	Ruth-NY .709	Ruth-NY 1172	Ruth-NY 211	Ruth-NY 92.1
Gehrig-NY 5.9	Manush-StL .378	Ruth-NY .463	Gehrig-NY .648	Gehrig-NY 1115	Gehrig-NY 196	Gehrig-NY 83.3
J.Sewell-Cle 5.3	Gehrig-NY .374	Goslin-Was .442	Goslin-Was .614	Goslin-Was 1056	Goslin-Was 176	Goslin-Was 50.7
Goslin-Was 4.9	Simmons-Phi .351	Bishop-Phi .438	Manush-StL .575	Manush-StL 989	Manush-StL 153	Manush-StL 46.3
Manush-StL 3.3	Lazzeri-NY .332	Manush-StL .414	Simmons-Phi .558	Simmons-Phi 954	Simmons-Phi 144	Foxx-Phi 28.9
RUNS	**HITS**	**DOUBLES**	**TRIPLES**	**HOME RUNS**	**TOTAL BASES**	**RUNS BATTED IN**
Ruth-NY 163	Manush-StL 241	Manush-StL 47	Combs-NY 21	Ruth-NY 54	Ruth-NY 380	Ruth-NY 142
Gehrig-NY 139	Gehrig-NY 210	Gehrig-NY 47	Manush-StL 20	Gehrig-NY 27	Manush-StL 367	Gehrig-NY 142
Combs-NY 118	Rice-Was 202	Meusel-NY 45	Gehringer-Det 16	Goslin-Was 17	Gehrig-NY 364	Meusel-NY 113
Blue-StL 116	Combs-NY 194	Schulte-StL 44		Hauser-Phi 16	Combs-NY 290	Manush-StL 108
Gehringer-Det 108	Gehringer-Det 193	Lind-Cle 42		Simmons-Phi 15	Heilmann-Det 283	
BASES ON BALLS	**STOLEN BASES**	**BASE STEALING RUNS**	**FIELDING RUNS-INFIELD**	**FIELDING RUNS-OUTFIELD**	**OUTFIELD ASSISTS**	**CATCHER CS PCT.**
Ruth-NY 137	Myer-Bos 30	Rice-Was 2.5	Gerber-StL-Bos 25.7	Jamieson-Cle 15.9	Jamieson-Cle 22	L.Sewell-Cle 47.6
Blue-StL 105	Mostil-Chi 23	Goslin-Was 2.5	J.Sewell-Cle 25.5	Mostil-Chi 11.9	Schulte-StL 21	Hargrave-Det 34.8
Bishop-Phi 100	Rice-Det 20	Reynolds-Chi 2.3	Regan-Bos 15.1	Schulte-StL 9.9	Taitt-Bos 19	Cochrane-Phi 32.4
Gehrig-NY 95	Cissell-Chi 18	Judge-Was 2.1	Tavener-Det 12.1	Goslin-Was 7.6	McNeely-StL 19	Schang-StL 31.5
Judge-Was 80	Bluege-Was 18		Bluege-Was 10.1	Taitt-Bos 6.0		
WINS	**WINNING PCT.**	**WINS ABOVE TEAM**	**GAMES STARTED**	**COMPLETE GAMES**	**FEWEST HITS/GAME**	**FEWEST BB/GAME**
Pipgras-NY 24	Crowder-StL .808	Crowder-StL 8.2	Pipgras-NY 38	Ruffing-Bos 25	Braxton-Was 7.30	Rommel-Phi 1.35
Grove-Phi 24	Hoyt-NY .767	Morris-Bos 6.0	Ruffing-Bos 34	Thomas-Chi 24	Grove-Phi 7.84	Quinn-Phi 1.45
Hoyt-NY 23	Grove-Phi .750	Grove-Phi 5.7	Thomas-Chi 32	Grove-Phi 24	Earnshaw-Phi 8.13	Pennock-NY 1.71
Crowder-StL 21	Pennock-NY .739	Jones-Was 5.7		Pipgras-NY 22	Jones-Was 8.37	Braxton-Was 1.81
Gray-StL 20	Quinn-Phi .720	Hoyt-NY 5.6			Johnson-NY 8.50	Russell-Bos 1.83
STRIKEOUTS	**STRIKEOUTS/GAME**	**GAMES**	**SAVES**	**BASE RUNNERS/9**	**ADJUSTED RELIEF RUNS**	**RELIEF RANKING**
Grove-Phi 183	Earnshaw-Phi 6.65	Marberry-Was 48	Hoyt-NY 8	Braxton-Was 9.32		
Pipgras-NY 139	Grove-Phi 6.29	Morris-Bos 47	Hudlin-Cle 7	Grove-Phi 10.08		
Thomas-Chi 129	Johnson-NY 4.97	Pipgras-NY 46	Lyons-Chi 6	Rommel-Phi 10.62		
Ruffing-Bos 118	Walberg-Phi 4.28	Rommel-Phi 43	Braxton-Was 6	Pennock-NY 10.88		
Earnshaw-Phi 117	Whitehill-Det 4.26			Heimach-NY 10.99		
INNINGS PITCHED	**OPPONENTS' AVG.**	**OPPONENTS' OBP**	**EARNED RUN AVERAGE**	**ADJUSTED ERA**	**ADJUSTED STARTER RUNS**	**PITCHER WINS**
Pipgras-NY 300.2	Braxton-Was .222	Braxton-Was .267	Braxton-Was 2.51	Braxton-Was 159	Grove-Phi 40.7	**Grove-Phi 4.7**
Ruffing-Bos 289.1	Grove-Phi .229	Grove-Phi .277	Pennock-NY 2.56	Grove-Phi 155	Braxton-Was 34.0	**Thomas-Chi 3.5**
Thomas-Chi 283.0	Earnshaw-Phi .240	Rommel-Phi .295	Grove-Phi 2.58	Pennock-NY 147	Thomas-Chi 30.7	**Jones-Was 3.3**
Hoyt-NY 273.0	Johnson-NY .250	Pennock-NY .302	Jones-Was 2.84	Jones-Was 141	Pennock-NY 30.6	**Braxton-Was 3.2**
Gray-StL 262.2	Jones-Was .252	Thomas-Chi .310	Quinn-Phi 2.90	Quinn-Phi 138	Jones-Was 27.1	**Pennock-NY 3.1**

MURDERERS' ROW SURVIVES A'S, KILLS CARDS

Once again the Yankees enjoyed a great attack, leading the league both individually and collectively in nearly every offensive category. Lou Gehrig was now Babe Ruth's equal at bat, and the supporting cast continued to shine. Rookie catcher Bill Dickey made his first appearance and would soon join the fearsome lineup. While the Yankees' pitching was not nearly as strong as in the previous season, they were deep enough to withstand the loss (and, later that year, death from heart disease) of veteran righty Urban Shocker.

It wasn't easy, however. The Athletics were a worthy opponent, and after a late-season hot streak actually took a half-game lead over New York on September 8. The next day, more than 85,000 fans crammed into Yankee Stadium to see the two teams meet in a doubleheader; it was the most important regular-season matchup that baseball had seen in years, and the largest crowd to that point ever to watch a major league game. New York swept the twin bill, and despite a late flurry by Philadelphia, clinched the flag on September 28.

The Athletics, a fascinating mix of young and old, had seven Hall of Famers on the club. Lefty Grove had become the league's best pitcher, and he was well supported by 28-year-old rookie George Earnshaw, who held opponents to a .240 average. Earnshaw and Grove were 1-2 in the league in strikeouts per game, while teammates Eddie Rommel and Jack Quinn were the two stingiest in walks.

Offensively, the entire A's lineup contributed, and the bench sported a group of all-time greats. Three of them retired after the season: pitcher "Bullet Joe" Bush and two of the game's greatest center fielders, Ty Cobb and Tris Speaker. Forty-year-old Eddie Collins would hang around with Philadelphia until 1930.

But it was still the Yankees' show. Showing no signs of weakness, New York blew by the St. Louis Cardinals in four straight World Series games. Babe Ruth, who batted .625, and Gehrig, who hit .545, homered in the same game three times.

1927 NATIONAL LEAGUE

TEAM	W	L	T	PCT	GB	HW	HL	R	OR	PA	H	2B	3B	HR	BB	SO	HB	SH	AVG	OBP	SLG	OPS	AOPS	BR	ABR	PF	SB	CS	BSA	BSR
Pit	94	60	2	.610	—	48	31	**817**	659	6077	**1648**	258	78	54	437	355	29	214	**.305**	**.361**	.412	773	106	100	46	107	65			
StL	92	61	0	.601	1.5	**55**	25	754	665	5888	1450	264	**79**	84	**484**	511	26	171	.278	.343	.408	751	104	50	27	103	**110**			
NY	92	62	1	.597	2	49	25	**817**	720	6045	1594	251	62	**109**	461	462	**32**	180	.297	.356	**.427**	**783**	**116**	**115**	**117**	100	73			
Chi	85	68	0	.556	8.5	50	28	750	661	6018	1505	**266**	63	74	481	492	27	207	.284	.346	.400	746	106	47	45	100	65			
Cin	75	78	0	.490	18.5	45	35	643	653	5827	1439	222	77	29	402	**332**	21	**219**	.278	.332	.367	699	96	-49	-28	97	62			
Bro	65	88	1	.425	28.5	34	39	541	**619**	5752	1314	195	74	39	368	494	25	166	.253	.306	.342	648	79	-157	-159	100	106			
Bos	60	94	1	.390	34	32	41	651	771	5941	1498	216	61	37	346	363	28	197	.279	.326	.363	689	98	-76	-23	92	100			
Phi	51	103	1	.331	43	34	43	678	903	5956	1487	216	46	57	434	482	28	177	.280	.337	.370	707	94	-30	-39	101	68			
Total	617	—	—	—	—	347	267	5651	—	47504	11935	1888	540	483	3413	3491	216	1531	.282	.339	.386	.725	—	—	—	—	649	—	—	—

TEAM	CG	SHO	GR	SV	IP	H	HR	BB	SO	BR/9	ERA	AERA	OAV	OOB	PR	APR	PF	OSB	OCS	FA	E	WPB	DP	FW	PW	BW	BSW	DIF
Pit	**90**	10	107	10	1385.0	1400	58	418	435	12.0	3.66	112	.267	.324	39	65	105	63	*36*	.969	187	32	130	.6	6.4	4.5	—	5.4
StL	89	**14**	110	11	1367.1	1416	72	363	394	**11.8**	3.57	110	.271	**.320**	52	56	101	85	*64*	.966	213	**21**	**170**	-1.0	5.5	2.7	—	8.3
NY	65	7	147	**16**	1381.2	1520	77	453	442	13.0	3.97	97	.283	.341	-8	-18	98	70	*54*	.969	195	34	160	.1	-1.8	**11.5**	—	5.1
Chi	75	11	114	5	1385.0	1439	50	514	465	12.9	3.65	106	.273	.342	40	32	99	**52**	*58*	.971	181	31	152	.8	3.2	4.4	—	.1
Cin	87	12	93	12	1368.0	1472	**36**	**316**	407	11.9	3.54	107	.281	.325	57	38	97	100	*31*	**.973**	**165**	34	160	**1.6**	3.8	-2.8	—	-4.1
Bro	74	7	131	10	1375.1	**1382**	63	418	**574**	11.9	**3.36**	**118**	**.265**	.323	**85**	**89**	101	99	*68*	.963	229	25	117	-1.8	**8.8**	-15.7	—	-2.8
Bos	52	3	**156**	11	1390.0	1602	43	468	402	13.6	4.22	88	.296	.356	-48	-83	95	81	***71***	.963	231	40	130	-1.8	-8.2	-2.3	—	-4.7
Phi	81	5	112	6	1355.1	1710	84	462	377	14.7	5.36	77	.317	.374	-218	-177	106	99	*42*	.972	169	35	152	1.5	-17.5	-3.8	—	-6.2
Total	613	69	970	81	11007.2	—	—	—	—	12.7	3.91	—	.282	.339	—	—	—	—	—	.969	1570	252	1171	—	—	—	—	—

BATTER-FIELDER WINS	BATTING AVERAGE	ON-BASE PERCENTAGE	SLUGGING AVERAGE	ON-BASE PLUS SLUGGING	ADJUSTED OPS	ADJUSTED BATTER RUNS
Frisch-StL 7.2	P.Waner-Pit .380	Hornsby-NY .448	Hafey-StL .590	Hornsby-NY 1035	Hornsby-NY 175	Hornsby-NY 64.1
Hornsby-NY 6.8	Hornsby-NY .361	P.Waner-Pit .437	Hornsby-NY .586	P.Waner-Pit .986	Wilson-Chi 159	P.Waner-Pit 47.1
Jackson-NY 5.4	L.Waner-Pit .355	Harper-NY .435	Wilson-Chi .579	Wilson-Chi .980	P.Waner-Pit 152	Wilson-Chi 46.1
P.Waner-Pit 3.9	Stephenson-Chi .344	Stephenson-Chi .415	P.Waner-Pit .549	Harper-NY .930	Harper-NY 149	Harper-NY 38.1
Dressen-Cin 3.3	Traynor-Pit .342	Harris-Pit .402	Terry-NY .529	Terry-NY .907	Stephenson-Chi 141	Stephenson-Chi 37.3

RUNS	HITS	DOUBLES	TRIPLES	HOME RUNS	TOTAL BASES	RUNS BATTED IN
L.Waner-Pit 133	P.Waner-Pit 237	Stephenson-Chi 46	P.Waner-Pit 18	Wilson-Chi 30	P.Waner-Pit 342	P.Waner-Pit 131
Hornsby-NY 133	L.Waner-Pit 223	P.Waner-Pit 42	Bottomley-StL 15	Williams-Phi 30	Hornsby-NY 333	Wilson-Chi 129
Wilson-Chi 119	Frisch-StL 208	Lindstrom-NY 36	Thompson-Phi 14	Hornsby-NY 26	Wilson-Chi 319	Hornsby-NY 125
P.Waner-Pit 114	Hornsby-NY 205	Dressen-Cin 36	Terry-NY 13	Terry-NY 20	Terry-NY 307	Bottomley-StL 124
Frisch-StL 112	Stephenson-Chi 199	Brown-Bos 35	Wilson-Chi 12	Bottomley-StL 19	Bottomley-StL 292	Terry-NY 121

BASES ON BALLS	STOLEN BASES	BASE STEALING RUNS	FIELDING RUNS-INFIELD	FIELDING RUNS-OUTFIELD	OUTFIELD ASSISTS	CATCHER CS PCT.
Hornsby-NY 86	Frisch-StL 48		Frisch-StL 49.3	Leach-Phi 16.3	Leach-Phi 26	Hartnett-Chi 51.2
Harper-NY 84	Carey-Bro 32		Jackson-NY 26.3	Statz-Bro 9.9	Welsh-Bos 24	Taylor-Bos-NY 42.4
Grantham-Pit 74	Hendrick-Bro 29		Friberg-Phi 20.3	Welsh-Bos 8.1	Williams-Phi 22	Gooch-Pit 38.5
Bottomley-StL 74	Adams-Chi 26		Traynor-Pit 14.3	P.Waner-Pit 6.7	P.Waner-Pit 20	Wilson-Phi 29.6
	Richbourg-Bos 24		Cooney-Chi-Phi 13.2	Bressler-Cin 5.2		Hargrave-Cin 25.0

WINS	WINNING PCT.	WINS ABOVE TEAM	GAMES STARTED	COMPLETE GAMES	FEWEST HITS/GAME	FEWEST BB/GAME
Root-Chi 26	Benton-Bos-NY .708	Haines-StL 5.3	Meadows-Pit 38	Vance-Bro 25	Vance-Bro 7.97	Alexander-StL 1.28
Haines-StL 24	Haines-StL .706	Root-Chi 4.7	Root-Chi 36	Meadows-Pit 25	Kremer-Pit 8.16	Lucas-Cin 1.46
Hill-Pit 22	Kremer-Pit .704	Benton-Bos-NY 4.4	Haines-StL 36	Haines-StL 25	Haines-StL 8.17	Donohue-Cin 1.51
Alexander-StL 21	Grimes-NY .704	Lucas-Cin 4.3	Grimes-NY 34	Hill-Pit 22	Bush-Chi 8.24	Carlson-Phi-Chi 1.63
	Alexander-StL .677	Grimes-NY 4.1	Aldridge-Pit 34	Alexander-StL 22	Hill-Pit 8.43	Henry-NY 1.70

STRIKEOUTS	STRIKEOUTS/GAME	GAMES	SAVES	BASE RUNNERS/9	ADJUSTED RELIEF RUNS	RELIEF RANKING
Vance-Bro 184	Vance-Bro 6.06	Scott-Phi 48	Sherdel-StL 6	Miljus-Pit 9.40	Clark-Bro 13.2	Clark-Bro 15.3
Root-Chi 145	Elliott-Bro 4.73	Root-Chi 48	Nehf-Cin-Chi 5	Alexander-StL 10.07	Ehrhardt-Bro 4.0	Ehrhardt-Bro 3.9
May-Cin 121	May-Cin 4.62	Ehrhardt-Bro 46	Mogridge-Bos 5	Lucas-Cin 10.14	Cvengros-Pit 3.6	Cvengros-Pit 2.0
Grimes-NY 102	Pruett-Phi 4.35	Henry-NY 45	Henry-NY 4	Kremer-Pit 10.27	Morrison-Pit 4	Morrison-Pit 4
Petty-Bro 101	Root-Chi 4.22	May-Cin 44		Vance-Bro 10.44		

INNINGS PITCHED	OPPONENTS' AVG.	OPPONENTS' OBP	EARNED RUN AVERAGE	ADJUSTED ERA	ADJUSTED STARTER RUNS	PITCHER WINS
Root-Chi 309.0	Vance-Bro .239	Alexander-StL .286	Kremer-Pit 2.47	Kremer-Pit 166	Alexander-StL 41.3	**Alexander-StL 5.0**
Haines-StL 300.2	Kremer-Pit .244	Lucas-Cin .287	Alexander-StL 2.52	Alexander-StL 157	Haines-StL 39.4	**Kremer-Pit 4.2**
Meadows-Pit 299.1	Haines-StL .245	Kremer-Pit .289	Vance-Bro 2.70	Vance-Bro 147	Kremer-Pit 39.0	**Haines-StL 4.1**
Hill-Pit 277.2	Hill-Pit .249	Vance-Bro .291	Haines-StL 2.72	Haines-StL 145	Vance-Bro 38.1	**Vance-Bro 3.9**
Vance-Bro 273.1	Bush-Chi .250	Petty-Bro .293	Petty-Bro 2.98	Petty-Bro 133	Petty-Bro 29.4	**Lucas-Cin 3.1**

Raising the Skull and Crossbones

Once again, the Pittsburgh Pirates showed their facility in developing young players by debuting two more future stars: outfielder Lloyd Waner and shortstop Dick Bartell. Waner, and older brother Paul, would star in Pittsburgh for many years, but Bartell, sent to Philly in a poor 1930 trade, did most of his damage for other clubs. The great seasons of the Waners, and a big year from obscure pitcher Carmen Hill, propelled Pittsburgh to its second flag in three seasons.

The Cardinals finished 1½ games out after dealing productive but cranky Rogers Hornsby to the Giants for another second sacker, Frankie Frisch. While Frisch played well offensively and defensively for St. Louis, Mound City fans lambasted the deal. New York was third, 2 games back, with mediocre starting pitching and a power-based offense.

Several Senior Circuit veterans played their final seasons. First baseman Jacques Fournier was gone after 1,503 games, while 38-year-old Heinie Groh was released by the Pirates. Rifle-armed outfielder Irish Meusel's career careened to a premature end in Brooklyn, while future Hall of Famer Zach Wheat bowed out with a .324 season as a part-timer in Philadelphia. In addition, August "Garry" Herrmann, president of the Reds since 1902 and a kingpin of the National League, bowed out due to poor health that would lead to his death in 1931.

The Chicago Cubs, reconsidering an earlier promise to keep Wrigley Field single decked, decided to double-deck their park, and as a result became the first NL team to break the million mark in attendance. Their 1,159,168 turnstile clicks helped the entire league once again set a new high. The last-place Phillies, meanwhile, had to play at the Athletics' home, Shibe Park, for a few games after a section of Baker Bowl bleachers collapsed on May 14. Forbes Field took in a club-record 869,720, plus another 83,000 for the World Series, but on the field the Pirates were no match for the Yankees.

1927 AMERICAN LEAGUE

TEAM	W	L	T	PCT	GB	HW	HL	R	OR	PA	H	2B	3B	HR	BB	SO	HB	SH	AVG	OBP	SLG	OPS	AOPS	BR	ABR	PF	SB	CS	BSA	BSR
NY	110	44	1	.714	—	**57**	19	**975**	**599**	6207	**1644**	291	**103**	**158**	**635**	605	22	203	**.307**	**.383**	**.489**	**872**	**135**	**236**	**268**	97	90	64	58	-3
Phi	91	63	1	.591	19	50	27	841	726	6094	1606	281	70	56	551	**326**	30	217	.303	.372	.414	786	103	80	35	106	101	63	62	0
Was	85	69	3	.552	25	51	28	782	730	6117	1549	268	87	29	498	359	31	199	.287	.351	.386	737	97	-27	-18	99	133	52	**72**	**11**
Det	82	71	3	.536	27.5	44	32	845	805	6112	1533	282	100	51	587	420	24	202	.289	.363	.409	772	105	46	35	101	**139**	73	66	5
Chi	70	83	0	.458	39.5	38	37	662	708	5910	1433	285	61	36	493	389	26	**234**	.278	.344	.378	722	94	-53	-35	98	89	75	54	-7
Cle	66	87	0	.431	43.5	35	42	668	766	5843	1471	**321**	52	26	381	366	**48**	212	.283	.337	.379	716	90	-68	-73	101	65	72	47	-11
StL	59	94	2	.386	50.5	38	38	724	904	5897	1440	262	59	55	443	420	43	191	.276	.338	.380	718	88	-69	-91	103	90	66	58	-3
Bos	51	103	0	.331	59	29	49	597	856	5867	1348	271	78	28	430	456	39	191	.259	.320	.357	677	82	-152	-139	98	81	46	64	2
Total	619	—	—	—	—	342	272	6094	—	48047	12024	2261	610	439	4018	3341	263	1649	.285	.351	.399	751	—	—	—	—	788	511	61	-5

TEAM	CG	SHO	GR	SV	IP	H	HR	BB	SO	BR/9	ERA	AERA	OAV	OOB	PR	APR	PF	OSB	OCS	FA	E	WPB	DP	FW	PW	BW	BSW	DIF
NY	82	**11**	109	20	1389.2	**1403**	42	**409**	431	**11.9**	**3.20**	**120**	**.267**	**.323**	**145**	**107**	93	94	44	.969	195	22	123	.7	**10.2**	**25.5**	-.2	-3.1
Phi	65	8	160	**24**	1384.0	1467	65	442	**553**	12.6	3.97	107	.278	.338	26	44	103	**84**	47	.970	190	27	124	1.0	4.2	3.3	.0	5.4
Was	62	10	**163**	23	1402.0	1434	53	491	497	12.6	3.97	102	.269	.335	26	14	98	86	55	.969	195	**18**	125	.8	1.3	-1.7	**1.1**	6.4
Det	75	5	131	17	1387.2	1542	52	577	421	14.0	4.14	102	.290	.364	0	9	102	100	62	.968	206	33	**173**	.1	.9	3.3	.5	.7
Chi	**85**	10	95	8	1367.0	1467	55	440	365	12.7	3.91	103	.283	.342	34	20	98	86	68	**.971**	**178**	20	131	**1.6**	1.9	-3.3	-.6	-6.0
Cle	72	5	132	8	1353.1	1542	**37**	508	366	13.9	4.27	98	.295	.361	-20	-11	102	86	91	.968	201	39	146	.2	-1.0	-6.9	-1.0	-1.7
StL	80	4	121	8	1353.1	1592	79	604	385	14.7	4.95	88	.304	.378	-122	-87	105	94	**92**	.960	248	48	166	-2.5	-8.3	-8.6	-.2	2.1
Bos	63	6	134	7	1366.1	1603	56	558	381	14.5	4.72	89	.305	.376	-88	-76	102	158	52	.964	228	34	167	-1.4	-7.2	-13.2	.3	-4.5
Total	584	59	1045	115	11003.1	—	—	—	—	13.4	4.14	—	.285	.351	—	—	—	—	—	.967	1641	241	1155	—	—	—	—	—

BATTER-FIELDER WINS	BATTING AVERAGE	ON-BASE PERCENTAGE	SLUGGING AVERAGE	ON-BASE PLUS SLUGGING	ADJUSTED OPS	ADJUSTED BATTER RUNS
Ruth-NY 8.8	Heilmann-Det .398	Ruth-NY .486	Ruth-NY .772	Ruth-NY 1258	Ruth-NY 229	Gehrig-NY 108.8
Gehrig-NY 8.4	Simmons-Phi .392	Heilmann-Det .475	Gehrig-NY .765	Gehrig-NY 1240	Gehrig-NY 224	Ruth-NY 108.0
Heilmann-Det 4.1	Gehrig-NY .373	Gehrig-NY .474	Simmons-Phi .645	Heilmann-Det 1091	Heilmann-Det 179	Heilmann-Det 62.6
Lazzeri-NY 3.5	Fothergill-Det .359	Bishop-Phi .442	Heilmann-Det .616	Fothergill-Det 929	Combs-NY 143	Combs-NY 40.3
Simmons-Phi 3.3	Cobb-Phi .357	Cobb-Phi .440	Williams-StL .525	Williams-StL 928	Fothergill-Det 138	Simmons-Phi 39.3
RUNS	**HITS**	**DOUBLES**	**TRIPLES**	**HOME RUNS**	**TOTAL BASES**	**RUNS BATTED IN**
Ruth-NY 158	Combs-NY 231	Gehrig-NY 52	Combs-NY 23	Ruth-NY 60	Gehrig-NY 447	Gehrig-NY 175
Gehrig-NY 149	Gehrig-NY 218	Burns-Cle 51	Manush-Det 18	Gehrig-NY 47	Ruth-NY 417	Ruth-NY 164
Combs-NY 137	Sisler-StL 201	Heilmann-Det 50	Gehrig-NY 18	Lazzeri-NY 18	Combs-NY 331	Heilmann-Det 120
Gehringer-Det 110	Heilmann-Det 201	J.Sewell-Cle 48	Goslin-Was 15	Williams-StL 17	Heilmann-Det 311	Goslin-Was 120
Heilmann-Det 106	Goslin-Was 194	Meusel-NY 47	Rice-Was 14	Simmons-Phi 15	Goslin-Was 300	Fothergill-Det 114
BASES ON BALLS	**STOLEN BASES**	**BASE STEALING RUNS**	**FIELDING RUNS-INFIELD**	**FIELDING RUNS-OUTFIELD**	**OUTFIELD ASSISTS**	**CATCHER CS PCT.**
Ruth-NY 137	Sisler-StL 27	Sisler-StL 3.5	Gehringer-Det 17.1	Falk-Chi 18.1	Rice-StL 26	L.Sewell-Cle 50.7
Gehrig-NY 109	Meusel-NY 24	Harris-Was 2.9	Bluege-Was 14.8	Rice-StL 10.9	Falk-Chi 22	Crouse-Chi 50.7
Bishop-Phi 105	Neun-Det 22	Goslin-Was 2.5	Sisler-StL 12.1	Metzler-Chi 7.2	Barrett-Chi 22	Woodall-Det 39.7
Heilmann-Det 72	Lazzeri-NY 22	Neun-Det 2.4	Koenig-NY 12.1	Barrett-Chi 6.9	Flagstead-Bos 19	Ruel-Was 39.6
Blue-Det 71	Cobb-Phi 22	Rice-Was 2.1	O'Rourke-StL 11.2	Williams-StL 5.8	Metzler-Chi 16	McCurdy-Chi 37.3
WINS	**WINNING PCT.**	**WINS ABOVE TEAM**	**GAMES STARTED**	**COMPLETE GAMES**	**FEWEST HITS/GAME**	**FEWEST BB/GAME**
Lyons-Chi 22	Hoyt-NY .759	Lyons-Chi 6.1	Thomas-Chi 36	Lyons-Chi 30	Moore-NY 7.82	Quinn-Phi 1.65
Hoyt-NY 22	Shocker-NY .750	Hudlin-Cle 5.2	Lyons-Chi 34	Thomas-Chi 24	Thomas-Chi 7.93	Shocker-NY 1.85
Grove-Phi 20	Moore-NY .731	Lisenbee-Was 4.0	Lisenbee-Was 34	Hoyt-NY 23	Pipgras-NY 8.01	Hoyt-NY 1.90
	Pennock-NY .704	Hadley-Was 3.6	Blankenship-Chi 34	Gaston-StL 21	Hadley-Was 8.02	Braxton-Was 1.91
	Lisenbee-Was .667	Rommel-Phi 3.5	Walberg-Phi 33		Lisenbee-Was 8.22	Lyons-Chi 1.96
STRIKEOUTS	**STRIKEOUTS/GAME**	**GAMES**	**SAVES**	**BASE RUNNERS/9**	**ADJUSTED RELIEF RUNS**	**RELIEF RANKING**
Grove-Phi 174	Grove-Phi 5.97	Braxton-Was 58	Moore-NY 13	Moore-NY 10.35	Braxton-Was 18.7	Braxton-Was 24.1
Walberg-Phi 136	Braxton-Was 5.56	Marberry-Was 56	Braxton-Was 13	Braxton-Was 10.37	Burke-Was 2.9	G.Smith-Det 1.7
Thomas-Chi 107	Walberg-Phi 4.91	Grove-Phi 51	Marberry-Was 9	Lyons-Chi 10.47	G.Smith-Det 2.7	Burke-Was 1.4
Lisenbee-Was 105	Pipgras-NY 4.38	Moore-NY 50	Grove-Phi 9	Hoyt-NY 10.53		
Braxton-Was 96	Ruffing-Bos 4.38	Walberg-Phi 46		Thomas-Chi 10.71		
INNINGS PITCHED	**OPPONENTS' AVG.**	**OPPONENTS' OBP**	**EARNED RUN AVERAGE**	**ADJUSTED ERA**	**ADJUSTED STARTER RUNS**	**PITCHER WINS**
Thomas-Chi 307.2	Moore-NY .234	Moore-NY .289	Moore-NY 2.28	Moore-NY 169	Thomas-Chi 42.0	**Lyons-Chi 4.7**
Lyons-Chi 307.2	Thomas-Chi .244	Braxton-Was .289	Hoyt-NY 2.63	Hoyt-NY 146	Moore-NY 38.8	**Moore-NY 4.5**
Hudlin-Cle 264.2	Hadley-Was .244	Lyons-Chi .292	Shocker-NY 2.84	Lyons-Chi 143	Lyons-Chi 38.2	**Hoyt-NY 3.8**
Grove-Phi 262.1	Lisenbee-Was .245	Hoyt-NY .294	Lyons-Chi 2.84	Hadley-Was 142	Hoyt-NY 37.6	**Thomas-Chi 3.8**
Hoyt-NY 256.1	Braxton-Was .246	Thomas-Chi .303	Hadley-Was 2.85	Braxton-Was 137	Hadley-Was 28.2	**Grove-Phi 3.0**

Murder by Bat

Some felt that Babe Ruth's better days were behind him. But in 1927, he exploded again, tagging 60 home runs to set a mark that lasted until 1961. Lou Gehrig chipped in 175 RBIs, which still tops the AL list. Earle Combs led the league in hits and triples. The remainder of the offense assisted in the bludgeoning, and Murderer's Row outscored its closest rivals by 134. In addition, the Yankees pitching staff was the stingiest in the league by a margin of 109 runs. This dominating team was one of the best in baseball history.

Needless to say, the rest of the AL provided no challenge to the Yankees, whose 110 wins set a league record. Ruth and Gehrig, together, smacked 107 homers; Washington, Cleveland, Chicago, and Boston *combined* for only 119. The Red Sox, Ruth's former employer, finished 59 games behind, last for the third straight season.

As the Yankees eradicated the rest of the league, some of the great players of the pre-Ruth era called it quits. Walter Johnson pitched his last game at 39; first baseman Stuffy McInnis and shortstop Roger Peckinpaugh hung 'em up; and hurler Bob Shawkey, a consistent winner for New York even before the Babe's arrival, pitched his last game. On the horizon were the second-place Athletics, who continued to improve as Lefty Grove, Al Simmons, Mickey Cochrane, and Jimmie Foxx developed. But they were two years away.

The Pirates were a fine club, winning a tight NL race with solid hitting from the Waner brothers. But Pittsburgh was no match for the Yankees in the World Series, losing in four. While two games were decided by one run, the Bucs scored just 10 times in the Series; the Yankees tallied 23. Ruth batted .400 and hit the lone 2 homers of the Series.

1926 NATIONAL LEAGUE

TEAM	W	L	T	PCT	GB	HW	HL	R	OR	PA	H	2B	3B	HR	BB	SO	HB	SH	AVG	OBP	SLG	OPS	AOPS	BR	ABR	PF	SB	CS	BSA	BSR
StL	89	65	2	.578	—	47	30	**817**	678	6104	**1541**	259	82	**90**	**478**	518	33	212	.286	.348	**.415**	**763**	107	**77**	48	104	83			
Cin	87	67	3	.565	2	**53**	23	747	651	6047	**1541**	242	**120**	35	454	**333**	**34**	**239**	**.290**	**.349**	.400	749	**110**	49	**70**	97	51			
Pit	84	69	4	.549	4.5	49	28	769	689	5969	1514	243	106	44	434	350	33	190	.285	.343	.396	739	99	25	-12	105	91			
Chi	82	72	1	.532	7	49	28	682	**602**	5902	1453	**291**	49	66	445	447	29	199	.278	.338	.390	728	100	12	4	101	85			
NY	74	77	0	.490	13.5	43	33	663	668	5667	1435	214	58	73	339	420	22	139	.278	.325	.384	709	97	-39	-31	99	**94**			
Bro	71	82	2	.464	17.5	38	38	623	705	5790	1348	246	62	40	475	464	27	158	.263	.328	.358	686	91	-63	-53	99	76			
Bos	66	86	1	.434	22	43	34	624	719	5870	1444	209	62	16	426	348	29	199	.277	.335	.350	685	99	-67	-5	91	81			
Phi	58	93	1	.384	29.5	33	42	687	900	5851	1479	244	50	75	422	479	22	153	.281	.337	.390	727	96	6	-28	105	47			
Total	618	—	—	—	—	355	256	5612	—	47200	11755	1948	589	439	3473	3359	229	1489	.280	.338	.386	724	—	—	—	—	608	—	—	—

TEAM	CG	SHO	GR	SV	IP	H	HR	BB	SO	BR/9	ERA	AERA	OAV	OOB	PR	APR	PF	OSB	OCS	FA	E	WPB	DP	FW	PW	BW	BSW	DIF
StL	**90**	10	118	6	1398.2	1423	76	397	365	11.8	3.67	106	**.269**	.322	24	35	102	60	*64*	.969	198	19	141	.3	3.5	4.7	—	3.5
Cin	88	**14**	107	8	1408.2	1449	40	**324**	424	**11.5**	3.42	108	.271	**.316**	64	44	97	76	*43*	.972	183	27	160	1.3	4.3	**6.9**	—	-2.6
Pit	83	12	131	**18**	1379.1	1422	50	455	387	12.5	3.67	107	.272	.334	24	41	103	63	*44*	.965	220	**18**	161	-.9	4.1	-1.2	—	5.5
Chi	77	13	114	14	1378.1	1407	**39**	486	508	12.6	**3.26**	**118**	.273	.340	**87**	**89**	101	**42**	*68*	**.974**	**162**	37	**174**	**2.4**	**8.8**	.4	—	-6.6
NY	61	4	135	15	1341.2	**1370**	70	427	419	12.2	3.77	100	**.269**	.328	8	-3	98	84	*54*	.970	186	36	150	.7	-.3	-3.1	—	1.2
Bro	83	5	108	9	1361.2	1440	50	472	**517**	12.8	3.82	100	.276	.339	1	0	100	97	*63*	.963	229	34	95	-1.5	.0	-5.2	—	1.3
Bos	60	9	132	9	1365.1	1536	46	455	408	13.4	4.01	88	.294	.354	-28	-76	93	92	***71***	.967	208	42	150	-.5	-7.5	-.5	—	-1.5
Phi	68	5	**171**	5	1334.1	1699	68	454	331	14.7	5.03	82	.315	.371	-179	-123	108	94	*56*	.964	224	46	153	-1.5	-12.2	-2.8	—	-1.1
Total	610	72	1016	84	10968.0	—	—	—	—	12.7	3.82	—	.280	.338	—	—	—	—	—	.968	1610	259	1184	—	—	—	—	—

BATTER-FIELDER WINS
O'Farrell-StL....... 3.2
Wilson-Chi 2.8
Waner-Pit............ 2.6
Bancroft-Bos 2.6
Adams-Chi.......... 2.6

BATTING AVERAGE
Hargrave-Cin 353
Christensen-Cin....350
Smith-Pit...............346
Williams-Phi..........345
Waner-Pit..............336

ON-BASE PERCENTAGE
Waner-Pit..............413
Blades-StL............409
Wilson-Chi 406
Grantham-Pit 400
Bancroft-Bos.........399

SLUGGING AVERAGE
Williams-Phi..........568
Wilson-Chi 539
Waner-Pit..............528
Hargrave-Cin 525
L.Bell-StL..............518

ON-BASE PLUS SLUGGING
Wilson-Chi 944
Waner-Pit..............941
L.Bell-StL..............901
Grantham-Pit 890
Herman-Bro..........875

ADJUSTED OPS
Wilson-Chi 150
Waner-Pit..............144
Herman-Bro..........136
L.Bell-StL..............135
Grantham-Pit 131

ADJUSTED BATTER RUNS
Wilson-Chi 39.2
Waner-Pit.............34.0
L.Bell-StL 27.6
Williams-Phi.........26.3
Herman-Bro.........24.3

RUNS
Cuyler-Pit.............113
Waner-Pit..............101
Southworth-NY-StL....99
Sand-Phi.................99

HITS
Brown-Bos 201
Cuyler-Pit..............197
Adams-Chi............193
L.Bell-StL 189

DOUBLES
Bottomley-StL 40
Roush-Cin...............37
Wilson-Chi 36

TRIPLES
Waner-Pit................22
Walker-Cin 20
Traynor-Pit 17

HOME RUNS
Wilson-Chi 21
Bottomley-StL 19
Williams-Phi............18
L.Bell-StL................17
Southworth-NY-StL....16

TOTAL BASES
Bottomley-StL 305
L.Bell-StL 301
Wilson-Chi 285
Waner-Pit..............283
Cuyler-Pit..............282

RUNS BATTED IN
Bottomley-StL 120
Wilson-Chi 109
L.Bell-StL 100
Southworth-NY-StL....99
Pipp-Cin..................99

BASES ON BALLS
Wilson-Chi 69
Waner-Pit................66
Sand-Phi.................66
Bancroft-Bos...........64
Blades-StL 62

STOLEN BASES
Cuyler-Pit................35
Adams-Chi..............27
Frisch-NY................23
Douthit-StL..............23
Youngs-NY..............21

BASE STEALING RUNS

FIELDING RUNS-INFIELD
Critz-Cin...............23.0
Friberg-Phi...........22.1
Adams-Chi...........20.1
Cooney-Chi..........17.8
Thevenow-StL......16.2

FIELDING RUNS-OUTFIELD
Heathcote-Chi........8.5
Welsh-Bos 8.2
Douthit-StL.............7.2
Cuyler-Pit...............6.7
Leach-Phi 6.0

OUTFIELD ASSISTS
Welsh-Bos 23
Heathcote-Chi.........22
Waner-Pit................21
Walker-Cin 21
Mueller-StL-NY 20

CATCHER CS PCT.
Hartnett-Chi 62.7
Gonzalez-Chi.......52.4
O'Farrell-StL 50.0
Wilson-Phi 45.9
Z.Taylor-Bos.........45.7

WINS
Rhem-StL 20
Meadows-Pit...........20
Kremer-Pit 20
Donohue-Cin 20
Mays-Cin 19

WINNING PCT.
Kremer-Pit 769
Rhem-StL 741
Meadows-Pit.........690
Mays-Cin 613
Donohue-Cin 588

WINS ABOVE TEAM
Kremer-Pit 7.0
Rhem-StL 5.8
Carlson-Phi............5.5
Meadows-Pit..........5.2
Haines-StL.............4.0

GAMES STARTED
Donohue-Cin 36
Rhem-StL 34
Carlson-Phi.............34
Petty-Bro.................33
Mays-Cin 33

COMPLETE GAMES
Mays-Cin 24
Petty-Bro.................23
Root-Chi 21
Rhem-StL 20
Carlson-Phi.............20

FEWEST HITS/GAME
Petty-Bro.............8.03
Greenfield-NY......8.33
Rhem-StL 8.41
Jones-Chi 8.48
Bush-Chi..............8.52

FEWEST BB/GAME
Donohue-Cin 1.23
Alexander-Chi-StL...1.39
Carlson-Phi..........1.58
Mays-Cin 1.70
Lucas-Cin 1.75

STRIKEOUTS
Vance-Bro............140
Root-Chi 127
May-Cin 103
Benton-Bos...........103
Petty-Bro...............101

STRIKEOUTS/GAME
Vance-Bro............7.46
May-Cin 5.53
Jones-Chi 4.49
Blake-Chi 4.33
Root-Chi 4.21

GAMES
Scott-NY 50
Willoughby-Phi........47
Donohue-Cin 47
Ulrich-Phi................45
May-Cin 45

SAVES
Davies-NY 6
Scott-NY 5
Kremer-Pit 5
Ehrhardt-Bro.............4

BASE RUNNERS/9
Alexander-Chi-StL.10.06
H.Bell-StL 10.69
Petty-Bro............10.71
Kremer-Pit 10.74
Bush-Pit.............10.90

ADJUSTED RELIEF RUNS
Hallahan-StL..........1.7

RELIEF RANKING
Hallahan-StL..........1.3

INNINGS PITCHED
Donohue-Cin 285.2
Mays-Cin 281.0
Petty-Bro...........275.2
Root-Chi 271.1
Carlson-Phi........267.1

OPPONENTS' AVG.
Petty-Bro..............240
Alexander-Chi-StL....250
Rhem-StL 250
Greenfield-NY.......251
Kremer-Pit 252

OPPONENTS' OBP
Alexander-Chi-StL....281
Petty-Bro..............296
Kremer-Pit 296
Donohue-Cin 298
Rhem-StL 305

EARNED RUN AVERAGE
Kremer-Pit 2.61
Root-Chi 2.82
Petty-Bro.............2.84
Bush-Chi..............2.86
Barnes-NY...........2.87

ADJUSTED ERA
Kremer-Pit 151
Root-Chi 136
Petty-Bro..............134
Bush-Chi...............134
Barnes-NY............131

ADJUSTED STARTER RUNS
Kremer-Pit 34.4
Root-Chi 30.1
Petty-Bro.............25.2
Carlson-Phi.........24.9
Mays-Cin 20.9

PITCHER WINS
Kremer-Pit.......... 3.9
Root-Chi............. 3.1
Mays-Cin............ 2.9
Carlson-Phi 2.6
Petty-Bro 2.4

Cardinals Nest at the Top

It had been a long upward crawl for the St. Louis Cardinals. Since joining the NL in 1892, the franchise had never won and rarely even contended. With slugging Rogers Hornsby taking the managerial reins, however, 1926 was different. St. Louis' powerful offense, led by Hornsby and Bottomley, bludgeoned its opponents into submission. Unheralded Les Bell (.325, 17 homers, 100 RBIs) turned in one of the best hitting performances by a third baseman to that time. Lowly Boston spiced things up by beating up on St. Louis in early September. The Braves in turn knocked Cincinnati, Chicago, and Pittsburgh out of the race.

Attendance again hit an all-time high. Since 1904, AL attendance had topped the NL's every season. But in 1926 the Senior Circuit outdrew its rival and would remain better attended for seven more seasons. Since five NL teams actually lost attendance in '26, the gains came from just three clubs: the Cardinals (60 percent increase), the Reds (69 percent), and the Cubs (70 percent).

Giants outfielder Ross Youngs came down with Bright's disease at midseason. He died in November 1927. However, 17-year-old Mel Ott moved in, hitting .383 in 35 games for the Giants. Two stellar Pittsburgh, hurlers, Babe Adams and Wilbur Cooper, ended their careers with 416 combined victories. But the Bucs welcomed outfielder Paul Waner, who had a tremendous start to his Hall of Fame career. He led the NL in on-base percentage and went 6-for-6 against St. Louis on August 26.

The Cardinals-Yankees World Series was a thriller. Down three games to two in New York, St. Louis blew out the Bombers in Game 6 and held on for a thrilling Game 7 victory. Summoned in relief, Grover Cleveland Alexander quelled two New York rallies in the final contest after winning Games 2 and 6. Babe Ruth hit 4 homers, but he was thrown out stealing second to end the Series!

1926 AMERICAN LEAGUE

TEAM	W	L	T	PCT	GB	HW	HL	R	OR	PA	H	2B	3B	HR	BB	SO	HB	SH	AVG	OBP	SLG	OPS	AOPS	BR	ABR	PF	SB	CS	BSA	BSR
NY	91	63	1	.591	—	**50**	25	**847**	713	6104	1508	262	75	**121**	**642**	580	23	218	.289	**.369**	**.437**	**806**	**119**	**124**	**138**	98	79	62	56	-4
Cle	88	66	0	.571	3	49	31	738	612	6005	1529	**333**	49	27	455	**332**	35	222	.289	.349	.386	735	97	-13	-19	101	88	42	**68**	**5**
Phi	83	67	0	.553	6	44	27	677	**570**	5833	1359	259	65	61	523	452	25	**239**	.269	.341	.383	724	90	-39	-75	106	56	45	55	-3
Was	81	69	2	.540	8	42	30	802	761	6011	1525	244	**97**	43	555	369	**38**	195	**.292**	.364	.401	765	109	46	66	98	117	91	56	-6
Chi	81	72	2	.529	9.5	47	31	730	665	6039	1508	314	60	32	556	381	34	229	.289	.361	.390	751	106	29	58	96	**123**	78	61	0
Det	79	75	3	.513	12	39	41	793	830	6184	**1547**	281	90	36	599	423	34	236	.291	.367	.398	765	105	53	43	101	88	71	55	-5
StL	62	92	1	.403	29	40	39	682	845	5936	1449	253	78	72	437	472	35	205	.276	.335	.394	729	92	-42	-73	105	64	66	49	-9
Bos	46	107	1	.301	44.5	25	51	562	835	5848	1325	249	54	32	465	454	33	165	.256	.321	.343	664	82	-158	-140	97	52	48	52	-5
Total	616	—	—	—	—	336	275	5831	—	47960	11750	2195	568	424	4232	3463	257	1709	.281	.351	.392	743	—	—	—	—	667	503	57	-29

TEAM	CG	SHO	GR	SV	IP	H	HR	BB	SO	BR/9	ERA	AERA	OAV	OOB	PR	APR	PF	OSB	OCS	FA	E	WPB	DP	FW	PW	BW	BSW	DIF
NY	63	4	147	20	1372.1	1442	56	478	486	12.8	3.86	100	.274	.337	24	-1	96	95	67	.966	210	36	117	-1.1	-.0	**13.4**	-.0	1.9
Cle	**96**	**11**	81	4	1374.0	1412	49	**450**	381	12.5	3.40	119	.271	.334	94	100	101	**49**	41	.972	173	28	153	1.1	9.7	-1.8	**.8**	1.3
Phi	62	10	156	16	1346.0	**1362**	**38**	451	**571**	**12.3**	**3.00**	**139**	**.268**	**.331**	**153**	**168**	104	78	64	.972	171	35	131	.9	**16.3**	-7.3	.0	-1.9
Was	65	5	143	**26**	1348.1	1489	45	566	418	14.0	4.34	89	.287	.361	-48	-74	96	80	59	.969	184	**21**	129	.2	-7.2	6.4	-.2	6.8
Chi	85	**11**	100	12	1380.0	1426	47	506	458	12.7	3.74	103	.271	.336	43	17	96	59	55	**.973**	**165**	**21**	122	**1.6**	1.6	5.6	.4	-4.7
Det	57	10	**164**	18	1394.2	1570	58	555	469	14.0	4.41	92	.292	.363	-61	-53	101	100	70	.969	193	24	151	.0	-5.1	4.2	-.1	3.0
StL	64	5	139	9	1368.0	1549	86	654	337	14.7	4.66	92	.297	.379	-98	-55	107	67	**86**	.963	235	38	**167**	-2.6	-5.3	-7.1	-.5	.5
Bos	53	6	163	5	1362.0	1520	45	546	336	13.9	4.72	86	.294	.365	-107	-99	101	139	59	.970	193	34	143	-.2	-9.6	-13.6	-.1	-7.1
Total	545	62	1093	110	10945.1	—	—	—	—	13.3	4.02	—	.281	.351	—	—	—	—	—	.969	1524	237	1113	—	—	—	—	—

BATTER-FIELDER WINS	BATTING AVERAGE	ON-BASE PERCENTAGE	SLUGGING AVERAGE	ON-BASE PLUS SLUGGING	ADJUSTED OPS	ADJUSTED BATTER RUNS
Ruth-NY 8.5	Manush-Det..........378	Ruth-NY................516	Ruth-NY................737	Ruth-NY.............1253	Ruth-NY................228	Ruth-NY............102.8
Goslin-Was......... 4.6	Ruth-NY................372	Heilmann-Det........445	Simmons-Phi........564	Manush-Det..........985	Goslin-Was...........155	Gehrig-NY............47.5
Rigney-Bos......... 4.3	Fothergill-Det........367	Bishop-Phi............431	Manush-Det..........564	Heilmann-Det........979	Gehrig-NY.............154	Goslin-Was..........45.0
Mostil-Chi........... 3.5	Heilmann-Det........367	Goslin-Was...........425	Gehrig-NY.............549	Gehrig-NY.............969	Manush-Det..........153	Heilmann-Det.......41.8
J.Sewell-Cle....... 3.4	Burns-Cle.............358	Manush-Det..........421	Goslin-Was...........542	Goslin-Was...........967	Heilmann-Det........153	Manush-Det.........37.3
RUNS	**HITS**	**DOUBLES**	**TRIPLES**	**HOME RUNS**	**TOTAL BASES**	**RUNS BATTED IN**
Ruth-NY................139	Rice-Was..............216	Burns-Cle...............64	Gehrig-NY..............20	Ruth-NY..................47	Ruth-NY................365	Ruth-NY................146
Gehrig-NY.............135	Burns-Cle.............216	Simmons-Phi..........53	Gehringer-Det.........17	Simmons-Phi..........19	Simmons-Phi........329	Lazzeri-NY............114
Mostil-Chi.............120	Goslin-Was...........201	Speaker-Cle...........52	Mostil-Chi...............15	Lazzeri-NY..............18	Gehrig-NY.............314	Burns-Cle.............114
Combs-NY............113	Simmons-Phi........199	Jacobson-StL-Bos..51	Goslin-Was.............15	Williams-StL............17	Goslin-Was...........308	Gehrig-NY.............112
Goslin-Was...........105	Mostil-Chi.............197	Gehrig-NY..............47		Goslin-Was.............17	Burns-Cle.............298	Simmons-Phi........109
BASES ON BALLS	**STOLEN BASES**	**BASE STEALING RUNS**	**FIELDING RUNS-INFIELD**	**FIELDING RUNS-OUTFIELD**	**OUTFIELD ASSISTS**	**CATCHER CS PCT.**
Ruth-NY................144	Mostil-Chi................35	Mostil-Chi..............2.8	Rigney-Bos..........21.1	Goslin-Was..........14.1	Rice-Was................25	Schalk-Chi...........46.8
Bishop-Phi............116	Rice-Was................24	Hunnefield-Chi.......2.1	Dykes-Phi............16.3	Rice-Was...............9.4	Goslin-Was.............25	L.Sewell-Cle........46.6
Rigney-Bos...........108	Hunnefield-Chi........24	McNeely-Was........1.9	Kamm-Chi............16.1	Falk-Chi.................8.3	Rice-StL..................22	Cochrane-Phi.......43.9
Gehrig-NY.............105	McNeely-Was.........18	Simmons-Phi.........1.4	Regan-Bos...........15.7	Rice-StL.................6.9	Speaker-Cle............20	Ruel-Was.............40.6
Speaker-Cle............94	J.Sewell-Cle...........17	J.Sewell-Cle..........1.3	McManus-StL......11.9	Mostil-Chi..............6.7		Collins-NY...........38.7
WINS	**WINNING PCT.**	**WINS ABOVE TEAM**	**GAMES STARTED**	**COMPLETE GAMES**	**FEWEST HITS/GAME**	**FEWEST BB/GAME**
Uhle-Cle..................27	Uhle-Cle...............711	Uhle-Cle.................7.4	Uhle-Cle..................36	Uhle-Cle..................32	Grove-Phi............7.92	Pennock-NY.........1.45
Pennock-NY............23	Pennock-NY..........676	Pate-Phi.................4.5	Whitehill-Det...........34	Lyons-Chi................24	Thomas-Chi.........8.13	Smith-Cle............1.48
Shocker-NY............19	Shocker-NY..........633	Pennock-NY...........4.3	Coveleski-Was........34	Johnson-Was.........22	Uhle-Cle..............8.48	Quinn-Phi............1.98
Lyons-Chi................18	Faber-Chi..............625	Dauss-Det.............3.1		Grove-Phi...............20	Lyons-Chi............8.50	Rommel-Phi.........2.22
	Hoyt-NY...............571	Faber-Chi..............2.8		Pennock-NY............19	Buckeye-Cle........8.69	Wingfield-Bos......2.36
STRIKEOUTS	**STRIKEOUTS/GAME**	**GAMES**	**SAVES**	**BASE RUNNERS/9**	**ADJUSTED RELIEF RUNS**	**RELIEF RANKING**
Grove-Phi..............194	Grove-Phi............6.77	Marberry-Was.........64	Marberry-Was.........22	Russell-Bos.......10.93	Pate-Phi..............19.6	Marberry-Was......21.2
Uhle-Cle................159	Thomas-Chi.........4.59	Pate-Phi..................47	Dauss-Det..................9	Pennock-NY.......11.52	Marberry-Was......13.3	Pate-Phi..............16.4
Thomas-Chi...........127	Uhle-Cle..............4.50	Grove-Phi................45	Pate-Phi.....................6	Rommel-Phi.......11.55	Braxton-NY............7.6	Braxton-NY............6.6
Johnson-Was........125	Johnson-Was.......4.32	Thomas-Chi............44	Grove-Phi...................6	Johnson-Was.....11.64	Russell-Bos...........7.6	Russell-Bos...........3.8
Whitehill-Det.........109	Whitehill-Det........3.89		Jones-NY....................5	Grove-Phi..........11.65		
INNINGS PITCHED	**OPPONENTS' AVG.**	**OPPONENTS' OBP**	**EARNED RUN AVERAGE**	**ADJUSTED ERA**	**ADJUSTED STARTER RUNS**	**PITCHER WINS**
Uhle-Cle.............318.1	Thomas-Chi..........244	Pennock-NY..........313	Grove-Phi............2.51	Grove-Phi.............166	Uhle-Cle..............44.6	**Uhle-Cle............. 5.4**
Lyons-Chi...........283.2	Grove-Phi.............244	Rommel-Phi..........314	Uhle-Cle..............2.83	Uhle-Cle................143	Grove-Phi............43.7	**Grove-Phi............ 3.7**
Pennock-NY.......266.1	Lyons-Chi.............252	Hoyt-NY................316	Lyons-Chi............3.01	Rommel-Phi..........135	Lyons-Chi............28.8	**Lyons-Chi............ 3.3**
Johnson-Was.....260.2	Uhle-Cle...............253	Johnson-Was........317	Rommel-Phi.........3.08	Buckeye-Cle.........131	Rommel-Phi.........27.1	**Walberg-Phi........ 2.3**
Shocker-NY.......258.1	Levsen-Cle...........261	Shocker-NY..........318	Buckeye-Cle........3.10	Lyons-Chi.............128	Walberg-Phi.........19.3	**Rommel-Phi....... 2.2**

The Yankees Are Back

Due to the calamitous (at least for pitchers) rise in offense, the rules committee decided that any flyball over an outfield fence less than 250 feet from home was a ground-rule double. Three clubs also tried to curb production; St. Louis, a home run haven in '25, pushed out the fences by 10 feet. Boston enlarged Fenway Park's right field by 45 feet, and the White Sox grew center field by 30. Philadelphia, however, hoping to spur on their young power, shrunk Shibe Park to all fields. The Senators also chopped Griffith Stadium's left field by 66 feet. But the upshot to all these moves was a decline in scoring by nearly half a run and a loss of more than 100 homers.

Into this environment moved the Yankees, bolstered by the hitting of a healthy Babe Ruth, rookie infielder Tony Lazzeri, and 23-year-old Lou Gehrig, making his first appearance among the league leaders—although he actually hit more triples than homers. Miller Huggins' lineup destroyed the competition, but they just held off second-place Cleveland, whose first baseman George Burns rapped out a major league record 64 doubles.

The Indians and third-place Athletics played in inhospitable home run parks, and couldn't compete with New York's firepower, and their pitching wasn't good enough to overcome this. Washington fell to fourth as Walter Johnson finally went over the hill.

Shortstop Everett Scott retired with the record for most consecutive games played (1,307), and Hall of Fame hurler Eddie Plank died at age 50 of a stroke. Joe Cronin, later a standout with the Senators, debuted for the Pittsburgh Pirates—who soon gave up on him.

In addition to the Yankees' tough World Series loss to the Cardinals, 1926 was an ignominious year for the Junior Circuit in another way: the NL moved ahead in attendance for the first time since 1903. The Senior Circuit remained ahead until 1934.

1925 NATIONAL LEAGUE

TEAM	W	L	T	PCT	GB	HW	HL	R	OR	PA	H	2B	3B	HR	BB	SO	HB	SH	AVG	OBP	SLG	OPS	AOPS	BR	ABR	PF	SB	CS	BSA	BSR
Pit	95	58	0	.621	—	**52**	25	**912**	715	6036	**1651**	**316**	**105**	78	**499**	363	30	135	**.307**	**.369**	**.449**	**818**	**108**	**120**	**62**	107	**159**	63	**72**	**13**
NY	86	66	0	.566	8.5	47	29	736	702	5858	1507	239	61	**114**	411	494	25	95	.283	.337	.415	752	101	-28	3	96	79	65	55	-5
Cin	80	73	0	.523	15	44	32	690	**643**	5838	1490	221	90	44	409	**327**	23	**173**	.285	.339	.387	726	93	-71	-54	98	108	107	50	-14
StL	77	76	0	.503	18	48	28	828	764	5936	1592	292	80	109	446	414	27	134	.299	.356	.445	801	**108**	75	56	102	70	51	58	-2
Bos	70	83	0	.458	25	37	39	708	802	5945	1567	260	70	41	405	380	30	145	.292	.345	.390	735	102	-48	22	91	77	72	52	-8
Phi	68	85	0	.444	27	38	39	812	930	6035	1598	288	58	100	456	542	**34**	133	.295	.354	.425	779	96	39	-28	109	48	59	45	-10
Bro	68	85	0	.444	27	40	37	786	866	6045	1617	250	80	64	437	383	26	114	.296	.351	.406	757	102	-8	14	97	37	30	55	-2
Chi	68	86	0	.442	27.5	37	40	723	773	5933	1473	254	70	86	397	470	33	150	.275	.329	.397	726	89	-78	-88	102	94	70	57	-4
Total	612	—	—	—	—	343	269	6195	—	47626	12495	2120	614	636	3460	3373	228	1079	.292	.348	.414	762	—	—	—	—	672	517	57	-33

TEAM	CG	SHO	GR	SV	IP	H	HR	BB	SO	BR/9	ERA	AERA	OAV	OOB	PR	APR	PF	OSB	OCS	FA	E	WPB	DP	FW	PW	BW	BSW	DIF
Pit	77	2	119	**13**	1354.2	1526	81	387	386	12.9	3.87	115	.287	.339	59	84	105	**54**	51	.964	224	36	**171**	-.9	7.9	**5.8**	**1.6**	4.1
NY	80	6	113	8	1354.0	1532	73	408	446	13.0	3.94	102	.289	.342	49	18	95	91	73	.968	199	**20**	129	.5	1.7	.3	-.0	7.6
Cin	**92**	**11**	103	12	1375.1	**1447**	**35**	**324**	437	**11.8**	**3.38**	**121**	**.272**	**.317**	**135**	**115**	96	107	52	.968	203	32	161	.3	**10.8**	-5.1	-.9	-1.6
StL	82	8	105	7	1335.2	1480	86	470	428	13.4	4.36	99	.283	.347	-14	-7	101	72	57	.966	204	25	156	.3	-.7	5.2	.2	-4.6
Bos	77	5	129	4	1366.2	1567	67	458	351	13.4	4.39	91	.291	.348	-19	-62	94	77	48	.964	221	29	145	-.7	-5.8	2.1	-.4	-1.7
Phi	69	8	**151**	9	1350.2	1753	117	444	371	14.8	5.02	95	.315	.368	-114	-34	112	89	54	.966	211	45	147	-.1	-3.2	-2.6	-.5	-2.0
Bro	82	4	128	4	1350.2	1608	75	477	**518**	14.1	4.77	88	.301	.362	-76	-92	98	122	**107**	.966	210	50	130	-.0	-8.6	1.3	.2	-1.3
Chi	75	5	115	10	1370.0	1575	102	485	435	13.7	4.41	98	.292	.353	-21	-13	101	60	75	**.969**	**198**	21	161	**.7**	-1.2	-8.2	.0	-.3
Total	634	49	963	67	10857.2	—	—	—	—	13.4	4.27	—	.292	.348	—	—	—	—	—	.966	1670	258	1200	—	—	—	—	—

BATTER-FIELDER WINS	BATTING AVERAGE	ON-BASE PERCENTAGE	SLUGGING AVERAGE	ON-BASE PLUS SLUGGING	ADJUSTED OPS	ADJUSTED BATTER RUNS
Hornsby-StL 6.8	Hornsby-StL .403	Hornsby-StL .489	Hornsby-StL .756	Hornsby-StL 1245	Hornsby-StL 208	Hornsby-StL 85.3
Fournier-Bro 4.2	Bottomley-StL .367	Fournier-Bro .446	Cuyler-Pit .598	Cuyler-Pit 1021	Fournier-Bro 162	Fournier-Bro 53.9
Bancroft-Bos 3.9	Wheat-Bro .359	Blades-StL .423	Wrightstone-Phi .591	Fournier-Bro 1015	Cuyler-Pit 148	Cuyler-Pit 44.1
Traynor-Pit 3.6	Cuyler-Pit .357	Cuyler-Pit .423	Bottomley-StL .578	Bottomley-StL 992	Bottomley-StL 147	Bottomley-StL 43.2
Cuyler-Pit 3.6	Fournier-Bro .350	Carey-Pit .418	Fournier-Bro .569	Blades-StL 958	Wheat-Bro 143	Wheat-Bro 38.8
RUNS	**HITS**	**DOUBLES**	**TRIPLES**	**HOME RUNS**	**TOTAL BASES**	**RUNS BATTED IN**
Cuyler-Pit 144	Bottomley-StL 227	Bottomley-StL 44	Cuyler-Pit 26	Hornsby-StL 39	Hornsby-StL 381	Hornsby-StL 143
Hornsby-StL 133	Wheat-Bro 221	Cuyler-Pit 43	Walker-Cin 16	Hartnett-Chi 24	Cuyler-Pit 369	Fournier-Bro 130
Wheat-Bro 125	Cuyler-Pit 220	Wheat-Bro 42	Roush-Cin 16	Fournier-Bro 22	Bottomley-StL 358	Bottomley-StL 128
Traynor-Pit 114	Hornsby-StL 203	Hornsby-StL 41	Fournier-Bro 16	Meusel-NY 21	Wheat-Bro 333	Wright-Pit 121
Blades-StL 112	Stock-Bro 202	Burrus-Bos 41		Bottomley-StL 21	Fournier-Bro 310	Barnhart-Pit 114
BASES ON BALLS	**STOLEN BASES**	**BASE STEALING RUNS**	**FIELDING RUNS-INFIELD**	**FIELDING RUNS-OUTFIELD**	**OUTFIELD ASSISTS**	**CATCHER CS PCT.**
Fournier-Bro 86	Carey-Pit 46	Carey-Pit 6.3	Adams-Chi 26.5	Felix-Bos 9.5	Welsh-Bos 27	Hartnett-Chi 58.0
Hornsby-StL 83	Cuyler-Pit 41	Cuyler-Pit 4.5	Traynor-Pit 23.3	Blades-StL 9.3	Youngs-NY 23	Smith-Pit 52.3
Moore-Pit 73	Adams-Chi 26	Smith-StL 3.7	Critz-Cin 19.7	Heathcote-Chi 8.3	Heathcote-Chi 21	Taylor-Bro 47.4
Youngs-NY 66	Roush-Cin 22	Moore-Pit 1.7	Kelly-NY 18.3	Neis-Bos 7.1	Cuyler-Pit 21	Snyder-NY 43.5
Carey-Pit 66	Frisch-NY 21	Grantham-Pit 1.7	Pinelli-Cin 17.0	Welsh-Bos 4.8	Carey-Pit 20	O'Farrell-Chi-StL 41.3
WINS	**WINNING PCT.**	**WINS ABOVE TEAM**	**GAMES STARTED**	**COMPLETE GAMES**	**FEWEST HITS/GAME**	**FEWEST BB/GAME**
Vance-Bro 22	Sherdel-StL .714	Vance-Bro 8.3	Donohue-Cin 38	Donohue-Cin 27	Luque-Cin 8.13	Alexander-Chi 1.11
Rixey-Cin 21	Vance-Bro .710	Rixey-Cin 5.3	Ring-Phi 37	Vance-Bro 26	Benton-Bos 8.35	Donohue-Cin 1.47
Donohue-Cin 21	Aldridge-Pit .682	Sherdel-StL 4.8	Rixey-Cin 36	Rixey-Cin 22	Vance-Bro 8.38	Rixey-Cin 1.47
Meadows-Pit 19	Kremer-Pit .680	Benton-Bos 4.4	Luque-Cin 36	Luque-Cin 22	Aldridge-Pit 9.20	Cooney-Bos 1.83
	Rixey-Cin .656	Alexander-Chi 3.6	Carlson-Phi 32	Ring-Phi 21	Donohue-Cin 9.27	Sherdel-StL 1.89
STRIKEOUTS	**STRIKEOUTS/GAME**	**GAMES**	**SAVES**	**BASE RUNNERS/9**	**ADJUSTED RELIEF RUNS**	**RELIEF RANKING**
Vance-Bro 221	Vance-Bro 7.50	Morrison-Pit 44	Morrison-Pit 4	Fitzsimmons-NY 10.61	Huntzinger-NY 3.9	Huntzinger-NY 3.3
Luque-Cin 140	Luque-Cin 4.33	Donohue-Cin 42	Bush-Chi 4	Luque-Cin 10.61		
Ring-Phi 93	Sothoron-StL 3.87	Bush-Chi 42		Donohue-Cin 10.79		
Blake-Chi 93	Bush-Chi 3.76	Osborne-Bro 41		Vance-Bro 10.96		
Aldridge-Pit 88	Aldridge-Pit 3.71	Kremer-Pit 40		Rixey-Cin 11.15		
INNINGS PITCHED	**OPPONENTS' AVG.**	**OPPONENTS' OBP**	**EARNED RUN AVERAGE**	**ADJUSTED ERA**	**ADJUSTED STARTER RUNS**	**PITCHER WINS**
Donohue-Cin 301.0	Luque-Cin .239	Luque-Cin .291	Luque-Cin 2.63	Luque-Cin 156	Luque-Cin 48.3	**Luque-Cin 5.9**
Luque-Cin 291.0	Benton-Bos .249	Donohue-Cin .299	Rixey-Cin 2.88	Rixey-Cin 143	Rixey-Cin 43.0	**Donohue-Cin 4.6**
Rixey-Cin 287.1	Vance-Bro .250	Vance-Bro .304	Reinhart-StL 3.05	Sherdel-StL 139	Donohue-Cin 38.3	**Rixey-Cin 4.1**
Ring-Phi 270.0	Donohue-Cin .268	Rixey-Cin .307	Donohue-Cin 3.08	Donohue-Cin 133	Sherdel-StL 28.5	**Scott-NY 3.5**
Vance-Bro 265.1	Scott-NY .269	Cooney-Bos .312	Benton-Bos 3.09	Benton-Bos 130	Scott-NY 25.5	**Sherdel-StL 2.8**

Fattening Up

NL hitters fattened up on Senior Circuit's hurlers in 1925. Each team averaged 5.06 runs per game, up 11 percent from '24. The biggest reason was the extra 137 home runs that NL batters slugged. The league ERA went up 40 points, and just two qualifying pitchers posted ERAs below 3.00.

The Pittsburgh Pirates shrunk right field at Forbes Field from 372 feet to just 300, which helped the Bucs score 188 more runs than in 1924, accounting for 40 percent of the league's increase. The cozier confines of Forbes Field did not harm Pittsburgh's crack staff at all; five Pirates had 15 or more victories. New York led the NL through June, but Pittsburgh—third-place finishers for the past three years—came on fast and took the lead for good in early July, eventually winning by $8^1/_2$ games. Kiki Cuyler scored 144 runs and smacked 26 triples and Max Carey stole 46 bases. The Bucs had seven .300 hitters.

The second-place Giants led the league in homers, with Irish Meusel hitting 21 and George Kelly 20, but their lineup featured several offensive dead spots. Perhaps the top 1-2 punch in the league was St. Louis' Rogers Hornsby (league MVP and Triple Crown winner) and Jim Bottomley (the NL leader in hits and doubles), but the rest of the team was thin.

The Washington Senators took three of the first four games of the World Series, but the Bucs weren't done. Pittsburgh won Game 5 at Washington, 6-3, then came from behind to take the final two contests at Forbes Field. Down 7-6 in the eighth inning of Game 7, the Pirates scored three times off 37-year-old Walter Johnson to capture the Series. It would be the Bucs' last World Series appearance until 1960.

1925 AMERICAN LEAGUE

TEAM	W	L	T	PCT	GB	HW	HL	R	OR	PA	H	2B	3B	HR	BB	SO	HB	SH	AVG	OBP	SLG	OPS	AOPS	BR	ABR	PF	SB	CS	BSA	BSR
Was	96	55	1	.636	—	**53**	22	829	**670**	5994	1577	251	71	56	533	427	47	208	.303	.373	.411	784	106	38	55	98	**135**	92	59	-2
Phi	88	64	1	.579	8.5	51	26	831	713	6071	**1659**	298	79	76	453	432	32	187	**.307**	.364	.434	798	101	53	0	107	67	60	53	-6
StL	82	71	1	.536	15	45	32	900	906	6110	1620	**304**	68	**110**	498	**375**	29	143	.298	.360	**.439**	**799**	103	53	11	105	85	78	52	-9
Det	81	73	2	.526	16.5	43	34	**903**	829	6264	1621	277	**84**	50	640	386	32	221	.302	**.379**	.413	792	**109**	**64**	**78**	99	97	63	**61**	**-1**
Chi	79	75	0	.513	18.5	44	33	811	770	6168	1482	299	59	38	**662**	405	**51**	**231**	.284	.370	.385	755	102	-2	43	95	131	87	60	-2
Cle	70	84	1	.455	27.5	37	39	782	817	6163	1613	285	58	52	520	379	27	180	.297	.361	.399	760	97	-12	-18	101	90	77	54	-7
NY	69	85	2	.448	28.5	42	36	706	774	6021	1471	247	74	**110**	470	482	24	174	.275	.336	.410	746	96	-65	-52	98	69	73	49	-10
Bos	47	105	0	.309	49.5	28	47	639	922	5845	1375	257	64	41	513	422	31	135	.266	.336	.364	700	83	-133	-132	100	42	56	43	-10
Total	616	—	—	—	—	343	269	6401	—	48636	12418	2218	557	533	4289	3308	273	1479	.292	.360	.408	768	—	—	—	—	716	586	55	-48

TEAM	CG	SHO	GR	SV	IP	H	HR	BB	SO	BR/9	ERA	AERA	OAV	OOB	PR	APR	PF	OSB	OCS	FA	E	WPB	DP	FW	PW	BW	BSW	DIF
Was	69	10	145	**21**	1358.1	**1434**	49	543	463	**13.3**	**3.70**	114	.278	.351	**105**	82	96	74	64	.972	170	**24**	**166**	1.8	7.6	5.1	.4	5.7
Phi	61	8	**161**	18	1381.2	1468	60	544	**495**	**13.3**	3.87	**120**	**.276**	**.347**	81	**113**	106	93	61	.966	211	41	148	-.6	**10.5**	.0	.0	2.1
StL	67	7	160	10	1379.2	1588	99	675	419	15.0	4.92	95	.298	.380	-80	-37	106	103	**94**	.964	226	44	164	-1.4	-3.4	1.0	-.3	9.6
Det	66	2	142	18	1383.2	1582	70	556	419	14.2	4.61	94	.296	.366	-32	-47	98	103	65	.972	173	34	143	1.9	-4.4	**7.2**	**.5**	-1.2
Chi	71	**12**	129	13	1385.2	1579	69	**489**	374	13.6	4.29	97	.295	.356	17	-23	95	**46**	88	.968	200	26	162	.2	-2.1	4.0	.4	-.4
Cle	**93**	6	103	9	1372.1	1604	**41**	493	345	14.0	4.49	98	.296	.359	-15	-9	101	71	57	.967	210	26	146	-.4	-.8	-1.7	-.0	-4.0
NY	80	8	123	13	1387.2	1560	78	505	492	13.6	4.33	98	.289	.353	10	-11	97	96	89	**.974**	**160**	32	150	**2.7**	-1.0	-4.8	-.4	-4.5
Bos	68	6	128	6	1326.2	1615	67	510	310	14.7	4.97	92	.308	.374	-84	-60	103	130	68	.957	271	28	150	-4.2	-5.6	-12.2	-.4	-6.6
Total	575	59	1091	108	10975.2	—	—	—	—	14.0	4.39	—	.292	.360	—	—	—	—	—	.968	1621	255	1229	—	—	—	—	—

BATTER-FIELDER WINS	BATTING AVERAGE	ON-BASE PERCENTAGE	SLUGGING AVERAGE	ON-BASE PLUS SLUGGING	ADJUSTED OPS	ADJUSTED BATTER RUNS
Speaker-Cle.......4.3	Heilmann-Det........393	Speaker-Cle..........479	Williams-StL..........613	Cobb-Det............1066	Cobb-Det..............171	Heilmann-Det.......55.5
J.Sewell-Cle.......3.9	Speaker-Cle..........389	Cobb-Det..............468	Simmons-Phi.........599	Speaker-Cle........1057	Speaker-Cle..........166	Cobb-Det.............47.9
Goslin-Was.........3.5	Simmons-Phi.........387	Collins-Chi............461	Cobb-Det..............598	Heilmann-Det......1026	Heilmann-Det........161	Speaker-Cle.........47.7
Cobb-Det............3.5	Cobb-Det..............378	Heilmann-Det........457	Speaker-Cle..........578	Simmons-Phi......1018	Wingo-Det.............151	Simmons-Phi........42.5
Heilmann-Det.....3.4	Wingo-Det.............370	Wingo-Det.............456	Heilmann-Det........569	Wingo-Det.............983	Simmons-Phi.........146	Wingo-Det............37.9

RUNS	HITS	DOUBLES	TRIPLES	HOME RUNS	TOTAL BASES	RUNS BATTED IN
Mostil-Chi.............135	Simmons-Phi........253	McManus-StL.........44	Goslin-Was.............20	Meusel-NY..............33	Simmons-Phi........392	Meusel-NY............138
Simmons-Phi........122	Rice-Was..............227	Simmons-Phi..........43	Mostil-Chi...............16	Williams-StL...........25	Meusel-NY............338	Heilmann-Det........134
Combs-NY.............117	Heilmann-Det........225	Sheely-Chi..............43	Sisler-StL...............15	Ruth-NY..................25	Goslin-Was............329	Simmons-Phi........129
Goslin-Was...........116	Sisler-StL..............224	Burns-Cle...............41		Simmons-Phi..........24	Heilmann-Det........326	Goslin-Was...........113
Rice-Was..............111	J.Sewell-Cle..........204			Gehrig-NY...............20	Sisler-StL..............311	Sheely-Chi............111

BASES ON BALLS	STOLEN BASES	BASE STEALING RUNS	FIELDING RUNS-INFIELD	FIELDING RUNS-OUTFIELD	OUTFIELD ASSISTS	CATCHER CS PCT.
Mostil-Chi...............90	Mostil-Chi...............43	Goslin-Was............3.1	J.Sewell-Cle.........15.8	Goslin-Was..........14.3	Goslin-Was.............24	Schalk-Chi...........65.6
Kamm-Chi...............90	Goslin-Was.............27	Mostil-Chi..............2.5	O'Rourke-Det.......14.7	Flagstead-Bos.....14.0	Flagstead-Bos........24	Bengough-NY......46.7
Collins-Chi.............87	Rice-Was................26	Blue-Det.................2.4	Sisler-StL.............10.4	Wingo-Det..............8.9	Rice-Was................20	Bassler-Det..........39.1
Bishop-Phi..............87		Collins-Chi.............2.1	Wambsganss-Bos..8.4	Rice-Was................6.8		Cochrane-Phi.......38.5
Blue-Det.................83		Haney-Det..............2.1	Davis-Chi...............6.9	Jamieson-Cle.........5.0		

WINS	WINNING PCT.	WINS ABOVE TEAM	GAMES STARTED	COMPLETE GAMES	FEWEST HITS/GAME	FEWEST BB/GAME
Rommel-Phi............21	Coveleski-Was......800	Coveleski-Was.......6.2	Zachary-Was.........33	Smith-Cle................22	Blankenship-Chi..8.46	Smith-Cle...............1.82
Lyons-Chi................21	Johnson-Was.........741	Lyons-Chi...............5.5	Whitehill-Det.........33	Ehmke-Bos.............22	Johnson-Was.........8.53	Quinn-Bos-Phi.....1.85
Johnson-Was..........20	Ruether-Was.........720	Blankenship-Chi....4.8	Harriss-Phi............33	Pennock-NY............21	Coveleski-Was.....8.59	Shocker-NY..........2.14
Coveleski-Was........20	Blankenship-Chi...680	Holloway-Det.........4.5		Lyons-Chi................19	Pennock-NY.........8.68	Faber-Chi.............2.23
Harriss-Phi..............19	Rommel-Phi..........677	Johnson-Was..........4.5		Wingfield-Bos.........18	Gray-Phi...............8.79	Pennock-NY.........2.31

STRIKEOUTS	STRIKEOUTS/GAME	GAMES	SAVES	BASE RUNNERS/9	ADJUSTED RELIEF RUNS	RELIEF RANKING
Grove-Phi..............116	Grove-Phi............5.30	Marberry-Was.........55	Marberry-Was.........15	Pennock-NY.......11.05	Marberry-Was........5.2	Marberry-Was........8.9
Johnson-Was.........108	Johnson-Was.......4.24	Walberg-Phi...........53	Doyle-Det..................8	Blankenship-Chi 11.13	Gregg-Was...............9	Gregg-Was...............5
Harriss-Phi..............95	Shawkey-NY.........3.92	Vangilder-StL.........52	Connally-Chi............8	Coveleski-Was...11.39		
Ehmke-Bos..............95	Walberg-Phi..........3.85	Rommel-Phi............52	Walberg-Phi.............7	Gray-Phi..............11.71		
Jones-NY.................92	Gray-Phi...............3.54	Pennock-NY...........47		Johnson-Was.....11.87		

INNINGS PITCHED	OPPONENTS' AVG.	OPPONENTS' OBP	EARNED RUN AVERAGE	ADJUSTED ERA	ADJUSTED STARTER RUNS	PITCHER WINS
Pennock-NY.......277.0	Johnson-Was........250	Pennock-NY..........303	Coveleski-Was.....2.84	Coveleski-Was......149	Coveleski-Was.....40.9	**Johnson-Was.....4.6**
Lyons-Chi...........262.2	Blankenship-Chi...253	Blankenship-Chi...308	Pennock-NY.........2.96	Pennock-NY..........144	Pennock-NY.........36.3	**Pennock-NY.......3.3**
Rommel-Phi.......261.0	Pennock-NY..........254	Coveleski-Was......312	Blankenship-Chi..3.03	Gray-Phi................142	Blankenship-Chi..31.2	**Harriss-Phi.........3.2**
Ehmke-Bos........260.2	Coveleski-Was......255	Johnson-Was........317	Johnson-Was.......3.07	Johnson-Was........138	Harriss-Phi...........30.6	**Rommel-Phi.......2.9**
Wingfield-Bos....254.1	Gray-Phi................260	Gray-Phi................319	Dauss-Det...........3.16	Blankenship-Chi...137	Johnson-Was.......30.1	**Coveleski-Was...2.9**

WALTER'S DISAPPOINTMENT

Has a team ever had a better set of players making their big league debuts than the 1925 A's? Both catcher Mickey Cochrane and pitcher Lefty Grove appeared for the first time on April 14, and first baseman Jimmie Foxx came up two weeks later. With Al Simmons rapping 253 hits in his sophomore season and Ed Rommel leading the league in wins for the second time, Philadelphia vaulted all the way to second.

But once again, it was Washington's year. The Senators broke away from the slumping Athletics in late August and won by $8\frac{1}{2}$ games. A superannuated pitching staff featuring Walter Johnson and Stan Coveleski (aided by Firpo Marberry) was good enough, and outfielder Goose Goslin was spectacular.

The Yankees were no factor; Babe Ruth's wild nightlife shelved him. He collapsed during spring training from an intestinal problem; he missed seven weeks. When he returned, Ruth wasn't the same hitter—he was suspended in September. The undermanned Yanks finished seventh. Lou Gehrig did play his first full season.

The relative pitching calm of 1924 was replaced by a stormy 1925 in which AL batters set a new homer record with 533—even with Ruth out of commission. The league batting and slugging averages were also the highest ever. AL teams scored 5.20 runs per game, the most since 1901.

Former "Clean Sox" outfielders Nemo Leibold and Shano Collins saw their final major league action, as did two other famous gardeners, Harry Hooper and Bobby Veach. In addition, Chief Bender, one of the great hurlers of the early century, pitched his last game.

The Senators went up three games to one on Pittsburgh in the World Series, but couldn't close the deal. With the Series knotted, Johnson started Game 7; he completed the contest, although he shouldn't have. He allowed all 9 runs (5 earned) and 15 hits in a game in which the Senators led 6-4 through the sixth.

1924 NATIONAL LEAGUE

TEAM	W	L	T	PCT	GB	HW	HL	R	OR	PA	H	2B	3B	HR	BB	SO	HB	SH	AVG	OBP	SLG	OPS	AOPS	BR	ABR	PF	SB	CS	BSA	BSR
NY	93	60	1	.608	—	**51**	26	**857**	641	6067	**1634**	269	81	**95**	467	479	28	127	**.300**	**.358**	**.432**	**790**	**120**	**127**	**151**	97	82	53	61	-1
Bro	92	62	0	.597	1.5	46	31	717	679	5951	1534	227	54	72	447	357	22	143	.287	.345	.391	736	105	21	45	97	34	46	43	-9
Pit	90	63	0	.588	3	49	28	724	586	5833	1517	222	**122**	44	366	396	28	151	.287	.336	.400	736	100	7	-4	102	**181**	92	**66**	**8**
Cin	83	70	0	.542	10	43	33	649	**579**	5835	1539	236	111	36	349	**334**	26	159	.290	.337	.397	734	103	5	16	99	103	98	51	-12
Chi	81	72	1	.529	12	46	31	698	699	5796	1419	207	59	66	**469**	521	30	**163**	.276	.340	.378	718	96	-9	-15	101	137	149	48	-22
StL	65	89	0	.422	28.5	40	37	740	750	5909	1552	**270**	87	67	382	418	33	145	.290	.341	.411	752	108	43	57	98	86	86	50	-11
Phi	55	96	1	.364	37	26	49	676	849	5855	1459	256	56	94	382	452	**36**	131	.275	.328	.397	725	88	-10	-84	112	57	67	46	-11
Bos	53	100	1	.346	40	28	48	520	798	5767	1355	194	52	25	354	451	26	104	.256	.306	.327	633	77	-184	-162	96	74	68	52	-8
Total	614	—	—	—	—	329	283	5581	—	47013	12009	1881	622	499	3216	3408	229	1123	.283	.337	.392	729	—	—	—	—	754	659	53	-65

TEAM	CG	SHO	GR	SV	IP	H	HR	BB	SO	BR/9	ERA	AERA	OAV	OOB	PR	APR	PF	OSB	OCS	FA	E	WPB	DP	FW	PW	BW	BSW	DIF
NY	71	4	148	**21**	1378.2	1464	77	392	406	12.2	3.62	101	.274	.326	38	7	95	96	74	.971	186	24	160	.4	.7	**15.0**	.7	-.3
Bro	**97**	10	84	5	1376.1	1432	58	403	**638**	12.2	3.64	103	.270	.326	35	17	97	108	95	.968	196	27	121	-.2	1.7	4.5	-.0	9.1
Pit	85	**15**	105	5	1382.0	**1387**	42	323	364	**11.3**	3.27	117	**.267**	.313	92	88	99	**56**	65	.971	183	31	161	.5	8.7	-.4	**1.6**	3.1
Cin	77	14	104	9	1378.0	1408	**30**	**293**	451	**11.3**	**3.12**	**121**	**.267**	**.309**	**115**	**102**	97	95	78	.966	217	**23**	142	-1.4	**10.1**	1.6	-.4	-3.4
Chi	85	4	107	6	1380.2	1459	89	438	416	12.5	3.83	102	.275	.333	6	11	101	76	80	.966	218	30	153	-1.4	1.1	-1.5	-1.4	7.7
StL	79	7	119	6	1364.2	1528	70	486	393	13.5	4.15	91	.290	.354	-43	-58	98	95	75	.969	188	32	162	.3	-5.8	5.7	-.3	-11.9
Phi	59	7	**154**	10	1354.1	1691	84	469	349	14.6	4.87	92	.314	.372	-151	-52	115	109	**97**	.972	175	43	**168**	.8	-5.2	-8.3	-.3	-7.6
Bos	66	10	123	4	1379.1	1607	49	402	364	13.3	4.46	86	.301	.353	-92	-101	99	119	95	**.973**	**168**	39	154	**1.4**	-10.0	-16.1	.0	1.2
Total	619	71	944	66	10994.0	—	—	—	—	12.6	3.87	—	.283	.337	—	—	—	—	—	.970	1531	249	1221	—	—	—	—	—

BATTER-FIELDER WINS
Hornsby-StL 9.3
Frisch-NY 6.0
Fournier-Bro 4.9
Wheat-Bro 4.5
Youngs-NY 3.5

BATTING AVERAGE
Hornsby-StL .424
Wheat-Bro .375
Youngs-NY .356
Cuyler-Pit .354
Roush-Cin .348

ON-BASE PERCENTAGE
Hornsby-StL .507
Youngs-NY .441
Fournier-Bro .428
Wheat-Bro .428
Williams-Phi .403

SLUGGING AVERAGE
Hornsby-StL .696
Williams-Phi .552
Wheat-Bro .549
Cuyler-Pit .539
Fournier-Bro .536

ON-BASE PLUS SLUGGING
Hornsby-StL 1203
Wheat-Bro 978
Fournier-Bro 965
Youngs-NY 962
Williams-Phi 955

ADJUSTED OPS
Hornsby-StL 223
Wheat-Bro 165
Fournier-Bro 162
Youngs-NY 161
Cuyler-Pit 147

ADJUSTED BATTER RUNS
Hornsby-StL 99.4
Wheat-Bro 53.7
Fournier-Bro 53.7
Youngs-NY 49.9
Kelly-NY 33.1

RUNS
Hornsby-StL 121
Frisch-NY 121
Carey-Pit 113
Youngs-NY 112
Williams-Phi 101

HITS
Hornsby-StL 227
Wheat-Bro 212
Frisch-NY 198
High-Bro 191
Fournier-Bro 188

DOUBLES
Hornsby-StL 43
Wheat-Bro 41
Kelly-NY 37

TRIPLES
Roush-Cin 21
Maranville-Pit 20
Wright-Pit 18
Cuyler-Pit 16
Frisch-NY 15

HOME RUNS
Fournier-Bro 27
Hornsby-StL 25
Williams-Phi 24
Kelly-NY 21

TOTAL BASES
Hornsby-StL 373
Wheat-Bro 311
Williams-Phi 308
Kelly-NY 303
Fournier-Bro 302

RUNS BATTED IN
Kelly-NY 136
Fournier-Bro 116
Wright-Pit 111
Bottomley-StL 111
Meusel-NY 102

BASES ON BALLS
Hornsby-StL 89
Fournier-Bro 83
Youngs-NY 77
Williams-Phi 67
Friberg-Chi 66

STOLEN BASES
Carey-Pit 49
Cuyler-Pit 32
Heathcote-Chi 26
Traynor-Pit 24
Smith-StL 24

BASE STEALING RUNS
Carey-Pit 6.2
Cuyler-Pit 3.2
Frisch-NY 1.7
Hartnett-Chi 1.5
Freigau-StL 1.1

FIELDING RUNS-INFIELD
Frisch-NY 27.6
Pinelli-Cin 24.3
Ford-Phi 8.9
Wright-Pit 8.7
Groh-NY 7.4

FIELDING RUNS-OUTFIELD
Smith-StL 8.8
Statz-Chi 8.8
Cunningham-Bos 5.3
Grigsby-Chi 4.5
Wheat-Bro 3.5

OUTFIELD ASSISTS
Statz-Chi 22
Cuyler-Pit 19
Smith-StL 18
Youngs-NY 17

CATCHER CS PCT.
Hartnett-Chi 52.8
Taylor-Bro 47.5
Gowdy-NY 46.8
Hargrave-Cin 44.9
O'Neil-Bos 43.4

WINS
Vance-Bro 28
Grimes-Bro 22
Mays-Cin 20
Cooper-Pit 20
Kremer-Pit 18

WINNING PCT.
Yde-Pit .842
Vance-Bro .824
Bentley-NY .762
Mays-Cin .690
Kremer-Pit .643

WINS ABOVE TEAM
Vance-Bro 10.6
Yde-Pit 6.2
Mays-Cin 5.4
Bentley-NY 4.5
Nehf-NY 4.2

GAMES STARTED
Grimes-Bro 36
Cooper-Pit 35
Vance-Bro 34
Barnes-Bos 32
Aldridge-Chi 32

COMPLETE GAMES
Vance-Bro 30
Grimes-Bro 30
Cooper-Pit 25
Barnes-Bos 21
Aldridge-Chi 20

FEWEST HITS/GAME
Vance-Bro 6.95
Yde-Pit 7.93
Morrison-Pit 8.07
Doak-StL-Bro 8.14
Rixey-Cin 8.27

FEWEST BB/GAME
Benton-Cin 1.33
Alexander-Chi 1.33
Cooper-Pit 1.34
Mays-Cin 1.43
Donohue-Cin 1.46

STRIKEOUTS
Vance-Bro 262
Grimes-Bro 135
Luque-Cin 86
Morrison-Pit 85
Kaufmann-Chi 79

STRIKEOUTS/GAME
Vance-Bro 7.65
Grimes-Bro 3.91
Nehf-NY 3.77
Luque-Cin 3.53
Kaufmann-Chi 3.41

GAMES
Morrison-Pit 41
Kremer-Pit 41
Keen-Chi 40
Sheehan-Cin 39

SAVES
May-Cin 6
Ryan-NY 5
Jonnard-NY 5

BASE RUNNERS/9
Vance-Bro 9.46
Ehrhardt-Bro 9.57
Rixey-Cin 10.12
Stone-Pit 10.13
Jonnard-NY 10.64

ADJUSTED RELIEF RUNS
Jonnard-NY 10.8
May-Cin 9.1
Stone-Pit 5.3

RELIEF RANKING
Jonnard-NY 10.0
May-Cin 6.2
Stone-Pit 4.4

INNINGS PITCHED
Grimes-Bro 310.2
Vance-Bro 308.1
Cooper-Pit 268.2
Barnes-Bos 267.2
Kremer-Pit 259.1

OPPONENTS' AVG.
Vance-Bro .213
Yde-Pit .244
Morrison-Pit .245
Rixey-Cin .246
Doak-StL-Bro .249

OPPONENTS' OBP
Vance-Bro .269
Rixey-Cin .285
Benton-Cin .297
Alexander-Chi .299
Nehf-NY .301

EARNED RUN AVERAGE
Vance-Bro 2.16
McQuillan-NY 2.69
Rixey-Cin 2.76
Benton-Cin 2.77
Yde-Pit 2.83

ADJUSTED ERA
Vance-Bro 173
Rixey-Cin 137
McQuillan-NY 136
Benton-Cin 136
Yde-Pit 136

ADJUSTED STARTER RUNS
Vance-Bro 56.6
Rixey-Cin 28.5
Yde-Pit 22.4
Kremer-Pit 21.1
McQuillan-NY 19.0

PITCHER WINS
Vance-Bro 5.9
Rixey-Cin 3.4
Mays-Cin 3.0
Cooper-Pit 2.7
Yde-Pit 2.2

Big Mac's Last Stand

NL pitchers gained a foothold in 1924 as the league ERA fell to 3.87. Brooklyn's Dazzy Vance won his third straight strikeout title (as well as the win and ERA championships) as his whiffs rose from 197 to 262.

The Giants, gunning for their fourth straight flag, dominated early but blew a 10-game lead over Pittsburgh by sleepwalking through August. Brooklyn rode Vance's golden arm to 15 straight wins—including 11 games in eight days—to establish a three-way tangle.

By late September, the Giants, who led the league in nearly every offensive category, regained their momentum while Brooklyn and Pittsburgh knocked each other around. New York eventually won by 1½ over Brooklyn; Pittsburgh, again using a speed-oriented offense, finished 3 games back.

The race raised attendance in Brooklyn and Pittsburgh, and as a result, NL tickets sold rose for the third straight year. Meanwhile, St. Louis saw a 19 percent decline even as Rogers Hornsby won his fifth batting title in a row—batting .424!—but his club ended sixth.

Two Hall of Famers debuted in 1924. Freddie Lindstrom was a utilityman for John McGraw's Giants, and Cardinals outfielder Chick Hafey got into 24 games down the stretch. Several prominent baseball figures died during the year. Candy Cummings, a 120-pound righty credited with inventing the curve in the 1860s, died at age 76. Pat Moran, 48, who guided the Phillies and the Reds to their first NL pennants, died from Bright's disease in spring training with Cincinnati. Hall of Famer Frank Chance died a year after managing the last-place Red Sox. Two notable active players also breathed their last. Third baseman Tony Boeckel of the Braves became the first player killed in a motor accident. Veteran first baseman Jake Daubert, Cincinnati's team captain who collected 2,326 hits, died October 9 following an appendectomy.

The Giants' loss in the World Series to Washington heralded the end of their dynasty. McGraw managed until 1932, but he never won another pennant.

1924 AMERICAN LEAGUE

TEAM	W	L	T	PCT	GB	HW	HL	R	OR	PA	H	2B	3B	HR	BB	SO	HB	SH	AVG	OBP	SLG	OPS	AOPS	BR	ABR	PF	SB	CS	BSA	BSR
Was	92	62	2	.597	—	**47**	30	755	**613**	6098	1558	255	**88**	22	513	392	**49**	**232**	.294	.361	.387	748	101	-10	14	97	116	85	58	-4
NY	89	63	1	.586	2	45	32	798	667	5936	1516	248	86	**98**	478	420	29	189	.289	.352	**.426**	**778**	106	25	27	100	69	67	51	-8
Det	86	68	2	.558	6	45	33	**849**	796	6262	**1604**	**315**	76	35	**607**	400	41	225	**.298**	**.373**	.404	777	**108**	**57**	**71**	98	100	77	56	-5
StL	74	78	1	.487	17	41	36	769	807	5923	1543	266	62	67	465	**349**	32	190	.295	.356	.408	764	96	9	-35	106	85	85	50	-11
Phi	71	81	0	.467	20	36	39	685	778	5749	1459	251	59	63	374	484	35	156	.281	.334	.389	723	90	-80	-86	101	77	68	53	-7
Cle	67	86	0	.438	24.5	37	38	755	814	6031	1580	306	59	41	492	371	44	163	.296	.361	.399	760	100	11	1	101	85	57	**60**	**-1**
Bos	67	87	3	.435	25	41	36	735	806	6185	1481	302	63	30	603	417	47	195	.277	.356	.374	730	94	-39	-40	100	78	61	56	-4
Chi	66	87	1	.431	25.5	37	39	793	858	6125	1512	254	58	41	604	421	34	**232**	.288	.365	.382	747	101	-5	20	97	**137**	92	**60**	-2
Total	617	—	—	—	—	329	283	6139	—	48309	12253	2197	551	397	4136	3254	311	1582	.290	.357	.397	754	—	—	—	—	747	592	56	-43

TEAM	CG	SHO	GR	SV	IP	H	HR	BB	SO	BR/9	ERA	AERA	OAV	OOB	PR	APR	PF	OSB	OCS	FA	E	WPB	DP	FW	PW	BW	BSW	DIF
Was	74	**13**	128	**25**	1383.0	**1329**	**34**	505	469	**12.2**	**3.34**	**121**	**.259**	**.330**	**136**	**112**	95	**62**	55	.972	171	18	149	1.3	**10.6**	1.3	.1	1.6
NY	76	**13**	112	13	1359.1	1483	59	522	**487**	13.4	3.86	108	.284	.353	56	45	98	88	74	**.974**	**156**	55	131	**2.0**	4.2	2.5	-.2	4.4
Det	60	5	158	20	1394.2	1586	55	**467**	441	13.5	4.19	98	.293	.354	5	-12	97	101	77	.971	187	**17**	142	.4	-1.1	**6.7**	.0	3.0
StL	66	11	**176**	7	1353.1	1511	68	517	386	13.8	4.57	99	.289	.358	-51	-9	107	100	82	.969	184	20	142	.3	-.8	-3.3	-.5	2.4
Phi	68	8	144	10	1345.0	1527	43	597	371	14.4	4.39	98	.292	.368	-24	-15	101	90	63	.971	180	31	**157**	.5	-1.4	-8.1	-.2	4.2
Cle	**87**	7	119	7	1349.0	1603	43	503	315	14.3	4.40	97	.300	.365	-25	-20	101	98	65	.967	205	43	130	-1.0	-1.9	.0	**.4**	-7.1
Bos	73	8	144	16	1391.1	1563	43	523	414	13.9	4.35	100	.290	.359	-19	2	103	100	82	.967	210	46	126	-1.0	.2	-3.8	.1	-5.5
Chi	76	1	118	11	1370.2	1635	52	512	360	14.3	4.74	87	.305	.368	-78	-98	97	108	**94**	.963	229	48	136	-2.4	-9.3	1.9	.3	-1.1
Total	580	66	1099	109	10946.1	—	—	—	—	13.7	4.23	—	.290	.357	—	—	—	—	—	.969	1522	278	1113	—	—	—	—	—

BATTER-FIELDER WINS	BATTING AVERAGE	ON-BASE PERCENTAGE	SLUGGING AVERAGE	ON-BASE PLUS SLUGGING	ADJUSTED OPS	ADJUSTED BATTER RUNS
Ruth-NY..............8.4	Ruth-NY................378	Ruth-NY................513	Ruth-NY................739	Ruth-NY.............1252	Ruth-NY................221	Ruth-NY.............104.0
J.Sewell-Cle..........4.5	Jamieson-Cle........359	Collins-Chi............441	Heilmann-Det........533	Heilmann-Det........961	Heilmann-Det........149	Heilmann-Det.......43.5
Heilmann-Det.....3.7	Falk-Chi................352	Speaker-Cle..........432	Williams-StL..........533	Williams-StL..........958	Goslin-Was...........145	Goslin-Was..........39.2
Rigney-Det.........3.5	Collins-Chi............349	Heilmann-Det........428	Jacobson-StL.........528	Speaker-Cle..........943	Speaker-Cle..........141	Collins-Chi...........34.9
Collins-Chi..........3.0	Bassler-Det...........346	Sheely-Chi.............426	Myatt-Cle..............518	Goslin-Was............937	Williams-StL..........138	Speaker-Cle.........32.2

RUNS	HITS	DOUBLES	TRIPLES	HOME RUNS	TOTAL BASES	RUNS BATTED IN
Ruth-NY................143	Rice-Was..............216	J.Sewell-Cle............45	Pipp-NY..................19	Ruth-NY..................46	Ruth-NY................391	Goslin-Was...........129
Cobb-Det..............115	Jamieson-Cle........213	Heilmann-Det..........45	Goslin-Was.............17	Hauser-Phi..............27	Jacobson-StL.........306	Ruth-NY................121
Collins-Chi............108	Cobb-Det..............211	Wambsganss-Bos...41	Heilmann-Det..........16	Jacobson-StL...........19	Heilmann-Det.........304	Meusel-NY............120
Hooper-Chi...........107	Ruth-NY................200	Jacobson-StL..........41	Rice-Was................14	Williams-StL............18	Goslin-Was...........299	Hauser-Phi............115
Heilmann-Det........107	Goslin-Was...........199	Meusel-NY..............40	Jacobson-StL..........12	Boone-Bos..............13	Hauser-Phi............290	

BASES ON BALLS	STOLEN BASES	BASE STEALING RUNS	FIELDING RUNS-INFIELD	FIELDING RUNS-OUTFIELD	OUTFIELD ASSISTS	CATCHER CS PCT.
Ruth-NY................142	Collins-Chi..............42	Collins-Chi..............3.3	J.Sewell-Cle.........21.8	Hooper-Chi...........10.4	Heilmann-Det..........31	Ruel-Was.............47.7
Rigney-Det............102	Meusel-NY..............26	Manush-Det............1.3	Lutzke-Cle...........16.6	Jacobson-StL..........9.9	Falk-Chi..................26	Severeid-StL.........45.6
Sheely-Chi..............95	Rice-Was................24	Burns-Cle..............1.3	Wambsganss-Bos13.0	Falk-Chi..................7.9	Hooper-Chi.............22	Crouse-Chi...........45.5
Collins-Chi..............89	Cobb-Det.................23	Heilmann-Det..........1.1	Peckinpaugh-Was11.0	Mostil-Chi................6.6	Speaker-Cle............20	Schang-NY...........44.4
Cobb-Det.................85	Jamieson-Cle..........21		Scott-NY..............10.3	Heilmann-Det..........6.5	Tobin-StL.................19	Bassler-Det...........43.7

WINS	WINNING PCT.	WINS ABOVE TEAM	GAMES STARTED	COMPLETE GAMES	FEWEST HITS/GAME	FEWEST BB/GAME
Johnson-Was..........23	Johnson-Was........767	Johnson-Was.........7.1	Johnson-Was..........38	Thurston-Chi...........28	Johnson-Was.......7.55	Smith-Cle.............1.53
Pennock-NY............21	Pennock-NY..........700	Thurston-Chi..........5.6	Thurston-Chi...........36	Ehmke-Bos.............26	Collins-Det...........8.29	Thurston-Chi..........1.86
Thurston-Chi...........20	Whitehill-Det.........654	Pennock-NY............4.8	Ehmke-Bos.............36	Pennock-NY............25	Marberry-Was........8.75	Shocker-StL..........1.90
Shaute-Cle..............20	Zachary-Was.........625	Shaute-Cle.............4.2		Shaute-Cle..............21	Zachary-Was.........8.79	Pennock-NY..........2.01
Ehmke-Bos.............19		Baumgartner-Phi....4.2		Rommel-Phi.............21	Wingard-StL..........8.88	Quinn-Bos..............2.05

STRIKEOUTS	STRIKEOUTS/GAME	GAMES	SAVES	BASE RUNNERS/9	ADJUSTED RELIEF RUNS	RELIEF RANKING
Johnson-Was........158	Johnson-Was.......5.12	Marberry-Was.........50	Marberry-Was.........15	Johnson-Was.....10.37	Speece-Was..........4.0	Speece-Was..........2.0
Ehmke-Bos...........119	Shawkey-NY........4.94	Holloway-Det..........49	Russell-Was.............8	Collins-Det.........11.08		
Shawkey-NY.........114	Ehmke-Bos..........3.40	Shaute-Cle..............46	Quinn-Bos.................7	Zachary-Was.....11.28		
Pennock-NY..........101	Shocker-StL.........3.22	Hoyt-NY..................46	Dauss-Det.................6	Smith-Cle...........11.48		
Shocker-StL............88	Pennock-NY.........3.17	Ehmke-Bos.............45	Connally-Chi.............6	Pennock-NY.......11.54		

INNINGS PITCHED	OPPONENTS' AVG.	OPPONENTS' OBP	EARNED RUN AVERAGE	ADJUSTED ERA	ADJUSTED STARTER RUNS	PITCHER WINS
Ehmke-Bos........315.0	Johnson-Was........224	Johnson-Was........284	Johnson-Was.......2.72	Baumgartner-Phi..149	Johnson-Was.......43.8	**Johnson-Was......4.9**
Thurston-Chi......291.0	Collins-Det............249	Collins-Det............307	Zachary-Was.......2.75	Johnson-Was........148	Pennock-NY.........42.5	**Pennock-NY.......3.8**
Pennock-NY.......286.1	Marberry-Was.......262	Smith-Cle..............312	Pennock-NY.........2.83	Pennock-NY..........147	Ehmke-Bos..........33.3	**Zachary-Was......3.7**
Shaute-Cle.........283.0	Wingard-StL..........262	Pennock-NY..........314	Baumgartner-Phi 2.88	Zachary-Was........147	Smith-Cle.............31.2	**Ehmke-Bos.........3.4**
Rommel-Phi.......278.0	Davis-StL..............263	Zachary-Was........315	Smith-Cle............3.02	Smith-Cle.............142	Zachary-Was.......30.2	**Bush-NY.............3.2**

First in War, First in Peace, First in Everything

Walter Johnson had pitched for a long time and never won a pennant. But in 1924, the Yankees were far from dominant, and the AL flag was ready for the picking. Washington, New York, and Detroit spent July and August twisted together. By September the Tigers had dropped out, and the Yankees chased the Senators to the end. Washington held on for its first flag thanks to the 36-year-old Johnson, the league's dominant hurler.

Playing in cavernous Griffith Stadium, the Senators lacked homers but hit plenty of triples, and Goose Goslin led the league in RBIs. Righty Firpo Marberry was credited (retroactively) with 15 saves and was the first reliever to lead the AL in appearances.

Homers declined to 397 as only nine players reached double figures. This was the final year in big-league history that either league hit fewer than 400. Fleet Walker, the first African American in the majors, died May 11, his legacy going unnoted for decades. Three Hall of Famers reached the majors in 1924. Al Simmons debuted for Philadelphia; as he became a top slugger, the Athletics returned to contention. Red Ruffing, who would pitch until 1947, bowed for the Red Sox. Charlie Gehringer got into a few games in second base for Detroit.

The Senators and Giants produced a memorable World Series; each of the seven games was close, with four decided by one run. New York appeared to have Game 7 wrapped up until the Senators, down 3-1 in the bottom of the eighth, tied it when a grounder by player-manager Bucky Harris hopped over the head of Giants third baseman Freddie Lindstrom. With the game still knotted in the 12th, the Senators had Muddy Ruel on second, and Johnson, on relief since the ninth, on first. Rookie Earl McNeely's grounder bounced over Lindstrom's head. Washington had its first, and as it would happen, only world champion.

1923 NATIONAL LEAGUE

TEAM	W	L	T	PCT	GB	HW	HL	R	OR	PA	H	2B	3B	HR	BB	SO	HB	SH	AVG	OBP	SLG	OPS	AOPS	BR	ABR	PF	SB	CS	BSA	BSR
NY	95	58	0	.621	—	**47**	30	**854**	679	6083	**1610**	248	76	85	**487**	406	31	113	**.295**	**.356**	**.415**	**771**	**110**	**73**	**84**	99	106	70	60	-1
Cin	91	63	0	.591	4.5	46	32	708	**629**	5935	1506	237	95	45	439	367	33	**185**	.285	.344	.392	736	102	-2	13	98	96	105	48	-16
Pit	87	67	0	.565	8.5	**47**	30	786	696	5943	1592	224	**111**	49	407	**362**	28	103	**.295**	.347	.404	751	102	22	6	102	154	75	**67**	**8**
Chi	83	71	0	.539	12.5	46	31	756	704	5896	1516	243	52	90	455	485	31	151	.288	.348	.406	754	104	35	34	100	**181**	143	56	-10
StL	79	74	1	.516	16	42	35	746	732	6137	1582	**274**	76	63	438	446	38	135	.286	.343	.398	741	103	7	24	98	89	61	59	-2
Bro	76	78	1	.494	19.5	37	40	753	741	6082	1559	214	81	62	425	382	33	148	.285	.340	.387	727	100	-23	-2	97	71	50	59	-2
Bos	54	100	1	.351	41.5	22	55	636	798	5957	1455	213	58	32	429	404	31	168	.273	.331	.353	684	90	-100	-73	96	57	80	42	-15
Phi	50	104	1	.325	45.5	20	55	748	1008	6054	1528	259	39	**112**	414	556	**39**	110	.278	.333	.401	734	89	-12	-89	112	70	73	49	-10
Total	617	—	—	—	—	307	308	5987	—	48087	12348	1912	588	538	3494	3408	264	1113	.286	.343	.395	737	—	—	—	—	824	657	56	-49

TEAM	CG	SHO	GR	SV	IP	H	HR	BB	SO	BR/9	ERA	AERA	OAV	OOB	PR	APR	PF	OSB	OCS	FA	E	WPB	DP	FW	PW	BW	BSW	DIF
NY	62	10	**159**	**18**	1378.0	1440	82	424	453	12.3	3.90	98	.271	.328	15	-14	96	**63**	69	**.972**	**176**	26	141	**2.4**	-1.3	**8.1**	.5	8.9
Cin	88	11	97	9	1391.1	1465	**28**	**359**	450	**12.0**	**3.21**	**120**	.273	**.322**	**121**	**102**	97	98	91	.969	202	31	144	.9	**9.8**	1.3	-1.0	3.0
Pit	92	5	99	9	1376.1	1513	53	402	414	12.7	3.87	103	.284	.337	19	19	100	78	70	.971	179	**25**	157	2.3	1.8	.6	**1.4**	4.0
Chi	80	8	107	11	1366.2	**1419**	86	435	408	12.4	3.82	105	**.269**	.329	27	25	100	80	69	.967	208	**25**	144	.5	2.4	3.3	-.4	.2
StL	77	9	126	7	1398.1	1539	70	456	398	13.1	3.87	101	.284	.344	20	5	98	111	71	.963	232	36	141	-.9	.5	2.3	.4	.2
Bro	**94**	8	92	5	1396.2	1503	55	476	**548**	13.0	3.74	103	.277	.340	39	21	97	131	103	.955	293	49	137	-4.4	2.0	-.2	.4	1.2
Bos	55	**13**	153	7	1392.2	1662	64	394	351	13.5	4.21	94	.302	.352	-34	-41	100	126	**105**	.964	230	32	157	-.7	-3.9	-7.0	-.9	-10.5
Phi	68	3	150	8	1376.1	1801	100	549	384	15.6	5.34	86	.322	.386	-205	-100	115	137	79	.966	217	60	**172**	.0	-9.6	-8.6	-.4	-8.5
Total	616	67	983	74	11076.1	—	—	—	—	13.1	3.99	—	.286	.343	—	—	—	—	—	.966	1737	284	1193	—	—	—	—	—

BATTER-FIELDER WINS	BATTING AVERAGE	ON-BASE PERCENTAGE	SLUGGING AVERAGE	ON-BASE PLUS SLUGGING	ADJUSTED OPS	ADJUSTED BATTER RUNS
Fournier-Bro....... 4.2	Hornsby-StL..........384	Hornsby-StL..........459	Hornsby-StL..........627	Hornsby-StL........1086	Hornsby-StL..........188	Hornsby-StL........55.7
O'Farrell-Chi....... 3.9	Wheat-Bro 375	Bottomley-StL 425	Fournier-Bro 588	Fournier-Bro 999	Fournier-Bro 165	Fournier-Bro 47.4
Hornsby-StL....... 3.8	Bottomley-StL 371	Youngs-NY............412	Williams-Phi..........576	Bottomley-StL 960	Bottomley-StL 155	Bottomley-StL 42.1
Hargrave-Cin...... 3.8	Fournier-Bro 351	Fournier-Bro 411	Barnhart-Pit 563	Williams-Phi..........947	Roush-Cin.............149	Roush-Cin............36.9
Traynor-Pit 3.6	Roush-Cin.............351	O'Farrell-Chi 408	Bottomley-StL 535	Roush-Cin.............938	Frisch-NY.............133	Frisch-NY.............30.0
RUNS	**HITS**	**DOUBLES**	**TRIPLES**	**HOME RUNS**	**TOTAL BASES**	**RUNS BATTED IN**
Youngs-NY............121	Frisch-NY..............223	Roush-Cin...............41	Traynor-Pit 19	Williams-Phi............41	Frisch-NY..............311	Meusel-NY............125
Carey-Pit...............120	Statz-Chi...............209	Tierney-Pit-Phi........36	Carey-Pit.................19	Fournier-Bro 22	Williams-Phi..........308	Williams-Phi..........114
Frisch-NY..............116	Traynor-Pit 208	Grantham-Chi 36	Roush-Cin...............18	Miller-Chi 20	Fournier-Bro 303	Frisch-NY.............111
Johnston-Bro 111	Johnston-Bro 203	Bottomley-StL 34	Southworth-Bos......16	Meusel-NY..............19	Traynor-Pit 301	Kelly-NY...............103
Statz-Chi...............110	Youngs-NY............200			Hornsby-StL............17	Statz-Chi...............288	Fournier-Bro 102
BASES ON BALLS	**STOLEN BASES**	**BASE STEALING RUNS**	**FIELDING RUNS-INFIELD**	**FIELDING RUNS-OUTFIELD**	**OUTFIELD ASSISTS**	**CATCHER CS PCT.**
Burns-Cin 101	Carey-Pit.................51	Carey-Pit................8.4	Tierney-Pit-Phi.....15.1	Carey-Pit.............12.1	Carey-Pit.................28	Snyder-NY 53.3
Sand-Phi.................82	Grantham-Chi 43	Smith-StL...............3.2	Johnston-Bro 14.4	Statz-Chi.............10.7	Statz-Chi.................26	O'Neil-Bos 48.5
Youngs-NY.............73	Smith-StL................32	Frisch-NY...............2.2	Bancroft-NY 12.4	Bigbee-Pit..............7.7	Youngs-NY..............22	Taylor-Bro 47.7
Carey-Pit.................73	Heathcote-Chi.........32	Rawlings-Pit...........2.0	B.Smith-Bos.........11.6	Smith-StL...............6.7	Southworth-Bos......22	O'Farrell-Chi 47.5
Grantham-Chi 71		Traynor-Pit 1.6	Maranville-Pit.......10.9	Barnhart-Pit 5.9	Neis-Bro..................20	Hargrave-Cin 46.9
WINS	**WINNING PCT.**	**WINS ABOVE TEAM**	**GAMES STARTED**	**COMPLETE GAMES**	**FEWEST HITS/GAME**	**FEWEST BB/GAME**
Luque-Cin...............27	Luque-Cin.............771	Luque-Cin..............8.8	Grimes-Bro 38	Grimes-Bro 33	Luque-Cin............7.80	Alexander-Chi.........89
Morrison-Pit............25	Ryan-NY...............762	Ring-Phi.................6.1	Cooper-Pit 38	Luque-Cin...............28	Vance-Bro............8.44	B.Adams-Pit.........1.42
Alexander-Chi.........22	Scott-NY...............696	Morrison-Pit 5.0	Rixey-Cin 37	Morrison-Pit............27	Morrison-Pit.........8.56	Genewich-Bos 1.82
Grimes-Bro 21	Morrison-Pit..........658	Alexander-Chi.........4.8	Morrison-Pit............37	Cooper-Pit 26	Keen-Chi..............8.59	Rixey-Cin 1.89
Donohue-Cin 21	Alexander-Chi.......647	Ryan-NY 4.3	Luque-Cin...............37	Alexander-Chi.........26	Aldridge-Chi.........8.67	Meadows-Phi-Pit .2.15
STRIKEOUTS	**STRIKEOUTS/GAME**	**GAMES**	**SAVES**	**BASE RUNNERS/9**	**ADJUSTED RELIEF RUNS**	**RELIEF RANKING**
Vance-Bro............197	Vance-Bro............6.32	Ryan-NY 45	Jonnard-NY 5	Alexander-Chi......9.97	Decatur-Bro 11.1	Decatur-Bro 6.9
Luque-Cin.............151	Luque-Cin............4.22	Jonnard-NY 45	Ryan-NY 4	Luque-Cin..........10.40	Jonnard-NY 3.6	Jonnard-NY 2.8
Grimes-Bro...........119	Bentley-NY 3.93	Oeschger-Bos.........44		Cooney-Bos.......10.74		
Morrison-Pit..........114	Osborne-Chi 3.46	J.Barnes-NY-Bos 43		Ryan-NY 11.31		
Ring-Phi................112	Morrison-Pit 3.40	Genewich-Bos 43		Aldridge-Chi.......11.49		
INNINGS PITCHED	**OPPONENTS' AVG.**	**OPPONENTS' OBP**	**EARNED RUN AVERAGE**	**ADJUSTED ERA**	**ADJUSTED STARTER RUNS**	**PITCHER WINS**
Grimes-Bro 327.0	Luque-Cin.............235	Alexander-Chi.......277	Luque-Cin............1.93	Luque-Cin.............200	Luque-Cin............70.4	**Luque-Cin 7.6**
Luque-Cin..........322.0	Vance-Bro.............250	Luque-Cin.............291	Rixey-Cin 2.80	Rixey-Cin 138	Rixey-Cin 36.7	**Rixey-Cin 3.3**
Rixey-Cin 309.0	Aldridge-Chi..........251	Aldridge-Chi..........307	Keen-Chi..............3.00	Keen-Chi...............133	Alexander-Chi......28.6	**Alexander-Chi.... 3.1**
Alexander-Chi....305.0	Morrison-Pit..........253	Ryan-NY 308	Kaufmann-Chi.......3.10	Kaufmann-Chi.......129	Ring-Phi...............25.0	**Kaufmann-Chi.... 2.0**
Ring-Phi.............304.1	Osborne-Chi 255	McQuillan-NY 315	Haines-StL...........3.11	Alexander-Chi.......125	Keen-Chi..............20.2	**Cooper-Pit 1.8**

GET OUT OF MY YARD

Going wire-to-wire, the New York Giants won their third straight NL crown, beating back occasional challenges from the Reds and Pirates. The Giants again had the league's best offense and pitching in road games, and played well at home as well. They paced the NL in runs by a margin of 68.

As only the Polo Grounds—expanded to 54,000 capacity—made any alterations to its field dimensions, NL pitchers began to gain some control and runs per game decreased by 3 percent. The Cardinals, who fell 5 games in the standings despite the monster season of Rogers Hornsby, suffered a 37 percent attendance drop. Five NL clubs posted double-digit gains, and league turnstile clicks were up.

Cincinnati, on its last legs as a contender, fielded a team comprised mostly of players in their 30s. Pitcher Dolf Luque was the best in the league at 27-8. Two other Reds pitchers won 20 (Eppa Rixey and Pete Donahue), but their second-line pitching was very poor.

Veteran outfielder Burt Shotton, who twice led the AL in walks, played in his last game (for the Cardinals), but he would re-emerge some five years later as a manager with the moribund Phillies. Two future Hall of Famers joined the major league fraternity: Bill Terry and Hack Wilson.

New York featured productive performers at nearly every position, with two youngsters—24-year-old second baseman Frankie Frisch and 19-year-old shortstop Travis Jackson—providing special fire. Platoon outfielder Casey Stengel hit .339 and batted .417 with 2 homers in the World Series. The Yankees reveled in their new home, which opened in 1923 because the Giants asked them to vacate the Polo Grounds, and knocked off the Giants on their third try in the World Series.

1923 AMERICAN LEAGUE

TEAM	W	L	T	PCT	GB	HW	HL	R	OR	PA	H	2B	3B	HR	BB	SO	HB	SH	AVG	OBP	SLG	OPS	AOPS	BR	ABR	PF	SB	CS	BSA	BSR
NY	98	54	0	.645	—	**46**	30	823	**622**	6047	1554	231	79	**105**	521	516	34	145	.291	.357	**.422**	779	108	71	57	102	69	74	48	-11
Det	83	71	1	.539	16	45	32	831	741	6173	1579	270	69	41	596	385	**55**	**256**	.300	.377	.401	778	113	94	111	98	87	62	58	-3
Cle	82	71	0	.536	16.5	42	36	**888**	746	6171	**1594**	**301**	75	59	**633**	**384**	49	199	**.301**	**.381**	.420	**801**	**117**	**141**	**143**	100	79	79	50	-10
Was	75	78	2	.490	23.5	43	34	720	747	6055	1436	224	**93**	26	532	448	47	232	.274	.346	.367	713	98	-49	-12	95	102	68	60	-1
StL	74	78	2	.487	24	40	36	688	720	5975	1489	248	62	82	442	423	26	209	.281	.339	.398	737	94	-17	-55	106	64	54	54	-5
Phi	69	83	1	.454	29	34	41	661	761	5853	1407	229	64	53	445	517	42	170	.271	.333	.370	703	89	-77	-85	101	72	62	54	-6
Chi	69	85	2	.448	30	30	45	692	741	6067	1463	254	57	42	532	458	40	249	.279	.350	.373	723	97	-25	-16	99	**191**	118	**62**	**1**
Bos	61	91	2	.401	37	37	40	584	809	5775	1354	253	54	34	391	480	42	161	.261	.318	.351	669	81	-144	-147	101	79	91	46	-14
Total	616	—	—	—	—	317	294	5887	—	48116	11876	2010	553	442	4092	3611	335	1621	.282	.351	.388	739	—	—	—	—	743	608	55	-49

TEAM	CG	SHO	GR	SV	IP	H	HR	BB	SO	BR/9	ERA	AERA	OAV	OOB	PR	APR	PF	OSB	OCS	FA	E	WPB	DP	FW	PW	BW	BSW	DIF
NY	**101**	9	68	10	1380.2	**1365**	68	491	**506**	**12.3**	**3.62**	**109**	**.263**	**.330**	**55**	**49**	99	**79**	58	**.977**	**144**	53	131	**3.3**	**4.7**	5.5	-.5	8.9
Det	61	9	**163**	12	1373.2	1502	58	**449**	447	13.1	4.09	94	.283	.345	-16	-35	97	84	**102**	.968	200	30	103	.0	-3.4	10.7	.3	-1.7
Cle	77	**10**	143	11	1376.0	1517	**36**	465	407	13.2	3.91	101	.285	.346	11	4	100	**79**	43	.964	226	28	143	-1.7	.4	**13.8**	-.4	-6.7
Was	71	8	130	**16**	1374.1	1527	56	563	474	14.0	3.98	95	.291	.364	0	-32	95	91	95	.966	216	31	**182**	-.9	-3.1	-1.2	.5	3.2
StL	83	**10**	126	10	1373.1	1430	59	528	488	13.2	3.93	106	.275	.348	9	35	105	99	79	.971	177	**23**	145	1.4	3.4	-5.3	.1	-1.6
Phi	65	7	131	12	1364.2	1465	68	550	400	13.5	4.08	101	.280	.352	-15	1	103	91	75	.965	221	42	127	-1.4	.0	-8.2	.0	2.5
Chi	74	5	126	11	1397.0	1512	49	534	467	13.4	4.05	98	.283	.353	-10	-13	99	105	66	.971	184	33	138	1.1	-1.3	-1.5	**.7**	-7.0
Bos	77	3	115	11	1372.0	1534	48	520	412	13.9	4.20	98	.294	.366	-33	-15	103	115	89	.963	232	41	126	-2.0	-1.5	-14.2	-.8	3.4
Total	609	61	1002	93	11011.2	—	—	—	—	13.3	3.98	—	.282	.351	—	—	—	—	—	.968	1600	281	1095	—	—	—	—	—

BATTER-FIELDER WINS	BATTING AVERAGE	ON-BASE PERCENTAGE	SLUGGING AVERAGE	ON-BASE PLUS SLUGGING	ADJUSTED OPS	ADJUSTED BATTER RUNS
Ruth-NY 10.1	Heilmann-Det........403	Ruth-NY................545	Ruth-NY................764	Ruth-NY..............1309	Ruth-NY................238	Ruth-NY.............119.2
Speaker-Cle 6.5	Ruth-NY................393	Heilmann-Det........481	Heilmann-Det........632	Heilmann-Det......1113	Heilmann-Det........195	Heilmann-Det.......75.5
J.Sewell-Cle 6.2	Speaker-Cle..........380	Speaker-Cle..........469	Williams-StL..........623	Speaker-Cle........1079	Speaker-Cle..........183	Speaker-Cle.........74.1
Heilmann-Det..... 6.0	Collins-Chi 360	J.Sewell-Cle..........456	Speaker-Cle..........610	Williams-StL........1062	Williams-StL..........168	Williams-StL.........54.7
Williams-StL....... 4.7	Williams-StL..........357	Collins-Chi 455	Harris-Bos.............520	J.Sewell-Cle..........935	J.Sewell-Cle..........147	J.Sewell-Cle.........44.9

RUNS	HITS	DOUBLES	TRIPLES	HOME RUNS	TOTAL BASES	RUNS BATTED IN
Ruth-NY................151	Jamieson-Cle........222	Speaker-Cle............59	Rice-Was 18	Ruth-NY..................41	Ruth-NY................399	Ruth-NY................131
Speaker-Cle..........133	Speaker-Cle..........218	Burns-Bos..............47	Goslin-Was 18	Williams-StL............29	Speaker-Cle..........350	Speaker-Cle..........130
Jamieson-Cle........130	Heilmann-Det........211	Ruth-NY..................45	Tobin-StL 15	Heilmann-Det..........18	Williams-StL..........346	Heilmann-Det........115
Heilmann-Det........121	Ruth-NY................205	Heilmann-Det..........44	Mostil-Chi................15	Speaker-Cle............17	Heilmann-Det........331	J.Sewell-Cle..........109
Rice-Was 117	Tobin-StL 202	J.Sewell-Cle............41		Hauser-Phi..............17	Tobin-StL 303	Pipp-NY 108

BASES ON BALLS	STOLEN BASES	BASE STEALING RUNS	FIELDING RUNS-INFIELD	FIELDING RUNS-OUTFIELD	OUTFIELD ASSISTS	CATCHER CS PCT.
Ruth-NY................170	Collins-Chi 48	Mostil-Chi...............3.4	Peckinpaugh-Was21.8	Mostil-Chi.............16.0	Flagstead-Det-Bos......31	Bassler-Det..........56.9
J.Sewell-Cle............98	Mostil-Chi................41	Rice-Was 1.6	Harris-Was...........18.6	Flagstead-Det-Bos...14.4	Speaker-Cle............26	Ruel-Was 51.3
Blue-Det..................96	Harris-Was..............23	Barrett-Chi 1.6	Lutzke-Cle 16.0	Williams-StL...........8.1	Goslin-Was 26	Schang-NY 45.1
Speaker-Cle............93	Rice-Was 20	Veach-Det.............1.1	Ward-NY................9.5	Rice-Was 6.7	Williams-StL............23	Picinich-Bos.........44.2
Collins-Chi 84			Judge-Was.............8.3	Ruth-NY.................6.4		Severeid-StL 44.2

WINS	WINNING PCT.	WINS ABOVE TEAM	GAMES STARTED	COMPLETE GAMES	FEWEST HITS/GAME	FEWEST BB/GAME
Uhle-Cle..................26	Pennock-NY..........760	Ehmke-Bos 5.3	Uhle-Cle..................44	Uhle-Cle..................29	Shawkey-NY........8.07	Shocker-StL.........1.59
Jones-NY................21	Jones-NY..............724	Shocker-StL...........5.1	Ehmke-Bos 39	Ehmke-Bos 28	Hoyt-NY 8.56	Coveleski-Cle.......1.66
Dauss-Det...............21	Hoyt-NY 654	Uhle-Cle.................4.9	Dauss-Det...............39	Shocker-StL............24	Bush-NY 8.59	Thurston-StL-Chi .1.75
Shocker-StL............20	Shocker-StL..........625	Pennock-NY...........4.6	Pillette-Det 36	Dauss-Det...............22	Russell-Was.........8.78	Quinn-Bos............1.96
Ehmke-Bos 20	Uhle-Cle................619	Cole-Det 3.8	Hasty-Phi 36	Bush-NY 22	Danforth-StL 8.79	Dauss-Det...........2.22

STRIKEOUTS	STRIKEOUTS/GAME	GAMES	SAVES	BASE RUNNERS/9	ADJUSTED RELIEF RUNS	RELIEF RANKING
Johnson-Was........130	Johnson-Det 4.75	Rommel-Phi............56	Russell-Was.............9	Shocker-StL 11.16		
Shawkey-NY 125	Johnson-Was.......4.48	Uhle-Cle..................54	Quinn-Bos.................7	Hoyt-NY 11.20		
Bush-NY 125	Shawkey-NY 4.35	Russell-Was............52	Harriss-Phi................6	Pennock-NY.......11.52		
Ehmke-Bos 121	Bush-NY 4.08	Cole-Det 52		Jones-NY...........11.63		
	Harriss-Phi...........3.83	Dauss-Det...............50		Coveleski-Cle.....11.64		

INNINGS PITCHED	OPPONENTS' AVG.	OPPONENTS' OBP	EARNED RUN AVERAGE	ADJUSTED ERA	ADJUSTED STARTER RUNS	PITCHER WINS
Uhle-Cle.............357.2	Shawkey-NY 246	Shocker-StL..........306	Coveleski-Cle.......2.76	Coveleski-Cle........143	Vangilder-StL.......27.8	**Uhle-Cle 3.4**
Ehmke-Bos 316.2	Hoyt-NY 253	Hoyt-NY 307	Hoyt-NY 3.02	Vangilder-StL 136	Coveleski-Cle.......26.2	**Rommel-Phi 3.2**
Dauss-Det..........316.0	Jones-NY..............257	Faber-Chi..............311	Russell-Was.........3.03	Hoyt-NY 131	Pennock-NY.........24.6	**Vangilder-StL..... 2.8**
Rommel-Phi.......297.2	Faber-Chi..............259	Jones-NY..............312	Vangilder-StL 3.06	Thurston-StL-Chi ..127	Shocker-StL.........24.1	**Bush-NY............. 2.6**
Vangilder-StL 282.1	Bush-NY 260	Pennock-NY..........314	Mogridge-Was 3.11	Rommel-Phi..........126	Rommel-Phi.........23.7	**Shocker-StL....... 2.6**

The Year the Yankees Were Born

Kicked out of the Polo Grounds by the Giants the year before, the New York Yankees built their own park, Yankee Stadium, which quickly became a palace of American sport.

The Bronx Bombers put on a show for the million-plus fans that filled the park, running away with the pennant. Babe Ruth had another spectacular season, leading the loop in runs, homers, and RBIs—all while drawing 170 walks to set an AL record that still stands.

While the Yankees didn't score as many runs as the Tigers or Indians, they had much better pitching; New York's deep, if unspectacular, staff was the only one in the league with more strikeouts than walks, and easily led in complete games. New York used rookie Lou Gehrig in a few games, and Earle Combs came up the next year. Both were clearly part of the Yankees' future. The 1923 season also saw the debut of the first great relief pitcher in the game's history, Washington's Firpo Marberry. Ted Lyons of Chicago began a playing career that would last—with three years as a Marine thrown in—until 1946.

The Tigers had a fine outfield. Harry Heilmann batted .403, and rookie Heinie Manush and 36-year-old Ty Cobb kicked in high averages, though Cobb continued to suffer from knee problems. For Cleveland, 35-year-old Tris Speaker set a new big-league record with 53 doubles and Charlie Jamieson notched 222 hits.

The Giants were again the Yankees' World Series opponents, and the NL won Game 1 on Casey Stengel's ninth-inning inside-the-park homer. But the story would end differently. The Yanks rebounded to win three times at their former home park. Trailing 4-1 at the Polo Grounds in Game 6, the Yankees put together a 5-run eighth to win the title. With another pennant, their first Series crown, a ballpark of their own, and the parts of a dynasty firmly coming into place, 1923 was the year the Yankees became the Yankees.

1922 NATIONAL LEAGUE

TEAM	W	L	T	PCT	GB	HW	HL	R	OR	PA	H	2B	3B	HR	BB	SO	HB	SH	AVG	OBP	SLG	OPS	AOPS	BR	ABR	PF	SB	CS	BSA	BSR
NY	93	61	2	.604	—	**51**	27	852	**658**	6109	1661	253	90	80	448	421	**48**	159	.305	**.363**	.428	791	109	79	72	101	116	83	58	-4
Cin	86	68	2	.558	7	48	29	766	677	5943	1561	226	99	45	436	381	36	189	.296	.353	.401	754	102	6	21	98	130	136	49	-19
StL	85	69	0	.552	8	42	35	863	819	6061	1634	**280**	88	107	447	425	28	161	.301	.357	**.444**	**801**	**118**	**94**	**137**	95	73	63	54	-6
Pit	85	69	1	.552	8	45	33	**865**	736	6151	**1698**	239	**110**	52	423	326	32	175	**.308**	.360	.419	779	106	54	44	101	**145**	59	**71**	**11**
Chi	80	74	2	.519	13	39	37	771	808	6092	1564	248	71	42	**525**	447	27	**205**	.293	.359	.390	749	97	10	-5	102	97	108	47	-16
Bro	76	78	1	.494	17	44	34	743	754	5955	1569	235	76	56	339	**318**	25	178	.290	.335	.392	727	94	-60	-54	99	79	60	57	-4
Phi	57	96	1	.373	35.5	35	41	738	920	6088	1537	268	55	**116**	450	611	39	140	.282	.341	.415	756	92	1	-67	110	48	60	44	-10
Bos	53	100	1	.346	39.5	32	43	596	822	5750	1355	162	73	32	387	451	28	174	.263	.317	.341	658	78	-184	-158	96	67	65	51	-8
Total	620	—	—	—	—	336	279	6194	—	48149	12579	1911	662	530	3455	3380	263	1381	.292	.348	.404	753	—	—	—	—	755	634	54	-56

TEAM	CG	SHO	GR	SV	IP	H	HR	BB	SO	BR/9	ERA	AERA	OAV	OOB	PR	APR	PF	OSB	OCS	FA	E	WPB	DP	FW	PW	BW	BSW	DIF
NY	76	7	135	**15**	1396.1	**1454**	71	393	388	12.0	**3.45**	**116**	**.272**	.324	**100**	**85**	98	**70**	58	**.970**	194	40	145	1.1	**8.0**	6.8	.3	-.2
Cin	**88**	8	93	3	1385.2	1481	**49**	**326**	357	**11.9**	3.53	113	.278	**.322**	87	71	97	77	69	.968	205	**18**	147	.4	6.7	2.0	-1.1	1.1
StL	60	8	**172**	12	1362.2	1609	61	447	465	13.9	4.44	87	.299	.358	-52	-93	94	90	83	.961	239	34	122	-2.0	-8.8	**12.9**	.0	5.8
Pit	**88**	**15**	114	7	1387.1	1613	52	358	490	13.0	3.98	102	.296	.343	18	14	99	92	64	**.970**	**187**	31	126	**1.5**	1.3	4.2	**1.7**	-.7
Chi	74	8	138	12	1397.2	1579	77	475	402	13.6	4.34	97	.292	.356	-38	-23	102	79	**104**	.968	204	35	**154**	.5	-2.2	-.5	-.9	6.0
Bro	82	12	115	8	1385.2	1574	74	490	**499**	13.6	4.05	100	.293	.356	8	2	99	128	82	.967	208	42	139	.1	.2	-5.1	.3	3.5
Phi	73	6	118	5	1372.0	1692	89	460	394	14.4	4.64	101	.307	.365	-82	6	114	123	76	.965	225	52	152	-1.1	.6	-6.3	-.3	-12.4
Bos	63	7	146	6	1348.0	1565	57	489	360	13.9	4.37	91	.298	.361	-41	-59	98	96	98	.965	215	34	121	-.4	-5.6	-14.9	-.0	-2.5
Total	604	71	1031	68	11035.1	—	—	—	—	13.3	4.10	—	.292	.348	—	—	—	—	—	.967	1677	286	1106	—	—	—	—	—

BATTER-FIELDER WINS	BATTING AVERAGE	ON-BASE PERCENTAGE	SLUGGING AVERAGE	ON-BASE PLUS SLUGGING	ADJUSTED OPS	ADJUSTED BATTER RUNS
Hornsby-StL.......8.9	Hornsby-StL.........401	Hornsby-StL.........459	Hornsby-StL.........722	Hornsby-StL........1181	Hornsby-StL..........210	Hornsby-StL......100.4
Bancroft-NY.......4.9	Grimes-Chi...........354	Grimes-Chi...........442	Grimes-Chi...........572	Grimes-Chi.........1014	Grimes-Chi...........157	Grimes-Chi..........46.8
O'Farrell-Chi......4.1	Miller-Chi.............352	O'Farrell-Chi.........439	Lee-Phi.................540	Williams-Phi..........905	Daubert-Cin..........130	Daubert-Cin.........25.3
Carey-Pit............3.5	Bigbee-Pit............350	Carey-Pit..............408	Tierney-Pit...........515	Miller-Chi.............899	Wheat-Bro............129	Wheat-Bro...........25.2
Grimes-Chi.........3.2	Tierney-Pit...........345	Bigbee-Pit............405	Williams-Phi..........514	Walker-Phi............899	Miller-Chi............128	Russell-Pit..........23.4

RUNS	HITS	DOUBLES	TRIPLES	HOME RUNS	TOTAL BASES	RUNS BATTED IN
Hornsby-StL..........141	Hornsby-StL.........250	Hornsby-StL...........46	Daubert-Cin............22	Hornsby-StL............42	Hornsby-StL..........450	Hornsby-StL..........152
Carey-Pit...............140	Bigbee-Pit.............215	Grimes-Chi............45	Meusel-NY..............17	Williams-Phi...........26	Meusel-NY............314	Meusel-NY............132
Smith-StL..............117	Bancroft-NY..........209	Duncan-Cin............44	Maranville-Pit..........15	Lee-Phi...................17	Wheat-Bro.............302	Wheat-Bro.............112
Bancroft-NY..........117	Carey-Pit..............207	Bancroft-NY...........41	Bigbee-Pit...............15	Kelly-NY..................17	Williams-Phi..........300	Kelly-NY................107
Maranville-Pit........115	Daubert-Cin...........205	Hollocher-Chi.........37			Daubert-Cin..........300	

BASES ON BALLS	STOLEN BASES	BASE STEALING RUNS	FIELDING RUNS-INFIELD	FIELDING RUNS-OUTFIELD	OUTFIELD ASSISTS	CATCHER CS PCT.
Carey-Pit.................80	Carey-Pit.................51	Carey-Pit.............10.5	Parkinson-Phi......27.9	Bigbee-Pit............13.7	Youngs-NY.............28	O'Farrell-Chi........57.9
O'Farrell-Chi...........79	Frisch-NY................31	Traynor-Pit............2.7	Bancroft-NY.........22.1	Carey-Pit...............9.9	Bigbee-Pit...............27	Wingo-Cin............53.3
Bancroft-NY............79	Burns-Cin................30	Kelly-NY.................1.6	Pinelli-Cin............21.9	Powell-Bos.............6.0	Walker-Phi..............24	O'Neil-Bos...........51.1
Burns-Cin................78	Maranville-Pit...........24	Smith-StL...............1.5	Bohne-Cin............12.5	Walker-Phi.............4.5	Carey-Pit.................22	Ainsmith-StL........46.9
Grimes-Chi..............75	Bigbee-Pit...............24	T.Griffith-Bro..........1.2	Kelly-NY.................9.3	Youngs-NY.............2.6	Burns-Cin...............20	Snyder-NY...........45.1

WINS	WINNING PCT.	WINS ABOVE TEAM	GAMES STARTED	COMPLETE GAMES	FEWEST HITS/GAME	FEWEST BB/GAME
Rixey-Cin................25	Donohue-Cin........667	Ruether-Bro...........5.5	Rixey-Cin................38	Cooper-Pit..............27	Douglas-NY.........8.79	Adams-Pit...............79
Cooper-Pit..............23	Rixey-Cin.............658	Rixey-Cin...............5.3	Cooper-Pit..............36	Ruether-Bro............26	Osborne-Chi........8.95	Alexander-Chi......1.25
Ruether-Bro............21	Couch-Cin.............640	Donohue-Cin..........3.8	Ruether-Bro............35	Rixey-Cin................26	Ryan-NY..............9.11	Rixey-Cin............1.29
Pfeffer-StL..............19	Ruether-Bro.........636	Vance-Bro..............3.7	Nehf-NY..................35		Luque-Cin............9.17	Donohue-Cin.......1.60
Nehf-NY..................19	Cooper-Pit............622	Cooper-Pit..............3.6			Vance-Bro............9.49	J.Barnes-NY........1.61

STRIKEOUTS	STRIKEOUTS/GAME	GAMES	SAVES	BASE RUNNERS/9	ADJUSTED RELIEF RUNS	RELIEF RANKING
Vance-Bro.............134	Vance-Bro............4.91	North-StL................53	Jonnard-NY..............5	McNamara-Bos..10.44	McNamara-Bos.....11.8	McNamara-Bos....10.5
Cooper-Pit.............129	Ring-Phi...............4.19	Sherdel-StL.............47	North-StL..................4	Douglas-NY.......11.02	Causey-NY............5.2	Causey-NY............4.8
Ring-Phi.................116	Osborne-Chi........3.96	Ryan-NY..................46		Adams-Pit...........11.03	Jonnard-NY...........3.9	Jonnard-NY...........3.0
Morrison-Pit...........104	Cooper-Pit............3.94	Oeschger-Bos.........46		Rixey-Cin............11.09	Mamaux-Bro...........2.6	Mamaux-Bro..........1.5
Grimes-Bro..............99	Doak-StL..............3.64	Morrison-Pit............45		Donohue-Cin.....11.34	Braxton-Bos...........2.4	Braxton-Bos...........1.2

INNINGS PITCHED	OPPONENTS' AVG.	OPPONENTS' OBP	EARNED RUN AVERAGE	ADJUSTED ERA	ADJUSTED STARTER RUNS	PITCHER WINS
Rixey-Cin...........313.1	Douglas-NY..........257	Douglas-NY..........302	Douglas-NY.........2.63	Douglas-NY..........152	Cooper-Pit...........27.3	**Cooper-Pit..........3.9**
Cooper-Pit.........294.2	Luque-Cin.............268	Rixey-Cin..............303	Ryan-NY...............3.01	Weinert-Phi...........137	Douglas-NY..........24.9	**Meadows-Phi.....2.6**
Morrison-Pit.......286.1	Ryan-NY...............269	Adams-Pit.............307	Donohue-Cin........3.12	Ryan-NY...............133	Donohue-Cin........21.6	**Nehf-NY.............2.5**
Nehf-NY............268.1	Osborne-Chi.........271	J.Barnes-NY.........311	Cooper-Pit...........3.18	Cooper-Pit............128	Nehf-NY...............21.1	**Ruether-Bro.......2.5**
Ruether-Bro.......267.1	Rixey-Cin..............275	Donohue-Cin.........312	Nehf-NY...............3.29	Donohue-Cin.........128	Morrison-Pit.........21.0	**Ryan-NY.............2.5**

Polo Grounds Potency

Team runs per game rose to 5.00, more than an entire run higher than 1920 and the century's top total to date. The league pounded 530 homers, another all-time high; four-baggers had more than doubled in two years. Meanwhile, the stolen base was at its lowest ebb yet at .61 per game. More runs meant fewer pitchers racking up big totals; just three pitchers won 20, compared to seven in 1920.

John McGraw's Giants, first or second every year since 1917, took their second straight NL flag. Only for a few days did the Giants trail, and they won easily over second-place Cincinnati, which featured 25-game winner Eppa Rixey. Three Giants hurlers graced the top five in ERA, and the club featured seven .300-hitting regulars.

Rogers Hornsby enjoyed arguably his greatest season in 1922, batting .401 and taking the Triple Crown. However, his Cardinals, otherwise weak offensively, tied for third with Pittsburgh. The Pirates topped the league in runs, bucking the trend by leading the loop in average and steals.

Three eventual Hall of Famers debuted. Cubs catcher Gabby Hartnett played the first of his 1,990 career games. Cardinals first baseman Jim Bottomley hit .325 after an August promotion. Finally, shortstop Travis Jackson began his fifteen-year career with a cameo appearance for the Giants. Two significant deaths bridged the old and the new. The great Cap Anson passed away at 70 on April 14. Meanwhile, 27-year-old Cardinals outfielder Austin McHenry, suffering from a brain tumor, died November 27.

The Giants again met—and vanquished—the Yankees at the Polo Grounds, making it 13 straight World Series games played at the same two-team venue. The Giants won in five (including one tie), allowing just 11 runs and batting .309. Nobody sensed that this would be the Giants' last world title for more than a decade.

1922 AMERICAN LEAGUE

TEAM	W	L	T	PCT	GB	HW	HL	R	OR	PA	H	2B	3B	HR	BB	SO	HB	SH	AVG	OBP	SLG	OPS	AOPS	BR	ABR	PF	SB	CS	BSA	BSR
NY	94	60	0	.610	—	50	27	758	**618**	6000	1504	220	75	95	497	532	40	218	.287	.353	.412	765	103	34	17	102	62	59	51	-7
StL	93	61	0	.604	1	**54**	23	**867**	643	6128	**1693**	291	**94**	98	473	381	36	203	**.313**	**.372**	**.455**	**827**	**117**	**159**	**128**	104	**136**	76	**64**	**3**
Det	79	75	1	.513	15	43	34	828	791	6170	1641	250	87	54	530	378	36	**244**	.306	**.372**	.415	787	115	94	122	97	78	62	56	-5
Cle	78	76	1	.506	16	44	35	768	817	6095	1544	**320**	73	32	**554**	**331**	45	203	.292	.364	.398	762	104	49	43	101	90	58	61	0
Chi	77	77	1	.500	17	43	34	691	691	6023	1463	243	62	45	482	463	43	231	.278	.343	.373	716	92	-52	-49	100	109	84	56	-5
Was	69	85	0	.448	25	40	39	650	706	5868	1395	229	76	45	458	442	**57**	152	.268	.334	.367	701	93	-86	-53	95	97	63	61	-1
Phi	65	89	1	.422	29	38	39	705	830	5854	1409	229	63	**111**	437	591	36	170	.270	.331	.402	733	94	-38	-55	103	60	69	47	-11
Bos	61	93	0	.396	33	31	42	598	769	5859	1392	250	55	45	366	455	44	161	.263	.316	.357	673	82	-151	-146	99	64	67	49	-9
Total	618	——		—	—	343	273	5865	—	47997	12041	2032	585	525	3797	3573	337	1582	.285	.348	.398	746	—	—	—	—	696	538	56	-35

TEAM	CG	SHO	GR	SV	IP	H	HR	BB	SO	BR/9	ERA	AERA	OAV	OOB	PR	APR	PF	OSB	OCS	FA	E	WPB	DP	FW	PW	BW	BSW	DIF
NY	**100**	7	69	14	1393.2	**1402**	73	423	458	**11.9**	3.39	118	**.268**	**.325**	99	92	99	67	72	**.975**	157	37	124	2.0	8.9	1.7	-.3	4.6
StL	79	8	115	**22**	1392.0	1412	71	**419**	**534**	12.1	**3.38**	**122**	**.268**	.327	**101**	**112**	103	**66**	**77**	.968	201	24	158	-.5	**10.9**	**12.4**	**.7**	-7.5
Det	67	7	133	15	1391.0	1554	62	473	461	13.7	4.27	91	.288	.354	-37	-67	96	112	60	.970	191	29	133	.2	-6.5	11.8	-.0	-3.4
Cle	76	**14**	135	7	1383.2	1605	58	464	489	13.7	4.59	87	.296	.356	-85	-93	99	106	48	.968	202	48	147	-.5	-9.0	4.2	.4	5.9
Chi	86	13	99	8	1403.2	1472	57	529	484	13.0	3.94	103	.278	.346	15	15	101	75	76	**.975**	**155**	**19**	143	**2.2**	1.5	-4.8	-.0	1.1
Was	84	13	97	10	1362.1	1485	49	500	422	13.4	3.81	101	.286	.354	33	6	96	85	74	.969	196	42	**168**	-.2	.6	-5.1	.3	-3.6
Phi	73	4	**147**	6	1362.1	1573	107	469	373	13.7	4.59	92	.297	.357	-85	-52	105	83	75	.966	215	38	118	-1.2	-5.0	-5.3	-.6	.2
Bos	71	10	130	6	1373.1	1508	**48**	503	359	13.5	4.30	95	.287	.354	-41	-31	102	102	56	.965	224	38	145	-1.8	-3.0	-14.2	-.4	3.4
Total	636	76	925	88	11062.0	—	—	—	—	13.1	4.03	—	.285	.348	—	—	—	—	—	.969	1541	275	1136	—	—	—	—	—

BATTER-FIELDER WINS	BATTING AVERAGE	ON-BASE PERCENTAGE	SLUGGING AVERAGE	ON-BASE PLUS SLUGGING	ADJUSTED OPS	ADJUSTED BATTER RUNS
Sisler-StL 6.3	Sisler-StL 420	Speaker-Cle 474	Ruth-NY 672	Ruth-NY 1106	Ruth-NY 181	Sisler-StL 60.0
Speaker-Cle 5.1	Cobb-Det 401	Sisler-StL 467	Williams-StL 627	Speaker-Cle 1080	Speaker-Cle 178	Cobb-Det 57.7
Cobb-Det 4.2	Speaker-Cle 378	Cobb-Det 462	Speaker-Cle 606	Sisler-StL 1061	Cobb-Det 172	Speaker-Cle 54.6
Williams-StL 4.1	Heilmann-Det 356	Ruth-NY 434	Heilmann-Det 598	Williams-StL 1040	Heilmann-Det 172	Williams-StL 52.1
Ruth-NY 3.5	Miller-Phi 335	Heilmann-Det 432	Sisler-StL 594	Heilmann-Det 1030	Sisler-StL 169	Ruth-NY 49.2

RUNS	HITS	DOUBLES	TRIPLES	HOME RUNS	TOTAL BASES	RUNS BATTED IN
Sisler-StL 134	Sisler-StL 246	Speaker-Cle 48	Sisler-StL 18	Williams-StL 39	Williams-StL 367	Williams-StL 155
Blue-Det 131	Cobb-Det 211	Pratt-Bos 44	Jacobson-StL 16	Walker-Phi 37	Sisler-StL 348	Veach-Det 126
Williams-StL 128	Tobin-StL 207	Sisler-StL 42	Cobb-Det 16	Ruth-NY 35	Walker-Phi 310	McManus-StL 109
Tobin-StL 122	Veach-Det 202	Cobb-Det 42	Judge-Was 15	Miller-Phi 21	Cobb-Det 297	Sisler-StL 105
			Mostil-Chi 14	Heilmann-Det 21	Tobin-StL 296	Jacobson-StL 102

BASES ON BALLS	STOLEN BASES	BASE STEALING RUNS	FIELDING RUNS-INFIELD	FIELDING RUNS-OUTFIELD	OUTFIELD ASSISTS	CATCHER CS PCT.
Witt-NY 89	Sisler-StL 51	Sisler-StL 4.6	Harris-Was 31.2	Veach-Det 9.7	Meusel-NY 24	Severeid-StL 54.1
Ruth-NY 84	Williams-StL 37	Jacobson-StL 2.1	Peckinpaugh-Was 18.3	Menosky-Bos 5.6	Rice-Was 23	Schang-NY 53.2
Blue-Det 82	Harris-Was 25	Evans-Cle 1.7	Scott-NY 16.6	Miller-Phi 5.2	Walker-Phi 19	Schalk-Chi 51.5
Speaker-Cle 77	Johnson-Chi 21	Harris-Was 1.7	Sisler-StL 11.7	Hooper-Chi 4.8	Miller-Phi 19	Gharrity-Was 48.2
Williams-StL 74		Veach-Det 1.6	Jones-Det 10.1	Harris-Bos 4.0	Hooper-Chi 19	Perkins-Phi 47.4

WINS	WINNING PCT.	WINS ABOVE TEAM	GAMES STARTED	COMPLETE GAMES	FEWEST HITS/GAME	FEWEST BB/GAME
Rommel-Phi 27	Bush-NY 788	Rommel-Phi 10.3	Uhle-Cle 40	Faber-Chi 31	Davis-StL 8.36	Shocker-StL 1.47
Bush-NY 26	Rommel-Phi 675	Bush-NY 8.5	Shocker-StL 38	Shocker-StL 29	Bush-NY 8.46	Vangilder-StL 1.76
Shocker-StL 24	Shawkey-NY 625	Mogridge-Was 4.4	Faber-Chi 38	Uhle-Cle 23	Faber-Chi 8.54	Mays-NY 1.88
Uhle-Cle 22	Pillette-Det 613	Kolp-StL 4.2	Pillette-Det 37	Johnson-Was 23	Shawkey-NY 8.59	Kolp-StL 1.91
Faber-Chi 21	Hoyt-NY 613	Zachary-Was 3.9			Wright-StL 8.65	Hasty-Phi 1.92

STRIKEOUTS	STRIKEOUTS/GAME	GAMES	SAVES	BASE RUNNERS/9	ADJUSTED RELIEF RUNS	RELIEF RANKING
Shocker-StL 149	Morton-Cle 4.53	Rommel-Phi 51	Jones-NY 8	Faber-Chi 10.82	Murray-NY 1.2	Murray-NY 1.0
Faber-Chi 148	Harriss-Phi 4.00	Uhle-Cle 50	Pruett-StL 7	Shocker-StL 11.02		
Shawkey-NY 130	Shawkey-NY 3.90	Shocker-StL 48	Wright-StL 5	Rommel-Phi 11.08		
Ehmke-Det 108	Shocker-StL 3.85	Harriss-Phi 47		Vangilder-StL 11.09		
Johnson-Was 105	Faber-Chi 3.78			Quinn-Bos 11.43		

INNINGS PITCHED	OPPONENTS' AVG.	OPPONENTS' OBP	EARNED RUN AVERAGE	ADJUSTED ERA	ADJUSTED STARTER RUNS	PITCHER WINS
Faber-Chi 352.0	Davis-StL 250	Faber-Chi 299	Faber-Chi 2.81	Faber-Chi 144	Faber-Chi 46.6	**Shocker-StL 4.9**
Shocker-StL 348.0	Bush-NY 252	Shocker-StL 304	Pillette-Det 2.85	Wright-StL 141	Shocker-StL 43.8	**Faber-Chi 4.6**
Shawkey-NY 299.2	Faber-Chi 252	Rommel-Phi 309	Shawkey-NY 2.91	Shocker-StL 139	Shawkey-NY 37.3	**Vangilder-StL 3.8**
Rommel-Phi 294.0	Shawkey-NY 256	Vangilder-StL 310	Wright-StL 2.92	Shawkey-NY 137	Pillette-Det 29.9	**Rommel-Phi 3.6**
Uhle-Cle 287.1	Pillette-Det 258	Quinn-Bos 311	Shocker-StL 2.97	Pillette-Det 136	Rommel-Phi 29.9	**Shawkey-NY 3.3**

Browns Come Close

Apparently deciding that if they couldn't beat 'em, they'd join 'em, the Athletics brought *in* the left-field fences at Shibe Park. As a result, Philadelphia hit the most homers in home games. Unfortunately, they also *allowed* the most, and finished seventh. These were hard years to be a Philadelphia baseball fan. The A's and Phillies both finished last in 1919, 1920, and 1921, and were seventh in 1922. Soon, Connie Mack's club would climb back to the top.

AL hitters pounded 525 homers, more than double the total of three years before. But this wasn't sloppy baseball; hitters still made contact (since 1918, no AL pitcher had notched 150 strikeouts). In addition, for the first time, the league's fielding percentage reached .970; it never again fell below .968. And as the 1910s faded into memory, so did two of the decade's standouts. Home Run Baker ended his career with the Yankees, and converted outfielder Smokey Joe Wood hit .297 in his final season for Cleveland.

The Yankees won the flag again. But one misconception about the Yankees teams of the 1920s is that they bludgeoned the opposition. It just isn't so; only twice in the '20s did they romp to the flag. In fact, in 1922, they almost lost—to the Browns. St. Louis was fueled by George Sisler, who set an AL record by hitting in 41 games. He also led the league in hits, runs, triples, while pounding out a .420 average (only surpassed in the AL by Nap Lajoie's .426 in 1901). The Browns scored 100 more runs than New York, had a better ERA, and stole more bases, but the Yankees moved ahead in August and eventually held on by 1 game.

The Yankees struggled without Babe Ruth and Bob Meusel, suspended a month for barnstorming. When the two returned, they carried the club's attack. They did little in October, though. The Yankees lost in five (four losses and one tie) to the pitching-rich Giants, who had served as their landlord at the Polo Grounds for a decade.

1921 NATIONAL LEAGUE

TEAM	W	L	T	PCT	GB	HW	HL	R	OR	PA	H	2B	3B	HR	BB	SO	HB	SH	AVG	OBP	SLG	OPS	AOPS	BR	ABR	PF	SB	CS	BSA	BSR
NY	94	59	0	.614	—	**53**	26	**840**	637	5946	1575	237	93	75	**469**	390	33	166	.298	**.359**	.421	780	112	97	95	100	**137**	114	55	-10
Pit	90	63	1	.588	4	45	31	692	**595**	5946	1533	231	**104**	37	341	371	23	203	.285	.330	.387	717	93	-40	-57	103	134	93	**59**	**-3**
StL	87	66	1	.569	7	48	29	809	681	5915	**1635**	**260**	88	83	382	452	29	195	**.308**	.358	**.437**	**795**	**118**	**116**	**134**	98	94	94	50	-12
Bos	79	74	0	.516	15	42	32	721	697	5982	1561	209	100	61	377	470	22	198	.290	.339	.400	739	107	3	45	95	94	100	48	-14
Bro	77	75	0	.507	16.5	41	37	667	681	5773	1476	209	85	59	325	400	21	164	.280	.325	.386	711	90	-54	-76	104	91	73	55	-6
Cin	70	83	0	.458	24	40	36	618	649	5727	1421	221	94	20	375	**308**	**45**	195	.278	.333	.370	703	96	-56	-26	95	117	120	49	-16
Chi	64	89	0	.418	30	32	44	668	773	5907	1553	234	56	37	343	374	35	**208**	.292	.339	.378	717	95	-29	-30	100	70	97	42	-19
Phi	51	103	0	.331	43.5	29	47	617	919	5760	1512	238	50	**88**	294	615	25	112	.284	.324	.397	721	89	-36	-84	108	66	80	45	-13
Total	613	—	—	—	—	330	282	5632	—	46956	12266	1839	670	460	2906	3380	233	1441	.289	.338	.397	736	—	—	—	—	803	771	51	-93

TEAM	CG	SHO	GR	SV	IP	H	HR	BB	SO	BR/9	ERA	AERA	OAV	OOB	PR	APR	PF	OSB	OCS	FA	E	WPB	DP	FW	PW	BW	BSW	DIF
NY	71	9	127	**18**	1372.1	1497	79	**295**	357	11.9	3.55	103	.286	.326	34	17	97	80	94	.971	187	29	**155**	1.3	1.7	9.4	.2	5.0
Pit	**88**	10	91	10	1415.2	**1448**	**37**	322	**500**	**11.5**	**3.17**	**121**	**.271**	**.316**	**96**	**103**	101	**73**	87	.973	172	27	129	2.3	**10.2**	-5.6	**.9**	5.8
StL	70	10	**155**	16	1371.2	1486	61	399	464	12.6	3.62	101	.282	.337	24	5	97	104	94	.965	219	52	130	-.6	.5	**13.2**	-.0	-2.6
Bos	74	**11**	124	12	1385.0	1488	54	420	382	12.6	3.90	94	.280	.337	-18	-40	97	90	**119**	.969	199	**16**	122	.5	-3.9	4.4	-.2	1.7
Bro	82	8	106	12	1363.1	1556	46	361	471	12.9	3.70	105	.293	.342	13	27	103	117	94	.964	232	37	142	-1.5	2.7	-7.5	.6	6.8
Cin	83	7	95	9	1363.0	1500	**37**	305	408	12.0	3.46	103	.287	.328	48	17	95	87	78	.969	193	32	139	.9	1.7	-2.6	-.4	-6.1
Chi	73	7	120	7	1363.0	1605	67	409	441	13.6	4.39	87	.303	.357	-93	-87	101	107	103	**.974**	**166**	24	129	**2.5**	-8.6	-3.0	-.7	-2.8
Phi	82	5	107	8	1348.2	1665	79	371	333	13.8	4.48	94	.308	.356	-105	-35	112	145	102	.955	295	55	127	-5.2	-3.5	-8.3	-.1	-8.9
Total	623	67	925	92	10982.2	—	—	—	—	12.6	3.78	—	.289	.338	—	—	—	—	—	.967	1663	272	1073	—	—	—	—	—

BATTER-FIELDER WINS	BATTING AVERAGE	ON-BASE PERCENTAGE	SLUGGING AVERAGE	ON-BASE PLUS SLUGGING	ADJUSTED OPS	ADJUSTED BATTER RUNS
Hornsby-StL 7.7	Hornsby-StL .397	Hornsby-StL .458	Hornsby-StL .639	Hornsby-StL 1097	Hornsby-StL 191	Hornsby-StL 79.2
Bancroft-NY 5.3	Roush-Cin .352	Youngs-NY .411	McHenry-StL .531	McHenry-StL 924	McHenry-StL 145	Fournier-StL 37.6
Frisch-NY 4.5	McHenry-StL .350	Fournier-StL .409	Kelly-NY .528	Fournier-StL 914	Fournier-StL 144	McHenry-StL 36.8
Johnston-Bro 3.0	Cruise-Bos .346	Grimes-Chi .406	Meusel-Phi-NY .515	Meusel-Phi-NY 895	Kelly-NY 131	Cruise-Bos 29.2
McHenry-StL 2.5	Fournier-StL .343	Carey-Pit .395	Mann-StL .512	Kelly-NY 884	Youngs-NY 129	Roush-Cin 27.2
RUNS	**HITS**	**DOUBLES**	**TRIPLES**	**HOME RUNS**	**TOTAL BASES**	**RUNS BATTED IN**
Hornsby-StL 131	Hornsby-StL 235	Hornsby-StL 44	Powell-Bos 18	Kelly-NY 23	Hornsby-StL 378	Hornsby-StL 126
Frisch-NY 121	Frisch-NY 211	Kelly-NY 42	Hornsby-StL 18	Hornsby-StL 21	Kelly-NY 310	Kelly-NY 122
Bancroft-NY 121	C.Bigbee-Pit 204	Johnston-Bro 41	Grimm-Pit 17	Williams-Phi 18	McHenry-StL 305	Youngs-NY 102
Powell-Bos 114	Johnston-Bro 203	Grimes-Chi 38	Frisch-NY 17	McHenry-StL 17	Meusel-Phi-NY 302	McHenry-StL 102
Burns-NY 111		McHenry-StL 37	C.Bigbee-Pit 17	Fournier-StL 16	Frisch-NY 300	Frisch-NY 100
BASES ON BALLS	**STOLEN BASES**	**BASE STEALING RUNS**	**FIELDING RUNS-INFIELD**	**FIELDING RUNS-OUTFIELD**	**OUTFIELD ASSISTS**	**CATCHER CS PCT.**
Burns-NY 80	Frisch-NY 49	Frisch-NY 6.2	Lavan-StL 20.5	C.Bigbee-Pit 11.8	Williams-Phi 29	O'Neil-Bos 59.8
Youngs-NY 71	Carey-Pit 37	Carey-Pit 3.9	Bancroft-NY 19.1	Williams-Phi 8.7	Meusel-Phi-NY 28	Snyder-NY 57.1
Grimes-Chi 70	Johnston-Bro 28	Stock-StL 1.4	Deal-Chi 12.8	Griffith-Bro 7.1	Griffith-Bro 27	Schmidt-Pit 55.0
Carey-Pit 70	Bohne-Cin 26	Cutshaw-Pit 1.3	Kelly-NY 11.7	McHenry-StL 5.2	C.Bigbee-Pit 27	Smith-NY 50.7
Bancroft-NY 66	Maranville-Pit 25	Maranville-Pit 1.3	Kilduff-Bro 11.5	Carey-Pit 5.1		O'Farrell-Chi 49.5
WINS	**WINNING PCT.**	**WINS ABOVE TEAM**	**GAMES STARTED**	**COMPLETE GAMES**	**FEWEST HITS/GAME**	**FEWEST BB/GAME**
Grimes-Bro 22	Doak-StL .714	Grimes-Bro 5.2	Cooper-Pit 38	Grimes-Bro 30	Glazner-Pit 8.23	Adams-Pit 1.01
Cooper-Pit 22	Nehf-NY .667	Doak-StL 3.9	Rixey-Cin 37	Cooper-Pit 29	Adams-Pit 8.72	Alexander-Chi 1.18
Oeschger-Bos 20	Grimes-Bro .629	Glazner-Pit 3.7	Oeschger-Bos 36	Luque-Cin 25	Oeschger-Bos 9.12	Barnes-NY 1.53
Nehf-NY 20	Barnes-NY .625	Adams-Pit 3.7	Marquard-Cin 36		Pertica-StL 9.16	Hubbell-Phi 1.55
Rixey-Cin 19	Toney-NY .621	Alexander-Chi 3.3	Luque-Cin 36		Nehf-NY 9.18	Doak-StL 1.60
STRIKEOUTS	**STRIKEOUTS/GAME**	**GAMES**	**SAVES**	**BASE RUNNERS/9**	**ADJUSTED RELIEF RUNS**	**RELIEF RANKING**
Grimes-Bro 136	Grimes-Bro 4.05	Scott-Bos 47	North-StL 7	Adams-Pit 9.73	North-StL 2.4	North-StL 2.4
Cooper-Pit 134	Cooper-Pit 3.69	Oeschger-Bos 46	Barnes-NY 6	J.Morrison-Pit 10.31		
Luque-Cin 102	Doak-StL 3.58	McQuillan-Bos 45	McQuillan-Bos 5	Ryan-NY 10.57		
McQuillan-Bos 94	Martin-Chi 3.56	Watson-Bos 44		Donohue-Cin 10.88		
	Glazner-Pit 3.38	Fillingim-Bos 44		Glazner-Pit 10.92		
INNINGS PITCHED	**OPPONENTS' AVG.**	**OPPONENTS' OBP**	**EARNED RUN AVERAGE**	**ADJUSTED ERA**	**ADJUSTED STARTER RUNS**	**PITCHER WINS**
Cooper-Pit 327.0	Glazner-Pit .250	Adams-Pit .272	Doak-StL 2.59	Adams-Pit 145	Grimes-Bro 32.8	**Grimes-Bro 4.0**
Luque-Cin 304.0	Adams-Pit .251	Glazner-Pit .306	Adams-Pit 2.64	Doak-StL 142	Glazner-Pit 26.4	**Adams-Pit 2.5**
Grimes-Bro 302.1	Pertica-StL .267	Nehf-NY .311	Glazner-Pit 2.77	Glazner-Pit 138	Rixey-Cin 22.6	**Rixey-Cin 2.2**
Rixey-Cin 301.0	Watson-Bos .270	Luque-Cin .312	Rixey-Cin 2.78	Grimes-Bro 137	Doak-StL 21.1	**Cooper-Pit 2.2**
Oeschger-Bos 299.0	Nehf-NY .271	Doak-StL .313	Grimes-Bro 2.83	Mitchell-Bro 134	Adams-Pit 20.5	**Mitchell-Bro 1.9**

A Powerful Visitation

The home run made a splash in the NL in 1921. Four-baggers nearly doubled, from 261 to 460 as runs per team per game rose 16 percent to 4.59, the highest since 1912. Batters struck out less often, despite the rise of the homer, and stolen bases continued to fade. Prior to 1921, the Braves shortened their left-field fence by 25 feet. Cubs Park, Cincinnati's Redland Field, and St. Louis' Sportsman's Park were also shrunk, though Redland Field remained a home run desert.

The change to power baseball caused casualties. After fifteen years, outfielder Dode Paskert played his last game. Perhaps the quintessential Dead Ball Era player, Paskert's singles, walks, and steals were no longer in vogue. Meanwhile, future Hall of Famer Kiki Cuyler began his eighteen-year career, going 0-for-3 in his only appearance of the season for the Pirates.

Seeking their first flag in twelve years, Pittsburgh topped the league most of the season. The pitching, led by Wilbur Cooper and 39-year-old Babe Adams, was the league's best, and their offense rated well, even in cavernous Forbes Field. Down the stretch, though, John McGraw's Giants came up winners. First baseman Bill Terry paced the NL with 23 homers, but New York did real damage by leading the loop in walks by a margin of nearly 100.

The Giants-Yankees World Series, the last best-of-nine affair, was classic. Each game was close into the late innings, with only two games settled by more than 2 runs. In the end, John McGraw's men were stronger as they gained their first world championship since 1905, in eight games.

1921 AMERICAN LEAGUE

TEAM	W	L	T	PCT	GB	HW	HL	R	OR	PA	H	2B	3B	HR	BB	SO	HB	SH	AVG	OBP	SLG	OPS	AOPS	BR	ABR	PF	SB	CS	BSA	BSR
NY	98	55	0	.641	—	**53**	25	**948**	708	6066	1576	285	87	**134**	588	569	40	189	.300	.375	**.464**	**839**	**116**	**146**	126	102	89	64	58	-3
Cle	94	60	0	.610	4.5	51	26	925	712	6275	1656	**355**	90	42	**623**	376	37	**232**	.308	.383	.430	813	111	121	107	102	51	42	55	-3
StL	81	73	0	.526	17.5	43	34	835	845	6096	1655	246	**106**	67	413	407	36	205	.304	.357	.425	782	98	24	-21	106	91	71	56	-5
Was	80	73	1	.523	18	46	30	704	738	6003	1468	240	96	42	462	472	**59**	188	.277	.342	.383	725	95	-83	-48	95	**112**	66	**63**	**2**
Bos	75	79	0	.487	23.5	41	36	668	**696**	5851	1440	248	69	17	428	**344**	31	186	.277	.335	.361	696	84	-134	-117	97	83	65	56	-4
Det	71	82	1	.464	27	37	40	883	852	6302	**1724**	268	100	58	582	376	29	230	**.316**	**.385**	.433	818	115	121	**130**	99	95	89	52	-10
Chi	62	92	0	.403	36.5	37	40	683	858	5997	1509	242	82	35	445	474	37	186	.283	.343	.379	722	90	-88	-79	99	94	93	50	-12
Phi	53	100	2	.346	45	28	47	657	894	6067	1497	256	64	82	424	565	43	135	.274	.331	.389	720	88	-103	-106	101	69	56	55	-4
Total	616	—	—	—	—	336	278	6303	—	48657	12525	2140	694	477	3965	3583	312	1551	.292	.357	.408	765	—	—	—	—	684	546	56	-41

TEAM	CG	SHO	GR	SV	IP	H	HR	BB	SO	BR/9	ERA	AERA	OAV	OOB	PR	APR	PF	OSB	OCS	FA	E	WPB	DP	FW	PW	BW	BSW	DIF
NY	**92**	8	96	15	1364.0	**1461**	51	470	**481**	13.1	**3.82**	**111**	**.277**	**.342**	**70**	**63**	99	82	61	.965	222	36	138	-.3	**5.9**	11.8	.2	3.9
Cle	81	**11**	114	14	1377.0	1534	**43**	**431**	475	**13.0**	3.90	109	.288	.344	58	55	100	96	52	.967	204	32	124	.8	5.1	10.0	.2	.8
StL	77	9	**142**	9	1379.0	1541	71	556	477	13.9	4.61	97	.288	.360	-51	-21	105	79	66	.964	224	**24**	127	-.3	-2.0	-2.0	.0	8.2
Was	80	10	108	10	1383.2	1568	51	442	452	13.3	3.97	104	.291	.349	47	23	96	**59**	67	.963	235	36	153	-.9	2.2	-4.5	**.7**	6.1
Bos	88	9	82	5	1364.1	1521	53	452	446	13.3	3.98	106	.291	.352	45	38	99	73	71	**.975**	**157**	27	151	**3.5**	3.6	-10.9	.1	1.8
Det	73	4	115	**17**	1386.1	1634	71	495	452	14.2	4.40	97	.297	.361	-18	-20	100	99	75	.963	232	34	107	-.8	-1.9	**12.2**	-.5	-14.6
Chi	84	7	106	9	1365.1	1603	52	549	392	14.4	4.94	86	.303	.372	-99	-109	99	98	79	.969	200	35	**155**	1.0	-10.2	-7.4	-.6	2.2
Phi	75	2	119	7	1400.1	1645	85	548	431	14.3	4.61	97	.300	.367	-52	-24	104	101	**90**	.958	274	48	144	-3.1	-2.2	-9.9	.1	-8.4
Total	650	60	882	86	11020.0	—	—	—	—	13.7	4.28	—	.292	.357	—	—	—	—	—	.965	1748	272	1099	—	—	—	—	—

BATTER-FIELDER WINS	BATTING AVERAGE	ON-BASE PERCENTAGE	SLUGGING AVERAGE	ON-BASE PLUS SLUGGING	ADJUSTED OPS	ADJUSTED BATTER RUNS
Ruth-NY 9.4	Heilmann-Det .394	Ruth-NY .512	Ruth-NY .846	Ruth-NY 1359	Ruth-NY 236	Ruth-NY 117.7
Cobb-Det 4.8	Cobb-Det .389	Cobb-Det .452	Heilmann-Det .606	Heilmann-Det 1051	Heilmann-Det 167	Heilmann-Det 60.7
Collins-Chi 4.4	Ruth-NY .378	Heilmann-Det .444	Cobb-Det .596	Cobb-Det 1048	Cobb-Det 167	Cobb-Det 52.2
Speaker-Cle 3.8	Sisler-StL .371	Speaker-Cle .439	Williams-StL .561	Williams-StL 990	Speaker-Cle 146	Speaker-Cle 38.5
Heilmann-Det 3.4	Speaker-Cle .362	Williams-StL .429	Sisler-StL .560	Speaker-Cle 977	Williams-StL 142	Williams-StL 36.3
RUNS	**HITS**	**DOUBLES**	**TRIPLES**	**HOME RUNS**	**TOTAL BASES**	**RUNS BATTED IN**
Ruth-NY 177	Heilmann-Det 237	Speaker-Cle 52	Tobin-StL 18	Ruth-NY 59	Ruth-NY 457	Ruth-NY 171
Tobin-StL 132	Tobin-StL 236	Ruth-NY 44	Sisler-StL 18	Williams-StL 24	Heilmann-Det 365	Heilmann-Det 139
Peckinpaugh-NY 128	Sisler-StL 216	Veach-Det 43	Shanks-Was 18	Meusel-NY 24	Meusel-NY 334	Meusel-NY 135
Sisler-StL 125	Jacobson-StL 211	Heilmann-Det 43		T.Walker-Phi 23	Tobin-StL 327	Veach-Det 128
Cobb-Det 124	Veach-Det 207	Meusel-NY 40		Heilmann-Det 19	Sisler-StL 326	Gardner-Cle 120
BASES ON BALLS	**STOLEN BASES**	**BASE STEALING RUNS**	**FIELDING RUNS-INFIELD**	**FIELDING RUNS-OUTFIELD**	**OUTFIELD ASSISTS**	**CATCHER CS PCT.**
Ruth-NY 145	Sisler-StL 35	Sisler-StL 3.8	Scott-Bos 41.2	Veach-Det 12.9	Tobin-StL 28	Gharrity-Was 55.3
Blue-Det 103	Harris-Was 29	Harris-Was 3.2	Collins-Chi 30.7	Speaker-Cle 9.2	Meusel-NY 28	Ruel-Bos 46.8
Peckinpaugh-NY 84	Rice-Was 26	Judge-Was 2.5	Dykes-Phi 21.1	Cobb-Det 6.0	Cobb-Det 27	Severeid-StL 46.1
J.Sewell-Cle 80	Johnson-Chi 22	Meusel-NY 1.6	Johnson-Chi 20.8	Rice-Was 5.9	Williams-StL 24	Perkins-Phi 46.1
Schang-NY 78	Cobb-Det 22	Rice-Was 1.5	Ward-NY 18.8	T.Walker-Phi 5.2	T.Walker-Phi 24	Schalk-Chi 45.7
WINS	**WINNING PCT.**	**WINS ABOVE TEAM**	**GAMES STARTED**	**COMPLETE GAMES**	**FEWEST HITS/GAME**	**FEWEST BB/GAME**
Shocker-StL 27	Mays-NY .750	Faber-Chi 8.9	Coveleski-Cle 40	Faber-Chi 32	Faber-Chi 7.97	Hasty-Phi 2.01
Mays-NY 27	Shocker-StL .692	Shocker-StL 8.2	Faber-Chi 39	Shocker-StL 30	Bush-Bos 8.63	Mays-NY 2.03
Faber-Chi 25	Bush-Bos .640	Mays-NY 6.6	Shocker-StL 38	Mays-NY 30	Mays-NY 8.88	Mogridge-Was 2.06
Jones-Bos 23	Coveleski-Cle .639	Jones-Bos 4.9	Mays-NY 38	Coveleski-Cle 28	Shawkey-NY 9.00	Bagby-Cle 2.07
Coveleski-Cle 23	Faber-Chi .625	Kerr-Chi 4.6	Jones-Bos 38		Johnson-Was 9.03	Zachary-Was 2.12
STRIKEOUTS	**STRIKEOUTS/GAME**	**GAMES**	**SAVES**	**BASE RUNNERS/9**	**ADJUSTED RELIEF RUNS**	**RELIEF RANKING**
Johnson-Was 143	Johnson-Was 4.88	Mays-NY 49	Middleton-Det 7	Faber-Chi 10.53		
Shocker-StL 132	Shawkey-NY 4.63	Shocker-StL 47	Mays-NY 7	Morton-Cle 11.03		
Shawkey-NY 126	Bayne-StL 4.50	Bayne-StL 47		Mays-NY 11.15		
Faber-Chi 124	Leonard-Det 4.41	Rommel-Phi 46		Mogridge-Was 11.69		
Leonard-Det 120	Mails-Cle 4.03			Shocker-StL 12.04		
INNINGS PITCHED	**OPPONENTS' AVG.**	**OPPONENTS' OBP**	**EARNED RUN AVERAGE**	**ADJUSTED ERA**	**ADJUSTED STARTER RUNS**	**PITCHER WINS**
Mays-NY 336.2	Faber-Chi .242	Faber-Chi .297	Faber-Chi 2.48	Faber-Chi 171	Faber-Chi 64.1	**Faber-Chi 6.8**
Faber-Chi 330.2	Mays-NY .257	Mays-NY .303	Mogridge-Was 3.00	Mays-NY 139	Mays-NY 42.6	**Mays-NY 5.4**
Shocker-StL 326.2	Bush-Bos .260	Mogridge-Was .313	Mays-NY 3.05	Mogridge-Was 137	Mogridge-Was 35.8	**Jones-Bos 4.3**
Coveleski-Cle 315.0	Shawkey-NY .263	Shocker-StL .319	Hoyt-NY 3.09	Hoyt-NY 137	Hoyt-NY 35.3	**Shocker-StL 4.2**
Kerr-Chi 308.2	Johnson-Was .263	Johnson-Was .326	Jones-Bos 3.22	Jones-Bos 131	Jones-Bos 34.3	**Hoyt-NY 3.3**

The First of Many

Resurgent New York, riding a one-man power wave, engaged with Cleveland in one of the decade's best races. Neck-and-neck from mid-May onward, the teams counter-punched their way through mid-September. With the two clubs tied on September 23, the Indians started a four-game set at New York. After splitting the first two, the Yankees destroyed Cleveland, 21-7, on September 25, won again the next day, and never looked back. This was the first pennant ever for the Yankees.

Once again, Babe Ruth outhomered most AL clubs. Bob Meusel, Wally Pipp, and Roger Peckinpaugh supported The Bambino ably, as did and a capable mound staff led by pariah Carl Mays. The game had changed almost overnight. Runs rose to 5.12 per team per game, and only Red Faber posted an ERA under 3.00. The overpowering force named Ruth set new major league marks for home runs and RBIs.

Stripped of talent by Judge Landis' lifetime suspensions, the White Sox fell to seventh. Due to the gambling scandal, the public lost confidence in baseball, especially in American League cities. Despite the excitement generated by Babe Ruth, attendance was down 9 percent in 1920; moreover, the perception of the AL as a "dirty league" helped the NL eventually surpass of the Junior Circuit in attendance as AL fans responded to the scandal by voting with their feet. AL attendance in 1930 was substantially less than the NL's, even though the AL had outdrawn the NL by 26 percent in 1920.

The Philadelphia A's expanded Shibe Park's right field by 40 feet in 1921, but that didn't stop the tide of home runs. New York, St. Louis, and Philadelphia were the league's big long-ball parks, but the Yankees led the loop in homers at home *and* on the road. In the crosstown World Series (the final best-of-nine classic), the Giants shut down the mighty Yankees, winning in eight.

1920 NATIONAL LEAGUE

TEAM	W	L	T	PCT	GB	HW	HL	R	OR	PA	H	2B	3B	HR	BB	SO	HB	SH	AVG	OBP	SLG	OPS	AOPS	BR	ABR	PF	SB	CS	BSA	BSR
Bro	93	61	1	.604	—	**49**	29	660	**528**	5966	1493	205	**99**	28	359	391	19	189	.277	.324	.367	691	100	17	-3	103	70	80	47	-13
NY	86	68	1	.558	7	45	35	**682**	543	5891	1427	210	76	46	**432**	545	26	124	.269	.327	.363	690	104	25	32	99	131	113	54	-11
Cin	82	71	1	.536	10.5	42	34	639	569	5799	1432	169	76	18	382	**367**	**47**	194	.277	.332	.349	681	102	10	19	99	158	128	55	-10
Pit	79	75	1	.513	14	42	35	530	552	5796	1342	162	90	16	374	405	29	174	.257	.310	.332	642	86	-71	-87	103	**181**	117	**61**	**-1**
StL	75	79	1	.487	18	38	38	675	682	6086	**1589**	**238**	96	32	373	484	26	192	**.289**	**.337**	**.385**	**722**	**117**	**84**	**112**	96	126	114	53	-12
Chi	75	79	0	.487	18	43	34	619	635	5811	1350	223	67	34	428	421	46	**220**	.264	.326	.354	680	98	11	-1	102	115	129	47	-20
Bos	62	90	1	.408	30	36	37	523	670	5802	1358	168	86	23	385	488	33	166	.260	.315	.339	654	97	-47	-22	96	88	98	47	-15
Phi	62	91	0	.405	30.5	32	45	565	714	5742	1385	229	54	**64**	283	531	36	159	.263	.305	.364	669	93	-28	-54	105	100	83	55	-7
Total	617	—	—	—	—	327	287	4893	—	46893	11376	1604	644	261	3016	3632	262	1418	.270	.322	.357	679	—	—	—	—	969	862	53	-89

TEAM	CG	SHO	GR	SV	IP	H	HR	BB	SO	BR/9	ERA	AERA	OAV	OOB	PR	APR	PF	OSB	OCS	FA	E	WPB	DP	FW	PW	BW	BSW	DIF
Bro	89	17	93	10	1427.1	1381	**25**	327	**553**	10.9	**2.62**	**122**	.259	.304	**81**	**89**	102	132	99	.966	226	47	118	-.2	**9.5**	-.3	-.2	7.2
NY	86	**18**	103	9	1408.2	1379	44	297	380	**10.8**	2.80	107	.261	.303	51	32	96	**95**	89	.969	210	37	**137**	.8	3.4	3.4	.0	1.4
Cin	90	12	82	9	1391.2	**1327**	26	393	435	11.3	2.90	105	**.256**	.313	36	23	97	108	111	.968	200	32	125	1.3	2.5	2.0	.1	-.4
Pit	92	17	85	10	1415.1	1389	**25**	**280**	444	**10.8**	2.89	111	.261	**.301**	39	49	103	120	99	**.971**	**186**	37	119	**2.2**	5.2	-9.3	**1.1**	2.8
StL	72	9	**135**	**12**	1426.2	1488	30	479	529	12.8	3.43	87	.277	.343	-47	-75	95	141	97	.961	256	39	136	-2.0	-8.0	**12.0**	-.1	-3.9
Chi	**95**	13	93	9	1388.2	1459	37	382	508	12.1	3.27	98	.276	.328	-21	-10	102	115	117	.965	225	**31**	112	-.2	-1.1	-.1	-1.0	.3
Bos	93	14	73	6	1386.1	1464	39	415	368	12.4	3.54	86	.280	.337	-62	-77	97	111	**143**	.964	239	32	125	-1.1	-8.2	-2.4	-.4	-1.9
Phi	77	8	102	11	1380.2	1480	35	444	419	12.8	3.63	94	.284	.345	-76	-32	109	147	107	.964	232	47	135	-.7	-3.4	-5.8	.4	-5.0
Total	694	108	766	76	11225.1	—	—	—	—	11.7	3.13	—	.270	.322	—	—	—	—	—	.966	1774	302	1007	—	—	—	—	—

BATTER-FIELDER WINS	BATTING AVERAGE	ON-BASE PERCENTAGE	SLUGGING AVERAGE	ON-BASE PLUS SLUGGING	ADJUSTED OPS	ADJUSTED BATTER RUNS
Hornsby-StL....... 7.9	Hornsby-StL..........370	Hornsby-StL..........431	Hornsby-StL..........559	Hornsby-StL..........990	Hornsby-StL..........190	Hornsby-StL.........69.0
Bancroft-Phi-NY 5.6	Nicholson-Pit 360	Youngs-NY...........427	Nicholson-Pit 530	Youngs-NY............904	Youngs-NY............161	Youngs-NY...........49.2
Youngs-NY.......... 4.1	Youngs-NY...........351	Roush-Cin............386	Williams-Phi..........497	Williams-Phi..........861	Roush-Cin.............142	Roush-Cin............30.7
Roush-Cin........... 3.1	Roush-Cin............339	Wheat-Bro 385	Youngs-NY............477	Wheat-Bro 848	Williams-Phi..........139	Wheat-Bro 29.1
Williams-Phi....... 3.0	Wheat-Bro 328	Groh-Cin..............375	Meusel-Phi............473	Roush-Cin.............839	Wheat-Bro 138	Williams-Phi.........28.4
RUNS	**HITS**	**DOUBLES**	**TRIPLES**	**HOME RUNS**	**TOTAL BASES**	**RUNS BATTED IN**
Burns-NY.............115	Hornsby-StL..........218	Hornsby-StL............44	Myers-Bro 22	Williams-Phi............15	Hornsby-StL..........329	Kelly-NY..................94
Bancroft-Phi-NY....102	Youngs-NY...........204	Bancroft-Phi-NY......36	Hornsby-StL............20	Meusel-Phi..............14	Williams-Phi..........293	Hornsby-StL............94
Daubert-Cin............97	Stock-StL 204	Williams-Phi............36	Roush-Cin...............16	Kelly-NY..................11	Youngs-NY...........277	Roush-Cin...............90
Hornsby-StL............96	Roush-Cin.............196	Myers-Bro...............36	Maranville-Bos........15	Robertson-Chi 10	Wheat-Bro 270	Duncan-Cin.............83
Youngs-NY.............92	Williams-Phi.........192	Burns-NY................35	Bigbee-Pit...............15	McHenry-StL 10	Myers-Bro 269	Myers-Bro 80
BASES ON BALLS	**STOLEN BASES**	**BASE STEALING RUNS**	**FIELDING RUNS-INFIELD**	**FIELDING RUNS-OUTFIELD**	**OUTFIELD ASSISTS**	**CATCHER CS PCT.**
Burns-NY................76	Carey-Pit.................52	Carey-Pit.................7.9	Bancroft-Phi-NY...36.8	Neale-Cin.............12.0	Youngs-NY..............26	Snyder-NY 50.5
Youngs-NY..............75	Roush-Cin...............36	Frisch-NY...............3.6	Terry-Chi..............17.4	Burns-NY.............10.9	Heathcote-StL.........26	O'Farrell-Chi 50.0
Paskert-Chi.............64	Frisch-NY................34	Neale-Cin...............2.2	Maranville-Bos.....15.3	Roush-Cin............10.2	Powell-Bos..............25	Smith-NY 45.7
Hornsby-StL............60	Bigbee-Pit...............31	Bigbee-Pit..............1.6	Fletcher-NY-Phi ...14.4	Williams-Phi.........10.2	Paskert-Chi.............23	Schmidt-Pit 45.7
Groh-Cin 60	Neale-Cin................29	Gowdy-Bos 1.0	Deal-Chi..............11.1	Heathcote-StL........9.8	Williams-Phi............22	Clemons-StL.........40.4
WINS	**WINNING PCT.**	**WINS ABOVE TEAM**	**GAMES STARTED**	**COMPLETE GAMES**	**FEWEST HITS/GAME**	**FEWEST BB/GAME**
Alexander-Chi.........27	Grimes-Bro 676	Alexander-Chi........8.3	Alexander-Chi.........40	Alexander-Chi.........33	Luque-Cin............7.28	Adams-Pit...............62
Cooper-Pit 24	Alexander-Chi.......659	Cooper-Pit 5.1	Vaughn-Chi.............38	Cooper-Pit 28	Ruether-Cin 7.96	Cooper-Pit 1.43
Grimes-Bro 23	Toney-NY.............656	Doak-StL................5.1		Rixey-Phi 25	Grimes-Bro 8.03	Nehf-NY...............1.44
Toney-NY................21	Pfeffer-Bro 640	Toney-NY...............4.2		Grimes-Bro 25	Mamaux-Bro 8.12	Benton-NY 1.44
Nehf-NY..................21	Nehf-NY...............636	Meadows-Phi.........3.8		Vaughn-Chi.............24	Adams-Pit............8.21	Marquard-Bro 1.66
STRIKEOUTS	**STRIKEOUTS/GAME**	**GAMES**	**SAVES**	**BASE RUNNERS/9**	**ADJUSTED RELIEF RUNS**	**RELIEF RANKING**
Alexander-Chi.......173	Mamaux-Bro........4.77	Haines-StL.............47	Sherdel-StL...............6	Adams-Pit............8.86		
Vaughn-Chi...........131	Alexander-Chi......4.29	Douglas-NY 46	McQuillan-Bos 5	Alexander-Chi....10.03		
Grimes-Bro 131	Schupp-StL..........4.27	Alexander-Chi.........46	Alexander-Chi...........5	Luque-Cin..........10.05		
Haines-StL............120	Marquard-Bro 4.22	Scott-Bos................44	Hubbell-NY-Phi 4	J.Barnes-NY 10.12		
Schupp-StL...........119	Sherdel-StL..........3.92	Cooper-Pit 44	Mamaux-Bro.............4	Grimes-Bro 10.14		
INNINGS PITCHED	**OPPONENTS' AVG.**	**OPPONENTS' OBP**	**EARNED RUN AVERAGE**	**ADJUSTED ERA**	**ADJUSTED STARTER RUNS**	**PITCHER WINS**
Alexander-Chi....363.1	Luque-Cin.............225	Adams-Pit.............259	Alexander-Chi......1.91	Alexander-Chi.......168	Alexander-Chi......51.6	**Alexander-Chi.... 6.9**
Cooper-Pit 327.0	Grimes-Bro 238	Grimes-Bro 282	Adams-Pit...........2.16	Adams-Pit.............149	Grimes-Bro 30.1	**Grimes-Bro......... 4.9**
Grimes-Bro 303.2	Adams-Pit.............244	Alexander-Chi.......285	Grimes-Bro 2.22	Grimes-Bro 144	Adams-Pit............27.6	**Smith-Bro 3.2**
Haines-StL.........301.2	Ponder-Pit.............246	Luque-Cin.............286	Cooper-Pit 2.39	Cooper-Pit 134	Cooper-Pit 26.1	**Cooper-Pit.......... 3.0**
Vaughn-Chi........301.0	Ruether-Cin 247	Ponder-Pit.............286	Ruether-Cin 2.47	Vaughn-Chi...........126	Ruether-Cin 19.5	**Vaughn-Chi......... 2.6**

Runs, Hits, and Robins

Runs per game rose 8 percent in 1920, but home runs were not the culprit; the league leader, Cy Williams, hit just 15, and he played in Philadelphia, the league's one home run haven. Stolen bases, meanwhile, dropped to their lowest level yet. The decision by the rules committee to disallow scuffed baseballs was the biggest contributor to increased scoring.

On July 1 the Cardinals moved into Sportsman's Park, owned by the AL Browns. Sportsman's was smaller than Robison Field, a change that helped second sacker Rogers Hornsby compile huge numbers in the coming years. On September 15 third baseman Pie Traynor played the first of his 1,941 major league games—all in Pittsburgh flannels.

The post-war attendance boom continued as league attendance leapt 40 percent. The biggest off-field news of the year, the Black Sox scandal, broke in September after rumors had circulated for a year. While the probe focused on the AL, the Senior Circuit was hit as well. Before the 1921 season started, NL veterans Claude Hendrix, Buck Herzog, and Benny Kauff were banned from baseball due to gambling or racketeering. The scandal also tainted the Reds' 1919 world championship victory.

The lowly Brooklyn Robins—who had managed only three first-division finishes since 1903—found themselves in a surprising September tangle with the mighty Giants and Reds. As the other two clubs treaded water, Brooklyn won 16 of 18 to clinch the pennant. Outfielders Hy Myers (22 triples) and Zack Wheat were the chief offensive weapons, as spitballing Burleigh Grimes paced the league in ERA. The Robins led the NL in ERA though the staff was a patchwork job—manager Wilbert Robinson used six starting pitchers. The 1920 campaign was only temporary balm for Brooklyn fans; the club immediately returned to the NL's nether regions and would not win again until 1941.

1920 AMERICAN LEAGUE

TEAM	W	L	T	PCT	GB	HW	HL	R	OR	PA	H	2B	3B	HR	BB	SO	HB	SH	AVG	OBP	SLG	OPS	AOPS	BR	ABR	PF	SB	CS	BSA	BSR
Cle	98	56	0	.636	—	51	27	**857**	642	6064	1574	**300**	95	35	**576**	379	36	**256**	.303	**.376**	.417	**793**	**113**	**130**	**104**	103	73	93	44	-16
Chi	96	58	0	.623	2	**52**	25	794	665	6032	1574	263	**98**	37	471	355	38	195	.295	.357	.402	759	107	49	49	100	109	96	53	-10
NY	95	59	0	.617	3	49	28	838	**629**	5911	1448	268	71	**115**	539	626	22	174	.280	.350	**.426**	776	107	74	47	104	64	82	44	-15
StL	76	77	1	.497	21.5	40	38	797	766	6032	**1651**	279	83	50	427	**339**	39	208	**.308**	.363	.419	782	110	94	70	103	121	79	**61**	**-1**
Bos	72	81	1	.471	25.5	41	35	650	698	5997	1397	216	71	22	533	429	46	219	.269	.342	.350	692	93	-71	-41	96	98	111	47	-17
Was	68	84	1	.447	29	37	38	723	802	5936	1526	233	81	36	433	543	**53**	199	.291	.351	.386	737	104	5	25	97	**160**	114	58	-5
Det	61	93	1	.396	37	32	46	652	833	5932	1408	228	72	30	479	391	19	219	.270	.334	.359	693	91	-82	-65	98	76	68	53	-7
Phi	48	106	2	.312	50	25	50	558	834	5823	1324	220	49	44	353	593	45	169	.252	.305	.338	643	74	-192	-197	101	50	67	43	-12
Total	617	——		—	—	327	287	5869	—	47727	11902	2007	620	369	3811	3655	298	1639	.284	.347	.387	735	—	—	—	—	751	710	51	-83

TEAM	CG	SHO	GR	SV	IP	H	HR	BB	SO	BR/9	ERA	AERA	OAV	OOB	PR	APR	PF	OSB	OCS	FA	E	WPB	DP	FW	PW	BW	BSW	DIF
Cle	94	11	100	7	1377.0	1448	**31**	**401**	466	**12.3**	3.41	111	.276	.331	57	58	100	84	70	.971	184	31	124	2.1	5.6	**10.1**	-.5	3.7
Chi	**109**	9	66	10	1386.2	1467	45	405	438	**12.3**	3.59	105	.280	.335	31	24	99	**61**	82	.968	198	27	**142**	1.2	2.3	4.8	.0	10.7
NY	88	**15**	93	11	1368.0	**1414**	48	420	480	**12.3**	**3.32**	**115**	**.270**	**.328**	**72**	**75**	101	87	58	.969	194	31	129	1.4	**7.3**	4.6	-.4	5.2
StL	84	9	102	**14**	1378.2	1481	53	578	444	13.7	4.03	97	.283	.359	-38	-22	103	95	89	.963	233	**23**	119	-1.2	-2.1	6.8	**.9**	-4.8
Bos	92	11	76	6	1395.1	1481	39	461	481	12.7	3.82	95	.279	.339	-5	-31	96	123	83	**.972**	**183**	45	131	**2.2**	-3.0	-4.0	-.6	.9
Was	81	10	102	10	1367.0	1521	51	520	418	13.7	4.17	89	.288	.357	-58	-71	98	91	99	.963	232	63	95	-1.3	-6.9	2.4	.5	-2.8
Det	74	9	**122**	7	1385.0	1487	46	561	**483**	13.7	4.04	92	.284	.359	-38	-52	98	107	96	.964	230	41	95	-.9	-5.0	-6.3	.3	-4.0
Phi	79	6	104	2	1380.1	1612	56	461	423	13.8	3.93	102	.302	.362	-21	11	106	103	**133**	.959	266	40	125	-3.3	1.1	-19.1	-.2	-7.5
Total	701	80	765	67	11038.0	—	—	—	—	13.1	3.79	—	.284	.347	—	—	—	—	—	.966	1720	301	960	—	—	—	—	—

BATTER-FIELDER WINS	BATTING AVERAGE	ON-BASE PERCENTAGE	SLUGGING AVERAGE	ON-BASE PLUS SLUGGING	ADJUSTED OPS	ADJUSTED BATTER RUNS
Ruth-NY 9.3	Sisler-StL .407	Ruth-NY .532	Ruth-NY .847	Ruth-NY 1379	Ruth-NY 252	Ruth-NY 110.5
Sisler-StL 7.9	Speaker-Cle .388	Speaker-Cle .483	Sisler-StL .632	Sisler-StL 1082	Sisler-StL 179	Sisler-StL 69.4
Speaker-Cle 5.4	Jackson-Chi .382	Sisler-StL .449	Jackson-Chi .589	Speaker-Cle 1045	Jackson-Chi 172	Speaker-Cle 63.9
E.Collins-Chi 5.4	Ruth-NY .376	Jackson-Chi .444	Speaker-Cle .562	Jackson-Chi 1033	Speaker-Cle 171	Jackson-Chi 59.0
Jackson-Chi 4.5	E.Collins-Chi .372	E.Collins-Chi .438	Felsch-Chi .540	E.Collins-Chi 932	E.Collins-Chi 146	E.Collins-Chi 43.1
RUNS	**HITS**	**DOUBLES**	**TRIPLES**	**HOME RUNS**	**TOTAL BASES**	**RUNS BATTED IN**
Ruth-NY 158	Sisler-StL 257	Speaker-Cle 50	Jackson-Chi 20	Ruth-NY 54	Sisler-StL 399	Ruth-NY 137
Speaker-Cle 137	E.Collins-Chi 224	Sisler-StL 49	Sisler-StL 18	Sisler-StL 19	Ruth-NY 388	Sisler-StL 122
Sisler-StL 137	Jackson-Chi 218	Jackson-Chi 42	Hooper-Bos 17	T.Walker-Phi 17	Jackson-Chi 336	Jacobson-StL 122
E.Collins-Chi 117	Jacobson-StL 216			Felsch-Chi 14	Speaker-Cle 310	Jackson-Chi 121
	Speaker-Cle 214				Jacobson-StL 305	Gardner-Cle 118
BASES ON BALLS	**STOLEN BASES**	**BASE STEALING RUNS**	**FIELDING RUNS-INFIELD**	**FIELDING RUNS-OUTFIELD**	**OUTFIELD ASSISTS**	**CATCHER CS PCT.**
Ruth-NY 150	Rice-Was 63	Rice-Was 3.4	Ward-NY 16.5	Rice-Was 17.0	T.Walker-Phi 26	Schalk-Chi 57.4
Speaker-Cle 97	Sisler-StL 42	Sisler-StL 3.3	Dykes-Phi 15.4	Veach-Det 13.6	Veach-Det 26	Severeid-StL 48.5
Hooper-Bos 88	Roth-Was 24	E.Collins-Chi 1.6	Sisler-StL 15.1	Felsch-Chi 12.4	Felsch-Chi 25	Stanage-Det 46.6
Young-Det 85	Menosky-Bos 23	Williams-StL 1.2	Scott-Bos 14.1	Jacobson-StL 9.6	Speaker-Cle 24	O'Neill-Cle 45.1
Roth-Was 75	Tobin-StL 21	Burns-Phi-Cle 1.1	Chapman-Cle 13.9	Speaker-Cle 6.0	Rice-Was 24	Hannah-NY 40.8
WINS	**WINNING PCT.**	**WINS ABOVE TEAM**	**GAMES STARTED**	**COMPLETE GAMES**	**FEWEST HITS/GAME**	**FEWEST BB/GAME**
Bagby-Cle 31	Bagby-Cle .721	Bagby-Cle 6.4	Faber-Chi 39	Bagby-Cle 30	Coveleski-Cle 8.11	Quinn-NY 1.71
Mays-NY 26	Mays-NY .703	Shocker-StL 5.8	Williams-Chi 38	Faber-Chi 28	Shocker-StL 8.21	Coveleski-Cle 1.86
Coveleski-Cle 24	Kerr-Chi .700	Mays-NY 5.1	Coveleski-Cle 38	Cicotte-Chi 28	Collins-NY 8.22	Bagby-Cle 2.09
Faber-Chi 23	Cicotte-Chi .677	Davis-StL 3.6	Bagby-Cle 38	Mays-NY 26	Shawkey-NY 8.27	Cicotte-Chi 2.20
Williams-Chi 22		Kerr-Chi 3.6	Mays-NY 37	Coveleski-Cle 26	Davis-StL 8.35	Perry-Phi 2.22
STRIKEOUTS	**STRIKEOUTS/GAME**	**GAMES**	**SAVES**	**BASE RUNNERS/9**	**ADJUSTED RELIEF RUNS**	**RELIEF RANKING**
Coveleski-Cle 133	Ayers-Det 4.44	Bagby-Cle 48	Shocker-StL 5	Coveleski-Cle 10.09		
Williams-Chi 128	Shawkey-NY 4.24	Ayers-Det 46	Kerr-Chi 5	Mails-Cle 10.23		
Shawkey-NY 126	Harper-Bos 3.93	Mays-NY 45	Burwell-StL 4	W.Johnson-Was 10.46		
Faber-Chi 108	Shocker-StL 3.92	Kerr-Chi 45		Shocker-StL 10.92		
Shocker-StL 107	Williams-Chi 3.85	Zachary-Was 44		Rommel-Phi 10.99		
INNINGS PITCHED	**OPPONENTS' AVG.**	**OPPONENTS' OBP**	**EARNED RUN AVERAGE**	**ADJUSTED ERA**	**ADJUSTED STARTER RUNS**	**PITCHER WINS**
Bagby-Cle 339.2	Coveleski-Cle .243	Coveleski-Cle .285	Shawkey-NY 2.45	Shawkey-NY 155	Coveleski-Cle 44.4	**Coveleski-Cle 5.5**
Faber-Chi 319.0	Collins-NY .247	Shocker-StL .305	Coveleski-Cle 2.49	Coveleski-Cle 153	Shawkey-NY 41.3	**Bagby-Cle 4.7**
Coveleski-Cle 315.0	Shawkey-NY .248	Shawkey-NY .308	Shocker-StL 2.71	Shocker-StL 144	Bagby-Cle 38.9	**Shawkey-NY 4.6**
Mays-NY 312.0	Shocker-StL .248	Quinn-NY .308	Rommel-Phi 2.85	Rommel-Phi 141	Shocker-StL 29.6	**Shocker-StL 3.7**
Cicotte-Chi 303.1	Ehmke-Det .253	Rommel-Phi .309	Bagby-Cle 2.89	Bagby-Cle 131	Mays-NY 28.0	**Mays-NY 3.5**

Scandal, Homers, and Clean Balls

Prior to the season, the major leagues decided that using discolored, lumpy baseballs could be dangerous for the players, offense, and attendance. The previous year's gains in runs per team per game continued, and the 1920 figure of 4.76 was the highest in eighteen years. The AL became the first league to draw five million fans, with the Yankees the first team to crack the million mark.

New rules preventing pitchers from defacing balls only increased the offense and excitement levels at the suddenly fuller parks. (Established spitball pitchers could continue their practice if they registered with the leagues.) St. Louis' George Sisler set an all-time record with 257 hits, and the 54 homers by new Yankee Babe Ruth made him a national hero.

The Indians, White Sox, and Yankees converged in June. Indians shortstop Ray Chapman was killed by an errant pitch thrown by Yankee Carl Mays on August 16, and for a time the Indians slumped. Cleveland, however, pulled shortstop Joe Sewell from the minors, and the Tribe regained its fire, winning seven straight while Chicago kayoed New York. The public outcry following Chapman's death forced umpires to keep clean baseballs in play at all times, which further increased scoring.

On September 27, with Chicago a half-game back, eight White Sox players were indicted for fixing 1919's World Series. Owner Charles Comiskey, who had conspired to squelch the investigation, was forced to suspend the players. The decimated White Sox crumbled while Cleveland clinched. To restore public confidence in baseball, the newly appointed Commissioner Kenesaw Mountain Landis barred the eight Sox, and several other miscreants.

After falling behind two games to one in the best-of-nine World Series, the Indians won four straight from Brooklyn to clinch the title. In those four wins, Brooklyn scored just twice. In Game 5, Cleveland's Elmer Smith hit the first Series grand slam. Four innings later, a line drive at Indians second baseman Bill Wambsganss turned into the second unassisted triple play of the century.

1919 NATIONAL LEAGUE

TEAM	W	L	T	PCT	GB	HW	HL	R	OR	PA	H	2B	3B	HR	BB	SO	HB	SH	AVG	OBP	SLG	OPS	AOPS	BR	ABR	PF	SB	CS	BSA	BSR
Cin	96	44	0	.686	—	**52**	19	577	**401**	5214	1204	135	**83**	20	**405**	368	33	**199**	.263	**.327**	.342	669	110	42	57	97	143			
NY	87	53	0	.621	9	46	23	**605**	470	5157	1254	204	64	40	328	407	37	128	**.269**	.322	**.366**	**688**	**113**	**67**	**73**	99	157			
Chi	75	65	0	.536	21	40	31	454	407	5088	1174	166	58	21	298	**359**	**42**	167	.256	.308	.332	640	97	-14	-17	101	150			
Pit	71	68	0	.511	24.5	40	30	472	466	5050	1132	130	82	17	344	381	24	144	.249	.306	.325	631	92	-28	-45	104	**196**			
Bro	69	71	1	.493	27	36	33	525	513	5283	**1272**	167	66	25	258	405	28	153	.263	.304	.340	644	97	-15	-25	102	112			
Bos	57	82	1	.410	38.5	29	38	465	563	5299	1201	142	62	24	355	481	**42**	156	.253	.311	.324	635	100	-18	4	96	145			
StL	54	83	1	.394	40.5	34	35	463	552	5053	1175	163	52	18	304	418	18	143	.256	.305	.326	631	101	-28	2	94	148			
Phi	47	90	1	.343	47.5	26	44	510	699	5220	1191	**208**	50	**42**	323	469	28	123	.251	.303	.342	645	92	-5	-39	107	114			
Total	558	—	—	—	—	303	253	4071	—	41364	9603	1315	517	207	2615	3288	252	1213	.258	.311	.337	648	—	—	—	—	1165	—	—	—

TEAM	CG	SHO	GR	SV	IP	H	HR	BB	SO	BR/9	ERA	AERA	OAV	OOB	PR	APR	PF	OSB	OCS	FA	E	WPB	DP	FW	PW	BW	BSW	DIF
Cin	89	**23**	74	9	1274.0	**1104**	21	298	407	**10.0**	2.23	124	**.239**	**.288**	96	79	95	133	*114*	**.974**	**151**	28	98	**2.7**	8.8	6.3	—	8.2
NY	72	11	96	**13**	1256.0	1153	34	305	340	10.6	2.70	104	.247	.296	29	14	96	147	*90*	.964	216	27	96	-1.0	1.6	**8.1**	—	8.4
Chi	80	21	79	5	1265.0	1127	**14**	294	**495**	10.3	**2.21**	**130**	.242	.291	**98**	**94**	99	140	*111*	.969	185	26	87	.7	**10.5**	-1.9	—	-4.3
Pit	91	17	54	4	1249.0	1113	23	**263**	391	10.2	2.88	104	.244	.290	4	17	104	**108**	*99*	.970	165	**24**	89	1.8	1.9	-5.0	—	2.8
Bro	**98**	12	50	1	1281.0	1256	21	292	476	11.1	2.73	109	.262	.309	25	32	102	172	*121*	.963	219	39	84	-1.1	3.6	-2.8	—	-.6
Bos	79	5	74	9	1270.1	1313	29	337	374	11.8	3.17	90	.276	.327	-36	-46	98	147	*133*	.966	204	41	111	-.4	-5.1	.4	—	-7.5
StL	55	6	**137**	8	1217.1	1146	25	415	414	11.9	3.23	86	.256	.326	-44	-63	96	137	*122*	.963	214	50	**112**	-1.1	-7.0	.2	—	-6.6
Phi	93	6	57	2	1252.0	1391	40	408	397	13.3	4.14	78	.294	.356	-171	-116	111	181	***135***	.963	218	53	**112**	-1.3	-12.9	-4.3	—	-2.9
Total	657	101	621	51	10064.2	—	—	—	—	11.2	2.91	—	.258	.311	—	—	—	—	—	.967	1572	288	789	—	—	—	—	—

BATTER-FIELDER WINS	BATTING AVERAGE	ON-BASE PERCENTAGE	SLUGGING AVERAGE	ON-BASE PLUS SLUGGING	ADJUSTED OPS	ADJUSTED BATTER RUNS
Hornsby-StL 5.1	Roush-Cin .321	Burns-NY .396	Myers-Bro .436	Groh-Cin .823	Hornsby-StL 154	Hornsby-StL 34.1
Maranville-Bos 4.6	Hornsby-StL .318	Groh-Cin .392	Doyle-NY .433	Hornsby-StL .814	Groh-Cin 151	Burns-NY 32.6
Stock-StL 4.4	Youngs-NY .311	Hornsby-StL .384	Groh-Cin .431	Roush-Cin .811	Roush-Cin 147	Groh-Cin 29.8
Fletcher-NY 3.4	Groh-Cin .310	Youngs-NY .384	Roush-Cin .431	Burns-NY .801	Burns-NY 142	Cravath-Phi 29.4
Groh-Cin 3.4	Stock-StL .307	Roush-Cin .380	Hornsby-StL .430	Youngs-NY .799	Youngs-NY 142	Roush-Cin 29.2

RUNS	HITS	DOUBLES	TRIPLES	HOME RUNS	TOTAL BASES	RUNS BATTED IN
Burns-NY 86	Olson-Bro 164	Youngs-NY 31	Southworth-Pit 14	Cravath-Phi 12	Myers-Bro 223	Myers-Bro 73
Groh-Cin 79	Hornsby-StL 163	Luderus-Phi 30	Myers-Bro 14	Kauff-NY 10	Hornsby-StL 220	Roush-Cin 71
Daubert-Cin 79	Roush-Cin 162	Burns-NY 30		Williams-Phi 9	Z.Wheat-Bro 219	Hornsby-StL 71
Rath-Cin 77	Burns-NY 162	Kauff-NY 27		Hornsby-StL 8	Roush-Cin 217	Kauff-NY 67
		Meusel-Phi 26		Doyle-NY 7	Burns-NY 216	Groh-Cin 63

BASES ON BALLS	STOLEN BASES	BASE STEALING RUNS	FIELDING RUNS-INFIELD	FIELDING RUNS-OUTFIELD	OUTFIELD ASSISTS	CATCHER CS PCT.
Burns-NY 82	Burns-NY 40		Maranville-Bos 26.3	Bigbee-Pit 14.5	Youngs-NY 23	Schmidt-Pit 51.1
Rath-Cin 64	Cutshaw-Pit 36		Fletcher-NY 25.3	Southworth-Pit 5.8	Roush-Cin 22	Wingo-Cin 49.6
Groh-Cin 66	Bigbee-Pit 31		Stock-StL 19.4	Roush-Cin 5.3	Powell-Bos 21	Snyder-StL-NY 49.3
Luderus-Phi 54	Smith-StL 30		Rath-Cin 12.9	McHenry-StL 4.4	Bigbee-Pit 21	Killefer-Chi 44.7
Boeckel-Pit-Bos 53			Luderus-Phi 9.3	Myers-Bro 3.7		Clemons-StL 44.5

WINS	WINNING PCT.	WINS ABOVE TEAM	GAMES STARTED	COMPLETE GAMES	FEWEST HITS/GAME	FEWEST BB/GAME
J.Barnes-NY 25	Ruether-Cin .760	J.Barnes-NY 6.2	Vaughn-Chi 37	Cooper-Pit 27	Alexander-Chi 6.89	Adams-Pit .79
Vaughn-Chi 21	Sallee-Cin .750	Nehf-Bos-NY 4.0	J.Barnes-NY 34	Pfeffer-Bro 26	Cooper-Pit 7.19	Sallee-Cin .79
Sallee-Cin 21	J.Barnes-NY .735	Adams-Pit 3.8	Rudolph-Bos 32	Vaughn-Chi 25	Ruether-Cin 7.23	J.Barnes-NY 1.07
	Eller-Cin .679	Ruether-Cin 3.4	Cooper-Pit 32	Rudolph-Bos 24	Carlson-Pit 7.28	Cadore-Bro 1.40
	Adams-Pit .630	Sallee-Cin 3.4	Nehf-Bos-NY 31		Fisher-Cin 7.28	Alexander-Chi 1.46

STRIKEOUTS	STRIKEOUTS/GAME	GAMES	SAVES	BASE RUNNERS/9	ADJUSTED RELIEF RUNS	RELIEF RANKING
Vaughn-Chi 141	Eller-Cin 4.97	Tuero-StL 45	Tuero-StL 4	Adams-Pit 8.17		
Eller-Cin 137	Alexander-Chi 4.63	Meadows-StL-Phi 40		Alexander-Chi 8.35		
Alexander-Chi 121	Meadows-StL-Phi 4.17	Vaughn-Chi 38		J.Barnes-NY 9.13		
Meadows-StL-Phi 116	Vaughn-Chi 4.14	Eller-Cin 38		Fisher-Cin 9.29		
Cooper-Pit 106	Grimes-Bro 4.07	J.Barnes-NY 38		Miller-Pit 9.33		

INNINGS PITCHED	OPPONENTS' AVG.	OPPONENTS' OBP	EARNED RUN AVERAGE	ADJUSTED ERA	ADJUSTED STARTER RUNS	PITCHER WINS
Vaughn-Chi 306.2	Alexander-Chi .211	Adams-Pit .241	Alexander-Chi 1.72	Alexander-Chi 167	Vaughn-Chi 36.3	**Alexander-Chi 4.6**
J.Barnes-NY 295.2	Adams-Pit .220	Alexander-Chi .245	Vaughn-Chi 1.79	Vaughn-Chi 161	Alexander-Chi 33.5	**Vaughn-Chi 4.3**
Cooper-Pit 286.2	Ruether-Cin .223	J.Barnes-NY .260	Ruether-Cin 1.82	Ruether-Cin 152	Adams-Pit 29.7	**Ruether-Cin 3.1**
Rudolph-Bos 273.2	Cooper-Pit .225	Fisher-Cin .271	Toney-NY 1.84	Toney-NY 152	Ruether-Cin 24.1	**Adams-Pit 3.0**
Nehf-Bos-NY 270.2	Nehf-Bos-NY .225	Miller-Pit .272	Adams-Pit 1.98	Adams-Pit 152	Sallee-Cin 20.2	**Sallee-Cin 2.5**

The Reds Were Cheated, Too

With the war's end, attendance shot up 109 percent across the league, rising more than 90 percent in five cities. However, the NL continued to lag behind the AL in attendance, as it had throughout the decade. On the field, teams stole more than one base per game for the last time in NL history. The home run age would soon render the old rules obsolete.

With former Philadelphia skipper Pat Moran at the helm, the Cincinnati Reds used deep pitching and a speed-and-contact offense to coast to the NL flag, leaving John McGraw's Giants behind in August. Classic Dead Ball Era players like Edd Roush, Heinie Groh, and Morrie Rath fueled the attack, while former slugger Sherry Magee ended his career on the Cincinnati bench.

Second-place New York brought up another quality rookie, infielder Frankie Frisch, who soon became a star. McGraw's intellect was certainly in question when he decided to employ veteran game-fixer Hal Chase as his regular first baseman. Not only did the 36-year-old Chase provide below-average offense, he also used his influence to help fix games. For this, he was finally bounced from baseball after the season.

The Phillies, contenders two years before, tumbled into the basement after a series of ill-advised trades. Once a proud franchise, they would be laughingstocks for most of the next four decades.

Oddly enough, the two times in the decade that everyone felt the AL was a World Series cinch, the NL club pulled off an upset. This time, the Reds—who, few people seem to recall, actually had eight more regular-season wins than the White Sox—beat Chicago in eight games in the best-of-nine format. Unfortunately for the Reds, several White Sox weren't playing on the level, so their first world championship would be forever tainted despite their best efforts.

1919 AMERICAN LEAGUE

TEAM	W	L	T	PCT	GB	HW	HL	R	OR	PA	H	2B	3B	HR	BB	SO	HB	SH	AVG	OBP	SLG	OPS	AOPS	BR	ABR	PF	SB	CS	BSA	BSR
Chi	88	52	0	.629	—	**48**	22	**667**	534	5359	**1343**	218	70	25	427	**358**	34	**223**	**.287**	.351	.380	731	111	71	68	100	**150**			
Cle	84	55	0	.604	3.5	44	25	636	537	5322	1268	**254**	72	24	**498**	367	38	221	.278	**.354**	**.381**	**735**	107	**83**	45	106	117			
NY	80	59	2	.576	7.5	46	25	578	**506**	5358	1275	193	49	**45**	386	479	32	165	.267	.326	.356	682	96	-21	-25	101	101			
Det	80	60	0	.571	8	46	24	618	578	5328	1319	222	**84**	23	429	427	25	209	.283	.346	**.381**	727	**113**	61	**76**	98	121			
StL	67	72	1	.482	20.5	40	30	533	567	5299	1234	187	73	31	391	443	35	201	.264	.326	.355	681	95	-24	-37	103	74			
Bos	66	71	1	.482	20.5	35	30	564	552	5254	1188	181	49	33	471	411	**45**	190	.261	.336	.344	680	103	-9	25	94	108			
Was	56	84	2	.400	32	32	40	533	570	5381	1238	177	63	24	416	511	40	168	.260	.325	.339	664	93	-49	-44	99	142			
Phi	36	104	0	.257	52	21	49	457	742	5230	1156	175	71	35	349	565	30	121	.244	.300	.334	634	82	-113	-118	101	103			
Total	560	—	—	—	—	312	245	4586	—	42531	10021	1607	531	240	3367	3561	279	1498	.268	.333	.359	692	—	—	—	—	916	—	—	—

TEAM	CG	SHO	GR	SV	IP	H	HR	BB	SO	BR/9	ERA	AERA	OAV	OOB	PR	APR	PF	OSB	OCS	FA	E	WPB	DP	FW	PW	BW	BSW	DIF
Chi	88	14	73	3	1265.2	1245	24	**342**	468	11.5	3.04	105	.262	.315	26	19	99	92	*84*	.969	176	**15**	116	1.6	2.0	7.1	—	7.2
Cle	79	10	93	**10**	1245.0	1242	19	362	432	11.8	2.94	**114**	.264	.321	39	51	104	**81**	*75*	.965	201	22	102	-.0	5.3	4.7	—	4.5
NY	85	14	90	7	1287.0	**1143**	47	433	500	**11.3**	**2.82**	113	**.240**	**.309**	**58**	**54**	99	111	*88*	.968	193	32	108	.7	**5.7**	-2.6	—	6.8
Det	85	10	74	4	1256.0	1254	35	436	428	12.4	3.30	97	.266	.333	-11	-14	99	128	*76*	.964	205	35	81	-.2	-1.5	**8.0**	—	3.7
StL	78	14	95	4	1256.0	1255	35	421	415	12.3	3.13	106	.263	.328	13	23	103	121	*94*	.963	215	35	98	-.8	2.4	-3.9	—	-.2
Bos	**89**	**15**	66	8	1224.1	1251	**16**	421	381	12.5	3.31	91	.275	.341	-12	-44	94	111	*97*	**.975**	**140**	56	**118**	**3.8**	-4.6	2.6	—	-4.3
Was	68	13	**97**	**10**	1274.1	1237	20	451	**536**	12.2	3.01	106	.259	.328	30	28	99	120	*104*	.960	227	50	86	-1.4	2.9	-4.6	—	-10.9
Phi	72	1	89	3	1239.1	1371	44	503	417	13.8	4.26	80	.292	.364	-143	-111	106	144	***118***	.956	257	36	96	-3.5	-11.6	-12.4	—	-6.5
Total	644	91	677	49	10047.2	—	—	—	—	12.2	3.22	—	.268	.333	—	—	—	—	—	.965	1614	281	805	—	—	—	—	—

BATTER-FIELDER WINS	BATTING AVERAGE	ON-BASE PERCENTAGE	SLUGGING AVERAGE	ON-BASE PLUS SLUGGING	ADJUSTED OPS	ADJUSTED BATTER RUNS
Ruth-Bos............7.3	Cobb-Det.............384	Ruth-Bos..............456	Ruth-Bos..............657	Ruth-Bos............1114	Ruth-Bos..............224	Ruth-Bos.............76.3
Peckinpaugh-NY5.1	Veach-Det............355	Cobb-Det.............429	Sisler-StL.............530	Cobb-Det..............944	Cobb-Det.............168	Cobb-Det............44.7
Veach-Det..........4.5	Sisler-StL.............352	Jackson-Chi.........422	Veach-Det............519	Jackson-Chi.........928	Veach-Det............160	Jackson-Chi.........41.9
Sisler-StL...........4.4	Jackson-Chi.........351	Leibold-Chi..........404	Cobb-Det.............515	Sisler-StL.............921	Jackson-Chi.........159	Veach-Det...........40.9
Jackson-Chi.......3.3	Flagstead-Det.......331	E.Collins-Chi.........400	Jackson-Chi..........506	Veach-Det............916	Sisler-StL.............153	Sisler-StL............33.3

RUNS	HITS	DOUBLES	TRIPLES	HOME RUNS	TOTAL BASES	RUNS BATTED IN
Ruth-Bos..............103	Veach-Det............191	Veach-Det..............45	Veach-Det..............17	Ruth-Bos.................29	Ruth-Bos..............284	Ruth-Bos..............114
Sisler-StL...............96	Cobb-Det.............191	Speaker-Cle...........38	Sisler-StL...............15	T.Walker-Phi...........10	Veach-Det............279	Veach-Det............101
Cobb-Det................92	Jackson-Chi..........181	Cobb-Det...............36	Heilmann-Det.........15	Sisler-StL...............10	Sisler-StL.............271	Jackson-Chi...........96
Weaver-Chi............89	Sisler-StL.............180	O'Neill-Cle.............35	Jackson-Chi...........14	Baker-NY................10	Jackson-Chi..........261	Heilmann-Det..........93
Peckinpaugh-NY.....89	Rice-Was.............179		Cobb-Det...............13	Smith-Cle.................9		Lewis-NY................89

BASES ON BALLS	STOLEN BASES	BASE STEALING RUNS	FIELDING RUNS-INFIELD	FIELDING RUNS-OUTFIELD	OUTFIELD ASSISTS	CATCHER CS PCT.
Graney-Cle...........105	E.Collins-Chi...........33		Peckinpaugh-NY..25.5	Felsch-Chi...........17.4	Felsch-Chi.............32	O'Neill-Cle...........48.5
Ruth-Bos..............101	Sisler-StL...............28		Pratt-NY..............24.6	Speaker-Cle.........14.8	Leibold-Chi.............26	Schalk-Chi...........47.7
Judge-Was..............81	Cobb-Det................28		Vitt-Bos................17.9	Ruth-Bos.................9.3	Speaker-Cle...........25	Ruel-NY...............46.7
Hooper-Bos............79	Rice-Was................26		Sisler-StL............13.1	Veach-Det...............9.0	Hooper-Bos............19	Schang-Bos.........46.3
Bush-Det.................75			Wambsganss-Cle 11.1	Leibold-Chi.............7.7	Cobb-Det................19	Severeid-StL........39.7

WINS	WINNING PCT.	WINS ABOVE TEAM	GAMES STARTED	COMPLETE GAMES	FEWEST HITS/GAME	FEWEST BB/GAME
Cicotte-Chi..............29	Cicotte-Chi............806	Cicotte-Chi..............9.9	Williams-Chi............40	Cicotte-Chi..............30	Johnson-Was.......7.28	Cicotte-Chi...........1.44
Coveleski-Cle..........24	Dauss-Det.............700	Johnson-Was.........6.4	Shaw-Was..............37	Williams-Chi............27	Thormahlen-NY...7.39	Johnson-Was.......1.58
Williams-Chi............23	Williams-Chi..........676	Sothoron-StL.........5.3	Cicotte-Chi..............35	Johnson-Was..........27	Shawkey-NY........7.51	Bagby-Cle............1.64
Dauss-Det...............21	Pennock-Bos........667	Dauss-Det..............5.3	Coveleski-Cle..........34	Mays-Bos-NY.........26	Cicotte-Chi...........7.51	Williams-Chi.........1.76
	Coveleski-Cle........667	Pennock-Bos.........4.8		Coveleski-Cle..........24	Mays-Bos-NY......7.68	Coveleski-Cle.......1.89

STRIKEOUTS	STRIKEOUTS/GAME	GAMES	SAVES	BASE RUNNERS/9	ADJUSTED RELIEF RUNS	RELIEF RANKING
Johnson-Was........147	Erickson-Det-Was5.52	Shaw-Was..............45	Russell-NY-Bos.........5	Cicotte-Chi...........9.01	Phillips-Cle............1.1	Phillips-Cle................9
Shaw-Was............128	Russell-NY-Bos....4.80	Russell-NY-Bos.......44	Shawkey-NY.............5	Johnson-Was.......9.08		
Williams-Chi..........125	Johnson-Was.......4.56	Kinney-Phi..............43	Shaw-Was................5	Williams-Chi.......10.12		
Shawkey-NY.........122	Kinney-Phi...........4.31	Coveleski-Cle..........43	Coveleski-Cle............4	Hoyt-Bos............10.34		
Coveleski-Cle........118	Leonard-Det.........4.22			Thormahlen-NY.10.49		

INNINGS PITCHED	OPPONENTS' AVG.	OPPONENTS' OBP	EARNED RUN AVERAGE	ADJUSTED ERA	ADJUSTED STARTER RUNS	PITCHER WINS
Shaw-Was.........306.2	Johnson-Was........219	Johnson-Was........259	Johnson-Was.......1.49	Johnson-Was........215	Johnson-Was.......52.4	**Johnson-Was.....6.7**
Cicotte-Chi.........306.2	Cicotte-Chi............228	Cicotte-Chi...........261	Cicotte-Chi...........1.82	Cicotte-Chi............175	Cicotte-Chi..........47.2	**Cicotte-Chi.........5.5**
Williams-Chi.......297.0	Thormahlen-NY....228	Williams-Chi..........289	Weilman-StL........2.07	Weilman-StL.........160	Sothoron-StL.......26.7	**Coveleski-Cle.....3.9**
Johnson-Was.....290.1	Shawkey-NY.........231	Morton-Cle............293	Mays-Bos-NY......2.10	Sothoron-StL........151	Coveleski-Cle.......26.2	**Mays-Bos-NY.....3.1**
Coveleski-Cle.....286.0	Mays-Bos-NY.......233	Quinn-NY..............295	Sothoron-StL.......2.20	Mays-Bos-NY.......147	Mays-Bos-NY......25.5	**Sothoron-StL.....2.5**

EARTHQUAKE

With the war over, and the players back to their teams, baseball could resume as normal. Except nothing about 1919 was normal. First of all, the schedule was set at 140 games, with a nine-game World Series proposed to recoup lost gates. The extra games gave the gamblers infiltrating baseball more incentive to push their agenda, but nobody could see this at the time.

The season's biggest story was the way baseballs flew out of the parks. With Babe Ruth given a chance to play every day for Boston, the game changed entirely as he clouted an amazing 29 homers to set an all-time mark. Other players followed his example; four-baggers increased by 150 percent to 240, setting a new league record that would be broken each of the next three years.

This rise in long balls came with no appreciable rise in strikeouts, but stolen bases—the run-creating method of the scratch-out-a-run Dead Ball Era—fell to a new low. Old-school baseball men pointed out that Ruth's team finished $20\frac{1}{2}$ games out, but part of the reason was because one of the league's best left-handers no longer took his regular turn in the Red Sox rotation. Boston's team ERA increased by a full run; the league ERA was up by half a run.

The peacetime economy and the excitement over Ruth's exploits caused attendance to rise in every AL city, increasing the league's turnstile clicks by 114 percent. Chicago and Detroit saw attendance increases of over 200 percent. While the White Sox had good battles from the Indians and Tigers, Chicago had the most talent in the league and pulled away, withstanding a late Cleveland charge to take the flag by $3\frac{1}{2}$. An aggressive, intelligent bunch, the Sox could hit, run, field, and pitch like nobody's business.

Few knew that this White Sox team, which played so well together, was divided by class, temperament, and greed. Chicago's surprise World Series loss to Cincinnati raised red flags.

1918 NATIONAL LEAGUE

TEAM	W	L	T	PCT	GB	HW	HL	R	OR	PA	H	2B	3B	HR	BB	SO	HB	SH	AVG	OBP	SLG	OPS	AOPS	BR	ABR	PF	SB	CS	BSA	BSR
Chi	84	45	2	.651	—	**49**	25	**538**	**393**	4900	1147	164	53	21	358	343	27	**190**	.265	.325	.342	667	106	50	37	103	159			
NY	71	53	0	.573	10.5	35	21	480	415	4589	1081	150	53	13	271	365	33	121	.260	.310	.330	640	103	2	11	98	130			
Cin	68	60	1	.531	15.5	46	24	530	496	4762	**1185**	**165**	**84**	15	304	303	31	162	**.278**	**.330**	**.366**	**696**	**120**	**86**	**96**	98	128			
Pit	65	60	1	.520	17	42	28	466	412	4667	1016	107	72	15	**371**	**285**	25	180	.248	.315	.321	636	96	-1	-16	103	**200**			
Bro	57	69	0	.452	25.5	33	21	360	463	4578	1052	121	62	10	212	326	**36**	118	.250	.291	.315	606	90	-57	-55	100	113			
Phi	55	68	2	.447	26	27	29	430	507	4677	1022	158	28	25	346	400	20	119	.244	.305	.313	618	88	-25	-52	107	97			
Bos	53	71	0	.427	28.5	23	29	424	469	4691	1014	107	59	13	350	438	28	151	.244	.307	.307	614	97	-33	-14	96	83			
StL	51	78	2	.395	33	32	40	454	527	4863	1066	147	64	**27**	329	461	24	141	.244	.301	.325	626	99	-22	-6	97	119			
Total	508	—	—	—	—	287	217	3682	—	37727	8583	1119	475	139	2541	2921	224	1182	.254	.311	.328	638	—	—	—	—	1029	—	—	—

TEAM	CG	SHO	GR	SV	IP	H	HR	BB	SO	BR/9	ERA	AERA	OAV	OOB	PR	APR	PF	OSB	OCS	FA	E	WPB	DP	FW	PW	BW	BSW	DIF
Chi	92	**23**	52	8	1197.0	1050	**13**	296	**472**	10.3	**2.18**	**128**	**.239**	.291	**77**	**80**	101	121	*100*	.966	188	31	91	.5	**8.9**	4.1	—	5.9
NY	74	18	71	**11**	1111.2	**1002**	20	**228**	330	**10.1**	2.64	100	.243	**.287**	15	-1	95	131	*63*	**.971**	**152**	30	78	**2.1**	-.1	1.2	—	5.8
Cin	84	14	62	6	1142.1	1136	19	381	321	12.1	3.00	89	.268	.332	-30	-44	97	118	*107*	.964	192	30	**127**	.0	-4.9	**10.7**	—	-1.9
Pit	85	10	52	7	1140.1	1005	**13**	299	367	10.5	2.48	116	.243	.300	36	49	104	**74**	*103*	.966	179	**19**	108	.6	5.5	-1.8	—	-1.8
Bro	85	17	51	2	1131.1	1024	22	320	395	10.9	2.81	99	.248	.307	-6	-4	101	144	*111*	.963	193	50	74	-.3	-.4	-6.1	—	.9
Phi	78	10	61	6	1139.2	1086	22	369	312	11.7	3.15	95	.258	.323	-49	-19	109	133	*99*	.961	211	38	91	-1.5	-2.1	-5.8	—	3.0
Bos	**96**	13	31	0	1117.1	1111	14	277	340	11.4	2.90	93	.266	.316	-17	-28	97	144	*101*	.965	184	21	89	.0	-3.1	-1.6	—	-4.4
StL	72	3	**79**	5	1193.0	1148	16	352	361	11.6	2.96	91	.261	.321	-27	-34	98	164	***119***	.962	220	21	116	-1.5	-3.8	-.7	—	-7.5
Total	666	108	459	45	9172.2	—	—	—	—	11.1	2.76	—	.254	.311	—	—	—	—	—	.965	1519	240	774	—	—	—	—	—

BATTER-FIELDER WINS	BATTING AVERAGE	ON-BASE PERCENTAGE	SLUGGING AVERAGE	ON-BASE PLUS SLUGGING	ADJUSTED OPS	ADJUSTED BATTER RUNS
Groh-Cin 4.1	Z.Wheat-Bro .... .335	Groh-Cin .... .395	Roush-Cin .... .455	Roush-Cin .... .823	Roush-Cin 153	Groh-Cin 29.5
Hornsby-StL 3.8	Roush-Cin .... .333	Hollocher-Chi .... .379	Daubert-Bro .... .429	Groh-Cin .... .791	Groh-Cin 144	Roush-Cin 25.5
Fletcher-NY 3.3	Groh-Cin .... .320	R.Smith-Bos .... .373	Hornsby-StL .... .416	Daubert-Bro .... .789	S.Magee-Cin 142	Hollocher-Chi 21.7
Fisher-StL 3.0	Hollocher-Chi .... .316	S.Magee-Cin .... .370	S.Magee-Cin .... .415	S.Magee-Cin .... .785	Daubert-Bro 141	S.Magee-Cin 20.2
R.Smith-Bos 2.9	Daubert-Bro .... .308	Z.Wheat-Bro .... .369	Wickland-Bos .... .398	Hollocher-Chi .... .775	Wickland-Bos 139	R.Smith-Bos 19.4
RUNS	**HITS**	**DOUBLES**	**TRIPLES**	**HOME RUNS**	**TOTAL BASES**	**RUNS BATTED IN**
Groh-Cin 86	Hollocher-Chi 161	Groh-Cin 28	Daubert-Bro 15	Cravath-Phi 8	Hollocher-Chi 202	S.Magee-Cin 76
Burns-NY 80	Groh-Cin 158	Mann-Chi 27	Wickland-Bos 13	Williams-Phi 6	Roush-Cin 198	Cutshaw-Pit 68
Flack-Chi 74	Roush-Cin 145	Cravath-Phi 27	S.Magee-Cin 13	Cruise-StL 6	Groh-Cin 195	Luderus-Phi 67
Hollocher-Chi 72	Youngs-NY 143	Meusel-Phi 25	L.Magee-Cin 13		Mann-Chi 188	R.Smith-Bos 65
	Merkle-Chi 143	Merkle-Chi 25			Merkle-Chi 187	Merkle-Chi 65
BASES ON BALLS	**STOLEN BASES**	**BASE STEALING RUNS**	**FIELDING RUNS-INFIELD**	**FIELDING RUNS-OUTFIELD**	**OUTFIELD ASSISTS**	**CATCHER CS PCT.**
Carey-Pit 62	Carey-Pit 58		Fletcher-NY 24.8	Carey-Pit 13.0	Carey-Pit 25	Schmidt-Pit 59.1
Flack-Chi 56	Burns-NY 40		Bancroft-Phi 16.3	Burns-NY 9.2	Flack-Chi 20	Burns-Phi 45.5
Groh-Cin 54	Hollocher-Chi 26		Blackburne-Cin 11.1	Myers-Bro 7.9	Cravath-Phi 19	Killefer-Chi 45.1
Cravath-Phi 54	Cutshaw-Pit 25		Doolan-Bro 9.5	Neale-Cin 6.8	Johnston-Bro 18	Wilson-Bos 41.0
Bancroft-Phi 54	Baird-StL 25		Hornsby-StL 9.4	Roush-Cin 5.0	Griffith-Cin 18	Adams-Phi 39.8
WINS	**WINNING PCT.**	**WINS ABOVE TEAM**	**GAMES STARTED**	**COMPLETE GAMES**	**FEWEST HITS/GAME**	**FEWEST BB/GAME**
Vaughn-Chi 22	Hendrix-Chi .... .741	Grimes-Bro 6.6	Vaughn-Chi 33	Nehf-Bos 28	Vaughn-Chi 6.70	Sallee-NY .... .82
Hendrix-Chi 20	Tyler-Chi .... .704	Mayer-Phi-Pit 5.0	Perritt-NY 31	Vaughn-Chi 27	Grimes-Bro 7.00	Perritt-NY 1.47
Tyler-Chi 19	Mayer-Phi-Pit .... .696	Hendrix-Chi 4.1	Nehf-Bos 31	Cooper-Pit 26	Cooper-Pit 7.21	G.Smith-Cin-NY-Bro 1.50
Grimes-Bro 19	Vaughn-Chi .... .688	Hamilton-Pit 3.0		Tyler-Chi 22	Tyler-Chi 7.28	Toney-Cin-NY 1.54
Cooper-Pit 19	Grimes-Bro .... .679	Cooper-Pit 2.5		Hendrix-Chi 21	Jacobs-Pit-Phi 7.50	Demaree-NY 1.58
STRIKEOUTS	**STRIKEOUTS/GAME**	**GAMES**	**SAVES**	**BASE RUNNERS/9**	**ADJUSTED RELIEF RUNS**	**RELIEF RANKING**
Vaughn-Chi 148	Vaughn-Chi 4.59	Grimes-Bro 40	Toney-Cin-NY 3	Sallee-NY 9.14		
Cooper-Pit 117	Cooper-Pit 3.85	Cooper-Pit 38	Oeschger-Phi 3	Vaughn-Chi 9.27		
Grimes-Bro 113	Grimes-Bro 3.77	Eller-Cin 37	Cooper-Pit 3	Harmon-Pit 9.62		
Tyler-Chi 102	Cheney-Bro 3.72		Anderson-NY 3	Grimes-Bro 9.67		
Nehf-Bos 96	May-StL 3.60			Cooper-Pit 9.68		
INNINGS PITCHED	**OPPONENTS' AVG.**	**OPPONENTS' OBP**	**EARNED RUN AVERAGE**	**ADJUSTED ERA**	**ADJUSTED STARTER RUNS**	**PITCHER WINS**
Vaughn-Chi 290.1	Vaughn-Chi .... .208	Sallee-NY .... .259	Vaughn-Chi 1.74	Vaughn-Chi 161	Vaughn-Chi 34.0	**Vaughn-Chi 4.5**
Nehf-Bos 284.1	Grimes-Bro .... .216	Vaughn-Chi .... .266	Tyler-Chi 2.00	Tyler-Chi 139	Tyler-Chi 26.6	**Tyler-Chi 3.2**
Cooper-Pit 273.1	Cooper-Pit .... .223	Grimes-Bro .... .276	Cooper-Pit 2.11	Cooper-Pit 136	Cooper-Pit 21.6	**Cooper-Pit 3.0**
Grimes-Bro 270.0	Tyler-Chi .... .226	Perritt-NY .... .278	Douglas-Chi 2.13	Douglas-Chi 131	Grimes-Bro 15.6	**Grimes-Bro 1.9**
Tyler-Chi 269.1	Jacobs-Pit-Phi ...... .233	Cooper-Pit .... .279	Grimes-Bro 2.13	Grimes-Bro 131	Hamilton-Pit 11.6	**Hogg-Phi 1.8**

The Abbreviated Race

World War I threatened to shut down the major leagues, and baseball saved face by agreeing to stop play on Labor Day. The loss of many regular players and pitchers to military jobs or combat assignments meant that expectations of who would win were completely thrown off.

The surprising Chicago Cubs, sparked by a big rookie season from infielder Charlie Hollocher, were up by 10½ games when the merry-go-round stopped. A good schedule, crammed with lots of early home games, helped; so did the great season of Jim "Hippo" Vaughn, the league's top pitcher.

The war, and its resultant drain on spectators and disposable income, brought league attendance down another 42 percent. Of course, there were fewer games, which decreased total tickets sold, but average attendance was down everywhere except Pittsburgh. For first time, batters' strikeouts declined to below three per game; they would remain less than three through 1929. Part of the reason strikeouts were down? Grover Cleveland Alexander had entered the service. The war forced some teams to use very old and very young players. Pittsburgh brought back 40-year-old Tommy Leach as a utilityman; 38-year-old Mickey Doolan hit .179 as Brooklyn's second sacker. The last-place Cardinals, hit very hard by the war, used both 19-year-old Charlie Grimm and 44-year-old Bobby Wallace.

In the World Series, played by special government order, the Cubs and Red Sox nearly boycotted over their low shares, but finally took the field. Boston won in six games in the only World Series to end before the second week of September.

First baseman Jack Beckley, owner of 2,934 career hits for four NL clubs, died at age 51, but his death didn't merit quite the attention given Eddie Grant, the first player killed in World War I. The veteran infielder died in October in the Argonne Forest of France.

1918 AMERICAN LEAGUE

TEAM	W	L	T	PCT	GB	HW	HL	R	OR	PA	H	2B	3B	HR	BB	SO	HB	SH	AVG	OBP	SLG	OPS	AOPS	BR	ABR	PF	SB	CS	BSA	BSR
Bos	75	51	0	.595	—	**49**	21	474	**380**	4609	990	159	54	15	407	**324**	27	**193**	.249	.322	.327	649	103	7	15	98	110			
Cle	73	54	2	.575	2.5	38	22	**504**	447	4869	1084	**176**	**67**	9	**491**	386	**42**	170	**.260**	**.344**	**.341**	**685**	102	**70**	23	110	**171**			
Was	72	56	2	.563	4	41	32	461	412	5017	**1144**	156	49	4	376	361	35	134	.256	.318	.315	633	98	-22	-14	98	137			
NY	60	63	3	.488	13.5	37	29	493	475	4785	1085	160	45	20	367	370	23	171	.257	.320	.330	650	99	2	-8	102	92			
StL	58	64	1	.475	15	23	30	426	448	4627	1040	152	40	5	397	340	35	176	.259	.331	.320	651	**105**	13	**28**	97	139			
Chi	57	67	0	.460	17	30	26	457	446	4698	1057	136	55	8	375	358	27	164	.256	.322	.321	643	98	-7	-11	101	119			
Det	55	71	2	.437	20	28	29	476	557	4879	1063	141	56	13	452	380	22	143	.249	.325	.318	643	103	-2	18	96	123			
Phi	52	76	2	.406	24	35	32	412	538	4777	1039	124	44	**22**	343	485	26	130	.243	.303	.308	611	88	-62	-66	101	83			
Total	508	—	—	—	—	281	221	3703	—	38261	8502	1204	410	96	3208	3004	237	1281	.254	.323	.322	646	—	—	—	—	974	—	—	—

TEAM	CG	SHO	GR	SV	IP	H	HR	BB	SO	BR/9	ERA	AERA	OAV	OOB	PR	APR	PF	OSB	OCS	FA	E	WPB	DP	FW	PW	BW	BSW	DIF
Bos	**105**	**26**	28	2	1120.0	**931**	**9**	380	392	10.8	2.31	116	**.231**	.302	58	49	97	112	*92*	**.971**	**152**	38	89	**2.5**	5.5	1.7	—	2.4
Cle	78	5	67	**13**	1161.0	1126	**9**	343	364	11.5	2.64	114	.262	.319	18	42	108	**93**	*93*	.962	207	**24**	82	-.7	4.7	2.6	—	2.9
Was	75	19	74	8	1228.0	1021	10	395	**505**	**10.6**	**2.14**	**127**	**.231**	**.298**	**86**	**81**	98	126	*101*	.960	226	53	95	-1.8	**9.0**	-1.6	—	2.3
NY	59	8	**88**	**13**	1157.1	1103	25	463	370	12.5	3.00	94	.261	.340	-30	-23	102	106	*92*	.970	161	25	**137**	1.9	-2.6	-.9	—	.0
StL	67	8	79	8	1111.1	993	11	402	346	11.5	2.75	99	.246	.319	2	-2	99	140	*96*	.963	190	25	86	-.2	-.2	**3.1**	—	-5.7
Chi	76	9	68	8	1126.0	1092	**9**	**300**	349	11.3	2.73	100	.261	.314	5	-3	99	97	*74*	.967	169	**24**	98	1.2	-.3	-1.2	—	-4.7
Det	74	8	76	7	1160.2	1130	10	437	374	12.4	3.40	78	.263	.335	-81	-104	96	157	*105*	.960	212	33	77	-1.1	-11.6	2.0	—	2.7
Phi	80	13	67	9	1156.0	1106	13	486	277	12.7	3.22	91	.266	.348	-58	-37	106	146	***124***	.959	228	27	136	-1.9	-4.1	-7.4	—	1.4
Total	614	96	547	68	9220.1	—	—	—	—	11.7	2.77	—	.254	.323	—	—	—	—	—	.964	1545	249	800	—	—	—	—	—

BATTER-FIELDER WINS	BATTING AVERAGE	ON-BASE PERCENTAGE	SLUGGING AVERAGE	ON-BASE PLUS SLUGGING	ADJUSTED OPS	ADJUSTED BATTER RUNS
T.Cobb-Det 4.3	T.Cobb-Det .382	T.Cobb-Det .440	Ruth-Bos .555	T.Cobb-Det .955	T.Cobb-Det 196	T.Cobb-Det 47.7
Sisler-StL 4.0	Burns-Phi .352	E.Collins-Chi .407	T.Cobb-Det .515	Burns-Phi .857	Sisler-StL 159	Ruth-Bos 37.5
Burns-Phi 3.8	Sisler-StL .341	Speaker-Cle .403	Burns-Phi .467	Sisler-StL .841	Burns-Phi 157	Burns-Phi 31.8
Chapman-Cle 3.0	Speaker-Cle .318	Sisler-StL .400	Sisler-StL .440	Speaker-Cle .839	Hooper-Bos 142	Sisler-StL 31.5
Baker-NY 2.9	Baker-NY .306	Hooper-Bos .391	Speaker-Cle .435	Hooper-Bos .796	Speaker-Cle 140	Hooper-Bos 27.3

RUNS	HITS	DOUBLES	TRIPLES	HOME RUNS	TOTAL BASES	RUNS BATTED IN
Chapman-Cle 84	Burns-Phi 178	Speaker-Cle 33	T.Cobb-Det 14	Walker-Phi 11	Burns-Phi 236	Veach-Det 78
T.Cobb-Det 83	T.Cobb-Det 161	Ruth-Bos 26	Veach-Det 13	Ruth-Bos 11	T.Cobb-Det 217	Burns-Phi 70
Hooper-Bos 81	Sisler-StL 154	Hooper-Bos 26	Hooper-Bos 13	Burns-Phi 6	Baker-NY 206	Wood-Cle 66
Bush-Det 74	Baker-NY 154	Baker-NY 24	Roth-Cle 12	Baker-NY 6	Speaker-Cle 205	Ruth-Bos 66
Speaker-Cle 73	Speaker-Cle 150				Sisler-StL 199	T.Cobb-Det 64

BASES ON BALLS	STOLEN BASES	BASE STEALING RUNS	FIELDING RUNS-INFIELD	FIELDING RUNS-OUTFIELD	OUTFIELD ASSISTS	CATCHER CS PCT.
Chapman-Cle 84	Sisler-StL 45		Peckinpaugh-NY 22.1	S.Collins-Chi 11.9	Demmitt-StL 25	Agnew-Bos 50.9
Bush-Det 79	Roth-Cle 36		Scott-Bos 20.8	Kopp-Phi 9.8	Walker-Phi 24	O'Neill-Cle 50.6
Hooper-Bos 75	Chapman-Cle 35		Dugan-Phi 16.7	Demmitt-StL 9.2	Tobin-StL 20	Hannah-NY 48.8
E.Collins-Chi 73	T.Cobb-Det 34		Gedeon-StL 15.6	Speaker-Cle 8.4	Kopp-Phi 20	Ainsmith-Was 47.1
Shotton-Was 67	Speaker-Cle 27		Gardner-Phi 12.8	Leibold-Chi 7.3	S.Collins-Chi 20	Schalk-Chi 43.1

WINS	WINNING PCT.	WINS ABOVE TEAM	GAMES STARTED	COMPLETE GAMES	FEWEST HITS/GAME	FEWEST BB/GAME
Johnson-Was 23	Jones-Bos .762	Jones-Bos 4.8	Perry-Phi 36	Perry-Phi 30	Sothoron-StL 6.55	Cicotte-Chi 1.35
Coveleski-Cle 22	Johnson-Was .639	Perry-Phi 4.7	Mays-Bos 33	Mays-Bos 30	Johnson-Was 6.65	Mogridge-NY 1.62
Mays-Bos 21	Coveleski-Cle .629	Johnson-Was 4.1	Coveleski-Cle 33	Johnson-Was 29	Harper-Was 6.71	Benz-Chi 1.64
Perry-Phi 20	Mays-Bos .618	Boland-Det 3.6	Harper-Was 32	Bush-Bos 26	Ruth-Bos 6.76	Enzmann-Cle 1.91
Bagby-Cle 17	Shaw-Was .571	Wright-StL 3.2		Coveleski-Cle 25	Mays-Bos 7.06	Johnson-Was 1.93

STRIKEOUTS	STRIKEOUTS/GAME	GAMES	SAVES	BASE RUNNERS/9	ADJUSTED RELIEF RUNS	RELIEF RANKING
Johnson-Was 162	Morton-Cle 5.16	Mogridge-NY 45	Mogridge-NY 7	Johnson-Was 8.81	Houck-StL 3.2	Houck-StL 2.6
Shaw-Was 129	Shaw-Was 4.81	Bagby-Cle 45	Bagby-Cle 6	Ruth-Bos 9.52		
Bush-Bos 125	Johnson-Was 4.47	Perry-Phi 44	Russell-NY 4	Sothoron-StL 9.56		
Morton-Cle 123	Bush-Bos 4.13	Shaw-Was 41	Geary-Phi 4	Matteson-Was 9.71		
Mays-Bos 114	Love-NY 3.74	Ayers-Was 40		Wright-StL 9.86		

INNINGS PITCHED	OPPONENTS' AVG.	OPPONENTS' OBP	EARNED RUN AVERAGE	ADJUSTED ERA	ADJUSTED STARTER RUNS	PITCHER WINS
Perry-Phi 332.1	Sothoron-StL .205	Johnson-Was .260	Johnson-Was 1.27	Johnson-Was 214	Johnson-Was 51.4	**Johnson-Was 7.6**
Johnson-Was 326.0	Johnson-Was .210	Sothoron-StL .274	Coveleski-Cle 1.82	Coveleski-Cle 164	Coveleski-Cle 35.0	**Coveleski-Cle 3.9**
Coveleski-Cle 311.0	Harper-Was .212	Ruth-Bos .277	Sothoron-StL 1.94	Perry-Phi 148	Perry-Phi 32.5	**Mays-Bos 3.7**
Mays-Bos 293.1	Ruth-Bos .214	Coveleski-Cle .279	Perry-Phi 1.98	Sothoron-StL 141	Harper-Was 17.3	**Perry-Phi 3.5**
Bush-Bos 272.2	Mays-Bos .221	Mays-Bos .284	Bush-Bos 2.11	Mogridge-NY 129	Sothoron-StL 16.9	**Ruth-Bos 2.9**

The Babe Does It All

Baseball's worst nightmare came true in 1918. Baseball had been declared a non-essential industry, forcing many players into military service or war-related jobs. The game shut down before it was forced to by the government. As a result, the Boston Red Sox were able to eke out a pennant when the abbreviated season ended on Labor Day. The defending champion White Sox lost Eddie Collins, Swede Risberg, Happy Felsch, Joe Jackson, Red Faber, and Lefty Williams; Chicago fell to sixth.

Boston had Carl Mays do the majority of heavy mound work, while Babe Ruth was 13-7 on the hill and hit .300 with 11 homers (tied for the league lead) in the outfield. Cleveland nearly scraped out a flag, but aside from Stan Coveleski, the pitching wasn't strong. Walter Johnson again was the league's top hurler, and the Senators were the only team with increased attendance.

This was a deadened form of baseball; homers fell to just .09 per game—only 1907 saw a lower percentage. Never again would a league hit fewer than the AL's 96 home runs. The average AL team tallied just 3.64 runs a game, the lowest production until 1968. The league's watered-down quality also meant parity. Last-place Philadelphia ended up just 24 out, a relative godsend for Connie Mack's sad crew. Eighteen-year-old Waite Hoyt debuted, and Smokey Joe Wood, forced to retire from the mound in 1915 because of a sore arm, resurrected his career as the right fielder for old pal Tris Speaker's Indians.

In a World Series held through special dispensation from the war department, the Red Sox won in six. Ruth and Mays each won twice as no team scored over 3 runs in a game. Boston took the Series despite being outscored (10-9), outhit (.210-.186), and outpitched (the Cubs' ERA was 1.04, Boston's 1.70). This bittersweet victory was one Boston would have to learn to savor. The club's fifth world championship in fifteen years would be their last of the century.

1917 NATIONAL LEAGUE

TEAM	W	L	T	PCT	GB	HW	HL	R	OR	PA	H	2B	3B	HR	BB	SO	HB	SH	AVG	OBP	SLG	OPS	AOPS	BR	ABR	PF	SB	CS	BSA	BSR
NY	98	56	4	.636	—	**50**	28	**635**	**457**	5787	1360	170	71	**39**	373	533	**52**	151	.261	**.317**	.343	660	113	**50**	70	97	**162**			
Phi	87	65	2	.572	10	46	29	578	500	5725	1262	**225**	60	38	**435**	533	20	186	.248	.310	.339	649	101	35	12	104	109			
StL	82	70	2	.539	15	38	38	531	567	5626	1271	159	93	26	359	652	24	160	.250	.303	.333	636	104	-1	14	97	159			
Cin	78	76	3	.506	20	39	38	601	611	5728	**1385**	196	**100**	26	312	**477**	34	131	**.264**	.309	**.354**	**663**	**114**	46	**72**	96	153			
Chi	74	80	3	.481	24	35	42	552	567	5775	1229	194	67	17	415	599	23	**202**	.239	.299	.313	612	86	-33	-71	108	127			
Bos	72	81	4	.471	25.5	35	42	536	552	5855	1280	169	75	22	427	587	45	182	.246	.309	.320	629	105	-2	32	94	155			
Bro	70	81	5	.464	26.5	36	38	511	559	5776	1299	159	78	25	334	527	29	162	.247	.296	.322	618	93	-35	-49	103	130			
Pit	51	103	3	.331	47	25	53	464	595	5788	1230	160	61	9	399	580	46	174	.238	.298	.298	596	86	-61	-76	103	150			
Total	625	—	—	—	—	304	308	4408	—	46060	10316	1432	605	202	3054	4488	273	1348	.249	.305	.328	633	—	—	—	—	1145	—	—	—

TEAM	CG	SHO	GR	SV	IP	H	HR	BB	SO	BR/9	ERA	AERA	OAV	OOB	PR	APR	PF	OSB	OCS	FA	E	WPB	DP	FW	PW	BW	BSW	DIF
NY	92	18	97	**14**	1426.2	**1221**	29	327	551	**9.9**	**2.27**	112	**.234**	**.283**	**69**	45	94	136	*63*	**.968**	**208**	**31**	122	**1.8**	5.1	7.9	—	6.2
Phi	102	**22**	65	5	1389.0	1258	25	**325**	616	10.5	2.46	**114**	.246	.295	38	**51**	104	125	*109*	.967	212	36	112	1.2	**5.8**	1.4	—	2.7
StL	66	16	**140**	10	1392.2	1257	29	421	502	11.1	3.03	89	.248	.311	-51	-55	99	**115**	*124*	.967	221	39	**153**	.6	-6.2	1.6	—	10.0
Cin	94	12	85	6	1397.1	1358	20	402	488	11.5	2.70	97	.260	.317	1	-15	97	159	*116*	.962	247	40	120	-.7	-1.7	**8.1**	—	-4.8
Chi	79	16	121	9	1404.0	1303	34	374	**654**	10.9	2.62	110	.253	.307	14	38	107	146	*127*	.959	267	63	121	-1.9	4.3	-8.0	—	2.6
Bos	**103**	21	81	3	1424.2	1309	19	371	593	10.8	2.77	92	.251	.304	-10	-40	94	126	*116*	.966	224	45	122	.7	-4.5	3.6	—	-4.3
Bro	99	8	81	9	1421.1	1288	32	405	582	11.0	2.78	100	.247	.307	-12	0	103	144	*106*	.962	245	40	102	-.7	.0	-5.5	—	.7
Pit	84	17	84	6	1417.2	1318	**14**	432	509	11.3	3.01	94	.253	.314	-48	-28	105	194	***129***	.961	251	43	119	-.9	-3.2	-8.6	—	-13.3
Total	719	130	754	62	11273.1	—	—	—	—	10.9	2.70	—	.249	.305	—	—	—	—	—	.964	1875	337	971	—	—	—	—	—

BATTER-FIELDER WINS	BATTING AVERAGE	ON-BASE PERCENTAGE	SLUGGING AVERAGE	ON-BASE PLUS SLUGGING	ADJUSTED OPS	ADJUSTED BATTER RUNS
Hornsby-StL 7.8	Roush-Cin .341	Groh-Cin .385	Hornsby-StL .484	Hornsby-StL .868	Hornsby-StL 170	Hornsby-StL 42.4
Groh-Cin 5.8	Hornsby-StL .327	Hornsby-StL .385	Cravath-Phi .473	Cravath-Phi .842	Roush-Cin 162	Groh-Cin 39.7
Fletcher-NY 4.5	Z.Wheat-Bro .312	Burns-NY .380	Roush-Cin .454	Roush-Cin .833	Cravath-Phi 151	Burns-NY 36.1
Bancroft-Phi 3.6	Kauff-NY .308	Roush-Cin .379	Z.Wheat-Bro .423	Groh-Cin .796	Groh-Cin 150	Roush-Cin 35.7
Burns-NY 3.5	Groh-Cin .304	Kauff-NY .379	Burns-NY .412	Burns-NY .792	Burns-NY 148	Cravath-Phi 31.8

RUNS	HITS	DOUBLES	TRIPLES	HOME RUNS	TOTAL BASES	RUNS BATTED IN
Burns-NY 103	Groh-Cin 182	Groh-Cin 39	Hornsby-StL 17	Robertson-NY 12	Hornsby-StL 253	Zimmerman-NY 102
Groh-Cin 91	Burns-NY 180	Merkle-Bro-Chi 31	Cravath-Phi 16	Cravath-Phi 12	Groh-Cin 246	Chase-Cin 86
Kauff-NY 89	Roush-Cin 178	Smith-Bos 31	Chase-Cin 15	Hornsby-StL 8	Burns-NY 246	Cravath-Phi 83
Hornsby-StL 86	Zimmerman-NY 174	Cravath-Phi 29	Roush-Cin 14		Cravath-Phi 238	Stengel-Bro 73
	Carey-Pit 174	Chase-Cin 28	Long-StL 14			Luderus-Phi 72

BASES ON BALLS	STOLEN BASES	BASE STEALING RUNS	FIELDING RUNS-INFIELD	FIELDING RUNS-OUTFIELD	OUTFIELD ASSISTS	CATCHER CS PCT.
Burns-NY 75	Carey-Pit 46		Bancroft-Phi 28.0	Carey-Pit 21.3	Stengel-Bro 30	Tragesser-Bos 44.4
Groh-Cin 71	Burns-NY 40		Fletcher-NY 27.8	Stengel-Bro 11.3	Carey-Pit 28	Wingo-Cin 42.8
Cravath-Phi 70	Kauff-NY 30		Hornsby-StL 19.0	Williams-Chi 10.8	Williams-Chi 23	Miller-Bro 42.6
Luderus-Phi 65	Maranville-Bos 27		Shean-Cin 17.4	King-Pit 7.6	Hickman-Bro 22	Rariden-NY 31.1
Paskert-Phi 62	Baird-Pit-StL 26		Miller-StL 17.2	Griffith-Cin 7.0	Mann-Chi 20	

WINS	WINNING PCT.	WINS ABOVE TEAM	GAMES STARTED	COMPLETE GAMES	FEWEST HITS/GAME	FEWEST BB/GAME
Alexander-Phi 30	Schupp-NY .750	Alexander-Phi 7.9	Alexander-Phi 44	Alexander-Phi 34	Schupp-NY 6.68	Alexander-Phi 1.30
Toney-Cin 24	Sallee-NY .720	Vaughn-Chi 6.6	Toney-Cin 42	Toney-Cin 31	Anderson-NY 6.78	Sallee-NY 1.42
Vaughn-Chi 23	Perritt-NY .708	Cooper-Pit 6.5	Schneider-Cin 42	Vaughn-Chi 27	Nehf-Bos 7.60	Nehf-Bos 1.50
Schupp-NY 21	Alexander-Phi .698	Nehf-Bos 5.5	Vaughn-Chi 38	Barnes-Bos 26	Pfeffer-Bro 7.61	Barnes-Bos 1.53
Schneider-Cin 20	Nehf-Bos .680	Marquard-Bro 5.1		Schupp-NY 25	Tyler-Bos 7.64	Douglas-Chi 1.53

STRIKEOUTS	STRIKEOUTS/GAME	GAMES	SAVES	BASE RUNNERS/9	ADJUSTED RELIEF RUNS	RELIEF RANKING
Alexander-Phi 200	Vaughn-Chi 5.94	Douglas-Chi 51	Sallee-NY 4	Anderson-NY 8.78		
Vaughn-Chi 195	Schupp-NY 4.86	Barnes-Bos 50		Schupp-NY 9.13		
Douglas-Chi 151	Alexander-Phi 4.64	Schneider-Cin 46		Alexander-Phi 9.23		
Schupp-NY 147	Douglas-Chi 4.63	Alexander-Phi 45		Nehf-Bos 9.26		
Schneider-Cin 138	Marquard-Bro 4.53	Doak-StL 44		Bender-Phi 9.32		

INNINGS PITCHED	OPPONENTS' AVG.	OPPONENTS' OBP	EARNED RUN AVERAGE	ADJUSTED ERA	ADJUSTED STARTER RUNS	PITCHER WINS
Alexander-Phi 388.0	Schupp-NY .209	Anderson-NY .255	Alexander-Phi 1.83	Anderson-NY 176	Alexander-Phi 39.3	**Alexander-Phi 5.4**
Toney-Cin 339.2	Anderson-NY .209	Schupp-NY .265	Anderson-NY 1.44	Alexander-Phi 153	Vaughn-Chi 25.3	**Vaughn-Chi 3.4**
Schneider-Cin 333.2	Nehf-Bos .231	Alexander-Phi .266	Perritt-NY 1.88	Vaughn-Chi 144	Schupp-NY 21.5	**Schupp-NY 2.2**
Cooper-Pit 297.2	Marquard-Bro .232	Nehf-Bos .268	Schupp-NY 1.95	Perritt-NY 135	Anderson-NY 18.1	**Rixey-Phi 1.8**
Vaughn-Chi 295.2	Pfeffer-Bro .234	Barnes-Bos .277	Vaughn-Chi 2.01	Schupp-NY 130	Toney-Cin 16.7	**Cadore-Bro 1.7**

Trouble Looming

The flag drive was never in doubt after June, as the Giants pulled away from the Phillies to win by 10 games. New York outfielder George Burns was the league's only 100-run man, and John McGraw used six quality starters. In Philadelphia, Grover Cleveland Alexander won 30 games for the third straight season, but his team didn't hit much.

Defending champion Brooklyn left the gate slowly and dropped all the way from first to seventh; their attack was too thin to help a decent pitching rotation. The Pirates dropped into the NL cellar for first time in the twentieth century, finishing 47 games from first place. Honus Wagner, a preseason holdout at 43, played his last season and hit just .265. St. Louis finished third, the franchise's best performance since joining the NL in 1892. Their top performer was infielder Rogers Hornsby. A 20-year-old outfielder named Ross Youngs debuted late in the year for the Giants. Room would be made for him in 1918.

In this, the twilight of the Dead Ball Era, even stolen bases fell to their lowest level yet as pitchers continued to deface, scuff, spit on, and otherwise render the baseball unhitable. No NL club had ever led the league with so few steals as New York's 162.

Following two years of gains, league attendance fell; only rejuvenated St. Louis reported an appreciable gain in tickets sold. For the Senior Circuit, at least, the hoped-for gains of the post-Federal League era had not yet materialized, and the coming conflict in Europe would take another bite out of baseball.

The phonograph record was a recent invention, and the World Series' platter was already skipping. Again the AL defeated the Senior Circuit's representative, with the White Sox putting lumps on the Giants' pitchers in a six-game set.

1917 AMERICAN LEAGUE

TEAM	W	L	T	PCT	GB	HW	HL	R	OR	PA	H	2B	3B	HR	BB	SO	HB	SH	AVG	OBP	SLG	OPS	AOPS	BR	ABR	PF	SB	CS	BSA	BSR
Chi	100	54	2	.649	—	**56**	21	**655**	463	5858	1281	152	**81**	18	522	479	**47**	232	.253	**.329**	.326	655	103	34	22	102	**219**			
Bos	90	62	5	.592	9	45	33	555	**455**	5858	1243	198	64	14	466	**473**	34	**310**	.246	.314	.319	633	100	-9	-3	99	105			
Cle	88	66	2	.571	12	43	34	584	543	5840	1224	**218**	64	13	**549**	596	35	262	.245	.324	.322	646	96	25	-16	107	210			
Det	78	75	1	.510	21.5	34	41	639	577	5814	**1317**	204	77	25	483	476	45	193	**.259**	.328	**.344**	**672**	**111**	**62**	**65**	100	163			
Was	74	79	4	.484	25.5	42	36	544	566	5861	1238	173	70	4	500	574	43	176	.241	.313	.304	617	95	-35	-28	99	166			
NY	71	82	2	.464	28.5	35	40	524	558	5858	1226	172	52	**27**	496	535	38	188	.239	.310	.308	618	93	-34	-39	101	136			
StL	57	97	1	.370	43	31	46	510	687	5694	1250	183	63	15	405	540	31	167	.246	.305	.315	620	98	-40	-20	96	157			
Phi	55	98	1	.359	44.5	29	47	529	691	5780	1296	177	62	17	435	519	33	203	.254	.316	.323	639	101	-2	6	99	112			
Total	622	—	—	—	—	315	298	4540	—	46563	10075	1477	533	133	3856	4192	306	1731	.248	.318	.320	638	—	—	—	—	1268	—	—	—

TEAM	CG	SHO	GR	SV	IP	H	HR	BB	SO	BR/9	ERA	AERA	OAV	OOB	PR	APR	PF	OSB	OCS	FA	E	WPB	DP	FW	PW	BW	BSW	DIF
Chi	78	**22**	112	21	1424.1	1236	**10**	**413**	517	10.6	**2.16**	**123**	.238	.298	**79**	**76**	100	**108**	*110*	.967	204	**22**	117	2.3	**8.5**	2.4	—	9.8
Bos	**115**	15	51	7	1421.1	**1197**	12	**413**	509	**10.5**	2.20	117	**.231**	**.295**	73	62	97	138	*120*	**.972**	**183**	51	116	**3.9**	6.9	-.3	—	3.5
Cle	73	20	129	**22**	1412.2	1270	17	438	451	11.1	2.52	112	.247	.310	22	45	106	144	*131*	.964	242	32	136	-.5	5.0	-1.8	—	8.3
Det	78	20	112	15	1396.1	1209	12	504	516	11.4	2.56	103	.240	.316	16	13	99	178	*112*	.964	234	39	95	-.1	1.4	**7.2**	—	-7.1
Was	84	21	98	10	1413.0	1217	12	537	**637**	11.4	2.75	95	.239	.316	-14	-20	99	179	*138*	.961	251	64	127	-1.0	-2.2	-3.1	—	3.9
NY	87	10	93	6	1411.1	1280	28	427	571	11.1	2.66	101	.252	.314	0	3	101	124	*131*	.965	225	35	129	.6	.3	-4.3	—	-2.1
StL	66	12	**143**	12	1385.1	1320	19	537	429	12.3	3.20	81	.257	.332	-83	-99	98	188	*130*	.957	281	55	**139**	-3.4	-11.0	-2.2	—	-3.3
Phi	80	8	95	8	1365.2	1310	23	562	516	12.5	3.27	84	.261	.338	-92	-77	103	209	***151***	.961	251	54	106	-1.4	-8.6	.7	—	-12.3
Total	661	128	833	101	11230.0	—	—	—	—	11.4	2.66	—	.248	.318	—	—	—	—	—	.964	1871	352	965	—	—	—	—	—

BATTER-FIELDER WINS	BATTING AVERAGE	ON-BASE PERCENTAGE	SLUGGING AVERAGE	ON-BASE PLUS SLUGGING	ADJUSTED OPS	ADJUSTED BATTER RUNS
Cobb-Det 7.4	Cobb-Det .383	Cobb-Det .444	Cobb-Det .570	Cobb-Det 1014	Cobb-Det 210	Cobb-Det 75.9
Chapman-Cle 5.8	Sisler-StL .353	Speaker-Cle .432	Speaker-Cle .486	Speaker-Cle .918	Speaker-Cle 168	Speaker-Cle 45.4
Sisler-StL 4.3	Speaker-Cle .352	Veach-Det .393	Veach-Det .457	Veach-Det .850	Sisler-StL 163	Veach-Det 41.2
Speaker-Cle 4.1	Veach-Det .319	Sisler-StL .390	Sisler-StL .453	Sisler-StL .843	Veach-Det 160	Sisler-StL 37.9
Veach-Det 4.0	Felsch-Chi .308	E.Collins-Chi .389	Jackson-Chi .429	Jackson-Chi .805	Jackson-Chi 142	Jackson-Chi 26.5
RUNS	**HITS**	**DOUBLES**	**TRIPLES**	**HOME RUNS**	**TOTAL BASES**	**RUNS BATTED IN**
Bush-Det 112	Cobb-Det 225	Cobb-Det 44	Cobb-Det 24	Pipp-NY 9	Cobb-Det 335	Veach-Det 103
Cobb-Det 107	Sisler-StL 190	Speaker-Cle 42	Jackson-Chi 17	Veach-Det 8	Veach-Det 261	Felsch-Chi 102
Chapman-Cle 98	Speaker-Cle 184	Veach-Det 31	Judge-Was 15	Bodie-Phi 7	Speaker-Cle 254	Cobb-Det 102
Jackson-Chi 91	Veach-Det 182	Sisler-StL 30	Chapman-Cle 13		Sisler-StL 244	Heilmann-Det 86
E.Collins-Chi 91		Roth-Cle 30			Bodie-Phi 233	Jackson-Chi 75
BASES ON BALLS	**STOLEN BASES**	**BASE STEALING RUNS**	**FIELDING RUNS-INFIELD**	**FIELDING RUNS-OUTFIELD**	**OUTFIELD ASSISTS**	**CATCHER CS PCT.**
Graney-Cle 94	Cobb-Det 55		Chapman-Cle 23.6	Felsch-Chi 14.6	Bodie-Phi 32	Schalk-Chi 51.8
E.Collins-Chi 89	E.Collins-Chi 53		Pratt-StL 17.8	Menosky-Was 10.5	Cobb-Det 27	Nunamaker-NY 50.7
Hooper-Bos 80	Chapman-Cle 52		Wambsganss-Cle 14.8	Shanks-Was 8.4	Rice-Was 26	O'Neill-Cle 46.5
Bush-Det 80	Roth-Cle 51		Lavan-StL 12.8	Bodie-Phi 7.5	Felsch-Chi 24	Agnew-Bos 46.0
Leibold-Chi 74	Sisler-StL 37		Baker-NY 9.4	Jackson-Chi 5.5	Speaker-Cle 23	Ainsmith-Was 45.7
WINS	**WINNING PCT.**	**WINS ABOVE TEAM**	**GAMES STARTED**	**COMPLETE GAMES**	**FEWEST HITS/GAME**	**FEWEST BB/GAME**
Cicotte-Chi 28	Russell-Chi .750	Mays-Bos 5.2	Davenport-StL 39	Ruth-Bos 35	Coveleski-Cle 6.09	Russell-Chi 1.52
Ruth-Bos 24	Mays-Bos .710	Johnson-Was 5.0	Ruth-Bos 38	Johnson-Was 30	Cicotte-Chi 6.39	Mogridge-NY 1.79
Johnson-Was 23	Cicotte-Chi .700	Klepfer-Cle 4.6	Bagby-Cle 37	Cicotte-Chi 29	Ruth-Bos 6.73	Cicotte-Chi 1.82
Bagby-Cle 23	Williams-Chi .680	Davenport-StL 4.2	Leonard-Bos 36	Mays-Bos 27	Johnson-Was 6.85	Johnson-Was 1.88
Mays-Bos 22	Ruth-Bos .649	Cicotte-Chi 3.7	Coveleski-Cle 36		Mays-Bos 7.16	Bagby-Cle 2.05
STRIKEOUTS	**STRIKEOUTS/GAME**	**GAMES**	**SAVES**	**BASE RUNNERS/9**	**ADJUSTED RELIEF RUNS**	**RELIEF RANKING**
Johnson-Was 188	Johnson-Was 5.19	Danforth-Chi 50	Danforth-Chi 9	Cicotte-Chi 8.28		
Cicotte-Chi 150	Harper-Was 4.97	Cicotte-Chi 49	Bagby-Cle 7	Coveleski-Cle 8.96		
Leonard-Bos 144	Bush-Phi 4.67	Bagby-Cle 49	Boland-Det 6	Johnson-Was 9.11		
Coveleski-Cle 133	Leonard-Bos 4.40	Sothoron-StL 48	Coumbe-Cle 5	Benz-Chi 9.60		
Ruth-Bos 128	Danforth-Chi 4.11			Russell-Chi 9.65		
INNINGS PITCHED	**OPPONENTS' AVG.**	**OPPONENTS' OBP**	**EARNED RUN AVERAGE**	**ADJUSTED ERA**	**ADJUSTED STARTER RUNS**	**PITCHER WINS**
Cicotte-Chi 346.2	Coveleski-Cle .194	Cicotte-Chi .248	Cicotte-Chi 1.53	Cicotte-Chi 173	Cicotte-Chi 44.8	**Cicotte-Chi 5.7**
Ruth-Bos 326.1	Cicotte-Chi .203	Coveleski-Cle .261	Mays-Bos 1.74	Coveleski-Cle 156	Coveleski-Cle 33.3	**Ruth-Bos 4.9**
Johnson-Was 326.0	Ruth-Bos .211	Johnson-Was .263	Coveleski-Cle 1.81	Mays-Bos 148	Bagby-Cle 30.2	**Mays-Bos 4.0**
Bagby-Cle 320.2	Johnson-Was .211	Russell-Chi .279	Faber-Chi 1.92	Bagby-Cle 142	Mays-Bos 24.7	**Bagby-Cle 3.9**
Coveleski-Cle 298.1	Mays-Bos .221	Mays-Bos .282	Russell-Chi 1.95	Faber-Chi 138	Ruth-Bos 22.2	**Coveleski-Cle 3.2**

White Sox Play Clean Ball

The waves of World War were causing the good ship baseball to list. America's economy sagged, and as a result, league attendance fell 17 percent. Speculation over an increased war effort led to cries of impending doom for baseball, which could lose much of its talent to conscription and military industry.

Despite a 1.79 ERA, 42-year-old Eddie Plank was 5-6 for seventh-place St. Louis, and his big-league career came to an end. Also finished at 36 was former White Sox ace "Big Ed" Walsh, whose arm was dead after leading the AL four times in a six-year span in innings pitched. No longer would pitchers be asked to shoulder the load that Walsh did in 1912, when he pitched 62 games and 393 innings (although that was actually a step back from his 464-inning, 40-win 1908 season).

Showing excellent all-around effort, Chicago pulled away from second-place Boston in September. The Red Sox were barely.500 down the stretch, while the White Sox came alive when they smelled the flag. Chicago won 100 games with an excellent attack, leading the league in runs scored, and 33-year-old spitballer Eddie Cicotte finally had his first 20-win season—28 to be precise.

Babe Ruth was 24-13 for the Bosox and hit .325, seeing extra duty as a pinch-hitter. The 1917 campaign was his final full season on the mound, as his bat would soon prove too hot to keep on the bench. Boston's attack was substandard; they didn't hit, draw walks, or steal bases.

The White Sox-Giants World Series started as a pitching paradise. Chicago allowed just 3 runs in winning the first pair at home. Back east, New York won the next two by shutouts. But Game 5 at Comiskey saw the Pale Hose outlast New York, 8-5, despite making 6 errors. Chicago then won the next game as the Giants made 3 miscues of their own. White Sox hurler Red Faber went 3-1 in 27 innings.

1916 NATIONAL LEAGUE

TEAM	W	L	T	PCT	GB	HW	HL	R	OR	PA	H	2B	3B	HR	BB	SO	HB	SH	AVG	OBP	SLG	OPS	AOPS	BR	ABR	PF	SB	CS	BSA	BSR
Bro	94	60	2	.610	—	**50**	27	585	471	5833	**1366**	195	80	28	355	**550**	41	**203**	**.261**	**.313**	**.345**	**658**	105	**46**	30	103	187			
Phi	91	62	1	.595	2.5	**50**	29	581	489	5597	1244	**223**	53	42	399	571	34	179	.250	.310	.341	651	102	39	19	104	149			
Bos	89	63	6	.586	4	41	31	542	**453**	5760	1181	166	73	22	**437**	646	46	202	.233	.299	.307	606	96	-38	-15	96	141			
NY	86	66	3	.566	7	47	30	**597**	504	5686	1305	188	74	42	356	558	44	134	.253	.307	.343	650	**112**	31	**63**	95	**206**			
Chi	67	86	3	.438	26.5	37	41	520	541	5778	1237	194	56	**46**	399	662	34	166	.239	.298	.325	623	88	-15	-66	111	133			
Pit	65	89	3	.422	29	37	40	484	586	5769	1246	147	**91**	20	372	618	**50**	166	.240	.298	.316	614	94	-36	-41	101	173			
StL	60	93	0	.392	33.5	36	40	476	629	5514	1223	155	74	25	335	651	33	116	.243	.295	.318	613	95	-38	-35	99	182			
Cin	60	93	2	.392	33.5	32	44	505	617	5783	1336	187	88	14	362	573	40	127	.254	.307	.331	638	105	11	25	98	157			
Total	622	—	—	—	—	330	282	4290	—	45720	10138	1455	589	239	3015	4829	322	1293	.247	.303	.328	632	—	—	—	—	1328	—	—	—

TEAM	CG	SHO	GR	SV	IP	H	HR	BB	SO	BR/9	ERA	AERA	OAV	OOB	PR	APR	PF	OSB	OCS	FA	E	WPB	DP	FW	PW	BW	BSW	DIF
Bro	96	22	92	9	1427.1	**1201**	**24**	372	634	10.2	**2.12**	**126**	**.232**	.289	**78**	**84**	102	162	119	.965	224	53	90	1.2	**9.6**	3.4	—	2.7
Phi	**97**	**25**	78	9	1382.1	1238	28	**295**	601	10.3	2.36	112	.244	.292	39	43	101	153	117	.963	234	60	119	.4	4.9	2.2	—	7.0
Bos	**97**	23	82	11	1415.2	1206	**24**	325	**644**	**9.9**	2.19	113	.235	**.285**	66	47	95	**100**	119	**.967**	**212**	**40**	124	**2.1**	5.4	-1.7	—	7.2
NY	88	22	103	12	1397.1	1267	41	310	638	10.4	2.60	93	.245	.293	2	-30	93	142	98	.966	217	55	108	1.5	-3.4	**7.2**	—	4.7
Chi	72	17	119	13	1416.2	1265	32	365	616	10.6	2.65	110	.244	.298	-6	35	111	177	134	.957	286	57	104	-2.6	4.0	-7.5	—	-3.4
Pit	88	11	102	7	1419.2	1277	**24**	443	596	11.1	2.76	97	.247	.311	-24	-14	103	192	142	.959	260	**40**	97	-.9	-1.6	-4.7	—	-4.8
StL	58	13	**127**	**15**	1355.0	1331	31	445	529	12.1	3.14	84	.265	.330	-80	-76	101	192	137	.957	278	51	124	-2.4	-8.7	-4.0	—	-1.4
Cin	86	7	98	6	1408.0	1356	35	461	569	11.9	3.10	84	.261	.326	-76	-82	99	210	**159**	.965	228	48	**126**	.9	-9.4	2.9	—	-10.9
Total	682	140	801	82	11222.0	—	—	—	—	10.8	2.61	—	.247	.303	—	—	—	—	—	.963	1939	404	892	—	—	—	—	—

BATTER-FIELDER WINS	BATTING AVERAGE	ON-BASE PERCENTAGE	SLUGGING AVERAGE	ON-BASE PLUS SLUGGING	ADJUSTED OPS	ADJUSTED BATTER RUNS
Groh-Cin 4.8	Chase-Cin .339	Cravath-Phi .379	Z.Wheat-Bro .461	Williams-Chi .831	Chase-Cin 155	Z.Wheat-Bro 32.6
Fletcher-NY 4.7	Daubert-Bro .316	Hinchman-Pit .378	Chase-Cin .459	Z.Wheat-Bro .828	Hornsby-StL 150	Chase-Cin 32.3
Doyle-NY-Chi 3.8	Hinchman-Pit .315	Williams-Chi .372	Williams-Chi .459	Chase-Cin .822	Z.Wheat-Bro 149	Hinchman-Pit 29.9
Hornsby-StL 3.7	Hornsby-StL .313	Daubert-Bro .371	Hornsby-StL .444	Cravath-Phi .819	Cravath-Phi 146	Hornsby-StL 28.2
Z.Wheat-Bro 3.6	Z.Wheat-Bro .312	Groh-Cin .370	Cravath-Phi .440	Hornsby-StL .814	Hinchman-Pit 146	Cravath-Phi 26.8

RUNS	HITS	DOUBLES	TRIPLES	HOME RUNS	TOTAL BASES	RUNS BATTED IN
Burns-NY 105	Chase-Cin 184	Niehoff-Phi 42	Hinchman-Pit 16	Williams-Chi 12	Z.Wheat-Bro 262	Zimmerman-Chi-NY 83
Carey-Pit 90	Robertson-NY 180	Z.Wheat-Bro 32	Roush-NY-Cin 15	Robertson-NY 12	Robertson-NY 250	Chase-Cin 82
Robertson-NY 88	Z.Wheat-Bro 177	Paskert-Phi 30	Kauff-NY 15	Cravath-Phi 11	Chase-Cin 249	Hinchman-Pit 76
Groh-Cin 85	Hinchman-Pit 175		Hornsby-StL 15	Z.Wheat-Bro 9	Hinchman-Pit 237	Kauff-NY 74
Paskert-Phi 82	Burns-NY 174			Kauff-NY 9	Burns-NY 229	Z.Wheat-Bro 73

BASES ON BALLS	STOLEN BASES	BASE STEALING RUNS	FIELDING RUNS-INFIELD	FIELDING RUNS-OUTFIELD	OUTFIELD ASSISTS	CATCHER CS PCT.
Groh-Cin 84	Carey-Pit 63	Carey-Pit 7.2	Betzel-StL 29.4	Carey-Pit 21.9	Carey-Pit 32	Gowdy-Bos 55.2
Saier-Chi 79	Kauff-NY 40	Bescher-StL 4.4	Bancroft-Phi 25.3	Snodgrass-Bos 8.9	Griffith-Cin 28	Wingo-Cin 46.7
Bancroft-Phi 74	Bescher-StL 39	Daubert-Bro 2.2	Maranville-Bos 23.3	Neale-Cin 6.6	Kauff-NY 22	Fischer-Chi-Pit 45.3
Kauff-NY 68	Burns-NY 37	Maranville-Bos 1.8	Fletcher-NY 21.6	Z.Wheat-Bro 6.2	Flack-Chi 22	Killefer-Phi 44.3
Cravath-Phi 64	Herzog-Cin-NY 34	Chase-Cin 1.0	Doyle-NY-Chi 18.0	Stengel-Bro 4.8	Neale-Cin 20	Rariden-NY 42.8

WINS	WINNING PCT.	WINS ABOVE TEAM	GAMES STARTED	COMPLETE GAMES	FEWEST HITS/GAME	FEWEST BB/GAME
Alexander-Phi 33	Hughes-Bos .842	Alexander-Phi 9.5	Alexander-Phi 45	Alexander-Phi 38	Cheney-Bro 6.33	Rudolph-Bos 1.10
Pfeffer-Bro 25	Alexander-Phi .733	Hughes-Bos 6.2	Toney-Cin 38	Pfeffer-Bro 30	Hughes-Bos 6.76	Alexander-Phi 1.16
Rixey-Phi 22	Pfeffer-Bro .694	Mamaux-Pit 6.0	Rudolph-Bos 38	Rudolph-Bos 27	Cooper-Pit 6.91	Demaree-Phi 1.52
Mamaux-Pit 21	Rixey-Phi .688	Pfeffer-Bro 4.8	Mamaux-Pit 37	Mamaux-Pit 26	Miller-Pit 7.02	Sallee-StL-NY 1.63
	Benton-NY .667	Rixey-Phi 4.4		Demaree-Phi 25	Ragan-Bos 7.07	Marquard-Bro 1.67

STRIKEOUTS	STRIKEOUTS/GAME	GAMES	SAVES	BASE RUNNERS/9	ADJUSTED RELIEF RUNS	RELIEF RANKING
Alexander-Phi 167	Cheney-Bro 5.91	Meadows-StL 51	Ames-StL 8	Schupp-NY 7.76		
Cheney-Bro 166	Hughes-Bos 5.42	Alexander-Phi 48	Packard-Chi 5	Rudolph-Bos 8.86		
Mamaux-Pit 163	Hendrix-Chi 4.83	Mamaux-Pit 45	Marquard-Bro 5	Alexander-Phi 8.86		
Toney-Cin 146	Mamaux-Pit 4.73	Ames-StL 45	Hughes-Bos 5	Prendergast-Chi 8.94		
Vaughn-Chi 144	Marquard-Bro 4.70			Marquard-Bro 9.09		

INNINGS PITCHED	OPPONENTS' AVG.	OPPONENTS' OBP	EARNED RUN AVERAGE	ADJUSTED ERA	ADJUSTED STARTER RUNS	PITCHER WINS
Alexander-Phi 389.0	Cheney-Bro .198	Rudolph-Bos .261	Alexander-Phi 1.55	Alexander-Phi 171	Alexander-Phi 47.0	**Alexander-Phi 7.2**
Pfeffer-Bro 328.2	Cooper-Pit .215	Alexander-Phi .262	Marquard-Bro 1.58	Marquard-Bro 169	Pfeffer-Bro 29.5	**Pfeffer-Bro 4.1**
Rudolph-Bos 312.0	Hughes-Bos .215	Marquard-Bro .267	Rixey-Phi 1.85	Cooper-Pit 144	Schupp-NY 23.7	**Rixey-Phi 2.5**
Mamaux-Pit 310.0	Ragan-Bos .218	Ragan-Bos .270	Cooper-Pit 1.87	Rixey-Phi 143	Marquard-Bro 23.1	**Tyler-Bos 2.3**
Toney-Cin 300.0	McConnell-Chi .223	McConnell-Chi .271	Pfeffer-Bro 1.92	Pfeffer-Bro 140	Rixey-Phi 21.0	**Cooper-Pit 2.1**

Ebbets Field's First Champeens

Offense continued its free fall as runs dropped for the fourth straight year. The average club tallied just 3.45 runs per game, the league's lowest total until 1968. The Federal League's demise meant fewer jobs for more players, and—as a result—lower salaries (and bigger profits) for the owners. The Cubs moved from West Side Grounds to Weeghman Park, and their attendance rose 109 percent.

Cy Williams led the NL in homers for first of four times, while the Pirates gave rookie Burleigh Grimes his first major league action; the right-hander lasted until 1934 and was the last to legally throw a spitball. The end of an era came on September 4, 1916: Three-Finger Brown, bowing out with the Cubs, and Christy Mathewson, now manager of Cincinnati, hooked up for their 25th and final duel. Matty's win gave each pitcher 12 wins against the other. It was the final big league game for both.

Grover Cleveland Alexander was the new breed. His 16 shutouts in '16 remain an all-time record and his 33 wins have not been matched since. "Alex" also paced the NL in strikeouts for the fourth time in five years. His 389 innings were 60 more than anyone else.

Alexander's Phillies opened September in a three-way race with Brooklyn and Boston. While the three clubs remained neck-and-neck into the last week, it was the Robins, so dubbed because of third-year manager Wilbert Robinson, who came out ahead. Philadelphia and Boston knocked each other out of the running. The late-charging Giants, who won a league-record 26 straight, fell just short in fourth.

This was big news for Brooklyn, which had spent most of the century as a league doormat. The Robins did it with balanced pitching and hitting. They had few stars (save Zack Wheat) but no weaknesses, and Jeff Pfeffer was arguably the league's second-best pitcher. In the World Series, however, the NL lost again as the Red Sox knocked out Brooklyn in five games.

1916 AMERICAN LEAGUE

TEAM	W	L	T	PCT	GB	HW	HL	R	OR	PA	H	2B	3B	HR	BB	SO	HB	SH	AVG	OBP	SLG	OPS	AOPS	BR	ABR	PF	SB	CS	BSA	BSR
Bos	91	63	2	.591	—	**49**	28	550	**480**	5758	1246	197	56	14	464	**482**	38	**238**	.248	.317	.318	635	97	-20	-22	100	129			
Chi	89	65	1	.578	2	**49**	28	601	497	5809	1277	194	**100**	17	447	591	**60**	221	.251	.319	.339	658	103	15	9	101	197			
Det	87	67	1	.565	4	**49**	28	**670**	595	5969	**1371**	202	96	17	545	529	29	202	**.264**	**.337**	**.350**	**687**	**109**	**78**	**56**	104	190			
NY	80	74	2	.519	11	46	31	577	561	5905	1277	194	59	**35**	516	632	36	155	.246	.318	.326	644	98	-4	-16	102	179			
StL	79	75	4	.513	12	45	32	588	545	5987	1262	181	50	14	**626**	638	42	164	.245	.331	.307	638	103	5	35	95	**234**			
Cle	77	77	3	.500	14	44	33	630	602	5853	1264	**233**	66	16	522	605	33	234	.250	.324	.331	655	97	21	-12	106	160			
Was	76	77	6	.497	14.5	**49**	28	536	543	5864	1238	170	60	12	535	597	50	165	.242	.320	.306	626	95	-30	-24	99	185			
Phi	36	117	1	.235	54.5	23	53	447	776	5604	1212	169	65	19	406	631	30	158	.242	.303	.313	616	96	-65	-40	95	151			
Total	625	—	—	—	—	354	261	4599	—	46749	10147	1540	552	144	4061	4705	318	1537	.248	.321	.324	645	—	—	—	—	1425	—	—	—

TEAM	CG	SHO	GR	SV	IP	H	HR	BB	SO	BR/9	ERA	AERA	OAV	OOB	PR	APR	PF	OSB	OCS	FA	E	WPB	DP	FW	PW	BW	BSW	DIF
Bos	76	**24**	103	16	1410.2	1221	**10**	463	584	11.0	2.48	112	.239	.307	55	45	98	134	124	**.972**	**183**	40	108	**3.0**	5.0	-2.4	—	8.4
Chi	73	20	140	15	1412.1	**1189**	14	**405**	644	**10.3**	**2.36**	**117**	**.236**	**.296**	**72**	**63**	98	**113**	118	.968	205	**28**	**134**	1.5	**7.0**	1.0	—	2.5
Det	81	8	126	13	1410.0	1254	12	578	531	12.1	2.97	96	.248	.333	-23	-18	101	202	113	.968	211	50	110	1.1	-2.0	**6.2**	—	4.6
NY	84	12	102	**17**	1428.0	1249	37	476	616	11.2	2.77	104	.244	.314	8	17	102	135	160	.967	219	32	119	.7	1.9	-1.8	—	2.2
StL	74	9	**141**	13	1443.2	1292	15	478	505	11.3	2.58	106	.248	.316	39	27	97	210	114	.963	248	38	120	-.9	3.0	3.9	—	-3.9
Cle	65	9	140	16	1410.0	1383	16	467	537	12.0	2.90	103	.264	.328	-13	15	106	167	123	.965	232	58	130	.0	1.7	-1.3	—	-.3
Was	85	11	107	7	1430.2	1271	14	490	**706**	11.3	2.67	104	.244	.314	25	18	99	178	125	.964	232	76	119	.2	2.0	-2.7	—	-.0
Phi	**94**	11	80	3	1343.2	1311	26	715	575	13.8	3.92	73	.267	.364	-163	-159	101	286	**184**	.951	314	70	126	-5.5	-17.6	-4.4	—	-13.0
Total	632	104	939	100	11289.0	—	—	—	—	11.6	2.82	—	.248	.321	—	—	—	—	—	.965	1844	392	966	—	—	—	—	—

BATTER-FIELDER WINS	BATTING AVERAGE	ON-BASE PERCENTAGE	SLUGGING AVERAGE	ON-BASE PLUS SLUGGING	ADJUSTED OPS	ADJUSTED BATTER RUNS
Speaker-Cle.......5.7	Speaker-Cle..........386	Speaker-Cle..........470	Speaker-Cle..........502	Speaker-Cle..........972	Speaker-Cle..........181	Speaker-Cle.........59.5
Cobb-Det............4.6	Cobb-Det..............371	Cobb-Det..............452	Jackson-Chi..........495	Cobb-Det..............944	Cobb-Det..............177	Cobb-Det.............54.6
Pratt-StL.............4.0	Jackson-Chi..........341	E.Collins-Chi.........405	Cobb-Det..............493	Jackson-Chi..........888	Jackson-Chi..........165	Jackson-Chi.........44.0
Jackson-Chi.......3.6	Strunk-Phi............316	Jackson-Chi..........393	Veach-Det.............433	Strunk-Phi............814	Strunk-Phi............152	Strunk-Phi...........35.8
Shotton-StL........3.0	Gardner-Bos.........308	Strunk-Phi............393	Baker-NY..............428	E.Collins-Chi.........802	E.Collins-Chi.........139	E.Collins-Chi........29.0

RUNS	HITS	DOUBLES	TRIPLES	HOME RUNS	TOTAL BASES	RUNS BATTED IN
Cobb-Det..............113	Speaker-Cle..........211	Speaker-Cle............41	Jackson-Chi............21	Pipp-NY..................12	Jackson-Chi..........293	Pratt-StL...............103
Graney-Cle...........106	Jackson-Chi..........202	Graney-Cle.............41	E.Collins-Chi...........17	Baker-NY................10	Speaker-Cle..........274	Pipp-NY..................93
Speaker-Cle..........102	Cobb-Det..............201	Jackson-Chi............40	Witt-Phi..................15	Schang-Phi...............7	Cobb-Det..............267	Veach-Det...............91
Shotton-StL.............97	Sisler-StL.............177	Pratt-StL.................35	Veach-Det...............15	Felsch-Chi................7	Veach-Det.............245	Speaker-Cle............79
Veach-Det...............92	Shotton-StL..........174	Veach-Det...............33				Jackson-Chi............78

BASES ON BALLS	STOLEN BASES	BASE STEALING RUNS	FIELDING RUNS-INFIELD	FIELDING RUNS-OUTFIELD	OUTFIELD ASSISTS	CATCHER CS PCT.
Shotton-StL...........110	Cobb-Det.................68	Cobb-Det...............6.6	Lajoie-Phi............26.7	Milan-Was............14.1	Milan-Was...............27	Nunamaker-NY....48.0
Graney-Cle...........102	Marsans-StL...........46	Hooper-Bos...........2.1	Vitt-Det.................26.3	Shanks-Was........13.5	Speaker-Cle............25	Schalk-Chi...........45.3
E.Collins-Chi...........86	Shotton-StL.............41	Schalk-Chi.............2.0	Lavan-StL.............25.9	Shotton-StL............8.1	Shotton-StL.............25	Thomas-Bos........42.9
Speaker-Cle............82	E.Collins-Chi...........40	Roth-Cle.................1.5	Pratt-StL..............19.6	Speaker-Cle...........5.6	Marsans-StL...........25	O'Neill-Cle...........41.7
Hooper-Bos.............80	Speaker-Cle............35	E.Collins-Chi..........1.5	McBride-Was.......13.6	Hooper-Bos...........5.2	Graney-Cle.............22	Henry-Was...........40.1

WINS	WINNING PCT.	WINS ABOVE TEAM	GAMES STARTED	COMPLETE GAMES	FEWEST HITS/GAME	FEWEST BB/GAME
Johnson-Was..........25	Cicotte-Chi............682	Shawkey-NY..........5.5	Ruth-Bos.................41	Johnson-Was..........36	Ruth-Bos.............6.40	Russell-Chi..........1.43
Shawkey-NY...........24	Ruth-Bos...............657	Bush-Phi................4.8	Coveleski-Det.........39	Myers-Phi...............31	Shawkey-NY........6.64	Cullop-NY............1.72
Ruth-Bos.................23	Coveleski-Det.......656	Myers-Phi..............4.3	Johnson-Was..........38	Bush-Phi.................25	Cicotte-Chi...........6.64	Coveleski-Det......1.75
Coveleski-Det.........21	Faber-Chi.............654	Coveleski-Det........4.0	Myers-Phi...............35	Ruth-Bos.................23	Bush-Phi..............6.97	Shore-Bos............1.95
Dauss-Det...............19	Shawkey-NY.........632	Johnson-Was.........3.6		Coveleski-Det.........22	Russell-Chi..........7.05	Johnson-Was.......2.00

STRIKEOUTS	STRIKEOUTS/GAME	GAMES	SAVES	BASE RUNNERS/9	ADJUSTED RELIEF RUNS	RELIEF RANKING
Johnson-Was........228	Johnson-Was.......5.55	Davenport-StL........59	Shawkey-NY.............8	Russell-Chi..........8.51		
Myers-Phi.............182	Williams-Chi.........5.54	Russell-Chi.............56	Russell-NY................6	Benz-Chi.............9.06		
Ruth-Bos...............170	Russell-NY...........5.46	Shawkey-NY...........53	Leonard-Bos.............6	Johnson-Was.......9.28		
Bush-Phi...............157	Harper-Was.........5.37	Gallia-Was.............49	Cicotte-Chi................5	Shawkey-NY........9.47		
Harper-Was..........149	Myers-Phi............5.20		Bagby-Cle.................5	Coveleski-Det......9.77		

INNINGS PITCHED	OPPONENTS' AVG.	OPPONENTS' OBP	EARNED RUN AVERAGE	ADJUSTED ERA	ADJUSTED STARTER RUNS	PITCHER WINS
Johnson-Was.....369.2	Ruth-Bos...............201	Russell-Chi...........254	Ruth-Bos.............1.75	Ruth-Bos...............158	Ruth-Bos.............35.1	**Ruth-Bos.............5.7**
Coveleski-Det....324.1	Shawkey-NY.........209	Johnson-Was........270	Cicotte-Chi...........1.78	Cicotte-Chi............155	Johnson-Was........34.9	**Johnson-Was.....5.2**
Ruth-Bos............323.2	Cicotte-Chi............218	Shawkey-NY.........273	Johnson-Was.......1.90	Johnson-Was........147	Coveleski-Det......26.2	**Shawkey-NY......3.4**
Myers-Phi..........315.0	Bush-Phi...............219	Ruth-Bos...............280	Coveleski-Det......1.97	Coveleski-Det.......145	Shawkey-NY.........23.6	**Coveleski-Det....3.1**
Davenport-StL...290.2	Johnson-Was........220	Coveleski-Det.......282	Faber-Chi.............2.02	Cullop-NY.............141	Cicotte-Chi...........18.3	**Mays-Bos............2.8**

Ruth Rises to the Occasion

Could Connie Mack's Athletics get worse? At 36-117, they set an AL record for losses and posted the worst team winning percentage of the twentieth century. Philadelphia dropped 20 in a row at one point. So many teams feasted on Philadelphia's misery that seventh-place Washington finished just one game under .500, and the Senators had even been in first place during May. Jack Nabors of the A's beat defending world champion Boston on May 22 for his first major league win; he lost his next 19 decisions and never won again. Nap Lajoie, 41, had an undignified finish to a great career, batting .246 for the pathetic A's.

On the other side of the pennant race, the Red Sox, White Sox, and Tigers clawed at each other into September. Despite trading Tris Speaker and Smokey Joe Wood to Cleveland in salary disputes, Boston held it together. While their attack was below par, Boston's five starters were extremely productive; Babe Ruth led the AL in ERA and shutouts.

Chicago had the better club on paper, featuring Eddie Collins and Joe Jackson, but lacked pitching depth (although Chisox righty Eddie Cicotte, at 15-7, led the loop in winning percentage and his 1.78 ERA was second). Detroit once again rode Ty Cobb's back into contention, as Sam Crawford began to slow up at age 36. Two future stars enjoyed excellent first full seasons. Stan Coveleski was 16-13 for Cleveland, while first baseman George Sisler won hearts in St. Louis. Both the Indians and Browns saw huge attendance gains as they began rebuilding. League attendance rose 42 percent.

Down the stretch, the Red Sox grabbed the flag with seven straight road victories against the White Sox, Tigers, and Indians. Boston was favored to win the World Series against Brooklyn, but after three one-run decisions—including a complete-game, 14-inning, 2-1 victory from Ruth in Game 2—the Red Sox barely led, two games to one. However, the Red Sox knocked out Rube Marquard and Jeff Pfeffer the next two games to repeat as champions.

1915 NATIONAL LEAGUE

TEAM	W	L	T	PCT	GB	HW	HL	R	OR	PA	H	2B	3B	HR	BB	SO	HB	SH	AVG	OBP	SLG	OPS	AOPS	BR	ABR	PF	SB	CS	BSA	BSR
Phi	90	62	1	.592	—	49	27	589	**463**	5591	1216	202	39	**58**	460	600	34	181	.247	.316	.340	**656**	104	**35**	29	101	121	113	52	-13
Bos	83	69	5	.546	7	49	27	582	545	5869	1219	**231**	57	17	**549**	620	**56**	**194**	.240	**.321**	.319	640	**105**	22	**50**	96	121	98	55	-8
Bro	80	72	2	.526	10	**51**	26	536	560	5635	1268	165	75	14	313	**496**	27	175	.248	.295	.317	612	89	-61	-70	102	131	126	51	-15
Chi	73	80	3	.477	17.5	42	34	570	620	5730	1246	212	66	53	393	639	41	182	.244	.303	**.342**	645	102	5	4	100	166	124	57	-7
Pit	73	81	2	.474	18	40	37	557	520	5743	1259	197	91	24	419	656	49	162	.246	.309	.334	643	102	7	15	99	**182**	111	**62**	**1**
StL	72	81	4	.471	18.5	42	36	**590**	601	5780	1297	159	**92**	20	457	658	42	175	**.254**	.320	.333	653	104	28	27	100	162	144	53	-15
Cin	71	83	6	.461	20	39	37	516	585	5836	**1323**	194	84	15	360	512	53	192	.253	.308	.331	639	98	-7	-17	102	156	142	52	-15
NY	69	83	3	.454	21	37	38	582	628	5703	1312	195	68	24	315	547	48	122	.251	.300	.329	629	103	-28	5	94	155	137	53	-14
Total	624	—	—	—	—	349	262	4522	—	45887	10140	1555	572	225	3266	4728	350	1383	.248	.309	.331	640	—	—	—	—	1194	995	55	-86

TEAM	CG	SHO	GR	SV	IP	H	HR	BB	SO	BR/9	ERA	AERA	OAV	OOB	PR	APR	PF	OSB	OCS	FA	E	WPB	DP	FW	PW	BW	BSW	DIF
Phi	**98**	**20**	67	8	1374.1	**1161**	26	342	652	**10.0**	**2.17**	**126**	**.234**	**.288**	**87**	**85**	100	134	*117*	**.966**	216	33	99	.8	**9.4**	3.2	-.3	.8
Bos	95	17	78	**13**	1405.2	1257	23	366	630	10.7	2.57	100	.246	.302	27	1	94	**110**	*124*	**.966**	**213**	34	115	**1.4**	.1	**5.6**	.3	-.4
Bro	87	16	91	8	1389.2	1252	29	473	499	11.6	2.66	104	.245	.318	14	17	101	172	*124*	.963	238	49	96	-.5	1.9	-7.8	-.5	10.9
Chi	71	18	**119**	8	1399.0	1272	28	480	**657**	11.6	3.11	89	.247	.316	-57	-54	101	151	***130***	.958	268	58	94	-2.3	-6.0	.4	.4	4.0
Pit	91	18	91	11	1380.0	1229	**21**	384	544	10.8	2.60	105	.246	.304	23	19	99	164	*126*	**.966**	214	**31**	100	1.2	2.1	1.7	**1.3**	-10.3
StL	79	13	103	9	1400.2	1320	30	402	538	11.3	2.89	96	.256	.314	-22	-17	101	133	*129*	.964	235	34	109	-.0	-1.9	3.0	-.5	-5.1
Cin	80	19	113	12	1432.1	1304	28	497	572	11.6	2.84	101	.250	.321	-15	1	104	163	*125*	**.966**	222	36	**148**	1.1	.1	-1.9	-.5	-4.9
NY	78	15	105	9	1385.0	1350	40	**325**	637	11.2	3.11	82	.260	.308	-57	-92	93	167	*120*	.960	256	56	119	-1.6	-10.2	.6	-.4	4.7
Total	679	136	767	78	11166.2	—	—	—	—	11.1	2.75	—	.248	.309	—	—	—	—	—	.964	1862	331	880	—	—	—	—	—

BATTER-FIELDER WINS	BATTING AVERAGE	ON-BASE PERCENTAGE	SLUGGING AVERAGE	ON-BASE PLUS SLUGGING	ADJUSTED OPS	ADJUSTED BATTER RUNS
Cravath-Phi........5.2	Doyle-NY..............320	Cravath-Phi...........393	Cravath-Phi...........510	Cravath-Phi...........902	Cravath-Phi...........170	Cravath-Phi..........47.3
Luderus-Phi........4.0	Luderus-Phi..........315	Luderus-Phi..........376	Luderus-Phi..........457	Luderus-Phi..........833	Doyle-NY..............150	Doyle-NY.............33.6
Herzog-Cin.........4.0	Griffith-Cin...........307	Daubert-Bro..........369	Long-StL...............446	Hinchman-Pit........807	Luderus-Phi..........150	Hinchman-Pit.......31.6
Snyder-StL.........3.8	Hinchman-Pit........307	Hinchman-Pit........368	Saier-Chi..............445	Doyle-NY..............799	Hinchman-Pit........146	Luderus-Phi.........30.7
Fletcher-NY........3.3	Daubert-Bro..........301	Doyle-NY..............358	Doyle-NY..............442	Saier-Chi..............795	Saier-Chi..............140	Saier-Chi..............24.7
RUNS	**HITS**	**DOUBLES**	**TRIPLES**	**HOME RUNS**	**TOTAL BASES**	**RUNS BATTED IN**
Cravath-Phi............89	Doyle-NY..............189	Doyle-NY................40	Long-StL.................25	Cravath-Phi.............24	Cravath-Phi...........266	Cravath-Phi...........115
Doyle-NY..................86	Griffith-Cin...........179	Luderus-Phi............36	H.Wagner-Pit..........17	Williams-Chi............13	Doyle-NY..............261	Magee-Bos.............87
Bancroft-Phi............85	Hinchman-Pit........177	Saier-Chi.................35	Griffith-Cin..............16	Schulte-Chi..............12	Griffith-Cin...........254	Griffith-Cin..............85
Burns-NY..................83	Groh-Cin...............170	Smith-Bos................34	Hinchman-Pit..........14	Saier-Chi.................11	Hinchman-Pit........253	H.Wagner-Pit..........78
O'Mara-Bro.............77	Burns-NY..............169	Magee-Bos.............34	Burns-NY.................14	Becker-Phi..............11	H.Wagner-Pit........239	Hinchman-Pit..........77
BASES ON BALLS	**STOLEN BASES**	**BASE STEALING RUNS**	**FIELDING RUNS-INFIELD**	**FIELDING RUNS-OUTFIELD**	**OUTFIELD ASSISTS**	**CATCHER CS PCT.**
Cravath-Phi............86	Carey-Pit.................36	Saier-Chi................3.2	Fletcher-NY.........34.8	Carey-Pit...............11.1	Cravath-Phi.............28	Gowdy-Bos............54.9
Bancroft-Phi............77	Herzog-Cin..............35	Bresnahan-Chi.......3.1	Herzog-Cin..........30.3	Wilson-StL............10.6	Schulte-Chi.............24	Snyder-StL...........50.2
Viox-Pit....................75	Saier-Chi.................29	Baird-Pit.................2.2	Maranville-Bos.....20.0	Z.Wheat-Bro..........9.1	Myers-Bro...............23	Killefer-Phi...........48.4
Huggins-StL............74	Baird-Pit..................29	Herzog-Cin.............2.1	Cutshaw-Bro........13.8	Cravath-Phi.............8.7	Carey-Pit.................21	Gibson-Pit.............43.0
Smith-Bos................67	Cutshaw-Bro...........28	Carey-Pit................2.0	Groh-Cin..............11.6	Magee-Bos..............6.3	Wilson-StL..............20	McCarty-Bro..........42.8
WINS	**WINNING PCT.**	**WINS ABOVE TEAM**	**GAMES STARTED**	**COMPLETE GAMES**	**FEWEST HITS/GAME**	**FEWEST BB/GAME**
Alexander-Phi.........31	Alexander-Phi.......756	Alexander-Phi.........9.8	Rudolph-Bos...........43	Alexander-Phi.........36	Alexander-Phi......6.05	Mathewson-NY.......97
Rudolph-Bos...........22	Toney-Cin.............739	Mamaux-Pit...........7.7	Alexander-Phi.........42	Rudolph-Bos...........30	Toney-Cin............6.47	Humphries-Chi.....1.21
Mayer-Phi...............21	Mamaux-Pit..........724	Toney-Cin..............6.4	Tesreau-NY.............39	Pfeffer-Bro..............26	Mamaux-Pit.........6.51	Adams-Pit............1.25
Mamaux-Pit............21	Vaughn-Chi...........625	Vaughn-Chi............5.3	Doak-StL.................36	Harmon-Pit.............25	Hughes-Bos.........6.68	Alexander-Phi......1.53
Vaughn-Chi.............20	Coombs-Bro..........600	Tesreau-NY............3.5		Tesreau-NY.............24	Zabel-Chi.............6.85	Rudolph-Bos.........1.69
STRIKEOUTS	**STRIKEOUTS/GAME**	**GAMES**	**SAVES**	**BASE RUNNERS/9**	**ADJUSTED RELIEF RUNS**	**RELIEF RANKING**
Alexander-Phi.......241	Alexander-Phi......5.76	Hughes-Bos............50	Hughes-Bos..............9	Alexander-Phi......7.82		
Tesreau-NY...........176	Hughes-Bos.........5.49	Dale-Cin..................49	Benton-Cin-NY.........5	Hughes-Bos.........8.89		
Hughes-Bos...........171	Mamaux-Pit.........5.44	Alexander-Phi.........49	Lavender-Chi............4	Tesreau-NY..........9.26		
Mamaux-Pit...........152	Douglas-Cin-Br-Chi.5.26	Schneider-Cin.........48	Cooper-Pit................4	Toney-Cin............9.54		
Vaughn-Chi...........148	Tesreau-NY..........5.18	Sallee-StL...............46		Nehf-Bos.............9.65		
INNINGS PITCHED	**OPPONENTS' AVG.**	**OPPONENTS' OBP**	**EARNED RUN AVERAGE**	**ADJUSTED ERA**	**ADJUSTED STARTER RUNS**	**PITCHER WINS**
Alexander-Phi....376.1	Alexander-Phi.......191	Alexander-Phi.......234	Alexander-Phi......1.22	Alexander-Phi.......224	Alexander-Phi......58.3	**Alexander-Phi....7.5**
Rudolph-Bos......341.1	Toney-Cin.............207	Hughes-Bos...........265	Toney-Cin.............1.58	Toney-Cin.............181	Toney-Cin............32.1	**Toney-Cin...........3.0**
Tesreau-NY........306.0	Mamaux-Pit..........208	Tesreau-NY...........269	Mamaux-Pit..........2.04	Mamaux-Pit...........134	Pfeffer-Bro...........21.6	**Pfeffer-Bro.........2.9**
Dale-Cin............296.2	Hughes-Bos..........213	Toney-Cin..............278	Pfeffer-Bro...........2.10	Pfeffer-Bro............132	Mamaux-Pit.........21.1	**Mayer-Phi...........2.5**
Pfeffer-Bro.........291.2	Tesreau-NY...........215	Adams-Pit.............280	Hughes-Bos.........2.12	Hughes-Bos..........122	Hughes-Bos.........16.0	**Mamaux-Pit.........2.0**

The Tightest Race Ever

On the field, the season was thrilling. Eddie Plank and Chief Bender escaped from Connie Mack after pitching the A's to the AL pennant a year earlier. Frank Allen of Pittsburgh pitched the first of four FL no-hitters. The Feds also outhomered the two established leagues in 1914–15, clubbing 545 as the NL hit 492 and the AL just 308. Dutch Zwilling, who would hit one career homer against non-FL pitching, smacked 29 in two years as the new league's home run king. Chicago, St. Louis, and Pittsburgh finished the year 1-2-3 as the Whales took the tightest race in major league history by exactly one percentage point; the Rebels were third by only .004.

Walter Johnson was the Whale that got away, even though Chicago Whales player-manager Joe Tinker signed Johnson to a three-year deal worth $58,500. Despite AL President Ban Johnson's assertion that The Big Train was "damaged goods," Washington owner Clark Griffith knew better. Aided by money from other AL clubs, he lured back his prized pitcher and later signed Johnson to a five-year, $80,000 contract, dimming the FL's long-term chances.

In January 1915 the FL sued the other two leagues for violating the Sherman Antitrust Act. They chose the U.S. District Court of Judge Kenesaw Mountain Landis, a noted trustbuster, as the venue. That proved to be as big a mistake as competing against two established leagues in a time of uncertainty because of the war in Europe. Landis, an ardent Cubs fan, effectively killed the Federal League by sitting on the case.

Absent a legal ruling, the competing leagues negotiated a complicated settlement that resulted in FL owners in St. Louis and Chicago buying the Browns and Cubs, bringing into the NL what would become Wrigley Field. The agreement paid off some—but not all—FL owners. FL players could return, but only eight former Feds later appeared in as many as 500 big league games.

1915 AMERICAN LEAGUE

TEAM	W	L	T	PCT	GB	HW	HL	R	OR	PA	H	2B	3B	HR	BB	SO	HB	SH	AVG	OBP	SLG	OPS	AOPS	BR	ABR	PF	SB	CS	BSA	BSR
Bos	101	50	4	.669	—	**55**	20	669	499	5865	1308	202	76	14	527	**476**	49	265	.260	.336	.339	675	110	48	69	97	118	117	50	-15
Det	100	54	2	.649	2.5	51	26	**778**	597	6046	**1372**	**207**	94	23	**681**	527	35	202	**.268**	**.357**	**.358**	**715**	**114**	**135**	**98**	105	**241**	146	62	2
Chi	93	61	1	.604	9.5	54	24	717	509	5838	1269	163	**102**	25	583	575	**71**	**270**	.258	.345	.348	693	110	82	62	103	233	183	56	-13
Was	85	68	2	.556	17	50	29	569	**491**	5719	1225	152	79	12	458	541	45	187	.244	.312	.312	624	90	-55	-65	102	186	106	**64**	**4**
NY	69	83	2	.454	32.5	37	43	584	588	5765	1162	167	50	**31**	570	669	44	169	.233	.317	.305	622	91	-45	-44	100	198	133	60	-3
StL	63	91	5	.409	39.5	35	38	522	680	5800	1255	166	65	19	472	765	43	173	.246	.315	.315	630	98	-46	-23	96	202	160	56	-12
Cle	57	95	2	.375	44.5	27	50	539	670	5738	1210	169	79	20	490	681	37	177	.240	.312	.317	629	91	-45	-55	102	138	117	54	-11
Phi	43	109	2	.283	58.5	19	53	545	889	5708	1204	183	72	16	436	634	54	137	.237	.304	.311	615	92	-75	-56	97	127	89	59	-3
Total	621	—	—	—	—	328	283	4923	—	46479	10005	1409	617	160	4217	4868	378	1580	.248	.325	.326	651	—	—	—	—	1443	1051	58	-50

TEAM	CG	SHO	GR	SV	IP	H	HR	BB	SO	BR/9	ERA	AERA	OAV	OOB	PR	APR	PF	OSB	OCS	FA	E	WPB	DP	FW	PW	BW	BSW	DIF
Bos	81	19	99	15	1397.0	1164	18	446	634	10.7	2.39	116	**.231**	.300	84	62	95	157	*125*	.964	226	51	95	2.5	6.6	7.3	-.9	10.1
Det	86	10	109	**19**	1413.1	1259	14	492	550	11.5	2.86	106	.243	.316	11	24	103	179	*121*	.961	258	62	107	.5	2.5	**10.4**	.9	8.7
Chi	91	16	91	9	1401.0	1242	14	**350**	635	**10.4**	2.43	122	.241	**.294**	78	83	101	**101**	*100*	.965	222	**38**	95	2.7	8.8	6.6	-.7	-1.4
Was	87	**21**	99	13	1393.2	**1161**	**12**	455	**715**	10.7	**2.31**	**129**	.232	.302	**97**	**101**	101	156	*123*	.964	230	50	101	2.2	**10.7**	-6.9	**1.1**	1.4
NY	**101**	12	66	1	1382.2	1272	41	517	559	12.0	3.06	96	.254	.329	-20	-20	100	188	*131*	**.966**	**217**	**38**	118	**2.9**	-2.1	-4.7	.4	-3.5
StL	76	6	131	6	1403.0	1256	21	612	566	12.4	3.04	94	.249	.338	-17	-32	98	196	*141*	.949	336	69	**144**	-4.3	-3.4	-2.4	-.6	-3.2
Cle	62	11	**138**	10	1372.0	1287	18	518	610	12.0	3.13	97	.256	.329	-30	-13	104	170	*135*	.957	280	54	82	-1.2	-1.4	-5.8	-.5	-10.1
Phi	78	6	95	2	1348.1	1358	22	827	588	15.0	4.29	68	.278	.388	-204	-207	100	295	***175***	.947	338	85	118	-5.0	-22.0	-5.9	.4	-.4
Total	662	101	828	75	11111.0	—	—	—	—	11.8	2.93	—	.248	.325	—	—	—	—	—	.959	2107	447	860	—	—	—	—	—

BATTER-FIELDER WINS	BATTING AVERAGE	ON-BASE PERCENTAGE	SLUGGING AVERAGE	ON-BASE PLUS SLUGGING	ADJUSTED OPS	ADJUSTED BATTER RUNS
E.Collins-Chi 6.6	Cobb-Det 369	Cobb-Det 486	Fournier-Chi..........491	Cobb-Det 973	Cobb-Det 182	Cobb-Det 66.6
Cobb-Det............ 5.7	E.Collins-Chi.........332	E.Collins-Chi.........460	Cobb-Det 487	Fournier-Chi..........920	Fournier-Chi..........170	E.Collins-Chi........49.8
Speaker-Bos 3.6	Fournier-Chi..........322	Fournier-Chi..........429	Kavanagh-Det.......452	E.Collins-Chi.........896	E.Collins-Chi.........163	Speaker-Bos........39.2
Fournier-Chi 3.6	Speaker-Bos.........322	Speaker-Bos.........416	J.Jackson-Cle-Chi.....445	J.Jackson-Cle-Chi.....830	Speaker-Bos.........152	Fournier-Chi.........38.4
Chapman-Cle 3.4	McInnis-Phi...........314	Shotton-StL...........409	Roth-Chi-Cle.........438	Speaker-Bos.........827	J.Jackson-Cle-Chi.....145	Shotton-StL..........32.3
RUNS	**HITS**	**DOUBLES**	**TRIPLES**	**HOME RUNS**	**TOTAL BASES**	**RUNS BATTED IN**
Cobb-Det 144	Cobb-Det 208	Veach-Det..............40	Crawford-Det 19	Roth-Chi-Cle............7	Cobb-Det 274	Veach-Det............112
E.Collins-Chi.........118	Crawford-Det 183	Pratt-StL 31	Fournier-Chi............18	Oldring-Phi...............6	Crawford-Det 264	Crawford-Det 112
Vitt-Det.................116	Veach-Det.............178	Lewis-Bos 31	Roth-Chi-Cle...........17		Veach-Det.............247	Cobb-Det 99
Speaker-Bos.........108	Speaker-Bos.........176	Crawford-Det 31	S.Collins-Chi...........17		Pratt-StL 237	S.Collins-Chi...........85
Chapman-Cle 101	Pratt-StL 175	Cobb-Det 31	Chapman-Cle 17		E.Collins-Chi.........227	J.Jackson-Cle-Chi.......81
BASES ON BALLS	**STOLEN BASES**	**BASE STEALING RUNS**	**FIELDING RUNS-INFIELD**	**FIELDING RUNS-OUTFIELD**	**OUTFIELD ASSISTS**	**CATCHER CS PCT.**
E.Collins-Chi.........119	Cobb-Det 96	Cobb-Det 7.8	Boone-NY 20.5	Strunk-Phi............11.1	T.Walker-StL 27	Schalk-Chi 51.7
Shotton-StL...........118	Maisel-NY 51	Maisel-NY 7.0	Lajoie-Phi............17.0	Hooper-Bos 8.7	Strunk-Phi...............24	Agnew-StL 46.8
Cobb-Det 118	E.Collins-Chi...........46	Moeller-Was...........3.5	Pratt-StL 16.0	T.Walker-StL 8.5	Hooper-Bos 23	O'Neill-Cle 44.6
Bush-Det...............118	Shotton-StL............43	Schang-Phi 2.9	Vitt-Det................12.9	Speaker-Bos..........7.8	Cobb-Det 22	Henry-Was...........44.5
Hooper-Bos 89	C.Milan-Was 40	Chapman-Cle 2.7	E.Collins-Chi........11.3	Shanks-Was 6.6	Speaker-Bos...........21	Thomas-Bos 43.9
WINS	**WINNING PCT.**	**WINS ABOVE TEAM**	**GAMES STARTED**	**COMPLETE GAMES**	**FEWEST HITS/GAME**	**FEWEST BB/GAME**
Johnson-Was..........27	Wood-Bos.............750	Johnson-Was.........6.6	Johnson-Was..........39	Johnson-Was..........35	Leonard-Bos........6.38	Johnson-Was.......1.50
Scott-Chi.................24	Shore-Bos.............704	Fisher-NY 5.1	Coveleski-Det 38	Caldwell-NY............31	Ruth-Bos.............6.86	Ayers-Was 1.62
Faber-Chi................24	Foster-Bos 704	Scott-Chi...............4.4	Scott-Chi.................35	Dauss-Det...............27	Wood-Bos...........6.86	Benz-Chi..............1.62
Dauss-Det...............24	Ruth-Bos...............692	Morton-Cle............4.2	Dauss-Det...............35	Scott-Chi.................23	Johnson-Was.......6.90	Russell-Chi 1.84
Coveleski-Det 22	Scott-Chi...............686	Caldwell-NY 3.5	Caldwell-NY............35	Dubuc-Det 22	Morton-Cle..........7.09	Cicotte-Chi..........1.93
STRIKEOUTS	**STRIKEOUTS/GAME**	**GAMES**	**SAVES**	**BASE RUNNERS/9**	**ADJUSTED RELIEF RUNS**	**RELIEF RANKING**
Johnson-Was........203	Leonard-Bos........5.69	Faber-Chi...............50	Mays-Bos.................7	Johnson-Was.......8.90		
Faber-Chi..............182	Mitchell-Cle..........5.68	Coveleski-Det 50		Morton-Cle...........9.41		
Wyckoff-Phi...........157	Faber-Chi.............5.47	Scott-Chi.................48		Wood-Bos............9.44		
Coveleski-Det 150	Johnson-Was.......5.43	Jones-Cle 48		Ayers-Was 9.50		
Mitchell-Cle...........149	Lowdermilk-StL-Det5.32			Benz-Chi.............9.63		
INNINGS PITCHED	**OPPONENTS' AVG.**	**OPPONENTS' OBP**	**EARNED RUN AVERAGE**	**ADJUSTED ERA**	**ADJUSTED STARTER RUNS**	**PITCHER WINS**
Johnson-Was.....336.2	Leonard-Bos.........208	Johnson-Was........260	Wood-Bos............1.49	Johnson-Was........191	Johnson-Was.......51.1	**Johnson-Was 7.4**
Coveleski-Det 312.2	Ruth-Bos...............212	Morton-Cle............268	Johnson-Was.......1.55	Wood-Bos.............186	Scott-Chi.............27.6	**Wood-Bos 3.9**
Dauss-Det..........309.2	Johnson-Was........214	Wood-Bos.............275	Shore-Bos............1.64	Shore-Bos.............169	Shore-Bos............27.2	**Scott-Chi............ 2.9**
Caldwell-NY.......305.0	Morton-Cle............216	Benz-Chi...............276	Scott-Chi.............2.03	Scott-Chi...............146	Morton-Cle...........25.0	**Foster-Bos 2.9**
Faber-Chi...........299.2	Wood-Bos..............216	Ayers-Was 276	Fisher-NY 2.11	Morton-Cle............142	Wood-Bos............24.9	**Ruth-Bos............ 2.8**

Alexander the Greatest

With Grover Cleveland Alexander dominating on the hill, the Phillies found themselves in first place in mid-July. Withstanding challenges from Boston and Brooklyn down the stretch, Philadelphia won the pennant by 7 games. Playing in a great home run park, the Phillies again paced the league in long balls; Gavvy Cravath slugged an unheard-of 24. Amazingly, pitching half his games in the Baker Bowl, Alexander allowed just *three* taters in 376 innings and posted a 1.22 ERA, the best mark in the majors until 1968.

The level of parity between NL teams was even greater in 1915. Pitchers had made adjustments to the lively ball, and the NL's average continued its drop to .248, the lowest since 1909. Only 21 games separated Philadelphia from last-place New York. The Giants' ignominious tumble to the basement was hell on manager John McGraw and veteran pitcher Christy Mathewson; again Matty was the league's stingiest pitcher with walks, but an 8-14 record marked his last full season. Meanwhile, sixth-place St. Louis saw a flash of better times ahead with the debut of infielder Rogers Hornsby.

Overall league attendance rose 42 percent, with gains of over 100 percent in Brooklyn, Philadelphia, and—surprisingly—seventh-place Cincinnati. Defending world champion Boston finished second, but attendance began a four-year decline just as the club opened cavernous Braves Field (the center-field fence was 550 feet from home plate). Across town, the AL's Red Sox capped off a big year by edging the Phillies in a five-game World Series in which four of the games were settled by one run and the other by two.

Two teammates from the NL's first Chicago club died. Pitcher and sporting goods entrepreneur Al Spalding passed away in San Diego at age 65. Ross Barnes, the National League's inaugural batting champion in 1876, died in Chicago.

1915 FEDERAL LEAGUE

TEAM	W	L	T	PCT	GB	HW	HL	R	OR	PA	H	2B	3B	HR	BB	SO	HB	SH	AVG	OBP	SLG	OPS	AOPS	BR	ABR	PF	SB	CS	BSA	BSR
Chi	86	66	3	.566	—	44	32	640	538	5784	1320	185	77	**50**	444	590	30	177	.257	.320	.352	672	101	-113	-82	94	161			
StL	87	67	5	.565	—	43	34	634	527	5990	1344	199	**81**	23	**576**	**502**	36	**233**	.261	**.340**	.345	685	94	-71	-98	105	195			
Pit	86	67	3	.562	0.5	45	31	592	**524**	5728	1318	180	80	20	448	561	38	202	.262	.326	.341	667	94	-113	-109	99	224			
KC	81	72	0	.529	5.5	**46**	31	547	551	5551	1206	200	66	28	368	503	46	200	.244	.303	.329	632	87	-185	-168	96	144			
New	80	72	3	.526	6	40	39	585	562	5771	1283	**210**	80	17	438	550	36	200	.252	.315	.334	649	93	-151	-123	94	184			
Buf	74	78	1	.487	12	37	40	574	634	5620	1261	193	68	40	420	587	19	116	.249	.309	.338	647	85	-161	-170	102	184			
Bro	70	82	1	.461	16	34	40	**647**	673	5707	**1348**	205	75	36	473	654	**47**	152	**.268**	.336	**.360**	**696**	**103**	**-57**	**-53**	99	**249**			
Bal	47	107	0	.305	40	24	51	550	760	5744	1235	196	53	36	470	641	37	177	.244	.313	.325	638	82	-168	-181	103	128			
Total	619	—	—	—	—	313	298	4769	—	45895	10315	1568	580	250	3637	4588	289	1457	.255	.320	.340	661	—	—	—	—	1469	—	—	—

TEAM	CG	SHO	GR	SV	IP	H	HR	BB	SO	BR/9	ERA	AERA	OAV	OOB	PR	APR	PF	OSB	OCS	FA	E	WPB	DP	FW	PW	BW	BSW	DIF
Chi	97	21	68	10	1397.2	1232	34	402	576	**10.7**	2.64	95	**.240**	**.299**	14	-22	92	164	*129*	.964	233	50	102	.4	-2.4	-8.8	—	20.8
StL	94	**24**	88	9	1426.0	1267	22	396	**698**	**10.7**	2.73	**105**	.243	.300	-1	**21**	105	182	*142*	.967	212	47	111	2.0	**2.3**	-10.5	—	16.3
Pit	88	16	88	12	1382.1	1273	36	441	517	11.4	2.79	97	.253	.317	-10	-13	99	**152**	*149*	**.971**	**182**	40	98	**3.5**	-1.4	-11.7	—	19.1
KC	95	16	75	11	1359.0	**1210**	29	**390**	526	10.8	2.82	93	.242	.301	-14	-31	96	192	*150*	.962	246	53	96	-.5	-3.3	-18.1	—	26.5
New	**100**	16	76	7	1406.2	1308	**15**	453	581	11.6	**2.60**	98	.253	.319	**19**	-8	94	154	*150*	.963	239	39	124	.0	-.9	-13.2	—	18.0
Buf	79	14	97	11	1360.0	1271	35	553	594	12.3	3.38	83	.254	.331	-99	-86	103	234	***166***	.964	232	48	112	.3	-9.3	-18.3	—	25.3
Bro	78	10	**99**	**16**	1355.2	1299	27	536	467	12.3	3.37	81	.258	.332	-96	-98	100	211	*148*	.955	290	60	103	-3.1	-10.5	**-5.7**	—	13.4
Bal	85	5	92	7	1360.1	1455	52	466	570	13.0	3.96	72	.284	.349	-186	-157	105	180	*147*	.957	273	**37**	**140**	-2.0	-16.9	-19.5	—	8.4
Total	716	122	683	83	11047.2	—	—	—	—	11.6	3.03	—	.255	.320	—	—	—	—	—	.963	1907	374	886	—	—	—	—	—

BATTER-FIELDER WINS	BATTING AVERAGE	ON-BASE PERCENTAGE	SLUGGING AVERAGE	ON-BASE PLUS SLUGGING	ADJUSTED OPS	ADJUSTED BATTER RUNS
Kauff-Bro 4.7	Kauff-Bro 342	Kauff-Bro 446	Kauff-Bro 509	Kauff-Bro 955	Kauff-Bro 170	Kauff-Bro 43.0
Rariden-New 4.3	Fischer-Chi 329	W.Miller-StL 400	Konetchy-Pit 483	Konetchy-Pit 846	Konetchy-Pit 138	Wilson-Chi 21.8
Wilson-Chi 2.6	Magee-Bro 323	Borton-StL 395	Chase-Buf 471	Evans-Bro-Bal 818	Zwilling-Chi 135	Konetchy-Pit 17.9
Cooper-Bro 2.0	Konetchy-Pit 314	Evans-Bro-Bal 392	Fischer-Chi 449	Zwilling-Chi 808	Mann-Chi 131	Zwilling-Chi 17.3
Louden-Buf 1.7	Flack-Chi 314	Cooper-Bro 388	Zwilling-Chi 442	Mann-Chi 795	Flack-Chi 129	Evans-Bro-Bal 16.1
RUNS	**HITS**	**DOUBLES**	**TRIPLES**	**HOME RUNS**	**TOTAL BASES**	**RUNS BATTED IN**
Borton-StL 97	Tobin-StL 184	Evans-Bro-Bal 34	Mann-Chi 19	Chase-Buf 17	Konetchy-Pit 278	Zwilling-Chi 94
Berghammer-Pit 96	Konetchy-Pit 181	Zwilling-Chi 32	Konetchy-Pit 18	Zwilling-Chi 13	Chase-Buf 267	Konetchy-Pit 93
Evans-Bro-Bal 94	Evans-Bro-Bal 171	Konetchy-Pit 31	Kelly-Pit 17	Kauff-Bro 12	Tobin-StL 254	Chase-Buf 89
Tobin-StL 92	Kauff-Bro 165	Chase-Buf 31	Gilmore-KC 15	Konetchy-Pit 10	Kauff-Bro 246	Kauff-Bro 83
Kauff-Bro 92	Chase-Buf 165			Walsh-Bal-StL 9	Zwilling-Chi 242	Borton-StL 83
BASES ON BALLS	**STOLEN BASES**	**BASE STEALING RUNS**	**FIELDING RUNS-INFIELD**	**FIELDING RUNS-OUTFIELD**	**OUTFIELD ASSISTS**	**CATCHER CS PCT.**
Borton-StL 92	Kauff-Bro 55		Doolan-Bal-Chi 31.0	Kelly-Pit 13.4	Kauff-Bro 32	Rariden-New 50.4
Kauff-Bro 85	Mowrey-Pit 40		Johnson-StL 16.4	Cooper-Bro 12.4	Kelly-Pit 27	Berry-Pit 48.6
Berghammer-Pit 83	Kelly-Pit 38		Louden-Buf 11.8	Kauff-Bro 11.2	Cooper-Bro 26	Owens-Bal 47.6
W.Miller-StL 79	Flack-Chi 37		Perring-KC 10.9	Mann-Chi 5.3	Flack-Chi 24	Fischer-Chi 46.4
	Magee-Bro 34		Halt-Bro 5.9	Gilmore-KC 5.1	Chadbourne-KC 24	Easterly-KC 43.0
WINS	**WINNING PCT.**	**WINS ABOVE TEAM**	**GAMES STARTED**	**COMPLETE GAMES**	**FEWEST HITS/GAME**	**FEWEST BB/GAME**
McConnell-Chi 25	McConnell-Chi 714	McConnell-Chi 7.1	Davenport-StL 46	Davenport-StL 30	Davenport-StL 6.88	Plank-StL 1.81
Allen-Pit 23	Brown-Chi 680	Reulbach-New 5.7	Schulz-Buf 38	Hendrix-Chi 26	Main-KC 7.08	Bender-Bal 1.87
Davenport-StL 22	Reulbach-New 677	Cullop-KC 5.7	Allen-Pit 37	Schulz-Buf 25	Plank-StL 7.11	Hearn-Pit 1.90
Cullop-KC 22	Cullop-KC 667	Schulz-Buf 4.7	Cullop-KC 36	Allen-Pit 24	Brown-Chi 7.20	Cullop-KC 1.99
	Plank-StL 656	Plank-StL 4.0	McConnell-Chi 35		Anderson-Buf 7.20	Quinn-Bal 2.07
STRIKEOUTS	**STRIKEOUTS/GAME**	**GAMES**	**SAVES**	**BASE RUNNERS/9**	**ADJUSTED RELIEF RUNS**	**RELIEF RANKING**
Davenport-StL 229	Anderson-Buf 5.33	Davenport-StL 55	Bedient-Buf 10	Plank-StL 9.02		
Schulz-Buf 160	Davenport-StL 5.25	Bedient-Buf 53	Barger-Pit 6	Davenport-StL 9.19		
McConnell-Chi 151	Plank-StL 4.93	Crandall-StL 51	Wiltse-Bro 5	Brown-Chi 9.90		
Plank-StL 147	Bailey-Bal-Chi 4.91	Johnson-KC 46		Anderson-Buf 10.01		
	Groom-StL 4.78			Reulbach-New ...10.17		
INNINGS PITCHED	**OPPONENTS' AVG.**	**OPPONENTS' OBP**	**EARNED RUN AVERAGE**	**ADJUSTED ERA**	**ADJUSTED STARTER RUNS**	**PITCHER WINS**
Davenport-StL ...392.2	Davenport-StL 215	Plank-StL 262	Moseley-New 1.91	Plank-StL 138	Davenport-StL 28.3	**Plank-StL 3.0**
Crandall-StL 312.2	Plank-StL 218	Davenport-StL 268	Plank-StL 2.08	Moseley-New 134	Plank-StL 22.7	**Crandall-StL 2.2**
Schulz-Buf 309.2	Brown-Chi 220	Brown-Chi 279	Brown-Chi 2.09	Davenport-StL 131	Moseley-New 17.3	**Brown-Chi 1.8**
McConnell-Chi ...303.0	Main-KC 222	Anderson-Buf 285	McConnell-Chi 2.20	Brown-Chi 120	Reulbach-New 12.2	**McConnell-Chi ... 1.7**
Cullop-KC 302.1	Anderson-Buf 222	Reulbach-New 287	Davenport-StL 2.20	Reulbach-New 115	Brown-Chi 10.7	**Moseley-New 1.3**

What Curse?

All season, the Red Sox and Tigers chased the flag together. For Boston, Smokey Joe Wood paced the league with a 1.49 ERA, while Babe Ruth was 18-6 and also hit .315. Peerless center fielder Tris Speaker served as the offense's one-man wrecking crew. Detroit's Sam Crawford, Bobby Veach, and Ty Cobb—who swiped 96 bases, establishing a big-league record that held until 1962—comprised the league's best outfield, an aggregation that helped make up for a very mediocre Tigers infield.

Chicago finished third, with newly acquired second baseman Eddie Collins enjoying another great season. His former team, the Athletics, declined an unprecedented 56 games from their 1914 performance, landing ignominiously in the AL basement. The club's attendance dropped 58 percent. While Mack divested himself of his talent, third sacker Frank Baker chose to hold out all year. Using a staggering 56 players in 1915, trying futilely to replace his formerly great team, Mack's club became the laughingstock of baseball and would finish last for the next *seven years*.

Walter Johnson's best efforts (he led the league in wins, strikeouts, and ERA) couldn't bring the Senators in above fourth, but Washington did give future Hall of Famer Sam Rice his first big-league action. Wally Pipp started his first season as New York's regular first baseman, a position he held for a decade until a headache forced him to sit out an afternoon in favor of Lou Gehrig.

The Red Sox held the cards in 1915. Rookie Carl Mays led the league with 7 saves, heading up a superb set of second-line pitchers who gave Boston much more mound depth that Detroit. The Tigers wound up $2^1/_2$ games back despite winning 100 games. Boston took on the NL's surprise champions, the Phillies, in the World Series. After Philadelphia's opening victory, the Red Sox won four straight one-run contests, three times scoring the deciding run in the ninth inning. Harry Hooper hit .350 with 2 home runs for the Red Sox.

1914 NATIONAL LEAGUE

TEAM	W	L	T	PCT	GB	HW	HL	R	OR	PA	H	2B	3B	HR	BB	SO	HB	SH	AVG	OBP	SLG	OPS	AOPS	BR	ABR	PF	SB	CS	BSA	BSR
Bos	94	59	5	.614	—	**51**	25	657	548	5979	1307	213	60	35	**502**	617	50	**221**	.251	.323	.335	658	103	20	24	99	139			
NY	84	70	2	.545	10.5	43	36	**672**	576	5789	1363	**222**	59	30	447	**479**	**57**	139	.265	**.330**	.348	678	**112**	56	**79**	97	**239**			
StL	81	72	4	.529	13	42	34	558	**540**	5720	1249	203	65	33	445	618	42	187	.248	.314	.333	647	100	-7	0	99	204			
Chi	78	76	2	.506	16.5	46	30	605	638	5784	1229	199	74	42	501	577	42	191	.243	.317	.337	654	101	8	10	100	164			
Bro	75	79	0	.487	19.5	45	34	622	618	5751	**1386**	172	**90**	31	376	559	33	190	**.269**	.323	.355	678	106	39	25	102	173			
Phi	74	80	0	.481	20.5	48	30	651	687	5770	1345	211	52	**62**	472	570	27	161	.263	.329	**.361**	**690**	105	**72**	31	107	145			
Pit	69	85	4	.448	25.5	39	36	503	**540**	5753	1197	148	79	18	416	608	36	156	.233	.295	.303	598	88	-106	-84	96	147			
Cin	60	94	3	.390	34.5	34	42	530	651	5635	1178	142	64	16	441	627	54	149	.236	.305	.300	605	83	-81	-96	103	224			
Total	625	—	—	—	—	348	267	4798	—	46181	10254	1510	543	267	3600	4655	341	1394	.251	.317	.334	651	—	—	—	—	1435	—	—	—

TEAM	CG	SHO	GR	SV	IP	H	HR	BB	SO	BR/9	ERA	AERA	OAV	OOB	PR	APR	PF	OSB	OCS	FA	E	WPB	DP	FW	PW	BW	BSW	DIF
Bos	**104**	19	69	6	1421.0	1272	38	477	606	11.4	2.74	100	.249	.319	7	1	99	139	*147*	.963	246	54	**143**	1.8	.1	2.6	—	13.0
NY	88	**20**	89	9	1390.2	1298	47	**367**	563	11.0	2.94	90	.253	**.306**	-25	-49	95	**129**	*121*	.961	254	**36**	119	1.1	-5.3	**8.5**	—	2.7
StL	84	16	96	12	1424.2	1279	**26**	422	531	11.1	**2.38**	**117**	.250	.313	**64**	**64**	100	176	*139*	.964	239	**36**	109	2.2	**6.9**	.0	—	-4.6
Chi	70	14	**110**	11	1389.1	**1169**	37	528	**651**	11.2	2.71	103	**.233**	.311	12	9	100	201	*145*	.951	310	89	87	-2.7	1.0	1.1	—	1.7
Bro	80	11	99	11	1368.1	1282	36	466	605	11.8	2.82	101	.255	.323	-5	7	103	199	*146*	.961	248	42	112	1.2	.8	2.7	—	-6.7
Phi	85	14	98	7	1379.1	1403	**26**	452	650	12.4	3.06	96	.270	.335	-42	-20	105	241	***170***	.950	324	38	81	-3.9	-2.2	3.3	—	-.3
Pit	86	10	97	11	1405.0	1272	27	392	488	**10.9**	2.70	98	.249	.308	13	-10	95	170	*133*	**.966**	**223**	39	96	**3.4**	-1.1	-9.1	—	-1.2
Cin	74	15	106	**15**	1387.1	1259	30	489	607	11.7	2.94	100	.248	.320	-24	-3	105	180	*146*	.952	314	79	113	-2.9	-.3	-10.4	—	-3.5
Total	671	119	764	82	11165.2	—	—	—	—	11.4	2.78	—	.251	.317	—	—	—	—	—	.958	2158	413	860	—	—	—	—	—

BATTER-FIELDER WINS	BATTING AVERAGE	ON-BASE PERCENTAGE	SLUGGING AVERAGE	ON-BASE PLUS SLUGGING	ADJUSTED OPS	ADJUSTED BATTER RUNS
Maranville-Bos .. 5.5	Daubert-Bro..........329	Stengel-Bro...........404	Magee-Phi...........509	Cravath-Phi...........901	Cravath-Phi...........157	Burns-NY.............39.3
Herzog-Cin 4.8	Becker-Phi............325	Burns-NY..............403	Cravath-Phi...........499	Magee-Phi............890	Magee-Phi............154	Cravath-Phi..........37.5
Magee-Phi 4.2	Dalton-Bro............319	Cravath-Phi...........402	Connolly-Bos.........494	Wheat-Bro............830	Burns-NY..............149	Magee-Phi...........35.4
Wheat-Bro 3.8	Wheat-Bro............319	Huggins-StL..........396	Wheat-Bro............452	Stengel-Bro...........829	Stengel-Bro...........143	Connolly-Bos.........32.5
Smith-Bro-Bos ... 3.8	Stengel-Bro...........316	Dalton-Bro............396	Becker-Phi............446	Burns-NY..............820	Wheat-Bro............143	Wheat-Bro...........27.7
RUNS	**HITS**	**DOUBLES**	**TRIPLES**	**HOME RUNS**	**TOTAL BASES**	**RUNS BATTED IN**
Burns-NY..............100	Magee-Phi............171	Magee-Phi..............39	Carey-Pit.................17	Cravath-Phi.............19	Magee-Phi...........277	Magee-Phi...........103
Magee-Phi..............96	Wheat-Bro............170	Zimmerman-Chi......36	Zimmerman-Chi......12	Saier-Chi.................18	Cravath-Phi...........249	Cravath-Phi..........100
Daubert-Bro............89	Burns-NY..............170	Burns-NY................35	Wilson-StL..............12	Magee-Phi..............15	Wheat-Bro............241	Wheat-Bro..............89
Saier-Chi.................87	Zimmerman-Chi....167	Connolly-Bos..........28	Cutshaw-Bro...........12	Luderus-Phi............12	Zimmerman-Chi....239	D.Miller-StL............88
Doyle-NY.................87	Becker-Phi............167				Burns-NY..............234	Zimmerman-Chi.......87
BASES ON BALLS	**STOLEN BASES**	**BASE STEALING RUNS**	**FIELDING RUNS-INFIELD**	**FIELDING RUNS-OUTFIELD**	**OUTFIELD ASSISTS**	**CATCHER CS PCT.**
Huggins-StL...........105	Burns-NY................62		Maranville-Bos.....49.8	Wheat-Bro............14.5	Wilson-StL..............34	Gonzalez-Cin.......50.9
Saier-Chi.................94	Herzog-Cin.............46		Herzog-Cin..........33.4	Wilson-StL...........12.1	Cravath-Phi.............34	Meyers-NY...........50.0
Burns-NY.................89	Dolan-StL................42		Cutshaw-Bro.........27.6	Mann-Bos..............9.5	Good-Chi.................25	Gibson-Pit............44.6
Evers-Bos.................87	Carey-Pit.................38		Smith-Bro-Bos.......18.3	Paskert-Phi............9.3	Mann-Bos...............24	Snyder-StL............44.2
Cravath-Phi.............83			Sweeney-Chi.......15.8	Carey-Pit................6.7	Carey-Pit.................23	Clarke-Cin............41.8
WINS	**WINNING PCT.**	**WINS ABOVE TEAM**	**GAMES STARTED**	**COMPLETE GAMES**	**FEWEST HITS/GAME**	**FEWEST BB/GAME**
Alexander-Phi.........27	James-Bos............788	James-Bos.............8.4	Tesreau-NY.............41	Alexander-Phi.........32	Tesreau-NY..........6.65	Mathewson-NY.......66
Tesreau-NY.............26	Doak-StL...............760	Tesreau-NY...........8.2	Cheney-Chi.............40	Rudolph-Bos...........31	Doak-StL..............6.79	Adams-Pit............1.24
Rudolph-Bos...........26	Tesreau-NY...........722	Alexander-Phi.........8.1	Alexander-Phi.........39	James-Bos..............30	Cheney-Chi..........6.91	Marquard-NY.......1.58
James-Bos..............26	Rudolph-Bos.........722	Pfeffer-Bro.............6.8	Mayer-Phi...............38	Mathewson-NY.......29	Douglas-Cin.........6.99	Rudolph-Bos........1.63
Mathewson-NY.......24	Pfeffer-Bro............657	Doak-StL................6.7		Pfeffer-Bro..............27	James-Bos............7.07	Alexander-Phi......1.93
STRIKEOUTS	**STRIKEOUTS/GAME**	**GAMES**	**SAVES**	**BASE RUNNERS/9**	**ADJUSTED RELIEF RUNS**	**RELIEF RANKING**
Alexander-Phi.......214	Alexander-Phi......5.43	Cheney-Chi.............50	Sallee-StL................6	Rudolph-Bos........9.45		
Tesreau-NY...........189	Tesreau-NY..........5.28	Mayer-Phi...............48	Ames-Cin..................6	Adams-Pit............9.51		
Vaughn-Chi...........165	Vaughn-Chi...........5.06	Ames-Cin................47	Cheney-Chi...............5	Mamaux-Pit.........9.57		
Cheney-Chi...........157	L.Tyler-Bos...........4.64		Pfeffer-Bro...............4	Mathewson-NY....9.78		
James-Bos............156	Ragan-Bro............4.58		McQuillan-Pit............4	Doak-StL............10.09		
INNINGS PITCHED	**OPPONENTS' AVG.**	**OPPONENTS' OBP**	**EARNED RUN AVERAGE**	**ADJUSTED ERA**	**ADJUSTED STARTER RUNS**	**PITCHER WINS**
Alexander-Phi....355.0	Tesreau-NY...........209	Adams-Pit.............276	Doak-StL..............1.72	Doak-StL...............162	James-Bos...........31.0	**James-Bos.......... 3.6**
Rudolph-Bos......336.1	Cheney-Chi...........215	Rudolph-Bos..........276	James-Bos............1.90	James-Bos.............145	Pfeffer-Bro...........30.4	**Pfeffer-Bro.......... 3.2**
James-Bos.........332.1	Doak-StL...............216	Mathewson-NY.....278	Pfeffer-Bro...........1.97	Pfeffer-Bro............145	Doak-StL..............27.2	**Alexander-Phi..... 3.1**
Tesreau-NY........322.1	Vaughn-Chi...........222	Alexander-Phi.......290	Vaughn-Chi...........2.05	Vaughn-Chi...........135	Sallee-StL............22.4	**Sallee-StL........... 3.1**
Mayer-Phi..........321.0	Douglas-Cin..........223	Doak-StL...............290	Sallee-StL............2.10	Sallee-StL.............133	Alexander-Phi......22.2	**Doak-StL............. 2.6**

A Federal Case

Chicago coal baron and machinery manufacturer Jim Gilmore, who had never even heard of the Federal League before August 1913, jumped in with both feet and took over the minor league's Chicago franchise late in the season. Gilmore then became league president and immediately escalated plans to become a major league, inducing well-to-do backers to support new franchises.

Robert B. Ward wanted to name his Brooklyn team the Tip-Tops, after his national bakery. Media outrage over such commercialism led to the alternate name Brookfeds. Restaurant chain owner Charles Weeghman took over the Chicago club, convinced by Gilmore it would take no more than $26,000. By the time new Weeghman Park opened in 1914, the franchise's backers had already spent $412,000.

Gilmore was better at landing big money than big players; Browns manager George Stovall was the first major league player to jump to the FL. The Feds also lured black sheep Hal Chase as well as Joe Tinker and Three Finger Brown, both past their prime.

From Terrapin Park in Baltimore, some of the 27,692 Opening Day patrons could see Oriole Park, where only 1,500 watched John McGraw's Giants play the International League Orioles in an exhibition game. Heavy FL-induced losses led Orioles owner Jack Dunn to offer Babe Ruth to Connie Mack; the A's said they couldn't afford Ruth, but new Red Sox owner Joe Lannin could. Dunn, who made $25,000 for selling Ruth and two others to Boston, moved his club to Richmond for 1915.

Good pitchers were rewarded with money, and victories. Ex-Pirates hurler Claude Hendrix won 29 and Jack Quinn, late of the Braves, won 26 in 1914. Chief Johnson, defying a permanent injunction to keep him from jumping from the Reds to the Feds, pitched through 1915 for Stovall's Kansas City Packers. Benny Kauff, whose major league experience consisted of 11 at bats with the Yankees in 1912, was an offensive force and led Indianapolis to the first FL pennant.

1914 AMERICAN LEAGUE

TEAM	W	L	T	PCT	GB	HW	HL	R	OR	PA	H	2B	3B	HR	BB	SO	HB	SH	AVG	OBP	SLG	OPS	AOPS	BR	ABR	PF	SB	CS	BSA	BSR
Phi	99	53	6	.651	—	**51**	24	**749**	529	5940	**1392**	165	80	**29**	545	**517**	**52**	**217**	**.272**	**.348**	**.352**	**700**	**123**	**113**	**142**	96	231	188	55	-15
Bos	91	62	6	.595	8.5	44	31	589	**510**	5816	1278	**226**	**85**	18	490	549	39	170	.250	.320	.338	658	105	28	28	100	177	176	50	-23
Was	81	73	4	.526	19	40	33	572	519	5801	1245	176	81	18	470	640	46	177	.244	.313	.320	633	93	-19	-40	104	220	163	57	-9
Det	80	73	4	.523	19.5	42	35	615	618	5908	1318	195	84	25	557	537	44	205	.258	.336	.344	680	109	78	58	103	211	154	**58**	**-7**
StL	71	82	6	.464	28.5	42	36	523	615	5706	1241	185	75	17	423	863	35	147	.243	.306	.319	625	99	-40	-19	96	233	189	55	-15
NY	70	84	3	.455	30	36	40	537	550	5756	1144	149	52	12	**577**	711	47	140	.229	.315	.287	602	88	-59	-57	100	**251**	191	57	-12
Chi	70	84	3	.455	30	43	37	487	560	5698	1205	161	71	19	408	609	46	204	.239	.302	.311	613	92	-62	-55	99	167	152	52	-16
Cle	51	102	4	.333	48.5	32	47	538	709	5800	1262	178	70	10	450	685	39	154	.245	.310	.312	622	90	-40	-60	104	167	157	52	-18
Total	631	—	—	—	—	330	283	4610	—	46425	10085	1435	598	148	3920	5111	348	1414	.248	.319	.323	642	—	—	—	—	1657	1370	55	-115

TEAM	CG	SHO	GR	SV	IP	H	HR	BB	SO	BR/9	ERA	AERA	OAV	OOB	PR	APR	PF	OSB	OCS	FA	E	WPB	DP	FW	PW	BW	BSW	DIF
Phi	89	24	95	16	1404.0	1264	18	521	720	11.6	2.78	94	.249	.322	-6	-29	95	228	*176*	**.966**	**213**	62	116	**3.5**	-3.2	**15.7**	-.0	7.1
Bos	88	24	92	7	1427.1	1207	18	393	602	**10.3**	**2.36**	**114**	.236	**.295**	**59**	**51**	98	172	*156*	.963	242	**41**	99	1.8	**5.6**	3.1	-1.0	4.9
Was	75	**25**	120	**19**	1420.2	**1170**	20	520	**784**	11.0	2.54	111	**.233**	.311	31	40	103	196	*166*	.961	254	68	116	1.0	4.4	-4.4	.6	2.4
Det	81	14	117	11	1412.0	1285	17	498	567	11.8	2.86	98	.249	.322	-19	-10	103	230	*171*	.958	286	54	101	-1.1	-1.1	6.4	**.8**	-1.6
StL	81	15	113	9	1410.2	1309	20	540	553	12.1	2.85	95	.251	.327	-17	-23	99	212	*171*	.952	317	71	114	-2.7	-2.5	-2.1	-.0	2.0
NY	**98**	9	83	2	1397.1	1277	30	**390**	563	10.9	2.81	98	.250	.308	-12	-10	101	216	*176*	.963	238	52	93	1.9	-1.1	-6.3	.3	-1.7
Chi	74	17	124	11	1398.2	1207	15	401	660	10.5	2.48	108	.239	.298	40	31	98	**164**	*164*	.955	299	47	90	-1.9	3.4	-6.1	-.2	-2.3
Cle	69	9	**129**	2	1391.2	1365	**10**	666	688	13.4	3.21	90	.267	.357	-74	-53	105	233	***190***	.953	300	76	**119**	-1.9	-5.9	-6.6	-.4	-10.7
Total	655	137	873	77	11262.1	—	—	—	—	11.5	2.73	—	.248	.319	—	—	—	—	—	.959	2149	471	848	—	—	—	—	—

BATTER-FIELDER WINS	BATTING AVERAGE	ON-BASE PERCENTAGE	SLUGGING AVERAGE	ON-BASE PLUS SLUGGING	ADJUSTED OPS	ADJUSTED BATTER RUNS
Speaker-Bos 7.3	Cobb-Det 368	Collins-Phi 452	Cobb-Det 513	Speaker-Bos 926	Collins-Phi 179	Collins-Phi 57.6
Collins-Phi 6.9	Collins-Phi 344	Speaker-Bos.........423	Speaker-Bos.........503	Collins-Phi 904	Speaker-Bos.........178	Speaker-Bos........56.7
Bush-Det............ 5.1	Speaker-Bos.........338	Jackson-Cle..........399	Crawford-Det 483	Crawford-Det 871	Crawford-Det 157	Cobb-Det 40.7
Baker-Phi............ 5.0	Jackson-Cle..........338	Crawford-Det 388	Jackson-Cle..........464	Jackson-Cle..........862	Baker-Phi..............153	Crawford-Det 38.0
T.Walker-StL 4.2	Baker-Phi..............319	Baker-Phi..............380	Collins-Phi 452	Baker-Phi..............822	Jackson-Cle..........153	Baker-Phi............35.3
RUNS	**HITS**	**DOUBLES**	**TRIPLES**	**HOME RUNS**	**TOTAL BASES**	**RUNS BATTED IN**
Collins-Phi 122	Speaker-Bos.........193	Speaker-Bos..........46	Crawford-Det 26	Baker-Phi..................9	Speaker-Bos.........287	Crawford-Det 104
Speaker-Bos.........101	Crawford-Det 183	Lewis-Bos 37	Gardner-Bos 19	Crawford-Det 8	Crawford-Det 281	McInnis-Phi.............95
Murphy-Phi 101	Baker-Phi..............182	Pratt-StL 34	Speaker-Bos...........18	T.Walker-StL 6	Baker-Phi..............252	Speaker-Bos............90
Bush-Det.................97	McInnis-Phi...........181	Collins-Chi 34	T.Walker-StL 16	Fournier-Chi.............6	Pratt-StL 240	Baker-Phi.................89
	Collins-Phi 181	Leary-StL.................28	Hooper-Bos 15		Collins-Phi 238	Collins-Phi 85
BASES ON BALLS	**STOLEN BASES**	**BASE STEALING RUNS**	**FIELDING RUNS-INFIELD**	**FIELDING RUNS-OUTFIELD**	**OUTFIELD ASSISTS**	**CATCHER CS PCT.**
Bush-Det...............112	Maisel-NY 74	Maisel-NY 10.3	Bush-Det..............31.8	Speaker-Bos........23.0	T.Walker-StL 30	Schalk-Chi 49.8
Collins-Phi 97	Collins-Phi 58	Peckinpaugh-NY....2.4	Gandil-Was..........23.3	T.Walker-StL 16.5	Speaker-Bos...........29	Agnew-StL 46.9
Murphy-Phi 87	Speaker-Bos...........42	Collins-Phi 2.3	Turner-Cle............22.3	Hooper-Bos 9.9	Demmitt-Det-Chi.....24	Henry-Was............46.4
Speaker-Bos...........77	Shotton-StL.............40	Moriarty-Det...........2.2	Boone-NY 17.7	Strunk-Phi..............6.3	Williams-StL...........24	Schang-Phi 45.2
Maisel-NY 76		Chapman-Cle 2.1	Moriarty-Det.........15.8	Graney-Cle 5.0	Hooper-Bos 23	Stanage-Det 44.6
WINS	**WINNING PCT.**	**WINS ABOVE TEAM**	**GAMES STARTED**	**COMPLETE GAMES**	**FEWEST HITS/GAME**	**FEWEST BB/GAME**
Johnson-Was..........28	Bender-Phi............850	Leonard-Bos..........6.3	Johnson-Was..........40	Johnson-Was..........33	Leonard-Bos........5.57	McHale-NY 1.55
Coveleski-Det 22	Leonard-Bos.........792	Bender-Phi.............6.0	Weilman-StL 36	Coveleski-Det 23	Caldwell-NY.........6.46	Russell-Chi 1.77
Collins-Bos 20	Plank-Phi 682	Caldwell-NY...........5.9	Coveleski-Det 36	Dauss-Det...............22	Shaw-Was 6.93	Johnson-Was.......1.79
Leonard-Bos...........19	Caldwell-NY..........667	Johnson-Was.........5.3		Caldwell-NY............22	Johnson-Was.......6.95	Warhop-NY 1.83
Dauss-Det...............19	Shawkey-Phi.........652	Coveleski-Det 5.3			Foster-Bos 6.97	Ayers-Was 1.83
STRIKEOUTS	**STRIKEOUTS/GAME**	**GAMES**	**SAVES**	**BASE RUNNERS/9**	**ADJUSTED RELIEF RUNS**	**RELIEF RANKING**
Johnson-Was........225	Leonard-Bos........7.05	Johnson-Was..........51	Shaw-Was 4	Leonard-Bos........8.29		
Mitchell-Cle...........179	Mitchell-Cle..........6.27	Ayers-Was 49	Mitchell-StL...............4	Caldwell-NY.........8.79		
Leonard-Bos.........176	Shaw-Was 5.74	Shaw-Was 48	Faber-Chi..................4	Johnson-Was.......9.01		
Shaw-Was 164	Johnson-Was.......5.45	Benz-Chi.................48	Bentley-Was 4	Shore-Bos............9.15		
Dauss-Det.............150	Bender-Phi...........5.38			Foster-Bos 9.48		
INNINGS PITCHED	**OPPONENTS' AVG.**	**OPPONENTS' OBP**	**EARNED RUN AVERAGE**	**ADJUSTED ERA**	**ADJUSTED STARTER RUNS**	**PITCHER WINS**
Johnson-Was.....371.2	Leonard-Bos.........180	Leonard-Bos.........246	Leonard-Bos...........96	Leonard-Bos.........279	Johnson-Was.......45.3	**Johnson-Was 7.2**
Coveleski-Det 303.1	Caldwell-NY..........205	Caldwell-NY..........260	Foster-Bos 1.70	Johnson-Was........163	Leonard-Bos 43.3	**Leonard-Bos 4.8**
Hamilton-StL......302.1	Shaw-Was 216	Johnson-Was........265	Johnson-Was.......1.72	Foster-Bos 158	Caldwell-NY.........21.0	**Caldwell-NY 3.0**
Dauss-Det..........302.0	Johnson-Was........217	Foster-Bos 274	Caldwell-NY.........1.94	Caldwell-NY..........142	Weilman-StL 20.6	**Coveleski-Det 2.3**
Weilman-StL 299.0	Foster-Bos 218	Benz-Chi...............282	Shore-Bos............2.00	Cicotte-Chi............131	Foster-Bos...........18.5	**Cicotte-Chi 2.1**

Hub Miracle

In last place on July 18, the Boston Braves suddenly began to win. Taking 34 of their last 44, they not only caught and passed the New York Giants, but they blew away the league and took the flag by an amazing $10^1/_2$ games. A three-man rotation carried the pitching load, and manager George Stallings made the most of a weak lineup by instituting a platoon system; this strategy was almost unknown at the time.

During the last month of the season, the Braves moved to Fenway Park due to suddenly huge crowds. Braves attendance had risen 72 percent in 1913, and went up another 84 percent in 1914; this led to the construction of massive Braves Field, which opened the following spring. Despite Boston's miracle victory, and the resulting excitement, overall league attendance fell a frightening 40 percent. Total turnstile clicks were under two million for the first time since 1902.

The birth of the Federal League led to player raids on the AL and NL. In the Senior Circuit, the lower talent level meant parity; the Braves' 94 wins were the lowest total for a flag winner in over a decade. But this didn't matter in October, as the heavily favored Philadelphia Athletics did a belly flop. Boston completed its ridiculous, unbelievable season with a four-game World Series sweep. It was the Senior Circuit's first Series win since 1909.

The Cubs' great 1900s infield was in the news in 1914. First baseman Frank Chance retired; second sacker Johnny Evers was the league MVP, hitting .279 with 87 walks for Boston; shortstop Joe Tinker managed the Federal League's Chicago club; and third baseman Harry Steinfeldt, out of the game since 1911, died at 36.

1914 FEDERAL LEAGUE

TEAM	W	L	T	PCT	GB	HW	HL	R	OR	PA	H	2B	3B	HR	BB	SO	HB	SH	AVG	OBP	SLG	OPS	AOPS	BR	ABR	PF	SB	CS	BSA	BSR
Ind	88	65	4	.575	—	**53**	23	**762**	622	5907	**1474**	**230**	**90**	33	470	668	38	**223**	**.285**	**.349**	**.383**	**732**	95	**-37**	-97	111	**273**			
Chi	87	67	3	.565	1.5	41	34	621	**517**	5821	1314	227	50	**52**	**520**	645	41	162	.258	.331	.352	683	**98**	-123	**-90**	94	171			
Bal	84	70	6	.545	4.5	**53**	26	645	628	5831	1374	222	67	32	487	589	**46**	178	.268	.337	.357	694	92	-105	-121	103	152			
Buf	80	71	4	.530	7	47	29	620	602	5649	1264	177	74	37	430	761	23	132	.250	.311	.336	647	80	-207	-216	102	228			
Bro	77	77	3	.500	11.5	47	32	662	677	5805	1402	225	85	42	404	665	45	135	.269	.326	.368	694	96	-120	-116	99	220			
KC	67	84	3	.444	20	38	37	644	683	5712	1369	226	77	39	399	621	36	150	.267	.324	.364	688	97	-129	-107	96	171			
Pit	64	86	4	.427	22.5	37	37	605	698	5751	1339	180	**90**	34	410	**575**	39	188	.262	.321	.352	673	90	-159	-155	99	153			
StL	62	89	3	.411	25	31	44	565	697	5791	1254	193	65	26	503	662	34	176	.247	.319	.326	645	77	-200	-222	105	113			
Total	624	—	—	—	—	347	262	5124	—	46267	10790	1680	598	295	3623	5186	302	1344	.263	.328	.355	682	—	—	—	—	1481	—	—	—

TEAM	CG	SHO	GR	SV	IP	H	HR	BB	SO	BR/9	ERA	AERA	OAV	OOB	PR	APR	PF	OSB	OCS	FA	E	WPB	DP	FW	PW	BW	BSW	DIF
Ind	**104**	15	67	9	1397.2	1352	**29**	476	664	12.1	3.06	102	.258	.325	-27	8	108	197	***159***	.956	289	45	113	-1.2	.8	-10.1	—	22.0
Chi	93	**17**	87	8	1420.1	**1204**	43	393	650	**10.3**	**2.44**	**109**	**.233**	**.291**	**70**	**36**	92	**135**	*144*	**.962**	249	**41**	114	1.1	**3.7**	**-9.4**	—	14.5
Bal	88	15	**93**	13	1392.0	1389	34	**392**	**732**	11.7	3.13	97	.268	.323	-38	-15	105	175	*144*	.960	263	55	105	.6	-1.6	-12.6	—	20.6
Buf	89	15	91	**16**	1387.0	1249	45	505	662	11.7	3.16	94	.245	.318	-42	-31	103	154	*149*	**.962**	**242**	55	109	**1.3**	-3.2	-22.5	—	28.9
Bro	91	11	92	9	1385.1	1375	31	559	636	12.9	3.33	86	.264	.341	-69	-71	100	216	*152*	.956	283	49	120	-.9	-7.4	-12.1	—	20.3
KC	82	10	92	12	1361.0	1387	37	445	600	12.4	3.41	82	.268	.331	-79	-99	96	196	*145*	.957	279	61	**135**	-.9	-10.3	-11.1	—	13.8
Pit	97	9	71	6	1370.0	1416	38	444	510	12.4	3.56	80	.273	.333	-103	-107	99	182	*151*	.960	253	45	92	.6	-11.1	-16.1	—	15.7
StL	97	9	73	6	1367.2	1418	38	409	661	12.3	3.59	85	.267	.324	-107	-79	105	226	*155*	.957	273	59	94	-.6	-8.2	-23.1	—	18.4
Total	741	101	666	79	11081.0	—	—	—	—	12.0	3.20	—	.263	.328	—	—	—	—	—	.959	2131	410	882	—	—	—	—	—

BATTER-FIELDER WINS	BATTING AVERAGE	ON-BASE PERCENTAGE	SLUGGING AVERAGE	ON-BASE PLUS SLUGGING	ADJUSTED OPS	ADJUSTED BATTER RUNS
Wilson-Chi 5.4	Kauff-Ind .370	Kauff-Ind .447	Evans-Bro .556	Kauff-Ind .981	Evans-Bro 165	Evans-Bro 39.0
Kenworthy-KC 5.1	Evans-Bro .348	Evans-Bro .416	Kauff-Ind .534	Evans-Bro .973	Kauff-Ind 150	Kauff-Ind 36.7
Kauff-Ind 3.7	Easterly-KC .335	Lennox-Pit .414	Kenworthy-KC .525	Lennox-Pit .907	Kenworthy-KC 148	Kenworthy-KC 25.7
Evans-Bro 3.3	Shaw-Bro .324	Meyer-Bal .395	Lennox-Pit .493	Kenworthy-KC .896	Lennox-Pit 148	Lennox-Pit 24.7
Doolan-Bal 1.7	Campbell-Ind .318	Wilson-Chi .394	Zwilling-Chi .485	Wilson-Chi .860	Wilson-Chi 142	Wilson-Chi 21.3

RUNS	HITS	DOUBLES	TRIPLES	HOME RUNS	TOTAL BASES	RUNS BATTED IN
Kauff-Ind 120	Kauff-Ind 211	Kauff-Ind 44	Evans-Bro 15	Zwilling-Chi 16	Kauff-Ind 305	LaPorte-Ind 107
McKechnie-Ind 107	Zwilling-Chi 185	Evans-Bro 41	Esmond-Ind 15	Kenworthy-KC 15	Zwilling-Chi 287	Evans-Bro 96
Duncan-Bal 99	Evans-Bro 179	Kenworthy-KC 40	Kenworthy-KC 14	Hanford-Buf 12	Kenworthy-KC 286	Zwilling-Chi 95
Kenworthy-KC 93	Oakes-Pit 178	Zwilling-Chi 38		Evans-Bro 12	Evans-Bro 286	Kauff-Ind 95
Evans-Bro 93	Hanford-Buf 174				Hanford-Buf 264	Kenworthy-KC 91

BASES ON BALLS	STOLEN BASES	BASE STEALING RUNS	FIELDING RUNS-INFIELD	FIELDING RUNS-OUTFIELD	OUTFIELD ASSISTS	CATCHER CS PCT.
Wickland-Chi 81	Kauff-Ind 75		Doolan-Bal 34.1	Chadbourne-KC 9.2	Chadbourne-KC 34	Wilson-Chi 52.2
Agler-Buf 77	McKechnie-Ind 47		McKechnie-Ind 22.5	Kauff-Ind 8.5	Tobin-StL 31	Blair-Buf 48.2
Kauff-Ind 72	Myers-Bro 43		Kenworthy-KC 22.4	Hanford-Buf 6.9	Kauff-Ind 31	Jacklitsch-Bal 47.5
	Chadbourne-KC 42		Wisterzil-Bro 16.1	Tobin-StL 5.6	Hanford-Buf 24	Berry-Pit 45.8
			Tinker-Chi 12.3	W.Miller-StL 4.7	Gilmore-KC 24	Rariden-Ind 44.8

WINS	WINNING PCT.	WINS ABOVE TEAM	GAMES STARTED	COMPLETE GAMES	FEWEST HITS/GAME	FEWEST BB/GAME
Hendrix-Chi 29	Ford-Buf .778	Hendrix-Chi 9.4	Falkenberg-Ind 43	Hendrix-Chi 34	Hendrix-Chi 6.51	Ford-Buf 1.49
Quinn-Bal 26	Hendrix-Chi .744	Ford-Buf 7.8	Quinn-Bal 42	Falkenberg-Ind 33	Ford-Buf 6.91	Suggs-Bal 1.61
Seaton-Bro 25	Quinn-Bal .650	Seaton-Bro 6.7	Suggs-Bal 38	Moseley-Ind 29	Krapp-Buf 7.05	Quinn-Bal 1.71
Falkenberg-Ind 25	Seaton-Bro .641	Knetzer-Pit 6.4	Seaton-Bro 38	Quinn-Bal 27	Fiske-Chi 7.32	Hendrix-Chi 1.91
Suggs-Bal 24	Suggs-Bal .632	Quinn-Bal 5.7	Moseley-Ind 38		Watson-Chi-StL 7.34	Keupper-StL 2.07

STRIKEOUTS	STRIKEOUTS/GAME	GAMES	SAVES	BASE RUNNERS/9	ADJUSTED RELIEF RUNS	RELIEF RANKING
Falkenberg-Ind 236	Davenport-StL 5.93	Hendrix-Chi 49	Ford-Buf 6	Hendrix-Chi 8.55		
Moseley-Ind 205	Moseley-Ind 5.83	Falkenberg-Ind 49	Wilhelm-Bal 5	Ford-Buf 8.66		
Hendrix-Chi 189	Falkenberg-Ind 5.63	Wilhelm-Bal 47	Packard-KC 5	Johnson-Chi 9.07		
Seaton-Bro 172	Groom-StL 5.36	Suggs-Bal 46	Hendrix-Chi 5	Falkenberg-Ind 10.16		
Groom-StL 167	Seaton-Bro 5.11	Quinn-Bal 46		Fiske-Chi 10.32		

INNINGS PITCHED	OPPONENTS' AVG.	OPPONENTS' OBP	EARNED RUN AVERAGE	ADJUSTED ERA	ADJUSTED STARTER RUNS	PITCHER WINS
Falkenberg-Ind 377.1	Hendrix-Chi .203	Hendrix-Chi .251	Johnson-Chi 1.57	Ford-Buf 163	Hendrix-Chi 42.2	**Hendrix-Chi 5.4**
Hendrix-Chi 362.0	Krapp-Buf .210	Ford-Buf .254	Hendrix-Chi 1.69	Hendrix-Chi 157	Falkenberg-Ind 33.1	**Falkenberg-Ind 3.2**
Quinn-Bal 342.2	Ford-Buf .214	Lange-Chi .282	Ford-Buf 1.82	Falkenberg-Ind 141	Ford-Buf 30.1	**Ford-Buf 3.0**
Suggs-Bal 319.1	Lange-Chi .224	Falkenberg-Ind .284	Watson-Chi-StL 2.01	Watson-Chi-StL 137	Watson-Chi-StL 19.7	**Quinn-Bal 2.5**
Moseley-Ind 316.2	Watson-Chi-StL .230	Anderson-Buf .297	Falkenberg-Ind 2.22	Lange-Chi 119	Quinn-Bal 15.4	**Suggs-Bal 1.7**

The End of an A's Era

Moundsmen came to terms with the cork-centered ball by developing techniques to increase movement on their pitches. As a result, in 1914 the AL's batting average dropped sharply for the third straight year to .248, where it would remain until 1918.

Only three players in the league scored 100 runs. Infielder Gus Williams of the Browns fanned 120 times to set new loop record. (His short career ended the next season.) Twenty-two-year-old southpaw Dutch Leonard of the Red Sox was spectacular, finishing 19-5 with an almost inconceivable 0.96 ERA, the best mark ever after the pitching mound was moved back to 60 feet, 6 inches.. The performance of Leonard, and the purchase from Baltimore of a young pitcher named George Ruth, helped the Red Sox improve to 91-62. Dominating Philadelphia remained out of reach, leading the league from June to the finish. Detroit debuted outfielder Harry Heilmann and improved to fourth, while the slumping Chisox got a good show from rookie hurler Red Faber.

Second baseman Eddie Collins of the Athletics led the AL in runs for the third straight season, cementing his reputation as one of baseball's smartest and most capable men. Once again, the entire A's infield was the class of the game, and seven of the eight regular position players hit at least .272. Seven Philadelphia pitchers had at least 10 wins.

Due to competition from the new Federal League, and a shrinking economy, AL attendance fell by nearly a quarter. Even in pennant-winning Philadelphia, without a Federal League competitor, crowds were down 39 percent. Perhaps the low attendance was a harbinger of doom. The heavily favored Athletics punted the World Series in four straight to the underdog Boston Braves. Conscious of his low box office receipts, and angry for his club's poor October play, the shrewd and thrifty Connie Mack chose to dismantle his dynasty.

1913 NATIONAL LEAGUE

TEAM	W	L	T	PCT	GB	HW	HL	R	OR	PA	H	2B	3B	HR	BB	SO	HB	SH	AVG	OBP	SLG	OPS	AOPS	BR	ABR	PF	SB	CS	BSA	BSR
NY	101	51	4	.664	—	**54**	23	684	**515**	5837	1427	226	70	31	444	**501**	**63**	112	**.273**	**.338**	.361	699	105	46	41	101	**296**	196	60	-3
Phi	88	63	8	.583	12.5	43	33	693	636	6001	**1433**	**257**	78	**73**	383	578	35	**183**	.265	.318	**.382**	700	102	31	4	104	156	122	56	-8
Chi	88	65	2	.575	13.5	51	25	**720**	630	5775	1289	195	**96**	59	**554**	634	41	158	.257	.335	.369	**704**	**107**	**53**	**52**	100	181	160	53	-16
Pit	78	71	6	.523	21.5	41	35	673	585	5830	1383	210	86	35	391	545	35	152	.263	.319	.356	675	103	-14	14	96	181	131	58	-6
Bos	69	82	3	.457	31.5	34	40	641	690	5845	1318	191	60	32	488	640	43	169	.256	.326	.335	661	93	-24	-36	102	177	153	54	-15
Bro	65	84	3	.436	34.5	29	47	595	613	5704	1394	193	86	39	361	555	31	147	.270	.321	.363	684	98	1	-16	103	188	150	56	-11
Cin	64	89	3	.418	37.5	32	44	607	717	5781	1339	170	**96**	27	458	579	29	162	.261	.325	.347	672	98	-13	-10	100	226	144	**61**	**-1**
StL	51	99	3	.340	49	25	48	528	755	5618	1229	152	72	15	451	573	44	156	.247	.316	.316	632	88	-80	-72	99	171	184	48	-27
Total	620	—	—	—	—	309	295	5141	—	46391	10812	1594	644	311	3530	4605	321	1239	.262	.325	.354	679	—	—	—	—	1576	1240	56	-87

TEAM	CG	SHO	GR	SV	IP	H	HR	BB	SO	BR/9	ERA	AERA	OAV	OOB	PR	APR	PF	OSB	OCS	FA	E	WPB	DP	FW	PW	BW	BSW	DIF
NY	82	12	94	**17**	1422.0	**1276**	38	**315**	651	**10.2**	**2.42**	**128**	**.243**	**.289**	**122**	**110**	97	**158**	133	.961	254	**34**	107	-.6	**11.4**	4.3	.8	9.1
Phi	77	**20**	**131**	11	1455.1	1407	40	512	**667**	12.1	3.15	105	.261	.330	7	26	104	193	**179**	**.968**	**214**	42	112	**2.2**	2.7	.4	.3	6.9
Chi	89	12	90	15	1373.0	1330	39	478	556	12.1	3.13	101	.260	.328	10	5	99	176	169	.959	260	58	106	-1.1	.5	**5.4**	-.5	7.2
Pit	74	9	109	7	1400.0	1344	**26**	434	590	11.6	2.90	104	.260	.320	46	18	94	222	151	.964	226	42	94	1.1	1.9	1.5	.5	-1.4
Bos	**105**	13	64	3	1373.1	1343	38	419	597	11.8	3.19	103	.263	.324	1	11	103	195	151	.957	273	43	82	-2.0	1.1	-3.7	-.4	-1.4
Bro	71	9	104	7	1373.0	1287	33	439	548	11.6	3.13	105	.255	.321	11	22	103	197	146	.961	243	37	**125**	-.3	2.3	-1.7	.0	-9.8
Cin	71	10	113	10	1380.0	1398	40	456	522	12.4	3.46	94	.273	.338	-40	-35	101	185	146	.961	251	52	104	-.4	-3.6	-1.0	**1.0**	-8.4
StL	74	6	114	11	1351.2	1426	57	477	465	13.0	4.23	76	.280	.348	-156	-150	101	250	165	.965	219	39	113	1.3	-15.6	-7.5	-1.7	-.5
Total	643	91	819	81	11128.1	—	—	—	—	11.9	3.20	—	.262	.325	—	—	—	—	—	.962	1940	347	843	—	—	—	—	—

BATTER-FIELDER WINS	BATTING AVERAGE	ON-BASE PERCENTAGE	SLUGGING AVERAGE	ON-BASE PLUS SLUGGING	ADJUSTED OPS	ADJUSTED BATTER RUNS
Tinker-Cin 3.8	Daubert-Bro .350	Huggins-StL .432	Cravath-Phi .568	Cravath-Phi .974	Cravath-Phi 169	Cravath-Phi 46.7
Evers-Chi 3.4	Cravath-Phi .341	Cravath-Phi .407	Becker-Cin-Phi .502	Zimmerman-Chi .868	Zimmerman-Chi 147	Viox-Pit 30.2
Zimmerman-Chi 3.3	Viox-Pit .317	Daubert-Bro .405	Zimmerman-Chi .490	Saier-Chi .850	Viox-Pit 142	Zimmerman-Chi 26.7
Cravath-Phi 3.0	Tinker-Cin .317	Viox-Pit .399	Saier-Chi .480	Magee-Phi .848	Saier-Chi 141	Saier-Chi 26.5
Meyers-NY 3.0	Becker-Cin-Phi .316	Leach-Chi .391	Magee-Phi .479	Daubert-Bro .829	Magee-Phi 135	Daubert-Bro 22.9

RUNS	HITS	DOUBLES	TRIPLES	HOME RUNS	TOTAL BASES	RUNS BATTED IN
Leach-Chi 99	Cravath-Phi 179	Smith-Bro 40	Saier-Chi 21	Cravath-Phi 19	Cravath-Phi 298	Cravath-Phi 128
Carey-Pit 99	Daubert-Bro 178	Burns-NY 37	Miller-Pit 20	Luderus-Phi 18	Luderus-Phi 254	Zimmerman-Chi 95
Lobert-Phi 98	Burns-NY 173	Magee-Phi 36	Konetchy-StL 17	Saier-Chi 14	Saier-Chi 249	Saier-Chi 92
Saier-Chi 94	Lobert-Phi 172	Cravath-Phi 34	Wilson-Pit 14	Magee-Phi 11	Miller-Pit 243	Miller-Pit 90
Magee-Phi 92	Carey-Pit 172		Cravath-Phi 14	Wilson-Pit 10	Lobert-Phi 243	Luderus-Phi 86

BASES ON BALLS	STOLEN BASES	BASE STEALING RUNS	FIELDING RUNS-INFIELD	FIELDING RUNS-OUTFIELD	OUTFIELD ASSISTS	CATCHER CS PCT.
Bescher-Cin 94	Carey-Pit 61	Carey-Pit 7.5	Evers-Chi 27.7	Paskert-Phi 11.2	Carey-Pit 28	Meyers-NY 47.9
Huggins-StL 92	Myers-Bos 57	Myers-Bos 6.2	Tinker-Cin 20.7	Carey-Pit 10.6	Murray-NY 24	Simon-Pit 46.6
Leach-Chi 77	Lobert-Phi 41	Marsans-Cin 4.3	Mowrey-StL 17.5	Murray-NY 8.9	Mitchell-Chi-Pit 23	Rariden-Bos 43.9
Bridwell-Chi 74	Burns-NY 40	Doyle-NY 3.5	Maranville-Bos 17.1	Magee-StL 8.7	Burns-NY 22	Clarke-Cin 41.7
	Cutshaw-Bro 39	Cutshaw-Bro 2.6	Cutshaw-Bro 16.9	Wheat-Bro 7.9	Bescher-Cin 22	

WINS	WINNING PCT.	WINS ABOVE TEAM	GAMES STARTED	COMPLETE GAMES	FEWEST HITS/GAME	FEWEST BB/GAME
Seaton-Phi 27	Humphries-Chi .800	Sallee-StL 6.6	Tesreau-NY 38	Tyler-Bos 28	Tesreau-NY 7.09	Mathewson-NY .62
Mathewson-NY 25	Alexander-Phi .733	Seaton-Phi 6.3	Adams-Pit 37	Mathewson-NY 25	Seaton-Phi 7.32	Humphries-Chi 1.19
Marquard-NY 23	Marquard-NY .697	Alexander-Phi 6.2	Cheney-Chi 36	Cheney-Chi 25	Allen-Bro 7.42	Adams-Pit 1.41
Tesreau-NY 22	Mathewson-NY .694	Adams-Pit 5.8	Alexander-Phi 36	Adams-Pit 24	Pierce-Chi 7.52	Marquard-NY 1.53
Alexander-Phi 22	Seaton-Phi .692	Humphries-Chi 5.6		Alexander-Phi 23	Tyler-Bos 7.59	Suggs-Cin 1.58

STRIKEOUTS	STRIKEOUTS/GAME	GAMES	SAVES	BASE RUNNERS/9	ADJUSTED RELIEF RUNS	RELIEF RANKING
Seaton-Phi 168	Tesreau-NY 5.33	Cheney-Chi 54	Cheney-Chi 11	Mathewson-NY 9.18	Crandall-NY 2.5	Crandall-NY 2.2
Tesreau-NY 167	Hendrix-Pit 5.15	Seaton-Phi 52	Crandall-NY 6	Adams-Pit 9.18		
Alexander-Phi 159	Marquard-NY 4.72	Sallee-StL 50	Brown-Cin 6	Marquard-NY 9.38		
Marquard-NY 151	Seaton-Phi 4.69	Alexander-Phi 47	Sallee-StL 5	Humphries-Chi 9.70		
Adams-Pit 144	Alexander-Phi 4.67	Camnitz-Pit-Phi 45		Demaree-NY 9.87		

INNINGS PITCHED	OPPONENTS' AVG.	OPPONENTS' OBP	EARNED RUN AVERAGE	ADJUSTED ERA	ADJUSTED STARTER RUNS	PITCHER WINS
Seaton-Phi 322.1	Tesreau-NY .220	Mathewson-NY .266	Mathewson-NY 2.06	Mathewson-NY 151	Mathewson-NY 36.8	**Mathewson-NY 4.6**
Adams-Pit 313.2	Seaton-Phi .226	Adams-Pit .267	Adams-Pit 2.15	Tesreau-NY 143	Adams-Pit 33.1	**Adams-Pit 4.1**
Alexander-Phi 306.1	Allen-Bro .231	Marquard-NY .273	Tesreau-NY 2.17	Demaree-NY 141	Tesreau-NY 27.8	**Tesreau-NY 3.6**
Mathewson-NY 306.0	Pierce-Chi .234	Humphries-Chi .277	Demaree-NY 2.21	Adams-Pit 140	Seaton-Phi 24.7	**Cheney-Chi 2.6**
Cheney-Chi 305.0	Tyler-Bos .235	Demaree-NY .286	Pierce-Chi 2.30	Brennan-Phi 139	Marquard-NY 23.0	**Marquard-NY 2.4**

Change of the Guard

The Phillies paced the loop through June, but the deeper Giants soon took over. Pitching again carried the day for New York, but they had a strong attack and the league's best manager, John McGraw. Despite New York's third straight pennant, and their fifth flag since 1904, it was a year of large-scale change in the Senior Circuit. The Phillies were a legitimate contender, riding the arm of Grover Cleveland Alexander and the bat of Gavvy Cravath, who led in homers with 19 (he learned to push the ball toward Baker Bowl's 272-foot right-field fence). In a decade that saw the Philadelphia's attendance wildly fluctuate each season, 1913 was a good year; fans came out in 80 percent greater numbers to greet the second-place club. On the other side of the state, though, Pittsburgh's attendance declined by 30 percent.

Brooklyn opened their new palace, Ebbets Field, and celebrated by beginning a steady improvement that would bring them the flag in 1916. Meanwhile, the Cubs began five years of misery by dumping several top players without talent ready to replace them. Owner Charlie Murphy caused so much bad PR for the franchise that in 1914 the Federal League was able to get a toehold, using Chicago as its bellwether.

The difference between athletics and baseball was clearly outlined in 1913. Debuting that year was Jim Thorpe, the world's greatest athlete; he could never hit the curve, however, and only exceeded 100 games played once in his six years in the majors. Edd Roush began a career that included three major leagues, two NL batting titles, and 2,376 hits. His only AL hit came with the 1913 White Sox.

Connie Mack's Athletics won the World Series against New York in five relatively easy games. It marked the third time since 1905 that the A's and Giants faced each other; the Mackmen took two of the matchups. It would be seventy-six years before they met again, when both teams resided in California's Bay Area.

1913 AMERICAN LEAGUE

TEAM	W	L	T	PCT	GB	HW	HL	R	OR	PA	H	2B	3B	HR	BB	SO	HB	SH	AVG	OBP	SLG	OPS	AOPS	BR	ABR	PF	SB	CS	BSA	BSR
Phi	96	57	0	.627	—	**50**	26	**794**	592	5817	**1412**	**223**	80	**33**	**534**	547	**65**	174	**.280**	**.356**	**.375**	**731**	**124**	**140**	**157**	98	221			
Was	90	64	1	.584	6.5	42	35	596	562	5667	1281	156	81	19	440	595	42	111	.252	.317	.326	643	93	-38	-50	102	**287**			
Cle	86	66	3	.566	9.5	45	32	633	536	5712	1349	206	74	16	420	557	53	**208**	.268	.331	.348	679	102	31	13	103	191			
Bos	79	71	1	.527	15.5	41	34	631	610	5649	1334	220	**101**	17	467	534	39	174	.268	.336	.364	700	109	67	51	103	189			
Chi	78	74	1	.513	17.5	40	37	488	**498**	5452	1139	157	66	24	398	550	36	196	.236	.299	.311	610	86	-97	-92	99	156			
Det	66	87	0	.431	30	34	42	625	716	5760	1344	180	**101**	24	496	**501**	46	154	.265	.336	.355	691	111	54	64	99	218			
NY	57	94	2	.377	38	27	47	529	668	5611	1157	155	45	8	**534**	617	57	140	.237	.320	.292	612	85	-73	-75	100	203			
StL	57	96	2	.373	39	31	46	528	642	5667	1193	179	73	18	455	769	43	138	.237	.306	.312	618	90	-81	-66	97	209			
Total	614	—	—	—	—	310	299	4824	—	45335	10209	1476	621	159	3744	4670	381	1295	.256	.325	.336	661	—	—	—	—	1674	—	—	—

TEAM	CG	SHO	GR	SV	IP	H	HR	BB	SO	BR/9	ERA	AERA	OAV	OOB	PR	APR	PF	OSB	OCS	FA	E	WPB	DP	FW	PW	BW	BSW	DIF
Phi	69	17	**124**	**22**	1351.1	1200	24	532	630	11.8	3.19	87	.243	.321	-39	-69	94	188	*162*	**.966**	**212**	59	108	**3.3**	-7.3	**16.7**	—	6.9
Was	78	**23**	120	20	1396.1	**1177**	35	465	**758**	**11.0**	2.73	108	**.233**	.306	31	34	101	177	*156*	.960	261	57	122	.4	3.6	-5.3	—	14.3
Cle	93	18	90	5	1386.2	1278	19	502	689	11.8	2.54	119	.251	.324	59	71	104	176	*169*	.962	242	56	124	1.6	7.6	1.4	—	-.5
Bos	83	12	95	10	1358.1	1323	**6**	442	710	11.9	2.94	100	.262	.325	-2	-3	100	229	*169*	.961	238	52	84	1.4	-.3	5.4	—	-2.5
Chi	84	17	98	8	1360.1	1190	10	**438**	602	**11.0**	**2.33**	**125**	.239	**.305**	**91**	**89**	100	**166**	*144*	.960	255	51	104	.5	**9.5**	-9.8	—	1.8
Det	90	4	87	7	1360.0	1359	13	504	468	12.6	3.38	86	.267	.339	-68	-71	100	256	*177*	.954	303	62	105	-2.5	-7.6	6.8	—	-7.2
NY	75	8	99	7	1344.0	1318	31	455	530	12.2	3.27	91	.262	.330	-51	-41	102	294	***192***	.954	293	56	94	-1.9	-4.4	-8.0	—	-4.2
StL	**104**	14	60	5	1382.1	1369	21	454	476	12.2	3.06	96	.269	.335	-20	-22	100	191	*184*	.954	301	**45**	**125**	-2.2	-2.3	-7.0	—	-7.9
Total	676	113	773	84	10939.1	—	—	—	—	11.8	2.93	—	.256	.325	—	—	—	—	—	.959	2105	438	866	—	—	—	—	—

BATTER-FIELDER WINS	BATTING AVERAGE	ON-BASE PERCENTAGE	SLUGGING AVERAGE	ON-BASE PLUS SLUGGING	ADJUSTED OPS	ADJUSTED BATTER RUNS
Collins-Phi 7.0	Cobb-Det 390	Cobb-Det 467	Jackson-Cle..........551	Jackson-Cle........1011	Cobb-Det 196	Jackson-Cle 63.4
Baker-Phi............6.6	Jackson-Cle..........373	Jackson-Cle..........460	Cobb-Det 535	Cobb-Det 1002	Jackson-Cle..........190	Speaker-Bos........53.6
Speaker-Bos 6.5	Speaker-Bos.........363	Collins-Phi 441	Speaker-Bos.........533	Speaker-Bos.........974	Speaker-Bos.........180	Cobb-Det 53.5
Jackson-Cle 5.9	Collins-Phi 345	Speaker-Bos.........441	Baker-Phi..............493	Baker-Phi..............906	Baker-Phi..............168	Baker-Phi..............49.9
Cobb-Det.............4.6	Baker-Phi..............337	Baker-Phi..............413	Crawford-Det 489	Collins-Phi 894	Collins-Phi 165	Collins-Phi 49.1
RUNS	**HITS**	**DOUBLES**	**TRIPLES**	**HOME RUNS**	**TOTAL BASES**	**RUNS BATTED IN**
Collins-Phi 125	Jackson-Cle..........197	Jackson-Cle............39	Crawford-Det 23	Baker-Phi................12	Crawford-Det 298	Baker-Phi..............117
Baker-Phi..............116	Crawford-Det 193	Speaker-Bos...........35	Speaker-Bos...........22	Crawford-Det 9	Jackson-Cle..........291	McInnis-Phi.............90
Jackson-Cle..........109	Baker-Phi..............190	Baker-Phi................34	Jackson-Cle............17	Bodie-Chi..................8	Baker-Phi..............278	Lewis-Bos 90
Shotton-StL...........105	Speaker-Bos.........189	Crawford-Det 32	Williams-StL............16	Jackson-Cle..............7	Speaker-Bos.........277	Pratt-StL 87
E.Murphy-Phi........105	Collins-Phi 184		Cobb-Det 16		Collins-Phi 242	Barry-Phi 85
BASES ON BALLS	**STOLEN BASES**	**BASE STEALING RUNS**	**FIELDING RUNS-INFIELD**	**FIELDING RUNS-OUTFIELD**	**OUTFIELD ASSISTS**	**CATCHER CS PCT.**
Shotton-StL.............99	Milan-Was...............75		Weaver-Chi..........35.5	Speaker-Bos........18.6	Speaker-Bos...........30	O'Neill-Cle 49.0
Collins-Phi 85	Moeller-Was............62		Collins-Phi 16.4	Lewis-Bos 11.2	Shotton-StL.............29	Carisch-Cle..........49.0
Wolter-NY 80	Collins-Phi 55		Lajoie-Cle 14.5	Johnston-StL 9.8	Lewis-Bos 29	Agnew-StL 48.9
Jackson-Cle............80	Cobb-Det 51		Turner-Cle............13.4	Hooper-Bos 7.7	Jackson-Cle............28	Henry-Was...........48.6
Bush-Det.................80	Speaker-Bos...........46		Baker-Phi...............9.3	Shotton-StL...........7.3	Moeller-Was...........27	Schalk-Chi 46.0
WINS	**WINNING PCT.**	**WINS ABOVE TEAM**	**GAMES STARTED**	**COMPLETE GAMES**	**FEWEST HITS/GAME**	**FEWEST BB/GAME**
Johnson-Was..........36	Johnson-Was........837	Johnson-Was.......14.7	Scott-Chi.................38	Johnson-Was..........29	Johnson-Was.......6.03	Johnson-Was..........99
Falkenberg-Cle 23	Bush-Phi...............714	Falkenberg-Cle 5.9	Russell-Chi 36	Russell-Chi 26	Mitchell-Cle..........6.35	Collins-Bos 1.35
Russell-Chi 22	Boehling-Was 708	Collins-Bos 5.7	Johnson-Was..........36	Scott-Chi.................25	Engel-Was 6.78	Mitchell-StL..........1.72
Bender-Phi..............21	Collins-Bos 704	Boehling-Was 4.0	Groom-Was 36		Leverenz-StL 7.06	Plank-Phi 2.11
	Falkenberg-Cle 697	Cicotte-Chi.............3.8	Falkenberg-Cle 36		Russell-Chi 7.11	Weilman-StL 2.15
STRIKEOUTS	**STRIKEOUTS/GAME**	**GAMES**	**SAVES**	**BASE RUNNERS/9**	**ADJUSTED RELIEF RUNS**	**RELIEF RANKING**
Johnson-Was........243	Johnson-Was.......6.32	Russell-Chi 52	Bender-Phi.............13	Johnson-Was.......7.26		
V.Gregg-Cle 166	Mitchell-Cle..........5.85	Scott-Chi.................48	Hughes-Was............6	Russell-Chi 9.55		
Falkenberg-Cle 166	Plank-Phi 5.60	Johnson-Was.........48	Bedient-Bos.............5	Scott-Chi...........10.00		
Scott-Chi...............158	Falkenberg-Cle 5.41	Bender-Phi.............48		Cicotte-Chi.........10.07		
Groom-Was 156	Groom-Was 5.31	V.Gregg-Cle 44		Plank-Phi 10.13		
INNINGS PITCHED	**OPPONENTS' AVG.**	**OPPONENTS' OBP**	**EARNED RUN AVERAGE**	**ADJUSTED ERA**	**ADJUSTED STARTER RUNS**	**PITCHER WINS**
Johnson-Was.....346.0	Johnson-Was........190	Johnson-Was........220	Johnson-Was.......1.14	Johnson-Was........258	Johnson-Was.......69.8	**Johnson-Was ...10.9**
Russell-Chi 316.2	Mitchell-Cle..........202	Russell-Chi 275	Cicotte-Chi...........1.58	Cicotte-Chi...........185	Russell-Chi 37.9	**Russell-Chi 4.7**
Scott-Chi...........312.1	Engel-Was 218	Cicotte-Chi...........283	Scott-Chi.............1.90	Mitchell-Cle..........159	Cicotte-Chi..........36.4	**Cicotte-Chi 4.1**
V.Gregg-Cle 285.2	Russell-Chi 220	Scott-Chi..............283	Russell-Chi 1.90	Scott-Chi..............154	Scott-Chi.............34.5	**Scott-Chi.............3.8**
Falkenberg-Cle ..276.0	Caldwell-NY 221	Bender-Phi...........287	Mitchell-Cle..........1.91	Russell-Chi 153	Falkenberg-Cle 27.0	**Falkenberg-Cle ..2.9**

Chief Saves the Day

Prior to the season, another big-market AL club shifted its headquarters as New York moved into the Giants' home, the Polo Grounds. The dimensions were smaller than those of Hilltop Park, but the potential gate receipts were much higher.

After a year off, the Athletics won once more, withstanding an August challenge from eventual third-place finishers Cleveland, who had a big year from Joe Jackson. Washington's Walter Johnson won 14 games in a row, helping his Senators finish second again. However, Boston slipped to fourth as Smokey Joe Wood broke his arm.

Chief Bender was 21-10 for the Athletics, and also was credited many years later with 13 saves, which tied the retroactive all-time record. Frank Baker paced the AL in homers and RBIs, and the entire club led the league in hits, doubles, homers, slugging, walks, and, of course, runs. Four Philadelphians scored 100 runs or more; among the other seven clubs, only three players could boast such a feat. It was a year of yet more star debuts for the A's. Pitcher Bob Shawkey, who would go one to glory with the Yankees, was 6-5 for the Mackmen, and catcher Wally Schang played 79 games.

In an entertaining five-game World Series, the A's defeated New York. The Giants' only win came in Game 2, a 10-inning shutout by Christy Mathewson, who drove in the game-deciding run. Three of the Philadelphia wins were by two or fewer runs. Both Mathewson and Eddie Plank were superb, posting identical 0.95 ERAs. Bender won both his games. Joe Bush, winner of Game 3, was the only other A's pitcher used.

Former Cleveland Spiders outfielder Lou "Chief" Sockalexis, who lost his potentially great career to drinking, died at 42 on Christmas Eve. While his life ended sadly, he had a legacy: a few years later, the city's American League club would become known as the "Indians."

1912 NATIONAL LEAGUE

TEAM	W	L	T	PCT	GB	HW	HL	R	OR	PA	H	2B	3B	HR	BB	SO	HB	SH	AVG	OBP	SLG	OPS	AOPS	BR	ABR	PF	SB	CS	BSA	BSR
NY	103	48	3	.682	—	**49**	25	**823**	571	5802	1451	231	89	**47**	514	497	**69**	152	**.286**	**.360**	.395	**755**	**110**	**92**	**69**	103	**319**			
Pit	93	58	1	.616	10	44	31	751	**565**	5879	**1493**	222	**129**	39	420	514	26	181	.284	.340	**.398**	738	**110**	39	50	99	177			
Chi	91	59	2	.607	11.5	46	30	756	668	5830	1398	**245**	91	42	**560**	615	40	**182**	.277	.354	.386	740	109	65	68	100	164			
Cin	75	78	2	.490	29	45	32	656	722	5794	1310	183	89	21	479	**492**	25	175	.256	.323	.339	662	90	-93	-74	97	248			
Phi	73	79	0	.480	30.5	34	41	670	688	5754	1354	244	68	43	464	615	34	179	.267	.332	.367	699	91	-21	-63	107	159			
StL	63	90	0	.412	41	37	40	659	830	5813	1366	190	77	27	508	620	47	166	.268	.340	.352	692	97	-28	-11	98	193			
Bro	58	95	0	.379	46	33	43	651	744	5830	1377	220	73	32	490	584	40	159	.268	.336	.358	694	100	-27	1	96	179			
Bos	52	101	2	.340	52	31	47	693	871	6031	1465	227	68	35	454	690	48	168	.273	.335	.361	696	94	-27	-39	102	137			
Total	613	—	—	—	—	319	289	5659	—	46733	11214	1762	684	286	3889	4627	329	1362	.272	.340	.369	710	—	—	—	—	1576	—	—	—

TEAM	CG	SHO	GR	SV	IP	H	HR	BB	SO	BR/9	ERA	AERA	OAV	OOB	PR	APR	PF	OSB	OCS	FA	E	WPB	DP	FW	PW	BW	BSW	DIF
NY	93	8	76	**16**	1369.2	1352	35	**338**	652	**11.3**	**2.58**	**130**	.259	**.307**	**124**	**120**	99	**141**	*113*	.956	280	49	123	-2.1	**11.8**	**6.8**	—	11.0
Pit	**94**	**18**	76	7	1385.0	**1268**	**28**	497	**664**	11.8	2.85	114	**.251**	.324	84	63	96	154	*137*	**.972**	**169**	38	125	**6.0**	6.2	4.9	—	.4
Chi	80	15	104	9	1358.2	1307	33	493	554	12.2	3.42	97	.259	.331	-4	-20	98	153	*150*	.960	249	46	125	-.0	-2.0	6.7	—	11.3
Cin	86	13	89	10	1377.2	1455	**28**	452	561	12.9	3.42	98	.279	.344	-4	-14	99	202	*153*	.960	249	**35**	102	.4	-1.4	-7.3	—	6.8
Phi	81	10	99	9	1355.0	1381	43	515	616	12.9	3.25	111	.272	.344	23	50	106	221	*173*	.963	231	61	98	1.3	4.9	-6.2	—	-3.1
StL	61	6	**134**	12	1353.0	1466	31	560	487	13.7	3.85	89	.286	.361	-68	-63	101	266	***188***	.957	274	41	113	-1.8	-6.2	-1.1	—	-4.5
Bro	71	10	99	8	1357.0	1399	45	510	553	12.9	3.64	92	.273	.343	-37	-50	98	214	*162*	.959	255	36	96	-.3	-4.9	.0	—	-13.3
Bos	88	5	94	5	1390.2	1544	43	521	542	13.6	4.17	86	.291	.359	-119	-94	105	225	*176*	.954	297	69	**129**	-3.2	-9.2	-3.8	—	-8.2
Total	654	85	771	76	10946.2	—	—	—	—	12.7	3.40	—	.272	.340	—	—	—	—	—	.960	2004	375	911	—	—	—	—	—

BATTER-FIELDER WINS	BATTING AVERAGE	ON-BASE PERCENTAGE	SLUGGING AVERAGE	ON-BASE PLUS SLUGGING	ADJUSTED OPS	ADJUSTED BATTER RUNS
Wagner-Pit..........5.9	Zimmerman-Chi....372	Evers-Chi..............431	Zimmerman-Chi....571	Zimmerman-Chi....989	Zimmerman-Chi....170	Zimmerman-Chi...51.1
Sweeney-Bos.....5.6	Meyers-NY...........358	Huggins-StL..........422	Wilson-Pit 513	Wagner-Pit............891	Wagner-Pit............145	Wagner-Pit...........34.0
Zimmerman-Chi 5.3	Sweeney-Bos 344	Paskert-Phi 420	Wagner-Pit............496	Evers-Chi..............873	Evers-Chi..............139	Evers-Chi.............30.1
Meyers-NY..........4.0	Evers-Chi..............341	Zimmerman-Chi....418	Meyers-NY............477	Doyle-NY 864	Wilson-Pit 134	Sweeney-Bos 29.5
Evers-Chi...........3.7	Doyle-NY 330	Sweeney-Bos 416	Doyle-NY 471	Titus-Phi-Bos........862	Konetchy-StL 134	Meyers-NY...........26.4
RUNS	**HITS**	**DOUBLES**	**TRIPLES**	**HOME RUNS**	**TOTAL BASES**	**RUNS BATTED IN**
Bescher-Cin..........120	Zimmerman-Chi....207	Zimmerman-Chi......41	Wilson-Pit 36	Zimmerman-Chi......14	Zimmerman-Chi....318	Wagner-Pit............102
Carey-Pit...............114	Sweeney-Bos 204	Paskert-Phi.............37	Wagner-Pit..............20	Schulte-Chi 12	Wilson-Pit 299	Sweeney-Bos 100
Paskert-Phi...........102	Campbell-Bos.......185	Wagner-Pit..............35	Murray-NY 20	Wilson-Pit 11	Wagner-Pit............277	Zimmerman-Chi......99
Campbell-Bos.......102	Doyle-NY 184	Miller-Pit..................33	Daubert-Bro............16	Merkle-NY...............11	Sweeney-Bos 264	Wilson-Pit 95
	Wagner-Pit............181	Doyle-NY 33		Cravath-Phi............11	Doyle-NY 263	Murray-NY 92
BASES ON BALLS	**STOLEN BASES**	**BASE STEALING RUNS**	**FIELDING RUNS-INFIELD**	**FIELDING RUNS-OUTFIELD**	**OUTFIELD ASSISTS**	**CATCHER CS PCT.**
Sheckard-Chi........122	Bescher-Cin............67		Tinker-Chi 26.3	Sheckard-Chi.........9.3	Sheckard-Chi..........26	Archer-Chi 49.1
Paskert-Phi 91	Carey-Pit.................45		Sweeney-Bos 26.0	Magee-StL 5.9	Cravath-Phi.............26	Gibson-Pit............47.6
Huggins-StL............87	Snodgrass-NY 43		Herzog-NY 20.1	Cravath-Phi............5.5	Snodgrass-NY 25	Killefer-Phi 46.4
Bescher-Cin............83	Murray-NY 38		Wagner-Pit...........17.1	Murray-NY 5.3	Moran-Bro...............24	Miller-Bro 45.6
Titus-Phi-Bos..........82			Fletcher-NY 14.5	Miller-Bos-Phi 4.3	Evans-StL 24	Meyers-NY...........45.4
WINS	**WINNING PCT.**	**WINS ABOVE TEAM**	**GAMES STARTED**	**COMPLETE GAMES**	**FEWEST HITS/GAME**	**FEWEST BB/GAME**
Marquard-NY 26	Hendrix-Pit............727	Cheney-Chi............6.4	Benton-Cin..............39	Cheney-Chi.............28	Tesreau-NY..........6.56	Mathewson-NY 99
Cheney-Chi.............26	Cheney-Chi...........722	Hendrix-Pit.............5.7	Marquard-NY 38	Mathewson-NY 27	Robinson-Pit........7.51	Robinson-Pit........1.54
Hendrix-Pit..............24	Tesreau-NY...........708	Harmon-StL 3.4	Fromme-Cin............37	Suggs-Cin...............25	O'Toole-Pit..........7.75	Suggs-Cin............1.66
Mathewson-NY 23	Marquard-NY 703	Rucker-Bro.............3.3	Cheney-Chi.............37	Hendrix-Pit..............25	Cheney-Chi..........7.77	Ames-NY 1.76
Camnitz-Pit.............22	Richie-Chi 667	Seaton-Phi.............2.9		Alexander-Phi 25	Brown-Bos 7.81	Adams-Pit............1.85
STRIKEOUTS	**STRIKEOUTS/GAME**	**GAMES**	**SAVES**	**BASE RUNNERS/9**	**ADJUSTED RELIEF RUNS**	**RELIEF RANKING**
Alexander-Phi 195	Alexander-Phi 5.66	Benton-Cin..............50	Sallee-StL 6	Robinson-Pit........9.57		
Hendrix-Pit............176	Hendrix-Pit...........5.49	Sallee-StL 48	Mathewson-NY 5	Mathewson-NY ..10.07		
Marquard-NY 175	Marquard-NY 5.35	Alexander-Phi 46	Rucker-Bro................4	Rucker-Bro.........10.49		
Benton-Cin............162	Tyler-Bos.............5.06	Rucker-Bro..............45	Reulbach-Chi............4	Tesreau-NY.........10.85		
Rucker-Bro............151	O'Toole-Pit 4.90	Seaton-Phi..............44		Adams-Pit..........10.94		
INNINGS PITCHED	**OPPONENTS' AVG.**	**OPPONENTS' OBP**	**EARNED RUN AVERAGE**	**ADJUSTED ERA**	**ADJUSTED STARTER RUNS**	**PITCHER WINS**
Alexander-Phi 310.1	Tesreau-NY...........204	Mathewson-NY 281	Tesreau-NY..........1.96	Tesreau-NY...........172	Mathewson-NY 43.1	**Mathewson-NY .. 5.3**
Mathewson-NY ..310.0	Cheney-Chi...........234	Robinson-Pit 284	Mathewson-NY 2.12	Mathewson-NY 159	Rucker-Bro...........37.3	**Rucker-Bro 5.1**
Cheney-Chi........303.1	Robinson-Pit 237	Rucker-Bro............298	Rucker-Bro...........2.21	Rucker-Bro............151	Tesreau-NY..........33.8	**Hendrix-Pit 4.0**
Suggs-Cin..........303.0	Brown-Bos 239	Tesreau-NY...........298	Robinson-Pit 2.26	Rixey-Phi 145	Marquard-NY 30.0	**Marquard-NY...... 3.5**
Benton-Cin.........302.0	O'Toole-Pit 241	Adams-Pit.............303	Ames-NY 2.46	Robinson-Pit 144	Alexander-Phi 27.2	**Alexander-Phi 3.0**

The Bats Take Over

Offense continued to increase in 1912 as runs scored reached 4.62 per game, the highest total in a decade. Honus Wagner led the league in RBIs at age 38, while Bob Bescher scored 120 runs and swiped 67 bases for the Reds. But the biggest numbers came from relative obscurities. Owen "Chief" Wilson, a 29-year-old Pittsburgh outfielder, rapped out an amazing 36 triples, the highest total before or since. Previously unheralded Cubs third baseman Heinie Zimmerman stomped the competition in batting average, slugging, hits, and doubles. Zimmerman's was one of the game's great fluke seasons.

There were pitchers of merit. Christy Mathewson, Rube Marquard, and rookie Jeff Tesreau combined to win 66 games for the Giants; Marquard's 19 wins in a row were the most in a season in the twentieth century and tied the all-time mark set by New York ace Tim Keefe in 1888. Two rookies made splashy entries in 1912: Eppa Rixey had 10 victories for Philadelphia, while Wilbur Cooper was a late-season sensation in Pittsburgh.

Two of the game's great personalities debuted, and one died. Casey Stengel started his career with Brooklyn, while Boston brought up 21-year-old shortstop Rabbit Maranville. Former Giants pitcher Bugs Raymond, who had partied his way out of the majors the year before, was beaten to death in September in an altercation during a semi-pro game.

The pennant race held little tension. The Giants won easily, capturing 16 straight at one point. The only early challenger, Cincinnati, dropped to fourth; their new digs, Redland Field, continuing a trend that saw five NL clubs open new parks during the decade. A lack of pennant-race excitement hurt attendance, which fell in six of eight cities and dropped by 15 percent. For the fifth consecutive year, New York, Pittsburgh, and Chicago ranked as the Senior Circuit's top clubs. However, the Giants again failed in the World Series, losing in five to Boston.

1912 AMERICAN LEAGUE

TEAM	W	L	T	PCT	GB	HW	HL	R	OR	PA	H	2B	3B	HR	BB	SO	HB	SH	AVG	OBP	SLG	OPS	AOPS	BR	ABR	PF	SB	CS	BSA	BSR
Bos	105	47	2	.691	—	**57**	20	**799**	**544**	5871	1404	**269**	84	**29**	**565**	—	45	190	.277	**.355**	**.380**	**735**	110	**111**	73	105	185			
Was	91	61	2	.599	14	45	32	699	581	5729	1298	202	86	20	472	—	38	144	.256	.324	.341	665	94	-32	-36	101	273			
Phi	90	62	1	.592	15	45	31	779	658	5835	**1442**	204	**108**	22	485	—	38	201	**.282**	.349	.377	726	**117**	82	**111**	96	258			
Chi	78	76	4	.506	28	34	43	639	648	5867	1321	174	80	17	423	—	51	**211**	.255	.317	.329	646	93	-71	-50	97	213			
Cle	75	78	2	.490	30.5	41	35	677	681	5798	1403	219	77	12	407	—	51	208	.273	.333	.353	686	98	6	-15	103	194			
Det	69	84	1	.451	36.5	37	39	720	777	5882	1376	189	86	19	530	—	58	151	.268	.343	.349	692	106	27	51	97	**277**			
StL	53	101	3	.344	53	27	50	552	764	5710	1262	166	71	19	449	—	42	139	.248	.315	.320	635	90	-89	-67	96	176			
NY	50	102	1	.329	55	31	44	630	842	5772	1320	168	79	18	463	—	**65**	152	.259	.329	.334	663	90	-33	-70	106	247			
Total	619	—	—	—	—	317	294	5495	—	46464	10826	1591	671	156	3794	5157	388	1396	.265	.333	.348	681	—	—	—	—	1823	—	—	—

TEAM	CG	SHO	GR	SV	IP	H	HR	BB	SO	BR/9	ERA	AERA	OAV	OOB	PR	APR	PF	OSB	OCS	FA	E	WPB	DP	FW	PW	BW	BSW	DIF
Bos	**108**	**18**	59	6	1362.0	1243	18	**385**	712	**11.0**	2.76	124	.248	**.306**	88	101	103	202	*163*	.957	267	**40**	88	2.4	10.1	7.3	—	9.2
Was	98	11	73	7	1376.2	**1219**	24	525	**828**	11.8	**2.69**	**125**	**.242**	.320	**99**	**104**	101	**164**	*178*	.954	297	70	92	.7	**10.4**	-3.6	—	7.6
Phi	95	11	81	9	1357.0	1273	**12**	518	601	12.3	3.32	93	.258	.336	2	-33	93	171	*172*	**.959**	**263**	55	115	**2.5**	-3.3	**11.1**	—	3.7
Chi	85	14	**101**	**16**	1413.0	1398	26	426	698	11.8	3.06	105	.264	.322	44	27	96	239	*190*	.956	291	50	102	1.5	2.7	-5.0	—	1.8
Cle	94	7	80	7	1352.2	1367	15	523	622	12.9	3.30	104	.272	.346	6	20	103	240	*190*	.954	287	65	124	1.4	2.0	-1.5	—	-3.4
Det	107	7	59	5	1367.1	1438	16	521	512	13.3	3.77	87	.277	.350	-66	-72	98	289	*192*	.950	338	83	91	-1.7	-7.2	5.1	—	-3.7
StL	85	8	89	5	1369.2	1433	17	442	547	12.7	3.71	90	.277	.341	-56	-55	100	271	***193***	.947	341	54	**127**	-1.6	-5.5	-6.7	—	-10.3
NY	105	5	60	3	1335.0	1448	28	436	637	13.0	4.13	88	.282	.344	-117	-66	108	248	*186*	.940	382	64	77	-4.4	-6.6	-7.0	—	-8.0
Total	777	81	602	58	10933.1	—	—	—	—	12.3	3.34	—	.265	.333	—	—	—	—	—	.952	2466	481	816	—	—	—	—	—

BATTER-FIELDER WINS	BATTING AVERAGE	ON-BASE PERCENTAGE	SLUGGING AVERAGE	ON-BASE PLUS SLUGGING	ADJUSTED OPS	ADJUSTED BATTER RUNS
Speaker-Bos......7.2	Cobb-Det..............409	Speaker-Bos.........464	Cobb-Det..............584	Cobb-Det...........1040	Cobb-Det..............203	Cobb-Det.............71.5
Jackson-Cle.......7.1	Jackson-Cle..........395	Jackson-Cle..........458	Jackson-Cle..........579	Jackson-Cle........1036	Jackson-Cle..........190	Speaker-Bos........68.2
Baker-Phi...........6.5	Speaker-Bos.........383	Cobb-Det..............456	Speaker-Bos.........567	Speaker-Bos.......1031	Speaker-Bos..........185	Jackson-Cle.........66.7
Collins-Phi.........6.4	Lajoie-Cle............368	Collins-Phi...........450	Baker-Phi..............541	Baker-Phi...............945	Baker-Phi...............176	Baker-Phi.............54.4
Cobb-Det............5.6	Collins-Phi...........348	Lajoie-Cle.............414	Crawford-Det........470	Collins-Phi............885	Collins-Phi............159	Collins-Phi...........49.6

RUNS	HITS	DOUBLES	TRIPLES	HOME RUNS	TOTAL BASES	RUNS BATTED IN
Collins-Phi............137	Jackson-Cle..........226	Speaker-Bos...........53	Jackson-Cle............26	Speaker-Bos...........10	Jackson-Cle..........331	Baker-Phi..............130
Speaker-Bos.........136	Cobb-Det..............226	Jackson-Cle............44	Cobb-Det................23	Baker-Phi................10	Speaker-Bos.........329	Lewis-Bos.............109
Jackson-Cle..........121	Speaker-Bos.........222	Baker-Phi................40	Crawford-Det..........21	Cobb-Det..................7	Cobb-Det..............323	Crawford-Det........109
Cobb-Det..............120	Baker-Phi..............200	Lewis-Bos...............36	Baker-Phi................21		Baker-Phi..............312	McInnis-Phi...........101
Baker-Phi..............116			Gardner-Bos...........18		Crawford-Det........273	

BASES ON BALLS	STOLEN BASES	BASE STEALING RUNS	FIELDING RUNS-INFIELD	FIELDING RUNS-OUTFIELD	OUTFIELD ASSISTS	CATCHER CS PCT.
Bush-Det...............117	Milan-Was...............88		McBride-Was.......27.8	Speaker-Bos........16.3	Speaker-Bos...........35	Lapp-Phi..............47.2
Collins-Phi............101	Collins-Phi.............63		Bush-Det..............27.0	Jackson-Cle.........13.9	Milan-Was...............31	Sweeney-NY.........43.7
Rath-Chi..................95	Cobb-Det................61		Louden-Det...........17.6	Hogan-StL.............9.8	Jackson-Cle............30	Carrigan-Bos.........43.3
Shotton-StL.............86	Speaker-Bos...........52		Rath-Chi..............16.2	Strunk-Phi..............8.1	Moeller-Was............25	Stanage-Det.........38.9
Speaker-Bos...........82	Zeider-Chi...............48		Collins-Phi...........14.0	Milan-Was..............6.8	Lewis-Bos...............23	

WINS	WINNING PCT.	WINS ABOVE TEAM	GAMES STARTED	COMPLETE GAMES	FEWEST HITS/GAME	FEWEST BB/GAME
Wood-Bos...............34	Wood-Bos.............872	Wood-Bos............12.8	Walsh-Chi...............41	Wood-Bos...............35	Johnson-Was.......6.32	Bender-Phi...........1.74
Johnson-Was..........33	Plank-Phi..............813	Plank-Phi...............9.6	Groom-Was.............40	Johnson-Was..........34	Wood-Bos.............6.99	Johnson-Was.......1.85
Walsh-Chi...............27	Johnson-Was........733	Johnson-Was.........9.4	Wood-Bos...............38	Walsh-Chi...............32	Houck-Phi............7.37	Collins-Bos..........1.90
Plank-Phi...............26	Bedient-Bos.........690	Walsh-Chi..............6.2	Johnson-Was..........37	Ford-NY..................30	Walsh-Chi............7.60	Powell-StL............1.99
Groom-Was.............24	Coombs-Phi..........677	Dubuc-Det..............5.0	Ford-NY..................35		O'Brien-Bos..........7.74	Warhop-NY...........2.06

STRIKEOUTS	STRIKEOUTS/GAME	GAMES	SAVES	BASE RUNNERS/9	ADJUSTED RELIEF RUNS	RELIEF RANKING
Johnson-Was........303	Johnson-Was.......7.39	Walsh-Chi...............62	Walsh-Chi...............10	Johnson-Was.......8.56		
Wood-Bos.............258	Wood-Bos............6.75	Johnson-Was..........50	Warhop-NY...............3	Wood-Bos.............9.44		
Walsh-Chi.............254	Gregg-Cle.............6.10	Wood-Bos...............43	Mogridge-Chi............3	Walsh-Chi.............9.78		
Gregg-Cle.............184	Walsh-Chi.............5.82	Groom-Was............43	Lange-Chi.................3	Bedient-Bos.......10.29		
Groom-Was...........179	Lange-Chi.............5.23	Benz-Chi.................42	Dubuc-Det................3	Collins-Bos........10.66		

INNINGS PITCHED	OPPONENTS' AVG.	OPPONENTS' OBP	EARNED RUN AVERAGE	ADJUSTED ERA	ADJUSTED STARTER RUNS	PITCHER WINS
Walsh-Chi..........393.0	Johnson-Was........196	Johnson-Was........248	Johnson-Was.......1.39	Johnson-Was........241	Johnson-Was.......77.1	**Johnson-Was...10.6**
Johnson-Was.....369.0	Wood-Bos.............216	Wood-Bos.............272	Wood-Bos............1.91	Wood-Bos.............179	Wood-Bos............53.1	**Wood-Bos...........7.6**
Wood-Bos..........344.0	Walsh-Chi.............231	Walsh-Chi.............279	Walsh-Chi............2.15	Walsh-Chi.............149	Walsh-Chi............49.0	**Walsh-Chi...........6.5**
Groom-Was.......316.0	Houck-Phi.............234	Bedient-Bos..........288	Plank-Phi.............2.22	Plank-Phi..............140	Gregg-Cle............27.5	**Plank-Phi.............3.2**
Ford-NY............291.2	Dubuc-Det............235	Collins-Bos...........297	Collins-Bos..........2.53	Collins-Bos...........135	Plank-Phi.............24.9	**Gregg-Cle...........2.8**

Glory on the Fens

It was quite a year in Boston. First, the Red Sox opened Fenway Park, a more intimate setting than cavernous Huntington Avenue Grounds. Second, pitcher Smokey Joe Wood finally got the support he needed to harness his dominating fastball. His heroics, and the spectacular play of Tris Speaker, propelled the Red Sox to the pennant. Wood's chief mound rival was Walter Johnson, who won 16 straight for surprising Washington. The two stars met September 5 in Boston, and Wood—also en route to winning 16 in a row—bested Johnson, 1-0.

A hitting slump dropped the Tigers to sixth, and the club fell lower in the public eye after striking in May to protest the suspension of Ty Cobb, who had severely beaten a heckler. With the club AWOL, a makeshift lineup of amateurs and Tigers coaches lost at Philadelphia, 24-2; Detroit ended the walkout the next day under pressure from AL President Ban Johnson. Rookie outfielder Bobby Veach would soon help the club regain its standing.

Earned runs for pitchers were first tabulated this year, but it would be until 1917 before ERA was an official statistic. Offensive players set two new league records: Joe Jackson of Cleveland hit 26 triples, while Washington's Clyde Milan swiped 88 bases. Buck Weaver and Ray Schalk made their debuts in Chicago, while Herb Pennock and Stan Coveleski pitched their first games, both for Philadelphia. Could Connie Mack pick 'em?

The Red Sox-New York Giants October matchup was the best World Series to date, going the full seven with a tie thrown in. Four one-run games kept fans on the edges of their seats. The Series ended with a thrilling duel between Christy Mathewson and Wood, on in relief of Hugh Bedient, went to the 10th before a wild series of plays gave the Red Sox a come-from-behind 3-2 win.

1911 NATIONAL LEAGUE

TEAM	W	L	T	PCT	GB	HW	HL	R	OR	PA	H	2B	3B	HR	BB	SO	HB	SH	AVG	OBP	SLG	OPS	AOPS	BR	ABR	PF	SB	CS	BSA	BSR
NY	99	54	1	.647	—	**49**	25	756	**542**	5781	1399	225	103	41	530	**506**	**85**	160	**.279**	**.358**	**.390**	**748**	**113**	**111**	**87**	103	**347**			
Chi	92	62	3	.597	7.5	**49**	32	**757**	607	5959	1335	218	101	54	585	617	42	**202**	.260	.341	.374	715	107	44	43	100	214			
Pit	85	69	1	.552	14.5	48	29	744	557	5907	1345	206	**106**	49	525	583	52	193	.262	.336	.372	708	101	27	1	104	160			
Phi	79	73	1	.520	19.5	42	34	658	669	5751	1307	214	56	**60**	490	588	31	186	.259	.328	.359	687	98	-10	-18	101	153			
StL	75	74	9	.503	22	36	38	671	745	5970	1295	199	86	26	**592**	650	65	181	.252	.337	.340	677	99	-17	2	97	175			
Cin	70	83	6	.458	29	38	42	682	706	6089	1379	180	105	21	578	594	35	185	.261	.337	.346	683	102	-13	13	96	289			
Bro	64	86	4	.427	33.5	31	42	539	659	5680	1198	151	71	28	425	683	39	157	.237	.301	.311	612	80	-157	-135	96	184			
Bos	44	107	5	.291	54	19	54	699	1021	6045	**1417**	**249**	54	37	554	577	31	152	.267	.340	.355	695	93	14	-40	108	169			
Total	623	—	—	—	—	312	296	5506	—	47182	10675	1642	682	316	4279	4798	380	1416	.260	.335	.356	691	—	—	—	—	1691	—	—	—

TEAM	CG	SHO	GR	SV	IP	H	HR	BB	SO	BR/9	ERA	AERA	OAV	OOB	PR	APR	PF	OSB	OCS	FA	E	WPB	DP	FW	PW	BW	BSW	DIF
NY	**95**	19	80	13	1368.0	1267	33	**369**	**771**	11.0	**2.69**	**125**	.246	**.300**	**106**	**101**	99	146	*117*	.959	256	41	86	.5	**10.1**	**8.7**	—	3.1
Chi	85	12	97	**16**	1411.0	1270	**26**	525	582	11.7	2.90	114	**.245**	.320	78	63	97	**133**	*152*	.960	260	46	114	.6	6.3	4.3	—	3.8
Pit	91	13	84	11	1380.1	**1249**	36	375	605	**10.8**	2.84	121	.248	.306	85	87	101	185	*154*	**.963**	232	43	**131**	**2.1**	8.7	.1	—	-2.9
Phi	90	**20**	78	10	1373.1	1285	43	598	697	12.7	3.30	104	.255	.340	14	19	101	243	*179*	**.963**	**231**	52	113	1.9	1.9	-1.8	—	1.0
StL	88	6	101	10	1402.1	1296	39	701	561	13.2	3.68	91	.254	.350	-46	-52	99	288	*190*	.960	261	51	106	.6	-5.2	.2	—	4.9
Cin	77	4	97	12	1425.0	1410	36	476	557	12.3	3.26	101	.265	.332	21	5	97	156	*163*	.955	295	38	108	-1.4	.5	1.3	—	-6.9
Bro	81	13	91	10	1371.2	1310	27	566	533	12.6	3.39	98	.263	.344	0	-13	98	256	*195*	.962	241	**25**	112	1.4	-1.3	-13.6	—	2.4
Bos	73	5	**115**	7	1374.0	1570	76	672	486	15.1	5.08	75	.296	.381	-258	-174	113	284	***201***	.947	347	55	110	-5.0	-17.5	-4.0	—	-5.0
Total	680	92	743	89	11105.2	—	—	—	—	12.4	3.39	—	.260	.335	—	—	—	—	—	.958	2123	351	880	—	—	—	—	—

BATTER-FIELDER WINS	BATTING AVERAGE	ON-BASE PERCENTAGE	SLUGGING AVERAGE	ON-BASE PLUS SLUGGING	ADJUSTED OPS	ADJUSTED BATTER RUNS
Sheckard-Chi 4.1	Wagner-Pit .334	Sheckard-Chi .434	Schulte-Chi .534	Wagner-Pit .930	Schulte-Chi 156	Schulte-Chi 40.4
Wagner-Pit 4.1	Miller-Bos .333	Wagner-Pit .423	Doyle-NY .527	Doyle-NY .924	Wagner-Pit 154	Doyle-NY 35.4
Meyers-NY 3.3	Meyers-NY .332	Bates-Cin .415	Wagner-Pit .507	Schulte-Chi .918	Doyle-NY 153	Wagner-Pit 35.2
Sweeney-Bos 3.1	Clarke-Pit .324	Sweeney-Bos .404	Clarke-Pit .492	Magee-Phi .849	Magee-Phi 135	Sheckard-Chi 33.5
Tinker-Chi 2.9	Fletcher-NY .319	Doyle-NY .397	Magee-Phi .483	Wilson-Pit .826	Konetchy-StL 132	Bates-Cin 28.6
RUNS	**HITS**	**DOUBLES**	**TRIPLES**	**HOME RUNS**	**TOTAL BASES**	**RUNS BATTED IN**
Sheckard-Chi 121	Miller-Bos 192	Konetchy-StL 38	Doyle-NY 25	Schulte-Chi 21	Schulte-Chi 308	Wilson-Pit 107
Huggins-StL 106	Hoblitzel-Cin 180	Miller-Bos 36	Mitchell-Cin 22	Luderus-Phi 16	Doyle-NY 277	Schulte-Chi 107
Bescher-Cin 106	Daubert-Bro 176	Wilson-Pit 34	Schulte-Chi 21	Magee-Phi 15	Luderus-Phi 260	Luderus-Phi 99
Schulte-Chi 105	Schulte-Chi 173	Herzog-Bos-NY 33	Zimmerman-Chi 17	Doyle-NY 13	Hoblitzel-Cin 258	Magee-Phi 94
Doyle-NY 102	Luderus-Phi 166	Sweeney-Bos 33	Byrne-Pit 17		Wilson-Pit 257	
BASES ON BALLS	**STOLEN BASES**	**BASE STEALING RUNS**	**FIELDING RUNS-INFIELD**	**FIELDING RUNS-OUTFIELD**	**OUTFIELD ASSISTS**	**CATCHER CS PCT.**
Sheckard-Chi 147	Bescher-Cin 81		Tinker-Chi 21.6	Sheckard-Chi 14.8	Sheckard-Chi 32	McLean-Cin 53.8
Bates-Cin 103	Devore-NY 61		Doolan-Phi 17.0	Mitchell-Cin 8.6	Snodgrass-NY 31	Gibson-Pit 46.1
Bescher-Cin 102	Snodgrass-NY 51		Merkle-NY 15.5	Ingerton-Bos 8.2	Devore-NY 29	Bergen-Bro 45.0
Huggins-StL 96	Merkle-NY 49		Huggins-StL 11.4	Leach-Pit 7.8	Oakes-StL 26	Meyers-NY 44.0
Knabe-Phi 94			Sweeney-Bos 11.2	Carey-Pit 7.1	Miller-Bos 26	
WINS	**WINNING PCT.**	**WINS ABOVE TEAM**	**GAMES STARTED**	**COMPLETE GAMES**	**FEWEST HITS/GAME**	**FEWEST BB/GAME**
Alexander-Phi 28	Marquard-NY .774	Alexander-Phi 8.5	Harmon-StL 41	Alexander-Phi 31	Alexander-Phi 6.99	Mathewson-NY 1.11
Mathewson-NY 26	Crandall-NY .750	Marquard-NY 6.4	Mathewson-NY 37	Mathewson-NY 29	Marquard-NY 7.16	Adams-Pit 1.29
Marquard-NY 24	Cole-Chi .720	Rucker-Bro 5.4	Leifield-Pit 37	Harmon-StL 28	Rucker-Bro 7.27	Steele-Pit-Bro 1.71
Harmon-StL 23	Alexander-Phi .683	Adams-Pit 4.4	Alexander-Phi 37	Leifield-Pit 26	Ames-NY 7.46	Brown-Chi 1.83
	Mathewson-NY .667	Harmon-StL 4.3	Adams-Pit 37	Adams-Pit 24	Harmon-StL 7.50	Wiltse-NY 1.87
STRIKEOUTS	**STRIKEOUTS/GAME**	**GAMES**	**SAVES**	**BASE RUNNERS/9**	**ADJUSTED RELIEF RUNS**	**RELIEF RANKING**
Marquard-NY 237	Marquard-NY 7.68	Brown-Chi 53	Brown-Chi 13	Adams-Pit 9.30		
Alexander-Phi 227	Alexander-Phi 5.57	Harmon-StL 51	Crandall-NY 5	Ames-NY 10.01		
Rucker-Bro 190	Rucker-Bro 5.42	Rucker-Bro 48		Mathewson-NY 10.03		
Moore-Phi 174	Ames-NY 5.18	Alexander-Phi 48		Steele-Pit-Bro 10.33		
Harmon-StL 144	Moore-Phi 5.08			Alexander-Phi 10.35		
INNINGS PITCHED	**OPPONENTS' AVG.**	**OPPONENTS' OBP**	**EARNED RUN AVERAGE**	**ADJUSTED ERA**	**ADJUSTED STARTER RUNS**	**PITCHER WINS**
Alexander-Phi 367.0	Alexander-Phi .219	Adams-Pit .271	Mathewson-NY 1.99	Mathewson-NY 168	Mathewson-NY 42.4	**Mathewson-NY 5.7**
Harmon-StL 348.0	Marquard-NY .219	Ames-NY .277	Richie-Chi 2.31	Adams-Pit 147	Alexander-Phi 37.0	**Rucker-Bro 3.9**
Leifield-Pit 318.0	Ames-NY .223	Mathewson-NY .283	Adams-Pit 2.33	Richie-Chi 143	Adams-Pit 35.4	**Adams-Pit 3.9**
Rucker-Bro 315.2	Rucker-Bro .226	Wiltse-NY .292	Marquard-NY 2.50	Marquard-NY 134	Leifield-Pit 29.7	**Alexander-Phi 3.7**
Moore-Phi 308.1	Keefe-Cin .229	Alexander-Phi .293	Alexander-Phi 2.57	Alexander-Phi 133	Rucker-Bro 29.6	**Leifield-Pit 3.4**

A Time of Giants

The introduction in both leagues of a new cork-centered baseball led to an increase in scoring. NL runs rose 9.7 percent and homers ballooned to 316, a league record until 1921. However, stolen bases were also up, to 1.36 per game, the highest in NL history. Bob Bescher of the Reds set a league record with 81 steals, while Jimmy Sheckard of the Cubs established a mark with 147 walks, the Senior Circuit's highest until 1947, though bases on balls for hitters were not widely recognized.

New York's Christy Mathewson had another amazing season, while his chief mound rival, Chicago's Mordecai Brown, notched 13 saves, which also set a record. Philadelphia rookie Grover Cleveland Alexander enjoyed one of the more spectacular debuts in history. The righty was 28-13, leading the NL in wins, shutouts, innings, and opponents' average.

On the other side, the last-place Braves became the only NL team until 1923 to allow more than 1,000 runs. In context, their staff rates as one of the worst of all time, posting a 5.08 ERA when the league ERA was 3.39, and leading in runs allowed by more than 250. Their hitters finished second in batting average and led in home runs, but it translated into 107 losses. Fans in the Hub showed an appropriate level of support; for the third straight year, attendance dropped more than 20 percent.

On June 28, the Giants moved into a new Polo Grounds, and experienced a huge gain in attendance. Gotham fans were rewarded in September when their club broke away from the Cubs to capture the flag. While much was made of New York's speed-based attack—they broke the league record with 347 swipes—the Giants won with the league's best pitching and hitters who led in batting average, on-base percentage, and slugging percentage. Unfortunately, the Giants didn't hit a lick in the World Series, losing to Philadelphia in five.

1911 AMERICAN LEAGUE

TEAM	W	L	T	PCT	GB	HW	HL	R	OR	PA	H	2B	3B	HR	BB	SO	HB	SH	AVG	OBP	SLG	OPS	AOPS	BR	ABR	PF	SB	CS	BSA	BSR
Phi	101	50	1	.669	—	**54**	20	**861**	**602**	5919	1540	237	93	**35**	424	—	65	**231**	**.296**	**.357**	**.398**	**755**	**119**	**109**	**124**	98	226			
Det	89	65	0	.578	13.5	51	25	831	777	5995	**1544**	230	**96**	30	471	—	49	181	.292	.355	.388	743	108	92	53	105	**276**			
Cle	80	73	3	.523	22	46	30	693	712	5885	1501	**238**	81	20	354	—	50	160	.282	.333	.369	702	101	1	-7	101	209			
Chi	77	74	3	.510	24	40	37	718	624	5850	1401	179	92	20	385	—	48	207	.269	.325	.350	675	97	-50	-28	97	201			
Bos	78	75	0	.510	24	39	37	680	643	5806	1379	203	66	**35**	**506**	—	74	212	.275	.350	.363	713	106	42	49	99	190			
NY	76	76	1	.500	25.5	36	40	684	723	5793	1374	190	**96**	25	493	—	64	184	.272	.344	.362	706	97	23	-21	107	269			
Was	64	90	0	.416	38.5	39	38	624	765	5760	1308	159	54	16	466	—	**80**	149	.258	.330	.320	650	89	-75	-63	98	215			
StL	45	107	0	.296	56.5	25	53	567	812	5631	1192	187	63	17	460	—	34	141	.239	.307	.311	618	81	-143	-121	96	125			
Total	614	—	—	—	—	330	280	5658	—	46639	11239	1623	641	198	3559	5093	464	1465	.273	.338	.358	696	—	—	—	—	1711	—	—	—

TEAM	CG	SHO	GR	SV	IP	H	HR	BB	SO	BR/9	ERA	AERA	OAV	OOB	PR	APR	PF	OSB	OCS	FA	E	WPB	DP	FW	PW	BW	BSW	DIF
Phi	97	13	77	**13**	1375.2	1343	**17**	487	739	12.5	3.01	105	.264	.338	50	22	94	184	*171*	**.964**	**225**	**48**	100	**4.9**	2.2	**12.2**	—	6.3
Det	**108**	8	67	3	1387.2	1514	28	460	538	13.3	3.73	93	.283	.348	-60	-43	104	203	*176*	.951	318	55	78	-.9	-4.2	5.2	—	12.0
Cle	93	6	74	6	1390.2	1382	**17**	552	675	12.9	3.36	101	.267	.345	-3	7	102	246	***193***	.954	303	88	**108**	.3	.7	-.7	—	3.2
Chi	85	**17**	**103**	11	1386.1	1349	22	**384**	**752**	**11.5**	2.97	108	**.255**	**.310**	57	39	96	**151**	*150*	.961	252	60	98	3.4	3.8	-2.8	—	-2.9
Bos	87	10	85	8	1351.2	**1309**	21	473	711	12.2	**2.74**	**119**	.262	.332	**89**	**80**	98	219	*177*	.949	323	60	93	-1.4	**7.9**	4.8	—	-9.8
NY	90	5	79	3	1360.2	1404	26	406	667	12.3	3.54	101	.270	.329	-30	9	108	219	*170*	.949	328	53	99	-1.7	.9	-2.1	—	2.9
Was	106	13	62	3	1353.1	1471	39	410	628	12.8	3.52	93	.277	.334	-27	-38	98	201	*178*	.953	305	96	90	-.0	-3.7	-6.2	—	-3.0
StL	92	8	80	1	1332.1	1465	28	463	383	13.4	3.86	87	.278	.342	-77	-73	101	291	*186*	.945	358	50	104	-3.8	-7.2	-11.9	—	-8.1
Total	758	80	627	48	10938.1	—	—	—	—	12.6	3.34	—	.273	.338	—	—	—	—	—	.953	2412	510	770	—	—	—	—	—

BATTER-FIELDER WINS	BATTING AVERAGE	ON-BASE PERCENTAGE	SLUGGING AVERAGE	ON-BASE PLUS SLUGGING	ADJUSTED OPS	ADJUSTED BATTER RUNS
Cobb-Det............6.6	Cobb-Det.............420	Jackson-Cle.........468	Cobb-Det.............621	Cobb-Det...........1088	Cobb-Det.............193	Cobb-Det............71.7
Jackson-Cle.......6.5	Jackson-Cle.........408	Cobb-Det.............467	Jackson-Cle.........590	Jackson-Cle........1058	Jackson-Cle.........192	Jackson-Cle.........71.5
Collins-Phi.........4.6	Crawford-Det........378	Collins-Phi...........451	Crawford-Det........526	Crawford-Det........964	Collins-Phi...........163	Crawford-Det.......47.0
Baker-Phi............3.5	Collins-Phi...........365	Crawford-Det........438	Cree-NY...............513	Collins-Phi...........932	Crawford-Det........160	Collins-Phi..........45.6
Gardner-Bos......3.3	Cree-NY...............348	Speaker-Bos.........418	Baker-Phi.............508	Cree-NY...............928	Speaker-Bos.........158	Speaker-Bos........40.5

RUNS	HITS	DOUBLES	TRIPLES	HOME RUNS	TOTAL BASES	RUNS BATTED IN
Cobb-Det.............147	Cobb-Det.............248	Cobb-Det...............47	Cobb-Det...............24	Baker-Phi...............11	Cobb-Det.............367	Cobb-Det.............127
Jackson-Cle.........126	Jackson-Cle.........233	Jackson-Cle...........45	Cree-NY.................22	Speaker-Bos............8	Jackson-Cle.........337	Crawford-Det........115
Bush-Det..............126	Crawford-Det........217	Baker-Phi...............42	Jackson-Cle...........19	Cobb-Det.................8	Crawford-Det........302	Baker-Phi..............115
Milan-Was............109	Baker-Phi.............198	Lord-Phi.................37	Lord-Chi.................18		Baker-Phi.............301	Bodie-Chi................97
Crawford-Det........109	Milan-Was............194	LaPorte-StL...........37	Wolter-NY..............15		Cree-NY...............267	Delahanty-Det.........94

BASES ON BALLS	STOLEN BASES	BASE STEALING RUNS	FIELDING RUNS-INFIELD	FIELDING RUNS-OUTFIELD	OUTFIELD ASSISTS	CATCHER CS PCT.
Bush-Det................98	Cobb-Det...............83		Tannehill-Chi........36.3	Hogan-Phi-StL.....12.6	Murphy-Phi............34	Sullivan-Chi.........52.2
Milan-Was..............74	Milan-Was.............58		McBride-Was.......27.4	Cobb-Det...............6.7	Milan-Was.............33	Thomas-Phi.........51.2
Gessler-Was...........74	Cree-NY.................48		Gardner-Bos........22.7	Milan-Was.............6.6	Jackson-Cle...........32	Stanage-Det........46.7
Hooper-Bos............73	Callahan-Chi..........45		Austin-StL............18.6	Hooper-Bos...........5.8	Hogan-Phi-StL........28	Sweeney-NY........42.0
Austin-StL..............69	Lord-Chi.................43		Bush-Det..............12.5	Jackson-Cle...........5.3		

WINS	WINNING PCT.	WINS ABOVE TEAM	GAMES STARTED	COMPLETE GAMES	FEWEST HITS/GAME	FEWEST BB/GAME
Coombs-Phi...........28	Bender-Phi...........773	Johnson-Was.........9.2	Coombs-Phi...........40	Johnson-Was.........36	Gregg-Cle...........6.33	White-Chi............1.47
Walsh-Chi..............27	Gregg-Cle............767	Gregg-Cle..............8.5	Walsh-Chi..............37	Walsh-Chi..............33	Wood-Bos...........7.38	Lake-StL.............1.67
Johnson-Was..........25	Plank-Phi.............742	Ford-NY................6.4	Johnson-Was.........37	Ford-NY.................26	Krapp-Cle...........7.62	Walsh-Chi............1.76
	Coombs-Phi..........700	Walsh-Chi..............5.5	Wood-Bos..............33	Coombs-Phi...........26	Morgan-Phi..........7.82	Warhop-NY..........1.89
	Morgan-Phi..........682	Plank-Phi...............4.1	Ford-NY.................33		Scott-Chi.............7.91	Powell-StL...........1.91

STRIKEOUTS	STRIKEOUTS/GAME	GAMES	SAVES	BASE RUNNERS/9	ADJUSTED RELIEF RUNS	RELIEF RANKING
Walsh-Chi............255	Wood-Bos...........7.54	Walsh-Chi..............56	Walsh-Chi.................4	Gregg-Cle...........9.86		
Wood-Bos............231	Walsh-Chi...........6.23	Coombs-Phi...........47	Plank-Phi.................4	Walsh-Chi...........9.91		
Johnson-Was........207	Lange-Chi...........5.79	Wood-Bos..............44	Hall-Bos...................4	Wood-Bos..........10.22		
Coombs-Phi.........185	Johnson-Was.......5.78	Caldwell-NY...........41	Wood-Bos.................3	Johnson-Was.....10.33		
Ford-NY...............158	Kahler-Cle...........5.66		Bender-Phi................3	Ford-NY............10.59		

INNINGS PITCHED	OPPONENTS' AVG.	OPPONENTS' OBP	EARNED RUN AVERAGE	ADJUSTED ERA	ADJUSTED STARTER RUNS	PITCHER WINS
Walsh-Chi.........368.2	Gregg-Cle............205	Walsh-Chi.............280	Gregg-Cle...........1.80	Gregg-Cle............189	Johnson-Was.......43.1	**Wood-Bos...........5.7**
Coombs-Phi.......336.2	Wood-Bos............223	Johnson-Was........283	Johnson-Was.......1.90	Johnson-Was........173	Gregg-Cle...........42.8	**Walsh-Chi...........5.5**
Johnson-Was.....322.1	Krapp-Cle............232	Wood-Bos.............284	Wood-Bos...........2.02	Wood-Bos.............162	Walsh-Chi...........42.1	**Johnson-Was.....5.4**
Ford-NY............281.1	Ford-NY...............237	Gregg-Cle............286	Plank-Phi............2.10	Ford-NY...............158	Wood-Bos...........33.7	**Gregg-Cle...........4.6**
Wood-Bos.........275.2	Johnson-Was........238	Ford-NY...............291	Bender-Phi..........2.16	Plank-Phi.............150	Ford-NY..............30.4	**Plank-Phi............3.2**

White Elephants on Parade

As the season opened, baseball fans were shocked by the death of Cleveland's mound ace, Addie Joss, from tuberculosis. The two-time league ERA leader died April 14, just two days after his 30th birthday. Cy Young threw his final pitch in the majors in 1911, going 7-9 for two clubs to raise his win total to 511.

The major leagues introduced a new cork-centered baseball, sending the previous rubber-centered ball to the trash bin. As a result, the league batting average rose 30 points. Home runs also increased and runs per game rose to 4.61, the highest total in a decade and the highest until 1920. Who better to benefit from this new ball than Ty Cobb, already the league's best player? The Georgia Peach set new AL marks in 1911 for hits, RBIs, runs, and total bases, and batted .420. Detroit started hot, leading by 9½ games in May, but from July through the end of the season played essentially .500 ball as the Athletics caught fire in August. Connie Mack's White Elephants pulled away and won by 13½ games.

Philadelphia's so-called "$100,000 Infield" of Stuffy McInnis, Eddie Collins, Jack Barry, and Frank Baker, showed good leather and fine stick, and the club's starting pitching was again excellent. The World Series went six games with the Athletics coming out on top for the second straight time. Baker hit two crucial long balls to gain the nickname "Home Run," and Chief Bender, Jack Coombs, and Eddie Plank bested the Giants. It was an exciting Series; the first five games were close, two of them extending into extra innings.

1910 NATIONAL LEAGUE

TEAM	W	L	T	PCT	GB	HW	HL	R	OR	PA	H	2B	3B	HR	BB	SO	HB	SH	AVG	OBP	SLG	OPS	AOPS	BR	ABR	PF	SB	CS	BSA	BSR
Chi	104	50	0	.675	—	**58**	19	712	**499**	5792	1333	219	**84**	**34**	542	501	39	**234**	.268	.344	**.366**	710	114	84	90	99	173			
NY	91	63	1	.591	13	52	26	**715**	567	5873	**1391**	204	83	31	562	**489**	57	193	**.275**	**.354**	**.366**	**720**	**116**	**108**	**107**	100	282			
Pit	86	67	1	.562	17.5	46	30	655	576	5794	1364	214	83	33	437	524	34	198	.266	.328	.360	688	100	30	-6	106	148			
Phi	78	75	4	.510	25.5	40	36	674	639	5925	1319	**223**	71	22	506	559	43	205	.255	.327	.338	665	97	-1	-21	103	199			
Cin	75	79	2	.487	29	39	37	620	684	5861	1326	150	79	23	529	515	29	182	.259	.332	.333	665	105	-3	26	96	**310**			
Bro	64	90	2	.416	40	39	39	497	623	5782	1174	166	73	25	434	706	40	183	.229	.294	.305	599	82	-136	-121	97	151			
StL	63	90	0	.412	40.5	35	41	639	718	5798	1217	167	70	15	**655**	581	**78**	153	.248	.345	.319	664	103	22	47	96	179			
Bos	53	100	4	.346	50.5	29	48	495	701	5710	1260	173	49	31	359	540	47	181	.246	.301	.317	618	81	-102	-124	105	152			
Total	621	—	—	—	—	338	276	5007	—	46535	10384	1516	592	214	4024	4415	367	1529	.256	.328	.338	666	—	—	—	—	1594	—	—	—

TEAM	CG	SHO	GR	SV	IP	H	HR	BB	SO	BR/9	ERA	AERA	OAV	OOB	PR	APR	PF	OSB	OCS	FA	E	WPB	DP	FW	PW	BW	BSW	DIF
Chi	100	**25**	74	13	1378.2	**1171**	18	474	609	**11.0**	**2.51**	**115**	**.235**	**.307**	**79**	**57**	95	**145**	*148*	.963	**230**	46	110	**2.1**	**6.0**	9.5	—	9.4
NY	96	9	80	10	1391.2	1290	30	397	**717**	11.2	2.68	110	.250	.308	54	45	98	192	*153*	.955	291	52	117	-1.7	4.7	**11.3**	—	-.3
Pit	73	13	100	12	1376.0	1254	20	**392**	479	11.1	2.83	109	.250	.311	29	37	102	168	*145*	.961	245	**23**	102	1.1	3.9	-.6	—	5.1
Phi	84	17	**107**	9	1411.1	1297	36	547	657	12.1	3.05	102	.253	.330	-5	9	103	213	*163*	.960	258	49	132	.6	.9	-2.2	—	2.1
Cin	86	16	88	11	1386.2	1334	27	528	497	12.5	3.08	94	.261	.338	-9	-30	96	153	*145*	.955	291	53	103	-1.6	-3.2	2.7	—	.0
Bro	**103**	15	65	5	1420.1	1331	**17**	545	555	12.1	3.07	99	.259	.335	-7	-9	100	215	*188*	**.964**	235	54	125	2.0	-.9	-12.7	—	-1.3
StL	81	4	96	**14**	1337.1	1396	30	541	466	13.3	3.78	79	.275	.350	-112	-122	98	264	*138*	.959	261	61	109	.0	-12.8	4.9	—	-5.6
Bos	72	12	**107**	9	1390.1	1328	36	599	531	12.8	3.22	103	.265	.349	-30	13	110	244	***192***	.954	305	57	**137**	-2.4	1.4	-13.1	—	-9.5
Total	695	111	717	83	11092.1	—	—	—	—	12.0	3.02	—	.256	.328	—	—	—	—	—	.959	2116	395	935	—	—	—	—	—

BATTER-FIELDER WINS	BATTING AVERAGE	ON-BASE PERCENTAGE	SLUGGING AVERAGE	ON-BASE PLUS SLUGGING	ADJUSTED OPS	ADJUSTED BATTER RUNS
Konetchy-StL.....3.9	Magee-Phi............331	Magee-Phi............445	Magee-Phi............507	Magee-Phi............952	Magee-Phi............172	Magee-Phi...........52.7
Mowrey-StL........3.6	Campbell-Pit.........326	Snodgrass-NY......440	Hofman-Chi..........461	Snodgrass-NY......871	Snodgrass-NY......154	Hofman-Chi..........33.3
Wagner-Pit..........3.5	Hofman-Chi..........325	Evers-Chi..............413	Schulte-Chi...........460	Hofman-Chi..........867	Hofman-Chi..........154	Snodgrass-NY.....33.1
Magee-Phi..........3.4	Snodgrass-NY......321	Hofman-Chi..........406	Merkle-NY.............441	Konetchy-StL........822	Konetchy-StL........145	Konetchy-StL.......31.9
Hofman-Chi........2.8	Wagner-Pit............320	Huggins-StL.........399	Campbell-Pit.........436	Wagner-Pit............822	Schulte-Chi...........137	Wagner-Pit...........23.7

RUNS	HITS	DOUBLES	TRIPLES	HOME RUNS	TOTAL BASES	RUNS BATTED IN
Magee-Phi............110	Wagner-Pit............178	Byrne-Pit.................43	Mitchell-Cin............18	Schulte-Chi............10	Magee-Phi............263	Magee-Phi............123
Huggins-StL..........101	Byrne-Pit...............178	Magee-Phi..............39	Magee-Phi..............17	Beck-Bos................10	Schulte-Chi...........257	Mitchell-Cin............88
Byrne-Pit...............101	Wheat-Bro............172	Wheat-Bro..............36	Konetchy-StL..........16	Doyle-NY..................8	Byrne-Pit...............251	Murray-NY..............87
Doyle-NY................97	Magee-Phi............172	Merkle-NY...............35	Hofman-Chi............16	Daubert-Bro.............8	Wheat-Bro............244	Hofman-Chi............86
Bescher-Cin............95	Hoblitzel-Cin.........170	Wagner-Pit..............34			Wagner-Pit...........240	Wagner-Pit..............81

BASES ON BALLS	STOLEN BASES	BASE STEALING RUNS	FIELDING RUNS-INFIELD	FIELDING RUNS-OUTFIELD	OUTFIELD ASSISTS	CATCHER CS PCT.
Huggins-StL..........116	Bescher-Cin............70		Shean-Bos..........43.2	Paskert-Cin............9.6	Murray-NY..............26	McLean-Cin.........49.5
Evers-Chi.............108	Murray-NY..............57		Doolan-Phi..........17.8	Sheckard-Chi.........8.1	Paskert-Cin............25	Kling-Chi.............48.7
Magee-Phi..............94	Paskert-Cin............51		Mowrey-StL.........14.3	Collins-Bos............8.1	Ellis-StL..................25	Bergen-Bro..........47.5
Titus-Phi.................93	Magee-Phi..............49		Tinker-Chi............14.3	Murray-NY.............5.9	Bates-Phi................24	Gibson-Pit...........46.9
Sheckard-Chi..........83	Devore-NY..............43		Knabe-Phi...........13.9	Bates-Phi..............5.4		Meyers-NY..........44.6

WINS	WINNING PCT.	WINS ABOVE TEAM	GAMES STARTED	COMPLETE GAMES	FEWEST HITS/GAME	FEWEST BB/GAME
Mathewson-NY.......27	Cole-Chi................833	Mathewson-NY......8.2	Rucker-Bro.............39	Rucker-Bro.............27	Cole-Chi...............6.53	Suggs-Cin............1.62
Brown-Chi...............25	Crandall-NY..........810	Cole-Chi.................6.3	Mattern-Bos...........37	Mathewson-NY.......27	Scanlan-Bro.........7.25	Mathewson-NY....1.70
Moore-Phi...............22	Mathewson-NY.....750	Crandall-NY...........6.0	Curtis-Bos..............37	Brown-Chi...............27	Moore-Phi...........7.25	Crandall-NY.........1.86
Suggs-Cin...............20	Adams-Pit............667	Phillippe-Pit...........5.9	Bell-Bro...................36	Bell-Bro...................25	Drucke-NY..........7.27	Brown-Chi............1.95
Cole-Chi..................20	Brown-Chi............641	Suggs-Cin.............5.1		Barger-Bro.............25	Ames-NY.............7.61	Wiltse-NY.............1.99

STRIKEOUTS	STRIKEOUTS/GAME	GAMES	SAVES	BASE RUNNERS/9	ADJUSTED RELIEF RUNS	RELIEF RANKING
Moore-Phi.............185	Drucke-NY...........6.31	Mattern-Bos............51	Gaspar-Cin...............7	Phillippe-Pit..........9.10		
Mathewson-NY.....184	Frock-Pit-Bos.......5.98	Gaspar-Cin.............48	Brown-Chi.................7	McQuillan-Phi......9.57		
Frock-Pit-Bos........171	Moore-Phi...........5.88		Crandall-NY.............5	Pfiester-Chi..........9.78		
Drucke-NY............151	Mathewson-NY....5.20		Richie-Bos-Chi..........4	Brown-Chi............9.87		
Rucker-Bro............147	Ames-NY............4.44		Phillippe-Pit.............4	Overall-Chi.........10.02		

INNINGS PITCHED	OPPONENTS' AVG.	OPPONENTS' OBP	EARNED RUN AVERAGE	ADJUSTED ERA	ADJUSTED STARTER RUNS	PITCHER WINS
Rucker-Bro.........320.1	Cole-Chi................211	Brown-Chi............277	McQuillan-Phi......1.60	Cole-Chi................159	Mathewson-NY....35.4	**Mathewson-NY..5.3**
Mathewson-NY..318.1	Drucke-NY............228	Mathewson-NY.....286	Cole-Chi..............1.80	Mathewson-NY.....156	Cole-Chi..............29.3	**Brown-Chi...........4.0**
Bell-Bro.............310.0	Moore-Phi............228	Crandall-NY.........289	Brown-Chi...........1.86	Brown-Chi............155	Brown-Chi...........28.6	**Cole-Chi.............3.1**
Mattern-Bos.......305.0	Brown-Chi............232	Adams-Pit............291	Mathewson-NY....1.89	Adams-Pit............138	McQuillan-Phi......22.8	**Moore-Phi...........2.6**
Brown-Chi.........295.1	Scanlan-Bro.........234	Bell-Bro................296	Ames-NY............2.22	Ames-NY.............133	Moore-Phi...........20.2	**Suggs-Cin...........2.4**

END OF AN ERA IN CHICAGO

The rules committee made two codifications that seem oddly obvious: The batting order must be presented before the game and followed, and substitutions can only come when time was out. In addition, the passed ball and wild pitch were first defined.

Christy Mathewson and Three Finger Brown were again the league's top pitchers, maintaining their touch even as team runs per game topped 4.00 for first time in five years. NL batters clubbed 214 homers in 1910, the highest total since 1901. But another runaway by the Cubs dropped attendance 16 percent; attendance would not reach its 1908 level again until 1920.

Jake Daubert debuted as Brooklyn's everyday first baseman, and went on to a fifteen-year career and two batting titles. Catcher Hank Gowdy, who would spend his entire seventeen-year skein with the Giants and Braves, plus another season in France during World War I, played his first game in September 1910. Pirates outfielder Max Carey, who would lead the NL ten times in steals, made The Show at age 20.

Infielder Alan Storke, who split '09 between Pittsburgh and St. Louis, underwent a lung operation in March but died from complications. He was 26. Others playing their last games (but not dying) included Hall of Famer "Wee" Willie Keeler, Pirates hurler Sam Leever, and Vic Willis, who won 249 games in thirteen years.

For the fourth time in five years, the Cubs won more than 100 games, pulling from the pack in May and never looking back. Neither the Pirates, whose pitching staff had aged dangerously, or the rebuilding Giants were serious threats. However, John McGraw had restocked New York with some excellent young players. A loss to the Athletics in the World Series ended the Cubs' era of dominance; they would only win one more flag in the next two decades.

1910 AMERICAN LEAGUE

TEAM	W	L	T	PCT	GB	HW	HL	R	OR	PA	H	2B	3B	HR	BB	SO	HB	SH	AVG	OBP	SLG	OPS	AOPS	BR	ABR	PF	SB	CS	BSA	BSR
Phi	102	48	5	.680	—	**57**	19	674	**442**	5809	**1373**	**191**	**105**	19	409	—	47	199	**.266**	.326	**.355**	**681**	**120**	**104**	**111**	99	207			
NY	88	63	5	.583	14.5	49	25	626	557	5762	1254	164	75	20	**464**	—	71	176	.248	.320	.322	642	101	45	11	106	**288**			
Det	86	68	1	.558	18	46	31	**679**	584	5746	1317	190	72	28	459	—	51	197	.261	**.329**	.344	673	110	99	57	107	249			
Bos	81	72	5	.529	22.5	51	28	641	564	5917	1350	175	87	**43**	430	—	56	**227**	.259	.323	.351	674	114	94	78	102	194			
Cle	71	81	9	.467	32	39	36	548	657	5988	1316	188	64	9	366	—	37	190	.244	.296	.308	604	94	-39	-46	101	189			
Chi	68	85	3	.444	35.5	41	37	457	479	5661	1058	115	58	7	403	—	44	190	.211	.275	.261	536	76	-154	-136	96	183			
Was	66	85	6	.437	36.5	38	35	501	551	5690	1175	145	47	9	449	—	**82**	170	.236	.309	.289	598	98	-30	-4	95	192			
StL	47	107	4	.305	57	26	51	451	743	5675	1105	131	60	12	415	—	36	147	.218	.281	.274	555	84	-120	-90	94	169			
Total	628	—	—	—	—	347	262	4577	—	46248	9948	1299	568	147	3395	5278	424	1496	.243	.308	.313	621	—	—	—	—	1671	—	—	—

TEAM	CG	SHO	GR	SV	IP	H	HR	BB	SO	BR/9	ERA	AERA	OAV	OOB	PR	APR	PF	OSB	OCS	FA	E	WPB	DP	FW	PW	BW	BSW	DIF
Phi	**123**	**24**	45	5	1421.2	**1103**	**8**	450	**789**	10.2	**1.79**	**133**	**.221**	.292	**116**	**97**	94	187	*168*	**.965**	**230**	49	**117**	**3.9**	**10.8**	**12.3**	—	.0
NY	110	14	57	**8**	1399.0	1238	16	**364**	654	10.7	2.61	102	.243	.300	-15	5	106	194	*152*	.956	286	**48**	95	.2	.6	1.2	—	10.5
Det	108	17	64	5	1380.1	1257	34	460	532	11.6	2.82	93	.248	.319	-47	-26	104	193	*168*	.956	288	**48**	79	-.0	-2.9	6.3	—	5.6
Bos	100	12	70	6	1430.0	1236	30	414	670	10.7	2.45	104	.235	.297	10	14	101	207	*141*	.954	309	52	80	-1.1	1.6	8.7	—	-4.6
Cle	92	13	**82**	5	1467.0	1392	10	488	617	11.9	2.88	90	.261	.330	-60	-49	103	259	*190*	.964	248	62	112	3.4	-5.4	-5.1	—	2.2
Chi	103	23	66	7	1421.0	1130	16	381	785	**9.8**	2.03	118	.222	**.281**	77	59	95	**175**	*158*	.954	314	**48**	100	-1.7	6.6	-15.1	—	1.8
Was	119	19	43	3	1373.1	1215	19	375	674	10.8	2.46	101	.244	.304	8	5	99	201	*170*	.959	264	84	99	1.8	.6	-.4	—	-11.4
StL	101	9	72	3	1391.0	1356	14	532	557	12.6	3.09	80	.265	.341	-89	-97	98	252	***196***	.943	385	**48**	113	-6.3	-10.8	-10.0	—	-2.9
Total	856	131	499	42	11283.1	—	—	—	—	11.0	2.52	—	.243	.308	—	—	—	—	—	.956	2324	439	795	—	—	—	—	—

BATTER-FIELDER WINS	BATTING AVERAGE	ON-BASE PERCENTAGE	SLUGGING AVERAGE	ON-BASE PLUS SLUGGING	ADJUSTED OPS	ADJUSTED BATTER RUNS
Lajoie-Cle 8.9	Cobb-Det .383	Cobb-Det .456	Cobb-Det .551	Cobb-Det 1008	Cobb-Det 202	Lajoie-Cle 69.3
Collins-Phi 7.0	Lajoie-Cle .384	Lajoie-Cle .445	Lajoie-Cle .514	Lajoie-Cle 960	Lajoie-Cle 198	Cobb-Det 61.5
Cobb-Det 6.3	Speaker-Bos .340	Speaker-Bos .404	Speaker-Bos .468	Speaker-Bos 873	Speaker-Bos 169	Speaker-Bos 42.5
Speaker-Bos 4.8	Collins-Phi .324	Collins-Phi .382	Murphy-Phi .436	Collins-Phi 800	Collins-Phi 152	Collins-Phi 33.9
McBride-Was 4.1	Knight-NY .312	Milan-Was .379	Oldring-Phi .430	Cree-NY 775	Murphy-Phi 143	Murphy-Phi 24.1

RUNS	HITS	DOUBLES	TRIPLES	HOME RUNS	TOTAL BASES	RUNS BATTED IN
Cobb-Det 106	Lajoie-Cle 227	Lajoie-Cle 51	Crawford-Det 19	Stahl-Bos 10	Lajoie-Cle 304	Crawford-Det 120
Lajoie-Cle 94	Cobb-Det 194	Cobb-Det 35	Lord-Cle-Phi 18	Lewis-Bos 8	Cobb-Det 279	Cobb-Det 91
Speaker-Bos 92	Collins-Phi 188	Lewis-Bos 29	Murphy-Phi 18	Cobb-Det 8	Speaker-Bos 252	Collins-Phi 81
Bush-Det 90	Speaker-Bos 183	Murphy-Phi 28	Stahl-Bos 16	Speaker-Bos 7	Crawford-Det 249	Stahl-Bos 77
Milan-Was 89	Crawford-Det 170	Oldring-Phi 27	Cree-NY 16	Crawford-Det 5	Murphy-Phi 244	Lajoie-Cle 76

BASES ON BALLS	STOLEN BASES	BASE STEALING RUNS	FIELDING RUNS-INFIELD	FIELDING RUNS-OUTFIELD	OUTFIELD ASSISTS	CATCHER CS PCT.
Bush-Det 78	Collins-Phi 81		McBride-Was 32.8	Lewis-Bos 11.5	Milan-Was 30	Stanage-Det 48.5
Milan-Was 71	Cobb-Det 65		Collins-Phi 29.8	Birmingham-Cle 10.3	Hooper-Bos 30	Street-Was 48.0
Wolter-NY 66	Zeider-Chi 49		Wallace-StL 22.6	Hooper-Bos 8.8	Lewis-Bos 28	Stephens-StL 42.8
Cobb-Det 64	Bush-Det 49		Lajoie-Cle 12.5	Speaker-Bos 8.6	Birmingham-Cle 24	Carrigan-Bos 40.4
	Milan-Was 44		Bush-Det 10.4	Milan-Was 7.6	Gessler-Was 23	

WINS	WINNING PCT.	WINS ABOVE TEAM	GAMES STARTED	COMPLETE GAMES	FEWEST HITS/GAME	FEWEST BB/GAME
Coombs-Phi 31	Bender-Phi .821	Ford-NY 9.7	Johnson-Was 42	Johnson-Was 38	Ford-NY 5.83	Walsh-Chi 1.49
Ford-NY 26	Ford-NY .813	Johnson-Was 7.4	Coombs-Phi 38	Coombs-Phi 35	Walsh-Chi 5.89	Young-Cle 1.49
Johnson-Was 25	Coombs-Phi .775	Coombs-Phi 7.3	Walsh-Chi 36	Walsh-Chi 33	Coombs-Phi 6.32	Collins-Bos 1.51
Bender-Phi 23	Donovan-Det .708	Bender-Phi 6.9	Morgan-Phi 34	Ford-NY 29	Johnson-Was 6.37	Bender-Phi 1.69
Mullin-Det 21	Mullin-Det .636	Donovan-Det 4.5	Ford-NY 33	Mullin-Det 27	Bender-Phi 6.55	Johnson-Was 1.85

STRIKEOUTS	STRIKEOUTS/GAME	GAMES	SAVES	BASE RUNNERS/9	ADJUSTED RELIEF RUNS	RELIEF RANKING
Johnson-Was 313	Johnson-Was 7.61	Walsh-Chi 45	Walsh-Chi 5	Walsh-Chi 7.47		
Walsh-Chi 258	Wood-Bos 6.64	Johnson-Was 45	Browning-Det 3	Ford-NY 8.17		
Coombs-Phi 224	Walsh-Chi 6.28	Coombs-Phi 45		Johnson-Was 8.54		
Ford-NY 209	Ford-NY 6.28	Scott-Chi 41		Bender-Phi 8.60		
Bender-Phi 155	Coombs-Phi 5.71			Collins-Bos 9.09		

INNINGS PITCHED	OPPONENTS' AVG.	OPPONENTS' OBP	EARNED RUN AVERAGE	ADJUSTED ERA	ADJUSTED STARTER RUNS	PITCHER WINS
Johnson-Was 370.0	Walsh-Chi .187	Walsh-Chi .226	Walsh-Chi 1.27	Walsh-Chi 189	Coombs-Phi 46.6	**Walsh-Chi 6.3**
Walsh-Chi 369.2	Ford-NY .188	Ford-NY .245	Coombs-Phi 1.30	Johnson-Was 183	Walsh-Chi 45.5	**Coombs-Phi 5.8**
Coombs-Phi 353.0	Coombs-Phi .201	Bender-Phi .255	Johnson-Was 1.36	Coombs-Phi 182	Johnson-Was 43.4	**Johnson-Was 5.5**
Ford-NY 299.2	Johnson-Was .205	Johnson-Was .257	Morgan-Phi 1.55	Ford-NY 161	Ford-NY 33.9	**Ford-NY 4.2**
Morgan-Phi 290.2	Hall-Bos .207	Collins-Bos .264	Bender-Phi 1.58	Collins-Bos 158	Bender-Phi 25.2	**Bender-Phi 4.1**

Chalmers Promotion Sparks Chicanery and Controversy

The Indians began the season in brand-new League Park, while on July 1, the White Sox moved into Comiskey Park, the "Palace of Baseball." In two years, half of the league had built new concrete-and-steel parks; one more step towards the AL's consolidation of power. Despite this, attendance fell nearly 13 percent.

One of the biggest controversies of the era focused on the batting title, a battle between Cleveland's popular Nap Lajoie and Detroit's *un*popular Ty Cobb. The Chalmers company promised a car to the batting titlist, and on the season's last day, the Browns had their third baseman play deep, allowing Lajoie to bunt for seven hits in a doubleheader and to finish at .384. Even so, Cobb won because of a clerical error that double-counted 2 of Cobb's hits, an error not corrected for 70 years. Chalmers awarded each man a car.

Connie Mack's Athletics pulled away from Detroit in early summer and coasted to the title. The Yankees moved from fifth to second with a speed-based attack and good pitching. The Tigers, disheartened by three straight World Series losses, ended third despite Cobb leading the league in runs, slugging, and on-base percentage, edging out Lajoie in those categories without any computation errors or uncontested bunts.

Two standouts played their last games. Outfielder Elmer Flick, a speed demon beset by injuries, was through at 34. Rube Waddell, the overpowering southpaw, could no longer get hitters out consistently, and was released by St. Louis. He would be dead within four years.

Setting an all-time AL record for team ERA at 1.79, Athletics pitchers—Jack Coombs and Chief Bender combined for 54 wins—did not allow a home run at Shibe Park *all season*. But they also had the league's best offense, as well as ERA, in road games. In the World Series, the Mackmen completely destroyed Chicago, mauling the Cubs for 35 runs in five games and allowing just 15.

1909 NATIONAL LEAGUE

TEAM	W	L	T	PCT	GB	HW	HL	R	OR	PA	H	2B	3B	HR	BB	SO	HB	SH	AVG	OBP	SLG	OPS	AOPS	BR	ABR	PF	SB	CS	BSA	BSR
Pit	110	42	2	.724	—	**56**	21	**699**	447	5855	**1332**	**218**	**92**	25	479	—	36	211	**.260**	.327	**.353**	**680**	**109**	**102**	50	108	185			
Chi	104	49	2	.680	6.5	47	29	635	**390**	5698	1227	203	60	20	420	—	31	**248**	.245	.308	.322	630	100	9	-4	102	187			
NY	92	61	5	.601	18.5	44	33	624	547	5951	1327	173	68	**26**	530	—	52	151	.254	**.329**	.328	657	**109**	71	61	102	240			
Cin	77	76	4	.503	33.5	39	38	606	599	5816	1273	159	72	22	478	—	38	212	.250	.319	.323	642	107	34	39	99	**280**			
Phi	74	79	1	.484	36.5	40	37	517	519	5696	1228	185	53	12	369	—	54	239	.244	.303	.309	612	95	-25	-29	101	185			
Bro	55	98	2	.359	55.5	34	45	444	627	5579	1157	176	59	16	330	—	20	173	.229	.279	.296	575	87	-100	-83	96	141			
StL	54	98	2	.355	56	26	48	583	731	5857	1242	148	56	15	**568**	—	**62**	119	.243	.326	.303	629	**109**	26	**66**	94	163			
Bos	45	108	2	.294	65.5	27	47	435	683	5636	1121	125	43	14	400	—	30	189	.223	.285	.274	559	76	-120	-139	105	135			
Total	621	—	—	—	—	313	298	4543	—	46088	9907	1387	503	150	3574	4437	323	1542	.244	.310	.314	624	—	—	—	—	1516	—	—	—

TEAM	CG	SHO	GR	SV	IP	H	HR	BB	SO	BR/9	ERA	AERA	OAV	OOB	PR	APR	PF	OSB	OCS	FA	E	WPB	DP	FW	PW	BW	BSW	DIF
Pit	93	21	82	11	1401.2	1174	12	**320**	490	9.9	2.07	131	.232	.284	81	95	105	**129**	*143*	**.964**	**228**	**24**	100	**3.5**	10.5	5.5	—	14.4
Chi	111	**32**	57	11	1399.1	**1094**	6	364	680	**9.6**	**1.75**	**145**	**.215**	**.272**	**131**	**127**	98	148	*146*	.962	244	37	95	2.6	**14.1**	-.4	—	11.2
NY	105	17	66	**15**	1440.2	1248	28	397	**735**	10.5	2.27	112	.238	.295	51	43	98	167	*153*	.954	307	55	99	-1.1	4.8	6.8	—	5.1
Cin	91	10	83	8	1407.0	1233	**5**	510	477	11.4	2.52	103	.240	.314	11	9	100	197	*148*	.952	309	56	**120**	-1.4	1.0	4.3	—	-3.5
Phi	89	17	84	6	1391.0	1190	23	472	612	11.0	2.44	106	.235	.304	23	20	100	184	*153*	.962	241	50	97	2.7	2.2	-3.2	—	-4.2
Bro	**126**	18	30	3	1384.1	1277	31	528	594	12.1	3.10	83	.256	.333	-79	-82	100	213	***185***	.955	282	34	86	.2	-9.1	-9.2	—	-3.4
StL	84	5	**92**	4	1379.2	1368	22	483	435	12.4	3.41	74	.263	.331	-126	-142	97	253	*161*	.950	322	61	90	-2.6	-15.7	**7.3**	—	-11.0
Bos	98	13	69	6	1370.2	1329	23	543	414	12.6	3.20	88	.263	.339	-93	-56	109	225	*169*	.948	342	67	101	-3.7	-6.2	-15.4	—	-6.1
Total	797	133	563	64	11174.1	—	—	—	—	11.2	2.59	—	.244	.310	—	—	—	—	—	.956	2275	384	788	—	—	—	—	—

BATTER-FIELDER WINS	BATTING AVERAGE	ON-BASE PERCENTAGE	SLUGGING AVERAGE	ON-BASE PLUS SLUGGING	ADJUSTED OPS	ADJUSTED BATTER RUNS
Wagner-Pit 5.6	Wagner-Pit .339	Wagner-Pit .420	Wagner-Pit .489	Wagner-Pit .909	Wagner-Pit 168	Wagner-Pit 41.7
Gibson-Pit 3.7	Mitchell-Cin .310	Bridwell-NY .386	Mitchell-Cin .430	Mitchell-Cin .808	Mitchell-Cin 152	Konetchy-StL 31.0
Konetchy-StL 3.6	Hoblitzel-Cin .308	Clarke-Pit .384	Doyle-NY .419	Hoblitzel-Cin .782	Konetchy-StL 145	Mitchell-Cin 30.5
Devlin-NY 3.5	Doyle-NY .302	Mitchell-Cin .378	Hoblitzel-Cin .418	Doyle-NY .779	Hoblitzel-Cin 144	Doyle-NY 25.2
Mitchell-Cin 3.2	Bridwell-NY .294	Evers-Chi .369	McCormick-NY .402	Konetchy-StL .762	Doyle-NY 140	Hoblitzel-Cin 25.1
RUNS	**HITS**	**DOUBLES**	**TRIPLES**	**HOME RUNS**	**TOTAL BASES**	**RUNS BATTED IN**
Leach-Pit 126	Doyle-NY 172	Wagner-Pit 39	Mitchell-Cin 17	Murray-NY 7	Wagner-Pit 242	Wagner-Pit 100
Clarke-Pit 97	Grant-Phi 170	Magee-Phi 33	Magee-Phi 14	Leach-Pit 6	Doyle-NY 239	Murray-NY 91
Byrne-StL-Pit 92	Wagner-Pit 168	D.Miller-Pit 31	Konetchy-StL 14	Doyle-NY 6	Konetchy-StL 228	D.Miller-Pit 87
Wagner-Pit 92	Konetchy-StL 165	Sheckard-Chi 29	D.Miller-Pit 13	Becker-Bos 6	Mitchell-Cin 225	Mitchell-Cin 86
	Burch-Bro 163	Leach-Pit 29		Wagner-Pit 5	D.Miller-Pit 222	Konetchy-StL 80
BASES ON BALLS	**STOLEN BASES**	**BASE STEALING RUNS**	**FIELDING RUNS-INFIELD**	**FIELDING RUNS-OUTFIELD**	**OUTFIELD ASSISTS**	**CATCHER CS PCT.**
Clarke-Pit 80	Bescher-Cin 54		Egan-Cin 23.7	Ellis-StL 12.9	Murray-NY 30	Gibson-Pit 52.9
Byrne-StL-Pit 78	Murray-NY 48		Doolan-Phi 23.5	Clarke-Pit 7.3	Ellis-StL 28	Schlei-NY 50.5
Evers-Chi 73	Egan-Cin 39		Tinker-Chi 18.3	Mitchell-Cin 5.3	Bates-Bos-Phi 27	Archer-Chi 49.0
Sheckard-Chi 72	Magee-Phi 38		Devlin-NY 16.9	O'Hara-NY 4.2	Becker-Bos 26	Bergen-Bro 48.9
Bridwell-NY 67	Burch-Bro 38		Byrne-StL-Pit 16.5	Bates-Bos-Phi 3.7		Dooin-Phi 44.9
WINS	**WINNING PCT.**	**WINS ABOVE TEAM**	**GAMES STARTED**	**COMPLETE GAMES**	**FEWEST HITS/GAME**	**FEWEST BB/GAME**
M.Brown-Chi 27	Mathewson-NY .806	Mathewson-NY 8.8	Willis-Pit 35	M.Brown-Chi 32	Mathewson-NY 6.28	Mathewson-NY 1.18
Mathewson-NY 25	H.Camnitz-Pit .806	H.Camnitz-Pit 5.4	Moore-Phi 34	Bell-Bro 29	Fromme-Cin 6.28	M.Brown-Chi 1.39
H.Camnitz-Pit 25	M.Brown-Chi .750	M.Brown-Chi 4.8	Fromme-Cin 34	Rucker-Bro 28	Overall-Chi 6.44	Wiltse-NY 1.70
Willis-Pit 22	Pfiester-Chi .739	Gaspar-Cin 4.6	M.Brown-Chi 34	Mathewson-NY 26	M.Brown-Chi 6.46	Maddox-Pit 1.73
	Leifield-Pit .704	Bell-Bro 4.5	Beebe-StL 34		H.Camnitz-Pit 6.58	McQuillan-Phi 1.96
STRIKEOUTS	**STRIKEOUTS/GAME**	**GAMES**	**SAVES**	**BASE RUNNERS/9**	**ADJUSTED RELIEF RUNS**	**RELIEF RANKING**
Overall-Chi 205	Overall-Chi 6.47	M.Brown-Chi 50	M.Brown-Chi 7	Mathewson-NY 7.45		
Rucker-Bro 201	Rucker-Bro 5.85	Mattern-Bos 47	Crandall-NY 6	Adams-Pit 7.89		
Moore-Phi 173	Ames-NY 5.75	Gaspar-Cin 44		M.Brown-Chi 8.04		
M.Brown-Chi 172	Marquard-NY 5.67	Beebe-StL 44		H.Camnitz-Pit 8.97		
Ames-NY 156	Moore-Phi 5.20			Curtis-Bos 9.22		
INNINGS PITCHED	**OPPONENTS' AVG.**	**OPPONENTS' OBP**	**EARNED RUN AVERAGE**	**ADJUSTED ERA**	**ADJUSTED STARTER RUNS**	**PITCHER WINS**
M.Brown-Chi 342.2	Overall-Chi .198	Mathewson-NY .228	Mathewson-NY 1.14	Mathewson-NY 223	M.Brown-Chi 45.2	**Mathewson-NY 6.6**
Mattern-Bos 316.1	Mathewson-NY .200	M.Brown-Chi .239	M.Brown-Chi 1.31	M.Brown-Chi 193	Mathewson-NY 42.2	**M.Brown-Chi 5.3**
Rucker-Bro 309.1	Fromme-Cin .201	Overall-Chi .262	Overall-Chi 1.42	Overall-Chi 178	Overall-Chi 35.5	**Overall-Chi 5.2**
Moore-Phi 299.2	M.Brown-Chi .202	H.Camnitz-Pit .267	H.Camnitz-Pit 1.62	H.Camnitz-Pit 167	H.Camnitz-Pit 31.3	**H.Camnitz-Pit 3.5**
Willis-Pit 289.2	Moore-Phi .210	McQuillan-Phi .271	Kroh-Chi 1.65	Reulbach-Chi 142	Reulbach-Chi 24.4	**Fromme-Cin 3.2**

The Great Cobb and Wagner Face Off

Offense increased slightly in the NL, due partly to park changes. On June 30, the Pirates opened Forbes Field, a slightly smaller field than their previous home, Exposition Park. Prior to the season, the Giants significantly reduced the size of center field at the Polo Grounds.

The NL's key rookie was 21-year-old Zack Wheat, who came up late in the season and joined Brooklyn's outfield. He remained with Brooklyn through 1926 before playing a final year with the Athletics while amassing 2,884 hits. John Clarkson, who three times led the NL in victories, died from pneumonia. His 49 wins in 1889, tops in the NL by 21 that year, remains the highest post-1885 total. Another who passed away was Herman Long, Boston's great shortstop of the 1890s, who died at 43 of consumption.

Pittsburgh, Chicago, and New York were again the class of the league. This time the Bucs emerged in May and floated away, finishing 6½ ahead of the Cubs, who themselves won 104 games. It was a return to glory for Honus Wagner, who won his fourth straight batting crown and led the NL in RBIs for the fourth time. Chicago again had the best pitching, but the Pirates sported the top four finishers in runs.

Then there was the league's doormat, the St. Louis Cardinals, who finished 50 or more games out of first for the fourth straight time. A somewhat respectable 43-57 on August 16, the Redbirds lost 15 straight down the stretch. As bad as the Cardinals were, Boston was even worse, ending up 65½ games out.

It was Babe Adams' turn to shine in the fall. The Pittsburgh righty, a fifth starter during the regular season, beat the Tigers three times in a World Series that went seven games. In the match-up of the game's two top stars, Wagner batted .333 with 6 RBIs, while Cobb hit .231 and scored just three times.

1909 AMERICAN LEAGUE

TEAM	W	L	T	PCT	GB	HW	HL	R	OR	PA	H	2B	3B	HR	BB	SO	HB	SH	AVG	OBP	SLG	OPS	AOPS	BR	ABR	PF	SB	CS	BSA	BSR
Det	98	54	6	.645	—	**57**	19	**666**	493	5763	**1360**	**209**	58	19	397	—	39	232	**.267**	**.325**	.342	**667**	113	**102**	75	104	**280**			
Phi	95	58	0	.621	3.5	49	27	605	**411**	5620	1257	186	**88**	**21**	403	—	64	**247**	.256	.321	**.343**	664	**115**	92	**80**	102	201			
Bos	88	63	1	.583	9.5	47	28	601	549	5575	1309	151	69	20	348	—	**77**	170	.263	.321	.333	654	112	73	60	102	215			
Chi	78	74	7	.513	20	42	34	492	464	5759	1109	145	56	4	**441**	—	57	243	.221	.291	.275	566	89	-72	-51	96	211			
NY	74	77	2	.490	23.5	41	35	589	587	5649	1234	143	61	16	407	—	63	198	.248	.313	.311	624	103	25	21	101	187			
Cle	71	82	2	.464	27.5	39	37	493	532	5536	1216	173	81	10	283	—	48	157	.241	.288	.313	601	92	-31	-50	104	173			
StL	61	89	4	.407	36	40	37	441	575	5487	1151	116	45	10	331	—	51	141	.232	.287	.279	566	91	-82	-48	93	136			
Was	42	110	4	.276	56	27	48	380	656	5541	1113	149	41	9	321	—	42	195	.223	.276	.275	551	84	-109	-88	95	136			
Total	620	—	—	—	—	342	265	4267	—	44930	9749	1272	499	109	2931	4918	441	1583	.244	.303	.309	612	—	—	—	—	1539	—	—	—

TEAM	CG	SHO	GR	SV	IP	H	HR	BB	SO	BR/9	ERA	AERA	OAV	OOB	PR	APR	PF	OSB	OCS	FA	E	WPB	DP	FW	PW	BW	BSW	DIF
Det	**117**	17	50	12	1420.1	1254	16	359	528	10.6	2.26	111	.238	.293	33	39	102	190	*155*	.959	276	**43**	87	.4	4.4	8.5	—	8.7
Phi	110	**27**	61	3	1378.0	**1069**	9	386	**728**	**9.9**	**1.93**	**124**	**.217**	**.282**	**82**	**74**	97	**152**	*162*	.961	**245**	45	92	1.8	**8.4**	**9.1**	—	-.8
Bos	75	11	**95**	**14**	1360.1	1213	18	384	555	10.9	2.59	96	.243	.303	-19	-15	101	167	*153*	.955	292	52	95	-1.3	-1.7	6.8	—	8.7
Chi	115	26	49	4	1430.1	1182	**8**	**340**	669	**9.9**	2.05	114	.229	.283	67	47	95	210	*158*	**.964**	246	54	101	**2.4**	5.3	-5.8	—	.0
NY	94	18	64	8	1350.1	1223	21	422	597	11.4	2.65	95	.248	.316	-26	-21	102	207	*156*	.948	330	52	94	-3.6	-2.4	2.4	—	2.1
Cle	110	15	51	3	1361.0	1212	9	348	568	10.6	2.40	106	.250	.307	11	20	103	180	*164*	.957	278	65	**110**	-.0	2.3	-5.7	—	-2.0
StL	105	21	55	4	1354.2	1287	16	383	620	11.4	2.88	84	.261	.319	-61	-74	98	203	***169***	.958	267	51	107	.5	-8.4	-5.5	—	-.6
Was	99	11	74	2	1374.2	1288	12	424	653	11.6	3.04	80	.248	.312	-87	-98	98	230	*159*	.957	280	72	100	-.0	-11.1	-10.0	—	-12.8
Total	825	146	499	50	11029.2	—	—	—	—	10.8	2.47	—	.244	.303	—	—	—	—	—	.957	2214	434	786	—	—	—	—	—

BATTER-FIELDER WINS	BATTING AVERAGE	ON-BASE PERCENTAGE	SLUGGING AVERAGE	ON-BASE PLUS SLUGGING	ADJUSTED OPS	ADJUSTED BATTER RUNS
Cobb-Det 6.0	Cobb-Det .377	Cobb-Det .431	Cobb-Det .517	Cobb-Det .947	Cobb-Det 190	Cobb-Det 59.2
Collins-Phi 5.9	Collins-Phi .347	Collins-Phi .416	Crawford-Det .452	Collins-Phi .866	Collins-Phi 170	Collins-Phi 48.1
Lajoie-Cle 5.7	Lajoie-Cle .324	Bush-Det .380	Collins-Phi .450	Crawford-Det .817	Stahl-Bos 153	Crawford-Det 33.2
Speaker-Bos 4.6	Lord-Bos .315	Lajoie-Cle .378	Baker-Phi .447	Stahl-Bos .812	Crawford-Det 151	Speaker-Bos 29.8
Engle-NY 2.3	Crawford-Det .314	Stahl-Bos .377	Speaker-Bos .443	Lajoie-Cle .809	Speaker-Bos 151	Stahl-Bos 27.2
RUNS	**HITS**	**DOUBLES**	**TRIPLES**	**HOME RUNS**	**TOTAL BASES**	**RUNS BATTED IN**
Cobb-Det 116	Cobb-Det 216	Crawford-Det 35	Baker-Phi 19	Cobb-Det 9	Cobb-Det 296	Cobb-Det 107
Bush-Det 114	Collins-Phi 198	Lajoie-Cle 33	Murphy-Phi 14	Speaker-Bos 7	Crawford-Det 266	Crawford-Det 97
Collins-Phi 104	Crawford-Det 185	Cobb-Det 33	Crawford-Det 14	Stahl-Bos 6	Collins-Phi 257	Baker-Phi 85
Lord-Bos 89	Speaker-Bos 168	Collins-Phi 30		Crawford-Det 6	Baker-Phi 242	Speaker-Bos 77
Crawford-Det 83	Lord-Bos 168	Murphy-Phi 28		Murphy-Phi 5	Speaker-Bos 241	Davis-Phi 75
BASES ON BALLS	**STOLEN BASES**	**BASE STEALING RUNS**	**FIELDING RUNS-INFIELD**	**FIELDING RUNS-OUTFIELD**	**OUTFIELD ASSISTS**	**CATCHER CS PCT.**
Bush-Det 88	Cobb-Det 76		Lajoie-Cle 23.3	Speaker-Bos 18.5	Speaker-Bos 35	Thomas-Phi 49.0
Collins-Phi 62	Collins-Phi 63		Parent-Chi 14.4	Engle-NY 14.9	Cobb-Det 24	Sullivan-Chi 43.9
Demmitt-NY 55	Bush-Det 53		McBride-Was 13.0	Hartzell-StL 8.5	Demmitt-NY 22	Street-Was 42.4
McIntyre-Det 54	Lord-Bos 36		Austin-NY 13.0	Milan-Was 4.7	Hartzell-StL 21	
	Dougherty-Chi 36		Wallace-StL 11.0	Niles-Bos 2.3	Niles-Bos 20	
WINS	**WINNING PCT.**	**WINS ABOVE TEAM**	**GAMES STARTED**	**COMPLETE GAMES**	**FEWEST HITS/GAME**	**FEWEST BB/GAME**
Mullin-Det 29	Mullin-Det .784	Mullin-Det 8.5	Smith-Chi 40	Smith-Chi 37	Morgan-Bos-Phi 6.26	Joss-Cle 1.15
Smith-Chi 25	Krause-Phi .692	Smith-Chi 4.6	Morgan-Bos-Phi 36	Young-Cle 30	Krause-Phi 6.38	White-Chi 1.57
Willett-Det 21	Bender-Phi .692	Cicotte-Bos 3.8	Johnson-Was 36	Mullin-Det 29	Walsh-Chi 6.49	Powell-StL 1.58
	Summers-Det .679	Young-Cle 3.7	Mullin-Det 35	Johnson-Was 27	Cicotte-Bos 6.49	Bender-Phi 1.62
	Willett-Det .677			Morgan-Bos-Phi 26	Wood-Bos 6.78	Summers-Det 1.66
STRIKEOUTS	**STRIKEOUTS/GAME**	**GAMES**	**SAVES**	**BASE RUNNERS/9**	**ADJUSTED RELIEF RUNS**	**RELIEF RANKING**
Smith-Chi 177	Berger-Cle 5.90	Smith-Chi 51	Arellanes-Bos 8	Walsh-Chi 8.60		
Johnson-Was 164	Krause-Phi 5.87	Arellanes-Bos 45	Powell-StL 3	Joss-Cle 8.64		
Berger-Cle 162	Bender-Phi 5.80	Groom-Was 44		Smith-Chi 8.73		
Bender-Phi 161	Waddell-StL 5.76	Willett-Det 41		Bender-Phi 8.86		
Waddell-StL 141	Bailey-StL 5.16			Krause-Phi 9.00		
INNINGS PITCHED	**OPPONENTS' AVG.**	**OPPONENTS' OBP**	**EARNED RUN AVERAGE**	**ADJUSTED ERA**	**ADJUSTED STARTER RUNS**	**PITCHER WINS**
Smith-Chi 365.0	Morgan-Bos-Phi .202	Walsh-Chi .253	Krause-Phi 1.39	Krause-Phi 172	Walsh-Chi 24.9	**Walsh-Chi 4.1**
Mullin-Det 303.2	Walsh-Chi .203	Bender-Phi .254	Walsh-Chi 1.41	Walsh-Chi 166	Morgan-Bos-Phi 24.3	**Smith-Chi 4.1**
Johnson-Was 296.1	Krause-Phi .204	Joss-Cle .255	Bender-Phi 1.66	Joss-Cle 149	Krause-Phi 23.3	**Bender-Phi 2.7**
Young-Cle 294.1	Cicotte-Bos .207	Smith-Chi .257	Joss-Cle 1.71	Killian-Det 147	Smith-Chi 22.9	**Krause-Phi 2.7**
Morgan-Bos-Phi 293.1	Wood-Bos .209	Krause-Phi .266	Killian-Det 1.71	Bender-Phi 145	Joss-Cle 20.9	**Plank-Phi 2.6**

Bengals Win Battle of Weak Bats

Detroit led the league almost the entire way as Cobb's Tigers captured their third straight AL pennant. Their challengers were the Athletics, led by second baseman Eddie Collins, and the Red Sox, led by center fielder Tris Speaker. Collins was an all-around standout, while Speaker set an AL mark with 35 outfield assists.

Chicago and Cleveland dropped from contention essentially because they couldn't score. Despite fielding just three quality offensive players—Ty Cobb, Donie Bush, and Sam Crawford—Detroit paced the AL in runs by more than 60. Cobb and Bush ranked first and second in runs, Cobb and Crawford first and second in RBIs. Cobb grabbed the Triple Crown and also led in on-base percentage, slugging, total bases, and steals. However, the Tigers magic wore off yet again in the World Series as Detroit fell to the Pirates.

Boston's Harry Hooper spent his rookie year as a part-time outfielder. Starting in 1910, he'd become a regular for sixteen years. Also for the Red Sox, star righty Jack Chesbro was done as a big leaguer at age 35. George Davis, a great shortstop of the nineteenth century, played his last game with the White Sox. Two active players died. Thirty-eight-year-old catcher Doc Powers passed away in April from complications of gangrene, while Jimmy Sebring, an outfielder who played one game for the Senators after five years in the NL, died in December from Bright's disease.

Two AL teams moved into shiny new digs. The Athletics built their revolutionary Shibe Park, which would serve them until they left the city in 1953, while the St. Louis Browns began playing in a new Sportsman's Park. The average AL team scored just 3.44 runs per game, the lowest mark until 1968; three starting pitchers had ERAs below 1.70. The fans apparently found the low-scoring style of play exciting enough, though, as attendance reached a pre-1920 peak.

1908 NATIONAL LEAGUE

TEAM	W	L	T	PCT	GB	HW	HL	R	OR	PA	H	2B	3B	HR	BB	SO	HB	SH	AVG	OBP	SLG	OPS	AOPS	BR	ABR	PF	SB	CS	BSA	BSR
Chi	99	55	4	.643	—	47	30	624	461	5813	1267	**196**	56	19	418	—	40	**270**	.249	.311	.321	632	105	53	29	104	**212**			
Pit	98	56	1	.636	1	42	35	585	468	5753	1263	162	**98**	25	420	—	40	184	.247	.309	.332	641	112	61	61	100	186			
NY	98	56	3	.636	1	**52**	25	**651**	455	5826	**1339**	182	43	20	**494**	—	**76**	250	**.267**	**.342**	**.333**	**675**	**117**	**144**	**113**	105	181			
Phi	83	71	1	.539	16	43	34	504	**445**	5612	1223	194	68	11	334	—	53	213	.244	.298	.316	614	100	13	-4	103	200			
Cin	73	81	1	.474	26	40	37	488	543	5511	1108	129	77	14	372	—	46	214	.227	.288	.294	582	95	-44	-31	97	196			
Bos	63	91	2	.409	36	35	42	537	622	5793	1228	137	43	17	414	—	54	194	.239	.303	.293	596	99	-12	-4	98	134			
Bro	53	101	0	.344	46	27	50	375	516	5415	1044	110	60	**28**	323	—	29	166	.213	.266	.277	543	82	-117	-102	96	113			
StL	49	105	0	.318	50	28	49	372	626	5450	1105	134	57	17	282	—	45	164	.223	.271	.283	554	87	-99	-79	95	150			
Total	622	—	—	—	—	314	302	4136	—	45173	9577	1244	502	151	3057	4180	383	1655	.239	.299	.306	605	—	—	—	—	1372	—	—	—

TEAM	CG	SHO	GR	SV	IP	H	HR	BB	SO	BR/9	ERA	AERA	OAV	OOB	PR	APR	PF	OSB	OCS	FA	E	WPB	DP	FW	PW	BW	BSW	DIF
Chi	108	**29**	60	12	1433.2	**1137**	20	437	**668**	10.1	2.14	109	**.221**	.287	33	30	100	158	*156*	**.969**	**205**	46	76	**3.7**	3.5	3.4	—	11.4
Pit	100	24	71	9	1402.1	1142	16	406	468	10.3	2.12	108	.223	.287	34	25	97	138	*104*	.964	226	**27**	74	1.9	2.9	7.1	—	9.1
NY	95	25	76	**18**	1411.0	1210	26	**288**	656	**9.8**	2.14	112	.232	**.277**	32	38	102	135	*125*	.962	250	41	79	.4	4.4	**13.1**	—	3.0
Phi	116	22	43	6	1393.0	1167	**8**	379	476	10.3	**2.10**	**115**	.234	.294	**38**	**44**	103	**128**	*154*	.963	238	45	75	1.0	**5.1**	-.5	—	.3
Cin	110	17	50	8	1384.0	1218	19	415	433	10.9	2.37	96	.243	.307	-4	-19	98	154	*137*	.959	255	40	72	-.2	-2.2	-3.6	—	2.0
Bos	92	14	**77**	1	1404.2	1262	29	423	416	11.2	2.79	86	.245	.310	-70	-66	102	199	*152*	.962	253	34	**90**	.0	-7.7	-.5	—	-6.0
Bro	**118**	20	43	4	1369.0	1165	17	444	535	11.0	2.47	94	.235	.306	-18	-24	99	203	*162*	.961	247	37	66	.3	-2.8	-11.9	—	-9.7
StL	97	13	72	4	1368.0	1217	16	430	528	11.1	2.64	89	.232	.296	-44	-51	100	257	***173***	.946	348	57	68	-6.8	-5.9	-9.2	—	-6.1
Total	836	164	492	62	11165.2	—	—	—	—	10.6	2.35	—	.239	.299	—	—	—	—	—	.961	2022	327	600	—	—	—	—	—

BATTER-FIELDER WINS	BATTING AVERAGE	ON-BASE PERCENTAGE	SLUGGING AVERAGE	ON-BASE PLUS SLUGGING	ADJUSTED OPS	ADJUSTED BATTER RUNS
Wagner-Pit.........6.9	Wagner-Pit...........354	Wagner-Pit...........415	Wagner-Pit...........542	Wagner-Pit...........957	Wagner-Pit...........205	Wagner-Pit..........66.3
Tinker-Chi..........4.5	Donlin-NY 334	Evers-Chi.............402	Donlin-NY 452	Donlin-NY 816	Donlin-NY 153	Donlin-NY 32.0
Dahlen-Bos.........4.5	Doyle-NY 308	Bresnahan-NY......401	Magee-Phi 417	Evers-Chi.............777	Lobert-Cin............145	Lobert-Cin...........26.5
Bresnahan-NY ...3.8	Bransfield-Phi 304	Titus-Phi 365	Lobert-Cin............407	Magee-Phi 776	Magee-Phi 143	Bresnahan-NY.....25.3
Ritchey-Bos........3.1	Evers-Chi.............300	Donlin-NY 364	Murray-StL...........400	Breshahan-NY......760	Evers-Chi.............143	Magee-Phi 25.3
RUNS	**HITS**	**DOUBLES**	**TRIPLES**	**HOME RUNS**	**TOTAL BASES**	**RUNS BATTED IN**
Tenney-NY...........101	Wagner-Pit...........201	Wagner-Pit.............39	Wagner-Pit.............19	Jordan-Bro.............12	Wagner-Pit...........308	Wagner-Pit...........109
Wagner-Pit...........100	Donlin-NY 198	Magee-Phi 30	Lobert-Cin...............18	Wagner-Pit.............10	Donlin-NY 268	Donlin-NY 106
Leach-Pit 93	Murray-StL...........167	Chance-Chi............27	Magee-Phi 16	Murray-StL...............7	Murray-StL...........237	Seymour-NY 92
Evers-Chi................83	Lobert-Cin............167	Knabe-Phi..............26	Leach-Pit 16	Tinker-Chi 6	Lobert-Cin............232	Bransfield-Phi 71
Clarke-Pit...............83	Bransfield-Phi 160	Donlin-NY 26		Donlin-NY 6	Leach-Pit 222	Tinker-Chi 68
BASES ON BALLS	**STOLEN BASES**	**BASE STEALING RUNS**	**FIELDING RUNS-INFIELD**	**FIELDING RUNS-OUTFIELD**	**OUTFIELD ASSISTS**	**CATCHER CS PCT.**
Bresnahan-NY 83	Wagner-Pit.............53		Dahlen-Bos..........37.5	Clarke-Pit............10.2	Seymour-NY 29	Dooin-Phi.............54.7
Tenney-NY 72	Murray-StL.............48		Tinker-Chi 26.4	Burch-Bro 8.5	Burch-Bro 24	Bresnahan-NY 47.2
Evers-Chi................66	Lobert-Cin..............47		Ritchey-Bos 12.9	Hummel-Bro 8.1	Shaw-StL 23	Schlei-Cin 45.9
Clarke-Pit...............65	Magee-Phi 40		Sweeney-Bos 12.2	Shaw-StL 7.3	Titus-Phi 22	Bergen-Bro 43.7
	Evers-Chi...............36		Devlin-NY 11.9	Seymour-NY 5.3	Murray-StL.............22	Gibson-Pit............42.8
WINS	**WINNING PCT.**	**WINS ABOVE TEAM**	**GAMES STARTED**	**COMPLETE GAMES**	**FEWEST HITS/GAME**	**FEWEST BB/GAME**
Mathewson-NY 37	Reulbach-Chi........774	Mathewson-NY 11.0	Mathewson-NY 44	Mathewson-NY 34	Brown-Chi............6.17	Mathewson-NY 97
Brown-Chi...............29	Mathewson-NY 771	Brown-Chi..............7.7	McQuillan-Phi 42	Wilhelm-Bro............33	Mathewson-NY 6.47	Brown-Chi............1.41
Reulbach-Chi..........24	Brown-Chi.............763	Reulbach-Chi.........6.5	Wiltse-NY................38	McQuillan-Phi 32	Raymond-StL.......6.55	Sparks-Phi...........1.74
	Maddox-Pit 742	Maddox-Pit 5.3	Willis-Pit..................38	Wiltse-NY................30	McQuillan-Phi 6.58	Ewing-Cin 1.75
	Leever-Pit 682	Rucker-Bro............4.3		Rucker-Bro.............30	Overall-Chi..........6.60	Campbell-Cin.......1.79
STRIKEOUTS	**STRIKEOUTS/GAME**	**GAMES**	**SAVES**	**BASE RUNNERS/9**	**ADJUSTED RELIEF RUNS**	**RELIEF RANKING**
Mathewson-NY 259	Overall-Chi...........6.68	Mathewson-NY 56	McGinnity-NY 5	Mathewson-NY 7.51		
Rucker-Bro............199	Mathewson-NY 5.97	Raymond-StL..........48	Mathewson-NY 5	Brown-Chi............7.72		
Overall-Chi............167	Rucker-Bro...........5.37	McQuillan-Phi 48	Brown-Chi.................5	McQuillan-Phi 9.01		
Raymond-StL........145	Camnitz-Pit..........4.49	Reulbach-Chi..........46	Overall-Chi................4	Willis-Pit..............9.28		
Reulbach-Chi........133	Ferguson-Bos 4.24		Ewing-Cin 3	Ewing-Cin 9.47		
INNINGS PITCHED	**OPPONENTS' AVG.**	**OPPONENTS' OBP**	**EARNED RUN AVERAGE**	**ADJUSTED ERA**	**ADJUSTED STARTER RUNS**	**PITCHER WINS**
Mathewson-NY ..390.2	Beebe-StL.............193	Mathewson-NY 222	Mathewson-NY 1.43	Mathewson-NY 168	Mathewson-NY 40.8	**Mathewson-NY .. 6.5**
McQuillan-Phi 359.2	Brown-Chi.............195	Brown-Chi.............232	Brown-Chi............1.47	Brown-Chi.............159	McQuillan-Phi 32.7	**Brown-Chi........... 4.4**
Rucker-Bro.........333.1	Mathewson-NY 197	Willis-Pit................262	McQuillan-Phi 1.53	McQuillan-Phi 158	Brown-Chi............32.0	**McQuillan-Phi 3.8**
Wilhelm-Bro 332.0	McQuillan-Phi 207	McQuillan-Phi 263	Camnitz-Pit..........1.56	Camnitz-Pit...........147	Reulbach-Chi.......13.9	**Reulbach-Chi 2.2**
Wiltse-NY..........330.0	Raymond-StL........207	Beebe-StL.............267	Coakley-Cin-Chi ..1.78	Richie-Phi 132	Wilhelm-Bro.........13.3	**Wiltse-NY........... 2.1**

Merkle's Boner Leads to Thrilling Three-Way

By decree, pitchers were no longer allowed to rub dirt on the baseball to deface it. Despite this, scoring dropped to just 3.32 runs per team per game, the lowest since 1901. The league batting average of .239 was also the lowest ever. Rookie Gavvy Cravath, future home run king, hit just one in 94 games, while pitchers Hippo Vaughn and Rube Marquard also debuted. Marquard, who played in New York, is now in the Hall of Fame, but Vaughn was clearly greater. Two old Baltimore Orioles ended their big-league tenure: "Iron Man" Joe McGinnity's arm gave out, while outfielder Joe Kelley was finished at 37.

Despite poor hitting, the first great NL pennant race of the century boosted attendance 33 percent. The Giants were up by $4^1/_2$ on September 18, but Philadelphia rookie left-hander Harry Coveleski beat New York thrice in the final week, drawing the race tighter. On a fateful September 23 in New York, the Giants scored in the ninth, apparently defeating Chicago, 2-1. While the "winning" run scored, however, Fred Merkle, who had been on first, failed to touch second base after the hit. Cubs infielder John Evers called for the ball; umpire Hank O'Day, who had ruled against the Cubs in a similar play weeks before, called Merkle out as fans poured onto the field. The game was later ruled a tie by NL President Harry Pulliam.

Chicago eliminated Pittsburgh on October 4, finishing the season knotted with the Giants. When the game was replayed on October 8, some 35,000 crazed fans at the Polo Grounds watched the Cubs defeat Christy Mathewson, 4-2. After this exhausting pennant race, Chicago's World Series win was almost anticlimactic. Ty Cobb hit .368, but Chicago took Detroit in five. Certainly, nobody at the time could have dreamed that this would be the mighty Cubs' last world championship of the century.

1908 AMERICAN LEAGUE

TEAM	W	L	T	PCT	GB	HW	HL	R	OR	PA	H	2B	3B	HR	BB	SO	HB	SH	AVG	OBP	SLG	OPS	AOPS	BR	ABR	PF	SB	CS	BSA	BSR
Det	90	63	1	.588	—	44	33	**647**	547	5668	**1347**	**199**	86	19	320	—	42	191	**.263**	**.312**	**.347**	**659**	**115**	**103**	**77**	104	165			
Cle	90	64	3	.584	0.5	**51**	26	569	**459**	5770	1221	188	58	18	364	—	55	**243**	.239	.297	.309	606	103	17	15	100	177			
Chi	88	64	4	.579	1.5	**51**	25	537	470	5788	1127	145	41	3	**463**	—	62	236	.224	.298	.271	569	91	-35	-27	98	209			
StL	83	69	3	.546	6.5	46	31	544	483	5726	1261	173	52	20	343	—	35	197	.245	.296	.310	606	102	14	11	101	126			
Bos	75	79	1	.487	15.5	37	40	564	513	5579	1239	117	**88**	14	289	—	**69**	173	.245	.295	.312	607	100	7	-8	103	156			
Phi	68	85	4	.444	22	46	30	486	562	5656	1131	183	50	**21**	368	—	37	186	.223	.281	.292	573	86	-43	-74	107	116			
Was	67	85	3	.441	22.5	43	32	479	539	5648	1186	132	74	8	368	—	43	196	.235	.293	.296	589	106	-17	30	92	170			
NY	51	103	1	.331	39.5	30	47	460	713	5533	1190	142	50	13	288	—	45	153	.236	.283	.291	574	91	-46	-51	101	**231**			
Total	622	—	—	—	—	348	264	4286	—	45368	9702	1279	499	116	2803	4930	388	1575	.239	.294	.304	598	—	—	—	—	1350	—	—	—

TEAM	CG	SHO	GR	SV	IP	H	HR	BB	SO	BR/9	ERA	AERA	OAV	OOB	PR	APR	PF	OSB	OCS	FA	E	WPB	DP	FW	PW	BW	BSW	DIF
Det	**119**	15	38	5	1374.1	1313	12	318	553	11.1	2.40	100	.255	.306	-3	2	101	176	*147*	.953	305	**40**	95	-2.1	.2	**8.8**	—	6.6
Cle	108	18	61	5	1424.1	1172	16	328	548	9.7	**2.02**	**118**	.229	.280	**59**	**56**	100	**123**	*127*	.962	257	46	95	1.6	**6.4**	1.7	—	3.3
Chi	107	**23**	62	**10**	1414.0	1165	11	**284**	623	**9.4**	2.22	104	**.225**	**.269**	26	14	97	149	*127*	**.966**	**232**	43	82	**3.2**	1.6	-3.1	—	10.3
StL	107	15	61	5	1397.0	**1151**	**7**	387	607	10.3	2.15	111	.230	.294	37	36	100	141	*138*	.964	237	45	**97**	2.7	4.1	1.3	—	-1.1
Bos	102	12	65	7	1380.1	1200	18	364	624	10.5	2.28	108	.238	.295	17	26	103	167	*155*	.955	297	63	71	-1.4	3.0	-.9	—	-2.6
Phi	102	**23**	74	4	1400.1	1194	10	410	**741**	10.6	2.56	100	.235	.298	-27	-4	107	242	***159***	.957	272	60	68	.6	-.5	-8.4	—	-.2
Was	106	15	60	7	1391.2	1236	16	348	649	10.5	2.34	97	.241	.294	7	-13	96	151	*136*	.958	275	63	89	.1	-1.5	3.4	—	-11.0
NY	90	11	**75**	3	1366.0	1293	26	458	585	12.0	3.16	78	.252	.322	-117	-102	104	201	*140*	.947	337	49	78	-4.1	-11.6	-5.8	—	-4.4
Total	841	132	496	46	11148.0	—	—	—	—	10.5	2.39	—	.239	.294	—	—	—	—	—	.958	2212	409	675	—	—	—	—	—

BATTER-FIELDER WINS	BATTING AVERAGE	ON-BASE PERCENTAGE	SLUGGING AVERAGE	ON-BASE PLUS SLUGGING	ADJUSTED OPS	ADJUSTED BATTER RUNS
Lajoie-Cle 8.0	Cobb-Det 324	Gessler-Bos..........394	Cobb-Det 475	Cobb-Det 842	Cobb-Det 166	Cobb-Det 40.0
McIntyre-Det...... 4.6	Crawford-Det 311	McIntyre-Det.........392	Crawford-Det 457	Gessler-Bos..........817	Gessler-Bos..........161	Crawford-Det 34.7
Cobb-Det............. 4.1	Gessler-Bos..........308	Hemphill-NY 374	Gessler-Bos..........423	Crawford-Det 812	Crawford-Det 157	McIntyre-Det........33.4
McBride-Was...... 3.7	Hemphill-NY 297	Hartsel-Phi............371	Rossman-Det........418	McIntyre-Det.........775	McIntyre-Det.........146	Gessler-Bos.........31.0
Wagner-Bos........ 3.2	McIntyre-Det.........295	Dougherty-Chi 367	McIntyre-Det.........383	Rossman-Det........748	Rossman-Det........137	Lajoie-Cle 24.3
RUNS	**HITS**	**DOUBLES**	**TRIPLES**	**HOME RUNS**	**TOTAL BASES**	**RUNS BATTED IN**
McIntyre-Det.........105	Cobb-Det 188	Cobb-Det 36	Cobb-Det 20	Crawford-Det 7	Cobb-Det 276	Cobb-Det 108
Crawford-Det 102	Crawford-Det 184	Rossman-Det..........33	Stahl-NY-Bos 16	Hinchman-Cle...........6	Crawford-Det 270	Crawford-Det 80
Schaefer-Det 96	McIntyre-Det.........168	Crawford-Det 33	Crawford-Det 16	Niles-NY-Bos 5	Rossman-Det........219	Lajoie-Cle 74
Jones-Chi 92	Lajoie-Cle 168	Lajoie-Cle 32	Gessler-Bos............14	Stone-StL.................5	McIntyre-Det.........218	Ferris-StL................74
Stone-StL................89	Stone-StL..............165	Stovall-Cle 29		Davis-Phi 5	Lajoie-Cle 218	Rossman-Det..........71
BASES ON BALLS	**STOLEN BASES**	**BASE STEALING RUNS**	**FIELDING RUNS-INFIELD**	**FIELDING RUNS-OUTFIELD**	**OUTFIELD ASSISTS**	**CATCHER CS PCT.**
Hartsel-Phi..............93	Dougherty-Chi 47		Lajoie-Cle 46.8	McIntyre-Det........16.4	Cobb-Det 23	N.Clarke-Cle 53.6
Jones-Chi 86	Hemphill-NY 42		McBride-Was 32.6	Murphy-Phi 5.3	Birmingham-Cle......20	Schmidt-Det.........49.0
McIntyre-Det...........83	Schaefer-Det 40		Wagner-Bos.........32.4	Hartzell-StL............5.0	Hoffman-StL 19	Street-Was...........48.2
J.Clarke-Cle............76	Cobb-Det 39		Tannehill-Chi........16.9	Milan-Was.............4.7	Milan-Was...............18	Criger-Bos 48.0
Davis-Phi 61	J.Clarke-Cle...........37		Wallace-StL 15.2	Stahl-NY-Bos 4.6		Spencer-StL.........47.9
WINS	**WINNING PCT.**	**WINS ABOVE TEAM**	**GAMES STARTED**	**COMPLETE GAMES**	**FEWEST HITS/GAME**	**FEWEST BB/GAME**
Walsh-Chi 40	Walsh-Chi 727	Walsh-Chi 12.7	Walsh-Chi 49	Walsh-Chi 42	Joss-Cle...............6.42	Joss-Cle..................83
Summers-Det 24	Donovan-Det.........720	Young-Bos 6.1	White-Chi................37	Young-Bos 30	Smith-Chi.............6.44	Burns-Was..............99
Joss-Cle..................24	Joss-Cle................686	Joss-Cle.................5.2	Waddell-StL 36	Joss-Cle..................29	Walsh-Chi 6.65	Walsh-Chi 1.09
Young-Bos 21	Summers-Det 667	Donovan-Det..........4.5	Smith-Chi................35	Howell-StL 27	Johnson-Was.......6.81	Young-Bos 1.11
Waddell-StL 19	Young-Bos 656	Summers-Det 4.2	Joss-Cle..................35	Mullin-Det 26	Berger-Cle 6.86	Summers-Det 1.64
STRIKEOUTS	**STRIKEOUTS/GAME**	**GAMES**	**SAVES**	**BASE RUNNERS/9**	**ADJUSTED RELIEF RUNS**	**RELIEF RANKING**
Walsh-Chi 269	Waddell-StL 7.31	Walsh-Chi 66	Walsh-Chi 6	Joss-Cle..............7.31		
Waddell-StL 232	Dygert-Phi 6.18	Vickers-Phi.............53	Hughes-Was.............4	Steele-Bos...........7.70		
Hughes-Was.........165	Johnson-Was.......5.62	Chesbro-NY............45	Waddell-StL 3	Walsh-Chi 7.91		
Dygert-Phi 164	Hughes-Was........5.37	Waddell-StL 43		Young-Bos 8.07		
Johnson-Was........160	Donovan-Det.......5.23	Hughes-Was...........43		Burns-Was...........8.62		
INNINGS PITCHED	**OPPONENTS' AVG.**	**OPPONENTS' OBP**	**EARNED RUN AVERAGE**	**ADJUSTED ERA**	**ADJUSTED STARTER RUNS**	**PITCHER WINS**
Walsh-Chi 464.0	Joss-Cle................197	Joss-Cle................218	Joss-Cle...............1.16	Joss-Cle................205	Walsh-Chi 42.7	**Walsh-Chi 6.8**
Joss-Cle.............325.0	Smith-Chi..............203	Walsh-Chi 232	Young-Bos 1.26	Young-Bos 194	Joss-Cle...............38.3	**Joss-Cle 5.0**
Howell-StL 324.1	Walsh-Chi 203	Young-Bos 240	Walsh-Chi 1.42	Walsh-Chi 163	Young-Bos 36.4	**Young-Bos 4.1**
Vickers-Phi.........317.0	Johnson-Was........211	Smith-Chi..............256	Summers-Det 1.64	Summers-Det 147	Johnson-Was.......17.0	**Rhoads-Cle......... 2.5**
Summers-Det 301.0	Young-Bos 213	Burns-Was............257	Johnson-Was.......1.65	Johnson-Was........138	Howell-StL 16.5	**Howell-StL.......... 2.2**

Rained Out of a Flag

Once again, pitchers asserted themselves. The AL's .239 batting average was the league's lowest until 1967, and the league's .598 OPS is the lowest in the history of baseball. Four clubs *slugged* under .300. Boston enlarged the already huge Huntington Avenue Grounds, but run production at the park was barely affected. Their 18-year-old pitching phenom, "Smokey Joe" Wood, made a successful debut.

The aging A's began to rebuild, falling to sixth, but what an eye Connie Mack had for talent! Making their major league debuts for Philly in 1908 were outfielders Joe Jackson and Amos Strunk and infielders Jack Barry and Frank "Home Run" Baker. Three of them would shortly help the club become great again. However, Mack and Jackson never quite got along, and "Shoeless Joe" ended up in Cleveland.

Cleveland, Chicago, and Detroit remained in the pennant chase until the last day. While Detroit led big in midsummer, Cleveland won 16 of 18 to climb ahead in late September. On October 2 the Indians' Addie Joss—whose 1.16 ERA set a league record—tossed a perfect game at Chicago while White Sox hurler Ed Walsh struck out 15 and allowed just 1 run.

The Tigers put on a spurt, though, and won the crown on the last day of the season, October 5. "Wild Bill" Donovan shut out Chicago to clinch the flag by a half-game over the Indians because Detroit was not required to make up a rainout. The ensuing flap led the leagues to establish a new rule mandating that all rainouts and ties critical to a pennant race be replayed.

Once again, Detroit had a fearsome attack, featuring four of the league's five top sluggers and pacing the league in runs by 78. Nevertheless, for the second straight year, the Cubs easily whipped the Tigers in the Fall Classic. This time Detroit won one game and Ty Cobb scored three times.

1907 NATIONAL LEAGUE

TEAM	W	L	T	PCT	GB	HW	HL	R	OR	PA	H	2B	3B	HR	BB	SO	HB	SH	AVG	OBP	SLG	OPS	AOPS	BR	ABR	PF	SB	CS	BSA	BSR
Chi	107	45	3	.704	—	**54**	19	574	**390**	5570	1224	**162**	48	13	435	—	48	195	.250	.318	.311	629	98	28	-5	106	235			
Pit	91	63	3	.591	17	47	29	**634**	510	5650	**1261**	133	78	19	469	—	46	178	**.254**	.325	**.324**	**649**	**109**	61	53	101	**264**			
Phi	83	64	2	.565	21.5	45	30	514	476	5320	1113	**162**	65	12	424	—	41	130	.236	.304	.305	609	99	-9	-1	99	154			
NY	82	71	2	.536	25.5	45	30	574	510	5624	1222	160	48	**23**	**516**	—	**69**	165	.251	**.331**	.317	648	107	**73**	**54**	103	205			
Bro	65	83	5	.439	40	37	38	446	522	5468	1135	142	63	18	336	—	40	**197**	.232	.287	.298	585	98	-64	-25	92	121			
Cin	66	87	3	.431	41.5	43	36	526	519	5567	1226	126	**90**	15	372	—	34	195	.247	.304	.318	622	98	-1	-22	104	158			
Bos	58	90	4	.392	47	31	42	502	652	5623	1222	142	61	22	413	—	57	133	.243	.308	.309	617	100	2	4	100	120			
StL	52	101	2	.340	55.5	31	47	419	610	5518	1163	121	52	18	312	—	42	156	.232	.283	.288	571	88	-91	-76	97	125			
Total	616	—	—	—	—	333	271	4189	—	44340	9566	1148	505	140	3277	4217	377	1349	.243	.308	.309	616	—	—	—	—	1382	—	—	—

TEAM	CG	SHO	GR	SV	IP	H	HR	BB	SO	BR/9	ERA	AERA	OAV	OOB	PR	APR	PF	OSB	OCS	FA	E	WPB	DP	FW	PW	BW	BSW	DIF
Chi	114	**32**	45	8	1373.1	**1054**	**11**	402	586	**9.8**	**1.73**	**144**	**.216**	**.281**	**112**	**114**	101	148	*132*	**.967**	**211**	31	110	**3.1**	**13.0**	-.6	—	15.5
Pit	111	24	51	5	1363.0	1207	12	**368**	497	10.7	2.30	106	.241	.299	25	19	99	**124**	*125*	.959	256	41	75	.2	2.2	6.0	—	5.6
Phi	110	21	46	4	1299.1	1095	13	422	499	10.9	2.43	99	.233	.304	5	-3	98	136	*139*	.957	256	40	104	-.7	-.3	-.1	—	10.6
NY	109	22	**63**	**13**	1371.0	1219	24	369	**655**	10.7	2.45	101	.238	.294	2	1	100	135	*121*	.963	232	60	75	1.6	.1	**6.1**	—	-2.4
Bro	125	20	29	1	1356.1	1218	16	463	479	11.4	2.38	98	.249	.319	12	-9	95	208	*152*	.959	262	41	94	-.7	-1.0	-2.8	—	-4.5
Cin	118	10	39	2	1351.1	1223	16	444	481	11.5	2.41	107	.251	.322	8	24	105	173	*150*	.963	227	**24**	118	2.1	2.7	-2.5	—	-12.8
Bos	121	9	38	2	1338.2	1324	28	458	426	12.4	3.33	76	.268	.339	-129	-115	103	238	*163*	.961	249	51	**128**	.1	-13.1	.5	—	-3.5
StL	**127**	19	29	2	1365.2	1212	20	500	594	11.6	2.70	93	.243	.318	-35	-32	101	220	***167***	.948	340	74	105	-5.8	-3.6	-8.6	—	-6.5
Total	935	157	340	37	10818.2	—	—	—	—	11.1	2.46	—	.243	.308	—	—	—	—	—	.960	2033	362	809	—	—	—	—	—

BATTER-FIELDER WINS	BATTING AVERAGE	ON-BASE PERCENTAGE	SLUGGING AVERAGE	ON-BASE PLUS SLUGGING	ADJUSTED OPS	ADJUSTED BATTER RUNS
Wagner-Pit.........6.7	Wagner-Pit...........350	Wagner-Pit...........408	Wagner-Pit...........513	Wagner-Pit...........921	Wagner-Pit...........186	Wagner-Pit..........50.3
Brain-Bos...........4.8	Magee-Phi 328	Magee-Phi 396	Magee-Phi 455	Magee-Phi 852	Magee-Phi 169	Magee-Phi 40.7
Magee-Phi 4.5	Beaumont-Bos......322	Clarke-Pit.............383	Lumley-Bro 425	Beaumont-Bos......790	Beaumont-Bos......148	Beaumont-Bos.....29.3
Mitchell-Cin........3.3	Leach-Pit 303	Devlin-NY 376	Beaumont-Bos......424	Clarke-Pit.............772	Lumley-Bro 144	Jordan-Bro...........26.3
Beaumont-Bos...3.0	Seymour-NY 294	Thomas-Phi 374	Brain-Bos..............420	Leach-Pit 756	Jordan-Bro............141	Clarke-Pit............25.8

RUNS	HITS	DOUBLES	TRIPLES	HOME RUNS	TOTAL BASES	RUNS BATTED IN
Shannon-NY 104	Beaumont-Bos......187	Wagner-Pit.............38	Ganzel-Cin.............16	Brain-Bos................10	Wagner-Pit...........264	Magee-Phi 85
Leach-Pit 102	Wagner-Pit...........180	Magee-Phi 28	Alperman-Bro 16	Lumley-Bro 9	Beaumont-Bos......246	Wagner-Pit..............82
Wagner-Pit.............98	Leach-Pit 166	Steinfeldt-Chi 25	Wagner-Pit.............14	Murray-StL 7	Magee-Phi 229	Abbaticchio-Pit........82
Clarke-Pit...............97	Magee-Phi 165	Seymour-NY 25	Beaumont-Bos........14	Wagner-Pit................6	Leach-Pit 221	Seymour-NY 75
Tenney-Bos.............83	Mitchell-Cin..........163	Brain-Bos...............:24	Clarke-Pit...............13	Browne-NY 5	Brain-Bos.............214	Steinfeldt-Chi 70

BASES ON BALLS	STOLEN BASES	BASE STEALING RUNS	FIELDING RUNS-INFIELD	FIELDING RUNS-OUTFIELD	OUTFIELD ASSISTS	CATCHER CS PCT.
Thomas-Phi 83	Wagner-Pit.............61		Evers-Chi 27.1	Mitchell-Cin..........25.1	Mitchell-Cin............39	Marshall-StL 45.4
Huggins-Cin............83	Magee-Phi 46		Brain-Bos............22.5	Leach-Pit 8.9	Beaumont-Bos........30	Ritter-Bro 40.0
Tenney-Bos............82	Evers-Chi...............46		Byrne-StL 20.6	Clarke-Pit...............7.8	Murray-StL.............25	
Shannon-NY 82	Leach-Pit 43		Doolan-Phi...........14.8	Magee-Phi 7.8	Titus-Phi 21	
Anderson-Pit...........80	Devlin-NY 38		Tinker-Chi 13.4	Beaumont-Bos.......4.1	Burch-StL-Bro.........19	

WINS	WINNING PCT.	WINS ABOVE TEAM	GAMES STARTED	COMPLETE GAMES	FEWEST HITS/GAME	FEWEST BB/GAME
Mathewson-NY 24	Reulbach-Chi........810	Sparks-Phi.............6.6	McGlynn-StL...........39	McGlynn-StL...........33	Lundgren-Chi.......5.65	Phillippe-Pit.........1.51
Overall-Chi.............23	Brown-Chi............:769	Mathewson-NY 6.1	Willis-Pit..................37	Ewing-Cin 32	Pfiester-Chi..........6.60	Mathewson-NY 1:51
Sparks-Phi 22	Overall-Chi...........767	Reulbach-Chi.........4.1	Ewing-Cin 37	Mathewson-NY 31	Overall-Chi..........6.74	Brown-Chi............1.55
Willis-Pit.................21	Sparks-Phi...........733	Pastorius-Bro.........3.9	Mathewson-NY 36	Karger-StL 29	Camnitz-Pit..........6.75	McGinnity-NY 1.68
	Lundgren-Chi........720	Overall-Chi............3.8	McGinnity-NY 34	Willis-Pit..................27	Reulbach-Chi.......6.89	Sparks-Phi...........1.73

STRIKEOUTS	STRIKEOUTS/GAME	GAMES	SAVES	BASE RUNNERS/9	ADJUSTED RELIEF RUNS	RELIEF RANKING
Mathewson-NY 178	Ames-NY 5.63	McGinnity-NY 47	McGinnity-NY 4	Mathewson-NY 8.71		
Ewing-Cin 147	Beebe-StL...........5.32	McGlynn-StL...........45	Overall-Chi................3	Brown-Chi............8.73		
Ames-NY 146	Mathewson-NY 5.09	Mathewson-NY 41	Brown-Chi.................3	Pfiester-Chi..........9.05		
Overall-Chi............141	Overall-Chi..........4.73	Ewing-Cin 41		Overall-Chi...........9.42		
Beebe-StL.............141	Reulbach-Chi.......4.50			Sparks-Phi 9.48		

INNINGS PITCHED	OPPONENTS' AVG.	OPPONENTS' OBP	EARNED RUN AVERAGE	ADJUSTED ERA	ADJUSTED STARTER RUNS	PITCHER WINS
McGlynn-StL......352.1	Lundgren-Chi........185	Mathewson-NY 247	Pfiester-Chi..........1.15	Pfiester-Chi...........215	Lundgren-Chi.......29.2	**Overall-Chi 3.9**
Ewing-Cin 332.2	Pfiester-Chi...........207	Brown-Chi.............262	Lundgren-Chi.......1.17	Lundgren-Chi........212	Brown-Chi............28.8	**Brown-Chi...........3.7**
Mathewson-NY ..315.0	Overall-Chi............208	Pfiester-Chi...........263	Brown-Chi............1.39	Brown-Chi.............179	Overall-Chi...........27.9	**Lundgren-Chi.....3.5**
Karger-StL 314.0	Camnitz-Pit...........211	Overall-Chi............268	Leever-Pit 1.66	Ewing-Cin 149	Ewing-Cin 26.1	**Mathewson-NY ..2.7**
McGinnity-NY 310.1	Mathewson-NY 212	Karger-StL 270	Overall-Chi...........1.68	Overall-Chi............148	Pfiester-Chi..........20.5	**Ewing-Cin 2.6**

Cubs are World Serious

Prior to the season, the rules committee voted that the strike zone should range from the knee to shoulder. With this on the books, runs continued to drop. The Cubs' 1.73 ERA set an all-time NL record.

Two soon-to-be-prominent New York Giants saw their first action in 1907. Second baseman "Laughing Larry" Doyle would play a dozen seasons for John McGraw, while first baseman Fred Merkle lasted sixteen years in the bigs despite being best remembered for a baserunning gaffe. Future batting star Heinie Zimmerman broke in with Chicago, while first baseman Ed Konetchy, a slick fielder who also collected 2,150 lifetime hits, came up at midseason to start for the Cardinals.

Appearing in their final games during 1907 were first baseman Jake Beckley (who collected 2,934 hits), veteran shortstop Tommy Corcoran, third baseman Lave Cross (who played 21 seasons), and Bobby Lowe (Boston's regular second baseman for eleven years). Boston outfielder Cozy Dolan fell ill at spring training with pneumonia and typhoid fever and died on March 29.

After a great start, the Giants crumbled in May. John McGraw worked quickly to reconstruct his aging club, and New York would be back in 1908. As the Giants rebuilt, the Cubs again ran away and hid from the competition, winning the flag by 17 games over Pittsburgh.

The Cubs steamrolled the Tigers in October in five games (one was a tie). Chicago outscored Detroit 19-6 in the World Series, with Ty Cobb crossing the plate just once. This was the last Series until 1918 when at least one team didn't hit a home run.

Finally, in the year's biggest lie, the Mills Commission—appointed to investigate the beginnings of baseball—concluded with not one iota of reliable evidence that Civil War General Abner Doubleday invented the game in Cooperstown, New York, in 1839. Doubleday, who passed away in 1893, was too dead to be able to deny anything.

1907 AMERICAN LEAGUE

TEAM	W	L	T	PCT	GB	HW	HL	R	OR	PA	H	2B	3B	HR	BB	SO	HB	SH	AVG	OBP	SLG	OPS	AOPS	BR	ABR	PF	SB	CS	BSA	BSR
Det	92	58	3	.613	—	**50**	27	**693**	531	5721	**1383**	179	**75**	11	315	—	44	158	**.266**	**.313**	**.335**	**648**	**108**	**62**	40	104	196			
Phi	88	57	5	.607	1.5	**50**	20	584	511	5596	1276	**220**	44	**22**	384	—	27	175	.255	.311	.329	640	106	57	**43**	102	137			
Chi	87	64	6	.576	5.5	48	29	588	**474**	5720	1205	149	33	5	**421**	—	48	**181**	.238	.302	.283	585	95	-35	-16	97	175			
Cle	85	67	6	.559	8	46	31	531	525	5636	1221	182	68	11	335	—	56	177	.241	.295	.310	605	97	-12	-16	101	193			
NY	70	78	4	.473	21	33	40	605	667	5530	1258	150	67	15	304	—	53	129	.249	.299	.315	614	93	-1	-42	108	206			
StL	69	83	3	.454	24	36	40	541	555	5784	1324	154	63	10	370	—	39	151	.253	.308	.313	621	103	17	19	100	144			
Bos	59	90	6	.396	32.5	34	41	466	558	5721	1224	154	48	18	305	—	35	146	.234	.281	.292	573	89	-78	-74	99	125			
Was	49	102	3	.325	43.5	27	47	506	693	5699	1243	134	57	12	390	—	**60**	137	.243	.304	.299	603	105	-10	37	92	**223**			
Total	617	—	—	—	—	324	275	4514	—	45407	10134	1322	455	104	2824	4479	362	1254	.247	.302	.309	611	—	—	—	—	1399	—	—	—

TEAM	CG	SHO	GR	SV	IP	H	HR	BB	SO	BR/9	ERA	AERA	OAV	OOB	PR	APR	PF	OSB	OCS	FA	E	WPB	DP	FW	PW	BW	BSW	DIF
Det	120	15	36	6	1370.2	1281	**8**	380	512	11.2	2.33	**112**	.251	.309	32	**39**	102	160	*137*	.959	260	46	79	1.0	**4.3**	4.4	—	7.3
Phi	106	**27**	65	6	1354.2	**1106**	13	378	**789**	10.3	2.35	111	**.226**	.290	29	37	102	181	*149*	.958	263	50	67	.4	4.1	**4.7**	—	6.3
Chi	112	17	53	**9**	1406.1	1279	13	**305**	604	10.3	**2.22**	108	.245	.290	**50**	28	94	**153**	*130*	**.966**	**233**	55	101	**3.4**	3.1	-1.8	—	6.8
Cle	127	20	36	5	1392.2	1253	**8**	362	513	10.8	2.26	111	.244	.300	43	36	99	174	*115*	.960	264	74	**137**	1.3	4.0	-1.8	—	5.5
NY	93	10	67	6	1333.2	1327	13	428	511	12.2	3.03	92	.262	.325	-73	-32	110	178	*143*	.947	334	52	79	-4.4	-3.5	-4.6	—	8.5
StL	**129**	15	28	**9**	1381.1	1254	17	352	463	10.8	2.61	96	.245	.300	-10	-16	99	198	*145*	.959	266	**33**	97	.8	-1.8	2.1	—	-8.1
Bos	100	17	**70**	7	1414.0	1222	22	337	517	**10.2**	2.45	105	.236	**.288**	14	18	101	160	***155***	.959	274	47	100	.2	2.0	-8.2	—	-9.5
Was	106	12	57	5	1351.1	1383	10	344	570	11.8	3.11	78	.268	.320	-86	-111	95	195	*137*	.951	310	76	69	-2.4	-12.3	4.1	—	-15.9
Total	893	133	412	53	11004.2	—	—	—	—	10.9	2.54	—	.247	.302	—	—	—	—	—	.958	2204	433	729	—	—	—	—	—

BATTER-FIELDER WINS	BATTING AVERAGE	ON-BASE PERCENTAGE	SLUGGING AVERAGE	ON-BASE PLUS SLUGGING	ADJUSTED OPS	ADJUSTED BATTER RUNS
Lajoie-Cle 7.0	Cobb-Det .350	Hartsel-Phi .405	Cobb-Det .468	Cobb-Det .848	Cobb-Det 164	Cobb-Det 40.4
Cobb-Det 4.9	Crawford-Det .323	Stone-StL .387	Crawford-Det .460	Crawford-Det .826	Crawford-Det 157	Stone-StL 35.5
Crawford-Det 3.9	Stone-StL .320	Flick-Cle .386	Flick-Cle .412	Flick-Cle .798	Flick-Cle 153	Crawford-Det 35.4
Flick-Cle 3.0	Flick-Cle .302	Cobb-Det .380	Stone-StL .399	Stone-StL .787	Stone-StL 151	Flick-Cle 34.6
Stone-StL 2.6	Nicholls-Phi .302	Crawford-Det .366	Davis-Phi .395	Hartsel-Phi .771	Hartsel-Phi 143	Hartsel-Phi 32.5

RUNS	HITS	DOUBLES	TRIPLES	HOME RUNS	TOTAL BASES	RUNS BATTED IN
Crawford-Det 102	Cobb-Det 212	Davis-Phi 35	Flick-Cle 18	Davis-Phi 8	Cobb-Det 283	Cobb-Det 119
D.Jones-Det 101	Stone-StL 191	Crawford-Det 34	Crawford-Det 17	Seybold-Phi 5	Crawford-Det 268	Seybold-Phi 92
Cobb-Det 97	Crawford-Det 188	Lajoie-Cle 30	Cobb-Det 14	Hoffman-NY 5	Stone-StL 238	Davis-Phi 87
Hartsel-Phi 93	Ganley-Was 167	J.Collins-Bos-Phi 29	Unglaub-Bos 13	Cobb-Det 5	Davis-Phi 230	Crawford-Det 81
Hahn-Chi 87	Flick-Cle 166	Seybold-Phi 29			Flick-Cle 226	Wallace-StL 70

BASES ON BALLS	STOLEN BASES	BASE STEALING RUNS	FIELDING RUNS-INFIELD	FIELDING RUNS-OUTFIELD	OUTFIELD ASSISTS	CATCHER CS PCT.
Hartsel-Phi 106	Cobb-Det 53		Lajoie-Cle 44.9	D.Jones-Det 12.8	Cobb-Det 30	Schmidt-Det 46.6
Hahn-Chi 84	Flick-Cle 41		Donahue-Chi 20.5	Birmingham-Cle 12.4	Birmingham-Cle 28	Clarke-Cle 40.9
Jones-Chi 67	Conroy-NY 41		Elberfeld-NY 12.8	Cobb-Det 12.0	Hahn-Chi 24	
Flick-Cle 64	Ganley-Was 40		Isbell-Chi 8.1	Crawford-Det 7.0	Ganley-Was 23	
D.Jones-Det 60	Altizer-Was 38		Wallace-StL 7.9	Ganley-Was 6.6		

WINS	WINNING PCT.	WINS ABOVE TEAM	GAMES STARTED	COMPLETE GAMES	FEWEST HITS/GAME	FEWEST BB/GAME
White-Chi 27	Donovan-Det .862	Donovan-Det 10.0	Walsh-Chi 46	Walsh-Chi 37	Dygert-Phi 6.88	White-Chi 1.18
Joss-Cle 27	Dygert-Phi .724	Joss-Cle 7.8	Mullin-Det 42	Mullin-Det 35	Winter-Bos 6.94	Altrock-Chi 1.31
Killian-Det 25	Joss-Cle .711	Young-Bos 6.7	Plank-Phi 40	Joss-Cle 34	Walsh-Chi 7.27	Young-Bos 1.34
Donovan-Det 25	Smith-Chi .697	White-Chi 5.9	Joss-Cle 38	Young-Bos 33	Howell-StL 7.34	Bender-Phi 1.40
	White-Chi .675	Smith-Chi 5.6		Plank-Phi 33	Donovan-Det 7.37	Joss-Cle 1.44

STRIKEOUTS	STRIKEOUTS/GAME	GAMES	SAVES	BASE RUNNERS/9	ADJUSTED RELIEF RUNS	RELIEF RANKING
Waddell-Phi 232	Waddell-Phi 7.33	Walsh-Chi 56	Dinneen-Bos-StL 4	Young-Bos 9.02		
Walsh-Chi 206	Dygert-Phi 5.19	White-Chi 46	Walsh-Chi 4	Joss-Cle 9.04		
Plank-Phi 183	Plank-Phi 4.79	Mullin-Det 46	Hughes-Was 4	Bender-Phi 9.11		
Dygert-Phi 151	Bender-Phi 4.60	Waddell-Phi 44		Winter-Bos 9.19		
Young-Bos 147	Walsh-Chi 4.39			Walsh-Chi 9.29		

INNINGS PITCHED	OPPONENTS' AVG.	OPPONENTS' OBP	EARNED RUN AVERAGE	ADJUSTED ERA	ADJUSTED STARTER RUNS	PITCHER WINS
Walsh-Chi 422.1	Dygert-Phi .214	Young-Bos .263	Walsh-Chi 1.60	Walsh-Chi 150	Walsh-Chi 32.8	**Walsh-Chi 4.6**
Mullin-Det 357.1	Winter-Bos .216	Joss-Cle .264	Killian-Det 1.78	Killian-Det 146	Joss-Cle 26.7	**Killian-Det 4.2**
Plank-Phi 343.2	Walsh-Chi .224	Bender-Phi .265	Joss-Cle 1.83	Joss-Cle 136	Young-Bos 24.9	**Joss-Cle 3.0**
Young-Bos 343.1	Howell-StL .225	Winter-Bos .267	Howell-StL 1.93	Howell-StL 130	Killian-Det 24.7	**Howell-StL 2.6**
Joss-Cle 338.2	Donovan-Det .226	Walsh-Chi .269	Young-Bos 1.99	Young-Bos 129	Plank-Phi 17.1	**Young-Bos 2.4**

A Peach Takes Root in Motown

Four teams entered September within striking distance of the pennant. While Chicago and Cleveland played .500 ball during the last month and Philadelphia peaked early, Detroit finished the season on a high to take the crown. Rarely has one player made such a difference to an entire league as Ty Cobb did in 1907. In his first season of more than 100 games, Cobb won the first of his 12 batting titles and led in slugging, hits, total bases, RBIs, and steals. His outfield mates, Sam Crawford and Davy Jones, were first and second in runs (Cobb was third). The Tigers leapt from sixth to first, edging the Athletics by 1½ games. Just as importantly, Cobb's speed-based game would usher in a new era of "attack" baseball.

The blow of a bad year can be softened by the gain of a Hall of Famer. Boston playing manager Chick Stahl committed suicide in spring training, but the club gained freshman outfielder Tris Speaker. Washington finished last while summoning 19-year-old pitcher Walter Johnson. While the rookie finished 5-9, his ERA was a sparkling 1.87. The Senators, as well as the Tigers, experienced huge attendance gains, and total spectators for the league increased by 16 percent.

Once again, Topsy Hartsel and Harry Davis provided the Philadelphia offense, and the deep pitching was nearly good enough to overcome the fearsome Tigers attack. In the World Series, however, the Tigers were toothless, as the Cubs completely shut them down in five games, including one tie.

At this time, the strike zone was defined, rather vaguely, as reaching from the knees to the shoulders (no "top" or "bottom" of either to make the definition more precise). Strikeouts fell a bit as homers dropped nearly 25 percent. The AL also ruled in 1907 that anyone appearing as a pinch hitter, pinch runner, or defensive substitute would now receive credit for a game played.

1906 NATIONAL LEAGUE

TEAM	W	L	T	PCT	GB	HW	HL	R	OR	PA	H	2B	3B	HR	BB	SO	HB	SH	AVG	OBP	SLG	OPS	AOPS	BR	ABR	PF	SB	CS	BSA	BSR
Chi	116	36	3	.763	—	**56**	21	**704**	**381**	5742	**1316**	181	**71**	20	448	—	45	**231**	**.262**	.328	**.339**	**667**	109	85	49	106	283			
NY	96	56	1	.632	20	51	24	625	509	5556	1217	162	53	14	**563**	—	**71**	154	.255	**.343**	.320	663	**112**	**96**	**82**	102	**288**			
Pit	93	60	1	.608	23.5	49	27	623	470	5686	1313	164	67	12	424	—	42	190	.261	.324	.327	651	105	56	30	104	162			
Phi	71	82	1	.464	45.5	37	40	528	564	5524	1183	**197**	47	12	432	—	36	145	.241	.307	.307	614	98	-6	-7	100	180			
Bro	66	86	1	.434	50	31	44	496	625	5483	1156	141	68	**25**	388	—	36	162	.236	.297	.308	605	103	-33	10	92	176			
Cin	64	87	4	.424	51.5	36	40	533	582	5642	1198	140	**71**	16	395	—	58	164	.238	.301	.304	605	91	-30	-52	104	170			
StL	52	98	4	.347	63	28	48	470	607	5613	1195	137	69	9	361	—	38	139	.235	.291	.295	586	93	-70	-49	96	110			
Bos	49	102	1	.325	66.5	28	47	408	649	5452	1115	136	43	16	356	—	52	119	.226	.286	.281	567	85	-97	-85	97	93			
Total	615	—	—	—	—	316	291	4387	—	44698	9693	1258	489	124	3367	4537	378	1304	.244	.310	.310	620	—	—	—	—	1462	—	—	—

TEAM	CG	SHO	GR	SV	IP	H	HR	BB	SO	BR/9	ERA	AERA	OAV	OOB	PR	APR	PF	OSB	OCS	FA	E	WPB	DP	FW	PW	BW	BSW	DIF
Chi	125	**30**	33	10	1388.1	**1018**	**12**	446	**702**	**9.8**	**1.75**	**150**	**.207**	**.280**	**135**	**135**	100	**107**	*143*	**.969**	**194**	**34**	100	**4.5**	**15.0**	5.4	—	15.0
NY	105	19	**55**	**18**	1334.1	1207	**12**	394	639	11.0	2.49	105	.241	.300	20	15	99	144	*154*	.963	233	50	84	1.8	1.7	**9.1**	—	7.4
Pit	116	27	42	2	1358.0	1234	13	**309**	532	10.5	2.21	120	.245	.294	62	69	102	157	*133*	.964	228	52	**109**	2.2	7.7	3.3	—	3.3
Phi	108	21	52	5	1354.1	1201	18	436	500	11.3	2.58	101	.235	.304	7	0	99	203	*119*	.956	271	46	83	-.6	.0	-.8	—	-4.1
Bro	119	22	36	11	1348.2	1255	15	453	476	11.7	3.13	80	.249	.316	-76	-97	96	192	*151*	.955	283	**34**	73	-1.5	-10.8	1.1	—	1.2
Cin	126	12	31	5	1369.2	1248	14	470	567	11.6	2.69	102	.250	.320	-10	5	105	184	*161*	.959	262	55	97	.0	.6	-5.8	—	-6.4
StL	118	4	37	2	1354.0	1246	16	479	559	11.9	3.04	86	.246	.318	-63	-65	100	250	*164*	.957	272	75	92	-.7	-7.2	-5.4	—	-9.7
Bos	**137**	10	16	0	1334.1	1291	24	436	562	12.0	3.14	85	.261	.328	-76	-69	102	225	***181***	.947	337	49	102	-5.2	-7.7	-9.4	—	-4.2
Total	954	145	302	53	10841.2	—	—	—	—	11.2	2.62	—	.244	.310	—	—	—	—	—	.959	2080	395	740	—	—	—	—	—

BATTER-FIELDER WINS	BATTING AVERAGE	ON-BASE PERCENTAGE	SLUGGING AVERAGE	ON-BASE PLUS SLUGGING	ADJUSTED OPS	ADJUSTED BATTER RUNS
Wagner-Pit......7.2	Wagner-Pit.......339	Bresnahan-NY......419	Lumley-Bro.......477	Wagner-Pit.......875	Lumley-Bro.......184	Lumley-Bro.......45.3
Devlin-NY.......6.6	Steinfeldt-Chi.......327	Chance-Chi.......419	Wagner-Pit.......459	Lumley-Bro.......864	Wagner-Pit.......166	Wagner-Pit.......42.2
Lumley-Bro.......4.5	Lumley-Bro.......324	Wagner-Pit.......416	Strang-NY.......435	Chance-Chi.......849	Chance-Chi.......156	Chance-Chi.......35.0
Bresnahan-NY...4.2	Strang-NY.......319	Devlin-NY.......396	Steinfeldt-Chi.......430	Steinfeldt-Chi.......825	Jordan-Bro.......153	Steinfeldt-Chi.......31.5
Huggins-Cin.......4.1	Chance-Chi.......319	Steinfeldt-Chi.......395	Chance-Chi.......430	Devlin-NY.......786	Steinfeldt-Chi.......149	Devlin-NY.......28.3
RUNS	**HITS**	**DOUBLES**	**TRIPLES**	**HOME RUNS**	**TOTAL BASES**	**RUNS BATTED IN**
Wagner-Pit.......103	Steinfeldt-Chi.......176	Wagner-Pit.......38	Schulte-Chi.......13	Jordan-Bro.......12	Wagner-Pit.......237	Steinfeldt-Chi.......83
Chance-Chi.......103	Wagner-Pit.......175	Magee-Phi.......36	Clarke-Pit.......13	Lumley-Bro.......9	Steinfeldt-Chi.......232	Nealon-Pit.......83
Sheckard-Chi.......90	Seymour-Cin-NY..165	Bransfield-Phi.......28	Nealon-Pit.......12	Seymour-Cin-NY......8	Lumley-Bro.......231	Seymour-Cin-NY....80
Nealon-Pit.......82	Magee-Phi.......159	Steinfeldt-Chi.......27	Lumley-Bro.......12	Schulte-Chi.......7	Magee-Phi.......229	Jordan-Bro.......78
	Huggins-Cin.......159	Sheckard-Chi.......27			Schulte-Chi.......223	
BASES ON BALLS	**STOLEN BASES**	**BASE STEALING RUNS**	**FIELDING RUNS-INFIELD**	**FIELDING RUNS-OUTFIELD**	**OUTFIELD ASSISTS**	**CATCHER CS PCT.**
Thomas-Phi.......107	Chance-Chi.......57		Devlin-NY.......28.8	Magee-Phi.......11.9	Dolan-Bos.......26	Gibson-Pit.......47.7
Bresnahan-NY.......81	Magee-Phi.......55		Brain-Bos.......25.0	Maloney-Bro.......9.1	Titus-Phi.......23	Bergen-Bro.......45.3
Titus-Phi.......78	Devlin-NY.......54		Gilbert-NY.......21.9	Thomas-Phi.......8.4	Maloney-Bro.......19	Dooin-Phi.......37.2
Dahlen-NY.......76	Wagner-Pit.......53		Huggins-Cin.......21.9	Titus-Phi.......6.8		
Devlin-NY.......74	Evers-Chi.......49		Wagner-Pit.......20.0	Clarke-Pit.......4.9		
WINS	**WINNING PCT.**	**WINS ABOVE TEAM**	**GAMES STARTED**	**COMPLETE GAMES**	**FEWEST HITS/GAME**	**FEWEST BB/GAME**
McGinnity-NY.......27	Reulbach-Chi.......826	Leever-Pit.......6.3	Young-Bos.......41	Young-Bos.......37	Reulbach-Chi.......5.33	Phillippe-Pit.......1.07
Brown-Chi.......26	Brown-Chi.......813	Weimer-Cin.......5.8	Weimer-Cin.......39	Pfeffer-Bos.......33	Pfiester-Chi.......6.21	Leever-Pit.......1.66
Willis-Pit.......23	Leever-Pit.......759	Scanlan-Bro.......4.7	Sparks-Phi.......37		Brown-Chi.......6.43	Sparks-Phi.......1.76
Mathewson-NY.......22	Lundgren-Chi.......739	McGinnity-NY.......4.1	McGinnity-NY.......37		Beebe-Chi-StL.....6.67	Ewing-Cin.......1.88
Leever-Pit.......22	Pfiester-Chi.......714	Brown-Chi.......4.0			Lundgren-Chi.......6.93	McGinnity-NY......1.88
STRIKEOUTS	**STRIKEOUTS/GAME**	**GAMES**	**SAVES**	**BASE RUNNERS/9**	**ADJUSTED RELIEF RUNS**	**RELIEF RANKING**
Beebe-Chi-StL......171	Ames-NY.......6.90	McGinnity-NY.......45	Ferguson-NY.......7	Brown-Chi.......8.53		
Pfeffer-Bos.......158	Beebe-Chi-StL.....6.67	Young-Bos.......43	Wiltse-NY.......6	Pfiester-Chi.......8.94		
Ames-NY.......156	Pfiester-Chi.......5.49	Sparks-Phi.......42	Stricklett-Bro.......5	Sparks-Phi.......8.98		
Pfiester-Chi.......153	Overall-Cin-Chi....5.05	Duggleby-Phi.......42		Reulbach-Chi.......9.66		
	Lush-Phi.......4.84			Ewing-Cin.......9.70		
INNINGS PITCHED	**OPPONENTS' AVG.**	**OPPONENTS' OBP**	**EARNED RUN AVERAGE**	**ADJUSTED ERA**	**ADJUSTED STARTER RUNS**	**PITCHER WINS**
Young-Bos.......358.1	Reulbach-Chi.......175	Brown-Chi.......252	Brown-Chi.......1.04	Brown-Chi.......253	Brown-Chi.......45.1	**Brown-Chi.......6.1**
McGinnity-NY....339.2	Pfiester-Chi.......194	Sparks-Phi.......257	Pfiester-Chi.......1.51	Pfiester-Chi.......174	Willis-Pit.......34.0	**Willis-Pit.......4.3**
Willis-Pit.......322.0	Brown-Chi.......202	Pfiester-Chi.......258	Reulbach-Chi.......1.65	Reulbach-Chi.......159	Pfiester-Chi.......29.9	**Reulbach-Chi.....2.8**
Sparks-Phi.......316.2	Beebe-Chi-StL......209	Phillippe-Pit.......276	Willis-Pit.......1.73	Willis-Pit.......154	Reulbach-Chi.......25.6	**Taylor-StL-Chi....2.8**
Lindaman-Bos...307.1	Sparks-Phi.......211	Reulbach-Chi.......278	Leifield-Pit.......1.87	Leifield-Pit.......143	Taylor-StL-Chi......20.0	**Weimer-Cin.......2.8**

A Chicago Revival

Staking their claim as the team of the decade, the Chicago Cubs walloped the rest of the league, going 116-36 to post the NL's best record ever while capturing the franchise's first flag since 1886. Chicago went 26-3 in August and easily held off a good New York team that won 96 games. Three Finger Brown had a 1.04 ERA, the best in modern NL history, and Ed Reulbach allowed just 5.33 hits per game, a record that would stand until 1968. The Cubs staff ERA was a spectacular 1.75.

The Cubs also had a productive offense headed by first baseman-manager Frank Chance and third sacker Harry Steinfeldt, one of baseball's first great offensive-minded third basemen. On the other hand, Boston (known as both the Doves and Beaneaters) lost 19 in a row and finished $66^1/_2$ games out, an all-time National League record for team futility. The Cubs had seven players score more often than Boston's runs leader, Fred Tenney.

Pitcher Babe Adams made his debut with the Cardinals. Purchased by Pittsburgh the next year, Adams remained with the club until 1926 and won 194 games. Hugh Duffy, who batted .440 in 1894, saw his last at bat at age 39, and John McGraw ended his playing days to concentrate fully on managing from the dugout. Kid Nichols, a 361-game winner who starred for Boston from 1980–1901, and who was arguably the greatest pitcher of the nineteenth century, retired. Buck Ewing, a pre-eminent star of nineteenth century ball, died at age 47.

Offense again dropped significantly in 1906. Small-ball techniques like the sacrifice bunt and the steal were at their apex. The orthodox little man's game became relevant in October's intra-city World Series, where the "Hitless Wonder" White Sox pulled off a surprise upset of the Cubs.

1906 AMERICAN LEAGUE

TEAM	W	L	T	PCT	GB	HW	HL	R	OR	PA	H	2B	3B	HR	BB	SO	HB	SH	AVG	OBP	SLG	OPS	AOPS	BR	ABR	PF	SB	CS	BSA	BSR
Chi	93	58	3	.616	—	**54**	23	570	**460**	5654	1133	152	52	7	**453**	—	**50**	**226**	.230	.301	.286	587	91	-45	-31	97	216			
NY	90	61	4	.596	3	53	23	640	543	5661	1354	166	**77**	17	331	—	46	189	.266	.316	.339	655	101	57	-1	110	192			
Cle	89	64	4	.582	5	47	30	**663**	481	5987	**1514**	**240**	73	12	330	—	41	191	**.279**	**.325**	**.357**	**682**	**121**	**114**	**124**	99	203			
Phi	78	67	4	.538	12	48	23	561	539	5475	1206	213	49	**32**	385	—	43	164	.247	.308	.330	638	102	35	17	103	165			
StL	76	73	5	.510	16	40	34	560	499	5614	1244	145	60	20	366	—	47	171	.247	.304	.312	616	102	-7	18	96	221			
Det	71	78	2	.477	21	42	34	518	598	5474	1195	154	64	10	333	—	33	178	.242	.295	.306	601	91	-38	-51	103	206			
Was	55	95	1	.367	37.5	33	41	519	665	5455	1180	144	65	26	306	—	49	144	.238	.289	.309	598	97	-46	-21	95	**233**			
Bos	49	105	1	.318	45.5	22	54	463	706	5645	1223	160	75	13	298	—	41	138	.237	.284	.304	588	89	-69	-68	100	99			
Total	613	—	—	—	—	339	262	4494	—	44965	10049	1374	515	137	2802	4561	350	1401	.249	.303	.318	621	—	—	—	—	1535	—	—	—

TEAM	CG	SHO	GR	SV	IP	H	HR	BB	SO	BR/9	ERA	AERA	OAV	OOB	PR	APR	PF	OSB	OCS	FA	E	WPB	DP	FW	PW	BW	BSW	DIF
Chi	117	**32**	43	4	1375.1	1212	11	**255**	543	**9.8**	2.13	119	.239	**.280**	85	66	94	**133**	*133*	.963	243	52	80	1.8	7.3	-3.4	—	11.8
NY	99	18	**68**	5	1357.2	1236	21	351	605	10.8	2.78	107	.246	.301	-13	25	110	184	*144*	.957	272	54	69	.1	2.7	-.1	—	11.7
Cle	**133**	27	27	4	1412.2	1197	16	365	530	10.3	**2.09**	**125**	.232	.289	**94**	**87**	97	170	*140*	**.967**	**217**	45	**111**	**3.8**	**9.6**	**13.6**	—	-14.5
Phi	107	19	51	4	1322.0	1135	**9**	425	**749**	11.0	2.60	105	.236	.305	13	16	101	192	*159*	.956	267	47	86	-.2	1.8	1.9	—	2.1
StL	**133**	17	21	5	1357.2	**1132**	14	314	558	10.0	2.23	116	**.230**	.284	70	56	96	211	*151*	.954	290	58	80	-1.1	6.2	2.0	—	-5.5
Det	128	7	25	4	1334.1	1398	14	389	469	12.4	3.06	90	.272	.330	-55	-42	103	171	*161*	.959	260	**34**	86	.4	-4.6	-5.6	—	6.3
Was	115	13	47	1	1322.2	1331	15	451	558	12.4	3.25	81	.265	.331	-83	-93	98	229	*161*	.955	279	54	78	-.8	-10.2	-2.3	—	-6.7
Bos	124	6	35	**6**	1382.0	1360	37	285	549	11.0	3.41	81	.262	.306	-111	-103	102	245	***182***	.949	335	57	84	-3.9	-11.3	-7.5	—	-5.3
Total	956	139	317	33	10864.1	—	—	—	—	11.0	2.69	—	.249	.303	—	—	—	—	—	.958	2163	401	674	—	—	—	—	—

BATTER-FIELDER WINS	BATTING AVERAGE	ON-BASE PERCENTAGE	SLUGGING AVERAGE	ON-BASE PLUS SLUGGING	ADJUSTED OPS	ADJUSTED BATTER RUNS
Lajoie-Cle 7.6	Stone-StL .... .358	Stone-StL .... .417	Stone-StL .... .501	Stone-StL .... .918	Stone-StL 195	Stone-StL 63.3
Stone-StL 5.9	Lajoie-Cle .... .355	Lajoie-Cle .... .392	Lajoie-Cle .... .465	Lajoie-Cle .... .857	Lajoie-Cle 170	Lajoie-Cle 48.2
Turner-Cle 4.2	Chase-NY .... .323	Flick-Cle .... .372	Davis-Phi .... .459	Davis-Phi .... .815	Flick-Cle 156	Flick-Cle 40.2
Davis-Phi 3.2	Congalton-Cle .... .320	Hartsel-Phi .... .363	Flick-Cle .... .441	Flick-Cle .... .813	Davis-Phi 150	Davis-Phi 32.1
Davis-Chi 3.2	Seybold-Phi .... .316	Davis-Phi .... .355	Hickman-Was .... .421	Crawford-Det .... .747	Hickman-Was 135	Seybold-Phi 20.0

RUNS	HITS	DOUBLES	TRIPLES	HOME RUNS	TOTAL BASES	RUNS BATTED IN
Flick-Cle 98	Lajoie-Cle 214	Lajoie-Cle 48	Flick-Cle 22	Davis-Phi 12	Stone-StL 291	Davis-Phi 96
Keeler-NY 96	Stone-StL 208	Davis-Phi 42	Stone-StL 20	Hickman-Was 9	Lajoie-Cle 280	Lajoie-Cle 91
Hartsel-Phi 96	Flick-Cle 194	Flick-Cle 34	Crawford-Det 16	Stone-StL 6	Flick-Cle 275	Davis-Chi 80
Davis-Phi 94	Chase-NY 193	Murphy-Phi 28	Ferris-Bos 13	Seybold-Phi 5	Davis-Phi 253	Williams-NY 77
Stone-StL 91	Keeler-NY 180	Turner-Cle 27			Chase-NY 236	Chase-NY 76

BASES ON BALLS	STOLEN BASES	BASE STEALING RUNS	FIELDING RUNS-INFIELD	FIELDING RUNS-OUTFIELD	OUTFIELD ASSISTS	CATCHER CS PCT.
Hartsel-Phi 88	Flick-Cle 39		Tannehill-Chi 32.4	Niles-StL 13.7	Niles-StL 34	Sullivan-Chi 51.8
Jones-Chi 83	Anderson-Was 39		Lajoie-Cle 21.3	McIntyre-Det 12.3	McIntyre-Det 25	Warner-Det-Was .. 51.0
E.Hahn-NY-Chi 72	Isbell-Chi 37		Turner-Cle 18.6	Anderson-Was 6.6	Stahl-Bos 24	Bemis-Cle 41.1
Wallace-StL 58	Altizer-Was 37		Schlafly-Was 16.2	Stahl-Bos 6.5	Jones-Chi 23	
McIntyre-Det 56	Donahue-Chi 36		Williams-NY 13.9	Crawford-Det 5.2	E.Hahn-NY-Chi 21	

WINS	WINNING PCT.	WINS ABOVE TEAM	GAMES STARTED	COMPLETE GAMES	FEWEST HITS/GAME	FEWEST BB/GAME
Orth-NY 27	Plank-Phi .... .760	Plank-Phi 6.6	Chesbro-NY 42	Orth-NY 36	Pelty-StL 6.53	Young-Bos .... .78
Chesbro-NY 23	White-Chi .... .750	Patten-Was 5.9	Mullin-Det 40	Mullin-Det 35	White-Chi 6.57	Altrock-Chi 1.31
Rhoads-Cle 22	Joss-Cle .... .700	Joss-Cle 4.9	Orth-NY 39	Hess-Cle 33	Walsh-Chi 6.95	Joss-Cle 1.37
Owen-Chi 22	Rhoads-Cle .... .688	Rhoads-Cle 4.8		Rhoads-Cle 31	Joss-Cle 7.02	White-Chi 1.56
	Owen-Chi .... .629	White-Chi 4.7			Powell-StL 7.23	Jacobson-StL 1.57

STRIKEOUTS	STRIKEOUTS/GAME	GAMES	SAVES	BASE RUNNERS/9	ADJUSTED RELIEF RUNS	RELIEF RANKING
Waddell-Phi 196	Waddell-Phi 6.47	Chesbro-NY 49	Hess-Cle 3	White-Chi 8.33		
Falkenberg-Was 178	Bender-Phi 6.00	Orth-NY 45	Bender-Phi 3	Joss-Cle 8.49		
Walsh-Chi 171	Walsh-Chi 5.53	Waddell-Phi 43		Patterson-Chi 8.87		
Hess-Cle 167	Falkenberg-Was ... 5.36	Hess-Cle 43		Walsh-Chi 9.05		
Bender-Phi 159	Powell-StL 4.87	Owen-Chi 42		Pelty-StL 9.18		

INNINGS PITCHED	OPPONENTS' AVG.	OPPONENTS' OBP	EARNED RUN AVERAGE	ADJUSTED ERA	ADJUSTED STARTER RUNS	PITCHER WINS
Orth-NY 338.2	Pelty-StL .... .206	White-Chi .... .249	White-Chi 1.52	White-Chi 167	Rhoads-Cle 28.5	**White-Chi 3.9**
Hess-Cle 333.2	White-Chi .... .207	Joss-Cle .... .252	Pelty-StL 1.59	Pelty-StL 163	Hess-Cle 28.3	**Joss-Cle 3.5**
Mullin-Det 330.0	Walsh-Chi .... .217	Walsh-Chi .... .265	Joss-Cle 1.72	Joss-Cle 152	White-Chi 28.3	**Orth-NY 3.4**
Chesbro-NY 325.0	Joss-Cle .... .218	Pelty-StL .... .267	Powell-StL 1.77	Powell-StL 146	Joss-Cle 28.1	**Hess-Cle 3.3**
Rhoads-Cle 315.0	Powell-StL .... .223	Powell-StL .... .275	Rhoads-Cle 1.80	Rhoads-Cle 145	Pelty-StL 26.9	**Pelty-StL 2.9**

Not Quite Hitless

As August began, six American League clubs boasted records over .500 (all but pathetic Washington and Boston, which had totally collapsed). When the dust cleared, it was the White Sox and the Highlanders jousting in the final weeks. While New York played middling ball down the stretch, the White Sox forged ahead and won by three games. Even with the good pennant race, attendance decreased for first time in the AL's short history.

The fourth-place Philadelphia Athletics debuted two future stars, pitcher Jack Coombs and second baseman Eddie Collins. And despite missing time to illness, sophomore outfielder Ty Cobb of Detroit showed that he would be a force to be reckoned with as he hit .316 in a league that batted just .249.

Although the White Sox were called "hitless wonders" while posting a .230 batting average (worst ever for a pennant winner), that appellation is truly a misnomer. The Chicago offense led the league in walks and actually ranked third in runs—second in scoring on the road. Spacious South Side Park kept their offense to just fifth in home contests, but it certainly helped their already excellent mound staff. Doc White paced the league in ERA, while Ed Walsh led in shutouts. Meanwhile, the second-place Yankees were outscored on the road but blew away their opposition at home.

When the World Series rolled around, it was a Second City delight—the Cubs had won 116 games during the regular season and were heavily favored against the White Sox. Nevertheless, the AL champs won two out of the first three, despite collecting just 9 hits in 27 innings off Cubs pitching.

After the Cubs' Three Finger Brown shut out the Sox on 2 hits to even the Series, the supposed "Hitless Wonders" opened up the baseball world's eyes by teeing off for 8-6 and 8-3 wins against Ed Reulbach and Brown to clinch the Series.

1905 NATIONAL LEAGUE

TEAM	W	L	T	PCT	GB	HW	HL	R	OR	PA	H	2B	3B	HR	BB	SO	HB	SH	AVG	OBP	SLG	OPS	AOPS	BR	ABR	PF	SB	CS	BSA	BSR
NY	105	48	2	.686	—	**54**	21	**780**	505	5839	1392	**191**	88	**39**	**517**	—	**90**	138	**.273**	**.351**	**.368**	**719**	**119**	**148**	**132**	102	**291**			
Pit	96	57	2	.627	9	49	28	692	570	5790	1385	190	91	22	382	—	36	159	.266	.320	.350	670	104	38	21	103	202			
Chi	92	61	2	.601	13	**54**	25	667	**442**	5810	1249	157	82	12	448	—	61	**193**	.245	.313	.314	627	90	-30	-53	104	267			
Phi	83	69	3	.546	21.5	39	36	708	603	5867	1362	187	82	16	406	—	44	174	.260	.318	.336	654	106	14	39	96	180			
Cin	79	74	2	.516	26	50	28	736	698	5865	**1401**	160	**101**	27	434	—	52	174	.269	.332	.354	686	101	73	3	111	181			
StL	58	96	0	.377	47.5	32	45	535	734	5609	1254	140	85	20	391	—	43	109	.248	.307	.321	628	97	-38	-19	97	162			
Bos	51	103	2	.331	54.5	29	46	468	733	5631	1217	148	52	17	302	—	54	85	.234	.284	.293	577	80	-137	-126	98	132			
Bro	48	104	3	.316	56.5	29	47	506	807	5604	1255	154	60	29	327	—	41	136	.246	.297	.317	614	97	-68	-23	93	186			
Total	620	—	—	—	—	336	276	5092	—	46015	10515	1327	641	182	3207	4462	421	1168	.255	.315	.332	647	—	—	—	—	1601	—	—	—

TEAM	CG	SHO	GR	SV	IP	H	HR	BB	SO	BR/9	ERA	AERA	OAV	OOB	PR	APR	PF	OSB	OCS	FA	E	WPB	DP	FW	PW	BW	BSW	DIF
NY	117	18	42	**15**	1370.0	1160	25	**364**	**760**	10.2	2.39	122	.229	**.284**	91	82	98	**123**	*138*	.960	258	82	93	2.3	8.5	**13.7**	—	4.0
Pit	113	12	**47**	6	1382.2	1270	**12**	389	512	11.2	2.86	104	.248	.308	20	16	100	164	*152*	.961	255	61	112	2.5	1.7	2.2	—	13.2
Chi	133	**23**	22	2	1407.1	**1135**	14	385	627	**10.0**	**2.04**	**146**	**.224**	.286	**149**	**145**	99	168	*150*	**.962**	**248**	45	99	**2.9**	**15.1**	-5.5	—	3.0
Phi	119	12	42	5	1398.2	1303	21	411	516	11.5	2.81	104	.252	.316	28	13	97	173	*160*	.957	275	**40**	99	1.2	1.4	4.1	—	.4
Cin	119	10	39	2	1365.2	1409	22	439	547	12.5	3.01	109	.272	.335	-3	38	110	203	*176*	.953	310	68	**122**	-1.0	3.9	.3	—	-.8
StL	135	10	19	2	1347.2	1431	28	367	411	12.3	3.59	83	.276	.329	-89	-93	99	238	*161*	.957	274	48	83	1.2	-9.7	-2.0	—	-8.5
Bos	**139**	14	18	0	1383.0	1390	36	433	533	12.1	3.52	88	.265	.326	-81	-66	103	278	***191***	.951	325	85	89	-1.8	-6.9	-13.1	—	-4.2
Bro	125	7	33	3	1347.0	1416	24	476	556	13.1	3.76	77	.274	.343	-114	-137	96	252	*182*	.937	408	**40**	101	-7.2	-14.2	-2.4	—	-4.2
Total	1000	106	262	35	11002.0	—	—	—	—	11.6	2.99	—	.255	.315	—	—	—	—	—	.954	2353	469	798	—	—	—	—	—

BATTER-FIELDER WINS	BATTING AVERAGE	ON-BASE PERCENTAGE	SLUGGING AVERAGE	ON-BASE PLUS SLUGGING	ADJUSTED OPS	ADJUSTED BATTER RUNS
Wagner-Pit..........7.5	Seymour-Cin.........377	Chance-Chi...........450	Seymour-Cin.........559	Seymour-Cin.........988	Seymour-Cin.........175	Seymour-Cin........52.3
Seymour-Cin........5.6	Wagner-Pit............363	Seymour-Cin..........429	Wagner-Pit............505	Wagner-Pit............932	Wagner-Pit............173	Wagner-Pit............50.4
Huggins-Cin.......4.7	Donlin-NY.............356	Wagner-Pit............427	Donlin-NY.............495	Donlin-NY.............908	Donlin-NY.............166	Donlin-NY............49.3
Titus-Phi.............4.1	Beaumont-Pit........328	Thomas-Phi..........417	Titus-Phi..............436	Chance-Chi..........883	Chance-Chi...........157	Titus-Phi..............40.4
Thomas-Phi........4.1	Thomas-Phi..........317	Donlin-NY.............413	Grady-StL.............434	Titus-Phi..............834	Titus-Phi..............154	Chance-Chi............34.8
RUNS	**HITS**	**DOUBLES**	**TRIPLES**	**HOME RUNS**	**TOTAL BASES**	**RUNS BATTED IN**
Donlin-NY.............124	Seymour-Cin.........219	Seymour-Cin..........40	Seymour-Cin...........21	Odwell-Cin................9	Seymour-Cin.........325	Seymour-Cin.........121
Thomas-Phi..........118	Donlin-NY.............216	Titus-Phi................36	Mertes-NY..............17	Seymour-Cin............8	Donlin-NY.............300	Mertes-NY............108
Huggins-Cin..........117	Wagner-Pit............199	Wagner-Pit..............32	Magee-Phi..............17	Lumley-Bro...............7	Wagner-Pit............277	Wagner-Pit............101
Wagner-Pit............114	Barry-Chi-Cin........182	Donlin-NY...............31	Smoot-StL...............16	Donlin-NY.................7	Magee-Phi.............253	Magee-Phi...............98
	Magee-Phi............180	Ritchey-Pit..............29	Donlin-NY...............16	Dahlen-NY................7	Titus-Phi...............239	Titus-Phi.................89
BASES ON BALLS	**STOLEN BASES**	**BASE STEALING RUNS**	**FIELDING RUNS-INFIELD**	**FIELDING RUNS-OUTFIELD**	**OUTFIELD ASSISTS**	**CATCHER CS PCT.**
Huggins-Cin..........103	Maloney-Chi...........59		Huggins-Cin.........36.8	Sheckard-Bro.......16.6	Thomas-Phi............27	Moran-Bos...........39.2
Slagle-Chi...............97	Devlin-NY...............59		Tenney-Bos..........22.1	Thomas-Phi.........14.8	Slagle-Chi...............27	
Thomas-Phi............93	Wagner-Pit..............57		Gilbert-NY............20.3	Seymour-Cin..........9.8	Seymour-Cin...........25	
Chance-Chi.............78	Mertes-NY..............52		Corcoran-Cin.......20.1	Magee-Phi.............9.7	Dunleavy-StL..........25	
Titus-Phi.................69	Magee-Phi..............48		Dahlen-NY...........19.8	Dunleavy-StL.........6.9		
WINS	**WINNING PCT.**	**WINS ABOVE TEAM**	**GAMES STARTED**	**COMPLETE GAMES**	**FEWEST HITS/GAME**	**FEWEST BB/GAME**
Mathewson-NY.......31	Leever-Pit.............800	Mathewson-NY......7.0	Young-Bos.............42	Young-Bos.............41	Reulbach-Chi.......6.42	Phillippe-Pit..........1.55
Pittinger-Phi...........23	Mathewson-NY.....775	Leever-Pit..............6.3	Willis-Bos................41	Willis-Bos................36	Mathewson-NY....6.70	Brown-Chi............1.59
Ames-NY................22	Ames-NY..............733	Young-Bos.............6.0	Overall-Cin.............39	Fraser-Bos..............35	Lundgren-Chi.......7.02	Young-Bos...........1.69
McGinnity-NY.........21	Wiltse-NY.............714	Ewing-Cin..............4.8	McGinnity-NY.........38	Taylor-StL...............34	Wicker-Chi...........7.03	Mathewson-NY....1.70
	Lynch-Pit..............680	Scanlan-Bro..........4.8			Wiltse-NY............7.22	McGinnity-NY......1.99
STRIKEOUTS	**STRIKEOUTS/GAME**	**GAMES**	**SAVES**	**BASE RUNNERS/9**	**ADJUSTED RELIEF RUNS**	**RELIEF RANKING**
Mathewson-NY.....206	Ames-NY.............6.78	Pittinger-Phi...........46	Elliott-NY...................6	Mathewson-NY....8.42		
Ames-NY..............198	Wiltse-NY............5.48	McGinnity-NY.........46	Wiltse-NY..................3	Reulbach-Chi.......9.23		
Overall-Cin............173	Mathewson-NY....5.47	Young-Bos.............43	McGinnity-NY...........3	Phillippe-Pit..........9.45		
Ewing-Cin.............164	Overall-Cin...........4.90	Mathewson-NY......43	Mathewson-NY.........3	Wicker-Chi...........9.46		
Young-Bos.............156	Scanlan-Bro.........4.87	Overall-Cin.............42		Hillebrand-Pit.......9.49		
INNINGS PITCHED	**OPPONENTS' AVG.**	**OPPONENTS' OBP**	**EARNED RUN AVERAGE**	**ADJUSTED ERA**	**ADJUSTED STARTER RUNS**	**PITCHER WINS**
Young-Bos.........378.0	Reulbach-Chi........201	Mathewson-NY.....245	Mathewson-NY....1.28	Mathewson-NY.....229	Mathewson-NY....56.6	**Mathewson-NY..8.5**
Willis-Bos...........342.0	Mathewson-NY.....205	Reulbach-Chi........266	Reulbach-Chi.......1.42	Reulbach-Chi........209	Reulbach-Chi.......48.0	**Reulbach-Chi.....4.6**
Mathewson-NY..338.2	Wiltse-NY.............219	Brown-Chi.............271	Wicker-Chi...........2.02	Wicker-Chi............147	Ewing-Cin............26.9	**Ewing-Cin...........2.9**
Pittinger-Phi.......337.1	Lundgren-Chi........220	Phillippe-Pit...........274	Briggs-Chi...........2.14	Briggs-Chi.............139	Wicker-Chi...........22.3	**Weimer-Chi........2.5**
Fraser-Bos.........334.1	Wicker-Chi............221	Wicker-Chi............276	Brown-Chi............2.17	Brown-Chi.............137	Phillippe-Pit.........22.1	**Wiltse-NY............2.3**

Christy Blanks A's

Four-time batting champion Pete Browning died at 44 from complications of mastoiditis, a disease that plagued him throughout his career. Outfielder Jesse "The Crab" Burkett and first baseman Dirty Jack Doyle played their final major league games, bringing to an end two great careers as well as two great nicknames. More were coming.

The Mahatma entered the major leagues on June 16, as the St. Louis Browns inserted 24-year-old catcher Branch Rickey into a game. Rickey's tenure as a player was brief, but he remained a fixture in the game for sixty years. Two weeks after Rickey's debut, New York Giants outfielder Moonlight Graham played his only game; he would languish in obscurity until revived nearly eighty years later by author W.P. Kinsella.

The suddenly unstoppable Giants again blew away the league, pacing the field wire to wire and surviving their only challenge, a brief August initiative from the Pirates. The Cubs, however, won 17 of their last 20, forecasting their great 1906 performance to come.

The Giants boasted few offensive leaders, but their lineup did everything well. Using the stolen base, the base on balls, and even the home run, New York led the league in runs by more than 40. Pittsburgh finished second; Honus Wagner failed to lead the league in a major offensive category for the only time between 1900 and 1912, but he was still the league's best hitter. Christy Mathewson was its best pitcher. New York's star captured 31 victories to lead the league by a margin of eight. On the other side, Vic Willis of seventh-place Boston dropped 29, the highest total of the twentieth century.

While the AL champion Philadelphia Athletics were an excellent club, they were clearly no match for the Giants in the World Series. Philadelphia won Game 2 with a shutout, as were all five games. However, Mathewson threw three of New York's four whitewashes in one of the greatest performances in postseason history.

1905 AMERICAN LEAGUE

TEAM	W	L	T	PCT	GB	HW	HL	R	OR	PA	H	2B	3B	HR	BB	SO	HB	SH	AVG	OBP	SLG	OPS	AOPS	BR	ABR	PF	SB	CS	BSA	BSR
Phi	92	56	4	.622	—	**51**	22	**623**	488	5721	1310	**256**	51	24	376	644	34	165	**.255**	**.310**	**.338**	**648**	**109**	**65**	**54**	102	190			
Chi	92	60	6	.605	2	50	29	612	**451**	5852	1213	200	55	11	439	613	58	**241**	.237	.305	.304	609	103	3	28	96	194			
Det	79	74	1	.516	15.5	45	30	512	604	5566	1209	190	54	13	375	583	40	180	.243	.302	.311	613	99	1	-3	101	129			
Bos	78	74	1	.513	16	44	32	579	565	5711	1179	165	69	**29**	**486**	553	37	139	.234	.305	.311	616	100	13	7	101	131			
Cle	76	78	1	.494	19	41	36	564	587	5655	**1318**	211	**72**	18	286	712	55	148	**.255**	.301	.334	635	106	32	24	101	188			
NY	71	78	3	.477	21.5	40	35	586	621	5535	1228	163	61	23	360	**537**	**67**	151	.248	.307	.319	626	93	24	-35	111	**200**			
Was	64	87	3	.424	29.5	33	42	559	623	5528	1121	193	68	22	298	824	54	161	.224	.274	.302	576	92	-72	-52	96	169			
StL	54	99	3	.353	40.5	34	42	512	608	5768	1205	153	49	16	362	639	52	150	.232	.288	.289	577	93	-66	-37	95	144			
Total	617	—	—	—	—	338	268	4547	—	45336	9783	1531	479	156	2982	5105	397	1335	.241	.299	.314	613	—	—	—	—	1345	—	—	—

TEAM	CG	SHO	GR	SV	IP	H	HR	BB	SO	BR/9	ERA	AERA	OAV	OOB	PR	APR	PF	OSB	OCS	FA	E	WPB	DP	FW	PW	BW	BSW	DIF
Phi	117	**19**	37	0	1383.1	**1137**	21	409	**895**	10.5	2.19	121	.227	.294	70	68	100	144	*124*	.957	265	61	64	.3	7.5	**5.9**	—	4.3
Chi	131	16	32	0	1427.0	1163	**11**	329	613	**9.6**	**1.99**	**124**	**.226**	**.277**	**105**	**78**	93	**132**	*126*	**.967**	**218**	58	**95**	**4.1**	**8.6**	3.1	—	.2
Det	124	17	31	1	1348.0	1226	**11**	474	578	11.7	2.83	96	.246	.318	-27	-18	103	232	*142*	.957	267	**38**	80	.4	-2.0	-.3	—	4.4
Bos	124	15	30	1	1356.1	1198	33	**292**	652	10.2	2.84	95	.238	.286	-29	-20	102	135	*132*	.953	296	51	75	-1.6	-2.2	.8	—	5.1
Cle	**140**	16	15	0	1363.1	1251	23	334	555	10.9	2.85	92	.245	.299	-30	-32	99	162	*125*	.963	233	56	84	2.8	-3.5	2.6	—	-2.9
NY	88	**19**	**76**	**4**	1353.2	1235	26	396	642	11.1	2.93	100	.246	.307	-42	-2	111	142	*120*	.952	293	69	88	-1.5	-.2	-3.8	—	2.1
Was	118	12	40	1	1362.1	1250	12	385	539	11.2	2.87	92	.247	.308	-33	-36	100	168	*150*	.951	318	43	76	-3.0	-4.0	-5.7	—	1.1
StL	134	11	22	2	1384.2	1245	19	389	633	11.0	2.74	93	.243	.304	-14	-34	96	225	***157***	.955	296	61	78	-1.3	-3.7	-4.1	—	-13.4
Total	976	125	283	9	10978.2	—	—	—	—	10.8	2.65	—	.241	.299	—	—	—	—	—	.957	2186	437	640	—	—	—	—	—

BATTER-FIELDER WINS	BATTING AVERAGE	ON-BASE PERCENTAGE	SLUGGING AVERAGE	ON-BASE PLUS SLUGGING	ADJUSTED OPS	ADJUSTED BATTER RUNS
Davis-Chi 4.4	Flick-Cle .308	Hartsel-Phi .409	Flick-Cle .462	Flick-Cle .845	Flick-Cle 165	Flick-Cle 37.7
Crawford-Det 4.2	Keeler-NY .302	Flick-Cle .383	Isbell-Chi .440	Crawford-Det .786	Crawford-Det 148	Hartsel-Phi 32.7
Wallace-StL 4.2	Bay-Cle .301	Keeler-NY .357	Crawford-Det .430	Stone-StL .756	Stone-StL 147	Stone-StL 32.0
Flick-Cle 3.3	Crawford-Det .297	Crawford-Det .357	Davis-Phi .422	Davis-Phi .756	Hartsel-Phi 138	Crawford-Det 31.4
Stone-StL 2.8	Isbell-Chi .296	Selbach-Bos .355	Stone-StL .410	Hartsel-Phi .755	Davis-Phi 137	Davis-Phi 25.1

RUNS	HITS	DOUBLES	TRIPLES	HOME RUNS	TOTAL BASES	RUNS BATTED IN
Davis-Phi 93	Stone-StL 187	Davis-Phi 47	Flick-Cle 18	Davis-Phi 8	Stone-StL 259	Davis-Phi 83
Jones-Chi 91	Davis-Phi 173	Crawford-Det 38	Ferris-Bos 16	Stone-StL 7	Davis-Phi 256	L.Cross-Phi 77
Bay-Cle 90	Crawford-Det 171	Hickman-Det-Was 37	Turner-Cle 14		Crawford-Det 247	Donahue-Chi 76
Hartsel-Phi 88	Keeler-NY 169	Seybold-Phi 37	Stone-StL 13		Hickman-Det-Was 232	Crawford-Det 75
Keeler-NY 81	Bay-Cle 166		Burkett-Bos 13		Flick-Cle 231	Turner-Cle 72

BASES ON BALLS	STOLEN BASES	BASE STEALING RUNS	FIELDING RUNS-INFIELD	FIELDING RUNS-OUTFIELD	OUTFIELD ASSISTS	CATCHER CS PCT.
Hartsel-Phi 121	Hoffman-Phi 46		Cassidy-Was 34.8	McIntyre-Det 17.8	Koehler-StL 24	Criger-Bos 51.6
Jones-Chi 73	Fultz-NY 44		Tannehill-Chi 25.3	Jones-Was 13.5	Jones-Was 24	Heydon-Was 47.8
Selbach-Bos 67	Stahl-Was 41		Wallace-StL 20.7	Crawford-Det 10.0	Jones-Chi 21	
Burkett-Bos 67	Hartsel-Phi 37		Davis-Chi 16.4	Seybold-Phi 7.9		
Davis-Chi 60			Ferris-Bos 14.6	Jones-Chi 7.1		

WINS	WINNING PCT.	WINS ABOVE TEAM	GAMES STARTED	COMPLETE GAMES	FEWEST HITS/GAME	FEWEST BB/GAME
Waddell-Phi 27	Waddell-Phi .730	Tannehill-Bos 7.1	Plank-Phi 41	Plank-Phi 35	Waddell-Phi 6.33	Young-Bos .84
Plank-Phi 24	Tannehill-Bos .710	Waddell-Phi 6.4	Mullin-Det 41	Mullin-Det 35	Smith-Chi 6.63	Joss-Cle 1.45
Killian-Det 23	Coakley-Phi .692	Killian-Det 5.0	Owen-Chi 38	Howell-StL 35	Young-Bos 6.96	Owen-Chi 1.51
Altrock-Chi 23	Plank-Phi .667	Joss-Cle 4.9	Chesbro-NY 38	Killian-Det 33	Howell-StL 7.02	Bernhard-Cle 1.76
Tannehill-Bos 22	Altrock-Chi .657	Rhoads-Cle 4.1		Owen-Chi 32	White-Chi 7.05	Altrock-Chi 1.80

STRIKEOUTS	STRIKEOUTS/GAME	GAMES	SAVES	BASE RUNNERS/9	ADJUSTED RELIEF RUNS	RELIEF RANKING
Waddell-Phi 287	Waddell-Phi 7.86	Waddell-Phi 46	Buchanan-StL 2	Young-Bos 8.03		
Young-Bos 210	Young-Bos 5.89	Mullin-Det 44		Griffith-NY 8.68		
Plank-Phi 210	Bender-Phi 5.58	Patten-Was 42		Patterson-Chi 9.03		
Howell-StL 198	Howell-StL 5.52	Owen-Chi 42		Waddell-Phi 9.06		
Smith-Chi 171	Hogg-NY 5.49			Owen-Chi 9.19		

INNINGS PITCHED	OPPONENTS' AVG.	OPPONENTS' OBP	EARNED RUN AVERAGE	ADJUSTED ERA	ADJUSTED STARTER RUNS	PITCHER WINS
Mullin-Det 347.2	Waddell-Phi .200	Young-Bos .241	Waddell-Phi 1.48	Waddell-Phi 179	Waddell-Phi 40.1	**Waddell-Phi 4.5**
Plank-Phi 346.2	Smith-Chi .208	Waddell-Phi .264	White-Chi 1.76	Young-Bos 147	Young-Bos 25.4	**Howell-StL 3.6**
Owen-Chi 334.0	Young-Bos .216	Owen-Chi .267	Young-Bos 1.82	Coakley-Phi 144	White-Chi 24.0	**White-Chi 2.9**
Waddell-Phi 328.2	Howell-StL .217	White-Chi .270	Coakley-Phi 1.84	White-Chi 140	Altrock-Chi 23.9	**Altrock-Chi 2.7**
Howell-StL 323.0	White-Chi .218	Joss-Cle .274	Altrock-Chi 1.88	Chesbro-NY 133	Plank-Phi 19.6	**Young-Bos 2.7**

Goose Eggs and Tough Guys

The Boston Americans and New York Highlanders sank from contention in 1905, falling to fourth and sixth places. After an early foray by Cleveland, the race settled into a battle between Philadelphia and Chicago. While both teams were hot down the stretch, the Athletics never trailed after early August.

The White Sox, finishing just 2 games out, were the first team since 1888 to post an ERA under 2.00. Of their six pitchers, the highest ERA belonged to Ed Walsh at 2.17. The White Sox hitters, an underrated bunch, were productive, with player-manager Fielder Jones scoring 91 runs—second in the league—despite hitting only .245.

Three influential players of great skill but questionable ethics made their debuts in 1905. On August 30, a Georgia freshman named Ty Cobb saw his first major league action for the Tigers. Two others with abundant talent but character even more dubious than that of Cobb made their first appearances: slick-fielding Hal Chase took over at first for New York, while 21-year-old pitcher Eddie Cicotte was 1-1 for Detroit. These two men would help to nearly destroy baseball in the next decade.

Enjoying another spectacular season in 1905, Philadelphia's Rube Waddell won the pitching "Triple Crown"; he also allowed just 6.33 hits per game, lowest in the AL until 1968. Eddie Plank, Andy Coakley, and Chief Bender rounded out one of the top rotations in history. However, the A's attack was equally strong; Topsy Hartsel led the league in walks for the second of five times as first sacker Harry Davis provided the punch, pacing the AL in doubles, homers, RBIs, and runs. In a year where just three AL regulars hit over .300, Philadelphia—the league's best offense—scored 4.06 runs per game. However, the A's tallied just three in a five-game World Series loss to the Giants.

1904 NATIONAL LEAGUE

TEAM	W	L	T	PCT	GB	HW	HL	R	OR	PA	H	2B	3B	HR	BB	SO	HB	SH	AVG	OBP	SLG	OPS	AOPS	BR	ABR	PF	SB	CS	BSA	BSR
NY	106	47	5	.693	—	**56**	26	**744**	**474**	5829	**1347**	**202**	65	**31**	**434**	—	**79**	**166**	**.262**	**.328**	**.344**	**672**	**109**	**92**	**62**	104	**283**			
Chi	93	60	3	.608	13	49	27	597	517	5697	1294	157	62	22	298	—	48	141	.248	.295	.315	610	94	-41	-42	100	227			
Cin	88	65	4	.575	18	49	27	695	547	5814	1332	189	92	21	399	—	49	135	.255	.313	.338	651	98	42	-12	109	180			
Pit	87	66	3	.569	19	48	30	675	592	5722	1333	164	**102**	15	391	—	47	124	.258	.316	.338	654	105	46	29	103	178			
StL	75	79	1	.487	31.5	39	36	602	595	5622	1292	175	66	24	343	—	46	129	.253	.306	.327	633	106	7	36	96	199			
Bro	56	97	1	.366	50	31	44	497	614	5499	1142	159	53	15	411	—	42	129	.232	.297	.295	592	91	-56	-42	98	205			
Bos	55	98	2	.359	51	34	45	491	749	5594	1217	153	50	24	316	—	42	101	.237	.287	.300	587	90	-80	-61	96	143			
Phi	52	100	3	.342	53.5	28	43	571	784	5639	1268	170	54	23	377	—	40	119	.248	.305	.316	621	102	-10	12	96	159			
Total	623	—	—	—	—	334	278	4872	—	45416	10225	1369	544	175	2969	4277	393	1044	.249	.306	.322	628	—	—	—	—	1574	—	—	—

TEAM	CG	SHO	GR	SV	IP	H	HR	BB	SO	BR/9	ERA	AERA	OAV	OOB	PR	APR	PF	OSB	OCS	FA	E	WPB	DP	FW	PW	BW	BSW	DIF
NY	127	**21**	**29**	**15**	1396.2	1151	36	349	**707**	**9.9**	**2.17**	**125**	**.222**	**.276**	**86**	**83**	100	**134**	*167*	**.956**	294	43	**93**	**2.3**	**8.8**	**6.6**	—	11.9
Chi	139	18	17	6	1383.2	**1150**	16	402	618	10.3	2.30	115	.224	.285	65	55	97	160	*164*	.954	298	49	89	1.8	5.8	-4.4	—	13.3
Cin	142	12	15	2	1392.2	1256	**13**	343	502	10.7	2.34	**125**	.241	.295	60	82	107	192	*176*	.954	301	60	81	1.7	8.7	-1.3	—	2.4
Pit	133	15	25	1	1348.1	1273	**13**	379	455	11.4	2.89	95	.248	.306	-24	-24	100	187	*160*	.955	**291**	49	**93**	2.2	-2.5	3.1	—	7.7
StL	**146**	7	8	2	1368.0	1286	23	**319**	529	10.8	2.64	102	.239	.286	13	5	99	235	*109*	.952	307	42	83	1.1	.5	3.8	—	-7.4
Bro	135	12	20	2	1337.1	1281	27	414	453	11.8	2.70	101	.255	.319	4	4	100	193	*180*	.945	343	**41**	87	-1.4	.4	-4.4	—	-15.1
Bos	136	13	20	0	1348.1	1405	25	500	544	13.1	3.43	80	.272	.343	-105	-104	101	230	***199***	.945	353	77	91	-1.9	-11.0	-6.5	—	-2.2
Phi	131	10	25	2	1339.1	1418	22	425	469	12.9	3.39	79	.270	.332	-99	-112	98	243	*183*	.937	403	50	**93**	-5.1	-11.9	1.3	—	-8.3
Total	1089	108	159	30	10914.1	—	—	—	—	11.3	2.73	—	.249	.306	—	—	—	—	—	.950	2590	411	710	—	—	—	—	—

BATTER-FIELDER WINS	BATTING AVERAGE	ON-BASE PERCENTAGE	SLUGGING AVERAGE	ON-BASE PLUS SLUGGING	ADJUSTED OPS	ADJUSTED BATTER RUNS
Wagner-Pit......... 5.3	Wagner-Pit...........349	Wagner-Pit...........423	Wagner-Pit...........520	Wagner-Pit...........944	Wagner-Pit...........186	Wagner-Pit...........51.7
Thomas-Phi........ 4.1	Donlin-Cin-NY.......329	Thomas-Phi..........416	Grady-StL............474	Chance-Chi...........812	Chance-Chi...........150	Thomas-Phi.........32.5
Leach-Pit........... 4.0	Beckley-StL...........325	Chance-Chi...........382	Donlin-Cin-NY.......457	Seymour-Cin.........790	Beckley-StL...........147	Beckley-StL..........30.2
Chance-Chi........ 3.8	Grady-StL.............313	Huggins-Cin..........377	Seymour-Cin.........439	Beckley-StL...........778	Thomas-Phi..........141	Chance-Chi..........27.3
Dahlen-NY.......... 3.2	Seymour-Cin.........313	Beckley-StL...........375	Chance-Chi...........430	Thomas-Phi..........761	Lumley-Bro...........137	Grady-StL............25.7

RUNS	HITS	DOUBLES	TRIPLES	HOME RUNS	TOTAL BASES	RUNS BATTED IN
Browne-NY.............99	Beaumont-Pit........185	Wagner-Pit.............44	Lumley-Bro.............18	Lumley-Bro..............9	Wagner-Pit............255	Dahlen-NY..............80
Wagner-Pit.............97	Beckley-StL...........179	Mertes-NY.............28	Wagner-Pit..............14	Brain-StL.................7	Lumley-Bro...........247	Mertes-NY..............78
Beaumont-Pit..........97	Wagner-Pit............171	Delahanty-Bos........27	Tinker-Chi...............13		Seymour-Cin.........233	Lumley-Bro.............78
Huggins-Cin............96	Browne-NY...........169	Seymour-Cin..........26	Seymour-Cin............13		Beaumont-Pit........230	Wagner-Pit..............75
	Seymour-Cin.........166	Dahlen-NY..............26	Kelley-Cin...............13		Beckley-StL...........222	Corcoran-Cin..........74

BASES ON BALLS	STOLEN BASES	BASE STEALING RUNS	FIELDING RUNS-INFIELD	FIELDING RUNS-OUTFIELD	OUTFIELD ASSISTS	CATCHER CS PCT.
Thomas-Phi..........102	Wagner-Pit.............53		Leach-Pit.............35.8	Thomas-Phi.........12.9	Sebring-Pit-Cin.......27	Warner-NY...........56.3
Huggins-Cin............88	Mertes-NY..............47		Evers-Chi.............28.2	Odwell-Cin...........12.3	Lumley-Bro.............26	Schlei-Cin............48.0
Devlin-NY...............62	Dahlen-NY..............47		Dahlen-NY...........25.0	Sheckard-Bro.......10.5	Titus-Phi.................21	
Wagner-Pit.............59	McGann-NY............42		Tinker-Chi............15.6	Sebring-Pit-Cin......9.8	Thomas-Phi............21	
Ritchey-Pit..............59	Chance-Chi.............42		Farrell-StL............14.5	Titus-Phi................9.7		

WINS	WINNING PCT.	WINS ABOVE TEAM	GAMES STARTED	COMPLETE GAMES	FEWEST HITS/GAME	FEWEST BB/GAME
McGinnity-NY.........35	McGinnity-NY.......814	McGinnity-NY......10.2	Mathewson-NY.......46	Willis-Bos................39	Brown-Chi............6.57	Hahn-Cin.............1.06
Mathewson-NY.......33	Mathewson-NY.....733	Harper-Cin.............6.3	McGinnity-NY.........44	Taylor-StL...............39	Weimer-Chi...........6.71	Phillippe-Pit..........1.40
Harper-Cin..............23	Harper-Cin............719	Nichols-StL............5.2	Willis-Bos................43	McGinnity-NY.........38	McGinnity-NY......6.77	Nichols-StL...........1.42
Taylor-NY................21	Flaherty-Pit...........679	Flaherty-Pit............4.1	Jones-Bro...............41	Jones-Bro...............38	Garvin-Bro............6.99	Kellum-Cin...........1.84
Nichols-StL.............21		Mathewson-NY......4.0	Taylor-StL...............39		Taylor-NY.............7.02	McFarland-StL......1.87

STRIKEOUTS	STRIKEOUTS/GAME	GAMES	SAVES	BASE RUNNERS/9	ADJUSTED RELIEF RUNS	RELIEF RANKING
Mathewson-NY.....212	Wiltse-NY.............5.74	McGinnity-NY.........51	McGinnity-NY...........5	Brown-Chi............8.94		
Willis-Bos.............196	Mathewson-NY....5.19	Mathewson-NY.......48	Wiltse-NY.................3	McGinnity-NY......8.96		
Weimer-Chi...........177	Weimer-Chi..........5.19	Jones-Bro...............46	Briggs-Chi................3	Robitaille-Pit........9.00		
Pittinger-Bos.........146	Willis-Bos.............5.04	Willis-Bos................43	Ames-NY..................3	Hahn-Cin.............9.07		
McGinnity-NY.......144	Phillippe-Pit..........4.43	Fraser-Phi..............42		Nichols-StL..........9.17		

INNINGS PITCHED	OPPONENTS' AVG.	OPPONENTS' OBP	EARNED RUN AVERAGE	ADJUSTED ERA	ADJUSTED STARTER RUNS	PITCHER WINS
McGinnity-NY....408.0	Brown-Chi............199	Brown-Chi............253	McGinnity-NY......1.61	McGinnity-NY.......169	McGinnity-NY......50.2	**McGinnity-NY.... 5.4**
Jones-Bro..........377.0	Weimer-Chi..........204	Nichols-StL...........256	Garvin-Bro...........1.68	Garvin-Bro...........162	Hahn-Cin.............27.2	**Mathewson-NY.. 4.2**
Mathewson-NY..367.2	McGinnity-NY.......206	McGinnity-NY.......256	Brown-Chi............1.86	Brown-Chi............142	Mathewson-NY....26.9	**Hahn-Cin............ 3.2**
Taylor-StL...........352.0	Taylor-NY.............214	Hahn-Cin..............262	Weimer-Chi..........1.91	Hahn-Cin..............142	Nichols-StL..........26.8	**Weimer-Chi........ 2.8**
Willis-Bos...........350.0	Garvin-Bro...........218	Mathewson-NY.....270	Nichols-StL..........2.02	Weimer-Chi..........139	Weimer-Chi..........25.9	**Nichols-StL........ 2.8**

Take a Giant Step

National League teams were first required to play a 154-game schedule in 1904, an arrangement that lasted for 58 years through 1961 (except for wartime changes). In addition, home teams were now required to provide more than one baseball for each game, and clubs had to wear different uniforms for home and road contests. Finally, outfield fences had to be at least 235 feet from home plate, and the distance from home plate to the backstop was first regulated.

The league's fielding average reached .950, and skyrocketed in the next two years. Oddly enough, shortstop Herman Long, a great defender in the nineteenth century, hung 'em up in 1904 at age 38. The Giants, meanwhile, brought back two popular 1880s stars for limited engagements. "Orator Jim" O'Rourke, who collected 2,304 hits in his 19-year career, was 1-for-4 in one game as a catcher at age 54, while 46-year-old outfielder Dan Brouthers, a five-time batting champ, went hitless in five tries. Two star outfielders, neither of whom was born when Brouthers won his first home run title, debuted in 1904. Frank Schulte became a key component of the Cubs' success, while Philadelphia's Sherry Magee led the NL four times in RBIs.

Team runs decreased to 3.91 per game (batters clubbed more homers, but batting average fell 20 points to .249). George Browne of the Giants topped the NL with 99 runs; no league leader had fewer until 1915. The Giants won 18 straight at one point, moving into first for good in June. Skipper John McGraw had world-class pitching with Christy Mathewson, Iron Joe McGinnity, Dummy Taylor, and rookie Hooks Wiltse. Offensively, New York led in runs, hits, doubles, homers, and walks.

Nevertheless, the proud Giants refused to play a World Series. Calling the Junior Circuit "bush," McGraw and Giants owner John Brush invited a hailstorm of criticism as the Giants refused to accept the AL, and defending world champion Boston, as a peer.

1904 AMERICAN LEAGUE

TEAM	W	L	T	PCT	GB	HW	HL	R	OR	PA	H	2B	3B	HR	BB	SO	HB	SH	AVG	OBP	SLG	OPS	AOPS	BR	ABR	PF	SB	CS	BSA	BSR
Bos	95	59	3	.617	—	49	30	608	**466**	5784	1294	194	**105**	26	347	570	51	155	.247	.301	.340	641	102	41	9	106	101			
NY	92	59	4	.609	1.5	46	29	598	526	5724	**1354**	195	91	27	312	**548**	57	135	.259	**.308**	.347	655	107	69	41	105	163			
Chi	89	65	2	.578	6	**50**	27	600	482	5638	1217	193	68	14	**373**	586	41	**197**	.242	.300	.316	616	104	6	29	96	**216**			
Cle	86	65	3	.570	7.5	44	31	**647**	482	5669	1340	**225**	90	27	307	714	46	164	**.260**	**.308**	**.354**	**662**	**116**	**80**	**86**	99	178			
Phi	81	70	4	.536	12.5	47	31	557	503	5578	1266	197	77	**31**	313	605	40	137	.249	.298	.336	634	101	29	1	105	137			
StL	65	87	4	.428	29	32	43	481	604	5817	1266	153	53	10	332	609	56	138	.239	.291	.294	585	96	-53	-19	94	150			
Det	62	90	10	.408	32	34	40	505	627	5853	1231	154	69	11	344	635	34	154	.231	.282	.292	574	90	-77	-61	97	112			
Was	38	113	6	.252	55.5	23	52	437	743	5606	1170	171	57	10	283	759	**59**	115	.227	.275	.288	563	84	-95	-88	98	150			
Total	626	—	—	—	—	325	283	4433	—	45669	10138	1482	610	156	2611	5026	384	1195	.244	.295	.321	616	—	—	—	—	1207	—	—	—

TEAM	CG	SHO	GR	SV	IP	H	HR	BB	SO	BR/9	ERA	AERA	OAV	OOB	PR	APR	PF	OSB	OCS	FA	E	WPB	DP	FW	PW	BW	BSW	DIF
Bos	**148**	21	9	1	1406.0	1208	31	**233**	612	**9.4**	**2.12**	**126**	.233	**.270**	**75**	**84**	103	118	*114*	.962	242	**41**	83	1.6	**9.4**	1.0	—	6.0
NY	123	15	**33**	1	1380.2	1180	29	311	684	10.0	2.57	106	.232	.282	4	21	104	161	*125*	.958	275	58	90	-.8	2.3	4.6	—	10.4
Chi	134	**26**	22	**3**	1380.0	1161	13	303	550	9.8	2.30	107	**.229**	.279	45	24	95	**112**	*111*	**.964**	**238**	57	95	**1.7**	2.7	3.2	—	4.4
Cle	141	20	15	0	1356.2	1273	**10**	285	627	10.6	2.22	114	.249	.294	56	48	98	121	*110*	.959	255	50	86	.4	5.4	**9.6**	—	-4.9
Phi	136	**26**	20	0	1361.1	**1149**	13	366	**887**	10.4	2.35	114	.230	.291	38	48	103	141	*104*	.959	250	44	67	.8	5.4	.1	—	-.8
StL	135	13	22	1	1410.0	1335	25	333	577	11.0	2.83	88	.251	.303	-36	-58	96	164	*128*	.960	267	44	78	-.2	-6.5	-2.1	—	-2.2
Det	143	15	21	0	1430.0	1345	16	433	556	11.6	2.77	92	.250	.314	-27	-36	98	188	*135*	.959	273	58	92	.0	-4.0	-6.8	—	-3.2
Was	137	7	20	**3**	1359.2	1487	19	347	533	12.5	3.62	73	.279	.330	-155	-142	102	202	***139***	.951	314	52	**97**	-3.1	-15.9	-9.8	—	-8.6
Total	1097	143	162	9	11084.1	—	—	—	—	10.7	2.60	—	.244	.295	—	—	—	—	—	.959	2114	404	688	—	—	—	—	—

BATTER-FIELDER WINS	BATTING AVERAGE	ON-BASE PERCENTAGE	SLUGGING AVERAGE	ON-BASE PLUS SLUGGING	ADJUSTED OPS	ADJUSTED BATTER RUNS
Lajoie-Cle..........7.4	Lajoie-Cle............376	Lajoie-Cle............413	Lajoie-Cle............546	Lajoie-Cle............959	Lajoie-Cle............204	Lajoie-Cle............64.3
Flick-Cle.............4.5	Keeler-NY............343	Keeler-NY............390	Davis-Phi............490	Flick-Cle..............820	Flick-Cle..............160	Flick-Cle..............40.2
Bradley-Cle..........4.0	Davis-Phi..............309	Flick-Cle..............371	Flick-Cle..............449	Keeler-NY............799	Keeler-NY............146	Keeler-NY............28.4
Murphy-Phi.........3.7	Flick-Cle..............306	Stahl-Bos............366	Murphy-Phi..........440	Stahl-Bos............782	Stahl-Bos............139	Stahl-Bos............27.8
Davis-Chi...........3.7	Bradley-Cle..........300	Burkett-StL...........363	Hickman-Cle-Det..437	Murphy-Phi..........760	Hickman-Cle-Det..137	Burkett-StL...........25.0

RUNS	HITS	DOUBLES	TRIPLES	HOME RUNS	TOTAL BASES	RUNS BATTED IN
Dougherty-Bos-NY.....113	Lajoie-Cle............208	Lajoie-Cle............49	Stahl-Bos..............19	Davis-Phi..............10	Lajoie-Cle............302	Lajoie-Cle............102
Flick-Cle.................97	Keeler-NY............186	Collins-Bos............33	Freeman-Bos..........19	Murphy-Phi..............7	Flick-Cle..............260	Freeman-Bos..........84
Bradley-Cle..............94	Bradley-Cle..........183	Bradley-Cle............32	Cassidy-Was..........19	Freeman-Bos...........7	Bradley-Cle..........249	Bradley-Cle............83
Lajoie-Cle...............92	Dougherty-Bos-NY...181		Murphy-Phi............17		Freeman-Bos........246	Anderson-NY..........82
	Flick-Cle..............177		Flick-Cle...............17			

BASES ON BALLS	STOLEN BASES	BASE STEALING RUNS	FIELDING RUNS-INFIELD	FIELDING RUNS-OUTFIELD	OUTFIELD ASSISTS	CATCHER CS PCT.
Barrett-Det.............79	Flick-Cle.................38		Tannehill-Chi........27.3	McIntyre-Det........12.4	Barrett-Det.............29	Sullivan-Chi..........52.2
Burkett-StL.............78	Bay-Cle...................38		Davis-Chi.............18.1	Donovan-Was.........8.8	Burkett-StL.............24	Criger-Bos............50.7
Hartsel-Phi.............75	Heidrick-StL...........35		Carr-Det-Cle........15.7	Barrett-Det.............8.5	Heidrick-StL...........22	Buelow-Det-Cle...43.7
Selbach-Was-Bos...72	Davis-Chi...............32		Williams-NY..........14.5	Heidrick-StL...........6.3	Flick-Cle.................19	Kittridge-Was.......41.0
Lush-Cle.................72	Conroy-NY..............30		Murphy-Phi..........14.2	Bay-Cle...................5.9		

WINS	WINNING PCT.	WINS ABOVE TEAM	GAMES STARTED	COMPLETE GAMES	FEWEST HITS/GAME	FEWEST BB/GAME
Chesbro-NY............41	Chesbro-NY..........774	Chesbro-NY.........14.0	Chesbro-NY............51	Chesbro-NY............48	Chesbro-NY.........6.69	Young-Bos..............69
Young-Bos..............26	Tannehill-Bos........656	Plank-Phi...............4.2	Waddell-Phi............46	Mullin-Det..............42	Owen-Chi.............6.94	Tannehill-Bos........1.05
Plank-Phi................26	Smith-Chi..............640	Glade-StL..............4.1	Powell-NY..............45	Young-Bos..............40	Smith-Chi.............6.98	Patterson-Chi.......1.31
Waddell-Phi............25	Bernhard-Cle..........639	Patten-Was.............3.9	Mullin-Det..............44	Waddell-Phi............39	Gibson-Bos..........7.12	Joss-Cle...............1.40
	Dinneen-Bos..........622	Bernhard-Cle..........3.6	Plank-Phi................43	Powell-NY..............38	Waddell-Phi.........7.21	Altrock-Chi...........1.41

STRIKEOUTS	STRIKEOUTS/GAME	GAMES	SAVES	BASE RUNNERS/9	ADJUSTED RELIEF RUNS	RELIEF RANKING
Waddell-Phi..........349	Waddell-Phi.........8.20	Chesbro-NY............55	Patten-Was...............3	Young-Bos...........8.53		
Chesbro-NY..........239	Bender-Phi...........6.58	Powell-NY..............47		Chesbro-NY.........8.57		
Powell-NY............202	Moore-Cle............5.49	Waddell-Phi............46		Owen-Chi.............9.00		
Plank-Phi..............201	Plank-Phi.............5.06	Patten-Was.............45		Joss-Cle...............9.22		
Young-Bos............200	Glade-StL............4.86	Mullin-Det..............45		Dinneen-Bos........9.33		

INNINGS PITCHED	OPPONENTS' AVG.	OPPONENTS' OBP	EARNED RUN AVERAGE	ADJUSTED ERA	ADJUSTED STARTER RUNS	PITCHER WINS
Chesbro-NY.......454.2	Chesbro-NY..........208	Young-Bos............251	Joss-Cle...............1.59	Waddell-Phi..........165	Chesbro-NY.........41.2	**Chesbro-NY........6.1**
Powell-NY..........390.1	Owen-Chi..............214	Chesbro-NY..........252	Waddell-Phi.........1.62	Joss-Cle...............159	Waddell-Phi.........39.7	**Waddell-Phi........4.1**
Waddell-Phi........383.0	Smith-Chi..............215	Owen-Chi..............261	Hess-Cle..............1.67	Chesbro-NY..........149	Young-Bos...........33.4	**Young-Bos............3.8**
Mullin-Det..........382.1	Gibson-Bos...........219	Joss-Cle................266	White-Chi.............1.78	White-Chi.............138	Plank-Phi.............23.4	**Plank-Phi............3.2**
Young-Bos.........380.0	Waddell-Phi..........221	Dinneen-Bos.........268	Chesbro-NY.........1.82	Young-Bos............136	Joss-Cle..............19.9	**Owen-Chi............3.2**

Pilgrims' Progress

AL offense continued to plummet in 1904, as scoring decreased another 14 percent due to substantial drops in both homers (almost 30 percent) and steals (which fell to less than one per game for the only time until 1918). Concomitantly, strikeouts continued to increase as Rube Waddell broke his own record by fanning 349, a major league mark that would last until 1965. Another top hurler, Ed Walsh of the White Sox, debuted at 23; he would eventually win 195 games.

The "First in War, First in Peace, Last in the American League" Washington Senators moved into a new stadium. However, there was nothing to celebrate about the move, as the club's .252 winning percentage was the majors' worst until 1916. The Tigers played 162 games, 10 of them ties; outfielder Jimmy Barrett took part in *all* of them, setting a games-played record that stood until 1961 (when the AL expanded and increased the schedule from 154 to 162 games).

The young but successful American League posted another huge attendance increase. Chicago, New York, and Boston—the league's three top performers—enjoyed large crowds as the new league's first real pennant race set the sporting world abuzz.

Jack Chesbro won 41 games, the most by anyone who played after the nineteenth century, but "Happy Jack" would be remembered more for a wild pitch that cost his team, the New York Highlanders, the pennant. New York and Boston, clinging together at the top of the standings for the final two months, met for a season-ending series at New York. With the Pilgrims up by 1½ and just two games remaining, Chesbro's ninth-inning wild pitch allowed the winning run—and resulted in a title—for Boston. Unfortunately, the obstinate New York Giants, perhaps afraid of losing, refused to agree to play in a World Series. This would be the only season without postseason baseball until 1994.

1903 NATIONAL LEAGUE

TEAM	W	L	T	PCT	GB	HW	HL	R	OR	PA	H	2B	3B	HR	BB	SO	HB	SH	AVG	OBP	SLG	OPS	AOPS	BR	ABR	PF	SB	CS	BSA	BSR
Pit	91	49	1	.650	—	**46**	24	**793**	613	5511	**1429**	208	**110**	**34**	364	—	50	109	.286	.341	**.393**	734	**113**	87	**64**	103	172			
NY	84	55	3	.604	6.5	41	27	729	**567**	5397	1290	181	49	20	379	—	**92**	**185**	.272	.338	.344	682	97	11	-13	104	264			
Chi	82	56	1	.594	8	45	28	695	599	5323	1300	191	62	9	422	—	50	118	.275	.340	.347	687	105	21	39	97	259			
Cin	74	65	2	.532	16.5	41	35	765	656	5379	1399	**228**	92	28	403	—	30	89	**.288**	.346	.390	**736**	104	**97**	20	111	151			
Bro	70	66	3	.515	19	40	33	667	682	5233	1201	177	56	15	**522**	—	53	124	.265	**.348**	.339	687	105	31	52	97	**273**			
Bos	58	80	2	.420	32	31	35	578	699	5240	1145	176	47	25	398	—	59	101	.245	.312	.318	630	90	-82	-58	96	159			
Phi	49	86	4	.363	39.5	25	33	617	738	5313	1283	186	62	12	338	—	39	155	.268	.322	.341	663	98	-34	-12	97	120			
StL	43	94	2	.314	46.5	22	45	505	795	5096	1176	138	65	8	277	—	34	96	.251	.297	.313	610	83	-130	-113	97	171			
Total	560	—	—	—	—	291	260	5349	—	42492	10223	1485	543	151	3103	3767	407	977	.269	.331	.349	679	—	—	—	—	1569	—	—	—

TEAM	CG	SHO	GR	SV	IP	H	HR	BB	SO	BR/9	ERA	AERA	OAV	OOB	PR	APR	PF	OSB	OCS	FA	E	WPB	DP	FW	PW	BW	BSW	DIF
Pit	117	**16**	26	5	1251.1	1215	**9**	384	454	11.8	2.91	111	.255	.316	48	44	99	**151**	*143*	**.951**	295	54	100	1.6	4.2	**6.1**	—	9.0
NY	115	8	**29**	**8**	1262.2	1257	20	371	**628**	11.9	2.95	113	.258	.316	43	54	102	163	*155*	**.951**	287	47	87	**2.3**	5.2	-1.2	—	8.3
Chi	117	6	24	6	1240.1	**1182**	14	**354**	451	**11.4**	**2.77**	113	**.250**	**.307**	**67**	48	96	161	*156*	.942	338	**32**	78	-1.6	4.6	3.7	—	6.3
Cin	**126**	11	16	1	1230.0	1277	14	378	480	12.6	3.07	**116**	.268	.331	26	**60**	109	166	*150*	.946	312	55	84	.4	**5.8**	1.9	—	-3.6
Bro	118	11	23	4	1221.1	1276	18	377	438	12.7	3.44	92	.275	.339	-25	-39	98	270	*154*	**.951**	**284**	46	98	2.0	-3.7	5.0	—	-1.3
Bos	125	8	15	1	1228.2	1310	30	460	516	13.4	3.34	96	.278	.348	-11	-21	98	206	***184***	.939	361	71	89	-3.0	-2.0	-5.6	—	-.4
Phi	**126**	5	13	3	1212.1	1347	21	425	381	13.6	3.96	82	.285	.352	-95	-97	100	235	*169*	.947	300	58	76	1.0	-9.3	-1.2	—	-9.0
StL	111	4	**29**	2	1212.1	1353	25	430	419	13.6	3.67	89	.284	.350	-55	-56	100	217	*178*	.940	354	51	**111**	-2.7	-5.4	-10.8	—	-6.6
Total	955	69	175	30	9859.0	—	—	—	—	12.6	3.26	—	.269	.331	—	—	—	—	—	.946	2531	414	723	—	—	—	—	—

BATTER-FIELDER WINS	BATTING AVERAGE	ON-BASE PERCENTAGE	SLUGGING AVERAGE	ON-BASE PLUS SLUGGING	ADJUSTED OPS	ADJUSTED BATTER RUNS
Sheckard-Bro 5.8	Wagner-Pit .355	Thomas-Phi .453	Clarke-Pit .532	Clarke-Pit .946	Clarke-Pit 164	Sheckard-Bro 44.6
Wagner-Pit 5.6	Clarke-Pit .351	Bresnahan-NY .443	Wagner-Pit .518	Donlin-Cin .936	Bresnahan-NY 161	Wagner-Pit 38.8
Thomas-Phi 3.9	Donlin-Cin .351	Chance-Chi .439	Donlin-Cin .516	Bresnahan-NY .936	Sheckard-Bro 160	Chance-Chi 37.9
Tenney-Bos 3.2	Bresnahan-NY .350	Sheckard-Bro .423	Bresnahan-NY .493	Wagner-Pit .931	Wagner-Pit 160	Bresnahan-NY 35.9
Chance-Chi 3.1	Seymour-Cin .342	Donlin-Cin .420	Steinfeldt-Cin .481	Sheckard-Bro .899	Chance-Chi 155	Thomas-Phi 35.2

RUNS	HITS	DOUBLES	TRIPLES	HOME RUNS	TOTAL BASES	RUNS BATTED IN
Beaumont-Pit 137	Beaumont-Pit 209	Steinfeldt-Cin 32	Wagner-Pit 19	Sheckard-Bro 9	Beaumont-Pit 272	Mertes-NY 104
Donlin-Cin 110	Seymour-Cin 191	Mertes-NY 32	Donlin-Cin 18		Seymour-Cin 267	Wagner-Pit 101
Browne-NY 105	Browne-NY 185	Clarke-Pit 32	Leach-Pit 17		Wagner-Pit 265	Doyle-Bro 91
Slagle-Chi 104	Wagner-Pit 182				Donlin-Cin 256	Leach-Pit 87
Strang-Bro 101	Donlin-Cin 174				Sheckard-Bro 245	Steinfeldt-Cin 83

BASES ON BALLS	STOLEN BASES	BASE STEALING RUNS	FIELDING RUNS-INFIELD	FIELDING RUNS-OUTFIELD	OUTFIELD ASSISTS	CATCHER CS PCT.
Thomas-Phi 107	Sheckard-Bro 67		Farrell-StL 21.1	Sheckard-Bro 25.2	Sheckard-Bro 36	Warner-NY 51.4
Dahlen-Bro 82	Chance-Chi 67		Dahlen-Bro 19.3	Thomas-Phi 12.0	Mertes-NY 24	Kling-Chi 50.3
Slagle-Chi 81	Wagner-Pit 46		Wagner-Pit 17.9	Mertes-NY 8.7	Keister-Phi 22	J.O'Neill-StL 46.2
Chance-Chi 78	Strang-Bro 46		Ritchey-Pit 16.5	Sebring-Pit 4.9	Stanley-Bos 21	
	Mertes-NY 45		Gremminger-Bos 16.3	Keister-Phi 4.8	Sebring-Pit 20	

WINS	WINNING PCT.	WINS ABOVE TEAM	GAMES STARTED	COMPLETE GAMES	FEWEST HITS/GAME	FEWEST BB/GAME
McGinnity-NY 31	Leever-Pit .781	Leever-Pit 7.0	McGinnity-NY 48	McGinnity-NY 44	Weimer-Chi 7.69	Phillippe-Pit .90
Mathewson-NY 30	Phillippe-Pit .735	Mathewson-NY 6.6	Mathewson-NY 42	Mathewson-NY 37	Mathewson-NY 7.89	Hahn-Cin 1.43
Phillippe-Pit 25	Weimer-Chi .714	Hahn-Cin 5.1	Pittinger-Bos 39	Pittinger-Bos 35	Taylor-Chi 7.98	Taylor-Chi 1.64
Leever-Pit 25	Mathewson-NY .698	Schmidt-Bro 5.1	Schmidt-Bro 36	Hahn-Cin 34	Leever-Pit 8.07	McFarland-StL 1.89
	Wicker-StL-Chi .690	Phillippe-Pit 5.1	Jones-Bro 36	Taylor-Chi 33	McGinnity-NY 8.11	Leever-Pit 1.90

STRIKEOUTS	STRIKEOUTS/GAME	GAMES	SAVES	BASE RUNNERS/9	ADJUSTED RELIEF RUNS	RELIEF RANKING
Mathewson-NY 267	Mathewson-NY 6.56	McGinnity-NY 55	Miller-NY 3	Phillippe-Pit 9.39		
McGinnity-NY 171	Piatt-Bos 4.97	Mathewson-NY 45	Lundgren-Chi 3	Taylor-Chi 9.77		
Garvin-Bro 154	Garvin-Bro 4.65	Pittinger-Bos 44		Leever-Pit 10.13		
Pittinger-Bos 140	Weimer-Chi 4.09	Schmidt-Bro 40		Mathewson-NY 10.59		
Weimer-Chi 128	Willis-Bos 4.05			Hahn-Cin 10.70		

INNINGS PITCHED	OPPONENTS' AVG.	OPPONENTS' OBP	EARNED RUN AVERAGE	ADJUSTED ERA	ADJUSTED STARTER RUNS	PITCHER WINS
McGinnity-NY 434.0	Weimer-Chi .225	Phillippe-Pit .263	Leever-Pit 2.06	Leever-Pit 157	McGinnity-NY 42.2	**Mathewson-NY 4.6**
Mathewson-NY 366.1	Mathewson-NY .231	Taylor-Chi .273	Mathewson-NY 2.26	Mathewson-NY 148	Mathewson-NY 39.2	**McGinnity-NY 4.0**
Pittinger-Bos 351.2	Taylor-Chi .235	Leever-Pit .282	Weimer-Chi 2.30	Hahn-Cin 141	Leever-Pit 37.5	**Leever-Pit 3.4**
Jones-Bro 324.1	McGinnity-NY .236	Mathewson-NY .287	Phillippe-Pit 2.43	McGinnity-NY 137	Hahn-Cin 32.4	**Hahn-Cin 3.1**
Taylor-Chi 312.1	Leever-Pit .238	McGinnity-NY .291	McGinnity-NY 2.43	Weimer-Chi 136	Weimer-Chi 27.7	**Phillippe-Pit 2.9**

The Makings of a Struggle

Largely on the strength of Honus Wagner, who captured the first of his eight batting titles, the Pirates were the class of the Senior Circuit for the third straight year. The Bucs, whose pitching staff had nearly twice as many shutouts as home runs allowed, emerged from a tangle with the Cubs and Giants in June. Despite playing just 104 games, Pittsburgh player-manager Fred Clarke paced the league in doubles.

The Giants finished 47 games closer to first place than in 1902, edging out the much-improved Cubs for second place. New York's metamorphosis led to a 91 percent rise in crowds at the Polo Grounds in 1903 as league attendance jumped 42 percent.

Mordecai "Three-Finger Brown," a 27-year-old rookie righty with two fingers missing from his pitching hand, entered the league with St. Louis. The Cubs would acquire him over the winter, fortifying an already excellent pitching staff and setting up one of the great pitching rivalries: "Three Fingers" against "The Big Six," New York's Christy Mathewson. Matty, still just 23, struck out 267 batters, 96 more than his nearest rival.

One of the least remembered nineteenth-century stars, outfielder Jimmy Ryan, retired with 2,513 hits under his belt, most of them collected with Chicago. Another little-recalled veteran outfielder, George Van Haltren, called it quits at age 37 with 2,544 hits.

Following the two-year slump in offense, NL hitters got well and team runs boomed to 4.78 per contest. Homers were way up, and stolen bases rose to 1.40 per game, the highest in NL history. Also at a peak was the interest level in a postseason AL-NL series, as the AL and NL champions agreed to a best-of-nine competition. Before it started, the Pirates lost 16-game winner Ed Doheny to a mental breakdown. His loss, and an injury to Sam Leever, stretched the Bucs' pitching staff to its breaking point as Boston won the first modern World Series in eight games.

1903 AMERICAN LEAGUE

TEAM	W	L	T	PCT	GB	HW	HL	R	OR	PA	H	2B	3B	HR	BB	SO	HB	SH	AVG	OBP	SLG	OPS	AOPS	BR	ABR	PF	SB	CS	BSA	BSR
Bos	91	47	3	.659	—	**49**	20	**708**	**504**	5365	**1336**	222	**113**	**48**	262	561	36	148	**.272**	.313	**.392**	**705**	111	**89**	55	105	141			
Phi	75	60	2	.556	14.5	44	21	597	519	5074	1236	227	68	32	268	513	32	101	.264	.309	.363	672	102	39	13	105	157			
Cle	77	63	0	.550	15	**49**	25	639	579	5225	1265	**231**	95	31	259	595	40	153	.265	.308	.373	681	**112**	51	**63**	98	175			
NY	72	62	2	.537	17	41	26	579	573	5091	1136	193	62	18	**332**	465	**65**	129	.249	.309	.330	639	92	-3	-36	106	160			
Det	65	71	1	.478	25	37	28	567	539	5090	1229	162	91	12	292	526	46	**170**	.268	**.318**	.351	669	110	37	55	97	128			
StL	65	74	0	.468	26.5	38	32	500	525	5047	1133	166	68	12	271	539	26	111	.244	.290	.317	607	90	-68	-54	97	101			
Chi	60	77	1	.438	30.5	41	28	516	613	5175	1152	176	49	14	325	537	38	142	.247	.301	.314	615	94	-45	-21	96	**180**			
Was	43	94	3	.314	47.5	29	40	437	691	4990	1066	172	72	17	257	**463**	39	81	.231	.277	.311	588	80	-100	-109	102	131			
Total	554	—	—	—	—	328	220	4543	—	41057	9553	1549	618	184	2266	4199	322	1035	.255	.303	.344	648	—	—	—	—	1173	—	—	—

TEAM	CG	SHO	GR	SV	IP	H	HR	BB	SO	BR/9	ERA	AERA	OAV	OOB	PR	APR	PF	OSB	OCS	FA	E	WPB	DP	FW	PW	BW	BSW	DIF
Bos	123	**20**	18	**4**	1255.0	1142	23	269	579	**10.4**	**2.57**	**118**	**.242**	**.288**	**55**	**63**	102	**123**	***130***	.959	239	44	86	2.3	**6.5**	5.7	—	7.5
Phi	112	10	**28**	1	1207.0	**1124**	20	315	**728**	11.3	2.98	103	.246	.305	-2	10	103	140	*122*	**.960**	**217**	58	66	**3.2**	1.0	1.3	—	1.9
Cle	**125**	**20**	15	0	1243.2	1161	**16**	271	521	10.6	2.73	105	.247	.293	32	18	96	135	*120*	.946	322	51	**99**	-3.2	1.9	**6.5**	—	1.8
NY	111	7	26	2	1201.1	1171	19	245	463	10.9	3.08	101	.255	.299	-16	5	105	133	*89*	.953	264	43	87	.0	.5	-3.7	—	8.2
Det	123	15	15	2	1196.0	1169	19	336	554	11.5	2.75	106	.256	.310	28	21	98	185	*126*	.950	281	40	82	-.9	2.2	5.7	—	-10.0
StL	124	12	16	3	1222.1	1220	26	**237**	511	11.0	2.77	105	.260	.300	26	19	98	127	*108*	.953	268	**34**	94	.2	2.0	-5.6	—	-1.0
Chi	114	9	26	**4**	1235.0	1233	23	287	391	11.5	3.02	93	.260	.309	-8	-30	95	131	*107*	.949	297	52	85	-1.8	-3.1	-2.2	—	-1.4
Was	122	6	18	3	1223.2	1333	38	306	452	12.4	3.82	82	.277	.325	-116	-89	106	199	*127*	.954	260	37	86	.8	-9.2	-11.3	—	-5.7
Total	954	99	162	19	9784.0	—	—	—	—	11.2	2.96	—	.255	.303	—	—	—	—	—	.953	2148	359	685	—	—	—	—	—

BATTER-FIELDER WINS	BATTING AVERAGE	ON-BASE PERCENTAGE	SLUGGING AVERAGE	ON-BASE PLUS SLUGGING	ADJUSTED OPS	ADJUSTED BATTER RUNS
Lajoie-Cle....8.1	Lajoie-Cle....344	Barrett-Det....407	Lajoie-Cle....518	Lajoie-Cle....896	Lajoie-Cle....170	Lajoie-Cle....40.6
Bradley-Cle....4.8	Crawford-Det....335	Hartsel-Phi....391	Bradley-Cle....496	Hartsel-Phi....868	Crawford-Det....159	Crawford-Det....36.3
Crawford-Det....3.6	Dougherty-Bos....331	Lajoie-Cle....379	Freeman-Bos....496	Crawford-Det....855	Bradley-Cle....154	Barrett-Det....32.8
Barrett-Det....3.4	Barrett-Det....315	Lush-Det....379	Crawford-Det....489	Bradley-Cle....844	Hartsel-Phi....152	Bradley-Cle....32.5
Collins-Bos....2.9	Bradley-Cle....313	Green-Chi....375	Hartsel-Phi....477	Freeman-Bos....823	Green-Chi....146	Green-Chi....30.0

RUNS	HITS	DOUBLES	TRIPLES	HOME RUNS	TOTAL BASES	RUNS BATTED IN
Dougherty-Bos....107	Dougherty-Bos....195	Seybold-Phi....45	Crawford-Det....25	Freeman-Bos....13	Freeman-Bos....281	Freeman-Bos....104
Bradley-Cle....101	Crawford-Det....184	Lajoie-Cle....41	Bradley-Cle....22	Hickman-Cle....12	Crawford-Det....269	Hickman-Cle....97
Keeler-NY....95	Parent-Bos....170	Freeman-Bos....39	Freeman-Bos....20	Ferris-Bos....9	Bradley-Cle....266	Lajoie-Cle....93
Barrett-Det....95	Bay-Cle....169	Bradley-Cle....36	Parent-Bos....17	Seybold-Phi....8	Lajoie-Cle....251	L.Cross-Phi....90
Bay-Cle....94	Bradley-Cle....168	Anderson-StL....34	Collins-Bos....17		Dougherty-Bos....250	Crawford-Det....89

BASES ON BALLS	STOLEN BASES	BASE STEALING RUNS	FIELDING RUNS-INFIELD	FIELDING RUNS-OUTFIELD	OUTFIELD ASSISTS	CATCHER CS PCT.
Barrett-Det....74	Bay-Cle....45		Lajoie-Cle....39.1	Lush-Det....12.8	Holmes-Was-Chi....19	Criger-Bos....53.1
Lush-Det....70	Pickering-Phi....40		Wallace-StL....18.4	Barrett-Det....6.7	Barrett-Det....19	
Pickering-Phi....53	Holmes-Was-Chi....35		Williams-NY....15.5	Holmes-Was-Chi....6.4		
Burkett-StL....52	Dougherty-Bos....35		Ferris-Bos....14.3	Crawford-Det....5.2		
Flick-Cle....51	Conroy-NY....33		Carr-Det....12.7	Robinson-Was....4.3		

WINS	WINNING PCT.	WINS ABOVE TEAM	GAMES STARTED	COMPLETE GAMES	FEWEST HITS/GAME	FEWEST BB/GAME
Young-Bos....28	Young-Bos....757	Young-Bos....6.5	Plank-Phi....40	Young-Bos....34	Moore-Cle....7.12	Young-Bos....97
Plank-Phi....23	Hughes-Bos....741	Moore-Cle....5.9	Waddell-Phi....38	Waddell-Phi....34	Donovan-Det....7.24	Bernhard-Cle....1.14
	Moore-Cle....714	Sudhoff-StL....4.9	White-Chi....36	Donovan-Det....34	Joss-Cle....7.36	Donahue-StL-Cle.1.14
	Dinneen-Bos....618	Bernhard-Cle....4.3	Mullin-Det....36		Waddell-Phi....7.61	Joss-Cle....1.17
	Plank-Phi....590	Hughes-Bos....3.8	Chesbro-NY....36		Dinneen-Bos....7.68	Tannehill-NY....1.28

STRIKEOUTS	STRIKEOUTS/GAME	GAMES	SAVES	BASE RUNNERS/9	ADJUSTED RELIEF RUNS	RELIEF RANKING
Waddell-Phi....302	Waddell-Phi....8.39	Plank-Phi....43	Young-Bos....2	Joss-Cle....8.82		
Donovan-Det....187	Donovan-Det....5.48	Mullin-Det....41	Powell-StL....2	Young-Bos....8.96		
Young-Bos....176	Moore-Cle....5.38	Young-Bos....40	Orth-Was....2	Bernhard-Cle....9.34		
Plank-Phi....176	Powell-StL....4.97	Flaherty-Chi....40	Mullin-Det....2	Moore-Cle....9.56		
Mullin-Det....170	Mullin-Det....4.77	Chesbro-NY....40	Dinneen-Bos....2	Dinneen-Bos....9.78		

INNINGS PITCHED	OPPONENTS' AVG.	OPPONENTS' OBP	EARNED RUN AVERAGE	ADJUSTED ERA	ADJUSTED STARTER RUNS	PITCHER WINS
Young-Bos....341.2	Moore-Cle....217	Joss-Cle....256	Moore-Cle....1.74	Moore-Cle....164	Young-Bos....34.0	**Young-Bos....4.8**
Plank-Phi....336.0	Donovan-Det....220	Young-Bos....259	Young-Bos....2.08	Young-Bos....146	Dinneen-Bos....27.8	**Mullin-Det....3.5**
Chesbro-NY....324.2	Joss-Cle....223	Bernhard-Cle....267	Bernhard-Cle....2.12	Bernhard-Cle....135	Moore-Cle....26.8	**Donovan-Det....3.0**
Waddell-Phi....324.0	Waddell-Phi....229	Moore-Cle....271	White-Chi....2.13	Dinneen-Bos....134	Donovan-Det....25.4	**Dinneen-Bos....2.9**
Mullin-Det....320.2	Dinneen-Bos....230	Dinneen-Bos....276	Joss-Cle....2.19	White-Chi....132	Waddell-Phi....23.2	**White-Chi....2.8**

UPSTART CHAMPIONS

Prior to the season, the NL weighed its options. After first proposing a merger with the AL, the Senior Circuit settled for a truce, and the two leagues agreed to respect each other's player contracts and to end their war. With the sale of the rubble of the Baltimore franchise to New York investors, the AL was now set with eight signature clubs, which remained in the same cities until 1953.

Two noteworthy players died. Tigers pitcher Win Mercer, apparently despondent at gambling losses, turned on the gas in a hotel room on January 13 and died at 28. He had recently been named Detroit's manager. In the year's oddest tragedy, slugging outfielder Ed Delahanty of Washington fell into the Niagara River on July 2 and was apparently swept over Niagara Falls to his death after being ejected from a train due to drunkenness. He was just 34.

On the field, the biggest story was the strikeout and the resulting huge 16 percent drop in scoring. The league's adoption of the foul-strike rule led, predictably, to K's rising by a whopping 58 percent. Rube Waddell of the Athletics shattered the big-league strikeout record by 63.

By the end of July, the AL race was essentially over. Boston, the league leader in runs and ERA, emerged from the pack and cruised to the pennant. Philadelphia's already good pitching was bolstered by rookie Chief Bender, but Boston had the league's best mound staff (ed by Cy Young) plus two first-rate hitters in Buck Freeman and Patsy Dougherty.

The first interleague championship since 1890 and the first modern World Series pitted the Boston Americans against NL champion Pittsburgh Pirates, with the newly "recognized" Junior Circuit winning the best-of-nine series, five games to three, after losing three of the first four games. Americans starter Bill Dinneen won thrice as Young took two more, besting the efforts of Pirates ace Deacon Phillippe, who pitched five complete games.

1902 NATIONAL LEAGUE

TEAM	W	L	T	PCT	GB	HW	HL	R	OR	PA	H	2B	3B	HR	BB	SO	HB	SH	AVG	OBP	SLG	OPS	AOPS	BR	ABR	PF	SB	CS	BSA	BSR
Pit	103	36	3	.741	—	**56**	15	**775**	**440**	5480	**1410**	**189**	**95**	18	372	446	**64**	118	**.286**	**.344**	**.374**	**718**	**124**	**154**	**129**	104	222			
Bro	75	63	3	.543	27.5	45	23	564	519	5344	1242	147	49	**19**	319	489	62	118	.256	.311	.319	630	99	-4	-8	101	145			
Bos	73	64	5	.533	29	42	27	572	516	5298	1178	142	39	14	**398**	481	43	131	.249	.313	.305	618	95	-13	-18	101	189			
Cin	70	70	1	.500	33.5	35	35	633	566	5342	1383	188	77	18	297	465	39	98	.282	.328	.362	690	109	96	38	110	131			
Chi	68	69	6	.496	34	31	38	544	505	5428	1224	133	40	6	358	572	44	**156**	.251	.308	.299	607	95	-37	-21	97	**229**			
StL	56	78	6	.418	44.5	28	38	517	695	5183	1226	116	37	10	273	**438**	52	107	.258	.306	.304	610	97	-39	-18	96	158			
Phi	56	81	1	.409	46	29	39	484	649	5125	1139	110	43	5	356	481	32	122	.247	.305	.293	598	90	-51	-51	100	108			
NY	48	88	5	.353	53.5	24	44	405	604	5034	1097	147	34	6	254	540	40	108	.237	.282	.287	569	81	-105	-101	99	187			
Total	564	—	—	—	—	290	259	4494	—	42234	9899	1172	414	96	2627	3912	376	958	.259	.313	.318	631	—	—	—	—	1369	—	—	—

TEAM	CG	SHO	GR	SV	IP	H	HR	BB	SO	BR/9	ERA	AERA	OAV	OOB	PR	APR	PF	OSB	OCS	FA	E	WPB	DP	FW	PW	BW	BSW	DIF
Pit	131	**21**	10	3	1264.2	1142	**4**	**250**	**564**	**10.3**	2.30	119	.241	**.288**	68	62	98	**117**	*116*	.958	247	39	87	3.4	6.5	**13.6**	—	10.0
Bro	131	14	10	3	1256.0	**1113**	10	363	536	10.8	2.69	103	**.238**	.298	12	9	99	217	*142*	.952	275	47	79	1.5	.9	-.8	—	4.4
Bos	124	14	18	**4**	1259.2	1233	16	372	523	11.8	2.61	108	.257	.316	24	29	102	156	*134*	**.959**	**240**	42	90	**3.8**	3.1	-1.9	—	-.5
Cin	130	9	13	1	1239.0	1228	15	352	430	11.9	2.67	112	.259	.318	15	41	108	143	*141*	.945	322	50	**118**	-1.4	4.3	4.0	—	-6.9
Chi	**134**	17	9	2	1293.1	1244	7	281	447	10.9	**2.19**	**123**	.253	.300	**85**	**75**	97	158	*138*	.946	331	48	113	-1.7	**7.9**	-2.2	—	-4.5
StL	112	7	**29**	**4**	1227.2	1399	16	338	400	13.0	3.47	79	.287	.338	-95	-103	99	188	*141*	.944	336	**35**	107	-2.4	-10.9	-1.9	—	4.2
Phi	118	8	21	3	1211.0	1323	12	334	504	12.7	3.50	80	.278	.333	-97	-92	101	217	*143*	.946	305	47	81	-.8	-9.7	-5.4	—	3.3
NY	120	11	21	1	1242.1	1217	16	337	508	11.6	2.86	98	.257	.313	-11	-9	101	173	***144***	.943	337	60	107	-2.3	-.9	-10.7	—	-6.1
Total	1000	101	131	21	9993.2	—	—	—	—	11.6	2.78	—	.259	.313	—	—	—	—	—	.949	2393	368	782	—	—	—	—	—

BATTER-FIELDER WINS	BATTING AVERAGE	ON-BASE PERCENTAGE	SLUGGING AVERAGE	ON-BASE PLUS SLUGGING	ADJUSTED OPS	ADJUSTED BATTER RUNS
Tenney-Bos 4.0	Beaumont-Pit .357	R.Thomas-Phi .414	Wagner-Pit .463	Wagner-Pit .857	Wagner-Pit 159	Wagner-Pit 37.1
Wagner-Pit 3.9	Crawford-Cin .333	Tenney-Bos .409	Crawford-Cin .461	Clarke-Pit .850	Clarke-Pit 157	Clarke-Pit 32.7
Leach-Pit 3.4	Keeler-Bro .333	Beaumont-Pit .404	Clarke-Pit .449	Crawford-Cin .848	Beaumont-Pit 148	Beaumont-Pit 31.3
Kling-Chi 2.7	Wagner-Pit .330	Clarke-Pit .401	Beckley-Cin .427	Beaumont-Pit .822	Crawford-Cin 147	Tenney-Bos 29.0
Farrell-StL 2.7	Beckley-Cin .330	Wagner-Pit .394	Leach-Pit .426	Beckley-Cin .804	Tenney-Bos 141	Crawford-Cin 28.9
RUNS	**HITS**	**DOUBLES**	**TRIPLES**	**HOME RUNS**	**TOTAL BASES**	**RUNS BATTED IN**
Wagner-Pit 105	Beaumont-Pit 193	Wagner-Pit 30	Leach-Pit 22	Leach-Pit 6	Crawford-Cin 256	Wagner-Pit 91
Clarke-Pit 103	Keeler-Bro 186	Clarke-Pit 27	Crawford-Cin 22	Beckley-Cin 5	Wagner-Pit 247	Leach-Pit 85
Beaumont-Pit 100	Crawford-Cin 185	Cooley-Bos 26	Wagner-Pit 16	Sheckard-Bro 4	Beckley-Cin 227	Crawford-Cin 78
Leach-Pit 97	Wagner-Pit 176	Dahlen-Bro 25	Clarke-Pit 14	McCreery-Bro 4	Beaumont-Pit 226	Dahlen-Bro 74
Crawford-Cin 92	Beckley-Cin 175	Beckley-Cin 23	Gremminger-Bos 12		Leach-Pit 219	
BASES ON BALLS	**STOLEN BASES**	**BASE STEALING RUNS**	**FIELDING RUNS-INFIELD**	**FIELDING RUNS-OUTFIELD**	**OUTFIELD ASSISTS**	**CATCHER CS PCT.**
R.Thomas-Phi 107	Wagner-Pit 42		Farrell-StL 31.8	Donovan-StL 8.9	Donovan-StL 30	Bergen-Cin 50.6
Lush-Bos 76	Slagle-Chi 41		Steinfeldt-Cin 21.9	Lush-Bos 8.6	Lush-Bos 24	Kittridge-Bos 46.3
Tenney-Bos 73	Donovan-StL 34		H.Long-Bos 19.8	Sheckard-Bro 8.5	Crawford-Cin 24	
Sheckard-Bro 57	Beaumont-Pit 33		Lowe-Chi 17.6	Dobbs-Cin-Chi 7.8	R.Thomas-Phi 23	
	Smith-NY 32		Leach-Pit 12.4	Brodie-NY 7.3	Brodie-NY 23	
WINS	**WINNING PCT.**	**WINS ABOVE TEAM**	**GAMES STARTED**	**COMPLETE GAMES**	**FEWEST HITS/GAME**	**FEWEST BB/GAME**
Chesbro-Pit 28	Chesbro-Pit .824	Taylor-Chi 7.2	Willis-Bos 46	Willis-Bos 45	Newton-Bro 7.08	Phillippe-Pit .86
Willis-Bos 27	Doheny-Pit .800	Hahn-Cin 6.6	Pittinger-Bos 40	Pittinger-Bos 36	McGinnity-NY 7.18	Tannehill-Pit .97
Pittinger-Bos 27	Tannehill-Pit .769	Chesbro-Pit 6.5	Yerkes-StL 37	Hahn-Cin 35	Taylor-Chi 7.36	Menefee-Chi 1.19
Taylor-Chi 23	Phillippe-Pit .690	Pittinger-Bos 5.8	Hahn-Cin 36	White-Phi 34	Donovan-Bro 7.56	Taylor-Chi 1.21
Hahn-Cin 23	Leever-Pit .682	Poole-Pit-Cin 4.2	White-Phi 35	Taylor-Chi 34	Chesbro-Pit 7.61	Leever-Pit 1.26
STRIKEOUTS	**STRIKEOUTS/GAME**	**GAMES**	**SAVES**	**BASE RUNNERS/9**	**ADJUSTED RELIEF RUNS**	**RELIEF RANKING**
Willis-Bos 225	White-Phi 5.44	Willis-Bos 51	Willis-Bos 3	Taylor-Chi 8.90		
White-Phi 185	Mathewson-NY 5.19	Pittinger-Bos 46	M.O'Neill-StL 2	Tannehill-Pit 9.27		
Pittinger-Bos 174	Donovan-Bro 5.14	Yerkes-StL 39	Newton-Bro 2	McGinnity-NY 9.59		
Donovan-Bro 170	Willis-Bos 4.94	Taylor-Chi 37	Leever-Pit 2	Hahn-Cin 9.70		
Mathewson-NY 164	Wicker-StL 4.61			Cronin-NY 9.71		
INNINGS PITCHED	**OPPONENTS' AVG.**	**OPPONENTS' OBP**	**EARNED RUN AVERAGE**	**ADJUSTED ERA**	**ADJUSTED STARTER RUNS**	**PITCHER WINS**
Willis-Bos 410.0	Newton-Bro .217	Taylor-Chi .258	Taylor-Chi 1.29	Taylor-Chi 209	Taylor-Chi 50.8	**Taylor-Chi 6.1**
Pittinger-Bos 389.1	McGinnity-NY .219	Tannehill-Pit .266	Hahn-Cin 1.77	Hahn-Cin 170	Hahn-Cin 40.6	**Hahn-Cin 4.4**
Taylor-Chi 333.2	Taylor-Chi .224	McGinnity-NY .273	Tannehill-Pit 1.95	Poole-Pit-Cin 142	Willis-Bos 27.9	**Willis-Bos 2.8**
Hahn-Cin 321.0	Donovan-Bro .228	Hahn-Cin .275	Lundgren-Chi 1.97	Tannehill-Pit 140	Chesbro-Pit 23.2	**Tannehill-Pit 2.7**
White-Phi 306.0	Chesbro-Pit .229	Phillippe-Pit .276	Phillippe-Pit 2.05	Lundgren-Chi 137	Phillippe-Pit 18.9	**Phillips-Cin 2.6**

Change is Gonna Come

By 1902 the old days were clearly gone. Jim "Pud" Galvin, a great nineteenth century hurler who once threw 72 complete games in a season, died at 46. Boston's Vic Willis topped the NL with 45 complete games as old-timers bemoaned pitchers' lack of stamina. Forty-year-old center fielder Dummy Hoy, who lived nearly sixty more years, played his final game.

The Reds opened The Palace of the Fans, which sported a 450-foot right-field line. Scoring decreased another 14 percent as foul bunts were also now counted as strikes. Homers dropped 58 percent as NL ERA dipped 51 points.

The already great Pirates further improved, taking the pennant by an amazing 27½ games. Leading from start to finish, Pittsburgh was 10 games up in mid-May. One of the dominant clubs of all time, the '02 Bucs led the league in runs by 142 and in runs allowed by 65. Competition would soon come from Chicago and New York as two pieces of a growing Cubs powerhouse, infielders Joe Tinker and Johnny Evers, debuted in 1902. In New York, young right-hander Christy Mathewson had his second spectacular season for a terrible team, going 14-17 with 8 shutouts for the Giants.

The most significant news occurred with the AL's Baltimore Orioles. As a result of a complicated conspiracy that included John McGraw, Reds owner John Brush, and Giants owner Andrew Freedman, the Orioles were stripped of their best players by nefarious means. Several Orioles—John McGraw, Roger Bresnahan, and pitcher Joe McGinnity among them—ended up in New York. Others wound up in Cincinnati. Brush purchased the Giants after the season, reaping the benefits as the moribund franchise was transformed overnight into a contender. The story did not end perfectly for masterminds Brush and McGraw, though. Infuriated, AL President Ban Johnson engineered the sale of what was left of the Orioles to New York investors the following year, bringing major league competition into the NL's biggest market.

1902 AMERICAN LEAGUE

TEAM	W	L	T	PCT	GB	HW	HL	R	OR	PA	H	2B	3B	HR	BB	SO	HB	SH	AVG	OBP	SLG	OPS	AOPS	BR	ABR	PF	SB	CS	BSA	BSR
Phi	83	53	1	.610	—	**56**	17	**775**	636	5261	1369	235	67	38	343	293	38	118	.287	.340	.389	729	104	**52**	23	104	201			
StL	78	58	4	.574	5	49	21	619	607	5251	1254	208	61	29	373	327	38	104	.265	.323	.353	676	94	-37	-28	99	137			
Bos	77	60	1	.562	6.5	43	27	664	**600**	5292	1356	195	95	42	275	375	42	100	.278	.322	.383	705	98	-4	-22	103	132			
Chi	74	60	4	.552	8	48	19	675	602	5255	1248	170	50	14	411	381	36	**154**	.268	.332	.335	667	95	-43	-14	96	**265**			
Cle	69	67	1	.507	14	40	25	686	667	5303	**1401**	248	68	33	308	356	35	120	**.289**	.336	.389	725	**111**	43	**73**	96	140			
Was	61	75	2	.449	22	40	28	707	790	5188	1338	**261**	66	**47**	329	296	44	81	.283	.335	**.395**	**730**	107	**52**	46	101	121			
Det	52	83	2	.385	30.5	35	33	566	657	5139	1167	141	55	22	359	**287**	53	83	.251	.312	.320	632	79	-112	-122	102	130			
Bal	50	88	3	.362	34	32	31	715	848	5348	1318	202	**107**	33	**417**	429	**54**	117	.277	**.342**	.385	727	103	50	19	104	189			
Total	553	—	—	—	—	343	201	5407	—	42037	10451	1660	569	258	2815	2744	340	877	.275	.331	.369	700	—	—	—	—	1315	—	—	—

TEAM	CG	SHO	GR	SV	IP	H	HR	BB	SO	BR/9	ERA	AERA	OAV	OOB	PR	APR	PF	OSB	OCS	FA	E	WPB	DP	FW	PW	BW	BSW	DIF
Phi	114	5	**25**	2	1216.1	1292	33	368	**455**	12.7	3.29	111	.273	.334	39	49	103	157	***147***	.953	270	41	75	1.4	4.6	2.2	—	6.8
StL	120	7	22	2	1244.0	1273	36	343	348	12.0	3.34	106	.266	.321	32	26	99	154	*124*	.953	274	45	122	1.5	2.5	-2.7	—	8.6
Bos	123	6	16	1	1238.0	1217	27	326	431	**11.5**	**3.02**	**118**	**.258**	**.311**	**75**	**75**	100	132	*135*	**.955**	263	**40**	101	2.0	**7.1**	-2.1	—	1.5
Chi	116	11	22	0	1221.2	1269	30	331	346	12.1	3.41	99	.269	.323	22	-5	95	**121**	*118*	**.955**	**257**	54	**125**	**2.3**	-.5	-1.3	—	6.5
Cle	116	**16**	23	**3**	1204.1	**1199**	26	411	361	12.4	3.28	105	.260	.327	39	21	96	183	*136*	.950	287	66	96	.3	2.0	**6.9**	—	-8.3
Was	**130**	2	8	0	1207.2	1403	56	**312**	300	13.2	4.36	85	.291	.341	-106	-85	104	173	*128*	.945	316	42	70	-1.3	-8.1	4.4	—	-2.0
Det	116	9	22	**3**	1190.2	1267	**20**	370	245	12.7	3.56	102	.274	.333	1	10	102	198	*136*	.943	332	44	111	-2.5	.9	-11.6	—	-2.4
Bal	119	3	22	1	1210.1	1531	30	354	258	14.3	4.33	87	.309	.360	-102	-73	106	197	*119*	.938	357	52	109	-3.5	-6.9	1.8	—	-10.4
Total	954	59	160	12	9733.0	—	—	—	—	12.6	3.57	—	.275	.331	—	—	—	—	—	.949	2356	384	809	—	—	—	—	—

BATTER-FIELDER WINS	BATTING AVERAGE	ON-BASE PERCENTAGE	SLUGGING AVERAGE	ON-BASE PLUS SLUGGING	ADJUSTED OPS	ADJUSTED BATTER RUNS
Lajoie-Phi-Cle....5.6	Delahanty-Was.....376	Delahanty-Was.....453	Delahanty-Was.....590	Delahanty-Was...1043	Delahanty-Was.....186	Delahanty-Was....57.7
Delahanty-Was..5.0	Lajoie-Phi-Cle.......378	Dougherty-Bos.....407	Lajoie-Phi-Cle.......565	Hickman-Bos-Cle..926	Hickman-Bos-Cle..159	Hickman-Bos-Cle.39.4
Bradley-Cle........4.8	Hickman-Bos-Cle..361	Barrett-Det...........397	Hickman-Bos-Cle..539	Bradley-Cle..........890	Bradley-Cle...........151	Lajoie-Phi-Cle......37.3
Hickman-Bos-Cle...2.6	Dougherty-Bos.....342	Selbach-Bal..........393	Bradley-Cle...........515	Seybold-Phi..........881	Seybold-Phi..........137	Bradley-Cle..........35.8
L.Cross-Phi.........2.3	L.Cross-Phi..........342	Jones-Chi.............390	Seybold-Phi..........506	Williams-Bal..........861	Freeman-Bos........131	Seybold-Phi.........24.5
RUNS	**HITS**	**DOUBLES**	**TRIPLES**	**HOME RUNS**	**TOTAL BASES**	**RUNS BATTED IN**
Hartsel-Phi............109	Hickman-Bos-Cle..193	Delahanty-Was.......43	Williams-Bal...........21	Seybold-Phi............16	Hickman-Bos-Cle..288	Freeman-Bos........121
Fultz-Phi..............109	L.Cross-Phi...........191	Davis-Phi...............43	Freeman-Bos..........19	Hickman-Bos-Cle....11	Freeman-Bos........283	Hickman-Bos-Cle..110
Strang-Chi............108	Bradley-Cle...........187	L.Cross-Phi............39	Ferris-Bos...............14	Freeman-Bos..........11	Bradley-Cle...........283	L.Cross-Phi..........108
Bradley-Cle...........104	Delahanty-Was.....178	Bradley-Cle............39	Delahanty-Was.......14	Bradley-Cle............11	Delahanty-Was.....279	Seybold-Phi............97
Delahanty-Was.....103	Freeman-Bos........174	Freeman-Bos..........38	Hickman-Bos-Cle....13	Delahanty-Was.......10	Seybold-Phi..........264	
BASES ON BALLS	**STOLEN BASES**	**BASE STEALING RUNS**	**FIELDING RUNS-INFIELD**	**FIELDING RUNS-OUTFIELD**	**OUTFIELD ASSISTS**	**CATCHER CS PCT.**
Hartsel-Phi.............87	Hartsel-Phi.............47		Ferris-Bos...........23.8	Selbach-Bal.........10.4	Mertes-Chi..............26	Clarke-Was..........44.3
Strang-Chi..............76	Mertes-Chi.............46		Padden-StL..........12.3	Jones-Chi.............9.8	Jones-Chi..............25	McGuire-Det........36.4
Barrett-Det.............74	Fultz-Phi................44		Bradley-Cle..........12.0	Barrett-Det............5.7	Barrett-Det............22	Robinson-Bal.......35.2
Burkett-StL.............71			Elberfeld-Det........11.6	Mertes-Chi............5.4	Stahl-Bos...............19	
Davis-Chi...............65			M.Cross-Phi...........9.3	Burkett-StL............5.2		
WINS	**WINNING PCT.**	**WINS ABOVE TEAM**	**GAMES STARTED**	**COMPLETE GAMES**	**FEWEST HITS/GAME**	**FEWEST BB/GAME**
Young-Bos.............32	Bernhard-Phi-Cle..783	Young-Bos...........10.9	Young-Bos.............43	Young-Bos.............41	Bernhard-Phi-Cle.7.01	Orth-Was............1.11
Waddell-Phi...........24	Waddell-Phi..........774	Waddell-Phi...........7.5	Dinneen-Bos..........42	Dinneen-Bos..........39	Waddell-Phi.........7.30	Young-Bos...........1.24
Powell-StL..............22	Young-Bos...........744	Bernhard-Phi-Cle...6.9	Powell-StL..............39	Powell-StL..............36	Joss-Cle..............7.52	Bernhard-Phi-Cle.1.47
R.Donahue-StL.......22	R.Donahue-StL.....667	R.Donahue-StL......4.4	Orth-Was...............37	Orth-Was...............36	Siever-Det...........7.93	Siever-Det...........1.53
Dinneen-Bos..........21	Griffith-Chi...........625	McGinnity-Bal........4.1	Wiltse-Phi-Bal.........35		Winter-Bos...........7.97	Plank-Phi............1.83
STRIKEOUTS	**STRIKEOUTS/GAME**	**GAMES**	**SAVES**	**BASE RUNNERS/9**	**ADJUSTED RELIEF RUNS**	**RELIEF RANKING**
Waddell-Phi..........210	Waddell-Phi.........6.84	Young-Bos.............45	Powell-StL.................2	Bernhard-Phi-Cle.8.68		
Young-Bos............160	Powell-StL...........3.76	Powell-StL..............42		Siever-Det...........9.56		
Powell-StL.............137	Young-Bos...........3.74	Dinneen-Bos..........42		Waddell-Phi.........9.71		
Dinneen-Bos.........136	Joss-Cle..............3.54	Wiltse-Phi-Bal.........38		Young-Bos...........9.73		
Plank-Phi..............107	Piatt-Chi..............3.51	Orth-Was...............38		Joss-Cle............10.46		
INNINGS PITCHED	**OPPONENTS' AVG.**	**OPPONENTS' OBP**	**EARNED RUN AVERAGE**	**ADJUSTED ERA**	**ADJUSTED STARTER RUNS**	**PITCHER WINS**
Young-Bos.........384.2	Bernhard-Phi-Cle..216	Bernhard-Phi-Cle..254	Siever-Det............1.91	Siever-Det............191	Young-Bos...........59.4	**Young-Bos..........6.0**
Dinneen-Bos......371.1	Waddell-Phi..........223	Siever-Det............273	Waddell-Phi.........2.05	Waddell-Phi..........179	Waddell-Phi.........48.3	**Waddell-Phi........5.8**
Powell-StL..........328.1	Joss-Cle...............228	Waddell-Phi..........276	Bernhard-Phi-Cle.2.15	Young-Bos...........166	Bernhard-Phi-Cle.33.3	**Bernhard-Phi-Cle...3.0**
Orth-Was...........324.0	Siever-Det............237	Young-Bos...........276	Young-Bos...........2.15	Bernhard-Phi-Cle..160	Dinneen-Bos........33.1	**Dinneen-Bos......2.3**
R.Donahue-StL..316.1	Winter-Bos...........238	Joss-Cle...............291	Garvin-Chi...........2.21	Garvin-Chi...........153	Siever-Det...........29.4	**Plank-Phi...........2.3**

Growing Pains

Prior to 1902 the poorly attended and unsuccessful Milwaukee franchise shifted to St. Louis to become the Browns. The fledgling AL's other sticky spot was Baltimore, a franchise that was ultimately ripped apart by its manager, John McGraw, as part of his blood feud with AL President Ban Johnson. The Orioles finished last, despite topping the loop in on-base percentage and triples, losing their best players—as well as McGraw—to the NL. Orioles catcher Wilbert Robinson retired, later to manage in Brooklyn for 18 years.

Boston outfielder Patsy Dougherty hit .342 in his first season, and Cleveland hurler Addie Joss was equally impressive (17-13 with a league-best 5 shutouts) as a rookie. Joss, just 22, was an exception to the rule—few regulars or starting pitchers of the time were younger than 25.

The defending champion White Sox led in July by as much as 5½ games but fell apart in August as a four-team scramble developed. Out of the chaos came the Philadelphia Athletics, who pulled away from St. Louis and Boston in September. The Browns' surprising second-place finish was the only time the franchise ended above fourth place until 1921.

Philadelphia's league-best offense was powered by slugger Socks Seybold, on-base threat Topsy Hartsel, and third baseman Lave Cross, who batted in 108 runs without a single homer. Pitcher Rube Waddell, a man-child who wore out welcomes with the Pirates and the Cubs, found a home under Connie Mack's wing. He went 24-7, leading the AL in strikeouts.

Although runs fell by 8 percent, home runs skyrocketed to 258, the AL's highest total until 1920. Seybold's 16 taters were two more than hit by the entire White Sox team, and his total stood as the league record until Babe Ruth broke it in 1919. Cleveland and Philadelphia saw their attendance rise more than 100 percent as, overall, the league saw a healthy sales increase of 31 percent in its second campaign.

1901 NATIONAL LEAGUE

TEAM	W	L	T	PCT	GB	HW	HL	R	OR	PA	H	2B	3B	HR	BB	SO	HB	SH	AVG	OBP	SLG	OPS	AOPS	BR	ABR	PF	SB	CS	BSA	BSR
Pit	90	49	1	.647	—	45	24	776	**534**	5468	1407	182	92	29	386	493	52	117	.286	**.345**	.379	**724**	113	**99**	77	103	203			
Phi	83	57	0	.593	7.5	**46**	23	668	543	5411	1275	194	58	24	**430**	549	62	126	.266	.334	.346	680	101	33	20	102	199			
Bro	79	57	1	.581	9.5	43	25	744	600	5312	1399	**206**	93	32	312	**449**	41	80	**.287**	.335	**.387**	722	112	86	67	103	178			
StL	76	64	2	.543	14.5	40	31	**792**	689	5565	**1430**	187	**94**	**39**	314	540	**90**	122	.284	.337	.381	718	**120**	86	**126**	95	190			
Bos	69	69	2	.500	20.5	41	29	531	556	5218	1180	135	36	28	303	519	34	**135**	.249	.298	.310	608	75	-105	-149	109	158			
Chi	53	86	1	.381	37	30	39	578	699	5277	1250	153	61	18	314	532	52	67	.258	.310	.326	636	93	-58	-36	96	**204**			
NY	52	85	4	.380	37	30	38	544	755	5260	1225	167	46	19	303	575	45	73	.253	.303	.318	621	90	-83	-60	96	133			
Cin	52	87	3	.374	38	27	43	561	818	5392	1232	173	70	38	323	584	42	113	.251	.303	.338	641	97	-57	-15	93	137			
Total	561	—	—	—	—	302	252	5194	—	42903	10398	1397	550	227	2685	4241	418	833	.267	.321	.348	669	—	—	—	—	1402	—	—	—

TEAM	CG	SHO	GR	SV	IP	H	HR	BB	SO	BR/9	ERA	AERA	OAV	OOB	PR	APR	PF	OSB	OCS	FA	E	WPB	DP	FW	PW	BW	BSW	DIF
Pit	119	**15**	21	4	1244.2	1198	20	**244**	505	**10.9**	**2.58**	**126**	.252	**.297**	**102**	**95**	98	**133**	*124*	.950	287	**44**	97	1.2	**9.3**	7.5	—	2.4
Phi	125	**15**	16	2	1246.2	1221	19	259	480	11.0	2.87	119	.255	.300	63	71	102	171	*135*	**.954**	**262**	61	65	**2.7**	7.0	2.0	—	1.4
Bro	111	7	26	**5**	1213.2	1244	**18**	435	583	12.8	3.14	107	.264	.333	24	27	101	213	*151*	.950	281	59	99	1.2	2.6	6.6	—	.6
StL	118	5	**29**	**5**	1269.2	1333	39	332	445	12.2	3.68	86	.268	.321	-51	-74	96	186	*146*	.949	305	63	**108**	.4	-7.3	**12.3**	—	.5
Bos	128	11	13	0	1263.0	**1196**	29	349	558	11.3	2.90	125	**.249**	.305	59	91	109	139	*128*	.952	282	45	89	1.5	8.9	-14.6	—	4.2
Chi	**131**	2	9	0	1241.2	1348	27	324	**586**	12.5	3.33	97	.275	.327	-2	-14	98	189	*143*	.943	336	61	87	-1.8	-1.4	-3.5	—	-9.8
NY	118	11	24	1	1232.0	1389	24	377	542	13.4	3.87	85	.283	.342	-75	-79	99	205	***154***	.941	348	97	81	-2.3	-7.7	-5.9	—	-.5
Cin	126	4	18	0	1265.2	1469	51	365	542	13.5	4.17	77	.289	.345	-120	-143	96	166	*143*	.940	355	**44**	102	-2.6	-14.0	-1.5	—	.6
Total	976	70	156	17	9977.0	—	—	—	—	12.2	3.32	—	.267	.321	—	—	—	—	—	.947	2456	474	728	—	—	—	—	—

BATTER-FIELDER WINS	BATTING AVERAGE	ON-BASE PERCENTAGE	SLUGGING AVERAGE	ON-BASE PLUS SLUGGING	ADJUSTED OPS	ADJUSTED BATTER RUNS
Burkett-StL.........5.5	Burkett-StL............376	Burkett-StL............440	Sheckard-Bro........534	Delahanty-Phi.......955	Burkett-StL............184	Burkett-StL...........66.1
Wallace-StL.........5.4	Delahanty-Phi.......354	Thomas-Phi..........437	Delahanty-Phi.......528	Burkett-StL............949	Delahanty-Phi.......173	Delahanty-Phi......52.1
Davis-NY.............4.6	Sheckard-Bro........354	Delahanty-Phi.......427	Crawford-Cin.........524	Sheckard-Bro........944	Crawford-Cin.........172	Hartsel-Chi..........47.7
Flick-Phi.............4.5	Wagner-Pit............353	Wagner-Pit............417	Burkett-StL............509	Wagner-Pit............911	Sheckard-Bro........168	Sheckard-Bro.......46.7
Wagner-Pit..........4.4	Keeler-Bro.............339	Hartsel-Chi...........414	Flick-Phi................500	Crawford-Cin.........903	Hartsel-Chi...........163	Crawford-Cin........44.0

RUNS	HITS	DOUBLES	TRIPLES	HOME RUNS	TOTAL BASES	RUNS BATTED IN
Burkett-StL............142	Burkett-StL............226	Delahanty-Phi.........38	Sheckard-Bro..........19	Crawford-Cin...........16	Burkett-StL............306	Wagner-Pit............126
Keeler-Bro.............123	Keeler-Bro.............202	Daly-Bro..................38	Flick-Phi..................17	Sheckard-Bro..........11	Sheckard-Bro........296	Delahanty-Phi.......108
Beaumont-Pit........120	Sheckard-Bro........196	Wagner-Pit.............37		Burkett-StL.............10	Delahanty-Phi.......286	Sheckard-Bro........104
Clarke-Pit..............118	Wagner-Pit............194	Beckley-Cin............36			Wagner-Pit............271	Crawford-Cin.........104
Sheckard-Bro........116	Delahanty-Phi.......192	Wallace-StL............34				

BASES ON BALLS	STOLEN BASES	BASE STEALING RUNS	FIELDING RUNS-INFIELD	FIELDING RUNS-OUTFIELD	OUTFIELD ASSISTS	CATCHER CS PCT.
Thomas-Phi..........100	Wagner-Pit.............49		Wallace-StL.........27.2	Flick-Phi..............13.9	Slagle-Phi-Bos........23	Kittridge-Bos........50.2
Hartsel-Chi.............74	Hartsel-Chi............41		Davis-NY............24.3	Sheckard-Bro.........9.2	VanHaltren-NY........23	Bergen-Cin..........47.9
Davis-Bro-Pit..........66	Strang-NY..............40		Dahlen-Bro..........13.6	Green-Chi..............6.6	Flick-Phi..................23	McFarland-Phi.....47.4
Delahanty-Phi.........65	Harley-Cin...............37		Daly-Bro...............10.3	VanHaltren-NY.......4.1	Harley-Cin...............20	Warner-NY...........42.9
Hamilton-Bos..........64	Beaumont-Pit..........36		Leach-Pit.............10.1	Nichols-StL............4.0	Crawford-Cin...........20	

WINS	WINNING PCT.	WINS ABOVE TEAM	GAMES STARTED	COMPLETE GAMES	FEWEST HITS/GAME	FEWEST BB/GAME
Donovan-Bro...........25	Chesbro-Pit...........677	Hahn-Cin................6.8	Taylor-NY................43	Hahn-Cin................41	Townsend-Phi......7.39	Orth-Phi...............1.02
Harper-StL..............23	Phillippe-Pit...........647	Mathewson-NY......6.0	Hahn-Cin................42	Taylor-NY................37	Mathewson-NY....7.71	Phillippe-Pit.........1.16
Phillippe-Pit............22	Tannehill-Pit..........643	Harper-StL.............4.7	Mathewson-NY.......38	Mathewson-NY.......36	Willis-Bos.............7.72	Tannehill-Pit.........1.28
Hahn-Cin.................22	Harper-StL............639	Donovan-Bro..........2.9	Donovan-Bro..........38	Donovan-Bro..........36	Orth-Phi...............7.99	Duggleby-Phi.......1.30
Chesbro-Pit.............21	Kitson-Bro.............633	Leever-Pit..............2.7			Chesbro-Pit..........8.17	Powell-StL............1.33

STRIKEOUTS	STRIKEOUTS/GAME	GAMES	SAVES	BASE RUNNERS/9	ADJUSTED RELIEF RUNS	RELIEF RANKING
Hahn-Cin.............239	Hughes-Chi..........6.57	Taylor-NY................45	Powell-StL.................3	Orth-Phi..............9.27		
Donovan-Bro.........226	Waddell-Pit-Chi....6.16	Powell-StL...............45	Donovan-Bro.............3	Phillippe-Pit.........9.79		
Hughes-Chi...........225	Mathewson-NY....5.92	Donovan-Bro...........45	Sudhoff-StL...............2	Tannehill-Pit.......10.20		
Mathewson-NY.....221	Donovan-Bro........5.79	Hahn-Cin.................42	Phillippe-Pit..............2	Chesbro-Pit........10.23		
Waddell-Pit-Chi.....172	Hahn-Cin.............5.73	Mathewson-NY.......40	Kitson-Bro.................2	Willis-Bos...........10.35		

INNINGS PITCHED	OPPONENTS' AVG.	OPPONENTS' OBP	EARNED RUN AVERAGE	ADJUSTED ERA	ADJUSTED STARTER RUNS	PITCHER WINS
Hahn-Cin...........375.1	Townsend-Phi.......223	Orth-Phi................264	Tannehill-Pit.........2.18	Willis-Bos.............153	Willis-Bos............38.5	**Orth-Phi.............4.4**
Taylor-NY...........353.1	Mathewson-NY.....230	Phillippe-Pit...........275	Phillippe-Pit.........2.22	Tannehill-Pit.........150	Orth-Phi...............33.1	**Willis-Bos...........4.2**
Donovan-Bro......351.0	Willis-Bos.............231	Tannehill-Pit.........284	Orth-Phi...............2.27	Orth-Phi................150	Phillippe-Pit..........33.0	**Phillippe-Pit.......4.1**
Powell-StL..........338.1	Orth-Phi................237	Chesbro-Pit...........284	Willis-Bos.............2.36	Phillippe-Pit..........147	Mathewson-NY....32.4	**Mathewson-NY..3.6**
Mathewson-NY..336.0	Chesbro-Pit...........241	Willis-Bos.............286	Chesbro-Pit..........2.38	Chesbro-Pit...........137	Chesbro-Pit..........32.1	**Tannehill-Pit.......3.3**

Contraction Leads to Competition as Scoring Drops

While the upstart AL's player raids damaged the Senior Circuit, the eight NL franchises were stable and remained in place until 1953. Their ballparks were not so durable. In-season fires damaged Cincinnati's League Park and St. Louis' Robison Field. Robison was repaired, but the Reds built a new ballpark—The Palace of the Fans—in the same location for 1902.

Contenders Brooklyn and Philadelphia were severely affected by the raiding: the Phillies lost Nap Lajoie, while Brooklyn did without Joe McGinnity and Lave Cross. Pittsburgh, though, came out relatively unscathed and passed New York in mid-June, cruising to the league crown. The Bucs had excellent pitching and a multidimensional offense. Future superstar Honus Wagner spent the year as a utility player yet still led the league in RBIs. In 1902, he'd take over fulltime at shortstop.

Two active players died in 1901. Tom O'Brien, Pittsburgh's first baseman in 1900, died February 4 from intestinal problems first suffered on a baseball trip to Cuba. Brooklyn pitcher Doc McJames, who lost the 1900 season to malaria, was 5-6 in 1901. Sent to South Carolina for rest, he fell from a moving carriage and died.

Two nineteenth century immortals ended their careers. "Sliding" Billy Hamilton, the previous century's top leadoff hitter, paced the NL four times in runs. Amos Rusie, a five-time strikeout champ who won 246 games from 1889–98, was traded at the end of 1900 to Cincinnati for young Christy Mathewson. Rusie's wing, however, was gone. During the season, two outstanding defensive catchers debuted. Pat Moran would later win a World Series as a manager, while Bill Bergen hit just .170 in his 947 big-league games.

NL teams scored only 4.63 runs per game, down more than 12 percent due to adoption of a rule counting foul balls as strikes. The league hit its most homers until 1911, with Sam Crawford's 16 the highest individual total for more than a decade.

1901 AMERICAN LEAGUE

TEAM	W	L	T	PCT	GB	HW	HL	R	OR	PA	H	2B	3B	HR	BB	SO	HB	SH	AVG	OBP	SLG	OPS	AOPS	BR	ABR	PF	SB	CS	BSA	BSR
Chi	83	53	1	.610	—	**49**	21	**819**	631	5397	1303	173	89	32	**475**	337	**62**	**135**	.276	.350	.370	720	**108**	42	**64**	97	**280**			
Bos	79	57	2	.581	4	**49**	20	759	**608**	5349	1353	183	104	**37**	331	**282**	47	105	.278	.330	.381	711	104	6	20	98	157			
Det	74	61	1	.548	8.5	42	27	741	694	5245	1303	180	80	29	380	346	54	**135**	.279	.340	.370	710	98	16	-16	105	204			
Phi	74	62	1	.544	9	42	24	805	760	5320	**1409**	**239**	87	35	301	344	52	85	.289	.337	.395	732	103	45	12	104	173			
Bal	68	65	2	.511	13.5	40	25	760	750	5111	1348	179	**111**	24	369	377	52	101	**.294**	**.353**	**.397**	**750**	**108**	**79**	46	104	207			
Was	61	72	5	.459	20.5	31	35	682	771	5259	1282	191	83	33	356	340	51	80	.269	.326	.364	690	97	-24	-13	99	127			
Cle	54	82	2	.397	29	28	39	666	831	5200	1311	197	68	12	243	326	48	76	.271	.313	.348	661	92	-83	-56	96	125			
Mil	48	89	2	.350	35.5	32	37	641	828	5288	1250	192	66	26	325	384	46	122	.261	.314	.345	659	91	-81	-47	95	176			
Total	549	—	—	—	—	313	228	5873	—	42169	10559	1534	688	228	2780	2736	412	839	.277	.333	.371	704	—	—	—	—	1449	—	—	—

TEAM	CG	SHO	GR	SV	IP	H	HR	BB	SO	BR/9	ERA	AERA	OAV	OOB	PR	APR	PF	OSB	OCS	FA	E	WPB	DP	FW	PW	BW	BSW	DIF
Chi	110	**11**	28	2	1218.1	1250	27	312	394	11.9	**2.98**	**117**	.263	.315	**93**	**71**	95	**153**	*135*	.941	345	55	100	.9	**6.4**	**5.8**	—	1.9
Bos	123	7	15	1	1217.0	**1178**	33	294	**396**	**11.2**	3.04	116	**.251**	**.301**	84	68	96	173	*157*	**.943**	337	35	104	1.6	6.1	1.8	—	1.5
Det	118	8	20	2	1188.2	1328	22	313	307	12.8	3.30	116	.280	.330	48	68	105	**153**	*141*	.930	410	38	**127**	-3.3	6.1	-1.4	—	5.1
Phi	**124**	6	14	1	1200.2	1346	**20**	374	350	13.3	4.00	94	.280	.339	-45	-31	103	187	*148*	.942	337	63	93	1.4	-2.8	1.1	—	6.3
Bal	115	4	21	3	1158.0	1313	21	344	271	13.3	3.73	104	.282	.338	-9	16	106	167	*112*	.926	401	49	76	-2.9	1.4	4.2	—	-1.2
Was	118	8	20	2	1183.0	1396	51	**284**	308	13.3	4.09	89	.291	.339	-57	-58	100	170	*134*	**.943**	**323**	**28**	97	**2.4**	-5.2	-1.2	—	-1.5
Cle	122	7	19	**4**	1182.1	1365	22	464	334	14.5	4.12	86	.286	.358	-60	-78	97	199	*152*	.942	329	77	99	2.1	-7.0	-5.1	—	-4.0
Mil	107	3	**34**	3	1218.0	1383	32	395	376	13.6	4.06	89	.283	.344	-53	-65	98	247	***171***	.934	393	64	106	-1.8	-5.9	-4.2	—	-8.6
Total	937	54	171	18	9566.0	—	—	—	—	13.0	3.66	—	.277	.333	—	—	—	—	—	.938	2875	409	802	—	—	—	—	—

BATTER-FIELDER WINS	BATTING AVERAGE	ON-BASE PERCENTAGE	SLUGGING AVERAGE	ON-BASE PLUS SLUGGING	ADJUSTED OPS	ADJUSTED BATTER RUNS
Lajoie-Phi 8.1	Lajoie-Phi.............426	Lajoie-Phi.............463	Lajoie-Phi.............643	Lajoie-Phi...........1106	Lajoie-Phi.............196	Lajoie-Phi............69.2
Collins-Bos.........4.2	Donlin-Bal............340	Jones-Chi 412	Freeman-Bos........520	Freeman-Bos........920	Freeman-Bos........157	Freeman-Bos.......37.0
Elberfeld-Det......3.5	Freeman-Bos........339	Donlin-Bal............409	Seybold-Phi..........503	Seybold-Phi..........901	Seybold-Phi..........142	Collins-Bos..........31.2
Freeman-Bos 2.7	Seybold-Phi..........334	Hoy-Chi................407	Williams-Bal.........495	Donlin-Bal............883	Collins-Bos...........142	McGraw-Bal.........29.1
Anderson-Mil 2.5	Collins-Bos...........332	Freeman-Bos........400	Collins-Bos...........495	Williams-Bal.........883	Donlin-Bal............138	Anderson-Mil 28.0
RUNS	**HITS**	**DOUBLES**	**TRIPLES**	**HOME RUNS**	**TOTAL BASES**	**RUNS BATTED IN**
Lajoie-Phi.............145	Lajoie-Phi.............232	Lajoie-Phi...............48	Williams-Bal...........21	Lajoie-Phi...............14	Lajoie-Phi.............350	Lajoie-Phi.............125
Jones-Chi 120	Anderson-Mil 190	Anderson-Mil 46	Keister-Bal 21	Freeman-Bos..........12	Collins-Bos...........279	Freeman-Bos.......114
Williams-Bal..........113	Collins-Bos 187	Collins-Bos 42	Mertes-Chi..............17	Grady-Was................9	Anderson-Mil 274	Anderson-Mil 99
Hoy-Chi.................112	Waldron-Mil-Was ..186	Farrell-Was 32	Stahl-Bos................16		Freeman-Bos........255	Mertes-Chi..............98
Barrett-Det............110	Dungan-Was..........179		Collins-Bos 16		Williams-Bal.........248	Williams-Bal............96
BASES ON BALLS	**STOLEN BASES**	**BASE STEALING RUNS**	**FIELDING RUNS-INFIELD**	**FIELDING RUNS-OUTFIELD**	**OUTFIELD ASSISTS**	**CATCHER CS PCT.**
Hoy-Chi...................86	Isbell-Chi................52		Clingman-Was 22.1	Seymour-Bal........13.9	Barrett-Det.............31	Buelow-Det..........50.4
Jones-Chi 84	Mertes-Chi..............46		Lajoie-Phi............22.0	Pickering-Cle 12.5	Seymour-Bal...........23	
Barrett-Det..............76	Seymour-Bal...........38		Elberfeld-Det........19.4	Barrett-Det...........11.4	Pickering-Cle 22	
McFarland-Chi 75	Jones-Chi 38		Conroy-Mil 16.9	Donlin-Bal..............6.9	Hemphill-Bos 22	
McGraw-Bal...........61			Collins-Bos 12.8	Farrell-Was 5.6	Hallman-Mil............21	
WINS	**WINNING PCT.**	**WINS ABOVE TEAM**	**GAMES STARTED**	**COMPLETE GAMES**	**FEWEST HITS/GAME**	**FEWEST BB/GAME**
Young-Bos 33	Griffith-Chi 774	Young-Bos 11.6	McGinnity-Bal 43	McGinnity-Bal 39	Young-Bos 7.85	Young-Bos 90
McGinnity-Bal 26	Young-Bos 767	Griffith-Chi 7.5	Young-Bos 41	Young-Bos 38	Callahan-Chi........8.15	Gear-Was 1.21
Griffith-Chi 24	Callahan-Chi.........652	Patten-Was 5.5	Fraser-Phi...............37	Miller-Det................35	Moore-Cle.............8.38	Lee-Was 1.55
Miller-Det................23	Patten-Was 643	Miller-Det 4.6	Carrick-Was............37	Fraser-Phi...............35	Lewis-Bos.............8.51	Griffith-Chi 1.69
Fraser-Phi...............22	Miller-Det 639	Moore-Cle...............4.1	Miller-Det................36	Carrick-Was............34	Winter-Bos............8.74	Cronin-Det 1.72
STRIKEOUTS	**STRIKEOUTS/GAME**	**GAMES**	**SAVES**	**BASE RUNNERS/9**	**ADJUSTED RELIEF RUNS**	**RELIEF RANKING**
Young-Bos 158	Garvin-Mil 4.27	McGinnity-Bal 48	Hoffer-Cle 3	Young-Bos 8.92		
Patterson-Chi........127	Patten-Was 3.86	Dowling-Mil-Cle 43		Callahan-Chi......10.62		
Dowling-Mil-Cle 124	Young-Bos 3.83	Young-Bos 43		Griffith-Chi 11.10		
Garvin-Mil 122	Patterson-Chi.......3.66	Carrick-Was............42		Lewis-Bos..........11.32		
Fraser-Phi.............110	Dowling-Mil-Cle ...3.65	Patterson-Chi..........41		Winter-Bos.........11.35		
INNINGS PITCHED	**OPPONENTS' AVG.**	**OPPONENTS' OBP**	**EARNED RUN AVERAGE**	**ADJUSTED ERA**	**ADJUSTED STARTER RUNS**	**PITCHER WINS**
McGinnity-Bal 382.0	Young-Bos 232	Young-Bos 256	Young-Bos 1.62	Young-Bos 217	Young-Bos 77.0	**Young-Bos 7.9**
Young-Bos 371.1	Callahan-Chi.........239	Callahan-Chi.........290	Callahan-Chi........2.42	Yeager-Det...........147	Miller-Det 32.9	**Griffith-Chi.........4.2**
Miller-Det...........332.0	Moore-Cle.............244	Griffith-Chi 300	Yeager-Det...........2.61	Callahan-Chi.........143	Griffith-Chi 28.6	**Callahan-Chi 3.7**
Fraser-Phi..........331.0	Lewis-Bos.............247	Lewis-Bos.............304	Griffith-Chi 2.67	Griffith-Chi 130	Callahan-Chi........25.5	**Miller-Det...........3.3**
Carrick-Was.......324.0	Winter-Bos............252	Winter-Bos............304	Winter-Bos...........2.80	Miller-Det.............130	Yeager-Det...........22.2	**Yeager-Det.........2.9**

Impressive Instant

Declaring itself a major league, and announcing the fact by recruiting top stars from NL clubs, the American League—formerly a minor league known as the Western League—broke in with a bang. The Philadelphia Athletics lured second baseman Nap Lajoie from the crosstown NL club and were rewarded when Lajoie won the AL's Triple Crown, taking the batting title by nearly 100 points. Others, including the Baltimore Orioles and their hard-boiled player-manager John McGraw, weren't happy with the high salaries paid by the Athletics.

Lajoie alone couldn't carry his team to victory; the Athletics came in fourth. Boston's Cy Young was the league's top pitcher, finishing with an ERA 0.80 lower than his nearest rival, but Boston's fellow moundsmen weren't worthy. The Red Sox finished second behind the White Sox, who had the league's best offense. Chicago's hitters led the league in walks and steals; 39-year-old Dummy Hoy paced the AL with 86 bases on balls and tallied a third-best 113 runs.

The prowess of Hoy, the overwhelming dominance of Young and Lajoie, and other factors reveal that the American League was a bit behind the talent curve in 1901. Runs per game were at 5.35, the loop's highest total until 1930, and fielding average was just .938, a figure that the NL had passed back in 1897. In 1902, however, the talent began to even out as stubborn and penurious NL owners failed to match the salaries offered by their new rivals. The Junior Circuit could soon call itself a peer—maybe even superior.

Several youngsters made their first major league appearances in 1901 due to the AL's need for players. Future Tigers outfielders Davy Jones and Matty McIntyre debuted at age 21, while lefty Eddie Plank finally got a chance to shine with Philadelphia, going 17-13 as a 26-year-old rookie. He would win 309 more games in the majors before retiring, all but 42 with Philadelphia.

1900 NATIONAL LEAGUE

TEAM	W	L	T	PCT	GB	HW	HL	R	OR	PA	H	2B	3B	HR	BB	SO	HB	SH	AVG	OBP	SLG	OPS	AOPS	BR	ABR	PF	SB	CS	BSA	BSR
Bro	82	54	6	.603	—	43	26	**816**	722	5440	1423	199	81	26	421	**272**	**81**	78	**.293**	**.359**	**.383**	**742**	104	**75**	29	106	**274**			
Pit	79	60	1	.568	4.5	42	28	733	**612**	5317	1312	185	**100**	26	327	321	63	110	.272	.327	.368	695	96	-27	-32	101	174			
Phi	75	63	3	.543	8	**45**	23	810	792	5594	**1439**	187	82	29	**440**	374	72	113	.290	.356	.378	734	**109**	60	**67**	99	205			
Bos	66	72	4	.478	17	42	29	778	739	5499	1403	163	68	**48**	395	278	45	107	.283	.342	.373	715	92	15	-69	112	182			
StL	65	75	2	.464	19	40	31	744	748	5444	1420	141	81	36	406	318	**81**	80	.291	.356	.375	731	108	50	56	99	243			
Chi	65	75	6	.464	19	**45**	30	635	751	5445	1276	**202**	51	33	343	383	65	**130**	.260	.317	.342	659	90	-85	-60	96	189			
Cin	62	77	5	.446	21.5	27	34	703	745	5517	1335	178	83	33	333	408	50	108	.266	.318	.354	672	92	-73	-56	98	183			
NY	60	78	3	.435	23	38	31	713	823	5229	1317	177	61	23	369	343	56	80	.279	.338	.357	695	102	-15	19	95	236			
Total	569	—	—	—	—	322	232	5932	—	43485	10925	1432	607	254	3034	2697	513	806	.279	.339	.366	705	—	—	—	—	1686	—	—	—

TEAM	CG	SHO	GR	SV	IP	H	HR	BB	SO	BR/9	ERA	AERA	OAV	OOB	PR	APR	PF	OSB	OCS	FA	E	WPB	DP	FW	PW	BW	BSW	DIF
Bro	104	8	**40**	**4**	1225.2	1370	30	405	300	13.6	3.89	98	.282	.346	-27	-9	104	213	*156*	.948	303	**51**	102	2.6	-.8	2.7	—	9.6
Pit	114	11	30	1	1229.0	**1232**	24	**295**	**415**	**11.7**	**3.06**	**119**	**.261**	**.313**	**87**	**79**	98	**166**	*151*	.945	322	71	106	1.1	**7.2**	-2.9	—	4.1
Phi	116	7	28	3	1248.2	1506	29	402	284	14.2	4.12	88	.298	.357	-59	-73	98	272	***185***	.945	330	80	**125**	.8	-6.7	**6.1**	—	5.8
Bos	116	8	29	2	1240.1	1263	59	463	340	12.9	3.72	111	.264	.335	-4	49	112	213	*165*	**.953**	**273**	85	86	**4.4**	4.5	-6.3	—	-5.6
StL	117	**12**	26	0	1217.1	1373	37	299	325	12.7	3.75	97	.284	.331	-7	-17	98	216	*167*	.943	331	55	73	.8	-1.6	5.1	—	-9.4
Chi	**137**	9	9	1	1271.0	1375	**21**	324	357	12.6	3.23	112	.276	.330	66	53	98	234	*172*	.933	418	63	98	-3.9	4.8	-5.5	—	-.4
Cin	118	9	28	1	1274.2	1383	28	404	399	13.0	3.83	96	.276	.338	-20	-24	99	190	*177*	.945	341	77	120	.5	-2.2	-5.1	—	-.7
NY	113	4	31	0	1207.1	1423	26	442	277	14.6	3.96	91	.293	.363	-35	-49	98	182	*177*	.928	439	69	124	-6.0	-4.5	1.7	—	-.3
Total	935	68	221	12	9914.0	—	—	—	—	13.2	3.69	—	.279	.339	—	—	—	—	—	.942	2757	551	834	—	—	—	—	—

BATTER-FIELDER WINS	BATTING AVERAGE	ON-BASE PERCENTAGE	SLUGGING AVERAGE	ON-BASE PLUS SLUGGING	ADJUSTED OPS	ADJUSTED BATTER RUNS
Flick-Phi ... 4.5	Wagner-Pit ... .381	McGraw-StL ... .505	Wagner-Pit ... .573	Wagner-Pit ... 1007	Wagner-Pit ... 175	Flick-Phi ... 55.6
Lajoie-Phi ... 4.4	Flick-Phi ... .367	Thomas-Phi ... .451	Flick-Phi ... .545	Flick-Phi ... 986	Flick-Phi ... 172	Wagner-Pit ... 53.3
Davis-NY ... 4.3	Burkett-StL ... .363	Hamilton-Bos ... .449	Lajoie-Phi ... .510	McGraw-StL ... 921	McGraw-StL ... 157	Selbach-NY ... 41.1
Wagner-Pit ... 4.1	Keeler-Bro ... .362	Flick-Phi ... .441	Kelley-Bro ... .485	Burkett-StL ... 904	Selbach-NY ... 151	Burkett-StL ... 39.3
Selbach-NY ... 3.7	McGraw-StL ... .344	Wagner-Pit ... .434	Hickman-NY ... .482	Selbach-NY ... 885	Burkett-StL ... 150	McGraw-StL ... 38.4

RUNS	HITS	DOUBLES	TRIPLES	HOME RUNS	TOTAL BASES	RUNS BATTED IN
Thomas-Phi ... 132	Keeler-Bro ... 204	Wagner-Pit ... 45	Wagner-Pit ... 22	Long-Bos ... 12	Wagner-Pit ... 302	Flick-Phi ... 110
Slagle-Phi ... 115	Burkett-StL ... 203	Lajoie-Phi ... 33	Kelley-Bro ... 17	Flick-Phi ... 11	Flick-Phi ... 297	Delahanty-Phi ... 109
VanHaltren-NY ... 114	Wagner-Pit ... 201	Flick-Phi ... 32	Hickman-NY ... 17	Donlin-StL ... 10	Burkett-StL ... 265	Wagner-Pit ... 100
Barrett-Cin ... 114	Flick-Phi ... 200	Delahanty-Phi ... 32	Stahl-Bos ... 16	Hickman-NY ... 9	Keeler-Bro ... 253	Collins-Bos ... 95
Wagner-Pit ... 107	Beckley-Cin ... 190	VanHaltren-NY ... 30	Flick-Phi ... 16	Sullivan-Bos ... 8	Beckley-Cin ... 242	Beckley-Cin ... 94

BASES ON BALLS	STOLEN BASES	BASE STEALING RUNS	FIELDING RUNS-INFIELD	FIELDING RUNS-OUTFIELD	OUTFIELD ASSISTS	CATCHER CS PCT.
Thomas-Phi ... 115	VanHaltren-NY ... 45		Davis-NY ... 28.7	Selbach-NY ... 12.4	VanHaltren-NY ... 28	Farrell-Bro ... 42.2
Hamilton-Bos ... 107	Donovan-StL ... 45		Lajoie-Phi ... 22.4	VanHaltren-NY ... 8.5	Selbach-NY ... 25	
McGraw-StL ... 85	Barrett-Cin ... 44		Dahlen-Bro ... 21.2	Keeler-Bro ... 5.7	Barrett-Cin ... 25	
Dahlen-Bro ... 73	Keeler-Bro ... 41		Steinfeldt-Cin ... 16.1	Burkett-StL ... 5.6	Flick-Phi ... 23	
			Childs-Chi ... 14.5	Stahl-Bos ... 4.5		

WINS	WINNING PCT.	WINS ABOVE TEAM	GAMES STARTED	COMPLETE GAMES	FEWEST HITS/GAME	FEWEST BB/GAME
McGinnity-Bro ... 28	McGinnity-Bro ... .778	McGinnity-Bro ... 9.3	Carrick-NY ... 41	Hawley-NY ... 34	Waddell-Pit ... 7.59	Young-StL ... 1.01
Tannehill-Pit ... 20	Tannehill-Pit ... .769	Tannehill-Pit ... 6.7	Hawley-NY ... 38	Dinneen-Bos ... 33	Garvin-Chi ... 8.22	Phillippe-Pit ... 1.35
Phillippe-Pit ... 20	Fraser-Phi ... .625	Dinneen-Bos ... 4.4			Nichols-Bos ... 8.36	Tannehill-Pit ... 1.65
Kennedy-Bro ... 20	Phillippe-Pit ... .606	Menefee-Chi ... 2.9			Dinneen-Bos ... 8.53	Griffith-Chi ... 1.85
Dinneen-Bos ... 20	Kennedy-Bro ... .606	Hawley-NY ... 2.7			Phillippe-Pit ... 8.84	Leever-Pit ... 1.86

STRIKEOUTS	STRIKEOUTS/GAME	GAMES	SAVES	BASE RUNNERS/9	ADJUSTED RELIEF RUNS	RELIEF RANKING
Hahn-Cin ... 132	Waddell-Pit ... 5.61	Carrick-NY ... 45	Kitson-Bro ... 4	Phillippe-Pit ... 10.42		
Waddell-Pit ... 130	Garvin-Chi ... 3.91	McGinnity-Bro ... 44	Bernhard-Phi ... 2	Waddell-Pit ... 10.52		
Young-StL ... 115	Hahn-Cin ... 3.82	Scott-Cin ... 42		Young-StL ... 10.53		
Garvin-Chi ... 107	Newton-Cin ... 3.40	Kennedy-Bro ... 42		Garvin-Chi ... 11.18		
Dinneen-Bos ... 107	Leever-Pit ... 3.25			Leever-Pit ... 11.30		

INNINGS PITCHED	OPPONENTS' AVG.	OPPONENTS' OBP	EARNED RUN AVERAGE	ADJUSTED ERA	ADJUSTED STARTER RUNS	PITCHER WINS
McGinnity-Bro ... 343.0	Waddell-Pit ... .229	Phillippe-Pit ... .289	Waddell-Pit ... 2.37	Waddell-Pit ... 153	Dinneen-Bos ... 31.8	**Dinneen-Bos ... 3.1**
Carrick-NY ... 341.2	Garvin-Chi ... .243	Waddell-Pit ... .291	Garvin-Chi ... 2.41	Garvin-Chi ... 149	Garvin-Chi ... 28.0	**Tannehill-Pit ... 2.7**
Hawley-NY ... 329.1	Nichols-Bos ... .246	Young-StL ... .291	Taylor-Chi ... 2.55	Taylor-Chi ... 141	Young-StL ... 27.8	**Young-StL ... 2.6**
Young-StL ... 321.1	Dinneen-Bos ... .250	Garvin-Chi ... .304	Leever-Pit ... 2.71	Nichols-Bos ... 134	Phillippe-Pit ... 25.7	**Leever-Pit ... 2.5**
Dinneen-Bos ... 320.2	Phillippe-Pit ... .257	Leever-Pit ... .306	Sudhoff-StL ... 2.76	Leever-Pit ... 134	Leever-Pit ... 24.8	**Garvin-Chi ... 2.4**

The Last One-Horse Town

In January 1900 Boston Beaneaters catcher Marty Bergen, injured the previous season and possibly despondent over finances, killed himself and his entire family. The horrific crime was the beginning of the end of a once-great Boston franchise.

The new century saw a streamlined, eight-club NL, free of syndicate ownership and with no team finishing more than 23 games out of first place. The rules committee changed home plate from a 12-inch square to a five-sided shape 17 inches wide, largely for the benefit of umpires.

Brooklyn, now named the Superbas, won the flag again, leading the league in scoring and benefiting from the strong arm of former Oriole "Iron Man" Joe McGinnity, who led the league in wins, but also in walks and hit batsmen (40, the most ever). Second-place Pittsburgh, fortified with stars Honus Wagner, who won his first bat crown, Deacon Phillippe, Rube Waddell, and Fred Clarke from Louisville, made it a close race and positioned themselves as an up-and-coming club.

In the last postseason series between NL clubs until 1969, the Superbas took on the Pirates. Like the Temple Cup this trophy originated in Pittsburgh, and it was even less popular than the first try earlier in the decade. Brooklyn won three of four games from the Pirates for the *Chronicle-Telegraph Cup. Only one crowd of more than 2,500 came out to see the series.*

St. Louis, having changed its name to the Cardinals, purchased John McGraw and Wilbert Robinson, who again refused the call to join Brooklyn after the Orioles disbanded. McGraw once more led the league in on-base percentage, but the Cards ended tied for fifth. A young pitcher with last-place New York went 0-3, but this was just the start for Christy Mathewson.

It was also the beginning of the American League, formerly the minor Western League. President Ban Johnson declared the AL a major for 1900 and fielded eight clubs, one in Chicago and seven in former National League or American Association cities. The new loop counted George Stallings, Connie Mack, and Charlie Comiskey among its skippers, and would soon enter into a fierce battle for talent with the NL—and help save baseball in the process.

1899 NATIONAL LEAGUE

TEAM	W	L	T	PCT	GB	HW	HL	R	OR	PA	H	2B	3B	HR	BB	SO	HB	SH	AVG	OBP	SLG	OPS	AOPS	BR	ABR	PF	SB	CS	BSA	BSR
Bro	101	47	2	.682	—	**60**	16	892	658	5614	1436	178	97	27	477	263	**125**	75	.291	**.368**	.383	751	110	89	70	102	271			
Bos	95	57	1	.625	8	53	26	858	**645**	5897	1517	178	90	39	431	269	43	133	.287	.345	.377	722	94	20	-53	110	185			
Phi	94	58	2	.618	9	58	25	**916**	743	5986	**1613**	**241**	83	31	441	341	75	117	**.301**	.363	**.395**	**758**	**118**	**100**	**134**	97	212			
Bal	86	62	4	.581	15	51	24	827	691	5707	1509	204	71	17	418	383	122	94	.297	.365	.376	741	104	73	30	105	**364**			
StL	84	67	4	.556	18.5	50	33	819	739	5913	1514	172	88	**47**	468	**262**	33	108	.285	.347	.378	725	102	27	8	102	210			
Cin	83	67	7	.553	19	57	29	861	777	5946	1448	195	106	13	**487**	300	67	133	.275	.344	.360	704	96	-5	-19	102	228			
Pit	76	73	6	.510	25.5	49	34	841	771	6079	1582	196	**121**	29	386	346	63	144	.288	.342	.384	726	104	22	25	100	179			
Chi	75	73	4	.507	26	44	39	812	763	5766	1428	173	82	27	406	342	64	148	.277	.338	.359	697	99	-26	-5	97	247			
Lou	75	77	4	.493	28	33	28	833	782	6014	1491	195	70	40	437	379	78	**163**	.279	.343	.365	708	100	-1	1	100	234			
NY	60	90	3	.400	42	35	38	741	868	5621	1441	165	66	23	389	361	46	61	.281	.337	.353	690	98	-38	-11	97	235			
Was	54	98	3	.355	49	35	43	743	983	5783	1429	162	87	**47**	350	341	87	90	.272	.328	.363	691	96	-48	-40	99	176			
Cle	20	134	0	.130	84	9	33	529	1252	5690	1333	142	50	12	289	280	65	57	.253	.299	.305	604	76	-213	-168	93	127			
Total	923	—	—	—	—	534	368	9672	—	70016	17741	2201	1011	352	4979	3867	868	1323	.282	.343	.366	710	—	—	—	—	2668	—	—	—

TEAM	CG	SHO	GR	SV	IP	H	HR	BB	SO	BR/9	ERA	AERA	OAV	OOB	PR	APR	PF	OSB	OCS	FA	E	WPB	DP	FW	PW	BW	BSW	DIF
Bro	121	9	30	**9**	1269.1	1320	32	463	331	13.0	**3.25**	120	.268	.337	85	91	102	229	*178*	.948	314	52	125	2.9	8.2	6.3	—	9.5
Bos	138	13	17	4	1348.0	**1273**	44	432	385	**11.8**	3.26	**127**	**.250**	**.317**	**87**	**123**	108	193	*169*	**.952**	**303**	58	124	**4.0**	**11.1**	-4.8	—	8.7
Phi	129	**15**	26	2	1333.1	1398	17	370	281	12.5	3.47	106	.270	.329	56	31	96	206	*178*	.940	379	85	110	-.3	2.8	**12.1**	—	3.3
Bal	132	9	20	5	1304.1	1403	**13**	349	294	12.6	3.31	119	.275	.330	78	90	103	**176**	*127*	.949	308	59	96	3.6	8.2	2.7	—	-2.4
StL	134	7	23	1	1340.2	1476	41	**321**	331	12.4	3.36	118	.280	.328	73	88	103	180	*173*	.939	397	48	117	-1.2	8.0	.7	—	1.0
Cin	131	8	28	5	1373.0	1494	26	372	361	12.7	3.70	106	.278	.334	23	30	102	177	*161*	.947	341	43	113	2.3	2.7	-1.7	—	4.7
Pit	118	9	**39**	4	1373.0	1471	27	438	338	13.0	3.61	105	.274	.337	36	30	99	195	*185*	.945	363	53	100	.8	2.7	2.3	—	-4.3
Chi	**147**	8	5	1	1331.1	1433	20	330	313	12.5	3.37	111	.275	.328	71	56	97	206	*171*	.935	428	33	**145**	-3.5	5.1	-.5	—	-.2
Lou	135	5	22	2	1360.1	1517	35	325	288	12.6	3.43	112	.282	.331	63	62	100	197	*171*	.939	399	**30**	103	-1.2	5.6	.0	—	-5.5
NY	139	4	14	0	1290.2	1463	19	630	**402**	15.3	4.27	88	.286	.375	-61	-80	97	249	*192*	.932	434	97	142	-3.7	-7.3	-1.0	—	-3.1
Was	131	3	28	0	1300.1	1649	35	422	328	14.9	4.93	79	.309	.368	-157	-147	102	288	*197*	.935	403	60	99	-1.6	-13.3	-3.6	—	-3.5
Cle	138	0	18	0	1264.0	1844	43	527	215	17.7	6.37	58	.340	.409	-354	-396	96	372	***218***	.937	388	66	121	-.8	-35.9	-15.2	—	-5.1
Total	1593	90	270	33	15888.1	—	—	—	—	13.4	3.85	—	.282	.343	—	—	—	—	—	.942	4457	684	1395	—	—	—	—	—

BATTER-FIELDER WINS	BATTING AVERAGE	ON-BASE PERCENTAGE	SLUGGING AVERAGE	ON-BASE PLUS SLUGGING	ADJUSTED OPS	ADJUSTED BATTER RUNS
G.Davis-NY........6.1	Delahanty-Phi.......410	McGraw-Bal..........547	Delahanty-Phi.......582	Delahanty-Phi.....1046	Delahanty-Phi.......193	Delahanty-Phi......76.5
Delahanty-Phi....5.6	Burkett-StL...........396	Delahanty-Phi.......464	Freeman-Was.......563	McGraw-Bal..........994	McGraw-Bal..........165	McGraw-Bal..........52.6
McGraw-Bal.......4.9	McGraw-Bal..........391	Burkett-StL...........463	Williams-Pit...........530	Burkett-StL............963	Burkett-StL............160	Burkett-StL...........49.2
Williams-Pit.......4.7	Keeler-Bro.............379	Thomas-Phi...........457	Wagner-Lou...........501	Williams-Pit...........946	Williams-Pit...........159	Williams-Pit..........48.7
Wallace-StL.......4.4	Williams-Pit...........354	Stahl-Bos...............426	Burkett-StL............500	Freeman-Was.......925	Freeman-Was.......154	Thomas-Phi.........36.6
RUNS	**HITS**	**DOUBLES**	**TRIPLES**	**HOME RUNS**	**TOTAL BASES**	**RUNS BATTED IN**
McGraw-Bal..........140	Delahanty-Phi.......238	Delahanty-Phi.........55	Williams-Pit............27	Freeman-Was.........25	Delahanty-Phi.......338	Delahanty-Phi.......137
Keeler-Bro.............140	Burkett-StL...........221	Wagner-Lou............45	Freeman-Was.........25	Wallace-StL............12	Freeman-Was.......331	Freeman-Was.......122
Thomas-Phi..........137	Williams-Pit...........220	Holmes-Bal..............31	Stahl-Bos.................19	Williams-Pit...............9	Williams-Pit...........329	Williams-Pit...........116
Delahanty-Phi.......135	Keeler-Bro.............216	Long-Bos..................30	Tenney-Bos.............17	Mertes-Chi.................9	Wagner-Lou..........288	Wagner-Lou..........114
Williams-Pit...........126	Tenney-Bos.............209	Duffy-Bos..................29	McCarthy-Pit...........17	Delahanty-Phi.............9	Stahl-Bos...............284	Wallace-StL...........108
BASES ON BALLS	**STOLEN BASES**	**BASE STEALING RUNS**	**FIELDING RUNS-INFIELD**	**FIELDING RUNS-OUTFIELD**	**OUTFIELD ASSISTS**	**CATCHER CS PCT.**
McGraw-Bal..........124	Sheckard-Bal..........77		G.Davis-NY..........46.3	Sheckard-Bal.......19.4	Heidrick-StL............34	McFarland-Phi.....47.2
Thomas-Phi..........115	McGraw-Bal............73		Cross-Cle-StL......35.6	Slagle-Was..........18.2	Sheckard-Bal..........33	Kittridge-Lou-Was...45.8
VanHaltren-NY........75	Heidrick-StL............55		Wallace-StL.........30.3	Selbach-Cin..........11.2	VanHaltren-NY.........31	Farrell-Was-Bro....45.4
Childs-StL...............74	Holmes-Bal..............50		Gleason-NY...........28.4	Kelley-Bro............10.1	Selbach-Cin............27	Robinson-Bal.......42.4
	Clarke-Lou..............49		Collins-Bos..........17.8	Lange-Chi...............8.5	Harley-Cle...............27	McGuire-Was-Bro41.8
WINS	**WINNING PCT.**	**WINS ABOVE TEAM**	**GAMES STARTED**	**COMPLETE GAMES**	**FEWEST HITS/GAME**	**FEWEST BB/GAME**
McGinnity-Bal.........28	Hughes-Bro..........824	Hughes-Bro............8.7	Powell-StL...............43	Young-StL...............40	Willis-Bos..............7.28	Young-StL.............1.07
Hughes-Bro............28	Willis-Bos..............771	Willis-Bos...............7.9	Carrick-NY...............43	Powell-StL...............40	Hughes-Bro..........7.71	Cuppy-StL.............1.36
Willis-Bos...............27	Hahn-Cin...............742	Hahn-Cin.................7.4	Young-StL................42	Carrick-NY..............40	Hahn-Cin..............8.16	Tannehill-Pit.........1.45
Young-StL...............26	Donahue-Phi.........724	Tannehill-Pit............5.8	McGinnity-Bal.........41	Taylor-Chi...............39	Seymour-NY.........8.28	Woods-Lou...........1.79
Tannehill-Pit............24	Kennedy-Bro..........710	Callahan-Chi...........5.2		McGinnity-Bal.........38	Leever-Pit.............8.38	Kitson-Bal.............1.79
STRIKEOUTS	**STRIKEOUTS/GAME**	**GAMES**	**SAVES**	**BASE RUNNERS/9**	**ADJUSTED RELIEF RUNS**	**RELIEF RANKING**
Hahn-Cin...............145	Seymour-NY........4.76	Leever-Pit...............51	Leever-Pit.................3	Young-StL..........10.19		
Seymour-NY.........142	Hahn-Cin.............4.22	Powell-StL...............48		Waddell-Lou.......10.37		
Leever-Pit.............121	Doheny-NY..........3.89	McGinnity-Bal.........48		Hahn-Cin............10.43		
Willis-Bos.............120	McJames-Bro.......3.43	Young-StL...............44		Orth-Phi..............10.64		
Doheny-NY...........120	Willis-Bos.............3.15	Carrick-NY..............44		Nichols-Bos.......10.85		
INNINGS PITCHED	**OPPONENTS' AVG.**	**OPPONENTS' OBP**	**EARNED RUN AVERAGE**	**ADJUSTED ERA**	**ADJUSTED STARTER RUNS**	**PITCHER WINS**
Leever-Pit..........379.0	Willis-Bos..............222	Young-StL..............285	Orth-Phi...............2.49	Willis-Bos..............166	Willis-Bos............58.2	**Young-StL...........5.1**
Powell-StL..........373.0	Hughes-Bro...........232	Hahn-Cin...............290	Willis-Bos.............2.50	Young-StL.............154	Young-StL............49.9	**Willis-Bos...........4.8**
Young-StL...........369.1	Hahn-Cin...............242	Nichols-Bos...........298	Young-StL.............2.58	McGinnity-Bal.......148	McGinnity-Bal......48.2	**Hughes-Bro.........4.6**
McGinnity-Bal....366.1	Seymour-NY.........245	Kitson-Bal.............303	Bernhard-Phi........2.65	Hahn-Cin..............146	Kitson-Bal............41.9	**McGinnity-Bal....4.5**
Carrick-NY.........361.2	Leever-Pit.............247	Willis-Bos.............304	McGinnity-Bal......2.68	Hughes-Bro...........145	Hahn-Cin.............41.1	**Tannehill-Pit.......4.3**

Syndicate Bosses

It was a year destroyed by syndicate ownership. The Robison brothers, detested owners of the Cleveland Spiders, decided to also buy the St. Louis Browns, and siphoned off Cleveland players to contribute to the Browns' effort. Public anger at this sham forced the Spiders, already a traveling team for much of 1898, back to the road. The horrible club finished 84 games out and lost 134 times, both all-time lows. The 6,088 who paid to see the club in Cleveland (the average crowd was 145), was the smallest turnstile count in NL history. It was only right that the Browns finished fifth, although they were second in attendance.

Baltimore suffered through a similar debacle. Orioles stars Ned Hanlon, Willie Keeler, Hughie Jennings, and Joe Kelley were transferred to Brooklyn. John McGraw, however, stayed behind, and took over as player-manager. Wilbert Robinson, who happened to be Mugsy's partner in a Baltimore billiard parlor and bowling alley, also stayed put and batted .284 as the club's regular catcher. McGraw posted a .547 on-base percentage—the highest in the majors until 1941—for his beloved Orioles, who played surprisingly well.

The Bridegrooms used their mother lode to win the crown. Keeler tied for the league lead (with McGraw) in runs, and pitcher Jim Hughes paced in wins. It was a team effort—Hanlon's club had few weaknesses. Boston finished second as Vic Willis became arguably the league's top starter, and Ed Delahanty's bat crown and 55 doubles (the most until 1923) powered the third-place Phillies.

To eliminate unnecessary trickery, catchers were required to stay in their box when pitches were delivered. And from this point on all players' uniforms on the same team had to conform. Several big names debuted, including Joe McGinnity, Deacon Phillippe, Jack Chesbro, Turkey Mike Donlin, and Sam Crawford.

Realizing the inevitable—that twelve teams made no sense, economically or otherwise—the NL contracted Louisville (owned by Barney Dreyfus, who also controlled Pittsburgh), Washington, Baltimore, and Cleveland for 1900. Such wisdom came too late, especially for the Spiders and their remaining fans. National League owners would reap the fruits of their poor stewardship of the game about a year later.

1898 NATIONAL LEAGUE

TEAM	W	L	T	PCT	GB	HW	HL	R	OR	PA	H	2B	3B	HR	BB	SO	HB	SH	AVG	OBP	SLG	OPS	AOPS	BR	ABR	PF	SB	CS	BSA	BSR
Bos	102	47	3	.685	—	**62**	15	872	**614**	5847	1531	190	55	**53**	405	303	32	134	.290	.344	**.377**	721	106	73	31	105	172			
Bal	96	53	5	.644	6	58	15	**933**	623	6000	**1584**	154	77	12	519	316	**160**	79	**.302**	**.382**	.368	**750**	**118**	**160**	**143**	102	**250**			
Cin	92	60	5	.605	11.5	58	28	831	740	5984	1448	207	**101**	19	455	**300**	59	136	.271	.335	.359	694	97	24	-28	107	165			
Chi	85	65	2	.567	17.5	58	31	828	679	5879	1431	175	84	18	476	394	71	113	.274	.343	.350	693	104	29	31	100	220			
Cle	81	68	7	.544	21	36	19	730	683	5962	1379	162	56	18	**545**	306	46	125	.263	.338	.325	663	96	-21	-10	99	93			
Phi	78	71	1	.523	24	49	31	823	784	5779	1431	**238**	81	33	472	382	69	120	.280	.348	**.377**	725	**118**	89	127	96	182			
NY	77	73	7	.513	25.5	45	28	837	800	5907	1422	190	86	34	428	372	69	61	.266	.328	.353	681	103	-5	20	97	214			
Pit	72	76	4	.486	29.5	39	35	634	694	5638	1313	140	88	14	336	343	74	**141**	.258	.313	.328	641	90	-83	-70	98	107			
Lou	70	81	3	.464	33	43	34	728	833	5775	1389	150	71	32	375	429	66	**141**	.267	.325	.342	667	97	-33	-22	99	235			
Bro	54	91	4	.372	46	30	41	638	811	5610	1314	156	66	17	328	314	65	91	.256	.309	.322	631	85	-101	-98	100	130			
Was	51	101	3	.336	52.5	34	44	704	939	5785	1423	177	80	36	370	386	70	88	.271	.327	.355	682	100	-6	-4	100	197			
StL	39	111	4	.260	63.5	20	44	571	929	5798	1290	149	55	13	383	402	84	117	.247	.309	.305	614	78	-128	-142	102	104			
Total	921	—	—	—	—	532	365	9129	—	69964	16955	2088	900	299	5092	4247	865	1346	.271	.334	.347	681	—	—	—	—	2069	—	—	—

TEAM	CG	SHO	GR	SV	IP	H	HR	BB	SO	BR/9	ERA	AERA	OAV	OOB	PR	APR	PF	OSB	OCS	FA	E	WPB	DP	FW	PW	BW	BSW	DIF
Bos	127	9	26	**8**	1340.0	**1186**	37	470	432	11.6	2.98	124	**.236**	**.310**	93	103	102	149	*125*	.950	310	87	102	3.1	9.6	2.9	—	11.9
Bal	138	12	15	0	1323.0	1236	17	400	422	**11.5**	2.90	123	.246	**.310**	104	99	99	146	*128*	.947	326	65	105	2.5	9.3	**13.4**	—	-3.6
Cin	131	10	**27**	2	1385.1	1484	16	449	294	13.0	3.50	109	.272	.336	17	47	106	**109**	*121*	.950	325	44	128	2.9	4.4	-2.6	—	11.3
Chi	137	**13**	15	0	1342.2	1357	17	364	323	12.1	**2.83**	**126**	.261	.319	**115**	**112**	99	111	*116*	.936	412	51	**149**	-2.9	**10.5**	2.9	—	-.5
Cle	**142**	9	15	0	1334.0	1429	26	**309**	339	12.1	3.20	113	.272	.320	59	60	100	159	*140*	**.952**	**301**	46	95	**4.2**	5.6	-.9	—	-2.4
Phi	129	10	22	0	1288.1	1440	23	399	325	13.4	3.72	92	.281	.342	-17	-45	95	151	*136*	.937	379	54	102	-1.2	-4.2	11.9	—	-3.0
NY	141	9	15	1	1353.2	1359	21	587	**558**	13.5	3.44	101	.260	.344	25	5	96	188	*156*	.932	447	119	113	-4.2	.5	1.9	—	3.9
Pit	131	10	22	3	1323.2	1400	**14**	346	330	12.3	3.41	104	.270	.323	29	22	99	170	*139*	.946	340	**42**	105	1.4	2.1	-6.5	—	1.1
Lou	137	4	19	0	1334.0	1457	33	470	271	13.6	4.24	84	.276	.346	-95	-100	99	205	*140*	.939	382	54	114	-.8	-9.3	-2.1	—	6.7
Bro	134	1	17	0	1298.2	1446	34	476	294	13.7	4.01	89	.280	.348	-59	-64	99	184	*140*	.947	334	56	125	1.3	-6.0	-9.2	—	-4.6
Was	129	0	**27**	1	1307.0	1577	29	450	371	14.5	4.52	81	.297	.360	-134	-125	102	256	***161***	.929	443	56	119	-4.2	-11.7	-.4	—	-8.7
StL	133	0	26	2	1324.1	1584	32	372	288	13.9	4.53	83	.295	.350	-137	-106	105	241	*158*	.939	388	56	97	-1.2	-9.9	-13.3	—	-11.6
Total	1609	87	246	17	15954.2	—	—	—	—	12.9	3.60	—	.271	.334	—	—	—	—	—	.942	4387	730	1354	—	—	—	—	—

BATTER-FIELDER WINS	BATTING AVERAGE	ON-BASE PERCENTAGE	SLUGGING AVERAGE	ON-BASE PLUS SLUGGING	ADJUSTED OPS	ADJUSTED BATTER RUNS
Jennings-Bal......4.9	Keeler-Bal.............385	Hamilton-Bos........480	Anderson-Br-Ws-Br .494	Hamilton-Bos........933	Hamilton-Bos........159	Delahanty-Phi......47.8
Dahlen-Chi..........4.3	Hamilton-Bos........369	McGraw-Bal..........475	Collins-Bos 479	Delahanty-Phi.......880	Delahanty-Phi.......159	McGraw-Bal.........43.7
Davis-NY.............4.0	McGraw-Bal..........342	Jennings-Bal.........454	Lajoie-Phi..............461	Flick-Phi...............878	Flick-Phi...............158	Jennings-Bal........43.7
Delahanty-Phi....3.9	Smith-Cin..............342	Flick-Phi...............430	Delahanty-Phi.......454	Jennings-Bal.........876	Jennings-Bal.........149	Flick-Phi..............40.9
Collins-Bos.........3.9	Burkett-Cle............341	Delahanty-Phi.......426	Hamilton-Bos........453	McGraw-Bal..........871	McGraw-Bal..........148	Hamilton-Bos.......39.2

RUNS	HITS	DOUBLES	TRIPLES	HOME RUNS	TOTAL BASES	RUNS BATTED IN
McGraw-Bal..........143	Keeler-Bal.............216	Lajoie-Phi................43	Anderson-Br-Ws-Br ...22	Collins-Bos 15	Collins-Bos 286	Lajoie-Phi..............127
Jennings-Bal.........135	Burkett-Cle............213	Delahanty-Phi.........36	VanHaltren-NY........16	Wagner-Lou............10	Lajoie-Phi..............280	Collins-Bos 111
VanHaltren-NY......129	VanHaltren-NY......204	Dahlen-Chi..............35	Hoy-Lou..................16	Joyce-NY................10	VanHaltren-NY......270	Kelley-Bal..............110
Keeler-Bal.............126	Lajoie-Phi..............197	Collins-Bos 35		Anderson-Br-Ws-Br 9	Anderson-Br-Ws-Br .257	Duffy-Bos..............108
Cooley-Phi............123		Anderson-Br-Ws-Br ...33		McKean-Cle.............9	Cooley-Phi............256	McGann-Bal..........106

BASES ON BALLS	STOLEN BASES	BASE STEALING RUNS	FIELDING RUNS-INFIELD	FIELDING RUNS-OUTFIELD	OUTFIELD ASSISTS	CATCHER CS PCT.
McGraw-Bal..........112	Delahanty-Phi.........58		Davis-NY 29.5	Selbach-Was 19.4	Harley-StL...............26	Donahue-Chi 51.4
Joyce-NY.................88	Hamilton-Bos..........54		Cross-StL.............20.4	Harley-StL..............8.3	Blake-Cle................25	Peitz-Cin..............50.7
Hamilton-Bos..........87	DeMontreville-Bal.......49		Dahlen-Chi...........20.1	Anderson-Br-Ws-Br ..7.4	Selbach-Was 24	Criger-Cle............47.9
Flick-Phi..................86	Dexter-Lou.............44		Wallace-Cle 18.3	Delahanty-Phi........7.0	Anderson-Br-Ws-Br ...23	McFarland-Phi 47.3
Jennings-Bal...........78	McGraw-Bal............43		Gleason-NY 17.6	F.Clarke-Lou 6.5	Miller-Cin 23	Robinson-Bal.......45.5

WINS	WINNING PCT.	WINS ABOVE TEAM	GAMES STARTED	COMPLETE GAMES	FEWEST HITS/GAME	FEWEST BB/GAME
Nichols-Bos 31	Lewis-Bos.............765	Cunningham-Lou...9.2	Taylor-StL................47	Taylor-StL................42	Nichols-Bos 7.33	Young-Cle...............98
Cunningham-Lou....28	Maul-Bal 741	Tannehill-Pit...........7.7	Seymour-NY 43	Cunningham-Lou....41	Willis-Bos.............7.64	Dwyer-Cin............1.58
McJames-Bal..........27	Nichols-Bos 721	Griffith-Chi 6.5		Young-Cle 40	Lewis-Bos 7.67	Cunningham-Lou.1.62
Hawley-Cin 27	Hawley-Cin 711	Hawley-Cin 6.2		Nichols-Bos 40	Maul-Bal 7.77	Tannehill-Pit.........1.74
Lewis-Bos 26	Griffith-Chi 706	Young-Cle..............5.9		McJames-Bal..........40	McJames-Bal.......7.87	Griffith-Chi 1.77

STRIKEOUTS	STRIKEOUTS/GAME	GAMES	SAVES	BASE RUNNERS/9	ADJUSTED RELIEF RUNS	RELIEF RANKING
Seymour-NY 239	Seymour-NY 6.03	Taylor-StL................50	Nichols-Bos 4	Nichols-Bos 9.63		
McJames-Bal........178	Willis-Bos............4.63	Nichols-Bos 50	Tannehill-Pit...............2	Maul-Bal 9.76		
Willis-Bos..............160	McJames-Bal.......4.28	Young-Cle 46	Lewis-Bos.................2	Young-Cle..........10.41		
Nichols-Bos 138	Doheny-NY 4.06		Hickman-Bos 2	Griffith-Chi 10.75		
Piatt-Phi................121	Piatt-Phi...............3.56		Dammann-Cin 2	McJames-Bal.....10.88		

INNINGS PITCHED	OPPONENTS' AVG.	OPPONENTS' OBP	EARNED RUN AVERAGE	ADJUSTED ERA	ADJUSTED STARTER RUNS	PITCHER WINS
Taylor-StL..........397.1	Nichols-Bos 221	Nichols-Bos 272	Griffith-Chi 1.88	Griffith-Chi 190	Griffith-Chi 63.3	**Nichols-Bos........ 6.4**
Nichols-Bos 388.0	Willis-Bos.............229	Maul-Bal 275	Maul-Bal 2.10	Nichols-Bos 173	Nichols-Bos 62.5	**Griffith-Chi.......... 5.9**
Young-Cle 377.2	Lewis-Bos.............229	Young-Cle.............288	Nichols-Bos 2.13	Maul-Bal 170	McJames-Bal.......49.2	**Maul-Bal............. 4.4**
McJames-Bal.....374.0	Maul-Bal 232	Griffith-Chi 294	McJames-Bal.......2.36	McJames-Bal........151	Maul-Bal 42.2	**Young-Cle........... 4.4**
Cunningham-Lou ..362.0	McJames-Bal........234	McJames-Bal........297	Callahan-Chi........2.46	Callahan-Chi.........145	Young-Cle 40.4	**McJames-Bal..... 4.3**

Beans in My Ears

In another move geared to make the game cleaner and more orderly, the NL voted to allow two umpires to be assigned to cover any game. The league also instituted a rule to prevent balks and began approaching the modern standard of what constitutes a stolen base.

Pitching continued to have the upper hand, as scoring per team dipped to 4.96 runs per game, the lowest mark in a decade. Clark Griffith's 1.88 ERA for Chicago was the game's best since the 1880s. Griffith was a fine pitcher—although a better manager and executive in the next century—and his '98 performance was by far the best of his career.

Helping to spell ace Kid Nichols, rookie hurler Vic Willis won 25 for Boston. The Beaneaters took their second straight flag by holding off a great Baltimore club. Boston's Jimmy Collins, the finest defensive third baseman of his day, also led in homers, and Hugh Duffy and Billy Hamilton were outstanding.

The Orioles led the league in scoring, with John McGraw, Willie Keeler, Hugh Jennings, and Joe Kelley providing the punch. A five-man pitching staff of obscurities and unexpected heroes kept Baltimore in the race until the end.

Giants outfielder George Van Haltren played 156 games, a mark that stood until 1904. Attendance fell, due in part to the Spanish-American War, and also because the twelve-team format hurt interest in many cities. Several clubs were so bad that their chances to win were finished by May. Crowds in Chicago rose dramatically as the Colts hosted more games than usual. The Cleveland Spiders, unpopular despite a winning record and the excellent pitching of Cy Young, were a traveling team much of the season.

Rookies included hurler Sam Leever, future Chicago standouts Harry Steinfeldt and Frank Chance, and two other up-and-comers, Elmer Flick and Tommy Leach. In his first full season, Honus Wagner led Louisville in homers and RBIs.

There was no Temple Cup in 1898—or ever again. Dwindling interest by fans and players alike led to the dissolution of the postseason series after four years.

1897 NATIONAL LEAGUE

TEAM	W	L	T	PCT	GB	HW	HL	R	OR	PA	H	2B	3B	HR	BB	SO	HB	SH	AVG	OBP	SLG	OPS	AOPS	BR	ABR	PF	SB	CS	BSA	BSR
Bos	93	39	3	.705	—	**54**	12	**1025**	**665**	5521	1574	230	83	**45**	423	262	47	114	.319	.378	**.426**	804	110	121	65	106	233			
Bal	90	40	6	.692	2	51	15	964	674	5496	**1584**	**243**	66	19	**437**	256	**115**	72	**.325**	**.394**	.414	**808**	**119**	**145**	**145**	100	**401**			
NY	83	48	7	.634	9.5	51	19	901	696	5395	1452	188	84	31	412	327	67	45	.298	.361	.390	751	106	22	46	97	332			
Cin	76	56	2	.576	17	49	18	763	705	5104	1311	219	69	22	380	**218**	65	**135**	.290	.353	.383	736	93	-2	-50	107	194			
Cle	69	62	1	.527	23.5	49	16	773	680	5175	1374	192	88	16	435	344	38	98	.298	.364	.389	753	99	27	-14	105	181			
Was	61	71	3	.462	32	40	26	781	793	5141	1376	194	77	36	374	348	59	72	.297	.357	.395	752	104	19	23	100	208			
Bro	61	71	4	.462	32	38	29	802	845	5334	1343	202	72	24	351	255	58	115	.279	.336	.366	702	95	-74	-32	95	187			
Pit	60	71	4	.458	32.5	38	27	676	835	5114	1266	140	**108**	25	359	334	67	98	.276	.337	.370	707	95	-67	-39	96	170			
Chi	59	73	6	.447	34	36	30	832	894	5385	1356	189	97	38	430	317	49	103	.282	.347	.386	733	94	-17	-46	104	264			
Phi	55	77	2	.417	38	32	34	752	792	5294	1392	213	83	40	399	299	42	97	.293	.353	.398	751	106	14	36	97	163			
Lou	52	78	6	.400	40	34	31	675	869	5131	1209	161	70	40	375	460	68	101	.264	.328	.355	683	88	-102	-79	97	200			
StL	29	102	2	.221	63.5	18	41	592	1088	5183	1285	151	67	32	354	314	76	80	.275	.336	.357	693	89	-86	-72	98	172			
Total	811	—	—	—	—	490	298	9536	—	63273	16522	2322	964	368	4729	3734	751	1130	.292	.354	.386	740	—	—	—	—	2705	—	—	—

TEAM	CG	SHO	GR	SV	IP	H	HR	BB	SO	BR/9	ERA	AERA	OAV	OOB	PR	APR	PF	OSB	OCS	FA	E	WPB	DP	FW	PW	BW	BSW	DIF
Bos	115	**8**	21	**7**	1194.1	1273	39	393	329	**12.9**	3.65	**122**	.271	**.333**	86	**102**	104	150	*104*	**.951**	272	56	80	3.9	**8.7**	5.6	—	8.8
Bal	118	3	20	0	1197.2	1296	**18**	382	361	13.2	3.55	117	.274	.338	99	83	97	211	*88*	**.951**	277	67	110	3.7	7.1	**12.4**	—	1.8
NY	119	**8**	19	3	1196.1	**1217**	26	490	**463**	13.3	**3.45**	120	**.262**	.341	**114**	95	96	**131**	*138*	.930	399	89	109	-3.4	8.1	3.9	—	8.8
Cin	100	4	**38**	2	1156.2	1375	**18**	329	270	13.7	4.09	111	.294	.347	28	54	106	145	*112*	.948	273	**30**	100	3.6	4.6	-4.3	—	6.0
Cle	111	6	20	0	1119.1	1297	32	**289**	277	13.1	3.95	114	.288	.337	44	63	104	194	*118*	.950	**261**	46	74	**4.1**	5.4	-1.2	—	-4.8
Was	102	7	34	6	1148.0	1383	27	400	348	14.6	4.01	108	.296	.362	37	39	101	278	***175***	.933	369	68	103	-2.0	3.3	2.0	—	-8.3
Bro	114	4	22	2	1194.2	1417	34	410	256	14.2	4.60	89	.293	.354	-40	-73	95	264	*164*	.936	364	50	99	-1.6	-6.3	-2.7	—	5.6
Pit	112	2	24	2	1153.1	1397	22	318	342	13.9	4.67	89	.297	.350	-48	-69	97	274	*116*	.936	346	54	70	-.6	-5.9	-3.3	—	4.4
Chi	**131**	2	7	1	1197.0	1485	30	433	361	14.9	4.53	98	.303	.367	-31	-12	104	261	*146*	.932	393	61	**112**	-3.0	-1.0	-3.9	—	1.0
Phi	115	4	19	2	1155.1	1415	28	364	253	14.3	4.60	91	.300	.356	-39	-55	97	222	*119*	.944	296	58	72	2.3	-4.7	3.1	—	-11.6
Lou	115	2	20	0	1155.0	1374	40	467	267	15.0	4.41	97	.294	.368	-14	-21	99	245	*145*	.930	399	91	87	-3.7	-1.8	-6.8	—	-.8
StL	110	1	25	1	1136.1	1594	54	454	207	16.8	6.17	71	.329	.394	-236	-221	102	330	*154*	.932	380	63	86	-3.0	-18.9	-6.2	—	-8.4
Total	1362	51	269	26	14004.0	—	—	—	—	14.1	4.30	—	.292	.354	—	—	—	—	—	.939	4029	733	1102	—	—	—	—	—

BATTER-FIELDER WINS	BATTING AVERAGE	ON-BASE PERCENTAGE	SLUGGING AVERAGE	ON-BASE PLUS SLUGGING	ADJUSTED OPS	ADJUSTED BATTER RUNS
Jennings-Bal...... 5.5	Keeler-Bal............424	McGraw-Bal..........471	Lajoie-Phi.............569	Keeler-Bal...........1003	F.Clarke-Lou 167	F.Clarke-Lou 54.5
Davis-NY............ 5.1	F.Clarke-Lou 390	Burkett-Cle............468	Keeler-Bal.............539	F.Clarke-Lou 992	Keeler-Bal.............164	Keeler-Bal.............51.9
F.Clarke-Lou....... 4.1	Burkett-Cle............383	Keeler-Bal.............464	Delahanty-Phi.......538	Delahanty-Phi.......981	Delahanty-Phi.......163	Delahanty-Phi......50.1
Delahanty-Phi.... 4.0	Delahanty-Phi.......377	Jennings-Bal.........463	F.Clarke-Lou 530	Lajoie-Phi.............960	Lajoie-Phi.............156	Lajoie-Phi.............39.3
Keeler-Bal 3.7	Kelley-Bal.............362	F.Clarke-Lou 461	Davis-NY 509	Burkett-Cle............944	Kelley-Bal.............147	Kelley-Bal.............38.7
RUNS	**HITS**	**DOUBLES**	**TRIPLES**	**HOME RUNS**	**TOTAL BASES**	**RUNS BATTED IN**
Hamilton-Bos........152	Keeler-Bal............239	Stenzel-Bal............43	Davis-Pit................28	Duffy-Bos................11	Lajoie-Phi.............310	Davis-NY 135
Keeler-Bal............145	F.Clarke-Lou 205	Lajoie-Phi...............40	Lajoie-Phi...............23	Davis-NY 10	Keeler-Bal.............304	Collins-Bos 132
Griffin-Bro.............136	Delahanty-Phi.......200	Delahanty-Phi.........40	Wallace-Cle 21	Lajoie-Phi..................9	Delahanty-Phi.......285	Duffy-Bos..............129
Jones-Bro 134	Burkett-Cle............198	Wallace-Cle 33	Keeler-Bal...............19	Grady-Phi-StL...........8	F.Clarke-Lou 279	Lajoie-Phi..............127
Jennings-Bal.........133	Lajoie-Phi.............197	Ryan-Chi.................33		Beckley-NY-Cin.........8		Kelley-Bal..............118
BASES ON BALLS	**STOLEN BASES**	**BASE STEALING RUNS**	**FIELDING RUNS-INFIELD**	**FIELDING RUNS-OUTFIELD**	**OUTFIELD ASSISTS**	**CATCHER CS PCT.**
Hamilton-Bos........105	Lange-Chi...............73		Clingman-Lou 30.3	Selbach-Was 12.3	VanHaltren-NY........31	Warner-NY...........52.3
McGraw-Bal............99	Stenzel-Bal 69		Cross-StL.............29.9	Delahanty-Phi........8.8	Ryan-Chi..................28	Grim-Bro...............40.2
Joyce-NY 81	Hamilton-Bos..........66		Jennings-Bal........23.0	Ryan-Chi.................7.4	McCreery-Lou-NY ..23	Zimmer-Cle...........38.9
Griffin-Bro 81	Davis-NY 65		Davis-NY 19.9	VanHaltren-NY.......6.7	Delahanty-Phi.........23	Kittridge-Chi.........33.5
Selbach-Was 80	Keeler-Bal...............64		Werden-Lou.........19.3	Hoy-Cin...................5.1	Jones-Bro 22	
WINS	**WINNING PCT.**	**WINS ABOVE TEAM**	**GAMES STARTED**	**COMPLETE GAMES**	**FEWEST HITS/GAME**	**FEWEST BB/GAME**
Nichols-Bos 31	Klobedanz-Bos 788	Rusie-NY 6.8	Mercer-Was 43	Killen-Pit 38	Seymour-NY 8.07	Young-Cle 1.31
Rusie-NY 28	Nops-Bal...............769	Klobedanz-Bos 5.7	Donahue-StL 42	Griffith-Chi 38	Rusie-NY 8.77	Tannehill-Pit.........1.52
Klobedanz-Bos 26	Corbett-Bal 750	Griffith-Chi 4.3	Killen-Pit 41	Donahue-StL 38	Nichols-Bos 8.85	Nichols-Bos 1.66
Corbett-Bal 24	Nichols-Bos 738	Breitenstein-Cin.....4.3	Nichols-Bos 40	Nichols-Bos 37	Hill-Lou 9.45	Cuppy-Cle............1.70
Breitenstein-Cin......23	Rusie-NY 737	Nops-Bal.................3.8	Kennedy-Bro...........40	Kennedy-Bro...........36	Corbett-Bal 9.49	Killen-Pit 2.03
STRIKEOUTS	**STRIKEOUTS/GAME**	**GAMES**	**SAVES**	**BASE RUNNERS/9**	**ADJUSTED RELIEF RUNS**	**RELIEF RANKING**
Seymour-NY 156	Seymour-NY 4.90	Mercer-Was 47	Nichols-Bos 3	Nichols-Bos 10.59		
McJames-Was......156	McJames-Was.....4.34	Young-Cle 46	Mercer-Was 3	Rusie-NY 11.48		
Corbett-Bal 149	Corbett-Bal 4.28	Nichols-Bos 46		Amole-Bal..........11.57		
Rusie-NY 135	Rusie-NY 3.77	Donahue-StL 46		Cuppy-Cle..........11.80		
Nichols-Bos 127	Nichols-Bos 3.11			Sullivan-Bos.......12.03		
INNINGS PITCHED	**OPPONENTS' AVG.**	**OPPONENTS' OBP**	**EARNED RUN AVERAGE**	**ADJUSTED ERA**	**ADJUSTED STARTER RUNS**	**PITCHER WINS**
Nichols-Bos 368.0	Seymour-NY.........238	Nichols-Bos 291	Rusie-NY 2.54	Nichols-Bos 169	Nichols-Bos 70.4	**Nichols-Bos........ 6.9**
Donahue-StL 348.0	Rusie-NY 254	Rusie-NY 308	Nichols-Bos 2.64	Rusie-NY 163	Rusie-NY 57.9	**Rusie-NY............. 5.9**
Griffith-Chi 343.2	Nichols-Bos 255	Cuppy-Cle.............314	Nops-Bal...............2.81	Nops-Bal...............148	Mercer-Was 33.2	**Mercer-Was........ 3.9**
Kennedy-Bro......343.1	Hill-Lou 268	Young-Cle 318	Corbett-Bal 3.11	Powell-Cle.............142	Breitenstein-Cin...31.4	**Breitenstein-Cin 2.9**
Mercer-Was 342.0	Corbett-Bal 269	Nops-Bal...............319	Powell-Cle............3.16	Cuppy-Cle.............140	Corbett-Bal 31.0	**Seymour-NY....... 2.9**

Clean Beaneaters

The league ruled before the season that pitchers could at no time intentionally deface the baseball, and that runners had to retouch bases when returning—ending the popular practice of simply cutting across the infield. These tactics were meant to clean up the game, but the best move toward making baseball more acceptable to the public was for "clean" teams to win.

This was accomplished when Frank Selee's Boston Beaneaters held off the Orioles to take the NL crown. Kid Nichols led the league in innings and wins, while Hugh Duffy, Fred Tenney, Jimmy Collins, and Billy Hamilton provided good defense as well as overpowering offensive punch—Boston was the last team to surpass 1,000 runs until 1930. Selee expertly combined youth and experience, and Beaneaters owner Arthur Soden challenged his club at midseason by forcing any player fined by an umpire to pay the tariff himself.

Baltimore didn't win despite runaway batting champ Willie Keeler's 44-game hitting streak and big years from Hughie Jennings and John McGraw. The Orioles had the last laugh, however, as they drubbed the Beantown nine in four of five high-scoring Temple Cup games.The Giants took third, with Amos Rusie returned from his holdout (other club owners, hip to Andrew Freedman's penury, kicked in to raise Rusie's salary). Eleventh-place Louisville didn't have much, but they did have .390-hitting Fred Clarke and versatile rookie Honus Wagner. Other 1897 rookies included Roger Bresnahan, Rube Waddell, and Jimmy Sheckard.

Prior to the season Brooklyn suffered the death of manager Dave Foutz, a 147-win pitcher and solid everyday hitter; he three times led his league in games played. Under replacement skipper Billy Barnie, the Bridegrooms improved three spots, to seventh.

The last original National Association player in the NL, Chicago's Cap Anson, retired at a ge 45. Anson left the club at the conclusion of a ten-year contract; Pop had been with the club for nineteen seasons as manager, and twenty-two years as a player. The sympathetic public dubbed the club the Orphans in his absence. He went to New York in 1898, but he lasted just two months at the helm.

As the nineteenth century hurtled to its conclusion, several other of the era's biggest stars, like Roger Connor, Buck Ewing, Silver King, Denny Lyons, and Fred Pfeffer took part in their last major league action.

1896 NATIONAL LEAGUE

TEAM	W	L	T	PCT	GB	HW	HL	R	OR	PA	H	2B	3B	HR	BB	SO	HB	SH	AVG	OBP	SLG	OPS	AOPS	BR	ABR	PF	SB	CS	BSA	BSR
Bal	90	39	3	.698	—	49	16	**995**	662	5323	**1548**	207	**100**	23	386	**201**	**120**	98	**.328**	**.393**	**.429**	**822**	**120**	**153**	**140**	101	**441**			
Cle	80	48	7	.625	9.5	43	19	840	650	5435	1463	207	72	28	436	316	37	106	.301	.363	.391	754	97	29	-18	106	175			
Cin	77	50	1	.606	12	**51**	15	783	**620**	4911	1283	204	73	20	382	226	42	**127**	.294	.357	.388	745	95	9	-38	107	350			
Bos	74	57	1	.565	17	42	24	865	761	5306	1421	175	75	36	414	275	51	118	.301	.364	.393	757	98	29	-17	106	243			
Chi	71	57	4	.555	18.5	42	24	815	804	5118	1311	182	97	34	409	290	35	92	.286	.349	.390	739	95	-8	-37	104	332			
Pit	66	63	2	.512	24	35	31	787	741	5254	1371	169	94	27	387	286	58	108	.292	.353	.385	738	103	-9	25	96	217			
NY	64	67	2	.489	27	39	26	829	821	5225	1383	159	87	40	439	271	53	72	.297	.364	.394	758	107	31	56	97	274			
Phi	62	68	0	.477	28.5	42	27	890	891	5273	1382	**234**	84	**49**	438	297	60	95	.295	.363	.413	776	110	62	73	99	191			
Was	58	73	2	.443	33	38	29	818	920	5315	1328	179	79	45	**516**	365	61	99	.286	.365	.388	753	103	32	32	100	258			
Bro	58	73	2	.443	33	35	28	692	764	5025	1292	174	87	28	344	269	39	94	.284	.340	.379	719	100	-47	-4	94	198			
StL	40	90	1	.308	50.5	27	34	593	929	4988	1162	134	78	37	332	300	35	101	.257	.313	.346	659	81	-154	-128	96	185			
Lou	38	93	3	.290	53	25	37	653	997	5057	1197	142	80	37	371	427	45	53	.261	.322	.351	673	85	-126	-101	96	195			
Total	792	—	—	—	—	468	310	9560	—	62230	16141	2166	1006	404	4854	3523	636	1163	.290	.354	.387	742	—	—	—	—	3059	—	—	—

TEAM	CG	SHO	GR	SV	IP	H	HR	BB	SO	BR/9	ERA	AERA	OAV	OOB	PR	APR	PF	OSB	OCS	FA	E	WPB	DP	FW	PW	BW	BSW	DIF
Bal	115	9	17	1	1168.1	1281	22	339	302	12.7	3.67	116	.277	.331	89	79	98	218	*118*	.945	296	58	114	2.7	6.7	**11.9**	—	4.3
Cle	113	9	24	**5**	1195.2	1363	27	**280**	336	**12.6**	**3.46**	**131**	.285	**.329**	**119**	**136**	104	183	*133*	.949	288	52	**117**	3.6	**11.5**	-1.5	—	2.4
Cin	105	**12**	26	4	1108.0	**1240**	27	310	219	13.0	3.67	125	.281	.335	85	108	106	**167**	*114*	**.951**	**252**	**42**	107	**4.7**	9.2	-3.2	—	2.9
Bos	110	6	24	3	1155.2	1254	57	397	277	13.1	3.78	120	**.275**	.337	75	93	104	228	*175*	.934	368	76	94	-1.7	7.9	-1.4	—	3.7
Chi	**118**	2	15	1	1161.1	1307	30	467	354	14.4	4.44	102	.282	.358	-11	11	104	271	*146*	.933	367	59	115	-1.6	.9	-3.1	—	10.8
Pit	108	8	26	1	1159.1	1286	**18**	439	**362**	13.9	4.30	97	.280	.351	7	-16	96	310	*168*	.941	317	68	103	1.2	-1.4	2.1	—	-.5
NY	104	1	30	2	1136.2	1303	33	403	312	14.0	4.54	92	.286	.352	-24	-46	96	265	*142*	.933	365	93	90	-1.3	-3.9	4.8	—	-1.0
Phi	107	3	25	2	1117.0	1473	39	387	243	15.4	5.20	83	.316	.375	-104	-113	99	245	*148*	.941	313	48	112	1.3	-9.6	6.2	—	-.9
Was	106	2	29	3	1136.2	1435	24	435	292	15.2	4.61	96	.306	.372	-32	-27	101	289	*152*	.927	398	79	99	-3.3	-2.3	2.7	—	-4.6
Bro	97	3	**38**	1	1144.0	1353	39	400	259	14.1	4.25	97	.292	.354	14	-18	95	248	*140*	.945	297	52	104	2.7	-1.5	-.3	—	-8.4
StL	115	1	18	1	1130.2	1448	40	456	279	15.5	5.33	82	.309	.376	-121	-125	100	303	***192***	.936	345	57	73	-.5	-10.6	-10.9	—	-3.1
Lou	108	1	29	4	1148.2	1398	48	541	288	15.9	5.12	84	.298	.381	-98	-103	99	332	*182*	.916	475	82	110	-7.8	-8.7	-8.6	—	-2.4
Total	1306	57	301	28	13762.0	—	—	—	—	14.1	4.36	—	.290	.354	—	—	—	—	—	.938	4081	766	1238	—	—	—	—	—

BATTER-FIELDER WINS	BATTING AVERAGE	ON-BASE PERCENTAGE	SLUGGING AVERAGE	ON-BASE PLUS SLUGGING	ADJUSTED OPS	ADJUSTED BATTER RUNS
Jennings-Bal......6.7	Burkett-Cle............410	Hamilton-Bos........478	Delahanty-Phi.......631	Delahanty-Phi.....1103	Delahanty-Phi.......192	Delahanty-Phi......68.4
Childs-Cle...........6.3	Jennings-Bal.........401	Jennings-Bal..........472	Dahlen-Chi............553	Kelley-Bal............1013	Kelley-Bal..............164	Kelley-Bal.............53.7
Delahanty-Phi....6.0	Delahanty-Phi.......397	Delahanty-Phi.......472	McCreery-Lou........546	Burkett-Cle...........1002	Joyce-Was-NY........162	Joyce-Was-NY......51.8
Dahlen-Chi..........5.5	Keeler-Bal.............386	Joyce-Was-NY......470	Kelley-Bal...............543	Dahlen-Chi.............990	Tiernan-NY...........159	Tiernan-NY.........48.5
Joyce-Was-NY ...4.3	Tiernan-NY...........369	Kelley-Bal..............469	Burkett-Cle............541	Joyce-Was-NY......988	E.Smith-Pit............158	Burkett-Cle...........46.3
RUNS	**HITS**	**DOUBLES**	**TRIPLES**	**HOME RUNS**	**TOTAL BASES**	**RUNS BATTED IN**
Burkett-Cle............160	Burkett-Cle............240	Delahanty-Phi.........44	VanHaltren-NY........21	Joyce-Was-NY.........13	Burkett-Cle............317	Delahanty-Phi.......126
Keeler-Bal.............153	Keeler-Bal.............210	Miller-Cin 38	McCreery-Lou.........21	Delahanty-Phi.........13	Delahanty-Phi.......315	Jennings-Bal.........121
Hamilton-Bos........153	Jennings-Bal.........209	Kelley-Bal................31	Kelley-Bal...............19	Thompson-Phi 12	Kelley-Bal..............282	Duffy-Bos..............113
Kelley-Bal..............148	Delahanty-Phi.......198	Dahlen-Chi..............30	Dahlen-Chi..............19	Connor-StL 11	VanHaltren-NY......272	McKean-Cle..........112
Dahlen-Chi............137	VanHaltren-NY......197		Clarke-Lou 18		Keeler-Bal.............270	
BASES ON BALLS	**STOLEN BASES**	**BASE STEALING RUNS**	**FIELDING RUNS-INFIELD**	**FIELDING RUNS-OUTFIELD**	**OUTFIELD ASSISTS**	**CATCHER CS PCT.**
Hamilton-Bos........110	Kelley-Bal................87		Childs-Cle............38.9	Thompson-Phi 17.5	Thompson-Phi.........28	Peitz-Cin 36.5
Joyce-Was-NY......101	Lange-Chi...............84		Jennings-Bal........31.2	Delahanty-Phi......14.7	VanHaltren-NY........25	Robinson-Bal.......32.5
Childs-Cle.............100	Hamilton-Bos..........83		Corcoran-Bro.......25.9	E.Smith-Pit.............7.9	Donovan-Pit............24	
Kelley-Bal...............91	Miller-Cin 76		Clingman-Lou 23.7	Selbach-Was 7.5	Brodie-Bal..............22	
Tiernan-NY............77	Doyle-Bal.................73		Dahlen-Chi...........21.8	Parrott-StL 7.1		
WINS	**WINNING PCT.**	**WINS ABOVE TEAM**	**GAMES STARTED**	**COMPLETE GAMES**	**FEWEST HITS/GAME**	**FEWEST BB/GAME**
Nichols-Bos 30	Hoffer-Bal 781	Meekin-NY.............8.0	Killen-Pit 50	Killen-Pit 44	Rhines-Cin............8.06	Young-Cle............1.35
Killen-Pit 30	Hemming-Bal........714	Nichols-Bos 7.8	Young-Cle 46	Young-Cle 42	Hawley-Pit............9.10	Clarke-NY............1.54
Young-Cle.................28	Dwyer-Cin.............686	Killen-Pit 7.8	Mercer-Was 45	Mercer-Was 38	Sullivan-NY..........9.13	Dwyer-Cin............1.87
Meekin-NY...............26	Nichols-Bos 682	Mercer-Was 7.1			Friend-Chi.............9.23	Cuppy-Cle............1.89
	Griffith-Chi 676	Griffith-Chi 5.8			Hoffer-Bal 9.23	Griffith-Chi 1.98
STRIKEOUTS	**STRIKEOUTS/GAME**	**GAMES**	**SAVES**	**BASE RUNNERS/9**	**ADJUSTED RELIEF RUNS**	**RELIEF RANKING**
Young-Cle 140	Briggs-Chi...........3.90	Killen-Pit 52	Young-Cle 3	Rhines-Cin.........11.64		
Hawley-Pit.............137	Pond-Bal 3.36	Young-Cle 51	Hill-Lou 2	Cuppy-Cle...........11.82		
Killen-Pit 134	McJames-Was.....3.31	Nichols-Bos 49	Fisher-Cin 2	Klobedanz-Bos ..11.94		
Breitenstein-StL....114	Hawley-Pit............3.26	Hawley-Pit...............49		Young-Cle 11.95		
Meekin-NY.............110	Young-Cle 3.04	Clarke-NY................48		Nichols-Bos 11.97		
INNINGS PITCHED	**OPPONENTS' AVG.**	**OPPONENTS' OBP**	**EARNED RUN AVERAGE**	**ADJUSTED ERA**	**ADJUSTED STARTER RUNS**	**PITCHER WINS**
Killen-Pit 432.1	Rhines-Cin............238	Rhines-Cin............311	Rhines-Cin...........2.45	Rhines-Cin.............188	Nichols-Bos 59.4	**Young-Cle 5.7**
Young-Cle 414.1	Hawley-Pit.............261	Cuppy-Cle.............314	Nichols-Bos 2.83	Nichols-Bos 160	Young-Cle 56.4	**Cuppy-Cle...........5.5**
Hawley-Pit..........378.0	Sullivan-NY...........261	Young-Cle 317	Cuppy-Cle.............3.12	Dwyer-Cin..............146	Cuppy-Cle.............55.0	**Nichols-Bos.........5.4**
Nichols-Bos 372.1	Friend-Chi.............264	Nichols-Bos 317	Dwyer-Cin.............3.15	Cuppy-Cle..............146	Dwyer-Cin.............42.4	**Dwyer-Cin............4.4**
Mercer-Was 366.1	Hoffer-Bal 264	Esper-Bal...............319	Young-Cle 3.24	Young-Cle 140	Hoffer-Bal 35.1	**Hoffer-Bal...........3.9**

Another Bird Victory

To aid the league's pitchers, the NL passed a rule allowing them to hide the baseball before or during their delivery. At least partially as a result, scoring decreased again, this time by half a run per game per team. The decrease in offense didn't stop everyone. Jesse Burkett's 240 hits set a mark that stood until 1911. Meanwhile, Hughie Jennings got hit by 51 pitches, an all-time high; he broke Curt Welch's 1891 record by 15. (Welch died in 1896, beset by the ravages of the bottle.)

The last player to hold out against wearing a fielder's glove, top shortstop Bid McPhee, finally gave in for 1896. The new innovation made him an even better shortstop. Meanwhile, two men who would go on to greater fame five years later, in the new American League, debuted: Fielder Jones, for Brooklyn, and Nap Lajoie, with Philadelphia.

Baltimore won its third straight league title. The club's offensive prowess put some distance between them and second-place Cleveland. Shortstop Jennings was an offensive and defensive force for the Orioles, and with the help of Willie Keeler, Joe Kelley, and Jack Doyle, the club batted .328, which was 27 points higher than the nearest rival. The Orioles scored 105 more runs and stole 91 more bases than anyone else. (Baltimore's 441 steals have never been surpassed, but there is a reason: through 1897 scorers also credited a stolen base if a runner advanced on a flyball or went two bases on a hit or infield out, as long as a palpable attempt was made to retire him.)

Cleveland again had Cy Young and Nig Cuppy on the hill, but the Spiders had little offense beyond the big three of Burkett, Ed McKean, and Cupid Childs. Surprising Cincinnati, under Buck Ewing, finished third, with Billy Rhines and Frank Dwyer finishing first and fourth in ERA. New York didn't contend, because mound mainstay Amos Rusie sat out the year rather than take a less-than-deserved pay cut.

The Orioles took revenge on Cleveland in their second Temple Cup match-up, sweeping them in four straight, with the *coup de grace* a 5-0 shutout in the finale. It was the only time that the first-place team in the regular season beat the second-place team in the four Temple Cup series.

Last-place Louisville increased its attendance by 30,000, but still drew barely 2,000 per game. The league's overall gate rose just 11,000, but the 2,900,973 tickets sold ranked as the highest total for any one league until 1904.

1895 NATIONAL LEAGUE

TEAM	W	L	T	PCT	GB	HW	HL	R	OR	PA	H	2B	3B	HR	BB	SO	HB	SH	AVG	OBP	SLG	OPS	AOPS	BR	ABR	PF	SB	CS	BSA	BSR
Bal	87	43	2	.669	—	**54**	12	1009	**646**	5311	1530	235	89	25	355	243	**106**	125	.324	.384	.427	811	110	94	68	103	310			
Cle	84	46	2	.646	3	47	13	921	725	5304	1433	194	69	29	476	365	49	87	.305	.375	.395	770	97	28	-22	106	188			
Phi	78	53	2	.595	9.5	51	21	**1068**	957	5689	**1664**	**272**	73	**61**	463	262	69	120	**.330**	**.394**	**.450**	**844**	**122**	**167**	**163**	100	276			
Chi	72	58	3	.554	15	43	26	866	854	5252	1401	171	85	55	422	344	42	80	.298	.361	.405	766	95	3	-50	107	260			
Bro	71	60	3	.542	16.5	43	22	879	838	5284	1346	191	78	41	397	319	63	67	.283	.346	.382	728	99	-64	6	92	184			
Bos	71	60	2	.542	16.5	48	19	911	829	5434	1377	198	57	54	505	**239**	52	**127**	.290	.364	.390	754	91	-3	-67	108	200			
Pit	71	61	3	.538	17	44	21	815	799	5226	1355	192	89	27	378	301	65	106	.290	.351	.386	737	99	-46	2	95	257			
Cin	66	64	2	.508	21	42	22	903	854	5190	1395	235	**105**	36	414	249	36	56	.298	.359	.416	775	99	18	-15	104	**326**			
NY	66	65	1	.504	21.5	40	27	852	834	5127	1324	191	90	32	454	292	30	38	.288	.355	.389	744	98	-30	-11	98	292			
Was	43	85	5	.336	43	31	34	840	1052	5258	1326	209	101	55	**522**	403	52	69	.287	.366	.412	778	105	33	44	99	238			
StL	39	92	5	.298	48.5	25	41	752	1036	5296	1356	155	88	39	388	283	30	64	.282	.339	.375	714	89	-97	-86	99	208			
Lou	35	96	2	.267	52.5	19	38	698	1090	5205	1320	171	73	34	346	323	77	58	.279	.339	.368	707	92	-103	-51	94	156			
Total	799	—	—	—	—	487	296	10514	—	63576	16827	2414	997	488	5120	3623	671	997	.296	.361	.400	761	—	—	—	—	2895	—	—	—

TEAM	CG	SHO	GR	SV	IP	H	HR	BB	SO	BR/9	ERA	AERA	OAV	OOB	PR	APR	PF	OSB	OCS	FA	E	WPB	DP	FW	PW	BW	BSW	DIF
Bal	104	**10**	30	4	1134.1	**1216**	31	430	244	13.4	**3.80**	125	**.271**	.340	**123**	119	100	**155**	*149*	**.946**	**288**	**43**	108	**5.3**	9.6	5.5	—	1.6
Cle	109	6	25	3	1151.2	1284	34	**350**	330	**13.0**	3.92	**127**	.278	**.334**	110	**130**	104	207	*130*	.936	351	84	77	1.7	**10.5**	-1.8	—	8.5
Phi	106	2	29	**7**	1161.0	1467	36	485	330	15.6	5.47	87	.304	.375	-89	-89	100	256	*110*	.933	369	68	93	.9	-7.2	**13.2**	—	5.6
Chi	**119**	3	14	1	1150.2	1422	38	432	297	15.0	4.67	109	.300	.366	13	49	107	254	*114*	.928	401	72	**113**	-.9	4.0	-4.1	—	8.0
Bro	104	5	29	6	1159.2	1366	42	397	218	14.0	4.93	89	.289	.350	-20	-75	92	188	*143*	.941	326	56	97	3.5	-6.1	.5	—	7.6
Bos	117	4	18	4	1185.1	1376	56	367	377	13.6	4.25	120	.287	.343	69	102	107	196	*140*	.935	365	76	106	1.1	8.3	-5.4	—	1.5
Pit	107	4	29	6	1179.2	1279	**19**	500	383	14.2	4.10	110	.273	.353	89	55	94	280	*144*	.930	394	83	95	-.2	4.5	.2	—	.6
Cin	97	2	35	6	1147.1	1451	39	362	245	14.7	4.81	103	.304	.361	-5	16	104	227	*145*	.931	377	54	112	.3	1.3	-1.2	—	.6
NY	115	6	18	1	1147.1	1359	34	415	**409**	14.3	4.51	103	.291	.354	33	16	97	247	*157*	.922	438	76	106	-3.1	1.3	-.9	—	3.2
Was	99	0	**38**	5	1111.1	1515	55	470	261	16.6	5.26	91	.321	.390	-60	-58	101	299	***191***	.917	450	53	97	-3.6	-4.7	3.6	—	-16.2
StL	106	1	30	1	1161.1	1572	64	443	284	16.0	5.73	84	.319	.381	-123	-116	101	320	*149*	.930	383	45	94	.6	-9.4	-7.0	—	-10.7
Lou	104	3	34	1	1117.1	1520	40	469	245	16.5	5.90	78	.320	.388	-139	-164	97	266	*126*	.913	477	79	104	-5.2	-13.3	-4.1	—	-7.9
Total	1287	46	329	45	13807.0	—	—	—	—	14.7	4.77	—	.296	.361	—	—	—	—	—	.930	4619	789	1202	—	—	—	—	—

BATTER-FIELDER WINS
- **Jennings-Bal......6.3**
- **Thompson-Phi ...5.0**
- **Delahanty-Phi....4.6**
- **Griffin-Bro...........3.8**
- **G.Davis-NY.........3.2**

BATTING AVERAGE
- Burkett-Cle............405
- Delahanty-Phi.......404
- Clements-Phi.........394
- Thompson-Phi......392
- Lange-Chi.............389

ON-BASE PERCENTAGE
- Delahanty-Phi.......500
- Hamilton-Phi.........490
- Burkett-Cle...........482
- McGraw-Bal...........459
- Lange-Chi.............456

SLUGGING AVERAGE
- Thompson-Phi......654
- Delahanty-Phi.......617
- Clements-Phi........612
- Lange-Chi.............575
- Kelley-Bal.............546

ON-BASE PLUS SLUGGING
- Delahanty-Phi.....1117
- Thompson-Phi....1085
- Lange-Chi...........1032
- Kelley-Bal...........1003
- Burkett-Cle..........1001

ADJUSTED OPS
- Delahanty-Phi.......186
- Thompson-Phi......177
- Stenzel-Pit............160
- Lange-Chi.............155
- Hamilton-Phi.........154

ADJUSTED BATTER RUNS
- Delahanty-Phi.:....68.7
- Thompson-Phi.....56.9
- Hamilton-Phi........50.4
- Stenzel-Pit...........50.3
- Burkett-Cle...........44.2

RUNS
- Hamilton-Phi.........166
- Keeler-Bal.............162
- Jennings-Bal.........159
- Burkett-Cle............153
- Delahanty-Phi........149

HITS
- Burkett-Cle............225
- Keeler-Bal.............213
- Thompson-Phi......211
- Jennings-Bal.........204
- Hamilton-Phi.........201

DOUBLES
- Delahanty-Phi.........49
- Thompson-Phi........45
- Jennings-Bal...........41
- Stenzel-Pit..............38
- Griffin-Bro...............38

TRIPLES
- Selbach-Was..........22
- Tiernan-NY.............21
- Thompson-Phi........21
- Cooley-StL..............20

HOME RUNS
- Thompson-Phi........18
- Joyce-Was..............17
- Clements-Phi..........13
- Delahanty-Phi.........11

TOTAL BASES
- Thompson-Phi......352
- Delahanty-Phi.......296
- Burkett-Cle...........288
- McKean-Cle...........284
- Kelley-Bal.............283

RUNS BATTED IN
- Thompson-Phi......165
- Kelley-Bal.............134
- Brodie-Bal.............134
- Jennings-Bal.........125
- McKean-Cle..........119

BASES ON BALLS
- Joyce-Was..............96
- Hamilton-Phi...........96
- Griffin-Bro...............93
- Delahanty-Phi.........86
- Kelley-Bal................77

STOLEN BASES
- Hamilton-Phi...........97
- Lange-Chi...............67
- McGraw-Bal.............61
- Kelley-Bal...............54

BASE STEALING RUNS

FIELDING RUNS-INFIELD
- Jennings-Bal........37.4
- Dahlen-Chi...........34.7
- Fuller-NY.............33.1
- Cross-Phi.............32.4
- Collins-Bos-Lou ...19.3

FIELDING RUNS-OUTFIELD
- Selbach-Was.......14.6
- Clarke-Lou...........13.2
- Thompson-Phi.....12.0
- Griffin-Bro...........11.8
- Miller-Cin.............10.4

OUTFIELD ASSISTS
- Abbey-Was............34
- Thompson-Phi.......31
- Bannon-Bos...........31
- Lange-Chi..............28
- VanHaltren-NY........26

CATCHER CS PCT.
- Robinson-Bal......48.2
- Clements-Phi.......32.9

WINS
- Young-Cle..............35
- Hoffer-Bal..............31
- Hawley-Pit..............31

WINNING PCT.
- Hoffer-Bal............838
- Young-Cle............778
- Rhines-Cin...........655

WINS ABOVE TEAM
- Hoffer-Bal............11.0
- Young-Cle............10.7
- Griffith-Chi.............5.7
- Rhines-Cin..............5.1
- Nichols-Bos 4.8

GAMES STARTED
- Breitenstein-StL.....51
- Hawley-Pit..............50
- Rusie-NY...............47
- Nichols-Bos 43
- Griffith-Chi 41

COMPLETE GAMES
- Breitenstein-StL......47
- Hawley-Pit..............44
- Nichols-Bos 43
- Rusie-NY...............42
- Griffith-Chi 39

FEWEST HITS/GAME
- Foreman-Pit..........8.44
- Hoffer-Bal 8.48
- Rusie-NY.............8.79
- Young-Cle............8.84
- Maul-Was.............9.02

FEWEST BB/GAME
- Young-Cle 1.83
- Clarke-NY.............1.92
- Nichols-Bos 2.07
- Staley-StL............2.21
- Taylor-Phi.............2.23

STRIKEOUTS
- Rusie-NY..............201
- Nichols-Bos 148
- Hawley-Pit.............142
- Breitenstein-StL....131
- Young-Cle.............121

STRIKEOUTS/GAME
- Rusie-NY 4.60
- McGill-Phi 4.32
- Foreman-Pit.........3.48
- Stivetts-Bos 3.43
- Nichols-Bos 3.41

GAMES
- Hawley-Pit..............56
- Breitenstein-StL......55
- Rusie-NY................49
- Nichols-Bos 48

SAVES
- Parrott-Cin 3
- Nichols-Bos 3
- Beam-Phi...................3

BASE RUNNERS/9
- McMahon-Bal 10.74
- Young-Cle..........10.86
- Maul-Was...........11.68
- Nichols-Bos 12.19
- Hawley-Pit..........12.23

ADJUSTED RELIEF RUNS

RELIEF RANKING

INNINGS PITCHED
- Hawley-Pit.........444.1
- Breitenstein-StL .438.2
- Rusie-NY 393.1
- Nichols-Bos 390.2
- Young-Cle 369.2

OPPONENTS' AVG.
- Foreman-Pit..........245
- Hoffer-Bal 246
- Rusie-NY 252
- Young-Cle.............253
- Maul-Was..............257

OPPONENTS' OBP
- Young-Cle 294
- Maul-Was..............310
- Nichols-Bos 319
- Hawley-Pit.............320
- Cuppy-Cle.............323

EARNED RUN AVERAGE
- Maul-Was............2.45
- McMahon-Bal 2.94
- Hawley-Pit...........3.18
- Hoffer-Bal 3.21
- Foreman-Pit.........3.22

ADJUSTED ERA
- Maul-Was.............195
- Young-Cle.............153
- Nichols-Bos 149
- Hoffer-Bal 148
- Hawley-Pit.............142

ADJUSTED STARTER RUNS
- Young-Cle 73.3
- Nichols-Bos 67.4
- Hawley-Pit............66.2
- Hoffer-Bal 55.9
- Cuppy-Cle............51.1

PITCHER WINS
- **Hawley-Pit..........7.4**
- **Young-Cle...........6.9**
- **Cuppy-Cle...........5.2**
- **Nichols-Bos.........5.2**
- **Hoffer-Bal...........4.6**

Refinement of the Formula

Pitchers got some relief in 1895, as scoring per game dipped nearly a run per team. The tight defense and strong teamwork of Baltimore led to as many imitators, as did their umpire-baiting and violence. For the first time the NL regulated the size and weight of fielders' gloves, except for those worn by catchers and first basemen. The league also inaugurated the infield fly rule to keep clubs from intentionally dropping popups. Those rules still couldn't keep the game from getting dirtier, though. The two most unscrupulous clubs, the Orioles and Cleveland Spiders, finished 1-2 in the league. Both clubs also had great talent, not just hardscrabble rowdies.

Despite injuries to many key players, the Orioles sported the best pitching (led by Bill Hoffer) and the second-most productive hitters; Willie Keeler and Hugh Jennings finished 2-3 in runs. Cleveland was carried by batting champ Jesse Burkett, shortstop Ed McKean, and hurlers Cy Young and Nig Cuppy. Spiders pitching overcame Baltimore bats to win the Temple Cup, 4 games to 1.

Boston fell to fifth but debuted future third base star Jimmy Collins, while shortstop Jack Glasscock, the 1890 batting champ, tumbled out of the league at age 36. First baseman Harry Davis, who would later win four straight AL home run titles, also made his first appearance.

Nine teams finished over .500, with three former American Association members, who barely drew flies, bringing up the rear. Parity and a decent pennant race raised league attendance 16 percent, due to huge gains in Boston, Chicago, Cincinnati, and especially Philadelphia. The Phillies were the NL's biggest draw—becoming the first team to pass 400,000 fans—and once again featured the league's highest-scoring offense.

Several clubs had by now adopted the monikers by which we know still them, including the Cincinnati Reds, Pittsburgh Pirates, New York Giants, and Philadelphia Phillies—although the league still had its Boston Beaneaters, Chicago Colts, and Brooklyn Bridegrooms (or Superbas, take your pick). Two NL clubs also carried names that their AL successors would adopt: the Orioles and the St. Louis Browns.

1894 NATIONAL LEAGUE

TEAM	W	L	T	PCT	GB	HW	HL	R	OR	PA	H	2B	3B	HR	BB	SO	HB	SH	AVG	OBP	SLG	OPS	AOPS	BR	ABR	PF	SB	CS	BSA	BSR
Bal	89	39	1	.695	—	**52**	15	1171	819	5564	1647	271	**150**	33	516	**200**	**98**	151	.343	**.418**	.483	**901**	116	**174**	124	104	324			
NY	88	44	7	.667	3	49	17	962	**801**	5480	1469	199	96	45	489	219	32	80	.301	.369	.409	778	92	-69	-63	99	326			
Bos	83	49	1	.629	8	44	19	**1220**	1002	5657	1658	**272**	94	**103**	535	261	47	64	.331	.401	**.484**	885	109	138	54	108	241			
Phi	71	57	4	.555	18	48	20	1179	995	5779	**1780**	259	137	40	508	254	60	122	**.350**	.415	.478	893	**122**	166	**195**	98	285			
Bro	70	61	4	.534	20.5	42	24	1024	1020	5452	1514	231	130	42	467	295	34	100	.312	.376	.439	815	108	-3	71	93	282			
Cle	68	61	1	.527	21.5	35	24	932	896	5336	1442	241	90	37	471	301	24	77	.303	.368	.414	782	89	-57	-91	104	220			
Pit	65	65	3	.500	25	46	28	965	981	5376	1465	223	125	48	444	210	69	**163**	.312	.379	.443	822	103	10	21	99	257			
Chi	57	75	5	.432	34	35	30	1056	1080	5643	1574	268	87	65	507	306	38	76	.313	.381	.440	821	97	15	-40	106	**332**			
StL	56	76	1	.424	35	34	32	771	953	5204	1320	171	113	54	442	289	40	112	.286	.354	.408	762	87	-107	-107	100	190			
Cin	55	75	4	.423	35	38	28	936	1108	5375	1407	228	71	61	517	255	43	62	.296	.370	.412	782	89	-53	-83	103	223			
Was	45	87	0	.341	46	32	30	882	1122	5325	1317	218	118	59	**617**	375	71	56	.287	.381	.425	806	101	-6	24	97	249			
Lou	36	94	1	.277	54	24	37	698	1019	5021	1216	173	89	42	355	368	54	93	.269	.330	.375	705	78	-207	-155	93	219			
Total	799	—	—	—	—	479	304	11796	—	65212	17809	2754	1300	629	5868	3333	610	1156	.309	.379	.435	814	—	—	—	—	3148	—	—	—

TEAM	CG	SHO	GR	SV	IP	H	HR	BB	SO	BR/9	ERA	AERA	OAV	OOB	PR	APR	PF	OSB	OCS	FA	E	WPB	DP	FW	PW	BW	BSW	DIF
Bal	97	1	**36**	**11**	1116.1	1371	**31**	472	275	15.2	5.00	109	.299	.371	41	56	103	202	*115*	**.944**	**293**	60	105	**5.7**	4.3	9.5	—	5.6
NY	113	5	30	5	1230.0	**1310**	37	546	**403**	**13.8**	**3.82**	**138**	**.271**	**.349**	**206**	**197**	99	256	***187***	.923	454	102	103	-1.8	**15.1**	-4.8	—	13.5
Bos	108	3	25	2	1166.0	1529	89	**411**	262	15.3	5.41	105	.314	.372	-11	31	107	223	*146*	.925	415	76	120	-.6	2.4	4.1	—	11.1
Phi	103	3	35	4	1151.2	1522	62	479	266	16.2	5.63	91	.315	.385	-38	-68	96	285	*118*	.934	351	82	114	2.9	-5.2	**14.9**	—	-5.6
Bro	106	3	30	5	1171.1	1465	41	558	290	16.0	5.56	89	.303	.383	-30	-85	93	294	*145*	.928	393	103	85	1.0	-6.5	5.4	—	4.6
Cle	106	**6**	28	2	1124.1	1390	54	435	254	14.9	4.97	110	.301	.366	45	60	103	**161**	*150*	.935	344	71	107	2.9	4.6	-7.0	—	3.0
Pit	106	2	31	0	1170.2	1563	39	466	308	15.9	5.62	93	.318	.381	-38	-52	98	261	*158*	.936	355	63	106	2.8	-4.0	1.6	—	-.4
Chi	**118**	0	20	0	1163.0	1575	43	569	284	17.1	5.72	98	.321	.398	-51	-12	106	323	*144*	.918	458	68	115	-2.4	-.9	-3.1	—	-2.7
StL	114	2	24	0	1161.0	1418	48	500	319	15.2	5.29	102	.299	.371	5	15	102	257	*173*	.923	426	79	109	-1.2	1.1	-8.2	—	-1.7
Cin	112	4	22	3	1165.1	1615	85	500	223	16.8	5.99	92	.326	.394	-85	-57	104	273	*155*	.925	430	**54**	122	-1.3	-4.4	-6.4	—	2.0
Was	102	0	35	4	1107.0	1573	59	446	190	16.9	5.51	96	.331	.396	-23	-30	99	355	*163*	.908	499	82	81	-5.6	-2.3	1.8	—	-15.0
Lou	114	2	17	1	1104.2	1478	41	486	259	16.4	5.50	93	.318	.387	-21	-52	96	258	***187***	.919	435	67	**131**	-2.1	-4.0	-11.9	—	-11.1
Total	1299	31	333	37	13831.1	—	—	—	—	15.8	5.33	—	.309	.379	—	—	—	—	—	.927	4853	907	1298	—	—	—	—	—

BATTER-FIELDER WINS	BATTING AVERAGE	ON-BASE PERCENTAGE	SLUGGING AVERAGE	ON-BASE PLUS SLUGGING	ADJUSTED OPS	ADJUSTED BATTER RUNS
Hamilton-Phi...... 4.5	Duffy-Bos.............440	Hamilton-Phi.........522	Thompson-Phi......696	Duffy-Bos............1196	Thompson-Phi......181	Hamilton-Phi........65.9
Duffy-Bos............ 4.5	Turner-Phi.............418	Kelley-Bal..............502	Duffy-Bos..............694	Thompson-Phi....1161	Joyce-Was............179	Duffy-Bos.............63.8
Dahlen-Chi.......... 4.5	Thompson-Phi......415	Duffy-Bos..............502	Joyce-Was............648	Joyce-Was..........1143	Duffy-Bos..............172	Thompson-Phi.....56.6
Joyce-Was.......... 4.3	E.Delahanty-Phi....404	Joyce-Was............496	Kelley-Bal..............602	Kelley-Bal............1104	Kelley-Bal..............158	Kelley-Bal.............54.9
E.Delahanty-Phi 4.2	Hamilton-Phi.........403	Childs-Cle.............475	E.Delahanty-Phi....584	E.Delahanty-Phi..1059	E.Delahanty-Phi....158	Joyce-Was...........52.4

RUNS	HITS	DOUBLES	TRIPLES	HOME RUNS	TOTAL BASES	RUNS BATTED IN
Hamilton-Phi.........198	Duffy-Bos.............237	Duffy-Bos...............51	Reitz-Bal.................31	Duffy-Bos................18	Duffy-Bos..............374	Thompson-Phi......147
Kelley-Bal.............165	Hamilton-Phi.........225	Kelley-Bal...............48	Thompson-Phi........28	Lowe-Bos................17	Lowe-Bos..............319	Duffy-Bos..............145
Keeler-Bal.............165	Keeler-Bal.............219	Wilmot-Chi..............45	Treadway-Bro..........26	Joyce-Was..............17	Thompson-Phi......314	E.Delahanty-Phi....133
Duffy-Bos..............160	Lowe-Bos..............212		Connor-NY-StL.......25	Dahlen-Chi..............15	Kelley-Bal..............305	Cross-Phi..............132
Lowe-Bos..............158			Brouthers-Bal..........23		Keeler-Bal.............305	Wilmot-Chi............130

BASES ON BALLS	STOLEN BASES	BASE STEALING RUNS	FIELDING RUNS-INFIELD	FIELDING RUNS-OUTFIELD	OUTFIELD ASSISTS	CATCHER CS PCT.
Hamilton-Phi.........128	Hamilton-Phi.........100		Jennings-Bal........33.0	Bannon-Bos.........16.7	Bannon-Bos............43	Zimmer-Cle..........50.9
Kelley-Bal.............107	McGraw-Bal............78		McPhee-Cin.........30.0	E.Delahanty-Phi...12.5	VanHaltren-NY........30	Mack-Pit...............36.5
Childs-Cle.............107	Wilmot-Chi..............76		Dahlen-Chi...........25.7	McCarthy-Bos........9.4	Hoy-Cin...................30	Robinson-Bal.......35.7
	Lange-Chi...............66		Cross-Phi.............25.0	Abbey-Was 7.7	McCarthy-Bos.........28	McGuire-Was.......31.4
	T.Brown-Lou 66		Reitz-Bal..............20.5	Lange-Chi.............6.7	Duffy-Bos................27	

WINS	WINNING PCT.	WINS ABOVE TEAM	GAMES STARTED	COMPLETE GAMES	FEWEST HITS/GAME	FEWEST BB/GAME
Rusie-NY................36	Meekin-NY............786	Meekin-NY.............9.4	Rusie-NY 50	Breitenstein-StL......46	Rusie-NY 8.64	Young-Cle 2.33
Meekin-NY..............33	McMahon-Bal 758	Breitenstein-StL.....7.2	Breitenstein-StL......50	Rusie-NY 45	Meekin-NY...........8.91	Menefee-Lou-Pit ..2.48
Nichols-Bos 32	Rusie-NY 735	Rusie-NY 7.1	Meekin-NY..............49	Young-Cle 44	Stein-Bro..............9.98	Gleason-StL-Bal ..2.54
Breitenstein-StL......27	Nichols-Bos 711	Nichols-Bos 6.8	Young-Cle 47	Meekin-NY..............41	Breitenstein-StL .10.00	Staley-Bos 2.63
		Stein-Bro................6.4	Nichols-Bos 46	Nichols-Bos 40	Clarkson-Cle......10.33	Nichols-Bos 2.68

STRIKEOUTS	STRIKEOUTS/GAME	GAMES	SAVES	BASE RUNNERS/9	ADJUSTED RELIEF RUNS	RELIEF RANKING
Rusie-NY 195	Rusie-NY 3.95	Breitenstein-StL......56	Mullane-Bal-Cle........4	Rusie-NY 12.79		
Breitenstein-StL....140	Hawke-Bal 2.97	Rusie-NY 54	Mercer-Was 3	Meekin-NY.........12.94		
Meekin-NY............137	Wadsworth-Lou....2.97	Meekin-NY..............53	Hawke-Bal 3	Clarkson-Cle......13.08		
Hawley-StL 120	Meekin-NY...........2.95	Hawley-StL 53		Young-Cle..........13.19		
Nichols-Bos 113	Chamberlain-Cin..2.89	Young-Cle 52		Nichols-Bos 13.67		

INNINGS PITCHED	OPPONENTS' AVG.	OPPONENTS' OBP	EARNED RUN AVERAGE	ADJUSTED ERA	ADJUSTED STARTER RUNS	PITCHER WINS
Breitenstein-StL .447.1	Rusie-NY 250	Rusie-NY 331	Rusie-NY 2.78	Rusie-NY 189	Rusie-NY 118.0	**Rusie-NY.......... 10.2**
Rusie-NY 444.0	Meekin-NY............256	Meekin-NY............333	Meekin-NY...........3.70	Meekin-NY............142	Meekin-NY............80.9	**Meekin-NY......... 6.2**
Meekin-NY.........418.0	Stein-Bro..............278	Clarkson-Cle.........336	Mercer-Was 3.85	Young-Cle 139	Young-Cle 65.3	**Young-Cle 5.0**
Young-Cle 408.2	Breitenstein-StL 279	Young-Cle 338	Young-Cle 3.94	Mercer-Was 137	Mercer-Was 40.8	**Mercer-Was 3.8**
Nichols-Bos 407.0	Clarkson-Cle.........285	Nichols-Bos 346	Taylor-Phi.............4.08	McMahon-Bal 130	Nichols-Bos 38.8	**Taylor-Phi 3.5**

Bird-Brained Baseball

Offense continued to rise. The league average went to a stratospheric .309, and clubs scored 7.38 runs per game, a mark that has never been bettered. Philadelphia's Billy Hamilton scored the most runs in history—198—and his .522 on-base percentage set a new standard. Boston's Hugh Duffy hit .440, an all-time high, and his record .694 slugging percentage lasted until 1921. Heinie Reitz smacked 31 triples to tie Dave Orr's 1886 mark, and that record wasn't broken until 1912. Bobby Lowe of Boston became the first player in history to homer four times in one game. The 629 home runs hit during the season would not be surpassed until 1925.

The move toward increased offense came in spite of a rule change; as of 1894, foul bunts were counted as strikes. Meanwhile, pity the pitchers. St. Louis' Ted Breitenstein was tagged for 497 hits and 320 runs, figures of terror that no moundsman has been unlucky enough to match. (Breitenstein still managed to win 27 times.) New York's Amos Rusie was the only pitcher with an ERA under 3.00.

Fans responded to the offense—the NL set another attendance record—but the game was changing for the worse. Greedy owners paid lower salaries, and as payoffs got lower, competition got tougher. Rule-breaking, fistfights, and umpire intimidation (and sometimes outright assault) became the rule.

The kings of this new era were the 1894 champion Baltimore Orioles, who were not above tripping or spiking opponents or stomping on an umpire's toes. Manager Ned Hanlon brought together a talented, smart, and tough club, including Joe Kelley, Hughie Jennings, Willie Keeler, Reitz, and John McGraw; these players would do anything, legal or not, to win. And as the Birds succeeded, other clubs followed. New York was a close second, with an ERA that was a full run better than any other team, led by strikeout pitchers Rusie and Joe Meekin. Boston was third, leading the league with 1,220 runs, but the club's pitchers allowed more than 1,000. Despite scoring 209 fewer runs while finishing second behind Baltimore, New York blasted the Orioles in the inaugural Temple Cup match-up. The Giants won all four games, including a 16-3 massacre in the last game.

While alcohol-related disease killed Ed Williamson and King Kelly, other players ended their careers: Pete Browning, John Clarkson, Charlie Comiskey, and John Ward. Future stars Fred Clarke and Bobby Wallace debuted.

1893 NATIONAL LEAGUE

TEAM	W	L	T	PCT	GB	HW	HL	R	OR	PA	H	2B	3B	HR	BB	SO	HB	SH	AVG	OBP	SLG	OPS	AOPS	BR	ABR	PF	SB	CS	BSA	BSR
Bos	86	43	2	.667	—	49	15	1008	795	5285	1358	178	50	65	**561**	292	46	—	.290	.372	.391	763	99	58	-9	108	243			
Pit	81	48	2	.628	5	**54**	19	970	**766**	5433	1447	176	**127**	37	537	274	62	—	.299	**.377**	.411	788	116	94	**114**	98	210			
Cle	73	55	1	.570	12.5	47	22	976	839	5309	1425	222	98	32	532	**229**	30	—	.300	.374	.408	782	106	87	33	106	252			
Phi	72	57	4	.558	14	43	22	**1011**	841	5690	**1553**	**246**	90	**80**	468	335	**71**	—	**.301**	.368	**.431**	**799**	**117**	**111**	112	100	202			
NY	68	64	4	.515	19.5	49	20	941	845	5418	1424	182	101	61	504	281	56	—	.293	.366	.410	776	110	67	62	101	**299**			
Cin	65	63	3	.508	20.5	37	27	759	814	5196	1195	161	65	29	531	257	48	—	.259	.341	.341	682	84	-88	-106	102	238			
Bro	65	63	2	.508	20.5	43	24	775	845	5024	1200	173	83	45	473	296	40	—	.266	.341	.371	712	97	-47	-10	95	213			
Bal	60	70	0	.462	26.5	36	24	820	893	5260	1281	164	86	27	539	323	70	—	.275	.359	.365	724	95	-12	-25	102	233			
Chi	56	71	1	.441	29	38	34	829	874	5166	1299	186	93	32	466	261	36	—	.279	.349	.379	728	99	-21	-9	99	255			
StL	57	75	3	.432	30.5	40	30	745	829	5466	1288	152	98	10	524	251	63	—	.264	.343	.341	684	86	-92	-94	100	250			
Lou	50	75	1	.400	34	24	28	759	942	5105	1185	177	73	19	485	306	54	—	.260	.338	.343	681	92	-93	-30	92	203			
Was	40	89	1	.310	46	21	27	722	1032	5328	1258	180	83	23	523	237	63	—	.265	.346	.353	699	92	-62	-40	97	154			
Total	785	—	—	—	—	481	292	10315	—	63680	15913	2197	1047	460	6143	3342	639	—	.280	.356	.379	736	—	—	—	—	2752	—	—	—

TEAM	CG	SHO	GR	SV	IP	H	HR	BB	SO	BR/9	ERA	AERA	OAV	OOB	PR	APR	PF	OSB	OCS	FA	E	WPB	DP	FW	PW	BW	BSW	DIF
Bos	**114**	2	20	2	1163.2	1314	66	402	253	**13.6**	4.43	111	.277	**.339**	30	60	106	**176**	*91*	.936	353	62	118	1.8	4.9	-.7	—	15.5
Pit	104	**8**	29	2	1167.0	**1232**	29	504	280	13.8	4.08	111	.263	.342	75	61	98	237	*133*	.938	347	77	112	2.1	5.0	**9.3**	—	.0
Cle	110	2	21	2	1140.1	1361	35	**356**	242	13.8	4.20	**116**	.288	.342	59	82	105	199	*151*	.929	395	98	92	-.9	6.7	2.7	—	.5
Phi	107	4	28	2	1189.0	1357	30	522	286	14.8	4.68	98	.279	.357	-2	-13	98	186	*108*	**.944**	**318**	**60**	121	**4.1**	-1.1	9.2	—	-4.7
NY	111	6	26	4	1211.1	1271	36	581	**395**	14.2	4.29	108	**.262**	.347	49	48	100	238	*174*	.927	432	137	95	-1.8	3.9	5.1	—	-5.2
Cin	97	4	**34**	**5**	1172.0	1305	38	549	258	14.8	4.55	105	.274	.357	15	29	103	211	*109*	.943	321	89	**138**	3.6	2.4	-8.7	—	3.7
Bro	109	3	23	3	1154.0	1262	41	547	297	14.4	4.55	97	.270	.352	15	-17	95	233	*118*	.930	385	83	88	-.2	-1.4	-.8	—	3.4
Bal	104	1	26	2	1123.2	1325	29	534	275	15.2	4.97	95	.285	.364	-39	-29	102	248	*100*	.929	384	111	95	-.1	-2.4	-2.0	—	-.4
Chi	101	4	31	**5**	1117.1	1278	**26**	553	273	15.3	4.81	96	.279	.365	-18	-24	99	242	*148*	.922	421	79	92	-2.5	-2.0	-.7	—	-2.3
StL	**114**	3	22	4	1207.0	1292	38	542	301	14.1	**4.06**	**116**	.266	.346	**80**	**87**	101	276	*152*	.930	398	107	110	-.0	**7.1**	-7.7	—	-8.3
Lou	113	4	13	1	1080.0	1431	38	479	190	16.3	5.90	74	.310	.380	-149	-194	94	206	*138*	.937	330	69	111	2.2	-15.9	-2.5	—	3.6
Was	110	2	20	0	1139.0	1485	54	574	292	16.7	5.56	83	.306	.387	-114	-121	99	300	***192***	.912	497	85	96	-6.5	-9.9	-3.3	—	-4.8
Total	1294	43	293	32	13864.1	—	—	—	—	14.7	4.66	—	.280	.356	—	—	—	—	—	.931	4581	1057	1268	—	—	—	—	—

BATTER-FIELDER WINS	BATTING AVERAGE	ON-BASE PERCENTAGE	SLUGGING AVERAGE	ON-BASE PLUS SLUGGING	ADJUSTED OPS	ADJUSTED BATTER RUNS
Delahanty-Phi....5.4	Thompson-Phi......370	Hamilton-Phi.........490	Delahanty-Phi.......583	Hamilton-Phi.......1014	Hamilton-Phi.........169	Delahanty-Phi......53.1
McPhee-Cin........3.6	Hamilton-Phi.........380	Childs-Cle............463	Davis-NY..............554	Delahanty-Phi.....1007	Delahanty-Phi.......166	Smith-Pit..............44.2
Childs-Cle...........3.4	Delahanty-Phi.......368	Burkett-Cle...........459	Thompson-Phi......530	Davis-NY..............964	Smith-Pit..............158	Thompson-Phi.....44.2
Davis-NY.............3.2	Duffy-Bos..............363	McGraw-Bal..........454	Smith-Pit...............525	Smith-Pit...............960	Davis-NY..............154	Hamilton-Phi........41.4
Hamilton-Phi......3.0	Davis-NY..............355	Smith-Pit..............435	Hamilton-Phi.........524	Thompson-Phi......954	Thompson-Phi......153	Davis-NY.............38.0
RUNS	**HITS**	**DOUBLES**	**TRIPLES**	**HOME RUNS**	**TOTAL BASES**	**RUNS BATTED IN**
Long-Bos..............149	Thompson-Phi......222	Thompson-Phi........37	Werden-StL............29	Delahanty-Phi.........19	Delahanty-Phi.......347	Delahanty-Phi.......146
Duffy-Bos..............147	Delahanty-Phi.......219	Delahanty-Phi.........35	Davis-NY................27	Clements-Phi..........17	Thompson-Phi......318	McKean-Cle..........133
Delahanty-Phi.......145	Duffy-Bos..............203	Tebeau-Cle.............32	McKean-Cle............24	Tiernan-NY.............14	Davis-NY..............304	Thompson-Phi......126
Childs-Cle.............145	Davis-NY..............195	Beckley-Pit.............32	Smith-Pit.................23	Lowe-Bos................14	Smith-Pit...............272	Nash-Bos..............123
Burkett-Cle...........145	Ward-NY...............193		Beckley-Pit.............19			Ewing-Cle.............122
BASES ON BALLS	**STOLEN BASES**	**BASE STEALING RUNS**	**FIELDING RUNS-INFIELD**	**FIELDING RUNS-OUTFIELD**	**OUTFIELD ASSISTS**	**CATCHER CS PCT.**
Crooks-StL............121	T.Brown-Lou...........66		McPhee-Cin.........31.4	T.Brown-Lou........25.7	T.Brown-Lou...........39	Kittridge-Chi.........38.1
Childs-Cle.............120	Dowd-StL................59		G.Smith-Cin.........16.4	Delahanty-Phi......23.7	Delahanty-Phi.........31	
Radford-Was.........104	Latham-Cin.............57		Long-Bos.............15.8	Treadway-Bal.........7.8	Radford-Was...........29	
McGraw-Bal..........101	Burke-NY................54		Wise-Was............15.5	Griffin-Bro..............7.3	McCarthy-Bos.........28	
Burkett-Cle.............98	Brodie-StL-Bal........49		Allen-Phi.............15.3	Radford-Was.........6.5		
WINS	**WINNING PCT.**	**WINS ABOVE TEAM**	**GAMES STARTED**	**COMPLETE GAMES**	**FEWEST HITS/GAME**	**FEWEST BB/GAME**
Killen-Pit.................36	Gastright-Pit-Bos.....750	Young-Cle.............9.0	Rusie-NY................52	Rusie-NY................50	Rusie-NY............8.42	Young-Cle............2.19
Young-Cle...............34	Killen-Pit..............720	Killen-Pit...............8.7	Killen-Pit.................48	Nichols-Bos............43	Breitenstein-StL...8.44	Nichols-Bos.........2.50
Nichols-Bos............34	Nichols-Bos..........708	Rusie-NY...............8.0	Young-Cle...............46	Young-Cle...............42	Killen-Pit.............8.70	Cuppy-Cle............2.77
Rusie-NY.................33	Young-Cle............680	McMahon-Bal........5.1	Gleason-StL............45	Kennedy-Bro...........40	Kennedy-Bro........8.84	Staley-Bos...........2.77
Kennedy-Bro...........25	Staley-Bos...........643	Nichols-Bos...........4.4			Stein-Bro.............8.87	Stratton-Lou.........2.86
STRIKEOUTS	**STRIKEOUTS/GAME**	**GAMES**	**SAVES**	**BASE RUNNERS/9**	**ADJUSTED RELIEF RUNS**	**RELIEF RANKING**
Rusie-NY.............208	Rusie-NY............3.88	Rusie-NY................56	Mullane-Cin-Bal........2	Young-Cle..........11.82		
Kennedy-Bro.........107	Meekin-Was.........3.34	Killen-Pit................55	Baldwin-Pit-NY.........2	Nichols-Bos.......11.84		
Young-Cle.............102	Hawley-StL.........2.89	Young-Cle...............53	Dwyer-Cin.................2	Killen-Pit............12.06		
Breitenstein-StL....102	Keefe-Phi............2.83	Nichols-Bos............52	Donnelly-Chi.............2	Breitenstein-StL.12.30		
Weyhing-Phi.........101	Terry-Pit..............2.75	Mullane-Cin-Bal......49	Colcolough-Pit..........2	Stein-Bro............12.70		
INNINGS PITCHED	**OPPONENTS' AVG.**	**OPPONENTS' OBP**	**EARNED RUN AVERAGE**	**ADJUSTED ERA**	**ADJUSTED STARTER RUNS**	**PITCHER WINS**
Rusie-NY...........482.0	Rusie-NY..............240	Young-Cle.............308	Breitenstein-StL...3.18	Breitenstein-StL....149	Rusie-NY.............74.0	**Rusie-NY.............6.8**
Nichols-Bos.......425.0	Breitenstein-StL....241	Nichols-Bos..........308	Rusie-NY.............3.23	Young-Cle.............145	Young-Cle............73.8	**Young-Cle...........6.5**
Young-Cle.........422.2	Killen-Pit...............246	Killen-Pit..............312	Young-Cle............3.36	Rusie-NY..............144	Breitenstein-StL...67.7	**Breitenstein-StL 5.6**
Killen-Pit...........415.0	Kennedy-Bro..........249	Breitenstein-StL....316	Ehret-Pit...............3.44	Nichols-Bos..........140	Nichols-Bos.........66.0	**Killen-Pit.............5.5**
	Stein-Bro...............250	Stein-Bro..............323	Clarkson-StL........3.48	Clarkson-StL.........136	Killen-Pit.............45.5	**Nichols-Bos........5.5**

Going Batty

League moguls decided to increase offense for 1893, and moved the mound 5 feet from the plate to its current distance of 60 feet, 6 inches. Pitchers were also now required to keep one foot on a rubber plate while delivering, effectively limiting them to just one stride. Some pitchers couldn't handle the new rules, including former mound stalwarts Gus Weyhing, Bill Hutchinson, and Silver King. On the other hand, Amos Rusie of New York made 52 starts, threw 482 innings, and walked 218 men. No hurler has matched these totals since.

Despite the league making flat-sided bats illegal, scoring duly increased 29 percent to 6.57 runs per game, a new high, with the loop average rising to an unprecedented .280. Five NL players scored 145 or more runs and two teams plated at least 1,000. St. Louis, which had the league's worst ERA in 1892 at 4.20, had the NL's best a year later at 4.06. (It translated into just one extra win for the Browns because of a mediocre offense.)

The Phillies, in a small park, were the league's top scoring club, and had the top three batting title contenders (Billy Hamilton, Sam Thompson, and Ed Delahanty). Philadelphia, though, finished a distant fourth because the team couldn't win on the road. Aside from the three big guns, the Phillies' offense was actually quite poor, and the team's pitching was below the necessary standard.

Although they lacked the big-name marquee stars of other clubs, Frank Selee's Boston Beaneaters took the prize, squeezing past Pittsburgh. Hugh Duffy, Bobby Lowe, and Herman Long provided offense and defense up the middle, and Kid Nichols adapted well to the new mound conditions. Three celebrated careers ended as Tim Keefe, King Kelly, and Curt Welch played their final games.

With more offense and a shorter schedule, fans had more interest in the league and attendance duly rose by 400,000, doubling in Chicago and New York. It marked the first time three teams attracted 300,000 fans, and the first time the league reached more than two million. There was no postseason tournament, however. With no rival league and no split schedule, the NL's moguls were at a loss for what to do after the end of the regular season. Thus, no postseason series was staged.

1892 NATIONAL LEAGUE

TEAM	W	L	T	PCT	GB	HW	HL	R	OR	PA	H	2B	3B	HR	BB	SO	HB	SH	AVG	OBP	SLG	OPS	AOPS	BR	ABR	PF	SB	CS	BSA	BSR
Bos	102	48	2	.680	—	54	21	862	649	5889	1325	203	51	34	526	492	**62**	—	.250	.325	.327	652	93	24	-43	109	338			
Cle	93	56	4	.624	8.5	54	24	855	**613**	6004	1376	196	96	26	552	538	40	—	.254	.328	.340	668	103	49	16	104	225			
Bro	95	59	4	.617	9	51	24	**935**	733	6168	**1439**	183	105	30	**629**	508	54	—	**.262**	**.344**	.350	694	**119**	**111**	**147**	96	**409**			
Phi	87	66	2	.569	16.5	**55**	26	860	690	5995	1420	**225**	95	**50**	528	515	54	—	**.262**	.334	**.367**	**701**	117	110	113	100	216			
Cin	82	68	5	.547	20	45	32	766	731	5890	1291	155	75	44	503	476	38	—	.241	.311	.323	634	98	-23	-12	99	270			
Pit	80	73	2	.523	23.5	52	34	802	796	5948	1288	143	108	38	435	**453**	44	—	.236	.297	.322	619	92	-65	-68	100	222			
Chi	70	76	1	.479	30	36	31	635	735	5526	1189	149	92	26	427	482	36	—	.235	.299	.316	615	90	-63	-70	101	233			
NY	71	80	2	.470	31.5	42	36	811	826	5835	1329	173	85	39	510	474	34	—	.251	.321	.338	659	106	26	39	98	301			
Lou	63	89	2	.414	40	37	31	649	804	5813	1209	133	61	18	433	508	46	—	.227	.290	.285	575	86	-138	-83	92	275			
Was	58	93	2	.384	44.5	34	36	731	869	5772	1246	149	78	37	529	555	39	—	.239	.314	.319	633	99	-19	3	97	276			
StL	56	94	5	.373	46	37	36	703	922	5918	1188	138	53	45	607	492	52	—	.226	.312	.298	610	94	-53	-15	95	209			
Bal	46	101	5	.313	54.5	29	46	779	1020	5857	1343	160	**111**	30	499	480	**62**	—	.254	.325	.343	668	104	41	19	103	227			
Total	921	—	—	—	—	526	377	9388	—	70615	15643	2007	1010	417	6178	5973	561	—	.245	.317	.328	644	—	—	—	—	3201	—	—	—

TEAM	CG	SHO	GR	SV	IP	H	HR	BB	SO	BR/9	ERA	AERA	OAV	OOB	PR	APR	PF	OSB	OCS	FA	E	WPB	DP	FW	PW	BW	BSW	DIF
Bos	142	**15**	11	1	1336.0	**1156**	41	460	514	11.1	2.86	123	**.224**	.292	64	90	107	**196**	*142*	.929	454	106	128	.5	8.3	-4.0	—	22.2
Cle	140	11	12	2	1336.0	1178	28	**413**	472	**10.9**	**2.41**	**140**	.228	**.289**	**130**	**139**	103	205	*131*	.935	407	**65**	95	3.4	**12.9**	1.5	—	.8
Bro	132	12	**26**	**5**	1405.2	1285	26	600	597	12.4	3.25	97	.234	.315	6	-14	96	258	*175*	**.940**	398	130	98	**4.8**	-1.3	**13.6**	—	.9
Phi	131	10	24	**5**	1379.0	1309	**24**	492	511	12.1	2.93	111	.241	.310	54	48	99	207	*108*	.939	**393**	84	128	4.5	4.4	10.5	—	-9.0
Cin	130	8	25	2	1377.1	1327	39	535	437	12.5	3.17	103	.243	.317	18	15	99	233	*119*	.939	402	111	**140**	4.0	1.4	-1.1	—	2.7
Pit	130	3	22	1	1347.1	1300	28	537	455	12.7	3.10	106	.244	.320	28	27	100	240	*201*	.927	483	108	113	-.7	2.5	-6.3	—	8.0
Chi	133	6	13	1	1298.0	1269	35	424	518	12.0	3.16	105	.246	.308	18	22	101	247	*152*	.932	424	81	85	1.3	2.0	-6.5	—	.1
NY	139	5	13	1	1322.2	1165	32	635	**650**	12.6	3.29	98	.227	.318	-1	-12	98	371	**223**	.912	565	216	97	-5.8	-1.1	3.6	—	-1.2
Lou	**147**	9	7	0	1346.0	1358	26	447	430	12.3	3.34	92	.252	.313	-8	-44	93	297	*164*	.928	471	112	133	-.2	-4.1	-7.7	—	-1.1
Was	129	5	**26**	3	1315.1	1293	40	556	479	13.1	3.46	94	.247	.327	-26	-32	99	386	*178*	.916	547	120	122	-4.8	-3.0	.3	—	-10.0
StL	139	4	22	1	1344.2	1466	47	543	478	13.8	4.20	76	.267	.339	-137	-156	97	287	*138*	.929	452	102	100	1.1	-14.4	-1.4	—	-4.3
Bal	131	2	22	2	1298.2	1537	51	536	437	14.7	4.28	80	.284	.353	-144	-119	104	274	*145*	.910	584	115	100	-7.1	-11.0	1.8	—	-11.1
Total	1623	90	223	24	16106.2	—	—	—	—	12.5	3.28	—	.245	.317	—	—	—	—	—	.928	5580	1350	1339	—	—	—	—	—

Split Season: First-half Winner BOS (52-22); Second-half Winner CLE (53-23)

BATTER-FIELDER WINS	BATTING AVERAGE	ON-BASE PERCENTAGE	SLUGGING AVERAGE	ON-BASE PLUS SLUGGING	ADJUSTED OPS	ADJUSTED BATTER RUNS
Brouthers-Bro.... 6.8	Brouthers-Bro 335	Childs-Cle 443	Delahanty-Phi.......495	Brouthers-Bro 911	Brouthers-Bro 182	Brouthers-Bro 63.5
McPhee-Cin........ 4.7	Hamilton-Phi 330	Brouthers-Bro 432	Brouthers-Bro 480	Connor-Phi 883	Connor-Phi 167	Connor-Phi 53.4
Connor-Phi 4.2	Childs-Cle 317	Hamilton-Phi 423	Ewing-NY.............473	Delahanty-Phi.......855	Burns-Bro 162	Burns-Bro 42.3
Childs-Cle.......... 3.9	Burns-Bro 315	Connor-Phi 420	Connor-Phi 463	Burns-Bro 849	Delahanty-Phi.......158	Childs-Cle............41.2
Hamilton-Phi...... 3.7	Ewing-NY.............310	Crooks-StL...........400	Burns-Bro 454	Childs-Cle.............841	Hamilton-Phi.........152	Hamilton-Phi.........40.4

RUNS	HITS	DOUBLES	TRIPLES	HOME RUNS	TOTAL BASES	RUNS BATTED IN
Childs-Cle.............136	Brouthers-Bro 197	Connor-Phi 37	Delahanty-Phi.........21	Holliday-Cin 13	Brouthers-Bro 282	Brouthers-Bro 124
Hamilton-Phi.........132	Thompson-Phi 186	Long-Bos 33	Virtue-Cle 20	Connor-Phi 12	Holliday-Cin 271	Thompson-Phi 104
Duffy-Bos..............125	Duffy-Bos..............184	Delahanty-Phi.........30	Brouthers-Bro 20	Ryan-Chi..................10	Thompson-Phi 263	Larkin-Was 96
Connor-Phi 123	Hamilton-Phi 183	Brouthers-Bro 30	Dahlen-Chi..............19	Beckley-Pit..............10	Connor-Phi 261	Burns-Bro 96
Brouthers-Bro 121	Long-Bos 181	Zimmer-Cle.............29	Beckley-Pit..............19	Thompson-Phi 9	Duffy-Bos..............251	Beckley-Pit..............96

BASES ON BALLS	STOLEN BASES	BASE STEALING RUNS	FIELDING RUNS-INFIELD	FIELDING RUNS-OUTFIELD	OUTFIELD ASSISTS	CATCHER CS PCT.
Crooks-StL............136	Ward-Bro 88		D.Richardson-Was ..44.8	Duffee-Was..........17.7	Brown-Lou 37	Zimmer-Cle..........38.4
Childs-Cle.............117	Brown-Lou 78		Shindle-Bal 36.5	Brown-Lou 15.6	Duffee-Was.............34	Clements-Phi.......34.2
Connor-Phi 116	Latham-Cin.............66		Bierbauer-Pit........29.1	Hamilton-Phi........12.3	McCarthy-Bos.........29	
McCarthy-Bos.........93	Hoy-Was.................60		Nash-Bos.............25.1	Griffin-Bro 9.6	VanHaltren-Bal-Pit......28	
	Dahlen-Chi..............60		Smith-Cin.............23.3	McAleer-Cle............8.5	Thompson-Phi 28	

WINS	WINNING PCT.	WINS ABOVE TEAM	GAMES STARTED	COMPLETE GAMES	FEWEST HITS/GAME	FEWEST BB/GAME
Young-Cle 36	Young-Cle 750	Young-Cle 10.2	Hutchison-Chi.........70	Hutchison-Chi.........67	Mullane-Cin 6.77	Stratton-Lou.........1.79
Hutchison-Chi 36	Terry-Bal-Pit..........692	Killen-Was..............8.9	Rusie-NY 62	Rusie-NY 59	Rusie-NY 6.82	Dwyer-StL-Cin 1.98
Stivetts-Bos 35	Haddock-Bro.........690	Terry-Bal-Pit...........5.2	Baldwin-Pit..............53	Nichols-Bos 49	Terry-Bal-Pit.........6.94	Sanders-Lou 2.08
Nichols-Bos 35	Staley-Bos 688	Haddock-Bro..........5.2	Killen-Was...............52	Young-Cle 48	Young-Cle 7.21	Young-Cle 2.34
		McMahon-Bal 5.1	Nichols-Bos 51		Duryea-Cin-Was ..7.25	Ehret-Pit..............2.36

STRIKEOUTS	STRIKEOUTS/GAME	GAMES	SAVES	BASE RUNNERS/9	ADJUSTED RELIEF RUNS	RELIEF RANKING
Hutchison-Chi.......314	Kennedy-Bro........5.09	Hutchison-Chi.........75	Weyhing-Phi 3	Young-Cle 9.77		
Rusie-NY 304	Rusie-NY 5.06	Rusie-NY 65	Duryea-Cin-Was 2	Nichols-Bos 10.63		
Weyhing-Phi 202	Hutchison-Chi......4.54	Killen-Was..............60		Stratton-Lou.......10.77		
Nichols-Bos 192	Stein-Bro.............4.53	Weyhing-Phi 59		Mullane-Cin 11.01		
Stein-Bro..............190	Crane-NY.............4.30	Baldwin-Pit..............56		Duryea-Cin-Was 11.08		

INNINGS PITCHED	OPPONENTS' AVG.	OPPONENTS' OBP	EARNED RUN AVERAGE	ADJUSTED ERA	ADJUSTED STARTER RUNS	PITCHER WINS
Hutchison-Chi....622.0	Mullane-Cin 201	Young-Cle 266	Young-Cle 1.93	Young-Cle 176	Young-Cle 73.5	**Young-Cle 6.4**
Rusie-NY 541.0	Rusie-NY 202	Nichols-Bos 283	Keefe-Phi 2.36	J.Clarkson-Bos-Cle...139	Cuppy-Cle............36.7	**Hutchison-Chi.... 4.0**
Weyhing-Phi 469.2	Terry-Bal-Pit..........205	Stratton-Lou..........286	J.Clarkson-Bos-Cle..2.48	Keefe-Phi 138	J.Clarkson-Bos-Cle..35.7	**Cuppy-Cle........... 3.7**
Killen-Was..........459.2	Young-Cle 211	Mullane-Cin 290	Cuppy-Cle............2.51	Cuppy-Cle.............135	Hutchison-Chi......35.6	**Stivetts-Bos 3.3**
	Duryea-Cin-Was...212	Duryea-Cin-Was...291	Terry-Bal-Pit.........2.57	Davies-Cle............131	Nichols-Bos 33.8	**Nichols-Bos........ 3.3**

Growing Overnight

The NL expanded to 12 teams by taking on former American Association franchises Baltimore, Louisville, St. Louis, and Washington. As the only "major league," League owners could now theoretically sit back, await the crowds, and print money. It didn't quite work out that way. First of all, the four "new" clubs were bad, already stripped of their best players. (Only St. Louis survived the century intact; Louisville merged with Pittsburgh in 1900.) In addition, the NL game soon became more violent and more crooked, partly due to syndicate ownership. Five teams, mostly terrible ones, went through multiple managers.

In 1892 most NL clubs adopted old Association policies of Sunday ball, selling alcohol, and charging as little as 25 cents for tickets. The league also expanded its schedule and played a "split season" in order to create a postseason tournament. Hitters could not attempt to be hit by pitches, and any pitches striking the hands or forearm were ruled strikes. In addition, fair balls hit over fences 235 or fewer feet away were doubles.

Boston, a solid two-way squad, rode its pitching to squeeze by Brooklyn for the first-half title. The Cleveland Spiders, featuring suddenly dominant hurler Cy Young and on-base machine Cupid Childs, barely won the second half. Boston easily took the postseason series. Slugging Roger Connor of Philadelphia set an all-time mark by playing in 155 games. St. Louis infielder Jack Crooks established a record of 136 walks that lasted until 1911. Fittingly, Crooks was also a stolen base threat, even though his club's 209 steals represented the lowest figure in the league—200 fewer than NL-leader Brooklyn.

With no AA, there were fewer major league jobs (and lower salaries). Ending their big league tenures were Jim Galvin, George Gore, Ned Hanlon, Hardy Richardson, and Mickey Welch. Future star "Wee Willie" Keeler debuted in New York. The addition of the new teams swelled league attendance totals, though crowds dwindled in Chicago, Boston, New York, and Philadelphia. The split season may have had something to do with this.

1891 NATIONAL LEAGUE

TEAM	W	L	T	PCT	GB	HW	HL	R	OR	PA	H	2B	3B	HR	BB	SO	HB	SH	AVG	OBP	SLG	OPS	AOPS	BR	ABR	PF	SB	CS	BSA	BSR
Bos	87	51	2	.630	—	**51**	20	**847**	**658**	5571	1264	181	81	53	**533**	537	**82**	—	.255	**.337**	.356	**693**	97	**54**	-35	112	289			
Chi	82	53	2	.607	3.5	43	22	832	730	5449	1231	159	88	**60**	526	457	50	—	.253	.332	.358	690	107	40	41	100	238			
NY	71	61	4	.538	13	39	28	754	711	5307	1271	189	72	46	438	**394**	36	—	**.263**	.329	**.360**	689	**111**	34	**68**	96	224			
Phi	68	69	1	.496	18.5	35	34	756	773	5469	1244	180	51	21	482	412	58	—	.252	.326	.322	648	92	-25	-43	103	232			
Cle	65	74	2	.468	22.5	40	28	835	888	5639	**1295**	183	88	22	519	464	46	—	.255	.330	.339	669	97	7	-25	104	242			
Bro	61	76	0	.445	25.5	41	31	765	820	5249	1233	**200**	69	23	465	435	36	—	.260	.330	.345	675	103	18	23	99	**337**			
Cin	56	81	1	.409	30.5	26	41	646	790	5249	1158	148	**90**	40	414	439	44	—	.242	.308	.335	643	92	-53	-58	101	244			
Pit	55	80	2	.407	30.5	32	34	679	744	5271	1148	148	71	29	427	503	50	—	.239	.308	.318	626	90	-75	-58	98	205			
Total	552	—	—	—	—	307	238	6114	—	43204	9844	1388	610	294	3804	3641	402	—	.252	.325	.342	667	—	—	—	—	2011	—	—	—

TEAM	CG	SHO	GR	SV	IP	H	HR	BB	SO	BR/9	ERA	AERA	OAV	OOB	PR	APR	PF	OSB	OCS	FA	E	WPB	DP	FW	PW	BW	BSW	DIF
Bos	**126**	9	15	**6**	1241.2	1223	51	**364**	525	**11.8**	**2.76**	**132**	.248	**.305**	**80**	**112**	109	197	*130*	**.938**	**358**	**79**	96	**4.7**	**10.0**	-3.1	—	6.5
Chi	114	6	24	3	1220.2	1207	53	475	477	12.7	3.47	96	.249	.322	-17	-21	100	**190**	*137*	.932	397	126	**119**	1.5	-1.9	3.7	—	11.2
NY	117	**11**	21	2	1204.0	**1098**	26	593	**651**	13.1	2.99	107	**.234**	.327	47	29	96	306	*174*	.933	384	136	104	2.2	2.6	**6.1**	—	-5.8
Phi	105	3	**34**	5	1229.1	1279	30	507	342	13.4	3.73	91	.259	.333	-53	-46	102	275	*128*	.925	443	102	108	-1.3	-4.1	-3.8	—	8.8
Cle	118	1	25	3	1244.0	1371	**24**	476	400	13.7	3.50	99	.270	.337	-22	-6	103	279	***203***	.920	485	111	86	-3.5	-.5	-2.2	—	1.7
Bro	121	8	16	3	1204.2	1272	40	459	407	13.4	3.86	86	.261	.332	-68	-76	99	244	*116*	.924	432	95	73	-.8	-6.8	2.1	—	-2.0
Cin	125	6	13	1	1218.2	1234	40	465	393	13.0	3.55	95	.253	.326	-28	-25	101	279	*134*	.931	409	120	101	.9	-2.2	-5.2	—	-6.0
Pit	122	7	16	3	1197.2	1160	30	465	446	12.7	2.89	114	.245	.320	61	52	98	241	*151*	.917	475	119	76	-3.6	4.6	-5.2	—	-8.3
Total	948	51	164	26	9760.2	—	—	—	—	13.0	3.34	—	.252	.325	—	—	—	—	—	.928	3383	888	763	—	—	—	—	—

BATTER-FIELDER WINS	BATTING AVERAGE	ON-BASE PERCENTAGE	SLUGGING AVERAGE	ON-BASE PLUS SLUGGING	ADJUSTED OPS	ADJUSTED BATTER RUNS
Hamilton-Phi 4.0	Hamilton-Phi .340	Hamilton-Phi .453	Stovey-Bos .498	Tiernan-NY .882	Tiernan-NY 163	Tiernan-NY 44.0
Richardson-NY 4.0	Holliday-Cin .319	Connor-NY .399	Tiernan-NY .494	Hamilton-Phi .874	Connor-NY 153	Hamilton-Phi 42.3
Latham-Cin 3.4	Browning-Pit-Cin .317	Childs-Cle .395	Holliday-Cin .473	Stovey-Bos .871	Hamilton-Phi 151	Connor-NY 36.6
Tiernan-NY 3.0	Clements-Phi .310	Browning-Pit-Cin .395	Connor-NY .449	Holliday-Cin .848	Holliday-Cin 145	Holliday-Cin 23.8
Pfeffer-Chi 3.0	Tiernan-NY .306	Tiernan-NY .388	Ryan-Chi .434	Connor-NY .848	Browning-Pit-Cin 139	Browning-Pit-Cin 23.0
RUNS	**HITS**	**DOUBLES**	**TRIPLES**	**HOME RUNS**	**TOTAL BASES**	**RUNS BATTED IN**
Hamilton-Phi 141	Hamilton-Phi 179	Griffin-Bro 36	Stovey-Bos 20	Tiernan-NY 16	Stovey-Bos 271	Anson-Chi 120
Long-Bos 129	McKean-Cle 170	Davis-Cle 35	Beckley-Pit 19	Stovey-Bos 16	Tiernan-NY 268	Stovey-Bos 95
Childs-Cle 120	Tiernan-NY 166	Stovey-Bos 31	McPhee-Cin 16	Wilmot-Chi 11	Long-Bos 235	O'Rourke-NY 95
Latham-Cin 119	Davis-Cle 165	Tiernan-NY 30	Ryan-Chi 15		Davis-Cle 233	Nash-Bos 95
Stovey-Bos 118	O'Rourke-NY 164		Virtue-Cle 14		Beckley-Pit 232	Connor-NY 94
BASES ON BALLS	**STOLEN BASES**	**BASE STEALING RUNS**	**FIELDING RUNS-INFIELD**	**FIELDING RUNS-OUTFIELD**	**OUTFIELD ASSISTS**	**CATCHER CS PCT.**
Hamilton-Phi 102	Hamilton-Phi 111		Richardson-NY 44.6	Griffin-Bro 20.0	Thompson-Phi 32	Kittridge-Chi 41.4
Childs-Cle 97	Latham-Cin 87		Pfeffer-Chi 23.6	Thompson-Phi 17.7	Griffin-Bro 31	Bennett-Bos 39.6
Connor-NY 83	Griffin-Bro 65		McPhee-Cin 23.5	Brodie-Bos 7.8	Davis-Cle 27	
Long-Bos 80	Long-Bos 60		Latham-Cin 21.3	Davis-Cle 7.8		
			Long-Bos 15.0	Stovey-Bos 6.6		
WINS	**WINNING PCT.**	**WINS ABOVE TEAM**	**GAMES STARTED**	**COMPLETE GAMES**	**FEWEST HITS/GAME**	**FEWEST BB/GAME**
Hutchison-Chi 44	J.Ewing-NY .724	Hutchison-Chi 11.4	Hutchison-Chi 58	Hutchison-Chi 56	Rusie-NY 7.03	Nichols-Bos 2.18
Rusie-NY 33	Hutchison-Chi .698	Rusie-NY 7.2	Rusie-NY 57	Rusie-NY 52	Baldwin-Pit 7.92	Staley-Pit-Bos 2.22
Clarkson-Bos 33	Staley-Pit-Bos .649	J.Ewing-NY 6.7	Clarkson-Bos 51	Baldwin-Pit 48	J.Ewing-NY 7.92	Galvin-Pit 2.26
Nichols-Bos 30	Nichols-Bos .638	Young-Cle 5.5	Baldwin-Pit 51	Clarkson-Bos 47	Hutchison-Chi 8.15	Radbourn-Cin 2.56
Young-Cle 27	Clarkson-Bos .635	Lovett-Bro 5.2	Nichols-Bos 48	Nichols-Bos 45	Mullane-Cin 8.23	Hutchison-Chi 2.86
STRIKEOUTS	**STRIKEOUTS/GAME**	**GAMES**	**SAVES**	**BASE RUNNERS/9**	**ADJUSTED RELIEF RUNS**	**RELIEF RANKING**
Rusie-NY 337	Rusie-NY 6.06	Hutchison-Chi 66	Nichols-Bos 3	Staley-Pit-Bos 11.08		
Hutchison-Chi 261	Nichols-Bos 5.08	Rusie-NY 61	Clarkson-Bos 3	Hutchison-Chi 11.12		
Nichols-Bos 240	J.Ewing-NY 4.61	Young-Cle 55	Young-Cle 2	Sharrott-NY 11.16		
Baldwin-Pit 197	Hutchison-Chi 4.19	Clarkson-Bos 55	Thornton-Phi 2	Nichols-Bos 11.28		
King-Pit 160	Baldwin-Pit 4.05			J.Ewing-NY 11.80		
INNINGS PITCHED	**OPPONENTS' AVG.**	**OPPONENTS' OBP**	**EARNED RUN AVERAGE**	**ADJUSTED ERA**	**ADJUSTED STARTER RUNS**	**PITCHER WINS**
Hutchison-Chi 561.0	Rusie-NY .207	Staley-Pit-Bos .292	J.Ewing-NY 2.27	Nichols-Bos 153	Nichols-Bos 48.2	**Nichols-Bos 4.5**
Rusie-NY 500.1	Baldwin-Pit .228	Hutchison-Chi .293	Nichols-Bos 2.39	J.Ewing-NY 141	Clarkson-Bos 41.0	**Clarkson-Bos 4.4**
Clarkson-Bos 460.2	J.Ewing-NY .228	Nichols-Bos .296	Rusie-NY 2.55	Staley-Pit-Bos 138	Rusie-NY 39.9	**Rusie-NY 3.9**
Baldwin-Pit 437.2	Hutchison-Chi .233	J.Ewing-NY .305	Staley-Pit-Bos 2.58	Clarkson-Bos 131	Staley-Pit-Bos 36.0	**Staley-Pit-Bos 3.3**
Mullane-Cin 426.1	Mullane-Cin .234	Clarkson-Bos .305	Baldwin-Pit 2.76	Rusie-NY 125	J.Ewing-NY 29.8	**J.Ewing-NY 2.5**

Disassociation

Following the Players' League's dissolution, the AA coaxed the PL's Boston and Philadelphia franchises to join, despite the NL's best efforts to prevent this. As a result, the NL and AA engaged in cataclysmic season-long battles and machinations to destroy each other. There would be no final postseason meeting between the leagues on the field.

Boston was the AA's best club, featuring such stars as Hugh Duffy, Tom Brown, and batting champ Dan Brouthers. Pitchers George Haddock and Charlie Buffinton provided the league's top hill work and just held off St. Louis' strong team. With Charlie Comiskey back in the fold, the Browns—buoyed by Jack Stivetts' pitching, Dummy Hoy and Tommy McCarthy's on-base ability, and Denny Lyons' power—wound up second.

Three future stars debuted in the AA's final season: Clark Griffith, Hugh Jennings, and John McGraw. Veterans Paul Hines—who dated back to the National Association of 1872—and Abner Dalrymple ended their major league careers.

With the PL out of the way, AA attendance rose by more than 300,000, seeing gains in most league cities, but the NL outdrew the Association. Consistent financial woes from the league's worst clubs led league management to seek a truce.

Therefore, postseason meetings between NL and AA moguls ended the Association for good. Four of the league's clubs were absorbed into the National League: St. Louis, Baltimore, Washington, and Louisville. The remaining teams (Boston, Milwaukee—who had replaced defunct Cincinnati in August—Columbus, and Philadelphia, which had replaced the AA's original Philadelphia Athletics) were hung out to dry. The Beer and Whiskey League, as NL supporters had mockingly called the AA because three of the original owners were liquor and beer barons, survived a decade as a major league, drawing practically 10 million fans (outdrawing the NL over the same span).

Though the American Association was history, several of its tenets were adopted by the new 12-team NL-AA amalgam, including Sunday ball, alcohol sales, a permanent core of umpires, and the option to sell tickets cheaply. Unfortunately, the logistics of a 12-team league would pose plenty of problems for the National League in the years ahead.

1891 AMERICAN ASSOCIATION

TEAM	W	L	T	PCT	GB	HW	HL	R	OR	PA	H	2B	3B	HR	BB	SO	HB	SH	AVG	OBP	SLG	OPS	AOPS	BR	ABR	PF	SB	CS	BSA	BSR
Bos	93	42	4	.689	—	51	17	**1028**	675	5606	**1341**	163	100	52	**651**	499	66	—	**.274**	**.367**	**.380**	**747**	**121**	**129**	**144**	99	**447**			
StL	85	51	3	.625	8.5	**52**	21	959	738	5640	1311	165	51	**57**	612	436	86	—	.265	.356	.354	710	94	66	-53	115	279			
Mil	21	15	0	.583	22.5	16	5	227	156	1407	332	58	15	13	107	114	29	—	.261	.333	.361	694	86	4	-32	120	47			
Bal	71	64	4	.526	22	44	24	850	798	5433	1217	142	99	30	551	553	**111**	—	.255	.346	.345	691	102	22	13	101	342			
Phi	73	66	4	.525	22	43	26	817	794	5560	1301	**182**	**123**	55	447	548	74	—	.258	.328	.376	704	106	20	17	100	149			
Col	61	76	1	.445	33	34	29	702	777	5263	1113	154	61	20	529	530	37	—	.237	.319	.308	627	89	-92	-50	94	280			
Cin	43	57	2	.430	32.5	24	20	549	**643**	4038	838	105	58	28	428	**385**	36	—	.234	.322	.320	642	81	-52	-95	108	164			
Lou	54	83	2	.394	40	39	32	698	873	5270	1229	127	68	17	438	465	68	—	.258	.329	.324	653	93	-54	-46	99	227			
Was	44	91	4	.326	49	28	40	691	1067	5259	1183	147	84	19	468	485	76	—	.251	.328	.330	658	97	-44	-8	95	219			
Total	557	—	—	—	—	331	214	6521	—	43476	9865	1243	659	291	4231	4015	583	—	.255	.338	.344	682	—	—	—	—	2154	—	—	—

TEAM	CG	SHO	GR	SV	IP	H	HR	BB	SO	BR/9	ERA	AERA	OAV	OOB	PR	APR	PF	OSB	OCS	FA	E	WPB	DP	FW	PW	BW	BSW	DIF
Bos	108	**9**	34	7	1219.2	1158	42	497	524	**12.6**	**3.03**	115	.242	**.321**	**92**	64	94	**176**	*173*	.934	392	133	115	4.1	5.5	**12.4**	—	3.5
StL	101	8	**38**	**10**	1206.2	**1088**	50	571	**613**	12.9	3.23	**130**	**.233**	.325	64	**113**	113	230	*134*	.920	459	155	91	.1	**9.7**	-4.6	—	11.7
Mil	35	3	1	0	309.2	291	6	120	137	12.2	2.50	175	.241	.314	42	54	118	58	*30*	.922	116	23	20	.2	4.7	-2.8	—	.9
Bal	118	6	21	2	1217.0	1238	33	472	408	13.1	3.43	108	.255	.329	37	39	100	185	*122*	.915	503	**123**	103	-2.5	3.4	1.1	—	1.5
Phi	**135**	3	7	0	1233.2	1274	35	520	533	13.6	4.01	94	.258	.338	-42	-31	102	270	*131*	.933	389	129	109	**5.1**	-2.7	1.5	—	-.3
Col	118	6	21	0	1213.1	1141	**29**	588	502	13.5	3.75	92	.241	.336	-5	-44	93	364	*172*	**.935**	**379**	132	**126**	4.7	-3.8	-4.3	—	-4.1
Cin	86	2	18	1	902.0	921	20	446	331	14.2	3.43	119	.256	.347	28	59	110	231	*163*	.913	389	84	68	-3.0	5.1	-8.2	—	-.9
Lou	126	**9**	12	1	1210.0	1334	32	**451**	481	13.8	4.22	87	.271	.340	-69	-79	98	332	***202***	.922	454	168	112	.4	-6.8	-4.0	—	-4.1
Was	123	2	17	2	1181.0	1420	44	566	486	15.9	4.83	77	.288	.374	-147	-145	101	308	*184*	.900	589	159	95	-7.6	-12.5	-.7	—	-2.7
Total	950	48	169	23	9693.0	—	—	—	—	13.6	3.71	—	.255	.338	—	—	—	—	—	.922	3670	1106	839	—	—	—	—	—

BATTER-FIELDER WINS	BATTING AVERAGE	ON-BASE PERCENTAGE	SLUGGING AVERAGE	ON-BASE PLUS SLUGGING	ADJUSTED OPS	ADJUSTED BATTER RUNS
Farrell-Bos..........4.4	Brouthers-Bos.......350	Brouthers-Bos.......471	Brouthers-Bos.......512	Brouthers-Bos.......983	Brouthers-Bos.......184	Brouthers-Bos......60.4
Brouthers-Bos ... 3.5	Duffy-Bos.............336	Lyons-StL.............445	Milligan-Phi...........505	Milligan-Phi...........903	Milligan-Phi...........158	Brown-Bos...........37.4
Milligan-Phi 3.2	O'Neill-StL 323	Hoy-StL................424	Farrell-Bos 474	Lyons-StL.............900	Brown-Bos 150	Duffy-Bos............34.4
Crooks-Col 3.2	Brown-Bos............321	Seery-Cin 423	Brown-Bos............469	Brown-Bos...........865	Duffy-Bos.............149	Milligan-Phi..........34.4
Duffy-Bos........... 2.7	VanHaltren-Bal 318	Duffy-Bos.............408	Cross-Phi..............458	Duffy-Bos.............861	Farrell-Bos 148	Joyce-Bos............29.0

RUNS	HITS	DOUBLES	TRIPLES	HOME RUNS	TOTAL BASES	RUNS BATTED IN
Brown-Bos............177	Brown-Bos............189	Milligan-Phi............35	Brown-Bos..............21	Farrell-Bos..............12	Brown-Bos............276	Farrell-Bos............110
VanHaltren-Bal 136	VanHaltren-Bal 180	Brown-Bos..............30	Brouthers-Bos.........19	Milligan-Phi.............11	VanHaltren-Bal 251	Duffy-Bos.............110
Hoy-StL.................134	Duffy-Bos.............180	O'Neill-StL 28	Canavan-Cin-Mil.....18	Lyons-StL................11	Brouthers-Bos.......249	Brouthers-Bos.......109
Duffy-Bos..............134	McCarthy-StL........176	Duffee-Col 28	Werden-Bal.............18		Duffy-Bos.............243	Milligan-Phi...........106
	Brouthers-Bos.......170	Larkin-Phi 27			Werden-Bal..........234	Werden-Bal...........104

BASES ON BALLS	STOLEN BASES	BASE STEALING RUNS	FIELDING RUNS-INFIELD	FIELDING RUNS-OUTFIELD	OUTFIELD ASSISTS	CATCHER CS PCT.
Hoy-StL.................117	Brown-Bos............106		Stricker-Bos 23.6	Andrews-Cin........:15.1	Duffee-Col 33	Kelly-Cin-Bos.......45.5
Crooks-Col............103	Duffy-Bos................85		Crooks-Col...........18.2	Weaver-Lou 13.8	Weaver-Lou 32	
McTamany-Col-Phi...101	VanHaltren-Bal 75		Eagan-StL............17.9	Wood-Phi...............9.9	Johnson-Bal............28	
Radford-Bos 96	Hoy-StL..................59		Radford-Bos 17.3	Welch-Bal 7.0	Wolf-Lou 27	
Johnson-Bal............89	Radford-Bos 55		Wheelock-Col 16.3	Duffee-Col 6.3	Hoy-StL...................26	

WINS	WINNING PCT.	WINS ABOVE TEAM	GAMES STARTED	COMPLETE GAMES	FEWEST HITS/GAME	FEWEST BB/GAME
McMahon-Bal 35	Buffinton-Bos........763	McMahon-Bal 6.7	McMahon-Bal 58	McMahon-Bal 53	Knell-Col..............7.07	Stratton-Lou.........1.78
Haddock-Bos..........34	Haddock-Bos........756	Haddock-Bos 6.5	Stivetts-StL 56	Weyhing-Phi 51	Stivetts-StL 7.30	Sanders-Phi.........2.30
Stivetts-StL 33	Weyhing-Phi 608	Weyhing-Phi 6.4	Carsey-Was............53	Knell-Col.................47	Buffinton-Bos.......7.50	McMahon-Bal 2.67
Weyhing-Phi 31	Stivetts-StL 600	Buffinton-Bos.........5.8	Knell-Col.................52	Carsey-Was............46	Crane-Cin 7.78	Ehret-Lou.............2.85
Buffinton-Bos..........29	McMahon-Bal 593	Foreman-Was........5.3	Weyhing-Phi 51	Chamberlain-Phi.....44	Haddock-Bos.......7.82	Griffith-StL-Bos....2.90

STRIKEOUTS	STRIKEOUTS/GAME	GAMES	SAVES	BASE RUNNERS/9	ADJUSTED RELIEF RUNS	RELIEF RANKING
Stivetts-StL 259	Meekin-Lou..........5.74	Stivetts-StL 64	Neale-StL..................3	Buffinton-Bos.....10.64		
Knell-Col...............228	Stivetts-StL 5.30	McMahon-Bal 61	Griffith-StL-Bos.........2	Haddock-Bos.....11.40		
Weyhing-Phi 219	McGill-Cin-StL 4.98	Knell-Col.................58	O'Brien-Bos.............2	Davies-Mil.........11.65		
McMahon-Bal 219	Daley-Bos............4.83	Carsey-Was............54	Daley-Bos................2	McMahon-Bal 11.79		
Chamberlain-Phi...204	Chamberlain-Phi..4.53	Weyhing-Phi 52		Killen-Mil...........11.82		

INNINGS PITCHED	OPPONENTS' AVG.	OPPONENTS' OBP	EARNED RUN AVERAGE	ADJUSTED ERA	ADJUSTED STARTER RUNS	PITCHER WINS
McMahon-Bal 503.0	Knell-Col..............209	Buffinton-Bos........285	Crane-Cin 2.45	Crane-Cin 167	Stivetts-StL 57.8	**Stivetts-StL 6.8**
Knell-Col............462.0	Stivetts-StL 215	Haddock-Bos 299	Haddock-Bos.......2.49	Stivetts-StL 146	McMahon-Bal 54.0	**Haddock-Bos 5.3**
Weyhing-Phi 450.0	Buffinton-Bos........219	McMahon-Bal 306	Buffinton-Bos.......2.55	Haddock-Bos........140	Buffinton-Bos.......45.3	**McMahon-Bal..... 4.9**
Stivetts-StL 440.0	Crane-Cin 225	Fitzgerald-Lou.......316	McMahon-Bal 2.81	Buffinton-Bos........136	Haddock-Bos.......44.6	**Buffinton-Bos..... 4.0**
Carsey-Was.......415.0	Haddock-Bos........226	Weyhing-Phi 317	Stivetts-StL 2.86	Mains-Cin-Mil........134	Crane-Cin 35.5	**Crane-Cin 2.6**

Winning the War

With the Players' League dissolved, the NL absorbed most of the players from the defunct loop's New York, Pittsburgh, Chicago, and Brooklyn clubs (including John Ward, who served as Brooklyn's player-manager). Boston claimed Harry Stovey from the Philadelphia AA team, citing a waiver error, and a committee ruled Boston did have such a right. The AA angrily responded by withdrawing from the National Agreement—the leagues were now officially at war. The AA's withdrawal from the agreement precluded even a financially rewarding postseason competition. The NL was happy with this decision, as it felt itself to be already winning the attendance war.

And this decision played itself out in the pennant race. Chicago led the NL hunt for most of the year, but an 18-game winning streak gave Boston the flag. Some sources now believe that Cap Anson's Chicago club, rumored despite the NL's objections to be willing to play AA champ Boston in a World Series, was jobbed out of the pennant by league-enforced umpire decisions.

Managed by Frank Selee, the Boston Beaneaters got power from Stovey, excellent all-around play from Herman Long, and top mound work from John Clarkson and Kid Nichols. Chicago, despite big seasons from Anson, rookie Bill Dahlen, and Bill Hutchinson, settled for an angry second. Philadelphia had Billy Hamilton, probably the NL's top player, but the Phillies lacked other offense and finished fourth. Despite the returning talent (at a much lower cost) to the NL, future stars Joe Kelley and Dahlen debuted. Hoss Radbourn pitched his last major league ball for seventh-place Cincinnati.

Following the end of the controversial season, the NL absorbed four AA franchises, and until 1901 there would be but one major league. The decade-long Association war yielded far-reaching spoils. Four NL teams that still exist today—Pittsburgh Pirates, Cincinnati Reds, St. Louis Cardinals, and Los Angeles Dodgers—came from the American Association. Two others current NL teams originated from the National Association (Atlanta Braves and Chicago Cubs), seven more resulted from expansion since 1962, and an eighth originated in the American League. The Philadelphia Phillies and San Francisco Giants, organized in 1883, are the lone nineteenth century teams to play their first games as NL franchises and continue to do so.

1890 NATIONAL LEAGUE

TEAM	W	L	T	PCT	GB	HW	HL	R	OR	PA	H	2B	3B	HR	BB	SO	HB	SH	AVG	OBP	SLG	OPS	AOPS	BR	ABR	PF	SB	CS	BSA	BSR
Bro	86	43	0	.667	—	**58**	16	**884**	620	4977	1166	184	75	43	517	**361**	41	—	.264	.346	**.369**	**715**	**113**	77	**74**	100	**349**			
Chi	84	53	2	.613	6	48	24	847	692	5453	**1271**	147	60	**67**	516	514	46	—	.260	.336	.356	692	102	37	5	104	329			
Phi	78	54	1	.591	9.5	54	22	823	707	5293	1267	**220**	78	23	522	403	64	—	**.269**	**.350**	.364	714	110	**84**	63	103	335			
Cin	77	55	2	.583	10.5	50	23	753	633	5128	1203	150	**120**	27	433	377	51	—	.259	.329	.360	689	106	20	24	100	312			
Bos	76	57	1	.571	12	43	23	763	**593**	5321	1220	175	62	31	**530**	515	**69**	—	.258	.342	.341	683	96	32	-27	108	285			
NY	63	68	4	.481	24	37	27	713	698	5232	1250	208	89	25	350	479	50	—	.259	.315	.354	669	99	-17	-18	100	289			
Cle	44	88	4	.333	43.5	30	37	630	832	5172	1073	132	59	21	497	474	42	—	.232	.312	.299	611	84	-98	-85	98	152			
Pit	23	113	2	.169	66.5	14	25	597	1235	5213	1088	160	43	20	408	458	66	—	.230	.300	.294	594	87	-134	-53	88	208			
Total	539	—	—	—	—	334	197	6010	—	41789	9538	1376	586	257	3773	3581	429	—	.254	.329	.342	671	—	—	—	—	2259	—	—	—

TEAM	CG	SHO	GR	SV	IP	H	HR	BB	SO	BR/9	ERA	AERA	OAV	OOB	PR	APR	PF	OSB	OCS	FA	E	WPB	DP	FW	PW	BW	BSW	DIF
Bro	115	6	14	2	1145.0	1102	27	401	403	12.2	3.06	112	.246	.315	64	49	96	304	*118*	**.940**	**320**	114	92	4.4	4.4	**6.6**	—	6.2
Chi	126	6	13	**3**	1237.1	1103	41	481	504	11.9	3.24	113	.234	.311	44	48	103	257	*145*	**.940**	344	138	89	**4.8**	4.3	.4	—	6.0
Phi	122	9	12	2	1194.2	1210	22	486	507	13.2	3.32	110	.255	.331	32	42	102	266	*139*	.929	398	102	**122**	.4	3.7	5.6	—	2.3
Cin	124	9	10	1	1190.2	1097	41	407	488	11.8	**2.79**	127	.238	.307	**102**	**100**	100	226	*162*	.932	382	116	106	1.5	**8.9**	2.1	—	-1.6
Bos	**132**	**13**	2	1	1187.0	1132	27	**354**	506	**11.5**	2.93	**128**	.245	**.303**	83	99	105	**220**	*150*	.935	359	**94**	77	2.9	8.8	-2.4	—	.2
NY	115	6	**20**	1	1177.0	**1029**	**14**	607	**612**	13.0	3.06	114	**.230**	.331	66	53	98	283	***209***	.922	440	164	104	-1.9	4.7	-1.6	—	-3.8
Cle	129	2	8	0	1184.1	1322	33	462	306	14.0	4.13	86	.275	.346	-75	-77	100	256	*198*	.929	405	108	108	.5	-6.8	-7.6	—	-8.1
Pit	119	3	**20**	0	1176.1	1520	52	573	381	16.6	5.97	55	.304	.384	-315	-379	92	447	*200*	.897	607	192	94	-11.6	-33.7	-4.7	—	5.0
Total	982	54	99	10	9492.1	—	—	—	—	13.0	3.56	—	.254	.329	—	—	—	—	—	.928	3255	1028	792	—	—	—	—	—

BATTER-FIELDER WINS	BATTING AVERAGE	ON-BASE PERCENTAGE	SLUGGING AVERAGE	ON-BASE PLUS SLUGGING	ADJUSTED OPS	ADJUSTED BATTER RUNS
Glasscock-NY....4.8	Glasscock-NY.......336	Anson-Chi............443	Tiernan-NY...........495	Tiernan-NY...........880	Tiernan-NY...........156	Tiernan-NY..........37.4
McPhee-Cin........3.9	Hamilton-Phi.........325	Hamilton-Phi.........430	Clements-Phi........472	Clements-Phi........864	Clements-Phi........148	Anson-Chi............33.9
Allen-Phi.............3.2	Clements-Phi........315	Pinkney-Bro..........411	Reilly-Cin.............472	Anson-Chi.............844	Pinkney-Bro..........145	McKean-Cle...........31.3
Clements-Phi.....3.0	O'Brien-Bro...........314	McKean-Cle..........401	Burns-Bro.............464	Pinkney-Bro..........842	Glasscock-NY........143	Pinkney-Bro.........31.1
Hamilton-Phi......2.6	Thompson-Phi......313	Glasscock-NY........395	Burkett-NY............461	Glasscock-NY.......834	McKean-Cle..........141	Hamilton-Phi........29.2

RUNS	HITS	DOUBLES	TRIPLES	HOME RUNS	TOTAL BASES	RUNS BATTED IN
Collins-Bro............148	Thompson-Phi......172	Thompson-Phi........41	Reilly-Cin...............26	Wilmot-Chi.............13	Tiernan-NY...........274	Burns-Bro.............128
Carroll-Chi............134	Glasscock-NY.......172	Glasscock-NY.........32	McPhee-Cin...........22	Tiernan-NY.............13	Reilly-Cin..............261	Anson-Chi.............107
Hamilton-Phi..........133	Tiernan-NY...........168	Collins-Bro.............32	Tiernan-NY.............21	Burns-Bro...............13	Thompson-Phi......243	Thompson-Phi......102
Tiernan-NY...........132	Reilly-Cin..............166	Myers-Phi...............29	Beard-Cin...............15	Long-Bos..................8	Wilmot-Chi............239	Wilmot-Chi..............99
McPhee-Cin..........125	Carroll-Chi............166	O'Brien-Bro............28			Glasscock-NY.......225	Foutz-Bro.................98

BASES ON BALLS	STOLEN BASES	BASE STEALING RUNS	FIELDING RUNS-INFIELD	FIELDING RUNS-OUTFIELD	OUTFIELD ASSISTS	CATCHER CS PCT.
Anson-Chi.............113	Hamilton-Phi..........102		Allen-Phi..............32.3	Davis-Cle.............12.3	Davis-Cle................35	Zimmer-Cle.........43.9
McKean-Cle............87	Collins-Bro..............85		McPhee-Cin.........26.4	Wilmot-Chi...........10.9	Sunday-Pit-Phi........30	Bennett-Bos.........39.1
Allen-Phi.................87	Sunday-Pit-Phi........84		Glasscock-NY......23.3	Carroll-Chi...........10.9	Thompson-Phi.........29	Kittridge-Chi.........38.5
Collins-Bro..............85	Wilmot-Chi..............76		Smalley-Cle.........20.2	Sunday-Pit-Phi.....10.3	Carroll-Chi..............28	
Hamilton-Phi...........83	Tiernan-NY..............56		Bassett-NY..........18.7	Gilks-Cle.................5.3	Wilmot-Chi..............26	

WINS	WINNING PCT.	WINS ABOVE TEAM	GAMES STARTED	COMPLETE GAMES	FEWEST HITS/GAME	FEWEST BB/GAME
Hutchison-Chi.........42	Lovett-Bro.............732	Gleason-Phi...........9.8	Hutchison-Chi.........66	Hutchison-Chi.........65	Rusie-NY.............7.15	Young-Cle............1.83
Gleason-Phi............38	Gleason-Phi..........691	Lovett-Bro..............5.4	Rusie-NY................62	Rusie-NY................56	Mullane-Cin.........7.54	Duryea-Cin..........1.97
Lovett-Bro...............30	Luby-Chi...............690	Beatin-Cle..............5.3	Gleason-Phi............55	Gleason-Phi............54	Hutchison-Chi.......7.54	Getzien-Bos.........2.11
Rusie-NY.................29	Caruthers-Bro.......676	Luby-Chi.................3.5	Beatin-Cle...............54	Beatin-Cle...............53	Rhines-Cin...........7.56	Nichols-Bos.........2.38
Rhines-Cin...............28	Hutchison-Chi........627	Rhines-Cin...............3.0	Nichols-Bos............47	Nichols-Bos............47	Luby-Chi...............7.60	Rhines-Cin...........2.53

STRIKEOUTS	STRIKEOUTS/GAME	GAMES	SAVES	BASE RUNNERS/9	ADJUSTED RELIEF RUNS	RELIEF RANKING
Rusie-NY..............341	Rusie-NY.............5.59	Hutchison-Chi.........71	Hutchison-Chi...........2	Rhines-Cin.........10.43		
Hutchison-Chi.......289	Nichols-Bos.........4.71	Rusie-NY.................67	Gleason-Phi.............2	Nichols-Bos.......10.55		
Nichols-Bos..........222	Terry-Bro.............4.50	Gleason-Phi............60	Foutz-Bro..................2	Hutchison-Chi....10.70		
Gleason-Phi..........222	Hutchison-Chi......4.31	Beatin-Cle...............54		Getzien-Bos.......10.98		
Terry-Bro..............185	Sharrott-NY..........4.11	Nichols-Bos............48		Duryea-Cin........11.10		

INNINGS PITCHED	OPPONENTS' AVG.	OPPONENTS' OBP	EARNED RUN AVERAGE	ADJUSTED ERA	ADJUSTED STARTER RUNS	PITCHER WINS
Hutchison-Chi....603.0	Rusie-NY..............212	Rhines-Cin...........282	Rhines-Cin...........1.95	Rhines-Cin...........182	Rhines-Cin..........67.5	**Rhines-Cin..........6.0**
Rusie-NY...........548.2	Mullane-Cin..........221	Nichols-Bos..........284	Nichols-Bos.........2.23	Nichols-Bos..........168	Nichols-Bos.........63.5	**Nichols-Bos.........5.9**
Gleason-Phi.......506.0	Hutchison-Chi.......221	Hutchison-Chi.......287	Mullane-Cin.........2.24	Mullane-Cin..........159	Hutchison-Chi.......51.3	**Rusie-NY.............5.9**
Beatin-Cle..........474.1	Rhines-Cin...........221	Getzien-Bos..........292	Rusie-NY.............2.56	Gleason-Phi..........139	Gleason-Phi.........50.9	**Hutchison-Chi....4.5**
Nichols-Bos.......424.0	Luby-Chi...............222	Duryea-Cin...........295	Gleason-Phi.........2.63	Rusie-NY..............137	Rusie-NY.............50.0	**Gleason-Phi.......4.0**

A Short-Lived Brotherhood

When John Ward and his associates broke away to form the Players' League, the magnates showed foresight. Their laudable and well-reasoned efforts to break the reserve clause, the use of two, rather than one, umpire to ensure fair play, and the decision to allow two free substitutes, rather than just one, foreshadowed future changes in the game. However, the league also used a substandard and much livelier ball, would not employ black players, did not sell alcohol in the parks, and refused to play ball on Sundays—ensuring that many working fans couldn't come to the games.

The Players' League went directly at the National League, setting up teams in seven NL cities—only Cincinnati was spared direct competition. Brooklyn and Philadelphia, also American Association cities, had three different major league teams simultaneously.

Hugh Duffy, formerly of the Chicago NL club, jumped to the PL's Chicago Pirates and led the new league in runs and hits. Pete Browning of Cleveland won his third big league batting title. Respected veterans like Ward, Ned Hanlon, Charlie Comiskey, and Buck Ewing served as PL managers.

But the league champ was Boston, featuring an all-time cast of characters: player-manager King Kelly, first baseman Dan Brouthers, slugging outfielders Hardy Richardson and outfielder Harry Stovey, plus 36-year-old pitcher Hoss Radbourn, enjoying his last hurrah despite a damaged wing. Brooklyn's club, Ward's Wonders, finished second. Despite Duffy's exploits and the fine pitching of Mark Baldwin and Silver King, Chicago ended up fourth. Veteran shortstop Jack Rowe and 43-year-old infielder Deacon White played their last seasons, for Buffalo. Former NL home run king Ed Williamson also ended his career in the PL, falling prey to the alcoholism that would end his life four years later.

Despite being shut out of any postseason play, the PL finished its first season as the people's choice, leading the three leagues in attendance. However, the costs of instituting a new league that paid players fairly proved daunting, and the league capitulated the following January. Some historians claim that the threat of the Players' League—coming at a cost of more than $250,000 for the National League—was the closest the NL ever came to toppling.

1890 AMERICAN ASSOCIATION

TEAM	W	L	T	PCT	GB	HW	HL	R	OR	PA	H	2B	3B	HR	BB	SO	HB	SH	AVG	OBP	SLG	OPS	AOPS	BR	ABR	PF	SB	CS	BSA	BSR
Lou	88	44	4	.667	—	**57**	13	819	**588**	5150	**1310**	156	65	15	410	460	53	—	**.279**	.344	.350	694	**112**	53	71	98	341			
Col	79	55	6	.590	10	47	22	831	617	5332	1225	159	77	16	**545**	557	46	—	.258	.341	.335	676	**112**	30	**90**	93	353			
StL	77	58	4	.570	12.5	45	25	**870**	736	5369	1308	178	73	**48**	474	490	**95**	—	.273	**.350**	**.370**	**720**	103	**102**	-8	114	307			
Tol	68	64	2	.515	20	40	27	739	689	5132	1152	152	**108**	24	486	558	71	—	.252	.333	.348	681	103	29	8	103	**421**			
Roc	63	63	7	.500	22	40	22	709	711	5056	1088	131	64	31	446	538	57	—	.239	.315	.316	631	98	-55	1	93	310			
Bal	15	19	4	.441	24	8	11	182	192	1366	278	34	16	2	125	152	28	—	.229	.316	.289	605	79	-24	-32	105	101			
Syr	55	72	1	.433	30.5	30	30	698	831	4961	1158	151	59	14	457	482	35	—	.259	.333	.329	662	**112**	1	85	90	292			
Phi	54	78	0	.409	34	36	36	702	945	5052	1057	**181**	51	24	475	540	87	—	.235	.320	.314	634	93	-37	-33	99	305			
Bro	26	72	2	.265	45	15	22	492	733	3834	769	116	47	13	328	**456**	31	—	.221	.294	.293	587	80	-99	-83	97	182			
Total	540	—	—	—	—	318	208	6042	—	41252	9345	1258	560	187	3746	4233	503	—	.253	.330	.332	662	—	—	—	—	2612	—	—	—

TEAM	CG	SHO	GR	SV	IP	H	HR	BB	SO	BR/9	ERA	AERA	OAV	OOB	PR	APR	PF	OSB	OCS	FA	E	WPB	DP	FW	PW	BW	BSW	DIF
Lou	114	13	20	**7**	1206.0	1120	18	**293**	587	**10.9**	**2.57**	**149**	.239	**.291**	**173**	**171**	100	**247**	*198*	**.934**	**380**	131	79	**2.8**	**15.0**	6.2	—	-2.1
Col	120	**14**	**22**	3	1214.2	**976**	20	471	624	11.2	2.99	120	**.214**	.297	118	87	93	321	*205*	.932	396	174	**101**	2.6	7.7	**7.9**	—	-6.2
StL	118	4	20	1	1195.1	1127	38	447	**733**	12.3	3.67	117	.242	.316	25	74	112	338	*205*	.916	478	158	93	-1.8	6.5	-.7	—	5.5
Tol	**122**	4	14	2	1159.1	1122	23	429	533	12.6	3.56	111	.247	.321	39	48	102	270	***221***	.925	419	173	75	.4	4.2	.7	—	-3.4
Roc	**122**	5	12	2	1161.2	1115	19	530	477	13.2	3.56	100	.246	.331	39	-2	92	284	*184*	.926	416	**125**	95	.4	-.2	.0	—	-.3
Bal	36	1	2	0	315.1	307	3	123	134	13.0	4.00	101	.248	.328	-5	2	105	75	*59*	.928	109	30	21	.6	.2	-2.8	—	.0
Syr	115	5	12	0	1089.2	1158	28	518	454	14.4	4.98	71	.265	.351	-135	-193	91	390	*170*	.925	391	142	90	.9	-17.0	7.5	—	.1
Phi	119	3	14	2	1132.0	1405	**17**	514	461	15.8	5.22	74	.296	.373	-171	-170	100	379	*169*	.918	452	145	93	-1.6	-15.0	-2.9	—	7.5
Bro	96	0	4	0	879.0	1011	21	421	230	15.2	4.71	83	.281	.365	-83	-80	101	308	*163*	.909	404	121	92	-4.4	-7.0	-7.3	—	-4.3
Total	962	49	120	17	9353.0	—	—	—	—	13.1	3.86	—	.253	.330	—	—	—	—	—	.923	3445	1199	739	—	—	—	—	—

BATTER-FIELDER WINS	BATTING AVERAGE	ON-BASE PERCENTAGE	SLUGGING AVERAGE	ON-BASE PLUS SLUGGING	ADJUSTED OPS	ADJUSTED BATTER RUNS
Childs-Syr...........6.8	Wolf-Lou 363	Lyons-Phi..............461	Lyons-Phi...............531	Lyons-Phi..............992	Lyons-Phi..............193	Childs-Syr............61.0
Lyons-Phi............4.7	Lyons-Phi..............354	Swartwood-Tol......444	Campau-StL 513	Childs-Syr.............915	Childs-Syr.............189	Wolf-Lou 46.8
Swartwood-Tol ..3.8	McCarthy-StL........350	Childs-Syr.............434	Childs-Syr.............481	Wolf-Lou 900	Wolf-Lou 169	Johnson-Col 46.2
O'Connor-Col 3.7	Johnson-Col 346	McCarthy-StL........430	Wolf-Lou 479	McCarthy-StL........898	Johnson-Col 168	Lyons-Phi.............43.9
Wolf-Lou..............3.6	Childs-Syr.............345	Wright-Syr.............428	McCarthy-StL........467	Swartwood-Tol......887	Swartwood-Tol......157	Swartwood-Tol.....38.4

RUNS	HITS	DOUBLES	TRIPLES	HOME RUNS	TOTAL BASES	RUNS BATTED IN
McTamany-Col......140	Wolf-Lou 197	Childs-Syr..............33	Werden-Tol 20	Campau-StL 9	Wolf-Lou 260	Johnson-Col 113
McCarthy-StL........137	McCarthy-StL........192	Wolf-Lou 29	Johnson-Col 18	Cartwright-StL 8	McCarthy-StL........256	Wolf-Lou 98
Fuller-StL..............118	Johnson-Col 186	Lyons-Phi.................29	Alvord-Tol................16	Stivetts-StL 7	Johnson-Col 248	Childs-Syr...............89
Sneed-Tol-Col.......117	Childs-Syr.............170		Sneed-Tol-Col.........15	Lyons-Phi..................7	Childs-Syr.............237	Knowles-Roc 84
Welch-Phi-Bal.......116	Taylor-Lou.............169				Werden-Tol 227	Shinnick-Lou...........82

BASES ON BALLS	STOLEN BASES	BASE STEALING RUNS	FIELDING RUNS-INFIELD	FIELDING RUNS-OUTFIELD	OUTFIELD ASSISTS	CATCHER CS PCT.
McTamany-Col......112	McCarthy-StL.........83		Gerhardt-Bro-StL .38.2	Welch-Phi-Bal......11.9	Scheffler-Roc..........29	
Crooks-Col..............96	Scheffler-Roc..........77		Reilly-Col 29.1	Lyons-Roc............10.9	Welch-Phi-Bal.........27	
Swartwood-Tol........80	VanDyke-Tol...........73		Tomney-Lou.........15.0	Scheffler-Roc.........8.1	Lyons-Roc...............26	
Werden-Tol 78	Welch-Phi-Bal.........72		Childs-Syr............14.4	Duffee-StL 7.0	Sneed-Tol-Col.........25	
Scheffler-Roc..........78			Lehane-Col 9.9	Swartwood-Tol 6.5		

WINS	WINNING PCT.	WINS ABOVE TEAM	GAMES STARTED	COMPLETE GAMES	FEWEST HITS/GAME	FEWEST BB/GAME
McMahon-Phi-Bal...36	Stratton-Lou..........708	McMahon-Phi-Bal 13.4	McMahon-Phi-Bal...57	McMahon-Phi-Bal...55	Knauss-Col..........6.73	Stratton-Lou.........1.27
Stratton-Lou............34	Chamberlain-SL-Col .682	Gastright-Col 6.6	Barr-Roc 54	Barr-Roc 52	Gastright-Col 7.00	Ehret-Lou.............1.98
Gastright-Col 30	Gastright-Col 682	Stratton-Lou...........4.4	Stratton-Lou............49	Stratton-Lou............44	Easton-Col...........7.50	Ramsey-StL.........2.63
Barr-Roc 28	Ehret-Lou..............641	Smith-Tol................3.3	Stivetts-StL 46	Healy-Tol.................44	Chamberlain-SL-Col 7.50	Smith-Tol..............2.83
Stivetts-StL 27	McMahon-Phi-Bal .632	Barr-Roc 3.2	Healy-Tol.................46		Healy-Tol.............7.54	McMahon-Phi-Bal 2.94

STRIKEOUTS	STRIKEOUTS/GAME	GAMES	SAVES	BASE RUNNERS/9	ADJUSTED RELIEF RUNS	RELIEF RANKING
McMahon-Phi-Bal .291	Ramsey-StL.........6.63	McMahon-Phi-Bal...60	Goodall-Lou..............4	Neale-StL............9.39		
Stivetts-StL 289	Stivetts-StL 6.20	Barr-Roc 57	Knauss-Col...............2	Stratton-Lou.........9.86		
Ramsey-StL..........257	Meakim-Lou.........5.77	Stivetts-StL 54	Ehret-Lou..................2	Gastright-Col 10.43		
Healy-Tol...............225	Chamberlain-SL-Col 5.49	Stratton-Lou............50		Knauss-Col........10.87		
Barr-Roc 209	Healy-Tol.............5.21	Gastright-Col 48		Healy-Tol...........11.04		

INNINGS PITCHED	OPPONENTS' AVG.	OPPONENTS' OBP	EARNED RUN AVERAGE	ADJUSTED ERA	ADJUSTED STARTER RUNS	PITCHER WINS
McMahon-Phi-Bal .509.0	Knauss-Col...........202	Stratton-Lou..........270	Stratton-Lou.........2.36	Stratton-Lou..........163	Stratton-Lou.........73.5	**Stratton-Lou.......8.9**
Barr-Roc 493.1	Gastright-Col 208	Gastright-Col 282	Ehret-Lou.............2.53	Ehret-Lou..............152	Ehret-Lou.............49.8	**Healy-Tol 4.3**
Stratton-Lou.......431.0	Easton-Col............220	Knauss-Col...........290	Knauss-Col..........2.81	Healy-Tol...............136	Healy-Tol.............40.2	**Stivetts-StL 4.2**
Stivetts-StL 419.1	Chamberlain-SL-Col .220	Healy-Tol...............293	Chamberlain-SL-Col 2.83	Meakim-Lou..........132	Stivetts-StL 30.6	**Ehret-Lou............4.1**
Gastright-Col 401.1	Healy-Tol...............221	Ehret-Lou..............296	Healy-Tol.............2.89	Chamberlain-SL-Col .131	Gastright-Col 29.9	**Gastright-Col 2.7**

Ball of Confusion

The Players' League rocked the NL and AA in 1890, but the Senior Circuit had its own share of intrigue, snaring two more Association franchises, Brooklyn and Cincinnati. The two new teams helped the NL survive; Cincinnati led in the early going and Brooklyn ended up on top at the end.

The Bridegrooms won despite significant injuries. Right fielder Oyster Burns and second baseman Hub Collins were the key offensive contributors, and Bob Caruthers, Tom Lovett, and Adonis Terry provided strong pitching. Second-place Chicago was weak in spots, though 42-game winner Bill Hutchinson certainly helped. Third-place Philadelphia got excellent pitching from Kid Gleason and big hitting from Sam Thompson and new recruit Billy Hamilton. Cincinnati received excellent pitching from rookie Billy Rhines, the only pitcher in the three major leagues to have an ERA below 2.00 in 1890.

Amos Rusie of New York set a new major league record by walking 293 hitters and led the league in losses, but he also paced the NL in strikeouts. His Giants finished sixth even with batting champ Jack Glasscock. Last-place Pittsburgh was so awful that 21 different pitchers started games, none more than 21 times. Billy Gumbert led with 4 wins. The club averaged just over 400 fans per game and soon became a traveling team.

Though the NL and AA had outlawed the pitcher's practice of intentionally defacing the ball with dirt, dilution of talent among the leagues allowed NL pitchers to lower their collective ERA by half a point. The loss of manpower to the PL pushed a great crop of rookies to debut: George Davis, Jesse Burkett, Bobby Lowe, Kid Nichols, and Cy Young.

The postseason, originally expected to be a cakewalk for Brooklyn, instead ended with each team winning three times before rain and low attendance caused the rest of the games to be cancelled. In truth, fans would have been more interested in the World Series had the Players' League champion Boston Reds been involved. Unsurprisingly, given the PL's competition, NL attendance fell by nearly half.

1890 PLAYERS LEAGUE

TEAM	W	L	T	PCT	GB	HW	HL	R	OR	PA	H	2B	3B	HR	BB	SO	HB	SH	AVG	OBP	SLG	OPS	AOPS	BR	ABR	PF	SB	CS	BSA	BSR
Bos	81	48	1	.628	—	**48**	21	992	**767**	5321	1306	**223**	76	54	**652**	435	43	—	.282	**.376**	.398	**774**	105	**97**	34	107	**412**			
Bro	76	56	1	.576	6.5	46	19	964	893	5431	1352	186	93	34	502	369	42	—	.277	.349	.374	723	92	-14	-66	106	272			
NY	74	57	1	.565	8	47	19	**1018**	875	5430	**1393**	204	97	**66**	486	364	31	—	.284	.352	**.405**	757	98	39	-38	109	231			
Chi	75	62	1	.547	10	46	23	886	770	5503	1311	200	95	31	492	410	43	—	.264	.335	.361	696	87	-67	-101	104	276			
Phi	68	63	1	.519	14	35	30	941	855	5337	1350	187	**113**	49	431	**321**	51	—	.278	.343	.393	736	100	-2	-22	102	203			
Pit	60	68	0	.469	20.5	37	28	835	892	5200	1192	168	**113**	35	569	375	54	—	.260	.349	.369	718	106	-17	60	92	249			
Cle	55	75	1	.423	26.5	31	30	849	1027	5362	1370	213	94	27	509	345	49	—	**.285**	.360	.386	746	**114**	31	**115**	92	180			
Buf	36	96	2	.273	46.5	23	42	793	1199	5432	1249	180	64	20	541	367	**96**	—	.260	.347	.337	684	96	-66	11	92	160			
Total	529	—	—	—	—	313	212	7278	—	43016	10523	1561	745	316	4182	2986	409	—	.274	.351	.378	729	—	—	—	—	1983	—	—	—

TEAM	CG	SHO	GR	SV	IP	H	HR	BB	SO	BR/9	ERA	AERA	OAV	OOB	PR	APR	PF	OSB	OCS	FA	E	WPB	DP	FW	PW	BW	BSW	DIF
Bos	105	6	**26**	4	1137.1	1291	49	467	345	14.3	3.79	116	.274	.346	55	73	104	**143**	*110*	.918	460	97	109	1.7	5.8	2.7	—	6.2
Bro	111	4	22	**7**	1184.0	1334	**26**	570	377	14.9	3.95	113	.273	.356	37	62	105	195	*142*	.909	531	110	114	-1.8	4.9	-5.3	—	12.1
NY	111	3	23	6	1172.1	**1216**	37	569	449	14.1	4.17	109	.257	.343	8	44	107	254	*152*	**.921**	**450**	147	94	**2.8**	3.5	-3.0	—	5.2
Chi	124	5	14	2	1219.1	1238	27	503	**460**	**13.2**	**3.39**	**128**	**.252**	**.327**	**114**	**125**	103	224	***179***	.918	492	**91**	107	1.6	**10.0**	-8.1	—	2.9
Phi	118	4	14	2	1154.1	1292	33	495	361	14.4	4.05	105	.271	.347	22	27	101	258	*151*	.910	510	106	**118**	-.7	2.2	-1.8	—	2.8
Pit	121	**7**	7	0	1116.2	1267	32	**334**	318	**13.2**	4.22	93	.274	.328	2	-43	92	231	*103*	.907	512	104	80	-1.7	-3.4	-4.8	—	-3.6
Cle	115	1	16	0	1143.2	1386	45	571	325	15.8	4.23	94	.287	.369	0	-35	94	361	*172*	.907	533	171	103	-2.3	-2.8	**9.2**	—	-14.1
Buf	**125**	2	9	0	1141.0	1499	67	673	351	17.5	6.11	67	.304	.393	-239	-265	97	317	*160*	.914	491	141	116	.8	-21.1	.9	—	-10.5
Total	930	32	131	21	9268.2	—	—	—	—	14.7	4.23	—	.274	.351	—	—	—	—	—	.913	3979	967	841	—	—	—	—	—

BATTER-FIELDER WINS	BATTING AVERAGE	ON-BASE PERCENTAGE	SLUGGING AVERAGE	ON-BASE PLUS SLUGGING	ADJUSTED OPS	ADJUSTED BATTER RUNS
Browning-Cle.....4.9	Browning-Cle........373	Brouthers-Bos.......466	Connor-NY............548	Connor-NY............998	Browning-Cle........175	Browning-Cle........60.1
Connor-NY..........2.8	Orr-Bro..................371	Browning-Cle........459	B.Ewing-NY..........545	Browning-Cle........976	Beckley-Pit............156	Larkin-Cle............42.7
Radford-Cle..........2.7	O'Rourke-NY..........360	Connor-NY............450	Beckley-Pit............535	Orr-Bro..................948	Larkin-Cle............153	Beckley-Pit...........39.6
Farrell-Chi...........2.6	Connor-NY............349	Robinson-Pit.........434	Orr-Bro..................534	Gore-NY 931	Connor-NY............152	Connor-NY...........36.5
B.Ewing-NY........2.5	Ryan-Chi...............340	Gore-NY 432	Browning-Cle........517	O'Rourke-NY........925	Orr-Bro..................144	Brouthers-Bos......32.0
RUNS	**HITS**	**DOUBLES**	**TRIPLES**	**HOME RUNS**	**TOTAL BASES**	**RUNS BATTED IN**
Duffy-Chi...............161	Duffy-Chi...............191	Browning-Cle..........40	Visner-Pit...............22	Connor-NY.............14	Shindle-Phi...........282	Richardson-Bos....146
Brown-Bos.............146	Shindle-Phi...........189	Beckley-Pit.............38	Beckley-Pit.............22	Richardson-Bos......13	Duffy-Chi...............280	Orr-Bro...................124
Stovey-Bos 142	Ward-Bro 188	O'Rourke-NY 37	Shindle-Phi.............21	Stovey-Bos 12	Beckley-Pit............276	Beckley-Pit............120
Ward-Bro...............134	Browning-Cle.........184	Duffy-Chi................36	Fields-Pit................20	Shindle-Phi.............10	Richardson-Bos....274	O'Rourke-NY 115
Connor-NY............133	Richardson-Bos....181	Brouthers-Bos.........36	Joyce-Bro 18	Gore-NY 10	Connor-NY............265	Larkin-Cle 112
BASES ON BALLS	**STOLEN BASES**	**BASE STEALING RUNS**	**FIELDING RUNS-INFIELD**	**FIELDING RUNS-OUTFIELD**	**OUTFIELD ASSISTS**	**CATCHER CS PCT.**
Joyce-Bro 123	Stovey-Bos 97		Bierbauer-Bro.....20.8	Wood-Phi.............14.2	Wood-Phi................35	
Robinson-Pit.........101	Brown-Bos..............79		Pfeffer-Chi...........20.0	Griffin-Phi............13.1	Duffy-Chi................34	
Brouthers-Bos.........99	Duffy-Chi.................78		Nash-Bos.............18.5	Duffy-Chi................9.4	Griffin-Phi...............33	
Hoy-Buf...................94	Hanlon-Pit...............65		White-Buf.............18.0	Seery-Bro 5.9	Brown-Bos 32	
	Ward-Bro 63		Ward-Bro 16.8	Fields-Pit.................5.5		
WINS	**WINNING PCT.**	**WINS ABOVE TEAM**	**GAMES STARTED**	**COMPLETE GAMES**	**FEWEST HITS/GAME**	**FEWEST BB/GAME**
Baldwin-Chi 33	Daley-Bos..............720	Knell-Phi 6.1	King-Chi..................56	Baldwin-Chi 53	King-Chi...............8.20	Staley-Pit 1.72
Weyhing-Bro...........30	Radbourn-Bos 692	Weyhing-Bro..........5.8	Baldwin-Chi 56	King-Chi..................48	Crane-NY..............8.80	Sanders-Phi.........1.79
King-Chi...................30	Knell-Phi 667	Radbourn-Bos 4.5	Weyhing-Bro...........46	Staley-Pit 44	Keefe-NY 8.84	Galvin-Pit.............2.03
Radbourn-Bos 27	Gumbert-Bos.........657	Gruber-Cle..............3.7	Staley-Pit 46	Gruber-Cle..............39	Hemming-Cle-Bro8.88	Morris-Pit 2.18
Gumbert-Bos 23	Weyhing-Bro.........652	Daley-Bos 3.6	Gruber-Cle..............44	Weyhing-Bro...........38	Knell-Phi 9.01	Radbourn-Bos 2.62
STRIKEOUTS	**STRIKEOUTS/GAME**	**GAMES**	**SAVES**	**BASE RUNNERS/9**	**ADJUSTED RELIEF RUNS**	**RELIEF RANKING**
Baldwin-Chi 206	J.Ewing-NY..........4.88	Baldwin-Chi 58	Hemming-Cle-Bro.....3	Staley-Pit..........11.07		
King-Chi.................185	Daley-Bos.............4.21	King-Chi..................56	O'Day-NY 3	King-Chi.............11.67		
Weyhing-Bro.........177	Weyhing-Bro........4.08	Weyhing-Bro...........49		Radbourn-Bos ...12.15		
Staley-Pit..............145	McGill-Cle 4.02	Gruber-Cle..............48		Keefe-NY 12.66		
J.Ewing-NY............145	Haddock-Buf.........3.81	Staley-Pit 46		Sanders-Phi.......12.75		
INNINGS PITCHED	**OPPONENTS' AVG.**	**OPPONENTS' OBP**	**EARNED RUN AVERAGE**	**ADJUSTED ERA**	**ADJUSTED STARTER RUNS**	**PITCHER WINS**
Baldwin-Chi 492.0	King-Chi................232	Staley-Pit 290	King-Chi...............2.69	King-Chi................161	King-Chi...............81.7	**King-Chi..............6.6**
King-Chi..............461.0	Crane-NY..............245	King-Chi.................301	Staley-Pit 3.23	Keefe-NY 134	Baldwin-Chi 48.7	**Baldwin-Chi.........4.1**
Weyhing-Bro......390.0	Keefe-NY 246	Radbourn-Bos 310	Radbourn-Bos 3.31	Radbourn-Bos 133	Radbourn-Bos 45.5	**Radbourn-Bos ... 3.9**
Staley-Pit 387.2	Hemming-Cle-Bro.247	Keefe-NY 318	Baldwin-Chi 3.35	Baldwin-Chi 130	Weyhing-Bro........40.2	**Weyhing-Bro 2.5**
Gruber-Cle.........383.1	Knell-Phi 250	Sanders-Phi..........320	Keefe-NY 3.38	Weyhing-Bro..........124	Staley-Pit 28.7	**Staley-Pit 2.5**

Barely There

Buffeted by defections and increased competition from the new Players' League, the AA struggled just to make it through 1890. Two top clubs, Brooklyn and Cincinnati, jumped to the NL, and Kansas City and Baltimore simply quit the league. New clubs in Toledo, Syracuse, and Rochester failed to garner much interest, and an expansion Brooklyn team lost its last 14 before disbanding in August. The Baltimore Orioles, who had deserted the American Association for the Atlantic Association, rejoined in order to help the AA finish the season.

Philadelphia ran out of money in August, and most of the club quit, forcing the recruitment of below-average substitutes. The dismal Athletics lost their final 22 games yet still had twice as many wins as miserable Brooklyn.

Many former Association players jumped to the NL and PL, including St. Louis' Charlie Comiskey, Arlie Latham, Tip O'Neill, and Silver King, Philadelphia slugger Harry Stovey, Kansas City shortstop Herman Long, and Louisville outfielder Pete Browning. The disemboweled Browns fell to third.

Perhaps the best indicator of the AA's quality is that the league champion, Louisville, had finished dead last the previous season with a .196 winning percentage and was the most games back of any team in league history. For 1890 the Colonels made few player changes and improved 67 games. Chicken Wolf, who had hit .300 just once in eight seasons, won the batting title at .363; pitcher Scott Stratton, 3-13 in 1889, went 34-14 and led the league in ERA. Columbus, leaping to second, couldn't provide enough of a challenge despite deep pitching and Jim McTamany's league-leading 140 runs.

Louisville was by far the league's top draw; St. Louis' attendance fell by 70,000, while Brooklyn's new club drew just 1,000 fans per game. Overall AA attendance sank to its lowest since its inaugural season in 1882. A postseason World Series between Louisville and turncoat Brooklyn was closer than expected, but rain postponed several contests. The games did not draw enough interest to continue play into November and the Series was called after six games.

1889 NATIONAL LEAGUE

TEAM	W	L	T	PCT	GB	HW	HL	R	OR	PA	H	2B	3B	HR	BB	SO	HB	SH	AVG	OBP	SLG	OPS	AOPS	BR	ABR	PF	SB	CS	BSA	BSR
NY	83	43	5	.659	—	47	15	**935**	708	5236	1319	208	**77**	52	**538**	386	27	—	**.282**	**.360**	**.393**	**753**	**116**	**105**	**103**	100	292			
Bos	83	45	5	.648	1	**48**	17	826	**626**	5140	1251	196	54	42	471	450	41	—	.270	.343	.363	706	97	22	-23	106	**331**			
Chi	67	65	4	.508	19	37	30	867	814	5397	1338	184	66	**79**	518	516	30	—	.276	.349	.390	739	107	76	34	105	243			
Phi	63	64	3	.496	20.5	43	24	742	748	5123	1248	215	52	44	393	**353**	35	—	.266	.327	.362	689	90	-17	-77	109	269			
Pit	61	71	2	.462	25	40	28	726	801	5212	1202	209	65	42	420	467	**44**	—	.253	.320	.351	671	103	-50	28	90	231			
Cle	61	72	3	.459	25.5	33	35	656	720	5140	1167	131	59	25	429	417	38	—	.250	.318	.319	637	85	-104	-91	98	237			
Ind	59	75	1	.440	28	32	36	819	894	5300	**1356**	**228**	35	62	377	447	**44**	—	.278	.335	.377	712	102	24	9	102	252			
Was	41	83	3	.331	41	24	29	632	892	4904	1105	151	57	25	466	456	43	—	.251	.329	.329	658	95	-56	-12	94	232			
Total	531	—	—	—	—	304	214	6203	—	41452	9986	1522	465	371	3612	3492	302	—	.266	.335	.361	696	—	—	—	—	2087	—	—	—

TEAM	CG	SHO	GR	SV	IP	H	HR	BB	SO	BR/9	ERA	AERA	OAV	OOB	PR	APR	PF	OSB	OCS	FA	E	WPB	DP	FW	PW	BW	BSW	DIF
NY	119	6	13	3	1150.0	**1067**	38	524	**558**	12.8	3.47	114	**.240**	.327	70	57	98	193	—	.919	437	102	90	-.3	4.9	**8.9**	—	6.5
Bos	121	**10**	12	**5**	1166.0	1152	41	413	497	**12.4**	**3.36**	**124**	.250	**.318**	**86**	**102**	104	**186**	—	.926	413	**77**	105	1.2	**8.8**	-2.0	—	10.9
Chi	123	6	13	2	1237.0	1313	71	408	434	12.8	3.73	112	.263	.324	41	62	104	301	—	.923	463	142	91	-.8	5.4	2.9	—	-6.5
Phi	106	4	27	2	1153.1	1288	**33**	428	443	13.6	4.00	109	.275	.339	3	39	108	229	—	.915	466	106	92	-2.0	3.4	-6.7	—	4.8
Pit	125	5	9	1	1130.2	1296	42	**374**	345	13.5	4.51	83	.272	.329	-60	-84	93	276	—	.931	385	140	94	2.8	-7.3	2.4	—	-3.0
Cle	**132**	6	5	1	1191.2	1182	36	519	435	13.2	3.66	110	.252	.332	48	47	100	271	—	**.936**	**365**	163	**108**	**4.2**	4.1	-7.9	—	-5.9
Ind	109	3	**29**	2	1174.1	1365	73	420	408	14.0	4.85	86	.282	.345	-108	-85	104	297	—	.926	420	117	102	1.2	-7.4	.8	—	-2.6
Was	113	1	16	0	1103.0	1261	37	527	388	14.9	4.68	85	.279	.360	-80	-92	98	334	—	.904	519	109	91	-5.2	-8.0	-1.0	—	-6.8
Total	948	41	124	16	9306.0	—	—	—	—	13.4	4.02	—	.266	.335	—	—	—	—	—	.923	3468	956	773	—	—	—	—	—

BATTER-FIELDER WINS	BATTING AVERAGE	ON-BASE PERCENTAGE	SLUGGING AVERAGE	ON-BASE PLUS SLUGGING	ADJUSTED OPS	ADJUSTED BATTER RUNS
Glasscock-Ind ... 5.8	Brouthers-Bos.......373	Carroll-Pit.............486	Connor-NY...........528	Carroll-Pit.............970	Carroll-Pit.............188	Carroll-Pit............49.6
Carroll-Pit.......... 3.7	Glasscock-Ind.......352	Brouthers-Bos.......462	Ryan-Chi...............516	Brouthers-Bos.......969	Connor-NY...........164	Tiernan-NY..........46.9
Ewing-NY........... 3.7	Anson-Chi............342	Tiernan-NY...........447	Brouthers-Bos.......507	Connor-NY...........955	Tiernan-NY...........162	Connor-NY..........46.1
Tiernan-NY......... 3.7	Tiernan-NY...........335	Anson-Chi............440	Tiernan-NY...........497	Tiernan-NY...........944	Brouthers-Bos.......160	Brouthers-Bos.....42.4
Wilmot-Was........ 3.1	Carroll-Pit.............330	Connor-NY...........426	Thompson-Phi......492	Ryan-Chi...............919	Ryan-Chi...............147	Anson-Chi...........36.5
RUNS	**HITS**	**DOUBLES**	**TRIPLES**	**HOME RUNS**	**TOTAL BASES**	**RUNS BATTED IN**
Tiernan-NY..........147	Glasscock-Ind.......205	Kelly-Bos................41	Wilmot-Was...........19	Thompson-Phi........20	Ryan-Chi...............297	Connor-NY............130
Duffy-Chi..............144	Ryan-Chi...............187	Glasscock-Ind........40	Fogarty-Phi............17	Denny-Ind..............18	Glasscock-Ind.......272	Brouthers-Bos.......118
Ryan-Chi...............140	Duffy-Chi...............182	Thompson-Phi........36	Connor-NY.............17	Ryan-Chi.................17	Thompson-Phi......262	Anson-Chi.............117
Gore-NY...............132	Brouthers-Bos.......181	O'Rourke-NY.........36	Tiernan-NY............14	Connor-NY.............13	Connor-NY...........262	Denny-Ind.............112
Glasscock-Ind.......128	Anson-Chi............177	Richardson-Bos......33	Ryan-Chi................14	Duffy-Chi................12	Duffy-Chi...............253	Thompson-Phi......111
BASES ON BALLS	**STOLEN BASES**	**BASE STEALING RUNS**	**FIELDING RUNS-INFIELD**	**FIELDING RUNS-OUTFIELD**	**OUTFIELD ASSISTS**	**CATCHER CS PCT.**
Tiernan-NY.............96	Fogarty-Phi.............99		Glasscock-Ind......38.1	Fogarty-Phi..........18.3	Fogarty-Phi............42	
Connor-NY.............93	Kelly-Bos.................68		Richardson-NY....14.9	Wilmot-Was.........14.3	Ryan-Chi.................36	
Radford-Cle............91	Brown-Bos..............63		Denny-Ind............12.7	Ryan-Chi................8.5	McGeachy-Ind........36	
Anson-Chi...............86	Ward-NY.................62		Bassett-Ind..........12.5	McGeachy-Ind.......7.8	McAleer-Cle...........29	
Carroll-Pit...............85	Glasscock-Ind.........57		Nash-Bos.............11.4	McAleer-Cle..........7.5	Hoy-Was................29	
WINS	**WINNING PCT.**	**WINS ABOVE TEAM**	**GAMES STARTED**	**COMPLETE GAMES**	**FEWEST HITS/GAME**	**FEWEST BB/GAME**
Clarkson-Bos..........49	Clarkson-Bos........721	Clarkson-Bos.......12.1	Clarkson-Bos..........72	Clarkson-Bos..........68	Keefe-NY............7.89	Galvin-Pit............2.06
Keefe-NY................28	Welch-NY............692	Buffinton-Phi.........8.2	Staley-Pit................47	Staley-Pit................46	Welch-NY............8.16	Boyle-Ind.............2.26
Buffinton-Phi...........28	Keefe-NY.............683	Galvin-Pit...............6.0	Keefe-NY................45	Welch-NY...............39	Clarkson-Bos.......8.55	Radbourn-Bos.....2.34
Welch-NY...............27	Radbourn-Bos......645	Ferson-Was...........5.4	Boyle-Ind................45	O'Brien-Cle............39	Crane-NY............8.62	Dwyer-Chi...........2.35
Galvin-Pit................23	Buffinton-Phi.........636	O'Brien-Cle............5.0	Getzien-Ind............44	Keefe-NY...............39	Hutchison-Chi......8.66	Sanders-Phi.........2.47
STRIKEOUTS	**STRIKEOUTS/GAME**	**GAMES**	**SAVES**	**BASE RUNNERS/9**	**ADJUSTED RELIEF RUNS**	**RELIEF RANKING**
Clarkson-Bos........284	Keefe-NY............5.56	Clarkson-Bos..........73	Sowders-Bos-Pit.......3	Clarkson-Bos.....11.74		
Keefe-NY..............225	Crane-NY.............5.07	Staley-Pit................49	Welch-NY.................2	Radbourn-Bos...11.76		
Staley-Pit..............159	Rusie-Ind............4.36	Keefe-NY................47	Bishop-Chi...............2	Staley-Pit...........11.94		
Buffinton-Phi.........153	Healy-Was-Chi.....4.35	Buffinton-Phi...........47		Welch-NY..........11.98		
Getzien-Ind...........139	Clarkson-Bos.......4.12	Boyle-Ind................46		Keefe-NY...........12.07		
INNINGS PITCHED	**OPPONENTS' AVG.**	**OPPONENTS' OBP**	**EARNED RUN AVERAGE**	**ADJUSTED ERA**	**ADJUSTED STARTER RUNS**	**PITCHER WINS**
Clarkson-Bos.....620.0	Keefe-NY.............228	Clarkson-Bos........306	Clarkson-Bos.......2.73	Clarkson-Bos........153	Clarkson-Bos.......92.8	**Clarkson-Bos..... 8.9**
Staley-Pit...........420.0	Welch-NY.............234	Radbourn-Bos......306	Bakely-Cle...........2.96	Bakely-Cle............136	Buffinton-Phi........44.6	**Buffinton-Phi...... 4.0**
Buffinton-Phi......380.0	Clarkson-Bos........243	Staley-Pit..............309	Welch-NY............3.02	Buffinton-Phi.........134	Welch-NY............40.8	**Welch-NY........... 3.1**
Boyle-Ind...........378.2	Crane-NY.............244	Welch-NY.............310	Buffinton-Phi........3.24	Welch-NY.............131	Bakely-Cle...........29.5	**Bakely-Cle......... 2.6**
Welch-NY..........375.0	Hutchison-Chi.......245	Keefe-NY.............312	Keefe-NY.............3.36	Sanders-Phi..........123	Keefe-NY............24.4	**Sanders-Phi....... 2.4**

Land of the Giants

The Detroit club left the NL, and Cleveland jumped from the American Association to fill the space. The new club finished sixth. The game itself underwent significant changes in 1889. First and forevermore, it now took four balls to draw a walk, which helped scoring increase by about 25 percent. In addition, the use of substitutes gained speed as teams were now allowed to change one player per game for any reason—not just injuries—at the end of any complete inning. Also, the owners' decision to institute a salary classification scheme infuriated players, who organized in secret.

New York won its second straight league title, edging out the Boston Beaneaters by 1 game. Tim Keefe's win on the season's last day clinched matters for the Giants, who sported the bats of Roger Connor, Mike Tiernan, and George Gore, and a great second starter in Mickey Welch. Boston contended largely on the arm of John Clarkson, who enjoyed one of the great ironman seasons by any pitcher. He led the league by huge margins in games, innings, wins, strikeouts, and ERA. His 68 complete games weren't quite a record, but no one has surpassed it since; the same can be said of his 49 wins, which still didn't match his career-high 53 victories in '85. Beaneaters teammate Dan Brouthers won his third batting title, but King Kelly, beginning to feel the effects of his dissipated lifestyle, fell off dramatically for Boston.

Future ace Amos Rusie debuted as a third starter for seventh-place Indianapolis. Sam Thompson led the league in homers and Jim Fogarty paced the NL in steals for Harry Wright's fourth-place Phillies.

The Giants took a hotly contested World Series from AA champ Brooklyn—New York's first "Subway Series," so to speak, even though the subway system did not open until 1904. The Bridegrooms, borrowing a tactic from AA St. Louis, won three times by stalling for darkness, but New York responded by outhitting Brooklyn, 102-67. Neither Keefe nor Welch had the strength to win a single contest—second-line hurlers Ed "Cannonball" Crane and Hank O'Day took over and saved the NL's bacon.

1889 AMERICAN ASSOCIATION

TEAM	W	L	T	PCT	GB	HW	HL	R	OR	PA	H	2B	3B	HR	BB	SO	HB	SH	AVG	OBP	SLG	OPS	AOPS	BR	ABR	PF	SB	CS	BSA	BSR
Bro	93	44	3	.679	—	50	18	**995**	706	5414	1265	188	79	47	**550**	**401**	49	—	.263	.344	.364	708	106	44	41	100	389			
StL	90	45	6	.667	2	**51**	18	957	**680**	5487	1312	211	64	**58**	493	477	55	—	.266	.339	.370	709	94	41	-63	113	336			
Phi	75	58	5	.564	16	46	22	880	787	5464	**1339**	**239**	65	43	534	496	62	—	**.275**	**.354**	.377	**731**	**114**	**92**	**105**	99	252			
Cin	76	63	2	.547	18	47	26	897	769	5356	1307	197	**96**	52	452	511	60	—	.270	.340	**.382**	722	107	56	30	103	462			
Bal	70	65	4	.519	22	41	23	791	795	5256	1209	155	68	20	418	536	**82**	—	.254	.325	.328	653	88	-58	-71	102	311			
Col	60	78	2	.435	33.5	36	33	779	924	5365	1247	171	95	36	507	609	42	—	.259	.335	.356	691	106	7	52	95	304			
KC	55	82	2	.401	38	35	35	852	1031	5443	1256	162	76	18	430	626	66	—	.254	.322	.328	650	84	-68	-113	106	**472**			
Lou	27	111	2	.196	66.5	18	47	632	1091	5316	1249	170	75	22	320	521	41	—	.252	.303	.330	633	86	-114	-100	98	203			
Total	559	—	—	—	—	324	222	6783	—	43101	10184	1493	618	296	3704	4177	457	—	.262	.333	.354	687	—	—	—	—	2729	—	—	—

TEAM	CG	SHO	GR	SV	IP	H	HR	BB	SO	BR/9	ERA	AERA	OAV	OOB	PR	APR	PF	OSB	OCS	FA	E	WPB	DP	FW	PW	BW	BSW	DIF
Bro	120	**10**	20	1	1212.2	1205	33	**400**	471	12.2	3.61	103	.251	.315	31	15	97	361	—	**.928**	**421**	**142**	92	**4.6**	1.3	3.5	—	15.2
StL	121	7	20	4	1237.2	**1166**	39	413	**617**	**11.9**	**3.00**	**141**	**.242**	**.309**	**116**	**152**	110	326	—	.925	438	196	100	3.8	**12.9**	-5.3	—	11.2
Phi	**130**	9	8	1	1199.1	1199	35	509	479	13.4	3.53	107	.253	.335	42	34	98	**280**	—	.920	465	152	120	1.7	2.9	**8.9**	—	-5.0
Cin	114	3	**27**	**8**	1243.0	1270	35	475	562	13.0	3.50	111	.257	.328	47	53	102	294	—	.926	440	187	**121**	3.7	4.5	2.5	—	-4.2
Bal	128	**10**	12	1	1192.0	1168	**27**	424	540	12.6	3.56	111	.249	.322	38	48	103	305	—	.907	536	195	104	-2.1	4.1	-6.0	—	6.5
Col	114	9	**27**	4	1199.0	1274	33	551	610	14.1	4.39	82	.264	.346	-73	-110	94	431	—	.915	497	275	92	.3	-9.3	4.4	—	-4.4
KC	128	0	11	2	1204.1	1373	51	457	447	14.1	4.36	97	.278	.347	-69	-15	110	363	—	.899	611	201	109	-6.3	-1.3	-9.6	—	3.6
Lou	127	2	13	1	1226.1	1529	43	475	451	15.1	4.81	80	.297	.362	-132	-133	100	369	—	.906	584	234	117	-4.5	-11.3	-8.5	—	-17.7
Total	982	50	138	22	9714.1	—	—	—	—	13.3	3.84	—	.262	.333	—	—	—	—	—	.916	3992	1582	855	—	—	—	—	—

BATTER-FIELDER WINS	BATTING AVERAGE	ON-BASE PERCENTAGE	SLUGGING AVERAGE	ON-BASE PLUS SLUGGING	ADJUSTED OPS	ADJUSTED BATTER RUNS
Stovey-Phi...5.0	Tucker-Bal...372	Tucker-Bal...450	Stovey-Phi...525	Tucker-Bal...934	Tucker-Bal...163	Tucker-Bal...46.3
Lyons-Phi...4.5	O'Neill-StL...335	Larkin-Phi...428	Holliday-Cin...497	Stovey-Phi...918	Stovey-Phi...162	Stovey-Phi...45.8
Bierbauer-Phi...4.3	Lyons-Phi...329	Lyons-Phi...426	Tucker-Bal...484	O'Neill-StL...897	Lyons-Phi...157	Lyons-Phi...43.3
Marr-Col...3.6	Orr-Col...327	O'Neill-StL...419	O'Neill-StL...478	Lyons-Phi...895	Larkin-Phi...145	Larkin-Phi...36.9
McPhee-Cin...3.6	Holliday-Cin...321	Hamilton-KC...413	Lyons-Phi...469	Holliday-Cin...869	Holliday-Cin...142	Marr-Col...35.2

RUNS	HITS	DOUBLES	TRIPLES	HOME RUNS	TOTAL BASES	RUNS BATTED IN
Stovey-Phi...152	Tucker-Bal...196	Welch-Phi...39	Marr-Col...15	Stovey-Phi...19	Stovey-Phi...292	Stovey-Phi...119
Griffin-Bal...152	Orr-Col...183	Stovey-Phi...38	Griffin-Bal...14	Holliday-Cin...19	Holliday-Cin...280	Foutz-Bro...113
O'Brien-Bro...146	Holliday-Cin...181	Lyons-Phi...36	Beard-Cin...14	Duffee-StL...16	Tucker-Bal...255	O'Neill-StL...110
Hamilton-KC...144	O'Neill-StL...179	O'Neill-StL...33		Milligan-StL...12	O'Neill-StL...255	Bierbauer-Phi...105
Collins-Bro...139	Shindle-Bal...178	Long-KC...32			Orr-Col...250	Holliday-Cin...104

BASES ON BALLS	STOLEN BASES	BASE STEALING RUNS	FIELDING RUNS-INFIELD	FIELDING RUNS-OUTFIELD	OUTFIELD ASSISTS	CATCHER CS PCT.
Robinson-StL...118	Hamilton-KC...111		McPhee-Cin...37.3	Stovey-Phi...17.7	Duffee-StL...43	
McTamany-Col...116	O'Brien-Bro...91		Bierbauer-Phi...36.4	Duffee-StL...15.7	Stovey-Phi...38	
Griffin-Bal...91	Long-KC...89		Long-KC...31.2	McCarthy-StL...13.0	McCarthy-StL...38	
Marr-Col...87	Nicol-Cin...80		Shindle-Bal...22.6	Hornung-Bal...12.3	Corkhill-Bro...35	
Hamilton-KC...87	Latham-StL...69		Tomney-Lou...21.6	Sommer-Bal...9.1	Hornung-Bal...32	

WINS	WINNING PCT.	WINS ABOVE TEAM	GAMES STARTED	COMPLETE GAMES	FEWEST HITS/GAME	FEWEST BB/GAME
Caruthers-Bro...40	Caruthers-Bro...784	Caruthers-Bro...11.2	Baldwin-Col...59	Kilroy-Bal...55	Stivetts-StL...7.18	Caruthers-Bro...2.10
King-StL...35	King-StL...686	Duryea-Cin...6.5	Kilroy-Bal...56	Baldwin-Col...54	Weyhing-Phi...7.66	Conway-KC...2.42
Duryea-Cin...32	Chamberlain-StL...681	Conway-KC...4.1	Weyhing-Phi...53	Weyhing-Phi...50	Terry-Bro...7.87	King-StL...2.46
Chamberlain-StL...32	Lovett-Bro...630	Mays-Col...2.5	King-StL...53	King-StL...47	Foreman-Bal...7.91	Lovett-Bro...2.55
Weyhing-Phi...30	Duryea-Cin...627	King-StL...2.3	Chamberlain-StL...51	Caruthers-Bro...46	Baldwin-Col...8.02	Swartzel-KC...2.57

STRIKEOUTS	STRIKEOUTS/GAME	GAMES	SAVES	BASE RUNNERS/9	ADJUSTED RELIEF RUNS	RELIEF RANKING
Baldwin-Col...368	Stivetts-StL...6.71	Baldwin-Col...63	Mullane-Cin...5	Stivetts-StL...10.61		
Kilroy-Bal...217	Baldwin-Col...6.45	Kilroy-Bal...59	Stivetts-StL...2	Caruthers-Bro...11.35		
Weyhing-Phi...213	Terry-Bro...5.13	King-StL...56		Duryea-Cin...11.56		
Chamberlain-StL...202	Sowders-KC...5.06	Caruthers-Bro...56		Foreman-Bal...11.76		
King-StL...188	Gastright-Col...4.65	Weyhing-Phi...54		Conway-KC...11.77		

INNINGS PITCHED	OPPONENTS' AVG.	OPPONENTS' OBP	EARNED RUN AVERAGE	ADJUSTED ERA	ADJUSTED STARTER RUNS	PITCHER WINS
Baldwin-Col...513.2	Stivetts-StL...212	Stivetts-StL...285	Stivetts-StL...2.25	Stivetts-StL...187	Chamberlain-StL...56.0	**Duryea-Cin...5.7**
Kilroy-Bal...480.2	Weyhing-Phi...223	Caruthers-Bro...299	Duryea-Cin...2.56	Duryea-Cin...152	King-StL...51.7	**Kilroy-Bal...5.7**
King-StL...458.0	Terry-Bro...228	Duryea-Cin...303	Kilroy-Bal...2.85	Chamberlain-StL...142	Duryea-Cin...50.6	**Chamberlain-StL4.6**
Weyhing-Phi...449.0	Foreman-Bal...229	Foreman-Bal...306	Weyhing-Phi...2.95	Kilroy-Bal...138	Kilroy-Bal...49.4	**Caruthers-Bro...4.6**
Caruthers-Bro...445.0	Baldwin-Col...231	Conway-KC...306	Chamberlain-StL...2.97	King-StL...134	Stivetts-StL...36.5	**King-StL...4.4**

Forfeiting a Title

Cleveland, a perennial doormat, left the league for the NL and was replaced by Columbus, which finished sixth. The big news in the AA was a dethroning of perennial champion St. Louis. The Browns' questionable on-field ethics, which included the tactic of stalling while ahead until darkness came and ended games, led to several forfeits. Brooklyn, white-hot down the stretch, grabbed the flag in the closet AA race since 1883.

The Bridegrooms led the league in runs despite lacking a single marquee star. Brooklyn moundsman Bob Caruthers paced the league in wins. St. Louis second baseman Yank Robinson broke his own record for walks and put together a .378 on-base percentage, but he hit just .208. Arlie Latham also disappointed at bat. Pitchers Silver King and Icebox Chamberlain were good, if unspectacular, though third arm Jack Stivetts paced the AA in ERA.

Once again, third-place Philadelphia had the AA's top power producer (this time Harry Stovey) as well as other bats in Curt Welch and Henry Larkin. Although the Athletics seem to have played in a good hitter's park, their offensive numbers, and their W-L record, were inadequate on the road.

With four balls once again required for a walk, Columbus pitcher Mark Baldwin set a record by passing 274 hitters. He also paced the league in games, strikeouts, and losses.

Baltimore improved 14 games, largely due to a great season from first baseman Tommy Tucker, who was the AA's surprise batting and on-base titlist in 1889. Seventh-place Kansas City installed rookie Herman Long at shortstop, and next to Billy Hamilton, Long was the team's best player. Meanwhile, last-place Louisville was almost unbelievably bad, finishing 66½ games out and running through four managers and five pitchers who made 18 or more starts.

League attendance rose by nearly 300,000, due to increases in Baltimore, Brooklyn, and Philadelphia. The Bridegrooms' tally of 353,690 was the highest attendance by any major league team to that point; it would not be surpassed for five years.

1888 NATIONAL LEAGUE

TEAM	W	L	T	PCT	GB	HW	HL	R	OR	PA	H	2B	3B	HR	BB	SO	HB	SH	AVG	OBP	SLG	OPS	AOPS	BR	ABR	PF	SB	CS	BSA	BSR
NY	84	47	7	.641	—	**44**	23	659	**479**	5046	1149	130	76	55	270	456	29	—	.242	.287	.336	623	105	18	26	99	314			
Chi	77	58	1	.570	9	43	27	**734**	659	4934	1201	147	**95**	**77**	290	563	28	—	.260	.308	**.383**	**691**	117	**125**	75	107	287			
Phi	69	61	2	.531	14.5	37	29	535	509	4847	1021	151	46	16	268	485	**51**	—	.225	.276	.290	566	82	-61	-89	105	246			
Bos	70	64	3	.522	15.5	36	30	669	619	5148	1183	167	89	56	282	524	32	—	.245	.291	.351	642	107	50	33	103	293			
Det	68	63	3	.519	16	40	26	721	629	5202	**1275**	177	72	51	**307**	**396**	46	—	**.263**	**.313**	.361	674	**120**	112	**104**	101	193			
Pit	66	68	5	.493	19.5	37	30	534	580	4953	1070	150	49	14	194	583	46	—	.227	.264	.289	553	90	-93	-44	91	287			
Ind	50	85	1	.370	36	31	35	603	731	4902	1100	**180**	33	34	236	492	43	—	.238	.281	.313	594	93	-20	-31	102	**350**			
Was	48	86	2	.358	37.5	26	38	482	731	4835	944	98	49	30	246	499	43	—	.208	.255	.271	526	78	-132	-99	93	331			
Total	544	—	—	—	—	294	238	4937	—	39867	8943	1200	509	333	2093	3998	318	—	.239	.285	.325	609	—	—	—	—	2301	—	—	—

TEAM	CG	SHO	GR	SV	IP	H	HR	BB	SO	BR/9	ERA	AERA	OAV	OOB	PR	APR	PF	OSB	OCS	FA	E	WPB	DP	FW	PW	BW	BSW	DIF
NY	133	**20**	4	1	1208.0	**907**	27	307	**726**	**9.3**	**1.96**	**139**	**.199**	**.255**	**117**	**107**	96	—	—	.924	432	193	76	1.2	**10.5**	2.6	—	4.2
Chi	123	13	**12**	1	1186.1	1139	63	308	588	11.4	2.96	102	.246	.301	-17	6	106	—	—	**.927**	417	186	**112**	1.7	.6	7.4	—	-.1
Phi	125	16	6	**3**	1167.0	1072	26	196	519	10.0	2.38	124	.236	.271	58	67	104	—	—	.923	424	128	70	.6	6.6	-8.8	—	5.6
Bos	134	7	3	0	1225.1	1104	36	269	484	10.4	2.61	110	.232	.280	30	30	101	—	—	.917	494	155	91	-2.2	3.0	3.2	—	-1.0
Det	130	10	4	1	1199.0	1115	44	**183**	522	10.0	2.74	101	.234	.266	12	2	98	—	—	.919	463	**101**	83	-1.1	.2	**10.2**	—	-6.8
Pit	**135**	13	3	0	1203.1	1190	**23**	223	367	10.8	2.67	98	.249	.287	22	-8	93	—	—	**.927**	**416**	141	88	**2.3**	-.8	-4.3	—	1.9
Ind	132	6	5	0	1187.2	1260	64	308	388	12.2	3.81	77	.263	.313	-129	-113	104	—	—	.921	449	183	84	-.0	-11.1	-3.0	—	-3.3
Was	133	6	3	0	1179.1	1157	50	298	406	11.5	3.54	78	.248	.300	-93	-110	97	—	—	.912	494	152	69	-2.4	-10.8	-9.7	—	4.0
Total	1045	91	40	6	9556.0	—	—	—	—	10.7	2.83	—	.239	.285	—	—	—	—	—	.921	3589	1239	673	—	—	—	—	—

BATTER-FIELDER WINS	BATTING AVERAGE	ON-BASE PERCENTAGE	SLUGGING AVERAGE	ON-BASE PLUS SLUGGING	ADJUSTED OPS	ADJUSTED BATTER RUNS
Pfeffer-Chi 4.4	Anson-Chi .344	Anson-Chi .400	Ryan-Chi .515	Anson-Chi .899	Connor-NY 178	Brouthers-Det 47.2
Nash-Bos 4.1	Ryan-Chi .332	Brouthers-Det .399	Anson-Chi .499	Ryan-Chi .892	Anson-Chi 172	Connor-NY 45.2
Ryan-Chi 3.8	Kelly-Bos .318	Connor-NY .389	Connor-NY .480	Connor-NY .869	Brouthers-Det 172	Ryan-Chi 42.1
Ewing-NY 3.8	Brouthers-Det .307	Ryan-Chi .377	Kelly-Bos .480	Brouthers-Det .862	Ryan-Chi 170	Anson-Chi 41.5
Anson-Chi 3.8	Ewing-NY .306	Hoy-Was .374	Johnston-Bos .472	Kelly-Bos .848	Kelly-Bos 164	Kelly-Bos 31.4
RUNS	**HITS**	**DOUBLES**	**TRIPLES**	**HOME RUNS**	**TOTAL BASES**	**RUNS BATTED IN**
Brouthers-Det 118	Ryan-Chi 182	Ryan-Chi 33	Johnston-Bos 18	Ryan-Chi 16	Ryan-Chi 283	Anson-Chi 84
Ryan-Chi 115	Anson-Chi 177	Brouthers-Det 33	Connor-NY 17	Connor-NY 14	Johnston-Bos 276	Nash-Bos 75
Johnston-Bos 102	Johnston-Bos 173	Johnston-Bos 31	Nash-Bos 15	Johnston-Bos 12	Anson-Chi 257	Rowe-Det 74
Anson-Chi 101	Brouthers-Det 160	Denny-Ind 27	Ewing-NY 15	Denny-Ind 12	Brouthers-Det 242	Williamson-Chi 73
Connor-NY 98	White-Det 157	Hines-Ind 26		Anson-Chi 12	Connor-NY 231	
BASES ON BALLS	**STOLEN BASES**	**BASE STEALING RUNS**	**FIELDING RUNS-INFIELD**	**FIELDING RUNS-OUTFIELD**	**OUTFIELD ASSISTS**	**CATCHER CS PCT.**
Connor-NY 73	Hoy-Was 82		Pfeffer-Chi 37.7	Sunday-Pit 15.1	Ryan-Chi 34	
Hoy-Was 69	Seery-Ind 80		Nash-Bos 18.3	Fogarty-Phi 14.1	Johnston-Bos 30	
Brouthers-Det 68	Sunday-Pit 71		Burns-Chi 17.4	Wilmot-Was 11.7	Sunday-Pit 27	
Williamson-Chi 65	Pfeffer-Chi 64		Denny-Ind 15.8	Seery-Ind 9.6	McGeachy-Ind 27	
Seery-Ind 64	Ryan-Chi 60		Glasscock-Ind 13.9	Hoy-Was 6.9		
WINS	**WINNING PCT.**	**WINS ABOVE TEAM**	**GAMES STARTED**	**COMPLETE GAMES**	**FEWEST HITS/GAME**	**FEWEST BB/GAME**
Keefe-NY 35	Keefe-NY .745	Conway-Det 9.6	Morris-Pit 55	Morris-Pit 54	Keefe-NY 6.57	Sanders-Phi 1.08
Clarkson-Bos 33	Conway-Det .682	Keefe-NY 9.1	Clarkson-Bos 54	Clarkson-Bos 53	Titcomb-NY 6.81	Galvin-Pit 1.09
Conway-Det 30	Sanders-Phi .655	Clarkson-Bos 8.1	Keefe-NY 51	Galvin-Pit 49	Welch-NY 6.94	Krock-Chi 1.19
Morris-Pit 29	Krock-Chi .641	Buffinton-Phi 6.1	Galvin-Pit 50	Keefe-NY 48	Conway-Det 7.25	Getzien-Det 1.20
Buffinton-Phi 28	Clarkson-Bos .623	Morris-Pit 5.0	Welch-NY 47	Welch-NY 47	Buffinton-Phi 7.28	Madden-Bos 1.31
STRIKEOUTS	**STRIKEOUTS/GAME**	**GAMES**	**SAVES**	**BASE RUNNERS/9**	**ADJUSTED RELIEF RUNS**	**RELIEF RANKING**
Keefe-NY 335	Keefe-NY 6.94	Morris-Pit 55	Wood-Phi 2	Keefe-NY 8.68		
Clarkson-Bos 223	Titcomb-NY 5.89	Clarkson-Bos 54	VanHaltren-Chi 1	Buffinton-Phi 8.70		
Getzien-Det 202	Baldwin-Chi 5.63	Keefe-NY 51	Tyng-Phi 1	Conway-Det 8.86		
Buffinton-Phi 199	VanHaltren-Chi 5.09	Galvin-Pit 50	Twitchell-Det 1	Sanders-Phi 9.02		
O'Day-Was 186	Getzien-Det 4.50	Welch-NY 47	Crane-NY 1	Gruber-Det 9.04		
INNINGS PITCHED	**OPPONENTS' AVG.**	**OPPONENTS' OBP**	**EARNED RUN AVERAGE**	**ADJUSTED ERA**	**ADJUSTED STARTER RUNS**	**PITCHER WINS**
Clarkson-Bos 483.1	Keefe-NY .196	Conway-Det .243	Keefe-NY 1.74	Keefe-NY 156	Keefe-NY 52.1	**Buffinton-Phi 5.1**
Morris-Pit 480.0	Titcomb-NY .201	Keefe-NY .243	Sanders-Phi 1.90	Sanders-Phi 156	Buffinton-Phi 44.8	**Keefe-NY 4.6**
Galvin-Pit 437.1	Welch-NY .207	Buffinton-Phi .244	Buffinton-Phi 1.91	Buffinton-Phi 155	Welch-NY 41.9	**Welch-NY 3.9**
Keefe-NY 434.1	Conway-Det .208	Gruber-Det .249	Welch-NY 1.93	Welch-NY 141	Sanders-Phi 29.8	**Conway-Det 3.9**
Welch-NY 425.1	Buffinton-Phi .213	Titcomb-NY .253	Sowders-Bos 2.07	Sowders-Bos 138	Krock-Chi 23.8	**Sanders-Phi 3.7**

Casey Debuts in Mudville

The NL went back to the three-strikes-and-you're-out rule. The new ruling rule helped pitchers dominate. As the NL's batting average dropped by nearly 30 points, scoring fell dramatically in 1888. Whiffs skyrocketed and walks, which still took five balls, dipped.

In this pitcher's year, only Chicago's Jimmy Ryan slugged over .500, and last-place Washington had seven regulars bat .225 or worse. By 1888 nearly all catchers were using a mitt; the 1884 ruling allowing pitchers to throw overhand made the mitt a necessity. And as new ways came in, old ones went out: Ezra Sutton, 38, one of the last remaining active players from the 1871 National Association, retired.

Washington became the first team to do its spring training in Florida. The warm setting might have helped rookie outfielder Dummy Hoy loosen up—he led the NL in stolen bases. Other important first-year men included future Hall of Famers Hugh Duffy of Chicago, Pittsburgh first baseman Jake Beckley, and Philadelphia's Ed Delahanty. Also debuting in Philadelphia was pitcher Kid Gleason, who later became a solid second baseman but is remembered as the blameless manager of the 1919 Black Sox.

The debut with the most lasting impact, though, belonged to a fictional batsman. Ernest Lawrence Thayer's epic baseball poem "Casey at the Bat" was an immediate success, with actors all over the land performing dramatic readings and spreading Casey's name.

Cap Anson won his second batting title, and once again Chicago had the league's top attack. But thanks to pitching Triple Crown winner Tim Keefe and his second, Mickey Welch, New York's mound work was outstanding. Roger Connor and Buck Ewing provided the Giants with enough offense to win easily.

Keefe was dominating in the World Series as the Giants easily breezed by AA champ St. Louis in a 10-game set. The Giants won six of the first seven, defusing any tension that the final games might have otherwise had. Keefe threw 4 complete-game victories, allowing just 2 earned runs in 35 innings.

1888 AMERICAN ASSOCIATION

TEAM	W	L	T	PCT	GB	HW	HL	R	OR	PA	H	2B	3B	HR	BB	SO	HB	SH	AVG	OBP	SLG	OPS	AOPS	BR	ABR	PF	SB	CS	BSA	BSR
StL	92	43	2	.681	—	**60**	21	789	**501**	5215	1189	149	47	**36**	**410**	521	50	—	**.250**	**.316**	.324	640	98	57	-20	111	468			
Bro	88	52	3	.629	6.5	53	20	758	584	5280	1177	172	70	25	353	**439**	56	—	.242	.300	.321	621	103	18	20	100	334			
Phi	81	52	3	.609	10	54	20	**827**	594	5208	**1209**	**183**	**89**	31	303	473	77	—	**.250**	.305	**.344**	**649**	**113**	**60**	**66**	99	434			
Cin	80	54	3	.597	11.5	56	25	745	628	5206	1161	132	82	32	345	555	60	—	.242	.301	.323	624	99	19	-18	105	**469**			
Bal	57	80	0	.416	36	30	26	653	779	5012	1068	162	70	19	298	479	58	—	.229	.284	.306	590	96	-37	-19	97	326			
Cle	50	82	3	.379	40.5	33	28	651	839	4997	1076	128	59	12	315	559	**79**	—	.234	.294	.295	589	96	-33	-13	97	353			
Lou	48	87	4	.356	44	27	29	689	870	5272	1177	**183**	67	14	322	604	69	—	.241	.297	.315	612	102	2	18	98	318			
KC	43	89	0	.326	47.5	23	34	579	896	4933	1000	142	61	19	288	604	57	—	.218	.273	.288	561	78	-85	-119	106	257			
Total	548	—	—	—	—	336	203	5691	—	41123	9057	1251	545	188	2634	4234	506	—	.238	.297	.315	612	—	—	—	—	2959	—	—	—

TEAM	CG	SHO	GR	SV	IP	H	HR	BB	SO	BR/9	ERA	AERA	OAV	OOB	PR	APR	PF	OSB	OCS	FA	E	WPB	DP	FW	PW	BW	BSW	DIF
StL	132	12	5	0	1212.2	**939**	19	**225**	517	**9.1**	**2.09**	**156**	**.206**	**.254**	**130**	**147**	107	**254**	—	**.924**	**430**	**167**	73	**3.4**	**13.6**	-1.8	—	9.3
Bro	**138**	9	5	0	1286.1	1059	15	285	577	9.7	2.33	128	.217	.266	104	94	97	345	—	.918	502	172	88	.6	8.7	1.8	—	6.9
Phi	133	**13**	3	0	1208.2	988	**14**	324	596	10.4	2.41	124	.216	.279	87	78	98	353	—	.919	475	267	73	.7	7.2	**6.1**	—	.5
Cin	132	10	5	**2**	1237.2	1103	19	310	539	10.8	2.73	116	.230	.288	46	58	104	289	—	.923	456	178	**100**	2.0	5.4	-1.7	—	7.3
Bal	130	3	**9**	0	1200.1	1162	23	419	525	12.5	3.78	79	.245	.318	-96	-111	97	434	—	.920	461	247	88	1.7	-10.3	-1.8	—	-1.2
Cle	131	6	4	1	1171.0	1235	38	389	500	12.9	3.72	83	.261	.324	-86	-82	101	388	—	.915	488	249	87	-.2	-7.6	-1.2	—	-7.0
Lou	133	6	6	0	1231.1	1265	28	281	**599**	11.7	3.25	95	.256	.304	-26	-24	100	384	—	.900	609	233	75	-6.2	-2.2	1.7	—	-12.7
KC	128	4	4	0	1157.2	1306	32	401	381	13.8	4.29	79	.275	.340	-159	-107	110	512	—	.914	507	222	95	-1.9	-9.9	-11.0	—	-.2
Total	1057	63	41	3	9705.2	—	—	—	—	11.3	3.06	—	.238	.297	—	—	—	—	—	.917	3928	1735	679	—	—	—	—	—

BATTER-FIELDER WINS	BATTING AVERAGE	ON-BASE PERCENTAGE	SLUGGING AVERAGE	ON-BASE PLUS SLUGGING	ADJUSTED OPS	ADJUSTED BATTER RUNS
Stovey-Phi 3.5	O'Neill-StL .335	Robinson-StL .400	Reilly-Cin .501	Reilly-Cin .864	Reilly-Cin 167	Stovey-Phi 38.8
Collins-Lou-Bro 3.2	Reilly-Cin .321	O'Neill-StL .390	Stovey-Phi .460	O'Neill-StL .836	Stovey-Phi 165	Reilly-Cin 36.0
McKean-Cle 3.1	Browning-Lou .313	Browning-Lou .380	O'Neill-StL .446	Stovey-Phi .825	Browning-Lou 164	Collins-Lou-Bro 35.8
Davis-KC 2.9	Collins-Lou-Bro .307	Collins-Lou-Bro .373	Browning-Lou .436	Browning-Lou .816	Collins-Lou-Bro 158	Burns-Bal-Bro 29.8
McPhee-Cin 2.8	Orr-Bro .305	Stovey-Phi .365	Burns-Bal-Bro .435	Collins-Lou-Bro .796	Burns-Bal-Bro 152	Browning-Lou 29.0
RUNS	**HITS**	**DOUBLES**	**TRIPLES**	**HOME RUNS**	**TOTAL BASES**	**RUNS BATTED IN**
Pinkney-Bro 134	O'Neill-StL 177	Collins-Lou-Bro 31	Stovey-Phi 20	Reilly-Cin 13	Reilly-Cin 264	Reilly-Cin 103
Collins-Lou-Bro 133	Reilly-Cin 169	Wolf-Lou 28	Burns-Bal-Bro 15	Stovey-Phi 9	Stovey-Phi 244	Larkin-Phi 101
Stovey-Phi 127	McKean-Cle 164	Reilly-Cin 28	McKean-Cle 15	Larkin-Phi 7	O'Neill-StL 236	Foutz-Bro 99
Welch-Phi 125	Collins-Lou-Bro 162	Larkin-Phi 28	Reilly-Cin 14		McKean-Cle 233	O'Neill-StL 98
Latham-StL 119	Corkhill-Cin-Bro 160		Foutz-Bro 13		Burns-Bal-Bro 230	Corkhill-Cin-Bro 93
BASES ON BALLS	**STOLEN BASES**	**BASE STEALING RUNS**	**FIELDING RUNS-INFIELD**	**FIELDING RUNS-OUTFIELD**	**OUTFIELD ASSISTS**	**CATCHER CS PCT.**
Robinson-StL 116	Latham-StL 109		Shindle-Bal 38.1	McCarthy-StL 25.5	McCarthy-StL 42	
Fennelly-Cin-Phi 72	Nicol-Cin 103		Davis-KC 28.5	Lyons-StL 6.2	Lyons-StL 32	
Nicol-Cin 67	Welch-Phi 95		Easterday-KC 26.0	Collins-Lou-Bro 6.1	McTamany-KC 27	
McTamany-KC 67	McCarthy-StL 93		McPhee-Cin 25.5	Griffin-Bal 4.9	Griffin-Bal 27	
Pinkney-Bro 66	Stovey-Phi 87		Stricker-Cle 23.1	Stovey-Phi 3.3	Welch-Phi 23	
WINS	**WINNING PCT.**	**WINS ABOVE TEAM**	**GAMES STARTED**	**COMPLETE GAMES**	**FEWEST HITS/GAME**	**FEWEST BB/GAME**
King-StL 45	Hudson-StL .714	Chamberlain-Lou-SL 8.5	King-StL 64	King-StL 64	Terry-Bro 6.69	King-StL 1.17
Seward-Phi 35	Chamberlain-Lou-SL .694	Seward-Phi 4.3	Bakely-Cle 61	Bakely-Cle 60	King-StL 6.70	Caruthers-Bro 1.22
Caruthers-Bro 29	King-StL .692	Viau-Cin 4.2	Seward-Phi 57	Seward-Phi 57	Seward-Phi 6.73	Hudson-StL 1.59
Weyhing-Phi 28	Caruthers-Bro .659	Bakely-Cle 4.1	Porter-KC 54	Porter-KC 53	Hughes-Bro 6.97	Ewing-Lou 1.60
Viau-Cin 27	Viau-Cin .659	Caruthers-Bro 2.5	Cunningham-Bal 51	Cunningham-Bal 50	Chamberlain-Lou-SL 6.98	Hecker-Lou 1.73
STRIKEOUTS	**STRIKEOUTS/GAME**	**GAMES**	**SAVES**	**BASE RUNNERS/9**	**ADJUSTED RELIEF RUNS**	**RELIEF RANKING**
Seward-Phi 272	Terry-Bro 6.37	King-StL 66	Mullane-Cin 1	King-StL 8.33		
King-StL 258	Ramsey-Lou 5.99	Bakely-Cle 61	Gilks-Cle 1	Caruthers-Bro 9.19		
Ramsey-Lou 228	Chamberlain-Lou-SL 5.14	Seward-Phi 57		Seward-Phi 9.32		
Bakely-Cle 212	Smith-Bal-Phi 4.90	Porter-KC 55		Foutz-Bro 9.51		
Weyhing-Phi 204	Seward-Phi 4.72	Cunningham-Bal 51		Hughes-Bro 9.55		
INNINGS PITCHED	**OPPONENTS' AVG.**	**OPPONENTS' OBP**	**EARNED RUN AVERAGE**	**ADJUSTED ERA**	**ADJUSTED STARTER RUNS**	**PITCHER WINS**
King-StL 584.2	Terry-Bro .200	King-StL .237	King-StL 1.63	King-StL 200	King-StL 95.3	**King-StL 10.2**
Bakely-Cle 532.2	King-StL .200	Caruthers-Bro .255	Seward-Phi 2.01	Seward-Phi 148	Seward-Phi 60.1	**Seward-Phi 5.1**
Seward-Phi 518.2	Seward-Phi .201	Seward-Phi .258	Terry-Bro 2.03	Terry-Bro 147	Hughes-Bro 31.5	**Caruthers-Bro 3.7**
Porter-KC 474.0	Hughes-Bro .206	Foutz-Bro .262	Hughes-Bro 2.13	Chamberlain-Lou-SL 143	Weyhing-Phi 30.2	**Weyhing-Phi 3.3**
Cunningham-Bal453.1	Chamberlain-Lou-SL .207	Hughes-Bro .262	Chamberlain-Lou-SL 2.19	Hughes-Bro 140	Caruthers-Bro 28.2	**Hudson-StL 2.9**

A Less Offensive League

Having lost the battle to the NL's Giants, the New York Metropolitans left the Association, replaced by Kansas City. The Blues duly finished last despite the debut of perhaps the greatest leadoff man of the century: "Sliding Billy" Hamilton. New rules, also adopted by the NL, increased strikeouts, chopped walks, and decreased scoring. Runs per team were down 1.5 per game in 1888 than the previous season. The top run-scoring team recorded 304 fewer runs than the in '87.

After dumping most of his high-salaried club over the winter, St. Louis owner Chris Von der Ahe was as surprised as anyone when his club took over the league lead in August and cruised to the title. Sporting the league's best pitching and second-best attack, the Browns were a complete club. Left fielder Tip O'Neill won his second straight batting title (although his average dropped an amazing 100 points), and unheralded Yank Robinson led the league in on-base percentage and garnered 116 bases on balls, the most walks in a season to that point. Arlie Latham, who paced in steals, was one of four Browns to score more than 100 runs. Silver King, given a bigger share of the load due to the sale of Dave Foutz and Bob Caruthers to Brooklyn, proved the league's top pitcher, posting the league's only ERA under 2.00.

George Pinkney of second-place Brooklyn played in 143 games, a new all-time record, and he led the league in runs. Foutz, when not pitching, was the right fielder for the Bridegrooms; his 99 RBIs were third-best in the league. Brooklyn didn't get much offense from anywhere else and couldn't hold the league lead.

Storm clouds were gathering. Perhaps aided by the decrease in hitting, league attendance dropped by more than 300,000 fans, and even in St. Louis, the crowds fell precipitously. For the first time AA attendance was significantly lower than that of the NL.

1887 NATIONAL LEAGUE

TEAM	W	L	T	PCT	GB	HW	HL	R	OR	PA	H	2B	3B	HR	BB	SO	HB	SH	AVG	OBP	SLG	OPS	AOPS	BR	ABR	PF	SB	CS	BSA	BSR
Det	79	45	3	.637	—	43	17	**969**	710	5079	**1404**	**213**	**126**	55	352	**258**	38	—	**.299**	**.353**	**.434**	**787**	**117**	**133**	**98**	104	267			
Phi	75	48	5	.610	3.5	38	23	901	**702**	5067	1269	**213**	89	47	385	346	**52**	—	.274	.337	.389	726	99	38	-10	106	355			
Chi	71	50	6	.587	6.5	**44**	18	813	716	4777	1177	178	98	**80**	**407**	400	20	—	.271	.336	.412	748	98	63	-32	113	382			
NY	68	55	6	.553	10.5	36	26	816	723	4924	1259	167	93	48	361	326	47	—	.279	.339	.389	728	111	36	76	95	**415**			
Bos	61	60	6	.504	16.5	38	21	834	792	4908	1255	185	94	53	340	392	37	—	.277	.333	.394	727	105	31	22	101	373			
Pit	55	69	1	.444	24	31	34	621	750	4771	1141	183	78	20	319	381	38	—	.258	.314	.349	663	95	-68	-14	93	221			
Was	46	76	4	.377	32	27	33	601	825	4624	1039	149	63	47	269	339	41	—	.241	.292	.337	629	83	-128	-87	94	334			
Ind	37	89	1	.294	43	24	39	628	965	4712	1080	162	70	33	300	379	44	—	.247	.302	.339	641	85	-105	-82	97	334			
Total	508	—	—	—	—	281	211	6183	—	38862	9624	1450	711	383	2733	2821	317	—	.269	.326	.381	707	—	—	—	—	2681	—	—	—

TEAM	CG	SHO	GR	SV	IP	H	HR	BB	SO	BR/9	ERA	AERA	OAV	OOB	PR	APR	PF	OSB	OCS	FA	E	WPB	DP	FW	PW	BW	BSW	DIF
Det	122	3	5	1	1116.1	1172	52	344	337	12.5	3.95	103	.264	.322	12	0	100	—	—	**.925**	**394**	**95**	92	**3.3**	.0	**8.3**	—	5.4
Phi	119	**7**	10	1	1132.2	1173	48	305	435	**12.0**	3.47	121	.259	**.311**	72	87	104	—	—	.912	471	152	76	-.4	7.4	-.8	—	7.4
Chi	117	4	**12**	**3**	1126.0	1156	55	338	**510**	12.4	**3.46**	**129**	.257	.317	**73**	**110**	110	—	—	.914	472	201	99	-.6	**9.3**	-2.7	—	4.5
NY	123	5	7	1	1111.2	**1096**	**27**	373	415	12.2	3.58	105	**.250**	.314	58	19	93	—	—	.920	431	196	83	1.8	1.6	6.4	—	-3.4
Bos	123	4	4	1	1100.2	1226	55	396	254	13.6	4.41	92	.273	.338	-44	-41	101	—	—	.905	522	154	94	-3.2	-3.5	1.9	—	5.3
Pit	123	4	2	0	1108.2	1287	39	**246**	248	12.7	4.12	93	.281	.322	-9	-40	94	—	—	.921	425	140	70	1.4	-3.4	-1.2	—	-3.8
Was	**124**	3	2	0	1090.1	1216	47	299	396	12.9	4.19	95	.272	.323	-18	-26	99	—	—	.909	483	194	77	-1.4	-2.2	-7.4	—	-4.1
Ind	118	4	10	1	1088.0	1289	60	431	245	14.6	5.24	79	.284	.352	-145	-135	102	—	—	.912	479	223	**105**	-1.0	-11.4	-6.9	—	-6.6
Total	969	34	52	8	8874.1	—	—	—	—	12.8	4.05	—	.269	.326	—	—	—	—	—	.915	3677	1355	696	—	—	—	—	—

BATTER-FIELDER WINS	BATTING AVERAGE	ON-BASE PERCENTAGE	SLUGGING AVERAGE	ON-BASE PLUS SLUGGING	ADJUSTED OPS	ADJUSTED BATTER RUNS
Ward-NY.............4.3	Anson-Chi............347	Brouthers-Det.......426	Thompson-Det......565	Brouthers-Det.......988	Brouthers-Det.......166	Brouthers-Det......46.3
Thompson-Det...4.2	Thompson-Det......372	Anson-Chi.............422	Brouthers-Det.......562	Thompson-Det......982	Connor-NY............164	Thompson-Det.....44.6
Glasscock-Ind ...4.0	Brouthers-Det.......338	Thompson-Det......416	Connor-NY...........541	Anson-Chi.............939	Thompson-Det......164	Connor-NY...........43.8
Denny-Ind...........3.9	Ward-NY...............338	Schomberg-Ind.....397	Wise-Bos.............522	Connor-NY...........933	Carroll-Pit.............154	Carroll-Pit............31.9
Richardson-Det.3.3	Wise-Bos.............334	Kelly-Bos.............393	Anson-Chi.............517	Wise-Bos.............913	Wise-Bos.............150	Wise-Bos............30.6
RUNS	**HITS**	**DOUBLES**	**TRIPLES**	**HOME RUNS**	**TOTAL BASES**	**RUNS BATTED IN**
Brouthers-Det.......153	Thompson-Det......203	Brouthers-Det.........36	Thompson-Det........23	B.O'Brien-Was........19	Thompson-Det......308	Thompson-Det......166
Rowe-Det.............135	Ward-NY...............184	Kelly-Bos.................34	Connor-NY.............22	Connor-NY.............17	Brouthers-Det.......281	Connor-NY...........104
Richardson-Det.....131	Richardson-Det.....178	Denny-Ind...............34	Johnston-Bos.........20	Pfeffer-Chi...............16	Richardson-Det.....263	Anson-Chi............102
Kelly-Bos.............120	Rowe-Det.............171	Anson-Chi...............33	Brouthers-Det.........20	Wood-Phi................14	Denny-Ind............256	Brouthers-Det.......101
	Brouthers-Det.......169		Wood-Phi................19		Connor-NY...........255	Denny-Ind...............97
BASES ON BALLS	**STOLEN BASES**	**BASE STEALING RUNS**	**FIELDING RUNS-INFIELD**	**FIELDING RUNS-OUTFIELD**	**OUTFIELD ASSISTS**	**CATCHER CS PCT.**
Fogarty-Phi............82	Ward-NY...............111		Glasscock-Ind......38.7	Fogarty-Phi..........30.1	Fogarty-Phi............39	
Connor-NY.............75	Fogarty-Phi...........102		Ward-NY..............32.4	Johnston-Bos.......22.5	Johnston-Bos..........34	
Williamson-Chi........73	Kelly-Bos.................84		Pfeffer-Chi...........22.9	Hornung-Bos 11.5	Ryan-Chi................33	
Seery-Ind...............71	Hanlon-Det 69		Denny-Ind...........21.8	Seery-Ind...............6.8	Seery-Ind...............25	
Brouthers-Det.........71	Glasscock-Ind.........62		Bassett-Ind 18.4	Thompson-Det.......6.4	Thompson-Det.......24	
WINS	**WINNING PCT.**	**WINS ABOVE TEAM**	**GAMES STARTED**	**COMPLETE GAMES**	**FEWEST HITS/GAME**	**FEWEST BB/GAME**
Clarkson-Chi...........38	Getzien-Det..........690	Keefe-NY...............8.8	Clarkson-Chi...........59	Clarkson-Chi...........56	Keefe-NY.............8.08	Whitney-Was..........93
Keefe-NY...............35	Ferguson-Phi........688	Galvin-Pit...............8.1	Keefe-NY...............56	Keefe-NY...............54	Conway-Det.........8.14	Galvin-Pit.............1.37
Getzien-Det............29	Casey-Phi.............683	Whitney-Was 7.8	Radbourn-Bos 50	Radbourn-Bos 48	Casey-Phi............8.69	Ferguson-Phi.......1.42
Galvin-Pit...............28	Keefe-NY.............648	Clarkson-Chi..........7.1	Galvin-Pit...............48	Galvin-Pit...............47	Welch-NY............8.82	Clarkson-Chi........1.58
Casey-Phi...............28	Clarkson-Chi.........644	Casey-Phi.............5.3	Whitney-Was..........47	Whitney-Was..........46	Clarkson-Chi........8.83	Boyle-Ind.............1.89
STRIKEOUTS	**STRIKEOUTS/GAME**	**GAMES**	**SAVES**	**BASE RUNNERS/9**	**ADJUSTED RELIEF RUNS**	**RELIEF RANKING**
Clarkson-Chi.........237	Baldwin-Chi 4.42	Clarkson-Chi..........60	8 players tied 1	Keefe-NY...........10.33		
Keefe-NY.............189	Gilmore-Was........4.37	Keefe-NY...............56		Clarkson-Chi......10.55		
Baldwin-Chi 164	Buffinton-Phi........4.33	Radbourn-Bos........50		Ferguson-Phi.....10.75		
Buffinton-Phi.........160	VanHaltren-Chi 4.25	Galvin-Pit...............49		Whitney-Was 10.85		
Whitney-Was 146	Clarkson-Chi........4.08	Whitney-Was 47		Welch-NY..........11.32		
INNINGS PITCHED	**OPPONENTS' AVG.**	**OPPONENTS' OBP**	**EARNED RUN AVERAGE**	**ADJUSTED ERA**	**ADJUSTED STARTER RUNS**	**PITCHER WINS**
Clarkson-Chi......523.0	Keefe-NY.............230	Keefe-NY.............276	Casey-Phi............2.86	Casey-Phi.............147	Clarkson-Chi........76.4	**Clarkson-Chi......7.5**
Keefe-NY..........476.2	Conway-Det..........235	Clarkson-Chi.........281	Conway-Det.........2.90	Clarkson-Chi.........145	Casey-Phi............56.6	**Ferguson-Phi......4.7**
Galvin-Pit..........440.2	Casey-Phi.............246	Whitney-Was 284	Ferguson-Phi.......3.00	Ferguson-Phi.........141	Keefe-NY.............40.5	**Keefe-NY...............4.3**
Radbourn-Bos ...425.0	Clarkson-Chi.........246	Ferguson-Phi 289	Clarkson-Chi........3.08	Conway-Det..........140	Ferguson-Phi.......40.2	**Whitney-Was......3.9**
Whitney-Was 404.2	Baldwin-Chi 248	Galvin-Pit.............299	Keefe-NY.............3.12	Baldwin-Chi 131	Baldwin-Chi 33.3	**Casey-Phi 3.6**

The Long October

Despite another National Agreement meeting in 1886, the gloves came off. For 1887 the NL lured over the AA's Pittsburgh franchise to replace bankrupt Kansas City. Both the NL and the AA used the same set of playing rules beginning in 1887, which at least helped in planning the World Series.

It was a year of rule changes. First of all, pitchers were prohibited from hiding the ball during their delivery or taking a running start before delivering. It once again took *four* strikes for a strikeout, while the number of balls needed for a walk was lowered to five.

Batters could no longer call for pitches in certain locations, and the strike zone was defined as ranging from the knee to the shoulder. For the first time NL batters hit by pitched balls were awarded first base—provided they at least tried to get out of the way.

For this year only, a walk truly was as good as a hit. Batters were given credits for hits if they drew bases on balls, leading to some stratospheric averages. Modern figures have Sam Thompson of pennant-winning Detroit taking the bat crown (after walks were removed from hit totals) and establishing a nineteenth century mark with 166 RBIs.

Thompson, Dan Brouthers, and Hardy Richardson supplied Detroit's offense, and the deep pitching staff did its best in what appears to have been a strong hitter's park. Second-place Philadelphia allowed the league's fewest runs.

Chicago owner Al Spalding jettisoned King Kelly, his most outspoken, and—not coincidentally—marketable talent. The outspoken, hard-drinking Kelly was sold to Boston for an unheard of $10,000. The White Stockings immediately slumped to third; Boston, with Kelly's 84 steals and 120 runs, did not budge from fifth. After the season, Spalding also dumped pitcher John Clarkson.

Detroit and AA champ St. Louis played a 15-game World Series, including stops at almost every major league city—one day the touring teams played a morning game in Washington and an afternoon tilt in Baltimore. Detroit won 10 to give the NL the crown. By the end of the interminable series, hardly anyone was watching.

1887 AMERICAN ASSOCIATION

TEAM	W	L	T	PCT	GB	HW	HL	R	OR	PA	H	2B	3B	HR	BB	SO	HB	SH	AVG	OBP	SLG	OPS	AOPS	BR	ABR	PF	SB	CS	BSA	BSR
StL	95	40	3	.704	—	**58**	15	**1131**	761	5557	**1550**	**261**	78	**39**	442	340	67	—	**.307**	**.371**	**.413**	**784**	111	**157**	52	111	**581**			
Cin	81	54	1	.600	14	46	27	892	**745**	5235	1285	179	**102**	37	382	366	56	—	.268	.329	.371	700	97	-15	-35	102	527			
Bal	77	58	6	.570	18	42	21	975	861	5362	1337	202	100	31	**469**	**334**	**68**	—	.277	.349	.380	729	**114**	51	**110**	94	545			
Lou	76	60	3	.559	19.5	45	23	956	854	5392	1420	194	98	27	436	356	40	—	.289	.352	.385	737	107	60	41	102	466			
Phi	64	69	4	.481	30	41	27	893	890	5326	1370	231	84	29	321	388	51	—	.277	.327	.375	702	99	-13	-14	100	476			
Bro	60	74	4	.448	34.5	36	38	904	918	5420	1281	200	82	25	456	365	51	—	.261	.330	.350	680	92	-40	-50	101	409			
NY	44	89	5	.331	50	25	34	754	1093	5310	1197	193	66	21	439	463	50	—	.248	.318	.329	647	88	-98	-61	96	305			
Cle	39	92	2	.298	54	22	36	729	1112	5070	1170	178	77	14	375	463	46	—	.252	.314	.332	646	87	-101	-78	97	355			
Total	550	—	—	—	—	315	221	7234	—	42672	10610	1638	687	223	3320	3075	429	—	.273	.336	.367	704	—	—	—	—	3664	—	—	—

TEAM	CG	SHO	GR	SV	IP	H	HR	BB	SO	BR/9	ERA	AERA	OAV	OOB	PR	APR	PF	OSB	OCS	FA	E	WPB	DP	FW	PW	BW	BSW	DIF
StL	132	6	5	2	1199.1	1254	19	**323**	334	**12.2**	3.77	120	.258	**.311**	69	94	106	**335**	—	**.916**	**481**	**171**	86	**3.6**	7.6	4.2	—	12.1
Cin	129	**11**	6	1	1182.2	**1202**	28	396	330	12.6	**3.58**	**121**	**.257**	.322	**93**	**98**	101	358	—	**.916**	484	203	**106**	3.0	**7.9**	-2.8	—	5.4
Bal	132	8	**9**	0	1220.0	1288	**16**	418	470	13.0	3.87	106	.262	.326	58	31	95	482	—	.907	549	229	66	.8	2.5	**8.9**	—	-2.7
Lou	**133**	3	4	1	1205.2	1274	31	357	**544**	12.5	3.82	115	.260	.316	63	73	102	462	—	.903	574	221	83	-.9	5.9	3.3	—	-.3
Phi	131	5	6	1	1186.1	1227	29	433	417	13.1	4.59	93	.259	.331	-39	-41	100	476	—	.907	528	300	95	1.0	-3.3	-1.1	—	.9
Bro	132	3	6	**3**	1185.1	1348	27	454	332	14.0	4.47	96	.281	.348	-24	-24	100	520	—	.905	562	202	88	-.5	-1.9	-4.1	—	-.5
NY	132	1	**9**	0	1180.1	1545	39	406	316	15.3	5.28	80	.308	.365	-130	-139	99	508	—	.894	632	194	102	-4.0	-11.3	-4.9	—	-2.3
Cle	127	2	6	1	1136.0	1472	34	533	332	16.4	4.99	87	.308	.384	-88	-83	101	523	—	.898	576	245	97	-2.2	-6.7	-6.3	—	-11.3
Total	1048	39	51	9	9495.2	—	—	—	—	13.6	4.29	—	.273	.336	—	—	—	—	—	.906	4386	1765	723	—	—	—	—	—

BATTER-FIELDER WINS	BATTING AVERAGE	ON-BASE PERCENTAGE	SLUGGING AVERAGE	ON-BASE PLUS SLUGGING	ADJUSTED OPS	ADJUSTED BATTER RUNS
O'Neill-StL 4.8	O'Neill-StL .435	O'Neill-StL .490	O'Neill-StL .691	O'Neill-StL 1180	O'Neill-StL 205	O'Neill-StL 70.6
Browning-Lou 3.8	Browning-Lou .402	Browning-Lou .464	Caruthers-StL .547	Browning-Lou 1011	Browning-Lou 178	Browning-Lou 58.5
Lyons-Phi 3.6	Orr-NY .368	Caruthers-StL .463	Browning-Lou .547	Caruthers-StL 1010	Burns-Bal 169	Burns-Bal 53.4
Burns-Bal 3.2	Lyons-Phi .367	Robinson-StL .445	Lyons-Phi .523	Lyons-Phi 943	Caruthers-StL 164	Lyons-Phi 47.8
McPhee-Cin 2.8	Caruthers-StL .357	Lyons-Phi .421	Burns-Bal .519	Burns-Bal 933	Lyons-Phi 162	Caruthers-StL 32.6
RUNS	**HITS**	**DOUBLES**	**TRIPLES**	**HOME RUNS**	**TOTAL BASES**	**RUNS BATTED IN**
O'Neill-StL 167	O'Neill-StL 225	O'Neill-StL 52	Poorman-Phi 19	O'Neill-StL 14	O'Neill-StL 357	O'Neill-StL 123
Latham-StL 163	Browning-Lou 220	Lyons-Phi 43	O'Neill-StL 19	Reilly-Cin 10	Browning-Lou 299	Browning-Lou 118
Griffin-Bal 142	Lyons-Phi 209	Reilly-Cin 35	McPhee-Cin 19	Burns-Bal 9	Lyons-Phi 298	Davis-Bal 109
Poorman-Phi 140	Latham-StL 198	Latham-StL 35	Kerins-Lou 19		Burns-Bal 286	Welch-StL 108
Comiskey-StL 139	Burns-Bal 188	Browning-Lou 35	Davis-Bal 19		Reilly-Cin 263	Foutz-StL 108
			Burns-Bal 19			
BASES ON BALLS	**STOLEN BASES**	**BASE STEALING RUNS**	**FIELDING RUNS-INFIELD**	**FIELDING RUNS-OUTFIELD**	**OUTFIELD ASSISTS**	**CATCHER CS PCT.**
Radford-NY 106	Nicol-Cin 138		Smith-Bro 30.1	Welch-StL 17.2	McTamany-Bro 32	
Robinson-StL 92	Latham-StL 129		McPhee-Cin 23.3	Corkhill-Cin 12.1	Welch-StL 29	
Nicol-Cin 86	Comiskey-StL 117		White-Lou 17.5	Wolf-Lou 8.8	Corkhill-Cin 29	
Mack-Lou 83	Browning-Lou 103		Pinkney-Bro 14.8	D.O'Brien-NY 7.1	Wolf-Lou 27	
Fennelly-Cin 82	McPhee-Cin 95		Stricker-Cle 11.1	Allen-Cle 6.2	Jones-Cin-NY 25	
WINS	**WINNING PCT.**	**WINS ABOVE TEAM**	**GAMES STARTED**	**COMPLETE GAMES**	**FEWEST HITS/GAME**	**FEWEST BB/GAME**
Kilroy-Bal 46	Caruthers-StL .763	Kilroy-Bal 15.4	Kilroy-Bal 69	Kilroy-Bal 66	Smith-Cin 8.05	Hecker-Lou 1.58
Ramsey-Lou 37	King-StL .727	Smith-Cin 6.2	Ramsey-Lou 64	Ramsey-Lou 61	Seward-Phi 8.51	Caruthers-StL 1.61
Smith-Cin 34	Kilroy-Bal .708	Caruthers-StL 4.9	Weyhing-Phi 55	Smith-Bal 54	Toole-Bro 8.63	Lynch-NY 1.73
King-StL 32	Foutz-StL .676	Mullane-Cin 4.0	Smith-Bal 55	Weyhing-Phi 53	Ramsey-Lou 8.73	Foutz-StL 2.39
Mullane-Cin 31	Smith-Cin .667	Toole-Bro 3.4		Seward-Phi 52	Caruthers-StL 8.89	Kilroy-Bal 2.40
STRIKEOUTS	**STRIKEOUTS/GAME**	**GAMES**	**SAVES**	**BASE RUNNERS/9**	**ADJUSTED RELIEF RUNS**	**RELIEF RANKING**
Ramsey-Lou 355	Ramsey-Lou 5.70	Kilroy-Bal 69	Terry-Bro 3	Smith-Cin 10.76		
Kilroy-Bal 217	Morrison-Cle 4.49	Ramsey-Lou 65		Caruthers-StL 10.93		
Smith-Bal 206	Terry-Bro 3.91	Smith-Bal 58		Kilroy-Bal 11.64		
Weyhing-Phi 193	Smith-Bal 3.77	Weyhing-Phi 55		Seward-Phi 11.65		
Smith-Cin 176	Weyhing-Phi 3.72	Seward-Phi 55		Ramsey-Lou 11.66		
INNINGS PITCHED	**OPPONENTS' AVG.**	**OPPONENTS' OBP**	**EARNED RUN AVERAGE**	**ADJUSTED ERA**	**ADJUSTED STARTER RUNS**	**PITCHER WINS**
Kilroy-Bal 589.1	Smith-Cin .230	Smith-Cin .286	Smith-Cin 2.94	Smith-Cin 148	Kilroy-Bal 71.6	**Kilroy-Bal 7.2**
Ramsey-Lou 561.0	Ramsey-Lou .242	Caruthers-StL .287	Kilroy-Bal 3.07	Caruthers-StL 137	Smith-Cin 71.0	**Smith-Cin 6.3**
Smith-Bal 491.1	Seward-Phi .244	Ramsey-Lou .299	Mullane-Cin 3.24	Mullane-Cin 134	Ramsey-Lou 57.8	**Caruthers-StL 5.9**
Seward-Phi 470.2	Caruthers-StL .247	Kilroy-Bal .306	Caruthers-StL 3.30	Kilroy-Bal 133	Mullane-Cin 51.1	**Mullane-Cin 4.6**
Weyhing-Phi 466.1	Kilroy-Bal .253	Foutz-StL .306	Ramsey-Lou 3.43	Ramsey-Lou 128	Caruthers-StL 45.5	**Ramsey-Lou 3.7**

Sitting in Coach

In agreeing to rewrite their rule book to match the NL's, owners of the American Association took a subordinate position. When the NL stole the AA's Pittsburgh franchise, it was war again. A Cleveland club was added to bring the Americans' total to eight teams.

Various rule changes served to elevate offense; the league's best pitching staff, second-place Cincinnati, had an ERA that would have ranked a poor fifth in the AA the previous season. The days of the one-pitcher team were long gone; all teams now had at least two pitchers (in Brooklyn's case, four) winning in double figures. To address charges that St. Louis' Arlie Latham was disgracing the game with his "coaching" routines, which involved running up and down the baselines shouting at the pitcher, coaches' boxes were installed. From this point, coaches were allowed only to address their own baserunners.

The loss of shouting privileges didn't seem to bother the Browns, who won again by a wide margin over Cincinnati. The Reds had one of the league's top hurlers, Elmer Smith, plus outfielder Hugh Nicol, who stole an all-time record 138 bases. But St. Louis was a juggernaut. The Browns plated a record 1,131 runs, and left fielder Tip O'Neill paced the league in nearly every significant offensive category. An unsung hero for the Browns? Bob Caruthers, who won 29 games on the hill and as a right fielder hit .357, fifth best in the AA.

While last-place Cleveland didn't have much talent, they could boast first baseman Jim Toy, the major leagues' first Native American player. Paul Radford of seventh-place New York became the first player in big league history to draw 100 walks in a season. Buoyed by gains in nearly every city, AA attendance rose to its all-time high, but the NL had caught up and passed its rival. The NL broke the one million mark for the first time and surpassed the AA's overall total for the first time since the Association's inaugural season in 1882.

1886 NATIONAL LEAGUE

TEAM	W	L	T	PCT	GB	HW	HL	R	OR	PA	H	2B	3B	HR	BB	SO	HB	SH	AVG	OBP	SLG	OPS	AOPS	BR	ABR	PF	SB	CS	BSA	BSR
Chi	90	34	2	.726	—	**52**	10	**900**	555	4838	1223	**198**	**87**	**53**	**460**	513	—	—	.279	**.348**	**.401**	**749**	116	**180**	69	115	213			
Det	87	36	3	.707	2.5	48	12	829	538	4875	**1260**	176	81	**53**	374	426	—	—	**.280**	.335	.390	725	**122**	137	**108**	104	194			
NY	75	44	5	.630	12.5	47	12	692	558	4535	1156	175	68	21	237	**410**	—	—	.269	.307	.356	663	106	29	22	101	155			
Phi	71	43	5	.623	14	45	14	621	**498**	4354	976	145	66	26	282	516	—	—	.240	.289	.327	616	91	-39	-44	101	**226**			
Bos	56	61	1	.479	30.5	32	25	657	661	4430	1085	151	59	24	250	537	—	—	.260	.301	.341	642	103	-1	16	97	156			
StL	43	79	4	.352	46	27	34	547	712	4485	1001	183	46	30	235	656	—	—	.236	.276	.321	597	92	-70	-31	94	156			
KC	30	91	5	.248	58.5	19	42	494	872	4505	967	177	48	19	269	608	—	—	.228	.274	.306	580	76	-91	-124	106	96			
Was	28	92	5	.233	60	19	42	445	791	4347	856	135	51	23	265	582	—	—	.210	.258	.285	543	75	-145	-107	93	143			
Total	495	—	—	—	—	289	191	5185	—	36369	8524	1340	506	249	2372	4248	—	—	.251	.300	.342	641	—	—	—	—	1339	—	—	—

TEAM	CG	SHO	GR	SV	IP	H	HR	BB	SO	BR/9	ERA	AERA	OAV	OOB	PR	APR	PF	OSB	OCS	FA	E	WPB	DP	FW	PW	BW	BSW	DIF
Chi	116	8	**10**	**3**	1097.2	988	49	262	**647**	**10.2**	2.54	**142**	.232	.277	91	**118**	110	—	—	.912	475	197	82	-1.8	**10.7**	6.3	—	12.8
Det	**122**	8	4	0	1103.2	995	**20**	270	592	10.3	2.85	116	.231	.276	53	55	101	—	—	.928	373	**138**	82	3.8	5.0	**9.8**	—	6.9
NY	119	3	5	1	1062.0	1029	23	280	588	11.1	2.86	111	.247	.294	50	39	97	—	—	**.929**	**359**	222	70	**4.2**	3.5	2.0	—	5.8
Phi	110	**10**	9	2	1045.2	**923**	29	264	540	**10.2**	**2.45**	134	**.224**	**.271**	**97**	95	100	—	—	.921	393	155	46	1.4	8.6	-4.0	—	8.0
Bos	116	3	2	0	1029.0	1049	33	298	511	11.8	3.24	99	.252	.302	5	-4	97	—	—	.905	465	217	63	-2.7	-.4	1.5	—	-.8
StL	118	6	8	0	1077.1	1050	34	392	501	12.0	3.24	99	.246	.309	6	-7	97	—	—	.914	452	293	**92**	-.5	-.6	-2.8	—	-14.0
KC	117	4	6	0	1066.2	1345	27	**246**	442	13.4	4.85	77	.295	.331	-185	-117	114	—	—	.910	482	230	79	-2.1	-10.6	-11.2	—	-6.5
Was	115	4	7	0	1041.0	1147	34	379	500	13.2	4.30	75	.271	.331	-117	-132	98	—	—	.910	458	211	69	-1.0	-12.0	-9.7	—	-9.3
Total	933	46	51	6	8523.0	—	—	—	—	11.5	3.29	—	.251	.300	—	—	—	—	—	.916	3457	1663	583	—	—	—	—	—

BATTER-FIELDER WINS	BATTING AVERAGE	ON-BASE PERCENTAGE	SLUGGING AVERAGE	ON-BASE PLUS SLUGGING	ADJUSTED OPS	ADJUSTED BATTER RUNS
Kelly-Chi 5.2	Kelly-Chi 388	Kelly-Chi 483	Brouthers-Det 581	Brouthers-Det 1026	Brouthers-Det 203	Brouthers-Det 62.6
Glasscock-StL 4.6	Anson-Chi 371	Brouthers-Det 445	Anson-Chi 544	Kelly-Chi 1018	Connor-NY 183	Kelly-Chi 48.1
Richardson-Det . 4.5	Brouthers-Det 370	Gore-Chi 434	Connor-NY 540	Anson-Chi 977	Kelly-Chi 182	Connor-NY 47.6
Connor-NY 4.2	Connor-NY 355	Anson-Chi 433	Kelly-Chi 534	Connor-NY 945	Anson-Chi 170	Richardson-Det 43.4
Brouthers-Det 3.9	Richardson-Det 351	Connor-NY 405	Richardson-Det 504	Richardson-Det 906	Richardson-Det 168	Anson-Chi 41.9

RUNS	HITS	DOUBLES	TRIPLES	HOME RUNS	TOTAL BASES	RUNS BATTED IN
Kelly-Chi 155	Richardson-Det 189	Brouthers-Det 40	Connor-NY 20	Richardson-Det 11	Brouthers-Det 284	Anson-Chi 147
Gore-Chi 150	Anson-Chi 187	Anson-Chi 35	Wood-Phi 15	Brouthers-Det 11	Anson-Chi 274	Pfeffer-Chi 95
Brouthers-Det 139	Brouthers-Det 181	Kelly-Chi 32	Brouthers-Det 15	Anson-Chi 10	Richardson-Det 271	Thompson-Det 89
Richardson-Det 125	Kelly-Chi 175	Hines-Was 30	Thompson-Det 13	Hines-Was 9	Connor-NY 262	Rowe-Det 87
Anson-Chi 117	Connor-NY 172			Denny-StL 9	Kelly-Chi 241	Ward-NY 81

BASES ON BALLS	STOLEN BASES	BASE STEALING RUNS	FIELDING RUNS-INFIELD	FIELDING RUNS-OUTFIELD	OUTFIELD ASSISTS	CATCHER CS PCT.
Gore-Chi 102	Andrews-Phi 56		Denny-StL 25.2	Johnston-Bos 13.5	Cahill-StL 34	
Kelly-Chi 83	Kelly-Chi 53		Knowles-Was 21.3	Lillie-KC 10.6	Lillie-KC 30	
Williamson-Chi 80	Hanlon-Det 50		Dunlap-StL-Det 17.4	Thompson-Det 8.2	Thompson-Det 29	
Brouthers-Det 66	Richardson-Det 42		Glasscock-StL 14.9	Richardson-Det 5.3	Radford-KC 29	
Radford-KC 58	Radford-KC 39		Burns-Chi 11.1	Hornung-Bos 5.1	Johnston-Bos 29	

WINS	WINNING PCT.	WINS ABOVE TEAM	GAMES STARTED	COMPLETE GAMES	FEWEST HITS/GAME	FEWEST BB/GAME
Keefe-NY 42	Flynn-Chi 793	Ferguson-Phi 9.6	Keefe-NY 64	Keefe-NY 62	Baldwin-Det 6.86	Whitney-KC 1.26
Baldwin-Det 42	Ferguson-Phi 769	Baldwin-Det 8.3	Welch-NY 59	Radbourn-Bos 57	Ferguson-Phi 7.21	Ferguson-Phi 1.57
Clarkson-Chi 36	Baldwin-Det 764	Keefe-NY 7.3	Radbourn-Bos 58	Welch-NY 56	Flynn-Chi 7.25	Clarkson-Chi 1.66
Welch-NY 33	McCormick-Chi 738	Flynn-Chi 4.3	Baldwin-Det 56	Baldwin-Det 55	Stemmeyer-Bos 7.74	Keefe-NY 1.72
McCormick-Chi 31	Getzien-Det 732	Stemmeyer-Bos 3.9	Clarkson-Chi 55	Clarkson-Chi 50	Boyle-StL 7.84	Baldwin-Det 1.85

STRIKEOUTS	STRIKEOUTS/GAME	GAMES	SAVES	BASE RUNNERS/9	ADJUSTED RELIEF RUNS	RELIEF RANKING
Baldwin-Det 323	Stemmeyer-Bos 6.17	Keefe-NY 64	Ferguson-Phi 2	Baldwin-Det 8.70		
Clarkson-Chi 313	Clarkson-Chi 6.04	Welch-NY 59	Williamson-Chi 1	Ferguson-Phi 8.78		
Keefe-NY 297	Baldwin-Det 5.97	Radbourn-Bos 58	Ryan-Chi 1	Flynn-Chi 9.46		
Welch-NY 272	Healy-StL 5.42	Baldwin-Det 56	Flynn-Chi 1	Gilmore-Was 9.48		
Stemmeyer-Bos 239	Flynn-Chi 5.11	Clarkson-Chi 55	Devlin-NY 1	Clarkson-Chi 9.74		

INNINGS PITCHED	OPPONENTS' AVG.	OPPONENTS' OBP	EARNED RUN AVERAGE	ADJUSTED ERA	ADJUSTED STARTER RUNS	PITCHER WINS
Keefe-NY 535.0	Baldwin-Det 202	Baldwin-Det 243	Boyle-StL 1.76	Boyle-StL 182	Ferguson-Phi 59.3	**Ferguson-Phi 6.5**
Radbourn-Bos 509.1	Ferguson-Phi 210	Ferguson-Phi 244	Ferguson-Phi 1.98	Ferguson-Phi 166	Baldwin-Det 55.4	**Baldwin-Det 5.7**
Welch-NY 500.0	Flynn-Chi 210	Flynn-Chi 257	Baldwin-Det 2.24	Flynn-Chi 161	Clarkson-Chi 50.2	**Clarkson-Chi 5.0**
Baldwin-Det 487.0	Stemmeyer-Bos 218	Boyle-StL 261	Flynn-Chi 2.24	Clarkson-Chi 149	Keefe-NY 39.1	**McCormick-Chi . 3.8**
Clarkson-Chi 466.2	Boyle-StL 220	Clarkson-Chi 264	Clarkson-Chi 2.41	Baldwin-Det 148	Casey-Phi 36.7	**Keefe-NY 3.8**

The Brotherhood of Man

When Providence and Buffalo folded following the 1885 season, the NL replaced them with Washington and Kansas City. They weren't inspired choices. The Kansas City Cowboys lasted one miserable year and the Washington Senators didn't see the next decade. The Senators, the first team to use that name, did provide 23-year-old catcher Connie Mack a start for his major league playing career. Finishing their careers, for the same poor club, were famous contract-jumper Davy Force and 43-year-old first baseman Joe Start, an original National Association player.

With salaries depressed by the end of the Union Association, the reserve clause in full effect, and owners ruling players with iron fists, New York Giants John Ward, Buck Ewing, and Tim Keefe were instrumental in establishing the Brotherhood of Professional Baseball Players, the game's first union.

The NL returned to the seven-ball walk, and also helped pitchers by allowing them to lift one foot when delivering the ball. This, and the lengthening of the pitcher's box, gave certain hard throwers an extra advantage, because they could get a running start to their delivery. While strikeouts increased, league ERA leapt by nearly half a run, mainly due to the incompetence of the expansion teams' pitching staffs.

The White Stockings won another close race, this one over Detroit. The Wolverines featured the bats of Dan Brouthers, Sam Thompson, and Hardy Richardson, as well as Lady Baldwin's pitching, but the club stalled in August. Cap Anson, King Kelly, and George Gore did the bat work for Chicago, while John Clarkson, Jim McCormick, and one-year wonder Jocko Flynn provided a top mound trio.

Kelly was one of the loop's dominant offensive performers, leading in runs, batting average, and on-base percentage. The charismatic, hard-living Kelly also finished second in the newly tabulated category of stolen bases, inspiring the popular song "Slide! Kelly! Slide!" However, Kelly and his Chicago teammates dropped a six-game World Series to the American Association champion St. Louis Browns.

1886 AMERICAN ASSOCIATION

TEAM	W	L	T	PCT	GB	HW	HL	R	OR	PA	H	2B	3B	HR	BB	SO	HB	SH	AVG	OBP	SLG	OPS	AOPS	BR	ABR	PF	SB	CS	BSA	BSR
StL	93	46	0	.669	—	**52**	18	**944**	**592**	5461	**1365**	**206**	85	20	400	**425**	52	—	**.273**	**.333**	**.360**	**693**	**116**	**117**	**75**	105	**336**			
Pit	80	57	3	.584	12	46	29	810	647	5370	1171	186	**96**	16	**478**	713	38	—	.241	.314	.329	643	106	33	37	100	260			
Bro	76	61	4	.555	16	43	25	832	832	5504	1261	196	80	16	433	523	18	—	.250	.311	.330	641	103	24	16	101	248			
Lou	66	70	2	.485	25.5	37	30	833	805	5357	1294	182	88	20	410	558	26	—	.263	.323	.348	671	108	75	28	106	202			
Cin	65	73	3	.471	27.5	40	31	883	865	5354	1225	145	95	**45**	374	633	**65**	—	.249	.311	.345	656	106	42	16	103	185			
Phi	63	72	4	.467	28	37	32	772	942	5275	1142	192	82	21	378	697	41	—	.235	.296	.321	617	95	-20	-28	101	284			
NY	53	82	2	.393	38	30	33	628	766	5046	1047	108	72	18	330	578	33	—	.224	.279	.289	568	88	-106	-47	92	120			
Bal	48	83	8	.366	41	30	31	625	878	5054	945	124	51	8	379	603	36	—	.204	.269	.258	527	70	-165	-150	98	269			
Total	557	—	—	—	—	315	229	6327	—	42421	9450	1339	649	164	3182	4730	309	—	.243	.305	.323	628	—	—	—	—	1904	—	—	—

TEAM	CG	SHO	GR	SV	IP	H	HR	BB	SO	BR/9	ERA	AERA	OAV	OOB	PR	APR	PF	OSB	OCS	FA	E	WPB	DP	FW	PW	BW	BSW	DIF
StL	134	14	5	**2**	1229.1	**1087**	13	329	583	**10.6**	**2.49**	**138**	**.227**	**.281**	**130**	**128**	100	188	—	.915	494	**163**	96	3.3	**11.2**	**6.6**	—	2.4
Pit	137	**15**	3	1	1226.0	1130	**10**	**299**	515	10.7	2.83	120	.235	.285	84	76	98	**140**	—	**.917**	**487**	220	90	**3.9**	6.7	3.2	—	-2.3
Bro	**138**	6	3	0	1234.2	1202	17	464	540	12.4	3.42	102	.243	.312	3	8	101	229	—	.900	610	232	87	-2.2	.7	1.4	—	7.6
Lou	131	5	7	**2**	1209.2	1109	16	432	720	11.7	3.07	118	.230	.297	51	71	106	229	—	.901	593	289	89	-2.0	6.2	2.5	—	-8.7
Cin	129	3	**14**	0	1247.2	1267	25	481	495	13.0	4.18	84	.255	.327	-103	-92	102	224	—	.905	582	247	**122**	-.8	-8.1	1.4	—	3.4
Phi	134	4	6	0	1218.2	1309	35	388	513	13.0	3.97	88	.259	.319	-72	-65	102	303	—	.894	637	317	99	-4.0	-5.7	-2.5	—	7.7
NY	134	5	3	0	1186.1	1148	23	386	559	11.8	3.50	93	.243	.304	-8	-36	95	271	—	.907	544	262	81	.3	-3.2	-4.1	—	-7.6
Bal	134	5	7	0	1206.2	1197	25	403	**805**	12.3	4.08	84	.244	.308	-85	-91	99	319	—	.910	523	367	59	1.8	-8.0	-13.2	—	1.8
Total	1071	57	48	5	9759.0	—	—	—	—	11.9	3.44	—	.243	.305	—	—	—	—	—	.906	4470	2097	723	—	—	—	—	—

BATTER-FIELDER WINS	BATTING AVERAGE	ON-BASE PERCENTAGE	SLUGGING AVERAGE	ON-BASE PLUS SLUGGING	ADJUSTED OPS	ADJUSTED BATTER RUNS
McPhee-Cin........4.2	Hecker-Lou...........341	Larkin-Phi...............390	Orr-NY.....................527	Orr-NY.....................890	Orr-NY....................193	Orr-NY.....................56.4
Orr-NY.................3.8	Browning-Lou........340	Browning-Lou........389	Caruthers-StL........527	Larkin-Phi................839	Larkin-Phi..............161	Larkin-Phi..............41.1
Kerins-Lou..........3.7	Orr-NY......................338	O'Neill-StL.............385	Larkin-Phi..............450	Browning-Lou........830	Stovey-Phi..............154	Caruthers-StL.......37.8
Larkin-Phi...........3.7	Caruthers-StL.......334	Stovey-Phi.............377	Hecker-Lou............446	O'Neill-StL.............826	O'Neill-StL.............151	O'Neill-StL.............33.1
O'Neill-StL..........3.2	O'Neill-StL.............328	Swartwood-Bro.....377	Browning-Lou........441	Stovey-Phi.............817	Browning-Lou........151	Stovey-Phi............32.1

RUNS	HITS	DOUBLES	TRIPLES	HOME RUNS	TOTAL BASES	RUNS BATTED IN
Latham-StL...........152	Orr-NY....................193	Larkin-Phi...............36	Orr-NY.....................31	McPhee-Cin..............8	Orr-NY....................301	O'Neill-StL.............107
McPhee-Cin..........139	O'Neill-StL.............190	McClellan-Bro.........33	Coleman-Phi-Pit.....17	Stovey-Phi.................7	O'Neill-StL.............255	Corkhill-Cin..............97
Larkin-Phi.............133	Larkin-Phi.............180	Welch-StL.................31	Kuehne-Pit...............17	Orr-NY.........................7	Larkin-Phi..............254	Welch-StL..................95
McClellan-Bro.......131	Latham-StL...........174	Barkley-Pit...............31	Fennelly-Cin............17		Welch-StL...............221	Orr-NY.........................91
Pinkney-Bro..........119	Phillips-Bro...........160	Browning-Lou..........29	Larkin-Phi.................16		McPhee-Cin............221	Reilly-Cin...................79

BASES ON BALLS	STOLEN BASES	BASE STEALING RUNS	FIELDING RUNS-INFIELD	FIELDING RUNS-OUTFIELD	OUTFIELD ASSISTS	CATCHER CS PCT.
Swartwood-Bro.......70	Stovey-Phi...............68		McPhee-Cin.........26.9	McTamany-Bro....11.3	Swartwood-Bro.......32	
Pinkney-Bro............70	Latham-StL..............60		Hankinson-NY.....26.8	Welch-StL............11.1	Brown-Pit.................30	
Mack-Lou.................68	Welch-StL.................59		Smith-Pit...............17.7	Wolf-Lou.................9.3	Wolf-Lou...................28	
Kerins-Lou...............66	Robinson-StL...........51		White-Lou.............16.7	O'Neill-StL..............7.7	McTamany-Bro.......27	
	McClellan-Bro..........43		Smith-Bro.............12.8	Sommer-Bal...........7.2		

WINS	WINNING PCT.	WINS ABOVE TEAM	GAMES STARTED	COMPLETE GAMES	FEWEST HITS/GAME	FEWEST BB/GAME
Morris-Pit...............41	Foutz-StL...............719	Ramsey-Lou........10.2	Kilroy-Bal.................68	Ramsey-Lou...........66	Ramsey-Lou........6.83	Galvin-Pit.............1.55
Foutz-StL.................41	Caruthers-StL.......682	Morris-Pit.............10.0	Ramsey-Lou...........67	Kilroy-Bal................66	Kilroy-Bal.............7.35	Morris-Pit.............1.91
Ramsey-Lou............38	Morris-Pit...............672	Kilroy-Bal................7.9	Morris-Pit................63	Morris-Pit................63	Morris-Pit.............7.37	Caruthers-StL.......2.00
Mullane-Cin............33	Hudson-StL............615	Mullane-Cin............7.1	Foutz-StL.................57	Mullane-Cin............55	Foutz-StL..............7.46	McGinnis-StL-Bal.2.27
Caruthers-StL.........30	Atkinson-Phi..........595	Foutz-StL.................6.6	Mullane-Cin............56	Foutz-StL.................55	Caruthers-StL.......7.51	Atkinson-Phi.........2.29

STRIKEOUTS	STRIKEOUTS/GAME	GAMES	SAVES	BASE RUNNERS/9	ADJUSTED RELIEF RUNS	RELIEF RANKING
Kilroy-Bal..............513	Kilroy-Bal.............7.92	Kilroy-Bal.................68	Morris-Pit....................1	Shaffer-NY...........9.13		
Ramsey-Lou..........499	Ramsey-Lou.........7.63	Ramsey-Lou...........67	Hudson-StL..................1	Morris-Pit.............9.40		
Morris-Pit..............326	Morris-Pit.............5.28	Morris-Pit.................64	Foutz-StL.....................1	Caruthers-StL.......9.67		
Foutz-StL...............283	Miller-Phi..............5.25	Mullane-Cin............63	Ely-Lou........................1	Handiboe-Pit......10.03		
Mullane-Cin...........250	Terry-Bro..............5.06	Foutz-StL.................59		Ramsey-Lou......10.18		

INNINGS PITCHED	OPPONENTS' AVG.	OPPONENTS' OBP	EARNED RUN AVERAGE	ADJUSTED ERA	ADJUSTED STARTER RUNS	PITCHER WINS
Ramsey-Lou......588.2	Ramsey-Lou.........198	Morris-Pit...............258	Foutz-StL.............2.11	Foutz-StL..............163	Ramsey-Lou........77.3	**Foutz-StL.............7.6**
Kilroy-Bal..........583.0	Kilroy-Bal..............210	Caruthers-StL........263	Caruthers-StL.......2.32	Ramsey-Lou..........148	Foutz-StL..............71.4	**Caruthers-StL.....7.2**
Morris-Pit...........555.1	Morris-Pit..............214	Ramsey-Lou..........269	Ramsey-Lou.........2.45	Caruthers-StL.......148	Morris-Pit.............61.6	**Ramsey-Lou.......6.7**
Mullane-Cin.......529.2	Foutz-StL...............216	Foutz-StL...............274	Morris-Pit.............2.45	Morris-Pit..............138	Caruthers-StL......50.8	**Morris-Pit............4.8**
Foutz-StL...........504.0	Caruthers-StL.......217	Kilroy-Bal..............274	Galvin-Pit.............2.67	Hecker-Lou...........127	Galvin-Pit.............31.2	**Hecker-Lou.........4.8**

"THE $15,000 SLIDE"

As the National League returned to the seven-ball walk, the AA reduced the free pass requirement to six. Walks nearly doubled. With the league also lengthening the pitching box and allowing hurlers to get running starts and deliver the ball with one foot off the ground, strikeouts soared as well.

The Baltimore Orioles finished last, but rookie pitcher Matt Kilroy set an all-time record by fanning 513 batters. Toad Ramsey of fourth-place Louisville came close to Kilroy, and his 499 is also second on the single-season list.

Rowdy, hard-bitten St. Louis cruised to an easy title. Pitchers Dave Foutz and Bob Caruthers won 71 games between themselves, better than all but two other teams. Arlie Latham scored 152 runs and was one of three Browns among the top four in stolen bases—an official statistic for the first time. Second-place Pittsburgh didn't have much offense, but pitchers Ed Morris and Jim Galvin carried the load.

The Browns took on the Chicago White Stockings in the World Series. Behind John Clarkson, Chicago won two of the first three at home. Then in St. Louis, the Browns whipped the White Stockings twice behind Foutz and third hurler Nat Hudson. Games 4 and 5 were plagued by charges that the White Stockings were "laying down" to extend the Series' gate receipts.

In Game 6, with the Browns up three games to two, the confident White Stockings had Clarkson on the hill and led 3-0 in the eighth. However, poor Chicago fielding and timely Browns hitting tied the game. St. Louis' Curt Welch and Foutz singled in the 10th, and then moved up a base on a sacrifice. On either a wild pitch or passed ball (sources differ), catcher King Kelly couldn't handle Clarkson's pitch and Welch scored the winning run. Some newspapers referred to Welch's plate-crossing as "The $15,000 Slide," referring to the Series' prize money, but it is still not certain whether Welch slid or scored standing up. Either way, the Association was vindicated yet again.

1885 NATIONAL LEAGUE

TEAM	W	L	T	PCT	GB	HW	HL	R	OR	PA	H	2B	3B	HR	BB	SO	HB	SH	AVG	OBP	SLG	OPS	AOPS	BR	ABR	PF	SB	CS	BSA	BSR
Chi	87	25	1	.777	—	42	14	**834**	470	4433	1079	**184**	75	**54**	**340**	429	—	—	.264	**.320**	**.385**	**705**	116	**146**	56	114				
NY	85	27	0	.759	2	**45**	10	691	**370**	4250	**1085**	150	**82**	16	221	**312**	—	—	**.269**	.307	.359	666	**122**	80	**89**	99				
Phi	56	54	1	.509	30	29	26	513	511	4113	891	156	35	20	220	401	—	—	.229	.270	.302	572	91	-44	-34	98				
Pro	53	57	0	.482	33	30	24	442	531	3992	820	114	30	6	265	430	—	—	.220	.272	.272	544	82	-74	-60	97				
Bos	46	66	1	.411	41	22	35	528	589	4140	915	144	53	22	190	522	—	—	.232	.267	.312	579	94	-42	-23	96				
Det	41	67	0	.380	44	29	23	514	582	3989	917	149	66	25	216	451	—	—	.243	.284	.337	621	105	17	16	100				
Buf	38	74	0	.339	49	19	38	495	761	4079	980	149	50	23	179	380	—	—	.251	.284	.333	617	100	10	-8	103				
StL	36	72	3	.333	49	23	33	390	593	3972	829	121	21	8	214	412	—	—	.221	.263	.270	533	81	-92	-62	94				
Total	445	—	—	—	—	239	203	4407	—	32968	7516	1167	412	174	1845	3337	—	—	.241	.284	.322	606	—	—	—	—	—	—	—	—

TEAM	CG	SHO	GR	SV	IP	H	HR	BB	SO	BR/9	ERA	AERA	OAV	OOB	PR	APR	PF	OSB	OCS	FA	E	WPB	DP	FW	PW	BW	BSW	DIF
Chi	108	14	**5**	**4**	1015.2	868	37	202	458	9.5	2.23	134	.221	.259	66	80	107	—	—	.903	496	133	80	-2.4	7.5	5.3	—	20.6
NY	109	**16**	3	1	994.0	**758**	**11**	265	**516**	**9.3**	**1.72**	**155**	**.205**	**.258**	**121**	**112**	95	—	—	**.929**	**331**	168	**85**	**6.0**	**10.5**	**8.4**	—	4.1
Phi	108	10	3	0	976.0	860	18	218	378	9.9	2.39	117	.224	.266	46	41	99	—	—	.905	447	167	66	-.3	3.9	-3.2	—	.6
Pro	108	8	3	0	960.2	912	18	235	371	10.7	2.71	99	.235	.278	12	-4	95	—	—	.903	459	165	70	-1.1	-.4	-5.6	—	5.1
Bos	**111**	10	2	0	981.0	1045	26	**188**	480	11.3	3.03	89	.261	.294	-23	-40	95	—	—	.901	478	184	79	-1.5	-3.8	-2.2	—	-2.6
Det	105	6	3	1	954.1	966	18	224	475	11.2	2.88	99	.249	.290	-6	-5	101	—	—	.901	462	**115**	61	-1.7	-.5	1.5	—	-12.4
Buf	107	4	**5**	1	956.0	1175	31	234	320	13.3	4.29	69	.289	.328	-157	-132	106	—	—	.901	464	196	65	-.9	-12.4	-.8	—	-3.9
StL	107	4	4	0	965.1	935	15	278	337	11.3	3.37	82	.245	.296	-59	-69	97	—	—	.916	398	178	67	2.3	-6.5	-5.8	—	-8.0
Total	863	72	28	7	7803.0	—	—	—	—	10.8	2.82	—	.241	.284	—	—	—	—	—	.908	3535	1306	573	—	—	—	—	—

BATTER-FIELDER WINS	BATTING AVERAGE	ON-BASE PERCENTAGE	SLUGGING AVERAGE	ON-BASE PLUS SLUGGING	ADJUSTED OPS	ADJUSTED BATTER RUNS
Connor-NY 4.3	Connor-NY .371	Connor-NY .435	Brouthers-Buf .543	Brouthers-Buf .951	Connor-NY 203	Connor-NY 53.8
Dunlap-StL 4.1	Brouthers-Buf .359	Brouthers-Buf .408	Connor-NY .495	Connor-NY .929	Brouthers-Buf 199	Brouthers-Buf 44.4
Glasscock-StL 3.5	Dorgan-NY .326	Gore-Chi .405	Ewing-NY .471	Gore-Chi .858	Bennett-Det 161	O'Rourke-NY 30.7
Bennett-Det 3.3	Richardson-Buf .319	Hanlon-Det .372	Anson-Chi .461	Anson-Chi .819	Ewing-NY 159	Gore-Chi 28.0
Brouthers-Buf 3.1	Gore-Chi .313	Anson-Chi .357	Richardson-Buf .458	Bennett-Det .812	O'Rourke-NY 158	Bennett-Det 25.1
RUNS	**HITS**	**DOUBLES**	**TRIPLES**	**HOME RUNS**	**TOTAL BASES**	**RUNS BATTED IN**
Kelly-Chi 124	Connor-NY 169	Anson-Chi 35	O'Rourke-NY 16	Dalrymple-Chi 11	Connor-NY 225	Anson-Chi 108
O'Rourke-NY 119	Brouthers-Buf 146	Brouthers-Buf 32	Connor-NY 15	Kelly-Chi 9	Brouthers-Buf 221	Kelly-Chi 75
Gore-Chi 115	Anson-Chi 144	Rowe-Buf 28	Gore-Chi 13		Dalrymple-Chi 219	Pfeffer-Chi 73
Dalrymple-Chi 109	Sutton-Bos 143	Dalrymple-Chi 27	Bennett-Det 13		Anson-Chi 214	Burns-Chi 71
Connor-NY 102	O'Rourke-NY 143	Mulvey-Phi 25			O'Rourke-NY 211	
BASES ON BALLS	**STOLEN BASES**	**BASE STEALING RUNS**	**FIELDING RUNS-INFIELD**	**FIELDING RUNS-OUTFIELD**	**OUTFIELD ASSISTS**	**CATCHER CS PCT.**
Williamson-Chi 75			Dunlap-StL 26.5	Fogarty-Phi 19.5	Kelly-Chi 29	
Gore-Chi 68			Pfeffer-Chi 22.3	Manning-Bos-Det 7.1	Shafer-StL 28	
Morrill-Bos 64			Glasscock-StL 21.1	Kelly-Chi 6,1	Radford-Pro 26	
Connor-NY 51			Williamson-Chi 9.1	Radford-Pro 5.0	Fogarty-Phi 26	
			Gerhardt-NY 8.8	Carroll-Pro 3.7	Thompson-Det 24	
WINS	**WINNING PCT.**	**WINS ABOVE TEAM**	**GAMES STARTED**	**COMPLETE GAMES**	**FEWEST HITS/GAME**	**FEWEST BB/GAME**
Clarkson-Chi 53	Welch-NY .800	Welch-NY 7.9	Clarkson-Chi 70	Clarkson-Chi 68	Keefe-NY 6.75	Whitney-Bos .75
Welch-NY 44	Clarkson-Chi .768	Radbourn-Pro 6.7	Welch-NY 55	Welch-NY 55	Welch-NY 6.80	Galvin-Buf 1.17
Keefe-NY 32	McCormick-Pro-Chi .750	Ferguson-Phi 4.2	Whitney-Bos 50	Whitney-Bos 50	Baldwin-Det 6.88	Clarkson-Chi 1.40
Radbourn-Pro 28	Keefe-NY .711	Baldwin-Det 3.2	Daily-Phi 50		Clarkson-Chi 7.18	Baldwin-Det 1.41
	Radbourn-Pro .571	Boyle-StL 3.0	Buffinton-Bos 50		Daily-Phi 7.57	C.Sweeney-StL 1.64
STRIKEOUTS	**STRIKEOUTS/GAME**	**GAMES**	**SAVES**	**BASE RUNNERS/9**	**ADJUSTED RELIEF RUNS**	**RELIEF RANKING**
Clarkson-Chi 308	Baldwin-Det 6.78	Clarkson-Chi 70	Williamson-Chi 2	Baldwin-Det 8.28		
Welch-NY 258	Keefe-NY 5.11	Welch-NY 56	Pfeffer-Chi 2	Clarkson-Chi 8.58		
Buffinton-Bos 242	Buffinton-Bos 5.01	Whitney-Bos 51	Welch-NY 1	Keefe-NY 9.05		
Keefe-NY 227	Welch-NY 4.72	Buffinton-Bos 51	Galvin-Buf 1	Richardson-NY 9.12		
Whitney-Bos 200	Clarkson-Chi 4.45	Daily-Phi 50	Baldwin-Det 1	Welch-NY 9.20		
INNINGS PITCHED	**OPPONENTS' AVG.**	**OPPONENTS' OBP**	**EARNED RUN AVERAGE**	**ADJUSTED ERA**	**ADJUSTED STARTER RUNS**	**PITCHER WINS**
Clarkson-Chi 623.0	Baldwin-Det .197	Baldwin-Det .228	Keefe-NY 1.58	Keefe-NY 169	Clarkson-Chi 70.8	**Clarkson-Chi 7.3**
Welch-NY 492.0	Welch-NY .203	Clarkson-Chi .239	Welch-NY 1.66	Clarkson-Chi 162	Welch-NY 59.7	**Welch-NY 6.0**
Radbourn-Pro 445.2	Keefe-NY .203	Shaw-Pro .254	Clarkson-Chi 1.85	Welch-NY 160	Keefe-NY 46.4	**Keefe-NY 4.5**
Whitney-Bos 441.1	Clarkson-Chi .208	Keefe-NY .255	Baldwin-Det 1.86	Baldwin-Det 153	Daily-Phi 28.8	**Ferguson-Phi 4.3**
Daily-Phi 440.0	Shaw-Pro .209	Daily-Phi .256	Radbourn-Pro 2.20	Daily-Phi 126	Ferguson-Phi 25.7	**Radbourn-Pro 3.4**

Back to Normal

The National League got sneaky, violating the National Agreement by adding the Union Association's St. Louis franchise (in place of Cleveland) to compete with the AA's popular Browns club. The AA laughed last, though, as the dreadful Maroons survived just two years in the NL and drew half the patrons of the Browns.

Syndicate ownership also reared its malformed head. The owner of both the AA and NL New York clubs transferred manager Jim Mutrie and top players Tim Keefe and Dude Esterbrook to the NL's Giants, ostensibly to field a better team for his 50-cent ticket prices. As a result, the Giants improved 23 games in the NL and the Mets fell 32 games in the AA standings.

For this season NL pitchers were constrained by an unusual rule—possibly instituted to balance their new permission to throw overhand—requiring moundsmen to keep both feet on the ground while delivering the ball. Catchers first wore chest protectors in 1885, and the new equipment allowed the receiver to play closer to the batter. Players were required to use round bats, though one section could be flat.

The NL also addressed Chicago infielder Ed Williamson's 27 homers in 1884, which doubled the previous mark. Since 25 of those homers were hit at a small home park, the NL ruled that, as had been common before 1884, fair balls clearing fences 210 feet or less from home plate were doubles.

The NL returned to its earlier form, with two outstanding contenders battling to the finish. New York had two spectacular hitters, Roger Connor and Buck Ewing, and strong pitching in Keefe and Mickey Welch, but couldn't quite match Chicago, who had ironman John Clarkson on the hill and powerful hitters at nearly every position. Unfortunately, the two best teams from the two biggest cities were followed by six also-rans; third-place Philadelphia finished 30 out. Sixth-place Detroit welcomed rookie outfielder Sam Thompson. Buffalo was seventh despite the best efforts of Dan Brouthers, Hardy Richardson, and pitcher Jim "Pud" Galvin. League attendance rose, led by increases in Chicago, New York, and Philadelphia.

1885 AMERICAN ASSOCIATION

TEAM	W	L	T	PCT	GB	HW	HL	R	OR	PA	H	2B	3B	HR	BB	SO	HB	SH	AVG	OBP	SLG	OPS	AOPS	BR	ABR	PF	SB	CS	BSA	BSR
StL	79	33	0	.705	—	**44**	11	677	**461**	4255	979	132	57	17	234	**282**	49	—	.246	.297	.321	618	96	2	-25	105				
Cin	63	49	0	.563	16	35	21	642	575	4254	1046	108	77	26	153	420	**51**	—	.258	.294	.342	636	103	16	4	102				
Pit	56	55	0	.505	22.5	37	20	547	539	4208	955	123	79	5	189	537	44	—	.240	.282	.315	597	94	-34	-26	99				
Phi	55	57	1	.491	24	33	23	**764**	691	4410	**1099**	**169**	76	**30**	223	410	45	—	**.265**	**.310**	**.365**	**675**	**111**	**80**	**39**	106				
Lou	53	59	0	.473	26	37	19	564	598	4146	986	126	**83**	19	152	448	25	—	.248	.281	.336	617	99	-13	-12	100				
Bro	53	59	0	.473	26	36	22	624	650	4223	966	121	65	14	238	324	42	—	.245	.295	.319	614	97	-4	-8	101				
NY	44	64	0	.407	33	28	24	526	688	3983	921	123	57	21	217	428	35	—	.247	.295	.327	622	105	5	30	96				
Bal	41	68	1	.376	36.5	29	25	541	683	4141	837	124	59	17	**279**	529	42	—	.219	.280	.296	576	87	-51	-43	99				
Total	445	—	—	—	—	279	165	4885	—	33620	7789	1026	553	149	1685	3378	333	—	.246	.292	.328	620	—	—	—	—	—	—	—	—

TEAM	CG	SHO	GR	SV	IP	H	HR	BB	SO	BR/9	ERA	AERA	OAV	OOB	PR	APR	PF	OSB	OCS	FA	E	WPB	DP	FW	PW	BW	BSW	DIF
StL	**111**	**11**	1	0	1002.0	**879**	12	**168**	378	**9.8**	**2.44**	**134**	**.228**	**.268**	**89**	**91**	101	—	—	**.920**	**381**	190	64	**3.0**	**8.2**	-2.3	—	14.1
Cin	102	7	**10**	1	999.1	998	24	250	330	11.9	3.26	100	.253	.309	-2	-1	100	—	—	.911	423	**172**	**86**	.8	-.0	.4	—	5.9
Pit	104	8	7	0	1011.0	918	14	201	454	10.3	2.92	110	.232	.275	36	33	99	—	—	.912	422	213	77	.6	3.0	-2.3	—	-.8
Phi	105	5	8	0	1003.1	1038	**11**	212	**506**	11.6	3.23	106	.255	.299	2	21	106	—	—	.901	483	242	79	-2.2	1.9	**3.5**	—	-4.2
Lou	109	3	4	1	1002.0	927	13	217	462	10.6	2.68	120	.232	.278	63	61	99	—	—	.905	460	248	75	-1.1	5.5	-1.1	—	-6.3
Bro	110	3	2	1	991.2	955	27	211	436	10.8	3.46	95	.240	.283	-24	-18	102	—	—	.910	434	219	56	.2	-1.6	-.7	—	-.9
NY	103	2	6	0	937.0	1015	36	204	408	11.9	4.15	75	.262	.303	-94	-113	96	—	—	.901	452	202	62	-1.6	-10.2	2.7	—	-1.0
Bal	103	2	7	**4**	971.0	1059	12	222	395	12.3	3.90	83	.269	.316	-71	-70	100	—	—	.909	419	272	71	.6	-6.3	-3.9	—	-3.9
Total	847	41	45	7	7917.1	—	—	—	—	11.1	3.24	—	.246	.292	—	—	—	—	—	.909	3474	1758	570	—	—	—	—	—

BATTER-FIELDER WINS	BATTING AVERAGE	ON-BASE PERCENTAGE	SLUGGING AVERAGE	ON-BASE PLUS SLUGGING	ADJUSTED OPS	ADJUSTED BATTER RUNS
Browning-Lou 4.2	Browning-Lou 362	Browning-Lou 393	Orr-NY 543	Browning-Lou 923	Browning-Lou 190	Browning-Lou 48.5
G.Smith-Bro 3.9	Orr-NY 342	Larkin-Phi 373	Browning-Lou 530	Orr-NY 901	Orr-NY 189	Orr-NY 42.4
Larkin-Phi 3.7	Larkin-Phi 329	Stovey-Phi 371	Larkin-Phi 525	Larkin-Phi 899	Larkin-Phi 171	Larkin-Phi 35.5
Jones-Cin 3.3	Jones-Cin 322	Brown-Pit 366	Stovey-Phi 488	Stovey-Phi 858	Stovey-Phi 160	Stovey-Phi 32.4
Nelson-NY 2.9	Stovey-Phi 315	Phillips-Bro 364	Jones-Cin 462	Jones-Cin 824	Jones-Cin 156	Jones-Cin 29.2

RUNS	HITS	DOUBLES	TRIPLES	HOME RUNS	TOTAL BASES	RUNS BATTED IN
Stovey-Phi 130	Browning-Lou 174	Larkin-Phi 37	Orr-NY 21	Stovey-Phi 13	Browning-Lou 255	Fennelly-Cin 89
Larkin-Phi 114	Jones-Cin 157	Browning-Lou 34	Kuehne-Pit 19	Fennelly-Cin 10	Orr-NY 241	Larkin-Phi 88
Jones-Cin 108	Stovey-Phi 153	Orr-NY 29	Wolf-Lou 17	Browning-Lou 9	Larkin-Phi 238	Orr-NY 77
Nelson-NY 98	Orr-NY 152	Stovey-Phi 27	Jones-Cin 17	Larkin-Phi 8	Stovey-Phi 237	Stovey-Phi 75
Browning-Lou 98	Larkin-Phi 149		Fennelly-Cin 17	Orr-NY 6	Jones-Cin 225	Browning-Lou 73

BASES ON BALLS	STOLEN BASES	BASE STEALING RUNS	FIELDING RUNS-INFIELD	FIELDING RUNS-OUTFIELD	OUTFIELD ASSISTS	CATCHER CS PCT.
Nelson-NY 61			G.Smith-Bro 40.3	Corkhill-Cin 15.9	Corkhill-Cin 35	
Macullar-Bal 49			Smith-Pit 28.7	Sommer-Bal 12.5	Nicol-StL 33	
Hotaling-Bro 49			Hankinson-NY 20.9	Welch-StL 12.0	Welch-StL 25	
Stovey-Phi 39			Houck-Phi 18.6	Nicol-StL 11.4	Larkin-Phi 23	
			Nelson-NY 16.8	Jones-Cin 11.2	Coleman-Phi 23	

WINS	WINNING PCT.	WINS ABOVE TEAM	GAMES STARTED	COMPLETE GAMES	FEWEST HITS/GAME	FEWEST BB/GAME
Caruthers-StL 40	Caruthers-StL 755	Morris-Pit 12.9	Morris-Pit 63	Morris-Pit 63	Morris-Pit 7.11	Lynch-NY 1.00
Morris-Pit 39	Foutz-StL 702	Porter-Bro 11.0	Henderson-Bal 61	Henderson-Bal 59	Mays-Lou 7.74	Hecker-Lou 1.01
Porter-Bro 33	Mathews-Phi 638	Mathews-Phi 9.7	Porter-Bro 54	Porter-Bro 53	Foutz-StL 7.75	Caruthers-StL 1.06
Foutz-StL 33	Morris-Pit 619	Hecker-Lou 7.7	Hecker-Lou 53	Caruthers-StL 53	McGinnis-StL 7.87	Mathews-Phi 1.21
	Porter-Bro 611	Caruthers-StL 7.3	Caruthers-StL 53	Hecker-Lou 51	Porter-Bro 7.98	McGinnis-StL 1.53

STRIKEOUTS	STRIKEOUTS/GAME	GAMES	SAVES	BASE RUNNERS/9	ADJUSTED RELIEF RUNS	RELIEF RANKING
Morris-Pit 298	Mathews-Phi 6.09	Morris-Pit 63	Burns-Bal 3	Ramsey-Lou 8.32		
Mathews-Phi 286	Cushman-Phi-NY .5.50	Henderson-Bal 61	Terry-Bro 1	Morris-Pit 8.89		
Henderson-Bal 263	Morris-Pit 4.62	Porter-Bro 54	Sommer-Bal 1	Caruthers-StL 9.44		
Hecker-Lou 209	Henderson-Bal 4.39	Hecker-Lou 53	Reccius-Lou 1	Hecker-Lou 9.86		
Porter-Bro 197	Harkins-Bro 4.33	Caruthers-StL 53	Corkhill-Cin 1	McGinnis-StL 9.88		

INNINGS PITCHED	OPPONENTS' AVG.	OPPONENTS' OBP	EARNED RUN AVERAGE	ADJUSTED ERA	ADJUSTED STARTER RUNS	PITCHER WINS
Morris-Pit 581.0	Morris-Pit 208	Morris-Pit 247	Caruthers-StL 2.07	Caruthers-StL 158	Caruthers-StL 61.3	**Caruthers-StL 6.3**
Henderson-Bal...539.1	Mays-Lou 219	Caruthers-StL 260	Hecker-Lou 2.17	Hecker-Lou 148	Morris-Pit 57.5	**Hecker-Lou 6.0**
Caruthers-StL 482.1	Porter-Bro 223	Hecker-Lou 265	Morris-Pit 2.35	Mathews-Phi 141	Hecker-Lou 51.4	**Morris-Pit 4.7**
Porter-Bro 481.2	McGinnis-StL 225	Cushman-Phi-NY ..266	Mathews-Phi 2.43	Morris-Pit 137	Mathews-Phi 42.1	**Foutz-StL 3.5**
Hecker-Lou 480.0	Foutz-StL 227	Mathews-Phi 267	Foutz-StL 2.63	Foutz-StL 124	Foutz-StL 29.3	**Mathews-Phi 3.3**

Gloves Off

With the Union Association dead, the two surviving leagues got dirty. The NL manipulated the rules and violated the National Agreement, then placated some aggrieved AA owners with cash payments, while the Association engaged in contract-breaking scams of its own. A midseason meeting resulted in the AA's sudden reversal on overhand pitching, which would now be permitted. This pushed the balance of power toward clubs with pitching and speed.

Therefore, the AA crowned a new champ: Charlie Comiskey's St. Louis Browns, a great defensive club sparked by aggressive baserunning and solid pitching. St. Louis moundsmen Bob Caruthers and Dave Foutz permitted the league's fewest hits, walks, and runs to breeze past Cincinnati by 16 games. Stripped by player transfers to the NL New York club, the defending champion Metropolitans sank to seventh.

The postseason "World Series" caused endless controversy and declared no champion. Game 1, in Chicago, was called by darkness shortly after the White Stockings tied the game in the eighth. The next contest in St. Louis was forfeited to the NL champion White Stockings when Comiskey pulled his team off the field in protest of a call. The Browns, however, won the next two in St. Louis. The teams then went to Pittsburgh for Game 5, which Chicago won, and Cincinnati the next day, resulting in another victory for the White Stockings by the same 9-2 score. The Browns won Game 7, also in Cincy, 13-4. The White Stockings ragged the umpiring, the games' locations, and the rules—all of which Chicago player-manager Cap Anson had agreed to beforehand.

Rival owners Chris Von der Ahe and Al Spalding benefited from the controversy—with no clear winner, the $1,000 purse was returned to them and never paid to the players. NL petulance provided a hearty laugh for AA supporters, but the ledgers supplied only indigestion. League attendance fell by 126,000, spiked by large dips in St. Louis and Baltimore.

1884 NATIONAL LEAGUE

TEAM	W	L	T	PCT	GB	HW	HL	R	OR	PA	H	2B	3B	HR	BB	SO	HB	SH	AVG	OBP	SLG	OPS	AOPS	BR	ABR	PF	SB	CS	BSA	BSR
Pro	84	28	2	.750	—	**45**	11	665	**388**	4393	987	153	43	21	**300**	469	—	—	.241	.293	.315	608	97	-16	-5	98				
Bos	73	38	5	.658	10.5	40	16	684	468	4396	1063	**179**	60	36	207	660	—	—	.254	.289	.351	640	105	18	21	100				
Buf	64	47	4	.577	19.5	37	18	700	626	4412	1099	163	**69**	39	215	**458**	—	—	.262	.298	.361	659	106	45	22	103				
NY	62	50	4	.554	22	34	22	693	623	4373	1053	149	68	22	249	492	—	—	.255	.298	.340	638	102	19	4	102				
Chi	62	50	1	.554	22	39	17	**834**	647	4446	**1176**	162	50	**142**	264	469	—	—	**.281**	**.324**	**.446**	**770**	**133**	**203**	**139**	108				
Phi	39	73	1	.348	45	19	37	549	824	4207	934	149	39	14	209	512	—	—	.234	.272	.301	573	88	-72	-45	95				
Cle	35	77	1	.313	49	22	34	458	716	4104	934	147	49	16	170	576	—	—	.237	.269	.312	581	83	-64	-82	103				
Det	28	84	2	.250	56	18	38	445	736	4177	825	114	47	31	207	699	—	—	.208	.247	.284	531	74	-134	-104	94				
Total	457	—	—	—	—	254	193	5028	—	34508	8071	1216	425	321	1821	4335	—	—	.247	.287	.340	626	—	—	—	—	—	—	—	—

TEAM	CG	SHO	GR	SV	IP	H	HR	BB	SO	BR/9	ERA	AERA	OAV	OOB	PR	APR	PF	OSB	OCS	FA	E	WPB	DP	FW	PW	BW	BSW	DIF
Pro	107	**16**	8	**2**	1036.1	**825**	**26**	172	639	**8.7**	**1.61**	**177**	**.209**	**.242**	**158**	**150**	96	—	—	.918	398	145	50	5.1	**13.4**	-.4	—	9.9
Bos	109	14	7	**2**	1037.0	932	30	**135**	**742**	9.3	2.47	117	.226	.250	58	51	97	—	—	**.922**	**384**	**138**	46	**6.3**	4.6	1.9	—	4.7
Buf	108	14	6	1	1001.0	1041	46	189	534	11.1	2.95	107	.254	.286	3	20	106	—	—	.905	462	167	71	1.9	1.8	2.0	—	2.8
NY	**111**	4	5	0	1014.0	1011	28	326	567	11.9	3.12	95	.245	.300	-16	-19	100	—	—	.895	514	200	69	-.6	-1.7	.4	—	8.0
Chi	106	9	**9**	0	997.1	1028	83	231	472	11.4	3.03	103	.250	.290	-6	10	105	—	—	.886	595	198	**107**	-5.6	.9	**12.4**	—	-1.7
Phi	106	3	7	1	981.0	1090	37	254	411	12.3	3.93	76	.261	.304	-103	-105	100	—	—	.888	536	326	67	-2.5	-9.4	-4.0	—	-1.1
Cle	107	7	6	0	994.2	1046	35	269	482	11.9	3.43	92	.256	.302	-50	-30	106	—	—	.897	512	230	75	-1.2	-2.7	-7.3	—	-9.8
Det	109	3	5	0	984.2	1097	36	245	488	12.3	3.38	86	.262	.302	-44	-55	97	—	—	.886	550	159	60	-3.0	-4.9	-9.3	—	-10.8
Total	863	70	53	6	8046.0	—	—	—	—	11.1	2.98	—	.247	.287	—	—	—	—	—	.899	3951	1563	545	—	—	—	—	—

BATTER-FIELDER WINS	BATTING AVERAGE	ON-BASE PERCENTAGE	SLUGGING AVERAGE	ON-BASE PLUS SLUGGING	ADJUSTED OPS	ADJUSTED BATTER RUNS
Pfeffer-Chi..........6.0	O'Rourke-Buf........347	Kelly-Chi..............414	Brouthers-Buf.......563	Brouthers-Buf.......941	Brouthers-Buf.......186	Kelly-Chi.............40.9
Williamson-Chi..4.7	Kelly-Chi..............354	Gore-Chi..............404	Williamson-Chi......554	Kelly-Chi..............938	Kelly-Chi..............178	Brouthers-Buf......38.0
Kelly-Chi............3.3	Sutton-Bos...........346	O'Rourke-Buf........392	Anson-Chi............543	Anson-Chi............916	Anson-Chi............170	Anson-Chi...........36.8
Ewing-NY............3.1	Anson-Chi............335	Sutton-Bos...........384	Kelly-Chi..............524	Williamson-Chi......898	O'Rourke-Buf........167	O'Rourke-Buf.......36.4
Sutton-Bos.........2.8	Brouthers-Buf.......327	Brouthers-Buf.......378	Pfeffer-Chi............514	O'Rourke-Buf........872	Williamson-Chi......164	Sutton-Bos..........34.7

RUNS	HITS	DOUBLES	TRIPLES	HOME RUNS	TOTAL BASES	RUNS BATTED IN
Kelly-Chi..............120	Sutton-Bos...........162	Hines-Pro...............36	Ewing-NY................20	Williamson-Chi........27	Dalrymple-Chi.......263	Anson-Chi............102
O'Rourke-Buf........119	O'Rourke-Buf........162	O'Rourke-Buf..........33	Brouthers-Buf.........15	Pfeffer-Chi..............25	Anson-Chi............258	Pfeffer-Chi............101
Hornung-Bos........119	Dalrymple-Chi.......161	Anson-Chi..............30	Rowe-Buf................14	Dalrymple-Chi.........22	Pfeffer-Chi............240	Kelly-Chi.................95
Dalrymple-Chi.......111	Kelly-Chi..............160	Manning-Phi...........29	McKinnon-NY.........13	Anson-Chi..............21	Kelly-Chi..............237	Williamson-Chi........84
Anson-Chi............108	Anson-Chi............159		Phillips-Cle.............12	Brouthers-Buf.........14	Williamson-Chi......231	Connor-NY..............82

BASES ON BALLS	STOLEN BASES	BASE STEALING RUNS	FIELDING RUNS-INFIELD	FIELDING RUNS-OUTFIELD	OUTFIELD ASSISTS	CATCHER CS PCT.
Gore-Chi.................61			Pfeffer-Chi...........43.3	Lillie-Buf..............15.8	Lillie-Buf.................41	
Kelly-Chi.................46			Williamson-Chi.....21.7	Hanlon-Det..........12.3	Kelly-Chi.................31	
Hines-Pro...............44			Mulvey-Phi...........12.9	Evans-Cle..............8.2	Hanlon-Det.............30	
Williamson-Chi........42			Ward-NY..............10.6	Fogarty-Phi............6.9	Radford-Pro............26	
			Richardson-Buf......5.2	G.Wood-Det...........4.0	Manning-Phi...........26	

WINS	WINNING PCT.	WINS ABOVE TEAM	GAMES STARTED	COMPLETE GAMES	FEWEST HITS/GAME	FEWEST BB/GAME
Radbourn-Pro.........59	Radbourn-Pro.......831	Radbourn-Pro......20.1	Radbourn-Pro.........73	Radbourn-Pro.........73	Sweeney-Pro.......6.23	Whitney-Bos...........72
Buffinton-Bos.........48	Buffinton-Bos........750	Galvin-Buf............15.1	Galvin-Buf...............72	Galvin-Buf...............71	Radbourn-Pro......7.00	Galvin-Buf...............89
Galvin-Buf..............46	Sweeney-Pro........680	Buffinton-Bos.......14.9	Buffinton-Bos..........67	Buffinton-Bos..........63	Clarkson-Chi........7.17	Buffinton-Bos.......1.17
Welch-NY...............39	Galvin-Buf.............676	Welch-NY............11.2	Welch-NY...............65	Welch-NY...............62	Getzien-Det.........7.21	Sweeney-Pro.......1.18
L.Corcoran-Chi.......35	Welch-NY..............650	McCormick-Cle......6.3	L.Corcoran-Chi.......59	L.Corcoran-Chi.......57	Whitney-Bos.........7.29	Coleman-Phi........1.28

STRIKEOUTS	STRIKEOUTS/GAME	GAMES	SAVES	BASE RUNNERS/9	ADJUSTED RELIEF RUNS	RELIEF RANKING
Radbourn-Pro.......441	Clarkson-Chi........7.78	Radbourn-Pro.........75	Morrill-Bos................2	Sweeney-Pro.......7.41		
Buffinton-Bos........417	Whitney-Bos........7.23	Galvin-Buf...............72	Sweeney-Pro............1	Whitney-Bos........8.01		
Galvin-Buf.............369	Getzien-Det.........6.54	Buffinton-Bos..........67	Radbourn-Pro...........1	Radbourn-Pro......8.30		
Welch-NY.............345	Buffinton-Bos.......6.39	Welch-NY...............65	O'Rourke-Buf...........1	Getzien-Det.........8.74		
L.Corcoran-Chi.....272	Sweeney-Pro.......5.90	L.Corcoran-Chi.......60	Ferguson-Phi............1	Galvin-Buf...........8.90		

INNINGS PITCHED	OPPONENTS' AVG.	OPPONENTS' OBP	EARNED RUN AVERAGE	ADJUSTED ERA	ADJUSTED STARTER RUNS	PITCHER WINS
Radbourn-Pro....678.2	Sweeney-Pro........187	Sweeney-Pro........215	Radbourn-Pro......1.38	Radbourn-Pro.......206	Radbourn-Pro....116.2	**Radbourn-Pro..10.7**
Galvin-Buf.........636.1	Getzien-Det..........204	Whitney-Bos........223	Sweeney-Pro.......1.55	Sweeney-Pro........184	Galvin-Buf...........80.9	**Galvin-Buf..........6.3**
Buffinton-Bos.....587.0	Radbourn-Pro.......205	Radbourn-Pro.......234	Getzien-Det.........1.95	Galvin-Buf.............158	Buffinton-Bos.......51.3	**Buffinton-Bos.....5.8**
Welch-NY.........557.1	Whitney-Bos.........207	Getzien-Det..........237	Galvin-Buf...........1.99	Getzien-Det..........148	Sweeney-Pro.......35.7	**Sweeney-Pro......4.4**
L.Corcoran-Chi..516.2	Clarkson-Chi.........208	Buffinton-Bos........244	Whitney-Bos........2.09	Clarkson-Chi.........147	L.Corcoran-Chi....34.6	**Whitney-Bos.......3.6**

Ride That Hoss

The National League expanded to 112 games, hoping to fight the new Union Association by garnering increased newspaper coverage. There were no franchise shifts. The league also first allowed its pitchers to throw overhand, although the Union and American Associations declined to make this change. Additionally, the NL cut the number of balls needed for a walk to six, while the other leagues held at seven.

The biggest story of the year was in Providence, which began the season with two star pitchers: Hoss Radbourn and Charlie Sweeney. When manager Frank Bancroft said that the two would share mound duties, an offended Radbourn loafed and earned a suspension.

Sweeney, receiving an offer from the wealthy St. Louis Union club, malingered and finagled a suspension as well. He then jumped to the outlaws, and Radbourn had the Grays where he wanted them. Radbourn pledged to pitch the rest of the season for Providence if the team would then allow him to depart via free agency. Radbourn went on to win 59 games, an all-time record. Unfortunately for Old Hoss, his arm was never quite the same, though he remained effective and had five 20-win seasons for Providence (he stayed through 1885) and Boston teams in two different leagues.

The '84 Grays had Paul Hines' big bat in center field, but offense wasn't their forte; four of the league's eight teams scored more runs. They still won by 10½ games, courtesy of Old Hoss. Providence then met American Association champs New York in a three-game tourney. Despite playing at New York's Polo Grounds and under Association rules, Radbourn won three straight—6-0, 3-1, and 11-2—to take what can legitimately be called the first World Series. The gate certainly wasn't great. Total attendance was less than 3,800, and just 300 people showed up for the inconsequential third game. Attendance for the whole NL season rose by just 5,000, despite the extra contests, and dropped precipitously in Detroit, Cleveland, and Chicago.

1884 AMERICAN ASSOCIATION

TEAM	W	L	T	PCT	GB	HW	HL	R	OR	PA	H	2B	3B	HR	BB	SO	HB	SH	AVG	OBP	SLG	OPS	AOPS	BR	ABR	PF	SB	CS	BSA	BSR
NY	75	32	5	.701	—	**42**	9	734	**423**	4250	1052	155	64	22	203	**315**	35	—	.262	**.304**	.349	653	120	73	90	98				
Col	69	39	2	.639	6.5	38	16	585	459	4014	901	107	96	**40**	196	629	59	—	.240	.288	.351	639	**121**	45	**98**	92				
Lou	68	40	2	.630	7.5	41	14	573	425	4137	1004	152	69	17	146	408	34	—	.254	.286	.340	626	112	29	58	96				
StL	67	40	3	.626	8	38	14	658	539	4163	987	151	60	11	172	339	39	—	.250	.288	.327	615	100	18	-3	104				
Cin	68	41	3	.624	8	40	16	**754**	512	4296	1037	109	96	36	154	409	52	—	.254	.289	.354	643	108	49	19	105				
Bal	63	43	2	.594	11.5	**42**	13	636	515	4120	896	133	84	32	**211**	545	**64**	—	.233	.284	.336	620	101	26	3	104				
Phi	61	46	1	.570	14	38	16	700	546	4152	**1057**	**167**	**100**	26	153	434	40	—	**.267**	.301	**.379**	**680**	117	**100**	59	106				
Tol	46	58	6	.442	27.5	28	25	463	571	3895	859	153	48	8	157	545	26	—	.231	.268	.305	573	87	-36	-53	104				
Bro	40	64	5	.385	33.5	23	26	476	644	3958	845	112	47	16	179	417	16	—	.225	.263	.292	555	83	-61	-64	101				
Ric	12	30	4	.286	30.5	5	15	194	294	1546	326	40	33	7	53	282	24	—	.222	.261	.308	569	89	-19	-17	99				
Pit	30	78	2	.278	45.5	18	37	406	725	3873	777	105	50	2	143	411	41	—	.211	.248	.268	516	73	-110	-105	99				
Ind	29	78	3	.271	46	17	39	462	755	3960	890	129	62	20	125	561	22	—	.233	.262	.315	577	93	-39	-25	97				
Was	12	51	0	.190	41	10	20	248	481	2282	434	61	24	6	100	377	16	—	.200	.241	.259	500	75	-76	-44	88				
Total	659	—	—	—	—	380	260	6889	—	48646	11065	1574	833	243	1992	5672	468	—	.240	.278	.326	604	—	—	—	—	—	—	—	—

TEAM	CG	SHO	GR	SV	IP	H	HR	BB	SO	BR/9	ERA	AERA	OAV	OOB	PR	APR	PF	OSB	OCS	FA	E	WPB	DP	FW	PW	BW	BSW	DIF
NY	110	9	2	0	985.0	**802**	15	115	628	**8.6**	2.46	127	**.209**	**.237**	86	75	96	—	—	.907	441	**137**	42	2.3	6.9	8.2	—	4.1
Col	102	8	8	**1**	962.1	815	22	172	526	9.5	2.68	113	.217	.256	60	38	93	—	—	.908	433	191	74	2.3	3.5	**9.0**	—	.3
Lou	101	6	9	0	989.2	837	**9**	**97**	470	8.8	**2.17**	**142**	.216	.241	**118**	**105**	95	—	—	**.912**	**426**	190	**84**	2.6	**9.6**	5.3	—	-3.5
StL	99	8	**11**	0	987.0	881	16	172	477	10.0	2.67	122	.226	.266	63	63	100	—	—	.900	490	174	65	-.2	5.8	-.3	—	8.2
Cin	**111**	**11**	1	0	983.2	955	27	181	308	11.1	3.33	100	.243	.289	-10	-1	103	—	—	.909	430	164	82	**2.8**	-.0	1.7	—	9.0
Bal	105	8	3	**1**	955.2	869	16	219	**635**	10.5	2.71	128	.224	.271	56	74	107	—	—	.899	461	210	61	.7	6.8	.3	—	2.3
Phi	105	5	3	0	948.2	920	16	127	530	10.3	3.42	99	.237	.269	-18	-4	104	—	—	.901	457	199	63	.9	-.4	5.4	—	1.6
Tol	103	9	6	**1**	946.0	885	12	169	501	10.5	3.06	111	.233	.275	19	34	105	—	—	.900	469	294	67	.7	3.1	-4.8	—	-5.0
Bro	105	6	4	0	948.2	996	20	163	378	11.2	3.79	87	.254	.288	-58	-50	102	—	—	.889	520	266	68	-1.6	-4.6	-5.8	—	.0
Ric	45	1	0	0	370.1	402	14	52	167	11.4	4.52	73	.257	.288	-53	-49	102	—	—	.874	239	82	27	-1.5	-4.5	-1.6	—	-1.4
Pit	108	4	2	0	943.1	1059	25	216	338	12.7	4.35	76	.265	.312	-116	-109	102	—	—	.889	523	218	71	-1.6	-10.0	-9.6	—	-2.9
Ind	107	2	3	0	937.2	1000	30	199	479	11.8	4.20	78	.254	.295	-100	-96	101	—	—	.889	515	250	45	-1.2	-8.8	-2.3	—	-12.2
Was	62	3	1	0	543.2	644	21	110	235	12.8	4.01	76	.273	.311	-46	-64	93	—	—	.858	400	165	40	-5.3	-5.8	-4.0	—	-4.4
Total	1263	80	53	3	11501.2	—	—	—	—	10.6	3.24	—	.240	.278	—	—	—	—	—	.897	5804	2540	789	—	—	—	—	—

BATTER-FIELDER WINS	BATTING AVERAGE	ON-BASE PERCENTAGE	SLUGGING AVERAGE	ON-BASE PLUS SLUGGING	ADJUSTED OPS	ADJUSTED BATTER RUNS
Barkley-Tol 4.8	Orr-NY 354	Jones-Cin 376	Reilly-Cin 551	Reilly-Cin 918	Orr-NY 195	Orr-NY 45.5
Fennelly-Was-Cin ... 4.2	Reilly-Cin 339	Nelson-NY 375	Stovey-Phi 545	Stovey-Phi 913	Reilly-Cin 186	Reilly-Cin 39.4
Smith-Col........... 4.1	Browning-Lou 336	Stovey-Phi 368	Orr-NY 539	Orr-NY 901	Fennelly-Was-Cin .186	Stovey-Phi 37.7
Latham-StL 4.1	Stovey-Phi 326	Fennelly-Was-Cin .367	Fennelly-Was-Cin .480	Fennelly-Was-Cin .847	Stovey-Phi 182	Browning-Lou 37.4
Esterbrook-NY ... 3.5	Lewis-StL..............323	Reilly-Cin 366	Browning-Lou 472	Jones-Cin 846	Browning-Lou 176	Fennelly-Was-Cin 37.3

RUNS	HITS	DOUBLES	TRIPLES	HOME RUNS	TOTAL BASES	RUNS BATTED IN
Stovey-Phi 124	Orr-NY 162	Barkley-Tol.............39	Stovey-Phi 23	Reilly-Cin 11	Reilly-Cin 247	
Jones-Cin 117	Reilly-Cin 152	Browning-Lou 33	Reilly-Cin 19	Stovey-Phi 10	Orr-NY 247	
Latham-StL............115	Esterbrook-NY......150	Orr-NY 32	Mann-Col.................18	Orr-NY 9	Stovey-Phi 244	
Reilly-Cin 114	Browning-Lou 150	Esterbrook-NY........29	Peltz-Ind..................17	Mann-Col...................7	Jones-Cin 222	
Nelson-NY 114	Jones-Cin 148	Lewis-StL.................25	Jones-Cin 17	Jones-Cin 7	Browning-Lou 211	

BASES ON BALLS	STOLEN BASES	BASE STEALING RUNS	FIELDING RUNS-INFIELD	FIELDING RUNS-OUTFIELD	OUTFIELD ASSISTS	CATCHER CS PCT.
Nelson-NY 74			Latham-StL..........37.2	Nicol-StL..............18.4	Nicol-StL.................48	
Geer-Bro..................38			Smith-Col.............29.8	Welch-Tol.............14.0	Knight-Phi...............36	
Jones-Cin 37			Barkley-Tol...........27.3	Knight-Phi............11.0	Poorman-Tol 29	
Macullar-Bal............36			Gerhardt-Lou.......22.5	Corkhill-Cin..........10.3	Corkhill-Cin.............29	
Richmond-Col.........35			Houck-Phi............22.0	Cline-Lou 6.1		

WINS	WINNING PCT.	WINS ABOVE TEAM	GAMES STARTED	COMPLETE GAMES	FEWEST HITS/GAME	FEWEST BB/GAME
Hecker-Lou 52	Morris-Col.............723	Hecker-Lou 18.0	Hecker-Lou 73	Hecker-Lou 72	Morris-Col............7.02	Driscoll-Lou.............62
Lynch-NY.................37	Hecker-Lou 722	Mullane-Tol 13.9	Mullane-Tol 65	Mullane-Tol 64	Hecker-Lou 7.06	Hecker-Lou 75
Keefe-NY 37	Foutz-StL 714	Morris-Col..............8.3	McKeon-Ind 60	McKeon-Ind 59	Keefe-NY 7.08	Lynch-NY..................76
Mullane-Tol 36	Lynch-NY..............712	Emslie-Bal 5.9	Keefe-NY 58	Keefe-NY 56	Mountain-Col 7.21	E.Dugan-Ric 81
	Keefe-NY 685	Mathews-Phi..........5.0	Terry-Bro..................55	Terry-Bro..................54	Foutz-StL 7.27	McGinnis-StL 89

STRIKEOUTS	STRIKEOUTS/GAME	GAMES	SAVES	BASE RUNNERS/9	ADJUSTED RELIEF RUNS	RELIEF RANKING
Hecker-Lou 385	Henderson-Bal.....7.09	Hecker-Lou 75	O'Day-Tol..................1	Hecker-Lou 8.02		
Henderson-Bal......346	Davis-StL 6.49	Mullane-Tol 67	Mountain-Col 1	Morris-Col............8.36		
Keefe-NY 334	Morris-Col............6.33	McKeon-Ind 61	T.Burns-Bal...............1	Lynch-NY.............8.56		
Mullane-Tol 325	Keefe-NY 6.22	Keefe-NY 58		Caruthers-StL 8.60		
McKeon-Ind 308	Mathews-Phi........5.98	Terry-Bro.................56		Keefe-NY 8.68		

INNINGS PITCHED	OPPONENTS' AVG.	OPPONENTS' OBP	EARNED RUN AVERAGE	ADJUSTED ERA	ADJUSTED STARTER RUNS	PITCHER WINS
Hecker-Lou 670.2	Keefe-NY 204	Hecker-Lou 226	Hecker-Lou 1.80	Hecker-Lou 171	Hecker-Lou 103.0	**Hecker-Lou 12.9**
Mullane-Tol 567.0	Hecker-Lou 204	Morris-Col.............234	Foutz-StL 2.18	Foutz-StL..............149	Mullane-Tol 54.6	**Mullane-Tol......... 7.1**
McKeon-Ind 512.0	Morris-Col.............204	Lynch-NY..............236	Morris-Col............2.18	Morris-Col.............139	Keefe-NY 46.2	**Keefe-NY 5.5**
Lynch-NY...........496.0	Mountain-Col 209	Keefe-NY 239	Keefe-NY 2.25	Keefe-NY 138	Morris-Col............45.7	**Morris-Col........... 4.5**
Keefe-NY 483.0	Foutz-StL 212	Foutz-StL 255	Mountain-Col 2.45	Mullane-Tol 135	Henderson-Bal.....36.7	**Henderson-Bal .. 3.9**

Mets Win New York's First Flag

While the National League believed it could live with the threat of the American Association, the threat from the new Union Association, whose owners did not respect the reserve clause, was another thing entirely. The NL supported Association expansion into four cities that the Unions might possibly inhabit: Brooklyn (which remains in the NL today as the Los Angeles Dodgers), Washington, Indianapolis, and Toledo.

While scrambling to keep their players from Union Association clutches, the AA debuted St. Louis pitchers Bob Caruthers and Dave Foutz , and Toledo outfielder Curt Welch and catcher Deacon McGuire. Brothers Moses and Welday Walker of Toledo became the first blacks ever to play major league baseball—and the last, thanks to various regressive thinkers, until 1947.

A five-team pennant race produced New York's first major league flag. Jim Mutrie's Metropolitans sported batting titlist Dave Orr and infielder Candy Nelson, whose 74 walks were *twice* the previous major league record. The Mets distributed the load equally on the mound. Tim Keefe and Jack Lynch each won 37 games, the first time in major league history two teammates ranked so high in this category. Columbus and Louisville, with Guy Hecker winning 52 times, finished 2-3 in pitching. St. Louis finished fourth, but when Charlie Comiskey took over the reins late in the year, the team immediately sparked. Cincinnati had slugger John Reilly but little else.

Washington defaulted in August, replaced by Richmond, a club from the Eastern League. About the only positive thing Richmond brought was 19-year-old third baseman Billy Nash, who went on to a long NL career. Following the 1883 season, Richmond, Indianapolis, and Toledo were asked to leave the league, and Columbus merged with Pittsburgh.

Despite increasing the schedule to more than 100 games, and adding extra teams, AA attendance rose by just 75,000. Philadelphia's attendance, the league's best in 1883, dipped by around 60 percent, even though the city's Union club defaulted in early August. Crowds were smaller but there was still plenty of life in them. On August 13 Baltimore management surrounded its field with barbed wire the day after fans surged out of the stands and roughed up the umpire.

1884 UNION ASSOCIATION

TEAM	W	L	T	PCT	GB	HW	HL	R	OR	PA	H	2B	3B	HR	BB	SO	HB	SH	AVG	OBP	SLG	OPS	AOPS	BR	ABR	PF	SB	CS	BSA	BSR
StL	94	19	1	.832	—	**50**	6	**887**	**429**	4466	**1251**	**259**	41	**32**	**181**	542	—	—	**.292**	**.321**	**.394**	**715**	**113**	**-31**	**-55**	104				
Mil	8	4	0	.667	35.5	8	4	53	34	415	88	25	0	0	20	70	—	—	.223	.260	.286	546	123	-26	5	55				
Cin	69	36	0	.657	21	35	17	703	466	3933	1027	118	**63**	26	147	**482**	—	—	.271	.298	.356	654	92	-119	-155	108				
Bal	58	47	1	.552	32	29	21	662	627	4027	952	150	26	17	144	652	—	—	.245	.272	.310	582	71	-219	-256	110				
Bos	58	51	2	.532	34	34	23	636	558	4068	928	168	32	19	128	787	—	—	.236	.260	.309	569	74	-245	-239	99				
CP	41	50	2	.451	42	21	18	438	482	3331	742	127	26	10	119	505	—	—	.231	.258	.296	554	70	-215	-212	99				
Was	47	65	2	.420	46.5	36	27	572	679	4044	931	120	26	4	118	558	—	—	.237	.259	.284	543	68	-278	-266	97				
Phi	21	46	0	.313	50	13	21	414	545	2621	618	108	35	7	103	405	—	—	.245	.275	.324	599	89	-128	-105	92				
StP	2	6	1	.250	39.5	0	0	24	57	279	49	13	1	0	7	47	—	—	.180	.201	.235	436	61	-30	-19	55				
Alt	6	19	0	.240	44	6	12	90	216	921	223	30	6	2	22	130	—	—	.248	.266	.301	567	72	-56	-57	101				
KC	16	63	3	.203	61	11	23	311	618	2925	557	104	15	6	123	529	—	—	.199	.232	.253	485	55	-258	-230	87				
Wil	2	16	0	.111	44.5	1	6	35	114	543	91	8	8	2	22	123	—	—	.175	.208	.232	440	33	-58	-59	103				
Total	428	—	—	—	—	244	178	4825	—	31573	7457	1230	279	125	1134	4830	—	—	.245	.272	.316	588	—	—	—	—	—	—	—	—

TEAM	CG	SHO	GR	SV	IP	H	HR	BB	SO	BR/9	ERA	AERA	OAV	OOB	PR	APR	PF	OSB	OCS	FA	E	WPB	DP	FW	PW	BW	BSW	DIF
StL	**104**	8	9	**6**	993.0	838	**9**	110	550	**8.6**	**1.96**	**122**	**.214**	**.235**	**53**	**47**	98	—	—	**.888**	554	**159**	**79**	**3.7**	**4.1**	**-4.8**	—	34.5
Mil	12	3	0	0	104.0	49	1	13	139	5.4	2.25	59	.132	.161	2	-20	55	—	—	.892	53	32	4	.6	-1.8	.4	—	2.7
Cin	95	**11**	8	1	914.1	831	17	**90**	503	9.1	2.38	107	.226	.245	5	16	105	—	—	.882	532	169	45	2.5	1.4	-13.6	—	26.1
Bal	92	4	14	0	946.2	1002	24	177	628	11.2	3.01	89	.254	.286	-61	-33	110	—	—	.872	616	259	53	-.8	-2.9	-22.4	—	31.6
Bos	100	5	9	1	953.1	885	17	110	**753**	9.4	2.70	88	.231	.252	-28	-36	98	—	—	.868	633	277	39	-.3	-3.2	-20.9	—	27.9
CP	86	6	6	0	803.2	**743**	12	137	679	9.9	2.72	89	.230	.261	-26	-27	100	—	—	.882	**459**	191	38	2.8	-2.4	-18.6	—	13.7
Was	94	5	**20**	0	953.2	992	16	168	684	10.9	3.43	70	.251	.282	-105	-111	98	—	—	.869	625	284	55	.7	-9.7	-23.3	—	23.3
Phi	64	1	3	0	593.1	726	7	105	310	12.6	4.63	50	.283	.311	-145	-161	95	—	—	.841	501	268	36	-5.2	-14.1	-9.2	—	16.0
StP	7	1	2	0	71.0	72	1	27	44	12.5	3.17	42	.248	.312	-6	-27	55	—	—	.872	47	12	6	.2	-2.4	-1.7	—	1.9
Alt	20	0	5	0	219.2	292	3	52	93	14.1	4.67	57	.300	.335	-55	-45	109	—	—	.862	156	63	4	-.6	-3.9	-5.0	—	3.1
KC	70	0	12	0	702.2	862	14	127	334	12.7	4.05	55	.283	.312	-126	-155	92	—	—	.861	520	209	51	-2.5	-13.6	-20.1	—	12.7
Wil	15	0	2	0	142.0	165	4	18	113	11.6	3.04	88	.273	.294	-10	-6	110	—	—	.860	104	62	10	-.1	-.5	-5.2	—	-1.2
Total	759	44	90	8	7397.1	—	—	—	—	10.5	3.04	—	.245	.272	—	—	—	—	—	.872	4800	1985	420	—	—	—	—	—

BATTER-FIELDER WINS	BATTING AVERAGE	ON-BASE PERCENTAGE	SLUGGING AVERAGE	ON-BASE PLUS SLUGGING	ADJUSTED OPS	ADJUSTED BATTER RUNS
Dunlap-StL 7.1	Dunlap-StL...........412	Dunlap-StL...........448	Dunlap-StL...........621	Dunlap-StL..........1069	Dunlap-StL...........213	Dunlap-StL...........50.1
Shafer-StL 1.9	Taylor-StL.............366	Shafer-StL 398	Taylor-StL.............548	Shafer-StL 899	Hoover-Phi............180	Shafer-StL 24.9
Hoover-Phi..........1.7	Dickerson-StL 365	Hoover-Phi............390	Shafer-StL 501	Hoover-Phi............885	Shafer-StL 165	Hoover-Phi...........19.4
Glasscock-Cin ...1.4	Hoover-Phi............364	Moore-Was 363	Hoover-Phi............495	Gleason-StL...........802	Moore-Was 140	Glasscock-Cin 13.6
Briody-Cin 1.1	Shafer-StL 360	Gleason-StL..........361	Burns-Cin 457	Moore-Was 777	Gleason-StL..........137	Taylor-StL.............12.1
RUNS	**HITS**	**DOUBLES**	**TRIPLES**	**HOME RUNS**	**TOTAL BASES**	**RUNS BATTED IN**
Dunlap-StL............160	Dunlap-StL............185	Shafer-StL 40	Burns-Cin 12	Dunlap-StL..............13	Dunlap-StL...........279	
Shafer-StL 130	Shafer-StL 168	Dunlap-StL...............39	Rowe-StL.................11	Crane-Bos 12	Shafer-StL 234	
Seery-Bal-KC 115	Moore-Was 155	Rowe-StL.................32	Shafer-StL 10	Levis-Bal-Was...........5	Rowe-StL...............208	
Robinson-Bal........101	Seery-Bal-KC 146	O'Brien-Bos 31			Crane-Bos 193	
Rowe-StL................95	Rowe-StL..............142	Gleason-StL.............30			Seery-Bal-KC 192	
BASES ON BALLS	**STOLEN BASES**	**BASE STEALING RUNS**	**FIELDING RUNS-INFIELD**	**FIELDING RUNS-OUTFIELD**	**OUTFIELD ASSISTS**	**CATCHER CS PCT.**
Robinson-Bal..........37			Dunlap-StL...........28.4	Wise-Was 8.3	Seery-Bal-KC 26	
Shafer-StL 30			Evers-Was 14.5	Boyle-StL 5.3	Slattery-Bos............26	
Dunlap-StL..............29			Robinson-Bal.......12.7	Harbridge-Cin 4.4	Shafer-StL 24	
Harbridge-Cin 25			Hackett-Bos.........11.6	Crane-Bos 4.1	Harbridge-Cin 24	
Gleason-StL............23			McCormick-Phi-Was .9.8	B.Sweeney-Bal 3.7	Sylvester-Cin 23	
WINS	**WINNING PCT.**	**WINS ABOVE TEAM**	**GAMES STARTED**	**COMPLETE GAMES**	**FEWEST HITS/GAME**	**FEWEST BB/GAME**
B.Sweeney-Bal 40	McCormick-Cin 875	B.Sweeney-Bal 12.7	B.Sweeney-Bal 60	B.Sweeney-Bal 58	McCormick-Cin....6.47	Sweeney-StL 43
Daily-CP-Was 28	Taylor-StL.............862	McCormick-Cin 8.3	Daily-CP-Was 58	Daily-CP-Was 56	Shaw-Bos 6.47	McCormick-Cin.......60
Taylor-StL...............25	Boyle-StL 833	Wise-Was 6.9	Bakely-Phi-Wil-KC......45	Bakely-Phi-Wil-KC......43	Sweeney-StL 6.87	Boyle-StL.................60
Bradley-Cin.............25	Sweeney-StL 774	Daily-CP-Was 5.4	Wise-Was 41	Bradley-Cin.............36	Boyle-StL 7.08	Bradley-Cin.............61
Sweeney-StL 24	B.Sweeney-Bal 656	Werden-StL 3.7	Burns-Cin 40	Shaw-Bos 35	Werden-StL 7.20	Murphy-Alt-Wil 62
STRIKEOUTS	**STRIKEOUTS/GAME**	**GAMES**	**SAVES**	**BASE RUNNERS/9**	**ADJUSTED RELIEF RUNS**	**RELIEF RANKING**
Daily-CP-Was 483	Shaw-Bos 8.81	B.Sweeney-Bal 62	Taylor-StL..................4	McCormick-Cin....7.07		
B.Sweeney-Bal 374	Daily-CP-Was 8.68	Daily-CP-Was 58	Sylvester-Cin 1	Sweeney-StL 7.31		
Shaw-Bos 309	Gagus-Was..........7.92	Wise-Was 50	Dunlap-StL..................1	Shaw-Bos 7.53		
Wise-Was 268	Robinson-Bal.......7.32	Bakely-Phi-Wil-KC......46	Brown-Bos.................1	Boyle-StL.............7.68		
Burke-Bos..............255	Burke-Bos............7.13	Bradley-Cin.............41	Boyle-StL 1	Werden-StL 8.60		
INNINGS PITCHED	**OPPONENTS' AVG.**	**OPPONENTS' OBP**	**EARNED RUN AVERAGE**	**ADJUSTED ERA**	**ADJUSTED STARTER RUNS**	**PITCHER WINS**
B.Sweeney-Bal ..538.0	McCormick-Cin 188	McCormick-Cin 202	McCormick-Cin 1.54	McCormick-Cin 165	McCormick-Cin....25.5	**Taylor-StL...........2.8**
Daily-CP-Was 500.2	Shaw-Bos 188	Sweeney-StL 207	Taylor-StL.............1.68	Taylor-StL..............142	Taylor-StL.............21.1	**Sweeney-StL......2.1**
Bakely-Phi-Wil-KC.394.2	Sweeney-StL 197	Shaw-Bos 212	Boyle-StL 1.74	Boyle-StL 137	Shaw-Bos 19.9	**McCormick-Cin .1.9**
Wise-Was 364.1	Boyle-StL 202	Boyle-StL 215	Shaw-Bos 1.77	Shaw-Bos 134	Sweeney-StL 16.4	**Shaw-Bos 1.3**
Bradley-Cin........342.0	Werden-StL 205	Werden-StL 235	Sweeney-StL 1.83	Sweeney-StL 130	Boyle-StL 9.5	**Boyle-StL.................7**

One-Shot Deal

The Union Association, set up ostensibly to challenge the reserve clause, sprang from the mind of St. Louis magnate Henry Lucas, who wanted to force his way into the big picture. It's no coincidence, then, that the St. Louis club was the class of the league, winning by 21 games. Several clubs, including Altoona, Philadelphia, and Chicago (which moved to Pittsburgh, *then* disbanded) weren't even around at the finish.

The Union owners went after low-level NL and AA players and the occasional regular, but almost immediately, contract-jumping and charges of game-throwing plagued the new league. Three good young players debuted in the Union Association before catching on elsewhere: shortstop Germany Smith and outfielders Tommy McCarthy and Oyster Burns. But the level of play was not high; journeyman pitcher Hugh "One Arm" Daily fanned 483 hitters, the third highest total ever. St. Louis' Fred Dunlap, the UA's star batter, hit .412 with 13 homers; he was a good hitter in the NL, but no superstar.

Much has been said about the league's thin qualifications as a major league. But the UA *operated* as a major league, raiding NL and AA rosters. It also played more games in 1884 than did clubs in any established minor league. The UA did, however, feature minor league teams. Wilmington, the champions of the Eastern League, jumped to the UA in August to replace Philadelphia. St. Paul joined the Union at the end of the Northwestern League season to finish out the season when Wilmington disbanded. The Milwaukee Grays, also of the Northwestern League, were the league's most successful replacement, going 8-4 in Pittsburgh's stead. Kansas City formed a team to replace Altoona, going 16-63. Only five teams were functioning at season's end.

The fragile league crumbled as soon as the NL accepted the St. Louis club for 1885 to provide competition for Chris Von der Ahe's successful AA franchise. Maroons dominated almost every UA statistical category and drew 116,000 of the league's 411,000 fans.

Vested-interest parties such as Al Spalding and Al Reach had nothing good to say about the Union Association. But many people hated the reserve clause, and it was only a few years until a more powerful league rose to combat it.

1883 NATIONAL LEAGUE

TEAM	W	L	T	PCT	GB	HW	HL	R	OR	PA	H	2B	3B	HR	BB	SO	HB	SH	AVG	OBP	SLG	OPS	AOPS	BR	ABR	PF	SB	CS	BSA	BSR
Bos	63	35	0	.643	—	**41**	8	669	456	3780	1010	209	**86**	**34**	123	423	—	—	.276	.300	**.408**	**708**	**114**	**68**	**53**	102				
Chi	59	39	0	.602	4	36	13	**679**	540	3787	1000	**277**	61	13	129	399	—	—	.273	.298	.393	691	104	55	7	108				
Pro	58	40	0	.592	5	34	15	636	**436**	3834	1001	189	59	21	149	309	—	—	.272	.300	.372	672	104	29	13	103				
Cle	55	42	3	.567	7.5	31	18	476	443	3596	852	184	38	8	139	374	—	—	.246	.276	.329	605	88	-52	-46	99				
Buf	52	45	1	.536	10.5	36	13	614	576	3876	**1058**	184	59	8	147	342	—	—	**.284**	**.311**	.371	682	108	44	30	102				
NY	46	50	2	.479	16	28	19	530	577	3651	900	139	69	24	127	**297**	—	—	.255	.281	.354	635	96	-23	-17	99				
Det	40	58	3	.408	23	23	26	524	650	3892	931	164	48	13	**166**	378	—	—	.250	.282	.330	612	93	-47	-21	95				
Phi	17	81	1	.173	46	9	40	437	887	3717	859	181	48	3	141	355	—	—	.240	.269	.320	589	90	-74	-27	91				
Total	395	—	—	—	—	238	152	4565	—	30133	7611	1527	468	124	1121	2877	—	—	.262	.290	.360	650	—	—	—	—	—	—	—	—

TEAM	CG	SHO	GR	SV	IP	H	HR	BB	SO	BR/9	ERA	AERA	OAV	OOB	PR	APR	PF	OSB	OCS	FA	E	WPB	DP	FW	PW	BW	BSW	DIF
Bos	89	**6**	9	**3**	860.0	853	11	**90**	**538**	9.9	2.55	121	.245	.264	56	53	99	—	—	.901	409	222	58	3.2	4.6	**4.6**	—	1.6
Chi	91	5	8	1	862.0	942	21	123	299	11.1	2.78	119	.260	.284	34	45	105	—	—	.879	543	137	76	-3.5	3.9	.6	—	8.9
Pro	88	4	10	1	871.0	827	12	111	376	**9.7**	2.37	130	.238	**.262**	74	69	98	—	—	.903	419	156	75	2.7	6.0	1.1	—	-.8
Cle	**92**	5	8	2	879.0	**818**	**7**	217	402	10.6	**2.22**	**142**	**.237**	.282	**89**	**92**	100	—	—	**.909**	**389**	135	69	**4.6**	**8.0**	-4.0	—	-2.1
Buf	90	5	9	2	859.1	971	12	101	362	11.2	3.32	96	.268	.288	-18	-9	101	—	—	.896	445	171	52	1.4	-.8	2.6	—	.3
NY	87	5	11	0	866.0	907	19	170	323	11.2	2.94	105	.253	.287	19	11	99	—	—	.889	468	181	52	.2	1.0	-1.5	—	-1.7
Det	89	5	**12**	2	894.1	1026	22	184	324	12.2	3.56	87	.270	.303	-42	-47	99	—	—	.893	470	**132**	**77**	.9	-4.1	-1.8	—	-3.9
Phi	91	3	9	0	864.2	1267	20	125	253	14.5	5.34	58	.318	.338	-212	-219	98	—	—	.858	639	179	62	-8.0	-19.1	-2.4	—	-2.5
Total	717	38	76	11	6956.1	—	—	—	—	11.3	3.13	—	.262	.290	—	—	—	—	—	.891	3782	1313	521	—	—	—	—	—

BATTER-FIELDER WINS
Farrell-Pro 3.5
Richardson-Buf . 3.1
Brouthers-Buf 3.0
Bennett-Det 3.0
Dunlap-Cle 2.9

BATTING AVERAGE
Brouthers-Buf 374
Connor-NY 357
Gore-Chi 334
Burdock-Bos 330
O'Rourke-Buf 328

ON-BASE PERCENTAGE
Brouthers-Buf 397
Connor-NY 394
Gore-Chi 377
Dunlap-Cle 361
Burdock-Bos 353

SLUGGING AVERAGE
Brouthers-Buf 572
Morrill-Bos 525
Connor-NY 506
Sutton-Bos 486
Ewing-NY 481

ON-BASE PLUS SLUGGING
Brouthers-Buf 969
Connor-NY 900
Morrill-Bos 868
Gore-Chi 849
Sutton-Bos 836

ADJUSTED OPS
Brouthers-Buf 186
Connor-NY 173
Morrill-Bos 155
Bennett-Det 155
Sutton-Bos 147

ADJUSTED BATTER RUNS
Brouthers-Buf 42.7
Connor-NY 35.9
Bennett-Det 26.3
Morrill-Bos 25.6
Dunlap-Cle 23.8

RUNS
Hornung-Bos 107
Gore-Chi 105
O'Rourke-Buf 102
Sutton-Bos 101
Hines-Pro 94

HITS
Brouthers-Buf 159
Connor-NY 146
O'Rourke-Buf 143
Sutton-Bos 134
Wood-Det 133

DOUBLES
Williamson-Chi 49
Brouthers-Buf 41
Burns-Chi 37
Anson-Chi 36

TRIPLES
Brouthers-Buf 17
Morrill-Bos 16
Sutton-Bos 15
Connor-NY 15

HOME RUNS
Ewing-NY 10
Hornung-Bos 8
Denny-Pro 8
Ward-NY 7
Morrill-Bos 6

TOTAL BASES
Brouthers-Buf 243
Morrill-Bos 212
Connor-NY 207
Sutton-Bos 201
Hornung-Bos 199

RUNS BATTED IN
Brouthers-Buf 97
Burdock-Bos 88
Sutton-Bos 73
Morrill-Bos 68
Anson-Chi 68

BASES ON BALLS
York-Cle 37
Hanlon-Det 34
Powell-Det 28
Shafer-Buf 27
Gore-Chi 27

STOLEN BASES

BASE STEALING RUNS

FIELDING RUNS-INFIELD
Farrell-Pro 24.7
Williamson-Chi 17.7
Glasscock-Cle 17.7
Pfeffer-Chi 16.3
Richardson-Buf 16.0

FIELDING RUNS-OUTFIELD
Shafer-Buf 16.2
Ward-NY 11.0
Gore-Chi 8.5
Kelly-Chi 8.3
Manning-Phi 7.1

OUTFIELD ASSISTS
Shafer-Buf 41
Kelly-Chi 38
Manning-Phi 37
Evans-Cle 29
Ward-NY 28

CATCHER CS PCT.

WINS
Radbourn-Pro 48
Galvin-Buf 46
Whitney-Bos 37
Corcoran-Chi 34
McCormick-Cle 28

WINNING PCT.
McCormick-Cle 700
Radbourn-Pro 658
Buffinton-Bos 641
Whitney-Bos 638
Corcoran-Chi 630

WINS ABOVE TEAM
Galvin-Buf 17.6
Radbourn-Pro 15.7
McCormick-Cle 8.6
Corcoran-Chi 3.8
Welch-NY 3.6

GAMES STARTED
Galvin-Buf 75
Radbourn-Pro 68
Coleman-Phi 61
Whitney-Bos 56
Corcoran-Chi 53

COMPLETE GAMES
Galvin-Buf 72
Radbourn-Pro 66
Coleman-Phi 59
Whitney-Bos 54
Corcoran-Chi 51

FEWEST HITS/GAME
Sawyer-Cle 7.60
Radbourn-Pro 8.01
McCormick-Cle 8.32
Daily-Cle 8.56
Whitney-Bos 8.61

FEWEST BB/GAME
Whitney-Bos 61
Galvin-Buf 69
Radbourn-Pro 80
Coleman-Phi 80
Goldsmith-Chi 92

STRIKEOUTS
Whitney-Bos 345
Radbourn-Pro 315
Galvin-Buf 279
Corcoran-Chi 216
Buffinton-Bos 188

STRIKEOUTS/GAME
Whitney-Bos 6.04
Buffinton-Bos 5.08
Sawyer-Cle 4.85
Radbourn-Pro 4.48
Corcoran-Chi 4.10

GAMES
Radbourn-Pro 76
Galvin-Buf 76
Coleman-Phi 65
Whitney-Bos 62
Corcoran-Chi 56

SAVES
Wiedman-Det 2
Whitney-Bos 2

BASE RUNNERS/9
Radbourn-Pro 8.81
Whitney-Bos 9.23
Galvin-Buf 9.96
McCormick-Cle ..10.03
Ward-NY 10.04

ADJUSTED RELIEF RUNS

RELIEF RANKING

INNINGS PITCHED
Galvin-Buf 656.1
Radbourn-Pro 632.1
Coleman-Phi 538.1
Whitney-Bos 514.0
Corcoran-Chi 473.2

OPPONENTS' AVG.
Sawyer-Cle 217
Radbourn-Pro 227
McCormick-Cle 233
Sweeney-Pro 237
Whitney-Bos 238

OPPONENTS' OBP
Radbourn-Pro 244
Whitney-Bos 251
Galvin-Buf 265
Ward-NY 267
McCormick-Cle 268

EARNED RUN AVERAGE
McCormick-Cle 1.84
Radbourn-Pro 2.05
Whitney-Bos 2.24
Sawyer-Cle 2.36
Daily-Cle 2.42

ADJUSTED ERA
McCormick-Cle 171
Radbourn-Pro 150
Whitney-Bos 138
Sawyer-Cle 133
Corcoran-Chi 132

ADJUSTED STARTER RUNS
Radbourn-Pro 73.5
McCormick-Cle 47.4
Whitney-Bos 44.4
Corcoran-Chi 36.8
Daily-Cle 34.0

PITCHER WINS
Radbourn-Pro 8.3
Whitney-Bos 5.6
McCormick-Cle .. 4.8
Corcoran-Chi 3.2
Galvin-Buf 2.4

Tiny Steps

After a reasonably successful 1882 campaign, the NL awarded franchises to Philadelphia and New York, each competing with AA franchises in the same cities. Both NL teams survive to this day. Prior to 1883 New York had not had any major league team since 1876. A meeting between NL and AA delegates in New York resulted in a peace agreement between the two warring leagues. Each club would now be able to reserve 11 players, rather than 10, and league contracts would be respected.

Abraham Mills was voted the league's new president, to be replaced in 1885 by Nicholas Young. The NL rules committee stated that pitches must not be delivered above the line of the shoulder. Any exception to this would result in a base-advancing "balk." In addition, the league ruled once and for all that a foul must be caught on the fly to register as an out. The AA retained the one-bounce exception.

Chicago again finished just ahead of Providence, but a September rush by the surprising Boston Beaneaters shoved both clubs aside. Boston, with a slugging offense led by Joe Hornung and John Morrill, featured a terrific pitcher in Jim Whitney. Although the White Stockings still led the league in runs, King Kelly and Fred Pfeffer had poor seasons, and Fred Goldsmith lost some of his touch on the hill. Perhaps 1883's most interesting debut came in Chicago, where outfielder and future evangelist Billy Sunday showed off legs that moved almost as quickly as his mouth—Cap Anson signed the 20-year-old outfielder because he "ran like a scared deer."

With two new clubs in large cities, NL attendance increased, but lagged far behind that of the AA. More than twice as many fans came out to see the AA's Philadelphia franchise than to see any NL club. Philadelphia's NL entry, which used an unheard-of 29 players, was allowed to cut its admission to 25 cents to match the AA's price. The last-place club drew 75,000, but that was still just one quarter of the Athletics' business.

1883 AMERICAN ASSOCIATION

TEAM	W	L	T	PCT	GB	HW	HL	R	OR	PA	H	2B	3B	HR	BB	SO	HB	SH	AVG	OBP	SLG	OPS	AOPS	BR	ABR	PF	SB	CS	BSA	BSR
Phi	66	32	0	.673	—	37	14	**720**	547	3912	**974**	**149**	50	20	**200**	268	—	—	**.262**	**.300**	.346	646	102	**49**	-4	109				
StL	65	33	0	.663	1	35	14	549	409	3619	891	118	46	7	124	**240**	—	—	.255	.280	.321	601	91	-13	-41	106				
Cin	61	37	0	.622	5	**38**	13	662	413	3808	961	122	74	**34**	139	261	—	—	**.262**	.289	**.363**	**652**	106	45	13	106				
NY	54	42	1	.563	11	29	17	498	**405**	3676	883	111	58	6	142	259	—	—	.250	.279	.319	598	91	-18	-40	104				
Lou	52	45	1	.536	13.5	29	18	564	562	3694	892	114	64	14	141	304	—	—	.251	.280	.331	611	**107**	-4	**40**	93				
Col	32	65	0	.330	33.5	18	29	476	659	3687	854	101	**79**	15	134	409	—	—	.240	.268	.326	594	102	-28	18	92				
Pit	31	67	0	.316	35	18	31	525	728	3771	892	120	58	13	164	345	—	—	.247	.280	.324	604	101	-10	14	96				
Bal	28	68	0	.292	37	18	31	471	742	3696	870	125	49	5	164	331	—	—	.246	.280	.314	594	91	-19	-35	103				
Total	390	—	—	—	—	222	167	4465	—	29863	7217	960	478	114	1208	2417	—	—	.252	.282	.331	613	—	—	—	—	—	—	—	—

TEAM	CG	SHO	GR	SV	IP	H	HR	BB	SO	BR/9	ERA	AERA	OAV	OOB	PR	APR	PF	OSB	OCS	FA	E	WPB	DP	FW	PW	BW	BSW	DIF
Phi	92	1	6	0	873.0	921	22	**95**	347	10.5	2.88	123	.254	.273	41	59	107	—	—	.865	584	168	40	-4.1	5.2	-.4	—	16.2
StL	93	**9**	5	**1**	879.1	**729**	**7**	150	325	**9.0**	**2.23**	**156**	**.211**	**.244**	**104**	**115**	106	—	—	**.909**	388	126	62	4.5	**10.1**	-3.6	—	5.0
Cin	96	8	2	0	866.2	766	17	168	215	9.7	2.26	143	.222	.258	100	95	98	—	—	.905	**383**	131	57	**4.7**	8.4	1.1	—	-2.2
NY	**97**	6	0	0	874.0	751	12	133	**478**	9.1	2.90	115	.218	.247	38	41	101	—	—	.905	391	**117**	45	4.1	3.6	-3.5	—	1.8
Lou	96	7	2	0	873.2	987	**7**	110	269	11.3	3.50	85	.267	.288	-20	-56	91	—	—	.886	478	156	67	.6	-4.9	**3.5**	—	4.3
Col	90	4	7	0	840.1	980	16	211	222	12.8	3.96	78	.274	.314	-62	-89	93	—	—	.874	535	170	**69**	-2.1	-7.8	1.6	—	-8.1
Pit	82	1	**18**	**1**	867.2	1140	21	151	271	13.4	4.62	70	.298	.325	-127	-135	99	—	—	.884	504	232	55	-.6	-11.9	1.2	—	-6.8
Bal	86	1	11	0	844.2	943	12	190	290	12.1	4.08	85	.265	.303	-74	-55	105	—	—	.855	624	277	44	-6.3	-4.8	-3.1	—	-5.8
Total	732	37	51	2	6919.1	—	—	—	—	11.0	3.30	—	.252	.282	—	—	—	—	—	.885	3887	1377	439	—	—	—	—	—

BATTER-FIELDER WINS	BATTING AVERAGE	ON-BASE PERCENTAGE	SLUGGING AVERAGE	ON-BASE PLUS SLUGGING	ADJUSTED OPS	ADJUSTED BATTER RUNS
Richmond-Col....3.8	Swartwood-Pit 357	Swartwood-Pit 394	Stovey-Phi 506	Swartwood-Pit 869	Swartwood-Pit 186	Swartwood-Pit 40.9
Smith-Col............3.4	Browning-Lou 338	Browning-Lou 378	Reilly-Cin 485	Stovey-Phi 852	Browning-Lou 183	Browning-Lou 34.4
Swartwood-Pit...2.8	Clinton-Bal 313	Moynahan-Phi 360	Swartwood-Pit 476	Browning-Lou 842	Stovey-Phi 156	Stovey-Phi 25.4
Gerhardt-Lou 2.4	Rowe-Bal 313	Clinton-Bal............357	Jones-Cin 471	Reilly-Cin 810	Reilly-Cin 149	Reilly-Cin 21.1
Holbert-NY 2.2	Reilly-Cin 311	Nelson-NY 353	Browning-Lou 464	Jones-Cin 799	Jones-Cin 146	Jones-Cin 18.2

RUNS	HITS	DOUBLES	TRIPLES	HOME RUNS	TOTAL BASES	RUNS BATTED IN
Stovey-Phi 110	Swartwood-Pit 147	Stovey-Phi 31	Smith-Col................17	Stovey-Phi 14	Stovey-Phi 213	
Reilly-Cin 103	Reilly-Cin 136	Swartwood-Pit 24	Reilly-Cin 14	Jones-Cin 10	Reilly-Cin 212	
Carpenter-Cin.........99	Carpenter-Cin.......130	Knight-Phi...............23	Kuehne-Col.............14	Reilly-Cin 9	Swartwood-Pit 196	
Knight-Phi...............98	Stovey-Phi 128	Hayes-Pit 23	Mansell-Pit..............13	Fulmer-Cin................5	Jones-Cin 184	
	Nelson-NY 127		Mann-Col................13	Brown-Col.................5	B.Gleason-StL 167	

BASES ON BALLS	STOLEN BASES	BASE STEALING RUNS	FIELDING RUNS-INFIELD	FIELDING RUNS-OUTFIELD	OUTFIELD ASSISTS	CATCHER CS PCT.
Stearns-Bal.............34			Battin-Pit..............28.8	Wolf-Lou 16.2	Nicol-StL.................31	
Nelson-NY 31			Richmond-Col......26.9	Nicol-StL 11.3	Wolf-Lou 29	
Moynahan-Phi 31			Latham-StL 21.3	Maskrey-Lou..........9.9	Dickerson-Pit 28	
J.Gleason-StL-Lou 29			Smith-Col.............19.5	Birchall-Phi 5.0		
			Gerhardt-Lou 18.4	Clinton-Bal.............4.8		

WINS	WINNING PCT.	WINS ABOVE TEAM	GAMES STARTED	COMPLETE GAMES	FEWEST HITS/GAME	FEWEST BB/GAME
White-Cin................43	Mullane-StL 700	Mountain-Col 9.9	Keefe-NY 68	Keefe-NY 68	Keefe-NY 7.10	Mathews-Phi...........73
Keefe-NY 41	Mathews-Phi.........698	Keefe-NY 8.8	White-Cin................64	White-Cin................64	Mullane-StL 7.27	Weaver-Lou 79
Mullane-StL 35	Bradley-Phi 696	White-Cin...............8.3	Mountain-Col 59	Mountain-Col 57	White-Cin.............7.38	Lynch-NY 88
Mathews-Phi...........30	White-Cin..............662	Driscoll-Pit 6.0	Hecker-Lou 52	Hecker-Lou 51	McGinnis-StL 7.64	Bradley-Phi 92
	McGinnis-StL 636	Mullane-StL 5.0	Mullane-StL 49	Mullane-StL 49	Deagle-Cin...........8.27	Driscoll-Pit 1.04

STRIKEOUTS	STRIKEOUTS/GAME	GAMES	SAVES	BASE RUNNERS/9	ADJUSTED RELIEF RUNS	RELIEF RANKING
Keefe-NY 359	Keefe-NY 5.22	Keefe-NY 68	Mullane-StL 1	Keefe-NY 8.67		
Mathews-Phi.........203	Mathews-Phi........4.80	White-Cin................65	Barr-Pit 1	Mullane-StL 8.71		
Mullane-StL 191	Lynch-NY.............4.20	Mountain-Col 59		Jones-Phi.............8.86		
Hecker-Lou 164	Mullane-StL 3.73	Mullane-StL 53		White-Cin.............9.00		
Mountain-Col 159	Henderson-Bal.....3.64	Hecker-Lou 53		McGinnis-StL 9.27		

INNINGS PITCHED	OPPONENTS' AVG.	OPPONENTS' OBP	EARNED RUN AVERAGE	ADJUSTED ERA	ADJUSTED STARTER RUNS	PITCHER WINS
Keefe-NY 619.0	Keefe-NY 203	Keefe-NY 237	White-Cin.............2.09	Mullane-StL 159	White-Cin.............74.8	**White-Cin............ 6.9**
White-Cin...........577.0	Mullane-StL 207	Mullane-StL 238	Mullane-StL 2.19	White-Cin..............155	Keefe-NY 60.8	**Keefe-NY 6.0**
Mountain-Col 503.0	White-Cin..............209	White-Cin..............244	Deagle-Cin...........2.31	McGinnis-StL 149	Mullane-StL 59.6	**Mullane-StL........ 5.5**
Hecker-Lou 469.0	McGinnis-StL 215	McGinnis-StL 249	McGinnis-StL 2.33	Mathews-Phi.........144	McGinnis-StL 49.3	**McGinnis-StL..... 4.2**
Mullane-StL 460.2	Deagle-Cin............229	Bradley-Phi 263	Keefe-NY 2.41	Deagle-Cin............140	Mathews-Phi........37.8	**Mathews-Phi...... 2.8**

Calm Before the Storm

After changing to the Reach baseball, the AA took the field for its second season with new clubs in New York City and Columbus, Ohio. The AA, like the NL, expanded its schedule to 98 games. Most clubs were going to larger rosters and deeper pitching staffs. The Athletics, Reds, and Baltimore used three pitchers for at least 16 starts, though New York (led by Tim Keefe, who completed all 68 of his starts) and Louisville made do with just two. Will White of Cincinnati was again the league's top hurler, but his club—despite leading the league in homers and batting average—was just 24-24 on the road, and finished third.

Philadelphia replaced first baseman Arlie Latham with Harry Stovey, and the new guy led the AA in runs, doubles, homers, and slugging. With fine pitching and an offense that led the league in walks and runs, the Athletics held off St. Louis by 1 game. The Browns, using fine pitching from Tony Mullane and solid defense, came close for garrulous owner Chris Von der Ahe and a fanatical fan base. The rough-and-tumble character of the team gained shape with the acquisition of Latham.

After eking out the league title, the Athletics were to meet the NL champion Boston Red Stockings in a postseason series, but suddenly reversed their decision after faring poorly in an October exhibition series against the NL's pathetic Philadelphia entry. Following this chain of events, the NL and AA met in New York that December and hammered out a "permanent" peace agreement with provisions for an annual postseason series between league champions.

The results of the AA's second season spoke loudly. The eight clubs combined to draw more than 1,000,000, with three clubs, (one of which was last-place Baltimore) pulling in more than 100,000 each. The entire NL drew just over 600,000—a nifty 35 percent increase—but not in the same league as the AA's 251 percent explosion.

1882 NATIONAL LEAGUE

TEAM	W	L	T	PCT	GB	HW	HL	R	OR	PA	H	2B	3B	HR	BB	SO	HB	SH	AVG	OBP	SLG	OPS	AOPS	BR	ABR	PF	SB	CS	BSA	BSR
Chi	55	29	0	.655	—	**35**	10	**604**	**353**	3367	**892**	**209**	54	15	**142**	262	—	—	**.277**	**.307**	**.389**	**696**	**118**	**87**	**61**	105				
Pro	52	32	0	.619	3	30	12	463	356	3206	776	121	53	11	102	255	—	—	.250	.274	.334	608	96	-17	-16	100				
Buf	45	39	0	.536	10	26	13	500	461	3244	858	146	47	18	116	**228**	—	—	.274	.300	.368	668	113	51	42	102				
Bos	45	39	1	.536	10	27	15	472	414	3252	823	114	50	15	134	244	—	—	.264	.294	.347	641	107	22	21	100				
Cle	42	40	2	.512	12	21	19	402	411	3131	716	139	40	**20**	122	261	—	—	.238	.268	.331	599	96	-23	-8	97				
Det	42	41	3	.506	12.5	24	18	407	488	3266	724	117	44	19	122	308	—	—	.230	.259	.314	573	84	-54	-53	100				
Tro	35	48	2	.422	19.5	22	20	430	522	3166	747	116	**59**	12	109	298	—	—	.244	.270	.333	603	99	-22	0	95				
Wor	18	66	0	.214	37	12	30	379	652	3097	689	109	57	16	113	303	—	—	.231	.259	.322	581	85	-45	-54	102				
Total	338	—	—	—	—	197	137	3657	—	25729	6225	1071	404	126	960	2159	—	—	.251	.279	.342	622	—	—	—	—	—	—	—	—

TEAM	CG	SHO	GR	SV	IP	H	HR	BB	SO	BR/9	ERA	AERA	OAV	OOB	PR	APR	PF	OSB	OCS	FA	E	WPB	DP	FW	PW	BW	BSW	DIF
Chi	**83**	7	1	0	763.2	**667**	13	102	279	**9.1**	**2.22**	**129**	**.221**	**.246**	**57**	**52**	99	—	—	.898	376	98	54	.1	**4.7**	**5.5**	—	2.6
Pro	80	**10**	4	**1**	752.0	690	12	87	273	9.3	2.27	123	.228	.250	51	48	97	—	—	.901	371	114	67	.4	4.4	-1.5	—	6.7
Buf	79	3	5	0	737.0	778	16	114	287	10.9	3.25	90	.254	.280	-30	-30	101	—	—	**.910**	315	136	42	3.3	-2.7	3.8	—	-1.4
Bos	81	4	4	0	749.0	738	**10**	**77**	352	9.8	2.80	102	.239	.258	7	4	99	—	—	**.910**	**314**	121	37	**3.6**	.4	1.9	—	-2.8
Cle	81	4	3	0	751.2	743	22	132	232	10.5	2.75	101	.249	.280	11	1	97	—	—	.905	358	163	**71**	1.1	.0	-.7	—	.6
Det	82	7	4	0	793.0	808	19	129	**354**	10.6	2.98	98	.248	.277	-9	-8	101	—	—	.893	396	**88**	44	-.4	-.7	-4.8	—	6.5
Tro	81	6	4	0	758.0	836	13	165	184	11.9	3.08	91	.267	.304	-16	-24	98	—	—	.887	432	106	70	-2.5	-2.2	.0	—	-1.8
Wor	75	0	**9**	0	738.1	964	21	151	195	13.6	3.75	82	.294	.325	-71	-51	107	—	—	.878	468	165	66	-4.6	-4.6	-4.9	—	-9.9
Total	642	41	34	1	6042.2	—	—	—	—	10.7	2.88	—	.251	.279	—	—	—	—	—	.897	3030	991	451	—	—	—	—	—

BATTER-FIELDER WINS	BATTING AVERAGE	ON-BASE PERCENTAGE	SLUGGING AVERAGE	ON-BASE PLUS SLUGGING	ADJUSTED OPS	ADJUSTED BATTER RUNS
Glasscock-Cle ... 4.1	Brouthers-Buf 368	Brouthers-Buf 403	Brouthers-Buf 547	Brouthers-Buf 950	Brouthers-Buf 198	Brouthers-Buf 37.9
Brouthers-Buf 2.8	Anson-Chi............362	Anson-Chi............397	Connor-Tro...........530	Anson-Chi............897	Connor-Tro...........188	Connor-Tro...........33.4
Dunlap-Cle.......... 2.8	Connor-Tro...........330	Whitney-Bos 382	Whitney-Bos 510	Whitney-Bos 892	Whitney-Bos 182	Anson-Chi............29.9
Bennett-Det........ 2.8	Start-Pro..............329	Gore-Chi..............369	Anson-Chi.............500	Connor-Tro...........884	Anson-Chi.............177	Whitney-Bos 24.1
Williamson-Chi .. 2.6	Whitney-Bos 323	Connor-Tro...........354	Hines-Pro.............467	Hines-Pro.............793	Hines-Pro.............151	Hines-Pro.............21.3

RUNS	HITS	DOUBLES	TRIPLES	HOME RUNS	TOTAL BASES	RUNS BATTED IN
Gore-Chi.................99	Brouthers-Buf 129	Kelly-Chi 37	Connor-Tro.............18	Wood-Det 7	Brouthers-Buf 192	Anson-Chi...............83
Dalrymple-Chi.........96	Anson-Chi.............126	Anson-Chi...............29	Wood-Det 12	Muldoon-Cle 6	Connor-Tro............185	Brouthers-Buf 63
Stovey-Wor 90		Hines-Pro................28	Corey-Wor 12	Brouthers-Buf 6	Hines-Pro..............177	Williamson-Chi........60
Kelly-Chi 81		Williamson-Chi........27			Anson-Chi.............174	Richardson-Buf.......57
Purcell-Buf..............79		Glasscock-Cle 27			Dalrymple-Chi.......167	Kelly-Chi 55

BASES ON BALLS	STOLEN BASES	BASE STEALING RUNS	FIELDING RUNS-INFIELD	FIELDING RUNS-OUTFIELD	OUTFIELD ASSISTS	CATCHER CS PCT.
Gore-Chi.................29			Glasscock-Cle 24.2	Evans-Wor...........14.6	Evans-Wor.............31	
Williamson-Chi........27			Richardson-Buf....19.3	Hornung-Bos 11.4	Nicol-Chi.................27	
Shafer-Cle 27			Dunlap-Cle...........17.9	Hanlon-Det 10.1	Knight-Det..............25	
Hanlon-Det 26			A.Irwin-Wor..........16.7	Kelly-Chi 8.2	Gore-Chi.................23	
			Williamson-Chi.....15.4	Stovey-Wor 3.2	Foley-Buf 22	

WINS	WINNING PCT.	WINS ABOVE TEAM	GAMES STARTED	COMPLETE GAMES	FEWEST HITS/GAME	FEWEST BB/GAME
McCormick-Cle.......36	Corcoran-Chi 692	McCormick-Cle......9.0	McCormick-Cle.......67	McCormick-Cle.......65	Corcoran-Chi 7.11	Mathews-Bos..........69
Radbourn-Pro.........33	Radbourn-Pro.......635	Richmond-Wor.......5.0	Radbourn-Pro.........51	Radbourn-Pro.........50	Radbourn-Pro......8.15	Galvin-Buf...............81
Goldsmith-Chi.........28	Goldsmith-Chi.......622	Wiedman-Det.........4.4	Galvin-Buf..............51	Galvin-Buf..............48	McCormick-Cle....8.31	Goldsmith-Chi.........84
Galvin-Buf..............28	Ward-Pro 594	Corcoran-Chi 3.6	Whitney-Bos 48	Whitney-Bos 46	Goldsmith-Chi......8.38	Wiedman-Det..........85
Corcoran-Chi 27	Mathews-Bos........559	Radbourn-Pro........2.6	Richmond-Wor........46	Goldsmith-Chi.........45	Ward-Pro 8.43	Whitney-Bos 88

STRIKEOUTS	STRIKEOUTS/GAME	GAMES	SAVES	BASE RUNNERS/9	ADJUSTED RELIEF RUNS	RELIEF RANKING
Radbourn-Pro.......201	Mathews-Bos.......4.83	McCormick-Cle.......68	Ward-Pro 1	Corcoran-Chi 8.70		
McCormick-Cle.....200	Derby-Det 4.52	Radbourn-Pro.........54		Radbourn-Pro......9.14		
Derby-Det 182	Corcoran-Chi 4.30	Galvin-Buf..............52		Goldsmith-Chi......9.22		
Whitney-Bos 180	Daily-Buf 4.08	Whitney-Bos 49		Wiedman-Det.......9.42		
Corcoran-Chi 170	Radbourn-Pro......3.88	Richmond-Wor........48		Mathews-Bos.......9.47		

INNINGS PITCHED	OPPONENTS' AVG.	OPPONENTS' OBP	EARNED RUN AVERAGE	ADJUSTED ERA	ADJUSTED STARTER RUNS	PITCHER WINS
McCormick-Cle..595.2	Corcoran-Chi 200	Corcoran-Chi 234	Corcoran-Chi 1.95	Corcoran-Chi 147	Radbourn-Pro......34.7	**Radbourn-Pro 3.2**
Radbourn-Pro....466.0	Radbourn-Pro.......226	Mathews-Bos.......246	Radbourn-Pro......2.11	Radbourn-Pro.......133	Corcoran-Chi 34.0	**Corcoran-Chi 2.9**
Galvin-Buf..........445.1	Ward-Pro 232	Radbourn-Pro.......247	McCormick-Cle....2.37	Goldsmith-Chi.......118	McCormick-Cle....30.3	**Whitney-Bos....... 2.8**
Whitney-Bos 420.0	Mathews-Bos........232	Wiedman-Det........253	Goldsmith-Chi......2.42	McCormick-Cle 117	Goldsmith-Chi......23.2	**McCormick-Cle.. 2.3**
	Daily-Buf 234	Goldsmith-Chi.......254	Keefe-Tro 2.49	Keefe-Tro 113	Wiedman-Det.......18.3	**Goldsmith-Chi.... 1.8**

The War Is On

In 1882, for the first time, the NL had no franchise shifts or new clubs. However, the ground was still quaking under the Senior Circuit. On William Hulbert's death in April, the league elected Boston owner Arthur Soden as president. Soden took office just as the new American Association, formed the previous winter and setting up shop in six cities forsaken by the NL, prepared for play.

For the third straight season, Chicago defeated Providence to win the NL title, but this time by a small margin. The White Stockings again had a murderous attack, with George Gore, Abner Dalrymple, and King Kelly rating 1-2-4 in runs, and pitchers Fred Goldsmith and Larry Corcoran were every bit the equal of Providence's Hoss Radbourn and John Ward. Dan Brouthers of third-place Buffalo led the NL in batting average, slugging percentage, on-base percentage, total bases, and hits.

Even though 1882 saw the first padded glove (worn by Providence shortstop Art Irwin, and later popularized by teammate John Ward), the NL's fielding percentage decreased by nearly 10 points. Chicago was last NL pennant winner to have a fielding average below .900.

Six NL clubs finished over .500. Only Worcester was a disaster, compiling a .214 winning percentage. Worcester drew just 11,000 fans all year, and on September 28 the club drew the smallest crowd in major league history: 6, that's right, 6. Worcester, and seventh-place Troy, were bounced from the NL for 1883 as Soden and the other league owners awarded franchises to magnates in Philadelphia and New York.

After a late-season schedule change appeared to give Chicago an unfair advantage, the White Stockings and Grays met in a nine-game series to determine the league champ. Cap Anson's White Stockings appeared to tank the first three games to increase interest in the remaining six, and the series indeed lasted nine games, with the White Stockings triumphing. Prior to their ill-advised postseason skirmish with Providence, the White Stockings split a two-game series with Association champion Cincinnati. The relevant parties duly noted the interest in this matchup.

1882 AMERICAN ASSOCIATION

TEAM	W	L	T	PCT	GB	HW	HL	R	OR	PA	H	2B	3B	HR	BB	SO	HB	SH	AVG	OBP	SLG	OPS	AOPS	BR	ABR	PF	SB	CS	BSA	BSR
Cin	55	25	0	.688	—	**31**	11	**489**	**268**	3109	**795**	95	47	5	102	204	—	—	**.264**	.289	.332	621	107	37	12	106				
Phi	41	34	0	.547	11.5	21	18	406	389	2832	660	89	21	5	125	**164**	—	—	.244	.277	.298	575	92	-3	-27	107				
Lou	42	38	0	.525	13	26	13	443	352	2934	728	**110**	28	9	**128**	193	—	—	.259	**.292**	.328	620	**120**	**40**	**66**	95				
Pit	39	39	1	.500	15	17	18	428	418	2994	730	**110**	**59**	**18**	90	183	—	—	.251	.274	**.348**	**622**	118	35	57	95				
StL	37	43	0	.463	18	24	20	399	496	2977	663	87	41	11	112	226	—	—	.231	.260	.302	562	90	-20	-35	104				
Bal	19	54	1	.260	32.5	9	25	273	515	2655	535	60	24	4	72	215	—	—	.207	.229	.254	483	72	-89	-66	92				
Total	234	—	—	—	—	128	105	2438	—	17501	4111	551	220	52	629	1185	—	—	.244	.271	.312	582	—	—	—	—	—	—	—	—

TEAM	CG	SHO	GR	SV	IP	H	HR	BB	SO	BR/9	ERA	AERA	OAV	OOB	PR	APR	PF	OSB	OCS	FA	E	WPB	DP	FW	PW	BW	BSW	DIF
Cin	**77**	**11**	3	0	721.1	**609**	7	125	165	**9.2**	**1.65**	**160**	**.214**	**.247**	**83**	**80**	98	—	—	**.907**	**332**	**102**	41	**3.7**	**7.3**	1.1	—	2.9
Phi	72	2	3	0	663.0	682	13	99	190	10.6	2.97	94	.249	.275	-21	-12	105	—	—	.895	361	119	36	1.2	-1.1	-2.5	—	5.9
Lou	73	6	7	0	693.1	637	6	112	240	9.7	2.03	122	.229	.259	51	37	92	—	—	.893	385	161	**57**	1.3	3.4	**6.1**	—	-8.7
Pit	**77**	2	2	0	696.2	694	**4**	**82**	**252**	10.0	2.79	93	.243	.264	-8	-15	97	—	—	.889	397	115	40	.5	-1.4	5.2	—	-4.3
StL	75	3	5	**1**	688.1	729	7	103	225	10.9	2.92	96	.254	.280	-18	-8	105	—	—	.875	446	205	41	-1.6	-.7	-3.2	—	2.5
Bal	64	1	**12**	0	646.1	760	15	108	113	12.1	3.88	71	.275	.302	-86	-80	102	—	—	.859	490	183	41	-5.0	-7.3	-6.1	—	.9
Total	438	25	32	1	4109.0	—	—	—	—	10.4	2.68	—	.244	.271	—	—	—	—	—	.886	2411	885	256	—	—	—	—	—

BATTER-FIELDER WINS
Browning-Lou....4.6
Snyder-Cin..........2.5
O'Brien-Phi.........2.2
Swartwood-Pit...1.8
Mansell-Pit.........1.6

BATTING AVERAGE
Browning-Lou 378
Carpenter-Cin.......342
Swartwood-Pit 329
O'Brien-Phi 303
Wolf-Lou 299

ON-BASE PERCENTAGE
Browning-Lou 430
Swartwood-Pit 370
Carpenter-Cin.......360
O'Brien-Phi 339
Sommer-Cin 333

SLUGGING AVERAGE
Browning-Lou 510
Swartwood-Pit 489
Taylor-Pit..............452
Mansell-Pit............438
Carpenter-Cin.......422

ON-BASE PLUS SLUGGING
Browning-Lou 940
Swartwood-Pit 859
Carpenter-Cin.......782
O'Brien-Phi 758
Taylor-Pit..............749

ADJUSTED OPS
Browning-Lou 228
Swartwood-Pit 197
Taylor-Pit..............157
Carpenter-Cin.......154
Mansell-Pit............150

ADJUSTED BATTER RUNS
Browning-Lou 40.9
Swartwood-Pit 33.4
Carpenter-Cin......18.5
Mansell-Pit...........17.1
Taylor-Pit..............16.9

RUNS
Swartwood-Pit 86
Sommer-Cin 82
Carpenter-Cin.........78
Browning-Lou 67
Birchall-Phi 65

HITS
Carpenter-Cin.......120
Browning-Lou 109
Swartwood-Pit 107
Sommer-Cin 102
B.Gleason-StL 100

DOUBLES
Swartwood-Pit 18
Mansell-Pit.............18
Browning-Lou 17
Taylor-Pit................16
Cuthbert-StL 16

TRIPLES
Mansell-Pit.............16
Taylor-Pit................13
Wheeler-Cin............11
Swartwood-Pit 11
Wolf-Lou 8

HOME RUNS
Walker-StL................7
Browning-Lou 5
Swartwood-Pit 4

TOTAL BASES
Swartwood-Pit 159
Mansell-Pit............152
Carpenter-Cin.......148
Browning-Lou 147
Taylor-Pit..............135

RUNS BATTED IN

BASES ON BALLS
J.Gleason-StL.........27
Browning-Lou 26
Sommer-Cin 24
J.Reccius-Lou.........23
Swartwood-Pit 21

STOLEN BASES

BASE STEALING RUNS

FIELDING RUNS-INFIELD
Stricker-Phi..........22.8
B.Gleason-StL 10.3
Browning-Lou 8.8
Peters-Pit...............5.7
Shetzline-Bal 4.1

FIELDING RUNS-OUTFIELD
Walker-StL.............5.7
O'Brien-Phi 4.6
Sommer-Cin 3.4
Blakiston-Phi..........3.2
Mansell-Pit.............2.8

OUTFIELD ASSISTS
Wolf-Lou 21
Walker-StL 18
Mansell-Pit.............16
Cline-Bal 16
Brown-Bal 16

CATCHER CS PCT.

WINS
White-Cin...............40
Mullane-Lou............30
Weaver-Phi.............26
McGinnis-StL..........25
Salisbury-Pit 20

WINNING PCT.
White-Cin.............769
Weaver-Phi 634
McGinnis-StL 581
Mullane-Lou..........556
Salisbury-Pit 526

WINS ABOVE TEAM
White-Cin............13.1
McGinnis-StL 8.2
Weaver-Phi 7.1
Mullane-Lou...........4.7
Driscoll-Pit 2.6

GAMES STARTED
Mullane-Lou............55
White-Cin................54
McGinnis-StL..........45
Landis-Phi-Bal 42
Weaver-Phi.............41

COMPLETE GAMES
White-Cin................52
Mullane-Lou............51
McGinnis-StL..........43
Weaver-Phi.............41
Salisbury-Pit 38

FEWEST HITS/GAME
Hecker-Lou 6.49
McCormick-Cin....7.25
Driscoll-Pit 7.25
White-Cin.............7.71
Geis-Bal...............7.90

FEWEST BB/GAME
Hecker-Lou 43
Driscoll-Pit 54
Weaver-Phi.............85
Salisbury-Pit 99
Landis-Phi-Bal 1.17

STRIKEOUTS
Mullane-Lou..........170
Salisbury-Pit 135
McGinnis-StL 134
White-Cin.............122
Weaver-Phi 104

STRIKEOUTS/GAME
Salisbury-Pit 3.63
Arundel-Pit...........3.53
Mullane-Lou.........3.32
McGinnis-StL 3.11
J.Reccius-Lou......2.94

GAMES
Mullane-Lou............55
White-Cin................54
McGinnis-StL..........45
Landis-Phi-Bal 44
Weaver-Phi.............42

SAVES
Fusselback-StL.........1

BASE RUNNERS/9
Hecker-Lou 6.92
Dorr-StL...............7.36
Driscoll-Pit 7.79
McCormick-Cin....8.97
White-Cin.............9.04

ADJUSTED RELIEF RUNS

RELIEF RANKING

INNINGS PITCHED
White-Cin..........480.0
Mullane-Lou.......460.1
McGinnis-StL.....388.1
Weaver-Phi........371.0
Landis-Phi-Bal...360.0

OPPONENTS' AVG.
Hecker-Lou 188
McCormick-Cin.....206
Driscoll-Pit 206
White-Cin..............216
Geis-Bal................220

OPPONENTS' OBP
Hecker-Lou 199
Driscoll-Pit 218
McCormick-Cin.....243
White-Cin..............244
Salisbury-Pit 253

EARNED RUN AVERAGE
Driscoll-Pit 1.21
Hecker-Lou 1.30
McCormick-Cin....1.52
White-Cin.............1.54
Mullane-Lou.........1.88

ADJUSTED ERA
Driscoll-Pit 216
Hecker-Lou 191
McCormick-Cin.....174
White-Cin..............172
Mullane-Lou..........132

ADJUSTED STARTER RUNS
White-Cin............60.3
Mullane-Lou.........34.3
Driscoll-Pit 26.6
McCormick-Cin....24.9
Hecker-Lou 11.1

PITCHER WINS
White-Cin............6.7
Mullane-Lou.......5.0
Driscoll-Pit 2.1
McCormick-Cin .1.8
Hecker-Lou 1.6

Association Baseball

The new American Association, in direct contrast to the NL, voted to allow Sunday ball and sale of alcohol at their parks, and allowed clubs to charge just a quarter for admission (the Senior Circuit's ticket prices were 50 cents). These attractions helped the new AA essentially match the NL in attendance for its premier season, even though the new league fielded just six clubs. Three original AA clubs—Cincinnati, Pittsburgh, and St. Louis—remain in operation today as National League franchises.

There were other differences between the leagues. The American Association did not fine pitchers who hit batters intentionally, but they did institute the practice of league-employed umpires, which the NL soon followed. Disdaining the NL's Spalding baseball, the AA used the Mahn ball.

Many of the new league's clubs had local flavors. The Cincinnati club had three regulars (Will White, Joe Sommer, and Hick Carpenter) who had played on the city's final NL entry back in 1880. Rather than go whole-hog to steal away "reserved" NL players, the AA instead used players who had enjoyed success in the minor leagues of the time or had previously washed out of the majors.

Nobody argued that the AA's talent was on an equal level to that of the major leagues, but several future stars got their start in the new loop. Among players making their major league debuts in the 1882 American Association were Louisville's Pete Browning (the league's top offensive player), St. Louis' Charlie Comiskey, and Bid McPhee of Cincinnati.

The Cincinnati Red Stockings ran away with the marbles, zooming out to a quick lead. The first-year league was fairly balanced, with four teams playing .500 ball or better, and St. Louis a respectable 18 games behind in fifth place; Baltimore was the league doormat. White was the AA's dominant pitcher, though he had competition from Tony Mullane of third-place Louisville. Hick Carpenter led the league in hits, while top defender McPhee anchored the infield.

1881 NATIONAL LEAGUE

TEAM	W	L	T	PCT	GB	HW	HL	R	OR	PA	H	2B	3B	HR	BB	SO	HB	SH	AVG	OBP	SLG	OPS	AOPS	BR	ABR	PF	SB	CS	BSA	BSR
Chi	56	28	0	.667	—	**32**	10	**550**	**380**	3254	**918**	**157**	36	12	140	224	—	—	**.295**	**.325**	**.380**	**705**	**119**	**88**	**63**	105				
Pro	47	37	1	.560	9	23	20	447	426	3223	780	144	37	11	**146**	214	—	—	.253	.287	.335	622	100	-3	5	98				
Buf	45	38	0	.542	10.5	25	16	440	447	3127	797	**157**	50	12	108	270	—	—	.264	.289	.361	650	109	22	28	99				
Det	41	43	0	.488	15	23	19	440	429	3131	780	131	**53**	**17**	136	250	—	—	.260	.293	.357	650	103	21	4	104				
Tro	39	45	1	.464	17	24	18	399	427	3186	754	124	31	5	140	240	—	—	.248	.281	.314	595	86	-32	-52	105				
Bos	38	45	0	.458	17.5	19	22	347	410	3026	733	121	27	5	110	193	—	—	.251	.279	.317	596	94	-32	-14	95				
Cle	36	48	1	.429	20	20	22	392	414	3249	796	120	39	7	132	224	—	—	.255	.286	.326	612	100	-17	7	95				
Wor	32	50	1	.390	23	19	22	410	492	3214	781	114	31	7	121	**169**	—	—	.253	.281	.316	597	86	-32	-54	106				
Total	336	—	—	—	—	185	149	3425	—	25410	6339	1068	304	76	1033	1784	—	—	.260	.290	.338	628	—	—	—	—	—	—	—	—

TEAM	CG	SHO	GR	SV	IP	H	HR	BB	SO	BR/9	ERA	AERA	OAV	OOB	PR	APR	PF	OSB	OCS	FA	E	WPB	DP	FW	PW	BW	BSW	DIF
Chi	81	9	3	0	744.2	**722**	14	122	228	**10.2**	2.43	**113**	**.243**	**.273**	29	**26**	99	—	—	.916	**309**	105	54	2.1	**2.4**	**5.9**	—	3.6
Pro	76	7	9	0	757.2	756	**5**	138	264	10.6	**2.40**	111	**.243**	.275	**32**	22	96	—	—	.896	390	139	66	-2.0	2.1	.5	—	4.5
Buf	72	5	**12**	0	742.1	881	9	**89**	185	11.8	2.84	98	.281	.301	-5	-5	100	—	—	.892	408	150	48	-3.4	-.5	2.6	—	4.8
Det	83	**10**	1	0	744.2	785	8	137	**265**	11.1	2.65	110	.257	.289	11	21	105	—	—	.906	338	**83**	**80**	.5	2.0	.4	—	-3.9
Tro	**85**	8	0	0	771.0	805	11	161	207	11.3	2.96	99	.263	.299	-16	-2	106	—	—	**.917**	311	85	70	**2.2**	-.2	-4.9	—	-.1
Bos	72	6	11	**3**	730.2	763	9	143	199	11.2	2.71	98	.258	.292	5	-4	96	—	—	.909	325	204	54	1.0	-.4	-1.3	—	-2.8
Cle	82	2	3	0	760.0	737	9	126	240	**10.2**	2.68	98	.244	.274	8	-5	94	—	—	.904	348	129	68	.2	-.5	.7	—	-6.4
Wor	80	5	3	0	737.1	882	11	120	196	12.2	3.54	85	.288	.315	-63	-39	109	—	—	.903	353	113	50	-.5	-3.6	-5.0	—	.2
Total	631	52	42	3	5988.1	—	—	—	—	11.1	2.77	—	.260	.290	—	—	—	—	—	.905	2782	1008	490	—	—	—	—	—

BATTER-FIELDER WINS	BATTING AVERAGE	ON-BASE PERCENTAGE	SLUGGING AVERAGE	ON-BASE PLUS SLUGGING	ADJUSTED OPS	ADJUSTED BATTER RUNS
Anson-Chi.......... 3.6	Anson-Chi............399	Anson-Chi............442	Brouthers-Buf 541	Anson-Chi............952	Anson-Chi............189	Anson-Chi............35.4
Dunlap-Cle......... 3.2	Powell-Det 338	York-Pro...............362	Anson-Chi............510	Brouthers-Buf 902	Brouthers-Buf 182	Brouthers-Buf 25.2
Bennett-Det........ 3.2	Rowe-Buf.............333	Brouthers-Buf 361	Rowe-Buf.............480	Bennett-Det 819	Dunlap-Cle............159	Dunlap-Cle...........24.8
Richardson-Buf . 2.8	Start-Pro..............328	Dunlap-Cle...........358	Bennett-Det 478	Dunlap-Cle............802	York-Pro...............150	York-Pro..............19.9
Williamson-Chi .. 2.1	Dunlap-Cle...........325	Gore-Chi..............354	Dunlap-Cle...........444	York-Pro...............790	Bennett-Det 149	O'Rourke-Buf.......16.5

RUNS	HITS	DOUBLES	TRIPLES	HOME RUNS	TOTAL BASES	RUNS BATTED IN
Gore-Chi................86	Anson-Chi............137	Kelly-Chi 27	Rowe-Buf...............11	Brouthers-Buf 8	Anson-Chi............175	Anson-Chi...............82
Kelly-Chi 84	Dalrymple-Chi.......117	Hines-Pro...............27	Phillips-Cle.............10	Bennett-Det 7	Dunlap-Cle...........156	Bennett-Det 64
Dalrymple-Chi.........72	Dickerson-Wor......116	Stovey-Wor 25		Farrell-Pro...............5	Kelly-Chi 153	Kelly-Chi 55
O'Rourke-Buf.........71		Dunlap-Cle.............25		Burns-Chi 4	Dalrymple-Chi.......150	
Farrell-Pro..............69		White-Buf...............24			Dickerson-Wor......149	

BASES ON BALLS	STOLEN BASES	BASE STEALING RUNS	FIELDING RUNS-INFIELD	FIELDING RUNS-OUTFIELD	OUTFIELD ASSISTS	CATCHER CS PCT.
Clapp-Cle...............35			Force-Buf............24.5	Richardson-Buf....22.3	Richardson-Buf.......45	
York-Pro.................29			Williamson-Chi.....21.3	Hornung-Bos 11.8	Kelly-Chi 31	
Ferguson-Tro 29			Glasscock-Cle 9.4	Evans-Tro 11.4	Evans-Tro 31	
Farrell-Pro..............29			Morrill-Bos 7.7	Dickerson-Wor.......9.2	Dickerson-Wor........28	
			Quest-Chi 7.6	Kelly-Chi 5.5	Shafer-Cle 24	

WINS	WINNING PCT.	WINS ABOVE TEAM	GAMES STARTED	COMPLETE GAMES	FEWEST HITS/GAME	FEWEST BB/GAME
Whitney-Bos 31	Radbourn-Pro.......694	Richmond-Wor.......8.7	Whitney-Bos 63	Whitney-Bos 57	McCormick-Cle....8.28	Galvin-Buf...............87
Corcoran-Chi 31	Corcoran-Chi 689	Radbourn-Pro........7.8	McCormick-Cle.......58	McCormick-Cle 57	Wiedman-Det.......8.45	Wiedman-Det..........94
Derby-Det 29	Goldsmith-Chi.......649	Whitney-Bos 5.9	Derby-Det...............55	Derby-Det 55	Radbourn-Pro......8.55	Goldsmith-Chi......1.20
Galvin-Buf...............28	Welch-Tro.............538	Derby-Det 5.3	Galvin-Buf...............53	Richmond-Wor........50	Corcoran-Chi 8.62	Richmond-Wor.....1.32
McCormick-Cle.......26	Galvin-Buf.............538	McCormick-Cle......4.7	Richmond-Wor........52	Galvin-Buf...............48	Ward-Pro 8.89	McCormick-Cle....1.44

STRIKEOUTS	STRIKEOUTS/GAME	GAMES	SAVES	BASE RUNNERS/9	ADJUSTED RELIEF RUNS	RELIEF RANKING
Derby-Det 212	Derby-Det 3.86	Whitney-Bos 66	Mathews-Pro-Bos.....2	Wiedman-Det.......9.39		
McCormick-Cle.....178	Corcoran-Chi 3.40	McCormick-Cle 59	Morrill-Bos 1	McCormick-Cle....9.72		
Whitney-Bos 162	Ward-Pro 3.25	Galvin-Buf...............56		Goldsmith-Chi....10.15		
Richmond-Wor......156	Radbourn-Pro......3.24	Derby-Det 56		Radbourn-Pro....10.32		
Corcoran-Chi 150	McCormick-Cle....3.05	Richmond-Wor........53		Ward-Pro 10.34		

INNINGS PITCHED	OPPONENTS' AVG.	OPPONENTS' OBP	EARNED RUN AVERAGE	ADJUSTED ERA	ADJUSTED STARTER RUNS	PITCHER WINS
Whitney-Bos 552.1	Radbourn-Pro.......235	Wiedman-Det........258	Wiedman-Det.......1.80	Wiedman-Det........162	Derby-Det 33.7	**Derby-Det 2.3**
McCormick-Cle..526.0	McCormick-Cle.....235	McCormick-Cle.....265	Ward-Pro 2.13	Derby-Det.............132	Galvin-Buf............18.3	**Whitney-Bos....... 2.1**
Derby-Det..........494.2	Wiedman-Det........238	Radbourn-Pro.......270	Derby-Det............2.20	Ward-Pro 125	Corcoran-Chi 15.8	**Galvin-Buf 2.0**
Galvin-Buf..........474.0	Corcoran-Chi 242	Goldsmith-Chi.......271	Corcoran-Chi 2.31	Corcoran-Chi 118	Ward-Pro 15.6	**Ward-Pro............ 1.9**
Richmond-Wor...462.1	Ward-Pro 242	Ward-Pro 271	Galvin-Buf............2.37	Galvin-Buf.............117	Radbourn-Pro......14.2	**Radbourn-Pro 1.4**

The Last Solo Flight

The season's most significant change was the decision to move the pitcher's box back 5 feet to a distance of 50 feet from home plate. As a result of this change, league batting average rose 15 points, and scoring increased by nearly half a run. In addition, only seven balls were now required for a walk, and bases on balls shot up 40 percent. Oddly, although the number of strikes for a whiff was also reduced to the present-day three, strikeouts actually decreased.

Much to the delight of William Hulbert, Chicago won again, breaking the race open late in the summer. They led the league in runs and fewest allowed, also making the league's fewest errors. The White Stockings' dominant lineup, held over from 1880, included the top three in runs: George Gore, King Kelly, and Abner Dalrymple. Cap Anson's .399 average topped the loop by 61 points.

Detroit, replacing Cincinnati, finished a surprising fourth, largely due to catcher Charlie Bennett's power hitting. Meanwhile, outfielder Dan Brouthers broke through for Buffalo after two trials with Troy, helping the Bisons rise from seventh to third. Despite great pitching from John Ward and Hoss Radbourn, Providence finished second because of several dead spots in the lineup. Overall, the league was much stronger and more balanced; for once, each team was competitive.

With greater competition came bigger crowds, and Detroit's admittance provided an unexpected attendance windfall. Chicago still led the NL in spectators for the fifth time in six seasons. League attendance surpassed 300,000 for the first time, although Troy and Worcester lagged far behind the rest.

Big changes were on the horizon. Several large cities were clamoring for big league ball, and in response, club owners from Philadelphia and Cincinnati founded the American Association in fall 1881. Not around to deal with this new threat was Hulbert, since 1876 the guiding force behind the National League, who died in spring 1882.

1880 NATIONAL LEAGUE

TEAM	W	L	T	PCT	GB	HW	HL	R	OR	PA	H	2B	3B	HR	BB	SO	HB	SH	AVG	OBP	SLG	OPS	AOPS	BR	ABR	PF	SB	CS	BSA	BSR
Chi	67	17	2	.798	—	**37**	5	**538**	317	3239	**876**	**164**	39	4	104	217	—	—	**.279**	**.303**	**.360**	**663**	**119**	**84**	**55**	106				
Pro	52	32	3	.619	15	31	12	419	**299**	3285	793	114	34	8	89	**186**	—	—	.248	.268	.313	581	101	-6	8	97				
Cle	47	37	1	.560	20	23	19	387	337	3078	726	130	**52**	7	76	237	—	—	.242	.261	.327	588	102	-2	6	98				
Tro	41	42	0	.494	25.5	20	21	392	438	3127	755	114	37	5	**120**	260	—	—	.251	.280	.319	599	100	15	-5	105				
Wor	40	43	2	.482	26.5	24	17	412	370	3105	699	129	**52**	8	81	278	—	—	.231	.251	.316	567	86	-22	-52	109				
Bos	40	44	2	.476	27	25	17	416	456	3185	779	134	41	**20**	105	221	—	—	.253	.278	.343	621	115	35	50	97				
Buf	24	58	3	.293	42	13	29	331	502	3052	669	104	37	3	90	327	—	—	.226	.249	.289	538	82	-49	-55	102				
Cin	21	59	3	.263	44	14	25	296	472	2970	649	91	36	7	75	267	—	—	.224	.244	.288	532	82	-56	-52	99				
Total	340	—	—	—	—	187	145	3191	—	25041	5946	980	328	62	740	1993	—	—	.245	.267	.320	587	—	—	—	—	—	—	—	—

TEAM	CG	SHO	GR	SV	IP	H	HR	BB	SO	BR/9	ERA	AERA	OAV	OOB	PR	APR	PF	OSB	OCS	FA	E	WPB	DP	FW	PW	BW	BSW	DIF
Chi	80	8	8	3	775.0	**622**	8	129	**367**	8.7	1.93	126	**.209**	.242	38	42	102	—	—	**.913**	**329**	141	41	**2.3**	4.1	**5.3**	—	13.3
Pro	75	**13**	12	3	799.0	663	7	**51**	286	**8.0**	**1.64**	**134**	.215	**.228**	**65**	**53**	93	—	—	.910	357	99	53	1.1	**5.2**	.8	—	3.0
Cle	**83**	7	2	1	759.2	685	4	98	289	9.3	1.90	124	.228	.253	40	39	99	—	—	.910	330	117	52	2.0	3.8	.6	—	-1.4
Tro	81	4	2	0	738.0	760	8	112	169	10.6	2.74	92	.255	.282	-30	-17	106	—	—	.900	366	160	**58**	-.3	-1.7	-.5	—	2.0
Wor	68	7	**18**	**5**	762.2	709	13	97	297	9.5	2.27	115	.233	.257	9	26	109	—	—	.906	355	**94**	49	.7	2.5	-5.1	—	.3
Bos	70	4	17	0	744.2	840	**2**	86	187	11.2	3.08	74	.276	.296	-59	-70	96	—	—	.901	367	132	54	.3	-6.8	4.9	—	-.4
Buf	72	6	13	1	739.0	879	10	78	186	11.7	3.09	79	.279	.297	-59	-50	104	—	—	.891	408	185	55	-2.1	-4.9	-5.3	—	-4.7
Cin	79	3	4	0	713.1	785	10	88	208	11.0	2.44	102	.259	.280	-5	5	105	—	—	.877	437	119	49	-4.1	.5	-5.1	—	-10.4
Total	608	52	76	13	6031.1	—	—	—	—	10.0	2.37	—	.245	.267	—	—	—	—	—	.901	2949	1047	411	—	—	—	—	—

BATTER-FIELDER WINS
- **Clapp-Cin 3.2**
- **Irwin-Wor 3.2**
- **Dunlap-Cle 2.6**
- **Gore-Chi 2.5**
- **Shafer-Cle 2.3**

BATTING AVERAGE
- Gore-Chi .360
- Anson-Chi .337
- Connor-Tro .332
- Dalrymple-Chi .330
- Burns-Chi .309

ON-BASE PERCENTAGE
- Gore-Chi .399
- Anson-Chi .362
- Connor-Tro .357
- Dalrymple-Chi .335
- Burns-Chi .333

SLUGGING AVERAGE
- Gore-Chi .463
- Connor-Tro .459
- Dalrymple-Chi .458
- Stovey-Wor .454
- J.O'Rourke-Bos .441

ON-BASE PLUS SLUGGING
- Gore-Chi .862
- Connor-Tro .816
- Dalrymple-Chi .793
- Anson-Chi .781
- J.O'Rourke-Bos .756

ADJUSTED OPS
- Gore-Chi 180
- Connor-Tro 166
- Jones-Bos 159
- J.O'Rourke-Bos 158
- Dalrymple-Chi 156

ADJUSTED BATTER RUNS
- Gore-Chi 27.3
- J.O'Rourke-Bos 22.4
- Connor-Tro 22.2
- Dalrymple-Chi 20.4
- Anson-Chi 19.9

RUNS
- Dalrymple-Chi 91
- Stovey-Wor 76
- Kelly-Chi 72
- J.O'Rourke-Bos 71
- Gore-Chi 70

HITS
- Dalrymple-Chi 126
- Anson-Chi 120
- Gore-Chi 116
- Hines-Pro 115
- Connor-Tro 113

DOUBLES
- Dunlap-Cle 27
- Dalrymple-Chi 25
- Anson-Chi 24
- Gore-Chi 23
- J.O'Rourke-Bos 22

TRIPLES
- Stovey-Wor 14
- Dalrymple-Chi 12
- J.O'Rourke-Bos 11
- Hornung-Buf 11
- Phillips-Cle 10

HOME RUNS
- Stovey-Wor 6
- J.O'Rourke-Bos 6
- Jones-Bos 5
- Dunlap-Cle 4

TOTAL BASES
- Dalrymple-Chi 175
- Stovey-Wor 161
- J.O'Rourke-Bos 160
- Dunlap-Cle 160
- Connor-Tro 156

RUNS BATTED IN
- Anson-Chi 74
- Kelly-Chi 60
- Gore-Chi 47
- Connor-Tro 47
- J.O'Rourke-Bos 45

BASES ON BALLS
- Ferguson-Tro 24
- J.O'Rourke-Bos 21
- Gore-Chi 21
- Clapp-Cin 21
- Crowley-Buf 19

STOLEN BASES

BASE STEALING RUNS

FIELDING RUNS-INFIELD
- Irwin-Wor 29.8
- Force-Buf 26.4
- Bradley-Pro 18.4
- Burdock-Bos 15.1
- Williamson-Chi 10.2

FIELDING RUNS-OUTFIELD
- Shafer-Cle 14.9
- Gillespie-Tro 6.3
- Bond-Bos 4.8
- J.O'Rourke-Bos 4.0
- Dalrymple-Chi 3.9

OUTFIELD ASSISTS
- Shafer-Cle 35
- Kelly-Chi 32
- Dorgan-Pro 25
- Crowley-Buf 23
- Knight-Wor 22

CATCHER CS PCT.

WINS
- McCormick-Cle 45
- Corcoran-Chi 43
- Ward-Pro 39
- Welch-Tro 34
- Richmond-Wor 32

WINNING PCT.
- Goldsmith-Chi .875
- Corcoran-Chi .754
- Ward-Pro .619
- McCormick-Cle .616
- Welch-Tro .531

WINS ABOVE TEAM
- McCormick-Cle 19.4
- Welch-Tro 8.3
- Galvin-Buf 7.0
- Goldsmith-Chi 5.6
- W.White-Cin 5.3

GAMES STARTED
- McCormick-Cle 74
- Ward-Pro 67
- Richmond-Wor 66
- Welch-Tro 64
- W.White-Cin 62

COMPLETE GAMES
- McCormick-Cle 72
- Welch-Tro 64
- Ward-Pro 59
- W.White-Cin 58

FEWEST HITS/GAME
- Keefe-Tro 5.83
- Corcoran-Chi 6.78
- Bradley-Pro 7.26
- Ward-Pro 7.58
- Corey-Wor 7.95

FEWEST BB/GAME
- Bradley-Pro .28
- Galvin-Buf .63
- Ward-Pro .68
- Wiedman-Buf .71
- Goldsmith-Chi .77

STRIKEOUTS
- Corcoran-Chi 268
- McCormick-Cle 260
- Richmond-Wor 243
- Ward-Pro 230
- W.White-Cin 161

STRIKEOUTS/GAME
- Corcoran-Chi 4.50
- Goldsmith-Chi 3.85
- Richmond-Wor 3.70
- McCormick-Cle 3.56
- Ward-Pro 3.48

GAMES
- Richmond-Wor 74
- McCormick-Cle 74
- Ward-Pro 70
- Welch-Tro 65

SAVES
- Richmond-Wor 3
- Corey-Wor 2
- Corcoran-Chi 2
- Bradley-Pro 2

BASE RUNNERS/9
- Keefe-Tro 7.20
- Bradley-Pro 7.53
- Ward-Pro 8.26
- Corcoran-Chi 8.44
- Goldsmith-Chi 8.86

ADJUSTED RELIEF RUNS

RELIEF RANKING

INNINGS PITCHED
- McCormick-Cle 657.2
- Ward-Pro 595.0
- Richmond-Wor 590.2
- Welch-Tro 574.0
- Corcoran-Chi 536.1

OPPONENTS' AVG.
- Keefe-Tro .178
- Corcoran-Chi .199
- Bradley-Pro .210
- Ward-Pro .217
- Corey-Wor .219

OPPONENTS' OBP
- Keefe-Tro .212
- Bradley-Pro .217
- Ward-Pro .232
- Corcoran-Chi .236
- Corey-Wor .239

EARNED RUN AVERAGE
- Keefe-Tro .86
- Bradley-Pro 1.38
- Ward-Pro 1.74
- Goldsmith-Chi 1.75
- McCormick-Cle 1.85

ADJUSTED ERA
- Keefe-Tro 294
- Bradley-Pro 160
- Goldsmith-Chi 138
- McCormick-Cle 127
- Ward-Pro 127

ADJUSTED STARTER RUNS
- McCormick-Cle 39.5
- Ward-Pro 34.6
- Corcoran-Chi 28.8
- Richmond-Wor 25.4
- Bradley-Pro 18.2

PITCHER WINS
- **McCormick-Cle 4.2**
- **Ward-Pro 3.5**
- **Corcoran-Chi 2.9**
- **Bradley-Pro 1.9**
- **Keefe-Tro 1.8**

Bound for Good

Owners unilaterally instituted a reserve clause after the 1879 season, which allowed each team to protect five players from other offers. This tactic neutralized player mobility and put a drain on salaries. William Hulbert also shoehorned through a provision prohibiting alcohol sales on the grounds of any league club. While these two policies made sense, given Hulbert's love of high class and high profit, they eventually helped give birth to the American Association. Empowered, some owners began fining players for non-existent infractions and, in the case of Boston, blacklisted slugger Charlie Jones in a financial dispute.

Despite the league's machinations, five clubs finished under .500 and pennant-winner Chicago—the NL's only good draw—ran away from the competition. With an offense sporting Cap Anson, King Kelly, Abner Dalrymple, and George Gore, the team topped the league in runs by more than 100. Their pitching permitted the fewest hits, and rookie Larry Corcoran led in strikeouts. Chicago's defense committed 3.82 errors per game, the best in the NL.

Debut players included slugger Roger Connor (the pre-Ruth career home run record holder), pitchers Hoss Radbourn and Tim Keefe, who, as a rookie, set an all-time mark with an 0.86 ERA, outfielder Ned Hanlon, third baseman Arlie Latham, and catcher Buck Ewing, considered by many the greatest player of the nineteenth century.

The league ruled that fouls could be caught on one bounce for an out. In addition, it now took just eight balls for a walk. The league batting average dropped to .245, and scoring fell dramatically. On June 12 Worcester's Lee Richmond threw the first perfect game in major league annals; Providence's John Ward tossed the second just five days later. The NL would not attain perfection again until 1964.

After the season Hulbert marshaled a 7-1 vote to expel Cincinnati from the league. The club's owners, unable to compete financially otherwise, had rented their park to other local teams and allowed them to play on Sundays and sell beer.

1879 NATIONAL LEAGUE

TEAM	W	L	T	PCT	GB	HW	HL	R	OR	PA	H	2B	3B	HR	BB	SO	HB	SH	AVG	OBP	SLG	OPS	AOPS	BR	ABR	PF	SB	CS	BSA	BSR
Pro	59	25	1	.702	—	**34**	8	**612**	355	3483	**1003**	142	**55**	12	**91**	**172**	—	—	**.296**	**.314**	**.381**	**695**	**134**	**111**	**121**	98				
Bos	54	30	0	.643	5	29	13	562	**348**	3307	883	138	51	**20**	90	222	—	—	.274	.294	.368	662	118	69	58	102				
Buf	46	32	1	.590	10	23	16	394	365	2984	733	105	54	2	78	314	—	—	.252	.272	.328	600	98	-1	-11	102				
Chi	46	33	4	.582	10.5	29	13	437	411	3189	808	**167**	32	3	73	294	—	—	.259	.276	.336	612	98	18	-8	106				
Cin	43	37	1	.538	14	21	16	485	464	3151	813	127	53	8	66	207	—	—	.264	.279	.347	626	115	26	50	95				
Cle	27	55	0	.329	31	15	27	322	461	3024	666	116	29	4	37	214	—	—	.223	.232	.285	517	73	-83	-80	99				
Syr	22	48	1	.314	30	11	22	276	462	2639	592	61	19	5	28	238	—	—	.227	.235	.270	505	78	-85	-50	89				
Tro	19	56	2	.253	35.5	12	27	321	543	2886	673	102	24	4	45	182	—	—	.237	.249	.294	543	87	-54	-29	93				
Total	321	—	—	—	—	174	142	3409	—	24663	6171	958	317	58	508	1843	—	—	.255	.271	.329	599	—	—	—	—	—	—	—	—

TEAM	CG	SHO	GR	SV	IP	H	HR	BB	SO	BR/9	ERA	AERA	OAV	OOB	PR	APR	PF	OSB	OCS	FA	E	WPB	DP	FW	PW	BW	BSW	DIF
Pro	73	3	**12**	**2**	776.0	765	9	62	**329**	9.6	**2.18**	108	.243	.258	**27**	16	94	—	—	.902	382	128	41	1.8	1.5	**11.2**	—	2.6
Bos	79	**13**	5	0	753.0	757	9	**46**	230	9.6	2.19	**114**	.251	.262	26	**25**	100	—	—	**.913**	**319**	108	58	**4.9**	**2.3**	5.3	—	-.5
Buf	78	8	1	0	713.0	**698**	**3**	47	198	**9.4**	2.34	112	**.242**	**.254**	13	21	105	—	—	.906	331	99	**62**	2.9	1.9	-1.0	—	3.2
Chi	**82**	6	1	0	744.0	762	5	57	211	9.9	2.46	105	.244	.258	3	9	103	—	—	.900	381	**93**	52	1.3	.8	-.7	—	5.1
Cin	79	4	3	0	726.0	756	11	81	246	10.4	2.29	102	.248	.267	16	4	93	—	—	.878	450	166	48	-2.9	.4	4.6	—	.9
Cle	79	3	3	0	741.0	818	4	116	287	11.3	2.65	95	.265	.292	-12	-12	100	—	—	.889	406	178	42	-.3	-1.1	-7.4	—	-5.2
Syr	64	5	7	0	649.0	775	4	52	132	11.5	3.19	74	.277	.290	-50	-62	95	—	—	.873	398	150	37	-2.7	-5.7	-4.6	—	.0
Tro	75	3	2	0	695.0	840	13	47	210	11.5	2.80	89	.275	.286	-23	-22	100	—	—	.875	460	217	44	-4.4	-2.0	-2.7	—	-9.3
Total	609	45	34	2	5797.0	—	—	—	—	10.4	2.50	—	.255	.271	—	—	—	—	—	.892	3127	1139	384	—	—	—	—	—

BATTER-FIELDER WINS	BATTING AVERAGE	ON-BASE PERCENTAGE	SLUGGING AVERAGE	ON-BASE PLUS SLUGGING	ADJUSTED OPS	ADJUSTED BATTER RUNS
Kelly-Cin............3.9	Anson-Chi............317	O'Rourke-Pro........371	O'Rourke-Bos.......521	O'Rourke-Bos.......877	Kelly-Cin..............188	Hines-Pro............34.7
Jones-Bos..........3.6	Hines-Pro.............357	Hines-Pro.............369	Jones-Bos............510	Jones-Bos............877	Jones-Bos............182	Kelly-Cin.............32.2
Williamson-Chi..3.3	O'Rourke-Pro........348	Jones-Bos............367	Kelly-Cin..............493	Kelly-Cin..............855	O'Rourke-Bos.......181	Jones-Bos...........31.9
Hines-Pro...........3.2	Kelly-Cin..............348	Kelly-Cin..............363	Hines-Pro.............482	Hines-Pro.............851	Hines-Pro.............181	O'Rourke-Pro.......28.7
Wright-Pro..........2.9	O'Rourke-Bos.......341	O'Rourke-Bos.......357	O'Rourke-Pro........459	O'Rourke-Pro........829	O'Rourke-Pro........174	O'Rourke-Bos......26.3

RUNS	HITS	DOUBLES	TRIPLES	HOME RUNS	TOTAL BASES	RUNS BATTED IN
Jones-Bos...............85	Hines-Pro.............146	Eden-Cle................31	Dickerson-Cin.........14	Jones-Bos................9	Hines-Pro.............197	O'Rourke-Bos.........62
Hines-Pro................81	O'Rourke-Pro........126	York-Pro..................25	Williamson-Chi........13	O'Rourke-Bos...........6	Jones-Bos............181	Jones-Bos..............62
Wright-Pro..............79	Kelly-Cin..............120	Hines-Pro................25	Kelly-Cin.................12	Brouthers-Tro...........4	Kelly-Cin..............170	Dickerson-Cin.........57
Kelly-Cin.................78	Jones-Bos............112	Dalrymple-Chi.........25	O'Rourke-Bos.........11	Eden-Cle..................3	O'Rourke-Pro.........166	McVey-Cin.............55
Dickerson-Cin.........73	D.White-Cin..........110	Houck-Bos..............24			O'Rourke-Bos.......165	

BASES ON BALLS	STOLEN BASES	BASE STEALING RUNS	FIELDING RUNS-INFIELD	FIELDING RUNS-OUTFIELD	OUTFIELD ASSISTS	CATCHER CS PCT.
Jones-Bos...............29			Wright-Pro...........19.6	Shafer-Chi...........19.2	Shafer-Chi..............50	
Williamson-Chi........24			Williamson-Chi.....18.9	Evans-Tro............17.6	Evans-Tro...............30	
York-Pro..................19			Fulmer-Buf..........18.2	M.Mansell-Syr......14.9	Hines-Pro...............24	
Richardson-Buf.......16			Quest-Chi...........16.0	Jones-Bos...........13.0	Eden-Cle.................21	
Barnes-Cin.............16			Hawkes-Tro.........14.5	Hines-Pro..............4.7	Jones-Bos...............20	

WINS	WINNING PCT.	WINS ABOVE TEAM	GAMES STARTED	COMPLETE GAMES	FEWEST HITS/GAME	FEWEST BB/GAME
Ward-Pro................47	Ward-Pro.............712	W.White-Cin.........21.5	W.White-Cin............75	W.White-Cin............75	McGunnigle-Buf...8.48	Bond-Bos................39
W.White-Cin............43	Bond-Bos.............694	Bond-Bos............12.0	Galvin-Buf..............66	Galvin-Buf..............65	Ward-Pro............8.75	Galvin-Buf..............47
Bond-Bos................43	Hankinson-Chi......600	McCormick-Syr......4.6	Bond-Bos................64	McCormick-Cle.......59	Bond-Bos............8.80	Bradley-Tro............48
Galvin-Buf..............37	W.White-Cin..........581	Ward-Pro..............4.5	Ward-Pro................60	Bond-Bos................59	Galvin-Buf...........8.88	Larkin-Chi...............53
Larkin-Chi...............31	Galvin-Buf............578	Salisbury-Tro..........1.1	McCormick-Cle.......60	Ward-Pro................58	W.White-Cin.........8.95	Ward-Pro................55

STRIKEOUTS	STRIKEOUTS/GAME	GAMES	SAVES	BASE RUNNERS/9	ADJUSTED RELIEF RUNS	RELIEF RANKING
Ward-Pro..............239	McGunnigle-Buf...4.65	W.White-Cin............76	Ward-Pro..................1	Goldsmith-Tro......8.86		
W.White-Cin..........232	Mathews-Pro.......4.29	Ward-Pro................70	Mathews-Pro............1	Bond-Bos............9.19		
McCormick-Cle.....197	Mitchell-Cle..........4.16	Galvin-Buf..............66		Ward-Pro............9.31		
Bond-Bos.............155	Ward-Pro............3.66	Bond-Bos................64		Galvin-Buf...........9.35		
Larkin-Chi.............142	McCormick-Cle....3.25	McCormick-Cle.......62		Larkin-Chi...........9.54		

INNINGS PITCHED	OPPONENTS' AVG.	OPPONENTS' OBP	EARNED RUN AVERAGE	ADJUSTED ERA	ADJUSTED STARTER RUNS	PITCHER WINS
W.White-Cin.......680.0	McGunnigle-Buf....235	Larkin-Chi............250	Bond-Bos............1.96	Bond-Bos.............127	Bond-Bos............38.8	**Bond-Bos............4.1**
Galvin-Buf..........593.0	W.White-Cin..........238	Ward-Pro.............250	W.White-Cin.........1.99	W.White-Cin..........117	W.White-Cin.........22.1	**Ward-Pro............2.7**
Ward-Pro...........587.0	Ward-Pro.............239	Galvin-Buf............253	Ward-Pro.............2.15	Galvin-Buf............115	Galvin-Buf...........20.5	**Galvin-Buf..........2.5**
Bond-Bos...........555.1	Larkin-Chi............240	W.White-Cin..........256	Salisbury-Tro........2.22	Salisbury-Tro.........112	Ward-Pro............12.9	**McCormick-Cle.... .6**
McCormick-Cle..546.1	Galvin-Buf............243	Bond-Bos.............259	Galvin-Buf...........2.28	Ward-Pro..............110	Larkin-Chi.............8.2	**Larkin-Chi............ .5**

The Last Free Season

To increase revenues, the NL expanded its schedule to 84 games and brought in four new teams: Troy, Cleveland, and two top International Association clubs, Buffalo and Syracuse. Despite these changes, however, league attendance was only a little higher for eight teams than it was for six clubs in 1878. Syracuse and Troy were abject failures on the field and at the gate, while Cincinnati's attendance fell dramatically.

Chicago once again had first-rate talent, including Cap Anson and Ed Williamson, and a maniacal fan base, but their pennant hopes evaporated when player-manager Anson went down in midsummer with a liver infection. Hard-charging Providence held off a late Boston rally to claim their first flag. George Wright, in his only season as a manager, bested his brother Harry, whose Boston clubs had won six titles in the last seven years in both the NA and NL. (After a salary dispute with Providence, George would return to play sparingly for Harry's Red Stockings.) Paul Hines and Jim O'Rourke provided most of the big hits for the Grays, while John Ward topped the league in wins and strikeouts.

Ward spent the year tossing a Spalding baseball. Former star hurler Al Spalding had retired to sell sporting goods, and he used his ties to get his ball named the official spheroid for all NL contests. Spalding also remained part owner of the Chicago White Stockings. The league adopted several new rules. A foul, hitherto an out if caught on a bounce, now had to be caught on the fly. Rules governing batting orders were established, and pitchers found to be intentionally hitting batters were fined, although batters were not yet allowed to take first base.

Boston's John O'Rourke, brother of Jim, was the league's top rookie, leading in RBIs and slugging (both calculated retroactively). Another freshman, Buffalo third baseman Hardy Richardson, eventually was the bigger star. Cincinnati pitcher Will White set the all-time record with 680 innings pitched, completing each of his 75 starts.

Only Syracuse was judged unfit for the NL. Worcester joined for 1880, giving Massachusetts, New York, and Ohio two teams apiece. Hulbert and his fellow owners had a new surprise up their sleeves: the reserve clause.

1878 NATIONAL LEAGUE

TEAM	W	L	T	PCT	GB	HW	HL	R	OR	PA	H	2B	3B	HR	BB	SO	HB	SH	AVG	OBP	SLG	OPS	AOPS	BR	ABR	PF	SB	CS	BSA	BSR
Bos	41	19	0	.683	—	23	7	298	**241**	2255	535	75	25	2	35	154	—	—	.241	.253	.300	553	79	-36	-55	108				
Cin	37	23	1	.617	4	**25**	8	333	281	2339	629	67	22	5	58	**141**	—	—	.276	.294	.331	625	**120**	20	**55**	91				
Pro	33	27	2	.550	8	17	13	353	337	2348	604	**107**	**30**	**8**	50	218	—	—	.263	.279	.346	625	109	20	21	100				
Chi	30	30	1	.500	11	17	18	**371**	331	2421	**677**	91	20	3	**88**	157	—	—	**.290**	**.316**	**.350**	**666**	115	**58**	34	107				
Ind	24	36	3	.400	17	10	17	293	328	2364	542	76	15	3	64	197	—	—	.236	.256	.286	542	95	-43	0	87				
Mil	15	45	1	.250	26	7	18	256	386	2281	552	65	20	2	69	214	—	—	.250	.272	.300	572	86	-19	-37	107				
Total	184	—	—	—	—	99	81	1904	—	14008	3539	481	132	23	364	1081	—	—	.259	.279	.319	598	—	—	—	—	—	—	—	—

TEAM	CG	SHO	GR	SV	IP	H	HR	BB	SO	BR/9	ERA	AERA	OAV	OOB	PR	APR	PF	OSB	OCS	FA	E	WPB	DP	FW	PW	BW	BSW	DIF
Bos	58	**9**	2	0	544.0	595	6	38	184	10.5	2.32	102	.272	.284	-1	2	102	—	—	**.914**	**228**	**62**	**48**	**3.5**	.2	-5.1	—	12.4
Cin	**61**	6	0	0	548.0	**546**	**2**	63	**220**	**10.0**	**1.84**	**116**	**.248**	.269	**28**	**19**	92	—	—	.900	269	99	37	1.5	**1.8**	**5.1**	—	-1.4
Pro	59	6	4	0	556.0	609	5	86	173	11.3	2.38	93	.265	.291	-5	-12	96	—	—	.892	311	133	42	-.5	-1.1	2.0	—	2.7
Chi	**61**	1	0	0	551.0	577	4	**35**	175	**10.0**	2.37	102	.253	**.265**	-4	3	105	—	—	.891	304	141	37	-.4	.3	3.2	—	-3.0
Ind	59	2	4	**1**	578.0	621	3	87	182	11.0	2.32	87	.262	.288	-1	-22	88	—	—	.898	290	95	37	.9	-2.1	.0	—	-4.8
Mil	54	1	**7**	0	547.0	589	3	55	147	10.6	2.60	101	.255	.272	-18	1	114	—	—	.866	376	149	32	-4.4	.0	-3.5	—	-7.2
Total	352	25	17	1	3324.0	—	—	—	—	10.6	2.30	—	.259	.279	—	—	—	—	—	.893	1778	679	233	—	—	—	—	—

BATTER-FIELDER WINS	BATTING AVERAGE	ON-BASE PERCENTAGE	SLUGGING AVERAGE	ON-BASE PLUS SLUGGING	ADJUSTED OPS	ADJUSTED BATTER RUNS
Shafer-Ind 3.3	Dalrymple-Mil .354	Ferguson-Chi .375	Hines-Pro .486	Hines-Pro .849	Shafer-Ind 196	Shafer-Ind 29.3
Ferguson-Chi 2.8	Hines-Pro .358	Anson-Chi .372	York-Pro .465	Shafer-Ind .824	Hines-Pro 177	Hines-Pro 20.4
Burdock-Bos 2.0	Ferguson-Chi .351	Shafer-Ind .369	Shafer-Ind .455	Start-Chi .794	Jones-Cin 163	Jones-Cin 17.5
Hines-Pro 1.7	Start-Chi .351	Dalrymple-Mil .368	Brown-Pro .453	York-Pro .793	York-Pro 159	York-Pro 16.5
Jones-Cin 1.7	Anson-Chi .341	Hines-Pro .363	Jones-Cin .441	Dalrymple-Mil .789	Brown-Pro 153	Clapp-Ind 15.6

RUNS	HITS	DOUBLES	TRIPLES	HOME RUNS	TOTAL BASES	RUNS BATTED IN
Higham-Pro 60	Start-Chi 100	Higham-Pro 22	York-Pro 10	Hines-Pro 4	York-Pro 125	Hines-Pro 50
Start-Chi 58	Dalrymple-Mil 96	Brown-Pro 21	O'Rourke-Bos 7	Jones-Cin 3	Start-Chi 125	Brown-Pro 43
York-Pro 56	Hines-Pro 92	York-Pro 19	Jones-Cin 7	McVey-Cin 2	Hines-Pro 125	Anson-Chi 40
Anson-Chi 55	Ferguson-Chi 91	Shafer-Ind 19		McKelvy-Ind 2	Shafer-Ind 121	Jones-Cin 39
Dalrymple-Mil 52		O'Rourke-Bos 17			Higham-Pro 117	Ferguson-Chi 39

BASES ON BALLS	STOLEN BASES	BASE STEALING RUNS	FIELDING RUNS-INFIELD	FIELDING RUNS-OUTFIELD	OUTFIELD ASSISTS	CATCHER CS PCT.
Remsen-Chi 17			Burdock-Bos 21.2	Shafer-Ind 7.6	Cassidy-Chi 30	
Larkin-Chi 17			Hague-Pro 19.1	Cassidy-Chi 7.3	Shafer-Ind 28	
Shafer-Ind 13			Ferguson-Chi 16.6	Dalrymple-Mil 6.8	Higham-Pro 27	
Clapp-Ind 13			Wright-Bos 10.3	Jones-Cin 4.4	Kelly-Cin 24	
Anson-Chi 13			Hankinson-Chi 7.9	Remsen-Chi 4.2	Holbert-Mil 19	

WINS	WINNING PCT.	WINS ABOVE TEAM	GAMES STARTED	COMPLETE GAMES	FEWEST HITS/GAME	FEWEST BB/GAME
Bond-Bos 40	Bond-Bos .678	Larkin-Chi 11.2	Bond-Bos 59	Bond-Bos 57	Mitchell-Cin 7.76	Weaver-Mil .49
W.White-Cin 30	Ward-Pro .629	Ward-Pro 5.9	Larkin-Chi 56	Larkin-Chi 56	Ward-Pro 8.30	Larkin-Chi .55
Larkin-Chi 29	W.White-Cin .588	Weaver-Mil 2.7	W.White-Cin 52	W.White-Cin 52	Weaver-Mil 8.72	Bond-Bos .56
Ward-Pro 22	Larkin-Chi .527	Wheeler-Pro 2.5	Weaver-Mil 43	Weaver-Mil 39	Larkin-Chi 9.09	Nichols-Pro .73
Nolan-Ind 13		Mitchell-Cin 2.1	Nolan-Ind 38		W.White-Cin 9.17	W.White-Cin .87

STRIKEOUTS	STRIKEOUTS/GAME	GAMES	SAVES	BASE RUNNERS/9	ADJUSTED RELIEF RUNS	RELIEF RANKING
Bond-Bos 182	Mitchell-Cin 5.74	Bond-Bos 59	Healey-Pro-Ind 1	Weaver-Mil 9.21		
W.White-Cin 169	Wheeler-Pro 3.63	Larkin-Chi 56		Ward-Pro 9.22		
Larkin-Chi 163	W.White-Cin 3.25	W.White-Cin 52		Larkin-Chi 9.64		
Nolan-Ind 125	Nolan-Ind 3.24	Weaver-Mil 45		Mitchell-Cin 9.79		
Ward-Pro 116	Ward-Pro 3.13	Nolan-Ind 38		W.White-Cin 10.04		

INNINGS PITCHED	OPPONENTS' AVG.	OPPONENTS' OBP	EARNED RUN AVERAGE	ADJUSTED ERA	ADJUSTED STARTER RUNS	PITCHER WINS
Bond-Bos 532.2	Mitchell-Cin .223	Weaver-Mil .247	Ward-Pro 1.51	Ward-Pro 146	Weaver-Mil 23.1	**Ward-Pro 2.2**
Larkin-Chi 506.0	Ward-Pro .231	Ward-Pro .251	McCormick-Ind 1.69	Weaver-Mil 134	Ward-Pro 21.8	**Weaver-Mil 2.1**
W.White-Cin 468.0	Weaver-Mil .237	Larkin-Chi .257	W.White-Cin 1.79	McCormick-Ind 120	W.White-Cin 15.7	**Larkin-Chi 1.9**
Weaver-Mil 383.0	Larkin-Chi .246	Mitchell-Cin .265	Weaver-Mil 1.95	W.White-Cin 119	Bond-Bos 13.8	**Bond-Bos .9**
Nolan-Ind 347.0	W.White-Cin .252	W.White-Cin .269	Bond-Bos 2.06	Bond-Bos 114	Larkin-Chi 9.6	**W.White-Cin .6**

A Good Defense

With new franchises in Providence, Indianapolis, and Milwaukee, the six-team National League took on an increasingly Midwestern look. (Newly organized "minor" leagues, chiefly the International Association, had started up to fill the need for organized baseball in the East.) Beginning in 1878 clubs used turnstiles to figure attendance, and team captains mutually determined which team would hit first. Batting orders were also required to remain consistent during the game.

Fortified by free agents Cal McVey, who managed and played third base, and Deacon White, the Cincinnati Red Stockings rose from last to second. Pitcher Will White, Deacon's brother, was outstanding in his first full year, helping the club post the league's best ERA. Paul Hines of third-place Providence won the league's first Triple Crown, but abysmal second-line pitching and poor defense scuttled his club's chances.

Boston won the flag by 4 games under legendary skipper Harry Wright. The starting lineup played nearly every inning—the team's substitute, Harry Schaefer, appeared in only 2 games. Boston's pitcher, Tommy Bond, was the NL's workhorse. He pitched in all but 1 Red Stockings game and won 40 times, 10 more than runner-up White in Cincinnati. Outstanding fielding helped the Red Stockings survive their mediocre offense. The club's .914 fielding percentage was a new record, shattering the old mark by 10 points. At this point, only a few players used gloves—Boston simply had great fielders.

Some top players made their debuts in 1878, including Milwaukee's catcher Charlie Bennett and outfielder Abner Dalrymple, Cincinnati outfielder King Kelly, Indianapolis third baseman Ed Williamson, and Providence pitcher John Montgomery Ward, who led the league with a 1.51 ERA.

Perhaps the greatest achievement from 1878 was that the NL became the first league to complete its entire schedule. It did not mean that everyone would be back on the '79 schedule, though. Indianapolis and Milwaukee, which brought up the rear of the loop in wins and attendance, were both dropped from the league after the season. NL President William Hulbert was in dire straits; despite being a Midwest chauvinist, he was forced to reach back to the East for new clubs to invite to his party.

1877 NATIONAL LEAGUE

TEAM	W	L	T	PCT	GB	HW	HL	R	OR	PA	H	2B	3B	HR	BB	SO	HB	SH	AVG	OBP	SLG	OPS	AOPS	BR	ABR	PF	SB	CS	BSA	BSR
Bos	42	18	1	.700	—	**27**	5	**419**	**263**	2433	**700**	**91**	**37**	4	65	121	—	—	**.296**	**.314**	**.370**	**684**	**114**	**49**	**35**	104				
Lou	35	25	1	.583	7	21	9	339	288	2413	659	75	36	**9**	58	140	—	—	.280	.297	.354	651	92	19	-37	118				
Har	31	27	2	.534	10	19	8	341	311	2388	637	63	31	4	30	**97**	—	—	.270	.279	.328	607	105	-18	22	89				
StL	28	32	0	.467	14	20	10	284	318	2235	531	51	36	1	57	147	—	—	.244	.263	.302	565	84	-48	-32	95				
Chi	26	33	1	.441	15.5	17	12	366	375	2330	633	79	30	0	57	111	—	—	.278	.296	.340	636	92	8	-29	112				
Cin	15	42	1	.263	25.5	12	17	291	485	2213	545	72	34	6	**78**	110	—	—	.255	.282	.329	611	107	-10	29	89				
Total	180	—	—	—	—	116	61	2040	—	14012	3705	431	204	24	345	726	—	—	.271	.289	.338	627	—	—	—	—	—	—	—	—

TEAM	CG	SHO	GR	SV	IP	H	HR	BB	SO	BR/9	ERA	AERA	OAV	OOB	PR	APR	PF	OSB	OCS	FA	E	WPB	DP	FW	PW	BW	BSW	DIF
Bos	**61**	**7**	0	0	548.0	**557**	5	**38**	**177**	**9.8**	**2.15**	130	**.249**	**.261**	**40**	40	100	—	—	.889	290	68	36	1.2	3.6	**3.1**	—	4.1
Lou	**61**	4	0	0	559.0	617	4	41	141	10.6	2.25	**147**	.270	.283	34	**56**	118	—	—	**.904**	**267**	80	37	**2.4**	**5.0**	-3.3	—	.9
Har	59	4	1	0	544.0	572	**2**	56	99	10.4	2.32	105	.253	.271	30	8	87	—	—	.885	313	**56**	32	-.2	.7	2.0	—	-.5
StL	52	1	8	0	541.0	582	**2**	92	132	11.2	2.66	98	.262	.291	9	-4	93	—	—	.892	281	110	29	1.4	-.4	-2.9	—	-.2
Chi	45	3	**16**	**3**	534.0	630	7	58	92	11.6	3.37	88	.274	.292	-33	-22	106	—	—	.883	313	119	**43**	-.2	-2.0	-2.6	—	1.2
Cin	48	1	10	1	515.0	747	4	61	85	14.1	4.19	63	.318	.335	-79	-94	94	—	—	.851	394	128	33	-4.7	-8.4	2.6	—	-3.0
Total	326	20	35	4	3241.0	—	—	—	—	11.2	2.81	—	.271	.289	—	—	—	—	—	.884	1858	561	210	—	—	—	—	—

BATTER-FIELDER WINS	BATTING AVERAGE	ON-BASE PERCENTAGE	SLUGGING AVERAGE	ON-BASE PLUS SLUGGING	ADJUSTED OPS	ADJUSTED BATTER RUNS
Jones-Cin-Chi-Cin.....2.6	D.White-Bos..........387	O'Rourke-Bos.......407	D.White-Bos..........545	D.White-Bos..........950	D.White-Bos.........190	D.White-Bos.........25.9
D.White-Bos 2.2	Cassidy-Har..........378	D.White-Bos..........405	Jones-Cin-Chi-Cin....471	O'Rourke-Bos.......852	Cassidy-Har..........184	Cassidy-Har.........24.2
Peters-Chi.......... 2.0	McVey-Chi 368	McVey-Chi 387	Cassidy-Har..........458	Cassidy-Har..........844	Jones-Cin-Chi-Cin....175	Jones-Cin-Chi-Cin...21.7
Gerhardt-Lou 1.7	O'Rourke-Bos.......362	Cassidy-Har..........386	McVey-Chi 455	McVey-Chi 842	O'Rourke-Bos.......162	O'Rourke-Bos......19.6
Cassidy-Har 1.6	Anson-Chi.............337	Anson-Chi.............360	O'Rourke-Bos.......445	Jones-Cin-Chi-Cin....824	Manning-Cin 157	Manning-Cin 17.2
RUNS	**HITS**	**DOUBLES**	**TRIPLES**	**HOME RUNS**	**TOTAL BASES**	**RUNS BATTED IN**
O'Rourke-Bos.........68	D.White-Bos..........103	Anson-Chi...............19	D.White-Bos...........11	Pike-Cin....................4	D.White-Bos..........145	D.White-Bos...........49
G.Wright-Bos..........58	McVey-Chi 98	York-Har..................16	Jones-Cin-Chi-Cin......10	Shafer-Lou.................3	McVey-Chi 121	Peters-Chi...............41
McVey-Chi 58	O'Rourke-Bos.........96	Manning-Cin 16	Hall-Lou 8	Jones-Cin-Chi-Cin........2	O'Rourke-Bos 118	Sutton-Bos..............39
Start-Har.................55	Cassidy-Har............95	G.Wright-Bos 15	Brown-Bos 8	D.White-Bos..............2	Hall-Lou 118	Jones-Cin-Chi-Cin......38
	Start-Har.................90	Hall-Lou 15		Snyder-Lou 2	Cassidy-Har............115	York-Har...................37
BASES ON BALLS	**STOLEN BASES**	**BASE STEALING RUNS**	**FIELDING RUNS-INFIELD**	**FIELDING RUNS-OUTFIELD**	**OUTFIELD ASSISTS**	**CATCHER CS PCT.**
O'Rourke-Bos.........20			Peters-Chi............20.0	Jones-Cin-Chi-Cin...12.8	Shafer-Lou..............21	
Jones-Cin-Chi-Cin......15			Gerhardt-Lou 18.6	Shafer-Lou...........12.7	Crowley-Lou 20	
Hall-Lou 12			Ferguson-Har 17.3	Crowley-Lou 7.5	Addy-Cin..................17	
Booth-Cin.................12			G.Wright-Bos 9.7	Addy-Cin................4.9	Cassidy-Har............16	
Force-StL 11			Foley-Cin 6.7	Pike-Cin 2.5	Jones-Cin-Chi-Cin.......15	
WINS	**WINNING PCT.**	**WINS ABOVE TEAM**	**GAMES STARTED**	**COMPLETE GAMES**	**FEWEST HITS/GAME**	**FEWEST BB/GAME**
Bond-Bos................40	Bond-Bos..............702	Devlin-Lou 17.5	Devlin-Lou 61	Devlin-Lou 61	Bond-Bos.............9.16	Bond-Bos.................62
Devlin-Lou 35	Devlin-Lou 583	Bond-Bos...............3.0	Bond-Bos.................58	Bond-Bos.................58	Larkin-Har...........9.16	Devlin-Lou 66
Larkin-Har...............29	Larkin-Har.............537	Mitchell-Cin............2.4	Larkin-Har...............56	Larkin-Har...............55	Nichols-StL 9.67	Cummings-Cin.........75
Nichols-StL 18	Nichols-StL 439	Larkin-Har..............2.0	Bradley-Chi.............44	Nichols-StL 35	Blong-StL..............9.75	Bradley-Chi.............89
Bradley-Chi..............18	Bradley-Chi...........439	Blong-StL...............1.5	Nichols-StL 39	Bradley-Chi..............35	Devlin-Lou 9.93	Larkin-Har...............95
STRIKEOUTS	**STRIKEOUTS/GAME**	**GAMES**	**SAVES**	**BASE RUNNERS/9**	**ADJUSTED RELIEF RUNS**	**RELIEF RANKING**
Bond-Bos..............170	Mitchell-Cin..........3.69	Devlin-Lou 61	McVey-Chi 2	Bond-Bos.............9.78		
Devlin-Lou 141	Bond-Bos.............2.94	Bond-Bos.................58	Spalding-Chi.............1	Larkin-Har..........10.11		
Larkin-Har...............96	Blong-StL.............2.45	Larkin-Har...............56	Manning-Cin 1	Devlin-Lou 10.59		
Nichols-StL 80	Devlin-Lou 2.27	Bradley-Chi.............50		Nichols-StL 11.03		
Bradley-Chi..............59	Nichols-StL 2.06	Nichols-StL 42		Bradley-Chi........11.22		
INNINGS PITCHED	**OPPONENTS' AVG.**	**OPPONENTS' OBP**	**EARNED RUN AVERAGE**	**ADJUSTED ERA**	**ADJUSTED STARTER RUNS**	**PITCHER WINS**
Devlin-Lou 559.0	Larkin-Har............245	Bond-Bos..............261	Bond-Bos.............2.11	Devlin-Lou 147	Devlin-Lou 55.5	**Devlin-Lou 5.0**
Bond-Bos............521.0	Bond-Bos..............249	Larkin-Har............264	Larkin-Har............2.14	Bond-Bos...............133	Bond-Bos.............39.8	**Bond-Bos............ 3.3**
Larkin-Har..........501.0	Blong-StL..............262	Devlin-Lou 283	Devlin-Lou 2.25	Larkin-Har.............114	Larkin-Har.............13.5	**Larkin-Har 1.6**
Bradley-Chi.........394.0	Nichols-StL 263	Bradley-Chi...........286	Nichols-StL 2.60	Nichols-StL 100	Reis-Chi..................7.8	**Reis-Chi 6**
Nichols-StL 350.0	Bradley-Chi...........269	Nichols-StL 289	Blong-StL..............2.74	Blong-StL................95	Nichols-StL 1.6	

Ramblin' Gamblin' Man

Jim Devlin was one of the finest pitchers in baseball during the 1870s. His great mound work—and the bat of outfielder George Hall—led the Louisville Grays to a big lead in the 1877 NL race. But an inexplicable late-season slump gave Boston the crown. An investigation of the Grays' desultory stretch performance led William Hulbert to ban, for life, four Louisville players—Devlin, Hall, Bill Craver, and Al Nichols—for throwing games. The troubled Devlin died six years later, still begging for reinstatement.

Boston, under Harry Wright, won a tainted title but had the league's top hitters in Deacon White and Jim O'Rourke. Chicago fell to fifth, becoming the only big league team ever to go an entire season without a homer. St. Louis barely missed joining the White Stockings in ignominy, but the Brown Stockings were spared by Jim Battin's lone career NL long ball.

The catcher's mask was first worn this year, and Chicago's Al Spalding, losing his mound skill, began wearing a glove on his catching hand when he played first base. Spalding retired after a final game in 1878 to sell sporting goods. Candy Cummings, purported inventor of the curveball, threw his last major league pitch for Cincinnati. Cummings was a success in the National Association—winning at least 28 games each season—but he was a flop in the new circuit.

The modified strike zone had a "low" pitch ranging from belt to knee and a "high" pitch above the belt and up to the shoulder. Runs declined, although batting average and OPS rose. Strikeouts increased as well. Other rules changes included the abolition of the "fair-foul rule," which helped end Ross Barnes' career, and the placement of home plate in fair territory. In 1877 the home team was allowed to bat first, and no substitutions were allowed, except for injury, after the start of the second inning.

Following the traumatic season, Louisville—along with Hartford and St. Louis—dropped out of the league, which therefore had to scramble for new clubs prior to the 1878 season.

1876 NATIONAL LEAGUE

TEAM	W	L	T	PCT	GB	HW	HL	R	OR	PA	H	2B	3B	HR	BB	SO	HB	SH	AVG	OBP	SLG	OPS	AOPS	BR	ABR	PF	SB	CS	BSA	BSR
Chi	52	14	0	.788	—	**25**	6	**624**	257	2818	**926**	**131**	32	8	**70**	45	—	—	**.337**	**.353**	**.417**	**770**	**140**	**164**	**102**	112				
StL	45	19	0	.703	6	24	6	386	**229**	2537	642	73	27	2	59	63	—	—	.259	.276	.313	589	102	-7	14	95				
Har	47	21	1	.691	6	23	9	429	261	2703	711	96	22	2	39	78	—	—	.267	.277	.322	599	92	2	-29	108				
Bos	39	31	0	.557	15	19	17	471	450	2780	723	96	24	**9**	58	98	—	—	.266	.281	.328	609	102	12	5	102				
Lou	30	36	3	.455	22	15	16	280	344	2594	641	68	14	6	24	98	—	—	.249	.256	.294	550	71	-43	-95	118				
NY	21	35	1	.375	26	13	20	260	412	2198	494	39	15	2	18	**35**	—	—	.227	.233	.261	494	75	-79	-42	87				
Phi	14	45	1	.237	34.5	10	24	378	534	2414	646	79	**35**	7	27	36	—	—	.271	.279	.342	621	108	15	18	99				
Cin	9	56	0	.138	42.5	6	24	238	579	2413	555	51	12	4	41	136	—	—	.234	.247	.271	518	86	-64	-14	86				
Total	260	—	—	—	—	135	122	3066	—	20457	5338	633	181	40	336	589	—	—	.265	.277	.321	598	—	—	—	—	—	—	—	—

TEAM	CG	SHO	GR	SV	IP	H	HR	BB	SO	BR/9	ERA	AERA	OAV	OOB	PR	APR	PF	OSB	OCS	FA	E	WPB	DP	FW	PW	BW	BSW	DIF
Chi	58	9	9	4	592.1	608	6	29	51	9.7	1.76	139	.247	.256	36	42	106	—	—	.899	282	**34**	33	6.0	3.7	**9.0**	—	.4
StL	63	**16**	1	0	577.0	**472**	3	39	103	**8.0**	**1.22**	**175**	**.210**	**.224**	**70**	**64**	93	—	—	**.902**	**268**	91	33	**6.1**	**5.6**	1.2	—	.0
Har	**69**	11	0	0	624.0	570	**2**	27	114	8.6	1.67	142	.227	.235	44	47	103	—	—	.888	337	46	27	4.0	4.1	-2.5	—	7.4
Bos	49	3	**21**	**7**	632.0	732	7	104	77	11.9	2.51	90	.268	.295	-14	-18	98	—	—	.860	442	108	42	-1.1	-1.6	.4	—	6.3
Lou	67	5	2	0	643.0	605	3	38	**125**	9.0	1.69	160	.229	.240	44	62	118	—	—	.875	397	70	44	.9	5.5	-8.4	—	-1.0
NY	56	2	1	0	530.0	718	8	**24**	37	12.6	2.94	73	.302	.309	-37	-50	93	—	—	.825	473	40	18	-6.8	-4.4	-3.7	—	7.9
Phi	53	1	7	2	550.0	783	**2**	41	22	13.5	3.22	75	.310	.321	-56	-46	105	—	—	.839	456	143	32	-5.0	-4.0	1.6	—	-8.1
Cin	57	0	9	0	591.0	850	9	34	60	13.5	3.62	61	.313	.322	-86	-99	95	—	—	.841	469	109	**45**	-4.1	-8.7	-1.2	—	-9.5
Total	472	47	50	13	4739.1	—	—	—	—	10.8	2.31	—	.265	.277	—	—	—	—	—	.866	3124	641	274	—	—	—	—	—

BATTER-FIELDER WINS
- **Barnes-Chi 4.2**
- **Anson-Chi........... 2.8**
- **G.Wright-Bos...... 2.5**
- **Battin-StL 2.3**
- **Hall-Phi 2.0**

BATTING AVERAGE
- Barnes-Chi 429
- Hall-Phi 366
- Anson-Chi.............356
- Peters-Chi.............351
- McVey-Chi 347

ON-BASE PERCENTAGE
- Barnes-Chi 462
- Hall-Phi 384
- Anson-Chi.............380
- White-Chi..............358
- O'Rourke-Bos.......358

SLUGGING AVERAGE
- Barnes-Chi 590
- Hall-Phi 545
- Pike-StL 472
- Anson-Chi.............450
- Meyerle-Phi 449

ON-BASE PLUS SLUGGING
- Barnes-Chi 1052
- Hall-Phi 929
- Anson-Chi.............830
- Pike-StL 813
- Meyerle-Phi 797

ADJUSTED OPS
- Barnes-Chi 222
- Hall-Phi 208
- Pike-StL 178
- Meyerle-Phi 165
- Jones-Cin 162

ADJUSTED BATTER RUNS
- Barnes-Chi 39.7
- Hall-Phi 29.0
- Pike-StL 23.5
- Jones-Cin 20.6
- O'Rourke-Bos......18.8

RUNS
- Barnes-Chi 126
- G.Wright-Bos..........72
- Peters-Chi...............70
- White-Chi.................66
- Burdock-Har 66

HITS
- Barnes-Chi 138
- Peters-Chi.............111
- Anson-Chi.............110
- McVey-Chi 107
- White-Chi..............104

DOUBLES
- Hines-Chi................21
- Higham-Har 21
- Barnes-Chi 21
- Pike-StL 19

TRIPLES
- Barnes-Chi 14
- Hall-Phi 13
- Pike-StL 10
- Meyerle-Phi 8

HOME RUNS
- Hall-Phi 5
- Jones-Cin 4

TOTAL BASES
- Barnes-Chi 190
- Hall-Phi 146
- Anson-Chi.............139
- Hines-Chi..............134

RUNS BATTED IN
- White-Chi.................60
- Hines-Chi.................59
- Barnes-Chi 59
- Anson-Chi...............59
- McVey-Chi 53

BASES ON BALLS
- Barnes-Chi 20
- O'Rourke-Bos.........15
- Burdock-Har 13
- Glenn-Chi 12
- Anson-Chi...............12

STOLEN BASES

BASE STEALING RUNS

FIELDING RUNS-INFIELD
- Somerville-Lou 27.6
- Force-Phi-NY.......19.8
- Battin-StL.............14.5
- G.Wright-Bos.......14.1
- Anson-Chi............13.7

FIELDING RUNS-OUTFIELD
- F.Treacey-NY.........9.1
- Remsen-Har 7.0
- Pierson-Cin............4.5
- Hines-Chi...............4.4
- Snyder-Cin.............3.8

OUTFIELD ASSISTS
- Higham-Har 16
- Pike-StL 13
- Blong-StL.................13
- Remsen-Har 12

CATCHER CS PCT.

WINS
- Spalding-Chi...........47
- Bradley-StL.............45
- Bond-Har 31
- Devlin-Lou 30
- Mathews-NY 21

WINNING PCT.
- Spalding-Chi.........797
- Manning-Bos 783
- Bond-Har 705
- Bradley-StL...........703
- Cummings-Har 667

WINS ABOVE TEAM
- Bradley-StL.........22.5
- Devlin-Lou 15.0
- Mathews-NY 10.5
- Spalding-Chi 8.5
- Manning-Bos 7.0

GAMES STARTED
- Devlin-Lou 68
- Bradley-StL.............64
- Spalding-Chi...........60
- Mathews-NY 56
- Bond-Har 45

COMPLETE GAMES
- Devlin-Lou 66
- Bradley-StL.............63
- Mathews-NY 55
- Spalding-Chi...........53
- Bond-Har 45

FEWEST HITS/GAME
- Bradley-StL..........7.38
- Bond-Har 7.83
- Devlin-Lou 8.19
- Cummings-Har 8.96
- Spalding-Chi........9.23

FEWEST BB/GAME
- Zettlein-Phi 23
- Fisher-Cin 24
- Bond-Har 29
- Mathews-NY 42
- Williams-Cin............43

STRIKEOUTS
- Devlin-Lou 122
- Bradley-StL...........103
- Bond-Har 88
- Spalding-Chi...........39
- Mathews-NY 37

STRIKEOUTS/GAME
- Bond-Har 1.94
- Devlin-Lou 1.77
- Bradley-StL..........1.62
- Borden-Bos..........1.40
- Fisher-Cin 1.14

GAMES
- Devlin-Lou 68
- Bradley-StL.............64
- Spalding-Chi...........61
- Mathews-NY 56
- Bond-Har 45

SAVES
- Manning-Bos 5
- Zettlein-Phi 2
- McVey-Chi 2

BASE RUNNERS/9
- Bradley-StL..........7.98
- Bond-Har 8.12
- Devlin-Lou 8.73
- Cummings-Har 9.54
- Spalding-Chi........9.67

ADJUSTED RELIEF RUNS

RELIEF RANKING

INNINGS PITCHED
- Devlin-Lou 622.0
- Bradley-StL........573.0
- Spalding-Chi......528.2
- Mathews-NY 516.0
- Bond-Har 408.0

OPPONENTS' AVG.
- Bradley-StL...........211
- Bond-Har 220
- Devlin-Lou 224
- Cummings-Har 239
- Spalding-Chi.........247

OPPONENTS' OBP
- Bradley-StL...........224
- Bond-Har 227
- Devlin-Lou 235
- Cummings-Har 251
- Spalding-Chi.........256

EARNED RUN AVERAGE
- Bradley-StL..........1.23
- Devlin-Lou 1.56
- Cummings-Har 1.67
- Bond-Har 1.68
- Spalding-Chi........1.75

ADJUSTED ERA
- Bradley-StL...........174
- Devlin-Lou 174
- Cummings-Har 142
- Bond-Har 141
- Spalding-Chi.........139

ADJUSTED STARTER RUNS
- Devlin-Lou 67.5
- Bradley-StL..........62.6
- Spalding-Chi........38.7
- Bond-Har 32.2
- Cummings-Har 15.0

PITCHER WINS
- **Devlin-Lou 6.2**
- **Bradley-StL 6.2**
- **Spalding-Chi 4.3**
- **Bond-Har 3.1**
- **McVey-Chi 7**

Get This Party Started

William Hulbert, owner of Chicago's National Association club, created a new league with the power and profits resting with the owners, rather than players. The National League began play on April 22, Boston beating Philadelphia, 6-5, with Jim O'Rourke connecting for the first hit. Boston (Atlanta Braves) and Chicago (Cubs), both former NA clubs, continue NL affiliations to this day.

Since 1870s baseball was about action, batters called for pitches where they wanted them (high, low, or "fair"). Nine balls were required for a batter to earn a walk. Home plate was square, rather than five-sided, and catchers stood straight up. Nobody used gloves.

Four strikes were required for a strikeout; after two strikes, a hitter ignoring a good ball was given a warning. Though the pitcher's box was just 45 feet away, pitchers were still required to throw underhand or sidearm, and didn't get much speed on the ball. In addition, batted balls bouncing foul before crossing first or third base were counted as fair in 1876. Many, including batting champ Ross Barnes, specialized in such trick hits, and scoring was the highest until 1887 and strikeouts at an all-time nadir.

Barnes was the league's dominant player, scoring 54 more runs than his nearest rival, George Wright. Barnes' lone home run in 1876 was the NL's first long ball, although he also led the league in doubles and triples. His White Stockings teammates were a nineteenth century "Who's Who of Baseball": Cap Anson, Paul Hines, Cal McVey, Deacon White, and pitcher Al Spalding. Pitcher George Bradley of St. Louis threw the NL's first no-hitter and led in ERA; he was also one of a handful of pitchers to exceed a strikeout per game.

Chicago ran away with the championship and, not surprisingly, led in attendance, despite 50-cent admissions (double the old rate), no alcohol, and no Sunday games—Hulbert strategies, adopted league-wide, to attract classier fans. And only the White Stockings made a profit, due to a runaway pennant race. New York and Philadelphia, finishing sixth and seventh, didn't make their final westward road trips, and Hulbert expelled them from the NL. Hulbert made his point clearly: This was not the National Association.

1875 NATIONAL ASSOCIATION

TEAM	W	L	T	PCT	GB	HW	HL	R	OR	PA	H	2B	3B	HR	BB	SO	HB	SH	AVG	OBP	SLG	OPS	AOPS	BR	ABR	PF	SB	CS	BSA	BSR
Bos	71	8	3	.899	—	**37**	0	**831**	**343**	3548	**1128**	**167**	51	**15**	33	52	—	—	**.321**	**.327**	**.410**	**737**	**153**	**195**	**169**	104	93	37	72	8
Har	54	28	4	.659	18.5	26	11	557	**343**	3390	871	92	35	2	34	64	—	—	.260	.267	.310	577	97	6	-20	105	65	33	66	3
Ath	53	20	4	.726	15	28	7	699	402	3288	941	124	**57**	7	**38**	55	—	—	.290	.298	.369	667	120	103	41	111	75	46	62	0
StL	39	29	2	.574	26.5	21	12	386	369	2706	643	85	29	0	32	102	—	—	.240	.249	.294	543	99	-23	17	91	**108**	36	**75**	**11**
Phi	37	31	2	.544	28.5	16	16	470	376	2742	683	67	27	5	21	58	—	—	.251	.257	.301	558	92	-13	-29	104	105	51	67	5
Mut	30	38	3	.441	35.5	13	21	328	425	2704	633	82	21	7	19	**47**	—	—	.236	.241	.290	531	82	-35	-55	105	20	24	45	-4
Chi	30	37	2	.448	35	16	16	379	416	2706	699	83	16	0	21	65	—	—	.260	.266	.303	569	99	0	-4	101	69	50	58	-2
NH	7	40	0	.149	48	3	24	170	397	1728	373	41	13	2	14	62	—	—	.218	.224	.260	484	80	-49	-17	87	35	16	69	2
Was	5	23	0	.179	40.5	2	10	107	338	1010	194	14	8	0	6	42	—	—	.193	.198	.223	421	50	-50	-46	96	23	7	77	3
RS	4	15	0	.211	37	3	11	60	161	700	137	20	1	0	12	45	—	—	.199	.213	.231	444	62	-28	-19	90	27	9	**75**	3
Cen	2	12	0	.143	36.5	0	7	70	138	540	125	22	3	0	10	25	—	—	.236	.250	.289	539	97	-5	2	92	4	0	0	1
Atl	2	42	0	.045	51.5	1	26	132	438	1570	304	33	6	2	8	36	—	—	.195	.199	.227	426	57	-75	-50	87	1	5	17	-2
Wes	1	12	0	.077	37	1	7	45	88	450	81	9	6	0	1	22	—	—	.180	.182	.227	409	41	-25	-27	105	4	6	40	-1
Total	345	—	—	—	—	167	168	4234	—	27082	6812	839	273	40	249	675	—	—	.254	.261	.310	571	—	—	—	—	629	320	66	26

TEAM	CG	SHO	GR	SV	IP	H	HR	BB	SO	BR/9	ERA	AERA	OAV	OOB	PR	APR	PF	OSB	OCS	FA	E	WPB	DP	FW	PW	BW	BSW	DIF
Bos	60	10	**24**	**17**	732.0	751	2	33	110	9.6	1.87	115	.248	.256	29	23	96	—	—	.870	483	113	**56**	4.3	2.0	**14.4**	.5	10.3
Har	**83**	**13**	3	0	770.0	708	4	**11**	**152**	**8.4**	**1.57**	**150**	**.228**	**.231**	**56**	**63**	105	—	—	**.881**	438	98	47	**7.8**	**5.4**	-1.7	.0	1.5
Ath	75	6	2	0	687.0	776	4	39	45	10.7	2.40	100	.268	.278	-13	0	107	—	—	.876	**419**	83	51	5.7	.0	3.5	-.2	7.5
StL	67	5	3	1	630.0	**636**	3	21	71	9.4	2.10	96	.241	.247	9	-7	90	—	—	.869	425	94	36	3.0	-.6	1.5	**.8**	.4
Phi	64	5	6	0	628.0	652	6	30	42	9.8	2.12	107	.243	.251	7	11	102	—	—	.848	477	**78**	32	.5	.9	-2.5	.3	3.8
Mut	70	3	1	0	636.2	718	4	21	77	10.4	2.46	95	.258	.264	-17	-9	105	—	—	.838	526	100	30	-1.5	-.8	-4.7	-.5	3.5
Chi	65	7	4	0	625.0	649	**0**	26	55	9.7	1.63	139	.243	.250	42	44	102	—	—	.853	478	147	30	.1	3.8	-.3	-.3	-6.7
NH	40	0	8	0	425.0	501	5	21	54	11.1	2.65	78	.254	.262	-20	-29	93	—	—	.814	447	103	24	-5.7	-2.5	-1.5	.0	-6.8
Was	23	0	5	0	250.2	397	6	10	6	14.6	3.77	63	.311	.317	-43	-37	107	—	—	.791	285	69	8	-4.3	-3.2	-3.9	.0	2.3
RS	16	2	3	0	171.0	209	**0**	3	21	11.2	2.63	83	.267	.269	-8	-9	98	—	—	.833	150	69	6	-.8	-.8	-1.6	.0	-2.3
Cen	14	0	0	0	126.0	169	**0**	5	6	12.4	2.71	80	.274	.280	-7	-8	98	—	—	.769	164	36	5	-3.2	-.7	.2	-.0	-1.2
Atl	31	0	14	0	396.0	535	6	17	16	12.5	3.16	66	.285	.291	-41	-51	94	—	—	.801	432	110	20	-6.0	-4.4	-4.3	-.3	-5.0
Wes	13	0	0	0	113.0	111	**0**	12	20	9.8	1.83	133	.225	.243	5	7	110	—	—	.860	78	46	5	.6	.6	-2.3	-.3	-4.1
Total	621	51	73	18	6190.1	—	—	—	—	10.3	2.23	—	.254	.261	—	—	—	—	—	.849	4802	1146	350	—	—	—	—	—

BATTER-FIELDER WINS	BATTING AVERAGE	ON-BASE PERCENTAGE	SLUGGING AVERAGE	ON-BASE PLUS SLUGGING	ADJUSTED OPS	ADJUSTED BATTER RUNS
Barnes-Bos 4.2	White-Bos .... .367	Barnes-Bos .... .375	McVey-Bos .... .517	McVey-Bos .... .873	Pike-StL 210	Pike-StL 35.1
White-Bos 3.9	Barnes-Bos .... .364	White-Bos .... .372	Pike-StL .... .494	Pike-StL .... .846	McVey-Bos 193	McVey-Bos 34.8
McVey-Bos 3.7	McVey-Bos .... .355	McVey-Bos .... .356	Craver-Cen-Ath ..... .455	White-Bos .... .824	White-Bos 178	Barnes-Bos 28.8
Pike-StL 2.8	Pike-StL .... .346	Pike-StL .... .352	White-Bos .... .453	Barnes-Bos .... .818	Barnes-Bos 177	White-Bos 27.8
G.Wright-Bos 2.1	G.Wright-Bos .... .333	G.Wright-Bos .... .337	Barnes-Bos .... .443	Craver-Cen-Ath ..... .779	G.Wright-Bos 159	G.Wright-Bos 22.4
RUNS	**HITS**	**DOUBLES**	**TRIPLES**	**HOME RUNS**	**TOTAL BASES**	**RUNS BATTED IN**
Barnes-Bos 115	Barnes-Bos 143	McVey-Bos 36	Craver-Cen-Ath 13	O'Rourke-Bos 6	McVey-Bos 201	McVey-Bos 87
G.Wright-Bos 106	McVey-Bos 138	White-Bos 23	Pike-StL 12	Start-Mut 4	G.Wright-Bos 176	Leonard-Bos 74
O'Rourke-Bos 97	G.Wright-Bos 136	Pike-StL 22	Hall-Ath 12	Hall-Ath 4	Barnes-Bos 174	O'Rourke-Bos 72
McVey-Bos 89	White-Bos 136	Force-Ath 22	McVey-Bos 9	Hallinan-Wes-Mut 3	White-Bos 168	Hall-Ath 62
Leonard-Bos 87	Leonard-Bos 127		Meyerle-Phi 8	McVey-Bos 3	Leonard-Bos 156	G.Wright-Bos 61
BASES ON BALLS	**STOLEN BASES**	**BASE STEALING RUNS**	**FIELDING RUNS-INFIELD**	**FIELDING RUNS-OUTFIELD**	**OUTFIELD ASSISTS**	**CATCHER CS PCT.**
Dehlman-StL 11	Murnane-Phi 30	Barnes-Bos 4.3	Barnes-Bos 23.0	Gedney-Mut 10.9	A.Allison-Was-Har 17	
O'Rourke-Bos 9	Barnes-Bos 29	Cuthbert-StL 3.6	Battin-StL 15.4	Anson-Ath 7.3	Booth-Mut 16	
Nelson-Mut 9	Pike-StL 25	Murnane-Phi 3.5	Sutton-Ath 13.2	A.Allison-Was-Har 5.0	Manning-Bos 15	
Hastings-Chi 9	Dehlman-StL 23	McGeary-Phi 2.8	Pearce-StL 11.3	York-Har 4.0	Addy-Phi 14	
Harbridge-Har 9	Burdock-Har 20	Battin-StL 2.3	Force-Ath 10.8	Eggler-Ath 3.8	Anson-Ath 13	
WINS	**WINNING PCT.**	**WINS ABOVE TEAM**	**GAMES STARTED**	**COMPLETE GAMES**	**FEWEST HITS/GAME**	**FEWEST BB/GAME**
Spalding-Bos 54	Spalding-Bos .... .915	Spalding-Bos 12.8	Mathews-Mut 70	Mathews-Mut 69	Borden-Phi 6.41	Cummings-Har .... .09
McBride-Ath 44	Manning-Bos .... .889	McBride-Ath 11.5	Spalding-Bos 62	McBride-Ath 59	Galvin-StL 7.69	Blong-RS .... .14
Cummings-Har 35	McBride-Ath .... .759	Cummings-Har 10.4	McBride-Ath 60	Bradley-StL 57	Bond-Har 7.72	Galvin-StL .... .15
Bradley-StL 33	Cummings-Har ..... .745	Zettlein-Chi-Phi 6.2	Bradley-StL 60	Spalding-Bos 52	Cummings-Har 8.59	Bond-Har .... .18
	Zettlein-Chi-Phi ..... .569	Parks-Was-Phi 1.7	Zettlein-Chi-Phi 52	Zettlein-Chi-Phi 49	Fisher-Phi 8.67	Fisher-Phi .... .23
STRIKEOUTS	**STRIKEOUTS/GAME**	**GAMES**	**SAVES**	**BASE RUNNERS/9**	**ADJUSTED RELIEF RUNS**	**RELIEF RANKING**
Cummings-Har 82	Manning-Bos 2.13	Spalding-Bos 72	Spalding-Bos 9	Borden-Phi 7.36		
Spalding-Bos 75	Bond-Har 1.79	Mathews-Mut 70	Manning-Bos 6	Galvin-StL 7.84		
Mathews-Mut 75	Cummings-Har 1.77	McBride-Ath 60	McVey-Bos 1	Bond-Har 7.90		
Bond-Har 70	Nichols-NH 1.50	Bradley-StL 60	Heifer-Bos 1	Cummings-Har 8.68		
Bradley-StL 60	Golden-Wes-Chi .. 1.32	Zettlein-Chi-Phi 52	Galvin-StL 1	Fisher-Phi 8.90		
INNINGS PITCHED	**OPPONENTS' AVG.**	**OPPONENTS' OBP**	**EARNED RUN AVERAGE**	**ADJUSTED ERA**	**ADJUSTED STARTER RUNS**	**PITCHER WINS**
Mathews-Mut 625.2	Borden-Phi .... .181	Borden-Phi .... .203	Galvin-StL 1.16	Galvin-StL 173	Cummings-Har 33.6	**Spalding-Bos 4.4**
Spalding-Bos 570.2	Galvin-StL .... .209	Galvin-StL .... .212	Bond-Har 1.41	Bond-Har 167	Spalding-Bos 33.2	**Bond-Har 3.1**
McBride-Ath 538.0	Bond-Har .... .216	Bond-Har .... .219	Borden-Phi 1.50	Borden-Phi 152	Bond-Har 32.7	**Cummings-Har .. 2.7**
Bradley-StL 535.2	Fisher-Phi .... .229	Fisher-Phi .... .233	Zettlein-Chi-Phi 1.59	Cummings-Har 146	Zettlein-Chi-Phi 23.7	**Zettlein-Chi-Phi . 1.4**
Zettlein-Chi-Phi .. 463.1	Cummings-Har ..... .235	Cummings-Har ..... .236	Spalding-Bos 1.59	Zettlein-Chi-Phi 143	Fisher-Phi 13.5	**Devlin-Chi 1.2**

Windup

Why did the National Association last only five seasons? There were several factors, including gambling, revolving players, and the inability of most clubs to turn a profit. Many of these problems stemmed from the league's big issue—the lack of competition. Harry Wright's Boston Red Stockings won the final 24 games of 1875 after starting the year without a loss in their first 22. On the other end of the standings was Brooklyn, which finished with an unfathomable .045 winning percentage.

The coming and going of franchises severely hurt the league's credibility. Twenty-three different teams played in the NA over five seasons. Only the Red Stockings, Atlantics, and Mutuals were around for the whole show. Because the franchise fee was just $10, there were always teams seemingly guaranteed to fail.

Just seven of 13 teams finished the 1875 season. The Westerns of Keokuk, Iowa, played on a former cornfield bounded by a lake known to swallow up outfielders; it was no surprise that the Westerns disbanded after 13 games. The Washington Nationals, back in the league after a two-year absence, learned one afternoon in St. Louis that the team could not pay their players' way back home. The St. Louis Brown Stockings, who drew a league record 78,000 fans in their only season in the NA, covered their fares back to Washington.

While Boston killed competition in the league, it was the breaking up of that club by Chicago owner William Hulbert (even as the Red Stockings continued drubbing his team) that spelled doom for the NA. Hulbert induced Al Spalding, still under contract to Boston, to join his club. With Spalding's help, Hulbert signed three of Boston's best hitters—Cal McVey, Ross Barnes, and James "Deacon" White—while also luring Cap Anson from the Athletics.

Hulbert had undercut the NA's lax organization and, seeking greater professionalism and profit, made his own arrangements with the owners of other clubs that winter. Six cities that had fielded NA ballclubs in 1875 played ball in an eight-team confederation the next spring. This was the birth of the National League.

1874 NATIONAL ASSOCIATION

TEAM	W	L	T	PCT	GB	HW	HL	R	OR	PA	H	2B	3B	HR	BB	SO	HB	SH	AVG	OBP	SLG	OPS	AOPS	BR	ABR	PF	SB	CS	BSA	BSR
Bos	52	18	1	.743	—	**27**	9	**735**	415	3163	**977**	**121**	**61**	**17**	34	**28**	—	—	**.312**	**.320**	**.406**	**726**	**128**	**113**	**77**	106	**45**	19	70	3
Mut	42	23	0	.646	7.5	**27**	8	501	377	2766	714	89	28	7	**36**	40	—	—	.262	.271	.322	593	90	-21	-35	103	36	4	**90**	**7**
Ath	33	22	0	.600	11.5	21	8	441	**344**	2283	647	83	18	6	24	51	—	—	.286	.294	.347	641	99	20	-14	109	36	14	72	3
Phi	29	29	0	.500	17	16	9	476	428	2463	677	78	50	2	28	33	—	—	.278	.286	.354	640	104	17	1	104	27	18	60	0
Chi	28	31	0	.475	18.5	18	10	418	480	2494	685	87	4	4	32	54	—	—	.278	.287	.322	609	97	-2	-6	101	32	12	73	3
Atl	22	33	1	.400	22.5	15	13	301	450	2200	498	45	8	1	31	51	—	—	.230	.240	.259	499	71	-85	-44	88	12	4	75	1
Har	16	37	0	.302	27.5	13	17	371	471	2175	591	86	18	2	31	63	—	—	.276	.286	.335	621	97	6	-13	105	42	21	67	2
Bal	9	38	0	.191	31.5	7	13	227	505	1798	435	45	7	1	22	37	—	—	.245	.254	.280	534	75	-48	-46	99	12	5	71	1
Total	232	—	—	—	—	144	87	3470	—	19342	5224	634	194	40	238	357	—	—	.273	.282	.333	616	—	—	—	—	242	97	71	19

TEAM	CG	SHO	GR	SV	IP	H	HR	BB	SO	BR/9	ERA	AERA	OAV	OOB	PR	APR	PF	OSB	OCS	FA	E	WPB	DP	FW	PW	BW	BSW	DIF
Bos	**65**	**4**	6	**3**	634.0	779	**1**	23	31	11.4	1.93	112	.274	.280	18	17	99	—	—	**.850**	489	50	**53**	4.5	1.3	**6.0**	.0	5.2
Mut	62	**4**	3	0	586.0	663	3	41	**101**	10.8	1.90	118	.261	.273	19	22	103	—	—	.847	438	91	22	**4.6**	1.7	-2.7	**.4**	5.6
Ath	55	0	0	0	487.0	**514**	6	32	37	**10.1**	**1.64**	**141**	**.240**	**.251**	**30**	**34**	106	—	—	.839	**396**	38	34	2.6	**2.6**	-1.1	.0	1.3
Phi	56	3	2	0	522.0	673	4	19	61	11.9	1.93	115	.278	.284	15	17	101	—	—	.809	518	**32**	38	-2.3	1.3	.0	-.2	1.1
Chi	58	3	1	0	533.2	684	7	45	26	12.3	2.65	84	.279	.292	-27	-24	102	—	—	.829	477	57	27	.2	-1.9	-.5	.0	.6
Atl	56	1	0	0	506.0	618	15	**11**	42	11.2	2.06	100	.266	.269	7	0	94	—	—	.822	500	79	15	-2.2	.0	-3.4	-.1	.3
Har	45	0	**8**	0	481.0	653	**1**	28	39	12.7	2.53	91	.284	.293	-18	-11	105	—	—	.797	521	85	17	-4.5	-.9	-1.0	-.0	-4.1
Bal	42	0	6	0	420.0	640	3	39	20	14.5	3.13	71	.305	.318	-44	-41	102	—	—	.812	436	54	15	-2.7	-3.2	-3.6	-.1	-4.9
Total	439	15	26	3	4169.2	—	—	—	—	11.8	2.19	—	.273	.282	—	—	—	—	—	.827	3775	486	221	—	—	—	—	—

BATTER-FIELDER WINS	BATTING AVERAGE	ON-BASE PERCENTAGE	SLUGGING AVERAGE	ON-BASE PLUS SLUGGING	ADJUSTED OPS	ADJUSTED BATTER RUNS
Barnes-Bos 1.9	Meyerle-Chi .394	Meyerle-Chi .401	Pike-Har .504	Meyerle-Chi .889	Meyerle-Chi 182	Meyerle-Chi 22.9
Pike-Har 1.8	McVey-Bos .359	Pike-Har .368	Craver-Phi .498	Pike-Har .872	Pike-Har 168	McVey-Bos 20.3
McVey-Bos 1.7	Pike-Har .355	McMullin-Ath .366	Meyerle-Chi .488	Craver-Phi .851	Craver-Phi 164	Craver-Phi 17.6
Craver-Phi 1.5	Manning-Bal-Har .346	McVey-Bos .360	McVey-Bos .481	McVey-Bos .842	McVey-Bos 158	Pike-Har 17.2
G.Wright-Bos 1.5	McMullin-Ath .346	Barnes-Bos .360	G.Wright-Bos .476	G.Wright-Bos .816	G.Wright-Bos 150	G.Wright-Bos 14.7

RUNS	HITS	DOUBLES	TRIPLES	HOME RUNS	TOTAL BASES	RUNS BATTED IN
McVey-Bos 91	McVey-Bos 123	Pike-Har 22	G.Wright-Bos 15	O'Rourke-Bos 5	McVey-Bos 165	McVey-Bos 71
O'Rourke-Bos 82	Spalding-Bos 119	McVey-Bos 21	Craver-Phi 11	White-Bos 3	O'Rourke-Bos 150	O'Rourke-Bos 61
Spalding-Bos 80	White-Bos 106	Meyerle-Chi 19	Holdsworth-Phi 9	McVey-Bos 3	G.Wright-Bos 149	Craver-Phi 56
G.Wright-Bos 76	Leonard-Bos 106	Craver-Phi 19		Clapp-Ath 3	White-Bos 134	Spalding-Bos 54
White-Bos 75	O'Rourke-Bos 104	Leonard-Bos 18			Spalding-Bos 134	White-Bos 52

BASES ON BALLS	STOLEN BASES	BASE STEALING RUNS	FIELDING RUNS-INFIELD	FIELDING RUNS-OUTFIELD	OUTFIELD ASSISTS	CATCHER CS PCT.
Nelson-Mut 9	Barlow-Har 17	Barlow-Har 2.3	White-Bal 27.3	Ryan-Bal 13.1	Treacey-Chi 14	
McMullin-Ath 8	O'Rourke-Bos 11	Cuthbert-Chi 1.8	Barnes-Bos 18.8	York-Phi 7.7	Remsen-Mut 12	
Barnes-Bos 8	Leonard-Bos 11	O'Rourke-Bos 1.7	Burdock-Mut 10.1	Eggler-Phi 6.8	Chapman-Atl 12	
	Craver-Phi 11	McGeary-Ath 1.5	Force-Chi 8.9	Hines-Chi 6.1	Cuthbert-Chi 10	
			Pearce-Atl 7.8	Hatfield-Mut 5.5	Bielaski-Bal 10	

WINS	WINNING PCT.	WINS ABOVE TEAM	GAMES STARTED	COMPLETE GAMES	FEWEST HITS/GAME	FEWEST BB/GAME
Spalding-Bos 52	Spalding-Bos .765	Spalding-Bos 26.0	Spalding-Bos 69	Spalding-Bos 65	McBride-Ath 9.50	Bond-Atl 14
Mathews-Mut 42	Mathews-Mut .656	Mathews-Mut 21.0	Mathews-Mut 65	Mathews-Mut 62	Mathews-Mut 10.15	Spalding-Bos 28
McBride-Ath 33	McBride-Ath .600	McBride-Ath 16.5	Zettlein-Chi 57	Zettlein-Chi 57	Bond-Atl 10.97	Cummings-Phi 34
Cummings-Phi 28	Cummings-Phi .519	Bond-Atl 11.0	McBride-Ath 55	McBride-Ath 55	Spalding-Bos 11.01	Fisher-Har 36
Zettlein-Chi 27	Zettlein-Chi .474	Cummings-Phi 9.7	Bond-Atl 55	Bond-Atl 55	Zettlein-Chi 11.17	McBride-Ath 59

STRIKEOUTS	STRIKEOUTS/GAME	GAMES	SAVES	BASE RUNNERS/9	ADJUSTED RELIEF RUNS	RELIEF RANKING
Mathews-Mut 101	Mathews-Mut 1.57	Spalding-Bos 71	H.Wright-Bos 3	McBride-Ath 10.09		
Cummings-Phi 61	Cummings-Phi 1.14	Mathews-Mut 65		Mathews-Mut 10.79		
Bond-Atl 42	Stearns-Har .79	Zettlein-Chi 57		Bond-Atl 11.12		
McBride-Ath 37	Bond-Atl .76	McBride-Ath 55		Spalding-Bos 11.28		
Spalding-Bos 31	Fisher-Har .70	Bond-Atl 55		Cummings-Phi 11.81		

INNINGS PITCHED	OPPONENTS' AVG.	OPPONENTS' OBP	EARNED RUN AVERAGE	ADJUSTED ERA	ADJUSTED STARTER RUNS	PITCHER WINS
Spalding-Bos 617.1	McBride-Ath .240	McBride-Ath .251	McBride-Ath 1.64	McBride-Ath 141	McBride-Ath 34.3	**Spalding-Bos 2.8**
Mathews-Mut 578.0	Mathews-Mut .261	Bond-Atl .268	Mathews-Mut 1.90	Mathews-Mut 118	Mathews-Mut 21.7	**McBride-Ath 1.9**
Zettlein-Chi 515.2	Bond-Atl .266	Mathews-Mut .273	Spalding-Bos 1.92	Cummings-Phi 113	Spalding-Bos 16.9	**Mathews-Mut 1.5**
Bond-Atl 497.0	Spalding-Bos .273	Spalding-Bos .278	Cummings-Phi 1.96	Spalding-Bos 113	Cummings-Phi 15.9	**Cummings-Phi .7**
McBride-Ath 487.0	Zettlein-Chi .273	Cummings-Phi .282	Bond-Atl 2.03	Bond-Atl 102	Fisher-Har 1.4	**Bond-Atl .6**

WHITE STOCKINGS TO THE RESCUE, SORT OF

Gambling was officially made against the rules in 1874. Players were threatened with expulsion if they bet on games they were playing in—this at least made gambling more covert. Athletics outfielder John Radcliffe was expelled during the season for offering an umpire $175 to help Chicago win a game (he played 5 games in 1875 for the Centennials).

The batter's box was first introduced in 1874. Walks were awarded on three "wide balls" or nine balls too high or low. A proposal by Henry Chadwick for ten men and ten innings was defeated at the annual league meeting in Boston.

Chicago returned after two years, and, no coincidence, the NA finally surpassed its overall attendance mark set in 1871. The White Stockings outdrew the Red Stockings at the gate but could not compete with them on the diamond; in a 38-1 loss to the Mutuals in June, Chicago committed 36 errors.

In midseason, Boston and the Athletics set sail for Great Britain. Harry Wright planned this tour to his native country, sending Red Stockings star Al Spalding to England to make arrangements. Wright, a professional cricketer less than a decade earlier, was embarrassed that Spalding had led his hosts to believe the American ballplayers were also fine cricketers—they weren't. The tour lost $3,000.

That was about all the Red Stockings lost. Boston did not miss a beat after six weeks away: Cal McVey led an attack that featured teammates in the top five spots in runs, hits, and total bases. (Boston swept the top five in these categories again in 1875.) For good measure, Boston's "Orator" Jim O'Rourke led the NA in home runs in 1874–75.

Boston took the title by 7½ games over New York, but it was only that close because their 9-1 mark against the Lord Baltimores was thrown out when that club did not complete its schedule. Despite the return of the White Stockings, only one midseason team failure, steps to limit gambling, and international press (some of it good), the NA was at a critical juncture. The decision to allow six more teams for 1875 was the fuel that caused the league to explode.

1873 NATIONAL ASSOCIATION

TEAM	W	L	T	PCT	GB	HW	HL	R	OR	PA	H	2B	3B	HR	BB	SO	HB	SH	AVG	OBP	SLG	OPS	AOPS	BR	ABR	PF	SB	CS	BSA	BSR
Bos	43	16	1	.729	—	**24**	8	**739**	460	2816	**933**	**144**	**44**	**13**	**68**	36	—	—	**.340**	**.355**	**.438**	**793**	**128**	**129**	**74**	108	**145**	48	75	**15**
Phi	36	17	0	.679	4	22	5	526	396	2388	645	83	20	8	62	41	—	—	.277	.296	.340	636	89	-18	-35	104	54	14	**79**	7
Bal	34	22	1	.607	7.5	19	6	644	451	2603	810	109	40	9	43	30	—	—	.316	.328	.401	729	121	59	62	100	28	13	68	2
Mut	29	24	0	.547	11	22	9	424	**385**	2254	622	51	36	5	43	**22**	—	—	.281	.295	.344	639	94	-20	-17	99	16	7	70	1
Ath	28	23	1	.549	11	21	6	474	403	2302	683	71	21	4	35	33	—	—	.301	.312	.356	668	95	6	-28	108	36	24	60	0
Atl	17	37	1	.315	23.5	14	14	366	549	2262	588	46	23	6	55	47	—	—	.266	.284	.316	600	92	-47	3	89	20	13	61	0
Was	8	31	0	.205	25	6	12	283	485	1580	408	40	19	2	20	36	—	—	.262	.271	.315	586	80	-42	-33	97	11	8	58	0
Res	2	21	0	.087	23	0	8	98	299	878	204	25	8	0	9	30	—	—	.235	.243	.282	525	64	-42	-30	92	4	4	50	-1
Mar	0	6	0	.000	16.5	0	1	26	152	211	33	1	0	0	0	3	—	—	.156	.156	.161	317	-5	-26	-21	77	0	0	0	0
Total	199	—	—	—	—	128	69	3580	—	17294	4926	570	211	47	335	278	—	—	.290	.304	.357	661	—	—	—	—	314	131	71	23

TEAM	CG	SHO	GR	SV	IP	H	HR	BB	SO	BR/9	ERA	AERA	OAV	OOB	PR	APR	PF	OSB	OCS	FA	E	WPB	DP	FW	PW	BW	BSW	DIF
Bos	46	1	**14**	**7**	536.0	708	5	**42**	55	12.6	3.07	113	.288	.300	19	23	102	—	—	.836	472	99	**54**	.6	1.6	**5.2**	**.9**	5.2
Phi	50	0	3	0	481.0	628	**3**	44	29	12.6	2.92	118	.285	.299	26	28	101	—	—	.849	378	**51**	43	2.4	2.0	-2.5	.3	7.3
Bal	**55**	1	2	0	508.2	680	4	43	37	12.8	3.08	110	.285	.298	18	18	100	—	—	**.862**	**345**	53	32	**5.6**	1.3	4.4	-.0	-5.3
Mut	48	2	5	0	477.0	**539**	5	68	**80**	**11.5**	**2.64**	**125**	**.255**	.278	**40**	**36**	97	—	—	.819	425	91	29	.1	**2.5**	-1.2	-.1	1.2
Ath	44	**3**	8	2	475.0	553	4	58	41	11.6	3.05	117	.257	**.276**	18	26	105	—	—	.840	390	84	30	1.4	1.8	-2.0	-.2	1.4
Atl	52	1	3	0	500.0	737	8	43	16	14.0	4.14	77	.305	.317	-41	-58	93	—	—	.817	515	53	34	-3.5	-4.1	.2	-.2	-2.4
Was	39	0	0	0	346.0	594	11	26	10	16.1	4.84	72	.337	.347	-55	-50	103	—	—	.812	348	80	27	-1.7	-3.5	-2.3	-.2	-3.8
Res	22	0	1	0	207.0	343	6	10	10	15.3	3.26	107	.312	.318	3	5	103	—	—	.789	244	22	14	-2.9	.4	-2.1	-.3	-4.6
Mar	6	0	0	0	54.0	144	1	1	0	24.2	8.00	42	.393	.395	-28	-28	100	—	—	.761	74	5	0	-1.3	-2.0	-1.5	-.2	1.9
Total	362	8	36	9	3584.2	—	—	—	—	13.2	3.40	—	.290	.304	—	—	—	—	—	.830	3191	538	263	—	—	—	—	—

BATTER-FIELDER WINS
Barnes-Bos........4.2
G.Wright-Bos......2.6
Ferguson-Atl......1.6
White-Bos..........1.4
Force-Bal............1.2

BATTING AVERAGE
Barnes-Bos..........431
Anson-Ath.............398
White-Bos.............392
G.Wright-Bos.......387
McVey-Bal.............380

ON-BASE PERCENTAGE
Barnes-Bos..........465
Anson-Ath.............409
G.Wright-Bos........404
White-Bos.............392
McVey-Bal.............390

SLUGGING AVERAGE
Barnes-Bos...........616
G.Wright-Bos........511
White-Bos.............508
McVey-Bal.............490
Meyerle-Phi..........479

ON-BASE PLUS SLUGGING
Barnes-Bos.........1080
G.Wright-Bos........914
White-Bos.............900
McVey-Bal.............879
Anson-Ath.............858

ADJUSTED OPS
Barnes-Bos..........200
McVey-Bal.............159
G.Wright-Bos........156
Pabor-Atl...............153
White-Bos.............152

ADJUSTED BATTER RUNS
Barnes-Bos..........38.2
G.Wright-Bos.......19.6
Pabor-Atl...............17.3
White-Bos............16.7
McVey-Bal............13.3

RUNS
Barnes-Bos..........125
G.Wright-Bos..........99
Spalding-Bos..........83
Eggler-Mut.............82
Leonard-Bos...........81

HITS
Barnes-Bos...........138
G.Wright-Bos........125
White-Bos.............122
Spalding-Bos........106
Anson-Ath.............101

DOUBLES
Barnes-Bos.............31
O'Rourke-Bos.........21
Mills-Bal.................20
Carey-Bal...............18

TRIPLES
Barnes-Bos.............11
Mills-Bal....................9
White-Bos..................8
Pike-Bal....................8
Holdsworth-Mut.........8

HOME RUNS
Pike-Bal......................4
G.Wright-Bos.............3
Meyerle-Phi................3

TOTAL BASES
Barnes-Bos...........197
G.Wright-Bos........165
White-Bos.............158
Pike-Bal................133

RUNS BATTED IN
White-Bos...............77
Spalding-Bos..........71
Leonard-Bos...........60
Barnes-Bos.............60
Meyerle-Phi.............59

BASES ON BALLS
Barnes-Bos.............20
O'Rourke-Bos.........15
Mack-Phi.................15
Malone-Phi.............14

STOLEN BASES
Barnes-Bos.............43
Leonard-Bos...........27
White-Bos...............19
Schafer-Bos...........14
Cuthbert-Phi...........14

BASE STEALING RUNS
Barnes-Bos............7.4
White-Bos..............3.1
Leonard-Bos..........2.8
Cuthbert-Phi..........2.4
Spalding-Bos.........2.0

FIELDING RUNS-INFIELD
Ferguson-Atl........27.4
G.Wright-Bos.......19.9
Barnes-Bos..........19.3
Fulmer-Phi...........18.0
Beals-Was.............9.0

FIELDING RUNS-OUTFIELD
Gedney-Mut.........14.2
York-Bal...............11.2
Bechtel-Phi............5.9
Fisher-Ath..............5.8
Eggler-Mut.............3.9

OUTFIELD ASSISTS
Leonard-Bos...........17
Fisher-Ath...............12

CATCHER CS PCT.

WINS
Spalding-Bos..........41
Zettlein-Phi.............36
Mathews-Mut...........29
Cummings-Bal........28
McBride-Ath............24

WINNING PCT.
Spalding-Bos........745
Zettlein-Phi...........706
Cummings-Bal......667
McBride-Ath..........558
Mathews-Mut........558

WINS ABOVE TEAM
Zettlein-Phi..........18.0
Mathews-Mut.......14.5
Spalding-Bos.......13.5
Cummings-Bal.......8.8
Britt-Atl..................8.5

GAMES STARTED
Spalding-Bos..........54
Britt-Atl....................54
Mathews-Mut..........52
Zettlein-Phi.............51
McBride-Ath............46

COMPLETE GAMES
Britt-Atl....................51
Zettlein-Phi.............49
Mathews-Mut..........47
Spalding-Bos..........46
Cummings-Bal........42

FEWEST HITS/GAME
Fisher-Ath............9.60
Mathews-Mut.........9.93
McBride-Ath.......10.65
Cummings-Bal...11.19
Zettlein-Phi.........11.62

FEWEST BB/GAME
H.Campbell-Res.....44
Stearns-Was...........51
Spalding-Bos..........65
Brainard-Bal............75
Britt-Atl....................77

STRIKEOUTS
Mathews-Mut...........79
Spalding-Bos..........50
Cummings-Bal........34
Zettlein-Phi.............29
McBride-Ath............25

STRIKEOUTS/GAME
Mathews-Mut.......1.60
Fisher-Ath...........1.49
Spalding-Bos..........91
Cummings-Bal........80
Greason-Was..........71

GAMES
Spalding-Bos..........60
Britt-Atl....................54
Mathews-Mut..........52
Zettlein-Phi.............51
McBride-Ath............46

SAVES
H.Wright-Bos............4
Spalding-Bos............3
Fisher-Ath.................2

BASE RUNNERS/9
Fisher-Ath..........10.67
Mathews-Mut.....11.19
McBride-Ath.......11.76
Cummings-Bal...11.97
Spalding-Bos.....12.30

ADJUSTED RELIEF RUNS

RELIEF RANKING

INNINGS PITCHED
Spalding-Bos.....496.2
Britt-Atl...............480.2
Zettlein-Phi........460.0
Mathews-Mut.....443.0
McBride-Ath.......382.2

OPPONENTS' AVG.
Fisher-Ath............231
Mathews-Mut.........251
McBride-Ath..........262
Cummings-Bal......274
Zettlein-Phi...........284

OPPONENTS' OBP
Fisher-Ath............250
Mathews-Mut.........274
McBride-Ath..........281
Cummings-Bal......287
Spalding-Bos........296

EARNED RUN AVERAGE
Fisher-Ath............1.81
Mathews-Mut.......2.58
Cummings-Bal......2.80
Zettlein-Phi..........2.86
H.Campbell-Res..2.95

ADJUSTED ERA
Fisher-Ath............197
Mathews-Mut.........128
Cummings-Bal......121
Zettlein-Phi...........121
H.Campbell-Res...119

ADJUSTED STARTER RUNS
Mathews-Mut.......36.8
Zettlein-Phi..........30.1
Cummings-Bal.....28.4
Spalding-Bos.......26.0
McBride-Ath.........15.0

PITCHER WINS
Spalding-Bos.....3.4
Mathews-Mut.......2.5
Cummings-Bal...2.1
Zettlein-Phi.........1.7
McBride-Ath.......1.2

NOT MUCH OF A HORSE RACE

Nine teams started 1873, but the Baltimore Marylands called it quits after going 0-6—the briefest of any team in the NA. The Resolutes of Elizabeth, New Jersey, stuck it out until August before quitting (although one of their two wins came against the powerhouse Red Stockings). League attendance was down 16 percent from 1871.

Lip Pike of the Lord Baltimores won his third successive home run crown in 1873. Although Pike homered just once more over the next two NA seasons, his 16 career long balls topped the circuit. Pike was also pretty fast, fast enough to beat a horse, outrunning a trotter in a 100-yard dash at Baltimore's Newington Park in August; "Clarence" had a 25-yard head start, but Pike took the race in 10 seconds flat.

Nearly 100 games into their existence, the Red Stockings were finally shut out. Unfazed, Boston marched to the pennant again, averaging almost 12 runs per game. The Red Stockings dominated every offensive category. Al Spalding not only won 41 times for Boston, he also drove in 71 runs in 60 games.

Cherokee Fisher had an interesting perspective on the NA. He pitched all five seasons in the league for a different team each year. In 1873, as an Athletic, he allowed the fewest runs per game for the second straight year, but he didn't pitch much because of the presence of veteran moundsman Dick McBride, the man who had finally shut out the mighty Red Stockings. Fisher played right field mostly and batted a career-best .262. The Athletics finished just 4 games behind Boston, the closest any NA team would ever get to the Red Stockings again.

Dick McBride managed every game the Athletics ever played as an NA club until October 9, 1875, when he had the rare distinction of being stripped of his job in the middle of a game against Boston. Following an on-field meeting by the club's board of directors, 23-year-old Adrian (not yet Cap) Anson made his managerial debut in the fifth inning.

1872 NATIONAL ASSOCIATION

TEAM	W	L	T	PCT	GB	HW	HL	R	OR	PA	H	2B	3B	HR	BB	SO	HB	SH	AVG	OBP	SLG	OPS	AOPS	BR	ABR	PF	SB	CS	BSA	BSR
Bos	39	8	1	.830	—	20	1	521	**236**	2155	673	**107**	30	7	29	26	—	—	**.317**	.326	**.405**	**731**	120	**62**	36	105	48	14	**77**	**6**
Bal	35	19	4	.648	7.5	20	7	**617**	434	2600	**753**	106	**31**	**14**	29	28	—	—	.293	.301	.375	676	104	25	0	105	53	18	75	5
Mut	34	20	2	.630	8.5	20	8	523	362	2484	670	87	14	4	58	52	—	—	.276	.293	.329	622	99	-17	18	94	**59**	22	73	5
Ath	30	14	3	.682	7.5	**22**	4	539	349	2211	679	79	25	4	**69**	47	—	—	**.317**	**.338**	.383	721	**124**	60	**58**	100	58	31	65	2
Tro	15	10	0	.600	13	6	6	273	191	1108	.330	58	8	5	9	14	—	—	.300	.306	.381	687	111	16	13	101	6	7	46	-1
Atl	9	28	0	.243	25	6	12	237	473	1476	377	35	10	1	19	**25**	—	—	.259	.268	.299	567	65	-40	-80	117	19	16	54	-1
Cle	6	16	0	.273	20.5	2	5	174	254	960	272	28	5	0	17	13	—	—	.288	.301	.329	630	102	-4	8	95	12	3	80	2
Man	5	19	0	.208	22.5	4	7	220	348	1023	275	36	9	2	10	13	—	—	.271	.279	.331	610	94	-13	0	94	6	7	46	-1
Eck	3	26	0	.103	27	3	11	152	413	1090	248	29	9	0	18	40	—	—	.231	.244	.275	519	72	-47	-14	85	8	13	38	-3
Oly	2	7	0	.222	18	1	6	54	140	369	91	10	3	0	4	4	—	—	.249	.257	.293	550	75	-12	-8	95	0	3	0	-1
Nat	0	11	0	.000	21	0	7	80	190	452	99	6	1	0	1	3	—	—	.220	.221	.237	458	37	-30	-39	117	0	0	0	0
Total	183	—	—	—	—	104	74	3390	—	15928	4467	581	145	37	263	265	—	—	.285	.297	.348	645	—	—	—	—	269	134	67	12

TEAM	CG	SHO	GR	SV	IP	H	HR	BB	SO	BR/9	ERA	AERA	OAV	OOB	PR	APR	PF	OSB	OCS	FA	E	WPB	DP	FW	PW	BW	BSW	DIF
Bos	41	**4**	7	**4**	430.1	**443**	**0**	27	29	**9.8**	**1.86**	**197**	**.243**	**.254**	**86**	**86**	100	—	—	**.875**	**280**	53	**44**	4.3	**6.0**	2.5	**.3**	2.3
Bal	48	1	**10**	1	516.0	573	3	63	**77**	11.1	2.90	127	.245	.265	43	45	101	—	—	.830	432	93	22	.4	3.1	.0	**.3**	4.2
Mut	**54**	3	2	1	512.0	622	2	33	46	11.5	3.02	112	.271	.282	36	22	93	—	—	.868	323	54	33	**5.2**	1.5	1.3	**.3**	-1.3
Ath	47	1	0	0	419.1	508	3	26	44	11.5	2.85	125	.265	.275	37	34	98	—	—	.858	298	**28**	20	3.0	2.4	**4.0**	.0	-1.5
Tro	17	2	8	1	225.0	277	2	10	19	11.5	2.60	140	.269	.276	26	26	100	—	—	.861	151	18	9	2.0	1.8	.9	-.1	-2.1
Atl	37	0	0	0	336.0	568	6	**21**	13	15.8	4.53	100	.326	.334	-33	0	124	—	—	.810	357	66	15	-4.0	.0	-5.6	-.1	.2
Cle	15	0	7	0	199.0	285	6	24	11	14.0	5.70	63	.290	.307	-45	-48	98	—	—	.816	184	53	17	-.9	-3.3	.6	.0	-1.4
Man	20	0	4	0	211.0	366	6	15	10	16.3	5.55	65	.326	.335	-44	-46	99	—	—	.804	231	18	11	-2.6	-3.2	.0	-.1	-1.1
Eck	28	0	1	0	259.1	484	7	36	13	18.0	5.55	61	.345	.361	-55	-66	93	—	—	.803	274	71	9	-2.8	-4.6	-1.0	-.3	-2.8
Oly	9	0	0	0	79.0	148	**0**	5	1	17.4	6.38	57	.333	.341	-24	-25	99	—	—	.786	96	30	7	-1.5	-1.7	-.6	-.1	1.4
Nat	11	0	0	0	99.0	193	2	3	2	17.8	6.18	75	.339	.343	-28	-13	127	—	—	.774	120	7	2	-1.9	-.9	-2.7	-.0	.1
Total	327	11	39	7	3286.0	—	—	—	—	13.0	3.65	—	.285	.297	—	—	—	—	—	.837	2746	491	189	—	—	—	—	—

BATTER-FIELDER WINS	BATTING AVERAGE	ON-BASE PERCENTAGE	SLUGGING AVERAGE	ON-BASE PLUS SLUGGING	ADJUSTED OPS	ADJUSTED BATTER RUNS
Barnes-Bos........3.5	Barnes-Bos..........430	Anson-Ath............455	Barnes-Bos...........583	Barnes-Bos.........1034	Barnes-Bos...........205	Barnes-Bos..........28.0
Eggler-Mut.........2.2	Force-Tro-Bal........418	Barnes-Bos...........452	Anson-Ath............525	Anson-Ath.............980	Anson-Ath.............200	Anson-Ath.............25.8
G.Wright-Bos......2.2	Anson-Ath.............415	Force-Tro-Bal........423	Wood-Tro-Eck.......500	Force-Tro-Bal........916	Force-Tro-Bal........176	Force-Tro-Bal.......19.0
Force-Tro-Bal.....1.8	Hastings-Cle-Bal...362	Hastings-Cle-Bal...376	Force-Tro-Bal........493	Wood-Tro-Eck.......833	Wood-Tro-Eck.......156	Eggler-Mut..........16.8
Ferguson-Atl......1.7	McGeary-Ath........360	McGeary-Ath........366	Meyerle-Ath..........486	G.Wright-Bos........816	Meyerle-Ath..........147	Hatfield-Mut..........14.7
RUNS	**HITS**	**DOUBLES**	**TRIPLES**	**HOME RUNS**	**TOTAL BASES**	**RUNS BATTED IN**
Eggler-Mut.............94	Barnes-Bos............99	Barnes-Bos............28	Gould-Bos................8	Pike-Bal....................7	Barnes-Bos...........134	Pike-Bal.....................60
G.Wright-Bos...........87	Eggler-Mut.............97	Eggler-Mut.............20	Anson-Ath................7	Gedney-Tro-Eck........3	Pike-Bal................131	Start-Mut..................48
Cuthbert-Ath...........83	Force-Tro-Bal.........94	Hall-Bal...................17	G.Wright-Bos...........6		G.Wright-Bos........120	Fisler-Ath.................48
Barnes-Bos.............81	Hatfield-Mut............93	G.Wright-Bos..........16	Hall-Bal....................6		Eggler-Mut............117	Anson-Ath.................48
Hatfield-Mut............76	Anson-Ath...............90				Hall-Bal.................116	
BASES ON BALLS	**STOLEN BASES**	**BASE STEALING RUNS**	**FIELDING RUNS-INFIELD**	**FIELDING RUNS-OUTFIELD**	**OUTFIELD ASSISTS**	**CATCHER CS PCT.**
Mack-Ath................23	Eggler-Mut..............18	Barnes-Bos............1.9	Ferguson-Atl........34.5	Eggler-Mut...........14.1	Eggler-Mut..............12	
Anson-Ath...............16	G.Wright-Bos..........14	Eggler-Mut.............1.9	Barnes-Bos..........25.5	York-Bal.................9.9	York-Bal....................7	
McMullin-Mut..........11	Cuthbert-Ath...........14	Pike-Bal.................1.9	G.Wright-Bos.......21.6	Reach-Ath..............4.4	Leonard-Bos.............7	
	McGeary-Ath..........13	G.Wright-Bos..........1.7	Fisler-Ath..............7.3	Meyerle-Ath...........3.0	Booth-Man-Atl...........6	
		Cuthbert-Ath..........1.7	Force-Tro-Bal.........7.2	McMullin-Mut..........2.9		
WINS	**WINNING PCT.**	**WINS ABOVE TEAM**	**GAMES STARTED**	**COMPLETE GAMES**	**FEWEST HITS/GAME**	**FEWEST BB/GAME**
Spalding-Bos..........38	Spalding-Bos........826	McBride-Ath.........15.0	Cummings-Mut.......55	Cummings-Mut.......53	Fisher-Bal............7.61	Stearns-Nat............27
Cummings-Mut.......33	McBride-Ath..........682	Zettlein-Tro-Eck.....5.1	Spalding-Bos..........48	McBride-Ath............47	Spalding-Bos.........9.27	Buttery-Man...........46
McBride-Ath............30	Cummings-Mut.....623	Britt-Atl...................4.5	McBride-Ath............47	Spalding-Bos..........41	Mathews-Bal......10.64	Zettlein-Tro-Eck......48
Mathews-Bal...........25	Mathews-Bal.........581	Fisher-Bal..............4.3	Mathews-Bal...........47	Mathews-Bal...........39	Zettlein-Tro-Eck .10.71	Brainard-Oly-Man...52
Zettlein-Tro-Eck......15	Zettlein-Tro-Eck....484	Buttery-Man...........1.4	Britt-Atl...................37	Britt-Atl...................37	McBride-Ath.......10.90	McBride-Ath............56
STRIKEOUTS	**STRIKEOUTS/GAME**	**GAMES**	**SAVES**	**BASE RUNNERS/9**	**ADJUSTED RELIEF RUNS**	**RELIEF RANKING**
Mathews-Bal...........57	Fisher-Bal............1.64	Cummings-Mut.......55	H.Wright-Bos............4	Fisher-Bal..............8.51	H.Wright-Bos.........5.2	H.Wright-Bos.........3.6
Cummings-Mut.......45	Mathews-Bal........1.26	Mathews-Bal...........49	Zettlein-Tro-Eck........1	Spalding-Bos.......9.87		
McBride-Ath............44	McBride-Ath.............94	Spalding-Bos..........48	McMullin-Mut............1	Zettlein-Tro-Eck .11.19		
Spalding-Bos..........28	Zettlein-Tro-Eck.......86	McBride-Ath............47	Fisher-Bal.................1	McBride-Ath.......11.46		
Zettlein-Tro-Eck......25	Cummings-Mut.......81	Britt-Atl...................37		Cummings-Mut..11.50		
INNINGS PITCHED	**OPPONENTS' AVG.**	**OPPONENTS' OBP**	**EARNED RUN AVERAGE**	**ADJUSTED ERA**	**ADJUSTED STARTER RUNS**	**PITCHER WINS**
Cummings-Mut..497.0	Fisher-Bal.............197	Fisher-Bal.............216	Fisher-Bal............1.80	Fisher-Bal.............205	Spalding-Bos.......80.9	**Spalding-Bos.....7.5**
McBride-Ath.......419.1	Spalding-Bos.........244	Spalding-Bos.........255	Spalding-Bos.......1.85	Spalding-Bos.........199	McBride-Ath.........34.0	**McBride-Ath.......2.6**
Mathews-Bal......406.0	Mathews-Bal.........257	Zettlein-Tro-Eck....273	Zettlein-Tro-Eck...2.57	Zettlein-Tro-Eck....139	Zettlein-Tro-Eck...30.2	**Zettlein-Tro-Eck 2.1**
Spalding-Bos.....404.2	Zettlein-Tro-Eck....265	McBride-Ath..........275	McBride-Ath.........2.85	McBride-Ath..........125	Mathews-Bal........26.0	**Fisher-Bal...........1.2**
Britt-Atl..............336.0	McBride-Ath..........265	Mathews-Bal.........277	Cummings-Mut....3.01	Mathews-Bal.........115	Cummings-Mut....23.3	**Cummings-Mut..1.1**

More Is Less

The NA increased to eleven teams in its second year, but several of the new clubs proved to be poor draws. Troy, Cleveland, the Brooklyn Eckfords, the Washington Olympics, and Mansfield of Middletown, Connecticut, wouldn't live to see 1873. Together they drew just 37,000; the six clubs that stuck it out had a combined attendance of 200,000. The Lord Baltimores, however, proved an inspired addition as they drew 40,500 fans and placed second to runaway winner Boston.

Harry Wright's Red Stockings were all business. In a league with questionable organization, officiating, and, in some cases, honesty of its participants, British-born Harry Wright was the pillar of class and professionalism. He had assembled the unbeatable Cincinnati Red Stockings of 1869, and he was hired to do the same thing in Boston in 1871. He brought several of his old Cincinnati players to Boston, including Cal McVey and Charlie Gould, but most important was Harry's brother, George. The Red Stockings finished 2 games back in 1871, but that failure would not happen again.

From 1872–75 Boston went 205-50 for an .804 winning percentage. Wright not only brought holdovers from Cincinnati, he also lured some of the best young talent to Boston. Al Spalding, who pitched in every one of Boston's games in 1872, and Ross Barnes, who averaged more than 2 hits per game during his NA career, both came from the Rockford club. Each was just 21.

Barnes and George Wright ranked 1-2 in runs, hits, doubles, total bases, and slugging. Defensively, second baseman Barnes and shortstop Wright were unmatched. Wright had superb hands and perfected the method of bending his elbows when catching the ball to cushion the shock. Barnes' .904 fielding average on the choppy NA fields was as impressive as his .430 batting average. Boston led the NA in double plays and fielding average as the Red Stockings lost just once in 21 tries at South End Grounds.

Baby-faced Candy Cummings, accused of signing contracts with three different teams before the season, dominated on the mound for the Mutuals. The reputed inventor of the curveball pitched in all but one of New York's games, completing 53. Cummings tossed more innings than every *team* except Baltimore.

1871 NATIONAL ASSOCIATION

TEAM	W	L	T	PCT	GB	HW	HL	R	OR	PA	H	2B	3B	HR	BB	SO	HB	SH	AVG	OBP	SLG	OPS	AOPS	BR	ABR	PF	SB	CS	BSA	BSR
Ath	21	7	0	.750	—	12	3	376	266	1327	410	66	27	9	46	23	—	—	**.320**	**.344**	**.435**	**779**	**125**	**39**	**43**	99	56	12	82	8
Bos	20	10	1	.667	2	12	5	**401**	303	1432	**426**	**70**	37	3	**60**	19	—	—	.310	.339	.422	761	115	34	22	103	**73**	16	82	**10**
Chi	19	9	0	.679	2	**13**	3	302	**241**	1256	323	52	21	**10**	**60**	22	—	—	.270	.305	.374	679	86	-6	-34	111	69	21	77	8
Mut	16	17	0	.485	7.5	12	7	302	313	1437	403	43	21	1	33	15	—	—	.287	.303	.350	653	97	-21	10	91	46	15	75	5
Oly	15	15	2	.500	7	8	5	310	303	1401	375	54	26	6	48	13	—	—	.277	.302	.369	671	98	-12	5	95	48	13	79	6
Tro	13	15	1	.464	8	7	9	351	362	1297	384	51	34	6	49	19	—	—	.308	.334	.417	751	114	25	20	101	62	24	72	5
Cle	10	19	0	.345	11.5	3	10	249	341	1212	328	35	**40**	7	26	25	—	—	.277	.292	.391	683	102	-10	6	95	18	8	69	1
Kek	7	12	0	.368	9.5	5	4	137	243	779	178	19	8	2	33	**9**	—	—	.239	.271	.294	565	63	-34	-37	102	16	4	80	2
Rok	4	21	0	.160	15.5	3	4	231	287	1074	274	44	25	3	38	30	—	—	.264	.291	.364	655	92	-16	-5	96	53	10	**84**	8
Total	127	—	—	—	—	75	50	2659	—	11215	3101	434	239	47	393	175	—	—	.287	.312	.384	695	—	—	—	—	441	123	78	54

TEAM	CG	SHO	GR	SV	IP	H	HR	BB	SO	BR/9	ERA	AERA	OAV	OOB	PR	APR	PF	OSB	OCS	FA	E	WPB	DP	FW	PW	BW	BSW	DIF
Ath	27	0	1	0	249.0	329	3	53	16	13.8	4.95	81	.284	.315	-20	-27	95	—	—	.845	**194**	**28**	13	1.1	-1.8	**2.8**	.1	4.7
Bos	22	**1**	**9**	**3**	276.0	367	**2**	42	23	13.3	3.55	117	.273	.296	20	19	99	—	—	.834	243	38	**24**	-.3	1.2	1.4	**.3**	2.3
Chi	25	0	3	1	251.0	**308**	6	**28**	22	**12.0**	**2.76**	**166**	**.264**	**.281**	**41**	**47**	109	—	—	.829	229	83	16	-.8	**3.1**	-2.2	.1	4.8
Mut	**32**	**1**	1	0	293.0	373	7	42	22	12.7	3.72	102	.271	.292	16	3	90	—	—	.840	235	98	14	1.0	.2	.7	-.0	-2.3
Oly	**32**	0	0	0	282.0	371	4	45	13	13.3	4.37	95	.281	.305	-5	-6	99	—	—	**.850**	218	49	20	**1.5**	-.4	.3	.0	-1.4
Tro	28	0	1	0	250.0	431	4	75	12	18.2	5.51	76	.342	.378	-36	-36	100	—	—	.845	198	96	22	1.3	-2.3	1.3	-.0	-1.2
Cle	23	0	6	0	254.0	346	13	53	**34**	14.1	4.11	100	.283	.312	3	0	98	—	—	.818	234	175	15	-.6	.0	.4	-.3	-3.9
Kek	19	**1**	0	0	169.0	261	5	21	17	15.0	5.17	88	.305	.322	-18	-10	108	—	—	.803	163	55	8	-.9	-.7	-2.4	-.3	1.7
Rok	23	**1**	2	0	226.0	315	3	34	16	13.9	4.30	95	.282	.303	-2	-6	97	—	—	.821	220	76	14	-1.5	-.4	-.3	.1	-6.4
Total	231	4	23	4	2250.0	—	—	—	—	14.0	4.22	—	.287	.312	—	—	—	—	—	.833	1934	698	146	—	—	—	—	—

BATTER-FIELDER WINS	BATTING AVERAGE	ON-BASE PERCENTAGE	SLUGGING AVERAGE	ON-BASE PLUS SLUGGING	ADJUSTED OPS	ADJUSTED BATTER RUNS
Barnes-Bos 1.8	Meyerle-Ath 492	Meyerle-Ath 500	Meyerle-Ath 700	Meyerle-Ath 1200	Meyerle-Ath 243	Meyerle-Ath 23.5
Wood-Chi 1.2	McVey-Bos............431	G.Wright-Bos........453	Pike-Tro 654	G.Wright-Bos......1078	G.Wright-Bos........200	Wolters-Mut 17.2
Force-Oly 1.2	Barnes-Bos...........401	Barnes-Bos...........447	Bass-Cle 640	Pike-Tro 1054	Pike-Tro 194	Barnes-Bos...........17.1
Pike-Tro 1.1	King-Tro 396	McVey-Bos............435	Barnes-Bos...........580	Barnes-Bos.........1027	Wolters-Mut 189	Pike-Tro 15.0
McVey-Bos 1.1	Wood-Chi..............378	Wood-Chi..............425	Treacey-Chi 573	McVey-Bos.............991	Barnes-Bos............186	McVey-Bos...........14.0

RUNS	HITS	DOUBLES	TRIPLES	HOME RUNS	TOTAL BASES	RUNS BATTED IN
Barnes-Bos.............66	McVey-Bos..............66	Anson-Rok.............11	Bass-Cle 10	Treacey-Chi 4	Meyerle-Ath 91	Wolters-Mut 44
Birdsall-Bos 51	Meyerle-Ath 64		Wolters-Mut 9	Pike-Tro 4	Barnes-Bos.............91	McVey-Bos..............43
Radcliff-Ath.............47	Barnes-Bos.............63		Barnes-Bos...............9	Meyerle-Ath 4	Pike-Tro 85	Meyerle-Ath 40
Cuthbert-Ath............47	Start-Mut.................58		Pratt-Cle 8		McVey-Bos..............85	Pike-Tro 39
Waterman-Oly 46	King-Tro 57				King-Tro 79	

BASES ON BALLS	STOLEN BASES	BASE STEALING RUNS	FIELDING RUNS-INFIELD	FIELDING RUNS-OUTFIELD	OUTFIELD ASSISTS	CATCHER CS PCT.
Pinkham-Chi...........18	McGeary-Tro...........20	Wood-Chi..............3.3	Force-Oly.............17.8	Treacey-Chi 6.6	Treacey-Chi 7	
H.Wright-Bos 13	Wood-Chi................18	McGeary-Tro..........3.0	Barnes-Bos..........12.3	Hall-Oly..................5.5	King-Tro 6	
Barnes-Bos.............13	Cuthbert-Ath 16	Cuthbert-Ath 2.8	Wood-Chi...............8.3	Eggler-Mut.............4.5	York-Tro 5	
Wood-Chi................11	Leonárd-Oly............14	Mack-Rok 2.6	Pinkham-Chi..........8.3	Cuthbert-Ath 3.3	H.Wright-Bos 5	
	Eggler-Mut..............14	Cone-Bos...............2.3	Craver-Tro.............6.4	King-Tro 3.0	Ham-Rok 5	

WINS	WINNING PCT.	WINS ABOVE TEAM	GAMES STARTED	COMPLETE GAMES	FEWEST HITS/GAME	FEWEST BB/GAME
Spalding-Bos 19	McBride-Ath..........783	Wolters-Mut 8.0	Wolters-Mut 32	Wolters-Mut 31	Wolters-Mut 10.97	Zettlein-Chi 93
Zettlein-Chi 18	Zettlein-Chi 667	McBride-Ath...........5.2	Spalding-Bos 31	Brainard-Oly 30	Zettlein-Chi 11.14	Mathews-Kek.......1.12
McBride-Ath............18	Spalding-Bos 655	Pratt-Cle 5.0	Brainard-Oly 30	McMullin-Tro 28	McBride-Ath.......11.55	Wolters-Mut 1.24
Wolters-Mut 16	Wolters-Mut 500	Fisher-Rok.............2.0	McMullin-Tro 29	Zettlein-Chi 25	Spalding-Bos 11.65	Brainard-Oly 1.26
		Stearns-Oly 1.0		McBride-Ath............25	Pratt-Cle 11.86	Fisher-Rok...........1.31

STRIKEOUTS	STRIKEOUTS/GAME	GAMES	SAVES	BASE RUNNERS/9	ADJUSTED RELIEF RUNS	RELIEF RANKING
Pratt-Cle 34	Pratt-Cle 1.36	Wolters-Mut 32	H.Wright-Bos 3	Zettlein-Chi 12.08	Pinkham-Chi..........1.8	Pinkham-Chi..........2.0
Spalding-Bos 23	Mathews-Kek..........91	Spalding-Bos 31	Pinkham-Chi.............1	Wolters-Mut 12.21		
Zettlein-Chi 22	Zettlein-Chi 82	Brainard-Oly 30		Spalding-Bos 12.98		
Wolters-Mut 22	Spalding-Bos 80	McMullin-Tro 29		McBride-Ath.......13.18		
Mathews-Kek..........17	Wolters-Mut 70			Brainard-Oly 13.57		

INNINGS PITCHED	OPPONENTS' AVG.	OPPONENTS' OBP	EARNED RUN AVERAGE	ADJUSTED ERA	ADJUSTED STARTER RUNS	PITCHER WINS
Wolters-Mut 283.0	Wolters-Mut 263	Zettlein-Chi 283	Zettlein-Chi 2.73	Zettlein-Chi 168	Zettlein-Chi 45.0	**Zettlein-Chi 2.6**
Brainard-Oly 264.0	Zettlein-Chi 267	Wolters-Mut 285	Spalding-Bos 3.36	Spalding-Bos 124	Spalding-Bos 22.3	**Wolters-Mut........ 2.0**
Spalding-Bos 257.1	Spalding-Bos 268	Spalding-Bos 290	Wolters-Mut 3.43	Wolters-Mut 110	Wolters-Mut 11.6	**Spalding-Bos 1.6**
McMullin-Tro 249.0	Pratt-Cle 277	Fisher-Rok............302	Pratt-Cle 3.77	Pratt-Cle 110	Pratt-Cle 7.2	**Pratt-Cle 8**
Zettlein-Chi 240.2	McBride-Ath..........280	McBride-Ath..........307	Fisher-Rok...........4.35	Fisher-Rok.............94	Stearns-Oly 3.4	**Stearns-Oly 1**

Up in Smoke

The Kekiongas of Fort Wayne won the first National Association game ever played as Bobby Mathews shut out Forest City of Cleveland, 2-0, on May 4, 1871. James "Deacon" White of Cleveland doubled for the first hit in the first professional baseball league. The Kekiongas lasted only 19 games into the season and drew just 3,500 fans. It was the start of a disaster-prone pattern that pervaded the NA's tenure: teams open with great fanfare, teams fare poorly, teams draw poorly, teams fold.

The NA had no set schedule, per se; clubs made their own arrangements. They were supposed to play five series of three games each, with the champion being declared based on winning percentage. Of course, not everyone played all the requisite series. Teams with little to gain and longer to travel didn't make every road trip—and the NA wasn't big on discipline for those who strayed. Clubs were often more interested in lucrative non-scheduled "exhibition games" than in fulfilling their league schedule. It was not uncommon for clubs to play twice as many nonleague contests as NA games.

The NA drew 266,500 in its inaugural season; the White Stockings' 69,000 led the circuit even though the Great Chicago Fire wiped out their ballpark and uniforms late in the season. The White Stockings (ancestors of today's Cubs) gamely continued their schedule on the road, wearing an odd assortment of uniforms and finishing a close second. Chicago did not return to the league for two seasons.

The Philadelphia Athletics won the first pennant, thanks in part to two forfeits by Rockford, which left the league after just one year. Rockford's 19-year-old third baseman, Cap Anson, would shift to the Athletics in 1872.

Philadelphia's Levi Meyerle, a notoriously horrendous fielder during a time of rough fields and rougher scorekeepers, began a long tradition of hapless defenders who played every day for a simple reason: they could hit. Numbers calculated years later confirmed eyewitness accounts: His 1871 fielding average was an incomprehensible .642, but he slugged .700 for his hometown Athletics. The brief NA season may have afforded Meyerle just 26 games, but his .492 batting average has never been approached by any batsman in the 132 years following.

The Foundation of the Game: The National Association of Base Ball Players, 1857–70

Near the midpoint of the nineteenth century, one of America's bat and ball games—as played by a coterie of New Yorkers—became the foundation of what we know as the National Pastime. This group, known as the Knickerbocker Club, played under a set of rules developed by two of its members, Alexander Cartwright and Daniel Adams. Beginning in 1845, this duo set down the basic rules of the game, determining the number of players, number of outs, distances between the bases, and the distance between the batter and the pitcher: all key elements making the game of "Base Ball" different than its predecessors.

After contesting other local clubs for several years, Adams suggested the next logical step would be the formation of a national body to govern the game. Following his lead, in May of 1857, 16 New York-area clubs met and formed baseball's first group. Formally organized the following spring, the "National Association of Base Ball Players" would govern the game for the next several years.

At first, the National Association was definitely a New York-centric entity. However, with the admittance of New Brunswick's (NJ) Liberty club, interest in baseball began to spread beyond its New York origins. By 1860, nearly 25 percent of the member clubs hailed from outside the metropolitan area, representing nearly two dozen cities in seven states. (See table)

During the Civil War, attendance at the National Convention was cut in half. Despite this setback, the War Between the States actually helped solidify baseball's place at the forefront of American sports. Before the hostilities, baseball shared equal billing with cricket in the sporting weeklies. Unlike baseball, though, cricket's accoutrements did not lend themselves well to the soldiers in the field. On the other hand, for baseball, all one really needed was a bat and a ball.

After the Civil War, membership in the National Association tripled in 1866, then tripled again the following year. It was now a truly national organization, with less than 20 percent of its membership hailing from the New York metropolitan area. Nor could New York claim to have a monopoly on the best players, as strong clubs fielded powerful nines in Philadelphia (Athletic), Chicago (White Stockings) and Washington, DC (National).

In some ways baseball in the 1860s bore little resemblance to the current game. For instance, until 1865 a fly ball caught on one bounce was an out. Also, if a ball landed fair it was forever fair, even if it spun into foul territory short of the bag. Statistics were kept for each player at a very simple level, with only runs and outs tabulated by most clubs. Later in the decade, spearheaded by Henry Chadwick, the game's first statistician, other elements like hits and total bases were added to the mix. Finally, championship teams were determined, not by won-lost record, but by defeating the current flag holder in a home-and-home series.

By 1869, with membership well over the 500 mark, several National Association clubs distanced themselves from the membership by publicly turning professional. Although technically outlawed by the NA, many ball players had been compensated throughout the 1860s, either by receiving a percentage of the gate receipts or by being given a lucrative "no-show" job. The big difference in 1869 was that a handful of clubs, led by the Red Stockings of Cincinnati, openly gave their players a yearly salary.

By the end of the following year, with the number of professional clubs at 15, the National Association was at a crossroads. On the one hand, most—if not all—amateur clubs wanted to remain just that: a club that was a source of recreation for its members. On the other hand, the professionals were out to make a buck, giving paying customers a chance to see the best ball players in the land. With such divergent agendas, the rift that developed in March 1871 was inevitable. At that time, most of the National Association's professional members banded together to become the forerunner of today's major leagues in the National Association of Professional Base Ball Players.

The remaining amateur clubs reformed under the banner of the National Association of Amateur Base Ball Players for a couple of years, then quietly faded out of existence. By then, it was readily apparent that widespread interest in the game revolved around the professional clubs, who clearly attracted the best players in the land.

Although lasting only a short while, the original National Association laid the foundation of the game we know today. All of the basic rules of the National Game, as well as the methods governing the sport, were laid out by our forefathers nearly 150 years ago.

National Association: 1857–1870

YEAR	CLUBS	NY%	CITIES	STATES	CHAMPIONSHIP CLUB	CITY	RECORD
1857	16	100%	3	1	Atlantic	Brooklyn	7-1-1*
1858	25	96%	4	2	Mutual	New York	11-1*
1859	50	88%	10	2	Atlantic	Brooklyn	11-1
1860	59	76%	22	7	Atlantic	Brooklyn	12-2-2
1861	55	69%	19	6	Atlantic	Brooklyn	5-2
1862	33	97%	7	2	Eckford	Brooklyn	14-2
1863	32	84%	8	3	Eckford	Brooklyn	10-0
1864	28	79%	9	4	Atlantic	Brooklyn	20-0-1
1865	30	67%	11	4	Atlantic	Brooklyn	18-0
1866	93	55%	48	11	Atlantic	Brooklyn	17-3
1867	340	16%	182	23	Union	Morrisania**	21-8
1868	514	12%	275	27	Mutual	New York	31-10
1869 professional	12	25%	9	5	Atlantic	Brooklyn	40-6-2
1869 amateur	(500+)	NA		24+	Star	Brooklyn	16-6*
1870 professional	15	27%	14	7	White Stockings	Chicago	65-8
1870 amateur	(500+)	NA		23+	Star	Brooklyn	24-9*

Notes

* *Unofficial champions*

** *Morrisania is now part of The Bronx*

NA records not complete for 1869-70; membership may well have included more clubs and states

1869-70 amateur membership also included one club from Ontario

THE SCIENCE OF HITTING: THE BATTER REGISTER

The two most commonly repeated things about hitting are both, not coincidentally, attributed to the late Ted Williams. The first statement was a trifle whose significance is overblown almost as often as it is paraphrased:

"Baseball is the only field of endeavor where a man can succeed three times out of ten and be considered a good performer."—sourced as "widely quoted" in Baseball's Greatest Quotations.

It should not have to be said that Williams was obviously indulging in hyperbole to make a point and not being literal here. After all, it is inconceivable that a player with a lifetime on-base percentage of .482 would think that the success of a batter was measured solely by his batting average.

On the very next page of that same book, the caption next to Williams' picture reads: "Ted Williams, who once termed his 2,019 career bases on balls (the equivalent of four seasons of walking) as my 'proudest record.' " (Williams was second to Babe Ruth in career walks when he retired; that figure has since been corrected to 2,021 walks and has been surpassed by both Rickey Henderson and Barry Bonds.)

No one ever accused "The Splendid Splinter" of being indecisive, so how does one reconcile these two seemingly divergent attitudes? The best way to view Williams' attitude about hitting is to understand that it wasn't reducible to the kind of catchy phrase so loved by the pundits.

The other oft-repeated Williams' comment on hitting—as quoted in Joe Falls' *Sporting News* column of February 8, 1969—is much more substantial and deserves much more scrutiny:

"First of all, the hardest single thing to do in sports is to hit a baseball. If this is true and it is, then it takes more hours of practice, more hours of dedication, more hours of desire to hit a baseball than it does to do anything else."

One reason that Teddy Ballgame is considered by many as the greatest hitter of all time was that he *studied* hitting. He turned it inside out, tested it, and thought constantly about how to improve his approach. For him, hitting *was* baseball. The study of hitting was serious science. Williams honed his bats to perfection, refined his ideas of the strike zone, thought about whether to swing down or up on the ball, and studied pitchers as if they were helpless butterflies he was about to pin to black paper.

Heeding the advice of Rogers Hornsby—often called the best right-handed batter of all time—Williams elected simply not to swing at bad pitches, either taking his walk or forcing the pitcher to come in to him and give him something truly good to swing at. The details are spelled out in *The Science of Hitting*, Williams' classic text (co-authored with John Underwood), which was first published in 1970 and remains in-print today.

Williams' scientific view of batting had little to do with that of the early part of the twentieth century, the era of great hitters like Ty Cobb and Joe Jackson. Players of that time used the term "scientific baseball" to describe things that *managers* told *players* to do. Called "little ball" today, it used stratagems such as sacrifice bunting, squeeze bunting, drag bunting, hitting-and-running, stealing, hitting behind the runner, and the like. Being *scientific* in those days meant employing the right *plays*, rather than how a batter approached his turn at bat.

F.C. Lane's classic work *Batting* was first published in 1925. It was reprinted by SABR in 2001 and is now available from the University of Nebraska Press (www.unp.unl.edu). The book is a treasure trove of insight into attitudes about hitting in the early twentieth century; all of the following quotations come from its pages.

Feared slugger Joe Jackson typified the view of the day, opining that hitters had little choice but to step up to the plate and whale away. "I don't care whether the ball is over the plate or not, so long as it looks good," he said, "Batters can't be choosers. They have to take what the pitcher gives them. And pitchers are not very accommodating."

The greatest hitter of his day, Ty Cobb, disagreed. Cobb believed that hitters controlled their destiny, and that they didn't have to take advantage of their first offering. "Many batters have the mistaken idea that the pitcher is working on them and that there is nothing they can do in self-defense . . . [T]hey reason, 'We have to hit what he gives us.' That's only partially true, however. The batter is seldom compelled to hit any particular ball. He has a choice."

Despite that clear-eyed assessment, Cobb didn't take many more free passes than Jackson on a year-by-year basis. Both of them, though, were smart enough to take a walk when they weren't offered anything to hit.

One of the most patient hitters of the era was Eddie Collins, the great second baseman who, according to Walter Johnson, would "never bite at a bad ball." However, most of the most patient hitters of the day were not stars.

Jack Graney, who twice led the AL in walks, knew what he was trying to accomplish. "Not only does waiting a pitcher out impair his confidence and his control," he said, "But it also makes him work harder . . . I believe the waiting game is the most effective batting system that could possibly be devised."

Another Dead Ball Era player who might be applying for a job as an Oakland or Boston hitting instructor if he were around today was Burt Shotton, who twice topped the AL in walks and later was a successful manager. "The very name baseball is almost the same as base on balls," Shotton noted. "The spectator at the game is likely to look upon the base on balls as a mere incident; a momentary wildness on the part of the pitcher, or a gift to a dangerous batter. This opinion is often justified, but just as often the base on balls is a real tribute to the batter's skill in working the pitcher."

Ted Williams' idea of science was to treat his precious at bats as lab experiments performed under controlled conditions. If he had good equipment, a good idea of the pitcher's strengths and weaknesses, and an eye for the strike zone, Williams believed he could hit anyone at any time. His approach had very little to do with the intricacies of what was—and still is—thought of as "strategic" baseball. Williams himself was the one who made the difference while in the batter's box.

Williams became a truly great hitter by combining a tremendously strong uppercut swing—which he practiced for hours and hours—with discerning strike-zone judgment. Power and plate discipline are still an unbeatable combination.

The science of hitting has certainly changed over time—like everything else in the game—though thoughtful and analytical hitters have followed similar approaches in different eras. When circumstances change dramatically in baseball, failure to make the appropriate adjustments is usually followed by a quick ticket out of the league.

Failure to adjust is a cardinal sin when analyzing baseball statistics. Baseball stats are certainly comparable over time, but they are not *directly* comparable. To take stats from twenty-five years ago and compare them directly to today's numbers is risky; to take stats from 1904 and compare them directly to today's stats is silly. To make judgments based simply on comparing raw stats is sheer folly.

The numbers in this Batter Register provide one with the opportunity to examine the raw stats, the ability to put them into the proper context, and a chance to make informed judgments. Barry Bonds can be compared to Willie Mays, Ted Williams to Joe DiMaggio, Babe Ruth to Ty Cobb. Context is not everything, but it is essential to understanding most things—including the game of baseball and the stats it produces.

Biographical Information

There are 16,642 major league players listed in *The Baseball Encyclopedia*: 9,353 in the Batter Register and 7,601 in the Pitcher Register, which means that 312 players are listed in both the Batter and Pitcher Registers.

▲ at the end of the biographical information indicates that the player is also listed in the Pitcher Register. A player whose primary position was not pitcher must have pitched at least 9 innings to appear in the Pitcher Register.

There is a wealth of biographical information in a single line atop each player entry. The biographical information answers questions about a player's life away from the batter's box: When was he born? Did he live to a ripe old age? How tall was he? Was he ever a manager, and for how long? Did he miss time to the military? And was he one of rare few to reach the Hall of Fame? The biographical line is a reminder that a player is more than just a collection of numbers. More details on many of the statistics and formulas shown in this register can be found in the glossary at the end of the encylopedia.

Every player in this register has (at least) a last name and a debut date. If a player has a matronymic name, it is placed in parentheses—for example, Roberto Clemente (Walker). Nicknames are included in the biographical line; if a nickname is what the player is known by during his career, it will be part of his listed name—such as, McInnis,

Stuffy. Other features and abbreviations for biographical information follow.

B (mm.dd.yyyy) is the date and place of birth.

D (mm.dd.yyyy) is the date and place of death, if death has occurred.

The side of the plate a player bats from is expressed *BR* (bats right), *BL* (bats left), or *BB* (bats both sides). The arm the player throws with is expressed *TR* (throws right), or *TL* (throws left). If a player changed his batting handedness for a substantial length of time during his career (e.g., from switch-hitting to batting left-handed or vice versa), that change is noted.

Height is shown by feet followed by inches. Weight is expressed in pounds. For many players who played for more than one season after 1949, additional information about their playing weights has been added to this edition. This new, more accurate information is based on extensive research conducted by the editors into year-by-year playing weight information as published in official and quasi-official sources. Those sources include annual team press or media guides, official league publications, and a variety of other reliable annual reference works.

An asterisk after a player's weight indicates that the player's listed weight for every season in his big-league career varied by less than 10 pounds from the weight shown in the encyclopedia.

If a player's weight varied by more than 10 pounds from the weight shown in the encyclopedia, a weight range for that player's career is shown in parentheses. That range represents the lowest and highest weights that he was listed at during his big-league career.

This new information is obviously not perfect, but it is substantially better than anything previous baseball encyclopedias have published. Previously, encyclopedias showed only a single player weight, whether that player played but one game in the majors or played 2,000 games over 15 years. Moreover, that weight was typically what was listed in the player's debut season and never updated. (In earlier editions of *The ESPN Baseball Encyclopedia*, player weights were updated based on research done by Pete Palmer for players whose careers were five years or longer, where Palmer attempted to estimate the midpoint weight for those players' careers.)

Research is ongoing to obtain more accurate player weights pre-1950. However, less information is available from then, so how much weight information will be added in future editions is unclear.

Complete draft information is shown in square brackets in the biographical line for all major league players that were selected in the annual amateur/first-year player drafts that began in 1965. This information has never before been published in a baseball encyclopedia.

The format for each player's draft information is [Team/League/Year Drafted/Round/Pick Number]. Teams and leagues are abbreviated in the same way as in the player registers. The year drafted is shown with two digits (e.g., "89" means 1989; "00" means 2000). The round number shown is the round designated by MLB. Therefore, so-called "sandwich" picks at the end of the first round are shown as first-rounders; ditto for second- and third-round sandwich picks. The pick number is the overall ordinal number of that pick in that draft, *not* the team's pick number. That is because a team's third pick in a particular draft might come in the first round at No. 35 or might come in the fourth round at No. 115.

The defunct Secondary Drafts of players who had been selected by a club in a previous draft but did not sign a professional contract are indicated by a capital *S* before the draft round number. The defunct January drafts (both Regular and Secondary) are indicated by an asterisk after the year; all other drafts were held in June.

The original amateur draft in 1965 had a unique format. From 1966–86, drafts were held in both January and June. After 1986, all four drafts were consolidated into a single June draft. In the late 1990s, MLB officially changed the name of the June amateur draft to the "First-Year Player Draft" after players like J.D. Drew signed pro contracts with independent league teams instead of signing with the major league club that had drafted them.

Team codes are shown as of the year the player was drafted, not the year of that player's major league debut and therefore, a player like Justin Baughman is shown as being drafted by California in 1995 [CalA95] even though he made his debut after the Angels had changed the team name to Anaheim.

Non-drafted players who started their pro careers after 1965, whether because they were ineligible for the draft (like most non-Americans) or because they weren't considered good enough prospects to be drafted, will have no draft information shown.

Debuts are marked *d* followed by the date the player made his first major league appearance. The debut year is the first year listed in the register, so it is not included in the biographical line.

Besides these basic pieces of information available in the biographical line, there are several other designations for players whose career, family, or duty took them beyond the norm.

If a player on a major league roster missed significant parts of any season serving the United States during wartime, the following abbreviations are used to identify how the player served:

Mil indicates military service in the army, navy, air force, or marines;

Mer indicates the merchant marine;

Def indicates defense plant work.

The seasons the player missed at least a part of are listed after the abbreviation for duty. At least one major leaguer missed time during the seasons below as a result of the following wars (dates include post-war service by some veterans):

Spanish-American War, 1898;
World War I, 1917–19;
World War II, 1941–46;
Korean War 1951–59;
Vietnam War 1962–72.

Many major league ballplayers served in the military after their playing days were over. That military service is not shown, which is why former New York Giants player Eddie Grant—who last played in 1915 and died in action World War I three years later—does not have a "Mil" in his bio info. A monument was erected to Grant at the Polo Grounds in 1921.

Negro Lg indicates a player played for a big-league caliber Negro League team prior to playing in the major leagues. The first and last years he played with such a Negro League team are shown. Because of the unstable nature of some Negro Leagues and of many Negro League teams—and because of the often-erratic schedules even in their best years—these dates do not necessarily indicate continuous service in the Negro Leagues. If a former Negro League player also served in the military during wartime, his military service will be shown even if it predates his major league debut.

For a list of all of the Negro Leagues that are considered to be of major league caliber, see the Black Baseball and Negro Leagues section of the encyclopedia.

If the player spent time as a coach, manager, or umpire, that is indicated by the following symbols which are followed by the number of seasons during which he performed those jobs. Abbreviations are:

C: Coach;
M: Manager;
U: Umpire.

HF indicates that the player is a member of the Hall of Fame; the year of election follows HF.

If the player had a close family member in the major leagues, the relative's relationship is identified by the codes listed below followed by the relative's first name (and, if it is different, the last name):

b: brother;
twb: twin brother;
f: father;
s: son;
gf: grandfather;
gs: grandson;
ggf: great grandfather;
ggs: great grandson.

Col indicates that the player played collegiate baseball at the university, college, or junior college shown. If a player played collegiate ball at more than one school, only the last school is shown. Typically, players transfer from two-years schools to four-year schools or from one four-years school to another, but a few have reversed that course and transferred from a four-year school to a junior or community college.

If a two-year school does not have *CC* for "Community College," *JC* for "Junior College," or *City* for "City College" as part of its name, we have appended [*JC*] to its name to indicate that. Note that, if a player attended a college but didn't play collegiate baseball there, no college is shown.

Because many colleges and universities have changed their names in the past, and because many of these older names would not be recognizable today, we show the institution's current name, not the name when that player played ball there. North Carolina State University—shown in the player registers as "North Carolina St."—is a good example why this is necessary:

- North Carolina College of Agriculture and Mechanic Arts 1887–1917
- North Carolina College of Agriculture and Engineering 1917–1963
- North Carolina State of the
- University of North Carolina at Raleigh 1963–1965
- North Carolina State University at Raleigh 1965–present

NC State has had a baseball team every year since 1903, except for 1916. More than a dozen major league players played ball at NCSU prior to 1963, yet almost no one except NC State alumni would recognize the earliest names of that institution if we showed them in a player's bio line.

A few players will have additional information shown in the biographical lines. DL information will be shown in the bio line for those years when that player didn't play in any games. Career games played at the three outfield positions (*LF/CF/RF*) will also be included at the end of the biographical information for some players if there is not enough room to place it in their Games at Position column.

STATISTICAL INFORMATION

Symbols in the first two columns:

† before the team name means he participated in Postseason Play that year;

★ after team name means he participated in All-Star game;

☆ after team name means he was selected to All-Star team but did not play;

✳ after team name means he was selected to All-Star team but replaced due to injury.

Boldface statistics in any category indicates a league-leading total or average.

The columns that appear in the player register after Year:

TM: Team. Each team is identified by a three-letter code that is usually the first three letters of the city, state, or area where the team is located.

LG: League. The leagues in this book include the National League (N), the American League (A), the Federal League (F), the Players League (P), the Union Association (U), the National Association (NA), and the American Association (AA).

G: Games. The number of games are boldfaced if the player appeared in all of his team's games for a given year.

AB: At Bats.

R: Runs.

H: Hits.

2B: Doubles.

3B: Triples.

HR: Home Runs.

RBI: Runs Batted In. RBI information is unavailable for 1882–84 American Association and 1884 Union Association. Since 1939, runs scoring on a groundball double play have not been counted as RBIs.

BB: Bases on Balls. Generally referred to today as walks.

IB: Intentional Base on Balls. Walking an opponent on purpose was first counted as a distinct category in 1955.

HP: Hit-by-Pitch. The rule awarding first base to batters hit by pitches was instituted in 1884 by the American Association. It was adopted in 1887 by the National League.

SO: Strikeouts. Strikeouts are available for batters in all years except for 1884 in the Union Association, from 1882–88 and 1890 in the American Association, from 1897–1909 in the National League, and 1901–12 in the American League.

AVG: Batting Average. Hits divided by at bats.

OBP: On-Base Percentage. The official definition of on-base percentage, which was established when OBP was made an official statistic in 1984, is: (hits plus walks plus hit-by-pitches) divided by (at bats plus walks plus hit-by-pitches plus sacrifice flies). This definition is used for 1954 and all later seasons. In the years prior to 1954, the definition depends on the data available.

SLG: Slugging Percentage. Total bases divided by at bats.

AOPS: Adjusted On-Base plus Slugging. On-base percentage and slugging average are added and normalized for the context of the offensive level of the league and the player's home park(s) and then converted to a scale in which 100 is average.

ABR: Adjusted Batting Runs. The linear weights values of the offensive events that the player's plate appearances precipitated are added and then normalized for the context of the offensive level of the league and the player's home park(s). It is then converted to a scale in which 0 is average and the output is the number of runs the player's batting added to or subtracted from his team compared what an average player would have done.

SB: Stolen Bases. Totals are available for all seasons in all leagues from 1886 on, as well as for all the seasons of the National Association.

CS: Caught Stealing. Totals are available for all American League players in 1914–15 and from 1920 on; caught stealing totals are available for all National League players in 1913, 1915, from 1920–26, and from 1951 on. Caught Stealing totals are also available for 1916 for all players who stole at least 20 bases.

FA: Fielding Average. Determined by the formula: (Assists plus Putouts) divided by (Assists plus Putouts plus Errors).

FR: Fielding Runs. This measures how many runs the player saves or loses for his team in the field compared to an average fielder. The formula takes into account assists, putouts, errors, and double plays, as well as passed balls for catchers. All of these defensive statistics are adjusted for context in several different ways. Defensive innings are based on play-by-play from 1969 forward and were estimated for previous years.

RNG: Range. This is calculated different ways for different positions. For infielders, range is based on assists per inning. For outfielders, range is based on putouts per inning. For catchers, range is based on stolen bases allowed per inning. The data is then adjusted in comparison to the league average, with 100 equaling league average—higher is always better. (Thus a 110 rating for a catcher means 10 percent fewer stolen bases allowed than average.) All statistics are adjusted for context, including the number of balls put into play and what direction the balls in play were likely to go in. Innings played data was calculated from play-by-play accounts from 1969 forward and is estimated for previous seasons. Outfielders are rated for their play at all outfield (weighted) positions, while infielders are only rated for their play at their primary position.

THR: Throwing. Throwing is calculated different ways for different positions. For infielders, throwing is based on double plays per inning. For outfielders, throwing is based on assists per inning. For catchers, throwing is based on caught stealing rates per inning. The data is then adjusted in comparison to league average, with 100 equaling league average. All statistics are adjusted for context by various methods. Innings played data was calculated from play-by-play accounts from 1969 forward and is estimated for previous seasons. Outfielders are rated for their play at all outfield positions, while infielders are only rated for their play at their primary position.

Stolen bases and caught stealing off catchers are italicized for both *range and throwing* for years prior to 1969 to indicate data was estimated from player and team data.

GAMES AT POSITION. Positions are listed left to right by decreasing number of games. The number of games played at each position is shown for every player—year-by-year and for his career.

Positions are identified by easily recognizable one- or two-letter abbreviations:

P: Pitcher.

1b: First Base.

2b: Second Base.

3b: Third Base.

S: Shortstop.

O: Outfield.

D: Designated Hitter.

M: Player-Manager (always at end of position codes),

/H: Pinch-Hitter (used only if player had no other position).

/R: Pinch-Runner (used only if player had no other position).

Position codes are followed by the number of games that the player played at that position during a season or in his career. Different positions are normally separated by commas, except when a slash (/) is used to indicate that the player played only one game at positions to the right of the slash. (No commas are used to separate such positions.)

Because the official statistics lump the three outfield positions into only one "outfield" position, the official number of games in the Outfield is always shown first with an *O*. If the player only played one outfield position in that year or in his career, that position will be identified by an *L*, *C*, or *R* after the number of games played.

If the player played two or three outfield positions in a year or in his career, a breakdown of the games in left, center, and right is presented in that order in parentheses, separated by slashes. When a player's career breakdown of games in left, center, and right won't fit in the Games at Position column totals line, that information has been added to the end of the player's biographical information. *If so, the primary outfield position played will be identified by L, C, or R following the number of games played in the outfield in the totals line.*

DL: Disabled List. This new category of information—never-before-published in an encyclopedia—shows the number of days spent on the major league disabled list, year-by-year and for each player's career. All DL assignments from 1941 to the present are shown. If a player was not disabled, his DL column will show zero for that year; if he was never disabled, his DL column will show zero for his career. Before 1941, when there was no DL, an em dash (—) is shown.

The **DL** column in the batter and pitcher registers shows the number of *days* (not *games*) missed by that player during the regular season while he was on the disabled list. If a player was assigned to the DL more than once during a particular season, the lengths of all his DL stints are combined. Time spent on the DL before Opening Day or after the last day of the regular season is not counted, which is why some players will have Days on DL data that is less than the minimum (currently 15 days).

A DL column entry of 166 or greater from 1941–58 indicates that a player spent the whole season on the DL since the length of the regular season in those years was 166–167 days. From 1959–68, the regular season was 171–174 days long, except for the 1960 AL (167 days), which opened almost a week later than the NL.

With expansion to two divisions in 1969, the regular season was stretched to 178–181 days, except in the strike year of 1972 (172 days). From 1982 to the present, the normal season has been 181–183 days long; in the last 20 years, the only seasons that were shorter than 182 days were due to lockouts or strikes in 1990 (178 days), 1994 (131), and 1995 (160). Because of the interruption of the season caused by September 11, the 2001 season went a week longer than its scheduled 183 days. (Note that the early season-opening series in Japan in 2000 and 2004 were not counted as part of the regular-season length.)

If a player spent all or part of any season on the major league DL but did not play in any games that year, his DL information is shown in square brackets at the end of his bio line. The format for these entries is [DL Year Tm Lg Days on DL]. If a player (e.g., Albert Belle) spent time on the DL in more than one season in which he never played, these DL stints will be separated by commas inside a single set of square brackets in his bio line.

In the rare cases when a player was traded while on the DL, the number of days he spent on the DL is shown separately for each team, but no total is shown for that year. There are also a small number of zero-day DL stints where players were put on the DL in the off-season (typically in the spring) but were activated on or before Opening Day and didn't miss any time during the regular season. If such a DL stint is the player's only time on the DL in a given season, we show a zero in the DL column.

The forerunner of the modern DL was instituted in 1941. Aside from a brief experiment by the NL in 1915–16 with a Disabled List (from which no records of disabled players have been found), seriously injured players were simply sent home by major league teams and told to report back when they were healthy enough to play again. If the club wanted to retain future rights to injured players, they simply placed them on the Suspended or Voluntary Retired lists—meaning that injured players were removed from major league rosters and didn't draw a salary, yet these same players still couldn't try to sign on with any other team in Organized Baseball.

The rules for using the DL in the 1940s were quite strict: Only two players from a club could be on the DL at any one time, players had to spend at least 60 days on the DL, and no one could be placed on the DL after August 1. Because of these strict rules and the depletion of top-flight talent during World War II, major league clubs very rarely used the DL before the 1950s. Fewer than a dozen players total ever spent time on the DL before 1946, and the first season that more than 12 players were assigned to the DL was 1950.

After the 1949 season, the rules were liberalized so that players needed to spend only 30 days on the DL. Many other changes to the rules governing disabled players have been made since 1960; 15-day DL stints were allowed for the first time in 1966.

BFW: Batter-Fielder Wins. The sum of a player's batting wins, basestealing wins, and fielding wins, this figure indicates how many games the player won or lost for his team compared to an average player.

For any missing data, such as CS, RBI or SO, the career total is underlined if it is a partial figure.

AARON, HANK Henry Louis "The Hammer"; B2.5.1934 Mobile AL; BR/TR/6´0˝/(170–180); d4.13; HF1982; b–Tommie; Negro Lg 1952; OF(313/293/2184)

YEAR	TM LG	G	AB	R	H	2B	3B	HR	RBI	BB-IB	HP	SO	AVG	OBP	SLG	AOPS	ABR	SB-CS	FA	FR	RNG	THR	GAMES AT POSITION	DL	BFW
1954	Mil N	122	468	58	131	27	6	13	69	28	3	39	.280	.322	.447	105	1	2-2	.970	-6	93	64	O116(105/0/11)	0	-1.2
1955	Mil N★	153	602	105	189	**37**	9	27	106	49-5	3	61	.314	.366	.540	144	37	3-1	.967	1	99	82	O126(26/0/105),2b27	0	3.4
1956	Mil N★	153	609	106	**200**	**34**	14	26	92	37-6	2	54	**.328**	.365	.558	154	43	2-4	.962	4	105	119	O152R	0	**4.1**
1957	†Mil N★	151	615	**118**	198	27	6	**44**	**132**	57-15	0	58	.322	.378	.600	170	58	1-1	.983	-5	97	77	O150(1/69/83)	0	4.7
1958	†Mil N★	153	601	109	196	34	4	30	95	59-16	1	49	.326	.386	.546	157	48	4-1	.984	-4	97	95	O153(0/39/120)	0	3.9
1959	Mil N★	154	629	116	**223**	46	7	39	123	51-17	4	54	**.355**	.401	**.636**	**188**	**77**	8-0	.982	-6	88	102	O152(0/13/144),3b5	0	**6.6**
1960	Mil N★	153	590	102	172	20	11	40	**126**	60-13	2	63	.292	.352	.566	160	46	16-7	.982	4	**108**	89	O153(0/3/151),2b2	0	4.5
1961	Mil N★	**155**	603	115	197	**39**	10	34	120	56-20	2	64	.327	.381	.594	**165**	**55**	21-9	.982	4	109	93	O154(0/71/88),3b2	0	**5.1**
1962	Mil N★	156	592	127	191	28	6	45	128	66-14	3	73	.323	.390	.618	171	58	15-7	.980	1	105	95	O153(0/83/71)/1	0	5.2
1963	Mil N★	161	631	**121**	201	29	4	**44**	**130**	78-18	0	94	.319	.391	**.586**	**180**	**66**	31-5	.979	-8	92	79	O161R	0	5.4
1964	Mil N★	145	570	103	187	30	2	24	95	62-9	0	46	.328	.393	.514	152	41	22-4	.983	7	115	133	O139R,2b11	0	4.5
1965	Mil N★	150	570	109	181	**40**	1	32	89	60-10	1	81	.318	.379	.560	161	47	24-4	.987	6	111	89	O148R	0	4.8
1966	Atl N★	158	603	117	168	23	1	**44**	**127**	76-15	1	96	.279	.356	.539	144	36	21-3	.988	8	**114**	109	O158(0/4/158),2b2	0	3.8
1967	Atl N★	155	600	**113**	184	37	3	**39**	109	63-19	0	97	.307	.369	**.573**	169	**53**	17-6	.979	6	110	106	O152(0/11/141)/2	0	5.4
1968	Atl N★	160	606	84	174	33	4	29	86	64-23	1	62	.287	.354	.498	154	40	28-5	.991	11	**121**	103	O151R,1b14	0	**5.0**
1969	†Atl N★	147	547	100	164	30	3	44	97	87-19	2	47	.300	.396	.607	176	57	9-10	.982	2	105	100	O144R,1b4	0	5.1
1970	Atl N★	150	516	103	154	26	1	38	118	74-15	2	63	.298	.385	.574	146	34	9-0	.977	2	110	74	O125R,1b11	0	3.0
1971	Atl N★	139	495	95	162	22	3	47	118	71-**21**	2	58	.327	.410	**.669**	**190**	58	1-1	.996	-9	77	92	1b71,O60(1/0/59)	0	4.2
1972	Atl N★	129	449	75	119	10	0	34	77	92-15	1	55	.265	.390	.514	143	28	4-0	.987	1	101	88	1b109,O15R	0	2.2
1973	Atl N★	120	392	84	118	12	1	40	96	68-13	1	51	.301	.402	.643	173	39	1-1	.977	1	91	63	O105(87/0/18)	0	3.5
1974	Atl N★	112	340	47	91	16	0	20	69	39-6	0	29	.268	.341	.491	127	11	1-0	.986	-3	89	54	O89L	0	0.5
1975	Mil A★	137	465	45	109	16	2	12	60	70-3	1	51	.234	.332	.355	95	-2	0-1	1.000	-1	38	0	D128,O3L	0	-0.6
1976	Mil A	85	271	22	62	8	0	10	35	35-1	0	38	.229	.315	.369	102	1	0-1	1.000	0	207	0	D74/lf	0	-0.1
Total	23	3298	12364	2174	3771	624	98	755	2297	1402-293	32	1383	.305	.374	.555	156	932	240-73	.980	17	103	93	O2760R,1b210,D202,2b43,3b7	0	83.0

AARON, TOMMIE Tommie Lee; B8.5.1939 Mobile AL; D8.16.1984 Atlanta GA; BR/TR/6´1˝/200; d4.10; C6; b–Hank

YEAR	TM LG	G	AB	R	H	2B	3B	HR	RBI	BB-IB	HP	SO	AVG	OBP	SLG	AOPS	ABR	SB-CS	FA	FR	RNG	THR	GAMES AT POSITION	DL	BFW
1962	Mil N	141	334	54	77	20	2	8	38	41-0	0	58	.231	.312	.374	86	-6	6-0	.989	4	**120**	**121**	1b110,O42L/23	0	-0.6
1963	Mil N	72	135	6	27	6	1	1	15	11-1	0	27	.200	.257	.281	57	-8	0-3	1.000	-3	61	151	1b45,O14(14/1/0),2b6/3	0	-1.5
1965	Mil N	8	16	1	3	0	0	0	1	1-0	0	2	.188	.235	.188	21	-2	0-0	.961	0	138	85	1b6	0	-0.2
1968	Atl N	98	283	21	69	10	3	1	25	21-1	0	37	.244	.295	.311	82	-6	3-4	.942	-2	88	87	O62L,1b28/3	0	-1.5
1969	†Atl N	49	60	13	15	2	0	1	5	6-0	0	6	.250	.318	.333	82	-1	0-1	1.000	0	50	113	1b16,O8L	0	-0.3
1970	Atl N	44	63	3	13	2	0	2	7	3-0	0	10	.206	.242	.333	50	-5	0-0	.955	-2	48	22	1b16,O12(10/0/2)	0	-0.7
1971	Atl N	25	53	4	12	2	0	0	3	3-1	0	5	.226	.268	.264	48	-4	0-0	.974	1	103	222	1b11,3b7	0	-0.3
Total	7	437	944	102	216	42	6	13	94	86-3	0	145	.229	.292	.327	75	-32	9-8	.990	-1	101	120	1b232,O138(136/1/2),3b10,2b7	0	-5.1

ABAD, ANDY Fausto Andres; B8.25.1972 Palm Beach FL; BL/TL/6´1˝/(184–210); [BosA93 16/443]; d9.10; Col Middle Georgia JC

YEAR	TM LG	G	AB	R	H	2B	3B	HR	RBI	BB-IB	HP	SO	AVG	OBP	SLG	AOPS	ABR	SB-CS	FA	FR	RNG	THR	GAMES AT POSITION	DL	BFW
2001	Oak A	1	1	0	0	0	0	0	0	0-0	0	0	.000	.000	.000	-99	0	0-0	1.000	0	0	1175	/1	0	0.0
2003	Bos A	9	17	1	2	0	0	0	0	2-0	0	5	.118	.211	.118	-10	-3	0-1	.973	-1	32	55	1b7/rf	0	-0.5
2006	Cin N	5	3	0	0	0	0	0	0	2-0	0	0	.000	.400	.000	15	0	0-0	ø	0	—	—	/H	0	-0.1
Total	3	15	21	1	2	0	0	0	0	4-0	0	5	.095	.240	.095	-7	-3	0-1	.974	-1	31	84	1b8/rf	0	-0.6

ABADIE, JOHN John; B11.4.1854 Philadelphia PA; D5.17.1905 Pemberton NJ; BR/TR/6´0˝/192; d4.26

YEAR	TM LG	G	AB	R	H	2B	3B	HR	RBI	BB-IB	HP	SO	AVG	OBP	SLG	AOPS	ABR	SB-CS	FA	FR	RNG	THR	GAMES AT POSITION	DL	BFW
1875	Cen NA	11	45	3	10	0	0	0	4	0	—	3	.222	.222	.222	60	-2	1-0	.912	-0	141	18	1b11	—	-0.1
	Atl NA	1	4	1	1	0	0	0	1	0	—	0	.250	.250	.250	85	0	0-0	.875	-0	0	0	/1	—	0.0
	Year	12	49	4	11	0	0	0	5	0	—	3	.224	.224	.224	62	-2	1-0	.910	-1	132	17	1b12	—	-0.1

ABBATICCHIO, ED Edward James "Batty"; B4.15.1877 Latrobe PA; D1.6.1957 Ft.Lauderdale FL; BR/TR/5´11˝/170; d9.4

YEAR	TM LG	G	AB	R	H	2B	3B	HR	RBI	BB-IB	HP	SO	AVG	OBP	SLG	AOPS	ABR	SB-CS	FA	FR	RNG	THR	GAMES AT POSITION	DL	BFW
1897	Phi N	3	10	0	3	0	0	0	0	1	0	—	.300	.364	.300	78	0	0	.875	-1	106	0	2b3	—	-0.1
1898	Phi N	25	92	9	21	4	0	0	14	7	1	—	.228	.290	.272	64	-4	4	.818	-10	50	0	3b20,2b4/rf	—	-1.3
1903	Bos N	136	489	61	111	18	5	1	46	52	4	—	.227	.306	.290	73	-16	23	.934	3	96	86	2b116,S17	—	-1.1
1904	Bos N	154	579	76	148	18	10	3	54	40	5	—	.256	.309	.337	103	1	24	.915	4	99	77	S154	—	1.0
1905	Bos N	153	610	70	170	25	12	3	41	35	8	—	.279	.326	.374	111	7	30	.919	-13	93	84	S152/cf	—	-0.2
1907	Pit N	147	496	63	130	14	7	2	82	65	8	—	.262	.357	.331	114	11	35	.951	-22	90	76	2b147	—	-1.1
1908	Pit N	146	500	43	125	16	7	1	61	58	7	—	.250	.336	.316	108	7	22	**.969**	-17	98	108	2b144	—	-1.0
1909	†Pit N	36	87	13	20	0	0	1	16	19	0	—	.230	.368	.264	89	0	2	.966	0	113	101	S18,2b4/cf	—	0.1
1910	Pit N	3	3	0	0	0	0	0	0	0	0	0	.000	.000	.000	-95	-1	0	.500	-0	96	0	/S	—	-0.1
	Bos N	52	178	20	44	4	2	0	10	12	0	16	.247	.295	.292	68	-8	2	.910	-2	107	97	S46/2	—	-0.8
	Year	55	181	20	44	4	2	0	10	12	0	16	.243	.290	.287	66	-8	2	.907	-2	107	96	S47/2	—	-0.9
Total	9	855	3044	355	772	99	43	11	324	289	33	16	.254	.325	.325	98	-3	142	.949	-59	94	88	2b419,S388,3b20,O3(0/2/1)	—	-4.6

ABBEY, CHARLIE Charles S.; B10.14.1866 Falls City NE; D4.27.1926 San Francisco CA; BL/TL/5´8.5˝/169; d8.16

YEAR	TM LG	G	AB	R	H	2B	3B	HR	RBI	BB-IB	HP	SO	AVG	OBP	SLG	AOPS	ABR	SB-CS	FA	FR	RNG	THR	GAMES AT POSITION	DL	BFW
1893	Was N	31	116	11	30	1	4	0	12	12	1	6	.259	.333	.336	80	-4	9	.937	3	113	76	O31L	—	-0.3
1894	Was N	129	523	95	164	26	18	7	101	58	7	38	.314	.389	.472	110	8	31	.909	8	113	99	O129(54/74/0)	—	0.5
1895	Was N	**133**	516	102	142	14	10	8	84	43	7	43	.275	.339	.388	88	-11	28	.902	7	166	152	O133(3/99/31)	—	-1.0
1896	Was N	79	301	47	79	12	6	1	49	27	4	20	.262	.331	.352	80	-9	16	.879	-3	125	112	O78(2/11/65)/P	—	-1.3
1897	Was N	80	300	52	78	14	8	3	34	27	4	—	.260	.329	.390	90	-5	9	.946	1	120	42	O80(2/1/77)	—	-0.7
Total	5	452	1756	307	493	67	46	19	280	167	23	107	.281	.351	.404	93	-21	93	.910	15	132	105	O451(92/185/173)/P	—	-2.8

ABBOTT, FRED Harry Frederick (b Harry Frederick Winbigler); B10.22.1874 Versailles OH; D6.11.1935 Los Angeles CA; BR/TR/5´10˝/180; d4.25

YEAR	TM LG	G	AB	R	H	2B	3B	HR	RBI	BB-IB	HP	SO	AVG	OBP	SLG	AOPS	ABR	SB-CS	FA	FR	RNG	THR	GAMES AT POSITION	DL	BFW
1903	Cle A	77	255	25	60	11	3	1	25	7	5	—	.235	.270	.314	76	-8	8	.958	5	*113*	*111*	C71,1b3	—	0.5
1904	Cle A	41	130	14	22	4	2	0	12	6	0	—	.169	.206	.231	38	-9	2	.953	-1	*115*	*109*	C33,1b7	—	-0.8
1905	Phi N	42	128	9	25	6	1	0	12	6	3	—	.195	.248	.258	53	-7	4	.954	2	*119*	*88*	C34,1b5	—	-0.3
Total	3	160	513	48	107	21	6	1	49	19	8	—	.209	.248	.279	61	-24	14	.956	6	*115*	*105*	C138,1b15	—	-0.6

ABBOTT, JEFF Jeffrey William; B8.17.1972 Atlanta GA; BR/TL/6´2˝/(190–200); [ChiA94 4/117]; d6.10; Col Kentucky

YEAR	TM LG	G	AB	R	H	2B	3B	HR	RBI	BB-IB	HP	SO	AVG	OBP	SLG	AOPS	ABR	SB-CS	FA	FR	RNG	THR	GAMES AT POSITION	DL	BFW
1997	Chi A	19	38	8	10	1	0	1	2	0-0	0	6	.263	.263	.368	65	-2	0-0	1.000	1	136	0	O10(5/1/4),D3	0	-0.2
1998	Chi A	89	244	33	68	14	1	12	41	9-1	0	28	.279	.298	.492	104	0	3-3	.971	-4	96	0	O76(20/38/27),D2	0	-0.5
1999	Chi A	17	57	5	9	0	0	2	6	5-0	0	12	.158	.222	.263	24	-7	1-1	.962	-2	81	0	O17L	0	-0.9
2000	†Chi A	80	215	31	59	15	1	3	29	21-1	2	38	.274	.343	.395	84	-5	2-1	.981	-5	85	67	O65(20/33/16),D7	0	-1.0
2001	Fla N	28	42	5	11	3	0	0	5	3-0	1	7	.262	.333	.333	74	-2	0-0	.963	0	116	0	O17(1/9/8)	72	-0.1
Total	5	233	596	82	157	33	2	18	83	38-2	3	91	.263	.307	.416	84	-16	6-5	.974	-10	93	25	O185(63/81/55),D12	72	-2.7

ABBOTT, KURT Kurt Thomas; B6.2.1969 Zanesville OH; BR/TR/6´0˝/(170–200); [OakA89 15/400]; d9.7; Col St. Petersburg (FL) JC; OF(32/4/8)

YEAR	TM LG	G	AB	R	H	2B	3B	HR	RBI	BB-IB	HP	SO	AVG	OBP	SLG	AOPS	ABR	SB-CS	FA	FR	RNG	THR	GAMES AT POSITION	DL	BFW
1993	Oak A	20	61	11	15	1	0	3	9	3-0	0	20	.246	.281	.410	88	-2	2-0	.971	1	129	136	O13L,S6,2b2	0	-0.1
1994	Fla N	101	345	41	86	17	3	9	33	16-1	5	98	.249	.291	.394	74	-14	3-0	.966	-4	95	99	S99	0	-1.0
1995	Fla N	120	420	60	107	18	7	17	60	36-4	5	110	.255	.318	.452	100	-2	4-3	.959	-16	89	96	S115	11	-0.9
1996	Fla N	109	320	37	81	18	7	8	33	22-1	3	99	.253	.307	.428	94	-4	3-3	.969	-3	99	130	S44,3b33,2b20	38	-0.4
1997	†Fla N	94	252	35	69	18	2	6	30	14-3	1	68	.274	.315	.433	97	-2	3-1	.969	0	95	78	2b54,O10L,S7,3b4,D2	0	0.1
1998	Oak A	35	123	17	33	7	1	2	9	10-0	1	34	.268	.326	.390	87	-2	2-1	.909	-7	90	92	S28,O5(5/0/1)/3D	16	-0.7
	Col N	42	71	9	18	6	0	3	15	2-0	1	19	.254	.276	.465	76	-2	0-0	.929	1	122	0	O9(4/0/5),2b7,S7,3b3/D	0	-0.2
1999	Col N	96	286	41	78	17	2	8	41	16-0	0	69	.273	.310	.430	68	-14	3-2	.989	-5	94	81	2b66,1b8,O4(0/2/2),S3	30	-1.6
2000	†NY N	79	157	22	34	7	1	6	12	14-2	1	51	.217	.283	.389	72	-8	1-1	.953	-6	89	59	S39,2b23,3b2,O2C	26	-1.1
2001	Atl N	6	9	0	2	0	0	0	0	0-0	0	3	.222	.222	.222	15	-1	1-0	1.000	2	245	0	/2S	177	0.1
Total	9	702	2044	273	523	109	23	62	242	133-11	17	571	.256	.305	.423	84	-51	22-11	.958	-38	93	99	S349,2b173,3b43,O43L,1b8,D6	298	-5.8

ABBOTT, ODY Ody Cleon; B9.5.1888 New Eagle PA; D4.13.1933 Washington DC; BR/TR/6´2˝/180; d9.10; Col Washington & Jefferson

YEAR	TM LG	G	AB	R	H	2B	3B	HR	RBI	BB-IB	HP	SO	AVG	OBP	SLG	AOPS	ABR	SB-CS	FA	FR	RNG	THR	GAMES AT POSITION	DL	BFW
1910	StL N	22	70	2	13	2	1	0	6	6	0	20	.186	.250	.243	46	-5	3	.982	1	109	70	O21C	—	-0.6

ABERCROMBIE, FRANCIS Francis Patterson; B1.2.1851 Fort Towson OK; D11.11.1939 Philadelphia PA; d10.21

YEAR	TM LG	G	AB	R	H	2B	3B	HR	RBI	BB-IB	HP	SO	AVG	OBP	SLG	AOPS	ABR	SB-CS	FA	FR	RNG	THR	GAMES AT POSITION	DL	BFW
1871	Tro NA	1	4	0	0	0	0	0	0	0	—	0	.000	.000	.000	-99	-1	0-0	.667	-0	88	0	/S	—	-0.1

ABERCROMBIE, REGGIE Reginald Demascus; B7.15.1980 Columbus GA; BR/TR/6´3˝/225; [LAN99 23/704]; d4.4; Col Lake City (FL) CC

YEAR	TM LG	G	AB	R	H	2B	3B	HR	RBI	BB-IB	HP	SO	AVG	OBP	SLG	AOPS	ABR	SB-CS	FA	FR	RNG	THR	GAMES AT POSITION	DL	BFW
2006	Fla N	111	255	39	54	12	2	5	24	18-2	3	78	.212	.271	.333	57	-18	6-5	.973	1	105	89	O93(3/87/13)	0	-1.7

YEAR	TM LG	G	AB	R	H	2B	3B	HR	RBI	BB-IB	HP	SO	AVG	OBP	SLG	AOPS	ABR	SB-CS	FA	FR	RNG	THR	GAMES AT POSITION	DL	BFW
ABERNATHY, BRENT	Michael Brent; B9.23.1977 Atlanta GA; BR/TR/6´1˝/185; [TorA96 2/44]; d6.25																								
2001	TB A	79	304	43	82	17	1	5	33	27-1	0	35	.270	.328	.382	88	-5	8-3	.981	-2	93	108	2b79	0	-0.2
2002	TB A	117	463	46	112	18	4	2	40	25-0	6	46	.242	.288	.311	61	-27	10-4	.979	-4	96	103	2b116/D	0	-2.4
2003	TB A	2	7	1	0	0	0	0	0	0-0	0	0	.000	.000	.000	-99	-2	1-0	.900	0	156	0	2b2	0	-0.2
	KC A	10	27	2	2	0	0	0	0	1-0	0	3	.074	.107	.074	-48	-6	0-0	1.000	-1	102	82	2b9	0	-0.6
	Year	12	34	3	2	0	0	0	0	1-0	0	3	.059	.086	.059	-58	-8	1-0	.976	-0	113	66	2b11	0	-0.8
2005	Min A	24	67	5	16	1	0	1	6	7-0	1	9	.239	.316	.299	65	-3	2-0	.968	-4	90	106	2b17,O5L,D2	16	-0.6
Total	4	232	868	97	212	36	5	8	79	60-1	7	93	.244	.297	.325	66	-43	21-7	.979	-10	95	104	2b223,O5L,D3	16	-4.0
ABERSON, CLIFF	Clifford Alexander "Kif"; B8.28.1921 Chicago IL; D6.23.1973 Vallejo CA; BR/TR/6´0˝/200; d7.18																								
1947	Chi N	47	140	24	39	6	3	4	20	20	0	32	.279	.369	.450	121	4	0	.920	-1	78	255	O40L	0	0.1
1948	Chi N	12	32	1	6	1	0	1	6	5	0	10	.188	.297	.313	68	-1	0	.867	-1	76	168	O8L	0	-0.3
1949	Chi N	4	7	0	0	0	0	0	0	0	0	2	.000	.000	.000	-99	-2	0	1.000	-0	97	0	/rf	0	-0.2
Total	3	63	179	25	45	7	3	5	26	25	0	44	.251	.343	.408	103	1	0	.913	-1	78	235	O49(48/0/1)	0	-0.4
ABNER, SHAWN	Shawn Wesley; B6.17.1966 Hamilton OH; BR/TR/6´1˝/(190–194); [NYN84 1/1]; d9.8																								
1987	SD N	16	47	5	13	3	1	2	7	2-0	0	8	.277	.306	.511	116	1	1-0	.926	1	101	257	O14(6/2/6)	0	0.1
1988	SD N	37	83	6	15	3	0	2	5	4-1	1	19	.181	.225	.289	48	-6	0-1	.982	-0	98	78	O35(10/11/17)	0	-0.8
1989	SD N	57	102	13	18	4	0	2	14	5-2	0	20	.176	.213	.275	39	-8	1-0	1.000	-0	101	0	O51(23/23/6)	0	-1.0
1990	SD N	91	184	17	45	9	0	1	15	9-1	2	28	.245	.286	.310	64	-9	2-3	.991	-2	99	36	O62(23/35/6)	0	-1.3
1991	SD N	53	115	15	19	4	1	1	5	7-4	1	25	.165	.218	.243	29	-11	0-0	1.000	2	117	58	O39(0/36/3)	0	-1.1
	Cal A	41	101	12	23	6	1	2	9	4-0	0	18	.228	.257	.366	70	-4	1-2	1.000	2	101	205	O38(0/31/7),D3	0	-0.4
1992	Chi A	97	208	21	58	10	1	1	16	12-2	3	35	.279	.323	.351	91	-3	1-2	1.000	3	115	49	O94(12/14/75)/D	0	-0.2
Total	6	392	840	89	191	39	4	11	71	43-10	7	153	.227	.269	.323	65	-40	6-8	.993	5	106	75	O333(74/152/120),D4	0	-4.7
ABRAMS, CAL	Calvin Ross; B3.2.1924 Philadelphia PA; D2.25.1997 Ft.Lauderdale FL; BL/TL/6´0˝/(185–195); d4.20																								
1949	Bro N	8	24	6	2	1	0	0	0	7	0	6	.083	.290	.125	15	-3	1	.833	-1	67	197	O7L	0	-0.4
1950	Bro N	38	44	5	9	1	0	0	4	9	0	13	.205	.340	.227	51	-3	0	1.000	0	114	0	O15(9/1/5)	0	-0.3
1951	Bro N	67	150	27	42	8	0	3	19	36	0	26	.280	.419	.393	118	6	3-2	.944	-2	89	101	O34L	0	0.2
1952	Bro N	10	10	1	2	0	0	0	0	2	0	4	.200	.333	.200	51	-1	0-0	ø	-0	0	0	/lf	0	-0.1
	Cin N	71	158	23	44	9	2	2	13	19	0	25	.278	.356	.399	109	2	1-0	1.000	1	110	33	O46(31/18/0)	0	0.1
	Year	81	168	24	46	9	2	2	13	21	0	29	.274	.354	.387	106	2	1-0	1.000	0	110	33	O47(32/18/0)	0	0.0
1953	Pit N	119	448	66	128	10	6	15	43	58	0	70	.286	.368	.435	109	6	4-4	.973	3	97	158	O112R	0	0.5
1954	Pit N	17	42	6	6	1	1	0	2	10	0	9	.143	.308	.214	39	-4	0-0	1.000	1	97	237	O13(5/3/5)	0	-0.3
	Bal A	115	423	67	124	22	7	6	25	72	4	67	.293	.400	.421	135	24	1-4	.977	1	109	68	O115(0/14/101)	0	2.0
1955	Bal A	118	309	56	75	12	3	6	32	89-2	3	69	.243	.413	.359	118	15	2-8	.985	-2	94	114	O96(13/58/46),1b4	0	0.7
1956	Chi A	4	3	0	1	0	0	0	0	2-0	0	1	.333	.600	.333	150	1	0-0	1.000	0	123	0	O2(1/0/1)	0	0.1
Total	8	567	1611	257	433	64	19	32	138	304-2	7	290	.269	.386	.392	113	43	12-18	.977	1	100	107	O441(101/94/270),1b4	0	2.5
ABREU, BOBBY	Bob Kelly; B3.11.1974 Aragua, Venezuela; BL/TR/6´0˝/(160–210); d9.1																								
1996	Hou N	15	22	1	5	1	0	0	1	2-0	0	3	.227	.292	.273	54	-1	0-0	1.000	-0	85	0	O7(6/0/1)	0	-0.2
1997	†Hou N	59	188	22	47	10	2	3	26	21-0	1	48	.250	.329	.372	86	-4	7-2	.978	-1	91	111	O53(10/1/43)	37	-0.6
1998	Phi N	151	497	68	155	29	6	17	74	84-14	0	133	.312	.409	.497	137	30	19-10	.973	6	101	177	O146R	0	2.9
1999	Phi N	152	546	118	183	35	**11**	20	93	109-8	3	113	.335	.446	.549	149	47	27-9	.989	-7	90	82	O146R,D5	0	3.3
2000	Phi N	154	576	103	182	42	10	25	79	100-9	1	116	.316	.416	.554	144	42	28-8	.989	11	111	136	O152R	0	4.5
2001	Phi N	**162**	588	118	170	48	4	31	110	106-11	1	137	.289	.393	.543	147	45	36-14	.976	-3	93	101	O162R	0	3.6
2002	Phi N	157	572	102	176	**50**	6	20	85	104-9	3	117	.308	.413	.521	155	51	31-12	.983	-6	90	97	O154(0/18/148)	0	4.0
2003	Phi N	158	577	99	173	35	1	20	101	109-13	2	126	.300	.409	.468	139	40	22-9	.981	-4	100	58	O158R	0	2.9
2004	Phi N★	159	574	118	173	47	1	30	105	127-10	5	116	.301	.428	.544	145	47	40-5	.982	2	98	127	O158R	0	4.6
2005	Phi N★	**162**	588	104	168	37	1	24	102	117-15	6	134	.286	.405	.474	126	29	31-9	.986	-7	92	81	O158R,D3	0	1.8
2006	Phi N	98	339	61	94	25	2	8	65	91-5	2	86	.277	.427	.434	117	15	20-4	.995	-3	93	84	O97(0/1/97)/D	0	1.0
	†NY A	58	209	37	69	16	0	7	42	33-1	1	52	.330	.419	.507	140	14	10-2	.984	4	108	185	O57(0/1/57)/D	0	1.6
Total	11	1485	5276	951	1595	375	44	205	883	1003-95	25	1181	.302	.412	.507	139	355	271-84	.983	-9	97	108	O1448(16/21/1426),D10	37	29.4
ABREU, JOE	Joseph Lawrence; B5.24.1913 Oakland CA; D3.17.1993 Hayward CA; BR/TR/5´8˝/160; d4.23																								
1942	Cin N	9	28	4	6	1	0	1	3	4	0	4	.214	.313	.357	96	0	0	.941	-1	85	97	3b6,2b2	0	0.0
ABSTEIN, BILL	William Henry "Big Bill"; B2.2.1883 St.Louis MO; D4.8.1940 St.Louis MO; BR/TR/6´0˝/185; d9.25																								
1906	Pit N	8	20	2	4	0	0	0	3	0	0	—	.200	.200	.200	24	-2	2	.769	-1	91	0	2b3,O2R	—	-0.3
1909	†Pit N	137	512	51	133	20	10	1	70	27	4	—	.260	.302	.344	93	-6	16	.982	-6	86	**118**	1b135	—	-1.7
1910	StL A	25	87	1	13	2	0	0	3	2	0	—	.149	.169	.172	7	-10	3	.963	1	148	104	1b23	—	-1.0
Total	3	170	619	54	150	22	10	1	76	29	4	—	.242	.281	.315	80	-18	21	.979	-6	95	116	1b158,2b3,O2R	—	-3.0
ACOSTA, MERITO	Baldomero Pedro (Fernandez); B5.19.1896 Bauta, Cuba; D11.17.1963 Miami FL; BL/TL/5´7˝/140; d6.15; b-Jose																								
1913	Was A	12	20	3	6	0	1	0	1	4	0	2	.300	.417	.400	136	1	2	.714	-1	62	0	O9(6/2/1)	—	-0.1
1914	Was A	39	74	10	19	2	2	0	4	11	0	18	.257	.353	.338	104	1	3-4	.857	1	79	268	O25(15/5/5)	—	0.0
1915	Was A	72	163	20	34	4	1	0	18	28	4	15	.209	.338	.245	73	-4	8-4	.963	0	106	78	O53(22/2/29)	—	-0.6
1916	Was A	5	8	0	1	0	0	0	0	2	0	0	.125	.300	.125	28	-1	0	1.000	1	148	231	O4L	—	0.0
1918	Was A	3	2	0	0	0	0	0	0	0	0	1	.000	.000	.000	-99	0	0	ø	0	—	—	/H	—	-0.1
	Phi A	49	169	23	51	3	3	0	14	18	0	10	.302	.369	.355	117	4	4	.944	-2	87	117	O45(5/20/21)	—	-0.1
	Year	52	171	23	51	3	3	0	14	18	0	11	.298	.365	.351	115	3	4	.944	-2	87	117	O45(5/20/21)	—	-0.2
Total	5	180	436	56	111	9	7	0	37	63	4	46	.255	.354	.307	97	1	17-8	.933	-1	94	124	O136(52/29/56)	—	-0.9
ADAIR, JIMMY	James Aubrey "Choppy"; B1.25.1907 Waxahachie TX; D12.9.1982 Dallas TX; BR/TR/5´10.5˝/154; d8.24; C11; Col East Texas Baptist/Marshall																								
1931	Chi N	18	76	9	21	3	1	0	3	1	0	8	.276	.286	.342	67	-4	1	.948	-1	97	76	S18	—	-0.4
ADAIR, JERRY	Kenneth Jerry; B12.17.1936 Sand Springs OK; D5.31.1987 Tulsa OK; BR/TR/6´0˝/(175–185); d9.2; C4; Col Oklahoma St.																								
1958	Bal A	11	19	1	2	0	0	0	0	1-0	0	7	.105	.150	.105	-30	-3	0-0	.967	2	120	94	S10/2	0	-0.1
1959	Bal A	12	35	3	11	0	1	0	2	1-0	0	5	.314	.333	.371	95	0	0-0	.932	-4	77	77	2b11/S	0	-0.4
1960	Bal A	3	5	1	1	0	0	1	1	0-0	0	0	.200	.200	.800	159	0	0-0	1.000	1	123	246	2b3	0	0.1
1961	Bal A	133	386	41	102	21	1	9	37	35-4	2	51	.264	.326	.394	95	-3	5-2	.987	-6	95	96	2b107,S27,3b2	0	0.2
1962	Bal A	139	538	67	153	29	4	11	48	27-1	2	77	.284	.319	.414	103	0	7-7	.969	0	95	116	S113,2b34/3	0	1.1
1963	Bal A	109	382	34	87	21	3	6	30	9-2	2	51	.228	.246	.346	67	-18	3-3	.985	3	99	109	2b103	0	-0.7
1964	Bal A	155	569	56	141	20	3	9	47	28-10	1	72	.248	.283	.341	73	-22	3-2	**.994**	13	101	117	2b153	0	0.4
1965	Bal A	157	582	51	151	26	3	7	66	35-7	2	65	.259	.303	.351	84	-13	6-4	**.986**	7	105	103	2b157	0	0.9
1966	Bal A	17	52	3	15	1	0	0	3	4-0	0	8	.288	.333	.308	89	-1	0-0	.969	-1	93	88	2b13	0	0.0
	Chi A	105	370	27	90	18	2	4	36	17-0	1	44	.243	.275	.335	81	-10	3-2	.975	8	121	99	S75,2b50	0	0.7
	Year	122	422	30	105	19	2	4	39	21-0	1	52	.249	.282	.332	82	-11	3-2	.975	7	121	99	S75,2b63	0	0.7
1967	Chi A	28	98	6	20	4	0	0	9	4-0	1	17	.204	.240	.245	46	-7	0-1	.985	1	96	156	2b27	0	-0.5
	†Bos A	89	316	41	92	13	1	3	26	13-0	2	35	.291	.321	.367	96	-2	1-4	.952	-7	107	161	3b35,S30,2b23	0	-0.7
	Year	117	414	47	112	17	1	3	35	17-0	3	52	.271	.302	.338	85	-8	1-5	.976	-6	86	126	2b50,3b35,S30	0	-1.2
1968	Bos A	74	208	18	45	1	0	2	12	9-2	1	28	.216	.252	.250	50	-13	0-0	.976	-5	92	71	S46,2b12,3b7/1	0	-1.6
1969	KC A	126	432	29	108	9	1	5	48	20-4	3	36	.250	.285	.310	66	-21	1-3	.984	-21	91	62	2b109,S8/3	0	-3.7
1970	KC A	7	27	0	4	0	0	0	1	5-1	0	3	.148	.281	.148	22	-3	0-1	1.000	-0	85	109	2b7	0	-0.3
Total	13	1165	4019	378	1022	163	19	57	366	208-31	17	499	.254	.292	.347	80	-116	29-29	.985	-9	97	100	2b810,S310,3b46/1	0	-4.6
ADAMS, SPARKY	Earl John; B8.26.1894 Zerbe PA; D2.24.1989 Pottsville PA; BR/TR/5´5.5˝/151; d9.18																								
1922	Chi N	11	44	5	11	0	1	0	3	4	0	3	.250	.313	.295	56	-3	1-2	.914	-2	98	89	2b11	—	-0.5
1923	Chi N	95	311	40	90	12	0	4	35	26	1	10	.289	.346	.367	88	-5	20-19	.935	-6	95	103	S79/rf	—	-0.5
1924	Chi N	117	418	66	117	11	5	1	27	40	1	20	.280	.344	.337	83	-9	15-17	.941	-5	97	117	S88,2b19	—	-0.8
1925	Chi N	149	627	95	180	29	8	2	48	44	7	15	.287	.341	.368	80	-19	26-12	**.983**	**27**	109	105	2b144,S5	—	1.3
1926	Chi N	154	624	95	193	35	3	0	39	52	5	27	.309	.367	.375	99	1	27	.965	20	105	120	2b136,3b19,S2	—	2.6
1927	Chi N	146	647	100	189	17	7	0	49	42	0	26	.292	.335	.340	81	-18	26	.994	4	95	97	2b60,3b53,S40	—	-0.5
1928	Pit N	135	539	91	149	14	6	0	38	64	4	18	.276	.357	.325	76	-17	8	.971	-7	97	79	2b107,S27/rf	—	-1.7
1929	Pit N	74	196	37	51	8	1	0	11	15	1	5	.260	.316	.311	55	-14	3	.901	-10	85	66	S30,2b20,3b15,O2L	—	-1.9

YEAR	TM LG	G	AB	R	H	2B	3B	HR	RBI	BB-IB	HP	SO	AVG	OBP	SLG	AOPS	ABR	SB-CS	FA	FR	RNG	THR	GAMES AT POSITION	DL	BFW
1930	†StL N	137	570	98	179	36	9	0	55	45	1	27	.314	.365	.409	84	-14	7	**.966**	-12	84	101	3b104,2b25,S7	—	-1.6
1931	†StL N	143	608	97	178	**46**	5	1	40	42	2	24	.293	.340	.390	92	-5	16	**.963**	-13	87	**122**	3b138,S6	—	-1.3
1932	StL N	31	127	22	35	3	1	0	13	14	1	5	.276	.352	.315	79	-3	0	.931	-2	81	215	3b30	—	-0.4
1933	StL N	8	30	1	5	1	0	0	0	1	1	3	.167	.219	.200	19	-3	0	.955	-1	101	66	S5,3b3	—	-0.4
	Cin N	137	538	59	141	21	1	1	22	44	2	30	.262	.320	.310	82	-11	3	.963	1	107	83	3b132,S8	—	-0.5
	Year	145	568	60	146	22	1	1	22	45	3	33	.257	.315	.305	78	-15	3	.959	0	**107**	87	3b135,S13	—	-0.9
1934	Cin N	87	278	38	70	16	1	0	14	20	2	10	.252	.307	.317	69	-12	2	.955	-1	102	175	3b38,2b29	—	-1.0
Total	13	1424	5557	844	1588	249	48	9	394	453	28	223	.286	.343	.353	82	-132	154-50	.974	-7	102	102	2b551,3b532,S297,O4(2/0/2)	—	-7.2
Adams, Buster	Elvin Clark; B6.24.1915 Trinidad CO; D9.1.1990 Rancho Mirage CA; BR/TR/6´0˝/180; d4.27																								
1939	StL N	2	1	1	0	0	0	0	0	0	0	0	.000	.000	.000	-94	0	0	ø	0	—	—	/H	—	0.0
1943	StL N	8	11	1	1	1	0	0	1	4	0	4	.091	.333	.182	48	0	0	1.000	0	111	0	O6C	0	-0.1
	Phi N	111	418	48	107	14	7	4	38	39	0	67	.256	.319	.352	98	-2	2	.984	0	106	59	O107(1/107/0)	0	-0.6
	Year	119	429	49	108	15	7	4	39	43	0	71	.252	.320	.347	96	-3	2	.984	0	106	57	O113(1/113/0)	0	-0.7
1944	Phi N	151	584	86	165	35	3	17	64	74	7	74	.283	.370	.440	132	27	2	.979	3	105	98	O151C	0	2.5
1945	Phi N	14	56	6	13	3	1	2	8	5	0	5	.232	.295	.429	103	0	0	1.000	-1	93	0	O14L	0	-0.2
	StL N	140	578	98	169	26	0	20	101	57	3	75	.292	.359	.441	119	14	3	.978	-6	96	74	O140(14/126/0)	0	0.3
	Year	154	634	104	182	29	1	22	109	62	3	80	.287	.353	.440	117	14	3	.979	-7	96	68	O154(27/126/0)	0	0.1
1946	StL N	81	173	21	32	6	0	5	22	29	3	27	.185	.312	.306	73	-6	3	.990	-2	97	27	O58(24/35/0)	0	-1.1
1947	Phi N	69	182	21	45	11	1	2	15	26	0	29	.247	.341	.352	88	-3	2	.954	-1	90	139	O51(6/1/44)	0	-0.5
Total	6	576	2003	282	532	96	12	50	249	234	13	281	.266	.346	.400	110	30	12	.979	-7	100	77	O527(58/426/44)	0	0.3
Adams, George	George; B Grafton MA; BR/TR/5´6˝/175; d6.14																								
1879	Syr N	4	13	0	3	0	0	0	0	1	—	1	.231	.286	.231	82	0	—	1.000	-1	0	0	O2C,1b2	—	-0.1
Adams, Glenn	Glenn Charles; B10.4.1947 Northbridge MA; BL/TR/6´0˝/(175–188); [HouN68*1/4]; d5.4; Col Springfield																								
1975	SF N	61	90	10	27	2	1	4	15	11-0	1	25	.300	.379	.478	133	4	1-0	.941	-1	92	77	O25(16/0/9)	0	0.2
1976	SF N	69	74	2	18	4	0	0	3	1-0	0	12	.243	.253	.297	54	-5	1-0	1.000	-1	44	0	O6(4/0/2)	0	-0.6
1977	Min A	95	269	32	91	17	0	6	49	18-3	0	30	.338	.376	.468	131	12	0-2	.969	0	96	131	D47,O44(16/0/28)	32	0.8
1978	Min A	116	310	27	80	18	1	7	35	17-0	0	32	.258	.297	.390	89	-5	0-1	1.000	1	289	0	D101,O5(2/0/3)	0	-0.8
1979	Min A	119	326	34	98	13	1	8	50	25-0	3	27	.301	.350	.420	104	2	2-2	.958	-4	81	67	D55,O53(45/0/8)	0	-0.6
1980	Min A	99	262	32	75	11	2	6	38	15-1	0	26	.286	.320	.412	94	-3	2-4	.947	-1	86	0	D81,O12L	15	-0.8
1981	Min A	72	220	13	46	10	0	2	24	20-4	0	26	.209	.273	.282	57	-12	0-1	ø	0	0	0	D62	0	-1.5
1982	Tor A	30	66	2	17	4	0	1	11	4-0	0	5	.258	.288	.364	75	-2	0-0	ø	0	0	0	D27	0	-0.3
Total	8	661	1617	152	452	79	5	34	225	111-8	4	183	.280	.324	.398	96	-9	6-10	.959	-7	88	79	D373,O145(95/0/50)	47	-3.6
Adams, Doug	Harold Douglas; B1.27.1943 Blue River WI; BL/TR/6´3˝/185; d9.8																								
1969	Chi A	8	14	1	3	0	0	0	1	1-0	0	3	.214	.267	.214	34	-1	0-0	1.000	-1	0	0	C4	0	-0.2
Adams, Herb	Herbert Loren; B4.14.1928 Hollywood CA; BL/TL/5´9˝/160; d9.17; Mil 1951–52; Col Northern Illinois																								
1948	Chi A	5	11	1	3	1	0	0	0	1	0	1	.273	.333	.364	88	0	0-0	1.000	2	111	706	O4(0/2/2)	0	0.1
1949	Chi A	56	208	26	61	5	3	0	16	9	0	16	.293	.323	.346	79	-8	1-2	.975	-1	93	120	O48(14/33/1)	0	-1.1
1950	Chi A	34	118	12	24	2	3	0	2	12	2	7	.203	.288	.271	45	-10	3-0	.978	-1	104	37	O33C	0	-1.1
Total	3	95	337	39	88	8	6	0	18	22	2	24	.261	.310	.320	67	-18	4-2	.978	-1	98	113	O85(14/68/3)	0	-2.1
Adams, Jim	James J.; B1868 E.St.Louis IL; TR; d4.21																								
1890	StL AA	1	4	0	1	0	0	0	0	0	0	—	.250	.250	.250	42	0	0	1.000	-0	*99*	*84*	/C	—	0.0
Adams, Bert	John Bertram; B6.21.1891 Wharton TX; D6.24.1940 Los Angeles CA; BB/TR/6´1˝/185; d8.30																								
1910	Cle A	5	13	1	3	0	0	0	0	0	0	—	.231	.231	.231	44	-1	0	.964	2	*99*	*250*	C5	—	0.1
1911	Cle A	2	5	0	1	0	0	0	0	1	0	—	.200	.333	.200	50	0	0	.900	-1	*74*	*111*	C2	—	-0.1
1912	Cle A	20	54	5	11	2	1	0	6	4	0	—	.204	.259	.278	52	-4	0	.942	1	*97*	*102*	C20	—	-0.1
1915	Phi N	24	27	1	3	0	0	0	2	2	0	3	.111	.172	.111	-13	-4	0	.974	-2	*99*	*70*	C23/1	—	-0.6
1916	Phi N	11	13	2	3	0	0	0	1	0	0	3	.231	.231	.231	40	-1	0	.929	0	111	116	C11	—	-0.1
1917	Phi N	43	107	4	22	4	1	1	7	0	0	20	.206	.206	.290	49	-7	0	.994	2	*112*	*111*	C38/1	—	-0.3
1918	Phi N	84	227	10	40	4	0	0	12	10	1	26	.176	.214	.194	23	-21	5	.976	-3	*102*	*83*	C76	—	-2.0
1919	Phi N	78	232	14	54	7	2	1	17	6	0	27	.233	.252	.293	59	-12	4	.966	-7	*82*	*112*	C73/1	—	-1.5
Total	8	267	678	37	137	17	4	2	45	23	1	79	.202	.229	.248	42	-50	9	.970	-9	*96*	*102*	C248,1b3	—	-4.6
Adams, Dick	Richard Leroy; B4.8.1920 Tuolumne CA; BR/TL/6´0˝/185; d5.20; b–Bobby																								
1947	Phi A	37	89	9	18	2	3	2	11	2	0	18	.202	.220	.360	58	-6	0-0	.995	1	119	114	1b24,O3(1/0/2)	0	-0.6
Adams, Ricky	Ricky Lee; B1.21.1959 Upland CA; BR/TR/6´2˝/180; [HouN77 1/14]; d9.15																								
1982	Cal A	8	14	1	2	0	0	0	0	0-0	1	2	.143	.200	.143	-4	-2	1-0	.947	-2	81	143	S8	0	-0.3
1983	Cal A	58	112	22	28	2	0	2	6	5-0	3	12	.250	.300	.321	71	-5	1-1	.960	13	127	135	S38,3b16,2b4	0	1.1
1985	SF N	54	121	12	23	3	1	2	10	5-3	1	23	.190	.228	.281	44	-10	1-1	.964	2	98	83	S25,3b16,2b6	0	-0.7
Total	3	120	247	35	53	5	1	4	16	10-3	5	37	.215	.260	.291	54	-17	3-2	.961	13	111	116	S71,3b32,2b10	0	0.1
Adams, Bobby	Robert Henry; B12.14.1921 Tuolumne CA; D2.13.1997 Gig Harbor WA; BR/TR/5´10˝/(162–170); d4.16; C6; b–Dick s–Mike																								
1946	Cin N	94	311	35	76	13	3	4	24	18	3	32	.244	.292	.344	83	-8	16	.967	22	123	177	2b74,O2R/3	0	1.8
1947	Cin N	81	217	39	59	11	2	4	20	25	4	23	.272	.358	.396	101	1	9	.967	6	103	110	2b69	0	1.0
1948	Cin N	87	262	33	78	20	3	1	21	25	1	23	.298	.361	.408	112	5	6	.965	-7	86	88	2b64,3b7	0	0.1
1949	Cin N	107	277	32	70	16	2	0	25	26	0	36	.253	.317	.325	72	-11	4	.984	-9	90	74	2b63,3b14	0	-1.6
1950	Cin N	115	348	57	98	21	8	3	25	43	0	29	.282	.361	.414	103	2	7	.981	-5	98	80	2b53,3b42	0	0.0
1951	Cin N	125	403	57	107	12	5	5	24	43	1	40	.266	.338	.357	86	-8	4-10	.956	-7	98	59	3b60,2b42/rf	0	-1.6
1952	Cin N	**154**	637	85	180	25	4	6	48	49	0	67	.283	.334	.363	93	-6	11-9	.962	7	**105**	105	3b154	0	0.0
1953	Cin N	150	607	99	167	14	6	8	49	58	0	67	.275	.338	.357	81	-17	3-2	.951	2	104	121	3b150	0	-1.5
1954	Cin N	110	390	69	105	25	6	3	23	55	3	46	.269	.362	.387	93	-2	2-5	.951	1	95	132	3b93,2b2	0	-0.3
1955	Cin N	64	150	23	41	11	2	2	20	20-1	3	21	.273	.368	.413	102	1	2-0	.969	4	113	158	3b42,2b5	0	0.5
	Chi A	28	21	8	2	0	1	0	3	4-0	0	4	.095	.240	.190	16	-3	0-0	.933	2	126	0	3b9/2	0	-0.1
1956	Bal A	41	111	19	25	6	1	0	7	25-0	0	15	.225	.362	.297	84	-1	1-1	.984	-5	94	119	3b24,2b18	0	-0.5
1957	Chi N	60	187	21	47	10	2	1	10	17-0	2	28	.251	.320	.342	79	-5	0-3	.949	-7	81	56	3b47/2	0	-1.4
1958	Chi N	62	96	14	27	4	4	0	4	6-0	0	15	.281	.324	.406	93	-1	2-0	.961	0	133	19	1b11,3b9,2b7	0	-0.1
1959	Chi N	3	2	0	0	0	0	0	0	0-0	0	1	.000	.000	.000	-99	-1	0-0	.667	-0	0	0	/1	0	-0.1
Total	14	1281	4019	591	1082	188	49	37	303	414-1	17	447	.269	.340	.368	90	-54	67-30	.955	3	99	102	3b652,2b399,1b12,O3R	0	-3.8
Adams, Bob	Robert Melvin; B1.6.1952 Pittsburgh PA; BR/TR/6´2˝/195; [DetA73 3/67]; d7.10; Col UCLA																								
1977	Det A	15	24	2	6	1	0	2	2	0-0	0	5	.250	.250	.542	103	0	0-0	1.000	-0	71	59	1b2/C	0	0.0
Adams, Mike	Robert Michael; B7.24.1948 Cincinnati OH; BR/TR/5´9˝/(180–200); [DetA67*S1/2]; d9.10; f–Bobby; Col Fullerton (CA) JC																								
1972	Min A	3	6	0	2	0	0	0	0	0-0	0	1	.333	.333	.333	94	0	0-0	1.000	-0	45	0	/lf	0	0.0
1973	Min A	55	66	21	14	2	0	3	6	17-0	1	18	.212	.381	.379	110	2	2-1	.978	-0	109	0	O24(23/1/0),D2	0	0.0
1976	Chi N	25	29	1	4	2	0	0	2	8-0	1	7	.138	.342	.207	54	-1	0-0	1.000	-1	60	0	O4(2/0/2),3b3/2	0	-0.3
1977	Chi N	2	2	0	0	0	0	0	0	0-0	0	1	.000	.000	.000	-90	-1	0-0	ø	-0	0	0	O2(1/1/0)	0	-0.1
1978	Oak A	15	15	5	3	1	0	0	1	7-0	0	2	.200	.455	.267	113	1	0-0	1.000	-0	58	134	2b6,3b3,D3	0	0.1
Total	5	100	118	27	23	5	0	3	9	32-0	2	29	.195	.375	.314	92	1	2-1	.980	-2	100	0	O31(27/2/2),2b7,3b6,D5	0	-0.3
Adams, Russ	Russ Moore; B8.30.1980 Laurinburg NC; BL/TR/6´1˝/180; [TorA02 1/14]; d9.3; Col North Carolina																								
2004	Tor A	22	72	10	22	2	1	4	10	5-0	1	5	.306	.359	.528	120	2	1-0	.936	-4	92	74	S21	0	0.0
2005	Tor A	139	481	68	123	27	5	8	63	50-1	3	57	.256	.325	.383	85	-10	11-2	.952	-23	90	87	S132	0	-2.1
2006	Tor A	90	251	31	55	14	1	3	28	22-0	1	41	.219	.282	.319	54	-17	1-2	.987	-7	94	72	2b50,S36	0	-2.0
Total	3	251	804	109	200	43	7	15	101	77-1	5	103	.249	.314	.376	78	-25	13-4	.946	-34	92	87	S189,2b50	0	-4.1

YEAR	TM LG	G	AB	R	H	2B	3B	HR	RBI	BB-IB	HP	SO	AVG	OBP	SLG	AOPS	ABR	SB-CS	FA	FR	RNG	THR	GAMES AT POSITION	DL	BFW
ADAMS, SPENCER	Spencer Dewey; B6.21.1898 Layton UT; D11.24.1970 Salt Lake City UT; BL/TR/5´9˝/158; d5.8																								
1923	Pit N	25	56	11	14	0	1	0	4	6	0	6	.250	.323	.286	60	-3	2-1	.879	-5	85	110	2b11,S6	—	-0.7
1925	†Was A	39	55	11	15	4	1	0	4	5	0	4	.273	.333	.382	83	-2	1-1	.941	-3	89	85	2b15,S8,3b3	—	-0.3
1926	†NY A	28	25	7	3	1	0	0	1	3	0	7	.120	.214	.160	-1	-4	1-0	1.000	2	109	163	2b4/3	—	-0.2
1927	StL A	88	259	32	69	11	3	0	29	24	2	33	.266	.333	.332	71	-11	1-8	.948	2	97	99	2b54,3b28	—	-0.9
Total	4	180	395	61	101	16	5	0	38	38	2	50	.256	.324	.322	66	-20	5-10	.944	-3	95	101	2b84,3b32,S14	—	-2.1
ADCOCK, JOE	Joseph Wilbur; B10.30.1927 Coushatta LA; D5.3.1999 Coushatta LA; BR/TR/6´4˝/(210–232); d4.23; M1; Col Louisiana St.																								
1950	Cin N	102	372	46	109	16	1	8	55	24	0	24	.293	.336	.406	94	-4	2	.968	2	107	106	O75L,1b24	0	-0.8
1951	Cin N	113	395	40	96	16	4	10	47	24	1	29	.243	.288	.380	77	-14	1-2	.983	3	107	94	O107L	0	-1.9
1952	Cin N	117	378	43	105	22	4	13	52	23	1	38	.278	.321	.460	115	6	1-4	.985	5	122	84	O85L,1b17	0	0.3
1953	Mil N	**157**	590	71	168	33	6	18	80	42	2	82	.285	.334	.453	110	7	3-2	.991	-3	90	111	1b157	0	-0.5
1954	Mil N	133	500	73	154	27	5	23	87	44	3	58	.308	.365	.520	137	26	1-4	.995	-11	68	108	1b133	0	0.5
1955	Mil N	84	288	40	76	14	0	15	45	31-3	2	44	.264	.339	.469	118	7	0-2	.990	-5	80	96	1b78	57	-0.3
1956	Mil N	137	454	76	132	23	1	38	103	32-6	1	86	.291	.337	.597	**154**	32	1-0	**.995**	-4	87	118	1b129	0	2.1
1957	†Mil N	65	209	31	60	13	2	12	38	20-3	1	51	.287	.351	.541	146	13	0-0	.996	-2	84	148	1b56	70	0.8
1958	†Mil N	105	320	40	88	15	1	19	54	21-1	1	63	.275	.317	.506	125	10	0-0	.989	-2	95	120	1b71,O22L	0	0.3
1959	Mil N	115	404	53	118	19	2	25	76	32-6	0	77	.292	.339	.535	141	22	0-0	.998	11	142	105	1b89,O21L	0	2.7
1960	Mil N★	138	514	55	153	21	4	25	91	46-7	1	86	.298	.354	.500	142	28	2-2	**.993**	3	108	97	1b136	0	2.3
1961	Mil N	152	562	77	160	20	0	35	108	59-4	2	94	.285	.354	.507	133	26	2-1	**.993**	-6	91	105	1b148	0	1.1
1962	Mil N	121	391	48	97	12	1	29	78	50-8	1	91	.248	.333	.506	126	13	2-0	**.997**	-2	91	95	1b112	0	0.6
1963	Cle A	97	283	28	71	7	1	13	49	30-4	0	53	.251	.320	.420	107	2	1-2	.995	-4	73	87	1b78	0	-0.7
1964	LA A	118	366	39	98	13	0	21	64	48-4	0	61	.268	.352	.475	142	20	0-2	.993	-4	83	125	1b105	0	1.0
1965	Cal A	122	349	30	84	14	0	14	47	37-3	1	74	.241	.315	.401	104	2	2-2	.996	-2	88	107	1b97	0	-0.6
1966	Cal A	83	231	33	63	10	3	18	48	31-6	0	48	.273	.355	.576	168	20	2-2	.997	0	100	125	1b71	0	1.7
Total	17	1959	6606	823	1832	295	35	336	1122	594-55	17	1059	.277	.337	.485	125	216	20-25	.994	-20	90	108	1b1501,O310L	127	8.6
ADDIS, BOB	Robert Gordon; B11.6.1925 Mineral OH; BL/TR/6´0˝/(175–185); d9.1																								
1950	Bos N	16	28	7	7	1	0	0	2	3	0	5	.250	.323	.286	66	-1	1	1.000	-1	82	0	O7(2/1/4)	0	-0.2
1951	Bos N	85	199	23	55	7	0	1	24	9	0	10	.276	.308	.327	76	-7	3-2	.982	-1	108	25	O46(31/10/5)	0	-1.1
1952	Chi N	93	292	38	86	13	2	1	20	23	0	30	.295	.346	.363	96	-1	4-4	.988	2	103	122	O79(3/42/37)	0	-0.2
1953	Chi N	10	12	2	2	1	0	0	1	2	0	0	.167	.286	.250	40	-1	0-0	1.000	1	122	475	O3(0/1/2)	0	0.0
	Pit N	4	3	0	0	0	0	0	0	0	0	2	.000	.000	.000	-99	-1	0-0	ø	0	—	—	/H	0	-0.1
	Year	14	15	2	2	1	0	0	1	2	0	2	.133	.235	.200	15	-2	0-0	1.000	1	122	475	O3(0/1/2)	0	-0.1
Total	4	208	534	70	150	22	2	2	47	37	0	47	.281	.327	.341	84	-11	8-6	.986	2	105	90	O135(36/54/48)	0	-1.6
ADDUCI, JIM	James David; B8.9.1959 Chicago IL; BL/TL/6´5˝/200; [StLN80 7/171]; d9.12; Col Southern Illinois																								
1983	StL N	10	20	0	1	0	0	0	0	1-0	0	6	.050	.095	.050	-58	-4	0-0	1.000	0	105	71	1b6/lf	0	-0.5
1986	Mil A	3	11	2	1	1	0	0	0	1-0	0	2	.091	.167	.182	-5	-2	0-0	1.000	0	142	42	1b3	0	-0.1
1988	Mil A	44	94	8	25	6	1	1	15	0-0	0	15	.266	.258	.383	78	-3	0-1	.969	1	100	117	O24(16/0/9),D10,1b3	0	-0.4
1989	Phi N	13	19	1	7	1	0	0	0	0-0	0	4	.368	.368	.421	125	1	0-0	1.000	1	170	49	1b4/lf	0	0.1
Total	4	70	144	11	34	8	1	1	15	2-0	0	27	.236	.242	.326	58	-8	0-1	.969	1	98	115	O26(18/0/9),1b16,D10	0	-0.9
ADDY, BOB	Robert Edward "Magnet"; B2.1845 Rochester NY; D4.9.1910 Pocatello ID; BL/TL/5´8˝/160; d5.6; M2																								
1871	Rok NA	**25**	118	30	32	6	0	0	13	4	—	0	.271	.295	.322	81	-2	8-1	.768	-1	**115**	65	2b22,S3	—	-0.2
1873	Phi NA	10	51	12	16	1	0	0	10	2	—	0	.314	.340	.333	96	0	1-1	.855	-2	87	54	2b10	—	-0.2
	Bos NA	31	152	37	54	6	3	1	32	2	—	1	.355	.364	.454	130	4	6-5	.702	-3	68	0	O31R	—	0.2
	Year	41	203	49	70	7	3	1	42	4	—	1	.345	.357	.424	121	4	7-6	.702	-5	68	0	O31R,2b10	—	0.0
1874	Har NA	50	213	25	51	9	2	0	22	1	—	1	.239	.243	.300	70	-8	4-2	.846	2	113	44	2b45,3b5/S	—	-0.7
1875	Phi NA	69	310	60	80	8	4	0	43	0	—	2	.258	.258	.310	93	-3	16-8	.761	-1	127	101	O68(0/1/67),2b2,M	—	0.0
1876	Chi N	32	142	36	40	4	1	0	16	5	—	0	.282	.306	.324	98	-1	—	.800	-1	108	0	O32(3/0/29)	—	-0.2
1877	Cin N	57	245	27	68	2	3	0	31	6	—	5	.278	.295	.310	102	1	—	.805	5	165	**229**	O57(0/1/56),M	—	0.6
Total	4NA	185	844	164	233	30	9	1	120	9	—	4	.276	.284	.336	93	-9	35-17	.746	-5	108	69	O99(0/1/98),2b79,3b5,S4	—	-0.9
Total	2	89	387	63	108	6	4	0	47	11	—	5	.279	.299	.315	100	0	—	.803	4	143	142	O89(3/1/85)	—	0.4
ADERHOLT, MORRIE	Morris Woodroe; B9.13.1915 Mt.Olive NC; D3.18.1955 Sarasota FL; BL/TR/6´1˝/188; d9.13; Col Wake Forest																								
1939	Was A	7	25	5	5	0	0	1	4	2	0	6	.200	.259	.320	51	-2	0-1	.872	-1	92	64	2b7	—	-0.3
1940	Was A	1	2	0	0	0	0	0	0	0	0	0	.000	.000	.000	-99	-1	0-0	1.000	0	59	237	/2	—	-0.1
1941	Was A	11	14	3	2	0	0	0	1	1	0	3	.143	.200	.143	-8	-2	0-0	.818	-1	45	97	2b2/3	0	-0.3
1944	Bro N	17	59	9	16	2	3	0	10	4	0	4	.271	.317	.407	105	0	0	.871	-1	92	94	O13(11/0/2)	0	-0.2
1945	Bro N	39	60	4	13	1	0	0	6	3	0	10	.217	.254	.233	36	-5	0	1.000	-1	66	0	O8(7/0/1)	0	-0.7
	Bos N	31	102	15	34	4	0	2	11	9	0	6	.333	.387	.431	127	4	3	.984	-0	108	0	O24L/2	0	0.2
	Year	70	162	19	47	5	0	2	17	12	0	16	.290	.339	.358	94	-1	3	.985	-1	101	0	O32(31/0/1)/2	0	-0.5
Total	5	106	262	36	70	7	3	3	32	19	0	29	.267	.317	.351	85	-6	3-1	.949	-5	98	29	O45(42/0/3),2b11/3	0	-1.4
ADKINS, DICK	Richard Earl; B3.3.1920 Electra TX; D9.12.1955 Electra TX; BR/TR/5´10˝/165; d9.19																								
1942	Phi A	3	7	2	1	0	0	0	0	2	0	2	.143	.333	.143	37	0	0-0	.875	-1	91	81	S3	0	-0.1
ADKINSON, HENRY	Henry Magee; B9.1.1874 Chicago IL; D5.1.1923 Salt Lake City UT; d9.25; Col Chicago																								
1895	StL N	1	5	1	2	0	0	0	0	0	0	2	.400	.400	.400	108	0	0	.667	-0	0	0	/lf	—	0.0
ADLESH, DAVE	David George; B7.15.1943 Long Beach CA; BR/TR/6´0˝/(185–190); d5.12																								
1963	Hou N	6	8	0	0	0	0	0	0	0-0	0	4	.000	.000	.000	-99	-2	0-0	.889	-1	74	0	C6	0	-0.4
1964	Hou N	3	10	0	2	0	0	0	0	0-0	0	5	.200	.200	.200	14	-1	0-0	1.000	-0	48	338	C3	0	-0.2
1965	Hou N	15	34	2	5	1	0	0	3	2-0	1	12	.147	.216	.176	13	-4	0-0	1.000	-1	102	124	C13	0	-0.5
1966	Hou N	3	6	0	0	0	0	0	0	0-0	0	4	.000	.000	.000	-99	-2	0-0	1.000	1	0	0	/C	0	0.0
1967	Hou N	39	94	4	17	1	0	1	4	11-3	0	28	.181	.264	.223	43	-7	0-0	.995	-4	69	67	C31	0	-1.1
1968	Hou N	40	104	3	19	1	1	0	4	5-2	1	27	.183	.227	.212	33	-9	0-0	.990	-7	49	74	C36	0	-1.7
Total	6	106	256	9	43	3	1	1	11	18-5	2	80	.168	.227	.199	26	-25	0-0	.992	-13	63	85	C90	0	-3.9
AFENIR, TROY	Michael Troy; B9.21.1963 Escondido CA; BR/TR/6´4˝/(185–210); [HouN83*S1/11]; d9.14; Col Palomar (CA) JC																								
1987	Hou N	10	20	1	6	1	0	0	1	0-0	0	12	.300	.300	.350	74	-1	0-0	.974	-3	49	44	C10	0	-0.4
1990	Oak A	14	14	0	2	0	0	0	2	0-0	0	6	.143	.133	.143	-21	-2	0-0	1.000	-2	0	78	C12/D	0	-0.4
1991	Oak A	5	11	0	1	0	0	0	0	0-0	0	2	.091	.091	.091	-52	-2	0-0	1.000	0	188	0	C4/D	0	-0.2
1992	Cin N	16	34	3	6	1	2	0	4	5-0	0	12	.176	.282	.324	69	-2	0-0	1.000	-3	166	26	C15	0	-0.5
Total	4	45	79	4	15	2	2	0	7	5-0	0	32	.190	.235	.266	40	-7	0-0	.992	-8	113	35	C41,D2	0	-1.5
AGBAYANI, BENNY	Benny Peter; B12.28.1971 Honolulu HI; BR/TR/6´0˝/225; [NYN93 30/836]; d6.17; Col Hawaii Pacific																								
1998	NY N	11	15	1	2	0	0	0	0	1-0	0	5	.133	.188	.133	-14	-3	0-2	1.000	-0	80	0	O9(1/2/6)	0	-0.4
1999	†NY N	101	276	42	79	18	3	14	42	32-4	3	60	.286	.363	.525	128	11	6-4	.984	-4	91	47	O80(47/4/45),D2	0	0.5
2000	†NY N	119	350	59	101	19	1	15	60	54-2	7	68	.289	.391	.477	126	16	5-5	.975	-3	98	56	O110(102/2/12)/D	0	0.8
2001	NY N	91	296	28	82	14	2	6	27	36-0	5	73	.277	.364	.399	105	3	4-5	.954	-4	97	21	O84L	35	-0.5
2002	Col N	48	117	10	24	5	0	4	19	10-0	0	35	.205	.266	.350	54	-8	1-0	1.000	0	105	58	O37L/D	24	-0.9
	Bos A	13	37	5	11	1	0	0	8	6-1	0	5	.297	.395	.324	93	0	0-0	.962	1	109	157	O13(11/1/3)	0	0.0
Total	5	383	1091	145	299	57	6	39	156	139-7	15	246	.274	.362	.445	109	19	16-16	.974	-11	97	48	O333(282/9/66),D4	59	-0.5
AGEE, TOMMIE	Tommie Lee; B8.9.1942 Magnolia AL; D1.22.2001 New York NY; BR/TR/5´11˝/(185–195); d9.14; Col Grambling St.																								
1962	Cle A	5	14	0	3	0	0	0	2	0-0	0	4	.214	.214	.214	16	-2	0-0	1.000	-1	62	0	O3(2/1/0)	0	-0.3
1963	Cle A	13	27	3	4	1	0	1	3	2-0	0	9	.148	.207	.296	39	-2	0-0	1.000	0	64	384	O13(4/3/6)	0	-0.3
1964	Cle A	13	12	0	2	0	0	0	0	0-0	0	3	.167	.167	.167	-7	-2	0-0	1.000	-1	56	0	O12(0/3/10)	0	-0.3
1965	Chi A	10	19	2	3	1	0	0	3	2-1	0	6	.158	.238	.211	30	-2	0-1	1.000	0	114	0	O9(0/5/6)	39	-0.2
1966	Chi A★	160	629	98	172	27	8	22	86	41-3	10	127	.273	.326	.447	129	21	44-18	.982	-3	96	116	O159(8/156/0)	0	1.7
1967	Chi A★	158	529	73	124	26	2	14	52	44-5	8	129	.234	.302	.371	102	1	28-10	.969	-6	101	65	O152(10/136/9)	0	-0.8
1968	NY N	132	368	30	80	12	3	5	17	15-3	4	103	.217	.255	.307	68	-15	13-8	.978	-2	96	93	O127(0/116/13)	0	-2.4
1969	†NY N	149	565	97	153	23	4	26	76	59-2	3	137	.271	.342	.464	121	15	12-9	.986	-1	104	78	O146(0/143/7)	0	1.0

YEAR	TM LG	G	AB	R	H	2B	3B	HR	RBI	BB-IB	HP	SO	AVG	OBP	SLG	AOPS	ABR	SB-CS	FA	FR	RNG	THR	GAMES AT POSITION	DL	BFW
1970	NY N	153	636	107	182	30	7	24	75	55-3	2	156	.286	.344	.469	114	11	31-15	.967	3	**115**	48	O150(0/149/2)	0	1.2
1971	NY N	113	425	58	121	19	0	14	50	50-2	2	84	.285	.362	.428	123	14	28-6	.978	6	114	118	O107(0/94/32)	15	2.2
1972	NY N	114	422	52	96	23	0	13	47	53-6	4	92	.227	.317	.374	98	0	8-9	.962	4	113	93	O109(6/91/20)	0	-0.1
1973	Hou N	83	204	30	48	5	2	8	15	16-1	1	55	.235	.294	.397	91	-4	2-5	.983	2	112	56	O67(34/18/17)	0	-0.6
	StL N	26	62	8	11	3	1	3	7	5-0	0	13	.177	.239	.403	74	-3	1-0	.981	3	147	111	O19(0/19/2)	0	0.0
	Year	109	266	38	59	8	3	11	22	21-1	1	68	.222	.281	.398	87	-6	3-5	.982	5	120	68	O86(34/37/19)	0	-0.6
Total	12	1129	3912	558	999	170	27	130	433	342-26	34	918	.255	.320	.412	108	32	167-81	.975	5	106	86	O1073(64/934/124)	54	1.1
Agganis, Harry	Harry "The Golden Greek"; B4.20.1929 Lynn MA; D6.27.1955 Cambridge MA; BL/TL/6´2˝/200; d4.13; Col Boston U.																								
1954	Bos A	132	434	54	109	13	8	11	57	47	0	57	.251	.321	.394	86	-9	6-3	.990	5	**118**	96	1b119	0	-1.0
1955	Bos A	25	83	11	26	10	1	0	10	10-0	0	10	.313	.383	.458	116	2	2-0	.987	-1	95	78	1b20	0	0.1
Total	2	157	517	65	135	23	9	11	67	57-0	0	67	.261	.331	.404	91	-7	8-3	.989	5	114	93	1b139	0	-0.9
Agler, Joe	Joseph Abram; B6.12.1887 Coshocton OH; D4.26.1971 Massillon OH; BL/TL/5´11˝/165; d10.1																								
1912	Was A	2	1	0	0	0	0	0	0	0	0	—	.000	.000	.000	-99	0	0	ø	0	0	0	/1	—	0.0
1914	Buf F	135	463	82	126	17	6	0	20	77	0	78	.272	.376	.335	93	-8	21	.985	3	123	114	1b76,O54(44/5/6)	—	-1.0
1915	Buf F	25	73	11	13	1	2	0	2	20	0	14	.178	.355	.247	69	-3	2	.973	-2	102	0	O20(6/3/11)/1	—	-0.7
	Bal F	72	214	28	46	4	2	0	14	34	1	38	.215	.325	.252	62	-13	15	.981	4	141	124	1b58,O4(2/1/1),2b3	—	-1.1
	Year	97	287	39	59	5	4	0	16	54	1	52	.206	.333	.251	64	-16	17	.981	2	140	123	1b59,O24(8/4/12),2b3	—	-1.8
Total	3	234	751	121	185	22	10	0	36	131	1	130	.246	.359	.302	81	-24	38	.983	5	130	118	1b136,O78(52/9/18),2b3	—	-2.8
Agnew, Sam	Samuel Lester "Slam"; B4.12.1887 Farmington MO; D7.19.1951 Sonoma CA; BR/TR/5´11˝/185; d4.10																								
1913	StL A	105	307	27	64	9	5	2	24	20	7	49	.208	.272	.290	66	-14	11	.952	5	*111*	*107*	C103	—	0.0
1914	StL A	115	311	22	66	5	4	0	16	24	5	63	.212	.279	.254	63	-15	10-8	.961	0	*98*	*108*	C115	—	-0.7
1915	StL A	104	295	18	60	4	2	0	19	12	5	36	.203	.247	.231	45	-21	5-2	.934	1	*94*	***127***	C102	—	-1.3
1916	Bos A	40	67	4	14	2	1	0	7	6	2	4	.209	.293	.269	69	-3	0	.952	5	155	150	C38	—	0.5
1917	Bos A	85	260	17	54	6	2	0	16	19	2	30	.208	.267	.246	57	-14	2	.965	-4	*118*	*89*	C85	—	-1.2
1918	†Bos A	72	199	11	33	8	0	0	6	11	3	26	.166	.221	.206	29	-17	0	.965	8	*113*	*115*	C72	—	-0.4
1919	Was A	42	98	6	23	7	0	0	10	10	1	8	.235	.312	.306	74	-3	1	.974	6	*97*	*133*	C36	—	0.6
Total	7	563	1537	105	314	41	14	2	98	102	25	216	.204	.265	.253	56	-87	29-10	.955	21	*108*	*113*	C551	—	-2.5
Aguayo, Luis	Luis (Muriel); B3.13.1959 Vega Baja, PR; BR/TR/5´9˝/(173–195); d4.19																								
1980	Phi N	20	47	7	13	1	2	1	8	2-0	0	3	.277	.300	.447	101	0	1-1	.962	3	101	121	2b14,S5	15	0.3
1981	†Phi N	45	84	11	18	4	0	1	7	6-0	2	15	.214	.283	.298	61	-4	1-0	.938	-6	79	93	2b21,S21,3b3	0	-0.9
1982	Phi N	50	56	11	15	1	2	3	7	5-1	1	7	.268	.339	.518	132	2	1-1	.966	-3	98	42	2b21,S15,3b5	0	0.0
1983	Phi N	2	4	1	1	0	0	0	0	1-0	0	2	.250	.400	.250	84	0	0-0	1.000	-2	0	0	S2	70	-0.2
1984	Phi N	58	72	15	20	4	0	3	11	8-2	0	16	.278	.350	.458	123	2	0-0	.909	4	149	104	3b14,2b12,S10	0	0.7
1985	Phi N	91	165	27	46	7	3	6	21	22-5	6	26	.279	.378	.467	133	8	1-0	.957	1	92	82	S60,2b17,3b7	0	1.5
1986	Phi N	62	133	17	28	6	1	4	13	8-0	3	26	.211	.267	.361	70	-6	1-1	.967	-9	99	81	2b31,S20/3	0	-1.3
1987	Phi N	94	209	25	43	9	1	12	21	15-1	5	56	.206	.273	.431	81	-7	0-0	.971	-2	96	94	S78,2b6,3b2	15	-0.3
1988	Phi N	49	97	9	24	3	0	3	5	13-2	0	17	.247	.336	.371	101	0	2-0	.967	4	104	110	S27,3b13,2b2	0	0.6
	NY A	50	140	12	35	4	0	3	8	7-1	1	33	.250	.289	.343	77	-5	0-2	.961	-7	97	83	3b33,2b13,S6	0	-1.2
1989	Cle A	47	97	7	17	4	1	1	8	7-0	2	19	.175	.239	.268	44	-7	0-0	.950	1	99	42	3b19,S15,2b10,D2	24	-0.6
Total	10	568	1104	142	260	43	10	37	109	94-12	20	220	.236	.304	.393	90	-17	7-5	.960	-16	92	90	S259,2b147,3b97,D2	124	-1.4
Aguila, Chris	Christopher Louis; B2.23.1979 Redwood City CA; BR/TR/5´11˝/180; [FlaN97 3/96]; d6.28																								
2004	Fla N	29	45	10	10	2	1	3	5	2-0	0	12	.222	.255	.511	96	-1	0-0	.909	0	99	163	O20(6/0/14)	0	-0.1
2005	Fla N	65	78	11	19	3	0	0	4	3-0	0	19	.244	.272	.282	48	-6	0-1	1.000	2	128	108	O42(27/2/14)	0	-0.5
2006	Fla N	47	95	5	22	8	1	0	7	9-1	0	26	.232	.298	.337	65	-5	2-1	1.000	1	97	196	O31(15/1/24)/D	0	-0.5
Total	3	141	218	26	51	13	2	3	16	14-1	0	57	.234	.280	.353	66	-12	2-2	.981	3	108	158	O93(48/3/52)/D	0	-1.1
Ahearn, Charlie	Charles; B Troy NY; d6.19																								
1880	Tro N	1	4	1	1	0	0	0	0	0	—	0	.250	.250	.250	67	0	—	.778	-0	—	—	/C	—	-0.1
Aikens, Willie	Willie Mays; B10.14.1954 Seneca SC; BL/TR/6´3˝/(220–225); [AnaA75*1/2]; d5.17; Col South Carolina St.																								
1977	Cal A	42	91	5	18	4	0	0	6	10-2	0	23	.198	.277	.242	44	-7	1-2	.971	-0	104	105	1b13,D13	0	-0.9
1979	Cal A	116	379	59	106	18	0	21	81	61-8	1	79	.280	.376	.493	138	22	1-3	.996	-4	73	94	1b55,D51	0	1.2
1980	†KC A	151	543	70	151	24	0	20	98	64-3	7	88	.278	.356	.433	115	13	1-0	.990	-8	81	85	1b138,D13	0	-0.3
1981	†KC A	101	349	45	93	16	0	17	53	62-**12**	3	47	.266	.377	.458	141	21	0-0	.992	-4	89	95	1b99	0	1.2
1982	KC A	134	466	50	131	29	1	17	74	45-7	3	70	.281	.345	.457	118	12	0-1	.994	1	105	96	1b128	15	0.6
1983	KC A	125	410	49	124	26	1	23	72	45-9	2	75	.302	.373	.539	147	27	0-0	.989	-1	100	111	1b112,D6	0	1.9
1984	Tor A	93	234	21	48	7	0	11	26	29-1	2	56	.205	.298	.376	82	-6	0-0	1.000	0	98	95	D81,1b2	0	-0.8
1985	Tor A	12	20	2	4	1	0	1	5	3-0	0	6	.200	.292	.400	88	0	0-0	ø	0	0	0	D11	0	-0.1
Total	8	774	2492	301	675	125	2	110	415	319-42	18	444	.271	.354	.455	122	82	3-6	.991	-15	92	96	1b547,D175	15	2.8
Ainge, Danny	Daniel Ray; B3.17.1959 Eugene OR; BR/TR (BB 1979p)/6´4˝/175; [TorA77 15/389]; d5.21																								
1979	Tor A	87	308	26	73	7	1	2	19	12-1	2	58	.237	.269	.286	49	-23	1-0	.977	1	102	103	2b86/D	0	-1.7
1980	Tor A	38	111	11	27	6	1	0	4	2-0	1	29	.243	.263	.315	55	-7	3-0	.986	0	92	152	O29(6/22/1),3b3/2D	0	-0.6
1981	Tor A	86	246	20	46	6	2	0	14	23-1	1	41	.187	.258	.228	39	-19	8-5	.949	2	103	148	3b77,S6,O4(0/3/1),2b2/D	0	-1.9
Total	3	211	665	57	146	19	4	2	37	37-2	4	128	.220	.264	.269	47	-49	12-5	.977	3	102	101	2b89,3b80,O33(6/25/2),S6,D4	0	-4.2
Ainsmith, Eddie	Edward Wilbur "Dorf" (b Edward Anshmedt); B2.4.1890 , Russia; D9.6.1981 Ft.Lauderdale FL; BR/TR/5´11˝/180; d8.9; Mil 1918																								
1910	Was A	33	104	4	20	1	2	0	9	6	0	—	.192	.236	.240	52	-6	0	.963	-2	*98*	*110*	C30	—	-0.6
1911	Was A	61	149	12	33	2	3	0	14	10	1	—	.221	.275	.275	55	-10	5	.952	2	*105*	*104*	C47	—	-0.4
1912	Was A	61	186	22	42	7	2	0	22	14	0	—	.226	.280	.285	61	-10	4	.958	15	*145*	*83*	C59	—	1.0
1913	Was A	84	229	26	49	4	4	2	20	12	3	41	.214	.262	.293	61	-13	17	.967	6	*120*	*83*	C79/P	—	-0.1
1914	Was A	62	151	11	34	7	0	0	13	9	1	28	.225	.273	.272	61	-7	8-5	.969	5	*112*	*82*	C51	—	0.2
1915	Was A	47	120	13	24	4	2	0	6	10	1	18	.200	.267	.267	59	-6	7-4	.988	6	*118*	*88*	C42	—	0.3
1916	Was A	51	100	11	17	4	0	0	8	8	0	14	.170	.231	.210	33	-8	3	.959	6	113	123	C46	—	0.1
1917	Was A	125	350	38	67	17	4	0	42	40	3	48	.191	.280	.263	66	-13	16	.971	8	*90*	*116*	C119	—	0.4
1918	Was A	96	292	22	62	10	9	0	20	29	0	44	.212	.283	.308	80	-8	6	.975	3	*102*	*109*	C89	—	0.3
1919	Det A	114	364	42	99	17	12	3	32	45	1	30	.272	.354	.409	117	8	9	.962	-11	*88*	*80*	C106	—	0.6
1920	Det A	69	186	19	43	5	3	1	19	14	0	19	.231	.285	.306	58	-12	4-3	.955	-6	*92*	*95*	C61/1	—	-1.3
1921	Det A	35	98	6	27	5	2	0	12	13	0	7	.276	.360	.367	87	-2	1-0	.947	-4	*87*	*109*	C34	—	-0.3
	StL N	27	62	5	18	0	1	0	5	3	0	4	.290	.323	.323	73	-3	0-0	.956	0	*109*	*87*	C23/1	—	-0.1
1922	StL N	119	379	46	111	14	4	13	59	28	1	43	.293	.343	.454	109	4	2-3	.963	-2	*108*	*98*	C116	—	0.8
1923	StL N	82	263	22	56	11	6	3	34	22	1	19	.213	.276	.335	62	-16	4-0	.980	-7	*93*	*83*	C80	—	-1.6
	Bro N	2	10	0	2	0	0	0	2	0	0	0	.200	.200	.200	6	-1	0-1	1.000	1	*94*	*66*	C2	—	-0.1
	Year	84	273	22	58	11	6	3	36	22	1	19	.212	.274	.330	60	-17	4-1	.981	-7	*93*	*82*	C82	—	-1.7
1924	NY N	10	5	0	3	0	0	0	0	0	0	0	.600	.600	.600	229	1	0-0	1.000	-0	*70*	*0*	C9	—	0.1
Total	15	1078	3048	299	707	108	54	22	317	263	12	315	.232	.296	.324	76	-102	86-16	.966	20	*104*	*96*	C993,1b2/P	—	-0.7
Aiton, George	George Wilson; B12.29.1890 Kingman KS; D8.16.1976 N.Hollywood CA; BB/TR/5´11.5˝/175; d6.29; Col Friends																								
1912	StL A	10	17	1	4	0	0	0	1	4	0	—	.235	.381	.235	80	0	0	.917	0	109	165	O7(5/2/0)	—	0.0
Ake, John	John Leckie; B8.29.1861 Altoona PA; D5.11.1887 LaCrosse WI; BR/TR/6´1˝/180; d5.12																								
1884	Bal AA	13	52	1	10	0	1	0	2	0	1	—	.192	.208	.231	41	-4	—	.677	-3	86	195	3b9,O3(2/0/1)/S	—	-0.6
Akers, Bill	William G. "Bump"; B12.25.1904 Chattanooga TN; D4.13.1962 Chattanooga TN; BR/TR/5´11˝/178; d9.8																								
1929	Det A	24	83	15	22	4	1	1	9	10	1	9	.265	.351	.373	86	-2	2-0	.935	-6	83	83	S24	—	-0.5
1930	Det A	85	233	36	65	8	5	9	40	36	0	34	.279	.375	.472	111	4	5-5	.944	6	104	123	S49,3b26	—	1.4
1931	Det A	29	66	5	13	2	2	0	3	7	0	6	.197	.274	.288	46	-5	0-1	.935	-4	82	79	S21,2b2	—	-0.8
1932	Bos N	36	93	8	24	3	1	1	17	10	0	15	.258	.330	.344	85	-2	0	.927	-5	95	30	3b20,2b5,S5	—	-0.5
Total	4	174	475	64	124	17	9	11	69	63	1	64	.261	.349	.404	93	-5	7-6	.936	-9	94	106	S99,3b46,2b7	—	-0.4

YEAR	TM LG	G	AB	R	H	2B	3B	HR	RBI	BB-IB	HP	SO	AVG	OBP	SLG	AOPS	ABR	SB-CS	FA	FR	RNG	THR	GAMES AT POSITION	DL	BFW
Alberts, Gus	Augustus Peter; B1861 Reading PA; D5.7.1912 Idaho Springs CO; BR/TR/5´6.5˝/180; d5.1																								
1884	Pit AA	2	5	1	1	0	0	0	—	0	0	—	.200	.200	.200	31	0	—	.500	-1	76	0	S2	—	-0.1
	Was U	4	16	4	4	0	0	0	—	4	—	—	.250	.400	.250	105	0	—	.870	1	113	132	S4	—	0.1
1888	Cle AA	102	364	51	75	10	6	1	48	41	7	—	.206	.299	.275	87	-3	26	.862	8	107	111	S53,3b49	—	0.6
1891	Mil AA	12	41	6	4	0	0	0	2	7	2	5	.098	.260	.098	2	-5	1	.814	-3	76	106	3b12	—	-0.8
Total	3	120	426	62	84	10	6	1	50	52	9	5	.197	.298	.256	76	-8	27	.880	5	97	119	3b61,S59	—	-0.2
Alberts, Butch	Francis Burt; B5.4.1950 Williamsport PA; BR/TR/6´2˝/205; [PitN72 28/642]; d9.7; Col Cincinnati																								
1978	Tor A	6	18	1	5	1	0	0	0	0-0	0	2	.278	.278	.333	70	-1	0-0	ø	0	—	—	D4	0	-0.1
Albright, Jack	Harold John; B6.30.1921 St.Petersburg FL; D7.22.1991 San Diego CA; BR/TR/5´9˝/175; d5.19; Col California																								
1947	Phi N	41	99	9	23	4	0	2	5	10	0	11	.232	.303	.333	71	-4	1	.943	1	106	96	S33	0	-0.2
Alcantara, Israel	Israel (Cristosomo); B5.6.1973 Bani, D.R.; BR/TR/6´2˝/(180–210); d6.25																								
2000	Bos A	21	45	9	13	1	0	4	7	3-0	0	7	.289	.333	.578	121	1	0-0	.889	-1	94	0	O7(1/0/7),1b5,D8	18	0.0
2001	Bos A	14	38	3	10	1	0	0	3	3-0	0	13	.263	.317	.289	61	-2	1-0	.900	-1	64	262	O8(6/0/2),1b4/D	0	-0.3
2002	Mil N	16	32	3	8	1	0	2	5	0-0	0	6	.250	.250	.469	84	-1	0-1	1.000	-1	76	0	O7(2/0/5),1b2	0	-0.3
Total	3	51	115	15	31	3	0	6	15	6-0	0	26	.270	.306	.452	92	-2	1-1	.923	-2	76	108	O22(9/0/14),1b11,D9	18	-0.6
Alcaraz, Luis	Angel Luis (Acosta); B6.20.1941 Humacao, PR; BR/TR/5´9˝/165; d9.13																								
1967	LA N	17	60	1	14	1	0	0	3	1-0	0	13	.233	.242	.250	46	-4	1-1	.990	3	106	164	2b17	0	0.0
1968	LA N	41	106	4	16	1	0	2	5	9-2	0	23	.151	.217	.217	33	-9	1-1	.979	0	98	78	2b20,3b13/S	0	-0.9
1969	KC A	22	79	15	20	2	1	1	7	7-0	0	9	.253	.314	.342	82	-2	0-0	.988	-4	91	44	2b19,3b2/S	0	-0.5
1970	KC A	35	120	10	20	5	1	1	14	4-0	0	13	.167	.192	.250	21	-13	0-0	.993	-12	76	58	2b31	0	-2.5
Total	4	115	365	30	70	9	2	4	29	21-2	0	58	.192	.235	.260	43	-28	2-2	.988	-12	90	81	2b87,3b15,S2	0	-3.9
Alcock, Scotty	John Forbes; B11.29.1885 Wooster OH; D1.30.1973 Wooster OH; BR/TR/5´9.5˝/160; d4.19																								
1914	Chi A	54	156	12	27	4	2	0	7	7	1	14	.173	.213	.224	32	-14	4-2	.905	1	104	169	3b48/2	—	-1.2
Aldrete, Mike	Michael Peter; B1.29.1961 Carmel CA; BL/TL/5´11˝/(180–185); [SFN83 7/174]; d5.28; C3; Col Stanford																								
1986	SF N	84	216	27	54	18	3	2	25	33-4	2	34	.250	.353	.389	110	4	1-3	1.000	3	148	149	1b37,O31(30/0/2)	0	0.4
1987	†SF N	126	357	50	116	18	2	9	51	43-5	0	50	.325	.396	.462	133	18	6-0	.986	1	107	67	O79(43/13/30),1b33	0	1.7
1988	SF N	139	389	44	104	15	0	3	50	56-13	0	65	.267	.357	.329	103	4	6-5	.982	3	108	89	O115(83/7/40),1b10	0	0.3
1989	Mon N	76	136	12	30	8	1	1	12	19-0	1	30	.221	.316	.316	81	-3	1-3	.980	1	95	148	O37(16/3/19),1b10	16	-0.4
1990	Mon N	96	161	22	39	7	1	1	18	37-2	1	31	.242	.385	.317	99	2	1-2	.982	1	91	207	O38(26/0/14),1b18	0	0.1
1991	SD N	12	15	2	0	0	0	0	1	3-0	0	4	.000	.167	.000	-48	-3	0-1	1.000	1	118	593	O5L	0	-0.3
	Cle A	85	183	22	48	6	1	1	19	36-1	0	37	.262	.380	.322	97	1	1-2	.994	-1	92	102	1b47,O16L,D7	0	-0.4
1993	Oak A	95	255	40	68	13	1	10	33	34-2	0	45	.267	.353	.443	119	7	1-1	.995	-4	74	84	1b59,O20(17/0/3),D6	0	-0.2
1994	Oak A	76	178	23	43	5	0	4	18	20-1	0	35	.242	.313	.337	75	-7	2-0	1.000	-2	85	0	O35(21/0/15),1b27/D	0	-1.1
1995	Oak A	60	125	18	34	8	0	4	21	19-1	1	23	.272	.367	.432	114	3	0-0	.989	-3	62	84	1b35,O16(9/1/6)	0	-0.2
	Cal A	18	24	1	6	0	0	0	3	0-0	0	8	.250	.240	.250	31	-3	0-0	1.000	1	390	0	O2L/1D	0	-0.2
	Year	78	149	19	40	8	0	4	24	19-1	1	31	.268	.349	.403	101	1	0-0	.989	-2	61	83	1b36,O18(11/1/6),D2	0	-0.4
1996	Cal A	31	40	5	6	1	0	3	8	5-0	0	4	.150	.239	.400	58	-3	0-0	.750	-1	46	0	O6(4/0/2)/1D	0	-0.4
	†NY A	32	68	11	17	5	0	3	12	9-0	0	15	.250	.338	.456	98	0	0-1	1.000	-2	70	0	O9(6/0/4),1b8/PD	28	-0.3
	Year	63	108	16	23	6	0	6	20	14-0	0	19	.213	.301	.435	83	-3	0-1	.909	-3	61	0	O15(10/0/6),D15,1b9/P	0	-0.7
Total	10	930	2147	277	565	104	9	41	271	314-29	5	381	.263	.356	.377	104	20	19-18	.983	-3	100	87	O409(278/24/135),1b286,D31/P	44	-1.0
Aldridge, Cory	Cory Jerome; B6.13.1979 San Angelo TX; BL/TR/6´0˝/210; [AtlN97 4/142]; d9.5; [DL 2002 Atl N 183]																								
2001	Atl N	8	5	1	0	0	0	0	0	0-0	0	4	.000	.000	.000	-99	-1	0-0	1.000	-0	64	0	O4(1/1/2)	0	-0.2
Aleno, Chuck	Charles; B2.19.1917 St.Louis MO; D2.10.2003 DeLand FL; BR/TR/6´1.5˝/215; d5.15																								
1941	Cin N	54	169	23	41	7	3	1	18	11	0	16	.243	.289	.337	76	-6	3	.975	-1	96	89	3b40,1b2	0	-0.6
1942	Cin N	7	14	1	2	1	0	0	0	3	0	3	.143	.294	.214	50	-1	0	.727	0	99	0	3b2/2	0	-0.1
1943	Cin N	7	10	0	3	0	0	0	1	2	0	1	.300	.417	.300	110	0	0	1.000	-0	69	0	O2L	0	0.0
1944	Cin N	50	127	10	21	3	0	1	15	15	1	15	.165	.259	.213	35	-11	0	.952	-4	85	102	3b42,1b3,S3	0	-1.5
Total	4	118	320	34	67	11	3	2	34	31	1	35	.209	.281	.281	60	-18	3	.954	-5	91	91	3b84,1b5,S3,O2L/2	0	-2.2
Alexander, Dale	David Dale "Moose"; B4.26.1903 Greeneville TN; D3.2.1979 Greeneville TN; BR/TR/6´3˝/210; d4.16; Col Milligan																								
1929	Det A	**155**	626	110	**215**	43	15	25	137	56	0	63	.343	.397	.580	148	42	5-9	.988	-4	92	87	1b155	—	2.4
1930	Det A	**154**	602	86	196	33	8	20	135	42	2	56	.326	.372	.507	118	15	6-5	.985	-6	83	106	1b154	—	-0.1
1931	Det A	135	517	75	168	47	3	3	87	64	2	35	.325	.401	.445	118	17	5-8	.987	-8	75	92	1b126,O4L	—	-0.4
1932	Det A	23	16	0	4	0	0	0	4	6	0	2	.250	.455	.250	84	0	0-0	1.000	-0	0	0	1b2	—	0.0
	Bos A	101	376	58	140	27	3	8	56	55	1	19	.372	.454	.524	157	35	4-5	.992	2	107	101	1b101	—	2.4
	Year	124	392	58	144	27	3	8	60	61	1	21	**.367**	.454	.513	152	34	4-5	.992	2	107	101	1b103	—	2.4
1933	Bos A	94	313	40	88	14	1	5	40	25	1	22	.281	.336	.380	90	-5	0-1	.992	3	118	84	1b79	—	-0.8
Total	5	662	2450	369	811	164	30	61	459	248	6	197	.331	.394	.497	128	104	20-28	.988	-13	92	95	1b617,O4L	—	3.5
Alexander, Gary	Gary Wayne; B3.27.1953 Los Angeles CA; BR/TR/6´2˝/(190–200); [SFN72*S2/36]; d9.12; Col Los Angeles Harbor (CA) JC																								
1975	SF N	3	3	1	0	0	0	0	0	1-0	0	2	.000	.250	.000	-25	0	0-0	1.000	-2	13	0	C2	0	-0.2
1976	SF N	23	73	12	13	1	1	2	7	10-1	0	16	.178	.274	.301	62	-4	1-0	.964	-6	52	78	C23	0	-0.9
1977	SF N	51	119	17	36	4	2	5	20	20-2	2	33	.303	.406	.496	142	8	3-1	.968	-10	53	53	C33/rf	0	0.0
1978	Oak A	58	174	18	36	6	1	10	22	22-2	1	66	.207	.298	.425	107	1	0-3	1.000	1	167	0	D45,O6(3/0/3)/C1	0	-0.1
	Cle A	90	324	39	76	14	3	17	62	35-3	1	100	.235	.308	.454	114	5	0-2	.983	-3	89	114	C66,D25	0	0.3
	Year	148	498	57	112	20	4	27	84	57-5	2	166	.225	.304	.444	111	6	0-5	.983	-2	89	114	D70,C67,O6(3/0/3)/1	0	0.2
1979	Cle A	110	358	54	82	9	2	15	54	46-3	1	100	.229	.313	.391	90	-6	4-2	.961	-22	70	82	C91,D13,O2(1/0/1)	0	-2.3
1980	Cle A	76	178	22	40	7	1	5	31	17-1	0	52	.225	.288	.360	77	-6	0-4	.971	-2	53	101	D40,C13,O2(1/0/1)	0	-1.0
1981	Pit N	21	47	6	10	4	1	1	6	3-0	0	12	.213	.255	.404	82	-1	0-0	.964	2	49	86	1b9,O8(7/0/2)	0	0.0
Total	7	432	1276	169	293	45	11	55	202	154-12	5	381	.230	.311	.411	99	-3	8-12	.969	-41	70	87	C229,D123,O19(12/0/8),1b10	0	-4.2
Alexander, Hugh	Hugh; B7.10.1917 Buffalo MO; D11.25.2000 Oklahoma City OK; BR/TR/6´0˝/190; d8.15																								
1937	Cle A	7	11	0	1	0	0	0	0	0	0	5	.091	.091	.091	-54	-3	1-0	.667	-1	65	0	O3(1/0/3)	—	-0.3
Alexander, Manny	Manuel De Jesus (b Manuel De Jesus (Alexander)); B3.20.1971 San Pedro de Macoris, D.R.; BR/TR/5´10˝/(150–180); d9.18; OF(4/0/2); [DL 1994 Bal A 29]																								
1992	Bal A	4	5	1	1	0	0	0	0	0-0	0	3	.200	.200	.200	12	-1	0-0	1.000	-0	68	109	S3	0	-0.1
1993	Bal A	3	0	1	0	0	0	0	0	0-0	0	0	ø	ø	ø	ø	0	0-0	ø	0	—	—	/R	0	0.0
1995	Bal A	94	242	35	57	9	1	3	23	20-0	2	30	.236	.299	.318	60	-15	11-4	.971	-5	86	122	2b81,S7,3b2/D	0	-1.4
1996	†Bal A	54	68	6	7	0	0	0	4	3-0	0	27	.103	.141	.103	-37	-15	3-3	.940	-2	111	89	S21,2b7,3b7,O3L/PD	0	-1.4
1997	NY N	54	149	26	37	9	3	2	15	9-1	1	38	.248	.294	.389	81	-5	11-0	.979	2	112	146	2b31,S26/3	46	0.2
	Chi N	33	99	11	29	3	1	1	7	8-2	2	16	.293	.358	.374	89	-2	2-1	.942	-2	110	71	S28,2b4	0	-0.1
	Year	87	248	37	66	12	4	3	22	17-3	3	54	.266	.320	.383	85	-6	13-1	.959	0	113	80	S54,2b35/3	0	0.1
1998	†Chi N	108	264	34	60	10	1	5	25	18-1	1	66	.227	.278	.330	57	-17	4-1	.964	-12	81	80	S50,2b27,3b19/lfD	0	-2.5
1999	Chi N	90	177	17	48	11	2	0	15	10-0	0	38	.271	.309	.356	68	-9	4-0	.988	1	114	86	S30,3b22,2b17,O2R	0	-0.5
2000	Bos A	101	194	30	41	4	3	4	19	13-0	0	41	.211	.261	.325	46	-17	2-0	.944	0	95	69	3b63,S20,2b7,D2	2	-1.4
2004	Tex A	21	21	3	5	2	0	0	3	1-0	0	7	.238	.273	.333	55	-1	0-0	.917	-1	124	0	2b11,S7,3b3	0	-0.2
2005	SD N	10	18	0	2	1	0	0	0	2-1	1	5	.111	.238	.167	9	-2	0-0	1.000	-3	59	0	2b5,S4/13	0	-0.5
2006	SD N	22	34	2	6	1	1	0	4	2-2	0	5	.176	.216	.265	25	-4	0-1	.900	2	103	158	3b13,S9	0	-0.2
Total	11	594	1271	166	293	50	12	15	115	86-7	7	276	.231	.282	.324	56	-88	37-10	.966	-18	104	88	S205,2b190,3b131,O6L,D6/1P	77	-8.1
Alexander, Matt	Matthew; B1.30.1947 Shreveport LA; BB/TR/5´11˝/(162–170); [ChiN68 2/35]; d8.23; Col Grambling St.																								
1973	Chi N	12	5	4	1	0	0	0	1	1-0	0	1	.200	.333	.200	47	0	2-0	1.000	-0	57	0	O3C	0	0.0
1974	Chi N	45	54	15	11	2	1	0	0	12-1	1	12	.204	.358	.278	76	-1	8-4	.921	-3	79	97	3b19,O4(0/2/1),2b2	0	-0.4
1975	Oak A	63	10	16	1	0	0	0	0	1-0	0	1	.100	.182	.100	-19	-2	17-10	1.000	-1	102	0	D17,O11(1/3/7),2b3,3b2	28	-0.3
1976	Oak A	61	30	16	1	0	0	0	0	0-0	0	5	.033	.033	.033	-84	-7	20-7	1.000	0	116	0	O23(7/7/11),D19	0	-0.6
1977	Oak A	90	42	24	10	1	0	0	2	4-0	0	6	.238	.304	.262	57	-2	26-14	1.000	-2	93	0	O31(7/17/8),S12,D12,2b4/3	0	-0.4
1978	Pit N	7	0	2	0	0	0	0	0	0-0	0	0	ø	ø	ø	ø	0	4-1	ø	0	—	—	/R	0	0.0
1979	†Pit N	44	13	16	7	0	1	0	1	0-0	0	0	.538	.538	.692	221	2	13-1	1.000	0	99	359	O11(6/3/3)/S	0	0.5

YEAR	TM LG	G	AB	R	H	2B	3B	HR	RBI	BB-IB	HP	SO	AVG	OBP	SLG	AOPS	ABR	SB-CS	FA	FR	RNG	THR	GAMES AT POSITION	DL	BFW
1980	Pit N	37	3	13	1	1	0	0	0	0-0	0	0	.333	.333	.667	167	0	10-3	1.000	0	189	0	O4(2/2/0)/2	15	0.2
1981	Pit N	15	11	5	4	0	0	0	0	0-0	0	1	.364	.364	.364	102	0	3-2	1.000	0	125	0	O6(2/3/1)	95	0.0
Total	9	374	168	111	36	4	2	0	4	18-1	1	26	.214	.294	.262	56	-10	103-42	1.000	-5	105	41	O93(25/40/31),D48,3b22,S13,2b10	138	-1.0
ALEXANDER, WALT	Walter Ernest; B3.5.1891 Atlanta GA; D12.29.1978 Fort Worth TX; BR/TR/5´10.5˝/165; d6.21																								
1912	StL A	37	97	5	17	4	0	0	5	8	1	—	.175	.245	.216	34	-8	1	.969	-3	*84*	*96*	C37	—	-0.9
1913	StL A	43	110	5	15	2	1	0	7	4	1	36	.136	.174	.173	2	-14	1	.947	3	*112*	*127*	C43	—	-0.9
1915	StL A	1	1	0	0	0	0	0	0	0	0	0	.000	.000	.000	-99	0	0	ø	-0	*0*	*0*	/C	—	0.0
	NY A	25	68	7	17	4	0	1	5	13	0	16	.250	.370	.353	117	2	2-1	.967	5	*105*	*118*	C24	—	1.0
	Year	26	69	7	17	4	0	1	5	13	0	16	.246	.366	.348	114	2	2-1	.967	5	*105*	*117*	C25	—	1.0
1916	NY A	36	78	8	20	6	1	0	3	13	2	20	.256	.376	.359	118	3	0	.960	2	133	134	C27	—	0.7
1917	NY A	20	51	1	7	2	1	0	4	4	0	11	.137	.200	.216	27	-5	1	.951	0	*140*	*74*	C20	—	-0.3
Total	5	162	405	26	76	18	3	1	24	42	4	83	.188	.271	.254	56	-22	5-1	.959	7	*111*	*112*	C152	—	-0.4
ALEXANDER, NIN	William Henry; B11.24.1858 Pana IL; D12.22.1933 Pana IL; BR/TR/5´4.5˝/163; d6.7																								
1884	KC U	19	65	2	9	0	0	0	—	1	—	—	.138	.152	.138	-13	-11	—	.907	-1	—	—	C17,S2,O2C	—	-0.9
	StL AA	1	4	0	0	0	0	0	—	0	0	—	.000	.000	.000	-97	-1	—	.667	-0	—	—	/Ccf	—	-0.1
Total	1	20	69	2	9	0	0	0	—	1	0	—	.130	.143	.130	-19	-12	—	.895	-1	—	—	C18,O3C,S2	—	-1.0
ALFARO, JASON	Jason; B11.29.1977 San Antonio TX; BR/TR/5´10˝/185; [HouN97 22/670]; d9.9; Col Hill (TX) JC																								
2004	Hou N	7	11	1	2	0	0	0	0	0-0	0	5	.182	.182	.182	-5	-2	0-0	1.000	-1	54	85	S3	0	-0.3
ALFONZO, EDGARDO	Edgardo Antonio; B8.11.1973 Santa Teresa, Miranda, Venez.; BR/TR/5´11˝/(187–225); d4.26																								
1995	NY N	101	335	26	93	13	5	4	41	12-1	1	37	.278	.301	.382	82	-10	1-1	.962	-9	100	103	3b58,2b29,S6	21	-1.7
1996	NY N	123	368	36	96	15	2	4	40	25-2	0	56	.261	.304	.345	76	-14	2-0	.974	-5	99	108	2b66,3b36,S15	0	-1.4
1997	NY N	151	518	84	163	27	2	10	72	63-0	5	56	.315	.391	.432	122	19	11-6	.967	8	113	**137**	3b143,S12,2b3	0	2.9
1998	NY N	144	557	94	155	28	2	17	78	65-1	3	77	.278	.355	.427	108	7	8-3	.976	-7	90	83	3b144/S	15	0.2
1999	†NY N	158	628	123	191	41	1	27	108	85-2	3	85	.304	.385	.502	129	30	9-2	**.993**	-9	95	102	2b158	0	2.8
2000	†NY N★	150	544	109	176	40	2	25	94	95-1	5	70	.324	.425	.542	151	48	3-2	.985	6	101	96	2b146,D2	0	5.6
2001	NY N	124	457	64	111	22	0	17	49	51-0	5	62	.243	.322	.403	93	-5	5-0	.987	-6	98	93	2b122	19	-0.4
2002	NY N	135	490	78	151	26	0	16	56	62-8	7	55	.308	.391	.459	131	24	6-0	.969	7	106	85	3b134	20	3.3
2003	†SF N	142	514	56	133	25	2	13	81	58-4	4	41	.259	.334	.391	88	-8	5-2	.966	-17	89	74	3b133,2b6	0	-2.4
2004	SF N	139	519	66	150	26	1	11	77	46-2	5	40	.289	.350	.407	92	-5	1-1	.965	-6	100	88	3b129,2b5	0	-1.0
2005	SF N	109	368	36	102	17	1	2	43	27-1	2	34	.277	.327	.345	75	-13	2-0	.967	-14	83	56	3b97,2b2	39	-2.6
2006	LA A	18	50	1	5	1	0	0	1	2-0	0	3	.100	.135	.120	-35	-10	0-0	1.000	-1	91	45	3b15,1b2/D	0	-1.1
	Tor A	12	37	4	6	1	0	0	4	5-0	1	1	.162	.279	.189	24	-4	0-0	1.000	-2	98	52	2b12	0	-0.6
	Year	30	87	5	11	2	0	0	5	7-0	1	4	.126	.200	.149	-8	-14	0-0	1.000	-3	91	45	3b15,2b12,1b2/D	0	-1.7
Total	12	1506	5385	777	1532	282	18	146	744	596-22	41	617	.284	.357	.425	106	59	53-17	.968	-53	98	90	3b889,2b549,S34,D3,1b2	114	3.6
ALFONZO, ELIEZER	Eliezer Jesus; B2.7.1979 Puerto La Cruz, Venezuela; BR/TR/6´0˝/225; d6.3																								
2006	SF N	87	286	27	76	17	2	12	39	9-7	7	74	.266	.302	.465	93	-4	1-0	.992	8	92	99	C84	0	0.9
ALICEA, LUIS	Luis Rene (De Jesus); B7.29.1965 Santurce, PR; BB/TR/5´9˝/(165–177); [StLN86 1/23]; d4.23; OF(10/0/1)																								
1988	StL N	93	297	20	63	10	4	1	24	25-4	2	32	.212	.276	.283	60	-15	1-1	.970	0	99	105	2b91	0	-1.4
1991	StL N	56	68	5	13	3	0	0	0	8-0	0	19	.191	.276	.235	45	-5	0-1	1.000	1	103	83	2b11,3b2/S	0	-0.4
1992	StL N	85	265	26	65	9	11	2	32	27-1	4	40	.245	.320	.385	103	0	2-5	.989	-7	105	90	2b75,S4	51	-0.7
1993	StL N	115	362	50	101	19	3	3	46	47-2	4	54	.279	.362	.373	100	2	11-1	.978	8	114	114	2b96,O4L/3	0	1.6
1994	StL N	88	205	32	57	12	5	5	29	30-4	3	38	.278	.373	.459	117	6	4-5	.986	8	108	120	2b53,O2L	0	1.5
1995	†Bos A	132	419	64	113	20	3	6	44	63-0	7	61	.270	.367	.375	93	-2	13-10	.977	15	**109**	117	2b132	0	1.7
1996	†StL N	129	380	54	98	26	3	5	42	52-10	5	78	.258	.350	.382	94	-1	11-3	.957	-11	93	108	2b125	0	-0.5
1997	Ana A	128	388	59	98	16	7	5	37	69-3	8	65	.253	.375	.369	95	0	22-8	.978	-5	96	89	2b105,3b12,D6	0	0.2
1998	†Tex A	101	259	51	71	15	3	6	33	37-0	5	40	.274	.372	.425	102	2	4-3	.970	1	97	101	2b45,3b26,D17,O2L	0	0.3
1999	Tex A	68	164	33	33	10	0	3	17	28-0	0	32	.201	.316	.317	59	-10	2-1	.980	-4	89	87	2b37,3b10/lfD	0	-1.2
2000	Tex A	139	540	85	159	25	8	6	63	59-1	5	75	.294	.365	.404	94	-4	1-3	.978	-13	95	91	2b130,3b8,S2,D4	0	-1.0
2001	KC A	113	387	44	106	16	4	4	32	23-0	4	56	.274	.320	.367	73	-15	8-6	.958	1	109	120	2b67,D22,3b18	0	-1.2
2002	KC A	94	237	28	54	8	2	1	23	32-1	1	34	.228	.322	.291	58	-14	2-3	.986	8	135	131	2b32,3b32,D16,1b2/SO(1/0/1)	0	-0.6
Total	13	1341	3971	551	1031	189	53	47	422	500-26	48	624	.260	.346	.369	88	-56	81-50	.975	2	102	105	2b999,3b109,D72,O10L,S8,1b2	51	-1.7
ALLANSON, ANDY	Andrew Neal; B12.22.1961 Richmond VA; BR/TR/6´5˝/(215–225); [CleA83 2/39]; d4.7; Col Richmond; [DL 1994 Cal A 41]																								
1986	Cle A	101	293	30	66	7	3	1	29	14-0	1	36	.225	.260	.280	49	-22	10-1	.960	-11	88	73	C99	0	-2.7
1987	Cle A	50	154	17	41	6	0	3	16	9-0	0	30	.266	.298	.364	76	-5	1-1	.986	-3	146	57	C50	0	-0.6
1988	Cle A	133	434	44	114	11	0	5	50	25-2	3	63	.263	.305	.323	74	-15	5-9	.986	4	114	104	C133	20	-0.5
1989	Cle A	111	323	30	75	9	1	3	17	23-2	4	47	.232	.289	.294	64	-16	4-4	.986	5	96	92	C111	0	-0.5
1991	Det A	60	151	10	35	10	0	1	16	7-0	0	31	.232	.266	.318	60	-8	0-1	.979	-1	143	107	C56,1b2/D	0	-0.8
1992	Mil A	9	25	6	8	1	0	0	0	1-0	0	2	.320	.346	.360	99	0	3-1	.943	-2	72	0	C9	43	-0.2
1993	SF N	13	24	3	4	1	0	0	2	1-0	0	2	.167	.200	.208	10	-3	0-0	1.000	-1	195	57	C8,1b2	0	-0.4
1995	Cal A	35	82	5	14	3	0	3	10	7-0	1	12	.171	.244	.317	45	-7	0-1	.994	2	73	139	C35	21	-0.4
Total	8	512	1486	145	357	48	4	16	140	87-4	9	223	.240	.283	.310	64	-76	23-18	.980	-7	109	90	C501,1b4/D	125	-6.1
ALLEN, NICK	Artemus Ward; B9.14.1888 Norton KS; D10.16.1939 Hines IL; BR/TR/6´0˝/180; d5.1; Mil 1918																								
1914	Buf F	32	63	3	15	1	0	0	4	3	0	12	.238	.273	.254	43	-6	4	.969	2	*117*	*105*	C26	—	-0.3
1915	Buf F	84	215	14	44	7	1	0	17	18	1	34	.205	.269	.247	45	-19	4	.956	-2	*80*	*110*	C80	—	-1.7
1916	Chi N	5	16	1	1	0	0	0	1	0	0	3	.063	.063	.063	-56	-3	0	.958	-0	107	60	C4	—	-0.4
1918	Cin N	37	96	6	25	2	2	0	5	4	1	7	.260	.297	.323	91	-1	0	.950	5	*122*	*133*	C31	—	0.6
1919	Cin N	15	25	7	8	0	1	0	5	2	1	6	.320	.393	.400	142	1	0	.958	2	*134*	*94*	C12	—	0.4
1920	Cin N	43	85	10	23	3	1	0	4	6	3	11	.271	.340	.329	94	0	0-0	.961	3	*118*	*127*	C36	—	0.6
Total	6	216	500	41	116	13	5	0	36	33	6	73	.232	.288	.278	62	-28	8-0	.958	9	*102*	*115*	C189	—	-0.8
ALLEN, BERNIE	Bernard Keith; B4.16.1939 E.Liverpool OH; BL/TR/6´0˝/(175–186); d4.10; Col Purdue																								
1962	Min A	159	573	79	154	27	7	12	64	62-10	0	82	.269	.338	.403	96	-3	0-1	.983	-9	94	110	2b158	0	0.1
1963	Min A	139	421	52	101	20	1	9	43	38-8	1	52	.240	.302	.356	83	-9	0-0	.976	-24	84	97	2b128	0	-2.5
1964	Min A	74	243	28	52	8	1	6	20	33-7	1	30	.214	.309	.329	78	-7	1-2	.979	-5	94	89	2b71	52	-0.7
1965	Min A	19	39	2	9	2	0	0	6	6-2	0	8	.231	.326	.282	73	-1	0-0	1.000	-1	91	125	2b10/3	53	-0.1
1966	Min A	101	319	34	76	18	1	5	30	26-5	2	40	.238	.299	.348	80	-7	2-3	.974	-5	92	93	2b89,3b2	0	-0.6
1967	Was A	87	254	13	49	5	1	3	18	18-1	0	43	.193	.244	.256	51	-16	1-2	.990	14	117	148	2b75	0	0.3
1968	Was A	120	373	31	90	12	4	6	40	28-5	4	35	.241	.301	.343	98	-2	2-0	**.991**	6	103	104	2b110,3b2	0	1.5
1969	Was A	122	365	33	90	17	4	9	45	50-3	0	35	.247	.337	.389	108	4	5-4	.974	9	106	112	2b110,3b6	0	1.9
1970	Was A	104	261	31	61	7	1	8	29	43-4	0	21	.234	.342	.360	98	0	0-2	.969	8	103	119	2b80,3b12	0	1.2
1971	Was A	97	229	18	61	11	1	4	22	33-1	0	27	.266	.359	.376	113	5	2-1	.961	-6	100	58	2b41,3b34	0	0.1
1972	NY A	84	220	26	50	9	0	9	21	23-4	0	42	.227	.296	.391	107	1	0-1	.940	0	104	122	3b44,2b20	0	0.3
1973	NY A	17	57	5	13	3	0	0	4	5-1	0	5	.228	.290	.281	63	-3	0-0	.985	0	102	87	2b13,D2	0	-0.2
	Mon N	16	50	5	9	1	0	2	9	5-1	0	4	.180	.255	.320	56	-3	0-0	.970	-3	80	41	2b9,3b8	0	-0.6
Total	12	1139	3404	357	815	140	21	73	351	370-52	8	424	.239	.314	.357	90	-41	13-16	.980	-16	98	106	2b914,3b109,D2	105	0.7
ALLEN, JACK	Cyrus Alban; B10.2.1855 Woodstock IL; D4.21.1915 Girard PA; BR/TR/?/160; d5.1; Col Case Western Reserve																								
1879	Syr N	11	48	7	9	2	1	0	3	1	—	5	.188	.204	.271	62	-2	—	.655	-5	30	0	3b8,O3R	—	-0.6
	Cle N	16	60	7	7	1	1	0	4	1	—	9	.117	.131	.167	-3	-6	—	.845	2	96	101	3b14,O2C	—	-0.3
	Year	27	108	14	16	3	2	0	7	2	—	14	.148	.164	.213	24	-8	—	.790	-3	73	66	3b22,O5(0/2/3)	—	-0.9
ALLEN, DUSTY	Dustin R.; B8.9.1972 Oklahoma City OK; BR/TR/6´4˝/215; [SDN95 30/817]; d7.1; Col Stanford																								
2000	SD N	9	12	0	0	0	0	0	0	2-0	0	5	.000	.143	.000	-64	-3	0-0	1.000	-0	64	0	O2L/1D	0	-0.3
	Det A	18	16	5	7	2	0	2	2	2-0	0	7	.438	.500	.938	255	4	0-0	1.000	-1	28	111	1b17/3lf	0	0.2
Total	1	27	28	5	7	2	0	2	2	4-0	0	12	.250	.344	.536	122	1	0-0	1.000	-1	27	109	1b18,O3L/3D	0	-0.1

YEAR	TM LG	G	AB	R	H	2B	3B	HR	RBI	BB-IB	HP	SO	AVG	OBP	SLG	AOPS	ABR	SB-CS	FA	FR	RNG	THR	GAMES AT POSITION	DL	BFW
ALLEN, ETHAN	Ethan Nathan; B1.1.1904 Cincinnati OH; D9.15.1993 Brookings OR; BR/TR/6´1˝/180; d6.21; Col Cincinnati																								
1926	Cin N	18	13	3	4	1	0	0	0	0	0	3	.308	.308	.385	88	0	0	1.000	1	172	0	O9(5/0/4)	—	0.0
1927	Cin N	111	359	54	106	26	4	2	20	14	2	23	.295	.325	.407	98	-2	12	.988	-3	100	58	O98(14/72/13)	—	-0.9
1928	Cin N	129	485	55	148	30	7	1	62	27	1	29	.305	.343	.402	96	-4	6	.981	-1	99	103	O129(1/128/0)	—	-1.0
1929	Cin N	143	538	69	157	27	11	6	64	20	0	21	.292	.317	.416	84	-17	21	**.988**	5	107	91	O137(24/134/10)	—	-1.7
1930	Cin N	21	46	10	10	1	0	3	7	5	0	2	.217	.294	.435	77	-2	1	.969	-0	109	0	O15(1/13/1)	—	-0.3
	NY N	76	238	48	73	9	2	7	31	12	0	23	.307	.340	.450	91	-4	5	.985	-2	87	130	O62(1/54/7)	—	-0.8
	Year	97	284	58	83	10	2	10	38	17	0	25	.292	.332	.447	89	-7	6	.981	-3	91	108	O77(2/67/8)	—	-1.1
1931	NY N	94	298	58	98	18	2	5	43	15	1	15	.329	.363	.453	121	8	6	.975	-3	98	40	O77(40/23/14)	—	0.2
1932	NY N	54	103	13	18	6	2	1	7	1	2	12	.175	.198	.301	33	-10	0	.957	-1	97	71	O24(11/13/0)	—	-1.2
1933	StL N	91	261	25	63	7	3	0	36	13	1	22	.241	.280	.291	60	-14	3	.984	7	114	163	O67(0/46/21)	—	-1.0
1934	Phi N	145	581	87	192	**42**	4	10	85	33	3	47	.330	.370	.468	108	8	6	.978	11	105	183	O145(87/47/16)	—	1.1
1935	Phi N	**156**	645	90	198	46	1	8	63	43	1	54	.307	.351	.419	96	-2	5	.980	13	102	**205**	O156(19/136/1)	—	0.6
1936	Phi N	30	125	21	37	3	1	1	9	4	0	8	.296	.318	.360	75	-5	4	.954	-1	108	39	O30(11/16/6)	—	-0.7
	Chi N	91	373	47	110	18	6	3	39	13	2	30	.295	.322	.399	91	-6	12	.980	-3	99	31	O89(73/16/0)	—	-1.3
	Year	121	498	68	147	21	7	4	48	17	2	38	.295	.321	.390	87	-11	16	.972	-4	101	33	O119(84/32/6)	—	-2.0
1937	StL A	103	320	39	101	18	1	0	31	21	1	17	.316	.360	.378	86	-7	3-4	.980	2	101	118	O78(12/54/14)	—	-0.8
1938	StL A	19	33	4	10	3	1	0	4	2	0	4	.303	.343	.455	98	0	0-0	1.000	-0	99	0	O7(2/5/0)	—	-0.1
Total	13	1281	4418	623	1325	255	45	47	501	223	14	310	.300	.336	.410	92	-57	84-4	.981	22	102	115	O1123(301/757/107)	—	-7.9
ALLEN, SLED	Fletcher Manson; B8.23.1886 West Plains MO; D10.16.1959 Lubbock TX; BR/TR/6´1˝/180; d5.4																								
1910	StL A	14	23	3	3	1	0	0	1	1	2	—	.130	.231	.174	29	-2	0	.903	-4	67	77	C12/1	—	-0.6
ALLEN, HAM	Frank Erwin; B4.20.1846 Augusta ME; D2.6.1881 Natick MA; 5´4˝/?; d4.27																								
1872	Man NA	17	70	9	19	3	0	0	11	0	—	1	.271	.271	.314	84	-1	0-0	.778	6	136	110	S9,O9(4/3/2),3b5	—	0.3
ALLEN, HANK	Harold Andrew; B7.23.1940 Wampum PA; BR/TR/6´0˝/(187–190); d9.9; b–Dick b–Ron; OF(137/95/72)																								
1966	Was A	9	31	2	12	0	0	1	6	3-0	0	6	.387	.441	.484	167	3	0-0	.917	0	131	0	O9(8/0/3)	0	0.3
1967	Was A	116	292	34	68	8	4	3	17	13-2	0	53	.233	.264	.318	75	-11	3-4	.980	-6	92	20	O99(59/65/1)	0	-2.3
1968	Was A	68	128	16	28	2	2	1	9	7-1	1	16	.219	.265	.289	70	-5	0-0	.895	-1	60	0	O25(12/0/13),3b16,2b11	0	-0.8
1969	Was A	109	271	42	75	9	3	1	17	13-1	1	28	.277	.311	.343	88	-6	12-3	.933	0	102	133	O91(48/16/42),3b6,2b3	24	-0.7
1970	Was A	22	38	3	8	2	0	0	4	5-1	0	9	.211	.295	.263	60	-2	0-0	1.000	-1	79	134	O17(5/3/10)	0	-0.3
	Mil A	28	61	4	14	4	0	0	4	7-0	0	5	.230	.309	.295	67	-2	0-1	1.000	2	82	318	O14(1/11/2),2b5,1b4	0	-0.1
	Year	50	99	7	22	6	0	0	8	12-1	0	14	.222	.304	.283	65	-4	0-1	1.000	2	80	220	O31(6/14/12),2b5,1b4	0	-0.4
1972	Chi A	9	21	1	3	0	0	0	0	0-0	0	2	.143	.143	.143	-15	-3	0-0	.905	2	120	443	3b6	0	-0.2
1973	Chi A	28	39	2	4	2	0	0	0	1-0	0	9	.103	.125	.154	-21	-6	0-1	1.000	-1	112	0	3b9,1b8,O5(4/0/1)/C2	0	-0.8
Total	7	389	881	104	212	27	9	6	57	49-5	2	128	.241	.281	.312	74	-32	15-9	.957	-4	93	76	O260L,3b37,2b20,1b12/C	24	-4.9
ALLEN, HEZEKIAH	Hezekiah "Ki"; B2.25.1863 Westport CT; D9.21.1916 Saugatuck CT; 5´11˝/160; d5.16																								
1884	Phi N	1	3	0	2	0	0	0	0	0	—	0	.667	.667	.667	337	1	—	1.000	-0	—	—	/C	—	0.0
ALLEN, HORACE	Horace Tanner "Pug"; B6.11.1899 DeLand FL; D7.5.1981 Canton NC; BL/TR/6´0˝/187; d6.15; Col Georgia Tech																								
1919	Bro N	4	7	0	0	0	0	0	0	0	0	2	.000	.000	.000	-98	-2	0	1.000	0	62	538	O2(1/1/0)	—	-0.2
ALLEN, JAMIE	James Bradley; B5.29.1958 Yakima WA; BR/TR/6´0˝/205; [SeaA79 2/27]; d5.1; Col Arizona St.																								
1983	Sea A	86	273	23	61	10	0	4	21	33-0	1	52	.223	.309	.304	67	-12	6-5	.959	-2	92	90	3b82,D2	0	-1.6
ALLEN, PETE	Jesse Hall; B5.1.1868 Columbiana OH; D4.16.1946 Philadelphia PA; BR/TR/5´8.5˝/185; d8.4; Col Amherst																								
1893	Cle N	1	4	0	0	0	0	0	0	0	0	0	.000	.000	.000	-94	-1	0	1.000	-1	*98*	*0*	/C	—	-0.1
ALLEN, CHAD	John Chad; B2.6.1975 Dallas TX; BR/TR/6´1˝/(195–200); [MinA96 4/97]; d4.6; Col Texas A&M																								
1999	Min A	137	481	69	133	21	3	10	46	37-1	2	89	.277	.330	.395	80	-15	14-7	.975	2	105	108	O133(133/0/1),D2	0	-1.6
2000	Min A	15	50	2	15	3	0	0	7	3-0	1	14	.300	.345	.360	76	-2	0-2	1.000	1	90	207	O15(2/0/13)	0	-0.2
2001	Min A	57	175	20	46	13	2	4	20	19-1	0	37	.263	.333	.429	94	-1	1-2	.968	2	107	176	O27(16/0/15),D23	69	-0.2
2002	Cle A	5	10	0	1	1	0	0	0	0-0	0	2	.100	.100	.200	-23	-2	0-0	1.000	-1	61	0	O4(3/0/1)	0	-0.2
2003	Fla N	12	24	2	5	1	1	0	0	0-0	1	5	.208	.240	.333	49	-2	0-0	1.000	1	141	323	O8(6/1/2)/D	0	-0.1
2004	Tex A	20	58	4	14	4	1	0	6	2-0	0	13	.241	.262	.345	55	-4	0-1	1.000	-2	65	0	O13(12/0/1),D5	0	-0.6
2005	Tex A	21	53	5	15	1	1	0	5	2-0	0	13	.283	.309	.340	71	-2	0-1	1.000	-0	48	0	D18,O2(1/0/1)	0	-0.4
Total	7	267	851	102	229	44	8	14	84	63-2	4	173	.269	.321	.389	79	-28	15-13	.978	3	102	122	O202(173/1/34),D49	69	-3.3
ALLEN, KIM	Kim Bryant; B4.5.1953 Fontana CA; BR/TR/5´11˝/(170–175); d9.2; Col California–Riverside																								
1980	Sea A	23	51	9	12	3	0	0	3	8-2	1	3	.235	.350	.294	77	-1	10-3	.970	-1	115	88	2b15,O4(3/0/2)/S	0	0.0
1981	Sea A	19	3	1	0	0	0	0	0	0-0	0	2	.000	.000	.000	-96	-1	2-1	ø	-1	0	0	2b2,O2C,D2	0	-0.2
Total	2	42	54	10	12	3	0	0	3	8-2	1	5	.222	.333	.278	69	-2	12-4	.970	-1	111	85	2b17,O6(3/2/2),D2/S	0	-0.2
ALLEN, LUKE	Lucas Gale; B8.4.1978 Covington GA; BL/TR/6´2˝/220; d9.10																								
2002	LA N	6	7	2	1	1	0	0	0	2-0	0	3	.143	.333	.286	69	0	0-0	1.000	0	110	0	O3R	0	0.0
2003	Col N	2	2	0	0	0	0	0	0	0-0	0	0	.000	.000	.000	-88	-1	0-0	ø	0	—	—	/H	0	-0.1
Total	2	8	9	2	1	1	0	0	0	2-0	0	3	.111	.273	.222	33	-1	0-0	1.000	0	110	0	O3R	0	-0.1
ALLEN, MYRON	Myron Smith "Zeke"; B3.22.1854 Kingston NY; D3.8.1924 Kingston NY; BR/TR/5´8˝/150; d7.19; ▲																								
1883	NY N	1	4	0	0	0	0	0	1	0	—	2	.000	.000	.000	-99	-1	—	1.000	-0	64	0	/P	—	0.0
1886	Bos N	1	3	0	0	0	0	0	0	0	—	1	.000	.000	.000	-99	-1	0	1.000	-0	82	0	/2	—	-0.1
1887	Cle AA	117	463	66	128	22	10	4	77	36	5	—	.276	.335	.393	106	3	26	.894	6	113	119	O115(73/1/41),3b3,S2,P2	—	0.6
1888	KC AA	37	136	23	29	6	4	0	10	9	1	—	.213	.267	.316	82	-3	4	.931	6	144	62	O35(33/2/0),P2	—	0.1
Total	4	156	606	89	157	28	14	4	88	45	6	3	.259	.317	.371	98	-2	30	.903	12	121	105	O150(106/3/41),P5,3b3,S2/2	—	0.6
ALLEN, DICK	Richard Anthony; B3.8.1942 Wampum PA; BR/TR/5´11˝/(185–190); d9.3; b–Hank b–Ron; OF(256/1/0)																								
1963	Phi N	10	24	6	7	2	1	0	2	0-0	0	5	.292	.280	.458	114	0	0-0	.833	-1	102	0	O7L/3	0	-0.1
1964	Phi N	**162**	632	**125**	201	38	**13**	29	91	67-13	0	138	.318	.382	.557	163	53	3-4	.921	6	103	**118**	3b162	0	5.9
1965	Phi N★	161	619	93	187	31	14	20	85	74-6	2	150	.302	.375	.494	146	39	15-2	.943	0	99	106	3b160,S2	0	4.2
1966	Phi N★	141	524	112	166	25	10	40	110	68-13	3	136	.317	.396	**.632**	**181**	**57**	10-6	.967	-6	95	85	3b91,O47L	0	5.0
1967	Phi N★	122	463	89	142	31	10	23	77	75-18	1	117	.307	**.404**	.566	**173**	46	20-5	.908	-4	99	114	3b121/2S	35	4.7
1968	Phi N	152	521	87	137	17	9	33	90	74-15	1	161	.263	.352	.520	161	38	7-7	.973	-4	98	59	O139(139/1/0),3b10	0	2.9
1969	Phi N	118	438	79	126	23	3	32	89	64-10	0	144	.288	.375	.573	167	39	9-3	.985	-8	77	99	1b117	0	2.4
1970	StL N★	122	459	88	128	17	5	34	101	71-16	2	118	.279	.377	.560	144	28	5-4	.993	-12	77	98	1b79,3b38,O3L	0	0.9
1971	LA N	155	549	82	162	24	1	23	90	93-13	1	113	.295	.395	.468	152	42	8-1	.918	-6	101	120	3b67,O60L,1b28	0	3.3
1972	Chi A★	148	506	90	156	28	5	**37**	**113**	**99**-16	1	126	.308	**.420**	**.603**	**198**	**65**	19-8	.995	-4	86	83	1b143,3b2	0	**5.8**
1973	Chi A✳	72	250	39	79	20	3	16	41	33-3	1	51	.316	.394	.612	175	25	7-2	.994	2	111	95	1b67,2b2/D	69	2.3
1974	Chi A★	128	462	84	139	23	1	**32**	88	57-9	1	89	.301	.375	**.563**	164	38	7-1	.986	-7	78	**106**	1b125/2D	0	2.4
1975	Phi N	119	416	54	97	21	3	12	62	58-4	2	109	.233	.327	.385	93	-3	11-2	.982	2	110	96	1b113	0	-0.9
1976	†Phi N	85	298	52	80	16	1	15	49	37-2	0	63	.268	.346	.480	129	11	11-4	.989	-1	93	124	1b85	55	0.5
1977	Oak A	54	171	19	41	4	0	5	31	24-0	1	36	.240	.330	.351	89	-2	1-3	.984	2	124	94	1b50/D	0	-0.3
Total	15	1749	6332	1099	1848	320	79	351	1119	894-138	16	1556	.292	.378	.534	156	476	133-52	.989	-42	90	100	1b807,3b652,O256L,2b4,D3,S3	159	39.0
ALLEN, BOB	Robert (b Alvah Charles Elliott); B10.13.1894 Muscoda WI; D12.18.1975 Naperville IL; BR/TR/5´10˝/180; d8.20; Col Wisconsin–Madison																								
1919	Phi A	9	22	3	3	1	0	0	0	3	1	7	.136	.269	.182	27	-2	0	.889	-1	76	0	O6C	—	-0.4
ALLEN, BOB	Robert Gilman; B7.10.1867 Marion OH; D5.14.1943 Little Rock AR; BR/TR/5´11˝/175; d4.19; M2																								
1890	Phi N	**133**	456	69	103	15	11	2	57	87	5	54	.226	.356	.320	95	0	13	.924	**32**	**108**	**138**	S133,M	—	3.2
1891	Phi N	118	438	46	97	7	4	1	51	43	0	44	.221	.291	.263	60	-23	12	.896	8	106	117	S118	—	-1.0
1892	Phi N	152	563	77	128	20	14	2	64	61	1	60	.227	.304	.323	90	-8	15	.919	15	104	129	S152	—	1.4
1893	Phi N	124	471	86	126	19	12	8	90	71	5	40	.268	.369	.410	107	5	8	.919	15	103	126	S124	—	2.2
1894	Phi N	41	154	27	40	10	4	0	19	17	1	11	.260	.337	.377	73	-7	4	.917	-3	95	85	S41	—	-0.6
1897	Bos N	34	119	33	38	5	0	1	24	18	0	—	.319	.409	.387	104	2	1	.924	5	111	113	S32/cf2	—	0.7

YEAR	TM LG	G	AB	R	H	2B	3B	HR	RBI	BB-IB	HP	SO	AVG	OBP	SLG	AOPS	ABR	SB-CS	FA	FR	RNG	THR	GAMES AT POSITION	DL	BFW
1900	Cin N	5	15	0	2	1	0	0	1	0	1	—	.133	.188	.200	7	-2	0	.864	-1	100	71	S5,M	—	-0.2
Total	7	607	2216	338	534	77	45	14	306	297	13	209	.241	.334	.335	88	-33	53	.915	72	105	124	S605/2cf	—	5.7
Allen, Rod	Roderick Bernet; B10.5.1959 Los Angeles CA; BR/TR/6´1˝/(185–200); [ChiA77 6/131]; d4.7																								
1983	Sea A	11	12	1	2	0	0	0	0	0-0	0	1	.167	.167	.167	-8	-2	0-0	1.000	0	133	0	O2R,D3	0	-0.2
1984	Det A	15	27	6	8	1	0	0	3	2-0	1	8	.296	.367	.333	95	0	1-0	1.000	0	391	0	D11,O2L	0	0.0
1988	Cle A	5	11	1	1	1	0	0	0	0-0	0	2	.091	.091	.182	-25	-2	0-0	ø	0	—	—	D4	0	-0.2
Total	3	31	50	8	11	2	0	0	3	2-0	1	11	.220	.264	.260	45	-4	1-0	1.000	0	160	0	D18,O4(2/0/2)	0	-0.4
Allen, Ron	Ronald Frederick; B12.23.1943 Wampum PA; BB/TR/6´3˝/205; d8.11; b–Hank b–Dick; Col Youngstown St.																								
1972	StL N	7	11	2	1	0	0	1	1	3-0	0	5	.091	.286	.364	84	0	0-0	.968	-1	52	42	1b5	0	-0.1
Allenson, Gary	Gary Martin; B2.4.1955 Culver City CA; BR/TR/5´11˝/(185–193); [BosA76 9/214]; d4.8; C6; Col Arizona St.																								
1979	Bos A	108	241	27	49	10	2	3	22	20-0	1	42	.203	.264	.299	50	-17	1-1	.980	3	100	93	C104,3b3	0	-1.1
1980	Bos A	36	70	9	25	6	0	0	10	13-0	0	11	.357	.452	.443	140	5	2-2	.981	1	111	62	C24,3b5,D6	0	0.7
1981	Bos A	47	139	23	31	8	0	5	25	23-0	1	33	.223	.335	.388	102	1	0-0	.969	-3	73	63	C47	25	0.1
1982	Bos A	92	264	25	54	11	0	6	33	38-1	1	39	.205	.306	.314	67	-11	0-3	.992	6	130	107	C91	0	-0.2
1983	Bos A	84	230	19	53	11	0	3	30	27-0	2	43	.230	.311	.317	70	-9	0-1	.984	-2	83	98	C84	0	-0.8
1984	Bos A	35	83	9	19	2	0	2	8	9-2	0	14	.229	.304	.325	71	-3	0-0	.987	-5	70	103	C35	0	-0.8
1985	Tor A	14	34	2	4	1	0	0	3	0-0	0	10	.118	.118	.147	-27	-6	0-0	1.000	-3	211	65	C14	0	-0.8
Total	7	416	1061	114	235	49	2	19	131	130-3	5	192	.221	.307	.325	71	-40	3-7	.984	-2	102	92	C399,3b8,D6	25	-2.9
Allensworth, Jermaine	Jermaine Lamont; B1.11.1972 Anderson IN; BR/TR/6´0˝/190; [PitN93 1/34]; d7.23; Col Purdue																								
1996	Pit N	61	229	32	60	9	3	4	31	23-0	4	50	.262	.337	.380	86	-4	11-6	.979	1	101	133	O61C	0	-0.3
1997	Pit N	108	369	55	94	18	2	3	43	44-1	7	79	.255	.340	.339	79	-10	14-7	.980	-7	87	109	O104C	38	-1.6
1998	Pit N	69	233	30	72	13	3	3	24	17-0	7	43	.309	.372	.429	110	4	8-4	.980	-1	98	102	O66C	0	0.3
	KC A	30	73	15	15	5	0	0	3	9-0	4	17	.205	.326	.274	56	-4	7-0	.982	-1	105	0	O27(1/24/2)	0	-0.3
	NY N	34	54	9	11	2	0	2	4	2-0	1	16	.204	.246	.352	56	-4	0-2	1.000	-2	73	0	O31(4/4/25)	0	-0.7
1999	NY N	40	73	14	16	2	0	3	9	9-0	1	23	.219	.310	.370	75	-3	2-1	1.000	2	117	87	O33(10/14/15)	0	-0.2
Total	4	342	1031	155	268	49	8	15	114	104-1	24	228	.260	.339	.367	84	-21	42-20	.982	-9	95	97	O322(15/273/42)	38	-2.8
Alley, Gene	Leonard Eugene; B7.10.1940 Richmond VA; BR/TR/6´0˝/(160–165); d9.4																								
1963	Pit N	17	51	3	11	1	0	0	0	2-0	0	12	.216	.245	.235	39	-4	0-1	.947	1	120	230	3b7,2b4,S4	0	-0.3
1964	Pit N	81	209	30	44	3	1	6	13	21-2	2	56	.211	.286	.321	72	-8	0-1	.966	15	119	122	S61,3b3/2	0	1.2
1965	Pit N	153	500	47	126	21	6	5	47	32-9	4	82	.252	.302	.348	82	-12	7-2	.968	24	**115**	**126**	S110,2b40/3	0	2.6
1966	Pit N	147	579	88	173	28	10	7	43	27-0	5	83	.299	.334	.418	108	5	8-8	.979	15	105	**148**	S143	0	3.2
1967	Pit N★	152	550	59	158	25	7	6	55	36-5	7	70	.287	.337	.391	108	5	10-5	.967	8	106	112	S146	0	2.9
1968	Pit N✳	133	474	48	116	20	2	4	39	39-6	5	78	.245	.307	.321	91	-5	13-5	.974	26	**118**	**146**	S109,2b24	0	3.7
1969	Pit N	82	285	28	70	3	2	8	32	19-1	1	48	.246	.293	.354	83	-8	4-0	.977	16	113	128	2b53,S25,3b5	29	1.5
1970	†Pit N	121	426	46	104	16	5	8	41	31-9	3	70	.244	.297	.362	77	-15	7-3	.975	**31**	113	128	S108,2b8,3b2	0	2.9
1971	†Pit N	114	348	38	79	8	7	6	28	35-14	0	43	.227	.296	.342	80	-10	9-2	.958	-8	98	86	S108/3	0	-0.5
1972	†Pit N	119	347	30	86	12	2	3	36	38-10	0	52	.248	.321	.320	84	-7	4-3	.970	11	107	**153**	S114,3b4	0	1.8
1973	Pit N	76	158	25	32	3	2	2	8	20-6	0	28	.203	.292	.285	62	-8	1-0	.981	5	106	80	S49,3b8	0	0.1
Total	11	1195	3927	442	999	140	44	55	342	300-62	27	622	.254	.310	.354	88	-67	63-30	.970	144	109	127	S977,2b130,3b31	29	19.1
Allie, Gair	Gair Roosevelt; B10.28.1931 Statesville NC; BR/TR/6´1˝/190; d4.13; Col Wake Forest																								
1954	Pit N	121	418	38	83	8	6	3	30	56	2	84	.199	.294	.268	49	-32	1-1	.952	-13	91	86	S95,3b19	0	-3.7
Allietta, Bob	Robert George; B5.1.1952 New Bedford MA; BR/TR/6´0˝/190; [AnaA71*A1/7]; d5.6																								
1975	Cal A	21	45	4	8	1	0	1	2	1-1	0	6	.178	.196	.267	32	-4	0-0	1.000	-1	73	73	C21	42	-0.5
Allison, Andy	Andrew K.; B1848 New York NY; 5´10˝/150; d5.7; M1																								
1872	Eck NA	22	92	9	15	2	0	0	10	1	—	2	.163	.172	.185	11	-8	0-0	.930	-1	80	53	1b22/rfM	—	-0.6
Allison, Art	Arthur Algernon; B1.29.1849 Philadelphia PA; D2.25.1916 Washington DC; 5´8˝/150; d5.4; b–Doug																								
1871	Cle NA	**29**	137	28	40	4	5	0	19	2	—	5	.292	.302	.394	104	1	3-1	.885	1	94	172	O29C,2b2	—	0.2
1872	Cle NA	19	87	13	23	4	0	0	8	0	—	2	.264	.264	.310	81	-1	0-0	.804	-1	90	200	O19(0/17/2)	—	-0.1
1873	Res NA	**23**	100	12	32	2	0	0	11	0	—	2	.320	.320	.340	103	1	0-0	.816	-2	64	142	O21(8/9/4),1b3/C	—	0.0
1875	Was NA	26	112	18	24	3	1	0	3	1	—	2	.214	.221	.259	69	-3	6-0	.924	-3	44	47	1b23,O3(0/1/2)/C	—	-0.4
	Har NA	40	175	26	42	4	1	1	19	0	—	3	.240	.240	.291	80	-4	1-2	.785	3	268	212	O37R,2b2/C1	—	0.1
	Year	66	287	44	66	7	2	1	22	1	—	5	.230	.233	.279	76	-7	7-2	.800	-0	255	202	O40(0/1/39),1b24,C2,2b2	—	-0.3
1876	Lou N	31	130	9	27	2	1	0	10	2	—	6	.208	.220	.238	45	-8	—	.789	3	230	115	O23R,1b8	—	-0.5
Total	4NA	137	611	97	161	17	7	1	60	3	—	14	.264	.267	.319	88	-6	10-3	.827	-2	146	182	O109(8/56/45),1b27,2b4,C3	—	-0.2
Allison, Doug	Douglas L.; B7.12.1846 Philadelphia PA; D12.19.1916 Washington DC; BR/TR/5´10.5˝/160; d5.5; M1; b–Art																								
1871	Oly NA	27	133	28	44	10	2	2	27	0	—	2	.331	.331	.481	137	7	1-1	.806	-3	—	—	C27	—	0.3
1872	Tro NA	23	114	23	35	4	2	0	20	1	—	3	.307	.313	.377	110	1	1-1	.897	6	—	—	C22/S	—	0.5
	Eck NA	18	83	18	28	2	1	0	4	1	—	5	.337	.345	.386	146	6	0-0	.863	-7	—	—	C18	—	-0.1
	Year	41	197	41	63	6	3	0	24	2	—	8	.320	.327	.381	124	6	1-1	.883	-1	—	—	C40/S	—	0.4
1873	Res NA	19	80	11	24	6	0	0	8	2	—	1	.300	.317	.375	113	2	0-0	.800	0	—	—	C18,O4(0/1/3),M	—	0.2
	Mut NA	11	48	6	10	0	0	0	3	1	—	0	.208	.224	.208	29	-4	0-0	.868	2	—	—	C11/rf	—	-0.1
	Year	30	128	17	34	6	0	0	11	3	—	1	.266	.282	.313	80	-2	0-0	.831	3	—	—	C29,O5(0/1/4)	—	0.1
1874	Mut NA	**65**	318	68	90	7	5	0	28	6	—	5	.283	.296	.336	99	-1	1-0	.800	1	81	0	O47(0/3/44),C34/2	—	0.2
1875	Har NA	61	269	38	67	7	0	0	21	6	—	3	.249	.265	.275	84	-5	2-0	**.896**	17	—	—	C59,1b2,O2R	—	1.1
1876	Har N	44	163	19	43	4	0	0	15	3	—	9	.264	.277	.288	82	-4	—	**.881**	10	—	—	C40,O6(0/1/5)	—	0.7
1877	Har N	29	115	14	17	2	0	0	6	3	—	7	.148	.169	.165	7	-11	—	.896	1	—	—	C29	—	-0.8
1878	Pro N	19	76	9	22	2	0	0	7	1	—	8	.289	.299	.316	102	0	—	.911	0	—	—	C19/P	—	0.1
1879	Pro N	1	5	0	0	0	0	0	0	0	—	1	.000	.000	.000	-99	-1	—	.833	-0	—	—	/C	—	-0.1
1883	Bal AA	1	3	2	2	0	0	0	—	0	—	—	.667	.667	.667	321	1	—	ø	-0	0	0	/cfC	—	0.1
Total	5NA	224	1045	192	298	36	10	2	111	17	—	19	.285	.297	.344	102	6	5-2	.863	18	—	—	C189,O54(0/4/50),1b2/2S	—	2.1
Total	5	94	362	44	84	8	0	0	28	7	—	25	.232	.247	.254	63	-15	—	.892	11	—	—	C90,O7(0/2/5)/P	—	-0.0
Allison, Milo	Milo Henry; B10.16.1889 Elk Rapids MI; D6.18.1957 Kenosha WI; BL/TR/5´10˝/155; d9.26																								
1913	Chi N	2	6	1	2	0	0	0	0	0	0	1	.333	.333	.333	91	0	1	1.000	-0	92	0	/cf	—	0.0
1914	Chi N	1	1	0	1	0	0	0	0	0	0	0	1.000	1.000	1.000	497	0	0	ø	0	—	—	/H	—	0.0
1916	Cle A	14	18	10	5	0	0	0	0	6	0	1	.278	.458	.278	115	1	0	1.000	-0	88	0	O5(1/0/4)	—	0.0
1917	Cle A	32	35	4	5	0	0	0	0	9	0	7	.143	.318	.143	38	-2	3	1.000	-1	76	96	O11(4/5/2)	—	-0.4
Total	4	49	60	15	13	0	0	0	0	15	0	9	.217	.373	.217	74	-1	4	1.000	-1	81	58	O17(5/6/6)	—	-0.4
Allison, Bill	William Andrew; d5.21																								
1872	Eck NA	5	19	5	3	0	0	0	1	0	—	1	.158	.158	.158	-3	-2	0-0	.500	-2	0	0	O2(0/1/1),1b2/2	—	-0.2
Allison, Bob	William Robert; B7.11.1934 Raytown MO; D4.9.1995 Rio Verde AZ; BR/TR/6´4˝/(205–223); d9.16; Col Kansas																								
1958	Was A	11	35	1	7	1	0	0	0	2-0	0	5	.200	.243	.229	31	-3	0-2	1.000	-0	105	0	O11(1/10/0)	0	-0.5
1959	Was A☆	150	570	83	149	18	**9**	30	85	60-1	2	92	.261	.333	.482	122	15	13-8	.974	-9	92	81	O149(7/134/9)	0	-0.1
1960	Was A	144	501	79	126	30	3	15	69	92-4	2	94	.251	.367	.413	113	12	11-9	.965	5	112	113	O140(0/4/139),1b4	0	1.2
1961	Min A	159	556	83	136	21	3	29	105	103-1	5	100	.245	.363	.450	111	11	2-7	.975	4	105	128	O150R,1b18	0	0.1
1962	Min A	149	519	102	138	24	8	29	102	84-0	4	115	.266	.370	.511	130	23	8-5	.977	4	107	123	O147(2/0/146)	0	1.7
1963	Min A★	148	527	**99**	143	25	4	35	91	90-2	3	109	.271	.378	.533	**150**	38	6-1	.971	9	115	113	O147(0/8/146)	0	3.8
1964	Min A★	149	492	90	141	27	4	32	86	92-4	7	99	.287	.404	.553	163	46	10-1	.986	4	99	88	1b93,O61(27/28/16)	0	4.5
1965	†Min A	135	438	71	102	14	5	23	78	73-4	2	114	.233	.342	.445	118	11	10-2	.972	8	108	151	O122L,1b3	0	1.5
1966	Min A	70	168	34	37	6	1	8	19	30-2	3	34	.220	.345	.411	110	3	6-0	.967	1	103	105	O56(44/1/11)	0	0.3
1967	Min A	153	496	73	128	21	6	24	75	74-2	2	114	.258	.356	.470	132	21	6-4	.978	-1	96	68	O145(138/0/9)	0	1.3
1968	Min A	145	469	63	116	16	8	22	52	52-5	2	98	.247	.324	.456	128	15	9-7	.966	-3	93	61	O117(116/1/1),1b17	0	0.5
1969	†Min A	81	189	18	43	8	2	8	27	29-5	1	39	.228	.333	.418	106	2	2-4	1.000	-1	94	49	O58L,1b3	0	-0.4

YEAR	TM LG	G	AB	R	H	2B	3B	HR	RBI	BB-IB	HP	SO	AVG	OBP	SLG	AOPS	ABR	SB-CS	FA	FR	RNG	THR	GAMES AT POSITION	DL	BFW
1970	†Min A	47	72	15	15	5	0	1	7	14-0	1	20	.208	.345	.319	83	-1	1-0	1.000	-0	100	0	O17(12/1/4),1b7	0	-0.2
Total	13	1541	5032	811	1281	216	53	256	796	795-30	34	1033	.255	.358	.471	126	193	84-50	.975	19	104	102	O1320(527/187/631),1b145	0	13.7
ALLRED, BEAU	Dale Le Beau; B6.4.1965 Mesa AZ; BL/TL/6´0˝/193; [CleA87 25/645]; d9.7; Col Lamar																								
1989	Cle A	13	24	0	6	3	0	0	1	2-0	0	10	.250	.308	.375	90	0	0-0	1.000	1	122	343	O5(3/0/2),D2	0	0.1
1990	Cle A	4	16	2	3	1	0	1	2	2-0	0	3	.188	.278	.438	97	0	0-0	.833	-1	64	0	O4(0/3/1)	0	-0.1
1991	Cle A	48	125	17	29	3	0	3	12	25-2	1	35	.232	.359	.328	92	0	2-2	.972	4	134	39	O42(20/0/27)/D	0	0.2
Total	3	65	165	19	38	7	0	4	15	29-2	1	48	.230	.345	.345	93	0	2-2	.969	4	128	65	O51(23/3/30),D3	0	0.2
ALMADA, MEL	Baldomero Melo (Quiros); B2.7.1913 Huatabampo, Sonora, Mexico; D8.13.1988 Caborca, Sonora, Mexico; BL/TL/6´0˝/170; d9.8																								
1933	Bos A	14	44	11	15	0	0	1	3	11	0	3	.341	.473	.409	137	3	3-1	1.000	0	98	98	O13(7/6/0)	—	0.3
1934	Bos A	23	90	7	21	2	1	0	10	6	0	8	.233	.281	.278	42	-8	3-2	.985	2	103	207	O23(0/16/7)	—	-0.7
1935	Bos A	151	607	85	176	27	9	3	59	55	1	34	.290	.350	.379	83	-16	20-9	.968	-1	88	190	O149(0/126/25),1b3	—	-1.9
1936	Bos A	96	320	40	81	16	4	1	21	24	0	15	.253	.305	.338	55	-24	2-4	.987	1	96	134	O81(11/3/69)	—	-2.5
1937	Bos A	32	110	17	26	6	2	1	9	15	0	6	.236	.328	.355	69	-5	0-1	.927	-3	88	53	O27(4/2/21),1b4	—	-1.0
	Was A	100	433	74	134	21	4	4	33	38	0	21	.309	.365	.404	98	-1	12-4	.964	10	109	162	O100(0/97/3)	—	0.6
	Year	132	543	91	160	27	6	5	42	53	0	27	.295	.357	.394	91	-7	12-5	.960	6	105	143	O127(4/99/24),1b4	—	-0.4
1938	Was A	47	197	24	48	7	4	1	15	8	1	16	.244	.277	.335	56	-15	4-1	.968	1	105	102	O47C	—	-1.3
	StL A	102	436	77	149	22	2	3	37	38	3	22	.342	.398	.422	106	5	9-5	.966	-3	96	99	O101C	—	0.0
	Year	149	633	101	197	29	6	4	52	46	4	38	.311	.362	.395	92	-9	13-6	.967	-1	99	100	O148C	—	-1.3
1939	StL A	42	134	17	32	2	1	1	7	10	0	8	.239	.292	.291	48	-11	1-0	.987	-1	93	80	O34(3/31/0)	—	-1.2
	Bro N	39	112	11	24	4	0	0	3	9	0	17	.214	.273	.250	40	-9	2	.977	1	111	82	O32C	—	-0.9
Total	7	646	2483	363	706	107	27	15	197	214	5	150	.284	.342	.367	79	-81	56-27	.970	8	98	138	O607(25/461/125),1b7	—	-8.6
ALMEIDA, RAFAEL	Rafael D. "Mike"; B6.30.1887 Havana, Cuba; D5.18.1969 Havana, Cuba; BR/TR/5´9˝/164; d7.4																								
1911	Cin N	36	96	9	30	5	1	0	15	9	2	16	.313	.383	.385	120	3	3	.890	-3	94	27	3b27/2S	—	0.0
1912	Cin N	16	59	9	13	4	3	0	10	5	0	8	.220	.281	.390	85	-2	0	.891	-1	101	101	3b15	—	-0.2
1913	Cin N	50	130	14	34	4	2	3	21	11	1	16	.262	.324	.392	104	0	4-5	.919	3	113	130	3b37,O3C,S2/2	—	0.4
Total	3	102	285	32	77	13	6	3	46	25	3	40	.270	.335	.389	106	1	7-5	.904	-1	104	88	3b79,O3C,S3,2b2	—	0.2
ALMON, BILL	William Francis; B11.21.1952 Providence RI; BR/TR/6´3˝/(170–191); [SDN74 1/1]; d9.2; Col Brown; OF(123/8/35)																								
1974	SD N	16	38	4	12	1	0	0	3	2-0	0	9	.316	.350	.342	99	0	1-0	.915	-4	86	53	S14	0	-0.3
1975	SD N	6	10	0	4	0	0	0	0	0-0	0	1	.400	.400	.400	131	0	0-0	1.000	-1	67	0	S2	0	0.0
1976	SD N	14	57	6	14	3	0	1	6	2-0	0	9	.246	.271	.351	82	-2	3-1	.962	4	124	103	S14	0	0.4
1977	SD N	155	613	75	160	18	11	2	43	37-1	0	114	.261	.303	.336	79	-21	20-9	.954	15	107	89	S155	0	1.1
1978	SD N	138	405	39	102	19	2	0	21	33-10	0	74	.252	.308	.309	78	-12	17-5	.933	-5	99	118	3b114,S15,2b7	0	-1.6
1979	SD N	100	198	20	45	3	0	1	8	21-7	0	48	.227	.299	.258	57	-12	6-5	.985	5	108	116	2b61,S25/cf	0	-0.3
1980	Mon N	18	38	2	10	1	1	0	3	1-0	0	5	.263	.275	.342	72	-2	0-0	.911	-3	84	19	S12/2	0	-0.3
	NY N	48	112	13	19	3	2	0	4	8-1	0	27	.170	.225	.232	28	-11	2-0	.967	5	100	131	S22,2b18,3b9	0	-0.4
	Year	66	150	15	29	4	3	0	7	9-1	0	32	.193	.237	.260	39	-13	2-0	.948	2	95	94	S34,2b19,3b9	0	-0.7
1981	Chi A	103	349	46	105	10	2	4	41	21-0	2	60	.301	.341	.375	109	3	16-6	.969	15	102	117	S103	0	3.2
1982	Chi A	111	308	40	79	10	4	4	26	25-0	1	49	.256	.313	.354	83	-8	10-8	.949	20	**113**	**130**	S108/D	0	2.1
1983	Oak A	143	451	45	120	29	1	4	63	26-3	2	67	.266	.302	.361	88	-7	26-8	.941	-17	88	63	S52,3b40,1b38,O23(9/0/15),2b5,D4	0	-2.0
1984	Oak A	106	211	24	47	11	0	7	16	10-0	0	42	.223	.253	.374	77	-7	5-7	1.000	-4	96	43	O48(33/1/17),1b44,D12,3b4/CS	0	-1.6
1985	Pit N	88	244	33	66	17	0	6	29	22-0	1	61	.270	.330	.414	109	3	10-7	.987	-7	93	86	S43,O32(26/6/0),1b7,3b7	0	-0.1
1986	Pit N	102	196	29	43	7	2	7	27	30-2	0	38	.219	.319	.383	91	-2	11-4	.983	-1	89	238	O54(53/0/2),3b28,S19,1b4	0	-0.3
1987	Pit N	19	20	5	4	1	0	0	1	1-0	0	5	.200	.238	.250	29	-2	0-0	.944	0	92	180	S4,O2L/3	0	-0.1
	NY N	49	54	8	13	3	0	0	4	8-0	0	16	.241	.339	.296	73	-2	1-0	.972	-2	112	65	S22,2b10,1b2/rf	0	-0.3
	Year	68	74	13	17	4	0	0	5	9-0	0	21	.230	.313	.284	61	-4	1-0	.963	-2	107	96	S26,2b10,O3(2/0/1),1b2/3	0	-0.4
1988	Phi N	20	26	1	3	2	0	0	1	3-0	0	11	.115	.207	.192	15	-3	0-0	.944	1	142	0	3b9,S5/1	0	-0.2
Total	15	1236	3330	390	846	138	25	36	296	250-24	6	636	.254	.305	.343	83	-85	128-60	.956	22	104	101	S616,3b212,O161L,2b102,1b96,D17/C	0	-0.7
ALMONTE, ERICK	Erick R.; B2.1.1978 Santo Domingo, D.R.; BR/TR/6´2˝/180; d9.4																								
2001	NY A	8	4	0	2	1	0	0	0	0-0	0	1	.500	.500	.750	221	1	2-0	.875	0	93	150	S4,D3	0	0.2
2003	NY A	31	100	17	26	6	0	1	11	8-0	1	24	.260	.321	.350	78	-3	1-0	.906	-7	81	74	S31	0	-0.7
Total	2	39	104	17	28	7	0	1	11	8-0	1	25	.269	.327	.365	84	-2	3-0	.904	-6	81	77	S35,D3	0	-0.5
ALOMAR, ROBERTO	Roberto (Velazquez); B2.5.1968 Ponce, PR; BB/TR (BL 1997p)/6´0˝/(155–190); d4.22; f-Sandy b-Sandy																								
1988	SD N	143	545	84	145	24	6	9	41	47-5	3	83	.266	.328	.382	105	3	24-6	.980	16	106	111	2b143	0	2.7
1989	SD N	158	623	82	184	27	1	7	56	53-4	1	76	.295	.347	.376	108	7	42-17	.967	6	104	104	2b157	0	2.1
1990	SD N★	147	586	80	168	27	5	6	60	48-1	2	72	.287	.340	.381	98	-2	24-7	.976	-0	100	99	2b137,S5	0	0.5
1991	†Tor A★	161	637	88	188	41	11	9	69	57-3	4	86	.295	.354	.436	114	12	53-11	.981	-16	93	78	2b160	0	0.8
1992	†Tor A★	152	571	105	177	27	8	8	76	87-5	5	52	.310	.405	.427	127	25	49-9	.993	-22	88	70	2b150/D	0	1.4
1993	†Tor A★	153	589	109	192	35	6	17	93	80-5	5	67	.326	.408	.492	139	35	55-15	.980	-9	97	91	2b150	0	3.9
1994	Tor A★	107	392	78	120	25	4	8	38	51-2	2	41	.306	.386	.452	114	10	19-8	.991	-2	91	107	2b106	0	1.3
1995	Tor A★	130	517	71	155	24	7	13	66	47-3	0	45	.300	.354	.449	108	5	30-3	**.994**	-6	94	90	2b128	0	1.0
1996	†Bal A★	153	588	132	193	43	4	22	94	90-10	1	65	.328	.411	.527	138	38	17-6	.985	22	**113**	111	2b141,D10	0	**6.1**
1997	†Bal A★	112	412	64	137	23	2	14	60	40-2	3	43	.333	.390	.500	136	22	9-3	.988	10	104	**108**	2b109,D2	27	3.6
1998	Bal A★	147	588	86	166	36	1	14	56	59-3	2	70	.282	.347	.418	100	1	18-5	.985	21	111	99	2b144,D3	16	2.9
1999	†Cle A★	159	563	**138**	182	40	3	24	120	99-3	7	96	.323	.422	.533	137	36	37-6	**.992**	7	102	100	2b156,D2	0	**5.1**
2000	Cle A★	155	610	111	189	40	2	19	89	64-4	6	82	.310	.378	.475	111	12	39-4	.980	14	99	103	2b155	0	3.7
2001	†Cle A★	157	575	113	193	34	12	20	100	80-5	4	71	.336	.415	.541	145	40	30-6	**.993**	8	99	88	2b157	0	5.6
2002	NY N	149	590	73	157	24	4	11	53	57-4	1	83	.266	.331	.376	91	-9	16-4	.983	-22	89	99	2b147	0	-2.2
2003	NY N	73	263	34	69	17	1	2	22	29-2	2	40	.262	.336	.357	86	-5	6-0	.981	-10	92	104	2b72	0	-1.0
	Chi A	67	253	42	64	11	1	3	17	30-1	1	37	.253	.330	.340	76	-8	6-2	.990	-2	93	94	2b67	0	-0.6
2004	Ari N	38	110	14	34	5	2	3	16	12-0	1	18	.309	.382	.473	112	2	0-2	.971	-4	84	63	2b28/D	61	-0.2
	Chi A	18	61	4	11	1	0	1	8	2-0	0	13	.180	.203	.246	17	-8	0-0	.982	1	97	190	2b13,D5	0	-0.6
Total	17	2379	9073	1508	2724	504	80	210	1134	1032-62	50	1140	.300	.371	.443	115	216	474-114	.984	10	99	97	2b2320,D24,S5	104	36.1
ALOMAR, SANDY	Santos Jr. (Velazquez); B6.18.1966 Salinas, PR; BR/TR/6´5˝/(200–235); d9.30; f-Sandy b-Roberto																								
1988	SD N	1	1	0	0	0	0	0	0	0-0	0	1	.000	.000	.000	-99	0	0-0	ø	0	—	—	/H	0	0.0
1989	SD N	7	19	1	4	1	0	1	6	3-1	0	3	.211	.318	.421	110	0	0-0	1.000	1	178	0	C6	0	0.2
1990	Cle A★	132	445	60	129	26	2	9	66	25-2	2	46	.290	.326	.418	108	4	4-1	.981	-5	102	98	C129	0	0.7
1991	Cle A★	51	184	10	40	9	0	0	7	8-1	4	24	.217	.264	.266	47	-13	0-4	.987	7	138	82	C46,D4	103	-0.5
1992	Cle A★	89	299	22	75	16	0	2	26	13-3	5	32	.251	.293	.324	74	-11	3-3	.996	3	140	114	C88/D	16	-0.3
1993	Cle A	64	215	24	58	7	1	6	32	11-0	6	28	.270	.318	.395	92	-3	3-1	.984	-4	94	71	C64	98	-0.2
1994	Cle A	80	292	44	84	15	1	14	43	25-2	2	31	.288	.347	.490	112	4	8-4	.996	3	119	93	C78	17	1.2
1995	†Cle A	66	203	32	61	6	0	10	35	7-0	3	26	.300	.332	.478	106	1	3-1	.995	7	93	94	C61	65	1.1
1996	†Cle A★	127	418	53	110	23	0	11	50	19-0	3	42	.263	.299	.397	74	-18	1-0	.988	1	90	114	C124/1	0	-0.8
1997	†Cle A★	125	451	63	146	37	0	21	83	19-2	3	48	.324	.354	.545	126	16	0-2	.985	-10	90	104	C119/D	0	1.3
1998	†Cle A★	117	409	45	96	26	2	6	44	18-0	3	45	.235	.270	.352	59	-26	0-3	.992	5	111	82	C111,D3	0	-1.3
1999	†Cle A	37	137	19	42	13	0	6	25	4-0	0	23	.307	.322	.533	109	1	0-1	.974	-1	77	38	C35/D	118	0.2
2000	Cle A	97	356	44	103	16	2	7	42	16-1	4	41	.289	.324	.404	81	-11	2-2	.989	-12	71	96	C95/D	18	-1.6
2001	Chi A	70	220	17	54	8	1	4	21	12-1	2	17	.245	.288	.345	63	-12	1-2	.990	-0	143	77	C69	40	-0.8
2002	Chi A	51	167	21	48	10	1	7	25	5-0	1	14	.287	.309	.485	104	0	0-0	.994	-2	70	84	C50	18	0.2
	Col N	38	116	8	31	4	0	0	12	4-0	0	19	.267	.292	.302	50	-8	0-0	1.000	-2	136	61	C38	0	-0.9
2003	Chi A	75	194	22	52	12	0	5	26	4-0	0	17	.268	.281	.407	76	-7	0-0	.997	-2	162	43	C75	23	-0.5
2004	Chi A	50	146	15	35	4	0	2	14	11-2	2	13	.240	.298	.308	58	-9	0-0	.990	-2	82	179	C49/D	16	-0.8
2005	Tex A	46	128	11	35	7	0	0	14	5-0	1	12	.273	.306	.328	67	-6	0-0	.992	-2	113	0	C46	0	-0.6
2006	LA N	27	62	3	20	5	0	0	9	0-0	0	7	.323	.323	.403	84	-1	0-0	.988	-5	54	35	C18	0	-0.5
	Chi A	19	46	5	10	3	0	1	8	3-0	0	7	.217	.255	.348	56	-3	0-0	.990	0	96	125	C17,D2	0	-0.2
Total	19	1369	4508	519	1233	248	10	112	588	212-15	41	496	.274	.310	.407	86	-102	25-24	.989	-19	106	90	C1318,D14/1	532	-4.1

YEAR	TM LG	G	AB	R	H	2B	3B	HR	RBI	BB-IB	HP	SO	AVG	OBP	SLG	AOPS	ABR	SB-CS	FA	FR	RNG	THR	GAMES AT POSITION	DL	BFW
Alomar, Sandy	Santos Sr. (Conde); B10.19.1943 Salinas, PR; BB/TR (BR 1964p, 65–66)/5´9˝/(140–170); d9.15; C12; s–Roberto s–Sandy; OF(5/0/3)																								
1964	Mil N	19	53	3	13	1	0	0	6	0-0	0	11	.245	.245	.264	43	-4	1-0	.967	4	123	89	S19	0	0.2
1965	Mil N	67	108	16	26	1	1	0	8	4-1	0	12	.241	.268	.269	51	-7	12-5	.964	1	95	77	S39,2b19	0	-0.2
1966	Atl N	31	44	4	4	1	0	0	2	1-1	0	10	.091	.111	.114	-37	-8	0-0	.981	-3	81	141	2b21,S5	0	-1.1
1967	NY N	15	22	1	0	0	0	0	0	0-0	0	6	.000	.000	.000	-99	-6	0-0	1.000	1	110	70	S10,3b3,2b2	0	-0.5
	Chi A	12	15	4	3	0	0	0	0	2-0	0	0	.200	.294	.200	50	-1	2-0	.952	1	106	280	S8,2b2	0	0.1
1968	Chi A	133	363	41	92	8	2	0	12	20-1	1	42	.253	.292	.287	76	-11	21-8	.958	-14	96	96	2b99,3b27,S9/lf	0	-1.8
1969	Chi A	22	58	8	13	2	0	0	4	4-0	0	6	.224	.274	.259	47	-4	2-0	.980	3	105	129	2b22	0	0.0
	Cal A	134	559	60	140	10	2	1	30	36-2	0	48	.250	.296	.281	65	-28	18-3	.969	-6	95	113	2b134	0	-2.3
	Year	156	617	68	153	12	2	1	34	40-2	0	54	.248	.294	.279	63	-32	20-3	.970	-3	96	115	2b156	0	-2.3
1970	Cal A★	**162**	672	82	169	18	2	2	36	49-2	1	65	.251	.302	.293	67	-31	35-12	.979	12	107	**125**	2b153,S10/3	0	-0.4
1971	Cal A	**162**	689	77	179	24	3	4	42	41-4	0	60	.260	.301	.321	82	-19	39-10	.989	23	**115**	110	2b137,S28	0	2.3
1972	Cal A	**155**	610	65	146	20	3	1	25	47-5	0	55	.239	.292	.287	77	-18	20-12	.977	7	98	95	2b154,S4	0	-0.1
1973	Cal A	136	470	45	112	7	1	0	28	34-1	0	44	.238	.288	.257	59	-26	25-10	.979	5	96	97	2b110,S31	0	-0.9
1974	Cal A	46	54	12	12	0	1	0	1	2-0	0	8	.222	.250	.259	49	-4	2-0	.977	1	85	135	S19,2b15,3b5/rfD	0	-0.1
	NY A	76	279	35	75	8	0	1	27	14-0	0	25	.269	.302	.308	77	-9	6-4	.977	-11	89	79	2b76	0	-1.5
	Year	122	333	47	87	8	1	1	28	16-0	0	33	.261	.293	.300	73	-12	8-4	.976	-10	92	78	2b91,S19,3b5/rfD	0	-1.6
1975	NY A	151	489	61	117	18	4	2	39	26-0	0	58	.239	.277	.305	65	-24	28-6	**.985**	-4	93	104	2b150/S	0	-1.5
1976	†NY A	67	163	20	39	4	0	1	10	13-0	0	12	.239	.295	.282	70	-6	12-7	.970	-3	103	83	2b38,S6,3b3/1rfD	0	-0.7
1977	Tex A	69	83	21	22	3	0	1	11	8-0	1	13	.265	.333	.337	83	-2	4-3	.973	-4	83	107	D26,2b18,S6,O5(4/0/1),1b4/3	0	-0.5
1978	Tex A	24	29	3	6	1	0	0	1	1-0	0	7	.207	.233	.241	33	-3	0-0	.975	1	146	128	1b9,2b6,3b3,S2,D3	100	-0.2
Total	15	1481	4760	558	1168	126	19	13	282	302-17	3	482	.245	.290	.288	68	-211	227-80	.977	14	100	105	2b1156,S197,3b43,D39,1b14,O8L	100	-9.2
Alou, Felipe	Felipe Rojas (b Felipe Rojas (Alou)); B5.12.1935 Haina, D.R.; BR/TR/6´0˝/(190–205); d6.8; M14/C5; b–Jesus b–Matty s–Moises; OF(434/484/736)																								
1958	SF N	75	182	21	46	9	2	4	16	19-2	1	34	.253	.325	.390	91	-2	4-2	.985	5	131	50	O70(28/3/44)	0	0.0
1959	SF N	95	247	38	68	13	2	10	33	17-1	0	38	.275	.318	.466	109	2	5-3	.974	-3	97	45	O69(0/10/64)	0	-0.3
1960	SF N	106	322	48	85	17	3	8	44	16-1	2	42	.264	.299	.410	99	-2	10-2	.958	-2	99	71	O95(68/7/24)	0	-0.7
1961	SF N	132	415	59	120	19	0	18	52	26-2	2	41	.289	.333	.465	113	7	11-4	.990	3	104	112	O122(42/6/87)	0	0.4
1962	†SF N★	154	561	96	177	30	3	25	98	33-2	5	66	.316	.356	.513	133	25	10-7	.971	-2	105	60	O150(11/2/141)	0	1.2
1963	SF N	157	565	75	159	31	9	20	82	27-3	6	87	.281	.319	.474	127	18	11-2	.986	2	108	82	O153(6/13/144)	0	1.3
1964	Mil N	121	415	60	105	26	3	9	51	30-5	4	41	.253	.306	.395	96	-2	5-2	.975	1	116	37	O92(14/60/27),1b18	31	-0.5
1965	Mil N	143	555	80	165	29	2	23	78	31-4	5	63	.297	.338	.481	128	19	8-4	.980	1	103	45	O91(66/24/9),1b69,3b2/S	0	1.4
1966	Atl N☆	154	666	**122**	**218**	32	6	31	74	24-6	12	51	.327	.361	.533	143	36	5-7	.988	6	103	95	1b90,O79(47/40/4),3b3/S	0	3.4
1967	Atl N	140	574	76	157	26	3	15	43	32-7	7	50	.274	.318	.408	108	5	6-5	.993	-12	54	104	1b85,O56(24/30/5)	0	-1.6
1968	Atl N★	160	662	72	**210**	37	5	11	57	48-14	4	56	.317	.365	.438	140	33	12-11	.980	-0	102	79	O158C	0	3.0
1969	†Atl N	123	476	54	134	13	1	5	32	23-4	4	23	.282	.319	.345	85	-10	4-6	.989	-0	106	56	O116(3/102/13)	0	-1.6
1970	Oak A	154	575	70	156	25	3	8	55	32-6	1	31	.271	.308	.367	89	-10	10-5	.977	8	109	119	O145(101/5/81)/1	0	-1.1
1971	Oak A	2	8	0	2	1	0	0	0	0-0	0	1	.250	.250	.375	76	0	0-0	1.000	1	195	0	O2L	0	0.0
	NY A	131	461	52	133	20	6	8	69	32-3	2	24	.289	.334	.410	116	8	5-5	.985	-11	79	57	O80(7/20/56),1b42	0	-1.2
	Year	133	469	52	135	21	6	8	69	32-3	2	25	.288	.333	.409	116	8	5-5	.986	-11	82	56	O82(9/20/56),1b42	0	-1.2
1972	NY A	120	324	33	90	18	1	6	37	22-1	2	27	.278	.326	.395	117	6	1-0	.990	5	146	120	1b95,O15R	0	0.6
1973	NY A	93	280	25	66	12	0	4	27	9-5	0	25	.236	.256	.321	64	-14	0-1	.988	-2	90	100	1b67,O22(1/1/21)	0	-2.3
	Mon N	19	48	4	10	1	0	1	4	2-1	0	4	.208	.240	.292	45	-4	0-1	1.000	3	123	275	O15(14/3/0)/1	0	-0.2
1974	Mil A	3	3	0	0	0	0	0	0	0-0	0	2	.000	.000	.000	-99	-1	0-0	.000	-0	0	0	/rf	0	-0.1
Total	17	2082	7339	985	2101	359	49	206	852	423-67	57	706	.286	.328	.433	114	114	107-67	.979	-1	104	82	O1531R,1b468,3b5,S2	31	1.7
Alou, Jesus	Jesus Maria Rojas (b Jesus Maria Rojas (Alou)); B3.24.1942 Haina, D.R.; BR/TR/6´2˝/(180–200); d9.10; C1; b–Felipe b–Matty																								
1963	SF N	16	24	3	6	1	0	0	5	0-0	1	3	.250	.280	.292	66	-1	0-1	.875	-1	73	0	O12(11/0/3)	0	-0.3
1964	SF N	115	376	42	103	11	0	3	28	13-2	4	35	.274	.305	.327	77	-12	6-6	.973	3	107	120	O108(9/4/99)	0	-1.7
1965	SF N	143	543	76	162	19	4	9	52	13-0	3	40	.298	.317	.398	98	-3	8-5	.980	1	105	81	O136(6/0/133)	0	-1.2
1966	SF N	110	370	41	96	13	1	1	20	9-1	2	22	.259	.279	.308	62	-19	5-5	.967	-7	85	61	O100(59/0/42)	0	-3.4
1967	SF N	129	510	55	149	15	4	5	30	14-2	4	39	.292	.316	.367	96	-4	1-7	.948	-6	94	63	O123(79/0/50)	0	-2.1
1968	SF N	120	419	26	110	15	4	0	39	9-3	1	23	.263	.278	.317	79	-12	1-4	.989	3	100	132	O105(49/0/65)	0	-2.0
1969	Hou N	115	452	49	112	19	4	5	34	15-6	4	30	.248	.276	.341	74	-18	4-6	.928	0	100	124	O112(65/0/58)	36	-2.6
1970	Hou N	117	458	59	140	27	3	1	44	21-4	1	15	.306	.335	.384	97	-3	3-2	.962	-5	89	84	O108(30/0/88)	0	-1.3
1971	Hou N	122	433	41	121	21	4	2	40	13-3	4	17	.279	.305	.360	91	-7	3-7	.983	8	105	87	O109(52/0/63)	0	-0.7
1972	Hou N	52	93	8	29	4	1	0	11	7-4	1	5	.312	.366	.376	115	2	0-2	.970	-1	108	0	O23(10/0/14)	0	0.0
1973	Hou N	28	55	7	13	2	0	1	8	1-1	2	6	.236	.276	.327	67	-3	0-0	.941	-1	91	0	O14(1/0/13)	0	-0.4
	†Oak A	36	108	10	33	3	0	1	11	2-1	0	6	.306	.318	.361	95	-1	0-0	1.000	1	109	75	O21(18/1/4),D6	0	-0.2
1974	†Oak A	96	220	13	59	8	0	2	15	5-1	2	9	.268	.288	.332	83	-6	0-0	1.000	4	132	301	D41,O25(9/0/16)	0	-0.4
1975	NY N	62	102	8	27	3	0	0	11	4-2	1	5	.265	.299	.294	67	-5	0-1	.963	1	82	279	O20(15/0/5)	0	-0.6
1978	Hou N	77	139	7	45	5	1	2	19	6-1	0	5	.324	.345	.417	122	3	0-0	.976	-1	88	52	O28(27/0/1)	0	0.1
1979	Hou N	42	43	3	11	4	0	0	10	6-1	0	7	.256	.347	.349	96	0	0-0	1.000	0	147	0	O6(5/0/1)/1	0	0.0
Total	15	1380	4345	448	1216	170	26	32	377	138-32	30	267	.280	.305	.353	86	-89	31-46	.968	-1	99	94	O1050(445/5/655),D47/1	36	-16.8
Alou, Matty	Mateo Rojas (b Mateo Rojas (Alou)); B12.22.1938 Haina, D.R.; BL/TL/5´9˝/160; d9.26; b–Felipe b–Jesus																								
1960	SF N	4	3	1	1	0	0	0	0	0-0	0	0	.333	.333	.333	88	0	0-0	1.000	0	239	0	/lf	0	0.0
1961	SF N	81	200	38	62	7	2	6	24	15-2	0	18	.310	.356	.455	118	5	3-2	.978	-2	100	50	O58(16/3/40)	0	0.0
1962	†SF N	78	195	28	57	8	1	3	14	14-0	3	17	.292	.349	.390	100	0	3-1	.976	-0	100	92	O57(35/9/21)	0	-0.2
1963	SF N	63	76	4	11	1	0	0	2	2-0	1	13	.145	.177	.158	-3	-10	0-1	.952	1	109	151	O20(13/2/7)	0	-1.2
1964	SF N	110	250	28	66	4	2	1	14	11-3	3	25	.264	.302	.308	71	-10	5-3	.976	2	115	52	O80(42/18/35)	36	-1.2
1965	SF N	117	324	37	75	12	2	2	18	17-2	2	28	.231	.274	.299	60	-17	10-2	.986	2	100	133	O103(72/11/23)/P	0	-2.0
1966	Pit N	141	535	86	183	18	9	2	27	24-4	4	44	**.342**	.373	.421	121	14	23-15	.972	-5	92	125	O136(1/135/0)	0	0.6
1967	Pit N	139	550	87	186	21	7	2	28	24-1	6	42	.338	.372	.413	124	16	16-10	.989	-6	85	124	O134C/1	0	0.6
1968	Pit N★	146	558	59	185	28	4	0	52	27-6	2	26	.332	.362	.396	130	20	18-10	.984	-7	91	89	O144C	0	1.0
1969	Pit N★	**162**	698	105	**231**	**41**	6	1	48	42-9	2	35	.331	.369	.411	121	20	22-8	.977	-4	96	106	O162(1/162/0)	0	1.4
1970	†Pit N	155	677	97	201	21	8	1	47	30-3	4	18	.297	.329	.356	84	-17	19-11	.975	-7	86	172	O153(0/152/1)	0	-2.7
1971	StL N	149	609	85	192	28	6	7	74	34-3	4	27	.315	.352	.415	112	10	19-10	.981	-2	101	158	O94(0/73/21),1b57	0	0.2
1972	StL N	108	404	46	127	17	2	3	31	24-2	1	23	.314	.353	.389	112	6	11-4	.988	-1	101	106	1b66,O39(1/0/38)	0	-0.1
	†Oak A	32	121	11	34	5	0	1	16	11-1	1	12	.281	.341	.347	112	2	2-1	1.000	-3	78	86	O32(2/0/31)/1	0	-0.2
1973	NY A	123	497	59	147	22	1	2	28	30-0	3	43	.296	.338	.356	98	-1	5-2	.974	-6	91	109	O85R,1b40/D	0	-1.4
	StL N	11	11	1	3	0	0	0	1	1-1	0	0	.273	.333	.273	69	0	0-0	1.000	1	102	0	/1cf	0	0.0
1974	SD N	48	81	8	16	3	0	0	3	5-1	0	6	.198	.241	.235	36	-7	0-0	.947	-2	83	0	O13L,1b2	0	-1.0
Total	15	1667	5789	780	1777	236	50	31	427	311-38	36	377	.307	.345	.381	104	31	156-80	.979	-37	93	117	O1312(197/844/302),1b168/DP	36	-6.2
Alou, Moises	Moises Rojas (b Moises Rojas); B7.3.1966 Atlanta GA; BR/TR/6´3˝/(175–220); [PitN86*1/2]; d7.26; f–Felipe; Col Canada (CA) JC; [DL 1991 Mon N 182, 1999 Hou N 182]																								
1990	Pit N	2	5	0	1	0	0	0	0	0-0	0	0	.200	.200	.200	11	-1	0-0	1.000	-0	102	0	O2L	0	-0.1
	Mon N	14	15	4	3	0	1	0	0	0-0	0	3	.200	.200	.333	46	-1	0-0	1.000	1	106	548	O5(1/2/2)	0	-0.1
	Year	16	20	4	4	0	1	0	0	0-0	0	3	.200	.200	.300	37	-2	0-0	1.000	1	105	360	O7(3/2/2)	0	-0.2
1992	Mon N	115	341	53	96	28	2	9	56	25-0	1	46	.282	.328	.455	122	9	16-2	.978	-0	96	138	O100(79/13/15)	20	1.0
1993	Mon N	136	482	70	138	29	6	18	85	38-9	5	53	.286	.340	.483	114	9	17-6	.985	1	99	116	O136(102/12/34)	16	0.7
1994	Mon N★	107	422	81	143	31	5	22	78	42-10	2	63	.339	.397	.592	153	33	7-6	.986	-2	100	57	O106(63/0/45)	0	2.5
1995	Mon N	93	344	48	94	22	0	14	58	29-6	9	56	.273	.342	.459	106	3	4-3	.981	-3	92	88	O92(61/4/30)	38	-0.3
1996	Mon N	143	540	87	152	28	2	21	96	49-7	2	83	.281	.339	.457	107	5	9-4	.989	2	102	93	O142(33/7/123)	15	0.1
1997	†Fla N★	150	538	88	157	29	5	23	115	70-9	4	85	.292	.373	.493	131	25	9-5	.988	-11	87	47	O150(89/55/22)	0	1.1
1998	†Hou N★	159	584	104	182	34	5	38	124	84-11	5	87	.312	.399	.582	159	52	11-3	.980	-8	83	109	O154(152/6/0)/D	0	3.9
2000	Hou N	126	454	82	161	28	2	30	114	52-4	2	45	.355	.416	.623	148	34	3-3	.970	-8	84	69	O121(59/0/64)/D	16	1.9
2001	†Hou N★	136	513	79	170	31	1	27	108	57-14	3	57	.331	.396	.554	133	27	5-1	.991	-6	83	121	O130R,D4	15	1.5
2002	Chi N	132	484	50	133	23	1	15	61	47-4	0	61	.275	.337	.419	98	-2	8-0	.991	1	98	88	O124(122/1/4),D2	15	-0.4
2003	†Chi N	151	565	83	158	35	1	22	91	63-7	7	67	.280	.357	.462	110	9	3-1	.972	-8	87	52	O142L,D9	0	-0.4
2004	Chi N★	155	601	106	176	36	3	39	106	68-2	0	80	.293	.361	.557	130	26	3-0	.969	-4	92	89	O154L/D	0	1.6
2005	SF N★	123	427	67	137	21	3	19	63	56-1	3	43	.321	.400	.518	136	24	5-1	.966	-1	101	75	O117(74/0/53),D3	31	1.8
2006	SF N	98	345	52	104	25	1	22	74	28-2	1	31	.301	.352	.571	131	15	2-1	.978	-1	104	24	O92(11/0/81)/D	49	1.0
Total	15	1840	6660	1054	2005	400	38	319	1229	708-86	44	860	.301	.368	.516	127	267	102-36	.980	-48	93	84	O1767(1144/100/603),D22	579	15.8

YEAR	TM LG	G	AB	R	H	2B	3B	HR	RBI	BB-IB	HP	SO	AVG	OBP	SLG	AOPS	ABR	SB-CS	FA	FR	RNG	THR	GAMES AT POSITION	DL	BFW
ALPERMAN, WHITEY	Charles Augustus; B11.11.1879 Etna PA; D12.25.1942 Pittsburgh PA; BR/TR/5´10˝/180; d4.13																								
1906	Bro N	128	441	38	111	15	7	3	46	6	14	—	.252	.284	.338	102	-2	13	.940	-3	102	72	2b103,S24/3	—	-0.4
1907	Bro N	141	558	44	130	23	**16**	2	39	13	12	—	.233	.266	.342	98	-6	5	.953	12	112	100	2b115,3b14,S12	—	0.9
1908	Bro N	70	213	17	42	3	1	1	15	9	7	—	.197	.253	.235	58	-10	2	.934	-3	102	77	2b42,3b9,O5R,S2	—	-1.5
1909	Bro N	111	420	35	104	19	12	1	41	2	6	—	.248	.262	.357	95	-7	7	.931	9	100	84	2b108	—	0.4
Total	4	450	1632	134	387	60	36	7	141	30	39	—	.237	.268	.331	93	-25	27	.941	16	105	85	2b368,S38,3b24,O5R	—	-0.6
ALSTON, TOM	Thomas Edison; B1.31.1926 Greensboro NC; D12.30.1993 Winston–Salem NC; BL/TR/6´5˝/(195–210); d4.13; Col North Carolina A&T																								
1954	StL N	66	244	28	60	14	2	4	34	24	2	41	.246	.317	.369	78	-8	3-5	.989	10	154	97	1b65	0	-0.3
1955	StL N	13	8	0	1	0	0	0	0	0-0	0	0	.125	.125	.125	-33	-2	0-0	1.000	0	141	109	1b7	0	-0.1
1956	StL N	3	2	0	0	0	0	0	0	0-0	0	0	.000	.000	.000	-99	-1	0-0	1.000	0	294	264	1b3	0	0.0
1957	StL N	9	17	2	5	1	0	0	2	1-0	0	5	.294	.333	.353	83	0	0-0	.947	-1	35	131	1b6	103	-0.2
Total	4	91	271	30	66	15	2	4	36	25-0	2	46	.244	.311	.358	74	-11	3-5	.987	9	148	100	1b81	103	-0.6
ALSTON, WALTER	Walter Emmons "Smokey"; B12.1.1911 Venice OH; D10.1.1984 Oxford OH; BR/TR/6´2˝/195; d9.27; M23; HF1983; Col Miami–Ohio																								
1936	StL N	1	1	0	0	0	0	0	0	0	0	1	.000	.000	.000	-99	0	0	.500	-0	0	0	/1	—	-0.1
ALSTON, DELL	Wendell; B9.22.1952 Valhalla NY; BL/TR/6´0˝/(174–175); d5.17; Col Concordia (NY)																								
1977	NY A	22	40	10	13	4	0	1	4	3-0	0	4	.325	.364	.500	136	2	3-3	1.000	0	58	806	D10,O2R	0	0.2
1978	NY A	3	3	0	0	0	0	0	0	0-0	0	2	.000	.000	.000	-99	-1	0-0	ø	0	—	—	/H	0	-0.1
	Oak A	58	173	17	36	2	0	1	10	10-0	0	21	.208	.250	.237	40	-14	11-10	.956	-3	99	0	O50(22/0/29),1b9,D3	0	-2.2
	Year	61	176	17	36	2	0	1	10	10-0	0	23	.205	.246	.233	37	-15	11-10	.956	-3	99	0	O50(22/0/29),1b9,D3	0	-2.3
1979	Cle A	54	62	10	18	0	2	1	12	10-1	0	10	.290	.384	.403	114	1	4-4	.969	0	94	178	O30(18/0/12),D7	0	0.0
1980	Cle A	52	54	11	12	1	2	0	9	5-2	2	7	.222	.302	.315	71	-2	2-4	.947	0	104	89	O26(12/4/11),D6	0	-0.4
Total	4	189	332	48	79	7	4	3	35	28-3	2	44	.238	.297	.310	71	-14	20-21	.957	-3	98	74	O108(52/4/54),D26,1b9	0	-2.5
ALTENBURG, JESSE	Jesse Howard; B1.2.1893 Ashley MI; D3.12.1973 Lansing MI; BL/TR/5´9˝/158; d9.19																								
1916	Pit N	8	14	2	6	1	1	0	0	1	0	1	.429	.467	.643	237	2	0	1.000	-0	85	0	O8(4/2/0)	—	0.2
1917	Pit N	11	17	1	3	0	0	0	3	0	0	4	.176	.176	.176	8	-2	0	1.000	-0	99	0	O4(1/0/3)	—	-0.3
Total	2	19	31	3	9	1	1	0	3	1	0	5	.290	.313	.387	112	0	0	1.000	-1	91	0	O12(5/2/3)	—	-0.1
ALTIZER, DAVE	David Tilden "Filipino"; B11.6.1876 Pearl IL; D5.14.1964 Pleasant Hill IL; BL/TR/5´10.5˝/160; d5.29; OF(4/53/52)																								
1906	Was A	115	433	56	111	9	5	1	27	35	8	—	.256	.324	.307	103	2	37	.931	-15	87	78	S113,O2R	—	-1.1
1907	Was A	147	540	60	145	15	5	2	42	34	6	—	.269	.319	.326	115	8	38	.923	-3	99	83	S80,1b50,O17C	—	0.8
1908	Was A	67	205	19	46	1	1	0	18	13	1	—	.224	.274	.239	73	-6	8	.959	-2	105	105	2b38,3b16,1b4/S	—	-0.9
	Cle A	29	89	11	19	1	2	0	5	7	1	—	.213	.278	.270	78	-2	7	.952	0	165	266	O24(0/20/4),S3	—	-0.4
	Year	96	294	30	65	2	3	0	23	20	2	—	.221	.275	.248	75	-8	15	.959	-2	105	105	2b38,O24(0/20/4),3b16,1b4,S4	—	-1.3
1909	Chi A	116	382	47	89	6	7	1	20	39	**16**	—	.233	.330	.293	101	2	27	.949	4	130	53	O61(4/14/45),1b46	—	0.2
1910	Cin N	3	10	3	6	0	0	0	0	3	0	0	.600	.692	.600	290	3	0	.933	-1	75	77	S3	—	0.2
1911	Cin N	37	75	8	17	4	1	0	4	9	1	5	.227	.318	.307	78	-2	2	.907	-0	106	55	S23/12rf	—	-0.1
Total	6	514	1734	204	433	36	21	4	116	140	33	5	.250	.318	.302	101	5	119	.925	-17	93	76	S223,O105C,1b101,2b39,3b16	—	-1.3
ALTMAN, GEORGE	George Lee; B3.20.1933 Goldsboro NC; BL/TR/6´4˝/(195–200); d4.11; Negro Lg 1955; Col Tennessee St.																								
1959	Chi N	135	420	54	103	14	4	12	47	34-4	7	80	.245	.312	.383	85	-10	1-0	.990	0	104	110	O121C	0	-1.5
1960	Chi N	119	334	50	89	16	4	13	51	32-6	1	67	.266	.330	.455	114	6	4-3	.993	-3	98	35	O79(26/32/23),1b21	0	-0.2
1961	Chi N★	138	518	77	157	28	**12**	27	96	40-3	4	92	.303	.353	.560	137	26	6-2	.978	-1	100	93	O130(1/25/115),1b3	0	1.6
1962	Chi N★	147	534	74	170	27	5	22	74	62-14	5	89	.318	.393	.511	136	29	19-7	.972	-4	101	73	O129(0/6/125),1b16	0	1.7
1963	StL N	135	464	62	127	18	7	9	47	47-2	2	93	.274	.339	.401	104	3	13-4	.979	2	108	91	O124(12/0/116)	0	-0.2
1964	NY N	124	422	48	97	14	1	9	47	18-4	1	70	.230	.262	.332	68	-19	4-2	.968	10	110	**173**	O109(95/0/14)	0	-1.6
1965	Chi N	90	196	24	46	7	1	4	23	19-2	0	36	.235	.302	.342	79	-5	3-2	.943	-2	98	0	O45(44/0/1),1b2	0	-1.1
1966	Chi N	88	185	19	41	6	0	5	17	14-3	0	37	.222	.276	.335	68	-8	2-2	.958	-1	72	168	O42(41/0/1),1b4	0	-1.2
1967	Chi N	15	18	1	2	2	0	0	1	2-0	0	8	.111	.200	.222	20	-2	0-0	1.000	-1	53	0	O4(3/0/1)/1	0	-0.3
Total	9	991	3091	409	832	132	34	101	403	268-38	20	572	.269	.329	.432	105	20	52-22	.977	-0	102	96	O783(222/184/396),1b47	0	-2.8
ALTOBELLI, JOE	Joseph Salvatore; B5.26.1932 Detroit MI; BL/TL/6´0˝/(180–185); d4.14; M7/C7																								
1955	Cle A	42	75	8	15	3	0	2	5	5-0	1	14	.200	.259	.320	53	-5	0-1	.992	-1	72	72	1b40	0	-0.9
1957	Cle A	83	87	9	18	3	2	0	9	5-0	1	14	.207	.253	.287	49	-6	3-2	.994	-0	73	81	1b56,O7(1/4/2)	0	-0.9
1961	Min A	41	95	10	21	2	1	3	14	13-0	0	14	.221	.312	.358	75	-3	0-0	.951	-1	104	0	O25L,1b2	0	-0.5
Total	3	166	257	27	54	8	3	5	28	23-0	2	42	.210	.277	.323	60	-14	3-3	.993	-3	74	74	1b98,O32(26/4/2)	0	-2.3
ALUSIK, GEORGE	George Joseph; B2.11.1935 Ashley PA; BR/TR/6´3.5˝/(170–180); d9.11																								
1958	Det A	2	2	0	0	0	0	0	0	0-0	0	1	.000	.000	.000	-93	-1	0-0	1.000	0	146	0	/lf	0	-0.1
1961	Det A	15	14	0	2	0	0	0	2	1-0	0	4	.143	.188	.143	-6	-2	0-0	ø	-0	0	0	/rf	0	-0.3
1962	Det A	2	2	0	0	0	0	0	0	0-0	0	0	.000	.000	.000	-97	-1	0-0	ø	0	—	—	/H	0	-0.1
	KC A	90	209	29	57	10	1	11	35	16-1	1	29	.273	.326	.488	111	3	1-1	.968	0	99	115	O50(35/0/22)/1	0	0.0
	Year	92	211	29	57	10	1	11	35	16-1	1	29	.270	.323	.483	109	2	1-1	.968	0	99	115	O50(35/0/22)/1	0	-0.1
1963	KC A	87	221	28	59	11	0	9	37	26-0	1	33	.267	.345	.439	112	4	0-1	1.000	1	93	133	O63(30/1/36)	31	0.1
1964	KC A	102	204	18	49	10	1	3	19	30-2	2	36	.240	.342	.343	89	-2	0-0	.984	-1	95	54	O44(43/0/3),1b12	0	-0.6
Total	5	298	652	75	167	31	2	23	93	73-3	4	103	.256	.333	.416	101	1	1-2	.985	-1	95	105	O159(109/1/62),1b13	31	-1.0
ALVARADO, LUIS	Luis Cesar (Martinez); B1.15.1949 Lajas, PR; D3.20.2001 Lajas, PR; BR/TR/5´9˝/(162–170); d9.13																								
1968	Bos A	11	46	3	6	2	0	0	1	1-0	1	11	.130	.167	.174	3	-5	0-0	.976	-4	75	92	S11	0	-1.1
1969	Bos A	6	5	0	0	0	0	0	0	0-0	0	2	.000	.000	.000	-96	-1	0-1	1.000	1	125	199	S5	0	-0.1
1970	Bos A	59	183	19	41	11	0	1	10	9-2	0	30	.224	.258	.301	51	-12	1-2	.929	-0	101	34	3b29,S27	0	-1.1
1971	Chi A	99	264	22	57	14	1	0	8	11-2	0	34	.216	.246	.277	47	-19	1-2	.959	7	99	96	S71,2b16	0	-0.5
1972	Chi A	103	254	30	54	4	1	4	29	13-5	1	36	.213	.254	.283	58	-14	2-2	.957	-3	98	70	S81,2b16,3b2	0	-1.0
1973	Chi A	80	203	21	47	7	2	0	20	4-0	1	20	.232	.250	.286	49	-14	6-2	.980	-1	99	83	2b45,S18,3b10/D	0	-1.2
1974	Chi A	8	10	1	1	0	0	0	0	0-0	0	1	.100	.100	.100	-41	-2	0-0	.667	-1	66	0	S4/23	0	-0.3
	StL N	17	36	3	5	2	0	0	1	2-0	0	6	.139	.179	.194	6	-5	0-0	.980	-3	86	112	S17	0	-0.7
	Cle A	61	114	12	25	2	0	0	12	6-0	0	14	.219	.256	.237	43	-8	1-1	.972	-0	102	101	2b46,S7,D3	0	-0.6
1976	StL N	16	42	5	12	1	0	0	3	3-1	0	6	.286	.333	.310	82	-1	0-0	.936	-8	65	38	2b16	0	-0.9
1977	NY N	1	2	0	0	0	0	0	0	0-0	0	0	.000	.000	.000	-99	-1	0-0	1.000	0	156	0	/2	0	0.0
	Det A	2	1	0	0	0	0	0	0	0-0	0	0	.000	.000	.000	-95	0	0-0	ø	-1	0	0	3b2	0	-0.1
Total	9	463	1160	116	248	43	4	5	84	49-10	3	160	.214	.247	.271	47	-82	11-10	.957	-13	98	88	S241,2b141,3b44,D4	0	-7.6
ALVAREZ, TONY	Antonio Enrique; B5.10.1979 Caracas, Distrito Capital, Venezuela; BR/TR/6´1˝/(200–202); d9.4																								
2002	Pit N	14	26	6	8	2	0	1	2	3-0	0	5	.308	.379	.500	127	1	1-0	1.000	-2	63	0	O8(2/6/1)	0	0.0
2004	Pit N	24	38	5	8	2	0	1	8	4-0	1	7	.211	.289	.342	66	-2	0-0	1.000	-1	86	0	O16(3/4/9)	0	-0.3
Total	2	38	64	11	16	4	0	2	10	7-0	1	12	.250	.324	.406	91	-1	1-0	1.000	-2	76	0	O24(5/10/10)	0	-0.3
ALVAREZ, CLEMENTE	Clemente Rafael; B5.18.1968 Anzoategul, Venezuela; BR/TR/5´11˝/180; d9.19																								
2000	Phi N	2	5	1	1	0	0	0	0	0-0	0	1	.200	.200	.200	1	-1	0-0	1.000	0	28	0	C2	0	0.0
ALVAREZ, GABE	Gabriel De Jesus; B3.6.1974 Navojoa, Sonora, Mexico; BR/TR/6´1˝/205; [SDN95 2/32]; d6.22; Col USC																								
1998	Det A	58	199	16	46	11	0	5	29	18-1	2	65	.231	.299	.362	71	-9	1-3	.873	-3	102	74	3b55,D2	0	-1.2
1999	Det A	22	53	5	11	3	0	2	4	3-0	0	9	.208	.250	.377	56	-4	0-0	1.000	-1	53	0	D12,O5R,3b2	0	-0.5
2000	Det A	1	1	0	0	0	0	0	0	2-0	0	1	.000	.667	.000	90	0	0-1	ø	0	—	—	/D	0	0.0
	SD N	11	13	1	2	1	0	0	0	1-0	0	1	.154	.214	.231	13	-2	0-0	1.000	-1	69	0	3b3,O2L	0	-0.2
Total	3	92	266	22	59	15	0	7	33	24-1	2	76	.222	.289	.357	66	-15	1-4	.875	-5	101	72	3b60,D15,O7(2/0/5)	0	-1.9
ALVAREZ, ORLANDO	Jesus Manuel Orlando (Monge); B2.28.1952 Rio Grande, PR; BR/TR/6´0˝/165; d9.1																								
1973	LA N	4	4	0	1	1	0	0	0	0-0	0	1	.250	.250	.500	106	0	0-0	ø	0	—	—	/H	0	0.0
1974	LA N	2	1	0	0	0	0	0	0	0-0	0	0	.000	.000	.000	-99	0	0-0	1.000	0	230	0	/lf	0	0.0
1975	LA N	4	4	0	0	0	0	0	0	0-0	0	1	.000	.000	.000	-99	-1	0-0	ø	0	—	—	/H	0	-0.1
1976	Cal A	15	42	4	7	1	0	2	8	0-0	0	3	.167	.167	.333	47	-3	0-0	1.000	-1	67	160	O11(10/1/0),D2	0	-0.5
Total	4	25	51	4	8	2	0	2	8	0-0	0	5	.157	.157	.314	36	-4	0-0	1.000	-1	71	156	O12(11/1/0),D2	0	-0.6

YEAR	TM LG	G	AB	R	H	2B	3B	HR	RBI	BB-IB	HP	SO	AVG	OBP	SLG	AOPS	ABR	SB-CS	FA	FR	RNG	THR	GAMES AT POSITION	DL	BFW
Alvarez, Ossie	Oswaldo (Gonzalez); B10.19.1933 Bolondron, Cuba; BR/TR/5´10˝/(156–165); d4.19																								
1958	Was A	87	196	20	41	3	0	0	5	16-0	0	26	.209	.269	.224	38	-17	1-1	.968	2	97	85	S64,2b14,3b3	0	-1.1
1959	Det A	8	2	0	1	0	0	0	0	0-0	0	1	.500	.500	.500	166	0	0-0	ø	0	—	—	/H	0	0.0
Total	2	95	198	20	42	3	0	0	5	16-0	0	27	.212	.271	.227	39	-17	1-1	.968	2	97	85	S64,2b14,3b3	0	-1.1
Alvarez, Rogelio	Rogelio (Hernandez); B4.18.1938 Pinar Del Rio, Cuba; BR/TR/5´11˝/185; d9.18																								
1960	Cin N	3	9	1	1	0	0	0	0	0-0	0	3	.111	.111	.111	-38	-2	0-0	1.000	-1	0	62	1b2	0	-0.3
1962	Cin N	14	28	1	6	0	0	0	2	1-0	0	10	.214	.241	.214	23	-3	0-0	.973	-1	76	126	1b13	0	-0.4
Total	2	17	37	2	7	0	0	0	2	1-0	0	13	.189	.211	.189	8	-5	0-0	.979	-1	60	112	1b15	0	-0.7
Alvis, Max	Roy Maxwell; B2.2.1938 Jasper TX; BR/TR/5´11˝/(185–190); d9.11; Col Texas																								
1962	Cle A	12	51	1	11	2	0	0	3	2-0	0	13	.216	.245	.255	36	-5	3-1	.935	-3	69	45	3b12	0	-0.8
1963	Cle A	158	602	81	165	32	7	22	67	36-2	**10**	109	.274	.324	.460	118	13	9-7	.942	-6	91	111	3b158	0	0.6
1964	Cle A	107	381	51	96	14	3	18	53	29-5	6	77	.252	.313	.446	110	4	5-5	.955	-7	91	94	3b105	35	-0.4
1965	Cle A★	159	604	88	149	24	2	21	61	47-4	**9**	121	.247	.308	.397	99	-2	12-8	.958	-17	80	57	3b156	0	-2.1
1966	Cle A	157	596	67	146	22	3	17	55	50-6	2	98	.245	.304	.378	95	-4	4-7	.958	-7	86	88	3b157	0	-1.5
1967	Cle A★	161	637	66	163	23	4	21	70	38-1	4	107	.256	.301	.403	106	2	3-10	.965	-10	86	74	3b161	0	-1.2
1968	Cle A	131	452	38	101	17	3	8	37	41-5	4	91	.223	.292	.327	90	-6	5-5	.960	-15	80	86	3b128	23	-2.6
1969	Cle A	66	191	13	43	6	0	1	15	14-1	0	26	.225	.275	.272	53	-12	1-1	.973	-4	84	88	3b58/S	59	-1.8
1970	Mil A	62	115	16	21	2	0	3	12	5-1	0	20	.183	.217	.278	35	-11	1-2	.909	-0	111	75	3b36	0	-1.2
Total	9	1013	3629	421	895	142	22	111	373	262-25	35	662	.247	.302	.390	97	-21	43-46	.956	-69	86	84	3b971/S	117	-11.0
Alvord, Billy	William Crawford "Uncle Bill"; B8.10.1863 St.Louis MO; D4.7.1927 St.Petersburg FL; 5´10˝/187; d4.30																								
1885	StL N	2	5	0	0	0	0	0	0	1	—	2	.000	.167	.000	-45	-1	—	.714	-1	27	0	3b2	—	-0.2
1889	KC AA	50	186	23	43	8	9	0	18	10	0	35	.231	.270	.371	77	-8	3	.877	3	132	122	3b34,S8,2b8	—	-0.3
1890	Tol AA	116	495	69	135	13	16	2	52	22	0	—	.273	.304	.376	97	-7	21	.872	4	98	76	3b116	—	0.0
1891	Cle N	13	59	7	17	2	2	1	7	0	1	7	.288	.300	.441	110	0	0	.814	-2	95	50	3b13	—	-0.1
	Was AA	81	312	28	73	8	3	0	30	11	0	38	.234	.260	.279	57	-19	3	.862	17	117	63	3b81	—	-0.1
1893	Cle N	3	12	2	2	0	0	0	2	0	0	1	.167	.167	.167	-11	-2	0	.875	-1	38	0	3b3	—	-0.3
Total	5	265	1069	129	270	31	30	3	109	44	1	83	.253	.283	.346	81	-37	27	.865	20	108	75	3b249,2b8,S8	—	-1.0
Alyea, Brant	Garrabrant Ryerson; B12.8.1940 Passaic NJ; BR/TR/6´3˝/215; d9.11; Col Hofstra																								
1965	Was A	8	13	3	3	0	0	2	6	1-0	0	4	.231	.286	.692	171	1	0-0	1.000	-1	0	0	1b3/lf	0	0.0
1968	Was A	53	150	18	40	11	1	6	23	10-0	1	39	.267	.317	.473	142	7	0-0	1.000	1	120	0	O39(16/0/24)	0	0.6
1969	Was A	104	237	29	59	4	0	11	40	34-4	1	67	.249	.341	.405	115	5	1-3	.938	-3	82	138	O69(36/0/36),1b3	0	-0.2
1970	†Min A	94	258	34	75	12	1	16	61	28-0	3	51	.291	.366	.531	142	15	3-3	.980	-1	90	110	O75(73/0/2)	0	1.0
1971	Min A	79	158	13	28	4	0	2	15	24-3	1	38	.177	.282	.241	50	-10	1-1	.962	-3	74	144	O48(47/0/1)	0	-1.6
1972	Oak A	10	13	1	3	1	0	0	0	1-0	0	0	.231	.286	.308	80	0	0-0	1.000	-0	104	0	O2L	21	-0.1
	StL N	13	19	0	3	1	0	0	1	0-0	0	6	.158	.158	.211	4	-2	0-0	1.000	1	152	769	O3(1/0/2)	0	-0.1
	Oak A	10	18	2	3	0	0	1	2	2-0	0	5	.167	.250	.333	76	-1	0-0	1.000	4	104	0	O6R	21	0.3
Total	6	371	866	100	214	33	2	38	148	100-7	6	210	.247	.326	.421	113	15	5-7	.972	-1	93	127	O243(176/0/71),1b6	42	-0.1
Amalfitano, Joey	John Joseph; B1.23.1934 San Pedro CA; BR/TR/5´11˝/(175–180); d5.2; M3/C31; Col Loyola Marymount																								
1954	NY N	9	5	2	0	0	0	0	0	0	0	4	.000	.000	.000	-99	-1	0-0	1.000	1	192	440	3b4/2	0	-0.1
1955	NY N	36	22	8	5	1	1	0	1	2-0	0	2	.227	.292	.364	72	-1	0-0	.957	4	194	129	S5,3b2	0	0.3
1960	SF N	106	328	47	91	15	3	1	27	26-1	3	31	.277	.335	.351	94	-3	2-3	.935	-1	112	93	3b63,2b33,S3/lf	0	-0.2
1961	SF N	109	384	64	98	11	4	2	23	44-2	0	59	.255	.331	.320	77	-12	7-4	.970	-15	87	79	2b95,3b6	0	-1.9
1962	Hou N	117	380	44	90	12	5	1	27	45-5	1	43	.237	.317	.303	73	-14	4-4	.967	-5	92	111	2b110,3b5	0	-1.0
1963	SF N	54	137	11	24	3	0	1	7	12-0	1	18	.175	.245	.219	36	-11	2-6	.980	-5	100	64	2b37,3b7	0	-1.7
1964	Chi N	100	324	51	78	19	6	4	27	40-1	5	42	.241	.333	.373	95	-1	2-7	.964	4	109	95	2b86/1S	0	0.9
1965	Chi N	67	96	13	26	4	0	0	8	12-0	2	14	.271	.364	.313	90	0	2-2	.989	5	145	93	2b24,S4	0	0.6
1966	Chi N	41	38	8	6	2	0	0	3	4-0	0	10	.158	.227	.211	26	-4	0-0	.977	-2	87	93	2b12,3b3,S2	0	-0.5
1967	Chi N	4	1	0	0	0	0	0	0	0-0	0	1	.000	.000	.000	-96	0	0-0	ø	0	—	—	/H	0	0.0
Total	10	643	1715	248	418	67	19	9	123	185-9	12	224	.244	.320	.321	78	-47	19-26	.970	-13	97	92	2b398,3b90,S15/1lf	0	-3.6
Amaral, Rich	Richard Louis; B4.1.1962 Visalia CA; BR/TR/6´0˝/175; [ChiN83 2/34]; d5.27; Col UCLA; OF(232/101/52)																								
1991	Sea A	14	16	2	1	0	0	0	0	1-0	1	5	.063	.167	.063	-34	-3	0-0	1.000	1	164	256	2b5,3b2,S2/1D	49	-0.2
1992	Sea A	35	100	9	24	3	0	1	7	5-0	0	16	.240	.276	.300	61	-6	4-2	.955	1	115	121	3b17,S17,O3(3/1/1),1b2/2	0	-0.4
1993	Sea A	110	373	53	108	24	1	1	44	33-0	3	54	.290	.348	.367	92	-3	19-11	.975	15	104	102	2b77,3b19,S14,1b3,D9	15	1.6
1994	Sea A	77	228	37	60	10	2	4	18	24-1	1	28	.263	.333	.377	82	-6	5-1	.943	2	103	79	2b42,O16(14/2/0),S7,1b2,D6	0	-0.2
1995	†Sea A	90	238	45	67	14	2	2	19	21-0	1	33	.282	.342	.382	87	-4	21-2	.992	3	102	187	O73(53/29/8)/D	0	0.1
1996	Sea A	118	312	69	91	11	3	1	29	47-0	5	55	.292	.392	.356	91	-2	25-6	1.000	-5	106	62	O91(63/26/5),2b15,1b10/3D	0	-0.4
1997	†Sea A	89	190	34	54	5	0	1	21	10-0	3	34	.284	.327	.326	72	-8	12-8	1.000	-3	94	0	O52(39/9/6),1b14,2b11/3SD	0	-1.1
1998	Sea A	73	134	25	37	6	0	1	4	13-0	1	24	.276	.342	.343	79	-4	11-1	1.000	-3	104	113	O52(43/4/9),2b11,1b7/3D	33	-0.5
1999	Bal A	91	137	21	38	8	1	0	11	15-0	1	20	.277	.348	.350	83	-3	9-6	1.000	1	112	0	O50(14/18/19),D18,1b2,2b2/3	0	-0.4
2000	Bal A	30	60	10	13	1	1	0	6	7-0	0	8	.217	.299	.267	47	-5	6-2	1.000	4	130	133	O19(3/12/4)/1D	42	-0.1
Total	10	727	1788	305	493	82	10	11	159	176-1	16	277	.276	.344	.351	82	-44	112-39	.996	16	104	89	O356L,2b164,D55,1b42,3b42,S41	139	-1.6
Amaro, Ruben	Ruben Jr.; B2.12.1965 Philadelphia PA; BB/TR/5´10˝/(170–191); [CalA87 11/291]; d6.8; f–Ruben; Col Stanford																								
1991	Cal A	10	23	0	5	1	0	0	2	3-1	0	3	.217	.308	.261	59	-1	0-0	1.000	-1	51	578	O5(3/0/2),2b4/D	0	-0.2
1992	Phi N	126	374	43	82	15	6	7	34	37-1	9	54	.219	.303	.348	84	-8	11-5	.992	5	111	85	O113(27/27/68)	0	-0.6
1993	Phi N	25	48	7	16	2	2	1	6	6-0	0	5	.333	.400	.521	149	3	0-0	.963	1	107	140	O16(3/8/6)	0	0.4
1994	Cle A	26	23	5	5	1	0	2	5	2-0	0	3	.217	.280	.522	100	0	2-1	.909	0	146	0	O12(1/10/1),D3	0	0.0
1995	†Cle A	28	60	5	12	3	0	1	7	4-0	2	6	.200	.273	.300	48	-5	1-3	1.000	-0	103	0	O22(5/14/6),D3	34	-0.6
1996	Phi N	61	117	14	37	10	0	2	15	9-0	3	18	.316	.380	.453	118	4	0-0	1.000	-0	108	0	O35(0/7/28)/1	0	0.2
1997	Phi N	117	175	18	41	6	1	2	21	21-0	2	24	.234	.320	.314	69	-8	1-1	.987	2	112	107	O72(26/37/15)/1	0	-0.7
1998	Phi N	92	107	7	20	5	0	1	10	6-0	0	15	.187	.224	.262	29	-11	0-0	1.000	0	76	258	O51(43/3/6)	0	-1.2
Total	8	485	927	99	218	43	9	16	100	88-2	16	128	.235	.310	.353	80	-26	15-10	.989	6	106	98	O326(108/106/132),D7,2b4,1b2	34	-2.7
Amaro, Ruben	Ruben Sr. (Mora); B1.6.1936 Nueva Laredo, Tamaulipas, Mexico; BR/TR/5´11˝/(165–175); d7.15; C6; s–Ruben																								
1958	StL N	40	76	8	17	2	1	0	0	5-1	0	8	.224	.272	.276	44	-6	0-1	.948	-3	89	104	S36/2	0	-0.8
1960	Phi N	92	264	25	61	9	1	0	16	21-2	2	32	.231	.292	.273	56	-16	0-1	.965	-8	95	94	S92	0	-1.8
1961	Phi N	135	381	34	98	14	9	1	32	53-2	2	59	.257	.351	.349	88	-5	1-0	.970	7	103	109	S132,1b3/2	0	1.2
1962	Phi N	79	226	24	55	10	0	0	19	30-4	1	28	.243	.330	.288	71	-8	5-2	.968	6	103	107	S78/1	0	0.5
1963	Phi N	115	217	25	47	9	2	2	19	19-6	0	31	.217	.276	.304	69	-9	0-1	.950	1	94	94	S63,3b45,1b5	0	-0.5
1964	Phi N	129	299	31	79	11	0	4	34	16-2	3	37	.264	.307	.341	84	-7	1-6	.971	-5	89	109	S79,1b58,2b3,3b3/lf	0	-0.9
1965	Phi N	118	184	26	39	7	0	0	15	27-3	1	22	.212	.312	.250	63	-8	1-1	.990	-6	162	101	1b60,S60,2b6	0	-1.1
1966	NY A	14	23	0	5	0	0	0	3	0-0	0	2	.217	.217	.217	26	-2	0-0	.977	2	108	177	S14	133	0.1
1967	NY A	130	417	31	93	12	0	1	17	43-4	1	49	.223	.297	.259	68	-16	3-2	.973	8	107	109	S123,3b3,1b2	0	0.2
1968	NY A	47	41	3	5	1	0	0	0	9-0	0	6	.122	.280	.146	33	-3	0-0	.962	-4	85	113	S23,1b22	0	-0.7
1969	Cal A	41	27	4	6	0	0	0	1	4-0	0	6	.222	.323	.222	57	-1	0-0	1.000	-2	0	37	1b18,2b9,S5,3b2	0	-0.4
Total	11	940	2155	211	505	75	13	8	156	227-24	10	280	.234	.309	.292	70	-81	11-14	.967	-6	98	105	S705,1b169,3b53,2b20/lf	133	-4.2
Ambler, Wayne	Wayne Harper; B11.8.1915 Abington PA; D1.3.1998 Ponte Vedra Beach FL; BR/TR/5´8.5˝/165; d6.4; Col Duke																								
1937	Phi A	56	162	3	35	5	0	0	11	13	0	8	.216	.274	.247	33	-17	1-0	.955	-1	102	102	2b56	—	-1.4
1938	Phi A	120	393	42	92	21	2	0	38	48	0	31	.234	.317	.298	56	-26	2-1	.942	-16	94	69	S116,2b4	—	-3.1
1939	Phi A	95	227	15	48	13	0	0	24	22	0	25	.211	.281	.269	42	-20	1-0	.954	-2	104	80	S77,2b19	—	-1.6
Total	3	271	782	60	175	39	2	0	73	83	0	64	.224	.298	.279	47	-63	4-1	.946	-20	97	73	S193,2b79	—	-6.1
Ambres, Chip	Raymond Payne; B12.19.1979 Beaumont TX; BR/TR/6´1˝/190; [FlaN98 1/27]; d7.20																								
2005	KC A	53	145	25	35	8	0	4	9	16-1	2	32	.241	.323	.379	90	-2	3-2	.988	-0	99	104	O47(23/24/0),D2	0	-0.3

YEAR	TM LG	G	AB	R	H	2B	3B	HR	RBI	BB-IB	HP	SO	AVG	OBP	SLG	AOPS	ABR	SB-CS	FA	FR	RNG	THR	GAMES AT POSITION	DL	BFW
AMELUNG, ED	Edward Allen; B4.13.1959 Fullerton CA; BL/TL/5´11˝/185; d7.28; Col San Diego St.																								
1984	LA N	34	46	7	10	0	0	0	4	2-0	0	4	.217	.250	.217	32	-4	3-2	1.000	1	136	0	O23(9/4/11)	0	-0.4
1986	LA N	8	11	0	1	0	0	0	0	0-0	0	4	.091	.091	.091	-53	-2	0-0	1.000	0	140	0	O4(0/2/2)	0	-0.2
Total	2	42	57	7	11	0	0	0	4	2-0	0	8	.193	.220	.193	17	-6	3-2	1.000	1	137	0	O27(9/6/13)	0	-0.6
AMEZAGA, ALFREDO	Alfredo (Delgado); B1.16.1978 Ciudad Obregon, Sonora, Mexico; BB/TR (BR 2002)/5´10˝/165; [AnaA99 13/401]; d5.24; Col St. Petersburg (FL) JC																								
2002	Ana A	12	13	3	7	2	0	0	2	0-0	0	1	.538	.538	.692	228	2	1-0	1.000	-0	100	44	S5	0	0.3
2003	Ana A	37	105	15	22	3	2	2	7	9-0	1	23	.210	.278	.333	63	-6	2-2	.970	-0	93	79	S24,3b13	0	-0.5
2004	†Ana A	73	93	12	15	2	0	2	11	3-0	3	24	.161	.212	.247	20	-11	3-2	.990	-0	109	43	S32,3b26,2b16	0	-0.9
2005	Col N	2	3	1	1	0	0	0	0	0-0	0	0	.333	.333	.333	68	0	0-0	ø	-0	0	0	/3	0	0.0
	Pit N	3	3	1	0	0	0	0	0	1-0	0	0	.000	.250	.000	-27	-1	1-0	1.000	0	147	323	/S	0	0.0
	Year	5	6	2	1	0	0	0	0	1-0	0	0	.167	.286	.167	22	-1	1-0	1.000	0	0	0	/3S	0	0.0
2006	Fla N	132	334	42	87	9	3	3	19	33-4	3	46	.260	.332	.332	75	-13	20-12	.977	4	109	65	O78(14/75/2),2b23,S11,3b4,1b2	0	-0.7
Total	5	259	551	74	132	16	5	7	39	46-4	7	94	.240	.306	.325	66	-29	27-16	.977	4	109	65	O78(14/75/2),S73,3b44,2b39,1b2	0	-1.8
AMOROS, SANDY	Edmundo (Isasi); B1.30.1930 Havana, Cuba; D6.27.1992 Miami FL; BL/TL/5´7.5˝/(163–170); d8.22; Negro Lg 1950																								
1952	†Bro N	20	44	10	11	3	1	0	3	5	0	14	.250	.327	.364	90	-1	1-0	1.000	-1	95	0	O10(3/4/7)	0	-0.2
1954	Bro N	79	263	44	72	18	6	9	34	31	1	24	.274	.353	.490	113	5	1-4	.987	1	99	128	O70(68/1/2)	0	0.1
1955	†Bro N	119	388	59	96	16	7	10	51	55-5	6	45	.247	.347	.402	96	-1	10-5	.972	-1	93	127	O109(102/8/5)	0	-0.8
1956	†Bro N	114	292	53	76	11	8	16	58	59-6	1	51	.260	.385	.517	130	14	3-4	.955	-7	83	60	O86(79/5/10)	0	0.2
1957	Bro N	106	238	40	66	7	1	7	26	46-3	3	42	.277	.399	.403	107	5	3-2	.984	0	105	50	O66(65/1/2)	0	0.1
1959	LA N	5	5	1	1	0	0	0	1	0-0	0	1	.200	.200	.200	6	-1	0-0	ø	0	—	—	/H	0	-0.1
1960	LA N	9	14	1	2	0	0	0	0	3-1	0	2	.143	.294	.143	23	-1	0-0	1.000	1	107	489	O3(0/1/3)	0	-0.1
	Det A	65	67	7	10	0	0	1	7	12-1	0	10	.149	.275	.194	29	-7	0-0	1.000	-1	95	0	O10(1/9/0)	0	-0.8
Total	7	517	1311	215	334	55	23	43	180	211-16	11	189	.255	.361	.430	105	13	18-15	.976	-7	94	94	O354(318/29/29)	0	-1.6
ANDERSON, ALF	Alfred Walton; B1.28.1914 Gainesville GA; D6.23.1985 Albany GA; BR/TR/5´11˝/165; d4.20; Mil 1944–45; Col Georgia																								
1941	Pit N	70	223	32	48	7	2	1	10	14	1	30	.215	.265	.278	53	-15	2	.931	-6	100	94	S58	0	-1.7
1942	Pit N	54	166	24	45	4	1	0	7	18	0	19	.271	.342	.307	89	-2	4	.942	-11	85	73	S48	0	-1.1
1946	Pit N	2	1	0	0	0	0	0	0	1	0	0	.000	.500	.000	47	0	0	ø	0	—	—	/H	0	0.0
Total	3	126	390	56	93	11	3	1	17	33	1	49	.238	.300	.290	68	-17	6	.936	-17	94	85	S106	0	-2.8
ANDERSON, ANDY	Andy Holm; B11.13.1922 Bremerton WA; D7.18.1982 Seattle WA; BR/TR/5´11˝/172; d5.10																								
1948	StL A	51	87	13	24	5	1	1	12	8	0	15	.276	.337	.391	91	-1	0-0	.917	-1	118	95	2b21,S10,1b2	0	-0.1
1949	StL A	71	136	10	17	3	0	1	5	14	0	21	.125	.207	.169	-0	-20	0-1	.957	-3	93	89	S44,2b8,3b8	0	-2.2
Total	2	122	223	23	41	8	1	2	17	22	0	36	.184	.257	.256	35	-21	0-1	.946	-4	90	93	S54,2b29,3b8,1b2	0	-2.3
ANDERSON, BRADY	Brady Kevin; B1.18.1964 Silver Spring MD; BL/TL/6´1˝/(185–202); [BosA85 10/257]; d4.4; Col California–Irvine																								
1988	Bos A	41	148	14	34	5	3	0	12	15-0	4	35	.230	.315	.304	72	-5	4-2	.989	0	95	141	O41(0/17/25)	0	-0.6
	Bal A	53	177	17	35	8	1	1	9	8-0	0	40	.198	.232	.271	41	-14	6-4	.981	4	121	46	O49C	0	-1.1
	Year	94	325	31	69	13	4	1	21	23-0	4	75	.212	.272	.286	56	-19	10-6	.984	4	108	92	O90(0/66/25)	0	-1.7
1989	Bal A	94	266	44	55	12	2	4	16	43-6	3	45	.207	.324	.312	82	-5	16-4	.985	-2	98	75	O79(3/75/1),D8	0	-0.5
1990	Bal A	89	234	24	54	5	2	3	24	31-2	5	46	.231	.327	.308	83	-5	15-2	.987	4	114	86	O63(44/21/1),D11	42	0.0
1991	Bal A	113	256	40	59	12	3	2	27	38-0	5	44	.230	.338	.324	88	-3	12-5	.981	-3	93	74	O101(75/26/9),D2	17	-0.6
1992	Bal A★	159	623	100	169	28	10	21	80	98-14	9	98	.271	.373	.449	127	25	53-16	.980	5	106	89	O158(148/7/3)	0	3.2
1993	Bal A	142	560	87	147	36	8	13	66	82-4	10	99	.262	.363	.425	107	8	24-12	.993	-3	98	81	O140(126/18/3),D2	15	0.1
1994	Bal A	111	453	78	119	25	5	12	48	57-3	10	75	.263	.356	.419	94	-3	31-1	.996	-2	101	55	O109(76/38/5)	0	-0.1
1995	Bal A	143	554	108	145	33	10	16	64	87-4	10	111	.262	.371	.444	109	9	26-7	.989	-12	91	11	O142(121/40/0)	0	-0.2
1996	†Bal A★	149	579	117	172	37	5	50	110	76-1	**22**	106	.297	.396	.637	157	51	21-8	.992	-8	92	113	O143C,D2	0	4.2
1997	†Bal A★	151	590	97	170	39	7	18	73	84-6	**19**	105	.288	.393	.469	128	28	18-12	.989	-12	89	32	O124C,D25	0	1.5
1998	Bal A	133	479	84	113	28	3	18	51	75-1	15	78	.236	.356	.420	103	4	21-7	.985	-14	87	13	O130C	18	-0.6
1999	Bal A	150	564	109	159	28	5	24	81	96-7	**24**	105	.282	.404	.477	129	30	36-7	.997	-11	91	35	O136(9/129/0),D10	0	2.3
2000	Bal A	141	506	89	130	26	0	19	50	92-5	8	103	.257	.375	.421	108	10	16-9	.997	-4	102	15	O127(16/88/24),D11	0	0.5
2001	Bal A	131	430	50	87	12	3	8	45	60-4	8	77	.202	.311	.300	66	-21	12-4	.988	4	105	111	O120(56/6/66),D4	0	-1.9
2002	Cle A	34	80	4	13	4	0	1	5	18-2	2	23	.162	.327	.250	56	-4	4-0	.981	-2	96	0	O29(14/16/2)/D	0	-0.5
Total	15	1834	6499	1062	1661	338	67	210	761	960-59	154	1190	.256	.362	.425	108	105	315-100	.989	-54	97	60	O1691(688/927/139),D76	92	5.7
ANDERSON, BRIAN	Brian Nikola; B3.11.1982 Tucson AZ; BR/TR/6´2˝/(205–215); [ChiA03 1/15]; d8.16; Col Arizona																								
2005	Chi A	13	34	3	6	1	0	2	3	0-0	0	12	.176	.176	.382	41	-3	1-0	1.000	0	86	193	O12(9/5/1)	0	-0.3
2006	Chi A	134	365	46	82	23	1	8	33	30-2	5	90	.225	.290	.359	66	-19	4-7	.994	1	107	53	O134C	0	-1.7
Total	2	147	399	49	88	24	1	10	36	30-2	5	102	.221	.281	.361	64	-22	5-7	.994	1	105	64	O146(9/139/1)	0	-2.0
ANDERSON, DAVE	David Carter; B8.1.1960 Louisville KY; BR/TR/6´2˝/(184–185); [LAN81 1/22]; d5.8; Col Memphis																								
1983	LA N	61	115	12	19	4	2	1	2	12-1	0	15	.165	.244	.261	40	-10	6-3	.969	-5	88	93	S53/3	0	-1.1
1984	LA N	121	374	51	94	16	2	3	34	45-4	2	55	.251	.331	.329	87	-5	15-5	.965	19	106	109	S111,3b11	0	2.7
1985	†LA N	77	221	24	44	6	0	4	18	35-3	1	42	.199	.310	.281	68	-9	5-4	.957	9	116	151	3b51,S25,2b2	66	0.2
1986	LA N	92	216	31	53	9	0	1	15	22-1	0	39	.245	.314	.301	76	-7	5-1	.976	0	101	116	3b51,S34,2b5	58	-0.4
1987	LA N	108	265	32	62	12	3	1	13	24-1	1	43	.234	.299	.313	64	-14	9-5	.977	3	99	87	S65,3b35,2b5	20	-0.4
1988	†LA N	116	285	31	71	10	2	2	20	32-4	1	45	.249	.325	.319	89	-4	4-2	.986	9	105	127	S82,3b12,2b11	0	1.2
1989	LA N	87	140	15	32	2	0	1	14	17-1	0	26	.229	.310	.264	67	-6	2-0	.990	-8	73	114	S33,3b18,2b7	0	-1.2
1990	SF N	60	100	14	35	5	1	1	6	3-0	0	20	.350	.369	.450	128	3	1-2	1.000	-4	97	65	S29,2b13,1b3,3b2	0	0.0
1991	SF N	100	226	24	56	5	2	2	13	12-2	0	35	.248	.286	.314	71	-10	2-4	.956	-0	97	133	S63,1b16,3b11,2b6	0	-0.9
1992	LA N	51	84	10	24	4	0	3	8	4-0	0	11	.286	.311	.440	114	1	0-4	.974	-1	82	106	3b26,S7	31	-0.1
Total	10	873	2026	244	490	73	12	19	143	206-17	5	331	.242	.312	.318	78	-61	49-30	.970	23	100	105	S502,3b218,2b49,1b19	175	0.0
ANDERSON, DREW	Drew Thomas; B6.9.1981 Kearney NE; BL/TR/6´2˝/195; [MilN03 24/699]; d9.11; Col Nebraska																								
2006	Mil N	9	9	3	1	0	0	0	0	1-0	0	4	.111	.200	.111	-17	-2	0-0	1.000	-0	53	0	O2(1/0/1)	0	-0.2
ANDERSON, DWAIN	Dwain Cleaven; B11.23.1947 Oakland CA; BR/TR/5´11˝/(165–180); d9.3																								
1971	Oak A	16	37	3	10	2	1	0	3	5-1	1	9	.270	.372	.378	115	1	0-1	.968	-2	92	112	S10,2b5/3	0	-0.1
1972	Oak A	3	7	2	0	0	0	0	0	1-0	0	4	.000	.125	.000	-64	-1	0-0	1.000	-1	60	0	/S3	0	-0.2
	StL N	57	135	12	36	4	1	1	8	8-1	1	23	.267	.313	.333	84	-3	0-1	.952	1	96	86	S43,3b13/2	0	0.1
1973	StL N	18	17	5	2	0	0	0	0	4-0	0	4	.118	.286	.118	16	-2	0-0	.500	-2	0	0	S3,O2C	0	-0.4
	SD N	53	107	11	13	0	0	0	3	14-0	0	29	.121	.223	.121	-2	-15	2-0	.932	-2	97	89	S39,3b6	0	-1.4
	Year	71	124	16	15	0	0	0	3	18-0	0	33	.121	.232	.121	1	-17	2-0	.919	-4	94	86	S42,3b6,O2C	0	-1.8
1974	Cle A	2	3	0	1	0	0	0	0	0-0	0	1	.333	.333	.333	93	0	0-0	1.000	-1	0	0	/2	0	-0.1
Total	4	149	306	33	62	6	2	1	14	32-2	2	70	.203	.282	.245	51	-20	2-2	.940	-6	94	87	S96,3b21,2b7,O2C	0	-2.1
ANDERSON, GOAT	Edward John; B1.13.1880 Cleveland OH; D3.15.1923 South Bend IN; BL/TR; d4.11																								
1907	Pit N	127	413	73	85	3	1	1	12	80	6	—	.206	.343	.225	77	-5	27	.953	-0	94	107	O117(2/24/91),2b5	—	-1.2
ANDERSON, FERRELL	Ferrell Jack "Andy"; B1.9.1918 Maple City KS; D3.12.1978 Joplin MO; BR/TR/6´1˝/200; d4.16; Col Kansas																								
1946	Bro N	79	199	19	51	10	0	2	14	18	4	21	.256	.330	.337	89	-3	1	.964	0	*147*	*116*	C70	0	0.1
1953	StL N	18	35	1	10	2	0	0	1	0	0	4	.286	.286	.343	63	-2	0-0	1.000	-1	*69*	*80*	C12	0	-0.2
Total	2	97	234	20	61	12	0	2	15	18	4	25	.261	.324	.338	85	-5	1-0	.968	-0	*138*	*112*	C82	0	-0.1
ANDERSON, GARRET	Garret Joseph; B6.30.1972 Los Angeles CA; BL/TL/6´3˝/(190–228); [CalA90 4/125]; d7.27																								
1994	Cal A	5	13	0	5	0	0	0	1	0-0	0	2	.385	.385	.385	98	0	0-0	1.000	1	160	0	O4L	0	0.0
1995	Cal A	106	374	50	120	19	1	16	69	19-4	1	65	.321	.352	.505	122	10	6-2	.978	5	115	109	O100(99/1/1)/D	0	1.1
1996	Cal A	150	607	79	173	33	2	12	72	27-5	0	84	.285	.314	.405	79	-21	7-9	.979	-2	105	48	O146(140/3/6)/D	0	-2.7
1997	Ana A	154	624	76	189	36	3	8	92	30-6	2	70	.303	.334	.409	93	-7	10-4	.992	10	111	149	O148(130/27/4),D4	0	-0.1
1998	Ana A	156	622	62	183	41	7	15	79	29-8	1	80	.294	.325	.455	99	-3	8-3	.983	5	108	104	O155(39/0/122)	0	-0.4
1999	Ana A	157	620	88	188	36	2	21	80	34-8	0	81	.303	.336	.469	104	2	3-4	.993	2	107	70	O153(32/116/6),D4	0	0.2
2000	Ana A	159	647	92	185	40	3	35	117	24-5	0	87	.286	.307	.519	102	-1	7-6	.990	-8	95	61	O148(0/137/15),D10	0	-0.9
2001	Ana A	161	672	83	194	39	2	28	123	27-4	0	100	.289	.314	.478	103	1	13-6	.994	1	100	94	O149(144/12/0),D12	0	-0.3
2002	†Ana A★	158	638	93	195	**56**	3	29	123	30-11	0	80	.306	.332	.539	130	25	6-4	.994	-2	97	80	O147(137/14/0),D10	0	1.7

YEAR	TM LG	G	AB	R	H	2B	3B	HR	RBI	BB-IB	HP	SO	AVG	OBP	SLG	AOPS	ABR	SB-CS	FA	FR	RNG	THR	GAMES AT POSITION	DL	BFW
2003	Ana A★	159	638	80	201	**49**	4	29	116	31-10	0	83	.315	.345	.541	134	30	6-3	.997	13	112	151	O144L,D15	0	3.5
2004	†Ana A	112	442	57	133	20	1	14	75	29-6	1	75	.301	.343	.446	109	5	2-1	.991	-3	95	92	O94C,D18	49	0.2
2005	†LA A★	142	575	68	163	34	1	17	96	23-8	0	84	.283	.308	.435	98	-3	1-1	.976	-2	96	72	O106L,D36	0	-1.1
2006	LA A	141	543	63	152	28	2	17	85	38-11	0	95	.280	.323	.433	98	-3	1-0	1.000	-1	105	15	O94L,D45	0	-0.9
Total	13	1760	7015	891	2081	431	31	241	1128	341-86	5	986	.297	.327	.470	105	35	70-43	.989	19	104	89	O1588(1069/404/154),D156	49	0.3

Anderson, George George Jendrus "Andy" (Born George Andrew Jendrus); B9.26.1889 Cleveland OH; D5.28.1962 Cleveland OH; BL/TR/5´8˝/160; d5.26

YEAR	TM LG	G	AB	R	H	2B	3B	HR	RBI	BB-IB	HP	SO	AVG	OBP	SLG	AOPS	ABR	SB-CS	FA	FR	RNG	THR	GAMES AT POSITION	DL	BFW
1914	Bro F	98	364	58	115	13	3	3	24	31	4	50	.316	.376	.393	110	0	16	.946	2	104	109	O92(70/21/1)	—	-0.2
1915	Bro F	136	511	70	135	23	9	2	39	52	8	54	.264	.342	.356	97	-9	20	.956	-4	91	97	O134(40/12/82)	—	-2.1
1918	StL N	35	132	20	39	4	5	0	6	15	3	7	.295	.380	.402	143	7	0	.956	-3	94	49	O35R	—	0.2
Total	3	269	1007	148	289	40	17	5	69	98	15	111	.287	.359	.375	108	-2	36	.952	-5	96	94	O261(110/33/118)	—	-2.1

Anderson, Sparky George Lee; B2.22.1934 Bridgewater SD; BR/TR/5´9˝/168; d4.10; M26/C1; HF2000

YEAR	TM LG	G	AB	R	H	2B	3B	HR	RBI	BB-IB	HP	SO	AVG	OBP	SLG	AOPS	ABR	SB-CS	FA	FR	RNG	THR	GAMES AT POSITION	DL	BFW
1959	Phi N	152	477	42	104	9	3	0	34	42-1	1	53	.218	.282	.249	43	-39	6-9	.984	0	97	78	2b152	0	-3.1

Anderson, Hal Harold; B2.10.1904 St.Louis MO; D5.1.1974 St.Louis MO; BR/TR/5´11˝/160; d4.12

YEAR	TM LG	G	AB	R	H	2B	3B	HR	RBI	BB-IB	HP	SO	AVG	OBP	SLG	AOPS	ABR	SB-CS	FA	FR	RNG	THR	GAMES AT POSITION	DL	BFW
1932	Chi A	9	32	4	8	0	0	0	2	0	0	1	.250	.250	.250	32	-3	0-1	1.000	1	103	162	O9C	—	-0.3

Anderson, Harry Harry Walter; B9.10.1931 North East MD; D6.11.1998 Greenville DE; BL/TR/6´3˝/(200–210); d4.18; Col West Chester

YEAR	TM LG	G	AB	R	H	2B	3B	HR	RBI	BB-IB	HP	SO	AVG	OBP	SLG	AOPS	ABR	SB-CS	FA	FR	RNG	THR	GAMES AT POSITION	DL	BFW
1957	Phi N	118	400	53	107	15	4	17	61	36-7	6	61	.268	.333	.452	113	7	2-3	.986	3	110	74	O109(107/0/2)	0	0.3
1958	Phi N	140	515	80	155	34	6	23	97	59-10	3	95	.301	.373	.524	137	28	0-2	.975	-7	92	63	O87L,1b49	0	1.3
1959	Phi N	142	508	50	122	28	6	14	63	43-14	5	95	.240	.304	.402	85	-11	1-1	.980	12	107	161	O137L	0	-0.8
1960	Phi N	38	93	10	23	2	0	5	12	10-1	2	19	.247	.333	.430	107	1	0-0	1.000	-1	92	86	O16L,1b12	0	-0.1
	Cin N	42	66	6	11	3	0	1	9	11-0	0	20	.167	.282	.258	49	-4	0-0	.990	-1	90	69	1b15,O4(2/0/2)	0	-0.6
	Year	80	159	16	34	5	0	6	21	21-1	2	39	.214	.311	.358	82	-4	0-0	.989	-2	89	57	1b27,O20(18/0/2)	0	-0.7
1961	Cin N	4	4	0	1	0	0	0	0	0-0	0	1	.250	.250	.250	33	0	0-0	ø	0	—	—	/H	0	0.0
Total	5	484	1586	199	419	82	16	60	242	159-32	16	291	.264	.334	.450	109	21	3-6	.982	7	103	105	O353(349/0/4),1b76	0	0.1

Anderson, Jim James Lea; B2.23.1957 Los Angeles CA; BR/TR/6´0˝/(170–180); [AnaA75 2/25]; d7.2

YEAR	TM LG	G	AB	R	H	2B	3B	HR	RBI	BB-IB	HP	SO	AVG	OBP	SLG	AOPS	ABR	SB-CS	FA	FR	RNG	THR	GAMES AT POSITION	DL	BFW
1978	Cal A	48	108	6	21	7	0	0	7	11-1	0	16	.194	.267	.259	51	-7	0-0	.955	-3	87	92	S47/2	0	-0.6
1979	†Cal A	96	234	33	58	13	1	3	23	17-0	1	31	.248	.298	.350	77	-7	3-2	.949	-2	95	94	S82,3b10,2b6,C3	0	-0.3
1980	Sea A	116	317	46	72	7	0	8	30	27-1	3	39	.227	.292	.325	68	-14	2-4	.958	7	113	105	S65,3b33,2b2/CD	0	-0.3
1981	Sea A	70	162	12	33	7	0	2	19	17-0	1	29	.204	.283	.284	61	-8	3-5	.947	1	104	115	S68,3b2	0	-0.3
1983	Tex A	50	102	8	22	1	1	0	6	5-0	0	8	.216	.252	.245	38	-9	1-2	.962	3	137	84	S27,2b17,3b3,O3(2/0/1)/CD	0	-0.4
1984	Tex A	39	47	2	5	0	0	0	1	4-0	0	7	.106	.176	.106	-19	-8	0-0	.989	4	106	127	S31,3b6/2	0	-0.2
Total	6	419	970	107	211	35	2	13	86	81-2	5	130	.218	.280	.298	60	-53	9-13	.955	10	103	103	S320,3b54,2b27,D7,C5,O3(2/0/1)	0	-2.1

Anderson, John John Joseph "Honest John"; B12.14.1873 Sarpsborg, Norway; D7.23.1949 Worcester MA; BB/TR/6´2˝/180; d9.8

YEAR	TM LG	G	AB	R	H	2B	3B	HR	RBI	BB-IB	HP	SO	AVG	OBP	SLG	AOPS	ABR	SB-CS	FA	FR	RNG	THR	GAMES AT POSITION	DL	BFW
1894	Bro N	17	63	14	19	1	3	1	19	3	0	3	.302	.333	.460	96	-1	7	.778	-3	0	0	O16(15/1/0)/3	—	-0.4
1895	Bro N	103	423	77	122	11	14	10	89	12	5	29	.288	.316	.452	105	-1	24	.882	-8	68	117	O102(90/0/12)	—	-1.5
1896	Bro N	108	430	70	135	23	17	1	55	18	2	23	.314	.344	.453	116	7	37	.942	-2	98	174	O68(33/9/26),1b42	—	0.1
1897	Bro N	117	492	93	160	28	12	4	85	17	7	—	.325	.357	.455	120	12	29	.936	-2	65	60	O115L,1b3	—	-0.1
1898	Bro N	6	21	1	3	2	0	0	2	1	1	—	.143	.217	.238	31	-2	0	1.000	-0	0	0	O5(2/1/2)	—	-0.2
	Was N	110	430	70	131	28	18	9	71	23	12	—	.305	.357	.516	150	24	18	.948	7	155	88	O93(13/78/2),1b17	—	2.3
	Bro N	19	69	11	19	3	4	0	8	5	1	—	.275	.333	.435	120	1	2	.966	0	0	0	O17L,1b2	—	0.0
	Year	135	520	82	153	33	**22**	9	81	29	14	—	.294	.348	**.494**	141	24	20	.952	7	**145**	98	O115(32/79/4),1b19	—	2.1
1899	Bro N	117	439	65	118	18	7	4	92	27	4	—	.269	.317	.369	86	-10	25	.933	-3	55	70	O76(7/61/8),1b41	—	-1.6
1901	Mil A	138	576	90	190	46	7	8	99	24	3	—	.330	.360	.476	137	28	35	**.982**	4	99	106	1b125,O13(12/0/1)	—	2.5
1902	StL A	126	524	60	149	29	6	4	85	21	3	—	.284	.316	.385	95	-5	15	.985	-9	67	110	1b126,O3(2/0/1)	—	-1.5
1903	StL A	138	550	65	156	34	8	2	78	23	0	—	.284	.312	.385	111	7	16	.986	5	111	**113**	1b133,O7(2/3/2)	—	1.0
1904	NY A	143	558	62	155	27	12	3	82	23	6	—	.278	.313	.385	115	8	20	.956	0	76	35	O112(46/52/13),1b33	—	0.2
1905	NY A	32	99	12	23	3	1	0	14	8	1	—	.232	.296	.283	75	-3	9	.900	-1	139	0	O22(1/19/2),1b3	—	-0.5
	Was A	101	400	50	116	21	6	1	38	22	2	—	.290	.330	.380	130	13	22	.960	-1	64	38	O97(16/3/78),1b4	—	0.7
	Year	133	499	62	139	24	7	1	52	30	3	—	.279	.323	.361	117	9	31	.949	-2	76	32	O119(17/22/80),1b7	—	0.2
1906	Was A	**151**	583	62	158	25	4	3	70	19	2	—	.271	.296	.343	105	1	**39**	.953	7	100	44	O151L	—	-0.1
1907	Was A	87	333	33	96	12	4	0	44	34	3	—	.288	.359	.348	136	15	19	.983	-1	85	45	1b61,O26L	—	1.3
1908	Chi A	123	355	36	93	17	1	0	47	30	1	—	.262	.321	.315	109	4	21	.963	-4	97	317	O87(13/2/72),1b9	—	-0.3
Total	14	1636	6345	871	1843	328	124	50	978	310	53	55	.290	.329	.405	114	98	338	.939	-11	86	87	O1010(561/229/219),1b599/3	—	1.9

Anderson, Kent Kent McKay; B8.12.1963 Florence SC; BR/TR/6´1˝/180; [CalA84 4/86]; d4.15; b–Mike; Col South Carolina

YEAR	TM LG	G	AB	R	H	2B	3B	HR	RBI	BB-IB	HP	SO	AVG	OBP	SLG	AOPS	ABR	SB-CS	FA	FR	RNG	THR	GAMES AT POSITION	DL	BFW
1989	Cal A	86	223	27	51	6	1	0	17	17-0	1	42	.229	.285	.265	57	-13	1-2	.972	8	109	134	S70,2b7,3b5,O2R/D	0	-0.1
1990	Cal A	49	143	16	44	6	1	1	5	13-1	1	19	.308	.369	.385	113	3	0-2	.964	7	97	116	S28,3b16,2b5	38	1.1
Total	2	135	366	43	95	12	2	1	22	30-1	2	61	.260	.318	.311	79	-10	1-4	.969	14	105	129	S98,3b21,2b12,O2R/D	38	1.0

Anderson, Marlon Marlon Ordell; B1.6.1974 Montgomery AL; BL/TR/5´11˝/(190–200); [PhiN95 2/42]; d9.8; Col South Alabama

YEAR	TM LG	G	AB	R	H	2B	3B	HR	RBI	BB-IB	HP	SO	AVG	OBP	SLG	AOPS	ABR	SB-CS	FA	FR	RNG	THR	GAMES AT POSITION	DL	BFW
1998	Phi N	17	43	4	14	3	0	1	4	1-0	0	6	.326	.333	.465	109	0	2-0	.978	1	112	103	2b9	0	0.2
1999	Phi N	129	452	48	114	26	4	5	54	24-1	2	61	.252	.292	.361	63	-27	13-2	.979	-7	95	86	2b121	0	-2.5
2000	Phi N	41	162	10	37	8	1	1	15	12-0	0	22	.228	.282	.309	49	-13	2-2	.989	-2	90	121	2b41	0	-1.3
2001	Phi N	147	522	69	153	30	2	11	61	35-5	2	74	.293	.337	.421	100	-1	8-5	.982	4	106	104	2b140	0	1.0
2002	Phi N	145	539	64	139	30	6	8	48	42-14	5	71	.258	.315	.380	88	-11	5-1	.970	-6	100	101	2b143	0	-0.9
2003	TB A	145	482	59	130	27	3	6	67	41-5	3	60	.270	.328	.376	88	-8	19-3	.973	-17	96	108	2b134,O3L,D4	0	-1.5
2004	†StL N	113	253	31	60	12	0	8	28	12-1	1	38	.237	.269	.379	66	-14	6-2	.969	-1	93	136	2b37,O36(28/0/11),1b2/D	0	-1.3
2005	NY N	123	235	31	62	9	0	7	19	18-0	1	45	.264	.316	.391	87	-5	6-1	.990	3	143	123	1b23,O23(9/0/14),2b20,D2	0	-0.3
2006	Was N	109	215	31	59	13	2	5	23	18-1	1	41	.274	.331	.423	96	-1	2-4	.961	-4	94	69	2b32,O17(0/7/10),1b2	0	-0.6
	†LA N	25	64	12	24	3	2	7	15	7-0	0	8	.375	.431	.813	209	10	2-2	.955	-2	76	0	O15(15/0/1)/2D	0	0.7
	Year	134	279	43	83	16	4	12	38	25-1	1	49	.297	.354	.513	124	9	4-6	.961	-6	95	68	2b33,O32(15/7/11),D3,1b2	0	0.1
Total	9	994	2967	359	792	161	20	59	334	210-27	15	426	.267	.316	.394	86	-70	65-22	.976	-31	99	102	2b678,O94(55/7/36),1b27,D10	0	-6.5

Anderson, Mike Michael Allen; B6.22.1951 Florence SC; BR/TR/6´2˝/(185–205); [PhiN69 1/6]; d9.2; b–Kent

YEAR	TM LG	G	AB	R	H	2B	3B	HR	RBI	BB-IB	HP	SO	AVG	OBP	SLG	AOPS	ABR	SB-CS	FA	FR	RNG	THR	GAMES AT POSITION	DL	BFW
1971	Phi N	26	89	11	22	5	1	2	5	13-0	0	28	.247	.343	.393	108	1	0-0	.986	0	107	69	O26C	0	0.1
1972	Phi N	36	103	8	20	5	1	2	5	19-1	0	36	.194	.317	.320	80	-2	1-0	.987	4	111	257	O35(0/3/34)	0	0.1
1973	Phi N	87	193	32	49	9	1	9	28	19-4	1	53	.254	.321	.451	109	2	0-3	.981	0	103	96	O67(0/12/57)	24	-0.1
1974	Phi N	145	395	35	99	22	2	5	34	37-13	0	75	.251	.313	.354	83	-9	2-1	.980	10	**117**	160	O133(1/2/131)/1	0	-0.5
1975	Phi N	115	247	24	64	10	3	4	28	17-3	2	66	.259	.307	.372	85	-6	1-2	.977	4	109	131	O105(0/24/88),1b3	0	-0.5
1976	StL N	86	199	17	58	8	1	1	12	26-4	1	30	.291	.371	.357	107	3	1-1	.982	3	108	131	O58(24/2/33),1b5	0	0.3
1977	StL N	94	154	18	34	4	1	4	17	14-0	0	31	.221	.286	.338	67	-8	2-3	.980	2	113	118	O77(2/1/74)	0	-0.8
1978	Bal A	53	32	2	3	0	1	0	3	3-0	0	10	.094	.171	.156	-8	-5	0-0	.962	-1	92	0	O47(41/2/6)	0	-0.7
1979	Phi N	79	78	12	18	4	0	1	2	13-0	0	14	.231	.341	.321	78	-2	1-2	.973	3	118	130	O70(47/6/20)/P	0	-0.1
Total	9	721	1490	159	367	67	11	28	134	161-25	4	343	.246	.319	.362	88	-26	8-12	.980	26	111	135	O618(115/78/443),1b9/P	24	-2.2

Andino, Robert Robert Lazaro; B4.25.1984 Miami FL; BR/TR/6´0˝/170; [FlaN02 2/52]; d9.4

YEAR	TM LG	G	AB	R	H	2B	3B	HR	RBI	BB-IB	HP	SO	AVG	OBP	SLG	AOPS	ABR	SB-CS	FA	FR	RNG	THR	GAMES AT POSITION	DL	BFW
2005	Fla N	17	44	4	7	4	0	0	1	5-1	0	8	.159	.245	.250	32	-4	1-0	.956	-7	62	76	S17	0	-1.0
2006	Fla N	11	24	0	4	1	0	0	2	1-0	0	6	.167	.185	.208	5	-3	1-0	.964	-0	107	48	S9	0	-0.3
Total	2	28	68	4	11	5	0	0	3	6-1	0	14	.162	.224	.235	23	-7	2-0	.959	-7	76	67	S26	0	-1.3

Andres, Ernie Ernest Henry "Junie"; B1.11.1918 Jeffersonville IN; BR/TR/6´1˝/200; d4.16; Col Indiana

YEAR	TM LG	G	AB	R	H	2B	3B	HR	RBI	BB-IB	HP	SO	AVG	OBP	SLG	AOPS	ABR	SB-CS	FA	FR	RNG	THR	GAMES AT POSITION	DL	BFW
1946	Bos A	15	41	0	4	2	0	0	1	3	0	5	.098	.159	.146	-14	-6	0-0	1.000	1	114	45	3b15	0	-0.6

Andrew, Kim Kim Darrell; B11.14.1953 Glendale CA; BR/TR/5´10˝/160; d4.16; Col Los Angeles Valley (CA) JC

YEAR	TM LG	G	AB	R	H	2B	3B	HR	RBI	BB-IB	HP	SO	AVG	OBP	SLG	AOPS	ABR	SB-CS	FA	FR	RNG	THR	GAMES AT POSITION	DL	BFW
1975	Bos A	2	2	0	1	0	0	0	0	0-0	0	0	.500	.500	.500	169	0	0-0	1.000	-0	76	0	2b2	0	0.0

Andrews, Shane Darrell Shane; B8.28.1971 Dallas TX; BR/TR/6´1˝/(215–220); [MonN90 1/11]; d4.26

YEAR	TM LG	G	AB	R	H	2B	3B	HR	RBI	BB-IB	HP	SO	AVG	OBP	SLG	AOPS	ABR	SB-CS	FA	FR	RNG	THR	GAMES AT POSITION	DL	BFW
1995	Mon N	84	220	27	47	10	1	8	31	17-2	1	68	.214	.271	.377	67	-11	1-1	.973	-1	104	32	3b51,1b29	0	-1.4
1996	Mon N	127	375	43	85	15	2	19	64	35-8	2	119	.227	.295	.429	86	-9	3-1	.955	16	115	81	3b123	0	0.8
1997	Mon N	18	64	10	13	3	0	4	9	3-0	0	20	.203	.232	.438	73	-3	0-0	.895	3	121	204	3b18	151	0.0
1998	Mon N	150	492	48	117	30	1	25	69	58-3	0	137	.238	.314	.455	103	1	1-6	.954	18	**118**	109	3b147	0	1.8

YEAR	TM LG	G	AB	R	H	2B	3B	HR	RBI	BB-IB	HP	SO	AVG	OBP	SLG	AOPS	ABR	SB-CS	FA	FR	RNG	THR	GAMES AT POSITION	DL	BFW
1999	Mon N	98	281	28	51	8	0	11	37	43-2	0	88	.181	.287	.327	58	-19	1-0	.932	-1	109	79	3b82,1b18/D	21	-1.9
	Chi N	19	67	13	17	4	0	5	14	7-1	1	21	.254	.329	.537	116	1	0-1	.955	-1	98	194	3b19/1	0	0.0
	Year	117	348	41	68	12	0	16	51	50-3	1	109	.195	.295	.368	70	-18	1-1	.936	-1	107	104	3b101,1b19/D	0	-1.9
2000	Chi N	66	192	25	44	5	0	14	39	27-1	2	59	.229	.329	.474	101	-1	1-1	.907	4	112	120	3b58,1b6	101	0.3
2002	Bos A	7	13	2	1	1	0	0	0	1-0	1	3	.077	.200	.154	-4	-2	0-0	1.000	1	147	287	3b4,1b2/lfD	0	-0.1
Total	7	569	1704	196	375	76	4	86	263	191-17	7	515	.220	.298	.421	86	-43	7-10	.946	40	113	100	3b502,1b56,D2/lf	273	-0.5
ANDREWS, FRED	Fred; B5.4.1952 Lafayette LA; BR/TR/5´8˝/152; [PhiN70 8/178]; d9.26																								
1976	Phi N	4	6	1	4	0	0	0	0	2-0	1	0	.667	.778	.667	301	2	1-1	1.000	-2	39	62	2b4	0	0.1
1977	Phi N	12	23	3	4	0	1	0	2	1-0	0	5	.174	.200	.261	24	-3	1-0	1.000	3	127	197	2b7	0	0.1
Total	2	16	29	4	8	0	1	0	2	3-0	1	5	.276	.353	.345	89	-1	2-1	1.000	1	97	151	2b11	0	0.2
ANDREWS, ED	George Edward; B4.5.1859 Painesville OH; D8.12.1934 W.Palm Beach FL; BR/TR/5´8˝/160; d5.1; U3; Col Case Western Reserve																								
1884	Phi N	109	420	74	93	21	2	0	23	9	—	42	.221	.238	.281	66	-16	—	.891	-20	95	78	2b109	—	-2.8
1885	Phi N	103	421	77	112	15	3	0	23	32	—	25	.266	.318	.316	108	5	—	.921	1	61	44	O99L,2b5	—	0.4
1886	Phi N	107	437	93	109	15	4	2	28	31	—	35	.249	.299	.316	86	-7	**56**	.903	3	118	73	O104(1/103/0),2b3	—	-0.6
1887	Phi N	104	464	110	151	19	7	4	67	21	3	21	.325	.359	.422	110	5	57	.902	-7	102	33	O99C,2b7/1	—	-0.4
1888	Phi N	124	528	75	126	14	4	3	44	21	3	41	.239	.272	.297	77	-14	35	.903	-6	111	129	O124C	—	-2.4
1889	Phi N	10	39	10	11	1	0	0	7	2	0	4	.282	.317	.308	68	-2	7	.808	-1	51	0	O9(8/0/1)/2	—	-0.3
	Ind N	40	173	32	53	11	0	0	22	5	1	10	.306	.330	.370	93	-2	7	.885	-2	140	75	O40C/2	—	-0.5
	Year	50	212	42	64	12	0	0	29	7	1	14	.302	.327	.358	88	-4	14	.867	-4	121	59	O49(8/40/1),2b2	—	-0.8
1890	Bro P	94	395	84	100	14	2	3	38	40	1	32	.253	.323	.322	68	-19	21	.912	-3	96	81	O94(1/89/4)	—	-2.0
1891	Cin AA	83	356	47	75	7	4	0	26	33	1	35	.211	.279	.253	48	-26	22	.961	15	165	118	O83L	—	-1.1
Total	8	774	3233	602	830	117	26	12	278	194	9	245	.257	.301	.320	82	-76	205	.912	-18	109	79	O652(192/455/5),2b126/1	—	-9.7
ANDREWS, JIM	James Pratt; B6.5.1865 Shelburne Falls MA; D12.27.1907 Chicago IL; d4.19																								
1890	Chi N	53	202	32	38	4	2	3	17	23	2	41	.188	.278	.272	58	-11	11	.900	1	109	58	O53R	—	-1.0
ANDREWS, MIKE	Michael Jay; B7.9.1943 Los Angeles CA; BR/TR/6´3˝/(185–195); d9.18; b–Rob																								
1966	Bos A	5	18	1	3	0	0	0	0	0-0	0	2	.167	.167	.167	-4	-2	0-0	1.000	2	130	61	2b5	0	0.0
1967	†Bos A	142	494	79	130	20	0	8	40	62-4	2	72	.263	.346	.352	99	2	7-7	.976	-3	99	87	2b139,S6	0	1.1
1968	Bos A	147	536	77	145	22	1	7	45	81-1	3	57	.271	.368	.354	113	13	3-8	.976	6	101	113	2b139,S4/3	0	3.3
1969	Bos A★	121	464	79	136	26	2	15	59	71-0	5	53	.293	.390	.455	130	22	1-1	.972	-0	98	97	2b120	0	3.0
1970	Bos A	151	589	91	149	28	1	17	65	81-0	3	63	.253	.344	.390	96	-1	2-1	.973	-30	83	73	2b148	0	-2.2
1971	Chi A	109	330	45	93	16	0	12	47	67-1	1	36	.282	.400	.439	135	19	3-5	.956	-1	100	107	2b76,1b25	0	2.2
1972	Chi A	148	505	58	111	18	0	7	50	70-3	2	78	.220	.313	.297	82	-9	2-2	.973	-8	90	79	2b145,1b5	0	-1.0
1973	Chi A	52	159	10	32	9	0	0	10	23-3	0	28	.201	.302	.258	57	-8	0-1	1.000	-1	89	20	D30,1b9,2b6,3b5	0	-1.1
	†Oak A	18	21	1	4	1	0	0	0	3-0	0	1	.190	.292	.238	53	-1	0-0	.944	-0	76	106	2b9,D2	0	-0.1
	Year	70	180	11	36	10	0	0	10	26-3	0	29	.200	.301	.256	57	-9	0-1	.974	-1	79	96	D32,2b15,1b9,3b5	0	-1.2
Total	8	893	3116	441	803	140	4	66	316	458-12	16	390	.258	.353	.369	104	35	18-25	.973	-35	95	91	2b787,1b39,D32,S10,3b6	0	5.2
ANDREWS, ROB	Robert Patrick; B12.11.1952 Santa Monica CA; BR/TR/6´0˝/180; [BalA70 10/247]; d4.7; b–Mike																								
1975	Hou N	103	277	29	66	5	4	0	19	31-4	0	34	.238	.310	.285	73	-11	12-5	.982	1	99	117	2b94,S6	0	-0.3
1976	Hou N	109	410	42	105	8	5	0	23	33-1	0	27	.256	.312	.300	81	-12	7-3	.977	9	109	92	2b107,S3	0	0.6
1977	SF N	127	436	60	115	11	3	0	25	56-0	0	33	.264	.345	.303	76	-13	5-6	.964	-11	97	94	2b115	0	-2.0
1978	SF N	79	177	21	39	3	3	1	11	20-1	0	18	.220	.299	.288	67	-8	5-1	.977	-0	99	83	2b62/S	0	-0.5
1979	SF N	75	154	22	40	3	0	2	13	8-0	0	9	.260	.289	.318	73	-6	4-1	.956	4	105	88	2b53,3b3	0	0.0
Total	5	493	1454	174	365	30	15	3	91	148-6	0	121	.251	.318	.298	75	-50	33-16	.972	2	102	96	2b431,S10,3b3	0	-2.2
ANDREWS, STAN	Stanley Joseph "Polo" (b Stanley Joseph Andruskewicz); B4.17.1917 Lynn MA; D6.10.1995 Bradenton FL; BR/TR/5´11˝/178; d6.11																								
1939	Bos N	13	26	1	6	0	0	0	1	1	0	2	.231	.259	.231	35	-2	0	.857	-2	*190*	*62*	C10	—	-0.4
1940	Bos N	19	33	1	6	0	0	0	2	0	0	3	.182	.182	.182	1	-5	1	.944	-1	*99*	*83*	C14	—	-0.5
1944	Bro N	4	8	1	1	0	0	0	1	1	0	2	.125	.222	.125	-1	-1	0	1.000	-0	*65*	*0*	C4	0	-0.1
1945	Bro N	21	49	5	8	0	1	0	2	5	1	4	.163	.255	.204	29	-5	0	.948	1	*99*	*178*	C21	0	-0.3
	Phi N	13	33	3	11	2	0	1	6	1	0	5	.333	.353	.485	135	1	1	.950	-1	*75*	*81*	C12	0	0.1
	Year	34	82	8	19	2	1	1	8	6	1	9	.232	.292	.317	70	-4	1	.949	-0	*90*	*142*	C33	0	-0.2
Total	4	70	149	11	32	2	1	1	12	8	1	16	.215	.259	.262	46	-12	2	.938	-3	*106*	*110*	C61	0	-1.2
ANDREWS, WALLY	William Walter; B9.18.1859 Philadelphia PA; D1.20.1940 Indianapolis IN; BR/TR/6´3˝/170; d5.22																								
1884	Lou AA	14	49	10	10	5	1	0	8	4	0	—	.204	.264	.347	102	1	—	.950	-1	138	61	1b9,3b3/lfS	—	-0.1
1888	Lou AA	26	93	12	18	6	3	0	6	13	0	—	.194	.292	.323	99	0	5	.997	1	103	128	1b26	—	-0.1
Total	2	40	142	22	28	11	4	0	14	17	0	—	.197	.283	.331	100	1	5	.985	0	111	112	1b35,3b3/Slf	—	-0.2
ANDRUS, FRED	Frederick Hotham; B8.23.1850 Washington MI; D11.10.1937 Detroit MI; BR/TR/6´2˝/185; d7.25; ▲																								
1876	Chi N	8	36	6	11	3	0	0	2	0	—	5	.306	.306	.389	116	0	—	.714	-2	0	0	O8(1/3/5)	—	-0.1
1884	Chi N	1	5	3	1	0	0	0	0	1	—	0	.200	.333	.200	67	0	—	1.000	0	163	0	/P	—	0.0
Total	2	9	41	9	12	3	0	0	2	1	—	5	.293	.310	.366	110	0	—	.714	-2	0	0	O8(1/3/5)/P	—	-0.1
ANDRUS, BILL	William Morgan "Andy"; B7.25.1907 Beaumont TX; D3.12.1982 Washington DC; BR/TR/6´0˝/185; d9.19																								
1931	Was A	3	7	0	0	0	0	0	1	0	0	1	.000	.000	.000	-99	-2	0-0	.750	-0	69	422	3b2	—	-0.2
1937	Phi N	3	2	0	0	0	0	0	0	0	0	2	.000	.000	.000	-93	-1	0	ø	-0	0	0	/3	—	-0.1
Total	2	6	9	0	0	0	0	0	1	0	0	3	.000	.000	.000	-98	-3	0-0	.750	-1	64	392	3b3	—	-0.3
ANDRUS, WIMAN	William Wiman; B10.14.1858 Orono ON, Can.; D6.17.1935 Miles City MT; 5´6.5˝/155; d9.15																								
1885	Pro N	1	4	0	0	0	0	0	0	0	—	1	.000	.000	.000	-99	-1	—	1.000	1	132	0	/3		0.0
ANGLEY, TOM	Thomas Samuel; B10.2.1904 Baltimore MD; D10.26.1952 Wichita KS; BL/TR/5´8˝/190; d4.23; Col Georgia Tech																								
1929	Chi N	5	16	1	4	1	0	0	6	2	0	2	.250	.333	.313	61	-1	0	.968	1	*157*	*175*	C5	—	0.0
ANKENMAN, PAT	Frederick Norman; B12.23.1912 Houston TX; D1.13.1989 Houston TX; BR/TR/5´4˝/125; d4.16; Mil 1943; Col Texas																								
1936	StL N	1	3	0	0	0	0	0	0	0	0	3	.000	.000	.000	-99	-1	0	.600	-1	31	0	/S	—	-0.2
1943	Bro N	1	2	1	1	0	0	0	0	0	0	0	.500	.500	.500	189	0	0	1.000	0	91	230	/S	0	0.1
1944	Bro N	13	24	1	6	1	0	0	3	0	0	2	.250	.250	.292	53	-2	0	.971	0	119	48	2b11,S2	0	-0.1
Total	3	15	29	2	7	1	0	0	3	0	0	5	.241	.241	.276	46	-3	0	.971	-1	119	48	2b11,S4	0	-0.2
ANNIS, BILL	William Perley; B3.8.1857 Stoneham MA; D6.10.1923 Kennebunkport ME; BR/5´7˝/150; d5.1																								
1884	Bos N	27	96	17	17	2	0	0	3	0	—	8	.177	.177	.198	18	-9	—	.900	-1	117	179	O27(4/15/8)	—	-1.0
ANSON, CAP	Adrian Constantine; B4.17.1852 Marshalltown IA; D4.14.1922 Chicago IL; BR/TR/6´0˝/227; d5.6; M21; HF1939; OF NA(1/5/31); OF(45/3/1)																								
1871	Rok NA	**25**	120	29	39	**11**	3	0	16	2	—	1	.325	.336	.467	134	6	6-2	.763	1	114	76	3b20,C5,2b2/1lf	—	0.4
1872	Ath NA	46	217	60	90	10	7	0	48	16	—	3	.415	**.455**	.525	200	26	6-6	.752	-10	74	99	3b46	—	1.0
1873	Ath NA	**52**	254	53	101	9	2	0	36	5	—	2	.398	.409	.449	143	12	1-2	.920	-4	107	120	1b36,3b11,C3,2b3,O3C	—	0.5
1874	Ath NA	**55**	260	51	87	8	3	0	37	4	—	1	.335	.345	.388	124	5	6-0	.936	-5	120	138	1b24,3b20,O8R,S6/C	—	0.1
1875	Ath NA	69	326	84	106	15	3	0	58	4	—	2	.325	.333	.390	135	9	11-6	.922	11	249	121	1b32,O25(0/2/23),C13,3b5,M	—	1.9
1876	Chi N	**66**	309	63	110	9	7	2	59	12	—	8	.356	.380	.450	157	16	—	.849	14	113	168	3b66,C2	—	2.8
1877	Chi N	59	255	52	86	**19**	1	0	32	9	—	3	.337	.360	.420	129	8	—	**.883**	7	105	**213**	3b40,C31	—	1.5
1878	Chi N	60	261	55	89	12	2	0	40	13	—	1	.341	.372	.402	145	12	—	.825	-7	48	0	O48(45/3/0),2b9,3b3,C3	—	0.3
1879	Chi N	51	227	40	72	20	1	0	34	2	—	2	**.317**	.323	.414	133	8	—	.975	0	62	121	1b51,M	—	0.6
1880	Chi N	**86**	356	54	120	24	1	1	**74**	14	—	12	.337	.362	.419	154	20	—	**.978**	0	72	89	1b81,3b9/S2M	—	1.6
1881	Chi N	**84**	343	67	**137**	21	7	1	**82**	26	—	4	**.399**	**.442**	.510	**189**	**35**	—	**.975**	7	**144**	112	1b84,C2/SM	—	**3.6**
1882	Chi N	82	348	69	126	29	8	1	**83**	20	—	7	.362	.397	.500	177	30	—	.949	-0	**119**	112	1b82/CM	—	2.0
1883	Chi N	**98**	413	70	127	36	5	0	68	18	—	9	.308	.336	.419	118	9	—	.964	3	**129**	117	1b98,P2/rfCM	—	0.3
1884	Chi N	**112**	475	108	159	30	3	21	**102**	29	—	13	.335	.373	.543	170	37	—	.956	-0	123	**166**	1b112,C3/SPM	—	2.3
1885	†Chi N	112	464	100	144	**35**	7	7	**108**	34	—	13	.310	.357	.461	143	21	—	.958	-4	100	117	1b112/CM	—	0.6
1886	†Chi N	125	504	117	187	35	11	10	**147**	55	—	19	.371	.433	.544	170	42	29	.963	9	144	**133**	1b125,C12,M	—	3.6
1887	Chi N	122	472	107	164	33	13	7	102	60	1	18	**.347**	.422	.517	141	26	27	.973	10	**156**	**114**	1b122/CM	—	2.1

YEAR	TM LG	G	AB	R	H	2B	3B	HR	RBI	BB-IB	HP	SO	AVG	OBP	SLG	AOPS	ABR	SB-CS	FA	FR	RNG	THR	GAMES AT POSITION	DL	BFW
1888	Chi N	134	515	101	177	20	12	12	**84**	47	1	24	**.344**	**.400**	.499	172	42	28	**.986**	9	133	**127**	1b134,M	—	3.8
1889	Chi N	134	518	100	177	32	7	7	117	86	5	19	.342	.440	.471	146	36	27	**.982**	8	**127**	98	1b134,M	—	2.8
1890	Chi N	**139**	504	95	157	14	5	7	107	**113**	6	23	.312	**.443**	.401	141	34	29	.978	1	**105**	95	1b135,C3,2b2,M	—	2.0
1891	Chi N	136	540	81	157	24	8	8	**120**	75	1	29	.291	.378	.409	129	22	17	.981	8	129	**123**	1b136,C2,M	—	1.6
1892	Chi N	**146**	559	62	152	25	9	1	74	67	4	30	.272	.354	.354	113	10	13	.973	-6	86	78	1b146,M	—	0.4
1893	Chi N	103	398	70	125	24	2	0	91	68	1	12	.314	.415	.384	115	13	13	.981	-4	79	88	1b101,M	—	0.8
1894	Chi N	84	343	85	133	29	4	5	100	41	3	15	.388	.457	.539	132	20	17	.990	3	104	94	1b83/2M	—	1.7
1895	Chi N	122	474	87	159	23	6	2	91	55	3	23	.335	.408	.422	107	6	12	.985	-1	91	110	1b122,M	—	0.4
1896	Chi N	108	402	72	133	18	2	2	90	49	3	10	.331	.407	.400	109	8	24	.983	-1	103	110	1b98,C10,M	—	0.6
1897	Chi N	114	424	67	121	17	3	3	75	60	4	—	.285	.379	.361	92	-2	11	.975	1	112	117	1b103,C11,M	—	0.0
Total	5NA	247	1177	277	423	53	18	0	195	31	—	9	.359	.376	.435	146	58	30-16	.765	-7	83	97	3b102,1b93,O37R,C22,S6,2b5	—	3.9
Total	22	2277	9104	1722	3012	529	124	97	1880	953	32	294	.331	.396	.448	139	453	247	.974	57	114	111	1b2059,3b118,C83,O49L,2b13,P3,S3	—	35.4

ANTHONY, ERIC Eric Todd; B11.8.1967 San Diego CA; BL/TL/6´2˝/195; [HouN86 34/795]; d7.28

YEAR	TM LG	G	AB	R	H	2B	3B	HR	RBI	BB-IB	HP	SO	AVG	OBP	SLG	AOPS	ABR	SB-CS	FA	FR	RNG	THR	GAMES AT POSITION	DL	BFW
1989	Hou N	25	61	7	11	2	0	4	7	9-2	0	16	.180	.286	.410	100	0	0-0	1.000	0	102	108	O21(3/0/18)	0	0.0
1990	Hou N	84	239	26	46	8	0	10	29	29-3	2	78	.192	.279	.351	76	-8	5-0	.970	-3	91	105	O71(13/0/59)	21	-1.2
1991	Hou N	39	118	11	18	6	0	1	7	12-1	0	41	.153	.227	.229	31	-11	1-0	.986	3	105	210	O37R	0	-0.9
1992	Hou N	137	440	45	105	15	1	19	80	38-5	1	98	.239	.298	.407	103	0	5-4	.973	-7	85	85	O115(1/2/113)	0	-1.2
1993	Hou N	145	486	70	121	19	4	15	66	49-2	2	88	.249	.319	.397	94	-5	3-5	.988	-7	93	67	O131(0/23/121)	0	-1.8
1994	Sea A	79	262	31	62	14	1	10	30	23-4	0	66	.237	.297	.412	79	-9	6-2	.985	-0	103	92	O71(62/5/10),D4	15	-1.0
1995	†Cin N	47	134	19	36	6	0	5	23	13-2	0	30	.269	.327	.425	97	-1	2-1	1.000	1	102	145	O24(4/1/20),1b17	88	-0.2
1996	Cin N	47	123	22	30	6	0	8	13	22-2	0	36	.244	.359	.488	119	4	0-1	.949	-5	59	99	O37(13/0/24)	44	-0.3
	Col N	32	62	10	15	2	0	4	9	10-0	0	20	.242	.342	.468	91	-1	0-1	1.000	-1	64	233	O19(1/9/10)	0	-0.3
	Year	79	185	32	45	8	0	12	22	32-2	0	56	.243	.353	.481	107	2	0-2	.967	-6	61	141	O56(14/9/34)	0	-0.6
1997	LA N	47	74	8	18	3	2	2	5	12-1	0	18	.243	.349	.419	107	1	2-0	.966	1	98	215	O21(17/0/4)	0	0.2
Total	9	682	1999	249	462	81	8	78	269	217-22	5	491	.231	.305	.397	90	-30	24-14	.981	-17	91	105	O547(114/40/416),1b17,D4	168	-6.7

ANTOLICK, JOE Joseph; B4.11.1916 Hokendauqua PA; D6.25.2002 Catasauqua PA; BR/TR/6´0˝/185; d9.20

YEAR	TM LG	G	AB	R	H	2B	3B	HR	RBI	BB-IB	HP	SO	AVG	OBP	SLG	AOPS	ABR	SB-CS	FA	FR	RNG	THR	GAMES AT POSITION	DL	BFW
1944	Phi N	4	6	1	2	0	0	0	0	1	0	0	.333	.429	.333	120	0	0	1.000	1	*57*	*0*	C3	0	0.1

ANTONELLI, JOHN John Lawrence; B7.15.1915 Memphis TN; D4.18.1990 Memphis TN; BR/TR/5´10.5˝/165; d9.16

YEAR	TM LG	G	AB	R	H	2B	3B	HR	RBI	BB-IB	HP	SO	AVG	OBP	SLG	AOPS	ABR	SB-CS	FA	FR	RNG	THR	GAMES AT POSITION	DL	BFW
1944	StL N	8	21	0	4	1	0	0	1	0	0	4	.190	.190	.238	20	-2	0	1.000	1	177	113	1b3,3b3,2b2	0	-0.2
1945	StL N	2	3	0	0	0	0	0	0	0	0	1	.000	.000	.000	-98	-1	0	.667	-1	0	0	/3	0	-0.1
	Phi N	125	504	50	129	27	2	1	28	24	2	24	.256	.292	.323	73	-20	1	.959	-4	95	109	3b108,2b23/1S	0	-2.1
	Year	127	507	50	129	27	2	1	28	24	2	25	.254	.291	.321	72	-20	1	.957	-4	94	108	3b109,2b23/1S	0	-2.2
Total	2	135	528	50	133	28	2	1	29	24	2	29	.252	.287	.318	70	-23	1	.958	-3	95	106	3b112,2b25,1b4/S	0	-2.4

ANTONELLO, BILL William James; B5.19.1927 Brooklyn NY; D3.4.1993 Fridley MN; BR/TR/5´11˝/185; d4.30

YEAR	TM LG	G	AB	R	H	2B	3B	HR	RBI	BB-IB	HP	SO	AVG	OBP	SLG	AOPS	ABR	SB-CS	FA	FR	RNG	THR	GAMES AT POSITION	DL	BFW
1953	Bro N	40	43	9	7	1	1	1	4	2	0	11	.163	.200	.302	28	-5	0-0	.964	1	133	0	O25(20/2/4)	0	-0.5

APARICIO, LUIS Luis Ernesto (Montiel); B4.29.1934 Maracaibo, Zulia, Venez.; BR/TR/5´9˝/(155–160); d4.17; HF1984

YEAR	TM LG	G	AB	R	H	2B	3B	HR	RBI	BB-IB	HP	SO	AVG	OBP	SLG	AOPS	ABR	SB-CS	FA	FR	RNG	THR	GAMES AT POSITION	DL	BFW
1956	Chi A	152	533	69	142	19	6	3	56	34-2	1	63	.266	.311	.341	71	-24	**21**-4	.954	-4	102	97	S152	0	-1.1
1957	Chi A	143	575	82	148	22	6	3	41	52-1	0	55	.257	.317	.332	78	-18	**28**-8	.972	-10	98	94	S142	0	-1.3
1958	Chi A★	145	557	76	148	20	9	2	40	35-2	1	38	.266	.309	.345	82	-15	**29**-6	.973	15	106	98	S145	0	1.6
1959	†Chi A★	152	612	98	157	18	5	6	51	53-1	3	40	.257	.316	.332	80	-17	**56**-13	**.970**	-3	99	97	S152	0	0.0
1960	Chi A★	153	600	86	166	20	7	2	61	43-3	1	39	.277	.323	.343	82	-16	**51**-8	**.979**	**34**	**114**	118	S153	0	**3.9**
1961	Chi A★	156	625	90	170	24	4	6	45	38-0	1	33	.272	.313	.352	79	-20	**53**-13	**.962**	12	**108**	94	S156	0	1.2
1962	Chi A★	153	581	72	140	23	5	7	40	32-1	1	36	.241	.280	.334	65	-30	**31**-12	**.973**	18	108	117	S152	0	0.3
1963	Bal A★	146	601	73	150	18	8	5	45	36-2	2	35	.250	.291	.331	78	-20	**40**-6	**.983**	-2	95	93	S145	0	-0.3
1964	Bal A✳	146	578	93	154	20	3	10	37	49-0	3	51	.266	.324	.363	92	-6	**57**-17	**.979**	10	104	124	S145	0	2.4
1965	Bal A	144	564	67	127	20	10	8	40	46-0	3	56	.225	.286	.339	76	-19	26-7	**.971**	3	105	113	S141	0	-0.1
1966	†Bal A	151	659	97	182	25	8	6	41	33-2	1	42	.276	.311	.366	95	-6	25-11	**.978**	9	96	118	S151	0	2.0
1967	Bal A	134	546	55	127	22	5	4	31	29-2	1	44	.233	.270	.313	73	-19	18-5	.957	-15	89	96	S131	0	-2.3
1968	Chi A	155	622	55	164	24	4	4	36	33-3	2	43	.264	.302	.334	92	-7	17-11	.977	20	115	110	S154	0	3.0
1969	Chi A	156	599	77	168	24	5	5	51	66-1	2	29	.280	.352	.362	96	-2	24-4	.976	33	**119**	102	S154	0	5.4
1970	Chi A★	146	552	86	173	29	3	5	43	53-1	1	34	.313	.372	.404	111	10	8-3	.976	25	116	108	S146	0	5.3
1971	Bos A★	125	491	56	114	23	0	4	45	35-0	2	43	.232	.284	.303	62	-24	6-4	.971	-18	91	75	S121	0	-3.0
1972	Bos A✳	110	436	47	112	26	3	3	39	26-0	2	28	.257	.299	.351	88	-6	3-3	.968	-10	91	79	S109	40	-0.4
1973	Bos A	132	499	56	135	17	1	0	49	43-1	0	33	.271	.324	.309	76	-15	13-1	.966	-12	95	87	S132	0	-1.0
Total	18	2599	10230	1335	2677	394	92	83	791	736-22	27	742	.262	.311	.343	82	-254	506-136	.972	104	103	102	S2581	40	15.6

APPLING, LUKE Lucius Benjamin "Old Aches and Pains"; B4.2.1907 High Point NC; D1.3.1991 Cumming GA; BR/TR/5´10˝/183; d9.10; Mil 1944–45; M1/C9; HF1964; Col Oglethorpe

YEAR	TM LG	G	AB	R	H	2B	3B	HR	RBI	BB-IB	HP	SO	AVG	OBP	SLG	AOPS	ABR	SB-CS	FA	FR	RNG	THR	GAMES AT POSITION	DL	BFW
1930	Chi A	6	26	2	8	2	0	0	2	0	0	0	.308	.308	.385	77	-1	2-0	.879	-2	92	26	S6	—	-0.2
1931	Chi A	96	297	36	69	13	4	1	28	29	1	27	.232	.303	.313	66	-15	9-2	.900	-9	102	79	S76/2	—	-1.6
1932	Chi A	139	489	66	134	20	10	3	63	40	0	36	.274	.329	.374	87	-11	9-8	.929	15	112	114	S85,2b30,3b14	—	1.1
1933	Chi A	**151**	612	90	197	36	10	6	85	56	0	29	.322	.379	.443	122	19	6-11	.939	9	**108**	119	S151	—	3.4
1934	Chi A	118	452	75	137	28	6	2	61	59	0	27	.303	.384	.405	100	2	3-1	.945	-7	98	74	S110,2b8	—	0.3
1935	Chi A	**153**	525	94	161	28	6	1	71	122	0	40	.307	.437	.389	112	18	12-6	.958	**25**	**113**	99	S153	—	5.1
1936	Chi A★	138	526	111	204	31	7	6	128	85	1	25	**.388**	.474	.508	137	37	10-6	.951	15	**108**	**129**	S137	—	5.4
1937	Chi A	**154**	574	98	182	42	8	4	77	86	1	28	.317	.407	.439	113	16	18-10	.944	17	**111**	**122**	S154	—	4.0
1938	Chi A	81	294	41	89	14	0	0	44	42	1	17	.303	.392	.350	85	-4	1-3	.953	2	112	72	S78	—	0.2
1939	Chi A☆	148	516	82	162	16	6	0	56	105	0	37	.314	.430	.368	103	9	16-9	.951	-1	**102**	95	S148	—	1.8
1940	Chi A★	150	566	96	197	27	13	0	79	69	1	35	.348	.420	.442	122	21	3-5	.953	-3	99	101	S150	—	2.6
1941	Chi A☆	154	592	93	186	26	8	1	57	82	1	32	.314	.399	.390	111	13	12-8	.948	-4	103	101	S154	0	1.9
1942	Chi A	142	543	78	142	26	4	3	53	63	3	23	.262	.342	.341	94	-3	17-5	.948	-3	103	93	S141	0	0.7
1943	Chi A☆	**155**	585	63	192	33	2	3	80	90	1	29	**.328**	**.419**	.407	142	37	27-8	.957	8	106	112	S155	0	6.3
1945	Chi A	18	57	12	21	2	2	1	10	12	0	7	.368	.478	.526	197	8	1-0	.930	-1	100	64	S17	0	0.9
1946	Chi A★	149	582	59	180	27	5	1	55	71	0	41	.309	.384	.378	118	17	6-4	.951	5	**113**	107	S149	0	3.2
1947	Chi A★	139	503	67	154	29	0	8	49	64	1	28	.306	.386	.412	126	20	8-6	.949	-9	104	91	S129,3b2	0	1.9
1948	Chi A	139	497	63	156	16	2	0	47	94	0	35	.314	.423	.354	112	15	10-4	.943	13	124	94	3b72,S64	0	3.2
1949	Chi A	142	492	82	148	21	5	5	58	121	0	24	.301	.439	.394	125	27	7-12	.964	-3	**105**	90	S141	0	2.8
1950	Chi A	50	128	11	30	3	4	0	13	12	0	8	.234	.300	.320	61	-8	2-0	.967	1	92	96	S20,1b13/2	0	-0.6
Total	20	2422	8856	1319	2749	440	102	45	1116	1302	11	528	.310	.399	.398	113	217	179-108	.948	68	106	101	S2218,3b88,2b40,1b13	0	42.4

ARAGON, ANGEL Angel (Valdes) "Pete"; B8.2.1890 Havana, Cuba; D1.24.1952 New York NY; BR/TR/5´5˝/150; d8.20; s–Jack

YEAR	TM LG	G	AB	R	H	2B	3B	HR	RBI	BB-IB	HP	SO	AVG	OBP	SLG	AOPS	ABR	SB-CS	FA	FR	RNG	THR	GAMES AT POSITION	DL	BFW
1914	NY A	6	7	1	1	0	0	0	0	1	1	2	.143	.333	.143	44	0	0	ø	-0	0	0	/cf	—	0.0
1916	NY A	12	24	1	5	0	0	0	3	2	0	2	.208	.269	.208	43	-2	2	.864	1	143	0	3b8,O2(1/0/1)	—	-0.1
1917	NY A	14	45	2	3	1	0	0	2	2	0	2	.067	.106	.089	-40	-8	0	.933	0	92	0	O6(4/2/0),3b4,S2	—	-0.9
Total	3	32	76	4	9	1	0	0	5	5	1	6	.118	.183	.132	-4	-10	2	.921	1	131	74	3b12,O9(5/3/1),S2	—	-1.0

ARAGON, JACK Angel Valdes (Reyes); B11.20.1915 Havana, Cuba; D4.4.1988 Clearwater FL; BR/TR/5´10˝/176; d8.13; Mil 1942–44; f–Angel

YEAR	TM LG	G	AB	R	H	2B	3B	HR	RBI	BB-IB	HP	SO	AVG	OBP	SLG	AOPS	ABR	SB-CS	FA	FR	RNG	THR	GAMES AT POSITION	DL	BFW
1941	NY N	1	0	0	0	0	0	0	0	0	0	0	ø	ø	ø	ø	0	0	ø	0	—	—	/R	0	0.0

ARCHDEACON, MAURICE Maurice John "Flash"; B12.14.1897 St.Louis MO; D9.5.1954 St.Louis MO; BL/TL/5´8˝/153; d9.17

YEAR	TM LG	G	AB	R	H	2B	3B	HR	RBI	BB-IB	HP	SO	AVG	OBP	SLG	AOPS	ABR	SB-CS	FA	FR	RNG	THR	GAMES AT POSITION	DL	BFW
1923	Chi A	22	87	23	35	5	1	0	4	6	0	8	.402	.441	.483	145	6	2-3	.918	-2	93	45	O20(0/18/2)	—	0.2
1924	Chi A	95	288	59	92	9	3	0	25	40	4	30	.319	.410	.372	106	5	11-7	.958	-1	96	126	O77C	—	0.1
1925	Chi A	10	9	2	1	0	0	0	0	2	0	1	.111	.273	.111	0	-1	0-0	1.000	0	113	0	/lf	—	-0.1
Total	3	127	384	84	128	14	4	0	29	48	4	39	.333	.413	.391	112	10	13-10	.950	-3	95	107	O98(1/95/2)	—	0.2

ARCHER, JIMMY James Patrick; B5.13.1883 Dublin, Ireland; D3.29.1958 Milwaukee WI; BR/TR/5´10˝/168; d9.6

YEAR	TM LG	G	AB	R	H	2B	3B	HR	RBI	BB-IB	HP	SO	AVG	OBP	SLG	AOPS	ABR	SB-CS	FA	FR	RNG	THR	GAMES AT POSITION	DL	BFW
1904	Pit N	7	20	1	3	0	0	0	1	0	0	—	.150	.150	.150	-7	-3	0	.919	0	*127*	*108*	C7/lf	—	-0.2
1907	†Det A	18	42	6	5	0	0	0	0	4	0	—	.119	.196	.119	1	-5	0	.975	1	*113*	*103*	C17/2	—	-0.2
1909	Chi N	80	261	31	60	9	2	1	30	12	1	—	.230	.266	.291	71	-10	5	.960	0	*129*	*89*	C80	—	-0.2
1910	†Chi N	98	313	36	81	17	6	2	41	14	1	49	.259	.293	.371	94	-4	6	.970	5	*143*	*104*	C49,1b40	—	0.5
1911	Chi N	116	387	41	98	18	5	4	41	18	1	43	.253	.288	.357	80	-13	5	.977	13	***160***	*84*	C102,1b10/2	—	0.9
1912	Chi N	120	385	35	109	20	2	5	58	22	5	36	.283	.330	.384	95	-3	7	.966	2	*131*	*92*	C118	—	0.9

YEAR	TM LG	G	AB	R	H	2B	3B	HR	RBI	BB-IB	HP	SO	AVG	OBP	SLG	AOPS	ABR	SB-CS	FA	FR	RNG	THR	GAMES AT POSITION	DL	BFW
1913	Chi N	111	368	38	98	14	7	2	44	19	5	27	.266	.311	.359	91	-5	4-5	.969	-0	112	109	C103,1b8	—	0.2
1914	Chi N	79	248	17	64	9	2	0	19	9	0	9	.258	.284	.310	77	-8	1	.973	-0	*93*	*101*	C76	—	-0.2
1915	Chi N	97	309	21	75	11	5	1	27	11	2	38	.243	.273	.320	79	-9	5-6	.977	-3	*97*	*104*	C88,1b4	—	-0.6
1916	Chi N	77	205	11	45	6	2	1	30	12	2	24	.220	.269	.283	63	-9	3	.979	-2	94	91	C61/3	—	-0.6
1917	Chi N	2	2	0	0	0	0	0	0	0	0	1	.000	.000	.000	-93	0	0	ø	0	—	—	/H	—	-0.1
1918	Pit N	24	58	4	9	1	2	0	3	1	2	6	.155	.197	.241	32	-5	0	.989	5	*155*	*133*	C21/1	—	0.2
	Bro N	9	22	3	6	0	1	0	0	1	0	5	.273	.304	.364	104	0	0	.968	0	*93*	*184*	C7	—	0.1
	Cin N	9	26	2	7	1	0	0	2	1	0	3	.269	.296	.308	86	0	0	1.000	1	*121*	*127*	C7/1	—	0.1
	Year	42	106	9	22	2	3	0	5	3	2	14	.208	.243	.283	59	-6	0	.987	7	*136*	*142*	C35,1b2	—	0.4
Total	12	847	2646	246	660	106	34	16	296	124	19	<u>241</u>	.249	.288	.333	80	-74	36-<u>11</u>	.971	25	*122*	*98*	C736,1b64,2b2/3lf	—	0.8
ARCHIE, GEORGE	George Albert; B4.27.1914 Nashville TN; D9.20.2001 Nashville TN; BR/TR/6´0˝/170; d9.14; Mil 1942–45																								
1938	Det A	3	2	1	0	0	0	0	0	0	0	1	.000	.000	.000	-95	-1	0-0	ø	0	—	—	/H	—	-0.1
1941	Was A	105	379	45	102	20	4	3	48	30	1	42	.269	.324	.367	87	-8	8-4	.936	-4	100	83	3b73,1b23	0	-1.1
	StL A	9	29	3	11	3	0	0	5	7	0	3	.379	.500	.483	156	3	2-0	.975	0	120	60	1b8	0	0.3
	Year	114	408	48	113	23	4	3	53	37	1	45	.277	.339	.375	92	-5	10-4	.936	-3	100	83	3b73,1b31	0	-0.8
1946	StL A	4	11	1	2	1	0	0	0	0	0	1	.182	.182	.273	25	-1	0-0	1.000	2	270	195	1b3	0	0.0
Total	3	121	421	50	115	24	4	3	53	37	1	47	.273	.333	.371	90	-7	10-4	.936	-2	100	83	3b73,1b34	0	-0.9
ARCIA, JOSE	Jose Raimundo (Orta); B8.22.1943 Havana, Cuba; BR/TR/6´3˝/170; d4.10																								
1968	Chi N	59	84	15	16	4	0	1	8	3-0	0	24	.190	.218	.274	44	-6	0-0	1.000	-4	84	0	O17(5/13/0),2b10,S7/3	0	-1.0
1969	SD N	120	302	35	65	11	3	0	10	14-0	2	47	.215	.255	.272	49	-21	14-7	.977	2	106	80	2b68,S37,3b8,O4L/1	0	-1.4
1970	SD N	114	229	28	51	9	3	0	17	12-1	7	36	.223	.282	.288	55	-15	3-6	.955	1	97	105	S67,2b20,3b9,O7L	0	-0.9
Total	3	293	615	78	132	24	6	1	35	29-1	9	107	.215	.260	.278	51	-42	17-13	.950	-1	98	91	S111,2b98,O28(16/13/0),3b18/1	0	-3.3
ARDELL, DAN	Daniel Miers; B5.27.1941 Seattle WA; BL/TL/6´2˝/185; d9.14; Col USC																								
1961	LA A	7	4	1	1	0	0	0	0	1-0	0	2	.250	.400	.250	70	0	0-0	1.000	-0	0	107	/1	0	0.0
ARDNER, JOE	Joseph A. "Old Hoss"; B2.27.1858 Mt.Vernon OH; D9.15.1935 Cleveland OH; BR/TR/?/160; d5.1																								
1884	Cle N	26	92	6	16	1	1	0	4	1	—	24	.174	.183	.207	21	-8	—	.866	-6	95	61	2b25/3	—	-1.2
1890	Cle N	84	323	28	72	13	1	0	35	17	2	40	.223	.266	.269	57	-18	9	.920	-6	98	118	2b84	—	-1.9
Total	2	110	415	34	88	14	2	0	39	18	2	64	.212	.248	.255	50	-26	9	.908	-12	97	106	2b109/3	—	-3.1
ARDOIN, DANNY	Daniel Wayne; B7.8.1974 Mamou LA; BR/TR/6´0˝/(215–220); [OakA95 5/120]; d8.2; Col McNeese St.																								
2000	Min A	15	32	4	4	1	0	1	5	8-0	0	10	.125	.300	.250	39	-3	0-0	.989	4	161	180	C15	0	0.1
2004	Tex A	6	8	1	1	0	0	0	1	3-0	0	2	.125	.364	.125	34	-1	0-0	.958	0	37	0	C6	0	0.0
2005	Col N	80	210	28	48	10	0	6	22	20-2	9	69	.229	.320	.362	71	-9	1-1	.988	14	153	155	C80	0	0.9
2006	Col N	35	109	12	21	5	1	0	2	8-2	2	27	.193	.261	.257	31	-11	0-0	.986	1	97	98	C35	67	-0.8
	Bal A	5	13	2	1	0	0	0	1	1-0	1	6	.077	.200	.077	-25	-2	0-0	1.000	1	207	0	C5	0	-0.1
Total	4	141	372	47	75	16	1	7	31	40-4	12	114	.202	.298	.306	53	-26	1-1	.987	20	137	133	C141	67	0.1
ARFT, HANK	Henry Irven "Bow Wow"; B1.28.1922 Manchester MO; D12.14.2002 St.Louis MO; BL/TL/5´10.5˝/190; d7.27																								
1948	StL A	69	248	25	59	10	3	5	38	45	0	43	.238	.355	.363	89	-3	1-2	.995	-0	96	111	1b69	0	-0.6
1949	StL A	6	5	1	1	1	0	0	2	0	0	1	.200	.200	.400	55	0	0-0	ø	0	—	—	/H	0	0.0
1950	StL A	98	280	45	75	16	4	1	32	46	2	48	.268	.375	.364	87	-4	3-2	.995	-1	96	67	1b84	0	-0.7
1951	StL A	112	345	44	90	16	5	7	42	41	0	34	.261	.339	.397	96	-3	4-6	.989	7	124	91	1b97	0	0.0
1952	StL A	15	28	1	4	3	1	0	4	5	0	7	.143	.273	.321	63	-1	0-0	.985	-0	81	164	1b10	0	-0.2
Total	5	300	906	116	229	46	13	13	118	137	2	133	.253	.352	.375	90	-11	8-10	.992	5	106	91	1b260	0	-1.5
ARIAS, ALEX	Alejandro; B11.20.1967 New York NY; BR/TR/6´3˝/(185–202); [ChiN87 3/62]; d5.12																								
1992	Chi N	32	99	14	29	6	0	0	7	11-0	2	13	.293	.375	.354	104	1	0-0	.967	-5	94	53	S30	0	-0.1
1993	Fla N	96	249	27	67	5	1	2	20	27-0	3	18	.269	.344	.321	76	-8	1-1	.987	-7	101	82	2b30,3b22,S18	0	-1.2
1994	Fla N	59	113	4	27	5	0	0	15	9-0	1	19	.239	.298	.283	51	-8	0-1	.985	-4	72	78	S20,3b15	0	-1.1
1995	Fla N	94	216	22	58	9	2	3	26	22-1	2	20	.269	.337	.370	86	-4	1-0	.947	-0	98	83	S36,3b21,2b6	0	-0.1
1996	Fla N	100	224	27	62	11	2	3	26	17-1	3	28	.277	.335	.384	92	-3	2-0	.956	2	99	144	3b59,S20/12	0	0.1
1997	†Fla N	74	93	13	23	2	0	1	11	12-0	3	12	.247	.352	.301	76	-3	0-1	.971	-2	70	116	3b37,S11	18	-0.4
1998	Phi N	56	133	17	39	8	0	1	16	13-3	1	18	.293	.358	.376	94	-1	2-0	.985	-3	96	54	S38,3b5/2	0	-0.1
1999	Phi N	118	347	43	105	20	1	4	48	36-6	4	31	.303	.373	.401	95	-1	2-2	.988	-18	86	81	S95,3b2/2	0	-1.2
2000	Phi N	70	155	17	29	9	0	2	15	16-2	3	28	.187	.271	.284	42	-14	1-0	.963	-6	90	90	S39,3b10/2	0	-1.7
2001	SD N	70	137	19	31	9	0	2	12	17-1	1	22	.226	.312	.336	74	-5	1-0	.957	-4	137	83	3b18,1b17,2b13,S13	15	-0.8
2002	NY A	6	7	0	0	0	0	0	0	1-0	0	2	.000	.125	.000	-63	-2	0-0	.750	-0	124	508	3b4/S	0	-0.2
Total	11	775	1773	203	470	84	6	18	196	181-14	23	211	.265	.338	.350	81	-48	10-5	.973	-47	89	81	S321,3b193,2b53,1b18	33	-6.8
ARIAS, GEORGE	George Alberto; B3.12.1972 Tucson AZ; BR/TR/5´11˝/190; [CalA93 7/187]; d4.2; Col Arizona																								
1996	Cal A	84	252	19	60	8	1	6	28	16-2	0	50	.238	.284	.349	58	-17	2-0	.960	22	136	137	3b83/D	0	0.5
1997	Ana A	3	6	1	2	0	0	0	1	0-0	0	0	.333	.333	.333	74	0	0-0	1.000	0	168	0	/3D	0	0.0
	SD N	11	22	2	5	1	0	0	2	0-0	0	1	.227	.227	.273	32	-2	0-0	.941	0	116	0	3b8	0	-0.2
1998	†SD N	20	36	4	7	1	1	1	4	3-0	2	16	.194	.293	.361	76	-1	0-0	.933	1	122	121	3b14/1	0	0.0
1999	SD N	55	164	20	40	8	0	7	20	6-0	0	54	.244	.271	.421	77	-7	0-0	.941	6	116	58	3b50	29	-0.1
Total	4	173	480	46	114	18	2	14	55	25-2	2	121	.237	.278	.371	65	-27	2-0	.952	29	128	104	3b156,D2/1	29	0.2
ARIAS, JOAQUIN	Joaquin; B9.21.1984 Santo Domingo, D.R.; BR/TR/6´1˝/165; d9.13																								
2006	Tex A	6	11	4	6	1	0	0	1	1-0	0	0	.545	.583	.636	216	2	0-1	1.000	3	138	131	S5/3	0	0.4
ARLETT, BUZZ	Russell Loris; B1.3.1899 Elmhurst CA; D5.16.1964 Minneapolis MN; BB/TR/6´2˝/210; d4.14																								
1931	Phi N	121	418	65	131	26	7	18	72	45	5	39	.313	.387	.538	135	21	3	.955	1	97	122	O94R,1b13	—	1.5
ARMAS, TONY	Antonio Rafael (Machado); B7.2.1953 Anzoategui, Venezuela; BR/TR/6´1˝/(182–224); d9.6; b–Marcos s–Tony																								
1976	Pit N	4	6	0	2	0	0	0	1	0-0	0	2	.333	.333	.333	88	0	0-0	1.000	0	101	0	O2(1/1/0)	0	0.0
1977	Oak A	118	363	26	87	8	2	13	53	20-2	0	99	.240	.274	.380	79	-12	1-2	.981	9	114	121	O112(3/84/30)/S	27	-0.6
1978	Oak A	91	239	17	51	6	1	2	13	10-2	2	62	.213	.250	.272	49	-17	1-2	.991	8	129	63	O85(2/40/47),D3	35	-1.2
1979	Oak A	80	278	29	69	9	3	11	34	16-2	1	67	.248	.290	.421	94	-4	1-0	.976	6	115	124	O80(12/17/53)	51	-0.1
1980	Oak A	158	628	87	175	18	8	35	109	29-4	2	128	.279	.310	.500	126	17	5-3	.975	11	114	137	O158(0/10/152)	0	1.9
1981	†Oak A★	**109**	440	51	115	24	3	**22**	76	19-6	2	115	.261	.294	.480	124	11	5-1	.993	5	110	95	O109(0/2/108)	0	1.0
1982	Oak A	138	536	58	125	19	2	28	89	33-5	1	128	.233	.275	.433	95	-7	2-2	.983	5	114	87	O135(0/5/133)/D	15	-0.9
1983	Bos A	145	574	77	125	23	2	36	107	29-0	2	131	.218	.254	.453	85	-15	0-1	.985	-1	103	70	O116C,D27	0	-1.8
1984	Bos A☆	157	639	107	171	29	5	**43**	**123**	32-9	1	156	.268	.300	.531	120	13	1-3	.974	-9	94	48	O126(0/126/1),D31	0	0.1
1985	Bos A	103	385	50	102	17	5	23	64	18-4	2	90	.265	.298	.514	113	5	0-0	.983	-6	88	63	O79(16/69/2),D19	29	-0.3
1986	†Bos A	121	425	40	112	21	4	11	58	24-1	2	77	.264	.305	.409	92	-6	0-3	.969	-6	93	70	O117(9/108/19)/D	15	-1.4
1987	Cal A	28	81	8	16	3	1	3	9	1-0	0	11	.198	.205	.370	50	-6	1-0	1.000	-2	87	0	O27(2/0/26)	0	-0.9
1988	Cal A	120	368	42	100	20	2	13	49	22-0	0	87	.272	.311	.443	112	4	1-3	.986	-3	92	91	O113(74/36/10),D5	0	-0.2
1989	Cal A	60	202	22	52	7	1	11	30	7-2	0	48	.257	.280	.465	109	1	0-0	.990	1	99	115	O47(5/1/42),1b2,D6	69	0.0
Total	14	1432	5164	614	1302	204	39	251	815	260-37	15	1201	.252	.287	.453	102	-16	18-20	.981	17	105	89	O1306(124/615/623),D93,1b2/S	241	-4.4
ARMAS, MARCOS	Marcos Rafael (Ruiz); B8.5.1969 Puerto Piritu, Anzoategui, Venez.; BR/TR/6´5˝/195; d5.25; b–Tony																								
1993	Oak A	15	31	7	6	2	0	1	1	1-0	1	12	.194	.242	.355	62	-2	1-0	1.000	-1	65	53	1b12/rfD	0	-0.3
ARMBRISTER, ED	Edison Rosanda; B7.4.1948 Nassau, Bahamas; BR/TR/5´11˝/160; d8.31																								
1973	†Cin N	18	37	5	8	3	1	1	5	2-0	0	8	.216	.250	.432	91	-1	0-0	.917	0	107	143	O14(3/4/7)	0	-0.1
1974	Cin N	9	7	0	2	0	0	0	0	1-0	0	1	.286	.375	.286	88	0	0-0	1.000	-0	65	0	O4(2/0/2)	0	0.0
1975	†Cin N	59	65	9	12	1	0	0	2	5-0	1	19	.185	.254	.200	27	-6	3-1	.867	-3	57	0	O19(10/4/7)	0	-1.0
1976	†Cin N	73	78	20	23	3	2	2	7	6-0	0	22	.295	.341	.462	124	2	7-3	.972	3	100	337	O32(20/0/13)	0	0.4
1977	Cin N	65	78	12	20	4	3	1	5	10-0	0	21	.256	.337	.423	101	0	5-6	.903	0	81	272	O27(20/0/7)	0	-0.1
Total	5	224	265	46	65	11	6	4	19	24-0	1	71	.245	.307	.377	88	-5	15-10	.925	-0	86	209	O96(55/8/36)	0	-0.8

YEAR	TM LG	G	AB	R	H	2B	3B	HR	RBI	BB-IB	HP	SO	AVG	OBP	SLG	AOPS	ABR	SB-CS	FA	FR	RNG	THR	GAMES AT POSITION	DL	BFW
Armbruster, Charlie	Charles Anthony; B8.30.1880 Cincinnati OH; D10.7.1964 Grants Pass OR; BR/TR/5´9˝/180; d7.17																								
1905	Bos A	35	91	13	18	4	0	0	6	18	1	—	.198	.336	.242	83	0	3	.944	-3	*123*	*75*	C35	—	-0.1
1906	Bos A	72	201	9	29	6	1	0	6	25	1	—	.144	.242	.184	34	-14	2	.955	-4	*82*	*112*	C66/1	—	-1.3
1907	Bos A	23	60	2	6	1	0	0	0	8	0	—	.100	.206	.117	3	-6	1	.935	1	*119*	*116*	C21	—	-0.3
	Chi A	1	3	0	0	0	0	0	0	1	0	—	.000	.250	.000	-20	0	0	1.000	0	*153*	*82*	/C	—	0.0
	Year	24	63	2	6	1	0	0	0	9	0	—	.095	.208	.111	2	-7	1	.940	2	*121*	*114*	C22	—	-0.3
Total	3	131	355	24	53	11	1	0	12	52	2	—	.149	.262	.186	42	-20	6	.949	-5	*101*	*102*	C123/1	—	-1.7
Armbruster, Harry	Henry Gregory "Army"; B3.20.1882 Liverpool (now Valley City) OH; D12.10.1953 Cincinnati OH; BL/TL/5´10˝/190; d4.30																								
1906	Phi A	91	265	40	63	6	3	2	24	43	4	—	.238	.353	.306	103	3	13	.971	0	98	51	O74(0/40/34)	—	0.0
Armstrong, George	Noble George "Dodo"; B6.3.1924 Orange NJ; D7.24.1993 Orange NJ; BR/TR/5´10˝/190; d4.26																								
1946	Phi A	8	6	0	1	1	0	0	0	1	0	1	.167	.286	.333	73	0	0-0	1.000	0	*0*	*392*	C4	0	0.0
Armstrong, Bob	Robert; B1850 Baltimore MD; 6´2˝/160; d6.26																								
1871	Kek NA	12	49	9	11	2	1	0	5	0	—	1	.224	.224	.306	50	-3	0-1	.816	1	132	0	O12(0/11/1)	—	-0.2
Arndt, Harry	Harry John; B2.12.1879 South Bend IN; D3.25.1921 South Bend IN; BR/TR/?/165; d7.2																								
1902	Det A	10	34	4	5	0	1	0	7	6	0	—	.147	.275	.206	34	-3	0	.958	0	0	0	O10(7/0/3)/1	—	-0.3
	Bal A	68	248	41	63	7	4	2	28	35	4	—	.254	.355	.339	89	-3	9	.872	1	121	52	O62(1/0/61),2b4,3b2/S	—	-0.4
	Year	78	282	45	68	7	5	2	35	41	4	—	.241	.346	.323	83	-5	9	.885	1	104	45	O72(8/0/64),2b4,3b2/1S	—	-0.7
1905	StL N	113	415	40	101	11	6	2	36	24	3	—	.243	.290	.313	82	-10	13	.951	-10	96	87	2b90,O9R,3b7,S5	—	-2.0
1906	StL N	69	256	30	69	7	9	2	26	19	0	—	.270	.320	.391	127	6	5	.965	10	106	191	3b65/1rf	—	2.0
1907	StL N	11	32	3	6	1	0	0	2	1	0	—	.188	.212	.219	36	-2	0	1.000	1	129	99	1b4,3b3	—	-0.2
Total	4	271	985	118	244	26	20	6	99	85	7	—	.248	.312	.333	91	-12	27	.952	2	97	85	2b94,O82(8/0/74),3b77,S6,1b6	—	-0.9
Arndt, Larry	Larry Wayne; B2.25.1963 Fremont OH; BR/TR/6´1˝/195; [OakA85 26/663]; d6.6; Col Bowling Green																								
1989	Oak A	2	6	1	1	0	0	0	0	0-0	0	1	.167	.167	.167	-6	-1	0-0	1.000	0	132	241	/13	0	-0.1
Arnold, Chris	Christopher Paul; B11.6.1947 Long Beach CA; BR/TR/5´10˝/(160–175); [SFN65 9/239]; d9.7																								
1971	SF N	6	13	2	3	0	0	1	3	1-0	0	2	.231	.286	.462	110	0	0-0	.917	-0	114	0	2b3	0	0.0
1972	SF N	51	84	8	19	3	1	1	4	8-1	0	12	.226	.293	.321	73	-3	0-1	.970	-1	119	211	3b17,2b7,S4	0	-0.3
1973	SF N	49	54	7	16	2	0	1	13	8-2	0	11	.296	.381	.389	111	1	0-0	.944	-3	48	0	C9/23	0	-0.1
1974	SF N	78	174	22	42	7	3	1	26	15-1	1	27	.241	.302	.333	75	-6	1-1	.974	-5	99	83	2b31,3b7/S	0	-0.9
1975	SF N	29	41	4	8	0	0	0	0	4-0	0	8	.195	.267	.195	29	-4	0-0	.923	1	93	230	2b4,O4(3/0/1)	0	-0.4
1976	SF N	60	69	4	15	0	1	0	5	6-1	0	16	.217	.276	.246	49	-5	0-0	1.000	4	188	67	2b8,3b4/1S	0	-0.1
Total	6	273	435	47	103	12	5	4	51	42-5	1	76	.237	.303	.315	72	-17	1-2	.971	-4	107	76	2b54,3b29,C9,S6,O4(3/0/1)/1	0	-1.8
Arnold, Billy	Willis S.; B3.2.1851 Middletown CT; D1.17.1899 Albany NY; d4.26																								
1872	Man NA	2	7	2	1	0	0	0	0	0	—	0	.143	.143	.143	-13	-1	1-0	1.000	0	0	0	O2R	—	0.0
Arnovich, Morrie	"Morris "Snooker"; B11.16.1910 Superior WI; D7.20.1959 Superior WI; BR/TR/5´10˝/168; d9.14; Mil 1942–45; Col Wisconsin–Superior																								
1936	Phi N	13	48	4	15	3	0	1	7	1	2	3	.313	.353	.438	102	0	0	1.000	1	120	92	O13L	—	0.1
1937	Phi N	117	410	60	119	27	4	10	60	34	3	32	.290	.349	.449	107	4	5	.972	7	110	130	O107(97/9/1)	—	0.5
1938	Phi N	139	502	47	138	29	0	4	72	42	2	37	.275	.333	.357	92	-4	2	.983	17	**118**	174	O133(130/1/3)	—	0.6
1939	Phi N☆	134	491	68	159	25	2	5	67	58	2	28	.324	.397	.413	122	18	7	.983	14	**122**	124	O132(131/2/0)	—	2.4
1940	Phi N	39	141	13	28	2	1	0	12	14	1	15	.199	.276	.227	42	-11	0	.959	1	105	102	O37(36/0/1)	—	-1.3
	†Cin N	62	211	17	60	10	2	0	21	13	0	10	.284	.326	.351	86	-4	1	1.000	3	105	120	O60(57/0/3)	—	-0.4
	Year	101	352	30	88	12	3	0	33	27	1	25	.250	.305	.301	68	-15	1	.983	4	105	112	O97(93/0/4)	—	-1.7
1941	NY N	85	207	25	58	8	3	2	22	23	0	14	.280	.352	.377	103	1	2	.982	1	98	148	O61L	0	0.0
1946	NY N	1	3	0	0	0	0	0	0	0	0	0	.000	.000	.000	-99	-1	0	1.000	-0	85	0	/lf	0	-0.1
Total	7	590	2013	234	577	104	12	22	261	185	10	139	.287	.350	.383	100	3	17	.981	45	113	137	O544(526/12/8)	0	1.8
Arundel, Tug	John Thomas; B6.30.1862 Romulus NY; D9.5.1912 Auburn NY; TR/5´10˝/175; d5.23																								
1882	Phi AA	1	5	0	0	0	0	0	—	0	—	—	.000	.000	.000	-94	-1	—	.800	-0	—	—	/C	—	-0.1
1884	Tol AA	15	47	6	4	0	0	0	—	3	0	—	.085	.140	.085	-24	-6	—	.946	5	—	—	C15	—	0.0
1887	Ind N	43	157	13	31	4	0	0	13	8	1	12	.197	.241	.223	31	-14	8	.865	-8	—	—	C42,O2R/1	—	-1.7
1888	Was N	17	51	2	10	0	1	0	3	5	0	10	.196	.268	.235	66	-2	1	.840	-6	—	—	C17	—	-0.6
Total	4	76	260	21	45	4	1	0	16	16	1	22	.173	.224	.196	25	-23	9	.882	-9	—	—	C75,O2R/1	—	-2.4
Asadoor, Randy	Randall Carl; B10.20.1962 Fresno CA; BR/TR/6´1˝/185; [TexA83 3/57]; d9.14; Col Cal St.–Fresno																								
1986	SD N	15	55	9	20	5	0	0	7	3-1	0	13	.364	.397	.455	137	3	1-2	.889	-0	103	41	3b15,2b2	0	0.2
Asbell, Jim	James Marion "Big Train"; B6.22.1914 Dallas TX; D7.6.1967 San Mateo CA; BR/TR/6´0˝/195; d5.8																								
1938	Chi N	17	33	6	6	2	0	0	3	3	0	9	.182	.250	.242	35	-3	0	1.000	1	94	171	O10(7/0/3)	—	-0.3
Asbjornson, Casper	Robert Anthony (Name Changed To Asby); B6.19.1909 Concord MA; D1.21.1970 Williamsport PA; BR/TR/6´1˝/196; d9.17																								
1928	Bos A	6	16	0	3	1	0	0	1	1	0	1	.188	.235	.250	28	-2	0-0	.917	-2	*69*	*134*	C6	—	-0.3
1929	Bos A	17	29	1	3	0	0	0	0	1	0	6	.103	.133	.103	-39	-6	0-0	.897	-2	*90*	*108*	C15	—	-0.7
1931	Cin N	45	118	13	36	7	1	0	22	7	1	23	.305	.349	.381	102	0	0	.981	-1	*83*	*132*	C31	—	0.1
1932	Cin N	29	58	5	10	2	0	1	4	0	1	15	.172	.186	.259	19	-7	0	.961	-1	*94*	*53*	C16	—	-0.7
Total	4	97	221	19	52	10	1	1	27	9	2	45	.235	.272	.303	56	-15	0-0	.960	-5	*86*	*110*	C68	—	-1.6
Ashburn, Richie	Don Richard "Whitey"; B3.19.1927 Tilden NE; D9.9.1997 New York NY; BL/TR/5´10˝/(170–175); d4.20; HF1995																								
1948	Phi N★	117	463	78	154	17	4	2	40	60	1	22	.333	.410	.400	122	17	**32**	.981	9	109	156	O116(15/102/0)	0	2.2
1949	Phi N	**154**	662	84	188	18	11	1	37	58	1	38	.284	.343	.349	88	-12	9	.980	10	**112**	108	O154C	0	-0.5
1950	†Phi N	151	594	84	180	25	**14**	2	41	63	2	32	.303	.372	.402	105	5	14	.988	-1	102	64	O147C	0	0.0
1951	Phi N★	**154**	643	92	**221**	31	5	4	63	50	2	37	.344	.393	.426	122	21	29-6	.988	**21**	**125**	107	O154C	0	4.2
1952	Phi N	**154**	613	93	173	31	6	1	42	75	2	30	.282	.362	.357	101	4	16-11	.980	8	103	147	O154C	0	0.7
1953	Phi N★	**156**	622	110	**205**	25	9	2	57	61	5	35	.330	.394	.408	110	12	14-6	.990	18	**115**	126	O156C	0	2.2
1954	Phi N	**153**	559	111	175	16	8	1	41	**125**	4	46	.313	**.441**	.376	116	23	11-8	.984	13	**116**	102	O153C	0	2.8
1955	Phi N	140	533	91	180	32	9	3	42	105-5	3	36	**.338**	**.449**	.448	142	41	12-10	.983	5	108	94	O140C	0	3.7
1956	Phi N	**154**	628	94	190	26	8	3	50	79-3	5	45	.303	.384	.384	110	12	10-1	.983	19	**124**	97	O154C	0	2.6
1957	Phi N	**156**	626	93	186	26	8	0	33	**94**-1	4	44	.297	.390	.364	108	13	13-10	.987	24	123	161	O156(0/156/1)	0	2.9
1958	Phi N☆	152	615	98	**215**	24	**13**	2	33	**97**-7	4	48	**.350**	**.440**	.441	136	39	30-12	.984	11	121	63	O152C	0	4.4
1959	Phi N	153	564	86	150	16	2	1	20	79-4	6	42	.266	.360	.307	79	-13	9-11	.971	-4	105	49	O149C	0	-2.7
1960	Chi N	151	547	99	159	16	5	0	40	**116**-1	1	50	.291	**.415**	.338	110	16	16-4	.976	-4	94	98	O146(45/106/0)	0	0.7
1961	Chi N	109	307	49	79	7	4	0	19	55-2	3	27	.257	.373	.306	83	-5	7-6	.978	-8	80	76	O76(14/62/0)	0	-1.6
1962	NY N★	135	389	60	119	7	3	7	28	81-2	0	39	.306	.424	.393	119	16	12-7	.975	1	97	131	O97(10/56/42),2b2	0	1.2
Total	15	2189	8365	1322	2574	317	109	29	586	1198-25	43	571	.308	.396	.382	111	189	234-92	.983	121	111	105	O2104(84/1995/43),2b2	0	22.8
Ashby, Alan	Alan Dean; B7.8.1951 Long Beach CA; BB/TR (BL 1976)/6´2˝/(170–195); [CleA69 3/63]; d7.3; C1																								
1973	Cle A	11	29	4	5	1	0	1	3	2-0	0	11	.172	.226	.310	49	-2	0-0	.978	-2	150	37	C11	0	-0.4
1974	Cle A	10	7	1	1	0	0	0	0	1-0	0	2	.143	.250	.143	15	-1	0-0	1.000	0	0	0	C9	0	-0.1
1975	Cle A	90	254	32	57	10	1	5	32	30-1	1	42	.224	.309	.331	80	-6	3-2	.990	-3	87	110	C87,1b2/3D	0	-0.6
1976	Cle A	89	247	26	59	5	1	4	32	27-4	0	49	.239	.310	.316	85	-4	0-2	.987	3	82	117	C86,1b2/3	24	0.2
1977	Tor A	124	396	25	83	16	3	2	29	50-3	2	51	.210	.301	.280	59	-22	0-2	.984	0	125	117	C124	0	-1.7
1978	Tor A	81	264	27	69	15	0	9	29	28-4	1	32	.261	.333	.420	109	3	1-1	.986	-5	107	103	C81	0	0.1
1979	Hou N	108	336	25	68	15	2	2	35	26-10	2	70	.202	.262	.277	51	-24	0-0	.987	1	102	83	C105	18	-1.9
1980	†Hou N	116	352	30	90	19	2	3	48	35-12	0	40	.256	.319	.347	95	-2	0-0	.991	-1	103	62	C114	0	0.1
1981	†Hou N	83	255	20	69	13	0	4	33	35-6	0	33	.271	.356	.369	113	6	0-2	.982	10	105	130	C81	0	2.0
1982	Hou N	100	339	40	87	14	2	12	49	27-4	1	53	.257	.311	.416	111	3	2-0	.977	-7	75	69	C95	0	0.1
1983	Hou N	87	275	31	63	18	1	8	34	31-4	0	38	.229	.303	.389	97	-1	0-0	.974	-8	83	86	C85	27	-0.6
1984	Hou N	66	191	16	50	7	0	4	27	20-2	1	22	.262	.330	.361	102	1	0-0	.986	-3	76	122	C63	34	-0.0
1985	Hou N	65	189	20	53	8	0	8	25	24-2	1	27	.280	.363	.450	129	8	0-0	.978	-2	78	108	C60	40	0.8
1986	†Hou N	120	315	24	81	15	0	7	38	39-9	0	56	.257	.333	.371	98	0	1-0	.985	-2	86	76	C103	0	0.2

YEAR	TM LG	G	AB	R	H	2B	3B	HR	RBI	BB-IB	HP	SO	AVG	OBP	SLG	AOPS	ABR	SB-CS	FA	FR	RNG	THR	GAMES AT POSITION	DL	BFW
1987	Hou N	125	386	53	111	16	0	14	63	50-2	1	52	.288	.367	.438	118	11	0-1	**.993**	-2	79	74	C110	0	1.3
1988	Hou N	73	227	19	54	10	0	7	33	29-3	0	36	.238	.319	.374	104	2	0-0	.991	-10	66	67	C66	69	-0.5
1989	Hou N	22	61	4	10	1	1	0	3	7-0	1	8	.164	.257	.213	38	-5	0-0	1.000	-4	87	65	C19	0	-0.8
Total	17	1370	4123	397	1010	183	13	90	513	461-66	11	622	.245	.320	.361	93	-33	7-10	.986	-35	92	92	C1299,1b4,3b2/D	212	-1.8
Ashford, Tucker	Thomas Steven; B12.4.1954 Memphis TN; BR/TR/6´1˝/(185–195); [SDN74*1/2]; d9.21; Col U. of Mississippi																								
1976	SD N	4	5	0	3	1	0	0	0	1-0	0	0	.600	.667	.800	341	2	2-0	1.000	-0	90	0	/3	0	0.2
1977	SD N	81	249	25	54	18	0	3	24	21-4	1	35	.217	.278	.325	69	-11	2-3	.937	-8	102	122	3b74,S10,2b4	0	-2.1
1978	SD N	75	155	11	38	11	0	3	26	14-1	0	31	.245	.301	.374	97	-1	1-0	.917	-11	47	68	3b32,2b18,1b14	0	-1.2
1980	Tex A	15	32	2	4	0	0	0	3	3-0	0	3	.125	.200	.125	-9	-5	0-0	.943	2	117	46	3b12,S2	0	-0.3
1981	NY A	3	0	0	0	0	0	0	0	0-0	0	0	ø	ø	ø	ø	0	0-0	ø	-1	0	0	2b2	0	-0.1
1983	NY N	35	56	3	10	0	1	0	2	7-1	0	4	.179	.270	.214	36	-5	0-0	.957	-0	90	117	3b15,2b13/C	0	-0.6
1984	KC A	9	13	1	2	1	0	0	0	1-0	0	2	.154	.214	.231	23	-1	0-0	.909	-1	86	125	3b9	0	-0.2
Total	7	222	510	42	111	31	1	6	55	47-6	1	75	.218	.282	.318	69	-21	5-3	.936	-19	93	105	3b143,2b37,1b14,S12/C	0	-4.3
Ashley, Billy	Billy Manual; B7.11.1970 Trenton MI; BR/TR/6´7˝/(220–242); [LAN88 3/62]; d9.1																								
1992	LA N	29	95	6	21	5	0	2	6	5-0	0	34	.221	.260	.337	69	-4	0-0	.857	-3	72	123	O27(1/0/26)	0	-0.9
1993	LA N	14	37	0	9	0	0	0	0	2-0	0	11	.243	.282	.243	45	-3	0-0	1.000	1	58	432	O11L	0	-0.3
1994	LA N	2	6	0	2	1	0	0	0	0-0	0	2	.333	.333	.500	120	0	0-0	1.000	-0	79	0	O2L	0	0.0
1995	†LA N	81	215	17	51	5	0	8	27	25-4	2	88	.237	.320	.372	89	-4	0-0	.972	0	103	60	O69L	0	-0.6
1996	†LA N	71	110	18	22	2	1	9	25	21-1	1	44	.200	.331	.482	119	3	0-0	.952	-1	85	141	O38L	22	0.1
1997	LA N	71	131	12	32	7	0	6	19	8-0	1	46	.244	.293	.435	93	-2	0-0	.911	-2	82	121	O35L	0	-0.5
1998	Bos A	13	24	3	7	3	0	3	7	2-0	0	11	.292	.346	.792	180	3	0-0	.857	0	0	377	1b2,O2L,D5	17	0.3
Total	7	281	618	56	144	23	1	28	84	63-5	4	236	.233	.307	.409	94	-7	0-0	.941	-5	87	130	O184(158/0/26),D5,1b2	39	-1.9
Asmussen, Tom	Thomas William; B9.26.1878 Chicago IL; D8.21.1963 Arlington Heights IL; TR; d8.10																								
1907	Bos N	2	5	0	0	0	0	0	0	0	0	—	.000	.000	.000	-99	-1	0	1.000	-1	*49*	*82*	C2	—	-0.2
Aspromonte, Ken	Kenneth Joseph; B9.22.1931 Brooklyn NY; BR/TR/6´0˝/180; d9.2; M3; b–Bob																								
1957	Bos A	24	78	9	21	5	0	0	4	17-0	0	10	.269	.396	.333	97	1	0-1	.965	-5	97	77	2b24	0	-0.3
1958	Bos A	6	16	0	2	0	0	0	0	3-0	0	1	.125	.263	.125	10	-2	0-0	.952	-3	51	72	2b6	0	-0.5
	Was A	92	253	15	57	9	1	5	27	25-1	1	28	.225	.296	.328	73	-9	1-1	.964	-6	99	88	2b72,3b11/S	0	-1.1
	Year	98	269	15	59	9	1	5	27	28-1	1	29	.219	.294	.316	69	-11	1-1	.963	-9	96	87	2b78,3b11/S	0	-1.6
1959	Was A	70	225	31	55	12	0	2	14	26-0	0	39	.244	.321	.324	79	-6	2-1	.960	-5	104	77	2b52,S12/1lf	0	-0.7
1960	Was A	4	3	0	0	0	0	0	0	0-0	0	1	.000	.000	.000	-99	-1	0-0	ø	0	—	—	/H	0	-0.1
	Cle A	117	459	65	133	20	1	10	48	53-0	2	32	.290	.364	.403	111	8	4-1	.976	-9	95	103	2b80,3b36	0	0.6
	Year	121	462	65	133	20	1	10	48	53-0	2	33	.288	.362	.400	110	7	4-1	.976	-9	95	103	2b80,3b36	0	0.5
1961	LA A	66	238	29	53	10	0	2	14	33-1	2	21	.223	.322	.290	58	-13	0-0	.970	20	119	123	2b62	0	1.2
	Cle A	22	70	5	16	6	1	0	5	6-0	0	3	.229	.286	.343	70	-3	0-0	.963	-3	106	67	2b21	0	-0.4
	Year	88	308	34	69	16	1	2	19	39-1	2	24	.224	.314	.302	61	-16	0-0	.969	17	116	111	2b83	0	0.8
1962	Cle A	20	28	4	4	2	0	0	1	6-1	0	5	.143	.286	.214	41	-2	0-0	1.000	-2	53	76	2b6,3b3	0	-0.3
	Mil N	34	79	11	23	2	0	0	7	6-0	1	5	.291	.341	.316	82	-2	0-1	1.000	0	99	92	2b12,3b6	0	-0.1
1963	Chi N	20	34	2	5	3	0	0	4	4-1	0	4	.147	.237	.235	35	-3	0-0	.951	2	134	106	2b7,1b2	0	0.0
Total	7	475	1483	171	369	69	3	19	124	179-4	6	149	.249	.330	.338	82	-32	7-5	.969	-10	102	95	2b342,3b56,S13,1b3/lf	0	-1.7
Aspromonte, Bob	Robert Thomas; B6.19.1938 Brooklyn NY; BR/TR/6´2˝/(180–190); d9.19; b–Ken; OF(60/0/2)																								
1956	Bro N	1	1	0	0	0	0	0	0	0-0	0	1	.000	.000	.000	-93	0	0-0	ø	0	—	—	/H	0	0.0
1960	LA N	21	55	1	10	1	0	1	6	0-0	1	6	.182	.196	.255	21	-6	1-0	.933	-4	60	77	S15,3b4	0	-1.0
1961	LA N	47	58	7	14	3	0	0	2	4-0	0	12	.241	.290	.293	51	-4	0-0	.917	1	121	0	3b9,S4,2b2	0	-0.3
1962	Hou N	149	534	59	142	18	4	11	59	46-4	8	54	.266	.332	.376	97	-2	4-5	.967	-0	92	85	3b142,S11/2	0	-0.3
1963	Hou N	136	468	42	100	9	5	8	49	40-4	1	57	.214	.276	.306	72	-18	3-1	.938	-8	91	22	3b131/1	0	-3.0
1964	Hou N	157	553	51	155	20	3	12	69	35-7	8	54	.280	.329	.392	109	6	6-7	**.973**	-8	95	43	3b155	0	-0.3
1965	Hou N	152	578	53	152	15	2	5	52	38-5	3	54	.263	.310	.322	85	-13	2-2	.962	8	107	106	3b146,1b6,S4	0	-0.6
1966	Hou N	152	560	55	141	16	3	8	52	35-7	2	63	.252	.297	.334	81	-16	0-4	**.962**	-9	90	62	3b149,1b2,S2	0	-2.8
1967	Hou N	137	486	51	143	24	5	6	58	45-11	2	44	.294	.354	.401	121	14	2-2	.963	-6	86	72	3b133	0	0.7
1968	Hou N	124	409	25	92	9	2	1	46	35-9	2	57	.225	.285	.264	68	-16	1-0	.973	-0	95	54	3b75,O36(35/0/2)/1S	0	-2.1
1969	†Atl N	82	198	16	50	8	1	3	24	13-1	2	19	.253	.304	.348	82	-5	0-1	.975	-5	106	88	O24L,3b23,S18,2b2	0	-1.1
1970	Atl N	62	127	5	27	3	0	0	7	13-0	0	13	.213	.282	.236	39	-11	0-0	.938	-0	102	112	3b30,S4/1lf	0	-1.1
1971	NY N	104	342	21	77	9	1	5	33	29-4	0	25	.225	.285	.301	66	-15	0-2	.965	-6	81	71	3b97	0	-2.5
Total	13	1324	4369	386	1103	135	26	60	457	333-52	29	459	.252	.308	.336	85	-86	19-24	.960	-38	93	65	3b1094,O61L,S59,1b11,2b5	0	-14.4
Asselstine, Brian	Brian Hanly; B9.23.1953 Santa Barbara CA; BL/TR/6´1˝/(170–190); [AtlN73*S1/15]; d9.14; Col Hancock (CA) JC																								
1976	Atl N	11	33	2	7	0	0	1	3	1-0	0	2	.212	.229	.303	49	-2	0-0	1.000	-1	91	0	O9(0/7/2)	0	-0.4
1977	Atl N	83	124	12	26	6	0	4	17	9-1	0	10	.210	.263	.355	58	-8	1-0	.983	1	114	64	O35(9/13/13)	0	-0.7
1978	Atl N	39	103	11	28	3	3	2	13	11-1	2	16	.272	.339	.417	104	0	2-1	.968	-1	100	47	O35(0/11/31)	122	-0.2
1979	Atl N	8	10	1	1	0	0	0	0	1-1	0	2	.100	.182	.100	-20	-2	0-0	1.000	-0	55	0	/lf	116	-0.2
1980	Atl N	87	218	18	62	13	1	3	25	11-3	1	37	.284	.318	.394	98	-1	1-3	.962	-9	79	0	O61(29/32/2)	15	-1.3
1981	Atl N	56	86	8	22	5	0	2	10	5-0	0	7	.256	.297	.384	92	-1	1-0	.958	-0	96	100	O16(4/0/12)	22	-0.2
Total	6	284	574	52	146	27	4	12	68	38-6	3	74	.254	.300	.378	84	-14	5-4	.971	-10	92	31	O157(43/63/60)	275	-3.0
Astroth, Joe	Joseph Henry; B9.1.1922 East Alton IL; BR/TR/5´9˝/187; d8.13; Col Illinois																								
1945	Phi A	10	17	1	1	0	0	0	1	0	1	1	.059	.111	.059	-50	-3	0-0	.857	-1	*96*	*137*	C8	0	-0.4
1946	Phi A	4	7	0	1	0	0	0	0	0	0	2	.143	.143	.143	-20	-1	0-0	.889	-0	*0*	*209*	C4	0	-0.1
1949	Phi A	55	148	18	36	4	1	0	12	21	0	13	.243	.337	.284	67	-7	1-0	.979	0	*105*	*115*	C44	0	-0.4
1950	Phi A	39	110	11	36	3	1	1	18	18	0	3	.327	.422	.400	113	3	0-0	.985	-5	*87*	*50*	C38	0	0.0
1951	Phi A	64	187	30	46	10	2	2	19	18	0	13	.246	.312	.353	78	-6	0-1	.992	4	*162*	*67*	C57	0	0.0
1952	Phi A	104	337	24	84	7	2	1	36	25	2	27	.249	.305	.291	62	-17	2-2	.992	-1	*121*	*84*	C102	0	-1.4
1953	Phi A	82	260	28	77	15	2	3	24	27	2	12	.296	.367	.404	104	2	1-0	.987	6	***151***	***130***	C79	0	1.2
1954	Phi A	77	226	22	50	8	1	1	23	21	3	19	.221	.296	.279	58	-13	0-0	.988	-3	*95*	*96*	C71	0	-1.3
1955	KC A	101	274	29	69	4	1	5	23	47-6	6	33	.252	.372	.328	89	-2	2-3	.989	-5	*120*	*82*	C100	0	-0.3
1956	KC A	8	13	0	1	0	0	0	0	0-0	0	1	.077	.077	.077	-59	-3	0-0	1.000	1	*108*	*256*	C8	0	-0.2
Total	10	544	1579	163	401	51	10	13	156	177-6	14	124	.254	.334	.324	77	-47	6-6	.987	-4	*122*	*94*	C511	0	-2.9
Atherton, Charlie	Charles Morgan Herbert "Prexy"; B11.19.1874 New Brunswick NJ; D12.19.1935 Vienna, Austria; BR/TR/5´10˝/160; d5.30; Col Penn St.																								
1899	Was N	65	242	28	60	5	6	0	23	21	2	—	.248	.313	.318	74	-9	2	.890	-5	86	69	3b63/rf	—	-1.2
Atkins, Garrett	Garrett Bernard; B12.12.1979 Orange CA; BR/TR/6´2˝/(190–215); [ColN00 5/137]; d8.3; Col UCLA																								
2003	Col N	25	69	6	11	2	0	0	4	3-0	1	14	.159	.205	.188	3	-10	0-0	.850	-5	82	0	3b19	0	-1.4
2004	Col N	15	28	3	10	2	0	1	8	4-0	0	3	.357	.424	.536	133	2	0-0	1.000	-1	63	152	3b4,1b3,O3L	0	0.1
2005	Col N	138	519	62	149	31	1	13	89	45-1	5	72	.287	.347	.426	91	-5	0-2	.950	-6	100	81	3b136	23	-1.1
2006	Col N	157	602	117	198	48	1	29	120	79-6	7	76	.329	.409	.556	133	34	4-0	.953	-15	93	115	3b157,1b3	0	1.9
Total	4	335	1218	188	368	83	2	43	221	131-7	13	165	.302	.373	.479	108	21	4-2	.947	-26	95	95	3b316,1b6,O3L	23	-0.5
Atkinson, Ed	Edward; B1851 Baltimore MD; d10.22																								
1873	Was NA	2	8	2	0	0	0	0	0	0	—	0	.000	.000	.000	-99	-2	0-0	1.000	-0	0	0	O2R	—	-0.1
Atkinson, Lefty	Hubert Berley; B6.2.1906 Chicago IL; D2.12.1961 Chicago IL; BL/TL/5´6.5˝/149; d8.5																								
1927	Was A	1	1	1	0	0	0	0	0	0	0	0	.000	.000	.000	-99	0	0-0	ø	0	—	—	/H	—	0.0
Attreau, Dick	Richard Gilbert; B4.8.1897 Chicago IL; D7.5.1964 Chicago IL; BL/TL/6´0˝/160; d9.14																								
1926	Phi N	17	61	9	14	1	1	0	5	6	0	5	.230	.299	.279	53	-4	0	.989	-2	62	77	1b17	—	-0.7
1927	Phi N	44	83	17	17	1	1	1	11	14	0	18	.205	.320	.277	60	-4	1	.989	-1	70	78	1b26	—	-0.7
Total	2	61	144	26	31	2	2	1	16	20	0	23	.215	.311	.278	57	-8	1	.989	-3	66	78	1b43	—	-1.4

YEAR	TM LG	G	AB	R	H	2B	3B	HR	RBI	BB-IB	HP	SO	AVG	OBP	SLG	AOPS	ABR	SB-CS	FA	FR	RNG	THR	GAMES AT POSITION	DL	BFW
Atwell, Toby	Maurice Dailey; B3.8.1924 Leesburg VA; D1.25.2003 Purcellville VA; BL/TR/5´9.5˝/185; d4.15; Col VPI																								
1952	Chi N☆	107	362	36	105	16	3	2	31	40	1	22	.290	.362	.367	102	2	2-1	.977	-9	58	81	C101	0	-0.1
1953	Chi N	24	74	10	17	2	0	1	8	13	0	7	.230	.345	.297	68	-3	0-0	.940	-1	90	165	C24	0	-0.3
	Pit N	53	139	11	34	6	0	0	17	20	3	12	.245	.352	.288	70	-5	0-0	.967	-4	69	108	C45	0	-0.7
	Year	77	213	21	51	8	0	1	25	33	3	19	.239	.349	.291	69	-8	0-0	.957	-5	77	129	C69	0	-1.0
1954	Pit N	96	287	36	83	8	4	3	26	43	3	21	.289	.384	.376	101	2	2-3	.990	-5	56	109	C88	0	0.1
1955	Pit N	71	207	21	44	8	0	1	18	40-9	1	16	.213	.337	.266	65	-8	0-1	.992	1	79	91	C67	0	-0.4
1956	Pit N	12	18	0	2	0	0	0	3	1-0	0	5	.111	.158	.111	-27	-3	0-0	1.000	1	154	109	C9	0	-0.2
	Mil N	15	30	2	5	1	0	2	7	4-1	0	1	.167	.265	.400	80	-1	0-0	1.000	-0	115	135	C10	0	-0.1
	Year	27	48	2	7	1	0	2	10	5-1	0	6	.146	.226	.292	40	-4	0-0	1.000	1	131	125	C19	0	-0.3
Total	5	378	1117	116	290	41	7	9	110	161-10	8	84	.260	.355	.333	86	-16	4-5	.980	-16	68	102	C344	0	-1.7
Atwood, Bill	William Franklin; B9.25.1911 Rome GA; D9.14.1993 Snyder TX; BR/TR/5´11.5˝/190; d4.15; Col Hardin–Simmons																								
1936	Phi N	71	192	21	58	9	2	2	29	11	2	15	.302	.346	.401	92	-2	0	.972	-1	99	77	C53	—	0.0
1937	Phi N	87	279	27	68	15	1	2	32	30	0	27	.244	.317	.326	69	-11	3	.968	-9	137	93	C80	—	-1.6
1938	Phi N	102	281	27	55	8	1	3	28	25	0	26	.196	.261	.263	46	-21	0	.969	-7	58	**125**	C94	—	-2.3
1939	Phi N	4	6	0	0	0	0	0	1	2	0	3	.000	.250	.000	-29	-1	1	1.000	-0	50	0	C2	—	-0.1
1940	Phi N	78	203	7	39	9	0	0	22	25	1	18	.192	.284	.236	47	-14	0	.989	0	91	105	C69	—	-1.0
Total	5	342	961	82	220	41	4	7	112	93	3	89	.229	.299	.302	63	-49	4	.974	-17	95	102	C298	—	-5.0
Atz, Jake	John Jacob (b Jacob Henry Atz); B7.1.1879 Washington DC; D5.22.1945 New Orleans LA; BR/TR/5´9˝/150; d9.24																								
1902	Was A	3	10	1	1	0	0	0	0	0	0	—	.100	.100	.100	-44	-2	0	1.000	1	147	93	2b3	—	-0.1
1907	Chi A	4	8	0	1	0	0	0	0	0	0	—	.125	.125	.125	-21	-1	0	1.000	1	177	469	3b2/cf	—	0.0
1908	Chi A	83	206	24	40	3	0	0	27	31	4	—	.194	.311	.209	71	-4	9	.936	-1	104	103	2b46,S18/3	—	-0.6
1909	Chi A	119	381	39	90	18	3	0	22	38	2	—	.236	.309	.299	96	-1	14	.954	-5	99	115	2b114,O3R/S	—	-0.5
Total	4	209	605	64	132	21	3	0	49	69	6	—	.218	.304	.263	83	-8	23	.949	-5	101	111	2b163,S19,O4(0/1/3),3b3	—	-1.2
Aubrey, Harry	Harry Herbert "Chub"; B7.5.1881 St.Joseph MO; D9.18.1953 Baltimore MD; BR/TR/5´7˝/130; d4.22																								
1903	Bos N	96	325	26	69	8	2	0	27	18	5	—	.212	.264	.249	49	-22	7	.868	-12	99	56	S94/2lf	—	-3.1
Aude, Rich	Richard Thomas; B7.13.1971 Van Nuys CA; BR/TR/6´5˝/(209–220); [PitN89 2/48]; d9.9																								
1993	Pit N	13	26	1	3	1	0	0	4	1-0	0	7	.115	.148	.154	-19	-4	0-0	1.000	-1	78	132	1b7/lf	0	-0.6
1995	Pit N	42	109	10	27	8	0	2	19	6-0	0	20	.248	.287	.376	71	-5	1-2	.996	-3	60	127	1b32	0	-1.0
1996	Pit N	7	16	0	4	0	0	0	1	0-0	0	8	.250	.250	.250	31	-2	0-0	.969	0	139	114	1b4	0	-0.2
Total	3	62	151	11	34	9	0	2	24	7-0	0	35	.225	.259	.325	52	-11	1-2	.994	-3	70	127	1b43/lf	0	-1.8
Auerbach, Rick	Frederick Steven; B2.15.1950 Woodland Hills CA; BR/TR/6´0˝/(165–175); [MilA69*S7/145]; d4.13; Col Los Angeles Pierce (CA) JC																								
1971	Mil A	79	236	22	48	10	0	1	9	20-1	2	40	.203	.271	.258	51	-15	3-2	.963	-11	91	72	S78	0	-1.9
1972	Mil A	153	554	50	121	16	3	2	30	43-5	2	62	.218	.277	.269	64	-25	24-8	.959	-17	96	97	S153	0	-2.5
1973	Mil A	6	10	2	1	1	0	0	0	0-0	0	1	.100	.100	.200	-18	-2	0-1	.833	-1	87	0	S2	0	-0.3
1974	†LA N	45	73	12	25	0	0	1	4	8-0	0	9	.342	.407	.384	127	3	4-2	.950	-2	86	84	S19,2b16,3b3	0	0.3
1975	LA N	85	170	18	38	9	0	0	12	18-3	0	22	.224	.298	.276	63	-8	3-2	.960	-20	77	62	S81/23	17	-2.3
1976	LA N	36	47	7	6	0	0	0	1	6-0	0	6	.128	.226	.128	2	-6	0-1	.943	1	89	154	S12,3b8,2b7	0	-0.4
1977	Cin N	33	45	5	7	2	0	0	3	4-0	0	7	.156	.216	.200	15	-5	0-0	.976	0	98	84	2b19,S12	0	-0.4
1978	Cin N	63	55	17	18	6	0	2	5	7-0	1	12	.327	.413	.545	165	5	1-0	.971	-0	102	103	S26,2b10,3b3	0	0.7
1979	†Cin N	62	100	17	21	8	1	1	12	14-1	0	19	.210	.304	.340	76	-3	0-1	.933	-3	112	95	3b18,S16,2b3	0	-0.5
1980	Cin N	24	33	5	11	1	1	1	4	3-0	0	5	.333	.389	.515	153	2	0-3	1.000	0	167	85	S3,3b3/2	0	0.2
1981	Sea A	38	84	12	13	3	0	1	6	4-0	1	15	.155	.200	.226	22	-9	1-1	.979	2	106	128	S38	53	-0.4
Total	11	624	1407	167	309	56	5	9	86	127-10	6	198	.220	.286	.286	65	-63	36-21	.960	-51	93	89	S440,2b57,3b36	70	-7.5
Augustine, Dave	David Ralph; B11.28.1949 Follansbee WV; BR/TR/6´2˝/172; d9.3; Col Miami–Dade Kendall (FL) CC																								
1973	Pit N	11	7	1	2	1	0	0	0	0-0	0	1	.286	.286	.429	97	0	0-0	1.000	0	72	578	O9(4/4/1)	0	0.0
1974	Pit N	18	22	3	4	0	0	0	0	0-0	0	5	.182	.182	.182	2	-3	0-1	1.000	3	132	483	O11(1/6/4)	0	-0.1
Total	2	29	29	4	6	1	0	0	0	0-0	0	6	.207	.207	.241	25	-3	0-1	1.000	3	115	511	O20(5/10/5)	0	-0.1
Aulds, Leslie	Leycester Doyle "Tex"; B12.28.1920 Farmerville LA; D10.13.1999 Hondo TX; BR/TR/6´2˝/185; d5.25																								
1947	Bos A	3	4	0	1	0	0	0	0	0	0	1	.250	.250	.250	37	0	0-0	1.000	0	0	0	C3	0	0.0
Ault, Doug	Douglas Reagan; B3.9.1950 Beaumont TX; D12.22.2004 Tarpon Springs FL; BR/TL/6´3˝/(200–205); d9.9; Col Texas Tech																								
1976	Tex A	9	20	0	6	1	0	0	0	1-0	0	3	.300	.333	.350	98	0	0-0	1.000	-1	0	57	1b4,D3	0	-0.1
1977	Tor A	129	445	44	109	22	3	11	64	39-5	4	68	.245	.310	.382	87	-8	4-4	.987	6	**120**	82	1b122,D4	0	-1.0
1978	Tor A	54	104	10	25	1	1	3	7	17-1	1	14	.240	.352	.356	98	0	0-0	.979	-2	81	78	1b25,O7(6/0/1),D5	0	-0.3
1980	Tor A	64	144	12	28	5	1	3	15	14-0	2	23	.194	.273	.306	57	-9	0-1	1.000	2	135	100	1b32,D21/lf	0	-0.9
Total	4	256	713	66	168	29	5	17	86	71-6	7	108	.236	.309	.362	82	-17	4-5	.988	6	116	84	1b183,D33,O8(7/0/1)	0	-2.3
Aurilia, Rich	Richard Santo; B9.2.1971 Brooklyn NY; BR/TR/6´1˝/(170–190); [TexA92 24/678]; d9.6; Col St. Johns																								
1995	SF N	9	19	4	9	3	0	2	4	1-0	0	2	.474	.476	.947	277	5	1-0	1.000	2	135	165	S6	0	0.7
1996	SF N	105	318	27	76	7	1	3	26	25-2	1	52	.239	.295	.296	58	-20	4-1	.973	-7	97	87	S93,2b11	6	-1.9
1997	SF N	46	102	16	28	8	0	5	19	8-0	0	15	.275	.321	.500	115	2	1-1	.979	8	119	122	S36	0	1.1
1998	SF N	122	413	54	110	27	2	9	49	31-3	2	62	.266	.319	.407	94	-4	3-3	.979	2	102	114	S120	16	0.5
1999	SF N	152	558	68	157	23	1	22	80	43-3	5	71	.281	.336	.444	103	0	2-3	.957	-3	99	108	S150	0	0.7
2000	†SF N	141	509	67	138	24	2	20	79	54-2	0	90	.271	.339	.444	103	1	1-2	.967	10	103	**130**	S140	0	2.0
2001	SF N★	156	636	114	**206**	37	5	37	97	47-2	0	83	.324	.369	.572	147	42	1-3	.975	-4	97	116	S149	0	4.6
2002	†SF N	133	538	76	138	35	2	15	61	37-0	4	90	.257	.305	.413	91	-9	1-2	**.980**	-10	90	**123**	S131	15	-1.0
2003	†SF N	129	505	65	140	26	1	13	58	36-0	1	82	.277	.325	.410	89	-9	2-2	.974	-19	89	109	S123/D	15	-1.8
2004	Sea A	73	261	27	63	13	0	4	28	22-1	2	43	.241	.304	.337	71	-11	1-0	.990	-11	88	85	S73	0	-1.6
	SD N	51	138	22	35	8	2	2	16	15-0	2	28	.254	.331	.384	90	-2	0-0	.919	-4	82	67	3b29,2b7,S6/1	0	-0.5
2005	Cin N	114	426	61	120	23	2	14	68	37-2	1	67	.282	.338	.444	103	1	2-0	.981	-2	101	86	2b68,S30,3b18	18	0.5
2006	Cin N	122	440	61	132	25	1	23	70	34-1	1	51	.300	.349	.518	112	8	3-0	.953	3	98	92	3b52,1b47,S26,2b10/D	15	1.0
Total	12	1353	4863	662	1352	259	19	169	655	390-16	19	736	.278	.332	.443	102	4	22-17	.974	-35	97	111	S1083,3b99,2b96,1b48,D2	85	4.3
Ausmus, Brad	Bradley David; B4.14.1969 New Haven CT; BR/TR/5´11˝/(185–195); [NYA87 48/1152]; d7.28																								
1993	SD N	49	160	18	41	8	1	5	12	6-0	0	28	.256	.283	.412	83	-5	2-0	.975	2	112	119	C49	0	0.1
1994	SD N	101	327	45	82	12	1	7	24	30-12	1	63	.251	.314	.358	78	-11	5-1	.991	-3	92	104	C99/1	0	-0.7
1995	SD N	103	328	44	96	16	4	5	34	31-3	2	56	.293	.353	.412	105	3	16-5	.992	5	134	127	C100/1	0	1.5
1996	SD N	50	149	16	27	4	0	1	13	13-0	3	27	.181	.261	.228	32	-15	1-4	.982	-3	104	116	C46	0	-1.6
	Det A	75	226	30	56	12	0	4	22	26-1	2	45	.248	.328	.354	73	-9	3-4	.992	-2	92	130	C73	0	-0.6
1997	†Hou N	130	425	45	113	25	1	4	44	38-4	3	78	.266	.326	.358	83	-10	14-6	.992	14	**187**	112	C129	0	1.2
1998	†Hou N	128	412	62	111	10	4	6	45	53-11	3	60	.269	.356	.357	91	-5	10-3	.992	5	128	91	C124	0	0.9
1999	Det A★	127	458	62	126	25	6	9	54	51-0	14	71	.275	.365	.415	97	-1	12-9	**.998**	-2	133	94	C127	0	0.4
2000	Det A	150	523	75	139	25	3	7	51	69-0	6	79	.266	.357	.365	84	-11	11-5	.992	21	196	106	C150/123	0	1.9
2001	†Hou N	128	422	45	98	23	4	5	34	30-6	1	64	.232	.284	.341	57	-28	4-1	**.997**	15	151	124	C127	0	-0.4
2002	Hou N	130	447	57	115	19	3	6	50	38-3	6	71	.257	.322	.353	72	-17	2-3	.997	8	110	92	C129	0	-0.1
2003	Hou N	143	450	43	103	12	2	4	47	46-1	4	66	.229	.303	.291	54	-30	5-3	.997	25	97	124	C143	0	0.3
2004	†Hou N	129	403	38	100	14	1	5	31	33-11	2	56	.248	.306	.325	62	-23	2-2	.995	4	79	115	C128	0	-1.2
2005	†Hou N	134	387	35	100	19	0	3	47	51-8	5	48	.258	.351	.331	79	-10	5-3	**.999**	18	157	72	C134/2S	0	1.7
2006	Hou N	139	439	37	101	16	1	2	39	45-2	6	71	.230	.308	.285	53	-31	3-1	**.998**	10	126	59	C138,2b2/1	0	-1.1
Total	14	1716	5556	652	1408	240	31	73	547	560-62	58	883	.253	.326	.347	74	-203	95-50	.994	116	131	103	C1696,2b4,1b4/S3	0	2.3
Austin, Henry	Henry C.; B10.1844 New York NY; D11.2.1904 Amityville NY; d4.28																								
1873	Res NA	**23**	101	10	25	3	3	0	11	0	—	5	.248	.248	.337	77	-2	1-1	.722	-1	114	251	O23(0/14/9)	—	-0.2
Austin, Jimmy	James Philip "Pepper"; B12.8.1879 Swansea, Wales; D3.6.1965 Laguna Beach CA; BB/TR/5´7.5˝/155; d4.19; M3/C18																								
1909	NY A	136	437	37	101	11	5	1	39	32	1	—	.231	.285	.286	80	-11	30	.928	13	105	**134**	3b111,S23/2	—	0.7
1910	NY A	133	432	46	94	11	4	2	36	47	7	—	.218	.305	.275	77	-10	22	.942	3	98	54	3b133	—	-0.4
1911	StL A	148	541	84	141	25	11	2	45	69	6	—	.261	.351	.359	102	3	26	.931	19	**116**	123	3b148	—	2.5

YEAR	TM LG	G	AB	R	H	2B	3B	HR	RBI	BB-IB	HP	SO	AVG	OBP	SLG	AOPS	ABR	SB-CS	FA	FR	RNG	THR	GAMES AT POSITION	DL	BFW
1912	StL A	149	536	57	135	14	8	2	44	38	4	—	.252	.306	.319	82	-14	28	.911	2	98	104	3b149	—	-0.9
1913	StL A	142	489	56	130	18	6	2	42	45	8	51	.266	.338	.339	101	1	37	**.944**	6	104	101	3b142,M	—	1.2
1914	StL A	130	466	55	111	16	4	0	30	40	1	59	.238	.300	.290	80	-12	20-23	.935	-1	99	98	3b127	—	-1.4
1915	StL A	141	477	61	127	6	6	1	30	64	2	60	.266	.355	.310	103	4	18-15	.917	10	104	**143**	3b141	—	1.7
1916	StL A	129	411	55	85	15	6	1	28	74	4	59	.207	.333	.280	89	-2	19	.939	-8	102	91	3b124	—	-0.8
1917	StL A	127	455	61	109	18	8	0	19	50	3	46	.240	.319	.314	97	-1	13	.947	7	102	118	3b121,S6	—	1.0
1918	StL A	110	367	42	97	14	4	0	20	53	1	32	.264	.359	.324	109	6	18	.939	-15	88	59	S57,3b48,M	—	-0.4
1919	StL A	106	396	54	94	9	9	1	21	42	2	31	.237	.314	.313	74	-14	8	.939	6	101	95	3b98	—	-0.5
1920	StL A	83	280	38	76	11	3	1	32	31	4	15	.271	.352	.343	82	-6	2-4	.943	0	96	106	3b75	—	-0.5
1921	StL A	27	66	8	18	2	1	0	2	4	1	7	.273	.324	.333	64	-4	2-1	.938	-2	87	0	S14,2b6,3b2	—	-0.4
1922	StL A	15	31	6	9	3	1	0	1	3	0	2	.290	.353	.452	105	0	0-0	.957	-2	62	0	3b9,2b2	—	-0.1
1923	StL A	1	0	0	0	0	0	0	0	0	0	0	ø	ø	ø	ø	0	0-0	ø	0	—	—	/RM	—	0.0
1925	StL A	1	1	0	0	0	0	0	0	0	0	0	.000	.000	.000	-95	0	0-0	1.000	-0	0	0	/3	—	0.0
1926	StL A	1	2	1	1	1	0	0	1	0	0	0	.500	.500	1.000	272	1	1-0	1.000	0	80	955	/3	—	0.1
1929	StL A	1	1	0	0	0	0	0	0	0	0	1	.000	.000	.000	-96	0	0-0	1.000	0	236	0	/3	—	0.0
Total	18	1580	5388	661	1328	174	76	13	390	592	44	363	.246	.326	.314	90	-59	244-43	.933	38	102	105	3b1431,S100,2b9	—	1.8
AUTRY, CHICK	Martin Gordon; B3.5.1903 Martindale TX; D1.26.1950 Savannah GA; BR/TR/6´0˝/180; d4.20																								
1924	NY A	2	0	1	0	0	0	0	0	0	1	0	ø	1.000	ø	172	0	0-0	1.000	-0	*0*	*0*	C2	—	0.0
1926	Cle A	3	7	1	1	0	0	0	0	1	0	0	.143	.250	.143	4	-1	0-0	1.000	-0	*97*	*130*	C3	—	-0.1
1927	Cle A	16	43	5	11	4	1	0	7	0	0	6	.256	.256	.395	66	-2	0-0	.933	1	*133*	*167*	C14	—	0.0
1928	Cle A	22	60	6	18	6	1	1	9	1	0	7	.300	.311	.483	105	0	0-0	.972	0	*100*	*64*	C18	—	0.1
1929	Chi A	43	96	7	20	6	0	1	12	1	1	8	.208	.224	.302	35	-10	0-0	.940	-3	*98*	*78*	C30	—	-1.1
1930	Chi A	34	71	1	18	1	1	0	5	4	0	8	.254	.293	.296	52	-5	0-0	.992	4	*108*	*139*	C29	—	0.0
Total	6	120	277	21	68	17	3	2	33	7	2	29	.245	.269	.350	59	-18	0-0	.965	2	*107*	*109*	C96	—	-1.1
AUTRY, CHICK	William Askew; B1.2.1885 Humboldt TN; D1.16.1976 Santa Rosa CA; BL/TL/5´11˝/168; d9.18																								
1907	Cin N	7	25	3	5	0	0	0	0	1	0	—	.200	.231	.200	34	-2	0	.929	-1	0	0	O7(4/3/0)	—	-0.4
1909	Cin N	9	33	3	6	2	0	0	4	2	0	—	.182	.229	.242	46	-2	1	.956	0	152	71	1b9	—	-0.2
	Bos N	65	199	16	39	4	0	0	13	21	2	—	.196	.279	.216	51	-11	5	.994	4	125	88	1b61,O4(4/1/0)	—	-0.9
	Year	74	232	19	45	6	0	0	17	23	2	—	.194	.272	.220	51	-13	6	.989	5	129	86	1b70,O4(4/1/0)	—	-1.1
Total	2	81	257	22	50	6	0	0	17	24	2	—	.195	.269	.218	49	-15	6	.989	4	129	86	1b70,O11(8/4/0)	—	-1.5
AVEN, BRUCE	David Bruce; B3.4.1972 Orange TX; BR/TR/5´9˝/180; [CleA94 30/829]; d8.27; Col Lamar																								
1997	Cle A	13	19	4	4	1	0	0	2	1-0	0	5	.211	.250	.263	33	-2	0-1	1.000	1	125	268	O13(10/1/2)	0	-0.1
1999	Fla N	137	381	57	110	19	2	12	70	44-1	9	82	.289	.370	.444	113	8	3-0	.984	1	103	73	O102(78/9/24),D6	0	0.7
2000	Pit N	72	148	18	37	11	0	5	25	5-0	0	31	.250	.275	.426	73	-7	2-3	.980	-3	87	0	O41(17/8/20)	17	-1.0
	LA N	9	20	2	5	0	0	2	4	3-0	0	8	.250	.348	.550	128	1	0-0	1.000	-0	93	0	O9L	0	0.0
	Year	81	168	20	42	11	0	7	29	8-0	0	39	.250	.284	.440	80	-6	2-3	.984	-3	88	0	O50(26/8/20)	0	-1.0
2001	LA N	21	24	3	8	2	0	1	2	0-0	2	5	.333	.385	.542	145	2	0-0	1.000	-0	78	0	O9(5/0/4)	0	0.1
2002	Cle A	7	17	1	2	0	0	0	0	4-0	0	4	.118	.286	.118	13	-2	1-0	1.000	-0	106	0	O7(5/1/1)	0	-0.2
Total	5	259	609	85	166	33	2	20	103	57-1	11	135	.273	.343	.432	99	0	6-4	.986	-1	100	58	O181(124/19/51),D6	17	-0.5
AVERILL, EARL	Earl Douglas; B9.9.1931 Cleveland OH; BR/TR/5´10˝/(190–200); d4.19; f–Earl; Col Oregon																								
1956	Cle A	42	93	12	22	6	0	3	14	14-1	1	25	.237	.343	.398	93	-1	0-1	.994	2	*83*	*131*	C34	0	0.3
1958	Cle A	17	55	2	10	1	0	2	7	4-0	1	7	.182	.250	.309	54	-4	1-0	.863	-0	113	98	3b17	0	-0.4
1959	Chi N	74	186	22	44	10	0	10	34	15-1	2	39	.237	.298	.452	98	-1	0-1	.963	5	56	82	C32,3b13,O5L,2b2	0	0.5
1960	Chi N	52	102	14	24	4	0	1	13	11-1	1	16	.235	.310	.304	71	-4	1-1	.979	-2	58	52	C34/3lf	0	-0.5
	Chi A	10	14	2	3	0	0	0	2	4-0	0	2	.214	.389	.214	68	0	0-0	1.000	2	80	159	C5	0	0.2
1961	LA A	115	323	56	86	9	0	21	59	62-1	2	70	.266	.384	.489	119	10	1-0	.991	1	67	99	C88,O9L/2	0	1.5
1962	LA A	92	187	21	41	9	0	4	22	43-3	1	47	.219	.366	.332	93	0	0-0	1.000	-2	87	85	O49L,C6	0	-0.3
1963	Phi N	47	71	8	19	2	0	3	8	9-1	0	14	.268	.341	.423	123	2	0-0	.966	3	81	170	C20,O8L/13	0	0.6
Total	7	449	1031	137	249	41	0	44	159	162-8	8	220	.242	.346	.409	101	2	3-3	.984	10	*68*	*107*	C219,O72L,3b32,2b3/1	0	1.9
AVERILL, EARL	Howard Earl "Rock","The Earl of Snohomish"; B5.21.1902 Snohomish WA; D8.16.1983 Everett WA; BL/TR/5´9.5˝/172; d4.16; HF1975; s–Earl																								
1929	Cle A	**152**	597	110	198	43	13	18	96	63	3	53	.332	.398	.538	134	30	13-14	.966	-11	89	85	O152C	—	1.0
1930	Cle A	139	534	102	181	33	8	19	119	56	2	48	.339	.404	.537	131	26	10-7	.949	-4	94	111	O134(0/132/2)	—	1.4
1931	Cle A	**155**	627	140	209	36	10	32	143	68	6	38	.333	.404	.576	147	41	9-9	.976	-4	98	76	O155C	—	3.0
1932	Cle A	**153**	631	116	198	37	14	32	124	75	**6**	40	.314	.392	.569	137	33	5-8	.964	-7	94	90	O153C	—	1.8
1933	Cle A★	**151**	599	83	180	39	16	11	92	54	5	29	.301	.363	.474	115	12	3-1	.971	-4	100	74	O149C	—	0.4
1934	Cle A★	**154**	598	128	187	48	6	31	113	99	4	44	.313	.414	.569	149	46	5-3	.970	3	104	98	O154C	—	4.1
1935	Cle A✱	140	563	109	162	34	13	19	79	70	1	58	.288	.368	.496	119	15	8-4	.982	-7	96	55	O139C	—	0.5
1936	Cle A★	152	614	136	**232**	39	**15**	28	126	65	1	35	.378	.438	.627	159	55	3-3	.969	-7	93	86	O150C	—	3.8
1937	Cle A★	**156**	609	121	182	33	11	21	92	88	0	65	.299	.387	.493	119	18	5-4	.976	-12	88	77	O156C	—	0.2
1938	Cle A★	134	482	101	159	27	15	14	93	81	3	48	.330	.429	.535	143	34	5-2	.975	1	98	115	O131(0/118/13)	—	2.8
1939	Cle A	24	55	8	15	8	0	1	7	6	0	12	.273	.344	.473	111	1	0-1	1.000	-1	72	0	O11R	—	-0.1
	Det A	87	309	58	81	20	6	10	58	43	1	30	.262	.354	.463	100	-1	4-2	.976	-3	94	59	O80(75/5/0)	—	-0.7
	Year	111	364	66	96	28	6	11	65	49	1	42	.264	.353	.464	102	1	4-3	.977	-5	92	53	O91(75/5/11)	—	-0.8
1940	†Det A	64	118	10	33	4	1	2	20	5	0	14	.280	.309	.381	71	-5	0-0	.962	-1	69	190	O22(7/11/5)	—	-0.7
1941	Bos N	8	17	2	2	0	0	0	2	1	1	4	.118	.211	.118	-6	-2	0	1.000	1	70	879	O4(1/3/0)	0	-0.2
Total	13	1669	6353	1224	2019	401	128	238	1164	774	33	518	.318	.395	.534	132	303	70-58	.970	-57	95	87	O1590(83/1477/31)	0	17.3
AVILA, BOBBY	Roberto Francisco (Gonzalez); B4.2.1924 Veracruz, Veracruz, Mexico; D10.26.2004 Veracruz, Veracruz, Mexico; BR/TR/5´10˝/(171–175); d4.30																								
1949	Cle A	31	14	3	3	0	0	0	3	1	0	3	.214	.267	.214	29	-1	0-0	1.000	2	187	110	2b5	0	0.0
1950	Cle A	80	201	39	60	10	2	1	21	29	1	17	.299	.390	.383	102	2	5-0	.983	-9	80	108	2b62,S2	0	-0.3
1951	Cle A	141	542	76	165	21	3	10	58	60	0	31	.304	.374	.410	118	14	14-8	.982	-3	97	88	2b136	0	1.9
1952	Cle A★	150	597	102	179	26	**11**	7	45	67	1	36	.300	.371	.415	127	21	12-10	.966	-23	94	76	2b149	0	0.6
1953	Cle A	141	559	85	160	22	3	8	55	58	2	27	.286	.355	.379	101	1	10-8	**.986**	13	**107**	108	2b140	0	2.3
1954	†Cle A★	143	555	112	189	27	2	15	67	59	1	31	**.341**	.402	.477	139	30	9-7	.976	7	**106**	**114**	2b141,S7	0	4.8
1955	Cle A★	141	537	83	146	22	4	13	61	82-1	2	47	.272	.368	.400	103	5	1-4	.982	-2	91	107	2b141	0	1.2
1956	Cle A	138	513	74	115	14	2	10	54	70-0	5	68	.224	.323	.318	68	-23	17-4	.977	-2	97	91	2b135	0	-1.3
1957	Cle A	129	463	60	124	19	3	5	48	46-2	1	47	.268	.334	.354	89	-6	2-4	.983	-10	92	87	2b107,3b16	0	-1.0
1958	Cle A	113	375	54	95	21	3	5	30	55-0	1	45	.253	.349	.365	100	2	5-7	.986	-6	92	106	2b82,3b33	0	0.0
1959	Bal A	20	47	1	8	0	0	0	0	4-0	0	5	.170	.235	.170	14	-6	0-0	1.000	-1	95	0	O10(1/0/9),2b8/3	0	-0.7
	Bos A	22	45	7	11	0	0	3	6	6-0	0	11	.244	.333	.444	107	0	0-0	.975	-4	72	109	2b11	0	-0.3
	Year	42	92	8	19	0	0	3	6	10-0	0	16	.207	.284	.304	61	-5	0-0	.967	-5	101	73	2b19,O10(1/0/9)/3	0	-1.0
	Mil N	51	172	29	41	3	2	3	19	24-0	0	31	.238	.330	.331	84	-4	3-0	.967	-4	101	73	2b51	0	-0.4
Total	11	1300	4620	725	1296	185	35	80	467	561-3	14	399	.281	.359	.388	104	35	78-52	.979	-42	97	96	2b1168,3b50,O10(1/0/9),S9	0	6.8
AVILES, RAMON	Ramon Antonio (Miranda); B1.22.1952 Manati, PR; BR/TR/5´9˝/155; d7.10																								
1977	Bos A	1	0	0	0	0	0	0	0	0-0	0	0	ø	ø	ø	ø	0	0-0	1.000	0	137	0	/2	0	0.0
1979	Phi N	27	61	7	17	2	0	0	12	8-1	1	8	.279	.371	.311	85	-1	0-0	.977	-6	80	66	2b27	0	-0.6
1980	†Phi N	51	101	12	28	6	0	2	9	10-2	0	9	.277	.336	.396	99	0	0-0	.944	-6	87	112	S29,2b15	0	-0.4
1981	†Phi N	38	28	2	6	1	0	0	3	3-0	0	5	.214	.290	.250	51	-2	0-0	1.000	1	118	90	2b20,3b13,S5	0	-0.1
Total	4	117	190	21	51	9	0	2	24	21-3	1	22	.268	.341	.347	88	-3	0-0	.971	-12	83	89	2b63,S34,3b13	0	-1.1
AYALA, BENNY	Benigno (Felix); B2.7.1951 Yauco, PR; BR/TR/6´1˝/(175–195); d8.27																								
1974	NY N	23	68	9	16	1	0	2	8	7-0	1	17	.235	.308	.338	83	-2	0-0	.927	-0	105	76	O20(18/0/2)	0	-0.3
1976	NY N	22	26	2	3	0	0	1	2	2-0	0	6	.115	.179	.231	16	-3	0-1	.889	1	111	410	O7(4/0/3)	0	-0.3
1977	StL N	1	3	0	1	0	0	0	0	0-0	0	1	.333	.333	.333	80	0	0-0	1.000	2	329	1378	/rf	0	0.2
1979	†Bal A	42	86	15	22	5	0	6	13	6-1	0	9	.256	.298	.523	123	2	0-0	.974	-0	116	0	O24(23/1/1),D10	0	0.1
1980	Bal A	76	170	28	45	8	1	10	33	19-3	0	21	.265	.335	.500	129	6	0-0	1.000	0	79	221	D41,O19(16/1/2)	0	0.5
1981	Bal A	44	86	12	24	2	0	3	13	11-0	1	9	.279	.364	.407	123	3	0-1	1.000	2	109	2196	D27,O4L	0	0.3
1982	Bal A	64	128	17	39	6	0	6	24	5-2	0	14	.305	.331	.492	123	4	1-1	.972	-1	103	0	O25L,D17,1b3	0	0.1
1983	†Bal A	47	104	12	23	7	0	4	13	9-0	0	18	.221	.278	.404	88	-2	0-0	.953	-1	101	0	O24(19/0/5),D11	0	-0.4

YEAR	TM LG	G	AB	R	H	2B	3B	HR	RBI	BB-IB	HP	SO	AVG	OBP	SLG	AOPS	ABR	SB-CS	FA	FR	RNG	THR	GAMES AT POSITION	DL	BFW
1984	Bal A	60	118	9	25	6	0	4	24	8-0	0	24	.212	.258	.364	72	-5	1-1	1.000	-1	74	0	D34,O13(11/0/2)	0	-0.7
1985	Cle A	46	76	10	19	7	0	2	15	4-1	0	17	.250	.284	.421	91	-1	0-0	.917	-1	86	132	O20L,D3	0	-0.2
Total	10	425	865	114	217	42	1	38	145	71-7	2	136	.251	.305	.434	104	2	2-4	.958	-1	101	106	O157(140/2/16),D143,1b3	0	-0.7
AYBAR, ERICK	Erick Johan; B1.14.1984 Bani, D.R.; BB/TR/5´10˝/170; d5.16; b–Willy																								
2006	LA A	34	40	5	10	1	1	0	2	0-0	0	8	.250	.250	.325	49	-3	1-0	.897	-1	91	114	S19,2b3,D5	0	-0.3
AYBAR, WILLY	Willy Del Jesus; B3.8.1983 Bani, D.R.; BB/TR/6´0˝/(175–200); d8.31; b–Erick																								
2005	LA N	26	86	12	28	8	0	1	10	18-0	1	11	.326	.448	.453	136	6	3-1	.962	-2	94	84	3b20,2b6	0	0.4
2006	LA N	43	128	15	32	12	0	3	22	18-0	3	17	.250	.356	.414	96	0	1-0	.922	3	108	44	3b29,2b15	0	0.4
	Atl N	36	115	17	36	6	0	1	8	10-0	1	19	.313	.373	.391	95	0	0-2	.947	-6	77	74	3b32	20	-0.7
	Year	79	243	32	68	18	0	4	30	28-0	4	36	.280	.364	.403	96	0	1-2	.934	-3	92	60	3b61,2b15	0	-0.3
Total	2	105	329	44	96	26	0	5	40	46-0	5	47	.292	.387	.416	106	6	4-3	.943	-5	92	67	3b81,2b21	20	0.1
AYLWARD, DICK	Richard John "Dandy"; B6.4.1925 Baltimore MD; D6.11.1983 Spring Valley CA; BR/TR/6´0˝/190; d5.1																								
1953	Cle A	4	3	0	0	0	0	0	0	0	0	1	.000	.000	.000	-99	-1	0-0	1.000	0	*0*	*0*	C4	0	-0.1
AYRAULT, JOE	Joseph Allen; B10.8.1971 Rochester MI; BR/TR/6´3˝/190; [AtlN90 5/129]; d9.1																								
1996	Atl N	7	5	0	1	0	0	0	0	0-0	1	1	.200	.333	.200	42	0	0-0	1.000	-0	0	0	C7	0	-0.1
AZCUE, JOE	Jose Joaquin (Lopez); B8.18.1939 Cienfuegos, Cuba; BR/TR/6´0˝/(195–200); d8.3																								
1960	Cin N	14	31	1	3	0	0	0	3	2-0	0	6	.097	.152	.097	-30	-6	0-1	1.000	5	108	132	C14	0	-0.1
1962	KC A	72	223	18	51	9	1	2	25	17-7	3	27	.229	.287	.305	58	-13	1-0	.985	4	90	126	C70	36	-0.6
1963	KC A	2	4	0	0	0	0	0	0	0-0	0	1	.000	.000	.000	-95	-1	0-0	1.000	0	0	0	/C	0	-0.1
	Cle A	94	320	26	91	16	0	14	46	15-1	0	46	.284	.314	.466	117	6	1-1	.992	6	111	138	C91	0	1.7
	Year	96	324	26	91	16	0	14	46	15-1	0	47	.281	.310	.460	114	5	1-1	.992	6	110	**137**	C92	0	1.6
1964	Cle A	83	271	20	74	9	1	4	34	16-2	2	38	.273	.314	.358	88	-5	0-2	.993	-4	101	117	C76	0	-0.6
1965	Cle A	111	335	16	77	7	0	2	35	27-8	3	54	.230	.290	.269	60	-17	2-1	.994	6	132	95	C108	0	-0.7
1966	Cle A	98	302	22	83	10	1	9	37	20-5	2	22	.275	.319	.404	108	3	0-2	.989	-3	**232**	120	C97	0	0.3
1967	Cle A	86	295	33	74	12	5	11	34	22-0	3	35	.251	.307	.437	117	5	0-3	**.999**	8	**184**	93	C86	0	1.8
1968	Cle A★	115	357	23	100	10	0	4	42	28-5	0	33	.280	.331	.342	106	3	1-1	**.996**	14	**177**	92	C97	0	2.4
1969	Cle A	7	24	1	7	0	0	1	1	4-0	0	3	.292	.393	.417	123	1	0-0	.980	1	118	100	C6	0	0.2
	Bos A	19	51	7	11	2	0	0	3	4-1	0	5	.216	.273	.255	46	-4	0-0	.981	3	205	114	C19	0	0.0
	Cal A	80	248	15	54	6	0	1	19	27-11	2	28	.218	.295	.254	59	-13	0-1	.992	9	128	111	C80	0	-0.1
	Year	106	323	23	72	8	0	2	23	35-12	2	36	.223	.299	.266	62	-16	0-1	.989	13	139	111	C105	0	0.1
1970	Cal A	114	351	19	85	13	1	2	25	24-4	2	40	.242	.292	.302	67	-16	0-0	.991	-4	105	81	C112	0	-1.6
1972	Cal A	3	2	0	0	0	0	0	0	0-0	0	1	.000	.000	.000	-99	-1	0-0	1.000	1	0	0	C2	0	0.0
	Mil A	11	14	0	2	0	0	0	0	1-1	0	5	.143	.200	.143	3	-2	0-0	1.000	1	98	250	C9	0	-0.1
	Year	14	16	0	2	0	0	0	0	1-1	0	6	.125	.176	.125	-9	-2	0-0	1.000	1	93	238	C11	0	-0.1
Total	11	909	2828	201	712	94	9	50	304	207-45	17	344	.252	.304	.344	85	-60	5-12	.992	46	142	108	C868	36	2.5
AZOCAR, OSCAR	Oscar Gregorio (Azocar); B2.21.1965 Soro, Sucre, Venez.; BL/TL/6´1˝/(170–195); d7.17																								
1990	NY A	65	214	18	53	8	0	5	19	2-0	1	15	.248	.257	.355	69	-10	7-0	.991	1	99	117	O57(47/0/12)/D	0	-1.0
1991	SD N	38	57	5	14	2	0	0	9	1-1	1	9	.246	.267	.281	54	-4	2-0	.875	-1	84	0	O13(12/0/1)/1	0	-0.5
1992	SD N	99	168	15	32	6	0	0	8	9-1	0	12	.190	.230	.226	30	-16	1-0	.942	0	111	68	O37(31/0/6)	0	-1.8
Total	3	202	439	38	99	16	0	5	36	12-2	2	36	.226	.248	.296	52	-30	10-0	.964	-0	102	90	O107(90/0/19)/1D	0	-3.3
BABB, CHARLIE	Charles Amos; B2.20.1873 Milwaukie OR; D3.19.1954 Portland OR; BB/TR/5´10˝/165; d4.17																								
1903	NY N	121	424	68	105	15	8	0	46	45	**22**	—	.248	.350	.321	88	-4	22	.912	-7	93	93	S113,3b8	—	-0.7
1904	Bro N	151	521	49	138	18	3	0	53	53	11	—	.265	.345	.311	106	7	34	.927	-2	97	81	S151	—	1.0
1905	Bro N	75	235	27	44	8	2	0	17	27	12	—	.187	.303	.238	67	-7	10	.923	-3	104	51	S36,1b31,3b5,2b2	—	-1.0
Total	3	347	1180	144	287	41	13	0	116	125	45	—	.243	.339	.300	92	-4	66	.921	-12	96	82	S300,1b31,3b13,2b2	—	-0.7
BABE, LOREN	Loren Rolland "Bee Bee"; B1.11.1928 Pisgah IA; D2.14.1984 Omaha NE; BL/TR/5´10˝/180; d8.19; C4																								
1952	NY A	12	21	1	2	1	0	0	0	4	0	4	.095	.240	.143	9	-3	1-0	.909	1	132	233	3b9	0	-0.1
1953	NY A	5	18	2	6	1	0	2	6	0	0	2	.333	.333	.722	185	2	0-0	.920	2	124	242	3b5	0	0.3
	Phi A	103	343	34	77	16	2	0	20	35	2	20	.224	.300	.283	56	-21	0-1	.950	0	100	108	3b93/S	0	-2.1
	Year	108	361	36	83	17	2	2	26	35	2	22	.230	.302	.305	62	-19	0-1	.948	2	101	116	3b98/S	0	-1.8
Total	2	120	382	37	85	18	2	2	26	39	2	26	.223	.298	.296	59	-22	1-1	.946	3	103	123	3b107/S	0	-1.9
BABINGTON, CHARLIE	Charles Percy; B5.4.1895 Cranston RI; D3.22.1957 Providence RI; BR/TR/6´0˝/170; d7.20; Col Brown																								
1915	NY N	28	33	5	8	3	1	0	2	0	1	4	.242	.265	.394	104	0	1	.909	-1	94	0	O12(2/11/1)/1	—	-0.1
BABITT, SHOOTY	Mack Neal; B3.9.1959 Oakland CA; BR/TR/5´8˝/174; [OakA77 25/623]; d4.9																								
1981	Oak A	54	156	10	40	1	3	0	14	13-1	0	13	.256	.314	.301	81	-4	5-4	.972	-21	81	38	2b52	0	-2.5
BACKMAN, WALLY	Walter Wayne; B9.22.1959 Hillsboro OR; BB/TR/5´9˝/(160–168); [NYN77 1/16]; d9.2																								
1980	NY N	27	93	12	30	1	1	0	9	11-1	1	14	.323	.396	.355	114	2	2-3	1.000	-9	73	58	2b20,S8	0	-0.6
1981	NY N	26	36	5	10	2	0	0	0	4-0	0	7	.278	.350	.333	95	0	1-0	.946	-1	102	49	2b11/3	0	0.0
1982	NY N	96	261	37	71	13	2	3	22	49-1	0	47	.272	.387	.372	113	7	8-7	.964	-4	98	68	2b88,3b6/S	24	0.7
1983	NY N	26	42	6	7	0	1	0	3	2-0	0	8	.167	.205	.214	16	-5	0-0	1.000	-2	75	58	2b14,3b2	0	-0.8
1984	NY N	128	436	68	122	19	2	1	26	56-2	0	63	.280	.360	.339	99	2	32-9	.981	-6	89	106	2b115,S8	0	0.7
1985	NY N	145	520	77	142	24	5	1	38	36-1	1	72	.273	.320	.344	88	-9	30-12	**.989**	-11	93	96	2b140/S	0	-1.1
1986	†NY N	124	387	67	124	18	2	1	27	36-1	0	32	.320	.376	.385	113	8	13-7	.966	-2	101	103	2b113	0	1.3
1987	NY N	94	300	43	75	6	1	1	23	25-0	0	43	.250	.307	.287	61	-17	11-3	.983	-9	94	95	2b87	20	-2.1
1988	†NY N	99	294	44	89	12	0	0	17	41-1	1	49	.303	.388	.344	117	9	9-5	.989	-9	92	83	2b92	15	0.2
1989	Min A	87	299	33	69	9	2	1	26	32-0	1	45	.231	.306	.284	63	-14	1-1	.982	-17	87	73	2b84/D	53	-3.0
1990	†Pit N	104	315	62	92	21	3	2	28	42-1	1	53	.292	.374	.397	117	9	6-3	.920	-11	89	63	3b71,2b15	0	-0.1
1991	Phi N	94	185	20	45	12	0	0	15	30-0	0	30	.243	.344	.308	87	-2	3-2	.981	-11	71	84	2b36,3b20	0	-1.3
1992	Phi N	42	48	6	13	1	0	0	6	6-1	0	9	.271	.352	.292	84	-1	1-0	.968	4	167	157	2b10,3b2	61	0.3
1993	Sea A	10	29	2	4	0	0	0	0	1-0	0	8	.138	.167	.138	-17	-5	0-0	.857	-1	100	0	3b9/2	16	-0.6
Total	14	1102	3245	482	893	138	19	10	240	371-9	5	480	.275	.349	.339	94	-16	117-52	.980	-88	92	90	2b826,3b111,S18/D	189	-6.4
BACON, EDDIE	Edgar Suter; B4.8.1895 Frankfort KY; D10.2.1963 Louisville KY; d8.13																								
1917	Phi A	4	6	1	3	1	0	0	2	0	0	0	.500	.500	.667	259	1	0	1.000	1	404	0	/P	—	0.0
BADER, ART	Arthur Herman; B9.21.1886 St.Louis MO; D4.5.1957 St.Louis MO; BR/TR/5´9˝/160; d8.2																								
1904	StL A	2	3	0	0	0	0	0	0	1	0	—	.000	.250	.000	-19	0	0	1.000	1	1002	0	/lf	—	0.0
BADGRO, RED	Morris Hiram; B12.1.1902 Orillia WA; D7.13.1998 Kent WA; BL/TR/6´0˝/190; d6.20; Col USC																								
1929	StL A	54	148	27	42	12	0	1	18	11	2	15	.284	.342	.385	84	-3	1-0	.983	-2	96	30	O37R	—	-0.7
1930	StL A	89	234	30	56	18	3	1	27	13	2	27	.239	.285	.355	59	-15	3-5	.952	-0	89	154	O61(4/14/43)	—	-1.9
Total	2	143	382	57	98	30	3	2	45	24	4	42	.257	.307	.366	69	-18	4-5	.962	-3	91	111	O98(4/14/80)	—	-2.6
BAERGA, CARLOS	Carlos Obed (Ortiz); B11.4.1968 Santurce, PR; BB/TR/5´11˝/(165–220); d4.14																								
1990	Cle A	108	312	46	81	17	2	7	47	16-2	4	57	.260	.300	.394	94	-3	0-2	.944	-5	112	108	3b50,S48,2b8	0	-0.8
1991	Cle A	158	593	80	171	28	2	11	69	48-5	6	74	.288	.346	.398	105	4	3-2	.944	17	114	88	3b89,2b75,S2	0	2.3
1992	Cle A★	161	657	92	205	32	1	20	105	35-10	13	76	.312	.354	.455	128	23	10-2	.979	8	99	**121**	2b160/D	0	3.7
1993	Cle A★	154	624	105	200	28	6	21	114	34-7	6	68	.321	.355	.486	125	20	15-4	.979	8	102	103	2b150,D4	0	3.5
1994	Cle A	103	442	81	139	32	2	19	80	10-1	6	45	.314	.333	.525	117	9	8-2	.973	4	104	101	2b102/D	0	1.8
1995	†Cle A★	135	557	87	175	28	2	15	90	35-6	3	31	.314	.355	.452	107	5	11-2	.973	10	107	121	2b134/D	0	2.1
1996	Cle A	100	424	54	113	25	0	10	55	16-0	7	25	.267	.302	.396	75	-17	1-1	.971	-1	101	96	2b100	0	-1.2
	NY N	26	83	5	16	3	0	2	11	5-0	2	2	.193	.253	.301	49	-7	0-0	.990	-4	49	72	1b16,3b6/2	0	-1.1
1997	NY N	133	467	53	131	25	1	9	52	20-1	3	54	.281	.311	.396	89	-9	2-6	.978	1	105	**122**	2b131	0	-0.4
1998	NY N	147	511	46	136	27	1	7	53	24-6	6	55	.266	.303	.364	78	-17	0-1	.986	-9	90	118	2b144	0	-2.0
1999	SD N	33	80	6	20	1	0	2	5	6-0	2	14	.250	.318	.338	71	-4	1-0	1.000	-3	85	136	2b13,3b13,1b2/D	0	-0.6
	Cle A	22	57	4	13	0	0	1	5	4-1	0	10	.228	.274	.281	41	-5	1-1	.964	-1	88	50	3b15,2b6/D	0	-0.6

YEAR	TM LG	G	AB	R	H	2B	3B	HR	RBI	BB-IB	HP	SO	AVG	OBP	SLG	AOPS	ABR	SB-CS	FA	FR	RNG	THR	GAMES AT POSITION	DL	BFW
2002	Bos A	73	182	17	52	11	0	2	19	7-1	2	20	.286	.316	.379	83	-4	6-0	.983	2	109	68	D32,2b17/3	24	-0.2
2003	Ari N	105	207	31	71	13	0	4	39	18-1	2	20	.343	.396	.464	115	6	1-1	.985	1	88	110	1b19,2b15,3b5,D6	0	0.6
2004	Ari N	79	85	6	20	2	0	2	11	6-0	3	12	.235	.309	.329	61	-5	0-0	1.000	1	155	55	1b6,D2	39	-0.5
2005	Was N	93	158	18	40	7	0	2	19	7-0	8	17	.253	.318	.335	75	-6	0-0	.920	-4	76	46	3b20,1b11,2b7/D	0	-1.0
Total	14	1630	5439	731	1583	279	17	134	774	291-41	73	580	.291	.332	.423	100	-10	59-24	.976	25	102	113	2b1063,3b199,1b54,D50,S50	63	5.6

BAEZ, JOSE Jose Antonio (b Jose Antonio Mota (Baez)); B12.31.1953 San Cristobal, D.R.; BR/TR/5´8˝/150; d4.6

YEAR	TM LG	G	AB	R	H	2B	3B	HR	RBI	BB-IB	HP	SO	AVG	OBP	SLG	AOPS	ABR	SB-CS	FA	FR	RNG	THR	GAMES AT POSITION	DL	BFW
1977	Sea A	91	305	39	79	14	1	1	17	19-1	1	20	.259	.305	.321	71	-12	6-1	.973	12	112	109	2b77/3D	0	0.5
1978	Sea A	23	50	8	8	0	1	0	2	6-1	0	7	.160	.250	.200	28	-5	1-0	.978	9	144	209	2b14,3b3/D	0	0.5
Total	2	114	355	47	87	14	2	1	19	25-2	1	27	.245	.297	.304	65	-17	7-1	.974	21	116	123	2b91,D4,3b4	0	1.0

BAEZ, KEVIN Kevin Richard; B1.10.1967 Brooklyn NY; BR/TR/6´0˝/(160–170); [NYN88 7/182]; d9.3; Col Dominican

YEAR	TM LG	G	AB	R	H	2B	3B	HR	RBI	BB-IB	HP	SO	AVG	OBP	SLG	AOPS	ABR	SB-CS	FA	FR	RNG	THR	GAMES AT POSITION	DL	BFW
1990	NY N	5	12	0	2	1	0	0	0	0-0	0	0	.167	.167	.250	13	-1	0-0	1.000	-0	79	66	S4	0	-0.2
1992	NY N	6	13	0	2	0	0	0	0	0-0	0	0	.154	.154	.154	-13	-2	0-0	.889	-0	98	95	S5	17	-0.2
1993	NY N	52	126	10	23	9	0	0	7	13-1	0	17	.183	.259	.254	38	-11	0-0	.967	-3	98	103	S52	0	-1.1
Total	3	63	151	10	27	10	0	0	7	13-1	0	17	.179	.244	.245	33	-14	0-0	.962	-3	97	100	S61	17	-1.5

BAGWELL, JEFF Jeffery Robert; B5.27.1968 Boston MA; BR/TR/6´0˝/(195–215); [BosA89 4/110]; d4.8; Col Hartford; [DL 2006 Hou N 182]

YEAR	TM LG	G	AB	R	H	2B	3B	HR	RBI	BB-IB	HP	SO	AVG	OBP	SLG	AOPS	ABR	SB-CS	FA	FR	RNG	THR	GAMES AT POSITION	DL	BFW
1991	Hou N	156	554	79	163	26	4	15	82	75-5	**13**	116	.294	.387	.437	140	33	7-4	.991	-4	89	89	1b155	0	1.8
1992	Hou N	**162**	586	87	160	34	6	18	96	84-13	12	97	.273	.368	.444	136	31	10-6	.995	4	107	95	1b159	0	2.6
1993	Hou N	142	535	76	171	37	4	20	88	62-6	3	73	.320	.388	.516	146	36	13-4	.993	4	106	103	1b140	0	2.9
1994	Hou N★	110	400	**104**	147	32	2	39	**116**	65-14	4	65	.368	.451	**.750**	**219**	**73**	15-4	.991	16	**148**	108	1b109/rf	0	**7.7**
1995	Hou N	114	448	88	130	29	0	21	87	79-12	6	102	.290	.399	.496	145	33	12-5	.994	**18**	**151**	84	1b114	32	4.0
1996	Hou N★	**162**	568	111	179	**48**	2	31	120	135-20	10	114	.315	.451	.570	182	79	21-7	.989	8	116	84	1b162	0	7.1
1997	†Hou N★	**162**	566	109	162	40	2	43	135	127-27	16	122	.286	.425	.592	170	65	31-10	.993	8	118	118	1b159/D	0	6.0
1998	†Hou N	147	540	124	164	33	1	34	111	109-8	7	90	.304	.424	.557	161	53	19-7	.995	11	125	102	1b147	15	5.1
1999	†Hou N★	**162**	562	**143**	171	35	0	42	126	**149**-16	11	127	.304	.454	.591	165	66	30-11	.994	3	102	**116**	1b161,D2	0	**5.3**
2000	Hou N	159	590	**152**	183	37	1	47	132	107-11	15	116	.310	.424	.615	148	47	9-6	.994	2	103	97	1b158/D	0	3.3
2001	†Hou N	161	600	126	173	43	4	39	130	106-5	6	135	.288	.397	.568	136	36	11-3	.992	15	**133**	101	1b160	0	3.6
2002	Hou N	158	571	94	166	33	2	31	98	101-8	10	130	.291	.401	.518	131	30	7-3	.995	6	110	93	1b153,D4	0	2.3
2003	Hou N	160	605	109	168	28	2	39	100	88-3	6	119	.278	.373	.524	124	23	11-4	.994	5	110	98	1b158	0	1.4
2004	†Hou N	156	572	104	152	29	2	27	89	96-6	8	131	.266	.377	.465	113	14	6-4	.995	0	93	90	1b152,D2	0	0.0
2005	†Hou N	39	100	11	25	4	0	3	19	18-1	1	21	.250	.358	.380	96	0	0-0	1.000	0	97	74	1b24	128	-0.2
Total	15	2150	7797	1517	2314	488	32	449	1529	1401-155	128	1558	.297	.408	.540	149	619	202-78	.993	96	114	98	1b2111,D10/rf	357	52.9

BAGWELL, BILL William Mallory "Big Bill"; B2.24.1895 Choudrant LA; D10.5.1976 Choudrant LA; BL/TL/6´1˝/175; d4.17

YEAR	TM LG	G	AB	R	H	2B	3B	HR	RBI	BB-IB	HP	SO	AVG	OBP	SLG	AOPS	ABR	SB-CS	FA	FR	RNG	THR	GAMES AT POSITION	DL	BFW
1923	Bos N	56	93	8	27	4	2	2	10	6	0	12	.290	.333	.441	107	0	0-0	1.000	0	105	71	O22L	—	0.0
1925	Phi A	36	50	4	15	2	1	0	10	2	0	2	.300	.327	.380	74	-2	0-0	.667	-1	34	0	O4L	—	-0.3
Total	2	92	143	12	42	6	3	2	20	8	0	14	.294	.331	.420	95	-2	0-0	.973	-1	94	60	O26L	—	-0.3

BAHRET, FRANK Frank F.; B1858 Poughkeepsie NY; D3.30.1888 Poughkeepsie NY; 6´1˝/184; d4.17

YEAR	TM LG	G	AB	R	H	2B	3B	HR	RBI	BB-IB	HP	SO	AVG	OBP	SLG	AOPS	ABR	SB-CS	FA	FR	RNG	THR	GAMES AT POSITION	DL	BFW
1884	Bal U	2	8	0	0	0	0	0	—	0	—	—	.000	.000	.000	-91	-2	—	1.000	-0	0	0	O2(0/1/1)	—	-0.2

BAILEY, GENE Arthur Eugene; B11.25.1893 Pearsall TX; D11.14.1973 Houston TX; BR/TR/5´8˝/160; d9.10; Mil 1918

YEAR	TM LG	G	AB	R	H	2B	3B	HR	RBI	BB-IB	HP	SO	AVG	OBP	SLG	AOPS	ABR	SB-CS	FA	FR	RNG	THR	GAMES AT POSITION	DL	BFW
1917	Phi A	5	12	1	1	0	0	0	0	1	0	1	.083	.154	.083	-28	-2	0	.833	-1	88	0	O4L	—	-0.3
1919	Bos N	4	6	0	2	0	0	0	1	0	0	2	.333	.333	.333	105	0	1	1.000	0	119	0	O3(0/1/1)	—	0.0
1920	Bos N	13	24	2	2	0	0	0	0	3	0	3	.083	.185	.083	-22	-4	0-1	.929	0	96	141	O8(5/4/1)	—	-0.5
	Bos A	46	135	14	31	2	0	0	5	9	1	15	.230	.283	.244	42	-11	2-7	.986	-1	97	70	O40(9/16/15)	—	-1.6
1923	Bro N	127	411	71	109	11	7	1	42	43	6	34	.265	.343	.333	81	-10	9-7	.959	-1	102	84	O100(25/60/17),1b5	—	-1.7
1924	Bro N	18	46	7	11	3	0	1	4	7	0	6	.239	.340	.370	93	0	1-0	1.000	1	109	117	O17(0/10/8)	—	0.0
Total	5	213	634	95	156	16	7	2	52	63	7	61	.246	.321	.303	69	-27	13-15	.965	-1	101	84	O172(43/91/42),1b5	—	-4.1

BAILEY, FRED Frederick Middleton "Penny"; B8.16.1895 Mt.Hope WV; D8.16.1972 Huntington WV; BL/TL/5´11˝/150; d8.19; Mil 1918; Col Washington and Lee

YEAR	TM LG	G	AB	R	H	2B	3B	HR	RBI	BB-IB	HP	SO	AVG	OBP	SLG	AOPS	ABR	SB-CS	FA	FR	RNG	THR	GAMES AT POSITION	DL	BFW
1916	Bos N	6	10	0	1	0	0	0	1	0	0	3	.100	.100	.100	-40	-2	0	1.000	-0	47	0	O2L	—	-0.2
1917	Bos N	50	110	9	21	2	1	1	5	9	3	25	.191	.270	.255	65	-4	3	.962	1	94	170	O27(9/15/4)	—	-0.6
1918	Bos N	4	4	1	1	0	0	0	0	0	0	1	.250	.250	.250	55	0	0	ø	0	—	—	/H	—	0.0
Total	3	60	124	10	23	2	1	1	6	9	3	29	.185	.257	.242	57	-6	3	.963	1	92	162	O29(10/15/4)	—	-0.8

BAILEY, BILL Harry Lewis; B11.19.1881 Shawnee OH; D10.27.1967 Seattle WA; BL/TR/5´10.5˝/170; d4.21

YEAR	TM LG	G	AB	R	H	2B	3B	HR	RBI	BB-IB	HP	SO	AVG	OBP	SLG	AOPS	ABR	SB-CS	FA	FR	RNG	THR	GAMES AT POSITION	DL	BFW
1911	NY A	5	9	1	1	0	0	0	0	0	0	—	.111	.111	.111	-36	-2	0	ø	0	0	0	O2/3	—	-0.1

BAILEY, MARK John Mark; B11.4.1961 Springfield MO; BB/TR/6´5˝/(195–200); [HouN82 6/147]; d4.27; C5; Col Missouri St.

YEAR	TM LG	G	AB	R	H	2B	3B	HR	RBI	BB-IB	HP	SO	AVG	OBP	SLG	AOPS	ABR	SB-CS	FA	FR	RNG	THR	GAMES AT POSITION	DL	BFW
1984	Hou N	108	344	38	73	16	1	9	34	53-4	2	71	.212	.318	.343	92	-2	0-1	.983	-4	83	97	C108	0	-0.2
1985	Hou N	114	332	47	88	14	0	10	45	67-13	1	70	.265	.389	.398	124	14	0-2	.979	-6	116	91	C110,1b2	0	1.3
1986	Hou N	57	153	9	27	5	0	4	15	28-6	0	45	.176	.302	.288	66	-7	1-1	.989	-0	80	131	C53/1	0	-0.5
1987	Hou N	35	64	5	13	1	0	0	3	10-0	0	21	.203	.311	.219	45	-5	1-0	.985	-1	84	119	C27	0	-0.5
1988	Hou N	8	23	1	3	0	0	0	0	5-0	0	6	.130	.286	.130	24	-2	0-1	.981	-0	87	80	C8	24	-0.3
1990	SF N	5	7	1	1	0	0	1	3	0-0	0	2	.143	.143	.571	90	0	0-0	1.000	0	0	0	/C	0	0.0
1992	SF N	13	26	0	4	1	0	0	1	3-0	0	7	.154	.241	.192	25	-3	0-0	1.000	-0	0	46	C7	31	-0.3
Total	7	340	949	101	209	37	1	24	101	166-23	3	222	.220	.337	.337	92	-5	2-5	.983	-11	93	100	C314,1b3	55	-0.5

BAILEY, ED Lonas Edgar; B4.15.1931 Strawberry Plains TN; BL/TR/6´2˝/(200–208); d9.26; b–Jim; Col Tennessee

YEAR	TM LG	G	AB	R	H	2B	3B	HR	RBI	BB-IB	HP	SO	AVG	OBP	SLG	AOPS	ABR	SB-CS	FA	FR	RNG	THR	GAMES AT POSITION	DL	BFW
1953	Cin N	2	8	1	3	1	0	0	1	1	0	3	.375	.444	.500	145	1	0-0	1.000	-1	*53*	*0*	C2	0	0.0
1954	Cin N	73	183	21	36	2	3	9	20	35	0	34	.197	.324	.388	83	-5	1-0	.973	-6	*167*	*84*	C61	0	-0.8
1955	Cin N	21	39	3	8	1	1	1	4	4-0	3	10	.205	.326	.359	77	-1	0-0	.962	2	*142*	*136*	C11	0	0.1
1956	Cin N★	118	383	59	115	8	2	28	75	52-11	3	50	.300	.385	.551	140	22	2-0	.984	1	*94*	*110*	C106	0	2.9
1957	Cin N★	122	391	54	102	15	2	20	48	73-9	2	69	.261	.377	.463	117	12	5-3	.991	-10	**167**	79	C115	0	0.8
1958	Cin N	112	360	39	90	23	1	11	59	47-10	1	61	.250	.337	.411	92	-3	2-2	.988	-3	**170**	88	C99	0	-0.1
1959	Cin N	121	379	43	100	13	0	12	40	62-6	2	53	.264	.370	.393	101	3	2-0	.990	7	186	113	C117	0	1.6
1960	Cin N★	133	441	52	115	19	3	13	67	59-9	2	70	.261	.346	.406	105	4	1-0	.990	-8	128	99	C129	0	0.3
1961	Cin N	12	43	4	13	4	0	0	2	3-1	0	5	.302	.348	.395	95	0	0-0	.967	-2	401	77	C12	0	-0.1
	SF N☆	107	340	39	81	9	1	13	51	42-6	4	41	.238	.324	.385	92	-4	1-5	.985	2	89	78	C103/lf	0	0.2
	Year	119	383	43	94	13	1	13	53	45-7	4	46	.245	.326	.386	93	-4	1-5	.984	1	121	78	C115/lf	0	0.1
1962	†SF N	96	254	32	59	9	1	17	45	42-5	6	42	.232	.351	.476	123	9	1-1	.987	-2	125	35	C75	0	1.0
1963	SF N★	105	308	41	81	8	0	21	68	50-11	1	64	.263	.366	.494	147	20	0-6	.987	-2	91	62	C88	0	2.2
1964	Mil N	95	271	30	71	10	1	5	34	34-2	1	39	.262	.343	.362	99	1	2-0	.982	-10	112	72	C80	0	-0.6
1965	SF N	24	28	1	3	0	0	0	3	6-1	0	7	.107	.250	.107	9	-3	0-0	1.000	3	275	127	C12,1b2	0	0.0
	Chi N	66	150	13	38	6	0	5	23	34-6	0	28	.253	.385	.393	119	6	0-1	.981	-4	74	71	C54,1b3	0	0.3
	Year	90	178	14	41	6	0	5	26	40-7	0	35	.230	.363	.348	102	2	0-1	.984	-1	98	78	C66,1b5	0	0.3
1966	Cal A	5	3	0	0	0	0	0	0	1-0	0	1	.000	.250	.000	-22	0	0-0	ø	0	—	—	/H	0	0.0
Total	14	1212	3581	432	915	128	15	155	540	545-77	25	577	.256	.355	.429	110	62	17-18	.986	-31	*134*	*85*	C1064,1b5/lf	0	7.8

BAILEY, BOB Robert Sherwood; B10.13.1942 Long Beach CA; BR/TR/6´0˝/(175–188); d9.14; OF(399/2/3)

YEAR	TM LG	G	AB	R	H	2B	3B	HR	RBI	BB-IB	HP	SO	AVG	OBP	SLG	AOPS	ABR	SB-CS	FA	FR	RNG	THR	GAMES AT POSITION	DL	BFW
1962	Pit N	14	42	6	7	2	1	0	6	6-0	0	10	.167	.271	.262	44	-3	1-1	.921	-0	105	89	3b12	0	-0.4
1963	Pit N	154	570	60	130	15	3	12	45	58-2	5	98	.228	.303	.328	82	-13	10-9	.933	12	113	**162**	3b153,S3	0	-0.3
1964	Pit N	143	530	73	149	26	3	11	51	44-1	1	78	.281	.336	.404	108	6	10-8	.943	8	114	117	3b105,O35(34/2/2),S2	0	1.2
1965	Pit N	159	626	87	160	28	3	11	49	70-1	0	93	.256	.330	.363	95	-3	10-14	.939	-13	95	118	3b142,O28L	0	-2.2
1966	Pit N	126	380	51	106	19	3	13	46	47-4	2	65	.279	.360	.447	123	13	5-3	.956	-4	103	109	3b96,O20L	0	0.9
1967	LA N	116	322	21	73	8	2	4	28	40-4	1	50	.227	.310	.301	84	-6	5-5	.941	-0	112	102	3b65,O27L,1b4/S	0	-1.0
1968	LA N	105	322	24	73	9	3	8	39	38-4	1	69	.227	.308	.348	105	2	1-2	.953	-5	90	87	3b90/Slf	0	-0.4
1969	Mon N	111	358	46	95	16	6	9	53	40-3	1	76	.265	.337	.419	111	5	3-3	.992	5	131	106	1b85,O12L/3	29	0.3
1970	Mon N	131	352	77	101	19	3	28	84	72-8	1	70	.287	.407	.597	166	35	5-3	.953	-2	95	62	3b48,O44L,1b18	0	2.9
1971	Mon N	157	545	65	137	21	4	14	83	97-8	0	105	.251	.359	.382	110	11	13-7	**.960**	-1	102	71	3b120,O51(51/0/1),1b9	0	0.8
1972	Mon N	143	489	55	114	10	4	16	57	59-7	1	112	.233	.315	.368	92	-5	6-7	.938	-1	103	97	3b134,O5L,1b3	0	-0.8
1973	Mon N	151	513	77	140	25	4	26	86	88-10	1	99	.273	.379	.489	134	26	5-8	.956	-1	102	88	3b146,O2L	0	2.4
1974	Mon N	152	507	69	142	20	2	20	73	100-9	1	107	.280	.396	.446	129	24	4-7	.974	-8	72	158	O78L,3b68	0	1.0

YEAR	TM LG	G	AB	R	H	2B	3B	HR	RBI	BB-IB	HP	SO	AVG	OBP	SLG	AOPS	ABR	SB-CS	FA	FR	RNG	THR	GAMES AT POSITION	DL	BFW
1975	Mon N	106	227	23	62	5	0	5	30	46-3	1	38	.273	.392	.361	106	4	4-4	.979	-1	89	103	O61L,3b3	20	0.0
1976	Cin N	69	124	17	37	6	1	6	23	16-1	0	26	.298	.376	.508	146	8	0-0	.974	-2	79	130	O31L,3b10	0	0.5
1977	Cin N	49	79	9	20	2	1	2	11	12-2	0	10	.253	.348	.380	94	0	1-1	.975	0	123	108	1b19,O3L	0	-0.2
	Bos A	2	2	0	0	0	0	0	0	0-0	0	1	.000	.000	.000	-90	-1	0-0	ø	0	—	—	/H	0	-0.1
1978	Bos A	43	94	12	18	3	0	4	9	19-0	1	19	.191	.328	.351	84	-2	2-1	1.000	0	109	0	D34/3lf	0	-0.2
Total	17	1931	6082	772	1564	234	43	189	773	852-67	17	1126	.257	.347	.403	110	101	85-83	.946	-13	103	104	3b1194,O399L,1b138,D34,S7	49	4.4
BAILOR, BOB	Robert Michael; B7.10.1951 Connellsville PA; BR/TR/5´11˝/(159–160); d9.6; C4; OF(79/105/254)																								
1975	Bal A	5	7	0	1	0	0	0	0	1-0	0	0	.143	.250	.143	14	-1	0-0	1.000	1	120	0	S2/2	0	0.0
1976	Bal A	9	6	2	2	0	1	0	0	0-0	0	0	.333	.333	.667	199	1	0-1	ø	-0	0	0	/SD	54	0.0
1977	Tor A	122	496	62	154	21	5	5	32	17-1	2	26	.310	.335	.403	99	-2	15-6	.988	5	102	226	O63(15/47/2),S53,D7	0	0.9
1978	Tor A	154	621	74	164	29	7	1	52	38-1	5	21	.264	.310	.338	81	-16	5-6	.964	11	109	165	O125(3/25/102),3b28,S4	0	-1.2
1979	Tor A	130	414	50	95	11	5	1	38	36-2	6	27	.229	.297	.287	59	-24	14-8	.987	5	96	**203**	O118(4/4/113),3b9/D	0	-2.3
1980	Tor A	117	347	44	82	14	2	1	16	36-3	2	33	.236	.311	.297	65	-16	12-8	.991	15	108	264	O98(41/28/33),S12,3b11,P3/2D	21	-0.3
1981	NY N	51	81	11	23	3	1	0	8	8-0	1	11	.284	.352	.346	100	0	2-0	.955	-2	99	66	S22,2b13,O13(10/0/3)/3	13	0.1
1982	NY N	110	376	44	104	14	1	0	31	20-0	2	17	.277	.313	.319	78	-11	20-3	.984	1	107	85	S60,2b56,3b21,O4(3/1/0)	0	-0.1
1983	NY N	118	340	33	85	8	0	1	30	20-2	1	23	.250	.290	.282	61	-18	18-3	.969	6	107	113	S75,2b50,3b11,O3(2/0/1)	16	-0.2
1984	LA N	65	131	11	36	4	0	0	8	8-1	0	1	.275	.317	.305	76	-4	3-1	.944	3	85	68	2b23,3b17,S16	65	0.1
1985	†LA N	74	118	8	29	3	1	0	7	3-0	1	5	.246	.270	.288	58	-7	1-0	.962	7	117	155	3b45,2b16,S5/lf	34	0.1
Total	11	955	2937	339	775	107	23	9	222	187-10	20	164	.264	.310	.325	76	-98	90-36	.980	54	105	207	O425R,S250,2b160,3b143,D10,P3	203	-2.9
BAINES, HAROLD	Harold Douglass; B3.15.1959 Easton MD; BL/TL/6´2˝/(175–215); [ChiA77 1/1]; d4.10; C3																								
1980	Chi A	141	491	55	125	23	6	13	49	19-7	1	65	.255	.281	.405	87	-11	2-4	.963	-9	88	62	O137R/D	0	-2.8
1981	Chi A	82	280	42	80	11	7	10	41	12-4	2	41	.286	.318	.482	130	9	6-2	.985	-0	82	197	O80R/D	0	0.5
1982	Chi A	161	608	89	165	29	8	25	105	49-10	0	95	.271	.321	.469	115	10	10-3	.980	-4	97	86	O161(1/3/160)	0	-0.1
1983	†Chi A	156	596	76	167	33	2	20	99	49-13	1	85	.280	.333	.443	108	6	7-5	.973	-4	97	88	O155(1/20/142)	0	-0.6
1984	Chi A	147	569	72	173	28	10	29	94	54-9	0	75	.304	.361	**.541**	140	29	1-2	.981	-2	100	87	O147(0/7/147)	0	1.9
1985	Chi A★	160	640	86	198	29	3	22	113	42-8	1	89	.309	.348	.467	117	14	1-1	.994	1	101	78	O159R/D	0	0.6
1986	Chi A★	145	570	72	169	29	2	21	88	38-9	2	89	.296	.338	.465	113	9	2-1	.984	8	105	153	O141R,D3	0	0.9
1987	Chi A★	132	505	59	148	26	4	20	93	46-2	1	82	.293	.352	.479	115	10	0-0	1.000	-1	83	0	D117,O8R	31	0.5
1988	Chi A	158	599	55	166	39	1	13	81	67-14	1	109	.277	.347	.411	113	12	0-0	.882	-1	67	167	D147,O9R	0	0.6
1989	Chi A★	96	333	55	107	20	1	13	56	60-13	1	52	.321	.423	.505	164	32	0-1	.981	-0	112	0	D70,O25R	0	2.9
	Tex A	50	172	18	49	9	0	3	16	13-0	0	27	.285	.333	.390	102	0	0-2	.667	-0	111	0	D46/rf	0	-0.2
	Year	146	505	73	156	29	1	16	72	73-13	1	79	.309	.395	.465	143	32	0-3	.964	-0	112	0	D116,O26R	0	2.7
1990	Tex A	103	321	41	93	10	1	13	44	47-9	0	63	.290	.377	.449	130	14	0-1	.833	0	181	0	D95,O2R	0	1.1
	†Oak A	32	94	11	25	5	0	3	21	20-1	0	17	.266	.381	.415	131	5	0-2	ø	0	0	0	D30	0	0.4
	Year	135	415	52	118	15	1	16	65	67-10	0	80	.284	.378	.441	131	19	0-3	.767	0	181	0	D125,O2R	0	1.5
1991	Oak A★	141	488	76	144	25	1	20	90	72-22	1	67	.295	.383	.473	144	32	0-1	.923	-0	77	198	D125,O12(1/0/10)	0	2.6
1992	†Oak A	140	478	58	121	18	0	16	76	59-6	0	61	.253	.331	.391	108	5	1-3	.964	-2	84	0	D116,O23(6/0/17)	0	-0.2
1993	Bal A	118	416	64	130	22	0	20	78	57-9	0	52	.313	.390	.510	135	22	0-0	ø	0	0	0	D116	22	1.5
1994	Bal A	94	326	44	96	12	1	16	54	30-6	1	49	.294	.356	.485	108	3	0-0	ø	0	0	0	D91	0	-0.2
1995	Bal A	127	385	60	115	19	1	24	63	70-13	0	45	.299	.403	.540	141	25	0-2	ø	0	0	0	D122	0	1.7
1996	Chi A	143	495	80	154	29	0	22	95	73-7	1	62	.311	.399	.503	132	27	3-1	ø	0	0	0	D141	0	1.8
1997	Chi A	93	318	40	97	18	0	12	52	41-10	0	47	.305	.382	.475	127	14	0-1	ø	0	0	0	D86	0	0.8
	†Bal A	44	134	15	39	5	0	4	15	14-1	0	15	.291	.356	.418	105	1	0-0	ø	-0	0	0	D35/rf	0	-0.1
	Year	137	452	55	136	23	0	16	67	55-11	0	62	.301	.375	.458	120	15	0-1	.577	-0	0	0	D121/rf	0	0.7
1998	Bal A	104	293	40	88	17	0	9	57	32-4	1	40	.300	.369	.451	114	7	0-0	ø	0	0	0	D80	24	0.2
1999	Bal A★	107	345	57	111	16	1	24	81	43-3	0	38	.322	.395	.583	151	26	1-2	ø	0	0	0	D96	0	1.9
	†Cle A	28	85	5	23	2	0	1	22	11-0	0	10	.271	.354	.329	72	-3	0-0	ø	0	0	0	D25	0	-0.4
	Year	135	430	62	134	18	1	25	103	54-3	0	48	.312	.387	.533	134	22	1-2	ø	0	0	0	D121	0	1.5
2000	Bal A	72	222	24	59	8	0	10	30	29-6	0	39	.266	.349	.437	103	1	0-0	ø	0	0	0	D62	0	-0.2
	†Chi A	24	61	2	13	5	0	1	9	7-1	0	11	.213	.294	.344	59	-4	0-0	ø	0	0	0	D16	0	-0.4
	Year	96	283	26	72	13	0	11	39	36-7	0	50	.254	.338	.417	92	-3	0-0	ø	0	0	0	D78	0	-0.6
2001	Chi A	32	84	3	11	1	0	0	6	8-0	0	16	.131	.202	.143	-5	-13	0-0	ø	0	0	0	D22	81	-1.4
Total	22	2830	9908	1299	2866	488	49	384	1628	1062-187	14	1441	.289	.356	.465	120	282	34-34	.978	-16	97	97	D1644,O1061(9/30/1039)	158	13.3
BAIRD, AL	Albert Wells; B6.2.1895 Cleburne TX; D11.27.1976 Shreveport LA; BR/TR/5´9˝/160; d9.10; Mil 1918; Col Louisiana St.																								
1917	NY N	10	24	1	7	0	0	0	4	2	0	2	.292	.346	.292	100	0	2	1.000	0	92	42	2b7,S3	—	0.1
1919	NY N	38	83	8	20	1	0	0	5	5	0	9	.241	.284	.253	63	-4	3	.898	5	120	127	2b24,S9,3b5	—	0.2
Total	2	48	107	9	27	1	0	0	9	7	0	11	.252	.298	.262	71	-4	5	.921	6	113	106	2b31,S12,3b5	—	0.3
BAIRD, DOUG	Howard Douglas; B9.27.1891 St.Charles MO; D6.13.1967 Thomasville GA; BR/TR/5´9.5˝/148; d4.18; Mil 1918; Col Westminster (MO)																								
1915	Pit N	145	512	49	112	26	12	1	53	37	4	88	.219	.277	.322	82	-12	29-12	.939	-2	95	83	3b120,O20C,2b3	—	-1.1
1916	Pit N	128	430	41	93	10	7	1	28	24	3	49	.216	.263	.279	66	-18	20-16	.933	-9	96	108	3b80,2b29,O16(10/5/1)	—	-3.1
1917	Pit N	43	135	17	35	6	1	0	18	20	0	19	.259	.355	.319	104	2	8	.935	-4	88	44	3b41,2b2	—	-0.1
	StL N	104	364	38	92	19	12	0	24	23	2	52	.253	.301	.371	108	2	18	.941	14	119	138	3b103,O2C	—	2.2
	Year	147	499	55	127	25	13	0	42	43	2	71	.255	.316	.357	107	4	26	.940	10	110	**112**	3b144,2b2,O2C	—	2.1
1918	StL N	82	316	41	78	12	8	2	25	25	1	42	.247	.304	.354	104	1	25	.967	11	118	81	3b81/Srf	—	1.6
1919	Phi N	66	242	33	61	13	3	2	30	22	1	28	.252	.317	.355	95	-1	13	.950	9	108	157	3b66	—	1.1
	StL N	16	33	4	7	0	1	0	4	2	0	3	.212	.257	.273	63	-2	2	.773	-3	80	0	3b8/2rf	—	-0.5
	Bro N	20	60	6	11	0	1	0	8	1	0	10	.183	.197	.217	24	-6	3	1.000	1	106	84	3b17	—	-0.5
	Year	102	335	43	79	13	5	2	42	25	1	41	.236	.291	.322	81	-8	18	.946	7	106	132	3b91/2rf	—	0.1
1920	Bro N	6	6	1	2	0	0	0	1	2	1	1	.333	.556	.333	154	1	0-0	.800	-0	98	0	3b2	—	0.1
	NY N	7	8	0	1	0	0	0	0	1	0	3	.125	.222	.125	1	-1	0-0	1.000	1	120	303	3b4	—	0.0
	Year	13	14	1	3	0	0	0	1	3	1	4	.214	.389	.214	76	0	0-0	.929	0	111	174	3b6	—	0.1
Total	6	617	2106	230	492	86	45	6	191	157	12	295	.234	.291	.326	88	-34	118-28	.944	18	105	104	3b522,O40(10/27/3),2b35/S	—	-0.3
BAKER, CHARLIE	Charles Arthur; B1.15.1856 W.Boylston MA; D1.15.1937 Manchester NH; BR/TR/5´4˝/140; d8.1																								
1884	CP U	15	57	5	8	2	0	1	—	0	—	—	.140	.140	.228	10	-8	—	.722	-1	128	0	O11R,S3/2	—	-0.8
BAKER, CHUCK	Charles Joseph; B12.6.1952 Seattle WA; BR/TR/5´11˝/(175–180); [SDN75*S2/43]; d4.7; Col Loyola Marymount																								
1978	SD N	44	58	8	12	1	0	0	3	2-0	0	15	.207	.233	.224	31	-6	0-0	.952	7	121	146	2b24,S12	0	0.3
1980	SD N	9	22	0	3	1	0	0	0	0-0	0	4	.136	.136	.182	-13	-3	0-0	.963	-0	116	83	S8	0	-0.3
1981	Min A	40	66	6	12	0	3	0	6	1-0	0	8	.182	.194	.273	31	-6	0-0	.969	4	110	80	S31,2b3/3D	0	-0.1
Total	3	93	146	14	27	2	3	0	9	3-0	0	27	.185	.201	.240	25	-15	0-0	.962	10	119	95	S51,2b27/D3	0	-0.1
BAKER, DAVE	David Glenn; B11.25.1957 Lacona IA; BL/TR/6´0˝/185; [TorA78 11/262]; d9.12; b–Doug; Col UCLA																								
1982	Tor A	9	20	3	5	1	0	0	2	3-0	2	3	.250	.400	.300	88	0	0-0	.808	1	127	154	3b8	0	0.0
BAKER, DEL	Delmer David; B5.3.1892 Sherwood OR; D9.11.1973 San Antonio TX; BR/TR/5´11.5˝/176; d4.16; M9/C20																								
1914	Det A	44	70	4	15	2	1	0	1	6	0	9	.214	.276	.271	63	-3	0-2	.920	-5	*88*	*86*	C38	—	-0.8
1915	Det A	68	134	16	33	3	3	0	15	15	1	15	.246	.327	.313	87	-2	3-1	.940	-5	*99*	*93*	C61	—	-0.3
1916	Det A	61	98	7	15	4	0	0	6	11	1	8	.153	.245	.194	31	-8	2	.975	-4	91	59	C59	—	-1.0
Total	3	173	302	27	63	9	4	0	22	32	2	32	.209	.289	.265	63	-13	5-3	.948	-15	*94*	*80*	C158	—	-2.1
BAKER, DOUG	Douglas Lee; B4.3.1961 Fullerton CA; BB/TR/5´9˝/165; [DetA82 9/230]; d7.2; b–Dave; Col Arizona St.																								
1984	†Det A	43	108	15	20	4	1	0	12	7-0	1	22	.185	.241	.241	34	-10	3-0	.969	-5	93	108	S39,2b5/D	0	-1.1
1985	Det A	15	27	4	5	1	0	0	1	0-0	0	9	.185	.185	.222	11	-3	0-0	.960	-3	62	50	S12/2	0	-0.6
1986	Det A	13	24	1	3	1	0	0	0	2-0	0	7	.125	.192	.167	-1	-3	0-0	.970	-2	87	106	S10,2b2/D	0	-0.4
1987	Det A	8	1	0	0	0	0	0	0	0-0	0	1	.000	.000	.000	-99	0	0-0	1.000	2	274	167	S6/23	0	0.1
1988	Min A	11	7	1	0	0	0	0	0	0-0	0	5	.000	.000	.000	-97	-2	0-0	1.000	-1	63	150	S9/23	0	-0.3
1989	Min A	43	78	17	23	5	1	0	9	9-0	2	18	.295	.378	.385	109	1	0-0	.982	-5	96	51	2b25,S19/D	0	-0.3
1990	Min A	3	1	0	0	0	0	0	0	0-0	0	0	.000	.000	.000	-94	0	0-0	1.000	0	120	0	2b3	0	0.0
Total	7	136	246	38	51	11	2	0	22	18-0	3	62	.207	.269	.268	49	-17	3-0	.973	-14	88	95	S95,2b38,D3,3b2	0	-2.6

YEAR	TM LG	G	AB	R	H	2B	3B	HR	RBI	BB-IB	HP	SO	AVG	OBP	SLG	AOPS	ABR	SB-CS	FA	FR	RNG	THR	GAMES AT POSITION	DL	BFW
BAKER, GENE	Eugene Walter; B6.15.1925 Davenport IA; D12.1.1999 Davenport IA; BR/TR/6´1˝/(170–177); d9.20; C1; Negro Lg 1948–50; Col St. Ambrose; [DL 1959 Pit N 46]																								
1953	Chi N	7	22	1	5	1	0	0	0	1	0	4	.227	.261	.273	39	-2	1-0	.917	-2	73	77	2b6	0	-0.4
1954	Chi N	135	541	68	149	32	5	13	61	47	2	55	.275	.333	.425	96	-4	4-5	.967	1	101	99	2b134	0	0.6
1955	Chi N★	**154**	609	82	163	29	7	11	52	49-1	2	57	.268	.323	.392	89	-10	9-7	.967	6	100	102	2b154	0	0.7
1956	Chi N	140	546	65	141	23	3	12	57	39-2	3	54	.258	.309	.377	85	-12	4-3	.969	13	**104**	101	2b140	0	1.2
1957	Chi N	12	44	4	11	3	1	1	10	6-0	1	3	.250	.353	.432	111	1	0-0	.867	-3	68	43	3b12	0	-0.3
	Pit N	111	365	36	97	19	4	2	36	29-5	1	29	.266	.318	.356	84	-8	3-2	.955	-2	100	113	3b60,S28,2b13	0	-0.7
	Year	123	409	40	108	22	5	3	46	35-5	2	32	.264	.322	.364	87	-7	3-2	.942	-5	95	101	3b72,S28,2b13	0	-1.0
1958	Pit N	29	56	3	14	2	1	0	7	8-0	0	6	.250	.338	.321	80	-1	0-0	1.000	1	92	0	3b11,2b3	70	0.0
1960	†Pit N	33	37	5	9	0	0	0	4	2-0	0	9	.243	.275	.243	45	-3	0-0	1.000	-0	82	221	3b7/2	0	-0.3
1961	Pit N	9	10	1	1	0	0	0	0	3-1	0	2	.100	.308	.100	15	-1	0-0	1.000	0	139	0	3b3	0	-0.1
Total	8	630	2230	265	590	109	21	39	227	184-9	9	219	.265	.321	.385	88	-40	21-17	.968	14	101	100	2b451,3b93,S28	116	0.7
BAKER, FLOYD	Floyd Wilson; B10.10.1916 Luray VA; D11.17.2004 Youngstown OH; BL/TR/5´9˝/160; d5.4; C4																								
1943	StL A	22	46	5	8	2	0	0	4	6	0	4	.174	.269	.217	42	-3	0-1	.961	-1	86	105	S10/3	0	-0.4
1944	†StL A	44	97	10	17	3	0	0	5	11	0	5	.175	.259	.206	32	-8	2-0	.979	-2	88	50	2b17,S16	0	-0.9
1945	Chi A	82	208	22	52	8	0	0	19	23	0	12	.250	.325	.288	81	-5	3-2	.971	1	104	68	3b58,2b11	0	-0.3
1946	Chi A	9	24	2	6	1	0	0	3	2	0	3	.250	.308	.292	71	-1	0-0	.962	0	102	68	3b6	0	-0.1
1947	Chi A	105	371	61	98	12	3	0	22	66	0	28	.264	.375	.313	96	1	9-7	.980	14	121	148	3b101/2S	0	1.5
1948	Chi A	104	335	47	72	8	3	0	18	73	2	26	.215	.359	.257	68	-12	4-10	.961	16	129	122	3b71,2b18/S	0	0.2
1949	Chi A	125	388	38	101	15	4	1	40	84	0	32	.260	.392	.327	94	1	3-1	**.977**	11	**115**	118	3b122,S3/2	0	1.2
1950	Chi A	83	186	26	59	7	0	0	11	32	0	10	.317	.417	.355	102	3	1-1	.987	3	105	71	3b53,2b3,O2L	0	0.5
1951	Chi A	82	133	24	35	6	1	0	14	25	0	12	.263	.380	.323	93	0	0-1	.924	-2	99	87	3b44,2b5,S3	0	-0.2
1952	Was A	79	263	27	69	8	0	0	33	30	2	17	.262	.342	.293	81	-6	1-0	.994	-15	91	75	2b68,S7/3	0	-1.7
1953	Was A	9	7	0	0	0	0	0	0	1	1	0	.000	.222	.000	-37	-1	0-0	.000	-1	0	0	/3	0	-0.2
	Bos A	81	172	22	47	4	2	0	24	24	1	10	.273	.365	.320	82	-4	0-2	.963	-1	100	97	3b37,2b16	0	-0.4
	Year	90	179	22	47	4	2	0	24	25	2	10	.263	.359	.307	78	-5	0-2	.952	-1	99	96	3b38,2b16	0	-0.6
1954	Bos A	21	20	1	4	2	0	0	3	0	0	1	.200	.200	.300	32	-2	0-0	.889	0	94	247	3b7/2	0	-0.2
	Phi N	23	22	0	5	0	0	0	0	5	0	4	.227	.370	.227	60	-1	0-0	1.000	2	140	0	3b7,2b2	0	0.1
1955	Phi N	5	8	0	0	0	0	0	0	0-0	0	1	.000	.000	.000	-99	-2	0-0	1.000	1	90	0	/3	0	-0.2
Total	13	874	2280	285	573	76	13	1	196	382-0	6	165	.251	.360	.297	82	-40	23-25	.971	26	114	111	3b510,2b143,S41,O2L	0	-1.1
BAKER, FRANK	Frank; B1.11.1944 Bartow FL; BL/TR/5´10˝/(180–190); d7.27																								
1969	Cle A	52	172	21	44	5	3	3	15	14-0	1	34	.256	.312	.372	89	-3	2-1	.950	-0	91	152	O46L	0	-0.6
1971	Cle A	73	181	18	38	12	1	1	23	12-3	1	34	.210	.262	.304	55	-11	1-3	.985	-4	77	72	O51(17/6/30)	0	-2.0
Total	2	125	353	39	82	17	4	4	38	26-3	2	68	.232	.286	.337	71	-14	3-4	.966	-4	84	112	O97(63/6/30)	0	-2.6
BAKER, FRANK	Frank Watts; B10.29.1946 Meridian MS; BL/TR/6´2˝/(178–185); d8.9; Col Southern Mississippi																								
1970	NY A	35	117	6	27	4	1	0	11	14-0	2	26	.231	.323	.282	71	-4	1-2	.973	5	116	117	S35	0	0.5
1971	NY A	43	79	9	11	2	0	0	2	16-3	0	22	.139	.281	.165	31	-7	3-0	.949	3	108	171	S38	0	0.1
1973	†Bal A	44	63	10	12	1	2	1	11	7-0	0	7	.190	.268	.317	65	-3	0-0	.964	-2	89	164	S32,2b7/13	0	-0.3
1974	†Bal A	24	29	3	5	1	0	0	0	3-0	0	5	.172	.250	.207	33	-2	0-0	.842	-3	101	93	S17,2b3/3	0	-0.4
Total	4	146	288	28	55	8	3	1	24	40-3	2	60	.191	.292	.250	56	-16	4-2	.953	3	107	142	S122,2b10,3b2/1	0	-0.1
BAKER, GEORGE	George F.; B1859 St.Louis MO; 5´11˝/162; d5.24																								
1883	Bal AA	7	22	0	5	0	0	0	—	0	—	—	.227	.227	.227	45	-1	—	.667	-2	67	192	S4,C3/rf	—	-0.3
1884	StL U	80	317	39	52	6	0	0	—	5	—	—	.164	.177	.183	9	-45	—	**.897**	15	—	—	C68,2b4,O4(2/1/2),3b3,S2	—	-2.2
1885	StL N	38	131	5	16	0	0	0	5	9	—	28	.122	.179	.122	-1	-14	—	.865	-10	—	—	C32,3b3,O2(1/1/0)/2	—	-2.1
1886	KC N	1	4	1	1	0	0	0	0	0	—	1	.250	.250	.250	49	0	0	.889	-0	—	—	/C	—	-0.1
Total	4	126	474	45	74	6	0	0	5	14	—	29	.156	.180	.169	8	-60	0	.887	2	—	—	C104,O7(3/2/3),3b6,S6,2b5	—	-4.7
BAKER, HOWARD	Howard Francis; B3.1.1888 Bridgeport CT; D1.16.1964 Bridgeport CT; BR/TR/5´11˝/175; d8.11																								
1912	Cle A	11	30	1	5	0	0	0	2	5	0	—	.167	.286	.167	29	-3	0	.964	-1	72	0	3b10	—	-0.3
1914	Chi A	15	47	4	13	1	1	0	5	3	0	8	.277	.320	.340	100	0	2-1	.879	-2	96	67	3b15	—	-0.2
1915	Chi A	2	2	0	0	0	0	0	0	0	0	2	.000	.000	.000	-97	0	0	ø	0	—	—	/H	—	-0.1
	NY N	1	3	0	0	0	0	0	0	0	0	0	.000	.000	.000	-99	-1	0	1.000	0	128	0	/3	—	-0.1
Total	3	29	82	5	18	1	1	0	7	8	0	10	.220	.289	.256	61	-4	2-1	.922	-3	88	38	3b26	—	-0.7
BAKER, JACK	Jack Edward; B5.4.1950 Birmingham AL; BR/TR/6´5˝/225; [BosA71 26/604]; d9.11; Col Auburn																								
1976	Bos A	12	23	1	3	0	0	1	2	1-0	0	5	.130	.160	.261	21	-2	0-0	.981	-1	74	134	1b8/D	0	-0.4
1977	Bos A	2	3	0	0	0	0	0	0	0-0	0	1	.000	.000	.000	-90	-1	0-0	.857	0	193	0	/1	0	-0.1
Total	2	14	26	1	3	0	0	1	2	1-0	0	6	.115	.143	.231	8	-3	0-0	.966	-1	87	119	1b9/D	0	-0.5
BAKER, JEFF	Jeffrey Glen; B6.21.1981 Bad Kissingen, West Germany; BR/TR/6´2˝/(210–220); [ColN02 4/111]; d4.4; Col Clemson																								
2005	Col N	12	38	6	8	4	0	1	4	5-0	0	12	.211	.302	.395	72	-1	0-0	.958	0	112	52	3b10	0	-0.1
2006	Col N	18	57	13	21	7	2	5	21	1-0	0	14	.368	.379	.825	180	6	2-0	1.000	-2	54	195	O12(2/0/10)/1	0	0.5
Total	2	30	95	19	29	11	2	6	25	6-0	0	26	.305	.347	.653	136	5	2-0	1.000	-2	54	195	O12(2/0/10),3b10/1	0	0.4
BAKER, JESSE	Jesse (b Michael Myron Silverman); B3.4.1895 Cleveland OH; D7.29.1976 W.Los Angeles CA; BR/TR/5´4˝/140; d9.14																								
1919	Was A	1	0	0	0	0	0	0	1	0	0	0	ø	ø	ø	ø	0	0	1.000	0	146	0	/S	—	0.0
BAKER, FRANK	John Franklin "Home Run"; B3.13.1886 Trappe MD; D6.28.1963 Trappe MD; BL/TR/5´11˝/173; d9.21; HF1955																								
1908	Phi A	9	31	5	9	3	0	0	2	0	0	—	.290	.290	.387	112	0	0	1.000	1	108	0	3b9	—	0.2
1909	Phi A	148	541	73	165	27	**19**	4	85	26	5	—	.305	.343	.447	146	25	20	.920	-10	89	95	3b146	—	2.2
1910	†Phi A	146	561	83	159	25	15	2	74	34	4	—	.283	.329	.392	127	15	21	.920	2	96	**179**	3b146	—	2.3
1911	†Phi A	148	592	96	198	42	14	**11**	115	40	2	—	.334	.379	.508	149	36	38	**.942**	-4	90	**125**	3b148	—	3.5
1912	Phi A	149	577	116	200	40	21	**10**	**130**	50	6	—	.347	.404	.541	176	54	40	.941	8	103	119	3b149	—	6.5
1913	†Phi A	149	564	116	190	34	9	**12**	**117**	63	10	31	.337	.413	.493	169	50	34	.921	9	100	95	3b149	—	6.6
1914	†Phi A	150	570	84	182	23	10	**9**	89	53	3	37	.319	.380	.442	153	35	19-20	.955	9	99	99	3b149	—	5.0
1916	NY A	100	360	46	97	23	2	10	52	36	5	30	.269	.344	.428	129	12	15	.940	1	100	90	3b96	—	1.7
1917	NY A	146	553	57	156	24	2	6	71	48	5	27	.282	.345	.365	116	10	18	.949	9	103	101	3b146	—	2.6
1918	NY A	**126**	504	65	154	24	5	6	62	38	2	13	.306	.357	.409	128	16	8	**.972**	7	103	117	3b126	—	2.9
1919	NY A	**141**	567	70	166	22	1	10	83	44	2	18	.293	.346	.388	105	3	13	.955	-5	95	**134**	3b141	—	0.3
1921	†NY A	94	330	46	97	16	2	9	71	26	4	12	.294	.353	.436	98	-2	8-5	.959	5	107	118	3b83	—	0.8
1922	†NY A	69	234	30	65	12	3	7	36	15	2	14	.278	.327	.444	97	-2	1-3	.962	-10	84	68	3b60	—	-0.9
Total	13	1575	5984	887	1838	315	103	96	987	473	50	182	.307	.363	.442	136	252	235-28	.943	25	98	114	3b1548	—	33.7
BAKER, DUSTY	Johnnie B; B6.15.1949 Riverside CA; BR/TR/6´2˝/(182–200); [AtlN67 26/504]; d9.7; M14/C5																								
1968	Atl N	6	5	0	2	0	0	0	0	0-0	0	1	.400	.400	.400	140	0	0-0	ø	-1	0	0	O3C	0	0.0
1969	Atl N	3	7	0	0	0	0	0	0	0-0	0	3	.000	.000	.000	-99	-2	0-0	1.000	-1	42	0	O3C	0	-0.3
1970	Atl N	13	24	3	7	0	0	0	4	2-0	0	4	.292	.333	.292	69	-1	0-0	.800	-1	87	221	O11(5/4/2)	0	-0.2
1971	Atl N	29	62	2	14	2	0	0	4	1-1	0	14	.226	.238	.258	38	-5	0-1	1.000	0	89	90	O18(1/4/16)	0	-0.6
1972	Atl N	127	446	62	143	27	2	17	76	45-2	4	68	.321	.383	.504	139	24	4-7	.989	12	111	104	O123(30/121/3)	0	3.3
1973	Atl N	159	604	101	174	29	4	21	99	67-8	5	72	.288	.359	.454	116	15	24-3	.983	-4	92	90	O156C	0	1.1
1974	Atl N	149	574	80	147	35	0	20	69	71-9	1	87	.256	.335	.422	108	7	18-7	.981	0	102	97	O148(0/102/112)	0	0.3
1975	Atl N	142	494	63	129	18	2	19	72	67-7	0	57	.261	.346	.421	110	7	12-7	.990	4	107	108	O136(0/12/129)	0	0.5
1976	LA N	112	384	36	93	13	0	4	39	31-3	1	54	.242	.298	.307	73	-14	2-4	.996	-6	97	43	O106(0/83/24)	0	-2.5
1977	†LA N	153	533	86	155	26	1	30	86	58-6	6	89	.291	.364	.512	132	24	2-6	.987	-8	82	84	O152(150/1/2)	0	0.8
1978	†LA N	149	522	62	137	24	1	11	66	47-2	3	66	.262	.325	.375	96	-3	12-3	.985	0	95	113	O145L	0	-0.8
1979	LA N	151	554	86	152	29	1	23	88	56-0	1	70	.274	.340	.455	118	13	11-4	.990	6	99	123	O150L	0	1.4
1980	LA N	153	579	80	170	26	4	29	97	43-4	3	66	.294	.339	.503	138	27	12-10	.991	-1	102	44	O151(151/1/1)	0	1.9
1981	†LA N★	103	400	48	128	17	3	9	49	29-1	1	43	.320	.363	.445	135	18	10-7	.990	-3	95	91	O101L	0	1.1
1982	LA N★	147	570	80	171	19	1	23	88	56-5	3	62	.300	.361	.458	133	25	17-10	.975	-14	81	59	O144(144/0/1)	0	0.5
1983	†LA N	149	531	71	138	25	1	15	73	72-2	2	59	.260	.346	.395	106	6	7-1	.981	-6	97	39	O143L	0	-0.5
1984	SF N	100	243	31	71	7	2	3	32	40-1	0	27	.292	.387	.374	120	8	4-1	.974	-2	101	24	O62(29/0/33)	0	0.4

YEAR	TM LG	G	AB	R	H	2B	3B	HR	RBI	BB-IB	HP	SO	AVG	OBP	SLG	AOPS	ABR	SB-CS	FA	FR	RNG	THR	GAMES AT POSITION	DL	BFW
1985	Oak A	111	343	48	92	15	1	14	52	50-0	0	47	.268	.359	.440	127	14	2-1	.993	-2	72	78	1b58,O35(32/0/5),D13	0	0.7
1986	Oak A	83	242	25	58	8	0	4	19	27-1	0	37	.240	.314	.322	80	-7	0-1	1.000	-1	86	133	O55(36/0/20),D15,1b3	0	-1.1
Total	19	2039	7117	964	1981	320	23	242	1013	762-52	30	926	.278	.347	.432	116	156	137-73	.985	-25	96	84	O1842(1117/490/348),1b61,D28	0	6.0
Baker, Phil	Philip; B9.19.1856 Philadelphia PA; D6.4.1940 Washington DC; BL/TL/5´8˝/152; d5.1																								
1883	Bal AA	28	121	22	33	2	1	1	—	8	—	—	.273	.318	.331	106	1	—	.883	-5	—	—	C19,O14(1/1/12)/S	—	-0.3
1884	Was U	86	371	75	107	12	5	1	—	11	—	—	.288	.309	.356	104	-9	—	.955	-3	111	98	1b39,O32C,C27	—	-1.3
1886	Was N	81	325	37	72	6	5	1	34	20	—	32	.222	.267	.280	72	-11	16	.967	-5	63	97	1b56,O21(1/7/14),C4	—	-1.9
Total	3	195	817	134	212	20	11	3	34	39	—	32	.259	.293	.322	92	-19	16	.963	-13	—	—	1b95,O67(2/40/26),C50/S	—	-3.5
Baker, Trace	Trace Lee; B11.7.1891 Pendleton OR; D3.14.1975 Placerville CA; BR/TR/6´1˝/180; d6.19; Col Washington																								
1911	Bos A	1	0	0	0	0	0	0	0	0	0	—	ø	ø	ø	ø	0	0	1.000	-0	0	0	/1	—	0.0
Baker, Bill	William Presley; B2.22.1911 Paw Creek NC; D4.13.2006 Myrtle Beach SC; BR/TR/6´0˝/200; d5.4; Mil 1944–45; C1																								
1940	†Cin N	27	69	5	15	1	1	0	7	4	0	8	.217	.260	.261	44	-6	2	1.000	2	*114*	*54*	C24	—	-0.2
1941	Cin N	2	1	0	0	0	0	0	0	1	0	1	.000	.500	.000	49	0	0	1.000	0	*0*	*0*	/C	0	0.0
	Pit N	35	67	5	15	3	0	0	6	11	0	0	.224	.333	.269	71	-2	0	.967	0	*113*	*102*	C33	0	-0.1
	Year	37	68	5	15	3	0	0	6	12	0	1	.221	.338	.265	71	-2	0	.967	0	*111*	*100*	C34	0	-0.1
1942	Pit N	18	17	1	2	0	0	0	2	1	0	0	.118	.167	.118	-16	-3	0	1.000	1	*126*	*0*	C11	0	-0.2
1943	Pit N	63	172	12	47	6	3	1	26	22	3	6	.273	.365	.360	106	2	3	.979	3	*138*	*101*	C56	0	0.8
1946	Pit N	53	113	7	27	4	0	1	8	12	0	6	.239	.312	.301	72	-4	0	.965	-4	*71*	*98*	C41/1	0	-0.7
1948	StL N	45	119	13	35	10	1	0	15	15	0	7	.294	.373	.395	102	1	1	.994	2	*311*	*72*	C36	0	0.5
1949	StL N	20	30	2	4	1	0	0	4	2	0	2	.133	.188	.167	-4	-4	0	1.000	-1	*146*	*0*	C10	0	-0.5
Total	7	263	588	45	145	25	5	2	68	68	3	30	.247	.328	.316	79	-16	6	.983	2	*155*	*83*	C212/1	0	-0.4
Bako, Paul	Gabor Paul; B6.20.1972 Lafayette LA; BL/TR/6´2˝/(205–215); [CinN93 5/148]; d4.30; Col Louisiana–Lafayette																								
1998	Det A	96	305	23	83	12	1	3	30	23-4	0	82	.272	.319	.348	74	-12	1-1	.989	-7	88	130	C94	0	-1.2
1999	Hou N	73	215	16	55	14	1	2	17	26-3	0	57	.256	.332	.358	77	-7	1-1	.988	7	130	103	C71	0	0.4
2000	Hou N	1	2	0	0	0	0	0	0	0-0	0	1	.000	.000	.000	-93	-1	0-0	1.000	0	0	0	/C	0	0.0
	Fla N	56	161	10	39	6	1	0	14	22-7	1	48	.242	.335	.292	64	-8	0-0	.991	-4	87	127	C56	0	-0.8
	†Atl N	24	58	8	11	4	0	2	6	5-3	0	15	.190	.254	.362	54	-4	0-0	.992	-0	116	80	C23/1	0	-0.3
	Year	81	221	18	50	10	1	2	20	27-10	1	64	.226	.312	.308	60	-14	0-0	.992	-4	94	114	C80/1	0	-1.1
2001	†Atl N	61	137	19	29	10	1	2	15	20-2	0	34	.212	.312	.343	69	-6	1-0	.991	2	70	153	C60	0	-0.1
2002	Mil N	87	234	24	55	8	1	4	20	20-3	0	46	.235	.295	.329	65	-13	0-2	.991	-10	85	91	C76	15	-1.9
2003	†Chi N	70	188	19	43	13	3	0	17	22-3	1	47	.229	.311	.330	66	-9	0-1	.987	-7	107	100	C69	0	-1.3
2004	Chi N	49	138	13	28	8	0	1	10	15-3	2	29	.203	.288	.283	48	-11	1-0	.989	-1	65	166	C47	0	-0.8
2005	LA N	13	40	1	10	2	0	0	4	7-1	0	12	.250	.362	.300	76	-1	0-0	.985	-3	642	117	C13	129	-0.3
2006	KC A	56	153	7	32	3	0	0	10	11-0	0	46	.209	.261	.229	29	-16	0-0	.993	-3	122	88	C53/D	31	-1.6
Total	9	586	1631	140	385	80	8	14	143	171-29	4	417	.236	.308	.321	63	-88	4-5	.990	-24	109	116	C563/D1	175	-7.9
Balaz, John	John Lawrence; B11.24.1950 Toronto ON, Can.; BR/TR/6´3˝/180; [AnaA70 5/108]; d9.10; Col San Diego (CA) City																								
1974	Cal A	14	42	4	10	0	0	1	5	2-0	1	10	.238	.289	.310	76	-1	0-0	1.000	-1	77	0	O12L	0	-0.4
1975	Cal A	45	120	10	29	8	1	1	10	5-0	0	25	.242	.270	.350	80	-4	0-0	1.000	1	93	188	O27(19/0/8),D11	0	-0.4
Total	2	59	162	14	39	8	1	2	15	7-0	1	35	.241	.275	.340	79	-5	0-0	1.000	-0	87	123	O39(31/0/8),D11	0	-0.8
Balboni, Steve	Stephen Charles; B1.16.1957 Brockton MA; BR/TR/6´3˝/(225–250); [NYA78 2/52]; d4.22; Col Eckerd																								
1981	NY A	4	7	2	2	1	1	0	2	1-0	0	4	.286	.375	.714	210	1	0-0	1.000	0	86	132	1b3/D	0	0.1
1982	NY A	33	107	8	20	2	1	2	4	6-0	0	34	.187	.228	.280	40	-9	0-0	.990	-0	96	115	1b26,D5	0	-1.1
1983	NY A	32	86	8	20	2	0	5	17	8-0	0	23	.233	.295	.430	101	0	0-0	.984	-1	82	121	1b23,D4	0	-0.2
1984	†KC A	126	438	58	107	23	2	28	77	45-5	4	139	.244	.320	.498	121	12	0-0	.987	-2	98	107	1b125/D	0	0.2
1985	†KC A	160	600	74	146	28	2	36	88	52-4	5	166	.243	.307	.477	110	7	1-1	.993	-5	90	101	1b160	0	-0.9
1986	KC A	138	512	54	117	25	1	29	88	43-2	1	146	.229	.286	.451	96	-5	0-0	.987	-4	94	103	1b137	0	-1.7
1987	KC A	121	386	44	80	11	1	24	60	34-1	2	97	.207	.273	.427	80	-13	0-0	.989	1	112	88	1b55,D52	0	-1.6
1988	KC A	21	63	2	9	2	0	2	5	1-0	0	20	.143	.156	.270	17	-7	0-0	.980	-1	67	123	1b13,D6	0	-1.0
	Sea A	97	350	44	88	15	1	21	61	23-2	1	67	.251	.298	.480	109	3	0-1	.994	-1	87	101	D56,1b40	0	-0.3
	Year	118	413	46	97	17	1	23	66	24-2	1	87	.235	.277	.448	96	-4	0-1	.991	-2	83	106	D62,1b53	0	-1.3
1989	NY A	110	300	33	71	12	2	17	59	25-5	3	67	.237	.296	.460	113	3	0-0	.994	-0	97	148	D82,1b20	0	0.0
1990	NY A	116	266	24	51	6	0	17	34	35-2	3	91	.192	.291	.406	93	-4	0-0	.984	-3	49	121	D72,1b28	0	-1.1
1993	Tex A	2	5	0	3	0	0	0	0	0-0	0	2	.600	.600	.600	231	1	0-0	ø	0	—	—	D2	0	0.1
Total	11	960	3120	351	714	127	11	181	495	273-21	19	856	.229	.293	.451	100	-11	1-2	.989	-16	93	105	1b630,D281	0	-7.5
Balcena, Bobby	Robert Rudolph; B8.1.1925 San Pedro CA; D1.5.1990 San Pedro CA; BR/TL/5´7˝/160; d9.16																								
1956	Cin N	7	2	2	0	0	0	0	0	0-0	0	1	.000	.000	.000	-94	-1	0-0	1.000	0	146	0	O2L	0	-0.1
Baldelli, Rocco	Rocco Dan; B9.25.1981 Woonsocket RI; BR/TR/6´4˝/(185–200); [TBA00 1/6]; d3.31; [DL 2005 TB A 183]																								
2003	TB A	156	637	89	184	32	8	11	78	30-4	8	128	.289	.326	.416	97	-4	27-10	.989	10	107	**197**	O154C,D2	0	1.0
2004	TB A	136	518	79	145	27	3	16	74	30-2	8	88	.280	.326	.436	99	-2	17-4	.978	10	112	**183**	O124C,D13	18	1.1
2006	TB A	92	364	59	110	24	6	16	57	14-1	7	70	.302	.339	.533	122	11	10-1	.979	3	105	140	O91C	65	1.5
Total	3	384	1519	227	439	83	17	43	209	74-7	23	286	.289	.329	.451	104	5	54-15	.983	23	108	179	O369C,D15	266	3.6
Baldwin, Kid	Clarence Geoghan; B11.1.1864 Newport KY; D7.10.1897 Cincinnati OH; BR/TR/5´6˝/147; d7.27; OF(11/13/8)																								
1884	KC U	50	191	19	37	6	3	0	—	4	—	—	.194	.210	.257	47	-18	—	.885	0	—	—	C44,O10(8/2/0)/23	—	-1.3
	CP U	1	1	0	1	0	0	0	—	0	—	—	1.000	1.000	1.000	513	0	—	1.000	-0	—	—	/C	—	0.0
	Year	51	192	19	38	6	3	0	—	4	—	—	.198	.214	.260	50	-18	—	.885	-0	—	—	C45,O10(8/2/0)/23	—	-1.3
1885	Cin AA	34	126	9	17	1	0	1	8	3	0	—	.135	.155	.167	2	-14	—	.863	-4	—	—	C25,O6(0/5/1),2b2,P2/3	—	-1.4
1886	Cin AA	87	315	41	72	8	7	3	32	8	2	—	.229	.252	.327	78	-10	12	.891	-7	—	—	C71,3b13,O6(0/5/1)	—	-1.0
1887	Cin AA	96	388	46	98	15	10	1	57	6	4	—	.253	.271	.351	71	-18	13	.874	-2	—	—	C96,O2L	—	-0.9
1888	Cin AA	67	271	27	59	11	3	1	25	3	3	—	.218	.235	.292	65	-12	4	.918	-4	—	—	C65,O2R/1	—	-0.9
1889	Cin AA	60	223	34	55	14	2	1	34	5	3	32	.247	.273	.341	72	-9	7	.912	-1	—	—	C55,O4(1/1/2)/31	—	-0.5
1890	Cin N	22	72	5	11	0	0	0	10	3	0	6	.153	.187	.153	-1	-9	2	.902	3	*125*	*119*	C20,O2R	—	-0.4
	Phi AA	24	90	5	21	1	2	0	12	4	1	—	.233	.274	.289	66	-4	2	.887	-4	*83*	*100*	C19,3b5	—	-0.6
Total	7	441	1677	186	371	56	27	7	178	36	13	38	.221	.243	.299	61	-94	40	.893	-17	*103*	*109*	C396,O32C,3b21,2b3,1b2,P2	—	-7.0
Baldwin, Frank	Frank De Witt; B12.25.1928 High Bridge NJ; D11.18.2004 Beaver OH; BR/TR/5´11˝/195; d4.22																								
1953	Cin N	16	20	0	2	0	0	0	0	1	0	9	.100	.143	.100	-35	-4	0-0	1.000	-1	*69*	*0*	C6	0	-0.5
Baldwin, Henry	Henry Clay "Ted"; B6.13.1894 Chadds Ford PA; D2.24.1964 West Chester PA; BR/TR/5´11˝/180; d5.22; Col Swarthmore																								
1927	Phi N	6	16	1	5	0	0	0	1	1	0	2	.313	.353	.313	78	0	0	.857	-1	98	94	S3,3b2	—	-0.1
Baldwin, Jeff	Jeffrey Allen; B9.5.1965 Milford DE; BL/TL/6´1˝/180; [HouN85*14/296]; d5.22; Col Camden Co. (NJ) JC																								
1990	Hou N	7	8	1	0	0	0	0	0	1-0	0	2	.000	.111	.000	-69	-2	0-0	1.000	-0	67	0	O3(2/0/1)	0	-0.2
Baldwin, Reggie	Reginald Conrad; B8.19.1954 River Rouge MI; BR/TR/6´1˝/195; [HouN76 3/49]; d5.25; Col Grambling St.																								
1978	Hou N	38	67	5	17	5	0	1	11	3-0	0	3	.254	.286	.373	88	-1	0-0	.955	-3	52	83	C17	0	-0.4
1979	Hou N	14	20	0	4	1	0	0	1	0-0	0	1	.200	.200	.250	23	-2	0-0	1.000	-0	0	0	C3/1	0	-0.3
Total	2	52	87	5	21	6	0	1	12	3-0	0	4	.241	.267	.345	73	-3	0-0	.956	-4	49	78	C20/1	0	-0.7
Baldwin, Billy	Robert Harvey; B6.9.1951 Tazewell VA; BL/TL/6´0˝/175; d7.29; Col Southern A&M																								
1975	Det A	30	95	8	21	3	0	4	8	5-0	0	14	.221	.260	.379	75	-4	2-1	.983	2	100	220	O25(0/13/13)/D	0	-0.3
1976	NY N	9	22	4	6	1	1	1	5	1-0	0	2	.273	.292	.545	144	1	0-0	.929	1	136	296	O5(3/0/2)	0	0.2
Total	2	39	117	12	27	4	1	5	13	6-0	0	16	.231	.266	.410	87	-3	2-1	.972	3	106	233	O30(3/13/15)/D	0	-0.1
Balenti, Mike	Michael Richard; B7.3.1886 Calumet OK; D8.4.1955 Altus OK; BR/TR/5´11˝/175; d7.19; Col Texas A&M																								
1911	Cin N	8	8	2	2	0	0	0	0	0	0	1	.250	.250	.250	42	-1	3	.857	0	127	248	S2/cf	—	0.0
1913	StL A	70	211	17	38	2	4	0	11	6	1	32	.180	.206	.227	28	-21	3	.923	-2	103	116	S56,O8L	—	-2.1
Total	2	78	219	19	40	2	4	0	11	6	1	33	.183	.208	.228	28	-22	6	.922	-2	103	119	S58,O9(8/1/0)	—	-2.1

THE BATTER REGISTER

YEAR	TM LG	G	AB	R	H	2B	3B	HR	RBI	BB-IB	HP	SO	AVG	OBP	SLG	AOPS	ABR	SB-CS	FA	FR	RNG	THR	GAMES AT POSITION	DL	BFW
Bales, Lee Wesley Owen; B12.4.1944 Los Angeles CA; BB/TR/5´10.5˝/(163–165); d8.7																									
1966	Atl N	12	16	4	1	0	0	0	0	0-0	0	5	.063	.063	.063	-64	-4	0-0	1.000	2	136	75	2b7,3b3	0	-0.1
1967	Hou N	19	27	4	3	0	0	0	2	8-0	0	7	.111	.306	.111	28	-2	1-1	.944	-2	69	0	2b6/S	0	-0.5
Total	2	31	43	8	4	0	0	0	2	8-0	0	12	.093	.231	.093	-3	-6	1-1	.978	-1	98	33	2b13,3b3/S	0	-0.6
Ball, Art Arthur Clark; B4.1876 KY; D12.26.1915 Chicago IL; TR/?/168; d8.1																									
1894	StL N	1	3	0	1	0	0	0	0	0	0	1	.333	.333	.333	61	0	0	.667	-1	0	0	/2	—	-0.1
1898	Bal N	32	81	7	15	2	0	0	8	7	1	—	.185	.258	.210	34	-7	2	.906	6	108	182	3b15,S14,2b2/cf	—	0.0
Total	2	33	84	7	16	2	0	0	8	7	1	1	.190	.261	.214	35	-7	2	.906	5	108	182	3b15,S14,2b3/cf	—	-0.1
Ball, Neal Cornelius; B4.22.1881 Grand Haven MI; D10.15.1957 Bridgeport CT; BR/TR/5´7˝/145; d9.12																									
1907	NY A	15	44	5	9	1	1	0	4	1	0	—	.205	.222	.273	53	-3	1	.817	-3	95	68	S11,2b5	—	-0.6
1908	NY A	132	446	35	110	16	2	0	38	21	2	—	.247	.284	.291	86	-7	32	.898	-6	100	62	S130/2	—	-1.1
1909	NY A	8	29	5	6	1	1	0	3	3	0	—	.207	.281	.310	86	-1	2	.917	-3	77	33	2b8	—	-0.4
	Cle A	96	324	29	83	13	2	1	25	17	1	—	.256	.295	.318	90	-4	17	.914	-10	91	129	S95	—	-1.2
	Year	104	353	34	89	14	3	1	28	20	1	—	.252	.294	.317	90	-5	19	.914	-13	91	129	S95,2b8	—	-1.6
1910	Cle A	54	123	13	25	3	1	0	12	9	0	—	.203	.258	.244	56	-6	4	.927	-3	88	101	S27,2b7,O6(0/5/1),3b3	—	-1.0
1911	Cle A	116	412	45	122	14	9	3	45	27	0	—	.296	.339	.396	104	0	21	.945	3	105	111	2b94,3b17/S	—	0.5
1912	Cle A	40	132	12	30	4	1	0	14	9	0	—	.227	.277	.273	55	-8	7	.938	0	93	98	2b37	—	-0.7
	†Bos A	18	45	10	9	2	0	0	6	3	0	—	.200	.250	.244	40	-4	5	.927	-2	96	35	2b17	—	-0.6
	Year	58	177	22	39	6	1	0	20	12	0	—	.220	.270	.266	51	-11	12	.936	-2	94	84	2b54	—	-1.3
1913	Bos A	23	58	9	10	2	0	0	4	9	1	13	.172	.294	.207	46	-4	3	.902	-3	88	124	2b10,S7/3	—	-0.6
Total	7	502	1613	163	404	56	17	4	151	99	4	13	.250	.295	.314	83	-37	92	.902	-28	96	89	S271,2b179,3b21,O6(0/5/1)	—	-5.7
Ball, Jim James Chandler; B2.22.1884 Harford Co. MD; D4.7.1963 Glendale CA; BR/TR/5´11˝/175; d9.21																									
1907	Bos N	10	36	3	6	2	0	0	3	2	0	—	.167	.211	.222	36	-3	0	.963	-2	*73*	*114*	C10	—	-0.5
1908	Bos N	6	15	1	1	0	0	0	0	1	0	—	.067	.125	.067	-39	-2	0	.917	-1	*83*	*142*	C6	—	-0.3
Total	2	16	51	4	7	2	0	0	3	3	0	—	.137	.185	.176	14	-5	0	.949	-3	*76*	*123*	C16	—	-0.8
Ball, Jeff Jeffery D.; B4.17.1969 Merced CA; BR/TR/5´10˝/185; [HouN90 12/332]; d6.10; Col San Jose St.																									
1998	SF N	2	4	0	1	0	0	0	0	0-0	0	0	.250	.250	.250	34	0	0-0	1.000	-0	0	158	/1	0	-0.1
Ballenger, Pelham Pelham Ashby; B2.6.1894 Gilreath Mill SC; D12.8.1948 Greenville SC; BR/TR/5´11˝/160; d5.7																									
1928	Was A	3	9	0	1	0	0	0	0	0	0	1	.111	.111	.111	-42	-2	0-0	1.000	1	161	236	3b3	—	-0.1
Bamberger, Hal Harold Earl "Dutch"; B10.29.1924 Lebanon PA; BL/TR/6´0˝/173; d9.15																									
1948	NY N	7	12	0	1	0	0	0	0	1	0	2	.083	.154	.083	-34	-2	0	1.000	-0	102	0	O3(0/1/2)	0	-0.3
Bancker, Stud John; B Philadelphia PA; d4.19																									
1875	NH NA	19	72	3	11	0	0	0	2	0	—	3	.153	.153	.153	7	-6	1-0	.796	-4	—	—	C14,2b4,3b3/S1	—	-0.8
Bancroft, Dave David James "Beauty"; B4.20.1891 Sioux City IA; D10.9.1972 Superior WI; BB/TR/5´9.5˝/160; d4.14; M4/C3; HF1971																									
1915	†Phi N	**153**	563	85	143	18	2	7	30	77	2	62	.254	.346	.330	104	6	15-27	.928	5	101	105	S153	—	1.7
1916	Phi N	142	477	53	101	10	0	3	33	74	4	57	.212	.323	.252	75	-10	15	.933	25	110	113	S142	—	2.8
1917	Phi N	127	478	56	116	22	5	4	43	44	0	42	.243	.307	.335	93	-3	14	.936	**28**	112	111	S120,2b3,O2L	—	3.6
1918	Phi N	**125**	499	69	132	19	4	0	26	54	1	36	.265	.338	.319	94	-1	11	.928	16	104	102	S125	—	2.6
1919	Phi N	92	335	45	91	13	7	0	25	31	0	30	.272	.333	.352	99	0	8	.951	6	99	96	S88	—	1.4
1920	Phi N	42	171	23	51	7	2	0	5	9	1	12	.298	.337	.363	96	-1	1-7	.981	9	106	131	S42	—	1.0
	NY N	108	442	79	132	29	7	0	31	33	1	32	.299	.349	.396	115	9	7-5	.946	28	118	143	S108	—	4.6
	Year	150	613	102	183	36	9	0	36	42	2	44	.299	.346	.387	109	8	8-12	**.955**	**37**	**115**	**140**	S150	—	5.6
1921	†NY N	**153**	606	121	193	26	15	6	67	66	4	23	.318	.389	.441	119	18	17-10	.960	19	104	**141**	S153	—	5.3
1922	†NY N	**156**	651	117	209	41	5	4	60	79	3	27	.321	.397	.418	109	14	16-11	.941	22	108	114	S156	—	4.9
1923	†NY N	107	444	80	135	33	3	1	31	62	1	23	.304	.391	.399	110	10	8-7	.936	12	107	94	S96,2b11	—	3.2
1924	Bos N	79	319	49	89	11	1	2	21	37	1	24	.279	.356	.339	91	-3	4-4	.961	-3	96	107	S79,M	—	0.3
1925	Bos N	128	479	75	153	29	8	2	49	64	0	22	.319	.400	.426	122	19	7-4	**.945**	10	**108**	101	S125,M	—	3.9
1926	Bos N	127	453	70	141	18	6	1	44	64	2	29	.311	.399	.384	122	18	3	.956	-5	96	92	S123,3b2,M	—	2.6
1927	Bos N	111	375	44	91	13	4	1	31	43	1	36	.243	.322	.307	75	-13	5	.939	5	100	100	S104/3M	—	0.3
1928	Bro N	149	515	47	127	19	5	0	51	59	2	20	.247	.326	.303	66	-24	7	.948	2	98	72	S149	—	-0.6
1929	Bro N	104	358	35	99	11	3	1	44	29	0	11	.277	.331	.332	66	-19	7	.955	-3	94	69	S102	—	-1.1
1930	NY N	10	17	0	1	1	0	0	0	2	0	1	.059	.158	.118	-33	-4	0	.966	-0	96	0	S8	—	-0.3
Total	16	1913	7182	1048	2004	320	77	32	591	827	23	487	.279	.355	.358	98	16	145-75	.944	178	104	105	S1873,2b14,3b3,O2L	—	36.2
Bando, Chris Christopher Michael; B2.4.1956 Cleveland OH; BB/TR/6´0˝/195; [CleA78 2/36]; d8.13; C3; b–Sal; Col Arizona St.																									
1981	Cle A	21	47	3	10	3	0	0	6	2-0	0	2	.213	.240	.277	50	-3	0-0	.967	-2	115	106	C15,D2	0	-0.5
1982	Cle A	66	184	13	39	6	1	3	16	24-1	0	30	.212	.299	.304	67	-8	0-0	.990	-6	107	108	C63,3b2	46	-1.2
1983	Cle A	48	121	15	31	3	0	4	15	15-0	0	19	.256	.336	.380	94	-1	0-1	.995	0	135	128	C43	0	0.1
1984	Cle A	75	220	38	64	11	0	12	41	33-5	0	35	.291	.377	.505	141	13	1-2	.982	-1	118	76	C63/13D	18	1.4
1985	Cle A	73	173	11	24	4	1	0	13	22-0	0	21	.139	.234	.173	14	-21	0-1	.986	-8	65	114	C67	0	-2.7
1986	Cle A	92	254	28	68	9	0	2	26	22-0	1	49	.268	.325	.327	80	-7	0-1	.990	-7	95	77	C86	0	-1.0
1987	Cle A	89	211	20	46	9	0	5	16	12-0	0	28	.218	.260	.332	55	-14	0-0	.990	-2	100	111	C86	0	-1.3
1988	Cle A	32	72	6	9	1	0	1	8	8-0	1	12	.125	.217	.181	14	-8	0-0	.979	2	111	128	C32	0	-0.5
	Det A	1	0	0	0	0	0	0	0	0-0	0	0	ø	ø	ø	ø	0	0-0	ø	-0	0	0	/C	0	0.0
	Year	33	72	6	9	1	0	1	8	8-0	1	12	.125	.217	.181	14	-8	0-0	.979	2	110	127	C33	0	-0.5
1989	Oak A	1	2	0	1	0	0	0	1	0-0	0	1	.500	.500	.500	189	0	0-0	1.000	1	0	0	/C	0	0.1
Total	9	498	1284	134	292	46	2	27	142	138-6	2	197	.227	.300	.329	73	-49	1-5	.987	-23	102	101	C457,3b3,D3/1	64	-5.6
Bando, Sal Salvatore Leonard; B2.13.1944 Cleveland OH; BR/TR/6´0˝/(195–200); [OakA65 6/119]; d9.3; C2; b–Chris; Col Arizona St.																									
1966	KC A	11	24	1	7	1	1	0	1	1-0	0	3	.292	.320	.417	113	0	0-0	.933	4	187	81	3b7	0	0.4
1967	KC A	47	130	11	25	3	2	0	6	16-0	3	24	.192	.295	.246	64	-6	1-0	.959	9	122	106	3b44	0	0.4
1968	Oak A	162	605	67	152	25	5	9	67	51-6	7	78	.251	.314	.354	107	5	13-4	.964	-4	89	97	3b162/lf	0	0.2
1969	Oak A★	**162**	609	106	171	25	3	31	113	111-5	11	82	.281	.400	.484	152	47	1-4	.954	-8	95	106	3b162	0	3.8
1970	Oak A	155	502	93	132	20	2	20	75	118-5	6	88	.263	.407	.430	136	32	6-10	.954	-13	88	76	3b152	0	1.7
1971	†Oak A	153	538	75	146	23	1	24	94	86-11	8	55	.271	.377	.452	137	29	3-7	.971	-20	82	77	3b153	0	0.8
1972	†Oak A★	152	535	64	126	20	3	15	77	78-17	9	55	.236	.341	.368	117	13	3-1	.960	0	102	108	3b151/2	0	1.5
1973	†Oak A★	**162**	592	97	170	**32**	3	29	98	82-5	4	84	.287	.375	.498	152	42	4-2	.949	-29	80	90	3b159,D3	0	1.3
1974	†Oak A✳	146	498	84	121	21	2	22	103	86-4	5	79	.243	.352	.426	133	24	2-3	.946	-14	89	102	3b141,D3	0	1.0
1975	†Oak A	160	562	64	129	24	1	15	78	87-2	5	80	.230	.337	.356	98	1	7-1	.967	-20	85	126	3b160	0	-1.9
1976	Oak A	158	550	75	132	18	2	27	84	76-1	4	74	.240	.335	.427	128	19	20-6	.962	-2	99	108	3b155,S5,D2	0	2.0
1977	Mil A	159	580	65	145	27	3	17	82	75-3	3	89	.250	.336	.395	99	1	4-2	.966	-1	100	120	3b135,D24/2S	0	-0.3
1978	Mil A	152	540	85	154	20	6	17	78	72-4	6	52	.285	.371	.439	127	21	3-2	.968	8	113	103	3b134,D12,1b5	0	2.7
1979	Mil A	130	476	57	117	14	3	9	43	57-3	3	42	.246	.330	.345	82	-11	2-0	.963	-11	94	81	3b109,D19,1b4/P2	0	-2.4
1980	Mil A	78	254	28	50	12	1	5	31	29-2	1	35	.197	.278	.311	64	-13	5-3	.934	-2	99	114	3b57,D15,1b7	0	-1.6
1981	†Mil A	32	65	10	13	4	0	2	9	6-1	0	3	.200	.268	.354	81	-2	1-1	.967	-1	94	145	3b15,1b9,D2	0	-0.4
Total	16	2019	7060	982	1790	289	38	242	1039	1031-69	75	923	.254	.352	.408	119	202	75-46	.959	-103	94	100	3b1896,D80,1b25,S6,2b3/Plf	0	9.2
Banister, Jeff Jeffery Todd; B1.15.1965 Weatherford OK; BR/TR/6´2˝/200; [PitN86 25/621]; d7.23; Col Houston																									
1991	Pit N	1	1	0	1	0	0	0	0	0-0	0	0	1.000	1.000	1.000	469	0	0-0	ø	0	—	—	/H	0	0.0
Banks, Brian Brian Glen; B9.28.1970 Mesa AZ; BB/TR/6´3˝/(200–210); [MilA93 2/43]; d9.9; Col Brigham Young																									
1996	Mil A	4	7	2	4	2	0	1	2	1-0	0	2	.571	.625	1.286	351	3	0-0	1.000	0	67	0	O3L/1	0	0.2
1997	Mil A	28	68	9	14	1	0	1	8	6-0	0	17	.206	.267	.265	40	-6	0-1	.950	-1	71	0	O15(15/0/1),1b5/3D	0	-0.8
1998	Mil N	24	24	3	7	2	0	1	5	4-0	0	7	.292	.393	.500	130	1	0-0	1.000	-1	39	0	C5,1b2/3lf	0	0.0
1999	Mil N	105	219	34	53	7	1	5	22	25-5	0	59	.242	.317	.352	69	-11	6-1	.992	-4	120	79	1b44,C40,O5(4/0/1)	0	-1.4
2002	Fla N	20	28	3	9	1	0	1	4	1-0	0	6	.321	.345	.464	115	0	0-0	1.000	-0	95	0	O8(3/0/5)/13	0	0.0
2003	†Fla N	92	149	14	35	6	2	4	23	25-1	2	38	.235	.348	.383	95	-1	2-1	.975	-2	89	69	O33(23/0/10),1b12/D	0	-0.4
Total	6	273	495	65	122	19	3	13	64	62-6	2	129	.246	.330	.376	83	-14	8-3	.989	-9	111	92	1b65,O65(49/0/17),C45,3b3,D2	0	-2.4

YEAR	TM LG	G	AB	R	H	2B	3B	HR	RBI	BB-IB	HP	SO	AVG	OBP	SLG	AOPS	ABR	SB-CS	FA	FR	RNG	THR	GAMES AT POSITION	DL	BFW
Banks, Ernie	Ernest "Mr. Cub"; B1.31.1931 Dallas TX; BR/TR/6´1˝/(170–185); d9.17; C7; HF1977; Negro Lg 1950–53 Mil 1951–52																								
1953	Chi N	10	35	3	11	1	1	2	6	4	0	5	.314	.385	.571	142	2	0-0	.981	2	112	133	S10	0	0.5
1954	Chi N	**154**	593	70	163	19	7	19	79	40	7	50	.275	.326	.427	94	-7	6-10	.959	-2	99	99	S154	0	0.2
1955	Chi N★	**154**	596	98	176	29	9	44	117	45-6	2	72	.295	.345	.596	145	35	9-3	**.972**	3	102	100	S154	0	5.1
1956	Chi N☆	139	538	82	160	25	8	28	85	52-18	0	62	.297	.358	.530	137	27	6-9	.962	-13	88	100	S139	0	2.4
1957	Chi N★	**156**	594	113	169	34	6	43	102	70-11	3	85	.285	.360	.579	150	41	8-4	.975	-11	90	86	S100,3b58	0	3.9
1958	Chi N★	**154**	617	119	193	23	11	**47**	**129**	52-12	4	87	.313	.366	**.614**	157	47	4-4	.960	0	99	89	S154	0	5.9
1959	Chi N★	**155**	589	97	179	25	6	45	**143**	64-**20**	7	72	.304	.374	.596	156	46	2-4	**.985**	7	**108**	103	S154	0	6.4
1960	Chi N★	**156**	597	94	162	32	7	**41**	117	71-**28**	4	69	.271	.350	.554	145	36	1-3	**.977**	12	107	99	S156	0	**6.0**
1961	Chi N★	138	511	75	142	22	4	29	80	54-21	2	75	.278	.346	.507	122	15	1-2	.965	20	**118**	100	S104,O23L,1b7	0	4.0
1962	Chi N★	154	610	87	164	20	6	37	104	30-3	7	71	.269	.306	.503	110	5	5-1	.993	-2	98	98	1b149,3b3	0	-0.5
1963	Chi N	130	432	41	98	20	1	18	64	39-16	4	73	.227	.292	.403	94	-3	0-3	.993	-2	95	110	1b125	0	-1.5
1964	Chi N	157	591	67	156	29	6	23	95	36-11	3	84	.264	.307	.450	107	4	1-2	.994	10	**126**	101	1b157	0	0.4
1965	Chi N★	163	612	79	162	25	3	28	106	55-19	6	64	.265	.328	.453	116	12	3-5	.992	-9	83	108	1b162	0	-0.8
1966	Chi N	141	511	52	139	23	7	15	75	29-10	5	59	.272	.315	.432	105	2	0-1	.992	2	110	83	1b130,3b8	0	-0.4
1967	Chi N★	151	573	68	158	26	4	23	95	27-8	3	93	.276	.310	.455	112	7	2-2	.993	1	102	101	1b147	0	-0.2
1968	Chi N	150	552	71	136	27	0	32	83	27-4	5	67	.246	.287	.469	117	9	2-0	.996	-0	97	**115**	1b147	0	0.1
1969	Chi N★	155	565	60	143	19	2	23	106	42-7	7	101	.253	.309	.416	91	-8	0-0	**.997**	-0	94	103	1b153	0	-2.1
1970	Chi N	72	222	25	56	6	2	12	44	20-3	1	33	.252	.313	.459	94	-3	0-0	.993	-2	86	119	1b62	30	-0.9
1971	Chi N	39	83	4	16	2	0	3	6	6-1	0	14	.193	.247	.325	53	-5	0-0	1.000	0	94	99	1b20	17	-0.7
Total	19	2528	9421	1305	2583	407	90	512	1636	763-198	70	1236	.274	.330	.500	122	262	50-53	.994	17	100	103	1b1259,S1125,3b69,O23L	47	27.8
Banks, George	George Edward; B9.24.1938 Pacolet Mills SC; D3.1.1985 Spartanburg SC; BR/TR/5´11˝/(180–185); d4.15																								
1962	Min A	63	103	22	26	0	2	4	15	21-0	1	27	.252	.372	.408	109	2	0-0	.962	-2	89	0	O17(7/0/11),3b6	0	-0.1
1963	Min A	25	71	5	11	4	0	3	8	9-1	1	21	.155	.259	.338	65	-3	0-0	.910	0	98	120	3b21	0	-0.3
1964	Min A	1	1	0	0	0	0	0	0	0-0	0	1	.000	.000	.000	-99	0	0-0	ø	0	—	—	/H	0	0.0
	Cle A	9	17	6	5	1	0	2	3	6-0	0	6	.294	.478	.706	226	3	0-0	1.000	-1	81	0	O3(3/0/1)/23	0	0.3
	Year	10	18	6	5	1	0	2	3	6-0	0	7	.278	.458	.667	210	3	0-0	1.000	-1	81	0	O3(3/0/1)/23	0	0.3
1965	Cle A	4	5	0	1	1	0	0	0	1-0	0	3	.200	.333	.400	107	0	0-1	1.000	0	94	523	/3	0	0.0
1966	Cle A	4	4	0	1	0	0	0	1	0-0	0	1	.250	.250	.250	44	0	0-0	ø	0	—	—	/H	0	0.0
Total	5	106	201	33	44	6	2	9	27	37-1	2	59	.219	.340	.403	102	2	0-1	.919	-2	98	130	3b29,O20(10/0/12)/2	0	-0.1
Bankston, Everett	Wilborn Everett; B5.25.1893 Barnesville GA; D2.26.1970 Griffin GA; BL/TR/5´11˝/180; d8.5																								
1915	Phi A	11	36	6	5	1	1	1	2	2	1	5	.139	.205	.306	55	-2	1	.882	-1	85	95	O8(4/4/0)	—	-0.4
Banning, Jim	James M.; B6.11.1865 New York NY; D10.14.1952 St.Paul MN; BL/TR/5´6˝/150; d9.27																								
1888	Was N	1	0	0	0	0	0	0	0	0	0	0	ø	ø	ø	ø	0	0	1.000	-0	—	—	/C	—	0.0
1889	Was N	2	1	0	0	0	0	0	0	0	0	0	.000	.000	.000	-99	0	0	1.000	1	—	—	C2	—	0.0
Total	2	3	1	0	0	0	0	0	0	0	0	0	.000	.000	.000	-99	0	0	1.000	1	—	—	C3	—	0.0
Bannister, Alan	Alan; B9.3.1951 Montebello CA; BR/TR/5´11˝/(170–175); [PhiN73*1/1]; d7.13; Col Arizona St.; OF(254/72/100)																								
1974	Phi N	26	25	4	3	0	0	0	1	3-0	1	7	.120	.241	.120	3	-3	0-0	1.000	-1	89	0	O8C,S2	0	-0.4
1975	Phi N	24	61	10	16	3	1	0	0	1-0	0	9	.262	.274	.344	67	-3	2-2	1.000	1	134	0	O18(4/14/1)/2S	0	-0.2
1976	Chi A	73	145	19	36	6	2	0	8	14-1	1	21	.248	.317	.317	86	-2	12-4	.988	1	120	46	O43(29/13/4),S14,2b4/3D	0	0.0
1977	Chi A	139	560	87	154	20	3	3	57	54-1	2	49	.275	.335	.338	86	-10	4-3	.936	-30	82	62	S133,2b3,O3(2/2/0)	0	-2.6
1978	Chi A	49	107	16	24	3	2	0	8	11-1	1	12	.224	.303	.290	66	-5	3-3	1.000	-1	102	0	D19,O15(8/7/0),S8,2b2	65	-0.6
1979	Chi A	136	506	71	144	28	8	2	55	43-1	3	40	.285	.342	.383	96	-3	22-6	.963	-15	92	68	2b65,O47(47/0/2),3b12/1D	0	-1.3
1980	Chi A	45	130	16	25	6	0	0	9	12-5	0	16	.192	.259	.238	38	-11	5-2	1.000	-0	98	0	O23(22/0/1),3b17	0	-1.2
	Cle A	81	262	41	86	17	4	1	32	28-1	0	25	.328	.388	.435	125	10	9-2	.968	-4	96	73	2b41,O40(9/9/26),3b3,S2	0	0.8
	Year	126	392	57	111	23	4	1	41	40-6	0	41	.283	.346	.370	97	-1	14-4	.981	-4	99	56	O63(31/9/27),2b41,3b20,S2	0	-0.4
1981	Cle A	68	232	36	61	11	1	1	17	16-2	0	19	.263	.309	.332	86	-4	16-2	.986	-3	108	93	O35(18/6/17),2b30,1b2/S	0	-0.4
1982	Cle A	101	348	40	93	16	1	4	41	42-1	1	41	.267	.347	.353	93	-2	18-5	.991	-3	113	35	O55(46/4/9),2b48,S2/3D	31	-0.2
1983	Cle A	117	377	51	100	25	4	5	45	31-0	3	43	.265	.323	.393	93	-3	6-6	.969	-1	91	123	O91(58/8/34),2b27,1b3,D3	0	-0.7
1984	Hou N	9	20	2	4	2	0	0	0	2-0	0	2	.200	.273	.300	65	-1	0-0	.947	-1	75	51	S4/lf	0	-0.1
	Tex A	47	112	20	33	2	1	2	9	21-0	1	17	.295	.407	.384	117	4	3-0	.959	-10	61	38	2b25,O3(1/1/1)13D	27	-0.5
1985	Tex A	57	122	17	32	4	1	1	6	14-0	0	17	.262	.338	.336	84	-2	8-2	1.000	-1	92	0	D21,O14(9/0/5),2b10,3b5,1b4	17	-0.3
Total	12	972	3007	430	811	143	28	19	288	292-13	13	318	.270	.334	.355	90	-35	108-37	.983	-65	103	72	O396L,2b256,S167,D66,3b40,1b11	140	-7.7
Bannon, Jimmy	James Henry "Foxy Grandpa"; B5.5.1871 Amesbury MA; D3.24.1948 Glen Rock NJ; BR/TR/5´5˝/160; d6.15; b–Tom; Col Holy Cross; ▲																								
1893	StL N	26	107	9	36	3	4	0	15	4	1	5	.336	.366	.439	113	1	8	.795	-5	59	0	O24(1/0/23),S2/P	—	-0.4
1894	Bos N	128	494	130	166	29	10	13	114	62	4	42	.336	.414	.514	114	10	47	.873	17	**200**	**242**	O128R/P	—	1.6
1895	Bos N	124	493	101	171	35	5	6	74	54	5	31	.347	.417	.475	120	16	28	.879	7	161	75	O123(1/0/122)/P	—	1.3
1896	Bos N	89	344	53	87	9	5	0	50	32	1	23	.253	.318	.308	62	-20	16	.901	-2	118	76	O76(2/1/73),2b6,S5,3b3	—	-2.1
Total	4	367	1438	293	460	76	24	19	253	152	11	101	.320	.389	.446	104	7	99	.877	17	160	131	O351(4/1/346),S7,2b6,3b3,P3	—	0.4
Bannon, Tom	Thomas Edward "Ward Six"; B5.8.1869 Amesbury MA; D1.26.1950 Lynn MA; BR/TR/5´8˝/175; d5.10; b–Jimmy																								
1895	NY N	37	159	33	43	6	2	0	8	7	0	8	.270	.301	.333	65	-9	20	.894	1	261	130	O21(13/0/8),1b16	—	-0.8
1896	NY N	2	7	1	1	1	0	0	0	1	0	1	.143	.250	.286	42	-1	0	.500	-1	0	0	O2(1/1/0)	—	-0.1
Total	2	39	166	34	44	7	2	0	8	8	0	9	.265	.299	.331	64	-10	20	.878	0	246	123	O23(14/1/8),1b16	—	-0.9
Barajas, Rod	Rodrigo Richard; B9.5.1975 Ontario CA; BR/TR/6´2˝/(220–230); d9.25; Col Cerritos (CA) JC																								
1999	Ari N	5	16	3	4	1	0	1	3	1-0	0	1	.250	.294	.500	95	0	0-0	1.000	-2	189	0	C5	0	-0.1
2000	Ari N	5	13	1	3	0	0	1	3	0-0	0	4	.231	.231	.462	66	-1	0-0	1.000	-0	0	0	C5	0	-0.1
2001	†Ari N	51	106	9	17	3	0	3	9	4-0	0	26	.160	.191	.274	17	-14	0-0	.995	-17	66	91	C50	0	-2.8
2002	†Ari N	70	154	12	36	10	0	3	23	10-4	3	25	.234	.288	.357	64	-8	1-0	.997	-15	147	81	C69/1	0	-2.0
2003	Ari N	80	220	19	48	15	0	3	28	14-7	1	43	.218	.265	.327	50	-16	0-0	1.000	11	130	113	C79	39	0.0
2004	Tex A	108	358	50	89	26	1	15	58	13-0	3	63	.249	.276	.453	83	-10	0-1	.990	0	128	88	C105,1b2	0	-0.3
2005	Tex A	120	410	53	104	24	0	21	60	26-0	6	70	.254	.306	.466	99	-1	0-0	.988	-6	142	84	C119/1	0	0.1
2006	Tex A	97	344	49	88	20	0	11	41	17-0	4	51	.256	.298	.410	81	-11	0-0	.984	1	136	87	C94,1b5	0	-0.3
Total	8	536	1621	196	389	99	1	58	225	85-11	17	283	.240	.282	.410	76	-61	1-1	.991	-26	131	88	C526,1b9	39	-5.5
Barbare, Walter	Walter Lawrence "Dinty"; B8.11.1891 Greenville SC; D10.28.1965 Greenville SC; BR/TR/6´0˝/162; d9.17																								
1914	Cle A	15	52	6	16	2	2	0	5	2	1	5	.308	.345	.423	126	1	1-4	.933	1	120	148	3b14/S	—	0.2
1915	Cle A	77	246	15	47	3	1	0	11	10	4	27	.191	.235	.211	33	-21	6-5	.960	6	104	104	3b68/1	—	-1.4
1916	Cle A	13	48	3	11	1	0	0	3	4	0	9	.229	.288	.250	58	-2	0	.977	2	122	88	3b12	—	0.0
1918	Bos A	13	29	2	5	3	0	0	2	0	0	1	.172	.172	.276	36	-2	1	.826	-3	79	73	3b11/S	—	-0.5
1919	Pit N	85	293	34	80	11	5	1	34	18	1	18	.273	.317	.355	98	-1	11	.961	-8	82	110	3b80/2	—	-0.7
1920	Pit N	57	186	9	51	5	2	0	12	9	0	11	.274	.308	.323	79	-5	5-3	.923	-4	92	102	S34,2b12,3b5	—	-0.7
1921	Bos N	134	550	66	166	22	7	0	49	24	0	28	.302	.331	.367	89	-9	11-4	.957	-15	94	89	S121,2b8,3b2	—	-1.0
1922	Bos N	106	373	38	86	5	4	0	40	21	0	22	.231	.272	.265	41	-34	2-0	.966	3	103	109	2b45,3b38,1b14	—	-2.7
Total	8	500	1777	173	462	52	21	1	156	88	6	121	.260	.297	.315	71	-73	37-16	.959	-18	96	105	3b230,S157,2b66,1b15	—	-6.8
Barbary, Red	Donald Odell; B6.20.1920 Simpsonville SC; D9.27.2003 Simpsonville SC; BR/TR/6´2˝/195; d5.22																								
1943	Was A	1	1	0	0	0	0	0	0	0	0	0	.000	.000	.000	-99	0	0-0	ø	0	—	—	/H	0	0.0
Barbeau, Jap	William Joseph; B6.10.1882 New York NY; D9.10.1969 Milwaukee WI; BR/TR/5´5˝/140; d9.27																								
1905	Cle A	11	37	1	10	1	1	0	2	1	0	—	.270	.289	.351	102	0	1	.905	0	106	213	2b11	—	0.0
1906	Cle A	42	129	8	25	5	3	0	12	9	2	—	.194	.257	.279	69	-5	5	.830	-8	87	204	3b32,S6	—	-1.3
1909	Pit N	91	350	60	77	16	3	0	25	37	4	—	.220	.302	.283	75	-9	19	.891	-18	83	89	3b85	—	-2.8
	StL N	48	175	23	44	3	0	0	5	28	5	—	.251	.370	.269	105	3	14	.901	-5	89	126	3b47	—	0.0
	Year	139	525	83	121	19	3	0	30	65	9	—	.230	.326	.278	85	-6	33	.895	-22	85	101	3b132	—	-2.8
1910	StL N	7	21	4	4	0	1	0	2	3	0	3	.190	.292	.286	71	-1	0	.917	2	155	0	3b6/2	—	0.1
Total	4	199	712	96	160	25	8	0	46	78	11	3	.225	.311	.282	82	-12	39	.884	-29	88	115	3b170,2b12,S6	—	-4.0

YEAR	TM LG	G	AB	R	H	2B	3B	HR	RBI	BB-IB	HP	SO	AVG	OBP	SLG	AOPS	ABR	SB-CS	FA	FR	RNG	THR	GAMES AT POSITION	DL	BFW
Barbee, Dave	David Monroe; B5.7.1905 Greensboro NC; D7.1.1968 Albemarle NC; BR/TR/5´11.5˝/178; d7.29; Col Oglethorpe																								
1926	Phi A	19	47	7	8	1	1	1	5	2	1	4	.170	.220	.298	32	-5	0-0	1.000	0	101	95	O10R		
1932	Pit N	97	327	37	84	22	6	5	55	18	2	38	.257	.300	.407	89	-6	1	.975	4	111	103	O78(77/1/0)	—	-0.6
Total	2	116	374	44	92	23	7	6	60	20	3	42	.246	.290	.393	82	-11	1-0	.977	4	110	102	O88(77/1/10)	—	-0.6
																								—	-1.2
Barber, Charlie	Charles D.; B1854 Philadelphia PA; D11.23.1910 Philadelphia PA; BR/TR; d4.17																								
1884	Cin U	55	204	38	41	1	4	0	—	11	—	—	.201	.242	.245	44	-21	—	.837	3	111	82	3b55	—	-1.5
Barber, Turner	Tyrus Turner; B7.9.1893 Lavinia TN; D10.20.1968 Milan TN; BL/TR/5´11˝/170; d8.19; Col Union (TN)																								
1915	Was A	20	53	9	16	1	1	0	6	6	1	7	.302	.383	.358	120	1	0-3	.952	0	78	177	O19(3/0/16)		
1916	Was A	15	33	3	7	0	1	1	5	2	0	3	.212	.257	.364	87	-1	0	.833	-1	90	0	O10(6/0/4)	—	0.0
1917	Chi N	7	28	2	6	1	0	0	2	2	0	8	.214	.267	.250	54	-1	1	1.000	1	90	242	O7(1/6/0)	—	-0.3
1918	†Chi N	55	123	11	29	3	2	0	10	9	1	16	.236	.293	.293	77	-3	3	.940	-2	92	62	O27(4/17/15),1b4	—	-0.1
1919	Chi N	76	230	26	72	9	4	0	21	14	1	17	.313	.355	.387	122	6	7	.949	-3	95	87	O68(53/13/2)	—	-0.8
1920	Chi N	94	340	27	90	10	5	0	50	9	3	26	.265	.290	.324	74	-12	5-6	.988	-6	73	85	1b69,O17(6/8/3),2b2	—	0.0
1921	Chi N	127	452	73	142	14	4	1	54	41	6	24	.314	.379	.369	99	1	5-9	.970	2	90	152	O123(90/20/14)	—	-2.3
1922	Chi N	84	226	35	70	7	4	0	29	30	0	9	.310	.391	.376	97	0	7-4	.953	-3	93	78	O47(31/0/16),1b16	—	-0.7
1923	Bro N	13	46	3	10	2	0	0	8	2	0	2	.217	.250	.261	36	-4	0-1	1.000	-1	84	86	O12C	—	-0.7
Total	9	491	1531	189	442	47	21	2	185	115	12	112	.289	.343	.351	93	-13	28-23	.959	-13	91	114	O330(194/76/70),1b89,2b2	—	-0.5
																								—	-5.4
Barberie, Bret	Bret Edward; B8.16.1967 Long Beach CA; BB/TR/5´11˝/(180–185); [MonN88 7/180]; d6.16; Col USC																								
1991	Mon N	57	136	16	48	12	2	2	18	20-2	2	22	.353	.435	.515	170	14	0-0	.931	-1	109	93	S19,2b10,3b10/1	0	1.5
1992	Mon N	111	285	26	66	11	0	1	24	47-3	8	62	.232	.354	.281	83	-3	9-5	.932	5	116	108	3b63,2b26/S	16	0.3
1993	Fla N	99	375	45	104	16	2	5	33	33-2	7	58	.277	.344	.371	87	-6	2-4	.982	7	105	102	2b97	68	0.5
1994	Fla N	107	372	40	112	20	2	5	31	23-3	9	65	.301	.356	.406	94	-2	2-0	.975	7	105	97	2b106	0	0.9
1995	Bal A	90	237	32	57	14	0	2	25	36-0	6	50	.241	.351	.325	77	-6	3-3	.977	4	101	119	2b74,3b3,D5	0	0.0
1996	Chi N	15	29	4	1	0	0	1	2	5-0	0	11	.034	.176	.138	-15	-5	0-1	1.000	-1	125	35	2b6,3b2/S	0	-0.6
Total	6	479	1434	163	388	73	6	16	133	164-10	32	268	.271	.356	.363	92	-8	16-13	.980	21	104	101	2b319,3b78,S21,D5/1	84	2.6
Barbieri, Jim	James Patrick; B9.15.1941 Schenectady NY; BL/TR/5´7˝/155; d7.5																								
1966	†LA N	39	82	9	23	5	0	0	3	9-1	0	7	.280	.352	.341	102	1	2-0	.939	1	108	187	O20(9/0/11)	0	0.1
Barclay, George	George Oliver "Deerfoot"; B5.16.1876 Millville PA; D4.3.1909 Philadelphia PA; BR/TR/5´10˝/162; d4.17; Col Lafayette																								
1902	StL N	137	543	79	163	14	2	3	53	31	6	—	.300	.345	.350	119	12	30	.904	-6	87	97	O137L	—	-0.2
1903	StL N	108	419	37	104	10	8	0	42	15	2	—	.248	.278	.310	70	-19	12	.901	-7	87	0	O107L	—	-3.2
1904	StL N	103	375	41	75	7	4	1	28	12	6	—	.200	.237	.248	52	-22	14	.947	-6	54	55	O103L	—	-3.7
	Bos N	24	93	5	21	3	1	0	10	2	2	—	.226	.258	.280	68	-4	3	.935	-2	74	110	O24(6/1/17)	—	-0.7
	Year	127	468	46	96	10	5	1	38	14	8	—	.205	.241	.254	55	-26	17	.945	-8	57	64	O127(109/1/17)	—	-4.4
1905	Bos N	29	108	5	19	1	0	0	7	2	2	—	.176	.205	.185	17	-11	2	.854	-4	54	109	O28L	—	-1.8
Total	4	401	1538	167	382	35	15	4	140	62	18	—	.248	.286	.298	79	-44	61	.911	-25	75	61	O399(381/1/17)	—	-9.6
Bard, Josh	Joshua David; B3.30.1978 Ithaca NY; BB/TR/6´3˝/(205–215); [ColN99 3/100]; d8.23; Col Texas Tech																								
2002	Cle A	24	90	9	20	5	0	3	12	4-0	0	13	.222	.255	.378	64	-5	0-0	.988	0	147	115	C24	0	-0.3
2003	Cle A	91	303	25	74	13	1	8	36	22-1	0	53	.244	.293	.373	75	-12	0-2	.991	11	110	125	C87/D	0	0.4
2004	Cle A	7	19	5	8	2	0	1	4	3-0	0	0	.421	.478	.684	212	3	0-0	1.000	1	77	142	C7	92	0.5
2005	Cle A	34	83	6	16	4	0	1	9	9-0	0	11	.193	.266	.277	48	-6	0-0	.983	2	193	71	C31	0	-0.3
2006	Bos A	7	18	2	5	1	0	0	0	3-0	0	3	.278	.381	.333	85	0	0-0	1.000	-3	28	71	C7	0	-0.2
	†SD N	93	231	28	78	19	0	9	40	27-1	1	39	.338	.406	.537	147	18	1-0	.993	1	79	78	C71	0	2.2
Total	5	256	744	75	201	44	1	22	101	68-2	1	119	.270	.329	.421	97	-2	1-2	.991	13	113	103	C227/D	92	2.3
Barfield, Jesse	Jesse Lee; B10.29.1959 Joliet IL; BR/TR/6´1˝/(170–206); [TorA77 9/233]; d9.3; C3; s–Josh																								
1981	Tor A	25	95	7	22	3	2	2	9	4-0	1	19	.232	.270	.368	78	-3	4-3	1.000	4	134	105	O25R	0	-0.1
1982	Tor A	139	394	54	97	13	2	18	58	42-3	3	79	.246	.323	.426	95	-3	1-4	.963	1	95	183	O137(1/3/136)/D	0	-0.9
1983	Tor A	128	388	58	98	13	3	27	68	22-0	4	110	.253	.296	.510	111	3	2-5	.966	8	107	**209**	O120(0/1/120),D5	0	0.4
1984	Tor A	110	320	51	91	14	1	14	49	35-5	2	81	.284	.357	.466	121	10	8-2	.952	6	113	178	O88(0/9/79),D9	0	1.2
1985	†Tor A	155	539	94	156	34	9	27	84	66-5	4	143	.289	.369	.536	141	31	22-8	.989	15	107	**206**	O154(0/8/147)	0	3.9
1986	Tor A★	158	589	107	170	35	2	**40**	108	69-5	8	146	.289	.368	.559	145	37	8-8	.992	16	112	182	O157(0/18/147)	0	4.3
1987	Tor A	159	590	89	155	25	3	28	84	58-7	3	141	.263	.331	.458	104	2	3-5	.992	13	112	163	O158(0/13/152)	0	0.7
1988	Tor A	137	468	62	114	21	5	18	56	41-6	1	108	.244	.302	.425	101	-1	7-3	.988	13	**114**	153	O136(0/13/132)/D	15	0.9
1989	Tor A	21	80	8	16	4	0	5	11	5-0	1	28	.200	.256	.438	93	-1	0-2	.979	2	94	246	O21(1/0/20)	0	-0.1
	NY A	129	441	71	106	19	1	18	56	82-6	2	122	.240	.360	.410	118	13	5-3	.972	8	106	166	O129(0/18/120)	0	1.8
	Year	150	521	79	122	23	1	23	67	87-6	3	150	.234	.345	.415	115	12	5-5	.973	10	104	177	O150(1/18/140)	0	1.7
1990	NY A	153	476	69	117	21	2	25	78	82-4	5	150	.246	.359	.456	126	19	4-3	.973	7	104	158	O151(0/4/151)	0	2.1
1991	NY A	84	284	37	64	12	0	17	48	36-6	0	80	.225	.312	.447	107	2	1-0	1.000	9	112	177	O81(1/0/81)	70	0.8
1992	NY A	30	95	8	13	2	0	2	7	9-2	0	27	.137	.210	.221	21	-10	1-1	.966	0	95	160	O30R	133	-1.2
Total	12	1428	4759	715	1219	216	30	241	716	551-49	34	1234	.256	.335	.466	116	99	66-47	.980	101	108	176	O1387(3/87/1340),D16	218	13.8
Barfield, Josh	Joshua Laroy; B12.17.1982 Barquisimeto, Lara, Venezuela; BR/TR/6´0˝/185; [SDN01 4/120]; d4.3; f–Jesse																								
2006	†SD N	150	539	72	151	32	3	13	58	30-7	2	81	.280	.318	.423	93	-7	21-5	.987	-19	89	99	2b147	0	-1.6
Barker, Al	Alfred L; B1.18.1839 Lost Creek Twp. IN; D9.15.1912 Rockford IL; d6.1																								
1871	Rok NA	1	4	0	1	0	0	0	2	1	—	0	.250	.400	.250	97	0	0-0	1.000	-0	0	0	/lf	—	0.0
Barker, Glen	Glen F.; B5.10.1971 Albany NY; BB/TR/5´10˝/180; [DetA93 11/305]; d4.7; Col St. Rose																								
1999	†Hou N	81	73	23	21	2	0	1	11	11-0	1	19	.288	.384	.356	91	0	17-6	.981	-0	94	158	O57(3/47/8)/D	15	0.1
2000	Hou N	84	67	18	15	2	1	2	6	7-0	1	23	.224	.307	.373	65	-4	9-6	.985	1	117	72	O69(2/63/4)	0	-0.3
2001	Hou N	70	24	12	2	0	0	0	1	3-0	2	6	.083	.233	.083	-10	-4	4-6	1.000	-0	112	0	O60C	0	-0.5
Total	3	235	164	53	38	4	1	3	18	21-0	4	48	.232	.330	.323	65	-8	30-18	.987	1	107	89	O186(5/170/12)/D	15	-0.7
Barker, Kevin	Kevin Stewart; B7.26.1975 Bristol VA; BL/TL/6´3˝/(205–235); [MilA96 3/73]; d8.19; Col VPI																								
1999	Mil N	38	117	13	33	3	0	3	23	9-1	0	19	.282	.331	.385	81	-4	1-0	.996	0	103	80	1b31	0	-0.6
2000	Mil N	40	100	14	22	5	0	2	9	20-0	1	21	.220	.352	.330	75	-3	1-0	.993	-3	73	96	1b32	0	-0.8
2002	SD N	7	19	0	3	0	0	0	0	1-0	0	6	.158	.200	.158	-5	-3	1-0	1.000	-1	30	108	1b6	0	-0.4
2006	Tor A	12	17	3	4	1	0	1	1	1-0	0	10	.235	.278	.471	85	0	0-0	1.000	-1	0	0	1b2/rfD	0	-0.1
Total	4	97	253	30	62	9	0	6	33	31-1	1	56	.245	.328	.352	74	-10	3-0	.995	-4	81	88	1b71,D5/rf	0	-1.9
Barker, Ray	Raymond Herrell "Buddy"; B3.12.1936 Martinsburg WV; BL/TR/6´0˝/(192–200); d9.13																								
1960	Bal A	5	6	0	0	0	0	0	0	0-0	0	3	.000	.000	.000	-99	-2	0-0	ø	-0	0	0	/lf	0	-0.2
1965	Cle A	11	6	0	0	0	0	0	0	2-1	0	2	.000	.250	.000	-22	-1	0-0	1.000	-0	0	0	1b3	0	-0.1
	NY A	98	205	21	52	11	0	7	31	20-5	3	46	.254	.326	.410	109	3	1-0	.991	6	149	110	1b61,3b3	0	0.6
	Year	109	211	21	52	11	0	7	31	22-6	3	48	.246	.324	.398	105	2	1-0	.991	6	148	109	1b64,3b3	0	0.5
1966	NY A	61	75	11	14	5	0	3	13	4-0	0	20	.187	.225	.373	72	-3	0-0	.987	4	178	65	1b47	0	0.0
1967	NY A	17	26	2	2	0	0	0	0	3-0	0	5	.077	.172	.077	-25	-4	0-0	.961	1	163	90	1b13	0	-0.4
Total	4	192	318	34	68	16	0	10	44	29-6	3	76	.214	.283	.358	84	-7	1-0	.987	11	158	95	1b124,3b3/lf	0	-0.1
Barkett, Andy	Andrew Jon; B9.5.1974 Miami FL; BL/TL/6´1˝/205; d5.28; Col North Carolina St.																								
2001	Pit N	17	46	5	14	2	0	1	3	4-1	1	7	.304	.373	.413	100	0	1-0	1.000	1	92	180	O10(9/0/2),1b4/D	0	0.0
Barkley, Red	John Duncan; B9.19.1912 Childress TX; D12.12.2000 Waco TX; BR/TR/5´11˝/160; d9.2; gs–Brian																								
1937	StL A	31	101	9	27	6	0	0	14	14	0	17	.267	.357	.327	73	-4	1-0	.969	-4	90	88	2b31	—	-0.5
1939	Bos N	12	11	1	0	0	0	0	0	1	0	2	.000	.083	.000	-82	-3	0	.842	2	158	0	S7,3b4	—	-0.1
1943	Bro N	20	51	6	16	3	0	0	7	4	0	7	.314	.364	.373	113	1	1	.894	-3	89	109	S18	0	-0.1
Total	3	63	163	16	43	9	0	0	21	19	0	26	.264	.341	.319	75	-6	2-0	.969	-5	90	88	2b31,S25,3b4	0	-0.7

YEAR	TM LG	G	AB	R	H	2B	3B	HR	RBI	BB-IB	HP	SO	AVG	OBP	SLG	AOPS	ABR	SB-CS	FA	FR	RNG	THR	GAMES AT POSITION	DL	BFW
Barkley, Sam	Samuel E; B5.24.1858 Wheeling WV; D4.20.1912 Wheeling WV; BR/TR/5´11.5˝/180; d5.1; M1																								
1884	Tol AA	104	435	71	133	**39**	9	1	—	22	2	—	.306	.342	.444	149	24	—	.930	26	111	106	2b103,C2	—	**4.8**
1885	†StL AA	106	418	67	112	18	10	3	53	25	2	—	.268	.312	.380	113	5	—	.921	12	111	106	2b96,1b11	—	1.7
1886	Pit AA	122	478	77	127	31	8	1	69	58	0	—	.266	.345	.370	125	16	22	.936	1	94	118	2b112,O8L,1b2	—	1.8
1887	Pit N	89	340	44	76	10	4	1	35	30	4	24	.224	.294	.285	66	-14	6	.979	-8	76	82	1b53,2b36	—	-2.2
1888	KC AA	116	482	67	104	21	6	4	51	26	4	—	.216	.262	.309	78	-14	15	.938	-8	92	89	2b116,M	—	-1.6
1889	KC AA	45	176	36	50	6	2	0	23	15	0	20	.284	.340	.341	89	-3	8	.923	-10	89	96	2b41,1b4	—	-1.0
Total	6	582	2329	362	602	125	39	10	231	176	12	44	.258	.314	.359	105	14	51	.929	13	100	103	2b504,1b70,O8L,C2	—	3.5
Barlow, Tom	Thomas H.; B1852 NY; d5.2																								
1872	Atl NA	**37**	171	34	54	1	0	0	8	3	—	2	.316	.328	.322	86	-5	7-5	.758	-10	—	—	C36,S4/3	—	-1.1
1873	Atl NA	**55**	269	48	74	0	2	1	12	5	—	1	.275	.288	.301	83	-3	3-4	.762	-16	—	—	C55/2S	—	-1.4
1874	Har NA	32	155	37	46	5	1	0	12	2	—	2	.297	.306	.342	102	0	**17**-4	.820	8	111	57	S32	—	0.7
1875	NH NA	1	5	1	1	0	0	0	0	0	—	0	.200	.200	.200	45	0	0-0	.800	0	109	0	/S	—	0.0
	Atl NA	1	4	0	0	0	0	0	0	0	—	0	.000	.000	.000	-99	-1	0-0	.500	-1	0	0	/2	—	-0.2
	Year	2	9	1	1	0	0	0	0	0	—	0	.111	.111	.111	-26	-1	0-0	.800	-1	109	0	/S2	—	-0.2
Total	4NA	126	604	120	175	6	3	1	32	10	—	5	.290	.301	.315	88	-9	27-13	.761	-18	—	—	C91,S38,2b2/3	—	-2.0
Barmes, Bruce	Bruce Raymond "Squeaky"; B10.23.1929 Vincennes IN; BL/TR/5´8˝/165; d9.13																								
1953	Was A	5	5	1	1	0	0	0	0	0	0	0	.200	.200	.200	8	-1	0-0	1.000	0	149	0	/rf	0	-0.1
Barmes, Clint	Clint Harold; B3.6.1979 Vincennes IN; BR/TR/6´0˝/(170–210); [ColN00 10/287]; d9.5; Col Indiana St.																								
2003	Col N	12	25	2	8	2	0	0	2	0-0	2	10	.320	.357	.400	89	0	0-0	.958	1	108	99	S12	0	0.2
2004	Col N	20	71	14	20	3	1	2	10	3-0	1	10	.282	.320	.437	83	-2	0-1	.979	8	135	91	2b9,S9	0	0.6
2005	Col N	81	350	55	101	19	1	10	46	16-1	6	36	.289	.330	.434	88	-6	6-4	.958	12	110	108	S80	88	1.1
2006	Col N	131	478	57	105	26	4	7	56	22-6	9	72	.220	.264	.335	49	-38	5-4	.969	6	105	112	S125,2b4	0	-2.2
Total	4	244	924	128	234	50	6	19	114	41-7	18	128	.253	.295	.382	67	-46	11-9	.965	27	108	110	S226,2b13	88	-0.3
Barna, Babe	Herbert Paul; B3.2.1915 Clarksburg WV; D5.18.1972 Charleston WV; BL/TR/6´2˝/210; d9.16; Col West Virginia																								
1937	Phi A	14	36	10	14	2	0	2	9	2	0	6	.389	.421	.611	159	3	1-0	.800	-1	74	0	O9L/1	—	0.2
1938	Phi A	9	30	4	4	0	0	0	2	3	0	5	.133	.212	.133	-12	-5	0-0	.917	-0	81	205	O7(4/0/3)	—	-0.6
1941	NY N	10	42	5	9	3	0	1	5	2	0	6	.214	.250	.357	68	-2	0	1.000	0	75	222	O10(2/0/8)	0	-0.3
1942	NY N	104	331	39	85	8	7	6	58	38	0	48	.257	.333	.378	107	2	3	.983	-4	91	67	O89(88/0/1)	0	-0.8
1943	NY N	40	113	11	23	5	1	1	12	16	0	9	.204	.302	.292	72	-4	3	.984	-1	97	72	O31L	0	-0.7
	Bos A	30	112	19	19	4	1	2	10	15	0	24	.170	.268	.277	58	-6	2-1	.940	-3	73	140	O29L	0	-1.1
Total	5	207	664	88	154	22	9	12	96	76	0	98	.232	.311	.346	88	-12	9-1	.969	-9	87	93	O175(163/0/12)/1	0	-3.3
Barnes, Ross	Charles Roscoe; B5.8.1850 Mount Morris NY; D2.5.1915 Chicago IL; BR/TR/5´8.5˝/145; d5.5; U1																								
1871	Bos NA	**31**	157	**66**	63	10	9	0	34	13	—	1	.401	.447	.580	186	17	11-6	.873	12	134	189	2b16,S15	—	**1.8**
1872	Bos NA	45	230	81	**99**	**28**	2	1	44	9	—	4	**.430**	.452	**.583**	**205**	**28**	12-2	**.904**	26	**130**	**261**	2b45	—	**3.5**
1873	Bos NA	**60**	320	**125**	**138**	**31**	**11**	2	60	**20**	—	2	**.431**	**.465**	**.616**	**200**	**38**	**43**-6	**.857**	19	**122**	127	2b47,3b13	—	**4.2**
1874	Bos NA	51	259	72	88	12	4	0	39	8	—	2	.340	.360	.417	140	11	8-7	**.856**	18	**117**	**201**	2b51/lf	—	**1.9**
1875	Bos NA	78	393	**115**	**143**	20	4	1	58	7	—	3	.364	**.375**	.443	177	29	29-6	.877	**22**	110	163	2b76,O3L,S2	—	**4.2**
1876	Chi N	**66**	322	**126**	**138**	**21**	**14**	1	59	**20**	—	8	**.429**	**.462**	**.590**	**222**	**40**	—	**.910**	7	106	118	2b66/P	—	**4.2**
1877	Chi N	22	92	16	25	1	0	0	5	7	—	4	.272	.323	.283	83	-2	—	.838	-7	93	60	2b22	—	-0.7
1879	Cin N	77	323	55	86	9	2	1	30	16	—	25	.266	.301	.316	109	4	—	.855	0	104	99	S61,2b16	—	0.7
1881	Bos N	69	295	42	80	14	1	0	17	16	—	16	.271	.309	.325	104	3	—	.854	-3	100	82	S63,2b7	—	0.3
Total	5NA	265	1359	459	531	101	30	4	235	57	—	12	.391	.415	.518	182	123	103-27	.873	97	119	184	2b235,S17,3b13,O4L	—	15.6
Total	4	234	1032	239	329	45	17	2	111	59	—	53	.319	.356	.401	143	45	—	.855	-3	102	90	S124,2b111/P	—	4.5
Barnes, Red	Emile; B12.25.1904 Suggsville AL; D7.3.1959 Mobile AL; BL/TR/5´10.5˝/158; d9.29; Col Alabama																								
1927	Was A	3	11	5	4	1	0	0	0	1	0	3	.364	.417	.455	127	1	0-0	1.000	0	57	383	O3(0/1/2)	—	0.1
1928	Was A	114	417	82	127	22	15	6	51	55	4	38	.305	.391	.472	127	17	7-3	.978	-4	88	131	O104(8/96/1)	—	0.8
1929	Was A	72	130	16	26	5	2	1	15	13	0	12	.200	.273	.292	45	-11	1-0	.877	-3	90	85	O30(8/14/9)	—	-1.4
1930	Was A	12	12	1	2	1	0	0	0	0	0	3	.167	.167	.250	4	-2	0-0	ø	0	—	—	/H	—	-0.2
	Chi A	85	266	48	66	12	7	1	31	26	1	20	.248	.317	.357	73	-11	4-2	.939	-1	95	119	O72(1/71/0)	—	-1.4
	Year	97	278	49	68	13	7	1	31	26	1	23	.245	.311	.353	70	-13	4-2	.939	-1	95	119	O72(1/71/0)	—	-1.6
Total	4	286	836	152	225	41	24	8	97	95	5	76	.269	.347	.404	95	-6	12-5	.953	-8	90	125	O209(17/182/12)	—	-2.1
Barnes, Eppie	Everett Duane; B12.1.1900 Ossining NY; D11.17.1980 Mineola NY; BL/TL/5´9˝/175; d9.25; Col Colgate																								
1923	Pit N	2	2	0	1	0	0	0	0	0	0	1	.500	.500	.500	161	0	0-0	1.000	0	568	382	/1	—	0.0
1924	Pit N	2	5	0	0	0	0	0	0	0	0	1	.000	.000	.000	-98	-1	0-0	1.000	0	205	0	/1	—	-0.1
Total	2	4	7	0	1	0	0	0	0	0	0	2	.143	.143	.143	-23	-1	0-0	1.000	1	304	104	1b2	—	-0.1
Barnes, John	John Delbert; B4.24.1976 San Diego CA; BR/TR/6´2˝/205; [BosA96 4/121]; d9.16; Col Grossmont (CA) JC																								
2000	Min A	11	37	5	13	4	0	0	2	2-0	2	6	.351	.415	.459	113	1	0-1	1.000	2	117	274	O11(2/2/8)	0	0.2
2001	Min A	9	21	1	1	0	0	0	0	1-0	1	3	.048	.130	.048	-48	-5	0-0	.895	1	119	230	O9(3/0/6)	71	-0.4
Total	2	20	58	6	14	4	0	0	2	3-0	3	9	.241	.313	.310	57	-4	0-1	.959	3	118	258	O20(5/2/14)	71	-0.2
Barnes, Honey	John Francis; B1.31.1900 Fulton NY; D6.18.1981 Lockport NY; BL/TR/5´10˝/175; d4.20; Col Colgate																								
1926	NY A	1	0	0	0	0	0	0	0	1	0	0	ø	1.000	ø	179	0	0-0	ø	0	0	0	/C	—	0.0
Barnes, Larry	Larry Richard; B7.23.1974 Bakersfield CA; BL/TL/6´1˝/195; d4.11; Col Cal St.–Fresno																								
2001	Ana A	16	40	2	4	0	0	1	2	1-0	0	9	.100	.122	.175	-23	-7	0-0	1.000	-0	93	53	1b16/lf	0	-0.8
2003	LA N	30	38	2	8	2	0	0	2	1-0	0	9	.211	.231	.263	29	-4	0-0	1.000	-0	57	95	1b8,O2L/D	0	-0.5
Total	2	46	78	4	12	2	0	1	4	2-0	0	18	.154	.175	.218	2	-11	0-0	1.000	-0	81	67	1b24,O3L/D	0	-1.3
Barnes, Lute	Luther Owens; B4.28.1947 Forest City IA; BR/TR/5´10˝/160; [NYN69 21/482]; d8.6; Col Oregon St.																								
1972	NY N	24	72	5	17	2	2	0	6	6-1	0	4	.236	.291	.319	76	-3	0-1	.959	1	95	140	2b14,S6	0	-0.1
1973	NY N	3	2	2	1	0	0	0	1	0-0	0	1	.500	.500	.500	179	0	0-0	ø	0	—	—	/H	0	0.0
Total	2	27	74	7	18	2	2	0	7	6-1	0	5	.243	.296	.324	78	-3	0-1	.959	1	95	140	2b14,S6	0	-0.1
Barnes, Sam	Samuel Thomas; B12.18.1899 Suggsville AL; D2.19.1981 Montgomery AL; BL/TR/5´8˝/150; d9.14; Col Auburn																								
1921	Det A	7	11	2	2	1	0	0	0	2	1	1	.182	.357	.273	63	0	0-0	.944	1	135	0	2b2	—	0.0
Barnes, Bill	William H.; B Indianapolis IN; d9.27																								
1884	StP U	8	30	2	6	1	0	0	—	0	—	—	.200	.200	.233	57	-2	—	.727	-2	0	290	O8C	—	-0.4
Barnes, Skeeter	William Henry; B3.3.1957 Cincinnati OH; BR/TR/5´10˝/(175–180); [CinN78 16/407]; d9.6; Col Cincinnati; OF(37/11/30)																								
1983	Cin N	15	34	5	7	0	0	1	4	7-0	2	3	.206	.372	.294	84	0	2-2	1.000	-0	129	103	1b7,3b7	0	-0.1
1984	Cin N	32	42	5	5	0	0	1	3	4-1	0	6	.119	.196	.190	8	-5	0-0	1.000	1	108	0	3b11,O3L	0	-0.5
1985	Mon N	19	26	0	4	1	0	0	0	0-0	0	2	.154	.154	.192	-4	-4	0-1	1.000	1	118	238	3b4,O3(1/0/2)/1	0	-0.3
1987	StL N	4	4	1	1	0	0	1	3	0-0	0	0	.250	.250	1.000	207	1	0-0	ø	-0	0	0	/3	0	0.0
1989	Cin N	5	3	1	0	0	0	0	0	0-0	0	0	.000	.000	.000	-97	-1	0-1	ø	0	—	—	/H	0	-0.1
1991	Det A	75	159	28	46	13	2	5	17	9-1	0	24	.289	.325	.491	121	4	10-7	1.000	-0	104	331	O33(13/5/17),3b17,1b9,2b7,D3	0	0.3
1992	Det A	95	165	27	45	8	1	3	25	10-1	2	18	.273	.318	.388	97	-1	3-1	.919	3	113	126	3b39,1b17,O15(4/6/5),2b7,D7	0	0.2
1993	Det A	84	160	24	45	8	1	2	27	11-0	0	19	.281	.318	.381	90	-3	5-5	.984	0	107	56	1b27,O18(12/0/6),3b13,D13,2b10,S2	0	-0.5
1994	Det A	24	21	4	6	0	0	1	4	0-0	0	2	.286	.286	.429	80	-1	0-1	1.000	-0	56	86	1b15,O4L/D	0	-0.2
Total	9	353	614	95	159	30	4	14	83	41-3	4	74	.259	.306	.389	90	-10	20-18	.938	3	108	107	3b92,O76L,1b76,D24,2b24,S2	0	-1.2
Barney, Ed	Edmund J.; B1.23.1890 Amery WI; D10.4.1967 Rice Lake WI; BL/TR/5´10.5˝/178; d7.22																								
1915	NY A	11	36	1	7	0	0	0	8	3	0	6	.194	.256	.194	35	-3	2-1	1.000	0	96	76	O10(3/7/0)	—	-0.4
	Pit N	32	99	16	27	1	2	0	5	11	3	12	.273	.363	.323	110	2	7-3	.972	0	109	61	O26(3/22/1)	—	0.1
1916	Pit N	45	137	16	27	4	0	0	9	23	0	15	.197	.313	.226	66	-4	8	.964	3	117	107	O40(20/20/0)	—	-0.4
Total	2	88	272	33	61	5	2	0	22	37	3	33	.224	.324	.257	78	-5	17-4	.971	4	112	87	O76(26/49/1)	—	-0.7

YEAR	TM LG	G	AB	R	H	2B	3B	HR	RBI	BB-IB	HP	SO	AVG	OBP	SLG	AOPS	ABR	SB-CS	FA	FR	RNG	THR	GAMES AT POSITION	DL	BFW
Barnhart, Clyde	Clyde Lee "Pooch"; B12.29.1895 Buck Valley PA; D1.21.1980 Hagerstown MD; BR/TR/5´10˝/155; d9.22; s–Vic; Col Shippensburg																								
1920	Pit N	12	46	5	15	4	2	0	5	1	0	2	.326	.340	.500	135	2	1-0	.971	0	107	176	3b12	—	0.3
1921	Pit N	124	449	66	116	15	13	3	62	32	3	36	.258	.312	.370	78	-15	3-3	.956	-19	84	94	3b118	—	-2.8
1922	Pit N	75	209	30	69	7	5	1	38	25	0	7	.330	.402	.426	112	5	3-2	.918	-7	64	96	3b30,O26(5/0/21)	—	-0.3
1923	Pit N	114	327	60	106	25	13	9	72	47	0	21	.324	.409	.563	151	24	5-7	.985	6	105	144	O92R	—	2.1
1924	Pit N	102	344	49	95	6	11	3	51	30	2	17	.276	.338	.384	91	-5	8-4	.970	1	108	76	O88R	—	-1.1
1925	†Pit N	142	539	85	175	32	11	4	114	59	0	25	.325	.391	.447	106	7	9-5	.962	-1	101	87	O138L	—	-0.4
1926	Pit N	76	203	26	39	3	0	0	10	23	1	13	.192	.278	.207	30	-20	1	.991	1	100	100	O61(54/0/8)	—	-2.3
1927	†Pit N	108	360	65	115	23	4	3	54	37	1	19	.319	.384	.431	110	7	2	.978	3	116	58	O94L	—	0.3
1928	Pit N	61	196	18	58	6	2	4	30	11	0	9	.296	.333	.408	89	-4	3	.971	-0	103	85	O48(45/0/4)/3	—	-0.7
Total	9	814	2673	404	788	121	61	27	436	265	7	149	.295	.360	.416	100	1	35-21	.973	-17	105	90	O547(336/0/213),3b161	—	-4.9
Barnhart, Vic	Victor Dee; B9.1.1922 Hagerstown MD; BR/TR/6´0˝/188; d10.1; f–Clyde																								
1944	Pit N	1	2	0	1	0	0	0	0	1	0	1	.500	.667	.500	222	0	0	.889	0	146	0	/S	0	0.1
1945	Pit N	71	201	21	54	7	0	0	19	9	0	11	.269	.300	.303	65	-10	2	.928	1	100	111	S60,3b4	0	-0.5
1946	Pit N	2	1	0	0	0	0	0	0	0	0	0	.000	.000	.000	-98	0	0	ø	0	—	—	/H	0	0.0
Total	3	74	204	21	55	7	0	0	19	10	0	12	.270	.304	.304	67	-10	2	.927	1	101	108	S61,3b4	0	-0.4
Barnie, Billy	William Harrison "Bald Billy"; B1.26.1853 New York NY; D7.15.1900 Hartford CT; TR/5´7˝/157; d5.7; M14/U1																								
1874	Har NA	45	190	21	35	4	2	0	20	1	—	13	.184	.188	.226	31	-15	2-2	.733	-8	—	—	C30,O29(0/4/25)/S	—	-1.7
1875	Wes NA	10	36	3	4	1	0	0	2	0	—	3	.111	.111	.139	-13	-4	0-0	.889	0	0	0	O7(0/3/4),C3	—	-0.3
	Mut NA	9	34	1	5	0	0	0	1	1	—	0	.147	.171	.147	11	-3	0-0	.750	-3	—	—	C6,O3(0/1/2)	—	-0.5
	Year	19	70	4	9	1	0	0	3	1	—	3	.129	.141	.143	-1	-7	0-0	.857	-2	0	0	O10(0/4/6),C9	—	-0.8
1883	Bal AA	17	55	7	11	0	0	0	—	2	—	—	.200	.228	.200	38	-4	—	.846	-2	—	—	C13,O6R/SM	—	-0.4
1886	Bal AA	2	6	0	0	0	0	0	0	1	0	—	.000	.143	.000	-55	-1	0	ø	-1	0	0	/cfC	—	-0.2
Total	2NA	64	260	25	44	5	2	0	23	2	—	16	.169	.176	.204	23	-22	2-2	.690	-10	—	—	O39(0/8/31),C39/S	—	-2.5
Total	2	19	61	7	11	0	0	0	0	3	0	0	.180	.219	.180	29	-5	0	.848	-3	—	—	C14,O7(0/1/6)/S	—	-0.6
Barnwell, Chris	Christopher Edward; B3.1.1979 Jacksonville FL; BR/TR/5´10˝/180; [MilN01 25/748]; d6.20; Col Flagler																								
2006	Mil N	13	30	2	2	0	0	0	1	1-0	0	6	.067	.097	.067	-56	-7	1-0	.960	1	114	147	S5,2b3,3b3	0	-0.5
Barone, Dick	Richard Anthony; B10.13.1932 San Jose CA; BR/TR/5´9˝/165; d9.22																								
1960	Pit N	3	6	0	0	0	0	0	0	0-0	0	1	.000	.000	.000	-99	-2	0-0	.875	-1	56	0	S2	0	-0.3
Barr, Scotty	Hyder Edward; B10.6.1886 Bristol TN; D12.2.1934 Ft.Worth TX; BR/TR/6´0˝/175; d8.22; Col Davidson																								
1908	Phi A	19	56	4	8	2	0	0	1	3	1	—	.143	.200	.179	22	-5	0	.923	-4	80	0	2b11,3b4,1b2,O2(1/1/0)	—	-1.0
1909	Phi A	22	51	5	4	1	0	0	1	11	1	—	.078	.254	.098	12	-5	2	.947	-1	0	0	O15(1/14/0),1b7	—	-0.7
Total	2	41	107	9	12	3	0	0	2	14	2	—	.112	.228	.140	17	-10	2	.947	-5	0	0	O17(2/15/0),2b11,1b9,3b4	—	-1.7
Barragan, Cuno	Facundo Anthony; B6.20.1932 Sacramento CA; BR/TR/5´11˝/180; d9.1; Col Cal St.–Sacramento																								
1961	Chi N	10	28	3	6	0	0	1	2	2-0	0	7	.214	.267	.321	54	-2	0-0	1.000	-1	0	102	C10	144	-0.2
1962	Chi N	58	134	11	27	6	1	0	12	21-1	0	28	.201	.306	.261	53	-8	0-2	.971	-6	88	126	C55	0	-1.3
1963	Chi N	1	1	0	0	0	0	0	0	0-0	0	1	.000	.000	.000	-95	0	0-0	1.000	-0	0	0	/C	0	-0.1
Total	3	69	163	14	33	6	1	1	14	23-1	0	36	.202	.298	.270	53	-10	0-2	.975	-7	73	121	C66	144	-1.6
Barranca, German	German (Costales); B10.19.1956 Veracruz, Veracruz, Mexico; BL/TR/6´0˝/(160–170); d9.2																								
1979	KC A	5	5	3	3	1	0	0	0	0-0	0	0	.600	.600	.800	268	1	3-1	1.000	2	231	412	/23D	0	0.4
1980	KC A	7	0	3	0	0	0	0	0	0-0	0	0	ø	ø	ø	ø	0	0-0	ø	0	—	—	/R	0	0.0
1981	Cin N	9	6	2	2	0	0	0	1	0-0	0	0	.333	.333	.333	90	0	0-0	ø	0	—	—	/H	0	0.0
1982	Cin N	46	51	11	13	1	3	0	2	2-0	0	9	.255	.283	.392	87	-1	2-0	.824	-2	80	44	2b6	0	-0.3
Total	4	67	62	19	18	2	3	0	3	2-0	0	9	.290	.313	.419	102	0	5-1	.893	0	113	125	2b7/D3	0	0.1
Barrett, Jimmy	James Erigena; B3.28.1875 Athol MA; D10.24.1921 Detroit MI; BL/TR/5´7˝/170; d9.13																								
1899	Cin N	26	92	30	34	2	4	0	10	18	1	—	.370	.477	.478	159	9	4	.936	-2	54	0	O26(3/0/23)	—	0.5
1900	Cin N	137	545	114	172	11	7	5	42	72	5	—	.316	.400	.389	121	19	44	.929	2	133	122	O137(0/115/22)	—	1.2
1901	Det A	**135**	542	110	159	16	9	4	65	76	5	—	.293	.385	.378	107	8	26	.940	11	**178**	175	O135C	—	1.2
1902	Det A	136	509	93	154	19	6	4	44	74	6	—	.303	.397	.387	116	15	24	.961	6	126	164	O136C	—	1.3
1903	Det A	136	517	95	163	13	10	2	31	**74**	6	—	.315	**.407**	.391	144	33	27	.955	7	128	182	O136C	—	3.4
1904	Det A	**162**	624	83	167	10	5	0	31	**79**	3	—	.268	.353	.300	111	12	15	.971	9	**163**	121	O162C	—	1.4
1905	Det A	20	67	2	17	1	0	0	3	6	1	—	.254	.324	.269	88	-1	0	1.000	-1	0	0	O18C	—	-0.3
1906	Cin N	5	12	1	0	0	0	0	0	2	0	—	.000	.143	.000	-53	-2	0	1.000	1	294	1194	O4R	—	-0.2
1907	Bos A	106	390	52	95	11	6	1	28	38	2	—	.244	.314	.310	100	1	3	.966	0	100	169	O99(96/3/0)	—	-0.6
1908	Bos A	3	8	0	1	0	0	0	1	1	0	—	.125	.222	.125	13	-1	0	1.000	-0	0	0	O2C	—	-0.1
Total	10	866	3306	580	962	83	47	16	255	440	29	—	.291	.379	.359	117	93	143	.954	31	135	150	O855(99/707/49)	—	7.8
Barrett, John	John; B Brooklyn NY; d9.18																								
1872	Atl NA	8	34	6	7	1	0	0	2	0	—	1	.206	.206	.235	30	-3	1-0	.808	-1	0	0	O8L	—	-0.2
Barrett, Johnny	John Joseph "Jack"; B12.18.1915 Lowell MA; D8.17.1974 Seabrook Beach NH; BL/TL/5´10.5˝/170; d4.14																								
1942	Pit N	111	332	56	82	11	6	0	26	48	3	42	.247	.347	.316	92	-2	10	.973	6	109	137	O94(15/5/74)	0	-0.1
1943	Pit N	130	290	41	67	12	3	1	32	32	4	23	.231	.316	.303	77	-8	5	.988	1	107	76	O99(4/3/92)	0	-1.3
1944	Pit N	149	568	99	153	24	**19**	7	83	86	1	56	.269	.366	.415	115	12	**28**	.972	-2	102	76	O147(1/67/92)	0	0.3
1945	Pit N	142	507	97	130	29	4	15	67	79	0	68	.256	.357	.418	111	9	25	.976	-6	98	68	O132(0/75/57)	0	-0.3
1946	Pit N	32	71	7	12	3	0	0	6	8	0	11	.169	.253	.211	32	-6	1	.919	-1	93	69	O21(0/12/9)	0	-0.9
	Bos N	24	43	3	10	3	0	0	6	12	0	1	.233	.400	.302	100	1	0	.962	-1	92	99	O17(2/11/4)	0	0.0
	Year	56	114	10	22	6	0	0	12	20	0	12	.193	.313	.246	59	-5	1	.937	-2	93	82	O38(2/23/13)	0	-0.9
Total	5	588	1811	303	454	82	32	23	220	265	8	201	.251	.349	.369	100	6	69	.974	-3	102	86	O510(22/173/328)	0	-2.3
Barrett, Marty	Martin F.; B11.1860 Port Henry NY; D1.29.1910 Holyoke MA; BR/TR/5´9˝/170; d6.24																								
1884	Bos N	3	6	0	0	0	0	0	0	0	—	4	.000	.000	.000	-99	-1	—	.900	-1	—	—	C3	—	-0.2
	Ind AA	5	13	1	1	1	0	0	—	1	0	—	.077	.143	.154	-3	-1	—	.808	-2	—	—	C4/rf	—	-0.3
Total	1	8	19	1	1	1	0	0	0	1	0	4	.053	.100	.105	-34	-2	—	.833	-3	—	—	C7/rf	—	-0.5
Barrett, Marty	Martin Glenn; B6.23.1958 Arcadia CA; BR/TR/5´10˝/(170–176); [BosA79 S1/1]; d9.6; b–Tom; Col Arizona St.																								
1982	Bos A	8	18	0	1	0	0	0	0	0-0	0	1	.056	.056	.056	-65	-4	0-0	1.000	4	157	124	2b7	0	0.0
1983	Bos A	33	44	7	10	1	1	0	2	3-0	0	1	.227	.271	.295	53	-3	0-0	.984	-4	75	83	2b23,D5	0	-0.6
1984	Bos A	139	475	56	144	23	3	3	45	42-2	1	25	.303	.358	.383	101	2	5-3	**.987**	0	103	72	2b136	0	1.0
1985	Bos A	156	534	59	142	26	0	5	56	56-3	2	50	.266	.336	.343	83	-11	7-5	.987	16	103	101	2b155	0	1.4
1986	†Bos A	158	625	94	179	39	4	4	60	65-0	1	31	.286	.353	.381	100	2	15-7	.982	-3	95	102	2b158	0	0.8
1987	Bos A	137	559	72	164	23	0	3	43	51-0	1	38	.293	.351	.351	85	-10	15-2	**.988**	**33**	108	116	2b137	16	3.0
1988	†Bos A	150	612	83	173	28	1	1	65	40-1	7	35	.283	.330	.337	84	-12	7-3	.990	5	90	100	2b150	0	-0.2
1989	Bos A	86	336	31	86	18	0	1	27	32-0	2	12	.256	.320	.318	77	-9	4-1	.975	-0	97	99	2b80,D4	61	-0.7
1990	†Bos A	62	159	15	36	4	0	0	13	15-1	1	13	.226	.294	.252	52	-10	4-0	.992	-2	97	79	2b60/3D	0	-1.0
1991	SD N	12	16	1	3	1	0	1	3	0-0	1	3	.188	.235	.438	82	0	0-0	1.000	1	101	291	2b2,3b2	33	0.1
Total	10	941	3378	418	938	163	9	18	314	304-7	16	209	.278	.337	.347	86	-55	57-21	.986	51	99	98	2b908,D10,3b3	110	3.8
Barrett, Michael	Michael Patrick; B10.22.1976 Atlanta GA; BR/TR/6´2˝/(185–210); [MonN95 1/28]; d9.19																								
1998	Mon N	8	23	3	7	2	0	1	2	3-0	1	6	.304	.407	.522	146	2	0-0	.963	1	41	268	C3,3b3	0	0.3
1999	Mon N	126	433	53	127	32	3	8	52	32-4	3	39	.293	.345	.436	100	0	0-2	.943	-5	102	40	3b66,C59,S2	18	-0.2
2000	Mon N	89	271	28	58	15	1	1	22	23-5	1	35	.214	.277	.288	43	-24	0-1	.891	-5	95	107	3b55,C28	0	-2.6
2001	Mon N	132	472	42	118	33	2	6	38	25-2	2	54	.250	.289	.367	69	-22	2-1	.993	-17	74	66	C131	0	-3.1
2002	Mon N	117	376	41	99	20	1	12	49	40-7	1	65	.263	.332	.418	92	-4	6-3	.989	10	101	88	C110,1b6	0	1.3
2003	Mon N	70	226	33	47	9	2	10	30	21-7	2	37	.208	.280	.398	73	-10	0-0	.998	-1	195	70	C68	45	-0.7
2004	Chi N	134	456	55	131	32	6	16	65	33-4	5	64	.287	.337	.489	108	5	1-4	.994	3	93	93	C130	0	1.5
2005	Chi N	133	424	48	117	32	3	16	61	40-3	7	61	.276	.345	.479	110	7	0-3	.994	-9	87	87	C122/D	0	0.5

YEAR	TM LG	G	AB	R	H	2B	3B	HR	RBI	BB-IB	HP	SO	AVG	OBP	SLG	AOPS	ABR	SB-CS	FA	FR	RNG	THR	GAMES AT POSITION	DL	BFW
2006	Chi N	107	375	54	115	25	3	16	53	33-2	5	41	.307	.368	.517	122	12	0-1	.994	-15	63	99	C102/D	29	0.3
Total	9	916	3056	357	819	200	21	86	372	250-34	27	402	.268	.326	.432	93	-34	9-15	.992	-38	93	85	C753,3b124,1b6,D2,S2	92	-2.7
BARRETT, BOB	Robert Schley "Jumbo"; B1.27.1899 Atlanta GA; D1.18.1982 Atlanta GA; BR/TR/5´11˝/175; d4.30																								
1923	Chi N	3	3	0	1	0	0	0	0	0	0	0	.333	.333	.333	76	0	0-0	ø	0	—	—	/H	—	0.0
1924	Chi N	54	133	12	32	2	3	5	21	7	0	29	.241	.279	.414	82	-4	1-0	.943	-2	98	93	2b25,1b10,3b8	—	-0.6
1925	Chi N	14	32	1	10	1	0	0	7	1	0	4	.313	.333	.344	72	-1	1-2	1.000	-1	35	356	3b6,2b4	—	-0.3
	Bro N	1	1	0	0	0	0	0	1	0	0	0	.000	.000	.000	-99	0	0-0	ø	0	—	—	/H	—	0.0
	Year	15	33	1	10	1	0	0	8	1	0	4	.303	.324	.333	67	-2	1-2	1.000	-1	35	356	3b6,2b4	—	-0.3
1927	Bro N	99	355	29	92	10	2	5	38	14	1	22	.259	.289	.341	68	-17	1	.920	-7	94	87	3b96	—	-1.8
1929	Bos A	68	126	15	34	10	0	0	19	10	0	6	.270	.324	.349	75	-4	3-1	.938	5	133	62	3b34,1b4,2b2/lf	—	0.2
Total	5	239	650	57	169	23	5	10	86	32	1	61	.260	.296	.357	72	-26	6-3	.924	-5	100	85	3b144,2b31,1b14/lf	—	-2.5
BARRETT, TOM	Thomas Loren; B4.2.1960 San Fernando CA; BB/TR/5´9˝/170; [NYA82 26/667]; d7.2; b–Marty; Col Arizona; [DL 1990 Phi N 178]																								
1988	Phi N	36	54	5	11	1	0	0	3	7-0	1	8	.204	.306	.222	53	-3	0-0	.959	2	123	104	2b10	0	-0.1
1989	Phi N	14	27	3	6	0	0	0	1	1-0	0	7	.222	.250	.222	36	-2	0-0	.978	2	86	197	2b9	0	0.0
1992	Bos A	4	3	1	0	0	0	0	0	2-0	0	0	.000	.400	.000	19	0	0-0	1.000	-1	76	0	2b2	0	-0.1
Total	3	54	84	9	17	1	0	0	4	10-0	1	15	.202	.295	.214	47	-5	0-0	.970	3	103	132	2b21	178	-0.2
BARRETT, BILL	William; B Washington DC; d7.8																								
1871	Kek NA	1	5	1	1	1	0	0	1	0	—	0	.200	.200	.400	66	0	0-0	1.000	1	—	—	/C3	—	0.0
1872	Oly NA	1	4	0	0	0	0	0	0	0	—	0	.000	.000	.000	-99	-1	0-0	.400	-2	—	—	/C	—	-0.2
1873	Bal NA	1	4	0	1	0	0	0	0	0	—	0	.250	.250	.250	49	0	0-1	.667	-1	31	0	/Srf	—	-0.1
Total	3NA	3	13	1	2	1	0	0	1	0	—	0	.154	.154	.231	12	-1	0-1	.769	-2	—	—	C2/rfS3	—	-0.3
BARRETT, BILL	William Joseph "Whispering Bill"; B5.28.1900 Cambridge MA; D1.26.1951 Cambridge MA; BR/TR/6´0˝/175; d5.13; OF(74/28/400)																								
1921	Phi A	14	30	3	7	2	1	0	3	0	0	5	.233	.233	.367	51	-2	0-0	.925	1	116	29	S8,P4,3b2/1	—	-0.1
1923	Chi A	44	162	17	44	7	2	2	23	9	0	24	.272	.310	.377	81	-5	12-3	.940	-1	100	100	O40(40/1/0)/3	—	-0.7
1924	Chi A	119	406	52	110	18	5	2	56	30	3	38	.271	.326	.355	78	-15	15-10	.904	-14	87	91	S77,O28(25/3/0),3b8	—	-2.1
1925	Chi A	81	245	44	89	23	3	3	40	24	0	27	.363	.420	.518	145	17	5-6	.943	-5	100	110	2b41,O27(3/1/23),S4,3b4	—	1.1
1926	Chi A	111	368	46	113	31	4	6	61	25	1	26	.307	.353	.462	115	7	9-7	.969	-2	103	78	O102(1/0/102),1b2	—	-0.2
1927	Chi A	147	556	62	159	35	9	4	83	52	0	46	.286	.347	.403	96	-3	20-13	.963	7	103	140	O147(0/12/136)	—	-0.7
1928	Chi A	76	235	34	65	11	2	3	26	14	1	30	.277	.320	.379	84	-6	8-4	.988	-1	104	187	O37(4/1/32),2b25	—	-0.9
1929	Chi A	3	1	0	0	0	0	0	0	2	0	0	.000	.667	.000	87	0	0-0	ø	0	—	—	/H	—	0.0
	Bos A	111	370	57	100	23	4	3	35	51	3	38	.270	.363	.378	93	-2	11-8	.974	7	104	164	O109(1/10/101)/3	—	-0.3
	Year	114	371	57	100	23	4	3	35	53	3	38	.270	.365	.377	94	-2	11-8	.974	7	104	164	O109(1/10/101)/3	—	-0.3
1930	Bos A	6	18	3	3	1	0	0	1	1	0	3	.167	.211	.222	10	-2	0-0	1.000	-1	71	0	O5R	—	-0.3
	Was A	6	4	0	0	0	0	0	0	1	0	2	.000	.200	.000	-44	-1	0-0	1.000	0	157	0	/rf	—	-0.1
	Year	12	22	3	3	1	0	0	1	2	0	5	.136	.208	.182	-0	-3	0-0	1.000	-1	78	0	O6R	—	-0.4
Total	9	718	2395	318	690	151	30	23	328	209	8	239	.288	.347	.405	97	-12	80-51	.964	-8	102	133	O496R,S89,2b66,3b16,P4,1b3	—	-4.3
BARRIOS, JOSE	Jose Manuel; B6.26.1957 New York NY; BR/TR/6´4˝/195; [SFN75 3/56]; d4.23																								
1982	SF N	10	19	2	3	0	0	0	0	1-0	0	4	.158	.200	.158	1	-3	0-0	1.000	-1	0	111	1b7	0	-0.4
BARRON, TONY	Anthony Dirk; B8.17.1966 Portland OR; BR/TR/6´0˝/185; [LAN87 7/170]; d6.2; Col Willamette																								
1996	Mon N	1	1	0	0	0	0	0	0	0-0	0	1	.000	.000	.000	-98	0	0-0	ø	0	—	—	/H	0	0.0
1997	Phi N	57	189	22	54	12	1	4	24	12-0	2	38	.286	.330	.423	98	-1	0-1	.983	3	121	82	O53R	0	0.0
Total	2	58	190	22	54	12	1	4	24	12-0	2	39	.284	.329	.421	97	-1	0-1	.983	3	121	82	O53R	0	0.0
BARRON, RED	David Irenus; B6.21.1900 Clarksville GA; D10.4.1982 Atlanta GA; BR/TR/5´11.5˝/185; d6.10; Col Georgia Tech																								
1929	Bos N	10	21	3	4	1	0	0	1	1	0	4	.190	.227	.238	16	-3	2	.929	1	114	291	O6L	—	-0.2
BARROWS, FRANK	Franklin Lee; B10.22.1844 Hudson OH; D2.6.1922 Fitchburg MA; d5.20																								
1871	Bos NA	18	86	13	13	2	1	0	11	0	—	0	.151	.151	.198	-1	-11	1-0	.829	-2	52	0	O17(13/0/4)/2	—	-0.8
BARROWS, CUKE	Roland; B10.20.1883 Gray ME; D2.10.1955 Gorham ME; BR/TL/5´8˝/158; d9.18																								
1909	Chi A	5	20	1	3	0	0	0	2	0	1	—	.150	.190	.150	8	-2	0	.923	1	228	562	O5L	—	-0.2
1910	Chi A	6	20	0	4	0	0	0	1	3	0	—	.200	.304	.200	61	-1	0	.875	-1	77	0	O6L	—	-0.2
1911	Chi A	13	46	5	9	2	0	0	4	7	1	—	.196	.315	.239	57	-2	2	1.000	-1	113	0	O13R	—	-0.4
1912	Chi A	8	13	0	3	0	0	0	2	2	0	—	.231	.333	.231	64	0	1	1.000	0	30	320	O3R	—	-0.1
Total	4	32	99	6	19	2	0	0	9	12	2	—	.192	.292	.212	50	-5	3	.950	-1	129	176	O27(11/0/16)	—	-0.9
BARRY, JEFF	Jeffrey Finas; B9.22.1969 Medford OR; BB/TR/6´1˝/(200–204); [MonN90 4/112]; d6.9; Col San Diego St.																								
1995	NY N	15	15	2	2	1	0	0	0	1-0	0	8	.133	.188	.200	2	-2	0-0	1.000	0	134	0	O2(1/0/1)	0	-0.2
1998	Col N	15	34	4	6	1	0	0	2	2-0	0	11	.176	.216	.206	11	-4	0-0	1.000	1	115	207	O10(1/8/5)	0	-0.3
1999	Col N	74	168	19	45	16	0	5	26	19-1	2	29	.268	.344	.452	80	-5	0-4	1.000	1	95	167	O56(14/32/15)	0	-0.5
Total	3	104	217	25	53	18	0	5	28	22-1	2	48	.244	.314	.396	66	-11	0-4	1.000	2	99	170	O68(16/40/21)	0	-1.0
BARRY, SHAD	John C.; B10.27.1878 Newburgh NY; D11.27.1936 Los Angeles CA; BR/TR; d5.30; Col Niagara; OF(214/39/371)																								
1899	Was N	78	247	31	71	7	5	1	33	12	3	—	.287	.328	.368	92	-4	11	.946	-9	81	0	O23(20/0/3),1b22,S13,3b13,2b7	—	-1.1
1900	Bos N	81	254	40	66	10	7	1	37	13	2	—	.260	.301	.366	74	-10	9	.956	-12	134	268	O24(22/1/1),S18,2b16,1b10/3	—	-2.1
1901	Bos N	11	40	3	7	2	0	0	6	2	1	—	.175	.233	.225	30	-4	1	.926	-0	68	0	O11L	—	-0.5
	Phi N	67	252	35	62	10	0	1	22	15	2	—	.246	.294	.298	70	-9	13	.903	-13	92	65	2b35,3b16,O13(3/9/1)/S	—	-2.2
	Year	78	292	38	69	12	0	1	28	17	3	—	.236	.285	.288	64	-13	14	.903	-13	92	65	2b35,O24(14/9/1),3b16/S	—	-2.7
1902	Phi N	**138**	543	65	156	20	6	3	58	44	2	—	.287	.343	.363	118	11	14	.939	-6	82	60	O137(7/0/130)/1	—	-0.1
1903	Phi N	138	550	75	152	24	5	1	60	30	6	—	.276	.321	.344	92	-6	26	.970	-2	94	52	O107(105/2/0),1b30/3	—	-1.4
1904	Phi N	35	122	15	25	2	0	0	3	11	2	—	.205	.281	.221	58	-6	2	.979	11	300	322	O32(11/6/15)/3	—	0.4
	Chi N	73	263	29	69	7	2	1	26	17	1	—	.262	.310	.316	93	-2	12	.917	-4	74	0	O30(0/13/17),1b18,3b16,S8,2b2	—	-0.8
	Year	108	385	44	94	9	2	1	29	28	3	—	.244	.300	.286	82	-8	14	.955	7	195	172	O62(11/19/32),1b18,3b17,S8,2b2	—	-0.4
1905	Chi N	27	104	10	22	2	0	0	10	5	1	—	.212	.255	.231	43	-7	5	.982	0	106	87	1b26	—	-0.8
	Cin N	125	494	90	160	11	12	1	56	33	5	—	.324	.372	.401	118	10	16	.982	-7	79	117	1b124,O2(1/1/0)	—	0.1
	Year	152	598	100	182	13	12	1	66	38	6	—	.304	.352	.371	105	3	21	.982	-6	84	**112**	1b150,O2(1/1/0)	—	-0.7
1906	Cin N	73	279	38	80	10	5	1	33	26	3	—	.287	.354	.369	120	7	11	.993	-0	90	113	1b43,O30(14/7/9)	—	0.4
	StL N	62	237	26	59	9	1	0	12	15	2	—	.249	.299	.295	89	-3	6	.930	-3	82	109	O35R,1b21,3b6	—	-0.9
	Year	135	516	64	139	19	6	1	45	41	5	—	.269	.329	.335	107	4	17	.922	-3	130	52	O65(14/7/44),1b64,3b6	—	-0.5
1907	StL N	81	294	30	73	5	2	0	19	28	3	—	.248	.320	.279	91	-2	4	.963	-5	103	0	O81R	—	-1.2
1908	StL N	74	268	24	61	8	1	0	11	19	3	—	.228	.286	.265	80	-6	9	.967	1	119	0	O69R,S2	—	-0.9
	NY N	37	67	5	10	1	1	0	5	9	1	—	.149	.260	.194	43	-4	1	.971	-2	0	0	O31(20/0/10)	—	-0.8
	Year	111	335	29	71	9	2	0	16	28	4	—	.212	.281	.251	71	-10	10	.968	-1	92	0	O100(20/0/79),S2	—	-1.7
Total	10	1100	4014	516	1073	128	47	10	391	279	37	—	.267	.321	.330	94	-35	140	.955	-50	106	58	O625R,1b295,2b60,3b54,S42	—	-11.9
BARRY, JACK	John Joseph; B4.26.1887 Meriden CT; D4.23.1961 Shrewsbury MA; BR/TR/5´9˝/158; d7.13; Mil 1918; M1; Col Holy Cross																								
1908	Phi A	40	135	13	30	4	3	0	8	10	3	—	.222	.291	.296	85	-2	5	.966	-7	102	53	2b20,S14,3b3	—	-0.9
1909	Phi A	124	409	56	88	11	2	1	23	44	10	—	.215	.307	.259	77	-8	17	.927	-26	88	**106**	S124	—	-3.5
1910	†Phi A	145	487	64	126	19	5	3	60	52	5	—	.259	.336	.337	112	8	14	.916	-27	87	**114**	S145	—	-1.6
1911	†Phi A	127	442	73	117	18	7	1	63	38	7	—	.265	.333	.344	90	-6	30	**.944**	-11	92	**108**	S127	—	-0.7
1912	Phi A	140	483	75	126	19	9	0	55	47	7	—	.261	.335	.337	96	-2	22	.925	-6	103	**125**	S139	—	0.1
1913	†Phi A	134	455	62	125	20	6	3	85	44	8	32	.275	.349	.365	111	7	15	.953	-5	96	116	S134	—	1.1
1914	†Phi A	140	467	57	113	12	0	0	42	53	4	34	.242	.324	.268	81	-9	22-13	.947	7	107	120	S140	—	0.9
1915	Phi A	54	194	16	43	6	2	0	15	15	2	9	.222	.284	.273	69	-8	6-5	.952	-2	95	87	S54	—	-0.7
	†Bos A	78	248	30	65	13	2	0	26	24	6	11	.262	.342	.331	104	2	0	.962	-4	100	76	2b78	—	-0.1
	Year	132	442	46	108	19	4	0	41	39	8	20	.244	.317	.305	89	-6	6-5	.962	-6	100	76	2b78,S54	—	-0.8
1916	Bos A	94	330	28	67	6	1	0	20	17	**17**	24	.203	.277	.227	52	-19	8	.974	1	102	81	2b94	—	-1.9
1917	Bos A	116	388	45	83	9	0	2	30	47	4	27	.214	.305	.253	71	-12	12	**.974**	-5	104	93	2b116,M	—	-1.7
1919	Bos A	31	108	13	26	5	1	0	2	5	3	5	.241	.293	.306	72	-4	2	.922	-5	99	106	2b31	—	-0.9
Total	11	1223	4146	532	1009	142	38	10	429	396	76	142	.243	.321	.303	88	-53	153-18	.935	-90	95	112	S877,2b339,3b3	—	-9.9

YEAR	TM LG	G	AB	R	H	2B	3B	HR	RBI	BB-IB	HP	SO	AVG	OBP	SLG	AOPS	ABR	SB-CS	FA	FR	RNG	THR	GAMES AT POSITION	DL	BFW
BARRY, RICH	Richard Donovan; B9.12.1940 Berkeley CA; BR/TR/6´4˝/205; d7.4																								
1969	Phi N	20	32	4	6	1	0	0	0	5-0	1	6	.188	.316	.219	53	-2	0-0	.938	0	134	0	O9L	0	-0.2
BARTEE, KIMERA	Kimera Anotchi; B7.21.1972 Omaha NE; BR/TR (BB 1998)/6´0˝/(175–200); [BalA93 14/399]; d4.3; Col Creighton																								
1996	Det A	110	217	32	55	6	1	1	14	17-0	0	77	.253	.308	.304	55	-15	20-10	.991	3	119	23	O99(4/95/2),D2	0	-1.0
1997	Det A	12	5	4	1	0	0	0	0	2-0	1	2	.200	.500	.200	93	0	3-1	1.000	-0	83	0	O6(3/3/0),D3	0	0.0
1998	Det A	57	98	20	19	5	1	3	15	6-0	0	35	.194	.238	.357	52	-7	9-5	.964	2	105	239	O29(11/18/1),D10	0	-0.6
1999	Det A	41	77	11	15	1	3	0	3	9-0	0	20	.195	.279	.286	44	-7	3-3	.985	0	113	0	O38C/D	0	-0.7
2000	Cin N	11	4	2	0	0	0	0	0	0-0	1	2	.000	.200	.000	-42	-1	1-0	1.000	-0	68	0	O3(2/1/0)	0	-0.1
2001	Col N	12	15	0	0	0	0	0	1	2-1	1	5	.000	.158	.000	-43	-3	0-0	.889	-1	92	0	O10(9/2/0)	0	-0.4
Total	6	243	416	69	90	12	5	4	33	36-1	3	141	.216	.282	.298	48	-33	36-19	.983	4	114	52	O185(29/157/3),D16	0	-2.8
BARTELL, DICK	Richard William "Rowdy Richard"; B11.22.1907 Chicago IL; D8.4.1995 Alameda CA; BR/TR/5´9˝/160; d10.2; Mil 1944–45; C7																								
1927	Pit N	1	2	0	0	0	0	0	0	2	0	0	.000	.500	.000	41	0	0	1.000	0	69	198	/S	—	0.0
1928	Pit N	72	233	27	71	8	4	1	36	21	6	18	.305	.377	.386	96	-1	4	.974	-2	96	110	2b39,S27/3	—	0.1
1929	Pit N	143	610	101	184	40	13	2	57	40	2	29	.302	.347	.420	87	-13	11	.953	-6	94	89	S74,2b70	—	-0.9
1930	Pit N	129	475	69	152	32	13	4	75	39	5	34	.320	.378	.467	102	2	8	.941	5	103	**115**	S126	—	1.8
1931	Phi N	135	554	88	160	43	7	0	34	27	3	38	.289	.325	.392	85	-11	6	.948	4	98	96	S133,2b3	—	0.3
1932	Phi N	**154**	614	118	189	48	7	1	53	64	6	47	.308	.379	.414	101	4	8	.963	9	102	82	S154	—	2.4
1933	Phi N★	**152**	587	78	159	25	5	1	37	56	5	46	.271	.340	.336	83	-11	6	.951	9	101	96	S152	—	0.9
1934	Phi N	146	604	102	187	30	4	0	37	64	**9**	59	.310	.384	.373	91	-4	13	.954	18	106	108	S146	—	2.4
1935	NY N	137	539	60	141	28	4	14	53	37	6	52	.262	.316	.406	94	-5	5	.954	7	101	102	S137	—	1.1
1936	†NY N	145	510	71	152	31	3	8	42	40	5	36	.298	.355	.418	109	7	6	.956	**43**	**122**	**125**	S144	—	**5.7**
1937	†NY N★	128	516	91	158	38	2	14	62	40	**10**	38	.306	.367	.469	124	18	5	.958	**36**	**114**	**134**	S128	—	**6.1**
1938	NY N	127	481	67	126	26	1	9	49	55	8	60	.262	.347	.376	98	1	4	.952	**26**	**111**	.115	S127	—	3.6
1939	Chi N	105	336	37	80	24	2	3	34	42	**7**	25	.238	.335	.348	82	-7	6	.943	-4	94	93	S101/3	—	-0.3
1940	†Det A	139	528	76	123	24	3	7	53	76	5	53	.233	.335	.330	67	-25	12-2	.953	13	100	89	S139	—	0.1
1941	Det A	5	12	0	2	1	0	0	1	2	1	2	.167	.333	.250	51	-1	0-1	.920	-0	84	67	S5	0	-0.1
	NY N	104	373	44	113	20	0	5	35	52	4	29	.303	.394	.397	121	13	6	.959	-5	96	102	3b84,S21	0	1.3
1942	NY N	90	316	53	77	10	3	5	24	44	**8**	34	.244	.351	.342	102	3	4	.965	3	109	140	3b52,S31	0	1.0
1943	NY N	99	337	48	91	14	0	5	28	47	**7**	27	.270	.371	.356	110	7	5	.980	15	115	84	3b54,S33	0	2.7
1946	NY N	5	2	0	0	0	0	0	0	0	0	0	.000	.000	.000	-99	-1	0	1.000	0	226	0	3b4,2b2	0	0.0
Total	18	2016	7629	1130	2165	442	71	79	710	748	97	627	.284	.355	.391	96	-24	109-3	.953	171	104	102	S1679,3b196,2b114	0	28.2
BARTIROME, TONY	Anthony Joseph; B5.9.1932 Pittsburgh PA; BL/TL/5´10˝/155; d4.19; Mil 1953–54; C3																								
1952	Pit N	124	355	32	78	10	3	0	16	26	0	37	.220	.273	.265	48	-25	3-3	.989	1	108	98	1b118	0	-2.9
BARTLETT, JASON	Jason Alan; B10.30.1979 Mountain View CA; BR/TR/6´0˝/(180–190); [SDN01 13/390]; d8.3; Col Oklahoma																								
2004	Min A	8	12	2	1	0	0	0	1	1-0	0	1	.083	.154	.083	-35	-2	2-0	.889	2	152	199	S5/2D	0	0.0
2005	Min A	74	224	33	54	10	1	3	16	21-0	4	37	.241	.316	.335	73	-8	4-0	.979	10	118	117	S68,D5	0	0.8
2006	†Min A	99	333	44	103	18	2	2	32	22-1	11	46	.309	.367	.393	98	0	10-5	.971	4	103	79	S99	0	1.1
Total	3	181	569	79	158	28	3	5	49	44-1	15	84	.278	.342	.364	85	-10	16-5	.972	16	110	96	S172,D6/2	0	1.9
BARTLEY, BOYD	Boyd Owen; B2.11.1920 Chicago IL; BR/TR/5´8.5˝/165; d5.30; Mil 1943–46; Col Illinois																								
1943	Bro N	9	21	0	1	0	0	0	1	1	0	3	.048	.091	.048	-59	-4	0	.897	-0	99	72	S9	0	-0.4
BARTLING, IRV	Henry Irving; B6.27.1914 Bay City MI; D6.12.1973 Westland MI; BR/TR/6´0˝/175; d9.8; Col Michigan St.																								
1938	Phi A	14	46	5	8	1	1	0	5	3	0	7	.174	.224	.239	17	-6	0-0	.914	-3	86	83	S13/3	—	-0.8
BARTON, HARRY	Harry Lamb; B1.20.1875 Chester PA; D1.25.1955 Upland PA; BB/TR/5´6.5˝/155; d4.15																								
1905	Phi A	29	60	5	10	2	1	0	3	3	0	—	.167	.206	.233	39	-4	2	.954	-4	*101*	*124*	C13,1b2,3b2/rf	—	-0.8
BARTON, BOB	Robert Wilbur; B7.30.1941 Norwood OH; BR/TR/6´0˝/(175–190); d9.17																								
1965	SF N	4	7	1	4	0	0	0	1	0-0	0	0	.571	.571	.571	217	1	0-0	1.000	1	0	0	C2	0	0.2
1966	SF N	43	91	1	16	2	1	0	3	5-2	0	5	.176	.216	.220	22	-10	0-0	.994	1	84	169	C39	0	-0.8
1967	SF N	7	19	0	4	0	0	0	1	0-0	1	2	.211	.250	.211	34	-2	0-0	1.000	1	230	66	C7	0	-0.1
1968	SF N	46	92	4	24	2	0	0	5	7-1	0	18	.261	.310	.283	80	-2	0-0	.995	6	109	131	C45	0	0.6
1969	SF N	49	106	5	18	2	0	0	1	9-1	1	19	.170	.241	.189	22	-11	0-0	.985	-8	76	60	C49	0	-1.9
1970	SD N	61	188	15	41	6	0	4	16	15-2	1	37	.218	.278	.314	61	-11	1-1	.995	4	71	148	C59	0	-0.5
1971	SD N	121	376	23	94	17	2	5	23	35-11	2	49	.250	.317	.346	94	-3	0-5	.981	10	89	**147**	C119	0	1.1
1972	SD N	29	88	1	17	1	0	0	9	2-0	0	19	.193	.209	.205	20	-10	2-0	.989	-3	125	110	C29	0	-1.3
1973	Cin N	3	1	0	0	0	0	0	0	1-0	0	0	.000	.500	.000	52	0	0-0	1.000	0	0	0	C2	0	0.0
1974	SD N	30	81	4	19	1	0	0	7	13-1	0	19	.235	.333	.247	69	-3	0-0	.981	6	87	245	C29	36	0.4
Total	10	393	1049	54	237	31	3	9	66	87-18	5	168	.226	.287	.287	64	-51	3-6	.987	17	91	141	C380	36	-2.3
BARTON, VINCE	Vincent David; B2.1.1908 Edmonton AL, Can.; D9.13.1973 Toronto ON, Can.; BL/TR/6´0˝/180; d7.17																								
1931	Chi N	66	239	45	57	10	1	13	50	21	**9**	40	.238	.323	.452	104	1	1	.964	-4	101	27	O61R	—	-0.7
1932	Chi N	36	134	19	30	2	3	3	15	8	1	22	.224	.273	.351	67	-7	0	1.000	-1	90	89	O34R	—	-1.0
Total	2	102	373	64	87	12	4	16	65	29	10	62	.233	.306	.416	91	-6	1	.976	-5	97	49	O95R	—	-1.7
BARTOSCH, DAVE	David Robert; B3.24.1917 St.Louis MO; D4.30.2006 Nashville TN; BR/TR/6´1˝/190; d4.28																								
1945	StL N	24	47	9	12	1	0	0	1	6	0	3	.255	.340	.277	71	-2	0	.964	-1	120	112	O11(4/0/7)	0	-0.1
BASGALL, MONTY	Romanus; B2.8.1922 Pfeifer KS; D9.22.2005 Sierra Vista AZ; BR/TR/5´10.5˝/175; d4.19; C14; Col Sterling																								
1948	Pit N	38	51	12	11	1	0	2	6	3	0	5	.216	.259	.353	63	-3	0	1.000	3	110	60	2b22	0	0.0
1949	Pit N	107	308	25	67	9	1	2	26	31	1	32	.218	.291	.273	51	-21	1	.972	-3	96	98	2b98,3b3	0	-2.0
1951	Pit N	55	153	15	32	5	2	0	9	12	1	14	.209	.271	.268	44	-12	0-0	.969	6	106	100	2b55	0	-0.4
Total	3	200	512	52	110	15	3	4	41	46	2	51	.215	.282	.279	50	-36	1-0	.973	5	100	96	2b175,3b3	0	-2.4
BASHANG, AL	Albert C. (b Albert C. Baschang); B8.22.1888 Cincinnati OH; D6.23.1967 Cincinnati OH; BB/TR/5´8˝/150; d7.30																								
1912	Det A	6	12	3	1	0	0	0	0	3	0	—	.083	.267	.083	2	-1	0	1.000	-0	92	0	O6(5/1/0)	—	-0.2
1918	Bro N	2	5	0	1	0	0	0	0	0	0	0	.200	.200	.200	22	0	0	1.000	1	0	0	/O	—	0.0
Total	2	8	17	3	2	0	0	0	0	3	0	0	.118	.250	.118	8	-1	0	1.000	0	89	0	O7(5/1/0)	—	-0.2
BASHORE, WALT	Walter Franklin (b Walter Franklin Beshore); B10.6.1909 Harrisburg PA; D9.26.1984 Sebring FL; BR/TR/6´0˝/170; d7.14																								
1936	Phi N	10	10	1	2	0	0	0	0	1	0	3	.200	.273	.200	26	-1	0	1.000	-1	58	0	O6C/3	—	-0.2
BASINSKI, EDDIE	Edwin Frank "Bazooka","Fiddler"; B11.4.1922 Buffalo NY; BR/TR/6´1˝/172; d5.20																								
1944	Bro N	39	105	13	27	4	1	0	9	6	2	10	.257	.310	.314	77	-3	1	.960	-3	89	73	2b37,S3	0	-0.5
1945	Bro N	108	336	30	88	9	4	0	33	11	4	33	.262	.293	.313	69	-15	0	.926	-10	92	119	S101,2b6	0	-1.9
1947	Pit N	56	161	15	32	6	2	4	17	18	0	27	.199	.279	.335	61	-10	0	.972	-5	95	102	2b56	0	-1.2
Total	3	203	602	58	147	19	7	4	59	35	6	70	.244	.292	.319	68	-28	1	.925	-19	92	117	S104,2b99	0	-3.6
BASS, JOHN	John Elias; B1848 Charleston SC; D9.25.1888 Denver CO; 5´6˝/150; d5.4																								
1871	Cle NA	22	89	18	27	1	**10**	3	18	3	—	4	.303	.326	.640	179	8	0-1	.779	-7	74	59	S22/C	—	0.1
1872	Atl NA	2	7	0	1	1	0	0	1	0	—	0	.143	.143	.286	24	-1	0-0	.500	-1	0	0	O2R	—	-0.1
1877	Har N	1	4	1	1	0	0	0	0	0	—	0	.250	.250	.250	65	0	—	ø	-0	0	0	/lf	—	0.0
Total	2NA	24	96	18	28	2	10	3	19	3	—	4	.292	.313	.615	166	7	0-1	.779	-7	74	59	S22,O2R/C	—	0.0
BASS, KEVIN	Kevin Charles; B5.12.1959 Redwood City CA; BB/TR/6´0˝/(180–190); [MilA77 2/29]; d4.9																								
1982	Mil A	18	9	4	0	0	0	0	0	1-0	0	1	.000	.100	.000	-73	-2	0-0	1.000	-1	72	0	O14(0/6/8),D2	0	-0.3
	Hou N	12	24	2	1	0	0	0	1	0-0	0	8	.042	.042	.042	-83	-6	0-0	.917	-1	72	0	O7(4/4/0)	0	-0.8
1983	Hou N	88	195	25	46	7	3	2	18	6-1	0	27	.236	.257	.333	67	-10	2-2	.945	-3	93	37	O52(0/5/47)	0	-1.6
1984	Hou N	121	331	33	86	17	5	2	29	6-1	3	57	.260	.279	.360	84	-9	5-5	.975	-0	101	93	O81(0/31/52)	11	-1.4
1985	Hou N	150	539	72	145	27	5	16	68	31-1	6	63	.269	.315	.427	108	4	19-8	**.997**	4	105	117	O141(10/105/39)	0	0.7
1986	†Hou N★	157	591	83	184	33	5	20	79	38-11	6	72	.311	.357	.486	134	26	22-13	.984	3	104	107	O155(2/41/133)	0	2.3

YEAR	TM LG	G	AB	R	H	2B	3B	HR	RBI	BB-IB	HP	SO	AVG	OBP	SLG	AOPS	ABR	SB-CS	FA	FR	RNG	THR	GAMES AT POSITION	DL	BFW
1987	Hou N	157	592	83	168	31	5	19	85	53-13	4	77	.284	.344	.449	113	10	21-8	.987	4	104	109	O155R	0	0.7
1988	Hou N	157	541	57	138	27	2	14	72	42-10	6	65	.255	.314	.390	106	3	31-6	.979	1	100	103	O147R	0	0.4
1989	Hou N	87	313	42	94	19	4	5	44	29-3	1	44	.300	.357	.435	131	13	11-4	.985	4	109	127	O84(31/0/53)	75	1.6
1990	SF N	61	214	25	54	9	1	7	32	14-3	2	26	.252	.303	.402	96	-2	2-2	.968	-7	79	51	O55R	99	-1.1
1991	SF N	124	361	43	84	10	4	10	40	36-8	4	56	.233	.307	.366	92	-5	7-4	.977	-0	90	142	O101(23/0/79)	34	-0.8
1992	SF N	89	265	25	71	11	3	7	30	16-1	1	53	.268	.310	.411	109	2	7-7	.983	-4	92	30	O72(56/0/21)	13	-0.5
	NY N	46	137	15	37	12	2	2	9	7-2	0	17	.270	.303	.431	107	1	7-2	.987	2	115	58	O39(28/0/13)	0	0.2
	Year	135	402	40	108	23	5	9	39	23-3	1	70	.269	.308	.418	108	3	14-9	.985	-2	100	40	O111(84/0/34)	0	-0.3
1993	Hou N	111	229	31	65	18	0	3	37	26-3	1	31	.284	.359	.402	107	3	7-1	.989	-2	89	85	O64(12/2/51)	0	0.0
1994	Hou N	82	203	37	63	15	1	6	35	28-6	1	24	.310	.393	.483	134	11	2-3	.977	-1	94	93	O57(11/0/47)	0	0.7
1995	Bal A	111	295	32	72	12	0	5	32	24-0	2	47	.244	.303	.336	65	-15	8-8	.984	-0	101	72	O77(32/0/53),D19	0	-2.0
Total	14	1571	4839	609	1308	248	40	118	611	357-63	37	668	.270	.323	.411	105	24	151-73	.982	-2	100	97	O1301(209/194/953),D21	232	-1.9
BASS, RANDY	Randy William; B3.13.1954 Lawton OK; BL/TR/6´1˝/(206–225); [MinA72 7/152]; d9.3																								
1977	Min A	9	19	0	2	0	0	0	0	0-0	0	5	.105	.105	.105	-43	-4	0-0	ø	0	—	—	D6	0	-0.4
1978	KC A	2	2	0	0	0	0	0	0	0-0	0	0	.000	.000	.000	-97	-1	0-0	ø	0	—	—	/H	0	-0.1
1979	Mon N	2	1	0	0	0	0	0	0	0-0	0	0	.000	.000	.000	-99	0	0-0	1.000	0	0	0	/1	0	0.0
1980	SD N	19	49	5	14	0	1	3	8	7-1	1	7	.286	.386	.510	159	4	0-0	.985	-1	83	104	1b15	0	0.2
1981	SD N	69	176	13	37	4	1	4	20	20-1	1	28	.210	.293	.313	79	-5	0-1	.993	3	124	101	1b50	0	-0.6
1982	SD N	13	30	1	6	0	0	1	8	2-0	1	4	.200	.265	.300	64	-2	0-0	1.000	-0	84	159	1b9	0	-0.2
	Tex A	16	48	5	10	2	0	1	6	1-0	1	7	.208	.231	.313	53	-3	0-0	1.000	-0	83	156	1b6,D7	0	-0.4
Total	6	130	325	24	69	6	2	9	42	30-2	4	51	.212	.284	.326	77	-11	0-1	.993	1	109	112	1b81,D13	0	-1.5
BASS, DOC	William Capers (Also Played One Game in 1918 Under Name of Johnson); B12.4.1898 Macon GA; D1.12.1970 Macon GA; BL/TL/5´10˝/165; d7.29; Col Mercer																								
1918	Bos N	2	1	1	1	0	0	0	0	0	0	0	1.000	1.000	1.000	533	0	1	ø	0	—	—	/H	—	0.1
BASSETT, CHARLEY	Charles Edwin; B2.9.1863 Central Falls RI; D5.28.1942 Pawtucket RI; BR/TR/5´10˝/150; d7.22; Col Brown																								
1884	Pro N	27	79	10	11	2	1	0	6	4	—	15	.139	.181	.190	17	-7	—	.815	-2	100	75	3b13,S7,O2(1/1/0)/2	—	-0.8
1885	Pro N	82	285	21	41	8	2	0	16	19	—	60	.144	.197	.186	25	-23	—	.900	3	103	114	2b39,S23,3b20/C	—	-1.6
1886	KC N	90	342	41	89	19	8	2	32	36	—	43	.260	.331	.380	109	4	6	.886	9	111	95	S82,3b8	—	1.3
1887	Ind N	119	452	41	104	14	6	1	47	25	5	31	.230	.278	.294	61	-23	25	**.931**	18	**115**	111	2b119	—	-0.1
1888	Ind N	128	481	58	116	20	3	2	60	32	6	41	.241	.297	.308	91	-4	24	.922	-14	103	84	2b128	—	-1.3
1889	Ind N	127	477	64	117	12	5	4	68	37	3	38	.245	.304	.317	71	-20	15	.937	13	**109**	**114**	2b127	—	-0.2
1890	NY N	100	410	52	98	13	8	0	54	29	7	25	.239	.300	.310	78	-13	14	**.952**	19	**109**	107	2b100	—	0.9
1891	NY N	130	524	60	136	19	8	4	68	36	4	29	.260	.312	.349	96	-4	16	**.908**	6	96	101	3b121,2b9	—	0.4
1892	NY N	35	130	9	27	2	3	0	16	6	2	11	.208	.254	.269	59	-7	0	.938	8	115	79	2b30,3b5	—	0.2
	Lou N	79	313	36	67	5	5	2	35	15	0	19	.214	.250	.281	66	-14	16	.861	-1	109	118	3b73,2b6	—	-1.3
	Year	114	443	45	94	7	8	2	51	21	2	30	.212	.251	.278	64	-22	16	.858	7	109	119	3b78,2b36	—	-1.1
Total	9	917	3493	392	806	114	49	15	402	239	27	312	.231	.285	.304	75	-111	116	.932	59	109	102	2b559,3b240,S112,O2(1/1/0)/C	—	-2.5
BASSLER, JOHNNY	John Landis; B6.3.1895 Mechanics Grove PA; D6.29.1979 Santa Monica CA; BL/TR/5´9˝/170; d7.11; C4																								
1913	Cle A	1	2	0	0	0	0	0	0	0	0	0	.000	.000	.000	-97	-1	0	.500	-1	62	*0*	/C	—	-0.2
1914	Cle A	43	77	5	14	1	1	0	6	15	0	8	.182	.323	.221	61	-3	3-2	.946	-2	*88*	*129*	C25/3rf	—	-0.3
1921	Det A	119	388	37	119	18	5	0	56	58	3	16	.307	.401	.379	101	4	2-1	.975	-4	*88*	*115*	C114	—	0.8
1922	Det A	121	372	41	120	14	0	0	41	62	2	12	.323	.422	.360	109	10	2-1	.980	-9	*80*	*106*	C118	—	0.9
1923	Det A	135	383	45	114	12	3	0	49	76	0	13	.298	.414	.345	103	7	2-2	.988	9	*113*	***140***	C128	—	2.2
1924	Det A	124	379	43	131	20	3	1	68	62	3	11	.346	.441	.422	125	19	2-1	.979	-6	*94*	*104*	C122	—	2.0
1925	Det A	121	344	40	96	19	3	0	52	74	1	6	.279	.408	.352	96	3	1-1	.983	-10	*87*	*87*	C118	—	0.0
1926	Det A	66	174	20	53	8	1	0	22	45	0	6	.305	.447	.362	111	7	0-0	1.000	1	*85*	*124*	C63	—	1.1
1927	Det A	81	200	19	57	7	0	0	24	45	0	9	.285	.416	.320	92	1	1-0	.974	-1	*91*	*101*	C67	—	0.4
Total	9	811	2319	250	704	99	16	1	318	437	10	81	.304	.416	.361	104	47	13-8	.980	-21	*92*	*112*	C756/rf3	—	6.9
BASTIAN, CHARLIE	Charles J.; B7.4.1860 Philadelphia PA; D1.18.1932 Pennsauken NJ; BR/TR/5´6.5˝/145; d8.18																								
1884	Wil U	**17**	60	6	12	1	3	2	—	3	—	—	.200	.238	.417	92	-3	—	.907	11	153	60	2b16/PS	—	0.8
	KC U	11	46	6	9	3	0	1	—	4	—	—	.196	.260	.326	88	-2	—	.950	1	108	83	2b11	—	-0.1
	Year	28	106	12	21	4	3	3	—	7	—	—	.198	.248	.377	90	-5	—	.923	12	135	69	2b27/PS	—	0.7
1885	Phi N	103	389	63	65	11	5	4	29	35	—	82	.167	.236	.252	59	-17	—	.890	8	102	117	S103	—	-0.6
1886	Phi N	105	373	46	81	9	11	2	38	33	—	73	.217	.281	.316	81	-9	29	**.945**	-5	**108**	59	2b87,S10,3b8	—	-1.0
1887	Phi N	60	221	33	47	11	1	1	21	19	3	29	.213	.284	.285	55	-13	11	.921	-11	92	95	2b39,S18,3b4	—	-1.9
1888	Phi N	80	275	30	53	4	1	1	17	27	7	41	.193	.282	.225	60	-11	12	.945	10	116	59	2b65,3b14/S	—	0.1
1889	Chi N	46	155	19	21	0	0	0	10	25	0	46	.135	.256	.135	10	-19	1	.919	-3	103	58	S45/2	—	-1.8
1890	Chi P	80	283	38	54	10	5	0	29	33	5	37	.191	.287	.261	45	-23	4	.880	-10	94	98	S64,2b12,3b4	—	-2.5
1891	Cin AA	1	4	0	0	0	0	0	0	0	0	0	.000	.000	.000	-92	-1	0	1.000	1	118	199	/2	—	0.0
	Phi N	1	0	0	0	0	0	0	0	0	0	0	ø	ø	ø	ø	0	0	1.000	0	133	0	/S	—	0.0
Total	8	504	1806	241	342	49	26	11	144	179	15	308	.189	.268	.264	57	-98	57	.892	1	99	106	S243,2b232,3b30/P	—	-7.0
BATCH, EMIL	Emil "Heinie","Ace"; B1.21.1880 Brooklyn NY; D8.23.1926 Brooklyn NY; BR/TR/5´7˝/170; d9.13																								
1904	Bro N	28	94	9	24	1	2	2	7	1	1	—	.255	.271	.372	100	-1	6	.880	-1	104	100	3b28	—	-0.2
1905	Bro N	145	568	64	143	20	11	5	49	26	0	—	.252	.285	.352	96	-6	21	.887	-5	91	116	3b145	—	-0.8
1906	Bro N	59	203	23	52	7	6	0	11	15	1	—	.256	.311	.350	115	2	3	.964	0	78	0	O50(47/0/3),3b2	—	0.0
1907	Bro N	116	388	38	96	10	3	0	31	23	1	—	.247	.291	.289	89	-6	7	.937	-4	95	109	O102(81/1/20),3b2/2S	—	-1.9
Total	4	348	1253	134	315	38	22	7	98	65	3	—	.251	.290	.334	98	-11	37	.886	-11	93	112	3b177,O152(128/1/23)/S2	—	-2.9
BATEMAN, JOHN	John Alvin; B7.21.1940 Killeen TX; D12.3.1996 Sand Springs OK; BR/TR/6´3˝/(200–225); d4.19																								
1963	Hou N	128	404	23	85	8	6	10	59	13-1	9	103	.210	.249	.334	71	-17	0-0	.971	-1	88	109	C115	0	-1.3
1964	Hou N	74	221	18	42	8	0	5	19	17-5	1	48	.190	.249	.294	56	-13	0-1	.987	5	70	67	C72	0	-0.5
1965	Hou N	45	142	15	28	3	1	7	14	12-3	0	37	.197	.256	.380	83	-4	0-1	.985	-0	144	97	C39	0	-0.3
1966	Hou N	131	433	39	121	24	3	17	70	20-9	5	74	.279	.315	.467	123	12	0-0	.981	2	103	75	C121	0	2.1
1967	Hou N	76	252	16	48	9	0	2	17	17-11	2	53	.190	.245	.250	44	-18	0-0	.989	1	90	85	C71	21	-1.6
1968	Hou N	111	350	28	87	19	0	4	33	23-16	3	46	.249	.297	.337	93	-3	1-1	.985	-2	80	63	C108	0	0.0
1969	Mon N	74	235	16	49	4	0	8	19	12-6	1	44	.209	.250	.328	60	-14	0-2	.985	-2	72	77	C66	21	-1.4
1970	Mon N	139	520	51	123	21	5	15	68	28-9	1	75	.237	.275	.383	75	-21	8-4	.983	6	143	115	C137	0	-0.9
1971	Mon N	139	492	34	119	17	3	10	56	19-3	4	87	.242	.273	.350	75	-18	1-0	.985	-6	83	110	C137	0	-1.9
1972	Mon N	18	29	0	7	1	0	0	3	3-0	0	4	.241	.313	.276	67	-1	0-0	1.000	-1	281	0	C7	0	-0.2
	Phi N	82	252	10	56	9	0	3	17	8-6	1	39	.222	.246	.294	52	-16	0-1	.972	-1	86	110	C80	0	-1.6
	Year	100	281	10	63	10	0	3	20	11-6	1	43	.224	.253	.292	54	-17	0-1	.973	-2	100	102	C87	0	-1.8
Total	10	1017	3330	250	765	123	18	81	375	172-69	27	610	.230	.271	.350	76	-113	10-10	.982	1	98	92	C953	42	-7.6
BATES, CHARLIE	Charles William; B9.17.1907 Philadelphia PA; D1.29.1980 Topeka KS; BR/TR/5´10˝/165; d9.22																								
1927	Phi A	9	38	5	9	2	2	0	2	3	0	5	.237	.293	.395	73	-2	3-1	.857	-1	91	98	O9(0/1/8)	—	-0.3
BATES, DEL	Delbert Oakley; B6.12.1940 Seattle WA; BL/TR/6´2˝/195; d5.6; Col Everett (WA) CC																								
1970	Phi N	22	60	1	8	2	0	0	1	6-1	4	15	.133	.257	.167	16	-7	0-1	.992	-0	62	125	C20	0	-0.7
BATES, BUD	Hubert Edgar; B3.16.1912 Los Angeles CA; D4.29.1987 Long Beach CA; BR/TR/6´0˝/165; d9.16																								
1939	Phi N	15	58	8	15	2	0	1	2	2	0	8	.259	.283	.345	70	-3	1	.978	1	116	82	O14(1/13/0)	—	-0.2
BATES, JASON	Jason Charles; B1.5.1971 Downey CA; BB/TR/5´11˝/(170–192); [ColN92 7/207]; d4.26; Col Arizona																								
1995	†Col N	116	322	42	86	17	4	8	46	42-3	2	70	.267	.355	.419	80	-8	3-6	.991	3	98	114	2b82,S20,3b15	0	-0.3
1996	Col N	88	160	19	33	8	1	1	9	23-1	2	34	.206	.312	.287	48	-11	2-1	.978	-3	111	93	2b37,S18,3b12	0	-1.2
1997	Col N	62	121	17	29	10	0	3	11	15-1	3	27	.240	.338	.397	75	-4	0-1	1.000	-4	71	148	2b22,S16,3b6	0	-0.7
1998	Col N	53	74	10	14	3	0	0	3	8-1	0	21	.189	.268	.230	27	-8	0-0	.974	-5	89	62	2b17,3b3,S3	24	-1.2
Total	4	319	677	88	162	38	5	12	69	88-6	7	152	.239	.332	.363	66	-31	5-8	.987	-9	97	108	2b158,S57,3b36	24	-3.4

YEAR	TM LG	G	AB	R	H	2B	3B	HR	RBI	BB-IB	HP	SO	AVG	OBP	SLG	AOPS	ABR	SB-CS	FA	FR	RNG	THR	GAMES AT POSITION	DL	BFW
BATES, JOHNNY	John William; B1.10.1884 Steubenville OH; D2.10.1949 Steubenville OH; BL/TL/5´7˝/168; d4.12																								
1906	Bos N	140	504	52	127	21	5	6	54	36	10	—	.252	.315	.349	110	5	9	.958	-11	70	91	O140(7/133/0)	—	-1.4
1907	Bos N	126	447	52	116	18	12	2	49	39	7	—	.260	.329	.367	118	9	11	.979	-3	107	111	O120(1/1/118)	—	0.0
1908	Bos N	127	445	48	115	14	6	1	29	35	2	—	.258	.315	.324	106	3	25	.948	-4	100	54	O117(101/8/8)	—	-0.9
1909	Bos N	63	236	27	68	15	3	1	23	20	4	—	.288	.354	.390	125	7	15	.945	5	178	0	O60L	—	0.9
	Phi N	77	266	43	78	11	1	1	15	28	2	—	.293	.365	.353	122	8	22	.959	-1	123	141	O73(11/62/0)	—	0.4
	Year	140	502	70	146	26	4	2	38	48	6	—	.291	.360	.371	123	15	37	.952	4	**149**	75	O133(71/62/0)	—	1.3
1910	Phi N	135	498	91	152	26	11	3	61	61	4	49	.305	.385	.420	130	20	31	.954	5	101	131	O131(25/103/3)	—	2.0
1911	Cin N	148	518	89	151	24	13	1	61	103	6	59	.292	.415	.394	131	29	33	.966	1	103	96	O147(0/145/2)	—	2.0
1912	Cin N	81	239	45	69	12	7	1	29	47	0	16	.289	.406	.410	127	11	10	.950	5	103	151	O65(1/64/0)	—	1.1
1913	Cin N	131	407	63	113	13	7	6	51	67	6	30	.278	.387	.388	122	15	21-9	.946	2	96	131	O111(0/24/88)	—	1.3
1914	Cin N	58	155	29	39	7	5	2	15	28	4	17	.252	.380	.400	128	7	4	.913	-6	85	71	O54C	—	-0.3
	Chi N	9	8	2	1	0	0	0	1	1	1	1	.125	.300	.125	28	-1	0	1.000	0	196	0	O3(0/2/1)	—	0.0
	Year	67	163	31	40	7	5	2	16	29	5	18	.245	.376	.387	124	6	4	.917	-5	99	92	O57(0/56/1)	—	-0.3
	Bal F	59	190	24	58	6	3	1	29	38	3	18	.305	.429	.384	119	5	6	.950	-1	99	92	O59(12/48/0)	—	0.0
Total	9	1154	3913	565	1087	167	73	25	417	503	49	190	.278	.367	.377	121	118	187-9	.955	-7	103	100	O1080(218/644/220)	—	5.1
BATES, RAY	Raymond; B2.8.1890 Paterson NJ; D8.15.1970 Tucson AZ; BR/TR/6´0˝/165; d5.31; Mil 1918																								
1913	Cle A	27	30	4	5	0	2	0	4	3	1	9	.167	.265	.300	63	-2	3	.905	0	114	244	3b12,O2C	—	-0.1
1917	Phi A	127	485	47	115	20	7	2	66	21	6	39	.237	.277	.320	83	-12	12	.933	9	104	86	3b124	—	0.0
Total	2	154	515	51	120	20	9	2	70	24	7	48	.233	.277	.318	82	-14	15	.932	9	104	93	3b136,O2C	—	-0.1
BATES, BILLY	William Derrick; B12.7.1963 Houston TX; BL/TR/5´7˝/(155–165); [MilA85 4/81]; d8.17; Col Texas																								
1989	Mil A	7	14	3	3	0	0	0	0	0-0	0	1	.214	.214	.214	21	-2	2-0	.938	3	125	251	2b7	20	0.2
1990	Mil A	14	29	6	3	1	0	0	2	4-0	0	7	.103	.206	.138	-0	-4	4-0	.962	-0	113	84	2b14	0	-0.3
	†Cin N	8	5	2	0	0	0	0	0	0-0	0	2	.000	.000	.000	-96	-1	2-1	1.000	-1	35	0	/2	0	-0.3
Total	2	29	48	11	6	1	0	0	2	4-0	0	10	.125	.189	.146	-4	-7	8-1	.953	1	111	125	2b22	20	-0.4
BATHE, BILL	William David; B10.14.1960 Downey CA; BR/TR/6´2˝/200; [OakA81 8/196]; d4.12; Col Pepperdine																								
1986	Oak A	39	103	9	19	3	0	5	11	2-0	1	20	.184	.208	.359	54	-7	0-0	.991	-3	64	92	C39	0	-0.9
1989	†SF N	30	32	3	9	1	0	0	6	0-0	0	7	.281	.273	.313	71	-1	0-0	1.000	1	54	203	C7	0	-0.1
1990	SF N	52	48	3	11	0	1	3	12	7-2	0	12	.229	.321	.458	118	1	0-0	1.000	-0	111	113	C8	59	0.1
Total	3	121	183	15	39	4	1	8	29	9-2	1	39	.213	.251	.377	75	-7	0-0	.992	-3	67	97	C54	59	-0.9
BATISTA, TONY	Leocadio Francisco; B12.9.1973 Puerto Plata, D.R.; BR/TR/6´0˝/(165–225); d6.3																								
1996	Oak A	74	238	38	71	10	2	6	25	19-0	1	49	.298	.350	.433	98	-1	7-3	.988	9	120	106	2b52,3b18,S4,D4	0	1.0
1997	Oak A	68	188	22	38	10	1	4	18	14-0	2	31	.202	.265	.330	54	-13	2-2	.970	7	112	96	S61,3b4/2D	16	-0.3
1998	Ari N	106	293	46	80	16	1	18	41	18-0	3	52	.273	.318	.519	116	5	1-1	.994	-1	93	116	2b41,S34,3b15	0	0.8
1999	Ari N	44	144	16	37	5	0	5	21	16-3	2	17	.257	.335	.396	85	-3	2-0	.979	9	114	123	S43	0	0.9
	Tor A	98	375	61	107	25	1	26	79	22-1	4	79	.285	.328	.565	121	10	2-0	.975	8	106	104	S98	0	2.4
2000	Tor A★	154	620	96	163	32	2	41	114	35-1	6	121	.263	.307	.519	101	-3	5-4	.963	12	107	**120**	3b154	0	0.9
2001	Tor A	72	271	29	56	11	1	13	45	13-1	4	66	.207	.251	.399	67	-14	0-1	.953	7	111	173	3b72	0	-0.7
	Bal A	84	308	41	82	16	5	12	42	19-0	0	47	.266	.305	.468	106	1	5-1	.934	2	103	102	D33,3b29,S20	0	0.3
	Year	156	579	70	138	27	6	25	87	32-1	4	113	.238	.280	.435	87	-14	5-2	.948	9	109	153	3b101,D33,S20	0	-0.4
2002	Bal A★	161	615	90	150	36	1	31	87	50-9	11	107	.244	.309	.457	106	4	5-4	.962	6	107	134	3b154,D7	0	1.0
2003	Bal A	161	631	76	148	20	1	26	99	28-4	5	102	.235	.270	.393	73	-28	4-3	.950	0	104	119	3b154,D7	0	-2.6
2004	Mon N	157	606	76	146	30	2	32	110	26-4	4	78	.241	.272	.455	81	-20	14-6	.954	3	109	**123**	3b155	0	-1.4
2006	Min A	50	178	24	42	12	0	5	21	15-1	2	27	.236	.303	.388	77	-6	0-1	.954	-2	95	65	3b50	0	-0.8
Total	10	1229	4467	615	1120	223	17	219	702	275-24	44	776	.251	.298	.455	93	-68	47-26	.956	59	106	123	3b805,S260,2b94,D52	16	1.5
BATISTA, RAFAEL	Rafael (Sanchez); B10.20.1947 San Pedro de Macoris, D.R.; BL/TL/6´1˝/195; d6.17																								
1973	Hou N	12	15	2	4	0	0	0	2	1-1	0	6	.267	.313	.267	62	-1	0-0	1.000	-0	56	40	1b8	0	-0.1
1975	Hou N	10	10	0	3	1	0	0	0	0-0	0	4	.300	.300	.400	100	0	0-0	ø	0	—	—	/H	0	0.0
Total	2	22	25	2	7	1	0	0	2	1-1	0	10	.280	.308	.320	77	-1	0-0	1.000	-0	56	40	1b8	0	-0.1
BATISTE, KEVIN	Kevin Wade; B10.21.1966 Galveston TX; BR/TR/6´2˝/187; [TorA85 2/53]; d6.13																								
1989	Tor A	6	8	1	2	0	0	0	0	0-0	0	5	.250	.250	.250	42	-1	0-0	1.000	0	135	0	O5(2/0/3)	0	0.0
BATISTE, KIM	Kimothy Emil; B3.15.1968 New Orleans LA; BR/TR/6´0˝/(175–200); [PhiN87 3/78]; d9.8																								
1991	Phi N	10	27	2	6	0	0	0	1	1-1	0	8	.222	.250	.222	34	-2	0-1	.970	1	111	113	S7	0	-0.2
1992	Phi N	44	136	9	28	4	0	1	10	4-1	0	18	.206	.224	.257	37	-12	0-0	.922	-11	76	79	S41	0	-2.2
1993	†Phi N	79	156	14	44	7	1	5	29	3-2	1	29	.282	.298	.436	96	-2	0-1	.956	5	86	51	3b58,S24	0	0.4
1994	Phi N	64	209	17	49	6	0	1	13	1-0	1	32	.234	.239	.278	34	-21	1-1	.919	-3	94	64	3b42,S17	0	-2.2
1996	SF N	54	130	17	27	6	0	3	11	5-1	0	33	.208	.235	.323	47	-11	3-3	.847	-5	85	188	3b25,S7	15	-1.6
Total	5	251	658	59	154	23	1	10	64	14-5	2	120	.234	.250	.318	52	-48	4-6	.908	-15	89	92	3b125,S96	15	-5.8
BATSCH, BILL	William McKinley; B5.18.1892 Mingo Junction OH; D12.31.1963 Canton OH; BR/TR/5´10.5˝/168; d9.9; Col Bethany																								
1916	Pit N	1	0	0	0	0	0	0	0	1	0	0	ø	1.000	ø	218	0	0	ø	0	—	—	/H	—	0.0
BATTAM, LARRY	Lawrence J.; B5.1.1876 Brooklyn NY; D1.27.1938 Brooklyn NY; 5´11˝/166; d9.28																								
1895	NY N	2	4	0	1	0	0	0	0	2	0	1	.250	.500	.250	99	0	0	.667	-1	83	0	3b2	—	0.0
BATTEN, GEORGE	George Burnett; B10.7.1891 Haddonfield NJ; D8.4.1972 New Port Richey FL; BR/TR/5´11˝/165; d9.28																								
1912	NY A	1	3	0	0	0	0	0	0	0	0	—	.000	.000	.000	-94	-1	0	1.000	-0	55	0	/2	—	-0.1
BATTEY, EARL	Earl Jesse; B1.5.1935 Los Angeles CA; D11.15.2003 Ocala FL; BR/TR/6´1˝/(205–225); d9.10																								
1955	Chi A	5	7	1	2	0	0	0	0	1-0	1	1	.286	.444	.286	97	0	0-0	1.000	1	*0*	*181*	C5	0	0.1
1956	Chi A	4	4	1	1	0	0	0	0	1-0	0	1	.250	.400	.250	74	0	0-0	.800	-1	*0*	*0*	C3	0	-0.1
1957	Chi A	48	115	12	20	2	3	3	6	11-1	0	38	.174	.246	.322	54	-8	0-2	.989	3	97	122	C43	0	-0.5
1958	Chi A	68	168	24	38	8	0	8	26	24-1	2	34	.226	.325	.417	106	2	1-0	.988	1	124	138	C49	0	0.5
1959	Chi A	26	64	9	14	1	2	2	7	8-0	0	13	.219	.306	.391	91	-1	0-0	.990	3	89	121	C20	0	0.2
1960	Was A	137	466	49	126	24	2	15	60	48-5	8	68	.270	.346	.427	110	7	4-5	.982	10	**154**	**141**	C136	0	2.3
1961	Min A	133	460	70	139	24	1	17	55	53-3	3	66	.302	.377	.470	118	13	3-3	.993	11	139	78	C131	0	2.9
1962	Min A★	148	522	58	146	20	3	11	57	57-3	0	48	.280	.348	.393	96	-2	0-0	.991	14	148	95	C147	0	1.9
1963	Min A★	147	508	64	145	17	1	26	84	61-8	8	75	.285	.369	.476	133	24	0-0	.994	8	133	79	C146	0	4.0
1964	Min A	131	405	33	110	17	1	12	52	51-6	1	49	.272	.348	.407	111	7	1-1	.990	-1	113	78	C125	0	1.2
1965	†Min A★	131	394	36	117	22	2	6	60	50-7	2	23	.297	.375	.409	119	12	0-0	.986	7	**158**	110	C128	0	2.6
1966	Min A★	115	364	30	93	12	1	4	34	43-7	3	30	.255	.337	.327	87	-5	4-1	.995	12	109	92	C113	0	1.4
1967	Min A	48	109	6	18	3	1	0	8	13-1	0	24	.165	.254	.211	36	-8	0-0	.987	-1	68	89	C41	23	-0.9
Total	13	1141	3586	393	969	150	17	104	449	421-42	28	470	.270	.349	.409	106	41	13-12	.990	66	*132*	*99*	C1087	23	15.6
BATTIN, JOE	Joseph V.; B11.11.1851 Philadelphia PA; D12.10.1937 Akron OH; BR/TR; d8.11; M2/U2																								
1871	Cle NA	1	3	0	0	0	0	0	0	1	—	0	.000	.250	.000	-21	0	0-0	1.000	0	0	0	/rf	—	0.0
1873	Ath NA	1	5	4	3	0	0	0	2	1	—	0	.600	.667	.600	258	1	0-0	.667	0	491	0	/cf	—	0.1
1874	Ath NA	51	226	40	52	11	1	0	27	1	—	7	.230	.233	.288	61	-11	3-2	.813	3	108	174	2b41,O7(0/2/5),S5	—	-0.8
1875	StL NA	67	284	31	71	6	3	0	33	0	—	6	.250	.250	.292	97	0	15-3	.861	14	**115**	130	2b62,3b6,C2/cf	—	1.0
1876	StL N	**64**	283	34	85	11	4	0	46	6	—	6	.300	.315	.367	134	11	—	**.867**	15	**115**	**203**	3b63/2	—	2.3
1877	StL N	57	226	28	45	3	7	1	22	6	—	17	.199	.220	.288	62	-10	—	.823	-3	114	161	3b32,2b21,O5C/P	—	-0.9
1882	Pit AA	34	133	13	28	5	1	1	—	3	—	—	.211	.228	.286	76	-3	—	.876	17	137	135	3b34	—	1.3
1883	Pit AA	**98**	388	42	83	9	6	1	—	11	—	—	.214	.236	.276	67	-14	—	**.891**	29	**127**	97	3b98,P2,M	—	1.5
1884	Pit AA	43	158	10	28	1	2	0	—	3	1	—	.177	.198	.209	33	-12	—	.919	8	122	73	3b43,M	—	-0.3
	CP U	18	69	8	13	2	0	0	—	0	—	—	.188	.188	.217	23	-9	—	.908	8	125	151	3b18,M	—	0.0
	Bal U	17	59	3	6	1	0	0	—	0	—	—	.102	.102	.119	-30	-11	—	.813	2	122	60	3b17	—	-0.8
	Year	35	128	11	19	3	0	0	—	0	—	—	.148	.148	.172	-3	-20	—	.868	10	124	112	3b35	—	-0.8
1890	Syr AA	29	119	15	25	2	1	0	13	8	0	—	.210	.260	.244	54	-7	8	.794	-6	89	39	3b29	—	-1.1

YEAR	TM LG	G	AB	R	H	2B	3B	HR	RBI	BB-IB	HP	SO	AVG	OBP	SLG	AOPS	ABR	SB-CS	FA	FR	RNG	THR	GAMES AT POSITION	DL	BFW
Total	4NA	120	518	75	126	17	4	0	62	3	—	13	.243	.248	.292	80	-10	18-5	.842	17	112	148	2b103,O10(0/4/6),3b6,S5,C2	—	0.3
Total	6	360	1435	153	313	34	21	3	81	37	1	23	.218	.238	.277	67	-55	8	.870	69	120	121	3b334,2b22,O5C,P3	—	2.0
BATTLE, ALLEN	Allen Zelmo; B11.29.1968 Grantham NC; BR/TR/6´0˝/170; [StLN91 10/259]; d4.26; Col South Alabama																								
1995	StL N	61	118	13	32	5	0	0	2	15-0	1	26	.271	.358	.314	78	-3	3-3	.984	1	121	0	O32(15/7/14)	0	-0.4
1996	Oak A	47	130	20	25	3	0	1	5	17-1	2	26	.192	.293	.238	38	-12	10-2	.988	-1	96	84	O47(24/27/0)	0	-1.1
Total	2	108	248	33	57	8	0	1	7	32-1	3	52	.230	.324	.274	56	-15	13-5	.986	-0	107	48	O79(39/34/14)	0	-1.5
BATTLE, HOWARD	Howard Dion; B3.25.1972 Biloxi MS; BR/TR/6´0˝/(197–208); [TorA90 4/123]; d9.5																								
1995	Tor A	9	15	3	3	0	0	0	0	4-0	0	8	.200	.368	.200	53	-1	1-0	1.000	-1	75	0	3b6/D	0	-0.2
1996	Phi N	5	5	0	0	0	0	0	0	0-0	0	2	.000	.000	.000	-99	-1	0-0	ø	-0	0	0	/3	0	-0.2
1999	†Atl N	15	17	2	6	0	0	1	5	2-0	0	3	.353	.421	.529	140	1	0-0	1.000	-0	76	0	3b6	0	0.1
Total	3	29	37	5	9	0	0	1	5	6-0	0	13	.243	.349	.324	75	-1	1-0	1.000	-2	73	0	3b13/D	0	-0.3
BATTLE, JIM	James Milton; B3.26.1901 Bailey TX; D9.30.1965 Chico CA; BR/TR/6´1˝/170; d9.9																								
1927	Chi A	6	8	1	3	0	1	0	0	0	0	1	.375	.375	.625	160	0	0-0	1.000	-1	68	0	3b4,S2	—	0.0
BATTS, MATT	Matthew Daniel; B10.16.1921 San Antonio TX; BR/TR/5´11˝/(200–214); d9.10; Col Baylor																								
1947	Bos A	7	16	3	8	1	0	1	5	1	0	1	.500	.529	.750	236	3	0-0	1.000	-0	*121*	*98*	C6	0	0.3
1948	Bos A	46	118	13	37	12	0	1	24	15	0	9	.314	.391	.441	115	3	0-0	.986	-1	*120*	*88*	C41	0	0.4
1949	Bos A	60	157	23	38	9	1	3	31	25	1	22	.242	.350	.369	84	-3	1-0	.977	1	*145*	*82*	C50	0	0.0
1950	Bos A	75	238	27	65	15	3	4	34	18	1	19	.273	.327	.412	80	-8	0-0	.994	1	*121*	*64*	C73	0	-0.3
1951	Bos A	11	29	1	4	1	0	0	2	1	0	2	.138	.167	.172	-8	-4	0-0	.975	-0	*138*	*148*	C11	0	-0.4
	StL A	79	248	26	75	17	1	5	31	21	0	21	.302	.357	.440	111	4	2-0	.960	-8	*91*	*113*	C64	0	-0.1
	Year	90	277	27	79	18	1	5	33	22	0	23	.285	.338	.412	98	-1	2-0	.962	-8	*96*	*117*	C75	0	-0.5
1952	Det A	56	173	11	41	4	1	3	13	14	1	22	.237	.298	.324	72	-7	1-0	.983	2	*104*	*134*	C55	33	-0.2
1953	Det A	116	374	38	104	24	3	6	42	24	0	36	.278	.322	.406	97	-3	2-3	.986	-15	*77*	*114*	C103	0	-1.4
1954	Det A	12	21	1	6	1	0	0	5	2	0	4	.286	.333	.333	89	0	0-0	.967	1	*153*	*167*	C8	0	0.1
	Chi A	55	158	16	36	7	1	3	19	17	0	15	.228	.299	.342	74	-6	0-1	.992	5	*124*	*104*	C42	0	0.1
	Year	67	179	17	42	8	1	3	24	19	0	19	.235	.303	.341	76	-6	0-1	.989	6	*127*	*111*	C50	0	0.2
1955	Cin N	26	71	4	18	4	1	0	13	4-0	0	11	.254	.286	.338	63	-4	0-0	.986	0	*119*	*81*	C21	0	-0.3
1956	Cin N	3	2	0	0	0	0	0	0	1-0	0	1	.000	.333	.000	0	0	0-0	ø	0	—	—	/H	0	0.0
Total	10	546	1605	163	432	95	11	26	219	143-0	3	163	.269	.329	.391	89	-25	6-4	.983	-15	*108*	*102*	C474	33	-1.8
BAUER, HANK	Henry Albert; B7.31.1922 E.St.Louis IL; BR/TR/6´0˝/(185–192); d9.6; M8/C1																								
1948	NY A	19	50	6	9	1	1	1	9	6	0	13	.180	.268	.300	51	-4	1-0	.964	0	103	115	O14(8/0/7)	0	-0.4
1949	†NY A	103	301	56	82	6	6	10	45	37	1	42	.272	.354	.432	107	1	2-2	.977	1	92	169	O95(21/25/60)	0	-0.1
1950	†NY A	113	415	72	133	16	2	13	70	35	5	41	.320	.380	.463	118	10	2-3	.987	2	105	93	O110(36/0/82)	0	0.7
1951	†NY A	118	348	53	103	19	3	10	54	42	1	39	.296	.373	.454	128	13	5-2	.990	2	103	108	O107(51/1/62)	0	1.1
1952	†NY A★	141	553	86	162	31	6	17	74	50	3	61	.293	.355	.463	134	23	6-7	.984	-3	89	141	O139(18/0/122)	0	1.5
1953	†NY A★	133	437	77	133	20	6	10	57	59	6	45	.304	.394	.446	131	21	2-3	.992	3	102	123	O126(3/1/124)	0	1.8
1954	NY A★	114	377	73	111	16	5	12	54	40	0	42	.294	.360	.459	128	13	4-4	.989	-2	97	85	O108(8/0/104)	0	0.7
1955	†NY A	139	492	97	137	20	5	20	53	56-1	8	65	.278	.360	.461	122	14	8-4	.981	5	106	136	O133(5/0/131)/C	0	1.5
1956	†NY A	147	539	96	130	18	7	26	84	59-3	2	72	.241	.316	.445	103	-1	4-2	.969	-6	90	98	O146(7/0/143)	0	-1.1
1957	†NY A	137	479	70	124	22	**9**	18	65	42-4	4	64	.259	.321	.455	112	6	7-2	.986	-6	91	78	O135(3/0/134)	0	-0.4
1958	†NY A	128	452	62	121	22	6	12	50	32-1	1	56	.268	.316	.423	106	2	3-2	.980	-6	89	75	O123(2/0/121)	0	-0.9
1959	NY A	114	341	44	81	20	0	9	39	33-1	2	54	.238	.307	.375	90	-5	4-2	.972	-8	87	40	O111(4/0/108)	0	-1.6
1960	KC A	95	255	30	70	15	0	3	31	21-1	1	36	.275	.326	.369	89	-4	1-0	.978	-5	79	107	O67R	0	-1.1
1961	KC A	43	106	11	28	3	1	3	18	9-0	0	8	.264	.319	.396	89	-2	1-0	.958	-2	85	103	O35(11/2/27),M	0	-0.5
Total	14	1544	5145	833	1424	229	57	164	703	521-11	34	638	.277	.346	.439	114	87	50-33	.982	-24	95	105	O1449(177/29/1292)/C	0	1.2
BAUGHMAN, JUSTIN	Justin Reis; B8.1.1974 Mountain View CA; BR/TR/5´11˝/180; [CalA95 5/116]; d5.17; Col Lewis & Clark; [DL 1999 Ana A 182]																								
1998	Ana A	63	196	24	50	9	1	1	20	6-0	1	36	.255	.277	.327	56	-13	10-4	.977	-1	101	64	2b59,S3/D	0	-1.0
2000	Ana A	16	22	4	5	2	0	0	0	1-0	0	2	.227	.261	.318	44	-2	3-0	.958	-0	132	147	2b5,S5,D4	0	-0.1
Total	2	79	218	28	55	11	1	1	20	7-0	1	38	.252	.275	.326	55	-15	13-4	.976	-2	103	70	2b64,S8,D5	182	-1.1
BAUMANN, PADDY	Charles John; B12.20.1885 Indianapolis IN; D11.20.1969 Indianapolis IN; BR/TR/5´9˝/160; d8.10																								
1911	Det A	26	94	8	24	2	4	0	11	6	1	—	.255	.307	.362	82	-3	1	.956	4	116	77	2b23,O3R	—	0.1
1912	Det A	16	42	3	11	1	0	0	7	6	0	—	.262	.354	.286	86	0	4	.786	-2	95	0	3b6,2b5,O2(1/1/0)	—	-0.3
1913	Det A	50	191	31	57	7	4	1	22	16	0	18	.298	.353	.393	120	4	4	.943	-6	98	83	2b49	—	-0.1
1914	Det A	3	11	1	0	0	0	0	0	2	0	1	.000	.154	.000	-52	-2	0	1.000	-1	93	101	2b3	—	-0.3
1915	NY A	76	219	30	64	13	1	2	28	28	3	32	.292	.380	.388	130	9	9-10	.978	1	96	113	2b43,3b19/cf	—	1.0
1916	NY A	79	237	35	68	5	3	1	25	19	5	16	.287	.352	.346	108	2	10	.958	-6	94	30	O28(12/1/15),3b26,2b9	—	-0.4
1917	NY A	49	110	10	24	2	1	0	8	4	0	9	.218	.246	.255	52	-7	2	.941	-6	70	126	2b18,O7(4/1/2)/3	—	-1.5
Total	7	299	904	118	248	30	13	4	101	81	9	76	.274	.340	.350	103	3	30-10	.953	-16	97	95	2b150,3b52,O41(17/4/20)	—	-1.5
BAUMER, JIM	James Sloan; B1.29.1931 Tulsa OK; D7.8.1996 Paoli PA; BR/TR/6´2˝/185; d9.14																								
1949	Chi A	8	10	2	4	1	1	0	2	2	2	1	.400	.571	.700	243	2	0-0	.938	1	126	170	S7	0	0.3
1961	Cin N	10	24	0	3	0	0	0	0	0-0	0	9	.125	.125	.125	-33	-5	0-0	1.000	-3	64	39	2b9	0	-0.8
Total	2	18	34	2	7	1	1	0	2	2-0	2	10	.206	.289	.294	55	-3	0-0	1.000	-3	64	39	2b9,S7	0	-0.5
BAUMGARTNER, JOHN	John Edward; B5.29.1931 Birmingham AL; BR/TR/6´1˝/190; d4.14; Col Alabama																								
1953	Det A	7	27	3	5	0	0	0	2	0	0	5	.185	.185	.185	0	-4	0-0	.913	-1	79	119	3b7	0	-0.5
BAUMHOLTZ, FRANK	Frank Conrad; B10.7.1918 Midvale OH; D12.14.1997 Winter Springs FL; BL/TL/5´10.5˝/175; d4.15; Col Ohio U.																								
1947	Cin N	151	643	96	182	32	9	5	45	56	1	53	.283	.341	.384	93	-7	6	.977	-7	84	136	O150(0/29/136)	0	-1.9
1948	Cin N	128	415	57	123	19	5	4	30	27	3	32	.296	.344	.395	103	1	8	.987	3	100	145	O110(20/23/67)	0	0.0
1949	Cin N	27	81	12	19	5	3	1	8	6	1	8	.235	.295	.407	86	-2	0	.964	1	115	53	O20(13/0/7)	0	-0.3
	Chi N	58	164	15	37	4	2	1	15	9	1	21	.226	.270	.293	52	-12	2	.986	-2	86	90	O43(0/7/38)	0	-1.5
	Year	85	245	27	56	9	5	2	23	15	2	29	.229	.279	.331	64	-14	2	.976	-1	97	77	O63(13/7/45)	0	-1.8
1951	Chi N	146	560	62	159	28	10	2	50	49	4	36	.284	.346	.380	94	-5	5-4	.975	-10	94	47	O140(17/64/60)	0	-2.1
1952	Chi N	103	409	59	133	17	4	4	35	27	3	27	.325	.371	.416	116	9	5-7	.974	3	107	99	O101(0/47/65)	38	0.7
1953	Chi N	133	520	75	159	36	7	3	25	42	1	36	.306	.359	.419	100	1	3-3	.980	-6	96	56	O130(0/69/64)	0	-1.0
1954	Chi N	90	303	38	90	12	6	4	28	20	1	15	.297	.340	.416	95	-3	1-3	.988	-4	95	37	O71(10/61/13)	0	-1.1
1955	Chi N	105	280	23	81	12	5	1	27	16-2	1	24	.289	.325	.379	88	-5	0-1	.993	0	105	61	O63(40/0/23)	0	-0.9
1956	Phi N	76	100	13	27	0	0	0	9	6-0	1	6	.270	.309	.270	61	-5	0-2	.962	1	98	185	O15(0/1/14)	0	-0.6
1957	Phi N	2	2	0	0	0	0	0	0	0-0	0	0	.000	.000	.000	-99	-1	0-0	ø	0	—	—	/H	0	-0.1
Total	10	1019	3477	450	1010	165	51	25	272	258-2	17	258	.290	.342	.389	95	-29	30-20	.980	-22	96	88	O843(100/301/487)	38	-8.8
BAUTISTA, DANNY	Daniel (Alcantara); B5.24.1972 Santo Domingo, D.R.; BR/TR/5´11˝/(170–225); d9.15																								
1993	Det A	17	61	6	19	3	0	1	9	1-0	0	10	.311	.317	.410	95	-1	3-1	1.000	1	103	207	O16(0/9/8)/D	0	0.1
1994	Det A	31	99	12	23	4	1	4	15	3-0	0	18	.232	.255	.414	68	-5	1-2	1.000	0	109	0	O30(0/14/16)/D	53	-0.6
1995	Det A	89	271	28	55	9	0	7	27	12-0	0	68	.203	.237	.314	42	-25	4-1	.988	-0	105	56	O86(2/0/84)/D	0	-2.7
1996	Det A	25	64	12	16	2	0	2	8	9-0	0	15	.250	.342	.375	81	-2	1-2	.974	-1	102	0	O22(12/0/12)/D	0	-0.4
	Atl N	17	20	1	3	0	0	0	1	2-0	1	5	.150	.261	.150	11	-3	0-0	1.000	-0	96	0	O14(2/2/10)	94	-0.3
1997	†Atl N	64	103	14	25	3	2	3	9	5-1	1	24	.243	.282	.398	75	-4	2-0	.984	1	110	51	O57(48/1/10)	22	-0.4
1998	†Atl N	82	144	17	36	11	0	3	17	7-0	0	21	.250	.281	.389	76	-5	1-0	.959	-4	79	0	O58(53/1/4)/D	43	-1.0
1999	Fla N	70	205	32	59	10	1	5	24	4-0	1	30	.288	.303	.420	86	-6	3-0	.979	7	137	98	O60(22/18/31)	0	0.1
2000	Fla N	44	89	9	17	4	0	4	12	5-0	0	20	.191	.234	.371	52	-7	1-0	.980	1	103	143	O38(25/5/17)	0	-0.6
	Ari N	87	262	45	83	16	7	7	47	20-4	3	30	.317	.366	.511	116	6	5-2	.987	3	103	148	O82(2/21/67)	0	0.6
	Year	131	351	54	100	20	7	11	59	25-4	3	50	.285	.333	.476	102	-1	6-2	.985	4	103	147	O120(27/26/84)	0	0.0
2001	†Ari N	100	222	26	67	11	2	5	26	14-1	1	31	.302	.346	.437	94	-2	3-2	1.000	2	101	146	O61(3/28/33)	0	-0.1
2002	Ari N	40	154	22	50	5	2	6	23	11-2	0	21	.325	.367	.500	115	3	4-2	.985	-3	92	0	O39(0/5/37)	130	-0.1
2003	Ari N	88	284	29	78	16	3	4	36	21-2	4	50	.275	.330	.394	82	-7	3-2	.961	-7	88	23	O79(3/18/59)	34	-1.7
2004	Ari N	141	539	64	154	27	1	11	65	35-2	4	66	.286	.332	.401	83	-13	6-2	.986	3	104	96	O137(0/2/135)D	0	-1.6
Total	12	895	2517	317	685	121	19	62	319	149-12	15	409	.272	.315	.409	83	-71	37-16	.984	3	103	76	O779(172/124/523),D6	376	-8.7

YEAR	TM LG	G	AB	R	H	2B	3B	HR	RBI	BB-IB	HP	SO	AVG	OBP	SLG	AOPS	ABR	SB-CS	FA	FR	RNG	THR	GAMES AT POSITION	DL	BFW
Bautista, Jose	Jose Antonio; B10.19.1980 Santo Domingo, D.R.; BR/TR/6´0˝/190; [PitN00 20/599]; d4.4																								
2004	Bal A	16	11	3	3	0	0	0	1	1-0	0	3	.273	.333	.273	61	-1	0-0	1.000	-0	71	542	O6R,3b4,D2	0	-0.1
	TB A	12	12	1	2	0	0	0	1	3-0	0	7	.167	.333	.167	37	-1	0-1	1.000	-0	63	0	O8(5/0/3),3b2/D	0	-0.2
	KC A	13	25	1	5	1	0	0	1	1-0	0	12	.200	.231	.240	23	-3	0-0	.957	2	130	172	3b11/rf	0	-0.1
	Year	41	48	5	10	1	0	0	2	5-0	0	22	.208	.283	.229	36	-5	0-1	.960	1	127	149	3b17,O15(5/0/10),D3	0	-0.4
	Pit N	23	40	1	8	2	0	0	0	2-0	0	18	.200	.238	.250	26	-4	0-0	.864	-1	110	0	O12(0/3/9)	0	-0.5
2005	Pit N	11	28	3	4	1	0	0	1	3-0	0	7	.143	.226	.179	8	-4	1-0	.952	0	99	150	3b8	0	-0.3
2006	Pit N	117	400	58	94	20	3	16	51	46-2	16	110	.235	.335	.420	91	-5	2-4	.988	-1	93	224	O85(6/57/25),3b33,2b3	0	-0.8
Total	3	192	516	67	116	24	3	16	54	56-2	16	157	.225	.318	.376	77	-18	3-5	.974	-1	93	204	O112(11/60/44),3b58,2b3,D3	0	-2.0
Baxes, Jim	Dimitrios Speros; B7.5.1928 San Francisco CA; D11.14.1996 Garden Grove CA; BR/TR/6´1˝/200; d4.11; b–Mike																								
1959	LA N	11	33	4	10	1	0	2	5	4-0	1	7	.303	.395	.515	130	2	1-0	.952	5	145	127	3b10	0	0.6
	Cle A	77	247	35	59	11	0	15	34	21-0	0	47	.239	.299	.466	111	2	0-1	.956	-11	85	94	2b48,3b22	0	-0.6
Total	1	88	280	39	69	12	0	17	39	25-0	1	54	.246	.310	.471	113	4	1-1	.956	-7	85	94	2b48,3b32	0	0.0
Baxes, Mike	Michael; B12.18.1930 San Francisco CA; BR/TR/5´10˝/175; d4.17; b–Jim																								
1956	KC A	73	106	9	24	3	1	1	5	18-1	0	15	.226	.339	.302	70	-4	0-1	.944	2	114	75	S62/2	0	0.0
1958	KC A	73	231	31	49	10	1	0	8	21-0	3	24	.212	.286	.264	52	-15	1-6	.969	-6	97	91	2b61,S4	0	-2.0
Total	2	146	337	40	73	13	2	1	13	39-1	3	39	.217	.303	.276	58	-19	1-7	.946	-5	114	71	S66,2b62	0	-2.0
Baxter, Moose	John Morris; B7.27.1876 Chippewa Falls WI; D8.7.1926 Portland OR; BL/TR/6´2˝/200; d4.19																								
1907	StL N	6	21	1	4	0	0	0	0	0	0	—	.190	.190	.190	20	-2	0	.921	-1	118	34	1b6	—	-0.3
Bay, Harry	Harry Elbert "Deerfoot"; B1.17.1878 Pontiac IL; D3.20.1952 Peoria IL; BL/TL/5´8˝/138; d7.23																								
1901	Cin N	41	157	25	33	1	2	1	3	13	1	—	.210	.275	.261	60	-8	4	.953	-1	60	217	O40(0/25/15)	—	-1.1
1902	Cin N	6	16	3	6	0	0	0	1	2	1	—	.375	.474	.375	148	1	0	.778	0	211	0	O3L	—	0.1
	Cle A	108	455	71	132	10	5	0	23	36	1	—	.290	.343	.334	92	-4	22	**.973**	1	92	105	O107(24/79/4)	—	-0.8
1903	Cle A	**140**	579	94	169	15	12	1	35	29	3	—	.292	.329	.364	110	6	**45**	.950	-5	83	79	O140(26/114/0)	—	-0.7
1904	Cle A	132	506	69	122	12	9	3	36	43	5	—	.241	.307	.318	99	0	**38**	**.987**	6	105	166	O132(5/127/0)	—	-0.1
1905	Cle A	144	552	90	166	18	10	0	22	36	5	—	.301	.349	.370	126	16	36	.970	-2	89	115	O144C	—	0.8
1906	Cle A	68	280	47	77	8	3	0	14	26	0	—	.275	.337	.325	109	3	17	.979	-5	91	117	O68C	—	-0.6
1907	Cle A	34	95	14	17	1	1	0	7	10	2	—	.179	.271	.211	53	-5	7	.968	2	143	127	O31(7/23/1)	—	-0.5
1908	Cle A	2	0	0	0	0	0	0	0	0	0	—	ø	ø	ø	ø	0	0	ø	0	—	—	/R	—	0.0
Total	8	675	2640	413	722	65	42	5	141	195	18	—	.273	.328	.336	103	9	169	.968	-4	93	122	O665(65/580/20)	—	-2.9
Bay, Jason	Jason Raymond; B9.20.1978 Trail BC, Can.; BR/TR/6´2˝/(200–205); [MonN00 22/645]; d5.23; Col Gonzaga																								
2003	SD N	3	8	2	2	1	0	1	2	1-0	1	1	.250	.400	.750	210	1	0-0	1.000	1	159	0	O3C	43	0.2
	Pit N	27	79	13	23	6	1	3	12	18-0	0	28	.291	.423	.506	139	6	3-1	.976	-2	85	67	O26(24/2/1)	0	0.3
	Year	30	87	15	25	7	1	4	14	19-0	1	29	.287	.421	.529	145	7	3-1	.980	-1	91	61	O29(24/5/1)	0	0.5
2004	Pit N	120	411	61	116	24	4	26	82	41-2	10	129	.282	.358	.550	131	18	4-6	.991	-0	106	49	O119(117/5/0)	33	1.2
2005	Pit N☆	**162**	599	110	183	44	6	32	101	95-9	6	142	.306	.402	.559	149	46	21-1	.988	-4	102	43	O162(146/30/0)	0	4.2
2006	Pit N★	159	570	101	163	29	3	35	109	102-9	8	156	.286	.396	.532	133	32	11-2	.991	7	110	120	O157L	0	3.3
Total	4	471	1667	287	487	104	14	97	306	257-20	25	456	.292	.390	.546	139	103	39-10	.989	2	105	72	O467(444/40/1)	76	9.2
Bayer, Chris	Christopher Andy; B12.19.1873 Louisville KY; D5.30.1933 Louisville KY; ?/175; d6.17																								
1899	Lou N	1	3	0	0	0	0	0	0	0	0	—	.000	.000	.000	-99	-1	0	.600	-1	36	0	/S	—	-0.2
Bayless, Dick	Harry Owen; B9.6.1883 Joplin MO; D12.16.1920 Santa Rita NM; BL/TR/5´9˝/178; d9.9																								
1908	Cin N	19	71	7	16	1	0	1	3	6	2	—	.225	.304	.282	90	-1	0	.946	3	251	345	O19(0/2/17)	—	0.1
Baylor, Don	Don Edward; B6.28.1949 Austin TX; BR/TR/6´1˝/(190–210); [BalA67 2/39]; d9.18; M9/C7																								
1970	Bal A	8	17	4	4	0	0	0	4	2-0	0	3	.235	.300	.235	53	-1	1-1	1.000	0	125	0	O6(3/4/0)	0	-0.1
1971	Bal A	1	2	0	0	0	0	0	0	2-0	1	1	.000	.600	.000	82	0	0-0	1.000	0	195	0	/rf	0	0.1
1972	Bal A	102	320	33	81	13	3	11	38	29-0	9	50	.253	.330	.416	117	7	24-2	.975	-4	100	35	O84(35/13/48),1b9	0	0.3
1973	†Bal A	118	405	64	116	20	4	11	51	35-3	**13**	48	.286	.357	.437	123	13	32-9	.981	-1	100	67	O110L,1b6/D	0	1.0
1974	†Bal A	137	489	66	133	22	1	10	59	43-6	10	56	.272	.341	.382	111	8	29-12	.978	-16	85	11	O129(112/2/26),1b8/D	0	-1.4
1975	Bal A	145	524	79	148	21	6	25	76	53-8	**13**	71	.282	.360	.489	147	32	32-17	.982	-6	91	77	O135(127/5/6),1b2,D7	0	1.9
1976	Oak A	157	595	85	147	25	1	15	68	58-4	**20**	72	.247	.329	.368	110	9	52-12	.981	-6	97	18	O76(27/2/50),1b69,D23	0	0.0
1977	Cal A	154	561	87	141	27	0	25	75	62-7	12	76	.251	.334	.433	113	11	26-12	.966	-2	97	59	O77(48/11/19),D61,1b18	0	0.4
1978	Cal A	158	591	103	151	26	0	34	99	56-9	**18**	71	.255	.332	.472	130	23	22-9	.974	-3	100	0	D102,O39L,1b17	0	1.6
1979	†Cal A★	**162**	628	**120**	186	33	3	36	**139**	71-6	11	51	.296	.371	.530	146	41	22-12	.976	-3	101	43	O97(78/0/19),D65/1	0	3.2
1980	Cal A	90	340	39	85	12	2	5	51	24-4	11	32	.250	.316	.341	82	-8	6-6	.969	1	106	99	O54(37/0/18),D36	46	-1.1
1981	Cal A	103	377	52	90	18	1	17	66	42-1	7	51	.239	.322	.427	115	7	3-3	1.000	1	116	60	D97,1b4/lf	0	0.5
1982	†Cal A	157	608	80	160	24	1	24	93	57-7	7	69	.263	.329	.424	105	4	10-4	ø	0	0	0	D155	0	0.0
1983	NY A	144	534	82	162	33	3	21	85	40-11	13	53	.303	.361	.494	138	28	17-7	1.000	0	101	0	D136,O5(2/0/4)/1	0	2.5
1984	NY A	134	493	84	129	29	1	27	89	38-6	**23**	68	.262	.341	.489	131	21	1-1	.889	-0	98	0	D127,O5(1/0/4)	0	1.7
1985	NY A	142	477	70	110	24	1	23	91	52-6	**24**	90	.231	.330	.430	110	8	0-4	ø	0	0	0	D140	0	0.2
1986	†Bos A	160	585	93	139	23	1	31	94	62-8	**35**	111	.238	.344	.439	111	11	3-5	.986	-2	43	74	D143,1b13,O3L	0	0.2
1987	Bos A	108	339	64	81	8	0	16	57	40-3	24	47	.239	.355	.404	99	1	5-2	ø	0	0	0	D97	0	-0.1
	†Min A	20	49	3	14	1	0	0	6	5-0	4	12	.286	.397	.306	87	0	0-1	ø	0	0	0	D14	0	-0.1
	Year	128	388	67	95	9	0	16	63	45-3	**28**	59	.245	.360	.392	98	1	5-3	ø	0	0	0	D111	0	-0.2
1988	†Oak A	92	264	28	58	7	0	7	34	34-2	12	44	.220	.332	.326	89	-3	0-1	ø	0	0	0	D80	0	-0.6
Total	19	2292	8198	1236	2135	366	28	338	1276	805-91	267	1069	.260	.342	.436	118	212	285-120	.977	-41	97	46	D1285,O822(623/37/195),1b148	46	10.2
Beach, Jack	Stonewall Jackson; B1862 Alexandria VA; D7.23.1896 Alexandria VA; d5.1																								
1884	Was AA	8	31	3	3	2	0	0	—	0	0	—	.097	.097	.161	-20	-4	—	.667	-1	128	335	O8(1/0/7)	—	-0.4
Beadle, Dave	David A.; B1.1864 New York NY; D9.22.1925 New York NY; BL/6´2˝/200; d6.17																								
1884	Det N	1	3	0	0	0	0	0	0	0	—	2	.000	.000	.000	-99	-1	—	.500	-1	0	0	/O(1/0/1)C	—	-0.1
Beall, Johnny	John Woolf; B3.12.1882 Beltsville MD; D6.13.1926 Beltsville MD; BL/TR/6´0˝/180; d4.17																								
1913	Cle A	6	6	0	1	0	0	0	1	0	0	2	.167	.167	.167	-2	-1	0	ø	0	—	—	/H	—	-0.1
	Chi A	17	60	10	16	0	1	2	3	0	1	0	.267	.279	.400	99	-1	1	.953	0	100	110	O17C	—	-0.2
	Year	23	66	10	17	0	1	2	4	0	1	2	.258	.269	.379	89	-2	1	.953	0	100	110	O17C	—	-0.3
1915	Cin N	10	34	3	8	1	0	0	3	5	1	10	.235	.350	.265	86	0	0-1	.960	1	99	153	O10(9/1/0)	—	0.0
1916	Cin N	6	21	3	7	2	0	1	4	3	0	7	.333	.417	.571	207	3	1	1.000	1	82	334	O6L	—	0.4
1918	StL N	19	49	2	11	1	0	0	6	3	0	6	.224	.269	.245	59	-2	0	1.000	-0	97	81	O18R	—	-0.4
Total	4	58	170	18	43	4	1	3	17	11	2	25	.253	.306	.341	95	-1	2-1	.972	1	97	136	O51(14/18/18)	—	-0.3
Beall, Bob	Robert Brooks; B4.24.1948 Portland OR; BB/TL/5´11˝/(175–180); [PhiN70 28/653]; d5.12; Col Oregon St.																								
1975	Atl N	20	31	2	7	2	0	0	1	6-0	0	9	.226	.351	.290	77	-1	0-0	.984	-0	91	104	1b8	0	-0.2
1978	Atl N	108	185	29	45	8	0	1	16	36-0	1	27	.243	.368	.303	81	-3	4-5	.987	1	119	87	1b40,O8(6/2/0)	0	-0.5
1979	Atl N	17	15	1	2	2	0	0	0	3-0	0	4	.133	.263	.267	46	-1	0-0	1.000	0	111	0	1b3	98	-0.1
1980	Pit N	3	3	0	0	0	0	0	0	0-0	0	1	.000	.000	.000	-97	-1	0-0	ø	0	—	—	/H	0	-0.1
Total	4	148	234	32	54	12	0	1	18	45-0	1	41	.231	.355	.295	76	-6	4-5	.987	0	114	87	1b51,O8(6/2/0)	98	-0.9
Beals, Tommy	Thomas L. (aka W.Thomas in 1871-1873); B8.1850 NY; D10.2.1915 San Francisco CA; BR/5´5˝/144; d7.27																								
1871	Oly NA	10	36	6	7	0	0	0	1	2	—	0	.194	.237	.194	27	-3	2-0	.778	2	92	0	O8(4/0/4),2b2	—	0.0
1872	Oly NA	**9**	36	6	11	1	1	0	5	1	—	1	.306	.324	.389	125	1	0-0	.853	1	146	95	2b5,S2,O2C	—	0.1
1873	Was NA	37	169	35	46	9	5	0	22	1	—	1	.272	.276	.385	96	0	3-0	.870	9	112	109	2b26,C13/lf	—	0.5
1874	Bos NA	19	97	20	19	3	4	0	17	0	—	2	.196	.196	.309	56	-5	0-1	.849	1	108	61	2b12,O9(1/2/6)	—	-0.4
1875	Bos NA	35	155	38	41	2	6	0	16	3	—	1	.265	.278	.355	114	1	1-0	.867	-0	43	126	O30(3/19/8),2b8	—	0.1
1880	Chi N	13	46	4	7	0	0	0	3	1	—	6	.152	.170	.152	10	-4	—	.889	-4	55	0	O10R,2b3	—	-0.9
Total	5NA	110	493	105	124	15	16	0	61	7	—	5	.252	.262	.347	90	-6	6-1	.864	13	112	115	2b53,O50(9/23/18),C13,S2	—	0.3

YEAR	TM LG	G	AB	R	H	2B	3B	HR	RBI	BB-IB	HP	SO	AVG	OBP	SLG	AOPS	ABR	SB-CS	FA	FR	RNG	THR	GAMES AT POSITION	DL	BFW
Beamon, Charlie	Charles Alfonzo Jr.; B12.4.1953 Oakland CA; BL/TL/6´1˝/(170–183); d9.11; f–Charlie; Col Laney (CA) JC																								
1978	Sea A	10	11	2	2	0	0	0	0	1-0	0	1	.182	.250	.182	23	-1	0-0	1.000	1	279	109	1b2,D6	0	0.0
1979	Sea A	27	25	5	5	1	0	0	0	0-0	0	5	.200	.200	.240	18	-3	1-0	1.000	-0	125	0	1b7,O2L,D5	0	-0.3
1981	Tor A	8	15	1	3	1	0	0	0	2-0	0	2	.200	.294	.267	59	-1	0-0	1.000	-0	0	0	D4/1	0	-0.1
Total	3	45	51	8	10	2	0	0	0	3-0	0	8	.196	.241	.235	32	-5	1-0	1.000	1	175	46	D15,1b10,O2L	0	-0.4
Beamon, Trey	Clifford; B2.11.1974 Dallas TX; BL/TR/6´3˝/(192–195); [PitN92 2/61]; d8.4																								
1996	Pit N	24	51	7	11	2	0	0	6	4-0	0	6	.216	.273	.255	39	-5	1-1	.960	-0	107	0	O14(5/0/10)	0	-0.6
1997	SD N	43	65	5	18	3	0	0	7	2-0	1	17	.277	.309	.323	70	-3	1-2	.909	0	76	368	O20(15/0/5)	0	-0.3
1998	Det A	28	42	4	11	4	0	0	2	5-0	0	13	.262	.340	.357	81	-1	1-0	1.000	1	200	0	D11,O4(2/0/2)	83	-0.1
Total	3	95	158	16	40	9	0	0	15	11-0	1	36	.253	.306	.310	63	-9	3-3	.944	1	99	172	O38(22/0/17),D11	83	-1.0
Bean, Joe	Joseph William; B3.18.1874 Boston MA; D2.15.1961 Atlanta GA; BR/TR/5´8˝/138; d4.28																								
1902	NY N	50	182	13	40	2	1	0	5	5	2	—	.220	.249	.242	52	-11	9	.880	-8	96	109	S50	—	-1.8
Bean, Billy	William Daro; B5.11.1964 Santa Ana CA; BL/TL/6´1˝/(185–190); [DetA86 4/99]; d4.25; Col Loyola Marymount																								
1987	Det A	26	66	6	17	2	0	0	4	5-0	0	11	.258	.310	.288	62	-4	1-1	1.000	3	129	111	O24(5/17/3)	0	-0.1
1988	Det A	10	11	2	2	0	1	0	0	0-0	0	2	.182	.182	.364	50	-1	0-0	1.000	0	83	0	O4(0/2/3),1b2/D	0	-0.1
1989	Det A	9	11	0	0	0	0	0	0	2-0	1	3	.000	.214	.000	-35	-2	0-0	.833	-1	88	0	O6(4/1/2),1b2	0	-0.3
	LA N	51	71	7	14	4	0	0	3	4-0	1	10	.197	.250	.254	45	-5	0-2	1.000	-0	103	0	O44(28/11/7)	0	-0.7
1993	SD N	88	177	19	46	9	0	5	32	6-1	2	29	.260	.284	.395	81	-5	2-4	.987	1	94	250	O54(11/17/32),1b12	0	-0.6
1994	SD N	84	135	7	29	5	1	0	14	7-1	0	25	.215	.248	.267	37	-13	0-1	1.000	0	110	0	O39(17/7/15),1b16	0	-1.5
1995	SD N	4	7	1	0	0	0	0	0	1-0	0	4	.000	.125	.000	-65	-2	0-0	.750	-1	72	0	O4L	0	-0.2
Total	6	272	478	42	108	20	2	5	53	25-2	4	84	.226	.266	.308	55	-32	3-8	.988	2	104	105	O175(69/55/62),1b32/D	0	-3.5
Beane, Billy	William Lamar; B3.29.1962 Orlando FL; BR/TR/6´4˝/(195–210); [NYN80 1/23]; d9.13																								
1984	NY N	5	10	0	1	0	0	0	0	0-0	0	2	.100	.100	.100	-44	-2	0-1	1.000	-0	55	0	O5(2/1/2)	0	-0.3
1985	NY N	8	8	0	2	1	0	0	1	0-0	0	3	.250	.250	.375	74	0	0-0	1.000	-0	39	0	O2(1/0/1)	0	-0.1
1986	Min A	80	183	20	39	6	0	3	15	11-0	0	54	.213	.258	.295	49	-13	2-3	1.000	2	120	0	O67(64/5/1),D5	14	-1.4
1987	Min A	12	15	1	4	2	0	0	1	0-0	0	6	.267	.267	.400	71	-1	0-0	1.000	0	152	0	O7R	0	0.0
1988	Det A	6	6	1	1	0	0	0	1	0-0	0	2	.167	.167	.167	-7	-1	0-0	1.000	-0	93	0	O6(4/1/1)	0	-0.1
1989	Oak A	37	79	8	19	5	0	0	11	0-0	0	13	.241	.237	.304	54	-5	3-1	1.000	1	114	0	O25(4/0/21),1b4/C3D	21	-0.5
Total	6	148	301	30	66	14	0	3	29	11-0	0	80	.219	.246	.296	48	-22	5-5	1.000	2	116	0	O112(75/7/33),D9,1b4/3C	35	-2.4
Beard, Ted	Cramer Theodore; B1.7.1921 Woodsboro MD; BL/TL/5´8˝/(160–165); d9.5																								
1948	Pit N	25	81	15	16	1	3	0	7	12	2	18	.198	.316	.284	62	-4	5	1.000	-1	105	0	O22C	0	-0.6
1949	Pit N	14	24	1	2	0	0	0	1	2	0	2	.083	.154	.083	-34	-5	0	.900	-1	91	0	O10R	0	-0.6
1950	Pit N	61	177	32	41	6	2	4	12	27	0	45	.232	.333	.356	79	-5	3	.983	2	109	108	O49(1/21/27)	38	-0.5
1951	Pit N	22	48	7	9	1	0	1	3	6	1	14	.188	.291	.271	51	-3	0-0	1.000	0	87	195	O15(12/4/0)	0	-0.4
1952	Pit N	15	44	5	8	2	1	0	3	7	0	9	.182	.294	.273	57	-3	2-0	1.000	0	103	83	O13(0/3/10)	0	-0.3
1957	Chi A	38	78	15	16	1	0	0	7	18-2	0	14	.205	.354	.218	59	-3	3-2	.974	1	80	309	O28(0/3/25)	0	-0.4
1958	Chi A	19	22	5	2	0	0	1	2	6-0	0	5	.091	.286	.227	44	-2	3-0	1.000	-0	107	0	O15(10/6/1)	0	-0.1
Total	7	194	474	80	94	11	6	6	35	78-2	3	107	.198	.315	.285	61	-25	16-2	.987	1	100	118	O152(23/59/73)	38	-2.9
Beard, Ollie	Oliver Perry; B5.2.1862 Lexington KY; D5.28.1929 Cincinnati OH; BR/TR/5´11˝/180; d4.17																								
1889	Cin AA	**141**	558	96	159	13	14	1	77	35	1	39	.285	.328	.364	94	-8	36	.896	18	109	**126**	S141	—	1.2
1890	Cin N	122	492	64	132	17	15	3	72	44	2	13	.268	.331	.382	108	3	30	.897	-1	**108**	117	S113,3b9	—	0.5
1891	Lou AA	68	257	35	62	4	5	0	24	33	1	9	.241	.330	.296	80	-6	7	.879	3	105	150	3b61,S7	—	-0.2
Total	3	331	1307	195	353	34	34	4	173	112	4	61	.270	.330	.357	97	-11	73	.896	20	109	121	S261,3b70	—	1.5
Beasley, Lew	Lewis Paige; B8.27.1948 Sparta VA; BL/TR/5´10˝/172; [BalA67*2/38]; d5.21																								
1977	Tex A	25	32	5	7	1	0	0	3	2-0	0	2	.219	.257	.250	41	-3	1-1	.833	-3	53	0	O18(14/0/4)/SD	0	-0.6
Beatty, Desmond	Desmond Aloysius "Desperate"; B4.7.1893 Baltimore MD; D10.6.1969 Norway ME; BR/TR/5´8.5˝/158; d9.28																								
1914	NY N	2	3	0	0	0	0	0	1	0	0	0	.000	.000	.000	-99	-1	0	.400	-1	47	0	/S3	—	-0.2
Beauchamp, Jim	James Edward; B8.21.1939 Vinita OK; BR/TR/6´2˝/(190–205); d9.22; C8																								
1963	StL N	4	3	0	0	0	0	0	0	0-0	0	2	.000	.000	.000	-91	-1	0-0	ø	0	—	—	/H	0	-0.1
1964	Hou N	23	55	6	9	2	0	2	4	5-0	1	16	.164	.246	.309	58	-3	0-0	.913	-1	86	0	O15(11/4/0),1b2	0	-0.5
1965	Hou N	24	53	5	10	1	0	0	4	5-0	0	11	.189	.259	.208	36	-5	0-2	1.000	1	70	199	O9L,1b3	0	-0.5
	Mil N	4	3	0	0	0	0	0	0	1-0	0	1	.000	.250	.000	-23	0	0-1	1.000	-0	0	123	1b2	0	-0.1
	Year	28	56	5	10	1	0	0	4	6-0	0	12	.179	.258	.196	32	-5	0-3	1.000	1	70	199	O9L,1b5	0	-0.6
1967	Atl N	4	3	0	0	0	0	0	1	0-0	0	0	.000	.000	.000	-99	-1	0-0	ø	0	—	—	/H	0	-0.1
1968	Cin N	31	57	10	15	2	0	2	14	4-1	0	19	.263	.306	.404	107	0	0-0	1.000	1	118	0	O13(1/11/1)/1	0	0.1
1969	Cin N	43	60	8	15	1	0	1	8	5-2	0	13	.250	.308	.317	71	-2	0-0	1.000	0	113	0	O9(5/4/0),1b3	0	-0.3
1970	Hou N	31	26	3	5	0	0	1	4	3-0	0	7	.192	.276	.308	58	-2	0-1	1.000	-1	83	0	O16(13/3/0)	0	-0.3
	StL N	44	58	8	15	2	0	1	6	8-0	0	11	.259	.338	.345	84	-1	2-0	1.000	1	113	245	O10(2/6/2),1b5	0	0.0
	Year	75	84	11	20	2	0	2	10	11-0	0	18	.238	.320	.333	77	-3	2-1	1.000	1	101	145	O26(15/9/2),1b5	0	-0.3
1971	StL N	77	162	24	38	8	3	2	16	9-1	1	26	.235	.274	.358	76	-6	3-1	.982	-2	85	87	1b44/lf	0	-1.1
1972	NY N	58	120	10	29	1	0	5	19	7-1	1	33	.242	.282	.375	89	-2	0-0	.979	-2	67	88	1b35,O5L	22	-0.7
1973	†NY N	50	61	5	17	1	1	0	14	7-1	0	11	.279	.343	.328	90	-1	1-0	.969	-1	73	123	1b11	0	-0.2
Total	10	393	661	79	153	18	4	14	90	54-6	3	150	.231	.288	.334	75	-24	6-5	.980	-4	91	90	1b106,O78(47/28/3)	22	-3.8
Beaumont, Ginger	Clarence Howeth; B7.23.1876 Rochester WI; D4.10.1956 Burlington WI; BL/TR/5´8˝/190; d4.21; Col Beloit																								
1899	Pit N	111	437	90	154	15	8	3	38	41	7	—	.352	.416	.444	136	23	31	.924	0	124	140	O100(3/96/1),1b2	—	1.5
1900	†Pit N	138	567	105	158	14	9	5	50	40	4	—	.279	.331	.362	90	-9	27	.944	-15	52	67	O138C	—	-3.0
1901	Pit N	133	558	120	185	14	5	8	72	44	2	—	.332	.382	.418	128	20	36	.943	-7	47	52	O133C	—	0.6
1902	Pit N	130	541	100	**193**	21	6	0	67	39	4	—	**.357**	.404	.418	148	31	33	.975	-2	85	204	O130C	—	2.4
1903	†Pit N	**141**	613	**137**	**209**	30	6	7	68	44	5	—	.341	.390	.444	133	26	23	.948	-11	76	45	O141C	—	0.8
1904	Pit N	153	615	97	**185**	12	12	3	54	34	1	—	.301	.338	.374	117	10	28	.968	-7	74	110	O153C	—	-0.4
1905	Pit N	103	384	60	126	12	8	3	40	22	0	—	.328	.365	.424	131	13	21	.972	0	99	178	O97C	—	0.9
1906	Pit N	80	310	48	82	9	3	2	32	19	2	—	.265	.311	.332	96	-2	1	.945	-5	63	96	O78C	—	-1.2
1907	Bos N	150	580	67	**187**	19	14	4	62	37	3	—	.322	.366	.424	148	29	25	.962	4	150	**224**	O149C	—	3.0
1908	Bos N	125	476	66	127	20	6	2	52	42	1	—	.267	.328	.347	117	9	13	.965	-3	112	80	O121C	—	0.0
1909	Bos N	123	407	35	107	11	4	0	60	35	0	—	.263	.321	.310	92	-4	12	.969	1	101	80	O111C	—	-0.9
1910	†Chi N	76	172	30	46	5	1	2	22	28	1	14	.267	.373	.343	110	3	4	.957	-2	98	73	O56(15/34/7)	—	-0.1
Total	12	1463	5660	955	1759	182	82	39	617	425	30	14	.311	.362	.393	122	149	254	.956	-48	89	114	O1407(18/1380/8),1b2	—	3.6
Beavens, Ed	Edward P. (aka Edward P. Bevens); B1848 Troy NY; TR/5´8˝/138; d5.9																								
1871	Tro NA	3	15	7	6	0	0	0	5	0	—	0	.400	.400	.400	129	0	2-0	.818	1	120	166	2b3	—	0.1
1872	Atl NA	10	43	6	9	2	0	0	2	1	—	0	.209	.227	.256	41	-3	0-0	.683	-6	92	50	2b10/Slf	—	-0.7
Total	2NA	13	58	13	15	2	0	0	7	1	—	0	.259	.271	.293	62	-3	2-0	.720	-5	99	78	2b13/lfS	—	-0.6
Bechtel, George	George A.; B1848 Philadelphia PA; 5´11˝/165; d5.20; ▲																								
1871	Ath NA	20	94	24	33	9	1	1	21	2	—	2	.351	.365	.500	147	6	4-0	.821	1	124	354	O15(1/3/11),P3,3b3	—	0.4
1872	Mut NA	51	247	61	74	11	3	0	42	7	—	3	.300	.319	.368	118	7	9-1	.823	-0	79	111	O50(13/0/37)/1	—	0.8
1873	Phi NA	**53**	258	53	63	12	1	1	39	9	—	1	.244	.270	.310	68	-10	2-1	.853	6	121	152	O52(0/2/50),P3	—	0.0
1874	Phi NA	32	151	29	42	4	5	1	34	2	—	1	.278	.288	.391	111	1	0-0	.731	-4	0	0	O28(1/0/28),P6	—	-0.1
1875	Cen NA	**14**	61	12	17	5	0	0	7	1	—	1	.279	.290	.361	136	4	0-0	.791	-1	91	138	P14	—	0.0
	Ath NA	35	164	33	46	6	2	0	20	1	—	3	.280	.285	.341	105	0	2-0	.810	0	73	101	O31(0/3/29),P4	—	0.2
	Year	49	225	45	63	11	2	0	27	2	—	4	.280	.286	.347	113	2	2-0	.810	-1	73	101	O31(0/3/29),P18	—	0.2
1876	Lou N	14	55	2	10	1	0	0	2	0	—	1	.182	.182	.200	23	-5	—	.882	-1	49	0	O14R	—	-0.5
	NY N	2	10	2	3	0	0	0	0	0	—	0	.300	.300	.300	115	0	—	.429	-2	0	0	O2C	—	-0.1
	Year	16	65	4	13	1	0	0	2	0	—	1	.200	.200	.215	34	-5	—	.750	-3	41	0	O16(0/2/14)	—	-0.6
Total	5NA	205	975	212	275	47	12	3	163	22	—	11	.282	.298	.364	104	8	17-2	.816	1	81	122	O176(15/8/155),P30,3b3/1	—	1.3

YEAR	TM LG	G	AB	R	H	2B	3B	HR	RBI	BB-IB	HP	SO	AVG	OBP	SLG	AOPS	ABR	SB-CS	FA	FR	RNG	THR	GAMES AT POSITION	DL	BFW
BECK, CLYDE	Clyde Eugene "Jersey"; B1.6.1900 Bassett CA; D7.15.1988 Temple City CA; BR/TR/5´10˝/176; d5.19																								
1926	Chi N	30	81	10	16	0	0	1	4	7	0	15	.198	.261	.235	34	-8	0	.993	8	107	150	2b30	—	0.1
1927	Chi N	117	391	44	101	20	5	2	44	43	0	37	.258	.332	.350	83	-9	0	.969	11	106	107	2b99,3b17/S	—	0.6
1928	Chi N	131	483	72	124	18	4	3	52	58	4	58	.257	.341	.329	77	-15	3	.958	3	92	161	3b87,S47/2	—	-0.2
1929	Chi N	54	190	28	40	7	0	0	9	19	0	24	.211	.282	.247	32	-20	3	.978	7	124	116	3b33,S14	—	-0.9
1930	Chi N	83	244	32	52	7	0	6	34	36	0	32	.213	.314	.316	53	-19	2	.953	-3	96	99	S57,2b24,3b2	—	-1.4
1931	Cin N	53	136	17	21	4	2	0	19	21	1	14	.154	.272	.213	34	-12	1	.960	0	103	204	3b38,S6	—	-1.1
Total	6	468	1525	203	354	56	11	12	162	184	5	180	.232	.317	.307	63	-83	9	.959	27	103	163	3b177,2b154,S125	—	-2.9
BECK, ERVE	Ervin Thomas "Dutch"; B7.19.1878 Toledo OH; D12.23.1916 Toledo OH; BR/TR/5´10˝/168; d9.19																								
1899	Bro N	8	24	2	4	2	0	0	2	0	0	—	.167	.167	.250	13	-3	0	.931	-1	126	52	2b6,S2	—	-0.3
1901	Cle A	135	539	78	156	26	8	6	79	23	1	—	.289	.320	.401	103	1	7	.927	-8	99	71	2b132	—	-0.6
1902	Cin N	48	187	19	57	10	3	1	20	3	1	—	.305	.319	.406	113	2	2	.936	-2	99	93	2b32,1b6,O6(3/0/3)	—	0.0
	Det A	41	162	23	48	4	0	2	22	4	0	—	.296	.313	.358	84	-4	3	.971	2	134	113	1b36,O5R	—	-0.3
Total	3	232	912	122	265	42	11	9	123	30	2	—	.291	.315	.390	99	-4	12	.929	-9	100	75	2b170,1b42,O11(3/0/8),S2	—	-1.2
BECK, FRED	Frederick Thomas; B11.17.1886 Havana IL; D3.12.1962 Havana IL; BL/TL/6´1˝/180; d4.14																								
1909	Bos N	96	334	20	66	5	6	2	27	17	4	—	.198	.245	.266	56	-19	5	.966	2	99	244	O57(12/42/2),1b33	—	-2.2
1910	Bos N	154	571	52	157	32	9	**10**	64	19	7	55	.275	.307	.415	105	0	8	.963	0	100	108	O134(2/125/7),1b19	—	-0.7
1911	Cin N	41	87	7	16	1	2	2	20	1	0	13	.184	.193	.310	41	-8	2	1.000	-0	99	109	O16(4/5/7),1b6	—	-0.9
	Phi N	66	210	26	59	8	3	3	25	17	4	21	.281	.346	.390	105	1	3	.957	-3	87	94	O61(11/1/50)	—	-0.5
	Year	107	297	33	75	9	5	5	45	18	4	34	.253	.304	.367	88	-7	5	.966	-3	89	97	O77(15/6/57),1b6	—	-1.4
1914	Chi F	**157**	555	51	155	23	4	11	77	44	8	66	.279	.341	.395	106	-5	9	.982	-13	66	119	1b157	—	-2.4
1915	Chi F	121	373	35	83	9	3	5	38	24	4	38	.223	.277	.303	67	-24	4	.992	-6	70	105	1b117	—	-3.6
Total	5	635	2130	191	536	78	27	33	251	122	27	193	.252	.301	.360	89	-55	31	.984	-20	72	110	1b332,O268(29/173/66)	—	-10.3
BECK, ZINN	Zinn Bertram; B9.30.1885 Steubenville OH; D3.19.1981 W.Palm Beach FL; BR/TR/5´10.5˝/160; d9.14																								
1913	StL N	10	30	4	5	1	0	0	2	4	0	10	.167	.265	.200	34	-2	1	.833	0	107	94	S5,3b5	—	-0.2
1914	StL N	137	457	42	106	15	11	3	45	28	4	32	.232	.282	.333	84	-12	14	.935	3	108	**150**	3b122,S16	—	-0.4
1915	StL N	70	223	21	52	9	4	0	15	12	3	31	.233	.282	.309	79	-6	3-10	.935	1	110	126	3b62,S4,2b2	—	-0.7
1916	StL N	62	184	8	41	7	1	0	10	14	1	21	.223	.281	.272	71	-6	3	.910	-2	98	100	3b52/12	—	-0.8
1918	NY A	11	8	0	0	0	0	0	1	0	0	1	.000	.000	.000	-98	-2	0	1.000	0	197	205	1b5/3	—	-0.2
Total	5	290	902	75	204	32	16	3	73	58	8	95	.226	.279	.307	76	-28	21-10	.932	2	107	132	3b242,S25,1b6,2b3	—	-2.3
BECKENDORF, HEINIE	Henry Ward; B6.15.1884 New York NY; D9.15.1949 Jackson Heights NY; BR/TR/5´9˝/174; d4.16																								
1909	Det A	15	27	1	7	1	0	0	1	2	0	—	.259	.310	.296	88	0	0	.957	-0	*96*	*88*	C15	—	0.0
1910	Det A	3	7	0	3	0	0	0	2	1	0	—	.429	.500	.429	179	1	0	.909	-0	*115*	*54*	C2	—	0.1
	Was A	37	103	8	15	1	0	0	10	5	3	—	.146	.207	.155	14	-10	0	.991	2	*103*	*64*	C36	—	-0.6
	Year	40	110	8	18	1	0	0	12	6	3	—	.164	.227	.173	26	-9	0	.988	1	*104*	*63*	C38	—	-0.5
Total	2	55	137	9	25	2	0	0	13	8	3	—	.182	.243	.197	39	-9	0	.983	1	*102*	*68*	C53	—	-0.5
BECKER, BEALS	David Beals; B7.5.1886 El Dorado KS; D8.16.1943 Huntington Park CA; BL/TL/5´9˝/170; d4.19																								
1908	Pit N	20	65	4	10	0	1	0	0	2	1	—	.154	.191	.185	20	-6	2	1.000	1	226	0	O17R	—	-0.7
	Bos N	43	171	13	47	3	1	0	7	7	0	—	.275	.303	.304	96	-1	7	.941	-1	182	93	O43(0/1/42)	—	-0.4
	Year	63	236	17	57	3	2	0	7	9	1	—	.242	.272	.271	74	-8	9	.958	-0	195	66	O60(0/1/59)	—	-1.1
1909	Bos N	152	562	60	138	15	6	6	24	47	1	—	.246	.305	.326	91	-7	21	.932	-2	123	150	O152R	—	-1.7
1910	NY N	80	126	18	36	2	4	3	24	14	0	25	.286	.357	.437	131	4	11	.972	3	107	178	O45(6/23/14)/1	—	0.6
1911	†NY N	88	172	28	45	11	1	1	20	26	0	22	.262	.359	.355	97	0	19	.975	1	101	129	O55(17/6/33)	—	-0.1
1912	†NY N	125	402	66	106	18	8	6	58	54	2	35	.264	.354	.393	101	1	30	.958	3	99	125	O117(1/93/26)	—	-0.3
1913	Cin N	30	108	11	32	5	3	0	14	6	0	12	.296	.333	.398	109	1	0-4	.971	1	110	77	O28(9/8/11)	—	-0.1
	Phi N	88	306	53	99	19	10	9	44	22	0	30	.324	.369	.539	151	19	11-12	.983	-1	103	58	O77(42/36/2)/1	—	1.2
	Year	118	414	64	131	24	13	9	58	28	0	42	.316	.360	.502	140	20	11-16	.980	-0	105	63	O105(51/44/13)/1	—	1.1
1914	Phi N	138	514	76	167	25	5	9	66	37	0	59	.325	.370	.446	133	20	16	.947	4	108	108	O126(87/32/8)	—	1.9
1915	†Phi N	112	338	38	83	16	4	11	35	26	1	48	.246	.301	.414	114	5	12-15	.943	-6	99	46	O98(90/0/8)	—	-0.9
Total	8	876	2764	367	763	114	43	45	292	241	5	231	.276	.335	.397	112	36	129-31	.955	4	114	106	O758(252/199/313),1b2	—	-0.5
BECKER, HEINZ	Heinz Reinhard "Dutch"; B8.26.1915 Berlin, Germany; D11.11.1991 Dallas TX; BB/TR (BL 1946)/6´2˝/200; d4.21																								
1943	Chi N	24	69	5	10	0	0	0	2	9	0	6	.145	.244	.145	14	-8	0	.983	1	132	66	1b18	0	-0.8
1945	†Chi N	67	133	25	38	8	2	2	27	17	2	16	.286	.375	.421	124	5	0	1.000	-1	72	132	1b28	0	0.2
1946	Chi N	9	7	0	2	0	0	0	1	1	0	1	.286	.375	.286	91	0	0	ø	0	—	—	/H	0	0.0
	Cle A	50	147	15	44	10	1	0	17	23	2	18	.299	.401	.381	127	7	1-0	.995	-0	91	95	1b44	0	0.6
1947	Cle A	2	2	0	0	0	0	0	0	0	0	1	.000	.000	.000	-99	-1	0-0	ø	0	—	—	/H	0	-0.1
Total	4	152	358	45	94	18	3	2	47	50	4	42	.263	.359	.346	102	3	1-0	.994	-0	94	100	1b90	0	-0.1
BECKER, JOE	Joseph Edward; B6.25.1908 St.Louis MO; D1.11.1998 Sunset Hills MO; BR/TR/6´1˝/180; d5.10; C16																								
1936	Cle A	22	50	5	9	3	1	1	11	5	0	4	.180	.255	.340	45	-5	0-0	.977	-2	*89*	*42*	C15	—	-0.6
1937	Cle A	18	33	3	11	2	1	0	2	3	1	4	.333	.405	.455	116	1	0-0	.949	-1	*82*	*205*	C12	—	0.1
Total	2	40	83	8	20	5	2	1	13	8	1	8	.241	.315	.386	73	-4	0-0	.964	-3	*86*	*112*	C27	—	-0.5
BECKER, MARTY	Martin Henry; B12.25.1893 Tiffin OH; D9.25.1957 Cincinnati OH; BB/TL/5´8.5˝/155; d9.8																								
1915	NY N	17	52	5	13	2	0	0	3	2	0	9	.250	.278	.288	76	-2	3	.917	1	86	230	O16(0/16/1)	—	-0.1
BECKER, RICH	Richard Godhard; B2.1.1972 Aurora IL; BL/TL (BB 1993–94, 95p)/5´10˝/(180–199); [MinA90 3/85]; d9.10																								
1993	Min A	3	7	3	2	2	0	0	0	5-0	0	4	.286	.583	.571	210	2	1-1	.875	-0	109	0	O3C	21	0.2
1994	Min A	28	98	12	26	3	0	1	8	13-0	0	25	.265	.351	.327	76	-3	6-1	.989	4	124	135	O26(1/23/2)/D	18	0.2
1995	Min A	106	392	45	93	15	1	2	33	34-0	4	95	.237	.303	.296	57	-25	8-9	.986	7	104	**227**	O105(2/99/5)	0	-1.7
1996	Min A	148	525	92	153	31	4	12	71	68-1	2	118	.291	.372	.434	102	3	19-5	.993	17	**114**	**209**	O146(15/121/10)	0	2.1
1997	Min A	132	443	61	117	22	3	10	45	62-1	1	130	.264	.354	.395	94	-3	17-5	.985	1	105	78	O128(9/114/14)	0	0.1
1998	NY N	49	100	15	19	4	2	3	10	21-2	0	42	.190	.331	.360	84	-2	3-1	.984	3	106	238	O41(17/14/13)	0	0.0
	Bal A	79	113	22	23	1	0	3	11	22-0	2	34	.204	.343	.292	69	-5	2-0	.984	-3	87	46	O60(5/13/43)/D	0	-0.7
1999	Mil N	89	139	15	35	5	2	5	16	33-0	0	38	.252	.395	.424	107	3	5-0	.970	0	93	160	O50(16/19/17),D2	0	0.3
	Oak A	40	125	21	33	3	0	1	10	25-0	2	43	.264	.395	.312	86	-1	3-2	.986	0	85	197	O39(17/32/8)	0	-0.1
2000	Oak A	23	47	11	11	2	0	1	5	11-0	1	17	.234	.390	.340	88	0	1-0	.949	2	111	306	O19(8/14/1),D2	0	0.2
	Det A	92	238	48	58	12	0	7	34	56-0	0	70	.244	.383	.382	97	1	1-2	.956	-3	94	78	O80(14/24/47),D3	0	-0.3
	Year	115	285	59	69	14	0	8	39	67-0	1	87	.242	.384	.375	96	1	2-2	.954	-1	97	116	O99(22/38/48),D5	0	-0.1
Total	8	789	2227	345	570	100	12	45	243	350-4	12	616	.256	.358	.372	88	-30	66-26	.983	29	104	158	O697(104/476/160),D9	39	0.3
BECKERT, GLENN	Glenn Alfred; B10.12.1940 Pittsburgh PA; BR/TR/6´1˝/(185–190); d4.12; Mil 1966; Col Allegheny																								
1965	Chi N	154	614	73	147	21	3	3	30	28-0	3	52	.239	.275	.298	60	-33	6-8	.973	5	108	102	2b153	0	-1.7
1966	Chi N	153	656	73	188	23	7	1	59	26-0	4	36	.287	.317	.348	84	-15	10-4	.970	-14	96	86	2b152/S	0	-1.6
1967	Chi N	146	597	91	167	32	3	5	40	30-1	0	25	.280	.314	.369	91	-7	10-3	.968	-2	103	100	2b144	0	0.4
1968	Chi N	155	643	**98**	189	28	4	4	37	31-0	2	20	.294	.326	.369	102	2	8-4	.977	10	104	117	2b155	0	2.9
1969	Chi N★	131	543	69	158	22	1	1	37	24-0	6	24	.291	.325	.341	78	-15	6-0	.965	11	**112**	91	2b129	21	0.6
1970	Chi N★	143	591	99	170	15	6	3	36	32-0	0	22	.288	.323	.349	71	-24	4-1	.970	13	107	105	2b138/cf	0	-0.1
1971	Chi N★	131	530	80	181	18	5	2	42	24-0	0	24	.342	.367	.406	104	3	3-2	.986	-1	100	89	2b129	0	1.2
1972	Chi N★	120	474	51	128	22	2	3	43	23-1	2	17	.270	.304	.344	76	-14	2-1	.976	15	**112**	101	2b118	0	0.9
1973	Chi N	114	372	38	95	13	0	0	29	30-1	2	15	.255	.313	.290	64	-17	0-2	.984	-7	98	88	2b88	22	-2.1
1974	SD N	64	172	11	44	1	0	0	7	11-0	0	8	.256	.301	.262	61	-9	0-0	.938	-10	84	67	2b36/3	69	-1.8
1975	SD N	9	16	2	6	1	0	0	0	1-0	0	0	.375	.412	.438	145	1	0-0	1.000	-0	106	0	3b4	0	0.1
Total	11	1320	5208	685	1473	196	31	22	360	260-3	19	243	.283	.318	.345	81	-128	49-25	.973	19	104	98	2b1242,3b5/cfS	112	-1.2
BECKLEY, JAKE	Jacob Peter "Eagle Eye"; B8.4.1867 Hannibal MO; D6.25.1918 Kansas City MO; BL/TL/5´10˝/200; d6.20; HF1971																								
1888	Pit N	71	283	35	97	15	3	0	27	7	2	22	.343	.363	.417	162	20	20	.979	-3	73	110	1b71	—	1.0
1889	Pit N	123	522	91	157	24	10	9	97	29	6	29	.301	.345	.437	129	19	11	.982	2	98	111	1b122/rf	—	0.8
1890	Pit P	121	516	109	167	38	**22**	9	120	42	6	32	.324	.381	.535	156	40	18	.976	-0	97	91	1b121	—	2.3

YEAR	TM LG	G	AB	R	H	2B	3B	HR	RBI	BB-IB	HP	SO	AVG	OBP	SLG	AOPS	ABR	SB-CS	FA	FR	RNG	THR	GAMES AT POSITION	DL	BFW
1891	Pit N	133	554	94	162	20	19	4	73	44	8	46	.292	.353	.419	128	18	13	.982	13	**147**	90	1b133	—	1.6
1892	Pit N	151	614	102	145	21	19	10	96	31	14	44	.236	.288	.381	102	-3	30	.978	20	**163**	101	1b151	—	1.5
1893	Pit N	**131**	542	108	164	32	19	5	106	54	20	26	.303	.386	.459	127	21	15	.986	11	**130**	106	1b131	—	2.5
1894	Pit N	132	537	123	185	36	19	7	122	43	19	16	.345	.412	.521	125	22	21	.978	5	115	94	1b132	—	2.0
1895	Pit N	130	534	104	175	31	19	5	111	24	21	20	.328	.380	.485	129	22	20	.978	-7	75	98	1b130	—	1.2
1896	Pit N	59	217	44	55	7	5	3	32	22	10	28	.253	.349	.373	94	-1	8	.982	-0	99	120	1b56,O3C/2	—	-0.2
	NY N	46	182	37	55	8	4	6	38	9	5	7	.302	.352	.489	124	5	11	.982	-1	96	69	1b45,O2L	—	0.4
	Year	105	399	81	110	15	9	9	70	31	15	35	.276	.351	.426	108	4	19	.982	-1	98	98	1b101,O5(2/3/0)/2	—	0.2
1897	NY N	17	68	8	17	2	3	1	11	2	3	—	.250	.301	.412	90	-2	2	.973	2	152	130	1b17	—	0.0
	Cin N	97	365	76	126	17	9	7	76	18	12	—	.345	.395	.499	127	12	23	.979	-3	85	114	1b97	—	0.8
	Year	114	433	84	143	19	12	8	87	20	15	—	.330	.380	.485	121	11	25	.978	-1	96	117	1b114	—	0.8
1898	Cin N	118	459	86	135	20	12	4	72	28	10	—	.294	.348	.416	111	5	6	.983	-1	92	107	1b118	—	0.3
1899	Cin N	135	517	87	172	27	16	3	99	40	10	—	.333	.392	.464	132	22	20	.986	5	107	97	1b135	—	2.4
1900	Cin N	141	558	98	190	26	10	2	94	40	4	—	.341	.389	.434	130	23	23	.980	5	115	**115**	1b140	—	2.5
1901	Cin N	140	580	78	178	36	13	3	79	28	7	—	.307	.346	.429	133	23	4	.977	-4	89	104	1b140	—	1.6
1902	Cin N	129	531	82	175	23	7	5	69	34	6	—	.330	.377	.427	135	21	15	.983	-2	87	**119**	1b129/P	—	1.7
1903	Cin N	120	459	85	150	29	10	2	81	42	1	—	.327	.384	.447	123	13	23	.976	4	114	96	1b119	—	1.4
1904	StL N	142	551	72	179	22	9	1	67	35	9	—	.325	.375	.403	147	30	17	.988	-12	67	113	1b142	—	1.7
1905	StL N	134	514	48	147	20	10	1	57	30	6	—	.286	.333	.370	113	7	12	.982	-8	80	79	1b134	—	-0.3
1906	StL N	87	320	29	79	16	6	0	44	13	3	—	.247	.283	.334	96	-3	3	.987	-4	78	90	1b85	—	-1.0
1907	StL N	32	115	6	24	3	0	0	7	1	1	—	.209	.222	.235	45	-8	0	.988	-2	71	107	1b32	—	-1.2
Total	20	2389	9538	1602	2934	473	244	87	1578	616	183	270	.308	.361	.436	126	306	315	.981	19	102	102	1b2380,O6(2/3/1)/P2	—	23.0
Becquer, Julio	Julio (Villegas); B12.20.1931 Havana, Cuba; BL/TL/5´11.5˝/(162–178); d9.13																								
1955	Was A	10	14	1	3	0	0	0	1	0-0	0	1	.214	.214	.214	16	-2	0-0	1.000	0	205	124	1b2	0	-0.1
1957	Was A	105	186	14	42	6	2	2	22	10-2	1	29	.226	.269	.312	59	-11	3-3	1.000	-0	90	87	1b43	0	-1.4
1958	Was A	86	164	10	39	3	0	0	12	8-3	0	21	.238	.270	.256	47	-12	1-2	.994	5	148	73	1b42/lf	0	-1.0
1959	Was A	108	220	20	59	12	5	1	26	8-2	1	17	.268	.296	.382	85	-5	3-2	.990	1	113	102	1b53	0	-0.7
1960	Was A	110	298	41	75	15	7	4	35	12-3	1	35	.252	.282	.389	81	-10	1-3	.989	-3	87	93	1b77/P	0	-1.8
1961	LA A	11	8	0	0	0	0	0	0	1-0	0	5	.000	.111	.000	-61	-2	0-0	1.000	0	92	0	1b5	0	-0.2
	Min A	57	84	13	20	1	2	5	18	2-1	0	12	.238	.253	.476	86	-3	0-1	1.000	-0	60	126	1b18,O5L/P	0	-0.4
	Year	68	92	13	20	1	2	5	18	3-1	0	17	.217	.240	.435	72	-5	0-1	1.000	-0	65	105	1b23,O5L/P	0	-0.6
1963	Min A	1	0	1	0	0	0	0	0	0-0	0	0	ø	ø	ø	ø	0	0-0	ø	0	—	—	/H	0	0.0
Total	7	488	974	100	238	37	16	12	114	41-11	3	120	.244	.276	.352	70	-45	8-11	.993	4	105	91	1b240,O6L,P2	0	-5.6
Bedell, Howie	Howard William; B9.29.1935 Clearfield PA; BL/TR/6´1˝/185; d4.10; C2; Col West Chester																								
1962	Mil N	58	138	15	27	1	2	0	2	11-0	0	22	.196	.255	.232	33	-14	1-0	.955	-1	108	0	O45(44/2/0)	0	-1.6
1968	Phi N	9	7	0	1	0	0	0	1	1-0	0	0	.143	.222	.143	20	-1	0-0	ø	0	—	—	/H	0	-0.1
Total	2	67	145	15	28	1	2	0	3	12-0	0	22	.193	.253	.228	32	-15	1-0	.955	-1	108	0	O45(44/2/0)	0	-1.7
Bedford, Gene	William Eugene; B12.2.1896 Dallas TX; D10.6.1977 San Antonio TX; BB/TR/5´8˝/170; d6.25; Col SMU																								
1925	Cle A	2	3	1	0	0	0	0	0	0	0	1	.000	.000	.000	-99	-1	0-0	1.000	-1	57	0	2b2	—	-0.2
Beecher, Ed	Edward Harry; B7.2.1860 Guilford CT; D9.12.1935 Hartford CT; BL/TL/5´10˝/185; d6.28																								
1887	Pit N	41	169	15	41	8	0	2	22	7	2	8	.243	.281	.325	73	-6	8	.915	5	167	79	O41(18/22/1)	—	-0.2
1889	Was N	42	179	20	53	9	0	0	30	5	1	4	.296	.319	.346	90	-2	3	.861	-2	93	64	O39(1/0/38),1b3	—	-0.4
1890	Buf P	126	536	69	159	22	10	3	90	29	7	23	.297	.341	.392	104	3	14	.810	-5	102	72	O126(119/0/7)/P	—	-0.4
1891	Was AA	58	235	35	57	11	3	2	28	27	5	9	.243	.333	.340	97	0	17	.824	0	116	142	O58(52/6/0)	—	-0.1
	Phi AA	16	71	9	15	2	4	0	7	3	0	4	.211	.243	.352	70	-4	7	1.000	-0	81	0	O16R	—	-0.4
	Year	74	306	44	72	13	7	2	35	30	5	13	.235	.314	.343	91	-4	24	.845	-0	110	116	O74(52/6/16)	—	-0.5
Total	4	283	1190	148	325	52	17	7	177	71	15	48	.273	.322	.363	94	-9	49	.843	-2	112	84	O280(190/28/62),1b3/P	—	-1.5
Beeler, Jodie	Joseph Sam; B11.26.1921 Dallas TX; D10.8.2002 Mesquite TX; BR/TR/6´0˝/170; d9.21																								
1944	Cin N	3	3	0	0	0	0	0	0	0	0	2	.000	.000	.000	-99	-1	0	.000	-1	0	0	/23	0	-0.2
Begley, Gene	Eugene T.; B6.7.1861 Brooklyn NY; d9.11																								
1886	NY N	5	16	1	2	0	0	0	1	1	—	3	.125	.176	.125	-7	-2	1	.864	-0	—	—	C3,O2R	—	-0.2
Begley, Jim	James Lawrence "Imp"; B9.19.1902 San Francisco CA; D2.22.1957 San Francisco CA; BR/TR/5´6˝/145; d5.28; Col San Francisco																								
1924	Cin N	2	5	1	1	0	0	0	0	2	0	0	.200	.429	.200	75	0	0-0	.933	0	118	0	2b2	—	0.0
Behel, Steve	Stephen Arnold Douglas; B11.6.1860 Earlville IL; D2.15.1945 Los Angeles CA; d9.27																								
1884	Mil U	9	33	5	8	1	0	0	—	3	—	—	.242	.306	.273	140	1	—	1.000	-0	64	0	O9L	—	0.1
1886	NY AA	59	224	32	46	5	2	0	17	22	1	—	.205	.279	.246	71	-6	16	.858	-4	76	0	O59(26/33/0)	—	-1.0
Total	2	68	257	37	54	6	2	0	17	25	1	—	.210	.283	.249	76	-5	16	.865	-4	75	0	O68(35/33/0)	—	-0.9
Bejma, Ollie	Alojzy Frank; B9.12.1907 South Bend IN; D1.3.1995 South Bend IN; BR/TR/5´10˝/165; d4.24																								
1934	StL A	95	262	39	71	16	3	2	29	40	4	36	.271	.376	.378	87	-4	3-2	.952	-6	93	107	S32,2b14,3b13,O9R	—	-0.6
1935	StL A	64	198	18	38	8	2	2	26	27	0	21	.192	.289	.283	46	-16	1-0	.952	-4	101	95	2b47,S8,3b2	—	-1.6
1936	StL A	67	139	19	36	2	3	2	18	27	0	21	.259	.380	.360	81	-4	0-0	.963	-9	88	43	2b32,3b7/S	—	-0.9
1939	Chi A	90	307	52	77	9	3	8	44	36	1	27	.251	.331	.378	79	-11	1-3	.981	-8	95	84	2b81/S3	—	-1.3
Total	4	316	906	128	222	35	11	14	117	130	5	105	.245	.343	.354	75	-35	5-5	.967	-26	94	78	2b174,S42,3b23,O9R	—	-4.4
Belanger, Mark	Mark Henry; B6.8.1944 Pittsfield MA; D10.6.1998 New York NY; BR/TR/6´1˝/(170–179); d8.7																								
1965	Bal A	11	3	1	1	0	0	0	0	0-0	0	0	.333	.333	.333	88	0	0-1	1.000	0	61	662	S4	0	0.0
1966	Bal A	8	19	2	3	1	0	0	0	0-0	0	3	.158	.158	.211	5	-2	0-0	1.000	3	136	106	S6	0	0.1
1967	Bal A	69	184	19	32	5	0	1	10	12-1	0	46	.174	.224	.217	31	-16	6-1	.952	2	93	90	S38,2b26,3b2	0	-1.0
1968	Bal A	145	472	40	98	13	0	2	21	40-2	4	114	.208	.272	.248	59	-23	10-1	.969	19	106	105	S145	0	1.2
1969	†Bal A	150	530	76	152	17	4	2	50	53-5	2	54	.287	.351	.345	95	-2	14-6	.968	-8	97	108	S148	0	0.8
1970	†Bal A	145	459	53	100	6	5	1	36	52-3	5	65	.218	.303	.259	56	-27	13-2	.970	-2	101	110	S143	0	-1.2
1971	†Bal A	150	500	67	133	19	4	0	35	73-6	7	48	.266	.365	.320	95	1	10-8	.978	-1	97	100	S149	0	1.8
1972	Bal A	113	285	36	53	9	1	2	16	18-1	2	53	.186	.236	.246	43	-20	6-3	.975	9	101	114	S105	0	-0.1
1973	†Bal A	154	470	60	106	15	1	0	27	49-1	5	54	.226	.302	.262	61	-23	13-6	.971	5	106	118	S154	0	0.0
1974	†Bal A	155	493	54	111	14	4	5	36	51-0	2	69	.225	.298	.300	75	-16	17-7	**.984**	3	**106**	110	S155	0	0.8
1975	Bal A	152	442	44	100	11	1	3	27	36-0	1	53	.226	.286	.276	63	-22	16-4	.978	**30**	**116**	**139**	S152	0	2.7
1976	Bal A★	153	522	66	141	22	2	1	40	51-0	2	64	.270	.336	.326	100	1	27-17	.982	16	**112**	111	S153	0	3.7
1977	Bal A	144	402	39	83	13	4	2	30	43-1	3	68	.206	.287	.274	57	-24	15-8	**.985**	19	108	117	S142	0	0.9
1978	Bal A	135	348	39	74	13	0	0	16	40-1	6	55	.213	.299	.250	61	-17	6-6	**.985**	**30**	**118**	119	S134	0	2.5
1979	†Bal A	101	198	28	33	6	2	0	9	29-0	1	33	.167	.273	.217	36	-17	5-1	.990	-4	93	99	S98	32	-1.3
1980	Bal A	113	268	37	61	7	3	0	22	12-0	0	25	.228	.261	.276	48	-20	6-3	.975	-3	97	92	S109	0	-1.4
1981	Bal A	64	139	9	23	3	2	1	10	12-0	2	25	.165	.242	.237	39	-11	2-1	.973	-0	102	64	S63	0	-0.6
1982	LA N	54	50	6	12	1	0	0	4	5-1	0	10	.240	.309	.260	62	-2	1-0	.953	-4	99	40	S44/2	0	-0.4
Total	18	2016	5784	676	1316	175	33	20	389	576-22	42	839	.228	.300	.280	67	-240	167-75	.977	114	105	109	S1942,2b27,3b2	32	8.5
Belardi, Wayne	Carroll Wayne; B9.5.1930 St.Helena CA; D10.21.1993 Santa Cruz CA; BL/TL/6´1˝/185; d4.18; Col Santa Clara																								
1950	Bro N	10	10	0	0	0	0	0	0	0	0	4	.000	.000	.000	-98	-3	0	1.000	-0	0	0	/1	0	-0.3
1951	Bro N	3	3	1	1	0	1	0	0	0	0	2	.333	.333	1.000	240	0	0-0	ø	0	—	—	/H	0	0.0
1953	†Bro N	69	163	19	39	3	2	11	34	16	1	40	.239	.311	.485	101	-1	0-0	.984	-1	95	124	1b38	30	-0.3
1954	Bro N	11	9	0	2	0	0	0	1	2	0	3	.222	.364	.222	55	-1	0-0	ø	0	—	—	/H	0	0.0
	Det A	88	250	27	58	7	1	11	24	33	5	34	.232	.330	.400	102	0	1-0	.988	2	111	89	1b79	0	-0.2
1955	Det A	3	3	0	0	0	0	0	0	0-0	0	1	.000	.000	.000	-99	-1	0-0	ø	0	—	—	/H	0	-0.1
1956	Det A	79	154	24	43	3	1	6	15	15-1	8	13	.279	.371	.429	111	3	0-0	.988	-1	94	78	1b31,O2(2/0/1)	0	0.0
Total	6	263	592	71	143	13	5	28	74	66-1	14	97	.242	.330	.422	100	-3	1-0	.987	-0	103	95	1b149,O2(2/0/1)	30	-0.9
Belcher, Kevin	Kevin Donnell; B8.8.1967 Waco TX; BR/TR/6´0˝/170; [TexA87 6/155]; d9.3; Col Navarro (TX) JC																								
1990	Tex A	16	15	4	2	1	0	0	0	2-0	0	6	.133	.235	.200	23	-2	0-0	1.000	0	115	0	O9(2/5/2)	0	-0.1

YEAR	TM LG	G	AB	R	H	2B	3B	HR	RBI	BB-IB	HP	SO	AVG	OBP	SLG	AOPS	ABR	SB-CS	FA	FR	RNG	THR	GAMES AT POSITION	DL	BFW
BELDEN, IRA	Ira Allison; B4.16.1874 Cleveland OH; D7.15.1916 Lakewood OH; BL/TR/5´11˝/175; d9.17																								
1897	Cle N	8	30	5	8	0	2	0	4	2	1	—	.267	.333	.400	88	-1	0	1.000	1	159	0	O8R	—	0.0
BELK, TIM	Timothy William; B4.6.1970 Cincinnati OH; BR/TR/6´3˝/200; [CinN92 15/409]; d6.25; Col Lubbock Christian																								
1996	Cin N	7	15	2	3	0	0	0	0	1-0	0	2	.200	.250	.200	20	-2	0-0	1.000	-1	0	57	1b6	0	-0.3
BELL, BUDDY	David Gus; B8.27.1951 Pittsburgh PA; BR/TR/6´2˝/(180–200); [CleA69 16/373]; d4.15; M8/C5; f–Gus s–David s–Mike; OF(11/64/66)																								
1972	Cle A	132	466	49	119	21	1	9	36	34-8	3	29	.255	.310	.363	96	-2	5-6	.990	5	104	120	O123(0/63/65),3b6	0	-0.3
1973	Cle A★	156	631	86	169	23	7	14	59	49-2	6	47	.268	.325	.393	100	-1	7-15	.958	27	117	**141**	3b154,O2(0/1/1)	0	2.1
1974	Cle A	116	423	51	111	15	1	7	46	35-1	3	29	.262	.322	.352	95	-3	1-3	.963	15	**115**	127	3b115/D	45	1.1
1975	Cle A	153	553	66	150	20	4	10	59	51-6	1	72	.271	.332	.376	100	0	6-5	.950	-0	98	95	3b153	0	-0.2
1976	Cle A	**159**	604	75	170	26	2	7	60	44-3	2	49	.281	.329	.366	105	3	3-8	.956	8	104	86	3b158,1b2	0	0.8
1977	Cle A	129	479	64	140	23	4	11	64	45-5	1	63	.292	.351	.426	115	10	1-8	.960	13	110	106	3b118,O11L	0	1.7
1978	Cle A	142	556	71	157	27	8	6	62	39-1	0	43	.282	.328	.392	103	1	1-3	.970	27	**116**	108	3b139/D	0	2.5
1979	Tex A	**162**	670	89	200	42	3	18	101	30-4	3	45	.299	.327	.451	110	7	5-4	.969	28	**123**	84	3b147,S33	0	3.4
1980	Tex A★	129	490	76	161	24	4	17	83	40-11	0	39	.329	.379	.498	142	28	3-1	**.981**	27	115	100	3b120,S3	15	5.1
1981	Tex A★	97	360	44	106	16	1	10	64	42-10	3	30	.294	.364	.428	137	18	3-3	.961	**34**	**144**	110	3b96/S	0	5.1
1982	Tex A★	148	537	62	159	27	2	13	67	70-8	2	50	.296	.376	.426	126	22	5-4	**.976**	**38**	**127**	113	3b145,S4	0	5.6
1983	Tex A	156	618	75	171	35	3	14	66	50-5	4	48	.277	.332	.411	105	5	3-5	.967	18	**113**	88	3b154	0	1.8
1984	Tex A★	148	553	88	174	36	5	11	83	63-8	3	54	.315	.382	.458	128	23	2-1	.958	24	**117**	104	3b147	0	4.5
1985	Tex A	84	313	33	74	13	3	4	32	33-1	1	21	.236	.308	.335	76	-10	3-2	.942	17	122	139	3b83	0	0.6
	Cin N	67	247	28	54	15	2	6	36	34-2	0	27	.219	.311	.368	86	-4	0-1	.946	-11	77	117	3b67	0	-1.7
1986	Cin N	155	568	89	158	29	3	20	75	73-4	5	49	.278	.362	.445	118	15	2-8	.975	-5	97	111	3b151/2	0	0.6
1987	Cin N	143	522	74	148	19	2	17	70	71-3	1	39	.284	.369	.425	106	6	4-1	**.979**	-24	82	73	3b142	0	-1.9
1988	Cin N	21	54	3	10	0	0	0	3	7-1	0	3	.185	.270	.185	34	-4	0-0	.968	-1	89	105	3b13,1b2	33	-0.6
	Hou N	74	269	24	68	10	1	7	37	19-1	0	29	.253	.301	.375	97	-2	1-1	.924	-10	88	79	3b66,1b7	15	-1.4
	Year	95	323	27	78	10	1	7	40	26-2	0	32	.241	.295	.344	86	-7	1-1	.931	-11	88	83	3b79,1b9	0	-2.0
1989	Tex A	34	82	4	15	4	0	0	3	7-0	0	10	.183	.247	.232	35	-7	0-0	1.000	0	96	0	D22,3b9/1	15	-0.8
Total	18	2405	8995	1151	2514	425	56	201	1106	836-84	38	776	.279	.341	.406	108	105	55-79	.964	229	110	104	3b2183,O136R,S41,D24,1b12/2	123	28.0
BELL, DAVID	David Michael; B9.14.1972 Cincinnati OH; BR/TR/5´10˝/(170–195); [CleA90 7/190]; d5.3; f–Buddy gf–Gus b–Mike																								
1995	Cle A	2	2	0	0	0	0	0	0	0-0	0	0	.000	.000	.000	-98	-1	0-0	1.000	0	252	0	3b2	0	0.0
	StL N	39	144	13	36	7	2	2	19	4-0	2	25	.250	.278	.368	68	-7	1-2	.967	-2	100	116	2b37,3b3	0	-0.8
1996	StL N	62	145	12	31	6	0	1	9	10-2	1	22	.214	.268	.276	44	-12	1-1	.953	4	110	24	3b45,2b20/S	0	-0.7
1997	StL N	66	142	9	30	7	2	1	12	10-2	0	28	.211	.261	.310	49	-11	1-0	.913	-4	99	34	3b35,2b23,S13	62	-1.4
1998	StL N	4	9	0	2	1	0	0	0	0-0	0	3	.222	.222	.333	44	-1	0-0	1.000	-1	53	0	3b4/2	0	-0.2
	Cle A	107	340	37	89	21	2	10	41	22-4	2	54	.262	.306	.424	85	-8	0-4	.982	13	107	99	2b101,3b6/1S	0	0.7
	Sea A	21	80	11	26	8	0	0	8	5-0	0	8	.325	.365	.425	104	1	0-0	.984	3	111	132	2b14,1b5,3b5/lf	0	0.4
	Year	128	420	48	115	29	2	10	49	27-4	2	62	.274	.317	.424	89	-7	0-4	.982	16	108	103	2b115,3b11,1b6/Slf	0	1.1
1999	Sea A	157	597	92	160	31	2	21	78	58-0	2	90	.268	.331	.432	95	-6	7-4	.978	2	101	105	2b154,1b4/S	0	0.3
2000	†Sea A	133	454	57	112	24	2	11	47	42-0	6	66	.247	.316	.381	78	-16	2-3	.944	-10	93	94	3b93,2b48,1b2/S	0	-2.3
2001	†Sea A	135	470	62	122	28	0	15	64	28-1	3	59	.260	.303	.415	92	-6	2-1	.961	2	102	112	3b134,1b2	0	-0.4
2002	†SF N	154	552	82	144	29	2	20	73	54-2	9	80	.261	.333	.429	103	2	1-2	.973	-7	98	86	3b139,2b12,S3,1b2	0	-0.4
2003	Phi N	85	297	32	58	14	0	4	37	41-1	4	40	.195	.296	.283	58	-18	0-0	.966	6	106	117	3b85,2b3	74	-1.1
2004	Phi N	143	533	67	155	33	1	18	77	57-4	6	75	.291	.363	.458	108	7	1-1	.943	3	109	89	3b142	0	1.1
2005	Phi N	150	557	53	138	31	1	10	61	47-6	5	69	.248	.310	.361	73	-22	0-1	.951	10	106	85	3b150	0	-1.1
2006	Phi N	92	324	39	90	17	2	6	34	32-2	3	38	.278	.345	.398	86	-6	1-0	.945	4	106	137	3b90	0	-0.1
	Mil N	53	180	21	46	10	2	4	29	18-1	1	30	.256	.323	.400	84	-4	2-1	.965	4	110	43	3b53	0	0.0
	Year	145	504	60	136	27	4	10	63	50-3	4	68	.270	.337	.399	86	-10	3-1	.952	8	107	103	3b143	0	-0.1
Total	12	1403	4826	587	1239	267	18	123	589	428-25	44	687	.257	.320	.396	85	-108	19-20	.955	26	104	93	3b986,2b413,S20,1b16/lf	136	-6.0
BELL, GUS	David Russell; B11.15.1928 Louisville KY; D5.7.1995 Montgomery OH; BL/TR/6´2˝/(190–199); d5.30; s–Buddy gs–David gs–Mike																								
1950	Pit N	111	422	62	119	22	11	8	53	28	4	46	.282	.333	.443	99	-2	4	.977	5	**109**	131	O104R	0	-0.1
1951	Pit N	149	600	80	167	27	**12**	16	89	42	4	41	.278	.330	.443	103	0	1-4	.986	1	95	136	O145R	0	-0.4
1952	Pit N	131	468	53	117	21	5	16	59	36	2	72	.250	.306	.419	97	-4	1-4	.972	-7	90	73	O123R	0	-1.7
1953	Cin N★	151	610	102	183	37	5	30	105	48	3	72	.300	.354	.525	124	21	0-2	.977	5	103	111	O151(0/145/6)	0	1.7
1954	Cin N★	153	619	104	185	38	7	17	101	48	4	58	.299	.349	.465	108	7	5-3	.986	-2	97	102	O153C	0	-0.2
1955	Cin N	**154**	610	88	188	30	6	27	104	54-2	0	57	.308	.361	.510	122	19	4-4	.987	-13	91	34	O154C	0	-0.2
1956	Cin N★	150	603	82	176	31	4	29	84	50-4	3	66	.292	.347	.501	117	15	6-2	.986	-11	84	110	O149C	0	-0.3
1957	Cin N★	121	510	65	149	20	3	13	61	30-5	3	54	.292	.332	.420	95	-4	0-1	.988	-7	93	76	O121C	0	-1.8
1958	Cin N	112	385	42	97	16	2	10	46	36-7	1	40	.252	.314	.382	80	-11	2-3	**.996**	-7	89	83	O107(20/87/0)	0	-2.5
1959	Cin N	148	580	59	170	27	2	19	115	29-1	2	44	.293	.325	.445	101	-1	2-3	**.996**	4	99	132	O145(6/0/141)	0	-0.2
1960	Cin N	143	515	65	135	19	5	12	62	29-3	1	40	.262	.300	.388	86	-11	4-3	.988	1	100	112	O131(41/0/97)	0	-1.6
1961	†Cin N	103	235	27	60	10	1	3	33	18-3	0	21	.255	.298	.345	72	-9	1-1	.991	-1	106	20	O75(43/1/33)	0	-1.4
1962	NY N	30	101	8	15	2	0	1	6	10-0	0	7	.149	.221	.198	14	-12	0-1	.979	3	90	327	O26R	0	-1.1
	Mil N	79	214	28	61	11	3	5	24	12-2	0	17	.285	.322	.435	104	0	0-0	.987	-1	93	90	O58(52/1/8)	0	-0.3
	Year	109	315	36	76	13	3	6	30	22-2	0	24	.241	.288	.359	74	-12	0-1	.984	3	92	173	O84(52/1/34)	0	-1.4
1963	Mil N	3	3	0	1	0	0	0	0	0-0	0	0	.333	.333	.333	94	0	0-0	ø	0	—	—	/H	130	0.0
1964	Mil N	3	3	0	0	0	0	0	0	0-0	0	1	.000	.000	.000	-99	-1	0-0	ø	0	—	—	/H	0	-0.1
Total	15	1741	6478	865	1823	311	66	206	942	470-27	27	636	.281	.330	.445	102	7	30-31	.985	-31	96	100	O1642(162/811/683)	130	-10.2
BELL, DEREK	Derek Nathaniel; B12.11.1968 Tampa FL; BR/TR/6´2˝/(200–215); [TorA87 2/49]; d6.28																								
1991	Tor A	18	28	5	4	0	0	0	1	6-0	1	5	.143	.314	.143	30	-2	3-2	.889	-2	75	0	O13(7/6/0)	0	-0.5
1992	†Tor A	61	161	23	39	6	3	2	15	15-1	5	34	.242	.324	.354	86	-3	7-2	1.000	2	104	139	O56(24/18/15)/D	29	-0.1
1993	SD N	150	542	73	142	19	1	21	72	23-5	12	122	.262	.303	.417	91	-9	26-5	.976	1	104	125	O125(1/119/6),3b19	0	-0.3
1994	SD N	108	434	54	135	20	0	14	54	29-5	1	88	.311	.354	.454	113	7	24-8	.962	-5	99	55	O108C	0	0.6
1995	Hou N	112	452	63	151	21	2	8	86	33-2	8	71	.334	.385	.442	127	18	27-9	.963	-4	87	132	O110(0/30/82)	0	1.3
1996	Hou N	158	627	84	165	40	3	17	113	40-8	8	123	.263	.311	.418	99	-3	29-3	.977	2	95	153	O157(0/2/157)	0	-0.3
1997	†Hou N	129	493	67	136	29	3	15	71	40-3	12	94	.276	.344	.438	107	4	15-7	.967	-8	92	61	O125(0/36/89)/D	30	-0.6
1998	†Hou N	156	630	111	198	41	2	22	108	51-0	4	126	.314	.364	.490	127	25	13-3	.973	-3	95	78	O154R	0	1.5
1999	†Hou N	128	509	61	120	22	0	12	66	50-1	4	129	.236	.306	.350	67	-26	18-6	.985	-14	79	49	O126R	15	-4.3
2000	†NY N	144	546	87	145	31	1	18	69	65-0	6	125	.266	.348	.425	100	0	8-4	.988	-7	90	58	O143(0/5/142)/P	0	-1.2
2001	Pit N	46	156	14	27	3	0	5	13	25-5	0	38	.173	.287	.288	48	-12	0-2	.988	-1	88	103	O46(5/1/43)	127	-1.6
Total	11	1210	4578	642	1262	232	15	134	668	377-30	61	955	.276	.336	.421	100	-1	170-51	.975	-39	93	92	O1163(37/325/814),3b19,D2/P	201	-5.5
BELL, FERN	Fernando Jerome Lee (b Fern Oran Bell) "Danny"; B1.21.1913 Ada OK; D8.29.2000 Rancho Mirage CA; BR/TR/6´0˝/180; d4.17																								
1939	Pit N	83	262	44	75	5	8	2	34	42	0	18	.286	.385	.389	110	5	2	.975	-1	100	120	O67(15/46/7)/3	—	0.2
1940	Pit N	6	3	0	0	0	0	0	1	1	0	1	.000	.250	.000	-26	0	0	ø	0	—	—	/H	—	0.0
Total	2	89	265	44	75	5	8	2	35	43	0	19	.283	.383	.385	109	5	2	.975	-1	100	120	O67(15/46/7)/3	—	0.2
BELL, FRANK	Frank Gustav; B1863 Cincinnati OH; D4.14.1891 Cincinnati OH; 6´0˝/?; d7.7; b–Charlie																								
1885	Bro AA	10	29	5	5	0	1	0	2	0	1	—	.172	.200	.241	39	-2	—	.739	-4	—	—	C5,O4(0/3/1),3b2	—	-0.5
BELL, GEORGE	George Antonio (Mathey); B10.21.1959 San Pedro de Macoris, D.R.; BR/TR/6´1˝/(185–210); d4.9; b–Juan																								
1981	Tor A	60	163	19	38	2	1	5	12	5-1	0	27	.233	.256	.350	69	-7	3-2	.969	2	110	108	O44(26/0/18),D8	0	-0.7
1983	Tor A	39	112	5	30	5	4	2	17	4-1	2	17	.268	.305	.438	95	-1	1-1	.954	-1	98	45	O34(28/0/6),D2	0	-0.4
1984	Tor A	159	606	85	177	39	4	26	87	24-2	8	86	.292	.326	.498	120	15	11-2	.971	-3	93	114	O147(66/0/90),3b3,D7	0	0.7
1985	†Tor A	157	607	87	167	28	6	28	95	43-6	8	90	.275	.327	.479	115	11	21-6	.968	-2	93	124	O157L,3b2	0	0.5
1986	Tor A	159	641	101	198	38	6	31	108	41-3	2	62	.309	.349	.532	133	27	7-8	.966	-3	85	173	O147L,D11,3b2	0	1.5
1987	Tor A★	156	610	111	188	32	4	47	**134**	39-9	7	75	.308	.352	.605	145	37	5-1	.960	-4	89	146	O148L/23D	0	2.5
1988	Tor A	156	614	78	165	27	5	24	97	34-5	1	66	.269	.304	.446	108	3	4-2	.946	-12	85	94	O149L,D7	0	-1.3
1989	†Tor A	153	613	88	182	41	2	18	104	33-3	4	60	.297	.330	.458	124	18	4-3	.963	-10	92	48	O134L,D19	0	0.3
1990	Tor A★	142	562	67	149	25	0	21	86	32-7	3	80	.265	.303	.422	100	-2	3-2	.979	-1	102	58	O106L,D36	0	-0.8
1991	Chi N★	149	558	63	159	27	0	25	86	32-6	4	62	.285	.323	.468	116	10	2-6	.962	-10	84	74	O146L	0	-0.5
1992	Chi A	155	627	74	160	27	0	25	112	31-8	6	97	.255	.294	.418	99	-4	5-2	.964	-2	87	0	D140,O15L	0	-1.1

YEAR	TM LG	G	AB	R	H	2B	3B	HR	RBI	BB-IB	HP	SO	AVG	OBP	SLG	AOPS	ABR	SB-CS	FA	FR	RNG	THR	GAMES AT POSITION	DL	BFW
1993	Chi A	102	410	36	89	17	2	13	64	13-2	4	49	.217	.243	.363	63	-24	1-1	ø	0	0	0	D102	41	-2.9
Total	12	1587	6123	814	1702	308	34	265	1002	331-53	49	771	.278	.316	.469	113	83	67-36	.964	-45	91	104	O1227(1123/0/114),D339,3b8/2	41	-2.2
Bell, Jay	Jay Stuart; B12.11.1965 Eglin A.F.B. FL; BR/TR/6´1˝/(180–185); [MinA84 1/8]; d9.29; C2																								
1986	Cle A	5	14	3	5	2	0	1	4	2-0	0	3	.357	.438	.714	210	2	0-0	.778	-0	148	101	2b2,D2	0	0.2
1987	Cle A	38	125	14	27	9	1	2	13	8-0	1	31	.216	.269	.352	62	-7	2-0	.947	-1	95	100	S38	0	-0.4
1988	Cle A	73	211	23	46	5	1	2	21	21-0	1	53	.218	.289	.280	59	-12	4-2	.965	-17	84	83	S72/D	0	-2.4
1989	Pit N	78	271	33	70	13	3	2	27	19-0	1	47	.258	.307	.351	91	-4	5-3	.968	-9	95	111	S78	0	-0.8
1990	†Pit N	159	583	93	148	28	7	7	52	65-0	3	109	.254	.329	.362	94	-4	10-6	.970	1	102	112	S159	0	0.9
1991	†Pit N	157	608	96	164	32	8	16	67	52-1	4	99	.270	.330	.428	113	9	10-6	.968	8	106	108	S156	0	3.0
1992	†Pit N	159	632	87	167	36	6	9	55	55-0	4	103	.264	.326	.383	101	1	7-5	.973	15	**112**	112	S159	0	3.0
1993	Pit N★	154	604	102	187	32	9	9	51	77-6	6	122	.310	.392	.437	122	22	16-10	**.986**	22	112	106	S154	0	5.4
1994	Pit N	110	424	68	117	35	4	9	45	49-1	3	82	.276	.353	.441	104	4	2-0	.973	18	**115**	99	S110	0	2.9
1995	Pit N	138	530	79	139	28	4	13	55	55-1	4	110	.262	.336	.404	92	-6	2-5	.978	11	105	105	S136,3b3	0	1.3
1996	Pit N	151	527	65	132	29	3	13	71	54-5	5	108	.250	.323	.391	85	-11	6-4	**.986**	6	**106**	82	S151	0	0.5
1997	KC A	153	573	89	167	28	3	21	92	71-2	4	101	.291	.368	.461	113	12	10-6	.985	8	106	111	S149,3b4	0	2.9
1998	Ari N	155	549	79	138	29	5	20	67	81-3	7	129	.251	.353	.432	105	6	3-5	.971	-11	101	99	S138,2b15	0	0.4
1999	†Ari N★	151	589	132	170	32	6	38	112	82-2	4	132	.289	.374	.557	132	28	7-4	.968	-19	87	99	2b148/SD	0	1.5
2000	Ari N	149	565	87	151	30	6	18	68	70-0	3	88	.267	.348	.437	94	-5	7-3	.988	-3	94	101	2b145/D	0	0.0
2001	†Ari N	129	428	59	106	24	1	13	46	65-3	4	79	.248	.349	.400	88	-6	0-1	.994	-11	84	105	2b80,3b40,D3	0	-1.3
2002	Ari N	32	49	3	8	1	0	2	11	5-0	1	9	.163	.250	.306	43	-4	0-0	1.000	0	81	234	3b6,1b5,2b2,S2	110	-0.4
2003	NY N	72	116	11	21	1	0	0	3	22-1	2	38	.181	.319	.190	39	-10	0-0	.952	-4	93	101	2b14,3b14,1b13,S12/D	15	-1.3
Total	18	2063	7398	1123	1963	394	67	195	860	853-25	57	1443	.265	.343	.416	101	15	91-60	.975	14	105	104	S1515,2b406,3b67,1b18,D10	125	15.4
Bell, Rudy	John (b Rudolph Fred Baerwald); B1.1.1881 Wausau WI; D7.28.1955 Albuquerque NM; BR/TR/5´8.5˝/158; d9.16																								
1907	NY A	17	52	4	11	2	1	0	3	3	1	—	.212	.268	.288	72	-2	4	.897	-1	0	0	O17(12/0/5)	—	-0.4
Bell, Juan	Juan (Mathey); B3.29.1968 San Pedro de Macoris, D.R.; BR/TR (BB 1995)/5´11˝/(157–176); d9.6; b–George																								
1989	Bal A	8	4	2	0	0	0	0	0	0-0	0	1	.000	.000	.000	-99	-1	1-0	1.000	1	172	263	2b2,S2,D4	0	0.0
1990	Bal A	5	2	1	0	0	0	0	0	0-0	0	1	.000	.000	.000	-99	-1	0-0	1.000	0	101	0	/SD	0	-0.1
1991	Bal A	100	209	26	36	9	2	1	15	8-0	0	51	.172	.201	.249	25	-22	0-0	.973	-2	106	97	2b77,S15/lfD	0	-2.3
1992	Phi N	46	147	12	30	3	1	1	8	18-5	1	29	.204	.292	.259	58	-8	5-0	.972	2	100	88	S46	0	-0.2
1993	Phi N	24	65	5	13	6	1	0	7	5-0	1	12	.200	.268	.323	58	-4	0-1	.909	-1	95	93	S22	0	-0.4
	Mil A	91	286	42	67	6	2	5	29	36-0	1	64	.234	.321	.322	74	-10	6-6	.983	-4	87	111	2b47,S40,O3(0/1/2),D2	0	-1.0
1994	Mon N	38	97	12	27	4	0	2	10	15-0	0	21	.278	.372	.381	97	0	4-0	.991	4	116	128	2b25,3b3/S	0	0.6
1995	Bos A	17	26	7	4	2	0	1	2	2-0	0	10	.154	.207	.346	42	-2	0-0	.857	-1	79	30	S6,2b5/3	0	-0.3
Total	7	329	836	107	177	30	6	10	71	84-5	3	189	.212	.284	.298	60	-48	16-7	.981	-2	102	110	2b156,S133,D11,3b4,O4(1/1/2)	0	-3.7
Bell, Kevin	Kevin Robert; B7.13.1955 Los Angeles CA; BR/TR/6´0˝/(185–195); [ChiA74*1/7]; d6.16; Col Mt. San Antonio (CA) JC																								
1976	Chi A	68	230	24	57	7	6	5	20	18-0	1	56	.248	.302	.396	104	0	2-1	.970	-1	91	84	3b67/D	0	-0.1
1977	Chi A	9	28	4	5	1	0	1	6	3-0	0	8	.179	.250	.321	57	-2	0-0	.909	1	87	159	S5,3b4/lf	100	-0.1
1978	Chi A	54	68	9	13	0	0	2	5	5-0	1	19	.191	.257	.279	50	-5	1-0	.946	6	121	124	3b52/D	0	0.1
1979	Chi A	70	200	20	49	8	1	4	22	15-0	0	43	.245	.296	.355	75	-7	2-4	.923	2	106	90	3b68,S2	0	-0.8
1980	Chi A	92	191	16	34	5	2	1	11	29-1	0	37	.178	.284	.241	46	-14	0-0	.925	2	109	91	3b83,S3,D3	0	-1.3
1982	Oak A	4	9	1	3	1	0	0	0	0-0	0	2	.333	.333	.444	115	0	0-0	.857	-0	71	216	3b3/D	0	0.0
Total	6	297	726	74	161	22	9	13	64	70-1	2	165	.222	.289	.331	73	-28	5-5	.940	9	104	97	3b277,S10,D6/lf	100	-2.2
Bell, Les	Lester Rowland; B12.14.1901 Harrisburg PA; D12.26.1985 Hershey PA; BR/TR/5´11˝/165; d9.18																								
1923	StL N	15	51	5	19	2	1	0	9	9	0	7	.373	.467	.451	146	4	1-0	.917	-2	97	94	S15	—	0.4
1924	StL N	17	57	5	14	3	2	1	5	3	1	7	.246	.295	.421	91	-1	0-0	.905	-4	78	75	S17	—	-0.3
1925	StL N	**153**	586	80	167	29	9	11	88	43	0	47	.285	.334	.422	89	-10	4-5	.924	1	99	143	3b153/S	—	-0.1
1926	†StL N	155	581	85	189	33	14	17	100	54	0	62	.325	.383	.518	135	28	9	.950	-24	83	100	3b155	—	1.3
1927	StL N	115	390	48	101	26	6	9	65	34	1	63	.259	.320	.426	95	-3	5	.904	-16	83	98	3b100,S10	—	-1.2
1928	Bos N	**153**	591	58	164	36	7	10	91	40	0	45	.277	.323	.413	96	-5	1	.948	7	102	122	3b153	—	1.1
1929	Bos N	139	483	58	144	23	5	9	72	50	0	42	.298	.364	.422	98	-1	4	.953	-21	83	79	3b127/2S	—	-1.3
1930	Chi N	74	248	35	69	15	4	5	47	24	0	27	.278	.342	.431	85	-6	1	.948	-2	90	126	3b70,1b2	—	-0.4
1931	Chi N	75	252	30	71	17	1	4	32	19	0	22	.282	.332	.405	95	-2	0	.944	4	103	162	3b70	—	0.5
Total	9	896	3239	404	938	184	49	66	509	276	2	322	.290	.346	.438	102	4	25-5	.939	-57	92	116	3b828,S44,1b2/2	—	0.0
Bell, Mike	Michael Allen; B4.22.1968 Lewiston NY; BL/TL/6´1˝/175; [AtlN86 4/86]; d5.2																								
1990	Atl N	36	45	8	11	5	1	1	5	2-0	1	9	.244	.292	.467	100	0	0-1	.981	1	130	79	1b24	0	-0.1
1991	Atl N	17	30	4	4	0	0	1	1	2-0	0	7	.133	.188	.233	17	-3	1-0	.975	-0	97	142	1b14	0	-0.4
Total	2	53	75	12	15	5	1	2	6	4-0	1	16	.200	.250	.373	67	-3	1-1	.979	0	116	107	1b38	0	-0.5
Bell, Mike	Michael John; B12.7.1974 Cincinnati OH; BR/TR/6´2˝/210; [TexA93 S1/30]; d7.20; f–Buddy gf–Gus b–David																								
2000	Cin N	19	27	5	6	0	0	2	4	4-0	0	7	.222	.323	.444	88	-1	0-0	.900	2	150	193	3b13	0	0.1
Bell, Beau	Roy Chester; B8.20.1907 Bellville TX; D9.14.1977 College Station TX; BR/TR/6´2˝/185; d4.16; Col Texas A&M																								
1935	StL A	76	220	20	55	8	2	3	17	16	1	16	.250	.304	.345	65	-12	1-1	.918	-4	92	68	O37(10/0/27),1b15,3b3	—	-1.9
1936	StL A	**155**	616	100	212	40	12	11	123	60	1	55	.344	.403	.502	119	18	4-1	.974	0	103	85	O142(12/0/133),1b17	—	0.8
1937	StL A☆	**156**	642	82	**218**	**51**	8	14	117	53	1	54	.340	.391	.509	124	24	2-2	.984	3	87	**178**	O131R,1b26,3b2	—	1.5
1938	StL A	147	526	91	138	35	3	13	84	71	0	46	.262	.350	.414	91	-7	1-3	.979	3	106	104	O132R,1b4	—	-1.2
1939	StL A	11	32	4	7	1	0	1	5	4	1	3	.219	.324	.344	69	-1	0-0	1.000	-0	105	0	O9L	—	-0.2
	Det A	54	134	14	32	4	2	0	24	24	1	16	.239	.358	.299	65	-7	0-1	1.000	2	99	179	O37L	—	-0.6
	Year	65	166	18	39	5	2	1	29	28	2	19	.235	.352	.307	66	-8	0-1	1.000	2	100	143	O46L	—	-0.8
1940	Cle A	120	444	55	124	22	2	4	58	34	1	41	.279	.332	.365	83	-11	2-2	.971	0	107	69	O97R,1b14	—	-1.7
1941	Cle A	48	104	12	20	4	3	0	9	10	1	8	.192	.270	.288	50	-8	1-2	1.000	-2	94	0	O14R,1b10	—	-1.2
Total	7	767	2718	378	806	165	32	46	437	272	7	239	.297	.362	.432	99	-4	11-12	.976	2	100	109	O599(68/0/534),1b86,3b5	0	-4.5
Bell, Terry	Terence William; B10.27.1962 Dayton OH; BR/TR/6´0˝/195; [SeaA83 1/17]; d9.3; Col Old Dominion																								
1986	KC A	8	3	0	0	0	0	0	0	2-0	0	1	.000	.400	.000	20	0	0-0	1.000	-1	117	0	C8	0	-0.1
1987	Atl N	1	1	0	0	0	0	0	0	0-0	0	1	.000	.000	.000	-96	0	0-0	ø	0	—	—	/H	0	0.0
Total	2	9	4	0	0	0	0	0	0	2-0	0	2	.000	.333	.000	-0	0	0-0	1.000	-1	117	0	C8	0	-0.1
Bella, Zeke	John; B8.23.1930 Greenwich CT; BR/TL/5´11˝/(180–185); d9.11																								
1957	NY A	5	10	0	1	0	0	0	0	1-0	0	2	.100	.182	.100	-21	-2	0-0	1.000	1	141	536	O4(1/0/3)	0	-0.1
1959	KC A	47	82	10	17	2	1	1	9	9-0	1	14	.207	.293	.293	60	-4	0-0	1.000	-1	72	208	O25(11/0/14)/1	0	-0.6
Total	2	52	92	10	18	2	1	1	9	10-0	1	16	.196	.282	.272	52	-6	0-0	1.000	1	82	255	O29(12/0/17)/1	0	-0.7
Bellan, Steve	Esteban Enrique; B1850 , Cuba; D8.8.1932 Havana, Cuba; 5´6˝/154; d5.9																								
1871	Tro NA	**29**	128	26	32	3	3	0	23	9	—	2	.250	.299	.320	77	-4	4-4	.713	-2	83	100	3b28/S	—	-0.4
1872	Tro NA	23	115	22	30	4	0	0	17	0	—	0	.261	.261	.296	70	-4	1-0	.673	-7	69	0	S9,3b8,O6C	—	-0.8
1873	Mut NA	8	32	4	7	2	0	0	3	2	—	0	.219	.265	.281	62	-1	0-0	.488	-6	46	327	3b7,2b3	—	-0.5
Total	3NA	60	275	52	69	9	3	0	43	11	—	2	.251	.280	.305	72	-9	5-4	.674	-14	76	141	3b43,S10,O6C,2b3	—	-1.7
Belle, Albert	Albert Jojuan "Joey"; B8.25.1966 Shreveport LA; BR/TR/6´2˝/(200–225); [CleA87 2/47]; d7.15; Col Louisiana St.; [DL 2001 Bal A 190, 2002 Bal A 183, 2003 Bal A 183]																								
1989	Cle A	62	218	22	49	8	4	7	37	12-0	2	55	.225	.269	.394	84	-6	2-2	.979	1	102	97	O44(15/0/31),D17	0	-0.8
1990	Cle A	9	23	1	4	0	0	1	3	1-0	0	6	.174	.208	.304	42	-2	0-0	ø	-0	0	0	/lfD	0	-0.2
1991	Cle A	123	461	60	130	31	2	28	95	25-2	5	99	.282	.323	.540	134	19	3-1	.952	1	98	168	O89(88/0/2),D32	0	1.7
1992	Cle A	153	585	81	152	23	1	34	112	52-5	4	128	.260	.320	.477	123	15	8-2	.969	-4	92	30	D100,O52L	0	0.8
1993	Cle A★	159	594	93	172	36	3	38	**129**	76-13	8	96	.290	.370	.552	146	39	23-12	.986	11	106	170	O150L,D9	0	4.3
1994	Cle A★	106	412	90	147	35	2	36	101	58-9	5	71	.357	.438	.714	190	57	9-6	.973	-3	89	103	O104L,D2	0	4.5
1995	†Cle A★	143	546	**121**	173	**52**	1	**50**	**126**	73-5	6	80	.317	.401	**.690**	174	60	5-2	.981	-1	99	70	O142L/D	0	5.0
1996	†Cle A★	158	602	124	187	38	3	48	**148**	99-15	7	87	.311	.410	.623	157	55	11-0	.970	-2	94	101	O152L,D6	0	4.5
1997	Chi A☆	**161**	634	90	174	45	1	30	116	53-6	6	105	.274	.332	.491	116	14	4-4	.972	2	116	10	O154L,D7	0	0.9
1998	Chi A	**163**	609	113	200	48	2	49	152	81-10	1	84	.328	.399	**.655**	**173**	**67**	6-4	.976	2	102	115	O159L,D4	0	**5.8**

YEAR	TM LG	G	AB	R	H	2B	3B	HR	RBI	BB-IB	HP	SO	AVG	OBP	SLG	AOPS	ABR	SB-CS	FA	FR	RNG	THR	GAMES AT POSITION	DL	BFW
1999	Bal A	161	610	108	181	36	1	37	117	101-15	7	82	.297	.400	.541	143	43	17-3	.985	-5	83	159	O154R,D7	0	3.0
2000	Bal A	141	559	71	157	37	1	23	103	52-11	4	68	.281	.342	.474	110	8	0-5	.986	-0	98	107	O110R,D31	0	-0.1
Total	12	1539	5853	974	1726	389	21	381	1239	683-91	55	961	.295	.369	.564	144	369	88-41	.976	1	99	106	O1311(1017/0/297),D222	556	29.4

BELLHORN, MARK Mark Christian; B8.23.1974 Boston MA; BB/TR/6´1˝/(190–209); [OakA95 2/35]; d6.10; Col Auburn; OF(1/3/4)

1997	Oak A	68	224	33	51	9	1	6	19	32-0	0	70	.228	.324	.357	78	-7	7-1	.951	7	103	114	3b40,2b17/SD	0	0.2
1998	Oak A	11	12	1	1	1	0	0	1	3-0	1	4	.083	.313	.167	30	-1	2-0	1.000	-0	144	0	3b5,S2/2D	0	-0.1
2000	Oak A	9	13	2	2	0	0	0	0	2-0	0	6	.154	.267	.154	10	-2	0-0	1.000	-1	37	0	2b2,3b2/S	0	-0.2
2001	Oak A	38	74	11	10	1	2	1	4	7-0	0	37	.135	.210	.243	19	-9	0-0	.953	-2	99	74	2b12,3b9,S5/rfD	0	-1.0
2002	Chi N	146	445	86	115	24	4	27	56	76-3	6	144	.258	.374	.512	130	21	7-5	.980	-8	93	98	2b77,3b36,1b22,S12/lf	0	1.6
2003	Chi N	51	139	15	29	7	1	2	22	29-1	1	46	.209	.341	.317	74	-4	3-3	.938	-1	96	58	3b42	0	-0.5
	Col N	48	110	12	26	3	0	0	4	21-0	2	32	.236	.368	.264	60	-5	2-3	.973	-1	105	59	2b20,3b15,S6,O5(0/3/2)/1	22	-0.6
	Year	99	249	27	55	10	1	2	26	50-1	3	78	.221	.353	.293	67	-10	5-6	.944	-1	98	56	3b57,2b20,S6,O5(0/3/2)/1	0	-1.1
2004	†Bos A	138	523	93	138	37	3	17	82	88-1	5	177	.264	.373	.444	106	8	6-1	.980	-4	97	84	2b124,3b16/S	18	1.0
2005	Bos A	85	283	41	61	20	0	7	28	49-1	0	109	.216	.328	.360	81	-6	3-0	.985	4	106	95	2b83/S	32	0.2
	†NY A	9	17	2	2	0	0	1	2	3-0	0	3	.118	.250	.294	44	-1	0-0	1.000	2	75	0	3b4,2b2,S2	0	0.1
	Year	94	300	43	63	20	0	8	30	52-1	0	112	.210	.324	.357	79	-8	3-0	.983	6	108	96	2b85,3b4,S3	0	0.3
2006	†SD N	115	253	26	48	11	2	8	27	32-0	2	90	.190	.285	.344	64	-15	0-0	.959	2	99	128	3b50,1b18,2b11/rfD	0	-1.3
Total	9	718	2093	322	483	113	13	69	245	342-6	17	718	.231	.342	.396	91	-21	30-13	.979	-2	101	91	2b349,3b219,1b41,S31,D11,O8R	72	-0.6

BELLIARD, RAFAEL Rafael Leonidas (Matias); B10.24.1961 Pueblo Nuevo, D.R.; BR/TR (BB 1982)/5´6˝/(139–160); d9.6; C1

1982	Pit N	9	2	3	1	0	0	0	0	0-0	0	0	.500	.500	.500	173	0	1-0	1.000	0	91	0	S4	0	0.1
1983	Pit N	4	1	1	0	0	0	0	0	0-0	0	1	.000	.000	.000	-97	0	0-0	1.000	1	170	300	S3	0	0.1
1984	Pit N	20	22	3	5	0	0	0	0	0-0	0	1	.227	.227	.227	28	-2	4-1	.889	-3	64	113	S12/2	61	-0.5
1985	Pit N	17	20	1	4	0	0	0	1	0-0	0	5	.200	.200	.200	12	-2	0-0	.947	1	112	72	S12	0	0.0
1986	Pit N	117	309	33	72	5	2	0	31	26-6	3	54	.233	.298	.262	55	-19	12-2	.970	10	114	90	S96,2b23	15	0.2
1987	Pit N	81	203	26	42	4	3	1	15	20-6	3	25	.207	.286	.271	48	-15	5-1	.979	2	99	85	S71,2b7	39	-0.6
1988	Pit N	122	286	28	61	0	4	0	11	26-3	4	47	.213	.288	.241	54	-17	7-1	**.977**	-11	96	101	S117,2b3	15	-2.2
1989	Pit N	67	154	10	33	4	0	0	8	8-2	0	22	.214	.253	.240	43	-12	5-2	.978	-4	101	82	S40,2b20,3b6	0	-1.4
1990	Pit N	47	54	10	11	3	0	0	6	5-0	1	13	.204	.283	.259	52	-3	1-2	1.000	-1	76	135	2b21,S10,3b5	0	-0.5
1991	†Atl N	149	353	36	88	9	2	0	27	22-2	2	63	.249	.296	.286	61	-18	3-1	.967	7	106	100	S145	0	-0.3
1992	†Atl N	144	285	20	60	6	1	0	14	14-4	3	43	.211	.255	.239	38	-23	0-1	.969	-1	100	93	S139/2	0	-1.9
1993	†Atl N	91	79	6	18	5	0	0	6	4-0	3	13	.228	.291	.291	55	-5	0-0	1.000	6	113	144	S58,2b24	0	0.2
1994	Atl N	46	120	9	29	7	1	0	9	2-1	2	29	.242	.264	.317	49	-9	0-2	.984	-7	72	78	S26,2b18	0	-1.4
1995	†Atl N	75	180	12	40	2	1	0	7	6-2	2	28	.222	.255	.244	31	-18	2-2	.992	2	92	64	S40,2b32	0	-1.3
1996	†Atl N	87	142	9	24	7	0	0	3	2-0	0	22	.169	.179	.218	4	-20	3-1	.983	7	105	115	S63,2b15	0	-0.9
1997	Atl N	72	71	9	15	3	0	1	3	1-0	0	17	.211	.219	.296	34	-7	0-1	.990	-4	85	106	S53,2b7	0	-0.9
1998	Atl N	7	20	1	5	0	0	0	1	0-0	0	1	.250	.250	.250	32	-2	0-0	.952	-1	75	128	S7	171	-0.3
Total	17	1155	2301	217	508	55	14	2	142	136-26	23	384	.221	.270	.259	45	-172	43-17	.974	2	100	95	S896,2b172,3b11	301	-11.6

BELLIARD, RON Ronald; B4.7.1975 Bronx NY; BR/TR/5´8˝/(180–200); [MilA94 8/207]; d9.12

1998	Mil N	8	5	1	1	0	0	0	0	0-0	0	0	.200	.200	.200	6	-1	0-0	ø	-0	0	0	/2	0	-0.1
1999	Mil N	124	457	60	135	29	4	8	58	64-0	0	59	.295	.379	.429	104	5	4-5	.978	-1	105	95	2b119/3S	0	0.8
2000	Mil N	152	571	83	150	30	9	8	54	82-4	3	84	.263	.354	.389	89	-8	7-5	.976	1	102	**125**	2b151	0	0.0
2001	Mil N	101	364	69	96	30	3	11	36	35-2	5	65	.264	.335	.453	104	2	5-2	.990	13	107	107	2b96	52	2.0
2002	Mil N	104	289	30	61	13	0	3	26	18-0	1	46	.211	.257	.287	44	-24	2-3	.975	-9	89	88	2b49,3b42	0	-3.2
2003	Col N	116	447	73	124	31	2	8	50	49-0	2	71	.277	.351	.409	86	-8	7-2	.973	-2	103	100	2b113	21	-0.4
2004	Cle A★	152	599	78	169	48	1	12	70	60-5	2	98	.282	.348	.426	104	6	3-2	.981	-6	99	90	2b151/D	0	0.6
2005	Cle A	145	536	71	152	36	1	17	78	35-0	1	72	.284	.325	.450	108	6	2-2	.981	3	102	112	2b141	0	1.5
2006	Cle A	93	350	43	102	21	0	8	44	21-0	4	45	.291	.337	.420	99	-1	2-0	.981	-3	102	87	2b91/3	0	0.1
	†StL N	54	194	20	46	9	1	5	23	15-2	1	36	.237	.295	.371	69	-10	0-3	.988	0	102	128	2b54	0	-0.8
Total	9	1049	3812	528	1036	247	21	80	439	379-13	19	576	.272	.338	.411	93	-33	32-24	.980	-4	102	104	2b966,3b44/DS	73	0.5

BELLINGER, CLAY Clayton Daniel; B11.18.1968 Oneonta NY; BR/TR/6´3˝/(195–215); [SFN89 2/44]; d4.9; Col Rollins; OF(32/36/7)

1999	†NY A	32	45	12	9	2	0	1	2	1-0	0	10	.200	.217	.311	33	-5	1-0	1.000	1	89	65	3b16,1b8,O2L/2SD	0	-0.4
2000	†NY A	98	184	33	38	8	2	6	21	17-1	5	48	.207	.288	.370	67	-10	5-0	.968	0	91	71	O46(17/26/5),2b21,3b18,1b10,S6	0	-0.8
2001	†NY A	51	81	12	13	1	1	5	12	4-0	1	23	.160	.207	.383	51	-7	1-2	1.000	3	81	0	O25(13/10/2),3b17,1b6,S2	0	-0.4
2002	Ana A	2	1	0	0	0	0	0	0	0-0	0	1	.000	.000	.000	-99	0	0-0	1.000	-0	0	0	1b2	0	0.0
Total	4	183	311	57	60	11	3	12	35	22-1	6	82	.193	.257	.363	58	-22	7-2	.977	4	88	48	O73C,3b51,1b26,2b22,S9,D4	0	-1.6

BELLMAN, JACK John Hutchins "Happy Jack"; B3.4.1864 Taylorsville KY; D12.8.1931 Louisville KY; d4.23

1889	StL AA	1	2	1	1	0	0	0	0	1	0	0	.500	.667	.500	207	0	0	1.000	-0	—	—	/C	—	0.0

BELLOIR, ROB Robert Edward; B7.13.1948 Heidelberg, Germany; BR/TR/5´10˝/(155–170); [CleA69 8/181]; d8.2; Col Mercer

1975	Atl N	43	105	11	23	2	1	0	9	7-0	0	8	.219	.268	.257	45	-8	0-0	.922	-6	100	81	S38/2	0	-1.1
1976	Atl N	30	60	5	12	2	0	0	4	5-1	0	7	.200	.262	.233	39	-5	0-0	.929	-5	80	114	S12,3b10,2b5	0	-0.9
1977	Atl N	6	1	2	0	0	0	0	0	0-0	0	0	.000	.000	.000	-90	0	0-0	1.000	0	141	0	S3	0	0.0
1978	Atl N	2	1	0	1	1	0	0	0	0-0	0	0	1.000	1.000	2.000	651	1	0-0	1.000	-0	141	0	/S3	0	0.1
Total	4	81	167	18	36	5	1	0	13	12-1	0	15	.216	.268	.257	46	-12	0-0	.924	-11	97	85	S54,3b11,2b6	0	-1.9

BELTRAN, CARLOS Carlos Ivan; B4.24.1977 Manati, PR; BB/TR/6´1˝/(175–190); [KCA95 2/49]; d9.14

1998	KC A	14	58	12	16	5	3	0	7	3-0	1	12	.276	.317	.466	98	0	3-0	.978	1	127	0	O14C	0	0.1
1999	KC A	156	663	112	194	27	7	22	108	46-2	4	123	.293	.337	.454	97	-5	27-8	.972	-1	96	158	O154C,D2	0	-0.1
2000	KC A	98	372	49	92	15	4	7	44	35-2	0	69	.247	.309	.366	67	-20	13-0	.975	-1	101	108	O88(2/83/3),D7	61	-1.5
2001	KC A	155	617	106	189	32	12	24	101	52-2	5	120	.306	.362	.514	116	14	31-1	.988	5	102	158	O152C,D3	0	2.5
2002	KC A	**162**	637	114	174	44	7	29	105	71-1	4	135	.273	.346	.501	109	8	35-7	.983	1	99	148	O149C,D12	0	1.5
2003	KC A	141	521	102	160	14	10	26	100	72-4	2	81	.307	.389	.522	130	23	41-4	.987	7	106	165	O130C,D8	19	3.6
2004	KC A	69	266	51	74	19	2	15	51	37-7	2	44	.278	.367	.534	132	13	14-3	.985	4	112	116	O69C	0	1.9
	†Hou N★	90	333	70	86	17	7	23	53	55-3	5	57	.258	.368	.559	132	16	28-0	.977	3	102	194	O89C	0	2.5
2005	NY N★	151	582	83	155	34	2	16	78	56-5	2	96	.266	.330	.414	97	-3	17-6	.990	1	107	65	O150C	0	0.2
2006	†NY N★	140	510	127	140	38	1	41	116	95-6	4	99	.275	.388	.594	151	42	18-3	.995	11	110	201	O136C/D	0	5.4
Total	9	1176	4559	826	1280	245	55	203	763	522-32	29	836	.281	.355	.492	113	88	227-32	.984	31	104	145	O1131(2/1126/3),D33	80	16.1

BELTRE, ADRIAN Adrian (Perez); B4.7.1979 Santo Domingo, D.R.; BR/TR/5´11˝/(165–220); d6.24

1998	LA N	77	195	18	42	9	0	7	22	14-0	3	37	.215	.278	.369	72	-9	3-1	.925	6	114	127	3b74,S2	0	-0.3
1999	LA N	152	538	84	148	27	5	15	67	61-12	6	105	.275	.352	.428	102	2	18-7	.932	-1	99	98	3b152	0	0.3
2000	LA N	138	510	71	148	30	2	20	85	56-2	2	80	.290	.360	.475	115	11	12-5	.944	17	**110**	124	3b138/S	19	2.8
2001	LA N	126	475	59	126	22	4	13	60	28-1	5	82	.265	.310	.411	90	-9	13-4	.952	6	100	88	3b124,S2	41	-0.1
2002	LA N	159	587	70	151	26	5	21	75	37-4	4	96	.257	.303	.426	95	-7	7-5	.954	-10	92	63	3b157	0	-1.7
2003	LA N	158	559	50	134	30	2	23	80	37-4	5	103	.240	.290	.424	86	-14	2-2	.957	9	98	**130**	3b157/S	0	-0.4
2004	†LA N	156	598	104	200	32	0	**48**	121	53-9	2	87	.334	.388	.629	160	51	7-2	.978	8	103	**123**	3b155/S	0	5.8
2005	Sea A	156	603	69	154	36	1	19	87	38-6	5	108	.255	.303	.413	95	-5	3-1	.967	-5	92	100	3b155/D	0	-0.9
2006	Sea A	156	620	88	166	39	4	25	89	47-4	10	118	.268	.328	.465	109	7	11-5	.968	4	98	98	3b155/2D	0	1.2
Total	9	1278	4685	613	1269	251	23	191	686	371-42	42	816	.271	.328	.457	106	27	76-32	.955	32	100	104	3b1267,S7,D2/2	60	6.7

BELTRE, ESTEBAN Esteban (Valera); B12.26.1967 Ingenio Quisquella, D.R.; BR/TR/5´10˝/(155–172); d9.3

1991	Chi A	8	6	0	1	0	0	0	0	1-0	0	1	.167	.286	.167	29	-1	1-0	1.000	-2	61	63	S8	0	-0.2
1992	Chi A	49	110	21	21	2	0	1	10	3-0	0	18	.191	.211	.236	26	-11	1-0	.924	-11	87	54	S43,D4	0	-2.0
1994	Tex A	48	131	12	37	5	0	0	12	16-0	0	25	.282	.358	.321	77	-4	2-5	.961	6	116	91	S41,3b5/2	0	0.3
1995	Tex A	54	92	7	20	8	0	0	7	4-0	0	15	.217	.250	.304	42	-8	0-0	.969	-4	85	93	S36,2b15/3	0	-0.9
1996	Bos A	27	62	6	16	2	0	0	6	4-0	0	14	.258	.299	.290	50	-5	1-0	1.000	-4	66	45	3b13,2b8,S6/D	0	-0.7
Total	5	186	401	46	95	17	0	1	35	28-0	0	73	.237	.285	.287	51	-29	5-5	.951	-15	95	75	S134,2b24,3b19,D5	0	-3.5

BEMIS, HARRY Harry Parker; B2.1.1874 Farmington NH; D5.23.1947 Cleveland OH; BR/TR/5´7.5˝/175; d4.23

1902	Cle A	93	317	42	99	12	7	1	29	19	8	—	.312	.366	.404	118	8	3	.964	1	93	***111***	C87,O2R/2	—	1.6

YEAR	TM LG	G	AB	R	H	2B	3B	HR	RBI	BB-IB	HP	SO	AVG	OBP	SLG	AOPS	ABR	SB-CS	FA	FR	RNG	THR	GAMES AT POSITION	DL	BFW
1903	Cle A	92	314	31	82	20	3	1	41	8	7	—	.261	.295	.354	96	-2	5	**.988**	-2	102	97	C74,1b10/2	—	0.3
1904	Cle A	97	336	35	76	11	6	0	25	8	7	—	.226	.259	.295	76	-10	6	.958	1	119	97	C79,1b13/2	—	-0.2
1905	Cle A	70	226	27	66	13	3	0	28	13	5	—	.292	.344	.376	127	7	3	.972	-4	102	81	C58,2b4,3b2/1	—	1.0
1906	Cle A	93	297	28	82	13	5	2	30	12	3	—	.276	.311	.374	116	4	8	.963	-3	116	75	C81	—	1.0
1907	Cle A	65	172	12	43	7	0	0	19	7	1	—	.250	.283	.291	82	-4	5	.957	-5	99	79	C51,1b2	—	-0.5
1908	Cle A	91	277	23	62	9	1	0	33	7	4	—	.224	.253	.264	68	-10	14	.964	-1	143	78	C76,1b2	—	-0.4
1909	Cle A	42	123	4	23	2	3	0	13	0	1	—	.187	.194	.252	39	-9	2	.971	1	109	77	C36	—	-0.6
1910	Cle A	61	167	12	36	5	1	1	16	5	0	—	.216	.238	.275	60	-8	3	.961	-7	84	101	C46	—	-1.2
Total	9	704	2229	214	569	92	29	5	234	79	36	—	.255	.292	.329	92	-24	49	.966	-18	109	90	C588,1b28,2b7,3b2,O2R	—	1.0
BENARD, MARVIN	Marvin Larry; B1.20.1971 Bluefields, Nicaragua; BL/TL/5´9˝/(180–191); [SFN92 50/1391]; d9.5; Col Lewis–Clark St.																								
1995	SF N	13	34	5	13	2	0	1	4	1-0	0	7	.382	.400	.529	146	2	1-0	1.000	0	124	0	O7C	0	0.3
1996	SF N	135	488	89	121	17	4	5	27	59-2	4	84	.248	.333	.330	78	-15	25-11	.984	6	110	104	O132(5/102/38)	0	-0.8
1997	†SF N	84	114	13	26	4	0	1	13	13-0	2	29	.228	.315	.289	62	-6	3-1	.967	-1	72	162	O36(14/6/18)/D	0	-0.8
1998	SF N	121	286	41	92	21	1	3	36	34-1	2	39	.322	.396	.434	125	12	11-4	.982	-5	89	24	O79(12/9/64),D2	0	0.5
1999	SF N	149	562	100	163	36	5	16	64	55-2	6	97	.290	.359	.457	112	10	27-14	.988	-3	100	67	O142(4/123/20)	0	0.8
2000	†SF N	149	560	102	147	27	6	12	55	63-0	6	97	.262	.342	.396	92	-7	22-7	.997	6	104	137	O141(21/128/38)	0	0.0
2001	SF N	129	392	70	104	19	2	15	44	29-2	4	66	.265	.320	.439	100	-1	10-5	.965	-0	101	94	O109(15/75/37)	0	-0.2
2002	SF N	65	123	16	34	9	2	1	13	7-0	1	26	.276	.321	.407	93	-2	5-1	1.000	3	113	213	O38(14/6/20)	61	0.1
2003	SF N	46	71	5	14	3	1	0	4	4-0	0	9	.197	.237	.268	32	-7	1-0	1.000	3	139	224	O21(17/0/4)	98	-0.5
Total	9	891	2630	441	714	138	21	54	260	265-7	25	454	.271	.343	.402	96	-14	105-43	.986	8	103	101	O705(102/456/239),D3	159	-0.6
BENAVIDES, FREDDIE	Alfredo; B4.7.1966 Laredo TX; BR/TR/6´2˝/(180–185); [CinN87 2/50]; d5.14; C1; Col TCU																								
1991	Cin N	24	63	11	18	1	0	0	3	1-1	1	15	.286	.303	.302	69	-3	1-0	.974	0	102	61	S20,2b3	0	-0.1
1992	Cin N	74	173	14	40	10	1	1	17	10-4	1	34	.231	.277	.318	66	-8	0-1	1.000	-1	93	61	2b37,S34/3	0	-0.8
1993	Col N	74	213	20	61	10	3	3	26	6-1	0	27	.286	.305	.404	75	-8	3-2	.937	-5	92	67	S48,2b19,3b5/1	41	-0.9
1994	Mon N	47	85	8	16	5	1	0	6	3-1	1	15	.188	.222	.271	28	-9	0-0	.976	-6	71	88	2b36,3b5,1b3,S3	0	-1.5
Total	4	219	534	53	135	26	5	4	52	20-7	3	91	.253	.282	.343	65	-28	4-3	.948	-12	95	92	S105,2b95,3b11,1b4	41	-3.3
BENCH, JOHNNY	Johnny Lee; B12.7.1947 Oklahoma City OK; BR/TR/6´1˝/(187–215); [CinN65 2/36]; d8.28; HF1989; OF(55/2/54)																								
1967	Cin N	26	86	7	14	3	1	1	6	5-0	0	19	.163	.207	.256	29	-8	0-1	.995	3	214	69	C26	0	-0.5
1968	Cin N★	154	564	67	155	40	2	15	82	31-8	2	96	.275	.311	.433	115	10	1-5	.991	9	130	111	C154	0	2.8
1969	Cin N★	148	532	83	156	23	1	26	90	49-7	4	86	.293	.353	.487	128	19	6-6	.992	6	**193**	104	C147	0	3.2
1970	†Cin N★	158	605	97	177	35	4	**45**	**148**	54-9	0	102	.293	.345	.587	145	36	5-2	.986	20	**211**	89	C139,O24(15/2/6),1b12/3	0	5.9
1971	Cin N★	149	562	80	134	19	2	27	61	49-7	0	83	.238	.299	.423	104	0	2-1	.988	11	162	83	C141,1b12,O12(10/0/3),3b3	0	1.7
1972	†Cin N★	147	538	87	145	22	2	**40**	**125**	100-**23**	2	84	.270	.379	.541	**169**	**51**	6-6	.992	7	**250**	86	C129,O17R,1b7,3b4	0	**6.5**
1973	†Cin N★	152	557	83	141	17	3	25	104	83-14	0	83	.253	.345	.429	120	15	4-1	.995	11	**204**	79	C134,O23R,1b4/3	0	3.2
1974	Cin N★	160	621	108	174	38	2	33	**129**	80-15	3	90	.280	.363	.507	144	36	5-4	.993	14	**212**	86	C137,3b36,1b5	0	5.7
1975	†Cin N★	142	530	83	150	39	1	28	110	65-12	2	108	.283	.359	.519	141	29	11-0	.989	18	**198**	82	C121,O19(16/0/3),1b9	0	5.4
1976	†Cin N★	135	465	62	109	24	1	16	74	81-6	2	95	.234	.348	.394	108	8	13-2	**.997**	7	136	101	C128,O5L/1	0	2.4
1977	Cin N★	142	494	67	136	34	2	31	109	58-8	1	95	.275	.348	.540	133	22	2-4	.987	3	143	81	C135,O8(7/0/1),1b4/3	0	2.9
1978	Cin N✳	120	393	52	102	17	1	23	73	50-10	1	83	.260	.340	.483	129	14	4-2	.989	8	**150**	100	C107,1b11,O2(1/0/1)	0	2.7
1979	†Cin N✳	130	464	73	128	19	0	22	80	67-8	0	73	.276	.364	.459	124	17	4-2	.986	5	134	92	C126,1b2	0	2.8
1980	Cin N★	114	360	52	90	12	0	24	68	41-2	2	64	.250	.327	.483	127	12	4-2	.991	-12	107	81	C105	0	0.4
1981	Cin N	52	178	14	55	8	0	8	25	17-3	0	21	.309	.369	.489	142	10	0-2	.983	-2	84	123	1b38,C7	85	0.5
1982	Cin N	119	399	44	103	16	0	13	38	37-2	0	58	.258	.320	.396	99	-1	1-2	.917	-17	80	62	3b107,1b8/C	0	-2.1
1983	Cin N★	110	310	32	79	15	2	12	54	24-1	0	38	.255	.308	.432	100	-1	0-1	.933	-7	87	85	3b42,1b32,C5/lf	0	-1.1
Total	17	2158	7658	1091	2048	381	24	389	1376	891-135	19	1278	.267	.342	.476	127	269	68-43	.990	82	173	91	C1742,3b195,1b145,O111L	85	42.4
BENEDICT, ART	Arthur Melville; B3.31.1862 Cornwall IL; D1.14.1948 Denver CO; BR/TR; d5.14																								
1883	Phi N	3	15	3	4	1	0	0	4	0	—	4	.267	.267	.333	89	0	—	.571	-3	62	0	2b3	—	-0.3
BENEDICT, BRUCE	Bruce Edwin; B8.18.1955 Birmingham AL; BR/TR/6´1˝/(175–195); [AtlN76 5/99]; d8.18; C3; Col Nebraska–Omaha																								
1978	Atl N	22	52	3	13	2	0	0	1	6-2	0	6	.250	.328	.288	66	-2	0-0	.990	-0	80	188	C22	0	-0.2
1979	Atl N	76	204	14	46	11	0	0	15	33-3	0	18	.225	.331	.279	65	-8	1-3	.984	-7	78	84	C76	0	-1.4
1980	Atl N	120	359	18	91	14	1	2	34	28-8	1	36	.253	.308	.315	74	-12	3-3	.988	6	**140**	93	C120	0	-0.3
1981	Atl N★	90	295	26	78	12	1	5	35	33-4	3	21	.264	.341	.363	100	1	1-1	.986	4	88	**131**	C90	0	0.9
1982	†Atl N	118	386	34	95	11	1	3	44	37-9	3	40	.246	.315	.303	73	-13	4-4	**.993**	4	110	93	C118	0	-0.6
1983	Atl N★	134	423	43	126	13	1	2	43	61-16	1	24	.298	.385	.348	98	2	1-3	.992	8	92	102	C134	0	1.6
1984	Atl N	95	300	26	67	8	1	4	25	34-3	1	25	.223	.301	.297	65	-14	1-2	.991	-7	96	71	C95	0	-1.8
1985	Atl N	70	208	12	42	6	0	0	20	22-1	1	12	.202	.279	.231	42	-16	0-1	.989	-7	85	102	C70	0	-2.2
1986	Atl N	64	160	11	36	10	1	0	13	15-1	2	10	.225	.298	.300	63	-8	1-0	.993	-4	173	86	C57	0	-1.0
1987	Atl N	37	95	4	14	1	0	1	5	17-0	0	15	.147	.277	.189	25	-10	0-1	.989	0	77	90	C35	0	-0.9
1988	Atl N	90	236	11	57	7	0	0	19	19-1	0	26	.242	.296	.271	62	-11	0-2	.989	3	109	120	C89	0	-0.5
1989	Atl N	66	160	12	31	3	0	1	6	23-4	1	18	.194	.299	.231	52	-9	0-0	.995	8	107	139	C65	0	0.2
Total	12	982	2878	214	696	98	6	18	260	328-52	13	251	.242	.320	.299	72	-100	12-20	.990	7	105	102	C971	0	-6.2
BENES, JOE	Joseph Anthony "Bananas"; B1.8.1901 Long Island City NY; D3.7.1975 Elmhurst NY; BR/TR/5´8.5˝/158; d5.9																								
1931	StL N	10	12	1	2	0	0	0	0	2	1	1	.167	.333	.167	37	-1	0	1.000	-0	109	78	S6,2b2/3	—	-0.1
BENGOUGH, BENNY	Bernard Oliver; B7.27.1898 Niagara Falls NY; D12.22.1968 Philadelphia PA; BR/TR/5´7.5˝/168; d5.18; C19; Col Niagara																								
1923	NY A	19	53	1	7	2	0	0	3	4	0	2	.132	.193	.170	-4	-8	0-0	.973	1	130	111	C19	—	-0.7
1924	NY A	11	16	4	5	1	1	0	3	2	0	0	.313	.389	.500	128	1	0-0	1.000	2	125	69	C11	—	0.3
1925	NY A	95	283	17	73	14	2	0	23	19	0	9	.258	.305	.322	60	-18	0-2	**.993**	6	96	114	C94	—	-0.7
1926	NY A	36	84	9	32	6	0	0	14	7	1	4	.381	.435	.452	134	5	1-0	.973	5	100	171	C35	—	1.1
1927	†NY A	31	85	6	21	3	3	0	10	4	0	4	.247	.281	.353	66	-5	0-3	.986	7	126	90	C30	—	0.3
1928	†NY A	58	161	12	43	3	1	0	9	7	1	8	.267	.302	.298	60	-10	0-0	.992	3	95	116	C58	—	-0.3
1929	NY A	23	62	5	12	2	1	0	7	0	0	2	.194	.194	.258	16	-8	0-0	.982	-3	90	71	C23	—	-1.0
1930	NY A	44	102	10	24	4	2	0	12	3	0	8	.235	.257	.314	46	-9	1-0	.990	4	103	97	C44	—	-0.2
1931	StL A	40	140	6	35	4	1	0	12	4	0	4	.250	.271	.293	46	-11	0-3	.986	1	104	98	C37	—	-0.8
1932	StL A	54	139	13	35	7	1	0	15	12	0	4	.252	.311	.317	60	-8	0-1	.989	5	118	135	C47	—	-0.1
Total	10	411	1125	83	287	46	12	0	108	62	2	45	.255	.295	.317	59	-71	2-9	.988	31	105	113	C398	—	-2.1
BENIQUEZ, JUAN	Juan Jose (Torres); B5.13.1950 San Sebastian, PR; BR/TR/5´11˝/(148–175); d9.4; OF(295/735/184)																								
1971	Bos A	16	57	8	17	2	0	0	4	3-0	0	4	.298	.333	.333	83	-1	3-1	.895	-8	61	56	S15	0	-0.8
1972	Bos A	33	99	10	24	4	1	1	8	7-0	0	11	.242	.287	.333	81	-2	2-0	.900	1	108	114	S27	0	0.3
1974	Bos A	106	389	60	104	14	3	5	33	25-2	1	61	.267	.313	.357	86	-7	19-11	.978	-2	104	58	O97(7/91/0),D4	25	-1.2
1975	†Bos A	78	254	43	74	14	4	2	17	25-1	2	26	.291	.358	.402	106	2	7-10	.991	1	119	104	O44(31/13/2),D20,3b14	16	-0.1
1976	Tex A	145	478	49	122	14	4	0	33	39-1	3	56	.255	.315	.301	80	-12	17-6	.986	13	109	**178**	O141C/2	0	-0.1
1977	Tex A	123	424	56	114	19	6	10	50	43-0	1	43	.269	.336	.413	102	1	26-18	.988	-2	96	115	O123C	15	-0.3
1978	Tex A	127	473	61	123	17	3	11	50	20-1	3	59	.260	.292	.378	87	-10	10-12	.972	-10	89	98	O126C	30	-2.3
1979	NY A	62	142	19	36	6	1	4	17	9-0	2	17	.254	.299	.394	89	-3	3-3	.981	1	95	137	O60(18/38/4),3b3	60	-0.3
1980	Sea A	70	237	26	54	10	0	6	21	17-0	0	25	.228	.278	.346	69	-10	2-3	.957	-1	104	70	O65(2/63/0)/D	74	-1.3
1981	Cal A	58	166	18	30	5	0	3	13	15-0	1	16	.181	.251	.265	49	-11	2-1	.959	-4	95	0	O55(15/36/7)/D	0	-1.8
1982	†Cal A	112	196	25	52	11	2	3	24	15-1	1	21	.265	.321	.388	92	-2	3-0	.983	-6	77	92	O107(37/25/51)	0	-1.0
1983	Cal A	92	315	44	96	15	0	3	34	15-0	4	29	.305	.343	.381	100	0	4-2	.968	-0	94	141	O84(38/30/31),D6	50	-0.3
1984	Cal A	110	354	60	119	17	0	8	39	18-0	3	43	.336	.370	.452	127	13	0-3	.971	0	104	85	O98(64/8/50)	0	0.8
1985	Cal A	132	411	54	125	13	5	8	42	34-3	5	46	.304	.364	.418	114	8	4-3	1.000	-9	84	26	O71(18/36/22),1b46,D14/3S	0	-0.6
1986	Bal A	113	343	48	103	15	0	6	36	40-1	3	49	.300	.372	.397	112	8	2-3	.963	-1	108	34	O54(44/3/9),3b25,D16,1b14	0	0.2
1987	KC A	57	174	14	41	7	0	3	26	11-1	1	26	.236	.282	.328	60	-10	0-0	1.000	-7	81	0	O22(17/2/4),D15,1b6,3b6	0	-1.9
	Tor A	39	81	6	23	5	1	5	21	5-0	1	13	.284	.330	.556	127	3	0-0	.875	-2	62	0	D15,O7(3/0/4),1b2	0	0.1
	Year	96	255	20	64	12	1	8	47	16-1	2	39	.251	.297	.400	81	-7	0-0	.976	-9	77	0	D30,O29(20/2/8),1b8,3b6	0	-1.8
1988	Tor A	27	58	9	17	2	0	1	8	8-0	0	6	.293	.373	.379	112	1	0-0	ø	-0	0	0	D19/lf	0	0.1
Total	17	1500	4651	610	1274	190	30	79	476	349-11	31	551	.274	.327	.379	95	-32	104-76	.977	-35	98	95	O1155C,D111,1b68,3b49,S43/2	270	-10.5

YEAR	TM LG	G	AB	R	H	2B	3B	HR	RBI	BB-IB	HP	SO	AVG	OBP	SLG	AOPS	ABR	SB-CS	FA	FR	RNG	THR	GAMES AT POSITION	DL	BFW
BENITEZ, YAMIL	Yamil Antonio; B10.5.1972 San Juan, PR; BR/TR/6´2˝/195; d9.15																								
1995	Mon N	14	39	8	15	2	1	2	7	1-0	0	7	.385	.400	.641	163	3	0-2	.950	0	101	160	O14(3/4/8)	0	0.2
1996	Mon N	11	12	0	2	0	0	0	2	0-0	0	4	.167	.167	.167	-11	-2	0-0	.500	-0	52	0	O4(3/0/1)	0	-0.2
1997	KC A	53	191	22	51	7	1	8	21	10-0	1	49	.267	.307	.440	89	-4	2-2	.965	-1	108	0	O52(31/0/22)	0	-0.7
1998	Ari N	91	206	17	41	7	1	9	30	14-1	4	46	.199	.262	.374	65	-12	2-2	.972	4	115	129	O62(49/0/13),D2	0	-1.0
Total	4	169	448	47	109	16	3	19	60	25-1	5	106	.243	.290	.420	82	-15	4-6	.963	2	110	69	O132(86/4/44),D2	0	-1.7
BENJAMIN, STAN	Alfred Stanley; B5.20.1914 Framingham MA; BR/TR/6´2˝/194; d9.16; Col McDaniel																								
1939	Phi N	12	50	4	7	2	1	0	2	1	0	6	.140	.157	.220	0	-7	1	.867	0	98	240	O7(4/2/2),3b5	—	-0.7
1940	Phi N	8	9	1	2	0	0	0	1	1	0	1	.222	.300	.222	48	-1	0	1.000	1	108	871	O2R	—	0.0
1941	Phi N	129	480	47	113	20	7	3	27	20	0	81	.235	.266	.325	68	-23	17	.980	-1	92	132	O110(2/26/86),1b8,2b2/3	0	-3.1
1942	Phi N	78	210	24	47	8	3	2	8	10	1	27	.224	.262	.319	73	-8	5	.976	1	92	207	O45(0/25/21),1b15	0	-1.1
1945	Cle A	14	21	1	7	2	0	0	3	0	0	0	.333	.333	.429	126	1	0-1	1.000	2	108	547	O4(3/0/1)	0	0.2
Total	5	241	770	77	176	32	11	5	41	32	1	115	.229	.260	.318	66	-38	23-1	.975	2	93	173	O168(9/53/112),1b23,3b6,2b2	0	-4.7
BENJAMIN, MIKE	Michael Paul; B11.22.1965 Euclid OH; BR/TR/6´0˝/(169–195); [SFN87 3/74]; d7.7; Col Arizona St.; [DL 2001 Pit N 190]																								
1989	SF N	14	6	6	1	0	0	0	0	0-0	0	1	.167	.167	.167	-5	-1	0-0	1.000	-1	74	0	S8	0	-0.1
1990	SF N	22	56	7	12	3	1	2	3	3-1	0	10	.214	.254	.411	82	-2	1-0	.988	4	122	117	S21	0	0.4
1991	SF N	54	106	12	13	3	0	2	8	7-2	2	26	.123	.188	.208	12	-13	3-0	.984	11	120	131	S51/3	0	0.1
1992	SF N	40	75	4	13	2	1	1	3	4-1	0	15	.173	.215	.267	38	-7	1-0	.991	-1	101	102	S33,3b2	60	-0.5
1993	SF N	63	146	22	29	7	0	4	16	9-2	4	23	.199	.264	.329	59	-9	0-0	.991	12	103	230	2b23,S23,3b16	29	0.5
1994	SF N	38	62	9	16	5	1	1	9	5-1	3	16	.258	.343	.419	101	0	5-0	.968	7	156	172	S18,2b10,3b5	0	0.9
1995	SF N	68	186	19	41	6	0	3	12	8-3	1	51	.220	.256	.301	47	-15	11-1	.964	1	114	53	3b43,S16,2b8	0	-1.1
1996	Phi N	35	103	13	23	5	1	4	13	12-5	2	21	.223	.316	.408	89	-2	3-1	.954	-2	99	78	S31/2	97	-0.1
1997	Bos A	49	116	12	27	9	1	0	7	4-0	1	27	.233	.262	.328	52	-8	2-3	.929	3	137	140	3b19,S16,2b5,1b4/PD	0	-0.4
1998	†Bos A	124	349	46	95	23	0	4	39	15-1	6	73	.272	.312	.372	76	-12	3-0	.994	4	89	95	2b87,S20,3b11,1b10,D2	0	-0.3
1999	Pit N	110	368	42	91	26	7	1	37	20-3	2	90	.247	.288	.364	64	-21	10-1	.982	**35**	128	148	S93,2b12,3b6	19	2.1
2000	Pit N	93	233	28	63	18	2	2	19	12-0	3	45	.270	.313	.391	77	-9	5-4	.974	25	150	116	3b34,S30,2b27/1	0	1.7
2002	Pit N	108	120	7	18	2	1	0	3	7-0	1	31	.150	.202	.183	3	-17	0-4	.979	4	104	91	3b62,S15,2b11/1rf	0	-1.4
Total	13	818	1926	227	442	109	15	24	169	106-19	25	429	.229	.277	.339	61	-116	44-14	.980	102	118	116	S375,3b199,2b184,1b16,D3/rfP	395	1.8
BENNERS, IKE	Isaac B.; B6.7.1856 Philadelphia PA; D4.18.1932 Philadelphia PA; BL/?/175; d5.1																								
1884	Bro AA	49	189	25	38	11	5	1	—	7	2	—	.201	.237	.328	82	-4	—	.821	-4	11	0	O49L	—	-0.8
	Wil U	6	22	0	1	0	0	0	—	1	—	—	.045	.087	.045	-57	-5	—	.750	-0	62	358	O6(0/3/3)	—	-0.5
Total	1	55	211	25	39	11	5	1	—	8	—	—	.185	.222	.299	66	-9	—	.813	-5	17	43	O55(49/3/3)	—	-1.3
BENNETT, CHARLIE	Charles Wesley; B11.21.1854 New Castle PA; D2.24.1927 Detroit MI; BR/TR/5´11˝/180; d5.1; OF(25/25/20)																								
1878	Mil N	49	184	16	45	9	0	1	12	10	—	26	.245	.284	.310	89	-2	—	.831	-12	—	—	C35,O20(0/16/4)	—	-1.3
1880	Wor N	51	193	20	44	9	3	0	18	10	—	30	.228	.266	.306	86	-3	—	.913	0	—	—	C46,O6(0/3/3)	—	-0.2
1881	Det N	76	299	44	90	18	7	7	64	18	—	37	.301	.341	.478	149	16	—	**.962**	17	—	—	C70,3b5,O3(1/2/0)	—	3.2
1882	Det N	84	342	43	103	16	10	5	51	20	—	33	.301	.340	.450	151	19	—	.945	6	—	—	C65,3b11,2b7/S1	—	2.8
1883	Det N	92	371	56	113	34	7	5	55	26	—	59	.305	.350	.474	155	26	—	**.944**	2	—	—	C72,2b15,O12(1/4/7)	—	3.0
1884	Det N	90	341	37	90	18	6	3	40	36	—	40	.264	.334	.378	132	15	—	.917	3	—	—	C80,O5(1/0/4),S4/321	—	2.2
1885	Det N	91	349	49	94	24	13	5	60	47	—	37	.269	.356	.456	161	25	—	.919	5	—	—	C62,O19(18/0/1),3b10	—	3.3
1886	Det N	72	235	37	57	13	5	4	34	48	—	29	.243	.371	.391	127	10	4	**.955**	13	—	—	C69,O4(3/0/1)/S	—	2.5
1887	†Det N	46	160	26	39	6	5	3	20	30	0	22	.244	.363	.400	108	2	7	.951	7	—	—	C45/lf1	—	1.0
1888	Det N	74	258	32	68	12	4	5	29	31	2	40	.264	.347	.399	136	12	4	**.966**	8	—	—	C73/1	—	2.5
1889	Bos N	82	247	42	57	8	2	4	28	21	2	43	.231	.296	.328	69	-11	7	**.955**	7	—	—	C82	—	0.2
1890	Bos N	85	281	59	60	17	2	3	40	72	2	56	.214	.377	.320	96	2	6	**.959**	19	***128***	*86*	C85	—	2.5
1891	Bos N	75	256	35	55	9	3	5	39	42	3	61	.215	.332	.332	84	-5	3	**.960**	18	*127*	*89*	C75	—	1.7
1892	†Bos N	35	114	19	23	4	0	1	16	27	0	23	.202	.355	.263	80	-1	6	.948	5	*132*	72	C35	—	0.6
1893	Bos N	60	191	34	40	6	0	4	27	40	2	36	.209	.352	.304	69	-8	5	.953	2	*131*	*58*	C60	—	-0.1
Total	15	1062	3821	549	978	203	67	55	533	478	11	572	.256	.340	.387	118	97	42	.942	100	*129*	*79*	C954,O70L,3b27,2b23,S6,1b4	—	23.9
BENNETT, GARY	Gary David; B4.17.1972 Waukegan IL; BR/TR/6´0˝/(190–210); [PhiN90 11/293]; d9.24																								
1995	Phi N	1	1	0	0	0	0	0	0	0-0	0	1	.000	.000	.000	-99	0	0-0	ø	0	—	—	/H	0	0.0
1996	Phi N	6	16	0	4	0	0	0	1	2-1	0	6	.250	.333	.250	56	-1	0-0	1.000	3	177	212	C5	0	0.2
1998	Phi N	9	31	4	9	0	0	0	3	5-0	0	5	.290	.378	.290	82	-1	0-0	1.000	-4	559	0	C9	0	-0.4
1999	Phi N	36	88	7	24	4	0	1	21	4-0	0	11	.273	.298	.352	65	-5	0-0	.971	-6	78	46	C32	0	-0.9
2000	Phi N	31	74	8	18	5	0	2	5	13-0	2	15	.243	.371	.392	93	0	0-0	.995	1	111	87	C31	0	0.2
2001	NY N	1	1	0	1	0	0	0	0	0-0	0	0	1.000	1.000	1.000	451	1	0-0	ø	0	—	—	/H	0	0.0
	Phi N	26	75	8	16	3	1	1	6	9-1	0	19	.213	.294	.320	63	-4	0-0	.987	-2	129	99	C24	0	-0.5
	Col N	19	55	7	15	3	0	1	4	3-3	1	5	.273	.317	.382	67	-3	0-0	1.000	-3	63	48	C19	0	-0.5
	Year	46	131	15	32	6	1	2	10	12-4	1	24	.244	.308	.351	67	-6	0-0	.992	-5	102	78	C43	0	-1.0
2002	Col N	90	291	26	77	10	2	4	26	15-2	6	45	.265	.314	.354	66	-14	1-3	.992	-14	115	55	C90	0	-2.3
2003	SD N	96	307	26	73	15	0	2	42	24-3	2	48	.238	.296	.306	63	-17	3-0	.996	-23	88	64	C91	36	-3.4
2004	Mil N	75	219	18	49	14	0	3	20	22-3	2	32	.224	.297	.329	62	-12	1-0	.993	-16	103	81	C75	0	-2.3
2005	Was N	68	199	11	44	7	0	1	21	21-3	2	37	.221	.298	.271	54	-13	0-1	.986	1	127	73	C64	0	-0.8
2006	†StL N	60	157	13	35	5	0	4	22	11-2	0	30	.223	.274	.331	54	-11	0-0	.988	-10	101	30	C56/1	0	-1.8
Total	11	518	1514	128	365	66	3	19	171	129-18	15	254	.241	.305	.326	64	-80	5-4	.991	-73	115	65	C496/1	36	-12.5
BENNETT, HERSCHEL	Herschel Emmett; B9.21.1896 Elwood MO; D9.9.1964 Springfield MO; BL/TR/5´9.5˝/160; d4.19																								
1923	StL A	5	4	0	0	0	0	0	0	1	0	1	.000	.200	.000	-42	-1	0-0	1.000	0	116	0	/cf	—	-0.1
1924	StL A	41	94	16	31	4	3	1	11	3	2	6	.330	.364	.468	107	0	1-0	.966	-1	84	109	O21(12/0/9)	—	-0.1
1925	StL A	93	298	46	83	11	6	2	37	18	2	16	.279	.324	.376	73	-13	4-10	.916	-1	91	155	O73(41/12/21)	—	-2.1
1926	StL A	80	225	33	60	14	2	1	26	22	2	21	.267	.337	.360	78	-7	2-1	.950	3	98	174	O50(36/6/9)	—	-0.8
1927	StL A	93	256	40	68	12	2	3	30	14	3	21	.266	.311	.363	72	-11	6-2	.946	1	110	86	O55(12/2/42)	—	-1.3
Total	5	312	877	135	242	41	13	7	104	58	9	65	.276	.327	.376	77	-32	13-13	.937	2	98	136	O200(101/21/81)	—	-4.4
BENNETT, FRED	James Fred "Red"; B3.15.1902 Atkins AR; D5.12.1957 Atkins AR; BR/TR/5´9˝/185; d4.13																								
1928	StL A	7	8	0	2	1	0	0	0	0	0	2	.250	.250	.375	60	0	0-0	1.000	0	158	0	/rf	—	0.0
1931	Pit N	32	89	6	25	5	0	1	7	7	0	4	.281	.333	.371	90	-1	0	.951	-0	90	143	O21(3/0/18)	—	-0.3
Total	2	39	97	6	27	6	0	1	7	7	0	6	.278	.327	.371	87	-1	0-0	.953	-0	93	138	O22(3/0/19)	—	-0.3
BENNETT, JOE	Joseph Rosenblum; B7.2.1900 New York NY; D7.11.1987 Morro Bay CA; BR/TR/5´9˝/168; d7.5; Col NYU																								
1923	Phi N	1	0	0	0	0	0	0	0	0	0	0	ø	ø	ø	ø	0	0-0	1.000	0	154	0	/3	—	0.0
BENNETT, PUG	Justin Titus; B2.20.1874 Ponca NE; D9.12.1935 Kirkland WA; BL/TR/5´11˝/165; d4.12; Col Blackburn																								
1906	StL N	153	595	66	156	16	7	1	34	56	8	—	.262	.334	.318	108	6	20	.948	-8	99	83	2b153	—	0.0
1907	StL N	87	324	20	72	8	2	0	21	21	1	—	.222	.272	.259	69	-12	7	.939	-10	89	88	2b83,3b3	—	-2.5
Total	2	240	919	86	228	24	9	1	55	77	9	—	.248	.312	.297	94	-6	27	.945	-18	96	85	2b236,3b3	—	-2.5
BENSON, VERN	Vernon Adair; B9.19.1924 Granite Quarry NC; BL/TR/5´11˝/180; d7.31; Mil 1943–45; M1/C18; Col Catawba																								
1943	Phi A	2	2	0	0	0	0	0	0	0	0	0	.000	.000	.000	-99	-1	0-0	ø	0	—	—	/H	0	-0.1
1946	Phi A	7	5	1	0	0	0	0	0	1	0	3	.000	.167	.000	-51	-1	0-0	1.000	0	203	0	O2L	0	-0.1
1951	StL N	13	46	8	12	3	1	1	7	6	0	8	.261	.346	.435	108	1	0-0	.950	1	125	190	3b9,O4L	0	0.1
1952	StL N	20	47	6	9	2	0	2	5	5	0	9	.191	.269	.362	73	-2	0-0	.889	-0	114	159	3b15	0	-0.2
1953	StL N	13	4	2	0	0	0	0	0	1	0	2	.000	.200	.000	-42	-1	0-0	ø	0	—	—	/H	0	-0.1
Total	5	55	104	17	21	5	1	3	12	13	0	22	.202	.291	.356	75	-4	0-0	.911	1	118	170	3b24,O6L	0	-0.4
BENTLEY, JACK	John Needles; B3.8.1895 Sandy Spring MD; D10.24.1969 Olney MD; BL/TL/5´11.5˝/200; d9.6; ▲																								
1913	Was A	3	3	0	0	0	0	0	0	0	0	0	.000	.000	.000	-98	0	0	1.000	0	154	0	P3	—	0.0
1914	Was A	30	40	7	11	2	0	0	4	0	0	5	.275	.275	.325	77	2	0	.930	-1	86	85	P30	—	0.0
1915	Was A	4	2	0	0	0	0	0	0	0	0	1	.000	.000	.000	-98	0	0	.750	-0	61	0	P4	—	0.0
1916	Was A	2	0	0	0	0	0	0	0	0	0	0	ø	ø	ø	ø	0	0	1.000	0	352	0	P2	—	0.0

YEAR	TM LG	G	AB	R	H	2B	3B	HR	RBI	BB-IB	HP	SO	AVG	OBP	SLG	AOPS	ABR	SB-CS	FA	FR	RNG	THR	GAMES AT POSITION	DL	BFW
1923	†NY N	52	89	9	38	6	2	1	14	3	0	4	.427	.446	.573	169	15	0-0	.977	-1	89	47	P31	—	0.0
1924	†NY N	46	98	12	26	5	1	0	6	3	0	13	.265	.287	.337	68	4	0-0	.979	-1	94	139	P28	—	0.0
1925	NY N	64	99	10	30	5	2	3	18	9	0	11	.303	.361	.485	119	3	0-0	.930	-1	89	91	P28,O3R/1	—	-0.1
1926	Phi N	75	240	19	62	12	3	2	27	5	0	4	.258	.273	.358	66	-12	0	.993	-1	90	81	1b56,P7	—	-1.6
	NY N	3	4	0	1	0	0	0	0	0	0	0	.250	.250	.250	35	0	0	ø	-0	0	0	/P	—	0.0
	Year	78	244	19	63	12	3	2	27	5	0	4	.258	.273	.357	65	-13	0	.993	-1	90	81	1b56,P8	—	-1.6
1927	NY N	8	9	1	2	0	0	1	2	1	0	1	.222	.300	.556	125	0	0	.750	-0	91	0	P4,1b2	—	0.0
Total	9	287	584	58	170	30	8	7	71	21	0	39	.291	.316	.406	91	12	0-0	.949	-5	90	84	P138,1b59,O3R	—	-1.7
BENTON, BUTCH	Alfred Lee; B8.24.1957 Tampa FL; BR/TR/6´1″/(193–195); [NYN75 1/6]; d9.14																								
1978	NY N	4	4	1	2	0	0	0	2	0-0	1	0	.500	.600	.500	216	1	0-0	1.000	-0	0	0	/C	0	0.1
1980	NY N	12	21	0	1	0	0	0	0	2-0	1	4	.048	.167	.048	-38	-4	0-0	.935	-2	96	47	C8	0	-0.6
1982	Chi N	4	7	0	1	0	0	0	1	0-0	0	1	.143	.143	.143	-19	-1	0-0	1.000	2	87	0	C4	0	0.1
1985	Cle A	31	67	5	12	4	0	0	7	3-2	0	9	.179	.208	.239	24	-7	0-0	.957	-5	118	95	C26	0	-1.1
Total	4	51	99	6	16	4	0	0	10	5-2	2	14	.162	.213	.202	16	-11	0-0	.959	-5	109	77	C39	0	-1.5
BENTON, STAN	Stanley W. "Rabbit"; B9.29.1901 Cannel City KY; D6.7.1984 Mesquite TX; BR/TR/5´7″/150; d9.13																								
1922	Phi N	6	19	1	4	1	0	0	3	2	0	1	.211	.286	.263	39	-2	0-0	.889	-1	103	0	2b5	—	-0.2
BENZINGER, TODD	Todd Eric; B2.11.1963 Dayton KY; BB/TR/6´1″/(185–195); [BosA81 4/96]; d6.21																								
1987	Bos A	73	223	36	62	11	1	8	43	22-3	2	41	.278	.344	.444	105	2	5-4	.987	9	131	157	O61(14/5/47),1b2	0	0.7
1988	†Bos A	120	405	47	103	28	1	13	70	22-4	1	80	.254	.293	.425	95	-4	2-3	.991	-3	78	89	1b85,O48(5/0/43)/D	19	-1.4
1989	Cin N	161	628	79	154	28	3	17	76	44-13	2	120	.245	.293	.381	89	-10	3-7	.995	-12	69	84	1b158	0	-3.8
1990	†Cin N	118	376	35	95	14	2	5	46	19-4	4	69	.253	.291	.340	72	-15	3-4	.992	-1	86	102	1b95,O10L	0	-2.5
1991	Cin N	51	123	7	23	3	2	1	11	10-2	0	20	.187	.244	.268	43	-10	2-0	.986	1	113	62	1b21,O15L	0	-1.1
	KC A	78	293	29	86	15	3	2	40	17-2	3	46	.294	.338	.386	99	-1	2-6	.996	-7	68	89	1b75/D	0	-1.4
1992	LA N	121	293	24	70	16	2	4	31	15-1	0	54	.239	.272	.348	76	-10	2-4	.989	-1	97	37	O51(18/0/33),1b42	0	-1.6
1993	SF N	86	177	25	51	7	2	6	26	13-1	0	35	.288	.332	.452	112	2	0-0	1.000	-3	66	120	1b40,O7L/3	0	-0.3
1994	SF N	107	328	32	87	13	2	9	31	17-4	2	84	.265	.304	.399	85	-9	2-1	.994	-5	83	102	1b99	0	-2.1
1995	SF N	9	10	2	2	0	0	1	2	2-1	0	3	.200	.308	.500	119	0	0-0	1.000	-1	0	200	1b5	0	0.0
Total	9	924	2856	316	733	135	18	66	376	181-35	14	552	.257	.301	.386	88	-55	21-29	.994	-22	77	94	1b622,O192(69/5/123),D2/3	19	-13.5
BERARDINO, JOHNNY	John "Bernie" (b Giovanni Berardino); B5.1.1917 Los Angeles CA; D5.19.1996 Los Angeles CA; BR/TR/6´0″/180; d4.22; Mil 1942–45; C1; Col USC																								
1939	StL A	126	468	42	120	24	5	5	58	37	2	36	.256	.314	.361	71	-22	6-2	.958	-1	99	76	2b114,3b8,S2	—	-1.4
1940	StL A	142	523	71	135	31	4	16	85	32	0	46	.258	.301	.424	84	-15	6-8	.939	10	**105**	112	S112,2b13,3b9	—	0.3
1941	StL A	128	469	48	127	30	4	5	89	41	2	27	.271	.332	.384	86	-10	3-5	.954	-10	91	104	S123/3	0	-1.2
1942	StL A	29	74	11	21	6	0	1	10	4	1	2	.284	.329	.405	104	0	3-1	.950	-0	73	76	S6,3b6,1b5,2b4	0	0.1
1946	StL A	144	582	70	154	29	5	5	68	34	1	58	.265	.306	.357	81	-16	2-4	.972	-2	101	91	2b143	0	-1.2
1947	StL A	90	306	29	80	22	1	1	20	44	2	26	.261	.358	.350	95	0	6-5	.977	-4	90	99	2b86	0	0.1
1948	Cle A	66	147	19	28	5	1	2	10	27	3	16	.190	.328	.279	64	-7	0-1	.988	2	99	110	2b20,1b18,S12,3b3	0	-0.5
1949	Cle A	50	116	11	23	6	1	0	13	14	2	14	.198	.295	.267	50	-8	0-1	.935	-3	97	68	3b25,2b8,S3	0	-1.1
1950	Cle A	4	5	1	2	0	0	0	3	1	0	0	.400	.500	.400	137	0	0-0	1.000	-0	66	86	/23	0	0.0
	Pit N	40	131	12	27	3	1	1	12	19	0	11	.206	.307	.267	51	-9	0	.964	2	112	102	2b36,3b3	0	-0.5
1951	StL A	39	119	13	27	7	1	0	13	17	0	18	.227	.324	.303	68	-5	1-1	.917	-5	77	84	3b31,2b2/1lf	0	-1.0
1952	Cle A	35	32	5	3	0	0	0	2	10	0	8	.094	.310	.094	17	-3	0-1	.960	1	138	66	2b8,S8,3b4,1b2	0	-0.2
	Pit N	19	56	2	8	4	0	0	4	4	0	6	.143	.200	.214	14	-6	0-0	.960	4	125	109	2b18	0	-0.2
Total	11	912	3028	334	755	167	23	36	387	284	13	268	.249	.316	.355	77	-101	27-29	.968	-6	101	91	2b453,S266,3b91,1b26/lf	0	-6.8
BERBERET, LOU	Louis Joseph; B11.20.1929 Long Beach CA; D4.6.2004 Las Vegas NV; BL/TR/5´11″/(200–212); d9.17; Col Santa Clara																								
1954	NY A	5	5	1	2	0	0	0	3	1	0	1	.400	.500	.400	154	0	0-0	1.000	1	*0*	*0*	C3	0	0.1
1955	NY A	2	5	1	2	0	0	0	2	1-0	0	0	.400	.500	.400	147	0	0-0	1.000	0	*0*	*0*	/C	0	0.1
1956	Was A	95	207	25	54	6	3	4	27	46-9	3	33	.261	.402	.377	107	4	0-0	.997	-2	*82*	*134*	C59	0	0.5
1957	Was A	99	264	24	69	11	2	7	36	41-5	2	38	.261	.359	.398	110	5	0-1	**1.000**	-4	84	130	C77	0	0.4
1958	Was A	5	6	0	1	0	0	0	0	4-0	0	1	.167	.500	.167	94	0	0-0	.917	0	27	226	C2	0	0.1
	Bos A	57	167	11	35	5	3	2	18	31-1	1	32	.210	.337	.311	74	-5	0-2	.984	-1	138	82	C49	0	-0.4
	Year	62	173	11	36	5	3	2	18	35-1	1	33	.208	.344	.306	76	-5	0-2	.981	-1	134	87	C51	0	-0.3
1959	Det A	100	338	38	73	8	2	13	44	35-1	0	59	.216	.284	.367	75	-13	0-0	.989	-7	**168**	110	C95	0	-1.5
1960	Det A	85	232	18	45	4	0	5	23	41-4	1	31	.194	.313	.276	60	-12	2-0	.993	1	111	116	C81	0	-0.7
Total	7	448	1224	118	281	34	10	31	153	200-20	7	195	.230	.337	.350	86	-21	2-3	.992	-12	*119*	*115*	C367	0	-1.4
BERBLINGER, JEFF	Jeffrey James; B11.19.1970 Wichita KS; BR/TR/6´0″/190; [StLN93 7/200]; d9.7; Col Kansas																								
1997	StL N	7	5	1	0	0	0	0	0	0-0	0	1	.000	.000	.000	-99	-1	0-0	1.000	1	108	258	2b4	0	-0.1
BERG, DAVE	David Scott; B9.3.1970 Roseville CA; BR/TR/5´11″/(185–196); [FlaN93 38/1079]; d4.2; Col Miami; OF(38/0/16)																								
1998	Fla N	81	182	18	57	11	0	2	21	26-1	0	46	.313	.393	.407	120	7	3-0	1.000	0	84	86	2b27,3b25,S17	0	0.9
1999	Fla N	109	304	42	87	18	1	3	25	27-0	2	59	.286	.348	.382	90	-5	2-2	.969	1	108	62	S37,2b29,3b19,O3L	0	0.0
2000	Fla N	82	210	23	53	14	1	1	21	25-0	5	46	.252	.340	.343	79	-6	3-0	.957	-5	98	110	S49,3b13,2b11	21	-0.6
2001	Fla N	82	215	26	52	12	1	4	16	14-0	2	39	.242	.292	.363	71	-10	0-1	.965	-7	101	111	2b34,S19,3b16	0	-1.4
2002	Tor A	109	374	42	101	26	2	4	39	26-1	5	57	.270	.322	.382	84	-8	0-2	.966	-3	99	115	2b52,3b20,S13,O13(3/0/10),1b10,D8	0	-1.0
2003	Tor A	61	161	26	41	6	1	4	18	11-0	0	34	.255	.301	.379	75	-6	0-1	.978	-6	92	61	2b24,3b17,O6(1/0/5),1b2/SD	30	-1.1
2004	Tor A	58	154	13	39	4	0	3	23	4-0	2	27	.253	.278	.338	57	-10	0-1	.974	-5	70	68	O31(31/0/1),1b7,2b4,3b3,D7	0	-1.6
Total	7	582	1600	190	430	91	6	21	163	133-2	16	308	.269	.328	.373	83	-38	8-7	.981	-24	98	94	2b181,S136,3b113,O53L,D22,1b19	51	-4.8
BERG, MOE	Morris; B3.2.1902 New York NY; D5.29.1972 Belleville NJ; BR/TR/6´1″/185; d6.27; C2; Col Princeton																								
1923	Bro N	49	129	9	24	3	2	0	6	2	0	5	.186	.198	.240	16	-16	1-0	.906	-5	93	83	S47/2	—	-1.6
1926	Chi A	41	113	4	25	6	0	0	7	6	0	9	.221	.261	.274	41	-10	0-2	.948	4	106	147	S31,2b2/3	—	-0.4
1927	Chi A	35	69	4	17	4	0	0	4	4	0	10	.246	.288	.304	55	-5	0-0	.952	-4	117	87	2b11,C10,S6,3b3	—	-0.7
1928	Chi A	76	224	25	55	16	0	0	29	14	4	25	.246	.302	.317	64	-12	3-1	.990	7	*139*	*96*	C73	—	0.0
1929	Chi A	107	352	32	101	7	0	0	47	17	2	16	.287	.323	.307	64	-19	5-1	.982	-1	*99*	*101*	C106	—	-1.2
1930	Chi A	20	61	4	7	3	0	0	7	1	0	5	.115	.129	.164	-27	-12	0-0	.986	-0	*95*	*126*	C20	—	-1.1
1931	Cle A	10	13	1	1	1	0	0	0	1	0	1	.077	.143	.154	-21	-2	0-0	.889	0	*174*	*247*	C8	—	-0.2
1932	Was A	75	195	16	46	8	1	1	26	8	0	13	.236	.266	.303	48	-16	1-1	1.000	6	*168*	*105*	C75	—	-0.6
1933	Was A	40	65	8	12	3	0	2	9	4	0	5	.185	.232	.323	46	-5	0-0	1.000	2	*221*	*72*	C35	—	-0.2
1934	Was A	33	86	5	21	4	0	0	6	6	1	4	.244	.301	.291	55	-6	2-0	.988	-3	*149*	*87*	C31	—	-0.6
	Cle A	29	97	4	25	3	1	0	9	1	0	7	.258	.265	.309	47	-8	0-0	.980	2	*127*	*68*	C28	—	-0.4
	Year	62	183	9	46	7	1	0	15	7	1	11	.251	.283	.301	51	-14	2-0	.983	-1	*137*	*76*	C59	—	-1.0
1935	Bos A	38	98	13	28	5	0	2	12	5	0	3	.286	.320	.398	79	-3	0-0	.991	3	*111*	*145*	C37	—	0.1
1936	Bos A	39	125	9	30	4	1	0	19	2	2	6	.240	.264	.288	34	-14	0-0	.986	9	*96*	*158*	C39	—	-0.2
1937	Bos A	47	141	13	36	3	1	0	20	5	0	4	.255	.281	.291	43	-13	0-0	.979	2	*115*	*91*	C47	—	-0.8
1938	Bos A	10	12	0	4	0	0	0	0	0	0	1	.333	.333	.333	64	-1	0-0	1.000	0	*113*	*155*	C7/1	—	0.0
1939	Bos A	14	33	3	9	1	0	1	5	2	0	3	.273	.314	.394	77	-1	0-0	.965	2	*101*	*178*	C13	—	0.1
Total	15	663	1813	150	441	71	6	6	206	78	9	117	.243	.278	.299	49	-143	12-5	.986	24	*127*	*107*	C529,S84,2b14,3b4/1	—	-7.8
BERGAMO, AUGIE	August Samuel; B2.14.1917 Detroit MI; D8.19.1974 Grosse Pointe MI; BL/TL/5´9″/165; d4.25																								
1944	†StL N	80	192	35	55	6	3	2	19	35	1	23	.286	.399	.380	118	6	0	.988	-4	94	0	O50(31/1/19),1b2	0	0.0
1945	StL N	94	304	51	96	17	2	3	44	43	0	21	.316	.401	.414	124	12	0	.969	2	101	140	O77(7/0/70),1b2	0	0.9
Total	2	174	496	86	151	23	5	5	63	78	1	44	.304	.400	.401	122	18	0	.975	-2	98	87	O127(38/1/89),1b4	0	0.9
BERGEN, MARTY	Martin; B10.25.1871 N.Brookfield MA; D1.19.1900 N.Brookfield MA; TR/5´10″/170; d4.17; b–Bill																								
1896	Bos N	65	245	39	66	6	4	4	37	11	3	22	.269	.309	.376	75	-10	6	.920	8	*113*	*115*	C63/1	—	0.3
1897	†Bos N	87	327	47	81	11	3	2	45	18	4	—	.248	.295	.318	58	-21	5	.963	14	*154*	*71*	C85/cf	—	0.1
1898	Bos N	120	446	62	125	16	5	3	60	13	1	—	.280	.302	.359	85	-11	9	.962	5	*117*	*92*	C117,1b2	—	0.4
1899	Bos N	72	260	32	67	11	3	1	34	10	2	—	.258	.290	.335	65	-13	4	.955	6	*119*	*96*	C72	—	-0.1
Total	4	344	1278	180	339	44	15	10	176	52	10	22	.265	.299	.347	72	-55	24	.954	33	*126*	*92*	C337,1b3/cf	—	0.7

BERGEN, BILL William Aloysius; B6.13.1878 N.Brookfield MA; D12.19.1943 Worcester MA; BR/TR/6´0˝/184; d5.6; b–Marty

YEAR	TM LG	G	AB	R	H	2B	3B	HR	RBI	BB-IB	HP	SO	AVG	OBP	SLG	AOPS	ABR	SB-CS	FA	FR	RNG	THR	GAMES AT POSITION	DL	BFW
1901	Cin N	87	308	15	55	6	4	1	17	8	0	—	.179	.199	.234	27	-30	2	.970	-3	110	105	C87	—	-2.5
1902	Cin N	89	322	19	58	8	3	0	36	14	0	—	.180	.214	.224	32	-26	2	.959	19	**125**	101	C89	—	0.2
1903	Cin N	58	207	21	47	4	2	0	19	7	0	—	.227	.252	.266	43	-16	2	.980	4	123	102	C58	—	-0.6
1904	Bro N	96	329	17	60	4	2	0	12	9	0	—	.182	.204	.207	28	-29	3	.959	13	100	111	C93/1	—	-0.7
1905	Bro N	79	247	12	47	3	2	0	22	7	0	—	.190	.213	.219	31	-22	4	.954	0	82	128	C76	—	-1.5
1906	Bro N	103	353	9	56	3	3	0	19	7	0	—	.159	.175	.184	13	-38	2	.977	1	97	104	C103	—	-2.9
1907	Bro N	51	138	2	22	3	0	0	14	1	0	—	.159	.165	.181	9	-15	1	.968	-2	87	123	C51	—	-1.5
1908	Bro N	99	302	8	53	8	2	0	15	5	0	—	.175	.189	.215	30	-25	1	**.989**	10	87	105	C99	—	-0.6
1909	Bro N	112	346	16	48	1	1	1	15	10	0	—	.139	.163	.156	-1	-42	4	.976	11	93	**125**	C112	—	-2.3
1910	Bro N	89	249	11	40	2	1	0	14	6	0	39	.161	.180	.177	4	-31	0	.981	13	99	**114**	C89	—	-1.1
1911	Bro N	84	227	8	30	3	1	0	10	14	0	42	.132	.183	.154	-6	-33	2	**.981**	5	87	**118**	C84	—	-2.2
Total	11	947	3028	138	516	45	21	2	193	88	0	81	.170	.194	.201	20	-307	23	.972	73	99	112	C941/1	—	-15.7

BERGER, BRANDON Brandon Charles; B2.21.1975 Covington KY; BR/TR/5´11˝/205; [KCA96 14/409]; d9.9; Col Eastern Kentucky

YEAR	TM LG	G	AB	R	H	2B	3B	HR	RBI	BB-IB	HP	SO	AVG	OBP	SLG	AOPS	ABR	SB-CS	FA	FR	RNG	THR	GAMES AT POSITION	DL	BFW
2001	KC A	6	16	4	5	1	1	2	2	2-0	0	2	.313	.389	.875	199	2	0-0	1.000	-1	69	0	O5L/D	0	0.1
2002	KC A	51	134	16	27	5	1	6	17	8-2	2	32	.201	.255	.388	61	-8	1-0	1.000	2	101	221	O36(14/4/21),D10/1	0	-0.7
2003	KC A	13	32	3	7	0	0	0	3	5-0	0	4	.219	.324	.219	44	-2	0-0	1.000	0	96	211	O11R/D	0	-0.2
2004	KC A	11	35	5	7	2	0	0	2	0-0	0	7	.200	.200	.257	18	-4	1-1	1.000	2	132	178	O11(10/0/1)	0	-0.3
Total	4	81	217	28	46	8	2	8	24	15-2	2	45	.212	.268	.378	63	-12	2-1	1.000	3	103	191	O63(29/4/33),D12/1	0	-1.1

BERGER, CLARENCE Clarence Edward; B11.1.1894 E.Cleveland OH; D6.30.1959 Washington DC; BL/TR/6´0˝/185; d9.23

YEAR	TM LG	G	AB	R	H	2B	3B	HR	RBI	BB-IB	HP	SO	AVG	OBP	SLG	AOPS	ABR	SB-CS	FA	FR	RNG	THR	GAMES AT POSITION	DL	BFW
1914	Pit N	6	13	2	1	0	0	0	0	1	0	4	.077	.143	.077	-36	-2	0	1.000	-1	53	0	O5R	—	-0.3

BERGER, JOHNNY John Henne; B8.27.1901 Philadelphia PA; D5.7.1979 Lake Charles LA; BR/TR/5´9˝/165; d4.20

YEAR	TM LG	G	AB	R	H	2B	3B	HR	RBI	BB-IB	HP	SO	AVG	OBP	SLG	AOPS	ABR	SB-CS	FA	FR	RNG	THR	GAMES AT POSITION	DL	BFW
1922	Phi A	2	1	0	1	0	0	0	0	0	0	0	1.000	1.000	1.000	412	0	1-0	1.000	0	0	0	C2	—	0.1
1927	Was A	9	15	1	4	0	0	0	1	2	0	3	.267	.353	.267	63	-1	0-0	.926	-0	144	0	C9	—	-0.1
Total	2	11	16	1	5	0	0	0	1	2	0	3	.313	.389	.313	85	-1	1-0	.935	0	129	0	C11	—	0.0

BERGER, TUN John Henry; B12.6.1867 Pittsburgh PA; D6.10.1907 Pittsburgh PA; TR/?/204; d5.9

YEAR	TM LG	G	AB	R	H	2B	3B	HR	RBI	BB-IB	HP	SO	AVG	OBP	SLG	AOPS	ABR	SB-CS	FA	FR	RNG	THR	GAMES AT POSITION	DL	BFW
1890	Pit N	104	391	64	104	18	4	0	40	35	7	23	.266	.337	.332	108	6	11	.912	-13	160	54	O41(4/3/36),S33,C21,2b6/3	—	-0.3
1891	Pit N	43	134	15	32	2	1	1	14	12	3	10	.239	.315	.291	79	-3	4	.920	-10	106	112	C18,2b17,S6,O2(0/1/1)	—	-1.0
1892	Was N	26	97	9	14	2	1	0	3	7	1	9	.144	.210	.186	20	-9	3	.872	-7	84	54	S18,C9	—	-1.4
Total	3	173	622	88	150	22	6	1	57	54	11	42	.241	.313	.301	87	-6	18	.837	-30	84	53	S57,C48,O43(4/4/37),2b23/3	—	-2.7

BERGER, JOE Joseph August "Fats"; B12.20.1886 St.Louis MO; D3.5.1956 Rock Island IL; BR/TR/5´10.5˝/170; d4.11

YEAR	TM LG	G	AB	R	H	2B	3B	HR	RBI	BB-IB	HP	SO	AVG	OBP	SLG	AOPS	ABR	SB-CS	FA	FR	RNG	THR	GAMES AT POSITION	DL	BFW
1913	Chi A	79	223	27	48	6	2	2	20	36	2	28	.215	.330	.287	82	-4	5	.959	3	111	82	2b71,S4/3	—	0.0
1914	Chi A	48	148	11	23	3	1	0	3	13	0	9	.155	.224	.189	25	-14	2-8	.922	0	104	86	S28,2b12,3b7	—	-1.6
Total	2	127	371	38	71	9	3	2	23	49	2	37	.191	.289	.248	60	-18	7-8	.956	3	110	89	2b83,S32,3b8	—	-1.6

BERGER, BOZE Louis William; B5.13.1910 Baltimore MD; D11.3.1992 Bethesda MD; BR/TR/6´2˝/180; d8.17; Col Maryland

YEAR	TM LG	G	AB	R	H	2B	3B	HR	RBI	BB-IB	HP	SO	AVG	OBP	SLG	AOPS	ABR	SB-CS	FA	FR	RNG	THR	GAMES AT POSITION	DL	BFW
1932	Cle A	1	1	0	0	0	0	0	0	0	0	1	.000	.000	.000	-94	0	0-0	1.000	0	98	0	/S	—	0.0
1935	Cle A	124	461	62	119	27	5	5	43	34	1	97	.258	.310	.371	74	-19	7-5	.964	12	106	119	2b120,S3,1b2/3	—	0.1
1936	Cle A	28	52	1	9	2	0	0	3	1	0	14	.173	.189	.212	-1	-9	0-0	.959	1	93	56	1b8,2b8,3b7,S2	—	-0.6
1937	Chi A	52	130	19	31	5	0	5	13	15	1	24	.238	.322	.392	79	-5	1-1	.931	-1	101	118	3b40/2S	—	-0.4
1938	Chi A	118	470	60	102	15	3	3	36	43	1	80	.217	.284	.281	41	-44	4-1	.946	-8	108	119	S67,2b42,3b9	—	-4.0
1939	Bos A	20	30	4	9	2	0	0	2	1	0	10	.300	.323	.367	73	-1	0-0	.947	1	97	48	S10,3b5,2b2	—	0.0
Total	6	343	1144	146	270	51	8	13	97	94	3	226	.236	.296	.329	57	-78	12-7	.954	5	104	111	2b173,S84,3b62,1b10	—	-4.9

BERGER, WALLY Walter Anton; B10.10.1905 Chicago IL; D11.30.1988 Redondo Beach CA; BR/TR/6´2˝/198; d4.15

YEAR	TM LG	G	AB	R	H	2B	3B	HR	RBI	BB-IB	HP	SO	AVG	OBP	SLG	AOPS	ABR	SB-CS	FA	FR	RNG	THR	GAMES AT POSITION	DL	BFW
1930	Bos N	151	555	98	172	27	14	38	119	54	4	69	.310	.375	.614	139	31	3	.966	3	106	98	O145L	—	2.0
1931	Bos N	**156**	617	94	199	44	8	19	84	55	2	70	.323	.380	.512	143	37	13	.977	4	102	118	O156C/1	—	3.6
1932	Bos N	145	602	90	185	34	6	17	73	33	3	66	.307	.346	.468	121	17	5	**.993**	-2	100	79	O134C,1b11	—	1.0
1933	Bos N★	137	528	84	165	37	8	27	106	41	3	77	.313	.365	.566	**177**	50	2	.977	-2	103	61	O136C	—	4.7
1934	Bos N★	150	615	92	183	35	8	34	121	49	3	65	.298	.352	.546	148	38	2	.978	-6	94	80	O150C	—	2.7
1935	Bos N★	150	589	91	174	39	4	**34**	**130**	50	4	80	.295	.355	.548	151	40	3	.965	9	**119**	67	O149C	—	4.4
1936	Bos N☆	138	534	88	154	23	3	25	91	53	8	84	.288	.361	.483	134	25	1	.966	-3	99	95	O133C	—	1.8
1937	Bos N	30	113	14	31	9	1	5	22	11	1	33	.274	.344	.504	140	6	0	1.000	-1	94	52	O28L	—	0.3
	†NY N	59	199	40	58	11	2	12	43	18	3	30	.291	.359	.548	141	11	3	.965	-3	88	97	O52(3/46/3)	—	0.6
	Year	89	312	54	89	20	3	17	65	29	4	63	.285	.354	.532	141	17	3	.976	-5	90	82	O80(31/46/3)	—	0.9
1938	NY N	16	32	5	6	0	0	0	4	2	0	4	.188	.235	.188	17	-4	0	1.000	0	120	0	O9(0/8/1)	—	-0.4
	Cin N	99	407	74	125	23	4	16	56	29	2	44	.307	.356	.501	137	19	2	.966	-2	95	94	O98L	—	1.2
	Year	115	439	79	131	23	4	16	60	31	2	48	.298	.347	.478	128	15	2	.970	-2	97	85	O107(98/8/1)	—	0.8
1939	†Cin N	97	329	36	85	15	1	14	44	36	5	63	.258	.341	.438	107	3	1	.970	-8	80	99	O95(66/29/0)	—	-0.9
1940	Cin N	2	2	0	0	0	0	0	0	0	0	1	.000	.000	.000	-99	-1	0	ø	0	—	—	/H	—	-0.1
	Phi N	20	41	3	13	2	0	1	5	4	0	7	.317	.378	.439	130	2	1	.947	-1	103	0	O11(4/2/5)/1	—	0.1
	Year	22	43	3	13	2	0	1	5	4	0	8	.302	.362	.419	119	1	1	.947	-1	103	0	O11(4/2/5)/1	—	0.0
Total	11	1350	5163	809	1550	299	59	242	898	435	38	693	.300	.359	.522	140	274	36	.974	-11	100	86	O1296(344/943/9),1b13	—	21.0

BERGERON, PETER Peter Francis; B11.9.1977 Greenfield MA; BL/TR/6´2˝/(185–190); [LAN96 4/118]; d9.7

YEAR	TM LG	G	AB	R	H	2B	3B	HR	RBI	BB-IB	HP	SO	AVG	OBP	SLG	AOPS	ABR	SB-CS	FA	FR	RNG	THR	GAMES AT POSITION	DL	BFW
1999	Mon N	16	45	12	11	2	0	0	1	9-0	0	5	.244	.370	.289	73	-1	0-0	.967	2	118	287	O13(13/3/0)	0	0.0
2000	Mon N	148	518	80	127	25	7	5	31	58-0	0	100	.245	.320	.349	69	-25	11-13	.985	5	99	**201**	O146(32/117/0)	0	-2.1
2001	Mon N	102	375	53	79	11	4	3	16	28-2	5	87	.211	.275	.285	45	-32	10-7	.996	-4	95	113	O101C	0	-3.4
2002	Mon N	31	123	24	23	3	2	0	7	22-0	0	44	.187	.310	.244	46	-9	10-3	.974	-2	100	0	O31C	0	-1.0
2004	Mon N	11	42	2	9	0	0	0	1	2-0	0	16	.214	.250	.214	21	-5	0-1	.913	-2	78	0	O11C	35	-0.7
Total	5	308	1103	171	249	41	13	8	56	119-2	5	252	.226	.303	.308	57	-72	31-24	.984	-1	98	143	O302(45/263/0)	35	-7.2

BERGH, JOHN John Baptist; B10.8.1857 Boston MA; D4.17.1883 Boston MA; d8.5

YEAR	TM LG	G	AB	R	H	2B	3B	HR	RBI	BB-IB	HP	SO	AVG	OBP	SLG	AOPS	ABR	SB-CS	FA	FR	RNG	THR	GAMES AT POSITION	DL	BFW
1876	Phi N	1	4	0	0	0	0	0	0	0	—	2	.000	.000	.000	-99	-1	—	1.000	-0	0	0	/cfC	—	-0.1
1880	Bos N	11	40	2	8	3	0	0	0	2	—	5	.200	.238	.275	76	-1	—	.844	-3	—	—	C11	—	-0.3
Total	2	12	44	2	8	3	0	0	0	2	—	7	.182	.217	.250	59	-2	—	.841	-3	—	—	C12/cf	—	-0.4

BERGHAMMER, MARTY Martin Andrew "Pepper"; B6.18.1888 Elliott PA; D12.21.1957 Pittsburgh PA; BL/TR/5´9˝/172; d9.8

YEAR	TM LG	G	AB	R	H	2B	3B	HR	RBI	BB-IB	HP	SO	AVG	OBP	SLG	AOPS	ABR	SB-CS	FA	FR	RNG	THR	GAMES AT POSITION	DL	BFW
1911	Chi A	2	5	0	0	0	0	0	0	0	1	—	.000	.167	.000	-54	-1	0	1.000	-0	51	0	2b2	—	-0.1
1913	Cin N	74	188	25	41	4	1	1	13	10	3	29	.218	.269	.266	53	-12	16-10	.909	4	107	97	S54,2b13	—	-0.5
1914	Cin N	77	112	15	25	2	0	0	6	10	0	18	.223	.287	.241	56	-6	4	.906	6	124	68	S33,2b13	—	0.1
1915	Pit F	132	469	96	114	10	6	0	33	83	12	44	.243	.371	.290	88	-9	26	**.943**	-15	90	113	S132	—	-1.6
Total	4	285	774	136	180	16	7	1	52	103	16	91	.233	.335	.275	75	-28	46-10	.931	-5	97	106	S219,2b28	—	-2.1

BERGMAN, AL Alfred Henry "Dutch"; B9.27.1890 Peru IN; D6.20.1961 Fort Wayne IN; BR/TR/5´7˝/155; d8.29; Col Notre Dame

YEAR	TM LG	G	AB	R	H	2B	3B	HR	RBI	BB-IB	HP	SO	AVG	OBP	SLG	AOPS	ABR	SB-CS	FA	FR	RNG	THR	GAMES AT POSITION	DL	BFW
1916	Cle A	8	14	2	3	0	1	0	0	2	0	4	.214	.313	.357	95	0	0	.889	-1	92	0	2b3	—	-0.1

BERGMAN, DAVE David Bruce; B6.6.1953 Evanston IL; BL/TL/6´1.5˝/(180–195); [NYA74 2/36]; d8.26; Col Illinois St.

YEAR	TM LG	G	AB	R	H	2B	3B	HR	RBI	BB-IB	HP	SO	AVG	OBP	SLG	AOPS	ABR	SB-CS	FA	FR	RNG	THR	GAMES AT POSITION	DL	BFW
1975	NY A	7	17	0	0	0	0	0	0	2-0	0	4	.000	.105	.000	-69	-4	0-0	.917	1	109	258	O6R	0	-0.4
1977	NY A	5	4	1	1	0	0	0	1	0-0	0	0	.250	.200	.250	37	0	0-0	1.000	0	157	0	O3(1/1/1),1b2	0	0.0
1978	Hou N	104	186	15	43	5	1	0	12	39-9	0	32	.231	.361	.269	85	-2	2-0	.993	-3	80	109	1b66,O29L	0	-0.7
1979	Hou N	13	15	4	6	0	0	1	2	0-0	0	3	.400	.400	.600	179	1	0-0	1.000	-0	0	93	1b4	0	0.1
1980	†Hou N	90	78	12	20	6	1	0	3	10-2	0	10	.256	.341	.359	104	1	1-0	.995	1	116	158	1b59,O5(3/0/2)	0	0.1
1981	Hou N	6	6	1	1	0	0	1	1	0-0	0	0	.167	.167	.667	135	0	0-0	1.000	0	626	0	/1	0	0.0
	SF N	63	145	16	37	9	0	3	13	19-3	0	18	.255	.339	.379	108	2	2-0	.992	2	136	99	1b33,O15L	0	0.2
	Year	69	151	17	38	9	0	4	14	19-3	0	18	.252	.333	.391	109	2	2-0	.992	2	140	98	1b34,O15L	0	0.2
1982	SF N	100	121	22	33	3	1	4	14	18-3	0	11	.273	.364	.413	119	3	3-0	.991	-0	92	76	1b69,O6(4/0/3)	0	0.2
1983	SF N	90	140	16	40	4	1	6	24	24-2	1	21	.286	.394	.457	139	8	2-1	.994	3	129	87	1b50,O6L	0	0.9
1984	†Det A	120	271	42	74	8	5	7	44	33-2	3	40	.273	.351	.417	114	5	3-4	.989	5	122	103	1b114,O2(1/0/1)	0	0.5
1985	Det A	69	140	8	25	2	0	3	7	14-0	0	15	.179	.250	.257	40	-12	0-0	.991	-1	93	88	1b44/lfD	37	-1.5
1986	Det A	65	130	14	30	6	1	1	9	21-0	0	16	.231	.338	.315	79	-3	0-0	.986	1	118	119	1b41,O2(1/0/1),D8	0	-0.4

YEAR	TM LG	G	AB	R	H	2B	3B	HR	RBI	BB-IB	HP	SO	AVG	OBP	SLG	AOPS	ABR	SB-CS	FA	FR	RNG	THR	GAMES AT POSITION	DL	BFW
1987	†Det A	91	172	25	47	7	3	6	22	30-4	1	23	.273	.379	.453	126	7	0-1	.992	-2	91	98	1b65,O7(3/0/4),D7	15	0.2
1988	Det A	116	289	37	85	14	0	5	35	38-2	0	34	.294	.372	.394	120	9	0-2	.990	1	110	86	1b64,D30,O13L	0	0.5
1989	Det A	137	385	38	103	13	1	7	37	44-3	2	44	.268	.345	.361	101	2	1-3	.993	5	**119**	88	1b123/lfD	0	-0.1
1990	Det A	100	205	21	57	10	1	2	26	33-3	0	17	.278	.375	.366	108	4	3-2	.995	-1	83	93	D51,1b27,O5L	0	-0.1
1991	Det A	86	194	23	46	10	1	7	29	35-2	0	40	.237	.351	.407	108	3	1-1	.997	-0	100	106	1b49,D13,O4L	0	-0.1
1992	Det A	87	181	17	42	3	0	1	10	20-1	0	19	.232	.305	.265	61	-9	1-0	.986	-3	80	84	1b55,D12/lf	0	-1.6
Total	17	1349	2679	312	690	100	16	54	289	380-36	7	347	.258	.348	.367	102	15	19-14	.992	8	107	97	1b866,D133,O106(88/1/18)	52	-2.2
BERGOLLA, WILLIAM	William Jose; B2.4.1983 Valencia, Venezuela; BR/TR/6´0˝/175; d5.9																								
2005	Cin N	17	38	3	5	0	0	0	1	0-0	0	10	.132	.132	.132	-31	-7	0-0	1.000	3	147	120	2b9/S	0	-0.4
BERKENSTOCK, NATE	Nathan; B1831 PA; D2.23.1900 Philadelphia PA; d10.30																								
1871	Ath NA	1	4	0	0	0	0	0	0	0	—	3	.000	.000	.000	-99	-1	0-0	1.000	0	0	0	/rf	—	0.0
BERKLEBACH, FRANK	Frank Pierce; B7.27.1853 Philadelphia PA; D6.10.1932 Merchantville NJ; 6´0˝/182; d7.4																								
1884	Cin AA	6	25	3	6	0	1	0	3	0	2	—	.240	.296	.320	96	0	—	.667	-1	0	0	O6L	—	-0.2
BERKMAN, LANCE	William Lance; B2.10.1976 Waco TX; BB/TL/6´1˝/(205–220); [HouN97 1/16]; d7.16; Col Rice																								
1999	Hou N	34	93	10	22	2	0	4	15	12-0	0	21	.237	.321	.387	80	-3	5-1	.955	-2	94	0	O27(22/0/8)/1	0	-0.5
2000	Hou N	114	353	76	105	28	1	21	67	56-1	1	73	.297	.388	.561	128	16	6-2	.968	0	99	107	O96(40/0/63),1b2	0	1.3
2001	†Hou N★	156	577	110	191	**55**	5	34	126	92-5	13	121	.331	.430	.620	157	54	7-9	.981	-2	100	61	O155(128/40/7)	0	4.4
2002	Hou N★	158	578	106	169	35	2	42	**128**	107-20	4	118	.292	.405	.578	144	40	8-4	.977	-10	88	70	O156(76/122/12)	0	2.9
2003	Hou N	153	538	110	155	35	6	25	93	107-13	9	108	.288	.412	.515	133	31	5-3	.989	-3	92	108	O153(153/1/0)	0	2.2
2004	†Hou N★	160	544	104	172	40	3	30	106	127-14	10	101	.316	.450	.566	156	55	9-7	.992	-5	86	124	O160(70/2/90),1b4	0	4.1
2005	†Hou N	132	468	76	137	34	1	24	82	91-12	4	72	.293	.411	.524	141	32	4-1	.994	-3	93	120	1b96,O49(39/0/11),D3	33	2.1
2006	Hou N★	152	536	95	169	29	0	45	136	98-22	4	106	.315	.420	.621	159	51	3-2	.994	1	111	120	1b112,O44(5/0/42),D3	0	3.9
Total	8	1059	3687	687	1120	258	18	225	753	690-87	45	720	.304	.416	.567	145	276	47-29	.979	-22	92	93	O840(533/165/233),1b215,D6	33	20.4
BERMAN, BOB	Robert Leon; B1.24.1899 New York NY; D8.2.1988 Bridgeport CT; BR/TR/5´7.5˝/158; d6.4; Col Fordham																								
1918	Was A	2	0	0	0	0	0	0	0	0	0	0	ø	ø	ø	ø	0	0	1.000	0	*0*	*0*	/C	—	0.0
BERNARD, CURT	Curtis Henry; B2.18.1878 Parkersburg WV; D4.10.1955 Culver City CA; BL/TR/5´10˝/150; d9.17																								
1900	NY N	20	71	9	18	2	0	0	8	6	2	—	.254	.329	.282	73	-2	1	.929	-2	39	0	O19R/S	—	-0.4
1901	NY N	23	76	11	17	0	2	0	6	7	0	—	.224	.289	.276	67	-3	2	.800	-2	189	0	O15(0/8/7),2b4,S2/3	—	-0.6
Total	2	43	147	20	35	2	2	0	14	13	2	—	.238	.309	.279	70	-5	3	.857	-4	110	0	O34(0/8/26),2b4,S3/3	—	-1.0
BERNAZARD, TONY	Antonio (Garcia); B8.24.1956 Caguas, PR; BB/TR/5´9˝/160; d7.13																								
1979	Mon N	22	40	11	12	2	0	1	8	15-0	1	12	.300	.500	.425	154	5	1-2	.982	-3	97	54	2b14	0	0.2
1980	Mon N	82	183	26	41	7	1	5	18	17-4	0	41	.224	.289	.355	78	-6	9-2	.976	-1	104	90	2b39,S22	0	-0.3
1981	Chi A	**106**	384	53	106	14	4	6	34	54-6	2	66	.276	.367	.380	118	11	4-4	.987	6	103	91	2b104/S	0	2.3
1982	Chi A	137	540	90	138	25	9	11	56	67-0	2	88	.256	.337	.396	101	1	11-0	.985	31	**112**	119	2b137	21	4.2
1983	Chi A	59	233	30	61	16	2	2	26	17-0	0	45	.262	.306	.373	84	-5	2-1	.976	2	111	99	2b59	0	0.0
	Sea A	80	300	35	80	18	1	6	30	38-3	2	52	.267	.351	.393	101	2	21-8	.971	5	100	89	2b79	0	1.3
	Year	139	533	65	141	34	3	8	56	55-3	2	97	.265	.332	.385	94	-3	23-9	.973	7	105	93	2b138	0	1.3
1984	Cle A	140	439	44	97	15	4	2	38	43-0	2	70	.221	.290	.287	60	-23	20-13	.971	2	103	101	2b136/D	0	-1.5
1985	Cle A	153	500	73	137	26	3	11	59	69-2	1	72	.274	.361	.404	110	9	17-9	.978	-10	97	83	2b147/S	0	0.8
1986	Cle A	146	562	88	169	28	4	17	73	53-5	6	77	.301	.362	.456	124	19	17-8	.979	3	104	91	2b146	0	3.0
1987	Cle A	79	293	39	70	12	1	11	30	25-2	1	49	.239	.300	.399	83	-8	7-4	.983	-14	90	71	2b78	0	-1.7
	Oak A	61	214	34	57	14	1	3	19	30-0	0	30	.266	.354	.383	103	2	4-4	.953	-15	85	64	2b59,D3	0	-1.0
	Year	140	507	73	127	26	2	14	49	55-2	1	79	.250	.323	.393	91	-6	11-8	.971	-30	88	68	2b137,D3	0	-2.7
1991	Det A	6	12	0	2	0	0	0	0	0-0	0	4	.167	.167	.167	-7	-2	0-0	.900	1	165	328	2b2,D2	0	-0.1
Total	10	1071	3700	523	970	177	30	75	391	428-22	17	606	.262	.339	.387	99	5	113-55	.978	7	102	92	2b1000,S24,D6	21	7.2
BERNHARDT, JUAN	Juan Ramon (Coradin); B8.31.1953 San Pedro de Macoris, D.R.; BR/TR/5´11˝/175; d7.10																								
1976	NY A	10	21	1	4	1	0	0	1	0-0	0	4	.190	.190	.238	25	-2	0-0	.800	-1	77	0	O4(1/0/3)/3D	0	-0.3
1977	Sea A	89	305	32	74	9	2	7	30	5-0	2	26	.243	.259	.354	66	-16	2-3	.982	1	102	28	D54,3b21,1b8	15	-1.8
1978	Sea A	54	165	13	38	9	0	2	12	9-1	1	10	.230	.270	.321	67	-7	1-1	.989	0	151	87	1b25,3b22,D2	0	-1.0
1979	Sea A	1	1	0	1	0	0	0	0	0-0	0	0	1.000	1.000	1.000	432	0	0-0	ø	0	—	—	/H	0	0.0
Total	4	154	492	46	117	19	2	9	43	14-1	3	40	.238	.261	.339	65	-25	3-4	.965	0	94	26	D58,3b44,1b33,O4(1/0/3)	15	-3.1
BERNIER, CARLOS	Carlos (Rodriguez); B1.28.1927 Juana Diaz, PR; D4.6.1989 Juana Diaz, PR; BR/TR/5´9˝/180; d4.22																								
1953	Pit N	105	310	48	66	7	8	3	31	51	4	53	.213	.332	.316	70	-13	15-14	.970	3	107	111	O86(11/57/18)	0	-1.5
BERO, JOHNNY	John George; B12.22.1922 Gary WV; D5.11.1985 Gardena CA; BL/TR/6´0˝/170; d9.26; Col Western Michigan																								
1948	Det A	4	9	2	0	0	0	0	0	1	0	1	.000	.100	.000	-70	-2	0-0	1.000	-1	59	0	2b2	0	-0.3
1951	StL A	61	160	24	34	5	0	5	17	26	0	30	.213	.323	.338	76	-5	1-1	.954	-7	97	73	S55/2	0	-0.9
Total	2	65	169	26	34	5	0	5	17	27	0	31	.201	.311	.320	69	-7	1-1	.954	-8	97	73	S55,2b3	0	-1.2
BERRA, DALE	Dale Anthony; B12.13.1956 Ridgewood NJ; BR/TR/6´0˝/(180–190); [PitN75 1/20]; d8.22; f–Yogi																								
1977	Pit N	17	40	0	7	1	0	0	3	1-0	0	8	.175	.195	.200	6	-5	0-0	.973	-0	88	62	3b14	0	-0.6
1978	Pit N	56	135	16	28	2	0	6	14	13-3	2	20	.207	.285	.356	75	-5	3-1	.908	-5	91	161	3b55,S2	0	-1.1
1979	Pit N	44	123	11	26	5	0	3	15	11-2	0	17	.211	.272	.325	60	-7	0-0	.940	-7	86	101	S22,3b22	0	-1.3
1980	Pit N	93	245	21	54	8	2	6	31	16-6	1	52	.220	.269	.343	68	-11	2-0	.968	-11	98	138	3b48,S45,2b4	0	-2.0
1981	Pit N	81	232	21	56	12	0	2	27	17-4	3	34	.241	.302	.319	72	-8	11-1	.976	-6	100	114	3b42,S30,2b18	0	-1.0
1982	Pit N	156	529	64	139	25	5	10	61	33-12	4	83	.263	.306	.386	90	-8	6-6	.961	5	103	90	S153,3b6	0	1.3
1983	Pit N	161	537	51	135	25	1	10	52	61-**19**	0	84	.251	.327	.358	87	-8	8-5	.963	14	100	108	S161	0	2.4
1984	Pit N	136	450	31	100	16	0	9	52	34-8	1	78	.222	.273	.318	67	-21	1-3	.955	-2	103	86	S135/3	15	-1.0
1985	NY A	48	109	8	25	5	1	1	8	7-0	0	20	.229	.276	.321	64	-6	1-1	.917	2	107	160	3b41,S6	0	-0.4
1986	NY A	42	108	10	25	7	0	2	13	9-0	1	14	.231	.294	.352	76	-4	0-0	.972	-0	93	88	S19,3b18,D4	0	-0.2
1987	Hou N	19	45	3	8	3	0	0	2	8-3	0	12	.178	.296	.244	49	-3	0-0	.963	-2	96	53	S18,2b3	0	-0.4
Total	11	853	2553	236	603	109	9	49	278	210-57	12	422	.236	.294	.344	76	-86	32-17	.959	-12	99	92	S591,3b247,2b25,D4	15	-4.3
BERRA, YOGI	Lawrence Peter; B5.12.1925 St.Louis MO; BL/TR/5´8˝/(183–194); d9.22; M7/C20; HF1972; s–Dale																								
1946	NY A	7	22	3	8	1	0	2	4	1	0	1	.364	.391	.682	193	2	0-0	1.000	2	*94*	*187*	C6	0	0.4
1947	†NY A	83	293	41	82	15	3	11	54	13	0	12	.280	.310	.464	115	3	0-1	.972	-5	*86*	*55*	C51,O24(12/0/12)	0	0.0
1948	NY A☆	125	469	70	143	24	10	14	98	25	1	24	.305	.341	.488	120	9	3-3	.979	-2	*92*	*115*	C71,O50R	0	0.8
1949	†NY A★	116	415	59	115	20	2	20	91	22	6	25	.277	.323	.480	111	2	2-1	.989	10	*81*	*108*	C109	0	1.7
1950	†NY A★	151	597	116	192	30	6	28	124	55	4	12	.322	.383	.533	136	29	4-2	.985	4	*128*	*103*	C148	0	3.8
1951	†NY A★	141	547	92	161	19	4	27	88	44	3	20	.294	.350	.492	131	19	5-4	.984	9	*115*	*124*	C141	0	3.5
1952	†NY A★	142	534	97	146	17	1	30	98	66	4	24	.273	.358	.478	139	26	2-3	.992	1	*93*	*102*	C140	0	3.5
1953	†NY A★	137	503	80	149	23	5	27	108	50	3	32	.296	.363	.523	142	27	0-3	.986	7	*122*	*85*	C133	0	3.8
1954	NY A★	151	584	88	179	28	6	22	125	56	4	29	.307	.367	.488	139	29	0-1	.990	7	***132***	*97*	C149/3	0	4.4
1955	†NY A★	147	541	84	147	20	3	27	108	60-6	7	20	.272	.349	.470	121	14	1-0	.984	4	***134***	*76*	C145	0	2.5
1956	†NY A★	140	521	93	155	29	2	30	105	65-7	5	29	.298	.378	.534	144	32	3-2	.986	6	*125*	*95*	C135/lf	0	4.3
1957	†NY A★	134	482	74	121	14	2	24	82	57-10	1	24	.251	.329	.438	110	6	1-2	.995	12	117	121	C121,O6(5/0/1)	0	2.3
1958	†NY A★	122	433	60	115	17	3	22	90	35-5	2	35	.266	.319	.471	120	10	3-0	**1.000**	10	103	**130**	C88,O21R,1b2	0	2.5
1959	NY A★	131	472	64	134	25	1	19	69	43-5	4	38	.284	.347	.462	125	16	1-2	**.997**	12	120	98	C116,O7(1/0/6)	0	3.3
1960	†NY A★	120	359	46	99	14	1	15	62	38-6	3	23	.276	.347	.446	120	10	2-1	.989	-2	120	99	C63,O36(20/0/17)	0	0.8
1961	†NY A★	119	395	62	107	11	0	22	61	35-4	2	28	.271	.330	.466	117	8	2-0	.988	4	103	114	O87(81/0/8),C15	0	0.8
1962	†NY A★	86	232	25	52	8	0	10	35	24-4	2	18	.224	.297	.388	87	-5	0-1	.990	5	154	83	C31,O28L	0	0.0
1963	†NY A	64	147	20	43	6	0	8	28	15-2	1	17	.293	.360	.497	139	8	1-0	.988	8	81	56	C35	0	1.8
1965	NY N	4	9	1	2	0	0	0	0	0-0	0	3	.222	.222	.222	27	-1	0-0	.941	0	49	0	C2	0	0.0
Total	19	2120	7555	1175	2150	321	49	358	1430	704-49	52	414	.285	.348	.482	126	244	30-26	.989	91	*114*	*101*	C1699,O260(148/0/115),1b2/3	0	40.2
BERRAN, DENNIS	Dennis Martin; B10.8.1887 Merrimac MA; D4.28.1943 Boston MA; BL/TL; d8.11																								
1912	Chi A	2	4	1	1	0	0	0	0	0	0	—	.250	.250	.250	44	0	0	1.000	-0	66	0	O2L	—	-0.1

YEAR	TM LG	G	AB	R	H	2B	3B	HR	RBI	BB-IB	HP	SO	AVG	OBP	SLG	AOPS	ABR	SB-CS	FA	FR	RNG	THR	GAMES AT POSITION	DL	BFW
Berres, Ray	Raymond Frederick; B8.31.1907 Kenosha WI; BR/TR/5´9˝/170; d4.24; C20																								
1934	Bro N	39	79	7	17	4	0	0	3	1	0	16	.215	.225	.266	32	-8	0	.969	-2	93	134	C37	—	-0.8
1936	Bro N	105	267	16	64	10	1	1	13	14	1	35	.240	.280	.296	55	-17	1	.988	10	65	125	C105	—	-0.3
1937	Pit N	2	6	0	1	0	0	0	0	0	0	0	.167	.167	.167	-9	-1	0	1.000	0	67	173	C2	—	0.0
1938	Pit N	40	100	7	23	2	0	0	6	8	0	10	.230	.287	.250	48	-7	0	.993	3	98	139	C40	—	-0.2
1939	Pit N	81	231	22	53	6	1	0	16	11	1	25	.229	.267	.264	44	-19	1	.993	0	112	88	C80	—	-1.5
1940	Pit N	21	32	2	6	0	0	0	2	1	0	1	.188	.212	.188	11	-4	0	.980	1	69	178	C21	—	-0.3
	Bos N	85	229	12	44	4	1	0	14	18	0	19	.192	.251	.218	32	-22	0	.981	1	102	121	C85	—	-1.7
	Year	106	261	14	50	4	1	0	16	19	0	20	.192	.246	.215	29	-26	0	.981	2	98	128	C106	—	-2.0
1941	Bos N	120	279	21	56	10	0	1	19	17	0	20	.201	.247	.247	41	-22	2	**.995**	4	93	117	C120	0	-1.3
1942	NY N	12	32	0	6	0	0	0	1	2	0	3	.188	.235	.188	24	-3	0	.973	-1	147	40	C12	0	-0.4
1943	NY N	20	28	1	4	1	0	0	0	1	0	2	.143	.172	.179	1	-4	0	.981	2	90	187	C17	0	-0.2
1944	NY N	16	17	4	8	0	0	1	2	1	1	0	.471	.526	.647	230	3	0	1.000	0	112	241	C12	0	0.4
1945	NY N	20	30	4	5	0	0	0	2	2	0	3	.167	.219	.167	8	-4	0	1.000	1	187	41	C20	0	-0.2
Total	11	561	1330	96	287	37	3	3	78	76	3	134	.216	.260	.255	43	-108	4	.989	19	95	118	C551	0	-6.5
Berroa, Angel	Angel Maria (Selmo); B1.27.1978 Santo Domingo, D.R.; BR/TR/6´0˝/(175–190); d9.18																								
2001	KC A	15	53	8	16	2	0	0	4	3-0	0	10	.302	.339	.340	72	-2	2-0	.953	1	114	108	S14	0	0.1
2002	KC A	20	75	8	17	7	1	0	5	7-1	1	10	.227	.301	.347	64	-4	3-0	.964	4	116	92	S20	0	0.2
2003	KC A	158	567	92	163	28	7	17	73	29-3	18	100	.287	.338	.451	100	-1	21-5	.968	3	105	98	S158	0	1.6
2004	KC A	134	512	72	134	27	6	8	43	23-0	12	87	.262	.308	.385	79	-17	14-8	.955	-4	100	105	S133	15	-0.9
2005	KC A	159	608	68	164	21	5	11	55	18-3	14	108	.270	.305	.375	83	-17	7-5	.965	-1	100	93	S159	0	-0.6
2006	KC A	132	474	45	111	18	1	9	54	14-1	3	88	.234	.259	.333	53	-35	3-1	.969	-7	99	102	S131	0	-3.0
Total	6	618	2289	293	605	103	20	45	234	94-8	48	403	.264	.305	.386	80	-76	50-19	.964	-3	102	99	S615	15	-2.6
Berroa, Geronimo	Geronimo Emiliano Letta (b Geronimo Emiliano Letta (Berroa)); B3.18.1965 Santo Domingo, D.R.; BR/TR/6´0˝/(195–210); d4.5																								
1989	Atl N	81	136	7	36	4	0	2	9	7-1	0	32	.265	.301	.338	81	-4	0-1	.971	3	135	72	O34(1/0/33)	0	-0.2
1990	Atl N	7	4	0	0	0	0	0	0	1-1	0	1	.000	.200	.000	-38	-1	0-0	1.000	-0	86	0	O3L	0	-0.1
1992	Cin N	13	15	2	4	1	0	0	0	2-0	1	1	.267	.389	.333	103	0	0-1	1.000	0	50	1067	O3L	0	0.0
1993	Fla N	14	34	3	4	1	0	0	0	2-0	0	7	.118	.167	.147	-14	-6	0-0	.833	-1	63	181	O9(1/0/8)	0	-0.7
1994	Oak A	96	340	55	104	18	2	13	65	41-0	3	62	.306	.379	.485	133	18	7-2	1.000	3	116	169	D44,O42(36/0/7),1b9	10	1.6
1995	Oak A	141	546	87	152	22	3	22	88	63-2	1	98	.278	.351	.451	113	10	7-4	.971	2	105	118	D72,O71(17/0/54)	0	0.5
1996	Oak A	153	586	101	170	32	1	36	106	47-0	4	122	.290	.344	.532	119	15	0-3	.980	-3	80	151	D91,O61(17/0/54)	0	0.4
1997	Oak A	73	261	40	81	12	0	16	42	36-2	1	58	.310	.395	.540	141	16	3-2	.986	-3	87	38	O43R,D32	0	0.9
	†Bal A	83	300	48	78	13	0	10	48	40-2	3	62	.260	.347	.403	100	1	1-2	.959	-2	95	43	D42,O40R	0	-0.6
	Year	156	561	88	159	25	0	26	90	76-4	4	120	.283	.369	.467	119	17	4-4	.955	-5	91	40	O83R,D74	0	0.3
1998	Cle A	20	65	6	13	3	1	0	3	7-0	0	17	.200	.278	.277	43	-6	1-0	1.000	1	104	130	O14L,D5	31	-0.5
	Det A	52	126	17	30	4	1	1	10	17-1	2	27	.238	.338	.310	69	-5	0-1	1.000	-0	101	0	D37,O4(2/0/2)	0	-0.7
	Year	72	191	23	43	7	2	1	13	24-1	2	44	.225	.318	.298	61	-11	1-1	1.000	1	104	113	D42,O18(16/0/2)	0	-1.2
1999	Tor A	22	62	11	12	3	0	1	6	9-0	2	15	.194	.315	.290	55	-4	0-0	1.000	0	111	0	D17,O2L	106	-0.5
2000	LA N	24	31	2	8	0	1	0	5	4-1	0	8	.258	.343	.323	73	-1	0-0	1.000	1	135	0	O6(4/0/2),1b2	123	-0.1
Total	11	779	2506	379	692	113	9	101	382	276-10	17	510	.276	.349	.449	109	33	19-16	.977	0	99	112	D340,O332(100/0/243),1b11	270	0.0
Berry, Ken	Allen Kent; B5.10.1941 Kansas City MO; BR/TR/5´11˝/(180–183); d9.9; Col Wichita St.																								
1962	Chi A	3	6	2	2	0	0	0	0	0-0	0	0	.333	.333	.333	80	0	0-0	1.000	1	120	1134	O2(1/1/1)	0	0.1
1963	Chi A	4	5	2	1	0	0	0	0	1-0	0	1	.200	.333	.200	55	0	0-0	.857	0	199	0	O2L/2	0	0.0
1964	Chi A	12	32	4	12	1	0	1	4	5-0	0	3	.375	.459	.500	171	3	0-1	1.000	-2	62	0	O12C	0	0.0
1965	Chi A	157	472	51	103	17	4	12	42	28-5	5	96	.218	.268	.347	79	-15	4-2	.980	-2	101	96	O156C	0	-2.3
1966	Chi A	147	443	50	120	20	2	8	34	28-4	2	63	.271	.316	.379	106	3	7-10	.991	-3	88	127	O141(101/13/41)	0	-1.0
1967	Chi A★	147	485	49	117	14	4	7	41	46-4	3	68	.241	.310	.330	93	-5	9-8	.992	-6	88	97	O143(50/38/86)	0	-2.2
1968	Chi A	153	504	49	127	21	2	7	32	25-1	1	64	.252	.288	.343	90	-7	6-6	.981	-2	98	108	O151(0/149/2)	0	-1.7
1969	Chi A	130	297	25	69	12	2	4	18	24-5	3	50	.232	.296	.327	71	-12	1-2	**1.000**	1	101	121	O120(2/116/2)	0	-1.5
1970	Chi A	141	463	45	128	12	2	7	50	43-10	6	61	.276	.344	.356	91	-5	6-4	.988	-1	102	103	O138C	0	-1.0
1971	Cal A	111	298	29	66	17	0	3	22	18-0	3	33	.221	.269	.309	69	-13	3-2	.988	4	111	91	O101(8/94/0)	15	-1.3
1972	Cal A	119	409	41	118	15	3	5	39	35-2	2	47	.289	.347	.377	122	11	5-3	**1.000**	8	106	**191**	O116C	0	1.8
1973	Cal A	136	415	48	118	11	2	3	36	26-0	1	50	.284	.327	.342	96	-3	1-6	**.997**	4	113	63	O129(15/111/4)	0	-0.5
1974	Mil A	98	267	21	64	9	2	1	24	18-0	3	26	.240	.295	.300	72	-10	3-1	.995	5	107	169	O82(5/74/5),D13	0	-0.7
1975	Cle A	25	40	6	8	1	0	0	1	1-0	1	7	.200	.238	.225	31	-4	0-1	.926	1	111	130	O18L,D5	0	-0.4
Total	14	1383	4136	422	1053	150	23	58	343	298-31	30	569	.255	.308	.344	90	-57	45-46	.989	8	100	114	O1311(202/1018/141),D18/2	15	-10.7
Berry, Charlie	Charles Francis; B10.18.1902 Phillipsburg NJ; D9.6.1972 Evanston IL; BR/TR/6´0˝/185; d6.15; C5/U21; f–Charlie; Col Lafayette																								
1925	Phi A	10	14	1	3	1	0	0	3	0	0	2	.214	.214	.286	24	-2	0-0	.900	-1	122	0	C4	—	-0.2
1928	Bos A	80	177	18	46	7	3	1	19	21	1	19	.260	.342	.350	84	-4	1-1	.959	-8	73	132	C63	—	-0.9
1929	Bos A	77	207	19	50	11	4	1	21	15	3	29	.242	.302	.348	69	-10	2-6	.983	3	106	130	C72	—	-0.5
1930	Bos A	88	256	31	74	9	6	6	35	16	0	22	.289	.331	.441	98	-2	2-0	.988	8	***165***	104	C85	—	1.0
1931	Bos A	111	357	41	101	16	2	6	49	29	0	38	.283	.337	.389	96	-3	4-0	.985	-0	116	98	C102	—	0.4
1932	Bos A	10	32	0	6	3	0	0	6	3	0	2	.188	.257	.281	40	-3	0-0	.944	-1	66	105	C10	—	-0.3
	Chi A	72	226	33	69	15	6	4	31	21	0	23	.305	.364	.478	124	8	3-0	.981	-2	81	156	C70	—	1.0
	Year	82	258	33	75	18	6	4	37	24	0	25	.291	.351	.453	114	5	3-0	.977	-3	79	***150***	C80	—	0.7
1933	Chi A	86	271	25	69	8	3	2	28	17	1	16	.255	.301	.328	70	-13	0-0	.987	-10	84	76	C83	—	-1.7
1934	Phi A	99	269	14	72	10	2	0	34	22	0	23	.268	.323	.320	69	-13	1-0	.987	-2	86	110	C99	—	-0.9
1935	Phi A	62	190	14	48	7	3	3	29	10	0	20	.253	.290	.368	70	-10	0-0	.987	-1	72	145	C56	—	-0.8
1936	Phi A	13	17	0	1	1	0	0	1	6	0	2	.059	.304	.118	8	-2	0-0	.971	-0	77	117	C12	—	-0.2
1938	Phi A	1	2	0	0	0	0	0	0	0	0	0	.000	.000	.000	-99	-1	0-0	1.000	0	0	857	/C	—	0.0
Total	11	709	2018	196	539	88	29	23	256	160	5	196	.267	.322	.374	83	-55	13-7	.982	-14	101	115	C657	—	-3.1
Berry, Charlie	Charles Joseph; B9.6.1860 Elizabeth NJ; D1.22.1940 Phillipsburg NJ; BR/TR/5´11˝/175; d4.30; s–Charlie																								
1884	Alt U	7	25	2	6	0	0	0	—	0	—	—	.240	.240	.240	45	-2	—	.862	-5	54	0	2b7	—	-0.6
	KC U	29	118	15	29	6	1	1	—	1	—	—	.246	.252	.339	89	-5	—	.887	1	102	83	2b22,O8(1/7/0)/3	—	-0.3
	CP U	7	27	4	3	2	0	0	—	0	—	—	.111	.111	.185	-12	-4	—	.833	-0	95	46	2b7	—	-0.4
	Year	43	170	21	38	8	1	1	—	1	—	—	.224	.228	.300	64	-13	—	.871	-4	92	59	2b36,O8(1/7/0)/3	—	-1.3
Berry, Claude	Claude Elzy "Admiral"; B2.14.1880 Losantville IN; D2.1.1974 Richmond IN; BR/TR/5´7˝/165; d4.22																								
1904	Chi A	3	1	1	0	0	0	0	0	1	0	—	.000	.500	.000	68	0	0	1.000	0	0	175	C3	—	0.1
1906	Phi A	10	30	2	7	0	0	0	2	2	0	—	.233	.281	.233	60	-1	1	.938	3	107	180	C10	—	0.3
1907	Phi A	8	19	2	4	2	0	0	1	2	0	—	.211	.286	.316	90	0	0	.944	-2	84	64	C8	—	-0.1
1914	Pit F	124	411	35	98	18	9	2	36	26	0	50	.238	.284	.341	70	-26	6	.970	1	103	101	C122	—	-1.5
1915	Pit F	100	292	32	56	11	1	1	26	29	2	42	.192	.269	.247	46	-25	7	.980	6	116	101	C99	—	-1.2
Total	5	245	753	72	165	31	10	3	65	60	2	92	.219	.279	.299	61	-52	14	.971	8	108	104	C242	—	-2.4
Berry, Neil	Cornelius John; B1.11.1922 Kalamazoo MI; BR/TR/5´10˝/170; d4.20; Col Western Michigan																								
1948	Det A	87	256	46	68	8	1	0	16	37	0	23	.266	.358	.305	75	-8	1-3	.930	-1	98	113	S41,2b26	0	-0.6
1949	Det A	109	329	38	78	9	1	0	18	27	2	24	.237	.299	.271	51	-24	4-2	.970	-8	93	86	2b95,S4	0	-2.6
1950	Det A	39	40	9	10	1	0	0	7	6	0	11	.250	.348	.275	59	-2	0-0	.944	2	100	181	S12,2b2/3	0	0.0
1951	Det A	67	157	17	36	5	2	0	9	10	0	15	.229	.275	.287	52	-11	4-2	.944	3	112	81	S38,2b10,3b7	0	-0.6
1952	Det A	73	189	22	43	4	3	0	13	22	1	19	.228	.311	.280	65	-9	1-3	.965	3	105	78	S66,3b2	0	-0.4
1953	StL A	57	99	14	28	1	2	0	11	9	0	10	.283	.343	.333	82	-3	1-2	.825	-3	77	35	3b18,2b15,S6	0	-0.5
	Chi A	5	8	1	1	0	0	0	0	1	0	1	.125	.222	.125	-4	-1	0-0	1.000	1	162	63	2b3	0	0.0
	Year	62	107	15	29	1	2	0	11	10	0	11	.271	.333	.318	75	-4	1-2	.825	-2	77	35	3b18,2b18,S6	0	-0.5
1954	Bal A	5	9	1	1	0	0	0	0	1	0	2	.111	.200	.111	-14	-1	0-0	1.000	0	90	113	S5	0	-0.1
Total	7	442	1087	148	265	28	9	0	74	113	3	105	.244	.317	.286	62	-59	11-12	.949	-4	105	95	S172,2b151,3b28	0	-4.8

YEAR	TM LG	G	AB	R	H	2B	3B	HR	RBI	BB-IB	HP	SO	AVG	OBP	SLG	AOPS	ABR	SB-CS	FA	FR	RNG	THR	GAMES AT POSITION	DL	BFW
BERRY, HOWARD	Joseph Howard Jr. "Nig"; B12.31.1894 Philadelphia PA; D4.29.1976 Philadelphia PA; BB/TR/5´10.5˝/159; d7.18; f–Howard; Col Penn																								
1921	NY N	9	6	0	2	0	1	0	2	1	0	1	.333	.429	.667	185	1	0-0	.875	0	155	0	2b7	—	0.1
1922	NY N	6	0	0	0	0	0	0	0	0	0	0	ø	ø	ø	ø	0	0-0	ø	0	—	—	/R	—	0.0
Total	2	15	6	0	2	0	1	0	2	1	0	1	.333	.429	.667	185	1	0-0	.875	0	155	0	2b7	—	0.1
BERRY, HOWARD	Joseph Howard Sr. "Hodge"; B9.10.1872 Wheeling WV; D3.13.1961 Allenwood NJ; BB/TR/5´9˝/172; d9.4; s–Howard																								
1902	Phi N	1	4	0	1	0	0	0	1	1	0	—	.250	.400	.250	101	0	1	1.000	-1	*57*	*0*	/C	—	-0.1
BERRY, SEAN	Sean Robert; B3.22.1966 Santa Monica CA; BR/TR/5´11˝/(200–210); [KCA86*S1/9]; d9.17; C1; Col UCLA																								
1990	KC A	8	23	2	5	1	1	0	4	2-0	0	5	.217	.280	.348	76	-1	0-0	.944	-0	78	148	3b8	0	-0.1
1991	KC A	31	60	5	8	3	0	0	1	5-0	1	23	.133	.212	.183	10	-7	0-0	.970	5	134	73	3b30	0	-0.2
1992	Mon N	24	57	5	19	1	0	1	4	1-0	0	11	.333	.345	.404	112	1	2-1	.879	-3	73	45	3b20	0	-0.3
1993	Mon N	122	299	50	78	15	2	14	49	41-6	2	70	.261	.348	.465	112	6	12-2	.936	1	101	105	3b96	0	0.9
1994	Mon N	103	320	43	89	19	2	11	41	32-7	3	50	.278	.347	.453	106	3	14-0	.938	-10	84	78	3b100	0	-0.3
1995	Mon N	103	314	38	100	22	1	14	55	25-1	2	53	.318	.367	.529	129	13	3-8	.947	2	97	153	3b83,1b3	0	1.3
1996	Hou N	132	431	55	121	38	1	17	95	23-1	9	58	.281	.328	.492	122	13	12-6	.922	-1	99	76	3b110	0	1.3
1997	†Hou N	96	301	37	77	24	1	8	43	25-1	5	53	.256	.318	.422	96	-2	1-5	.921	-1	102	94	3b85,D3	30	-0.4
1998	†Hou N	102	299	48	94	17	1	13	52	31-3	7	50	.314	.387	.508	138	17	3-1	.953	-0	97	105	3b87/D	0	1.7
1999	Mil N	106	259	26	59	11	1	2	23	17-0	3	50	.228	.281	.301	48	-21	0-0	.989	-3	80	109	1b64	0	-2.8
2000	Mil N	32	46	1	7	2	0	1	2	4-0	0	13	.152	.220	.261	21	-6	0-1	1.000	-3	36	82	3b9	0	-0.9
	Bos A	1	4	0	0	0	0	0	0	0-0	0	2	.000	.000	.000	-97	-1	0-0	ø	-1	0	0	/3	0	-0.2
Total	11	860	2413	310	657	153	10	81	369	206-19	32	438	.272	.334	.445	104	15	47-24	.937	-15	96	98	3b629,1b67,D4	30	-0.0
BERRY, TOM	Thomas Haney; B12.31.1842 Chester PA; D6.6.1915 Chester PA; 5´6˝/140; d9.2																								
1871	Ath NA	1	4	0	1	0	0	0	0	0	—	0	.250	.250	.250	45	0	0-0	.000	-0	0	0	/rf	—	0.0
BERRYHILL, DAMON	Damon Scott; B12.3.1963 South Laguna CA; BB/TR/6´0˝/(205–210); [ChiN84*1/4]; d9.5; Col Orange Coast (CA) JC																								
1987	Chi N	12	28	2	5	1	0	0	1	3-0	0	5	.179	.258	.214	26	-3	0-1	.909	-5	80	34	C11	0	-0.8
1988	Chi N	95	309	19	80	19	1	7	38	17-5	0	56	.259	.295	.395	93	-3	1-0	.982	-0	113	**149**	C90	15	0.2
1989	Chi N	91	334	37	86	13	0	5	41	16-4	2	54	.257	.291	.341	76	-11	1-0	.992	0	179	90	C89	69	-0.6
1990	Chi N	17	53	6	10	4	0	1	9	5-1	0	14	.189	.254	.321	55	-3	0-0	.978	-2	109	37	C15	128	-0.5
1991	Chi N	62	159	13	30	7	0	5	14	11-1	1	41	.189	.244	.327	57	-9	1-2	.967	-7	101	61	C48	0	-1.5
	Atl N	1	1	0	0	0	0	0	0	0-0	0	1	.000	.000	.000	-95	0	0-0	1.000	0	0	0	/C	0	0.0
	Year	63	160	13	30	7	0	5	14	11-1	1	42	.188	.243	.325	56	-10	1-2	.967	-7	100	60	C49	0	-1.5
1992	†Atl N	101	307	21	70	16	1	10	43	17-4	1	67	.228	.268	.384	79	-9	0-2	.998	-9	83	71	C84	0	-1.5
1993	†Atl N	115	335	24	82	18	2	8	43	21-1	2	64	.245	.291	.382	77	-11	0-0	.990	8	105	92	C105	0	0.2
1994	Bos A	82	255	30	67	17	2	6	34	19-0	0	59	.263	.312	.416	82	-7	0-1	.995	-1	70	111	C67,D6	0	-0.4
1995	Cin N	34	82	6	15	3	0	2	11	10-2	0	19	.183	.260	.293	48	-6	0-0	.988	1	109	80	C29/1	39	-0.4
1997	†SF N	73	167	17	43	8	0	3	23	20-5	0	29	.257	.335	.359	84	-4	0-0	.990	1	101	112	C51/1	38	0.0
Total	10	683	2030	175	488	106	6	47	257	139-23	6	409	.240	.288	.368	77	-66	3-6	.988	-14	111	96	C590,D6,1b2	289	-5.3
BERTE, HARRY	Harry Thomas; B5.10.1872 Covington KY; D5.6.1952 Los Angeles CA; TR/5´10˝/160; d9.17																								
1903	StL N	4	15	1	5	0	0	0	1	1	0	—	.333	.375	.333	106	0	0	.778	-3	67	137	2b3/S	—	-0.3
BERTELL, DICK	Richard George; B11.21.1935 Oak Park IL; D12.20.1999 Mission Viejo CA; BR/TR/6´0.5˝/200; d9.22; Col Iowa St.; [DL 1966 SF N 67]																								
1960	Chi N	5	15	0	2	0	0	0	2	3-0	0	1	.133	.263	.133	17	-2	0-0	1.000	-1	68	146	C5	0	-0.3
1961	Chi N	92	267	20	73	7	1	2	33	15-3	0	33	.273	.308	.330	70	-12	0-0	.982	3	113	111	C90	0	-0.5
1962	Chi N	77	215	19	65	6	2	2	18	13-5	1	30	.302	.343	.377	90	-3	0-1	.986	-10	71	115	C76	0	-1.0
1963	Chi N	100	322	15	75	7	2	2	14	24-6	0	41	.233	.284	.286	62	-16	0-2	.988	17	**137**	**162**	C99	0	0.6
1964	Chi N	112	353	29	84	11	3	4	35	33-8	2	67	.238	.305	.320	74	-12	2-1	.981	-3	137	132	C110	0	-1.0
1965	Chi N	34	84	6	18	2	0	0	7	11-2	0	10	.214	.302	.238	54	-5	0-0	.981	1	113	217	C34	0	-0.3
	SF N	22	48	1	9	1	0	0	3	7-3	0	5	.188	.291	.208	42	-3	0-0	.992	0	66	95	C22	0	-0.3
	Year	56	132	7	27	3	0	0	10	18-5	0	15	.205	.298	.227	50	-8	0-0	.986	1	96	172	C56	0	-0.6
1967	Chi N	2	6	1	1	0	1	0	0	0-0	0	1	.167	.167	.500	80	0	0-0	1.000	0	0	0	C2	0	0.0
Total	7	444	1310	91	327	34	9	10	112	106-27	3	188	.250	.305	.312	70	-53	2-4	.985	7	116	137	C438	67	-2.8
BERTHRONG, HARRY	Henry Washburn; B1.1.1844 Mumford NY; D4.28.1928 Chelsea MA; TR/5´6.5˝/140; d5.5																								
1871	Oly NA	17	73	17	17	1	1	0	8	4	—	2	.233	.273	.274	61	-3	3-1	.806	-4	0	0	O12(11/1/0),2b5/C	—	-0.4
BERTOIA, RENO	Reno Peter; B1.8.1935 St.Vito Udine, Italy; BR/TR/5´11.5˝/185; d9.22																								
1953	Det A	1	1	0	0	0	0	0	0	0	0	1	.000	.000	.000	-99	0	0-0	.500	-1	0	0	/2	0	-0.1
1954	Det A	54	37	13	6	2	0	1	2	5	0	9	.162	.262	.297	54	-2	1-0	.969	8	175	109	2b15,3b8,S3	0	0.6
1955	Det A	38	68	13	14	2	1	1	10	5-1	0	11	.206	.253	.309	54	-5	0-0	.923	3	113	196	3b14,2b6,S5	0	-0.1
1956	Det A	22	66	7	12	2	0	1	5	6-0	1	12	.182	.260	.258	37	-6	0-0	.982	5	111	122	2b18,3b2	0	0.0
1957	Det A	97	295	28	81	16	2	4	28	19-2	4	43	.275	.326	.383	91	-4	2-3	.953	-23	76	56	3b83,S7,2b2	0	-2.8
1958	Det A	86	240	28	56	6	0	6	27	20-2	2	35	.233	.290	.333	68	-10	5-2	.950	3	108	104	3b68,S5/lf	0	-0.7
1959	Was A	90	308	33	73	10	0	8	29	29-3	1	48	.237	.302	.347	79	-9	2-5	.971	-7	101	83	2b71,3b5/S	0	-1.2
1960	Was A	121	460	44	122	17	7	4	45	26-2	8	58	.265	.313	.359	83	-12	3-5	.961	-5	100	80	3b112,2b21	0	-1.9
1961	Min A	35	104	17	22	2	0	1	8	20-1	0	12	.212	.333	.260	59	-5	0-0	.900	-6	86	46	3b32	0	-1.2
	KC A	39	120	12	29	2	0	0	13	9-0	0	15	.242	.286	.258	48	-9	1-0	.942	4	118	93	3b29,2b6	0	-0.5
	Det A	24	46	6	10	1	0	1	4	3-0	0	8	.217	.265	.304	50	-3	2-0	.931	-2	77	100	3b13,2b7/S	0	-0.5
	Year	98	270	35	61	5	0	2	25	32-1	0	35	.226	.302	.267	53	-18	3-0	.923	-4	97	73	3b74,2b13/S	0	-2.2
1962	Det A	5	0	3	0	0	0	0	0	0-0	0	0	ø	ø	ø	ø	0	0-0	1.000	0	162	0	/2S3	0	0.0
Total	10	612	1745	204	425	60	10	27	171	142-11	16	252	.244	.303	.336	73	-65	16-15	.949	-20	96	82	3b367,2b148,S23/lf	0	-8.4
BESCHER, BOB	Robert Henry; B2.25.1884 London OH; D11.29.1942 London OH; BB/TL/6´1˝/200; d9.5; Col Wittenberg																								
1908	Cin N	32	114	16	31	5	5	0	17	9	2	—	.272	.336	.404	140	5	10	1.000	3	46	190	O32L	—	0.6
1909	Cin N	124	446	73	107	17	6	1	34	56	8	—	.240	.335	.312	102	3	**54**	.953	0	85	105	O117(115/0/2)	—	-0.4
1910	Cin N	150	589	95	147	20	10	4	48	81	4	75	.250	.344	.338	104	4	**70**	.947	2	108	81	O150L	—	-0.3
1911	Cin N	153	599	106	165	32	10	1	45	102	5	78	.275	.385	.367	115	18	**81**	.954	-8	87	95	O153L	—	0.3
1912	Cin N	145	548	**120**	154	29	11	4	38	83	6	61	.281	.381	.396	116	16	**67**	.963	2	**110**	68	O143L	—	1.1
1913	Cin N	141	511	86	132	22	11	1	37	**94**	3	68	.258	.377	.350	109	11	38-23	.968	4	100	119	O138L	—	1.0
1914	NY N	135	512	82	138	23	4	6	35	45	6	48	.270	.336	.365	112	8	36	.960	1	103	90	O126(15/111/0)	—	0.0
1915	StL N	130	486	71	128	15	7	4	34	52	6	53	.263	.342	.348	109	6	27-19	.971	-2	100	78	O129(128/0/1)	—	-0.2
1916	StL N	151	561	78	132	24	8	6	43	60	6	50	.235	.316	.339	102	2	39-12	.953	-0	98	114	O151(151/2/1)	—	0.0
1917	StL N	42	110	10	17	1	1	1	8	20	1	13	.155	.290	.209	56	-5	3	.984	-5	88	0	O32(27/4/0)	—	-1.3
1918	Cle A	25	60	12	20	2	1	0	6	17	1	5	.333	.487	.400	153	6	3	.969	0	92	135	O17(0/3/14)	—	0.5
Total	11	1228	4536	749	1171	190	74	28	345	619	48	<u>451</u>	.258	.353	.351	109	74	428-<u>54</u>	.960	-3	97	94	O1188(1052/120/18)	—	1.3
BESTICK, WILLIAM	William; B New York NY; d6.20																								
1872	Eck NA	4	14	0	4	0	0	0	0	0	—	0	.286	.286	.286	90	0	0-0	.760	-2	—	—	C4/S	—	-0.1
BESWICK, JIM	James William; B2.12.1958 Wilkinsburg PA; BB/TR/6´1˝/180; [SDN76 5/101]; d8.9																								
1978	SD N	17	20	2	1	0	0	0	0	1-0	0	7	.050	.095	.050	-63	-4	0-0	1.000	-0	99	0	O6(0/2/4)	0	-0.5
BETANCOURT, YUNIESKY	Yuniesky (Perez); B1.31.1982 Santa Clara, Cuba; BR/TR/5´10˝/190; d7.28																								
2005	Sea A	60	211	24	54	11	5	1	15	11-0	2	24	.256	.296	.370	83	-6	1-3	.978	-3	93	102	S53,2b9	0	-0.6
2006	Sea A	157	558	68	161	28	6	8	47	17-0	1	54	.289	.310	.403	88	-12	11-8	.971	-7	94	93	S157	0	-0.7
Total	2	217	769	92	215	39	11	9	62	28-0	3	78	.280	.306	.394	87	-18	12-11	.973	-11	94	95	S210,2b9	0	-1.3
BETCHER, FRANK	Franklin Lyle (b Franklin Lyle Bettger); B2.15.1888 Philadelphia PA; D11.27.1981 Wynnewood PA; BB/TR/5´11˝/173; d5.21																								
1910	StL N	35	89	7	18	2	0	0	6	7	2	14	.202	.276	.225	48	-6	1	.928	0	105	72	S12,3b7,2b6,O2(1/1/0)	—	-0.6

YEAR	TM LG	G	AB	R	H	2B	3B	HR	RBI	BB-IB	HP	SO	AVG	OBP	SLG	AOPS	ABR	SB-CS	FA	FR	RNG	THR	GAMES AT POSITION	DL	BFW
BETEMIT, WILSON	Wilson; B11.2.1981 Santo Domingo, D.R.; BB/TR/6´2˝/(155–200); d9.18																								
2001	Atl N	8	3	1	0	0	0	0	0	2-0	0	3	.000	.400	.000	17	0	1-0	ø	-0	0	0	/S	0	0.0
2004	†Atl N	22	47	2	8	0	0	0	3	4-0	0	16	.170	.231	.170	7	-7	0-1	.933	0	122	95	S11,3b7	0	-0.6
2005	†Atl N	115	246	36	75	12	4	4	20	22-4	0	55	.305	.359	.435	107	2	1-3	.952	-8	98	65	3b63,S25/2	0	-0.5
2006	Atl N	88	199	30	56	16	0	9	29	19-3	0	57	.281	.344	.497	111	3	2-1	.941	1	91	198	3b30,S18,2b10	0	0.5
	†LA N	55	174	19	42	7	0	9	24	17-3	0	45	.241	.306	.437	88	-4	1-0	.964	-3	96	106	3b49/D	0	-0.6
	Year	143	373	49	98	23	0	18	53	36-6	0	102	.263	.326	.469	100	-1	3-1	.957	-2	94	137	3b79,S18,2b10/D	0	-0.1
Total	4	288	669	88	181	35	4	22	76	64-10	0	176	.271	.332	.433	96	-6	5-5	.956	-10	95	112	3b149,S55,2b11/D	0	-1.2
BETHEA, BILL	William Lamar "Spot"; B1.1.1942 Houston TX; BR/TR/6´0˝/175; d9.13; Col Texas																								
1964	Min A	10	30	4	5	1	0	0	2	4-0	0	4	.167	.265	.200	31	-3	0-0	1.000	-2	83	129	2b7,S3	0	-0.4
BETTENCOURT, LARRY	Lawrence Joseph; B9.22.1905 Newark CA; D9.15.1978 New Orleans LA; BR/TR/5´11˝/195; d6.2; Col St. Marys (CA)																								
1928	StL A	67	159	30	45	9	4	4	24	22	2	19	.283	.377	.465	117	4	2-1	.946	-6	88	59	3b41,O2R/C	—	0.0
1931	StL A	74	206	27	53	9	2	3	26	31	1	35	.257	.357	.364	87	-3	4-3	.963	-1	94	118	O58(2/0/56)	—	-0.7
1932	StL A	27	30	4	4	1	0	1	3	7	0	6	.133	.297	.267	45	-2	1-0	1.000	0	122	0	O4(2/0/3),3b2	—	-0.2
Total	3	168	395	61	102	19	6	8	53	60	3	60	.258	.360	.397	95	-1	7-4	.966	-6	95	111	O64(4/0/61),3b43/C	—	-0.9
BETZEL, BRUNO	Christian Frederick Albert John Henry David; B12.6.1894 Chattanooga OH; D2.7.1965 W.Hollywood FL; BR/TR/5´9˝/158; d9.3																								
1914	StL N	7	9	2	0	0	0	0	0	1	0	1	.000	.100	.000	-70	-2	0	1.000	1	157	0	2b4/3	—	-0.1
1915	StL N	117	367	42	92	12	4	0	27	18	3	48	.251	.291	.305	80	-9	10-13	.937	4	112	74	3b105,2b3,S2	—	-0.6
1916	StL N	142	510	49	119	15	11	1	37	39	0	77	.233	.288	.312	85	-10	22-16	.960	**29**	**112**	132	2b113,3b33,O7(1/2/4)	—	2.3
1917	StL N	106	328	24	71	4	3	1	17	20	2	47	.216	.266	.256	62	-15	9	.962	12	113	138	2b75,O23(12/1/9),3b4	—	-0.4
1918	StL N	76	230	18	51	6	7	0	13	12	0	16	.222	.260	.309	76	-8	8	.914	-2	103	60	3b34,O21(1/7/15),2b10	—	-1.2
Total	5	448	1444	135	333	37	25	2	94	90	5	189	.231	.278	.295	76	-44	49-29	.956	44	113	132	2b205,3b177,O51(14/10/28),S2	—	-0.0
BEVACQUA, KURT	Kurt Anthony; B1.23.1947 Miami Beach FL; BR/TR/6´1˝/(180–195); [CinN67 S2/26]; d6.22; Col Miami–Dade North (FL) CC; OF(47/0/25)																								
1971	Cle A	55	137	9	28	3	1	3	13	4-1	0	28	.204	.222	.307	46	-10	0-0	.971	-3	91	53	2b36,O5(2/0/3),3b3,S2	0	-1.3
1972	Cle A	19	35	2	4	0	0	1	1	3-1	0	10	.114	.184	.200	14	-4	0-0	.900	0	65	0	O11(8/0/3)/3	0	-0.5
1973	KC A	99	276	39	71	8	3	2	40	25-1	1	42	.257	.317	.330	78	-8	2-3	.935	-10	81	92	3b40,2b16,D16,O10(5/0/5),1b9	0	-2.0
1974	Pit N	18	35	1	4	1	0	0	0	2-1	0	10	.114	.162	.143	-15	-5	0-0	.955	-2	71	0	3b8/lf	0	-0.8
	KC A	39	90	10	19	0	0	0	3	9-0	1	20	.211	.290	.211	44	-6	1-1	.987	-3	54	154	1b14,3b13,2b7,S2,D3	0	-1.1
1975	Mil A	104	258	30	59	14	0	2	24	26-1	1	45	.229	.300	.306	72	-9	3-4	.948	-6	90	108	3b60,2b32,S5,1b3/D	0	-1.4
1976	Mil A	12	7	3	1	0	0	0	0	0-0	0	0	.143	.143	.143	-16	-1	0-0	1.000	1	257	0	2b2,D3	0	0.0
1977	Tex A	39	96	13	32	7	2	5	28	6-1	0	13	.333	.365	.604	159	7	0-1	1.000	-1	61	0	O14(6/0/8),3b11,1b5,2b5,D3	0	0.6
1978	Tex A	90	248	21	55	12	0	6	30	18-0	0	31	.222	.271	.343	72	-10	1-2	.877	-5	95	88	3b49,D16,2b13/1	0	-1.6
1979	SD N	114	297	23	75	12	4	1	34	38-2	0	25	.253	.331	.330	88	-4	2-5	.954	2	105	135	3b64,2b16,1b8,O8L	0	-0.5
1980	SD N	62	71	4	19	6	1	0	12	6-0	0	1	.268	.321	.380	103	0	1-1	.929	-0	109	127	3b13,O4L,2b2/1	0	0.0
	Pit N	22	43	1	7	1	0	0	4	6-0	1	7	.163	.280	.186	31	-4	0-0	.958	1	117	90	3b9,1b2	0	-0.4
	Year	84	114	5	26	7	1	0	16	12-0	1	8	.228	.305	.307	75	-4	1-1	.947	0	114	105	3b22,O4L,1b3,2b2	0	-0.4
1981	Pit N	29	27	2	7	1	0	1	4	4-0	0	6	.259	.333	.407	110	0	0-0	.941	1	128	214	2b4,3b2	0	0.2
1982	SD N	64	123	15	31	9	0	0	24	17-4	0	22	.252	.333	.325	93	0	2-0	.989	-1	94	72	1b30,O3(2/0/1)/3	0	-0.3
1983	SD N	74	156	17	38	7	0	2	24	18-1	0	33	.244	.320	.327	83	-3	0-3	.995	1	89	93	1b27,3b12,O12(9/0/3)	0	-0.5
1984	†SD N	59	80	7	16	3	0	1	9	14-1	1	19	.200	.326	.275	70	-3	0-0	1.000	-2	87	114	1b20,3b10,O3(1/0/2)	0	-0.6
1985	SD N	71	138	17	33	6	0	3	25	25-5	0	17	.239	.349	.348	98	1	0-0	.946	0	93	145	3b33,1b9/lf	0	0.0
Total	15	970	2117	214	499	90	11	27	275	221-19	5	329	.236	.305	.327	78	-59	12-20	.938	-28	94	121	3b329,2b133,1b129,O72L,D42,S9	0	-10.2
BEVAN, HAL	Harold Joseph; B11.15.1930 New Orleans LA; D10.5.1968 New Orleans LA; BR/TR/6´2˝/198; d4.24																								
1952	Bos A	1	1	0	0	0	0	0	0	0	0	0	.000	.000	.000	-93	0	0-0	ø	-0	0	0	/3	0	0.0
	Phi A	8	17	1	6	0	0	0	4	0	0	1	.353	.353	.353	91	0	2-0	1.000	0	105	0	3b6	106	0.0
	Year	9	18	1	6	0	0	0	4	0	0	1	.333	.333	.333	81	-1	2-0	1.000	0	102	0	3b7	0	0.0
1955	KC A	3	3	0	0	0	0	0	0	0-0	0	0	.000	.000	.000	-99	-1	0-0	1.000	-0	0	0	/3	0	-0.1
1961	Cin N	3	3	1	1	0	0	1	1	0-0	0	2	.333	.333	1.333	311	1	0-0	ø	0	—	—	/H	0	0.1
Total	3	15	24	2	7	0	0	1	5	0-0	0	3	.292	.292	.417	89	0	2-0	1.000	0	97	0	3b8	106	0.0
BEVILLE, MONTE	Henry Monte; B2.24.1875 Dublin IN; D1.24.1955 Grand Rapids MI; BL/TR/5´11˝/180; d4.24																								
1903	NY A	82	258	23	50	14	1	0	29	16	4	—	.194	.252	.256	49	-15	4	.960	-7	*105*	*81*	C75,1b3	—	-1.6
1904	NY A	9	22	2	6	2	0	0	2	2	0	—	.273	.333	.364	115	1	0	.906	-2	56	0	1b4,C3	—	-0.1
	Det A	54	174	14	36	5	1	0	13	8	2	—	.207	.250	.247	59	-8	2	.957	-4	*86*	*82*	C30,1b24	—	-1.1
	Year	63	196	16	42	7	1	0	15	10	2	—	.214	.260	.260	66	-7	2	.950	-5	*86*	*83*	C33,1b28	—	-1.2
Total	2	145	454	39	92	21	2	0	44	26	6	—	.203	.255	.258	56	-22	6	.957	-12	*99*	*82*	C108,1b31	—	-2.8
BIANCALANA, BUDDY	Roland Americo; B2.2.1960 Larkspur CA; BB/TR/5´11˝/(155–160); [KCA78 1/25]; d9.12; [DL 1989 KC A 182]																								
1982	KC A	3	2	0	1	0	1	0	0	1-0	0	0	.500	.667	1.500	471	1	0-0	1.000	2	199	137	S3	0	0.3
1983	KC A	6	15	2	3	0	0	0	0	0-0	0	7	.200	.200	.200	10	-2	1-0	.914	2	138	97	S6	0	0.1
1984	†KC A	66	134	18	26	6	1	2	9	6-0	0	44	.194	.229	.299	44	-11	1-2	.946	-2	116	85	S33,2b29/D	0	-0.9
1985	†KC A	81	138	21	26	5	1	1	6	17-0	0	34	.188	.277	.261	48	-10	1-4	.961	4	110	98	S74,2b4,D2	18	-0.1
1986	KC A	100	190	24	46	4	4	2	8	15-0	0	50	.242	.298	.337	71	-8	5-1	.946	-5	97	102	S89,2b12	0	-0.6
1987	KC A	37	47	4	10	1	0	1	7	1-0	0	10	.213	.229	.298	37	-4	0-0	.886	-3	102	73	S22,2b12/D	15	-0.6
	Hou N	18	24	1	1	0	0	0	0	1-0	0	12	.042	.080	.042	-69	-6	0-0	.889	-2	78	53	S16,2b3	0	-0.8
Total	6	311	550	70	113	16	7	6	30	41-0	0	157	.205	.261	.293	50	-40	8-7	.945	-4	106	95	S243,2b60,D4	215	-2.6
BIANCO, TOMMY	Thomas Anthony; B12.16.1952 Rockville Centre NY; BB/TR/5´11˝/190; [MilA71 1/3]; d5.28																								
1975	Mil A	18	34	6	6	1	0	0	0	3-0	1	7	.176	.263	.206	34	-3	0-0	.941	-0	108	0	3b7,1b5,D2	0	-0.4
BIASATTI, HANK	Henry Arcado; B1.14.1922 Beano, Italy; D4.20.1996 Dearborn MI; BL/TL/5´11˝/175; d4.23																								
1949	Phi A	21	24	6	2	2	0	0	2	8	0	5	.083	.313	.167	30	-2	0-0	.979	-1	59	78	1b8	0	-0.3
BICHETTE, DANTE	Alphonse Dante; B11.18.1963 W.Palm Beach FL; BR/TR/6´3˝/(212–238); [CalA84 17/424]; d9.5; Col Palm Beach (FL) CC																								
1988	Cal A	21	46	1	12	2	0	0	8	0-0	0	7	.261	.240	.304	59	-3	0-0	.979	2	107	261	O21(3/17/5)	0	-0.1
1989	Cal A	48	138	13	29	7	0	3	15	6-0	0	24	.210	.240	.326	60	-8	3-0	.990	6	116	232	O40(12/6/23)/D	0	-0.2
1990	Cal A	109	349	40	89	15	1	15	53	16-1	3	79	.255	.292	.433	102	-1	5-2	.965	2	93	195	O105(51/16/53)	0	-0.1
1991	Mil A	134	445	53	106	18	3	15	59	22-4	1	107	.238	.272	.393	84	-12	14-8	.976	9	109	160	O127(1/7/120)/3	0	-0.6
1992	Mil A	112	387	37	111	27	2	5	41	16-3	3	74	.287	.318	.406	103	1	18-7	.990	-5	90	87	O101(0/1/101),D4	0	-0.6
1993	Col N	141	538	93	167	43	5	21	89	28-2	7	99	.310	.348	.526	113	10	14-8	.973	9	112	137	O137(0/9/134)	0	1.3
1994	Col N★	116	484	74	147	33	2	27	95	19-3	4	70	.304	.334	.548	107	5	21-8	.991	-1	94	116	O116R	0	0.0
1995	†Col N★	139	579	102	**197**	38	2	**40**	**128**	22-5	4	96	.340	.364	**.620**	121	17	13-9	.986	-8	82	103	O136(120/0/35)	0	0.3
1996	Col N★	159	633	114	198	39	3	31	141	45-4	6	105	.313	.359	.531	107	7	31-12	.967	-12	87	49	O156(19/0/138)	0	-1.0
1997	Col N	151	561	81	173	31	2	26	118	30-1	3	90	.308	.343	.510	98	-1	6-5	.987	-6	89	46	O139(128/0/16),D5	0	-1.3
1998	Col N★	161	662	97	**219**	48	2	22	122	28-2	2	76	.331	.357	.509	103	4	14-4	.965	6	99	138	O156(134/0/29)/D	0	0.5
1999	Col N	151	593	104	177	38	2	34	133	54-3	2	84	.298	.354	.541	98	-1	6-6	.951	0	87	193	O144L,D2	0	-0.7
2000	Cin N	125	461	67	136	27	2	16	76	41-3	4	69	.295	.353	.466	103	2	5-2	.969	3	101	148	O121R	0	0.0
	Bos A	30	114	13	33	5	0	7	14	8-0	0	22	.289	.336	.518	109	1	0-0	ø	0	0	0	D30	0	-0.1
2001	Bos A	107	391	45	112	30	1	12	49	20-1	3	76	.286	.325	.460	104	2	2-2	.955	-2	85	137	O53(37/0/16),D46	0	-0.4
Total	14	1704	6381	934	1906	401	27	274	1141	355-32	41	1078	.299	.336	.499	104	23	152-73	.974	2	95	128	O1552(649/56/907),D89/3	0	-3.0
BIECHER, ED	Edward "Scrap Iron"; B8.27.1875 St.Louis MO; D7.15.1939 St.Louis MO; d9.26																								
1897	StL N	3	12	1	4	0	0	0	1	0	0	—	.333	.333	.333	78	0	1	1.000	-0	0	0	O3L	—	-0.1
1898	Cle N	8	25	1	5	2	0	0	0	0	0	—	.200	.200	.280	38	-2	0	.846	-1	121	0	O8C	—	-0.3
Total	2	11	37	2	9	2	0	0	1	0	0	—	.243	.243	.297	51	-2	1	.895	-1	83	0	O11(3/8/0)	—	-0.4
BIELASKI, OSCAR	Oscar; B3.21.1847 Washington DC; D11.8.1911 Washington DC; BR/TR/5´10.5˝/170; d4.24																								
1872	Nat NA	10	46	13	8	0	0	0	3	0	—	0	.174	.174	.174	6	-6	0-0	.737	-1	0	0	O10R	—	-0.4
1873	Was NA	38	173	35	49	3	2	0	20	4	—	6	.283	.299	.324	87	-2	1-3	.755	2	128	0	O38(2/0/36)	—	0.1
1874	Bal NA	43	187	24	45	0	0	0	8	2	—	4	.241	.249	.241	58	-9	3-1	.806	5	156	72	O43(0/1/43)/1	—	-0.1
1875	Chi NA	51	201	21	48	1	0	0	11	2	—	5	.239	.246	.244	70	-6	5-5	.748	-1	140	130	O51(4/0/48)	—	-0.4

YEAR	TM LG	G	AB	R	H	2B	3B	HR	RBI	BB-IB	HP	SO	AVG	OBP	SLG	AOPS	ABR	SB-CS	FA	FR	RNG	THR	GAMES AT POSITION	DL	BFW
1876	Chi N	32	139	24	29	3	0	0	10	2	—	3	.209	.220	.230	45	-9	—	.763	-3	76	106	O32R	—	-1.0
Total	4NA	142	607	93	150	4	2	0	42	8	—	15	.247	.257	.260	66	-23	9-9	.767	5	132	68	O142(6/1/137)/1	—	-0.8
BIERBAUER, LOU	Louis W.; B9.28.1865 Erie PA; D1.31.1926 Erie PA; BL/TR/5´8˝/140; d4.17; ▲																								
1886	Phi AA	137	522	56	118	17	5	2	47	21	0	—	.226	.256	.289	70	-20	19	.910	-5	**104**	85	2b133,C4,S2,P2	—	-1.7
1887	Phi AA	126	530	74	144	19	7	1	82	13	0	—	.272	.289	.340	75	-20	40	.921	-7	99	87	2b126/P	—	-1.8
1888	Phi AA	134	535	83	143	20	9	0	80	25	1	—	.267	.301	.338	105	2	34	.916	22	**110**	95	2b121,3b13/P	—	2.6
1889	Phi AA	130	549	80	167	27	7	7	105	29	4	30	.304	.344	.417	118	11	17	.941	36	107	127	2b130/C	—	4.3
1890	Bro P	**133**	589	128	180	31	11	7	99	40	0	15	.306	.350	.431	102	-2	16	.931	21	**112**	113	2b133	—	1.9
1891	Pit N	121	500	60	103	13	6	1	47	28	3	19	.206	.252	.262	51	-33	12	.929	-0	98	82	2b121	—	-2.6
1892	Pit N	**152**	649	81	153	20	9	8	65	25	0	29	.236	.264	.331	79	-20	11	.950	29	**117**	102	2b152	—	1.4
1893	Pit N	128	528	84	150	19	11	4	94	36	4	12	.284	.335	.384	93	-8	11	**.959**	14	105	123	2b128	—	1.0
1894	Pit N	131	528	87	160	20	13	3	109	26	2	10	.303	.338	.407	80	-20	19	.939	6	109	93	2b131	—	-0.6
1895	Pit N	118	470	54	122	13	11	1	71	19	2	8	.260	.291	.340	66	-26	18	.947	9	**108**	102	2b118	—	-0.9
1896	Pit N	59	258	33	74	10	6	0	39	5	0	7	.287	.300	.372	80	-9	7	.966	8	108	127	2b59	—	0.1
1897	StL N	12	46	1	10	0	0	0	1	0	0	—	.217	.217	.217	15	-6	2	.921	-1	97	91	2b12	—	-0.6
1898	StL N	4	9	0	0	0	0	0	0	1	0	—	.000	.100	.000	-69	-2	0	.429	-1	83	0	2b2/S3	—	-0.3
Total	13	1385	5713	821	1524	209	95	34	839	268	16	130	.267	.301	.354	84	-153	206	.935	130	107	102	2b1366,3b14,C5,P4,S3	—	2.8
BIERMAN, CHARLIE	Charles S.; B1845 Hoboken NJ; D8.4.1879 Hoboken NJ; 6´0˝/180; d6.21																								
1871	Kek NA	1	2	0	0	0	0	0	0	1	—	0	.000	.333	.000	6	0	0-0	.818	-0	0	0	/1	—	0.0
BIESER, STEVE	Steven Ray; B8.4.1967 Perryville MO; BL/TR/5´10˝/170; [PhiN89 32/820]; d4.1; Col Southeast Missouri																								
1997	NY N	47	69	16	17	3	0	0	4	7-1	4	20	.246	.346	.290	73	-2	2-3	1.000	2	112	287	O21(9/13/1),C2	0	-0.1
1998	Pit N	13	11	2	3	1	0	0	1	2-0	0	2	.273	.385	.364	97	0	0-0	ø	-0	0	0	/lf	0	0.0
Total	2	60	80	18	20	4	0	0	5	9-1	4	22	.250	.351	.300	77	-2	2-3	1.000	2	109	279	O22(10/13/1),C2	0	-0.1
BIGBEE, CARSON	Carson Lee "Skeeter"; B3.31.1895 Lebanon OR; D10.17.1964 Portland OR; BL/TR/5´9˝/157; d8.24; b–Lyle; Col Oregon																								
1916	Pit N	43	164	17	41	3	6	0	3	7	1	14	.250	.285	.341	91	-3	8	.946	-5	85	85	2b23,O19L/3	—	-0.9
1917	Pit N	133	469	46	112	11	6	0	21	37	5	16	.239	.301	.288	79	-11	19	.961	-4	107	64	O107(85/5/17),2b16,S2	—	-2.3
1918	Pit N	92	310	47	79	11	3	1	19	42	0	10	.255	.344	.319	99	2	19	.958	0	93	129	O92(87/0/5)	—	-0.3
1919	Pit N	125	478	61	132	11	4	2	27	37	3	26	.276	.332	.328	95	-2	31	.971	15	**119**	128	O124(50/75/0)	—	0.6
1920	Pit N	137	550	78	154	19	15	4	32	45	6	28	.280	.341	.391	106	4	31-15	.971	3	103	104	O133(128/6/0)	—	0.3
1921	Pit N	147	632	100	204	23	17	3	42	41	0	19	.323	.364	.427	106	5	21-20	.977	12	105	142	O146(133/13/0)	—	0.3
1922	Pit N	150	614	113	215	29	15	5	99	56	1	13	.350	.405	.471	124	23	24-15	.956	14	**111**	**146**	O150(146/4/0)	—	2.3
1923	Pit N	123	499	79	149	18	7	0	54	43	1	15	.299	.355	.363	88	-8	10-9	.990	8	111	105	O122L	—	-1.1
1924	Pit N	89	282	42	74	4	1	0	15	26	3	12	.262	.331	.284	65	-13	15-7	.943	1	101	118	O75L	—	-1.7
1925	†Pit N	66	126	31	30	7	0	0	8	7	0	8	.238	.278	.294	43	-11	2-2	.942	1	106	105	O42(30/2/10)	—	-1.2
1926	Pit N	42	68	15	15	3	1	2	4	3	1	0	.221	.264	.382	69	-3	2	.966	1	101	175	O21(17/4/0)	—	-0.4
Total	11	1147	4192	629	1205	139	75	17	324	344	21	161	.287	.345	.369	96	-17	182-68	.966	44	107	119	O1031(892/109/32),2b39,S2/3	—	-4.4
BIGBEE, LYLE	Lyle Randolph "Al"; B8.22.1893 Waterloo OR; D8.5.1942 Portland OR; BL/TR/6´0˝/180; d4.15; b–Carson; Col Oregon; ▲																								
1920	Phi A	38	75	5	14	2	0	1	8	9	1	12	.187	.282	.253	42	-6	1-0	.857	-3	85	0	O13(11/0/1),P12	—	-0.8
1921	Pit N	5	2	0	0	0	0	0	0	0	0	1	.000	.000	.000	-97	0	0-0	1.000	-0	96	0	P5	—	0.0
Total	2	43	77	5	14	2	0	1	8	9	1	13	.182	.276	.247	39	-6	1-0	1.000	-3	103	0	P17,O13(11/0/1)	—	-0.8
BIGBIE, LARRY	Larry Robert; B11.4.1977 Hobart IN; BL/TR/6´4˝/(190–210); [BalA99 1/21]; d6.23; Col Ball St.																								
2001	Bal A	47	131	15	30	6	0	2	11	17-1	0	42	.229	.318	.321	73	-5	4-1	1.000	-2	91	91	O40(5/18/17)	0	-0.6
2002	Bal A	16	34	1	6	1	0	0	3	1-0	0	11	.176	.194	.206	9	-5	1-0	1.000	0	117	0	O12(6/1/6)	0	-0.4
2003	Bal A	83	287	43	87	15	1	9	31	29-3	0	60	.303	.365	.456	116	7	7-1	.994	2	102	105	O80(76/2/5)	66	0.7
2004	Bal A	139	478	76	134	23	1	15	68	45-0	1	113	.280	.341	.427	100	0	8-3	.993	1	107	42	O134(114/30/0),D2	16	-0.2
2005	Bal A	67	206	22	51	9	1	5	21	21-1	0	49	.248	.314	.374	83	-5	3-3	1.000	-2	92	96	O62(57/6/0)	17	-0.9
	Col N	23	66	5	14	1	1	0	2	3-0	1	18	.212	.257	.258	32	-7	2-0	1.000	1	108	127	O15(0/11/5)	16	-0.5
2006	StL N	17	25	2	6	1	0	0	1	3-0	0	9	.240	.321	.280	56	-2	0-0	1.000	-0	85	0	O12(11/0/1)	154	-0.2
Total	6	392	1227	164	328	56	4	31	137	119-5	2	302	.267	.331	.395	91	-17	25-8	.996	-0	101	74	O355(269/68/34),D2	269	-2.1
BIGELOW, ELLIOT	Elliot Allardice "Babe","Gilly"; B10.13.1897 Tarpon Springs FL; D8.13.1933 Tampa FL; BL/TL/5´11˝/185; d4.18																								
1929	Bos A	100	211	23	60	16	0	1	26	23	1	18	.284	.357	.374	91	-2	1-4	.944	-2	85	125	O59(2/2/55)	—	-0.8
BIGGIO, CRAIG	Craig Alan; B12.14.1965 Smithtown NY; BR/TR/5´11˝/(180–185); [HouN87 1/22]; d6.26; Col Seton Hall; OF(109/255/2)																								
1988	Hou N	50	123	14	26	6	1	3	5	7-2	0	29	.211	.254	.350	74	-5	6-1	.991	6	67	121	C50	0	0.5
1989	Hou N	134	443	64	114	21	2	13	60	49-8	6	64	.257	.336	.402	115	9	21-3	.990	-20	66	67	C125,O5(1/4/0)	0	0.0
1990	Hou N	150	555	53	153	24	2	4	42	53-1	3	79	.276	.342	.348	93	-4	25-11	.985	-5	78	104	C113,O50(17/34/2)	0	-0.2
1991	Hou N★	149	546	79	161	23	4	4	46	53-3	2	71	.295	.358	.374	112	10	19-6	.990	-9	89	84	C139,2b3,O2(1/1/0)	0	1.1
1992	Hou N★	**162**	613	96	170	32	3	6	39	94-9	7	95	.277	.378	.369	117	19	38-15	.984	-27	84	84	2b161	0	-0.1
1993	Hou N	155	610	98	175	41	5	21	64	77-7	10	93	.287	.373	.474	130	28	15-17	.982	-0	95	101	2b155	0	3.2
1994	Hou N★	114	437	88	139	**44**	5	6	56	62-1	8	58	.318	.411	.483	139	30	**39**-4	.988	-4	98	89	2b113	0	3.7
1995	Hou N★	141	553	**123**	167	30	2	22	77	80-1	**22**	85	.302	.406	.483	144	40	33-8	.986	-6	100	82	2b141	0	4.4
1996	Hou N★	**162**	605	113	174	24	4	15	75	75-0	**27**	72	.288	.386	.415	122	23	25-7	.988	-2	96	70	2b162	0	3.2
1997	†Hou N★	**162**	619	**146**	191	37	8	22	81	84-6	**34**	107	.309	.415	.501	144	46	47-10	.979	25	**111**	116	2b160/D	0	**8.2**
1998	†Hou N★	160	646	123	210	**51**	2	20	88	64-6	23	113	.325	.403	.503	141	42	50-8	.980	-0	102	98	2b159/D	0	5.6
1999	†Hou N	160	639	123	188	**56**	0	16	73	88-9	11	107	.294	.386	.457	114	19	28-14	.985	19	100	**124**	2b155,O6L,D2	0	4.3
2000	Hou N	101	377	67	101	13	5	8	35	61-3	16	73	.268	.388	.393	92	-2	12-2	.987	-5	99	87	2b100	60	0.0
2001	†Hou N	155	617	118	180	35	3	20	70	66-4	**28**	100	.292	.382	.455	108	11	7-4	.984	-16	90	96	2b154/D	0	0.2
2002	Hou N	145	577	96	146	36	3	15	58	50-2	17	111	.253	.330	.404	85	-11	16-2	.988	-4	88	96	2b142/lf	0	-0.6
2003	Hou N	153	628	102	166	44	2	15	62	57-3	**27**	116	.264	.350	.412	93	-4	8-4	.997	-5	94	111	O150C	0	-0.6
2004	†Hou N	156	633	100	178	47	0	24	63	40-0	15	94	.281	.337	.469	102	2	7-2	.966	-8	92	58	O149(83/66/0)/D	0	-0.6
2005	†Hou N	155	590	94	156	40	1	26	69	37-2	17	90	.264	.325	.468	103	2	11-1	.976	11	104	104	2b141,D5	0	2.1
2006	Hou N	145	548	79	135	33	0	21	62	40-1	9	84	.246	.306	.422	82	-15	3-2	.989	-6	99	109	2b129,D5	0	-1.5
Total	19	2709	10359	1776	2930	637	52	281	1125	1137-68	282	1641	.283	.367	.436	113	240	410-121	.984	-56	97	97	2b1875,C427,O363C,D16	60	32.9
BIGLER, PETE	Ivan Edward; B12.13.1892 Bradford OH; D4.1.1975 Coldwater MI; BR/TR/5´9˝/150; d5.6; Col Springfield																								
1917	StL A	1	0	0	0	0	0	0	0	0	0	0	ø	ø	ø	ø	0	0	ø	0	—	—	/R	—	0.0
BIGNELL, GEORGE	George William; B7.18.1858 Taunton MA; D1.16.1925 Providence RI; 5´9˝/160; d9.27																								
1884	Mil U	4	9	4	2	0	0	0	—	1	—	—	.222	.300	.222	111	0	—	.951	1	—	—	C4	—	0.1
BIITTNER, LARRY	Lawrence David; B7.27.1945 Pocahontas IA; BL/TL/6´2˝/(200–205); [TexA68 10/212]; d7.17; Col Buena Vista																								
1970	Was A	2	2	0	0	0	0	0	0	0-0	0	0	.000	.000	.000	-99	-1	0-0	ø	0	—	—	/H	0	-0.1
1971	Was A	66	171	12	44	4	1	0	16	16-3	1	20	.257	.323	.292	79	-5	1-0	.940	1	95	227	O41(7/0/38),1b3	0	-0.6
1972	Tex A	137	382	34	99	18	1	3	31	29-5	2	37	.259	.313	.335	97	-2	1-3	.991	1	126	82	1b65,O65(28/8/32)	0	-1.0
1973	Tex A	83	258	19	65	8	2	1	12	20-0	1	21	.252	.307	.310	77	-8	1-0	.980	3	93	177	O57(19/2/38),1b20,D3	0	-0.9
1974	Mon N	18	26	2	7	1	0	0	3	0-0	0	2	.269	.269	.308	58	-2	0-0	1.000	1	107	444	O4L	0	-0.1
1975	Mon N	121	346	34	109	13	5	3	28	34-8	0	33	.315	.376	.408	112	6	2-1	.972	-0	95	127	O93(35/4/55)	0	0.1
1976	Mon N	11	32	2	6	1	0	0	1	0-0	0	3	.188	.188	.219	14	-4	0-0	.947	1	125	189	O7(3/0/4)	0	-0.3
	Chi N	78	192	21	47	13	1	0	17	10-3	1	6	.245	.286	.323	66	-8	0-2	.985	5	174	92	1b33,O24(22/0/3)	15	-0.8
	Year	89	224	23	53	14	1	0	18	10-3	1	9	.237	.272	.308	59	-12	0-2	.985	6	174	92	1b33,O31(25/0/7)	0	-1.1
1977	Chi N	138	493	74	147	28	1	12	62	35-2	1	36	.298	.345	.432	97	-2	2-1	.987	4	139	93	1b80,O52L/P	0	-0.4
1978	Chi N	120	343	32	88	15	1	4	50	23-4	1	37	.257	.300	.341	72	-13	0-1	.987	5	149	120	1b62,O29L	0	-1.4
1979	Chi N	111	272	35	79	13	3	3	50	21-1	0	23	.290	.339	.393	91	-3	1-1	.925	-3	70	113	O44(23/1/21),1b32	0	-0.9
1980	Chi N	127	273	21	68	12	2	1	34	18-2	2	33	.249	.294	.319	67	-12	1-3	.996	2	105	62	1b41,O38(20/0/17)	0	-1.5
1981	Cin N	42	61	1	13	4	0	0	8	4-1	0	4	.213	.258	.279	54	-4	0-0	1.000	1	75	48	1b8,O3R	0	-0.3
1982	Cin N	97	184	18	57	9	2	2	24	17-2	2	16	.310	.369	.413	120	5	1-0	.978	1	96	113	O31(26/0/6),1b15	0	0.5
1983	Tex A	66	116	5	32	5	1	0	18	9-5	0	16	.276	.323	.336	84	-2	0-0	.987	1	139	99	1b22,O2R,D9	0	-0.2
Total	14	1217	3151	310	861	144	20	29	354	236-36	11	287	.273	.324	.359	87	-55	10-12	.970	23	91	133	O490(268/15/219),1b381,D12/P	15	-7.9

YEAR	TM LG	G	AB	R	H	2B	3B	HR	RBI	BB-IB	HP	SO	AVG	OBP	SLG	AOPS	ABR	SB-CS	FA	FR	RNG	THR	GAMES AT POSITION	DL	BFW
BILARDELLO, DANN	Dann James; B5.26.1959 Santa Cruz CA; BR/TR/6´0˝/(185–190); [LAN78 S1/7]; d4.11; Col Cabrillo (CA) JC																								
1983	Cin N	109	298	27	71	18	0	9	38	15-3	1	49	.238	.274	.389	80	-9	2-1	.991	-1	104	121	C105	0	-0.7
1984	Cin N	68	182	16	38	7	0	2	10	19-3	1	34	.209	.287	.280	57	-10	0-1	.992	3	121	129	C68	0	-0.5
1985	Cin N	42	102	6	17	0	0	1	9	4-1	1	15	.167	.206	.196	12	-12	0-0	.986	7	122	179	C42	0	-0.4
1986	Mon N	79	191	12	37	5	0	4	17	14-3	0	32	.194	.249	.283	46	-15	1-0	.982	-1	104	80	C77	0	-1.3
1989	Pit N	33	80	11	18	6	0	2	8	2-0	0	18	.225	.244	.375	77	-3	1-2	.970	2	76	134	C33	0	0.0
1990	Pit N	19	37	1	2	0	0	0	3	4-1	0	10	.054	.146	.054	-44	-7	0-0	1.000	3	192	128	C19	0	-0.4
1991	SD N	15	26	4	7	2	1	0	5	3-0	0	4	.269	.345	.423	111	0	0-0	1.000	4	109	128	C13	0	0.5
1992	SD N	17	33	2	4	1	0	0	1	4-1	0	8	.121	.216	.152	6	-4	0-0	1.000	1	51	173	C14	57	-0.2
Total	8	382	949	79	194	39	1	18	91	65-12	3	170	.204	.257	.305	55	-60	4-4	.988	18	109	124	C371	57	-3.0
BILKO, STEVE	Stephen Thomas; B11.13.1928 Nanticoke PA; D3.7.1978 Wilkes–Barre PA; BR/TR/6´1˝/(230–235); d9.22																								
1949	StL N	6	17	3	5	2	0	0	2	5	0	6	.294	.455	.412	128	1	0	1.000	0	109	26	1b5	0	0.1
1950	StL N	10	33	1	6	1	0	0	2	4	0	10	.182	.270	.212	27	-3	0	.989	1	123	98	1b9	0	-0.3
1951	StL N	21	72	5	16	4	0	2	12	9	0	10	.222	.309	.361	79	-2	0-0	.984	0	106	104	1b19	0	-0.3
1952	StL N	20	72	7	19	6	1	1	6	4	0	15	.264	.303	.417	97	0	0-0	.995	5	184	83	1b20	0	0.4
1953	StL N	154	570	72	143	23	3	21	84	70	1	125	.251	.334	.412	93	-6	0-1	.991	9	**121**	106	1b154	0	-0.5
1954	StL N	8	14	1	2	0	0	0	1	3	0	1	.143	.294	.143	18	-2	0-0	1.000	2	299	102	1b6	0	0.0
	Chi N	47	92	11	22	8	1	4	12	11	0	24	.239	.320	.478	104	0	0-0	1.000	6	200	94	1b22	0	0.5
	Year	55	106	12	24	8	1	4	13	14	0	25	.226	.317	.434	92	-1	0-0	1.000	8	214	95	1b28	0	0.5
1958	Cin N	31	87	12	23	4	2	4	17	10-0	0	20	.264	.330	.494	111	1	0-0	.995	-1	83	109	1b21	0	-0.1
	LA N	47	101	13	21	1	2	7	18	8-0	0	37	.208	.264	.465	86	-3	0-0	.995	2	123	97	1b25	0	-0.3
	Year	78	188	25	44	5	4	11	35	18-0	0	57	.234	.295	.479	98	-2	0-0	.995	1	104	103	1b46	0	-0.4
1960	Det A	78	222	20	46	11	2	9	25	27-0	0	31	.207	.292	.396	82	-6	0-1	.991	-0	97	95	1b62	0	-1.0
1961	LA A	114	294	49	82	16	1	20	59	58-2	0	81	.279	.395	.544	134	16	1-1	.989	3	112	82	1b86,O3R	0	1.3
1962	LA A	64	164	26	47	9	1	8	38	25-0	2	35	.287	.374	.500	141	10	1-1	.995	-1	90	97	1b50	31	0.7
Total	10	600	1738	220	432	85	13	76	276	234-2	3	395	.249	.336	.444	103	6	2-4	.992	25	119	97	1b479,O3R	31	0.5
BILLINGS, JOSH	John Augustus; B11.30.1892 Grantville KS; D12.30.1981 Santa Monica CA; BR/TR/5´11˝/165; d9.9; Mil 1918; Col Oklahoma St.																								
1913	Cle A	1	3	0	0	0	0	0	0	0	0	3	.000	.000	.000	-97	-1	0	.857	0	*125*	*99*	/C	—	-0.1
1914	Cle A	11	8	3	2	1	0	0	0	1	0	1	.250	.333	.375	109	0	1	.813	1	*0*	*147*	C3	—	0.1
1915	Cle A	8	21	2	4	1	0	0	0	0	0	6	.190	.190	.238	28	-2	1	1.000	-0	*94*	*63*	C7/cf	—	-0.2
1916	Cle A	22	31	2	5	0	0	0	1	2	0	11	.161	.212	.161	12	-3	0	.981	2	126	76	C12	—	-0.1
1917	Cle A	66	129	8	23	3	2	0	9	8	3	21	.178	.243	.233	42	-9	2	.974	2	*108*	*118*	C48	—	-0.4
1918	Cle A	2	3	0	1	0	0	0	0	0	0	0	.333	.333	.333	92	0	0	1.000	0	*0*	*0*	/C	—	0.0
1919	StL A	38	76	9	15	1	1	0	3	1	1	12	.197	.218	.237	27	-8	0	.982	3	*102*	*128*	C26/1	—	-0.3
1920	StL A	66	155	19	43	5	2	0	11	11	7	10	.277	.353	.335	80	-4	1-0	.967	-4	*92*	*104*	C40	—	-0.5
1921	StL A	20	46	2	10	0	0	0	4	0	0	7	.217	.217	.217	11	-6	0-0	.982	1	*110*	*88*	C12	—	-0.5
1922	StL A	5	7	0	3	1	0	0	1	0	0	0	.429	.429	.571	153	1	0-0	1.000	-0	*64*	*191*	C3	—	0.0
1923	StL A	4	9	0	0	0	0	0	0	0	0	2	.000	.000	.000	-95	-3	0-0	.917	0	*141*	*173*	C4	—	-0.2
Total	11	243	488	45	106	12	5	0	29	23	11	73	.217	.268	.262	47	-35	5-0	.970	4	*102*	*109*	C157/1cf	—	-2.2
BILLINGS, DICK	Richard Arlin; B12.4.1942 Detroit MI; BR/TR/6´1˝/(190–195); [TexA65 16/622]; d9.11; Col Michigan St.																								
1968	Was A	12	33	3	6	1	0	1	3	5-0	0	13	.182	.282	.303	82	-1	0-0	.929	1	93	219	O8L,3b4	0	-0.1
1969	Was A	27	37	3	5	0	0	0	0	6-0	0	8	.135	.256	.135	13	-4	0-1	1.000	0	78	0	O6(5/1/0)/3	0	-0.5
1970	Was A	11	24	3	6	2	0	1	1	2-0	0	3	.250	.308	.458	113	0	0-0	1.000	-2	86	178	C8	0	-0.1
1971	Was A	116	349	32	86	14	0	6	48	21-1	5	54	.246	.296	.338	84	-8	2-5	.992	-3	62	121	C62,O32(22/0/12),3b2	0	-1.2
1972	Tex A	133	469	41	119	15	1	5	58	29-5	2	77	.254	.296	.322	88	-8	1-5	.981	-1	77	136	C92,O41(39/0/2),3b5/1	0	-1.0
1973	Tex A	81	280	17	50	11	0	3	32	20-2	2	43	.179	.237	.250	39	-23	1-1	.975	-16	66	110	C72,O4(3/0/1),1b3,D2	16	-3.8
1974	Tex A	16	31	2	7	1	0	0	0	4-0	0	6	.226	.314	.258	68	-1	2-0	1.000	0	136	91	C13/lfD	50	0.0
	StL N	1	5	0	1	0	0	0	0	0-0	0	1	.200	.200	.200	12	-1	0-0	1.000	0	0	0	/C	0	-0.1
1975	StL N	3	3	0	0	0	0	0	0	0-0	0	2	.000	.000	.000	-96	-1	0-0	ø	0	—	—	/H	0	-0.1
Total	8	400	1231	101	280	44	1	16	142	87-8	9	207	.227	.281	.304	72	-47	6-12	.984	-21	72	122	C248,O92(78/1/15),3b12,1b4,D3	66	-6.9
BINKS, GEORGE	George Alvin "Bingo" (b George Alvin Binkowski); B7.11.1914 Chicago IL; BL/TL/6´0˝/175; d9.23																								
1944	Was A	5	12	0	3	0	0	0	0	0	0	1	.250	.250	.250	45	-1	0-0	1.000	-0	97	0	O3R	0	-0.1
1945	Was A	145	550	62	153	32	6	6	81	34	3	52	.278	.324	.391	117	9	11-7	.977	5	106	117	O128(27/79/26),1b20	0	0.8
1946	Was A	65	134	13	26	3	0	0	12	6	0	16	.194	.229	.216	26	-14	1-0	1.000	1	112	53	O28(15/9/5)	0	-1.5
1947	Phi A	104	333	33	86	19	4	2	34	23	1	36	.258	.308	.357	83	-8	8-2	.965	2	101	149	O75(25/0/51),1b13	0	-1.0
1948	Phi A	17	41	2	4	1	0	0	2	2	0	2	.098	.140	.122	-30	-8	1-0	1.000	0	92	146	O14(2/0/12)	0	-0.8
	StL A	15	23	2	5	0	0	0	1	2	0	1	.217	.280	.217	32	-2	0-0	1.000	-1	96	0	O5(2/0/3),1b4	0	-0.3
	Year	32	64	4	9	1	0	0	3	4	0	3	.141	.191	.156	-7	-10	1-0	1.000	-1	93	106	O19(4/0/15),1b4	0	-1.1
Total	5	351	1093	112	277	55	10	8	130	67	4	108	.253	.299	.344	86	-24	21-9	.977	7	104	118	O253(71/88/100),1b37	0	-2.9
BIRAS, STEVE	Stephen Alexander; B2.26.1922 E.St.Louis IL; D4.21.1965 St.Louis MO; BR/TR/5´11˝/185; d9.15																								
1944	Cle A	2	2	0	2	0	0	0	2	0	0	0	1.000	1.000	1.000	491	1	0-0	.667	-0	77	0	/2	0	0.1
BIRCHALL, JUD	Adoniram Judson; B9.12.1855 Philadelphia PA; D12.22.1887 Philadelphia PA; d5.2																								
1882	Phi AA	**75**	338	65	89	12	1	0	27	8	—	—	.263	.280	.305	91	-4	—	.860	0	80	0	O74L/2	—	-0.5
1883	Phi AA	96	448	95	108	10	1	1	24	20	—	—	.241	.274	.275	70	-16	—	.809	5	116	0	O96L	—	-1.2
1884	Phi AA	54	221	36	57	2	2	0	—	4	5	—	.258	.287	.285	82	-5	—	.838	2	65	62	O52(51/0/1),3b2	—	-0.4
Total	3	225	1007	196	254	24	4	1	51	32	5	—	.252	.279	.287	80	-25	—	.832	7	92	15	O222(221/0/1),3b2/2	—	-2.1
BIRD, FRANK	Frank Zepherin "Dodo"; B3.10.1869 Spencer MA; D5.20.1958 Worcester MA; BR/TR/5´10˝/195; d4.16																								
1892	StL N	17	50	9	10	3	1	1	1	6	0	11	.200	.286	.360	100	0	2	.920	-3	*96*	*96*	C17	—	-0.2
BIRD, GEORGE	George Raymond; B6.23.1850 Stillman Valley IL; D11.9.1940 Rockford IL; BR/TR/5´9˝/150; d5.6																								
1871	Rok NA	**25**	106	19	28	2	5	0	13	3	—	2	.264	.284	.377	92	-1	1-0	.756	-5	66	0	O25(1/25/0)	—	-0.4
BIRDSALL, DAVE	David Solomon; B7.16.1838 New York NY; D12.30.1896 Boston MA; BR/TR/5´9˝/126; d5.5																								
1871	Bos NA	29	152	51	46	3	3	0	24	4	—	4	.303	.321	.362	93	-2	6-0	.769	0	110	208	O27R,C7	—	0.0
1872	Bos NA	16	76	11	16	3	0	0	15	1	—	0	.211	.221	.250	42	-5	0-2	.826	2	—	—	C12,O7(4/0/3)	—	-0.3
1873	Bos NA	3	11	4	1	0	0	0	0	2	—	0	.091	.231	.091	-1	-1	1-0	.200	-2	0	0	O3(1/0/3)	—	-0.2
Total	3NA	48	239	66	63	6	3	0	39	7	—	4	.264	.285	.314	73	-8	7-2	.720	0	—	—	O37(5/0/33),C19	—	-0.5
BIRMINGHAM, JOE	Joseph Leo "Dode"; B8.6.1884 Elmira NY; D4.24.1946 Tampico, Tamaulipas, Mexico; BR/TR/5´10˝/185; d9.12; M4; Col Cornell																								
1906	Cle A	10	40	5	11	2	1	0	6	1	0	—	.275	.293	.375	110	0	2	1.000	1	155	0	O9L/3	—	0.0
1907	Cle A	137	476	55	112	10	9	1	33	16	3	—	.235	.265	.300	79	-13	23	.949	12	**168**	213	O133(17/101/16),S3	—	-0.8
1908	Cle A	122	413	32	88	10	1	2	38	19	3	—	.213	.253	.257	65	-16	15	.957	4	**148**	**179**	O121(1/119/1)/S	—	-2.0
1909	Cle A	100	343	29	99	10	5	1	38	19	4	—	.289	.333	.356	113	4	12	.948	2	124	75	O98C	—	0.2
1910	Cle A	104	367	41	84	11	2	0	35	23	5	—	.229	.284	.270	72	-12	18	.961	11	107	**159**	O103(1/102/0)/3	—	-0.6
1911	Cle A	125	447	55	136	18	5	2	51	15	5	—	.304	.334	.380	98	-3	16	.973	3	101	110	O102(3/96/3),3b16	—	-0.6
1912	Cle A	107	369	49	94	19	3	1	45	26	4	—	.255	.311	.331	81	-9	15	.952	2	93	129	O96(3/93/0),1b9,M	—	-1.4
1913	Cle A	47	131	16	37	9	1	0	15	8	0	22	.282	.324	.366	99	0	7	.974	-2	102	39	O36(4/32/0),M	—	-0.5
1914	Cle A	19	47	2	6	0	0	0	4	2	0	5	.128	.163	.128	-12	-7	0-1	1.000	-0	92	90	O14(0/6/8),M	—	-0.9
Total	9	771	2633	284	667	89	27	7	265	129	24	27	.253	.294	.316	84	-56	108-1	.958	33	125	141	O712(38/647/28),3b18,1b9,S4	—	-6.6
BISCHOFF, JOHN	John George "Smiley"; B10.28.1894 Granite City IL; D12.28.1981 Granite City IL; BR/TR/5´7˝/165; d4.18																								
1925	Chi A	7	11	1	1	0	0	0	0	1	0	5	.091	.167	.091	-35	-2	0-0	1.000	-0	*110*	*212*	C4	—	-0.2
	Bos A	41	133	13	37	9	1	1	16	6	0	11	.278	.309	.383	75	-6	1-2	.952	-4	*70*	*100*	C40	—	-0.7
	Year	48	144	14	38	9	1	1	16	7	0	16	.264	.298	.361	67	-8	1-2	.955	-4	*72*	*106*	C44	—	-0.9
1926	Bos A	59	127	6	33	11	2	0	19	15	1	16	.260	.343	.378	91	-2	1-3	.974	-4	*66*	*87*	C46	—	-0.4
Total	2	107	271	20	71	20	3	1	35	22	1	32	.262	.320	.369	78	-10	2-5	.964	-8	*69*	*97*	C90	—	-1.3
BISHOP, FRANK	Frank H.; B9.21.1860 Belvidere IL; D6.18.1929 Chicago IL; d5.27																								
1884	CP U	4	16	1	3	1	0	0	—	0	—	—	.188	.188	.250	32	-2	—	.667	-2	49	0	3b3/S	—	-0.3

Bishop, Max Max Frederick "Tilly","Camera Eye"; B9.5.1899 Waynesboro PA; D2.24.1962 Waynesboro PA; BL/TR/5´8.5˝/165; d4.15; Col CC of Baltimore (MD)

YEAR	TM LG	G	AB	R	H	2B	3B	HR	RBI	BB-IB	HP	SO	AVG	OBP	SLG	AOPS	ABR	SB-CS	FA	FR	RNG	THR	GAMES AT POSITION	DL	BFW
1924	Phi A	91	294	52	75	13	2	2	21	54	5	30	.255	.380	.333	84	-4	4-3	.969	10	114	108	2b80	—	0.7
1925	Phi A	105	368	66	103	18	4	4	27	87	2	37	.280	.420	.383	98	4	5-9	.957	5	**109**	90	2b104	—	0.9
1926	Phi A	122	400	77	106	20	2	0	33	116	1	41	.265	.431	.325	94	5	4-5	**.987**	6	102	95	2b119	—	1.3
1927	Phi A	117	372	80	103	15	1	0	22	105	5	28	.277	.442	.323	95	6	8-6	.967	2	103	85	2b106	—	1.0
1928	Phi A	126	472	104	149	27	5	6	50	100	3	36	.316	.438	.432	126	25	6-10	**.978**	-6	92	92	2b125	—	1.9
1929	†Phi A	129	475	102	110	19	6	3	36	**128**	3	44	.232	.398	.316	83	-5	1-4	.970	-20	88	77	2b129	—	-2.1
1930	†Phi A	130	441	117	111	27	6	10	38	128	6	60	.252	.426	.408	108	13	3-2	.976	-1	101	81	2b127	—	1.4
1931	†Phi A	130	497	115	146	30	4	5	37	112	2	51	.294	.426	.400	111	15	3-1	.984	2	98	116	2b130	—	2.4
1932	Phi A	114	409	89	104	24	2	5	37	110	0	43	.254	.412	.359	98	6	2-2	**.988**	-1	100	106	2b106	—	1.1
1933	Phi A	117	391	80	115	27	1	4	42	106	1	46	.294	.446	.399	124	23	1-5	.975	-7	101	70	2b113	—	2.0
1934	Bos A	97	253	65	66	13	1	1	22	82	2	22	.261	.445	.332	96	5	3-2	.990	3	98	105	2b57,1b15	—	0.9
1935	Bos A	60	122	19	28	3	1	1	14	28	1	14	.230	.377	.295	71	-4	0-2	.978	-3	93	55	2b34,1b11,S2	—	-0.6
Total	12	1338	4494	966	1216	236	35	41	379	1156	31	452	.271	.423	.366	102	89	40-51	.976	-10	100	91	2b1230,1b26,S2	—	10.9

Bishop, Mike Michael David; B11.5.1958 Santa Maria CA; D2.8.2005 Bakersfield CA; BR/TR/6´2˝/225; [AnaA76 12/270]; d4.16

YEAR	TM LG	G	AB	R	H	2B	3B	HR	RBI	BB-IB	HP	SO	AVG	OBP	SLG	AOPS	ABR	SB-CS	FA	FR	RNG	THR	GAMES AT POSITION	DL	BFW
1983	NY N	3	8	2	1	1	0	0	0	3-0	0	4	.125	.364	.250	73	0	0-0	.944	-0	86	79	C3	0	0.0

Bisland, Rivington Rivington Martin; B2.17.1890 New York NY; D1.11.1973 Salzburg, Austria; BR/TR/5´9˝/155; d9.13

YEAR	TM LG	G	AB	R	H	2B	3B	HR	RBI	BB-IB	HP	SO	AVG	OBP	SLG	AOPS	ABR	SB-CS	FA	FR	RNG	THR	GAMES AT POSITION	DL	BFW
1912	Pit N	1	1	0	0	0	0	0	0	0	0	0	.000	.000	.000	-99	0	0	ø	0	—	—	/H	—	0.0
1913	StL A	12	44	3	6	0	0	0	3	2	1	5	.136	.191	.136	-4	-6	0	.963	-3	89	66	S12	—	-0.9
1914	Cle A	18	57	9	6	1	0	0	2	6	0	2	.105	.190	.123	-5	-7	2-5	.962	0	100	92	S15/3	—	-0.8
Total	3	31	102	12	12	1	0	0	5	8	1	7	.118	.189	.127	-6	-13	2-5	.962	-2	95	81	S27/3	—	-1.7

Bissonette, Del Delphia Louis; B9.6.1899 Winthrop ME; D6.9.1972 Augusta ME; BL/TL/5´11˝/180; d4.11; M1/C2; Col Georgetown

YEAR	TM LG	G	AB	R	H	2B	3B	HR	RBI	BB-IB	HP	SO	AVG	OBP	SLG	AOPS	ABR	SB-CS	FA	FR	RNG	THR	GAMES AT POSITION	DL	BFW
1928	Bro N	**155**	587	90	188	30	13	25	106	70	4	75	.320	.396	.543	145	38	5	.987	-3	90	74	1b155	—	2.4
1929	Bro N	116	431	68	121	28	10	12	75	46	1	58	.281	.351	.476	105	2	2	.987	-9	67	74	1b113	—	-1.3
1930	Bro N	146	572	102	192	33	13	16	113	56	1	66	.336	.396	.523	121	19	4	.987	-9	78	**118**	1b146	—	0.1
1931	Bro N	152	587	90	170	19	14	12	87	59	0	53	.290	.354	.431	111	8	4	.990	-6	79	104	1b152	—	-1.3
1933	Bro N	35	114	9	28	7	0	1	10	2	0	17	.246	.259	.333	71	-5	2	.988	-0	97	100	1b32	—	-0.8
Total	5	604	2291	359	699	117	50	66	391	233	6	269	.305	.371	.486	119	62	17	.988	-28	80	94	1b598	—	-0.9

Bittman, Red Henry Peter; B7.22.1862 Cincinnati OH; D11.8.1929 Cincinnati OH; d10.10

YEAR	TM LG	G	AB	R	H	2B	3B	HR	RBI	BB-IB	HP	SO	AVG	OBP	SLG	AOPS	ABR	SB-CS	FA	FR	RNG	THR	GAMES AT POSITION	DL	BFW
1889	KC AA	4	14	2	4	0	0	0	2	1	0	1	.286	.333	.286	72	-1	1	1.000	1	112	104	2b4	—	0.0

Bjorkman, George George Anton; B8.26.1956 Ontario CA; BR/TR/6´2˝/190; [StLN78 4/93]; d7.10; Col Oral Roberts

YEAR	TM LG	G	AB	R	H	2B	3B	HR	RBI	BB-IB	HP	SO	AVG	OBP	SLG	AOPS	ABR	SB-CS	FA	FR	RNG	THR	GAMES AT POSITION	DL	BFW
1983	Hou N	29	75	8	17	4	0	2	14	16-4	1	29	.227	.370	.360	109	2	0-0	.993	-3	95	73	C29	0	0.0

Black, John John Falcnor "Jack" (b John Falcnor Haddow); B2.23.1890 Covington KY; D3.20.1962 Rutherford NJ; BR/TR/6´1˝/185; d6.20

YEAR	TM LG	G	AB	R	H	2B	3B	HR	RBI	BB-IB	HP	SO	AVG	OBP	SLG	AOPS	ABR	SB-CS	FA	FR	RNG	THR	GAMES AT POSITION	DL	BFW
1911	StL A	54	186	13	28	4	0	0	7	10	2	—	.151	.202	.172	5	-24	4	.972	0	111	121	1b54	—	-2.6

Black, Bill John William "Jigger"; B8.12.1899 Philadelphia PA; D1.14.1968 Philadelphia PA; BL/TR/5´11˝/168; d5.4

YEAR	TM LG	G	AB	R	H	2B	3B	HR	RBI	BB-IB	HP	SO	AVG	OBP	SLG	AOPS	ABR	SB-CS	FA	FR	RNG	THR	GAMES AT POSITION	DL	BFW
1924	Chi A	6	5	0	1	0	0	0	0	0	0	0	.200	.200	.200	3	-1	0-0	ø	-0	0	0	/2	—	-0.1

Black, Bob Robert Benjamin; B12.10.1862 Cincinnati OH; D3.21.1933 Sioux City IA; 5´5.5˝/155; d8.19; ▲

YEAR	TM LG	G	AB	R	H	2B	3B	HR	RBI	BB-IB	HP	SO	AVG	OBP	SLG	AOPS	ABR	SB-CS	FA	FR	RNG	THR	GAMES AT POSITION	DL	BFW
1884	KC U	38	146	25	36	14	2	1	—	10	—	—	.247	.295	.390	122	0	—	.784	-0	94	0	O19(5/7/7),P16,2b6/S	—	-0.1

Blackaby, Ethan Ethan Allen; B7.24.1940 Cincinnati OH; BL/TL/5´11˝/(190–194); d9.6; Col Illinois

YEAR	TM LG	G	AB	R	H	2B	3B	HR	RBI	BB-IB	HP	SO	AVG	OBP	SLG	AOPS	ABR	SB-CS	FA	FR	RNG	THR	GAMES AT POSITION	DL	BFW
1962	Mil N	6	13	0	2	1	0	0	0	1-0	0	8	.154	.214	.231	20	-1	0-0	1.000	-1	50	0	O3(2/1/0)	0	-0.2
1964	Mil N	9	12	0	1	0	0	0	1	1-0	0	2	.083	.154	.083	-31	-2	0-0	.500	-1	21	0	O5(2/0/3)	0	-0.4
Total	2	15	25	0	3	1	0	0	1	2-0	0	10	.120	.185	.160	-4	-3	0-0	.800	-2	36	0	O8(4/1/3)	0	-0.6

Blackburn, Earl Earl Stuart; B11.1.1892 Leesville OH; D8.3.1966 Mansfield OH; BR/TR/5´11˝/180; d9.17

YEAR	TM LG	G	AB	R	H	2B	3B	HR	RBI	BB-IB	HP	SO	AVG	OBP	SLG	AOPS	ABR	SB-CS	FA	FR	RNG	THR	GAMES AT POSITION	DL	BFW
1912	Pit N	1	0	0	0	0	0	0	0	0	0	0	ø	ø	ø	ø	0	0	1.000	0	*0*	*0*	/C	—	0.0
	Cin N	1	0	0	0	0	0	0	0	1	0	0	ø	1.000	ø	191	0	0	1.000	0	*0*	*0*	/C	—	0.1
	Year	2	0	0	0	0	0	0	0	1	0	0	ø	1.000	ø	190	0	0	1.000	0	*0*	*0*	C2	—	0.1
1913	Cin N	17	27	1	7	0	0	0	3	2	0	5	.259	.310	.259	64	-1	2-1	.848	-2	108	86	C12	—	-0.2
1915	Bos N	3	6	0	1	0	0	0	0	2	0	1	.167	.375	.167	70	0	0	1.000	-0	*94*	*126*	C3	—	0.0
1916	Bos N	47	110	12	30	4	4	0	7	9	0	21	.273	.328	.382	123	3	2	.972	3	173	67	C44	—	1.0
1917	Chi N	2	2	0	0	0	0	0	0	0	0	0	.000	.000	.000	-93	0	0	ø	0	—	—	/H	—	-0.1
Total	5	71	145	13	38	4	4	0	10	14	0	27	.262	.327	.345	107	2	4-1	.954	2	*156*	*71*	C61	—	0.8

Blackburne, Lena Russell Aubrey "Slats"; B10.23.1886 Clifton Heights PA; D2.29.1968 Riverside NJ; BR/TR/5´11˝/160; d4.14; M2/C13

YEAR	TM LG	G	AB	R	H	2B	3B	HR	RBI	BB-IB	HP	SO	AVG	OBP	SLG	AOPS	ABR	SB-CS	FA	FR	RNG	THR	GAMES AT POSITION	DL	BFW
1910	Chi A	75	242	16	42	3	1	0	10	19	4	—	.174	.245	.194	39	-17	4	.911	11	107	117	S74	—	-0.4
1912	Chi A	5	1	0	0	0	0	0	0	1	0	—	.000	.500	.000	48	0	1	.800	0	57	570	S4/3	—	0.0
1914	Chi A	144	474	52	105	10	5	1	35	66	6	58	.222	.324	.270	80	-9	25-15	.963	4	**109**	67	2b143	—	-0.3
1915	Chi A	96	283	33	61	5	1	0	25	35	1	34	.216	.304	.240	61	-13	13-11	.949	-9	88	108	3b83,S9	—	-2.2
1918	Cin N	125	435	34	99	8	10	1	45	25	1	30	.228	.271	.299	75	-15	6	.938	11	99	**126**	S125	—	0.5
1919	Bos N	31	80	5	21	3	1	0	4	6	1	7	.262	.322	.325	99	0	3	.948	1	96	103	3b24/12S	—	0.2
	Phi N	72	291	32	58	10	5	2	19	10	1	22	.199	.228	.289	51	-18	2	.933	7	114	94	3b72/1	—	-1.0
	Year	103	371	37	79	13	6	2	23	16	2	29	.213	.249	.296	61	-18	5	.937	8	**110**	96	3b96,1b2/2S	—	-0.8
1927	Chi A	1	1	1	1	0	0	0	1	0	0	0	1.000	1.000	1.000	431	0	0-0	ø	0	—	—	/H	—	0.0
1929	Chi A	1	0	0	0	0	0	0	0	0	0	0	ø	ø	ø	ø	0	0-0	ø	0	0	0	/PM	—	0.0
Total	8	550	1807	173	387	39	23	4	139	162	14	151	.214	.284	.268	67	-72	54-26	.927	25	102	124	S213,3b180,2b144,1b2/P	—	-3.2

Blackerby, George George Franklin; B11.10.1903 Luther OK; D5.30.1987 Wichita Falls TX; BR/TR/6´1˝/176; d8.10

YEAR	TM LG	G	AB	R	H	2B	3B	HR	RBI	BB-IB	HP	SO	AVG	OBP	SLG	AOPS	ABR	SB-CS	FA	FR	RNG	THR	GAMES AT POSITION	DL	BFW
1928	Chi A	30	83	8	21	0	0	0	12	4	0	10	.253	.287	.253	44	-7	2-1	.953	-1	95	54	O20L	—	-0.9

Blackwell, Fred Fredrick William "Blacky"; B9.7.1891 Bowling Green KY; D12.8.1975 Morgantown KY; BL/TR/5´11.5˝/160; d9.25; Mil 1918

YEAR	TM LG	G	AB	R	H	2B	3B	HR	RBI	BB-IB	HP	SO	AVG	OBP	SLG	AOPS	ABR	SB-CS	FA	FR	RNG	THR	GAMES AT POSITION	DL	BFW
1917	Pit N	3	10	1	2	0	0	0	2	0	0	3	.200	.200	.200	22	-1	0	1.000	0	*84*	*102*	C3	—	-0.1
1918	Pit N	8	13	1	2	0	0	0	4	3	0	4	.154	.313	.154	42	-1	0	.926	0	*148*	*87*	C8	—	0.0
1919	Pit N	24	65	3	14	3	0	0	4	3	1	9	.215	.261	.262	55	-3	0	.964	0	*135*	*75*	C22	—	-0.1
Total	3	35	88	5	18	3	0	0	10	6	1	16	.205	.263	.239	50	-5	0	.961	1	*132*	*80*	C33	—	-0.2

Blackwell, Tim Timothy P; B8.19.1952 San Diego CA; BB/TR/5´11˝/(170–185); [BosA70 13/311]; d7.3

YEAR	TM LG	G	AB	R	H	2B	3B	HR	RBI	BB-IB	HP	SO	AVG	OBP	SLG	AOPS	ABR	SB-CS	FA	FR	RNG	THR	GAMES AT POSITION	DL	BFW
1974	Bos A	44	122	9	30	1	1	0	8	10-1	1	21	.246	.308	.270	63	-6	1-1	.971	-4	82	105	C44	0	-0.8
1975	Bos A	59	132	15	26	3	2	0	6	19-0	1	13	.197	.303	.250	53	-8	0-0	.984	1	82	104	C57,D2	0	-0.5
1976	Phi N	4	8	0	2	0	0	0	1	0-0	0	1	.250	.250	.250	41	-1	0-0	1.000	1	0	0	C4	0	0.1
1977	Phi N	1	0	1	0	0	0	0	0	0-0	0	0	ø	ø	ø	ø	0	0-0	1.000	0	0	0	/C	0	0.0
	Mon N	16	22	3	2	1	0	0	0	2-1	0	7	.091	.167	.136	-18	-4	0-0	.925	-3	48	0	C14	0	-0.7
	Year	17	22	4	2	1	0	0	0	2-1	0	7	.091	.167	.136	-18	-4	0-0	.929	-3	46	0	C15	0	-0.7
1978	Chi N	49	103	8	23	3	0	0	7	23-1	1	17	.223	.367	.252	69	-3	0-0	.987	4	101	44	C49	0	0.3
1979	Chi N	63	122	8	20	3	1	0	12	32-1	1	25	.164	.338	.205	48	-7	0-0	.975	-4	85	105	C63	0	-1.0
1980	Chi N	103	320	24	87	16	4	5	30	41-6	0	62	.272	.352	.394	100	1	0-1	.982	14	99	**158**	C103	0	2.0
1981	Chi N	58	158	21	37	10	2	1	11	23-4	0	23	.234	.331	.342	86	-2	2-1	.993	-6	61	115	C56	0	-0.6
1982	Mon N	23	42	2	8	2	1	0	3	3-0	0	11	.190	.244	.286	46	-3	0-0	.985	-1	71	86	C18	0	-0.4
1983	Mon N	6	15	0	3	1	0	0	2	1-0	0	3	.200	.250	.267	43	-1	0-0	.935	-2	39	0	C5	0	-0.3
Total	10	426	1044	91	238	40	11	6	80	154-14	4	183	.228	.328	.305	73	-34	3-3	.981	1	84	110	C414,D2	0	-1.9

Blades, Ray Francis Raymond; B8.6.1896 Mt.Vernon IL; D5.18.1979 Lincoln IL; BR/TR/5´7.5˝/163; d8.19; M3/C11

YEAR	TM LG	G	AB	R	H	2B	3B	HR	RBI	BB-IB	HP	SO	AVG	OBP	SLG	AOPS	ABR	SB-CS	FA	FR	RNG	THR	GAMES AT POSITION	DL	BFW
1922	StL N	37	130	27	39	2	4	3	21	25	4	21	.300	.428	.446	132	8	3-3	.931	-1	103	169	O29(28/0/1),S4/3	—	0.4
1923	StL N	98	317	48	78	21	5	5	44	37	9	46	.246	.342	.391	95	-1	4-2	.967	6	110	138	O83(81/1/3),3b4	—	-0.1
1924	StL N	131	456	86	142	21	13	11	68	35	10	38	.311	.373	.487	131	19	7-9	.956	-1	**114**	55	O109(106/3/1),2b7,3b7	—	0.9
1925	StL N	122	462	112	158	37	8	12	57	59	6	47	.342	.423	.535	140	30	6-8	.979	9	**114**	127	O114L/3	—	2.7
1926	StL N	107	416	81	127	17	12	8	43	62	**11**	57	.305	.409	.462	129	19	6	.980	0	101	94	O105L	—	1.1
1927	StL N	61	180	33	57	8	5	2	29	28	2	22	.317	.414	.450	127	8	3	.914	-9	74	0	O50(29/0/21)	—	-0.4

YEAR	TM LG	G	AB	R	H	2B	3B	HR	RBI	BB-IB	HP	SO	AVG	OBP	SLG	AOPS	ABR	SB-CS	FA	FR	RNG	THR	GAMES AT POSITION	DL	BFW
1928	†StL N	51	85	9	20	7	1	1	19	20	2	26	.235	.393	.376	100	1	0	.972	-1	87	56	O19(4/0/15)	—	-0.1
1930	†StL N	45	101	26	40	6	2	4	25	21	1	15	.396	.504	.614	163	12	1	.957	-1	107	33	O32(13/0/21)	—	0.7
1931	†StL N	35	67	10	19	4	0	1	5	10	2	7	.284	.392	.388	106	1	1	.871	-2	83	70	O20(7/0/13)	—	-0.2
1932	StL N	80	201	35	46	10	1	3	29	34	0	31	.229	.340	.333	80	-5	2	.975	-1	106	42	O62(13/0/49)/3	—	-0.9
Total	10	767	2415	467	726	133	51	50	340	331	47	310	.301	.395	.460	123	92	33-22	.963	-1	105	87	O623(500/4/124),3b14,2b7,S4	—	4.1
Bladt, Rick	Richard Alan; B12.9.1946 Santa Cruz CA; BR/TR/6´1˝/160; d6.15; Col Foothill (CA) JC																								
1969	Chi N	10	13	1	2	0	0	0	1	0-0	0	5	.154	.154	.154	-12	-2	0-0	1.000	1	141	401	O7(2/5/1)	0	-0.1
1975	NY A	52	117	13	26	3	1	1	11	11-0	1	8	.222	.292	.291	66	-5	6-2	.973	2	106	154	O51C	0	-0.4
Total	2	62	130	14	28	3	1	1	12	11-0	1	13	.215	.280	.277	58	-7	6-2	.976	3	109	178	O58(2/56/1)	0	-0.5
Blaemire, Rae	Rae Bertrum; B2.8.1911 Gary IN; D12.23.1975 Champaign IL; BR/TR/6´0˝/178; d9.13																								
1941	NY N	2	5	0	2	0	0	0	0	0	0	0	.400	.400	.400	123	0	0	1.000	-0	*0*	*0*	C2	0	0.0
Blair, Footsie	Clarence Vick; B7.13.1900 Enterprise OK; D7.1.1982 Texarkana TX; BL/TR/6´1˝/180; d4.28																								
1929	†Chi N	26	72	10	23	5	0	1	8	3	0	4	.319	.347	.431	91	-1	1	.897	-0	88	0	3b8,1b7,2b2	—	-0.1
1930	Chi N	134	578	97	158	24	12	6	59	20	7	58	.273	.306	.388	66	-35	9	.958	4	105	101	2b115,3b13	—	-2.4
1931	Chi N	86	240	31	62	19	4	3	29	14	1	26	.258	.302	.408	88	-5	1	.956	-7	89	67	2b44,1b23/3	—	-1.1
Total	3	246	890	138	243	48	16	10	96	37	8	88	.273	.308	.397	73	-41	11	.958	-4	101	94	2b161,1b30,3b22	—	-3.6
Blair, Buddy	Louis Nathan; B9.10.1910 Columbia MS; D6.7.1996 Monroe LA; BL/TR/6´0˝/186; d4.14; Mil 1943–45; Col Louisiana St.																								
1942	Phi A	137	484	48	135	26	8	5	66	30	3	30	.279	.325	.397	103	0	1-6	.931	-5	95	84	3b126	0	-0.3
Blair, Paul	Paul L D; B2.1.1944 Cushing OK; BR/TR (BB 1971p)/6´0˝/(168–177); d9.9; OF(31/1801/58)																								
1964	Bal A	8	1	0	0	0	0	0	0	0-0	0	1	.000	.000	.000	-99	0	0-1	1.000	-0	83	0	O6C	0	-0.1
1965	Bal A	119	364	49	85	19	2	5	25	32-3	4	52	.234	.302	.338	80	-9	8-5	.992	-1	101	110	O116C	0	-1.4
1966	†Bal A	133	303	35	84	20	2	6	33	15-0	0	36	.277	.309	.416	109	3	5-6	.990	-3	98	73	O127(2/125/0)	0	-0.4
1967	Bal A	151	552	72	162	27	**12**	11	64	50-3	5	68	.293	.353	.446	137	25	8-6	.985	9	113	151	O146C	0	3.2
1968	Bal A	141	421	48	89	22	1	7	38	37-4	2	60	.211	.277	.318	80	-10	4-2	.993	4	104	135	O132C/3	0	-1.0
1969	†Bal A★	150	625	102	178	32	5	26	76	40-0	2	72	.285	.327	.477	122	15	20-6	.988	12	114	144	O150C	0	2.6
1970	†Bal A	133	480	79	128	24	2	18	65	56-1	3	93	.267	.344	.438	113	9	24-11	.990	11	121	122	O128C/3	21	1.9
1971	†Bal A	141	516	75	135	24	8	10	44	32-2	1	94	.262	.306	.397	97	-4	14-11	.991	-4	101	48	O138C	0	-1.3
1972	Bal A	142	477	47	111	20	8	8	49	25-0	0	78	.233	.267	.358	83	-12	7-8	.991	5	109	122	O139C	0	-1.3
1973	†Bal A★	146	500	73	140	25	3	10	64	43-4	0	72	.280	.334	.402	107	4	18-8	.990	6	105	139	O144C/D	0	0.8
1974	†Bal A	151	552	77	144	27	4	17	62	43-0	2	59	.261	.313	.417	112	7	27-9	.985	-1	106	62	O151C	0	0.5
1975	Bal A	140	440	51	96	13	4	5	31	25-0	0	82	.218	.257	.300	61	-24	17-11	.991	-1	101	93	O138C/1D	0	-3.0
1976	Bal A	145	375	29	74	16	0	3	16	22-2	2	49	.197	.245	.264	52	-23	15-6	.979	-1	104	71	O139C/D	0	-2.7
1977	†NY A	83	164	20	43	4	3	4	25	9-1	2	16	.262	.303	.396	91	-3	3-2	.969	-1	101	28	O79(6/42/33)/D	0	-0.5
1978	†NY A	75	125	10	22	5	0	2	13	9-0	0	17	.176	.231	.264	40	-10	1-1	.989	-2	98	84	O64(1/49/16),2b5,S4,3b3	0	-1.4
1979	NY A	2	5	0	1	0	0	0	0	0-0	0	1	.200	.200	.200	8	-1	0-0	1.000	0	173	0	O2(0/1/1)	0	0.0
	Cin N	75	140	7	21	4	1	2	15	11-3	0	27	.150	.209	.236	22	-16	0-0	.992	2	109	96	O67(16/56/2)	0	-1.5
1980	NY A	12	2	2	0	0	0	0	0	0-0	0	0	.000	.000	.000	-99	-1	0-0	1.000	0	155	0	O12(6/1/6)	0	0.0
Total	17	1947	6042	776	1513	282	55	134	620	449-23	23	877	.250	.302	.382	96	-50	171-93	.988	37	107	104	O1878C,2b5,3b5,S4,D4/1	21	-5.6
Blair, Walter	Walter Allen "Heavy"; B10.13.1883 Landrus PA; D8.20.1948 Lewisburg PA; BR/TR/6´0˝/185; d9.17; M1; Col Bucknell																								
1907	NY A	7	22	1	4	0	0	0	1	2	0	—	.182	.250	.182	35	-2	0	.922	1	*99*	*112*	C7	—	0.0
1908	NY A	76	211	9	40	5	1	1	13	11	2	—	.190	.237	.237	53	-11	4	.956	-12	*74*	*99*	C60,O9(2/0/7),1b3	—	-2.1
1909	NY A	42	110	5	23	2	2	0	11	7	2	—	.209	.269	.264	68	-4	2	.964	-5	*86*	*87*	C42	—	-0.7
1910	NY A	6	22	2	5	0	1	0	2	0	0	—	.227	.227	.318	67	-1	0	.970	-1	*87*	*125*	C6	—	-0.2
1911	NY A	85	222	18	43	9	2	0	26	16	3	—	.194	.257	.252	40	-18	2	.970	2	*96*	*105*	C84/1	—	-1.0
1914	Buf F	128	378	22	92	11	2	0	33	32	1	64	.243	.304	.283	59	-27	6	.984	11	*114*	*100*	C128	—	-0.6
1915	Buf F	98	290	23	65	15	3	2	20	18	2	32	.224	.274	.317	65	-19	4	**.981**	-2	*75*	***119***	C97,M	—	-1.4
Total	7	442	1255	80	272	42	11	3	106	86	10	96	.217	.272	.275	56	-82	18	.974	-6	*93*	*105*	C424,O9(2/0/7),1b4	—	-6.0
Blake, Harry	Harry Cooper; B6.16.1874 Portsmouth OH; D10.14.1919 Chicago IL; BR/TR/5´7˝/165; d7.7																								
1894	Cle N	73	296	51	78	15	4	1	51	30	2	22	.264	.335	.351	63	-18	1	.932	2	133	148	O73(0/4/69)	—	-1.5
1895	†Cle N	85	318	50	88	10	1	3	45	31	1	33	.277	.343	.343	73	-13	11	.898	-5	99	113	O84R	—	-1.8
1896	†Cle N	104	383	66	92	12	5	1	43	46	0	30	.240	.322	.305	62	-21	10	.944	-2	111	145	O103(0/12/92)/S	—	-2.5
1897	Cle N	32	117	17	30	3	1	1	15	12	1	—	.256	.331	.325	70	-5	5	.989	3	63	238	O32(2/25/5)	—	-0.4
1898	Cle N	136	474	65	116	18	7	0	58	69	1	—	.245	.342	.312	89	-4	12	.952	6	133	74	O136(1/22/114),1b2	—	-0.4
1899	StL N	97	292	50	70	9	4	2	41	43	2	—	.240	.341	.318	80	-7	16	.979	1	85	100	O87(9/69/9),2b4/S1C	—	-1.0
Total	6	527	1880	299	474	67	22	8	253	231	7	85	.252	.336	.324	73	-68	55	.948	6	111	121	O515(12/132/373),2b4,1b3,S2/C	—	-7.6
Blake, Casey	William Casey; B8.23.1973 Des Moines IA; BR/TR/6´2˝/(195–210); [TorA96 7/189]; d8.14; Col Wichita St.																								
1999	Tor A	14	39	6	10	2	0	1	1	2-0	0	7	.256	.293	.385	70	-2	0-0	1.000	3	119	230	3b14	0	0.1
2000	Min A	7	16	1	3	2	0	0	1	3-0	1	7	.188	.333	.313	65	-1	0-0	1.000	-1	70	0	3b5/1D	0	-0.2
2001	Min A	13	22	1	7	1	0	0	2	3-1	0	8	.318	.400	.364	98	0	1-0	.800	-0	83	0	3b5,1b3,D4	0	0.0
	Bal A	6	15	2	2	0	0	1	2	1-0	0	4	.133	.188	.333	35	-2	2-0	.967	-1	0	80	1b5/D	0	-0.3
	Year	19	37	3	9	1	0	1	4	4-1	0	12	.243	.317	.351	74	-1	3-0	.979	-2	49	77	1b8,3b5,D5	0	-0.3
2002	Min A	9	20	2	4	1	0	0	1	2-0	0	7	.200	.273	.250	39	-2	0-0	.846	-2	64	128	3b5,1b3	0	-0.3
2003	Cle A	152	557	80	143	35	0	17	67	38-1	10	109	.257	.312	.411	90	-8	7-9	.952	6	108	128	3b140,1b31	0	-0.4
2004	Cle A	152	587	93	159	36	3	28	88	68-2	9	139	.271	.354	.486	121	18	5-8	.939	-2	99	92	3b152,1b8	0	1.5
2005	Cle A	147	523	72	126	32	1	23	58	43-3	10	116	.241	.308	.438	100	-1	4-5	.973	-0	105	38	O138R,3b6,1b4	0	-0.9
2006	Cle A	109	401	63	113	20	1	19	68	45-5	4	93	.282	.356	.479	119	12	6-0	.986	2	109	102	O93R,1b9,D8	48	1.0
Total	8	609	2180	320	567	129	5	89	288	205-12	34	490	.260	.330	.446	105	14	25-22	.945	5	103	112	3b327,O231R,1b64,D14	48	0.5
Blakely, Linc	Lincoln Howard; B2.12.1912 Oakland CA; D9.28.1976 Oakland CA; BR/TR/6´0˝/180; d4.29																								
1934	Cin N	34	102	11	23	1	1	0	10	5	1	14	.225	.269	.255	42	-9	1	.987	3	109	211	O28(6/22/0)	—	-0.6
Blakiston, Bob	Robert J. (b Robert J. Blackstone); B10.2.1855 San Francisco CA; D12.25.1918 San Francisco CA; 5´8.5˝/180; d5.2																								
1882	Phi AA	72	281	40	64	4	1	0	20	9	—	—	.228	.252	.249	65	-11	—	.855	-1	154	0	O38(0/4/34),3b34/2	—	-1.1
1883	Phi AA	44	167	26	41	3	3	0	26	9	—	—	.246	.284	.299	81	-4	—	.857	-1	93	0	O37(2/35/0),1b6,3b5	—	-0.5
1884	Phi AA	32	128	21	33	6	0	0	—	11	4	—	.258	.336	.305	104	1	—	.911	-3	53	119	O28(0/27/1),3b2/12S	—	-0.2
	Ind AA	6	18	0	4	1	0	0	—	1	0	—	.222	.263	.278	79	0	—	.884	-1	155	0	1b5/rf	—	-0.1
	Year	38	146	21	37	7	0	0	—	12	4	—	.253	.327	.301	101	1	—	.914	-3	51	115	O29(0/27/3),1b6,3b2/2S	—	-0.3
Total	3	154	594	87	142	14	4	0	46	30	4	—	.239	.280	.276	79	-14	—	.874	-5	103	37	O104(2/66/37),3b41,1b12,2b2/S	—	-1.9
Blalock, Hank	Hank Joe; B11.21.1980 San Diego CA; BL/TR/6´1˝/(192–200); [TexA99 3/105]; d4.1																								
2002	Tex A	49	147	16	31	8	0	3	17	20-1	1	43	.211	.306	.327	68	-7	0-0	.943	-5	88	86	3b46	0	-1.1
2003	Tex A★	143	567	89	170	33	3	29	90	44-1	1	97	.300	.350	.522	118	14	2-3	.959	6	99	128	3b141,2b4	0	1.9
2004	Tex A★	159	624	107	172	38	3	32	110	75-7	6	149	.276	.355	.500	116	15	2-2	.957	-5	98	123	3b159	0	1.0
2005	Tex A	161	647	80	170	34	0	25	92	51-1	3	132	.263	.318	.431	95	-5	1-0	**.973**	-6	99	76	3b158,D2	0	-1.0
2006	Tex A	152	591	76	157	26	3	16	89	51-6	2	98	.266	.325	.401	87	-12	1-0	.963	-8	97	76	3b122,D29	0	-2.0
Total	5	664	2576	368	700	139	9	105	398	241-16	13	519	.272	.335	.455	102	5	6-5	.962	-18	98	100	3b626,D31,2b4	0	-1.2
Blanchard, Johnny	John Edwin; B2.26.1933 Minneapolis MN; BL/TR/6´1˝/(195–204); d9.25																								
1955	NY A	1	3	0	0	0	0	0	0	1-0	0	0	.000	.250	.000	-29	-1	0-0	1.000	0	*0*	*0*	/C	0	0.0
1959	NY A	49	59	6	10	1	0	2	4	7-0	0	12	.169	.258	.288	51	-4	0-0	.963	-2	31	94	C12,O8(1/0/7)/1	0	-0.6
1960	†NY A	53	99	8	24	3	1	4	14	6-1	1	17	.242	.292	.414	94	-2	0-0	.988	5	100	37	C28	32	0.5
1961	†NY A	93	243	38	74	10	1	21	54	27-9	4	28	.305	.382	.613	170	23	1-0	.990	-1	96	52	C48,O15(8/0/7)	0	2.4
1962	†NY A	93	246	33	57	7	0	13	39	28-0	1	32	.232	.309	.419	98	-1	0-0	.987	-7	90	78	O47(15/0/32),C15,1b2	0	-1.1
1963	†NY A	76	218	22	49	4	0	16	45	26-3	0	30	.225	.305	.463	114	3	0-0	.987	-6	74	54	O64(22/0/42)	0	-0.7
1964	†NY A	77	161	18	41	8	0	7	28	24-4	0	24	.255	.344	.435	115	4	1-0	.984	-5	120	68	C25,O14(6/0/8),1b3	0	-0.1
1965	NY A	12	34	1	5	1	0	1	3	7-2	0	3	.147	.286	.265	60	-2	0-0	.961	-1	100	79	C12	0	-0.2
	KC A	52	120	10	24	2	0	2	11	8-1	1	16	.200	.250	.267	49	-8	0-0	1.000	-5	84	0	O20(1/0/19),C14	0	-1.4
	Year	64	154	11	29	3	0	3	14	15-3	1	19	.188	.259	.266	52	-10	0-0	.971	-6	72	64	C26,O20(1/0/19)	0	-1.6

YEAR	TM LG	G	AB	R	H	2B	3B	HR	RBI	BB-IB	HP	SO	AVG	OBP	SLG	AOPS	ABR	SB-CS	FA	FR	RNG	THR	GAMES AT POSITION	DL	BFW
	Mil N	10	10	1	1	0	0	1	2	2-0	0	1	.100	.250	.400	79	0	0-0	ø	-0	0	0	/lf	0	-0.1
Total	8	516	1193	137	285	36	2	67	200	136-20	7	163	.239	.317	.441	109	12	2-0	.987	-22	83	56	O169(54/0/115),C155,1b6	32	-1.3
BLANCO, ANDRES	Andres Eloy (Perez); B4.11.1984 Urama, Carabobo, Venezuela; BB/TR/5´10˝/(150–185); d4.17																								
2004	KC A	19	60	9	19	2	2	0	5	5-0	1	6	.317	.379	.417	107	1	1-2	.959	4	116	135	S19	0	0.5
2005	KC A	26	79	6	17	0	1	0	5	0-0	1	5	.215	.220	.241	25	-9	0-1	.977	7	110	140	2b24,S7	0	-0.1
2006	KC A	33	87	9	21	4	1	0	9	5-0	1	14	.241	.290	.310	57	-6	0-1	.956	4	116	150	S25,2b7	0	-0.1
Total	3	78	226	24	57	6	4	0	19	10-0	3	25	.252	.290	.314	60	-14	1-4	.960	15	114	140	S51,2b31	0	0.3
BLANCO, DAMASO	Damaso (Caripe); B11.12.1941 Curiepe, Miranda, Venez; BR/TR/5´10˝/165; d5.26																								
1972	SF N	39	20	5	7	1	0	0	2	4-0	0	3	.350	.440	.400	143	2	2-1	.889	-1	91	182	3b19,S8,2b3	0	0.1
1973	SF N	28	12	4	0	0	0	0	0	1-0	0	2	.000	.077	.000	-74	-3	0-0	1.000	-1	50	0	3b7,S5,2b3	0	-0.4
1974	SF N	5	1	0	0	0	0	0	0	0-0	0	1	.000	.000	.000	-96	0	1-0	ø	0	—	—	/H	0	0.0
Total	3	72	33	9	7	1	0	0	2	5-0	0	6	.212	.308	.242	58	-1	3-1	.929	-2	81	139	3b26,S13,2b6	0	-0.3
BLANCO, HENRY	Henry Ramon; B8.29.1971 Caracas, Distrito Capital, Venez; BR/TR/5´11˝/(168–225); d7.25; [DL 1998 LA N 120]																								
1997	LA N	3	5	1	2	0	0	1	1	0-0	0	1	.400	.400	1.000	269	1	0-0	1.000	-0	0	0	/13	0	0.1
1999	Col N	88	263	30	61	12	3	6	28	34-1	1	38	.232	.320	.369	59	-16	1-1	.992	19	102	**161**	C86/lf	0	0.7
2000	Mil N	93	284	29	67	24	0	7	31	36-6	0	60	.236	.318	.394	80	-8	0-3	.991	14	184	**165**	C88	16	1.0
2001	Mil N	104	314	33	66	18	3	6	31	34-6	2	72	.210	.290	.344	65	-17	3-1	.992	10	131	113	C102	0	0.0
2002	†Atl N	81	221	17	45	9	1	6	22	20-5	1	51	.204	.267	.335	59	-14	0-2	.993	-1	106	115	C79	15	-1.1
2003	Atl N	55	151	11	30	8	0	1	13	10-2	1	21	.199	.252	.272	37	-14	0-0	.996	-4	67	109	C52	0	-1.5
2004	†Min A	114	315	36	65	19	1	10	37	21-0	3	56	.206	.260	.368	60	-19	0-3	.991	10	**160**	127	C114	0	-0.3
2005	Chi N	54	161	16	39	6	0	6	25	11-1	0	24	.242	.287	.391	74	-7	0-0	.998	13	126	189	C54	0	1.0
2006	Chi N	74	241	23	64	15	2	6	37	14-1	0	38	.266	.304	.419	82	-7	0-0	.998	7	143	137	C69,1b6	0	0.4
Total	9	666	1955	196	439	111	10	49	225	180-22	8	361	.225	.290	.367	66	-101	4-10	.993	69	133	138	C644,1b7/lf3	151	0.3
BLANCO, OSSIE	Oswaldo Carlos (Diaz); B9.8.1945 Caracas, Distrito Capital, Venez; BR/TR/6´0˝/185; d5.26																								
1970	Chi A	34	66	4	13	0	0	0	8	3-0	0	14	.197	.225	.197	19	-7	0-1	.993	-0	103	83	1b22/lf	0	-0.9
1974	Cle A	18	36	1	7	0	0	0	2	7-0	0	4	.194	.326	.194	53	-2	0-3	.992	-2	50	104	1b16/D	0	-0.6
Total	2	52	102	5	20	0	0	0	10	10-0	0	18	.196	.263	.196	31	-9	0-4	.993	-2	76	94	1b38/Dlf	0	-1.5
BLANCO, TONY	Tony Hemiphere (Cabrera); B11.10.1981 San Juan de Maguana, D.R.; BR/TR/6´1˝/175; d4.4																								
2005	Was N	56	62	7	11	3	0	1	7	2-0	1	19	.177	.215	.274	28	-7	1-0	1.000	-0	86	288	O11(9/0/2),3b5,1b3	25	-0.7
BLANK, COONIE	Frank Ignatz; B10.18.1892 St.Louis MO; D12.8.1961 St.Louis MO; BR/TR/5´11˝/165; d8.15																								
1909	StL N	1	2	0	0	0	0	0	0	0	0	—	.000	.000	.000	-99	0	0	1.000	-0	*55*	*0*	/C	—	-0.1
BLANKENSHIP, CLIFF	Clifford Douglas; B4.10.1880 Columbus GA; D4.26.1956 Oakland CA; BR/TR/5´10.5˝/165; d4.17																								
1905	Cin N	19	56	8	11	1	1	0	7	4	0	—	.196	.250	.250	44	-4	1	.960	-3	47	97	1b15	—	-0.7
1907	Was A	37	102	4	23	2	0	0	6	3	0	—	.225	.248	.245	62	-5	3	.991	-1	*85*	*123*	C22,1b9	—	-0.4
1909	Was A	39	60	4	15	1	0	0	9	0	0	—	.250	.250	.267	66	-3	2	.907	-6	*69*	*83*	C17,O4(1/1/2)	—	-0.8
Total	3	95	218	16	49	4	1	0	22	7	0	—	.225	.249	.252	58	-12	6	.964	-9	*80*	*110*	C39,1b24,O4(1/1/2)	—	-1.9
BLANKENSHIP, LANCE	Lance Robert; B12.6.1963 Portland OR; BR/TR/6´0˝/185; [OakA86 10/249]; d9.4; Col California; OF(71/66/71); [DL 1994 Oak A 131]																								
1988	Oak A	10	3	1	0	0	0	0	0	0-0	0	1	.000	.000	.000	-99	-1	0-1	1.000	-1	42	0	2b4,D4	0	-0.2
1989	†Oak A	58	125	22	29	5	1	1	4	8-0	0	31	.232	.276	.312	68	-6	5-1	1.000	1	120	80	O25(4/0/21),2b24,D10	0	-0.5
1990	†Oak A	86	136	18	26	3	0	0	10	20-0	0	23	.191	.295	.213	46	-9	3-1	.947	-2	99	62	3b28,O28(10/1/17),2b20/1D	0	-1.1
1991	Oak A	90	185	33	46	8	0	3	21	23-0	3	42	.249	.336	.341	94	-1	12-3	.983	10	107	107	2b45,O28(18/0/11),3b14,D6	0	1.1
1992	†Oak A	123	349	59	84	24	1	3	34	82-2	6	57	.241	.393	.341	113	13	21-7	.992	7	104	117	2b78,O51(22/16/20),1b7,D3	33	2.3
1993	Oak A	94	252	43	48	8	1	2	23	67-0	2	64	.190	.363	.254	73	-6	13-5	.994	-0	109	29	O66(17/49/2),2b19,1b6,S2,D5	49	-0.4
Total	6	461	1050	176	233	48	3	9	92	200-2	11	218	.222	.350	.299	86	-10	54-18	.987	15	112	33	O198L,2b190,3b42,D34,1b14,S2	213	1.2
BLANKS, LARVELL	Larvell; B1.28.1950 Del Rio TX; BR/TR/5´8˝/(165–167); [AtlN69 3/60]; d7.19																								
1972	Atl N	33	85	10	28	5	0	1	7	7-0	0	12	.329	.376	.424	118	2	0-0	1.000	5	116	113	2b18,S4,3b2	0	0.9
1973	Atl N	17	18	1	4	0	0	0	0	1-0	0	3	.222	.263	.222	33	-2	0-0	ø	-1	0	0	3b3,2b2,S2	0	-0.3
1974	Atl N	3	8	0	2	0	0	0	1	0-0	0	0	.250	.250	.250	39	-1	0-0	.889	-1	111	0	S2	0	-0.1
1975	Atl N	141	471	49	110	13	3	3	38	38-1	2	43	.234	.292	.293	61	-25	4-3	.960	-8	106	85	S129,2b12	0	-1.9
1976	Cle A	104	328	45	92	8	7	5	41	30-0	0	31	.280	.337	.393	115	5	1-2	.977	-7	86	116	S56,2b46,3b2,D3	0	0.6
1977	Cle A	105	322	43	92	10	4	6	38	19-1	1	37	.286	.324	.398	99	-1	3-0	.960	-11	83	75	S66,3b18,2b12,D6	0	-0.6
1978	Cle A	70	193	19	49	10	0	2	20	10-0	0	16	.254	.285	.337	77	-6	0-0	.926	-4	98	100	S43,2b17,3b3/D	0	-0.6
1979	Tex A	68	120	13	24	5	0	1	15	11-0	0	9	.200	.259	.267	45	-9	0-0	.972	-7	90	108	S49,2b16/D	0	-1.3
1980	Atl N	88	221	23	45	6	0	2	12	16-1	0	27	.204	.255	.258	44	-17	1-2	.947	13	117	138	S56,3b43/2	0	-0.3
Total	9	629	1766	203	446	57	14	20	172	132-3	3	178	.253	.302	.335	78	-54	9-7	.957	-21	99	94	S407,2b124,3b71,D11	0	-3.6
BLASINGAME, DON	Don Lee; B3.16.1932 Corinth MS; D4.13.2005 Fountain Hills AZ; BL/TR/5´10˝/(160–165); d9.20																								
1955	StL N	5	16	4	6	1	0	0	0	6-1	0	0	.375	.545	.438	165	2	1-1	.955	0	124	37	2b3,S2	0	0.3
1956	StL N	150	587	94	153	22	7	0	27	72-0	3	52	.261	.344	.322	81	-14	8-8	.986	17	106	132	2b98,S49,3b2	0	1.3
1957	StL N	**154**	650	108	176	25	7	8	58	71-4	1	49	.271	.343	.368	89	-8	21-9	.984	20	**110**	125	2b154	0	2.5
1958	StL N★	143	547	71	150	19	10	2	36	57-2	1	47	.274	.343	.356	83	-13	20-5	.964	-1	100	96	2b137	0	-0.2
1959	StL N	150	615	90	178	26	7	1	24	67-2	2	42	.289	.361	.359	87	-9	15-15	.979	**20**	107	103	2b150	0	2.0
1960	SF N	136	523	72	123	12	8	2	31	49-1	2	53	.235	.302	.300	70	-22	14-2	.979	-4	95	84	2b133	0	-1.5
1961	SF N	3	1	1	0	0	0	0	0	2-0	0	1	.000	.667	.000	100	0	0-0	ø	0	—	—	/H	0	0.0
	†Cin N	123	450	59	100	18	4	1	21	39-0	2	38	.222	.286	.287	52	-31	4-3	.972	-15	90	68	2b116	0	-3.7
	Year	126	451	60	100	18	4	1	21	41-0	2	39	.222	.288	.286	53	-30	4-3	.972	-15	90	68	2b116	0	-3.7
1962	Cin N	141	494	77	139	9	7	2	35	63-2	2	44	.281	.364	.340	88	-7	4-3	.976	-4	96	79	2b137	0	0.1
1963	Cin N	18	31	4	5	2	0	0	0	7-0	0	5	.161	.316	.226	57	-1	0-1	.974	-1	70	126	2b11,3b2	0	-0.3
	Was A	69	254	29	65	10	2	2	12	24-1	0	18	.256	.320	.335	84	-5	3-2	.991	10	110	130	2b64	0	1.1
1964	Was A	143	506	56	135	17	2	1	34	40-1	0	44	.267	.320	.314	78	-15	8-5	.977	-12	102	88	2b135	0	-1.7
1965	Was A	129	403	47	90	8	8	1	18	35-1	2	45	.223	.287	.290	66	-19	5-4	.984	2	100	105	2b110	0	-1.0
1966	Was A	68	200	18	43	9	0	1	11	18-0	0	21	.215	.280	.275	61	-10	2-1	.984	-1	100	105	2b58/S	0	-0.6
	KC A	12	19	1	3	0	0	0	1	2-0	0	3	.158	.238	.158	17	-2	0-1	1.000	1	122	112	2b4	0	-0.2
	Year	80	219	19	46	9	0	1	12	20-0	0	24	.210	.276	.265	57	-12	2-2	.985	0	101	105	2b62/S	0	-0.8
Total	12	1444	5296	731	1366	178	62	21	308	552-15	15	462	.258	.329	.327	78	-154	105-60	.979	32	101	100	2b1310,S52,3b4	0	-1.9
BLATNIK, JOHNNY	John Louis; B3.10.1921 Bridgeport OH; D1.21.2004 Lansing OH; BR/TR/6´0˝/195; d4.21																								
1948	Phi N	121	415	56	108	27	8	6	45	31	2	77	.260	.315	.407	96	-4	3	.946	-0	100	110	O105L	0	-1.2
1949	Phi N	6	8	3	1	0	0	0	0	4	0	1	.125	.417	.125	53	0	0	1.000	-0	84	0	O2R	0	0.0
1950	Phi N	4	4	0	1	0	0	0	0	2	0	3	.250	.500	.250	106	0	0	1.000	0	114	0	/lf	0	0.0
	StL N	7	20	0	3	0	0	0	1	3	0	2	.150	.261	.150	11	-3	0	.875	-0	66	279	O7(2/0/7)	0	-0.3
	Year	11	24	0	4	0	0	0	1	5	0	5	.167	.310	.167	29	-2	0	.900	-0	73	239	O8(3/0/7)	0	-0.3
Total	3	138	447	59	113	27	8	6	46	40	2	83	.253	.317	.389	91	-7	3	.945	-1	98	115	O115(108/0/9)	0	-1.5
BLATTNER, BUDDY	Robert Garnett; B2.8.1920 St.Louis MO; BR/TR/6´0.5˝/180; d4.18; Mil 1943–45																								
1942	StL N	19	23	3	1	0	0	0	1	3	1	6	.043	.185	.043	-29	-4	0	.900	-1	92	68	S13,2b3	0	-0.4
1946	NY N	126	420	63	107	18	6	11	49	56	**6**	52	.255	.351	.405	113	8	12	.976	4	101	93	2b114/1	0	1.9
1947	NY N	55	153	28	40	9	2	0	13	21	0	19	.261	.351	.346	85	-3	4	.947	-1	110	64	2b34,3b11	0	-0.2
1948	NY N	8	20	3	4	1	0	0	0	3	0	2	.200	.304	.250	51	-1	2	1.000	2	152	129	2b7	0	0.1
1949	Phi N	64	97	15	24	6	0	5	21	19	0	17	.247	.371	.464	126	4	0	.981	-6	87	69	2b15,3b12/S	0	-0.1
Total	5	272	713	112	176	34	8	16	84	102	7	96	.247	.347	.384	102	4	18	.971	-1	103	87	2b173,3b23,S14/1	0	1.3
BLAUSER, JEFF	Jeffrey Michael; B11.8.1965 Los Gatos CA; BR/TR/6´0˝/(170–190); [AtlN84 S1/5]; d7.5; Col Sacramento (CA) City																								
1987	Atl N	51	165	11	40	6	3	2	15	18-1	3	34	.242	.328	.352	77	-5	7-3	.962	4	116	93	S50	0	0.4
1988	Atl N	18	67	7	16	3	1	2	7	2-0	1	11	.239	.268	.403	88	-1	0-1	.967	1	143	69	2b9,S8	0	0.0
1989	Atl N	142	456	63	123	24	2	12	46	38-2	1	101	.270	.325	.410	107	4	5-2	.929	-16	97	85	3b78,2b39,S30,O2C	0	-1.0
1990	Atl N	115	386	46	104	24	3	8	39	35-1	5	70	.269	.338	.409	99	0	3-5	.961	-3	100	90	S93,2b14,3b9/cf	16	0.4

YEAR	TM LG	G	AB	R	H	2B	3B	HR	RBI	BB-IB	HP	SO	AVG	OBP	SLG	AOPS	ABR	SB-CS	FA	FR	RNG	THR	GAMES AT POSITION	DL	BFW
1991	†Atl N	129	352	49	91	14	3	11	54	54-4	2	59	.259	.358	.409	109	6	5-6	.948	-14	83	91	S85,2b32,3b18	0	-0.5
1992	†Atl N	123	343	61	90	19	3	14	46	46-2	4	82	.262	.354	.458	121	11	5-5	.968	-14	91	75	S106,2b21/3	0	0.1
1993	†Atl N★	161	597	110	182	29	2	15	73	85-0	**16**	109	.305	.401	.436	122	24	16-6	.970	-16	93	106	S161	0	2.1
1994	Atl N	96	380	56	98	21	4	6	45	38-0	5	64	.258	.329	.382	83	-9	1-3	.970	4	100	85	S96	18	0.2
1995	†Atl N	115	431	60	91	16	2	12	31	57-2	12	107	.211	.319	.341	71	-17	8-5	.970	3	97	102	S115	0	-0.6
1996	†Atl N	83	265	48	65	14	1	10	35	40-3	6	54	.245	.356	.419	98	0	6-0	.926	-14	89	95	S79	67	-0.7
1997	†Atl N★	151	519	90	160	31	4	17	70	70-6	20	101	.308	.405	.482	131	27	5-1	.973	-18	88	107	S149/D	0	2.0
1998	†Chi N	119	361	49	79	11	3	4	26	60-1	8	93	.219	.340	.299	68	-15	2-2	.965	-22	88	58	S106	15	-2.9
1999	Chi N	104	200	41	48	5	2	9	26	26-0	8	52	.240	.347	.420	94	-2	2-2	.961	-5	78	92	2b25,S22,3b18/lf	0	-0.5
Total	13	1407	4522	691	1187	217	33	122	513	569-22	91	937	.262	.354	.406	101	23	65-41	.964	-110	93	91	S1100,2b140,3b124,O4(1/3/0)/D	116	-1.0
BLAYLOCK, MARV	Marvin Edward; B9.30.1929 Ft.Smith AR; D10.23.1993 Conway AR; BL/TL/6´1.5˝/175; d9.26; Col Arkansas–Fort Smith [JC]																								
1950	NY N	1	1	0	0	0	0	0	0	0	0	0	.000	.000	.000	-99	0	0	ø	0	—	—	/H	0	0.0
1955	Phi N	113	259	30	54	7	7	3	24	31-2	1	43	.208	.293	.324	66	-13	6-1	.991	2	98	69	1b77,O6(4/0/2)	0	-1.4
1956	Phi N	136	460	61	117	14	8	10	50	50-2	2	86	.254	.327	.385	93	-5	5-1	.992	-4	85	91	1b124/rf	0	-1.5
1957	Phi N	37	26	5	4	0	0	2	4	3-0	3	8	.154	.313	.385	89	0	0-0	1.000	0	58	0	1b12/rf	0	-0.1
Total	4	287	746	96	175	21	15	15	78	84-4	6	137	.235	.314	.363	83	-18	11-2	.992	-2	89	82	1b213,O8(4/0/5)	0	-3.0
BLEFARY, CURT	Curtis Le Roy; B7.5.1943 Brooklyn NY; D1.28.2001 Pompano Beach FL; BL/TR/6´2˝/(195–210); d4.14; Col Wagner; OF(323/0/232)																								
1965	Bal A	144	462	72	120	23	4	22	70	88-4	3	73	.260	.381	.470	138	26	4-2	.979	1	96	121	O136(63/0/73)	0	2.0
1966	†Bal A	131	419	73	107	14	3	23	64	73-3	6	56	.255	.371	.468	142	26	1-4	.976	-2	92	82	O109L,1b20	0	1.7
1967	Bal A	155	554	69	134	19	5	22	81	73-11	8	94	.242	.337	.413	122	16	4-4	.968	11	94	188	O103(86/0/19),1b52	0	1.9
1968	Bal A	137	451	50	90	8	1	15	39	65-11	4	66	.200	.301	.322	90	-4	6-3	.962	-6	102	183	O92(55/0/46),C40,1b12	0	-1.6
1969	Hou N	155	542	66	137	26	7	12	67	77-10	4	79	.253	.347	.393	109	8	8-7	.987	6	**109**	96	1b152/lf	0	0.1
1970	NY A	99	269	34	57	6	0	9	37	43-3	3	37	.212	.324	.335	87	-4	1-3	.972	-9	80	21	O79R,1b6	0	-1.9
1971	NY A	21	36	4	7	1	0	1	2	3-0	0	5	.194	.256	.306	61	-2	0-0	.875	-0	70	335	O6R,1b4	0	-0.3
	†Oak A	50	101	15	22	2	0	5	12	15-2	1	15	.218	.325	.386	103	0	0-1	.975	-2	63	112	C14,O14(8/0/6),3b5,2b2	0	-0.2
	Year	71	137	19	29	3	0	6	14	18-2	1	20	.212	.308	.365	92	-2	0-1	.958	-2	85	233	O20(8/0/12),C14,3b5,1b4,2b2	0	-0.5
1972	Oak A	8	11	1	5	2	0	0	1	0-0	0	1	.455	.417	.636	233	2	0-0	ø	-0	0	0	/12lf	0	0.2
	SD N	74	102	10	20	3	0	3	9	19-3	0	18	.196	.320	.314	88	-1	0-0	.982	-3	50	125	C12,1b6,3b3,O3R	0	-0.5
Total	8	974	2947	394	699	104	20	112	382	456-47	29	444	.237	.342	.400	115	67	24-24	.972	-5	93	126	O544L,1b253,C66,3b8,2b3	0	1.4
BLESSITT, IKE	Isaiah; B9.30.1949 Detroit MI; BR/TR/5´11˝/185; [DetA67 15/295]; d9.7																								
1972	Det A	4	5	0	0	0	0	0	0	0-0	0	2	.000	.000	.000	-97	-1	0-0	1.000	0	168	0	/O(1/0/1)	0	-0.1
BLIGH, NED	Edwin Forrest; B6.30.1864 Brooklyn NY; D4.18.1892 Brooklyn NY; BR/TR/5´11˝/172; d6.26																								
1886	Bal AA	3	9	0	0	0	0	0	0	1	0	—	.000	.100	.000	-69	-2	0	.833	-1	—	—	C3	—	-0.3
1888	Cin AA	3	5	0	0	0	0	0	0	0	0	—	.000	.000	.000	-95	-1	0	1.000	-0	—	—	C2/rf	—	-0.1
1889	Col AA	28	93	6	13	1	1	0	5	4	3	14	.140	.200	.172	7	-12	2	.927	-3	—	—	C28	—	-1.1
1890	Col AA	8	29	2	6	2	0	0	5	2	0	—	.207	.258	.276	62	-1	0	.933	1	*105*	*141*	C8	—	0.0
	†Lou AA	24	73	9	15	0	0	1	9	9	0	—	.205	.293	.247	60	-4	1	.921	2	*135*	*82*	C24	—	0.0
	Year	32	102	11	21	2	0	1	14	11	0	—	.206	.283	.255	61	-5	1	.925	3	*127*	*98*	C32	—	0.0
Total	4	66	209	17	34	3	1	1	19	16	3	14	.163	.232	.201	28	-20	3	.923	-2	*127*	*98*	C65/rf	—	-1.5
BLISS, FRANK	Frank Eugene; B12.10.1852 Chicago IL; D1.8.1929 Nashville TN; d6.20; Col Michigan																								
1878	Mil N	2	8	1	1	0	0	0	0	0	—	0	.125	.125	.125	-17	-1	—	1.000	-1	93	0	/3C	—	-0.1
BLISS, JACK	John Joseph Albert; B1.9.1882 Vancouver WA; D10.23.1968 Temple City CA; BR/TR/5´9˝/185; d5.10; Col California																								
1908	StL N	44	136	9	29	4	0	1	5	8	2	—	.213	.267	.265	73	-4	3	.992	-2	*67*	*117*	C43	—	-0.2
1909	StL N	35	113	12	25	2	1	1	8	12	2	—	.221	.307	.283	89	-1	2	.951	-2	*79*	*96*	C32	—	-0.1
1910	StL N	16	33	2	2	0	0	0	3	4	0	8	.061	.162	.061	-36	-6	0	.980	-2	*73*	*80*	C13	—	-0.7
1911	StL N	97	258	36	59	6	4	1	27	42	2	25	.229	.341	.295	81	-5	5	.952	-15	*75*	*105*	C84/S	—	-1.4
1912	StL N	49	114	11	28	3	1	0	18	19	4	14	.246	.372	.289	84	-1	3	.973	-6	*69*	*96*	C41	—	-0.4
Total	5	241	654	70	143	15	6	3	61	85	10	47	.219	.318	.274	76	-17	13	.966	-27	*73*	*103*	C213/S	—	-2.8
BLOCK, BRUNO	James John (b James John Blochowicz); B3.13.1885 Wisconsin Rapids WI; D8.6.1937 S.Milwaukee WI; BR/TR/5´9˝/185; d8.5																								
1907	Was A	24	57	3	8	2	1	0	2	2	0	—	.140	.169	.211	23	-5	0	.949	-4	*78*	*102*	C21	—	-0.9
1910	Chi A	55	152	12	32	1	1	0	9	13	0	—	.211	.273	.230	60	-7	3	.964	2	*120*	*102*	C47	—	0.0
1911	Chi A	39	115	11	35	6	1	1	18	6	0	—	.304	.339	.400	109	1	0	.972	0	*145*	*74*	C38	—	0.4
1912	Chi A	46	136	8	35	5	6	0	26	7	0	—	.257	.294	.382	96	-2	1	.980	2	*99*	*93*	C46	—	0.3
1914	Chi F	45	106	8	21	4	1	0	14	11	0	17	.198	.274	.255	47	-10	1	.966	3	*140*	*88*	C34	—	-0.5
Total	5	209	566	42	131	18	10	1	69	39	0	17	.231	.281	.304	74	-23	5	.969	3	*120*	*91*	C186	—	-0.7
BLOCK, CY	Seymour; B5.4.1919 Brooklyn NY; D9.22.2004 Manhasset NY; BR/TR/6´0˝/180; d9.7; Mil 1943–45																								
1942	Chi N	9	33	6	12	1	1	0	4	3	0	3	.364	.417	.455	161	2	2	.917	-2	70	59	3b8/2	0	0.1
1945	†Chi N	2	7	1	1	0	0	0	1	0	0	0	.143	.143	.143	-21	-1	0	1.000	1	147	0	/23	0	-0.1
1946	Chi N	6	13	2	3	0	0	0	0	4	0	0	.231	.412	.231	86	0	0	1.000	1	105	582	3b4	0	0.1
Total	3	17	53	9	16	1	1	0	5	7	0	3	.302	.383	.358	118	1	2	.947	-1	82	195	3b13,2b2	0	0.1
BLOCKER, TERRY	Terry Fennell; B8.18.1959 Columbia SC; BL/TL/6´2˝/195; [NYN81 1/4]; d4.11; Col Tennessee St.																								
1985	NY N	18	15	1	1	0	0	0	0	1-0	0	2	.067	.125	.067	-46	-3	0-0	1.000	-0	75	0	O5(3/1/1)	15	-0.4
1988	Atl N	66	198	13	42	4	2	2	10	10-3	0	20	.212	.250	.283	51	-13	1-1	.994	1	108	37	O61C	0	-1.4
1989	Atl N	26	31	1	7	1	0	0	1	1-0	0	5	.226	.250	.258	45	-2	1-0	1.000	-0	93	0	O8(2/2/4)/P	0	-0.2
Total	3	110	244	15	50	5	2	2	11	12-3	0	27	.205	.242	.266	44	-18	2-1	.994	0	106	33	O74(5/64/5)/P	15	-2.0
BLOGG, WES	Wesley Collins; B1855 Norfolk VA; D3.10.1897 Baltimore MD; 5´8˝/155; d6.20																								
1883	Pit AA	9	34	0	5	0	0	0	—	0	—	—	.147	.147	.147	-5	-4	—	.881	-2	—	—	C6,O3R	—	-0.5
BLOMBERG, RON	Ronald Mark "Boomer"; B8.23.1948 Atlanta GA; BL/TR/6´1˝/(185–205); [NYA67 1/1]; d9.10; [DL 1977 NY A 180]																								
1969	NY A	4	6	0	3	0	0	0	0	1-0	0	0	.500	.571	.500	209	1	0-0	1.000	-0	70	0	O2L	0	0.1
1971	NY A	64	199	30	64	6	2	7	31	14-3	0	23	.322	.363	.477	144	10	2-4	.970	-4	91	27	O57R	0	0.3
1972	NY A	107	299	36	80	22	1	14	49	38-4	3	26	.268	.355	.488	153	20	0-2	.985	-7	72	127	1b95	0	0.6
1973	NY A	100	301	45	99	13	1	12	57	34-4	0	25	.329	.395	.498	154	22	2-0	.980	1	122	128	D55,1b41	0	1.9
1974	NY A	90	264	39	82	11	2	10	48	29-2	2	33	.311	.375	.481	149	17	2-1	1.000	1	108	175	D58,O19(2/0/17)	0	1.6
1975	NY A	34	106	18	27	8	2	4	17	13-1	0	10	.255	.336	.481	130	4	0-0	1.000	0	112	0	D27/rf	106	0.3
1976	NY A	1	2	0	0	0	0	0	0	0-0	0	0	.000	.000	.000	-99	-1	0-0	ø	0	—	—	/D	148	-0.1
1978	Chi A	61	156	16	36	7	0	5	22	11-2	0	17	.231	.280	.372	81	-4	0-0	.986	-1	69	35	D36,1b7	0	-0.7
Total	8	461	1333	184	391	67	8	52	224	140-16	5	134	.293	.360	.473	140	69	6-7	.983	-10	86	122	D177,1b143,O79(4/0/75)	434	4.0
BLONG, JOE	Joseph Myles; B9.17.1853 St.Louis MO; D9.17.1892 St.Louis MO; BR/TR; d5.4; ▲																								
1875	RS NA	16	68	3	10	2	0	0	5	0	—	7	.147	.147	.176	13	-5	1-0	.927	3	134	82	P15,O4(2/2/0)	—	0.1
1876	StL N	62	264	30	62	7	4	0	30	2	—	9	.235	.241	.292	81	-5	—	.895	-1	124	123	O62R/P	—	-0.5
1877	StL N	58	218	17	47	8	3	0	13	4	—	22	.216	.230	.280	63	-8	—	.835	-2	86	0	O40(13/4/23),P25	—	-0.7
Total	2	120	482	47	109	15	7	0	43	6	—	31	.226	.236	.286	72	-13	—	.867	-3	110	77	O102(13/4/85),P26	—	-1.2
BLOODWORTH, JIMMY	James Henry; B7.26.1917 Tallahassee FL; D8.17.2002 Apalachicola FL; BR/TR/5´11˝/180; d9.14; Mil 1944–46																								
1937	Was A	15	50	3	11	2	1	0	8	5	0	8	.220	.291	.300	51	-4	0-1	.946	-1	102	98	2b14	—	-0.4
1939	Was A	83	318	34	92	24	1	4	40	10	1	26	.289	.313	.409	90	-6	3-1	.972	12	101	135	2b73,O5R	—	0.9
1940	Was A	119	469	47	115	17	8	11	70	16	1	71	.245	.272	.386	73	-23	3-1	.978	14	97	106	2b96,1b17,3b6	—	-0.4
1941	Was A	142	506	59	124	24	3	7	66	41	1	58	.245	.303	.346	75	-20	1-1	.971	**27**	**109**	114	2b132,3b6/S	0	1.5
1942	Det A	137	533	62	129	23	1	13	57	35	5	63	.242	.295	.362	78	-17	2-8	.972	10	**104**	75	2b134,S2	0	-0.1
1943	Det A	129	474	41	114	23	4	6	52	29	3	59	.241	.289	.344	79	-14	4-7	.972	15	104	86	2b129	0	0.8
1946	Det A	76	249	25	61	8	1	5	36	12	2	26	.245	.285	.345	71	-10	3-3	.974	-1	94	107	2b71	0	-0.8
1947	Pit N	88	316	27	79	9	0	7	48	16	2	39	.250	.290	.345	66	-16	1	.979	-16	84	95	2b87	0	-2.8
1949	Cin N	134	452	40	118	27	1	9	59	27	1	36	.261	.304	.385	83	-12	1	.981	-4	100	93	2b92,1b23,3b8	0	-1.2
1950	Cin N	4	14	1	3	1	0	0	1	2	0	0	.214	.313	.286	58	-1	0	1.000	-2	58	0	2b4	0	-0.2

YEAR	TM LG	G	AB	R	H	2B	3B	HR	RBI	BB-IB	HP	SO	AVG	OBP	SLG	AOPS	ABR	SB-CS	FA	FR	RNG	THR	GAMES AT POSITION	DL	BFW
	†Phi N	54	96	6	22	2	0	0	13	6	0	12	.229	.275	.250	40	-9	0	1.000	-1	96	100	2b27,1b7,3b2	0	-0.8
	Year	58	110	7	25	3	0	0	14	8	0	12	.227	.280	.255	42	-9	0	1.000	-3	91	86	2b31,1b7,3b2	0	-1.0
1951	Phi N	21	42	2	6	0	0	0	1	3	0	9	.143	.200	.143	-6	-6	1-0	1.000	-1	99	64	2b8,1b6	0	-0.7
Total	11	1002	3519	347	874	160	20	62	451	202	16	407	.248	.292	.358	74	-138	19-22	.975	52	100	98	2b867,1b53,3b22,O5R,S3	0	-4.2
Bloomfield, Bud	Clyde Stalcup; B1.5.1936 Oklahoma City OK; BR/TR/5´11.5˝/175; d9.25; Col Tulsa																								
1963	StL N	1	0	0	0	0	0	0	0	0-0	0	0	ø	ø	ø	ø	0	0-0	ø	-0	0	0	/3	0	0.0
1964	Min A	7	7	1	1	0	0	0	0	0-0	0	0	.143	.143	.143	-20	-1	0-0	1.000	0	119	197	2b3,S2	0	-0.1
Total	2	8	7	1	1	0	0	0	0	0-0	0	0	.143	.143	.143	-20	-1	0-0	1.000	-0	119	197	2b3,S2/3	0	-0.1
Bloomquist, Willie	William Paul; B11.27.1977 Bremerton WA; BR/TR/5´11˝/(185–195); [SeaA99 3/95]; d9.1; Col Arizona St.; OF(29/64/13)																								
2002	Sea A	12	33	11	15	4	0	0	7	5-0	0	2	.455	.526	.576	199	5	3-1	1.000	1	121	0	O7L,2b4	0	0.6
2003	Sea A	89	196	30	49	7	2	1	14	19-1	1	39	.250	.317	.321	74	-7	4-1	.970	-6	80	65	3b37,S18,D12,O11(10/0/1),2b7,1b3	0	-1.2
2004	Sea A	93	188	27	46	10	0	2	18	10-0	0	48	.245	.283	.330	62	-11	13-2	.923	-7	76	145	3b31,S20,1b19,O9(8/1/0)/2D	19	-1.4
2005	Sea A	82	249	27	64	15	2	0	22	11-0	1	38	.257	.289	.333	71	-11	14-1	.986	-9	96	113	2b32,S24,O15(1/15/0),3b6/1D	34	-1.4
2006	Sea A	102	251	36	62	6	2	1	15	24-0	4	40	.247	.320	.299	67	-12	16-3	1.000	-7	97	88	O59(3/48/12),S17,2b15,3b12,1b4,D2	0	-1.5
Total	5	378	917	131	236	42	6	4	76	69-1	6	167	.257	.312	.329	73	-36	50-8	.994	-28	100	79	O101C,3b86,S79,2b59,1b27,D21	53	-4.9
Blosser, Greg	Gregory Brent; B6.26.1971 Manatee FL; BL/TL/6´3˝/205; [BosA89 1/16]; d9.5																								
1993	Bos A	17	28	1	2	1	0	0	1	2-0	0	7	.071	.133	.107	-32	-5	1-0	1.000	1	105	328	O9L/D	0	-0.5
1994	Bos A	5	11	2	1	0	0	0	1	4-0	0	4	.091	.333	.091	16	-1	0-0	.727	0	184	0	O3(1/0/2)/D	0	-0.1
Total	2	22	39	3	3	1	0	0	2	6-0	0	11	.077	.200	.103	-16	-6	1-0	.870	1	129	229	O12(10/0/2),D2	0	-0.6
Blott, Jack	John Leonard; B8.24.1902 Girard OH; D6.11.1964 Ann Arbor MI; BR/TR/6´0˝/210; d7.30; Col Michigan																								
1924	Cin N	2	1	0	0	0	0	0	0	0	0	0	.000	.000	.000	-99	0	0-0	1.000	-0	*0*	*0*	/C	—	0.0
Blowers, Mike	Michael Roy; B4.24.1965 Wurzburg, West Germany; BR/TR/6´2˝/(190–210); [MonN86 10/252]; d9.1; Col Washington																								
1989	NY A	13	38	2	10	0	0	0	3	3-0	0	13	.263	.317	.263	66	-2	0-0	.852	-4	62	148	3b13	0	-0.5
1990	NY A	48	144	16	27	4	0	5	21	12-1	1	50	.188	.255	.319	59	-8	1-0	.899	-11	74	51	3b45,D2	0	-2.0
1991	NY A	15	35	3	7	0	0	1	1	4-0	0	3	.200	.282	.286	57	-2	0-0	.870	-3	77	49	3b14	0	-0.5
1992	Sea A	31	73	7	14	3	0	1	2	6-0	0	20	.192	.253	.274	47	-5	0-0	.984	1	90	193	3b29,1b3	0	-0.5
1993	Sea A	127	379	55	106	23	3	15	57	44-3	2	98	.280	.357	.475	119	10	1-5	.951	7	107	75	3b117,O2(1/0/1)/C1D	0	1.6
1994	Sea A	85	270	37	78	13	0	9	49	25-2	1	60	.289	.348	.437	99	0	2-2	.939	5	108	64	3b48,1b20,O9(8/0/1),D9	0	0.3
1995	†Sea A	134	439	59	113	24	1	23	96	53-0	0	128	.257	.335	.474	107	4	2-1	.947	-14	79	43	3b126,1b7,O5(2/0/3)	0	-0.9
1996	LA N	92	317	31	84	19	2	6	38	37-2	1	77	.265	.341	.394	100	1	0-0	.951	-18	72	66	3b90,1b6/S	74	-1.7
1997	†Sea A	68	150	22	44	5	0	5	20	21-1	0	33	.293	.376	.427	110	3	0-0	.990	1	125	93	1b49,3b10,O6(5/0/1)/D	0	0.1
1998	Oak A	129	409	56	97	24	2	11	71	39-1	1	116	.237	.302	.386	79	-13	1-0	.927	-9	96	95	3b120,1b8,D2	0	-2.0
1999	Sea A	19	46	2	11	1	0	2	7	4-0	0	12	.239	.300	.391	75	-2	0-0	1.000	1	125	163	1b14,3b4/D	0	-0.2
Total	11	761	2300	290	591	116	8	78	365	248-10	6	610	.257	.329	.416	96	-14	7-8	.938	-44	89	74	3b616,1b108,O22(16/0/6),D18/SC	74	-6.3
Blue, Bert	Bird Wayne; B12.9.1877 Bettsville OH; D9.2.1929 Detroit MI; BR/TR/6´3˝/200; d6.15																								
1908	StL A	11	24	2	9	1	2	0	1	3	0	—	.375	.444	.583	232	3	0	.942	1	*141*	*57*	C8	—	0.5
	Phi A	6	18	2	3	0	0	0	1	0	0	—	.167	.167	.167	8	-2	0	1.000	0	*73*	*123*	C6	—	-0.1
	Year	17	42	4	12	1	2	0	2	3	0	—	.286	.333	.405	136	1	0	.967	1	*113*	*84*	C14	—	0.4
Blue, Lu	Luzerne Atwell; B3.5.1897 Washington DC; D7.28.1958 Alexandria VA; BB/TL/5´10˝/165; d4.14																								
1921	Det A	153	585	103	180	33	11	5	75	103	5	47	.308	.416	.427	116	20	13-17	.990	-6	85	68	1b152	—	0.1
1922	Det A	145	584	131	175	31	9	6	45	82	7	48	.300	.392	.414	114	15	8-5	.991	0	101	101	1b144	—	0.6
1923	Det A	129	504	100	143	27	7	1	46	96	4	40	.284	.402	.371	106	11	10-11	.992	5	113	79	1b129	—	0.5
1924	Det A	108	395	81	123	26	7	2	53	64	4	26	.311	.413	.428	119	14	9-4	.986	3	114	93	1b108	—	1.0
1925	Det A	150	532	91	163	18	9	3	94	83	3	29	.306	.403	.391	104	6	19-5	.988	1	102	94	1b148	—	0.0
1926	Det A	128	429	92	123	24	14	1	52	90	2	18	.287	.413	.415	115	13	13-7	.985	-6	82	108	1b109/cf	—	0.0
1927	Det A	112	365	71	95	17	9	1	42	71	2	28	.260	.384	.364	94	-1	13-7	.984	-2	98	**120**	1b104	—	-0.8
1928	StL A	**154**	549	116	154	32	11	14	80	105	4	43	.281	.400	.455	120	20	12-7	.989	2	106	103	1b154	—	1.2
1929	StL A	151	573	111	168	40	10	6	61	126	2	32	.293	.422	.429	115	21	12-6	.994	-3	92	107	1b151	—	0.7
1930	StL A	117	425	85	100	27	5	4	42	81	4	44	.235	.363	.351	79	-11	12-7	.987	-0	104	100	1b111	—	-1.6
1931	Chi A	155	589	119	179	23	15	1	62	127	3	60	.304	.430	.399	126	32	13-3	.990	-3	95	81	1b155	—	1.5
1932	Chi A	112	373	51	93	21	2	0	43	64	3	21	.249	.364	.316	83	-6	17-6	.986	8	**138**	**116**	1b105	—	-0.5
1933	Bro N	1	1	0	0	0	0	0	0	0	0	0	.000	.000	.000	-99	0	0	1.000	-0	0	0	/1	—	0.0
Total	13	1615	5904	1151	1696	319	109	44	695	1092	43	436	.287	.402	.401	109	134	151-85	.989	-2	101	96	1b1571/cf	—	2.7
Bluege, Ossie	Oswald Louis; B10.24.1900 Chicago IL; D10.14.1985 Edina MN; BR/TR/5´11˝/162; d4.24; M5/C3; b–Otto																								
1922	Was A	19	61	5	12	1	0	0	2	7	2	7	.197	.300	.213	37	-5	1-0	.925	-2	95	101	3b17,S2	—	-0.6
1923	Was A	109	379	48	93	15	7	2	42	48	8	53	.245	.343	.338	84	-8	5-3	.936	4	103	**144**	3b106,2b4	—	0.3
1924	†Was A	117	402	59	113	15	4	2	49	39	9	36	.281	.358	.353	86	-8	7-5	.943	-13	92	65	3b102,2b10,S4	—	-1.4
1925	†Was A	145	522	77	150	27	4	4	79	59	2	56	.287	.362	.377	89	-7	16-15	.953	1	100	108	3b144,S4	—	0.1
1926	Was A	139	487	69	132	19	8	3	65	70	5	46	.271	.368	.361	93	-3	12-9	.952	-16	91	64	3b134,S8	—	-1.0
1927	Was A	146	503	71	138	21	10	1	66	57	5	47	.274	.354	.362	87	-9	15-5	.961	15	**112**	71	3b146	—	1.5
1928	Was A	146	518	78	154	33	7	2	75	46	**8**	27	.297	.364	.400	101	2	18-6	.960	10	**110**	**133**	3b144/2	—	2.2
1929	Was A	64	220	35	65	6	0	5	31	19	1	15	.295	.354	.391	91	-3	6-4	.967	4	117	132	3b35,2b14,S10	—	0.4
1930	Was A	134	476	64	138	27	7	3	69	51	8	40	.290	.368	.395	93	-3	15-8	.964	-1	101	91	3b134	—	0.4
1931	Was A	152	570	82	155	25	7	8	98	50	5	39	.272	.336	.382	88	-11	16-10	**.960**	-7	94	97	3b152/S	—	-1.1
1932	Was A	149	507	64	131	22	4	5	64	83	4	41	.258	.367	.347	87	-6	9-7	.970	5	105	**119**	3b149	—	0.3
1933	†Was A	140	501	63	131	14	0	6	71	55	3	34	.261	.338	.325	77	-15	6-7	.965	-10	97	116	3b138	—	-2.1
1934	Was A	99	285	39	70	9	2	0	11	23	2	15	.246	.306	.291	57	-19	2-1	.950	7	120	136	3b41,S30,2b5,O5L	—	-0.7
1935	Was A★	100	320	44	84	14	3	0	34	37	1	21	.262	.341	.325	75	-11	2-2	.967	2	99	85	S58,3b25,2b4	—	-0.4
1936	Was A	90	319	43	92	12	1	1	55	38	6	16	.288	.375	.342	83	-7	5-3	.993	4	97	108	2b52,S23,3b15	—	0.2
1937	Was A	42	127	12	36	4	2	1	13	13	1	9	.283	.355	.370	87	-3	1-1	.952	-2	96	100	S28,1b2,3b2	—	-0.2
1938	Was A	58	184	25	48	12	1	0	21	21	1	11	.261	.340	.337	75	-7	3-1	.990	0	104	101	2b38,S10/13	—	-0.3
1939	Was A	18	59	5	9	0	0	0	3	7	0	2	.153	.242	.153	3	-9	1-0	.989	0	127	114	1b11,2b2,S2,3b2	—	-0.8
Total	18	1867	6440	883	1751	276	67	43	848	723	71	515	.272	.352	.356	85	-132	140-87	.957	3	102	104	3b1487,S180,2b130,1b14,O5L	—	-3.2
Bluege, Otto	Otto Adam "Squeaky"; B7.20.1909 Chicago IL; D6.28.1977 Chicago IL; BR/TR/5´10˝/154; d4.12; b–Ossie																								
1932	Cin N	1	0	1	0	0	0	0	0	0	0	0	ø	ø	ø	ø	0	0	ø	0	—	—	/R	—	0.0
1933	Cin N	108	291	17	62	6	2	0	18	26	0	29	.213	.278	.247	52	-18	0	.937	-8	99	98	S95,2b10/3	—	-2.1
Total	2	109	291	18	62	6	2	0	18	26	0	29	.213	.278	.247	52	-18	0	.937	-8	99	98	S95,2b10/3	—	-2.1
Bluhm, Red	Harvey Fred; B6.27.1894 Cleveland OH; D5.7.1952 Flint MI; BR/TR/5´11˝/165; d7.3																								
1918	Bos A	1	1	0	0	0	0	0	0	0	0	0	.000	.000	.000	-99	0	0	ø	0	—	—	/H	—	0.0
Blum, Geoff	Geoffrey Edward; B4.26.1973 Redwood City CA; BB/TR/6´3˝/(195–200); [MonN94 7/196]; d8.9; Col California; OF(52/0/5)																								
1999	Mon N	45	133	21	32	7	2	8	18	17-3	0	25	.241	.327	.504	110	1	1-0	.928	-13	82	48	S42,2b2	0	-0.8
2000	Mon N	124	343	40	97	20	2	11	45	26-2	3	60	.283	.335	.449	96	-3	1-4	.952	12	117	70	3b55,S44,2b13,1b11	0	1.0
2001	Mon N	148	453	57	107	25	0	9	50	43-8	10	94	.236	.313	.351	73	-18	9-5	.966	2	103	105	3b72,O35L,2b25,1b14,S4	0	-1.6
2002	Hou N	130	368	45	104	20	4	10	52	49-5	1	70	.283	.367	.440	104	3	2-0	.971	15	113	147	3b104,O10(9/0/3),S2/12	0	1.8
2003	Hou N	123	420	51	110	19	0	10	52	20-1	2	50	.262	.295	.379	71	-18	0-0	.971	-7	96	144	3b83,2b25,S11,1b6,O2(1/0/1)	0	-2.4
2004	TB A	112	339	38	73	21	0	8	35	24-1	0	58	.215	.266	.348	60	-21	2-3	.934	-10	98	108	3b59,2b52,O7L,1b2/SD	0	-2.8
2005	SD N	78	224	26	54	13	1	5	22	24-0	3	28	.241	.321	.375	86	-5	3-2	.965	1	125	144	3b34,2b19,S14,1b2	18	-0.2
	†Chi A	31	95	6	19	2	1	1	3	4-0	0	15	.200	.232	.274	33	-9	0-1	1.000	0	91	88	1b12,3b12,S6,2b2	0	-1.0
2006	†SD N	109	276	27	70	17	1	4	34	17-1	0	51	.254	.293	.366	72	-12	0-1	.971	3	104	113	S49,3b34,1b2/2rf	0	-0.6
Total	8	900	2651	311	666	144	11	66	311	224-21	19	451	.251	.312	.389	80	-82	18-16	.963	2	107	118	3b453,S173,2b140,O55L,1b50,D2	18	-6.6
Boak, Chet	Chester Robert; B6.19.1935 New Castle PA; D11.28.1983 Emporium PA; BR/TR/6´0˝/180; d9.18																								
1960	KC A	5	13	1	2	0	0	0	1	0-0	1	2	.154	.200	.154	1	-2	0-0	.957	-0	95	125	2b5	0	-0.2
1961	Was A	5	7	0	0	0	0	0	0	1-0	0	1	.000	.125	.000	-64	-2	1-0	1.000	-1	71	0	/2	0	-0.2
Total	2	10	20	1	2	0	0	0	1	1-0	1	3	.100	.174	.100	-22	-4	1-0	.962	-1	90	100	2b6	0	-0.4

YEAR	TM LG	G	AB	R	H	2B	3B	HR	RBI	BB-IB	HP	SO	AVG	OBP	SLG	AOPS	ABR	SB-CS	FA	FR	RNG	THR	GAMES AT POSITION	DL	BFW
Boardman, Frederick	Frederick; d8.29																								
1874	Bal NA	1	4	0	1	0	0	0	0	0	—	0	.250	.250	.250	61	0	0-0	ø	0	0	0	/rf	—	0.0
Bobb, Randy	Mark Randall; B1.1.1948 Los Angeles CA; D6.13.1982 Carnelian Bay CA; BR/TR/6´1˝/(190–200); [ChiN67 S1/2]; d8.15; Col Arizona St.																								
1968	Chi N	7	8	0	1	0	0	0	0	1-0	0	2	.125	.222	.125	6	-1	0-0	1.000	-0	0	258	C7	0	-0.1
1969	Chi N	3	2	0	0	0	0	0	0	0-0	0	1	.000	.000	.000	-89	0	0-0	1.000	-1	35	0	C2	0	-0.1
Total	2	10	10	0	1	0	0	0	0	1-0	0	3	.100	.182	.100	-14	-1	0-0	1.000	-1	8	200	C9	0	-0.2
Bocachica, Hiram	Hiram (Colon); B3.4.1976 Ponce, PR; BR/TR/5´11˝/(165–195); [MonN94 1/21]; d9.13																								
2000	LA N	8	10	2	3	0	0	0	0	0-0	0	2	.300	.300	.300	55	-1	0-0	1.000	3	252	255	2b2	0	0.2
2001	LA N	75	133	15	31	11	1	2	9	9-0	1	33	.233	.287	.376	74	-5	4-1	.941	-4	100	95	2b19,O13(10/0/3),3b8	17	-0.8
2002	LA N	49	65	12	14	3	0	4	9	5-0	0	19	.215	.271	.446	90	-1	1-1	.960	-1	99	0	O22(19/3/2)	0	-0.3
	Det A	34	103	14	23	4	0	4	8	5-0	0	22	.223	.259	.379	69	-5	2-2	.966	0	91	235	O32(1/27/4),2b2/D	0	-0.5
2003	Det A	6	22	1	1	1	0	0	0	0-0	0	7	.045	.045	.091	-68	-5	0-0	1.000	0	80	377	O6(1/5/0)	0	-0.5
2004	Sea A	50	90	9	22	5	0	3	6	12-0	1	27	.244	.337	.400	96	0	5-4	1.000	-2	93	0	O44(1/32/12),D3	0	-0.2
2005	Oak A	9	19	2	2	0	0	0	0	0-0	0	7	.105	.105	.105	-44	-4	0-0	1.000	-0	92	0	O6(0/1/5),3b2/D	0	-0.4
2006	Oak A	8	13	3	3	0	0	0	0	3-0	0	4	.231	.375	.231	64	-1	1-0	1.000	-1	50	0	O8(1/4/3)	0	-0.2
Total	7	239	455	58	99	24	1	13	32	34-0	2	121	.218	.274	.360	68	-22	13-8	.978	-6	91	88	O131(33/72/29),2b23,3b10,D5	17	-2.7
Boccabella, John	John Dominic; B6.29.1941 San Francisco CA; BR/TR/6´1˝/(195–210); d9.2; Col Santa Clara																								
1963	Chi N	24	74	7	14	4	1	1	5	6-0	0	21	.189	.247	.311	57	-4	0-1	.996	-1	82	183	1b24	0	-0.7
1964	Chi N	9	23	4	9	2	1	0	6	0-0	0	3	.391	.391	.565	159	2	0-0	1.000	-0	121	104	1b5,O2L	0	0.1
1965	Chi N	6	12	2	4	0	0	2	4	1-0	0	2	.333	.385	.833	227	2	0-0	1.000	-0	107	0	1b2/lf	0	0.2
1966	Chi N	75	206	22	47	9	0	6	25	14-1	0	39	.228	.274	.359	74	-7	0-1	.981	3	101	155	O33L,1b30,C5	39	-0.8
1967	Chi N	25	35	0	6	1	1	0	8	3-1	1	7	.171	.250	.257	45	-3	0-0	1.000	-1	131	0	O9(4/0/5),1b3/C	0	-0.4
1968	Chi N	7	14	0	1	0	0	0	1	2-0	0	2	.071	.176	.071	-19	-2	0-0	1.000	0	47	0	C4/lf	0	-0.2
1969	Mon N	40	86	4	9	2	0	1	6	6-1	1	30	.105	.170	.163	-6	-12	1-0	1.000	-1	79	181	C32	0	-1.3
1970	Mon N	61	145	18	39	3	1	5	17	11-2	0	24	.269	.321	.407	93	-2	0-1	.993	6	178	111	1b33,C24/3	0	0.3
1971	Mon N	74	177	15	39	11	0	3	15	14-2	1	26	.220	.278	.333	72	-6	0-1	.979	-3	118	97	C37,1b37,3b2	0	-1.1
1972	Mon N	83	207	14	47	8	1	1	10	9-3	1	29	.227	.259	.290	56	-12	1-2	.983	6	99	164	C73,1b7/3	0	-0.6
1973	Mon N	118	403	25	94	13	0	7	46	26-8	1	57	.233	.279	.318	63	-21	1-1	.980	5	100	119	C117/1	22	-1.2
1974	SF N	29	80	6	11	3	0	0	5	4-2	0	6	.138	.176	.175	-1	-11	0-0	.991	-1	110	46	C26	0	-1.1
Total	12	551	1462	117	320	56	5	26	148	96-20	5	246	.219	.267	.317	62	-76	3-7	.984	14	101	125	C319,1b142,O46(41/0/5),3b4	61	-6.8
Bocek, Milt	Milton Francis; B7.16.1912 Chicago IL; BR/TR/6´1˝/185; d9.3																								
1933	Chi A	11	22	3	8	1	0	1	3	4	0	6	.364	.462	.545	173	3	0-0	1.000	-1	76	0	O6(3/1/2)	—	0.2
1934	Chi A	19	38	3	8	1	0	0	3	5	0	5	.211	.302	.237	39	-3	0-0	1.000	2	117	238	O10(9/1/0)	—	-0.2
Total	2	30	60	6	16	2	0	1	6	9	0	11	.267	.362	.350	86	0	0-0	1.000	1	106	175	O16(12/2/2)	—	0.0
Bochte, Bruce	Bruce Anton; B11.12.1950 Pasadena CA; BL/TL/6´3˝/(195–200); [AnaA72 2/34]; d7.19; Col Santa Clara																								
1974	Cal A	57	196	24	53	4	1	5	26	18-0	1	23	.270	.332	.378	110	2	6-3	.985	-3	96	87	O39(32/5/3),1b24	0	-0.4
1975	Cal A	107	375	41	107	19	3	3	48	45-5	2	43	.285	.362	.376	118	10	3-4	.987	-6	75	103	1b105/D	50	-0.5
1976	Cal A	146	466	53	120	17	1	2	49	64-11	2	53	.258	.346	.311	101	3	4-5	.988	1	104	55	O86(71/0/18),1b59/D	0	-0.6
1977	Cal A	25	100	12	29	4	0	2	8	7-0	0	4	.290	.336	.390	101	0	3-2	1.000	0	79	304	O24C/D	0	0.0
	Cle A	112	392	52	119	19	1	5	43	40-3	0	38	.304	.364	.395	111	7	3-2	.966	3	109	130	O76(74/3/1),1b36/D	0	0.5
	Year	137	492	64	148	23	1	7	51	47-3	0	42	.301	.358	.394	109	7	6-4	.974	3	102	173	O100(74/27/1),1b36,D2	0	0.5
1978	Sea A	140	486	58	128	25	3	11	51	60-3	1	47	.263	.342	.395	108	6	3-4	.984	-5	84	114	O91(82/19/0),D43/1	0	-0.4
1979	Sea A★	150	554	81	175	38	6	16	100	67-8	2	64	.316	.385	.493	134	28	2-2	.991	5	114	103	1b147	0	2.4
1980	Sea A	148	520	62	156	34	4	13	78	72-13	0	81	.300	.381	.456	127	22	2-3	.996	7	119	116	1b133,D11	0	2.0
1981	Sea A	99	335	39	87	16	0	6	30	47-5	2	53	.260	.354	.361	102	3	1-3	.995	-4	94	97	1b82,O14L/D	0	-0.8
1982	Sea A	144	509	58	151	21	0	12	70	67-5	3	71	.297	.380	.409	113	12	8-5	.988	-5	83	91	O99(99/1/0),1b34,D12	0	0.0
1984	Oak A	148	469	58	124	23	0	5	52	52-3	0	59	.264	.333	.345	95	-1	2-5	.993	-13	68	98	1b144,D2	0	-2.4
1985	Oak A	137	424	48	125	17	1	14	60	49-6	0	58	.295	.367	.439	129	17	3-1	.990	-10	73	86	1b128	0	0.1
1986	Oak A	125	407	57	104	13	1	6	43	65-3	0	68	.256	.357	.337	97	1	3-2	.991	0	100	86	1b115/D	0	-0.5
Total	12	1538	5233	643	1478	250	21	100	658	653-65	13	662	.282	.360	.396	113	110	43-41	.992	-29	93	98	1b1008,O429(372/52/22),D74	50	-0.6
Bochy, Bruce	Bruce Douglas; B4.16.1955 Landes de Bussac, France; BR/TR/6´4˝/(205–234); [HouN75 S1/23]; d7.19; M12/C2; Col Brevard (FL) CC																								
1978	Hou N	54	154	8	41	8	0	3	15	11-4	0	35	.266	.311	.377	99	-1	0-0	.974	-1	71	128	C53	0	0.1
1979	Hou N	56	129	11	28	4	0	1	6	13-4	1	25	.217	.294	.271	59	-7	0-0	.970	-3	80	121	C55	0	-0.9
1980	†Hou N	22	22	0	4	1	0	0	0	5-1	1	7	.182	.357	.227	72	0	0-0	1.000	-1	74	0	C10/1	0	-0.1
1982	NY N	17	49	4	15	4	0	2	8	4-0	0	6	.306	.358	.510	140	3	0-0	.961	0	82	139	C16/1	0	0.4
1983	SD N	23	42	2	9	1	1	0	3	0-0	0	9	.214	.205	.286	39	-4	0-0	1.000	1	151	186	C11	0	-0.2
1984	†SD N	37	92	10	21	5	1	4	15	3-0	0	21	.228	.250	.435	89	-2	0-1	.988	1	98	69	C36	0	0.0
1985	SD N	48	112	16	30	2	0	6	13	6-1	0	30	.268	.305	.446	109	0	0-0	.988	-4	76	88	C46	0	-0.2
1986	SD N	63	127	16	32	9	0	8	22	14-3	0	23	.252	.326	.512	130	5	1-0	.991	1	91	107	C48	0	0.8
1987	SD N	38	75	8	12	3	0	2	11	11-1	0	21	.160	.264	.280	47	-6	0-1	.962	-5	86	15	C23	23	-1.1
Total	9	358	802	75	192	37	2	26	93	67-14	2	177	.239	.298	.388	92	-12	1-2	.979	-10	85	103	C298,1b2	23	-1.2
Bockman, Eddie	Joseph Edward; B7.26.1920 Santa Ana CA; BR/TR/5´9˝/175; d9.11																								
1946	NY A	4	12	2	1	1	0	0	0	1	0	4	.083	.154	.167	-10	-2	0-0	.933	1	77	375	3b4	0	-0.1
1947	Cle A	46	66	8	17	2	2	1	14	5	0	17	.258	.310	.394	97	-1	0-0	.946	5	135	241	3b12,2b4/Slf	0	0.4
1948	Pit N	70	176	23	42	7	1	4	23	17	1	35	.239	.309	.358	79	-6	2	.962	7	119	129	3b51/2	0	0.2
1949	Pit N	79	220	21	49	6	1	6	19	23	0	31	.223	.296	.341	69	-10	3	.959	5	108	120	3b68,2b5	0	-0.5
Total	4	199	474	54	109	16	4	11	56	46	1	87	.230	.299	.350	74	-19	5-0	.958	18	114	143	3b135,2b10/lfS	0	0.0
Bodie, Ping	Frank Stephan (b Francesco Stephano Pezzolo); B10.8.1887 San Francisco CA; D12.17.1961 San Francisco CA; BR/TR/5´8˝/195; d4.22																								
1911	Chi A	145	551	75	159	27	13	4	97	49	1	—	.289	.348	.407	114	9	14	.969	-2	94	111	O128(0/107/21),2b16	—	-0.2
1912	Chi A	138	472	58	139	24	7	5	72	43	4	—	.294	.358	.407	123	14	12	.969	-10	88	62	O130(8/72/50)	—	-0.4
1913	Chi A	127	406	39	107	14	8	8	48	35	2	57	.264	.325	.397	112	4	5	.968	-5	94	81	O119(43/76/0)	—	-0.8
1914	Chi A	107	327	21	75	9	5	3	29	21	1	35	.229	.278	.315	79	-10	12-11	.959	-3	89	120	O95(2/92/1)	—	-2.2
1917	Phi A	148	557	51	162	28	11	7	74	53	3	40	.291	.356	.418	138	24	13	.963	7	93	**168**	O145L/1	—	2.8
1918	NY A	91	324	36	83	12	6	3	46	27	3	24	.256	.319	.358	102	0	6	.971	4	97	139	O90L	—	-0.1
1919	NY A	134	475	45	132	27	8	6	59	36	4	46	.278	.334	.406	107	3	15	.959	-11	89	68	O134(0/129/5)	—	-1.8
1920	NY A	129	471	63	139	26	12	7	79	40	0	30	.295	.350	.446	106	3	6-14	.968	-12	88	77	O129C	—	-2.1
1921	NY A	31	87	5	15	2	2	0	12	8	0	8	.172	.242	.241	23	-11	0-1	.944	-3	75	90	O25(5/20/0)	—	-1.4
Total	9	1050	3670	393	1011	169	72	43	516	312	18	240	.275	.335	.396	110	36	83-26	.965	-35	91	102	O995(293/625/77),2b16/1	—	-6.2
Boeckel, Tony	Norman Doxie; B8.25.1892 Los Angeles CA; D2.16.1924 LaJolla CA; BR/TR/5´10.5˝/175; d7.23; Mil 1918																								
1917	Pit N	64	219	16	58	11	1	0	23	8	2	31	.265	.297	.324	88	-3	6	.935	-3	95	89	3b62	—	-0.5
1919	Pit N	45	152	18	38	9	2	0	16	18	1	20	.250	.333	.336	98	0	11	.930	-7	88	38	3b45	—	-0.5
	Bos N	95	365	42	91	11	5	1	26	35	1	13	.249	.317	.315	94	-2	10	.960	1	104	85	3b93	—	0.1
	Year	140	517	60	129	20	7	1	42	53	2	33	.250	.322	.321	95	-2	21	.951	-6	99	70	3b138	—	-0.4
1920	Bos N	**153**	582	70	156	28	5	3	62	38	1	50	.268	.314	.349	94	-5	18-15	.936	-6	91	110	3b149,S3/2	—	-0.8
1921	Bos N	**153**	592	93	185	20	13	10	84	52	2	41	.313	.370	.441	120	17	20-15	.933	-13	91	67	3b153	—	1.3
1922	Bos N	119	402	61	116	19	6	6	47	35	2	32	.289	.349	.410	99	-1	14-8	.952	-9	86	75	3b106	—	-0.2
1923	Bos N	148	568	72	169	32	4	7	79	51	2	31	.298	.357	.405	105	5	11-8	.939	-9	94	100	3b147/S	—	0.4
Total	6	777	2880	372	813	130	36	27	337	237	11	218	.282	.339	.381	102	11	90-46	.941	-45	93	86	3b755,S4/2	—	-0.2
Boehmer, Len	Leonard Joseph Stephen; B6.28.1941 Flint Hill MO; BR/TR/6´1˝/192; d6.18; Col St. Louis																								
1967	Cin N	2	3	0	0	0	0	0	0	0-0	0	0	.000	.000	.000	-90	-1	0-0	1.000	0	149	0	/2	0	-0.1
1969	NY A	45	108	5	19	4	0	0	7	8-2	0	10	.176	.233	.213	26	-11	0-1	.995	1	98	103	1b21,3b8/2S	0	-1.2
1971	NY A	3	5	0	0	0	0	0	0	0-0	0	0	.000	.000	.000	-99	-1	0-0	1.000	-0	51	0	/3	0	-0.2
Total	3	50	116	5	19	4	0	0	7	8-2	0	10	.164	.218	.198	18	-13	0-1	.995	1	98	103	1b21,3b9,2b2/S	0	-1.5

BOGAR, TIM Timothy Paul; B10.28.1966 Indianapolis IN; BR/TR/6´2˝/198; [NYN87 8/212]; d4.21; Col Eastern Illinois

YEAR	TM LG	G	AB	R	H	2B	3B	HR	RBI	BB-IB	HP	SO	AVG	OBP	SLG	AOPS	ABR	SB-CS	FA	FR	RNG	THR	GAMES AT POSITION	DL	BFW
1993	NY N	78	205	19	50	13	0	3	25	14-2	3	29	.244	.300	.351	75	-7	0-1	.972	9	109	99	S66,3b7,2b6	16	0.6
1994	NY N	50	52	5	8	0	0	2	5	4-1	0	11	.154	.211	.269	25	-6	1-0	.909	5	81	0	3b22,1b14,S7/2lf	34	-0.1
1995	NY N	78	145	17	42	7	0	1	21	9-0	0	25	.290	.329	.359	85	-3	1-0	.971	3	97	55	S27,3b25,1b10,2b7/lf	0	0.1
1996	NY N	91	89	17	19	4	0	0	6	8-0	2	20	.213	.287	.258	49	-6	1-3	1.000	1	70	113	1b32,3b25,S19,2b8	0	-0.6
1997	Hou N	97	241	30	60	14	4	4	30	24-1	3	42	.249	.320	.390	89	-4	4-1	.985	11	109	140	S80,3b14/1	24	1.2
1998	Hou N	79	156	12	24	4	1	1	8	9-2	2	36	.154	.208	.212	11	-21	2-1	.989	5	116	77	S55,2b11,3b11/D	0	-1.3
1999	†Hou N	106	309	44	74	16	2	4	31	38-5	4	52	.239	.328	.343	72	-13	3-5	.977	26	117	144	S90,3b12/2	0	1.7
2000	Hou N	110	304	32	63	9	2	7	33	35-7	3	56	.207	.292	.319	51	-24	1-1	.971	3	106	102	S95,2b2,P2/3	0	-1.3
2001	LA N	12	15	4	5	2	0	2	2	2-0	0	1	.333	.412	.867	232	3	0-0	1.000	-2	0	128	1b3,S2/3	168	0.1
Total	9	701	1516	180	345	69	9	24	161	143-18	17	272	.228	.298	.332	64	-81	13-12	.978	61	111	116	S441,3b118,1b60,2b36,P2,O2L/D	242	0.4

BOGENER, TERRY Terry Wayne; B9.28.1955 Hannibal MO; BL/TL/6´0˝/193; [TexA78 6/150]; d6.14; Col Oklahoma

YEAR	TM LG	G	AB	R	H	2B	3B	HR	RBI	BB-IB	HP	SO	AVG	OBP	SLG	AOPS	ABR	SB-CS	FA	FR	RNG	THR	GAMES AT POSITION	DL	BFW
1982	Tex A	24	60	6	13	2	1	1	4	4-0	2	8	.217	.288	.333	73	-2	2-0	1.000	-1	84	0	O16(4/10/2),D4	0	-0.4

BOGGS, WADE Wade Anthony; B6.15.1958 Omaha NE; BL/TR/6´2˝/(185–197); [BosA76 7/166]; d4.10; C1; HF2005

YEAR	TM LG	G	AB	R	H	2B	3B	HR	RBI	BB-IB	HP	SO	AVG	OBP	SLG	AOPS	ABR	SB-CS	FA	FR	RNG	THR	GAMES AT POSITION	DL	BFW
1982	Bos A	104	338	51	118	14	1	5	44	35-4	0	21	.349	.406	.441	126	14	1-0	.994	20	156	95	1b49,3b44/lfD	0	2.9
1983	Bos A	153	582	100	210	44	7	5	74	92-2	1	36	**.361**	**.444**	.486	146	43	3-3	.947	4	103	112	3b153	0	4.4
1984	Bos A	158	625	109	203	31	4	6	55	89-6	0	44	.325	.407	.416	123	24	3-2	.959	22	111	100	3b156,D2	0	4.4
1985	Bos A★	161	653	107	**240**	42	3	8	78	96-5	4	61	**.368**	**.450**	.478	148	51	2-1	.965	9	104	94	3b161	0	5.6
1986	†Bos A★	149	580	107	207	47	2	8	71	**105**-14	0	44	**.357**	**.453**	.486	155	54	0-4	.953	6	99	118	3b149	0	**5.4**
1987	Bos A★	147	551	108	200	40	6	24	89	105-**19**	2	48	**.363**	**.461**	.588	**172**	**65**	1-3	.965	8	102	129	3b145/1D	0	**6.5**
1988	†Bos A★	155	584	**128**	214	**45**	6	5	58	**125-18**	3	34	**.366**	**.476**	.490	165	**62**	2-3	.971	3	92	69	3b151,D3	0	**6.4**
1989	Bos A★	156	621	**113**	205	**51**	7	3	54	107-**19**	7	51	.330	**.430**	.449	140	41	2-6	.958	3	95	111	3b152,D3	0	4.3
1990	†Bos A★	155	619	89	187	44	5	6	63	87-**19**	1	68	.302	.386	.418	120	21	0-0	.946	-15	86	63	3b152,D3	0	0.6
1991	Bos A★	144	546	93	181	42	2	8	51	89-**25**	0	32	.332	.421	.460	137	33	1-2	.968	5	99	133	3b140	0	3.8
1992	Bos A★	143	514	62	133	22	4	7	50	74-**19**	4	31	.259	.353	.358	94	-2	1-3	.952	-0	98	**118**	3b117,D21	0	-0.4
1993	NY A★	143	560	83	169	26	1	2	59	74-4	0	49	.302	.378	.363	104	7	0-1	**.970**	21	**121**	**131**	3b134,D8	0	2.8
1994	NY A★	97	366	61	125	19	1	11	55	61-3	1	29	.342	.433	.489	143	27	2-1	.962	9	**116**	137	3b93,1b4	0	3.3
1995	†NY A★	126	460	76	149	22	4	5	63	74-5	0	50	.324	.412	.422	120	18	1-1	**.981**	-2	96	62	3b117,1b9	0	1.5
1996	†NY A★	132	501	80	156	29	2	2	41	67-7	0	32	.311	.389	.389	99	2	1-2	.974	-4	91	116	3b123,D4	0	-0.1
1997	†NY A	104	353	55	103	23	1	4	28	48-3	0	38	.292	.373	.397	103	4	0-1	.978	2	100	131	3b76,D19/P	0	0.4
1998	TB A	123	435	51	122	23	4	7	52	46-6	0	54	.280	.348	.400	92	-5	3-2	.973	1	101	108	3b78,D33	21	-0.5
1999	TB A	90	292	40	88	14	1	2	29	38-2	0	23	.301	.377	.377	93	-2	1-0	.942	-7	83	116	3b74,1b4/PD	46	-0.8
Total	18	2440	9180	1513	3010	578	61	118	1014	1412-180	23	745	.328	.415	.443	129	457	24-35	.962	84	101	107	3b2215,D107,1b67,P2/lf	67	50.5

BOHN, T.J. Thomas Joseph; B1.17.1980 St.Louis Park MN; BR/TR/6´5˝/210; [SeaA02 30/910]; d8.22; Col Bellevue

YEAR	TM LG	G	AB	R	H	2B	3B	HR	RBI	BB-IB	HP	SO	AVG	OBP	SLG	AOPS	ABR	SB-CS	FA	FR	RNG	THR	GAMES AT POSITION	DL	BFW
2006	Sea A	18	14	2	2	0	0	1	2	2-0	0	8	.143	.250	.357	58	-1	0-0	.875	-1	64	0	O18(1/0/17)	0	-0.2

BOHNE, SAM Samuel Arthur (b Samuel Arthur Cohen); B10.22.1896 San Francisco CA; D5.23.1977 Palo Alto CA; BR/TR/5´8.5˝/175; d9.9

YEAR	TM LG	G	AB	R	H	2B	3B	HR	RBI	BB-IB	HP	SO	AVG	OBP	SLG	AOPS	ABR	SB-CS	FA	FR	RNG	THR	GAMES AT POSITION	DL	BFW
1916	StL N	14	38	3	9	0	0	0	0	4	0	6	.237	.310	.237	69	-1	3	.870	-3	98	63	S14	—	-0.4
1921	Cin N	**153**	613	98	175	28	16	3	44	54	4	38	.285	.347	.398	101	1	26-22	.973	10	97	120	2b102,3b53	—	1.6
1922	Cin N	112	383	53	105	14	5	3	51	39	2	18	.274	.344	.360	83	-9	13-8	.958	13	114	128	2b85,S20	—	0.8
1923	Cin N	139	539	77	136	18	10	3	47	48	2	37	.252	.316	.340	74	-21	16-19	.975	9	104	86	2b96,3b35,S9/1	—	-0.8
1924	Cin N	100	349	42	89	15	9	4	46	18	1	24	.255	.293	.384	81	-11	9-6	.941	-5	95	74	2b48,S40,3b12	—	-1.0
1925	Cin N	73	214	24	55	9	1	2	24	14	0	14	.257	.303	.336	65	-12	6-4	.933	-5	98	102	S49,2b10,O4(1/0/4),1b2,3b2	—	-1.1
1926	Cin N	25	54	8	11	0	2	0	5	4	0	8	.204	.259	.278	46	-5	1	.931	-2	100	91	S20	—	-0.5
	Bro N	47	125	4	25	3	2	1	11	12	0	9	.200	.270	.280	49	-9	1	.965	5	109	60	2b31,3b15	—	-0.3
	Year	72	179	12	36	3	4	1	16	16	0	17	.201	.267	.279	48	-14	2	.965	3	109	60	2b31,S20,3b15	—	-0.8
Total	7	663	2315	309	605	87	45	16	228	193	9	154	.261	.321	.359	81	-67	75-59	.966	23	103	102	2b372,S152,3b117,O4(1/0/4),1b3	—	-1.7

BOISCLAIR, BRUCE Bruce Armand; B12.9.1952 Putnam CT; BL/TL/6´2˝/(185–200); [NYN70 20/486]; d9.11

YEAR	TM LG	G	AB	R	H	2B	3B	HR	RBI	BB-IB	HP	SO	AVG	OBP	SLG	AOPS	ABR	SB-CS	FA	FR	RNG	THR	GAMES AT POSITION	DL	BFW
1974	NY N	7	12	0	3	1	0	0	1	1-0	0	4	.250	.308	.333	80	0	0-0	.923	2	112	837	O5(2/3/0)	0	0.1
1976	NY N	110	286	42	82	13	3	2	13	28-5	0	55	.287	.350	.374	111	4	9-5	.981	0	104	66	O87(35/39/20)	0	0.2
1977	NY N	127	307	41	90	21	1	4	44	31-0	1	57	.293	.359	.407	109	5	6-4	.959	-4	101	20	O91(30/9/55),1b9	0	-0.3
1978	NY N	107	214	24	48	7	1	4	15	23-3	0	43	.224	.293	.322	76	-7	3-3	.983	2	115	71	O69(12/2/58)/1	0	-0.9
1979	NY N	59	98	7	18	5	1	0	4	3-0	1	24	.184	.210	.255	29	-10	0-2	1.000	0	97	137	O24(8/0/17)/1	60	-1.2
Total	5	410	917	114	241	47	6	10	77	86-8	2	183	.263	.324	.360	93	-8	18-14	.975	0	105	71	O276(87/53/150),1b11	60	-2.1

BOKEN, BOB Robert Anthony; B2.23.1908 Maryville IL; D10.6.1988 Las Vegas NV; BR/TR/6´2˝/165; d4.25

YEAR	TM LG	G	AB	R	H	2B	3B	HR	RBI	BB-IB	HP	SO	AVG	OBP	SLG	AOPS	ABR	SB-CS	FA	FR	RNG	THR	GAMES AT POSITION	DL	BFW
1933	Was A	55	133	19	37	5	2	3	26	9	0	16	.278	.324	.414	95	-2	0-0	.969	-3	103	94	2b31,3b19,S10	—	-0.2
1934	Was A	11	27	5	6	1	1	0	6	3	0	1	.222	.300	.333	66	-2	2-0	.864	1	112	268	3b6/2	—	0.0
	Chi A	81	297	30	70	9	1	3	40	15	1	32	.236	.275	.303	47	-24	2-1	.929	-15	92	69	2b57,S22	—	-3.2
	Year	92	324	35	76	10	2	3	46	18	1	33	.235	.277	.306	49	-26	4-1	.929	-14	92	73	2b58,S22,3b6	—	-3.2
Total	2	147	457	54	113	15	4	6	72	27	1	49	.247	.291	.337	62	-28	4-1	.941	-17	95	79	2b89,S32,3b25	—	-3.4

BOLAND ; d9.4

YEAR	TM LG	G	AB	R	H	2B	3B	HR	RBI	BB-IB	HP	SO	AVG	OBP	SLG	AOPS	ABR	SB-CS	FA	FR	RNG	THR	GAMES AT POSITION	DL	BFW
1875	Atl NA	1	4	0	0	0	0	0	0	0	—	0	.000	.000	.000	-99	-1	0-0	.750	-0	55	0	/3	—	-0.1

BOLAND, ED Edward John; B4.18.1908 Long Island City NY; D2.5.1993 Clearwater FL; BL/TL/5´10˝/165; d9.18

YEAR	TM LG	G	AB	R	H	2B	3B	HR	RBI	BB-IB	HP	SO	AVG	OBP	SLG	AOPS	ABR	SB-CS	FA	FR	RNG	THR	GAMES AT POSITION	DL	BFW
1934	Phi N	8	30	2	9	1	1	0	5	0	0	2	.300	.300	.400	76	-1	1	.778	-1	55	207	O7R	—	-0.2
1935	Phi N	30	47	5	10	0	0	0	4	4	0	6	.213	.275	.213	30	-5	1	.833	-2	88	0	O10(2/2/6)	—	-0.6
1944	Was A	19	59	4	16	4	0	0	14	0	0	6	.271	.271	.339	77	-2	0-0	.889	0	92	245	O14R	0	-0.3
Total	3	57	136	11	35	5	1	0	23	4	0	14	.257	.279	.309	59	-8	2-0	.852	-2	83	161	O31(2/2/27)	0	-1.1

BOLD, CHARLIE Charles Dickens "Dutch"; B10.27.1894 Karlskrona, Sweden; D7.29.1978 Chelsea MA; BR/TR/6´2˝/185; d8.24; Col Georgetown

YEAR	TM LG	G	AB	R	H	2B	3B	HR	RBI	BB-IB	HP	SO	AVG	OBP	SLG	AOPS	ABR	SB-CS	FA	FR	RNG	THR	GAMES AT POSITION	DL	BFW
1914	StL A	2	1	0	0	0	0	0	0	0	0	1	.000	.000	.000	-99	0	0	.500	-0	0	0	/1	—	-0.1

BOLES, CARL Carl Theodore; B10.31.1934 Center Point AR; BR/TR/5´11˝/188; d8.2; Col Arkansas–Pine Bluff

YEAR	TM LG	G	AB	R	H	2B	3B	HR	RBI	BB-IB	HP	SO	AVG	OBP	SLG	AOPS	ABR	SB-CS	FA	FR	RNG	THR	GAMES AT POSITION	DL	BFW
1962	SF N	19	24	4	9	0	0	0	1	0-0	0	6	.375	.375	.375	104	0	0-0	.833	-1	75	0	O7L	0	-0.1

BOLEY, JOE John Peter (b John Peter Bolinsky); B7.19.1896 Mahanoy City PA; D12.30.1962 Mahanoy City PA; BR/TR/5´11˝/170; d4.12

YEAR	TM LG	G	AB	R	H	2B	3B	HR	RBI	BB-IB	HP	SO	AVG	OBP	SLG	AOPS	ABR	SB-CS	FA	FR	RNG	THR	GAMES AT POSITION	DL	BFW
1927	Phi A	118	370	49	115	18	8	1	52	26	3	14	.311	.361	.411	95	-4	8-5	.951	-7	97	88	S114	—	0.1
1928	Phi A	132	425	49	112	20	3	0	49	32	1	11	.264	.317	.325	67	-20	5-1	.949	-17	87	78	S132	—	-2.3
1929	†Phi A	91	303	36	76	17	6	2	47	24	2	16	.251	.310	.366	71	-14	1-0	.963	-11	87	104	S88/3	—	-1.4
1930	†Phi A	121	420	41	116	22	2	4	55	32	5	26	.276	.335	.367	74	-16	0-0	**.970**	-6	88	99	S120	—	-0.9
1931	†Phi A	67	224	26	51	9	3	0	20	15	2	13	.228	.282	.295	49	-17	1-1	.954	-8	87	111	S62/2	—	-2.0
1932	Phi A	10	34	2	7	2	0	0	4	1	0	4	.206	.229	.265	26	-4	0-1	.897	-4	76	44	S10	—	-0.7
	Cle A	1	4	0	1	0	0	0	0	0	0	0	.250	.250	.250	28	0	0-0	ø	-0	0	0	/S	—	-0.1
	Year	11	38	2	8	2	0	0	4	1	0	4	.211	.231	.263	27	-4	0-1	.897	-4	75	43	S11	—	-0.8
Total	6	540	1780	203	478	88	22	7	227	130	13	84	.269	.323	.354	72	-75	15-8	.957	-53	89	93	S527/23	—	-7.3

BOLGER, JIM James Cyril "Dutch"; B2.23.1932 Cincinnati OH; BR/TR/6´2˝/(180–185); d6.24

YEAR	TM LG	G	AB	R	H	2B	3B	HR	RBI	BB-IB	HP	SO	AVG	OBP	SLG	AOPS	ABR	SB-CS	FA	FR	RNG	THR	GAMES AT POSITION	DL	BFW
1950	Cin N	2	1	0	0	0	0	0	0	0	0	0	.000	.000	.000	-99	0	0	ø	-0	0	0	O2L	0	0.0
1951	Cin N	2	0	1	0	0	0	0	0	0	0	0	ø	ø	ø	ø	0	1-0	ø	0	—	—	/R	0	0.0
1954	Cin N	5	3	1	1	0	0	0	0	0	0	1	.333	.333	.333	72	0	0-0	ø	-0	0	0	O2C	0	0.0
1955	Chi N	64	160	19	33	5	4	0	7	9-1	2	17	.206	.257	.287	45	-13	2-2	.955	-2	105	28	O51(3/49/0)	0	-1.8
1957	Chi N	112	273	28	75	4	1	5	29	10-1	3	36	.275	.303	.352	78	-9	0-1	.987	4	121	99	O63(24/28/17),3b3	0	-0.8
1958	Chi N	84	120	15	27	4	1	1	11	9-0	1	20	.225	.285	.300	56	-8	0-1	.940	0	113	66	O37(28/6/5)	0	-0.9
1959	Cle A	8	7	0	0	0	0	0	0	1-0	0	1	.000	.125	.000	-65	-2	0-0	ø	0	—	—	/H	0	-0.2
	Phi N	35	48	1	4	1	0	0	1	3-1	0	8	.083	.135	.104	-34	-9	0-0	.938	-0	114	0	O9(7/1/1)	0	-1.0
Total	7	312	612	65	140	14	6	6	48	32-3	6	83	.229	.272	.301	54	-41	3-4	.966	3	114	64	O164(64/86/23),3b3	0	-4.7

YEAR	TM LG	G	AB	R	H	2B	3B	HR	RBI	BB-IB	HP	SO	AVG	OBP	SLG	AOPS	ABR	SB-CS	FA	FR	RNG	THR	GAMES AT POSITION	DL	BFW
Bolick, Frank	Frank Charles; B6.28.1966 Ashland PA; BB/TR/5´10˝/(180–200); [MilA87 9/227]; d4.5; Col Georgia Tech																								
1993	Mon N	95	213	25	45	13	0	4	24	23-2	4	37	.211	.298	.329	65	-10	1-0	.992	4	135	106	1b51,3b24	0	-0.9
1998	Ana A	21	45	3	7	2	0	1	2	11-0	0	8	.156	.321	.267	54	-3	0-0	1.000	-1	72	0	3b7/1rfD	0	-0.3
Total	2	116	258	28	52	15	0	5	26	34-2	4	45	.202	.302	.318	63	-13	1-0	.992	3	134	109	1b52,3b31,D9/rf	0	-1.2
Bolling, Frank	Frank Elmore; B11.16.1931 Mobile AL; BR/TR/6´1˝/(170–175); d4.13; Mil 1955; b–Milt; Col Spring Hill																								
1954	Det A	117	368	46	87	15	2	6	38	36	0	51	.236	.302	.337	77	-12	3-5	.974	-20	88	77	2b113	0	-2.8
1956	Det A	102	366	53	103	21	7	7	45	42-1	2	51	.281	.354	.434	108	4	6-2	.978	-9	95	92	2b102	0	0.3
1957	Det A	146	576	72	149	27	6	15	40	57-3	2	64	.259	.327	.405	96	-3	4-9	.980	-3	99	107	2b146	0	0.3
1958	Det A	**154**	610	91	164	25	4	14	75	54-1	4	54	.269	.328	.392	92	-6	6-4	**.985**	12	107	96	2b154	0	1.7
1959	Det A	127	459	56	122	18	3	13	55	45-2	7	37	.266	.339	.403	98	-1	2-2	.987	2	98	100	2b126	0	1.0
1960	Det A	139	536	64	136	20	4	9	59	40-2	2	48	.254	.308	.356	77	-18	7-4	.978	-2	97	93	2b138	0	-1.0
1961	Mil N★	148	585	86	153	16	4	15	56	57-1	3	62	.262	.329	.379	93	-6	7-3	**.988**	-1	110	107	2b148	0	0.6
1962	Mil N★	122	406	45	110	17	4	9	43	35-3	4	45	.271	.333	.399	99	-1	2-2	**.989**	-7	99	104	2b119	0	0.2
1963	Mil N	142	542	73	132	18	2	5	43	41-3	3	47	.244	.299	.312	77	-16	2-1	.981	2	101	133	2b141	0	-0.2
1964	Mil N	120	352	35	70	11	1	5	34	21-3	2	44	.199	.245	.278	48	-25	0-1	**.985**	-5	94	117	2b117	0	-2.4
1965	Mil N	148	535	55	141	26	3	7	50	24-6	0	41	.264	.295	.363	84	-12	0-4	.976	-11	94	97	2b147	0	-1.3
1966	Atl N	75	227	16	48	7	0	1	18	10-3	1	14	.211	.244	.256	40	-18	1-1	.983	-9	90	92	2b67	0	-2.5
Total	12	1540	5562	692	1415	221	40	106	556	462-28	30	558	.254	.313	.366	85	-114	40-38	.982	-51	99	102	2b1518	0	-6.1
Bolling, Jack	John Edward; B2.20.1917 Mobile AL; D4.13.1998 Panama City FL; BL/TL/5´11˝/168; d6.10; Mil 1944–46; Col Alabama																								
1939	Phi N	69	211	27	61	11	0	3	13	11	0	10	.289	.324	.384	92	-3	6	.982	2	123	77	1b48	—	-0.5
1944	Bro N	56	131	21	46	14	1	1	25	14	1	4	.351	.418	.496	159	11	0	.991	1	114	30	1b27	0	1.1
Total	2	125	342	48	107	25	1	4	38	25	1	14	.313	.361	.427	118	8	6	.985	3	120	60	1b75	0	0.6
Bolling, Milt	Milton Joseph; B8.9.1930 Mississippi City MS; BR/TR/6´1˝/(180–185); d9.10; b–Frank																								
1952	Bos A	11	36	4	8	1	0	1	3	3	0	5	.222	.282	.333	66	-2	0-1	.984	3	124	80	S11	0	0.2
1953	Bos A	109	323	30	85	12	1	5	28	23	3	41	.263	.318	.353	77	-11	1-4	.956	5	104	110	S109	0	0.1
1954	Bos A	113	370	42	92	20	3	6	36	47	4	55	.249	.337	.368	84	-7	2-4	.946	9	**111**	97	S107,3b5	0	1.1
1955	Bos A	6	5	0	1	0	0	0	0	0-0	0	1	.200	.200	.200	7	-1	0-0	.800	-0	109	0	S2	63	-0.1
1956	Bos A	45	118	19	25	3	2	3	8	18-1	1	20	.212	.319	.347	68	-6	0-1	.947	-4	94	78	S26,3b11/2	0	-0.9
1957	Bos A	1	1	0	0	0	0	0	0	0-0	0	0	.000	.000	.000	-95	0	0-0	ø	0	—	—	/H	0	0.0
	Was A	91	277	29	63	12	1	4	19	18-0	2	59	.227	.277	.321	64	-14	2-2	.982	4	108	92	2b53,S37/3	0	-0.5
	Year	92	278	29	63	12	1	4	19	18-0	2	59	.227	.276	.320	64	-14	2-2	.982	4	108	92	2b53,S37/3	0	-0.5
1958	Det A	24	31	3	6	2	0	0	0	5-0	0	7	.194	.306	.258	53	-2	0-0	.946	0	89	140	S13/23	0	-0.1
Total	7	400	1161	127	280	50	7	19	94	114-1	10	188	.241	.313	.345	74	-43	5-12	.952	16	107	99	S305,2b55,3b18	63	-0.2
Bollweg, Don	Donald Raymond; B2.12.1921 Wheaton IL; D5.26.1996 Wheaton IL; BL/TL/6´1˝/190; d9.28																								
1950	StL N	4	11	1	2	0	0	0	1	1	0	1	.182	.250	.182	15	-1	0	1.000	-1	0	115	1b4	0	-0.2
1951	StL N	6	9	1	1	1	0	0	2	0	0	1	.111	.111	.222	-13	-1	0-0	.941	-1	0	155	1b2	0	-0.2
1953	†NY A	70	155	24	46	6	4	6	24	21	1	31	.297	.384	.503	143	9	1-0	.983	-4	66	116	1b43	0	0.4
1954	Phi A	103	268	35	60	15	3	5	24	35	3	33	.224	.319	.358	85	-5	1-0	.978	2	119	83	1b71	0	-0.7
1955	KC A	12	9	1	1	0	0	0	2	3-2	0	2	.111	.333	.111	23	-1	0-0	1.000	-0	0	377	1b3	0	-0.1
Total	5	195	452	62	110	22	7	11	53	60-2	4	68	.243	.337	.396	100	1	2-0	.980	-3	95	98	1b123	0	-0.8
Bolton, Cecil	Cecil Glenford "Glenn"; B2.13.1904 Booneville MS; D8.25.1993 Jackson MS; BL/TL/6´4˝/195; d9.21; Col Mississippi St.																								
1928	Cle A	4	13	1	2	0	2	0	0	2	0	2	.154	.267	.462	87	-1	0-0	.955	-1	42	93	1b4	—	-0.2
Bolton, Cliff	William Clifton; B4.10.1907 High Point NC; D4.21.1979 Lexington NC; BL/TR/5´9˝/160; d4.20																								
1931	Was A	23	43	3	11	1	1	0	6	1	0	5	.256	.273	.326	56	-3	0-0	.947	-3	*103*	*92*	C13	—	-0.5
1933	†Was A	33	39	4	16	1	1	0	6	6	1	3	.410	.500	.487	164	4	0-0	.889	-1	*160*	*75*	C9/rf	—	0.3
1934	Was A	42	148	12	40	9	1	1	17	11	0	9	.270	.321	.365	80	-5	2-0	.981	-3	*152*	*120*	C39	—	-0.4
1935	Was A	110	375	47	114	18	11	2	55	58	1	13	.304	.399	.427	117	11	0-1	.971	-23	*75*	*87*	C106	—	-0.5
1936	Was A	86	289	41	84	18	4	2	51	25	1	12	.291	.349	.401	90	-5	1-2	.979	-2	*86*	***114***	C83	—	-0.2
1937	Det A	27	57	6	15	2	0	1	7	8	0	6	.263	.354	.351	76	-2	0-0	.982	0	*89*	*121*	C13	—	-0.1
1941	Was A	14	11	0	0	0	0	0	1	1	0	2	.000	.083	.000	-80	-3	0-0	1.000	0	*0*	*0*	C3	0	-0.3
Total	7	335	962	113	280	49	18	6	143	110	3	50	.291	.366	.398	98	-3	3-3	.974	-32	*94*	*102*	C266/rf	0	-1.7
Bond, Walt	Walter Franklin; B10.19.1937 Denmark TN; D9.14.1967 Houston TX; BL/TR/6´7˝/(222–235); d4.19; Col Lane																								
1960	Cle A	40	131	19	29	2	1	5	18	13-2	3	14	.221	.302	.366	84	-3	4-1	1.000	1	110	93	O36(5/11/20)	0	-0.3
1961	Cle A	38	52	7	9	1	1	2	7	6-0	1	10	.173	.267	.346	65	-3	1-0	1.000	0	98	155	O12(0/1/11)	0	-0.3
1962	Cle A	12	50	10	19	3	0	6	17	4-1	0	9	.380	.426	.800	228	9	1-0	1.000	-0	107	0	O12(3/0/10)	0	0.8
1964	Hou N	148	543	63	138	16	7	20	85	38-8	8	90	.254	.310	.420	110	5	2-2	.989	-10	75	83	1b76,O71(28/1/42)	0	-1.4
1965	Hou N	117	407	46	107	17	2	7	47	42-8	5	51	.263	.337	.366	106	4	2-1	.983	-5	96	92	1b74,O38(18/0/21)	0	-0.8
1967	Min A	10	16	4	5	1	0	1	5	3-0	0	1	.313	.400	.563	174	2	0-0	.875	0	160	0	O3L	0	0.2
Total	6	365	1199	149	307	40	11	41	179	106-19	17	175	.256	.323	.410	110	14	10-4	.974	-13	99	37	O172(57/13/104),1b150	0	-1.8
Bonds, Barry	Barry Lamar; B7.24.1964 Riverside CA; BL/TL/6´1˝/(185–230); [PitN85 1/6]; d5.30; f–Bobby; Col Arizona St.																								
1986	Pit N	113	413	72	92	26	3	16	48	65-2	2	102	.223	.330	.416	102	2	36-7	.983	4	108	140	O110C	0	1.1
1987	Pit N	150	551	99	144	34	9	25	59	54-3	3	88	.261	.329	.492	113	9	32-10	.986	16	117	172	O145(101/46/1)	0	2.4
1988	Pit N	144	538	97	152	30	5	24	58	72-14	2	82	.283	.368	.491	146	33	17-11	.980	2	107	60	O136(135/3/0)	0	3.3
1989	Pit N	159	580	96	144	34	6	19	58	93-22	1	93	.248	.351	.426	126	22	32-10	.984	12	111	154	O156L	0	3.5
1990	†Pit N★	151	519	104	156	32	3	33	114	93-15	3	83	.301	.406	**.565**	**171**	**54**	52-13	.983	8	107	126	O150(149/2/0)	0	**6.4**
1991	†Pit N	153	510	95	149	28	5	25	116	107-25	4	73	.292	**.410**	.514	**162**	**48**	43-13	.991	6	106	147	O150(150/4/0)	0	5.6
1992	†Pit N★	140	473	**109**	147	36	5	34	103	**127-32**	5	69	.311	**.456**	**.624**	**205**	**75**	39-8	.991	-0	104	57	O139L	19	**7.9**
1993	SF N★	159	539	129	181	38	4	**46**	**123**	126-**43**	2	79	.336	**.458**	**.677**	**207**	**90**	29-12	.984	-3	100	59	O157L	0	**8.0**
1994	SF N★	112	391	89	122	18	1	37	81	**74-18**	6	43	.312	.426	.647	182	50	29-9	.986	1	92	144	O112L	0	4.8
1995	SF N★	**144**	506	109	149	30	7	33	104	**120-22**	5	83	.294	**.431**	.577	168	**56**	31-10	.980	5	104	130	O143L	0	**5.6**
1996	SF N★	158	517	122	159	27	3	42	129	**151-30**	1	76	.308	.461	.615	186	75	40-7	.980	4	104	114	O152(149/6/0)	0	**7.6**
1997	†SF N★	159	532	123	155	26	5	40	101	**145-34**	8	87	.291	.446	.585	172	65	37-8	.984	-0	100	95	O159L	0	6.2
1998	SF N★	156	552	120	167	44	7	37	122	130-**29**	8	92	.303	.438	.609	182	74	28-12	.984	-1	105	20	O155L	0	6.7
1999	SF N	102	355	91	93	20	2	34	83	73-9	3	62	.262	.389	.617	160	34	15-2	.984	-0	100	69	O96L,D4	52	3.0
2000	†SF N✳	143	480	129	147	28	4	49	106	**117**-22	3	77	.306	.440	.688	**193**	**73**	11-3	.989	5	104	99	O141L	0	**6.8**
2001	SF N★	153	476	129	156	32	2	**73**	137	**177**-35	9	93	.328	**.515**	**.863**	**263**	**133**	13-3	.977	-4	94	82	O143L,D6	0	**11.7**
2002	†SF N★	143	403	117	149	31	2	46	110	**198-68**	9	47	**.370**	**.582**	**.799**	**269**	**126**	9-2	.968	-2	100	49	O135L,D5	0	**11.5**
2003	†SF N★	130	390	111	133	22	1	45	90	**148-61**	10	58	.341	**.529**	**.749**	**226**	**87**	7-0	.992	2	106	67	O123L,D6	0	**8.2**
2004	SF N★	147	373	129	135	27	3	45	101	**232-120**	9	41	**.362**	**.609**	**.812**	**255**	**119**	6-1	.983	-2	91	150	O133L,D7	0	**10.7**
2005	SF N	14	42	8	12	1	0	5	10	9-3	0	6	.286	.404	.667	172	5	0-0	1.000	-1	87	0	O13L	162	0.3
2006	SF N	130	367	74	99	23	0	26	77	**115-38**	10	51	.270	**.454**	.545	154	39	3-0	.985	0	95	111	O116L,D5	0	3.4
Total	21	2860	9507	2152	2841	587	77	734	1930	2426-645	103	1485	.299	.443	.608	182	1269	509-141	.984	51	103	101	O2764(2605/171/1),D33	233	124.7
Bonds, Bobby	Bobby Lee; B3.15.1946 Riverside CA; D8.23.2003 San Carlos CA; BR/TR/6´1˝/(188–198); d6.25; C8; s–Barry; Col Riverside (CA) CC																								
1968	SF N	81	307	55	78	10	5	9	35	38-0	1	84	.254	.336	.407	123	9	16-7	.978	1	105	98	O80(0/35/62)	0	0.8
1969	SF N	158	622	**120**	161	25	6	32	90	81-3	10	187	.259	.351	.473	131	26	45-4	.978	-1	104	77	O155(0/77/99)	0	2.8
1970	SF N	157	663	134	200	36	10	26	78	77-7	2	189	.302	.375	.504	135	32	48-10	.969	6	105	131	O157(1/32/141)	0	3.7
1971	†SF N★	155	619	110	178	32	4	33	102	62-6	5	137	.288	.355	.512	145	36	26-8	**.994**	2	104	92	O154(0/33/133)	0	3.5
1972	SF N	153	626	118	162	29	5	26	80	60-4	5	137	.259	.326	.446	116	12	44-6	.978	5	115	70	O153(0/12/143)	0	1.8
1973	SF N★	160	643	**131**	182	34	4	39	96	87-9	4	148	.283	.370	.530	141	36	43-17	.970	6	115	84	O158(0/2/158)	0	3.9
1974	SF N	150	567	97	145	22	8	21	71	95-8	4	134	.256	.364	.434	118	16	41-11	.966	2	107	106	O148(0/8/141)	0	1.6
1975	NY A★	145	529	93	143	26	3	32	85	89-8	3	137	.270	.375	.512	151	38	30-17	.987	5	107	122	O129(1/44/90),D12	0	3.8
1976	Cal A	99	378	48	100	10	3	10	54	41-6	3	90	.265	.337	.386	120	9	30-15	.977	3	101	130	O98R/D	67	0.9
1977	Cal A	158	592	103	156	23	9	37	115	74-5	2	141	.264	.342	.520	138	29	41-18	.986	-0	104	53	O140R,D18	0	2.3
1978	Chi A	26	90	8	25	4	0	2	8	10-1	0	10	.278	.347	.389	106	1	6-2	.956	0	89	188	O22R,D3	0	0.1
	Tex A	130	475	85	126	15	4	29	82	69-6	2	110	.265	.356	.497	138	24	37-20	.970	-1	90	154	O111R,D18	0	1.8
	Year	156	565	93	151	19	4	31	90	79-7	2	120	.267	.355	.480	133	25	43-22	.968	-1	90	159	O133R,D21	0	1.9

YEAR	TM LG	G	AB	R	H	2B	3B	HR	RBI	BB-IB	HP	SO	AVG	OBP	SLG	AOPS	ABR	SB-CS	FA	FR	RNG	THR	GAMES AT POSITION	DL	BFW
1979	Cle A	146	538	93	148	24	1	25	85	74-4	8	135	.275	.367	.463	123	19	34-23	.979	7	116	107	O116R,D29	0	1.8
1980	StL N	86	231	37	47	5	3	5	24	33-3	2	74	.203	.305	.316	71	-9	15-5	.967	-0	97	107	O70(63/0/15)	22	-1.1
1981	Chi N	45	163	26	35	7	1	6	19	24-5	2	44	.215	.323	.380	93	-1	5-6	.982	-3	94	65	O45(0/42/3)	65	-0.5
Total	14	1849	7043	1258	1886	302	66	332	1024	914-75	53	1757	.268	.353	.471	129	277	461-169	.977	32	106	100	O1736(65/285/1472),D81	154	27.2
BONE, GEORGE	George Drummond; B8.28.1874 New Haven CT; D5.26.1918 West Haven CT; BB/TR/5´7˝/152; d9.18																								
1901	Mil A	12	43	6	13	2	0	0	6	4	0	—	.302	.362	.349	103	0	0	.869	-1	87	148	S12	—	0.0
BONGIOVANNI, NINO	Anthony Thomas; B12.21.1911 New Orleans LA; BL/TL/5´10˝/175; d4.23																								
1938	Cin N	2	7	0	2	1	0	0	0	0	0	0	.286	.286	.429	97	0	0	1.000	0	123	0	O2L	—	0.0
1939	†Cin N	66	159	17	41	6	0	0	16	9	0	8	.258	.298	.296	60	-9	0	.989	1	119	31	O39(6/1/32)	—	-1.0
Total	2	68	166	17	43	7	0	0	16	9	0	8	.259	.297	.301	61	-9	0	.990	1	119	29	O41(8/1/32)	—	-1.0
BONILLA, JUAN	Juan Guillermo; B2.12.1955 Santurce, PR; BR/TR/5´9˝/170; d4.9; Col Florida St.																								
1981	SD N	99	369	30	107	13	2	1	25	25-5	2	23	.290	.337	.344	102	1	4-9	.976	-8	98	108	2b97	0	-0.4
1982	SD N	45	182	21	51	6	2	0	8	11-0	1	15	.280	.325	.335	90	-3	0-1	.975	-4	100	100	2b45	124	-0.5
1983	SD N	152	556	55	132	17	4	4	45	50-11	3	40	.237	.301	.304	71	-22	3-0	.986	-9	97	104	2b149	0	-2.3
1985	NY A	8	16	0	2	1	0	0	2	0-0	0	3	.125	.125	.188	-16	-3	0-0	.955	0	109	105	2b7	0	-0.2
1986	Bal A	102	284	33	69	10	1	1	18	25-0	3	21	.243	.311	.296	67	-13	0-0	.981	-4	90	107	2b70,3b33,D2	0	-1.3
1987	NY A	23	55	6	14	3	0	1	3	5-0	0	6	.255	.317	.364	80	-2	0-0	.965	-2	91	89	2b22/3D	0	-0.3
Total	6	429	1462	145	375	50	9	7	101	116-16	9	108	.256	.314	.317	79	-42	7-10	.980	-27	96	104	2b390,3b34,D3	124	-5.0
BONILLA, BOBBY	Roberto Martin Antonio; B2.23.1963 Bronx NY; BB/TR/6´3˝/(210–240); d4.9; OF(206/10/698); [DL 1985 Pit N 102]																								
1986	Chi A	75	234	27	63	10	2	2	26	33-2	1	49	.269	.361	.355	93	-1	4-1	.989	1	110	79	O43(39/4/4),1b30	0	-0.3
	Pit N	63	192	28	46	6	2	1	17	29-1	1	39	.240	.342	.307	78	-5	4-4	.974	-0	85	94	O51(37/6/24),1b4,3b4	0	-0.8
1987	Pit N	141	466	58	140	33	3	15	77	39-4	2	64	.300	.351	.481	118	12	3-5	.932	-10	92	93	3b89,O46(17/0/34),1b6	0	-0.2
1988	Pit N★	159	584	87	160	32	7	24	100	85-19	4	82	.274	.366	.476	142	34	3-5	.935	3	108	66	3b159	0	3.8
1989	Pit N★	163	616	96	173	37	10	24	86	76-20	1	93	.281	.358	.490	146	36	8-8	.929	5	108	121	3b156,1b8/rf	0	4.2
1990	†Pit N★	160	625	112	175	39	7	32	120	45-9	1	103	.280	.322	.518	134	25	4-3	.961	-5	91	73	O149R,3b14,1b3	0	1.6
1991	†Pit N★	157	577	102	174	**44**	6	18	100	90-8	2	67	.302	.391	.492	150	43	2-4	.989	3	93	113	O104R,3b67,1b4	0	4.3
1992	NY N	128	438	62	109	23	0	19	70	66-10	1	73	.249	.348	.432	121	13	4-3	.992	4	108	93	O121R,1b6	16	1.4
1993	NY N★	139	502	81	133	21	3	34	87	72-11	0	96	.265	.352	.522	134	23	3-3	.969	-2	88	125	O85R,3b52,1b6	0	1.7
1994	NY N	108	403	60	117	24	1	20	67	55-9	0	101	.290	.374	.504	128	18	1-3	.942	6	111	153	3b107	0	2.3
1995	NY N★	80	317	49	103	25	4	18	53	31-10	1	48	.325	.385	.599	161	27	0-3	.882	-5	88	122	3b46,O31L,1b10	0	1.9
	Bal A	61	237	47	79	12	4	10	46	23-0	1	31	.333	.392	.544	139	13	0-2	.971	1	94	83	O39(1/0/38),3b24	0	1.0
1996	†Bal A	159	595	107	171	27	5	28	116	75-7	5	85	.287	.363	.491	116	15	1-3	.975	-8	86	107	O108R,D44,1b9,3b4	0	-0.1
1997	†Fla N	153	562	77	167	39	3	17	96	73-8	5	94	.297	.378	.468	127	24	6-6	.938	-17	81	115	3b149,1b2,D3	0	0.8
1998	Fla N	28	97	11	27	5	0	4	15	12-1	0	22	.278	.355	.454	119	3	0-1	.922	-4	84	117	3b26	12	-0.1
	LA N	72	236	28	56	6	1	7	30	29-3	0	37	.237	.315	.360	83	-6	1-1	.912	-9	80	85	3b59,O12L	36	-1.5
	Year	100	333	39	83	11	1	11	45	41-4	0	59	.249	.326	.387	93	-4	1-2	.915	-13	81	95	3b85,O12L	0	-1.6
1999	†NY N	60	119	12	19	5	0	4	18	19-1	1	16	.160	.277	.303	50	-10	0-1	.974	1	100	168	O25(2/0/23),1b4,D3	80	-1.0
2000	†Atl N	114	239	23	61	13	3	5	28	37-2	1	51	.255	.356	.397	91	-3	0-0	.927	-10	57	34	O64(63/0/1)/3D	0	-1.4
2001	StL N	93	174	17	37	7	0	5	21	23-3	1	53	.213	.308	.339	66	-9	1-1	.992	-2	61	139	1b33,O10(4/0/6)/PD	8	-1.3
Total	16	2113	7213	1084	2010	408	61	287	1173	912-128	28	1204	.279	.358	.472	124	252	45-57	.931	-49	100	108	3b957,O889R,1b125,D53/P	254	16.3
BONIN, LUTHER	Ernest Luther "Bonnie"; B1.13.1888 Greenhill IN; D1.3.1966 Sycamore OH; BL/TR/5´9.5˝/178; d4.13																								
1913	StL A	1	1	0	0	0	0	0	0	0	0	0	.000	.000	.000	-99	0	0	ø	0	—	—	/H	—	0.0
1914	Buf F	20	76	6	14	4	1	0	4	7	0	11	.184	.253	.263	40	-8	3	.970	0	94	122	O20R	—	-0.9
Total	2	21	77	6	14	4	1	0	4	7	0	11	.182	.250	.260	38	-8	3	.970	0	94	122	O20R	—	-0.9
BONNELL, BARRY	Robert Barry; B10.27.1953 Mariemont OH; BR/TR/6´3˝/(190–208); [PhiN75*S1/1]; d5.4; Col Ohio St.; OF(395/344/214)																								
1977	Atl N	100	360	41	108	11	0	1	45	37-8	2	32	.300	.368	.339	82	-7	7-5	.989	6	124	76	O75(2/63/10),3b32	22	-0.3
1978	Atl N	117	304	36	73	11	3	1	16	20-1	0	30	.240	.287	.306	59	-16	12-6	.984	7	105	159	O105(53/55/11),3b15	0	-1.2
1979	Atl N	127	375	47	97	20	3	12	45	26-2	3	55	.259	.311	.424	93	-4	8-7	.983	-1	92	106	O124(77/74/0)/3	0	-0.9
1980	Tor A	130	463	55	124	22	4	13	56	37-2	2	59	.268	.322	.417	98	-2	3-4	.973	-1	92	164	O122(5/57/61),D3	19	-0.7
1981	Tor A	66	227	21	50	7	4	4	28	12-0	1	25	.220	.262	.339	68	-10	4-3	.975	1	103	112	O66(9/18/41)	0	-1.3
1982	Tor A	140	437	59	128	26	3	6	49	32-4	3	51	.293	.342	.407	97	-1	14-2	.979	-6	93	45	O125(99/39/7),3b9,D6	0	-0.8
1983	Tor A	121	377	49	120	21	3	10	54	33-5	0	52	.318	.369	.469	122	12	10-7	.986	-1	94	95	O117(62/22/51),3b4/D	0	0.6
1984	Sea A	110	363	42	96	15	4	8	48	25-3	2	51	.264	.315	.394	95	-3	5-2	.994	-3	89	153	O94(70/16/20),3b10,1b5,D8	0	-1.0
1985	Sea A	48	111	9	27	8	0	1	10	6-1	0	19	.243	.282	.342	69	-5	1-2	.976	-0	101	164	O22(9/0/13),1b5,D2	30	-0.6
1986	Sea A	17	51	4	10	2	0	0	4	1-0	0	13	.196	.208	.235	21	-6	0-1	.941	1	99	0	O9L,1b8,D2	0	-0.6
Total	10	976	3068	363	833	143	24	56	355	229-26	13	387	.272	.323	.389	90	-42	64-39	.982	2	97	114	O859L,3b71,D22,1b18	71	-6.8
BONNER, FRANK	Frank J; B8.20.1869 Lowell MA; D12.31.1905 Kansas City MO; BR/TR/5´7.5˝/169; d4.26																								
1894	†Bal N	33	118	27	38	10	2	0	24	17	1	5	.322	.412	.441	101	1	12	.904	-9	82	74	2b27,O4(2/1/1),3b2/S	—	-0.5
1895	Bal N	11	42	9	14	1	1	0	7	5	0	1	.333	.404	.405	106	0	4	.742	-4	76	159	3b11	—	-0.2
	StL N	15	59	3	8	0	1	1	8	1	1	8	.136	.164	.220	-1	-10	2	.656	-5	72	0	3b10,O5R/C	—	-1.2
	Year	26	101	12	22	1	2	1	15	6	1	9	.218	.269	.297	46	-9	6	.698	-8	74	83	3b21,O5R/C	—	-1.4
1896	Bro N	9	34	8	6	2	0	0	5	2	2	8	.176	.263	.235	34	-3	1	.915	0	129	84	2b9	—	-0.2
1899	Was N	85	347	41	95	20	4	2	44	18	2	—	.274	.313	.372	88	-6	6	.940	3	102	94	2b85	—	0.1
1902	Cle A	34	132	14	37	6	0	0	14	5	1	—	.280	.312	.326	80	-4	1	.907	-6	95	39	2b34	—	-0.9
	Phi A	11	44	2	8	0	0	0	3	0	1	—	.182	.200	.182	6	-6	0	.937	-1	95	80	2b11	—	-0.7
	Year	45	176	16	45	6	0	0	17	5	2	—	.256	.284	.290	61	-10	1	.915	-7	95	50	2b45	—	-1.6
1903	Bos N	48	173	11	38	5	0	1	10	7	3	—	.220	.262	.266	53	-11	2	.957	-1	99	145	2b24,S22	—	-1.0
Total	6	246	949	115	244	44	8	4	115	55	11	22	.257	.305	.333	73	-39	28	.931	-21	99	87	2b190,S23,3b23,O9(2/1/6)/C	—	-4.6
BONNER, BOBBY	Robert Averill; B8.12.1956 Uvalde TX; BR/TR/6´0˝/185; [BalA78 3/74]; d9.12; Col Texas A&M																								
1980	Bal A	4	4	1	0	0	0	0	1	0-0	0	0	.000	.000	.000	-99	-1	0-0	.889	-0	110	91	S3	0	-0.1
1981	Bal A	10	27	6	8	2	0	0	2	1-0	0	4	.296	.310	.370	99	0	1-0	.976	2	109	163	S9	0	0.3
1982	Bal A	41	77	8	13	3	1	0	5	3-0	0	12	.169	.198	.234	19	-9	0-0	.959	-12	76	62	S38,2b3	0	-1.8
1983	Bal A	6	0	0	0	0	0	0	0	0-0	0	0	ø	ø	ø	ø	0	0-0	1.000	-1	0	0	2b5/D	0	-0.1
Total	4	61	108	15	21	5	1	0	8	4-0	0	16	.194	.219	.259	34	-10	1-0	.960	-10	85	85	S50,2b8/D	0	-1.7
BONURA, ZEKE	Henry John; B9.20.1908 New Orleans LA; D3.9.1987 New Orleans LA; BR/TR/6´0˝/210; d4.17; Mil 1941–45																								
1934	Chi A	127	510	86	154	35	4	27	110	64	0	31	.302	.380	.545	132	23	0-2	**.996**	4	109	81	1b127	—	1.3
1935	Chi A	138	550	107	162	34	4	21	92	57	3	28	.295	.364	.485	115	11	4-0	.994	2	105	93	1b138	—	0.1
1936	Chi A	148	587	120	194	39	7	12	138	94	4	29	.330	.426	.482	119	22	4-2	**.996**	11	**134**	**118**	1b146	—	1.7
1937	Chi A	116	447	79	154	41	2	19	100	49	2	24	.345	.412	.573	146	32	5-1	.989	-2	97	**132**	1b115	—	1.9
1938	Was A	137	540	72	156	27	3	22	114	44	3	29	.289	.346	.472	111	6	2-2	**.993**	3	109	107	1b129	—	-0.4
1939	NY N	123	455	75	146	26	6	11	85	46	4	22	.321	.388	.477	130	20	1	.992	6	118	104	1b122	—	1.5
1940	Was A	79	311	41	85	16	3	3	45	40	1	13	.273	.358	.373	96	-1	2-0	.982	-4	85	97	1b79	—	-1.1
	Chi N	49	182	20	48	14	0	4	20	10	0	4	.264	.302	.407	96	-1	1	.991	6	151	99	1b44	—	0.0
Total	7	917	3582	600	1099	232	29	119	704	404	17	180	.307	.380	.487	121	112	19-7	.992	26	112	104	1b900	—	5.0
BOOE, EVERETT	Everett Little; B9.28.1891 Mocksville NC; D5.21.1969 Kenedy TX; BL/TR/5´8.5˝/165; d4.13; Col Davidson																								
1913	Pit N	29	80	9	16	0	2	0	2	6	0	9	.200	.256	.250	47	-6	2-4	1.000	1	89	162	O22(1/21/0)	—	-0.8
1914	Ind F	20	31	5	7	1	0	0	6	7	0	6	.226	.368	.258	65	-2	4	.778	-1	96	0	O5(4/1/0),S3	—	-0.3
	Buf F	76	241	29	54	9	2	0	14	21	1	50	.224	.289	.278	54	-19	8	.959	-3	97	90	O58(23/0/35),S8,3b2/2	—	-2.6
	Year	96	272	34	61	10	2	0	20	28	1	56	.224	.299	.276	55	-21	12	.944	-5	97	84	O63(27/1/35),S11,3b2/2	—	-2.9
Total	2	125	352	43	77	10	4	0	22	34	1	65	.219	.289	.270	54	-27	14-4	.959	-4	95	102	O85(28/22/35),S11,3b2/2	—	-3.7
BOOKER, BUDDY	Richard Lee; B5.28.1942 Lynchburg VA; BL/TR/5´10˝/(170–185); d6.4																								
1966	Cle A	18	28	6	6	1	0	2	5	2-0	0	6	.214	.267	.464	105	0	0-0	.964	-4	85	66	C12	0	-0.4
1968	Chi A	5	5	0	0	0	0	0	0	1-0	0	2	.000	.167	.000	-46	-1	0-0	1.000	-1	28	0	C3	0	-0.2
Total	2	23	33	6	6	1	0	2	5	3-0	0	8	.182	.250	.394	83	-1	0-0	.967	-4	80	60	C15	0	-0.6

Booker, Rod Roderick Stewart; B9.4.1958 Los Angeles CA; BL/TR/6´0˝/(175–178); [MinA80 4/90]; d4.29; Col California

YEAR	TM LG	G	AB	R	H	2B	3B	HR	RBI	BB-IB	HP	SO	AVG	OBP	SLG	AOPS	ABR	SB-CS	FA	FR	RNG	THR	GAMES AT POSITION	DL	BFW
1987	StL N	44	47	9	13	1	1	0	8	7-1	0	7	.277	.370	.340	88	-1	2-0	.960	1	105	57	2b18,3b4/S	0	0.2
1988	StL N	18	35	6	12	3	0	0	3	4-0	0	3	.343	.410	.429	139	2	2-2	.889	-2	85	0	3b13/2	0	0.0
1989	StL N	10	8	1	2	0	0	0	0	0-0	0	1	.250	.250	.250	42	-1	0-0	.867	1	149	177	2b5/3	0	0.0
1990	Phi N	73	131	19	29	5	2	0	10	15-7	0	26	.221	.301	.290	64	-6	3-1	.976	-11	76	93	S27,2b23,3b10	0	-1.6
1991	Phi N	28	53	3	12	1	0	0	7	1-1	0	7	.226	.236	.245	37	-5	0-0	1.000	-5	75	29	S20,3b3	0	-0.9
Total	5	173	274	38	68	10	3	0	28	27-9	0	44	.248	.315	.307	72	-11	7-3	.985	-16	76	68	S48,2b47,3b31	0	-2.3

Bool, Al Albert; B8.24.1897 Lincoln NE; D9.27.1981 Lincoln NE; BR/TR/5´11˝/180; d9.29

YEAR	TM LG	G	AB	R	H	2B	3B	HR	RBI	BB-IB	HP	SO	AVG	OBP	SLG	AOPS	ABR	SB-CS	FA	FR	RNG	THR	GAMES AT POSITION	DL	BFW
1928	Was A	2	7	0	1	0	0	0	1	0	0	0	.143	.143	.143	-25	-1	0-0	1.000	0	*111*	*121*	C2	—	-0.1
1930	Pit N	78	216	30	56	12	4	7	46	25	0	29	.259	.336	.449	87	-5	0	.967	1	*95*	*135*	C65	—	0.0
1931	Bos N	49	85	5	16	1	0	0	6	9	0	13	.188	.266	.200	28	-9	0	.989	-0	*103*	*101*	C37	—	-0.8
Total	3	129	308	35	73	13	4	7	53	34	0	42	.237	.313	.373	71	-15	0-0	.973	1	*98*	*125*	C104	—	-0.9

Boone, Aaron Aaron John; B3.9.1973 LaMesa CA; BR/TR/6´2˝/(190–200); [CinN94 3/72]; d6.20; b–Bret f–Bob gf–Ray; Col USC; [DL 2004 Cle A 100]

YEAR	TM LG	G	AB	R	H	2B	3B	HR	RBI	BB-IB	HP	SO	AVG	OBP	SLG	AOPS	ABR	SB-CS	FA	FR	RNG	THR	GAMES AT POSITION	DL	BFW
1997	Cin N	16	49	5	12	1	0	0	5	2-0	0	5	.245	.275	.265	41	-4	1-0	.917	-0	100	0	3b13/2	0	-0.4
1998	Cin N	58	181	24	51	13	2	2	28	15-1	5	36	.282	.350	.409	99	0	6-1	.950	0	103	82	3b52/2S	0	0.1
1999	Cin N	139	472	56	132	26	5	14	72	30-2	8	79	.280	.330	.445	92	-7	17-6	.958	2	103	89	3b136,S6	0	-0.3
2000	Cin N	84	291	44	83	18	0	12	43	24-1	10	52	.285	.356	.471	104	2	6-1	.964	3	103	144	3b84,S2	83	0.6
2001	Cin N	103	381	54	112	26	2	14	62	29-1	8	71	.294	.351	.483	108	5	6-3	.936	5	114	94	3b103	62	1.0
2002	Cin N	**162**	606	83	146	38	2	26	87	56-4	10	111	.241	.314	.439	93	-7	32-8	.954	16	**122**	**142**	3b154,S16	0	1.5
2003	Cin N★	106	403	61	110	19	3	18	65	35-2	5	74	.273	.339	.469	113	6	15-3	.945	10	114	124	3b83,2b19,S5	0	2.0
	†NY A	54	189	31	48	13	0	6	31	11-0	3	30	.254	.302	.418	89	-3	8-0	.961	5	109	83	3b54	0	0.4
2005	Cle A	143	511	61	124	19	1	16	60	35-3	9	92	.243	.299	.378	82	-14	9-3	.955	2	105	88	3b142/D	0	-1.0
2006	Cle A	104	354	50	89	19	1	7	46	27-1	6	62	.251	.314	.370	80	-11	5-4	.938	-12	92	79	3b101/2D	0	-2.1
Total	9	969	3437	469	907	192	16	115	499	264-15	64	612	.264	.325	.429	94	-33	105-29	.951	31	108	103	3b922,S30,2b22,D2	245	1.8

Boone, Bret Bret Robert; B4.6.1969 El Cajon CA; BR/TR/5´10˝/(180–190); [SeaA90 5/134]; d8.19; b–Aaron f–Bob gf–Ray; Col USC

YEAR	TM LG	G	AB	R	H	2B	3B	HR	RBI	BB-IB	HP	SO	AVG	OBP	SLG	AOPS	ABR	SB-CS	FA	FR	RNG	THR	GAMES AT POSITION	DL	BFW
1992	Sea A	33	129	15	25	4	0	4	15	4-0	1	34	.194	.224	.318	50	-9	1-1	.965	1	104	94	2b32,3b6	0	-0.8
1993	Sea A	76	271	31	68	12	2	12	38	17-1	4	52	.251	.301	.443	96	-3	2-3	.991	-5	89	116	2b74/D	0	-0.5
1994	Cin N	108	381	59	122	25	2	12	68	24-1	8	74	.320	.368	.491	123	13	3-4	.974	-18	88	95	2b106,3b2	0	0.0
1995	†Cin N	138	513	63	137	34	2	15	68	41-0	6	84	.267	.326	.429	97	-3	5-1	**.994**	-8	94	**127**	2b138	0	-0.3
1996	Cin N	142	520	56	121	21	3	12	69	31-0	3	100	.233	.275	.354	65	-28	3-2	**.991**	3	98	95	2b141	15	-1.9
1997	Cin N	139	443	40	99	25	1	7	46	45-4	4	101	.223	.298	.332	64	-23	5-5	**.997**	-4	94	95	2b136	0	-2.1
1998	Cin N☆	157	583	76	155	38	1	24	95	48-3	4	104	.266	.324	.458	102	1	6-4	.988	-7	94	101	2b156	0	0.2
1999	†Atl N	152	608	102	153	38	1	20	63	47-0	5	112	.252	.310	.416	82	-18	14-9	.982	2	**107**	90	2b151	0	-0.9
2000	SD N	127	463	61	116	18	2	19	74	50-7	5	97	.251	.326	.421	94	-6	8-4	.977	-5	94	102	2b126	35	-0.4
2001	†Sea A★	158	623	118	206	37	3	37	**141**	40-5	9	110	.331	.372	.578	156	49	5-5	.986	-16	93	106	2b156,D2	0	3.7
2002	Sea A	155	608	88	169	34	3	24	107	53-4	6	102	.278	.339	.462	115	12	12-5	**.989**	-18	91	94	2b153/D	0	0.2
2003	Sea A★	159	622	111	183	35	5	35	117	68-3	7	125	.294	.366	.535	142	38	16-3	.990	-15	91	**117**	2b158	0	3.1
2004	Sea A	148	593	74	149	30	0	24	83	56-2	3	135	.251	.317	.423	96	-5	10-5	.978	-35	84	94	2b148	0	-3.0
2005	Sea A	74	273	30	63	15	3	7	34	24-2	3	52	.231	.299	.385	87	-6	4-2	.979	-15	89	87	2b74	0	-1.6
	Min A	14	53	3	9	0	0	0	3	4-0	1	13	.170	.241	.170	12	-7	0-0	.974	1	91	132	2b14	0	-0.5
	Year	88	326	33	72	15	3	7	37	28-2	4	65	.221	.290	.350	74	-13	4-2	.978	-14	89	94	2b88	0	-2.1
Total	14	1780	6683	927	1775	366	28	252	1021	552-32	69	1295	.266	.325	.442	101	5	94-53	.986	-140	93	102	2b1763,3b8,D4	50	-4.8

Boone, Ike Isaac Morgan; B2.17.1897 Samantha AL; D8.1.1958 Northport AL; BL/TR/6´0˝/195; d4.22; b–Dan; Col Alabama

YEAR	TM LG	G	AB	R	H	2B	3B	HR	RBI	BB-IB	HP	SO	AVG	OBP	SLG	AOPS	ABR	SB-CS	FA	FR	RNG	THR	GAMES AT POSITION	DL	BFW
1922	NY N	2	2	0	1	0	0	0	0	0	0	1	.500	.500	.500	157	0	0-0	ø	0	—	—	/H	—	0.0
1923	Bos A	5	15	1	4	0	1	0	2	1	0	0	.267	.313	.400	86	0	0-1	.929	-0	114	0	O4C	—	-0.1
1924	Bos A	128	487	72	164	31	4	13	98	54	1	32	.337	.404	.497	131	23	2-2	.976	-9	82	96	O124R	—	0.3
1925	Bos A	133	476	79	157	34	5	9	68	60	1	19	.330	.406	.479	124	19	1-4	.941	-9	90	73	O118R	—	-0.0
1927	Chi A	29	53	10	12	4	0	1	11	3	0	4	.226	.268	.358	63	-3	0-0	1.000	-1	100	0	O11(1/0/10)	—	-0.4
1930	Bro N	40	101	13	30	9	1	3	13	14	0	8	.297	.383	.495	111	2	0	.960	-0	105	63	O27L	—	0.0
1931	Bro N	6	5	0	1	0	0	0	0	1	0	1	.200	.333	.200	47	0	0	ø	0	—	—	/H	—	0.0
1932	Bro N	13	21	2	3	1	0	0	2	5	0	2	.143	.308	.190	38	-2	0	1.000	0	83	245	O8(2/0/6)	—	-0.1
Total	8	356	1160	177	372	79	11	26	194	138	2	67	.321	.394	.475	121	39	3-7	.960	-19	88	82	O292(30/4/258)	—	-0.3

Boone, Lute Lute Joseph "Danny"; B5.6.1890 Pittsburgh PA; D7.29.1982 Pittsburgh PA; BR/TR/5´9˝/160; d9.9

YEAR	TM LG	G	AB	R	H	2B	3B	HR	RBI	BB-IB	HP	SO	AVG	OBP	SLG	AOPS	ABR	SB-CS	FA	FR	RNG	THR	GAMES AT POSITION	DL	BFW
1913	NY A	6	12	3	4	0	0	0	1	3	0	1	.333	.467	.333	134	1	0	.857	-1	87	0	S4	—	0.0
1914	NY A	106	370	34	82	8	2	0	21	31	2	41	.222	.285	.254	63	-17	10-18	.960	18	111	115	2b90,3b9/rf	—	-0.2
1915	NY A	130	431	44	88	12	2	5	43	41	8	53	.204	.285	.276	68	-17	14-17	.965	**21**	**117**	**140**	2b115,S11,3b4	—	0.3
1916	NY A	46	124	14	23	4	0	1	8	8	3	10	.185	.252	.242	47	-8	7	.973	3	119	148	3b25,S12,2b8	—	-0.4
1918	Pit N	27	91	7	18	3	0	0	3	8	0	6	.198	.263	.231	49	-5	1	.921	-3	95	60	S26/2	—	-0.8
Total	5	315	1028	102	215	27	4	6	76	91	13	111	.209	.282	.261	63	-46	32-35	.964	37	114	128	2b214,S53,3b38/rf	—	-1.1

Boone, Ray Raymond Otis "Ike"; B7.27.1923 San Diego CA; D10.17.2004 San Diego CA; BR/TR/6´1˝/(185–190); d9.3; s–Bob gs–Bret gs–Aaron

YEAR	TM LG	G	AB	R	H	2B	3B	HR	RBI	BB-IB	HP	SO	AVG	OBP	SLG	AOPS	ABR	SB-CS	FA	FR	RNG	THR	GAMES AT POSITION	DL	BFW
1948	†Cle A	6	5	0	2	1	0	0	1	0	0	1	.400	.400	.600	168	0	0-0	.889	0	129	0	S4	0	0.1
1949	Cle A	86	258	39	65	4	4	4	26	38	2	17	.252	.352	.345	87	-5	0-2	.947	0	97	117	S76	0	-0.1
1950	Cle A	109	365	53	110	14	6	7	58	56	2	27	.301	.397	.430	116	10	4-3	.945	-7	93	96	S102	0	0.8
1951	Cle A	151	544	65	127	14	1	12	51	48	5	36	.233	.302	.329	75	-21	5-3	.957	-1	98	106	S151	0	-1.3
1952	Cle A	103	316	57	83	8	2	7	45	53	2	33	.263	.372	.367	113	7	0-1	.941	-4	98	102	S96,3b2/2	0	0.9
1953	Cle A	34	112	21	27	1	2	4	21	24	0	21	.241	.375	.393	110	2	1-2	.952	1	100	122	S31	0	0.6
	Det A	101	385	73	120	16	6	22	93	48	5	47	.312	.395	.556	156	30	2-1	.958	1	99	125	3b97,S3	0	3.0
	Year	135	497	94	147	17	8	26	114	72	5	68	.296	.390	.519	146	32	3-3	.958	3	99	125	3b97,S34	0	3.6
1954	Det A★	148	543	76	160	19	7	20	85	71	2	53	.295	.376	.466	133	24	4-2	.964	2	103	80	3b148/S	0	2.6
1955	Det A	135	500	61	142	22	7	20	**116**	50-2	1	49	.284	.346	.476	123	14	1-1	.953	-2	98	133	3b126	0	1.2
1956	Det A★	131	481	77	148	14	6	25	81	77-8	3	46	.308	.403	.518	142	30	0-0	.959	-4	91	83	3b130	0	2.5
1957	Det A	129	462	48	126	25	3	12	65	57-6	3	47	.273	.353	.418	108	6	1-1	.990	-11	60	99	1b117,3b4	0	-1.2
1958	Det A	39	114	16	27	4	1	6	20	14-1	1	13	.237	.323	.447	103	0	0-2	.988	-1	82	101	1b32	0	-0.3
	Chi A	77	246	25	60	12	1	7	41	18-1	1	33	.244	.295	.386	89	-4	1-1	.986	-2	90	85	1b63	0	-1.1
	Year	116	360	41	87	16	2	13	61	32-2	2	46	.242	.304	.406	93	-4	1-3	.986	-3	87	90	1b95	0	-1.4
1959	Chi A	9	21	3	5	0	0	1	5	7-0	0	5	.238	.400	.381	126	1	1-0	.955	0	141	45	1b6	0	0.1
	KC A	61	132	19	36	6	0	2	12	27-2	0	17	.273	.396	.364	108	3	1-0	.983	3	128	77	1b38,3b3	0	0.5
	Year	70	153	22	41	6	0	3	17	34-2	0	22	.268	.397	.366	111	4	2-0	.980	3	60	213	1b44,3b3	0	0.6
	Mil N	13	15	3	3	0	0	1	2	4-0	0	2	.200	.368	.400	114	0	0-0	1.000	-0	60	213	1b3	0	0.0
1960	Mil N	7	12	3	3	1	0	0	4	5-0	0	1	.250	.471	.333	135	1	0-0	1.000	0	121	108	1b4	0	0.1
	Bos A	34	78	6	16	1	0	1	11	11-0	0	15	.205	.300	.256	51	-5	0-0	.994	-0	90	107	1b22	0	-0.7
Total	13	1373	4589	645	1260	162	46	151	737	608-20	27	463	.275	.361	.429	115	93	21-19	.958	-25	98	103	3b510,S464,1b285/2	0	7.7

Boone, Bob Robert Raymond; B11.19.1947 San Diego CA; BR/TR/6´2˝/(195–210); [PhiN69 6/124]; d9.10; M6/C1; f–Ray s–Bret s–Aaron; Col Stanford

YEAR	TM LG	G	AB	R	H	2B	3B	HR	RBI	BB-IB	HP	SO	AVG	OBP	SLG	AOPS	ABR	SB-CS	FA	FR	RNG	THR	GAMES AT POSITION	DL	BFW
1972	Phi N	16	51	4	14	1	0	1	4	5-2	0	7	.275	.333	.353	94	0	1-0	.936	-4	140	101	C14	0	-0.4
1973	Phi N	145	521	42	136	20	2	10	61	41-8	0	36	.261	.311	.365	85	-11	3-4	.990	14	120	**138**	C145	0	0.9
1974	Phi N	146	488	41	118	24	3	3	52	35-9	4	29	.242	.295	.322	70	-20	3-1	.976	-2	89	112	C146	0	-1.6
1975	Phi N	97	289	28	71	14	2	2	20	32-6	1	14	.246	.322	.329	77	-8	1-3	.990	2	138	117	C92,3b3	0	-0.3
1976	†Phi N★	121	361	40	98	18	2	4	54	45-14	1	44	.271	.348	.366	100	2	2-5	.993	-8	125	62	C108,1b4	0	-0.3
1977	†Phi N	132	440	55	125	26	4	11	66	42-5	2	54	.284	.343	.436	104	3	5-5	.989	7	119	85	C131,3b2	0	1.5
1978	†Phi N★	132	435	48	123	18	4	12	62	46-10	1	37	.283	.347	.425	114	8	2-5	**.991**	-1	133	84	C129,1b3/lf	0	1.2
1979	Phi N★	119	398	38	114	21	3	9	58	49-9	2	33	.286	.367	.422	110	7	1-4	.988	-2	**152**	101	C117,3b2	0	0.8
1980	†Phi N	141	480	34	110	23	1	9	55	48-12	1	41	.229	.299	.338	73	-17	3-4	.979	3	102	108	C138	0	-0.9
1981	†Phi N	76	227	19	48	7	0	4	24	22-2	0	16	.211	.279	.295	60	-12	2-2	.985	-12	72	78	C75	0	-2.3
1982	†Cal A	143	472	42	121	17	0	7	58	39-2	0	34	.256	.310	.337	78	-14	0-2	.989	15	**193**	**130**	C143	0	0.7
1983	Cal A★	142	468	46	120	18	0	9	52	24-1	0	42	.256	.289	.353	77	-16	4-3	.980	10	148	111	C142	0	0.0
1984	Cal A	139	450	33	91	16	1	3	32	25-1	0	45	.202	.242	.262	40	-37	3-3	.984	9	148	93	C137	0	-2.3
1985	Cal A	150	460	37	114	17	0	5	55	37-2	3	35	.248	.306	.317	72	-18	1-2	.987	10	**154**	104	C147	0	-0.2
1986	†Cal A	144	442	48	98	12	2	7	49	43-1	0	30	.222	.287	.305	63	-23	1-0	.988	20	**210**	94	C144	0	0.3

YEAR	TM LG	G	AB	R	H	2B	3B	HR	RBI	BB-IB	HP	SO	AVG	OBP	SLG	AOPS	ABR	SB-CS	FA	FR	RNG	THR	GAMES AT POSITION	DL	BFW
1987	Cal A	128	389	42	94	18	0	3	33	35-0	1	36	.242	.304	.311	66	-18	0-2	.983	5	**207**	92	C127/D	0	-0.9
1988	Cal A	122	352	38	104	17	0	5	39	29-2	2	26	.295	.352	.386	109	5	2-2	.986	-3	118	127	C121	0	0.8
1989	KC A	131	405	33	111	13	2	1	43	49-4	2	37	.274	.351	.323	93	-2	3-2	.991	11	138	110	C129	0	1.7
1990	KC A	40	117	11	28	3	0	0	9	17-0	0	12	.239	.336	.265	71	-4	1-1	.985	-3	78	78	C40	64	-0.4
Total	19	2264	7245	679	1838	303	26	105	826	663-90	20	608	.254	.315	.346	82	-175	38-50	.986	70	140	104	C2225,1b7,3b7/Dlf	64	-1.7
Booth	; d5.1																								
1875	NH NA	1	2	0	0	0	0	0	0	0	—	1	.000	.000	.000	-99	0	0-0	.500	-0	66	0	/S	—	-0.1
Booth, Amos	Amos Smith "Darling"; B9.14.1848 Lebanon OH; D7.1.1921 Miamisburg OH; BR/TR/5´9˝/159; d4.25; ▲																								
1876	Cin N	63	272	31	71	3	0	0	14	9	—	11	.261	.285	.272	101	3	—	.760	-16	77	0	3b24,C24,S22,O3R,P3	—	-1.0
1877	Cin N	44	157	16	27	2	1	0	13	12	—	10	.172	.231	.197	41	-9	—	.853	-5	107	28	S13,C12,P12,2b10,3b3/lf	—	-0.9
1880	Cin N	1	2	0	0	0	0	0	0	0	—	0	.000	.000	.000	-99	0	—	ø	-0	0	0	/3	—	-0.1
1882	Bal AA	1	3	0	0	0	0	0	—	0	—	—	.000	.000	.000	-99	-1	—	1.000	0	66	0	/3	—	-0.1
	Lou AA	1	4	0	0	0	0	0	—	0	—	—	.000	.000	.000	-99	-1	—	1.000	-0	103	0	/2	—	-0.1
	Year	2	7	0	0	0	0	0	—	0	—	—	.000	.000	.000	-99	-1	—	1.000	0	66	0	/32	—	-0.2
Total	4	110	438	47	98	5	1	0	27	21	—	21	.224	.259	.240	73	-8	—	.746	-21	—	—	C36,S35,3b29,P15,2b11,O4(1/0/3)	—	-2.2
Booth, Eddie	Edward H.; B Brooklyn NY; d4.26																								
1872	Man NA	**24**	116	25	37	5	2	0	15	0	—	1	.319	.319	.397	126	4	0-2	.775	4	120	92	2b20,O4(0/3/1)	—	0.4
	Atl NA	15	62	10	19	4	0	0	7	0	—	0	.306	.306	.371	92	-1	0-2	.808	2	358	0	O14(6/0/8)/2	—	0.0
	Year	39	178	35	56	9	2	0	22	0	—	1	.315	.315	.388	111	2	0-4	.780	6	121	97	2b21,O18(6/3/9)	—	0.4
1873	Res NA	18	74	11	21	5	2	0	6	0	—	1	.284	.284	.405	110	1	0-0	.875	-3	41	0	O17(15/0/2)/2	—	-0.1
	Atl NA	16	70	8	14	3	1	0	7	2	—	0	.200	.222	.271	51	-3	0-1	.788	0	130	0	O16(0/4/12)	—	-0.2
	Year	34	144	19	35	8	3	0	13	2	—	1	.243	.253	.340	81	-2	0-1	.831	-3	84	0	O33(15/4/14)/2	—	-0.3
1874	Atl NA	44	185	24	47	4	3	1	16	3	—	3	.254	.266	.324	100	2	0-0	.809	-8	48	0	O44L/2	—	-0.4
1875	Mut NA	68	281	33	56	3	4	0	18	0	—	2	.199	.199	.238	49	-15	4-3	.827	1	**158**	103	O63(3/1/60),2b8	—	-0.9
1876	NY N	**57**	228	17	49	2	1	0	7	2	—	4	.215	.222	.232	59	-8	—	.764	-5	132	0	O53(0/2/51),2b5/P	—	-1.2
Total	4NA	185	788	111	194	24	12	1	69	5	—	7	.246	.251	.311	81	-12	4-8	.824	-3	130	41	O158(68/8/83),2b31	—	-1.2
Booty, Josh	Joshua Gibson; B4.29.1975 Starkville MS; BR/TR/6´3˝/(210–220); [FlaN94 1/5]; d9.24																								
1996	Fla N	2	2	1	1	0	0	0	0	0-0	0	0	.500	.500	.500	169	0	0-0	ø	-0	0	0	/3	0	0.0
1997	Fla N	4	5	2	3	0	0	0	1	1-0	0	1	.600	.667	.600	246	1	0-0	.857	1	174	387	3b4	0	0.2
1998	Fla N	7	19	0	3	1	0	0	3	3-0	0	8	.158	.273	.211	31	-2	0-0	.833	-1	95	83	3b7	0	-0.3
Total	3	13	26	3	7	1	0	0	4	4-0	0	9	.269	.367	.308	84	-1	0-0	.840	-0	109	143	3b12	0	-0.1
Borchard, Joe	Joseph Edward; B11.25.1978 Los Angeles CA; BB/TR/6´5˝/(220–230); [ChiA00 1/12]; d9.2; Col Stanford																								
2002	Chi A	16	36	5	8	0	0	2	5	1-0	0	14	.222	.243	.389	62	-2	0-0	1.000	-1	90	0	O15(10/5/3)	0	-0.3
2003	Chi A	16	49	5	9	1	0	1	5	5-0	0	18	.184	.246	.265	37	-5	0-1	1.000	-2	83	0	O16C	0	-0.7
2004	Chi A	63	201	26	35	4	1	9	20	19-1	1	57	.174	.249	.338	49	-16	1-0	.972	-2	92	112	O56(0/2/54),D4	0	-1.9
2005	Chi A	7	12	0	5	2	0	0	0	0-0	0	4	.417	.417	.583	156	1	0-1	1.000	0	184	0	O2R,D3	0	0.1
2006	Sea A	6	9	3	2	0	0	0	0	0-0	0	3	.222	.222	.222	17	-1	0-1	1.000	1	87	1097	O3C/D	0	-0.1
	Fla N	108	230	30	53	7	1	10	28	28-3	3	66	.230	.322	.400	88	-5	0-2	.982	6	111	305	O63(15/0/55)/1D	0	-0.2
Total	5	216	537	69	112	14	2	22	58	53-4	4	162	.209	.283	.365	67	-28	1-5	.982	2	98	174	O155(25/26/114),D10/1	0	-3.1
Bordagaray, Frenchy	Stanley George; B1.3.1910 Coalinga CA; D4.13.2000 Ventura CA; BR/TR/5´7.5˝/175; d4.17; Col Cal St.–Fresno																								
1934	Chi A	29	87	12	28	3	1	0	2	3	0	8	.322	.344	.379	84	-2	1-2	.938	-1	86	156	O17(2/1/14)	—	-0.4
1935	Bro N	120	422	69	119	19	6	1	39	17	6	29	.282	.319	.363	85	-10	18	.980	2	95	164	O105(17/61/27)	—	-1.1
1936	Bro N	125	372	63	117	21	3	4	31	17	1	42	.315	.346	.419	104	2	12	.991	2	111	117	O92(14/46/33),2b11,3b6	—	0.1
1937	StL N	96	300	43	88	11	4	1	37	15	2	25	.293	.331	.367	88	-6	11	.942	-6	82	32	3b50,O28(3/7/15)	—	-1.1
1938	StL N	81	156	19	44	5	1	0	21	8	2	9	.282	.325	.327	76	-5	2	.959	0	112	133	O29(6/14/9),3b4	—	-0.6
1939	†Cin N	63	122	19	24	5	1	0	12	9	0	10	.197	.252	.254	36	-11	3	1.000	-0	104	47	O43(21/3/19),2b2	—	-1.3
1941	†NY A	36	73	10	19	1	0	0	4	6	1	8	.260	.325	.274	61	-4	1-0	.967	-1	94	75	O19(6/0/13)	0	-0.5
1942	Bro N	48	58	11	14	2	0	0	5	3	0	3	.241	.279	.276	62	-3	2	1.000	0	117	0	O17(0/10/7)	0	-0.3
1943	Bro N	89	268	47	81	18	2	0	19	30	3	15	.302	.379	.384	120	9	6	.989	-7	99	147	O53(28/6/20),3b25	0	0.0
1944	Bro N	130	501	85	141	26	4	6	51	36	1	22	.281	.331	.385	103	1	3	.945	-15	79	78	3b98,O25(5/15/8)	0	-1.4
1945	Bro N	113	273	32	70	9	6	2	49	29	0	15	.256	.328	.355	91	-4	7	.886	-9	86	72	3b57,O22(9/7/6)	0	-1.3
Total	11	930	2632	410	745	120	28	14	270	173	16	186	.283	.331	.366	91	-33	66-2	.982	-32	103	113	O450(111/170/171),3b240,2b13	0	-7.9
Borders, Pat	Patrick Lance; B5.14.1963 Columbus OH; BR/TR/6´2˝/(190–205); [TorA82 6/134]; d4.6																								
1988	Tor A	56	154	15	42	6	3	5	21	3-0	0	24	.273	.285	.448	101	-1	0-0	.973	2	120	160	C43/23D	45	0.4
1989	†Tor A	94	241	22	62	11	1	3	29	11-2	1	45	.257	.290	.349	81	-7	2-1	.980	1	88	136	C68,D18	0	-0.4
1990	Tor A	125	346	36	99	24	2	15	49	18-2	0	57	.286	.319	.497	123	9	0-1	.993	4	110	128	C115/D	0	1.9
1991	†Tor A	105	291	22	71	17	0	5	36	11-1	1	45	.244	.271	.354	70	-13	0-0	.993	13	98	107	C102	0	0.5
1992	†Tor A	138	480	47	116	26	2	13	53	33-3	2	75	.242	.290	.385	84	-11	1-1	.991	5	83	103	C137	0	0.1
1993	†Tor A	138	488	38	124	30	0	9	55	20-2	2	66	.254	.285	.371	74	-19	2-2	.986	2	80	102	C138	0	-0.8
1994	Tor A	85	295	24	73	13	1	3	26	15-0	0	50	.247	.284	.329	57	-20	1-1	.988	6	84	128	C85	0	-0.7
1995	KC A	52	143	14	33	8	1	4	13	7-1	0	22	.231	.267	.385	66	-8	0-0	1.000	1	196	97	C45,D3	0	-0.4
	Hou N	11	35	1	4	0	0	0	0	2-1	0	7	.114	.162	.114	-27	-7	0-0	.987	1	118	198	C11	0	-0.5
1996	StL N	26	69	3	22	3	0	0	4	1-0	0	14	.319	.329	.362	82	-2	0-1	.984	5	198	127	C17/1	0	0.3
	Cal A	19	57	6	13	3	0	2	8	3-0	0	11	.228	.267	.386	61	-4	0-1	.984	2	69	113	C19	0	0.0
	Chi A	31	94	6	26	1	0	3	6	5-0	0	18	.277	.313	.383	78	-4	0-0	.982	-3	75	129	C30/D	0	-0.4
	Year	50	151	12	39	4	0	5	14	8-0	0	29	.258	.296	.384	72	-7	0-1	.983	-0	73	123	C49/D	0	-0.4
1997	Cle A	55	159	17	47	7	1	4	15	9-0	2	27	.296	.341	.428	95	-1	0-2	1.000	0	84	96	C53	0	0.1
1998	Cle A	54	160	12	38	6	0	0	6	10-0	2	40	.237	.289	.275	47	-13	0-2	.974	-4	97	88	C53/3	0	-1.4
1999	Cle A	6	20	2	6	0	1	0	3	0-0	0	3	.300	.300	.400	73	-1	0-1	.943	-2	36	0	C5	0	-0.3
	Tor A	6	14	1	3	0	0	1	3	1-0	0	2	.214	.267	.429	72	-1	0-0	1.000	-0	0	200	C3/3D	0	-0.1
	Year	12	34	3	9	0	1	1	6	1-0	0	5	.265	.286	.412	73	-2	0-1	.955	-3	27	51	C8,D3/3	0	-0.4
2001	Sea A	5	6	1	3	0	0	0	0	0-0	0	1	.500	.500	.500	174	1	0-0	.923	-0	150	153	C5	0	0.0
2002	Sea A	4	4	0	2	1	0	0	1	0-0	0	1	.500	.500	.750	234	1	0-0	1.000	-0	0	0	C2,D2	0	0.1
2003	Sea A	12	14	1	2	1	0	0	1	1-0	0	5	.143	.200	.214	10	-2	0-0	1.000	1	111	308	C7,3b2	0	-0.1
2004	Sea A	19	53	6	10	2	0	1	5	1-0	0	12	.189	.204	.283	26	-6	1-1	.992	5	131	187	C19	0	0.0
	†Min A	19	42	3	12	4	0	0	5	0-0	1	10	.286	.302	.381	74	-2	2-0	.968	-1	69	153	C19	0	-0.1
	Year	38	95	9	22	6	0	1	10	1-0	1	22	.232	.247	.326	48	-7	3-1	.982	3	102	171	C38	0	-0.1
2005	Sea A	39	117	12	23	5	0	1	7	4-1	1	22	.197	.228	.265	34	-11	0-0	.990	-8	74	128	C39	0	-1.6
Total	17	1099	3282	289	831	168	12	69	346	155-13	12	557	.253	.288	.375	76	-122	9-14	.988	28	96	117	C1015,D35,3b5/12	45	-3.4
Bordick, Mike	Michael Todd; B7.21.1965 Marquette MI; BR/TR/5´11˝/(170–175); d4.11; Col Maine																								
1990	†Oak A	25	14	0	1	0	0	0	0	1-0	0	4	.071	.133	.071	-43	-3	0-0	1.000	-3	79	0	3b10,S9,2b7	0	-0.6
1991	Oak A	90	235	21	56	5	1	0	21	14-0	3	37	.238	.289	.268	58	-14	3-4	.972	-6	96	89	S84,2b5/3	0	-1.5
1992	†Oak A	154	504	62	151	19	4	3	48	40-2	9	59	.300	.358	.371	111	8	12-6	.987	5	101	98	2b95,S70	0	2.1
1993	Oak A	159	546	60	136	21	2	3	48	60-2	11	58	.249	.332	.311	79	-14	10-10	.982	-15	92	99	S159/2	0	-1.8
1994	Oak A	**114**	391	38	99	18	4	2	37	38-1	3	44	.253	.320	.335	76	-14	7-2	.974	6	98	95	S112,2b4	0	0.1
1995	Oak A	126	428	46	113	13	0	8	44	35-2	5	48	.264	.325	.350	80	-13	11-3	.983	8	95	113	S126/D	19	0.6
1996	Oak A	155	525	46	126	18	4	5	54	52-0	1	59	.240	.307	.318	60	-33	5-6	.979	10	108	113	S155	0	-1.2
1997	†Bal A	153	509	55	120	19	1	7	46	33-1	2	66	.236	.283	.318	59	-32	0-2	.980	-3	97	105	S153	0	-2.3
1998	Bal A	151	465	59	121	29	1	13	51	39-0	10	65	.260	.328	.411	93	-5	6-7	.990	21	107	102	S150	0	2.4
1999	Bal A	160	631	93	175	35	7	10	77	54-1	5	102	.277	.334	.403	91	-9	14-4	**.989**	**35**	114	**125**	S159	0	3.6
2000	Bal A★	100	391	70	116	22	1	16	59	34-0	1	71	.297	.350	.481	114	8	6-5	.979	-13	89	81	S100	0	0.2
	†NY N	56	192	18	50	8	0	4	21	15-0	2	28	.260	.321	.365	77	-7	3-1	.968	-7	90	77	S56	0	-1.0
2001	Bal A	58	229	32	57	13	0	7	30	17-1	6	36	.249	.314	.397	92	-3	9-3	.977	-5	92	76	S58	116	-0.3
2002	Bal A	117	367	37	85	19	3	8	36	35-0	3	63	.232	.302	.365	81	-10	7-4	**.998**	**26**	**117**	**125**	S117	32	2.3
2003	Tor A	102	343	39	94	18	2	5	54	33-0	2	60	.274	.340	.382	87	-6	3-1	.987	12	100	124	S69,3b22,2b13/D	0	1.1
Total	14	1720	5770	676	1500	257	30	91	626	500-10	63	800	.260	.323	.362	83	-147	96-58	.982	71	101	105	S1577,2b125,3b33,D2	167	3.7

YEAR	TM LG	G	AB	R	H	2B	3B	HR	RBI	BB-IB	HP	SO	AVG	OBP	SLG	AOPS	ABR	SB-CS	FA	FR	RNG	THR	GAMES AT POSITION	DL	BFW
BORGMANN, GLENN	Glenn Dennis; B5.25.1950 Paterson NJ; BR/TR/6´4˝/210; [MinA71 D1/9]; d7.1; Col South Alabama																								
1972	Min A	56	175	11	41	4	0	3	14	25-8	0	25	.234	.325	.309	86	-2	0-0	.965	2	124	91	C56	0	0.2
1973	Min A	12	34	7	9	2	0	0	9	6-0	0	10	.265	.375	.324	94	0	0-0	1.000	-4	90	76	C12	0	-0.3
1974	Min A	128	345	33	87	8	1	3	45	39-0	1	44	.252	.323	.307	82	-7	2-1	**.997**	-2	89	108	C128	0	-0.4
1975	Min A	125	352	34	73	15	2	2	33	47-1	2	59	.207	.303	.278	65	-15	0-1	.989	2	102	**120**	C125	0	-0.9
1976	Min A	24	65	10	16	3	0	1	6	19-0	0	7	.246	.417	.338	121	3	1-1	.976	-2	68	117	C24	0	0.2
1977	Min A	17	43	12	11	1	0	2	7	11-0	0	9	.256	.407	.419	127	2	0-0	1.000	-3	53	98	C17	73	0.0
1978	Min A	49	123	16	26	4	1	3	15	18-0	0	17	.211	.306	.333	80	-3	0-0	.990	1	129	120	C46/D	0	0.0
1979	Min A	31	70	4	14	3	0	0	8	12-0	0	11	.200	.317	.243	51	-4	1-0	.993	3	78	81	C31	0	0.0
1980	Chi A	32	87	10	19	2	0	2	14	14-0	0	9	.218	.320	.310	76	-3	0-0	1.000	5	106	169	C32	0	0.3
Total	9	474	1294	137	296	42	4	16	151	191-9	3	191	.229	.325	.304	79	-29	4-3	.989	0	99	112	C471/D	73	-0.9
BORKOWSKI, BOB	Robert Vilarian; B1.27.1926 Dayton OH; BR/TR/6´0˝/(180–182); d4.22																								
1950	Chi N	85	256	27	70	7	4	4	29	16	1	30	.273	.319	.379	84	-7	1	.975	-2	99	56	O65(7/29/30)/1	0	-1.2
1951	Chi N	58	89	9	14	1	0	0	10	3	0	16	.157	.185	.169	-4	-13	0-0	.933	-0	109	68	O25(7/9/9)	0	-1.4
1952	Cin N	126	377	42	95	11	4	4	24	26	0	53	.252	.300	.334	76	-13	1-3	.991	-2	103	58	O103(15/64/26),1b5	0	-2.0
1953	Cin N	94	249	32	67	11	1	7	29	21	1	41	.269	.328	.406	89	-4	0-1	.982	-3	94	71	O67(3/3/61),1b2	0	-0.9
1954	Cin N	73	162	13	43	12	1	1	19	8	1	18	.265	.299	.370	73	-6	0-2	1.000	1	107	114	O36(13/0/23),1b3	0	-0.8
1955	Cin N	25	18	1	3	1	0	0	1	1-0	0	2	.167	.211	.222	14	-2	0-0	1.000	0	151	0	O11L/1	0	-0.2
	Bro N	9	19	2	2	0	0	0	0	1-0	0	6	.105	.150	.105	-30	-4	0-0	1.000	-1	84	0	O9(3/2/4)	0	-0.4
	Year	34	37	3	5	1	0	0	1	2-0	0	8	.135	.179	.162	-8	-6	0-0	1.000	-0	103	0	O20(14/2/4)/1	0	-0.6
Total	6	470	1170	126	294	43	10	16	112	76-0	3	166	.251	.298	.346	71	-49	2-6	.982	-6	101	66	O316(59/107/153),1b12	0	-6.9
BOROM, RED	Edward Jones; B10.30.1916 Spartanburg SC; BL/TR/5´10˝/175; d4.23																								
1944	Det A	7	14	1	1	0	0	0	1	2	0	2	.071	.188	.071	-23	-2	0-0	.950	0	154	44	2b4/S	0	-0.2
1945	†Det A	55	130	19	35	4	0	0	9	7	0	8	.269	.307	.300	72	-5	4-2	.966	4	119	96	2b28,3b4,S2	0	0.1
Total	2	62	144	20	36	4	0	0	10	9	0	10	.250	.294	.278	62	-7	4-2	.964	5	123	90	2b32,3b4,S3	0	-0.1
BOROS, STEVE	Stephen; B9.3.1936 Flint MI; BR/TR/6´0˝/185; d6.19; M3/C10; Col Michigan																								
1957	Det A	24	41	4	6	1	0	0	2	1-0	0	8	.146	.167	.171	-7	-6	0-0	.906	-0	122	63	3b9,S5	0	-0.7
1958	Det A	6	2	0	0	0	0	0	0	0-0	0	0	.000	.000	.000	-93	-1	0-0	1.000	-0	0	0	/2	0	-0.1
1961	Det A	116	396	51	107	18	2	5	62	68-2	8	42	.270	.382	.364	99	3	4-2	.953	-21	80	69	3b116	39	-1.8
1962	Det A	116	356	46	81	14	1	16	47	53-3	3	62	.228	.331	.407	95	-2	3-1	.931	-17	77	87	3b105,2b6	0	-1.9
1963	Chi N	41	90	9	19	5	1	3	7	12-0	0	19	.211	.304	.389	93	-1	0-2	.975	-1	82	77	1b14,O11R	0	-0.4
1964	Cin N	117	370	31	95	12	3	2	31	47-14	2	43	.257	.342	.322	86	-5	4-1	.961	-3	90	107	3b114	0	-0.9
1965	Cin N	2	0	0	0	0	0	0	0	0-0	0	0	ø	ø	ø	ø	0	0-0	1.000	0	114	0	3b2	0	0.0
Total	7	422	1255	141	308	50	7	26	149	181-19	13	174	.245	.344	.359	90	-12	11-6	.948	-42	84	87	3b346,1b14,O11R,2b7,S5	39	-5.8
BORTON, BABE	William Baker; B8.14.1888 Marion IL; D7.29.1954 Berkeley CA; BL/TL/6´0˝/178; d9.2																								
1912	Chi A	31	105	15	39	3	1	0	17	8	0	—	.371	.416	.419	143	6	1	.997	0	92	103	1b30	—	0.5
1913	Chi A	28	80	9	22	5	0	0	13	23	1	5	.275	.442	.338	130	6	1	.991	-2	71	136	1b26	—	0.3
	NY A	33	108	8	14	2	0	0	11	18	1	19	.130	.260	.148	20	-10	1	.978	4	157	87	1b33	—	-0.8
	Year	61	188	17	36	7	0	0	24	41	2	24	.191	.342	.229	68	-5	2	.984	2	118	109	1b59	—	-0.5
1915	StL F	**159**	549	**97**	157	20	14	3	83	**92**	7	64	.286	.395	.390	115	8	17	.993	-10	65	**113**	1b159	—	-0.6
1916	StL A	66	98	10	22	1	2	1	12	19	0	13	.224	.350	.306	102	1	1	.991	-1	73	69	1b22	—	-0.1
Total	4	317	940	139	254	31	17	4	136	160	9	101	.270	.381	.352	108	11	21	.991	-8	80	108	1b270	—	-0.7
BOSCH, DON	Donald John; B7.15.1942 San Francisco CA; BB/TR/5´10˝/(160–165); d9.19																								
1966	Pit N	3	2	0	0	0	0	0	0	0-0	0	0	.000	.000	.000	-99	-1	0-0	ø	-0	0	0	/cf	0	-0.1
1967	NY N	44	93	7	13	0	1	0	2	5-0	0	24	.140	.184	.161	-0	-12	3-1	1.000	-1	89	131	O39C	0	-1.5
1968	NY N	50	111	14	19	1	0	3	7	9-1	0	33	.171	.231	.261	48	-7	0-2	.974	3	120	174	O33(4/30/0)	0	-0.6
1969	Mon N	49	112	13	20	5	0	1	4	8-0	0	20	.179	.233	.250	35	-10	1-0	.964	-1	98	67	O32(2/29/1)	0	-1.2
Total	4	146	318	34	52	6	1	4	13	22-1	0	77	.164	.217	.226	28	-30	4-3	.979	2	102	126	O105(6/99/1)	0	-3.4
BOSETTI, RICK	Richard Alan; B8.5.1953 Redding CA; BR/TR/5´11˝/(175–185); [PhiN73*7/114]; d9.9; Col Shasta (CA) JC																								
1976	Phi N	13	18	6	5	1	0	0	0	1-0	0	3	.278	.316	.333	81	0	3-0	1.000	0	86	377	O6(1/4/1)	0	0.0
1977	StL N	41	69	12	16	0	0	0	3	6-0	1	11	.232	.303	.232	46	-5	4-4	1.000	2	100	227	O35(27/7/3)	0	-0.5
1978	Tor A	136	568	61	147	25	5	5	42	30-0	3	65	.259	.299	.347	80	-16	6-10	.986	14	112	194	O135C	15	-0.5
1979	Tor A	**162**	619	59	161	35	2	8	65	22-0	3	70	.260	.286	.362	73	-24	13-12	.974	9	105	167	O162C	0	-1.7
1980	Tor A	53	188	24	40	7	1	4	18	15-1	2	29	.213	.277	.324	62	-10	4-6	.985	-4	88	112	O51C	105	-1.5
1981	Tor A	25	47	5	11	2	0	0	4	2-0	0	6	.234	.265	.277	53	-3	0-2	1.000	0	107	0	O19(5/13/2)/D	0	-0.4
	†Oak A	9	19	4	2	0	0	0	1	3-0	0	3	.105	.227	.105	-2	-2	0-0	1.000	0	129	0	O5(0/4/1),D2	0	-0.2
	Year	34	66	9	13	2	0	0	5	5-0	0	9	.197	.254	.227	38	-5	0-2	1.000	0	111	0	O24(5/17/3),D3	0	-0.6
1982	Oak A	6	15	1	3	0	0	0	0	0-0	0	1	.200	.200	.200	11	-2	0-0	1.000	2	116	643	O6C	0	0.0
Total	7	445	1543	172	385	70	8	17	133	79-1	9	188	.250	.288	.338	71	-62	30-34	.982	25	105	173	O419(33/382/7),D3	120	-4.8
BOSLEY, THAD	Thaddis; B9.17.1956 Oceanside CA; BL/TL/6´3˝/(165–175); [CalA74 4/82]; d6.29; C5																								
1977	Cal A	58	212	19	63	10	2	0	19	16-0	1	32	.297	.346	.363	98	0	5-4	.963	-1	110	28	O55(20/35/1)	27	-0.2
1978	Chi A	66	219	25	59	5	1	2	13	13-1	0	32	.269	.308	.329	79	-7	12-11	.975	3	114	82	O64(15/39/14)	18	-0.6
1979	Chi A	36	77	13	24	1	1	1	8	9-0	0	14	.312	.384	.390	109	1	4-1	.967	4	149	143	O28(22/1/5)/D	0	0.5
1980	Chi A	70	147	12	33	2	0	2	14	10-3	0	27	.224	.272	.279	52	-10	3-2	.958	-0	108	38	O52(32/18/4)	55	-1.2
1981	†Mil A	42	105	11	24	2	0	0	3	6-0	0	13	.229	.270	.248	52	-7	2-1	.966	-2	93	54	O37(7/8/22)/D	0	-1.0
1982	Sea A	22	46	3	8	1	0	0	2	4-0	0	8	.174	.240	.196	21	-5	3-1	1.000	-3	44	128	O19(15/3/2)	0	-0.8
1983	Chi N	43	72	12	21	4	1	2	12	10-1	0	12	.292	.373	.458	125	3	1-1	1.000	1	102	102	O20(16/1/3)	0	0.3
1984	†Chi N	55	98	17	29	2	2	2	14	13-2	0	22	.296	.375	.418	114	2	5-1	.976	0	99	139	O33(11/2/21)	0	0.2
1985	Chi N	108	180	25	59	6	3	7	27	20-1	0	29	.328	.391	.511	138	9	5-1	.988	2	133	0	O55(46/7/8)	0	1.1
1986	Chi N	87	120	15	33	4	1	1	9	18-3	0	24	.275	.370	.350	93	-1	3-0	.969	-2	86	0	O41(32/2/8)	0	-0.3
1987	KC A	80	140	13	39	6	1	1	16	9-2	0	26	.279	.318	.357	78	-5	0-0	.966	-1	96	0	O28(13/1/14),D13	0	-0.7
1988	KC A	15	21	1	4	0	0	0	2	2-1	0	6	.190	.250	.190	28	-2	0-0	1.000	-0	83	0	O6(1/4/1),D4	16	-0.2
	Cal A	35	75	9	21	5	0	0	7	6-0	0	12	.280	.321	.347	93	-1	1-1	.965	1	120	0	O26(24/0/2),D2	0	0.0
	Year	50	96	10	25	5	0	0	9	8-1	0	18	.260	.306	.313	78	-3	1-1	.967	1	117	0	O32(25/4/3),D6	0	-0.2
1989	Tex A	37	40	5	9	2	0	1	9	3-0	0	11	.225	.273	.350	75	-1	2-0	1.000	2	216	603	O8(6/0/2),D5	0	0.1
1990	Tex A	30	29	3	4	0	0	1	3	4-1	0	7	.138	.242	.241	36	-3	1-0	1.000	-1	51	0	O9(7/1/1),D4	0	-0.4
Total	14	784	1581	183	430	50	12	20	158	143-15	1	275	.272	.330	.357	89	-27	47-24	.972	4	109	57	O481(267/122/108),D30	116	-3.2
BOSS, HARLEY	Elmer Harley "Lefty"; B11.19.1908 Hodge LA; D5.15.1964 Nashville TN; BL/TL/5´11.5˝/185; d7.19; Col Louisiana Tech																								
1928	Was A	12	12	1	3	0	0	0	2	3	0	1	.250	.400	.250	75	0	0-0	.970	-1	0	106	1b5	—	-0.1
1929	Was A	28	66	9	18	2	1	0	6	2	0	6	.273	.294	.333	61	-4	0-0	.977	0	117	126	1b18	—	-0.5
1930	Was A	3	3	0	0	0	0	0	0	0	0	0	.000	.000	.000	-99	-1	0-0	1.000	-0	0	0	/1	—	-0.1
1933	Cle A	112	438	54	118	17	7	1	53	25	1	27	.269	.310	.347	71	-20	2-5	.994	5	119	112	1b110	—	-2.5
Total	4	155	519	64	139	19	8	1	61	30	1	34	.268	.309	.341	69	-25	2-5	.992	5	116	113	1b134	—	-3.2
BOSTICK, HENRY	Henry Landers (b Henry Lipschitz); B1.12.1895 Boston MA; D9.16.1968 Denver CO; BR/TR; d5.18; Col Denver																								
1915	Phi A	2	7	0	0	0	0	0	2	1	0	1	.000	.125	.000	-65	-1	0	1.000	-1	78	0	3b2	—	-0.2
BOSTOCK, LYMAN	Lyman Wesley; B11.22.1950 Birmingham AL; D9.23.1978 Gary IN; BL/TR/6´1˝/180; [MinA72 26/596]; d4.8; Col Cal St.–Northridge																								
1975	Min A	98	369	52	104	21	5	0	29	28-2	0	42	.282	.331	.366	96	-2	2-3	.985	-5	97	43	O92(12/28/55)/D	31	-1.2
1976	Min A	128	474	75	153	21	9	4	60	33-5	1	37	.323	.364	.430	131	17	12-6	.988	1	99	115	O124(0/121/3)	0	1.6
1977	Min A	153	593	104	199	36	12	14	90	51-5	6	59	.336	.389	.508	145	38	16-7	.989	-2	99	93	O149(60/90/3)	0	3.3
1978	Cal A	147	568	74	168	24	4	5	71	59-8	2	36	.296	.362	.379	113	11	15-12	.989	4	109	69	O146(0/58/90)/D	0	0.9
Total	4	526	2004	305	624	102	30	23	250	171-20	9	174	.311	.365	.427	124	64	45-28	.988	-2	102	82	O511(72/297/151),D2	31	4.6

Boston, Daryl Daryl Lamont; B1.4.1963 Cincinnati OH; BL/TL/6´3˝/(185–210); [ChiA81 1/7]; d5.13

YEAR	TM LG	G	AB	R	H	2B	3B	HR	RBI	BB-IB	HP	SO	AVG	OBP	SLG	AOPS	ABR	SB-CS	FA	FR	RNG	THR	GAMES AT POSITION	DL	BFW
1984	Chi A	35	83	8	14	3	1	0	3	4-0	0	20	.169	.207	.229	19	-9	6-0	.910	-2	95	130	O34(0/30/5)/D	0	-1.0
1985	Chi A	95	232	20	53	13	1	3	15	14-1	0	44	.228	.271	.332	62	-12	8-6	.989	3	101	168	O93(0/90/4),D2	0	-1.1
1986	Chi A	56	199	29	53	11	3	5	22	21-3	0	33	.266	.335	.427	102	1	9-5	.969	1	107	105	O53C/D	0	0.2
1987	Chi A	103	337	51	87	21	2	10	29	25-2	0	68	.258	.307	.421	89	-6	12-6	.991	-1	100	58	O92(51/45/0),D5	0	-0.8
1988	Chi A	105	281	37	61	12	2	15	31	21-5	0	44	.217	.271	.434	94	-4	9-3	.951	-1	101	97	O85(44/43/1),D5	0	-0.5
1989	Chi A	101	218	34	55	3	4	5	23	24-3	0	31	.252	.325	.372	98	-1	7-2	.971	1	110	54	O75(57/2/21),D9	0	-0.1
1990	Chi A	5	1	0	0	0	0	0	0	0-0	0	0	.000	.000	.000	-99	0	1-0	ø	-0	0	0	/rfD	0	0.0
	NY N	115	366	65	100	21	2	12	45	28-2	2	50	.273	.328	.440	109	4	18-7	.986	-5	95	65	O109(1/108/0)	0	0.0
1991	NY N	137	255	40	70	16	4	4	21	30-0	0	42	.275	.350	.416	115	6	15-8	.981	-0	104	52	O115(9/74/37)	0	0.5
1992	NY N	130	289	37	72	14	2	11	35	38-6	3	60	.249	.338	.426	117	7	12-6	.993	-2	90	141	O95(66/16/14)	0	0.4
1993	Col N	124	291	46	76	15	1	14	40	26-1	2	57	.261	.325	.464	93	-3	1-6	.985	-4	85	111	O79(41/31/9)	0	-1.0
1994	NY A	52	77	11	14	2	0	4	14	6-0	1	20	.182	.250	.364	58	-5	0-1	1.000	-0	74	221	O16(7/7/2),D9	0	-0.6
Total	11	1058	2629	378	655	131	22	83	278	237-23	8	469	.249	.312	.410	94	-22	98-50	.977	-10	98	96	O847(276/499/94),D35	0	-4.0

Boswell, Ken Kenneth George; B2.23.1946 Austin TX; BL/TR/6´0˝/(170–178); [NYN65 4/66]; d9.18; Col Sam Houston St.

YEAR	TM LG	G	AB	R	H	2B	3B	HR	RBI	BB-IB	HP	SO	AVG	OBP	SLG	AOPS	ABR	SB-CS	FA	FR	RNG	THR	GAMES AT POSITION	DL	BFW
1967	NY N	11	40	2	9	3	0	1	4	1-0	0	5	.225	.233	.375	76	-1	0-0	.971	3	139	76	2b6,3b4	0	0.2
1968	NY N	75	284	37	74	7	2	4	11	16-0	1	27	.261	.300	.342	92	-3	7-2	.965	-1	101	93	2b69	56	0.3
1969	†NY N	102	362	48	101	14	7	3	32	36-3	2	47	.279	.347	.381	101	1	7-3	.959	-14	92	100	2b96	0	-0.7
1970	NY N	105	351	32	89	13	2	5	44	41-8	2	32	.254	.331	.345	81	-9	5-4	.996	-10	91	86	2b101	0	-1.3
1971	NY N	116	392	46	107	20	1	5	40	36-4	2	31	.273	.334	.367	100	1	5-2	.973	-26	78	86	2b109	0	-2.0
1972	NY N	100	355	35	75	9	1	9	33	32-1	0	35	.211	.274	.318	70	-15	2-2	.990	-23	72	97	2b94	0	-3.5
1973	†NY N	76	110	12	25	2	1	2	14	12-2	0	11	.227	.303	.318	73	-4	0-0	.973	0	90	116	3b17,2b3	0	-0.4
1974	NY N	96	222	19	48	6	1	2	15	18-1	1	19	.216	.277	.279	57	-13	0-1	1.000	5	92	69	2b28,3b20,O7(2/0/5)	0	-0.8
1975	Hou N	86	178	16	43	8	2	0	21	30-7	1	12	.242	.349	.309	92	-1	0-3	.991	-5	102	74	2b31,3b23	0	-0.6
1976	Hou N	91	126	12	33	8	1	0	18	8-2	0	8	.262	.301	.341	91	-2	1-0	.933	-4	81	152	3b16,2b3/lf	0	-0.5
1977	Hou N	72	97	7	21	1	1	0	12	10-1	0	12	.216	.287	.247	50	-7	0-0	1.000	-1	81	118	2b26,3b2	0	-0.8
Total	11	930	2517	266	625	91	19	31	244	240-29	9	239	.248	.313	.337	84	-53	27-17	.979	-76	87	90	2b566,3b82,O8(3/0/5)	56	-10.1

Bottarini, John John Charles; B9.14.1908 Crockett CA; D10.8.1976 Jemez Springs NM; BR/TR/6´0˝/190; d4.22

YEAR	TM LG	G	AB	R	H	2B	3B	HR	RBI	BB-IB	HP	SO	AVG	OBP	SLG	AOPS	ABR	SB-CS	FA	FR	RNG	THR	GAMES AT POSITION	DL	BFW
1937	Chi N	26	40	3	11	3	0	1	7	5	1	10	.275	.370	.425	111	1	0	1.000	0	*115*	*134*	C18/lf	—	0.2

Bottomley, Jim James Leroy "Sunny Jim"; B4.23.1900 Oglesby IL; D12.11.1959 St.Louis MO; BL/TL/6´0˝/180; d8.18; M1/C1; HF1974

YEAR	TM LG	G	AB	R	H	2B	3B	HR	RBI	BB-IB	HP	SO	AVG	OBP	SLG	AOPS	ABR	SB-CS	FA	FR	RNG	THR	GAMES AT POSITION	DL	BFW
1922	StL N	37	151	29	49	8	5	5	35	6	2	13	.325	.358	.543	136	7	3-1	.986	-3	65	81	1b34	—	0.2
1923	StL N	134	523	79	194	34	14	8	94	45	4	44	.371	.425	.535	155	42	4-6	.986	-12	61	88	1b130	—	1.9
1924	StL N	137	528	87	167	31	12	14	111	35	3	35	.316	.362	.500	131	22	5-4	.982	-11	67	94	1b133/2	—	0.1
1925	StL N	**153**	619	92	**227**	**44**	12	21	128	47	2	36	.367	.413	.578	147	43	3-4	.987	-3	91	107	1b153	—	2.7
1926	†StL N	154	603	98	180	**40**	14	19	**120**	58	4	52	.299	.364	.506	127	22	4	.989	-15	61	101	1b154	—	-0.3
1927	StL N	152	574	95	174	31	15	19	124	74	5	49	.303	.387	.509	134	28	8	.989	-12	73	**130**	1b152	—	0.6
1928	†StL N	149	576	123	187	42	**20**	**31**	**136**	71	3	54	.325	.402	.628	163	51	10	.987	-14	61	94	1b148	—	2.5
1929	StL N	146	560	108	176	31	12	29	137	70	1	54	.314	.391	.568	133	28	3	.991	-5	83	102	1b145	—	1.2
1930	†StL N	131	487	92	148	33	7	15	97	44	5	36	.304	.368	.493	102	1	5	.990	-14	53	111	1b124	—	-1.8
1931	†StL N	108	382	73	133	34	5	9	75	34	1	24	.348	.403	.534	144	25	3	.987	-4	81	118	1b93	—	1.2
1932	StL N	91	311	45	92	16	3	11	48	25	1	32	.296	.350	.473	115	7	2	.986	-3	81	108	1b74	—	-0.4
1933	Cin N	145	549	57	137	23	9	13	83	42	7	28	.250	.311	.395	102	0	3	.991	-9	78	102	1b145	—	-2.4
1934	Cin N	142	556	72	158	31	11	11	78	33	0	40	.284	.324	.439	105	2	1	.989	-4	93	92	1b139	—	-1.5
1935	Cin N	107	399	44	103	21	1	1	49	18	2	24	.258	.294	.323	68	-18	3	.992	-2	88	101	1b97	—	-2.9
1936	StL A	140	544	72	162	39	11	12	95	44	3	55	.298	.354	.476	100	-2	0-0	.992	-9	67	80	1b140	—	-2.1
1937	StL A	65	109	11	26	7	0	1	12	18	0	15	.239	.346	.330	71	-4	1-0	.995	1	113	86	1b24,M	—	-0.5
Total	16	1991	7471	1177	2313	465	151	219	1422	664	43	591	.310	.369	.500	124	254	58-15	.988	-120	74	101	1b1885/2	—	-1.5

Botts, Jason Jason Carl; B7.26.1980 Paso Robles CA; BB/TR/6´6˝/250; [TexA99 46/1375]; d9.14; Col Glendale (CA) JC

YEAR	TM LG	G	AB	R	H	2B	3B	HR	RBI	BB-IB	HP	SO	AVG	OBP	SLG	AOPS	ABR	SB-CS	FA	FR	RNG	THR	GAMES AT POSITION	DL	BFW
2005	Tex A	10	27	4	8	0	0	0	3	3-0	0	13	.296	.367	.296	78	-1	0-0	.900	0	87	398	O7L,D3	0	-0.1
2006	Tex A	20	50	8	11	4	0	1	6	8-1	0	18	.220	.317	.360	78	-1	0-0	1.000	0	435	0	D13/lf	0	-0.2
Total	2	30	77	12	19	4	0	1	9	11-1	0	31	.247	.333	.338	78	-2	0-0	.909	1	95	388	D16,O8L	0	-0.3

Bouchee, Ed Edward Francis; B3.7.1933 Livingston MT; BL/TL/6´1˝/(200–210); d9.19; Col Washington St.

YEAR	TM LG	G	AB	R	H	2B	3B	HR	RBI	BB-IB	HP	SO	AVG	OBP	SLG	AOPS	ABR	SB-CS	FA	FR	RNG	THR	GAMES AT POSITION	DL	BFW
1956	Phi N	9	22	0	6	2	0	0	1	5-0	0	6	.273	.407	.364	112	1	0-0	1.000	-0	69	123	1b6	0	0.0
1957	Phi N	154	574	78	168	35	8	17	76	84-6	**14**	91	.293	.394	.470	136	33	1-0	.988	6	**111**	78	1b154	0	3.1
1958	Phi N	89	334	55	86	19	5	9	39	51-4	0	74	.257	.355	.425	107	5	1-0	.993	-1	94	73	1b89	0	-0.2
1959	Phi N	136	499	75	142	29	4	15	74	70-4	5	74	.285	.375	.449	117	15	0-4	.986	-2	96	89	1b134	0	0.4
1960	Phi N	22	65	1	17	4	0	0	8	9-2	1	11	.262	.355	.323	89	0	0-0	.994	0	105	79	1b22	0	-0.1
	Chi N	98	299	33	71	11	1	5	44	45-4	2	51	.237	.335	.331	86	-4	2-0	.991	-0	100	88	1b80	0	-0.9
	Year	120	364	34	88	15	1	5	52	54-6	3	62	.242	.339	.330	86	-5	2-0	.992	0	101	86	1b102	0	-1.0
1961	Chi N	112	319	49	79	12	3	12	38	58-7	5	77	.248	.371	.417	108	6	1-4	.983	1	109	112	1b107	0	-0.1
1962	NY N	50	87	7	14	2	0	3	10	18-2	0	17	.161	.302	.287	59	-5	0-0	.976	4	208	106	1b19	0	-0.2
Total	7	670	2199	298	583	114	21	61	290	340-29	27	401	.265	.368	.419	112	51	5-8	.988	8	105	88	1b611	0	2.0

Boucher, Al Alexander Francis "Bo"; B11.13.1881 Franklin MA; D6.23.1974 Torrance CA; BR/TR/5´8.5˝/156; d4.16

YEAR	TM LG	G	AB	R	H	2B	3B	HR	RBI	BB-IB	HP	SO	AVG	OBP	SLG	AOPS	ABR	SB-CS	FA	FR	RNG	THR	GAMES AT POSITION	DL	BFW
1914	StL F	147	516	62	119	26	4	2	49	52	2	88	.231	.304	.308	64	-33	13	.916	-4	95	79	3b147	—	-3.6

Boucher, Medric Medric Charles Francis; B3.12.1886 St.Louis MO; D3.12.1974 Martinez CA; BR/TR/5´10˝/165; d5.20

YEAR	TM LG	G	AB	R	H	2B	3B	HR	RBI	BB-IB	HP	SO	AVG	OBP	SLG	AOPS	ABR	SB-CS	FA	FR	RNG	THR	GAMES AT POSITION	DL	BFW
1914	Bal F	16	16	2	5	1	1	0	2	1	0	1	.313	.353	.500	127	0	0	.950	0	*151*	*41*	C7/1rf	—	0.1
	Pit F	1	1	0	0	0	0	0	0	0	0	0	.000	.000	.000	-99	0	0	ø	0	—	—	/H	—	0.0
	Year	17	17	2	5	1	1	0	2	1	0	1	.294	.333	.471	114	0	0	.950	0	*151*	*41*	C7/1rf	—	0.1

Boudreau, Lou Louis; B7.17.1917 Harvey IL; D8.20.2001 Olympia Fields IL; BR/TR/5´11˝/185; d9.9; M16; HF1970; Col Illinois

YEAR	TM LG	G	AB	R	H	2B	3B	HR	RBI	BB-IB	HP	SO	AVG	OBP	SLG	AOPS	ABR	SB-CS	FA	FR	RNG	THR	GAMES AT POSITION	DL	BFW
1938	Cle A	1	1	0	0	0	0	0	0	1	0	0	.000	.500	.000	36	0	0-0	ø	-0	0	0	/3	—	0.0
1939	Cle A	53	225	42	58	15	4	0	19	28	0	24	.258	.340	.360	82	-6	2-1	.953	6	109	95	S53	—	0.4
1940	Cle A★	**155**	627	97	185	46	10	9	101	73	2	39	.295	.370	.443	113	14	6-3	**.968**	12	100	**134**	S155	—	3.5
1941	Cle A★	148	579	95	149	**45**	8	10	56	85	3	57	.257	.355	.415	108	9	9-4	**.966**	13	103	101	S147	0	3.2
1942	Cle A★	147	506	57	143	18	10	2	58	75	4	39	.283	.379	.370	118	15	7-16	**.965**	-2	101	124	S146,M	0	2.0
1943	Cle A☆	152	539	69	154	32	7	3	67	90	0	31	.286	.388	.388	135	29	4-7	**.970**	**25**	108	**126**	S152/CM	0	**6.8**
1944	Cle A☆	150	584	91	191	**45**	5	3	67	73	5	39	**.327**	.406	.437	146	39	11-3	**.978**	20	103	123	S149/CM	0	**7.5**
1945	Cle A✳	97	345	50	106	24	1	3	48	35	2	20	.307	.374	.409	133	15	0-4	.983	4	94	120	S97,M	0	2.7
1946	Cle A	140	515	51	151	30	6	6	62	40	1	14	.293	.345	.410	118	11	6-7	**.970**	17	99	105	S139,M	0	3.7
1947	Cle A★	150	538	79	165	**45**	3	4	67	67	4	10	.307	.388	.424	129	24	1-0	**.982**	19	106	**123**	S148,M	0	5.3
1948	†Cle A★	152	560	116	199	34	6	18	106	98	2	9	.355	.453	.534	166	58	3-2	**.975**	8	103	**121**	S151/CM	0	**7.1**
1949	Cle A	134	475	53	135	20	3	4	60	70	4	10	.284	.381	.364	100	2	0-1	.982	8	105	131	S88,3b38,1b6/2M	0	1.5
1950	Cle A	81	260	23	70	13	2	1	29	31	1	5	.269	.349	.346	81	-7	1-2	.986	2	95	106	S61,1b8,2b2,3b2,M	0	-0.2
1951	Bos A	82	273	37	73	18	1	5	47	30	6	12	.267	.353	.396	93	-2	1-0	.951	1	104	126	S52,3b15,1b2	0	0.2
1952	Bos A	4	2	1	0	0	0	0	2	0	0	0	.000	.000	.000	-93	-1	0-0	1.000	-0	151	0	/S3M	0	-0.1
Total	15	1646	6029	861	1779	385	66	68	789	796	34	309	.295	.380	.415	121	200	51-50	.973	134	102	119	S1539,3b57,1b16,2b3,C3	0	43.6

Bourjos, Chris Christopher; B10.16.1955 Chicago IL; BR/TR/6´0˝/187; d8.31; Col Northern Illinois

YEAR	TM LG	G	AB	R	H	2B	3B	HR	RBI	BB-IB	HP	SO	AVG	OBP	SLG	AOPS	ABR	SB-CS	FA	FR	RNG	THR	GAMES AT POSITION	DL	BFW
1980	SF N	13	22	4	5	1	0	1	2	2-0	0	7	.227	.292	.409	97	0	0-0	1.000	-1	67	0	O6(2/0/4)	0	-0.1

Bourn, Michael Michael Ray; B12.27.1982 Houston TX; BL/TR/5´11˝/180; [PhiN03 4/115]; d7.30; Col Houston

YEAR	TM LG	G	AB	R	H	2B	3B	HR	RBI	BB-IB	HP	SO	AVG	OBP	SLG	AOPS	ABR	SB-CS	FA	FR	RNG	THR	GAMES AT POSITION	DL	BFW
2006	Phi N	17	8	2	1	0	0	0	0	1-0	0	3	.125	.222	.125	-7	-1	1-2	1.000	-0	99	0	O15(1/0/14)	0	-0.2

Bournigal, Rafael Rafael Antonio (Pelletier); B5.12.1966 Azua, D.R.; BR/TR/5´11˝/(160–176); [LAN87 19/482]; d9.1; Col Florida St.

YEAR	TM LG	G	AB	R	H	2B	3B	HR	RBI	BB-IB	HP	SO	AVG	OBP	SLG	AOPS	ABR	SB-CS	FA	FR	RNG	THR	GAMES AT POSITION	DL	BFW
1992	LA N	10	20	1	3	1	0	0	0	1-0	1	2	.150	.227	.200	22	-2	0-0	.967	0	91	157	S9	0	-0.1
1993	LA N	8	18	0	9	1	0	0	3	0-0	0	2	.500	.500	.556	192	2	0-0	1.000	0	47	0	2b4,S4	0	0.3
1994	LA N	40	116	2	26	3	1	0	11	9-1	2	5	.224	.291	.267	50	-9	0-0	.981	-4	87	109	S40	0	-1.0
1996	Oak A	88	252	33	61	14	2	0	18	16-0	1	19	.242	.290	.313	53	-18	4-3	.993	3	109	99	2b64,S23	0	-1.1

THE BATTER REGISTER

YEAR	TM LG	G	AB	R	H	2B	3B	HR	RBI	BB-IB	HP	SO	AVG	OBP	SLG	AOPS	ABR	SB-CS	FA	FR	RNG	THR	GAMES AT POSITION	DL	BFW
1997	Oak A	79	222	29	62	9	0	1	20	16-1	4	19	.279	.339	.333	76	-7	2-1	.980	5	114	91	S74,2b7	30	0.3
1998	Oak A	85	209	23	47	11	0	1	19	10-1	2	11	.225	.265	.292	46	-17	6-1	1.000	-3	93	102	2b48,S38/D	0	-1.5
1999	Sea A	55	95	16	26	5	0	2	14	7-0	0	6	.274	.317	.389	82	-3	0-0	.987	2	105	116	S28,2b17,3b8/lfD	0	0.1
Total	7	365	932	104	234	44	3	4	85	59-3	10	64	.251	.301	.318	62	-54	12-5	.986	3	103	101	S216,2b140,3b8,D2/lf	30	-3.0

BOURQUE, PAT Patrick Daniel; B3.23.1947 Worcester MA; BL/TL/6´0˝/210; d9.6; Col Holy Cross

YEAR	TM LG	G	AB	R	H	2B	3B	HR	RBI	BB-IB	HP	SO	AVG	OBP	SLG	AOPS	ABR	SB-CS	FA	FR	RNG	THR	GAMES AT POSITION	DL	BFW
1971	Chi N	14	37	3	7	0	1	1	3	3-0	0	9	.189	.250	.324	54	-2	0-0	.957	2	187	73	1b11	0	-0.2
1972	Chi N	11	27	3	7	1	0	0	5	2-0	0	2	.259	.310	.296	66	-1	0-0	1.000	1	148	162	1b7	0	-0.1
1973	Chi N	57	139	11	29	6	0	7	20	16-1	2	21	.209	.297	.403	86	-3	1-1	.986	4	145	109	1b38	0	-0.2
	†Oak A	23	42	8	8	4	1	2	9	15-2	0	10	.190	.390	.476	154	4	0-0	1.000	-1	0	111	D15,1b5	0	0.3
1974	Oak A	73	96	6	22	4	0	1	16	15-1	0	20	.229	.327	.302	89	-1	0-2	.988	-1	83	127	1b39,D8	0	-0.4
	Min A	23	64	5	14	2	0	1	8	7-0	0	11	.219	.296	.297	69	-2	0-0	.987	3	168	99	1b21	0	-0.1
	Year	96	160	11	36	6	0	2	24	22-1	0	31	.225	.315	.300	82	-3	0-2	.988	2	125	113	1b60,D8	0	-0.5
Total	4	201	405	36	87	17	2	12	61	58-4	2	73	.215	.313	.356	87	-5	1-3	.985	9	138	110	1b121,D23	0	-0.7

BOWA, LARRY Lawrence Robert; B12.6.1945 Sacramento CA; BB/TR/5´10˝/(155–159); d4.7; M6/C14; Col Sacramento (CA) City

YEAR	TM LG	G	AB	R	H	2B	3B	HR	RBI	BB-IB	HP	SO	AVG	OBP	SLG	AOPS	ABR	SB-CS	FA	FR	RNG	THR	GAMES AT POSITION	DL	BFW
1970	Phi N	145	547	50	137	17	6	0	34	21-1	0	48	.250	.277	.303	57	-35	24-13	.979	-23	91	79	S143/2	0	-4.1
1971	Phi N	159	650	74	162	18	5	0	25	36-2	5	61	.249	.293	.292	66	-30	28-11	**.987**	5	105	95	S157	0	-0.3
1972	Phi N	152	579	67	145	11	**13**	1	31	32-1	2	51	.250	.291	.320	72	-24	17-9	**.987**	2	101	97	S150	0	-0.4
1973	Phi N	122	446	42	94	11	3	0	23	24-8	1	31	.211	.252	.249	38	-38	10-6	.979	2	96	113	S122	37	-2.3
1974	Phi N★	**162**	669	97	184	19	10	1	36	23-0	1	52	.275	.298	.338	75	-25	39-11	**.984**	-13	90	103	S162	0	-1.4
1975	Phi N★	136	583	79	178	18	9	2	38	24-0	2	32	.305	.334	.377	93	-8	24-6	.962	-11	90	104	S135	27	0.1
1976	†Phi N★	156	624	71	155	15	9	0	49	32-3	0	31	.248	.283	.301	64	-31	30-8	.975	-14	95	105	S156	0	-2.4
1977	†Phi N	154	624	93	175	19	3	4	41	32-2	0	32	.280	.313	.340	72	-25	32-3	.983	3	103	111	S154	0	0.0
1978	†Phi N★	156	654	78	192	31	5	3	43	24-1	1	40	.294	.319	.370	90	-10	27-5	**.986**	6	102	112	S156	0	1.7
1979	Phi N★	147	539	74	130	17	11	0	31	61-5	1	32	.241	.316	.314	70	-22	20-9	**.991**	-6	96	96	S146	15	-1.2
1980	†Phi N	147	540	57	144	16	4	2	39	24-7	3	28	.267	.300	.322	70	-22	21-6	.975	-20	92	80	S147	0	-2.6
1981	†Phi N	103	360	34	102	14	3	0	31	26-2	0	17	.283	.331	.339	86	-6	16-7	.975	-7	99	83	S102	0	-0.2
1982	Chi N	142	499	50	123	15	7	0	29	39-5	1	38	.246	.302	.305	68	-22	8-3	.973	-22	93	81	S140	0	-3.0
1983	Chi N	147	499	73	133	20	5	2	43	35-1	0	30	.267	.312	.339	77	-16	7-3	**.984**	26	**112**	122	S145	0	2.6
1984	†Chi N	133	391	33	87	14	2	0	17	28-5	0	24	.223	.274	.269	49	-26	10-4	.974	12	106	93	S132	0	-0.1
1985	Chi N	72	195	13	48	6	4	0	13	11-2	0	20	.246	.285	.318	63	-10	5-1	.970	4	107	93	S66	0	0.0
	NY N	14	19	2	2	1	0	0	2	2-0	0	2	.105	.190	.158	-2	-3	0-0	.882	-2	50	140	S9,2b4	0	-0.4
	Year	86	214	15	50	7	4	0	15	13-2	0	22	.234	.276	.304	58	-12	5-1	.965	2	103	96	S75,2b4	0	-0.4
Total	16	2247	8418	987	2191	262	99	15	525	474-45	17	569	.260	.300	.320	70	-353	318-105	.980	-58	98	99	S2222,2b5	79	-14.0

BOWCOCK, BENNY Benjamin James; B10.28.1879 Fall River MA; D6.16.1961 Taunton MA; BR/TR/5´7˝/150; d9.18

YEAR	TM LG	G	AB	R	H	2B	3B	HR	RBI	BB-IB	HP	SO	AVG	OBP	SLG	AOPS	ABR	SB-CS	FA	FR	RNG	THR	GAMES AT POSITION	DL	BFW
1903	StL A	14	50	7	16	3	1	1	10	3	0	—	.320	.358	.480	154	3	1	.885	-6	79	85	2b14	—	-0.2

BOWDEN, TIM David Timon; B8.15.1891 McDonough GA; D10.25.1949 Emory (now part of Atlanta) GA; BL/TR/5´10˝/175; d9.17; Col Georgia

YEAR	TM LG	G	AB	R	H	2B	3B	HR	RBI	BB-IB	HP	SO	AVG	OBP	SLG	AOPS	ABR	SB-CS	FA	FR	RNG	THR	GAMES AT POSITION	DL	BFW
1914	StL A	7	9	0	2	0	0	0	0	1	0	6	.222	.300	.222	60	0	0	1.000	0	123	0	O4(0/1/3)	—	-0.1

BOWEN, CHICK Emmons Joseph; B7.26.1897 New Haven CT; D8.9.1948 New Haven CT; BR/TR/5´7˝/165; d9.15; Col Holy Cross

YEAR	TM LG	G	AB	R	H	2B	3B	HR	RBI	BB-IB	HP	SO	AVG	OBP	SLG	AOPS	ABR	SB-CS	FA	FR	RNG	THR	GAMES AT POSITION	DL	BFW
1919	NY N	3	5	0	1	0	0	0	1	1	0	2	.200	.333	.200	63	0	0	1.000	-0	108	0	O2(0/1/1)	—	0.0

BOWEN, ROB Robert McClure; B2.24.1981 Bedford TX; BB/TR/6´2˝/(210–225); [MinA99 2/56]; d9.1

YEAR	TM LG	G	AB	R	H	2B	3B	HR	RBI	BB-IB	HP	SO	AVG	OBP	SLG	AOPS	ABR	SB-CS	FA	FR	RNG	THR	GAMES AT POSITION	DL	BFW
2003	Min A	7	10	0	1	0	0	0	1	0-0	0	4	.100	.091	.100	-45	-2	0-0	.944	-2	18	0	C7	0	-0.4
2004	Min A	17	27	1	3	0	0	1	2	4-0	0	10	.111	.226	.222	17	-3	0-0	.985	-1	78	45	C15	0	-0.4
2006	†SD N	94	94	22	23	5	0	3	13	13-0	1	26	.245	.339	.394	93	-1	0-1	.994	-1	165	19	C65/1	16	0.0
Total	3	118	131	23	27	5	0	4	16	17-0	1	40	.206	.298	.336	66	-6	0-1	.988	-4	131	25	C87/1	16	-0.8

BOWEN, SAM Samuel Thomas; B9.18.1952 Brunswick GA; BR/TR/5´9˝/167; [BosA74 7/164]; d8.25; Col Valdosta St.

YEAR	TM LG	G	AB	R	H	2B	3B	HR	RBI	BB-IB	HP	SO	AVG	OBP	SLG	AOPS	ABR	SB-CS	FA	FR	RNG	THR	GAMES AT POSITION	DL	BFW
1977	Bos A	3	2	0	0	0	0	0	0	0-0	0	2	.000	.000	.000	-90	-1	0-0	1.000	0	229	0	O3(2/1/0)	0	0.0
1978	Bos A	6	7	3	1	0	0	1	1	1-0	0	2	.143	.250	.571	113	0	0-0	1.000	-1	28	0	O4(1/3/0)	0	-0.1
1980	Bos A	7	13	0	2	0	0	0	0	2-0	0	3	.154	.267	.154	17	-1	1-0	1.000	2	142	290	O6(1/4/1)	0	0.0
Total	3	16	22	3	3	0	0	1	1	3-0	0	7	.136	.240	.273	38	-2	1-0	1.000	1	110	172	O13(4/8/1)	0	-0.1

BOWENS, SAM Samuel Edward; B3.23.1939 Wilmington NC; D3.28.2003 Wilmington NC; BR/TR/6´1.5˝/(190–209); d9.7; Negro Lg 1957–58; Col Tennessee St.

YEAR	TM LG	G	AB	R	H	2B	3B	HR	RBI	BB-IB	HP	SO	AVG	OBP	SLG	AOPS	ABR	SB-CS	FA	FR	RNG	THR	GAMES AT POSITION	DL	BFW
1963	Bal A	15	48	8	16	3	1	1	9	4-1	0	5	.333	.385	.500	151	3	1-1	.952	-2	86	0	O13R	0	0.1
1964	Bal A	139	501	58	132	25	2	22	71	42-1	4	99	.263	.323	.453	114	9	4-3	.981	3	107	103	O135(32/0/120)	0	0.3
1965	Bal A	84	203	16	33	4	1	7	20	10-0	0	41	.163	.199	.296	39	-17	7-1	.982	1	105	82	O68(11/0/58)	0	-2.1
1966	Bal A	89	243	26	51	9	1	6	20	17-2	5	52	.210	.275	.329	74	-8	9-3	.960	3	102	192	O68(32/4/41)	0	-0.9
1967	Bal A	62	120	13	22	2	1	5	12	11-0	1	43	.183	.258	.342	76	-4	3-4	.977	-1	86	111	O32(16/0/16)	0	-0.8
1968	Was A	57	115	14	22	4	0	4	7	11-0	0	39	.191	.262	.330	81	-3	0-0	.957	0	100	142	O27(11/3/14)	0	-0.5
1969	Was A	33	57	6	11	1	0	0	4	5-0	0	14	.193	.258	.211	34	-5	1-1	.971	-0	102	77	O30(6/3/22)	0	-0.7
Total	7	479	1287	141	287	48	6	45	143	100-4	10	293	.223	.283	.375	87	-25	25-13	.974	4	102	114	O373(108/10/284)	0	-4.6

BOWERMAN, FRANK Frank Eugene "Mike"; B12.5.1868 Romeo MI; D11.30.1948 Romeo MI; BR/TR/6´2˝/190; d8.24; M1; Col Michigan

YEAR	TM LG	G	AB	R	H	2B	3B	HR	RBI	BB-IB	HP	SO	AVG	OBP	SLG	AOPS	ABR	SB-CS	FA	FR	RNG	THR	GAMES AT POSITION	DL	BFW
1895	Bal N	1	1	0	0	0	0	0	0	0	0	0	.000	.000	.000	-97	0	0	1.000	0	*0*	*0*	/C	—	0.0
1896	Bal N	4	16	0	2	0	0	0	4	1	0	0	.125	.176	.125	-20	-3	0	.900	-0	*118*	*167*	C3/1	—	-0.2
1897	†Bal N	38	130	16	41	5	0	1	21	1	2	—	.315	.331	.377	87	-3	3	.948	-0	*103*	*76*	C36	—	0.0
1898	Bal N	5	16	5	7	1	0	0	1	2	1	—	.438	.526	.500	191	2	1	.950	-0	*115*	*163*	C4	—	0.2
	Pit N	69	241	17	66	6	3	0	29	7	1	—	.274	.297	.324	79	-8	4	.946	2	*104*	*106*	C59,1b9	—	0.0
	Year	74	257	22	73	7	3	0	30	9	2	—	.284	.313	.335	87	-5	5	.946	2	*105*	*110*	C63,1b9	—	0.2
1899	Pit N	110	427	51	111	16	10	3	53	12	5	—	.260	.288	.365	79	-15	10	.947	13	*121*	*109*	C80,1b28	—	0.5
1900	NY N	80	270	25	65	5	3	1	42	6	4	—	.241	.268	.293	57	-17	10	.929	11	*110*	***125***	C75,S2	—	0.1
1901	NY N	59	191	20	38	5	3	0	14	7	2	—	.199	.235	.257	44	-14	3	.950	4	*96*	*113*	C46,2b3,S3,3b3/1	—	-0.6
1902	NY N	109	373	38	93	14	6	0	27	13	1	—	.249	.276	.319	85	-8	12	.954	2	*96*	***111***	C100,1b3	—	0.3
1903	NY N	64	210	22	58	6	2	1	31	6	3	—	.276	.306	.338	81	-6	5	.977	3	*118*	*85*	C55,1b4/cf	—	0.2
1904	NY N	93	289	38	67	11	4	2	27	16	7	—	.232	.288	.318	84	-6	7	.977	8	***143***	*98*	C79,1b9,2b2/P	—	1.0
1905	NY N	98	297	37	80	8	1	3	41	12	11	—	.269	.322	.333	93	-2	6	.982	5	*150*	*80*	C72,1b17/2	—	0.9
1906	NY N	103	285	23	65	7	3	1	42	15	3	—	.228	.274	.284	72	-10	5	.984	7	*113*	*109*	C67,1b20	—	0.3
1907	NY N	96	311	31	81	8	2	0	32	17	5	—	.260	.309	.299	88	-5	11	.990	-2	*127*	*91*	C62,1b29	—	-0.1
1908	Bos N	86	254	16	58	8	1	1	25	13	3	—	.228	.274	.280	78	-7	4	.971	-3	*88*	*94*	C63,1b11	—	-0.5
1909	Bos N	33	99	6	21	2	0	0	4	2	0	—	.212	.228	.232	41	-7	0	.928	-1	*91*	*90*	C27,M	—	-0.6
Total	15	1048	3410	345	853	102	38	13	393	130	48	0	.250	.287	.314	77	-109	81	.963	48	*114*	*102*	C829,1b132,2b6,S5,3b3/Pcf	—	1.5

BOWERS, BRENT Brent Raymond; B5.2.1971 Bridgeview IL; BL/TR/6´3˝/200; [TorA89 2/60]; d8.16

YEAR	TM LG	G	AB	R	H	2B	3B	HR	RBI	BB-IB	HP	SO	AVG	OBP	SLG	AOPS	ABR	SB-CS	FA	FR	RNG	THR	GAMES AT POSITION	DL	BFW
1996	Bal A	21	39	6	12	2	0	0	3	0-0	0	7	.308	.308	.359	68	-2	0-0	1.000	1	95	250	O21L	0	-0.1

BOWERS, BILLY Grover Bill; B3.25.1922 Parkin AR; D9.17.1996 Wynne AR; BL/TR/5´9.5˝/176; d4.24

YEAR	TM LG	G	AB	R	H	2B	3B	HR	RBI	BB-IB	HP	SO	AVG	OBP	SLG	AOPS	ABR	SB-CS	FA	FR	RNG	THR	GAMES AT POSITION	DL	BFW
1949	Chi A	26	78	5	15	2	1	0	6	4	0	5	.192	.232	.244	27	-9	1-1	.980	0	102	132	O20(3/10/8)	0	-0.9

BOWES, FRANK Frank M.; B1865 Bath NY; D1.21.1895 New York NY; TR/5´9˝/160; d4.17

YEAR	TM LG	G	AB	R	H	2B	3B	HR	RBI	BB-IB	HP	SO	AVG	OBP	SLG	AOPS	ABR	SB-CS	FA	FR	RNG	THR	GAMES AT POSITION	DL	BFW
1890	Bro AA	61	232	28	51	5	2	0	24	7	1	—	.220	.246	.259	50	-16	11	.813	-11	*82*	*96*	C25,O19(4/2/13),3b13,1b3,S2	—	-2.2

BOWIE, JIM James R.; B2.17.1965 Tokyo, Japan; BL/TL/6´0˝/205; [SeaA86 12/297]; d8.3; Col Louisiana St.

YEAR	TM LG	G	AB	R	H	2B	3B	HR	RBI	BB-IB	HP	SO	AVG	OBP	SLG	AOPS	ABR	SB-CS	FA	FR	RNG	THR	GAMES AT POSITION	DL	BFW
1994	Oak A	6	14	0	3	0	0	0	0	0-0	0	2	.214	.214	.214	12	-2	0-0	1.000	-0	66	138	1b6	0	-0.2

BOWLIN, WELDON Lois Weldon "Hoss"; B12.10.1940 Paragould AR; BR/TR/5´9˝/155; d9.16; Col Arkansas St.

YEAR	TM LG	G	AB	R	H	2B	3B	HR	RBI	BB-IB	HP	SO	AVG	OBP	SLG	AOPS	ABR	SB-CS	FA	FR	RNG	THR	GAMES AT POSITION	DL	BFW
1967	KC A	2	5	0	1	0	0	0	0	0-0	0	0	.200	.200	.200	19	-1	0-0	1.000	0	133	0	3b2	0	0.0

BOWLING, STEVE Stephen Shaddon; B6.26.1952 Tulsa OK; BR/TR/6´0˝/185; [MilA74 7/150]; d9.7; Col Tulsa

YEAR	TM LG	G	AB	R	H	2B	3B	HR	RBI	BB-IB	HP	SO	AVG	OBP	SLG	AOPS	ABR	SB-CS	FA	FR	RNG	THR	GAMES AT POSITION	DL	BFW
1976	Mil A	14	42	4	7	2	0	0	2	2-0	0	5	.167	.205	.214	23	-4	0-0	.975	1	118	116	O13C/D	0	-0.3
1977	Tor A	89	194	19	40	8	1	1	13	37-1	0	42	.206	.330	.273	67	-7	2-3	.987	8	98	304	O87(20/24/47)	0	-0.3
Total	2	103	236	23	47	10	1	1	15	39-1	0	47	.199	.310	.263	60	-11	2-3	.985	9	101	276	O100(20/37/47)/D	0	-0.6

YEAR	TM LG	G	AB	R	H	2B	3B	HR	RBI	BB-IB	HP	SO	AVG	OBP	SLG	AOPS	ABR	SB-CS	FA	FR	RNG	THR	GAMES AT POSITION	DL	BFW
BOWMAN, ELMER	Elmari Wilhelm "Big Bow"; B3.19.1897 Proctor VT; D12.17.1985 Los Angeles CA; BR/TR/6´0.5˝/193; d8.3; Col Vermont																								
1920	Was A	2	1	0	0	0	0	0	0	1	0	0	.000	.500	.000	42	0	0-0	ø	0	—	—	/H	—	0.0
BOWMAN, ERNIE	Ernest Ferrell; B7.28.1935 Johnson City TN; BR/TR/5´10˝/(160–165); d4.12																								
1961	SF N	38	38	10	8	0	2	0	2	1-0	0	8	.211	.231	.316	45	-3	2-0	.885	-4	81	57	2b13,S12,3b7	0	-0.6
1962	†SF N	46	42	9	8	1	0	1	4	1-0	1	10	.190	.227	.286	37	-4	0-1	1.000	-5	76	19	2b17,3b11,S10	0	-0.9
1963	SF N	81	125	10	23	3	0	0	4	0-0	0	15	.184	.181	.208	13	-14	1-2	.952	-8	79	75	S40,2b26,3b12	0	-2.1
Total	3	165	205	29	39	4	2	1	10	2-0	1	33	.190	.200	.244	24	-21	3-3	.950	-17	83	68	S62,2b56,3b30	0	-3.6
BOWMAN, BOB	Robert Leroy; B5.10.1931 Laytonville CA; BR/TR/6´1˝/195; d4.16; Col San Jose St.																								
1955	Phi N	3	3	0	0	0	0	0	0	0-0	0	0	.000	.000	.000	-99	-1	0-0	1.000	0	134	0	O2(1/0/1)	0	-0.1
1956	Phi N	6	16	2	3	0	1	1	2	0-0	0	6	.188	.188	.500	78	-1	0-0	.833	-1	75	0	O5(0/1/4)	0	-0.2
1957	Phi N	99	237	31	63	8	2	6	23	27-1	6	50	.266	.352	.392	104	2	0-0	.929	1	101	166	O81(3/0/79)	0	0.1
1958	Phi N	91	184	31	53	11	2	8	24	16-2	0	30	.288	.343	.500	122	5	0-1	.988	-2	102	29	O57(20/1/37)	0	0.2
1959	Phi N	57	79	7	10	0	0	2	5	5-0	0	23	.127	.176	.203	1	-12	0-0	1.000	1	107	95	O20(11/2/7),P5	0	-1.1
Total	5	256	519	71	129	19	5	17	54	48-3	6	109	.249	.317	.403	93	-7	0-1	.955	0	102	107	O165(35/4/128),P5	0	-1.1
BOWMAN, BILL	William George; B1869 Chicago IL; 5´11˝/180; d6.18																								
1891	Chi N	15	45	2	4	1	0	0	5	5	1	9	.089	.196	.111	-10	-6	0	.915	-2	*130*	*99*	C15	—	-0.7
BOWSER, RED	James Harvey; B9.20.1881 Freeport PA; D5.22.1943 Moundsville WV; d9.13																								
1910	Chi A	1	2	0	0	0	0	0	0	0	0	—	.000	.000	.000	-99	0	0	ø	0	0	0	/O	—	-0.1
BOYD, FRANK	Frank Jay; B4.2.1868 West Middletown PA; D12.16.1937 Oil City PA; BR/TR/?/168; d5.18																								
1893	Cle N	2	5	3	1	1	0	0	3	1	0	0	.200	.333	.400	89	0	0	1.000	0	*98*	*174*	C2	—	0.0
BOYD, JAKE	Jacob Henry; B1.19.1874 Martinsburg WV; D8.12.1932 Gettysburg PA; TL/?/160; d9.20; ▲																								
1894	Was N	6	21	1	3	0	0	0	1	1	0	4	.143	.182	.143	-22	-4	2	.833	1	410	0	O3(1/0/2),P3	—	-0.1
1895	Was N	52	159	29	43	5	1	1	16	20	7	28	.270	.376	.333	85	-2	2	.786	-7	82	160	O21(3/0/18),P15,2b10,S8/3	—	-0.8
1896	Was N	4	13	1	1	0	0	0	1	1	1	1	.077	.200	.077	-25	-1	0	.909	0	113	0	P4	—	0.0
Total	3	62	193	31	47	5	1	1	18	22	8	33	.244	.345	.295	66	-7	4	.794	-6	132	136	O24(4/0/20),P22,2b10,S8/3	—	-0.9
BOYD, BOB	Robert Richard "The Rope"; B10.1.1919 Potts Camp MS; D9.7.2004 Wichita KS; BL/TL/5´10˝/(160–170); d9.8; Negro Lg 1946–50																								
1951	Chi A	12	18	3	3	0	1	0	4	3	0	3	.167	.286	.278	54	-1	0-0	1.000	-1	38	244	1b6	0	-0.2
1953	Chi A	55	165	20	49	6	2	3	23	13	1	11	.297	.352	.412	103	0	1-4	1.000	-1	84	97	1b29,O16(15/0/1)	0	-0.4
1954	Chi A	29	56	10	10	3	0	0	5	4	0	3	.179	.233	.232	27	-6	2-0	.955	-0	108	175	O13L,1b12	0	-0.6
1956	Bal A	70	225	28	70	8	3	2	11	30-2	1	14	.311	.395	.400	119	7	0-5	.990	-4	68	92	1b60,O8(3/0/5)	85	-0.2
1957	Bal A	141	485	73	154	16	8	4	34	55-3	2	31	.318	.388	.408	126	18	2-4	.991	-3	92	100	1b132/lf	0	0.8
1958	Bal A	125	401	58	124	21	5	7	36	25-1	2	24	.309	.350	.439	123	12	1-1	.994	0	99	108	1b99	0	0.7
1959	Bal A	128	415	42	110	20	2	3	41	29-1	1	14	.265	.312	.345	83	-10	3-1	.985	-8	73	**110**	1b109	0	-2.4
1960	Bal A	71	82	9	26	5	2	0	9	6-1	0	5	.317	.364	.427	114	2	0-0	1.000	-0	82	144	1b17	0	0.1
1961	KC A	26	48	7	11	2	0	0	9	1-0	0	2	.229	.240	.271	37	-4	0-2	1.000	-1	44	66	1b8	0	-0.6
	Mil N	36	41	3	10	0	0	0	3	1-0	0	7	.244	.256	.244	38	-4	0-0	1.000	1	280	149	1b3	0	-0.3
Total	9	693	1936	253	567	81	23	19	175	167-8	7	114	.293	.349	.388	105	14	9-17	.991	-17	85	104	1b475,O38(32/0/6)	85	-3.1
BOYD, BILL	William J.; B12.22.1852 New York NY; D10.1.1912 Jamaica NY; d4.22; M1/U1																								
1872	Mut NA	36	170	27	44	6	1	1	32	6	—	7	.259	.284	.324	92	0	4-2	.730	-12	75	54	3b34/2rf	—	-0.9
1873	Atl NA	48	228	31	63	5	4	1	30	2	—	4	.276	.283	.346	95	1	1-1	.716	3	172	84	O43R,3b8	—	0.4
1874	Har NA	26	117	22	41	8	4	0	19	1	—	2	.350	.356	.487	160	7	1-0	.664	-9	75	159	3b25/rf	—	-0.2
1875	Atl NA	36	151	14	44	11	0	1	10	1	—	0	.291	.296	.384	154	10	0-0	.774	-7	95	59	2b15,O12R,3b9,1b2/PSM	—	0.2
Total	4NA	146	666	94	192	30	9	3	91	10	—	13	.288	.299	.374	118	18	6-3	.704	-24	79	88	3b76,O57R,2b16,1b2/SP	—	-0.5
BOYER, CLETE	Cletis Leroy; B2.9.1937 Cassville MO; BR/TR/6´0˝/(165–188); d6.5; C10; b–Cloyd b–Ken																								
1955	KC A	47	79	3	19	1	0	0	6	3-0	0	17	.241	.268	.253	40	-7	0-0	.963	2	89	120	S12,3b11,2b10	0	-0.4
1956	KC A	67	129	15	28	3	1	1	4	11-1	1	24	.217	.284	.279	49	-10	1-1	.971	11	120	117	2b51,3b7	0	0.3
1957	KC A	10	0	0	0	0	0	0	0	0-0	0	0	ø	ø	ø	ø	0	0-0	ø	-0	0	0	/23	0	0.0
1959	NY A	47	114	4	20	2	0	0	3	6-2	0	23	.175	.215	.193	14	-14	1-0	.990	2	93	102	S26,3b16	0	-1.0
1960	†NY A	124	393	54	95	20	1	14	46	23-1	3	85	.242	.285	.405	90	-7	2-3	.967	24	120	132	3b99,S33	0	1.8
1961	†NY A	148	504	61	113	19	5	11	55	63-4	2	83	.224	.308	.347	80	-14	1-3	.967	**28**	**118**	**140**	3b141,S12/rf	0	1.3
1962	†NY A	158	566	85	154	24	1	18	68	51-8	3	106	.272	.331	.413	104	2	3-2	.964	34	**122**	**151**	3b157	0	3.6
1963	†NY A	152	557	59	140	20	3	12	54	33-11	2	91	.251	.295	.363	84	-13	4-2	.954	22	**108**	134	3b141,S9/2	0	1.0
1964	†NY A	147	510	43	111	10	5	8	52	36-11	1	93	.218	.269	.304	59	-30	6-1	.968	8	**110**	139	3b123,S21	0	-2.0
1965	NY A	148	514	69	129	23	6	18	58	39-10	2	79	.251	.304	.424	106	2	4-1	.968	21	**114**	**160**	3b147,S2	0	2.5
1966	NY A	144	500	59	120	22	4	14	57	46-4	2	48	.240	.303	.384	101	0	6-0	.966	20	127	80	3b85,S59	0	2.8
1967	Atl N	154	572	63	140	18	3	26	96	39-3	2	81	.245	.292	.423	105	1	6-3	**.970**	7	97	123	3b150,S6	0	0.8
1968	Atl N	71	273	19	62	7	2	4	17	16-3	2	32	.227	.275	.311	75	-9	2-0	.981	4	101	141	3b69	25	-0.6
1969	†Atl N	144	496	57	124	16	1	14	57	55-6	4	87	.250	.328	.371	95	-3	3-7	**.965**	7	104	83	3b141	0	0.1
1970	Atl N	134	475	44	117	14	1	16	62	41-8	1	71	.246	.305	.381	79	-15	2-5	.954	11	112	94	3b126,S5	0	-0.6
1971	Atl N	30	98	10	24	1	0	6	19	8-2	0	11	.245	.299	.439	101	0	0-0	.961	2	113	133	3b25/S	0	0.1
Total	16	1725	5780	645	1396	200	33	162	654	470-74	25	931	.242	.299	.372	87	-117	41-28	.965	202	112	126	3b1439,S186,2b63/rf	25	9.7
BOYER, KEN	Kenton Lloyd; B5.20.1931 Liberty MO; D9.7.1982 St.Louis MO; BR/TR/6´2˝/(190–200); d4.12; M3/C2; b–Clete b–Cloyd																								
1955	StL N	147	530	78	140	27	2	18	62	37-5	1	67	.264	.311	.425	94	-6	22-17	.952	2	103	**104**	3b139,S18	0	-0.4
1956	StL N★	150	595	91	182	30	2	26	98	38-7	1	65	.306	.347	.494	123	18	8-3	.961	9	**109**	**149**	3b149	0	2.8
1957	StL N	142	544	79	144	18	3	19	62	44-8	1	77	.265	.318	.414	94	-6	12-8	**.996**	2	101	27	O105C,3b41	0	-0.8
1958	StL N	150	570	101	175	21	9	23	90	49-8	3	53	.307	.360	.496	121	16	11-6	.962	25	**116**	**136**	3b144,O6C/S	0	4.0
1959	StL N★	149	563	86	174	18	5	28	94	67-7	2	77	.309	.384	.508	127	22	12-6	.956	12	**111**	**135**	3b143,S12	0	3.5
1960	StL N★	151	552	95	168	26	10	32	97	56-10	4	77	.304	.370	.562	139	30	8-7	.959	16	107	**149**	3b146	0	4.5
1961	StL N★	153	589	109	194	26	11	24	95	68-9	1	91	.329	.397	.533	132	28	6-3	.951	14	**116**	76	3b153	0	4.1
1962	StL N★	160	611	92	178	27	5	24	98	75-7	1	104	.291	.369	.470	113	12	12-7	.956	4	102	**120**	3b160	0	1.6
1963	StL N★	159	617	86	176	28	2	24	111	70-10	2	90	.285	.358	.454	121	19	1-0	.925	-16	91	97	3b159	0	0.3
1964	†StL N★	**162**	628	100	185	30	10	24	**119**	70-12	2	85	.295	.365	.489	128	24	3-5	.951	0	102	**118**	3b162	0	2.3
1965	StL N	144	535	71	139	18	2	13	75	57-3	1	73	.260	.328	.374	90	-6	2-7	**.968**	-12	91	79	3b143	0	-2.2
1966	NY N	136	496	62	132	28	2	14	61	30-5	0	64	.266	.304	.415	101	0	4-3	.951	14	**116**	126	3b130,1b2	0	1.4
1967	NY N	56	166	17	39	7	2	3	13	26-3	0	22	.235	.335	.355	100	1	2-1	.949	-0	104	97	3b44,1b8	0	0.0
	Chi A	57	180	17	47	5	1	4	21	7-0	0	25	.261	.287	.367	96	-2	0-2	.957	-1	101	87	3b33,1b18	0	-0.5
1968	Chi A	10	24	0	3	0	0	0	0	1-0	0	6	.125	.160	.125	-13	-3	0-0	.900	-1	84	140	3b5/1	0	-0.5
	LA N	83	221	20	60	7	2	6	41	16-3	1	34	.271	.317	.403	126	6	2-2	.922	1	108	92	3b34,1b32	0	0.6
1969	LA N	25	34	0	7	2	0	0	4	2-0	0	7	.206	.250	.265	47	-2	0-0	.971	-0	91	236	1b4	0	-0.3
Total	15	2034	7455	1104	2143	318	68	282	1141	713-97	20	1017	.287	.349	.462	115	151	105-77	.952	69	106	115	3b1785,O111C,1b65,S31	0	20.4
BOYLAND, DOE	Dorian Scott; B1.6.1955 Chicago IL; BL/TL/6´4˝/(200–204); [PitN76 2/45]; d9.4; Col Wisconsin–Oshkosh																								
1978	Pit N	6	8	1	2	0	0	0	1	0-0	0	1	.250	.250	.250	38	-1	0-0	1.000	-0	0	0	/1	0	-0.1
1979	Pit N	4	3	0	0	0	0	0	0	0-0	0	2	.000	.000	.000	-95	-1	0-0	ø	0	—	—	/H	0	-0.1
1981	Pit N	11	8	0	0	0	0	0	0	1-0	0	3	.000	.111	.000	-63	-2	0-0	ø	0	—	—	/H	0	-0.2
Total	3	21	19	1	2	0	0	0	1	1-0	0	6	.105	.150	.105	-26	-4	0-0	1.000	-0	0	0	/1	0	-0.4
BOYLE, EDDIE	Edward J.; B5.8.1874 Cincinnati OH; D2.9.1941 Cincinnati OH; BR/TR/6´3˝/200; d4.17; b–Jack																								
1896	Lou N	3	9	0	0	0	0	0	0	2	0	2	.000	.182	.000	-52	-2	0	.938	-0	*78*	*93*	C3	—	-0.2
	Pit N	2	5	0	0	0	0	0	0	0	0	1	.000	.000	.000	-99	-1	0	.833	-1	*75*	*75*	C2	—	-0.2
	Year	5	14	0	0	0	0	0	0	2	0	3	.000	.125	.000	-68	-3	0	.909	-1	77	*88*	C5	—	-0.4
BOYLE, HENRY	Henry J. "Handsome Henry"; B9.20.1860 Philadelphia PA; D5.25.1932 Philadelphia PA; BR/TR; d7.9; OF(54/18/13); ▲																								
1884	StL U	65	262	41	68	10	3	4	—	9	—	—	.260	.284	.366	92	-11	—	.885	4	137	140	O43(40/2/2),P19,3b4/S21	—	-0.4
1885	StL N	72	258	24	52	9	1	1	21	13	—	38	.202	.240	.256	64	-9	—	.907	-4	86	172	P42,O31(12/10/9),2b2	—	-0.8
1886	StL N	30	108	8	27	2	2	1	13	5	—	19	.250	.283	.333	93	-1	0	.852	0	112	90	P25,O6(0/5/1)	—	0.0
1887	Ind N	41	141	17	27	9	1	2	13	9	2	18	.191	.250	.312	57	-8	2	.912	-6	67	134	P38,O4(2/1/1)	—	-0.4

YEAR	TM LG	G	AB	R	H	2B	3B	HR	RBI	BB-IB	HP	SO	AVG	OBP	SLG	AOPS	ABR	SB-CS	FA	FR	RNG	THR	GAMES AT POSITION	DL	BFW
1888	Ind N	37	125	13	18	2	0	1	6	6	1	31	.144	.189	.184	19	-11	1	.933	2	120	59	P37/1	—	0.1
1889	Ind N	46	155	17	38	10	0	1	17	9	1	23	.245	.291	.329	71	-6	4	.958	-5	69	0	P46/3	—	-0.2
Total	6	291	1049	120	230	42	7	10	70	51	4	129	.219	.258	.301	69	-46	7	.912	-8	87	103	P207,O84L,3b5,2b3,1b2/S	—	-1.7
Boyle, Jim	James John; B1.19.1904 Cincinnati OH; D12.24.1958 Cincinnati OH; BR/TR/6´0˝/180; d6.20; b–Buzz; Col Xavier																								
1926	NY N	1	0	0	0	0	0	0	0	0	0	0	ø	ø	ø	ø	0	0	ø	0	*0*	*0*	/C	—	0.0
Boyle, Jack	John Anthony "Honest Jack"; B3.22.1866 Cincinnati OH; D1.7.1913 Cincinnati OH; BR/TR/6´4˝/190; d10.8; b–Eddie; OF(6/2/7)																								
1886	Cin AA	1	5	0	1	0	0	0	0	0	0	—	.200	.200	.200	25	0	0	.769	-1	—	—	/C	—	-0.1
1887	†StL AA	88	350	48	66	3	1	2	41	20	2	—	.189	.237	.220	25	-38	7	**.897**	-9	—	—	C86,O2R,1b2/3	—	-3.3
1888	†StL AA	71	257	33	62	8	1	1	23	13	3	—	.241	.286	.292	77	-8	11	**.932**	13	—	—	C70/cf	—	1.1
1889	StL AA	99	347	54	85	11	5	3	42	21	7	42	.245	.301	.331	71	-16	5	.947	9	—	—	C80,3b12,O5(3/0/2),1b4/2	—	-0.1
1890	Chi P	100	369	56	96	9	5	1	49	44	5	29	.260	.347	.320	76	-13	11	.940	-2	*116*	*98*	C50,3b30,S16,1b7,O2R	—	-0.8
1891	StL AA	121	434	76	122	18	8	5	79	44	12	35	.281	.363	.394	102	-1	18	.936	-3	*116*	*78*	C91,S25,3b7,O3(1/1/1),2b3,1b3	—	0.3
1892	NY N	120	436	52	80	8	8	0	32	36	4	41	.183	.252	.239	49	-28	10	.922	-3	*70*	***152***	C79,1b40,O2L,S2	—	-2.3
1893	Phi N	116	504	105	144	29	9	4	81	41	10	30	.286	.351	.403	100	-1	22	.988	6	119	101	1b112,C6,2b2	—	0.4
1894	Phi N	117	510	103	152	23	10	4	89	46	3	27	.298	.360	.406	86	-12	23	.982	0	98	106	1b117/32	—	-0.9
1895	Phi N	**133**	565	90	143	17	4	0	67	35	5	23	.253	.302	.297	55	-39	13	.973	-6	84	82	1b133	—	-3.7
1896	Phi N	40	145	17	43	4	1	1	28	6	5	7	.297	.346	.359	87	-3	3	.920	-7	*102*	*81*	C28,1b12	—	-0.6
1897	Phi N	75	288	37	73	9	1	2	36	19	3	—	.253	.306	.313	65	-15	3	.962	-6	*103*	*89*	C50,1b24	—	-1.4
1898	Phi N	6	22	0	2	0	1	0	3	1	0	—	.091	.130	.182	-11	-3	0	.919	-1	120	94	1b4,C3	—	-0.4
Total	13	1087	4232	671	1069	139	54	23	570	326	59	234	.253	.315	.327	72	-177	126	.929	-9	*100*	*103*	C544,1b458,3b51,S43,O15R,2b7	—	-11.8
Boyle, Jack	John Bellew; B7.9.1889 Morris IL; D4.3.1971 Ft.Lauderdale FL; BL/TR/5´11.5˝/165; d6.28; Col Chicago																								
1912	Phi N	15	25	4	7	1	0	0	2	1	0	5	.280	.308	.320	67	-1	0	.905	3	164	292	3b6,S2	—	0.2
Boyle, Buzz	Ralph Francis; B2.9.1908 Cincinnati OH; D11.12.1978 Cincinnati OH; BL/TL/5´11.5˝/170; d9.11; b–Jim; Col Xavier																								
1929	Bos N	17	57	8	15	2	1	1	2	6	0	11	.263	.333	.386	81	-2	2	1.000	1	106	101	O17L	—	-0.2
1930	Bos N	1	1	0	0	0	0	0	0	0	0	1	.000	.000	.000	-99	0	0	ø	-0	0	0	/cf	—	0.0
1933	Bro N	93	338	38	101	13	4	0	31	16	0	24	.299	.331	.361	102	0	7	.975	-3	103	32	O90(45/34/10)	—	-0.7
1934	Bro N	128	472	88	144	26	10	7	48	51	3	44	.305	.376	.447	126	18	8	.970	9	103	**189**	O121(18/19/86)	—	1.9
1935	Bro N	127	475	51	129	17	9	4	44	43	0	45	.272	.332	.371	90	-7	7	.963	4	99	152	O124(0/17/107)	—	-0.9
Total	5	366	1343	185	389	58	24	12	125	116	3	125	.290	.347	.395	105	9	24	.970	11	102	135	O353(80/71/203)	—	0.1
Brack, Gibby	Gilbert Herman; B3.29.1908 Chicago IL; D1.20.1960 Greenville TX; BR/TR/5´9˝/170; d4.23																								
1937	Bro N	112	372	60	102	27	9	5	38	44	0	93	.274	.351	.435	111	6	9	.969	2	102	130	O101(37/44/21)	—	0.4
1938	Bro N	40	56	10	12	2	1	1	6	4	0	14	.214	.267	.339	64	-3	1	1.000	3	124	350	O13(7/0/6)	—	-0.1
	Phi N	72	282	40	81	20	4	4	28	18	1	30	.287	.332	.429	111	4	2	.964	-0	103	88	O68(12/38/24)	—	0.1
	Year	112	338	50	93	22	5	5	34	22	1	44	.275	.321	.414	102	0	3	.969	3	106	123	O81(19/38/30)	—	0.0
1939	Phi N	91	270	40	78	21	4	6	41	26	0	49	.289	.351	.463	121	8	1	.959	-3	98	102	O48(2/6/40),1b19	—	0.0
Total	3	315	980	150	273	70	18	16	113	92	1	186	.279	.341	.436	111	15	13	.967	2	103	122	O230(58/88/91),1b19	—	0.4
Bradford, Buddy	Charles William; B7.25.1944 Mobile AL; BR/TR/5´11˝/(170–191); d9.9																								
1966	Chi A	14	28	3	4	0	0	0	0	2-0	0	6	.143	.200	.143	0	-4	0-0	.833	-2	37	0	O9(5/0/4)	0	-0.7
1967	Chi A	24	20	6	2	1	0	0	1	1-1	0	7	.100	.143	.150	-14	-3	1-0	.900	-1	75	0	O14(6/1/8)	0	-0.5
1968	Chi A	103	281	32	61	11	0	5	24	23-2	2	67	.217	.277	.310	78	-7	8-4	.965	-1	103	78	O99(35/25/58)	0	-1.5
1969	Chi A	93	273	36	70	8	2	11	27	34-4	4	75	.256	.347	.421	109	3	5-2	.961	-5	89	91	O88(0/48/59)	0	-0.5
1970	Chi A	32	91	8	17	3	0	2	8	10-0	0	30	.187	.265	.286	51	-6	1-2	.979	-2	86	65	O27(2/20/9)	0	-1.0
	Cle A	75	163	25	32	6	1	7	23	21-1	1	43	.196	.290	.374	79	-5	0-1	.984	1	115	36	O64(1/58/5)/3	0	-0.6
	Year	107	254	33	49	9	1	9	31	31-1	1	73	.193	.281	.343	69	-11	1-3	.982	-1	105	46	O91(3/78/14)/3	0	-1.6
1971	Cle A	20	38	4	6	2	1	0	3	6-1	0	10	.158	.273	.263	48	-3	0-0	.930	1	122	123	O18C	0	-0.2
	Cin N	79	100	17	20	3	0	2	12	14-4	3	23	.200	.316	.290	73	-3	4-2	.986	-0	89	98	O66(36/26/5)	0	-0.5
1972	Chi A	35	48	13	13	2	0	2	8	4-0	1	13	.271	.340	.438	127	2	3-2	1.000	0	100	109	O28(3/22/3)	0	0.1
1973	Chi A	53	168	24	40	3	1	8	15	17-1	2	43	.238	.316	.411	100	-1	4-5	.992	3	94	257	O51(1/48/2)	32	0.0
1974	Chi A	39	96	16	32	2	0	5	10	13-0	1	11	.333	.414	.510	162	8	1-2	.980	1	103	118	O32(10/0/24)/D	82	0.7
1975	Chi A	25	58	8	9	3	1	2	15	8-0	3	22	.155	.274	.345	78	-2	3-2	.966	-0	98	90	O18(3/0/15),D4	0	-0.3
	StL N	50	81	12	22	1	0	4	15	12-0	0	24	.272	.366	.432	115	2	0-2	.935	1	123	85	O25(3/1/21)	0	0.1
1976	Chi A	55	160	20	35	5	2	4	14	19-2	2	37	.219	.309	.350	92	-2	6-0	.978	-2	104	0	O48(2/0/46),D3	0	-0.4
Total	11	697	1605	224	363	50	8	52	175	184-16	19	411	.226	.311	.364	91	-21	36-24	.971	-7	99	91	O587(107/267/259),D8/3	114	-5.3
Bradford, Vic	Henry Victor; B3.5.1915 Brownsville TN; D6.10.1994 Paris KY; BR/TR/6´2˝/190; d5.1; Mil 1944–46; Col Alabama																								
1943	NY N	6	5	1	1	0	0	0	1	1	0	1	.200	.333	.200	55	0	0	1.000	0	185	0	/lf	0	0.0
Bradley, Al	Albert Joseph; B5.23.1856 Bradys Bend PA; D2.5.1937 Altoona PA; 5´10˝/185; d5.21																								
1884	Was U	1	3	0	0	0	0	0	—	2	—	—	.000	.400	.000	32	0	—	1.000	0	0	0	/cf	—	0.0
Bradley, George	George Washington "Grin"; B7.13.1852 Reading PA; D10.2.1931 Philadelphia PA; BR/TR/5´10.5˝/175; d5.4; OF(11/19/16); ▲																								
1875	StL NA	60	254	28	62	7	3	0	24	1	—	19	.244	.247	.295	96	0	3-3	.896	0	108	193	P60,S2/2lf	—	-0.1
1876	StL N	**64**	265	29	66	7	6	0	28	3	—	12	.249	.257	.321	97	3	—	.919	2	96	188	P64	—	0.0
1877	Chi N	55	214	31	52	7	3	0	12	6	—	19	.243	.264	.304	70	-8	—	**.950**	-2	101	100	P50,3b16,1b3/rf	—	-0.3
1879	Tro N	63	251	36	62	9	5	0	23	1	—	20	.247	.250	.323	93	-2	—	.867	6	130	0	P54,3b5,1b3/rfS	—	0.3
1880	Pro N	82	309	32	70	7	6	0	23	5	—	38	.227	.239	.288	80	-7	—	.858	17	**147**	**166**	3b57,P28,O7(1/0/6),1b2	—	1.2
1881	Det N	1	4	0	0	0	0	0	0	0	—	0	.000	.000	.000	-96	-1	—	.667	-1	38	396	/S	—	-0.1
	Cle N	60	241	21	60	10	1	2	18	4	—	25	.249	.261	.324	88	-3	—	.865	-12	76	83	3b48,P6,S6/lf	—	-1.2
	Year	61	245	21	60	10	1	2	18	4	—	25	.245	.257	.318	84	-4	—	.865	-12	76	83	3b48,S7,P6/lf	—	-1.3
1882	Cle N	30	115	16	21	5	0	0	6	4	—	16	.183	.210	.226	41	-7	—	.897	3	**151**	**607**	P18,O9(5/4/0),1b6	—	-0.2
1883	Cle N	4	16	0	5	0	1	0	1	0	—	1	.313	.313	.438	126	0	—	.792	-1	79	178	S4	—	0.0
	Phi AA	76	312	47	73	8	5	1	36	8	—	—	.234	.253	.301	71	-11	—	.779	1	118	129	3b44,P26,O11C,1b2	—	-0.5
1884	Cin U	58	226	31	43	4	7	0	—	7	—	—	.190	.215	.270	43	-24	—	.912	-1	105	152	P41,O16(4/4/8),S5,1b2	—	-1.0
1886	Phi AA	13	48	1	4	0	1	0	1	1	0	—	.083	.102	.125	-29	-7	2	.849	1	115	49	S13	—	-0.6
1888	Bal AA	1	3	0	0	0	0	0	0	0	0	—	.000	.000	.000	-99	-1	0	.600	-1	34	0	/S	—	-0.2
Total	10	507	2004	244	456	57	35	3	148	39	0	131	.228	.242	.295	72	-68	2	.896	12	110	136	P287,3b170,O46C,S31,1b18	—	-2.6
Bradley, George	George Washington; B4.1.1914 Greenwood AR; D10.19.1982 Lawrenceburg TN; BR/TR/6´1.5˝/185; d4.28																								
1946	StL A	4	12	2	2	1	0	0	3	0	0	1	.167	.167	.250	15	-1	0-0	1.000	-0	86	0	O3C	0	-0.2
Bradley, Hugh	Hugh Frederick "Corns"; B5.23.1885 Grafton MA; D1.26.1949 Worcester MA; BR/TR/5´10˝/175; d4.25; Col Holy Cross																								
1910	Bos A	32	83	8	14	6	2	0	7	5	0	—	.169	.216	.289	57	-4	2	.995	-1	69	115	1b21,C3/rf	—	-0.7
1911	Bos A	12	41	9	13	2	0	1	4	2	1	—	.317	.364	.439	125	1	1	.993	1	101	126	1b12	—	0.1
1912	Bos A	40	137	16	26	11	1	1	19	15	1	—	.190	.275	.307	63	-7	3	.989	0	94	80	1b40	—	-0.7
1914	Pit F	118	427	41	131	20	6	0	61	27	8	27	.307	.359	.382	103	-5	7	.990	-0	98	83	1b118	—	-0.8
1915	Pit F	26	66	3	18	4	1	0	6	4	0	5	.273	.314	.364	91	-2	2	.952	-1	99	0	O15R	—	-0.4
	Bro F	37	126	7	31	3	2	0	18	4	0	9	.246	.269	.302	61	-9	6	.996	3	156	47	1b26,O7R/C	—	-0.8
	New F	12	33	0	5	0	0	0	2	2	2	3	.152	.243	.152	13	-4	2	.986	-1	23	94	1b8	—	-0.7
	Year	75	225	10	54	7	3	0	26	10	2	17	.240	.278	.298	63	-15	10	.994	0	125	58	1b34,O22R/C	—	-1.9
Total	5	277	913	84	238	46	12	2	117	59	12	44	.261	.314	.344	84	-30	23	.991	-1	99	84	1b225,O23R,C4	—	-4.0
Bradley, Jack	John Thomas; B9.20.1893 Denver CO; D3.18.1969 Tulsa OK; BR/TR/5´11˝/175; d6.18; Col Illinois																								
1916	Cle A	2	3	0	0	0	0	0	0	0	0	1	.000	.000	.000	-94	-1	0	1.000	-0	51	0	/C	—	-0.1
Bradley, Mark	Mark Allen; B12.3.1956 Elizabethtown KY; BR/TR/6´1˝/(180–185); [LAN75 1/24]; d9.3																								
1981	LA N	9	6	2	1	1	0	0	0	0-0	0	1	.167	.167	.333	41	0	0-0	1.000	1	91	704	O6(1/0/5)	0	0.0
1982	LA N	8	3	1	1	0	0	0	0	0-0	0	0	.333	.333	.333	90	0	0-0	1.000	-0	76	0	O3(1/0/2)	0	0.0
1983	NY N	73	104	10	21	4	0	3	5	11-1	0	35	.202	.278	.327	67	-5	4-2	1.000	-0	91	133	O35(14/7/16)	0	-0.6
Total	3	90	113	13	23	5	0	3	5	11-1	0	36	.204	.274	.327	67	-5	4-2	1.000	0	91	171	O44(16/7/23)	0	-0.6

BRADLEY, MILTON Milton Obelle; B4.15.1978 Harbor City CA; BB/TR/6´0˝/(180–205); [MonN96 2/40]; d7.19

YEAR	TM LG	G	AB	R	H	2B	3B	HR	RBI	BB-IB	HP	SO	AVG	OBP	SLG	AOPS	ABR	SB-CS	FA	FR	RNG	THR	GAMES AT POSITION	DL	BFW
2000	Mon N	42	154	20	34	8	1	2	15	14-0	1	32	.221	.288	.325	55	-11	2-1	.979	1	96	262	O40C	0	-0.9
2001	Mon N	67	220	19	49	16	3	1	19	19-0	1	62	.223	.287	.336	61	-13	7-4	.988	4	111	145	O65(13/52/2)	0	-0.9
	Cle A	10	18	3	4	1	0	0	0	2-0	0	3	.222	.300	.278	52	-1	1-1	.929	0	98	361	O9(0/8/1)/D	0	-0.1
2002	Cle A	98	325	48	81	18	3	9	38	32-2	0	58	.249	.317	.406	89	-6	6-3	.982	3	99	205	O94C/D	51	-0.1
2003	Cle A	101	377	61	121	34	2	10	56	64-8	5	73	.321	.421	.501	144	29	17-7	.992	-2	94	133	O93C,D8	65	2.8
2004	†LA N	141	516	72	138	24	0	19	67	71-3	6	123	.267	.362	.424	104	5	15-11	.977	5	109	109	O138(17/93/31)	0	0.8
2005	LA N	75	283	49	82	14	1	13	38	25-1	2	47	.290	.350	.484	115	6	6-1	.989	3	105	161	O72C	95	1.1
2006	†Oak A	96	351	53	97	14	2	14	52	51-1	2	65	.276	.370	.447	113	8	10-2	.980	-2	101	68	O94R/D	69	0.3
Total	7	630	2244	325	606	129	12	68	285	278-15	17	463	.270	.354	.429	103	17	64-30	.983	12	103	143	O605(30/452/128),D11	280	3.0

BRADLEY, PHIL Philip Poole; B3.11.1959 Bloomington IN; BR/TR/6´0˝/(175–190); [SeaA81 3/53]; d9.2; Col Missouri

YEAR	TM LG	G	AB	R	H	2B	3B	HR	RBI	BB-IB	HP	SO	AVG	OBP	SLG	AOPS	ABR	SB-CS	FA	FR	RNG	THR	GAMES AT POSITION	DL	BFW
1983	Sea A	23	67	8	18	2	0	0	5	8-0	0	5	.269	.342	.299	76	-2	3-1	.974	-3	76	94	O21C/D	0	-0.4
1984	Sea A	124	322	49	97	12	4	0	24	34-2	3	61	.301	.373	.363	105	4	21-8	.992	1	105	51	O117(48/68/14),D3	0	0.4
1985	Sea A★	159	641	100	192	33	8	26	88	55-4	12	129	.300	.365	.498	132	28	22-9	.986	-1	97	99	O159(126/28/10)	0	2.2
1986	Sea A	143	526	88	163	27	4	12	50	77-1	8	134	.310	.405	.445	130	26	21-12	.996	-6	85	120	O140(138/5/0)	17	1.4
1987	Sea A	158	603	101	179	38	10	14	67	84-2	8	119	.297	.387	.463	119	19	40-10	.983	-5	87	122	O158L	0	1.2
1988	Phi N	154	569	77	150	30	5	11	56	54-0	**16**	106	.264	.341	.392	108	8	11-9	.990	5	102	151	O153(153/3/1)	0	0.8
1989	Bal A	144	545	83	151	23	10	11	55	70-4	7	103	.277	.364	.417	123	18	20-6	.990	-6	93	46	O140L,D2	0	1.0
1990	Bal A	72	289	39	78	9	1	4	26	30-2	7	35	.270	.352	.349	100	1	10-4	.987	-1	98	65	O70L,D2	26	-0.1
	Chi A	45	133	20	30	5	1	0	5	20-3	4	26	.226	.344	.278	78	-3	7-3	.973	-1	100	54	O38(23/14/6),D7	0	-0.4
	Year	117	422	59	108	14	2	4	31	50-5	**11**	61	.256	.349	.327	93	-2	17-7	.982	-1	99	62	O108(93/14/6),D9	0	-0.5
Total	8	1022	3695	565	1058	179	43	78	376	432-18	65	718	.286	.369	.421	117	99	155-62	.988	-17	94	98	O996(856/139/31),D15	43	6.1

BRADLEY, SCOTT Scott William; B3.22.1960 Glen Ridge NJ; BL/TR/5´11˝/(175–185); [NYA81 3/64]; d9.9; Col North Carolina

YEAR	TM LG	G	AB	R	H	2B	3B	HR	RBI	BB-IB	HP	SO	AVG	OBP	SLG	AOPS	ABR	SB-CS	FA	FR	RNG	THR	GAMES AT POSITION	DL	BFW
1984	NY A	9	21	3	6	1	0	0	2	1-0	0	1	.286	.318	.333	83	0	0-0	1.000	-0	103	0	O5L,C3	0	-0.1
1985	NY A	19	49	4	8	2	1	0	1	1-0	1	5	.163	.196	.245	20	-6	0-0	.923	-2	56	118	C3,D9	54	-0.7
1986	Chi A	9	21	3	6	0	0	0	0	1-0	2	0	.286	.375	.286	80	0	0-2	ø	-0	0	0	/lfD	0	-0.1
	Sea A	68	199	17	60	8	3	5	28	12-4	2	7	.302	.344	.447	113	3	1-0	.990	-6	103	75	C59,D3	0	0.0
	Year	77	220	20	66	8	3	5	28	13-4	4	7	.300	.347	.432	110	3	1-2	.990	-6	103	75	C59,D9/lf	0	-0.1
1987	Sea A	102	342	34	95	15	1	5	43	15-1	3	18	.278	.310	.371	77	-12	0-1	.983	-3	84	86	C82,3b8,O2R,D6	0	-1.2
1988	Sea A	103	335	45	86	17	1	4	33	17-1	2	16	.257	.295	.349	77	-11	1-1	.991	5	84	102	C85,O4R,3b3,1b2,D4	0	-0.1
1989	Sea A	103	270	21	74	16	0	3	37	21-4	1	23	.274	.322	.367	93	-2	1-1	.993	-0	74	75	C70,1b2/lfD	0	0.1
1990	Sea A	101	233	11	52	9	0	1	28	15-2	0	20	.223	.264	.275	52	-15	0-1	.995	2	78	97	C63,3b5/1D	0	-1.1
1991	Sea A	83	172	10	35	7	0	0	11	19-2	0	19	.203	.280	.244	47	-12	0-0	.993	-5	80	46	C65,3b4/1D	0	-1.5
1992	Sea A	2	1	0	0	0	0	0	0	1-0	0	1	.000	.500	.000	50	0	0-0	1.000	1	0	0	/C	0	0.1
	Cin N	5	5	1	2	0	0	0	1	1-0	0	0	.400	.500	.400	154	0	0-0	1.000	-1	36	0	C2	0	0.0
Total	9	604	1648	149	424	75	6	18	184	104-14	11	110	.257	.302	.343	76	-55	3-6	.990	-10	83	83	C433,D42,3b20,O13(7/0/6),1b6	54	-4.6

BRADLEY, BILL William Joseph; B2.13.1878 Cleveland OH; D3.11.1954 Cleveland OH; BR/TR/6´0˝/185; d8.26; M2

YEAR	TM LG	G	AB	R	H	2B	3B	HR	RBI	BB-IB	HP	SO	AVG	OBP	SLG	AOPS	ABR	SB-CS	FA	FR	RNG	THR	GAMES AT POSITION	DL	BFW
1899	Chi N	35	129	26	40	6	1	2	18	12	2	—	.310	.378	.419	121	4	4	.884	-4	97	157	3b30,S5	—	0.1
1900	Chi N	122	444	63	125	21	8	5	49	27	5	—	.282	.330	.399	104	1	14	.882	14	**111**	75	3b106,1b15	—	1.6
1901	Cle A	133	516	95	151	28	13	1	55	26	8	—	.293	.336	.403	109	5	15	**.930**	12	102	125	3b133/P	—	1.9
1902	Cle A	**137**	550	104	187	39	12	11	77	27	4	—	.340	.375	.515	151	36	11	.923	12	107	107	3b137	—	4.8
1903	Cle A	136	536	101	168	36	22	6	68	25	3	—	.313	.348	.496	154	33	21	.924	11	**114**	130	3b136	—	4.8
1904	Cle A	**154**	609	94	183	32	8	6	83	26	5	—	.300	.334	.409	136	23	23	**.955**	9	104	132	3b154	—	4.0
1905	Cle A	146	541	63	145	34	6	0	51	27	15	—	.268	.321	.353	112	8	22	**.945**	13	108	141	3b146,M	—	2.7
1906	Cle A	82	302	32	83	16	2	2	25	18	4	—	.275	.324	.361	116	6	13	.966	1	103	80	3b82	—	1.0
1907	Cle A	139	498	48	111	20	1	0	34	35	9	—	.223	.286	.267	76	-12	20	**.938**	6	**101**	**130**	3b139	—	-0.3
1908	Cle A	148	548	70	133	24	7	1	46	29	13	—	.243	.297	.318	99	-1	18	.939	-25	88	110	3b118,S30	—	-2.5
1909	Cle A	95	334	30	62	6	3	0	22	19	3	—	.186	.236	.222	43	-22	8	.957	-5	94	164	3b87,1b3,2b3	—	-2.9
1910	Cle A	61	214	12	42	3	0	0	12	10	1	—	.196	.236	.210	39	-15	6	.956	-2	95	86	3b61	—	-1.8
1914	Bro F	7	6	1	3	1	0	0	3	0	0	0	.500	.500	.667	218	1	0	ø	0	—	—	/HM	—	0.1
1915	KC F	66	203	15	38	9	1	0	9	9	1	18	.187	.225	.241	33	-22	6	.949	-3	98	60	3b61	—	-2.6
Total	14	1461	5430	754	1471	275	84	34	552	290	73	18	.271	.317	.371	108	45	181	.933	40	103	118	3b1390,S35,1b18,2b3/P	—	10.9

BRADSHAW, DALLAS Dallas Carl "Windy"; B11.23.1895 Wolf Creek IL; D12.11.1939 Herrin IL; BL/TR/5´7˝/145; d6.5

YEAR	TM LG	G	AB	R	H	2B	3B	HR	RBI	BB-IB	HP	SO	AVG	OBP	SLG	AOPS	ABR	SB-CS	FA	FR	RNG	THR	GAMES AT POSITION	DL	BFW
1917	Phi A	2	4	0	0	0	0	0	0	0	0	1	.000	.000	.000	-99	-1	0	1.000	0	61	196	/2	—	-0.1

BRADSHAW, GEORGE George Thomas; B9.12.1924 Salisbury NC; D11.4.1994 Hendersonville NC; BR/TR/6´2˝/185; d8.10

YEAR	TM LG	G	AB	R	H	2B	3B	HR	RBI	BB-IB	HP	SO	AVG	OBP	SLG	AOPS	ABR	SB-CS	FA	FR	RNG	THR	GAMES AT POSITION	DL	BFW
1952	Was A	10	23	3	5	2	0	0	6	1	1	2	.217	.280	.304	65	-1	0-0	.917	-2	*83*	*0*	C9	0	-0.3

BRADSHAW, TERRY Terry Leon; B2.3.1969 Franklin VA; BL/TR/6´0˝/(180–195); [StLN90 9/249]; d5.4; Col Norfolk St.

YEAR	TM LG	G	AB	R	H	2B	3B	HR	RBI	BB-IB	HP	SO	AVG	OBP	SLG	AOPS	ABR	SB-CS	FA	FR	RNG	THR	GAMES AT POSITION	DL	BFW
1995	StL N	19	44	6	10	1	1	0	2	2-0	0	10	.227	.261	.295	45	-4	1-2	.952	1	121	202	O10(6/3/1)	0	-0.3
1996	StL N	15	21	4	7	1	0	0	3	3-0	0	2	.333	.417	.381	112	1	0-1	1.000	-1	50	0	O7(4/3/1)	0	-0.1
Total	2	34	65	10	17	2	1	0	5	5-0	0	12	.262	.314	.323	68	-3	1-3	.960	-0	97	135	O17(10/6/2)	0	-0.4

BRADY, BRIAN Brian Phelan; B7.11.1962 Elmhurst NY; BL/TL/5´11˝/185; [CalA84 6/138]; d4.16; Col New York Tech

YEAR	TM LG	G	AB	R	H	2B	3B	HR	RBI	BB-IB	HP	SO	AVG	OBP	SLG	AOPS	ABR	SB-CS	FA	FR	RNG	THR	GAMES AT POSITION	DL	BFW
1989	Cal A	2	2	0	1	1	0	0	1	0-0	0	1	.500	.500	1.000	318	1	0-0	ø	-0	0	0	/rf	0	0.1

BRADY, CLIFF Clifford Francis; B3.6.1897 St.Louis MO; D9.25.1974 Belleville IL; BR/TR/5´5.5˝/140; d8.8

YEAR	TM LG	G	AB	R	H	2B	3B	HR	RBI	BB-IB	HP	SO	AVG	OBP	SLG	AOPS	ABR	SB-CS	FA	FR	RNG	THR	GAMES AT POSITION	DL	BFW
1920	Bos A	53	180	16	41	5	1	0	12	13	1	12	.228	.284	.267	48	-14	0-1	.974	11	124	95	2b53	—	-0.2

BRADY, SPIKE Michael T.; B12.1854 Chicago IL; d9.25

YEAR	TM LG	G	AB	R	H	2B	3B	HR	RBI	BB-IB	HP	SO	AVG	OBP	SLG	AOPS	ABR	SB-CS	FA	FR	RNG	THR	GAMES AT POSITION	DL	BFW
1875	Chi NA	1	4	1	1	0	1	0	0	0	—	0	.250	.250	.750	231	0	0-0	.625	-0	247	0	/cf	—	0.0

BRADY, BOB Robert Jay; B11.8.1922 Lewistown PA; D4.22.1996 Manchester CT; BL/TR/6´1˝/175; d8.24

YEAR	TM LG	G	AB	R	H	2B	3B	HR	RBI	BB-IB	HP	SO	AVG	OBP	SLG	AOPS	ABR	SB-CS	FA	FR	RNG	THR	GAMES AT POSITION	DL	BFW
1946	Bos N	3	5	0	1	0	0	0	0	1	0	1	.200	.333	.200	52	0	0	.857	-0	*47*	*275*	/C	0	0.0
1947	Bos N	1	1	0	0	0	0	0	0	0	0	0	.000	.000	.000	-99	0	0	ø	0	—	—	/H	0	0.0
Total	2	4	6	0	1	0	0	0	0	1	0	1	.167	.286	.167	29	0	0	.857	-0	*47*	*275*	/C	0	0.0

BRADY, STEVE Stephen A.; B7.14.1851 Worcester MA; D11.1.1917 Hartford CT; 5´9.5˝/165; d7.23

YEAR	TM LG	G	AB	R	H	2B	3B	HR	RBI	BB-IB	HP	SO	AVG	OBP	SLG	AOPS	ABR	SB-CS	FA	FR	RNG	THR	GAMES AT POSITION	DL	BFW
1874	Har NA	27	118	19	37	5	1	0	14	2	—	10	.314	.325	.373	117	2	1-2	.662	-9	58	0	3b16,O11(0/5/6)/S	—	-0.6
1875	Was NA	21	91	7	13	0	0	0	3	0	—	4	.143	.143	.143	-0	-9	5-0	.815	-5	107	26	2b18,O2(1/0/1)/C1	—	-1.2
	Har NA	1	4	0	0	0	0	0	0	0	—	1	.000	.000	.000	-95	-1	0-0	1.000	1	454	0	/cf	—	0.0
	Year	22	95	7	13	0	0	0	3	0	—	5	.137	.137	.137	-5	-10	5-0	.815	-4	107	26	2b18,O3(1/1/1)/C1	—	-1.2
1883	NY AA	**97**	432	69	117	12	6	0	—	11	—	—	.271	.289	.326	94	-4	—	.961	3	121	101	1b81,O16R	—	-0.8
1884	†NY AA	**112**	485	102	122	11	3	1	—	21	0	—	.252	.283	.293	90	-5	—	.918	2	124	38	O110R,1b5/2	—	-0.4
1885	NY AA	**108**	434	60	128	14	5	3	58	25	6	—	.295	.342	.371	131	16	—	.879	-5	58	88	O105R,1b4,2b2/3	—	0.9
1886	NY AA	124	466	56	112	8	5	0	39	35	3	—	.240	.298	.279	88	-4	16	.836	-4	123	27	O123R/1	—	-0.8
Total	2NA	49	213	26	50	5	1	0	17	2	—	15	.235	.242	.268	68	-8	6-2	.815	-13	107	26	2b18,3b16,O14(1/6/7)/1CS	—	-1.8
Total	4	441	1817	287	479	45	19	4	97	92	9	0	.264	.302	.316	100	3	16	.877	-4	102	63	O354R,1b91,2b3/3	—	-1.1

BRADY, DOUG Stephen Douglas; B11.23.1969 Jacksonville IL; BB/TR/5´11˝/165; [ChiA91 12/332]; d9.5; Col Liberty

YEAR	TM LG	G	AB	R	H	2B	3B	HR	RBI	BB-IB	HP	SO	AVG	OBP	SLG	AOPS	ABR	SB-CS	FA	FR	RNG	THR	GAMES AT POSITION	DL	BFW
1995	Chi A	12	21	4	4	1	0	0	3	2-0	0	4	.190	.261	.238	32	-2	0-1	1.000	3	141	108	2b6,D3	0	0.1

BRAGAN, BOBBY Robert Randall "Nig"; B10.30.1917 Birmingham AL; BR/TR/5´10.5˝/175; d4.16; Mil 1945–46; M7/C2

YEAR	TM LG	G	AB	R	H	2B	3B	HR	RBI	BB-IB	HP	SO	AVG	OBP	SLG	AOPS	ABR	SB-CS	FA	FR	RNG	THR	GAMES AT POSITION	DL	BFW
1940	Phi N	132	474	36	105	14	1	7	44	28	0	34	.222	.265	.300	58	-29	2	.936	4	105	100	S132,3b2	—	-1.5
1941	Phi N	154	557	37	140	19	3	4	69	26	0	29	.251	.285	.318	72	-23	7	.944	-7	95	88	S154,2b2/3	0	-2.0
1942	Phi N	109	335	17	73	12	2	2	15	20	1	21	.218	.264	.284	63	-17	0	.939	8	108	106	S78,C22,2b4,3b3	0	-0.2
1943	Bro N	74	220	17	58	7	2	2	24	15	0	16	.264	.311	.341	88	-4	0	.973	0	*97*	*114*	C57,3b12	0	-0.1
1944	Bro N	94	266	26	71	8	4	0	17	13	1	14	.267	.304	.327	79	-8	2	.954	-3	91	64	S51,C35,3b6/2	0	-0.7
1947	†Bro N	25	36	3	7	2	0	0	3	7	0	3	.194	.326	.250	53	-2	1	1.000	2	*88*	*94*	C21	0	0.1
1948	Bro N	9	12	0	2	0	0	0	0	1	0	0	.167	.231	.167	9	-2	0	1.000	-0	*70*	*214*	C5	0	-0.2
Total	7	597	1900	136	456	62	12	15	172	110	2	117	.240	.282	.309	69	-85	12	.941	4	100	93	S415,C140,3b24,2b7	0	-4.6

YEAR	TM LG	G	AB	R	H	2B	3B	HR	RBI	BB-IB	HP	SO	AVG	OBP	SLG	AOPS	ABR	SB-CS	FA	FR	RNG	THR	GAMES AT POSITION	DL	BFW
Bragg, Darren	Darren William; B9.7.1969 Waterbury CT; BL/TR/5´9˝/180; [SeaA91 22/578]; d4.12; Col Georgia Tech																								
1994	Sea A	8	19	4	3	1	0	0	2	2-1	0	5	.158	.238	.211	17	-2	0-0	1.000	-0	47	0	O3L,D3	0	-0.3
1995	Sea A	52	145	20	34	5	1	3	12	18-1	4	37	.234	.331	.345	77	-5	9-0	.989	6	112	280	O47(32/0/17),D2	0	0.1
1996	Sea A	69	195	36	53	12	1	7	25	33-4	2	35	.272	.376	.451	109	4	8-5	.992	4	106	186	O63(48/5/16)	0	0.6
	Bos A	58	222	38	56	14	1	3	22	36-2	2	39	.252	.357	.365	83	-5	6-4	.986	2	100	140	O58(7/47/29)	0	-0.3
	Year	127	417	74	109	26	2	10	47	69-6	4	74	.261	.366	.405	95	-1	14-9	.989	6	103	162	O121(55/52/45)	0	0.3
1997	Bos A	153	513	65	132	35	2	9	57	61-5	3	102	.257	.337	.386	87	-8	10-6	.987	6	105	142	O150(1/118/41)/3	0	-0.3
1998	†Bos A	129	409	51	114	29	3	8	57	42-0	6	99	.279	.351	.423	99	0	5-3	**.996**	-3	97	75	O124(7/12/112),D4	0	-0.7
1999	StL N	93	273	38	71	12	1	6	26	44-1	3	67	.260	.369	.377	88	-4	3-0	.982	0	95	157	O88(22/43/33)	62	-0.4
2000	Col N	71	149	16	33	7	1	3	21	17-1	0	41	.221	.296	.342	50	-11	4-1	1.000	-3	84	0	O43(34/0/9)	0	-1.4
2001	NY N	18	57	4	15	6	0	0	5	4-0	1	23	.263	.323	.368	84	-1	3-2	1.000	-1	78	114	O16(8/2/10)	0	-0.3
	NY A	5	4	1	1	1	0	0	0	0-0	0	1	.250	.250	.500	90	0	0-0	1.000	0	118	0	O3R	0	0.0
2002	†Atl N	109	212	34	57	15	2	3	15	24-0	2	52	.269	.347	.401	97	0	5-2	.971	-1	100	67	O63(12/18/36),D3	0	-0.3
2003	†Atl N	104	162	21	39	5	1	0	9	13-1	2	38	.241	.305	.284	55	-11	2-1	.988	-4	86	36	O78(29/21/35)	0	-1.6
2004	SD N	9	7	2	1	0	0	0	0	2-0	0	2	.143	.333	.143	31	-1	0-0	ø	0	—	—	/H	0	-0.1
	Cin N	38	94	11	18	3	1	4	9	8-1	0	29	.191	.255	.372	61	-6	1-0	.984	3	126	164	O26(2/14/11)	0	-0.3
	Year	47	101	13	19	3	1	4	9	10-1	0	31	.188	.261	.356	59	-7	1-0	.984	3	126	164	O26(2/14/11)	0	-0.4
Total	11	916	2461	341	627	145	14	46	260	304-17	25	570	.255	.340	.381	84	-50	56-24	.988	9	100	124	O762(205/280/352),D12/3	62	-5.3
Braggs, Glenn	Glenn Erick; B10.17.1962 San Bernardino CA; BR/TR/6´3˝/(210–220); [MilA83 2/54]; d7.18; Col Hawaii–Manoa																								
1986	Mil A	58	215	19	51	8	2	4	18	11-0	1	47	.237	.274	.349	67	-11	1-1	.910	-0	103	141	O56(51/3/5),D2	0	-1.3
1987	Mil A	132	505	67	136	28	7	13	77	47-7	4	96	.269	.332	.430	98	-1	12-5	.972	10	**128**	71	O123R,D8	0	0.3
1988	Mil A	72	272	30	71	14	0	10	42	14-0	5	60	.261	.307	.423	102	0	6-4	.978	1	114	29	O54R,D18	93	-0.1
1989	Mil A	144	514	77	127	12	3	15	66	42-4	4	111	.247	.305	.370	91	-8	17-5	.972	-1	100	77	O132(127/0/9),D13	0	-1.2
1990	Mil A	37	113	17	28	5	0	3	13	12-2	3	21	.248	.328	.372	98	0	5-3	.965	3	131	48	O32(13/0/20),D2	0	0.2
	†Cin N	72	201	22	60	9	1	6	28	26-1	3	43	.299	.385	.443	123	7	3-4	.968	6	102	266	O60(26/0/35)	0	1.1
1991	Cin N	85	250	36	65	10	0	11	39	23-3	2	46	.260	.323	.432	107	2	11-3	.966	1	112	52	O74(55/0/27)	42	0.3
1992	Cin N	92	266	40	63	16	3	8	38	36-5	2	48	.237	.330	.410	106	3	3-1	.946	-7	78	85	O79(56/0/29)	15	-0.6
Total	7	692	2336	308	601	102	16	70	321	211-22	24	472	.257	.322	.405	98	-8	58-26	.963	13	108	92	O610(328/3/302),D43	150	-1.3
Brain, Dave	David Leonard; B1.24.1879 Hereford, England; D5.25.1959 Los Angeles CA; BR/TR/5´10˝/170; d4.24; OF(26/15/5)																								
1901	Chi A	5	20	2	7	1	0	0	5	1	0	—	.350	.381	.400	120	1	0	.909	0	96	189	2b5	—	0.1
1903	StL N	119	464	44	107	8	15	1	60	25	0	—	.231	.270	.319	70	-22	21	.908	7	104	121	S72,3b46	—	-1.1
1904	StL N	127	488	57	130	24	12	7	72	17	0	—	.266	.291	.408	120	8	18	.927	-3	100	108	S59,3b30,O19(7/11/1),2b13,1b4	—	0.8
1905	StL N	44	158	11	36	4	5	1	17	8	1	—	.228	.269	.335	82	-4	4	.910	-7	83	36	S29,3b6,O6(0/4/2)	—	-1.1
	Pit N	85	307	31	79	17	6	3	46	15	2	—	.257	.296	.381	99	-2	8	.923	6	116	152	3b78,S4	—	0.7
	Year	129	465	42	115	21	11	4	63	23	3	—	.247	.287	.366	93	-6	12	.929	-1	117	141	3b84,S33,O6(0/4/2)	—	-0.4
1906	Bos N	139	525	43	131	19	5	5	45	29	3	—	.250	.293	.333	98	-4	11	.917	25	116	**152**	3b139	—	2.8
1907	Bos N	133	509	60	142	24	9	**10**	56	29	5	—	.279	.324	.420	134	17	10	.916	24	**121**	**148**	3b130,O3L	—	4.8
1908	Cin N	16	55	4	6	0	0	0	1	8	0	—	.109	.222	.109	7	-6	0	.947	-1	0	0	O16L	—	-0.8
	NY N	11	17	2	3	0	0	0	1	2	0	—	.176	.263	.176	39	-1	1	.867	-2	92	0	2b3,O3R,3b2/S	—	-0.4
	Year	27	72	6	9	0	0	0	2	10	0	—	.125	.232	.125	14	-7	1	.947	-3	0	0	O19(16/0/2),2b3,3b2/S	—	-1.2
Total	7	679	2543	254	641	97	52	27	303	134	11	—	.252	.292	.363	101	-13	73	.913	50	116	142	3b431,S165,O47L,2b21,1b4	—	5.8
Brainard, Fred	Frederick F.; B2.17.1892 Champaign IL; D4.17.1959 Galveston TX; BR/TR/6´0˝/176; d10.6; Col Illinois																								
1914	NY N	2	5	1	1	0	0	0	0	1	0	0	.200	.333	.200	62	0	0	.923	0	94	130	2b2	—	0.0
1915	NY N	91	249	31	50	7	2	1	21	21	1	44	.201	.266	.257	62	-12	6-7	.988	4	149	141	1b43,3b15,S9/2cf	—	-1.0
1916	NY N	2	7	0	0	0	0	0	0	0	0	0	.000	.000	.000	-99	-2	0	.625	-1	46	0	3b2	—	-0.4
Total	3	95	261	32	51	7	2	1	21	22	1	44	.195	.261	.249	58	-14	6-7	.988	3	149	141	1b43,3b17,S9,2b3/cf	—	-1.4
Bramhall, Art	Arthur Washington; B2.22.1909 Oak Park IL; D9.4.1985 Madison WI; BR/TR/5´11˝/170; d4.18; Col DePaul																								
1935	Phi N	2	1	0	0	0	0	0	0	0	0	0	.000	.000	.000	-91	0	0	1.000	0	146	0	/S3	—	0.0
Brancato, Al	Albert "Bronk"; B5.29.1919 Philadelphia PA; BR/TR/5´9.5˝/188; d9.7; Mil 1942–45																								
1939	Phi A	21	68	12	14	5	0	1	8	8	1	4	.206	.299	.324	60	-4	1-0	.939	-1	106	48	3b20/S	—	-0.4
1940	Phi A	107	298	42	57	11	2	1	23	28	2	36	.191	.265	.252	36	-29	3-1	.949	-3	96	85	S80,3b25	—	-2.5
1941	Phi A	144	530	60	124	20	9	2	49	59	0	49	.234	.311	.317	68	-25	1-5	.915	-17	101	88	S139,3b7	0	-3.3
1945	Phi A	10	34	3	4	1	0	0	0	1	0	3	.118	.143	.147	-16	-5	0-0	.959	-1	88	86	S10	0	-0.6
Total	4	282	930	117	199	37	11	4	80	96	3	92	.214	.290	.290	54	-63	5-6	.927	-21	99	87	S230,3b52	0	-6.8
Brand, Ron	Ronald George; B1.13.1940 Los Angeles CA; BR/TR/5´8˝/(164–172); d5.26; Col Los Angeles Valley (CA) JC																								
1963	Pit N	46	66	8	19	2	0	1	7	10-0	1	11	.288	.390	.364	118	2	0-0	.968	5	115	121	C33,2b2,3b2	0	0.8
1965	Hou N	117	391	27	92	6	3	2	37	19-2	6	34	.235	.281	.281	63	-20	10-5	.988	-6	96	87	C102,3b6,O5L	0	-2.3
1966	Hou N	56	123	12	30	2	0	0	10	9-3	2	13	.244	.301	.260	64	-6	0-2	.986	1	100	72	C25,2b9,O3L/3	0	-0.4
1967	Hou N	84	215	22	52	8	1	0	18	23-7	2	17	.242	.321	.288	78	-5	4-0	.998	-2	94	119	C67/2lf	21	-0.4
1968	Hou N	43	81	7	13	2	0	0	4	9-0	2	11	.160	.261	.185	36	-6	1-1	1.000	3	95	51	C29/3rf	0	-0.2
1969	Mon N	103	287	19	74	12	0	0	20	30-4	1	19	.258	.327	.300	77	-8	2-3	.985	-7	75	118	C84,O2(1/1/0)	0	-1.3
1970	Mon N	72	126	10	30	2	3	0	9	9-0	0	16	.238	.287	.302	58	-8	2-1	.952	1	117	120	S19,3b12,C9,O5(1/3/1),2b3	0	-0.5
1971	Mon N	47	56	3	12	0	0	0	1	3-0	0	5	.214	.254	.214	33	-5	1-1	.957	5	126	135	S22,3b4,O4(3/1/0)/C2	0	0.1
Total	8	568	1345	108	322	34	7	3	106	112-16	14	126	.239	.303	.282	68	-56	20-13	.988	0	91	100	C350,S41,3b26,021(14/5/2),2b16	21	-4.2
Brandt, Jackie	John George; B4.28.1934 Omaha NE; BR/TR/5´11˝/(165–185); d4.21; Mil 1957–58																								
1956	StL N	27	42	9	12	3	0	1	3	4-0	1	5	.286	.362	.429	111	1	0-1	1.000	1	115	81	O26(3/3/20)	0	0.1
	NY N	98	351	45	105	16	8	11	47	17-2	0	31	.299	.330	.484	116	6	3-4	.989	1	98	130	O96(86/3/26)	0	0.2
	Year	125	393	54	117	19	8	12	50	21-2	1	36	.298	.333	.478	116	7	3-5	**.990**	2	100	123	O122(89/6/46)	0	0.3
1958	SF N	18	52	7	13	1	0	0	3	6-0	0	5	.250	.328	.269	62	-3	1-0	1.000	-0	107	0	O14(11/1/3)	0	-0.4
1959	SF N	137	429	63	116	16	5	12	57	35-2	0	69	.270	.324	.415	98	-3	11-4	.984	2	102	141	O116(111/4/6),3b18,1b3/2	0	-0.5
1960	Bal A	145	511	73	130	24	6	15	65	47-3	3	69	.254	.317	.413	98	-3	5-3	.983	0	101	127	O142(17/102/51),3b2/1	0	-0.9
1961	Bal A★	139	516	93	153	18	5	16	72	62-0	1	51	.297	.371	.444	122	16	10-2	.974	-7	95	74	O136(21/120/34)/3	0	0.5
1962	Bal A	143	505	76	129	29	5	19	75	55-2	4	64	.255	.330	.446	115	10	9-3	.976	1	104	135	O138(0/109/30),3b2	0	0.7
1963	Bal A	142	451	49	112	15	5	15	61	34-3	0	85	.248	.298	.404	99	-2	4-5	.986	2	105	114	O134(30/92/39)/3	0	-0.7
1964	Bal A	137	523	66	127	25	1	13	47	45-5	3	104	.243	.305	.369	87	-9	1-4	.981	13	116	156	O134(10/131/0)	0	-0.2
1965	Bal A	96	243	35	59	17	0	8	24	21-0	0	40	.243	.303	.412	99	0	1-2	.961	4	111	167	O84(39/37/22)	0	0.0
1966	Phi N	82	164	16	41	6	1	1	15	17-2	0	36	.250	.317	.317	78	-4	0-2	.988	-4	82	95	O71(17/49/6)	0	-1.1
1967	Phi N	16	19	1	2	1	0	0	1	0-0	0	6	.105	.105	.158	-25	-3	0-0	1.000	-0	53	0	O3L	0	-0.4
	Hou N	41	89	7	21	4	1	1	15	8-1	0	9	.236	.296	.337	85	-2	0-0	.991	-2	76	46	1b14,O6L/3	0	-0.5
	Year	57	108	8	23	5	1	1	16	8-1	0	15	.213	.265	.306	65	-5	0-0	.991	-2	76	46	1b14,O9L/3	0	-0.9
Total	11	1221	3895	540	1020	175	37	112	485	351-20	12	574	.262	.323	.412	102	4	45-30	.980	11	103	123	O1100(354/651/237),3b25,1b18/2	0	-3.2
Brannan, Otis	Otis Owen; B3.13.1899 Greenbrier AR; D6.6.1967 Little Rock AR; BL/TR/5´9˝/160; d4.11; Col Arkansas St.																								
1928	StL A	135	483	68	118	18	3	10	66	60	4	19	.244	.333	.356	79	-15	3-9	.964	-6	101	98	2b135	—	-1.9
1929	StL A	23	51	4	15	1	0	1	8	4	0	4	.294	.345	.373	82	-1	0-0	.975	0	105	76	2b19	—	-0.1
Total	2	158	534	72	133	19	3	11	74	64	4	23	.249	.334	.358	79	-16	3-9	.966	-6	101	96	2b154	—	-2.0
Brannock, Mike	Michael J.; B10.25.1851 Douglas MA; D10.7.1881 Chicago IL; 5´8˝/162; d10.21																								
1871	Chi NA	3	14	2	1	0	0	0	0	0	—	0	.071	.071	.071	-53	-3	0-0	.500	-2	40	0	3b3	—	-0.3
1875	Chi NA	2	9	2	1	0	0	0	0	0	—	0	.111	.111	.111	-22	-1	2-0	.500	-1	83	0	3b2	—	-0.2
Total	2NA	5	23	4	2	0	0	0	0	0	—	0	.087	.087	.087	-43	-4	2-0	.500	-3	59	0	3b5	—	-0.5
Branom, Dud	Edgar Dudley; B11.30.1897 Sulphur Springs TX; D2.4.1980 Sun City AZ; BL/TL/6´1˝/190; d4.12																								
1927	Phi A	30	94	8	22	1	0	0	13	2	0	5	.234	.250	.245	27	-10	2-1	.973	-0	108	105	1b26	—	-1.2

YEAR	TM LG	G	AB	R	H	2B	3B	HR	RBI	BB-IB	HP	SO	AVG	OBP	SLG	AOPS	ABR	SB-CS	FA	FR	RNG	THR	GAMES AT POSITION	DL	BFW
BRANSFIELD, KITTY	William Edward; B1.7.1875 Worcester MA; D5.1.1947 Worcester MA; BR/TR/5´11˝/207; d8.22; U1																								
1898	Bos N	5	9	2	2	0	1	0	1	0	0	—	.222	.222	.444	85	0	0	.889	-1	97	*0*	C4/1	—	-0.1
1901	Pit N	139	566	92	167	26	16	0	91	29	5	—	.295	.335	.398	109	5	23	.981	-10	66	117	1b139	—	-0.8
1902	Pit N	102	413	49	126	21	8	0	69	17	2	—	.305	.336	.395	121	9	23	.984	-7	69	82	1b101	—	0.0
1903	†Pit N	127	505	69	134	23	7	2	57	33	3	—	.265	.314	.350	87	-10	13	.981	5	117	**136**	1b127	—	-0.7
1904	Pit N	139	520	47	116	17	9	0	60	22	3	—	.223	.259	.290	68	-21	11	.981	-2	97	**121**	1b139	—	-2.8
1905	Phi N	151	580	55	150	23	9	3	76	27	2	—	.259	.294	.345	93	-7	27	.985	-2	94	99	1b151	—	-1.2
1906	Phi N	140	524	47	144	28	5	1	60	16	3	—	.275	.300	.353	104	0	12	.980	-1	100	86	1b139	—	-0.5
1907	Phi N	94	348	25	81	15	2	0	38	14	0	—	.233	.262	.287	73	-12	8	.978	-3	93	101	1b92	—	-1.8
1908	Phi N	144	527	53	160	25	7	3	71	23	2	—	.304	.335	.395	128	15	30	.986	-1	98	111	1b143	—	1.3
1909	Phi N	140	527	47	154	27	6	1	59	18	3	—	.292	.319	.372	114	6	17	**.989**	7	**117**	108	1b138	—	1.1
1910	Phi N	123	427	39	102	17	4	3	52	20	1	34	.239	.275	.319	71	-18	10	.982	-4	83	**130**	1b110	—	-2.6
1911	Phi N	23	43	4	11	1	1	0	3	0	0	5	.256	.256	.326	61	-3	1	.987	0	95	47	1b8	—	-0.3
	Chi N	3	10	0	4	2	0	0	0	2	0	2	.400	.500	.600	207	2	0	1.000	-0	62	398	1b3	—	0.1
	Year	26	53	4	15	3	1	0	3	2	0	7	.283	.309	.377	91	-1	1	.991	-0	86	143	1b11	—	-0.2
Total	12	1330	4999	529	1351	225	75	13	637	221	24	41	.270	.304	.353	97	-34	175	.983	-18	94	110	1b1291,C4	—	-8.3
BRANSON, JEFF	Jeffery Glenn; B1.26.1967 Waynesboro MS; BL/TR/6´0˝/180; [CinN88 2/45]; d4.12; Col West Alabama																								
1992	Cin N	72	115	12	34	7	1	0	15	5-2	0	16	.296	.322	.374	95	-1	0-1	.946	2	103	161	2b33,3b8/S	0	0.1
1993	Cin N	125	381	40	92	15	1	3	22	19-2	0	73	.241	.275	.310	57	-24	4-1	.978	0	96	94	S59,2b45,3b14/1	0	-1.8
1994	Cin N	58	109	18	31	4	1	6	16	5-2	0	16	.284	.316	.505	110	1	0-0	.980	-5	69	57	2b19,3b18,S8,1b2	0	-0.4
1995	†Cin N	122	331	43	86	18	2	12	45	44-14	2	69	.260	.345	.435	104	3	2-1	.971	13	107	**191**	3b98,S32,2b6/1	0	1.7
1996	Cin N	129	311	34	76	16	4	9	37	31-4	1	67	.244	.312	.408	87	-6	2-0	.932	-4	102	157	3b64,S38,2b31	0	-0.7
1997	Cin N	65	98	9	15	3	1	1	5	7-1	0	23	.153	.210	.235	16	-13	1-0	.971	-0	95	202	3b27,2b14,S11	0	-1.2
	†Cle A	29	72	5	19	4	0	2	7	7-0	1	17	.264	.329	.403	89	-1	0-2	.986	-1	104	91	2b19,3b6,S2/D	0	-0.1
1998	†Cle A	63	100	6	20	4	1	1	9	3-0	0	21	.200	.221	.290	31	-11	0-0	.960	0	88	155	2b31,3b20,1b3,S2	30	-0.9
2000	LA N	18	17	3	4	1	0	0	0	1-0	0	6	.235	.278	.294	47	-1	0-0	1.000	-1	68	0	S7,2b3,3b3	0	-0.2
2001	LA N	13	21	3	6	0	0	0	0	0-0	0	4	.286	.286	.286	52	-2	0-0	1.000	-1	96	93	2b6,S2/3	0	-0.2
Total	9	694	1555	173	383	72	11	34	156	122-25	4	312	.246	.300	.372	77	-55	9-5	.957	2	103	161	3b259,2b207,S162,1b7/D	30	-3.7
BRANT, MARSHALL	Marshall Lee; B9.17.1955 Garberville CA; BR/TR/6´5˝/185; [NYN75*4/73]; d10.1; Col Sonoma St.																								
1980	NY A	3	6	0	0	0	0	0	0	0-0	0	3	.000	.000	.000	-99	-2	0-0	1.000	0	135	181	1b2/D	0	-0.2
1983	Oak A	5	14	2	2	0	0	0	2	0-0	0	3	.143	.143	.143	-22	-2	0-0	.905	-1	0	161	1b3/D	0	-0.4
Total	2	8	20	2	2	0	0	0	2	0-0	0	6	.100	.100	.100	-47	-4	0-0	.935	-1	44	167	1b5,D2	0	-0.6
BRANTLEY, MICKEY	Michael Charles; B6.17.1961 Catskill NY; BR/TR/5´10˝/180; [SeaA83 2/35]; d8.9; C3; Col Coastal Carolina; [DL 1990 Sea A 6]																								
1986	Sea A	27	102	12	20	3	2	3	7	10-0	0	21	.196	.268	.353	66	-5	1-1	.983	-1	81	222	O25(1/25/0)	0	-0.7
1987	Sea A	92	351	52	106	23	2	14	54	24-0	0	44	.302	.344	.499	114	7	13-4	.982	-5	89	68	O82(6/51/35),D8	46	0.1
1988	Sea A	149	577	76	152	25	4	15	56	26-0	2	64	.263	.296	.399	89	-10	18-7	.982	-0	103	65	O147(118/49/4),D2	0	-1.3
1989	Sea A	34	108	14	17	5	0	0	8	7-0	0	7	.157	.207	.204	16	-12	2-2	1.000	1	109	68	O23(12/0/11),D7	0	-1.3
Total	4	302	1138	154	295	56	8	32	125	67-0	2	136	.259	.300	.407	89	-20	34-14	.984	-6	97	81	O277(137/125/50),D17	52	-3.2
BRANYAN, RUSSELL	Russell Oles; B12.19.1975 Warner Robins GA; BL/TR/6´3˝/195; [CleA94 7/185]; d9.26																								
1998	Cle A	1	4	0	0	0	0	0	0	0-0	0	2	.000	.000	.000	-96	-1	0-0	1.000	-0	75	0	/3	0	-0.1
1999	Cle A	11	38	4	8	2	0	1	6	3-0	1	19	.211	.286	.342	56	-3	0-0	.960	3	159	0	3b8,D3	0	0.0
2000	Cle A	67	193	32	46	7	2	16	38	22-1	4	76	.238	.327	.544	112	2	0-0	.968	1	114	123	O33(18/0/15),D23/3	0	0.1
2001	†Cle A	113	315	48	73	16	2	20	54	38-1	3	132	.232	.316	.486	104	1	1-1	.930	-2	95	77	3b72,O33(31/0/2),D7	0	-0.1
2002	Cle A	50	161	16	33	4	0	8	17	17-0	0	65	.205	.278	.379	72	-7	1-2	.986	-2	87	180	O42L,3b8/D	0	-1.0
	Cin N	84	217	34	53	9	1	16	39	34-3	2	86	.244	.349	.516	121	6	3-1	.951	-0	93	235	O25L,1b18,3b16,D4	0	0.4
2003	Cin N	74	176	22	38	12	0	9	26	27-0	1	69	.216	.322	.438	101	0	0-0	.968	6	153	153	3b20,O17L,1b14/D	75	0.5
2004	Mil N	51	158	21	37	11	1	11	27	20-0	2	68	.234	.324	.525	114	3	1-0	.962	5	114	96	3b44,1b2	0	0.8
2005	Mil N	85	202	23	52	11	0	12	31	39-10	0	80	.257	.378	.490	125	8	1-0	.946	-7	77	104	3b59,1b5,O3L/D	32	0.1
2006	TB A	64	169	23	34	10	0	12	27	19-0	2	62	.201	.286	.473	94	-2	2-0	.969	0	105	191	O55(1/0/54),3b5,1b2	0	-0.3
	†SD N	27	72	14	21	1	0	6	9	15-1	1	27	.292	.416	.556	155	7	0-0	.933	-4	75	86	3b26	0	0.2
Total	9	627	1705	237	395	83	6	111	274	234-16	16	686	.232	.327	.483	107	14	9-4	.940	1	97	90	3b260,O208(137/0/71),1b41,D40	107	0.6
BRASHEAR, ROY	Roy Parks; B1.3.1874 Ashtabula OH; D4.20.1951 Los Angeles CA; BR/TR/5´11˝/190; d4.25; b–Kitty																								
1902	StL N	110	388	36	107	8	2	1	40	32	1	—	.276	.333	.314	104	2	9	.980	-5	92	120	1b67,2b21,O16(1/7/8),S3	—	-0.4
1903	Phi N	20	75	9	17	3	0	0	4	6	0	—	.227	.284	.267	59	-4	2	.918	-3	84	124	2b18,1b2	—	-0.7
Total	2	130	463	45	124	11	2	1	44	38	1	—	.268	.325	.307	96	-2	11	.978	-8	92	119	1b69,2b39,O16(1/7/8),S3	—	-1.1
BRATCHER, JOE	Joseph Warlick "Goobers"; B7.22.1898 Grand Saline TX; D10.13.1977 Fort Worth TX; BL/TR/5´8.5˝/140; d8.26																								
1924	StL N	4	1	1	0	0	0	0	0	0	0	0	.000	.000	.000	-99	0	0-0	ø	-0	0	0	/cf	—	0.0
BRATSCHI, FRED	Frederick Oscar "Fritz"; B1.16.1892 Alliance OH; D1.10.1962 Massillon OH; BR/TR/5´10˝/170; d7.24																								
1921	Chi A	16	28	0	8	1	0	0	3	0	0	2	.286	.286	.321	55	-2	0-0	1.000	1	88	350	O5(1/0/4)	—	-0.1
1926	Bos A	72	167	12	46	10	1	0	19	14	1	15	.275	.335	.347	81	-5	0-1	.949	-5	80	30	O37(29/0/8)	—	-1.2
1927	Bos A	1	1	0	0	0	0	0	0	0	0	0	.000	.000	.000	-99	0	0-0	ø	0	—	—	/H	—	0.0
Total	3	89	196	12	54	11	1	0	22	14	1	17	.276	.327	.342	76	-7	0-1	.956	-4	81	66	O42(30/0/12)	—	-1.3
BRAUN, STEVE	Stephen Russell; B5.8.1948 Trenton NJ; BL/TR/5´10˝/(175–180); [MinA66 10/200]; d4.6; C1; OF(465/0/35)																								
1971	Min A	128	343	51	87	12	2	5	35	48-4	5	50	.254	.350	.344	95	0	8-3	.933	-10	81	54	3b73,2b28,S10,O2L	0	-0.8
1972	Min A	121	402	40	116	21	0	2	50	45-1	2	38	.289	.360	.356	109	7	4-5	.970	-10	100	103	3b74,2b20,S11,O9(8/0/1)	0	-0.3
1973	Min A	115	361	46	102	28	5	6	42	74-8	3	48	.283	.408	.438	133	20	4-3	.941	-7	91	114	3b102,O6L	0	1.2
1974	Min A	129	453	53	127	12	1	8	40	56-4	2	51	.280	.361	.364	106	5	4-4	.964	2	89	143	O108L,3b17	0	0.1
1975	Min A	136	453	70	137	18	3	11	45	66-5	1	55	.302	.389	.426	130	21	0-2	.971	-2	96	84	O106L,1b9,3b2/2D	0	1.2
1976	Min A	122	417	73	120	12	3	3	61	67-2	1	43	.288	.384	.353	116	12	12-4	.971	2	111	203	D71,O32(30/0/3),3b16	0	1.3
1977	Sea A	139	451	51	106	19	1	5	31	80-2	2	59	.235	.351	.315	84	-6	8-3	.975	4	98	159	O100L,D32/3	0	-0.7
1978	Sea A	32	74	11	17	4	0	3	15	9-1	0	5	.230	.310	.405	101	0	1-0	1.000	-0	81	0	D14,O4(2/0/2)	0	-0.1
	†KC A	64	137	16	36	10	1	0	14	28-1	0	16	.263	.386	.350	106	3	3-2	.964	-2	108	63	O33L,3b11	0	0.0
	Year	96	211	27	53	14	1	3	29	37-2	0	21	.251	.360	.370	104	3	4-2	.967	-2	105	56	O37(35/0/2),D14,3b11	0	-0.1
1979	KC A	58	116	15	31	2	0	4	10	22-2	0	11	.267	.384	.388	106	2	0-0	1.000	1	85	353	O18L,D11,3b2	34	0.2
1980	KC A	14	23	0	1	0	0	0	1	2-0	0	2	.043	.120	.043	-52	-5	0-0	1.000	-1	27	0	O5(3/0/2)/D	0	-0.6
	Tor A	37	55	4	15	2	0	1	9	8-1	0	5	.273	.365	.364	96	0	0-0	1.000	0	437	0	D13/3	0	0.0
	Year	51	78	4	16	2	0	1	10	10-1	0	7	.205	.295	.269	54	-5	0-0	1.000	-1	27	0	D14,O5(3/0/2)/3	0	-0.6
1981	StL N	44	46	9	9	2	1	0	2	15-0	0	7	.196	.393	.283	90	0	1-0	1.000	1	114	346	O12(6/0/6)/3	0	0.2
1982	†StL N	58	62	6	17	4	0	0	4	11-0	0	10	.274	.384	.339	101	1	0-0	1.000	-2	62	0	O8(6/0/2),3b5	15	-0.1
1983	StL N	78	92	8	25	2	1	3	7	21-0	0	7	.272	.404	.413	127	4	0-1	1.000	0	84	0	O22(18/0/5),3b4	0	0.4
1984	StL N	86	98	6	27	3	1	0	16	17-0	0	17	.276	.383	.327	103	1	0-0	1.000	-2	48	123	O19(12/0/7)/3	0	-0.1
1985	†StL N	64	67	7	16	4	0	1	6	10-1	1	9	.239	.342	.343	94	0	0-0	1.000	1	107	205	O14(7/0/7)	0	0.0
Total	15	1425	3650	466	989	155	19	52	388	579-32	17	433	.271	.371	.367	108	65	45-27	.973	-23	94	136	O498L,3b310,D151,2b49,S21,1b9	49	1.9
BRAVO, ANGEL	Angel Alfonso (Urdaneta); B8.4.1942 Maracaibo, Zulia, Venez; BL/TL/5´8˝/(150–155); d6.6																								
1969	Chi A	27	90	10	26	4	2	1	3	3-0	1	5	.289	.319	.411	98	-1	2-0	.978	-2	90	0	O25(2/24/3)	0	-0.3
1970	†Cin N	65	65	10	18	1	1	0	3	9-0	0	13	.277	.365	.323	85	-1	0-1	.947	0	100	204	O22(5/12/5)	0	-0.1
1971	Cin N	5	5	0	1	0	0	0	0	0-0	0	1	.200	.200	.200	14	-1	0-0	ø	0	—	—	/H	0	-0.1
	SD N	52	58	6	9	2	0	0	6	8-1	1	12	.155	.265	.190	34	-5	0-1	.833	-2	41	0	O9(5/3/1)	0	-0.8
	Year	57	63	6	10	2	0	0	6	8-1	1	13	.159	.260	.190	32	-5	0-1	.833	-2	41	0	O9(5/3/1)	0	-0.9
Total	3	149	218	26	54	7	3	1	12	20-1	2	31	.248	.315	.321	77	-8	2-2	.957	-4	84	46	O56(12/39/9)	0	-1.3
BRAY, BUSTER	Clarence Wilbur; B4.1.1913 Birmingham AL; D9.4.1982 Evansville IN; BL/TL/6´0˝/170; d4.18																								
1941	Bos N	4	11	2	1	1	0	0	1	1	0	2	.091	.167	.182	-2	-2	0	1.000	-0	98	0	O3C	0	-0.2
BRAZELL, CRAIG	Craig Walter; B5.10.1980 Montgomery AL; BL/TR/6´3˝/210; [NYN98 5/154]; d8.17																								
2004	NY N	24	34	3	9	2	0	1	3	1-0	0	7	.265	.286	.412	79	-1	0-0	.974	0	158	30	1b7	0	-0.1

YEAR	TM LG	G	AB	R	H	2B	3B	HR	RBI	BB-IB	HP	SO	AVG	OBP	SLG	AOPS	ABR	SB-CS	FA	FR	RNG	THR	GAMES AT POSITION	DL	BFW
Brazill, Frank	Frank Leo; B8.11.1899 Spangler PA; D11.3.1976 Oakland CA; BL/TR/5´11.5˝/175; d4.13																								
1921	Phi A	66	177	17	48	3	1	0	19	23	2	21	.271	.361	.299	70	-7	2-4	.984	-2	98	114	1b36,3b9	—	-1.1
1922	Phi A	6	13	0	1	0	0	0	1	0	0	1	.077	.077	.077	-58	-3	0-0	.750	-1	50	0	3b2	—	-0.4
Total	2	72	190	17	49	3	1	0	20	23	2	22	.258	.344	.284	62	-10	2-4	.984	-4	98	114	1b36,3b11	—	-1.5
Bream, Sid	Sidney Eugene; B8.3.1960 Carlisle PA; BL/TL/6´4˝/(215–220); [LAN81 2/48]; d9.1; Col Liberty																								
1983	LA N	15	11	0	2	0	0	0	2	2-0	0	2	.182	.308	.182	39	-1	0-0	1.000	-0	0	116	1b4	0	-0.1
1984	LA N	27	49	2	9	3	0	0	6	6-2	0	9	.184	.263	.245	46	-3	1-0	1.000	2	153	102	1b14	0	-0.2
1985	LA N	24	53	4	7	0	0	3	6	7-3	0	10	.132	.230	.302	50	-4	0-0	.994	2	151	72	1b16	0	-0.3
	Pit N	26	95	14	27	7	0	3	15	11-2	0	14	.284	.355	.453	126	4	0-2	.992	2	124	102	1b25	0	0.3
	Year	50	148	18	34	7	0	6	21	18-5	0	24	.230	.310	.399	99	0	0-2	.993	4	134	91	1b41	0	0.0
1986	Pit N	154	522	73	140	37	5	16	77	60-5	1	73	.268	.341	.450	114	11	13-7	.989	21	**152**	95	1b153,O2L	0	2.4
1987	Pit N	149	516	64	142	25	3	13	65	49-11	0	69	.275	.336	.411	96	-3	9-8	.988	8	122	106	1b144	0	-0.5
1988	Pit N	148	462	50	122	37	0	10	65	47-6	1	64	.264	.328	.409	113	9	9-9	.995	19	**152**	98	1b138	0	1.9
1989	Pit N	19	36	3	8	3	0	0	4	12-0	0	10	.222	.417	.306	113	2	0-4	.992	-0	94	66	1b13	149	-0.1
1990	†Pit N	147	389	39	105	23	2	15	67	48-5	2	65	.270	.349	.455	125	14	8-4	.993	10	133	**113**	1b142	0	1.6
1991	†Atl N	91	265	32	67	12	0	11	45	25-5	0	31	.253	.313	.423	100	0	0-3	.996	1	103	114	1b85	61	-0.6
1992	†Atl N	125	372	30	97	25	1	10	61	46-2	1	51	.261	.340	.414	107	5	6-0	.989	0	103	97	1b120	0	-0.1
1993	†Atl N	117	277	33	72	14	1	9	35	31-3	0	43	.260	.332	.415	97	-1	4-2	.996	6	123	122	1b90	0	-0.2
1994	Hou N	46	61	7	21	5	0	0	7	9-1	0	9	.344	.429	.426	130	3	0-1	.986	2	207	141	1b10	31	0.5
Total	12	1088	3108	351	819	191	12	90	455	353-45	5	450	.264	.336	.420	107	36	50-40	.992	72	130	104	1b954,O2L	241	4.6
Breazeale, Jim	James Leo; B10.3.1949 Houston TX; BL/TR/6´2˝/(195–215); [AtlN68*1/8]; d9.13; [DL 1973 Atl N 53]																								
1969	Atl N	2	1	1	0	0	0	0	0	2-0	0	0	.000	.667	.000	100	0	0-0	.833	-0	0	0	/1	0	0.0
1971	Atl N	10	21	1	4	0	0	1	3	0-0	0	3	.190	.182	.333	43	-2	0-0	1.000	-0	68	82	1b4	0	-0.3
1972	Atl N	52	85	10	21	2	0	5	17	6-1	0	12	.247	.297	.447	100	0	0-1	1.000	-2	36	95	1b16/3	0	-0.4
1978	Chi A	25	72	8	15	3	0	3	13	8-0	0	10	.208	.284	.375	84	-2	0-0	.992	-3	29	75	1b19,D4	0	-0.6
Total	4	89	179	20	40	5	0	9	33	16-1	0	25	.223	.284	.402	88	-4	0-1	.993	-6	36	82	1b40,D4/3	53	-1.3
Brede, Brent	Brent David; B9.13.1971 Belleville IL; BL/TL/6´4˝/(190–208); [MinA90 5/140]; d9.8																								
1996	Min A	10	20	2	6	0	1	0	2	1-0	0	5	.300	.333	.400	83	-1	0-0	1.000	1	127	304	O7R	0	0.0
1997	Min A	61	190	25	52	11	1	3	21	21-0	1	38	.274	.347	.389	91	-2	7-2	.957	-3	90	0	O42(3/0/40),1b15/D	0	-0.7
1998	Ari N	98	212	23	48	9	3	2	17	24-2	2	43	.226	.311	.325	67	-10	1-0	.964	-2	92	67	O58(26/0/39),1b12/D	0	-1.4
Total	3	169	422	50	106	20	5	5	40	46-2	3	86	.251	.328	.358	79	-13	8-2	.964	-4	93	52	O107(29/0/86),1b27,D2	0	-2.1
Breeden, Danny	Danny Richard; B6.27.1942 Albany GA; BR/TR/5´11.5˝/(180–185); d7.24; b–Hal; Col Troy St.																								
1969	Cin N	3	8	0	1	0	0	0	1	0-0	0	3	.125	.125	.125	-28	-1	0-0	.941	-1	65	0	C3	0	-0.2
1971	Chi N	25	65	3	10	1	0	0	4	9-0	1	18	.154	.263	.169	22	-6	0-0	.975	3	101	56	C25	0	-0.2
Total	2	28	73	3	11	1	0	0	5	9-0	1	21	.151	.250	.164	18	-7	0-0	.972	3	96	49	C28	0	-0.4
Breeden, Hal	Harold Noel; B6.28.1944 Albany GA; BR/TL/6´2˝/(195–200); d4.7; b–Danny																								
1971	Chi N	23	36	1	5	1	0	1	2	2-0	0	7	.139	.184	.250	19	-4	0-0	.982	1	164	39	1b8	0	-0.4
1972	Mon N	42	87	6	20	2	0	3	10	7-1	0	15	.230	.281	.356	80	-2	0-0	.994	-0	91	84	1b26/lf	0	-0.5
1973	Mon N	105	258	36	71	10	6	15	43	29-3	2	45	.275	.353	.535	138	12	0-1	.991	3	118	99	1b66	0	1.0
1974	Mon N	79	190	14	47	13	0	2	20	24-0	0	35	.247	.330	.347	85	-3	0-1	.987	0	104	127	1b56	0	-0.7
1975	Mon N	24	37	4	5	2	0	0	1	7-3	0	5	.135	.273	.189	28	-3	0-0	.989	-1	77	72	1b12	0	-0.5
Total	5	273	608	61	148	28	6	21	76	69-7	2	107	.243	.321	.413	99	0	0-2	.990	3	110	102	1b168/lf	0	-1.1
Breeding, Marv	Marvin Eugene; B3.8.1934 Decatur AL; BR/TR/6´0˝/175; d4.19; Col Samford																								
1960	Bal A	152	551	69	147	25	2	3	43	35-2	3	80	.267	.313	.336	77	-18	10-4	.977	9	102	112	2b152	0	0.2
1961	Bal A	90	244	32	51	8	0	1	16	14-1	0	33	.209	.250	.254	37	-22	5-2	.970	4	99	123	2b80	0	-1.2
1962	Bal A	95	240	27	59	10	1	2	18	8-0	1	41	.246	.273	.321	63	-13	2-2	.977	10	113	120	2b73/S3	0	0.2
1963	Was A	58	197	20	54	7	2	1	14	7-0	0	21	.274	.299	.345	80	-6	1-1	.914	-1	100	20	3b29,2b22,S2	0	-0.5
	LA N	20	36	6	6	0	0	0	1	2-0	0	5	.167	.211	.167	11	-4	1-0	.972	-5	74	0	2b17/S3	0	-1.0
Total	4	415	1268	154	317	50	5	7	92	66-3	4	180	.250	.288	.314	65	-63	19-9	.975	18	103	112	2b344,3b31,S4	0	-2.3
Bremer, Herb	Herbert Frederick; B10.26.1913 Chicago IL; D11.28.1979 Columbus GA; BR/TR/6´0˝/195; d9.16																								
1937	StL N	11	33	2	7	1	0	0	3	2	0	4	.212	.257	.242	36	-3	0	.979	-0	*81*	*107*	C10	—	-0.3
1938	StL N	50	151	14	33	5	1	2	14	9	0	36	.219	.262	.305	53	-10	1	.977	2	*91*	*123*	C50	—	-0.6
1939	StL N	9	9	0	1	0	0	0	1	0	0	2	.111	.111	.111	-38	-2	0	1.000	0	*67*	*0*	C8	—	-0.2
Total	3	70	193	16	41	6	1	2	18	11	0	42	.212	.255	.285	45	-15	1	.979	2	*88*	*115*	C68	—	-1.1
Brenegan, Sam	Olaf Selmar; B9.1.1890 Galesville WI; D4.20.1956 Galesville WI; BL/TR/6´2˝/185; d4.24																								
1914	Pit N	1	0	0	0	0	0	0	0	0	0	0	ø	ø	ø	ø	0	0	ø	-0	*0*	*0*	/C	—	0.0
Brenly, Bob	Robert Earl; B2.25.1954 Coshocton OH; BR/TR/6´2˝/(200–210); d8.14; M4/C4; Col Ohio U.																								
1981	SF N	19	45	5	15	2	1	1	4	6-0	1	4	.333	.423	.489	163	4	0-1	.964	-4	104	50	C14,3b3/lf	0	0.0
1982	SF N	65	180	26	51	4	1	4	15	18-4	1	26	.283	.348	.383	107	2	6-2	.961	-3	85	143	C61/3	38	0.1
1983	SF N	104	281	36	63	12	2	7	34	37-6	2	48	.224	.317	.356	89	-4	10-7	.983	6	110	**132**	C90,1b10,O2(1/0/1)	0	0.5
1984	SF N★	145	506	74	147	28	0	20	80	48-3	3	52	.291	.352	.464	132	22	6-9	.986	-13	100	125	C127,1b22,O3(1/0/2)	0	1.1
1985	SF N	133	440	41	97	16	1	19	56	57-5	2	62	.220	.311	.391	100	-1	1-4	.984	-4	99	103	C110,3b17,1b10	0	-0.2
1986	SF N	149	472	60	116	26	0	16	62	74-10	3	97	.246	.350	.403	113	10	10-6	**.995**	2	126	121	C101,3b45,1b19	0	1.5
1987	†SF N	123	375	55	100	19	1	18	51	47-3	3	85	.267	.348	.467	121	11	10-7	.988	13	115	140	C108,1b6,3b2	0	2.7
1988	SF N	73	206	13	39	7	0	5	22	20-3	2	40	.189	.265	.296	64	-10	1-2	.984	-1	118	73	C69	0	-0.8
1989	Tor A	48	88	9	15	3	1	1	6	10-0	0	17	.170	.255	.261	46	-6	1-0	.975	-3	53	81	D28,C13,1b5	0	-1.0
	SF N	12	22	2	4	2	0	0	3	1-1	0	7	.182	.208	.273	40	-2	0-0	1.000	0	278	39	C12	0	-0.1
Total	9	871	2615	321	647	119	7	91	333	318-35	17	438	.247	.330	.403	107	26	45-38	.984	-7	109	118	C705,1b72,3b68,D28,O6(3/0/3)	38	3.8
Brennan, Jim	Jack (b John Gottlieb Dorn); B1862 St.Louis MO; ?/155; d4.20																								
1884	StL U	56	231	38	50	6	1	0	—	12	—	—	.216	.255	.251	52	-20	—	.891	2	—	—	C33,O16(7/4/6),3b7/S	—	-1.4
1885	StL N	3	10	0	1	0	0	0	1	1	—	1	.100	.182	.100	-7	-1	—	.750	-1	0	0	O2L/3	—	-0.2
1888	KC AA	34	118	5	20	2	0	0	6	3	2	—	.169	.203	.186	24	-10	3	.884	-2	—	—	C25,O5(2/1/2),3b5	—	-0.9
1889	Phi AA	31	113	12	25	4	0	0	15	10	0	15	.221	.285	.257	55	-6	1	.818	-2	—	—	C13,O7(0/4/3),2b7,3b4	—	-0.6
1890	Cle P	59	233	32	59	3	7	0	26	13	4	29	.253	.304	.326	74	-9	8	.845	-12	*70*	*104*	C42,3b14,O6(2/0/4)	—	-1.5
Total	5	183	705	87	155	15	8	0	48	39	6	45	.220	.267	.264	55	-46	12	.869	-15	*70*	*104*	C113,O36(13/9/15),3b31,2b7/S	—	-4.6
Brenzel, Bill	William Richard; B3.3.1910 Oakland CA; D6.12.1979 Oakland CA; BR/TR/5´10˝/173; d4.13																								
1932	Pit N	9	24	0	1	1	0	0	2	0	0	4	.042	.042	.083	-69	-6	0	1.000	1	*89*	*46*	C9	—	-0.5
1934	Cle A	15	51	4	11	3	0	0	3	2	0	1	.216	.245	.275	33	-5	0-0	1.000	2	*112*	*103*	C15	—	-0.3
1935	Cle A	52	142	12	31	5	1	0	14	6	0	10	.218	.250	.268	33	-15	2-2	.975	-4	*105*	*113*	C51	—	-1.6
Total	3	76	217	16	43	9	1	0	19	8	0	15	.198	.227	.249	23	-26	2-2	.985	-2	*105*	*102*	C75	—	-2.4
Bresnahan, Roger	Roger Philip "The Duke of Tralee"; B6.11.1879 Toledo OH; D12.4.1944 Toledo OH; BR/TR/5´9˝/200; d8.27; M5/C6; HF1945; OF(19/221/41); ▲																								
1897	Was N	6	16	1	6	0	0	0	3	1	0	—	.375	.412	.375	109	0	0	1.000	-1	75	0	P6/cf	—	0.0
1900	Chi N	2	2	0	0	0	0	0	0	0	0	—	.000	.000	.000	-99	-1	0	ø	-0	*0*	*0*	/C	—	-0.1
1901	Bal A	86	295	40	79	9	9	1	32	23	1	—	.268	.323	.369	88	-6	10	.919	-12	*98*	*85*	C69,O8(7/0/1),3b4,P2,2b2	—	-1.1
1902	Bal A	65	235	30	64	8	6	4	34	21	2	—	.272	.337	.409	102	0	12	.880	-7	92	89	3b30,C22,O15C	—	-0.5
	NY N	51	178	16	51	9	3	1	22	16	2	—	.287	.352	.388	130	6	6	.946	0	191	126	O27R,C16,1b4,S4/3	—	0.8
1903	NY N	113	406	87	142	30	8	4	55	61	7	—	.350	.443	.493	161	36	34	.965	-0	122	235	O84(4/79/1),1b13,C11,3b4	—	3.1
1904	NY N	109	402	81	114	22	7	5	33	58	5	—	.284	.381	.410	138	21	13	.954	-1	123	314	O93(7/81/5),1b10,S4/23	—	1.6
1905	†NY N	104	331	58	100	18	3	0	46	50	11	—	.302	.411	.375	132	18	11	.970	8	***152***	*100*	C87,O8(0/2/4)	—	3.4
1906	NY N	124	405	69	114	22	4	0	43	81	**15**	—	.281	**.419**	.356	139	26	25	.974	6	*118*	***120***	C82,O40(0/39/3)	—	4.2
1907	NY N	110	328	57	83	9	7	4	38	61	6	—	.253	.380	.360	128	14	15	.986	-2	*125*	*81*	C95,1b6,O2C/3	—	2.3
1908	NY N	140	449	70	127	25	3	1	54	**83**	6	—	.283	.401	.359	136	25	14	.985	-5	*125*	*85*	C139	—	3.8
1909	StL N	72	234	27	57	4	1	0	23	46	1	—	.244	.370	.269	105	5	11	.960	-9	*74*	*118*	C59,2b9/3M	—	0.1

YEAR	TM LG	G	AB	R	H	2B	3B	HR	RBI	BB-IB	HP	SO	AVG	OBP	SLG	AOPS	ABR	SB-CS	FA	FR	RNG	THR	GAMES AT POSITION	DL	BFW
1910	StL N	88	234	35	65	15	3	0	27	55	2	17	.278	.419	.368	135	15	13	.961	-15	*74*	*99*	C77,O2(1/1/0)/PM	—	0.8
1911	StL N	81	227	22	63	17	8	3	41	45	3	19	.278	.404	.463	146	16	4	.968	-10	*76*	*110*	C77,2b2,M	—	1.2
1912	StL N	48	108	8	36	7	2	1	15	14	2	9	.333	.419	.463	145	7	4	.974	2	*79*	*125*	C28,M	—	1.1
1913	Chi N	69	162	20	37	5	2	1	21	21	2	11	.228	.324	.302	79	-4	7-1	.963	-2	109	98	C58	—	0.0
1914	Chi N	101	248	42	69	10	4	0	24	49	2	20	.278	.401	.351	125	11	14	.978	-4	*88*	*101*	C85,2b14/cf	—	1.5
1915	Chi N	77	221	19	45	8	1	1	19	29	0	23	.204	.296	.262	70	-7	19-3	.982	1	*99*	*101*	C68,M	—	0.3
Total	17	1446	4481	682	1252	218	71	26	530	714	67	99	.279	.386	.377	126	182	212-4	.971	-52	*106*	*99*	C974,O281C,3b42,1b33,2b28,P9,S8	—	22.5
Bressler, Rube	Raymond Bloom; B10.23.1894 Coder PA; D11.7.1966 Cincinnati OH; BR/TL/6´0˝/187; d4.24; Mil 1918; ▲																								
1914	Phi A	29	51	6	11	1	1	0	4	6	1	7	.216	.310	.275	79	4	0	.941	-3	61	138	P29	—	0.0
1915	Phi A	33	55	9	8	0	1	1	4	9	1	13	.145	.277	.236	56	1	0	.900	0	106	0	P32	—	0.0
1916	Phi A	4	5	1	1	0	1	0	1	0	0	0	.200	.200	.600	147	1	0	1.000	-0	47	0	P4	—	0.0
1917	Cin N	3	5	0	1	0	0	0	0	0	0	2	.200	.200	.200	24	0	0	1.000	-0	39	0	P2	—	0.0
1918	Cin N	23	62	10	17	5	0	0	6	5	0	4	.274	.328	.355	110	1	0	.982	3	137	152	P17,O3(3/0/1)	—	0.1
1919	Cin N	61	165	22	34	3	4	2	17	23	2	15	.206	.311	.309	89	-2	2	.965	1	111	63	O48(41/0/7),P13	—	-0.4
1920	Cin N	21	30	4	8	1	0	0	3	1	0	4	.267	.290	.300	71	-1	1-0	1.000	-1	109	502	P10,O3(0/1/2),1b2	—	-0.2
1921	Cin N	109	323	41	99	18	6	1	54	39	2	20	.307	.385	.409	115	9	5-5	.953	-5	100	56	O85(9/0/76),1b6	—	-0.3
1922	Cin N	52	53	7	14	0	2	0	8	4	0	4	.264	.316	.340	70	-3	1-0	1.000	-1	0	0	1b3,O2(1/0/1)	—	-0.3
1923	Cin N	54	119	25	33	3	1	0	18	20	4	4	.277	.399	.319	93	0	3-1	.983	-2	79	73	1b22,O6(3/0/3)	—	-0.2
1924	Cin N	115	383	41	133	14	13	4	49	22	4	20	.347	.389	.483	134	17	9-10	.990	2	122	104	1b50,O49(45/0/4)	—	1.0
1925	Cin N	97	319	43	111	17	6	4	61	40	2	16	.348	.424	.476	133	18	9-5	.982	-5	79	126	1b52,O38(36/0/2)	—	0.7
1926	Cin N	86	297	58	106	15	9	1	51	37	3	20	.357	.433	.478	149	22	3	.970	-5	95	52	O80L,1b4	—	1.1
1927	Cin N	124	467	43	136	14	8	3	77	32	1	22	.291	.338	.375	94	-5	4	.972	5	104	132	O120L	—	-0.9
1928	Bro N	145	501	78	148	29	13	4	70	80	5	33	.295	.398	.429	118	16	2	**.985**	-6	93	68	O137L	—	-0.1
1929	Bro N	136	456	72	145	22	8	9	77	67	1	27	.318	.406	.461	117	14	4	.954	1	107	87	O122L	—	0.5
1930	Bro N	109	335	53	100	12	8	3	52	51	2	19	.299	.394	.409	96	-1	4	.995	7	118	83	O90L,1b7	—	-0.1
1931	Bro N	67	153	22	43	4	5	0	26	11	0	10	.281	.329	.373	89	-3	0	.982	-2	91	58	O35(23/7/3)/1	—	-0.6
1932	Phi N	27	83	9	19	6	1	0	6	2	0	5	.229	.247	.325	47	-6	0	1.000	3	110	360	O18L	—	-0.4
	StL N	10	19	0	3	0	0	0	2	0	0	1	.158	.158	.158	-14	-3	0	1.000	-0	104	0	O4L	—	-0.3
	Year	37	102	9	22	6	1	0	8	2	0	6	.216	.231	.294	37	-9	0	1.000	3	109	298	O22L	—	-0.7
Total	19	1305	3881	544	1170	164	87	32	586	449	28	246	.301	.378	.413	110	79	47-21	.971	-8	102	85	O840(732/8/99),1b147,P107	—	-0.4
Bressoud, Eddie	Edward Francis; B5.2.1932 Los Angeles CA; BR/TR/6´1˝/(175–185); d6.14																								
1956	NY N	49	163	15	37	4	2	0	9	12-1	1	20	.227	.284	.276	52	-11	1-0	.950	-8	92	90	S48	0	-1.6
1957	NY N	49	127	11	34	2	2	5	10	4-1	2	19	.268	.299	.433	94	-2	0-1	.940	-5	95	80	S33,3b12	0	-0.5
1958	SF N	66	137	19	36	5	3	0	8	14-1	0	22	.263	.331	.343	81	-4	0-1	.966	-7	90	84	2b57,3b6,S4	0	-0.8
1959	SF N	104	315	36	79	17	2	9	26	28-6	0	55	.251	.311	.403	91	-5	0-0	.974	-9	95	71	S92/123	0	-0.6
1960	SF N	116	386	37	87	19	6	9	43	35-12	2	72	.225	.290	.376	87	-8	1-2	.960	2	102	83	S115	0	0.3
1961	SF N	59	114	14	24	6	0	3	11	11-4	0	23	.211	.276	.342	66	-6	1-1	.964	-10	72	71	S34,3b3/2	0	-1.3
1962	Bos A	153	599	79	166	40	9	14	68	46-4	2	118	.277	.329	.444	103	2	2-3	.965	23	**109**	106	S153	0	3.7
1963	Bos A	140	497	61	129	23	6	20	60	52-2	2	93	.260	.329	.451	113	9	1-1	.962	-13	88	94	S137	0	0.8
1964	Bos A☆	158	566	86	166	41	3	15	55	72-4	1	99	.293	.372	.456	123	21	1-1	.972	-8	92	78	S158	0	2.7
1965	Bos A	107	296	29	67	11	1	8	25	29-4	1	77	.226	.297	.351	79	-8	0-1	.963	0	94	101	S86,3b2/lf	0	-0.2
1966	NY N	133	405	48	91	15	5	10	49	47-4	1	107	.225	.304	.360	87	-7	2-2	.960	10	110	109	S94,3b32,1b9,2b7	0	1.0
1967	†StL N	52	67	8	9	1	1	1	1	9-1	0	18	.134	.237	.224	33	-6	0-0	.929	-9	77	92	S48/3	0	-1.5
Total	12	1186	3672	443	925	184	40	94	365	359-44	12	723	.252	.319	.401	96	-25	9-13	.963	-34	96	90	S1002,2b66,3b57,1b10/lf	0	2.0
Breton, Jim	John Frederick; B7.15.1891 Chicago IL; D5.30.1973 Beloit WI; BR/TR/5´10.5˝/178; d8.25; Col Illinois																								
1913	Chi A	12	30	1	5	1	1	0	2	1	0	5	.167	.194	.267	35	-3	0	.938	2	152	112	S7,3b3	—	0.0
1914	Chi A	81	231	21	49	7	2	0	24	24	2	42	.212	.292	.260	67	-9	9-6	.910	0	107	63	3b79	—	-0.7
1915	Chi A	16	36	3	5	1	0	0	1	5	1	9	.139	.262	.167	27	-3	2-1	.882	-2	74	126	3b14/2S	—	-0.5
Total	3	109	297	25	59	9	3	0	27	30	3	56	.199	.279	.249	59	-15	11-7	.906	1	103	69	3b96,S8/2	—	-1.2
Brett, George	George Howard; B5.15.1953 Glen Dale WV; BL/TR/6´0˝/(180–205); [KCA71 2/29]; d8.2; HF1999; b–Ken; OF(22/0/14)																								
1973	KC A	13	40	2	5	2	0	0	0	0-0	0	5	.125	.125	.175	-15	-6	0-0	.974	2	126	88	3b13	0	-0.4
1974	KC A	133	457	49	129	21	5	2	47	21-3	0	38	.282	.313	.363	89	-7	8-5	.948	-7	102	56	3b132/S	0	-1.6
1975	KC A	159	634	84	**195**	35	**13**	11	89	46-6	2	49	.308	.353	.456	125	19	13-10	.949	2	104	86	3b159/S	0	2.0
1976	†KC A★	159	645	94	**215**	34	**14**	7	67	49-4	1	36	**.333**	.377	.462	145	35	21-11	.948	3	103	86	3b157,S4	0	4.1
1977	†KC A★	139	564	105	176	32	13	22	88	55-9	2	24	.312	.373	.532	142	32	14-12	.957	18	114	**137**	3b135/SD	0	4.6
1978	†KC A★	128	510	79	150	**45**	8	9	62	39-6	1	35	.294	.342	.467	123	15	23-7	.961	4	104	108	3b128/S	33	2.0
1979	KC A★	154	645	119	**212**	42	**20**	23	107	51-14	0	36	.329	.376	.563	146	40	17-10	.944	14	114	99	3b149,1b8/D	0	4.9
1980	†KC A✳	117	449	87	175	33	9	24	118	58-16	1	22	**.390**	**.454**	**.664**	**201**	**64**	15-6	.955	4	106	123	3b112/1	29	**6.5**
1981	†KC A★	89	347	42	109	27	7	6	43	27-7	1	23	.314	.361	.484	143	19	14-6	.946	-10	91	46	3b88	0	0.9
1982	KC A★	144	552	101	166	32	9	21	82	71-14	1	51	.301	.378	.505	140	31	6-1	.959	-7	96	83	3b134,O12L	0	2.2
1983	KC A★	123	464	90	144	38	2	25	93	57-13	1	39	.310	.385	**.563**	156	37	0-1	.919	-16	87	117	3b102,1b14,O13(6/0/7)/D	21	1.7
1984	†KC A★	104	377	42	107	21	3	13	69	38-6	0	37	.284	.344	.459	120	10	0-2	.949	4	110	114	3b101	46	1.2
1985	†KC A★	155	550	108	184	38	5	30	112	103-**31**	3	49	.335	.436	**.585**	**177**	**64**	9-1	.967	5	105	116	3b152/D	0	6.6
1986	KC A✳	124	441	70	128	28	4	16	73	80-**18**	4	45	.290	.401	.481	136	26	1-2	.952	-1	99	88	3b115,S2,D7	0	2.3
1987	KC A	115	427	71	124	18	2	22	78	72-14	1	47	.290	.388	.496	130	21	6-3	.993	-3	88	101	1b83,D21,3b11	50	1.1
1988	KC A★	157	589	90	180	42	3	24	103	82-15	3	51	.306	.389	.509	149	41	14-3	.992	-7	81	102	1b124,D33/S	0	2.7
1989	KC A	124	457	67	129	26	3	12	80	59-14	3	47	.282	.362	.431	125	17	14-4	.998	4	106	82	1b104,D17,O2L	41	1.4
1990	KC A	142	544	82	179	**45**	7	14	87	56-14	0	63	**.329**	.387	.515	153	40	9-2	.993	-3	86	98	1b102,D32,O9(2/0/7)/3	0	3.0
1991	KC A	131	505	77	129	40	2	10	61	58-10	0	75	.255	.327	.402	101	2	2-0	.989	-1	69	72	D118,1b10	31	-0.3
1992	KC A	152	592	55	169	35	5	7	61	35-6	6	69	.285	.330	.397	100	-1	8-6	.987	-0	109	70	D132,1b15,3b3	0	-0.7
1993	KC A	145	560	69	149	31	3	19	75	39-9	3	67	.266	.312	.434	93	-7	7-5	ø	0	0	0	D140	0	-1.4
Total	21	2707	10349	1583	3154	665	137	317	1595	1096-229	33	908	.305	.369	.487	134	492	201-97	.951	4	103	98	3b1692,D506,1b461,O36L,S11	251	42.8
Brewer, Tony	Anthony Bruce; B11.25.1957 Coushatta LA; BR/TR/5´11˝/190; d8.1; b–Mike; Col Miami																								
1984	LA N	24	37	3	4	1	0	1	4	4-1	0	9	.108	.195	.216	15	-4	1-0	1.000	-1	72	0	O10(8/0/2)	0	-0.6
Brewer, Mike	Michael Quinn; B10.24.1959 Shreveport LA; BR/TR/6´5˝/190; [KCA79*1/22]; d6.11; b–Tony; Col Foothill (CA) JC																								
1986	KC A	12	18	0	3	1	0	0	0	2-0	0	6	.167	.250	.222	29	-2	0-1	1.000	-1	85	0	O9R/D	0	-0.3
Brewer, Rod	Rodney Lee; B2.24.1966 Eustis FL; BL/TL/6´3˝/(208–218); [StLN87 5/124]; d9.5; Col Florida																								
1990	StL N	14	25	4	6	1	0	0	2	0-0	0	4	.240	.240	.280	42	-2	0-0	.981	1	167	143	1b9	0	-0.2
1991	StL N	19	13	0	1	0	0	0	1	0-0	0	5	.077	.077	.077	-56	-3	0-0	1.000	0	107	86	1b15,O3R	0	-0.3
1992	StL N	29	103	11	31	6	0	0	10	8-0	1	12	.301	.354	.359	106	1	0-1	1.000	1	102	102	1b27,O4L	0	0.0
1993	StL N	110	147	15	42	8	0	2	20	17-5	1	26	.286	.359	.381	100	1	1-0	.960	-2	103	57	O33(15/0/19),1b32/P	0	-0.3
Total	4	172	288	30	80	15	0	2	33	25-5	2	47	.278	.336	.351	91	-3	1-1	.995	-0	100	117	1b83,O40(19/0/22)/P	0	-0.8
Brewster, Charlie	Charles Lawrence; B12.27.1916 Marthaville LA; D10.1.2000 Alma GA; BR/TR/5´8.5˝/175; d5.2																								
1943	Cin N	7	8	0	1	0	0	0	0	0	0	1	.125	.125	.125	-28	-1	0	1.000	-0	72	177	2b2	0	-0.1
	Phi N	49	159	13	35	2	0	0	12	10	2	19	.220	.275	.233	49	-11	1	.901	-18	79	70	S46	0	-2.7
	Year	56	167	13	36	2	0	0	12	10	2	20	.216	.268	.228	45	-12	1	.901	-18	79	70	S46,2b2	0	-2.8
1944	Chi N	10	44	4	11	2	0	0	2	5	0	7	.250	.327	.295	76	-1	0	.903	-1	86	148	S10	0	-0.1
1946	Cle A	3	2	0	0	0	0	0	0	1	0	1	.000	.333	.000	-1	0	0-0	1.000	0	151	0	/S	0	0.0
Total	3	69	213	17	47	4	0	0	14	16	2	28	.221	.281	.239	52	-13	1-0	.902	-18	81	85	S57,2b2	0	-2.9
Brickell, Fritz	Fritz Darrell; B3.19.1935 Wichita KS; D10.15.1965 Wichita KS; BR/TR/5´5.5˝/(157–160); d4.30; f–Fred																								
1958	NY A	2	0	0	0	0	0	0	0	0-0	0	0	ø	ø	ø	ø	0	0-0	1.000	-0	110	0	2b2	0	0.0
1959	NY A	18	39	4	10	1	0	1	4	1-0	0	10	.256	.275	.359	75	-2	0-0	.925	-2	105	44	S15,2b3	0	-0.3
1961	LA A	21	49	3	6	0	0	0	3	6-0	0	9	.122	.218	.122	-6	-7	0-0	.901	-1	86	123	S17	0	-0.7
Total	3	41	88	7	16	1	0	1	7	7-0	0	19	.182	.242	.227	26	-9	0-0	.911	-3	94	88	S32,2b5	0	-1.0

THE BATTER REGISTER

BRICKELL, FRED George Frederick; B11.9.1906 Saffordville KS; D4.8.1961 Wichita KS; BL/TR/5´7˝/160; d8.19; s–Fritz

YEAR	TM LG	G	AB	R	H	2B	3B	HR	RBI	BB-IB	HP	SO	AVG	OBP	SLG	AOPS	ABR	SB-CS	FA	FR	RNG	THR	GAMES AT POSITION	DL	BFW
1926	Pit N	24	55	11	19	3	1	0	4	3	2	6	.345	.400	.436	119	2	0	.920	1	88	279	O14L	—	0.2
1927	†Pit N	32	21	6	6	1	0	1	4	1	0	0	.286	.318	.476	103	0	0	1.000	0	208	0	O3(0/1/2)	—	0.0
1928	Pit N	81	202	34	65	4	4	3	41	20	0	18	.322	.383	.426	107	2	5	.958	3	108	157	O50(44/0/8)	—	0.1
1929	Pit N	60	118	13	37	4	2	0	17	7	0	12	.314	.352	.381	80	-4	3	1.000	2	110	151	O27(14/0/13)	—	-0.3
1930	Pit N	68	219	36	65	9	3	1	14	15	0	20	.297	.342	.379	74	-9	3	.951	-1	102	73	O61(11/50/0)	—	-1.1
	Phi N	53	240	33	59	12	6	0	17	13	2	21	.246	.290	.346	49	-20	1	.963	2	104	135	O53C	—	-1.9
	Year	121	459	69	124	21	9	1	31	28	2	41	.270	.315	.362	61	-30	4	.958	1	103	105	O114(11/103/0)	—	-3.0
1931	Phi N	130	514	77	130	14	5	1	31	42	5	39	.253	.316	.305	63	-26	5	.978	0	103	79	O122C	—	-3.0
1932	Phi N	45	66	9	22	6	1	0	2	4	2	5	.333	.389	.455	112	2	2	.935	1	99	230	O12(1/11/0)	—	0.2
1933	Phi N	8	13	2	4	1	1	0	1	1	0	0	.308	.357	.538	136	1	0	1.000	1	130	354	O4L	—	0.1
Total	8	501	1448	221	407	54	23	6	131	106	11	121	.281	.335	.363	75	-52	19	.967	9	104	119	O346(88/237/23)	—	-5.7

BRICKLEY, GEORGE George Vincent; B7.19.1894 Everett MA; D2.23.1947 Everett MA; BR/TR/5´9˝/180; d9.26

YEAR	TM LG	G	AB	R	H	2B	3B	HR	RBI	BB-IB	HP	SO	AVG	OBP	SLG	AOPS	ABR	SB-CS	FA	FR	RNG	THR	GAMES AT POSITION	DL	BFW
1913	Phi A	5	12	0	2	0	1	0	0	0	1	4	.167	.231	.333	66	-1	0	1.000	-0	66	0	O4R	—	-0.1

BRIDEWESER, JIM James Ehrenfeld; B2.13.1927 Lancaster OH; D8.25.1989 El Toro CA; BR/TR/6´0˝/165; d9.29; Col USC

YEAR	TM LG	G	AB	R	H	2B	3B	HR	RBI	BB-IB	HP	SO	AVG	OBP	SLG	AOPS	ABR	SB-CS	FA	FR	RNG	THR	GAMES AT POSITION	DL	BFW
1951	NY A	2	8	1	3	0	0	0	0	0	0	1	.375	.375	.375	107	0	0-0	.818	-0	87	225	S2	0	0.0
1952	NY A	42	38	12	10	0	0	0	2	3	0	5	.263	.317	.263	67	-2	0-0	.935	1	132	94	S22,2b4/3	0	-0.1
1953	NY A	7	3	3	3	0	1	0	3	1	0	0	1.000	1.000	1.667	631	2	0-0	.833	-0	0	0	S3	0	0.2
1954	Bal A	73	204	18	54	7	2	0	12	15	1	27	.265	.317	.319	81	-6	1-1	.944	-8	95	89	S48,2b19	0	-1.0
1955	Chi A	34	58	6	12	3	2	0	4	3-0	0	7	.207	.246	.328	52	-4	0-0	.949	3	108	142	S26,3b3,2b2	0	0.0
1956	Chi A	10	11	0	2	1	0	0	1	0-0	1	3	.182	.250	.273	37	-1	0-0	.938	-0	110	50	S10	0	-0.1
	Det A	70	156	23	34	4	0	0	10	20-2	0	19	.218	.307	.244	47	-12	3-1	.987	6	113	117	S32,2b31,3b4	0	-0.2
	Year	80	167	23	36	5	0	0	11	20-2	1	22	.216	.303	.246	46	-13	3-1	.979	5	112	105	S42,2b31,3b4	0	-0.3
1957	Bal A	91	142	16	38	7	1	1	18	21-2	0	16	.268	.362	.352	102	1	2-0	.943	-2	97	111	S74,3b3/2	0	0.4
Total	7	329	620	79	156	22	6	1	50	63-4	2	78	.252	.322	.311	75	-22	6-2	.946	-2	101	108	S217,2b57,3b11	0	-0.8

BRIDGES, ROCKY Everett Lamar; B8.7.1927 Refugio TX; BR/TR/5´8˝/(170–175); d4.17; C7

YEAR	TM LG	G	AB	R	H	2B	3B	HR	RBI	BB-IB	HP	SO	AVG	OBP	SLG	AOPS	ABR	SB-CS	FA	FR	RNG	THR	GAMES AT POSITION	DL	BFW
1951	Bro N	63	134	13	34	7	0	1	15	10	0	10	.254	.306	.328	69	-6	0-0	.871	-1	98	148	3b40,2b10,S9	0	-0.6
1952	Bro N	51	56	9	11	3	0	0	2	7	0	9	.196	.286	.250	49	-4	0-1	.986	6	112	162	2b24,S13,3b6	0	0.3
1953	Cin N	122	432	52	98	13	2	1	21	37	0	42	.227	.288	.273	47	-34	6-3	.976	14	106	**122**	2b115,S6,3b3	0	-1.1
1954	Cin N	53	52	4	12	1	0	0	2	7	0	7	.231	.322	.250	50	-4	0-1	1.000	6	122	73	S20,2b19,3b13	0	0.3
1955	Cin N	95	168	20	48	4	0	1	18	15-2	0	19	.286	.341	.327	75	-6	1-1	.965	4	106	95	3b59,S26,2b9	0	-0.1
1956	Cin N	71	19	9	4	0	0	0	1	4-0	0	3	.211	.348	.211	52	-1	1-2	.966	3	97	85	3b51,2b8,S7/lf	0	0.2
1957	Cin N	5	1	1	0	0	0	0	0	1-0	0	1	.000	.500	.000	46	0	0-0	1.000	-1	0	0	2b2/S3	0	-0.1
	Was A	120	391	40	89	17	2	3	47	40-4	2	32	.228	.298	.304	67	-17	0-2	.971	**28**	**116**	98	S108,2b14/3	0	2.0
1958	Was A☆	116	377	38	99	14	3	5	28	27-1	3	32	.263	.315	.355	86	-8	0-3	.976	12	109	100	S112,2b3,3b3	0	1.3
1959	Det A	116	381	38	102	16	3	3	35	30-2	1	35	.268	.320	.349	80	-10	1-2	.952	8	98	**115**	S110,2b5	0	0.6
1960	Det A	10	5	0	1	0	0	0	0	0-0	0	0	.200	.200	.200	8	-1	0-0	1.000	1	126	0	3b7,S3	0	0.0
	Cle A	10	27	1	9	0	0	0	3	1-1	0	2	.333	.357	.333	91	0	0-0	1.000	2	127	81	S7,3b3	0	0.2
	Year	20	32	1	10	0	0	0	3	1-1	0	2	.313	.333	.313	76	-1	0-0	1.000	3	120	114	3b10,S10	0	0.2
	StL N	3	0	0	0	0	0	0	0	0-0	0	0	ø	ø	ø	ø	0	0-0	1.000	1	80	360	2b3	0	0.1
1961	LA A	84	229	20	55	5	1	2	15	26-0	1	37	.240	.320	.297	59	-13	1-0	.988	5	105	64	2b58,S25,3b4	0	-0.1
Total	11	919	2272	245	562	80	11	16	187	205-10	7	229	.247	.310	.313	67	-104	10-15	.968	87	109	103	S447,2b270,3b191/lf	0	3.0

BRIDWELL, AL Albert Henry; B1.4.1884 Friendship OH; D1.23.1969 Portsmouth OH; BL/TR/5´9˝/170; d4.16; OF(3/2/14)

YEAR	TM LG	G	AB	R	H	2B	3B	HR	RBI	BB-IB	HP	SO	AVG	OBP	SLG	AOPS	ABR	SB-CS	FA	FR	RNG	THR	GAMES AT POSITION	DL	BFW
1905	Cin N	82	254	17	64	3	1	0	17	19	2	—	.252	.309	.272	66	-10	8	.944	4	105	122	3b43,O18(3/2/13),2b7,S5/1	—	-0.6
1906	Bos N	120	459	41	104	9	1	0	22	44	2	—	.227	.297	.251	73	-14	6	.930	18	104	101	S119/rf	—	0.9
1907	Bos N	140	509	49	111	8	2	0	26	61	6	—	.218	.309	.242	73	-13	17	**.942**	5	102	111	S140	—	-0.5
1908	NY N	147	467	53	133	14	1	0	46	52	6	—	.285	.364	.319	113	10	20	.933	9	103	98	S147	—	2.7
1909	NY N	145	476	59	140	11	5	0	55	67	4	—	.294	.386	.338	123	16	32	.940	2	99	115	S145	—	2.5
1910	NY N	142	492	74	136	15	7	0	48	73	4	23	.276	.374	.335	107	8	14	.946	4	95	96	S141	—	1.7
1911	NY N	76	263	28	71	10	1	0	31	33	3	10	.270	.358	.316	86	-3	8	.917	5	104	96	S76	—	0.6
	Bos N	51	182	29	53	5	0	0	10	33	1	8	.291	.403	.319	95	1	2	.950	-4	100	83	S51	—	0.0
	Year	127	445	57	124	15	1	0	41	66	4	18	.279	.377	.317	90	-2	10	.929	0	102	91	S127	—	0.6
1912	Bos N	31	106	6	25	5	1	0	14	5	0	5	.236	.270	.302	55	-7	2	.936	-5	89	112	S31	—	-1.0
1913	Chi N	136	405	35	97	6	6	1	37	74	1	28	.240	.358	.291	87	-4	12-16	.948	3	100	96	S136	—	0.5
1914	StL F	117	381	46	90	6	5	1	33	71	2	18	.236	.359	.286	73	-17	9	.944	-4	96	96	S103,2b11	—	-1.4
1915	StL F	65	175	20	40	3	2	0	9	25	1	6	.229	.328	.269	65	-10	6	.952	1	104	76	2b42,3b15/1	—	-0.9
Total	11	1252	4169	457	1064	95	32	2	348	557	32	98	.255	.347	.295	89	-43	136-16	.939	36	100	102	S1094,2b60,3b58,O19R,1b2	—	4.5

BRIEF, BUNNY Anthony Vincent (b Anthony John Grzeszkowski); B7.3.1892 Remus MI; D2.11.1963 Milwaukee WI; BR/TR/6´0˝/185; d9.22

YEAR	TM LG	G	AB	R	H	2B	3B	HR	RBI	BB-IB	HP	SO	AVG	OBP	SLG	AOPS	ABR	SB-CS	FA	FR	RNG	THR	GAMES AT POSITION	DL	BFW
1912	StL A	15	42	9	13	3	0	0	5	6	1	—	.310	.408	.381	131	2	2	.826	-1	108	0	O9L,1b4	—	0.1
1913	StL A	85	258	24	56	11	6	1	26	21	3	46	.217	.284	.318	78	-8	3	.986	-1	93	122	1b62,O8L	—	-1.2
1915	Chi A	48	154	13	33	6	2	2	17	16	4	28	.214	.305	.318	84	-3	8-6	.986	-2	86	104	1b46	—	-0.7
1917	Pit N	36	115	15	25	5	1	2	11	15	2	21	.217	.318	.330	96	0	4	.988	2	121	107	1b34	—	0.1
Total	4	184	569	61	127	25	9	5	59	58	10	95	.223	.306	.325	87	-9	17-6	.987	-3	98	114	1b146,O17L	—	-1.7

BRIGGS, CHARLIE Charles R.; B9.1860 Batavia IL; D3.10.1920 Seattle WA; 5´7˝/170; d5.2

YEAR	TM LG	G	AB	R	H	2B	3B	HR	RBI	BB-IB	HP	SO	AVG	OBP	SLG	AOPS	ABR	SB-CS	FA	FR	RNG	THR	GAMES AT POSITION	DL	BFW
1884	CP U	49	182	29	31	8	2	1	—	11	—	—	.170	.218	.253	43	-18	—	.814	-6	69	79	O37(3/28/6),2b12,S2	—	-2.2

BRIGGS, DAN Dan Lee; B11.18.1952 Scotia CA; BL/TL/6´0˝/(175–180); [AnaA70 2/34]; d9.10

YEAR	TM LG	G	AB	R	H	2B	3B	HR	RBI	BB-IB	HP	SO	AVG	OBP	SLG	AOPS	ABR	SB-CS	FA	FR	RNG	THR	GAMES AT POSITION	DL	BFW
1975	Cal A	13	31	3	7	1	0	1	3	2-0	0	6	.226	.273	.355	82	-1	0-2	.953	-1	36	111	1b6,O5L,D2	0	-0.3
1976	Cal A	77	248	19	53	13	2	1	14	13-3	1	47	.214	.254	.294	65	-12	0-3	.993	1	101	122	1b44,O40(2/32/9)/D	0	-1.7
1977	Cal A	59	74	6	12	2	0	1	4	8-1	0	14	.162	.241	.230	31	-7	0-0	.993	0	110	75	1b45,O13(0/12/1)	0	-0.8
1978	Cle A	15	49	4	8	0	1	1	1	4-0	0	9	.163	.226	.265	38	-4	0-0	1.000	2	120	90	O15R	0	-0.4
1979	SD N	104	227	34	47	4	3	8	30	18-5	5	45	.207	.277	.357	77	-9	2-1	.986	5	137	72	1b50,O44(25/16/3)	0	-0.7
1981	Mon N	9	11	0	1	0	0	0	0	0-0	0	3	.091	.091	.091	-47	-2	0-1	1.000	0	161	81	1b3,O3(1/2/1)	0	-0.3
1982	Chi N	48	48	1	6	0	0	0	1	0-0	1	9	.125	.143	.125	-24	-8	0-0	.875	1	77	800	O10(8/1/1),1b4	0	-0.8
Total	7	325	688	67	134	20	6	12	53	45-9	7	133	.195	.249	.294	55	-43	2-7	.989	8	114	94	1b152,O130(41/63/30),D3	0	-5.0

BRIGGS, GRANT Grant; B3.16.1865 Pittsburgh PA; D5.31.1928 Pittsburgh PA; 5´11˝/170; d4.17

YEAR	TM LG	G	AB	R	H	2B	3B	HR	RBI	BB-IB	HP	SO	AVG	OBP	SLG	AOPS	ABR	SB-CS	FA	FR	RNG	THR	GAMES AT POSITION	DL	BFW
1890	Syr AA	86	316	44	57	6	5	0	21	16	1	—	.180	.222	.231	37	-26	7	.928	-10	*78*	*101*	C46,O33(4/25/4),3b5,S4	—	-2.9
1891	Lou AA	1	4	0	1	0	0	0	0	0	0	0	.250	.250	.250	44	0	0	1.000	-0	*79*	*103*	/C	—	0.0
1892	StL N	22	55	2	4	1	0	0	1	5	1	14	.073	.164	.091	-24	-8	2	.902	-8	*96*	*81*	C15,O8(2/1/5)	—	-1.5
1895	Lou N	1	3	0	0	0	0	0	0	0	0	1	.000	.000	.000	-99	-1	0	1.000	-0	*108*	*0*	/C	—	-0.1
Total	4	110	378	46	62	7	5	0	22	21	2	15	.164	.212	.209	27	-35	9	.925	-19	*82*	*96*	C63,O41(6/26/9),3b5,S4	—	-4.5

BRIGGS, JOHNNY John Edward; B3.10.1944 Paterson NJ; BL/TL/6´1˝/(190–198); d4.17; Col Seton Hall

YEAR	TM LG	G	AB	R	H	2B	3B	HR	RBI	BB-IB	HP	SO	AVG	OBP	SLG	AOPS	ABR	SB-CS	FA	FR	RNG	THR	GAMES AT POSITION	DL	BFW
1964	Phi N	61	66	16	17	2	0	1	6	9-0	0	12	.258	.347	.333	94	0	1-1	.957	1	114	164	O19(9/9/1)/1	0	0.0
1965	Phi N	93	229	47	54	9	4	4	23	42-1	0	44	.236	.349	.362	104	3	3-2	.982	-3	95	66	O66(4/62/0)	0	-0.2
1966	Phi N	81	255	43	72	13	5	10	23	41-3	0	55	.282	.380	.490	140	15	3-2	.977	-5	90	70	O69(2/68/0)	48	0.9
1967	Phi N	106	332	47	77	12	4	9	30	41-1	0	72	.232	.315	.373	96	-2	3-5	.979	-1	104	41	O94(31/65/1)	0	-0.8
1968	Phi N	110	338	36	86	13	1	7	31	58-4	1	72	.254	.364	.361	119	11	8-5	.968	-3	100	24	O65(10/34/21),1b36	0	0.4
1969	Phi N	124	361	51	86	20	3	12	46	64-3	0	78	.238	.351	.410	116	10	9-6	.971	4	112	107	O108(76/32/12),1b2	0	0.9
1970	Phi N	110	341	43	92	15	7	9	47	39-5	0	65	.270	.342	.434	110	4	5-4	.980	7	120	113	O95(79/11/15)	32	0.6
1971	Phi N	10	22	3	4	1	0	0	3	6-1	0	2	.182	.357	.227	68	-1	0-0	.846	-0	89	246	O8L	0	-0.1
	Mil A	125	375	51	99	11	1	21	59	71-7	1	79	.264	.378	.467	141	22	1-2	.958	5	113	127	O65(55/0/11),1b60	0	2.0
1972	Mil A	135	418	58	111	14	1	21	65	54-4	1	67	.266	.347	.455	141	21	1-2	.980	0	104	82	O106(98/12/0),1b28	0	1.5
1973	Mil A	142	488	78	120	20	7	18	57	87-6	2	83	.246	.361	.426	123	17	15-9	.968	3	101	90	O137L/D	0	1.2
1974	Mil A	154	554	72	140	30	8	17	73	71-2	0	102	.253	.337	.428	119	14	9-7	.973	0	98	91	O149(148/1/0),D2	0	0.6
1975	Mil A	28	74	12	22	1	0	3	5	20-0	0	13	.297	.447	.432	148	6	0-2	.962	2	110	204	O21L/D	0	0.7
	Min A	87	264	44	61	9	2	7	39	60-10	0	41	.231	.371	.360	107	5	6-2	.983	9	165	97	1b49,O35(20/0/17),D2	0	0.9

YEAR	TM LG	G	AB	R	H	2B	3B	HR	RBI	BB-IB	HP	SO	AVG	OBP	SLG	AOPS	ABR	SB-CS	FA	FR	RNG	THR	GAMES AT POSITION	DL	BFW
	Year	115	338	56	83	10	2	10	44	80-10	0	54	.246	.388	.376	116	11	6-4	.983	11	108	134	O56(41/0/17),1b49,D3	0	1.6
Total	12	1366	4117	601	1041	170	43	139	507	663-47	5	785	.253	.355	.416	120	125	64-49	.973	19	104	88	O1037(698/294/78),1b176,D6	80	8.6
Bright, Harry	Harry James; B9.22.1929 Kansas City MO; D3.13.2000 Sacramento CA; BR/TR/6´0˝/(184–190); d8.7																								
1958	Pit N	15	24	4	6	1	0	1	3	1-0	0	6	.250	.269	.417	84	-1	0-0	1.000	-1	93	0	3b7	0	-0.2
1959	Pit N	40	48	4	12	1	0	3	8	5-0	0	10	.250	.321	.458	105	0	0-0	1.000	-0	48	0	O4(3/0/1),3b3/2	0	0.0
1960	Pit N	4	4	0	0	0	0	0	0	0-0	0	2	.000	.000	.000	-99	-1	0-0	ø	0	—	—	/H	0	-0.1
1961	Was A	72	183	20	44	6	0	4	21	19-1	0	23	.240	.310	.339	75	-7	0-2	.928	7	123	174	3b40,C8/2	0	0.0
1962	Was A	113	392	55	107	15	4	17	67	26-0	2	51	.273	.319	.462	109	3	2-1	.989	0	108	106	1b99,C3/3	0	-0.3
1963	Cin N	1	1	0	0	0	0	0	0	0-0	0	1	.000	.000	.000	-97	0	0-0	1.000	0	0	0	/1	0	0.0
	†NY A	60	157	15	37	7	0	7	23	13-1	1	31	.236	.297	.414	98	-1	0-0	.985	-4	42	159	1b35,3b12	0	-0.7
1964	NY A	4	5	0	1	0	0	0	0	1-0	0	1	.200	.333	.200	52	0	0-0	1.000	-0	0	0	1b2	0	-0.1
1965	Chi N	27	25	1	7	1	0	0	4	0-0	0	8	.280	.269	.320	67	-1	0-0	ø	0	—	—	/H	0	-0.1
Total	8	336	839	99	214	31	4	32	126	65-2	3	133	.255	.309	.416	96	-8	2-3	.988	1	92	117	1b137,3b63,C11,O4(3/0/1),2b2	0	-1.5
Briley, Greg	Gregory "Peewee"; B5.24.1965 Greenville NC; BL/TR/5´8˝/(165–180); [SeaA86 S1/12]; d6.27; Col North Carolina St.																								
1988	Sea A	13	36	6	9	2	0	1	4	5-1	0	6	.250	.333	.389	99	0	0-1	.929	-2	64	0	O11L	0	-0.3
1989	Sea A	115	394	52	105	22	4	13	52	39-1	5	82	.266	.336	.442	115	8	11-5	.958	1	96	92	O105(96/0/10),2b10,D2	0	0.7
1990	Sea A	125	337	40	83	18	2	5	29	37-0	1	48	.246	.319	.356	88	-5	16-4	.989	-1	100	67	O107(43/0/67),D4	0	-0.7
1991	Sea A	139	381	39	99	17	3	2	26	27-0	0	51	.260	.307	.336	78	-12	23-11	.980	-4	93	82	O125(94/4/46)/23D	0	-1.8
1992	Sea A	86	200	18	55	10	0	5	12	4-0	1	31	.275	.290	.400	91	-3	9-2	.967	-5	89	56	O42(27/13/4),D12,2b4,3b4	48	-0.8
1993	Fla N	120	170	17	33	6	0	3	12	12-0	1	42	.194	.250	.282	40	-15	6-2	.986	1	107	80	O67(32/1/36)	0	-1.5
Total	6	598	1518	172	384	75	9	29	135	124-2	8	260	.253	.310	.372	88	-27	65-25	.975	-10	96	76	O457(303/18/163),D20,2b15,3b5	48	-4.4
Brinker, Bill	William Hutchinson "Dode"; B8.30.1883 Warrensburg MO; D2.5.1965 Arcadia CA; BB/TR/6´1˝/190; d4.24; Col Washington																								
1912	Phi N	9	18	1	4	1	0	0	2	2	0	3	.222	.300	.278	55	-1	0	.778	-1	84	0	3b2,O2(1/1/0)	—	-0.2
Brinkman, Chuck	Charles Ernest; B9.16.1944 Cincinnati OH; BR/TR/6´1˝/185; [ChiA66 16/318]; d7.10; b–Ed; Col Ohio St.																								
1969	Chi A	14	15	2	1	0	0	0	0	1-0	0	5	.067	.125	.067	-43	-3	0-0	1.000	-1	103	57	C14	0	-0.4
1970	Chi A	9	20	4	5	1	0	0	0	3-0	0	3	.250	.348	.300	77	0	0-0	.974	0	303	101	C9	0	0.0
1971	Chi A	15	20	0	4	0	0	0	1	3-1	0	5	.200	.304	.200	44	-1	0-0	1.000	-2	33	196	C14	0	-0.3
1972	Chi A	35	52	1	7	0	0	0	0	4-0	0	7	.135	.196	.135	-0	-6	0-0	.985	3	80	150	C33	0	-0.3
1973	Chi A	63	139	13	26	6	0	1	10	11-0	1	37	.187	.252	.252	41	-11	0-0	.987	4	105	114	C63	0	-0.5
1974	Chi A	8	14	1	2	0	0	0	0	1-0	0	3	.143	.200	.143	-0	-2	0-0	1.000	-2	73	57	C8	15	-0.4
	Pit N	4	7	1	1	0	0	0	1	0-0	0	0	.143	.125	.143	-20	-1	0-0	1.000	-1	157	0	C4	0	-0.2
Total	6	148	267	22	46	7	0	1	12	23-1	1	60	.172	.240	.210	28	-24	0-0	.988	2	109	117	C145	15	-2.1
Brinkman, Ed	Edwin Albert; B12.8.1941 Cincinnati OH; BR/TR/6´0˝/170; d9.6; C8; b–Chuck; Col Cincinnati																								
1961	Was A	4	11	0	1	0	0	0	0	1-0	0	1	.091	.167	.091	-30	-2	0-0	.889	-0	104	166	3b3	0	-0.2
1962	Was A	54	133	8	22	7	1	0	4	11-0	0	28	.165	.228	.233	25	-14	1-0	.942	-8	86	101	S38,3b10	0	-1.9
1963	Was A	145	514	44	117	20	3	7	45	31-4	4	86	.228	.276	.319	67	-24	5-3	.950	4	111	109	S143	0	-0.7
1964	Was A	132	447	54	100	20	3	8	34	26-1	4	99	.224	.271	.336	68	-20	2-2	.969	2	104	104	S125	0	-0.8
1965	Was A	154	444	35	82	13	2	5	35	38-7	2	82	.185	.251	.257	46	-32	1-2	.964	0	95	93	S150	0	-2.2
1966	Was A	158	582	42	133	18	9	7	48	29-4	0	105	.229	.263	.326	70	-25	7-9	.965	7	106	94	S158	0	-0.6
1967	Was A	109	320	21	60	9	2	1	18	24-1	4	58	.188	.252	.237	47	-21	1-3	**.979**	2	**108**	100	S109	0	-1.2
1968	Was A	77	193	12	36	3	0	0	6	19-5	0	31	.187	.259	.202	43	-13	0-0	.967	-4	105	74	S74,2b2/lf	0	-1.4
1969	Was A	151	576	71	153	18	5	2	43	50-3	5	42	.266	.328	.325	88	-9	2-2	.976	20	113	104	S150	0	2.9
1970	Was A	158	625	63	164	17	2	1	40	60-0	5	41	.262	.330	.301	79	-17	8-9	.974	**31**	**117**	105	S157	0	3.3
1971	Det A	159	527	40	120	18	2	1	37	44-7	7	54	.228	.293	.275	60	-27	1-4	.980	4	102	94	S159	0	-0.5
1972	†Det A	**156**	516	42	105	19	1	6	49	38-9	3	51	.203	.259	.279	59	-26	0-0	**.990**	2	98	89	S156	0	-0.6
1973	Det A★	**162**	515	55	122	16	4	7	40	34-1	1	79	.237	.284	.324	67	-24	0-1	.968	-17	90	89	S162	0	-2.2
1974	Det A	153	502	55	111	15	3	14	54	29-0	3	71	.221	.266	.347	73	-19	2-0	.972	6	101	92	S151,3b2	0	0.6
1975	StL N	28	75	6	18	4	0	1	6	7-2	1	10	.240	.306	.333	76	-2	0-0	.948	0	97	108	S24	0	0.0
	Tex A	1	2	0	0	0	0	0	0	0-0	0	1	.000	.000	.000	-99	-1	0-0	1.000	-0	82	0	/3	0	-0.1
	NY A	44	63	2	11	4	1	0	2	3-0	1	6	.175	.224	.270	39	-5	0-0	.933	-6	84	112	S39,2b3,3b3	0	-0.9
	Year	45	65	2	11	4	1	0	2	3-0	1	7	.169	.217	.262	35	-6	0-0	.933	-6	84	112	S39,3b4,2b3	0	-1.0
Total	15	1845	6045	550	1355	201	38	60	461	444-44	40	845	.224	.280	.300	65	-281	30-35	.970	46	103	97	S1795,3b19,2b5/lf	0	-6.5
Brinkopf, Leon	Leon Clarence; B10.20.1926 Cape Girardeau MO; D7.2.1998 Cape Girardeau MO; BR/TR/5´11.5˝/185; d4.18																								
1952	Chi N	9	22	1	4	0	0	0	2	4	0	5	.182	.308	.182	38	-2	0-0	.955	-1	110	30	S6	0	-0.3
Briody, Fatty	Charles F. "Alderman"; B8.13.1858 Lansingburg NY; D6.22.1903 Chicago IL; TR/5´8.5˝/190; d6.16																								
1880	Tro N	1	4	0	0	0	0	0	0	0	—	0	.000	.000	.000	-95	-1	—	.700	-1	—	—	/C	—	-0.2
1882	Cle N	53	194	30	50	13	0	0	13	9	—	13	.258	.291	.325	101	1	—	.902	1	—	—	C53	—	0.6
1883	Cle N	40	145	23	34	5	1	0	10	3	—	13	.234	.250	.283	62	-7	—	.900	5	—	—	C33,2b4,1b2/3	—	0.1
1884	Cle N	43	148	17	25	6	0	1	12	6	—	19	.169	.201	.230	34	-11	—	.922	10	—	—	C42/rf	—	0.3
	Cin U	22	89	11	30	2	2	0	—	1	—	—	.337	.344	.404	117	-1	—	.943	12	—	—	C22	—	1.1
1885	StL N	62	215	14	42	9	0	1	17	12	—	23	.195	.238	.251	62	-8	—	.893	-7	—	—	C60/cf32	—	-1.0
1886	KC N	56	215	14	51	10	3	0	29	3	—	35	.237	.248	.312	65	-10	0	.919	-1	—	—	C54,O2(0/1/1)/1	—	-0.6
1887	Det N	33	128	24	29	6	1	1	26	9	1	10	.227	.283	.313	63	-7	6	.907	6	—	—	C33	—	0.2
1888	KC AA	13	48	1	10	1	0	0	8	1	0	—	.208	.224	.229	43	-3	0	.896	-3	—	—	C13	—	-0.5
Total	8	323	1186	134	271	52	7	3	115	44	1	113	.228	.257	.292	68	-47	6	.910	21	—	—	C311,2b5,O4(0/2/2),1b3,3b2	—	0.0
Bristow, George	George T.; B5.1870 Paw Paw IL; TR; d4.15																								
1899	Cle N	3	8	0	1	1	0	0	0	0	1	—	.125	.222	.250	32	-1	0	1.000	1	281	0	O3(1/0/2)	—	0.0
Brito, Bernardo	Bernardo; B12.4.1963 San Cristobal, D.R.; BR/TR/6´1˝/(190–210); d9.15																								
1992	Min A	8	14	1	2	1	0	0	2	0-0	0	4	.143	.133	.214	-1	-2	0-1	.750	-0	86	0	O3L/D	0	-0.3
1993	Min A	27	54	8	13	2	0	4	9	1-0	0	20	.241	.255	.500	97	-1	0-0	1.000	1	97	272	O10L,D7	0	-0.1
1995	Min A	5	5	1	1	0	0	1	1	0-0	1	3	.200	.333	.800	182	1	0-0	ø	0	—	—	D3	0	0.0
Total	3	40	73	10	16	3	0	5	12	1-0	1	27	.219	.237	.466	85	-2	0-1	.941	0	95	211	O13L,D11	0	-0.4
Brito, Jorge	Jorge Manuel (Uceta); B6.22.1966 Moncion, D.R.; BR/TR/6´1˝/190; d4.30																								
1995	Col N	18	51	5	11	3	0	0	7	2-0	1	17	.216	.259	.275	32	-5	1-0	.991	4	160	108	C18	0	0.0
1996	Col N	8	14	1	1	0	0	0	0	1-0	2	8	.071	.235	.071	-12	-2	0-0	1.000	3	97	64	C8	27	0.1
Total	2	26	65	6	12	3	0	0	7	3-0	3	25	.185	.254	.231	23	-7	1-0	.994	6	143	96	C26	27	0.1
Brito, Juan	Juan Ramon; B11.7.1979 Santiago Rodriguez, D.R.; BR/TR/5´11˝/205; d5.3																								
2002	KC A	9	23	1	7	2	0	0	1	0-0	0	3	.304	.304	.391	74	-1	0-0	.978	-1	53	230	C9	0	-0.1
2004	Ari N	54	171	17	35	7	0	3	12	9-1	1	41	.205	.246	.298	38	-16	1-0	.990	-0	82	146	C54	0	-1.3
Total	2	63	194	18	42	9	0	3	13	9-1	1	44	.216	.252	.309	42	-17	1-0	.989	-1	79	156	C63	0	-1.4
Brito, Tilson	Tilson Manuel (Jiminez); B5.28.1972 Santo Domingo, D.R.; BR/TR/6´0˝/(170–180); d4.1																								
1996	Tor A	26	80	10	19	7	0	1	7	10-0	3	18	.237	.344	.363	79	-2	1-1	.956	-1	99	124	2b18,S5,D2	0	-0.1
1997	Tor A	49	126	9	28	3	0	0	8	9-0	2	28	.222	.281	.246	40	-11	1-0	.989	-2	96	103	2b25,3b17,S8	0	-1.1
	Oak A	17	46	8	13	2	1	2	6	1-0	0	10	.283	.298	.500	103	0	0-0	.920	2	124	151	3b10,S6,2b2	22	0.2
	Year	66	172	17	41	5	1	2	14	10-0	2	38	.238	.285	.314	57	-11	1-0	.961	-1	100	124	2b27,3b27,S14	0	-0.9
Total	2	92	252	27	60	12	1	3	21	20-0	5	56	.238	.305	.329	64	-13	2-1	.974	-1	100	124	2b45,3b27,S19,D2	22	-1.0
Brittain, Gus	August Schuster; B11.29.1909 Wilmington NC; D2.16.1974 Wilmington NC; BR/TR/5´10˝/192; d7.22																								
1937	Cin N	3	6	0	1	0	0	0	0	0	0	3	.167	.167	.167	-10	-1	0	1.000	0	*0*	*0*	/C	—	-0.1
Britton, Gil	Stephen Gilbert; B9.21.1891 Parsons KS; D6.20.1983 Parsons KS; BR/TR/5´10˝/160; d9.20																								
1913	Pit N	3	12	0	0	0	0	0	0	0	0	2	.000	.000	.000	-99	-3	0	.824	-1	95	183	S3	—	-0.4

YEAR	TM LG	G	AB	R	H	2B	3B	HR	RBI	BB-IB	HP	SO	AVG	OBP	SLG	AOPS	ABR	SB-CS	FA	FR	RNG	THR	GAMES AT POSITION	DL	BFW
Brock, Greg	Gregory Allen; B6.14.1957 McMinnville OR; BL/TR/6´3˝/(200–205); [LAN79 13/336]; d9.1; Col Wyoming																								
1982	LA N	18	17	1	2	1	0	0	1	1-1	0	5	.118	.167	.176	-4	-2	0-0	1.000	-0	0	0	1b3	0	-0.3
1983	†LA N	146	455	64	102	14	2	20	66	83-12	1	81	.224	.343	.396	105	5	5-1	.991	6	114	94	1b140	0	0.3
1984	LA N	88	271	33	61	6	0	14	34	39-3	0	37	.225	.319	.402	103	1	8-0	.995	7	129	99	1b83	26	0.5
1985	†LA N	129	438	64	110	19	0	21	66	54-4	0	72	.251	.332	.438	117	9	4-2	.994	5	113	97	1b122	0	0.7
1986	LA N	115	325	33	76	13	0	16	52	37-5	0	60	.234	.309	.422	108	2	2-5	.996	13	148	70	1b99	21	0.8
1987	Mil A	141	532	81	159	29	3	13	85	57-4	6	63	.299	.371	.438	111	10	5-4	.993	5	112	95	1b141	15	0.6
1988	Mil A	115	364	53	77	16	1	6	50	63-16	3	48	.212	.329	.310	80	-7	6-2	.993	10	**135**	110	1b114/D	46	-0.4
1989	Mil A	107	373	40	99	16	0	12	52	43-8	3	49	.265	.345	.405	112	6	6-1	.995	-4	87	106	1b100,D7	58	-0.3
1990	Mil A	123	367	42	91	23	0	7	50	43-9	2	45	.248	.324	.368	95	-1	4-2	.995	-4	89	96	1b115	0	-1.3
1991	Mil A	31	60	9	17	4	0	1	6	14-1	0	9	.283	.419	.400	130	4	1-1	1.000	-1	76	116	1b25	0	0.1
Total	10	1013	3202	420	794	141	6	110	462	434-63	15	469	.248	.338	.399	104	27	41-18	.994	37	114	96	1b942,D8	166	0.7
Brock, John	John Roy; B10.16.1896 Hamilton IL; D10.27.1951 Clayton MO; BR/TR/5´6.5˝/165; d8.10																								
1917	StL N	7	15	4	6	1	0	0	2	0	0	2	.400	.400	.467	170	1	2	.944	-0	*140*	*92*	C4	—	0.1
1918	StL N	27	52	9	11	2	0	0	4	3	0	10	.212	.255	.250	56	-3	5	.951	-2	*81*	*137*	C18/rf	—	-0.4
Total	2	34	67	13	17	3	0	0	6	3	0	12	.254	.286	.299	81	-2	7	.949	-2	*93*	*128*	C22/rf	—	-0.3
Brock, Lou	Louis Clark; B6.18.1939 El Dorado AR; BL/TL/5´11.5˝/(170–175); d9.10; HF1985; Col Southern A&M																								
1961	Chi N	4	11	1	1	0	0	0	0	1-0	0	3	.091	.167	.091	-29	-2	0-0	.750	-1	101	0	O3C	0	-0.3
1962	Chi N	123	434	73	114	24	7	9	35	35-4	3	96	.263	.319	.412	92	-5	16-7	.965	-3	98	101	O106C	0	-1.0
1963	Chi N	148	547	79	141	19	11	9	37	31-2	4	122	.258	.300	.382	91	-8	24-12	.973	10	112	160	O140R	0	-0.6
1964	Chi N	52	215	30	54	9	2	2	14	13-0	2	40	.251	.300	.340	77	-7	10-3	.959	0	88	197	O52(0/2/51)	0	-0.9
	†StL N	103	419	81	146	21	9	12	44	27-0	2	87	.348	.387	.527	143	24	33-15	.949	2	103	105	O102(99/2/4)	0	2.3
	Year	155	634	111	200	30	11	14	58	40-0	4	127	.315	.358	.464	121	18	43-18	.953	3	98	136	O154(99/4/55)	0	1.4
1965	StL N	155	631	107	182	35	8	16	69	45-6	10	116	.288	.345	.445	110	9	63-27	.959	4	103	126	O153(150/2/7)	0	0.9
1966	StL N	156	643	94	183	24	12	15	46	31-6	3	134	.285	.320	.429	106	3	**74**-18	.936	-2	99	83	O154(122/0/34)	0	0.1
1967	†StL N★	159	689	**113**	206	32	12	21	76	24-6	6	109	.299	.327	.472	128	21	**52**-18	.956	2	102	121	O157L	0	2.1
1968	†StL N	159	660	92	184	**46**	**14**	6	51	46-7	3	124	.279	.328	.418	125	19	**62**-12	.952	1	105	88	O156L	0	2.3
1969	StL N	157	655	97	195	33	10	12	47	50-15	2	115	.298	.349	.434	117	14	**53**-14	.949	-3	94	81	O157L	0	0.9
1970	StL N	155	664	114	202	29	5	13	57	60-12	1	99	.304	.361	.422	106	6	51-15	.962	-7	91	78	O152(149/0/3)	0	-0.4
1971	StL N★	157	640	**126**	200	37	7	7	61	76-5	1	107	.313	.385	.425	124	23	**64**-19	.951	-7	92	68	O157(156/0/1)	0	1.5
1972	StL N☆	153	621	81	193	26	8	3	42	47-12	1	93	.311	.359	.393	115	12	**63**-18	.952	-7	88	60	O149L	0	0.4
1973	StL N	160	650	110	193	29	8	7	63	71-15	0	112	.297	.364	.398	111	11	**70**-20	.963	-6	93	27	O159L	0	0.4
1974	StL N★	153	635	105	194	25	7	3	48	61-16	2	88	.306	.368	.381	110	9	**118**-33	.967	-4	93	73	O152L	0	1.1
1975	StL N★	136	528	78	163	27	6	3	47	38-6	3	64	.309	.359	.400	105	4	56-16	.966	-2	101	53	O128L	0	0.1
1976	StL N	133	498	73	150	24	5	4	67	35-7	1	75	.301	.344	.394	108	5	56-19	.983	-3	94	72	O123L	0	0.1
1977	StL N	141	489	69	133	22	6	2	46	30-2	2	74	.272	.317	.354	80	-14	35-24	.954	-6	91	29	O130L	0	-2.7
1978	StL N	92	298	31	66	9	0	0	12	17-2	0	29	.221	.263	.252	45	-22	17-5	.975	-5	86	36	O79L	0	-3.1
1979	StL N★	120	405	56	123	15	4	5	38	23-1	3	43	.304	.342	.398	100	0	21-12	.958	-4	84	100	O98L	0	-0.8
Total	19	2616	10332	1610	3023	486	141	149	900	761-124	49	1730	.293	.343	.410	108	102	938-307	.959	-40	96	85	O2507(2164/115/240)	0	2.4
Brock, Tarrik	Tarrik Jumaan; B12.25.1973 Goleta CA; BL/TL/6´3˝/185; [DetA91 2/59]; d3.29																								
2000	Chi N	13	12	1	2	0	0	0	0	4-0	0	4	.167	.375	.167	44	-1	1-1	.889	-0	97	0	O10(9/2/0)	0	-0.1
Broderick, Matt	Matthew Thomas; B12.1.1877 Lattimer PA; D2.26.1940 Freeland PA; BR/TR/5´6.5˝/135; d5.1; Col Villanova																								
1903	Bro N	2	2	0	0	0	0	0	0	0	0	—	.000	.000	.000	-99	-1	0	1.000	0	0	1331	/2	—	0.0
Brodie, Steve	Walter Scott; B9.11.1868 Warrenton VA; D10.30.1935 Baltimore MD; BL/TR/5´11˝/180; d4.21																								
1890	Bos N	132	514	77	152	19	9	0	67	66	11	20	.296	.387	.368	111	9	29	**.953**	2	82	140	O132(2/19/114)	—	0.8
1891	Bos N	133	523	84	136	13	6	2	78	63	10	39	.260	.351	.319	85	-10	25	.951	8	122	**294**	O133(1/102/31)	—	-0.5
1892	StL N	154	602	85	153	10	9	4	60	52	4	31	.254	.318	.321	98	-2	28	.943	3	92	77	O137(1/121/17),2b16,3b2	—	-0.7
1893	StL N	107	469	71	149	16	8	2	79	33	11	16	.318	.376	.399	106	3	41	.951	5	112	181	O107(0/102/5)	—	0.1
	Bal N	25	97	18	35	7	2	0	19	12	3	2	.361	.446	.474	142	7	8	.963	-1	55	0	O25(2/24/0)	—	0.3
	Year	**132**	566	89	184	23	10	2	98	45	14	18	.325	.389	.412	112	10	49	.953	4	103	152	O132(2/126/5)	—	0.4
1894	†Bal N	**129**	573	134	210	25	11	3	113	18	13	8	.366	.399	.464	103	1	42	.950	-7	65	81	O129C	—	-1.1
1895	†Bal N	**131**	528	85	184	27	10	2	134	26	14	15	.348	.394	.449	114	10	35	.965	3	119	51	O131C	—	0.4
1896	†Bal N	**132**	516	98	153	19	11	2	87	36	18	17	.297	.363	.388	96	-3	25	.972	7	117	139	O132C	—	-0.4
1897	Pit N	100	370	47	108	7	12	2	53	25	7	—	.292	.348	.392	99	-2	11	**.983**	2	83	39	O100C	—	-0.5
1898	Pit N	42	156	15	41	5	0	0	21	6	3	—	.263	.303	.295	73	-6	3	.958	2	67	76	O42C	—	-0.6
	Bal N	23	98	12	30	3	2	0	19	5	1	—	.306	.346	.378	105	0	3	.923	1	144	0	O23C	—	0.0
	Year	65	254	27	71	8	2	0	40	11	4	—	.280	.320	.327	86	-5	6	.946	3	95	48	O65C	—	-0.6
1899	Bal N	137	531	82	164	26	1	3	87	31	23	—	.309	.373	.379	101	2	19	**.979**	-1	73	95	O137(0/136/1)	—	-0.7
1901	Bal A	83	306	41	95	6	6	2	41	25	8	—	.310	.378	.389	108	4	9	.963	-2	40	0	O83(11/72/0)	—	-0.2
1902	NY N	110	420	37	118	8	2	3	42	22	6	—	.281	.326	.331	104	1	11	.953	7	157	**215**	O110C	—	0.4
Total	12	1438	5703	886	1728	191	89	25	900	420	132	148	.303	.365	.381	102	14	289	.959	28	97	119	O1421(17/1243/168),2b16,3b2	—	-2.7
Brogna, Rico	Rico Joseph; B4.18.1970 Turners Falls MA; BL/TL/6´2˝/(200–205); [DetA88 1/26]; d8.8																								
1992	Det A	9	26	3	5	1	0	1	3	3-0	0	5	.192	.276	.346	72	-1	0-0	.982	0	126	151	1b8,D2	0	-0.1
1994	NY N	39	131	16	46	11	2	7	20	6-0	0	29	.351	.380	.626	158	11	1-0	.997	1	110	112	1b35	0	0.8
1995	NY N	134	495	72	143	27	2	22	76	39-7	2	111	.289	.342	.485	119	12	0-0	**.998**	0	100	101	1b131	0	0.2
1996	NY N	55	188	18	48	10	1	7	30	19-1	0	50	.255	.318	.431	102	0	0-0	.996	-2	84	114	1b52	102	-0.7
1997	Phi N	148	543	68	137	36	1	20	81	33-4	0	116	.252	.293	.433	89	-11	12-3	.994	9	114	89	1b145	0	-1.3
1998	Phi N	153	565	77	150	36	3	20	104	49-8	0	125	.265	.319	.446	100	-1	7-7	.996	13	126	89	1b151	0	-0.2
1999	Phi N	157	619	90	172	29	4	24	102	54-7	2	132	.278	.336	.454	97	-5	8-5	.995	8	120	96	1b157	0	-1.0
2000	Phi N	38	129	12	32	14	0	1	13	7-1	2	28	.248	.295	.380	70	-6	1-0	.996	-1	83	86	1b34	70	-0.9
	Bos A	43	56	8	11	3	0	1	8	3-0	0	13	.196	.237	.304	35	-6	0-0	.983	-2	74	87	1b37,D2	0	-0.8
2001	Atl N	72	206	15	51	9	0	3	21	14-1	1	46	.248	.297	.335	63	-12	3-1	.994	3	122	73	1b67	0	-1.3
Total	9	848	2958	379	795	176	13	106	458	227-29	7	655	.269	.320	.445	97	-19	32-16	.995	30	112	94	1b817,D4	172	-5.3
Brohamer, Jack	John Anthony; B2.26.1950 Maywood CA; BL/TR (BB 1972p)/5´10˝/(165–170); [CleA67 34/638]; d4.18																								
1972	Cle A	136	527	49	123	13	2	5	35	27-0	1	46	.233	.271	.294	66	-23	3-2	.977	4	106	103	2b132/3	0	-1.2
1973	Cle A	102	300	29	66	12	1	4	29	32-3	0	23	.220	.291	.307	68	-12	0-2	.971	10	108	103	2b97	0	0.3
1974	Cle A	101	315	33	85	11	1	2	30	26-0	3	22	.270	.329	.330	91	-3	2-1	.987	4	107	107	2b99	31	0.7
1975	Cle A	69	217	15	53	5	0	6	16	14-0	0	14	.244	.289	.350	80	-7	2-2	.976	-1	91	123	2b66	30	-0.4
1976	Chi A	119	354	33	89	12	2	7	40	44-9	3	28	.251	.333	.356	103	2	1-3	.984	14	106	98	2b117/3	0	2.3
1977	Chi A	59	152	26	39	10	3	2	20	21-4	1	8	.257	.347	.401	104	2	0-0	.923	-3	112	146	3b38,2b18/D	0	-0.1
1978	Bos A	81	244	34	57	14	1	1	25	25-1	0	13	.234	.300	.311	67	-10	1-3	.974	-6	91	97	3b30,D25,2b23	0	-1.8
1979	Bos A	64	192	25	51	7	1	1	11	15-1	0	15	.266	.316	.328	71	-8	0-3	.982	-1	95	92	2b36,3b22	17	-0.8
1980	Bos A	21	57	5	18	2	0	1	6	4-0	0	3	.316	.361	.404	103	0	0-0	.900	-1	92	150	3b13,2b4,D3	0	-0.1
	Cle A	53	142	13	32	5	1	1	15	14-4	0	6	.225	.291	.296	62	-7	0-1	.979	-4	93	90	2b47/D	0	-1.0
	Year	74	199	18	50	7	1	2	21	18-4	0	9	.251	.311	.327	74	-7	0-1	.981	-5	95	83	2b51,3b13,D4	0	-1.1
Total	9	805	2500	262	613	91	12	30	227	222-22	8	178	.245	.306	.327	79	-66	9-17	.979	14	102	102	2b639,3b105,D30	78	-2.1
Bronkie, Herman	Herman Charles "Dutch"; B3.31.1885 S.Manchester CT; D5.27.1968 Somers CT; BR/TR/5´9˝/165; d9.20																								
1910	Cle A	5	10	1	2	0	0	0	0	1	0	—	.200	.273	.200	48	-1	1	.625	-2	46	0	3b3/S	—	-0.3
1911	Cle A	2	6	0	1	0	0	0	0	0	0	—	.167	.167	.167	-7	-1	0	1.000	-0	37	0	3b2	—	-0.1
1912	Cle A	6	16	1	0	0	0	0	0	1	0	—	.000	.059	.000	-80	-4	0	.917	1	128	120	3b6	—	-0.2
1914	Chi N	1	1	1	1	1	0	0	1	0	0	0	1.000	1.000	2.000	786	1	0	.000	-1	0	0	/3	—	0.0
1918	StL N	18	68	7	15	3	0	1	7	2	0	4	.221	.243	.309	70	-3	0	.984	0	107	63	3b18	—	-0.2
1919	StL A	67	196	23	50	6	4	0	14	23	1	23	.255	.336	.327	84	-4	2	.939	4	115	133	3b34,2b16,1b2	—	0.1
1922	StL A	23	64	7	18	4	1	0	2	6	0	7	.281	.343	.375	84	-1	0-2	.917	-0	88	245	3b18	—	-0.1
Total	7	122	361	40	87	14	5	1	24	33	1	34	.241	.306	.316	74	-13	3-2	.931	2	105	132	3b82,2b16,1b2/S	—	-0.8

YEAR	TM LG	G	AB	R	H	2B	3B	HR	RBI	BB-IB	HP	SO	AVG	OBP	SLG	AOPS	ABR	SB-CS	FA	FR	RNG	THR	GAMES AT POSITION	DL	BFW
Brookens, Tom	Thomas Dale; B8.10.1953 Chambersburg PA; BR/TR/5´10˝/170; [DetA75*1/4]; d7.10; Col Mansfield; OF(0/2/6)																								
1979	Det A	60	190	23	50	5	2	4	21	11-0	2	40	.263	.309	.374	81	-6	10-3	.945	8	123	148	3b42,2b19/D	0	0.4
1980	Det A	151	509	64	140	25	9	10	66	32-3	1	71	.275	.315	.418	98	-3	13-11	.931	6	105	100	3b138,2b9/SD	0	0.1
1981	Det A	71	239	19	58	10	1	4	25	14-0	2	43	.243	.284	.343	79	-7	5-3	.952	3	104	114	3b71	0	-0.5
1982	Det A	140	398	40	92	15	3	9	58	27-0	0	63	.231	.277	.352	72	-16	5-9	.939	5	113	112	3b113,2b26,S9/cf	0	-1.4
1983	Det A	138	332	50	71	13	3	6	32	29-2	2	46	.214	.276	.325	68	-15	10-4	.928	6	101	129	3b103,S30,2b10/D	0	-0.8
1984	†Det A	113	224	32	55	11	4	5	26	19-0	1	33	.246	.306	.397	93	-2	6-6	.969	6	104	172	3b68,S28,2b26/D	16	0.6
1985	Det A	156	485	54	115	34	6	7	47	27-0	0	78	.237	.277	.375	77	-16	14-5	.943	3	99	106	3b151,S8,2b3/CD	0	-1.4
1986	Det A	98	281	42	76	11	2	3	25	20-0	1	42	.270	.319	.356	84	-6	11-8	.955	-8	99	76	3b35,2b31,S14,D14,O3(0/1/3)	0	-1.3
1987	†Det A	143	444	59	107	15	3	13	59	33-3	2	63	.241	.295	.376	80	-14	7-4	.954	-4	101	73	3b122,S16,2b11	0	-1.7
1988	Det A	136	441	62	107	23	5	5	38	44-2	3	74	.243	.313	.351	90	-6	4-4	.952	-4	96	78	3b136,S3/2	0	-1.0
1989	NY A	66	168	14	38	6	0	4	14	11-1	0	27	.226	.272	.333	71	-7	1-3	.926	-5	95	60	3b51,S7,2b5,O3R,D3	39	-1.3
1990	Cle A	64	154	18	41	7	2	1	20	14-1	0	25	.266	.322	.357	91	-2	0-0	.923	3	122	103	3b35,2b21,S3,1b2/D	15	0.1
Total	12	1336	3865	477	950	175	40	71	431	281-12	14	605	.246	.296	.367	82	-100	86-60	.943	19	103	102	3b1065,2b162,S119,D23,O7R,1b2/C	70	-8.2
Brooks, Hubie	Hubert; B9.24.1956 Los Angeles CA; BR/TR/6´0˝/(178–205); [NYN78 1/3]; d9.4; Col Arizona St.; OF(7/0/576)																								
1980	NY N	24	81	8	25	2	1	1	10	5-0	2	9	.309	.364	.395	113	1	1-1	.966	-1	91	58	3b23	0	0.0
1981	NY N	98	358	34	110	21	2	4	38	23-2	1	65	.307	.345	.411	116	7	9-5	.924	1	104	93	3b93,O3(1/0/2)/S	0	0.8
1982	NY N	126	457	40	114	21	2	2	40	28-5	5	76	.249	.297	.317	72	-17	6-3	.931	-9	95	78	3b126	24	-2.9
1983	NY N	150	586	53	147	18	4	5	58	24-2	4	96	.251	.284	.321	68	-27	6-4	.950	6	**112**	106	3b145,2b7	0	-2.5
1984	NY N	153	561	61	159	23	2	16	73	48-15	2	79	.283	.341	.417	114	9	6-5	.929	-12	87	102	3b129,S26	0	-0.3
1985	Mon N	156	605	67	163	34	7	13	100	34-6	5	79	.269	.310	.413	107	3	6-9	.958	-35	90	89	S155	0	-1.7
1986	Mon N★	80	306	50	104	18	5	14	58	25-3	2	60	.340	.388	.569	163	25	4-2	.958	-7	96	82	S80	65	2.7
1987	Mon N★	112	430	57	113	22	3	14	72	24-2	1	72	.263	.301	.426	87	-9	4-3	.953	-23	87	91	S109	44	-2.2
1988	Mon N	151	588	61	164	35	2	20	90	35-3	1	108	.279	.318	.447	112	8	7-3	.968	-5	93	111	O149R	0	0.0
1989	Mon N	148	542	56	145	30	1	14	70	39-2	4	108	.268	.317	.404	104	3	6-11	.964	-6	92	84	O140R	0	-1.1
1990	LA N	153	568	74	151	28	1	20	91	33-10	6	108	.266	.307	.424	103	1	2-5	.964	-7	90	90	O150R	0	-1.3
1991	NY N	103	357	48	85	11	1	16	50	44-8	3	62	.238	.324	.409	106	3	3-1	.972	-2	96	90	O100R	49	-0.2
1992	Cal A	82	306	28	66	13	0	8	36	12-3	1	46	.216	.247	.337	61	-17	3-3	.986	-0	97	71	D70,1b6	76	-2.1
1993	KC A	75	168	14	48	12	0	1	24	11-1	1	27	.286	.331	.375	84	-3	0-1	.966	1	98	157	O40(6/0/34),1b3,D9	0	-0.4
1994	KC A	34	61	5	14	2	0	1	14	2-0	0	10	.230	.239	.311	43	-5	1-0	1.000	-0	45	117	D19,1b4	0	-0.6
Total	15	1645	5974	656	1608	290	31	149	824	387-62	38	1005	.269	.315	.403	99	-18	64-56	.966	-99	93	97	O582R,3b516,S371,D98,1b13,2b7	258	-11.8
Brooks, Jerry	Jerome Edward; B3.23.1967 Syracuse NY; BR/TR/6´0˝/195; [LAN88 12/296]; d9.6; Col Clemson																								
1993	LA N	9	9	2	2	1	0	1	1	0-0	0	2	.222	.222	.667	134	0	0-0	ø	-0	0	0	O2R	0	0.0
1996	Fla N	8	5	2	2	0	1	0	3	1-0	1	1	.400	.571	.800	264	1	0-0	1.000	-0	129	0	O2R/1	0	0.1
Total	2	17	14	4	4	1	1	1	4	1-0	1	3	.286	.375	.714	190	1	0-0	1.000	-1	75	0	O4R/1	0	0.1
Brooks, Mandy	Jonathan Joseph (b Jonathan Joseph Brozek); B8.18.1897 Milwaukee WI; D6.17.1962 Kirkwood MO; BR/TR/5´9˝/165; d5.30																								
1925	Chi N	90	349	55	98	25	7	14	72	19	2	28	.281	.322	.513	108	2	10-3	.977	3	105	111	O89C	—	0.3
1926	Chi N	26	48	7	9	1	0	1	6	5	1	5	.188	.278	.271	48	-4	0	1.000	1	97	161	O18(4/5/9)	—	-0.3
Total	2	116	397	62	107	26	7	15	78	24	3	33	.270	.316	.484	101	-2	10-3	.979	4	104	117	O107(4/94/9)	—	0.0
Brooks, Bobby	Robert; B11.1.1945 Los Angeles CA; D10.11.1994 Harbor City CA; BR/TR/5´8.5˝/165; [OakA65 9/256]; d9.1; Col Los Angeles Harbor (CA) JC																								
1969	Oak A	29	79	13	19	5	0	3	10	20-1	1	24	.241	.396	.418	134	5	0-2	1.000	-1	84	116	O21(16/0/5)	0	0.3
1970	Oak A	7	18	2	6	1	0	2	5	1-0	0	7	.333	.368	.722	200	2	0-1	1.000	-1	53	0	O5(4/0/2)	0	0.1
1972	Oak A	15	39	4	7	0	0	0	5	8-1	0	8	.179	.319	.179	54	-2	0-1	.930	1	137	0	O11C	0	-0.2
1973	Cal A	4	7	0	1	0	0	0	0	0-0	0	3	.143	.143	.143	-21	-1	0-0	ø	-0	0	0	/lf	0	-0.2
Total	4	55	143	19	33	6	0	5	20	29-2	1	42	.231	.362	.378	115	4	0-4	.964	-1	95	65	O38(21/11/7)	0	0.0
Brosius, Scott	Scott David; B8.15.1966 Hillsboro OR; BR/TR/6´1˝/(185–202); [OakA87 20/511]; d8.7; Col Linfield; OF(37/68/74)																								
1991	Oak A	36	68	9	16	5	0	2	4	3-0	0	11	.235	.268	.397	86	-2	3-1	1.000	-1	67	59	2b18,O13(5/0/10),3b7/D	0	-0.2
1992	Oak A	38	87	13	19	2	0	4	13	3-1	2	13	.218	.258	.379	81	-3	3-0	1.000	-3	75	112	O20(4/0/19),3b12,1b3/SD	45	-0.6
1993	Oak A	70	213	26	53	10	1	6	25	14-0	1	37	.249	.296	.390	88	-5	6-0	.991	-2	97	81	O46(8/34/6),1b11,3b10,S6,D2	0	-0.5
1994	Oak A	96	324	31	77	14	1	14	49	24-0	2	57	.238	.289	.417	87	-8	2-6	.946	5	102	125	3b93,O7(2/2/4)/1	18	-0.4
1995	Oak A	123	389	69	102	19	2	17	46	41-0	8	67	.262	.342	.452	111	6	4-2	.918	-2	107	89	3b60,O49(8/22/22),1b18,2b3,S3,D2	0	0.2
1996	Oak A	114	428	73	130	25	0	22	71	59-4	7	85	.304	.393	.516	130	21	7-2	.969	15	121	124	3b109,1b10,O4(3/2/0)	51	3.3
1997	Oak A	129	479	59	97	20	1	11	41	34-1	4	102	.203	.259	.317	50	-37	9-4	.977	17	122	124	3b107,S30,O22(6/6/11)	22	-1.8
1998	†NY A★	152	530	86	159	34	0	19	98	52-1	10	97	.300	.371	.472	123	19	11-8	.948	9	106	145	3b150,1b3/rf	0	2.7
1999	†NY A	133	473	64	117	26	1	17	71	39-2	6	74	.247	.307	.414	85	-12	9-3	**.962**	4	100	97	3b132/D	15	-0.6
2000	†NY A	135	470	57	108	20	0	16	64	45-1	2	73	.230	.299	.374	70	-23	0-3	.968	-3	92	99	3b134,1b2,O2(1/0/1)/D	20	-2.4
2001	†NY A	120	428	57	123	25	2	13	49	34-2	5	83	.287	.343	.446	106	4	3-1	.935	2	97	107	3b120,O2C	36	0.6
Total	11	1146	3889	544	1001	200	8	141	531	348-12	47	699	.257	.323	.422	94	-40	57-30	.956	41	105	114	3b934,O166R,1b48,S40,2b21,D8	207	0.3
Broskie, Sig	Sigmund Theodore "Chops"; B3.23.1911 Iselin PA; D5.17.1975 Canton OH; BR/TR/5´11.5˝/200; d9.11																								
1940	Bos N	11	22	1	6	1	0	0	4	1	0	2	.273	.304	.318	76	-1	0	.935	0	*125*	*148*	C11	—	0.0
Brottem, Tony	Anton Christian; B4.30.1891 Halstad MN; D8.5.1929 Chicago IL; BR/TR/6´0.5˝/176; d4.17; Mil 1918																								
1916	StL N	26	33	3	6	1	0	0	4	3	0	10	.182	.250	.212	43	-2	1	.950	-1	75	172	C15,O2(0/1/1)	—	-0.3
1918	StL N	2	4	0	0	0	0	0	0	1	0	0	.000	.200	.000	-39	-1	0	1.000	1	384	0	1b2	—	0.0
1921	Was A	4	7	1	1	0	0	0	0	2	0	1	.143	.333	.143	26	-1	0-0	1.000	1	*143*	*81*	C4	—	0.0
	Pit N	30	91	6	22	2	0	0	9	3	0	11	.242	.266	.264	40	-8	0-1	.983	-0	*135*	*86*	C29	—	-0.7
Total	3	62	135	10	29	3	0	0	13	9	0	22	.215	.264	.237	38	-12	1-1	.977	1	*124*	*103*	C48,1b2,O2(0/1/1)	—	-1.0
Broughton, Cal	Cecil Calvert; B12.28.1860 Magnolia WI; D3.15.1939 Evansville WI; BR/TR/5´10˝/180; d5.2																								
1883	Cle N	4	10	2	2	0	0	0	1	2	—	2	.200	.333	.200	68	0	—	.950	0	—	—	C4	—	0.0
	Bal AA	9	32	1	6	0	0	0	—	1	—	—	.188	.212	.188	29	-3	—	.825	-2	—	—	C8/rf	—	-0.4
1884	Mil U	11	39	5	12	5	0	0	—	0	—	—	.308	.308	.436	226	5	—	.937	-0	—	—	C7,O5(1/4/0)	—	0.4
1885	StL AA	4	17	1	1	0	0	0	1	0	0	—	.059	.059	.059	-60	-3	—	.889	-1	—	—	C4	—	-0.3
	NY AA	11	41	1	6	1	0	0	1	1	0	—	.146	.167	.171	7	-4	—	.860	-1	—	—	C11	—	-0.4
	Year	15	58	2	7	1	0	0	2	1	0	—	.121	.136	.138	-14	-7	—	.867	-2	—	—	C15	—	-0.7
1888	Det N	1	4	0	0	0	0	0	0	0	0	0	.000	.000	.000	-99	-1	0	1.000	1	—	—	/C	—	0.0
Total	4	40	143	10	27	6	0	0	3	4	0	2	.189	.211	.231	43	-6	0	.887	-4	—	—	C35,O6(1/4/1)	—	-0.7
Brouhard, Mark	Mark Steven; B5.22.1956 Burbank CA; BR/TR/6´1˝/(200–210); [AnaA76*4/74]; d4.12; Col Los Angeles Pierce (CA) JC																								
1980	Mil A	45	125	17	29	6	0	5	16	7-0	1	24	.232	.278	.400	86	-3	1-0	.964	0	121	0	D21,O12(4/0/8),1b10	0	-0.4
1981	Mil A	60	186	19	51	6	3	2	20	7-1	2	41	.274	.305	.371	99	-1	1-1	.990	3	95	206	O51(7/0/46),D7	0	-0.1
1982	†Mil A	40	108	16	29	4	1	4	10	9-0	2	17	.269	.336	.435	116	2	0-3	.986	2	119	103	O30(7/0/23),D7	0	0.2
1983	Mil A	56	185	25	51	10	1	7	23	9-0	2	39	.276	.315	.454	117	4	0-4	.991	3	122	30	O42(38/0/8),D11	20	0.3
1984	Mil A	66	197	20	47	7	0	6	22	16-3	2	36	.239	.298	.365	87	-4	0-3	.983	5	107	186	O52(48/0/4),D8	0	-0.2
1985	Mil A	37	108	11	28	7	2	1	13	5-1	1	26	.259	.298	.389	86	-2	0-0	.964	-2	98	0	O29(10/0/21)/D	0	-0.5
Total	6	304	909	108	235	40	7	25	104	53-5	10	183	.259	.305	.400	98	-4	2-11	.983	11	109	112	O216(114/0/110),D55,1b10	20	-0.7
Broussard, Ben	Benjamin Isaac; B9.24.1976 Beaumont TX; BL/TL/6´2˝/220; [CinN99 2/65]; d6.22; Col McNeese St.																								
2002	Cle A	39	112	10	27	4	0	4	9	7-1	1	25	.241	.292	.384	76	-4	0-0	.960	-2	91	66	O32L,1b4,D3	0	-0.7
2003	Cle A	116	386	53	96	21	3	16	55	32-2	5	75	.249	.312	.443	97	-2	5-2	.991	-2	96	98	1b114	7	-1.3
2004	Cle A	139	418	57	115	28	5	17	82	52-3	12	95	.275	.370	.488	126	17	4-2	.994	1	103	109	1b133	0	0.8
2005	Cle A	142	466	59	119	30	5	19	68	32-5	4	98	.255	.307	.464	105	2	2-2	.992	-6	80	**122**	1b138,D2	0	-1.5
2006	Cle A	88	268	44	86	14	0	13	46	17-1	1	58	.321	.361	.519	130	11	0-1	.989	5	137	99	1b80	0	0.9
	Sea A	56	164	17	39	7	0	8	17	9-2	2	45	.238	.282	.427	86	-4	2-0	.976	1	172	164	D45,1b10	0	-0.6
	Year	144	432	61	125	21	0	21	63	26-3	3	103	.289	.331	.484	114	7	2-1	.980	6	141	106	1b90,D45	0	0.3
Total	5	580	1814	240	482	104	13	77	277	149-14	25	396	.266	.328	.465	109	20	13-7	.992	-3	101	109	1b479,D50,O32L	7	-2.4
Brouthers, Art	Arthur Henry; B11.25.1882 Montgomery AL; D9.28.1959 Charleston SC; BR/TR/6´1˝/?; d4.14																								
1906	Phi A	37	144	18	30	5	1	0	14	5	1	—	.208	.240	.257	54	-8	4	.900	-3	86	0	3b35/2	—	-1.1

YEAR	TM LG	G	AB	R	H	2B	3B	HR	RBI	BB-IB	HP	SO	AVG	OBP	SLG	AOPS	ABR	SB-CS	FA	FR	RNG	THR	GAMES AT POSITION	DL	BFW
BROUTHERS, DAN	Dennis Joseph "Big Dan"; B5.8.1858 Sylvan Lake NY; D8.2.1932 E.Orange NJ; BL/TL/6´2˝/207; d6.23; HF1945; ▲																								
1879	Tro N	39	168	17	46	12	1	4	17	1	—	18	.274	.278	.429	138	7	—	.926	-5	63	59	1b37,P3	—	0.1
1880	Tro N	3	12	0	2	0	0	0	1	1	—	0	.167	.231	.167	35	-1	—	.893	-1	0	70	1b3	—	-0.2
1881	Buf N	65	270	60	86	18	9	**8**	45	18	—	22	.319	.361	**.541**	182	25	—	.797	-6	72	62	O35(33/0/2),1b30	—	1.5
1882	Buf N	**84**	351	71	**129**	23	11	6	63	21	—	7	**.368**	**.403**	**.547**	**198**	**38**	—	**.974**	1	84	84	1b84	—	2.8
1883	Buf N	**98**	425	85	**159**	41	**17**	3	**97**	16	—	17	**.374**	**.397**	**.572**	**186**	**43**	—	.961	1	108	82	1b97/3P	—	3.0
1884	Buf N	94	398	82	130	22	15	14	79	33	—	20	.327	.378	**.563**	**186**	38	—	.964	0	112	93	1b93/3	—	2.7
1885	Buf N	98	407	87	146	32	11	7	59	34	—	10	.359	.408	**.543**	199	44	—	.975	-2	76	92	1b98	—	3.1
1886	Det N	121	489	139	181	**40**	15	**11**	72	66	—	16	.370	.445	**.581**	**203**	**63**	21	.968	-8	58	123	1b121	—	3.9
1887	†Det N	123	500	**153**	169	**36**	20	12	101	71	6	9	.338	**.426**	.562	**166**	**46**	34	.969	-4	80	103	1b123	—	2.6
1888	Det N	129	522	**118**	160	**33**	11	9	66	68	12	13	.307	.399	.464	172	**47**	34	.971	-2	101	94	1b129	—	3.3
1889	Bos N	126	485	105	181	26	9	7	118	66	**14**	6	**.373**	.462	.507	160	42	22	.974	1	104	**119**	1b126	—	2.8
1890	Bos P	123	460	117	152	36	9	1	97	99	18	17	.330	**.466**	.454	137	32	28	.963	2	119	109	1b123	—	1.8
1891	Bos AA	130	486	117	170	26	19	5	109	87	24	20	**.350**	**.471**	**.512**	**184**	**60**	31	.978	-7	63	121	1b130	—	3.5
1892	Bro N	152	588	121	**197**	30	20	5	**124**	84	16	30	**.335**	.432	.480	**182**	**64**	31	.982	12	129	82	1b152	—	**6.8**
1893	Bro N	77	282	57	95	21	11	2	59	52	6	10	.337	.450	.511	163	29	9	.986	4	113	110	1b77	—	2.6
1894	†Bal N	123	525	137	182	39	23	9	128	67	5	9	.347	.425	.560	130	25	38	.976	-2	95	110	1b123	—	1.7
1895	Bal N	5	23	2	6	2	0	0	5	1	0	1	.261	.292	.348	63	-1	0	1.000	0	119	322	1b5	—	-0.1
	Lou N	24	97	13	30	10	1	2	15	11	0	2	.309	.380	.495	133	5	1	.953	-2	79	87	1b24	—	0.2
	Year	29	120	15	36	12	1	2	20	12	0	3	.300	.364	.467	119	4	1	.960	-2	86	126	1b29	—	0.1
1896	Phi N	57	218	42	75	13	3	1	41	44	4	11	.344	.462	.445	141	17	7	.983	-3	74	116	1b57	—	1.2
1904	NY N	2	5	0	0	0	0	0	0	0	0	—	.000	.000	.000	-96	-1	0	1.000	-0	0	0	/1	—	-0.1
Total	19	1673	6711	1523	2296	460	205	106	1296	840	105	238	.342	.423	.519	169	622	256	.971	-20	94	102	1b1633,O35(33/0/2),P4,3b2	—	43.2
BROVIA, JOE	Joseph John "Ox" (b Giuseppe Giovanni Brovia); B2.18.1922 Davenport CA; D8.15.1994 Santa Cruz CA; BL/TR/6´3˝/195; d7.3																								
1955	Cin N	21	18	0	2	0	0	0	4	1-0	0	6	.111	.150	.111	-25	-3	0-0	ø	0	—	—	/H	0	-0.3
BROWER, FRANK	Frank Willard "Turkeyfoot"; B3.26.1893 Gainesville VA; D11.20.1960 Baltimore MD; BL/TR/6´2˝/180; d8.14; Col Washington and Lee; ▲																								
1920	Was A	36	119	21	37	7	2	1	13	9	3	11	.311	.374	.429	115	3	1-1	.900	-1	85	141	O20(1/0/19),1b9/3	—	0.1
1921	Was A	83	203	31	53	12	3	1	35	18	3	7	.261	.330	.365	81	-6	1-1	.917	4	112	148	O46R,1b4	—	-0.6
1922	Was A	139	471	61	138	20	6	9	71	52	10	25	.293	.375	.418	112	9	8-6	.978	-3	100	70	O121R,1b7	—	-0.3
1923	Cle A	126	397	77	113	25	8	16	66	62	8	32	.285	.392	.509	136	21	6-5	.988	-1	100	110	1b112,O4(1/0/3)	—	1.3
1924	Cle A	66	107	16	30	10	1	3	20	27	2	9	.280	.434	.477	133	7	1-1	.990	1	117	67	1b26,P4,O3(2/0/1)	—	0.5
Total	5	450	1297	206	371	74	20	30	205	168	26	84	.286	.379	.443	117	34	17-14	.952	-0	101	96	O194(4/0/190),1b158,P4/3	—	1.0
BROWER, LOUIS	Louis Lester; B7.1.1900 Cleveland OH; D3.4.1994 Tyler TX; BR/TR/5´10˝/155; d6.13																								
1931	Det A	21	62	3	10	1	0	0	6	8	2	5	.161	.278	.177	21	-7	1-0	.886	-6	71	95	S20,2b2	—	-1.1
BROWER, BOB	Robert Richard; B1.10.1960 Jamaica NY; BR/TR/5´11˝/190; d9.3; Col Duke																								
1986	Tex A	21	9	3	1	1	0	0	0	0-0	0	3	.111	.111	.222	-12	-1	1-2	1.000	-1	79	0	O17(16/1/1)/D	0	-0.3
1987	Tex A	127	303	63	79	10	3	14	46	36-0	0	66	.261	.338	.452	107	2	15-9	.964	-4	95	47	O106(45/67/6),D7	0	-0.3
1988	Tex A	82	201	29	45	7	0	1	11	27-0	0	38	.224	.316	.274	65	-9	10-5	.972	-3	89	81	O59(26/33/4),D13	23	-1.3
1989	NY A	26	69	9	16	3	0	2	3	6-0	0	11	.232	.293	.362	84	-2	3-1	.970	3	131	142	O25(1/9/15)/D	13	0.2
Total	4	256	582	104	141	21	3	17	60	69-0	0	118	.242	.322	.376	88	-10	29-17	.968	-4	97	68	O207(88/110/26),D22	36	-1.7
BROWN, ADRIAN	Adrian Demond; B2.7.1974 McComb MS; BB/TR (BR 2002p)/6´0˝/(175–200); [PitN92 48/1351]; d5.16																								
1997	Pit N	48	147	17	28	6	0	1	10	13-0	4	18	.190	.273	.252	38	-13	8-4	.987	-1	90	169	O38(0/35/3)	0	-1.4
1998	Pit N	41	152	20	43	4	1	0	5	9-0	0	18	.283	.323	.322	70	-7	4-0	.977	1	103	137	O38(3/34/1)	0	-0.5
1999	Pit N	116	226	34	61	5	2	4	17	33-2	1	39	.270	.364	.363	85	-5	5-3	.966	-4	90	82	O96(4/29/66)	0	-0.9
2000	Pit N	104	308	64	97	18	3	4	28	29-1	0	34	.315	.373	.432	103	2	13-1	.976	-1	93	164	O92(7/71/15)	51	0.3
2001	Pit N	8	31	3	6	0	0	1	2	3-0	0	3	.194	.265	.290	42	-3	2-1	1.000	-0	104	0	O7C	179	-0.3
2002	Pit N	91	208	20	45	10	2	1	21	19-0	1	34	.216	.284	.298	53	-14	10-6	.974	-4	92	34	O71(0/64/9)	0	-1.9
2003	†Bos A	9	15	2	3	0	0	0	1	1-0	0	4	.200	.250	.200	20	-2	2-0	1.000	-0	85	0	O9(3/6/0)	0	-0.2
2004	KC A	5	11	0	3	0	0	0	0	0-0	0	2	.273	.273	.273	43	-1	0-0	1.000	0	141	0	O5(4/0/1)	0	-0.1
2006	Tex A	25	36	6	7	1	0	0	2	2-0	0	9	.194	.231	.222	20	-4	1-0	.971	3	122	494	O24(3/10/11)	0	-0.1
Total	9	447	1134	166	293	44	8	11	86	109-3	6	161	.258	.325	.340	72	-47	45-15	.976	-6	95	124	O380(24/256/106)	230	-5.1
BROWN, BRANT	Brant Michael; B6.22.1971 Porterville CA; BL/TL/6´3˝/(205–220); [ChiN92 3/79]; d6.15; Col Cal St.–Fresno																								
1996	Chi N	29	69	11	21	1	0	5	9	2-1	1	17	.304	.329	.536	120	2	3-3	1.000	2	151	35	1b18	0	0.2
1997	Chi N	46	137	15	32	7	1	5	15	7-0	3	28	.234	.286	.409	77	-5	2-1	1.000	0	102	204	O27L,1b12	0	-0.7
1998	†Chi N	124	347	56	101	17	7	14	48	30-2	1	95	.291	.348	.501	116	7	4-5	.963	-3	101	20	O102(48/69/0),1b7	29	0.2
1999	Pit N	130	341	49	79	20	3	16	58	22-3	4	114	.232	.283	.449	82	-12	3-4	.981	1	108	96	O82(0/23/59),1b7,D6	0	-1.3
2000	Fla N	41	73	4	14	6	0	2	6	3-0	0	33	.192	.224	.356	46	-7	1-0	.923	-1	85	0	O13(8/0/5),1b5	0	-0.7
	Chi N	54	89	7	14	1	0	3	10	10-0	1	29	.157	.248	.270	32	-10	2-1	1.000	1	110	0	O28(18/9/3),1b7	0	-1.0
	Year	95	162	11	28	7	0	5	16	13-0	1	62	.173	.237	.309	38	-16	3-1	.980	-0	102	0	O41(26/9/8),1b12	0	-1.7
Total	5	424	1056	142	261	52	11	45	146	74-6	10	316	.247	.301	.445	88	-25	15-14	.975	1	104	65	O252(101/101/67),1b56,D6	29	-3.3
BROWN, CURTIS	Curtis; B9.14.1945 Sacramento CA; BR/TR/5´11˝/180; d5.27; b–Leon																								
1973	Mon N	1	4	0	0	0	0	0	0	0-0	0	0	.000	.000	.000	-96	-1	0-0	1.000	0	159	0	/lf	0	-0.1
BROWN, DARRELL	Darrell Wayne; B10.29.1955 Oklahoma City OK; BB/TR/6´0˝/(180–184); [DetA77 3/57]; d4.11; Col Cal St.–Los Angeles																								
1981	Det A	16	4	4	1	0	0	0	0	0-0	0	1	.250	.250	.250	43	0	1-0	1.000	-0	70	0	O6(1/2/3),D4	0	0.0
1982	Oak A	8	18	2	6	0	1	0	3	1-0	0	2	.333	.368	.444	126	0	1-0	1.000	-1	90	0	O7(1/0/6)/D	0	0.0
1983	Min A	91	309	40	84	6	2	0	22	10-0	1	28	.272	.297	.304	63	-16	3-3	.995	-4	95	44	O81(5/76/0),D3	0	-2.1
1984	Min A	95	260	36	71	9	3	1	19	14-1	0	16	.273	.309	.342	76	-9	4-1	.993	3	109	115	O55(19/35/0),D13	0	-0.7
Total	4	210	591	82	162	15	6	1	44	25-1	1	47	.274	.304	.325	71	-25	9-4	.994	-2	100	70	O149(26/113/9),D21	0	-2.8
BROWN, DELOS	Delos Hight; B10.4.1892 Anna IL; D12.21.1964 Carbondale IL; BR/TR/5´9˝/160; d6.12; Col Millikin																								
1914	Chi A	1	1	0	0	0	0	0	0	0	0	1	.000	.000	.000	-99	0	0	ø	0	—	—	/H	—	0.0
BROWN, DEE	Dermal Bram; B3.27.1978 Bronx NY; BL/TR/6´0˝/(210–225); [KCA96 1/14]; d9.14																								
1998	KC A	5	3	2	0	0	0	0	0	0-0	0	1	.000	.000	.000	-96	-1	0-0	1.000	0	144	0	O2R,D3	0	-0.1
1999	KC A	12	25	1	2	0	0	0	0	2-0	0	7	.080	.148	.080	-38	-5	0-0	.929	2	195	501	O3L,D2	0	-0.4
2000	KC A	15	25	4	4	1	0	0	4	3-0	0	9	.160	.250	.200	15	-3	0-0	1.000	1	145	0	O5L	0	-0.3
2001	KC A	106	380	39	93	19	0	7	40	22-4	1	81	.245	.286	.350	61	-22	5-3	.988	-3	91	58	O83(77/4/3),D20	40	-2.8
2002	KC A	16	51	5	12	3	1	1	7	4-0	0	20	.235	.291	.392	70	-2	0-0	.923	-1	71	0	O8L,D5	0	-0.4
2003	KC A	50	132	16	30	7	0	2	14	8-1	2	37	.227	.280	.326	56	-8	1-1	.985	3	120	132	O33(17/0/17),D11	52	-0.7
2004	KC A	59	195	19	49	7	0	4	24	11-0	1	50	.251	.293	.349	67	-10	2-2	.970	-0	98	143	O53L/D	24	-1.2
Total	7	263	811	86	190	37	1	14	89	50-5	4	205	.234	.281	.334	57	-51	8-6	.978	-0	100	97	O187(163/4/22),D42	116	-5.9
BROWN, DRUMMOND	Drummond Nicol; B1.31.1885 Los Angeles CA; D1.27.1927 Parkville MO; BR/TR/6´0˝/180; d4.25																								
1913	Bos N	15	34	3	11	1	0	1	2	2	0	9	.324	.361	.441	126	1	0	.960	-3	92	58	C12	—	-0.1
1914	KC F	31	58	4	11	3	0	0	5	7	0	6	.190	.277	.241	44	-5	1	.954	2	*106*	*116*	C23,1b2	—	-0.2
1915	KC F	77	227	13	55	10	1	1	26	12	3	23	.242	.289	.308	71	-13	3	.961	-2	*94*	*103*	C65/1	—	-1.0
Total	3	123	319	20	77	14	1	2	33	21	3	38	.241	.294	.310	72	-17	4	.960	-3	*96*	*101*	C100,1b3	—	-1.3
BROWN, ED	Edward P.; B Chicago IL; TR/?/178; d8.19; ▲																								
1882	StL AA	17	60	4	11	0	0	0	—	4	—	—	.183	.234	.183	41	-4	—	.808	-2	92	0	O15(2/0/13),2b2/P	—	-0.5
1884	Tol AA	42	153	13	27	3	0	0	—	2	0	—	.176	.187	.196	24	-13	—	.815	-8	77	24	3b40,O2L/CP	—	-1.8
Total	2	59	213	17	38	3	0	0	—	6	0	—	.178	.201	.192	29	-17	—	.815	-10	77	24	3b40,O17(4/0/13),P2,2b2/C	—	-2.3
BROWN, EDDIE	Edward William "Glass Arm Eddie"; B7.17.1891 Milligan NE; D9.10.1956 Vallejo CA; BR/TR/6´3˝/190; d9.26; Col Syracuse																								
1920	NY N	3	8	1	1	1	0	0	0	0	0	3	.125	.125	.250	6	-1	0-0	1.000	-0	97	0	O2C	—	-0.2
1921	NY N	70	128	16	36	6	2	0	12	4	4	11	.281	.324	.359	80	-4	1-0	.956	-1	101	56	O30(2/26/2)	—	-0.6
1924	Bro N	114	455	56	140	30	4	5	78	26	0	15	.308	.345	.424	108	5	3-5	.975	-4	106	26	O114C	—	-0.4
1925	Bro N	**153**	618	88	189	39	11	5	99	22	2	18	.306	.332	.429	95	-6	3-4	.972	1	108	49	O153C	—	-1.2

YEAR	TM LG	G	AB	R	H	2B	3B	HR	RBI	BB-IB	HP	SO	AVG	OBP	SLG	AOPS	ABR	SB-CS	FA	FR	RNG	THR	GAMES AT POSITION	DL	BFW
1926	Bos N	**153**	612	71	**201**	31	8	2	84	23	2	20	.328	.355	.415	117	12	5	.965	3	110	69	O153(73/80/0)	—	0.6
1927	Bos N	**155**	558	64	171	35	6	2	75	28	0	20	.306	.340	.401	106	4	11	.980	3	**111**	74	O150L/1	—	-0.4
1928	Bos N	142	523	45	140	28	2	2	59	24	4	22	.268	.305	.340	72	-22	6	.960	-3	103	58	O129(80/50/1)/1	—	-3.3
Total	7	790	2902	341	878	170	33	16	407	127	12	109	.303	.334	.400	99	-12	29-9	.970	-1	108	56	O731(305/425/3),1b2	—	-5.5
Brown, Randy	Edwin Randolph; B8.29.1944 Leesburg FL; BL/TR/5´7˝/170; [AnaA66 18/348]; d9.11; Col Florida St.																								
1969	Cal A	13	25	3	4	1	0	0	0	6-0	0	1	.160	.323	.200	51	-1	0-0	1.000	0	77	143	C10/cf	0	-0.1
1970	Cal A	5	4	0	0	0	0	0	0	0-0	0	0	.000	.000	.000	-99	-1	0-0	1.000	-2	42	0	C5	0	-0.3
Total	2	18	29	3	4	1	0	0	0	6-0	0	1	.138	.286	.172	32	-2	0-0	1.000	-2	70	113	C15/cf	0	-0.4
Brown, Emil	Emil Quincy; B12.29.1974 Chicago IL; BR/TR/6´2˝/(192–210); [OakA94 6/149]; d4.3; Col Indian River (FL) CC																								
1997	Pit N	66	95	16	17	2	1	2	6	10-1	7	32	.179	.304	.284	54	-6	5-1	.948	2	117	134	O42(30/8/4)	0	-0.5
1998	Pit N	13	39	2	10	1	0	0	3	1-0	1	11	.256	.293	.282	52	-3	0-0	1.000	2	119	333	O10(9/1/1)	0	-0.1
1999	Pit N	6	14	0	2	1	0	0	0	0-0	0	3	.143	.143	.214	-11	-2	0-0	1.000	0	113	-0	O6L	0	-0.2
2000	Pit N	50	119	13	26	5	0	3	16	11-0	3	34	.218	.299	.336	60	-7	3-1	1.000	0	90	165	O38(14/12/18)	14	-0.8
2001	Pit N	61	123	18	25	4	1	3	13	15-1	2	42	.203	.300	.325	60	-7	10-4	.988	1	99	216	O54(2/51/2)	0	-0.5
	SD N	13	14	3	1	0	0	0	0	1-0	0	7	.071	.133	.071	-49	-3	2-0	1.000	-1	83	0	O11(4/6/2)	0	-0.3
	Year	74	137	21	26	4	1	3	13	16-1	2	49	.190	.284	.299	51	-10	12-4	.989	1	97	188	O65(6/57/4)	0	-0.8
2005	KC A	150	545	75	156	31	5	17	86	48-1	8	108	.286	.349	.455	117	13	10-1	.958	-2	98	115	O139(11/0/129),D10	0	0.6
2006	KC A	147	527	77	151	41	2	15	81	59-3	5	95	.287	.358	.457	113	12	6-3	.990	3	104	109	O134(87/0/54),D10	0	0.9
Total	7	506	1476	204	388	85	9	40	205	145-6	26	332	.263	.336	.414	97	-3	36-10	.977	6	101	130	O434(163/78/210),D20	14	-0.9
Brown, Fred	Fred Herbert; B4.12.1879 Ossipee NH; D2.3.1955 Somersworth NH; BR/TR/5´10.5˝/190; d5.4; Col Dartmouth																								
1901	Bos N	7	14	1	2	0	0	0	2	0	0	—	.143	.143	.143	-16	-2	0	1.000	1	205	0	O5(3/0/2)	—	-0.2
1902	Bos N	2	6	1	2	1	0	0	0	0	0	—	.333	.333	.500	155	0	0	1.000	0	726	0	O2R	—	0.1
Total	2	9	20	2	4	1	0	0	2	0	0	—	.200	.200	.250	30	-2	0	1.000	1	314	0	O7(3/0/4)	—	-0.1
Brown, Ike	Isaac; B4.13.1942 Memphis TN; D5.17.2001 Memphis TN; BR/TR/6´1˝/(205–210); d6.17; Negro Lg 1960–61; OF(44/0/7)																								
1969	Det A	70	170	24	39	4	3	5	12	26-4	2	43	.229	.338	.376	96	-1	2-3	.962	-8	96	77	2b45,3b12,O3(1/0/2)/S	0	-0.7
1970	Det A	56	94	17	27	5	0	4	15	13-0	1	26	.287	.376	.468	131	4	0-0	.935	-7	65	65	2b23,O4(3/0/1)/3	0	-0.2
1971	Det A	59	110	20	28	1	0	8	19	19-1	0	25	.255	.359	.482	132	5	0-1	1.000	-0	92	45	1b17,O9(8/0/1),2b8,3b4/S	0	0.3
1972	†Det A	51	84	12	21	3	0	2	10	17-1	0	23	.250	.376	.357	115	2	1-2	1.000	5	188	104	O22(20/0/3),1b13,2b3/S3	0	0.6
1973	Det A	42	76	12	22	2	1	1	9	15-1	0	13	.289	.407	.382	116	2	0-1	.983	-0	123	87	1b21,O12L,3b2,D2	0	0.0
1974	Det A	2	2	0	0	0	0	0	0	0-0	0	0	.000	.000	.000	-97	-1	0-0	1.000	0	64	0	3b2	0	0.0
Total	6	280	536	85	137	15	4	20	65	90-7	3	130	.256	.364	.410	115	11	3-7	.956	-11	89	75	2b79,1b51,O50L,3b22,S3,D2	0	0.0
Brown, Jim	James Donaldson "Don","Moose"; B3.31.1893 Laurel MD; BR/TR/6´0˝/178; d9.13																								
1915	StL N	1	2	0	1	0	0	0	0	2	0	1	.500	.750	.500	281	1	0	1.000	-0	61	0	/cf	—	0.1
1916	Phi A	14	42	6	10	2	1	1	5	4	0	9	.238	.304	.405	119	1	0	.895	-1	79	155	O12(0/6/6)	—	-0.1
Total	2	15	44	6	11	2	1	1	5	6	0	10	.250	.340	.409	131	2	0	.900	-1	78	145	O13(0/7/6)	—	0.0
Brown, Jimmy	James Roberson; B4.25.1910 Jamesville NC; D12.29.1977 Bath NC; BB/TR/5´8.5˝/165; d4.23; Mil 1944–45; C3; Col North Carolina St.																								
1937	StL N	138	525	86	145	20	9	2	53	27	1	29	.276	.313	.360	81	-15	10	.964	-14	101	85	2b112,S25/3	—	-2.1
1938	StL N	108	382	50	115	12	6	0	38	27	2	9	.301	.350	.364	91	-4	7	.968	-0	100	120	2b49,S30,3b24	—	0.1
1939	StL N	147	645	88	192	31	8	3	51	32	4	18	.298	.335	.384	87	-12	4	.957	-4	101	98	S104,2b50	—	-0.6
1940	StL N	107	454	56	127	17	4	0	30	24	1	15	.280	.317	.335	76	-15	9	.977	-17	93	107	2b48,3b41,S28	—	-2.7
1941	StL N	132	549	81	168	28	9	3	56	45	4	22	.306	.363	.406	109	7	2	.965	2	101	102	3b123,2b11	0	1.4
1942	†StL N★	145	606	75	155	28	4	1	71	52	0	11	.256	.315	.320	80	-15	4	.970	-7	89	125	2b82,3b66,S12	0	-1.5
1943	StL N	34	110	6	20	4	2	0	8	6	0	1	.182	.224	.255	37	-9	0	.978	2	98	102	2b19,3b9,S6	0	-0.7
1946	Pit N	79	241	23	58	6	0	0	12	18	0	5	.241	.293	.266	58	-13	3	.960	-2	99	82	S30,2b21,3b9	0	-1.3
Total	8	890	3512	465	980	146	42	9	319	231	12	110	.279	.326	.352	84	-76	39	.968	-42	97	103	2b392,3b273,S235	0	-7.4
Brown, Jim	James W. H.; B12.12.1860 Clinton Co. PA; D4.6.1908 Williamsport PA; d4.17; ▲																								
1884	Alt U	21	88	12	22	2	2	1	—	1	—	—	.250	.258	.352	82	-5	—	.615	-3	60	0	O14(2/4/8),P11	—	-0.6
	NY N	1	3	0	0	0	0	0	0	0	—	1	.000	.000	.000	-98	-1	—	.333	-0	54	0	/P	—	0.0
	StP U	6	16	5	5	4	0	0	—	1	—	—	.313	.353	.563	318	4	—	.706	0	148	0	P6/1rf	—	0.1
1886	Phi AA	1	3	0	0	0	0	0	0	0	0	—	.000	.000	.000	-99	-1	0	1.000	-0	73	0	/P	—	0.0
Total	2	29	110	17	27	6	2	1	0	2	0	1	.245	.259	.364	93	-3	0	.741	-4	117	0	P19,O15(2/4/9)/1	—	-0.5
Brown, Jarvis	Jarvis Ardel; B3.26.1967 Waukegan IL; BR/TR/5´7˝/(165–170); [MinA86*1/9]; d7.2; Col Triton (IL) JC																								
1991	†Min A	38	37	10	8	0	0	0	0	2-0	0	8	.216	.256	.216	31	-4	7-1	.955	-2	74	0	O32(3/11/19),D4	0	-0.5
1992	Min A	35	15	8	1	0	0	0	0	2-0	1	4	.067	.222	.067	-15	-2	2-2	.952	-0	108	0	O31(4/9/18),D2	0	-0.3
1993	SD N	47	133	21	31	9	2	0	8	15-0	6	26	.233	.335	.331	79	-3	3-3	.982	4	121	104	O43(5/40/0)	0	0.0
1994	Atl N	17	15	3	2	1	0	1	1	0-0	0	2	.133	.133	.400	31	-2	0-0	1.000	0	108	0	O9(3/4/2)	0	-0.2
1995	Bal A	18	27	2	4	1	0	0	1	7-0	0	9	.148	.324	.185	36	-2	1-1	1.000	-2	73	0	O17(0/13/5)	24	-0.4
Total	5	155	227	44	46	11	2	1	10	26-0	7	49	.203	.303	.282	57	-13	13-7	.978	-0	104	53	O132(15/77/44),D6	24	-1.4
Brown, Jake	Jerald Ray; B3.22.1948 Sumrall MS; D12.18.1981 Houston TX; BR/TR/6´2˝/198; [SFN69 S1/2]; d5.17; Col Southern A&M																								
1975	SF N	41	43	6	9	3	0	0	4	5-0	0	13	.209	.292	.279	57	-2	0-0	.857	-0	87	211	O14(9/1/4)	0	-0.3
Brown, Jeremy	Jeremy Scott; B10.25.1979 Birmingham AL; BR/TR/5´10˝/225; [OakA02 1/35]; d9.3; Col Alabama																								
2006	Oak A	5	10	1	3	2	0	0	0	1-0	0	1	.300	.364	.500	123	0	0-0	1.000	0	0	0	/CD	0	0.1
Brown, Chris	John Christopher; B8.15.1961 Jackson MS; BR/TR/6´2˝/(185–210); [SFN79 2/44]; d9.3																								
1984	SF N	23	84	6	24	7	0	1	11	9-0	1	19	.286	.358	.405	118	3	2-1	.900	-2	88	72	3b23	0	0.0
1985	SF N	131	432	50	117	20	3	16	61	38-4	**11**	78	.271	.345	.442	124	13	2-3	**.971**	4	97	74	3b120	0	1.5
1986	SF N★	116	416	57	132	16	3	7	49	33-4	9	43	.317	.376	.421	127	15	13-9	.933	-10	88	100	3b111,S2	0	0.3
1987	SF N	38	132	17	32	6	0	6	17	9-1	3	16	.242	.306	.424	95	-1	1-3	.905	-3	88	87	3b37/S	44	-0.6
	SD N	44	155	17	36	3	0	6	23	11-0	3	30	.232	.294	.368	77	-6	3-1	.942	-4	88	170	3b43	0	-1.0
	Year	82	287	34	68	9	0	12	40	20-1	6	46	.237	.299	.394	86	-7	4-4	.923	-7	88	132	3b80/S	0	-1.6
1988	SD N	80	247	14	58	6	0	2	19	19-3	3	49	.235	.295	.283	69	-10	0-0	.949	2	101	143	3b72	0	-0.8
1989	Det A	17	57	3	11	3	0	0	4	1-0	0	17	.193	.203	.246	28	-6	0-0	.909	-1	84	138	3b17	0	-0.7
Total	6	449	1523	164	410	61	6	38	184	120-12	30	252	.269	.333	.392	105	8	21-17	.943	-15	93	105	3b423,S3	44	-1.3
Brown, Lindsay	John Lindsay "Red"; B7.22.1911 Mason TX; D1.1.1967 San Antonio TX; BR/TR/5´10˝/160; d7.13																								
1937	Bro N	48	115	16	31	3	1	0	6	3	0	17	.270	.288	.313	62	-6	1	.937	2	100	123	S45	—	-0.2
Brown, Joe	Joseph E.; B4.4.1859 Warren PA; D6.28.1888 Warren PA; 5´10˝/162; d8.16; ▲																								
1884	Chi N	15	61	6	13	1	0	0	3	0	—	15	.213	.213	.230	36	-5	—	.750	-1	98	0	O9(0/1/9),P7/1C	—	-0.3
1885	Bal AA	5	19	2	3	0	0	0	0	0	0	—	.158	.158	.158	-0	-2	—	1.000	0	80	0	P4/2	—	0.0
Total	2	20	80	8	16	1	0	0	3	0	0	15	.200	.200	.213	28	-7	—	.895	-1	96	0	P11,O9(0/1/9)/2C1	—	-0.3
Brown, Kevin	Kevin Lee; B4.21.1973 Valparaiso IN; BR/TR/6´2˝/(200–224); [TexA94 2/56]; d9.12; Col Southern Indiana																								
1996	Tex A	3	4	1	0	0	0	0	1	2-0	1	2	.000	.375	.000	20	0	0-0	1.000	1	0	221	C2/D	0	0.1
1997	Tex A	4	5	1	2	0	0	1	1	0-0	0	0	.400	.400	1.000	234	1	0-0	.900	-0	101	0	C4	0	0.1
1998	Tor A	52	110	17	29	7	1	2	15	9-0	2	31	.264	.320	.400	89	-2	0-0	.993	3	84	107	C52	17	0.3
1999	Tor A	2	9	1	4	2	0	0	1	0-0	0	3	.444	.444	.667	175	1	0-0	1.000	-1	130	155	C2	0	0.1
2000	Mil N	5	17	3	4	3	0	0	1	1-0	0	5	.235	.278	.412	72	-1	0-0	.957	-2	70	0	C5	0	-0.3
2001	Mil N	17	43	7	9	0	1	4	12	2-0	1	18	.209	.261	.535	100	-1	0-0	1.000	-2	77	131	C16	0	-0.1
2002	Bos A	2	1	0	0	0	0	0	0	0-0	0	0	.000	.000	.000	-98	0	0-0	1.000	-0	0	0	C2	0	0.0
Total	7	85	189	30	48	12	2	7	31	14-0	4	59	.254	.311	.450	96	-2	0-0	.990	-2	81	105	C83/D	17	0.2
Brown, Larry	Larry Leslie; B3.1.1940 Shinnston WV; BR/TR/5´11˝/(157–168); d7.6; b–Dick																								
1963	Cle A	74	247	28	63	6	0	5	18	22-0	1	27	.255	.316	.340	85	-5	4-3	.938	-9	97	68	S46,2b27	0	-0.9
1964	Cle A	115	335	33	77	12	1	12	40	24-3	2	55	.230	.283	.379	84	-8	1-2	.981	7	108	92	2b103,S4	0	0.6
1965	Cle A	124	438	52	111	22	2	8	40	38-0	2	62	.253	.315	.368	93	-4	5-7	.977	1	96	110	S95,2b26	0	0.6

YEAR	TM LG	G	AB	R	H	2B	3B	HR	RBI	BB-IB	HP	SO	AVG	OBP	SLG	AOPS	ABR	SB-CS	FA	FR	RNG	THR	GAMES AT POSITION	DL	BFW
1966	Cle A	105	340	29	78	12	0	3	17	36-3	3	58	.229	.309	.291	73	-11	0-1	.961	-6	91	90	S90,2b10	42	-1.0
1967	Cle A	152	485	38	110	16	2	7	37	53-6	6	62	.227	.308	.311	84	-9	4-4	.967	-3	93	109	S150	0	0.1
1968	Cle A	154	495	43	116	18	3	6	35	43-10	5	46	.234	.300	.319	90	-6	1-1	.966	-16	84	95	S154	0	-1.0
1969	Cle A	132	469	48	112	10	2	4	24	44-2	1	43	.239	.304	.294	66	-21	5-3	.959	-8	92	99	S101,3b29,2b5	0	-1.8
1970	Cle A	72	155	17	40	5	2	0	15	20-1	0	14	.258	.339	.316	79	-4	1-0	.950	0	91	108	S27,3b17,2b16	0	0.0
1971	Cle A	13	50	4	11	1	0	0	5	3-0	1	3	.220	.278	.240	44	-4	0-0	.980	-6	61	45	S13	0	-0.9
	Oak A	70	189	14	37	2	1	1	9	7-0	1	19	.196	.228	.233	31	-18	1-2	.959	-1	93	134	S31,2b23,3b10	0	-1.6
	Year	83	239	18	48	3	1	1	14	10-0	2	22	.201	.239	.234	35	-21	1-2	.965	-7	82	104	S44,2b23,3b10	0	-2.5
1972	Oak A	47	142	11	26	2	0	0	4	13-1	0	8	.183	.250	.197	36	-11	0-0	.974	-2	96	117	2b46/3	108	-1.2
1973	†Bal A	17	28	4	7	0	0	1	5	5-0	0	4	.250	.353	.357	103	0	0-0	.880	-2	77	155	3b15/2	0	-0.2
1974	Tex A	54	76	10	15	2	0	0	5	9-0	0	13	.197	.279	.224	48	-5	0-0	.931	3	119	171	3b47,2b8/S	0	-0.2
Total	12	1129	3449	331	803	108	13	47	254	317-26	22	414	.233	.300	.313	76	-106	22-23	.964	-41	91	99	S712,2b265,3b119	150	-7.5
Brown, Leon	Leon; B11.16.1949 Sacramento CA; BR/TR/6´0˝/185; [BalA66 9/176]; d5.19; b–Curtis; Col Cal St.–Sacramento																								
1976	NY N	64	70	11	15	3	0	0	2	4-0	0	4	.214	.257	.257	48	-5	2-4	1.000	3	102	254	O43(39/28/6)	0	-0.4
Brown, Lew	Lewis J. "Blower"; B2.1.1858 Leominster MA; D1.15.1889 Boston MA; BR/TR/5´10.5˝/185; d6.17																								
1876	Bos N	45	195	23	41	6	6	2	21	3	—	22	.210	.222	.333	82	-4	—	.856	1	—	—	C45/O(0/1/1)	—	-0.2
1877	Bos N	58	221	27	56	12	8	1	31	6	—	33	.253	.273	.394	104	0	—	.897	15	—	—	C55,1b4	—	1.5
1878	Pro N	58	243	44	74	21	6	1	43	7	—	37	.305	.324	.453	153	14	—	.880	3	—	—	C45,1b15/rfP	—	1.6
1879	Pro N	53	229	23	59	13	4	2	38	4	—	24	.258	.270	.376	112	3	—	.847	-6	—	—	C48,O6R	—	-0.1
	Chi N	6	21	2	6	1	0	0	3	1	—	4	.286	.318	.333	109	0	—	.974	0	138	206	1b6	—	0.0
	Year	59	250	25	65	14	4	2	41	5	—	28	.260	.275	.372	112	3	—	.847	-5	—	—	C48,O6R,1b6	—	-0.1
1881	Det N	27	108	16	26	3	1	3	14	3	—	16	.241	.261	.370	93	-1	—	.959	-1	84	134	1b27	—	-0.3
	Pro N	18	75	9	18	3	1	0	10	4	—	13	.240	.278	.307	85	-1	—	.833	-2	42	0	O13R,1b5	—	-0.3
	Year	45	183	25	44	6	2	3	24	7	—	29	.240	.268	.344	90	-2	—	.960	-3	80	136	1b32,O13R	—	-0.6
1883	Bos N	14	54	5	13	4	1	0	9	3	—	6	.241	.281	.352	89	-1	—	.943	-2	43	111	1b14	—	-0.3
	Lou AA	14	60	6	11	2	1	0	—	1	—	—	.183	.197	.250	46	-3	—	.891	-2	121	91	1b14/C	—	-0.6
1884	Bos U	85	325	50	75	18	3	1	—	13	—	—	.231	.260	.314	74	-20	—	.914	10	—	—	C54,1b33,O2R/P	—	-0.7
Total	7	378	1531	205	379	83	31	10	169	45	—	155	.248	.269	.362	99	-13	—	.884	17	—	—	C248,1b118,O23(0/1/23),P2	—	0.6
Brown, Marty	Marty Leo; B1.23.1963 Lawton OK; BR/TR/6´1˝/(190–195); [CinN85 12/292]; d9.4; Col Georgia																								
1988	Cin N	10	16	0	3	1	0	0	2	1-0	0	2	.188	.235	.250	38	-1	0-1	1.000	-0	100	0	3b8	0	-0.2
1989	Cin N	16	30	2	5	1	0	0	4	4-0	0	9	.167	.257	.200	34	-3	0-0	.913	0	116	147	3b11	0	-0.2
1990	Bal A	9	15	1	3	0	0	0	0	1-0	0	7	.200	.250	.200	28	-1	0-0	1.000	-1	47	0	2b3,3b2,D4	0	-0.3
Total	3	35	61	3	11	2	0	0	6	6-0	0	18	.180	.250	.213	34	-5	0-1	.943	-1	108	88	3b21,D4,2b3	0	-0.7
Brown, Mike	Michael Charles; B12.29.1959 San Francisco CA; BR/TR/6´2˝/(195–196); [CalA80 7/176]; d7.21; Col San Jose St.																								
1983	Cal A	31	104	12	24	5	1	3	9	7-0	0	20	.231	.279	.385	81	-3	1-0	.949	-2	76	167	O31(18/3/11)	0	-0.6
1984	Cal A	62	148	19	42	8	3	7	22	13-1	0	23	.284	.342	.520	135	6	0-2	.968	-2	78	181	O44(2/0/43),D3	0	0.2
1985	Cal A	60	153	23	41	9	1	4	20	7-0	1	21	.268	.304	.418	96	-1	0-1	1.000	1	100	115	O48(1/1/46),D7	0	-0.3
	Pit N	57	205	29	68	18	2	5	33	22-4	0	27	.332	.391	.512	153	15	2-2	.938	-4	85	81	O56R	0	0.8
1986	Pit N	87	243	18	53	7	0	4	26	27-3	0	32	.218	.293	.296	62	-12	2-3	.973	-3	92	59	O71R	0	-2.1
1988	Cal A	18	50	4	11	2	0	0	3	1-0	0	12	.220	.235	.260	39	-4	0-0	.946	1	103	226	O18(18/0/2)	0	-0.4
Total	5	315	903	105	239	49	7	23	113	77-8	1	135	.265	.321	.411	101	1	5-8	.964	-10	88	115	O268(39/4/229),D10	0	-2.4
Brown, Oliver	Oliver S.; B1849 Brooklyn NY; D9.23.1932 Brooklyn NY; BR/TR; d8.1																								
1872	Atl NA	4	15	0	2	0	0	0	0	0	—	1	.133	.133	.133	-15	-2	0-0	.889	0	0	0	O4R	—	-0.1
1875	Atl NA	3	10	0	0	0	0	0	0	0	—	0	.000	.000	.000	-99	-2	0-0	.833	-1	0	0	1b2,O2(0/1/1)	—	-0.2
Total	2NA	7	25	0	2	0	0	0	0	0	—	1	.080	.080	.080	-46	-4	0-0	.846	-0	0	0	O6(0/1/5),1b2	—	-0.3
Brown, Ollie	Ollie Lee "Downtown"; B2.11.1944 Tuscaloosa AL; BR/TR/6´3˝/(175–200); d9.10; b–Oscar																								
1965	SF N	6	10	0	2	1	0	0	0	0-0	0	2	.200	.200	.300	38	-1	0-0	1.000	-0	88	0	O4R	0	-0.1
1966	SF N	115	348	32	81	7	1	7	33	33-7	2	66	.233	.303	.319	71	-13	2-5	.978	-2	88	167	O114(1/16/107)	0	-2.4
1967	SF N	120	412	44	110	12	1	13	53	25-7	4	65	.267	.312	.396	104	1	0-2	.985	-6	91	63	O115(0/10/111)	0	-1.4
1968	SF N	40	95	7	22	4	0	0	11	3-0	2	23	.232	.270	.274	64	-4	1-0	1.000	-3	71	51	O35(3/3/30)	0	-1.0
1969	SD N	151	568	76	150	18	3	20	61	44-3	3	97	.264	.319	.412	107	3	10-6	.976	2	100	122	O148R	0	-0.2
1970	SD N	139	534	79	156	34	1	23	89	34-8	0	78	.292	.331	.489	122	14	5-3	.964	1	99	126	O137R	0	0.9
1971	SD N	145	484	36	132	16	0	9	55	52-5	3	74	.273	.346	.362	108	6	3-3	.982	2	96	88	O134(0/1/134)	0	0.0
1972	SD N	23	70	3	12	2	0	0	3	5-2	0	9	.171	.224	.200	24	-7	0-0	1.000	0	108	80	O17R	0	-0.9
	Oak A	20	54	5	13	1	0	1	4	6-1	0	14	.241	.317	.315	93	0	1-1	1.000	-1	97	0	O16(0/9/9)	0	-0.2
	Mil A	66	179	21	50	8	0	3	25	17-3	1	24	.279	.342	.374	116	4	0-2	.992	8	124	225	O56R/3	0	1.0
	Year	86	233	26	63	9	0	4	29	23-4	1	38	.270	.336	.361	111	3	1-3	.994	7	118	174	O72(0/9/65)/3	0	0.8
1973	Mil A	97	296	28	83	10	1	7	32	33-1	2	53	.280	.355	.392	112	5	4-1	1.000	-1	21	0	D82,O4R	0	0.3
1974	Hou N	27	69	8	15	1	0	3	6	4-0	0	15	.217	.260	.362	76	-3	0-0	1.000	1	132	0	O20R	0	-0.3
	Phi N	43	99	11	24	5	2	4	13	6-1	0	20	.242	.286	.455	100	-1	0-1	.921	-2	83	67	O33(24/0/9)	0	-0.5
	Year	70	168	19	39	6	2	7	19	10-1	0	35	.232	.275	.417	91	-3	0-1	.961	-1	103	39	O53(24/0/29)	0	-0.8
1975	Phi N	84	145	19	44	12	0	6	26	15-1	0	29	.303	.369	.510	135	7	1-1	1.000	-1	103	0	O63(23/0/48)	0	0.4
1976	†Phi N	92	209	30	53	10	1	5	30	33-5	0	33	.254	.350	.383	105	3	2-1	.949	2	100	162	O75(9/0/69)	0	0.2
1977	†Phi N	53	70	5	17	3	1	1	13	4-1	0	14	.243	.280	.357	67	-3	1-1	1.000	-1	79	135	O21(15/0/7)	0	-0.5
Total	13	1221	3642	404	964	144	11	102	454	314-45	17	616	.265	.324	.394	103	11	30-27	.977	1	97	110	O992(75/39/910),D82/3	0	-4.7
Brown, Oscar	Oscar Lee; B2.8.1946 Long Beach CA; BR/TR/6´0˝/(175–180); [AtlN66 S1/7]; d9.3; b–Ollie; Col USC																								
1969	Atl N	7	4	2	1	0	0	0	0	0-0	0	1	.250	.250	.250	40	0	0-0	1.000	-0	90	0	O3(0/2/1)	0	0.0
1970	Atl N	28	47	6	18	2	1	1	7	7-0	1	7	.383	.464	.532	159	4	0-2	.960	-1	93	0	O25(8/12/5)	0	0.2
1971	Atl N	27	43	4	9	4	0	0	5	3-0	0	8	.209	.261	.302	55	-2	0-0	1.000	0	66	118	O15(6/7/3)	0	-0.3
1972	Atl N	76	164	19	37	5	1	3	16	4-0	0	29	.226	.244	.323	55	-10	0-2	.899	4	111	254	O59(28/3/28)	0	-1.0
1973	Atl N	22	58	3	12	3	0	0	0	3-0	0	10	.207	.246	.259	37	-5	0-0	1.000	1	119	102	O13(5/3/5)	65	-0.5
Total	5	160	316	34	77	14	2	4	28	17-0	1	55	.244	.284	.339	69	-13	0-4	.939	4	104	164	O115(47/27/42)	65	-1.6
Brown, Dick	Richard Ernest; B1.17.1935 Shinnston WV; D4.17.1970 Baltimore MD; BR/TR/6´3˝/(175–190); d6.20; b–Larry																								
1957	Cle A	34	114	10	30	4	0	4	22	4-1	0	23	.263	.281	.404	88	-3	1-1	.986	-1	49	102	C33	0	-0.2
1958	Cle A	68	173	20	41	5	0	7	20	14-1	3	27	.237	.304	.387	91	-2	1-0	.987	1	66	124	C62	0	0.2
1959	Cle A	48	141	15	31	7	0	5	16	11-1	3	39	.220	.288	.376	85	-3	0-0	.996	3	124	106	C48	0	0.2
1960	Chi A	16	43	4	7	0	0	3	5	3-0	0	11	.163	.217	.372	57	-3	0-0	.986	2	54	39	C14	0	-0.1
1961	Det A	93	308	32	82	12	2	16	45	22-2	0	57	.266	.312	.474	105	0	0-2	.990	6	142	**148**	C91	47	1.0
1962	Det A	134	431	40	104	12	0	12	40	21-7	2	66	.241	.279	.353	67	-22	0-1	.994	8	131	57	C132	0	-0.8
1963	Bal A	59	171	13	42	7	0	2	13	15-6	1	35	.246	.310	.322	80	-4	1-0	.986	2	123	85	C58	0	0.1
1964	Bal A	88	230	24	59	6	0	8	32	12-4	1	45	.257	.294	.387	89	-4	2-0	.988	-1	106	107	C84	0	-0.2
1965	Bal A	96	255	17	59	9	1	5	30	17-8	1	53	.231	.278	.333	73	-10	2-2	.983	2	107	**147**	C92	0	-0.4
Total	9	636	1866	175	455	62	3	62	223	119-30	11	356	.244	.291	.380	83	-51	7-6	.989	23	112	105	C614	47	-0.2
Brown, Robert	Robert; d7.29																								
1874	Bal NA	2	9	0	0	0	0	0	0	0	—	0	.000	.000	.000	-99	-2	0-0	.727	-1	78	0	S2	—	-0.2
Brown, Bobby	Robert William "Doc"; B10.25.1924 Seattle WA; BL/TR/6´1˝/180; d9.22; Mil 1952–54; Col Tulane																								
1946	NY A	7	24	1	8	1	0	0	1	4	0	0	.333	.429	.375	124	1	0-0	1.000	-2	73	39	S5,3b2	0	0.0
1947	†NY A	69	150	21	45	6	1	1	18	21	1	9	.300	.390	.373	114	4	0-2	.932	-7	73	73	3b27,S11,O3(0/2/1)	0	-0.4
1948	NY A	113	363	62	109	19	5	3	48	48	1	16	.300	.383	.405	111	7	0-1	.946	-13	84	104	3b41,S26,2b17,O4(3/0/1)	0	-0.4
1949	†NY A	104	343	61	97	14	4	6	61	38	3	18	.283	.359	.399	101	0	4-3	.949	-3	94	88	3b86,O3(1/0/2)	0	-0.4
1950	†NY A	95	277	33	74	4	2	4	37	39	1	18	.267	.360	.339	82	-7	3-1	.958	-4	94	89	3b82	0	-1.0
1951	†NY A	103	313	44	84	15	2	6	51	47	3	18	.268	.369	.387	108	5	1-1	.955	-6	91	86	3b90	0	-0.1
1952	NY A	29	89	6	22	2	0	1	14	9	1	6	.247	.323	.303	80	-2	1-1	.894	2	118	73	3b24	0	-0.1
1954	NY A	28	60	5	13	1	0	1	7	8	0	3	.217	.304	.283	65	-3	0-1	1.000	1	102	78	3b17	0	-0.3
Total	8	548	1619	233	452	62	14	22	237	214	10	88	.279	.367	.376	100	5	9-10	.948	-32	93	87	3b369,S42,2b17,O10(4/2/4)	0	-2.7

Brown, Bobby Rogers Lee; B5.24.1954 Norfolk VA; BB/TR (BL 1979)/6´1˝/(198–231); [BalA72 11/264]; d4.5

YEAR	TM LG	G	AB	R	H	2B	3B	HR	RBI	BB-IB	HP	SO	AVG	OBP	SLG	AOPS	ABR	SB-CS	FA	FR	RNG	THR	GAMES AT POSITION	DL	BFW
1979	Tor A	4	10	1	0	0	0	0	0	2-0	0	1	.000	.167	.000	-50	-2	0-0	1.000	0	110	0	O4(2/0/2)	0	-0.2
	NY A	30	68	7	17	3	1	0	3	2-0	0	17	.250	.271	.324	61	-4	2-1	.949	-0	113	0	O27(7/20/0)/D	0	-0.5
	Year	34	78	8	17	3	1	0	3	4-0	0	18	.218	.256	.282	46	-6	2-1	.955	-0	113	0	O31(9/20/2)/D	0	-0.7
1980	†NY A	137	412	65	107	12	5	14	47	29-4	0	82	.260	.306	.415	98	-3	27-8	.972	3	105	88	O131(28/81/25)/D	0	0.0
1981	†NY A	31	62	5	14	1	0	0	6	5-0	0	15	.226	.279	.242	53	-4	4-2	.949	3	126	166	O29(6/11/14),D2	0	-0.2
1982	Sea A	79	245	29	59	7	1	4	17	17-2	0	32	.241	.288	.327	67	-12	28-6	.968	2	105	128	O68(51/14/4),D3	21	-0.8
1983	SD N	57	225	40	60	5	3	5	22	23-0	0	38	.267	.333	.382	101	0	27-9	.963	-4	97	24	O54(52/4/0)	0	-0.4
1984	†SD N	85	171	28	43	7	2	3	29	11-0	0	33	.251	.292	.368	85	-4	16-4	.971	2	115	69	O53(27/13/16)	0	-0.2
1985	SD N	79	84	8	13	3	0	0	6	5-0	0	20	.155	.200	.190	10	-10	6-4	1.000	0	79	246	O28(9/9/12)	0	-1.1
Total	7	502	1277	183	313	38	12	26	130	94-6	0	238	.245	.295	.355	80	-39	110-34	.968	6	106	87	O394(182/152/73),D7	21	-3.4

Brown, Roosevelt Roosevelt Lawayne; B8.3.1975 Vicksburg MS; BL/TR/5´11˝/(195–200); [AtlN93 20/572]; d5.18

YEAR	TM LG	G	AB	R	H	2B	3B	HR	RBI	BB-IB	HP	SO	AVG	OBP	SLG	AOPS	ABR	SB-CS	FA	FR	RNG	THR	GAMES AT POSITION	DL	BFW
1999	Chi N	33	64	6	14	6	1	1	10	2-0	0	14	.219	.239	.391	57	-5	1-0	.955	-2	70	122	O18(13/5/1)	0	-0.6
2000	Chi N	45	91	11	32	8	0	3	14	4-0	1	22	.352	.378	.538	132	4	0-1	1.000	2	110	104	O28(24/1/5)	0	0.5
2001	Chi N	39	83	13	22	6	1	4	22	7-0	1	12	.265	.326	.506	115	2	0-0	.952	-2	77	0	O22(21/1/3),D3	0	-0.1
2002	Chi N	111	204	14	43	12	0	3	23	23-0	3	50	.211	.299	.314	62	-11	2-2	.975	-1	99	42	O64(48/13/4)/D	0	-1.3
Total	4	228	442	44	111	32	2	11	69	36-0	5	98	.251	.311	.407	86	-10	3-3	.975	-2	93	58	O132(106/20/13),D4	0	-1.5

Brown, Sam Samuel Wakefield; B5.21.1878 Webster PA; D11.8.1931 Mount Pleasant PA; BR/TR; d4.21; Col Grove City

YEAR	TM LG	G	AB	R	H	2B	3B	HR	RBI	BB-IB	HP	SO	AVG	OBP	SLG	AOPS	ABR	SB-CS	FA	FR	RNG	THR	GAMES AT POSITION	DL	BFW
1906	Bos N	71	231	12	48	6	1	0	20	13	4	—	.208	.262	.242	59	-11	4	.970	-2	*85*	*124*	C35,O13(6/4/1),3b12,1b3,2b2	—	-1.1
1907	Bos N	70	208	17	40	6	0	0	14	12	4	—	.192	.250	.221	48	-12	0	.970	-4	*80*	*111*	C63,1b2	—	-1.1
Total	2	141	439	29	88	12	1	0	34	25	8	—	.200	.256	.232	54	-23	4	.970	-6	*82*	*116*	C98,O13(6/4/1),3b12,1b5,2b2	—	-2.2

Brown, Tommy Thomas Michael "Buckshot"; B12.6.1927 Brooklyn NY; BR/TR/6´1˝/(170–172); d8.3; Mil 1946–47; OF(87/0/6)

YEAR	TM LG	G	AB	R	H	2B	3B	HR	RBI	BB-IB	HP	SO	AVG	OBP	SLG	AOPS	ABR	SB-CS	FA	FR	RNG	THR	GAMES AT POSITION	DL	BFW
1944	Bro N	46	146	17	24	4	0	0	8	8	0	17	.164	.208	.192	13	-17	0	.925	-10	82	87	S46	0	-2.5
1945	Bro N	57	196	13	48	3	4	2	19	6	0	16	.245	.267	.332	66	-11	3	.918	-6	97	92	S55/rf	0	-1.2
1947	Bro N	15	34	3	8	1	0	0	2	1	0	6	.235	.257	.265	37	-3	0	1.000	1	102	0	3b6,O3L/S	0	-0.2
1948	Bro N	54	145	18	35	4	0	2	20	7	1	17	.241	.281	.310	58	-9	1	.936	-3	84	120	3b43/1	0	-1.2
1949	†Bro N	41	89	14	27	2	0	3	18	6	0	8	.303	.347	.427	102	0	0	.931	-0	110	55	O27L	0	-0.2
1950	Bro N	48	86	15	25	2	1	8	20	11	1	9	.291	.378	.616	153	6	0	.917	1	101	191	O16L	0	0.5
1951	Bro N	11	25	2	4	2	0	0	1	2	0	4	.160	.222	.240	24	-3	0-0	.909	-0	83	224	O5L	0	-0.3
	Phi N	78	196	24	43	2	1	10	32	15	1	21	.219	.278	.393	80	-7	1-2	.966	-6	106	0	O32L,2b14,1b12/3	0	-1.6
	Year	89	221	26	47	4	1	10	33	17	1	25	.213	.272	.376	73	-10	1-2	.957	-7	102	39	O37L,2b14,1b12/3	0	-1.9
1952	Phi N	18	25	2	4	1	0	1	2	4	0	3	.160	.276	.320	65	-1	0-0	1.000	0	142	0	1b3,O3L	0	-0.1
	Chi N	61	200	24	64	11	0	3	24	12	0	24	.320	.358	.420	114	4	1-2	.911	-16	82	75	S39,2b10,1b5	0	-1.1
	Year	79	225	26	68	12	0	4	26	16	0	27	.302	.349	.409	109	3	1-2	.911	-16	82	75	S39,2b10,1b8,O3L	0	-1.2
1953	Chi N	65	138	19	27	7	1	2	13	13	3	17	.196	.279	.304	51	-10	1-0	.903	-5	92	77	S25,O6(1/0/5)	0	-1.2
Total	9	494	1280	151	309	39	7	31	159	85	6	142	.241	.292	.355	74	-51	7-4	.916	-45	89	86	S166,O93L,3b50,2b24,1b21	0	-9.1

Brown, Tom Thomas Tarlton; B9.21.1860 Liverpool, England; D10.25.1927 Washington DC; BL/TR/5´10˝/168; d7.6; M2/U4; ▲

YEAR	TM LG	G	AB	R	H	2B	3B	HR	RBI	BB-IB	HP	SO	AVG	OBP	SLG	AOPS	ABR	SB-CS	FA	FR	RNG	THR	GAMES AT POSITION	DL	BFW
1882	Bal AA	45	181	30	55	5	2	1	23	6	—	—	.304	.326	.370	146	9	—	.728	-1	155	82	O45R,P2	—	0.7
1883	Col AA	**97**	420	69	115	12	7	5	32	20	—	—	.274	.307	.371	127	14	—	.808	-1	121	123	O96R,P3	—	1.1
1884	Col AA	107	451	93	123	9	11	5	32	24	4	—	.273	.315	.375	135	18	—	.847	-6	88	180	O107R,P4	—	1.0
1885	Pit AA	108	437	81	134	16	12	4	68	34	7	—	.307	.366	.426	152	27	—	.828	-5	111	61	O108R,P2	—	1.8
1886	Pit AA	115	460	106	131	11	11	1	51	56	2	—	.285	.365	.363	129	17	30	.837	6	**156**	**381**	O115(1/1/115)/P	—	1.9
1887	Pit N	47	192	30	47	3	4	0	6	11	1	40	.245	.289	.302	69	-8	12	.870	2	112	0	O47C	—	-0.7
	Ind N	36	140	20	25	3	0	2	9	8	1	25	.179	.228	.243	32	-13	13	.813	-3	110	156	O36(0/17/19)	—	-1.4
	Year	83	332	50	72	6	4	2	15	19	2	65	.217	.263	.277	53	-21	25	.851	-1	111	65	O83(0/64/19)	—	-2.1
1888	Bos N	107	420	62	104	10	7	9	49	30	1	68	.248	.299	.369	109	4	46	.896	-6	94	80	O107(6/2/99)	—	-0.4
1889	Bos N	90	362	93	84	10	5	2	24	59	1	56	.232	.341	.304	76	-11	63	.901	2	73	33	O90(88/0/2)	—	-1.0
1890	Bos P	128	543	146	149	23	14	4	61	86	3	84	.274	.377	.390	98	-1	79	.911	2	136	172	O128C	—	-0.3
1891	Bos AA	137	589	**177**	**189**	30	**21**	5	72	70	4	96	.321	.397	.469	150	37	**106**	.878	-12	95	150	O137C	—	1.8
1892	Lou N	153	660	105	150	16	8	2	45	47	5	94	.227	.284	.285	78	-18	78	.919	16	151	156	O153C	—	-1.1
1893	Lou N	122	529	104	127	15	7	5	54	56	5	63	.240	.319	.323	77	-17	**66**	.929	26	**192**	**273**	O122C	—	0.1
1894	Lou N	**130**	541	123	137	22	14	9	57	60	3	74	.253	.331	.396	80	-19	66	.912	2	97	147	O130C	—	-2.0
1895	StL N	84	355	73	78	11	4	1	31	48	2	44	.220	.316	.282	56	-23	34	.951	7	120	166	O84(1/83/0)	—	-1.7
	Was N	34	134	25	32	8	3	2	16	18	0	16	.239	.329	.388	85	-3	8	.909	-5	23	0	O34C	—	-0.8
	Year	118	489	98	110	19	7	3	47	66	2	60	.225	.320	.311	64	-26	42	.942	2	95	123	O118(1/117/0)	—	-2.5
1896	Was N	116	435	87	128	17	6	2	59	58	6	49	.294	.385	.375	101	3	28	.928	-4	46	47	O116(0/114/2)	—	-0.6
1897	Was N	116	469	91	137	17	2	5	45	52	1	—	.292	.364	.369	94	-3	25	.928	-2	102	149	O115C,M	—	-1.0
1898	Was N	16	55	8	9	1	0	0	2	5	0	—	.164	.233	.182	19	-6	3	.925	0	49	0	O15C,M	—	-0.6
Total	17	1788	7373	1523	1954	239	138	64	736	748	46	709	.265	.336	.361	101	7	657	.890	18	114	144	O1785(96/1098/593),P12	—	-3.2

Brown, Tom Thomas William; B12.12.1940 Laureldale PA; BB/TL/6´1˝/190; d4.8; Col Maryland

YEAR	TM LG	G	AB	R	H	2B	3B	HR	RBI	BB-IB	HP	SO	AVG	OBP	SLG	AOPS	ABR	SB-CS	FA	FR	RNG	THR	GAMES AT POSITION	DL	BFW
1963	Was A	61	116	8	17	4	0	1	4	11-0	1	45	.147	.227	.207	23	-12	2-1	1.000	-2	82	0	O16(10/5/1),1b14	0	-1.6

Brown, Willard Willard Jessie; B6.26.1915 Shreveport LA; D8.4.1996 Houston TX; BR/TR/5´11.5˝/200; d7.19; Negro Lg 1934–51 Mil 1944–45

YEAR	TM LG	G	AB	R	H	2B	3B	HR	RBI	BB-IB	HP	SO	AVG	OBP	SLG	AOPS	ABR	SB-CS	FA	FR	RNG	THR	GAMES AT POSITION	DL	BFW
1947	StL A	21	67	4	12	3	0	1	6	0	0	7	.179	.179	.269	23	-7	2-2	1.000	1	124	0	O18(0/1/17)	0	-0.8

Brown, Gates William James "Gator"; B5.2.1939 Crestline OH; BL/TR/5´11˝/(200–225); d6.19; C7

YEAR	TM LG	G	AB	R	H	2B	3B	HR	RBI	BB-IB	HP	SO	AVG	OBP	SLG	AOPS	ABR	SB-CS	FA	FR	RNG	THR	GAMES AT POSITION	DL	BFW
1963	Det A	55	82	16	22	3	1	2	14	8-0	1	13	.268	.333	.402	104	0	2-1	1.000	4	138	320	O16L	0	0.4
1964	Det A	123	426	65	116	22	6	15	54	31-0	4	53	.272	.326	.458	114	7	11-4	.981	6	116	78	O106L	0	0.9
1965	Det A	96	227	33	58	14	2	10	43	17-1	0	33	.256	.305	.467	115	4	6-0	.973	3	121	33	O56(49/0/7)	0	0.5
1966	Det A	88	169	27	45	5	1	7	27	18-2	2	19	.266	.337	.432	119	4	3-0	.980	-2	71	177	O43L	0	0.1
1967	Det A	51	91	17	17	1	1	2	9	13-0	0	15	.187	.286	.286	68	-4	0-0	1.000	-0	85	102	O20L	63	-0.5
1968	†Det A	67	92	15	34	7	2	6	15	12-1	0	4	.370	.442	.685	231	15	0-0	1.000	-1	78	120	O17L/1	0	1.5
1969	Det A	60	93	13	19	1	2	1	6	5-0	1	17	.204	.250	.290	49	-7	0-0	.906	1	127	108	O14L	0	-0.7
1970	Det A	81	124	18	28	3	0	3	24	20-0	1	14	.226	.331	.323	82	-2	0-0	.950	-0	102	76	O26L	0	-0.4
1971	Det A	82	195	37	66	2	3	11	29	21-2	2	17	.338	.408	.549	162	15	4-2	.986	-2	90	78	O56L	24	1.2
1972	†Det A	103	252	33	58	5	0	10	31	26-3	2	28	.230	.304	.369	97	-1	3-0	.977	5	123	118	O72L	0	0.1
1973	Det A	125	377	48	89	11	1	12	50	52-6	1	41	.236	.328	.366	90	-4	1-1	1.000	-0	43	0	D119,O2L	0	-0.8
1974	Det A	73	99	7	24	2	0	4	17	10-2	0	15	.242	.312	.384	96	-1	0-0	ø	0	0	0	D13	0	-0.1
1975	Det A	47	35	1	6	2	0	1	3	9-1	1	6	.171	.356	.314	87	0	0-0	ø	0	—	—	/H	0	-0.1
Total	13	1051	2262	330	582	78	19	84	322	242-18	15	275	.257	.330	.420	109	26	30-8	.977	13	108	100	O428(421/0/7),D132/1	87	2.1

Brown, Willard William M. "Big Bill","California"; B1866 San Francisco CA; D12.20.1897 San Francisco CA; BR/TR/6´2˝/190; d5.10

YEAR	TM LG	G	AB	R	H	2B	3B	HR	RBI	BB-IB	HP	SO	AVG	OBP	SLG	AOPS	ABR	SB-CS	FA	FR	RNG	THR	GAMES AT POSITION	DL	BFW
1887	NY N	49	170	17	37	3	2	0	25	10	3	15	.218	.273	.259	51	-11	10	.914	-2	—	—	C46,3b3,O2R	—	-0.8
1888	†NY N	20	59	4	16	1	0	0	6	1	0	8	.271	.283	.288	84	-1	1	.893	-1	—	—	C20	—	-0.1
1889	†NY N	40	139	16	36	10	0	1	29	9	3	9	.259	.318	.353	86	-2	6	.846	-5	—	—	C37,O3C	—	-0.5
1890	NY P	60	230	47	64	8	4	4	43	13	1	13	.278	.320	.400	84	-7	5	.900	-4	*100*	*107*	C34,O13(2/0/11),1b9,3b3,2b2	—	-0.8
1891	Phi N	115	441	62	107	20	4	0	50	34	4	35	.243	.303	.306	75	-14	7	**.989**	4	111	113	1b97,C19,O2C	—	-1.6
1893	Bal N	7	32	5	4	3	0	0	5	1	0	3	.125	.152	.219	-2	-5	0	.985	-0	80	67	1b7	—	-0.4
	Lou N	111	461	80	140	23	7	1	85	50	1	32	.304	.373	.390	112	10	9	.989	-1	86	103	1b111/C	—	0.7
	Year	118	493	85	144	26	7	1	90	51	1	35	.292	.360	.379	104	5	9	**.988**	-1	86	101	1b118/C	—	0.3
1894	Lou N	13	48	5	10	2	0	0	9	5	0	7	.208	.283	.250	31	-5	1	.977	4	231	67	1b13	—	-0.1
	StL N	3	9	0	1	0	0	0	0	0	0	2	.111	.111	.111	-46	-2	0	1.000	0	120	107	1b3	—	-0.2
	Year	16	57	5	11	2	0	0	9	5	0	9	.193	.258	.228	19	-8	1	.982	4	211	74	1b16	—	-0.3
Total	7	418	1589	236	415	70	17	6	252	123	12	124	.261	.319	.338	82	-37	39	.987	-5	105	103	1b240,C157,O20(2/5/13),3b6,2b2	—	-3.8

Brown, Bill William Verna "Verna"; B7.8.1893 Coleman TX; D5.13.1965 Lubbock TX; BL/TL/5´8˝/185; d8.15

YEAR	TM LG	G	AB	R	H	2B	3B	HR	RBI	BB-IB	HP	SO	AVG	OBP	SLG	AOPS	ABR	SB-CS	FA	FR	RNG	THR	GAMES AT POSITION	DL	BFW
1912	StL A	9	20	0	4	0	0	0	1	0	0	—	.200	.200	.200	15	-2	0	.909	-0	111	0	O7(6/1/0)	—	-0.3

YEAR	TM LG	G	AB	R	H	2B	3B	HR	RBI	BB-IB	HP	SO	AVG	OBP	SLG	AOPS	ABR	SB-CS	FA	FR	RNG	THR	GAMES AT POSITION	DL	BFW
BROWNE, BYRON	Byron Ellis; B12.27.1942 St.Joseph MO; BR/TR/6´2˝/(185–200); d9.9; Col Missouri Western																								
1965	Chi N	4	6	0	0	0	0	0	0	0-0	0	2	.000	.000	.000	-98	-2	0-0	.667	-0	67	0	O4L	0	-0.2
1966	Chi N	120	419	46	102	15	7	16	51	40-1	5	143	.243	.316	.427	103	1	3-3	.967	-8	91	38	O114(67/42/10)	0	-1.3
1967	Chi N	10	19	3	3	2	0	0	2	4-1	0	5	.158	.304	.263	61	-1	1-1	1.000	-0	103	0	O8(0/2/6)	0	-0.2
1968	Hou N	10	13	0	3	0	0	0	1	4-0	0	6	.231	.412	.231	99	0	0-0	1.000	2	192	604	O2R	0	0.2
1969	StL N	22	53	9	12	0	1	1	7	11-1	0	14	.226	.359	.321	91	0	0-0	1.000	4	130	320	O16(5/5/8)	0	0.3
1970	Phi N	104	270	29	67	17	2	10	36	33-5	0	72	.248	.327	.437	106	2	1-2	.975	1	105	86	O88(6/23/61)	0	0.0
1971	Phi N	58	68	5	14	3	0	3	5	8-0	0	23	.206	.289	.382	89	-1	0-0	1.000	-2	79	0	O30(17/4/10)	0	-0.4
1972	Phi N	21	21	2	4	0	0	0	0	1-0	0	8	.190	.227	.190	19	-2	0-0	1.000	-1	37	0	O9(0/3/6)	0	-0.3
Total	8	349	869	94	205	37	10	30	102	101-8	5	273	.236	.318	.405	98	-3	5-6	.973	-5	98	72	O271(99/79/103)	0	-1.9
BROWNE, EARL	Earl James "Snitz"; B3.5.1911 Louisville KY; D1.12.1993 Whittier CA; BL/TL/6´0˝/175; d9.12																								
1935	Pit N	9	32	6	8	2	0	0	6	2	0	8	.250	.294	.313	61	-2	0	1.000	0	93	70	1b9	—	-0.2
1936	Pit N	8	23	7	7	1	2	0	3	1	0	4	.304	.333	.522	124	0	0	1.000	1	95	385	O4L/1	—	0.1
1937	Phi N	105	332	42	97	19	3	6	52	21	4	41	.292	.342	.422	98	-1	4	.980	3	94	146	O54(8/5/43),1b23	—	-0.3
1938	Phi N	21	74	4	19	4	0	0	8	5	0	11	.257	.304	.311	71	-3	0	.978	-0	101	78	1b16,O2L	—	-0.5
Total	4	143	461	59	131	26	5	6	69	29	4	64	.284	.332	.401	93	-6	4	.983	4	96	156	O60(14/5/43),1b49	—	-0.9
BROWNE, GEORGE	George Edward; B1.12.1876 Richmond VA; D12.9.1920 Hyde Park NY; BL/TR/5´10.5˝/160; d9.27																								
1901	Phi N	8	26	2	5	1	0	0	4	1	1	—	.192	.250	.231	39	-2	2	1.000	-0	0	0	O8(6/1/1)	—	-0.3
1902	Phi N	70	281	41	73	7	1	0	26	16	2	—	.260	.304	.292	84	-5	11	.910	6	137	36	O70L	—	-0.4
	NY N	53	216	30	69	9	5	0	14	9	3	—	.319	.355	.407	137	8	13	.895	-1	92	52	O53(51/0/2)	—	0.4
	Year	123	497	71	142	16	6	0	40	25	5	—	.286	.326	.342	107	3	24	.904	4	118	43	O123(121/0/2)	—	0.0
1903	NY N	141	591	105	185	20	3	3	45	43	4	—	.313	.364	.372	106	5	27	.918	-6	66	91	O141(1/0/140)	—	-0.7
1904	NY N	150	596	**99**	169	16	5	4	39	39	4	—	.284	.332	.347	105	3	24	.925	-6	106	148	O149R	—	-1.0
1905	†NY N	127	536	95	157	16	14	4	43	20	2	—	.293	.321	.397	111	4	26	.915	-9	54	29	O127R	—	-1.1
1906	NY N	122	477	61	126	10	4	0	38	27	0	—	.264	.304	.302	87	-9	32	.934	-5	113	87	O121R	—	-2.1
1907	NY N	127	458	54	119	11	10	5	37	31	1	—	.260	.308	.360	106	1	15	.941	-7	88	137	O121R	—	-1.2
1908	Bos N	138	536	61	122	10	6	1	34	36	0	—	.228	.276	.274	77	-15	17	.950	2	111	181	O138(12/17/109)	—	-2.3
1909	Chi N	12	39	7	8	0	1	0	1	5	0	—	.205	.295	.256	70	-1	3	.944	-1	73	0	O12(0/11/1)	—	-0.3
	Was A	103	393	40	107	15	5	1	16	17	3	—	.272	.308	.344	111	3	13	.935	-3	92	96	O101(63/4/34)	—	-0.5
1910	Was A	7	22	1	4	0	0	0	0	1	0	—	.182	.217	.182	26	-2	0	.667	-1	64	0	O5L	—	-0.4
	Chi A	30	112	17	27	4	1	0	4	12	0	—	.241	.315	.295	95	0	5	.952	-3	79	53	O29(0/20/9)	—	-0.6
	Year	37	134	18	31	4	1	0	4	13	0	—	.231	.299	.276	84	-2	5	.917	-5	77	46	O34(5/20/9)	—	-1.0
1911	Bro N	8	12	1	4	0	0	0	2	1	0	1	.333	.385	.333	106	0	2	1.000	-0	121	0	O2R	—	0.0
1912	Phi N	6	5	0	1	0	0	0	0	1	0	0	.200	.333	.200	45	0	0	ø	0	—	—	/H	—	0.0
Total	12	1102	4300	614	1176	119	55	18	303	259	20	1	.273	.318	.339	100	-10	190	.927	-36	93	100	O1077(208/53/816)	—	-10.5
BROWNE, JERRY	Jerome Austin; B2.13.1966 Christiansted, V.I.; BB/TR/5´10˝/(165–170); d9.6; OF(98/67/25)																								
1986	Tex A	12	24	6	10	2	0	0	3	1-0	0	4	.417	.440	.500	151	2	0-2	.923	-2	86	97	2b8	0	0.0
1987	Tex A	132	454	63	123	16	6	1	38	61-0	2	50	.271	.358	.339	86	-7	27-17	.980	-4	92	77	2b130/D	15	-0.4
1988	Tex A	73	214	26	49	9	2	1	17	25-0	0	32	.229	.308	.304	71	-8	7-5	.958	-25	75	62	2b70/D	0	-3.3
1989	Cle A	153	598	83	179	31	4	5	45	68-10	1	64	.299	.370	.390	113	12	14-6	.979	-38	87	70	2b151,D2	0	-2.2
1990	Cle A	140	513	92	137	26	5	6	50	72-1	2	46	.267	.353	.372	105	6	12-7	.985	-11	96	73	2b139	0	-0.2
1991	Cle A	107	290	28	66	5	2	1	29	27-0	1	29	.228	.292	.269	57	-17	2-4	.964	-3	98	65	2b47,O17L,3b15,D7	0	-2.1
1992	†Oak A	111	324	43	93	12	2	3	40	40-0	4	40	.287	.366	.364	112	7	3-3	.965	-7	89	108	3b58,O43(17/23/6),2b19/SD	0	-0.1
1993	Oak A	76	260	27	65	13	0	2	19	22-0	0	17	.250	.306	.323	74	-10	4-0	.985	-0	109	33	O56(30/26/4),3b13,2b3,1b2	90	-1.0
1994	Fla N	101	329	42	97	17	4	3	30	52-3	2	23	.295	.392	.398	103	4	3-0	.931	-1	90	118	3b62,O30(23/7/4),2b15	0	0.4
1995	Fla N	77	184	21	47	4	0	1	17	25-0	1	20	.255	.346	.293	70	-7	1-1	.959	6	109	158	O29(11/11/11),2b27,3b7	43	-0.1
Total	10	982	3190	431	866	135	25	23	288	393-14	13	325	.271	.351	.351	93	-18	73-45	.977	-85	90	71	2b609,O175L,3b155,D12,1b2/S	148	-9.0
BROWNE, PIDGE	Prentice Almont; B3.21.1929 Peekskill NY; D6.3.1997 Houston TX; BL/TL/6´1˝/190; d4.13																								
1962	Hou N	65	100	8	21	4	2	1	10	13-0	0	9	.210	.298	.320	72	-4	0-0	.983	1	117	74	1b26	0	-0.4
BROWNING, PETE	Louis Rogers "The Gladiator"; B6.17.1861 Louisville KY; D9.10.1905 Louisville KY; BR/TR/6´0˝/180; d5.2; OF(477/490/35)																								
1882	Lou AA	69	288	67	109	17	3	5	—	26	—	—	**.378**	**.430**	**.510**	**229**	**41**	—	.890	9	104	117	2b42,S18,3b13	—	**4.6**
1883	Lou AA	84	358	95	121	15	9	4	—	23	—	—	.338	.378	.464	183	34	—	.861	-9	48	81	O48(34/11/3),S26,3b10,2b3/1	—	2.2
1884	Lou AA	103	447	101	150	33	8	4	47	13	2	—	.336	.357	.472	176	37	—	.806	-12	67	81	3b52,O24(1/23/0),1b23,2b4/P	—	2.1
1885	Lou AA	**112**	481	98	**174**	34	10	9	73	25	0	—	**.362**	**.393**	.530	**190**	**48**	—	.900	3	104	115	O112C	—	**4.2**
1886	Lou AA	112	467	86	159	29	6	2	68	30	7	—	.340	.389	.441	151	27	26	.791	-13	74	29	O112(31/82/0)	—	0.9
1887	Lou AA	134	547	137	220	35	16	4	118	55	8	—	.402	.464	.547	178	59	103	.868	-6	93	152	O134C	—	3.8
1888	Lou AA	99	383	58	120	22	8	3	72	37	4	—	.313	.380	.436	164	29	36	.888	-1	104	226	O99(20/79/0)	—	2.3
1889	Lou AA	83	324	39	83	19	5	2	32	34	0	30	.256	.327	.364	98	0	21	.882	-4	74	96	O83L	—	-0.6
1890	Cle P	118	493	112	184	**40**	8	5	93	75	3	36	**.373**	.459	.517	**175**	**60**	35	.893	5	82	82	O118L	—	**4.9**
1891	Pit N	50	203	35	59	14	1	4	28	27	1	31	.291	.377	.429	138	11	4	.904	3	92	0	O50(48/0/2)	—	1.1
	Cin N	55	216	29	74	10	3	0	33	24	2	23	.343	.413	.417	141	12	12	.924	-2	65	128	O55(54/1/0)	—	0.8
	Year	105	419	64	133	24	4	4	61	51	3	54	.317	.395	.422	139	23	16	.913	1	78	66	O105(102/1/2)	—	1.9
1892	Lou N	21	77	10	19	4	0	0	4	12	0	7	.247	.348	.299	104	1	5	.911	-1	28	273	O21L	—	-0.2
	Cin N	83	307	47	93	12	5	3	52	40	0	26	.303	.383	.404	140	16	8	.917	-2	99	0	O82(23/46/16),1b2	—	0.8
	Year	104	384	57	112	16	5	3	56	52	0	33	.292	.376	.383	133	18	13	.916	-3	84	58	O103(44/46/16),1b2	—	0.6
1893	Lou N	57	220	38	78	11	3	1	37	44	2	15	.355	.466	.445	155	22	8	.881	-4	51	44	O57(44/0/13)	—	1.2
1894	StL N	2	7	1	1	0	0	0	0	0	0	0	.143	.143	.143	-31	-2	0	1.000	-0	0	0	O2C	—	-0.2
	Bro N	1	2	1	2	0	0	0	2	1	0	0	1.000	1.000	1.000	412	1	0	1.000	-0	0	0	/rf	—	0.1
	Year	3	9	2	3	0	0	0	2	1	0	0	.333	.400	.333	80	0	0	1.000	-1	0	0	O3(0/2/1)	—	-0.1
Total	13	1183	4820	954	1646	295	85	46	659	466	29	168	.341	.403	.467	164	396	258	.883	-35	82	103	O998C,3b75,2b49,S44,1b26/P	—	28.0
BRUBAKER, BILL	Wilbur Lee; B11.7.1910 Cleveland OH; D4.2.1978 Laguna Hills CA; BR/TR/6´2˝/185; d9.8; gs–Dennis Rasmussen; Col UCLA																								
1932	Pit N	7	24	3	10	3	0	0	4	3	0	4	.417	.481	.542	178	3	1	.909	0	103	176	3b7	—	0.3
1933	Pit N	2	2	0	0	0	0	0	0	0	0	0	.000	.000	.000	-99	-1	0	1.000	0	148	0	/3	—	0.0
1934	Pit N	3	6	0	2	1	0	0	1	1	0	0	.333	.429	.500	144	-0	0	1.000	1	139	395	3b3	—	0.1
1935	Pit N	6	11	1	0	0	0	0	0	2	0	5	.000	.154	.000	-53	-2	0	.889	-0	96	0	3b5	—	-0.3
1936	Pit N	145	554	77	160	27	4	6	102	50	4	96	.289	.352	.384	96	-2	5	.940	-12	90	49	3b145	—	-0.9
1937	Pit N	120	413	57	105	20	4	6	48	47	3	51	.254	.335	.366	90	-5	2	.952	5	**108**	116	3b115,S3/1	—	0.4
1938	Pit N	45	112	18	33	5	0	3	19	9	0	14	.295	.347	.420	109	1	2	.875	-3	85	137	3b18,1b9,S3/lf	—	-0.1
1939	Pit N	100	345	41	80	23	1	7	43	29	3	51	.232	.297	.365	78	-11	3	.950	5	102	100	2b65,3b32/S	—	-0.1
1940	Pit N	38	78	8	15	3	1	0	7	8	0	16	.192	.267	.256	45	-6	0	.955	4	117	133	3b19,S8,1b4	—	-0.2
1943	Bos N	13	19	3	8	3	0	0	1	2	0	2	.421	.476	.579	207	3	0	.778	-1	95	0	3b5,1b3	0	0.2
Total	10	479	1564	208	413	85	10	22	225	151	10	239	.264	.333	.373	90	-20	13	.938	-2	102	85	3b350,2b65,1b17,S15/lf	0	-0.6
BRUCE, LOU	Louis R.; B1.16.1877 St.Regis NY; D2.9.1968 Ilion NY; BL/TR/5´5˝/145; d6.22; Col Syracuse; ▲																								
1904	Phi A	30	101	9	27	3	0	0	8	5	0	—	.267	.302	.297	85	-2	2	.969	-0	131	350	O25(11/10/5),P2/23	—	-0.3
BRUCKER, EARLE	Earle Francis Jr.; B8.29.1925 Los Angeles CA; BL/TR/6´2˝/210; d10.2; f–Earle; Col San Diego St.																								
1948	Phi A	2	6	0	1	1	0	0	0	1	0	1	.167	.286	.333	64	0	0-0	1.000	0	*0*	*0*	C2	0	0.0
BRUCKER, EARLE	Earle Francis Sr.; B5.6.1901 Albany NY; D5.8.1981 San Diego CA; BR/TR/5´11˝/175; d4.19; M1/C11; s–Earle																								
1937	Phi A	102	317	40	82	16	5	6	37	48	0	30	.259	.356	.397	91	-4	1-2	.971	-5	*87*	*106*	C92	—	-0.4
1938	Phi A	53	171	26	64	21	1	3	35	19	0	16	.374	.437	.561	152	15	1-1	.986	-4	*79*	*87*	C44/1	—	1.2
1939	Phi A	62	172	18	50	15	1	3	31	24	1	16	.291	.381	.442	112	4	0-1	1.000	-6	*72*	*84*	C47	—	0.1
1940	Phi A	23	46	3	9	1	1	0	2	6	0	3	.196	.288	.261	44	-4	0-0	.966	0	*71*	*134*	C13	—	-0.3
1943	Phi A	1	1	0	0	0	0	0	0	0	0	0	.000	.000	.000	-99	0	0-0	ø	0	—	—	/H	0	0.0
Total	5	241	707	87	205	53	8	12	105	97	1	65	.290	.376	.438	108	11	2-4	.980	-15	*81*	*98*	C196/1	0	0.6

YEAR	TM LG	G	AB	R	H	2B	3B	HR	RBI	BB-IB	HP	SO	AVG	OBP	SLG	AOPS	ABR	SB-CS	FA	FR	RNG	THR	GAMES AT POSITION	DL	BFW
Bruett, J. T.	Joseph Timothy; B10.8.1967 Milwaukee WI; BL/TL/5´11˝/175; [MinA88 11/285]; d6.3; Col Minnesota																								
1992	Min A	56	76	7	19	4	0	0	2	6-1	1	12	.250	.313	.303	71	-3	6-3	.979	-1	94	81	O45(5/20/22),D3	0	-0.4
1993	Min A	17	20	2	5	2	0	0	1	1-0	1	4	.250	.318	.350	79	-1	0-0	.857	-1	105	0	O13(2/4/8)	0	-0.1
Total	2	73	96	9	24	6	0	0	3	7-1	2	16	.250	.314	.313	72	-4	6-3	.952	-1	96	64	O58(7/24/30),D3	0	-0.5
Bruggy, Frank	Frank Leo; B5.4.1891 Elizabeth NJ; D4.5.1959 Elizabeth NJ; BR/TR/5´11˝/195; d4.13; Col Seton Hall																								
1921	Phi N	96	277	28	86	11	2	5	28	23	3	37	.310	.370	.419	100	1	6-2	.953	-11	*69*	*104*	C86,1b2	—	-0.4
1922	Phi A	53	111	10	31	7	0	0	9	6	1	11	.279	.322	.342	71	-5	1-2	.925	-2	*113*	*121*	C31	—	-0.5
1923	Phi A	54	105	4	22	3	0	1	6	4	1	9	.210	.245	.267	34	-10	1-1	.950	-1	*110*	*131*	C34,1b5	—	-1.0
1924	Phi A	50	113	9	30	6	0	0	8	8	0	15	.265	.314	.319	63	-6	4-0	.928	-6	*98*	*83*	C44	—	-0.9
1925	Cin N	6	14	2	3	0	0	0	1	2	0	0	.214	.313	.214	38	-1	0-0	.870	-1	*85*	*107*	C6	—	-0.2
Total	5	259	620	53	172	27	2	6	52	43	5	72	.277	.329	.356	76	-21	12-5	.941	-19	*88*	*106*	C201,1b7	—	-3.0
Brumbaugh, Cliff	Clifford Michael; B4.21.1974 Wilmington DE; BR/TR/6´2˝/205; [TexA95 13/346]; d5.30; Col Delaware																								
2001	Tex A	7	10	1	0	0	0	0	0	1-0	0	5	.000	.091	.000	-71	-3	0-0	1.000	-0	84	0	O6(2/0/4)	0	-0.3
	Col N	14	36	5	10	2	0	1	4	2-0	0	9	.278	.316	.417	72	-1	0-1	1.000	-1	94	0	O11(4/0/8)	0	-0.3
Total	1	21	46	6	10	2	0	1	4	3-0	0	14	.217	.265	.326	45	-4	0-1	1.000	-1	91	0	O17(6/0/12)	0	-0.6
Brumfield, Jacob	Jacob Donnell; B5.27.1965 Bogalusa LA; BR/TR/6´0˝/(170–190); [ChiN83 7/164]; d4.6																								
1992	Cin N	24	30	6	4	0	0	0	2	2-1	1	4	.133	.212	.133	-0	-4	6-0	1.000	2	132	279	O16(7/8/1)	0	-0.1
1993	Cin N	103	272	40	73	17	3	6	23	21-4	1	47	.268	.321	.419	96	-2	20-8	.978	3	101	156	O96(24/68/5),2b4	0	0.3
1994	Cin N	68	122	36	38	10	2	4	11	15-0	0	18	.311	.381	.525	135	7	6-3	.987	2	117	65	O43(14/24/6)	0	0.8
1995	Pit N	116	402	64	109	23	2	4	26	37-0	5	71	.271	.339	.368	85	-8	22-12	.969	5	109	159	O104C	15	-0.1
1996	Pit N	29	80	11	20	9	0	2	8	5-1	0	17	.250	.291	.438	87	-2	3-1	.946	-2	82	110	O22C	0	-0.3
	Tor A	90	308	52	79	19	2	12	52	24-1	4	58	.256	.316	.448	92	-5	12-3	.982	1	96	165	O83(18/39/37),D5	0	-0.4
1997	Tor A	58	174	22	36	5	1	2	20	14-0	1	31	.207	.268	.282	44	-15	4-4	1.000	3	98	266	O47(14/24/10),D4	15	-1.3
1999	LA N	18	17	4	5	0	1	0	1	0-0	0	5	.294	.294	.412	80	-1	0-0	1.000	0	122	0	O11(7/4/0)	0	-0.1
	Tor A	62	170	25	40	8	3	2	19	19-0	0	39	.235	.307	.353	68	-9	1-2	.978	3	110	161	O53(10/36/8),D6	0	-0.6
Total	7	568	1575	260	404	91	14	32	162	137-7	12	290	.257	.318	.393	84	-39	74-33	.979	17	104	163	O475(94/329/67),D15,2b4	30	-1.8
Brumley, Mike	Anthony Michael; B4.9.1963 Oklahoma City OK; BB/TR/5´10˝/(165–175); [BosA83 2/33]; d6.16; f–Mike; Col Texas																								
1987	Chi N	39	104	8	21	2	2	1	9	10-1	1	30	.202	.276	.288	48	-8	7-1	.965	1	101	123	S34/2	0	-0.2
1989	Det A	92	212	33	42	5	2	1	11	14-0	1	45	.198	.251	.255	44	-16	8-4	.980	-14	86	49	S42,2b24,3b11,O4(1/1/2),D8	0	-2.8
1990	Sea A	62	147	19	33	5	4	0	7	10-0	0	22	.224	.272	.313	63	-8	2-0	.983	-2	92	88	S47,2b6,3b3,O2(1/1/0)/D	35	-0.6
1991	Bos A	63	118	16	25	5	0	0	5	10-0	0	22	.212	.273	.254	44	-9	2-0	.950	7	119	69	S31,3b17,2b7,O4C,D2	0	0.1
1992	Bos A	2	1	0	0	0	0	0	0	0-0	0	0	.000	.000	.000	-93	0	0-0	ø	0	—	—	/H	0	0.0
1993	Hou N	8	10	1	3	0	0	0	2	1-0	0	3	.300	.364	.300	83	0	0-1	ø	-0	0	0	/3SO(1/0/1)	0	-0.1
1994	Oak A	11	25	0	6	0	0	0	2	1-0	0	8	.240	.269	.240	35	-3	0-0	.929	-2	86	102	2b4,3b4,O3L/S	0	-0.4
1995	Hou N	18	18	1	1	0	0	1	2	0-0	0	6	.056	.056	.222	-33	-4	1-0	1.000	-1	42	0	S3,O3L/13	0	-0.4
Total	8	295	635	78	131	17	8	3	38	46-1	2	136	.206	.261	.272	47	-48	20-6	.972	-10	97	82	S159,2b42,3b37,O17(9/6/3),D11/1	35	-4.4
Brumley, Mike	Tony Mike; B7.10.1938 Granite OK; BL/TR/5´10˝/(195–205); d4.18; s–Mike; Col Oklahoma																								
1964	Was A	136	426	36	104	19	2	2	35	40-6	1	54	.244	.309	.312	74	-14	1-1	.991	-4	114	102	C132	0	-1.3
1965	Was A	79	216	15	45	4	0	3	15	20-6	2	33	.208	.280	.269	58	-12	1-1	.990	1	74	112	C66	0	-0.9
1966	Was A	9	18	1	2	1	0	0	0	0-0	0	2	.111	.111	.167	-22	-3	0-0	1.000	-0	0	89	C7	0	-0.3
Total	3	224	660	52	151	24	2	5	50	60-12	3	89	.229	.295	.294	67	-29	2-2	.991	-4	98	105	C205	0	-2.5
Brummer, Glenn	Glenn Edward; B11.23.1954 Olney IL; BR/TR/6´0˝/(185–200); d5.25; Col Lake Land (IL) JC																								
1981	StL N	21	30	2	6	1	0	0	2	1-0	0	2	.200	.219	.233	29	-3	0-0	1.000	-1	84	98	C19	0	-0.4
1982	†StL N	35	64	4	15	4	0	0	8	0-0	0	12	.234	.234	.297	46	-5	2-0	.970	-1	161	49	C32	0	-0.5
1983	StL N	45	87	7	24	7	0	0	9	10-1	0	11	.276	.351	.356	96	0	1-3	.978	-4	99	68	C41	0	-0.4
1984	StL N	28	58	3	12	0	0	1	3	3-0	0	7	.207	.246	.259	43	-5	0-0	.973	2	164	117	C26	46	-0.2
1985	Tex A	49	108	7	30	4	0	0	5	11-1	2	22	.278	.355	.315	84	-2	1-5	.989	-8	84	40	C47/rfD	0	-1.0
Total	5	178	347	23	87	16	0	1	27	25-2	2	54	.251	.304	.305	69	-15	4-8	.981	-12	115	66	C165/Drf	46	-2.5
Brunansky, Tom	Thomas Andrew; B8.20.1960 Covina CA; BR/TR/6´4˝/(205–220); [CalA78 1/14]; d4.9																								
1981	Cal A	11	33	7	5	0	0	3	6	8-0	0	10	.152	.317	.424	111	1	1-0	.938	2	107	363	O11L	0	0.2
1982	Min A	127	463	77	126	30	1	20	46	71-0	8	101	.272	.377	.471	127	20	1-2	.986	11	123	91	O127(3/38/97)	0	2.6
1983	Min A	151	542	70	123	24	5	28	82	61-4	4	95	.227	.308	.445	101	-1	2-5	.985	13	114	146	O146(0/38/119),D4	0	0.5
1984	Min A	155	567	75	144	21	0	32	85	57-2	0	94	.254	.320	.460	108	5	4-5	.984	0	95	135	O153R/D	0	-0.4
1985	Min A★	157	567	71	137	28	4	27	90	71-7	0	86	.242	.320	.448	103	2	5-3	.984	1	96	135	O155(0/1/155)	0	-0.5
1986	Min A	157	593	69	152	28	1	23	75	53-4	1	98	.256	.315	.423	97	-3	12-4	.982	3	105	97	O152(0/1/152),D2	0	-0.7
1987	†Min A	155	532	83	138	22	2	32	85	74-5	4	104	.259	.352	.489	116	13	11-11	.990	3	104	108	O138(58/0/107),D17	0	0.7
1988	Min A	14	49	5	9	1	0	1	6	7-0	0	11	.184	.286	.265	54	-3	1-2	.864	-3	70	0	O13(1/0/12)/D	0	-0.7
	StL N	143	523	69	128	22	4	22	79	79-6	4	82	.245	.345	.428	120	15	16-6	**.996**	-1	92	136	O143(1/0/143)	0	1.1
1989	StL N	158	556	67	133	29	3	20	85	59-3	2	107	.239	.312	.410	102	1	5-9	.977	-2	96	107	O155(0/1/155)/1	0	-0.8
1990	StL N	19	57	5	9	3	0	1	2	12-0	1	10	.158	.310	.263	60	-3	0-0	.950	0	106	83	O17R	0	-0.3
	†Bos A	129	461	61	123	24	5	15	71	54-7	3	105	.267	.342	.438	113	8	5-10	.982	4	113	83	O121(0/1/121),D7	0	0.6
1991	Bos A	142	459	54	105	24	1	16	70	49-2	3	72	.229	.303	.390	87	-9	1-2	.989	0	105	56	O137(0/1/136)/D	0	-1.3
1992	Bos A	138	458	47	122	31	3	15	74	66-2	0	96	.266	.354	.445	115	11	2-5	.980	0	101	99	O92R,1b28,D17	0	0.5
1993	Mil A	80	224	20	41	7	3	6	29	25-0	0	59	.183	.265	.321	57	-15	3-4	.987	3	113	86	O71R,D6	60	-1.5
1994	Mil A	16	28	2	6	2	0	0	0	1-0	0	9	.214	.241	.286	34	-3	0-0	1.000	-1	46	0	O6R,1b2,D2	0	-0.4
	Bos A	48	177	22	42	10	1	10	34	23-1	0	48	.237	.319	.475	98	-1	0-2	.989	-2	101	33	O42(14/0/33),1b5,D3	0	-0.6
	Year	64	205	24	48	12	1	10	34	24-1	0	57	.234	.309	.449	89	-4	0-2	.989	-3	98	31	O48(14/0/39),1b7,D5	0	-1.0
Total	14	1800	6289	804	1543	306	33	271	919	770-43	30	1187	.245	.327	.434	105	38	69-70	.984	33	104	108	O1679(88/81/1569),D61,1b36	60	-1.0
Brunsberg, Arlo	Arlo Adolph; B8.15.1940 Fertile MN; BL/TR/6´0˝/190; d9.23; Col Concordia College (MN)																								
1966	Det A	2	3	1	1	1	0	0	0	0-0	1	0	.333	.500	.667	227	1	0-0	1.000	-0	0	0	C2	0	0.1
Bruntlett, Eric	Eric Kevin; B3.29.1978 Lafayette IN; BR/TR/6´0˝/(190–200); [HouN00 9/277]; d6.27; Col Stanford																								
2003	Hou N	31	54	3	14	3	0	1	4	0-0	0	10	.259	.255	.370	58	-3	0-0	.963	-2	66	68	S10,2b9,O2(1/1/0)/3	0	-0.4
2004	†Hou N	45	52	14	13	2	0	4	8	7-0	0	13	.250	.328	.519	114	1	4-0	.938	-5	68	103	S33,2b5,O2(1/1/0)	0	-0.2
2005	†Hou N	91	109	19	24	5	2	4	14	10-0	1	25	.220	.292	.413	81	-4	7-2	.929	2	62	56	2b28,O26(11/14/1),S10,3b8/1	0	-0.1
2006	Hou N	73	119	11	33	8	0	0	10	13-1	1	21	.277	.351	.345	78	-3	3-1	.938	4	111	151	2b23,S21,O18(6/8/5),3b2	0	0.2
Total	4	240	334	47	84	18	2	9	36	30-1	2	69	.251	.314	.398	82	-9	14-3	.957	-1	95	97	S74,2b65,O48(19/24/6),3b11/1	0	-0.5
Brush, Bob	Robert; B3.8.1875 Osage IA; D4.2.1944 San Bernardino CA; 5´10˝/?; d4.20																								
1907	Bos N	2	2	0	0	0	0	0	0	0	0	—	.000	.000	.000	-99	0	0	1.000	-0	0	0	/1	—	-0.1
Bruton, Bill	William Haron; B11.9.1925 Panola AL; D12.5.1995 Marshallton DE; BL/TR/6´0.5˝/(165–169); d4.13																								
1953	Mil N	151	613	82	153	18	14	1	41	44	6	100	.250	.306	.330	70	-29	**26**-11	.979	0	98	111	O150C	0	-3.3
1954	Mil N	142	567	89	161	20	7	4	30	40	4	78	.284	.336	.365	88	-11	**34**-13	.981	-1	94	**134**	O141C	0	-1.6
1955	Mil N	149	636	106	175	30	12	9	47	43-6	4	72	.275	.325	.403	97	-5	**25**-11	.968	9	106	148	O149C	0	-0.2
1956	Mil N	147	525	73	143	23	**15**	8	56	26-11	1	63	.272	.304	.419	99	-4	8-6	.969	-3	100	92	O145C	0	-1.4
1957	Mil N	79	306	41	85	16	9	5	30	19-4	1	35	.278	.317	.438	110	3	11-4	.981	-3	96	85	O79C	73	-0.3
1958	†Mil N	100	325	47	91	11	3	3	28	27-4	2	37	.280	.336	.360	93	-4	4-1	.977	-6	92	88	O96C	40	-1.3
1959	Mil N	133	478	72	138	22	6	6	41	35-2	1	54	.289	.338	.397	104	2	13-5	.991	0	106	87	O133C	0	-0.3
1960	Mil N	151	629	**112**	180	27	**13**	12	54	41-1	2	97	.286	.330	.428	115	10	22-13	.986	-6	94	89	O149C	0	-0.3
1961	Det A	160	596	99	153	15	5	17	63	61-0	3	66	.257	.327	.384	87	-12	22-6	.988	4	114	51	O155C	0	-0.9
1962	Det A	147	561	90	156	27	5	16	74	55-0	5	67	.278	.346	.430	104	4	14-7	.983	8	**119**	74	O145C	0	0.8
1963	Det A	145	524	84	134	21	8	8	48	59-3	0	70	.256	.330	.372	93	-4	14-7	.991	1	110	72	O138C	0	-0.6
1964	Det A	106	296	42	82	11	5	5	33	32-1	0	54	.277	.347	.399	105	2	14-5	.987	1	95	155	O81(10/70/1)	0	0.2
Total	12	1610	6056	937	1651	241	102	94	545	482-32	29	793	.273	.328	.393	96	-48	207-89	.981	5	103	97	O1561(10/1550/1)	113	-9.2

YEAR	TM LG	G	AB	R	H	2B	3B	HR	RBI	BB-IB	HP	SO	AVG	OBP	SLG	AOPS	ABR	SB-CS	FA	FR	RNG	THR	GAMES AT POSITION	DL	BFW
Bruyette, Ed	Edward T.; B8.31.1874 Manawa WI; D8.5.1940 Peshastin WA; BL/TR/5´10˝/170; d8.6																								
1901	Mil A	26	82	7	15	3	0	0	4	12	1	—	.183	.295	.220	46	-5	1	.778	-4	45	0	O21C,2b3/S3	—	-1.0
Bryan, Billy	William Ronald; B12.4.1938 Morgan GA; BL/TR/6´4˝/(200–215); d9.12																								
1961	KC A	9	19	2	3	0	0	1	2	2-0	0	7	.158	.238	.316	46	-2	0-0	1.000	-1	0	0	C4	0	-0.2
1962	KC A	25	74	5	11	2	1	2	7	5-0	0	32	.149	.203	.284	28	-8	0-0	.976	-3	59	25	C22	0	-1.1
1963	KC A	24	65	11	11	1	1	3	7	9-5	0	22	.169	.270	.354	69	-3	0-0	.981	2	101	30	C24	0	0.1
1964	KC A	93	220	19	53	9	2	13	36	16-1	0	69	.241	.290	.477	107	1	0-0	.991	-9	74	86	C65	0	-0.6
1965	KC A	108	325	36	82	11	5	14	51	29-5	2	87	.252	.315	.446	116	6	0-0	.984	-4	84	89	C95	0	0.6
1966	KC A	32	76	0	10	4	0	0	7	6-0	0	17	.132	.193	.184	10	-9	0-0	.965	1	36	107	C21,1b3	0	-0.8
	NY A	27	69	5	15	2	0	4	5	5-0	0	19	.217	.270	.420	99	0	0-0	.988	-0	80	181	C14,1b3	0	0.0
	Year	59	145	5	25	6	0	4	12	11-0	0	36	.172	.229	.297	52	-9	0-0	.975	1	58	144	C35,1b6	0	-0.8
1967	NY A	16	12	1	2	0	0	1	2	5-0	0	3	.167	.412	.417	151	1	0-0	1.000	0	0	0	/C	0	0.1
1968	Was A	40	108	7	22	3	0	3	8	14-2	1	27	.204	.301	.315	90	-1	0-1	.983	-3	85	107	C28	0	-0.3
Total	8	374	968	86	209	32	9	41	125	91-13	3	283	.216	.284	.395	91	-15	0-1	.984	-17	77	85	C274,1b6	0	-2.2
Bryant, Derek	Derek Roszell; B10.9.1951 Lexington KY; BR/TR/5´11˝/185; [OakA73 8/191]; d4.24; Col Kentucky																								
1979	Oak A	39	106	8	19	2	1	0	13	10-1	0	10	.179	.246	.217	29	-11	0-0	1.000	-1	93	94	O33(25/0/10),D2	0	-1.3
Bryant, Don	Donald Ray; B7.13.1941 Jasper FL; BR/TR/6´5˝/(200–205); d7.17; C7																								
1966	Chi N	13	26	2	8	2	0	0	4	1-0	1	4	.308	.357	.385	105	0	1-0	.978	-0	58	51	C10	0	0.1
1969	Hou N	31	59	2	11	1	0	1	6	4-1	1	13	.186	.250	.254	42	-5	0-0	.993	-1	59	21	C28	0	-0.5
1970	Hou N	15	24	2	5	0	0	0	3	1-0	0	8	.208	.231	.208	22	-3	0-0	.957	-2	26	125	C13	0	-0.5
Total	3	59	109	6	24	3	0	1	13	6-1	2	25	.220	.271	.275	53	-8	1-0	.983	-4	52	48	C51	0	-0.9
Bryant, George	George F.; B2.10.1857 Bridgeport CT; D6.12.1907 Boston MA; d8.6																								
1885	Det N	1	4	0	0	0	0	0	1	0	—	2	.000	.000	.000	-99	-1	—	1.000	-0	46	339	/2	—	-0.1
Bryant, Ralph	Ralph Wendell; B5.20.1961 Fort Gaines GA; BL/TR/6´2˝/(200–205); [LAN81 S1/22]; d9.8; Col Abraham Baldwin (GA) JC																								
1985	LA N	6	6	0	2	0	0	0	1	0-0	0	2	.333	.333	.333	89	0	0-0	ø	-0	0	0	O3(2/0/1)	0	0.0
1986	LA N	27	75	15	19	4	2	6	13	5-0	1	25	.253	.305	.600	155	5	0-1	.953	1	110	131	O26R	0	0.4
1987	LA N	46	69	7	17	2	1	2	10	10-2	1	24	.246	.346	.391	98	0	2-1	.917	-1	97	0	O19(8/0/12)	0	-0.2
Total	3	79	150	22	38	6	3	8	24	15-2	2	51	.253	.325	.493	125	5	2-2	.940	-0	103	79	O48(10/0/39)	0	0.2
Brye, Steve	Stephen Robert; B2.4.1949 Alameda CA; BR/TR/6´0˝/(188–190); [MinA67 1/17]; d9.3																								
1970	Min A	9	11	1	2	1	0	0	2	2-0	0	4	.182	.308	.273	60	-1	0-0	1.000	-1	66	0	O6(6/0/1)	0	-0.1
1971	Min A	28	107	10	24	1	0	3	11	7-0	0	15	.224	.270	.318	65	-5	3-1	.966	1	93	231	O28(25/7/0)	0	-0.6
1972	Min A	100	253	18	61	9	3	0	12	17-1	1	38	.241	.292	.300	73	-9	3-1	.994	9	114	166	O93(74/20/2)	0	-0.4
1973	Min A	92	278	39	73	9	5	6	33	35-1	0	43	.263	.343	.396	104	1	3-5	.986	2	108	71	O87(12/72/4)/D	0	0.0
1974	Min A	135	488	52	138	32	1	2	41	22-1	5	59	.283	.319	.365	94	-4	1-3	**.997**	-2	97	120	O129(0/128/1)	0	-1.0
1975	Min A	86	246	41	62	13	1	9	34	21-2	2	37	.252	.315	.423	106	1	2-1	.983	-0	93	146	O72(19/5/48),D6	21	-0.2
1976	Min A	87	258	33	68	11	0	2	23	13-0	0	31	.264	.295	.329	82	-6	1-2	.987	-6	88	21	O78(11/57/17),D3	0	-1.6
1977	Mil A	94	241	27	60	14	3	7	28	16-0	1	39	.249	.297	.419	93	-3	1-0	1.000	7	111	173	O83(29/43/17),D6	0	0.2
1978	Pit N	66	115	16	27	7	0	1	9	11-1	1	10	.235	.305	.322	72	-4	2-1	.983	-1	96	85	O47(28/7/12)	0	-0.6
Total	9	697	1997	237	515	97	13	30	193	144-6	10	276	.258	.309	.365	90	-30	16-14	.991	9	101	120	O623(204/339/102),D16	21	-4.3
Bubela, Jaime	Jaime Lee; B6.6.1978 Houston TX; BL/TR/6´1˝/200; [SeaA00 7/206]; d9.15; Col Baylor																								
2005	Sea A	11	19	3	2	0	0	0	0	1-0	0	4	.105	.150	.105	-33	-4	1-0	1.000	1	125	0	O7(1/6/0)/D	0	-0.3
Bubser, Hal	Harold Frederick; B9.28.1895 Chicago IL; D6.22.1959 Melrose Park IL; BR/TR/5´11˝/170; d4.15																								
1922	Chi A	3	3	0	0	0	0	0	0	0	0	2	.000	.000	.000	-99	-1	0-0	ø	0	—	—	/H	—	-0.1
Bucha, Johnny	John George; B1.22.1925 Allentown PA; D4.28.1996 Bethlehem PA; BR/TR/5´11˝/190; d5.2																								
1948	StL N	2	1	0	0	0	0	0	0	1	0	0	.000	.500	.000	43	0	0	1.000	-0	*0*	*0*	/C	0	0.0
1950	StL N	22	36	1	5	1	0	0	1	4	0	7	.139	.225	.167	5	-5	0	.959	-0	*146*	*86*	C17	0	-0.5
1953	Det A	60	158	17	35	9	0	1	14	20	0	14	.222	.309	.297	65	-7	1-1	.984	-6	*81*	*118*	C56	0	-1.1
Total	3	84	195	18	40	10	0	1	15	25	0	21	.205	.295	.272	53	-12	1-1	.980	-6	*92*	*112*	C74	0	-1.6
Buchanan, Brian	Brian James; B7.21.1973 Miami FL; BR/TR/6´4˝/230; [NYA94 1/24]; d5.19; Col Virginia																								
2000	Min A	30	82	10	19	3	0	1	8	8-0	1	22	.232	.301	.305	52	-6	0-2	1.000	-2	77	67	O25(2/0/24),D2	0	-0.9
2001	Min A	69	197	28	54	12	0	10	32	19-0	2	58	.274	.342	.487	110	3	1-1	.973	-0	105	45	O46(7/0/39),D19	15	0.0
2002	Min A	44	135	19	34	5	1	5	15	6-0	2	33	.252	.294	.415	83	-4	2-1	1.000	1	127	0	O24R,D17	15	-0.4
	SD N	48	92	12	27	5	0	6	13	9-0	1	26	.293	.363	.543	147	6	0-1	1.000	-0	108	79	1b15,O14R	0	0.4
2003	SD N	115	198	29	52	10	2	8	29	24-1	3	51	.263	.346	.455	119	5	6-2	1.000	1	114	144	O43(15/0/29),1b24,D5	0	0.4
2004	SD N	38	60	7	12	2	0	2	6	6-2	1	19	.200	.279	.333	62	-4	0-0	1.000	-2	58	0	O18(15/0/3),1b3	25	-0.6
	NY N	2	3	0	0	0	0	0	0	1-0	0	1	.000	.250	.000	-28	-1	0-0	1.000	0	154	115	/1	0	-0.1
	Year	40	63	7	12	2	0	2	6	7-2	1	20	.190	.278	.317	57	-4	0-0	1.000	-2	58	0	O18(15/0/3),1b4	0	-0.7
Total	5	346	767	105	198	37	3	32	103	73-3	10	210	.258	.328	.439	100	-1	9-7	.987	-3	99	65	O170(39/0/133),1b43,D43	55	-1.2
Buchek, Jerry	Gerald Peter; B5.9.1942 St.Louis MO; BR/TR/5´11˝/(180–185); d6.30																								
1961	StL N	31	90	6	12	2	0	0	9	0-0	2	28	.133	.151	.156	-16	-15	0-0	.912	-8	78	115	S31	0	-2.1
1963	StL N	3	4	0	1	0	0	0	0	0-0	0	2	.250	.250	.250	41	0	0-0	1.000	-0	59	309	/S	0	0.0
1964	†StL N	35	30	7	6	0	2	0	1	3-0	0	11	.200	.273	.333	64	-2	0-0	.929	2	116	70	S20,2b9/3	0	0.2
1965	StL N	55	166	17	41	8	3	3	21	13-2	0	46	.247	.300	.386	84	-4	1-0	.994	8	105	120	2b33,S18/3	30	0.9
1966	StL N	100	284	23	67	10	4	4	25	23-4	0	71	.236	.288	.342	75	-10	0-5	.974	-6	105	132	2b49,S48,3b4	0	-1.1
1967	NY N	124	411	35	97	11	2	14	41	26-5	2	101	.236	.283	.375	89	-8	3-5	.977	-3	96	90	2b95,3b17,S9	0	-0.4
1968	NY N	73	192	8	35	4	0	1	11	10-5	3	53	.182	.234	.219	36	-15	1-1	.935	-1	101	117	3b37,2b12,O9L	0	-1.9
Total	7	421	1177	96	259	35	11	22	108	75-16	7	312	.220	.269	.325	67	-54	5-11	.978	-8	100	105	2b198,S127,3b60,O9L	30	-4.4
Bucher, Jim	James Quinter; B3.24.1911 Manassas VA; D10.21.2004 Elizabethtown PA; BL/TR/5´11˝/170; d4.18																								
1934	Bro N	47	84	12	19	5	2	0	8	4	0	7	.226	.261	.333	61	-5	1	.920	-2	93	117	2b20,3b6	—	-0.6
1935	Bro N	123	473	72	143	22	1	7	58	10	0	33	.302	.317	.397	93	-6	4	.950	-2	100	113	2b41,3b39,O37(21/0/16)	—	-0.7
1936	Bro N	110	370	49	93	12	8	2	41	29	0	27	.251	.306	.343	74	-15	5	.910	-6	108	86	3b39,2b32,O30(7/0/23)	—	-2.0
1937	Bro N	125	380	44	96	11	2	4	37	20	3	18	.253	.295	.324	67	-18	5	.951	-10	79	97	2b49,3b43,O6(4/1/1)	—	-2.4
1938	StL N	17	57	7	13	3	1	0	7	2	0	2	.228	.254	.316	53	-4	0	.955	-3	81	115	2b14/3	—	-0.6
1944	Bos A	80	277	39	76	9	2	4	31	19	2	13	.274	.326	.365	98	-1	3-3	.958	-4	96	119	3b44,2b21	0	-0.4
1945	Bos A	52	151	19	34	4	3	0	11	7	1	13	.225	.264	.291	60	-8	1-3	.940	1	111	125	3b32,2b2	0	-0.9
Total	7	554	1792	242	474	66	19	17	193	91	6	113	.265	.302	.351	78	-57	19-6	.939	-25	102	102	3b204,2b179,O73(32/1/40)	0	-7.6
Buck, John	Johnathan R.; B7.7.1980 Kemmerer WY; BR/TR/6´3˝/(210–220); [HouN98 7/212]; d6.25																								
2004	KC A	71	238	36	56	9	0	12	30	15-0	0	79	.235	.280	.424	80	-8	1-1	.992	-6	114	91	C68,D3	0	-1.0
2005	KC A	118	401	40	97	21	1	12	47	23-2	3	94	.242	.287	.389	81	-12	2-2	.996	-9	100	123	C117	0	-1.3
2006	KC A	114	371	37	91	21	1	11	50	26-2	7	84	.245	.306	.396	82	-11	0-2	.991	-8	175	70	C112	0	-1.2
Total	3	303	1010	113	244	51	2	35	127	64-4	10	257	.242	.292	.400	81	-31	3-5	.993	-24	131	96	C297,D3	0	-3.5
Buckley, Kevin	Kevin John; B1.16.1959 Quincy MA; BR/TR/6´1˝/200; [TexA81 17/424]; d9.4; Col Maine																								
1984	Tex A	5	7	1	2	1	0	0	0	2-0	0	4	.286	.444	.429	138	1	0-0	ø	0	—	—	D3	0	0.0
Buckley, Dick	Richard D.; B9.21.1858 Troy NY; D12.12.1929 Pittsburgh PA; BR/TR/5´10˝/195; d4.20																								
1888	Ind N	71	260	28	71	9	3	5	22	6	0	24	.273	.289	.388	112	3	4	.898	-14	—	—	C51,3b22/rf1	—	-0.7
1889	Ind N	68	260	35	67	11	0	8	41	15	1	32	.258	.301	.392	90	-5	5	.877	-13	—	—	C55,3b12/lf1	—	-1.2
1890	NY N	70	266	39	68	11	0	2	26	23	4	35	.256	.324	.320	88	-4	3	.931	7	*98*	*127*	C62,3b8	—	0.7
1891	NY N	75	253	23	55	9	1	4	31	11	3	30	.217	.258	.308	67	-11	3	.958	4	*82*	*106*	C74/3	—	-0.1
1892	StL N	121	410	43	93	17	4	5	52	22	5	34	.227	.275	.324	85	-9	7	.937	-9	*95*	*85*	C119,1b2	—	-0.7
1893	StL N	9	23	2	4	1	0	0	1	0	0	0	.174	.174	.217	4	-3	0	.914	0	*86*	*100*	C9	—	-0.2
1894	StL N	29	89	5	16	1	2	1	3	6	1	3	.180	.240	.270	23	-12	1	.936	2	*106*	*118*	C27/1	—	-0.6

YEAR	TM LG	G	AB	R	H	2B	3B	HR	RBI	BB-IB	HP	SO	AVG	OBP	SLG	AOPS	ABR	SB-CS	FA	FR	RNG	THR	GAMES AT POSITION	DL	BFW
	Phi N	43	160	18	47	7	3	1	26	6	2	13	.294	.327	.394	75	-7	0	.966	-1	*92*	*90*	C42/1	—	-0.4
	Year	72	249	23	63	8	5	2	29	12	3	16	.253	.295	.349	56	-20	1	.954	1	*97*	*100*	C69,1b2	—	-1.0
1895	Phi N	38	112	20	28	6	1	0	14	9	5	17	.250	.333	.321	69	-5	2	.919	-1	*93*	*84*	C38	—	-0.2
Total	8	524	1833	213	449	72	14	26	216	98	21	188	.245	.291	.342	81	-53	25	.931	-25	*93*	*100*	C477,3b43,1b6,O2(1/0/1)	—	-3.4
Buckner, Bill	William Joseph; B12.14.1949 Vallejo CA; BL/TL/6´0˝/(182–195); [LAN68 2/25]; d9.21; C2																								
1969	LA N	1	1	0	0	0	0	0	0	0-0	0	0	.000	.000	.000	-99	0	0-0	ø	0	—	—	/H	0	0.0
1970	LA N	28	68	6	13	3	1	0	4	3-1	0	7	.191	.225	.265	32	-7	0-1	1.000	1	121	81	O20(19/0/1)/1	0	-0.7
1971	LA N	108	358	37	99	15	1	5	41	11-4	5	18	.277	.306	.366	95	-4	4-1	.994	4	110	91	O86(6/0/81),1b11	0	-0.5
1972	LA N	105	383	47	122	14	3	5	37	17-2	1	13	.319	.348	.410	117	7	10-3	.992	2	112	24	O61(19/0/52),1b35	0	0.5
1973	LA N	140	575	68	158	20	0	8	46	17-5	3	34	.275	.297	.351	82	-16	12-2	.998	-2	94	137	1b93,O48(35/0/13)	0	-2.7
1974	†LA N	145	580	83	182	30	3	7	58	30-10	4	24	.314	.351	.412	117	12	31-13	.976	-6	94	44	O137(134/0/4),1b6	0	-0.1
1975	LA N	92	288	30	70	11	2	6	31	17-7	2	15	.243	.286	.358	82	-8	8-3	.986	2	108	80	O72L	21	-1.0
1976	LA N	154	642	76	193	28	4	7	60	26-6	1	26	.301	.326	.389	104	1	28-9	.985	-2	99	62	O153(149/0/5)/1	0	-0.8
1977	Chi N	122	426	40	121	27	0	11	60	21-2	1	23	.284	.314	.425	88	-7	7-5	.990	-2	92	102	1b99	13	-1.6
1978	Chi N	117	446	47	144	26	1	5	74	18-5	0	17	.323	.345	.419	102	1	7-5	.995	7	128	103	1b105	15	0.2
1979	Chi N	149	591	72	168	34	7	14	66	30-6	2	28	.284	.319	.437	95	-5	9-4	.995	15	136	103	1b140	0	0.2
1980	Chi N	145	578	69	187	41	3	10	68	30-11	0	18	**.324**	.353	.457	116	13	1-2	.993	5	123	91	1b94,O50(42/0/12)	0	1.0
1981	Chi N★	**106**	421	45	131	**35**	3	10	75	26-9	1	16	.311	.349	.480	127	15	5-2	.984	0	105	99	1b105	0	0.9
1982	Chi N	161	657	93	201	34	5	15	105	36-7	5	26	.306	.342	.441	115	12	15-5	.993	12	125	72	1b161	0	1.6
1983	Chi N	153	626	79	175	**38**	6	16	66	25-5	5	30	.280	.310	.436	101	-1	12-4	.992	22	**153**	116	1b144,O15L	0	1.3
1984	Chi N	21	43	3	9	0	0	0	2	1-1	1	1	.209	.239	.209	26	-4	0-0	1.000	1	126	114	1b7,O2L	0	-0.3
	Bos A	114	439	51	122	21	2	11	67	24-5	5	38	.278	.321	.410	96	-3	2-2	.986	6	117	75	1b113	0	-0.4
1985	Bos A	162	673	89	201	46	3	16	110	30-5	2	36	.299	.325	.447	106	5	18-4	.992	**25**	**150**	96	1b162	0	2.2
1986	†Bos A	153	629	73	168	39	2	18	102	40-9	4	25	.267	.311	.421	98	-3	6-4	.989	20	**142**	93	1b138,D15	0	0.7
1987	Bos A	75	286	23	78	6	1	2	42	13-1	0	19	.273	.299	.322	64	-15	1-3	.991	2	109	88	1b74	16	-1.7
	Cal A	57	183	16	56	12	1	3	32	9-1	0	7	.306	.337	.432	106	1	1-0	1.000	-0	62	30	D39,1b5	0	0.0
	Year	132	469	39	134	18	2	5	74	22-2	0	26	.286	.314	.365	80	-14	2-3	.992	2	106	85	1b79,D39	0	-1.7
1988	Cal A	19	43	1	9	0	0	0	9	4-0	0	0	.209	.271	.209	39	-4	2-0	1.000	0	1146	972	D11/1	0	-0.3
	KC A	89	242	18	62	14	0	3	34	13-5	0	19	.256	.290	.351	79	-7	3-1	.994	-0	91	70	D42,1b21	0	-1.0
	Year	108	285	19	71	14	0	3	43	17-5	0	19	.249	.287	.330	73	-10	5-1	.973	0	97	75	D53,1b22	0	-1.3
1989	KC A	79	176	7	38	4	1	1	16	6-2	0	11	.216	.240	.267	43	-14	1-0	.985	-1	89	113	1b24,D19	0	-1.7
1990	Bos A	22	43	4	8	0	0	1	3	3-2	0	2	.186	.234	.256	37	-4	0-0	1.000	-0	86	73	1b15	0	-0.5
Total	22	2517	9397	1077	2715	498	49	174	1208	450-111	42	453	.289	.321	.408	99	-35	183-73	.992	112	125	97	1b1555,O644(493/0/168),D126	65	-4.7
Budaska, Mark	Mark David; B12.27.1952 Sharon PA; BB/TL/6´0˝/180; d6.6; Col Los Angeles Pierce (CA) JC																								
1978	Oak A	4	4	0	1	1	0	0	0	1-0	0	2	.250	.400	.500	159	0	0-0	.500	-1	42	0	O2(1/0/1)	0	0.0
1981	Oak A	9	32	3	5	1	0	0	2	4-0	0	10	.156	.250	.188	29	-3	0-1	ø	0	—	—	D9	0	-0.4
Total	2	13	36	3	6	2	0	0	2	5-0	0	12	.167	.268	.222	44	-3	0-1	.500	-1	42	0	D9,O2(1/0/1)	0	-0.4
Budd	B Cleveland OH; d9.10																								
1890	Cle P	1	4	0	0	0	0	0	0	0	0	3	.000	.000	.000	-99	-1	0	1.000	0	0	0	/lf	—	-0.1
Buddin, Don	Donald Thomas; B5.5.1934 Turbeville SC; BR/TR/5´11˝/178; d4.17																								
1956	Bos A	114	377	49	90	24	0	5	37	65-1	4	62	.239	.352	.342	76	-11	2-0	.953	7	105	**123**	S113	0	0.6
1958	Bos A	136	497	74	118	25	2	12	43	82-1	4	106	.237	.349	.368	92	-3	0-4	.958	19	110	109	S136	0	2.6
1959	Bos A	151	485	75	117	24	1	10	53	92-0	5	99	.241	.366	.357	95	1	6-1	.949	-7	97	96	S150	0	0.7
1960	Bos A	124	428	62	105	21	5	6	36	62-5	1	59	.245	.338	.360	87	-6	4-2	.951	-2	96	91	S124	0	0.2
1961	Bos A	115	339	58	89	22	3	6	42	72-7	2	45	.263	.394	.398	110	9	2-1	.956	-2	96	99	S109	0	1.6
1962	Hou N	40	80	10	13	4	1	2	10	17-2	1	17	.162	.316	.313	75	-2	0-0	.952	-1	92	94	S27,3b9	0	-0.1
	Det A	31	83	14	19	3	0	0	4	20-0	1	16	.229	.385	.265	76	-2	1-0	.978	-2	94	118	S19,2b5,3b2	0	-0.2
Total	6	711	2289	342	551	123	12	41	225	410-16	18	404	.241	.358	.359	90	-14	15-8	.954	11	100	104	S678,3b11,2b5	0	5.4
Budzinski, Mark	Mark Joseph; B8.26.1973 Baltimore MD; BL/TL/6´2˝/180; [CleA95 21/586]; d8.3; Col Richmond																								
2003	Cin N	4	7	0	0	0	0	0	0	0-0	0	4	.000	.000	.000	-99	-2	0-0	1.000	0	133	0	/cf	0	-0.2
Buechele, Steve	Steven Bernard; B9.26.1961 Lancaster CA; BR/TR/6´2˝/(190–200); [TexA82 5/122]; d7.19; Col Stanford																								
1985	Tex A	69	219	22	48	6	3	6	21	14-2	2	38	.219	.271	.356	69	-10	3-2	.969	7	107	132	3b69/2	0	-0.5
1986	Tex A	153	461	54	112	19	2	18	54	35-1	5	98	.243	.302	.410	89	-8	5-8	.968	15	108	81	3b137,2b33,O2L	0	0.5
1987	Tex A	136	363	45	86	20	0	13	50	28-3	1	66	.237	.290	.399	81	-11	2-2	.964	-5	97	65	3b123,2b18,O2L	0	-1.6
1988	Tex A	155	503	68	126	21	4	16	58	65-6	5	79	.250	.342	.404	105	4	2-4	.962	7	106	97	3b153,2b2	0	1.0
1989	Tex A	155	486	60	114	22	2	16	59	36-0	5	107	.235	.294	.387	89	-8	1-3	.969	19	106	98	3b145,2b18/SD	0	1.0
1990	Tex A	91	251	30	54	10	0	7	30	27-1	2	63	.215	.294	.339	77	-8	1-0	.966	5	104	48	3b88,2b4	65	-0.2
1991	Tex A	121	416	58	111	17	2	18	66	39-4	5	69	.267	.335	.447	117	9	0-4	**.991**	15	115	92	3b111,2b13,S4	0	2.3
	†Pit N	31	114	16	28	5	1	4	19	10-0	2	28	.246	.315	.412	105	0	0-1	.956	-0	100	106	3b31	0	0.0
1992	Pit N	80	285	27	71	14	1	8	43	34-4	2	61	.249	.331	.389	104	2	0-2	.957	1	109	80	3b80	0	0.3
	Chi N	65	239	25	66	9	3	1	21	18-2	5	44	.276	.338	.351	93	-2	1-1	.960	1	105	59	3b63,2b2	0	-0.1
	Year	145	524	52	137	23	4	9	64	52-6	7	105	.261	.334	.372	99	0	1-3	.958	3	**107**	71	3b143,2b2	0	0.2
1993	Chi N	133	460	53	125	27	2	15	65	48-5	5	87	.272	.345	.437	109	6	1-1	**.975**	-2	99	121	3b129,1b6	15	0.5
1994	Chi N	104	339	33	82	11	1	14	52	39-2	4	80	.242	.325	.404	89	-6	1-0	.974	-11	84	90	3b99,1b6/2	0	-1.6
1995	Chi N	32	106	10	20	2	0	1	9	11-0	0	19	.189	.265	.236	33	-10	0-0	.942	-2	93	59	3b32	24	-1.2
	Tex A	9	24	0	3	0	0	0	0	4-1	0	3	.125	.250	.125	1	-4	0-0	1.000	-0	84	161	3b9	0	-0.3
Total	11	1334	4266	501	1046	183	21	137	547	408-31	43	842	.245	.316	.394	93	-46	17-28	.968	50	103	90	3b1269,2b92,1b12,S5,O4L/D	104	0.1
Buelow, Charlie	Charles John; B1.12.1877 Dubuque IA; D5.4.1951 Dubuque IA; BR/TR; d6.1																								
1901	NY N	22	72	3	8	4	0	0	4	2	1	—	.111	.147	.167	-10	-10	0	.853	3	131	109	3b17,2b2	—	-0.7
Buelow, Fritz	Frederick William Alexander; B2.13.1876 Berlin, Germany; D12.27.1933 Detroit MI; BR/TR/5´10.5˝/170; d9.28																								
1899	StL N	7	15	4	7	0	2	0	2	2	1	—	.467	.556	.733	246	3	0	1.000	-0	*141*	*30*	C4,O2L	—	0.3
1900	StL N	6	17	2	4	0	0	0	3	0	0	—	.235	.235	.235	30	-2	0	.864	-1	*100*	*104*	C4/lf	—	-0.2
1901	Det A	70	231	28	52	5	5	2	29	11	3	—	.225	.269	.316	59	-14	2	.967	6	*118*	*108*	C69	—	-0.1
1902	Det A	66	224	23	50	5	2	2	29	9	1	—	.223	.256	.290	50	-16	3	.927	-5	*84*	*119*	C63,1b2	—	-1.4
1903	Det A	63	192	24	41	3	6	1	13	6	3	—	.214	.249	.307	68	-8	4	.961	-3	*79*	*112*	C60,1b2	—	-0.7
1904	Det A	42	136	6	15	1	1	0	5	8	0	—	.110	.160	.132	-7	-17	2	.975	-1	*87*	*110*	C42	—	-1.6
	Cle A	42	119	11	21	4	1	0	5	11	1	—	.176	.252	.227	52	-6	2	.979	2	*118*	*85*	C42	—	0.0
	Year	84	255	17	36	5	2	0	10	19	1	—	.141	.204	.176	21	-23	4	.977	1	*102*	*98*	C84	—	-1.6
1905	Cle A	75	239	11	41	4	1	1	18	6	2	—	.172	.198	.209	29	-20	7	.960	-4	*102*	*105*	C60,O8R,1b3,3b2	—	-2.0
1906	Cle A	34	86	7	14	2	0	0	7	9	1	—	.163	.250	.186	38	-6	0	.938	1	*128*	*115*	C33/1	—	-0.2
1907	StL A	26	75	9	11	1	0	0	1	7	0	—	.147	.220	.160	21	-6	0	.983	-0	*89*	*126*	C25	—	-0.5
Total	9	431	1334	125	256	25	18	6	112	69	12	—	.192	.238	.251	46	-92	20	.960	-5	*100*	*109*	C402,O11(3/0/8),1b8,3b2	—	-6.4
Bues, Art	Arthur Frederick; B3.3.1888 Milwaukee WI; D11.7.1954 Whitefish Bay WI; BR/TR/5´11˝/184; d4.17																								
1913	Bos N	2	1	0	0	0	0	0	0	0	0	1	.000	.000	.000	-98	0	0	ø	-0	0	0	/23	—	-0.1
1914	Chi N	14	45	3	10	1	1	0	4	5	0	6	.222	.300	.289	76	-1	1	.968	-2	76	0	3b12	—	-0.3
Total	2	16	46	3	10	1	1	0	4	5	0	7	.217	.294	.283	72	-1	1	.968	-2	75	0	3b13/2	—	-0.4
Buffinton, Charlie	Charles G.; B6.14.1861 Fall River MA; D9.23.1907 Fall River MA; BR/TR/6´1˝/180; d5.17; M1; ▲																								
1882	Bos N	15	50	5	13	1	0	0	4	2	—	3	.260	.288	.280	83	-1	—	.615	-2	108	0	O7R,P5,1b4	—	-0.3
1883	Bos N	86	341	28	81	8	3	1	26	6	—	24	.238	.251	.287	62	-16	—	.756	-6	93	197	O51(0/13/40),P43,1b2	—	-1.4
1884	Bos N	87	352	48	94	18	3	1	39	16	—	12	.267	.299	.344	102	1	—	.946	-3	98	64	P67,O13(0/13/1),1b11	—	-0.4
1885	Bos N	82	338	26	81	12	3	1	33	3	—	26	.240	.246	.302	79	-8	—	.912	1	121	178	P51,O18(1/11/6),1b15	—	-0.6
1886	Bos N	44	176	27	51	4	1	1	30	6	—	12	.290	.313	.341	102	0	3	.968	-5	54	73	1b19,P18,O9(0/1/8)	—	-0.6
1887	Phi N	66	269	34	72	12	1	1	46	11	1	3	.268	.299	.331	70	-11	8	.931	3	144	236	P40,O22(7/7/8),1b10	—	-0.5
1888	Phi N	46	160	14	29	4	1	0	12	7	0	5	.181	.216	.219	37	-11	1	.939	9	**141**	168	P46/lf	—	0.4
1889	Phi N	47	154	16	32	2	0	0	21	9	1	5	.208	.256	.221	31	-15	0	.916	1	107	131	P47/lf	—	0.0
1890	Phi P	42	150	24	41	3	2	1	24	9	1	3	.273	.319	.340	74	-6	1	.864	1	105	210	P36,O5(1/2/2),1b3,M	—	0.0

YEAR	TM LG	G	AB	R	H	2B	3B	HR	RBI	BB-IB	HP	SO	AVG	OBP	SLG	AOPS	ABR	SB-CS	FA	FR	RNG	THR	GAMES AT POSITION	DL	BFW
1891	Bos AA	58	181	16	34	2	1	1	16	19	1	15	.188	.269	.227	43	-14	0	.934	5	134	119	P48,O10(5/0/6),1b4	—	0.0
1892	Bal N	13	43	7	15	1	1	0	4	3	0	6	.349	.391	.419	141	4	1	.892	1	138	115	P13	—	0.0
Total	11	586	2214	245	543	67	16	7	255	91	4	114	.245	.276	.299	71	-77	14	.916	6	116	147	P414,O137(16/47/78),1b68	—	-3.4

BUFORD, DAMON Damon Jackson; B6.12.1970 Baltimore MD; BR/TR/5´10˝/(170–180); [BalA90 10/283]; d5.4; f–Don; Col USC

YEAR	TM LG	G	AB	R	H	2B	3B	HR	RBI	BB-IB	HP	SO	AVG	OBP	SLG	AOPS	ABR	SB-CS	FA	FR	RNG	THR	GAMES AT POSITION	DL	BFW
1993	Bal A	53	79	18	18	5	0	2	9	9-0	1	19	.228	.315	.367	79	-2	2-2	.984	1	98	146	O30(5/24/1),D17	0	-0.3
1994	Bal A	4	2	2	1	0	0	0	0	0-0	0	1	.500	.500	.500	151	0	0-0	ø	-0	0	0	/lfD	0	0.0
1995	Bal A	24	32	6	2	0	0	0	2	6-0	0	7	.063	.205	.063	-24	-6	3-1	1.000	1	126	0	O24(0/15/9)	0	-0.4
	NY N	44	136	24	32	5	0	4	12	19-0	5	28	.235	.346	.360	91	-1	7-7	.972	-2	92	93	O39(25/16/0)	0	-0.4
1996	†Tex A	90	145	30	41	9	0	6	20	15-0	0	34	.283	.348	.469	98	0	8-5	1.000	-1	95	101	O80(14/25/44)	0	-0.2
1997	Tex A	122	366	49	82	18	0	8	39	30-0	3	83	.224	.287	.339	59	-22	18-7	.990	3	105	129	O117C,D3	0	-1.6
1998	†Bos A	86	216	37	61	14	4	10	42	22-1	1	43	.282	.349	.523	121	6	5-5	1.000	-1	94	116	O67C,D15/23	31	0.4
1999	†Bos A	91	297	39	72	15	2	6	38	21-0	2	74	.242	.294	.367	66	-16	9-2	.985	1	100	127	O84(5/82/0),D5	17	-1.2
2000	Chi N	150	495	64	124	18	3	15	48	47-3	8	118	.251	.324	.390	81	-16	4-6	.986	-4	103	49	O148(2/140/7)	0	-1.9
2001	Chi N	35	85	11	15	2	0	3	8	4-0	0	23	.176	.213	.306	33	-9	0-0	1.000	-1	101	0	O34(0/33/1)	0	-1.0
Total	9	699	1853	280	448	86	9	54	218	173-4	20	430	.242	.311	.385	77	-66	56-35	.989	-3	101	93	O624(52/519/62),D41/32	48	-6.6

BUFORD, DON Donald Alvin; B2.2.1937 Linden TX; BB/TR/5´8˝/(160–175); d9.14; C6; s–Damon; Col USC

YEAR	TM LG	G	AB	R	H	2B	3B	HR	RBI	BB-IB	HP	SO	AVG	OBP	SLG	AOPS	ABR	SB-CS	FA	FR	RNG	THR	GAMES AT POSITION	DL	BFW
1963	Chi A	12	42	9	12	1	2	0	5	5-0	0	7	.286	.354	.405	116	1	1-0	.955	-4	62	65	3b9,2b2	0	-0.3
1964	Chi A	135	442	62	116	14	6	4	30	46-2	5	62	.262	.337	.348	94	-3	12-7	.968	-2	92	133	2b92,3b37	0	0.2
1965	Chi A	155	586	93	166	22	5	10	47	67-4	4	76	.283	.358	.389	120	17	17-7	.981	22	108	**129**	2b139,3b41	0	**5.3**
1966	Chi A	**163**	607	85	148	26	7	8	52	69-3	3	71	.244	.323	.349	100	1	51-22	.939	11	**117**	**119**	3b133,2b37,O11(8/0/3)	0	1.9
1967	Chi A	156	535	61	129	10	9	4	32	65-3	1	51	.241	.322	.316	93	-4	34-21	.948	6	108	100	3b121,2b51/lf	0	0.5
1968	Bal A	130	426	65	120	13	4	15	46	57-5	4	46	.282	.367	.437	144	24	27-12	1.000	2	107	106	O65(27/41/2),2b58,3b2	0	3.3
1969	†Bal A	144	554	99	161	31	3	11	64	96-7	5	62	.291	.397	.417	127	26	19-18	.983	-4	93	67	O128L,2b10,3b6	0	1.3
1970	†Bal A	144	504	99	137	15	2	17	66	109-8	8	55	.272	.406	.411	125	23	16-8	.987	2	98	160	O130L,2b3,3b3	0	1.9
1971	†Bal A★	122	449	**99**	130	19	4	19	54	89-15	7	62	.290	.413	.477	151	35	15-7	.987	0	103	84	O115(114/0/1)	0	3.1
1972	Bal A	125	408	46	84	6	2	5	22	69-10	4	83	.206	.326	.267	75	-10	8-3	.989	-4	91	75	O105(104/0/1)	0	-2.3
Total	10	1286	4553	718	1203	157	44	93	418	672-57	41	575	.264	.362	.379	115	110	200-105	.988	28	98	100	O555(512/41/7),2b392,3b352	0	14.9

BUHNER, JAY Jay Campbell; B8.13.1964 Louisville KY; BR/TR/6´3˝/(205–222); [PitN84*S2/36]; d9.11; Col McLennan (TX) CC

YEAR	TM LG	G	AB	R	H	2B	3B	HR	RBI	BB-IB	HP	SO	AVG	OBP	SLG	AOPS	ABR	SB-CS	FA	FR	RNG	THR	GAMES AT POSITION	DL	BFW
1987	NY A	7	22	0	5	2	0	0	1	1-0	0	6	.227	.261	.318	53	-1	0-0	1.000	0	78	259	O7(2/3/2)	0	-0.2
1988	NY A	25	69	8	13	0	0	3	13	3-0	3	25	.188	.250	.319	59	-4	0-0	.964	1	107	218	O22(3/16/3)	0	-0.3
	Sea A	60	192	28	43	13	1	10	25	25-1	3	68	.224	.320	.458	111	3	1-1	.993	7	112	206	O59(1/2/55)	0	0.8
	Year	85	261	36	56	13	1	13	38	28-1	6	93	.215	.302	.421	98	-1	1-1	.985	8	111	209	O81(4/18/58)	0	0.5
1989	Sea A	58	204	27	56	15	1	9	33	19-0	2	55	.275	.341	.490	128	7	1-4	.966	-1	90	140	O57(0/2/56)	51	0.3
1990	Sea A	51	163	16	45	12	0	7	33	17-1	4	50	.276	.357	.479	130	7	2-2	.966	-5	77	41	O40(0/1/39),D10	120	0.1
1991	Sea A	137	406	64	99	14	4	27	77	53-5	6	117	.244	.337	.498	128	14	0-1	.981	7	102	177	O131(1/3/131)	0	1.8
1992	Sea A	152	543	69	132	16	3	25	79	71-2	6	146	.243	.333	.422	110	7	0-6	.994	4	97	135	O150(0/2/150)	0	0.4
1993	Sea A	158	563	91	153	28	3	27	98	100-11	2	144	.272	.379	.476	127	24	2-5	.978	-9	88	75	O148R,D10	0	0.6
1994	Sea A	101	358	74	100	23	4	21	68	66-3	5	63	.279	.394	.542	136	21	0-1	.990	3	96	166	O96(0/1/95),D4	0	1.8
1995	†Sea A	126	470	86	123	23	0	40	121	60-7	1	120	.262	.343	.566	131	19	0-1	.989	-9	82	67	O120R,D4	16	0.4
1996	Sea A★	150	564	107	153	29	0	44	138	84-5	9	159	.271	.369	.557	131	27	0-1	.989	-6	87	90	O142R,D8	0	1.2
1997	†Sea A	157	540	104	131	18	2	40	109	119-3	5	175	.243	.383	.506	130	27	0-0	**.997**	-2	97	53	O154R,D2	0	1.7
1998	Sea A	72	244	33	59	7	1	15	45	38-0	1	71	.242	.344	.463	107	2	0-0	.985	1	100	110	O70R/D	85	0.0
1999	Sea A	87	266	37	59	11	0	14	38	69-0	5	100	.222	.388	.421	108	6	0-0	.993	-4	79	126	O85R/1	57	-0.2
2000	†Sea A	112	364	50	92	20	0	26	82	59-3	4	98	.253	.361	.522	123	13	0-2	1.000	-3	94	63	O104R/D	14	0.4
2001	†Sea A	19	45	4	10	2	0	2	5	8-0	0	9	.222	.340	.400	99	0	0-0	1.000	-1	88	0	O12(10/0/2),D4	153	-0.1
Total	15	1472	5013	798	1273	233	19	310	965	792-41	56	1406	.254	.359	.494	123	172	6-24	.988	-17	93	109	O1397(17/30/1356),D44/1	496	8.7

BUKER, HARRY Henry L. "Happy"; B1859 Chicago IL; D8.10.1899 Chicago IL; ?/140; d6.11

YEAR	TM LG	G	AB	R	H	2B	3B	HR	RBI	BB-IB	HP	SO	AVG	OBP	SLG	AOPS	ABR	SB-CS	FA	FR	RNG	THR	GAMES AT POSITION	DL	BFW
1884	Det N	30	111	5	15	1	0	0	3	4	—	15	.135	.165	.144	-2	-13	—	.867	1	109	106	S19,O11R	—	-1.0

BULLARD, GEORGE George Donald "Curly"; B10.24.1928 Lynn MA; D12.23.2002 Lynn MA; BR/TR/5´9.5˝/165; d9.17

YEAR	TM LG	G	AB	R	H	2B	3B	HR	RBI	BB-IB	HP	SO	AVG	OBP	SLG	AOPS	ABR	SB-CS	FA	FR	RNG	THR	GAMES AT POSITION	DL	BFW
1954	Det A	4	1	0	0	0	0	0	0	0	0	0	.000	.000	.000	-99	0	0-0	.800	0	116	0	/S	0	0.0

BULLAS, SIM Simeon Edward; B4.10.1861 Cleveland OH; D1.14.1908 Cleveland OH; BR/TR/5´7.5˝/150; d5.2

YEAR	TM LG	G	AB	R	H	2B	3B	HR	RBI	BB-IB	HP	SO	AVG	OBP	SLG	AOPS	ABR	SB-CS	FA	FR	RNG	THR	GAMES AT POSITION	DL	BFW
1884	Tol AA	13	45	4	4	0	1	0	—	1	0	—	.089	.109	.133	-21	-6	—	.909	-3	—	—	C12,O2L	—	-0.8

BULLETT, SCOTT Scott Douglas; B12.25.1968 Martinsburg WV; BL/TL (BB 1993)/6´2˝/(190–220); d9.3

YEAR	TM LG	G	AB	R	H	2B	3B	HR	RBI	BB-IB	HP	SO	AVG	OBP	SLG	AOPS	ABR	SB-CS	FA	FR	RNG	THR	GAMES AT POSITION	DL	BFW
1991	Pit N	11	4	2	0	0	0	0	0	0-0	1	3	.000	.200	.000	-39	-1	1-1	1.000	-0	82	0	O3(1/1/1)	0	-0.1
1993	Pit N	23	55	2	11	0	2	0	4	3-0	0	15	.200	.237	.273	37	-5	3-2	1.000	-1	92	124	O19(0/18/1)	0	-0.6
1995	Chi N	104	150	19	41	5	7	3	22	12-2	1	30	.273	.331	.460	106	0	8-3	.968	-2	94	51	O64(54/12/0)	0	-0.1
1996	Chi N	109	165	26	35	5	0	3	16	10-0	0	54	.212	.256	.297	44	-14	7-3	.986	3	119	111	O58(28/11/22)	21	-1.1
Total	4	247	374	49	87	10	9	6	42	25-2	2	102	.233	.283	.356	67	-20	19-9	.983	1	103	87	O144(83/42/24)	21	-1.9

BULLING, BUD Terry Charles "Terry"; B12.15.1952 Lynwood CA; BR/TR/6´1˝/(195–210); [MinA74 14/326]; d7.3; Col Cal St.–Los Angeles

YEAR	TM LG	G	AB	R	H	2B	3B	HR	RBI	BB-IB	HP	SO	AVG	OBP	SLG	AOPS	ABR	SB-CS	FA	FR	RNG	THR	GAMES AT POSITION	DL	BFW
1977	Min A	15	32	2	5	1	0	0	5	5-1	0	5	.156	.270	.188	28	-3	0-0	.952	-1	57	34	C10,D3	0	-0.4
1981	Sea A	62	154	15	38	3	0	2	15	21-0	1	20	.247	.341	.305	83	-3	0-0	.977	-6	80	103	C62	0	-0.7
1982	Sea A	56	154	17	34	7	0	1	8	19-2	0	16	.221	.306	.286	62	-8	2-1	.991	2	103	123	C56	15	-0.3
1983	Sea A	5	5	0	0	0	0	0	0	0-0	0	0	.000	.000	.000	-96	-1	0-0	1.000	0	155	0	C5	0	-0.1
Total	4	138	345	34	77	11	0	3	28	45-3	1	41	.223	.315	.281	66	-15	2-1	.983	-5	90	105	C133,D3	15	-1.5

BULLOCK, ERIC Eric Gerald; B2.16.1960 Los Angeles CA; BL/TL/5´11˝/185; [HouN81 S1/20]; d8.26; Col Los Angeles Harbor (CA) JC

YEAR	TM LG	G	AB	R	H	2B	3B	HR	RBI	BB-IB	HP	SO	AVG	OBP	SLG	AOPS	ABR	SB-CS	FA	FR	RNG	THR	GAMES AT POSITION	DL	BFW
1985	Hou N	18	25	3	7	2	0	0	2	1-0	0	3	.280	.308	.360	88	0	0-1	.750	-1	83	0	O7(4/0/3)	0	-0.2
1986	Hou N	6	21	0	1	0	0	0	1	0-0	0	3	.048	.048	.048	-76	-5	2-0	.875	-1	71	0	O6L	0	-0.6
1988	Min A	16	17	3	5	0	0	0	3	3-0	0	1	.294	.400	.294	95	0	1-0	.875	0	175	0	O4(3/0/2),D2	0	0.1
1989	Phi N	6	4	1	0	0	0	0	0	0-0	0	2	.000	.000	.000	-99	-1	0-0	1.000	0	194	0	O3(0/1/2)	0	-0.1
1990	Mon N	4	2	0	1	0	0	0	0	0-0	0	0	.500	.500	.500	182	0	0-0	ø	0	—	—	/H	0	0.0
1991	Mon N	73	72	6	16	4	0	1	6	9-0	0	13	.222	.305	.319	78	-2	6-1	1.000	0	100	0	O9(6/0/3),1b3	0	-0.1
1992	Mon N	8	5	0	0	0	0	0	0	0-0	0	1	.000	.000	.000	-99	-1	0-0	ø	0	—	—	/H	0	-0.2
Total	7	131	146	13	30	6	0	1	12	13-0	0	23	.205	.269	.267	52	-9	9-2	.892	-1	98	0	O29(19/1/10),1b3,D2	0	-1.1

BUMBRY, AL Alonza Benjamin (b Alonza Benjamin Bumbrey); B4.21.1947 Fredericksburg VA; BL/TR/5´8˝/(170–175); [BalA68 11/238]; d9.5; C9; Col Virginia St.

YEAR	TM LG	G	AB	R	H	2B	3B	HR	RBI	BB-IB	HP	SO	AVG	OBP	SLG	AOPS	ABR	SB-CS	FA	FR	RNG	THR	GAMES AT POSITION	DL	BFW
1972	Bal A	9	11	5	4	0	1	0	0	0-0	0	0	.364	.364	.545	161	1	1-1	1.000	0	119	0	O2L	0	0.1
1973	†Bal A	110	356	73	120	15	**11**	7	34	34-0	3	49	.337	.398	.500	151	24	23-10	.978	-7	86	36	O86(62/1/29),D7	0	1.4
1974	†Bal A	94	270	35	63	10	3	1	19	21-2	1	46	.233	.288	.304	73	-10	12-4	.953	0	96	159	O67L,D7	0	-1.3
1975	Bal A	114	349	47	94	19	4	2	32	32-3	4	81	.269	.336	.364	104	2	16-3	1.000	-2	87	70	D48,O39(35/3/1)	0	-0.1
1976	Bal A	133	450	71	113	15	7	9	36	43-2	1	76	.251	.316	.376	108	4	42-10	.989	0	99	113	O116(82/57/0),D10	0	0.5
1977	Bal A	133	518	74	164	31	3	4	41	45-4	2	88	.317	.371	.411	120	16	19-8	.991	1	102	76	O130(52/112/0)	15	1.6
1978	Bal A	33	114	21	27	5	2	2	6	17-0	2	15	.237	.346	.368	107	2	5-3	.985	-1	93	111	O28(16/17/0)	112	0.0
1979	†Bal A	148	569	80	162	29	1	7	49	43-3	3	74	.285	.336	.376	96	-3	37-12	.982	-4	97	76	O146(5/146/0)	0	-0.4
1980	Bal A★	160	645	118	205	29	9	9	53	78-8	3	75	.318	.392	.433	128	28	44-11	.990	5	110	62	O160(1/160/0)	0	3.6
1981	Bal A	101	392	61	107	18	2	1	27	51-2	2	51	.273	.358	.337	102	3	22-15	.992	-2	96	100	O100C	0	0.0
1982	Bal A	150	562	77	147	20	4	5	40	44-4	0	77	.262	.314	.338	80	-16	10-5	.986	6	108	98	O147(3/146/0)/D	0	-1.1
1983	†Bal A	124	378	63	104	14	4	3	31	31-2	0	33	.275	.328	.357	90	-5	12-5	.988	-2	99	54	O104(17/99/0),D11	0	-0.8
1984	Bal A	119	344	47	93	12	1	3	24	25-0	0	35	.270	.317	.337	83	-8	9-5	.988	3	101	125	O99(28/82/0),D9	0	-0.6
1985	SD N	68	95	6	19	3	0	1	10	7-0	0	9	.200	.255	.263	46	-7	2-0	.939	0	126	0	O17(12/5/1)	0	-0.7
Total	14	1496	5053	778	1422	220	52	54	402	471-30	21	709	.281	.343	.378	104	31	254-92	.986	-4	100	85	O1241(382/928/31),D93	127	2.2

BUNCE, JOSH Joshua; B5.10.1847 Brooklyn NY; D4.28.1912 Brooklyn NY; d8.27

YEAR	TM LG	G	AB	R	H	2B	3B	HR	RBI	BB-IB	HP	SO	AVG	OBP	SLG	AOPS	ABR	SB-CS	FA	FR	RNG	THR	GAMES AT POSITION	DL	BFW
1877	Har N	1	4	0	0	0	0	0	0	0	—	0	.000	.000	.000	-99	-1	—	1.000	-0	0	0	/lf	—	-0.1

BURBRINK, NELSON Nelson Edward; B12.28.1921 Cincinnati OH; D4.12.2001 Largo FL; BR/TR/5´10˝/195; d6.5

YEAR	TM LG	G	AB	R	H	2B	3B	HR	RBI	BB-IB	HP	SO	AVG	OBP	SLG	AOPS	ABR	SB-CS	FA	FR	RNG	THR	GAMES AT POSITION	DL	BFW
1955	StL N	58	170	11	47	8	1	0	15	14-1	1	13	.276	.333	.335	79	-5	1-1	.979	-2	*106*	*118*	C55	0	-0.5

YEAR	TM LG	G	AB	R	H	2B	3B	HR	RBI	BB-IB	HP	SO	AVG	OBP	SLG	AOPS	ABR	SB-CS	FA	FR	RNG	THR	GAMES AT POSITION	DL	BFW
Burch, Al	Albert William; B10.7.1883 Albany NY; D10.5.1926 Brooklyn NY; BL/TR/5´8.5˝/160; d6.19																								
1906	StL N	91	335	40	89	5	1	0	11	37	0	—	.266	.339	.287	99	1	15	.934	-1	131	210	O91(0/58/33)	—	-0.5
1907	StL N	48	154	18	35	3	1	0	5	17	0	—	.227	.304	.260	79	-3	7	.922	-1	152	235	O48C	—	-0.7
	Bro N	40	120	12	35	2	2	0	12	11	0	—	.292	.351	.342	127	4	5	.890	2	180	0	O36(27/5/5)/2	—	0.4
	Year	88	274	30	70	5	3	0	17	28	0	—	.255	.325	.296	100	0	12	.908	1	164	134	O84(27/53/5)/2	—	-0.3
1908	Bro N	123	456	45	111	8	4	2	18	33	0	—	.243	.294	.292	91	-6	15	.971	9	**151**	156	O116(47/44/28)	—	-0.4
1909	Bro N	152	601	80	163	20	6	1	30	51	1	—	.271	.329	.329	108	5	38	.955	2	106	77	O151(41/102/9)/1	—	0.0
1910	Bro N	103	352	41	83	8	3	1	20	22	0	30	.236	.281	.284	67	-16	13	.957	-2	91	110	O70(0/26/45),1b13	—	-2.3
1911	Bro N	54	167	18	38	2	3	0	7	15	0	22	.228	.291	.275	61	-9	3	.972	1	102	97	O43(0/41/3),2b3	—	-1.1
Total	6	611	2185	254	554	48	20	4	103	186	1	52	.254	.312	.299	91	-24	96	.950	11	126	130	O555(115/324/123),1b14,2b4	—	-4.6
Burch, Ernie	Ernest A.; B9.9.1856 DeKalb Co. IL; D10.12.1892 Guthrie OK; BL/5´10˝/190; d8.15																								
1884	Cle N	32	124	9	26	4	0	0	7	5	—	24	.210	.240	.242	50	-7	—	.899	5	162	94	O32(23/0/9)	—	-0.3
1886	Bro AA	113	456	78	119	22	6	2	72	39	1	—	.261	.321	.349	109	5	16	.884	-10	56	89	O113L	—	-0.7
1887	Bro AA	49	188	47	55	4	4	2	26	29	3	—	.293	.395	.388	118	6	15	.899	1	101	56	O49L	—	0.4
Total	3	194	768	134	200	30	10	4	105	73	4	24	.260	.328	.341	102	4	31	.891	-4	85	81	O194(185/0/9)	—	-0.6
Burda, Bob	Edward Robert; B7.16.1938 St.Louis MO; BL/TL/5´11˝/(175–180); d8.25; Col Illinois																								
1962	StL N	7	14	0	1	0	0	0	0	3-0	0	1	.071	.235	.071	-12	-2	1-0	.917	0	145	0	O6(1/0/5)	0	-0.2
1965	SF N	31	27	0	3	0	0	0	5	5-0	0	6	.111	.235	.111	6	-3	0-0	.969	-1	0	37	1b11/lf	0	-0.5
1966	SF N	37	43	3	7	3	0	0	2	2-0	0	5	.163	.196	.233	19	-5	0-0	1.000	-1	132	0	1b7,O4(3/0/1)	0	-0.6
1969	SF N	97	161	20	37	8	0	6	27	21-3	0	12	.230	.317	.391	99	0	0-1	.995	-0	92	93	1b45,O19(5/0/15)	0	-0.3
1970	SF N	28	23	1	6	0	0	0	3	5-2	1	2	.261	.414	.261	86	0	0-0	.933	-1	0	63	1b8/lf	0	-0.1
	Mil A	78	222	19	55	9	0	4	20	16-1	3	17	.248	.303	.342	79	-7	1-0	.987	-5	76	87	O64R,1b7	0	-1.5
1971	StL N	65	71	6	21	0	0	1	12	10-2	1	11	.296	.386	.338	103	1	0-0	1.000	1	127	61	1b13/rf	0	0.1
1972	Bos A	45	73	4	12	1	0	2	9	8-3	0	11	.164	.241	.260	48	-5	0-0	.992	-0	81	103	1b15/lf	0	-0.7
Total	7	388	634	53	142	21	0	13	78	70-11	5	65	.224	.302	.319	74	-21	2-1	.992	-7	83	81	1b106,O97(12/0/86)	0	-3.8
Burdock, Jack	John Joseph "Black Jack"; B4.1852 Brooklyn NY; D11.27.1931 Brooklyn NY; BR/TR/5´9.5˝/158; d5.2; M1/U3																								
1872	Atl NA	**37**	174	27	47	3	0	0	14	1	—	1	.270	.274	.287	62	-10	0-1	.743	-7	94	22	S36,C4,2b2	—	-1.3
1873	Atl NA	**55**	245	56	62	7	1	2	36	7	—	4	.253	.274	.314	82	-2	3-2	.818	-0	105	94	2b55,C2	—	-0.5
1874	Mut NA	61	273	45	75	11	4	1	26	1	—	5	.275	.277	.355	98	-1	4-1	**.820**	10	93	97	3b60,O3(2/1/0)	—	0.6
1875	Har NA	74	350	72	103	12	5	0	35	3	—	13	.294	.300	.357	121	6	20-11	**.895**	-3	84	134	2b73,3b2/C	—	-0.1
1876	Har N	**69**	309	66	80	9	1	0	23	13	—	16	.259	.289	.294	87	-5	—	.895	2	89	98	2b69/3	—	0.0
1877	Har N	58	277	35	72	6	0	0	9	2	—	16	.260	.265	.282	81	-5	—	**.903**	7	99	128	2b55,3b3	—	0.4
1878	Bos N	**60**	246	37	64	12	6	0	25	3	—	17	.260	.269	.358	97	-2	—	**.918**	**21**	**103**	**151**	2b60	—	2.0
1879	Bos N	**84**	359	64	86	10	3	0	36	9	—	28	.240	.258	.284	77	-9	—	.911	12	100	147	2b84	—	0.6
1880	Bos N	**86**	356	58	90	17	4	2	35	8	—	26	.253	.269	.340	108	3	—	**.923**	15	100	101	2b86	—	2.1
1881	Bos N	73	282	36	67	12	4	1	24	7	—	18	.238	.256	.319	84	-5	—	.911	-8	91	98	2b72/S	—	-1.0
1882	Bos N	83	319	36	76	6	7	0	27	9	—	24	.238	.259	.301	79	-8	—	**.932**	6	99	82	2b83	—	0.0
1883	Bos N	96	400	80	132	27	8	5	88	14	—	35	.330	.353	.475	145	21	—	.921	1	93	103	2b96,M	—	2.2
1884	Bos N	87	361	65	97	14	4	6	49	15	—	52	.269	.298	.380	112	5	—	**.922**	2	100	82	2b87/3	—	0.9
1885	Bos N	45	169	18	24	5	0	0	7	8	—	18	.142	.181	.172	15	-15	—	.917	-3	96	83	2b45	—	-1.6
1886	Bos N	59	221	26	48	6	1	0	25	11	—	27	.217	.254	.253	56	-11	3	.904	-10	92	87	2b59	—	-1.8
1887	Bos N	65	237	36	61	6	0	0	29	18	4	22	.257	.320	.283	68	-9	19	.882	-16	94	124	2b65	—	-2.0
1888	Bos N	22	79	5	16	0	0	0	4	2	1	5	.203	.232	.203	38	-6	1	.903	-1	100	116	2b22	—	-0.6
	Bro AA	70	246	15	30	1	2	1	8	8	5	—	.122	.166	.154	3	-27	9	.904	-3	104	101	2b70	—	-2.5
1891	Bro N	3	12	1	1	0	0	0	1	1	0	1	.083	.154	.083	-31	-2	0	1.000	-0	106	88	2b3	—	-0.2
Total	4NA	227	1042	200	287	33	10	3	111	12	—	23	.275	.284	.335	95	-7	27-15	.859	-1	93	116	2b130,3b62,S36,C7,O3(2/1/0)	—	-1.3
Total	14	960	3873	578	944	131	40	15	390	128	10	305	.244	.270	.310	83	-75	32	.912	26	97	106	2b956,3b5/S	—	-1.5
Burg, Joe	Joseph Peter; B6.4.1882 Chicago IL; D4.28.1969 Joliet IL; BR/TR/5´10˝/150; d9.26																								
1910	Bos N	13	46	7	15	0	1	0	10	7	0	12	.326	.415	.370	124	2	5	.867	1	123	58	3b12/S	—	0.3
Burgess, Smoky	Forrest Harrill; B2.6.1927 Caroleen NC; D9.15.1991 Asheville NC; BL/TR/5´8˝/(171–198); d4.19																								
1949	Chi N	46	56	4	15	0	0	1	12	4	0	4	.268	.317	.321	73	-2	0	1.000	1	*78*	*250*	C8	0	-0.1
1951	Chi N	94	219	21	55	4	2	2	20	21	0	12	.251	.317	.315	69	-10	2-0	.980	-4	*58*	*129*	C64	0	-1.1
1952	Phi N	110	371	49	110	27	2	6	56	49	1	21	.296	.380	.429	125	15	3-1	.978	-4	*94*	*97*	C104	0	1.8
1953	Phi N	102	312	31	91	17	5	4	36	37	2	17	.292	.370	.417	105	4	3-2	**.993**	-4	*102*	*46*	C95	0	0.4
1954	Phi N★	108	345	41	127	27	5	4	46	42	0	11	.368	.432	.510	146	26	1-5	.975	-3	*111*	*69*	C91	0	2.5
1955	Phi N	7	21	4	4	2	0	1	1	3-1	0	1	.190	.292	.429	90	0	0-0	1.000	1	*90*	*0*	C6	0	0.1
	Cin N★	116	421	67	129	15	3	20	77	47-4	1	35	.306	.373	.499	123	14	1-1	.986	-3	*120*	*62*	C107	0	1.6
	Year	123	442	71	133	17	3	21	78	50-5	1	36	.301	.369	.495	122	14	1-1	.987	-3	*118*	*59*	C113	0	1.7
1956	Cin N	90	229	28	63	10	0	12	39	26-4	0	18	.275	.346	.476	112	4	0-1	1.000	-2	*91*	77	C55	0	0.5
1957	Cin N	90	205	29	58	14	1	14	39	24-5	0	16	.283	.353	.566	134	10	0-0	.988	-5	58	69	C45	0	0.7
1958	Cin N	99	251	28	71	12	1	6	31	22-3	1	20	.283	.343	.410	93	-2	0-0	.988	7	114	99	C58	0	0.7
1959	Pit N★	114	377	41	112	28	5	11	59	31-9	2	16	.297	.349	.485	122	12	0-0	.984	-8	112	105	C101	0	0.8
1960	†Pit N★	110	337	33	99	15	2	7	39	35-12	0	13	.294	.356	.412	110	5	0-1	**.994**	5	163	91	C89	0	1.5
1961	Pit N★	100	323	37	98	17	3	12	52	30-8	2	16	.303	.365	.486	123	11	1-0	**.991**	-5	**167**	61	C92	0	1.0
1962	Pit N	103	360	38	118	19	2	13	61	31-9	0	19	.328	.375	.500	134	17	0-1	.988	-3	106	76	C101	0	1.8
1963	Pit N	91	264	20	74	10	1	6	37	24-8	1	14	.280	.338	.394	111	4	0-1	.990	-6	76	102	C72	0	0.1
1964	Pit N☆	68	171	9	42	3	1	2	17	13-3	1	14	.246	.303	.310	73	-6	2-1	.992	-5	82	67	C44	0	-1.0
	Chi A	7	5	1	1	0	0	1	1	2-2	0	0	.200	.429	.800	239	1	0-0	ø	0	—	—	/H	0	0.1
1965	Chi A	80	77	2	22	4	0	2	24	11-4	0	7	.286	.371	.416	132	4	0-0	1.000	1	130	155	C5	0	0.5
1966	Chi A	79	67	0	21	5	0	0	15	11-2	1	8	.313	.412	.388	143	5	0-0	1.000	0	0	0	C2	0	0.5
1967	Chi A	77	60	2	8	1	0	2	11	14-6	1	8	.133	.303	.250	69	-2	0-0	ø	0	—	—	/H	0	-0.2
Total	18	1691	4471	485	1318	230	33	126	673	477-80	13	270	.295	.362	.446	116	110	13-14	.988	-38	*109*	*82*	C1139	0	12.2
Burgess, Tom	Thomas Roland "Tim"; B9.1.1927 London ON, Can.; BL/TL/6´0˝/(175–180); d4.17; C2																								
1954	StL N	17	21	2	1	1	0	0	1	3	0	9	.048	.167	.095	-29	-4	0-0	.750	-1	65	0	O4R	0	-0.5
1962	LA A	87	143	17	28	7	1	2	13	36-8	0	20	.196	.354	.301	82	-2	2-0	.997	-3	68	101	1b35,O2L	0	-0.6
Total	2	104	164	19	29	8	1	2	14	39-8	0	29	.177	.332	.274	67	-6	2-0	.997	-3	68	101	1b35,O6(2/0/4)	0	-1.1
Burgo, Bill	William Ross; B11.15.1919 Johnstown PA; D10.19.1988 Morgan City LA; BR/TR/5´8˝/185; d9.22																								
1943	Phi A	17	70	12	26	4	2	1	9	4	2	1	.371	.421	.529	178	7	0-2	.979	1	108	137	O17L	0	0.7
1944	Phi A	27	88	6	21	2	0	1	3	7	3	3	.239	.316	.295	76	-3	1-3	.955	1	119	52	O22(14/0/8)	0	-0.4
Total	2	44	158	18	47	6	2	2	12	11	5	4	.297	.362	.399	121	4	1-5	.965	2	114	88	O39(31/0/8)	0	0.3
Burich, Bill	William Max; B5.29.1918 Calumet MI; BR/TR/6´0˝/180; d4.15; Mil 1943–46																								
1942	Phi N	25	80	3	23	1	0	0	7	6	0	13	.287	.337	.300	92	-1	2	.917	-4	83	54	S19,3b3	0	-0.3
1946	Phi N	2	1	1	0	0	0	0	0	0	0	0	.000	.000	.000	-99	0	0	ø	-0	0	0	/3	0	0.0
Total	2	27	81	4	23	1	0	0	7	6	0	13	.284	.333	.296	89	-1	2	.917	-4	83	54	S19,3b4	0	-0.3
Burk, Mack	Mack Edwin; B4.21.1935 Nacogdoches TX; BR/TR/6´4˝/180; d5.25; Mil 1957–58; Col Texas																								
1956	Phi N	15	1	3	1	0	0	0	0	0-0	0	0	1.000	1.000	1.000	449	0	0-0	1.000	0	*0*	*0*	/C	0	0.0
1958	Phi N	1	1	0	0	0	0	0	0	0-0	0	1	.000	.000	.000	-99	0	0-0	ø	0	—	—	/H	0	0.0
Total	2	16	2	3	1	0	0	0	0	0-0	0	1	.500	.500	.500	171	0	0-0	1.000	0	*0*	*0*	/C	0	0.0
Burkam, Chris	Chauncey De Pew; B10.13.1892 Benton Harbor MI; D5.9.1964 Kalamazoo MI; BL/TR/5´11˝/175; d6.24																								
1915	StL A	1	1	0	0	0	0	0	0	0	0	1	.000	.000	.000	-99	0	0	ø	0	—	—	/H	—	0.0

YEAR	TM LG	G	AB	R	H	2B	3B	HR	RBI	BB-IB	HP	SO	AVG	OBP	SLG	AOPS	ABR	SB-CS	FA	FR	RNG	THR	GAMES AT POSITION	DL	BFW
BURKE, CHRIS	Christopher Allen; B3.11.1980 Louisville KY; BR/TR/5´11˝/180; [HouN01 1/10]; d7.4; Col Tennessee																								
2004	Hou N	17	17	2	1	0	0	0	0	3-0	0	3	.059	.200	.059	-27	-3	0-0	1.000	3	174	164	2b7	0	0.0
2005	†Hou N	108	318	49	79	19	2	5	26	23-0	6	62	.248	.309	.368	76	-11	11-6	.992	-4	90	73	O84(83/6/0),2b18	0	-1.7
2006	Hou N	123	366	58	101	23	1	9	40	27-0	14	77	.276	.347	.418	93	-3	11-1	.974	-5	106	109	2b69,O61(19/38/7),S8	15	-0.5
Total	3	248	701	109	181	42	3	14	66	53-0	20	142	.258	.326	.387	82	-17	22-7	.991	-6	88	76	O145(102/44/7),2b94,S8	15	-2.2
BURKE, DAN	Daniel L.; B10.25.1868 Abington MA; D3.20.1933 Taunton MA; BR/TR/5´10˝/190; d4.18																								
1890	Roc AA	32	102	14	22	1	0	0	9	17	1	—	.216	.333	.225	70	-2	2	.944	-1	189	122	O29(0/19/10),C4,1b2	—	-0.3
	Syr AA	9	20	1	0	0	0	0	0	5	1	—	.000	.231	.000	-35	-3	0	.900	-1	*79*	*65*	C9	—	-0.3
	Year	41	122	15	22	1	0	0	9	22	2	—	.180	.315	.189	53	-5	2	.944	-2	189	122	O29(0/19/10),C13,1b2	—	-0.6
1892	Bos N	1	4	0	0	0	0	0	0	0	0	2	.000	.000	.000	-92	-1	0	.900	0	*107*	*80*	/C	—	0.0
Total	2	42	126	15	22	1	0	0	9	22	2	2	.175	.307	.183	48	-6	2	.944	-2	189	122	O29(0/19/10),C14,1b2	—	-0.6
BURKE, EDDIE	Edward D.; B10.6.1866 Northumberland PA; D11.26.1907 Utica NY; BL/TR/5´6˝/161; d4.19																								
1890	Phi N	100	430	85	113	16	11	4	50	49	8	40	.263	.349	.379	109	5	38	.904	1	138	113	O96C,2b4	—	0.2
	Pit N	31	124	17	26	5	2	1	7	14	1	9	.210	.295	.306	85	-2	6	.911	0	38	71	O31C	—	-0.2
	Year	131	554	102	139	21	13	5	57	63	9	49	.251	.337	.363	105	3	44	.906	1	114	103	O127C,2b4	—	0.0
1891	Mil AA	35	144	31	34	9	0	2	21	12	10	19	.236	.337	.340	78	-5	7	.918	2	131	254	O35C	—	-0.3
1892	Cin N	15	41	6	6	1	0	0	4	9	0	4	.146	.300	.171	44	-2	2	1.000	-1	138	334	O14(3/5/6)/3	—	-0.3
	NY N	89	363	81	94	10	5	6	41	46	5	37	.259	.350	.364	118	9	42	.857	-5	98	74	2b59,O30L	—	0.4
	Year	104	404	87	100	11	5	6	45	55	5	41	.248	.345	.344	110	7	44	.857	-6	98	74	2b59,O44(33/5/6)/3	—	0.1
1893	NY N	135	537	122	150	23	10	9	80	51	**25**	32	.279	.369	.410	106	5	54	.911	0	82	41	O135L	—	-0.6
1894	†NY N	138	574	124	176	23	11	4	77	39	10	35	.307	.361	.406	85	-15	36	.934	-6	71	58	O138L	—	-2.6
1895	NY N	39	167	38	43	6	2	1	12	7	3	9	.257	.299	.335	65	-9	14	.914	1	128	144	O39L	—	-1.0
	Cin N	56	228	52	61	8	6	1	28	22	4	14	.268	.343	.368	80	-7	19	.899	1	89	99	O56(56/0/1)	—	-0.9
	Year	95	395	90	104	14	8	2	40	29	7	23	.263	.325	.354	74	-16	33	.905	2	105	117	O95(95/0/1)	—	-1.9
1896	Cin N	122	521	120	177	24	9	1	52	41	4	29	.340	.392	.426	108	6	53	.935	2	74	74	O122(116/5/1)	—	-0.3
1897	Cin N	95	387	71	103	17	1	1	41	29	6	—	.266	.327	.323	67	-18	22	.940	5	78	152	O95(94/0/1)	—	-1.9
Total	8	855	3516	747	983	142	57	30	413	319	76	228	.280	.352	.378	94	-33	293	.921	0	90	93	O791(611/172/9),2b63/3	—	-7.5
BURKE, FRANK	Frank Aloysius; B2.16.1880 Carbon Co. PA; D9.17.1946 Los Angeles CA; TR; d9.14																								
1906	NY N	8	9	2	3	1	1	0	1	1	0	—	.333	.400	.667	227	1	1	.667	-1	0	0	O4(0/3/1)	—	0.1
1907	Bos N	43	129	6	23	0	1	0	8	11	0	—	.178	.243	.194	37	-9	3	.955	-3	60	0	O36(32/4/1)	—	-1.7
Total	2	51	138	8	26	1	2	0	9	12	0	—	.188	.253	.225	50	-8	4	.942	-4	57	0	O40(32/7/2)	—	-1.6
BURKE, GLENN	Glenn Lawrence; B11.16.1952 Oakland CA; D5.30.1995 San Leandro CA; BR/TR/6´0˝/205; [LAN72 17/401]; d4.9; Col Merritt (CA) JC; [DL 1980 Oak A 33]																								
1976	LA N	25	46	9	11	2	0	0	5	3-0	1	8	.239	.300	.283	67	-2	3-2	.971	-2	89	0	O20(5/15/0)	0	-0.5
1977	†LA N	83	169	16	43	8	0	1	13	5-1	1	22	.254	.280	.320	60	-10	13-5	.971	-7	81	31	O74(5/64/6)	0	-1.7
1978	LA N	16	19	2	4	0	0	0	2	0-0	0	4	.211	.211	.211	18	-2	1-0	1.000	-1	69	0	O15(4/11/0)	0	-0.3
	Oak A	78	200	19	47	6	1	1	14	10-1	0	26	.235	.270	.290	61	-11	15-8	.987	0	109	27	O67(13/45/14)/1D	23	-1.2
1979	Oak A	23	89	4	19	2	1	0	4	4-1	0	10	.213	.247	.258	38	-8	3-1	1.000	0	93	115	O23(22/0/2)	0	-0.9
Total	4	225	523	50	124	18	2	2	38	22-3	2	70	.237	.270	.291	56	-33	35-16	.983	-10	94	38	O199(49/135/22),D2/1	56	-4.6
BURKE, JAMIE	James Eugene; B9.24.1971 Roseburg OR; BR/TR/6´0˝/(195–220); [AnaA93 9/243]; d5.9; Col Oregon St.																								
2001	Ana A	9	5	1	1	0	0	0	0	0-0	0	2	.200	.200	.200	6	-1	0-0	1.000	1	82	0	C8/1D	0	0.0
2003	Chi A	6	8	0	3	0	0	0	2	0-0	0	0	.375	.375	.375	95	0	0-0	1.000	-1	57	0	C4/1D	0	-0.1
2004	Chi A	57	120	22	40	9	0	0	15	10-0	1	13	.333	.386	.408	105	2	0-0	.987	0	156	103	C45,1b2,3b2,O2R,D3	0	0.4
2005	Chi A	1	1	0	0	0	0	0	0	0-0	0	0	.000	.000	.000	-96	0	0-0	ø	0	0	0	/1	0	0.0
Total	4	73	134	23	44	9	0	0	17	10-0	1	15	.328	.377	.396	99	1	0-0	.988	-0	148	94	C57,D5,1b5,O2R,3b2	0	0.3
BURKE, JIMMY	James Timothy "Sunset Jimmy"; B10.12.1874 St.Louis MO; D3.26.1942 St.Louis MO; BR/TR/5´7˝/160; d10.6; M4/C15																								
1898	Cle N	13	38	1	4	1	0	0	1	2	0	—	.105	.150	.132	-19	-6	1	.853	-2	93	0	3b13	—	-0.8
1899	StL N	2	6	1	2	0	0	0	0	1	0	—	.333	.429	.333	108	0	0	.923	1	131	277	2b2	—	0.1
1901	Mil A	64	233	24	48	8	0	0	26	17	2	—	.206	.266	.240	43	-17	6	.860	-8	92	53	3b64	—	-2.1
	Chi A	42	148	20	39	5	0	0	21	12	2	—	.264	.327	.297	76	-4	11	.867	-4	98	97	S31,3b11	—	-0.6
	Year	106	381	44	87	13	0	0	47	29	4	—	.228	.290	.262	56	-21	17	.859	-12	124	224	3b75,S31	—	-2.7
	Pit N	14	51	4	10	0	0	0	4	4	1	—	.196	.268	.196	35	-4	0	.877	2	124	224	3b14	—	-0.1
1902	Pit N	60	203	24	60	12	2	0	26	17	3	—	.296	.359	.374	122	6	9	.895	-3	102	88	2b27,O18(7/0/11),3b9,S4	—	0.3
1903	StL N	115	431	55	123	13	3	0	42	23	3	—	.285	.326	.329	90	-6	28	.911	9	107	**138**	3b93,2b15,O5(4/0/1)	—	0.5
1904	StL N	118	406	37	92	10	3	0	37	15	10	—	.227	.271	.266	69	-15	17	.897	-7	94	84	3b118	—	-2.0
1905	StL N	122	431	34	97	9	5	1	30	21	9	—	.225	.275	.276	67	-18	15	.924	4	104	90	3b122,M	—	-1.2
Total	7	550	1947	200	475	58	13	1	187	112	30	—	.244	.295	.289	73	-64	87	.899	-8	101	91	3b444,2b44,S35,O23(11/0/12)	—	-5.9
BURKE, JOE	Joseph Aloysius; B12.7.1867 Nashville TN; D11.3.1940 Cincinnati OH; 5´7˝/160; d9.26																								
1890	StL AA	2	6	3	4	0	0	0	2	1	1	—	.667	.750	.667	278	2	0	.750	-0	131	0	3b2	—	0.1
1891	Cin AA	1	4	0	1	0	0	0	1	0	0	2	.250	.250	.250	40	0	0	1.000	1	134	0	/2	—	0.0
Total	2	3	10	3	5	0	0	0	3	1	1	2	.500	.583	.500	193	2	0	.750	1	131	0	3b2/2	—	0.1
BURKE, LEO	Leo Patrick; B5.6.1934 Hagerstown MD; BR/TR/5´10˝/(175–190); d9.7; Col VPI																								
1958	Bal A	7	11	4	5	1	0	1	4	1-0	0	2	.455	.500	.818	271	3	0-0	1.000	-1	75	0	O3(1/1/1)/3	0	0.2
1959	Bal A	5	10	0	2	0	0	0	1	0-0	1	5	.200	.273	.200	33	-1	0-0	1.000	-1	73	0	2b2,3b2	0	-0.2
1961	LA A	6	5	0	0	0	0	0	0	0-0	0	1	.000	.000	.000	-90	-1	0-0	ø	0	—	—	/H	0	-0.1
1962	LA A	19	64	8	17	1	0	4	14	5-1	1	11	.266	.329	.469	115	1	0-0	.958	-1	108	0	O12(4/0/8),3b4/S	0	-0.1
1963	StL N	30	49	6	10	2	1	1	5	4-0	0	12	.204	.264	.347	68	-2	0-0	1.000	0	136	0	O11(2/0/9),3b5	0	-0.3
	Chi N	27	49	4	9	0	0	2	7	4-1	0	13	.184	.241	.306	55	-3	0-1	.925	3	128	140	2b10,1b4	0	0.0
	Year	57	98	10	19	2	1	3	12	8-1	0	25	.194	.252	.327	61	-5	0-1	1.000	3	136	0	O11(2/0/9),2b10,3b5,1b4	0	-0.3
1964	Chi N	59	103	11	27	3	1	1	14	7-1	1	31	.262	.315	.340	81	-3	0-0	1.000	-1	113	107	O18R,2b5,3b4,1b2/C	0	-0.5
1965	Chi N	12	10	0	2	0	0	0	0	0-0	0	4	.200	.200	.200	13	-1	0-0	1.000	-0	0	0	C2/rf	0	-0.1
Total	7	165	301	33	72	7	2	9	45	21-3	3	79	.239	.294	.365	81	-7	0-1	.985	-2	113	43	O45(7/1/37),2b17,3b16,1b6,C3/S	0	-1.1
BURKE, LES	Leslie Kingston "Buck"; B12.18.1902 Lynn MA; D5.6.1975 Danvers MA; BL/TR/5´9˝/168; d5.2																								
1923	Det A	7	10	2	1	0	0	0	2	0	0	1	.100	.100	.100	-48	-2	0-0	.500	-1	44	0	3b2/2	—	-0.3
1924	Det A	72	241	30	61	10	4	0	17	22	2	20	.253	.321	.328	69	-12	2-4	.957	-2	102	102	2b58,S6	—	-1.3
1925	Det A	77	180	32	52	6	3	0	24	17	2	8	.289	.357	.356	82	-5	4-1	.962	4	105	115	2b52	—	0.0
1926	Det A	38	75	9	17	1	0	0	4	7	1	3	.227	.301	.240	42	-6	1-2	.942	1	106	123	2b15,3b7/S	—	-0.5
Total	4	194	506	73	131	17	7	0	47	46	5	32	.259	.327	.320	67	-25	7-7	.958	1	104	109	2b126,3b9,S7	—	-2.1
BURKE, MIKE	Michael E.; B1854 NY; D6.9.1889 Albany NY; BR/TR/6´0˝/190; d5.1																								
1879	Cin N	28	117	13	26	3	0	0	8	2	—	5	.222	.235	.248	63	-4	—	.786	-6	87	70	S19,O5(0/1/4),3b5	—	-0.9
BURKE, PAT	Patrick Edward; B5.13.1901 St.Louis MO; D7.7.1965 St.Louis MO; BR/TR/5´10.5˝/170; d9.23																								
1924	StL A	1	3	0	0	0	0	0	0	1	0	0	.000	.000	.000	-94	-1	0-0	ø	-0	0	0	/3	—	-0.1
BURKETT, JESSE	Jesse Cail "Crab"; B12.4.1868 Wheeling WV; D5.27.1953 Worcester MA; BL/TL/5´8˝/155; d4.22; C1; HF1946; ▲																								
1890	NY N	101	401	67	124	23	13	4	60	33	3	52	.309	.366	.461	140	19	14	.824	1	142	115	O90(11/2/77),P21	—	1.3
1891	Cle N	40	167	29	45	7	4	0	13	23	0	19	.269	.358	.359	105	1	1	.892	-2	82	90	O40(6/2/35)	—	-0.1
1892	†Cle N	145	608	119	167	15	14	6	66	67	1	59	.275	.348	.375	114	9	36	.904	2	86	161	O145L	—	-0.2
1893	Cle N	125	511	145	178	25	15	6	82	98	7	23	.348	.459	.491	144	36	39	.849	-7	89	115	O125L	—	1.4
1894	Cle N	125	523	138	187	27	14	8	94	84	1	27	.358	.447	.509	125	24	28	.915	-4	81	106	O125L/P	—	0.7
1895	†Cle N	**132**	555	153	**225**	22	13	5	83	74	8	32	**.405**	.482	.519	149	44	41	.884	-4	84	98	O132(131/0/1)	—	2.3
1896	†Cle N	133	586	**160**	**240**	27	16	6	72	49	7	19	**.410**	.461	.541	155	46	34	.926	-4	94	92	O133L	—	2.5
1897	Cle N	127	517	129	198	28	7	2	60	76	7	—	.383	.468	.476	142	37	28	.949	-1	100	94	O127(127/1/0)	—	2.1
1898	Cle N	150	624	114	213	18	9	0	42	69	9	—	.341	.415	.399	135	32	19	.938	-7	81	67	O150(148/1/1)	—	1.2
1899	StL N	141	558	116	221	21	8	7	71	67	2	—	.396	.463	.500	160	49	25	.938	-2	93	54	O140(139/0/1)/2	—	3.1
1900	StL N	**141**	559	88	203	11	15	7	68	62	3	—	.363	.429	.474	150	39	32	.934	6	89	123	O141(140/1/0)	—	3.0

THE BATTER REGISTER

YEAR	TM LG	G	AB	R	H	2B	3B	HR	RBI	BB-IB	HP	SO	AVG	OBP	SLG	AOPS	ABR	SB-CS	FA	FR	RNG	THR	GAMES AT POSITION	DL	BFW
1901	StL N	**142**	601	**142**	**226**	20	15	10	75	59	10	—	**.376**	**.440**	.509	**184**	**66**	27	.923	-1	93	88	O142L	—	**5.5**
1902	StL A	138	553	97	169	29	9	5	52	71	5	—	.306	.390	.418	126	22	23	.924	5	94	144	O137L/PS3	—	1.9
1903	StL A	132	515	73	151	20	7	3	40	52	3	—	.293	.361	.377	125	18	17	.941	-3	69	112	O132L	—	0.7
1904	StL A	147	575	72	156	15	10	2	27	78	5	—	.271	.363	.343	132	25	12	.942	5	145	92	O147L	—	2.4
1905	Bos A	148	573	78	147	12	13	4	47	67	4	—	.257	.339	.344	115	11	13	.929	-2	67	0	O148L	—	0.1
Total	16	2067	8426	1720	2850	320	182	75	952	1029	75	231	.338	.415	.446	140	478	389	.917	-19	93	96	O2054(1936/7/115),P23/3S2	—	27.9
BURKHART, MORGAN	Morgan; B1.29.1972 St.Louis MO; BB/TL/5´11˝/(220–225); d6.27; Col Central Missouri																								
2000	Bos A	25	73	16	21	3	0	4	18	17-1	4	25	.288	.442	.493	134	5	0-0	.964	-1	52	42	D19,1b5/lf	0	0.3
2001	Bos A	11	33	3	6	1	0	1	4	1-0	0	11	.182	.206	.303	32	-3	0-0	1.000	-0	68	117	1b5,D6	0	-0.4
2003	KC A	6	15	1	3	0	0	0	1	1-0	0	2	.200	.250	.200	20	-2	0-0	1.000	-0	0	140	1b2,D2	0	-0.2
Total	3	42	121	20	30	4	0	5	23	19-1	4	38	.248	.366	.405	96	0	0-0	.986	-1	50	96	D27,1b12/lf	0	-0.3
BURKS, ELLIS	Ellis Rena; B9.11.1964 Vicksburg MS; BR/TR/6´2˝/(175–209); [BosA83*1/20]; d4.30; Col Ranger (TX) JC																								
1987	Bos A	133	558	94	152	30	2	20	59	41-0	2	98	.272	.324	.441	97	-3	27-6	.988	7	99	**269**	O132C/D	0	0.7
1988	†Bos A	144	540	93	159	37	5	18	92	62-1	3	89	.294	.367	.481	131	23	25-9	.977	3	103	147	O142C,D2	8	2.7
1989	Bos A	97	399	73	121	19	6	12	61	36-2	5	52	.303	.365	.471	127	14	21-5	.977	-0	98	137	O95C/D	47	1.6
1990	†Bos A✻	152	588	89	174	33	8	21	89	48-4	1	82	.296	.349	.486	125	18	9-11	.994	-10	88	97	O143C,D6	0	0.6
1991	Bos A	130	474	56	119	33	3	14	56	39-2	6	81	.251	.314	.422	97	-2	6-11	.993	-10	91	33	O126C,D2	0	-1.5
1992	Bos A	66	235	35	60	8	3	8	30	25-2	1	48	.255	.327	.417	100	0	5-2	.984	-10	72	88	O63C/D	102	-1.1
1993	†Chi A	146	499	75	137	24	4	17	74	60-2	4	97	.275	.352	.441	115	11	6-9	.982	-0	106	60	O146(0/21/132)	0	0.3
1994	Col N	42	149	33	48	8	3	13	24	16-3	0	39	.322	.388	.678	146	10	3-1	.964	-4	85	98	O39C	74	0.7
1995	†Col N	103	278	41	74	10	6	14	49	39-0	2	72	.266	.359	.496	96	-2	7-3	.970	1	109	83	O80(23/65/1)	10	0.0
1996	Col N★	156	613	**142**	211	45	8	40	128	61-2	6	114	.344	.408	**.639**	139	35	32-6	.983	-2	97	71	O152(129/32/0)	0	3.3
1997	Col N	119	424	91	123	19	2	32	82	47-0	3	75	.290	.363	.571	114	9	7-2	.982	-5	87	104	O112(66/89/0)	31	0.3
1998	Col N	100	357	54	102	22	5	16	54	39-0	2	80	.286	.355	.510	103	2	3-7	.975	-5	89	84	O98(45/78/0)	0	-0.5
	SF N	42	147	22	45	6	1	5	22	19-1	3	31	.306	.387	.463	132	7	8-1	.989	-3	96	39	O41(0/36/10)	0	0.6
	Year	142	504	76	147	28	6	21	76	58-1	5	111	.292	.365	.496	110	8	11-8	.979	-8	91	70	O139(45/114/10)	0	0.1
1999	SF N	120	390	73	110	19	0	31	96	69-2	6	86	.282	.394	.569	151	32	7-5	.991	-0	105	45	O107R,D3	17	2.5
2000	†SF N	122	393	74	135	21	5	24	96	56-5	1	49	.344	.419	.606	168	42	5-1	.982	2	109	64	O108R,D2	14	3.7
2001	†Cle A	124	439	83	123	29	1	28	74	62-2	5	85	.280	.369	.542	133	22	5-1	1.000	-0	79	202	D102,O20(18/0/2)	16	1.5
2002	Cle A	138	518	92	156	28	0	32	91	44-3	6	108	.301	.362	.541	133	24	2-3	1.000	-1	66	0	D127,O6L	0	1.5
2003	Cle A	55	198	27	52	11	1	6	28	27-2	3	46	.263	.360	.419	105	2	1-1	1.000	0	154	0	D51,O2L	113	0.0
2004	Bos A	11	33	6	6	0	0	1	1	3-0	1	8	.182	.270	.273	40	-3	2-0	ø	0	—	—	D9	150	-0.3
Total	18	2000	7232	1253	2107	402	63	352	1206	793-33	60	1340	.291	.363	.510	123	241	181-84	.983	-35	96	100	O1612(289/1062/360),D307	582	16.6
BURLESON, RICK	Richard Paul "Rooster"; B4.29.1951 Lynwood CA; BR/TR/5´10˝/160; [BosA70*S1/5]; d5.4; C5; [DL 1985 Cal A 182]																								
1974	Bos A	114	384	36	109	22	0	4	44	21-0	2	34	.284	.320	.372	93	-3	3-3	.957	-3	99	86	S88,2b31,3b2	0	0.6
1975	†Bos A	158	580	66	146	25	1	6	62	45-1	3	44	.252	.305	.329	74	-20	8-5	.963	2	103	110	S158	0	0.1
1976	Bos A	152	540	75	157	27	1	7	42	60-2	5	37	.291	.365	.383	107	7	14-9	.957	3	103	101	S152	0	2.9
1977	Bos A★	154	663	80	194	36	7	3	52	47-1	2	69	.293	.338	.382	87	-11	13-12	.970	20	107	**125**	S154	0	2.4
1978	Bos A✻	145	626	75	155	32	5	5	49	40-2	4	71	.248	.295	.339	71	-24	8-8	.981	20	109	113	S144	14	1.0
1979	Bos A★	153	627	93	174	32	5	5	60	35-0	3	54	.278	.315	.368	80	-18	9-5	**.980**	30	113	108	S153	0	2.8
1980	Bos A	155	644	89	179	29	2	8	51	62-0	2	51	.278	.341	.366	90	-8	12-13	.974	**31**	110	**136**	S155	0	3.7
1981	Cal A★	109	430	53	126	17	1	5	33	42-2	3	38	.293	.357	.372	110	7	4-6	.979	27	115	123	S109	0	4.5
1982	Cal A	11	45	4	7	1	0	0	2	6-2	0	3	.156	.255	.178	21	-5	0-0	.986	4	126	157	S11	169	0.1
1983	Cal A	33	119	22	34	7	0	0	11	12-0	0	12	.286	.348	.345	93	-1	0-2	.969	2	110	82	S31	102	0.3
1984	Cal A	7	4	2	0	0	0	0	0	0-0	0	2	.000	.000	.000	-99	-1	0-0	ø	0	—	—	/H	152	-0.1
1986	†Cal A	93	271	35	77	14	0	5	29	33-1	1	32	.284	.363	.391	107	4	1-3	.984	-5	96	72	D38,S37,2b6,3b4	0	0.0
1987	Bal A	62	206	26	43	14	1	2	14	17-0	3	30	.209	.279	.316	59	-12	0-2	.977	-6	93	109	2b55,D7	0	-1.5
Total	13	1346	5139	656	1401	256	23	50	449	420-11	28	477	.273	.328	.361	87	-85	72-68	.971	126	108	113	S1192,2b92,D45,3b6	619	16.8
BURNETT, HERCULES	Hercules H.; B8.13.1865 Louisville KY; D10.4.1936 Louisville KY; BR/5´11˝/177; d6.26																								
1888	Lou AA	1	4	1	0	0	0	0	0	1	0	—	.000	.200	.000	-34	-1	1	.667	-0	0	0	/rf	—	-0.1
1895	Lou N	5	17	6	7	0	1	2	3	2	0	2	.412	.474	.882	262	4	2	.769	-1	147	0	O4C/1	—	0.2
Total	2	6	21	7	7	0	1	2	3	3	0	2	.333	.417	.714	212	3	3	.750	-1	110	0	O5(0/4/1)/1	—	0.1
BURNETT, JOHNNY	John Henderson; B11.1.1904 Bartow FL; D8.12.1959 Tampa FL; BL/TR/5´11˝/175; d5.7; Col Florida																								
1927	Cle A	17	8	5	0	0	0	0	0	0	0	3	.000	.000	.000	-99	-2	1-0	.833	1	163	284	2b2	—	-0.2
1928	Cle A	3	10	3	5	0	0	0	1	0	0	1	.500	.500	.500	162	1	0-0	.867	0	95	189	S2	—	0.1
1929	Cle A	19	33	2	5	1	0	0	2	1	1	2	.152	.200	.182	-1	-5	0-0	.923	2	135	64	S10,2b8	—	-0.2
1930	Cle A	54	170	28	53	13	0	0	20	17	1	8	.312	.378	.388	91	-1	2-2	.973	-1	107	42	3b27,S19	—	0.1
1931	Cle A	111	427	85	128	25	5	1	52	39	1	25	.300	.360	.389	92	-5	5-2	.938	-1	99	108	S63,2b35,3b21/rf	—	0.1
1932	Cle A	129	512	81	152	23	5	4	53	46	4	27	.297	.359	.385	87	-9	2-5	.946	-19	97	83	S103,2b26	—	-1.9
1933	Cle A	83	261	39	71	11	2	1	29	23	1	14	.272	.333	.341	76	-9	3-2	.938	-2	101	98	S41,2b17,3b12	—	-0.7
1934	Cle A	72	208	28	61	11	2	3	30	18	1	11	.293	.352	.409	94	-2	1-1	.981	-6	85	88	3b42,S9,2b3,O2(1/0/1)	—	-0.6
1935	StL A	70	206	17	46	10	1	0	26	19	0	16	.223	.289	.282	46	-17	1-0	.939	-3	104	123	3b31,S18,2b12	—	-1.6
Total	9	558	1835	288	521	94	15	9	213	163	9	107	.284	.345	.366	81	-49	15-12	.935	-29	100	95	S265,3b133,2b103,O3(1/0/2)	—	-4.9
BURNETT, JACK	John Jeirus (b John Jeirus Barnett); B12.16.1879 Ventura CA; D9.3.1923 Modoc Co. CA; BB; d7.2																								
1907	StL N	59	206	18	49	8	4	0	12	15	2	—	.238	.296	.316	95	-2	5	.955	-5	102	49	O59C	—	-1.0
BURNITZ, JEROMY	Jeromy Neal; B4.15.1969 Westminster CA; BL/TR/6´0˝/(180–216); [NYN90 1/17]; d6.21; Col Oklahoma St.																								
1993	NY N	86	263	49	64	10	6	13	38	38-4	1	66	.243	.339	.475	117	6	3-6	.977	1	101	113	O79(0/20/61)	0	0.3
1994	NY N	45	143	26	34	4	0	3	15	23-0	1	45	.238	.347	.329	78	-4	1-1	.970	-6	77	32	O42R	0	-1.2
1995	Cle A	9	7	4	4	1	0	0	0	0-0	0	0	.571	.571	.714	227	1	0-0	1.000	1	191	0	O6(5/1/0),D2	0	0.2
1996	Cle A	71	128	30	36	10	0	7	26	25-1	2	31	.281	.406	.523	133	8	2-1	1.000	-1	105	0	O30(10/6/14),D15	0	0.5
	Mil A	23	72	8	17	4	0	2	14	8-1	2	16	.236	.321	.375	74	-3	2-0	.975	-2	81	71	O22(0/8/14)	0	-0.5
	Year	94	200	38	53	14	0	9	40	33-2	4	47	.265	.377	.470	112	5	4-1	.988	-3	93	36	O52(10/14/28),D15	0	0.0
1997	Mil A	153	494	85	139	37	8	27	85	75-8	5	111	.281	.382	.553	138	29	20-13	.975	-3	89	153	O149(5/26/124)	0	2.0
1998	Mil N	161	609	92	160	28	1	38	125	70-7	4	158	.263	.339	.499	116	13	7-4	.972	-2	98	92	O161(0/1/161)	0	0.3
1999	Mil N★	130	467	87	126	33	2	33	103	91-7	16	124	.270	.402	.561	141	33	7-3	.982	0	100	92	O127R,D3	33	2.5
2000	Mil N	161	564	91	131	29	2	31	98	99-10	14	121	.232	.356	.456	105	6	6-4	.979	-2	96	113	O158R/D	0	-0.4
2001	Mil N	154	562	104	141	32	4	34	100	80-9	5	150	.251	.347	.504	119	16	0-4	.981	1	97	127	O153R	0	0.8
2002	NY N	154	479	65	103	15	0	19	54	58-5	10	135	.215	.311	.365	82	-13	10-7	.966	-4	96	80	O140R/D	0	-2.4
2003	NY N	65	234	38	64	18	0	18	45	21-6	4	55	.274	.344	.581	141	13	1-4	.986	-1	104	50	O65(10/21/48)	30	0.9
	LA N	61	230	25	47	4	0	13	32	14-3	1	57	.204	.252	.391	66	-13	4-0	.946	-5	79	90	O60(54/12/2)	0	-2.0
	Year	126	464	63	111	22	0	31	77	35-9	5	112	.239	.299	.487	104	0	5-4	.970	-6	92	69	O125(64/33/50)	0	-1.1
2004	Col N	150	540	94	153	30	4	37	110	58-7	5	124	.283	.356	.559	117	14	5-6	.974	-7	85	126	O143(21/69/79),D3	0	0.2
2005	Chi N	160	605	84	156	31	2	24	87	57-3	3	109	.258	.322	.435	94	-6	5-4	.984	2	109	71	O160(0/3/158)	0	-1.2
2006	Pit N	111	313	35	72	12	0	16	49	22-4	5	74	.230	.289	.422	78	-12	1-1	.984	-7	81	28	O84R	0	-2.2
Total	14	1694	5710	917	1447	298	29	315	981	739-75	78	1376	.253	.345	.481	111	88	74-58	.977	-34	95	96	O1579(105/167/1365),D25	63	-2.2
BURNS, C.B.	Charles Brittingham; B5.15.1879 Bay View MD; D6.6.1968 Havre de Grace MD; BR/TR/6´0˝/175; d8.19																								
1902	Bal A	1	1	0	1	0	0	0	0	0	0	—	1.000	1.000	1.000	436	0	0	ø	0	—	—	/H	—	0.0
BURNS, ED	Edward James; B10.31.1887 San Francisco CA; D5.30.1942 Monterey CA; BR/TR/5´6˝/165; d6.25; Col St. Marys (CA)																								
1912	StL N	1	1	0	0	0	0	0	1	0	0	0	.000	.000	.000	-99	0	0	ø	0	*0*	*0*	/C	—	0.0
1913	Phi N	17	30	3	6	3	0	0	3	6	1	3	.200	.351	.300	83	0	2	.980	-2	94	90	C15	—	-0.1
1914	Phi N	70	139	8	36	3	4	0	16	20	0	12	.259	.352	.338	99	0	5	.947	-5	*73*	*122*	C55	—	-0.2
1915	†Phi N	67	174	11	42	5	0	0	16	20	2	12	.241	.327	.270	81	-3	1	.981	-1	*106*	*93*	C62	—	0.1
1916	Phi N	78	219	14	51	8	1	0	14	16	3	18	.233	.294	.279	74	-6	3	.981	-6	105	90	C75/Scf	—	-0.7
1917	Phi N	20	49	2	10	1	0	0	6	1	0	5	.204	.220	.224	35	-4	2	.971	-0	*108*	*131*	C15	—	-0.4
1918	Phi N	68	184	10	38	1	1	0	9	20	1	9	.207	.288	.223	53	-10	1	.981	-4	*96*	*111*	C68	—	-1.0
Total	7	321	796	48	183	21	6	0	65	83	7	59	.230	.308	.271	73	-23	14	.974	-19	*97*	*103*	C291/cfS	—	-2.3

BURNS, GEORGE George Henry "Tioga George"; B1.31.1893 Niles OH; D1.7.1978 Kirkland WA; BR/TR/6´1.5˝/180; d4.14

YEAR	TM LG	G	AB	R	H	2B	3B	HR	RBI	BB-IB	HP	SO	AVG	OBP	SLG	AOPS	ABR	SB-CS	FA	FR	RNG	THR	GAMES AT POSITION	DL	BFW
1914	Det A	137	478	55	139	22	5	5	57	32	**12**	56	.291	.351	.389	119	10	23-13	.982	-6	91	106	1b137	—	0.2
1915	Det A	105	392	49	99	18	3	5	50	22	5	51	.253	.301	.352	91	-6	9-3	.986	-4	90	123	1b104	—	-1.2
1916	Det A	135	479	60	137	22	6	4	73	22	7	30	.286	.327	.382	109	3	12	.985	-10	72	97	1b124	—	-1.1
1917	Det A	119	407	42	92	14	10	1	40	15	6	33	.226	.264	.317	77	-14	3	.990	-4	84	72	1b104	—	-2.3
1918	Phi A	**130**	505	61	**178**	22	9	6	70	23	**8**	25	.352	.390	.467	157	32	8	.983	6	**124**	**132**	1b128,O2(1/0/1)	—	3.8
1919	Phi A	126	470	63	139	29	9	8	57	19	**12**	18	.296	.339	.447	118	9	15	.980	2	120	83	1b86,O34R	—	0.7
1920	Phi A	22	60	1	14	3	0	1	7	6	1	7	.233	.313	.333	71	-2	4-0	.958	0	84	164	O13R	—	-0.2
	†Cle A	44	56	7	15	4	1	0	13	4	2	3	.268	.339	.375	86	-1	1-0	.979	1	159	21	1b12/rf	—	0.0
	Year	66	116	8	29	7	1	1	20	10	3	10	.250	.326	.353	78	-4	5-0	.958	1	83	161	O14R,1b12	—	-0.2
1921	Cle A	84	244	52	88	21	4	0	49	13	2	19	.361	.398	.480	121	8	3-1	.990	2	111	108	1b73	—	0.6
1922	Bos A	147	558	71	171	32	5	12	73	20	9	28	.306	.341	.446	104	1	8-2	.987	-1	103	101	1b140	—	-0.7
1923	Bos A	146	551	91	181	47	5	7	82	45	7	33	.328	.386	.470	124	20	9-7	.990	-1	97	90	1b146	—	0.8
1924	Cle A	129	462	64	143	37	5	4	68	29	15	27	.310	.370	.437	106	4	14-5	.987	9	**130**	90	1b127	—	0.6
1925	Cle A	127	488	69	164	41	4	6	79	24	3	24	.336	.371	.473	112	8	16-11	.989	1	102	92	1b126	—	0.0
1926	Cle A	151	603	97	**216**	**64**	3	4	114	28	8	33	.358	.394	.494	130	27	13-7	.988	1	107	115	1b151	—	1.8
1927	Cle A	140	549	84	175	51	2	3	78	42	7	27	.319	.375	.435	109	9	13-11	.990	4	112	99	1b139	—	0.3
1928	Cle A	82	209	29	52	12	1	5	30	17	6	11	.249	.323	.388	85	-5	2-3	.984	2	126	108	1b53	—	-0.6
	NY A	4	4	1	2	0	0	0	0	0	0	1	.500	.500	.500	169	0	0-0	1.000	-0	0	0	1b2	—	0.0
	Year	86	213	30	54	12	1	5	30	17	6	12	.254	.326	.390	87	-4	2-3	.985	2	125	107	1b55	—	-0.6
1929	NY A	9	9	0	0	0	0	0	0	0	0	4	.000	.000	.000	-99	-3	0-0	ø	0	—	—	/H	—	-0.3
	†Phi A	29	49	5	13	5	0	1	11	2	0	3	.265	.294	.429	81	-1	1-0	1.000	-0	77	110	1b19	—	-0.2
	Year	38	58	5	13	5	0	1	11	2	0	7	.224	.250	.362	55	-4	1-0	1.000	-0	77	110	1b19	—	-0.5
Total	16	1866	6573	901	2018	444	72	72	951	363	110	433	.307	.354	.429	112	99	154-63	.987	2	104	101	1b1671,O50(1/0/49)	—	2.2

BURNS, GEORGE George Joseph; B11.24.1889 Utica NY; D8.15.1966 Gloversville NY; BR/TR/5´7˝/160; d10.3; C1

YEAR	TM LG	G	AB	R	H	2B	3B	HR	RBI	BB-IB	HP	SO	AVG	OBP	SLG	AOPS	ABR	SB-CS	FA	FR	RNG	THR	GAMES AT POSITION	DL	BFW
1911	NY N	6	17	2	1	0	0	0	0	1	0	0	.059	.111	.059	-50	-3	0	1.000	-1	89	0	O6(1/4/1)	—	-0.4
1912	NY N	29	51	11	15	4	0	0	3	8	1	8	.294	.400	.373	109	1	7	1.000	1	94	163	O23(13/5/5)	—	0.2
1913	†NY N	150	605	81	173	37	4	2	54	58	4	74	.286	.352	.370	106	7	40-35	.963	1	101	102	O150(119/0/32)	—	-0.3
1914	NY N	154	561	**100**	170	35	10	3	60	89	5	53	.303	.403	.417	149	**39**	**62**	.950	0	106	82	O154(102/0/54)	—	3.4
1915	NY N	**155**	622	83	169	27	14	3	51	56	1	57	.272	.333	.375	121	15	27-20	.960	-7	93	72	O155(140/0/15)	—	-0.1
1916	NY N	**155**	623	**105**	174	24	8	5	41	63	1	47	.279	.346	.368	126	20	37-26	.962	-0	97	117	O155L	—	1.4
1917	†NY N	152	597	**103**	180	25	13	5	45	**75**	1	55	.302	.380	.412	148	36	40	.974	2	105	83	O152L	—	3.5
1918	NY N	119	465	80	135	22	6	4	51	43	3	37	.290	.354	.389	129	17	40	.965	9	**125**	80	O119L	—	2.3
1919	NY N	139	534	**86**	162	30	9	2	46	**82**	0	37	.303	**.396**	.404	142	33	**40**	**.990**	2	105	85	O139L	—	3.1
1920	NY N	154	631	**115**	181	35	9	6	46	**76**	2	48	.287	.365	.399	121	20	22-22	.983	11	**123**	74	O154(154/1/0)	—	2.3
1921	†NY N	149	605	111	181	28	9	4	61	**80**	6	24	.299	.386	.395	107	10	19-20	.972	-7	96	75	O149(90/59/0)/3	—	-0.9
1922	Cin N	**156**	631	104	180	20	10	1	53	78	2	38	.285	.366	.353	88	-9	30-23	.976	-4	95	97	O156(0/109/47)	—	-2.2
1923	Cin N	**154**	614	99	168	27	13	3	45	**101**	0	46	.274	.376	.375	101	5	12-14	.960	-6	101	60	O154(0/3/151)	—	-1.5
1924	Cin N	93	336	43	86	19	2	2	33	29	0	21	.256	.315	.342	77	-10	3-6	.963	2	99	129	O90(12/1/79)	—	-1.7
1925	Phi N	88	349	65	102	29	1	1	22	33	0	20	.292	.353	.390	82	-8	4-8	.990	2	102	99	O88(66/4/22)	—	-1.4
Total	15	1853	7241	1188	2077	362	108	41	611	872	26	565	.287	.366	.384	115	173	383-174	.970	6	103	88	O1844(1262/186/406)/3	—	7.7

BURNS, JIM James M.; B St.Louis MO; D2.17.1909 Chicago IL; 5´7˝/168; d9.25

YEAR	TM LG	G	AB	R	H	2B	3B	HR	RBI	BB-IB	HP	SO	AVG	OBP	SLG	AOPS	ABR	SB-CS	FA	FR	RNG	THR	GAMES AT POSITION	DL	BFW
1888	KC AA	15	66	13	20	0	0	0	4	1	3	—	.303	.343	.303	101	0	6	.853	1	155	300	O15L	—	0.1
1889	KC AA	134	579	103	176	23	11	5	97	20	7	68	.304	.335	.408	105	-1	56	.913	-8	44	65	O134C/3	—	-1.1
1891	Was AA	20	82	15	26	6	0	0	10	6	2	10	.317	.378	.390	126	3	2	.771	-4	31	0	O20(0/5/16)/S	—	-0.1
Total	3	169	727	131	222	29	11	5	111	27	12	78	.305	.341	.396	107	2	64	.897	-10	53	81	O169(15/139/16)/S3	—	-1.1

BURNS, JACK John Irving "Slug"; B8.31.1907 Cambridge MA; D4.18.1975 Brighton MA; BL/TL/5´10.5˝/175; d9.17; C5

YEAR	TM LG	G	AB	R	H	2B	3B	HR	RBI	BB-IB	HP	SO	AVG	OBP	SLG	AOPS	ABR	SB-CS	FA	FR	RNG	THR	GAMES AT POSITION	DL	BFW
1930	StL A	8	30	5	9	3	0	0	2	5	0	5	.300	.400	.400	100	0	0-0	1.000	1	138	165	1b8	—	0.1
1931	StL A	144	570	75	148	27	7	4	70	42	1	58	.260	.312	.353	72	-25	19-12	.993	19	**159**	114	1b143	—	-1.8
1932	StL A	150	617	111	188	33	8	11	70	61	1	43	.305	.368	.438	102	2	17-11	.992	5	111	99	1b150	—	-0.7
1933	StL A	144	556	89	160	43	4	7	71	56	0	51	.288	.353	.417	97	-1	11-11	.992	3	108	114	1b143	—	-1.3
1934	StL A	**154**	612	86	157	28	8	13	73	62	2	47	.257	.327	.392	78	-22	9-3	.992	-0	97	98	1b154	—	-3.3
1935	StL A	143	549	77	157	28	1	5	67	68	1	49	.286	.366	.368	86	-9	3-2	.992	-9	74	92	1b141	—	-2.9
1936	StL A	9	14	2	3	1	0	0	1	3	0	1	.214	.353	.286	58	-1	0-0	1.000	-0	73	120	1b2	—	-0.1
	Det A	138	558	96	158	36	3	4	63	79	3	45	.283	.375	.380	87	-9	4-8	.994	1	99	109	1b138	—	-2.1
	Year	147	572	98	161	37	3	4	64	82	3	46	.281	.374	.378	86	-10	4-8	.994	1	99	109	1b140	—	-2.2
Total	7	890	3506	541	980	199	31	44	417	376	8	299	.280	.351	.392	87	-65	63-47	.992	19	108	105	1b879	—	-12.1

BURNS, JACK John Joseph; B5.13.1880 Avoca PA; D6.24.1957 Waterford CT; BR/TR/5´10˝/160; d9.11

YEAR	TM LG	G	AB	R	H	2B	3B	HR	RBI	BB-IB	HP	SO	AVG	OBP	SLG	AOPS	ABR	SB-CS	FA	FR	RNG	THR	GAMES AT POSITION	DL	BFW
1903	Det A	11	37	2	10	0	0	0	3	1	2	—	.270	.325	.270	82	-1	0	.981	2	109	135	2b11	—	0.1
1904	Det A	4	16	3	2	0	0	0	1	1	0	—	.125	.176	.125	-4	-2	1	.952	-1	72	77	2b4	—	-0.4
Total	2	15	53	5	12	0	0	0	4	2	2	—	.226	.281	.226	57	-3	1	.973	0	98	118	2b15	—	-0.3

BURNS, JOE Joseph Francis; B3.26.1889 Ipswich MA; D7.12.1987 Beverly MA; BL/TL/5´11˝/170; d6.19

YEAR	TM LG	G	AB	R	H	2B	3B	HR	RBI	BB-IB	HP	SO	AVG	OBP	SLG	AOPS	ABR	SB-CS	FA	FR	RNG	THR	GAMES AT POSITION	DL	BFW
1910	Cin N	1	1	0	1	0	0	0	0	0	0	0	1.000	1.000	1.000	506	0	1	ø	0	—	—	/H	—	0.1
1913	Det A	4	13	0	5	0	0	0	1	2	1	4	.385	.500	.385	162	1	0	1.000	-0	99	0	O4L	—	0.1
Total	2	5	14	0	6	0	0	0	1	2	1	4	.429	.529	.429	184	1	1	1.000	-0	99	0	O4L	—	0.2

BURNS, JOE Joseph Francis; B2.25.1900 Trenton NJ; D1.7.1986 Trenton NJ; BR/TR/6´0˝/175; d4.18

YEAR	TM LG	G	AB	R	H	2B	3B	HR	RBI	BB-IB	HP	SO	AVG	OBP	SLG	AOPS	ABR	SB-CS	FA	FR	RNG	THR	GAMES AT POSITION	DL	BFW
1924	Chi A	8	19	1	2	0	0	0	0	0	0	2	.105	.105	.105	-47	-4	0-0	.933	-1	*72*	*56*	C6	—	-0.5

BURNS, JOE Joseph James; B6.17.1916 Bryn Mawr PA; D6.24.1974 Bryn Mawr PA; BR/TR/5´10.5˝/175; d4.24

YEAR	TM LG	G	AB	R	H	2B	3B	HR	RBI	BB-IB	HP	SO	AVG	OBP	SLG	AOPS	ABR	SB-CS	FA	FR	RNG	THR	GAMES AT POSITION	DL	BFW
1943	Bos N	52	135	12	28	3	0	1	5	8	2	25	.207	.262	.252	49	-9	2	.933	2	116	125	3b34,O4(1/1/2)	0	-0.7
1944	Phi A	28	75	5	18	2	0	1	8	4	0	8	.240	.278	.307	68	-3	0-1	.919	-5	79	98	3b17,2b9	0	-0.9
1945	Phi A	31	90	7	23	1	1	0	3	4	0	17	.256	.287	.289	68	-4	0-1	1.000	-2	83	63	O19R,3b5/1	0	-0.8
Total	3	111	300	24	69	6	1	2	16	16	2	50	.230	.274	.277	60	-16	2-2	.920	-5	104	110	3b56,O23(1/1/21),2b9/1	0	-2.4

BURNS, PAT Patrick; d8.11

YEAR	TM LG	G	AB	R	H	2B	3B	HR	RBI	BB-IB	HP	SO	AVG	OBP	SLG	AOPS	ABR	SB-CS	FA	FR	RNG	THR	GAMES AT POSITION	DL	BFW
1884	Bal AA	6	25	3	5	2	1	0	—	3	0	—	.200	.286	.360	105	0	—	.953	-1	46	70	1b6	—	-0.1
	Bal U	1	4	0	2	0	0	0	—	0	—	—	.500	.500	.500	185	0	—	.917	-0	0	238	/1	—	0.0
Total	1	7	29	3	7	2	1	0	—	3	—	—	.241	.313	.379	117	0	—	.947	-1	39	96	1b7	—	-0.1

BURNS, DICK Richard Simon; B12.26.1863 Holyoke MA; D11.16.1937 Holyoke MA; BL/TL/5´7˝/140; d5.3; ▲

YEAR	TM LG	G	AB	R	H	2B	3B	HR	RBI	BB-IB	HP	SO	AVG	OBP	SLG	AOPS	ABR	SB-CS	FA	FR	RNG	THR	GAMES AT POSITION	DL	BFW
1883	Det N	37	140	11	26	7	1	0	5	2	—	22	.186	.197	.250	36	-10	—	.758	-4	89	132	O24(1/1/23),P17	—	-0.9
1884	Cin U	79	350	84	107	17	**12**	4	—	5	—	—	.306	.315	.457	122	-3	—	.827	-2	95	78	O44(6/33/7),P40,S2	—	-0.4
1885	StL N	14	54	2	12	2	1	0	4	3	—	8	.222	.263	.296	86	-1	—	.682	-2	93	334	O14C/P	—	-0.3
Total	3	130	544	97	145	26	14	4	9	10	—	30	.267	.280	.388	98	-14	—	.785	-8	93	135	O82(7/48/30),P58,S2	—	-1.6

BURNS, TOM Thomas Everett; B3.30.1857 Honesdale PA; D3.19.1902 Jersey City NJ; BR/TR/5´7˝/152; d5.1; M3/U1; OF(10/2/2)

YEAR	TM LG	G	AB	R	H	2B	3B	HR	RBI	BB-IB	HP	SO	AVG	OBP	SLG	AOPS	ABR	SB-CS	FA	FR	RNG	THR	GAMES AT POSITION	DL	BFW
1880	Chi N	85	333	47	103	17	3	0	43	12	—	23	.309	.333	.378	133	11	—	.864	-25	76	54	S79,3b9,C2/P	—	-1.1
1881	Chi N	**84**	342	41	95	20	3	4	42	14	—	22	.278	.306	.389	112	4	—	.870	-4	96	88	S80,3b3,2b3	—	0.4
1882	Chi N	**84**	355	55	88	23	6	0	48	15	—	28	.248	.278	.346	95	-2	—	.911	-2	93	119	2b43,S41	—	-0.1
1883	Chi N	97	405	69	119	37	7	2	67	13	—	31	.294	.316	.435	116	7	—	.872	3	106	113	S79,2b19/lf	—	1.1
1884	Chi N	83	343	54	84	14	2	7	44	13	—	50	.245	.272	.359	89	-5	—	.838	-4	**103**	113	S80,3b3	—	-0.6
1885	†Chi N	111	445	82	121	23	9	7	71	16	—	48	.272	.297	.411	112	3	—	.844	-4	101	114	S111/2	—	0.2
1886	†Chi N	112	445	64	123	18	10	3	65	14	—	40	.276	.298	.382	92	-7	15	.890	11	106	101	3b112	—	0.5
1887	Chi N	115	424	57	112	20	10	3	60	34	1	32	.264	.320	.380	83	-12	32	.872	17	110	**134**	3b107,O8(6/2/0)	—	0.6
1888	Chi N	134	483	60	115	12	6	3	70	26	3	49	.238	.281	.306	81	-11	34	.905	17	105	89	3b134	—	0.8
1889	Chi N	**136**	525	64	135	27	6	4	66	32	2	57	.257	.302	.354	78	-18	18	.880	-3	100	**124**	3b136	—	-1.6
1890	Chi N	**139**	538	86	149	17	6	5	86	57	2	45	.277	.348	.359	102	1	44	.898	2	101	**122**	3b139	—	0.4
1891	Chi N	59	243	36	55	8	1	1	17	21	0	21	.226	.288	.280	66	-11	18	.892	-1	90	150	3b53,S4,O2L	—	-1.0

YEAR	TM LG	G	AB	R	H	2B	3B	HR	RBI	BB-IB	HP	SO	AVG	OBP	SLG	AOPS	ABR	SB-CS	FA	FR	RNG	THR	GAMES AT POSITION	DL	BFW
1892	Pit N	12	39	7	8	0	0	0	4	3	0	8	.205	.262	.205	41	-3	1	.690	-4	58	0	3b8,O3(1/0/2),M	—	-0.7
Total	13	1251	4920	722	1307	236	69	39	683	270	8	454	.266	.305	.365	96	-43	162	.886	2	102	115	3b704,S474,2b66,O14L,C2/P	—	-1.1
Burns, Tommy	Thomas P. "Oyster"; B9.6.1864 Philadelphia PA; D11.11.1928 Brooklyn NY; BL/TR/5´8˝/183; d8.18; OF(100/15/781); ▲																								
1884	Wil U	2	7	0	1	0	1	0	—	1	—	—	.143	.250	.429	99	0	—	.778	-0	101	0	S2	—	0.0
	Bal AA	35	131	34	39	2	6	6	23	7	3	—	.298	.348	.542	179	10	—	.826	-4	64	210	O24R,2b10,P2/3	—	0.6
1885	Bal AA	78	321	47	74	11	6	5	37	16	6	—	.231	.280	.349	99	0	—	.908	1	193	254	O45(1/0/44),P15,S10,3b6,2b6/1	—	0.1
1887	Bal AA	140	551	122	188	33	**19**	9	99	63	5	—	.341	.414	.519	169	53	58	.841	-17	84	85	S98,3b42,P3/2	—	3.2
1888	Bal AA	79	325	54	97	18	9	4	42	24	1	—	.298	.349	.446	158	21	23	.855	-7	29	42	O56(46/0/10),S23,P5,3b2/2	—	1.1
	Bro AA	52	204	40	58	9	6	2	25	14	3	—	.284	.339	.417	142	9	21	.851	-9	90	84	S36,O14C,2b3	—	0.1
	Year	131	529	94	155	27	15	6	67	38	4	—	.293	.345	.435	152	30	44	.847	-16	24	35	O70(46/14/10),S59,P5,2b4,3b2	—	1.2
1889	†Bro AA	131	504	105	153	19	13	5	100	68	4	26	.304	.391	.423	131	22	32	.920	-7	97	113	O113R,S19	—	1.2
1890	†Bro N	119	472	102	134	22	12	**13**	**128**	51	4	42	.284	.359	.464	139	21	21	.941	-2	120	108	O116R,3b3	—	1.6
1891	Bro N	123	470	75	134	24	13	4	83	53	0	30	.285	.358	.417	126	15	21	.922	-1	91	164	O113R,S6,3b5	—	1.2
1892	Bro N	141	542	88	171	27	18	4	96	65	6	42	.315	.395	.454	162	42	33	.937	-12	79	96	O129(2/0/127),3b7,S5	—	2.2
1893	Bro N	109	415	68	112	22	8	7	60	36	4	16	.270	.334	.412	103	0	14	.932	-0	109	136	O108(0/1/108)/S	—	-0.4
1894	Bro N	126	513	107	182	32	14	5	109	44	3	18	.355	.409	.501	127	24	30	.949	-5	72	78	O126R	—	1.0
1895	Bro N	20	76	7	14	0	1	0	7	8	1	2	.184	.271	.211	27	-8	0	.918	1	132	156	O19L	—	-0.8
	NY N	33	114	21	35	5	3	1	25	14	1	6	.307	.388	.430	113	3	10	.870	-2	123	0	O32L/1	—	-0.1
	Year	53	190	28	49	5	4	1	32	22	2	8	.258	.341	.342	80	-5	10	.893	-1	127	67	O51L/1	—	-0.9
Total	11	1188	4645	870	1392	224	129	65	<u>834</u>	464	41	<u>182</u>	.300	.368	.445	135	212	263	.920	-64	94	114	O895R,S200,3b66,P25,2b21,1b2	—	11.0
Burr, Alex	Alexander Thomson; B11.1.1893 Chicago IL; D10.12.1918 Cazaux, France; BR/TR/6´3.5˝/190; d4.21; Col Williams																								
1914	NY A	1	0	0	0	0	0	0	0	0	0	0	ø	ø	ø	ø	0	0	ø	-0	0	0	/cf	—	0.0
Burrell, Buster	Frank Andrew; B12.22.1866 Weymouth MA; D5.8.1962 Weymouth MA; BR/TR/5´10˝/165; d8.1																								
1891	NY N	15	53	1	5	0	0	0	1	3	1	12	.094	.158	.094	-27	-9	2	.856	-6	82	104	C15/cf	—	-1.3
1895	Bro N	12	28	7	4	0	0	1	5	4	0	3	.143	.250	.250	32	-3	0	.838	-1	129	77	C12	—	-0.3
1896	Bro N	62	206	19	62	11	3	0	23	15	0	13	.301	.348	.383	98	0	1	.928	-6	104	74	C60	—	-0.1
1897	Bro N	33	103	15	25	2	0	2	18	10	0	—	.243	.310	.320	70	-4	1	.884	-5	89	93	C27,1b4	—	-0.6
Total	4	122	390	42	96	13	3	3	47	32	1	<u>28</u>	.246	.305	.318	70	-16	4	.896	-18	100	83	C114,1b4/cf	—	-2.3
Burrell, Pat	Patrick Brian; B10.10.1976 Eureka Springs AR; BR/TR/6´4˝/(222–230); [PhiN98 1/1]; d5.24; Col Miami																								
2000	Phi N	111	408	57	106	27	1	18	79	63-2	1	139	.260	.359	.463	107	5	0-0	.988	-6	60	80	1b58,O48L,D4	0	-0.7
2001	Phi N	155	539	70	139	29	2	27	89	70-7	5	162	.258	.346	.469	114	11	2-1	.972	0	87	186	O146L,D5	0	0.6
2002	Phi N	157	586	96	165	39	2	37	116	89-9	3	153	.282	.376	.544	149	43	1-0	.979	-5	92	80	O157L	0	3.2
2003	Phi N	146	522	57	109	31	4	21	64	72-2	4	142	.209	.309	.404	91	-8	0-0	.976	-4	94	84	O140L,D2	0	-1.7
2004	Phi N	127	448	66	115	17	0	24	84	78-7	2	130	.257	.365	.455	108	7	2-0	.983	1	100	132	O122L	30	0.4
2005	Phi N	154	562	78	158	27	1	32	117	99-6	3	160	.281	.389	.504	128	26	0-0	.972	-4	87	121	O153L	0	1.6
2006	Phi N	144	462	80	119	24	1	29	95	98-5	3	131	.258	.388	.502	121	17	0-0	.986	1	95	134	O126L,D6	0	1.3
Total	7	994	3527	504	911	194	11	188	644	569-38	21	1017	.258	.362	.479	118	101	5-1	.978	-16	92	127	O892L,1b58,D17	30	4.7
Burright, Larry	Larry Allen "Possum"; B7.10.1937 Roseville IL; BR/TR/5´11˝/170; d4.12; Col Fullerton (CA) JC																								
1962	LA N	115	249	35	51	6	5	4	30	21-5	0	67	.205	.264	.317	60	-15	4-3	.962	-1	99	71	2b109/S	0	-1.0
1963	NY N	41	100	9	22	2	1	0	3	8-1	2	25	.220	.291	.260	59	-5	1-0	.946	10	131	90	S19,2b15/3	0	0.8
1964	NY N	3	7	0	0	0	0	0	0	0-0	0	0	.000	.000	.000	-99	-2	0-0	1.000	4	191	215	2b3	0	0.2
Total	3	159	356	44	73	8	6	4	33	29-6	2	92	.205	.267	.295	56	-22	5-3	.964	13	105	83	2b127,S20/3	0	0.0
Burris, Paul	Paul Robert; B7.21.1923 Hickory NC; D10.3.1999 Charlotte NC; BR/TR/6´0˝/(180–190); d10.2																								
1948	Bos N	2	4	0	2	0	0	0	0	0	0	0	.500	.500	.500	174	0	0	1.000	1	0	0	C2	0	0.1
1950	Bos N	10	23	1	4	1	0	0	3	1	0	2	.174	.208	.217	13	-3	0	1.000	1	87	0	C8	0	-0.2
1952	Bos N	55	168	14	37	4	0	2	21	7	1	19	.220	.256	.280	50	-12	0-0	1.000	-3	91	68	C50	0	-1.3
1953	Mil N	2	1	0	0	0	0	0	0	0	0	0	.000	.000	.000	-99	0	0-0	1.000	0	0	0	C2	77	0.0
Total	4	69	196	15	43	5	0	2	24	8	1	21	.219	.254	.276	47	-15	0-<u>0</u>	1.000	-2	88	57	C62	77	-1.4
Burroughs, Henry	Henry S.; B1845 NJ; D3.31.1878 Newark NJ; 5´8˝/147; d5.5																								
1871	Oly NA	12	63	11	15	2	3	1	14	1	—	1	.238	.250	.413	91	-1	0-0	.706	-2	107	0	O8(4/0/4),3b5/2	—	-0.1
1872	Oly NA	2	7	1	1	0	0	0	0	1	—	0	.143	.250	.143	25	-1	0-0	.625	-0	305	0	O2C	—	-0.1
Total	2NA	14	70	12	16	2	3	1	14	2	—	1	.229	.250	.386	85	-2	0-0	.680	-2	162	0	O10(4/2/4),3b5/2	—	-0.2
Burroughs, Jeff	Jeffrey Alan; B3.7.1951 Long Beach CA; BR/TR/6´1˝/200; [TexA69 1/1]; d7.20; s-Sean																								
1970	Was A	6	12	1	2	0	0	0	1	2-0	0	5	.167	.286	.167	29	-1	0-0	1.000	-0	89	0	O3R	0	-0.2
1971	Was A	59	181	20	42	9	0	5	25	22-0	1	55	.232	.319	.365	98	0	1-0	.966	-2	90	98	O50(34/0/23)	0	-0.5
1972	Tex A	22	65	4	12	1	0	1	3	5-0	0	22	.185	.243	.246	47	-4	0-2	.935	-1	85	155	O19(17/0/2)/1	19	-0.8
1973	Tex A	151	526	71	147	17	1	30	85	67-3	1	88	.279	.355	.487	142	29	0-0	.975	10	112	139	O148(43/0/106),1b3/D	0	3.1
1974	Tex A★	152	554	84	167	33	2	25	**118**	91-12	5	104	.301	.397	.504	164	**50**	2-3	.972	-13	81	89	O150R,1b2/D	0	3.0
1975	Tex A	152	585	81	132	20	0	29	94	79-11	1	155	.226	.315	.409	105	4	4-4	.966	-15	83	77	O148R,D3	0	-2.0
1976	Tex A	158	604	71	143	22	2	18	86	69-4	2	93	.237	.315	.369	98	-1	0-0	.987	-6	89	104	O155R,D3	0	-1.6
1977	Atl N	154	579	91	157	19	1	41	114	86-2	0	126	.271	.362	.520	121	17	4-1	.974	-12	86	77	O154R	0	-0.2
1978	Atl N☆	153	488	72	147	30	6	23	77	**117**-12	0	92	.301	**.432**	.529	152	41	1-2	.975	-4	85	115	O146L	0	3.2
1979	Atl N	116	397	49	89	14	1	11	47	73-7	3	75	.224	.347	.348	85	-5	2-2	.963	-3	86	102	O110L	0	-1.4
1980	Atl N	99	278	35	73	14	0	13	51	35-6	2	57	.263	.347	.453	121	8	1-1	.977	-7	89	0	O73L	0	-0.2
1981	Sea A	89	319	32	81	13	1	10	41	41-3	0	64	.254	.339	.395	106	3	0-1	.985	-11	72	65	O87(1/0/86)/D	0	-1.3
1982	Oak A	113	285	42	79	13	2	16	48	45-0	0	61	.277	.372	.505	144	18	1-3	.981	-2	97	0	D48,O34(17/0/18)	0	1.3
1983	Oak A	121	401	43	108	15	1	10	56	47-4	0	79	.269	.341	.387	107	5	0-2	ø	0	0	0	D114	0	0.0
1984	Oak A	58	71	5	15	1	0	2	8	18-0	0	23	.211	.367	.310	96	1	0-0	1.000	-0	55	0	D23,O4L	0	0.0
1985	†Tor A	86	191	19	49	9	3	6	28	34-1	0	36	.257	.366	.429	114	5	0-1	ø	0	0	0	D75	0	0.2
Total	16	1689	5536	720	1443	230	20	240	882	831-65	15	1135	.261	.355	.439	121	170	16-22	.974	-65	88	90	O1281(445/0/845),D269,1b6	19	2.6
Burroughs, Sean	Sean Patrick; B9.12.1980 Atlanta GA; BL/TR/6´2˝/(180–200); [SDN98 1/9]; d4.2; f-Jeff																								
2002	SD N	63	192	18	52	5	1	1	11	12-1	1	30	.271	.317	.323	75	-8	2-0	.935	0	93	61	3b48,2b13	47	-0.7
2003	SD N	146	517	62	148	27	6	7	58	44-4	11	75	.286	.352	.402	106	5	7-2	.966	1	95	105	3b137	0	0.7
2004	SD N	130	523	76	156	23	3	2	47	31-4	9	52	.298	.348	.365	89	-9	5-4	.957	-5	91	121	3b125	0	-1.3
2005	†SD N	93	284	20	71	7	2	1	17	24-4	5	41	.250	.318	.299	67	-14	4-0	.962	3	103	116	3b78/SP	0	-1.0
2006	TB A	8	21	3	4	1	0	0	1	4-0	0	7	.190	.320	.238	48	-1	1-0	.963	3	148	264	3b7	11	0.2
Total	5	440	1537	179	431	63	12	11	134	115-13	26	205	.280	.340	.358	88	-27	19-6	.959	3	96	111	3b395,2b13/PS	58	-2.1
Burrus, Dick	Maurice Lennon; B1.29.1898 Hatteras NC; D2.2.1972 Elizabeth City NC; BL/TL/5´11˝/175; d6.23; Col North Carolina St.																								
1919	Phi A	70	194	17	50	3	4	0	8	9	1	25	.258	.294	.314	70	-9	2	.986	-3	91	72	1b38,O10(0/2/8)	—	-1.4
1920	Phi A	71	135	11	25	8	0	0	10	5	2	7	.185	.225	.244	24	-15	0-3	.989	-1	97	142	1b31,O2R	—	-1.7
1925	Bos N	152	588	82	200	41	4	5	87	51	3	29	.340	.396	.449	126	26	8-9	**.990**	1	102	87	1b151	—	1.4
1926	Bos N	131	486	59	131	21	1	3	61	37	2	16	.270	.324	.335	85	-10	4	.991	12	**140**	88	1b128	—	-0.6
1927	Bos N	72	220	22	70	8	3	0	32	17	1	10	.318	.370	.382	110	3	3	.972	1	120	103	1b61	—	0.0
1928	Bos N	64	137	15	37	6	0	3	13	19	2	8	.270	.367	.380	101	1	1	.977	-2	87	101	1b32	—	-0.3
Total	6	560	1760	206	513	87	12	11	211	138	11	95	.291	.347	.373	97	-4	18-<u>12</u>	.986	8	114	92	1b441,O12(0/2/10)	—	-2.6
Burt, Frank	Frank J.; B Camden NJ; d5.2																								
1882	Bal AA	10	36	2	4	2	1	0	—	1	—	—	.111	.135	.222	20	-3	—	.815	-1	40	335	O10L	—	-0.4
Burton, Ellis	Ellis Narrington; B8.12.1936 Los Angeles CA; BB/TR/5´11˝/(150–165); d9.18																								
1958	StL N	8	30	5	7	0	1	2	4	3-0	1	8	.233	.324	.500	110	0	0-1	1.000	-1	92	0	O7(5/0/2)	0	-0.1
1960	StL N	29	28	5	6	1	0	0	2	4-0	0	14	.214	.313	.250	52	-2	0-2	1.000	-2	54	0	O23(14/5/4)	0	-0.5
1963	Cle A	26	31	6	6	3	0	1	1	4-0	0	4	.194	.286	.387	87	0	0-0	1.000	-1	53	182	O16(9/0/7)	0	-0.2
	Chi N	93	322	45	74	16	1	12	41	36-1	4	59	.230	.311	.398	98	0	6-3	.975	-9	79	101	O90(1/76/21)	0	-1.3
1964	Chi N	42	105	12	20	3	2	2	7	17-0	0	22	.190	.303	.314	71	-4	4-0	.981	-2	95	0	O29(1/21/11)	0	-0.7

YEAR	TM LG	G	AB	R	H	2B	3B	HR	RBI	BB-IB	HP	SO	AVG	OBP	SLG	AOPS	ABR	SB-CS	FA	FR	RNG	THR	GAMES AT POSITION	DL	BFW
1965	Chi N	17	40	6	7	1	0	0	4	1-0	0	10	.175	.186	.200	11	-5	1-0	1.000	1	109	214	O12(2/10/0)	0	-0.4
Total	5	215	556	79	120	24	4	17	59	65-1	5	117	.216	.300	.365	85	-11	11-6	.981	-13	81	84	O177(32/112/45)	0	-3.2
Busby, Jim	James Franklin; B1.8.1927 Kenedy TX; D7.8.1996 Augusta GA; BR/TR/6´1″/175; d4.23; C18; Col TCU																								
1950	Chi A	18	48	5	10	0	0	0	4	1	0	5	.208	.224	.208	12	-7	0-2	.964	1	92	233	O12(0/12/1)	0	-0.7
1951	Chi A★	143	477	59	135	15	2	5	68	40	4	46	.283	.344	.354	91	-7	26-11	.982	7	106	127	O139C	0	-0.1
1952	Chi A	16	39	5	5	0	0	0	0	2	0	7	.128	.171	.128	-16	-6	0-2	1.000	1	118	0	O16C	0	-0.7
	Was A	129	512	58	125	24	4	2	47	22	4	48	.244	.281	.318	69	-24	5-6	.993	6	114	38	O128C	0	-2.3
	Year	145	551	63	130	24	4	2	47	24	4	55	.236	.273	.305	62	-30	5-8	.994	7	**114**	35	O144C	0	-3.0
1953	Was A	150	586	68	183	28	7	6	82	38	4	45	.312	.358	.415	111	8	13-6	.988	13	113	112	O150C	0	1.4
1954	Was A	**155**	628	83	187	22	7	7	80	43	3	56	.298	.342	.389	107	3	17-2	.988	5	**114**	40	O155C	0	0.4
1955	Was A	47	191	23	44	6	2	6	14	13-1	0	22	.230	.279	.377	79	-7	5-0	.993	-1	104	35	O47C	0	-0.9
	Chi A	99	337	38	82	13	4	1	27	25-0	0	37	.243	.294	.315	62	-19	7-3	.984	1	100	111	O99C	0	-2.2
	Year	146	528	61	126	19	6	7	41	38-1	0	59	.239	.289	.337	68	-26	12-3	.987	0	101	85	O146C	0	-3.1
1956	Cle A	135	494	72	116	17	3	12	50	43-2	4	47	.235	.301	.354	71	-22	8-3	.989	0	109	37	O133C	0	-2.7
1957	Cle A	30	74	9	14	2	1	2	4	1-0	0	8	.189	.200	.324	41	-7	0-1	.978	-1	94	78	O26(2/25/0)	0	-0.9
	Bal A	86	288	31	72	10	1	3	19	23-0	0	36	.250	.304	.323	77	-10	6-3	.984	6	114	141	O85C	0	-0.7
	Year	116	362	40	86	12	2	5	23	24-0	0	44	.238	.284	.323	69	-17	6-4	.983	5	110	129	O111(2/110/0)	0	-1.6
1958	Bal A	113	215	32	51	7	2	3	19	24-0	3	37	.237	.320	.330	84	-4	6-4	**.995**	4	**124**	27	O103C/3	0	-0.4
1959	Bos A	61	102	16	23	8	0	1	5	5-0	1	18	.225	.266	.333	61	-5	0-1	.980	-1	92	67	O34(8/25/1)	0	-0.8
1960	Bos A	1	0	0	0	0	0	0	0	0-0	0	0	ø	ø	ø	ø	0	0-0	ø	-0	0	0	/lf	0	0.0
	Bal A	79	159	25	41	7	1	0	12	20-1	0	14	.258	.341	.314	79	-4	2-3	.985	2	115	70	O71C	0	-0.5
	Year	80	159	25	41	7	1	0	12	20-1	0	14	.258	.341	.314	79	-4	2-3	.985	2	115	70	O72(1/71/0)	0	-0.5
1961	Bal A	75	89	15	23	3	1	0	6	8-0	0	10	.258	.316	.315	73	-3	2-0	.987	0	105	127	O71C	0	-0.4
1962	Hou N	15	11	2	2	0	0	0	1	2-0	0	3	.182	.308	.182	38	-1	0-1	1.000	-1	60	0	O10(1/8/1)/C	0	-0.2
Total	13	1352	4250	541	1113	162	35	48	438	310-4	23	439	.262	.314	.350	82	-115	97-48	.988	41	110	77	O1280(12/1267/3)/C3	0	-11.7
Busby, Paul	Paul Miller "Red"; B8.25.1918 Waynesboro MS; BL/TR/6´1″/175; d9.14																								
1941	Phi N	10	16	3	5	0	0	0	2	0	0	1	.313	.313	.313	79	-1	0	1.000	-0	78	0	O3(0/2/1)	0	-0.1
1943	Phi N	26	40	13	10	1	0	0	5	2	0	1	.250	.286	.275	65	-2	2	1.000	0	121	0	O10(2/0/8)	0	-0.3
Total	2	36	56	16	15	1	0	0	7	2	0	2	.268	.293	.286	69	-3	2	1.000	-0	115	0	O13(2/2/9)	0	-0.4
Busch, Ed	Edgar John; B11.16.1917 Lebanon IL; D1.17.1987 St.Clair Co. IL; BR/TR/5´10″/175; d9.30																								
1943	Phi A	4	17	2	5	0	0	0	0	1	1	2	.294	.368	.294	95	0	0-1	.941	-2	55	39	S4	0	-0.2
1944	Phi A	140	484	41	131	11	3	0	40	29	1	17	.271	.313	.306	78	-15	5-3	.940	-21	93	74	S111,2b27,3b4	0	-2.7
1945	Phi A	126	416	37	104	10	3	0	35	32	1	9	.250	.305	.288	73	-15	2-3	.952	1	105	93	S116,2b2,3b2/1	0	-0.6
Total	3	270	917	80	240	21	6	0	75	62	3	28	.262	.311	.298	76	-30	7-7	.946	-22	98	83	S231,2b29,3b6/1	0	-3.5
Busch, Mike	Michael Anthony; B7.7.1968 Davenport IA; BR/TR/6´5″/(175–220); [LAN90 4/110]; d8.30; Col Iowa St.																								
1995	LA N	13	17	3	4	0	0	3	6	0-0	0	7	.235	.235	.765	162	1	0-0	.875	-1	76	0	3b10,1b2	0	0.0
1996	LA N	38	83	8	18	4	0	4	17	5-0	0	33	.217	.261	.410	78	-3	0-0	.932	-3	73	36	3b23/1	34	-0.6
Total	2	51	100	11	22	4	0	7	23	5-0	0	40	.220	.257	.470	92	-2	0-0	.923	-4	73	30	3b33,1b3	34	-0.6
Bush, Homer	Homer Giles; B11.12.1972 East St.Louis IL; BR/TR/5´11″/(175–185); [SDN91 7/185]; d8.16; [DL 1996 SD N 133]																								
1997	NY A	10	11	2	4	0	0	0	3	0-0	0	0	.364	.364	.364	91	0	0-0	.913	1	137	92	2b8/D	0	0.1
1998	†NY A	45	71	17	27	3	0	1	5	5-0	0	19	.380	.421	.465	136	4	6-3	.971	-3	73	50	2b24,D12,3b3,S2	0	0.1
1999	Tor A	128	485	69	155	26	4	5	55	21-0	6	82	.320	.353	.421	95	-4	32-8	.984	10	109	107	2b109,S18	33	1.6
2000	Tor A	76	297	38	64	8	0	1	18	18-0	5	60	.215	.271	.253	33	-31	9-4	.986	18	113	128	2b75	76	-0.8
2001	Tor A	78	271	32	83	11	1	3	27	8-1	6	50	.306	.336	.387	89	-4	13-4	.990	19	115	141	2b78	79	1.9
2002	Tor A	23	78	9	18	2	0	1	2	2-0	2	12	.231	.268	.295	48	-6	2-0	.990	-2	95	84	2b22/D	0	-0.6
	Fla N	40	54	7	12	0	0	0	5	3-0	0	13	.222	.263	.222	31	-6	2-1	.962	-7	64	37	2b12,S4	0	-1.3
2004	NY A	9	7	2	0	0	0	0	0	0-0	1	2	.000	.125	.000	-63	-2	1-0	1.000	-1	50	184	2b4,D2	0	-0.2
Total	7	409	1274	176	363	50	5	11	115	57-1	20	238	.285	.324	.358	75	-49	65-20	.985	35	107	115	2b332,S24,D16,3b3	321	0.8
Bush, Donie	Owen Joseph; B10.8.1887 Indianapolis IN; D3.28.1972 Indianapolis IN; BB/TR/5´6″/140; d9.18; M7																								
1908	Det A	20	68	13	20	1	1	0	4	7	0	—	.294	.360	.338	122	2	2	.938	-2	93	140	S20	—	0.1
1909	†Det A	157	532	114	145	18	2	0	33	**88**	4	—	.273	.380	.314	114	15	53	.925	0	**110**	73	S157	—	2.3
1910	Det A	142	496	90	130	13	4	3	34	**78**	2	—	.262	.365	.323	108	8	49	**.940**	10	**110**	61	S141/3	—	2.6
1911	Det A	150	561	126	130	18	5	1	36	**98**	3	—	.232	.349	.287	74	-15	40	.925	13	**112**	72	S150	—	0.8
1912	Det A	144	511	107	118	14	8	2	38	**117**	3	—	.231	.377	.301	98	6	37	.929	27	**121**	88	S144	—	4.2
1913	Det A	152	597	98	150	19	10	1	40	80	4	32	.251	.344	.322	96	-1	44	.938	2	106	94	S152	—	1.2
1914	Det A	**157**	596	97	150	18	4	0	32	**112**	3	54	.252	.373	.295	98	6	35-26	.944	**32**	**114**	106	S157	—	5.1
1915	Det A	155	561	99	128	12	8	1	44	118	2	44	.228	.364	.283	89	-1	35-27	.937	6	105	109	S155	—	1.4
1916	Det A	145	550	73	124	5	9	0	34	75	1	42	.225	.319	.267	74	-16	19	.954	-16	96	73	S144	—	-2.5
1917	Det A	147	581	**112**	163	18	3	0	24	80	2	40	.281	.370	.322	111	12	34	.932	-17	95	64	S147	—	0.6
1918	Det A	**128**	500	74	117	10	3	0	22	79	1	31	.234	.340	.266	86	-5	9	.931	-20	91	54	S128	—	-1.7
1919	Det A	129	509	82	124	11	6	0	26	75	2	36	.244	.343	.289	80	-11	22	.943	-10	95	80	S129	—	-1.2
1920	Det A	141	506	85	133	18	5	1	33	73	1	32	.263	.357	.324	83	-9	15-7	.938	-15	95	69	S140	—	-1.4
1921	Det A	104	402	72	113	6	5	0	27	45	1	23	.281	.355	.321	74	-15	8-11	.949	-6	101	87	S81,2b23	—	-1.2
	Was A	23	84	15	18	1	0	0	2	12	0	4	.214	.313	.226	41	-7	2-2	.932	-2	99	119	S21	—	-0.7
	Year	127	486	87	131	7	5	0	29	57	1	27	.270	.347	.305	69	-22	10-13	.946	-8	101	93	S102,2b23	—	-1.9
1922	Was A	41	134	17	32	4	1	0	7	21	0	7	.239	.342	.284	68	-6	1-1	.957	2	106	183	3b37/2	—	-0.2
1923	Was A	10	22	6	9	0	0	0	0	0	0	1	.409	.409	.409	122	1	1-1	.813	-1	90	0	3b5,2b2,M	—	0.0
Total	16	1945	7210	1280	1804	186	74	9	436	1158	29	346	.250	.356	.300	91	-36	406-75	.936	3	104	81	S1866,3b43,2b26	—	9.4
Bush, Randy	Robert Randall; B10.5.1958 Dover DE; BL/TL/6´1″/(184–190); [MinA79 2/37]; d5.1; Col New Orleans																								
1982	Min A	55	119	13	29	6	1	4	13	8-0	3	28	.244	.305	.412	92	-1	0-0	1.000	-0	88	0	D26,O6L	0	-0.3
1983	Min A	124	373	43	93	24	3	11	56	34-8	7	51	.249	.323	.418	98	-1	0-1	1.000	1	165	38	D103,1b3	0	-0.4
1984	Min A	113	311	46	69	17	1	11	43	31-6	4	60	.222	.292	.389	85	-6	1-2	1.000	-0	0	154	D89,1b2	0	-1.0
1985	Min A	97	234	26	56	13	3	10	35	24-1	5	30	.239	.321	.449	102	1	3-0	.969	-3	92	0	O41(39/0/4),D28/1	0	-0.4
1986	Min A	130	357	50	96	19	7	7	45	39-2	4	63	.269	.347	.420	105	3	5-3	.977	-3	100	37	O102(90/0/13),1b3,D6	0	-0.4
1987	†Min A	122	293	46	74	10	2	11	46	43-5	3	49	.253	.349	.413	99	0	10-3	.982	-4	99	25	O75(2/0/72),1b9,D9	0	-0.5
1988	Min A	136	394	51	103	20	3	14	51	58-14	9	49	.261	.365	.434	120	13	8-6	.979	-1	101	56	O109(1/0/108),1b6,D7	0	0.8
1989	Min A	141	391	60	103	17	4	14	54	48-6	3	73	.263	.347	.435	112	7	5-8	.986	3	109	111	O109(34/1/88),1b25,D5	0	0.4
1990	Min A	73	181	17	44	8	0	6	18	21-2	6	27	.243	.338	.387	97	0	0-3	1.000	0	103	57	O32(2/0/32),D29,1b6	76	-0.3
1991	†Min A	93	165	21	50	10	1	6	23	24-3	3	25	.303	.401	.485	137	9	0-2	1.000	-1	95	54	O38(7/0/32),1b12,D10	0	0.6
1992	Min A	100	182	14	39	8	1	2	22	11-3	2	37	.214	.263	.302	57	-11	1-1	1.000	-0	110	0	O24(3/0/21),D24,1b8	0	-1.3
1993	Min A	35	45	1	7	2	0	0	3	7-1	0	13	.156	.269	.200	28	-4	0-0	1.000	-1	0	132	1b4/rfD	0	-0.5
Total	12	1219	3045	388	763	154	26	96	409	348-51	49	505	.251	.334	.413	101	10	33-29	.983	-9	101	53	O537(184/1/371),D341,1b79	76	-3.3
Bushong, Doc	Albert John; B9.15.1856 Philadelphia PA; D8.19.1908 Brooklyn NY; BR/TR/5´11″/165; d7.19; Col Penn																								
1875	Atl NA	1	5	0	3	0	1	0	0	0	—	0	.600	.600	1.000	511	2	0-0	.800	-0	—	—	/C	—	0.1
1876	Phi N	5	21	4	1	0	0	0	1	0	—	0	.048	.048	.048	-69	-4	—	.769	-2	—	—	C5	—	-0.5
1880	Wor N	41	146	13	25	3	0	0	19	1	—	16	.171	.177	.192	23	-12	—	.918	13	—	—	C40/rf3	—	0.2
1881	Wor N	76	275	35	64	7	4	0	21	21	—	23	.233	.287	.287	77	-7	—	.918	9	—	—	C76	—	0.4
1882	Wor N	69	253	20	40	4	1	1	15	5	—	17	.158	.174	.194	18	-23	—	.897	-3	—	—	C69	—	-1.8
1883	Cle N	63	215	15	37	5	0	0	9	7	—	19	.172	.198	.195	21	-20	—	.909	13	—	—	C63	—	-0.1
1884	Cle N	62	203	24	48	6	1	0	10	17	—	11	.236	.295	.276	78	-5	—	.886	0	—	—	C62/cf	—	0.1
1885	†StL AA	85	300	42	80	13	5	0	21	11	2	—	.267	.297	.343	97	-2	—	.932	12	—	—	C85/3	—	1.6
1886	†StL AA	107	386	56	86	8	0	1	31	31	0	—	.223	.281	.251	64	-16	12	**.942**	15	—	—	C106/1	—	0.7
1887	†StL AA	53	201	35	51	4	0	0	26	11	2	—	.254	.299	.274	55	-13	14	.927	4	—	—	C52,O2R,3b2	—	-0.4
1888	Bro AA	69	253	23	53	5	1	0	16	5	2	—	.209	.231	.237	50	-15	9	.915	-4	—	—	C69	—	-1.2
1889	†Bro AA	25	84	15	13	1	0	0	8	9	0	7	.155	.237	.167	16	-9	2	.894	-0	—	—	C25	—	-0.7
1890	†Bro N	16	55	5	13	2	0	0	7	6	0	4	.236	.311	.273	70	-2	2	.913	-2	*86*	62	C15,O2C	—	-0.2
Total	12	671	2392	287	511	58	12	2	184	124	6	97	.214	.254	.250	55	-128	39	.916	57	*86*	62	C667,O6(0/3/3),3b4/1	—	-1.9

YEAR	TM LG	G	AB	R	H	2B	3B	HR	RBI	BB-IB	HP	SO	AVG	OBP	SLG	AOPS	ABR	SB-CS	FA	FR	RNG	THR	GAMES AT POSITION	DL	BFW
Buskey, Joe Joseph Henry "Jazzbow"; B12.18.1902 Cumberland MD; D4.11.1949 Cumberland MD; BR/TR/5´10˝/175; d4.19																									
1926	Phi N	5	8	1	0	0	0	0	0	1	0	1	.000	.111	.000	-65	-2	0	.810	-1	93	48	S5	—	-0.3
Buskey, Mike Michael Thomas; B1.13.1949 San Francisco CA; BR/TR/5´11˝/165; d9.5; Col San Francisco																									
1977	Phi N	6	7	1	2	0	1	0	1	0-0	1	1	.286	.375	.571	142	0	0-0	.882	1	102	227	S6	0	0.1
Busse, Ray Raymond Edward; B9.25.1948 Daytona Beach FL; BR/TR/6´4˝/175; d7.24; Col Daytona Beach (FL) JC																									
1971	Hou N	10	34	2	5	3	0	0	4	2-0	0	9	.147	.194	.235	22	-3	0-0	.929	-6	56	0	S5,3b3	0	-1.0
1973	StL N	24	70	6	10	4	2	2	5	5-2	0	21	.143	.200	.343	47	-6	0-1	.898	1	107	136	S23	0	-0.3
	Hou N	15	17	1	1	0	0	0	0	1-0	0	12	.059	.111	.059	-52	-4	0-0	1.000	1	120	89	S5,3b3	15	-0.3
	Year	39	87	7	11	4	2	2	5	6-2	0	33	.126	.183	.287	28	-9	0-1	.906	1	108	132	S28,3b3	0	-0.6
1974	Hou N	19	34	3	7	1	0	0	0	3-0	0	12	.206	.270	.235	44	-3	0-0	.864	-0	120	77	3b8	0	-0.3
Total	3	68	155	12	23	8	2	2	9	11-2	0	54	.148	.205	.265	30	-16	0-1	.908	-5	98	107	S33,3b14	15	-1.9
Butcher, Hank Henry Joseph; B7.12.1886 Chicago IL; D12.28.1979 Hazel Crest IL; BR/TR/5´10˝/180; d7.8																									
1911	Cle A	38	133	22	32	7	3	1	11	11	1	—	.241	.303	.361	84	-3	9	.984	1	104	102	O34(24/4/6)	—	-0.3
1912	Cle A	26	82	9	16	4	1	1	10	6	0	—	.195	.250	.305	57	-5	1	.920	1	106	112	O21L	—	-0.5
Total	2	64	215	31	48	11	4	2	21	17	1	—	.223	.283	.340	74	-8	10	.956	2	105	106	O55(45/4/6)	—	-0.8
Butera, Sal Salvatore Philip; B9.25.1952 Richmond Hill NY; BR/TR/6´0˝/(189–192); d4.10; C2; Col Suffolk (NY) CC																									
1980	Min A	34	85	4	23	1	0	0	2	3-0	1	6	.271	.300	.282	57	-5	0-0	.950	-6	115	111	C32,D2	0	-1.0
1981	Min A	62	167	13	40	7	1	0	18	22-0	0	14	.240	.325	.293	75	-4	0-0	.970	5	131	147	C59/1D	0	0.3
1982	Min A	54	126	9	32	2	0	0	8	17-0	1	12	.254	.347	.270	70	-5	0-0	.988	3	91	101	C53	0	0.0
1983	Det A	4	5	1	1	0	0	0	0	0-0	0	0	.200	.200	.200	11	-1	0-0	.929	1	107	0	C4	0	0.0
1984	Mon N	3	3	0	0	0	0	0	0	1-0	0	0	.000	.250	.000	-26	0	0-0	1.000	1	90	0	C2	0	0.0
1985	Mon N	67	120	11	24	1	0	3	12	13-1	1	12	.200	.281	.283	62	-6	0-0	.984	-6	64	76	C66/P	0	-1.1
1986	Cin N	56	113	14	27	6	1	2	16	21-3	0	10	.239	.356	.363	96	0	0-0	.979	-2	105	86	C53/P	0	-0.1
1987	Cin N	5	11	1	2	0	0	1	2	1-0	0	6	.182	.250	.455	79	0	0-0	.920	0	49	240	C5	0	0.0
	†Min A	51	111	7	19	5	0	1	12	7-0	0	16	.171	.217	.243	22	-13	0-0	.983	-5	65	123	C51	0	-1.6
1988	Tor A	23	60	3	14	2	1	1	6	1-0	0	9	.233	.246	.350	64	-3	0-0	.991	-0	110	71	C23	0	-0.3
Total	9	359	801	63	182	24	3	8	76	86-4	3	85	.227	.302	.295	65	-37	0-0	.978	-11	97	107	C348,D3,P2/1	0	-3.8
Butka, Ed Edward Luke "Babe"; B1.7.1916 Canonsburg PA; D4.21.2005 Pittsburgh PA; BR/TR/6´3˝/193; d9.26																									
1943	Was A	3	9	0	3	1	0	0	1	0	0	3	.333	.333	.444	132	0	0-0	1.000	1	217	57	1b3	0	0.1
1944	Was A	15	41	1	8	1	0	0	1	2	0	11	.195	.233	.220	31	-4	0-0	.972	-0	109	84	1b14	0	-0.5
Total	2	18	50	1	11	2	0	0	2	2	0	14	.220	.250	.260	48	-4	0-0	.977	1	127	80	1b17	0	-0.4
Butler, Art Arthur Edward (b Arthur Edward Bouthillier); B12.19.1887 Fall River MA; D10.7.1984 Fall River MA; BR/TR/5´9˝/160; d4.14																									
1911	Bos N	27	68	11	12	2	0	0	2	6	2	6	.176	.263	.206	30	-6	0	.930	-2	107	45	3b14,2b4/S	—	-0.9
1912	Pit N	43	154	19	42	4	2	1	17	15	0	13	.273	.337	.344	88	-3	2	.960	-15	80	75	2b43	—	-1.7
1913	Pit N	82	214	40	60	9	3	0	20	32	2	14	.280	.379	.350	114	6	9-5	.919	-15	82	75	2b28,S26,3b2,O2R	—	-0.7
1914	StL N	86	274	29	55	12	3	1	24	39	5	23	.201	.311	.277	76	-6	14	.927	-16	93	90	S83/cf	—	-1.8
1915	StL N	130	469	73	119	12	5	1	31	47	1	34	.254	.323	.307	91	-4	26-14	.916	-32	88	84	S125,2b2	—	-3.1
1916	StL N	86	110	9	23	5	0	0	7	7	0	12	.209	.256	.255	57	-5	3	.882	-3	77	0	O15(2/9/4),2b8/S3	—	-1.0
Total	6	454	1289	181	311	44	13	3	101	146	10	102	.241	.323	.303	85	-18	54-19	.919	-83	89	82	S236,2b85,O18(2/10/6),3b17	—	-9.2
Butler, Brett Brett Morgan; B6.15.1957 Los Angeles CA; BL/TL/5´10˝/(160–161); [AtlN79 23/573]; d8.20; C1; Col Southeastern Oklahoma																									
1981	Atl N	40	126	17	32	2	3	0	4	19-0	0	17	.254	.352	.317	91	-1	9-1	.987	-0	103	70	O37(25/11/5)	0	-0.1
1982	†Atl N	89	240	35	52	2	0	0	7	25-0	0	35	.217	.291	.225	45	-17	21-8	1.000	-6	87	56	O77C	0	-2.3
1983	Atl N	151	549	84	154	21	**13**	5	37	54-3	2	56	.281	.344	.393	98	-2	39-23	.987	6	101	140	O143(109/38/4)	0	0.0
1984	Cle A	159	602	108	162	25	9	3	49	86-1	4	62	.269	.361	.355	98	2	52-22	.991	2	101	123	O156(0/155/1)	0	0.6
1985	Cle A	152	591	106	184	28	14	5	50	63-2	1	42	.311	.377	.431	122	19	47-20	**.998**	14	108	199	O150C/D	0	3.4
1986	Cle A	161	587	92	163	17	**14**	4	51	70-1	4	65	.278	.356	.375	101	2	32-15	.993	1	101	104	O159C	0	0.3
1987	Cle A	137	522	91	154	25	8	9	41	91-0	1	55	.295	.399	.425	118	18	33-16	.990	7	112	66	O136C	19	2.4
1988	SF N	157	568	**109**	163	27	9	6	43	97-4	4	64	.287	.393	.398	134	30	43-20	.988	-3	101	43	O155C	0	3.0
1989	†SF N	154	594	100	168	22	4	4	36	59-2	3	69	.283	.349	.354	105	5	31-16	.986	4	104	137	O152C	0	0.9
1990	SF N	160	622	108	**192**	20	9	3	44	90-1	6	62	.309	.397	.384	121	22	51-19	.986	-8	99	44	O159C	0	1.8
1991	LA N★	161	615	**112**	182	13	5	2	38	**108-4**	1	79	.296	.401	.343	113	17	38-28	**1.000**	-5	97	91	O161C	0	1.0
1992	LA N	157	553	86	171	14	11	3	39	95-2	3	67	.309	.413	.391	130	27	41-21	.995	-7	92	108	O155C	0	2.2
1993	LA N	156	607	80	181	21	10	1	42	86-1	5	69	.298	.387	.371	111	13	39-19	**1.000**	-11	90	72	O155C	0	0.6
1994	LA N	111	417	79	131	13	**9**	8	33	68-0	2	52	.314	.411	.446	131	22	27-8	.993	1	99	138	O111C	0	2.6
1995	NY N	90	367	54	114	13	7	1	25	43-2	0	42	.311	.381	.392	109	5	21-7	.995	-0	98	124	O90C	0	0.8
	†LA N	39	146	24	40	5	2	0	13	24-0	0	9	.274	.368	.336	96	0	11-1	.987	-4	87	0	O38C	0	-0.1
	Year	129	513	78	154	18	**9**	1	38	67-2	0	51	.300	.377	.376	105	6	32-8	.993	-5	95	87	O128C	0	0.7
1996	LA N	34	131	22	35	1	1	0	8	9-0	1	22	.267	.313	.290	66	-7	8-3	.987	-1	101	62	O34C	127	-0.6
1997	LA N	105	343	52	97	8	3	0	18	42-0	1	40	.283	.363	.324	87	-5	15-10	1.000	-1	95	88	O91(47/49/0)/D	27	-0.8
Total	17	2213	8180	1359	2375	277	131	54	578	1129-23	38	907	.290	.377	.376	110	150	558-257	.992	-13	99	100	O2159(181/1986/10),D2	173	15.7
Butler, Frank Frank Dean "Stuffy","Goldbrick"; B7.18.1860 Savannah GA; D7.10.1945 Jacksonville FL; BL/TL/5´7˝/155; d7.30																									
1895	NY N	5	22	5	6	1	0	0	2	1	0	1	.273	.304	.318	62	-1	0	1.000	-0	0	0	O5(4/0/1)	—	-0.2
Butler, Kid Frank Edward; B5.1861 Boston MA; D4.9.1921 S.Boston MA; 5´6˝/140; d5.20																									
1884	Bos U	71	255	36	43	15	0	0	—	12	—	—	.169	.206	.227	32	-29	—	.810	-4	67	58	O53(37/7/9),2b12,S6,3b2	—	-3.0
Butler, John John Albert (aka Frederick King in 1901); B7.26.1879 Boston MA; D2.2.1950 Boston MA; BR/TR/5´7˝/170; d9.28; Col Fordham																									
1901	Mil A	1	3	0	0	0	0	0	0	1	0	—	.000	.250	.000	-28	0	0	1.000	-1	*46*	*0*	/C	—	-0.1
1904	StL N	12	37	0	6	1	0	0	1	4	1	—	.162	.262	.189	42	-2	0	.968	-2	*82*	*67*	C12	—	-0.4
1906	Bro N	1	0	0	0	0	0	0	0	0	0	—	ø	ø	ø	ø	0	0	1.000	0	*0*	*297*	/C	—	0.0
1907	Bro N	30	79	6	10	1	0	0	2	9	0	—	.127	.216	.139	12	-8	0	.946	-5	*85*	*99*	C28/lf	—	-1.2
Total	4	44	119	6	16	2	0	0	3	14	1	—	.134	.231	.151	21	-10	0	.953	-8	*83*	*90*	C42/lf	—	-1.7
Butler, Johnny John Stephen "Trolley Line"; B3.20.1893 Fall River KS; D4.29.1967 Seal Beach CA; BR/TR/6´0˝/175; d4.18; C1																									
1926	Bro N	147	501	54	135	27	5	1	68	54	5	44	.269	.346	.349	89	-6	6	.949	-2	95	68	S102,3b42,2b8	—	0.5
1927	Bro N	149	521	39	124	13	6	2	57	34	6	33	.238	.292	.298	58	-32	9	.959	-5	87	98	S90,3b60	—	-2.3
1928	Chi N	62	174	17	47	7	0	0	16	19	3	7	.270	.352	.310	75	-5	2	.950	5	109	93	3b59,S2	—	0.3
1929	StL N	17	55	5	9	1	1	0	5	4	0	5	.164	.220	.218	9	-8	0	.964	-1	78	0	3b9,S8	—	-0.7
Total	4	375	1251	115	315	48	12	3	146	111	14	89	.252	.320	.317	70	-51	17	.954	-3	91	82	S202,3b170,2b8	—	-2.2
Butler, Brent Justin Brent; B2.11.1978 Laurinburg NC; BR/TR/6´0˝/180; [StLN96 3/68]; d7.4																									
2001	Col N	53	119	17	29	7	1	1	14	7-0	1	7	.244	.287	.345	53	-8	1-1	.959	-2	103	118	2b23,S10,3b9	0	-0.9
2002	Col N	113	344	55	89	18	4	9	42	10-3	5	40	.259	.287	.413	72	-14	2-6	.974	-9	101	101	2b72,3b33,S13	0	-2.1
2003	Col N	37	90	13	19	3	1	1	4	7-2	1	13	.211	.276	.300	44	-7	1-0	.988	-4	99	74	2b20,3b8,S4	0	-1.0
Total	3	203	553	85	137	28	6	11	60	24-5	7	60	.248	.285	.380	63	-29	4-7	.973	-14	101	99	2b115,3b50,S27	0	-4.0
Butler, Rich Richard Dwight; B5.1.1973 Toronto ON, Can.; BL/TR/6´1˝/(190–205); d9.6; b–Rob																									
1997	Tor A	7	14	3	4	1	0	0	2	2-0	0	3	.286	.375	.357	92	0	0-1	1.000	-0	83	0	O3L/D	0	-0.1
1998	TB A	72	217	25	49	3	3	7	20	15-0	2	37	.226	.278	.364	65	-13	4-2	1.000	1	100	109	O61(39/0/22)	36	-1.3
1999	TB A	7	20	2	3	1	0	0	0	2-0	0	4	.150	.227	.200	10	-3	0-0	1.000	-1	80	0	O6(2/0/4)	11	-0.3
Total	3	86	251	30	56	5	3	7	22	19-0	2	44	.223	.280	.351	62	-16	4-3	1.000	-0	98	95	O70(44/0/26)/D	47	-1.7
Butler, Dick Richard H.; B12.1869 Brooklyn NY; D7.16.1917 New York NY; d6.16																									
1897	Lou N	10	38	3	7	0	0	0	2	0	0	—	.184	.184	.184	-3	-6	1	.818	-3	*93*	*119*	C10	—	-0.7
1899	Was N	12	36	4	10	0	1	0	1	2	0	—	.278	.316	.333	79	-1	1	.892	-4	*77*	*133*	C11	—	-0.4
Total	2	22	74	7	17	0	1	0	3	2	0	—	.230	.250	.257	37	-7	2	.852	-6	*85*	*126*	C21	—	-1.1

YEAR	TM LG	G	AB	R	H	2B	3B	HR	RBI	BB-IB	HP	SO	AVG	OBP	SLG	AOPS	ABR	SB-CS	FA	FR	RNG	THR	GAMES AT POSITION	DL	BFW
Butler, Rob	Robert Frank John; B4.10.1970 E.York ON, Can.; BL/TL/5´11˝/185; d6.12; b–Rich																								
1993	†Tor A	17	48	8	13	4	0	0	2	7-0	1	12	.271	.375	.354	95	0	2-2	.970	0	118	0	O16(15/1/0)	70	0.0
1994	Tor A	41	74	13	13	0	1	0	5	7-0	1	8	.176	.250	.203	20	-9	0-1	.977	-1	96	0	O31(17/13/2)/D	0	-1.0
1997	Phi N	43	89	10	26	9	1	0	13	5-0	0	8	.292	.326	.416	95	-1	1-0	1.000	2	92	334	O25(4/14/8)	22	0.1
1999	Tor A	8	7	1	1	0	0	0	1	0-0	1	0	.143	.250	.143	4	-1	0-0	1.000	-0	49	0	O2L,D3	76	-0.1
Total	4	109	218	32	53	13	2	0	21	19-0	3	28	.243	.309	.321	66	-11	3-3	.982	1	99	113	O74(38/28/10),D4	168	-1.0
Butler, Bill	William J.; B1861 New Orleans LA; d6.29																								
1884	Ind AA	9	31	7	7	3	2	0	—	1	0	—	.226	.250	.452	128	1	—	.700	-1	157	0	O9(1/1/7)	—	0.0
Butler, Kid	Willis Everett; B8.9.1887 Franklin PA; D2.22.1964 Richmond CA; BR/TR/5´11˝/155; d4.30																								
1907	StL A	20	59	4	13	2	0	0	6	2	0	—	.220	.246	.254	60	-3	1	.940	0	118	70	2b11,3b5/S	—	-0.2
Buttery, Frank	Frank; B5.13.1851 Silvermine CT; D12.16.1902 Norwalk CT; d4.26; ▲																								
1872	Man NA	18	93	16	20	0	0	0	7	0	—	2	.215	.215	.215	35	-7	0-0	.842	-0	131	0	P8,O8R,3b5	—	-0.3
Buzas, Joe	Joseph John; B10.2.1919 Alpha NJ; D3.19.2003 Salt Lake City UT; BR/TR/6´1˝/180; d4.17; Col Bucknell																								
1945	NY A	30	65	8	17	2	1	0	6	2	0	5	.262	.284	.323	73	-3	2-0	.898	-2	100	89	S12	0	-0.4
Byers, Bill	James William; B10.3.1877 Bridgeton IN; D9.8.1948 Baltimore MD; BL/TR/5´7˝/210; d4.15																								
1904	StL N	19	60	3	13	0	0	0	4	1	0	—	.217	.230	.217	40	-4	0	.971	-2	*89*	*55*	C16/1	—	-0.5
Byers, Randy	Randell Parker; B10.2.1964 Bridgeton NJ; BL/TR/6´2˝/180; [SDN84*S1/8]; d9.7; Col CC of Baltimore (MD)																								
1987	SD N	10	16	1	5	1	0	0	1	1-0	0	5	.313	.353	.375	97	0	1-0	1.000	0	83	391	O5L	0	0.0
1988	SD N	11	10	0	2	1	0	0	0	0-0	0	5	.200	.200	.300	43	-1	0-0	ø	-0	0	0	O2(1/0/1)	0	-0.1
Total	2	21	26	1	7	2	0	0	1	1-0	0	10	.269	.296	.346	77	-1	1-0	1.000	0	80	379	O7(6/0/1)	0	-0.1
Bynum, Freddie	Freddie Lee; B3.15.1980 Wilson NC; BL/TR/6´1˝/(180–185); [OakA00 2/60]; d8.30; Col Pitt Co. (NC) CC																								
2005	Oak A	7	7	0	2	1	0	0	1	0-0	0	3	.286	.286	.429	87	0	0-0	ø	-1	0	0	2b3,O2(1/1/0)	0	-0.1
2006	Chi N	71	136	20	35	5	5	4	12	9-0	1	44	.257	.308	.456	90	-3	8-4	.931	-1	114	0	O22(13/2/8),2b15	57	-0.3
Total	2	78	143	20	37	6	5	4	13	9-0	1	47	.259	.307	.455	90	-3	8-4	.941	-2	119	0	O24(14/3/8),2b18	57	-0.4
Byrd, Jim	James Edward; B10.3.1968 Wewahitchka FL; BR/TR/6´1˝/185; [BosA87 8/214]; d5.31; Col Seminole St. (OK) JC																								
1993	Bos A	2	0	0	0	0	0	0	0	0-0	0	0	ø	ø	ø	ø	0	0-0	ø	0	—	—	/R	0	0.0
Byrd, Marlon	Marlon Jerrard; B8.30.1977 Boynton Beach FL; BR/TR/6´0˝/(225–235); [PhiN99 10/306]; d9.8; Col Georgia Perimeter JC																								
2002	Phi N	10	35	2	8	2	0	1	1	1-0	0	8	.229	.250	.371	65	-2	0-2	1.000	-1	82	0	O10(0/8/2)	0	-0.4
2003	Phi N	135	495	86	150	28	4	7	45	44-3	7	94	.303	.366	.418	113	10	11-1	.984	-4	99	72	O131C	15	1.0
2004	Phi N	106	346	48	79	13	2	5	33	22-1	7	68	.228	.287	.321	55	-23	2-2	.990	-4	93	92	O92C	0	-2.6
2005	Was N	74	216	20	57	15	2	2	26	18-1	1	47	.264	.318	.380	87	-4	5-1	.985	4	109	155	O65(54/11/4),D2	0	-0.1
	Phi N	5	13	0	4	0	0	0	0	1-0	1	3	.308	.400	.308	86	0	0-0	1.000	-1	67	0	O5C	30	-0.1
	Year	79	229	20	61	15	2	2	26	19-1	2	50	.266	.323	.376	87	-4	5-1	.985	4	106	145	O70(54/16/4),D2	0	-0.2
2006	Was N	78	197	28	44	8	1	5	18	22-1	6	47	.223	.317	.350	75	-7	3-3	.987	2	113	36	O71(3/57/18)	0	-0.6
Total	5	408	1302	184	342	66	9	20	123	108-6	22	267	.263	.327	.373	85	-26	21-9	.986	-3	101	82	O374(57/304/24),D2	45	-2.8
Byrd, Sammy	Samuel Dewey "Babe Ruth's Legs"; B10.15.1906 Bremen GA; D5.11.1981 Mesa AZ; BR/TR/5´10.5˝/175; d5.11																								
1929	NY A	62	170	32	53	12	0	5	28	28	0	18	.312	.409	.471	135	10	1-4	.950	3	110	128	O54(6/16/32)	—	0.8
1930	NY A	92	218	46	62	12	2	6	31	30	0	18	.284	.371	.440	110	4	5-1	.992	1	110	48	O85(47/12/26)	—	0.1
1931	NY A	115	248	51	67	18	2	3	32	29	1	26	.270	.349	.395	101	1	5-0	.974	0	106	58	O88(26/34/34)	—	-0.1
1932	†NY A	105	209	49	62	12	1	8	30	30	0	20	.297	.385	.478	129	10	1-2	.964	-1	98	96	O91(11/70/11)	—	0.6
1933	NY A	85	107	26	30	6	1	2	11	15	0	12	.280	.369	.411	113	2	0-1	.987	3	131	42	O71(23/15/35)	—	0.3
1934	NY A	106	191	32	47	8	0	3	23	18	2	22	.246	.318	.335	73	-8	1-2	**.988**	6	**132**	44	O104(34/13/59)	—	-0.5
1935	Cin N	121	416	51	109	25	4	9	52	37	0	51	.262	.322	.406	97	-2	4	.970	-1	98	109	O115(39/76/0)	—	-0.7
1936	Cin N	59	141	17	35	8	0	2	13	11	0	11	.248	.303	.348	80	-4	0	.989	1	112	43	O37(15/22/0)	—	-0.4
Total	8	745	1700	304	465	101	10	38	220	198	3	178	.274	.350	.412	104	13	17-10	.975	11	109	78	O645(201/258/197)	—	0.1
Byrne, Bobby	Robert Matthew; B12.31.1884 St.Louis MO; D12.31.1964 Wayne PA; BR/TR/5´7.5˝/145; d4.11																								
1907	StL N	149	559	55	143	11	5	0	29	35	6	—	.256	.307	.293	91	-7	21	.920	21	112	117	3b148/S	—	2.0
1908	StL N	127	439	27	84	7	1	0	14	23	4	—	.191	.238	.212	46	-27	16	.925	10	105	91	3b122,S4	—	-1.6
1909	StL N	105	421	61	90	13	6	1	33	46	7	—	.214	.302	.280	86	-6	21	.922	13	116	74	3b105	—	1.1
	†Pit N	46	168	31	43	6	2	0	7	32	4	—	.256	.387	.315	109	4	8	.987	3	115	60	3b46	—	1.0
	Year	151	589	92	133	19	8	1	40	78	11	—	.226	.327	.290	93	-1	29	.939	16	**116**	70	3b151	—	2.1
1910	Pit N	148	602	101	**178**	**43**	12	2	52	66	1	27	.296	.366	.417	121	17	36	.929	-7	101	56	3b148	—	1.4
1911	Pit N	153	598	96	155	24	17	2	52	67	8	41	.259	.342	.366	94	-5	23	.930	-2	100	112	3b152	—	-0.3
1912	Pit N	130	528	99	152	31	11	3	35	54	4	40	.288	.358	.405	110	8	20	**.948**	-24	76	90	3b130	—	-1.2
1913	Pit N	113	448	54	121	22	0	1	47	29	5	28	.270	.322	.326	89	-6	10-16	.940	-10	83	96	3b110	—	-1.7
	Phi N	19	58	9	13	1	0	1	4	5	2	3	.224	.308	.293	69	-2	2-3	.963	0	104	0	3b15	—	-0.2
	Year	132	506	63	134	23	0	2	51	34	7	31	.265	.320	.322	86	-8	12-19	.943	-10	86	84	3b125	—	-1.9
1914	Phi N	126	467	61	127	12	1	0	26	45	2	44	.272	.339	.302	85	-7	9	.934	-1	109	47	2b101,3b22	—	-0.6
1915	†Phi N	105	387	50	81	6	4	0	21	39	5	28	.209	.290	.245	62	-17	4-12	**.969**	-5	94	75	3b105	—	-2.5
1916	Phi N	48	141	22	33	10	1	0	9	14	1	7	.234	.308	.319	89	-1	6	.933	1	99	149	3b40	—	0.1
1917	Phi N	13	14	1	5	0	0	0	0	1	0	2	.357	.400	.357	128	0	0	1.000	-1	33	0	3b4	—	0.0
	Chi A	1	1	0	0	0	0	0	0	0	0	0	.000	.000	.000	-98	0	0	1.000	0	154	0	/2	—	0.0
Total	11	1283	4831	667	1225	186	60	10	329	456	49	220	.254	.324	.323	91	-49	176-31	.934	-1	99	90	3b1147,2b102,S5	—	-2.5
Byrnes, Eric	Eric James; B2.16.1976 Redwood City CA; BR/TR/6´2˝/(205–210); [OakA98 8/225]; d8.22; Col UCLA																								
2000	Oak A	10	10	5	3	0	0	0	0	0-0	1	1	.300	.364	.300	72	0	2-1	1.000	0	131	0	O4(1/0/3),D2	0	0.0
2001	†Oak A	19	38	9	9	1	0	3	5	4-0	1	6	.237	.326	.500	113	1	1-0	.933	-2	74	0	O12(8/2/5),D5	0	-0.1
2002	†Oak A	90	94	24	23	4	2	3	11	4-0	3	17	.245	.291	.426	90	-2	3-0	.982	-3	84	56	O79(52/10/22),D6	0	-0.5
2003	†Oak A	121	414	64	109	27	9	12	51	42-4	2	71	.263	.333	.459	106	3	10-2	.991	-11	80	92	O117(44/82/2),D2	0	-0.6
2004	Oak A	143	569	91	161	39	3	20	73	46-0	12	111	.283	.347	.467	111	10	17-1	.989	-5	90	136	O141(109/33/20)/D	0	0.4
2005	Oak A	59	192	30	51	15	2	7	24	14-0	7	27	.266	.336	.474	114	4	2-2	.984	5	120	153	O54(51/2/4),D4	0	0.7
	Col N	15	53	2	10	2	0	0	5	7-0	0	11	.189	.283	.226	32	-5	2-0	.976	3	144	133	O14(4/4/8)	0	-0.3
	Bal A	52	167	17	32	7	1	3	11	11-0	1	33	.192	.246	.299	44	-14	3-0	.969	1	108	87	O51(51/1/1)	0	-1.4
2006	Ari N	143	562	82	150	37	3	26	79	34-2	5	88	.267	.313	.482	94	-6	25-3	.997	-7	93	76	O137(12/123/10)	0	-0.7
Total	7	652	2099	324	548	132	20	74	259	162-6	32	365	.261	.322	.449	97	-9	65-9	.988	-17	94	102	O609(332/257/75),D20	0	-2.5
Byrnes, Jim	James Joseph; B1.5.1880 San Francisco CA; D7.31.1941 San Francisco CA; BR/TR/5´9˝/150; d4.19																								
1906	Phi A	10	23	2	4	0	1	0	0	0	0	—	.174	.174	.261	34	-2	0	.889	-0	*103*	*122*	C9	—	-0.2
Byrnes, Milt	Milton John "Skippy"; B11.15.1916 St.Louis MO; D2.1.1979 St.Louis MO; BL/TL/5´10.5˝/170; d4.21																								
1943	StL A	129	429	58	120	28	7	4	50	53	2	49	.280	.362	.406	122	13	1-4	**.997**	7	104	150	O114(23/66/26)	0	1.4
1944	†StL A	128	407	63	120	20	4	4	45	68	0	50	.295	.396	.393	119	13	1-7	.976	0	105	73	O122(41/52/36)	0	0.6
1945	StL A	133	442	53	110	29	4	8	59	78	1	84	.249	.363	.387	112	10	1-3	.988	7	111	105	O125(31/56/47),1b2	0	1.0
Total	3	390	1278	174	350	77	15	16	154	199	3	183	.274	.373	.395	117	36	3-14	.987	14	107	109	O361(95/174/109),1b2	0	3.0
Caballero, Putsy	Ralph Joseph; B11.5.1927 New Orleans LA; BR/TR/5´11˝/(168–175); d9.14																								
1944	Phi N	4	4	0	0	0	0	0	0	0	0	1	.000	.000	.000	-99	-1	0	.889	1	119	0	3b2	0	-0.1
1945	Phi N	9	1	1	0	0	0	0	1	0	0	0	.000	.000	.000	-99	0	0	.857	0	87	417	3b5	0	0.0
1947	Phi N	2	7	2	1	0	0	0	0	1	0	0	.143	.250	.143	7	-1	0	1.000	0	117	102	2b2/3	0	-0.1
1948	Phi N	113	351	33	86	12	1	0	19	24	0	18	.245	.293	.285	58	-21	7	.962	5	103	114	3b79,2b23	0	-1.5
1949	Phi N	29	68	8	19	3	0	0	3	0	0	3	.279	.279	.324	63	-4	0	.981	0	92	106	2b21/S	0	-0.2
1950	†Phi N	46	24	12	4	0	0	0	0	2	0	2	.167	.231	.167	7	-3	1	.950	2	127	146	2b5,3b4,S2	0	-0.1
1951	Phi N	84	161	15	30	3	2	1	11	12	0	7	.186	.243	.248	33	-16	1-2	.985	-1	95	109	2b54,3b3/S	0	-1.5
1952	Phi N	35	42	10	10	3	0	0	6	2	0	3	.238	.273	.310	62	-2	1-0	.857	-0	110	148	S8,2b7,3b7	0	-0.2
Total	8	322	658	81	150	21	3	1	40	41	0	34	.228	.273	.274	49	-48	10-2	.968	7	96	104	2b112,3b101,S12	0	-3.7

YEAR	TM LG	G	AB	R	H	2B	3B	HR	RBI	BB-IB	HP	SO	AVG	OBP	SLG	AOPS	ABR	SB-CS	FA	FR	RNG	THR	GAMES AT POSITION	DL	BFW
CABELL, ENOS	Enos Milton; B10.8.1949 Fort Riley KS; BR/TR/6´5˝/(172–190); d9.17; Col Los Angeles Harbor (CA) JC; OF(42/1/72)																								
1972	Bal A	3	5	-0	0	0	0	0	1	0-0	0	0	.000	.000	.000	-96	-1	0-0	1.000	-0	0	134	/1	0	-0.2
1973	Bal A	32	47	12	10	2	0	1	3	3-0	0	7	.213	.250	.319	62	-2	1-3	.991	-2	54	149	1b23/3	0	-0.6
1974	†Bal A	80	174	24	42	4	2	3	17	7-1	0	20	.241	.269	.339	76	-6	5-3	.995	-0	109	118	1b28,O22(1/0/22),3b19/2D	0	-0.9
1975	Hou N	117	348	43	92	17	6	2	43	18-1	3	53	.264	.303	.365	92	-6	12-3	.973	3	85	231	O67(37/0/32),1b25,3b22	0	-0.5
1976	Hou N	144	586	85	160	13	7	2	43	29-1	2	79	.273	.309	.329	89	-12	35-8	.958	-2	97	88	3b143,1b3	0	-1.0
1977	Hou N	150	625	101	176	36	7	16	68	27-2	3	55	.282	.313	.438	108	3	42-22	.948	-1	97	76	3b144,1b8/S	0	0.2
1978	Hou N	**162**	660	92	195	31	8	7	71	22-1	5	80	.295	.321	.398	108	3	33-15	.958	-7	91	58	3b153,1b14/S	0	-0.5
1979	Hou N	155	603	60	164	30	5	6	67	21-7	3	68	.272	.299	.368	86	-14	37-18	.957	-20	76	54	3b132,1b51	0	-3.8
1980	†Hou N	152	604	69	167	23	8	2	55	26-6	1	84	.276	.305	.351	91	-11	21-13	.927	-12	89	71	3b150/1	0	-2.6
1981	SF N	96	396	41	101	20	1	2	36	10-0	1	47	.255	.274	.326	72	-16	6-7	.987	-2	**134**	99	1b69,3b22	0	-2.6
1982	Det A	125	464	45	121	17	3	2	37	15-2	1	48	.261	.284	.323	66	-22	15-6	.992	-1	123	127	1b83,3b59,O3(1/0/2)	0	-2.7
1983	Det A	121	392	62	122	23	5	5	46	16-2	1	41	.311	.335	.434	114	6	4-8	.997	5	121	108	1b106,3b4/SD	0	0.4
1984	Hou N	127	436	52	135	17	3	8	44	21-5	1	47	.310	.341	.417	120	10	8-11	.993	-1	95	**123**	1b112	0	0.0
1985	Hou N	60	143	20	35	8	1	2	14	16-0	0	15	.245	.321	.357	91	-2	3-1	.994	-1	92	106	1b49	0	-0.4
	†LA N	57	192	20	56	11	0	0	22	14-1	0	21	.292	.340	.349	95	-1	6-2	.920	3	117	137	3b32,1b21,O4(1/0/3)	0	0.1
	Year	117	335	40	91	19	1	2	36	30-1	0	36	.272	.332	.352	93	-2	9-3	.993	2	79	90	1b70,3b32,O4(1/0/3)	0	-0.3
1986	LA N	107	277	27	71	11	0	2	29	14-2	2	26	.256	.294	.318	75	-10	10-4	.987	3	105	85	1b61,O16(2/1/13),3b7	0	-1.1
Total	15	1688	5952	753	1647	263	56	60	596	259-31	23	691	.277	.308	.370	93	-81	238-124	.944	-33	92	74	3b888,1b655,O112R,D9,S3/2	0	-16.2
CABRERA, ALEX	Alexander Alberto; B12.24.1971 Caripito, Monagas, Venez.; BR/TR/6´2˝/217; d6.26																								
2000	Ari N	31	80	10	21	2	1	5	14	4-0	1	21	.262	.299	.500	95	-1	0-0	1.000	1	84	104	1b15,O12(1/0/11)	14	-0.1
CABRERA, AL	Alfredo A.; B5.11.1881 Canary Islands, Spain; D1964 Batabano, Cuba; TR; d5.16																								
1913	StL N	1	2	0	0	0	0	0	0	0	0	0	.000	.000	.000	-99	-1	0	ø	-0	0	0	/S	—	-0.1
CABRERA, FRANCISCO	Francisco (Paulino); B10.10.1966 Santo Domingo, D.R.; BR/TR/6´4˝/(193–195); d7.24																								
1989	Tor A	3	12	1	2	1	0	0	0	1-0	0	3	.167	.231	.250	36	-1	0-0	ø	0	—	—	D3	0	-0.1
	Atl N	4	14	0	3	2	0	0	0	0-0	0	3	.214	.214	.357	59	-1	0-0	1.000	-1	69	68	1b2/C	0	-0.2
1990	Atl N	63	137	14	38	5	1	7	25	5-0	0	21	.277	.301	.482	106	0	1-0	.990	-1	90	64	1b48,C3	0	-0.2
1991	†Atl N	44	95	7	23	6	0	4	23	6-0	0	20	.242	.284	.432	94	-1	1-1	.987	-1	104	78	C17,1b14	0	-0.2
1992	†Atl N	12	10	2	3	0	0	2	3	1-0	0	1	.300	.364	.900	232	2	0-0	ø	-0	0	0	/C	0	0.1
1993	†Atl N	70	83	8	20	3	0	4	11	8-1	0	21	.241	.308	.422	91	-1	0-0	1.000	2	174	69	1b12,C2	0	0.0
Total	5	196	351	32	89	17	1	17	62	21-1	0	69	.254	.294	.453	99	-2	2-1	.989	-1	113	66	1b76,C24,D3	0	-0.6
CABRERA, JOLBERT	Jolbert Alexis; B12.8.1972 Cartagena, Colombia; BR/TR/6´0˝/(177–195); d4.12; b–Orlando; OF(124/128/66)																								
1998	Cle A	1	2	0	0	0	0	0	0	0-0	0	1	.000	.000	.000	-96	-1	0-0	1.000	0	122	0	/S	0	0.0
1999	Cle A	30	37	6	7	1	0	0	0	1-0	1	8	.189	.231	.216	14	-5	3-0	.957	1	109	0	O16(4/12/0),2b6	0	-0.3
2000	Cle A	100	175	27	44	3	1	2	15	8-0	2	15	.251	.290	.314	52	-13	6-4	.989	4	105	145	O74(24/26/29),2b19,S8,D2	0	-0.9
2001	†Cle A	141	287	50	75	16	3	1	38	16-0	6	41	.261	.312	.348	72	-12	10-4	.978	-0	93	40	O83(36/35/18),2b28,3b27,S14/D	0	-1.0
2002	Cle A	38	72	5	8	1	0	0	7	5-0	1	13	.111	.177	.125	-17	-12	1-1	1.000	-1	89	0	O34(5/16/13),2b3/D	32	-1.3
	LA N	10	12	3	4	1	0	0	1	2-0	0	2	.333	.429	.417	131	1	0-0	1.000	1	158	0	O4(3/0/1),3b3/2	0	0.1
2003	LA N	128	347	43	98	32	2	6	37	17-3	10	62	.282	.332	.438	102	1	6-4	.967	-4	67	143	O63(31/38/4),2b59,S9,1b8,3b5	0	-0.2
2004	Sea A	113	359	38	97	19	2	6	47	16-1	8	70	.270	.312	.384	85	-8	10-3	.970	-4	106	135	3b36,1b23,O23(21/1/1),2b18,S14,D5	0	-1.1
Total	7	561	1291	172	333	73	8	15	145	65-4	28	212	.258	.305	.362	74	-49	36-16	.981	-4	94	97	O297C,2b134,3b71,S46,1b31,D9	32	-4.7
CABRERA, MIGUEL	Jose Miguel (Torres); B4.18.1983 Maracay, Aragua, Venezuela; BR/TR/6´2˝/(180–210); d6.20																								
2003	†Fla N	87	314	39	84	21	3	12	62	25-3	2	84	.268	.325	.468	108	3	0-2	.972	-4	102	151	O55L,3b34	0	-0.3
2004	Fla N★	160	603	101	177	31	1	33	112	68-5	6	148	.294	.366	.512	132	28	5-2	.968	-3	91	142	O158(59/0/100)/D	0	1.8
2005	Fla N★	158	613	106	198	43	2	33	116	64-12	2	125	.323	.385	.561	153	47	1-0	.976	-6	81	168	O134L,3b29	0	3.6
2006	Fla N★	158	576	112	195	50	2	26	114	86-27	10	108	.339	.430	.568	161	58	9-6	.957	-10	87	108	3b157/D	0	4.7
Total	4	563	2106	358	654	145	8	104	404	243-47	20	465	.311	.384	.535	143	136	15-10	.971	-22	89	153	O347(248/0/100),3b220,D2	0	9.8
CABRERA, MELKY	Melky; B8.11.1984 Santo Domingo, D.R.; BB/TL/5´11˝/170; d7.7																								
2005	NY A	6	19	1	4	0	0	0	0	0-0	0	2	.211	.211	.211	13	-2	0-0	1.000	-1	64	0	O6C	0	-0.4
2006	†NY A	130	460	75	129	26	2	7	50	56-3	2	59	.280	.360	.391	95	-2	12-5	.992	3	98	134	O127(116/4/8)	0	-0.3
Total	2	136	479	76	133	26	2	7	50	56-3	2	61	.278	.355	.384	92	-4	12-5	.993	1	97	128	O133(116/10/8)	0	-0.7
CABRERA, ORLANDO	Orlando Luis; B11.2.1974 Cartagena, Colombia; BR/TR/5´10˝/(150–190); d9.3; b–Jolbert																								
1997	Mon N	16	18	4	4	0	0	0	2	1-0	0	3	.222	.263	.222	29	-2	1-2	.875	1	150	126	S6,2b4	0	-0.1
1998	Mon N	79	261	44	73	16	5	3	22	18-1	0	27	.280	.325	.414	96	-2	6-2	.984	-5	91	69	S52,2b28	0	-0.2
1999	Mon N	104	382	48	97	23	5	8	39	18-4	3	38	.254	.293	.403	77	-16	2-2	.979	15	107	98	S102	56	0.6
2000	Mon N	125	422	47	100	25	1	13	55	25-3	1	28	.237	.279	.393	67	-23	4-4	.981	8	108	104	S124/2	30	-0.6
2001	Mon N	**162**	626	64	173	41	6	14	96	43-5	4	54	.276	.324	.428	94	-7	19-7	**.986**	29	**113**	105	S162	0	3.5
2002	Mon N	153	563	64	148	43	1	7	56	48-4	2	53	.263	.321	.380	80	-15	25-7	.962	21	113	103	S153	0	2.1
2003	Mon N	**162**	626	95	186	47	2	17	80	52-3	1	64	.297	.347	.460	107	7	24-2	.975	6	101	104	S162	0	2.9
2004	Mon N	103	390	41	96	19	2	4	31	28-0	2	31	.246	.298	.336	62	-22	12-3	.984	4	103	109	S101	0	-0.9
	†Bos A	58	228	33	67	19	1	6	31	11-0	1	23	.294	.320	.465	98	-1	4-1	.966	-6	94	68	S57	0	-0.2
2005	†LA A	141	540	70	139	28	3	8	57	38-4	3	50	.257	.309	.365	81	-15	21-2	**.988**	-15	87	96	S140	19	-1.5
2006	LA A	153	607	95	171	45	1	9	72	51-0	3	58	.282	.335	.404	95	-3	27-3	.975	-4	89	**110**	S152	0	0.8
Total	10	1256	4663	605	1254	306	27	89	541	333-24	20	429	.269	.317	.403	86	-99	145-35	.978	54	102	101	S1211,2b33	105	6.4
CACEK, CRAIG	Craig Thomas; B9.10.1954 Hollywood CA; BR/TR/6´1˝/195; [NYN72 9/205]; d6.18																								
1977	Hou N	7	20	0	1	0	0	0	1	1-0	0	3	.050	.095	.050	-65	-5	0-0	.981	-1	31	161	1b6	0	-0.7
CACERES, EDGAR	Edgar Fidel; B6.6.1964 Barquisimeto, Lara, Venez.; BB/TR/6´1˝/170; d6.8																								
1995	KC A	55	117	13	28	6	2	1	17	8-0	1	15	.239	.291	.350	65	-6	2-2	.992	0	102	66	2b36,S8,1b6,3b3,D3	15	-0.5
CADY, CHARLIE	Charles B.; B12.1865 Chicago IL; D6.7.1909 Kankakee IL; 5´11˝/180; d9.5; ▲																								
1883	Cle N	3	11	0	0	0	0	0	0	1	—	5	.000	.083	.000	-73	-2	—	1.000	-0	0	0	O2R/P	—	-0.1
1884	CP U	6	20	4	2	1	1	0	—	1	—	—	.100	.143	.250	17	-3	—	.909	-0	76	0	P4,O2C	—	-0.1
	KC U	2	3	0	0	0	0	0	—	0	—	—	.000	.000	.000	-99	-1	—	.600	-2	—	—	/C2	—	-0.3
	Year	8	23	4	2	1	1	0	—	1	—	—	.087	.125	.217	2	-4	—	.909	-2	76	0	P4,O2C/C2	—	-0.4
Total	2	11	34	4	2	1	1	0	0	2	—	5	.059	.111	.147	-23	-6	—	.917	-3	—	—	P5,O4(0/2/2)/2C	—	-0.5
CADY, HICK	Forrest Leroy (b Forrest Leroy Bergland); B1.26.1886 Bishop Hill IL; D3.3.1946 Cedar Rapids IA; BR/TR/6´2˝/179; d4.26																								
1912	†Bos A	47	135	19	35	13	2	0	9	10	3	—	.259	.324	.385	98	0	0	.990	9	*126*	*93*	C43,1b4	—	1.2
1913	Bos A	40	96	10	24	5	2	0	6	5	1	14	.250	.294	.344	84	-2	1	.992	4	*98*	*91*	C39	—	0.4
1914	Bos A	61	159	14	41	6	1	0	8	12	0	22	.258	.310	.308	86	-3	2-1	.971	2	*121*	*109*	C58	—	0.4
1915	†Bos A	78	205	25	57	10	2	0	17	19	1	25	.278	.342	.346	109	2	0-2	.980	4	*117*	*87*	C77	—	1.2
1916	†Bos A	78	162	5	31	6	3	0	13	15	1	16	.191	.264	.265	59	-9	0	.967	-5	126	72	C63,1b3	—	-1.1
1917	Bos A	17	46	4	7	1	1	0	2	1	0	6	.152	.170	.217	18	-5	0	.959	1	*125*	*99*	C14	—	-0.4
1919	Phi N	34	98	6	21	6	0	1	19	4	1	8	.214	.252	.306	63	-4	1	.984	-6	*74*	*111*	C29	—	-0.9
Total	7	355	901	83	216	47	11	1	74	66	7	91	.240	.297	.320	82	-21	4-3	.979	8	*115*	*93*	C323,1b7	—	0.8
CAFEGO, TOM	Thomas; B8.21.1911 Whipple WV; D10.29.1961 Detroit MI; BL/TR/5´10˝/160; d9.3																								
1937	StL A	4	4	1	0	0	0	0	0	0	0	1	.000	.000	.000	-99	-1	0-0	.500	-0	83	0	/lf	—	-0.1
CAFFIE, JOE	Joseph Clifford "Rabbit"; B2.14.1931 Ramer AL; BL/TR/5´10.5˝/180; d9.13; Negro Lg 1950																								
1956	Cle A	12	38	7	13	0	0	0	1	4-0	2	8	.342	.432	.342	104	1	3-2	1.000	1	106	134	O10L	0	0.1
1957	Cle A	32	89	14	24	2	1	3	10	4-2	0	11	.270	.301	.416	95	-1	0-1	.976	0	120	0	O19(3/0/18)	0	-0.2
Total	2	44	127	21	37	2	1	3	11	8-2	2	19	.291	.343	.394	99	0	3-3	.984	1	115	47	O29(13/0/18)	0	-0.1
CAFFYN, BEN	Benjamin Thomas; B2.10.1880 Peoria IL; D11.22.1942 Peoria IL; BL/TL/5´10˝/175; d8.21																								
1906	Cle A	30	103	16	20	4	0	0	3	12	2	—	.194	.291	.233	65	-3	2	.909	-3	60	308	O29(28/1/0)	—	-0.9

YEAR	TM LG	G	AB	R	H	2B	3B	HR	RBI	BB-IB	HP	SO	AVG	OBP	SLG	AOPS	ABR	SB-CS	FA	FR	RNG	THR	GAMES AT POSITION	DL	BFW
CAGE, WAYNE	Wayne Levell; B11.23.1951 Monroe LA; BL/TL/6´4˝/175; [CleA71 3/55]; d4.22																								
1978	Cle A	36	98	11	24	6	1	4	13	9-0	0	28	.245	.308	.449	111	1	1-2	.988	1	140	131	D20,1b11	0	0.0
1979	Cle A	29	56	6	13	2	0	1	6	5-0	0	16	.232	.295	.321	66	-3	0-2	1.000	0	126	72	1b7,D9	0	-0.3
Total	2	65	154	17	37	8	1	5	19	14-0	0	44	.240	.304	.403	94	-2	1-4	.992	1	135	111	D29,1b18	0	-0.3
CAHILL, JOHN	John Patrick Parnell "Patsy"; B4.30.1865 San Francisco CA; D10.31.1901 Pleasanton CA; BR/TR/5´7.5˝/168; d5.31; ▲																								
1884	Col AA	59	210	28	46	3	3	0	—	6	2	—	.219	.248	.262	72	-6	—	.843	-0	79	0	O56L,S5,P2	—	-0.7
1886	StL N	125	463	43	92	17	6	1	32	9	—	79	.199	.214	.268	49	-28	16	.866	2	141	131	O124(0/1/123),P2/S3	—	-2.5
1887	Ind N	68	263	22	54	4	3	0	26	9	1	5	.205	.234	.243	34	-24	34	.826	-5	108	49	O56(0/3/53),3b9,P6/S	—	-2.4
Total	3	252	936	93	192	24	12	1	58	24	3	84	.205	.227	.260	49	-58	50	.851	-4	119	81	O236(56/4/176),3b10,P10,S7	—	-5.6
CAHILL, TOM	Thomas H.; B10.1868 Fall River MA; D12.25.1894 Scranton PA; 5´7˝/150; d4.9; Col Penn																								
1891	Lou AA	119	430	68	109	17	7	3	44	41	6	51	.253	.327	.347	94	-4	38	.930	-8	*83*	*122*	C55,S49,O12(9/2/1),2b6,3b2	—	-0.5
CAIRO, MIGUEL	Miguel Jesus; B5.4.1974 Anaco, Anzoategui, Venez.; BR/TR/6´1˝/(160–210); d4.17; OF(50/0/12)																								
1996	Tor A	9	27	5	6	2	0	0	1	2-0	1	9	.222	.300	.296	52	-2	0-0	1.000	-1	77	95	2b9	0	-0.2
1997	Chi N	16	29	7	7	1	0	0	1	2-0	1	3	.241	.313	.276	54	-2	0-0	1.000	0	83	129	2b9,S2	0	-0.1
1998	TB A	150	515	49	138	26	5	5	46	24-0	6	44	.268	.307	.367	73	-21	19-8	.978	17	107	122	2b148,D2	0	0.4
1999	TB A	120	465	61	137	15	5	3	36	24-0	7	46	.295	.335	.368	79	-15	22-7	.986	27	**111**	**117**	2b117,D2	39	1.8
2000	TB A	119	375	49	98	18	2	1	34	29-0	2	34	.261	.314	.328	65	-20	28-7	.983	5	99	111	2b108,D2	0	-0.6
2001	Chi N	66	123	20	35	3	1	2	9	16-1	0	21	.285	.364	.374	95	-1	2-1	.900	-4	73	145	3b40,2b11/S	0	-0.4
	†StL N	27	33	5	11	5	0	1	7	2-0	0	2	.333	.371	.576	137	2	0-0	1.000	-0	174	0	O6L,2b5,3b3/1S	0	0.2
	Year	93	156	25	46	8	1	3	16	18-1	0	23	.295	.366	.417	104	1	2-1	.882	-5	71	142	3b43,2b16,O6L,S2/1	0	-0.2
2002	†StL N	108	184	28	46	9	2	2	23	13-2	3	36	.250	.307	.353	74	-7	1-1	.905	-2	94	0	O24(19/0/5),2b18,3b7,S6,1b4,D3	0	-0.9
2003	StL N	92	261	41	64	15	2	5	32	13-1	6	30	.245	.289	.375	75	-10	4-1	.986	-14	87	75	2b40,O27(22/0/6),3b12,S7,1b3	40	-2.3
2004	†NY A	122	360	48	105	17	5	6	42	18-1	14	49	.292	.346	.417	99	-1	11-3	.987	-5	93	97	2b113,3b8,S3/1	0	0.1
2005	NY N	100	327	31	82	18	0	2	19	19-2	4	31	.251	.296	.324	65	-17	13-3	.984	-1	99	122	2b82,1b8,3b3,O3(2/0/1)	17	-1.3
2006	NY A	81	222	28	53	12	3	0	30	13-0	1	31	.239	.280	.320	56	-15	13-1	.990	3	108	112	2b45,1b16,S14,3b8/lfD	36	-0.7
Total	11	1010	2921	372	782	141	25	27	280	175-7	45	336	.268	.316	.361	75	-109	113-32	.984	27	102	112	2b705,3b81,O61L,S34,1b33,D11	132	-4.0
CAITHAMER, GEORGE	George Theodore "Sidee"; B7.22.1910 Chicago IL; D6.1.1954 Chicago IL; BR/TR/5´10˝/168; d9.17																								
1934	Chi A	5	19	1	6	1	0	0	3	1	0	5	.316	.350	.368	83	0	0-0	.958	-1	*59*	*75*	C5	—	-0.1
CALDERON, IVAN	Ivan (Perez); B3.19.1962 Fajardo, PR; D12.27.2003 Loiza, PR; BR/TR/6´1˝/(160–221); d8.10																								
1984	Sea A	11	24	2	5	1	0	1	1	2-0	0	5	.208	.269	.375	77	-1	1-0	1.000	0	110	0	O11(4/6/1)	17	-0.1
1985	Sea A	67	210	37	60	16	4	8	28	19-1	2	45	.286	.349	.514	132	9	4-2	.981	1	95	151	O53(33/1/22),1b2,D3	0	0.7
1986	Sea A	37	131	13	31	5	0	2	13	6-0	1	33	.237	.275	.321	61	-7	3-1	.937	-1	86	187	O32(2/2/31)	0	-0.9
	Chi A	13	33	3	10	2	1	0	2	3-1	0	6	.303	.361	.424	109	0	0-0	.900	0	135	0	O5L,D6	0	0.0
	Year	50	164	16	41	7	1	2	15	9-1	1	39	.250	.293	.341	71	-7	3-1	.932	-1	90	170	O37(7/2/31),D6	0	-0.9
1987	Chi A	144	542	93	159	38	2	28	83	60-6	1	109	.293	.362	.526	129	23	10-5	.984	-1	101	76	O139(6/0/135),D3	15	1.4
1988	Chi A	73	264	40	56	14	0	14	35	34-2	0	66	.212	.299	.424	101	0	4-4	.954	-1	96	119	O67(4/0/63),D3	79	-0.3
1989	Chi A	157	622	83	178	34	9	14	87	43-7	3	94	.286	.332	.437	118	13	7-1	.978	-2	99	104	O103(17/0/89),D36,1b26	0	0.7
1990	Chi A	158	607	85	166	44	2	14	74	51-7	1	79	.273	.327	.422	111	9	32-16	.975	-1	100	84	O130(130/0/3),D27,1b2	0	0.5
1991	Mon N★	134	470	69	141	22	3	19	75	53-4	3	64	.300	.368	.481	140	26	31-16	.974	-1	104	43	O122L,1b4	0	2.3
1992	Mon N	48	170	19	45	14	2	3	24	14-1	1	22	.265	.323	.424	111	2	1-2	.988	-1	92	100	O46L	119	-0.1
1993	Bos A	73	213	25	47	8	2	1	19	21-1	1	28	.221	.291	.291	54	-14	4-2	1.000	1	111	69	O47(9/2/39),D19	19	-1.5
	Chi A	9	26	1	3	2	0	0	3	0-0	0	5	.115	.115	.192	-19	-4	0-0	ø	0	—	—	D6	0	-0.5
	Year	82	239	26	50	10	2	1	22	21-1	1	33	.209	.274	.280	47	-18	4-2	1.000	1	111	69	O47(9/2/39),D25	0	-2.0
Total	10	924	3312	470	901	200	25	104	444	306-30	13	556	.272	.333	.442	113	56	97-49	.976	-5	100	90	O755(378/11/383),D103,1b34	249	2.2
CALDERONE, SAM	Samuel Francis; B2.6.1926 Beverly NJ; BR/TR/5´10.5˝/(180–185); d4.19; Mil 1951–52																								
1950	NY N	34	67	9	20	1	0	1	12	2	0	5	.299	.319	.358	77	-2	0	.972	-2	*156*	*81*	C33	0	-0.3
1953	NY N	35	45	4	10	2	0	0	8	1	0	4	.222	.239	.267	31	-5	0-0	.966	0	*157*	*101*	C31	0	-0.4
1954	Mil N	22	29	3	11	2	0	0	5	4	0	4	.379	.441	.448	146	2	0-0	1.000	2	*102*	*67*	C16	0	0.4
Total	3	91	141	16	41	5	0	1	25	7	0	13	.291	.322	.348	76	-5	0-0	.978	-0	*144*	*84*	C80	0	-0.3
CALDWELL, BRUCE	Bruce; B2.8.1906 Ashton RI; D2.15.1959 West Haven CT; BR/TR/6´0˝/195; d6.30; Col Yale																								
1928	Cle A	18	27	2	6	1	1	0	3	2	1	2	.222	.300	.333	66	-1	1-0	1.000	0	97	159	O10R/1	—	-0.2
1932	Bro N	7	11	2	1	0	0	0	2	2	0	2	.091	.231	.091	-10	-2	0	.875	-1	0	53	1b6	—	-0.3
Total	2	25	38	4	7	1	1	0	5	4	1	4	.184	.279	.263	44	-3	1-0	1.000	-1	97	159	O10R,1b7	—	-0.5
CALDWELL, RAY	Raymond Benjamin "Rube","Sum"; B4.26.1888 Corydon PA; D8.17.1967 Salamanca NY; BL/TR/6´2˝/190; d9.9; ▲																								
1910	NY A	6	6	0	0	0	0	0	0	0	0	—	.000	.000	.000	-95	-1	0	1.000	-0	66	0	P6	—	0.0
1911	NY A	59	147	14	40	4	1	0	17	11	0	—	.272	.323	.313	73	-5	5	.953	-2	76	103	P41,O11(5/0/5)	—	-0.3
1912	NY A	44	76	18	18	1	2	0	6	5	0	—	.237	.284	.303	64	-4	4	.938	1	111	125	P30/lf	—	0.0
1913	NY A	59	97	10	28	3	2	0	11	3	0	15	.289	.310	.361	96	-1	3	**1.000**	-1	87	63	P27,O3(0/1/2)	—	-0.1
1914	NY A	59	113	9	22	4	0	0	10	7	1	24	.195	.248	.230	44	-8	2-1	.967	-4	74	101	P31,1b6	—	-0.5
1915	NY A	72	144	27	35	4	1	4	20	9	0	32	.243	.288	.368	96	-8	4-3	**.988**	-3	80	161	P36	—	0.0
1916	NY A	45	93	6	19	2	0	0	4	2	0	17	.204	.221	.226	34	-8	1	.960	-0	93	111	P21,O2	—	0.0
1917	NY A	63	124	12	32	6	1	2	12	16	0	16	.258	.343	.371	117	3	2	.973	-2	88	43	P32,O8(0/5/3)	—	-0.1
1918	NY A	65	151	14	44	10	0	1	18	13	1	23	.291	.352	.377	117	3	2	.977	-3	73	49	P24,O19(2/12/5)	—	-0.1
1919	Bos A	33	48	5	13	1	1	0	4	0	0	9	.271	.271	.333	73	-2	0	.950	-2	78	0	P18,O2L	—	-0.1
	Cle A	6	23	4	8	4	0	0	2	0	0	4	.348	.348	.522	134	3	0	.900	-1	56	0	P6	—	0.0
	Year	39	71	9	21	5	1	0	6	0	0	13	.296	.296	.394	97	-1	0	.933	-3	70	0	P24,O2L	—	-0.1
1920	†Cle A	41	89	17	19	3	0	0	7	10	1	13	.213	.300	.247	45	1	0-2	.917	-3	80	0	P34	—	0.0
1921	Cle A	38	53	2	11	4	0	1	3	2	0	5	.208	.236	.340	45	0	0-0	.930	-0	93	83	P37	—	0.0
Total	12	590	1164	138	289	46	8	8	114	78	3	158	.248	.297	.322	78	-11	23-6	.960	-21	83	80	P343,O46(11/18/15),1b6	—	-1.2
CALHOUN, JACK	John Charles "Red"; B12.14.1879 Pittsburgh PA; D2.27.1947 Cincinnati OH; BR/TR/6´0˝/185; d6.27																								
1902	StL N	20	64	3	10	2	1	0	8	8	1	—	.156	.260	.219	50	-4	1	.972	-1	89	66	3b12,1b5/rf	—	-0.5
CALHOUN, BILL	William Davitte "Mary"; B6.23.1890 Rockmart GA; D1.28.1955 Sandersville GA; BL/TL/6´0˝/180; d4.24; Col Georgia Tech																								
1913	Bos N	6	13	0	1	0	0	0	0	0	0	3	.077	.077	.077	-55	-3	0	.970	-0	67	70	1b3	—	-0.3
CALLAGHAN, MARTY	Martin Francis; B6.9.1900 Norwood MA; D6.23.1975 Norfolk MA; BL/TL/5´10˝/157; d4.13																								
1922	Chi N	74	175	31	45	7	4	0	20	17	1	17	.257	.326	.343	71	-7	2-3	.946	-4	96	38	O53(12/10/31)	—	-1.4
1923	Chi N	61	129	18	29	1	3	0	14	8	1	18	.225	.275	.279	47	-10	2-5	.969	-0	100	98	O38(19/0/19)	—	-1.4
1928	Cin N	81	238	29	69	11	4	0	24	27	0	10	.290	.362	.370	93	-2	5	.980	-1	97	97	O69(48/22/1)	—	-0.6
1930	Cin N	79	225	28	62	9	2	0	16	19	1	25	.276	.335	.333	66	-12	1	.986	1	106	71	O54(16/38/0)	—	-1.3
Total	4	295	767	106	205	28	13	0	74	71	3	70	.267	.332	.338	72	-31	10-8	.973	-4	100	77	O214(95/70/51)	—	-4.7
CALLAGHAN, PAT	Patrick J.; B New York NY; d5.1																								
1884	Ind AA	61	258	38	67	8	5	2	—	8	0	—	.260	.282	.353	109	2	—	.812	-9	83	67	3b61	—	-0.5
CALLAHAN, DAVE	David Joseph; B7.20.1888 Seneca IL; D10.28.1969 Ottawa IL; BL/TR/5´10˝/165; d9.14																								
1910	Cle A	13	44	6	8	1	0	0	2	4	1	—	.182	.265	.205	47	-3	5	1.000	-0	123	0	O12L	—	-0.4
1911	Cle A	6	16	1	4	0	1	0	0	1	0	—	.250	.294	.375	85	-1	0	.875	1	64	342	O4C	—	0.0
Total	2	19	60	7	12	1	1	0	2	5	1	—	.200	.273	.250	58	-4	5	.972	1	111	71	O16(12/4/0)	—	-0.4
CALLAHAN, ED	Edward Joseph; B12.11.1857 Boston MA; D2.5.1947 New York NY; d7.19																								
1884	StL U	1	3	0	0	0	0	0	—	0	—	—	.000	.000	.000	-96	-1	—	1.000	1	708	0	/lf	—	0.0
	KC U	3	11	0	4	0	0	0	—	0	—	—	.364	.364	.364	139	0	—	.800	1	139	192	S3	—	0.1
	Bos U	4	13	2	5	0	0	0	—	1	—	—	.385	.429	.385	150	1	—	.750	-1	0	0	O4(1/0/3)	—	0.0
	Year	8	27	2	9	0	0	0	—	1	—	—	.333	.357	.333	116	0	—	.778	1	86	0	O5(2/0/3),S3	—	0.1

YEAR	TM LG	G	AB	R	H	2B	3B	HR	RBI	BB-IB	HP	SO	AVG	OBP	SLG	AOPS	ABR	SB-CS	FA	FR	RNG	THR	GAMES AT POSITION	DL	BFW
CALLAHAN, NIXEY	James Joseph; B3.18.1874 Fitchburg MA; D10.4.1934 Boston MA; BR/TR/5´10.5˝/180; d5.12; M7; OF(401/30/59); ▲																								
1894	Phi N	9	21	4	5	0	0	0	0	0	0	7	.238	.238	.238	15	-1	0	.923	1	125	0	P9	—	0.0
1897	Chi N	94	360	60	105	18	6	3	47	10	5	—	.292	.320	.400	86	-9	12	.918	3	102	95	2b30,P23,O21(12/9/0),S18,3b2	—	-0.3
1898	Chi N	43	164	27	43	7	5	0	22	4	0	—	.262	.280	.366	85	-5	3	.947	-2	93	145	P31,O9(1/0/8)/S21	—	-0.3
1899	Chi N	47	150	21	39	4	3	0	18	8	2	—	.260	.306	.327	76	-5	9	.904	4	128	95	P35,O9(0/7/2),S2/2	—	0.0
1900	Chi N	32	115	16	27	3	2	0	9	6	0	—	.235	.273	.296	59	2	5	.975	6	131	104	P32	—	0.0
1901	Chi A	45	118	15	39	7	3	1	19	10	0	—	.331	.383	.466	138	6	10	.944	4	**135**	159	P27,3b6,2b2	—	0.2
1902	Chi A	70	218	27	51	7	2	0	13	6	2	—	.234	.261	.284	53	-14	4	.941	4	129	**250**	P35,O23(6/3/15)/S	—	-0.4
1903	Chi A	118	439	47	128	26	5	2	56	20	1	—	.292	.324	.387	118	9	24	.895	-5	106	47	3b102,O8(6/0/2),P3,M	—	0.6
1904	Chi A	132	482	66	126	23	2	0	54	39	1	—	.261	.318	.317	105	5	29	.977	-13	81	0	O104L,2b28,M	—	-1.5
1905	Chi A	96	345	50	94	18	6	1	43	29	4	—	.272	.336	.368	128	11	26	.956	-5	104	0	O93(71/1/21)	—	0.2
1911	Chi A	120	466	64	131	13	5	3	60	15	2	—	.281	.306	.350	86	-12	45	.963	-11	85	56	O114(93/10/11)	—	-2.8
1912	Chi A	111	408	45	111	9	7	1	52	12	3	—	.272	.298	.336	84	-11	19	.939	-16	81	22	O107L,M	—	-3.2
1913	Chi A	6	9	0	2	0	0	0	1	0	0	2	.222	.222	.222	30	-1	0	1.000	-0	108	0	/lfM	—	-0.1
Total	13	923	3295	442	901	135	46	11	394	159	20	9	.273	.311	.352	94	-25	186	.953	-30	94	26	O489L,P195,3b110,2b62,S22/1	—	-7.6
CALLAHAN, JIM	James Timothy "Red" (b James Timothy Callaghan); B1.12.1881 Allegheny Co. PA; D3.9.1968 Carnegie PA; BR/TR/5´9˝/145; d5.25																								
1902	NY N	1	4	0	0	0	0	0	0	1	0	—	.000	.200	.000	-38	-1	0	ø	0	0	0	/rf	—	-0.1
CALLAHAN, LEO	Leo David; B8.9.1890 Jamaica Plain MA; D5.2.1982 Erie PA; BL/TL/5´8˝/142; d4.9																								
1913	Bro N	33	41	6	7	3	1	0	3	4	0	5	.171	.244	.293	52	-3	0	.857	-1	105	0	O8(2/4/2)	—	-0.4
1919	Phi N	81	235	26	54	14	4	1	9	29	1	19	.230	.317	.336	90	-2	5	.950	2	91	162	O58(12/9/38)	—	-0.4
Total	2	114	276	32	61	17	5	1	12	33	1	24	.221	.306	.330	84	-5	5	.941	1	92	148	O66(14/13/40)	—	-0.8
CALLAHAN, WESLEY	Wesley Leroy; B7.3.1888 Lyons IN; D9.13.1953 Dayton OH; BR/TR/5´7.5˝/155; d9.7																								
1913	StL N	7	14	0	4	0	0	0	1	2	0	2	.286	.375	.286	91	0	1	.920	0	112	119	S6	—	0.1
CALLASPO, ALBERTO	Alberto Jose; B4.19.1983 Maracay, Venezuela; BB/TR/5´10˝/175; d8.6																								
2006	Ari N	23	42	2	10	1	1	0	6	4-0	0	6	.238	.298	.310	55	-3	0-1	.929	-0	84	83	S4,2b3,3b2	0	-0.3
CALLAWAY, FRANK	Frank Burnett; B2.26.1898 Knoxville TN; D8.21.1987 Knoxville TN; BR/TR/6´0˝/170; d9.17; Col Tennessee																								
1921	Phi A	14	50	7	12	1	1	0	4	2	1	11	.240	.283	.300	49	-4	1-0	.878	-5	96	28	S14	—	-0.7
1922	Phi A	29	48	5	13	0	2	0	4	0	0	13	.271	.271	.354	60	-3	0-0	.880	0	126	112	2b11,3b5,S4	—	-0.2
Total	2	43	98	12	25	1	3	0	8	2	1	24	.255	.277	.327	54	-7	1-0	.889	-5	96	26	S18,2b11,3b5	—	-0.9
CALLISON, JOHNNY	John Wesley; B3.12.1939 Qualls OK; D10.12.2006 Abington PA; BL/TR/5´10˝/(170–180); d9.9																								
1958	Chi A	18	64	10	19	4	2	1	12	6-0	0	14	.297	.352	.469	128	2	1-0	.976	1	104	173	O18L	0	0.3
1959	Chi A	49	104	12	18	3	0	3	12	13-0	1	20	.173	.271	.288	54	-7	0-1	.983	-1	84	147	O41L	0	-1.0
1960	Phi N	99	288	36	75	11	5	9	30	45-2	0	70	.260	.360	.427	114	7	0-4	.989	6	115	104	O86(32/16/47)	32	0.7
1961	Phi N	138	455	74	121	20	11	9	47	69-5	3	76	.266	.363	.418	109	7	10-4	.967	1	101	98	O124(90/1/35)	0	0.2
1962	Phi N★	157	603	107	181	26	**10**	23	83	54-1	6	96	.300	.363	.491	131	25	10-3	.980	22	**125**	**194**	O152(3/5/151)	0	3.7
1963	Phi N	157	626	96	178	36	11	26	78	50-4	2	111	.284	.339	.502	140	31	8-3	.994	19	114	**225**	O157(2/1/156)	0	4.2
1964	Phi N★	**162**	654	101	179	30	10	31	104	36-3	6	95	.274	.316	.492	126	19	6-3	.988	14	114	161	O162(2/0/162)	0	2.3
1965	Phi N☆	160	619	93	162	25	**16**	32	101	57-2	6	117	.262	.328	.509	135	26	6-5	.982	15	**112**	**199**	O159R	0	3.1
1966	Phi N	155	612	93	169	**40**	7	11	55	56-4	3	83	.276	.338	.418	109	9	8-8	.990	2	102	111	O154R	0	-0.1
1967	Phi N	149	556	62	145	30	5	14	64	55-17	3	63	.261	.329	.408	109	7	6-12	.977	5	107	113	O147R	0	-0.1
1968	Phi N	121	398	46	97	18	4	14	40	42-4	3	70	.244	.319	.415	120	10	4-3	**1.000**	2	100	117	O109R	0	0.4
1969	Phi N	134	495	66	131	29	5	16	64	49-11	3	73	.265	.332	.440	118	11	2-1	.990	12	**119**	124	O129R	20	1.7
1970	Chi N	147	477	65	126	23	2	19	68	60-11	3	63	.264	.348	.440	98	0	7-2	.973	-0	100	90	O144(0/3/143)	0	-0.7
1971	Chi N	103	290	27	61	12	1	8	38	36-8	2	55	.210	.298	.341	71	-10	2-1	.982	-2	102	51	O89(1/0/88)	0	-1.8
1972	NY A	92	275	28	71	10	0	9	34	18-1	0	34	.258	.299	.393	108	2	3-0	.992	-2	92	78	O74R	0	-0.4
1973	NY A	45	136	10	24	4	0	1	10	4-0	0	24	.176	.197	.228	21	-15	1-1	.960	-2	82	103	O32R,D10	0	-2.0
Total	16	1886	6652	926	1757	321	89	226	840	650-73	41	1064	.264	.331	.441	114	124	74-51	.984	90	108	137	O1777(189/26/1586),D10	52	10.5
CALLOWAY, RON	Ronald Isiah; B9.4.1976 San Jose CA; BL/TL/6´1˝/(200–210); [AriN97 8/263]; d3.31; Col Canada (CA) JC																								
2003	Mon N	126	340	36	81	17	1	9	52	20-1	2	80	.238	.282	.374	68	-17	9-2	.983	1	105	76	O97(50/2/47)	0	-1.8
2004	Mon N	46	84	4	14	2	0	1	10	5-0	0	22	.167	.211	.226	13	-11	2-0	1.000	-1	90	0	O20(6/0/15)	0	-1.3
Total	2	172	424	40	95	19	1	10	62	25-1	2	102	.224	.268	.344	57	-28	11-2	.985	-1	103	64	O117(56/2/62)	0	-3.1
CALVO, JACK	Jacinto (Gonzalez) (Born Jacinto Del Calvo); B6.11.1894 Havana, Cuba; D6.15.1965 Miami FL; BL/TL/5´10˝/156; d5.9																								
1913	Was A	17	33	5	8	0	0	1	2	1	0	4	.242	.265	.333	73	-1	0	.900	-0	64	212	O13(6/0/7)	—	-0.2
1920	Was A	17	23	5	1	0	1	0	2	2	0	2	.043	.120	.130	-35	-5	0-0	1.000	-1	79	0	O10(6/1/3)	—	-0.6
Total	2	34	56	10	9	0	1	1	4	3	0	6	.161	.203	.250	27	-6	0-0	.938	-1	69	137	O23(12/1/10)	—	-0.8
CALZADO, NAPOLEON	Napolean; B2.9.1977 Santo Domingo, D.R.; BR/TR/6´3˝/200; d5.29																								
2005	Bal A	4	5	0	1	0	0	0	0	0-0	0	1	.200	.200	.200	7	-1	0-0	1.000	-0	99	0	O2(1/1/0)	0	-0.1
CAMELLI, HANK	Henry Richard; B12.12.1914 Gloucester MA; D7.14.1996 Wellesley MA; BR/TR/5´11˝/190; d10.3																								
1943	Pit N	1	3	1	0	0	0	0	0	1	0	0	.000	.250	.000	-24	0	0	1.000	0	*0*	*0*	/C	0	0.0
1944	Pit N	63	125	14	37	5	1	1	10	18	0	12	.296	.385	.376	110	2	0	.959	2	*100*	*85*	C61	0	0.7
1945	Pit N	1	2	0	0	0	0	0	0	1	0	0	.000	.333	.000	-3	0	0	1.000	0	*0*	*0*	/C	0	0.0
1946	Pit N	42	96	8	20	2	2	0	5	8	0	9	.208	.269	.271	52	-6	0	.971	1	*69*	*117*	C39	0	-0.4
1947	Bos N	52	150	10	29	8	1	1	11	18	0	18	.193	.280	.280	50	-11	0	.977	2	*83*	*90*	C51	0	-0.6
Total	5	159	376	33	86	15	4	2	26	46	0	39	.229	.313	.306	70	-15	0	.970	5	*84*	*93*	C153	0	-0.3
CAMERON, JACK	John Stanley "Happy Jack"; B9.22.1884 Sydney NS, Can.; D7.12.1963 Charlotte NC; BR/TR/5´10˝/170; d9.13																								
1906	Bos N	18	61	3	11	0	0	0	4	2	0	—	.180	.206	.180	21	-6	0	.852	-1	150	193	O16(15/0/1),P2	—	-0.8
CAMERON, MIKE	Michael Terrance; B1.8.1973 LaGrange GA; BR/TR/6´2˝/(190–200); [ChiA91 18/488]; d8.27																								
1995	Chi A	28	38	4	7	2	0	1	2	3-0	0	15	.184	.244	.316	46	-3	0-0	1.000	1	111	108	O28(0/3/26)	0	-0.3
1996	Chi A	11	11	1	1	0	0	0	0	1-0	0	3	.091	.167	.091	-34	-2	0-1	1.000	-0	79	0	O8(2/4/5),D2	0	-0.3
1997	Chi A	116	379	63	98	18	3	14	55	55-1	5	105	.259	.356	.433	109	6	23-2	.985	13	**124**	88	O112(0/102/37),D4	0	2.2
1998	Chi A	141	396	53	83	16	5	8	43	37-0	6	101	.210	.285	.336	62	-23	27-11	.988	2	106	83	O138(0/136/2)	0	-1.7
1999	Cin N	146	542	93	139	34	9	21	66	80-2	6	145	.256	.357	.469	104	3	38-12	.979	-1	104	88	O146C	0	0.8
2000	†Sea A	155	543	96	145	28	4	19	78	78-0	9	133	.267	.365	.438	105	6	24-7	.985	1	106	68	O155(0/155/1)	0	1.0
2001	†Sea A★	150	540	99	144	30	5	25	110	69-3	10	155	.267	.353	.480	125	21	34-5	.986	5	110	96	O149C/D	0	3.2
2002	Sea A	158	545	84	130	26	5	25	80	79-3	7	176	.239	.340	.442	110	9	31-8	.988	3	107	76	O155C	0	1.7
2003	Sea A	147	534	74	135	31	5	18	76	70-1	5	137	.253	.344	.431	109	8	17-7	.992	16	**126**	45	O147C	0	2.6
2004	NY N	140	493	76	114	30	1	30	76	57-2	8	143	.231	.319	.479	105	3	22-6	.978	2	106	86	O135C	0	0.9
2005	NY N	76	308	47	84	23	2	12	39	29-0	4	85	.273	.342	.477	115	6	13-1	.962	-3	98	68	O76(0/10/68)	84	0.3
2006	†SD N	141	552	88	148	34	9	22	83	71-2	6	142	.268	.355	.482	119	15	25-9	.984	1	105	86	O141C	20	1.9
Total	12	1409	4881	778	1228	272	48	195	708	629-14	66	1340	.252	.342	.447	106	49	254-69	.985	39	109	79	O1390(2/1283/139),D7	104	12.3
CAMILLI, DOLPH	Adolph Louis; B4.23.1907 San Francisco CA; D10.21.1997 San Mateo CA; BL/TL/5´10˝/185; d9.9; s–Doug																								
1933	Chi N	16	58	8	13	2	1	2	7	4	0	11	.224	.274	.397	90	-1	3	.994	2	130	166	1b16	—	-0.1
1934	Chi N	32	120	17	33	8	0	4	19	5	2	25	.275	.315	.442	102	0	1	.988	2	123	108	1b32	—	-0.1
	Phi N	102	378	52	100	20	3	12	68	48	2	69	.265	.350	.429	95	-2	3	.985	-3	92	97	1b102	—	-1.4
	Year	134	498	69	133	28	3	16	87	53	4	94	.267	.342	.432	96	-2	4	.986	-1	99	100	1b134	—	-1.5
1935	Phi N	**156**	602	88	157	23	5	25	83	65	3	113	.261	.336	.440	97	-3	9	.987	-2	98	92	1b156	—	-1.9
1936	Phi N	151	530	106	167	29	13	28	102	116	3	84	.315	.441	.577	156	47	5	.988	-11	77	93	1b150	—	2.2
1937	Phi N	131	475	101	161	23	7	27	80	90	2	82	.339	**.446**	.587	165	47	6	**.994**	4	108	92	1b131	—	3.8
1938	Bro N	146	509	106	128	25	11	24	100	**119**	0	101	.251	.393	.485	137	30	6	.995	-1	95	104	1b145	—	1.5
1939	Bro N★	**157**	565	105	164	30	12	26	104	**110**	4	107	.290	.409	.524	144	38	1	.990	9	122	106	1b157	—	3.2
1940	Bro N	142	512	92	147	29	13	23	96	89	4	83	.287	.397	.529	145	33	9	.992	-5	84	79	1b140	—	1.4
1941	†Bro N✳	149	529	92	151	29	6	**34**	**120**	104	4	115	.285	.407	.556	162	**46**	3	.989	1	101	99	1b148	0	3.3
1942	Bro N	150	524	89	132	23	7	26	109	97	3	85	.252	.372	.471	144	31	10	.992	-1	94	121	1b150	0	1.7

THE BATTER REGISTER

YEAR	TM LG	G	AB	R	H	2B	3B	HR	RBI	BB-IB	HP	SO	AVG	OBP	SLG	AOPS	ABR	SB-CS	FA	FR	RNG	THR	GAMES AT POSITION	DL	BFW
1943	Bro N	95	353	56	87	15	6	6	43	65	1	48	.246	.365	.374	113	8	2	.992	-1	94	91	1b95	0	0.3
1945	Bos A	63	198	24	42	5	2	2	19	35	0	38	.212	.330	.288	78	-4	2-0	.991	2	110	132	1b54	0	-0.5
Total	12	1490	5353	936	1482	261	86	239	950	947	28	961	.277	.388	.492	134	270	60-0	.990	-5	98	100	1b1476	0	13.4
CAMILLI, DOUG	Douglas Joseph; B9.22.1936 Philadelphia PA; BR/TR/5´11˝/(180–195); d9.25; C6; f–Dolph; Col Stanford																								
1960	LA N	6	24	4	8	2	0	1	3	1-0	1	4	.333	.385	.542	141	1	0-0	.980	-0	121	0	C6	0	0.1
1961	LA N	13	30	3	4	0	0	3	4	1-0	0	9	.133	.161	.433	47	-3	0-0	.986	2	91	57	C12	0	0.0
1962	LA N	45	88	16	25	5	2	4	22	12-1	0	21	.284	.366	.523	145	6	0-0	.983	-5	82	66	C39	0	0.1
1963	LA N	49	117	9	19	1	1	3	10	11-6	0	22	.162	.234	.265	47	-9	0-0	.977	3	99	29	C47	0	-0.4
1964	LA N	50	123	1	22	3	0	0	10	8-1	0	19	.179	.226	.203	25	-12	0-0	.990	2	128	109	C46	0	-0.9
1965	Was A	75	193	13	37	6	1	3	18	16-2	1	34	.192	.257	.280	53	-12	0-0	.980	1	123	127	C59	0	-0.9
1966	Was A	44	107	5	22	4	0	2	8	3-0	1	19	.206	.234	.299	53	-7	0-0	.990	2	127	167	C39	66	-0.4
1967	Was A	30	82	5	15	1	0	2	5	4-0	0	16	.183	.221	.268	46	-6	0-0	.993	-5	76	117	C24	0	-1.0
1969	Was A	1	3	0	1	0	0	0	0	0-0	0	2	.333	.333	.333	92	0	0-0	1.000	0	0	0	/C	0	0.0
Total	9	313	767	56	153	22	4	18	80	56-10	3	146	.199	.256	.309	61	-42	0-0	.984	-2	109	99	C273	66	-3.4
CAMILLI, LOU	Louis Steven; B9.24.1946 El Paso TX; BB/TR/5´10˝/(170–180); [CleA67 S3/55]; d8.9; Col Texas A&M																								
1969	Cle A	13	14	0	0	0	0	0	0	0-0	0	3	.000	.000	.000	-97	-4	0-0	1.000	2	91	83	3b13	0	-0.2
1970	Cle A	16	15	0	0	0	0	0	0	2-0	0	2	.000	.118	.000	-62	-3	0-0	1.000	1	143	0	S3,2b2/3	0	-0.3
1971	Cle A	39	81	5	16	2	0	0	0	8-1	0	10	.198	.270	.222	37	-7	0-0	.938	-3	95	50	S23,2b16	0	-0.8
1972	Cle A	39	41	2	6	2	0	0	3	3-0	0	8	.146	.205	.195	19	-4	0-0	1.000	-1	79	91	S8,2b2	0	-0.5
Total	4	107	151	7	22	4	0	0	3	13-1	0	23	.146	.213	.172	11	-18	0-0	.951	-2	94	56	S34,2b20,3b14	0	-1.8
CAMINITI, KEN	Kenneth Gene; B4.21.1963 Hanford CA; D10.10.2004 Bronx NY; BB/TR/6´0˝/200; [HouN84 3/71]; d7.16; Col San Jose St.																								
1987	Hou N	63	203	10	50	7	1	3	23	12-1	0	44	.246	.287	.335	67	-10	0-0	.949	2	92	127	3b61	0	-0.9
1988	Hou N	30	83	5	15	2	0	1	7	5-0	0	18	.181	.225	.241	36	-7	0-0	.948	-1	96	57	3b28	0	-0.9
1989	Hou N	161	585	71	149	31	3	10	72	51-9	3	93	.255	.316	.369	99	-1	4-1	.954	11	108	103	3b160	0	1.2
1990	Hou N	153	541	52	131	20	2	4	51	48-7	0	97	.242	.302	.309	71	-22	9-4	.945	-9	93	108	3b149	0	-3.1
1991	Hou N	152	574	65	145	30	3	13	80	46-7	5	85	.253	.312	.383	100	-1	4-5	.948	14	107	114	3b152	0	1.3
1992	Hou N	135	506	68	149	31	2	13	62	44-13	1	68	.294	.350	.441	128	18	10-4	.966	-7	88	88	3b129	22	1.3
1993	Hou N	143	543	75	142	31	0	13	75	49-10	0	88	.262	.321	.390	93	-6	8-5	.942	11	103	106	3b143	0	0.6
1994	Hou N★	111	406	63	115	28	2	18	75	43-13	2	71	.283	.352	.495	125	14	4-3	.969	5	103	102	3b108	0	1.9
1995	SD N	143	526	74	159	33	0	26	94	69-8	1	94	.302	.380	.513	138	30	12-5	.936	14	106	122	3b143	0	4.4
1996	†SD N★	146	546	109	178	37	2	40	130	78-16	4	99	.326	.408	.621	176	62	11-5	.954	15	112	128	3b145	0	7.4
1997	SD N★	137	486	92	141	28	0	26	90	80-9	3	118	.290	.389	.508	143	33	11-2	.941	16	**121**	84	3b133	15	5.0
1998	†SD N	131	452	87	114	29	0	29	82	71-4	4	108	.252	.353	.509	134	23	6-2	.931	-9	90	80	3b126	21	1.5
1999	†Hou N	78	273	45	78	11	1	13	56	46-4	3	58	.286	.386	.476	120	10	6-2	.932	4	103	150	3b75	86	1.4
2000	Hou N	59	208	42	63	13	0	15	45	42-8	1	37	.303	.419	.582	139	14	3-0	.915	-7	85	77	3b58	107	0.7
2001	Tex A	54	185	24	43	8	1	9	25	22-2	2	41	.232	.318	.432	93	-2	0-0	.940	-1	97	105	3b53	15	-0.3
	†Atl N	64	171	12	38	9	0	6	16	21-1	0	44	.222	.306	.380	76	-6	0-1	.977	-3	80	91	1b33,3b13/D	0	-1.2
Total	15	1760	6288	894	1710	348	17	239	983	727-112	29	1163	.272	.347	.447	116	149	88-39	.946	53	102	106	3b1676,1b33/D	266	20.3
CAMP, HOWIE	Howard Lee "Red"; B7.1.1893 Hopeful AL; D5.8.1960 Eastaboga AL; BL/TR/5´9˝/169; d9.19; Mil 1918																								
1917	NY A	5	21	3	6	1	0	0	0	1	0	2	.286	.318	.333	98	0	0	.857	0	82	263	O5(0/4/1)	—	0.0
CAMP, LEW	Robert Plantagenet Llewellan; B2.23.1868 Columbus OH; D10.1.1948 Omaha NE; BL/TR/6´0˝/175; d8.26; b–Kid																								
1892	StL N	42	145	19	30	3	1	2	13	17	1	27	.207	.294	.283	79	-3	12	.780	-13	78	68	3b39,O3(0/2/1)	—	-1.5
1893	Chi N	38	156	37	41	7	7	2	17	19	1	19	.263	.347	.436	109	1	30	.847	-5	79	71	3b16,O11C,2b9,S3	—	-0.3
1894	Chi N	8	33	1	6	2	0	0	1	1	0	6	.182	.206	.242	7	-5	0	.830	-4	68	92	2b8	—	-0.7
Total	3	88	334	57	77	12	8	4	31	37	2	52	.231	.311	.350	85	-7	42	.801	-22	78	69	3b55,2b17,O14(0/13/1),S3	—	-2.5
CAMPANELLA, ROY	Roy; B11.19.1921 Philadelphia PA; D6.26.1993 Woodland Hills CA; BR/TR/5´8˝/(200–215); d4.20; HF1969; Negro Lg 1937–45; [DL 1958 LA N 168]																								
1948	Bro N	83	279	32	72	11	3	9	45	36	1	45	.258	.345	.416	102	1	3	.981	8	*130*	*146*	C78	0	1.2
1949	†Bro N★	130	436	65	125	22	2	22	82	67	3	36	.287	.385	.498	130	20	3	.985	5	***140***	*110*	C127	0	3.1
1950	Bro N★	126	437	70	123	19	3	31	89	55	2	51	.281	.364	.551	134	21	1	.985	-3	*126*	*92*	C123	0	2.4
1951	Bro N★	143	505	90	164	33	1	33	108	53	4	51	.325	.393	.590	158	41	1-2	.986	12	***254***	*107*	C140	0	5.9
1952	†Bro N★	128	468	73	126	18	1	22	97	57	3	59	.269	.352	.453	120	13	8-4	**.994**	-3	*147*	*101*	C122	0	1.8
1953	†Bro N★	144	519	103	162	26	3	41	**142**	67	4	58	.312	.395	.611	154	41	4-2	.989	5	***166***	*98*	C140	0	5.0
1954	Bro N★	111	397	43	82	14	3	19	51	42	2	49	.207	.285	.401	74	-17	1-4	.989	-1	*148*	*109*	C111	0	-1.3
1955	†Bro N✻	123	446	81	142	20	1	32	107	56-9	6	41	.318	.395	.583	153	35	2-3	.992	4	*118*	*73*	C121	0	4.3
1956	†Bro N★	124	388	39	85	6	1	20	73	66-15	1	61	.219	.333	.394	88	-6	1-0	.985	4	*134*	*88*	C121	0	0.5
1957	Bro N	103	330	31	80	9	0	13	62	34-6	4	50	.242	.316	.388	81	-8	1-0	**.993**	20	137	*77*	C100	0	1.7
Total	10	1215	4205	627	1161	178	18	242	856	533-30	30	501	.276	.360	.500	123	141	25-15	.988	52	*153*	*99*	C1183	168	24.6
CAMPANERIS, BERT	Dagoberto (Blanco) "Campy" (b Dagoberto Campaneria (Blanco)); B3.9.1942 Pueblo Nuevo, Cuba; BR/TR/5´10˝/(155–160); d7.23; OF(68/2/1)																								
1964	KC A	67	269	27	69	14	3	4	22	15-0	4	41	.257	.306	.375	86	-5	10-2	.981	-7	89	59	S38,O27L,3b6	0	-0.9
1965	KC A	144	578	67	156	23	**12**	6	42	41-0	**9**	71	.270	.326	.382	103	1	**51**-19	.938	-9	93	82	S109,O39(38/2/1)/PC123	0	0.3
1966	KC A	142	573	82	153	29	10	5	42	25-1	5	72	.267	.302	.379	98	-3	**52**-10	.971	-15	89	92	S138	0	0.2
1967	KC A	147	601	85	149	29	6	3	32	36-2	7	82	.248	.297	.331	89	-9	**55**-16	.954	-13	89	92	S145	0	-0.3
1968	Oak A★	159	642	87	**177**	25	9	4	38	50-2	4	69	.276	.330	.361	115	10	**62**-22	.956	8	102	106	S155,O3L	0	4.2
1969	Oak A	135	547	71	142	15	2	2	25	30-2	4	62	.260	.302	.305	73	-21	62-8	.967	-3	103	100	S125	0	0.2
1970	Oak A	147	603	97	168	28	4	22	64	36-1	4	73	.279	.321	.448	114	9	**42**-10	.973	2	99	115	S143	0	3.4
1971	†Oak A	134	569	80	143	18	4	5	47	29-1	2	64	.251	.287	.323	75	-21	34-7	.960	3	98	120	S133	20	0.4
1972	†Oak A☆	149	625	85	150	25	2	8	32	32-0	2	88	.240	.278	.325	83	-15	**52**-14	.977	5	101	113	S148	0	1.6
1973	†Oak A★	151	601	89	150	17	6	4	46	50-1	4	79	.250	.308	.318	81	-16	34-10	.969	-3	101	103	S149	0	0.3
1974	†Oak A★	134	527	77	153	18	8	2	41	47-2	0	81	.290	.347	.366	112	8	34-15	.966	-2	98	104	S133/D	15	2.4
1975	†Oak A★	137	509	69	135	15	3	4	46	50-2	7	71	.265	.337	.330	92	-5	24-12	.962	-16	93	82	S137	0	-0.4
1976	Oak A	149	536	67	137	14	1	1	52	63-0	3	80	.256	.331	.291	88	-5	54-12	.969	-1	106	79	S149	0	1.9
1977	Tex A★	150	552	77	140	19	7	5	46	47-1	4	86	.254	.314	.341	78	-17	27-20	.968	26	**113**	113	S149	0	2.3
1978	Tex A	98	269	30	50	5	3	1	17	20-0	2	36	.186	.245	.238	37	-23	22-4	.954	4	104	93	S89,D4	18	-0.7
1979	Tex A	8	9	2	1	0	0	0	0	1-0	0	3	.111	.200	.111	-14	-1	1-0	.962	3	117	219	S8	0	0.2
	†Cal A	85	239	27	56	4	4	0	15	19-0	2	32	.234	.294	.285	59	-14	12-4	.957	11	102	142	S82/D	0	0.6
	Year	93	248	29	57	4	4	0	15	20-0	2	35	.230	.290	.278	56	-16	13-4	.957	14	103	146	S90/D	0	0.8
1980	Cal A	77	210	32	53	8	1	2	18	14-0	1	33	.252	.300	.329	74	-8	10-5	.957	-9	86	99	S64/2D	0	-1.0
1981	Cal A	55	82	11	21	2	1	1	10	5-0	0	10	.256	.295	.341	83	-2	5-2	.900	-8	83	106	3b45,S3,2b2	0	-1.1
1983	NY A	60	143	19	46	5	0	0	11	8-0	0	9	.322	.355	.357	100	0	6-7	.964	-1	119	127	2b32,3b24	15	-0.2
Total	19	2328	8684	1181	2249	313	86	79	646	618-15	64	1142	.259	.311	.342	89	-137	649-199	.964	-24	99	101	S2097,3b76,O69L,2b36,D8/1CP	68	13.4
CAMPANIS, AL	Alexander Sebastian (b Alessandro Campani); B11.2.1916 Kos, Dodecanese Islands; D6.21.1998 Fullerton CA; BB/TR/6´0˝/185; d9.23; Mil 1944–45; s–Jim; Col NYU																								
1943	Bro N	7	20	3	2	0	0	0	0	4	0	5	.100	.250	.100	3	-2	0	1.000	1	90	106	2b7	0	-0.1
CAMPANIS, JIM	James Alexander; B2.9.1944 New York NY; BR/TR/6´0˝/(195–205); d9.20; f–Al																								
1966	LA N	1	1	0	0	0	0	0	0	0-0	0	0	.000	.000	.000	-99	0	0-0	1.000	0	0	0	/C	0	0.0
1967	LA N	41	62	3	10	1	0	2	2	9-1	0	14	.161	.268	.274	60	-3	0-0	.990	1	69	54	C23	0	-0.2
1968	LA N	4	11	0	1	0	0	0	0	1-0	0	2	.091	.167	.091	-23	-2	0-0	.960	0	51	206	C4	0	-0.2
1969	KC A	30	83	4	13	5	0	0	5	5-1	0	19	.157	.202	.217	18	-9	0-0	.982	1	67	78	C26	0	-0.8
1970	KC A	31	54	6	7	0	0	2	2	4-1	1	14	.130	.203	.241	22	-6	0-0	.986	-3	36	162	C13/rf	0	-0.9
1973	Pit N	6	6	0	1	0	0	0	0	0-0	0	0	.167	.167	.167	-8	-1	0-0	ø	0	—	—	/H	0	-0.1
Total	6	113	217	13	32	6	0	4	9	19-3	1	49	.147	.218	.230	27	-21	0-0	.983	-1	59	99	C67/rf	0	-2.2
CAMPAU, COUNT	Charles Columbus; B10.17.1863 Detroit MI; D4.3.1938 New Orleans LA; BL/TR/5´11˝/160; d7.7; M1																								
1888	Det N	70	251	28	51	5	3	1	18	19	0	36	.203	.259	.259	65	-10	27	.933	-4	85	138	O70R	—	-1.4
1890	StL AA	75	314	68	101	9	12	**9**	75	26	0	—	.322	.374	.513	141	12	36	.934	2	106	36	O74(39/2/33)/31M	—	1.1
1894	Was N	2	7	1	1	0	0	0	0	1	0	4	.143	.250	.143	-3	-1	0	1.000	-0	0	0	O2L	—	-0.1
Total	3	147	572	97	153	14	15	10	93	46	0	40	.267	.322	.397	109	1	63	.934	-2	95	84	O146(41/2/103)/13	—	-0.4

YEAR	TM LG	G	AB	R	H	2B	3B	HR	RBI	BB-IB	HP	SO	AVG	OBP	SLG	AOPS	ABR	SB-CS	FA	FR	RNG	THR	GAMES AT POSITION	DL	BFW
CAMPBELL, VIN	Arthur Vincent; B1.30.1888 St.Louis MO; D11.16.1969 Towson MD; BL/TR/6´0˝/185; d6.6; Col Vanderbilt																								
1908	Chi N	1	1	0	0	0	0	0	0	0	0	—	.000	.000	.000	-96	0	0	ø	0	—	—	/H	—	0.0
1910	Pit N	97	282	42	92	9	5	4	21	26	4	23	.326	.391	.436	133	12	17	.895	-4	100	83	O74(38/17/18)	—	0.5
1911	Pit N	42	93	12	29	3	1	0	10	8	0	7	.312	.366	.366	101	0	6	.923	-2	101	38	O21(9/1/11)	—	-0.2
1912	Bos N	145	624	102	185	32	9	3	48	32	3	44	.296	.334	.391	96	-5	19	.938	-5	99	89	O144C	—	-2.0
1914	Ind F	134	544	92	173	23	11	7	44	37	6	47	.318	.368	.439	108	-2	26	.925	-8	88	95	O132(1/94/37)	—	-1.8
1915	New F	127	525	78	163	18	10	1	44	29	5	35	.310	.352	.389	115	1	24	.947	-9	87	84	O126(0/12/115)	—	-1.7
Total	6	546	2069	326	642	85	36	15	167	132	18	156	.310	.357	.408	109	6	92	.929	-27	93	86	O497(48/268/181)	—	-5.2
CAMPBELL, BRUCE	Bruce Douglas; B10.20.1909 Chicago IL; D6.17.1995 Ft.Myers Beach FL; BL/TR/6´1˝/185; d9.12; Mil 1942–45																								
1930	Chi A	5	10	4	5	1	1	0	5	1	0	2	.500	.545	.800	245	2	0-0	1.000	0	128	0	O4L	—	0.2
1931	Chi A	4	17	4	7	2	0	2	5	0	1	4	.412	.444	.882	256	4	0-0	.900	-0	101	0	O4L	—	0.3
1932	Chi A	7	18	3	4	1	0	0	2	0	0	2	.222	.222	.278	31	-2	0-1	1.000	-0	81	0	O4(3/0/1)	—	-0.3
	StL A	139	593	83	169	35	11	14	85	40	6	102	.285	.336	.452	97	-5	7-5	.935	4	107	119	O139R	—	-0.9
	Year	146	611	86	173	36	11	14	87	40	**6**	104	.283	.333	.447	95	-6	7-6	.935	3	106	117	O143(3/0/140)	—	-1.2
1933	StL A	148	567	87	157	38	8	16	106	69	2	77	.277	.357	.457	108	6	10-4	.950	-5	87	134	O144R	—	-0.6
1934	StL A	138	481	62	134	25	6	9	74	51	2	64	.279	.350	.412	88	-9	5-4	.935	1	97	147	O123R	—	-1.5
1935	Cle A	80	308	56	100	26	3	7	54	31	2	33	.325	.390	.497	126	12	2-1	.992	-7	88	32	O75R	—	0.1
1936	Cle A	76	172	35	64	15	2	6	30	19	2	17	.372	.440	.587	150	14	2-1	.960	0	95	121	O47R	—	1.1
1937	Cle A	134	448	82	135	42	11	4	61	67	0	49	.301	.392	.471	116	13	4-5	.978	-0	91	129	O123R	—	0.4
1938	Cle A	133	511	90	148	27	12	12	72	53	3	57	.290	.360	.460	106	3	11-7	.967	1	97	124	O122R	—	-0.4
1939	Cle A	130	450	84	129	23	13	8	72	67	3	48	.287	.383	.449	116	12	7-6	.942	-4	87	134	O115R	—	0.0
1940	†Det A	103	297	56	84	15	5	8	44	45	2	28	.283	.381	.448	104	3	2-7	.959	-1	97	108	O74R	—	-0.4
1941	Det A	141	512	72	141	28	10	15	93	68	3	67	.275	.364	.457	105	4	3-3	.976	-8	95	41	O133R	0	-1.2
1942	Was A	122	378	41	105	17	5	5	63	37	1	34	.278	.344	.389	107	3	0-6	.955	0	109	63	O87(20/0/68)	0	-0.4
Total	13	1360	4762	759	1382	295	87	106	766	548	27	584	.290	.367	.455	108	60	53-50	.956	-20	95	107	O1194(31/0/1164)	0	-3.6
CAMPBELL, SOUP	Clarence; B3.7.1915 Sparta VA; D2.16.2000 Sparta VA; BL/TR/6´1˝/188; d4.21; Mil 1942–46; Col Hampden-Sydney																								
1940	Cle A	35	62	8	14	1	0	0	2	7	0	12	.226	.304	.242	45	-5	0-0	1.000	1	121	0	O16(8/5/4)	—	-0.5
1941	Cle A	104	328	36	82	10	4	3	35	31	1	21	.250	.317	.332	75	-12	1-9	.981	0	101	92	O78(20/59/0)	0	-1.7
Total	2	139	390	44	96	11	4	3	37	38	1	33	.246	.315	.318	70	-17	1-9	.984	1	104	80	O94(28/64/4)	0	-2.2
CAMPBELL, DAVE	David Wilson; B1.14.1942 Manistee MI; BR/TR/6´0˝/(180–185); d9.17; Col Michigan																								
1967	Det A	2	2	0	0	0	0	0	0	0-0	0	1	.000	.000	.000	-97	0	0-0	.500	-0	0	0	/1	0	-0.1
1968	Det A	9	8	1	1	0	0	1	2	1-0	0	3	.125	.222	.500	111	0	0-0	1.000	-1	64	113	2b5	0	0.0
1969	Det A	32	39	4	4	1	0	0	2	4-0	1	15	.103	.205	.128	-5	-5	0-1	.967	-2	41	137	1b13,2b5/3	0	-0.9
1970	SD N	154	581	71	127	28	2	12	40	40-2	1	115	.219	.268	.336	64	-32	18-6	.974	18	111	96	2b153	0	-0.2
1971	SD N	108	365	38	83	14	2	7	29	37-0	0	75	.227	.299	.334	84	-8	9-6	.968	2	111	95	2b69,3b40,S4,1b2,O2L	0	-0.3
1972	SD N	33	100	6	24	5	0	0	3	11-2	0	12	.240	.315	.290	79	-3	0-4	.988	1	101	53	3b31/2	97	-0.4
1973	SD N	33	98	2	22	3	0	0	8	7-1	0	15	.224	.271	.255	52	-6	1-1	.979	4	103	107	2b27,1b3,3b2	0	-0.2
	StL N	13	21	1	0	0	0	0	1	1-0	0	6	.000	.043	.000	-86	-5	0-0	.933	-3	68	41	2b6	0	-0.8
	Hou N	9	15	1	4	2	0	0	2	0-0	0	4	.267	.267	.400	83	0	0-0	1.000	2	161	146	3b5,1b2/lf	0	0.1
	Year	55	134	4	26	5	0	0	11	8-1	0	25	.194	.234	.231	33	-12	1-1	.975	3	98	98	2b33,3b7,1b5/lf	0	-0.9
1974	Hou N	35	23	4	2	1	0	0	2	1-0	0	8	.087	.125	.130	-30	-4	1-0	.895	2	102	198	2b9,1b6,3b2/lf	44	-0.2
Total	8	428	1252	128	267	54	4	20	89	102-5	2	254	.213	.272	.311	63	-63	29-18	.971	22	109	96	2b275,3b81,1b27,O4L,S4	141	-3.0
CAMPBELL, JIM	James Robert; B6.24.1937 Palo Alto CA; BR/TR/6´0˝/190; d7.17																								
1962	Hou N	27	86	6	19	4	0	3	6	6-0	0	23	.221	.272	.372	77	-3	0-0	.970	3	70	133	C25	0	0.1
1963	Hou N	55	158	9	35	3	0	4	19	10-3	0	40	.222	.268	.316	72	-6	0-0	.979	-3	77	86	C42	0	-0.8
Total	2	82	244	15	54	7	0	7	25	16-3	0	63	.221	.269	.336	74	-9	0-0	.975	-0	74	103	C67	0	-0.7
CAMPBELL, JIM	James Robert; B1.10.1943 Hartsville SC; BL/TR/6´0˝/205; d4.11																								
1970	StL N	13	13	0	3	0	0	0	1	0-0	0	3	.231	.231	.231	23	-1	0-0	ø	0	—	—	/H	0	-0.1
CAMPBELL, JOE	Joseph Earl; B3.10.1944 Louisville KY; BR/TR/6´1˝/175; [NYN65 26/808]; d5.3; Col Morehead St.																								
1967	Chi N	1	3	0	0	0	0	0	0	0-0	0	3	.000	.000	.000	-96	-1	0-0	ø	-0	0	0	/rf	0	-0.1
CAMPBELL, HUTCH	Marc Thaddeus; B11.29.1884 Punxsutawney PA; D2.13.1946 New Bethlehem PA; BB/TR/5´9˝/155; d9.30; Col Lock Haven																								
1907	Pit N	2	4	0	1	0	0	0	1	1	0	—	.250	.400	.250	102	0	0	.889	0	132	0	S2	—	0.0
CAMPBELL, MAT	Mathew; B8.1.1850 , Ireland; D1.12.1926 Scotch Plains NJ; d4.28; b-Hugh																								
1873	Res NA	21	84	9	12	2	0	0	2	2	—	6	.143	.163	.167	-3	-10	1-0	.938	-2	75	89	1b18,S3/rf	—	-0.8
CAMPBELL, PAUL	Paul McLaughlin; B9.1.1917 Paw Creek NC; D6.22.2006 Charlotte NC; BL/TL/5´10˝/185; d4.15; Mil 1943–45																								
1941	Bos A	1	0	0	0	0	0	0	0	0	0	0	ø	ø	ø	ø	0	0-0	ø	0	—	—	/R	0	0.0
1942	Bos A	26	15	4	1	0	0	0	0	1	0	5	.067	.125	.067	-44	-3	1-0	1.000	0	162	0	O4C	0	-0.3
1946	†Bos A	28	26	3	3	1	0	0	0	2	0	7	.115	.179	.154	-6	-4	0-0	1.000	-0	50	81	1b5	0	-0.4
1948	Det A	59	83	15	22	1	1	1	11	1	0	10	.265	.274	.337	60	-5	0-0	.969	2	164	71	1b27	0	-0.4
1949	Det A	87	255	38	71	15	4	3	30	24	1	32	.278	.343	.404	97	-2	3-3	.988	-3	83	108	1b74	0	-0.7
1950	Det A	3	1	1	0	0	0	0	0	0	0	0	.000	.000	.000	-97	0	0-0	ø	0	—	—	/H	0	0.0
Total	6	204	380	61	97	17	5	4	41	28	1	54	.255	.308	.358	76	-14	4-3	.984	-1	98	99	1b106,O4C	0	-1.8
CAMPBELL, RON	Ronald Thomas; B4.5.1940 Chattanooga TN; BR/TR/6´1˝/(180–185); d9.1; Col Tennessee Wesleyan																								
1964	Chi N	26	92	7	25	6	1	1	10	1-0	0	21	.272	.277	.391	83	-2	0-1	.941	8	134	100	2b26	0	0.8
1965	Chi N	2	2	0	0	0	0	0	0	0-0	0	0	.000	.000	.000	-98	-1	0-0	ø	0	—	—	/H	0	-0.1
1966	Chi N	24	60	4	13	1	0	0	4	6-2	0	5	.217	.284	.233	46	-4	1-1	.980	4	133	104	S11,3b7	0	0.0
Total	3	52	154	11	38	7	1	1	14	7-2	0	26	.247	.276	.325	67	-7	1-2	.941	12	134	100	2b26,S11,3b7	0	0.7
CAMPBELL, SAM	Samuel; B Philadelphia PA; d10.11																								
1890	Phi AA	2	5	0	0	0	0	0	0	1	0	—	.000	.167	.000	-51	-1	0	.833	-1	25	0	2b2	—	-0.2
CAMPBELL, GILLY	William Gilthorpe; B2.13.1908 Kansas City KS; D2.21.1973 Los Angeles CA; BL/TR/5´7.5˝/182; d4.25																								
1933	Chi N	46	89	11	25	3	1	1	10	7	2	4	.281	.347	.371	105	1	0	.949	-1	*142*	*83*	C20	—	0.1
1935	Cin N	88	218	26	56	7	0	3	30	42	1	7	.257	.379	.330	95	1	3	.986	-1	*90*	*117*	C66,1b5/lf	—	0.3
1936	Cin N	89	235	28	63	13	1	1	40	43	1	14	.268	.384	.345	104	4	2	.984	3	*97*	*119*	C71/1	—	1.1
1937	Cin N	18	40	3	11	2	0	0	2	5	0	1	.275	.356	.325	90	0	0	.967	-1	*80*	*86*	C17	—	0.0
1938	Bro N	54	126	10	31	5	0	0	11	19	2	9	.246	.354	.286	76	-3	0	.958	-1	*82*	*121*	C44	—	-0.1
Total	5	295	708	78	186	30	2	5	93	116	6	35	.263	.371	.332	96	3	5	.975	0	*95*	*113*	C218,1b6/lf	—	1.4
CAMPOS, FRANK	Francisco Jose (Lopez); B5.11.1924 Havana, Cuba; D1.28.2006 Miami FL; BL/TL/5´11˝/180; d9.11; [DL 1954 Was A 64]																								
1951	Was A	8	26	4	11	3	1	0	3	0	0	1	.423	.423	.615	182	3	0-0	1.000	-1	74	0	O7R	0	0.2
1952	Was A	53	112	9	29	6	1	0	8	1	2	13	.259	.278	.330	71	-5	0-0	.978	-1	104	0	O23(13/1/10)	0	-0.7
1953	Was A	10	9	0	1	0	0	0	2	1	0	0	.111	.200	.111	-14	-1	0-0	ø	0	—	—	/H	0	-0.1
Total	3	71	147	13	41	9	2	0	13	2	2	14	.279	.298	.367	86	-3	0-0	.981	-2	99	0	O30(13/1/17)	64	-0.6
CAMPUSANO, SIL	Silvestre (Diaz); B12.31.1965 Santo Domingo, D.R.; BR/TR/6´0˝/(160–190); d4.4																								
1988	Tor A	73	142	14	31	10	2	2	12	9-0	4	33	.218	.282	.359	78	-4	0-0	.934	-2	96	82	O69(15/35/19),D2	29	-0.7
1990	Phi N	66	85	10	18	1	1	2	9	6-0	1	16	.212	.269	.318	62	-5	1-0	.976	-3	78	78	O47(16/25/7)	0	-0.8
1991	Phi N	15	35	2	4	0	0	1	2	1-0	0	10	.114	.139	.200	-6	-5	0-0	1.000	1	111	177	O15(1/15/0)	18	-0.5
Total	3	154	262	26	53	11	3	5	23	16-0	5	59	.202	.260	.324	62	-14	1-0	.953	-4	93	94	O131(32/75/26),D2	47	-2.0
CANALE, GEORGE	George Anthony; B8.11.1965 Memphis TN; BL/TR/6´1˝/190; [MilA86 6/139]; d9.3; Col VPI																								
1989	Mil A	13	26	5	5	1	0	1	3	2-0	0	3	.192	.250	.346	67	-1	0-1	.989	-1	70	58	1b11	0	-0.3
1990	Mil A	10	13	4	1	1	0	0	0	2-0	0	6	.077	.200	.154	0	-2	0-1	1.000	0	124	24	1b6,D3	0	-0.2
1991	Mil A	21	34	6	6	2	0	3	10	8-0	0	6	.176	.318	.500	130	1	0-0	.983	2	166	85	1b19	0	0.3
Total	3	44	73	15	12	4	0	4	13	12-0	0	15	.164	.276	.384	85	-2	0-2	.988	2	127	65	1b36,D3	0	-0.2

YEAR	TM LG	G	AB	R	H	2B	3B	HR	RBI	BB-IB	HP	SO	AVG	OBP	SLG	AOPS	ABR	SB-CS	FA	FR	RNG	THR	GAMES AT POSITION	DL	BFW
CANATE, WILLIE	Emisael William (Librada); B12.11.1971 Maracaibo, Zulia, Venez.; BR/TR/6´0˝/170; d4.16																								
1993	†Tor A	38	47	12	10	0	0	1	3	6-0	1	15	.213	.309	.277	59	-3	1-1	1.000	2	111	205	O31(17/6/9)/D	32	-0.1
CANAVAN, JIM	James Edward; B11.26.1866 New Bedford MA; D5.27.1949 New Bedford MA; BR/TR/5´8˝/160; d4.8; OF(105/10/106)																								
1891	Cin AA	101	426	74	97	13	14	7	66	27	5	44	.228	.282	.373	80	-16	21	.860	-14	95	85	S101	—	-2.3
	Mil AA	35	142	33	38	2	4	3	21	16	0	10	.268	.342	.401	94	-3	7	.864	-2	107	44	2b24,S11	—	-0.3
	Year	136	568	107	135	15	18	10	87	43	5	54	.238	.297	.380	84	-18	28	.860	-15	96	80	S112,2b24	—	-2.6
1892	Chi N	118	439	48	73	10	11	0	32	48	0	48	.166	.248	.239	47	-29	33	.923	-11	96	86	2b112,O4(1/3/0),S2	—	-3.3
1893	Cin N	121	461	65	104	13	7	5	64	51	2	20	.226	.305	.317	64	-26	31	.931	-0	76	0	O117(96/6/16),2b5/3	—	-2.9
1894	Cin N	103	364	81	100	16	10	13	74	64	0	25	.275	.383	.481	104	1	13	.897	-1	64	153	O97(8/1/90),S3,3b2/21	—	-0.4
1897	Bro N	63	240	25	52	9	3	2	34	26	2	—	.217	.299	.304	63	-13	9	.909	-17	84	84	2b63	—	-2.4
Total	5	541	2072	326	464	63	49	30	291	232	9	147	.224	.305	.345	74	-86	114	.917	-45	73	66	O218R,2b205,S117,3b3/1	—	-11.6
CANCEL, ROBINSON	Robinson Castro; B5.4.1976 Lajas, PR; BR/TR/6´0˝/195; [MilA94 16/431]; d9.3; [DL 2000 Mil N 149]																								
1999	Mil N	15	44	5	8	2	0	0	5	2-0	1	12	.182	.234	.227	17	-6	0-0	.980	3	83	107	C15	0	-0.2
CANDAELE, CASEY	Casey Todd; B1.12.1961 Lompoc CA; BB/TR/5´9˝/(160–165); d6.5; Col Arizona; OF(86/78/38)																								
1986	Mon N	30	104	9	24	4	1	0	6	5-0	0	15	.231	.264	.288	53	-7	3-5	.983	1	103	96	2b24,3b4	0	-0.6
1987	Mon N	138	449	62	122	23	4	1	23	38-3	2	28	.272	.330	.347	77	-14	7-10	.985	3	106	77	2b68,O67(8/45/16),S25/1	0	-1.0
1988	Mon N	36	116	9	20	5	1	0	4	10-1	0	11	.172	.238	.233	34	-10	1-0	.988	-1	100	94	2b35	0	-1.1
	Hou N	21	31	2	5	3	0	0	1	1-0	0	6	.161	.188	.258	28	-3	0-1	1.000	2	121	105	2b10,O5(0/3/2)/3	0	-0.1
	Year	57	147	11	25	8	1	0	5	11-1	0	17	.170	.228	.238	33	-13	1-1	.990	1	104	96	2b45,O5(0/3/2)/3	0	-1.2
1990	Hou N	130	262	30	75	8	6	3	22	31-5	1	42	.286	.364	.397	112	5	7-5	1.000	1	111	55	O58(36/12/13),2b49,S13/3	0	0.6
1991	Hou N	151	461	44	121	20	7	4	50	40-7	0	49	.262	.319	.362	97	-3	9-3	.982	5	100	94	2b109,O26(18/5/4),3b11	0	0.5
1992	Hou N	135	320	19	68	12	1	1	18	24-3	3	36	.213	.269	.266	56	-19	7-1	.968	8	107	124	S65,3b29,O21(20/1/1),2b9	0	-0.7
1993	Hou N	75	121	18	29	8	0	1	7	10-0	0	14	.240	.298	.331	70	-5	2-3	1.000	-2	69	57	2b19,O17(4/12/2),S14,3b4	23	-0.7
1996	†Cle A	24	44	8	11	2	0	1	4	1-0	0	9	.250	.267	.364	57	-3	0-0	1.000	6	130	219	2b11,3b3/S	0	0.3
1997	Cle A	14	26	5	8	1	0	0	4	1-0	0	1	.308	.333	.346	75	-1	1-0	1.000	4	174	124	2b9/3D	0	0.4
Total	9	754	1934	206	483	86	20	11	139	161-19	6	211	.250	.308	.332	77	-60	37-28	.987	26	102	94	2b343,O194L,S118,3b54/D1	23	-2.4
CANGELOSI, JOHN	John Anthony; B3.10.1963 Brooklyn NY; BB/TL/5´8˝/(150–160); [ChiA82*4/91]; d6.30; Col Miami–Dade North (FL) CC																								
1985	Chi A	5	2	2	0	0	0	0	0	0-0	1	1	.000	.333	.000	1	0	0-0	1.000	-1	31	0	O3C,D2	0	-0.1
1986	Chi A	137	438	65	103	16	3	2	32	71-0	7	61	.235	.349	.299	76	-12	50-17	.969	-7	90	102	O129(29/98/5),D3	0	-1.6
1987	Pit N	104	182	44	50	8	3	4	18	46-1	3	33	.275	.427	.418	124	9	21-6	.962	0	99	129	O47(27/16/8)	0	1.1
1988	Pit N	75	118	18	30	4	1	0	8	17-0	1	16	.254	.353	.305	91	-1	9-4	.963	0	117	0	O24(11/12/3)/P	21	0.0
1989	Pit N	112	160	18	35	4	2	0	9	35-2	3	20	.219	.365	.269	88	0	11-8	.973	1	114	67	O46(12/24/10)	0	0.0
1990	Pit N	58	76	13	15	2	0	0	1	11-0	1	12	.197	.307	.224	50	-5	7-2	1.000	-1	86	0	O12(3/9/0)	0	-0.6
1992	Tex A	73	85	12	16	2	0	1	6	18-0	0	16	.188	.330	.247	66	-3	6-5	.964	3	106	212	O65(36/24/10),D6	0	-0.2
1994	NY N	62	111	14	28	4	0	0	4	19-1	2	20	.252	.371	.288	76	-3	5-1	1.000	4	104	264	O50(24/13/19)	0	0.1
1995	Hou N	90	201	46	64	5	2	2	18	48-2	4	42	.318	.457	.393	136	15	21-5	.950	-1	95	116	O59(26/32/1)/P	0	1.6
1996	Hou N	108	262	49	69	11	4	1	16	44-0	5	41	.263	.378	.347	101	3	17-9	.975	1	97	156	O78(53/29/0)	0	0.3
1997	†Fla N	103	192	28	47	8	0	1	12	19-1	3	33	.245	.321	.302	68	-9	5-1	1.000	1	112	46	O58(34/23/6)/P	0	-0.8
1998	Fla N	104	171	19	43	8	0	1	10	30-0	1	23	.251	.365	.316	87	-2	2-3	.969	-1	96	56	O45(9/33/8)/D	0	-0.4
1999	Col N	7	6	0	1	1	0	0	0	0-0	0	4	.167	.167	.333	18	-1	0-0	1.000	0	226	0	/lf	0	-0.1
Total	13	1038	2004	328	501	73	15	12	134	358-7	31	322	.250	.370	.319	90	-9	154-61	.972	-1	99	114	O617(265/317/70),D12,P3	21	-0.7
CANIZARO, JAY	Jason Kyle; B7.4.1973 Beaumont TX; BR/TR/5´9˝/(170–178); [SFN93 4/106]; d4.28; Col Oklahoma St.; [DL 2001 Min A 190]																								
1996	SF N	43	120	11	24	4	1	2	8	9-0	1	38	.200	.260	.300	49	-9	0-2	.972	-1	103	89	2b35,S7	0	-0.9
1999	SF N	12	18	5	8	2	0	1	9	1-0	0	2	.444	.474	.722	211	3	1-0	1.000	-1	89	74	2b4	0	0.2
2000	Min A	102	346	43	93	21	1	7	40	24-0	1	57	.269	.318	.396	74	-14	4-2	.982	-24	86	71	2b90,D2	0	-3.1
2002	Min A	38	112	14	24	8	1	0	11	10-0	1	22	.214	.280	.304	55	-7	0-1	.990	-4	91	90	2b30,3b8	0	-1.0
Total	4	195	596	73	149	35	3	10	68	44-0	3	119	.250	.303	.369	70	-27	5-5	.981	-29	90	78	2b159,3b8,S7,D2	190	-4.8
CANNELL, RIP	Virgin Wirt; B1.23.1880 S.Bridgton ME; D8.26.1948 Bridgton ME; BL/TR/5´10.5˝/180; d4.14; Col Tufts																								
1904	Bos N	100	346	32	81	5	1	0	18	23	2	—	.234	.286	.254	70	-12	10	.897	-10	44	26	O93(15/10/69)	—	-2.9
1905	Bos N	154	567	52	140	14	4	0	36	51	2	—	.247	.311	.286	80	-13	17	.935	-11	69	117	O154(3/149/3)	—	-3.3
Total	2	254	913	84	221	19	5	0	54	74	4	—	.242	.302	.274	76	-25	27	.923	-21	60	83	O247(18/159/72)	—	-6.2
CANNIZARO, ANDY	Andrew Lee; B12.19.1978 New Orleans LA; BR/TR/5´10˝/170; [NYA01 7/215]; d9.5; Col Tulane																								
2006	NY A	13	8	5	2	0	0	1	1	1-0	0	1	.250	.333	.625	140	0	0-0	.909	-2	90	0	S10,2b2,3b2	0	-0.2
CANNIZZARO, CHRIS	Christopher John; B5.3.1938 Oakland CA; BR/TR/6´0˝/(180–190); d4.17; C3																								
1960	StL N	7	9	0	2	0	0	0	1	1-0	0	3	.222	.273	.222	42	-1	0-0	1.000	1	134	0	C6	0	0.0
1961	StL N	6	2	0	1	0	0	0	0	0-0	0	0	.500	.500	.500	151	0	0-0	1.000	-0	0	0	C5	0	0.0
1962	NY N	59	133	9	32	2	1	0	9	19-1	1	26	.241	.335	.271	65	-6	1-1	.973	-1	131	193	C56/rf	0	-0.5
1963	NY N	16	33	4	8	1	0	0	4	1-0	0	8	.242	.257	.273	54	-2	0-0	1.000	-1	421	139	C15	0	-0.2
1964	NY N	60	164	11	51	10	0	0	10	14-2	1	28	.311	.367	.372	112	3	0-5	.988	1	168	135	C53	0	0.5
1965	NY N	114	251	17	46	8	2	0	7	28-4	2	60	.183	.270	.231	44	-18	0-2	.977	3	**152**	136	C112	0	-1.2
1968	Pit N	25	58	5	14	2	2	1	7	9-4	0	13	.241	.343	.397	123	2	0-0	.976	0	145	119	C25	0	0.3
1969	SD N☆	134	418	23	92	14	3	4	33	42-8	0	81	.220	.290	.297	67	-19	0-1	.988	-9	92	118	C132	0	-2.4
1970	SD N	111	341	27	95	13	3	5	42	48-8	1	49	.279	.366	.378	104	4	2-7	.980	-8	116	89	C110	0	-0.2
1971	SD N	21	63	2	12	1	0	1	8	11-0	1	10	.190	.320	.254	69	-2	0-0	.992	-0	118	68	C19	0	-0.2
	Chi N	71	197	18	42	8	1	5	23	28-2	1	24	.213	.311	.340	74	-6	0-0	.983	-12	81	99	C70	0	-1.6
	Year	92	260	20	54	9	1	6	31	39-2	2	34	.208	.314	.319	73	-8	0-0	.985	-12	90	92	C89	0	-1.8
1972	LA N	73	200	14	48	6	0	2	18	31-5	0	38	.240	.341	.300	85	-3	0-1	.983	-6	99	56	C72	0	-0.6
1973	LA N	17	21	0	4	0	0	0	3	3-1	0	3	.190	.280	.190	37	-2	0-0	1.000	-2	100	0	C13	0	-0.4
1974	SD N	26	60	2	11	1	0	0	4	6-0	0	11	.183	.258	.200	31	-6	0-0	.979	-2	93	87	C26	0	-0.7
Total	13	740	1950	132	458	66	12	18	169	241-35	7	354	.235	.319	.309	77	-56	3-17	.983	-36	121	110	C714/rf	0	-7.2
CANNON, JOE	Joseph Jerome; B7.13.1953 Camp Lejeune NC; BL/TR/6´3˝/185; [HouN74*1/16]; d9.22; Col Pensacola (FL) JC																								
1977	Hou N	9	17	3	2	2	0	0	1	0-0	0	5	.118	.118	.235	-9	-3	1-1	1.000	0	125	0	O3L	0	-0.3
1978	Hou N	8	18	1	4	0	0	0	1	0-0	0	1	.222	.222	.222	26	-2	0-1	.778	-1	87	0	O5(3/2/0)	0	-0.3
1979	Tor A	61	142	14	30	1	1	1	5	1-0	0	34	.211	.217	.254	26	-15	12-2	1.000	3	104	176	O50(17/0/40)	0	-1.2
1980	Tor A	70	50	16	4	0	0	0	4	0-0	1	14	.080	.098	.080	-49	-10	2-2	.968	-1	80	96	O33(18/16/0)/D	0	-1.2
Total	4	148	227	34	40	3	1	1	11	1-0	1	54	.176	.183	.211	7	-30	15-6	.977	1	98	136	O91(41/18/40)/D	0	-3.0
CANO, ROBINSON	Robinson Jose (Mercedes); B10.22.1982 San Pedro de Macoris, D.R.; BL/TR/6´0˝/(170–175); d5.3; f–Jose																								
2005	†NY A	132	522	78	155	34	4	14	62	16-1	3	68	.297	.320	.458	105	2	1-3	.974	4	103	87	2b131	0	1.2
2006	†NY A✳	122	482	62	165	41	1	15	78	18-3	2	54	.342	.365	.525	128	19	5-2	.984	-2	99	93	2b118,D4	43	2.2
Total	2	254	1004	140	320	75	5	29	140	34-4	5	122	.319	.342	.490	116	21	6-5	.979	3	101	90	2b249,D4	43	3.4
CANSECO, JOSE	Jose (Capas); B7.2.1964 Havana, Cuba; BR/TR/6´4˝/(195–240); [OakA82 15/392]; d9.2; twb–Ozzie																								
1985	Oak A	29	96	16	29	3	0	5	13	4-0	0	31	.302	.330	.490	130	3	1-1	.951	1	104	117	O26(13/1/16)	0	0.2
1986	Oak A☆	157	600	85	144	29	1	33	117	65-1	8	175	.240	.318	.457	117	14	15-7	.958	-7	98	39	O155(124/0/46)/D	0	0.1
1987	Oak A	159	630	81	162	35	3	31	113	50-2	2	157	.257	.310	.470	111	8	15-3	.975	6	104	141	O130L,D30	0	0.9
1988	†Oak A★	158	610	120	187	34	0	**42**	**124**	78-10	10	128	.307	.391	**.569**	**171**	60	40-16	.978	2	99	123	O144R,D13	0	5.9
1989	†Oak A✳	65	227	40	61	9	1	17	57	23-4	2	69	.269	.333	.542	150	14	6-3	.976	2	105	120	O56R,D5	101	1.4
1990	†Oak A★	131	481	83	132	14	2	37	101	72-8	5	158	.274	.371	.543	159	38	19-10	.995	1	102	109	O88R,D43	15	3.6
1991	Oak A	154	572	115	152	32	1	**44**	122	78-7	9	152	.266	.359	.556	159	46	26-6	.965	-7	96	54	O131R,D24	0	3.7
1992	Oak A✳	97	366	66	90	11	0	22	72	48-1	3	104	.246	.335	.456	127	12	5-7	.988	1	103	95	O77R,D20	15	0.9
	Tex A	22	73	8	17	4	0	4	15	15-1	3	24	.233	.385	.452	138	5	1-0	.970	1	126	0	O13R,D8	0	0.5
	Year	119	439	74	107	15	0	26	87	63-2	6	128	.244	.344	.456	129	17	6-7	.985	2	106	81	O90R,D28	0	1.4
1993	Tex A	60	231	30	59	14	1	10	46	16-2	3	62	.255	.308	.455	107	1	6-6	.970	-1	92	110	O49R/P	102	-0.3
1994	Tex A	111	429	88	121	19	2	31	90	69-8	5	114	.282	.386	.552	137	24	15-8	ø	0	0	0	D111	0	1.7
1995	†Bos A	102	396	64	121	25	1	24	81	42-4	7	93	.306	.378	.556	136	21	4-0	1.000	-0	64	0	D101/rf	36	1.5

YEAR	TM LG	G	AB	R	H	2B	3B	HR	RBI	BB-IB	HP	SO	AVG	OBP	SLG	AOPS	ABR	SB-CS	FA	FR	RNG	THR	GAMES AT POSITION	DL	BFW
1996	Bos A	96	360	68	104	22	1	28	82	63-3	6	82	.289	.400	.589	144	26	3-1	1.000	-1	80	140	D84,O11(10/0/2)	68	1.9
1997	Oak A	108	388	56	91	19	0	23	74	51-1	3	122	.235	.325	.461	103	1	8-2	.938	-4	86	73	D56,O44(19/0/27)	52	-0.6
1998	Tor A	151	583	98	138	26	0	46	107	65-5	6	159	.237	.318	.518	112	8	29-17	.960	-1	95	101	D78,O73(50/0/26)	0	0.1
1999	TB A✱	113	430	75	120	18	1	34	95	58-3	7	135	.279	.369	.563	132	20	3-0	1.000	0	77	338	D106,O6L	41	1.4
2000	TB A	61	218	31	56	15	0	9	30	41-1	4	65	.257	.383	.450	112	6	2-0	ø	0	0	0	D60	53	0.3
	†NY A	37	111	16	27	3	0	6	19	23-1	0	37	.243	.365	.432	105	1	0-0	.818	-0	118	0	D26,O5(4/0/1)	0	-0.1
	Year	98	329	47	83	18	0	15	49	64-2	4	102	.252	.377	.444	109	7	2-0	.866	-0	118	0	D86,O5(4/0/1)	0	-0.2
2001	Chi A	76	256	46	66	8	0	16	49	45-1	1	75	.258	.366	.477	114	6	2-1	1.000	-1	34	0	D68,O2R	0	0.2
Total	17	1887	7057	1186	1877	340	14	462	1407	906-63	84	1942	.266	.353	.515	132	314	200-88	.971	-8	99	94	O1011(356/1/679),D834/P	483	23.3
CANSECO, OZZIE	Osvaldo (Capas); B7.2.1964 Havana, Cuba; BR/TR/6´2˝/220; [NYA83*2/40]; d7.18; twb–Jose; Col Miami–Dade Kendall (FL) CC; [DL 1989 Oak A 24]																								
1990	Oak A	9	19	1	2	1	0	0	1	1-0	0	10	.105	.150	.158	-14	-3	0-0	1.000	-0	86	0	O2(1/0/1),D4	0	-0.3
1992	StL N	9	29	7	8	5	0	0	3	7-0	0	4	.276	.417	.448	148	3	0-0	.889	-2	48	0	O8(7/0/1)	0	0.0
1993	StL N	6	17	0	3	0	0	0	0	1-0	0	3	.176	.222	.176	8	-2	0-0	.500	-2	13	0	O5L	0	-0.4
Total	3	24	65	8	13	6	0	0	4	9-0	0	17	.200	.297	.292	66	-2	0-0	.857	-4	42	0	O15(13/0/2),D4	24	-0.7
CANTU, JORGE	Jorge Luis (Guzman); B1.30.1982 McAllen TX; BR/TR/6´1˝/(180–185); d7.17																								
2004	TB A	50	173	25	52	20	1	2	17	9-0	2	44	.301	.341	.462	110	3	0-0	.964	-4	95	91	2b33,3b11/SD	0	0.1
2005	TB A	150	598	73	171	40	1	28	117	19-1	6	83	.286	.311	.497	113	9	1-0	.971	-35	85	70	2b80,3b62,D13	0	-2.2
2006	TB A	107	413	40	103	18	2	14	62	26-2	3	91	.249	.295	.404	80	-13	1-1	.973	-18	86	81	2b103,D2	43	-2.6
Total	3	307	1184	138	326	78	4	44	196	54-3	11	218	.275	.310	.459	101	-1	2-1	.971	-57	87	78	2b216,3b73,D19/S	43	-4.7
CANTZ, BART	Bartholomew L.; B1.29.1860 Philadelphia PA; D2.12.1943 Philadelphia PA; TR; d7.25																								
1888	Bal AA	37	126	7	21	2	1	0	9	2	0	—	.167	.180	.198	22	-11	0	.904	-7	—	—	C33,O4(1/0/3)	—	-1.5
1889	Bal AA	20	69	6	12	2	0	0	8	4	0	14	.174	.219	.203	20	-7	2	.860	-5	—	—	C18,O2R	—	-0.9
1890	Phi AA	5	22	1	1	0	0	0	1	0	0	—	.045	.045	.045	-74	-5	0	.893	-2	*84*	*127*	C5	—	-0.6
Total	3	62	217	14	34	4	1	0	18	6	0	14	.157	.179	.184	11	-23	2	.890	-14	*84*	*127*	C56,O6(1/0/5)	—	-3.0
CAPRA, NICK	Nick Lee; B3.8.1958 Denver CO; BR/TR/5´8˝/165; [TexA79 3/69]; d9.6; Col Oklahoma																								
1982	Tex A	13	15	2	4	0	0	1	1	3-0	1	4	.267	.421	.467	150	1	2-1	1.000	2	131	586	O9(4/1/4)	0	0.3
1983	Tex A	8	2	2	0	0	0	0	0	0-0	0	0	.000	.000	.000	-99	-1	0-0	ø	-0	0	0	O4(1/1/2)	0	-0.1
1985	Tex A	8	8	1	1	0	0	0	0	0-0	0	0	.125	.125	.125	-31	-1	0-0	1.000	1	158	0	O8(1/3/4)	0	-0.1
1988	KC A	14	29	3	4	1	0	0	0	2-0	0	3	.138	.194	.172	3	-4	1-0	1.000	-1	77	0	O11(2/7/2)/D	0	-0.5
1991	Tex A	2	0	1	0	0	0	0	0	1-0	0	0	ø	1.000	ø	205	0	0-0	1.000	0	242	0	O2(1/1/0)	0	0.1
Total	5	45	54	9	9	1	0	1	1	6-0	1	7	.167	.262	.241	41	-5	3-1	1.000	2	111	175	O34(9/13/12)/D	0	-0.3
CAPRI, PAT	Patrick Nicholas; B11.27.1918 New York NY; D6.14.1989 New York NY; BR/TR/6´0.5˝/170; d7.16; Col Brooklyn																								
1944	Bos N	7	1	1	0	0	0	0	0	0	0	1	.000	.000	.000	-96	0	0	1.000	1	287	732	/2	0	0.0
CAPRON, RALPH	Ralph Earl; B6.16.1889 Minneapolis MN; D9.19.1980 Los Angeles CA; BL/TR/5´11.5˝/165; d4.25; Col Minnesota																								
1912	Pit N	1	0	0	0	0	0	0	0	0	0	0	ø	ø	ø	ø	0	0	ø	0	—	—	/R	—	0.0
1913	Phi N	2	1	1	0	0	0	0	0	0	0	0	.000	.000	.000	-96	0	0	ø	-0	0	0	/lf	—	0.0
Total	2	3	1	1	0	0	0	0	0	0	0	0	.000	.000	.000	-96	0	0	.000	-0	0	0	/lf	—	0.0
CARABALLO, RAMON	Ramon (Sanchez); B5.23.1969 Rio San Juan, D.R.; BB/TR/5´7˝/150; d9.9																								
1993	Atl N	6	0	0	0	0	0	0	0	0-0	0	0	ø	ø	ø	ø	0	0-0	1.000	1	116	0	2b5	0	0.1
1995	StL N	34	99	10	20	4	1	2	3	6-0	3	33	.202	.269	.323	54	-7	3-2	.956	4	115	139	2b24	0	-0.1
Total	2	40	99	10	20	4	1	2	3	6-0	3	33	.202	.269	.323	54	-7	3-2	.958	5	115	134	2b29	0	0.0
CARBINE, JOHN	John C.; B10.12.1855 Syracuse NY; D9.11.1915 Chicago IL; 6´0˝/187; d5.8																								
1875	Wes NA	10	36	0	3	0	0	0	2	0	—	1	.083	.083	.083	-40	-5	0-0	.950	1	154	111	1b10	—	-0.4
1876	Lou N	7	25	3	4	0	0	0	1	0	—	0	.160	.160	.160	6	-3	—	.878	-0	88	219	1b6/rf	—	-0.3
CARBO, BERNIE	Bernardo; B8.5.1947 Detroit MI; BL/TR/6´0˝/(175–185); [CinN65 1/16]; d9.2																								
1969	Cin N	4	3	0	0	0	0	0	0	0-0	0	2	.000	.000	.000	-95	-1	0-0	ø	0	—	—	/H	0	-0.1
1970	†Cin N	125	365	54	113	19	3	21	63	94-9	4	77	.310	.454	.551	167	41	10-4	.979	-1	93	101	O119(118/0/1)	0	3.4
1971	Cin N	106	310	33	68	20	1	5	20	54-4	2	56	.219	.338	.339	93	0	2-1	.982	1	94	118	O90L	0	-0.5
1972	Cin N	19	21	2	3	0	0	0	0	6-1	1	3	.143	.357	.143	49	-1	0-0	1.000	0	146	0	O4R	0	-0.1
	StL N	99	302	42	78	13	1	7	34	57-9	5	56	.258	.381	.377	118	11	0-1	.967	7	103	236	O92R/3	0	1.3
	Year	118	323	44	81	13	1	7	34	63-10	6	59	.251	.380	.362	114	10	0-1	.969	7	105	228	O96R/3	0	1.2
1973	StL N	111	308	42	88	18	0	8	40	58-7	1	52	.286	.397	.422	127	15	2-0	.978	3	104	139	O94(2/0/93)	0	1.4
1974	Bos A	117	338	40	84	20	0	12	61	58-7	4	90	.249	.364	.414	116	9	4-3	.994	0	100	82	O87(33/0/56),D15	0	0.5
1975	†Bos A	107	319	64	82	21	3	15	50	83-5	1	69	.257	.409	.483	140	21	2-4	.976	1	100	114	O85(38/0/47),D13	0	1.7
1976	Bos A	17	55	5	13	4	0	2	6	8-1	0	17	.236	.333	.418	107	1	1-0	1.000	0	100	0	D15/lf	0	0.0
	Mil A	69	183	20	43	7	0	3	15	33-3	0	55	.235	.352	.322	100	2	1-2	1.000	5	122	243	O33(4/0/29),D24	0	0.5
	Year	86	238	25	56	11	0	5	21	41-4	0	72	.235	.348	.345	102	2	2-2	1.000	5	122	239	D39,O34(5/0/29)	0	0.5
1977	Bos A	86	228	36	66	6	1	15	34	47-3	0	72	.289	.409	.522	137	13	1-2	.951	2	111	115	O67(8/0/59),D7	0	1.2
1978	Bos A	17	46	7	12	3	0	1	6	8-0	0	8	.261	.370	.391	104	1	1-1	1.000	1	155	0	O9(1/0/8),D8	0	0.1
	Cle A	60	174	21	50	8	0	4	16	20-1	1	31	.287	.362	.402	116	4	1-0	1.000	-1	23	0	D49,O4R	0	0.2
	Year	77	220	28	62	11	0	5	22	28-1	1	39	.282	.364	.400	113	5	2-1	.850	1	127	0	D57,O13(1/0/12)	0	0.3
1979	StL N	52	64	6	18	1	0	3	12	10-0	0	22	.281	.368	.438	120	2	1-0	1.000	-2	57	0	O17(4/0/13)	0	0.0
1980	StL N	14	11	0	2	0	0	0	0	1-0	0	0	.182	.250	.182	21	-1	0-0	ø	0	—	—	/H	0	-0.2
	Pit N	7	6	0	2	0	0	0	1	1-0	0	1	.333	.429	.333	111	0	0-0	ø	0	—	—	/H	0	0.0
	Year	21	17	0	4	0	0	0	1	2-0	0	1	.235	.316	.235	54	-1	0-0	ø	0	—	—	0	—	-0.2
Total	12	1010	2733	372	722	140	9	96	358	538-50	19	611	.264	.387	.427	125	117	26-18	.978	17	101	131	O702(299/0/406),D131/3	0	9.4
CARDENAL, JOSE	Jose Rosario Domec (b Jose Rosario Domec (Cardenal)); B10.7.1943 Matanzas, Cuba; BR/TR/5´10˝/(150–160); d4.14; C11; OF(427/847/549)																								
1963	SF N	9	5	1	1	0	0	0	2	1-0	0	1	.200	.333	.200	58	0	0-1	ø	-0	0	0	O2(0/1/1)	0	-0.1
1964	SF N	20	15	3	0	0	0	0	0	2-0	0	3	.000	.118	.000	-62	-3	2-0	.909	1	83	549	O16(8/2/6)	0	-0.2
1965	Cal A	134	512	58	128	23	2	11	57	27-1	2	72	.250	.287	.367	87	-10	37-15	.964	3	100	**221**	O129C,3b2/2	0	-0.8
1966	Cal A	154	561	67	155	15	3	16	48	34-5	4	69	.276	.320	.399	109	5	24-11	.992	3	105	113	O146(7/140/0)	0	0.6
1967	Cal A	108	381	40	90	13	5	6	27	15-0	2	63	.236	.268	.344	83	-10	10-5	.986	3	102	173	O101(27/70/17)	0	-1.1
1968	Cle A	157	583	78	150	21	7	7	44	39-3	2	74	.257	.305	.353	101	-1	40-18	.974	7	108	124	O153C	0	0.4
1969	Cle A	146	557	75	143	26	3	11	45	49-3	0	58	.257	.314	.373	90	-8	36-6	.982	2	108	109	O142(1/141/0),3b5	0	-0.4
1970	StL N	148	552	73	162	32	6	10	74	45-0	1	70	.293	.348	.428	104	3	26-9	.969	-9	91	78	O134(0/133/1)	0	-0.7
1971	StL N	89	301	37	73	12	4	7	48	29-1	0	35	.243	.303	.379	90	-4	12-3	.969	7	118	162	O83(0/8/78)	0	0.0
	Mil A	53	198	20	51	10	0	3	32	13-0	1	20	.258	.297	.354	87	-4	9-5	.979	3	107	183	O52(0/45/7)	0	-0.2
1972	Chi N	143	533	96	155	24	6	17	70	55-3	1	58	.291	.356	.454	117	12	25-14	.971	-9	85	112	O137(8/16/125)	0	-0.3
1973	Chi N	145	522	80	158	33	2	11	68	58-9	5	62	.303	.375	.437	116	14	19-7	.980	-5	92	106	O142(1/2/142)	0	0.4
1974	Chi N	143	542	75	159	35	3	13	72	56-3	1	67	.293	.359	.441	118	14	23-9	.965	4	101	157	O137(32/1/108)	0	1.3
1975	Chi N	154	574	85	182	30	2	9	68	77-5	4	50	.317	.397	.423	123	22	34-12	.976	9	107	126	O151(137/0/18)	0	2.7
1976	Chi N	136	521	64	156	25	2	8	47	32-0	1	39	.299	.339	.401	101	1	23-14	.981	3	97	116	O128(127/0/2)	0	-0.3
1977	Chi N	100	226	33	54	12	1	3	18	28-2	1	30	.239	.324	.341	71	-8	5-4	.989	-4	84	30	O62(54/6/2)/2S	18	-1.6
1978	†Phi N	87	201	27	50	12	0	4	33	23-2	0	16	.249	.323	.368	92	-2	2-3	.990	-5	71	136	1b50,O13(10/0/4)	0	-1.0
1979	Phi N	29	48	4	10	3	0	0	9	8-1	0	8	.208	.321	.271	61	-2	1-0	1.000	-1	85	0	O12(9/0/6)/1	0	-0.4
	NY N	11	37	8	11	4	0	2	4	6-0	1	3	.297	.409	.568	168	4	1-0	1.000	-1	102	0	O9R,1b2	40	0.3
	Year	40	85	12	21	7	0	2	13	14-1	1	11	.247	.360	.400	104	1	2-0	1.000	-2	93	0	O21(9/0/15),1b3	0	-0.1
1980	NY N	26	42	4	7	1	0	0	4	6-0	0	4	.167	.265	.190	31	-4	0-1	1.000	1	141	268	O6(2/0/4),1b5	0	-0.4
	†KC A	25	53	8	18	2	0	0	5	5-0	0	5	.340	.377	.377	112	1	0-0	.970	-1	84	150	O23(4/0/19)	0	0.0
Total	18	2017	6964	936	1913	333	46	138	775	608-38	26	807	.275	.333	.395	102	20	329-137	.976	13	100	129	O1778C,1b58,3b7,2b2/S	58	-1.8
CARDENAS, LEO	Leonardo Lazaro (Alfonso) "Chico"; B12.17.1938 Matanzas, Cuba; BR/TR/5´10˝/(150–163); d7.25																								
1960	Cin N	48	142	13	33	2	4	1	12	6-0	0	32	.232	.264	.324	59	-9	0-0	.958	0	103	130	S47	0	-0.5
1961	†Cin N	74	198	23	61	18	1	5	24	15-1	0	39	.308	.353	.485	119	6	1-0	.973	-11	87	66	S63	0	0.0
1962	Cin N	153	589	77	173	31	4	10	60	39-4	5	99	.294	.341	.411	98	-1	2-5	.972	-11	94	89	S149	0	0.0
1963	Cin N	158	565	42	133	22	4	7	48	23-6	4	101	.235	.270	.326	69	-23	3-5	**.972**	-3	92	99	S157	0	-1.5

YEAR	TM LG	G	AB	R	H	2B	3B	HR	RBI	BB-IB	HP	SO	AVG	OBP	SLG	AOPS	ABR	SB-CS	FA	FR	RNG	THR	GAMES AT POSITION	DL	BFW
1964	Cin N★	**163**	597	61	150	32	2	9	69	41-10	2	110	.251	.299	.357	82	-14	4-4	.960	-11	85	97	S163	0	-1.2
1965	Cin N★	156	557	65	160	25	11	11	57	60-**25**	1	100	.287	.355	.431	113	11	1-4	.975	-2	90	93	S155	0	2.2
1966	Cin N★	**160**	568	59	145	25	4	20	81	45-**18**	1	87	.255	.309	.419	93	-6	9-4	**.980**	-14	87	88	S160	0	-0.5
1967	Cin N	108	379	30	97	14	3	2	21	34-16	2	77	.256	.320	.325	76	-10	4-5	.971	-10	90	87	S108	60	-1.3
1968	Cin N★	137	452	45	106	13	2	7	41	36-18	2	83	.235	.292	.319	79	-11	2-1	.955	-22	91	82	S136	0	-2.6
1969	†Min A	160	578	67	162	24	4	10	70	66-12	4	96	.280	.353	.388	106	6	5-6	.965	23	112	**134**	S160	0	4.9
1970	†Min A	160	588	67	145	34	4	11	65	42-2	4	101	.247	.300	.374	84	-14	2-5	.978	5	100	100	S160	0	0.9
1971	Min A☆	153	554	59	146	25	4	18	75	51-5	1	69	.264	.321	.421	107	4	3-3	**.985**	0	95	96	S153	0	2.4
1972	Cal A	150	551	25	123	11	2	6	42	35-4	2	73	.223	.272	.283	69	-23	1-2	.970	8	98	90	S150	0	0.2
1973	Cle A	72	195	9	42	4	0	0	12	13-0	0	42	.215	.264	.236	41	-15	1-4	.964	-12	84	86	S67,3b5	0	-2.2
1974	Tex A	34	92	5	25	3	0	0	7	2-1	0	14	.272	.287	.304	72	-4	1-0	1.000	2	106	29	3b21,S10,D4	0	-0.1
1975	Tex A	55	102	15	24	2	0	1	5	14-0	0	12	.235	.328	.284	75	-3	0-0	.956	8	122	153	3b43,S5,2b3	0	0.5
Total	16	1941	6707	662	1725	285	49	118	689	522-122	28	1135	.257	.311	.367	88	-106	39-48	.971	-49	94	96	S1843,3b69,D4,2b3	60	1.2
CARDONA, JAVIER	Javier Peterson; B9.15.1975 Santurce, PR; BR/TR/6´1˝/185; [DetA94 23/641]; d5.31; Col Lake Land (IL) JC																								
2000	Det A	26	40	1	7	1	0	1	2	0-0	1	9	.175	.190	.275	17	-5	0-0	.973	-3	99	58	C26	0	-0.7
2001	Det A	46	96	10	25	8	0	1	10	2-0	1	12	.260	.280	.375	73	-4	0-1	.980	-7	199	111	C44/D	0	-0.9
2002	SD N	15	39	2	4	1	0	0	2	2-0	0	10	.103	.143	.128	-29	-8	0-0	.976	-2	134	131	C14	0	-0.9
Total	3	87	175	13	36	10	0	2	14	4-0	2	31	.206	.228	.297	38	-17	0-1	.977	-12	161	102	C84/D	0	-2.5
CAREW, ROD	Rodney Cline; B10.1.1945 Gatun, Canal Zone; BL/TR/6´0˝/(170–182); d4.11; C10; HF1991																								
1967	Min A★	137	514	66	150	22	7	8	51	37-4	2	91	.292	.341	.409	112	7	5-9	.976	-2	97	86	2b134	0	1.6
1968	Min A★	127	461	46	126	27	2	1	42	26-1	1	71	.273	.312	.347	95	-3	12-4	.968	-5	96	77	2b117,S4	0	0.5
1969	†Min A★	123	458	79	152	30	4	8	56	37-0	3	72	**.332**	.386	.467	134	21	19-8	.970	-6	102	116	2b118	0	2.5
1970	†Min A✳	51	191	27	70	12	3	4	28	11-0	2	28	.366	.407	.524	152	13	4-6	.961	-5	101	99	2b45/1	69	1.0
1971	Min A★	147	577	88	177	16	10	2	48	45-1	1	81	.307	.356	.380	106	4	6-7	.976	-21	87	80	2b142,3b2	0	-1.0
1972	Min A★	142	535	61	170	21	6	0	51	43-9	2	60	**.318**	.369	.379	118	12	12-6	.978	2	100	103	2b139	0	2.6
1973	Min A★	149	580	98	**203**	30	**11**	6	62	62-9	2	55	**.350**	.411	.471	143	34	41-16	.984	10	98	96	2b147	0	**5.8**
1974	Min A★	153	599	86	**218**	30	5	3	55	74-9	1	49	**.364**	**.433**	.446	149	42	38-16	.960	13	100	104	2b148	0	**6.9**
1975	Min A★	143	535	89	192	24	4	14	80	64-**18**	1	40	**.359**	**.421**	.497	159	44	35-9	.973	12	106	95	2b123,1b14,D2	0	6.7
1976	Min A★	156	605	97	200	29	12	9	90	67-14	1	52	.331	.395	.463	149	38	49-22	.989	-3	97	**113**	1b152,2b7	0	2.7
1977	Min A★	155	616	**128**	**239**	38	**16**	14	100	69-**15**	3	55	**.388**	**.449**	.570	**178**	**69**	23-13	.994	7	114	**124**	1b151,2b4/D	0	**6.5**
1978	Min A★	152	564	85	188	26	10	5	70	78-**19**	1	62	**.333**	**.411**	.441	138	32	27-7	.989	-0	105	111	1b148,2b4/lf	0	2.6
1979	†Cal A✳	110	409	78	130	15	3	3	44	73-7	0	46	.318	.419	.391	124	19	18-8	.988	-8	72	108	1b103,D6	46	0.5
1980	Cal A★	144	540	74	179	34	7	3	59	59-7	1	38	.331	.396	.437	131	25	23-15	.994	-4	82	81	1b103,D32	0	1.3
1981	Cal A★	93	364	57	111	17	1	2	21	45-7	0	45	.305	.380	.374	117	10	16-9	.995	-1	98	114	1b90,D2	0	0.4
1982	†Cal A✳	138	523	88	167	25	5	3	44	67-5	2	49	.319	.396	.403	120	17	10-17	.992	1	106	105	1b134	0	0.6
1983	Cal A★	129	472	66	160	24	2	2	44	57-9	1	48	.339	.409	.411	128	21	6-7	.994	-9	72	112	1b89,D24,2b2	0	0.5
1984	Cal A★	93	329	42	97	8	1	3	31	40-1	0	39	.295	.367	.353	102	2	4-3	.981	-3	99	108	1b83/D	23	-0.6
1985	Cal A	127	443	69	124	17	3	2	39	64-9	1	47	.280	.371	.345	98	2	5-5	.994	-10	73	**128**	1b116	21	-1.6
Total	19	2469	9315	1424	3053	445	112	92	1015	1018-144	25	1028	.328	.393	.429	130	409	353-187	.991	-32	94	111	1b1184,2b1130,D68,S4,3b2/lf	159	39.5
CAREY, ANDY	Andrew Arthur (b Andrew Arthur Hexem); B10.18.1931 Oakland CA; BR/TR/6´1˝/(185–198); d5.2; Col St. Marys (CA)																								
1952	NY A	16	40	6	6	0	0	0	1	3	0	10	.150	.209	.150	1	-5	0-0	.889	-1	102	185	3b14/S	0	-0.7
1953	NY A	51	81	14	26	5	0	4	8	9	0	12	.321	.389	.531	152	6	2-1	.988	5	121	172	3b40,S2/2	0	1.1
1954	NY A	122	411	60	124	14	6	8	65	43	7	38	.302	.373	.423	123	13	5-5	.967	13	105	**141**	3b120	0	2.5
1955	†NY A	135	510	73	131	19	**11**	7	47	44-6	1	51	.257	.313	.378	88	-11	3-3	.954	10	102	**138**	3b135	0	-0.2
1956	†NY A	132	422	54	100	18	2	7	50	45-4	2	53	.237	.310	.339	75	-16	9-6	.947	-3	101	**102**	3b131	0	-1.9
1957	†NY A	85	247	30	63	6	5	6	33	15-3	5	42	.255	.309	.393	92	-4	2-2	.977	-0	99	70	3b81	0	-0.5
1958	†NY A	102	315	39	90	19	4	12	45	34-4	6	43	.286	.363	.486	137	16	1-2	.961	8	104	122	3b99	0	2.4
1959	NY A	41	101	11	26	1	0	3	9	7-0	0	17	.257	.306	.356	84	-3	1-1	.916	-1	83	200	3b34	70	-0.4
1960	NY A	4	3	1	1	0	0	0	1	0-0	0	1	.333	.333	.333	86	0	0-0	1.000	0	143	0	3b2/lf	0	0.0
	KC A	102	343	30	80	14	4	12	53	26-0	1	52	.233	.287	.402	84	-9	0-0	.975	3	100	135	3b91	0	-0.7
	Year	106	346	31	81	14	4	12	54	26-0	1	53	.234	.287	.402	85	-9	0-0	.975	3	100	134	3b93/lf	0	-0.7
1961	KC A	39	123	20	30	6	2	3	11	15-0	2	23	.244	.336	.398	94	-1	0-0	.944	-3	93	147	3b39	0	-0.4
	Chi A	56	143	21	38	12	3	0	14	11-0	2	24	.266	.323	.392	93	-1	0-1	.961	-10	81	49	3b54	0	-1.2
	Year	95	266	41	68	18	5	3	25	26-0	4	47	.256	.329	.395	93	-2	0-1	.953	-13	87	94	3b93	0	-1.6
1962	LA N	53	111	12	26	5	1	2	13	16-1	1	23	.234	.333	.351	90	-1	0-0	.932	-3	88	71	3b42	0	-0.4
Total	11	938	2850	371	741	119	38	64	350	268-18	27	389	.260	.327	.396	97	-16	23-21	.958	18	100	121	3b882,S3/lf2	70	-0.4
CAREY, SCOOPS	George C.; B12.4.1870 Pittsburgh PA; D12.17.1916 E.Liverpool OH; BR/TR/5´11˝/175; d4.26; Col West Virginia																								
1895	†Bal N	123	490	59	128	21	6	1	75	27	4	32	.261	.305	.335	63	-29	2	**.987**	-7	65	**112**	1b123/cfS3	—	-2.9
1898	Lou N	8	32	1	6	1	1	0	1	1	0	—	.188	.212	.281	42	-3	0	.961	-0	118	92	1b8	—	-0.3
1902	Was A	120	452	46	142	35	11	0	60	20	5	—	.314	.350	.440	117	10	3	**.989**	4	107	76	1b120	—	1.1
1903	Was A	48	183	8	37	3	2	0	23	4	1	—	.202	.223	.240	38	-14	0	.977	-3	81	75	1b47	—	-1.9
Total	4	299	1157	114	313	60	20	1	159	52	10	32	.271	.308	.360	80	-36	5	.986	-5	86	91	1b298/3Scf	—	-4.0
CAREY, MAX	Max George "Scoops" (b Maximilian Carnarius); B1.11.1890 Terre Haute IN; D5.30.1976 Miami FL; BB/TR/5´11.5˝/170; d10.3; M2/C1; HF1961																								
1910	Pit N	2	6	2	3	0	1	0	2	2	0	1	.500	.625	.833	307	2	0	1.000	1	149	239	O2L	—	0.3
1911	Pit N	129	427	77	110	15	10	5	43	44	7	75	.258	.337	.375	95	-4	27	.975	7	**121**	66	O122(46/76/0)	—	-0.3
1912	Pit N	150	587	114	177	23	8	5	66	61	5	79	.302	.372	.394	111	10	45	.968	3	106	77	O150(145/6/0)	—	0.6
1913	Pit N	154	620	**99**	172	23	10	5	49	55	3	67	.277	.339	.371	107	6	**61**-17	.961	11	107	127	O154(144/11/0)	—	1.7
1914	Pit N	156	593	76	144	25	**17**	1	31	59	2	56	.243	.313	.347	101	-1	38	.966	7	105	117	O154L	—	-0.1
1915	Pit N	140	564	76	143	26	5	3	27	57	4	58	.254	.326	.333	101	2	**36**-17	.982	11	109	126	O139L	—	1.0
1916	Pit N	154	599	90	158	23	11	7	42	59	7	58	.264	.337	.374	117	13	**63**-19	.983	22	113	**166**	O154(21/134/0)	—	3.6
1917	Pit N	155	588	82	174	21	12	1	51	58	10	38	.296	.369	.378	125	20	**46**	.979	21	**121**	136	O153C	—	3.4
1918	Pit N	**126**	468	70	128	14	6	3	48	**62**	4	25	.274	.363	.348	113	10	**58**	.958	13	110	**146**	O126C	—	1.6
1919	Pit N	66	244	41	75	10	2	0	9	25	2	24	.307	.376	.365	119	7	18	.947	1	114	63	O63C	—	0.4
1920	Pit N	130	485	74	140	18	4	1	35	59	3	31	.289	.369	.348	104	5	**52**-10	.967	-5	103	52	O129C	—	-0.1
1921	Pit N	140	521	85	161	34	4	7	56	70	4	30	.309	.395	.430	115	16	37-12	.957	5	**115**	71	O139C	—	1.8
1922	Pit N	**155**	629	140	207	28	12	10	70	**80**	4	26	.329	.408	.459	122	23	**51**-2	.969	10	109	116	O155(3/152/0)	—	3.5
1923	Pit N	153	610	120	188	32	**19**	6	63	73	7	28	.308	.388	.452	119	18	**51**-8	.962	12	108	137	O153C	—	3.0
1924	Pit N	149	599	113	178	30	9	8	55	58	7	17	.297	.366	.417	108	8	**49**-13	.965	2	103	97	O149C	—	1.0
1925	†Pit N	133	542	109	186	39	13	5	44	66	4	19	.343	.418	.491	123	22	**46**-11	.950	4	99	**160**	O130C	—	2.4
1926	Pit N	86	324	46	72	14	5	0	28	30	0	14	.222	.288	.296	55	-21	10	.943	1	104	104	O82C	—	-2.3
	Bro N	27	100	18	26	3	1	0	7	8	0	5	.260	.315	.310	70	-4	0	.933	-3	100	0	O27C	—	-0.8
	Year	113	424	64	98	17	6	0	35	38	0	19	.231	.294	.300	58	-25	10	.941	-2	103	78	O109C	—	-3.1
1927	Bro N	144	538	70	143	30	10	1	54	64	1	18	.266	.345	.364	90	-6	32	.970	3	101	112	O141(1/38/108)	—	-1.4
1928	Bro N	108	296	41	73	11	0	2	19	47	2	24	.247	.354	.304	74	-9	18	.986	1	102	109	O95(1/75/35)	—	-1.2
1929	Bro N	19	23	2	7	0	0	0	1	3	1	2	.304	.407	.304	81	0	0	1.000	-0	101	0	O4(0/2/2)	—	-0.1
Total	20	2476	9363	1545	2665	419	159	70	800	1040	77	695	.285	.361	.386	107	117	738-109	.966	127	108	111	O2421(656/1645/145)	—	18.0
CAREY, PAUL	Paul Stephan; B1.8.1968 Boston MA; BL/TR/6´4˝/215; [Mial90 3/100]; d5.25; Col Stanford; [DL 1994 Bal A 99]																								
1993	Bal A	18	47	1	10	1	0	0	3	5-0	0	14	.213	.288	.234	40	-4	0-0	.970	-2	21	122	1b9,D5	0	-0.6
CAREY, ROGER	Roger J.; B1865 NY; D2.8.1895 New York NY; d7.9																								
1887	NY N	1	4	0	0	0	0	0	2	0	0	1	.000	.000	.000	-99	-1	0	.800	0	143	193	/2	—	-0.1
CAREY, TOM	Thomas Francis Aloysius "Scoops"; B10.11.1906 Hoboken NJ; D2.21.1970 Rochester NY; BR/TR/5´8.5˝/170; d7.19; Mil 1943–45; C2																								
1935	StL A	76	296	29	86	18	4	0	42	13	0	11	.291	.320	.378	77	-11	0-2	.961	-3	100	93	2b76	—	-1.0
1936	StL A	134	488	58	133	27	6	1	57	27	3	25	.273	.315	.359	64	-29	2-1	.967	-1	**105**	86	2b128/S	—	-2.0
1937	StL A	130	487	54	134	24	1	1	40	21	1	26	.275	.306	.335	61	-30	1-2	.983	-2	99	89	2b87,S44/3	—	-2.2
1939	Bos A	54	161	17	39	6	2	0	20	3	2	9	.242	.265	.304	44	-14	0-0	1.000	6	111	106	2b35,S10	—	-0.6
1940	Bos A	43	62	4	20	4	0	0	7	2	0	1	.323	.344	.387	86	-1	0-0	.953	3	121	162	S20,2b4,3b4	—	0.3
1941	Bos A	25	21	7	4	0	0	0	2	0	0	2	.190	.190	.190	1	-3	0-0	1.000	2	105	169	2b9,S8/3	0	-0.1

YEAR	TM LG	G	AB	R	H	2B	3B	HR	RBI	BB-IB	HP	SO	AVG	OBP	SLG	AOPS	ABR	SB-CS	FA	FR	RNG	THR	GAMES AT POSITION	DL	BFW
1942	Bos A	1	1	0	1	0	0	0	1	0	0	0	1.000	1.000	1.000	448	0	0-0	1.000	-0	0	0	/2	0	0.0
1946	Bos A	3	5	0	1	0	0	0	0	0	0	1	.200	.200	.200	11	-1	0-0	.900	1	139	202	2b3	0	0.0
Total	8	466	1521	169	418	79	13	2	169	66	6	75	.275	.308	.348	63	-89	3-5	.973	5	103	91	2b343,S83,3b6	0	-5.6
Carey, Tom	Thomas John; B3.1846 Brooklyn NY; D8.16.1906 San Francisco CA; BR/TR/5´8˝/145; d5.4; M2/U2																								
1871	Kek NA	19	87	16	20	2	0	0	10	2	—	1	.230	.247	.253	43	-6	5-0	.857	0	96	74	2b19	—	-0.4
1872	Bal NA	42	196	42	57	7	0	2	27	2	—	2	.291	.298	.357	96	-2	4-1	.815	-13	63	39	2b29,S9,3b3,O3R/1	—	-1.1
1873	Bal NA	56	291	76	98	18	3	1	55	1	—	4	.337	.339	.430	126	10	2-3	.847	-3	94	106	2b54,3b4,S3,M	—	0.2
1874	Mut NA	64	287	56	82	10	3	1	38	2	—	4	.286	.291	.352	102	0	3-0	.776	-19	80	61	S51,2b13,M	—	-1.6
1875	Har NA	86	382	63	101	6	2	0	38	1	—	3	.264	.266	.291	89	-6	13-3	.844	-13	83	136	S86/2	—	-1.7
1876	Har N	68	289	51	78	7	0	0	26	3	—	4	.270	.277	.294	84	-6	—	.882	0	99	84	S68	—	-0.2
1877	Har N	60	274	38	70	3	2	1	20	0	—	9	.255	.255	.292	81	-5	—	.826	-7	107	84	S60	—	-0.8
1878	Pro N	61	253	33	60	10	3	0	24	0	—	14	.237	.237	.300	76	-7	—	.874	2	107	55	S61	—	-0.2
1879	Cle N	80	335	30	80	14	1	0	32	5	—	20	.239	.250	.287	77	-8	—	.864	-3	99	67	S80	—	-0.7
Total	5NA	267	1243	253	358	43	8	4	168	8	—	14	.288	.293	.345	99	-4	27-7	.813	-47	82	105	S149,2b116,3b7,O3R/1	—	-4.6
Total	4	269	1151	152	288	34	6	1	102	8	—	47	.250	.255	.293	79	-26	—	.862	-8	103	72	S269	—	-1.9
Carfrey, Ed	Ed; d4.19																								
1890	Phi AA	1	4	0	1	0	0	0	0	0	0	—	.250	.250	.250	48	0	0	.750	-1	59	0	/S	—	-0.1
Cargo, Bobby	Robert J.; B10.1868 Pittsburgh PA; D4.27.1904 Atlanta GA; BR/TR; d10.6																								
1892	Pit N	2	4	0	1	0	0	0	0	0	0	0	.250	.250	.250	51	0	0	.636	-0	109	404	S2	—	-0.1
Carisch, Fred	Frederick Behlmer; B11.14.1881 Fountain City WI; D4.19.1977 San Gabriel CA; BR/TR/5´10.5˝/174; d8.31; C2																								
1903	Pit N	5	18	4	6	4	0	1	5	0	0	—	.333	.333	.722	192	2	0	.969	1	143	102	C4	—	0.3
1904	Pit N	37	125	9	31	3	1	0	8	9	0	—	.248	.299	.288	79	-3	3	.984	2	108	109	C22,1b14	—	0.1
1905	Pit N	32	107	7	22	0	3	0	8	2	1	—	.206	.227	.262	44	-8	1	.973	3	126	97	C30	—	-0.3
1906	Pit N	4	12	0	1	0	0	0	0	1	0	—	.083	.154	.083	-25	-2	1	.909	-1	114	107	C4	—	-0.2
1912	Cle A	24	69	4	19	3	1	0	5	1	0	—	.275	.286	.348	78	-2	3	.952	4	103	125	C23	—	0.4
1913	Cle A	82	222	11	48	4	2	0	26	21	1	19	.216	.287	.252	56	-12	6	.971	14	126	94	C79	—	0.8
1914	Cle A	40	102	8	22	3	2	0	5	12	0	18	.216	.298	.284	72	-3	2-2	.962	-1	89	90	C38	—	-0.2
1923	Det A	2	0	0	0	0	0	0	0	0	0	0	ø	ø	ø	ø	0	0-0	1.000	-0	0	0	C2	—	0.0
Total	8	226	655	43	149	17	9	1	57	46	2	37	.227	.280	.285	66	-28	16-2	.968	22	115	99	C202,1b14	—	0.9
Carl, Fred	Frederick E.; B9.8.1858 Baltimore MD; D1.13.1899 Baltimore MD; BL/TL/5´6˝/158; d7.25																								
1889	Lou AA	25	99	13	20	2	2	0	13	16	0	22	.202	.313	.263	66	-4	0	.735	0	128	125	O18(2/4/12),2b6/3	—	-0.3
Carl, Lew	Lewis Adolph; B1836 Baltimore MD; D5.19.1885 Newark NJ; d9.9																								
1874	Bal NA	1	3	0	0	0	0	0	0	0	—	0	.000	.000	.000	-99	-1	0-0	.250	-1	—	—	/C	—	-0.1
Carleton, Jim	James Leslie; B8.20.1848 NY; D4.25.1910 Detroit MI; 5´8˝/155; d5.4																								
1871	Cle NA	29	127	31	32	8	1	0	18	8	—	3	.252	.296	.331	85	-1	2-1	.898	-3	87	78	1b29	—	-0.2
1872	Cle NA	7	38	8	12	1	0	0	4	1	—	0	.316	.333	.342	114	1	1-0	.956	2	483	135	1b7	—	0.2
Total	2NA	36	165	39	44	9	1	0	22	9	—	3	.267	.305	.333	91	0	3-1	.908	-1	165	89	1b36	—	0.0
Carlin, Jim	James Arthur; B2.23.1918 Wylam AL; BR/TR/5´11˝/165; d7.26; Mil 1942–45; Col Southeastern Louisiana																								
1941	Phi N	16	21	2	3	1	0	1	2	3	0	4	.143	.250	.333	66	-1	0	1.000	-1	55	0	O9(0/4/5),3b2	0	-0.2
Carlisle, Walter	Walter "Rosy"; B7.6.1881 Yorkshire, England; D5.27.1945 Los Angeles CA; BB/TR/5´9˝/154; d5.8																								
1908	Bos A	3	10	0	1	0	0	0	0	1	0	—	.100	.182	.100	-8	-1	1	1.000	1	298	0	O3L	—	-0.1
Carlstrom, Swede	Albin Oscar; B10.26.1886 Elizabeth NJ; D4.28.1935 Elizabeth NJ; BR/TR/6´0˝/167; d9.12																								
1911	Bos A	2	6	0	1	0	0	0	0	0	0	—	.167	.167	.167	-7	-1	0	1.000	0	108	165	S2	—	0.0
Carlyle, Cleo	Hiram Cleo; B9.7.1902 Fairburn GA; D11.12.1967 Los Angeles CA; BL/TR/6´0˝/170; d5.16; b–Roy																								
1927	Bos A	95	278	31	65	12	8	1	28	36	1	40	.234	.324	.345	75	-11	4-4	.965	-2	88	132	O83(30/3/50)	—	-1.8
Carlyle, Roy	Roy Edward "Dizzy"; B12.10.1900 Buford GA; D11.22.1956 Norcross GA; BL/TR/6´2.5˝/195; d4.16; b–Cleo; Col Oglethorpe																								
1925	Was A	1	1	0	0	0	0	0	0	0	0	1	.000	.000	.000	-99	-1	0-0	ø	0	—	—	/H	—	0.0
	Bos A	93	276	36	90	20	3	7	49	16	1	28	.326	.365	.496	117	6	1-1	.909	-5	93	70	O67(43/0/24)	—	-0.4
	Year	94	277	36	90	20	3	7	49	16	1	29	.325	.364	.495	116	6	1-1	.909	-5	93	70	O67(43/0/24)	—	-0.4
1926	Bos A	45	165	22	47	6	2	2	16	4	2	18	.285	.310	.382	82	-5	0-0	.904	-5	81	88	O38R	—	-1.3
	NY A	35	62	3	20	5	1	0	11	4	1	9	.323	.373	.435	112	1	0-0	.941	-1	85	96	O15R	—	0.0
	Year	80	227	25	67	11	3	2	27	8	3	27	.295	.328	.396	91	-4	0-0	.911	-5	82	90	O53R	—	-1.3
Total	2	174	504	61	157	31	6	9	76	24	4	56	.312	.348	.450	105	2	1-1	.910	-11	88	78	O120(43/0/77)	—	-1.7
Carman, George	George Wartman; B3.29.1866 Philadelphia PA; D6.16.1929 Lancaster PA; d9.4																								
1890	Phi AA	27	93	9	16	2	0	0	7	8	1	—	.172	.245	.194	30	-8	5	.768	-8	88	80	S14,O10R,2b2/3	—	-1.4
Carmel, Duke	Leon James; B4.23.1937 New York NY; BL/TL/6´3˝/(197–202); d9.10																								
1959	StL N	10	23	2	3	1	0	0	3	1-0	0	6	.130	.167	.174	-9	-4	0-1	1.000	-0	101	0	O10(2/8/3)	0	-0.5
1960	StL N	4	3	0	0	0	0	0	0	1-0	0	1	.000	.250	.000	-23	0	1-1	1.000	0	225	102	1b2/rf	0	0.0
1963	StL N	57	44	9	10	1	0	1	2	9-0	0	11	.227	.358	.318	88	0	0-0	.974	2	159	0	O38(26/6/8)/1	0	0.1
	NY N	47	149	11	35	5	3	3	18	16-2	0	37	.235	.307	.369	93	-1	2-2	.980	-2	99	74	O21C,1b18	0	-0.6
	Year	104	193	20	45	6	3	4	20	25-2	0	48	.233	.320	.358	90	-2	2-2	.977	0	123	45	O59(26/27/8),1b19	0	-0.5
1965	NY A	6	8	0	0	0	0	0	0	0-0	0	5	.000	.000	.000	-99	-2	0-0	1.000	0	127	0	1b2	0	-0.2
Total	4	124	227	22	48	7	3	4	23	27-2	0	60	.211	.294	.322	73	-7	3-4	.981	0	119	37	O70(28/35/12),1b23	0	-1.2
Carnett, Eddie	Edwin Elliott "Lefty"; B10.21.1916 Springfield MO; BL/TL/6´0˝/185; d4.19; Mil 1945–46; Col Santa Ana (CA) JC																								
1941	Bos N	2	0	0	0	0	0	0	0	0	0	0	ø	ø	ø	ø	0	0	ø	0	0	0	P2	0	0.0
1944	Chi A	126	457	51	126	18	8	1	60	26	5	35	.276	.322	.357	95	-4	5-2	.949	-5	97	92	O88(62/25/6),1b25,P2	0	-1.5
1945	Cle A	30	73	5	16	7	0	0	7	2	1	9	.219	.250	.315	66	-3	0-1	.971	-0	100	68	O16(8/1/7),P2	0	-0.5
Total	3	158	530	56	142	25	8	1	67	28	6	44	.268	.312	.351	91	-7	5-3	.952	-5	97	88	O104(70/26/13),1b25,P6	0	-2.0
Carney, John	John Joseph "Handsome Jack"; B11.10.1866 Salem MA; D10.19.1925 Litchfield NH; BR/TR/5´10.5˝/175; d4.24																								
1889	Was N	69	273	25	63	7	0	1	29	14	1	14	.231	.271	.267	53	-17	12	.957	-6	67	85	1b53,O16(1/0/15)	—	-2.5
1890	Buf P	28	107	11	29	3	0	0	13	7	3	14	.271	.333	.299	76	-3	2	.972	-1	79	107	1b24,O4(1/0/3)	—	-0.5
	Cle P	25	89	15	31	5	3	0	21	14	1	5	.348	.442	.472	157	8	6	.857	-2	97	0	O19R,1b6	—	0.4
	Year	53	196	26	60	8	3	0	34	21	4	19	.306	.385	.378	113	5	8	.969	-4	72	115	1b30,O23(1/0/22)	—	-0.1
1891	Cin AA	99	367	47	102	10	8	3	43	35	3	18	.278	.346	.373	98	-3	15	.974	1	111	71	1b99	—	-1.0
	Mil AA	31	110	22	33	5	2	3	23	13	3	8	.300	.389	.464	120	2	5	.986	4	160	101	1b31	—	0.3
	Year	130	477	69	135	15	10	6	66	48	6	26	.283	.356	.394	103	-1	20	.977	4	123	78	1b130	—	-0.7
Total	3	252	946	120	258	30	13	7	129	83	11	59	.273	.338	.354	92	-13	40	.971	-5	102	85	1b213,O39(2/0/37)	—	-3.3
Carney, Pat	Patrick Joseph "Doc"; B8.7.1876 Holyoke MA; D1.9.1953 Worcester MA; BL/TL/6´0˝/200; d9.20; Col Holy Cross; ▲																								
1901	Bos N	13	55	6	16	2	1	0	6	3	1	—	.291	.339	.364	95	0	0	.933	-2	0	0	O13R	—	-0.3
1902	Bos N	137	522	75	141	17	4	2	65	42	12	—	.270	.339	.330	105	5	27	.930	-8	106	158	O137(3/0/135),P2	—	-1.0
1903	Bos N	110	392	37	94	12	4	1	49	28	4	—	.240	.297	.298	73	-14	10	.953	-3	86	135	O92(3/0/90),P10/1	—	-1.9
1904	Bos N	78	279	24	57	5	2	0	11	12	1	—	.204	.240	.237	49	-17	6	.953	-1	145	181	O71(2/9/60),P4/1	—	-2.1
Total	4	338	1248	142	308	36	11	3	131	85	18	—	.247	.304	.300	82	-26	43	.942	-14	105	151	O313(8/9/298),P16,1b2	—	-5.3
Carney, Bill	William John; B3.25.1874 St.Paul MN; D7.31.1938 Hopkins MN; BB/TR/5´10˝/?; d8.22																								
1904	Chi N	2	7	0	0	0	0	0	0	1	0	—	.000	.125	.000	-60	-1	0	1.000	0	580	0	O2R	—	-0.1
Carpenter, Bubba	Charles Sydney; B7.23.1968 Dallas TX; BL/TL/6´1˝/185; d5.13; Col Arkansas																								
2000	Col N	15	27	4	6	0	0	3	5	4-0	0	13	.222	.323	.556	94	0	0-0	1.000	-1	39	0	O6(5/0/1),D2	0	-0.2

YEAR	TM LG	G	AB	R	H	2B	3B	HR	RBI	BB-IB	HP	SO	AVG	OBP	SLG	AOPS	ABR	SB-CS	FA	FR	RNG	THR	GAMES AT POSITION	DL	BFW
CARPENTER, HICK	Warren William; B8.16.1855 Grafton MA; D4.18.1937 San Diego CA; BR/TL/5´11˝/186; d5.1																								
1879	Syr N	65	261	30	53	6	0	0	20	2	—	15	.203	.209	.226	49	-13	—	.948	-5	117	72	1b34,3b18,O11R,2b3	—	-1.7
1880	Cin N	77	300	32	72	6	4	0	23	2	—	15	.240	.245	.287	80	-7	—	.853	-0	89	109	3b67,1b9/S	—	-0.5
1881	Wor N	**83**	347	40	75	12	2	2	31	3	—	19	.216	.223	.280	54	-19	—	.848	3	104	100	3b83	—	-1.3
1882	Cin AA	**80**	351	78	**120**	15	5	1	67	10	—	—	.342	.360	.422	154	18	—	**.835**	-3	92	93	3b80	—	1.5
1883	Cin AA	95	435	99	130	18	4	3	40	19	—	—	.299	.328	.379	120	9	—	.870	-5	92	68	3b95	—	0.5
1884	Cin AA	108	474	80	121	16	2	4	60	6	4	—	.255	.271	.323	89	-7	—	.881	-9	86	135	3b108/rf	—	-1.3
1885	Cin AA	**112**	473	89	131	12	8	2	61	9	3	—	.277	.295	.349	101	-1	—	.860	-7	90	104	3b112	—	-0.6
1886	Cin AA	111	458	67	101	8	5	2	61	18	8	—	.221	.262	.273	66	-20	8	.841	-7	99	136	3b111	—	-2.2
1887	Cin AA	127	498	70	124	12	6	1	50	19	4	—	.249	.282	.303	62	-28	44	.846	-14	95	95	3b127	—	-3.2
1888	Cin AA	136	551	68	147	14	5	3	67	5	5	—	.267	.280	.327	89	-10	59	.866	-14	97	81	3b136	—	-2.0
1889	Cin AA	123	486	67	127	23	6	0	63	18	4	41	.261	.293	.333	76	-17	47	.835	-25	82	87	3b121,1b2	—	-3.5
1892	StL N	1	3	0	1	0	0	0	0	1	0	1	.333	.500	.333	161	0	0	.714	-0	90	0	/3	—	0.0
Total	12	1118	4637	720	1202	142	47	18	543	112	28	91	.259	.281	.322	86	-95	158	.853	-86	92	98	3b1059,1b45,O12R,2b3/S	—	-14.3
CARR, CHARLIE	Charles Carbitt; B12.27.1876 Coatesville PA; D11.25.1932 Memphis TN; BR/TR/6´2˝/195; d9.15; Col Lehigh																								
1898	Was N	20	73	6	14	2	0	0	4	2	0	—	.192	.213	.219	24	-7	2	.950	-2	84	114	1b20	—	-0.9
1901	Phi A	2	8	0	1	0	0	0	0	0	0	—	.125	.125	.125	-29	-1	0	.926	0	174	0	1b2	—	-0.1
1903	Det A	135	548	59	154	23	11	2	79	10	2	—	.281	.296	.374	103	0	10	.982	13	**134**	90	1b135	—	1.0
1904	Det A	92	360	29	77	13	3	0	40	14	1	—	.214	.245	.267	64	-15	6	.983	16	169	109	1b92	—	-0.1
	Cle A	32	120	9	27	5	1	0	7	4	0	—	.225	.250	.283	69	-4	0	.973	-0	105	94	1b32	—	-0.6
	Year	124	480	38	104	18	4	0	47	18	1	—	.217	.246	.271	65	-20	6	.980	16	**152**	105	1b124	—	-0.7
1905	Cle A	89	306	29	72	12	4	1	31	13	0	—	.235	.266	.310	82	-7	12	.991	-1	89	96	1b87	—	-1.1
1906	Cin N	22	94	9	18	2	3	0	10	2	1	—	.191	.216	.277	51	-6	0	.983	1	112	147	1b22	—	-0.6
1914	Ind F	115	441	44	129	11	10	3	69	26	1	47	.293	.333	.383	86	-16	19	**.991**	1	98	110	1b115	—	-1.9
Total	7	507	1950	185	492	68	32	6	240	71	5	47	.252	.280	.329	81	-56	49	.984	27	120	102	1b505	—	-4.3
CARR, CHUCK	Charles Lee Glenn; B8.10.1967 San Bernardino CA; BB/TR (BR 1995p)/5´10˝/165; [CinN86 9/228]; d4.28																								
1990	NY N	4	2	0	0	0	0	0	0	0-0	0	2	.000	.000	.000	-99	-1	1-0	ø	-0	0	0	/lf	0	0.0
1991	NY N	12	11	1	2	0	0	0	1	0-0	0	2	.182	.182	.182	3	-1	1-0	1.000	1	153	0	O9C	15	-0.1
1992	StL N	22	64	8	14	3	0	0	3	9-0	0	6	.219	.315	.266	68	-2	10-2	1.000	-0	100	98	O19(5/9/6)	0	-0.2
1993	Fla N	142	551	75	147	19	2	4	41	49-0	2	74	.267	.327	.330	73	-20	**58**-22	.985	7	112	99	O139C	17	-0.7
1994	Fla N	106	433	61	114	19	2	2	30	22-1	5	71	.263	.305	.330	64	-23	32-8	.980	6	118	72	O104C	0	-1.1
1995	Fla N	105	308	54	70	20	0	2	20	46-1	2	49	.227	.330	.312	70	-12	25-11	.987	6	111	**179**	O103C	27	-0.3
1996	Mil A	27	106	18	29	6	1	1	11	6-0	0	21	.274	.310	.377	70	-5	5-4	1.000	5	123	271	O27C	141	0.0
1997	Mil A	26	46	3	6	3	0	0	0	2-0	1	11	.130	.184	.196	-1	-7	1-0	1.000	-1	77	152	O23C/D	0	-0.8
	†Hou N	63	192	34	53	11	2	4	17	15-2	2	37	.276	.333	.417	98	-1	11-5	.966	-1	98	126	O59(1/58/0)	0	-0.1
Total	8	507	1713	254	435	81	7	13	123	149-4	12	273	.254	.316	.332	70	-72	144-52	.984	22	111	122	O484(7/472/6)/D	200	-3.3
CARR, LEW	Lewis Smith; B8.15.1872 Union Springs NY; D6.15.1954 Moravia NY; BR/TR/6´2˝/200; d7.4; Col Hobart and William Smith																								
1901	Pit N	9	28	2	7	1	1	0	4	2	2	—	.250	.344	.357	100	0	0	.886	-3	82	130	S9/3	—	-0.3
CARRASQUEL, CHICO	Alfonso (Colon); B1.23.1928 Caracas, Distrito Capital, Venez.; D5.26.2005 Caracas, Distrito Capital, Venez.; BR/TR/6´0˝/(170–172); d4.18																								
1950	Chi A	141	524	72	148	21	5	4	46	66	5	46	.282	.368	.365	91	-6	0-2	.961	11	**107**	106	S141	0	1.2
1951	Chi A★	147	538	41	142	22	4	2	58	46	3	39	.264	.325	.331	79	-16	14-4	**.975**	12	**110**	108	S147	0	0.6
1952	Chi A	100	359	36	89	7	4	1	42	33	2	27	.248	.315	.298	71	-15	2-2	.964	-11	89	88	S99	0	-2.1
1953	Chi A★	149	552	72	154	30	4	2	47	38	4	47	.279	.330	.359	83	-13	5-3	**.976**	5	100	94	S149	0	0.5
1954	Chi A★	**155**	620	106	158	28	3	12	62	85	5	67	.255	.348	.368	93	-4	7-6	**.975**	13	103	110	S155	0	2.3
1955	Chi A★	145	523	83	134	11	2	11	52	61-0	4	59	.256	.335	.348	83	-13	1-1	.973	4	101	102	S144	0	0.3
1956	Cle A	141	474	60	115	15	1	7	48	52-0	6	61	.243	.323	.323	70	-20	0-4	.967	-20	84	85	S141/3	0	-3.0
1957	Cle A	125	392	37	108	14	1	8	57	41-2	8	53	.276	.351	.378	102	2	0-2	.960	-4	95	86	S122	0	0.7
1958	Cle A	49	156	14	40	6	0	2	21	14-1	0	12	.256	.318	.333	81	-4	0-0	.931	-14	78	82	S32,3b14	0	-1.7
	KC A	59	160	19	34	5	1	2	13	21-0	0	15	.213	.304	.294	64	-8	0-1	.976	-3	100	190	3b32,S22	0	-1.0
	Year	108	316	33	74	11	1	4	34	35-1	0	27	.234	.311	.313	72	-12	0-1	.947	-18	82	72	S54,3b46	0	-2.7
1959	Bal A	114	346	28	77	13	0	4	28	34-1	1	41	.223	.292	.295	64	-17	2-3	.970	-6	99	136	S89,2b22,3b2/1	0	-1.7
Total	10	1325	4644	568	1199	172	25	55	474	491-4	38	467	.258	.333	.342	82	-114	31-28	.969	-15	99	100	S1241,3b49,2b22/1	0	-3.9
CARREON, CAM	Camilo; B8.6.1937 Colton CA; D9.2.1987 Tucson AZ; BR/TR/6´0˝/(185–198); d9.27; s–Mark																								
1959	Chi A	1	1	0	0	0	0	0	0	0-0	0	0	.000	.000	.000	-99	0	0-0	1.000	0	0	0	/C	0	0.0
1960	Chi A	8	17	2	4	0	0	0	2	1-0	0	3	.235	.278	.235	41	-1	0-0	1.000	0	0	197	C7	0	-0.1
1961	Chi A	78	229	32	62	5	1	4	27	21-2	0	24	.271	.331	.354	85	-5	0-1	.995	9	97	74	C71	0	0.7
1962	Chi A	106	313	31	80	19	1	4	37	33-2	1	37	.256	.328	.361	86	-6	1-1	.995	6	86	61	C93	0	0.5
1963	Chi A	101	270	28	74	10	1	2	35	23-2	1	32	.274	.332	.341	91	-3	1-1	.987	-1	91	100	C92	0	0.0
1964	Chi A	37	95	12	26	5	0	0	4	7-3	1	13	.274	.330	.326	86	-2	0-0	.987	-1	264	63	C34	32	-0.2
1965	Cle A	19	52	6	12	2	1	1	7	9-3	0	6	.231	.344	.365	101	0	1-1	1.000	-1	115	82	C19	0	0.0
1966	Bal A	4	9	2	2	2	0	0	2	3-0	0	2	.222	.417	.444	150	1	0-0	1.000	0	61	278	C3	0	0.1
Total	8	354	986	113	260	43	4	11	114	97-12	3	117	.264	.331	.349	87	-16	3-4	.993	13	106	80	C320	32	1.0
CARREON, MARK	Mark Steven; B7.19.1963 Chicago IL; BR/TL/6´0˝/(170–195); [NYN81 8/185]; d9.8; f–Cam																								
1987	NY N	9	12	0	3	0	0	0	1	1-0	0	1	.250	.308	.250	52	-1	0-1	.800	-0	87	0	O5L	0	-0.2
1988	NY N	7	9	5	5	2	0	1	1	2-0	0	1	.556	.636	1.111	409	4	0-0	1.000	-1	26	0	O4L	0	0.3
1989	NY N	68	133	20	41	6	0	6	16	12-0	1	17	.308	.370	.489	150	8	2-3	.983	-1	103	0	O39(18/0/21)	21	0.6
1990	NY N	82	188	30	47	12	0	10	26	15-0	2	29	.250	.312	.473	113	3	1-0	1.000	-3	92	40	O60(16/36/13)	44	-0.1
1991	NY N	106	254	18	66	6	0	4	21	12-2	2	26	.260	.297	.331	77	-8	2-1	.971	-4	82	122	O77(43/22/22)	0	-1.4
1992	Det A	101	336	34	78	11	1	10	41	22-2	1	57	.232	.278	.360	77	-12	3-1	.979	1	105	91	O83(64/1/19),D13	18	-1.3
1993	SF N	78	150	22	49	9	1	7	33	13-2	1	16	.327	.373	.540	149	10	1-0	.943	-3	76	90	O41(9/5/30),1b3	0	0.6
1994	SF N	51	100	8	27	4	0	3	20	7-0	2	20	.270	.324	.400	93	-1	0-0	.978	-2	98	0	O33(10/0/24)	16	-0.4
1995	SF N	117	396	53	119	24	0	17	65	23-1	4	37	.301	.343	.490	120	10	0-1	.993	-7	79	103	1b81,O22(3/0/19)	0	-0.4
1996	SF N	81	292	40	76	22	3	9	51	22-2	3	33	.260	.317	.449	102	0	2-3	.986	-5	77	114	1b73,O5(3/0/2)	0	-1.2
	Cle A	38	142	16	46	12	0	2	14	11-0	3	9	.324	.385	.451	110	3	1-1	.994	-2	85	88	1b34,O5(0/4/1),D2	37	-0.2
Total	10	738	2012	246	557	108	5	69	289	140-9	19	246	.277	.327	.438	107	16	12-11	.974	-25	92	74	O374(175/68/151),1b191,D15	136	-3.7
CARRIGAN, BILL	William Francis "Rough"; B10.22.1883 Lewiston ME; D7.8.1969 Lewiston ME; BR/TR/5´9˝/175; d7.7; M7; Col Holy Cross																								
1906	Bos A	37	109	5	23	0	0	0	10	5	1	—	.211	.252	.211	45	-7	3	.940	-4	*84*	*104*	C35	—	-0.8
1908	Bos A	57	149	13	35	5	2	0	14	3	1	—	.235	.255	.295	77	-4	1	.955	5	*102*	*118*	C47,1b3	—	0.5
1909	Bos A	94	280	25	83	13	2	1	36	17	2	—	.296	.341	.368	121	7	2	.972	2	*112*	*105*	C77,1b8	—	1.9
1910	Bos A	114	342	36	85	11	1	3	53	23	6	—	.249	.307	.313	92	-3	10	.962	-16	*100*	*84*	C110	—	-1.0
1911	Bos A	72	232	29	67	6	1	1	30	26	5	—	.289	.373	.336	99	1	5	.972	-0	*96*	*106*	C62,1b6	—	0.6
1912	†Bos A	87	266	34	70	7	1	0	24	38	2	—	.263	.359	.297	84	-4	7	**.970**	-4	*110*	*86*	C87	—	-0.1
1913	Bos A	87	256	17	62	15	5	0	28	27	2	26	.242	.319	.340	91	-3	6	.979	-7	*87*	*109*	C82,M	—	-0.3
1914	Bos A	82	178	18	45	5	1	1	22	40	2	18	.253	.395	.309	112	6	1-2	**.984**	8	*126*	*83*	C78,M	—	2.1
1915	†Bos A	46	95	10	19	3	0	0	7	16	1	12	.200	.321	.232	68	-3	0	.975	7	*128*	*106*	C44,M	—	0.8
1916	†Bos A	33	63	7	17	2	1	0	11	11	0	3	.270	.378	.333	113	2	2	1.000	5	151	58	C27,M	—	0.9
Total	10	709	1970	194	506	67	14	6	235	206	22	59	.257	.334	.314	94	-8	37-2	.971	-3	*107*	*96*	C649,1b17	—	4.6
CARRILLO, MATIAS	Matias (Garcia); B2.24.1963 Los Mochis, Sinaloa, Mexico; BL/TL/5´11˝/190; d5.23																								
1991	Mil A	3	0	0	0	0	0	0	0	0-0	0	0	ø	ø	ø	ø	0	0-0	ø	-0	0	0	O3L	0	0.0
1993	Fla N	24	55	4	14	6	0	0	3	1-0	1	7	.255	.281	.364	67	-2	0-0	1.000	-1	85	0	O16(4/5/9)	0	-0.4
1994	Fla N	80	136	13	34	7	0	0	9	9-0	0	31	.250	.295	.301	54	-9	3-3	.982	0	81	246	O49(20/8/25)	0	-1.0
Total	3	107	191	17	48	13	0	0	12	10-0	1	38	.251	.291	.319	58	-11	3-3	.987	-1	81	174	O68(27/13/34)	0	-1.4
CARROLL	; d4.17																								
1884	Was U	4	16	1	4	0	0	0	—	0	—	—	.250	.250	.250	54	-1	—	.500	-1	98	0	O4L	—	-0.2

YEAR	TM LG	G	AB	R	H	2B	3B	HR	RBI	BB-IB	HP	SO	AVG	OBP	SLG	AOPS	ABR	SB-CS	FA	FR	RNG	THR	GAMES AT POSITION	DL	BFW
CARROLL, DIXIE Dorsey Lee; B5.19.1891 Paducah KY; D10.13.1984 Jacksonville FL; BL/TR/5´11˝/165; d9.12																									
1919	Bos N	15	49	10	13	3	1	0	7	7	2	1	.265	.379	.367	130	2	5	.921	1	89	255	O13(6/8/1)	—	0.3
CARROLL, FRED Frederick Herbert; B7.2.1864 Sacramento CA; D11.7.1904 San Rafael CA; BR/TR/5´11˝/185; d5.1; Col St. Marys (CA); OF(144/67/108)																									
1884	Col AA	69	252	46	70	13	5	6	—	13	5	—	.278	.326	.440	161	18	—	.944	7	—	—	C54,O15(12/2/1)	—	2.6
1885	Pit AA	71	280	45	75	13	8	0	30	7	5	—	.268	.298	.371	112	3	—	.926	1	—	—	C60,O12(10/2/0)	—	0.8
1886	Pit AA	122	486	92	140	28	11	5	64	52	4	—	.288	.362	.422	146	27	20	.921	0	—	—	C70,O27(15/10/2),1b25/S	—	2.7
1887	Pit N	102	421	71	138	24	15	6	54	36	2	21	.328	.383	.499	154	32	23	.833	-16	114	0	O46(8/33/5),C40,1b17/S	—	1.4
1888	Pit N	97	366	62	91	14	5	2	48	32	10	31	.249	.326	.331	120	11	18	.897	-11	—	—	C54,O38(31/2/5),1b5/3	—	0.4
1889	Pit N	91	318	80	105	21	11	2	51	85	11	26	.330	**.486**	.484	**188**	**50**	19	.930	-8	—	—	C43,O41(24/12/5),1b7/3	—	3.7
1890	Pit P	111	416	95	124	20	7	2	71	75	11	22	.298	.418	.394	128	25	35	.856	-13	*103*	*69*	C56,O49(42/6/1),1b7	—	1.2
1891	Pit N	91	353	55	77	13	4	4	48	48	2	36	.218	.315	.312	85	-6	22	.915	4	81	80	O91(2/0/89)	—	-0.2
Total	8	754	2892	546	820	146	66	27	366	348	50	136	.284	.370	.408	137	160	137	.913	-35	*103*	*69*	C377,O319L,1b61,3b2,S2	—	12.6
CARROLL, JAMEY Jamey Blake; B2.18.1974 Evansville IN; BR/TR/5´10˝/(170–175); [MonN96 14/400]; d9.11; Col Evansville																									
2002	Mon N	16	71	16	22	5	3	1	6	4-0	0	12	.310	.347	.507	115	1	1-0	.917	-1	98	71	3b13,S3/2	0	0.1
2003	Mon N	105	227	31	59	10	1	1	10	19-0	3	39	.260	.323	.326	69	-10	5-2	.969	10	128	93	3b67,S14,2b11/D	0	0.2
2004	Mon N	102	218	36	63	14	2	0	16	32-1	1	21	.289	.378	.372	92	-1	5-1	.995	-3	84	125	2b51,3b13,S10,O2L	0	0.0
2005	Was N	113	303	44	76	8	1	0	22	34-1	5	55	.251	.333	.284	68	-13	3-4	.980	-9	99	102	2b63,S41,3b12	0	-1.8
2006	Col N	136	463	84	139	23	5	5	36	56-1	3	66	.300	.377	.404	93	-3	10-12	**.995**	**41**	**139**	**138**	2b109,S10,3b8	0	3.9
Total	5	472	1282	211	359	60	12	7	90	145-3	12	193	.280	.356	.362	85	-26	24-19	.991	39	116	126	2b235,3b113,S78,O2L/D	0	2.4
CARROLL, SCRAPPY John E.; B8.27.1860 Buffalo NY; D11.14.1942 Buffalo NY; BR/5´7.5˝/?; d9.27																									
1884	StP U	**9**	31	3	3	1	0	0	—	2	—	—	.097	.152	.129	-26	-6	—	.824	3	305	334	O8R,3b2	—	-0.2
1885	Buf N	13	40	1	3	0	0	0	1	2	—	8	.075	.119	.075	-35	-6	—	.917	2	202	0	O13(7/6/0)	—	-0.4
1887	Cle AA	57	216	30	43	5	1	0	19	15	4	—	.199	.264	.231	40	-17	19	.843	-3	86	47	O54(14/0/40),3b3/2	—	-1.7
Total	3	79	287	34	49	6	1	0	20	19	4	8	.171	.232	.199	26	-29	19	.853	1	126	68	O75(21/6/48),3b5/2	—	-2.3
CARROLL, PAT Patrick; B3.1853 Philadelphia PA; D2.14.1916 Philadelphia PA; d5.10																									
1884	Alt U	11	49	4	13	1	0	0	—	1	—	—	.265	.280	.286	71	-3	—	.920	-2	—	—	C8,O3R	—	-0.4
	Phi U	5	19	1	3	1	0	0	—	0	—	—	.158	.158	.211	12	-3	—	.804	-2	—	—	C5	—	-0.4
	Year	16	68	5	16	2	0	0	—	1	—	—	.235	.246	.265	56	-6	—	.865	-4	—	—	C13,O3R	—	-0.8
CARROLL, DOC Ralph Arthur "Red"; B12.28.1891 Worcester MA; D6.27.1983 Worcester MA; BR/TR/6´0˝/170; d6.27; Col Tufts																									
1916	Phi A	10	22	1	2	0	0	0	0	1	1	8	.091	.167	.091	-24	-3	0	.942	-2	63	214	C10	—	-0.5
CARROLL, CLIFF Samuel Clifford; B10.18.1859 Clay Grove IA; D6.12.1923 Portland OR; BB/TR/5´8˝/163; d8.3																									
1882	Pro N	10	41	4	5	0	0	0	2	0	—	4	.122	.122	.122	-21	-5	—	1.000	1	94	508	O10(2/0/8)	—	-0.4
1883	Pro N	58	238	37	63	12	3	1	20	4	—	28	.265	.277	.353	87	-4	—	.902	3	80	209	O58(56/1/1)	—	-0.2
1884	†Pro N	113	452	90	118	16	4	3	54	29	—	39	.261	.306	.334	103	2	—	.904	0	46	34	O113L	—	0.0
1885	Pro N	104	426	62	99	12	3	1	40	29	—	29	.232	.281	.282	85	-6	—	.886	4	51	75	O104L	—	-0.5
1886	Was N	111	433	73	99	11	6	2	22	44	—	26	.229	.300	.296	88	-4	31	.862	-0	101	106	O111(109/1/1)	—	-0.6
1887	Was N	103	420	79	104	17	4	4	37	17	9	30	.248	.291	.336	79	-11	40	.902	1	105	183	O103(102/1/0)	—	-1.1
1888	Pit N	5	20	1	0	0	0	0	0	0	0	8	.000	.000	.000	-99	-5	2	.667	-1	128	0	O5(1/0/4)	—	-0.6
1890	Chi N	136	582	134	166	16	6	7	65	53	7	34	.285	.352	.369	106	3	34	.936	11	114	151	O136(112/0/24)	—	1.0
1891	Chi N	130	515	87	132	20	8	7	80	50	15	42	.256	.340	.367	106	4	31	.915	-5	75	153	O130(0/1/130)	—	-0.1
1892	StL N	101	407	82	111	14	8	4	49	47	11	22	.273	.363	.376	130	17	30	.901	5	121	28	O101(99/0/3)	—	1.2
1893	Bos N	120	438	80	98	7	5	2	54	88	5	28	.224	.360	.276	65	-20	29	.917	2	89	127	O120(33/0/89)	—	-2.1
Total	11	991	3972	729	995	125	47	31	423	361	47	290	.251	.320	.329	93	-29	197	.905	21	88	119	O991(731/4/260)	—	-3.4
CARROLL, TOM Thomas Edward; B9.17.1936 Jamaica NY; BR/TR/6´3˝/(186–190); d5.7; Mil 1958; Col Notre Dame																									
1955	†NY A	14	6	3	2	0	0	0	0	0-0	0	2	.333	.333	.333	81	0	0-0	.875	1	177	0	S4	0	0.1
1956	NY A	36	17	11	6	0	0	0	0	1-0	0	3	.353	.389	.353	100	0	1-0	.857	3	262	452	3b11/S	0	0.3
1959	KC A	14	7	1	1	0	0	0	1	0-0	0	1	.143	.143	.143	-21	-1	0-0	1.000	1	115	53	S9,3b3	0	0.0
Total	3	64	30	15	9	0	0	0	1	1-0	0	6	.300	.323	.300	69	-1	1-0	.813	4	245	390	3b14,S14	0	0.4
CARSON, KIT Walter Lloyd; B11.15.1912 Colton CA; D6.21.1983 Long Beach CA; BL/TL/6´0˝/180; d7.21																									
1934	Cle A	5	18	4	5	2	1	0	1	2	0	3	.278	.350	.500	115	0	0-0	1.000	-1	41	0	O4R	—	0.0
1935	Cle A	16	22	1	5	2	0	0	1	2	0	6	.227	.292	.318	57	-1	0-1	1.000	-0	105	0	O4R	—	-0.2
Total	2	21	40	5	10	4	1	0	2	4	0	9	.250	.318	.400	83	-1	0-1	1.000	-1	78	0	O8R	—	-0.2
CARSWELL, FRANK Frank Willis "Tex","Wheels"; B11.6.1919 Palestine TX; D10.16.1998 Houston TX; BR/TR/6´0˝/185; d4.17; Col Rice																									
1953	Det A	16	15	2	4	0	0	0	2	3	0	1	.267	.389	.267	81	0	0-0	1.000	-0	60	0	O3L	0	0.0
CARTER, GARY Gary Edmund; B4.8.1954 Culver City CA; BR/TR/6´2˝/(205–215); [MonN72 3/53]; d9.16; HF2003																									
1974	Mon N	9	27	5	11	0	1	1	6	1-0	0	2	.407	.414	.593	174	2	2-0	1.000	0	338	58	C6,O2R	0	0.3
1975	Mon N★	144	503	58	136	20	1	17	68	72-8	1	83	.270	.360	.416	110	8	5-2	.974	-8	92	17	O92R,C66/3	0	-0.1
1976	Mon N	91	311	31	68	8	1	6	38	30-2	1	43	.219	.287	.309	67	-14	0-2	.994	11	146	138	C60,O36(2/0/34)	46	-0.3
1977	Mon N	154	522	86	148	29	2	31	84	58-5	5	103	.284	.356	.525	137	27	5-5	.990	4	103	87	C146/lf	0	3.7
1978	Mon N	157	533	76	136	27	1	20	72	62-11	5	70	.255	.336	.422	112	9	10-6	.989	23	149	104	C152/1	0	3.9
1979	Mon N★	141	505	74	143	26	5	22	75	40-3	5	62	.283	.338	.485	123	14	3-2	.989	22	138	122	C138	0	4.3
1980	Mon N★	154	549	76	145	25	5	29	101	58-11	1	78	.264	.331	.486	124	16	3-2	**.993**	26	138	103	C149	0	5.1
1981	†Mon N★	100	374	48	94	20	2	16	68	35-4	1	35	.251	.313	.444	110	4	1-5	.993	14	157	108	C100/1	0	2.2
1982	Mon N★	154	557	91	163	32	1	29	97	78-11	6	64	.293	.381	.510	143	34	2-5	.991	26	133	109	C153	0	**6.8**
1983	Mon N★	145	541	63	146	37	3	17	79	51-7	7	57	.270	.336	.444	116	12	1-1	**.995**	25	151	115	C144/1	0	4.4
1984	Mon N★	159	596	75	175	32	1	27	**106**	64-9	6	57	.294	.366	.487	144	35	2-2	.993	4	112	91	C143,1b25	0	4.5
1985	NY N✱	149	555	83	156	17	1	32	100	69-16	6	46	.281	.365	.488	140	29	1-1	.992	9	120	98	C143,1b6/rf	0	4.6
1986	†NY N★	132	490	81	125	14	2	24	105	62-9	6	63	.255	.337	.439	117	11	1-0	.991	8	102	82	C122,1b9,O4(2/0/2)/3	15	2.5
1987	NY N★	139	523	55	123	18	2	20	83	42-1	1	73	.235	.290	.392	83	-15	0-0	.991	2	99	91	C135,1b4/rf	0	-0.8
1988	†NY N★	130	455	39	110	16	2	11	46	34-1	7	52	.242	.301	.358	93	-5	0-2	.990	-9	75	74	C119,1b10/3	0	-0.9
1989	NY N	50	153	14	28	8	0	2	15	12-0	0	15	.183	.241	.275	50	-10	0-0	.980	-5	68	132	C47/1	74	-1.4
1990	SF N	92	244	24	62	10	0	9	27	25-3	1	31	.254	.324	.406	103	1	1-1	.992	-5	85	93	C80,1b3	16	0.0
1991	LA N	101	248	22	61	14	0	6	26	22-1	7	26	.246	.323	.375	98	0	2-2	.988	4	81	121	C68,1b10	0	0.6
1992	Mon N	95	285	24	62	18	1	5	29	33-4	2	37	.218	.299	.340	82	-6	0-4	.989	-3	58	135	C85,1b5	0	-0.6
Total	19	2296	7971	1025	2092	371	31	324	1225	848-106	68	997	.262	.335	.439	115	152	39-42	.991	148	120	104	C2056,O137(5/0/132),1b76,3b3	151	38.8
CARTER, HOWIE John Howard; B10.13.1904 New York NY; D7.24.1991 New York NY; BR/TR/5´10˝/154; d6.21; Col Fordham																									
1926	Cin N	5	1	0	0	0	0	0	0	0	0	0	.000	.000	.000	-99	0	0	1.000	0	172	0	2b3/S	—	0.0
CARTER, JOE Joseph Chris; B3.7.1960 Oklahoma City OK; BR/TR/6´3˝/(215–230); [ChiN81 1/2]; d7.30; Col Wichita St.; OF(775/432/624)																									
1983	Chi N	23	51	6	9	1	1	0	1	0-0	0	21	.176	.176	.235	13	-6	1-0	1.000	-0	100	0	O16(14/2/1)	0	-0.7
1984	Cle A	66	244	32	67	6	1	13	41	11-0	1	48	.275	.307	.467	109	2	2-4	.956	4	103	253	O59(48/14/0),1b7	15	0.2
1985	Cle A	143	489	64	128	27	0	15	59	25-2	2	74	.262	.298	.409	92	-6	24-6	.983	7	108	137	O135(122/4/30),1b11/23D	0	-0.1
1986	Cle A	162	663	108	200	36	9	29	**121**	32-3	5	95	.302	.335	.514	130	24	29-7	.976	4	113	114	O104(45/9/78),1b70	0	2.3
1987	Cle A	149	588	83	155	27	2	32	106	27-6	9	105	.264	.304	.480	103	0	31-6	.983	-7	77	86	1b84,O62(42/13/14),D5	0	-0.9
1988	Cle A	157	621	85	168	36	6	27	98	35-6	7	82	.271	.314	.478	116	11	27-5	.985	0	101	106	O156C	0	1.4
1989	Cle A	**162**	651	84	158	32	4	35	105	39-8	8	112	.243	.292	.465	109	4	13-5	.978	-2	96	72	O146(56/103/1),1b11,D8	0	-0.1
1990	SD N	**162**	634	79	147	27	1	24	115	48-18	7	93	.232	.290	.391	86	-14	22-6	.988	2	104	143	O150(51/112/0),1b14	0	-1.3
1991	†Tor A★	**162**	638	89	174	42	3	33	108	49-12	**10**	112	.273	.330	.503	123	19	20-9	.974	-3	91	127	O151(57/0/100),D11	0	1.1
1992	†Tor A★	158	622	97	164	30	7	34	119	36-4	11	109	.264	.309	.498	119	12	12-5	.971	1	100	119	O129(6/0/123),D24,1b4	0	0.9
1993	†Tor A★	155	603	92	153	33	5	33	121	47-5	9	113	.254	.312	.489	111	7	8-3	.974	-5	97	70	O151(55/0/96),D3	0	-0.4
1994	Tor A★	111	435	70	118	25	2	27	103	33-6	2	64	.271	.317	.524	113	6	11-0	.991	-3	100	53	O110R/D	0	0.0
1995	Tor A	139	558	70	141	23	0	25	76	37-5	3	87	.253	.300	.428	87	-13	12-1	.975	0	99	108	O128(116/20/0),1b7,D5	0	-1.4
1996	Tor A★	157	625	84	158	35	7	30	107	44-2	7	106	.253	.306	.475	95	-8	7-6	.961	-13	74	94	O115L,1b41,D15	0	-2.7
1997	Tor A	157	612	76	143	30	4	21	102	40-5	7	105	.234	.284	.399	77	-23	8-2	.972	-2	108	33	D65,O51(41/0/10),1b42	0	-3.3
1998	Bal A	85	283	36	70	15	1	11	34	18-4	2	48	.247	.297	.424	86	-7	3-1	.962	3	115	132	O50(3/0/47),D32/1	0	-0.7

YEAR	TM LG	G	AB	R	H	2B	3B	HR	RBI	BB-IB	HP	SO	AVG	OBP	SLG	AOPS	ABR	SB-CS	FA	FR	RNG	THR	GAMES AT POSITION	DL	BFW
	SF N	41	105	15	31	7	0	7	29	6-0	0	13	.295	.322	.562	137	5	1-0	1.000	-3	62	0	O17(4/0/14),1b16	0	0.1
Total	16	2189	8422	1170	2184	432	53	396	1445	527-86	90	1387	.259	.306	.464	104	13	231-66	.977	-18	99	103	O1730L,1b308,D176/32	15	-5.6
CARTER, BLACKIE	Otis Leonard; B9.30.1902 Langley SC; D9.10.1976 Greenville SC; BR/TR/5´10˝/175; d10.3; Col Furman																								
1925	NY N	1	4	0	0	0	0	0	0	0	0	1	.000	.000	.000	-99	-1	0-0	1.000	1	46	1047	/lf	—	-0.1
1926	NY N	5	17	4	4	1	0	1	1	1	0	0	.235	.278	.471	100	0	0	.917	-0	112	0	O4(3/0/1)	—	-0.1
Total	2	6	21	4	4	1	0	1	1	1	0	1	.190	.227	.381	61	-1	0-0	.929	0	100	185	O5(4/0/1)	—	-0.2
CARTER, STEVE	Steven Jerome; B12.3.1964 Charlottesville VA; BL/TR/6´4˝/200; [PitN87 17/424]; d4.16; Col Georgia																								
1989	Pit N	9	16	2	2	1	0	1	3	2-1	0	5	.125	.222	.375	70	-1	0-0	1.000	-1	51	0	O5R	0	-0.2
1990	Pit N	5	5	0	1	0	0	0	0	0-0	0	1	.200	.200	.200	11	-1	0-0	1.000	0	155	0	O3(1/2/1)	0	0.0
Total	2	14	21	2	3	1	0	1	3	2-1	0	6	.143	.217	.333	56	-2	0-0	1.000	-1	73	0	O8(1/2/6)	0	-0.2
CARTWRIGHT, ED	Edward Charles "Jumbo"; B10.6.1859 Johnstown PA; D9.3.1933 St.Petersburg FL; BR/TR/5´10˝/220; d7.10																								
1890	StL AA	75	300	70	90	12	4	8	60	29	3	—	.300	.367	.447	123	6	26	.976	-1	85	101	1b75	—	-0.1
1894	Was N	**132**	507	88	149	35	13	12	106	57	8	43	.294	.374	.485	109	7	31	.973	-1	100	71	1b132	—	0.4
1895	Was N	122	472	95	156	34	17	3	90	54	1	41	.331	.400	.494	131	22	50	.984	15	**149**	86	1b122	—	2.9
1896	Was N	**133**	499	76	138	15	10	1	62	54	2	44	.277	.350	.353	85	-10	28	.978	0	100	86	1b133	—	-0.9
1897	Was N	33	124	19	29	4	0	0	15	8	1	—	.234	.286	.266	46	-10	9	.963	2	143	92	1b33	—	-0.7
Total	5	495	1902	348	562	100	44	24	333	202	15	128	.295	.368	.432	106	15	144	.977	16	113	85	1b495	—	1.6
CARTY, RICO	Ricardo Adolfo Jacobo (b Ricardo Adolfo Jacobo (Carty)); B9.1.1939 San Pedro de Macoris, D.R.; BR/TR/6´3˝/(190–210); d9.15; [DL 1968 Atl N 175, 1971 Atl N 122]																								
1963	Mil N	2	2	0	0	0	0	0	0	0-0	0	2	.000	.000	.000	-99	-1	0-0	ø	0	—	—	/H	0	-0.1
1964	Mil N	133	455	72	150	28	4	22	88	43-4	3	78	.330	.388	.554	162	38	1-2	.978	-0	97	72	O121(118/1/2)	0	3.2
1965	Mil N	83	271	37	84	18	1	10	35	17-0	3	44	.310	.355	.494	136	13	1-4	.958	1	106	86	O73L	0	1.0
1966	Atl N	151	521	73	170	25	2	15	76	60-7	0	74	.326	.391	.468	137	28	4-6	.971	4	106	95	O126(126/0/1),C17,1b2/3	0	2.6
1967	Atl N	134	444	41	113	16	2	15	64	49-10	1	70	.255	.329	.401	110	6	4-3	.959	1	105	98	O112(97/0/15),1b9	0	-0.1
1969	†Atl N	104	304	47	104	15	0	16	58	32-3	0	28	.342	.401	.549	164	26	0-2	.952	-3	96	0	O79L	22	1.8
1970	Atl N★	136	478	84	175	23	3	25	101	77-6	2	46	**.366**	**.454**	.584	167	49	1-2	.974	-0	105	57	O133L	0	4.0
1972	Atl N	86	271	31	75	12	2	6	29	44-4	0	33	.277	.378	.402	112	6	0-0	.979	2	104	63	O78L	33	0.5
1973	Tex A	86	306	24	71	12	0	3	33	36-2	1	39	.232	.311	.301	77	-9	2-0	1.000	-1	96	62	O53L,D31	22	-1.3
	Chi N	22	70	4	15	0	0	1	8	6-0	0	10	.214	.276	.257	45	-5	0-0	.947	-0	104	0	O19L	0	-0.7
	Oak A	7	8	1	2	1	0	1	1	2-0	0	1	.250	.400	.750	228	1	0-0	ø	0	—	—	D2	0	0.1
1974	Cle A	33	91	6	33	5	0	1	16	5-0	0	9	.363	.396	.451	144	5	0-0	.985	-2	22	147	D14,1b8	0	0.3
1975	Cle A	118	383	57	118	19	1	18	64	45-3	2	31	.308	.378	.504	149	25	2-2	.990	-1	100	113	D72,1b26,O12L	0	2.0
1976	Cle A	152	552	67	171	34	0	13	83	67-9	0	45	.310	.379	.442	142	32	1-1	1.000	-1	41	97	D137,1b12/lf	0	2.7
1977	Cle A	127	461	50	129	23	1	15	80	56-6	0	51	.280	.355	.432	117	12	1-2	1.000	1	226	263	D123,1b2	19	0.9
1978	Tor A	104	387	51	110	16	0	20	68	36-5	0	41	.284	.340	.481	127	13	1-1	ø	0	0	0	D101	0	1.0
	Oak A	41	141	19	39	5	1	11	31	21-2	0	16	.277	.368	.560	166	12	0-0	ø	0	0	0	D41	0	1.1
	Year	145	528	70	149	21	1	31	99	57-7	0	57	.282	.348	.502	137	25	1-1	.853	0	0	0	D142	0	2.1
1979	Tor A	132	461	48	118	26	0	12	55	46-4	1	45	.256	.322	.390	91	-6	3-1	ø	0	0	0	D129	0	-0.9
Total	15	1651	5606	712	1677	278	17	204	890	642-65	13	663	.299	.369	.464	131	245	21-26	.970	-0	102	68	O807(789/1/18),D650,1b59,C17/3	393	18.1
CARUSO, MIKE	Michael John; B5.27.1977 Queens NY; BL/TR/6´1˝/172; [SFN96 2/42]; d3.31; [DL 2000 Chi A 52]																								
1998	Chi A	133	523	81	160	17	6	5	55	14-0	7	38	.306	.331	.390	89	-10	22-6	.944	-8	98	107	S131	0	-0.6
1999	Chi A	136	529	60	132	11	4	2	35	20-0	3	36	.250	.280	.297	47	-44	12-14	.957	-23	92	94	S132,D2	0	-5.6
2002	KC A	12	20	3	2	0	0	0	0	1-0	0	2	.100	.143	.100	-30	-4	0-0	1.000	-1	135	0	S5,2b4,3b2	0	-0.4
Total	3	281	1072	144	294	28	10	7	90	35-0	10	76	.274	.302	.339	65	-58	34-20	.951	-32	95	99	S268,2b4,3b2,D2	52	-6.6
CARUTHERS, BOB	Robert Lee "Parisian Bob"; B1.5.1864 Memphis TN; D8.5.1911 Peoria IL; BL/TR/5´7˝/138; d9.7; M1/U2; ▲																								
1884	StL AA	23	82	15	22	2	0	2	—	4	0	—	.268	.302	.366	113	1	—	.750	-4	47	0	O16R,P13	—	-0.3
1885	†StL AA	60	222	37	50	10	2	1	12	20	0	—	.225	.289	.302	83	-4	—	.902	-1	97	**233**	P53,O7(6/0/1)	—	-0.1
1886	†StL AA	87	317	91	106	21	14	4	61	64	1	—	.334	.448	.527	196	38	26	.897	-4	80	112	P44,O43(1/0/42),2b2	—	1.3
1887	†StL AA	98	364	102	130	23	11	8	73	66	6	—	.357	.463	.547	164	33	49	.903	8	121	56	O54(3/2/50),P39,1b7	—	1.8
1888	Bro AA	94	335	58	77	10	5	5	53	45	4	—	.230	.328	.334	113	7	23	.899	-1	58	183	O51(4/16/31),P44	—	0.1
1889	†Bro AA	59	172	45	43	8	3	2	31	44	2	17	.250	.408	.366	121	8	9	.968	1	103	166	P56,O3(0/1/2),1b2	—	0.0
1890	†Bro N	71	238	46	63	7	4	1	29	47	5	18	.265	.397	.340	115	8	13	.860	-1	74	0	O39(37/1/1),P37	—	0.0
1891	Bro N	56	171	24	48	5	3	2	23	25	0	13	.281	.372	.380	120	5	4	.940	-1	108	91	P38,O17(1/2/14)/2	—	0.0
1892	StL N	143	513	76	142	16	8	3	69	86	5	29	.277	.386	.357	131	25	24	.892	-9	75	47	O122(6/7/110),P16,2b6,1b4,M	—	0.8
1893	Chi N	1	3	0	0	0	0	0	0	1	0	0	.000	.250	.000	-32	-1	0	1.000	-0	0	0	/cf	—	-0.1
	Cin N	13	48	14	14	2	0	1	8	15	1	2	.292	.469	.396	128	3	4	.857	-1	45	0	O13R	—	0.1
	Year	14	51	14	14	2	0	1	8	16	1	2	.275	.456	.373	119	3	4	.862	-1	43	0	O14(0/1/13)	—	0.0
Total	10	705	2465	508	695	104	50	29	359	417	24	79	.282	.391	.400	135	123	152	.875	-14	90	87	O366(58/30/280),P340,1b13,2b9	—	3.6
CASANOVA, PAUL	Paulino (Ortiz); B12.21.1941 Colon, Cuba; BR/TR/6´4˝/(190–200); d9.18																								
1965	Was A	5	13	2	4	1	0	0	1	1-0	0	3	.308	.357	.385	112	0	0-0	.938	-2	53	0	C4	0	-0.2
1966	Was A	122	429	45	109	16	5	13	44	14-2	1	78	.254	.278	.406	95	-5	1-2	.981	-2	142	102	C119	0	-0.2
1967	Was A☆	141	528	47	131	19	1	9	53	17-5	2	65	.248	.273	.339	84	-13	1-1	.984	1	153	92	C137	0	-0.6
1968	Was A	96	322	19	63	6	0	4	25	7-1	0	52	.196	.210	.252	42	-24	0-1	.989	-8	119	87	C92	0	-3.3
1969	Was A	124	379	26	82	9	2	4	37	18-7	3	52	.216	.254	.282	54	-25	0-0	.992	-2	110	85	C122	0	-2.4
1970	Was A	104	328	25	75	17	3	6	30	10-2	1	47	.229	.251	.354	69	-16	0-0	.988	1	166	96	C100	0	-1.2
1971	Was A	94	311	19	63	9	1	5	26	14-1	1	52	.203	.238	.286	51	-22	0-3	.985	-3	112	75	C83	0	-2.4
1972	Atl N	49	136	8	28	3	0	2	10	4-2	0	28	.206	.229	.272	38	-11	0-1	.975	-8	176	78	C43	0	-1.9
1973	Atl N	82	236	18	51	7	0	7	18	11-3	1	36	.216	.254	.335	58	-14	0-2	.977	-7	54	153	C78	0	-2.0
1974	Atl N	42	104	5	21	0	0	0	8	5-2	0	17	.202	.232	.202	23	-11	0-0	.986	-2	101	134	C33	0	-1.2
Total	10	859	2786	214	627	87	12	50	252	101-25	9	430	.225	.252	.319	64	-141	2-10	.985	-32	128	96	C811	0	-15.4
CASANOVA, RAUL	Raul; B8.23.1972 Humacao, PR; BB/TR/6´0˝/(192–230); [NYN90 8/226]; d5.24; [DL 1999 Det A 98]																								
1996	Det A	25	85	6	16	1	0	4	9	6-0	0	18	.188	.242	.341	45	-8	0-0	.978	-4	45	150	C22,D3	55	-1.0
1997	Det A	101	304	27	74	10	1	5	24	26-1	3	48	.243	.308	.332	68	-15	1-1	.985	1	74	108	C92/D	0	-0.7
1998	Det A	16	42	4	6	2	0	1	3	5-0	1	10	.143	.250	.262	33	-4	0-0	.967	1	78	182	C14	101	-0.2
2000	Mil N	86	231	20	57	13	3	6	36	26-1	4	48	.247	.331	.407	86	-5	1-2	.990	-3	95	65	C72,D3	0	-0.4
2001	Mil N	71	192	21	50	10	0	11	33	12-2	1	29	.260	.303	.484	102	0	0-0	.991	-6	71	90	C56,D2	58	-0.3
2002	Mil N	31	87	3	16	1	0	1	8	10-4	1	18	.184	.273	.230	35	-8	0-0	.994	-2	68	137	C28	98	-0.9
	Bal A	2	1	0	0	0	0	0	0	0-0	0	1	.000	.000	.000	-99	0	0-0	1.000	0	0	0	C2	0	0.0
2005	Chi A	6	5	0	1	0	0	0	0	0-0	0	1	.200	.200	.200	7	-1	0-0	1.000	-0	0	0	C6	0	-0.1
Total	7	338	947	81	220	37	4	28	113	85-8	10	173	.232	.300	.369	72	-41	2-3	.987	-12	75	103	C292,D9	410	-3.6
CASE, GEORGE	George Washington; B11.11.1915 Trenton NJ; D1.23.1989 Trenton NJ; BR/TR/6´0˝/183; d9.8; C4																								
1937	Was A	22	90	14	26	6	2	0	11	3	0	5	.289	.312	.400	82	-3	2-1	.945	-0	112	50	O22(8/1/14)	—	-0.4
1938	Was A	107	433	69	132	27	3	2	40	39	0	28	.305	.362	.395	96	-2	11-6	.964	-6	93	73	O101(0/19/82)	—	-1.2
1939	Was A☆	128	530	103	160	20	7	2	35	56	0	36	.302	.369	.377	98	-1	**51**-17	.955	-2	103	66	O123(7/79/38)	—	-0.2
1940	Was A	**154**	656	109	192	29	5	5	56	52	5	39	.293	.349	.375	94	-6	**35**-10	.970	-3	99	86	O154(0/118/36)	—	-0.9
1941	Was A	153	649	95	176	32	8	2	53	51	1	37	.271	.325	.354	84	-17	**33**-9	.975	12	108	153	O151(115/0/36)	0	-0.9
1942	Was A	125	513	101	164	26	2	5	43	44	3	30	.320	.377	.407	122	15	**44**-6	.951	-3	105	43	O120(86/0/34)	0	1.3
1943	Was A★	141	613	**102**	180	36	5	1	52	41	3	27	.294	.341	.374	113	9	**61**-14	.985	2	106	76	O140(18/0/122)	0	1.1
1944	Was A✱	119	464	63	116	14	2	2	32	49	3	22	.250	.326	.302	83	-9	49-18	.970	2	108	70	O114(83/7/28)	0	-1.1
1945	Was A✱	123	504	72	148	19	5	1	31	49	3	27	.294	.360	.357	118	12	30-16	.979	9	108	137	O123(87/15/27)	0	1.5
1946	Cle A	118	484	46	109	23	4	1	22	34	3	38	.225	.280	.295	65	-24	**28**-11	.983	-6	90	65	O118L	0	-3.9
1947	Was A	36	80	11	12	1	0	0	2	8	0	8	.150	.227	.162	10	-10	5-1	.963	1	113	73	O21(12/4/5)	0	-1.0
Total	11	1226	5016	785	1415	233	43	21	377	426	21	297	.282	.341	.358	95	-36	349-109	.970	5	103	87	O1187(534/243/422)	0	-5.7

Casey, Dennis Dennis Patrick; B3.30.1858 Binghamton NY; D1.19.1909 Binghamton NY; BL/TR/5´9˝/164; d8.18; b–Dan

YEAR	TM LG	G	AB	R	H	2B	3B	HR	RBI	BB-IB	HP	SO	AVG	OBP	SLG	AOPS	ABR	SB-CS	FA	FR	RNG	THR	GAMES AT POSITION	DL	BFW
1884	Wil U	2	8	1	2	1	0	0	—	0	—	—	.250	.250	.375	85	0	—	1.000	0	0	0	O2C	—	0.0
	Bal AA	37	149	20	37	7	4	3	—	5	0	—	.248	.273	.409	115	2	—	.898	0	79	208	O37C	—	0.1
1885	Bal AA	63	264	50	76	10	5	3	29	21	3	—	.288	.347	.398	137	12	—	.821	-5	96	0	O63C	—	0.4
Total	2	102	421	71	115	18	9	6	29	26	3	—	.273	.320	.401	128	14	—	.847	-5	89	71	O102C	—	0.5

Casey, Doc James Patrick; B3.15.1870 Lawrence MA; D12.31.1936 Detroit MI; BB/TR/5´6˝/157; d9.14; Col Maryland

YEAR	TM LG	G	AB	R	H	2B	3B	HR	RBI	BB-IB	HP	SO	AVG	OBP	SLG	AOPS	ABR	SB-CS	FA	FR	RNG	THR	GAMES AT POSITION	DL	BFW
1898	Was N	28	112	13	31	2	0	0	15	3	1	—	.277	.302	.295	71	-4	15	.893	-2	101	120	3b22,S4,C3	—	-0.5
1899	Was N	9	34	3	4	2	0	0	2	2	0	—	.118	.167	.176	-6	-5	1	.853	-1	87	209	3b9	—	-0.5
	Bro N	134	525	75	141	14	8	1	43	25	9	—	.269	.313	.331	75	-19	27	.892	-16	88	107	3b134	—	-3.0
	Year	143	559	78	145	16	8	1	45	27	9	—	.259	.304	.322	70	-24	28	.889	-16	88	113	3b143	—	-3.5
1900	Bro N	1	3	0	1	0	0	0	1	0	1	—	.333	.500	.333	125	0	0	1.000	0	103	0	/3	—	0.0
1901	Det A	128	540	105	153	16	9	2	46	32	10	—	.283	.335	.357	88	-9	34	.887	3	**112**	137	3b127	—	-0.3
1902	Det A	132	520	69	142	18	7	3	55	44	7	—	.273	.338	.352	90	-7	22	.904	3	106	87	3b132	—	0.0
1903	Chi N	112	435	56	126	8	3	1	40	19	3	—	.290	.324	.329	88	-8	11	.915	-19	84	47	3b112	—	-2.3
1904	Chi N	136	548	71	147	20	4	1	43	18	7	—	.268	.300	.325	93	-6	21	.911	-10	91	84	3b134,C2	—	-1.3
1905	Chi N	144	526	66	122	21	10	1	56	41	6	—	.232	.295	.316	79	-14	22	**.949**	-10	94	50	3b142/S	—	-2.2
1906	Bro N	149	571	71	133	17	8	0	34	52	8	—	.233	.306	.291	93	-4	22	.919	-16	93	64	3b149	—	-1.8
1907	Bro N	141	527	55	122	19	3	0	19	34	3	—	.231	.282	.279	82	-11	16	.955	-7	95	87	3b138	—	-1.7
Total	10	1114	4341	584	1122	137	52	9	354	270	55	—	.258	.310	.320	85	-87	191	.915	-74	96	84	3b1100,C5,S5	—	-13.6

Casey, Joe Joseph Felix; B8.15.1887 Boston MA; D6.2.1966 Melrose MA; BR/TR/5´9˝/180; d10.1; Col Boston College

YEAR	TM LG	G	AB	R	H	2B	3B	HR	RBI	BB-IB	HP	SO	AVG	OBP	SLG	AOPS	ABR	SB-CS	FA	FR	RNG	THR	GAMES AT POSITION	DL	BFW
1909	Det A	3	5	1	0	0	0	0	0	1	0	—	.000	.167	.000	-45	-1	0	1.000	1	*125*	*193*	C3	—	0.0
1910	Det A	23	62	3	12	3	0	0	2	2	1	—	.194	.231	.242	45	-4	1	.964	3	*114*	*104*	C22	—	0.2
1911	Det A	15	33	2	5	0	0	0	3	3	0	—	.152	.222	.152	5	-4	0	.956	-2	*103*	*84*	C12,O3C	—	-0.5
1918	Was A	9	17	3	4	0	0	0	2	2	0	2	.235	.316	.235	67	-1	0	1.000	1	*105*	*72*	C8	—	0.1
Total	4	50	117	9	21	3	0	0	7	8	1	2	.179	.238	.205	32	-10	1	.970	4	*111*	*100*	C45,O3C	—	-0.2

Casey, Bob Orrin Robinson; B1.26.1859 Adolphustown ON, Can.; D11.28.1936 Syracuse NY; BR/5´11˝/190; d7.17

YEAR	TM LG	G	AB	R	H	2B	3B	HR	RBI	BB-IB	HP	SO	AVG	OBP	SLG	AOPS	ABR	SB-CS	FA	FR	RNG	THR	GAMES AT POSITION	DL	BFW
1882	Det N	9	39	5	9	2	1	1	7	0	—	15	.231	.231	.410	101	0	—	.667	-5	58	0	3b8/2	—	-0.5

Casey, Sean Sean Thomas; B7.2.1974 Willingboro NJ; BL/TR/6´4˝/(215–235); [CleA95 2/53]; d9.12; Col Richmond

YEAR	TM LG	G	AB	R	H	2B	3B	HR	RBI	BB-IB	HP	SO	AVG	OBP	SLG	AOPS	ABR	SB-CS	FA	FR	RNG	THR	GAMES AT POSITION	DL	BFW
1997	Cle A	6	10	1	2	0	0	0	1	1-0	1	2	.200	.333	.200	42	-1	0-0	1.000	-0	0	0	/1D	0	-0.1
1998	Cin N	96	302	44	82	21	1	7	52	43-3	3	45	.272	.365	.417	105	4	1-1	.994	-8	62	104	1b86	32	-1.2
1999	Cin N★	151	594	103	197	42	3	25	99	61-13	9	88	.332	.399	.539	131	30	0-2	.995	-15	59	101	1b148/D	0	0.1
2000	Cin N	133	480	69	151	33	2	20	85	52-4	7	80	.315	.385	.517	123	18	1-0	.995	-10	72	107	1b129	15	-0.3
2001	Cin N★	145	533	69	165	40	0	13	89	43-8	9	63	.310	.369	.458	107	7	3-1	.994	-10	74	84	1b136,D3	0	-1.4
2002	Cin N	120	425	56	111	25	0	6	42	43-6	5	47	.261	.334	.362	81	-11	2-1	.993	-2	96	101	1b108/D	37	-2.2
2003	Cin N	147	573	71	167	19	3	14	80	51-4	2	58	.291	.350	.408	102	1	4-0	.996	-10	78	87	1b144	0	-2.0
2004	Cin N✳	146	571	101	185	44	2	24	99	46-5	10	36	.324	.381	.534	137	32	2-0	.994	-18	57	70	1b145/D	16	0.2
2005	Cin N	137	529	75	165	32	0	9	58	48-3	5	48	.312	.371	.423	108	8	2-0	**.998**	-9	70	76	1b134/D	0	-1.2
2006	Pit N	59	213	30	63	15	0	3	29	23-5	6	22	.296	.377	.408	100	1	0-0	1.000	-3	69	92	1b55	44	-0.6
	†Det A	53	184	17	45	7	0	5	30	10-4	1	21	.245	.286	.364	68	-9	0-1	.996	-5	53	101	1b51	0	-1.8
Total	10	1193	4414	636	1333	278	11	126	664	421-55	58	510	.302	.368	.456	111	80	15-6	.995	-89	70	91	1b1137,D10	144	-10.5

Cash, Dave David; B6.11.1948 Utica NY; BR/TR/5´11˝/(165–172); [PitN66 5/95]; d9.13; C3

YEAR	TM LG	G	AB	R	H	2B	3B	HR	RBI	BB-IB	HP	SO	AVG	OBP	SLG	AOPS	ABR	SB-CS	FA	FR	RNG	THR	GAMES AT POSITION	DL	BFW
1969	Pit N	18	61	8	17	3	1	0	4	9-0	0	9	.279	.371	.361	108	1	2-0	.990	6	129	82	2b17	0	0.9
1970	†Pit N	64	210	30	66	7	6	1	28	17-3	1	25	.314	.365	.419	111	3	5-2	.974	8	103	127	2b55	0	1.5
1971	†Pit N	123	478	79	138	17	4	2	34	46-0	0	33	.289	.349	.354	99	0	13-5	.987	-1	102	120	2b105,3b24,S3	0	0.8
1972	†Pit N	99	425	58	120	22	4	3	30	22-1	0	31	.282	.316	.374	97	-3	9-9	.992	25	114	136	2b97	0	2.9
1973	Pit N	116	436	59	118	21	2	2	31	38-0	0	36	.271	.328	.342	88	-7	2-5	.979	5	103	75	2b92,3b17	0	0.3
1974	Phi N★	**162**	687	89	206	26	11	2	58	46-4	9	33	.300	.351	.378	100	-1	20-8	.977	31	109	127	2b162	0	4.4
1975	Phi N★	**162**	699	111	**213**	40	3	4	57	56-5	4	34	.305	.356	.388	102	4	13-6	.981	18	104	**123**	2b162	0	3.4
1976	†Phi N★	160	666	92	189	14	**12**	1	56	54-3	2	13	.284	.337	.345	91	-8	10-12	**.988**	10	96	**126**	2b158	0	1.0
1977	Mon N	153	650	91	188	42	7	0	43	52-5	2	33	.289	.343	.375	95	-4	21-12	.986	-15	96	79	2b153	0	-1.0
1978	Mon N	159	658	66	166	26	3	3	43	37-2	0	29	.252	.291	.315	70	-28	12-6	**.986**	-7	98	103	2b159	0	-2.8
1979	Mon N	76	187	24	60	11	1	2	19	12-0	0	12	.321	.358	.422	113	3	7-4	.971	-5	99	75	2b47	0	0.1
1980	SD N	130	397	25	90	14	2	1	23	35-5	0	21	.227	.287	.280	64	-20	6-5	.987	6	104	102	2b123	0	-0.8
Total	12	1422	5554	732	1571	243	56	21	426	424-28	18	309	.283	.334	.358	92	-60	120-74	.984	81	103	110	2b1330,3b41,S3	0	10.7

Cash, Kevin Kevin Forrest; B12.6.1977 Tampa FL; BR/TR/6´0˝/(185–190); d9.6; Col Florida St.

YEAR	TM LG	G	AB	R	H	2B	3B	HR	RBI	BB-IB	HP	SO	AVG	OBP	SLG	AOPS	ABR	SB-CS	FA	FR	RNG	THR	GAMES AT POSITION	DL	BFW
2002	Tor A	7	14	1	2	0	0	0	0	1-0	0	4	.143	.200	.143	-6	-2	0-0	.968	0	79	88	C7	0	-0.2
2003	Tor A	34	106	10	15	3	0	1	8	4-0	1	22	.142	.179	.198	-0	-16	0-0	.995	-3	130	78	C34	0	-1.6
2004	Tor A	60	181	18	35	9	0	4	21	10-0	4	59	.193	.249	.309	43	-16	0-0	.994	8	145	118	C60	17	-0.4
2005	TB A	13	31	4	5	1	0	2	2	1-0	1	13	.161	.212	.387	56	-2	0-0	1.000	0	167	135	C13	34	-0.1
Total	4	114	332	33	57	13	0	7	31	16-0	6	98	.172	.221	.274	28	-36	0-0	.994	5	140	106	C114	51	-2.3

Cash, Norm Norman Dalton; B11.10.1934 Justiceburg TX; D10.12.1986 Beaver Island MI; BL/TL/6´0˝/(165–190); d6.18; Col Sul Ross St.

YEAR	TM LG	G	AB	R	H	2B	3B	HR	RBI	BB-IB	HP	SO	AVG	OBP	SLG	AOPS	ABR	SB-CS	FA	FR	RNG	THR	GAMES AT POSITION	DL	BFW
1958	Chi A	13	8	2	2	0	0	0	0	0-0	0	1	.250	.250	.250	39	-1	0-0	1.000	-0	68	0	O4(1/0/3)	0	-0.1
1959	†Chi A	58	104	16	25	0	1	4	16	18-3	5	9	.240	.372	.375	109	2	1-1	.984	-1	86	92	1b31	0	-0.1
1960	Det A	121	353	64	101	16	3	18	63	65-1	6	58	.286	.402	.501	140	22	4-2	.991	-1	98	85	1b99,O4(3/0/1)	0	1.6
1961	Det A★	159	535	119	**193**	22	8	41	132	124-**19**	9	85	**.361**	**.487**	.662	198	83	11-5	.992	5	109	97	1b157	0	**7.6**
1962	Det A	148	507	94	123	16	2	39	89	104-12	**13**	82	.243	.382	.513	134	28	6-3	.992	8	114	80	1b146,O3R	0	2.7
1963	Det A	147	493	67	133	19	1	26	79	89-8	6	76	.270	.386	.471	135	27	2-3	.994	3	105	88	1b142	0	2.2
1964	Det A	144	479	63	123	15	5	23	83	70-4	3	66	.257	.351	.453	121	15	2-1	**.997**	4	107	93	1b137	0	1.1
1965	Det A	142	467	79	124	23	1	30	82	77-5	4	62	.266	.371	.512	147	31	6-6	.992	6	**115**	96	1b139	0	3.0
1966	Det A★	160	603	98	168	18	3	32	93	66-4	4	91	.279	.351	.478	133	26	2-1	.988	4	108	96	1b158	0	2.1
1967	Det A	152	488	64	118	16	5	22	72	81-9	4	100	.242	.352	.430	127	19	3-2	**.995**	10	121	99	1b146	0	2.2
1968	†Det A	127	411	50	108	15	1	25	63	39-7	3	70	.263	.329	.487	141	20	1-1	.992	9	**127**	91	1b117	0	2.4
1969	Det A	142	483	81	135	15	4	22	74	63-5	6	80	.280	.368	.464	127	18	2-1	.994	7	**114**	98	1b134	0	1.4
1970	Det A	130	370	58	96	18	2	15	53	72-6	5	58	.259	.383	.441	127	17	0-1	.989	3	110	83	1b114	0	1.1
1971	Det A★	135	452	72	128	10	3	32	91	59-7	7	86	.283	.372	.531	148	28	1-0	.992	1	101	96	1b131	0	2.0
1972	†Det A★	137	440	51	114	16	0	22	61	50-13	4	64	.259	.338	.445	128	15	0-2	.993	2	102	103	1b134	0	0.7
1973	Det A	121	363	51	95	19	0	19	40	47-7	8	73	.262	.357	.471	124	12	1-0	.991	2	107	85	1b114,D3	0	0.7
1974	Det A	53	149	17	34	3	2	7	12	19-2	3	30	.228	.327	.416	109	2	1-1	.985	-0	101	83	1b44	0	-0.2
Total	17	2089	6705	1046	1820	241	41	377	1103	1043-112	90	1091	.271	.374	.488	138	364	43-30	.992	61	109	92	1b1943,O11(4/0/7),D3	0	30.4

Cash, Ron Ronald Forrest; B11.20.1949 Atlanta GA; BR/TR/6´0˝/180; d9.4; Col Florida St.

YEAR	TM LG	G	AB	R	H	2B	3B	HR	RBI	BB-IB	HP	SO	AVG	OBP	SLG	AOPS	ABR	SB-CS	FA	FR	RNG	THR	GAMES AT POSITION	DL	BFW
1973	Det A	14	39	8	16	1	1	0	6	5-0	0	5	.410	.467	.487	162	3	0-0	.900	0	104	357	O7L,3b6	0	0.4
1974	Det A	20	62	6	14	2	0	0	5	0-0	0	11	.226	.222	.258	38	-5	0-1	.979	-1	87	93	1b15,3b4	23	-0.9
Total	2	34	101	14	30	3	1	0	11	5-0	0	16	.297	.324	.347	89	-2	0-1	.979	-1	87	93	1b15,3b10,O7L	23	-0.5

Casilla, Alexi Alexi; B7.20.1984 San Cristobal, D.R.; BB/TR/5´9˝/160; d9.1

YEAR	TM LG	G	AB	R	H	2B	3B	HR	RBI	BB-IB	HP	SO	AVG	OBP	SLG	AOPS	ABR	SB-CS	FA	FR	RNG	THR	GAMES AT POSITION	DL	BFW
2006	Min A	9	4	1	1	0	0	0	0	2-0	0	1	.250	.500	.250	103	0	0-0	1.000	4	188	432	2b4,S2,D2	0	0.4

Casimiro, Carlos Carlos Rafael; B11.8.1976 San Pedro de Macoris, D.R.; BR/TR/5´11˝/179; d7.31

YEAR	TM LG	G	AB	R	H	2B	3B	HR	RBI	BB-IB	HP	SO	AVG	OBP	SLG	AOPS	ABR	SB-CS	FA	FR	RNG	THR	GAMES AT POSITION	DL	BFW
2000	Bal A	2	8	0	1	1	0	0	3	0-0	0	2	.125	.125	.250	-9	-1	0-0	ø	0	—	—	D2	0	-0.1

Caskin, Ed Edward James; B12.30.1851 Danvers MA; D10.9.1924 Danvers MA; BR/TR/5´9.5˝/165; d5.1

YEAR	TM LG	G	AB	R	H	2B	3B	HR	RBI	BB-IB	HP	SO	AVG	OBP	SLG	AOPS	ABR	SB-CS	FA	FR	RNG	THR	GAMES AT POSITION	DL	BFW
1879	Tro N	70	304	32	78	13	2	0	21	2	—	14	.257	.261	.313	95	-1	—	.902	6	121	94	S42,C22,2b6	—	0.7
1880	Tro N	82	333	36	75	5	4	0	28	7	—	24	.225	.241	.264	68	-12	—	.885	6	112	73	S82,C2	—	-0.2
1881	Tro N	63	234	33	53	7	1	0	21	13	—	29	.226	.267	.265	65	-9	—	.906	3	102	94	S63	—	-0.4
1883	NY N	95	383	47	91	11	2	1	40	14	—	25	.238	.264	.285	68	-15	—	.855	-5	98	62	S81,2b13/C	—	-1.5
1884	NY N	100	351	49	81	11	1	1	40	34	—	55	.231	.299	.276	80	-7	—	.883	5	98	**125**	S96,C6	—	0.1
1885	StL N	71	262	31	47	3	0	0	12	12	—	22	.179	.215	.191	34	-18	—	.884	-3	101	56	3b69,C2/S	—	-1.9

YEAR	TM LG	G	AB	R	H	2B	3B	HR	RBI	BB-IB	HP	SO	AVG	OBP	SLG	AOPS	ABR	SB-CS	FA	FR	RNG	THR	GAMES AT POSITION	DL	BFW
1886	NY N	1	4	1	2	0	0	0	1	0	—	1	.500	.500	.500	203	0	0	1.000	-1	0	0	/S	—	0.0
Total	7	482	1871	229	427	50	10	2	163	82	—	170	.228	.261	.269	70	-62	0	.883	11	104	90	S366,3b69,C33,2b19	—	-3.2

CASSADY, HARRY Harry Delbert (b Harry Delbert Cassaday); B7.20.1880 Bellflower IL; D4.19.1969 Fresno CA; BL/TL/5´8˝/145; d8.8; Col Illinois Wesleyan

YEAR	TM LG	G	AB	R	H	2B	3B	HR	RBI	BB-IB	HP	SO	AVG	OBP	SLG	AOPS	ABR	SB-CS	FA	FR	RNG	THR	GAMES AT POSITION	DL	BFW
1904	Pit N	12	44	8	9	0	0	0	3	2	0	—	.205	.239	.205	36	-3	2	.867	-0	243	0	O12R	—	-0.4
1905	Was A	10	30	1	4	0	0	0	1	0	0	—	.133	.133	.133	-16	-4	0	1.000	1	113	0	O9R	—	-0.4
Total	2	22	74	9	13	0	0	0	4	2	0	—	.176	.197	.176	17	-7	2	.933	1	184	0	O21R	—	-0.8

CASSIDY, JOHN John P.; B1857 Brooklyn NY; D7.2.1891 Brooklyn NY; BR/TL/5´8˝/168; d4.24; OF(1/147/411); ▲

YEAR	TM LG	G	AB	R	H	2B	3B	HR	RBI	BB-IB	HP	SO	AVG	OBP	SLG	AOPS	ABR	SB-CS	FA	FR	RNG	THR	GAMES AT POSITION	DL	BFW
1875	Atl NA	41	166	14	29	3	2	1	6	0	—	4	.175	.175	.235	47	-7	0-0	.782	-4	110	43	P30,O12(1/0/11),1b10,2b2	—	-0.5
	NH NA	6	22	3	3	1	0	0	1	0	—	1	.136	.136	.182	11	-2	0-1	.988	1	84	149	1b6	—	-0.1
	Year	**47**	188	17	32	4	2	1	7	0	—	5	.170	.170	.229	43	-9	0-1	.782	-3	110	43	P30,1b16,O12(1/0/11),2b2	—	-0.6
1876	Har N	12	47	6	13	2	0	0	8	1	—	0	.277	.292	.319	95	0	—	1.000	1	189	0	O8R,1b4	—	0.1
1877	Har N	**60**	251	43	95	10	5	0	27	3	—	3	.378	.386	.458	185	24	—	.722	-5	147	117	O58(0/1/57),P2	—	1.6
1878	Chi N	60	256	33	68	7	1	0	29	9	—	11	.266	.291	.301	89	-3	—	.810	7	190	**265**	O60R/C	—	0.3
1879	Tro N	9	37	4	7	1	0	0	1	2	—	4	.189	.231	.216	52	-2	—	.889	-1	76	0	O8(0/3/5),1b2	—	-0.3
1880	Tro N	**83**	352	40	89	14	8	0	29	12	—	34	.253	.277	.338	102	0	—	.880	-4	95	28	O82(0/47/35)/2	—	-0.5
1881	Tro N	**85**	370	57	82	13	3	1	11	18	—	21	.222	.258	.281	66	-15	—	.872	-12	87	0	O84C/S	—	-2.8
1882	Tro N	29	121	14	21	3	1	0	9	3	—	16	.174	.194	.215	32	-9	—	.778	-8	66	140	O16(0/12/4),3b13	—	-1.6
1883	Pro N	89	366	46	87	16	5	0	42	9	—	38	.238	.256	.309	69	-14	—	.864	-0	133	73	O88(1/0/87)/21	—	-1.3
1884	Bro AA	106	433	57	109	11	6	2	—	19	2	—	.252	.286	.319	96	-2	—	.847	-8	132	162	O101R,3b4/S	—	-1.0
1885	Bro AA	54	221	36	47	6	2	1	28	8	3	—	.213	.250	.271	64	-9	—	.852	-6	83	197	O54R	—	-1.4
Total	10	587	2454	336	618	83	31	4	184	84	5	127	.252	.278	.316	89	-30	—	.845	-35	122	108	O559R,3b17,1b7,S2,2b2,P2/C	—	-6.9

CASSIDY, JOE Joseph Phillip; B2.8.1883 Chester PA; D3.25.1906 Chester PA; BR/TR; d4.18; Col Villanova

YEAR	TM LG	G	AB	R	H	2B	3B	HR	RBI	BB-IB	HP	SO	AVG	OBP	SLG	AOPS	ABR	SB-CS	FA	FR	RNG	THR	GAMES AT POSITION	DL	BFW
1904	Was A	152	581	63	140	12	**19**	1	33	15	4	—	.241	.265	.332	90	-10	17	.937	7	96	111	S99,O32(1/20/11),3b23	—	-0.1
1905	Was A	151	576	67	124	16	4	1	43	25	2	—	.215	.250	.262	65	-24	23	.934	**35**	**115**	104	S151	—	1.7
Total	2	303	1157	130	264	28	23	2	76	40	6	—	.228	.258	.297	78	-34	40	.935	42	108	107	S250,O32(1/20/11),3b23	—	1.6

CASSIDY, PETE Peter Francis; B4.8.1873 Wilmington DE; D7.9.1929 Wilmington DE; BR/TR/5´10˝/165; d4.18

YEAR	TM LG	G	AB	R	H	2B	3B	HR	RBI	BB-IB	HP	SO	AVG	OBP	SLG	AOPS	ABR	SB-CS	FA	FR	RNG	THR	GAMES AT POSITION	DL	BFW
1896	Lou N	49	184	16	39	1	1	0	12	7	4	7	.212	.256	.228	29	-19	5	.973	-7	89	56	1b38,S11	—	-2.2
1899	Bro N	6	20	2	3	1	0	0	4	1	2	—	.150	.261	.200	27	-2	1	1.000	-2	77	0	3b3,S2	—	-0.4
	Was N	46	178	21	56	13	0	3	32	9	5	—	.315	.365	.438	121	5	5	.970	-2	92	111	1b37,3b6,S3	—	0.3
	Year	52	198	23	59	14	0	3	36	10	7	—	.298	.353	.414	111	3	6	.970	-5	92	111	1b37,3b9,S5	—	-0.1
Total	2	101	382	39	98	15	1	3	48	17	11	7	.257	.307	.325	72	-16	11	.972	-11	91	84	1b75,S16,3b9	—	-2.3

CASSINI, JACK Jack Dempsey "Gabby","Scat"; B10.26.1919 Dearborn MI; BR/TR/5´10˝/175; d4.19

YEAR	TM LG	G	AB	R	H	2B	3B	HR	RBI	BB-IB	HP	SO	AVG	OBP	SLG	AOPS	ABR	SB-CS	FA	FR	RNG	THR	GAMES AT POSITION	DL	BFW
1949	Pit N	8	0	3	0	0	0	0	0	0	0	0	ø	ø	ø	ø	0	0	ø	0	—	—	/R	0	0.0

CASTELLANO, PEDRO Pedro Orlando (Arrieta); B3.11.1970 Barquisimeto, Lara, Venez.; BR/TR/6´1˝/(175–180); d5.30

YEAR	TM LG	G	AB	R	H	2B	3B	HR	RBI	BB-IB	HP	SO	AVG	OBP	SLG	AOPS	ABR	SB-CS	FA	FR	RNG	THR	GAMES AT POSITION	DL	BFW
1993	Col N	34	71	12	13	2	0	3	7	8-0	0	16	.183	.266	.338	52	-5	1-1	.909	-2	97	61	3b13,1b10,S5,2b4	0	-0.7
1995	Col N	4	5	0	0	0	0	0	0	2-0	0	3	.000	.286	.000	-13	-1	0-0	1.000	-1	0	0	3b3	0	-0.1
1996	Col N	13	17	1	2	0	0	0	2	3-1	1	6	.118	.286	.118	9	-2	0-0	1.000	1	167	136	2b3/3lf	0	-0.1
Total	3	51	93	13	15	2	0	3	9	13-1	1	25	.161	.271	.280	40	-8	1-1	.917	-2	89	53	3b17,1b10,2b7,S5/lf	0	-0.9

CASTIGLIA, JIM James Vincent; B9.30.1918 Passaic NJ; BL/TR/5´11˝/200; d4.14; Mil 1942–45; Col Georgetown

YEAR	TM LG	G	AB	R	H	2B	3B	HR	RBI	BB-IB	HP	SO	AVG	OBP	SLG	AOPS	ABR	SB-CS	FA	FR	RNG	THR	GAMES AT POSITION	DL	BFW
1942	Phi A	16	18	2	7	0	0	0	2	1	0	3	.389	.421	.389	129	1	0-0	.875	-1	*72*	*198*	C3	0	0.0

CASTIGLIONE, PETE Peter Paul; B2.13.1921 Greenwich CT; BR/TR/5´11˝/(170–175); d9.10

YEAR	TM LG	G	AB	R	H	2B	3B	HR	RBI	BB-IB	HP	SO	AVG	OBP	SLG	AOPS	ABR	SB-CS	FA	FR	RNG	THR	GAMES AT POSITION	DL	BFW
1947	Pit N	13	50	6	14	0	0	0	1	2	0	5	.280	.308	.280	55	-3	0	.970	-0	100	74	S13	0	-0.3
1948	Pit N	4	2	0	0	0	0	0	0	0	0	0	.000	.000	.000	-98	-1	1	1.000	0	145	0	/S	0	-0.1
1949	Pit N	118	448	57	120	20	2	6	43	20	0	43	.268	.299	.362	74	-17	2	.957	4	103	128	3b98,S17,O2R	0	-1.3
1950	Pit N	94	263	29	67	10	3	3	22	23	1	23	.255	.317	.350	73	-11	1	.970	-11	86	115	3b35,S29,2b9,1b3	0	-2.0
1951	Pit N	132	482	62	126	19	4	7	42	34	1	28	.261	.311	.361	78	-16	2-2	.957	8	115	103	3b99,S28	0	-0.7
1952	Pit N	67	214	27	57	9	1	4	18	17	1	8	.266	.323	.374	90	-3	3-3	.951	4	111	64	3b57/1lf	0	0.0
1953	Pit N	45	159	14	33	2	1	4	21	5	1	14	.208	.236	.308	41	-15	1-1	.978	4	113	64	3b43	0	-1.1
	StL N	67	52	9	9	2	0	0	3	2	0	5	.173	.204	.212	9	-7	0-0	.967	4	121	211	3b51,2b9,S3	0	-0.3
	Year	112	211	23	42	4	1	4	24	7	1	19	.199	.228	.284	33	-22	1-1	.976	8	114	90	3b94,2b9,S3	0	-1.4
1954	StL N	5	0	1	0	0	0	0	0	0	0	0	ø	ø	ø	ø	0	0-0	1.000	0	142	0	3b5	0	0.0
Total	8	545	1670	205	426	62	11	24	150	103	4	126	.255	.300	.349	71	-73	10-6	.960	12	108	102	3b388,S91,2b18,1b4,O3(1/0/2)	0	-5.8

CASTILLA, VINNY Vinicio (Soria); B7.4.1967 Oaxaca, Oaxaca, Mexico; BR/TR/6´1˝/(175–205); d9.1

YEAR	TM LG	G	AB	R	H	2B	3B	HR	RBI	BB-IB	HP	SO	AVG	OBP	SLG	AOPS	ABR	SB-CS	FA	FR	RNG	THR	GAMES AT POSITION	DL	BFW
1991	Atl N	12	5	1	1	0	0	0	0	0-0	0	2	.200	.200	.200	12	-1	0-0	1.000	-1	65	0	S12	0	-0.2
1992	Atl N	9	16	1	4	1	0	0	1	1-1	1	4	.250	.333	.313	79	0	0-0	.875	-0	72	0	3b4,S4	0	0.0
1993	Col N	105	337	36	86	9	7	9	30	13-4	2	45	.255	.283	.404	71	-15	2-5	.975	4	103	105	S104	15	-0.6
1994	Col N	52	130	16	43	11	1	3	18	7-1	0	23	.331	.357	.500	105	1	2-1	.984	-0	98	119	S18,2b14,3b9,1b2	0	0.3
1995	†Col N★	139	527	82	163	34	2	32	90	30-2	4	87	.309	.347	.564	106	5	2-8	.958	-7	99	87	3b137,S5	0	-0.3
1996	Col N	160	629	97	191	34	0	40	113	35-7	5	88	.304	.343	.548	106	5	7-2	.960	**34**	**130**	**150**	3b160	0	3.9
1997	Col N	159	612	94	186	25	2	40	113	44-9	8	108	.304	.356	.547	108	7	2-4	.954	12	116	135	3b157	0	1.8
1998	Col N★	**162**	645	108	206	28	4	46	144	40-7	6	89	.319	.362	.589	120	18	5-9	.970	0	102	125	3b162/S	0	1.7
1999	Col N	158	615	83	169	24	1	33	102	53-7	1	75	.275	.331	.478	81	-18	2-3	.954	-1	101	107	3b157	0	-1.8
2000	TB A	85	331	22	73	9	1	6	42	14-3	3	41	.221	.254	.308	43	-30	1-2	.967	14	126	135	3b83	60	-1.5
2001	TB A	24	93	7	20	6	0	2	9	3-0	1	22	.215	.247	.344	55	-6	0-0	.934	2	101	119	3b24	0	-0.4
	†Hou N	122	445	62	120	28	1	23	82	32-3	3	86	.270	.320	.492	99	-1	1-4	.963	9	107	91	3b121,S3	0	0.7
2002	†Atl N	143	543	56	126	23	2	12	61	22-4	7	69	.232	.268	.348	62	-32	4-1	**.982**	-18	91	90	3b139	0	-5.0
2003	†Atl N	147	542	65	150	28	3	22	76	26-3	3	86	.277	.310	.461	99	-3	1-2	.955	0	104	106	3b147	0	-0.3
2004	Col N	148	583	93	158	43	3	35	**131**	51-6	6	113	.271	.332	.535	107	6	0-0	**.987**	7	104	96	3b148	0	1.3
2005	Was N	142	494	53	125	36	1	12	66	43-7	7	82	.253	.319	.403	93	-6	4-2	.970	-10	85	91	3b138	0	-1.5
2006	SD N	72	254	24	59	10	0	4	23	9-0	2	46	.232	.260	.319	51	-20	0-0	.971	-2	95	72	3b69	0	-2.1
	Col N	15	21	2	4	0	0	1	4	0-0	1	3	.190	.227	.333	38	-2	0-0	1.000	-0	0	143	1b7/3	0	-0.2
	Year	87	275	26	63	10	0	5	27	9-0	3	49	.229	.258	.320	49	-22	0-0	.971	-2	96	71	3b70,1b7	0	-2.3
Total	16	1854	6822	902	1884	349	28	320	1105	423-64	60	1069	.276	.321	.476	93	-92	33-43	.965	43	105	108	3b1656,S147,2b14,1b9	75	-4.2

CASTILLO, ALBERTO Alberto Terrero; B2.10.1970 San Juan de la Maguana, D.R.; BR/TR/6´0˝/(184–215); d5.28

YEAR	TM LG	G	AB	R	H	2B	3B	HR	RBI	BB-IB	HP	SO	AVG	OBP	SLG	AOPS	ABR	SB-CS	FA	FR	RNG	THR	GAMES AT POSITION	DL	BFW
1995	NY N	13	29	2	3	0	0	0	0	3-0	1	9	.103	.212	.103	-14	-5	1-0	.974	3	198	154	C12	0	-0.1
1996	NY N	6	11	1	4	0	0	0	0	0-0	0	4	.364	.364	.364	97	0	0-0	1.000	-1	76	0	C6	0	-0.1
1997	NY N	35	59	3	12	1	0	0	7	9-0	0	16	.203	.304	.220	44	-5	0-1	.987	2	159	42	C34	0	-0.1
1998	NY N	38	83	13	17	4	0	2	7	9-0	1	17	.205	.290	.325	64	-4	0-2	.990	2	137	188	C35/D	0	-0.1
1999	StL N	93	255	21	67	8	0	4	31	24-1	2	48	.263	.326	.341	69	-12	0-0	.991	11	159	157	C91	0	0.4
2000	Tor A	66	185	14	39	7	0	1	16	21-0	0	36	.211	.287	.265	41	-17	0-0	.993	8	133	116	C66	0	-0.4
2001	Tor A	66	131	9	26	4	0	1	4	7-0	3	30	.198	.255	.252	34	-13	1-1	.989	7	98	103	C66	0	-0.3
2002	NY A	15	37	3	5	1	1	0	4	1-0	0	12	.135	.158	.216	-2	-6	0-0	.990	3	79	166	C14	0	-0.2
2003	SF N	11	15	2	3	1	0	1	4	0-0	0	5	.200	.200	.467	66	-1	0-0	.975	2	219	0	C10	30	0.1
2004	KC A	29	89	12	24	6	0	1	11	14-0	0	10	.270	.365	.371	94	0	0-2	.995	7	103	123	C29	0	0.8
2005	KC A	34	100	13	21	5	1	1	14	12-0	0	21	.210	.292	.310	63	-5	1-0	.992	8	285	84	C34	0	0.5
	Oak A	1	1	0	0	0	0	0	0	0-0	0	1	.000	.000	.000	-99	0	0-0	1.000	0	0	0	/C	0	0.0
	Year	35	101	13	21	5	1	1	14	12-0	0	22	.208	.289	.307	62	-5	1-0	.992	8	282	83	C35	0	0.5
Total	11	407	995	93	221	37	2	11	98	100-1	7	209	.222	.295	.296	54	-68	3-6	.990	52	149	123	C398/D	30	0.5

CASTILLO, TONY Anthony; B6.14.1957 San Jose CA; BR/TR/6´4˝/185; [SDN75 3/50]; d9.22

YEAR	TM LG	G	AB	R	H	2B	3B	HR	RBI	BB-IB	HP	SO	AVG	OBP	SLG	AOPS	ABR	SB-CS	FA	FR	RNG	THR	GAMES AT POSITION	DL	BFW
1978	SD N	5	8	0	1	0	0	0	1	0-0	0	2	.125	.125	.125	-32	-1	0-0	.950	1	226	187	C5	0	0.0

CASTILLO, BRAULIO Braulio Robinson Medrano (b Braulio Robinson Medrano (Castillo)); B5.13.1968 Elias Pina, D.R.; BR/TR/6´0˝/160; d8.18

YEAR	TM LG	G	AB	R	H	2B	3B	HR	RBI	BB-IB	HP	SO	AVG	OBP	SLG	AOPS	ABR	SB-CS	FA	FR	RNG	THR	GAMES AT POSITION	DL	BFW
1991	Phi N	28	52	3	9	3	0	0	2	1-0	0	15	.173	.189	.231	17	-6	1-1	.977	0	98	208	O26(0/24/2)	0	-0.6
1992	Phi N	28	76	12	15	3	1	2	7	4-0	0	15	.197	.237	.342	62	-4	1-0	.956	-1	102	0	O24(2/6/16)	0	-0.6
Total	2	56	128	15	24	6	1	2	9	5-0	0	30	.188	.218	.297	44	-10	2-1	.966	-1	100	98	O50(2/30/18)	0	-1.2

YEAR	TM LG	G	AB	R	H	2B	3B	HR	RBI	BB-IB	HP	SO	AVG	OBP	SLG	AOPS	ABR	SB-CS	FA	FR	RNG	THR	GAMES AT POSITION	DL	BFW
Castillo, Manny	Esteban Manuel Antonio (Cabrera); B4.1.1957 Santo Domingo, D.R.; BB/TR/5´9˝/(160–180); d9.1																								
1980	KC A	7	10	1	2	0	0	0	0	0-0	0	0	.200	.200	.200	10	-1	0-0	1.000	0	103	0	3b3/2D	0	-0.1
1982	Sea A	138	506	49	130	29	1	3	49	22-2	2	35	.257	.286	.336	69	-21	2-8	.938	-16	81	74	3b130,2b9	0	-4.2
1983	Sea A	91	203	13	42	6	3	0	24	7-2	1	20	.207	.233	.266	37	-18	1-1	.971	8	112	94	3b55,1b11,2b5/PD	0	-1.1
Total	3	236	719	63	174	35	4	3	73	29-4	3	55	.242	.270	.314	59	-40	3-9	.949	-8	89	78	3b188,2b15,1b11,D8/P	0	-5.4
Castillo, Jose	Jose (Rondon); B3.19.1981 Las Mercedes, Guarico, Venezuela; BR/TR/6´1˝/(200–210); d4.7																								
2004	Pit N	129	383	44	98	15	2	8	39	23-5	1	92	.256	.298	.368	71	-17	3-2	.980	4	100	113	2b123,S2	0	-0.8
2005	Pit N	101	370	49	99	16	3	11	53	23-3	0	59	.268	.307	.416	88	-8	2-3	.977	16	108	139	2b100	69	1.2
2006	Pit N	148	518	54	131	25	0	14	65	32-8	5	98	.253	.299	.382	72	-22	6-4	.975	-1	95	103	2b145	0	-1.6
Total	3	378	1271	147	328	56	5	33	157	78-16	6	249	.258	.301	.388	77	-47	11-9	.977	20	100	116	2b368,S2	69	-1.2
Castillo, Juan	Juan (Bryas); B1.25.1962 San Pedro de Macoris, D.R.; BB/TR (BR 1988–89)/5´11˝/(155–162); d4.12																								
1986	Mil A	26	54	6	9	0	1	0	5	5-0	1	12	.167	.250	.204	24	-6	1-1	1.000	-2	83	77	2b17,S4,3b2/rfD	0	-0.7
1987	Mil A	116	321	44	72	11	4	3	28	33-0	3	76	.224	.302	.312	61	-18	15-7	.973	-11	90	93	2b97,S13,3b7	15	-2.2
1988	Mil A	54	90	10	20	0	0	0	2	3-0	0	14	.222	.247	.222	32	-8	2-0	.932	0	129	105	2b18,3b17,S13/lfD	38	-0.7
1989	Mil A	3	4	0	0	0	0	0	3	0-0	0	2	.000	.000	.000	-99	-1	0-0	1.000	0	90	83	2b3	0	-0.1
Total	4	199	469	60	101	11	5	3	38	41-0	4	104	.215	.282	.279	51	-33	18-8	.972	-13	93	92	2b135,S30,3b26,D5,O2(1/0/1)	53	-3.7
Castillo, Luis	Luis Antonio (Donato); B9.12.1975 San Pedro de Macoris, D.R.; BB/TR (BR 1998p)/5´11˝/(155–196); d8.8																								
1996	Fla N	41	164	26	43	2	1	1	8	14-0	0	46	.262	.320	.305	68	-8	17-4	.986	7	104	143	2b41	0	0.3
1997	Fla N	75	263	27	63	8	0	0	8	27-0	0	53	.240	.310	.270	56	-17	16-10	.971	-3	94	106	2b70	15	-1.6
1998	Fla N	44	153	21	31	3	2	1	10	22-0	1	33	.203	.307	.268	56	-10	3-0	.970	-1	93	105	2b44	0	-0.7
1999	Fla N	128	487	76	147	23	4	0	28	67-0	0	85	.302	.384	.366	97	1	50-17	.976	-12	97	88	2b126	0	-0.1
2000	Fla N	136	539	101	180	17	3	2	17	78-0	0	86	.334	.418	.388	111	13	**62**-22	.983	-4	98	92	2b136	19	2.1
2001	Fla N	134	537	76	141	16	10	2	45	67-0	1	90	.263	.344	.341	81	-15	33-16	.980	10	104	**118**	2b133	0	0.3
2002	Fla N★	146	606	86	185	18	5	2	39	55-4	2	76	.305	.364	.361	96	-3	**48**-15	.981	-12	97	94	2b144	0	-0.3
2003	†Fla N★	152	595	99	187	19	6	6	39	63-0	2	60	.314	.381	.397	108	8	21-19	.986	4	103	99	2b152	0	1.7
2004	Fla N	150	564	91	164	12	7	2	47	75-2	1	68	.291	.373	.348	93	-4	21-4	.991	1	99	111	2b148	0	0.7
2005	Fla N★	122	439	72	132	12	4	4	30	65-1	1	32	.301	.391	.374	108	7	10-7	.988	20	109	109	2b120	0	3.2
2006	†Min A	142	584	84	173	22	6	3	49	56-0	1	58	.296	.358	.370	89	-8	25-11	.991	-4	93	88	2b142	0	-0.4
Total	11	1270	4931	759	1446	152	48	23	320	589-7	9	687	.293	.369	.358	93	-36	306-125	.983	6	99	102	2b1256	34	5.2
Castillo, Marty	Martin Horace; B1.16.1957 Long Beach CA; BR/TR/6´1˝/(190–205); [DetA78 5/116]; d8.19; Col Chapman																								
1981	Det A	6	8	1	1	0	0	0	0	0-0	0	2	.125	.125	.125	-27	-1	0-0	1.000	2	147	642	3b4/Clf	0	0.1
1982	Det A	1	0	0	0	0	0	0	0	0-0	0	0	ø	ø	ø	ø	0	0-0	1.000	-0	7	0	/C	0	0.0
1983	Det A	67	119	10	23	4	0	2	10	7-0	0	22	.193	.238	.277	42	-10	2-0	.990	0	94	82	3b58,C10	0	-1.0
1984	†Det A	70	141	16	33	5	2	4	17	10-0	0	33	.234	.285	.383	83	-4	1-0	.970	-6	101	111	C36,3b33/D	0	-0.8
1985	Det A	57	84	4	10	2	0	2	5	2-0	0	19	.119	.138	.214	-5	-12	0-2	.977	0	109	157	C32,3b25	0	-1.2
Total	5	201	352	31	67	11	2	8	32	19-0	0	76	.190	.231	.301	46	-27	3-2	.978	-3	97	91	3b120,C80/Dlf	0	-2.9
Castillo, Carmen	Monte Carmelo; B6.8.1958 San Pedro de Macoris, D.R.; BR/TR/6´1˝/(185–201); d7.17																								
1982	Cle A	47	120	11	25	4	0	2	11	6-2	2	17	.208	.258	.292	50	-8	0-0	.978	1	123	0	O43(19/8/20),D2	0	-0.9
1983	Cle A	23	36	9	10	2	1	1	3	4-0	1	6	.278	.366	.472	124	1	1-1	.929	1	99	343	O19R/D	0	0.2
1984	Cle A	87	211	36	55	9	2	10	36	21-0	2	32	.261	.329	.464	116	4	1-3	.933	-2	106	57	O70R,D2	0	-0.1
1985	Cle A	67	184	27	45	5	1	11	25	11-0	3	40	.245	.298	.462	105	0	3-0	.953	-0	116	0	O51R,D9	0	-0.2
1986	Cle A	85	205	34	57	9	0	8	32	9-0	1	48	.278	.310	.439	103	0	2-1	.939	2	106	209	O37R,D35	0	0.0
1987	Cle A	89	220	27	55	17	0	11	31	16-0	0	52	.250	.296	.477	101	0	1-1	1.000	1	92	264	D43,O23(1/0/22)	0	-0.1
1988	Cle A	66	176	12	48	8	0	4	14	5-1	1	31	.273	.297	.386	87	-4	6-2	.933	-2	96	49	O45(30/0/16),D9	0	-0.6
1989	Min A	94	218	23	56	13	3	8	33	15-1	1	40	.257	.305	.454	105	1	1-2	.976	2	113	81	O67(7/0/61),D16	0	0.1
1990	Min A	64	137	11	30	4	0	0	12	3-1	1	23	.219	.239	.248	35	-12	0-1	.923	-1	104	0	D35,O21(2/0/21)	0	-1.5
1991	Min A	9	12	0	2	0	1	0	0	0-0	1	2	.167	.231	.333	52	-1	0-0	1.000	0	126	0	O4(1/0/3),D2	0	-0.1
Total	10	631	1519	190	383	71	8	55	197	90-5	13	291	.252	.298	.418	93	-19	15-11	.953	3	109	80	O380(60/8/320),D154	0	-3.2
Castino, John	John Anthony; B10.23.1954 Evanston IL; BR/TR/5´11˝/(169–178); [MinA76 3/58]; d4.6; Col Rollins; [DL 1985 Min A 181]																								
1979	Min A	148	393	49	112	13	8	5	52	27-0	1	72	.285	.331	.397	92	-6	5-2	.963	9	109	**136**	3b143,S5	0	0.2
1980	Min A	150	546	67	165	17	7	13	64	29-1	0	67	.302	.336	.430	101	-1	7-5	.961	21	114	122	3b138,S18	0	2.0
1981	Min A	101	381	41	102	13	**9**	6	36	18-3	1	52	.268	.301	.396	94	-5	4-5	**.975**	17	113	125	3b98,2b4	0	1.1
1982	Min A	117	410	48	99	12	6	6	37	36-1	2	51	.241	.304	.344	76	-14	2-5	.995	-0	90	100	2b96,3b21,O6(5/1/0)/D	14	-1.2
1983	Min A	142	563	83	156	30	4	11	57	62-1	1	54	.277	.348	.403	102	3	4-2	.990	10	104	92	2b132,3b8/D	0	2.0
1984	Min A	8	27	5	12	1	0	0	3	5-2	0	2	.444	.531	.481	173	3	0-0	1.000	-1	81	74	3b8	140	0.2
Total	6	666	2320	293	646	86	34	41	249	177-8	5	298	.278	.329	.398	95	-20	22-19	.967	56	112	126	3b416,2b232,S23,O6(5/1/0),D2	335	4.3
Castino, Vince	Vincent Charles; B10.11.1917 Willisville IL; D3.6.1967 Sacramento CA; BR/TR/5´9˝/175; d6.24																								
1943	Chi A	33	101	14	23	1	0	2	16	12	0	11	.228	.310	.297	78	-3	0-0	.971	-5	*88*	*47*	C30	0	-0.6
1944	Chi A	29	78	8	18	5	0	0	3	10	1	13	.231	.326	.295	79	-2	0-1	.990	1	*120*	*137*	C26	0	0.1
1945	Chi A	26	36	2	8	1	0	0	4	3	0	7	.222	.282	.250	56	-2	0-0	.951	-1	*160*	*111*	C25	0	-0.3
Total	3	88	215	24	49	7	0	2	23	25	1	31	.228	.311	.288	75	-7	0-1	.976	-5	*112*	*92*	C81	0	-0.8
Castle, Don	Donald Hardy; B2.1.1950 Kokomo IN; BL/TL/6´1˝/195; [TexA68 1/8]; d9.11																								
1973	Tex A	4	13	0	4	1	0	0	2	1-0	0	3	.308	.357	.385	113	0	0-0	ø	0	—	—	D3	0	0.0
Castle, John	John Francis; B6.1.1879 Honey Brook PA; D4.13.1929 Philadelphia PA; 5´10.5˝/?; d4.25																								
1910	Phi N	3	4	1	1	0	0	0	0	0	0	0	.250	.250	.250	44	0	1	ø	-0	0	0	O2(1/1/0)	—	0.0
Castleman, Foster	Foster Ephraim; B1.1.1931 Nashville TN; BR/TR/6´0˝/175; d8.4																								
1954	NY N	13	12	0	3	0	0	0	1	0	1	3	.250	.308	.250	47	-1	0-0	ø	-0	0	0	3b2	0	-0.1
1955	NY N	15	28	3	6	1	0	2	4	2-0	0	4	.214	.267	.464	89	-1	0-0	1.000	-2	73	57	2b6/3	0	-0.2
1956	NY N	124	385	33	87	16	3	14	45	15-2	2	50	.226	.256	.392	72	-17	2-1	.947	3	108	61	3b107,S2/2	0	-1.4
1957	NY N	18	37	7	6	2	0	1	1	2-0	0	8	.162	.205	.297	33	-4	0-0	.867	-2	79	82	3b7/2S	0	-0.5
1958	Bal A	98	200	15	34	5	0	3	14	16-2	3	34	.170	.242	.240	35	-18	2-0	.964	-12	85	95	S91,2b4,3b4/lf	0	-2.5
Total	5	268	662	58	136	24	3	20	65	35-4	6	99	.205	.250	.341	60	-41	4-1	.944	-12	106	62	3b121,S94,2b12/lf	0	-4.7
Castro, Bernie	Bernabel; B7.14.1979 Santo Domingo, D.R.; BB/TR/5´10˝/165; d9.1																								
2005	Bal A	24	80	14	23	3	1	0	7	9-0	0	10	.287	.360	.350	90	-1	6-2	.941	-1	99	92	2b11/lfD	0	-0.1
2006	Was N	42	110	18	25	1	3	0	10	9-0	0	18	.227	.286	.291	51	-9	7-2	.984	-7	77	70	2b29,O2L	0	-1.3
Total	2	66	190	32	48	4	4	0	17	18-0	0	28	.253	.317	.316	68	-10	13-4	.972	-8	84	77	2b40,D9,O3L	0	-1.4
Castro, Juan	Juan Gabriel; B6.20.1972 Los Mochis, Sinaloa, Mexico; BR/TR/5´10˝/(163–195); d9.2																								
1995	LA N	11	4	0	1	0	0	0	0	1-0	0	1	.250	.400	.250	82	0	0-0	1.000	1	153	0	3b7,S4	0	0.1
1996	†LA N	70	132	16	26	5	3	0	5	10-0	0	27	.197	.254	.280	43	-11	1-0	.982	-5	90	137	S30,3b23,2b9/lf	0	-1.4
1997	LA N	40	75	3	11	3	1	0	4	7-1	0	20	.147	.220	.213	15	-10	0-0	1.000	-2	82	77	S22,2b14,3b3	58	-1.1
1998	LA N	89	220	25	43	7	0	2	14	15-0	0	37	.195	.245	.255	34	-22	0-0	.954	3	102	143	S47,2b38,3b12	0	-1.5
1999	LA N	2	1	0	0	0	0	0	0	0-0	0	1	.000	.000	.000	-99	0	0-0	1.000	1	408	463	/2S	0	0.1
2000	Cin N	82	224	20	54	12	2	4	23	14-1	0	33	.241	.283	.366	61	-14	0-2	.994	-7	95	101	S57,2b21,3b7	0	-1.6
2001	Cin N	96	242	27	54	10	0	3	13	13-2	0	50	.223	.261	.302	43	-21	0-0	.944	-14	89	68	S46,2b37,3b19/1	0	-3.1
2002	Cin N	54	82	5	18	3	0	2	11	7-0	0	18	.220	.278	.329	58	-5	0-0	.964	-0	96	125	S25,2b17/13	62	-0.4
2003	Cin N	113	320	28	81	14	1	9	33	18-1	0	58	.253	.290	.387	79	-11	2-3	.984	-1	108	94	2b56,3b30,S24/1	15	-0.9
2004	Cin N	111	299	36	73	21	2	5	26	14-1	0	51	.244	.277	.378	69	-15	1-0	.958	3	91	84	3b78,S31,2b12,1b4	21	-0.9
2005	Min A	97	272	27	70	18	1	5	33	9-1	0	39	.257	.279	.386	74	-11	0-1	.985	15	124	134	S73,3b22,2b5	22	0.9
2006	Min A	50	156	10	36	5	2	1	14	6-0	0	23	.231	.258	.308	46	-13	1-1	.968	8	110	104	S50	0	-0.2
	Cin N	54	95	8	27	5	1	2	14	5-0	0	13	.284	.320	.421	83	-3	0-1	.985	-1	90	111	S27,3b20/2	0	-0.3
Total	12	869	2122	205	494	103	13	33	190	119-7	0	371	.233	.272	.340	59	-136	5-8	.977	0	103	115	S437,3b222,2b211,1b7/lf	178	-10.3
Castro, Louis	Louis Manuel "Jud"; B1877 , Colombia; D9.24.1941 New York NY; BR/TR/5´7˝/?; d4.23; Col Manhattan																								
1902	Phi A	42	143	18	35	8	1	1	15	4	0	—	.245	.265	.336	63	-8	2	.918	-11	82	70	2b36,O3(0/2/1)/S	—	-1.8

YEAR	TM LG	G	AB	R	H	2B	3B	HR	RBI	BB-IB	HP	SO	AVG	OBP	SLG	AOPS	ABR	SB-CS	FA	FR	RNG	THR	GAMES AT POSITION	DL	BFW
CASTRO, RAMON	Ramon Abraham; B3.1.1976 Vega Baja, PR; BR/TR/6´3˝/(225–235); [HouN94 1/17]; d8.27																								
1999	Fla N	24	67	4	12	4	0	2	4	10-3	0	14	.179	.282	.328	58	-4	0-0	.992	-1	141	143	C24	0	-0.4
2000	Fla N	50	138	10	33	4	0	2	14	16-7	1	36	.239	.318	.312	65	-8	0-0	.980	-1	93	128	C50	0	-0.6
2001	Fla N	7	11	0	2	0	0	0	1	1-0	0	1	.182	.250	.182	15	-1	0-0	1.000	-1	94	0	C3	0	-0.2
2002	Fla N	54	101	11	24	4	0	6	18	14-3	0	24	.238	.322	.455	108	1	0-0	1.000	-4	78	119	C37/D	22	-0.1
2003	Fla N	40	53	6	15	2	0	5	8	4-0	0	11	.283	.333	.604	143	3	0-0	.982	-1	176	0	C18/D	0	0.3
2004	Fla N	32	96	9	13	3	0	3	8	11-2	1	30	.135	.231	.260	28	-11	0-0	.990	1	163	89	C31	124	-0.8
2005	NY N	99	209	26	51	16	0	8	41	25-2	0	58	.244	.321	.435	99	0	1-0	.993	-3	133	80	C99	18	0.2
2006	NY N	40	126	13	30	7	0	4	12	15-2	1	40	.238	.322	.389	83	-3	0-0	.996	5	116	115	C37	62	0.4
Total	8	346	801	79	180	40	0	30	106	96-19	3	214	.225	.307	.387	82	-23	1-0	.991	-4	123	102	C299,D2	226	-1.2
CASTRO, RAMON	Ramon Alfredo; B10.23.1979 Valencia, Carabobo, Venezuela; BR/TR/6´0˝/195; d6.21																								
2004	Oak A	9	15	2	2	1	0	0	3	1-1	0	3	.133	.188	.200	1	-2	0-0	1.000	-1	60	0	3b6/SD	0	-0.3
CATALANOTTO, FRANK	Frank John; B4.27.1974 Smithtown NY; BL/TR/6´0˝/(170–195); [DetA92 10/280]; d9.3; OF(418/0/60)																								
1997	Det A	13	26	2	8	2	0	0	3	3-0	0	7	.308	.379	.385	101	0	0-0	1.000	-2	81	0	2b6,D3	0	-0.1
1998	Det A	89	213	23	60	13	2	6	25	12-1	4	39	.282	.325	.446	99	-1	3-2	.974	-0	86	108	2b31,D23,1b18,3b3	0	-0.3
1999	Det A	100	286	41	79	19	0	11	35	15-1	9	49	.276	.327	.458	97	-2	3-4	1.000	-10	72	130	1b32,2b32,3b21,D9	0	-1.2
2000	Tex A	103	282	55	82	13	2	10	42	33-0	6	36	.291	.375	.457	108	4	6-2	.966	-5	101	73	2b49,D20,1b17/rf	22	0.0
2001	Tex A	133	463	77	153	31	5	11	54	39-3	8	55	.330	.391	.490	127	19	15-5	.995	-1	106	36	O92(78/0/15),2b13,3b11,1b5,D5	0	1.6
2002	Tex A	68	212	42	57	16	6	3	23	25-0	8	27	.269	.364	.443	111	4	9-5	.971	-3	84	0	O26L,2b23,1b15,D8	92	0.0
2003	Tor A	133	489	83	146	34	6	13	59	35-1	6	62	.299	.351	.472	111	8	2-2	.993	-8	79	74	O100(61/0/43),D21,1b5	0	-0.6
2004	Tor A	75	249	27	73	19	1	1	26	17-1	4	33	.293	.344	.390	87	-4	1-0	.971	-1	95	51	O41L,D29	95	-0.8
2005	Tor A	130	419	56	126	29	5	8	59	37-0	10	53	.301	.367	.451	112	8	0-2	**1.000**	-3	94	84	O111L,D15	0	0.1
2006	Tor A	128	437	56	131	36	2	7	56	52-0	4	37	.300	.376	.439	107	7	1-3	.994	-1	86	162	O102(101/0/1),D20	0	0.1
Total	10	972	3076	462	915	212	29	70	382	268-7	59	398	.297	.362	.454	108	43	40-25	.992	-32	91	81	O473L,2b154,D153,1b92,3b35	209	-1.2
CATER, DANNY	Danny Anderson; B2.25.1940 Austin TX; BR/TR/5´11.5˝/(170–198); d4.14; OF(293/2/16)																								
1964	Phi N	60	152	13	45	9	1	1	13	7-1	0	15	.296	.325	.388	102	0	1-0	.981	2	98	218	O39(36/1/2),1b7/3	40	0.0
1965	Chi A	142	514	74	139	18	4	14	55	33-0	3	65	.270	.316	.403	110	5	3-3	.978	-10	80	82	O127(127/1/0),3b11,1b3	0	-1.3
1966	Chi A	21	60	3	11	1	1	0	4	0-0	1	10	.183	.194	.233	25	-6	3-1	.909	-3	70	0	O18(16/0/3)	0	-1.0
	KC A	116	425	47	124	16	3	7	52	28-2	1	37	.292	.334	.393	113	6	1-4	.994	-2	100	111	1b53,3b42,O22(21/0/1)	0	-0.2
	Year	137	485	50	135	17	4	7	56	28-2	2	47	.278	.317	.373	102	0	4-5	.994	-5	100	111	1b53,3b42,O40(37/0/4)	0	-1.2
1967	KC A	142	529	55	143	17	4	4	46	34-9	4	56	.270	.317	.340	98	-2	4-5	.916	-10	76	36	3b56,O55L,1b44	0	-2.0
1968	Oak A	147	504	53	146	28	3	6	62	35-3	2	43	.290	.336	.393	126	15	8-7	**.995**	-3	87	108	1b121,O20(19/0/2)/2	0	0.4
1969	Oak A	152	584	64	153	24	2	10	76	28-3	2	40	.262	.296	.361	87	-13	1-4	.992	2	112	114	1b132,O20(19/0/1),2b4	0	-2.5
1970	NY A	155	582	64	175	26	5	6	76	34-6	2	44	.301	.340	.393	107	4	4-2	.992	-4	98	96	1b131,3b42,O7R	0	-1.0
1971	NY A	121	428	39	118	16	5	4	50	19-4	2	25	.276	.308	.364	95	-5	0-3	.995	10	159	110	1b78,3b52	0	-0.1
1972	Bos A	92	317	32	75	17	1	8	39	15-2	2	33	.237	.270	.372	86	-6	0-1	.993	5	121	88	1b90	0	-0.9
1973	Bos A	63	195	30	61	12	0	1	24	10-1	1	22	.313	.348	.390	102	1	0-0	.997	2	88	134	1b37,3b21,D3	0	-0.1
1974	Bos A	56	126	14	31	5	0	5	20	10-1	2	13	.246	.309	.405	98	0	1-0	1.000	0	100	63	1b23,D14	0	-0.2
1975	StL N	22	35	3	8	2	0	0	2	1-1	0	3	.229	.250	.286	46	-3	0-0	.981	-0	99	80	1b12	0	-0.3
Total	12	1289	4451	491	1229	191	29	66	519	254-33	22	406	.276	.316	.377	101	-4	26-30	.994	-12	108	105	1b731,O308L,3b225,D17,2b5	40	-9.2
CATES, ELI	Eli Eldo; B1.26.1877 Greens Fork IN; D5.29.1964 Anderson IN; BR/TR/5´9.5˝/175; d4.20; ▲																								
1908	Was A	40	59	5	11	1	1	0	3	6	1	—	.186	.273	.237	72	-2	0	.907	-0	118	107	P19,2b3	—	-0.1
CATHER, TED	Theodore Physick; B5.20.1889 Chester PA; D4.9.1945 Elkton MD; BR/TR/5´10.5˝/178; d9.23																								
1912	StL N	5	19	4	8	1	1	0	2	0	0	4	.421	.421	.579	176	2	1	.944	1	110	213	O5(0/4/1)	—	0.2
1913	StL N	67	183	16	39	8	4	0	12	9	0	24	.213	.250	.301	58	-11	7-6	.915	-2	86	139	O57(14/1/42)/P1	—	-1.6
1914	StL N	39	99	11	27	7	0	0	13	3	0	15	.273	.294	.343	90	-1	4	.981	1	99	129	O28(23/5/0)	—	-0.2
	†Bos N	50	145	19	43	11	2	0	27	7	2	28	.297	.338	.400	120	3	7	.953	-3	85	81	O48(23/7/20)	—	-0.1
	Year	89	244	30	70	18	2	0	40	10	2	43	.287	.320	.377	108	2	11	.966	-2	91	101	O76(46/12/20)	—	-0.3
1915	Bos N	40	102	10	21	3	1	2	18	15	2	19	.206	.319	.314	96	0	2-4	.902	-3	75	72	O32(31/0/2)	—	-0.6
Total	4	201	548	60	138	30	8	2	72	34	4	90	.252	.300	.347	91	-7	21-10	.938	-6	87	113	O170(91/17/65)/1P	—	-2.3
CATON, HOWDY	James Howard "Buster"; B7.16.1896 Zanesville OH; D1.8.1948 Zanesville OH; BR/TR/5´6˝/165; d9.17; Mil 1918																								
1917	Pit N	14	57	6	12	1	2	0	4	6	0	7	.211	.286	.298	77	-2	0	.895	-3	99	75	S14	—	-0.4
1918	Pit N	80	303	37	71	5	7	0	17	32	2	16	.234	.312	.297	83	-6	12	.928	-7	101	112	S79	—	-0.9
1919	Pit N	39	102	13	18	1	2	0	5	12	0	10	.176	.263	.225	46	-7	2	.927	-9	65	65	S17,3b14/cf	—	-1.6
1920	Pit N	98	352	29	83	11	5	0	27	33	2	19	.236	.305	.295	71	-13	4-9	.929	-22	89	97	S96	—	-3.3
Total	4	231	814	85	184	18	16	0	53	83	4	52	.226	.301	.287	72	-28	18-9	.926	-41	93	99	S206,3b14/cf	—	-6.2
CATTERSON, TOM	Thomas Henry; B8.25.1884 Warwick RI; D2.5.1920 Portland ME; BL/TL/5´10˝/170; d9.19; Col Villanova																								
1908	Bro N	19	68	5	13	1	1	1	2	5	1	—	.191	.257	.279	74	-2	0	.976	0	42	0	O18L	—	-0.4
1909	Bro N	9	18	0	4	0	0	0	1	3	0	—	.222	.333	.222	75	0	0	.833	-1	0	0	O6C	—	-0.2
Total	2	28	86	5	17	1	1	1	3	8	1	—	.198	.274	.267	75	-2	0	.957	-1	35	0	O24(18/6/0)	—	-0.6
CAULFIELD, JAKE	John Joseph; B11.23.1917 Los Angeles CA; D12.16.1986 San Francisco CA; BR/TR/5´11˝/170; d4.24; Col San Francisco																								
1946	Phi A	44	94	13	26	8	0	0	10	4	0	11	.277	.306	.362	87	-2	0-0	.929	-4	85	87	S31/3	0	-0.4
CAUSEY, WAYNE	James Wayne; B12.26.1936 Ruston LA; BL/TR/5´10.5˝/175; d6.5																								
1955	Bal A	68	175	14	34	2	1	1	9	17-1	1	25	.194	.269	.234	39	-16	0-1	.912	-6	101	122	3b55,2b7/S	0	-2.2
1956	Bal A	53	88	7	15	0	1	1	4	8-0	0	23	.170	.237	.227	26	-10	0-0	.980	1	117	130	3b30,2b7	0	-0.9
1957	Bal A	14	10	2	2	0	0	0	1	5-2	1	2	.200	.471	.200	105	1	0-0	.960	2	133	86	2b6,3b5	0	0.3
1961	KC A	104	312	37	86	14	1	8	49	37-0	0	28	.276	.348	.404	100	0	0-0	.955	17	121	116	3b88,S11,2b9	0	1.8
1962	KC A	117	305	40	77	14	1	4	38	41-5	2	30	.252	.340	.344	82	-6	2-0	.953	3	102	71	S51,3b26,2b9	0	0.1
1963	KC A	139	554	72	155	32	4	8	44	56-3	0	54	.280	.345	.395	101	3	4-2	.978	12	106	101	S135,3b2	0	2.7
1964	KC A	157	604	82	170	31	4	8	49	88-3	7	65	.281	.377	.386	110	13	0-1	.967	2	95	89	S131,2b17,3b9	0	2.9
1965	KC A	144	513	48	134	17	8	3	34	61-4	2	48	.261	.341	.343	97	-1	1-3	.972	-16	94	93	S62,2b45,3b35	0	-1.0
1966	KC A	28	79	1	18	0	0	0	5	7-1	0	6	.228	.284	.228	53	-5	1-0	.871	-6	46	114	3b15,S10	0	-1.1
	Chi A	78	164	23	40	8	2	0	13	24-0	0	13	.244	.333	.317	97	0	2-0	.980	-4	102	65	2b60/S3	0	0.1
	Year	106	243	24	58	8	2	0	18	31-1	0	19	.239	.318	.288	83	-5	3-0	.980	-10	102	65	2b60,3b16,S11	0	-1.0
1967	Chi A	124	292	21	66	10	3	1	28	32-4	1	35	.226	.302	.291	80	-7	2-5	.978	-4	109	94	2b96,S2	0	-0.7
1968	Chi A	59	100	8	18	2	0	0	7	14-2	1	7	.180	.284	.200	49	-6	0-0	.971	-5	93	87	2b41	0	-1.0
	Cal A	4	11	0	0	0	0	0	0	0-0	0	1	.000	.000	.000	-99	-3	0-0	1.000	1	132	184	2b4	0	-0.2
	Year	63	111	8	18	2	0	0	7	14-2	1	8	.162	.260	.180	36	-8	0-0	.975	-4	62	59	2b45	0	-1.2
	Atl N	16	37	2	4	0	1	1	4	0-0	0	4	.108	.103	.243	3	-5	0-0	1.000	-4	62	59	2b6,S2,3b2	0	-1.0
Total	11	1105	3244	357	819	130	26	35	285	390-25	15	341	.252	.333	.341	89	-42	12-12	.969	-6	100	91	S406,2b307,3b268	0	-0.2
CAVANAUGH, JOHN	John Joseph; B6.5.1900 Scranton PA; D1.14.1961 New Brunswick NJ; BR/TR/5´9˝/158; d7.7																								
1919	Phi N	1	1	0	0	0	0	0	0	0	0	1	.000	.000	.000	-93	0	0	ø	-0	0	0	/3	—	0.0
CAVARRETTA, PHIL	Philip Joseph; B7.19.1916 Chicago IL; BL/TL/5´11.5˝/175; d9.16; M3/C4																								
1934	Chi N	7	21	5	8	0	1	1	6	2	0	3	.381	.435	.619	182	2	1	1.000	1	148	151	1b5	—	0.2
1935	†Chi N	146	589	85	162	28	12	8	82	39	2	61	.275	.322	.404	93	-7	4	.986	2	108	**128**	1b145	—	-1.8
1936	Chi N	124	458	55	125	18	1	9	56	17	5	36	.273	.306	.376	81	-14	8	.987	-2	95	113	1b115	—	-2.5
1937	Chi N	106	329	43	94	18	7	5	56	32	0	35	.286	.349	.429	106	3	7	.972	-2	90	191	O55(7/47/1),1b43	—	0.0
1938	†Chi N	92	268	29	64	11	4	1	28	14	4	27	.239	.287	.321	65	-13	4	.962	-2	84	138	O52(7/8/37),1b28	—	-2.0
1939	Chi N	22	55	4	15	3	1	0	0	4	0	3	.273	.322	.364	82	-1	2	.991	-1	76	94	1b13/rf	—	-0.3
1940	Chi N	65	193	34	54	11	4	2	22	31	3	18	.280	.388	.409	122	7	3	.991	-1	94	138	1b52	—	0.2
1941	Chi N	107	346	46	99	18	4	6	40	53	2	28	.286	.384	.413	129	15	2	.992	-5	97	69	O66(8/53/6),1b33	0	0.6
1942	Chi N	136	482	59	130	28	4	3	54	71	1	42	.270	.365	.363	118	14	7	.989	0	97	72	O70(4/67/0),1b61	0	0.7
1943	Chi N	143	530	93	154	27	9	8	73	75	3	42	.291	.382	.421	134	25	3	.987	-11	74	95	1b134,O7C	0	0.7
1944	Chi N★	152	614	106	**197**	35	15	5	82	67	3	42	.321	.390	.451	137	31	4	.992	-7	80	107	1b139,O13C	0	1.7

YEAR	TM LG	G	AB	R	H	2B	3B	HR	RBI	BB-IB	HP	SO	AVG	OBP	SLG	AOPS	ABR	SB-CS	FA	FR	RNG	THR	GAMES AT POSITION	DL	BFW
1945	†Chi N✱	132	498	94	177	34	10	6	97	81	4	34	**.355**	**.449**	.500	167	50	5	.993	-1	92	104	1b120,O11L	0	4.1
1946	Chi N★	139	510	89	150	28	10	8	78	88	3	54	.294	.401	.435	140	30	2	.967	3	108	80	O86(7/13/78),1b51	0	3.0
1947	Chi N★	127	459	56	144	22	5	2	63	58	0	35	.314	.391	.397	114	11	2	.977	-2	90	149	O100(69/26/8),1b24	0	0.3
1948	Chi N	111	334	41	93	16	5	3	40	35	1	29	.278	.349	.383	102	1	4	.998	1	110	147	1b41,O40(30/0/10)	0	-0.2
1949	Chi N	105	360	46	106	22	4	8	49	45	1	31	.294	.374	.444	122	12	2	.993	9	142	89	1b70,O25(3/0/21)	0	1.7
1950	Chi N	82	256	49	70	11	1	10	31	40	2	31	.273	.376	.441	115	7	1	.986	0	107	88	1b67,O3R	0	0.5
1951	Chi N	89	206	24	64	7	1	6	28	27	1	28	.311	.393	.442	122	7	0-0	.994	3	122	110	1b53,M	0	0.9
1952	Chi N	41	63	7	15	1	1	1	8	9	0	3	.238	.333	.333	84	-1	0-0	.991	1	129	136	1b13,M	0	-0.1
1953	Chi N	27	21	3	6	3	0	0	3	6	0	3	.286	.444	.429	126	1	0-0	ø	0	—	—	/HM	0	0.1
1954	Chi A	71	158	21	50	6	0	3	24	26	2	12	.316	.417	.411	124	7	4-0	.993	-2	83	114	1b44,O9(2/0/7)	0	0.4
1955	Chi A	6	4	1	0	0	0	0	0	0-0	0	1	.000	.000	.000	-97	-1	0-0	1.000	-0	0	0	1b3	0	-0.1
Total	22	2030	6754	990	1977	347	99	95	920	820-0	37	598	.293	.372	.416	118	186	65-0	.990	-10	99	105	1b1254,O538(148/234/172)	0	8.1

CAVENEY, IKE James Christopher; B12.10.1894 San Francisco CA; D7.6.1949 San Francisco CA; BR/TR/5´9˝/168; d4.12

YEAR	TM LG	G	AB	R	H	2B	3B	HR	RBI	BB-IB	HP	SO	AVG	OBP	SLG	AOPS	ABR	SB-CS	FA	FR	RNG	THR	GAMES AT POSITION	DL	BFW
1922	Cin N	118	394	41	94	12	9	3	54	29	6	33	.239	.301	.338	66	-21	6-6	.934	-5	100	**121**	S118	—	-1.3
1923	Cin N	138	488	58	135	21	9	4	63	26	1	41	.277	.315	.381	84	-13	5-4	.942	-1	98	109	S138	—	0.1
1924	Cin N	95	337	36	92	19	1	4	32	14	4	21	.273	.310	.371	83	-8	2-3	.924	-3	99	112	S90,2b5	—	-0.2
1925	Cin N	115	358	38	89	9	5	2	47	28	0	31	.249	.303	.318	60	-22	2-0	.941	5	105	**129**	S111	—	-0.6
Total	4	466	1577	173	410	61	24	13	196	97	11	126	.260	.307	.354	74	-64	15-13	.936	-4	100	117	S457,2b5	—	-2.0

CEDENO, ANDUJAR Andujar (Donastorg); B8.21.1969 LaRomana, D.R.; D10.28.2000 Santo Domingo, D.R.; BR/TR/6´1˝/(168–170); d9.2; b–Domingo

YEAR	TM LG	G	AB	R	H	2B	3B	HR	RBI	BB-IB	HP	SO	AVG	OBP	SLG	AOPS	ABR	SB-CS	FA	FR	RNG	THR	GAMES AT POSITION	DL	BFW
1990	Hou N	7	8	0	0	0	0	0	0	0-0	0	5	.000	.000	.000	-99	-2	0-0	.833	-2	39	0	S3	0	-0.4
1991	Hou N	67	251	27	61	13	2	9	36	9-1	1	74	.243	.270	.418	96	-3	4-3	.930	-18	80	104	S66	0	-1.7
1992	Hou N	71	220	15	38	13	2	2	13	14-2	3	71	.173	.232	.277	45	-16	2-0	.959	-8	96	77	S70	0	-2.1
1993	Hou N	149	505	69	143	24	4	11	56	48-9	3	97	.283	.346	.412	106	5	9-7	.955	-21	91	99	S149/3	0	-0.6
1994	Hou N	98	342	38	90	26	0	9	49	29-15	8	79	.263	.334	.418	100	0	1-1	.947	1	101	**122**	S95	0	0.8
1995	SD N	120	390	42	82	16	2	6	31	28-7	5	92	.210	.271	.308	54	-27	5-3	.965	-3	96	93	S116/3	0	-2.2
1996	SD N	49	154	10	36	2	1	3	18	9-2	1	32	.234	.279	.318	60	-10	3-2	.946	-1	106	115	S47,3b2	0	-0.8
	Det A	52	179	19	35	4	2	7	20	4-0	0	37	.196	.213	.358	41	-18	2-1	.948	-2	106	70	S51/3	0	-1.5
	Hou N	3	2	1	0	0	0	0	0	2-0	0	1	.000	.500	.000	50	0	0-0	1.000	2	194	440	S2/3	0	0.2
Total	7	616	2051	221	485	98	13	47	223	143-36	21	488	.236	.292	.366	77	-71	26-17	.952	-52	95	99	S599,3b6	0	-8.3

CEDENO, CESAR Cesar (Encarnacion); B2.25.1951 Santo Domingo, D.R.; BR/TR/6´2˝/(175–200); d6.20

YEAR	TM LG	G	AB	R	H	2B	3B	HR	RBI	BB-IB	HP	SO	AVG	OBP	SLG	AOPS	ABR	SB-CS	FA	FR	RNG	THR	GAMES AT POSITION	DL	BFW
1970	Hou N	90	355	46	110	21	4	7	42	15-2	2	57	.310	.340	.451	115	6	17-4	.968	-2	108	19	O90(0/75/17)	0	0.4
1971	Hou N	161	611	85	161	**40**	6	10	81	25-5	3	102	.264	.293	.398	98	-4	20-9	.989	-6	85	59	O157(11/125/30),1b2	0	-1.5
1972	Hou N★	139	559	103	179	**39**	8	22	82	56-5	5	62	.320	.385	.537	165	47	55-21	.981	2	103	108	O137C	0	5.3
1973	Hou N★	139	525	86	168	35	2	25	70	41-7	7	79	.320	.376	.537	152	36	56-15	.981	6	109	117	O136C	0	4.6
1974	Hou N★	160	610	95	164	29	5	26	102	64-6	4	103	.269	.338	.461	129	21	57-17	.993	6	109	110	O157C	0	3.1
1975	Hou N	131	500	93	144	31	3	13	63	62-9	7	52	.288	.371	.440	135	25	50-17	.982	-4	96	96	O131C	19	2.3
1976	Hou N★	150	575	89	171	26	5	18	83	55-9	1	51	.297	.357	.454	141	29	58-15	.980	-2	99	119	O146C	0	3.3
1977	Hou N	141	530	92	148	36	8	14	71	47-7	11	50	.279	.346	.457	124	18	61-14	**.997**	1	98	156	O137C	7	2.7
1978	Hou N	50	192	31	54	8	2	7	23	15-1	0	24	.281	.333	.453	126	6	23-2	.987	4	118	73	O50C	104	1.4
1979	Hou N	132	470	57	123	27	4	6	54	64-8	3	52	.262	.348	.374	105	5	30-13	.981	-10	55	122	1b91,O40C	0	-0.9
1980	†Hou N	137	499	71	154	32	8	10	73	66-11	1	72	.309	.389	.465	150	35	48-15	.977	-5	95	98	O136C	0	3.6
1981	†Hou N	82	306	42	83	19	0	5	34	24-2	1	31	.271	.321	.382	106	2	12-7	.991	-3	88	88	1b46,O34C	0	-0.4
1982	Cin N	138	492	52	142	35	1	8	57	41-2	4	41	.289	.346	.413	112	9	16-11	.990	-6	97	53	O131C/1	0	0.1
1983	Cin N	98	332	40	77	16	0	9	39	33-2	3	53	.232	.302	.361	82	-8	13-9	.993	0	110	106	O73(0/1/73),1b17	0	-1.4
1984	Cin N	110	380	59	105	24	2	10	47	25-4	1	54	.276	.321	.429	105	2	19-3	.980	2	108	143	O77(52/14/19),1b44	15	0.2
1985	Cin N	83	220	24	53	12	0	3	30	19-1	3	35	.241	.307	.336	77	-6	9-5	.990	1	116	32	O53(46/4/4),1b34	0	-0.8
	†StL N	28	76	14	33	4	1	6	19	5-2	0	7	.434	.463	.750	237	13	5-1	.993	-3	46	132	1b23,O2(1/0/1)	0	1.0
	Year	111	296	38	86	16	1	9	49	24-3	3	42	.291	.347	.443	116	6	14-6	.993	-2	69	126	1b57,O55(47/4/5)	0	0.2
1986	LA N	37	78	5	18	2	1	0	6	7-0	0	13	.231	.294	.282	64	-4	1-1	.944	-2	85	76	O31(28/3/0)	0	-0.7
Total	17	2006	7310	1084	2087	436	60	199	976	664-83	56	938	.285	.347	.443	124	232	550-179	.985	-21	101	94	O1718(138/1457/144),1b258	145	22.3

CEDENO, DOMINGO Domingo Antonio (Donastorg); B11.4.1968 LaRomana, D.R.; BB/TR/6´1˝/(165–170); d5.19; b–Andujar

YEAR	TM LG	G	AB	R	H	2B	3B	HR	RBI	BB-IB	HP	SO	AVG	OBP	SLG	AOPS	ABR	SB-CS	FA	FR	RNG	THR	GAMES AT POSITION	DL	BFW
1993	Tor A	15	46	5	8	0	0	0	7	1-0	0	10	.174	.188	.174	-1	-7	1-0	.973	-2	107	69	S10,2b5	0	-0.7
1994	Tor A	47	97	14	19	2	3	0	10	10-0	0	31	.196	.261	.278	42	-9	1-2	.935	-7	87	78	2b28,S8,3b6/lf	0	-1.4
1995	Tor A	51	161	18	38	6	1	4	14	10-0	2	35	.236	.289	.360	68	-8	0-1	.980	3	106	88	S30,2b20/3	0	-0.3
1996	Tor A	77	282	44	79	10	2	2	17	15-0	2	60	.280	.320	.351	70	-13	5-3	.969	3	95	118	2b62,3b6,S5	0	-0.6
	Chi A	12	19	2	3	2	0	0	3	0-0	0	4	.158	.143	.263	4	-3	1-0	ø	-2	0	0	2b2,S2/D	0	-0.4
	Year	89	301	46	82	12	2	2	20	15-0	2	64	.272	.308	.346	67	-16	6-3	.969	1	93	116	2b64,S7,3b6/D	0	-1.0
1997	Tex A	113	365	49	103	19	6	4	36	27-0	2	77	.282	.334	.400	85	-8	3-3	.960	-6	102	76	2b65,S43,3b3,D2	37	-0.9
1998	Tex A	61	141	19	37	9	1	2	21	10-0	0	32	.262	.309	.383	75	-5	2-1	.963	-7	87	79	S35,D14,2b7	0	-1.0
1999	Sea A	21	42	4	9	2	0	2	8	5-0	1	9	.214	.313	.405	82	-1	1-1	.941	2	120	112	S20/23	0	0.1
	Phi N	32	66	5	10	4	0	1	5	5-0	0	22	.152	.211	.258	18	-9	0-1	.982	-2	88	68	S19/2	0	-1.0
Total	7	429	1219	160	306	54	13	15	121	83-0	7	280	.251	.300	.354	67	-63	14-12	.964	-19	97	90	2b191,S172,D17,3b17/lf	37	-6.2

CEDENO, ROGER Roger Leandro; B8.16.1974 Valencia, Carabobo, Venez.; BB/TR/6´1˝/(165–205); d6.20

YEAR	TM LG	G	AB	R	H	2B	3B	HR	RBI	BB-IB	HP	SO	AVG	OBP	SLG	AOPS	ABR	SB-CS	FA	FR	RNG	THR	GAMES AT POSITION	DL	BFW
1995	LA N	40	42	4	10	2	0	0	3	3-0	0	10	.238	.283	.286	56	-3	1-0	.977	2	135	0	O36(19/13/5)	0	-0.1
1996	LA N	86	211	26	52	11	1	2	18	24-0	1	47	.246	.326	.336	80	-6	5-1	.983	1	105	73	O71(20/50/4)	0	-0.5
1997	LA N	80	194	31	53	10	2	3	17	25-2	3	44	.273	.362	.392	105	2	9-1	.987	5	131	38	O71(13/55/4)	54	0.9
1998	LA N	105	240	33	58	11	1	2	17	27-2	0	57	.242	.317	.321	72	-10	8-2	.978	-4	77	117	O77(45/29/10)	24	-1.3
1999	†NY N	155	453	90	142	23	4	4	36	60-3	3	100	.313	.396	.408	109	9	66-17	.989	4	105	118	O149(13/21/127)/2	0	1.6
2000	Hou N	74	259	54	73	2	5	6	26	43-0	0	47	.282	.383	.398	91	-3	25-11	.978	-3	100	26	O67(23/29/17)	83	-0.5
2001	Det A	131	523	79	153	14	11	6	48	36-1	2	83	.293	.337	.396	96	-5	55-15	.953	-12	87	68	O120(0/67/55),D7	0	-1.2
2002	NY N	149	511	65	133	19	2	7	41	42-1	2	92	.260	.318	.346	80	-16	25-4	.966	-5	100	26	O132L	0	-2.2
2003	NY N	148	484	70	129	25	4	7	37	38-3	1	86	.267	.320	.378	85	-12	14-9	.987	1	104	71	O128(0/17/111)	0	-1.5
2004	†StL N	95	200	22	53	9	2	3	23	19-2	0	41	.265	.327	.375	80	-6	5-1	1.000	-5	64	85	O54(23/0/35)/D	32	-1.2
2005	StL N	37	57	4	9	1	0	0	8	2-0	1	6	.158	.197	.175	-0	-9	0-2	.818	-2	53	0	O16(6/0/10)	18	-1.2
Total	11	1100	3174	478	865	127	32	40	274	319-14	13	613	.273	.340	.371	88	-59	213-63	.976	-19	99	67	O921(294/281/378),D8/2	211	-7.2

CEDENO, RONNY Ronny Alexander (Salazar); B2.2.1983 Carabobo, Venezuela; BR/TR/6´0˝/180; d4.23

YEAR	TM LG	G	AB	R	H	2B	3B	HR	RBI	BB-IB	HP	SO	AVG	OBP	SLG	AOPS	ABR	SB-CS	FA	FR	RNG	THR	GAMES AT POSITION	DL	BFW
2005	Chi N	41	80	13	24	3	0	1	6	5-1	2	11	.300	.356	.375	89	-1	1-0	.986	-3	75	72	S29/2	0	-0.3
2006	Chi N	151	534	51	131	18	7	6	41	17-4	3	109	.245	.271	.339	54	-39	8-8	.956	-6	96	78	S134,2b15	0	-3.5
Total	2	192	614	64	155	21	7	7	47	22-5	5	120	.252	.283	.344	59	-40	9-8	.960	-9	93	77	S163,2b16	0	-3.8

CEPEDA, ORLANDO Orlando Manuel (Penne) "Baby Bull","Cha Cha"; B9.17.1937 Ponce, PR; BR/TR/6´2˝/(200–210); d4.15; C1; HF1999

YEAR	TM LG	G	AB	R	H	2B	3B	HR	RBI	BB-IB	HP	SO	AVG	OBP	SLG	AOPS	ABR	SB-CS	FA	FR	RNG	THR	GAMES AT POSITION	DL	BFW
1958	SF N	148	603	88	188	**38**	4	25	96	29-7	3	84	.312	.342	.512	126	21	15-11	.989	-2	96	95	1b147	0	0.9
1959	SF N★	151	605	92	192	35	4	27	105	33-10	5	100	.317	.355	.522	134	27	23-9	.984	-8	96	88	1b122,O44L,3b4	0	1.2
1960	SF N★	151	569	81	169	36	3	24	96	34-9	8	91	.297	.343	.497	135	26	15-6	.983	-2	104	143	O91L,1b63	0	1.7
1961	SF N★	152	585	105	182	28	4	**46**	**142**	39-11	9	91	.311	.362	.609	158	45	12-8	.997	-3	85	79	1b81,O80(64/0/17)	0	3.2
1962	†SF N★	162	625	105	191	26	1	35	114	37-8	6	97	.306	.347	.518	132	26	10-4	.991	-7	83	99	1b160,O2(1/0/1)	0	1.0
1963	SF N☆	156	579	100	183	33	4	34	97	37-11	10	70	.316	.366	.563	166	48	8-3	.985	-10	82	80	1b150,O3L	0	3.2
1964	SF N★	142	529	75	161	27	2	31	97	43-7	8	83	.304	.361	.539	148	33	9-4	.986	-7	84	85	1b139/lf	0	1.9
1965	SF N	33	34	1	6	1	0	1	5	3-1	0	9	.176	.225	.294	49	-2	0-0	1.000	0	131	64	1b4,O2L	103	-0.2
1966	SF N	19	49	5	14	2	0	3	15	4-2	1	11	.286	.352	.510	132	2	0-1	.778	-2	64	0	O8L,1b6	0	-0.1
	StL N	123	452	65	137	24	0	17	58	34-10	13	68	.303	.362	.469	130	20	9-8	.989	-5	85	119	1b120	0	0.7
	Year	142	501	70	151	26	0	20	73	38-12	**14**	79	.301	.361	.473	130	22	9-9	.990	-7	83	120	1b126,O8L	0	0.6
1967	†StL N★	151	563	91	183	37	0	25	**111**	62-23	**12**	75	.325	.399	.524	166	51	11-2	.993	0	99	91	1b151	0	4.6
1968	†StL N	157	600	71	149	26	2	16	73	43-13	9	96	.248	.306	.378	107	4	8-6	.988	-5	91	99	1b154	0	-1.2
1969	†Atl N	154	573	74	147	28	2	22	88	55-10	5	76	.257	.325	.428	109	6	12-5	.994	1	103	84	1b153	0	-0.4
1970	Atl N	148	567	87	173	33	0	34	111	47-11	9	75	.305	.365	.543	133	26	6-5	.992	4	107	87	1b148	0	1.7
1971	Atl N	71	250	31	69	10	1	14	44	22-7	0	29	.276	.330	.492	123	7	3-6	.992	1	108	107	1b63	36	0.1
1972	Atl N	28	84	6	25	3	0	4	9	7-1	0	17	.298	.352	.476	122	2	0-0	1.000	1	106	88	1b22	0	0.1
	Oak A	3	3	0	0	0	0	0	0	0-0	0	0	.000	.000	.000	-99	-1	0-0	ø	0	—	—	/H	85	-0.1

YEAR	TM LG	G	AB	R	H	2B	3B	HR	RBI	BB-IB	HP	SO	AVG	OBP	SLG	AOPS	ABR	SB-CS	FA	FR	RNG	THR	GAMES AT POSITION	DL	BFW
1973	Bos A	142	550	51	159	25	0	20	86	50-13	3	81	.289	.350	.444	116	11	0-2	ø	0	0	0	D142	0	0.7
1974	KC A	33	107	3	23	5	0	1	18	9-0	1	16	.215	.282	.290	61	-5	1-0	ø	0	0	0	D26	0	-0.6
Total	17	2124	7927	1131	2351	417	27	379	1365	588-154	102	1169	.297	.350	.499	133	347	142-80	.990	-44	92	92	1b1683,O231(214/0/18),D168,3b4	224	18.4
CEPICKY, MATT	Matthew William; B11.10.1977 St.Louis MO; BL/TR/6´2˝/215; [MonN99 4/120]; d7.31; Col Missouri St.																								
2002	Mon N	32	74	7	16	3	0	3	15	4-1	0	21	.216	.256	.378	61	-4	0-0	1.000	-2	76	0	O17(16/0/1)	0	-0.7
2003	Mon N	5	8	0	2	1	0	0	0	0-0	0	2	.250	.250	.375	59	0	0-0	1.000	-1	27	0	O4(3/0/1)	0	-0.1
2004	Mon N	32	60	4	13	4	0	1	3	1-0	0	18	.217	.230	.333	41	-5	1-0	1.000	1	147	0	O11(9/0/2),D2	0	-0.4
2005	Was N	11	25	1	6	3	0	0	3	1-0	0	8	.240	.269	.360	66	-1	0-1	1.000	1	175	0	O6(5/0/1)	0	0.0
2006	Fla N	9	18	0	2	0	0	0	0	1-0	0	4	.111	.158	.111	-31	-4	0-0	1.000	0	108	0	O6(1/0/5)	0	-0.4
Total	5	89	185	12	39	11	0	4	21	7-1	0	53	.211	.240	.335	47	-14	1-1	1.000	0	110	0	O44(34/0/10),D2	0	-1.6
CERMAK, ED	Edward Hugo; B3.10.1882 Cleveland OH; D11.22.1911 Cleveland OH; BR/TR/5´11˝/170; d9.9																								
1901	Cle A	1	4	0	0	0	0	0	0	0	0	—	.000	.000	.000	-99	-1	0	1.000	1	450	1792	/rf	—	0.0
CERONE, RICK	Richard Aldo; B5.19.1954 Newark NJ; BR/TR/5´11˝/(184–195); [CleA75 1/7]; d8.17; Col Seton Hall																								
1975	Cle A	7	12	1	3	1	0	0	0	1-0	0	0	.250	.308	.333	81	0	0-0	1.000	-1	126	68	C7	0	-0.1
1976	Cle A	7	16	1	2	0	0	0	1	0-0	0	2	.125	.125	.125	-27	-3	0-0	.963	-1	86	59	C6/D	0	-0.3
1977	Tor A	31	100	7	20	4	0	1	10	6-0	0	12	.200	.245	.270	40	-8	0-0	.994	2	183	86	C31	0	-0.6
1978	Tor A	88	282	25	63	8	2	3	20	23-0	1	32	.223	.284	.298	63	-14	0-3	.992	1	112	103	C84,D2	0	-1.1
1979	Tor A	136	469	47	112	27	4	7	61	37-1	1	40	.239	.294	.358	75	-17	1-4	.980	3	129	97	C136	0	-0.9
1980	†NY A	147	519	70	144	30	4	14	85	32-2	6	56	.277	.321	.432	108	4	1-3	.990	18	**172**	116	C147	0	2.8
1981	†NY A	71	234	23	57	13	2	2	21	12-0	0	24	.244	.276	.342	79	-7	0-2	.992	-3	116	80	C69	35	-0.8
1982	NY A	89	300	29	68	10	0	5	28	19-1	1	27	.227	.271	.310	61	-16	0-2	.989	-11	100	69	C89	64	-2.4
1983	NY A	80	246	18	54	7	0	2	22	15-1	1	29	.220	.267	.272	50	-17	0-0	.991	-5	103	60	C78/3	0	-1.9
1984	NY A	38	120	8	25	3	0	2	13	9-0	1	15	.208	.269	.283	55	-8	1-0	.996	-1	120	104	C38	59	-0.7
1985	Atl N	96	282	15	61	9	0	3	25	29-1	1	25	.216	.288	.280	57	-16	0-3	.986	-5	99	100	C91	15	-2.0
1986	Mil A	68	216	22	56	14	0	4	18	15-0	1	28	.259	.304	.380	84	-5	1-1	.991	4	109	168	C68	0	0.2
1987	NY A	113	284	28	69	12	1	4	23	30-0	4	46	.243	.320	.335	76	-9	0-1	**.998**	8	123	109	C111,P2,1b2	0	0.2
1988	Bos A	84	264	31	71	13	1	3	27	20-0	3	32	.269	.326	.360	88	-4	0-0	**1.000**	-2	91	71	C83/D	0	-0.2
1989	Bos A	102	296	28	72	16	1	4	48	34-1	2	40	.243	.320	.345	84	-6	0-0	.984	-3	73	116	C97/rfD	0	-0.3
1990	NY A	49	139	12	42	6	0	2	11	5-0	0	13	.302	.324	.388	98	-1	0-0	.995	2	146	158	C35/2D	64	0.3
1991	NY N	90	227	18	62	13	0	2	16	30-2	1	24	.273	.360	.357	103	2	1-1	.987	2	**138**	121	C81	0	0.8
1992	Mon N	33	63	10	17	4	0	1	7	3-0	1	5	.270	.313	.381	96	0	1-2	1.000	-1	82	66	C28	0	-0.1
Total	18	1329	4069	393	998	190	15	59	436	320-9	24	450	.245	.301	.343	78	-125	6-22	.990	8	120	102	C1279,D11,1b2,P2/2rf3	237	-7.1
CERV, BOB	Robert Henry; B5.5.1926 Weston NE; BR/TR/6´0˝/(202–226); d8.1; Col Nebraska																								
1951	NY A	12	28	4	6	1	0	0	2	4	0	6	.214	.313	.250	55	-2	0-0	.875	-1	101	0	O9R	0	-0.3
1952	NY A	36	87	11	21	3	2	1	8	9	0	22	.241	.313	.356	91	-1	0-1	1.000	0	102	68	O27(15/12/0)	0	-0.3
1953	NY A	8	6	0	0	0	0	0	0	1	0	1	.000	.143	.000	-61	-1	0-0	ø	0	—	—	/H	0	-0.1
1954	NY A	56	100	14	26	6	0	5	13	11	0	17	.260	.330	.470	122	3	0-2	.897	-2	73	94	O24L	0	-0.1
1955	†NY A	55	85	17	29	4	2	3	22	7-0	3	16	.341	.411	.541	157	7	4-0	1.000	-1	88	105	O20(13/7/1)	0	0.6
1956	†NY A	54	115	16	35	5	6	3	25	18-0	0	13	.304	.396	.530	148	8	0-1	.984	1	93	190	O44(29/15/1)	0	0.7
1957	KC A	124	345	35	94	14	2	11	44	20-1	1	57	.272	.312	.420	97	-3	1-1	.964	-3	92	117	O89(40/35/22)	0	-1.0
1958	KC A★	141	515	93	157	20	7	38	104	50-10	5	82	.305	.371	.592	158	39	3-3	.985	13	113	155	O136L	0	4.4
1959	KC A	125	463	61	132	22	4	20	87	35-5	3	87	.285	.332	.479	120	11	3-2	.980	3	100	108	O119L	0	0.7
1960	KC A	23	78	14	20	1	1	6	12	10-1	0	17	.256	.337	.526	130	3	0-0	.977	2	92	279	O21L	0	0.4
	†NY A	87	216	32	54	11	1	8	28	30-2	3	36	.250	.349	.421	114	5	0-0	.982	4	103	182	O51(50/1/1),1b3	0	0.6
	Year	110	294	46	74	12	2	14	40	40-3	3	53	.252	.346	.449	119	8	0-0	.980	6	100	211	O72(71/1/1),1b3	0	1.0
1961	LA A	18	57	3	9	3	0	2	6	1-0	0	8	.158	.169	.316	25	-6	0-0	.944	-2	68	0	O15L	0	-1.0
	NY A	57	118	17	32	5	1	6	20	12-0	1	17	.271	.344	.483	125	4	1-0	.983	3	117	112	O30(28/2/0),1b3	0	0.5
	Year	75	175	20	41	8	1	8	26	13-0	1	25	.234	.289	.429	91	-3	1-0	.974	0	100	72	O45(43/2/0),1b3	0	-0.5
1962	NY A	14	17	1	2	1	0	0	0	2-0	1	3	.118	.250	.176	18	-2	0-0	1.000	-0	82	0	O3(1/0/2)	0	-0.2
	Hou N	19	31	2	7	0	0	2	3	2-0	0	10	.226	.273	.419	89	-1	0-0	.833	-1	47	297	O6L	0	-0.2
Total	12	829	2261	320	624	96	26	105	374	212-19	17	392	.276	.340	.481	122	64	12-10	.976	17	100	134	O594(497/72/36),1b6	0	4.7
CEY, RON	Ronald Charles "The Penguin"; B2.15.1948 Tacoma WA; BR/TR/5´10˝/185; [LAN68 S3/53]; d9.3; Col Washington St.																								
1971	LA N	2	2	0	0	0	0	0	0	0-0	0	2	.000	.000	.000	-99	-1	0-0	ø	0	—	—	/H	0	-0.1
1972	LA N	11	37	3	10	1	0	1	3	7-0	1	10	.270	.400	.378	124	2	0-0	.900	-2	84	60	3b11	0	-0.1
1973	LA N	152	507	60	124	18	4	15	80	74-7	2	77	.245	.338	.385	105	4	1-1	.961	5	101	159	3b146	0	0.9
1974	†LA N★	159	577	88	151	20	2	18	97	76-13	7	68	.262	.349	.397	114	12	1-1	.959	14	103	91	3b158	0	2.5
1975	LA N★	158	566	72	160	29	2	25	101	78-15	7	74	.283	.372	.473	140	32	5-2	.960	-3	94	100	3b158	0	3.0
1976	LA N★	145	502	69	139	18	3	23	80	89-13	3	74	.277	.386	.462	142	31	0-4	.965	9	111	91	3b144	0	3.9
1977	†LA N★	153	564	77	136	22	3	30	110	93-6	2	106	.241	.347	.450	112	11	3-4	.964	12	105	129	3b153	0	2.0
1978	†LA N★	159	555	84	150	32	0	23	84	96-9	7	96	.270	.380	.452	133	29	2-5	.966	3	102	107	3b158	0	2.9
1979	LA N★	150	487	77	137	20	1	28	81	86-8	2	85	.281	.389	.499	144	32	3-3	**.977**	6	101	102	3b150	0	3.6
1980	LA N	157	551	81	140	25	0	28	77	69-5	5	92	.254	.342	.452	123	17	2-2	.972	6	101	109	3b157	0	2.2
1981	†LA N	85	312	42	90	15	2	13	50	40-3	3	55	.288	.372	.474	146	19	0-2	.941	4	100	119	3b84	0	2.2
1982	LA N	150	556	62	141	23	1	24	79	57-6	4	99	.254	.323	.428	113	9	3-2	.963	-1	100	103	3b149	0	0.6
1983	Chi N	159	581	73	160	33	1	24	90	62-11	5	85	.275	.346	.460	117	14	0-0	.955	-13	95	47	3b157	0	-0.2
1984	†Chi N	146	505	71	121	27	0	25	97	61-10	6	108	.240	.324	.442	106	4	3-2	**.967**	-12	88	96	3b144	0	-1.1
1985	Chi N	145	500	64	116	18	2	22	63	58-9	4	106	.232	.316	.408	92	-5	1-1	.943	-8	99	87	3b140	0	-1.7
1986	Chi N	97	256	42	70	21	0	13	36	44-1	3	66	.273	.384	.508	134	14	0-0	.952	-6	92	59	3b77	0	0.7
1987	Oak A	45	104	12	23	6	0	4	11	22-1	1	32	.221	.359	.394	107	2	0-0	.982	-2	25	71	D30,1b7,3b3	0	-0.1
Total	17	2073	7162	977	1868	328	21	316	1139	1012-117	62	1235	.261	.354	.445	121	226	24-29	.961	11	100	101	3b1989,D30,1b7	0	21.2
CHACON, ELIO	Elio (Rodriguez); B10.26.1936 Caracas, Distrito Capital, Venez.; D4.24.1992 Caracas, Distrito Capital, Venez.; BR/TR/5´9˝/170; d4.20																								
1960	Cin N	49	116	14	21	1	0	0	7	14-1	1	23	.181	.271	.190	29	-11	7-1	.980	1	99	114	2b43,O2R	0	-0.6
1961	†Cin N	61	132	26	35	4	2	2	5	21-0	2	22	.265	.374	.371	97	0	1-4	.989	-0	100	90	2b42,O7(3/0/5)	0	0.2
1962	NY N	118	368	49	87	10	3	2	27	76-3	1	64	.236	.368	.296	80	-7	12-7	.961	-2	103	88	S110,2b2/3	0	0.0
Total	3	228	616	89	143	15	5	4	39	111-4	4	109	.232	.351	.292	74	-18	20-12	.961	-1	103	88	S110,2b87,O9(3/0/7)/3	0	-0.4
CHADBOURNE, CHET	Chester James "Pop"; B10.28.1884 Parkman ME; D6.21.1943 Los Angeles CA; BL/TR/5´9˝/170; d9.17																								
1906	Bos A	11	43	7	13	1	0	0	3	3	0	—	.302	.348	.326	111	1	1	.926	2	131	78	2b11/S	—	0.3
1907	Bos A	10	38	0	11	0	0	0	1	7	0	—	.289	.400	.289	121	1	1	1.000	-0	78	0	O10L	—	0.1
1914	KC F	147	581	92	161	22	8	1	37	69	5	49	.277	.359	.348	97	-10	42	.965	9	95	**157**	O146L	—	-0.7
1915	KC F	152	587	75	133	16	9	1	35	62	6	29	.227	.307	.290	71	-32	29	**.979**	-4	91	109	O152(5/147/0)	—	-5.1
1918	Bos N	27	104	9	27	2	1	0	6	5	1	5	.260	.300	.298	86	-2	5	.925	-3	90	57	O27C	—	-0.8
Total	5	347	1353	183	345	41	18	2	82	146	12	83	.255	.333	.316	86	-42	78	.969	4	92	123	O335(161/174/0),2b11/S	—	-6.2
CHALK, DAVE	David Lee; B8.30.1950 Del Rio TX; BR/TR/5´10˝/(170–175); [AnaA72 1/10]; d9.4; Col Texas; [DL 1979 Cal A 30]																								
1973	Cal A	24	69	14	16	2	0	0	6	9-0	1	13	.232	.329	.261	73	-2	0-0	.962	2	96	148	S22	0	0.3
1974	Cal A★	133	465	44	117	9	3	5	31	30-1	7	57	.252	.304	.316	84	-11	10-10	.938	6	91	93	S99,3b38	0	0.5
1975	Cal A☆	149	513	59	140	24	2	3	56	66-4	2	49	.273	.353	.345	107	7	6-9	.976	5	99	100	3b149	0	1.0
1976	Cal A	142	438	39	95	14	1	0	33	49-3	10	62	.217	.308	.253	70	-14	0-0	.971	3	98	83	S102,3b49	0	0.0
1977	Cal A	149	519	58	144	27	2	3	45	52-2	5	69	.277	.345	.355	96	-1	12-8	.948	-2	93	81	3b141,2b7,S4	0	-0.5
1978	Cal A	135	470	42	119	12	0	1	34	38-0	7	34	.253	.318	.285	73	-16	5-8	.955	-11	88	86	S97,2b29,3b22/D	0	-2.0
1979	Tex A	9	8	0	2	0	0	0	0	0-0	0	0	.250	.250	.250	36	-1	0-0	1.000	0	210	0	S3/2D	0	0.0
	Oak A	66	212	15	47	6	0	2	13	29-0	1	14	.222	.317	.278	66	-9	2-1	.988	-10	89	78	2b37,S16,3b16	0	-1.6
	Year	75	220	15	49	6	0	2	13	29-0	1	14	.223	.315	.277	64	-10	2-1	.988	-10	88	77	2b38,S19,3b16,D2	0	-1.6
1980	†KC A	69	167	19	42	10	1	1	20	18-0	2	27	.251	.326	.341	83	-3	1-1	.964	-7	95	54	3b33,2b17/SD	0	-1.0
1981	KC A	27	49	2	11	3	0	0	5	4-0	0	2	.224	.283	.286	64	-2	0-1	.955	-4	66	203	3b14,2b10/S	0	-0.7
Total	9	903	2910	292	733	107	9	15	243	295-10	35	327	.252	.325	.310	84	-52	36-38	.962	-19	95	101	3b462,S345,2b101,D9	30	-4.0
CHAMBERLAIN, JOE	Joseph Jeremiah; B5.10.1910 San Francisco CA; D1.28.1983 San Francisco CA; BR/TR/6´1˝/175; d4.17																								
1934	Chi A	43	141	13	34	5	1	2	17	6	0	38	.241	.272	.333	54	-10	1-1	.896	-5	112	66	S26,3b14/2	—	-1.3

YEAR	TM LG	G	AB	R	H	2B	3B	HR	RBI	BB-IB	HP	SO	AVG	OBP	SLG	AOPS	ABR	SB-CS	FA	FR	RNG	THR	GAMES AT POSITION	DL	BFW
CHAMBERLAIN, WES	Wesley Polk; B4.13.1966 Chicago IL; BR/TR/6´2˝/(210–230); [PitN87 4/86]; d8.31; Col Jackson St.																								
1990	Phi N	18	46	9	13	3	0	2	4	1-0	0	9	.283	.298	.478	110	0	4-0	.958	-0	111	0	O10(10/0/2)	0	0.1
1991	Phi N	101	383	51	92	16	3	13	50	31-0	2	73	.240	.300	.399	96	-3	9-4	.985	-1	99	70	O98(95/0/3)	0	-0.7
1992	Phi N	76	275	26	71	18	0	9	41	10-2	1	55	.258	.285	.422	98	-2	4-0	.971	-2	97	72	O73(28/0/48)	47	-0.5
1993	†Phi N	96	284	34	80	20	2	12	45	17-3	1	51	.282	.320	.493	117	6	2-1	.993	6	103	207	O76R	18	0.9
1994	Phi N	24	69	7	19	5	0	2	6	3-0	0	12	.275	.306	.435	89	-1	0-0	1.000	1	93	272	O18R	16	-0.1
	Bos A	51	164	13	42	9	1	4	20	12-2	0	38	.256	.307	.396	76	-6	0-2	1.000	3	105	207	O34R,D12	0	-0.6
1995	Bos A	19	42	4	5	1	0	1	1	3-0	0	11	.119	.178	.214	1	-6	1-0	.955	1	109	158	O12R,D5	0	-0.6
Total	6	385	1263	144	322	72	6	43	167	77-7	4	249	.255	.299	.424	95	-12	20-7	.984	8	100	126	O321(133/0/193),D17	81	-1.5
CHAMBERS, AL	Albert Eugene; B3.24.1961 Harrisburg PA; BL/TL/6´4˝/(215–217); [SeaA79 1/1]; d7.23																								
1983	Sea A	31	67	11	14	3	0	1	7	18-1	0	20	.209	.376	.299	85	0	0-1	1.000	-1	52	0	D22,O3L	0	-0.2
1984	Sea A	22	49	4	11	1	0	1	4	3-0	0	12	.224	.269	.306	59	-3	2-1	.947	-1	89	0	O13L/D	0	-0.4
1985	Sea A	4	4	0	0	0	0	0	0	0-0	0	2	.000	.000	.000	-99	-1	0-0	ø	0	—	—	/H	0	-0.1
Total	3	57	120	15	25	4	0	2	11	21-1	0	34	.208	.326	.292	70	-4	2-2	.955	-2	81	0	D23,O16L	0	-0.7
CHAMBLEE, JIM	James Nathaniel; B5.6.1975 Denton TX; BR/TR/6´4˝/170; [BosA95 12/326]; d8.24; Col Odessa (TX) JC																								
2003	Cin N	2	2	0	0	0	0	0	0	0-0	0	2	.000	.000	.000	-99	-1	0-0	ø	-0	0	0	/3	0	-0.1
CHAMBLISS, CHRIS	Carroll Christopher; B12.26.1948 Dayton OH; BL/TR/6´1˝/(195–225); [CleA70*1/1]; d5.28; C12; Col UCLA																								
1971	Cle A	111	415	49	114	20	4	9	48	40-1	2	83	.275	.341	.407	102	1	2-0	.992	-6	77	83	1b108	0	-1.4
1972	Cle A	121	466	51	136	27	2	6	44	26-2	0	63	.292	.327	.397	111	6	3-4	.993	-8	74	109	1b119	0	-1.4
1973	Cle A	155	572	70	156	30	2	11	53	58-8	3	76	.273	.342	.390	104	4	4-8	.991	4	110	107	1b154	0	-0.7
1974	Cle A	17	67	8	22	4	0	0	7	5-1	0	5	.328	.375	.388	121	2	0-1	.982	-3	53	93	1b17	0	-0.3
	NY A	110	400	38	97	16	3	6	43	23-1	0	43	.243	.282	.343	80	-11	0-0	.992	6	120	101	1b106	0	-1.5
	Year	127	467	46	119	20	3	6	50	28-2	0	48	.255	.296	.349	86	-9	0-1	.990	3	110	100	1b123	0	-1.8
1975	NY A	150	562	66	171	38	4	9	72	29-9	1	50	.304	.336	.434	118	12	0-1	.991	4	106	97	1b147	0	0.4
1976	†NY A★	156	641	79	188	32	6	17	96	27-1	3	80	.293	.323	.441	124	16	1-0	.994	-2	98	106	1b155/D	0	0.1
1977	†NY A	157	600	90	172	32	6	17	90	45-5	2	73	.287	.336	.445	112	9	4-0	.989	-3	94	106	1b157	0	-0.3
1978	†NY A	162	625	81	171	26	3	12	90	41-3	5	60	.274	.321	.382	99	-1	2-1	**.997**	4	105	102	1b155,D7	0	-0.7
1979	NY A	149	554	61	155	27	3	18	63	34-4	5	53	.280	.324	.437	106	3	3-2	.995	3	107	118	1b134,D16	0	-0.3
1980	Atl N	158	602	83	170	37	2	18	72	49-6	4	73	.282	.338	.440	115	12	7-3	.993	-2	97	**120**	1b158	0	0.1
1981	Atl N	**107**	404	44	110	25	2	8	51	44-10	1	41	.272	.343	.403	112	7	4-1	.997	6	117	97	1b107	0	0.7
1982	†Atl N	157	534	57	144	25	2	20	86	57-13	0	57	.270	.337	.436	113	9	7-3	.993	11	**126**	**132**	1b151	0	1.2
1983	Atl N	131	447	59	125	24	3	20	78	63-15	0	68	.280	.366	.481	125	16	2-7	.996	0	98	123	1b126	15	0.7
1984	Atl N	135	389	47	100	14	0	9	44	58-12	1	54	.257	.350	.362	95	0	1-2	.993	-1	97	106	1b109	0	-0.9
1985	Atl N	101	170	16	40	7	0	3	21	18-4	0	22	.235	.307	.329	74	-6	0-0	.997	1	110	109	1b39	0	-0.7
1986	Atl N	97	122	13	38	8	0	2	14	15-4	0	24	.311	.384	.426	119	4	0-2	.993	-2	53	124	1b20	0	0.0
1988	NY A	1	1	0	0	0	0	0	0	0-0	0	1	.000	.000	.000	-99	0	0-0	ø	0	—	—	/H	0	0.0
Total	17	2175	7571	912	2109	392	42	185	972	632-99	27	926	.279	.334	.415	108	83	40-35	.993	12	101	108	1b1962,D24	15	-5.0
CHAMPION, MIKE	Robert Michael; B2.10.1955 Montgomery AL; BR/TR/6´0˝/180; [SDN73 2/28]; d9.14																								
1976	SD N	11	38	4	9	2	0	1	2	1-0	0	3	.237	.256	.368	82	-1	0-0	.940	-3	87	31	2b11	0	-0.4
1977	SD N	150	507	35	116	14	6	1	43	27-3	2	85	.229	.271	.286	55	-35	3-3	.974	-29	90	86	2b149	0	-5.8
1978	SD N	32	53	3	12	0	2	0	4	5-0	0	13	.226	.293	.302	72	-2	0-0	.932	1	120	151	2b20,3b4	0	-0.1
Total	3	193	598	42	137	16	8	2	49	33-3	2	101	.229	.272	.293	58	-38	3-3	.968	-31	92	88	2b180,3b4	0	-6.3
CHANCE, FRANK	Frank Leroy "Husk","The Peerless Leader"; B9.9.1876 Fresno CA; D9.15.1924 Los Angeles CA; BR/TR/6´0˝/190; d4.29; M11; HF1946																								
1898	Chi N	53	147	32	41	4	3	1	14	7	6	—	.279	.338	.367	102	0	7	.950	-1	*155*	*74*	C33,O17(1/1/15),1b3	—	-0.1
1899	Chi N	64	192	37	55	6	2	1	22	15	4	—	.286	.351	.354	96	-1	10	.950	0	*108*	*105*	C57/lf1	—	0.4
1900	Chi N	56	149	26	44	9	3	0	13	15	15	—	.295	.413	.396	129	8	8	.932	-3	*94*	*109*	C51/1	—	0.8
1901	Chi N	69	241	38	67	12	4	0	36	29	9	—	.278	.376	.361	119	8	27	.932	-2	125	0	O51(4/1/46),C13,1b6	—	0.5
1902	Chi N	76	242	40	70	9	4	1	31	37	8	—	.289	.401	.372	143	15	29	.969	-2	89	105	1b38,C30,O4R	—	1.6
1903	Chi N	125	441	83	144	24	10	2	81	78	10	—	.327	.439	.440	155	38	**67**	.972	-3	97	89	1b121,C2	—	3.1
1904	Chi N	124	451	89	140	16	10	6	49	36	16	—	.310	.382	.430	150	27	42	.990	11	**128**	101	1b123/C	—	3.8
1905	Chi N	118	392	92	124	16	12	2	70	78	17	—	.316	**.450**	.434	157	35	38	.990	2	99	105	1b115,M	—	3.5
1906	†Chi N	136	474	**103**	151	24	10	3	71	70	12	—	.319	.419	.430	156	35	**57**	.989	-1	92	125	1b136,M	—	3.4
1907	†Chi N	111	382	58	112	19	2	1	49	51	13	—	.293	.395	.361	129	17	35	**.992**	7	119	**135**	1b109,M	—	2.5
1908	†Chi N	129	452	65	123	27	4	2	55	37	8	—	.272	.338	.363	119	11	27	.989	5	110	111	1b126,M	—	1.5
1909	Chi N	93	324	53	88	16	4	0	46	30	4	—	.272	.341	.346	110	4	29	.994	-2	82	115	1b92,M	—	0.1
1910	†Chi N	88	295	54	88	12	8	0	36	37	10	15	.298	.395	.393	131	13	16	.996	-1	83	111	1b87,M	—	1.1
1911	Chi N	31	88	23	21	6	3	1	17	25	5	13	.239	.432	.409	136	6	9	.990	-2	66	77	1b29,M	—	0.4
1912	Chi N	2	5	2	1	0	0	0	0	3	0	0	.200	.500	.200	96	0	1	1.000	-0	0	88	1b2,M	—	0.0
1913	NY A	12	24	3	5	0	0	0	6	8	0	1	.208	.406	.208	81	0	1	1.000	0	106	47	1b7,M	—	0.0
1914	NY A	1	0	0	0	0	0	0	0	0	0	0	ø	ø	ø	ø	0	0	1.000	-0	0	0	/1M	—	0.0
Total	17	1288	4299	798	1274	200	79	20	596	556	137	29	.296	.394	.394	135	216	403	.987	8	101	109	1b997,C187,O73(6/2/65)	—	22.6
CHANCE, BOB	Robert; B9.10.1940 Statesboro GA; BL/TR/6´2˝/(196–219); d9.4																								
1963	Cle A	16	52	5	15	4	0	2	7	1-0	0	10	.288	.302	.481	116	1	0-1	.909	-1	95	0	O14R	0	-0.1
1964	Cle A	120	390	45	109	16	1	14	75	40-8	3	101	.279	.346	.433	118	10	3-3	.988	-11	51	78	1b81,O31(1/0/30)	0	-0.8
1965	Was A	72	199	20	51	9	0	4	14	18-2	0	44	.256	.317	.362	94	-1	0-1	.988	-2	86	100	1b48,O3R	0	-0.7
1966	Was A	37	57	1	10	3	0	1	8	2-0	0	23	.175	.200	.281	38	-5	0-0	.974	-1	53	89	1b13	0	-0.7
1967	Was A	27	42	5	9	2	0	3	7	7-0	1	13	.214	.340	.476	144	3	0-0	1.000	-0	87	97	1b10	0	0.2
1969	Cal A	5	7	0	1	0	0	0	1	0-0	0	4	.143	.143	.143	-21	-1	0-0	.909	-0	0	0	/1	0	-0.2
Total	6	277	747	76	195	34	1	24	112	68-10	4	195	.261	.323	.406	106	7	3-5	.987	-16	65	87	1b153,O48(1/0/47)	0	-2.3
CHANEY, DARREL	Darrel Lee; B3.9.1948 Hammond IN; BB/TR (BL 1973p, 74–75)/6´1˝/(190–195); [CinN66 2/33]; d4.11																								
1969	Cin N	93	209	21	40	5	2	0	15	24-4	1	75	.191	.278	.234	43	-16	1-0	.947	-14	91	102	S91	0	-2.3
1970	†Cin N	57	95	7	22	3	0	1	4	3-1	1	26	.232	.263	.295	49	-7	1-1	.941	1	92	46	S30,2b18,3b3	0	-0.4
1971	Cin N	10	24	2	3	0	0	0	1	1-0	0	3	.125	.160	.125	-19	-4	0-1	1.000	-1	86	26	S7/23	0	-0.5
1972	†Cin N	83	196	29	49	7	2	2	19	29-7	0	28	.250	.345	.337	100	1	1-3	.963	-12	90	84	S64,2b12,3b10	0	-0.6
1973	†Cin N	105	227	27	41	7	1	0	14	26-5	1	50	.181	.267	.220	38	-19	4-3	.964	2	105	119	S75,2b14,3b12	0	-0.9
1974	Cin N	117	135	27	27	6	1	2	16	26-6	0	33	.200	.327	.304	79	-3	1-2	.952	-1	86	49	3b81,2b38,S12	0	-0.2
1975	†Cin N	71	160	18	35	6	0	2	26	14-2	0	38	.219	.280	.294	59	-9	3-0	.961	9	122	116	S34,2b23,3b13	0	0.5
1976	Atl N	153	496	42	125	20	8	1	50	54-7	1	92	.252	.324	.331	82	-11	5-7	.950	5	102	93	S151/23	0	1.0
1977	Atl N	74	209	22	42	7	2	3	15	17-2	0	44	.201	.260	.297	44	-17	0-0	.979	9	104	72	S41,2b24	54	-0.3
1978	Atl N	89	245	27	55	9	1	3	20	25-7	0	48	.224	.295	.306	62	-12	1-0	.976	-2	98	81	S77,3b8/2	0	-0.8
1979	Atl N	63	117	15	19	5	0	0	10	19-2	0	34	.162	.277	.205	32	-10	2-1	.945	-5	92	86	S39,2b5,3b4/C	0	-1.3
Total	11	915	2113	237	458	75	17	14	190	238-43	4	471	.217	.296	.288	61	-107	19-18	.959	-10	100	93	S621,2b137,3b133/C	54	-5.8
CHANNELL, LES	Lester Clark "Goat","Gint"; B3.3.1886 Crestline OH; D5.8.1954 Denver CO; BL/TL/6´0˝/180; d5.11																								
1910	NY A	6	19	3	6	0	0	0	3	2	0	—	.316	.381	.316	112	0	2	1.000	-0	111	0	O6L	—	0.0
1914	NY A	1	1	0	1	1	0	0	0	0	0	0	1.000	1.000	2.000	803	1	0	ø	0	—	—	/H	—	0.1
Total	2	7	20	3	7	1	0	0	3	2	0	0	.350	.409	.400	145	1	2	1.000	-0	111	0	O6L	—	0.1
CHANT, CHARLIE	Charles Joseph; B8.7.1951 Bell CA; BR/TR/6´0˝/185; [OakA69 19/439]; d9.12																								
1975	Oak A	5	5	1	0	0	0	0	0	0-0	0	0	.000	.000	.000	-99	-1	0-0	1.000	-0	36	0	O5(3/0/2)/D	0	-0.2
1976	StL N	15	14	0	2	0	0	0	0	0-0	0	4	.143	.143	.143	-18	-2	0-0	1.000	2	149	270	O14(7/2/5)	0	-0.1
Total	2	20	19	1	2	0	0	0	0	0-0	0	4	.105	.105	.105	-40	-3	0-0	1.000	1	124	210	O19(10/2/7)/D	0	-0.3
CHAPLIN, ED	Bert Edgar (b Bert Edgar Chapman); B9.25.1893 Pelzer SC; D8.15.1978 Sanford FL; BL/TR/5´7˝/158; d9.4; Col South Carolina																								
1920	Bos A	4	5	2	1	1	0	0	1	4	0	1	.200	.556	.400	163	1	0-0	.900	-0	*108*	*0*	C2	—	0.1
1921	Bos A	3	2	0	0	0	0	0	0	0	0	1	.000	.000	.000	-99	-1	0-0	1.000	0	*0*	*968*	/C	—	-0.1
1922	Bos A	28	69	8	13	1	1	0	6	9	0	9	.188	.282	.232	35	-7	2-1	.960	-2	*80*	*78*	C21	—	-0.7
Total	3	35	76	10	14	2	1	0	7	13	0	11	.184	.303	.237	43	-7	2-1	.953	-2	*82*	*81*	C24	—	-0.7

YEAR	TM LG	G	AB	R	H	2B	3B	HR	RBI	BB-IB	HP	SO	AVG	OBP	SLG	AOPS	ABR	SB-CS	FA	FR	RNG	THR	GAMES AT POSITION	DL	BFW
CHAPMAN, CALVIN	Calvin Louis; B12.20.1910 Courtland MS; D4.1.1983 Batesville MS; BL/TR/5´9˝/160; d9.10; b–Ed																								
1935	Cin N	15	53	6	18	1	0	0	3	4	0	5	.340	.386	.358	105	0	2	.949	-1	96	141	S12,2b4	—	0.0
1936	Cin N	96	219	35	54	7	3	1	22	16	1	19	.247	.301	.320	72	-9	5	.961	-5	81	129	O31(21/1/9),2b23/3	—	-1.5
Total	2	111	272	41	72	8	3	1	25	20	1	24	.265	.317	.327	78	-9	7	.961	-7	81	129	O31(21/1/9),2b27,S12/3	—	-1.5
CHAPMAN, GLENN	Glenn Justice "Pete"; B1.21.1906 Cambridge City IN; D11.5.1988 Richmond IN; BR/TR/5´11.5˝/170; d4.18																								
1934	Bro N	67	93	19	26	5	1	1	10	7	0	19	.280	.330	.387	96	-1	1	1.000	2	123	0	O40(27/0/14),2b14	—	0.1
CHAPMAN, HARRY	Harry E.; B10.26.1887 Severance KS; D10.21.1918 Nevada MO; BR/TR/5´11˝/160; d10.6																								
1912	Chi N	1	4	1	1	0	1	0	1	0	0	0	.250	.250	.750	169	0	1	1.000	1	*177*	*142*	/C	—	0.1
1913	Cin N	2	2	0	1	0	0	0	0	0	0	1	.500	.500	.500	187	0	0	ø	0	—	—	/H	—	0.0
1914	StL F	64	181	16	38	2	1	0	14	13	2	27	.210	.270	.232	36	-19	2	.973	-5	*83*	*98*	C51/12cf	—	-2.1
1915	StL F	62	186	19	37	6	3	1	29	22	0	24	.199	.284	.280	56	-14	4	.989	6	*107*	*98*	C53	—	-0.4
1916	StL A	18	31	2	3	0	0	0	0	2	0	5	.097	.152	.097	-27	-5	0	.981	1	96	155	C14	—	-0.4
Total	5	147	404	38	80	8	5	1	44	37	2	57	.198	.269	.250	43	-38	7	.982	2	*97*	*103*	C119/cf21	—	-2.8
CHAPMAN, JACK	John Curtis "Death To Flying Things"; B5.8.1843 Brooklyn NY; D6.10.1916 Brooklyn NY; TR/5´11˝/170; d5.5; M11																								
1874	Atl NA	53	242	32	64	10	2	0	24	4	—	11	.264	.276	.322	103	4	2-1	.741	1	**167**	0	O53(0/1/52)/1	—	0.6
1875	StL NA	43	195	28	44	5	3	0	30	1	—	7	.226	.230	.282	84	-2	4-1	.733	-5	81	159	O43R/1	—	-0.3
1876	Lou N	17	67	4	16	1	0	0	5	1	—	3	.239	.250	.254	58	-3	—	.750	-3	78	0	O17(5/1/11)/3M	—	-0.6
Total	2NA	96	437	60	108	15	5	0	54	5	—	18	.247	.256	.304	95	2	6-2	.738	-4	126	75	O96(0/1/95),1b2	—	0.3
CHAPMAN, JOHN	John Joseph; B10.15.1899 Centralia PA; D11.3.1953 Philadelphia PA; BR/TR/5´10.5˝/175; d6.28; Col Mount St. Marys																								
1924	Phi A	19	71	7	20	4	1	0	7	4	1	8	.282	.329	.366	78	-2	0-0	.958	-5	73	116	S19	—	-0.6
CHAPMAN, KELVIN	Kelvin Keith; B6.2.1956 Willits CA; BR/TR/5´11˝/(172–173); d4.5; Col Santa Rosa (CA) JC																								
1979	NY N	35	80	7	12	1	2	0	4	5-0	0	15	.150	.198	.213	13	-10	0-0	.980	-2	86	121	2b22/3	0	-1.1
1984	NY N	75	197	27	57	13	0	3	23	19-0	2	30	.289	.356	.401	114	4	8-7	.979	-4	87	103	2b57,3b3	0	0.3
1985	NY N	62	144	16	25	3	0	0	7	9-0	2	15	.174	.231	.194	21	-15	5-4	.970	-10	82	79	2b48/3	0	-2.6
Total	3	172	421	50	94	17	2	3	34	33-0	4	60	.223	.284	.295	63	-21	13-11	.976	-16	85	98	2b127,3b5	0	-3.4
CHAPMAN, RAY	Raymond Johnson; B1.15.1891 Beaver Dam KY; D8.17.1920 New York NY; BR/TR/5´10˝/170; d8.30																								
1912	Cle A	31	109	29	34	6	3	0	19	10	1	—	.312	.375	.422	124	3	10	.904	-7	77	98	S31	—	-0.2
1913	Cle A	141	508	78	131	19	7	3	39	46	2	51	.258	.322	.341	91	-6	29	.936	-9	92	106	S138/rf	—	-0.6
1914	Cle A	106	375	59	103	16	10	2	42	48	1	48	.275	.358	.387	119	9	24-9	.913	-13	86	77	S72,2b33	—	0.5
1915	Cle A	**154**	570	101	154	14	17	3	67	70	3	82	.270	.353	.370	114	9	36-15	.944	10	100	66	S154	—	3.4
1916	Cle A	109	346	50	80	10	5	0	27	50	1	46	.231	.330	.289	81	-7	21-14	.935	7	102	92	S52,3b36,2b16	—	0.6
1917	Cle A	**156**	563	98	170	28	13	2	36	61	0	65	.302	.370	.409	128	19	52	.938	**24**	**111**	107	S156	—	5.8
1918	Cle A	128	446	**84**	119	19	8	1	32	**84**	6	46	.267	.390	.352	113	12	35	.936	7	101	85	S128/cf	—	3.0
1919	Cle A	115	433	75	130	23	10	3	53	31	3	38	.300	.351	.420	109	4	18	.944	2	100	107	S115	—	1.4
1920	Cle A	111	435	97	132	27	8	3	49	52	2	38	.303	.380	.423	109	7	13-9	.959	14	**106**	106	S111	—	2.7
Total	9	1051	3785	671	1053	162	81	17	364	452	19	<u>414</u>	.278	.358	.377	110	50	238-<u>47</u>	.939	34	100	94	S957,2b49,3b36,O2(0/1/1)	—	16.6
CHAPMAN, SAM	Samuel Blake; B4.11.1916 Tiburon CA; BR/TR/6´1˝/190; d5.16; Mil 1942–45; Col California																								
1938	Phi A	114	406	60	105	17	7	17	63	55	4	94	.259	.353	.461	105	1	3-4	.952	0	102	103	O110(103/8/0)	—	-0.4
1939	Phi A	140	498	74	134	24	6	15	64	51	1	62	.269	.338	.432	98	-4	11-4	.955	1	106	107	O117C,1b19	—	-0.6
1940	Phi A	134	508	88	140	26	3	23	75	46	1	96	.276	.337	.474	110	6	2-6	.963	5	104	142	O129C	—	0.5
1941	Phi A	143	552	97	178	29	9	25	106	47	2	49	.322	.378	.543	145	32	6-9	.967	12	106	**174**	O141(0/140/1)	0	3.7
1945	Phi A	9	30	3	6	2	0	0	1	2	0	4	.200	.250	.267	50	-2	0-0	1.000	-1	90	0	O8C	0	-0.3
1946	Phi A★	146	545	77	142	22	5	20	67	54	0	66	.261	.327	.429	111	6	1-3	.970	-8	108	134	O145(89/59/0)	0	0.5
1947	Phi A	149	551	84	139	18	5	14	83	65	0	70	.252	.331	.379	95	-4	3-4	.987	8	103	161	O146(12/134/0)	0	-0.1
1948	Phi A	123	445	58	115	18	6	13	70	55	1	50	.258	.341	.413	100	-2	6-1	.982	1	104	79	O118C	0	-0.3
1949	Phi A	**154**	589	89	164	24	4	24	108	80	2	68	.278	.367	.455	121	16	3-4	.979	3	104	101	O154C	0	1.4
1950	Phi A	144	553	93	139	20	6	23	95	68	4	79	.251	.338	.434	98	-4	3-3	.978	5	108	90	O140C	0	-0.3
1951	Phi A	18	65	7	11	1	0	0	5	12	0	12	.169	.299	.185	32	-6	0-0	.957	-2	91	57	O17C	0	-0.8
	Cle A	94	246	24	56	9	1	6	36	27	0	32	.228	.304	.346	80	-8	3-0	.985	-4	93	40	O84(38/44/7)/1	0	-1.4
	Year	112	311	31	67	10	1	6	41	39	0	44	.215	.303	.312	69	-14	3-0	.978	-6	93	44	O101(38/61/7)/1	0	-2.2
Total	11	1368	4988	754	1329	210	52	180	773	562	15	682	.266	.342	.438	107	31	41-38	.972	36	104	117	O1309(242/1068/8),1b20	0	1.9
CHAPMAN, TRAVIS	Travis Adrian; B6.5.1978 Jacksonville FL; BR/TR/6´2˝/180; [PhiN00 17/505]; d9.9; Col Mississippi St.																								
2003	Phi N	1	1	0	0	0	0	0	0	0-0	0	0	.000	.000	.000	-99	0	0-0	ø	-0	0	0	/3	0	-0.1
CHAPMAN, BEN	William Benjamin; B12.25.1908 Nashville TN; D7.7.1993 Hoover AL; BR/TR/6´0˝/190; d4.15; M4/C1; OF(404/583/541); ▲																								
1930	NY A	138	513	74	162	31	10	10	81	43	2	58	.316	.371	.474	118	13	14-6	.912	-9	92	71	3b91,2b45	—	1.1
1931	NY A	149	600	120	189	28	11	17	122	75	5	77	.315	.396	.483	138	34	**61**-23	.963	6	106	125	O137(90/0/50),2b11	—	3.4
1932	†NY A	151	581	101	174	41	15	10	107	71	5	55	.299	.381	.473	126	24	**38**-18	.949	4	106	122	O150(81/0/86)	—	1.9
1933	NY A★	147	565	112	176	36	4	9	98	72	4	45	.312	.393	.437	127	25	**27**-18	.975	14	107	**190**	O147(76/0/77)	—	2.9
1934	NY A★	149	588	82	181	21	**13**	5	86	67	3	68	.308	.381	.413	113	11	26-16	.967	4	106	100	O149(41/87/23)	—	0.9
1935	NY A★	140	553	118	160	38	8	8	74	61	1	39	.289	.361	.430	110	8	17-10	.964	13	103	**243**	O138C	—	1.7
1936	NY A	36	139	19	37	14	3	1	21	15	0	20	.266	.338	.432	92	-2	1-2	.965	1	106	93	O36C	—	-0.2
	Was A★	97	401	91	133	36	7	4	60	69	1	18	.332	.431	.486	133	25	19-7	.959	-1	97	112	O97C	—	2.1
	Year	133	540	110	170	50	10	5	81	84	1	38	.315	.408	.472	123	23	20-9	.961	-0	99	107	O133C	—	1.9
1937	Was A	35	130	23	34	7	1	0	12	26	0	7	.262	.385	.331	86	-1	8-0	.957	-1	104	34	O32C	—	-0.2
	Bos A	113	423	76	130	23	11	7	57	57	1	35	.307	.391	.463	110	7	27-12	.985	5	114	85	O112(2/10/100)/S	—	0.6
	Year	148	553	99	164	30	12	7	69	83	1	42	.297	.389	.432	105	6	**35**-12	.978	4	**112**	74	O144(2/42/100)/S	—	0.4
1938	Bos A	127	480	92	163	40	8	6	80	65	0	33	.340	.418	.494	122	19	13-6	.966	5	106	130	O126(1/0/125)/3	—	1.6
1939	Cle A	149	545	101	158	31	9	6	82	87	2	30	.290	.390	.413	109	11	18-6	.971	-6	93	100	O146(2/137/9)	—	0.3
1940	Cle A	143	548	82	157	40	6	4	50	78	2	45	.286	.377	.403	105	8	13-7	.964	1	103	94	O140(62/18/62)	—	0.2
1941	Was A	28	110	9	28	6	0	1	10	10	0	6	.255	.317	.336	76	-4	2-2	.983	1	100	142	O26L	0	-0.4
	Chi A	57	190	26	43	9	1	2	19	19	0	14	.226	.297	.316	63	-10	2-2	.992	0	100	91	O49(21/22/7)	0	-1.2
	Year	85	300	35	71	15	1	3	29	29	0	20	.237	.304	.323	68	-14	4-4	.989	1	100	108	O75(47/22/7)	0	-1.6
1944	Bro N	20	38	11	14	4	0	0	11	5	0	4	.368	.442	.474	161	7	1	.900	-2	40	0	P11	0	0.0
1945	Bro N	13	22	2	3	0	0	0	3	2	0	1	.136	.208	.136	-3	-1	0	.938	1	123	172	P10	0	0.0
	Phi N	24	51	4	16	2	0	0	4	2	0	1	.314	.340	.353	95	0	0	.933	-1	80	183	O10(2/6/2),3b4,P3,M	0	-0.2
	Year	37	73	6	19	2	0	0	7	4	0	2	.260	.299	.288	65	-4	0	.941	-1	117	152	P13,O10(2/6/2),3b4	0	-0.2
1946	Phi N	1	1	0	0	0	0	0	0	0	0	0	.000	.000	.000	-99	0	0	ø	0	0	0	/PM	0	0.0
Total	15	1717	6478	1144	1958	407	107	90	977	824	26	556	.302	.383	.440	115	174	287-<u>135</u>	.967	36	104	127	O1495C,3b96,2b56,P25/S	0	14.5
CHAPMAN, FRED	William Fred "Chappie"; B7.17.1916 Liberty NC; D3.27.1997 Kannapolis NC; BR/TR/6´1˝/185; d9.15; Mil 1943–45																								
1939	Phi A	15	49	5	14	1	1	0	1	1	0	3	.286	.300	.347	66	-3	1-0	.899	-3	98	59	S15	—	-0.4
1940	Phi A	26	69	6	11	1	0	0	4	6	0	10	.159	.227	.174	6	-10	1-1	.862	-6	88	88	S25	—	-1.4
1941	Phi A	35	69	1	11	1	0	0	4	4	0	15	.159	.205	.174	1	-10	1-2	.917	-1	121	66	S28,3b2/2	0	-1.1
Total	3	76	187	12	36	3	1	0	9	11	0	28	.193	.237	.219	20	-23	3-3	.889	-10	101	74	S68,3b2/2	0	-2.9
CHAPPAS, HARRY	Harry Perry; B10.26.1957 Mt.Rainier MD; BB/TR/5´3˝/150; [ChiA76*S6/94]; d9.7; Col Miami–Dade North (FL) CC																								
1978	Chi A	20	75	11	20	1	0	0	6	6-0	1	11	.267	.318	.280	72	-3	1-2	1.000	1	107	66	S20	0	0.0
1979	Chi A	26	59	9	17	1	0	1	4	5-0	1	5	.288	.354	.356	92	-1	1-1	.929	1	107	104	S23	0	0.2
1980	Chi A	26	50	6	8	2	0	0	2	4-0	1	10	.160	.236	.200	21	-5	0-2	.981	3	113	139	S19/2D	0	-0.2
Total	3	72	184	26	45	4	0	1	12	15-0	3	26	.245	.307	.283	65	-9	2-5	.967	5	108	95	S62,D2/2	0	0.0
CHAPPELL, LARRY	La Verne Ashford; B2.19.1890 McClusky IL; D11.8.1918 San Francisco CA; BL/TR/6´0˝/186; d7.18																								
1913	Chi A	60	208	20	48	8	1	0	15	18	1	22	.231	.295	.279	69	-8	7	.952	-3	98	59	O59(52/7/0)	—	-1.6
1914	Chi A	21	39	3	9	0	0	0	1	4	0	11	.231	.302	.231	61	-2	0	.929	-1	93	0	O9(7/0/2)	—	-0.4
1915	Chi A	1	1	0	0	0	0	0	0	0	0	0	.000	.000	.000	-97	0	0	ø	0	—	—	/H	—	0.0
1916	Cle A	3	2	0	0	0	0	0	0	1	0	0	.000	.333	.000	1	0	1	ø	0	—	—	/H	—	0.0

YEAR	TM LG	G	AB	R	H	2B	3B	HR	RBI	BB-IB	HP	SO	AVG	OBP	SLG	AOPS	ABR	SB-CS	FA	FR	RNG	THR	GAMES AT POSITION	DL	BFW
	Bos N	20	53	4	12	1	1	0	9	2	1	8	.226	.268	.283	72	-2	1	.957	-2	93	0	O14(12/0/2)	—	-0.5
1917	Bos N	4	2	0	0	0	0	0	1	0	0	1	.000	.000	.000	-99	0	0	ø	-0	0	0	/cf	—	-0.1
Total	5	109	305	27	69	9	2	0	26	25	2	42	.226	.289	.269	66	-12	9	.951	-6	97	44	O83(71/8/4)	—	-2.6
CHARBONEAU, JOE	Joseph; B6.17.1955 Belvidere IL; BR/TR/6´2˝/200; [PhiN76 S2/35]; d4.11; Col West Valley (CA) CC																								
1980	Cle A	131	453	76	131	17	2	23	87	49-0	3	70	.289	.358	.488	129	18	2-4	.963	-1	95	128	O67(67/0/1),D57	0	1.2
1981	Cle A	48	138	14	29	7	1	4	18	7-0	0	22	.210	.247	.362	74	-5	1-0	.963	-1	97	58	O27(24/0/5),D14	0	-0.8
1982	Cle A	22	56	7	12	2	1	2	9	5-0	1	7	.214	.286	.393	85	-1	0-0	.955	-3	72	0	O18(9/0/8)/D	0	-0.5
Total	3	201	647	97	172	26	4	29	114	61-0	4	99	.266	.329	.453	115	12	3-4	.962	-4	92	94	O112(100/0/14),D72	0	-0.1
CHARLES, ED	Edwin Douglas; B4.29.1933 Daytona Beach FL; BR/TR/5´10˝/170; d4.11																								
1962	KC A	147	535	81	154	24	7	17	74	54-0	4	70	.288	.356	.454	111	9	20-4	.964	14	110	102	3b140,2b2	0	2.5
1963	KC A	158	603	82	161	28	2	15	79	58-7	5	79	.267	.332	.395	99	0	15-8	.949	-1	104	62	3b158	0	-0.1
1964	KC A	150	557	69	134	25	2	16	63	64-2	4	92	.241	.321	.379	92	-5	12-7	.954	-14	89	86	3b147	0	-2.1
1965	KC A	134	480	55	129	19	7	8	56	44-0	4	72	.269	.332	.387	106	4	13-4	.971	5	98	104	3b128/2S	0	1.0
1966	KC A	118	385	52	110	18	8	9	42	30-2	0	53	.286	.337	.444	127	12	12-5	.963	-1	104	108	3b104/1lf	0	1.2
1967	KC A	19	61	5	15	1	0	0	5	12-1	1	13	.246	.378	.262	95	1	1-0	.966	3	117	35	3b18	0	0.4
	NY N	101	323	32	77	13	2	3	31	24-1	7	58	.238	.300	.319	80	-8	4-1	.944	14	119	106	3b89	0	0.7
1968	NY N	117	369	41	102	11	1	15	53	28-4	2	57	.276	.328	.434	127	11	5-4	.954	1	103	114	3b106,1b2	0	1.3
1969	†NY N	61	169	21	35	8	1	3	18	18-3	1	31	.207	.286	.320	68	-7	4-2	.946	-1	96	131	3b52	0	-0.9
Total	8	1005	3482	438	917	147	30	86	421	332-20	28	525	.263	.330	.397	103	17	86-35	.957	19	103	95	3b942,1b3,2b3/lfS	0	4.0
CHARLES, FRANK	Franklin Scott; B2.23.1969 Fontana CA; BR/TR/6´4˝/210; [SFN91 17/453]; d9.5; Col Cal St.–Fullerton																								
2000	Hou N	4	7	1	3	1	0	0	2	0-0	0	2	.429	.429	.571	139	0	0-0	1.000	1	61	0	/C	0	0.1
CHARLES, CHAPPY	Raymond (b Charles Shuh Achenbach); B3.25.1881 Phillipsburg NJ; D8.4.1959 Bethlehem PA; BR/TR/5´11˝/175; d4.15																								
1908	StL N	121	454	39	93	14	3	1	17	19	1	—	.205	.238	.256	61	-22	15	.921	-6	98	26	2b65,S31,3b23	—	-3.0
1909	StL N	99	339	33	80	7	3	0	29	31	5	—	.236	.309	.274	87	-5	7	.918	-8	96	108	2b71,S26,3b2	—	-1.2
	Cin N	13	43	3	11	2	0	0	5	4	0	—	.256	.319	.302	94	0	2	.932	-1	107	34	2b10,S3	—	-0.1
	Year	112	382	36	91	9	3	0	34	35	5	—	.238	.310	.277	87	-5	9	.920	-9	97	100	2b81,S29,3b2	—	-1.3
1910	Cin N	4	15	1	2	0	1	0	0	0	0	1	.133	.133	.267	17	-2	0	.818	-1	82	119	S4	—	-0.3
Total	3	237	851	76	186	23	7	1	51	54	6	1	.219	.270	.266	72	-29	24	.920	-15	98	68	2b146,S64,3b25	—	-4.6
CHARTAK, MIKE	Michael George "Shotgun"; B4.28.1916 Brooklyn NY; D7.25.1967 Cedar Rapids IA; BL/TL/6˝2˝/180; d9.13																								
1940	NY A	11	15	2	2	1	0	0	3	5	0	5	.133	.350	.200	49	-1	0-0	1.000	-0	87	0	O3R	—	-0.1
1942	NY A	5	5	0	0	0	0	0	0	0	0	0	.000	.000	.000	-99	-1	0-0	ø	0	—	—	/H	0	-0.1
	Was A	24	92	11	20	4	2	1	8	14	0	16	.217	.321	.337	86	-2	0-1	.926	0	103	116	O24R	0	-0.4
	StL A	73	237	37	59	11	2	9	43	40	2	27	.249	.362	.426	119	7	3-3	.974	5	104	199	O64R	0	0.8
	Year	102	334	48	79	15	4	10	51	54	2	43	.237	.346	.395	107	4	3-4	.962	5	104	177	O88R	0	0.3
1943	StL A	108	344	38	88	16	2	10	37	39	1	55	.256	.333	.401	112	5	1-3	.970	-0	109	78	O77R,1b18	0	-0.2
1944	†StL A	35	72	8	17	2	1	1	7	6	1	9	.236	.304	.333	77	-2	0-0	1.000	0	88	63	1b12,O7(4/0/3)	0	-0.3
Total	4	256	765	96	186	34	7	21	98	104	4	112	.243	.337	.388	105	6	4-7	.967	5	106	127	O175(4/0/171),1b30	0	-0.3
CHASE, HAL	Harold Homer "Prince Hal"; B2.13.1883 Los Gatos CA; D5.18.1947 Colusa CA; BR/TL/6´0˝/175; d4.14; M2; Col Santa Clara																								
1905	NY A	128	465	60	116	16	6	3	49	15	3	—	.249	.277	.329	83	-11	22	.976	-9	78	125	1b124,S2/2	—	-2.4
1906	NY A	151	597	84	193	23	10	0	76	13	3	—	.323	.341	.395	118	10	28	.980	-2	95	89	1b150/2	—	0.6
1907	NY A	125	498	72	143	23	3	2	68	19	1	—	.287	.315	.357	106	2	32	.973	0	103	84	1b121,O4L	—	0.0
1908	NY A	106	405	50	104	11	3	1	36	15	1	—	.257	.285	.306	91	-5	27	.980	-3	91	73	1b98,2b3,O3L/3P	—	-1.2
1909	NY A	118	474	60	134	17	3	4	63	20	4	—	.283	.317	.357	112	5	25	.978	-2	100	89	1b118/S	—	0.1
1910	NY A	130	524	67	152	20	5	3	73	16	1	—	.290	.312	.365	106	1	40	.981	-4	88	120	1b130,M	—	-0.6
1911	NY A	133	527	82	166	32	7	3	62	21	1	—	.315	.342	.419	105	2	36	.974	-2	101	108	1b124,O7C,2b2,M	—	-0.3
1912	NY A	131	522	61	143	21	9	4	58	17	2	—	.274	.299	.372	86	-12	33	.979	-1	**111**	80	1b122,2b7	—	-1.7
1913	NY A	39	146	15	31	2	4	0	9	11	0	13	.212	.268	.281	60	-8	5	.982	-4	88	97	1b29,2b5,O5C	—	-1.4
	Chi A	102	384	49	110	11	10	2	39	16	3	41	.286	.320	.383	107	0	9	.976	1	114	104	1b102	—	-0.1
	Year	141	530	64	141	13	14	2	48	27	3	54	.266	.305	.355	94	-8	14	.977	-3	108	102	1b131,2b5,O5C	—	-1.5
1914	Chi A	58	206	27	55	10	5	0	20	23	1	19	.267	.343	.364	114	4	9-4	.981	2	116	103	1b58	—	0.5
	Buf F	75	291	43	101	19	9	3	48	6	2	31	.347	.365	.505	133	7	10	.980	-1	99	89	1b73	—	0.5
1915	Buf F	145	567	85	165	31	10	**17**	89	20	1	50	.291	.316	.471	118	1	23	.983	0	103	101	1b143/rf	—	-0.3
1916	Cin N	142	542	66	**184**	29	12	4	82	19	1	48	**.339**	.363	.459	**155**	32	22-11	.986	-5	79	116	1b98,O25(14/14/0),2b16	—	2.8
1917	Cin N	152	602	71	167	28	15	4	86	15	1	49	.277	.296	.394	115	7	21	.983	-3	98	103	1b151	—	0.0
1918	Cin N	74	259	30	78	12	6	2	38	13	2	15	.301	.339	.417	133	9	5	.980	-2	93	146	1b67,O2L	—	0.6
1919	NY N	110	408	58	116	17	7	5	45	17	3	40	.284	.318	.397	115	6	16	.984	-1	101	**111**	1b107	—	0.2
Total	15	1919	7417	980	2158	322	124	57	941	276	30	306	.291	.319	.391	110	50	363-15	.980	-35	98	102	1b1815,O47(23/26/1),2b35,S3/P3	—	-2.7
CHATHAM, BUSTER	Charles L; B12.25.1901 West TX; D12.15.1975 Waco TX; BR/TR/5´5˝/150; d6.1																								
1930	Bos N	112	404	48	108	20	11	5	56	37	2	41	.267	.332	.408	80	-14	8	.920	-11	88	158	3b92,S17	—	-1.6
1931	Bos N	17	44	4	10	1	0	1	3	6	0	6	.227	.320	.318	75	-2	0	.762	-4	51	99	S6,3b6	—	-0.5
Total	2	129	448	52	118	21	11	6	59	43	2	47	.263	.331	.400	80	-16	8	.924	-15	90	155	3b98,S23	—	-2.1
CHATTERTON, JIM	James M.; B10.14.1864 Brooklyn NY; D12.15.1944 Tewksbury MA; d6.7																								
1884	KC U	4	15	4	2	1	0	0	—	2	—	—	.133	.235	.200	38	-1	—	1.000	1	590	0	O2R,1b2/P	—	-0.1
CHAVARRIA, OSSIE	Osvaldo (Quijano); B8.5.1940 Colon, Pan; BR/TR/5´11˝/155; d4.14																								
1966	KC A	86	191	26	46	10	0	2	10	18-1	0	43	.241	.306	.325	84	-4	3-2	.939	-3	83	82	O26(19/0/7),S23,2b14,1b8,3b5	0	-0.6
1967	KC A	38	59	2	6	2	0	0	4	7-0	1	16	.102	.209	.136	4	-7	1-0	1.000	1	105	144	2b17,3b7,O3(2/0/1),S2	0	-0.5
Total	2	124	250	28	52	12	0	2	14	25-1	1	59	.208	.283	.280	65	-11	4-2	.990	-2	100	108	2b31,O29(21/0/8),S25,3b12,1b8	0	-1.1
CHAVEZ, ANGEL	Angel Aristides (Castro); B7.22.1981 David, Pan; BR/TR/6´1˝/195; d8.30																								
2005	SF N	10	19	1	5	1	0	0	1	0-0	0	3	.263	.263	.316	50	-1	0-0	1.000	-4	63	0	2b5,S4/3	0	-0.5
CHAVEZ, ENDY	Endy De Jesus; B2.7.1978 Valencia, Carabobo, Venez.; BL/TL/6´0˝/(155–165); d5.29																								
2001	KC A	29	77	4	16	2	0	0	5	3-0	0	8	.208	.237	.234	23	-9	0-2	1.000	0	91	162	O28(22/5/2)	0	-0.9
2002	Mon N	36	125	20	37	8	5	1	9	5-0	0	16	.296	.321	.464	99	-1	3-5	.989	5	109	402	O35C	0	0.4
2003	Mon N	141	483	66	121	25	5	5	47	31-3	0	59	.251	.294	.354	67	-24	18-7	.990	1	99	138	O135C	0	-2.0
2004	Mon N	132	502	65	139	20	6	5	34	30-0	1	40	.277	.318	.371	74	-20	32-7	.984	2	100	144	O127C	0	-1.1
2005	Was N	7	9	2	2	1	0	0	1	3-0	0	1	.222	.417	.333	105	0	0-1	1.000	-1	68	0	O6C	0	0.0
	Phi N	91	107	17	23	3	3	0	10	4-0	0	13	.215	.243	.299	40	-10	2-1	.980	3	100	365	O51(20/28/5)	0	-0.8
	Year	98	116	19	25	4	3	0	11	7-0	0	14	.216	.260	.302	45	-10	2-2	.981	2	100	365	O57(20/34/5)	0	-0.8
2006	†NY N	133	353	48	108	22	5	4	42	24-3	0	44	.306	.348	.431	101	0	12-3	**1.000**	8	108	195	O120(43/39/46)	0	0.7
Total	6	569	1656	222	446	81	24	15	148	100-6	1	181	.269	.310	.374	75	-64	67-26	.990	18	102	185	O502(85/375/53)	0	-3.7
CHAVEZ, ERIC	Eric Cesar; B12.7.1977 Los Angeles CA; BL/TR/6´0˝/(195–210); [OakA96 1/10]; d9.8																								
1998	Oak A	16	45	6	14	4	1	0	6	3-1	0	5	.311	.354	.444	107	0	1-1	1.000	2	109	119	3b13	0	0.2
1999	Oak A	115	356	47	88	21	2	13	50	46-4	0	56	.247	.333	.427	95	-3	1-1	.961	-8	90	81	3b105,S2,D3	29	-0.9
2000	†Oak A	153	501	89	139	23	4	26	86	62-8	1	94	.277	.355	.495	115	10	2-2	.951	-6	99	66	3b146,S2	0	0.5
2001	†Oak A	151	552	91	159	43	0	32	114	41-9	4	99	.288	.338	.540	127	21	8-2	**.972**	12	**108**	119	3b149/1SD	0	3.3
2002	†Oak A	153	585	87	161	31	3	34	109	65-13	1	119	.275	.348	.513	126	21	8-3	.961	12	**108**	105	3b143/lfD	0	3.3
2003	†Oak A	156	588	94	166	39	5	29	101	62-10	1	89	.282	.350	.514	124	20	8-3	.971	23	**112**	**137**	3b154	0	4.2
2004	Oak A	125	475	87	131	20	0	29	77	**95**-10	3	99	.276	.397	.501	134	27	6-3	.968	14	**109**	**150**	3b125/lf	37	3.9
2005	Oak A	160	625	92	168	40	1	27	101	58-4	2	129	.269	.329	.466	110	9	6-0	.966	8	102	111	3b153,D6	0	1.8
2006	†Oak A	137	485	74	117	24	2	22	72	84-6	1	100	.241	.351	.435	105	5	3-0	**.987**	8	103	**153**	3b134,D3	0	1.3
Total	9	1166	4212	667	1143	245	18	212	716	516-65	13	790	.271	.350	.489	118	110	43-15	.968	65	105	116	3b1122,D22,S5,O2L/1	66	17.6

THE BATTER REGISTER

YEAR	TM LG	G	AB	R	H	2B	3B	HR	RBI	BB-IB	HP	SO	AVG	OBP	SLG	AOPS	ABR	SB-CS	FA	FR	RNG	THR	GAMES AT POSITION	DL	BFW
CHAVEZ, RAUL	Raul Alexander; B3.18.1973 Valencia, Carabobo, Venez.; BR/TR/5´11˝/(175–215); d8.30																								
1996	Mon N	4	5	1	1	0	0	0	0	1-0	0	1	.200	.333	.200	44	0	1-0	1.000	1	0	0	C3	0	0.0
1997	Mon N	13	26	0	7	0	0	0	2	0-0	0	5	.269	.259	.269	42	-2	1-0	1.000	1	121	108	C13	0	-0.1
1998	Sea A	1	1	0	0	0	0	0	0	0-0	0	0	.000	.000	.000	-99	0	0-0	1.000	-0	0	0	/C	0	0.0
2000	Hou N	14	43	3	11	2	0	1	5	3-2	0	6	.256	.298	.372	65	-2	0-0	.986	-4	83	57	C14	0	-0.6
2002	Hou N	2	4	1	1	1	0	0	0	1-0	1	0	.250	.500	.500	152	1	0-0	1.000	-1	0	0	C2	0	0.0
2003	Hou N	19	37	5	10	1	1	1	4	1-0	0	6	.270	.289	.432	81	-1	0-0	1.000	-1	223	150	C16	0	-0.2
2004	†Hou N	64	162	9	34	8	0	0	23	10-3	0	38	.210	.256	.259	33	-16	0-1	.991	6	112	109	C61	0	-0.7
2005	†Hou N	37	99	6	17	3	0	2	6	4-0	1	18	.172	.210	.263	23	-12	1-0	.991	8	207	185	C36	0	-0.2
2006	Bal A	16	28	1	5	0	0	0	0	1-0	0	4	.179	.207	.179	1	-4	0-0	.985	2	222	153	C15	0	-0.2
Total	9	170	405	26	86	15	1	4	40	21-5	2	78	.212	.253	.284	38	-36	3-1	.992	11	146	125	C161	0	-2.0
CHEEK, HARRY	Harry G.; B1879 Sedalia MO; D6.25.1956 Paramus NJ; TR; d4.30																								
1910	Phi N	2	4	1	2	1	0	0	0	0	0	0	.500	.500	.750	255	1	0	1.000	-1	*87*	*0*	C2	—	0.0
CHEN, CHIN-FENG	Chin-Feng; B10.28.1977 Tainan City, Taiwan; BR/TR/6´1˝/(189–190); d9.14																								
2002	LA N	3	5	1	0	0	0	0	0	1-0	0	3	.000	.167	.000	-54	-1	0-0	1.000	0	164	0	/lf	0	-0.1
2003	LA N	1	1	0	0	0	0	0	0	0-0	0	0	.000	.000	.000	-99	0	0-0	ø	0	—	—	/H	0	0.0
2004	LA N	8	8	1	0	0	0	0	0	2-0	0	3	.000	.200	.000	-42	-2	0-0	1.000	1	247	0	O3L	0	-0.1
2005	LA N	7	8	1	2	0	0	0	2	0-0	0	4	.250	.250	.250	31	-1	0-0	1.000	-0	82	0	O3L	0	-0.1
Total	4	19	22	3	2	0	0	0	2	3-0	0	10	.091	.200	.091	-21	-4	0-0	1.000	1	176	0	O7L	0	-0.3
CHERVINKO, PAUL	Paul; B7.23.1910 Trauger PA; D6.3.1976 Danville IL; BR/TR/5´8˝/185; d5.30; Col Illinois																								
1937	Bro N	30	48	1	7	0	1	0	2	3	0	16	.146	.196	.188	5	-7	0	1.000	0	*81*	*85*	C26	—	-0.5
1938	Bro N	12	27	0	4	0	0	0	3	2	0	0	.148	.207	.148	-1	-4	0	.974	0	*102*	*120*	C12	—	-0.3
Total	2	42	75	1	11	0	1	0	5	5	0	16	.147	.200	.173	3	-11	0	.990	0	*90*	*99*	C38	—	-0.8
CHILDS, CUPID	Clarence Lemuel; B8.14.1867 Calvert Co. MD; D11.8.1912 Baltimore MD; BL/TR/5´8˝/185; d4.23																								
1888	Phi N	2	4	0	0	0	0	0	0	0	0	0	.000	.000	.000	-95	-1	0	.857	0	108	248	2b2	—	-0.1
1890	Syr AA	126	493	109	170	**33**	14	2	89	72	6	—	.345	.434	.481	189	**61**	56	.928	14	105	103	2b125/S	—	**6.8**
1891	Cle N	**141**	551	120	155	21	12	2	83	97	7	32	.281	.395	.374	119	18	39	.910	-12	99	84	2b141	—	0.9
1892	†Cle N	145	558	**136**	177	14	11	3	53	117	9	20	.317	**.443**	.398	149	41	26	.938	-5	99	97	2b145	—	3.9
1893	Cle N	124	485	145	158	19	10	3	65	120	4	12	.326	.463	.425	129	28	23	.926	9	107	101	2b123	—	3.4
1894	Cle N	118	479	143	169	21	12	2	52	107	5	11	.353	.475	.459	121	24	17	.916	-1	101	99	2b118	—	2.2
1895	†Cle N	120	466	96	134	15	4	4	90	74	6	24	.288	.392	.363	90	-5	20	.921	10	106	91	2b120	—	0.9
1896	†Cle N	132	498	106	177	24	9	1	106	100	4	18	.355	.467	.446	133	31	25	.942	**39**	**117**	**147**	2b132	—	6.3
1897	Cle N	114	444	105	150	15	9	1	61	74	2	—	.338	.435	.419	119	16	25	.944	18	106	116	2b114	—	3.3
1898	Cle N	110	413	90	119	9	4	1	31	69	4	—	.288	.395	.337	112	11	9	.931	12	**110**	95	2b110	—	2.5
1899	StL N	125	464	73	123	11	11	1	48	74	2	—	.265	.369	.343	93	-2	11	.934	-14	91	97	2b125	—	-0.9
1900	Chi N	137	531	67	128	14	5	0	44	57	7	—	.241	.323	.286	71	-19	15	.935	15	110	105	2b137	—	0.2
1901	Chi N	63	236	24	61	9	0	0	21	30	7	—	.258	.359	.297	95	1	3	.939	9	106	154	2b63	—	1.0
Total	13	1457	5622	1214	1721	205	101	20	743	.991	63	117	.306	.416	.389	119	204	269	.930	94	105	106	2b1455/S	—	30.4
CHILDS, PETE	Peter Pierre; B11.15.1871 Philadelphia PA; D2.15.1922 Philadelphia PA; TR; d4.24																								
1901	StL N	29	79	12	21	1	0	0	8	14	2	—	.266	.389	.278	100	1	0	.907	-5	94	66	2b19,O2(1/1/0)/S	—	-0.3
	Chi N	60	210	23	48	5	1	0	14	26	2	—	.229	.319	.262	72	-6	4	.958	12	116	92	2b60	—	0.6
	Year	89	289	35	69	6	1	0	22	40	4	—	.239	.339	.266	80	-5	4	.947	7	111	86	2b79,O2(1/1/0)/S	—	0.3
1902	Phi N	123	403	25	78	5	0	0	25	34	0	—	.194	.256	.206	43	-26	6	.945	-8	97	53	2b123	—	-3.6
Total	2	212	692	60	147	11	1	0	47	74	4	—	.212	.292	.231	59	-31	10	.946	-1	102	66	2b202,O2(1/1/0)/S	—	-3.3
CHILDS, SAM	Samuel Beresford; B11.6.1861 East Hartford CT; D5.21.1938 Denver CO; d5.31; Col Yale																								
1883	Col AA	1	4	0	0	0	0	0	—	0	—	—	.000	.000	.000	-99	-1	—	1.000	0	0	0	/1	—	-0.1
CHILES, PEARCE	Pearce Nuget "What's the Use"; B5.28.1867 Deepwater MO; BR/TR/5´11˝/185; d4.18																								
1899	Phi N	97	338	57	108	28	7	2	76	16	1	—	.320	.352	.462	127	11	6	.944	-10	96	247	O46(13/2/31),1b25,2b16	—	0.0
1900	Phi N	33	111	13	24	6	2	1	23	6	0	—	.216	.256	.333	63	-6	4	.987	-1	102	132	1b16,2b12,O3R	—	-0.6
Total	2	130	449	70	132	34	9	3	99	22	1	—	.294	.328	.430	111	5	10	.947	-11	90	232	O49(13/2/34),1b41,2b28	—	-0.6
CHILES, RICH	Richard Francis; B11.22.1949 Sacramento CA; BL/TL/5´11˝/(170–175); [HouN68 2/23]; d4.20																								
1971	Hou N	67	119	12	27	5	1	2	15	6-0	1	20	.227	.268	.336	73	-5	0-1	1.000	-1	67	0	O27(25/0/2)	0	-0.8
1972	Hou N	9	11	0	3	1	0	0	2	1-0	0	1	.273	.333	.364	101	0	0-0	1.000	0	149	0	O2L	0	0.0
1973	NY N	8	25	2	3	2	0	0	1	0-0	0	2	.120	.120	.200	-13	-4	0-0	1.000	2	143	249	O8C	0	-0.2
1976	Hou N	5	4	1	2	1	0	0	0	0-0	0	0	.500	.500	.750	273	1	0-0	1.000	0	427	0	/lf	19	0.1
1977	Min A	108	261	31	69	16	1	3	36	23-2	2	17	.264	.323	.368	90	-3	0-1	.946	-2	97	0	D61,O22(1/0/21)	0	-0.7
1978	Min A	87	198	22	53	12	0	1	22	20-2	2	25	.268	.333	.343	91	-2	1-2	.965	0	101	88	O61(58/0/3),D8	0	-0.4
Total	6	284	618	68	157	37	2	6	76	50-4	5	65	.254	.310	.350	85	-13	1-4	.972	-1	97	62	O121(87/8/26),D69	19	-2.0
CHIOZZA, DINO	Dino Joseph "Dynamo"; B6.30.1912 Memphis TN; D4.23.1972 Memphis TN; BL/TR/6´0˝/170; d7.14; b–Lou																								
1935	Phi N	2	0	1	0	0	0	0	0	0	0	0	ø	ø	ø	ø	0	0	1.000	-0	0	0	S2	—	0.0
CHIOZZA, LOU	Louis Peo; B5.17.1910 Tallulah LA; D2.28.1971 Memphis TN; BL/TR/6´0˝/172; d4.17; b–Dino																								
1934	Phi N	134	484	66	147	28	5	0	44	34	6	35	.304	.357	.382	86	-8	9	.938	-18	93	73	2b85,3b26,O17(13/0/4)	—	-2.1
1935	Phi N	124	472	71	134	26	6	3	47	33	2	44	.284	.333	.383	84	-10	5	.947	4	**106**	74	2b120,3b2	—	0.1
1936	Phi N	144	572	83	170	32	6	1	48	37	6	39	.297	.346	.379	87	-10	17	.972	-6	100	108	O90(4/85/1),2b33,3b26	—	-1.5
1937	†NY N	117	439	49	102	11	2	4	29	20	0	30	.232	.266	.294	51	-31	6	.939	-4	96	81	3b93,O12C,2b2	—	-3.2
1938	NY N	57	179	15	42	7	2	3	17	12	0	7	.235	.283	.346	72	-8	5	.944	-3	109	49	2b34,O16(5/10/0)/3	—	-0.9
1939	NY N	40	142	19	38	3	1	3	12	9	0	10	.268	.311	.366	81	-4	3	.915	-2	97	137	3b30,S8	—	-0.5
Total	6	616	2288	303	633	107	22	14	197	145	14	165	.277	.324	.361	78	-71	45	.943	-28	102	70	2b274,3b178,O135(22/107/5),S8	—	-8.1
CHIPPLE, WALT	Walter John (b Walter John Chlipala); B9.26.1918 Utica NY; D6.8.1988 Tonawanda NY; BR/TR/6´0.5˝/168; d4.17																								
1945	Was A	18	44	4	6	0	0	0	5	5	0	6	.136	.224	.136	6	-5	0-1	.978	2	121	172	O13(1/11/1)	0	-0.4
CHISM, TOM	Thomas Raymond; B5.9.1955 Chester PA; BL/TL/6´1˝/190; [BalA74 S4/36]; d9.13; Col Widener																								
1979	Bal A	6	3	0	0	0	0	0	0	0-0	0	0	.000	.000	.000	-99	-1	0-0	1.000	-0	0	0	1b4	0	-0.1
CHITI, HARRY	Harry; B11.16.1932 Kincaid IL; D1.31.2002 Haines City FL; BR/TR/6´3˝/(220–225); d9.27; Mil 1953–54																								
1950	Chi N	3	6	0	2	0	0	0	0	0	0	0	.333	.333	.333	77	0	0	1.000	-0	*0*	*534*	/C	0	-0.1
1951	Chi N	9	31	1	11	2	0	0	5	2	0	2	.355	.394	.419	117	1	0-0	.913	-1	*63*	*188*	C8	0	0.0
1952	Chi N	32	113	14	31	5	0	5	13	5	0	8	.274	.305	.451	106	0	0-1	.984	2	*66*	*65*	C32	0	0.4
1955	Chi N	113	338	24	78	6	1	11	41	25-8	1	68	.231	.282	.352	68	-17	0-0	.984	-4	*66*	***131***	C113	0	-1.5
1956	Chi N	72	203	17	43	6	4	4	18	19-3	1	35	.212	.281	.340	68	-10	0-0	.981	0	*78*	*136*	C67	0	-0.7
1958	KC A	103	295	32	79	11	3	9	44	18-4	3	48	.268	.311	.417	98	-2	3-2	.987	4	126	76	C83	0	0.6
1959	KC A	55	162	20	44	11	1	5	25	17-1	1	26	.272	.344	.444	113	3	0-1	.988	2	125	110	C47	0	0.7
1960	KC A	58	190	16	42	7	0	5	28	17-0	1	33	.221	.288	.337	68	-9	1-0	.983	-1	76	70	C52	0	-0.7
	Det A	37	104	9	17	0	0	2	5	10-1	0	12	.163	.235	.221	24	-11	0-3	.984	-2	69	95	C36	0	-1.3
	Year	95	294	25	59	7	0	7	33	27-1	1	45	.201	.269	.296	52	-20	1-3	.984	-3	73	80	C88	0	-2.0
1961	Det A	5	12	0	1	0	0	0	0	1-0	0	2	.083	.154	.083	-34	-2	0-0	1.000	-0	69	364	C5	0	-0.3
1962	NY N	15	41	2	8	1	0	0	0	1-0	0	8	.195	.233	.220	22	-5	0-0	.971	-1	64	79	C14	0	-0.5
Total	10	502	1495	135	356	49	9	41	179	115-17	8	242	.238	.294	.365	77	-52	4-7	.983	-1	*86*	*107*	C458	0	-3.4
CHOI, HEE-SEOP	Hee-Seop; B3.16.1979 Chun-Nam, South Korea; BL/TL/6´5˝/(235–240); d9.3; [DL 2006 Bos A 31]																								
2002	Chi N	24	50	6	9	1	0	2	4	7-0	0	15	.180	.281	.320	58	-3	0-0	.983	-1	81	133	1b22	0	-0.5
2003	Chi N	80	202	31	44	17	0	8	28	37-1	4	71	.218	.350	.421	98	1	1-1	.991	2	103	97	1b69	22	-0.3
2004	Fla N	95	281	48	76	16	1	15	40	52-4	3	78	.270	.388	.495	133	16	1-0	.990	-6	75	93	1b89	0	0.3
	†LA N	31	62	5	10	5	0	0	6	11-2	1	18	.161	.289	.242	42	-5	0-0	.994	-1	89	141	1b23	0	-0.7
	Year	126	343	53	86	21	1	15	46	63-6	4	96	.251	.370	.449	116	10	1-0	.990	-6	78	102	1b112	0	-0.4

YEAR	TM LG	G	AB	R	H	2B	3B	HR	RBI	BB-IB	HP	SO	AVG	OBP	SLG	AOPS	ABR	SB-CS	FA	FR	RNG	THR	GAMES AT POSITION	DL	BFW
2005	LA N	133	320	40	81	15	2	15	42	34-1	8	80	.253	.336	.453	105	2	1-3	.997	5	124	94	1b83	0	0.0
Total	4	363	915	130	220	54	3	40	120	141-8	16	262	.240	.349	.437	105	11	3-4	.992	0	98	100	1b286	53	-1.2
CHOO, SHIN-SOO	Shin-Soo; B7.13.1982 Pusan, South Korea; BL/TL/5´11˝/(180–210); d4.21																								
2005	Sea A	10	18	1	1	0	0	0	1	3-0	0	4	.056	.190	.056	-32	-3	0-0	1.000	1	139	0	O5L	0	-0.2
2006	Sea A	4	11	0	1	1	0	0	0	0-0	1	4	.091	.167	.182	-11	-2	0-0	.944	2	154	488	O4C	0	0.0
	Cle A	45	146	23	43	11	3	3	22	18-2	1	46	.295	.373	.473	123	5	5-3	.976	0	104	80	O39(9/0/30)/D	0	0.4
	Year	49	157	23	44	12	3	3	22	18-2	2	50	.280	.360	.452	114	4	5-3	.971	2	109	120	O43(9/4/30)/D	0	0.4
Total	2	59	175	24	45	12	3	3	23	21-2	2	54	.257	.342	.411	99	0	5-3	.975	3	112	108	O48(14/4/30)/D	0	0.2
CHOUINARD, FELIX	Felix George; B10.5.1887 Chicago IL; D4.28.1955 Hines IL; BR/TR/5´7˝/150; d9.11																								
1910	Chi A	24	82	6	16	3	2	0	9	8	1	—	.195	.275	.280	77	-2	4	.962	2	90	197	O23C/2	—	-0.1
1911	Chi A	14	17	3	3	0	0	0	0	0	0	—	.176	.176	.176	-2	-2	0	.857	1	103	313	2b4,O4(0/3/1)	—	-0.2
1914	Pit F	9	30	2	9	1	0	1	3	0	0	4	.300	.300	.433	99	-1	1	.917	-0	101	189	2b4,O3(2/1/0)/S	—	-0.1
	Bro F	32	79	7	20	1	2	0	8	4	0	13	.253	.289	.316	65	-6	3	.929	1	106	119	O20(5/14/2)	—	-0.6
	Bal F	5	9	3	4	0	0	0	1	0	0	1	.444	.444	.444	138	0	0	1.000	-0	96	0	O2(1/1/0)	—	0.0
	Year	46	118	12	33	2	2	1	12	4	0	18	.280	.303	.356	79	-6	4	.941	0	102	123	O25(8/16/2),2b4/S	—	-0.7
1915	Bro F	4	4	1	2	0	0	0	2	0	0	0	.500	.500	.500	183	0	0	1.000	-0	61	0	O2(1/1/0)	—	0.0
Total	4	88	221	22	54	5	4	1	23	12	1	18	.244	.286	.317	75	-11	8	.948	3	96	161	O54(9/43/3),2b9/S	—	-1.0
CHOZEN, HARRY	Harry; B9.27.1915 Winnebago MN; D9.16.1994 Houston TX; BR/TR/5´9.5˝/190; d9.21																								
1937	Cin N	1	4	0	1	0	0	0	0	0	0	0	.250	.250	.250	38	0	0	.833	-0	42	0	/C	—	-0.1
CHRISLEY, NEIL	Barbra O'Neil; B12.16.1931 Calhoun Falls SC; BL/TR/6´3˝/187; d4.15																								
1957	Was A	26	51	6	8	2	1	0	3	7-0	0	7	.157	.259	.235	36	-5	0-0	.810	-1	82	144	O11(4/0/7)	0	-0.6
1958	Was A	105	233	19	50	7	4	5	26	16-2	0	18	.215	.265	.343	67	-12	1-3	.992	3	103	153	O69(38/7/25)/3	0	-1.3
1959	Det A	65	106	7	14	3	0	6	11	12-0	1	10	.132	.225	.330	48	-8	0-0	1.000	-1	90	0	O21(3/1/17)	0	-1.0
1960	Det A	96	220	27	56	10	3	5	24	19-0	1	26	.255	.311	.395	89	-4	2-0	.981	1	110	66	O47(31/4/12),1b2	0	-0.5
1961	Mil N	10	9	1	2	0	0	0	0	1-0	0	1	.222	.300	.222	44	-1	0-0	ø	0	—	—	/H	0	-0.1
Total	5	302	619	60	130	22	8	16	64	55-2	2	62	.210	.275	.349	69	-30	3-3	.975	2	102	101	O148(76/12/61),1b2/3	0	-3.5
CHRISTENBURY, LLOYD	Lloyd Reid "Low"; B10.19.1893 Mecklenburg Co. NC; D12.13.1944 Birmingham AL; BL/TR/5´7˝/165; d9.20; Col Davidson																								
1919	Bos N	7	31	5	9	1	0	0	4	2	0	2	.290	.333	.323	102	0	0	.941	1	93	208	O7L	—	0.1
1920	Bos N	65	106	17	22	2	2	0	14	13	1	12	.208	.300	.264	66	-4	0-1	.895	-3	84	86	O14(0/7/7),S7,2b6,3b2	—	-0.8
1921	Bos N	62	125	34	44	6	2	3	16	21	1	7	.352	.449	.504	161	12	3-4	.914	-10	81	69	2b32,S2,3b2	—	0.3
1922	Bos N	71	152	22	38	5	2	1	13	18	2	11	.250	.337	.329	76	-5	2-4	.946	2	109	139	O32(30/0/2),2b5,3b2	—	-0.6
Total	4	205	414	78	113	14	6	4	47	54	4	32	.273	.362	.365	101	3	5-9	.936	-10	102	141	O53(37/7/9),2b43,S9,3b6	—	-1.0
CHRISTENSEN, BRUCE	Bruce Ray; B2.22.1948 Madison WI; BL/TR/5´11˝/165; [AnaA66 17/328]; d7.17																								
1971	Cal A	29	63	4	17	1	0	0	3	6-1	0	5	.270	.333	.286	82	-1	0-1	.988	-2	97	123	S24	0	-0.1
CHRISTENSEN, JOHN	John Lawrence; B9.5.1960 Downey CA; BR/TR/6´0˝/180; [NYN81 2/38]; d9.13; Col Cal St.–Fullerton																								
1984	NY N	5	11	2	3	2	0	0	3	1-0	0	2	.273	.308	.455	121	0	0-1	.500	-1	20	0	O5(3/0/2)	0	-0.1
1985	NY N	51	113	10	21	4	1	3	13	19-1	0	23	.186	.303	.319	75	-4	1-2	.956	-4	69	93	O38(6/2/31)	0	-1.0
1987	Sea A	53	132	19	32	6	1	2	12	12-0	0	28	.242	.306	.348	69	-6	2-0	1.000	1	98	136	O43(2/0/41),D8	39	-0.6
1988	Min A	23	38	5	10	4	0	0	5	3-1	2	5	.263	.349	.368	98	0	0-0	1.000	-0	99	0	O17R/D	0	0.0
Total	4	132	294	36	66	16	2	5	33	35-2	2	58	.224	.310	.344	77	-10	3-3	.977	-5	83	95	O103(11/2/91),D9	39	-1.7
CHRISTENSEN, MC KAY	McKay Andrew; B8.14.1975 Upland CA; BL/TL/5´11˝/180; [AnaA94 1/6]; d4.6																								
1999	Chi A	28	53	10	12	1	0	1	6	4-0	0	7	.226	.271	.302	48	-4	2-1	.943	-0	116	0	O27C	0	-0.4
2000	†Chi A	32	19	4	2	0	0	0	1	2-0	1	6	.105	.227	.105	-11	-3	1-1	1.000	0	91	235	O29C	0	-0.3
2001	Chi A	7	4	0	1	0	0	0	0	0-0	1	2	.250	.400	.250	73	0	0-0	1.000	-1	37	0	O6C	0	-0.1
	LA N	28	49	7	16	2	0	1	7	3-0	3	10	.327	.400	.429	122	2	3-2	.917	-1	88	0	O14(3/11/0)	0	0.0
2002	NY N	4	3	1	1	0	0	0	0	1-0	0	1	.333	.500	.333	132	0	0-0	1.000	0	190	0	O3(2/1/0)	0	0.0
Total	4	99	128	22	32	3	0	2	14	10-0	5	26	.250	.324	.320	68	-5	6-4	.951	-2	100	51	O79(5/74/0)	0	-0.8
CHRISTENSEN, CUCKOO	Walter Niels "Seacap"; B10.24.1899 San Francisco CA; D12.20.1984 Menlo Park CA; BL/TL/5´6.5˝/156; d4.13																								
1926	Cin N	114	329	41	115	15	7	0	41	40	4	18	.350	.426	.438	136	19	8	.978	-5	92	71	O93(72/19/9)	—	0.9
1927	Cin N	57	185	25	47	6	0	0	16	20	1	16	.254	.330	.286	68	-8	4	.957	-2	87	119	O50(11/35/4)	—	-1.2
Total	2	171	514	66	162	21	7	0	57	60	5	34	.315	.392	.383	112	11	12	.970	-7	90	88	O143(83/54/13)	—	-0.3
CHRISTENSON, RYAN	Ryan Alan; B3.28.1974 Redlands CA; BR/TR/6´0˝/(175–191); [OakA95 10/260]; d4.20; Col Pepperdine																								
1998	Oak A	117	370	56	95	22	2	5	40	36-0	1	106	.257	.321	.368	80	-10	5-6	.983	2	104	105	O116(1/113/4)	0	-0.8
1999	Oak A	106	268	41	56	12	1	4	24	38-0	1	58	.209	.305	.306	59	-16	7-5	.969	-1	105	60	O104C/D	0	-1.6
2000	†Oak A	121	129	31	32	2	2	4	18	19-0	1	33	.248	.349	.388	87	-3	1-2	.951	-2	92	78	O114(76/27/14)	0	-0.5
2001	Ari N	19	4	3	1	1	0	0	1	1-0	0	1	.250	.400	.500	122	0	1-0	1.000	-0	69	0	O5(4/1/0)	0	0.0
	Oak A	7	4	1	0	0	0	0	0	0-0	0	1	.000	.000	.000	-99	-1	0-0	1.000	-0	61	0	O4(1/1/3)/D	0	-0.1
2002	Mil N	22	58	5	9	4	0	1	3	5-0	0	13	.155	.222	.276	30	-6	0-0	1.000	-1	103	0	O21(6/16/0)	0	-0.7
2003	Tex A	60	165	22	29	7	0	2	16	15-0	3	44	.176	.255	.255	33	-16	2-2	1.000	-0	107	0	O59C	0	-1.5
Total	6	452	998	159	222	48	5	16	102	114-0	6	256	.222	.303	.329	64	-52	16-15	.979	-2	103	65	O423(88/321/21),D2	0	-5.2
CHRISTIAN, BOB	Robert Charles; B10.17.1945 Chicago IL; D2.20.1974 San Diego CA; BR/TR/5´10˝/180; d9.2; Col Grossmont (CA) JC																								
1968	Det A	3	3	0	1	1	0	0	0	0-0	0	0	.333	.333	.667	192	0	0-0	1.000	-0	0	0	/1rf	0	0.0
1969	Chi A	39	129	11	28	4	0	3	16	10-1	1	19	.217	.273	.318	63	-7	3-0	.958	-0	99	105	O38(37/0/1)	0	-0.9
1970	Chi A	12	15	3	4	0	0	1	3	1-0	0	4	.267	.313	.467	108	0	0-0	1.000	-1	51	0	O4L	0	-0.1
Total	3	54	147	14	33	5	0	4	19	11-1	1	23	.224	.278	.340	70	-7	3-0	.959	-1	96	98	O43(41/0/2)/1	0	-1.0
CHRISTMAN, MARK	Marquette Joseph; B10.21.1913 Maplewood MO; D10.9.1976 St.Louis MO; BR/TR/5´11˝/180; d4.20																								
1938	Det A	95	318	35	79	6	4	1	44	27	0	21	.248	.307	.302	50	-25	5-2	.983	10	109	118	3b69,S21	—	-1.1
1939	Det A	6	16	0	4	2	0	0	0	0	0	2	.250	.250	.375	54	-1	0-0	.900	-1	72	155	3b5	—	-0.1
	StL A	79	222	27	48	6	3	0	20	20	0	10	.216	.281	.270	41	-20	2-1	.960	14	112	103	S64/2	—	-0.2
	Year	85	238	27	52	8	3	0	20	20	0	12	.218	.279	.277	42	-22	2-1	.960	13	112	103	S64,3b5/2	—	-0.3
1943	StL A	98	336	31	91	11	5	2	35	19	4	19	.271	.318	.351	94	-4	0-3	.991	2	111	78	3b37,S24,1b20,2b14	0	-0.2
1944	†StL A	148	547	56	148	25	1	6	83	47	3	37	.271	.332	.353	90	-6	5-2	**.972**	4	98	**125**	3b145,1b3	0	-0.1
1945	StL A	78	289	32	80	7	4	4	34	19	3	19	.277	.328	.370	98	-2	1-0	.973	-1	94	94	3b77	0	-0.2
1946	StL A	128	458	40	118	22	2	1	41	22	2	29	.258	.295	.321	68	-20	0-2	.975	9	116	125	3b77,S47	0	-0.9
1947	Was A	110	374	27	83	15	2	1	33	32	2	16	.222	.287	.281	60	-21	4-4	.978	-6	94	100	S106/2	0	-2.2
1948	Was A	120	409	38	106	17	2	1	40	25	1	19	.259	.303	.318	67	-21	0-3	.969	-25	85	75	S102,3b9,2b3	0	-4.0
1949	Was A	49	112	8	24	2	0	3	18	8	1	7	.214	.273	.313	56	-8	0-0	.967	3	122	157	3b23,1b6,S4/2	0	-0.5
Total	9	911	3081	294	781	113	23	19	348	219	16	179	.253	.306	.324	71	-128	17-17	.975	8	104	115	3b442,S368,1b29,2b20	0	-9.5
CHRISTMAS, STEVE	Stephen Randall; B12.9.1957 Orlando FL; BL/TR/6´0˝/190; d9.1; Col Southwestern Oklahoma																								
1983	Cin N	9	17	0	1	0	0	0	1	1-0	0	3	.059	.105	.059	-50	-4	0-0	1.000	1	122	168	C7	0	-0.2
1984	Chi A	12	11	1	4	1	0	1	4	0-0	0	2	.364	.364	.727	184	1	0-0	1.000	0	6	0	/C	0	0.1
1986	Chi N	3	9	0	1	1	0	0	2	0-0	0	1	.111	.111	.222	-10	-1	0-0	1.000	0	32	224	/C1	69	-0.1
Total	3	24	37	1	6	2	0	1	7	1-0	0	6	.162	.179	.297	30	-4	0-0	1.000	1	102	175	C9/1	69	-0.2
CHRISTOPHER, JOE	Joseph O'Neal; B12.13.1935 Frederiksted, V.I.; BR/TR/5´10˝/(175–182); d5.26																								
1959	Pit N	15	12	6	0	0	0	0	0	1-0	0	4	.000	.077	.000	-78	-3	0-0	1.000	-1	66	0	O9R	0	-0.4
1960	†Pit N	50	56	21	13	2	0	1	3	5-0	0	8	.232	.295	.321	68	-2	1-0	1.000	-1	92	0	O17(11/5/1)	0	-0.4
1961	Pit N	76	186	25	49	7	3	0	14	18-0	0	24	.263	.327	.333	76	-6	6-4	.978	-1	98	53	O55(45/5/5)	0	-1.0
1962	NY N	119	271	36	66	10	2	6	32	35-0	4	42	.244	.338	.362	87	-4	11-3	.972	-3	90	89	O94(19/34/42)	0	-1.0
1963	NY N	64	149	19	33	5	1	1	8	13-0	3	21	.221	.295	.289	68	-6	1-3	.983	-2	97	39	O45(6/0/40)	0	-1.1
1964	NY N	154	543	78	163	26	8	16	76	48-5	6	92	.300	.360	.466	135	25	6-5	.974	-3	96	93	O145(7/10/129)	0	1.3
1965	NY N	148	437	38	109	18	3	5	40	35-3	6	82	.249	.311	.339	87	-7	4-4	.989	-5	94	44	O112(62/0/51)	0	-2.0

YEAR	TM LG	G	AB	R	H	2B	3B	HR	RBI	BB-IB	HP	SO	AVG	OBP	SLG	AOPS	ABR	SB-CS	FA	FR	RNG	THR	GAMES AT POSITION	DL	BFW
1966	Bos A	12	13	1	1	0	0	0	0	2-0	0	4	.077	.200	.077	-15	-2	0-0	1.000	-0	47	0	O2L	0	-0.2
Total	8	638	1667	224	434	68	17	29	173	157-8	19	277	.260	.329	.374	96	-5	29-19	.979	-16	94	67	O479(152/54/277)	0	-4.8
CHRISTOPHER, LOYD	Loyd Eugene; B12.31.1919 Richmond CA; D9.5.1991 Richmond CA; BR/TR/6´2˝/190; d4.20; b–Russ																								
1945	Bos A	8	14	4	4	0	0	0	4	3	0	2	.286	.412	.286	101	0	0-0	1.000	-0	78	0	O3C	0	0.0
	Chi N	1	0	0	0	0	0	0	0	0	0	0	ø	ø	ø	ø	0	0	ø	-0	0	0	/lf	0	0.0
1947	Chi A	7	23	1	5	0	1	0	0	2	0	4	.217	.280	.304	65	-1	0-1	1.000	1	114	192	O7L	0	-0.1
Total	2	16	37	5	9	0	1	0	4	5	0	6	.243	.333	.297	80	-1	0-1	1.000	1	104	143	O11(8/3/0)	0	-0.1
CHURCH, HI	Hiram Lincoln; B11.23.1863 Central Square NY; D2.23.1926 Jacksonville FL; d8.23; Col Syracuse																								
1890	Bro AA	3	9	1	1	0	0	0	0	0	0	—	.111	.111	.111	-36	-2	0	1.000	-1	0	0	O3L	—	-0.2
CHURCH, RYAN	Ryan Matthew; B10.14.1978 Santa Barbara CA; BL/TL/6´1˝/190; [CleA00 14/426]; d8.21; Col Nevada–Reno																								
2004	Mon N	30	63	6	11	1	0	1	6	7-1	0	16	.175	.257	.238	28	-7	0-0	1.000	3	124	360	O18(12/2/6)	0	-0.4
2005	Was N	102	268	41	77	15	3	9	42	24-0	5	70	.287	.353	.466	119	7	3-2	1.000	4	118	50	O85(51/20/21)	35	0.9
2006	Was N	71	196	22	54	17	1	10	35	26-0	3	60	.276	.366	.526	131	10	6-1	.986	2	112	74	O62(2/51/14)	0	1.2
Total	3	203	527	69	142	33	4	20	83	57-1	8	146	.269	.347	.461	112	10	9-3	.994	10	116	92	O165(65/73/41)	35	1.7
CHURRY, JOHN	John; B11.26.1900 Johnstown PA; D2.8.1970 Zanesville OH; BR/TR/5´9˝/172; d5.24																								
1924	Chi N	6	7	0	1	1	0	0	0	2	0	0	.143	.333	.286	67	0	0-0	1.000	0	*90*	*135*	C3	—	0.0
1925	Chi N	3	6	1	3	0	0	0	1	0	0	0	.500	.500	.500	154	0	0-0	1.000	0	*61*	*422*	C3	—	0.0
1926	Chi N	2	4	0	0	0	0	0	0	1	0	2	.000	.200	.000	-42	-1	0	1.000	0	*0*	*0*	/C	—	-0.1
1927	Chi N	1	1	0	1	0	0	0	0	0	0	0	1.000	1.000	1.000	436	0	0	1.000	0	*0*	*0*	/C	—	0.1
Total	4	12	18	1	5	1	0	0	1	3	0	2	.278	.381	.333	89	-1	0-0	1.000	0	*52*	*170*	C8	—	0.0
CIAFFONE, LARRY	Lawrence Thomas "Symphony Larry"; B8.17.1924 Brooklyn NY; D12.14.1991 Brooklyn NY; BR/TR/5´9.5˝/185; d4.17																								
1951	StL N	5	5	0	0	0	0	0	0	1	0	2	.000	.167	.000	-51	-1	0-0	1.000	0	103	0	/lf	0	-0.1
CIANFROCCO, ARCHI	Angelo Dominic; B10.6.1966 Rome NY; BR/TR/6´5˝/(200–215); [MonN87 5/122]; d4.8; Col Purdue; OF(8/0/17)																								
1992	Mon N	86	232	25	56	5	2	6	30	11-0	1	66	.241	.276	.358	79	-8	3-0	.993	1	117	81	1b56,3b19,O5L	0	-1.0
1993	Mon N	12	17	3	4	1	0	1	1	0-0	0	5	.235	.235	.471	80	-1	0-0	1.000	-0	62	173	1b11	0	-0.1
	SD N	84	279	27	68	10	2	11	47	17-1	3	64	.244	.289	.412	86	-7	2-0	.932	-7	76	85	3b64,1b31	0	-1.5
	Year	96	296	30	72	11	2	12	48	17-1	3	69	.243	.287	.416	85	-7	2-0	.932	-7	76	85	3b64,1b42	0	-1.6
1994	SD N	59	146	9	32	8	0	4	13	3-0	4	39	.219	.252	.356	59	-9	2-0	.920	3	106	42	3b37,1b16/S	0	-0.7
1995	SD N	51	118	22	31	7	0	5	31	11-1	2	28	.263	.333	.449	108	1	0-2	1.000	0	88	84	1b30,S15,O7(2/0/5),2b3,3b3	0	0.1
1996	†SD N	79	192	21	54	13	3	2	32	8-0	2	56	.281	.315	.411	94	-2	1-0	1.000	-5	96	83	1b33,3b11,S10,O8(1/0/7),2b6/C	31	-0.8
1997	SD N	89	220	25	54	12	0	4	26	25-1	3	80	.245	.328	.355	85	-5	7-1	.983	7	110	80	1b39,3b38,2b12,S5,O2R	0	0.2
1998	SD N	40	72	4	9	3	0	1	5	5-0	1	22	.125	.192	.208	6	-10	1-0	1.000	1	138	136	1b19,3b13,2b3,O3R	29	-1.0
Total	7	500	1276	136	308	59	7	34	185	80-3	16	360	.241	.292	.379	80	-41	16-3	.994	0	113	91	1b235,3b185,S31,O25R,2b24/C	60	-4.8
CIAS, DARRYL	Darryl Richard; B4.23.1957 New York NY; BR/TR/5´11˝/188; [BalA75 6/143]; d4.27																								
1983	Oak A	19	18	1	6	1	0	0	1	2-0	0	4	.333	.400	.389	125	1	1-0	.967	-3	55	45	C19	0	-0.2
CICERO, JOE	Joseph Francis "Dode"; B11.18.1910 Atlantic City NJ; D3.30.1983 Clearwater FL; BR/TR/5´8˝/167; d9.20																								
1929	Bos A	10	32	6	10	2	2	0	4	0	0	2	.313	.313	.500	108	0	0-0	1.000	-0	101	0	O7(1/6/0)	—	-0.1
1930	Bos A	18	30	5	5	1	2	0	4	1	0	5	.167	.194	.333	32	-4	0-0	ø	-0	0	0	O5(1/0/4),3b2	—	-0.3
1945	Phi A	12	19	3	3	0	0	0	0	1	1	6	.158	.238	.158	16	-2	0-0	1.000	-0	91	0	O7(1/0/6)	0	-0.3
Total	3	40	81	14	18	3	4	0	8	2	1	13	.222	.250	.358	60	-6	0-0	1.000	-1	94	0	O19(3/6/10),3b2	0	-0.7
CIESLAK, TED	Thaddeus Walter; B11.22.1912 Milwaukee WI; D5.9.1993 Milwaukee WI; BR/TR/5´10˝/175; d4.18																								
1944	Phi N	85	220	18	54	10	0	2	11	21	1	17	.245	.314	.318	81	-5	1	.877	-12	81	14	3b48,O5L	0	-1.8
CIHOCKI, AL	Albert Joseph; B5.7.1924 Nanticoke PA; BR/TR/5´11˝/185; d4.17																								
1945	Cle A	92	283	21	60	9	3	0	24	11	0	48	.212	.241	.265	49	-20	2-1	.946	-2	100	117	S41,3b29,2b23	0	-1.9
CIHOCKI, ED	Edward Joseph "Cy"; B5.9.1907 Wilmington DE; D11.9.1987 Newark DE; BR/TR/5´8˝/163; d5.29																								
1932	Phi A	1	1	0	0	0	0	0	0	0	0	0	.000	.000	.000	-97	0	0-0	ø	0	—	—	/H	—	0.0
1933	Phi A	33	97	6	14	2	3	0	9	7	0	16	.144	.202	.227	13	-13	0-0	.904	-2	95	120	S28/23	—	-1.3
Total	2	34	98	6	14	2	3	0	9	7	0	16	.143	.200	.224	12	-13	0-0	.904	-2	95	120	S28/32	—	-1.3
CIMOLI, GINO	Gino Nicholas (b Gino Anichletto Cimoli); B12.18.1929 San Francisco CA; BR/TR/6´2˝/(180–205); d4.19																								
1956	†Bro N	73	36	3	4	1	0	0	4	1-1	0	8	.111	.135	.139	-24	-6	1-0	.946	1	132	0	O62(52/8/3)	0	-0.6
1957	Bro N★	142	532	88	156	22	5	10	57	39-1	4	86	.293	.343	.410	93	-4	3-1	.979	0	97	116	O138(81/24/51)	0	-1.1
1958	LA N	109	325	35	80	6	3	9	27	18-0	3	49	.246	.292	.366	71	-15	3-3	.974	0	95	154	O104(34/68/12)	0	-2.0
1959	StL N	143	519	61	145	40	7	8	72	37-2	2	83	.279	.327	.430	94	-4	7-0	.979	4	103	132	O141(43/45/55)	0	-0.5
1960	†Pit N	101	307	36	82	14	4	0	28	32-3	1	43	.267	.336	.339	85	-5	1-0	.964	-3	99	76	O91(27/58/17)	0	-1.2
1961	Pit N	21	67	4	20	3	1	0	6	2-0	0	13	.299	.319	.373	83	-2	0-0	.971	-0	100	76	O19(14/5/0)	0	-0.3
	Mil N	37	117	12	23	5	0	3	4	11-0	0	15	.197	.266	.316	57	-7	1-0	.985	-4	88	0	O31(0/30/1)	0	-1.2
	Year	58	184	16	43	8	1	3	10	13-0	0	28	.234	.284	.337	67	-9	1-0	.980	-4	92	28	O50(14/35/1)	0	-1.5
1962	KC A	152	550	67	151	20	**15**	10	71	40-2	2	89	.275	.323	.420	95	-6	2-1	.968	-7	89	101	O147(5/10/138)	0	-2.3
1963	KC A	145	529	56	139	19	11	4	48	39-3	2	72	.263	.313	.363	85	-11	3-1	.985	4	100	156	O136(2/13/130)	0	-1.7
1964	KC A	4	9	1	0	0	0	0	0	0-0	0	1	.000	.000	.000	-97	-2	0-0	1.000	0	152	0	O4(1/0/3)	0	-0.2
	Bal A	38	58	6	8	3	2	0	3	2-1	0	13	.138	.164	.259	16	-7	0-0	.893	-2	84	0	O35(11/2/23)	0	-1.1
	Year	42	67	7	8	3	2	0	3	2-1	0	14	.119	.143	.224	1	-9	0-0	.912	-2	92	0	O39(12/2/26)	0	-1.3
1965	Cal A	4	5	1	0	0	0	0	1	0-0	0	2	.000	.000	.000	-99	-1	0-0	1.000	0	162	0	/rf	0	-0.1
Total	10	969	3054	370	808	133	48	44	321	221-13	14	474	.265	.315	.383	84	-70	21-6	.974	-7	97	113	O909(270/263/434)	0	-12.3
CINTRON, ALEX	Alexander; B12.17.1978 Humacao, PR; BB/TR/6´1˝/(170–205); [AriN97 36/1103]; d7.24																								
2001	Ari N	8	7	0	2	0	1	0	0	0-0	0	0	.286	.286	.571	106	0	0-0	1.000	0	112	0	S7	0	0.0
2002	†Ari N	38	75	11	16	6	0	0	4	12-2	0	13	.213	.322	.293	58	-4	0-0	1.000	-0	76	103	2b18,3b9,S8	0	-0.3
2003	Ari N	117	448	70	142	26	6	13	51	29-0	2	33	.317	.359	.489	110	6	2-3	.979	-2	89	101	S93,3b16,2b9	0	1.1
2004	Ari N	154	564	56	148	31	7	4	49	31-2	2	59	.262	.301	.363	67	-28	3-3	.972	-1	103	72	S133,2b19/3	0	-1.9
2005	Ari N	122	330	36	90	19	2	8	48	12-3	1	33	.273	.298	.415	81	-10	1-2	.966	-3	111	92	S39,3b32,2b23	0	-1.0
2006	Chi A	91	288	35	82	10	3	5	41	10-0	2	35	.285	.310	.392	79	-10	10-3	.973	-10	91	85	S41,2b26,3b11,D8	0	-1.4
Total	6	530	1712	208	480	92	19	30	193	94-7	7	173	.280	.318	.409	83	-46	16-11	.974	-16	98	86	S321,2b95,3b69,D8	0	-3.5
CIPRIANI, FRANK	Frank Dominick; B4.14.1941 Buffalo NY; BR/TR/6´0˝/185; d9.8; Col Fordham																								
1961	KC A	13	36	2	9	0	0	0	2	2-0	0	4	.250	.289	.250	45	-3	0-0	1.000	-0	109	0	O11R	0	-0.4
CIRILLO, JEFF	Jeffrey Howard; B9.23.1969 Pasadena CA; BR/TR/6´2˝/(180–200); [MilA91 11/286]; d5.11; Col USC																								
1994	Mil A	39	126	17	30	9	0	3	12	11-0	2	16	.238	.309	.381	73	-5	0-1	.965	-3	92	144	3b37/2	0	-0.8
1995	Mil A	125	328	57	91	19	4	9	39	47-0	4	42	.277	.371	.442	105	4	7-2	.938	10	117	**168**	3b108,2b25,1b3,S2	0	1.5
1996	Mil A	158	566	101	184	46	5	15	83	58-0	7	69	.325	.391	.504	120	19	4-9	.950	-14	92	69	3b154,1b2/2D	0	0.3
1997	Mil A★	154	580	74	167	46	2	10	82	60-0	14	74	.288	.367	.426	105	7	4-3	.963	**24**	**117**	119	3b150,D2	0	3.0
1998	Mil N	156	604	97	194	31	1	14	68	79-3	4	88	.321	.402	.445	121	22	10-4	.976	22	113	**164**	3b149,1b6	0	4.3
1999	Mil N	157	607	98	198	35	1	15	88	75-4	5	83	.326	.401	.461	118	20	7-4	.967	7	105	130	3b155	0	2.6
2000	Col N★	157	598	111	195	53	2	11	115	67-4	6	72	.326	.392	.477	97	1	3-4	.964	7	106	**144**	3b155	0	0.8
2001	Col N	138	528	72	165	26	4	17	83	43-6	5	63	.313	.364	.473	96	-2	12-2	**.982**	18	**117**	105	3b137	16	1.8
2002	Sea A	146	485	51	121	20	0	6	54	31-0	9	67	.249	.301	.328	71	-20	8-4	**.973**	1	92	118	3b141,1b11	0	-1.8
2003	Sea A	87	258	24	53	11	0	2	23	24-1	5	32	.205	.284	.271	51	-18	1-1	.977	-10	78	60	3b85/1	26	-2.7
2004	SD N	33	75	12	16	3	0	1	7	5-0	0	14	.213	.259	.293	46	-6	0-0	1.000	-3	59	66	3b11,1b10,2b4/lf	37	-1.0
2005	Mil N	77	185	29	52	15	0	4	23	23-0	4	22	.281	.373	.427	108	3	4-2	.951	-5	82	104	3b53,2b3/1	68	-0.1
2006	Mil N	112	263	33	84	16	0	3	23	21-0	1	33	.319	.369	.414	100	1	1-1	.978	4	101	153	3b42,1b13,2b12,S3	0	0.5
Total	13	1539	5203	776	1550	330	19	110	700	544-18	66	675	.298	.368	.432	101	26	61-37	.967	58	103	121	3b1377,1b47,2b46,D5,S5/lf	147	8.4
CISAR, GEORGE	George Joseph; B8.25.1912 Chicago IL; BR/TR/6´0˝/175; d9.9																								
1937	Bro N	20	29	8	6	0	0	0	4	2	0	6	.207	.258	.207	27	-3	3	1.000	0	119	0	O13(9/0/4)	—	-0.3

YEAR	TM LG	G	AB	R	H	2B	3B	HR	RBI	BB-IB	HP	SO	AVG	OBP	SLG	AOPS	ABR	SB-CS	FA	FR	RNG	THR	GAMES AT POSITION	DL	BFW
CISSELL, BILL	Chalmer William; B1.3.1904 Perryville MO; D3.15.1949 Chicago IL; BR/TR/5´11˝/170; d4.11																								
1928	Chi A	125	443	66	115	22	3	1	60	29	1	41	.260	.307	.330	68	-21	18-6	.938	1	102	107	S123	—	-0.5
1929	Chi A	**152**	618	83	173	27	12	5	62	28	1	53	.280	.312	.387	80	-22	25-17	.937	-3	100	97	S152	—	-0.8
1930	Chi A	141	562	82	152	28	9	2	48	28	2	32	.270	.307	.363	72	-26	16-9	.948	-9	97	88	2b107,3b24,S10	—	-2.7
1931	Chi A	109	409	42	90	13	5	1	46	16	4	26	.220	.256	.284	44	-35	18-6	.944	-7	97	96	S83,2b23/3	—	-3.2
1932	Chi A	12	43	7	11	1	1	1	5	1	0	0	.256	.273	.395	76	-2	0-0	.928	-1	72	120	S12	—	-0.2
	Cle A	131	541	78	173	35	6	6	93	28	1	25	.320	.354	.440	98	-2	18-15	.964	5	**106**	99	2b129,S6	—	0.9
	Year	143	584	85	184	36	7	7	98	29	1	25	.315	.349	.437	97	-4	18-15	.964	4	**106**	99	2b129,S18	—	0.7
1933	Cle A	112	409	53	94	21	3	6	33	31	0	29	.230	.284	.340	62	-24	6-6	.947	-3	98	68	2b62,S46/3	—	-1.9
1934	Bos A	102	416	71	111	13	4	4	44	28	1	23	.267	.315	.346	66	-22	11-4	.959	-3	96	94	2b96,S7,3b2	—	-1.7
1937	Phi A	34	117	15	31	7	0	1	14	17	0	10	.265	.358	.350	81	-3	0-0	.962	1	107	69	2b33	—	0.0
1938	NY N	38	149	19	40	6	0	2	18	6	0	11	.268	.297	.349	76	-5	1	.977	8	115	99	2b33,3b6	—	0.5
Total	9	956	3707	516	990	173	43	29	423	212	10	250	.267	.308	.360	73	-162	113-63	.958	-12	101	88	2b483,S439,3b34	—	-9.6
CLABAUGH, MOOSE	John William; B11.13.1901 Albany MO; D7.11.1984 Tucson AZ; BL/TR/6´0˝/185; d8.30																								
1926	Bro N	11	14	2	1	1	0	0	1	0	1	1	.071	.133	.143	-26	-3	0	.600	-1	84	0	O2L	—	-0.3
CLACK, BOBBY	Robert Suter "Gentlemanly Bob"; B6.13.1850 , England; D10.22.1933 Danvers MA; BR/TR/5´9˝/153; d5.13																								
1874	Atl NA	33	135	22	23	1	0	0	13	4	—	2	.170	.194	.178	23	-10	0-0	.779	-3	110	0	O31(1/30/0),1b2	—	-1.0
1875	Atl NA	17	59	1	6	0	0	0	1	0	—	3	.102	.102	.102	-33	-7	0-0	.867	2	154	325	O17(0/16/1)/1	—	-0.4
1876	Cin N	32	118	10	19	0	1	0	5	5	—	12	.161	.195	.178	29	-8	—	.736	-2	90	0	O17(0/3/14),2b8,1b5,3b3/P	—	-0.8
Total	2NA	50	194	23	29	1	0	0	14	4	—	5	.149	.167	.155	7	-17	0-0	.811	-0	125	108	O48(1/46/1),1b3	—	-1.4
CLAIRE, DAVEY	David Matthew; B11.17.1897 Ludington MI; D1.7.1956 Las Vegas NV; BR/TR/5´8˝/164; d9.17																								
1920	Det A	3	7	1	1	0	0	0	0	0	0	0	.143	.143	.143	-25	-1	0-0	.800	-1	105	0	S3	—	-0.2
CLANCY, AL	Albert Harrison; B8.14.1888 Santa Fe NM; D10.17.1951 Las Cruces NM; BR/TR/5´10.5˝/175; d6.20																								
1911	StL A	3	5	0	0	0	0	0	0	0	1	—	.000	.167	.000	-54	-1	0	.800	0	120	532	3b2	—	-0.1
CLANCY, BUD	John William; B9.15.1900 Odell IL; D9.26.1968 Ottumwa IA; BL/TL/6´0˝/170; d8.29																								
1924	Chi A	13	35	5	9	1	0	0	6	3	0	2	.257	.316	.286	58	-2	3-2	.947	-2	54	67	1b8	—	-0.4
1925	Chi A	4	3	0	0	0	0	0	0	1	0	0	.000	.250	.000	-34	-1	0-0	ø	0	—	—	/H	—	-0.1
1926	Chi A	12	38	3	13	2	2	0	7	1	1	1	.342	.375	.500	132	1	0-0	.991	-0	94	153	1b10	—	0.1
1927	Chi A	130	464	46	139	21	2	3	53	24	2	24	.300	.337	.373	86	-10	4-3	.991	-1	97	85	1b123	—	-1.9
1928	Chi A	130	487	64	132	19	11	2	37	42	2	25	.271	.331	.368	85	-12	6-9	.991	4	**112**	104	1b128	—	-1.8
1929	Chi A	92	290	36	82	14	6	3	45	16	0	19	.283	.320	.403	86	-7	3-1	.991	2	113	83	1b74	—	-0.9
1930	Chi A	68	234	28	57	8	3	3	27	12	2	18	.244	.286	.342	61	-15	3-1	.995	-3	72	79	1b60	—	-2.0
1932	Bro N	53	196	14	60	4	2	0	16	6	0	13	.306	.327	.347	83	-5	0	.996	3	116	126	1b53	—	-0.7
1934	Phi N	20	49	8	12	0	0	1	7	6	1	4	.245	.339	.306	65	-2	0	1.000	-1	65	134	1b10	—	-0.4
Total	9	522	1796	204	504	69	26	12	198	111	8	106	.281	.325	.368	82	-53	19-16	.992	2	101	96	1b466	—	-8.1
CLANCY, BILL	William Edward; B4.12.1879 Redfield NY; D2.10.1948 Oriskany NY; BR/TR/6´2˝/180; d4.14																								
1905	Pit N	56	227	23	52	11	3	2	34	4	1	—	.229	.246	.330	69	-10	3	.983	-3	81	118	1b52,O4R	—	-1.4
CLANTON, UKE	Eucal "Cat"; B2.19.1898 Powell MO; D2.24.1960 Antlers OK; BL/TL/5´8˝/165; d9.21; Col Oklahoma																								
1922	Cle A	1	1	0	0	0	0	0	0	0	0	1	.000	.000	.000	-99	0	0-0	.500	-0	0	0	/1	—	-0.1
CLAPINSKI, CHRIS	Christopher Alan; B8.20.1971 Buffalo NY; BB/TR/6´0˝/175; d7.17; Col California																								
1999	Fla N	36	56	6	13	1	2	0	2	9-0	1	12	.232	.348	.321	75	-2	1-0	.882	-1	65	72	3b9,S6,O3L,2b2/D	0	-0.2
2000	Fla N	34	49	12	15	4	1	1	7	5-0	0	7	.306	.370	.490	121	2	0-0	.933	-1	97	65	2b14,3b3,O3L/S	0	0.1
Total	2	70	105	18	28	5	3	1	9	14-0	1	19	.267	.358	.400	97	0	1-0	.935	-2	101	64	2b16,3b12,S7,O6L/D	0	-0.1
CLAPP, AARON	Aaron Bronson; B7.1856 Ithaca NY; D1.13.1914 Sayre PA; TR/5´8˝/175; d5.1; b–John																								
1879	Tro N	36	146	24	39	9	3	0	18	6	—	10	.267	.296	.370	126	5	—	.935	-3	63	80	1b25,O11(7/1/3)	—	0.0
CLAPP, JOHN	John Edgar; B7.17.1851 Ithaca NY; D12.18.1904 Ithaca NY; BR/TR/5´7˝/194; d4.26; M6; b–Aaron; OF(62/19/21)																								
1872	Man NA	19	97	30	27	7	1	1	16	1	—	0	.278	.286	.402	116	2	2-1	.845	-1	—	—	C19,S2/1cfM	—	0.1
1873	Ath NA	45	204	36	62	10	2	1	27	2	—	2	.304	.311	.387	98	-2	4-5	.893	2	—	—	C43,S6/2cf	—	0.0
1874	Ath NA	39	165	46	48	7	4	3	19	1	—	1	.291	.295	.436	121	3	2-0	.861	7	—	—	C27,O15(0/1/14)/S	—	0.8
1875	Ath NA	60	292	65	77	8	7	0	39	7	—	1	.264	.281	.339	103	-1	9-5	.874	18	—	—	C60	—	1.5
1876	StL N	**64**	298	60	91	4	2	0	29	8	—	2	.305	.324	.332	125	9	—	.874	10	—	—	C61,O4(0/1/3)/2	—	1.8
1877	StL N	**60**	255	47	81	6	6	0	34	8	—	6	.318	.338	.388	135	10	—	.887	-5	—	—	C53,O10(2/0/9)/1	—	0.6
1878	Ind N	**63**	263	42	80	10	2	0	29	13	—	8	.304	.337	.357	148	16	—	.890	-3	48	0	O44L,1b12,C9,S3/2M	—	0.9
1879	Buf N	70	292	47	77	12	5	1	36	11	—	11	.264	.290	.349	107	2	—	.906	-8	—	—	C63,O7R,M	—	-0.4
1880	Cin N	80	323	33	91	16	4	1	20	21	—	10	.282	.326	.365	135	13	—	.897	19	—	—	C73,O10(1/9/0),M	—	**3.2**
1881	Cle N	68	261	47	66	12	2	0	25	**35**	—	6	.253	.341	.314	113	7	—	.890	-3	—	—	C48,O21(15/6/0),M	—	0.4
1883	NY N	20	73	6	13	0	0	0	5	5	—	4	.178	.231	.178	27	-6	—	.895	3	—	—	C16,O5(0/3/2),M	—	-0.2
Total	4NA	163	758	177	214	32	14	5	101	11	—	4	.282	.293	.381	107	2	17-11	.873	26	—	—	C149,O17(0/3/14),S9/21	—	2.4
Total	7	425	1765	282	499	60	21	2	178	101	—	47	.283	.322	.344	122	51	—	.892	14	—	—	C323,O101L,1b13,S3,2b2	—	6.3
CLAPP, STUBBY	Richard Keith; B2.24.1973 Windsor ON, Can.; BL/TR/5´8˝/175; [StLN96 36/1058]; d6.18; Col Texas Tech																								
2001	StL N	23	25	0	5	2	0	0	1	1-0	0	7	.200	.231	.280	30	-3	0-0	1.000	0	174	0	2b4,O4L	0	-0.2
CLARE, DENNY	Dennis J.; B1.1853 Brooklyn NY; D11.26.1928 Brooklyn NY; d9.14																								
1872	Atl NA	2	7	1	1	0	0	0	0	0	—	0	.143	.143	.143	-10	-1	0-0	.857	-1	195	0	2b2/S	—	-0.2
CLAREY, DOUG	Douglas William; B4.20.1954 Los Angeles CA; BR/TR/6´0˝/180; [MinA72 6/128]; d4.20																								
1976	StL N	9	4	2	1	0	0	1	2	0-0	0	1	.250	.250	1.000	238	1	0-0	1.000	-1	27	0	2b7	0	-0.1
CLARK, ALLIE	Alfred Aloysius; B6.16.1923 S.Amboy NJ; BR/TR/5´11˝/185; d8.5																								
1947	†NY A	24	67	9	25	5	0	1	14	5	0	2	.373	.417	.493	154	5	0-0	1.000	0	115	0	O16(6/0/10)	0	0.4
1948	†Cle A	81	271	43	84	5	2	9	38	23	0	13	.310	.364	.443	117	5	0-2	.982	-3	89	95	O65(21/0/44),3b5/1	0	-0.2
1949	Cle A	35	74	8	13	4	0	1	9	4	0	7	.176	.218	.270	29	-8	0-0	1.000	-2	65	98	O17(1/0/16)/1	0	-1.0
1950	Cle A	59	163	19	35	6	1	6	21	11	0	10	.215	.264	.374	64	-10	0-1	.987	-1	97	70	O41(25/0/17)	0	-1.3
1951	Cle A	3	10	3	3	2	0	1	3	1	0	2	.300	.364	.800	221	2	0-0	1.000	-0	73	0	O3R	0	0.1
	Phi A	56	161	20	40	10	1	4	22	15	2	7	.248	.320	.398	91	-2	2-0	.984	0	102	95	O32(1/1/30),3b10	0	-0.2
	Year	59	171	23	43	12	1	5	25	16	2	9	.251	.323	.421	98	-1	2-0	.985	0	100	88	O35(1/1/33),3b10	0	-0.1
1952	Phi A	71	186	23	51	12	0	7	29	10	1	19	.274	.315	.452	105	0	0-2	.988	-1	100	61	O48(7/2/39),1b2	0	-0.3
1953	Phi A	20	74	6	15	4	0	3	13	3	0	5	.203	.234	.378	61	-5	0-0	1.000	-0	92	117	O19R	0	-0.6
	Chi A	9	15	0	1	0	0	0	0	0	0	5	.067	.067	.067	-62	-3	0-0	1.000	-0	0	279	/1lf	0	-0.4
	Year	29	89	6	16	4	0	3	13	3	0	10	.180	.207	.326	40	-8	0-0	1.000	-1	91	113	O20(1/0/19)/1	0	-1.0
Total	7	358	1021	131	267	48	4	32	149	72	3	70	.262	.312	.410	92	-16	2-5	.988	-8	95	78	O242(62/3/178),3b15,1b5	0	-3.5
CLARK, DAD	Alfred Robert "Fred"; B7.16.1873 San Francisco CA; D7.26.1956 Ogden UT; BL/TL/5´11˝/170; d7.3																								
1902	Chi N	12	43	1	8	1	0	0	2	4	0	—	.186	.255	.209	45	-3	1	.938	-2	88	147	1b12	—	-0.5
CLARK, TONY	Anthony Christopher; B6.15.1972 Newton KS; BB/TR/6´7˝/(205–250); [DetA90 1/2]; d9.3																								
1995	Det A	27	101	10	24	5	1	3	11	8-0	0	30	.238	.294	.396	77	-4	0-0	.985	-1	94	99	1b27	0	-0.7
1996	Det A	100	376	56	94	14	0	27	72	29-1	0	127	.250	.299	.503	99	-3	0-1	.993	-2	90	92	1b86,D12	0	-1.3
1997	Det A	159	580	105	160	28	3	32	117	93-13	3	144	.276	.376	.500	127	25	1-3	.993	-3	94	101	1b158/D	0	0.7
1998	Det A	157	602	84	175	37	0	34	103	63-5	3	128	.291	.358	.522	124	21	3-3	.991	-0	104	111	1b142,D15	0	0.7
1999	Det A	143	536	74	150	29	0	31	99	64-7	6	133	.280	.361	.507	117	14	2-1	.992	2	106	95	1b132,D11	15	0.3
2000	Det A	60	208	32	57	14	0	13	37	24-2	0	51	.274	.349	.529	119	6	0-0	.993	3	121	104	1b58/D	90	0.3
2001	Det A★	126	428	67	123	29	3	16	75	62-10	1	108	.287	.374	.481	128	19	0-1	.996	-1	99	108	1b78,D42	0	0.9
2002	Bos A	90	275	25	57	12	1	3	29	21-0	1	57	.207	.265	.291	47	-21	0-0	.992	4	118	99	1b85,D2	0	-2.3
2003	NY N	125	254	29	59	13	0	16	43	24-2	1	73	.232	.300	.472	102	-1	0-0	.992	-4	71	83	1b80/lf	0	-1.0

YEAR	TM LG	G	AB	R	H	2B	3B	HR	RBI	BB-IB	HP	SO	AVG	OBP	SLG	AOPS	ABR	SB-CS	FA	FR	RNG	THR	GAMES AT POSITION	DL	BFW
2004	†NY A	106	253	37	56	12	0	16	49	26-3	2	92	.221	.297	.458	93	-3	0-0	.994	0	99	112	1b99/D	0	-0.9
2005	Ari N	130	349	47	106	22	2	30	87	37-6	1	88	.304	.366	.636	150	24	0-0	.997	-1	95	90	1b83,D7	0	1.7
2006	Ari N	79	132	13	26	4	0	6	16	13-2	2	40	.197	.279	.364	59	-9	0-0	.993	0	106	111	1b53	39	-1.0
Total	12	1302	4094	579	1087	219	10	227	738	464-51	20	1071	.266	.341	.490	112	68	6-9	.993	-3	100	101	1b1081,D92/lf	144	-2.6
CLARK, EARL	Bailey Earl; B11.6.1907 Washington DC; D1.16.1938 Washington DC; BR/TR/5´10˝/160; d8.17																								
1927	Bos N	13	44	6	12	1	0	0	3	2	0	4	.273	.304	.295	66	-2	0	1.000	-0	114	0	O13(10/3/0)	—	-0.3
1928	Bos N	28	112	18	34	9	1	0	10	4	2	8	.304	.339	.402	98	0	0	.987	-2	103	0	O27C	—	-0.3
1929	Bos N	84	279	43	88	13	3	1	30	12	1	30	.315	.346	.394	86	-6	6	.978	4	109	100	O74(4/70/1)	—	-0.6
1930	Bos N	82	233	29	69	11	3	3	28	7	1	22	.296	.320	.408	77	-10	3	.977	3	118	55	O63(1/40/22)	—	-0.8
1931	Bos N	16	50	8	11	2	0	0	4	7	0	4	.220	.316	.260	58	-3	1	.970	1	98	257	O14L	—	-0.3
1932	Bos N	50	44	11	11	2	0	0	4	2	0	7	.250	.283	.295	58	-3	1	1.000	3	136	394	O16(6/3/6)	—	0.0
1933	Bos N	7	23	3	8	1	0	0	1	2	0	1	.348	.400	.391	138	1	0	1.000	-1	81	0	O6(3/3/0)	—	0.0
1934	StL A	13	41	4	7	2	0	0	1	1	0	3	.171	.190	.220	5	-6	0-0	1.000	0	115	0	O9(2/0/7)	—	-0.6
Total	8	293	826	122	240	41	7	4	81	37	4	79	.291	.324	.372	78	-29	11-0	.981	8	111	81	O222(40/146/36)	—	-2.9
CLARK, BRADY	Brady William; B4.18.1973 Portland OR; BR/TR/6´2˝/(195–205); d9.3; Col San Diego																								
2000	Cin N	11	11	1	3	1	0	0	2	0-0	0	2	.273	.273	.364	57	-1	0-0	1.000	1	237	0	O5(2/0/3)	0	0.0
2001	Cin N	89	129	22	34	3	0	6	18	22-1	1	16	.264	.373	.426	101	1	4-1	.981	-1	103	0	O43(26/7/14)/D	0	-0.1
2002	Cin N	51	66	6	10	3	0	0	9	6-2	1	9	.152	.233	.197	14	-8	1-2	.938	-1	78	0	O22(15/3/6)	0	-1.1
	NY N	10	12	3	5	1	0	0	1	1-0	0	2	.417	.462	.500	162	1	0-0	1.000	-0	93	0	O6(1/2/3)	0	0.1
	Year	61	78	9	15	4	0	0	10	7-2	1	11	.192	.267	.244	35	-7	1-2	.950	-2	81	0	O28(16/5/9)	0	-1.0
2003	Mil N	128	315	33	86	21	1	6	40	21-0	9	40	.273	.330	.403	92	-3	13-2	.973	5	114	100	O105(25/6/82)	16	0.0
2004	Mil N	138	353	41	99	18	1	7	46	53-2	9	48	.280	.385	.397	103	4	15-8	.984	10	**127**	82	O133(3/9/123)	0	1.0
2005	Mil N	145	599	94	183	31	1	13	53	47-1	18	55	.306	.372	.426	108	9	10-13	.995	11	**119**	69	O145C	15	1.9
2006	Mil N	138	415	51	109	14	2	4	29	43-4	14	60	.263	.348	.335	77	-13	3-4	.985	-2	104	40	O119(3/114/7)	0	-1.5
Total	7	710	1900	251	529	92	5	36	198	193-10	52	232	.278	.358	.389	94	-10	46-30	.986	22	115	65	O578(75/286/238)/D	31	0.3
CLARK, DANNY	Daniel Curran; B1.18.1894 Meridian MS; D5.23.1937 Meridian MS; BL/TR/5´9˝/167; d4.12																								
1922	Det A	83	185	31	54	11	3	3	26	15	0	11	.292	.345	.432	105	1	1-0	.945	-3	101	88	2b38,O5R/3	—	-0.1
1924	Bos A	104	325	36	90	23	3	2	54	51	2	19	.277	.378	.385	97	1	4-7	.943	-0	105	56	3b94	—	0.4
1927	StL N	58	72	8	17	2	2	0	13	8	0	7	.236	.313	.319	67	-3	0	.929	1	118	81	O9R	—	-0.4
Total	3	245	582	75	161	36	8	5	93	74	2	37	.277	.360	.392	96	-1	5-7	.943	-2	105	56	3b95,2b38,O14R	—	-0.1
CLARK, DAVE	David Earl; B9.3.1962 Tupelo MS; BL/TR/6´2˝/(198–213); [CleA83 1/11]; d9.3; C2; Col Jackson St.																								
1986	Cle A	18	58	10	16	1	0	3	9	7-0	0	11	.276	.348	.448	118	1	1-0	1.000	1	127	0	O10R,D7	0	0.2
1987	Cle A	29	87	11	18	5	0	3	12	2-0	0	24	.207	.225	.368	53	-6	1-0	1.000	1	118	136	O13(1/0/12),D12	0	-0.6
1988	Cle A	63	156	11	41	4	1	3	18	17-2	0	28	.263	.333	.359	92	-2	0-2	.947	-2	89	0	D27,O23(10/1/15)	0	-0.6
1989	Cle A	102	253	21	60	12	0	8	29	30-5	0	63	.237	.317	.379	94	-2	0-2	.964	-3	70	0	D55,O21(12/0/11)	0	-0.8
1990	Chi N	84	171	22	47	4	2	5	20	8-1	0	40	.275	.304	.409	89	-3	7-1	1.000	-1	87	85	O39L	0	-0.4
1991	KC A	11	10	1	2	0	0	0	1	1-0	0	1	.200	.273	.200	33	-1	0-0	ø	-0	0	0	/rfD	0	-0.1
1992	Pit N	23	33	3	7	0	0	2	7	6-0	0	8	.212	.325	.394	106	0	0-0	1.000	-1	71	0	O8(1/0/7)	0	-0.1
1993	Pit N	110	277	43	75	11	2	11	46	38-5	1	58	.271	.358	.444	114	6	1-0	.957	-6	90	53	O91(40/0/53)	0	-0.2
1994	Pit N	86	223	37	66	11	1	10	46	22-0	0	48	.296	.355	.489	116	5	2-2	.974	2	102	130	O57(10/0/48)	0	0.4
1995	Pit N	77	196	30	55	6	0	4	24	24-1	1	38	.281	.359	.372	92	-2	3-3	.961	0	113	32	O61(34/0/29)	47	-0.4
1996	Pit N	92	211	28	58	12	2	8	35	31-3	0	51	.275	.366	.464	114	5	2-1	.988	-1	93	102	O61(34/0/28)	0	0.2
	†LA N	15	15	0	3	0	0	0	1	3-0	0	2	.200	.333	.200	48	-1	0-0	ø	-0	0	0	/lf	0	-0.1
	Year	107	226	28	61	12	2	8	36	34-3	0	53	.270	.364	.447	110	4	2-1	.988	-1	91	100	O62(35/0/28)	0	0.1
1997	Chi N	102	143	19	43	8	0	5	32	19-3	2	34	.301	.386	.462	118	4	1-0	.953	2	113	165	O25(24/0/1),D4	0	0.5
1998	†Hou N	93	131	12	27	7	0	0	4	14-1	1	45	.206	.288	.260	47	-10	1-1	.885	-2	79	102	O22(9/0/13),D4	0	-1.2
Total	13	905	1964	248	518	81	8	62	284	222-21	5	451	.264	.338	.408	98	-6	19-12	.969	-11	96	73	O433(215/1/228),D110	47	-3.2
CLARK, DOUG	Douglas Dwyer; B3.5.1976 Springfield MA; BL/TR/6´2˝/205; [SFN98 7/218]; d9.14; Col Massachusetts																								
2005	SF N	8	5	2	0	0	0	0	0	1-0	0	2	.000	.167	.000	-50	-1	0-0	ø	0	—	—	/H	0	-0.2
2006	Oak A	6	6	0	1	0	0	0	0	0-0	0	3	.167	.167	.167	-14	-1	1-0	ø	0	0	0	/lf	0	-0.1
Total	2	14	11	2	1	0	0	0	0	1-0	0	5	.091	.167	.091	-30	-2	1-0	.000	0	0	0	/lf	0	-0.3
CLARK, GLEN	Glen Ester; B3.7.1941 Austin TX; BB/TR/6´1˝/190; d6.3																								
1967	Atl N	4	4	0	0	0	0	0	0	0-0	0	1	.000	.000	.000	-99	-1	0-0	ø	0	—	—	/H	0	-0.1
CLARK, PEP	Harry; B3.20.1883 Union City OH; D6.8.1965 Milwaukee WI; BR/TR/5´7.5˝/175; d9.11																								
1903	Chi A	15	65	7	20	4	2	0	9	2	1	—	.308	.338	.431	135	3	5	.877	-1	118	58	3b15	—	0.3
CLARK, HOWIE	Howard Roddy; B2.13.1974 San Diego CA; BL/TR/5´10˝/(180–195); [BalA92 27/744]; d7.16; OF(17/0/12)																								
2002	Bal A	14	53	3	16	5	0	0	4	3-0	2	6	.302	.362	.396	107	1	0-0	1.000	0	119	0	O4L/1D	0	0.1
2003	Tor A	38	70	9	25	3	1	0	7	3-0	2	6	.357	.400	.429	114	2	0-1	.957	1	114	239	3b13,O5(4/0/1),2b3,1b2/SD	0	0.2
2004	Tor A	40	115	17	25	6	0	3	12	13-0	0	15	.217	.292	.348	64	-6	0-0	.972	-1	108	214	O19(9/0/11),1b11/23D	0	-0.8
2006	Bal A	7	7	1	1	0	0	0	0	2-0	0	2	.143	.333	.143	31	-1	0-0	ø	-0	0	0	/3D	0	-0.1
Total	4	99	245	30	67	14	1	3	23	21-0	4	29	.273	.338	.376	86	-4	0-1	.980	0	105	148	O28L,D20,3b15,1b14,2b4/S	0	-0.6
CLARK, JACK	Jack Anthony; B11.10.1955 New Brighton PA; BR/TR/6´2˝/(170–210); [SFN73 13/294]; d9.12; C3; OF(11/23/1014)																								
1975	SF N	8	17	3	4	0	0	0	2	1-0	0	2	.235	.263	.235	42	-1	1-0	1.000	0	110	0	O3(1/2/1),3b2	0	-0.1
1976	SF N	26	102	14	23	6	2	2	10	8-0	0	18	.225	.277	.382	85	-2	6-2	.987	3	113	168	O26(5/20/8)	0	0.0
1977	SF N	136	413	64	104	17	4	13	51	49-2	2	73	.252	.332	.407	97	-2	12-4	.975	6	110	135	O114(0/1/113)	0	0.0
1978	SF N★	156	592	90	181	46	8	25	98	50-8	3	72	.306	.358	.537	154	41	15-11	.982	8	107	127	O152R	0	4.1
1979	SF N★	143	527	84	144	25	2	26	86	63-6	1	95	.273	.348	.476	133	23	11-8	.982	2	97	118	O140R,3b2	0	1.8
1980	SF N	127	437	77	124	20	8	22	82	74-13	2	52	.284	.382	.517	156	35	2-5	.967	-4	98	66	O120R	16	2.4
1981	SF N	99	385	60	103	19	2	17	53	45-6	1	45	.268	.341	.460	131	15	1-1	.981	5	99	**168**	O98R	0	1.6
1982	SF N	157	563	90	154	30	3	27	103	90-7	1	91	.274	.372	.481	139	32	6-9	.980	-4	96	89	O155R	0	1.9
1983	SF N	135	492	82	132	25	0	20	66	74-6	1	79	.268	.361	.441	126	19	5-3	.967	6	101	**183**	O133R,1b2	0	1.9
1984	SF N	57	203	33	65	9	1	11	44	43-7	0	29	.320	.434	.537	178	23	1-1	.990	-1	90	82	O54R,1b4	72	2.0
1985	†StL N★	126	442	71	124	26	3	22	87	83-14	2	88	.281	.393	.502	151	33	1-4	.988	-9	81	**112**	1b121,O12R	15	1.7
1986	StL N	65	232	34	55	12	2	9	23	45-4	1	61	.237	.362	.422	116	7	1-1	.995	-6	75	137	1b64	103	-0.3
1987	†StL N★	131	419	93	120	23	1	35	106	**136**-13	0	139	.286	**.459**	**.597**	**173**	53	1-2	.989	-5	92	116	1b126/rf	0	3.9
1988	NY A	150	496	81	120	14	0	27	93	113-6	2	141	.242	.381	.433	129	24	3-2	.951	-1	99	91	D112,O19(5/0/14),1b10	11	1.9
1989	SD N	142	455	76	110	19	1	26	94	**132**-18	1	145	.242	.410	.459	149	37	6-2	.988	2	107	**119**	1b131,O12R	0	3.2
1990	SD N	115	334	59	89	12	1	25	62	**104**-11	2	91	.266	.441	.533	166	37	4-3	.994	-1	95	104	1b109	29	2.9
1991	Bos A	140	481	75	120	18	1	28	87	96-3	3	133	.249	.374	.466	125	19	0-2	ø	0	0	0	D135	0	1.4
1992	Bos A	81	257	32	54	11	0	5	33	56-3	2	87	.210	.350	.311	82	-4	1-1	.992	0	106	74	D64,1b13	0	-0.7
Total	18	1994	6847	1118	1826	332	39	340	1180	1262-127	24	1441	.267	.379	.476	137	389	77-61	.978	1	101	122	O1039R,1b580,D311,3b4	246	29.6
CLARK, JIM	James (b James Petrosky); B9.21.1927 Baggaley PA; D10.24.1990 Santa Monica CA; BR/TR/5´9˝/150; d8.17																								
1948	Was A	9	12	1	3	0	0	0	0	0	0	2	.250	.250	.250	34	-1	0-0	1.000	-0	95	0	/S3	0	-0.1
CLARK, JIM	James Edward; B4.30.1947 Kansas City KS; BR/TR/6´1˝/190; d7.16																								
1971	Cle A	13	18	2	3	0	1	0	0	2-0	0	7	.167	.250	.278	45	-1	0-0	1.000	0	150	0	O3(2/0/1)/1	0	-0.1
CLARK, JIM	James Francis; B12.26.1887 Brooklyn NY; D3.20.1969 Beaumont TX; BR/TR/5´11˝/175; d9.2; Col Bucknell																								
1911	StL N	14	18	2	3	0	1	0	3	3	0	4	.167	.286	.278	60	-1	2	1.000	-1	83	0	O8(1/6/1)	—	-0.2
1912	StL N	2	1	0	0	0	0	0	0	0	0	1	.000	.000	.000	-99	0	0	ø	0	—	—	/H	—	0.0
Total	2	16	19	2	3	0	1	0	3	3	0	5	.158	.273	.263	51	-1	2	1.000	-1	83	0	O8(1/6/1)	—	-0.2
CLARK, JERALD	Jerald Dwayne; B8.10.1963 Crockett TX; BR/TR/6´4˝/(189–205); [SDN85 12/310]; d9.19; b–Phil; Col Lamar																								
1988	SD N	6	15	0	3	1	0	0	3	0-0	0	4	.200	.200	.267	33	-1	0-0	1.000	1	152	496	O4L	0	0.0
1989	SD N	17	41	5	8	2	0	1	7	3-0	0	9	.195	.250	.317	61	-2	0-1	.947	0	80	356	O14(10/0/4)	0	-0.3
1990	SD N	53	101	12	27	4	1	5	11	5-0	0	24	.267	.299	.475	109	1	0-0	1.000	0	93	49	1b15,O13(5/0/9)	0	0.0

YEAR	TM LG	G	AB	R	H	2B	3B	HR	RBI	BB-IB	HP	SO	AVG	OBP	SLG	AOPS	ABR	SB-CS	FA	FR	RNG	THR	GAMES AT POSITION	DL	BFW
1991	SD N	118	369	26	84	16	0	10	47	31-2	6	90	.228	.295	.352	80	-10	2-1	.994	-5	86	91	O96(85/0/13),1b16	19	-2.0
1992	SD N	146	496	45	120	22	6	12	58	22-3	4	97	.242	.278	.383	84	-12	3-0	.990	7	110	153	O134(115/1/22),1b11	0	-1.0
1993	Col N	140	478	65	135	26	6	13	67	20-2	10	60	.282	.324	.444	89	-8	9-6	.966	-1	105	100	O96(80/0/17),1b37	0	-1.6
1995	Min A	36	109	17	37	8	3	3	15	2-0	1	11	.339	.354	.550	131	4	3-0	1.000	-1	99	77	O23(12/10/5),1b11,D3	106	0.3
Total	7	516	1609	170	414	79	16	44	208	83-7	21	295	.257	.301	.408	89	-28	17-8	.983	2	102	124	O380(311/11/70),1b90,D3	125	-4.6
CLARK, JERMAINE	Jermaine Marcel; B9.29.1976 Berkeley CA; BL/TR/5´10˝/(170–175); [SeaA97 5/163]; d4.3; Col San Francisco																								
2001	Det A	3	0	1	0	0	0	0	0	0-0	0	0	ø	ø	ø	ø	0	0-0	ø	0	—	—	R2	0	0.0
2003	Tex A	10	9	0	0	0	0	0	0	3-0	0	0	.000	.250	.000	-24	-2	0-0	1.000	-8	16	0	O6(5/1/0),2b2/D	0	-1.0
	SD N	1	2	0	0	0	0	0	1	0-0	0	1	.000	.000	.000	-99	-1	0-1	1.000	0	107	0	/lf	0	-0.1
	Tex A	14	37	2	8	2	0	0	6	3-0	0	4	.216	.268	.270	42	-3	2-1	1.000	-1	16	0	O11L,2b5/D	0	-0.4
2004	Cin N	14	30	4	4	1	0	0	2	1-0	2	8	.133	.212	.167	-0	-5	1-0	1.000	0	106	333	O8(1/1/6),2b2	0	-0.4
2005	Oak A	4	0	2	0	0	0	0	0	1-0	0	0	ø	1.000	ø	202	0	0-0	ø	-0	0	0	2b2/lf	0	0.0
Total	4	46	78	9	12	3	0	0	9	8-0	2	13	.154	.244	.192	18	-11	3-2	1.000	-9	68	164	O27(19/2/6),2b11,D2	0	-1.9
CLARK, CAP	John Carrol; B9.19.1906 Snow Camp NC; D2.16.1957 Fayetteville NC; BL/TR/5´11˝/180; d4.23; Col Elon																								
1938	Phi N	52	74	11	19	1	1	0	4	9	0	10	.257	.337	.297	78	-2	0	.936	-4	*57*	*107*	C29	—	-0.5
CLARK, MEL	Melvin Earl; B7.7.1926 Letart WV; BR/TR/6´0˝/180; d9.11; Col Ohio U.																								
1951	Phi N	10	31	2	10	1	0	1	3	0	0	3	.323	.323	.452	108	0	0-1	1.000	-0	102	0	O7(1/0/6)	0	-0.1
1952	Phi N	47	155	20	52	6	4	1	15	6	1	13	.335	.364	.445	125	4	2-1	1.000	3	108	146	O38(12/0/27)/3	0	0.6
1953	Phi N	60	198	31	59	10	4	0	19	11	1	17	.298	.338	.389	89	-3	1-0	.991	1	109	53	O51(1/0/51)	0	-0.4
1954	Phi N	83	233	26	56	9	7	1	24	17	0	21	.240	.291	.352	67	-12	0-1	.961	4	101	192	O63(21/0/42)	0	-1.2
1955	Phi N	10	32	3	5	3	0	0	1	3-0	0	4	.156	.229	.250	27	-3	0-0	1.000	3	114	401	O8R	0	-0.1
1957	Det A	5	7	0	0	0	0	0	1	0-0	0	3	.000	.000	.000	-97	-2	0-0	1.000	0	191	0	O2L	0	-0.2
Total	6	215	656	82	182	29	15	3	63	37-0	2	61	.277	.318	.381	85	-16	3-3	.983	9	106	141	O169(37/0/134)/3	0	-1.4
CLARK, SPIDER	Owen F.; B9.16.1867 Brooklyn NY; D2.8.1892 Brooklyn NY; TR/5´10˝/150; d5.2; OF(5/4/34)																								
1889	Was N	38	145	19	37	7	2	3	22	6	0	18	.255	.285	.393	93	-2	8	.887	4	—	—	C14,S13,O9R,3b2,2b2	—	0.3
1890	Buf P	69	260	45	69	11	1	2	25	20	3	16	.265	.325	.338	84	-5	8	.938	-3	106	149	O34(5/4/25),C14,2b13,1b6,3b3/SP	—	-0.5
Total	2	107	405	64	106	18	3	5	47	26	3	34	.262	.311	.358	88	-7	16	.952	2	—	—	O43R,C28,2b15,S14,1b6,3b5/P	—	-0.2
CLARK, PHIL	Phillip Benjamin; B5.6.1968 Crockett TX; BR/TR/6´0˝/(180–205); [DetA86 1/18]; d5.27; b–Jerald																								
1992	Det A	23	54	3	22	4	0	1	5	6-1	0	9	.407	.467	.537	178	6	1-0	.931	1	138	0	O13(4/0/9),D7	0	0.7
1993	SD N	102	240	33	75	17	0	9	33	8-2	5	31	.313	.345	.496	122	7	2-0	.963	10	142	254	O36(22/0/15),1b24,C11,3b5	0	1.5
1994	SD N	61	149	14	32	6	0	5	20	5-1	3	17	.215	.250	.356	59	-10	1-2	.992	-2	100	104	1b24,O17(12/0/5),C5/3	0	-1.4
1995	SD N	75	97	12	21	3	0	2	7	8-1	1	18	.216	.278	.309	58	-6	0-2	1.000	-2	86	0	O34(14/0/21),1b2	0	-0.9
1996	Bos A	3	3	0	0	0	0	0	0	0-0	0	1	.000	.000	.000	-98	-1	0-0	1.000	0	0	0	/13D	0	-0.1
Total	5	264	543	62	150	30	0	17	65	27-5	9	76	.276	.317	.425	97	-4	4-4	.951	7	121	103	O100(52/0/50),1b51,C16,D8,3b7	0	-0.2
CLARK, BOBBY	Robert Cale; B6.13.1955 Sacramento CA; BR/TR/6´0˝/190; [AnaA75*S5/87]; d8.21; Col California–Riverside																								
1979	†Cal A	19	54	8	16	2	2	1	5	5-0	0	11	.296	.356	.463	122	1	1-1	.978	4	132	372	O19(16/3/2)	0	0.5
1980	Cal A	78	261	26	60	10	1	5	23	11-0	2	42	.230	.266	.333	64	-14	0-1	.982	8	122	119	O77(33/46/0)	0	-0.7
1981	Cal A	34	88	12	22	2	1	4	19	7-0	0	18	.250	.305	.432	109	1	0-0	1.000	4	112	290	O34(27/8/1)	0	0.4
1982	†Cal A	102	90	11	19	1	0	2	8	0-0	0	29	.211	.209	.289	35	-8	1-0	1.000	1	101	80	O102(24/24/57)	0	-0.9
1983	Cal A	76	212	17	49	9	1	5	21	9-0	0	45	.231	.261	.354	68	-10	0-0	1.000	-5	93	0	O72(43/4/28)/3D	45	-1.8
1984	Mil A	58	169	17	44	7	2	2	16	16-0	1	35	.260	.326	.361	94	-1	1-5	.981	-8	80	0	O56(3/42/16)	30	-1.2
1985	Mil A	29	93	6	21	3	0	0	8	7-0	0	19	.226	.277	.258	49	-7	1-1	1.000	2	116	61	O27(1/17/12)	0	-0.6
Total	7	396	967	97	231	34	7	19	100	55-0	3	199	.239	.281	.347	73	-38	4-8	.990	6	105	91	O387(147/144/116),D2/3	75	-4.3
CLARK, BOB	Robert H.; B3.18.1863 Covington KY; D8.21.1919 Covington KY; BR/TR/5´10˝/175; d4.17																								
1886	Bro AA	71	269	37	58	8	2	0	26	17	0	—	.216	.262	.260	63	-12	14	.864	-7	—	—	C44,O17(6/1/11),S12	—	-1.3
1887	Bro AA	48	177	24	47	3	1	0	18	7	1	—	.266	.297	.294	64	-9	15	.871	-2	—	—	C45,O3R	—	-0.6
1888	Bro AA	45	150	23	36	5	3	1	20	9	2	—	.240	.292	.333	100	0	11	.884	-2	—	—	C36,O8(1/1/6)/1	—	0.1
1889	†Bro AA	53	182	32	50	5	2	0	22	26	1	7	.275	.368	.324	98	1	18	.870	-0	—	—	C53	—	0.4
1890	†Bro N	43	151	24	33	3	3	0	15	15	4	8	.219	.306	.278	70	-6	10	.836	-15	*86*	*76*	C42/rf	—	-1.5
1891	Cin N	16	54	2	6	0	0	0	3	6	1	9	.111	.213	.111	-5	-7	3	.868	-4	*91*	*91*	C16	—	-0.9
1893	Lou N	12	28	3	3	1	0	0	3	5	0	5	.107	.242	.143	4	-4	0	.947	-1	*102*	*149*	C10/rfS	—	-0.3
Total	7	288	1011	145	233	25	11	1	107	85	9	29	.230	.296	.280	71	-37	71	.867	-31	*89*	*86*	C246,O30(7/2/22),S13/1	—	-4.1
CLARK, RON	Ronald Bruce; B1.14.1943 Ft.Worth TX; BR/TR/5´10˝/(165–175); d9.11; C6																								
1966	Min A	5	1	1	1	0	0	0	1	0-0	0	0	1.000	.500	1.000	448	0	0-0	ø	-0	0	0	/3	0	0.0
1967	Min A	20	60	7	10	3	1	2	11	4-0	0	9	.167	.215	.350	61	-3	0-0	.891	-2	101	0	3b16	81	-0.5
1968	Min A	104	227	14	42	5	1	1	13	16-2	2	44	.185	.245	.229	42	-16	3-2	.932	-4	113	109	3b52,S43,2b10	0	-1.9
1969	Min A	5	8	0	1	0	0	0	0	0-0	0	0	.125	.125	.125	-29	-1	0-0	1.000	-1	31	0	3b2	0	-0.3
	Sea A	57	163	9	32	5	0	0	12	13-2	1	29	.196	.258	.227	37	-14	1-0	.966	-9	83	69	S38,3b15,2b5/1	0	-2.0
	Year	62	171	9	33	5	0	0	12	13-2	1	29	.193	.253	.222	34	-15	1-0	.966	-10	83	69	S38,3b17,2b5/1	0	-2.3
1971	Oak A	2	1	0	0	0	0	0	0	1-0	0	0	.000	.500	.000	53	0	0-0	ø	0	—	—	/H	0	0.0
1972	Oak A	14	15	1	4	2	0	0	1	2-0	0	4	.267	.353	.400	130	1	0-0	1.000	1	93	211	2b11,3b3	0	0.2
	Mil A	22	54	8	10	1	1	2	5	5-0	0	11	.185	.250	.352	80	-2	0-0	.963	4	142	108	2b11,3b10	0	0.3
	Year	36	69	9	14	3	1	2	6	7-0	0	15	.203	.273	.362	92	-1	0-0	.974	5	126	142	2b22,3b13	0	0.5
1975	Phi N	1	1	0	0	0	0	0	0	0-0	0	1	.000	.000	.000	-95	0	0-0	ø	0	—	—	/H	0	0.0
Total	7	230	530	40	100	16	3	5	43	41-4	3	98	.189	.249	.258	48	-35	4-2	.904	-12	105	89	3b99,S81,2b37/1	81	-4.2
CLARK, ROY	Roy Elliott "Pepper"; B5.11.1874 New Haven CT; D11.1.1925 Bridgeport CT; BL/TR/5´8˝/170; d4.19; Col Brown																								
1902	NY N	22	80	4	12	1	0	0	3	1	0	—	.150	.160	.162	-0	-10	5	.964	-1	88	174	O21(3/9/9)	—	-1.2
CLARK, WILL	William Nuschler; B3.13.1964 New Orleans LA; BL/TL/6´1˝/(185–200); [SFN85 1/2]; d4.8; Col Mississippi St.																								
1986	SF N	111	408	66	117	27	2	11	41	34-10	3	76	.287	.343	.444	122	12	4-7	.989	-3	93	102	1b102	50	0.1
1987	†SF N	150	529	89	163	29	5	35	91	49-11	5	98	.308	.371	.580	155	40	5-17	.991	1	104	**125**	1b139	0	2.7
1988	SF N★	**162**	575	102	162	31	6	29	**109**	**100-27**	4	129	.282	.386	.508	163	**51**	9-1	.993	-3	94	**120**	1b158	0	4.0
1989	†SF N★	159	588	**104**	196	38	9	23	111	74-14	5	103	.333	.407	.546	176	60	8-3	.994	-1	100	115	1b158	0	5.1
1990	SF N★	154	600	91	177	25	5	19	95	62-9	3	97	.295	.357	.448	126	21	8-2	.992	-1	101	108	1b153	0	1.0
1991	SF N★	148	565	84	170	32	7	29	116	51-12	2	91	.301	.359	**.536**	153	38	4-2	**.997**	5	109	**119**	1b144	0	3.4
1992	SF N★	144	513	69	154	40	1	16	73	73-23	4	82	.300	.384	.476	152	39	12-7	.993	1	103	**132**	1b141	0	3.1
1993	SF N	132	491	82	139	27	2	14	73	63-6	6	68	.283	.367	.432	118	15	2-2	.988	-2	98	**127**	1b129	15	0.1
1994	Tex A★	110	389	73	128	24	2	13	80	71-11	3	59	.329	.431	.501	139	27	5-1	.990	2	108	95	1b107/D	0	1.8
1995	Tex A	123	454	85	137	27	3	16	92	68-6	4	50	.302	.389	.480	123	18	0-1	.994	1	102	**117**	1b122/D	0	0.6
1996	†Tex A	117	436	69	124	25	1	13	72	64-5	5	67	.284	.377	.436	100	2	2-1	.996	-2	93	90	1b117	48	-0.9
1997	Tex A	110	393	56	128	29	1	12	51	49-11	3	62	.326	.400	.496	125	16	0-0	.996	-1	95	101	1b100,D7	52	0.6
1998	†Tex A	149	554	98	169	41	1	23	102	72-5	3	97	.305	.384	.507	124	21	1-0	.989	-9	79	98	1b134,D15	0	0.0
1999	Bal A	77	251	40	76	15	0	10	29	38-2	2	42	.303	.395	.482	128	12	2-2	.995	2	111	101	1b63,D3	87	0.8
2000	Bal A	79	256	49	77	15	1	9	28	47-3	4	45	.301	.413	.473	131	15	4-2	.991	-1	93	90	1b72,D6	14	0.7
	†StL N	51	171	29	59	15	1	12	42	22-0	3	24	.345	.426	.655	165	18	1-0	.992	-2	84	94	1b50	0	1.1
Total	15	1976	7173	1186	2176	440	47	284	1205	937-155	59	1190	.303	.384	.497	137	405	67-48	.992	-14	98	111	1b1889,D33	266	24.2
CLARK, WILLIE	William Otis "Wee Willie"; B8.16.1872 Pittsburgh PA; D11.13.1932 Pittsburgh PA; BL/TL/6´0˝/195; d6.20																								
1895	NY N	23	88	9	23	3	2	0	16	5	0	6	.261	.301	.341	67	-5	1	.974	1	119	124	1b23	—	-0.3
1896	NY N	72	247	38	72	12	4	0	33	15	8	12	.291	.352	.372	94	-2	8	.975	-4	75	105	1b65	—	-0.5
1897	NY N	116	431	63	122	17	12	1	75	37	9	—	.283	.352	.385	97	-2	18	.984	3	106	122	1b107,O7L/3	—	0.0
1898	Pit N	57	209	29	64	9	7	1	31	22	2	—	.306	.378	.431	134	9	0	.984	1	98	90	1b57	—	0.9
1899	Pit N	81	300	49	85	13	10	0	44	35	10	—	.283	.377	.393	112	6	11	.989	0	89	78	1b79	—	0.5
Total	5	349	1275	188	366	54	35	2	199	114	29	18	.287	.359	.389	104	6	38	.983	0	95	102	1b331,O7L/3	—	0.6
CLARK, WIN	William Winfield; B4.11.1875 Circleville OH; D4.15.1959 Los Angeles CA; BR/TR/5´10˝/175; d7.12																								
1897	Lou N	4	16	2	3	0	0	0	2	1	0	—	.188	.235	.188	13	-2	1	.810	-2	75	80	2b3/3	—	-0.3

YEAR	TM LG	G	AB	R	H	2B	3B	HR	RBI	BB-IB	HP	SO	AVG	OBP	SLG	AOPS	ABR	SB-CS	FA	FR	RNG	THR	GAMES AT POSITION	DL	BFW
CLARKE, ARTIE	Arthur Franklin; B5.6.1865 Providence RI; D11.14.1949 Brookline MA; BR/TR/5´8˝/155; d4.19; Col Williams																								
1890	NY N	101	395	55	89	12	8	0	49	32	4	38	.225	.290	.296	71	-16	44	.908	-2	*98*	*146*	C36,O33(3/1/30),3b16,2b15/S	—	-1.3
1891	NY N	48	174	17	33	2	2	0	21	15	0	16	.190	.254	.224	41	-13	5	.916	-11	*82*	*120*	C42,3b5,O2(0/1/1)	—	-1.9
Total	2	149	569	72	122	14	10	0	70	47	4	54	.214	.279	.274	62	-29	49	.912	-13	*90*	*132*	C78,O35(3/2/31),3b21,2b15/S	—	-3.2
CLARKE, FRED	Fred Clifford "Cap"; B10.3.1872 Winterset IA; D8.14.1960 Winfield KS; BL/TR/5´10.5˝/165; d6.30; M19/C1; HF1945; b–Josh																								
1894	Lou N	76	314	55	86	11	7	7	48	26	4	27	.274	.337	.420	88	-8	26	.886	4	118	62	O76L	—	-0.8
1895	Lou N	**132**	550	96	191	21	5	4	82	34	10	24	.347	.396	.425	119	18	40	.881	13	103	80	O132L	—	1.6
1896	Lou N	131	517	96	168	15	18	9	79	43	14	34	.325	.392	.476	133	24	34	.908	2	101	38	O131L	—	1.2
1897	Lou N	130	526	122	205	30	13	6	67	45	25	—	.390	.461	.530	**167**	**55**	59	.927	5	96	0	O129(128/3/0),M	—	4.1
1898	Lou N	149	599	116	184	23	12	3	47	48	15	—	.307	.373	.401	123	19	40	.940	7	90	58	O149(148/0/2),M	—	1.1
1899	Lou N	149	606	122	206	23	9	5	70	49	16	—	.340	.404	.432	130	26	49	.964	-1	89	34	O145L,S3,M	—	1.2
1900	Pit N	106	399	84	110	15	12	3	32	51	7	—	.276	.368	.396	110	6	21	.944	2	55	58	O104L,M	—	-0.1
1901	Pit N	129	527	118	171	24	15	6	60	51	10	—	.324	.395	.461	143	30	23	.970	2	80	0	O127L/S3M	—	2.4
1902	Pit N	113	459	103	145	27	14	2	53	51	**14**	—	.316	.401	.449	157	33	29	.958	-1	83	57	O113(110/0/4),M	—	2.6
1903	†Pit N	104	427	88	150	**32**	15	5	70	41	5	—	.351	.414	**.532**	**164**	35	21	.962	-8	71	95	O101L,S2,M	—	2.0
1904	Pit N	72	278	51	85	7	11	0	25	22	5	—	.306	.367	.410	136	11	11	.979	-1	44	76	O70L,M	—	0.7
1905	Pit N	141	525	95	157	18	15	2	51	55	2	—	.299	.368	.402	126	17	24	.976	5	9	9	O137L,M	—	1.5
1906	Pit N	118	417	69	129	14	**13**	1	39	40	1	—	.309	.371	.412	138	18	18	.974	5	107	98	O110L,M	—	1.8
1907	Pit N	148	501	97	145	18	13	2	59	68	8	—	.289	.383	.389	140	26	37	**.987**	8	77	44	O144L,M	—	2.9
1908	Pit N	151	551	83	146	18	15	2	53	65	6	—	.265	.349	.363	127	18	24	.973	10	79	47	O151(150/1/0),M	—	2.3
1909	†Pit N	152	550	97	158	16	11	3	68	**80**	6	—	.287	.384	.373	124	19	31	**.987**	7	79	47	O152L,M	—	1.9
1910	Pit N	123	429	57	113	23	9	2	63	53	4	23	.263	.350	.373	105	3	12	.967	3	**113**	64	O118L,M	—	0.0
1911	Pit N	110	392	73	127	25	13	5	49	53	2	27	.324	.407	.492	146	24	10	.970	-1	108	56	O101L,M	—	1.9
1913	Pit N	9	13	0	1	1	0	0	0	0	0	0	.077	.077	.154	-37	-2	0	1.000	-0	77	0	O2L,M	—	-0.3
1914	Pit N	2	2	0	0	0	0	0	0	0	0	0	.000	.000	.000	-99	-1	0	ø	0	—	—	/HM	—	-0.1
1915	Pit N	1	2	0	1	0	0	0	0	0	0	0	.500	.500	.500	206	0	0	ø	-0	0	0	/lfM	—	0.0
Total	21	2246	8584	1622	2678	361	220	67	1015	875	154	135	.312	.386	.429	132	371	509	.952	62	83	49	O2193(2187/4/6),S6/3	—	27.9
CLARKE, HARRY	Harry Corson; B1.13.1861 New York NY; D3.3.1923 Los Angeles CA; d8.28																								
1889	Was N	1	3	0	0	0	0	0	0	0	0	1	.000	.000	.000	-99	-1	0	1.000	1	915	0	/rf	—	0.0
CLARKE, HORACE	Horace Meredith; B6.2.1940 Frederiksted, V.I.; BB/TR/5´9˝/(170–182); d5.13																								
1965	NY A	51	108	13	28	1	0	1	9	6-0	0	6	.259	.296	.296	70	-4	2-1	.923	2	134	129	3b17,2b7/S	0	-0.3
1966	NY A	96	312	37	83	10	4	6	28	27-4	1	24	.266	.324	.381	107	2	5-3	.970	-11	86	106	S63,2b16,3b4	0	-0.2
1967	NY A	143	588	74	160	17	0	3	29	42-2	0	64	.272	.321	.316	92	-6	21-4	**.990**	16	**116**	97	2b140	0	2.8
1968	NY A	148	579	52	133	6	1	2	26	23-0	0	46	.230	.258	.254	58	-32	20-7	.984	**29**	**119**	103	2b139	0	1.3
1969	NY A	156	641	82	183	26	7	4	48	53-1	0	41	.285	.339	.367	101	0	33-13	.982	2	101	**119**	2b156	0	1.6
1970	NY A	158	686	81	172	24	2	4	46	35-5	2	35	.251	.286	.309	68	-32	23-7	.979	-8	104	96	2b157	0	-2.7
1971	NY A	159	625	76	156	23	7	2	41	64-2	2	43	.250	.321	.318	86	-12	17-7	.981	-3	106	98	2b156	0	-0.3
1972	NY A	147	547	65	132	20	2	3	37	56-4	4	44	.241	.315	.302	86	-8	18-6	.985	15	**115**	116	2b143	0	2.0
1973	NY A	148	590	60	155	21	0	2	35	47-0	2	48	.263	.317	.308	79	-16	11-10	.979	16	107	111	2b147	0	0.9
1974	NY A	24	47	3	11	1	0	0	1	4-0	0	5	.234	.294	.255	60	-2	1-0	1.000	-1	88	62	2b20/D	0	-0.3
	SD N	42	90	5	17	1	0	0	4	8-0	0	6	.189	.255	.200	30	-9	0-0	.978	-0	100	51	2b21	0	-0.8
Total	10	1272	4813	548	1230	150	23	27	304	365-18	11	362	.256	.308	.313	82	-119	151-58	.983	58	109	104	2b1102,S64,3b21/D	0	4.0
CLARKE, NIG	Jay Justin; B12.15.1882 Amherstburg ON, Can.; D6.15.1949 River Rouge MI; BL/TR (BB 1907)/5´8˝/165; d4.26																								
1905	Cle A	5	9	2	1	1	0	0	1	1	0	—	.111	.200	.222	33	-1	0	1.000	-1	*76*	*55*	C5	—	-0.2
	Det A	3	7	1	3	0	0	1	1	0	1	—	.429	.500	.857	326	2	0	1.000	0	*71*	*116*	C2	—	0.2
	Cle A	37	114	9	23	5	1	0	8	10	0	—	.202	.266	.263	67	-4	0	.961	-2	*76*	*55*	C37	—	-0.3
	Year	45	130	12	27	6	1	1	10	11	1	—	.208	.275	.292	79	-3	0	.965	-3	*103*	*92*	C44	—	-0.3
1906	Cle A	57	179	22	64	12	4	1	21	13	1	—	.358	.404	.486	181	17	3	.982	2	*117*	*93*	C54	—	2.5
1907	Cle A	120	390	44	105	19	6	3	33	35	2	—	.269	.333	.372	123	11	3	.961	-8	*100*	*87*	C115	—	1.5
1908	Cle A	97	290	34	70	8	6	1	27	30	1	—	.241	.315	.321	106	2	6	.969	-1	***137***	*101*	C90	—	1.1
1909	Cle A	55	164	15	45	4	2	0	14	9	1	—	.274	.316	.323	98	-1	1	.952	-1	*106*	*111*	C44	—	0.3
1910	Cle A	21	58	4	9	2	0	0	2	8	0	—	.155	.258	.190	40	-4	0	.974	-0	*90*	*121*	C17	—	-0.2
1911	StL A	82	256	22	55	10	1	0	18	26	0	—	.215	.287	.262	56	-15	2	.926	-12	*76*	*104*	C73,1b4	—	-2.1
1919	Phi N	26	62	4	15	3	0	0	2	4	1	5	.242	.299	.290	72	-2	1	.969	-2	*83*	*138*	C22	—	-0.2
1920	Pit N	3	7	0	0	0	0	0	0	2	0	4	.000	.222	.000	-32	-1	0-0	1.000	1	*101*	*105*	C3	—	0.0
Total	9	506	1536	157	390	64	20	6	127	138	7	9	.254	.318	.333	102	4	16-0	.960	-23	*105*	*99*	C462,1b4	—	2.6
CLARKE, JOSH	Joshua Baldwin "Pepper"; B3.8.1879 Winfield KS; D7.2.1962 Ventura CA; BL/TR/5´10˝/180; d6.15; b–Fred																								
1898	Lou N	6	18	0	3	0	0	0	0	1	0	—	.167	.211	.167	9	-2	0	.917	-0	0	0	O5(2/0/4)	—	-0.3
1905	StL N	50	167	31	43	3	2	3	18	27	0	—	.257	.361	.353	117	4	8	.942	-8	29	0	O26(2/5/19),2b16,S4	—	-0.4
1908	Cle A	131	492	70	119	8	4	1	21	76	4	—	.242	.348	.280	104	7	37	.963	-3	84	26	O131(130/1/0)	—	-0.5
1909	Cle A	4	12	1	0	0	0	0	0	2	0	—	.000	.143	.000	-52	-2	0	.600	-1	0	0	O4L	—	-0.4
1911	Bos N	32	120	16	28	7	3	1	4	29	1	22	.233	.387	.367	103	2	6	.938	3	107	153	O30L	—	0.3
Total	5	223	809	118	193	18	9	5	43	135	5	22	.239	.351	.302	102	9	51	.949	-10	77	42	O196(168/6/23),2b16,S4	—	-1.3
CLARKE, GREY	Richard Grey "Noisy"; B9.26.1912 Fulton AL; D11.25.1993 Kannapolis NC; BR/TR/5´9˝/183; d4.19																								
1944	Chi A	63	169	14	44	10	1	0	27	22	2	6	.260	.352	.331	97	0	0-4	.941	1	110	77	3b45	0	0.0
CLARKE, SUMPTER	Sumpter Mills; B10.18.1897 Savannah GA; D3.16.1962 Knoxville TN; BR/TR/5´11˝/170; d9.27; b–Rufe; Col South Carolina																								
1920	Chi N	1	3	0	1	0	0	0	0	0	0	1	.333	.333	.333	90	0	0-0	1.000	-0	91	0	/3	—	0.0
1923	Cle A	1	3	0	0	0	0	0	0	0	0	0	.000	.000	.000	-99	-1	0-0	1.000	0	0	0	/O	—	-0.1
1924	Cle A	35	104	17	24	6	1	0	11	6	0	12	.231	.273	.308	49	-8	0-0	1.000	-1	97	67	O33(2/9/22)	—	-1.0
Total	3	37	110	17	25	6	1	0	11	6	0	13	.227	.267	.300	46	-9	0-0	1.000	-1	97	67	O34(2/9/22)/3	—	-1.1
CLARKE, TOMMY	Thomas Aloysius; B5.9.1888 New York NY; D8.14.1945 Corona NY; BR/TR/5´11˝/175; d8.26; C5																								
1909	Cin N	18	52	8	13	3	2	0	10	6	0	—	.250	.328	.385	122	1	3	.965	2	*102*	*119*	C17	—	0.5
1910	Cin N	64	151	19	42	6	5	1	20	19	3	17	.278	.370	.404	131	6	1	.971	2	*123*	*85*	C56	—	1.3
1911	Cin N	86	203	20	49	6	7	1	25	25	1	22	.241	.328	.355	94	-2	4	.970	8	*133*	*86*	C81/1	—	1.1
1912	Cin N	72	146	19	41	7	2	0	22	28	1	14	.281	.400	.356	111	4	9	.983	3	*98*	*99*	C63	—	1.1
1913	Cin N	114	330	29	87	11	8	1	38	39	2	40	.264	.345	.355	100	1	2-1	.979	-5	99	89	C100	—	0.4
1914	Cin N	113	313	30	82	13	7	2	25	31	2	30	.262	.332	.367	105	2	6	.973	2	*92*	*98*	C106	—	1.2
1915	Cin N	96	226	23	65	7	2	0	21	33	1	22	.288	.381	.336	116	6	7-3	.981	-3	*93*	*91*	C72	—	1.0
1916	Cin N	78	177	10	42	10	1	0	17	24	0	20	.237	.328	.305	97	1	8	.965	-9	75	96	C51	—	-0.6
1917	Cin N	58	110	11	32	3	3	1	13	11	1	12	.291	.361	.400	139	5	2	.991	-3	*81*	*82*	C29	—	0.4
1918	Chi N	1	0	0	0	0	0	0	0	0	0	0	ø	ø	ø	ø	0	0	ø	0	*0*	*0*	/C	—	0.0
Total	10	700	1708	169	453	66	37	6	191	216	11	177	.265	.351	.358	109	24	42-4	.975	-4	*100*	*93*	C576/1	—	6.4
CLARKE, BOILERYARD	William Jones; B10.18.1868 New York NY; D7.29.1959 Princeton NJ; BR/TR/5´11.5˝/170; d5.1																								
1893	Bal N	49	183	23	32	1	3	1	24	19	6	14	.175	.274	.230	34	-18	2	.909	-5	*90*	*100*	C38,1b11	—	-1.6
1894	Bal N	28	100	18	24	8	0	1	19	16	3	14	.240	.361	.350	69	-5	2	.903	-1	*121*	*89*	C23,1b5	—	-0.2
1895	†Bal N	67	241	38	70	15	3	0	35	13	9	18	.290	.350	.378	85	-5	8	.938	15	*149*	*115*	C60,1b6	—	1.2
1896	Bal N	80	300	48	89	14	7	2	71	14	8	12	.297	.345	.410	97	-2	7	.948	-3	*111*	*86*	C67,1b14	—	0.0
1897	†Bal N	64	241	32	65	7	1	1	38	9	9	—	.270	.320	.320	69	-11	5	.939	-9	*102*	*64*	C59,1b4	—	-1.2
1898	Bal N	82	285	26	69	5	2	0	27	4	15	—	.242	.289	.274	60	-15	2	.962	3	*113*	*96*	C70,1b10	—	-0.5
1899	Bos N	60	223	25	50	3	2	2	32	10	4	—	.224	.270	.283	47	-17	2	.940	3	*119*	*88*	C60	—	-0.8
1900	Bos N	81	270	35	85	5	2	1	30	9	3	—	.315	.344	.359	84	-7	0	.928	4	*101*	*107*	C67,1b8	—	0.3
1901	Was A	110	422	58	118	15	5	3	54	23	12	—	.280	.335	.360	94	-3	7	.952	-5	*108*	*96*	C107,1b3	—	0.2
1902	Was A	87	291	31	78	15	0	6	40	23	4	—	.268	.330	.381	96	-1	1	**.972**	-4	*99*	*102*	C87	—	0.3
1903	Was A	126	465	35	111	14	6	2	38	15	7	—	.239	.273	.308	72	-16	12	.981	-14	80	94	1b88,C37	—	-2.9
1904	Was A	85	275	23	58	8	1	0	17	17	5	—	.211	.269	.247	65	-10	5	.977	-4	*73*	*125*	C52,1b29	—	-1.1

YEAR	TM LG	G	AB	R	H	2B	3B	HR	RBI	BB-IB	HP	SO	AVG	OBP	SLG	AOPS	ABR	SB-CS	FA	FR	RNG	THR	GAMES AT POSITION	DL	BFW
1905	NY N	31	50	2	9	0	0	1	4	4	0	—	.180	.241	.240	42	-4	1	.973	-1	66	96	1b15,C12	—	-0.4
Total	13	950	3346	394	858	110	32	20	429	176	85	58	.256	.310	.326	75	-114	54	.947	-18	*106*	*98*	C739,1b193	—	-6.7
Clarke, Stu	William Stuart; B1.24.1906 San Francisco CA; D8.26.1985 Hayward CA; BR/TR/5´8.5˝/160; d7.17																								
1929	Pit N	57	178	20	47	5	7	2	21	19	1	21	.264	.338	.404	81	-6	3	.919	-9	97	78	S41,3b15/2	—	-0.9
1930	Pit N	4	9	2	4	0	1	0	2	1	0	0	.444	.500	.667	178	1	0	1.000	-1	64	0	2b2	—	0.0
Total	2	61	187	22	51	5	8	2	23	20	1	21	.273	.346	.417	86	-5	3	.919	-9	97	78	S41,3b15,2b3	—	-0.9
Clarkson, Bus	James Buster; B3.13.1915 Hopkins SC; D1.18.1989 Jeannette PA; BR/TR/5´11˝/210; d4.30; Negro Lg 1937–50 Mil 1943–45; Col Wilberforce																								
1952	Bos N	14	25	3	5	0	0	0	1	3	0	3	.200	.286	.200	38	-2	0-0	.938	-2	60	0	S6,3b2	0	-0.4
Clary, Ellis	Ellis "Cat"; B9.11.1916 Valdosta GA; D6.2.2000 Valdosta GA; BR/TR/5´8˝/160; d6.7; C7																								
1942	Was A	76	240	34	66	9	0	0	16	45	2	25	.275	.394	.313	101	4	2-0	.969	-15	86	75	2b69,3b2	0	-0.7
1943	Was A	73	254	36	65	19	1	0	19	44	2	31	.256	.370	.339	112	7	8-4	.945	-6	90	49	3b68/S	0	0.3
	StL A	23	69	15	19	2	0	0	5	11	0	6	.275	.375	.304	98	0	1-2	.972	0	107	135	3b14,2b3	0	0.1
	Year	96	323	51	84	21	1	0	24	55	2	37	.260	.371	.331	109	7	9-6	.949	-5	93	62	3b82,2b3/S	0	0.4
1944	†StL A	25	49	6	13	1	1	0	4	12	0	9	.265	.410	.327	106	1	1-0	1.000	-0	94	118	3b11,2b6	0	0.1
1945	StL A	26	38	6	8	1	0	1	2	2	0	3	.211	.250	.316	61	-2	0-2	.947	0	106	171	3b16,2b3	0	-0.3
Total	4	223	650	97	171	32	2	1	46	114	4	74	.263	.376	.323	103	10	12-8	.953	-20	94	78	3b111,2b81/S	0	-0.5
Clay, Dain	Dain Elmer "Sniffy","Ding-A-Ling"; B7.10.1919 Hicksville OH; D8.28.1994 Chula Vista CA; BR/TR/5´10.5˝/160; d6.12; Col Kent St.																								
1943	Cin N	49	93	19	25	2	4	0	9	8	1	14	.269	.333	.376	106	0	1	.936	-2	81	103	O33(1/29/3)	0	-0.3
1944	Cin N	110	356	51	89	15	0	0	17	17	3	18	.250	.290	.292	67	-16	8	.993	-2	103	45	O98(5/93/0)	0	-2.2
1945	Cin N	153	656	81	184	29	2	1	50	37	2	58	.280	.321	.335	84	-15	19	.989	1	104	77	O152C	0	-1.9
1946	Cin N	121	435	52	99	17	0	2	22	53	5	40	.228	.318	.280	73	-14	11	**.988**	-5	94	85	O120(11/107/2)	0	-2.5
Total	4	433	1540	203	397	63	6	3	98	115	11	130	.258	.314	.312	79	-45	39	.987	-9	99	73	O403(17/381/5)	0	-6.9
Clay, Bill	Frederick C.; B11.23.1874 Baltimore MD; D10.12.1917 York PA; TL/?/175; d8.8																								
1902	Phi N	3	8	1	2	0	0	0	1	0	0	—	.250	.250	.250	54	0	0	.750	-1	0	0	O3L	—	-0.1
Clayton, Royce	Royce Spencer; B1.2.1970 Burbank CA; BR/TR/6´0˝/(175–200); [SFN88 1/15]; d9.20																								
1991	SF N	9	26	0	3	1	0	0	2	1-0	0	6	.115	.148	.154	-15	-4	0-0	.880	-6	30	29	S8	0	-1.0
1992	SF N	98	321	31	72	7	4	4	24	26-3	0	63	.224	.281	.308	71	-14	8-4	.973	-2	99	107	S94/3	0	-0.9
1993	SF N	153	549	54	155	21	5	6	70	38-2	5	91	.282	.331	.372	92	-7	11-10	.963	4	98	126	S153	0	0.7
1994	SF N	108	385	38	91	14	6	3	30	30-2	3	74	.236	.295	.327	65	-21	23-3	.973	8	106	105	S108	0	-0.1
1995	SF N	138	509	56	124	29	3	5	58	38-1	3	109	.244	.298	.342	70	-22	24-9	.969	3	104	115	S136	0	-0.7
1996	†StL N	129	491	64	136	20	4	6	35	33-4	1	89	.277	.321	.371	82	-13	33-15	.972	0	101	101	S113	0	-0.2
1997	StL N★	154	576	75	153	39	5	9	61	33-4	3	109	.266	.306	.398	83	-15	30-10	.973	11	106	107	S153	0	1.0
1998	StL N	90	355	59	83	19	1	4	29	40-1	2	51	.234	.313	.327	69	-15	19-6	.970	5	111	96	S89	15	-0.1
	†Tex A	52	186	30	53	12	1	5	24	13-0	1	32	.285	.330	.441	94	-2	5-5	.972	0	102	76	S52	0	0.2
1999	†Tex A	133	465	69	134	21	5	14	52	39-1	4	100	.288	.346	.445	95	-4	8-6	.961	5	107	100	S133	20	0.9
2000	Tex A	148	513	70	124	21	5	14	54	42-1	3	92	.242	.301	.384	71	-24	11-7	.977	-6	95	87	S148	0	-1.8
2001	Chi A	135	433	62	114	21	4	9	60	33-2	3	72	.263	.315	.393	81	-12	10-7	.988	-1	103	94	S133	0	-0.4
2002	Chi A	112	342	51	86	14	2	7	35	20-0	3	67	.251	.295	.365	73	-14	5-1	.989	6	101	113	S109	0	0.0
2003	Mil N	146	483	49	110	16	1	11	39	49-10	3	92	.228	.301	.333	66	-25	5-2	.977	-15	96	82	S141	0	-2.8
2004	Col N	146	574	95	160	36	4	8	54	48-0	4	125	.279	.338	.397	79	-16	10-5	**.986**	-6	100	86	S144	0	-1.1
2005	Ari N	143	522	59	141	28	4	2	44	38-0	1	105	.270	.320	.351	72	-21	13-3	.982	-1	104	101	S141	0	-1.0
2006	Was N	87	305	36	82	22	1	0	27	19-3	4	53	.269	.315	.348	75	-11	8-3	.970	-6	103	71	S86	0	-1.0
	Cin N	50	149	13	35	8	0	2	13	11-0	1	32	.235	.290	.329	56	-10	6-3	.958	-6	90	63	S43	0	-1.2
	Year	137	454	49	117	30	1	2	40	30-3	5	85	.258	.307	.341	68	-22	14-6	.966	-11	0	0	S129	0	-2.2
Total	16	2031	7184	911	1856	349	55	109	711	551-34	44	1362	.258	.313	.368	77	-250	229-99	.974	-5	102	98	S1984/3	35	-9.5
Clemens, Chet	Chester Spurgeon; B5.10.1917 San Fernando CA; D2.10.2002 San Clemente CA; BR/TR/6´0˝/175; d9.13; Mil 1944–46																								
1939	Bos N	9	23	2	5	0	0	0	1	1	0	3	.217	.250	.217	29	-2	1	.867	-1	102	0	O7L	—	-0.3
1944	Bos N	19	17	7	3	1	1	0	2	2	0	2	.176	.263	.353	69	-1	0	1.000	0	123	0	O7L	0	-0.1
Total	2	28	40	9	8	1	1	0	3	3	0	5	.200	.256	.275	46	-3	1	.905	-1	108	0	O14L	0	-0.4
Clemens, Clem	Clement Lambert "Count" (b Clement Lambert Ulatowski); B11.21.1886 Chicago IL; D11.2.1967 St.Petersburg FL; BR/TR/5´11˝/176; d5.15; Col Notre Dame																								
1914	Chi F	13	27	4	4	0	0	0	2	3	0	0	.148	.233	.148	6	-4	0	.950	-0	*144*	*69*	C8	—	-0.4
1915	Chi F	11	22	3	3	1	0	0	3	1	0	0	.136	.174	.182	0	-3	0	1.000	-0	*122*	*61*	C9,2b2	—	-0.3
1916	Chi N	10	15	0	0	0	0	0	0	1	0	6	.000	.063	.000	-72	-3	0	.941	0	128	101	C9	—	-0.3
Total	3	34	64	7	7	1	0	0	5	5	0	6	.109	.174	.125	-15	-10	0	.962	0	*132*	*76*	C26,2b2	—	-1.0
Clemens, Doug	Douglas Horace; B6.9.1939 Leesport PA; BL/TR/6´0˝/180; d10.2; Col Syracuse																								
1960	StL N	1	0	0	0	0	0	0	0	0-0	0	0	ø	ø	ø	ø	0	0-0	1.000	0	330	0	/rf	0	0.0
1961	StL N	6	12	1	2	1	0	0	0	3-0	0	1	.167	.333	.250	53	-1	0-0	.667	-1	41	0	O3(2/0/2)	0	-0.2
1962	StL N	48	93	12	22	1	1	1	12	17-1	0	19	.237	.355	.301	71	-3	0-0	.974	-3	90	0	O34(7/1/27)	0	-0.7
1963	StL N	5	6	1	1	0	0	1	2	1-0	0	2	.167	.286	.667	151	0	0-0	1.000	1	96	809	O3(2/0/1)	0	0.1
1964	StL N	33	78	8	16	4	3	1	9	6-0	1	16	.205	.271	.372	73	-3	0-0	.970	0	93	158	O22(17/0/5)	0	-0.4
	Chi N	54	140	23	39	10	2	2	12	18-2	1	22	.279	.363	.421	116	4	0-0	.923	2	106	191	O40(1/2/38)	30	0.3
	Year	87	218	31	55	14	5	3	21	24-2	2	38	.252	.331	.404	100	1	0-0	.937	2	101	179	O62(18/2/43)	0	-0.1
1965	Chi N	128	340	36	75	11	0	4	26	38-4	2	53	.221	.300	.288	66	-14	5-8	.981	-4	86	122	O105(44/13/49)	0	-2.7
1966	Phi N	79	121	10	31	1	0	1	15	16-0	2	25	.256	.353	.289	81	-2	1-0	1.000	2	112	71	O28(24/2/3)/1	0	-0.2
1967	Phi N	69	73	2	13	5	0	0	4	8-0	1	15	.178	.262	.247	48	-5	0-0	1.000	-1	52	0	O10(9/0/1)	0	-0.7
1968	Phi N	29	57	6	12	1	1	2	8	7-1	0	13	.211	.292	.368	99	0	0-0	1.000	-1	93	83	O17(3/0/15)	0	-0.2
Total	9	452	920	99	211	34	7	12	88	114-8	7	166	.229	.317	.321	78	-24	6-8	.969	-4	92	116	O263(109/18/142)/1	30	-4.7
Clemens, Bob	Robert Baxter; B8.9.1886 Odessa MO; D4.5.1964 Marshall MO; BR/TR/5´9˝/163; d9.17; Col Missouri Valley																								
1914	StL A	7	13	1	3	0	1	0	3	2	1	1	.231	.375	.385	134	1	0-2	.750	-0	76	201	O5(2/1/2)	—	-0.1
Clement, Wally	Wallace Oakes; B7.21.1881 Auburn ME; D11.1.1953 Coral Gables FL; BL/TR/5´11˝/175; d8.17; Col Tufts																								
1908	Phi N	16	36	0	8	3	0	0	1	0	0	—	.222	.222	.306	66	-1	2	1.000	2	71	312	O8L	—	0.0
1909	Phi N	3	3	0	0	0	0	0	0	0	0	—	.000	.000	.000	-99	-1	0	ø	0	—	—	/H	—	-0.1
	Bro N	92	340	35	88	8	4	0	17	18	0	—	.259	.296	.306	90	-5	11	.965	2	108	129	O88(84/0/4)	—	-0.9
	Year	95	343	35	88	8	4	0	17	18	0	—	.257	.294	.303	88	-6	11	.965	2	108	129	O88(84/0/4)	—	-1.0
Total	2	111	379	35	96	11	4	0	18	18	0	—	.253	.287	.303	86	-7	13	.970	4	104	149	O96(92/0/4)	—	-1.0
Clemente, Edgard	Edgard Alexis (Velazquez) (b Edgard Alexis Velazquez); B12.15.1975 Santurce, PR; BR/TR/5´11˝/188; [ColN93 10/296]; d9.10																								
1998	Col N	11	17	2	6	0	1	0	2	2-0	0	8	.353	.421	.471	111	0	0-0	.857	-1	56	0	O7(0/1/6)	0	-0.1
1999	Col N	57	162	24	41	10	2	8	25	7-0	0	46	.253	.282	.488	72	-7	0-0	.972	0	104	91	O49(2/45/4)	0	-0.7
2000	Ana A	46	78	4	17	2	0	0	5	0-0	1	27	.218	.228	.244	19	-10	0-1	1.000	0	95	180	O32(15/5/12),D11	0	-1.0
Total	3	114	257	30	64	12	3	8	32	9-0	1	81	.249	.276	.412	61	-17	0-1	.974	-1	97	108	O88(17/51/22),D11	0	-1.8
Clemente, Roberto	Roberto (Walker) "Bob"; B8.18.1934 Carolina, PR; D12.31.1972 San Juan, PR; BR/TR/5´11˝/(175–180); d4.17; HF1973																								
1955	Pit N	124	474	48	121	23	11	5	47	18-3	2	60	.255	.284	.382	76	-18	2-5	.978	11	**109**	181	O118(1/10/111)	0	-1.3
1956	Pit N	147	543	66	169	30	7	7	60	13-2	4	58	.311	.330	.431	105	3	6-6	.957	3	102	**152**	O139(26/22/101),2b2/3	0	-0.1
1957	Pit N	111	451	42	114	17	7	4	30	23-1	0	45	.253	.288	.348	72	-19	0-4	.979	11	**126**	109	O109(0/14/97)	0	-1.4
1958	Pit N	140	519	69	150	24	10	6	50	31-1	0	41	.289	.327	.408	96	-4	8-2	.982	21	**128**	**199**	O135R	0	1.4
1959	Pit N	105	432	60	128	17	7	4	50	15-2	3	51	.296	.322	.396	91	-7	2-3	.948	6	**115**	120	O104R	40	-0.5
1960	†Pit N★	144	570	89	179	22	6	16	94	39-4	2	72	.314	.357	.458	121	16	4-5	.971	-1	91	141	O142R	0	0.9
1961	Pit N★	146	572	100	201	30	10	23	89	35-10	3	59	**.351**	.390	.559	148	38	4-1	.969	9	97	**205**	O144(0/1/144)	0	3.7
1962	Pit N★	144	538	95	168	28	9	10	74	35-9	1	73	.312	.352	.454	115	11	6-4	.973	10	111	163	O142R	0	1.0
1963	Pit N★	152	600	77	192	23	8	17	76	31-6	4	64	.320	.356	.470	135	26	12-2	.958	-7	92	97	O151(0/8/143)	0	1.2
1964	Pit N★	155	622	95	**211**	40	7	12	87	51-16	2	87	**.339**	.388	.484	145	38	5-2	.968	4	107	115	O154R	0	3.3
1965	Pit N★	152	589	91	194	21	14	10	65	43-14	5	78	**.329**	.378	.463	136	27	8-0	.968	7	106	157	O145(0/5/143)	0	2.7
1966	Pit N★	154	638	105	202	31	11	29	119	46-13	0	109	.317	.360	.536	146	38	7-5	.965	10	113	152	O154(0/1/154)	0	3.7

YEAR	TM LG	G	AB	R	H	2B	3B	HR	RBI	BB-IB	HP	SO	AVG	OBP	SLG	AOPS	ABR	SB-CS	FA	FR	RNG	THR	GAMES AT POSITION	DL	BFW
1967	Pit N★	147	585	103	**209**	26	10	23	110	41-17	3	103	**.357**	.400	.554	170	51	9-1	.970	5	100	158	O145(0/2/144)	0	5.1
1968	Pit N	132	502	74	146	18	12	18	57	51-**27**	1	77	.291	.355	.482	152	31	2-3	.984	7	120	79	O131R	0	3.2
1969	Pit N★	138	507	87	175	20	**12**	19	91	56-16	3	73	.345	.411	.544	170	47	4-1	.980	6	104	152	O135R	0	4.8
1970	†Pit N★	108	412	65	145	22	10	14	60	38-14	2	66	.352	.407	.556	156	32	3-0	.966	3	98	171	O104R	0	3.0
1971	†Pit N★	132	522	82	178	29	8	13	86	26-5	0	65	.341	.370	.502	144	28	1-2	.993	7	**112**	122	O124R	0	3.0
1972	†Pit N✳	102	378	68	118	19	7	10	60	29-7	0	49	.312	.356	.479	139	18	0-0	1.000	3	115	72	O94R	0	1.7
Total	18	2433	9454	1416	3000	440	166	240	1305	621-167	35	1230	.317	.359	.475	130	356	83-46	.973	116	108	143	O2370(27/63/2302),2b2/3	40	35.4
CLEMENTS, ED	Edward; B Philadelphia PA; d6.24																								
1890	Pit N	1	1	0	0	0	0	0	0	0	0	0	.000	.000	.000	-99	0	0	.400	-1	52	0	/S	—	-0.1
CLEMENTS, JACK	John J.; B7.24.1864 Philadelphia PA; D5.23.1941 Norristown PA; BL/TL/5´8.5˝/204; d4.22; M1																								
1884	Phi U	41	177	37	50	13	2	3	—	9	—	—	.282	.317	.429	135	3	—	.764	-2	210	156	O22(5/0/17),C20/S	—	0.1
	Phi N	9	30	3	7	0	0	0	0	4	—	8	.233	.324	.233	82	0	—	.827	-2	—	—	C9	—	-0.1
1885	Phi N	52	188	14	36	11	3	1	14	2	—	30	.191	.200	.298	61	-8	—	.891	-4	—	—	C41,O11(2/7/2)	—	-0.9
1886	Phi N	54	185	15	38	5	1	0	11	7	—	34	.205	.234	.243	45	-12	4	.930	7	—	—	C47,O7(1/0/6)	—	-0.2
1887	Phi N	66	246	48	69	13	7	1	47	9	4	24	.280	.317	.402	93	-3	7	.940	8	—	—	C59,3b4,S3	—	0.8
1888	Phi N	86	326	26	80	8	4	1	32	10	4	36	.245	.276	.304	80	-8	3	.927	0	—	—	C85/rf	—	0.0
1889	Phi N	78	310	51	88	17	1	4	35	29	1	21	.284	.347	.384	95	-3	3	.916	-6	—	—	C78	—	-0.2
1890	Phi N	97	381	64	120	23	8	7	74	45	3	30	.315	.392	.472	148	23	10	.944	4	*105*	*80*	C91,1b5,M	—	3.0
1891	Phi N	107	423	58	131	29	4	4	75	43	5	19	.310	.380	.426	131	18	3	.927	-6	*93*	*86*	C107,1b2	—	1.8
1892	Phi N	109	402	50	106	25	6	8	76	43	3	40	.264	.339	.415	128	14	7	.950	13	***135***	*66*	C109	—	3.3
1893	Phi N	94	376	64	107	20	3	17	80	39	5	29	.285	.360	.489	125	12	3	.942	-3	***128***	*69*	C92/1	—	1.4
1894	Phi N	48	171	26	60	6	5	3	36	26	9	9	.351	.461	.497	134	12	6	.940	-5	*91*	*70*	C48	—	0.8
1895	Phi N	88	322	64	127	27	2	13	75	22	8	7	.394	.446	.612	170	34	3	.969	-8	*94*	*89*	C88	—	2.6
1896	Phi N	57	184	35	66	5	7	5	45	17	5	14	.359	.427	.543	157	15	2	.966	-3	*104*	*103*	C53	—	1.4
1897	Phi N	55	185	18	44	4	2	6	36	12	6	—	.238	.305	.378	82	-6	3	.962	-2	*103*	*80*	C49	—	-0.3
1898	StL N	99	335	39	86	19	5	3	41	21	7	—	.257	.314	.370	94	-4	1	**.971**	-12	*74*	*90*	C86	—	-0.7
1899	Cle N	4	12	1	3	0	0	0	0	0	1	—	.250	.308	.250	58	-1	0	.938	-1	*61*	*155*	C4	—	-0.1
1900	Bos N	16	42	6	13	1	0	1	10	3	1	—	.310	.370	.405	101	0	0	.948	1	*99*	*63*	C10	—	0.2
Total	17	1160	4295	619	1231	226	60	77	687	341	62	301	.287	.348	.421	116	86	55	.937	-21	*105*	*80*	C1076,O41(8/7/26),1b8,3b4,S4	—	12.9
CLEMONS, VERNE	Verne James "Stinger","Tubby"; B9.8.1891 Clemons IA; D5.5.1959 Bay Pines FL; BR/TR/5´9.5˝/190; d4.22																								
1916	StL A	4	7	0	1	1	0	0	0	0	0	1	.143	.143	.286	30	-1	0	.889	-0	85	160	C2	—	-0.1
1919	StL N	88	239	14	63	13	2	2	22	26	0	13	.264	.336	.360	116	6	4	.982	3	*104*	*97*	C75	—	1.6
1920	StL N	112	338	17	95	10	6	1	36	30	0	12	.281	.340	.355	103	2	1-1	.977	-7	*85*	*90*	C103	—	0.3
1921	StL N	117	341	29	109	16	2	2	48	33	0	17	.320	.380	.396	108	5	0-0	.985	-1	*95*	*95*	C107	—	1.0
1922	StL N	71	160	9	41	4	0	0	15	18	0	5	.256	.331	.281	62	-8	1-0	.996	2	*106*	*121*	C63	—	-0.3
1923	StL N	57	130	6	37	9	1	0	13	10	2	11	.285	.345	.369	90	-1	0-0	.981	1	*105*	*102*	C41	—	0.2
1924	StL N	25	56	3	18	3	0	0	6	2	0	3	.321	.345	.375	94	0	0-0	.983	-1	*98*	*90*	C17	—	-0.1
Total	7	474	1271	78	364	56	11	5	140	119	2	62	.286	.348	.360	99	3	6-1	.983	-4	*96*	*98*	C408	—	2.6
CLENDENON, DONN	Donn Alvin; B7.15.1935 Neosho MO; D9.17.2005 Sioux Falls SD; BR/TR/6´3.5˝/(201–220); d9.22; Col Morehouse																								
1961	Pit N	9	35	7	11	1	1	0	2	5-0	0	10	.314	.400	.400	113	1	0-0	1.000	-0	91	123	O8(1/0/7)	0	0.0
1962	Pit N	80	222	39	67	8	5	7	28	26-3	1	58	.302	.376	.477	128	9	16-4	.990	-2	79	122	1b52,O19(16/1/2)	0	0.5
1963	Pit N	154	563	65	155	28	7	15	57	39-3	5	136	.275	.326	.430	116	11	22-13	.991	5	**112**	**130**	1b151	0	0.7
1964	Pit N	133	457	53	129	23	8	12	64	26-2	2	96	.282	.321	.446	115	8	12-8	.989	-1	99	**124**	1b119	0	0.0
1965	Pit N	162	612	89	184	32	14	14	96	48-7	5	128	.301	.351	.467	129	23	9-9	.984	2	112	**132**	1b158/3	0	1.5
1966	Pit N	155	571	80	171	22	10	28	98	52-7	2	142	.299	.358	.520	141	30	8-7	.985	-1	103	**147**	1b152	0	2.0
1967	Pit N	131	478	46	119	15	2	13	56	34-4	1	107	.249	.298	.370	90	-7	4-4	.988	5	**121**	**118**	1b123	0	-1.1
1968	Pit N	158	584	63	150	20	6	17	87	47-4	1	163	.257	.309	.399	114	9	10-3	.990	8	**123**	112	1b155	0	0.9
1969	Mon N	38	129	14	31	6	1	4	14	6-1	0	32	.240	.272	.395	85	-3	0-2	.987	3	144	112	1b24,O11(9/1/1)	0	-0.3
	†NY N	72	202	31	51	5	0	12	37	19-4	2	62	.252	.321	.455	113	3	3-2	.984	-3	81	131	1b58/lf	0	-0.5
	Year	110	331	45	82	11	1	16	51	25-5	2	94	.248	.303	.432	102	0	3-4	.985	0	100	125	1b82,O12(10/1/1)	0	-0.8
1970	NY N	121	396	65	114	18	3	22	97	39-4	1	91	.288	.348	.515	128	14	4-1	.991	-0	96	102	1b100	0	0.7
1971	NY N	88	263	29	65	10	0	11	37	21-3	1	78	.247	.302	.411	101	0	1-2	.985	-2	88	101	1b72	0	-0.8
1972	StL N	61	136	13	26	4	0	4	9	17-4	0	37	.191	.279	.309	68	-6	1-2	.986	2	127	132	1b36	0	-0.7
Total	12	1362	4648	594	1273	192	57	159	682	379-46	21	1140	.274	.328	.442	116	92	90-57	.988	16	108	124	1b1200,O39(27/2/10)/3	0	2.9
CLEVELAND, ELMER	Elmer Ellsworth; B9.15.1862 Washington DC; D10.8.1913 Zimmerman PA; BR/TR/5´11˝/190; d8.29																								
1884	Cin U	29	115	24	37	9	2	0	—	4	—	—	.322	.345	.435	125	0	—	.843	1	99	0	3b29	—	0.1
1888	NY N	9	34	6	8	0	2	2	7	3	0	1	.235	.297	.529	161	2	1	.667	-4	42	0	3b9	—	-0.2
	Pit N	30	108	10	24	2	1	2	9	5	2	23	.222	.270	.315	94	-1	3	.831	-5	90	86	3b30	—	-0.6
	Year	39	142	16	32	2	3	4	16	8	2	24	.225	.276	.366	111	2	4	.806	-10	80	67	3b39	—	-0.8
1891	Col AA	12	41	12	7	0	0	0	4	12	1	9	.171	.370	.171	59	-1	4	.843	1	111	43	3b12	—	0.0
Total	3	80	298	52	76	11	5	4	20	24	3	33	.255	.317	.366	110	0	8	.830	-8	93	37	3b80	—	-0.7
CLEVLEN, BRENT	Brent Aaron; B10.27.1983 Austin TX; BR/TR/6´2˝/190; [DetA02 2/49]; d7.30																								
2006	Det A	31	39	9	11	1	2	3	6	2-0	0	15	.282	.317	.641	142	2	0-0	1.000	2	97	418	O29(8/13/13)	0	0.4
CLIBURN, STAN	Stanley Gene; B12.19.1956 Jackson MS; BR/TR/6´0˝/190; [AnaA74 5/106]; d5.6; twb–Stew																								
1980	Cal A	54	56	7	10	2	0	2	6	3-0	0	9	.179	.217	.321	47	-4	0-0	.971	-1	60	93	C54	0	-0.5
CLIFT, HARLOND	Harlond Benton "Darkie"; B8.12.1912 El Reno OK; D4.27.1992 Yakima WA; BR/TR/5´11˝/180; d4.17																								
1934	StL A	147	572	104	149	30	10	14	56	84	2	100	.260	.357	.421	92	-7	7-2	.929	-14	89	98	3b141	—	-1.4
1935	StL A	137	475	101	140	26	4	11	69	83	6	39	.295	.406	.436	113	12	0-3	.934	-6	102	63	3b127,2b6	—	0.9
1936	StL A	152	576	145	174	40	11	20	73	115	7	68	.302	.424	.514	127	28	12-4	.951	5	105	99	3b152	—	3.4
1937	StL A☆	155	571	103	175	36	7	29	118	98	6	80	.306	.413	.546	139	36	8-5	.947	**41**	**129**	**141**	3b155	—	**7.4**
1938	StL A	149	534	119	155	25	7	34	118	118	5	67	.290	.423	.554	143	39	10-5	**.962**	15	102	105	3b149	—	5.3
1939	StL A	151	526	90	142	25	2	15	84	**111**	5	55	.270	.402	.411	106	10	4-3	.953	13	107	99	3b149	—	2.6
1940	StL A	150	523	92	143	29	5	20	87	104	2	62	.273	.396	.463	119	19	9-8	**.959**	9	**110**	104	3b147	—	3.0
1941	StL A	154	584	108	149	33	9	17	84	113	0	93	.255	.376	.430	109	10	6-4	.959	5	104	94	3b154	0	2.0
1942	StL A	143	541	108	148	39	4	7	55	106	2	48	.274	.394	.399	122	22	6-4	.941	-1	101	106	3b141/S	0	2.6
1943	StL A	105	379	43	88	11	3	3	25	54	1	37	.232	.329	.301	83	-7	5-4	.950	16	118	98	3b104	0	1.1
	Was A	8	30	4	9	0	0	0	4	5	1	3	.300	.417	.300	115	1	0-0	.968	-1	69	0	3b8	0	0.0
	Year	113	409	47	97	11	3	3	29	59	2	40	.237	.336	.301	85	-6	5-4	.951	15	**114**	91	3b112	0	1.1
1944	Was A	12	44	4	7	3	0	0	3	3	0	3	.159	.213	.227	27	-4	0-0	.842	-2	90	95	3b12	0	-0.7
1945	Was A	119	375	49	79	12	0	8	53	76	4	58	.211	.349	.307	99	4	2-1	.934	-4	98	95	3b111	0	0.1
Total	12	1582	5730	1070	1558	309	62	178	829	1070	41	713	.272	.390	.441	115	163	69-43	.948	75	106	100	3b1550,2b6/S	0	26.3
CLIFTON, FLEA	Herman Earl; B12.12.1909 Cincinnati OH; D12.22.1997 Cincinnati OH; BR/TR/5´10˝/160; d4.29																								
1934	Det A	16	16	3	1	0	0	0	1	1	0	2	.063	.118	.063	-52	-4	0-0	1.000	1	141	0	3b4/2	—	-0.3
1935	†Det A	43	110	15	28	5	0	0	9	5	1	13	.255	.293	.300	56	-7	2-1	.934	-1	89	74	3b21,2b5,S4	—	-0.7
1936	Det A	13	26	5	5	1	0	0	1	4	0	3	.192	.300	.231	33	-3	0-1	.926	-1	84	95	S6,3b2/2	—	-0.3
1937	Det A	15	43	4	5	1	0	0	2	7	0	10	.116	.240	.140	-2	-7	3-0	.958	-2	94	66	3b7,S4,2b3	—	-0.7
Total	4	87	195	27	39	7	0	0	13	17	1	28	.200	.268	.236	30	-21	5-2	.937	-3	94	85	3b34,S14,2b10	—	-2.0
CLINE, MONK	John P.; B3.3.1858 Louisville KY; D9.23.1916 Louisville KY; BL/TL/5´4˝/150; d7.4																								
1882	Bal AA	44	172	18	38	6	2	0	—	3	—	—	.221	.234	.279	79	-3	—	.825	4	165	87	O39(1/38/0),S8,2b2/3	—	-0.1
1884	Lou AA	94	396	91	115	16	7	2	39	27	4	—	.290	.342	.381	142	20	—	.875	4	142	44	O90(8/81/3),S6	—	1.9
1885	Lou AA	2	9	0	2	1	0	0	2	0	0	—	.222	.222	.333	74	0	—	1.000	-0	0	0	/lf3	—	0.0
1888	KC AA	73	293	45	69	13	2	0	19	20	2	—	.235	.289	.294	82	-6	29	.883	5	192	135	O70(32/0/38),2b3/3	—	-0.2
1891	Lou AA	19	70	11	21	3	1	0	11	16	0	2	.300	.430	.371	131	4	2	.929	-1	72	0	O19L	—	0.2
Total	5	232	940	165	245	39	12	2	71	66	6	2	.261	.313	.334	110	15	31	.868	12	157	78	O219(61/119/41),S14,2b5,3b3	—	1.8

YEAR	TM LG	G	AB	R	H	2B	3B	HR	RBI	BB-IB	HP	SO	AVG	OBP	SLG	AOPS	ABR	SB-CS	FA	FR	RNG	THR	GAMES AT POSITION	DL	BFW
Cline, Ty	Tyrone Alexander; B6.15.1939 Hampton SC; BL/TL/6´0.5˝/(168–170); d9.14; Col Clemson																								
1960	Cle A	7	26	2	8	1	1	0	2	0-0	0	4	.308	.308	.423	99	0	0-0	1.000	1	161	0	O6C	0	0.1
1961	Cle A	12	43	9	9	2	1	0	1	6-0	2	1	.209	.333	.302	73	-1	1-0	1.000	-2	70	0	O12C	0	-0.4
1962	Cle A	118	375	53	93	15	5	2	28	28-0	5	50	.248	.308	.331	74	-14	5-4	.992	1	109	67	O107C	0	-1.6
1963	Mil N	72	174	17	41	2	1	0	10	10-0	2	31	.236	.283	.259	58	-9	2-1	.992	5	114	173	O62C	0	-0.6
1964	Mil N	101	116	22	35	4	2	1	13	8-0	3	22	.302	.359	.397	113	2	0-1	.982	2	106	286	O54(3/49/2),1b6	0	0.3
1965	Mil N	123	220	27	42	5	3	0	10	16-2	0	50	.191	.246	.241	37	-19	2-2	.969	5	120	178	O86(17/58/12),1b5	0	-1.7
1966	Chi N	7	17	3	6	0	0	0	2	0-0	0	2	.353	.353	.353	96	0	1-0	1.000	-0	97	0	O5C	0	0.0
	Atl N	42	71	12	18	0	0	0	6	3-0	2	11	.254	.303	.254	56	-4	2-1	1.000	-1	111	142	O19(7/5/10),1b6	0	-0.6
	Year	49	88	15	24	0	0	0	8	3-0	2	13	.273	.312	.273	63	-4	3-1	1.000	-1	108	108	O24(7/10/10),1b6	0	-0.6
1967	Atl N	10	8	0	0	0	0	0	0	0-0	1	3	.000	.111	.000	-66	-2	0-0	1.000	0	514	0	/lf	0	-0.2
	SF N	64	122	18	33	5	5	0	4	9-0	1	13	.270	.326	.393	106	1	2-1	1.000	-2	90	0	O37(17/21/3)	21	-0.3
	Year	74	130	18	33	5	5	0	4	9-0	2	16	.254	.312	.369	96	-1	2-1	1.000	-2	92	0	O38(18/21/3)	0	-0.5
1968	SF N	116	291	37	65	6	3	1	28	11-1	1	26	.223	.253	.275	59	-15	0-2	.971	1	99	170	O70(48/13/10),1b24	0	-2.2
1969	Mon N	101	209	26	50	5	3	2	12	32-1	2	22	.239	.346	.321	87	-3	4-3	.988	1	110	103	O41(7/35/0),1b17	0	-0.4
1970	Mon N	2	2	0	1	0	0	0	0	0-0	0	0	.500	.500	.500	168	0	0-0	ø	0	—	—	/H	65	0.0
	†Cin N	48	63	13	17	7	1	0	8	12-1	0	11	.270	.387	.413	114	2	1-2	.966	1	124	138	O20(6/8/6),1b2	0	0.2
	Year	50	65	13	18	7	1	0	8	12-1	0	11	.277	.390	.415	115	2	1-2	.966	1	124	138	O20(6/8/6),1b2	0	0.2
1971	Cin N	69	97	12	19	1	0	0	1	18-0	2	16	.196	.333	.206	56	-5	2-2	1.000	-1	95	0	O28(6/21/1),1b2	0	-0.7
Total	12	892	1834	251	437	53	25	6	125	153-5	21	262	.238	.304	.304	72	-67	22-19	.986	12	108	116	O548(112/402/44),1b62	86	-8.1
Clines, Gene	Eugene Anthony; B10.6.1946 San Pablo CA; BR/TR/5´9˝/(170–171); [PitN66 6/115]; d6.28; C20																								
1970	Pit N	31	37	4	15	2	0	0	3	2-0	0	5	.405	.436	.459	141	2	2-1	1.000	-1	45	0	O7(2/2/3)	0	0.1
1971	†Pit N	97	273	52	84	12	4	1	24	22-0	3	36	.308	.366	.392	114	5	15-6	.981	4	100	202	O74(20/43/13)	0	0.8
1972	†Pit N	107	311	52	104	15	6	0	17	16-1	2	47	.334	.369	.421	126	10	12-6	.958	-2	91	138	O83(38/17/39)	0	0.6
1973	Pit N	110	304	42	80	11	3	1	23	26-0	3	36	.263	.327	.329	84	-6	8-7	.968	-2	96	121	O77(7/45/25)	21	-1.2
1974	†Pit N	107	276	29	62	5	1	0	14	30-2	4	40	.225	.307	.250	59	-14	14-2	.989	5	111	137	O78(19/51/11)	0	-1.0
1975	NY N	82	203	25	46	6	3	0	10	11-1	1	21	.227	.269	.286	56	-13	4-4	.982	5	95	297	O60(35/34/2)	0	-1.2
1976	Tex A	116	446	52	123	12	3	0	38	16-0	4	52	.276	.304	.316	81	-12	11-9	.987	3	103	126	O103(96/5/4),D10	0	-1.6
1977	Chi N	101	239	27	70	12	2	3	41	25-2	1	25	.293	.358	.397	93	-1	1-2	.986	-6	68	88	O63(50/3/11)	16	-1.0
1978	Chi N	109	229	31	59	10	2	0	17	21-1	1	28	.258	.321	.319	71	-8	4-3	.978	-1	85	155	O66(35/10/24)	0	-1.2
1979	Chi N	10	10	0	2	0	0	0	0	0-0	0	1	.200	.200	.200	9	-1	0-0	ø	0	—	—	/H	0	-0.2
Total	10	870	2328	314	645	85	24	5	187	169-7	19	291	.277	.329	.341	87	-38	71-40	.979	6	95	151	O611(302/210/132),D10	37	-5.9
Clingman, Billy	William Frederick; B11.21.1869 Cincinnati OH; D5.14.1958 Cincinnati OH; BB/TR/5´11˝/150; d9.9																								
1890	Cin N	7	27	2	7	1	0	0	5	1	0	0	.259	.286	.296	70	-1	0	.892	-1	107	181	S6/2	—	-0.1
1891	Cin AA	1	5	0	1	1	0	0	0	0	0	0	.200	.200	.400	66	0	0	.667	-1	84	0	/2	—	-0.1
1895	Pit N	107	386	69	99	16	4	0	45	41	2	43	.256	.331	.319	72	-15	19	.888	12	114	102	3b107	—	0.0
1896	Lou N	121	423	57	99	10	2	2	37	57	3	51	.234	.329	.281	64	-20	19	.925	24	**114**	104	3b121	—	0.5
1897	Lou N	115	403	61	92	14	7	2	47	37	5	—	.228	.301	.313	64	-21	14	**.947**	30	**124**	106	3b115	—	0.9
1898	Lou N	**154**	538	65	138	12	6	0	50	51	5	—	.257	.327	.301	81	-12	15	.914	7	112	101	3b79,S74/cf2	—	0.0
1899	Lou N	110	369	68	97	15	5	2	45	46	3	—	.263	.349	.347	91	-3	13	.913	-3	106	112	S110	—	-0.1
1900	Chi N	47	159	15	33	6	0	0	11	17	2	—	.208	.292	.245	51	-10	6	.872	-11	91	107	S47	—	-1.8
1901	Was A	137	480	66	116	10	7	2	55	42	4	—	.242	.308	.304	71	-18	10	**.932**	**22**	**107**	112	S137	—	0.7
1903	Cle A	21	64	10	18	1	1	0	7	11	0	—	.281	.387	.328	118	2	2	.932	1	114	64	2b11,S7,3b3	—	0.4
Total	10	820	2854	413	700	86	32	8	302	303	24	94	.245	.323	.306	74	-98	98	.919	81	116	103	3b425,S381,2b14/cf	—	0.4
Clinton, Jim	James Lawrence "Big Jim"; B8.10.1850 New York NY; D9.3.1921 Brooklyn NY; BR/TR/5´8.5˝/174; d5.18; U1; OF NA(0/8/9); ▲																								
1872	Eck NA	25	98	11	24	4	1	0	6	0	—	3	.245	.245	.306	81	-1	0-1	.712	-4	105	0	3b11,O9(0/7/2),2b3,C2,S2/P	—	-0.4
1873	Res NA	9	39	5	9	2	0	0	4	0	—	2	.231	.231	.282	55	-2	0-0	.687	-2	84	58	3b9	—	-0.3
1874	Atl NA	2	11	3	2	1	0	0	2	0	—	2	.182	.182	.273	49	0	0-0	.444	-1	72	0	/2cf	—	-0.1
1875	Atl NA	22	81	3	10	0	0	0	0	0	—	0	.123	.123	.123	-16	-8	0-0	.830	3	125	75	P17,O7R,1b5/2	—	0.0
1876	Lou N	16	65	8	22	2	0	0	0	0	—	0	.338	.338	.369	115	0	—	.783	0	168	231	O14R/1P	—	0.0
1882	Wor N	26	98	9	16	2	0	0	3	7	—	13	.163	.219	.184	30	-7	—	.734	-4	67	63	O26(21/1/4)	—	-1.1
1883	Bal AA	94	399	69	125	16	8	0	—	27	—	—	.313	.357	.393	137	17	—	.842	4	102	85	O92L,2b2	—	1.6
1884	Bal AA	104	437	82	118	12	6	4	—	29	13	—	.270	.334	.352	119	10	—	.807	-4	83	161	O104(37/67/0)/2	—	0.3
1885	Cin AA	105	408	48	97	5	5	0	34	15	7	—	.238	.277	.275	73	-13	—	.877	-2	78	114	O105C	—	-1.7
1886	Bal AA	23	83	8	15	1	0	0	6	4	1	—	.181	.227	.193	33	-6	3	.894	-1	26	142	O23C	—	-0.7
Total	4NA	58	229	22	45	7	1	0	12	0	—	7	.197	.197	.236	43	-11	0-1	.698	-4	94	29	3b20,P18,O17R,1b5,2b5,S2,C2	—	-0.8
Total	6	368	1490	224	393	38	19	4	43	82	21	13	.264	.311	.323	101	1	3	.838	-6	85	123	O364(150/196/18),2b3/P1	—	-1.6
Clinton, Lou	Luciean Louis; B10.13.1937 Ponca City OK; D12.6.1997 Wichita KS; BR/TR/6´1˝/(185–195); d4.22																								
1960	Bos A	96	298	37	68	17	5	6	37	20-1	3	66	.228	.278	.379	75	-11	4-3	.966	2	113	78	O89R	0	-1.3
1961	Bos A	17	51	4	13	2	1	0	3	2-0	0	10	.255	.283	.333	63	-3	0-0	1.000	3	121	308	O13R	0	-0.1
1962	Bos A	114	398	63	117	24	10	18	75	34-3	1	79	.294	.349	.540	132	16	2-1	.979	1	103	106	O103R	0	1.0
1963	Bos A	148	560	71	130	23	7	22	77	49-6	1	118	.232	.294	.416	94	-6	0-0	.982	7	**118**	73	O146R	0	-1.0
1964	Bos A	37	120	15	31	4	3	3	6	9-1	0	33	.258	.310	.417	95	-1	1-0	1.000	5	115	333	O35R	0	0.2
	LA A	91	306	30	76	18	0	9	38	31-0	1	40	.248	.317	.395	108	3	3-0	.985	1	84	235	O86R	0	-0.1
	Year	128	426	45	107	22	3	12	44	40-1	1	73	.251	.315	.401	104	2	4-0	.990	6	92	**262**	O121R	0	0.1
1965	Cal A	89	222	29	54	12	3	1	8	23-1	1	37	.243	.316	.338	88	-3	2-3	.983	1	96	151	O73(1/0/72)	0	-0.8
	KC A	1	1	0	0	0	0	0	0	0-0	0	0	.000	.000	.000	-99	0	0-0	ø	-0	0	0	/rf	0	0.0
	Cle A	12	34	2	6	1	0	1	2	3-0	0	7	.176	.243	.294	51	-2	0-0	.941	0	91	189	O9(9/1/1)	0	-0.3
	Year	102	257	31	60	13	3	2	10	26-1	1	44	.233	.305	.331	83	-6	2-3	.977	1	95	155	O83(10/1/74)	0	-1.1
1966	NY A	80	159	18	35	10	2	5	21	16-1	0	27	.220	.288	.403	101	0	0-0	.976	-1	97	77	O63(5/1/57)	0	-0.4
1967	NY A	6	4	1	2	1	0	0	2	1-1	0	1	.500	.600	.750	308	1	0-0	ø	-0	0	0	/lf	0	0.1
Total	8	691	2153	270	532	112	31	65	269	188-14	7	418	.247	.308	.418	99	-6	12-7	.980	18	105	133	O619(16/2/603)	0	-2.7
Closser, J.D.	Jeffrey Darrin; B1.15.1980 Beech Grove IN; BB/TR/5´10˝/(175–200); [AriN98 5/163]; d6.30																								
2004	Col N	36	113	5	36	6	0	1	10	6-0	2	22	.319	.364	.398	86	-2	0-0	.986	2	85	147	C32	0	0.2
2005	Col N	92	237	31	52	12	2	7	27	32-1	1	48	.219	.314	.376	72	-10	1-0	.982	-9	64	81	C80	0	-1.4
2006	Col N	32	97	10	19	3	1	2	11	12-2	1	23	.196	.288	.309	50	-7	0-1	.989	3	95	134	C29	0	-0.3
Total	3	160	447	46	107	21	3	10	48	50-3	4	93	.239	.320	.367	70	-19	1-1	.985	-4	76	109	C141	0	-1.5
Clough, Ed	Edgar George "Big Ed","Spec"; B10.28.1906 Wiconisco PA; D1.30.1944 Harrisburg PA; BL/TL/6´0˝/188; d8.28; ▲																								
1924	StL N	7	14	0	1	0	0	0	1	0	0	3	.071	.071	.071	-63	-3	0-0	1.000	1	139	227	O6(5/0/1)	—	-0.2
1925	StL N	3	4	0	1	0	0	0	0	0	0	0	.250	.250	.250	28	0	0-0	1.000	-0	42	0	P3	—	0.0
1926	StL N	1	1	0	0	0	0	0	0	0	0	0	.000	.000	.000	-96	0	0	ø	-0	0	0	/P	—	0.0
Total	3	11	19	0	2	0	0	0	1	0	0	3	.105	.105	.105	-44	-3	0-0	1.000	1	139	227	O6(5/0/1),P4	—	-0.2
Clyburn, Danny	Danny; B4.6.1974 Lancaster SC; BR/TR/6´3˝/(217–220); [PitN92 2/47]; d9.15																								
1997	Bal A	2	3	0	0	0	0	0	0	0-0	0	2	.000	.000	.000	-99	-1	0-0	ø	-0	0	0	/lf	0	-0.1
1998	Bal A	11	25	6	7	0	0	1	3	1-0	0	10	.280	.308	.400	84	-1	0-0	1.000	-0	108	0	O8(5/0/5)/D	77	-0.1
1999	TB A	28	81	8	16	4	0	3	5	7-0	1	21	.198	.270	.358	57	-6	0-0	1.000	2	106	244	O24(14/0/10),D4	0	-0.4
Total	3	41	109	14	23	4	0	4	8	8-0	1	33	.211	.271	.358	59	-8	0-0	1.000	2	105	188	O33(20/0/15),D5	77	-0.6
Clymer, Otis	Otis Edgar; B1.27.1876 Pine Grove PA; D2.27.1926 St.Paul MN; BB/TR/5´11˝/180; d4.14																								
1905	Pit N	96	365	74	108	11	5	0	23	19	1	—	.296	.332	.353	102	0	23	.986	-2	61	188	O89(4/0/85)/1	—	-0.6
1906	Pit N	11	45	7	11	0	1	0	1	3	0	—	.244	.292	.289	78	-1	1	.900	-1	69	0	O11R	—	-0.3
1907	Pit N	22	66	8	15	2	0	0	4	5	3	—	.227	.311	.258	77	-1	4	.923	-2	0	0	O15R/1	—	-0.5
	Was A	57	206	30	65	5	5	1	16	18	4	—	.316	.382	.403	163	15	18	.912	-2	64	0	O51(27/1/24)/1	—	1.1
1908	Was A	110	368	32	93	11	4	1	35	20	0	—	.253	.291	.313	105	1	19	.933	-1	185	299	O82(1/0/81),2b13,3b2	—	-0.4
1909	Was A	45	138	11	27	5	2	0	6	17	0	—	.196	.284	.261	76	-3	7	.922	-2	65	91	O41(0/1/40)	—	-0.8
1913	Chi N	30	105	16	24	5	1	0	7	14	0	18	.229	.319	.295	76	-3	9-5	.933	-3	92	57	O26(0/24/2)	—	-0.7
	Bos N	14	37	4	12	3	1	0	6	3	0	3	.324	.375	.459	135	2	2-1	.880	-1	104	0	O11(1/7/4)	—	0.0

YEAR TM LG	G	AB	R	H	2B	3B	HR	RBI	BB-IB	HP	SO	AVG	OBP	SLG	AOPS	ABR	SB-CS	FA	FR	RNG	THR	GAMES AT POSITION	DL	BFW
Year	44	142	20	36	8	2	0	13	17	0	21	.254	.333	.338	91	-1	11-6	.918	-4	95	41	O37(1/31/6)	—	-0.7
Total 6	385	1330	182	355	42	19	2	98	99	8	21	.267	.322	.332	106	10	83-6	.939	-15	94	142	O326(33/33/262),2b13,1b3,3b2	—	-2.2
Clymer, Bill William Johnston "Derby Day Bill"; B12.18.1873 Philadelphia PA; D12.26.1936 Philadelphia PA; d6.25; C1																								
1891 Phi AA	3	11	0	0	0	0	0	0	1	1	2	.000	.154	.000	-55	-2	1	.867	-1	55	0	S3	—	-0.3
Coachman, Pete Bobby Dean; B11.11.1961 Cottonwood AL; BR/TR/5´9˝/175; [CalA84 11/268]; d8.18; Col South Alabama																								
1990 Cal A	16	45	3	14	3	0	0	5	1-0	2	7	.311	.354	.378	107	0	0-1	.958	0	100	183	3b9,2b2,D2	0	0.0
Coan, Gil Gilbert Fitzgerald; B5.18.1922 Monroe NC; BL/TR/6´0˝/180; d4.27																								
1946 Was A	59	134	17	28	3	2	3	9	7	4	37	.209	.269	.328	70	-6	2-2	.969	-1	102	0	O29(27/0/2)	0	-1.0
1947 Was A	11	42	5	21	3	2	0	3	5	0	6	.500	.553	.667	245	8	2-1	1.000	1	103	128	O11R	0	0.9
1948 Was A	138	513	56	119	13	9	7	60	41	7	78	.232	.298	.333	70	-26	23-9	.970	12	**119**	116	O131L	0	-2.1
1949 Was A	111	358	36	78	7	8	3	25	29	1	58	.218	.278	.307	56	-26	9-6	.975	-0	98	115	O97(68/29/0)	0	-3.1
1950 Was A	104	366	58	111	17	4	7	50	28	4	46	.303	.359	.429	106	2	10-5	.970	-0	105	55	O98(95/3/1)	35	-0.4
1951 Was A	135	538	85	163	25	7	9	62	39	6	62	.303	.357	.426	113	8	8-5	.965	**18**	**121**	**162**	O132L	0	1.6
1952 Was A	107	332	50	68	11	6	5	20	32	1	35	.205	.277	.319	68	-16	9-4	.984	0	101	77	O86L	0	-2.2
1953 Was A	68	168	28	33	1	4	2	17	22	3	23	.196	.301	.286	60	-10	7-0	1.000	3	114	62	O46(45/1/0)	0	-0.8
1954 Bal A	94	265	29	74	11	1	2	20	16	1	17	.279	.320	.351	91	-4	9-4	.968	-3	100	21	O67(36/32/0)	0	-1.1
1955 Bal A	61	130	18	31	7	1	1	11	13-0	1	15	.238	.313	.331	79	-4	4-2	.983	0	85	201	O43(42/0/1)	0	-0.5
Chi A	17	17	0	3	0	0	0	1	0-0	0	5	.176	.176	.176	-5	-3	0-0	1.000	0	127	0	O3(1/0/2)	0	-0.3
Year	78	147	18	34	7	1	1	12	13-0	1	20	.231	.298	.313	68	-7	4-2	.984	0	88	0	O46(43/0/3)	0	-0.8
NY N	9	13	0	2	0	0	0	0	0-0	0	1	.154	.154	.154	-18	-2	0-0	1.000	-0	88	0	O6(1/2/4)	0	-0.3
1956 NY N	4	1	2	0	0	0	0	0	0-0	0	1	.000	.000	.000	-99	0	0-0	ø	0	—	—	/H	0	0.0
Total 11	918	2877	384	731	98	44	39	278	232-0	28	384	.254	.316	.359	84	-79	83-38	.973	29	108	99	O749(664/67/21)	35	-9.3
Coats, Buck Buck; B6.9.1982 Fort Benning GA; BL/TR/6´3˝/195; [ChiN00 18/523]; d8.22																								
2006 Chi N	18	18	2	3	1	0	1	1	0-0	0	6	.167	.167	.389	35	-2	0-0	1.000	-0	109	0	O4(0/3/1)	0	-0.2
Cobb, Joe Joseph Stanley (b Joseph Stanley Serafin); B1.24.1895 Hudson PA; D12.24.1947 Allentown PA; BR/TR/5´9˝/170; d4.25; Mil 1918																								
1918 Det A	1	0	0	0	0	0	0	0	1	0	0	ø	1.000	ø	210	0	0	ø	0	—	—	/H	—	0.0
Cobb, Ty Tyrus Raymond "The Georgia Peach"; B12.18.1886 Narrows (Banks Co.) GA; D7.17.1961 Atlanta GA; BL/TR/6´1˝/175; d8.30; M6; HF1936; OF(35/2194/706)																								
1905 Det A	41	150	19	36	6	0	1	15	10	0	—	.240	.287	.300	86	-2	2	.958	2	141	96	O41(2/39/0)	—	-0.2
1906 Det A	98	358	45	113	15	5	1	34	19	3	—	.316	.355	.394	131	12	23	.961	4	112	134	O96(18/55/24)	—	1.2
1907 †Det A	150	605	97	**212**	28	14	5	**119**	24	5	—	**.350**	.380	**.468**	**164**	**40**	**53**	.961	12	156	**267**	O150R	—	4.9
1908 †Det A	150	581	88	**188**	**36**	**20**	4	**108**	34	6	—	**.324**	.367	**.475**	**166**	**40**	39	.944	3	132	101	O150R	—	4.1
1909 †Det A	156	573	**116**	**216**	33	10	**9**	**107**	48	6	—	**.377**	**.431**	**.517**	**190**	**59**	**76**	.946	2	120	162	O156R	—	**6.0**
1910 Det A	140	506	**106**	194	35	13	8	91	64	4	—	**.383**	**.456**	**.551**	**202**	61	65	.958	3	112	87	O137(0/111/26)	—	6.3
1911 Det A	146	591	**147**	**248**	**47**	**24**	8	**127**	44	8	—	**.420**	.467	**.621**	**193**	**72**	**83**	.957	7	111	95	O146C	—	**6.6**
1912 Det A	140	553	120	**226**	30	23	7	83	43	5	—	**.409**	.456	**.584**	**203**	**72**	61	.940	-4	98	96	O140C	—	5.6
1913 Det A	122	428	70	167	18	16	4	67	58	4	31	**.390**	**.467**	.535	**196**	54	51	.947	-1	97	112	O118(0/116/2)/2	—	4.6
1914 Det A	98	345	69	127	22	11	2	57	57	6	22	**.368**	.466	**.513**	188	41	35-17	.949	-14	79	61	O96C	—	2.3
1915 Det A	**156**	563	**144**	**208**	31	13	3	99	118	10	43	**.369**	**.486**	.487	**182**	**67**	**96**-38	.951	-9	88	95	O156C	—	5.7
1916 Det A	145	542	**113**	201	31	10	5	68	78	2	39	.371	.452	.493	177	55	**68**-24	.953	-8	93	85	O143C/1	—	4.6
1917 Det A	152	588	107	**225**	**44**	**24**	6	102	61	4	34	**.383**	**.444**	**.570**	**210**	**76**	**55**	.973	4	100	116	O152(0/123/29)	—	**7.4**
1918 Det A	111	421	83	161	19	**14**	3	64	41	2	21	**.382**	**.440**	.515	**196**	**48**	34	.975	-1	99	88	O95(0/92/3),1b13,P2/23	—	**4.3**
1919 Det A	124	497	92	**191**	36	13	1	70	38	1	22	**.384**	.429	.515	168	45	28	.973	-6	88	107	O123C	—	3.1
1920 Det A	112	428	86	143	28	8	2	63	58	2	28	.334	.416	.451	133	23	15-10	.966	-11	90	57	O112C	—	0.4
1921 Det A	128	507	124	197	37	16	12	101	56	3	19	.389	.452	.596	167	52	22-15	.970	6	96	**169**	O121C,M	—	4.8
1922 Det A	137	526	99	211	42	16	4	99	55	4	24	.401	.462	.565	172	58	9-13	.980	-5	93	96	O134(0/133/1),M	—	4.2
1923 Det A	145	556	103	189	40	7	6	88	66	3	14	.340	.413	.469	135	30	9-10	.969	3	107	92	O141C,M	—	2.5
1924 Det A	155	625	115	211	38	10	4	79	85	1	18	.338	.418	.450	126	27	23-14	**.986**	0	101	82	O155C,M	—	2.0
1925 Det A	121	415	97	157	31	12	12	102	65	5	12	.378	.468	.598	**171**	48	13-9	.948	-5	96	82	O105(0/101/4)/PM	—	3.5
1926 Det A	79	233	48	79	18	5	4	62	26	1	2	.339	.408	.511	137	13	9-4	.950	-4	89	80	O55(15/39/1),M	—	0.7
1927 Phi A	133	490	104	175	32	7	5	93	67	5	12	.357	.440	.482	131	26	22-16	.969	-5	96	73	O127(0/52/75)	—	1.2
1928 Phi A	95	353	54	114	27	4	1	40	34	4	16	.323	.389	.431	112	8	6-8	.964	-1	104	85	O85R	—	-0.1
Total 24	3034	11434	2246	4189	724	295	117	1938	1249	94	357	.366	.433	.512	167	1025	897-178	.961	-28	104	108	O2934C,1b14,P3,2b2/3	—	85.7
Coble, Dave David Lamar; B12.24.1912 Monroe NC; D10.15.1971 Orlando FL; BR/TR/6´1˝/183; d5.1; Col South Carolina																								
1939 Phi N	15	25	2	7	1	0	0	0	0	0	3	.280	.280	.320	63	-1	0	.938	-2	*49*	*121*	C13	—	-0.3
Cochran, George George Leslie; B2.12.1889 Rusk TX; D5.21.1960 Harbor City CA; TR; d7.29																								
1918 Bos A	24	60	7	7	0	0	0	3	10	2	6	.117	.264	.117	15	-6	3	.960	-1	102	133	3b22/S	—	-0.7
Cochrane, Dave David Carter; B1.31.1963 Riverside CA; BB/TR/6´2˝/180; [NYN81 4/81]; d9.2; OF(42/0/12)																								
1986 Chi A	19	62	4	12	2	0	1	2	5-1	0	22	.194	.254	.274	42	-5	0-0	.872	-4	95	33	3b18/S	0	-0.9
1989 Sea A	54	102	13	24	4	1	3	7	14-0	1	27	.235	.333	.382	98	0	0-2	.905	-5	89	151	S30,1b9,3b9,2b4,O3L,C2	0	-0.6
1990 Sea A	15	20	0	3	0	0	0	0	0-0	0	8	.150	.150	.150	-16	-3	0-0	1.000	1	58	0	S5,1b3,3b3/C	0	-0.2
1991 Sea A	65	178	16	44	13	0	2	22	9-0	1	38	.247	.286	.354	76	-6	0-1	.969	-6	84	0	O26(23/0/3),C19,3b13,1b4/D	0	-1.2
1992 Sea A	65	152	10	38	5	0	2	12	12-0	1	34	.250	.309	.322	76	-5	1-0	.879	-1	83	293	O25(16/0/9),C21,3b10,1b3,S3,D2/2	66	-0.6
Total 5	218	514	43	121	24	1	8	43	40-1	3	129	.235	.294	.333	73	-19	1-3	.925	-15	82	125	O54L,3b53,C43,S39,1b19,2b5,D3	66	-3.5
Cochrane, Mickey Gordon Stanley; B4.6.1903 Bridgewater MA; D6.28.1962 Lake Forest IL; BL/TR/5´10.5˝/180; d4.14; M5/C1; HF1947; Col Boston U.																								
1925 Phi A	134	420	69	139	21	5	6	55	44	2	19	.331	.397	.448	107	5	7-4	.984	-5	*96*	*80*	C133	—	0.7
1926 Phi A	120	370	50	101	8	9	8	47	56	0	15	.273	.369	.408	97	-2	5-2	.975	12	*109*	*96*	C115	—	1.7
1927 Phi A	126	432	80	146	20	6	12	80	50	2	7	.338	.409	.495	127	17	9-6	.986	5	***117***	*72*	C123	—	2.8
1928 Phi A	131	468	92	137	26	12	10	57	76	3	25	.293	.395	.464	122	17	7-5	.966	5	*109*	*63*	C130	—	2.8
1929 †Phi A	135	514	113	170	37	8	7	95	69	2	8	.331	.412	.475	123	21	7-7	.983	6	*93*	*62*	C135	—	3.3
1930 †Phi A	130	487	110	174	42	5	10	85	55	1	18	.357	.424	.526	133	27	5-0	**.993**	6	*99*	*77*	C130	—	3.8
1931 †Phi A	122	459	87	160	31	6	17	89	56	3	21	.349	.423	.553	146	31	2-3	.986	11	***128***	*89*	C117	—	4.5
1932 Phi A	139	518	118	152	35	4	23	112	100	4	22	.293	.412	.510	132	29	0-1	**.993**	9	*107*	*92*	C137/lf	—	4.2
1933 Phi A	130	429	104	138	30	4	15	60	106	3	22	.322	**.459**	.515	156	43	8-6	.989	-6	*88*	*82*	C128	—	4.1
1934 †Det A★	129	437	74	140	32	1	2	76	78	4	26	.320	.428	.412	117	17	8-4	.988	1	***135***	*119*	C124,M	—	2.4
1935 †Det A☆	115	411	93	131	33	3	5	47	96	4	15	.319	.452	.450	139	32	5-5	.989	-0	***129***	*83*	C110,M	—	3.6
1936 Det A	44	126	24	34	8	0	2	17	46	0	15	.270	.465	.381	111	6	1-1	.983	-6	*118*	*61*	C42,M	—	0.2
1937 Det A	27	98	27	30	10	1	2	12	25	1	4	.306	.452	.490	134	7	0-1	1.000	-2	*89*	*69*	C27,M	—	0.6
Total 13	1482	5169	1041	1652	333	64	119	832	857	29	217	.320	.419	.478	127	250	64-45	.985	37	*109*	*82*	C1451/lf	—	34.7
Cockman, Jim James; B4.26.1873 Guelph ON, Can.; D9.28.1947 Guelph ON, Can.; BR/TR/5´6˝/145; d9.28																								
1905 NY A	13	38	5	4	0	0	0	2	4	0	—	.105	.190	.105	-5	-4	2	.875	-2	90	0	3b13	—	-0.6
Cockrell, Alan Atlee Alan; B12.5.1962 Kansas City KS; BR/TR/6´2˝/212; [SFN84 1/9]; d9.7; C1; Col Tennessee																								
1996 Col N	9	8	0	2	1	0	0	2	0-0	0	4	.250	.222	.375	50	-1	0-0	ø	-0	0	0	/rf	0	-0.1
Coffey, Jack John Francis; B1.28.1887 New York NY; D2.14.1966 Bronx NY; BR/TR/5´11˝/178; d6.23; Col Fordham																								
1909 Bos N	73	257	21	48	4	4	0	20	11	3	—	.187	.229	.233	41	-19	2	.896	-7	102	67	S73	—	-2.6
1918 Det A	22	67	7	14	0	2	0	4	8	1	6	.209	.303	.269	75	-2	2	.957	-2	89	64	2b22	—	-0.4
Bos A	15	44	5	7	1	0	1	2	3	0	2	.159	.213	.250	40	-3	2	.955	1	115	0	3b14/2	—	-0.2
Year	37	111	12	21	1	2	1	6	11	1	8	.189	.268	.261	62	-6	4	.959	-0	93	61	2b23,3b14	—	-0.6
Total 2	110	368	33	69	5	6	1	26	22	4	8	.188	.241	.242	48	-24	6	.896	-7	102	67	S73,2b23,3b14	—	-3.2
Coffie, Ivanon Ivanon Angelino; B5.16.1977 Willemstad, Curacao, Netherlands Antilles; BL/TR/6´1˝/192; d7.15																								
2000 Bal A	23	60	6	13	4	1	0	6	5-0	1	11	.217	.284	.317	56	-4	1-0	.971	0	113	40	3b15,S4/D	0	-0.3

THE BATTER REGISTER

YEAR	TM LG	G	AB	R	H	2B	3B	HR	RBI	BB-IB	HP	SO	AVG	OBP	SLG	AOPS	ABR	SB-CS	FA	FR	RNG	THR	GAMES AT POSITION	DL	BFW
COGGINS, FRANK	Franklin; B5.22.1944 Griffin GA; BB/TR/6´2˝/(185–187); d9.10																								
1967	Was A	19	75	9	23	3	0	1	8	2-0	0	17	.307	.321	.387	114	1	1-0	.964	3	121	101	2b19	0	0.6
1968	Was A	62	171	15	30	6	1	0	7	9-2	0	33	.175	.215	.222	34	-14	1-1	.953	-5	92	109	2b52	0	-1.7
1972	Chi N	6	1	1	0	0	0	0	0	1-0	0	0	.000	.500	.000	48	0	0-0	ø	0	—	—	/H	0	0.0
Total	3	87	247	25	53	9	1	1	15	12-2	0	50	.215	.249	.271	59	-13	2-1	.957	-2	100	107	2b71	0	-1.1
COGGINS, RICH	Richard Allen; B12.7.1950 Indianapolis IN; BL/TL/5´8˝/170; [BalA68 21/475]; d8.29																								
1972	Bal A	16	39	5	13	4	0	0	1	1-0	0	6	.333	.350	.436	128	1	0-2	1.000	4	172	148	O13(0/9/6)	0	0.4
1973	†Bal A	110	389	54	124	19	9	7	41	28-2	0	24	.319	.363	.468	132	15	17-9	.987	1	102	88	O101(0/39/76)/D	0	1.3
1974	†Bal A	113	411	53	100	13	3	4	32	29-3	5	31	.243	.299	.319	80	-11	26-6	.984	-3	102	37	O105(2/30/87)	0	-1.6
1975	Mon N	13	37	1	10	3	1	0	4	1-0	0	7	.270	.289	.405	87	-1	0-0	1.000	-1	89	0	O10(9/0/2)	45	-0.2
	NY A	51	107	7	24	1	0	1	6	7-0	0	16	.224	.272	.262	52	-7	3-3	.970	1	105	118	O36(3/25/8),D9	0	-0.7
1976	NY A	7	4	1	1	0	0	0	1	0-0	0	1	.250	.250	.250	47	0	1-0	1.000	0	201	0	O2(0/1/1)/D	0	0.0
	Chi A	32	96	4	15	2	0	0	5	6-0	0	15	.156	.206	.177	13	-11	3-1	1.000	-3	81	52	O26(6/2/23)	0	-1.6
	Year	39	100	5	16	2	0	0	6	6-0	0	16	.160	.208	.180	14	-11	4-1	1.000	-2	84	51	O28(6/3/24)/D	0	-1.6
Total	5	342	1083	125	287	42	13	12	90	72-5	5	100	.265	.312	.361	93	-14	50-21	.986	-1	103	67	O293(20/106/203),D11	45	-2.4
COGSWELL, ED	Edward; B2.25.1854 , England; D7.27.1888 Fitchburg MA; BR/TR/5´8˝/150; d7.11																								
1879	Bos N	49	236	51	76	8	1	1	18	8	—	5	.322	.344	.377	135	9	—	.967	1	78	120	1b49	—	0.6
1880	Tro N	47	209	41	63	7	3	0	13	11	—	10	.301	.336	.364	130	6	—	.961	1	117	76	1b47	—	0.5
1882	Wor N	13	51	10	7	1	0	0	1	6	—	6	.137	.228	.157	26	-4	—	.937	-1	82	128	1b13	—	-0.6
Total	3	109	496	102	146	16	4	1	32	25	—	21	.294	.328	.349	121	11	—	.960	1	95	102	1b109	—	0.5
COHEN, ALTA	Alta Albert "Schoolboy"; B12.25.1908 New York NY; D3.11.2003 Maplewood NJ; BL/TL/5´10.5˝/170; d4.15																								
1931	Bro N	1	3	1	2	0	0	0	0	0	0	0	.667	.667	.667	261	1	0	1.000	1	46	1623	/rf	—	0.2
1932	Bro N	9	32	1	5	1	0	0	1	3	0	7	.156	.229	.188	14	-4	0	.850	1	73	517	O8(5/3/0)	—	-0.4
1933	Phi N	19	32	6	6	1	0	0	1	6	0	4	.188	.316	.219	49	-2	0	1.000	0	116	0	O7L	—	-0.2
Total	3	29	67	8	13	2	0	0	2	9	0	11	.194	.289	.224	42	-5	0	.925	2	90	369	O16(12/3/1)	—	-0.4
COHEN, ANDY	Andrew Howard; B10.25.1904 Baltimore MD; D10.29.1988 El Paso TX; BR/TR/5´8˝/155; d6.6; M1/C1; b–Syd; Col Alabama																								
1926	NY N	32	35	4	9	0	1	0	8	1	0	2	.257	.278	.314	60	-2	0	.792	0	123	0	2b10,S10,3b2	—	-0.2
1928	NY N	129	504	64	138	24	7	9	59	31	2	17	.274	.318	.403	87	-11	3	.969	2	103	115	2b126,S3/3	—	-0.6
1929	NY N	101	347	40	102	12	2	5	47	11	2	15	.294	.319	.383	73	-16	3	.964	10	108	106	2b94/S3	—	-0.3
Total	3	262	886	108	249	36	10	14	114	43	4	34	.281	.317	.392	81	-29	6	.964	11	105	110	2b230,S14,3b4	—	-1.1
COKER, JIMMIE	Jimmie Goodwin; B3.28.1936 Holly Hill SC; D10.29.1991 Throckmorton TX; BR/TR/5´11˝/(190–196); d9.11																								
1958	Phi N	2	6	0	1	0	0	0	0	0-0	0	0	.167	.167	.167	-12	-1	0-0	1.000	-1	0	0	C2	0	-0.1
1960	Phi N	81	252	18	54	5	3	6	34	23-2	4	45	.214	.289	.329	69	-11	0-3	.982	-1	54	116	C76	0	-1.0
1961	Phi N	11	25	3	10	1	0	1	4	7-1	0	4	.400	.531	.560	193	4	1-0	.984	-0	34	52	C11	0	0.4
1962	Phi N	5	3	0	0	0	0	0	1	1-0	0	2	.000	.200	.000	-27	-1	0-0	ø	0	—	—	/H	0	-0.1
1963	SF N	4	5	0	1	0	0	0	0	1-0	0	2	.200	.333	.200	58	0	0-0	1.000	-1	12	0	C2	0	-0.1
1964	Cin N	11	32	3	10	2	0	1	4	3-1	0	5	.313	.371	.469	130	1	0-0	1.000	1	86	293	C11	0	0.3
1965	Cin N	24	61	3	15	2	0	2	9	8-1	0	16	.246	.329	.377	93	0	0-0	.993	3	53	115	C19	0	0.3
1966	Cin N	50	111	9	28	3	0	4	14	8-1	0	5	.252	.300	.387	83	-3	0-1	.979	1	85	165	C39,O2L	0	-0.1
1967	Cin N	45	97	8	18	2	1	2	4	4-1	0	20	.186	.218	.289	39	-8	0-1	.976	-2	80	92	C34	0	-1.0
Total	9	233	592	44	137	15	4	16	70	55-7	4	99	.231	.299	.351	77	-19	1-5	.983	-0	63	127	C194,O2L	0	-1.4
COLANGELO, MIKE	Michael Gus; B10.22.1976 Teaneck NJ; BR/TR/6´1˝/185; [AnaA97 21/627]; d6.13; Col George Mason; [DL 2000 Ana A 181]																								
1999	Ana A	1	2	0	1	0	0	0	0	1-0	0	0	.500	.667	.500	204	0	0-0	1.000	1	72	2192	/lf	112	0.1
2001	SD N	50	91	10	22	3	3	2	8	8-0	1	30	.242	.310	.407	90	-2	0-0	.979	-0	95	74	O40(25/14/4)	0	-0.3
2002	Oak A	20	23	2	4	1	0	0	0	1-0	1	2	.174	.240	.217	23	-3	0-0	1.000	-1	95	0	O19(14/1/5)	0	-0.3
Total	3	71	116	12	27	4	3	2	8	10-0	2	32	.233	.305	.371	79	-5	0-0	.985	-0	94	100	O60(40/15/9)	293	-0.5
COLAVITO, ROCKY	Rocco Domenico; B8.10.1933 New York NY; BR/TR/6´3˝/(183–199); d9.10; C6																								
1955	Cle A	5	9	3	4	2	0	0	0	0-0	0	2	.444	.444	.667	189	1	0-0	1.000	1	133	463	O2R	0	0.2
1956	Cle A	101	322	55	89	11	4	21	65	49-0	2	46	.276	.372	.531	134	15	0-1	.968	-1	99	89	O98R	0	1.0
1957	Cle A	134	461	66	116	26	0	25	84	71-0	1	80	.252	.348	.471	124	16	1-6	.962	9	**119**	128	O130R	0	1.9
1958	Cle A	143	489	80	148	26	3	41	113	84-6	2	89	.303	.405	**.620**	183	57	0-2	.981	-2	96	124	O129(1/0/129),1b11/P	0	5.0
1959	Cle A★	**154**	588	90	151	24	0	**42**	111	71-8	2	86	.257	.337	.512	135	27	3-3	.985	5	114	81	O154R	0	2.5
1960	Det A	145	555	67	138	18	1	35	87	53-4	4	80	.249	.317	.474	108	4	3-6	.976	1	100	118	O144R	0	-0.2
1961	Det A★	**163**	583	129	169	30	2	45	140	113-2	2	75	.290	.402	.580	156	49	1-2	.975	7	103	129	O161(150/0/20)	0	4.6
1962	Det A★	**161**	601	90	164	30	2	37	112	96-7	2	68	.273	.371	.514	132	29	2-0	.992	12	111	105	O161L	0	3.2
1963	Det A	160	597	91	162	29	2	22	91	84-9	1	78	.271	.358	.437	119	18	0-0	.988	6	105	89	O159(142/0/23)	0	1.4
1964	KC A★	160	588	89	161	31	2	34	102	83-4	5	56	.274	.366	.507	136	31	3-1	.973	-2	99	104	O159(3/0/157)	0	1.9
1965	Cle A★	**162**	592	92	170	25	2	26	**108**	**93**-11	3	63	.287	.383	.468	140	35	1-1	**1.000**	-1	98	92	O162(1/0/162)	0	2.3
1966	Cle A★	151	533	68	127	13	0	30	72	76-4	3	81	.238	.336	.432	119	14	2-1	.982	3	104	127	O146R	0	0.8
1967	Cle A	63	191	10	46	9	0	5	21	24-0	1	31	.241	.329	.366	104	2	2-2	.962	-2	93	65	O50(28/0/31)	0	-0.4
	Chi A	60	190	20	42	4	1	3	29	25-2	0	10	.221	.306	.300	85	-3	1-1	.977	-4	87	56	O58(11/0/54)	0	-1.2
	Year	123	381	30	88	13	1	8	50	49-2	1	41	.231	.317	.333	95	-2	3-3	.970	-5	90	60	O108(39/0/85)	0	-1.6
1968	LA N	40	113	8	23	3	0	3	11	15-1	0	18	.204	.295	.310	89	-1	0-1	1.000	-1	91	95	O33(21/0/13)	0	-0.5
	NY A	39	91	13	20	2	2	5	13	14-0	1	17	.220	.330	.451	139	4	0-0	.933	-4	63	69	O28(6/0/22)/P	0	-0.2
Total	14	1841	6503	971	1730	283	21	374	1159	951-58	29	880	.266	.359	.489	132	298	19-27	.980	27	103	105	O1774(524/0/1285),1b11,P2	0	22.3
COLBERN, MIKE	Michael Malloy; B4.19.1955 Santa Monica CA; BR/TR/6´3˝/205; [ChiA76 2/32]; d7.18; Col Arizona St.																								
1978	Chi A	48	141	11	38	5	1	2	20	1-0	2	36	.270	.281	.362	80	-4	0-1	.969	-1	96	104	C47/D	0	-0.4
1979	Chi A	32	83	5	20	5	1	0	8	4-0	0	25	.241	.276	.325	61	-5	0-0	.971	-1	77	161	C32	30	-0.4
Total	2	80	224	16	58	10	2	2	28	5-0	2	61	.259	.279	.348	73	-9	0-1	.970	-2	89	126	C79/D	30	-0.8
COLBERT, CRAIG	Craig Charles; B2.13.1965 Iowa City IA; BR/TR/6´0˝/(190–214); [SFN86 20/500]; d4.6; Col Oral Roberts																								
1992	SF N	49	126	10	29	5	2	1	16	9-0	0	22	.230	.277	.325	75	-5	1-0	.994	-3	122	98	C35,3b9,2b2	15	-0.6
1993	SF N	23	37	2	6	2	0	1	5	3-1	0	13	.162	.225	.297	40	-3	0-0	.982	2	271	81	C10,2b2/3	79	-0.1
Total	2	72	163	12	35	7	2	2	21	12-1	0	35	.215	.266	.319	67	-8	1-0	.990	-1	156	94	C45,3b10,2b4	94	-0.7
COLBERT, NATE	Nathan; B4.9.1946 St.Louis MO; BR/TR/6´2˝/(190–209); d4.14																								
1966	Hou N	19	7	3	0	0	0	0	0	0-0	0	4	.000	.000	.000	-99	-2	0-0	ø	0	—	—	/H	16	-0.2
1968	Hou N	20	53	5	8	1	0	0	4	1-0	0	23	.151	.164	.170	1	-6	1-1	.952	-1	107	163	O11(3/5/3),1b5	0	-1.0
1969	SD N	139	483	64	123	20	9	24	66	45-7	3	123	.255	.322	.482	127	14	6-4	.990	0	107	85	1b134	0	0.4
1970	SD N	156	572	84	148	17	6	38	86	56-8	4	150	.259	.328	.509	125	17	3-5	.991	-8	84	95	1b153/3	0	-0.4
1971	SD N★	156	565	81	149	25	3	27	84	63-6	4	119	.264	.339	.462	134	24	5-2	.993	3	104	92	1b153	0	1.6
1972	SD N★	151	563	87	141	27	2	38	111	70-14	2	127	.250	.333	.508	147	33	15-6	.996	6	112	88	1b150	0	2.9
1973	SD N★	145	529	73	143	25	2	22	80	54-9	8	146	.270	.343	.450	130	21	9-8	.992	5	111	100	1b144	0	1.3
1974	SD N	119	368	53	76	16	0	14	54	62-6	1	108	.207	.319	.364	96	-1	10-2	.988	9	133	80	1b79,O48L	0	0.2
1975	Det A	45	156	16	23	4	2	4	18	17-0	0	52	.147	.231	.276	41	-13	0-2	.982	-4	72	80	1b44/D	0	-2.2
	Mon N	38	81	10	14	4	1	4	11	5-3	1	31	.173	.230	.395	67	-4	0-0	.988	-1	83	123	1b22	0	-0.7
1976	Mon N	14	40	5	8	2	0	2	6	9-1	0	16	.200	.347	.400	106	1	3-1	1.000	1	90	644	O7L,1b6	0	0.2
	Oak A	2	5	0	0	0	0	0	0	1-1	0	3	.000	.167	.000	-50	-1	0-0	ø	0	—	—	D2	0	-0.1
Total	10	1004	3422	481	833	141	25	173	520	383-55	23	902	.243	.322	.451	120	83	52-31	.991	10	103	91	1b890,O66(58/5/3),D3/3	16	2.0
COLBRUNN, GREG	Gregory Joseph; B7.26.1969 Fontana CA; BR/TR/6´0˝/(190–215); [MonN87 6/148]; d7.9; [DL 2005 Tex A 183]																								
1992	Mon N	52	168	12	45	8	0	2	18	6-1	2	34	.268	.294	.351	85	-4	3-2	.992	-1	90	81	1b47	16	-0.9
1993	Mon N	70	153	15	39	9	0	4	23	6-1	1	33	.255	.282	.392	76	-5	4-2	.995	-1	94	101	1b61	100	-0.9
1994	Fla N	47	155	17	47	10	0	6	31	9-0	2	27	.303	.345	.484	110	2	1-1	.988	-2	91	92	1b41	63	-0.3
1995	Fla N	138	528	70	146	22	1	23	89	22-4	6	69	.277	.311	.453	97	-4	11-3	.996	-3	90	97	1b134	0	-1.8
1996	Fla N	141	511	60	146	26	2	16	69	25-1	14	76	.286	.333	.438	105	3	4-5	.995	4	111	**124**	1b134	15	-0.5
1997	Min A	70	217	24	61	14	0	5	26	8-1	1	38	.281	.307	.415	85	-5	1-2	.988	-0	103	135	1b64,D2	0	-1.0

YEAR	TM LG	G	AB	R	H	2B	3B	HR	RBI	BB-IB	HP	SO	AVG	OBP	SLG	AOPS	ABR	SB-CS	FA	FR	RNG	THR	GAMES AT POSITION	DL	BFW
	†Atl N	28	54	3	15	3	0	2	9	2-0	1	11	.278	.316	.444	95	-1	0-0	.984	0	120	60	1b14,D3	0	-0.1
1998	Col N	62	122	12	38	8	2	2	13	8-0	1	23	.311	.359	.459	93	-1	3-3	.992	1	125	93	1b27,O5R/C	0	-0.2
	†Atl N	28	44	6	13	3	0	1	10	2-0	3	11	.295	.367	.432	110	1	1-0	1.000	0	84	41	1b9/rfD	0	0.0
	Year	90	166	18	51	11	2	3	23	10-0	4	34	.307	.361	.452	98	0	4-3	.993	1	115	81	1b36,O6R,D3/C	0	-0.2
1999	†Ari N	67	135	20	44	5	3	5	24	12-0	4	23	.326	.392	.519	128	6	1-1	.996	1	116	105	1b39,3b2,D2	0	0.4
2000	Ari N	116	329	48	103	22	1	15	57	43-2	10	45	.313	.405	.523	128	16	0-1	.989	1	102	96	1b99/3D	0	0.8
2001	†Ari N	59	97	12	28	8	0	4	18	9-0	4	14	.289	.373	.495	114	2	0-0	.987	-1	160	107	1b14,3b10	70	0.1
2002	†Ari N	72	171	30	57	16	2	10	27	13-1	0	19	.333	.378	.626	145	11	0-0	.993	-4	64	71	1b40,3b5,D3	25	0.5
2003	Sea A	22	58	7	16	1	1	3	7	4-0	0	16	.276	.323	.483	114	1	0-1	.989	-1	68	64	1b14,D4	107	-0.1
2004	Ari N	20	27	1	3	0	0	0	1	1-0	0	5	.111	.143	.111	-31	-5	0-0	1.000	0	155	0	1b2,D2	114	-0.5
Total	13	992	2769	337	801	155	12	98	422	170-11	49	444	.289	.338	.460	105	17	29-21	.993	-4	99	102	1b739,D21,3b18,O6R/C	693	-4.5
Cole, Alex	Alexander; B8.17.1965 Fayetteville NC; BL/TL/6´0˝/(170–184); [StLN85*2/43]; d7.27; Col Manatee (FL) CC																								
1990	Cle A	63	227	43	68	5	4	0	13	28-0	1	38	.300	.379	.357	107	3	40-9	.961	-1	99	104	O59C/D	0	0.7
1991	Cle A	122	387	58	114	17	3	0	21	58-2	1	47	.295	.386	.354	106	6	27-17	.970	0	102	118	O107(8/101/0),D6	22	0.5
1992	Cle A	41	97	11	20	1	0	0	5	10-0	1	21	.206	.284	.216	43	-7	9-2	.971	-2	80	81	O24(18/5/2),D4	0	-0.9
	†Pit N	64	205	33	57	3	7	0	10	18-1	0	46	.278	.335	.361	98	-1	7-4	.989	-1	87	151	O53(0/1/52)	0	-0.3
1993	Col N	126	348	50	89	9	4	0	24	43-3	2	58	.256	.339	.305	64	-17	30-13	.982	-1	98	111	O93C	0	-1.5
1994	Min A	105	345	68	102	15	5	4	23	44-2	1	60	.296	.375	.403	100	1	29-8	.969	1	107	79	O100(16/84/0)/D	0	0.6
1995	Min A	28	79	10	27	3	2	1	14	8-0	1	15	.342	.409	.468	127	3	1-3	.938	-1	93	109	O23C,D2	111	0.1
1996	Bos A	24	72	13	16	5	1	0	7	8-0	0	11	.222	.296	.319	56	-5	5-3	.974	-2	79	90	O24C	0	-0.6
Total	7	573	1760	286	493	58	26	5	117	217-8	7	296	.280	.360	.351	90	-17	148-59	.971	-8	98	107	O483(42/390/54),D14	133	-1.4
Cole, Dick	Richard Roy; B5.6.1926 Long Beach CA; BR/TR/6´2˝/175; d4.27; C1																								
1951	StL N	15	36	4	7	1	0	0	3	6	0	5	.194	.310	.222	45	-3	0-0	.969	3	142	125	2b14	0	0.1
	Pit N	42	106	9	25	4	0	1	11	15	0	9	.236	.331	.302	69	-4	0-1	.981	-1	92	77	2b34,S8	0	-0.4
	Year	57	142	13	32	5	0	1	14	21	0	14	.225	.325	.282	63	-7	0-1	.978	2	105	90	2b48,S8	0	-0.3
1953	Pit N	97	235	29	64	13	1	0	23	38	0	26	.272	.374	.336	87	-2	2-2	.965	-5	95	85	S77,2b7/1	0	-0.2
1954	Pit N	138	486	40	131	22	5	1	40	41	0	48	.270	.323	.342	75	-17	0-0	.949	-8	100	68	S66,3b55,2b17	0	-1.9
1955	Pit N	77	239	16	54	8	3	0	21	18-1	2	22	.226	.285	.285	53	-16	0-0	.935	1	103	112	3b33,2b24,S12	0	-1.3
1956	Pit N	72	99	7	21	2	1	0	9	11-0	0	9	.212	.291	.253	49	-7	0-0	.947	-3	106	163	3b18,2b12,S6	0	-1.0
1957	Mil N	15	14	1	1	0	0	0	0	3-1	0	5	.071	.235	.071	-13	-2	0-0	.952	-1	81	194	2b10/13	0	-0.3
Total	6	456	1215	106	303	50	10	2	107	132-2	2	124	.249	.322	.312	69	-51	2-3	.961	-14	98	78	S169,2b118,3b107,1b2	0	-5.0
Cole, Stu	Stewart Bryan; B2.7.1966 Charlotte NC; BR/TR/6´1˝/175; [KCA87 3/67]; d9.5; Col North Carolina–Charlotte																								
1991	KC A	9	7	1	1	0	0	0	0	2-0	0	2	.143	.333	.143	36	-1	0-0	1.000	-1	111	0	2b5/SD	0	-0.2
Cole, Willis	Willis Russell; B1.6.1882 Milton Junction WI; D10.11.1965 Madison WI; BR/TR/5´8˝/170; d8.22																								
1909	Chi A	46	165	17	39	7	3	0	16	16	1	—	.236	.308	.315	101	0	3	.889	-5	85	84	O46C	—	-0.8
1910	Chi A	22	80	6	14	2	1	0	2	4	1	—	.175	.224	.225	42	-6	0	.974	1	77	205	O22C	—	-0.7
Total	2	68	245	23	53	9	4	0	18	20	2	—	.216	.281	.286	82	-6	3	.912	-5	82	122	O68C	—	-1.5
Coleman, Choo Choo	Clarence; B8.25.1937 Orlando FL; BL/TR/5´9˝/(160–165); d4.16																								
1961	Phi N	34	47	3	6	1	0	0	4	2-0	1	8	.128	.180	.149	-12	-8	0-0	.977	-2	49	55	C14	0	-0.9
1962	NY N	55	152	24	38	7	2	6	17	11-2	1	24	.250	.303	.441	96	-1	2-4	.995	-4	90	102	C44	0	-0.5
1963	NY N	106	247	22	44	0	0	3	9	24-3	5	49	.178	.264	.215	39	-19	5-5	.969	7	103	141	C91/lf	0	-1.1
1966	NY N	6	16	2	3	0	0	0	0	0-0	0	4	.188	.188	.188	5	-2	0-0	.963	-2	36	143	C5	0	-0.4
Total	4	201	462	51	91	8	2	9	30	37-5	7	85	.197	.266	.281	52	-30	7-9	.977	-1	93	123	C154/lf	0	-2.9
Coleman, Curt	Curtis Hancock; B2.18.1887 Salem OR; D7.1.1980 Newport OR; BL/TR/5´11˝/180; d4.13; Col Oregon																								
1912	NY A	12	37	8	9	4	0	0	4	7	0	—	.243	.364	.351	99	0	0	.865	-0	113	67	3b10	—	0.1
Coleman, Dave	David Lee; B10.26.1950 Dayton OH; BR/TR/6´3˝/195; [BosA69 18/419]; d4.13																								
1977	Bos A	11	12	1	0	0	0	0	0	1-0	0	3	.000	.077	.000	-69	-3	0-0	1.000	-1	59	0	O9(3/5/1)	0	-0.4
Coleman, Jerry	Gerald Francis; B9.14.1924 San Jose CA; BR/TR/6´0˝/(167–170); d4.20; Mil 1952–53; M1																								
1949	†NY A	128	447	54	123	21	5	2	42	63	2	44	.275	.367	.358	92	-4	8-6	**.981**	5	95	111	2b122,S4	0	0.7
1950	†NY A★	153	522	69	150	19	6	6	69	67	3	38	.287	.372	.381	96	-2	3-2	.977	-12	89	111	2b152,S6	0	-0.6
1951	†NY A	121	362	48	90	11	2	3	43	31	4	36	.249	.315	.315	73	-14	6-1	.968	6	96	123	2b102,S18	0	-0.2
1952	NY A	11	42	6	17	2	1	0	4	5	0	4	.405	.468	.500	180	5	0-1	.971	2	98	200	2b11	0	0.7
1953	NY A	8	10	1	2	0	0	0	0	0	0	2	.200	.200	.200	9	-1	0-0	1.000	1	102	191	2b7/S	0	0.0
1954	NY A	107	300	39	65	7	1	3	21	26	0	29	.217	.278	.277	54	-20	3-0	.977	**15**	114	132	2b79,S30/3	0	0.2
1955	†NY A	43	96	12	22	5	0	0	8	11-0	2	11	.229	.321	.281	64	-4	0-2	.966	-1	84	142	S29,2b13/3	88	-0.4
1956	†NY A	80	183	15	47	5	1	0	18	12-2	1	33	.257	.305	.295	61	-11	1-2	.979	8	111	136	2b41,S24,3b18	0	0.1
1957	†NY A	72	157	23	42	7	2	2	12	20-0	1	21	.268	.354	.376	101	1	1-1	.969	-2	97	141	2b45,3b21,S4	0	0.1
Total	9	723	2119	267	558	77	18	16	217	235-2	13	218	.263	.340	.339	83	-50	22-15	.976	21	97	122	2b572,S116,3b41	88	0.6
Coleman, Gordy	Gordon Calvin; B7.5.1934 Rockville MD; D3.12.1994 Cincinnati OH; BL/TR/6´2˝/(208–220); d9.19																								
1959	Cle A	6	15	5	8	0	1	0	2	1-0	0	2	.533	.563	.667	245	3	0-0	.955	0	156	39	1b3	0	0.3
1960	Cin N	66	251	26	68	10	1	6	32	12-1	2	32	.271	.308	.390	89	-4	1-1	.998	7	135	132	1b66	0	-0.2
1961	†Cin N	150	520	63	149	27	4	26	87	45-11	2	67	.287	.341	.504	120	14	1-3	.991	6	113	78	1b150	0	1.1
1962	Cin N	136	476	73	132	13	1	28	86	36-4	3	68	.277	.331	.485	113	7	2-3	.989	-1	95	95	1b128	0	-0.3
1963	Cin N	123	365	38	90	20	2	14	59	29-1	2	51	.247	.303	.427	105	2	1-0	.987	2	105	96	1b107	0	-0.1
1964	Cin N	89	198	18	48	6	2	5	27	13-1	1	30	.242	.291	.369	82	-5	2-0	.990	3	126	92	1b49	0	-0.4
1965	Cin N	108	325	39	98	19	0	14	57	24-4	1	38	.302	.348	.489	125	11	0-0	.991	0	94	82	1b89	0	0.7
1966	Cin N	91	227	20	57	7	0	5	37	16-2	0	45	.251	.299	.348	73	-8	2-1	.986	-1	88	76	1b65	0	-1.3
1967	Cin N	4	7	0	0	0	0	0	0	1-1	0	0	.000	.125	.000	-55	-1	0-0	1.000	0	122	0	1b2	0	-0.2
Total	9	773	2384	282	650	102	11	98	387	177-25	11	333	.273	.324	.448	106	19	9-8	.990	16	107	91	1b659	0	-0.4
Coleman, John	John Francis; B3.6.1863 Saratoga Springs NY; D5.31.1922 Detroit MI; BL/TR (BB 1887)/5´9.5˝/170; d5.1; Col Syracuse; ▲																								
1883	Phi N	90	354	33	83	12	8	0	32	15	—	39	.234	.266	.314	83	-7	—	.886	6	111	53	P65,O31(19/12/0)/2	—	0.2
1884	Phi N	43	171	16	42	7	2	0	22	8	—	20	.246	.279	.310	89	-2	—	.844	3	120	224	O27(3/19/5),P21,1b2	—	0.0
	Phi AA	28	107	16	22	2	3	2	—	5	0	—	.206	.241	.336	81	-3	—	.743	-1	147	165	O24(11/13/0),P3,1b2	—	-0.4
1885	Phi AA	96	398	71	119	15	11	3	70	25	3	—	.299	.345	.415	131	13	—	.844	1	153	170	O93(1/17/76),P8	—	1.0
1886	Phi AA	121	492	67	121	18	16	0	65	33	2	—	.246	.296	.348	100	-2	28	.862	2	122	160	O115(0/5/110),1b6,P3/2	—	-0.1
	Pit AA	11	43	3	15	2	1	0	9	2	0	—	.349	.378	.442	157	3	1	.786	-1	69	0	O11L	—	0.1
	Year	132	535	70	136	20	17	0	74	35	2	—	.254	.302	.355	105	1	29	.858	0	118	148	O126(11/5/110),1b6,P3/2	—	0.0
1887	Pit N	115	475	75	139	21	11	2	54	31	1	40	.293	.337	.396	111	8	25	.899	-1	83	83	O115(0/2/113),1b2	—	0.5
1888	Pit N	116	438	49	101	11	4	0	26	29	4	52	.231	.285	.274	86	-5	15	.928	2	130	66	O91(0/3/88),1b25	—	-0.6
1889	Phi AA	6	19	1	1	0	0	0	1	1	0	3	.053	.100	.053	-57	-4	1	.929	0	148	0	P5/lf	—	0.0
1890	Pit N	3	11	1	2	0	0	0	0	3	0	0	.182	.357	.182	66	0	1	1.000	-1	0	0	O2(1/0/1),P2	—	0.0
Total	8	629	2508	332	645	88	56	7	279	152	10	154	.257	.302	.345	101	1	71	.873	10	123	132	O510(47/71/393),P107,1b37,2b2	—	0.7
Coleman, Michael	Michael Donnell; B8.16.1975 Nashville TN; BR/TR/5´11˝/(180–225); [BosA94 18/495]; d9.1; [DL 2000 Bos A 96, 2002 Bos A 25]																								
1997	Bos A	8	24	2	4	1	0	0	2	0-0	0	11	.167	.167	.208	-3	-4	1-0	.941	-1	90	0	O7C	0	-0.4
1999	Bos A	2	5	1	1	0	0	0	0	1-0	0	0	.200	.333	.200	39	0	0-0	ø	-1	0	0	O2(1/1/0)	0	-0.1
2001	NY A	12	38	5	8	0	0	1	7	0-0	0	15	.211	.205	.289	30	-4	0-1	1.000	-2	51	0	O9(1/7/3),D3	0	-0.6
Total	3	22	67	8	13	1	0	1	9	1-0	0	26	.194	.203	.254	19	-8	1-1	.960	-4	63	0	O18(2/15/3),D3	121	-1.1
Coleman, Ed	Parke Edward; B12.1.1901 Canby OR; D8.5.1964 Oregon City OR; BL/TR/6´2˝/200; d4.15; Col Oregon St.																								
1932	Phi A	26	73	13	25	7	1	1	13	1	0	6	.342	.351	.507	115	1	1-0	1.000	2	92	299	O16R	—	0.2
1933	Phi A	102	388	48	109	26	3	6	68	19	2	51	.281	.318	.410	91	-6	0-0	.948	-2	105	63	O89(1/0/88)	—	-1.3
1934	Phi A	101	329	53	92	14	6	14	60	29	2	34	.280	.342	.486	116	5	0-1	.980	1	94	134	O86R	—	0.1
1935	Phi A	10	13	0	1	0	0	0	0	0	0	3	.077	.077	.077	-61	-3	0-0	ø	-0	0	0	/rf	—	-0.3
	StL A	108	397	66	114	15	9	17	71	53	1	41	.287	.373	.499	118	9	0-2	.974	-2	90	131	O102R	—	0.1
	Year	118	410	66	115	15	9	17	71	53	1	44	.280	.364	.485	113	7	0-2	.974	-2	90	131	O103R	—	-0.2

YEAR	TM LG	G	AB	R	H	2B	3B	HR	RBI	BB-IB	HP	SO	AVG	OBP	SLG	AOPS	ABR	SB-CS	FA	FR	RNG	THR	GAMES AT POSITION	DL	BFW
1936	StL A	92	137	13	40	5	4	2	34	15	1	17	.292	.366	.431	93	-2	0-0	.939	-2	93	0	O18R	—	-0.4
Total	5	439	1337	193	381	67	23	40	246	117	6	152	.285	.345	.459	105	4	1-3	.966	-4	96	112	O312(1/0/311)	—	-1.6
Coleman, Ray	Raymond Leroy; B6.4.1922 Dunsmuir CA; BL/TR/5´11˝/170; d4.22																								
1947	StL A	110	343	34	89	9	7	2	30	26	1	32	.259	.314	.344	81	-10	2-5	.984	1	100	115	O93(21/0/73)	0	-1.4
1948	StL A	17	29	2	5	0	1	0	2	2	0	5	.172	.226	.241	24	-3	1-0	.889	-1	88	0	O5R	0	-0.4
	Phi A	68	210	32	51	6	6	0	21	31	0	17	.243	.340	.329	78	-7	4-3	.978	1	92	166	O53(0/32/21)	0	-0.8
	Year	85	239	34	56	6	7	0	23	33	0	22	.234	.327	.318	72	-10	5-3	.972	0	92	153	O58(0/32/26)	0	-1.2
1950	StL A	117	384	54	104	25	6	8	55	32	2	37	.271	.330	.430	90	-7	7-5	.985	3	107	86	O98(27/43/28)	0	-0.8
1951	StL A	91	341	41	96	16	5	5	55	24	0	32	.282	.329	.402	94	-4	3-4	.975	2	100	138	O87(47/5/42)	0	-0.7
	Chi A	51	181	21	50	8	7	3	21	15	0	14	.276	.332	.448	112	1	2-3	.980	3	117	69	O51(23/29/12)	0	0.2
	Year	142	522	62	146	24	12	8	76	39	0	46	.280	.330	.418	100	-3	5-7	.977	5	106	113	O138(70/34/54)	0	-0.5
1952	Chi A	85	195	19	42	7	1	2	14	13	0	17	.215	.264	.292	54	-13	0-0	.978	2	104	129	O73(28/33/15)	0	-1.4
	StL A	20	46	5	9	3	0	0	1	5	1	4	.196	.288	.261	52	-3	0-0	1.000	-0	107	0	O16(5/5/6)	0	-0.4
	Year	105	241	24	51	10	1	2	15	18	1	21	.212	.269	.286	54	-15	0-0	.982	2	105	107	O89(33/38/21)	0	-1.8
Total	5	559	1729	208	446	74	33	20	199	148	4	158	.258	.318	.374	84	-46	19-20	.980	11	103	112	O476(151/147/202)	0	-5.7
Coleman, Bob	Robert Hunter; B9.26.1890 Huntingburg IN; D7.16.1959 Boston MA; BR/TR/6´2˝/190; d6.13; M3/C3																								
1913	Pit N	24	50	5	9	2	0	0	9	7	0	8	.180	.281	.220	46	-3	0	.978	-3	83	89	C24	—	-0.5
1914	Pit N	73	150	11	40	4	1	1	14	15	0	32	.267	.333	.327	101	0	3	.977	2	*113*	*89*	C72	—	0.7
1916	Cle A	19	28	3	6	2	0	0	4	7	0	6	.214	.371	.286	92	0	0	.972	-1	99	136	C12	—	0.0
Total	3	116	228	19	55	8	1	1	27	29	0	46	.241	.327	.298	87	-3	3	.976	-2	*105*	*94*	C108	—	0.2
Coleman, Vince	Vincent Maurice; B9.22.1961 Jacksonville FL; BB/TR/6´0˝/(170–195); [StLN82 10/257]; d4.18; Col Florida A&M																								
1985	†StL N	151	636	107	170	20	10	1	40	50-1	0	115	.267	.320	.335	84	-15	**110**-25	.979	5	101	143	O150(138/17/10)	0	0.0
1986	StL N	154	600	94	139	13	8	0	29	60-0	2	98	.232	.301	.280	62	-31	**107**-14	.972	-1	96	111	O149(131/20/0)	0	-2.1
1987	†StL N	151	623	121	180	14	10	3	43	70-0	3	126	.289	.363	.358	90	-8	**109**-22	.970	-0	93	146	O150L	0	0.1
1988	StL N★	153	616	77	160	20	10	3	38	49-4	1	111	.260	.313	.339	86	-12	**81**-27	.971	-3	92	152	O150(127/24/0)	0	-1.1
1989	StL N★	145	563	94	143	21	9	2	28	50-0	2	90	.254	.316	.334	83	-12	**65**-10	.962	-10	86	63	O142L	0	-1.7
1990	StL N	124	497	73	145	18	9	6	39	35-1	2	88	.292	.340	.400	102	1	**77**-17	.981	2	96	135	O120(118/0/2)	0	1.0
1991	NY N	72	278	45	71	7	5	1	17	39-0	0	47	.255	.347	.327	91	-3	37-14	.979	-7	82	135	O70C	84	-0.7
1992	NY N	71	229	37	63	11	1	2	21	27-3	2	41	.275	.355	.358	104	2	24-9	.991	-2	93	73	O61(41/21/0)	77	0.1
1993	NY N	92	373	64	104	14	8	2	25	21-1	0	58	.279	.316	.375	86	-9	38-13	.982	-3	96	76	O90L	0	-1.1
1994	KC A	104	438	61	105	14	12	2	33	29-0	1	72	.240	.285	.340	58	-29	50-8	.962	-4	79	155	O99L,D5	0	-2.7
1995	KC A	75	293	39	84	13	4	4	20	27-1	1	48	.287	.348	.399	92	-4	26-9	.975	-5	74	143	O69(57/2/13),D4	0	-0.8
	†Sea A	40	162	27	47	10	2	1	9	10-1	1	32	.290	.335	.395	88	-3	16-7	.988	2	116	84	O38L	0	-0.1
	Year	115	455	66	131	23	6	5	29	37-2	2	80	.288	.343	.398	91	-7	42-16	.980	-3	89	122	O107(95/2/13),D4	0	-0.9
1996	Cin N	33	84	10	13	1	1	1	4	9-0	0	31	.155	.237	.226	22	-10	12-2	.968	0	92	203	O20L	0	-0.8
1997	Det A	6	14	0	1	0	0	0	0	1-0	0	3	.071	.133	.071	-45	-3	0-0	1.000	-0	84	0	O3(2/1/0)/D	0	-0.3
Total	13	1371	5406	849	1425	176	89	28	346	477-12	15	960	.264	.324	.345	83	-136	752-177	.974	-26	92	123	O1311(1153/155/25),D10	161	-10.2
Coles, Cad	Cadwallader; B1.17.1886 Rock Hill SC; D6.30.1942 Miami FL; BL/TR/6´0.5˝/174; d4.16; Col Clemson																								
1914	KC F	78	194	17	49	7	3	1	25	5	0	30	.253	.271	.335	67	-13	6	.889	-5	77	82	O39(3/31/6),1b3	—	-2.2
Coles, Chuck	Charles Edward; B6.27.1931 Fredericktown PA; D1.25.1996 Myrtle Beach SC; BL/TL/5´9˝/180; d9.19; Col Waynesburg																								
1958	Cin N	5	11	0	2	1	0	0	2	2-0	0	6	.182	.308	.273	52	-1	0-0	1.000	1	169	0	O4(3/1/0)	0	0.0
Coles, Darnell	Darnell; B6.2.1962 San Bernardino CA; BR/TR/6´1˝/(170–190); [SeaA80 1/6]; d9.4; OF(123/0/228)																								
1983	Sea A	27	92	9	26	7	0	1	6	7-0	0	12	.283	.333	.391	95	0	0-3	.941	-2	84	136	3b26	0	-0.4
1984	Sea A	48	143	15	23	3	1	0	6	17-0	2	26	.161	.259	.196	28	-14	2-1	.918	-4	82	130	3b42,O3L,D3	22	-1.9
1985	Sea A	27	59	8	14	4	0	1	5	9-0	1	17	.237	.338	.356	92	0	0-1	.918	1	113	130	S15,3b7,O2L,D2	0	0.2
1986	Det A	142	521	67	142	30	2	20	86	45-3	6	84	.273	.333	.453	112	9	6-2	.938	-4	97	105	3b133,S2,O2R,D7	15	0.3
1987	Det A	53	149	14	27	5	1	4	15	15-1	2	23	.181	.263	.309	54	-10	0-1	.847	-1	109	87	3b36,1b9,O8(2/0/6)/SD	33	-1.2
	Pit N	40	119	20	27	8	0	6	24	19-2	1	20	.227	.333	.445	104	1	1-3	1.000	-4	63	60	O26(1/0/26),3b10/1	0	-0.5
1988	Pit N	68	211	20	49	13	1	5	36	20-1	3	41	.232	.299	.374	96	-1	1-1	.990	-5	92	0	O55R/13	0	-0.8
	Sea A	55	195	32	57	10	1	10	34	17-0	4	26	.292	.356	.508	134	9	3-2	.986	-4	75	122	O47(43/0/4)/1D	0	0.4
1989	Sea A	146	535	54	135	21	3	10	59	27-1	6	61	.252	.294	.359	81	-15	5-4	.975	7	101	136	O89(7/0/83),3b26,1b18,D12	0	-1.2
1990	Sea A	37	107	9	23	5	1	2	16	4-1	1	17	.215	.248	.336	62	-6	0-0	.970	1	91	0	O20R,3b6,1b4/D	0	-0.6
	Det A	52	108	13	22	2	0	1	4	12-1	0	21	.204	.281	.250	50	-7	0-4	1.000	2	96	0	D30,O11(4/0/9),3b8	0	-0.8
	Year	89	215	22	45	7	1	3	20	16-2	1	38	.209	.265	.293	56	-13	0-4	.977	3	92	0	O31(4/0/29),D31,3b14,1b4	0	-1.4
1991	SF N	11	14	1	3	0	0	0	0	0-0	0	2	.214	.214	.214	21	-2	0-0	ø	-1	0	0	O3R/1	0	-0.2
1992	Cin N	55	141	16	44	11	2	3	18	3-0	0	15	.312	.322	.482	123	4	1-0	1.000	0	103	38	3b23,1b20,O5(3/0/2)	40	0.3
1993	Tor A	64	194	26	49	9	1	4	26	16-1	4	29	.253	.319	.371	84	-4	1-1	.957	-6	91	45	O44(31/0/13),3b16/1D	0	-1.2
1994	Tor A	48	143	15	30	6	1	4	15	10-0	1	25	.210	.263	.350	56	-10	0-0	.980	-2	108	63	O29(24/0/5),1b10,3b7/D	0	-1.3
1995	StL N	63	138	13	31	7	0	3	16	16-1	3	20	.225	.316	.341	73	-5	0-0	.951	-8	64	32	3b22,1b18/lf	0	-1.4
1997	Col N	21	22	1	7	1	0	1	2	0-0	1	6	.318	.348	.500	97	0	0-0	1.000	-0	123	0	3b3,O2L	0	0.0
Total	14	957	2891	333	709	142	14	75	368	237-12	35	445	.245	.307	.382	88	-51	20-23	.923	-30	97	93	3b366,O347R,1b84,D67,S18	110	-10.3
Coletta, Chris	Christopher Michael; B8.2.1944 Brooklyn NY; BL/TL/5´11˝/190; d8.15																								
1972	Cal A	14	30	5	9	1	0	1	7	1-0	0	4	.300	.323	.433	130	1	0-0	1.000	-1	35	0	O7(5/0/2)	0	-0.1
Colgan, Ed	William H.; B E.St.Louis IL; D8.8.1895 Great Falls MT; ?/180; d5.3																								
1884	Pit AA	48	161	10	25	4	1	0	—	3	0	—	.155	.171	.193	18	-14	—	.906	1	—	—	C44,O4(2/0/2)	—	-0.9
Colina, Alvin	Alvin Enrique; B12.26.1982 Puerto Cabello, Venezuela; BR/TR/6´3˝/210; d9.18																								
2006	Col N	2	5	0	1	0	0	0	1	0-0	0	1	.200	.200	.200	3	-1	0-0	1.000	0	0	0	/C	0	0.0
Collier, Lou	Louis Keith; B8.21.1973 Chicago IL; BR/TR/5´10˝/(180–191); [PitN92 31/875]; d6.28; Col Triton (IL) JC																								
1997	Pit N	18	37	3	5	0	0	0	3	1-0	0	11	.135	.158	.135	-22	-7	1-0	1.000	1	116	106	S18	0	-0.5
1998	Pit N	110	334	30	82	13	6	2	34	31-6	6	70	.246	.316	.338	73	-13	2-2	.960	1	100	96	S107	16	-0.5
1999	Mil N	74	135	18	35	9	0	2	21	14-0	0	32	.259	.325	.370	76	-5	3-2	.948	-8	88	52	S31,O10(9/0/1),3b7,2b4	0	-1.1
2000	Mil N	14	32	9	7	1	0	1	2	6-0	0	4	.219	.333	.344	75	-1	0-0	1.000	1	86	401	O10(5/7/0)/3	0	-0.1
2001	Mil N	50	127	19	32	8	1	2	14	17-0	1	30	.252	.340	.378	89	-2	5-1	.976	1	108	99	O23(12/11/0),3b16/D	0	0.0
2002	Mon N	13	11	3	1	1	0	0	0	1-1	1	3	.091	.231	.182	10	-1	0-0	1.000	-1	90	0	O7(3/3/1),2b2/3	0	-0.2
2003	Bos A	4	1	0	0	0	0	0	0	0-0	0	0	.000	.000	.000	-96	0	0-1	1.000	0	167	0	3b2,O2(1/1/0)	0	-0.1
2004	Phi N	32	36	7	10	1	0	1	4	5-0	1	10	.278	.381	.389	97	0	1-0	1.000	-1	41	0	O8L/3	0	-0.1
Total	8	315	713	89	172	33	7	8	78	75-7	9	160	.241	.317	.341	72	-29	12-6	.962	-6	99	90	S156,O60(38/22/2),3b28,2b6/D	16	-2.6
Collins	; d9.12																								
1892	StL N	1	2	0	0	0	0	0	0	0	0	2	.000	.000	.000	-99	0	0	1.000	0	0	0	/rf	—	-0.1
Collins, Chub	Charles Augustine; B10.12.1857 Dundas ON, Can.; D5.20.1914 Dundas ON, Can.; BB/TR/5´11.5˝/165; d5.1																								
1884	Buf N	45	169	24	30	6	0	0	20	14	—	36	.178	.240	.213	42	-11	—	.914	2	105	94	2b42,S3	—	-0.6
	Ind AA	38	138	18	31	3	1	0	—	9	0	—	.225	.272	.261	77	-3	—	.886	-6	90	58	2b38	—	-0.7
1885	Det N	14	55	8	10	0	2	0	6	0	—	11	.182	.182	.255	40	-4	—	.792	-5	83	73	S14	—	-0.9
Total	2	97	362	50	71	9	3	0	<u>26</u>	23	—	<u>47</u>	.196	.244	.238	55	-18	—	.901	-9	98	77	2b80,S17	—	-2.2
Collins, Wilson	Cyril Wilson; B5.7.1889 Pulaski TN; D2.28.1941 Knoxville TN; BR/TR/5´9.5˝/165; d5.12; Col Vanderbilt																								
1913	Bos N	16	3	3	1	0	0	0	0	0	0	1	.333	.333	.333	89	0	0	1.000	0	180	0	O9(5/3/1)	—	0.0
1914	Bos N	27	35	5	9	0	0	0	1	2	0	8	.257	.297	.257	66	-2	0	.917	-0	120	0	O19(9/3/7)	—	-0.3
Total	2	43	38	8	10	0	0	0	1	2	0	9	.263	.300	.263	68	-2	0	.926	-0	125	0	O28(14/6/8)	—	-0.3
Collins, Dan	Daniel Thomas; B7.12.1854 St.Louis MO; D9.21.1883 New Orleans LA; d6.8; ▲																								
1874	Chi NA	3	12	1	1	1	0	0	0	0	—	2	.083	.083	.167	-22	-2	1-0	1.000	0	243	0	P2,O2R/S	—	-0.1
1876	Lou N	7	28	3	4	1	0	0	9	0	—	2	.143	.143	.179	5	-3	—	.909	1	179	492	O7(0/2/5)	—	-0.2

YEAR	TM LG	G	AB	R	H	2B	3B	HR	RBI	BB-IB	HP	SO	AVG	OBP	SLG	AOPS	ABR	SB-CS	FA	FR	RNG	THR	GAMES AT POSITION	DL	BFW
COLLINS, DAVE	David S; B10.20.1952 Rapid City SD; BB/TL/5´11˝/(170–175); [CalA72 S1/6]; d6.7; C9; Col Mesa (AZ) CC																								
1975	Cal A	93	319	41	85	13	4	3	29	36-1	1	55	.266	.340	.361	106	3	24-10	.988	3	112	59	O75(74/1/0),D12	0	0.3
1976	Cal A	99	365	45	96	12	1	4	28	40-2	0	55	.263	.335	.334	103	2	32-19	.994	2	110	64	O71(52/19/0),D22	0	0.0
1977	Sea A	120	402	46	96	9	3	5	28	33-0	3	66	.239	.299	.313	68	-18	25-10	.985	1	95	127	O73(67/3/3),D40	0	-2.0
1978	Cin N	102	102	13	22	1	0	0	7	15-0	0	18	.216	.311	.225	53	-6	7-7	.969	1	103	140	O24(3/17/4)	0	-0.6
1979	†Cin N	122	396	59	126	16	4	3	35	27-2	2	48	.318	.364	.402	109	5	16-9	.976	-4	101	31	O91(45/3/50),1b10	0	-0.3
1980	Cin N	144	551	94	167	20	4	3	35	53-2	3	68	.303	.366	.370	108	8	79-21	.986	4	112	60	O141(18/119/6)	0	2.1
1981	Cin N	95	360	63	98	18	6	3	23	41-1	6	41	.272	.355	.381	110	6	26-10	.977	0	108	60	O94(1/0/93)	0	0.4
1982	NY A	111	348	41	88	12	3	3	25	28-3	5	49	.253	.315	.330	79	-10	13-8	.992	-1	98	145	O60(20/20/25),1b52/D	0	-1.5
1983	Tor A	118	402	55	109	12	4	1	34	43-1	2	67	.271	.343	.328	81	-9	31-7	.989	10	**115**	105	O112(112/2/1),1b5/D	18	0.0
1984	Tor A	128	441	59	136	24	**15**	2	44	33-0	9	41	.308	.366	.444	119	11	60-14	.991	-2	87	110	O108(106/2/0),1b6,D4	0	1.3
1985	Oak A	112	379	52	95	16	4	4	29	29-2	1	37	.251	.303	.346	84	-9	29-8	.978	2	113	17	O91L	0	-0.8
1986	Det A	124	419	44	113	18	2	1	27	44-0	2	49	.270	.340	.329	84	-8	27-12	.995	1	109	34	O94(76/10/11),D24	0	-1.0
1987	Cin N	57	85	19	25	5	0	0	5	11-0	2	12	.294	.388	.353	94	0	9-0	1.000	1	135	0	O21(18/2/1)	0	0.3
1988	Cin N	99	174	12	41	6	2	0	14	11-0	2	27	.236	.286	.293	65	-8	7-2	.965	-1	96	139	O35(13/5/18),1b3	0	-1.0
1989	Cin N	78	106	12	25	4	0	0	7	10-0	0	17	.236	.302	.274	64	-5	3-1	1.000	3	165	0	O16L	0	-0.2
1990	StL N	99	58	12	13	1	0	0	3	13-2	0	10	.224	.366	.241	70	-2	7-1	1.000	-4	0	72	1b49,O12(4/1/8)	0	-0.5
Total	16	1701	4907	667	1335	187	52	32	373	467-16	38	660	.272	.338	.351	93	-40	395-139	.986	15	107	71	O1118(716/204/220),1b125,D104	18	-3.5
COLLINS, EDDIE	Edward Trowbridge Jr.; B11.23.1916 Lansdowne PA; D11.2.2000 Jennersville PA; BL/TR/5´10˝/175; d7.4; Mil 1942–45; f–Eddie; Col Yale																								
1939	Phi A	32	21	6	5	1	0	0	0	0	0	3	.238	.238	.286	34	-2	1-0	1.000	0	202	0	O6R/2	—	-0.2
1941	Phi A	80	219	29	53	6	3	0	12	20	0	24	.242	.305	.297	61	-13	2-1	.968	1	113	65	O50(4/9/38)	0	-1.4
1942	Phi A	20	34	6	8	2	0	0	4	4	0	2	.235	.316	.294	72	-1	1-0	.800	-1	70	0	O9(1/3/6)	0	-0.3
Total	3	132	274	41	66	9	3	0	16	24	0	29	.241	.302	.296	61	-16	4-1	.959	0	113	56	O65(5/12/50)/2	0	-1.9
COLLINS, EDDIE	Edward Trowbridge Sr. "Cocky" (aka Sullivan in 1906); B5.2.1887 Millerton NY; D3.25.1951 Boston MA; BL/TR/5´9˝/175; d9.17; Mil 1918; M3/C2; HF1939; s–Eddie; Col Columbia																								
1906	Phi A	6	15	2	3	0	0	0	0	0	0	—	.200	.200	.200	25	-1	1	.900	-1	91	0	S3/23	—	-0.2
1907	Phi A	14	23	0	8	0	1	0	2	0	0	—	.348	.348	.435	146	1	0	.833	-1	78	99	S6	—	0.0
1908	Phi A	102	330	39	90	18	7	1	40	16	3	—	.273	.312	.379	116	5	8	.944	-10	89	34	2b47,S28,O10(2/3/5)	—	-0.5
1909	Phi A	**153**	571	104	198	30	10	3	56	62	6	—	.347	.416	.450	170	48	63	**.967**	4	93	114	2b152/S	—	5.9
1910	†Phi A	153	581	81	188	16	15	3	81	49	6	—	.324	.382	.418	152	34	**81**	**.972**	30	**104**	**136**	2b153	—	7.0
1911	†Phi A	132	493	92	180	22	13	3	73	62	15	—	.365	.451	.481	163	46	38	.967	-0	90	107	2b132	—	4.6
1912	Phi A	**153**	543	**137**	189	25	11	0	64	101	0	—	.348	.450	.435	159	50	63	.955	14	103	**125**	2b153	—	6.4
1913	†Phi A	148	534	**125**	184	23	13	3	73	85	7	37	.345	.441	.453	165	49	55	.965	16	**106**	107	2b148	—	**7.0**
1914	†Phi A	152	526	**122**	181	23	14	2	85	97	6	31	.344	**.452**	.452	**179**	**58**	58-30	**.970**	2	91	116	2b152	—	6.9
1915	Chi A	**155**	521	118	173	22	10	4	77	**119**	5	27	.332	.460	.436	163	50	46-30	**.974**	11	104	103	2b155	—	**6.6**
1916	Chi A	**155**	545	87	168	14	17	0	52	86	3	36	.308	.405	.396	139	29	40-21	**.976**	-7	91	**131**	2b155	—	2.9
1917	†Chi A	**156**	564	91	163	18	12	0	67	89	3	16	.289	.389	.363	127	22	53	.969	-26	85	110	2b156	—	-0.1
1918	Chi A	97	330	51	91	8	2	2	30	73	0	13	.276	.407	.330	121	14	22	.974	-1	95	131	2b96	—	1.6
1919	†Chi A	**140**	518	87	165	19	7	4	80	68	2	27	.319	.400	.405	126	20	**33**	.974	3	97	**125**	2b140	—	2.7
1920	Chi A	153	602	117	224	38	13	3	76	69	2	19	.372	.438	.493	146	43	20-8	**.976**	10	99	115	2b153	—	5.4
1921	Chi A	139	526	79	177	20	10	2	58	66	2	11	.337	.412	.424	115	15	12-10	**.968**	31	**112**	115	2b136	—	4.4
1922	Chi A	154	598	92	194	20	12	1	69	73	3	16	.324	.401	.403	110	12	20-12	**.976**	-13	93	87	2b154	—	0.4
1923	Chi A	145	505	89	182	22	5	5	67	84	4	8	.360	.455	.453	141	37	**48**-29	.975	-6	99	93	2b142	—	3.4
1924	Chi A	152	556	108	194	27	7	6	86	89	3	16	.349	.441	.455	136	35	**42**-17	**.977**	-10	95	94	2b150,M	—	3.0
1925	Chi A	118	425	80	147	26	3	3	80	87	4	8	.346	.461	.442	137	32	19-6	.970	-13	93	110	2b116,M	—	2.3
1926	Chi A	106	375	66	129	32	4	1	62	62	3	8	.344	.441	.459	140	27	13-8	.973	-8	93	99	2b101,M	—	2.1
1927	Phi A	95	226	50	76	12	1	1	15	56	0	9	.336	.468	.412	123	12	6-2	.965	-5	88	107	2b56/S	—	0.9
1928	Phi A	36	33	3	10	3	0	0	7	4	0	4	.303	.378	.394	100	0	0-0	ø	-1	0	0	2b2/S	—	-0.1
1929	Phi A	9	7	0	0	0	0	0	0	2	0	0	.000	.222	.000	-37	-1	0-0	ø	0	—	—	/H	—	-0.1
1930	Phi A	3	2	1	1	0	0	0	0	0	0	0	.500	.500	.500	148	0	0-0	ø	0	—	—	/H	—	0.0
Total	25	2826	9949	1821	3315	438	187	47	1300	1499	77	286	.333	.424	.429	142	637	741-173	.970	21	97	111	2b2650,S40,O10(2/3/5)/3	—	72.5
COLLINS, HUB	Hubert B.; B4.15.1864 Louisville KY; D5.21.1892 Brooklyn NY; BR/TR/5´8˝/160; d9.4; OF(241/31/0)																								
1886	Lou AA	27	101	12	29	3	2	0	10	5	0	—	.287	.321	.356	106	0	7	.885	-2	46	0	O24(22/2/0),3b2/S21	—	-0.2
1887	Lou AA	130	559	122	162	22	8	1	66	39	2	—	.290	.338	.363	94	-6	71	.887	-7	103	27	O109L,2b10,1b8,S4/3	—	-1.2
1888	Lou AA	116	485	117	149	26	11	2	50	41	4	—	.307	.366	.419	154	30	62	.890	3	124	162	O82(57/26/0),2b19,S15	—	2.8
	Bro AA	12	42	16	13	5	1	0	3	9	1	—	.310	.442	.476	195	5	9	.897	-2	88	106	2b12	—	0.3
	Year	128	527	133	162	**31**	12	2	53	50	5	—	.307	.373	.423	158	36	71	.890	0	124	162	O82(57/26/0),2b31,S15	—	3.1
1889	†Bro AA	**138**	560	139	149	18	3	2	73	80	7	41	.266	.365	.320	95	0	65	.929	-3	101	91	2b138	—	0.2
1890	†Bro N	**129**	510	**148**	142	32	7	3	69	85	3	47	.278	.385	.386	124	20	85	.945	3	104	118	2b129	—	2.4
1891	Bro N	107	435	82	120	16	5	3	31	59	2	63	.276	.365	.356	111	8	32	.910	-21	91	58	2b72,O35(32/3/0)	—	-1.0
1892	Bro N	21	87	17	26	5	1	0	17	14	0	13	.299	.396	.379	140	5	4	.925	-2	0	0	O21L	—	0.1
Total	7	680	2779	653	790	127	38	11	319	332	19	164	.284	.365	.369	115	62	335	.928	-32	99	92	2b381,O271L,S20,1b9,3b3	—	3.4
COLLINS, RIPPER	James Anthony; B3.30.1904 Altoona PA; D4.15.1970 New Haven CT; BB/TL/5´9˝/165; d4.18; C3																								
1931	†StL N	89	279	34	84	20	10	4	59	18	3	24	.301	.350	.487	118	6	1	.995	4	123	104	1b68,O3(1/0/2)	—	0.4
1932	StL N	149	549	82	153	28	8	21	91	38	3	67	.279	.329	.474	110	6	4	.999	-1	83	107	1b81,O60(15/0/45)	—	-0.6
1933	StL N	132	493	66	153	26	7	10	68	38	3	49	.310	.363	.452	125	16	7	.994	3	102	83	1b123	—	0.8
1934	†StL N	**154**	600	116	200	40	12	**35**	128	57	2	50	.333	.393	**.615**	155	46	2	.991	8	**118**	99	1b154	—	3.7
1935	StL N★	150	578	109	181	36	10	23	122	65	3	45	.313	.385	.529	138	31	0	.987	1	102	102	1b150	—	1.7
1936	StL N★	103	277	48	81	15	3	13	48	48	1	30	.292	.399	.509	143	18	1	.990	-1	93	104	1b61,O9(1/0/8)	—	1.1
1937	Chi N★	115	456	77	125	16	5	16	71	32	5	46	.274	.329	.436	102	0	2	.991	1	101	106	1b111	—	-1.0
1938	†Chi N	143	490	78	131	22	8	13	61	54	3	48	.267	.344	.424	107	5	1	**.996**	8	118	108	1b135	—	0.0
1941	Pit N	49	62	5	13	2	2	0	11	6	0	14	.210	.279	.306	65	-3	0	.947	1	180	85	1b11,O3R	0	-0.3
Total	9	1084	3784	615	1121	205	65	135	659	356	23	373	.296	.360	.492	125	125	18	.992	23	107	101	1b894,O75(17/0/58)	0	5.8
COLLINS, JIMMY	James Joseph; B1.16.1870 Buffalo NY; D3.6.1943 Buffalo NY; BR/TR/5´9˝/178; d4.19; M6; HF1945																								
1895	Bos N	11	38	10	8	3	0	1	8	4	1	4	.211	.302	.368	67	-2	0	.714	-2	81	0	O10R	—	-0.3
	Lou N	96	373	65	104	17	5	6	49	33	9	16	.279	.352	.399	100	1	12	.926	20	116	95	3b77,O18(0/7/11),2b2/S	—	1.7
	Year	107	411	75	112	20	5	7	57	37	10	20	.273	.347	.397	96	-2	12	.926	19	116	95	3b77,O28(0/7/21),2b2/S	—	1.4
1896	Bos N	84	304	48	90	10	9	1	46	30	8	12	.296	.374	.398	98	-1	10	.909	16	118	137	3b80,S4	—	1.4
1897	†Bos N	134	529	103	183	28	13	6	132	41	7	—	.346	.400	.482	125	18	14	.917	19	113	129	3b134	—	3.3
1898	Bos N	**152**	597	107	196	35	5	**15**	111	40	7	—	.328	.377	.479	138	27	12	.932	12	101	104	3b152	—	3.9
1899	Bos N	151	599	98	166	28	11	5	92	40	12	—	.277	.335	.386	89	-11	12	.943	18	109	115	3b151	—	0.8
1900	Bos N	**142**	586	104	178	25	5	6	95	34	10	—	.304	.352	.394	94	-6	23	.935	10	96	113	3b141/S	—	0.6
1901	Bos A	**138**	564	108	187	42	16	6	94	34	5	—	.332	.375	.495	142	31	19	.914	13	106	**142**	3b138,M	—	4.2
1902	Bos A	108	429	71	138	21	10	6	61	24	2	—	.322	.360	.459	123	12	18	**.954**	8	105	96	3b107,M	—	2.1
1903	†Bos A	130	540	88	160	33	17	5	72	24	2	—	.296	.329	.448	125	14	23	**.952**	10	103	**149**	3b130,M	—	2.9
1904	Bos A	156	631	85	171	33	13	3	67	27	5	—	.271	.306	.379	110	6	19	.945	5	104	121	3b156,M	—	1.7
1905	Bos A	131	508	66	140	26	5	4	65	37	4	—	.276	.330	.370	120	12	18	.923	5	103	115	3b131,M	—	2.2
1906	Bos A	37	142	17	39	8	4	1	16	4	0	—	.275	.295	.408	120	2	1	.911	2	107	64	3b32,M	—	0.5
1907	Bos A	41	158	13	46	8	0	0	10	10	0	—	.291	.333	.342	116	3	4	.874	-6	89	53	3b41	—	-0.2
	Phi A	99	364	38	99	21	0	0	35	24	8	—	.272	.331	.330	108	5	4	.904	-2	94	116	3b98	—	0.5
	Year	140	522	51	145	29	0	0	45	34	8	—	.278	.332	.333	110	8	8	.895	-9	93	98	3b139	—	0.3
1908	Phi A	115	433	34	94	14	3	0	30	20	4	—	.217	.258	.263	65	-17	5	.928	-7	92	109	3b115	—	-2.3
Total	14	1725	6795	1055	1999	352	116	65	983	426	84	32	.294	.343	.409	112	94	194	.929	122	104	117	3b1683,O28(0/7/21),S6,2b2	—	23.0
COLLINS, ZIP	John Edgar; B5.4.1892 Brooklyn NY; D12.19.1983 Manassas VA; BL/TL/5´11˝/152; d7.31																								
1914	Pit N	49	182	14	44	2	0	0	15	8	1	10	.242	.277	.253	61	-9	3	.962	1	103	107	O49(0/11/40)	—	-1.2
1915	Pit N	101	354	51	104	8	5	1	23	24	1	38	.294	.340	.353	112	4	6-7	.942	1	104	103	O89C	—	-0.2
	Bos N	5	14	3	4	1	1	0	0	2	0	1	.286	.375	.500	171	1	1	1.000	0	88	245	O4L	—	0.2
	Year	106	368	54	108	9	6	1	23	26	1	39	.293	.342	.359	114	5	7-7	.944	2	103	108	O93(4/89/0)	—	0.0
1916	Bos N	93	268	39	56	1	6	1	18	18	1	42	.209	.261	.269	66	-12	4	.947	-1	89	131	O78(26/27/27)	—	-2.0

YEAR	TM LG	G	AB	R	H	2B	3B	HR	RBI	BB-IB	HP	SO	AVG	OBP	SLG	AOPS	ABR	SB-CS	FA	FR	RNG	THR	GAMES AT POSITION	DL	BFW
1917	Bos N	9	27	3	4	0	1	0	2	0	0	4	.148	.148	.222	14	-3	0	1.000	-0	118	0	O5(1/0/4)	—	-0.4
1921	Phi A	24	71	14	20	5	1	0	5	6	2	5	.282	.354	.380	87	-1	1-2	.915	-0	100	116	O20C	—	-0.3
Total	5	281	916	124	232	17	14	2	63	58	5	100	.253	.301	.309	85	-20	15-9	.946	1	99	112	O245(31/147/71)	—	-3.9
COLLINS, SHANO	John Francis; B12.4.1885 Charlestown MA; D9.10.1955 Newton MA; BR/TR/6´0˝/185; d4.21; M2; gs–Bob Gallagher																								
1910	Chi A	97	315	29	62	10	8	1	24	25	1	—	.197	.258	.289	74	-11	10	.949	2	96	118	O66(19/7/40),1b28	—	-1.4
1911	Chi A	106	370	48	97	16	12	4	48	20	5	—	.262	.309	.403	101	-2	14	.978	4	118	117	1b98,2b3,O3L	—	-0.1
1912	Chi A	153	579	75	168	34	10	2	81	29	5	—	.290	.330	.394	110	5	27	.969	0	100	70	O105(1/17/85),1b46	—	-0.2
1913	Chi A	148	535	53	128	26	9	1	47	32	3	60	.239	.286	.327	80	-16	22	.949	2	111	87	O147(2/0/145)	—	-2.3
1914	Chi A	154	598	61	164	34	9	3	65	27	6	49	.274	.312	.376	108	3	30-24	.970	1	100	103	O154(7/45/103)	—	-0.7
1915	Chi A	153	576	73	148	24	17	2	85	28	6	50	.257	.298	.368	96	-7	38-19	.963	-0	106	96	O104(20/21/64),1b47	—	-1.3
1916	Chi A	143	527	74	128	28	12	0	42	59	3	51	.243	.323	.342	98	-1	16	.959	5	104	119	O137(23/2/112),1b4	—	-0.4
1917	†Chi A	82	252	38	59	13	3	1	14	10	2	27	.234	.269	.321	78	-8	14	.992	3	119	72	O73(9/0/64)	—	-0.9
1918	Chi A	103	365	30	100	18	11	1	56	17	2	19	.274	.310	.392	111	2	7	.973	12	117	151	O93(16/34/42),1b5	—	0.9
1919	†Chi A	63	179	21	50	6	3	1	16	7	3	11	.279	.317	.363	90	-3	3	.957	4	115	135	O46(2/7/37),1b8	—	-0.1
1920	Chi A	133	495	70	150	21	10	1	63	23	4	24	.303	.339	.392	93	-7	12-9	.988	-7	82	106	1b116,O13(2/1/10)	—	-1.7
1921	Bos A	141	542	63	155	29	12	4	69	18	4	38	.286	.314	.406	85	-16	15-8	.966	4	99	124	O139(1/44/94),1b3	—	-1.9
1922	Bos A	135	472	33	128	24	7	1	52	7	5	30	.271	.289	.358	68	-24	7-9	.951	-4	104	49	O117(11/45/63)/1	—	-3.7
1923	Bos A	97	342	41	79	10	5	0	18	11	5	29	.231	.265	.289	46	-29	7-8	.953	-0	86	172	O89(0/57/32)	—	-3.4
1924	Bos A	89	240	37	70	17	5	0	28	18	3	17	.292	.349	.404	94	-3	4-6	.957	-8	79	66	O56(18/11/27),1b12	—	-1.5
1925	Bos A	2	3	1	1	0	0	0	1	0	0	0	.333	.333	.333	70	0	0-0	ø	-0	0	0	/cf	—	0.0
Total	16	1799	6390	747	1687	310	133	22	709	331	57	405	.264	.306	.364	90	-117	226-83	.962	17	103	103	O1343(133/292/918),1b368,2b3	—	-18.7
COLLINS, JOE	Joseph Edward (b Joseph Edward Kollonige); B12.3.1922 Scranton PA; D8.30.1989 Union NJ; BL/TL/6´0˝/(185–192); d9.25																								
1948	NY A	5	5	0	1	1	0	0	2	0	0	1	.200	.200	.400	58	0	0-0	ø	0	—	—	/H	0	0.0
1949	NY A	7	10	2	1	0	0	0	4	6	0	2	.100	.438	.100	46	0	0-0	.920	-1	0	60	1b5	0	-0.1
1950	†NY A	108	205	47	48	8	3	8	28	31	0	34	.234	.335	.420	95	-2	5-0	.987	0	101	111	1b99,O2R	0	-0.3
1951	†NY A	125	262	52	75	8	5	9	48	34	0	23	.286	.368	.458	127	9	9-7	.987	5	126	110	1b114,O15R	0	1.1
1952	†NY A	122	428	69	120	16	8	18	59	55	1	47	.280	.364	.481	142	23	4-2	.990	-3	90	**124**	1b119	0	1.7
1953	†NY A	127	387	72	104	11	2	17	44	59	0	36	.269	.365	.439	121	11	2-6	.989	1	106	116	1b113,O4R	0	0.5
1954	NY A	130	343	67	93	20	2	12	46	51	0	37	.271	.365	.446	126	13	2-2	.992	2	108	**142**	1b117	0	1.0
1955	†NY A	105	278	40	65	9	1	13	45	44-2	2	32	.234	.339	.414	104	2	0-2	.998	7	135	146	1b73,O27R	0	0.4
1956	†NY A	100	262	38	59	5	3	7	43	34-2	1	33	.225	.313	.347	78	-9	3-1	.990	5	103	60	O51(25/7/24),1b43	0	-0.7
1957	†NY A	79	149	17	30	1	0	2	10	24-2	0	18	.201	.310	.248	56	-9	2-1	.987	-0	97	112	1b32,O15(2/2/11)	0	-1.1
Total	10	908	2329	404	596	79	24	86	329	338-6	4	263	.256	.350	.421	112	38	27-21	.990	16	110	125	1b715,O114(27/9/83)	0	2.5
COLLINS, KEVIN	Kevin Michael "Casey"; B8.4.1946 Springfield MA; BL/TR/6´2˝/(180–190); d9.1																								
1965	NY N	11	23	3	4	1	0	0	0	1-0	0	9	.174	.208	.217	21	-2	0-1	1.000	-2	101	128	3b7,S3	132	-0.5
1967	NY N	4	10	1	1	0	0	0	0	0-0	0	3	.100	.100	.100	-43	-2	1-0	1.000	-0	117	0	2b2	0	-0.2
1968	NY N	58	154	12	31	5	2	1	13	7-2	0	37	.201	.233	.279	54	-9	0-1	.955	-5	77	110	3b40,2b6/S	0	-1.7
1969	NY N	16	40	1	6	3	0	1	2	3-1	0	10	.150	.209	.300	40	-3	0-0	.925	1	113	114	3b14	0	-0.2
	Mon N	52	96	5	23	5	1	2	12	8-0	0	16	.240	.292	.375	87	-2	0-0	1.000	-5	76	40	2b20,3b16	0	-0.7
	Year	68	136	6	29	8	1	3	14	11-1	0	26	.213	.268	.353	73	-5	0-0	.917	-4	93	95	3b30,2b20	0	-0.9
1970	Det A	25	24	2	5	1	0	1	3	1-0	0	10	.208	.240	.375	66	-1	0-0	1.000	0	158	0	/1	0	-0.1
1971	Det A	35	41	6	11	2	1	1	4	0-0	0	12	.268	.268	.439	93	-1	0-0	1.000	1	114	0	3b4,O2(1/0/1)/2	23	0.0
Total	6	201	388	30	81	17	4	6	34	20-3	0	97	.209	.245	.320	62	-20	1-2	.944	-11	85	103	3b81,2b29,S4,O2(1/0/1)/1	155	-3.4
COLLINS, ORTH	Orth Stein "Buck"; B4.27.1880 Lafayette IN; D12.13.1949 Ft.Lauderdale FL; BL/TR/6´0˝/150; d6.1																								
1904	NY A	5	17	3	6	1	1	0	1	1	0	—	.353	.389	.529	180	1	0	1.000	3	1145	0	O5(0/5/1)	—	0.4
1909	Was A	8	7	0	0	0	0	0	0	0	0	—	.000	.000	.000	-99	-2	0	1.000	-0	0	0	O2(0/1/1)/P	—	-0.2
Total	2	13	24	3	6	1	1	0	1	1	0	—	.250	.280	.375	104	-1	0	1.000	3	954	0	O7(0/6/2)/P	—	0.2
COLLINS, RIP	Robert Joseph; B9.18.1909 Pittsburgh PA; D4.19.1969 Pittsburgh PA; BR/TR/5´11˝/176; d4.28																								
1940	Chi N	47	120	11	25	3	0	1	14	14	1	18	.208	.296	.258	55	-7	4	.951	-3	*104*	*109*	C42	—	-0.8
1944	NY A	3	3	0	1	0	0	0	0	1	0	0	.333	.500	.333	136	0	0-0	1.000	0	*0*	*0*	C3	0	0.1
Total	2	50	123	11	26	3	0	1	14	15	1	18	.211	.302	.260	58	-7	4-0	.953	-3	*101*	*105*	C45	0	-0.7
COLLINS, PAT	Tharon Leslie; B9.13.1896 Sweet Sprgs. MO; D5.20.1960 Kansas City KS; BR/TR/5´9˝/178; d9.5																								
1919	StL A	11	21	2	3	1	0	0	1	4	0	2	.143	.280	.190	32	-2	0	.929	-0	*107*	*87*	C5	—	-0.2
1920	StL A	23	28	5	6	1	0	0	6	3	0	5	.214	.290	.250	43	-2	0-0	1.000	-1	*82*	*61*	C7	—	-0.3
1921	StL A	58	111	9	27	3	0	1	10	16	0	17	.243	.339	.297	60	-6	1-0	.961	-1	*113*	*80*	C31	—	-0.5
1922	StL A	63	127	14	39	6	0	8	23	21	0	21	.307	.405	.543	140	8	0-1	.980	4	*133*	*92*	C28,1b5	—	1.2
1923	StL A	85	181	9	32	8	0	3	30	15	0	45	.177	.240	.271	32	-18	0-0	.980	-0	*96*	*102*	C47	—	-1.6
1924	StL A	32	54	9	17	2	0	1	11	11	0	14	.315	.431	.407	110	1	0-1	.969	-1	*95*	*107*	C20	—	0.1
1926	†NY A	102	290	41	83	11	3	7	35	73	2	57	.286	.433	.417	124	15	3-2	.971	1	*89*	*95*	C100	—	2.2
1927	†NY A	92	251	38	69	9	3	7	36	54	2	24	.275	.407	.418	118	9	0-1	.976	-3	*103*	*59*	C89	—	1.1
1928	†NY A	70	136	18	30	5	0	6	14	35	0	16	.221	.380	.390	106	3	0-0	.977	-4	*88*	*100*	C70	—	0.2
1929	Bos N	7	5	1	0	0	0	0	2	3	0	1	.000	.375	.000	2	-1	0	1.000	0	*91*	*75*	C6	—	0.0
Total	10	543	1204	146	306	46	6	33	168	235	4	202	.254	.378	.385	98	7	4-5	.974	-5	*99*	*87*	C403,1b5	—	2.2
COLLINS, BILLY	William J.; B1863 Dublin, Ireland; D6.8.1893 Brooklyn NY; BR/?/150; d8.1																								
1887	NY AA	1	4	0	1	0	0	0	0	0	0	—	.250	.250	.250	42	0	0	.250	-2	—	—	/C	—	-0.2
1889	Phi AA	1	4	0	1	0	0	0	1	1	0	0	.250	.400	.250	88	0	1	.800	-1	—	—	/C	—	0.0
1890	Phi AA	1	1	0	0	0	0	0	0	0	0	—	.000	.000	.000	-99	0	0	.500	-1	59	0	/S	—	-0.1
1891	Cle N	2	3	0	0	0	0	0	0	0	0	0	.000	.000	.000	-96	-1	0	ø	1	0	0	/rfC	—	0.0
Total	4	5	12	0	2	0	0	0	1	1	0	0	.167	.231	.167	14	-1	1	.737	-2	—	—	C3/rfS	—	-0.3
COLLINS, BILL	William Shirley; B3.27.1882 Chesterton IN; D6.26.1961 San Bernardino CA; BB/TR/6´0˝/170; d4.14																								
1910	Bos N	151	584	67	141	6	7	3	40	43	13	48	.241	.308	.291	72	-22	36	**.977**	8	108	109	O151(129/10/13)	—	-2.4
1911	Bos N	17	44	8	6	1	1	0	8	1	0	8	.136	.156	.205	0	-6	4	1.000	1	127	61	O13(3/8/2)/3	—	-0.6
	Chi N	7	3	2	1	1	0	0	0	1	0	0	.333	.500	.667	225	1	0	1.000	0	101	0	O4(2/2/0)	—	0.1
	Year	24	47	10	7	2	1	0	8	2	0	8	.149	.184	.234	16	-6	4	1.000	1	126	59	O17(5/10/2)/3	—	-0.5
1913	Bro N	32	95	8	18	1	0	0	4	8	2	11	.189	.267	.200	33	-8	2-4	.921	-2	102	29	O27(13/15/0)	—	-1.4
1914	Buf F	21	47	6	7	2	2	0	2	1	0	8	.149	.167	.277	19	-7	0	.864	1	75	260	O15(2/1/13)	—	-0.6
Total	4	228	773	91	173	11	10	3	54	54	15	75	.224	.287	.276	60	-42	42-4	.966	8	106	105	O210(149/36/28)/3	—	-4.9
COLLVER, BILL	William J.; B3.21.1867 Clyde OH; D3.24.1888 Detroit MI; d7.4																								
1885	Bos N	1	4	0	0	0	0	0	0	0	—	1	.000	.000	.000	-99	-1	—	ø	-0	0	0	/rf	—	-0.1
COLMAN, FRANK	Frank Lloyd; B3.2.1918 London ON, Can.; D2.19.1983 London ON, Can.; BL/TL/5´11˝/188; d9.12																								
1942	Pit N	10	37	2	5	0	0	1	2	2	0	2	.135	.179	.216	15	-4	0	1.000	1	93	285	O8R	0	-0.4
1943	Pit N	32	59	9	16	2	2	0	4	8	0	7	.271	.358	.373	108	1	0	1.000	-0	111	0	O11R	0	-0.1
1944	Pit N	99	226	30	61	9	5	6	53	25	1	27	.270	.345	.434	113	4	0	.964	-1	103	77	O53(3/0/50),1b6	0	0.0
1945	Pit N	77	153	18	32	11	1	4	30	9	0	16	.209	.253	.373	70	-7	0	.993	1	131	83	1b22,O12(6/0/5)	0	-0.8
1946	Pit N	26	53	3	9	3	0	1	6	2	1	7	.170	.214	.283	39	-4	0	1.000	0	100	142	O8(4/0/4),1b2	0	-0.5
	NY A	5	15	2	4	0	0	1	5	1	0	1	.267	.313	.467	114	0	0-0	1.000	-0	110	0	O5R	0	0.0
1947	NY A	22	28	2	3	0	0	2	6	2	0	6	.107	.167	.321	34	-3	0-0	1.000	1	96	450	O6L	0	-0.3
Total	6	271	571	66	130	25	8	15	106	49	2	66	.228	.291	.378	85	-13	0-0	.980	1	102	93	O103(19/0/83),1b30	0	-2.1
COLON, CRIS	Cristobal; B1.3.1969 LaGuaira, Vargas, Venez.; BB/TR/6´2˝/180; d9.18																								
1992	Tex A	14	36	5	6	0	0	0	1	1-0	0	8	.167	.189	.167	0	-5	0-0	.946	0	104	63	S14	0	-0.4
COLUCCIO, BOB	Robert Pasquali; B10.2.1951 Centralia WA; BR/TR/5´11˝/(180–185); [MilA69 17/403]; d4.15																								
1973	Mil A	124	438	65	98	21	8	15	58	54-2	3	92	.224	.311	.411	104	1	13-6	.992	8	110	165	O108(18/14/79),D11	0	0.5
1974	Mil A	138	394	42	88	13	4	6	31	43-2	3	61	.223	.305	.322	81	-10	15-9	.989	6	108	109	O131(4/103/34),D2	0	-0.8
1975	Mil A	22	62	8	12	0	1	1	5	11-0	1	11	.194	.320	.274	70	-2	1-4	1.000	-0	102	67	O22C	0	-0.4

YEAR	TM LG	G	AB	R	H	2B	3B	HR	RBI	BB-IB	HP	SO	AVG	OBP	SLG	AOPS	ABR	SB-CS	FA	FR	RNG	THR	GAMES AT POSITION	DL	BFW
	Chi A	61	161	22	33	4	2	4	13	13-1	1	34	.205	.269	.329	67	-8	4-0	.980	1	104	113	O59(14/3/44)/D	36	-0.8
	Year	83	223	30	45	4	3	5	18	24-1	2	45	.202	.284	.314	68	-10	5-4	.987	1	103	98	O81(14/25/44)/D	0	-1.2
1977	Chi A	20	37	4	10	0	0	0	7	6-0	0	2	.270	.356	.270	78	-1	0-2	1.000	1	101	113	O19(9/8/3)	0	-0.1
1978	StL N	5	3	0	0	0	0	0	0	1-0	0	2	.000	.250	.000	-25	0	0-0	1.000	-0	91	0	O2(1/0/1)	0	-0.1
Total	5	370	1095	141	241	38	15	26	114	128-5	8	202	.220	.305	.353	87	-20	33-21	.990	15	107	126	O341(46/150/161),D14	36	-1.7
Combs, Earle	Earle Bryan "The Kentucky Colonel"; B5.14.1899 Pebworth KY; D7.21.1976 Richmond KY; BL/TR/6´0˝/185; d4.16; C16; HF1970; Col Eastern Kentucky																								
1924	NY A	24	35	10	14	5	0	0	2	4	0	2	.400	.462	.543	159	3	0-1	1.000	-1	98	0	O11(5/3/3)	—	0.2
1925	NY A	150	593	117	203	36	13	3	61	65	4	43	.342	.411	.462	123	23	12-13	.979	-5	98	73	O150(12/138/0)	—	0.8
1926	†NY A	145	606	113	181	31	12	8	55	47	3	23	.299	.352	.429	105	2	8-6	.970	-3	103	57	O145C	—	-0.7
1927	†NY A	152	648	137	**231**	36	**23**	6	64	62	2	31	.356	.414	.511	143	40	15-6	.968	-6	104	39	O152C	—	2.8
1928	†NY A	149	626	118	194	33	**21**	7	56	77	2	33	.310	.387	.463	127	24	11-8	.980	0	106	66	O149C	—	1.7
1929	NY A	142	586	119	202	33	15	3	65	69	0	32	.345	.414	.468	135	33	12-7	.966	-7	94	69	O141C	—	1.9
1930	NY A	137	532	129	183	30	**22**	7	82	74	0	26	.344	.424	.523	145	38	16-10	.969	-4	99	51	O135(60/45/30)	—	2.3
1931	NY A	138	563	120	179	31	13	5	58	68	3	34	.318	.394	.446	128	24	11-3	.974	-8	95	49	O129C	—	1.3
1932	†NY A	144	591	143	190	32	10	9	65	81	2	16	.321	.405	.455	129	28	3-9	.967	-9	94	52	O139(42/115/1)	—	1.1
1933	NY A	122	417	86	125	22	16	5	64	47	1	19	.300	.372	.465	128	16	6-4	.975	-5	98	41	O104(23/80/2)	—	0.7
1934	NY A	63	251	47	80	13	5	2	25	40	0	9	.319	.412	.434	127	12	3-1	.993	-3	99	21	O62(12/51/0)	—	0.7
1935	NY A	89	298	47	84	7	4	3	35	36	0	10	.282	.359	.362	92	-3	1-3	.993	-1	102	39	O70(57/13/1)	—	-0.8
Total	12	1455	5746	1186	1866	309	154	58	632	670	17	278	.325	.397	.462	127	240	98-71	.974	-51	99	53	O1387(211/1161/37)	—	12.0
Combs, Merl	Merrill Russell; B12.11.1919 Los Angeles CA; D7.7.1981 Riverside CA; BL/TR/6´0˝/172; d9.12; C2; Col USC																								
1947	Bos A	17	68	8	15	1	0	1	6	9	2	9	.221	.329	.279	65	-3	0-0	1.000	3	117	181	3b17	0	0.0
1949	Bos A	14	24	5	5	1	0	0	1	9	0	0	.208	.424	.250	75	0	0-0	.923	-1	81	120	3b9/S	0	-0.1
1950	Bos A	1	0	0	0	0	0	0	0	1	0	0	ø	1.000	ø	158	0	0-0	ø	0	—	—	/H	0	0.0
	Was A	37	102	19	25	1	0	0	6	22	0	16	.245	.379	.255	68	-4	0-0	.966	0	107	89	S30	0	-0.2
	Year	38	102	19	25	1	0	0	6	23	0	16	.245	.384	.255	69	-3	0-0	.966	0	107	89	S30	0	-0.2
1951	Cle A	19	28	2	5	2	0	0	2	2	0	3	.179	.233	.250	32	-3	0-0	.960	3	131	87	S16	0	0.0
1952	Cle A	52	139	11	23	1	1	1	10	14	0	15	.165	.242	.209	28	-14	0-1	.972	8	115	113	S49,2b3	0	-0.4
Total	5	140	361	45	73	6	1	2	25	57	2	43	.202	.314	.241	52	-24	0-1	.968	13	113	101	S96,3b26,2b3	0	-0.7
Comer, Wayne	Harry Wayne; B2.3.1944 Shenandoah VA; BR/TR/5´10˝/175; d9.17																								
1967	Det A	4	3	0	1	0	0	0	0	0-0	0	0	.333	.333	.333	95	0	0-0	ø	-0	0	0	/cf	0	0.0
1968	†Det A	48	48	8	6	0	1	1	3	2-0	0	7	.125	.160	.229	16	-5	0-0	1.000	0	113	0	O27(26/0/1)/C	0	-0.6
1969	Sea A	147	481	88	118	18	1	15	54	82-2	1	79	.245	.354	.380	107	7	18-7	.980	7	105	**161**	O139(20/92/46)/C3	0	1.1
1970	Mil A	13	17	1	1	0	0	0	1	0-0	0	3	.059	.059	.059	-67	-4	0-0	1.000	0	109	0	O5(1/2/2)	0	-0.4
	Was A	77	129	21	30	4	0	0	8	22-0	1	16	.233	.346	.264	75	-3	4-1	.960	-2	91	84	O58(18/21/20)/3	21	-0.7
	Year	90	146	22	31	4	0	0	9	22-0	1	19	.212	.318	.240	59	-7	4-1	.962	-2	92	79	O63(19/23/22)/3	0	-1.1
1972	Det A	27	9	1	1	0	0	0	1	0-0	0	1	.111	.100	.111	-33	-1	0-1	1.000	-1	69	0	O17(15/1/1)	0	-0.3
Total	5	316	687	119	157	22	2	16	67	106-2	2	106	.229	.331	.336	89	-6	22-9	.978	4	102	131	O247(80/117/70),3b2,C2	21	-0.9
Comiskey, Charlie	Charles Albert "Commy","The Old Roman"; B8.15.1859 Chicago IL; D10.26.1931 Eagle River WI; BR/TR/6´0˝/180; d5.2; M12; HF1939; ▲																								
1882	StL AA	78	329	58	80	9	5	1	45	4	—	—	.243	.252	.310	85	-6	—	.967	-1	73	73	1b77,P2	—	-1.3
1883	StL AA	96	401	87	118	17	9	2	64	11	—	—	.294	.313	.397	120	7	—	.963	-1	70	**135**	1b96/lfM	—	-0.2
1884	StL AA	108	460	76	109	17	6	2	84	5	5	—	.237	.253	.313	81	-11	—	.969	2	101	116	1b108/2PM	—	-1.7
1885	†StL AA	83	340	68	87	15	7	2	44	14	4	—	.256	.293	.359	101	-1	—	.969	1	110	92	1b83,M	—	-0.6
1886	†StL AA	131	578	95	147	15	9	3	76	10	0	—	.254	.267	.327	82	-16	41	.975	5	125	125	1b122,2b9,O2R,M	—	-2.0
1887	†StL AA	125	538	139	180	22	5	4	103	27	7	—	.335	.374	.416	109	3	117	.976	4	**135**	115	1b116,2b9,O3R,M	—	-0.2
1888	†StL AA	**137**	576	102	157	22	5	6	83	12	4	—	.273	.292	.359	98	-5	72	.970	-4	95	109	1b133,O5(0/2/3),2b3,M	—	-2.0
1889	StL AA	137	587	105	168	28	10	3	102	19	3	19	.286	.312	.383	86	-16	65	.970	-1	95	106	1b134,O3(0/1/2),2b3/PM	—	-2.4
1890	Chi P	88	377	53	92	11	3	0	59	14	3	17	.244	.277	.289	49	-29	34	.965	-3	92	106	1b88,M	—	-3.2
1891	StL AA	**139**	572	84	148	16	2	2	88	33	7	25	.259	.307	.304	65	-29	38	.979	4	110	106	1b139,O2L,M	—	-3.3
1892	Cin N	141	551	61	125	14	6	3	71	32	4	16	.227	.274	.290	72	-20	30	.984	1	96	**132**	1b141,M	—	-1.9
1893	Cin N	64	259	38	57	12	1	0	26	11	2	2	.220	.257	.274	40	-23	9	.979	-6	59	143	1b64,M	—	-2.5
1894	Cin N	63	228	26	61	9	0	0	38	5	4	5	.268	.295	.307	44	-22	10	.973	-3	82	101	1b62/rfM	—	-1.9
Total	13	1390	5796	992	1529	207	68	28	883	197	43	84	.264	.293	.337	81	-168	416	.973	-3	99	113	1b1363,2b25,O17(3/3/11),P4	—	-23.2
Command, Jim	James Dalton "Igor"; B10.15.1928 Grand Rapids MI; BL/TR/6´2˝/200; d6.20																								
1954	Phi N	9	18	1	4	1	0	1	6	2	0	4	.222	.300	.444	91	0	0-0	.929	-0	96	0	3b6	0	-0.1
1955	Phi N	5	5	0	0	0	0	0	0	0-0	0	0	.000	.000	.000	-99	-1	0-0	ø	0	—	—	/H	0	-0.1
Total	2	14	23	1	4	1	0	1	6	2-0	0	4	.174	.240	.348	52	-1	0-0	.929	-0	96	0	3b6	0	-0.2
Comorosky, Adam	Adam Anthony; B12.9.1905 Swoyersville PA; D3.2.1951 Swoyersville PA; BR/TR/5´10˝/167; d9.13																								
1926	Pit N	8	15	2	4	1	1	0	0	1	0	2	.267	.313	.467	102	0	1	1.000	-0	108	0	O6L	—	0.0
1927	Pit N	18	61	5	14	1	0	0	4	3	0	1	.230	.266	.246	35	-6	0	.978	1	123	65	O16(15/1/0)	—	-0.6
1928	Pit N	51	176	22	52	6	3	2	34	15	1	6	.295	.354	.398	92	-2	1	.968	1	113	52	O49(38/9/5)	—	-0.4
1929	Pit N	127	473	86	152	26	11	6	97	40	2	22	.321	.377	.461	104	2	19	.963	-1	102	73	O121L	—	-0.7
1930	Pit N	152	597	112	187	47	**23**	12	119	51	4	33	.313	.371	.529	114	12	14	.969	2	102	107	O152(130/30/0)	—	0.3
1931	Pit N	99	350	37	85	12	1	1	48	34	0	28	.243	.310	.291	63	-18	11	.978	3	110	81	O90(89/0/1)	—	-2.0
1932	Pit N	108	370	54	106	18	4	4	46	25	3	20	.286	.337	.389	96	-2	7	.981	5	116	62	O92(74/18/0)	—	-0.1
1933	Pit N	64	162	18	46	8	1	1	15	4	0	9	.284	.301	.364	89	-3	2	1.000	-1	101	42	O30L	—	-0.5
1934	Cin N	127	446	46	115	12	6	0	40	34	3	23	.258	.315	.312	70	-19	1	.970	-1	107	48	O122(47/9/66)	—	-2.7
1935	Cin N	59	137	22	34	3	1	2	14	7	1	14	.248	.290	.328	68	-7	1	.953	1	105	116	O40(25/10/5)	—	-0.7
Total	10	813	2787	404	795	134	51	28	417	214	14	158	.285	.339	.400	91	-43	57	.972	10	107	74	O718(575/77/77)	—	-7.4
Compton, Pete	Anna Sebastian "Bash"; B9.28.1889 San Marcos TX; D2.3.1978 Kansas City MO; BL/TL/5´11˝/170; d9.6																								
1911	StL A	28	107	9	29	4	0	0	5	8	0	—	.271	.322	.308	79	-3	2	.917	1	94	149	O28R	—	-0.3
1912	StL A	103	268	26	75	6	4	2	30	22	2	—	.280	.339	.354	102	0	11	.925	2	112	98	O72(50/0/22)	—	-0.1
1913	StL A	63	100	14	18	5	2	2	17	13	0	13	.180	.274	.330	79	-3	2	.862	-2	79	85	O21(8/5/8)	—	-0.6
1915	StL F	2	8	0	2	0	0	0	3	0	0	0	.250	.250	.250	39	-1	0	1.000	-0	62	0	O2C	—	-0.1
	Bos N	35	116	10	28	7	1	1	12	8	0	11	.241	.290	.345	96	-1	4-1	.971	0	108	58	O31(0/20/11)	—	-0.2
1916	Bos N	34	98	13	20	2	0	0	8	7	1	7	.204	.264	.224	53	-5	5	.939	-1	101	64	O30(3/26/1)	—	-0.9
	Pit N	5	16	1	1	0	0	0	0	2	1	5	.063	.211	.063	-14	-2	0	.917	-0	120	0	O5R	—	-0.3
	Year	39	114	14	21	2	0	0	8	9	2	12	.184	.256	.202	43	-7	5	.936	-1	104	53	O35(3/26/6)	—	-1.2
1918	NY N	21	60	5	13	0	1	0	5	5	0	4	.217	.277	.250	62	-3	2	.971	1	106	169	O19(12/2/5)	—	-0.2
Total	6	291	773	78	186	24	8	5	80	65	4	40	.241	.303	.312	83	-18	26-1	.933	1	104	95	O208(73/55/80)	—	-2.7
Compton, Mike	Michael Lynn; B8.15.1944 Stamford TX; BR/TR/5´10˝/180; d4.17; Col Sul Ross St.																								
1970	Phi N	47	110	8	18	0	1	1	7	9-3	2	22	.164	.240	.209	22	-13	0-0	.986	-1	87	119	C40	0	-1.2
Conatser, Clint	Clinton Astor "Connie" (b Astor Clinton Conatser); B7.24.1921 Los Angeles CA; BR/TR/5´11˝/182; d4.21; Col Los Angeles (CA) City																								
1948	†Bos N	90	224	30	62	9	3	3	23	32	1	27	.277	.370	.384	106	3	0	.974	-2	99	68	O76(24/52/0)	0	-0.1
1949	Bos N	53	152	10	40	6	0	3	16	14	0	19	.263	.325	.362	89	-3	0	.951	1	103	151	O44(15/13/16)	0	-0.3
Total	2	143	376	40	102	15	3	6	39	46	1	46	.271	.352	.375	99	0	0	.965	-1	101	102	O120(39/65/16)	0	-0.4
Concepcion, Dave	David Ismael (Benitez); B6.17.1948 Aragua, Venezuela; BR/TR/6´1˝/(155–200); d4.6																								
1970	†Cin N	101	265	38	69	6	3	1	19	23-5	3	45	.260	.324	.317	73	-10	10-2	.945	-3	101	110	S93,2b3	0	-0.2
1971	Cin N	130	327	24	67	4	4	1	20	18-2	0	51	.205	.246	.251	42	-26	9-3	.974	-2	99	**115**	S112,2b10,3b7,O5C	15	-1.8
1972	†Cin N	119	378	40	79	13	2	2	29	32-8	2	65	.209	.272	.270	58	-21	13-6	.969	1	103	122	S114,3b9/2	0	-0.7
1973	Cin N✳	89	328	39	94	18	3	8	46	21-3	1	55	.287	.327	.433	115	6	22-5	.974	6	104	110	S88,O2C	72	2.5
1974	Cin N	160	594	70	167	25	1	14	82	44-10	6	79	.281	.335	.397	106	4	41-6	.963	11	105	113	S160/cf	0	4.1
1975	†Cin N★	140	507	62	139	23	1	5	49	39-4	2	51	.274	.326	.353	88	-8	33-6	.977	17	109	**141**	S130,3b6	0	3.0
1976	†Cin N★	152	576	74	162	28	7	9	69	49-11	1	68	.281	.335	.401	106	4	21-10	.968	17	105	105	S150	0	4.2
1977	Cin N★	156	572	59	155	26	3	8	64	46-6	0	77	.271	.322	.369	84	-13	29-7	**.986**	16	100	115	S156	0	2.3
1978	Cin N★	153	565	75	170	33	4	6	67	51-4	1	83	.301	.357	.405	113	11	23-10	.969	4	100	83	S152	0	3.3
1979	†Cin N✳	149	590	91	166	25	3	16	84	64-5	0	73	.281	.348	.415	109	7	19-7	.967	20	107	120	S148	0	4.5

YEAR	TM LG	G	AB	R	H	2B	3B	HR	RBI	BB-IB	HP	SO	AVG	OBP	SLG	AOPS	ABR	SB-CS	FA	FR	RNG	THR	GAMES AT POSITION	DL	BFW
1980	Cin N★	156	622	72	162	31	8	5	77	37-2	1	107	.260	.300	.360	86	-13	12-2	.978	-9	91	112	S155/2	0	-0.4
1981	Cin N★	106	421	57	129	28	0	5	67	37-1	1	61	.306	.358	.409	119	12	4-5	.960	8	98	113	S106	0	3.2
1982	Cin N★	147	572	48	164	25	4	5	53	45-4	0	61	.287	.337	.371	98	-1	13-6	.977	19	101	112	S145/13	0	3.4
1983	Cin N	143	528	54	123	22	0	1	47	56-9	0	81	.233	.303	.280	61	-26	14-9	.979	-6	93	83	S139,3b6/1	0	-1.9
1984	Cin N	154	531	46	130	26	1	4	58	52-5	0	72	.245	.307	.320	74	-17	22-6	.978	-27	83	71	S104,3b54,1b6	0	-3.5
1985	Cin N	155	560	59	141	19	2	7	48	50-3	3	67	.252	.314	.330	77	-17	16-12	.962	-31	87	75	S151,3b5	0	-3.5
1986	Cin N	90	311	42	81	13	2	3	30	26-1	0	43	.260	.314	.344	79	-9	13-2	.965	-1	101	97	S60,1b12,2b10,3b10	52	-0.2
1987	Cin N	104	279	32	89	15	0	1	33	28-5	0	24	.319	.377	.384	100	1	4-3	.992	5	102	126	2b59,1b26,3b13,S2	0	0.7
1988	Cin N	84	197	11	39	9	0	0	8	18-5	0	23	.198	.265	.244	45	-14	3-2	.994	3	99	127	2b46,1b16,S13,3b9/P	15	-1.0
Total	19	2488	8723	993	2326	389	48	101	950	736-93	21	1186	.267	.322	.357	89	-130	321-109	.971	47	99	106	S2178,2b130,3b120,1b62,O8C/P	154	18.0
CONCEPCION, ONIX	Onix Cardona (Cardona); B10.5.1957 Dorado, PR; BR/TR/5´6˝/(160–180); d8.30; [DL 1986 KC A 45]																								
1980	†KC A	12	15	1	2	0	0	0	2	0-0	0	1	.133	.133	.133	-26	-3	0-0	.833	-2	81	39	S6	0	-0.5
1981	KC A	2	0	0	0	0	0	0	0	0-0	0	0	ø	ø	ø	ø	0	0-0	ø	-0	0	0	/S	0	0.0
1982	KC A	74	205	17	48	9	1	0	15	5-0	1	18	.234	.256	.288	49	-15	2-1	.948	-8	100	100	S46,2b24/D	18	-1.8
1983	KC A	80	219	22	53	11	3	0	20	12-0	1	12	.242	.282	.320	65	-11	10-3	.913	-7	89	132	3b31,2b28,S21/D	0	-1.4
1984	†KC A	90	287	36	81	9	2	1	23	14-0	3	33	.282	.319	.338	82	-7	9-6	.972	9	114	114	S85,2b6/3	41	1.1
1985	†KC A	131	314	32	64	5	1	2	20	16-0	6	29	.204	.255	.245	38	-27	4-4	.959	6	**114**	94	S128,2b2	0	-1.1
1987	Pit N	1	1	0	1	0	0	0	0	0-0	0	0	1.000	1.000	1.000	427	0	0-0	ø	0	—	—	/H	68	0.0
Total	7	390	1041	108	249	34	7	3	80	47-0	11	93	.239	.278	.294	57	-63	25-14	.960	-3	109	100	S287,2b60,3b32,D2	172	-3.7
CONDE, RAMON	Ramon Luis (Roman) "Wito"; B12.29.1934 Juana Diaz, PR; BR/TR/5´8˝/172; d7.17																								
1962	Chi A	14	16	0	0	0	0	0	1	3-0	0	3	.000	.158	.000	-54	-4	0-0	.889	-1	57	0	3b7	0	-0.5
CONE, FRED	Joseph Frederick; B5.1848 Rockford IL; D4.13.1909 Chicago IL; 5´9.5˝/171; d5.5																								
1871	Bos NA	19	77	17	20	3	1	0	16	8	—	2	.260	.329	.325	86	-1	12-1	.854	-1	90	0	O18(18/0/1)	—	0.1
CONGALTON, BUNK	William Millar; B1.24.1875 Guelph ON, Can.; D8.19.1937 Cleveland OH; BL/TL/5´11˝/190; d4.17																								
1902	Chi N	47	188	16	45	3	0	1	27	7	0	—	.239	.267	.271	68	-8	4	.988	0	96	67	O47(0/5/43)	—	-1.0
1905	Cle A	12	47	4	17	0	0	0	5	2	0	—	.362	.388	.362	136	2	3	.923	-1	152	0	O12R	—	0.0
1906	Cle A	117	419	51	134	13	5	3	50	24	3	—	.320	.361	.396	139	18	12	.957	-9	41	0	O114(21/1/93)	—	0.4
1907	Cle A	9	22	2	4	0	0	0	2	4	0	—	.182	.308	.182	56	-1	0	1.000	0	125	0	O6R	—	-0.1
	Bos A	124	496	44	142	11	8	2	47	20	3	—	.286	.318	.353	115	6	13	.969	-3	113	119	O123R	—	-0.3
	Year	133	518	46	146	11	8	2	49	24	3	—	.282	.317	.346	112	5	13	.971	-2	114	113	O129R	—	-0.4
Total	4	309	1172	117	342	27	13	6	131	57	6	—	.292	.328	.352	116	17	32	.967	-12	85	59	O302(21/6/277)	—	-1.0
CONIGLIARO, TONY	Anthony Richard; B1.7.1945 Revere MA; D2.24.1990 Salem MA; BR/TR/6´3˝/(185–205); d4.16; b–Billy; [DL 1968 Bos A 175]																								
1964	Bos A	111	404	69	117	21	2	24	52	35-1	5	78	.290	.354	.530	135	19	2-4	.973	1	97	134	O106(81/25/2)	37	1.4
1965	Bos A	138	521	82	140	21	5	**32**	82	51-6	5	116	.269	.338	.512	131	20	4-2	.976	9	**117**	128	O137(0/2/135)	0	2.1
1966	Bos A	150	558	77	148	26	7	28	93	52-8	5	112	.265	.330	.487	120	14	0-2	.973	-5	93	95	O146R	0	-0.1
1967	Bos A★	95	349	59	100	11	5	20	67	27-2	5	58	.287	.341	.519	141	17	4-6	.983	3	114	86	O95R	40	1.3
1969	Bos A	141	506	57	129	21	3	20	82	48-6	4	111	.255	.321	.427	104	2	2-4	.981	-11	88	39	O137R	0	-1.9
1970	Bos A	146	560	89	149	20	1	36	116	43-4	8	93	.266	.324	.498	117	11	4-2	.977	-3	98	75	O146R	0	0.0
1971	Cal A	74	266	23	59	18	0	4	15	23-1	1	52	.222	.285	.335	81	-7	3-3	.994	4	109	122	O72R	80	-0.7
1975	Bos A	21	57	8	7	1	0	2	9	8-0	0	9	.123	.221	.246	32	-5	1-0	ø	0	0	0	D15	0	-0.6
Total	8	876	3221	464	849	139	23	166	516	287-28	33	629	.264	.327	.476	118	71	20-23	.979	-2	101	94	O839(81/27/733),D15	332	1.5
CONIGLIARO, BILLY	William Michael; B8.15.1947 Revere MA; BR/TR/6´0˝/(180–190); [BosA65 1/5]; d4.11; b–Tony																								
1969	Bos A	32	80	14	23	6	2	4	7	9-0	1	23	.287	.367	.563	150	5	1-1	.926	-5	57	0	O24(3/18/6)	0	-0.1
1970	Bos A	114	398	59	108	16	3	18	58	35-0	7	73	.271	.339	.462	112	6	3-7	.968	2	102	122	O108(77/25/20)	0	0.0
1971	Bos A	101	351	42	92	26	1	11	33	25-4	0	68	.262	.310	.436	102	1	3-2	.983	-1	101	81	O100(1/79/20)	0	-0.4
1972	Mil A	52	191	22	44	6	2	7	16	8-0	0	54	.230	.261	.393	94	-3	1-0	.992	5	121	137	O50(2/6/45)	0	0.0
1973	†Oak A	48	110	5	22	2	2	0	14	9-1	0	26	.200	.252	.255	48	-8	1-0	1.000	3	104	227	O40(21/18/3)/2	59	-0.7
Total	5	347	1130	142	289	56	10	40	128	86-5	8	244	.256	.311	.429	103	1	9-10	.980	3	102	114	O322(104/146/94)/2	59	-1.2
CONINE, JEFF	Jeffrey Guy; B6.26.1966 Tacoma WA; BR/TR/6´1˝/(200–225); [KCA87 58/1226]; d9.16; Col UCLA																								
1990	KC A	9	20	3	5	2	0	0	2	2-0	0	5	.250	.318	.350	88	0	0-0	.977	-0	99	146	1b9	0	-0.1
1992	KC A	28	91	10	23	5	2	0	9	8-1	0	23	.253	.313	.352	83	-2	0-0	1.000	-1	88	71	O23(22/0/1),1b4	0	-0.5
1993	Fla N	**162**	595	75	174	24	3	12	79	52-2	5	135	.292	.351	.403	97	-2	2-2	.992	-2	90	104	O147L,1b43	0	-1.1
1994	Fla N☆	**115**	451	60	144	27	6	18	82	40-4	1	92	.319	.373	.525	127	17	1-2	.974	1	103	71	O97L,1b46	0	1.2
1995	Fla N★	133	483	72	146	26	2	25	105	66-5	1	94	.302	.379	.520	134	25	2-0	.976	0	96	101	O118L,1b14	0	2.0
1996	Fla N	157	597	84	175	32	2	26	95	62-1	4	121	.293	.360	.484	124	21	1-4	.975	2	86	114	O128L,1b48	0	1.3
1997	†Fla N	151	405	46	98	13	1	17	61	57-3	2	89	.242	.337	.405	98	-1	2-0	.992	9	**127**	112	1b145/lf	0	-0.2
1998	KC A	93	309	30	79	26	0	8	43	26-1	2	68	.256	.312	.417	86	-6	3-0	.993	-4	92	84	O80(50/0/31),1b12,D3	58	-1.3
1999	Bal A	139	444	54	129	31	1	13	75	30-0	3	40	.291	.335	.453	103	2	0-3	.993	-3	88	130	1b99,D20,O13(7/0/6),3b4	0	-1.1
2000	Bal A	119	409	53	116	20	2	13	46	36-1	2	53	.284	.341	.438	101	0	4-3	.932	4	107	136	3b44,1b39,D20,O19(7/0/12)	0	-0.1
2001	Bal A	139	524	75	163	23	2	14	97	64-6	5	75	.311	.386	.443	126	22	12-8	.994	-2	83	94	1b80,O36(22/0/16),3b17,D12	0	1.0
2002	Bal A	116	451	44	123	26	4	15	63	25-6	2	66	.273	.307	.448	105	1	8-0	.990	-8	79	115	1b103,O6L,D7	53	-1.4
2003	Bal A	124	493	75	143	33	3	15	80	37-5	5	60	.290	.338	.460	111	8	5-0	.992	-2	97	102	1b118,O8(6/0/2)/3	0	-0.3
	†Fla N	25	84	13	20	3	0	5	15	13-0	0	10	.238	.337	.452	109	1	0-0	1.000	2	105	210	O25L	0	0.2
2004	Fla N	140	521	55	146	35	1	14	83	48-3	2	78	.280	.340	.432	104	3	5-5	.994	13	122	114	O83L,1b57	0	0.7
2005	Fla N	131	335	42	102	20	2	3	33	38-2	3	58	.304	.374	.403	111	7	2-0	.973	1	111	70	O61(37/0/28),1b45,D3	0	0.4
2006	Bal A	114	389	43	103	20	3	9	49	35-2	2	53	.265	.325	.401	90	-6	3-2	.996	-0	102	97	1b73,O57(56/0/1)/3D	0	-1.2
	Phi N	28	100	11	28	6	1	1	17	5-2	2	12	.280	.327	.390	79	-3	0-0	.973	-3	82	0	O26(12/0/25)	0	-0.7
Total	16	1923	6701	845	1917	372	35	208	1034	644-44	41	1132	.286	.348	.445	109	87	50-29	.992	8	104	108	1b935,O928(824/0/122),D68,3b67	111	-1.2
CONLAN, JOCKO	John Bertrand; B12.6.1899 Chicago IL; D4.16.1989 Scottsdale AZ; BL/TL/5´7.5˝/165; d7.6; U24; HF1974																								
1934	Chi A	63	225	35	56	11	3	0	16	19	1	7	.249	.310	.324	62	-13	2-2	.955	-3	89	116	O54(0/54/4)	—	-1.7
1935	Chi A	65	140	20	40	7	1	0	15	14	1	6	.286	.355	.350	81	-4	3-3	.961	-0	96	120	O37(0/21/16)	—	-0.5
Total	2	128	365	55	96	18	4	0	31	33	2	13	.263	.327	.334	69	-17	5-5	.957	-3	92	117	O91(0/75/20)	—	-2.2
CONLON, JOCKO	Arthur Joseph; B12.10.1897 Woburn MA; D8.5.1987 Falmouth MA; BR/TR/5´7˝/145; d4.17; Col Harvard																								
1923	Bos N	59	147	23	32	3	0	0	17	11	6	11	.218	.299	.238	45	-11	0-3	.955	-2	102	77	2b36,S6,3b4	—	-1.2
CONN, BERT	Albert Thomas; B9.22.1879 Philadelphia PA; D11.2.1944 Philadelphia PA; TR/6´0˝/178; d9.16; ▲																								
1898	Phi N	1	3	1	1	0	1	0	1	0	0	—	.333	.333	1.000	291	1	0	1.000	-0	58	0	/P	—	0.0
1900	Phi N	6	9	4	3	1	0	0	1	0	0	—	.333	.333	.444	115	1	0	.667	-1	23	0	P4	—	0.0
1901	Phi N	5	18	2	4	1	0	0	0	0	1	—	.222	.263	.278	56	-1	0	.880	-2	93	0	2b5	—	-0.2
Total	3	12	30	7	8	2	1	0	2	0	1	—	.267	.290	.400	95	1	0	.880	-2	93	0	2b5,P5	—	-0.2
CONNALLY, FRITZIE	Fritzie Lee; B5.19.1958 Bryan TX; BR/TR/6´3˝/210; [ChiN80 7/167]; d9.9; Col Baylor																								
1983	Chi N	8	10	0	1	0	0	0	0	0-0	0	5	.100	.100	.100	-42	-2	0-0	1.000	0	109	0	3b3	0	-0.2
1985	Bal A	50	112	16	26	4	0	3	15	19-0	1	21	.232	.346	.348	94	0	0-0	.976	-2	96	50	3b46,1b2/D	0	-0.2
Total	2	58	122	16	27	4	0	3	15	19-0	1	26	.221	.329	.328	83	-2	0-0	.977	-2	97	48	3b49,1b2/D	0	-0.4
CONNATSER, BRUCE	Broadus Milburn; B9.19.1902 Sevierville TN; D1.27.1971 Terre Haute IN; BR/TR/5´11.5˝/170; d9.15; Col Alabama																								
1931	Cle A	12	49	5	14	3	0	0	4	2	1	3	.286	.327	.347	73	-2	0-0	1.000	1	138	41	1b12	—	-0.2
1932	Cle A	23	60	8	14	3	1	0	4	4	0	8	.233	.281	.317	51	-4	1-0	1.000	0	108	75	1b14	—	-0.5
Total	2	35	109	13	28	6	1	0	8	6	1	11	.257	.302	.330	61	-6	1-0	1.000	2	123	58	1b26	—	-0.7
CONNAUGHTON, FRANK	Frank Henry; B1.1.1869 Clinton MA; D12.1.1942 Boston MA; BR/TR/5´9˝/165; d5.28																								
1894	Bos N	46	171	42	59	9	2	2	33	16	2	8	.345	.407	.456	100	0	3	.892	0	106	87	S33,C7,O4(2/2/0)	—	0.2
1896	NY N	88	315	53	82	3	2	2	43	25	2	7	.260	.319	.302	66	-16	22	.892	5	116	88	S54,O30L	—	-0.9
1906	Bos N	12	44	3	9	0	0	0	1	3	1	—	.205	.271	.205	50	-3	1	.918	-1	88	54	S11/2	—	-0.4
Total	3	146	530	98	150	12	4	4	77	44	5	15	.283	.344	.343	78	-19	26	.894	5	110	84	S98,O34(32/2/0),C7/2	—	-1.1

YEAR	TM LG	G	AB	R	H	2B	3B	HR	RBI	BB-IB	HP	SO	AVG	OBP	SLG	AOPS	ABR	SB-CS	FA	FR	RNG	THR	GAMES AT POSITION	DL	BFW
Connell, Gene	Eugene Joseph; B5.10.1906 Hazleton PA; D8.31.1937 Waverly NY; BR/TR/6´0.5˝/180; d7.4; b–Joe; Col Penn																								
1931	Phi N	6	12	1	3	0	0	0	0	0	0	3	.250	.250	.250	32	-1	0	1.000	-1	*57*	*104*	C6	—	-0.2
Connell, Joe	Joseph Bernard; B1.16.1902 Bethlehem PA; D9.21.1977 Trexlertown PA; BL/TL/5´8˝/165; d6.15; b–Gene; Col Villanova																								
1926	NY N	2	1	1	0	0	0	0	0	0	0	0	.000	.000	.000	-99	0	0	ø	0	—	—	/H	—	0.0
Connell, Pete	Peter J. (b Patrick J. O'Connell); B1862 Brooklyn NY; D5.5.1892 Brooklyn NY; 6´1˝/180; d9.3																								
1886	NY AA	1	5	0	0	0	0	0	0	0	0	—	.000	.000	.000	-99	-1	0	.667	-1	55	0	/3	—	-0.2
1890	Bro AA	11	40	7	9	2	1	0	3	7	0	—	.225	.340	.325	100	0	3	.830	-1	100	106	3b10/1	—	-0.1
Total	2	12	45	7	9	2	1	0	3	7	0	—	.200	.308	.289	80	-1	3	.820	-2	96	97	3b11/1	—	-0.3
Connell, Terry	Terence G.; B6.17.1855 Philadelphia PA; D3.25.1924 Narberth PA; d6.20																								
1874	Chi NA	1	4	0	0	0	0	0	0	0	—	0	.000	.000	.000	-99	-1	0-0	.429	-1	—	—	/C	—	-0.1
Connelly, Tom	Thomas Martin; B10.20.1897 Chicago IL; D2.18.1941 Hines IL; BL/TR/5´11.5˝/165; d9.24																								
1920	NY A	1	1	0	0	0	0	0	0	0	0	0	.000	.000	.000	-97	0	0-0	ø	0	—	—	/H	—	0.0
1921	NY A	4	5	0	1	0	0	0	0	1	0	0	.200	.333	.200	38	0	0-0	1.000	0	146	0	O3(0/1/2)	—	0.0
Total	2	5	6	0	1	0	0	0	0	1	0	0	.167	.286	.167	18	0	0-0	1.000	0	146	0	O3(0/1/2)	—	0.0
Connolly, Ed	Edward Joseph Sr.; B7.17.1908 Brooklyn NY; D11.12.1963 Pittsfield MA; BR/TR/5´8.5˝/180; d9.20; s–Ed																								
1929	Bos A	5	8	0	0	0	0	0	0	0	0	2	.000	.000	.000	-99	-2	0-0	.889	-0	*104*	*124*	C5	—	-0.3
1930	Bos A	27	48	1	9	2	0	0	7	4	0	3	.188	.250	.229	23	-6	0-0	1.000	0	*141*	*122*	C26	—	-0.4
1931	Bos A	42	93	3	7	1	0	0	3	5	1	18	.075	.131	.086	-44	-20	0-0	.981	-1	*116*	*82*	C41	—	-1.8
1932	Bos A	75	222	9	50	8	4	0	21	20	0	27	.225	.289	.297	54	-16	0-1	.957	-2	*69*	*130*	C75	—	-1.3
Total	4	149	371	13	66	11	4	0	31	29	1	50	.178	.239	.229	23	-44	0-1	.966	-3	*90*	*117*	C147	—	-3.8
Connolly, Red	John.M.; B1863 New York NY; D3.2.1896 New York NY; BB; d7.1																								
1886	StL N	2	7	0	0	0	0	0	0	0	—	3	.000	.000	.000	-99	-2	0	ø	-0	0	0	O2C	—	-0.2
Connolly, Joey	Joseph Francis; B2.1.1884 N.Smithfield RI; D9.1.1943 N.Smithfield RI; BL/TR/5´7.5˝/165; d4.10																								
1913	Bos N	126	427	79	120	18	11	5	57	66	1	47	.281	.379	.410	123	15	18-21	.954	-5	88	100	O124L	—	0.0
1914	†Bos N	120	399	64	122	28	10	9	65	49	8	36	.306	.393	.494	164	33	12	.974	-1	84	144	O118(115/0/5)	—	2.9
1915	Bos N	104	305	48	91	14	8	0	23	39	5	35	.298	.387	.397	144	18	13-12	.971	1	98	103	O93(81/3/9)	—	1.4
1916	Bos N	62	110	11	25	5	2	0	12	14	1	13	.227	.320	.309	98	0	5	.980	1	98	138	O31(14/4/12)	—	0.0
Total	4	412	1241	202	358	65	31	14	157	168	15	131	.288	.380	.425	139	66	48-33	.967	-5	90	117	O366(334/7/26)	—	4.3
Connolly, Joe	Joseph H. "Coaster Joe"; B6.27.1894 San Francisco CA; D3.30.1960 San Francisco CA; BR/TR/6´0˝/170; d10.1																								
1921	NY N	2	4	0	0	0	0	0	0	1	0	1	.000	.200	.000	-42	-1	0-0	1.000	-0	101	0	/lf	—	-0.1
1922	Cle A	12	45	6	11	2	1	0	6	5	0	8	.244	.320	.333	70	-2	1-0	.972	1	103	153	O12C	—	-0.2
1923	Cle A	52	109	25	33	10	1	3	25	13	0	7	.303	.377	.495	129	5	1-2	.957	-3	82	60	O39(2/3/34)	—	-0.1
1924	Bos A	14	10	1	1	0	0	0	1	2	0	2	.100	.250	.100	-7	-2	0-0	1.000	0	130	0	O3R	—	-0.2
Total	4	80	168	32	45	12	2	3	32	21	0	18	.268	.349	.417	100	0	2-2	.966	-2	91	86	O55(3/15/37)	—	-0.6
Connolly, Bud	Mervin Thomas "Mike"; B5.25.1901 San Francisco CA; D6.12.1964 Berkeley CA; BR/TR/5´8˝/154; d5.3																								
1925	Bos A	43	107	12	28	7	1	0	21	23	0	9	.262	.392	.346	88	-1	0-3	.950	-4	88	75	S34,3b2	—	-0.2
Connolly, Tom	Thomas Francis "Blackie","Ham"; B12.30.1892 Boston MA; D5.14.1966 Boston MA; BL/TR/5´11˝/175; d5.12; Col Georgetown																								
1915	Was A	50	141	14	26	3	2	0	7	14	2	19	.184	.268	.234	49	-9	5-4	.970	-2	88	102	3b24,O19(11/0/8),S4	—	-1.2
Connor, Ned	Edward; B1850 NY; D1.28.1898 Philadelphia PA; 5´9˝/156; d5.18																								
1871	Tro NA	7	33	6	7	0	0	0	2	0	—	0	.212	.212	.212	22	-3	0-0	.878	-1	167	50	1b4,O3R	—	-0.2
Connor, Jim	James Matthew (b James Matthew O'Connor); B5.11.1863 Port Jervis NY; D9.3.1950 Providence RI; BR/TR/5´10.5˝/179; d7.11																								
1892	Chi N	9	34	0	2	0	0	0	0	1	1	7	.059	.111	.059	-48	-6	0	.917	-4	76	0	2b9	—	-1.0
1897	Chi N	77	285	40	83	10	5	3	38	24	4	—	.291	.355	.393	94	-3	10	.936	19	118	138	2b76	—	1.6
1898	Chi N	138	505	51	114	9	9	0	67	42	3	—	.226	.289	.279	63	-25	11	.946	-7	100	143	2b138	—	-2.4
1899	Chi N	69	234	26	48	7	1	0	24	18	1	—	.205	.265	.244	41	-19	6	.942	2	111	126	2b44,3b25	—	-1.3
Total	4	293	1058	117	247	26	15	3	129	85	9	7	.233	.296	.295	64	-53	27	.942	10	106	135	2b267,3b25	—	-3.1
Connor, Joe	Joseph Francis; B12.8.1874 Waterbury CT; D11.8.1957 Waterbury CT; BR/TR/6´2˝/185; d9.9; b–Roger																								
1895	StL N	2	7	0	0	0	0	0	1	0	0	2	.000	.000	.000	-99	-2	0	1.000	1	138	0	3b2	—	-0.1
1900	Bos N	7	19	2	4	0	0	0	4	2	0	—	.211	.286	.211	34	-2	1	.971	2	*98*	*127*	C7	—	0.0
1901	Mil A	38	102	10	28	3	1	1	9	6	1	—	.275	.321	.353	91	-1	4	.949	-3	*74*	*120*	C30/23cf	—	-0.2
	Cle A	37	121	13	17	3	1	0	6	7	2	—	.140	.200	.182	7	-15	2	.942	-1	*94*	*93*	C32,O4R/S	—	-1.3
	Year	75	223	23	45	6	2	1	15	13	3	—	.202	.255	.260	45	-17	6	.946	-4	*85*	*105*	C62,O5(0/1/4)/23S	—	-1.5
1905	NY A	8	22	4	5	1	0	0	2	3	0	—	.227	.320	.273	79	0	1	.978	1	*117*	*142*	C6,1b2	—	0.2
Total	4	92	271	29	54	7	2	1	22	18	3	2	.199	.257	.251	43	-20	8	.952	-1	*89*	*111*	C75,O5(0/1/4),3b3,1b2/S2	—	-1.4
Connor, Roger	Roger; B7.1.1857 Waterbury CT; D1.4.1931 Waterbury CT; BL/TL/6´3˝/220; d5.1; M1; HF1976; b–Joe																								
1880	Tro N	**83**	340	53	113	18	8	3	47	13	—	21	.332	.357	.459	166	22	—	.821	-11	93	108	3b83	—	1.3
1881	Tro N	**85**	367	55	107	17	6	2	31	15	—	20	.292	.319	.387	115	6	—	.950	2	128	105	1b85	—	0.3
1882	Tro N	81	349	65	115	22	**18**	4	42	13	—	20	.330	.354	.530	188	33	—	.951	0	183	123	1b43,O24(5/19/0),3b14	—	2.6
1883	NY N	**98**	409	80	146	28	15	1	50	25	—	16	.357	.394	.506	173	36	—	.958	3	125	75	1b98	—	2.6
1884	NY N	**116**	477	98	151	28	4	4	82	38	—	32	.317	.367	.417	143	24	—	.860	-1	94	103	2b67,O37C,3b12	—	2.2
1885	NY N	110	455	102	**169**	23	15	1	65	51	—	8	**.371**	**.435**	.495	**203**	**54**	—	.975	3	**109**	**138**	1b110	—	**4.3**
1886	NY N	118	485	105	172	29	**20**	7	71	41	—	15	.355	.405	.540	183	48	17	.973	10	**147**	104	1b118	—	4.2
1887	NY N	127	471	113	134	26	22	17	104	75	8	50	.285	.392	.541	164	44	43	**.993**	5	96	100	1b127	—	3.1
1888	†NY N	134	481	98	140	15	17	14	71	**73**	4	44	.291	.389	.480	**178**	45	27	.982	1	88	100	1b133/2	—	3.3
1889	†NY N	**131**	496	117	157	32	17	13	**130**	93	2	46	.317	.426	**.528**	164	46	21	.977	-8	56	96	1b131/3	—	2.3
1890	NY P	123	484	133	169	24	15	**14**	103	88	1	32	.349	.450	**.548**	152	37	22	**.985**	10	**129**	**111**	1b123	—	2.8
1891	NY N	129	479	112	139	29	13	7	94	83	4	39	.290	.399	.449	153	37	27	.983	1	96	112	1b129	—	2.3
1892	Phi N	**155**	564	123	166	**37**	11	12	73	116	6	39	.294	.420	.463	167	53	22	**.985**	-6	71	118	1b155	—	4.2
1893	NY N	135	511	111	156	25	8	11	105	91	3	26	.305	.413	.450	129	24	24	.974	2	110	83	1b135/3	—	2.1
1894	NY N	22	82	10	24	7	0	1	14	8	0	0	.293	.356	.415	86	-2	2	.976	2	131	108	1b21/rf	—	0.0
	StL N	99	380	83	122	28	25	7	79	51	6	17	.321	.410	.582	137	21	17	.974	5	122	114	1b99	—	1.9
	Year	121	462	93	146	35	25	8	93	59	6	17	.316	.400	.552	128	19	19	.974	6	**123**	**113**	1b120/rf	—	1.9
1895	StL N	104	401	78	131	29	9	8	78	63	3	10	.327	.422	.504	140	27	9	.986	5	111	90	1b104	—	2.5
1896	StL N	126	483	71	137	21	9	11	72	52	2	14	.284	.356	.433	112	8	10	**.988**	13	**139**	57	1b126,M	—	1.7
1897	StL N	22	83	13	19	3	1	1	12	13	0	—	.229	.333	.325	76	-3	3	.984	-0	95	41	1b22	—	-0.3
Total	18	1998	7797	1620	2467	441	233	138	1323	1002	39	449	.316	.397	.486	154	560	244	.978	33	109	100	1b1759,3b111,2b68,O62(5/56/1)	—	43.4
Connors, Jerry	Jeremiah; B Cleveland OH; d7.11																								
1892	Phi N	1	3	0	0	0	0	0	0	0	0	1	.000	.000	.000	-99	-1	0	ø	-0	0	0	/rf	—	-0.1
Connors, Chuck	Kevin Joseph Aloysius; B4.10.1921 Brooklyn NY; D11.10.1992 Los Angeles CA; BL/TL/6´5˝/190; d5.1; Col Seton Hall																								
1949	Bro N	1	1	0	0	0	0	0	0	0	0	0	.000	.000	.000	-96	0	0	ø	0	—	—	/H	0	0.0
1951	Chi N	66	201	16	48	5	1	2	18	12	0	25	.239	.282	.303	56	-13	4-0	.984	-2	95	84	1b57	0	-1.5
Total	2	67	202	16	48	5	1	2	18	12	0	25	.238	.280	.302	56	-13	4-0	.984	-2	95	84	1b57	0	-1.5
Connors, Merv	Mervin James; B1.23.1914 Berkeley CA; D1.8.2006 Berkeley CA; BR/TR/6´2˝/192; d9.4																								
1937	Chi A	28	103	12	24	4	1	2	12	14	0	19	.233	.325	.350	70	-5	2-1	.926	-2	98	158	3b28	—	-0.5
1938	Chi A	24	62	14	22	4	0	6	13	9	0	17	.355	.437	.710	178	7	0-0	.979	0	117	131	1b16	—	0.6
Total	2	52	165	26	46	8	1	8	25	23	0	36	.279	.367	.485	111	2	2-1	.926	-1	98	158	3b28,1b16	—	0.1
Conroy, Ben	Bernard Patrick; B3.14.1871 Philadelphia PA; D11.25.1937 Philadelphia PA; ?/160; d4.21																								
1890	Phi AA	117	404	45	69	13	1	0	21	45	5	—	.171	.262	.208	39	-30	17	.893	-1	107	98	S74,2b42/cf	—	-2.5

YEAR	TM LG	G	AB	R	H	2B	3B	HR	RBI	BB-IB	HP	SO	AVG	OBP	SLG	AOPS	ABR	SB-CS	FA	FR	RNG	THR	GAMES AT POSITION	DL	BFW
Conroy, Wid	William Edward; B4.5.1877 Philadelphia PA; D12.6.1959 Mt.Holly NJ; BR/TR/5´9˝/158; d4.25; C1; OF(224/76/10)																								
1901	Mil A	131	503	74	129	20	6	5	64	36	8	—	.256	.316	.350	89	-7	21	.922	17	106	97	S118,3b12	—	1.3
1902	Pit N	99	365	55	89	10	6	1	47	24	5	—	.244	.299	.312	86	-7	10	.925	8	104	**132**	S95,O3(2/0/1)	—	0.4
1903	NY A	126	503	74	137	23	12	1	45	32	5	—	.272	.322	.372	101	1	33	.919	3	104	88	3b123,S4	—	0.7
1904	NY A	140	489	58	119	18	12	1	52	43	7	—	.243	.314	.335	100	1	30	.944	7	108	86	3b110,S27,O3C	—	1.2
1905	NY A	101	385	55	105	19	11	2	25	32	0	—	.273	.329	.395	116	6	25	.928	0	87	23	3b48,O25(20/3/2),S17,1b10,2b3	—	0.7
1906	NY A	148	567	67	139	17	10	4	54	47	0	—	.245	.303	.332	89	-7	32	.968	-2	95	38	O97(37/66/0),S49,3b2	—	-1.4
1907	NY A	140	530	58	124	12	11	3	51	30	3	—	.234	.279	.315	83	-12	41	.955	8	76	60	O100L,S38	—	-1.0
1908	NY A	141	531	44	126	22	3	1	39	14	1	—	.237	.258	.296	79	-14	23	.939	14	107	83	3b119,2b12,O10(5/1/4)	—	0.3
1909	Was A	139	488	44	119	13	4	1	20	37	1	—	.244	.298	.293	91	-5	24	.938	3	103	95	3b120,2b13,O5(2/3/0)/S	—	0.1
1910	Was A	103	351	36	89	11	3	1	27	30	1	—	.254	.314	.311	100	0	11	.961	1	94	102	3b46,O46(44/0/2),2b5	—	0.0
1911	Was A	106	349	40	81	11	4	2	28	20	4	—	.232	.282	.304	64	-18	12	.930	8	116	102	3b85,O15(14/0/1)/2	—	-0.9
Total	11	1374	5061	605	1257	176	82	22	452	345	35	—	.248	.301	.329	91	-62	262	.934	67	104	86	3b665,S349,O304L,2b34,1b10	—	1.4
Conroy, Bill	William Frederick "Pep"; B1.9.1899 Chicago IL; D1.23.1970 Chicago IL; BR/TR/5´8.5˝/160; d4.18																								
1923	Was A	18	60	6	8	2	2	0	2	4	0	9	.133	.188	.233	11	-8	0-0	.926	-1	67	0	3b10,1b6/cf	—	-0.9
Conroy, Bill	William Gordon; B2.26.1915 Bloomington IL; D11.13.1997 Citrus Heights CA; BR/TR/6´0˝/185; d9.21; Mil 1945; Col Illinois Wesleyan																								
1935	Phi A	1	4	0	1	1	0	0	0	1	0	0	.250	.400	.500	133	0	0-0	1.000	0	*73*	*0*	/C	—	0.0
1936	Phi A	1	2	0	1	0	0	0	0	0	0	1	.500	.500	.500	151	0	0-0	1.000	-0	*0*	*0*	/C	—	0.0
1937	Phi A	26	60	4	12	1	1	0	3	7	0	9	.200	.284	.250	36	-6	1-0	1.000	-1	*87*	*79*	C18/1	—	-0.5
1942	Bos A	83	250	22	50	4	2	4	20	40	2	47	.200	.315	.280	66	-11	2-0	.971	-0	*113*	*93*	C83	0	-0.6
1943	Bos A	39	89	13	16	5	0	1	6	18	3	19	.180	.336	.270	77	-1	0-0	.969	0	*108*	*92*	C38	0	0.1
1944	Bos A	19	47	6	10	2	0	0	4	11	0	9	.213	.362	.255	79	-1	0-0	.972	-0	*103*	*105*	C19	0	0.0
Total	6	169	452	45	90	13	3	5	33	77	5	85	.199	.322	.274	66	-19	3-0	.974	-2	*107*	*91*	C160/1	0	-1.0
Consolo, Billy	William Angelo; B8.18.1934 Cleveland OH; BR/TR/5´11˝/180; d4.20; C15																								
1953	Bos A	47	65	9	14	2	1	1	6	2	0	23	.215	.239	.323	48	-5	1-2	.808	5	121	185	3b16,2b11	0	0.0
1954	Bos A	91	242	23	55	7	1	1	11	33	2	69	.227	.324	.277	59	-12	2-1	.953	-2	97	84	S50,3b18,2b12	0	-1.0
1955	Bos A	8	18	4	4	0	0	0	0	5-0	0	4	.222	.391	.222	63	-1	0-0	.889	-3	49	35	2b4	0	-0.3
1956	Bos A	48	11	13	2	0	0	0	1	3-0	0	5	.182	.357	.182	41	-1	0-0	.920	4	207	215	2b25	0	0.3
1957	Bos A	68	196	26	53	6	1	4	19	23-0	0	48	.270	.345	.372	91	-2	1-3	.933	6	119	106	S42,2b16,3b2	0	0.7
1958	Bos A	46	72	13	9	2	1	0	5	6-0	0	14	.125	.192	.181	3	-10	0-0	.925	-3	70	96	2b13,S11/3	0	-1.1
1959	Bos A	10	14	3	3	1	0	0	0	2-0	0	5	.214	.313	.286	63	-1	0-0	.818	-1	48	73	S2	0	-0.2
	Was A	79	202	25	43	5	3	0	10	36-0	0	54	.213	.332	.267	67	-8	1-0	.952	15	119	110	S75,2b4	0	1.3
	Year	89	216	28	46	6	3	0	10	38-0	0	59	.213	.331	.269	66	-9	1-0	.948	14	117	109	S77,2b4	0	1.1
1960	Was A	100	174	23	36	4	2	3	15	25-1	1	29	.207	.310	.305	68	-8	1-1	.938	-10	94	100	S82,2b12,3b2	0	-1.3
1961	Min A	11	5	1	0	0	0	0	0	0-0	0	1	.000	.000	.000	-95	-1	0-0	1.000	-1	34	0	2b3,S3/3	0	-0.3
1962	Phi N	13	5	3	2	0	0	0	0	0-0	0	1	.400	.400	.400	119	0	0-0	ø	-0	0	0	/3	0	0.0
	LA A	28	20	4	2	0	0	0	0	3-0	0	11	.100	.217	.100	-12	-3	2-0	.917	0	69	207	3b20,S4/2	0	-0.2
	KC A	54	154	11	37	4	2	0	16	23-2	0	33	.240	.337	.292	68	-6	1-3	.950	-3	98	88	S48	0	-0.7
	Year	82	174	15	39	4	2	0	16	26-2	0	44	.224	.323	.270	61	-9	3-3	.944	-3	102	84	S52,3b20/2	0	-0.9
Total	10	603	1178	158	260	31	11	9	83	161-3	3	297	.221	.315	.289	63	-58	9-10	.945	7	106	98	S317,2b101,3b61	0	-2.8
Conti, Jason	Stanley Jason; B1.27.1975 Pittsburgh PA; BL/TR/5´11˝/(174–180); [AriN96 32/965]; d6.29; Col Pittsburgh																								
2000	Ari N	47	91	11	21	4	3	1	15	7-2	1	30	.231	.293	.374	64	-5	3-0	.983	4	117	290	O35(2/4/33)	0	-0.2
2001	Ari N	5	4	1	1	0	0	0	0	1-0	0	2	.250	.400	.250	69	0	0-0	ø	-0	0	0	/rf	0	0.0
2002	TB A	78	222	26	57	15	2	3	21	18-1	1	55	.257	.315	.383	86	-4	4-2	.966	7	114	214	O74(21/28/28)	0	0.1
2003	Mil N	30	48	3	11	2	0	2	7	2-0	0	18	.229	.255	.396	68	-3	0-1	.909	1	133	139	O20(1/1/19)	0	-0.2
2004	Tex A	22	55	6	10	3	0	0	4	5-0	0	19	.182	.250	.236	27	-6	0-2	1.000	1	116	0	O21(1/20/0)	0	-0.6
Total	5	182	420	47	100	24	5	6	47	33-3	2	124	.238	.296	.362	71	-18	7-5	.968	12	117	192	O151(25/53/81)	0	-0.9
Conway, Charlie	Charles Connell; B4.28.1886 Youngstown OH; D9.12.1968 Youngstown OH; BR/TR; d4.15																								
1911	Was A	2	3	0	1	0	1	0	0	0	0	—	.333	.333	1.000	272	0	0	.000	-0	0	0	O2	—	0.0
Conway, Jack	Jack Clements; B7.30.1918 Bryan TX; D6.11.1993 Waco TX; BR/TR/5´11.5˝/175; d9.9; Mil 1942–45; Col Texas																								
1941	Cle A	2	2	0	1	0	0	0	1	0	0	0	.500	.500	.500	174	0	0-0	1.000	1	151	0	S2	0	0.1
1946	Cle A	68	258	24	58	6	2	0	18	20	0	36	.225	.281	.264	56	-16	2-2	.955	-9	85	74	2b50,S14,3b3	0	-2.4
1947	Cle A	34	50	3	9	2	0	0	5	3	0	8	.180	.226	.220	25	-5	0-0	.877	-1	106	131	S24,2b5/3	0	-0.5
1948	NY N	24	49	8	12	2	1	1	3	5	0	10	.245	.315	.388	89	-1	0	.985	4	120	143	2b13,S6,3b3	0	0.3
Total	4	128	359	35	80	10	3	1	27	28	0	54	.223	.279	.276	57	-22	2-2	.962	-6	91	84	2b68,S46,3b7	0	-2.5
Conway, Owen	Owen Sylvester; B10.23.1890 New York NY; D3.12.1942 Philadelphia PA; TR; d6.21																								
1915	Phi A	4	15	2	1	0	0	0	0	0	0	3	.067	.067	.067	-62	-3	0	.750	0	115	197	3b4	—	-0.3
Conway, Pete	Peter J.; B10.30.1866 Burmont PA; D1.13.1903 Clifton Heights PA; BR/TR/5´10.5˝/162; d8.10; b–Jim; ▲																								
1885	Buf N	29	90	7	10	5	0	1	7	5	—	28	.111	.158	.200	15	-8	—	.889	-1	112	0	P27,O2R/S1	—	-0.1
1886	KC N	51	194	22	47	8	2	1	18	5	—	34	.242	.261	.320	71	-7	3	.857	-3	122	172	O31(3/20/8),P23	—	-0.6
	Det N	12	43	10	8	1	0	2	3	1	—	8	.186	.205	.349	63	-2	0	.846	-1	101	0	P11/lf	—	0.0
	Year	63	237	32	55	9	2	3	21	6	—	42	.232	.251	.325	70	-9	3	.826	-3	89	49	P34,O32(4/20/8)	—	-0.6
1887	†Det N	24	95	16	22	5	1	1	7	2	0	9	.232	.247	.337	58	-6	0	**.979**	1	131	0	P17,O8L	—	-0.2
1888	Det N	45	167	28	46	4	2	3	23	8	3	25	.275	.320	.377	120	4	1	.938	2	114	230	P45/lf	—	0.1
1889	Pit N	3	10	2	1	0	0	1	2	1	0	3	.100	.182	.400	66	-1	1	.875	0	139	0	P3/lf	—	0.0
Total	5	164	599	85	134	23	5	9	60	22	3	107	.224	.255	.324	73	-20	5	.907	-0	110	99	P126,O44(14/20/10)/1S	—	-0.8
Conway, Rip	Richard Daniel; B4.18.1896 White Bear Lake MN; D12.2.1972 St.Paul MN; BL/TR/5´6˝/160; d4.16; Mil 1918; Col St. Thomas (MN)																								
1918	Bos N	14	24	4	4	0	0	0	2	2	0	4	.167	.231	.167	23	-2	1	.810	-3	61	0	2b5/3	—	-0.6
Conway, Bill	William F.; B11.28.1861 Lowell MA; D12.18.1943 Somerville MA; BR/TR/5´8˝/170; d7.28; b–Dick																								
1884	Phi N	1	4	0	0	0	0	0	0	0	—	1	.000	.000	.000	-99	-1	—	1.000	0	—	—	/C	—	-0.1
1886	Bal AA	7	14	4	2	0	0	0	3	7	0	—	.143	.429	.143	84	1	0	.925	-3	—	—	C7	—	-0.2
Total	2	8	18	4	2	0	0	0	3	7	0	1	.111	.360	.111	52	0	0	.936	-3	—	—	C8	—	-0.3
Conwell, Ed	Edward James "Irish"; B1.29.1890 Chicago IL; D5.1.1926 Chicago IL; BR/TR/5´11˝/155; d9.22																								
1911	StL N	1	1	0	0	0	0	0	0	0	0	1	.000	.000	.000	-99	0	0	.000	-1	0	0	/3	—	-0.1
Conyers, Herb	Herbert Leroy; B1.8.1921 Cowgill MO; D9.16.1964 Cleveland OH; BL/TR/6´4˝/205; d4.18																								
1950	Cle A	7	9	2	3	0	0	1	1	1	0	2	.333	.400	.667	175	1	1-0	1.000	-0	0	0	/1	0	0.1
Coogan, Dale	Dale Roger; B8.14.1930 Los Angeles CA; D3.8.1989 Mission Viejo CA; BL/TL/6´1˝/190; d4.22																								
1950	Pit N	53	129	19	31	6	1	1	13	17	2	24	.240	.338	.326	73	-5	0	.980	2	135	96	1b32	0	-0.3
Coogan, Dan	Daniel George; B2.16.1875 Philadelphia PA; D10.28.1942 Philadelphia PA; 5´8˝/128; d4.25; Col Penn																								
1895	Was N	26	77	9	17	2	1	0	7	13	0	6	.221	.333	.273	58	-4	1	.746	-9	81	71	S18,C5,O2R/3	—	-1.0
Cook, Jim	James Fitchie; B11.10.1879 Dundee IL; D6.17.1949 St.Louis MO; BR/TR/5´9˝/163; d7.2; Col Illinois																								
1903	Chi N	8	26	3	4	1	0	0	2	2	1	—	.154	.241	.192	25	-2	1	1.000	-1	0	0	O5C,2b2/1	—	-0.4
Cook, Doc	Luther Almus; B6.24.1886 Whitt TX; D6.30.1973 Lawrenceburg TN; BL/TR/6´0˝/170; d8.7; Col Vanderbilt																								
1913	NY A	20	72	9	19	2	1	0	1	10	2	4	.264	.369	.319	101	1	1	.939	-0	101	88	O20(0/13/7)	—	-0.1
1914	NY A	132	470	59	133	11	3	1	40	44	9	60	.283	.356	.326	105	4	26-32	.949	-3	94	97	O127(1/10/116)	—	-1.2
1915	NY A	132	476	70	129	16	5	2	33	62	8	43	.271	.364	.338	111	8	29-18	.959	-1	93	123	O131R	—	0.1
1916	NY A	4	10	0	1	0	0	0	1	0	0	2	.100	.100	.100	-39	-2	0	1.000	-0	98	0	O3R	—	-0.2
Total	4	288	1028	138	282	29	9	3	75	116	19	109	.274	.359	.329	106	11	56-50	.953	-5	94	108	O281(1/23/257)	—	-1.4

YEAR	TM LG	G	AB	R	H	2B	3B	HR	RBI	BB-IB	HP	SO	AVG	OBP	SLG	AOPS	ABR	SB-CS	FA	FR	RNG	THR	GAMES AT POSITION	DL	BFW
Cook, Paul	Paul; B5.5.1863 Caledonia NY; D5.25.1905 Rochester NY; BR/TR/5´10˝/185; d9.13																								
1884	Phi N	3	12	0	1	0	0	0	0	0	—	2	.083	.083	.083	-50	-2	—	.818	-2	—	—	C3	—	-0.4
1886	Lou AA	66	262	28	54	5	2	0	14	10	0	—	.206	.235	.240	46	-17	6	.945	-7	98	104	1b43,C21,O2(1/0/1)	—	-2.3
1887	Lou AA	61	223	34	55	4	2	0	17	11	4	—	.247	.294	.283	60	-12	15	.916	-4	—	—	C55,1b6	—	-1.0
1888	Lou AA	57	185	20	34	2	0	0	13	5	4	—	.184	.222	.195	35	-13	9	.901	-8	—	—	C53,O4(1/0/3)/S	—	-1.6
1889	Lou AA	81	286	34	65	10	1	0	15	15	9	48	.227	.287	.269	60	-15	11	.925	3	—	—	C74,O7(0/2/5)/S1	—	-0.5
1890	Bro P	58	218	32	55	3	3	0	31	14	2	18	.252	.303	.294	56	-15	7	.890	3	129	120	C36,1b21/rf	—	-0.8
1891	Lou AA	45	153	21	35	3	1	0	23	11	1	17	.229	.285	.261	57	-9	4	.909	-10	83	105	C35,1b10	—	-1.5
	StL AA	7	25	3	5	0	0	0	1	1	1	2	.200	.259	.200	28	-2	0	.921	1	116	88	C7	—	0.0
	Year	52	178	24	40	3	1	0	24	12	2	19	.225	.281	.253	52	-11	4	.912	-8	90	101	C42,1b10	—	-1.5
Total	7	378	1364	172	304	27	9	0	114	67	21	87	.223	.270	.256	52	-85	52	.906	-22	109	110	C284,1b81,O14(2/2/10),S2	—	-8.1
Cook, Cliff	Raymond Clifford; B8.20.1936 Dallas TX; BR/TR/6´0˝/(187–190); d9.9																								
1959	Cin N	9	21	3	8	2	1	0	5	2-1	0	8	.381	.435	.571	161	2	1-0	.909	1	118	216	3b9	0	0.3
1960	Cin N	54	149	9	31	7	0	3	13	8-1	0	51	.208	.247	.315	52	-10	0-0	.954	-2	91	108	3b47,O4(3/1/0)	0	-1.3
1961	Cin N	4	5	0	0	0	0	0	0	0-0	0	4	.000	.000	.000	-99	-1	0-0	1.000	0	186	0	/3	0	-0.1
1962	Cin N	6	5	0	0	0	0	0	0	0-0	0	2	.000	.000	.000	-97	-1	0-0	1.000	-1	0	0	3b4	0	-0.2
	NY N	40	112	12	26	6	1	2	9	4-0	3	34	.232	.275	.357	68	-5	1-0	.875	-6	73	66	3b16,O10R	33	-1.1
	Year	46	117	12	26	6	1	2	9	4-0	3	36	.222	.264	.342	61	-7	1-0	.878	-6	68	61	3b20,O10R	0	-1.3
1963	NY N	50	106	9	15	2	1	2	8	12-4	0	37	.142	.229	.236	34	-9	0-1	1.000	3	92	174	O21(8/1/12),3b9,1b5	0	-0.8
Total	5	163	398	33	80	17	3	7	35	26-6	3	136	.201	.254	.312	54	-24	2-1	.937	-4	97	96	3b86,O35(11/2/22),1b5	33	-3.2
Cooke, Dusty	Allen Lindsey; B6.23.1907 Swepsonville NC; D11.21.1987 Raleigh NC; BL/TR/6´1˝/205; d4.15; M1/C5																								
1930	NY A	92	216	43	55	12	3	6	29	32	1	61	.255	.353	.421	100	0	4-6	.978	1	111	47	O73(21/28/24)	—	-0.3
1931	NY A	27	39	10	13	1	0	1	6	8	0	11	.333	.447	.436	141	3	4-1	1.000	1	136	0	O11(7/0/6)	—	0.3
1932	NY A	3	0	1	0	0	0	0	0	1	0	0	ø	1.000	ø	191	0	0-0	ø	0	—	—	/H	—	0.0
1933	Bos A	119	454	86	133	35	10	5	54	67	2	71	.293	.386	.447	121	16	7-5	.956	-5	98	62	O118(47/70/30)	—	0.6
1934	Bos A	74	168	34	41	8	5	1	26	36	0	25	.244	.377	.369	87	-2	7-2	.976	-2	95	33	O44(9/14/21)	—	-0.5
1935	Bos A	100	294	51	90	18	6	3	34	46	0	24	.306	.400	.439	109	5	6-8	.972	-2	100	66	O82(7/35/44)	—	-0.1
1936	Bos A	111	341	58	93	20	3	6	47	72	1	48	.273	.401	.402	93	-1	4-3	.972	-1	108	35	O91(24/1/67)	—	-0.7
1938	Cin N	82	233	41	64	15	1	2	33	28	1	36	.275	.355	.373	103	2	0	.963	1	106	89	O51(46/0/7)	—	0.0
Total	8	608	1745	324	489	109	28	24	229	290	5	276	.280	.384	.416	106	23	32-25	.969	-7	104	55	O470(161/148/199)	—	-0.7
Cooke, Fred	Frederick B.; B Paulding OH; D1.22.1923 Gallipolis OH; 5´10˝/164; d7.30																								
1897	Cle N	5	17	2	5	2	0	0	3	3	0	—	.294	.400	.412	109	0	0	.857	1	490	0	O5R	—	0.1
Cookson, Brent	Brent Adam; B9.7.1969 Van Nuys CA; BR/TR/5´11˝/(195–200); [OakA91 15/411]; d8.12; Col Cal St.–Long Beach																								
1995	KC A	22	35	2	5	1	0	0	5	2-0	0	7	.143	.189	.171	-5	-6	1-0	1.000	-0	98	0	O12(10/0/2),D2	0	-0.6
1999	LA N	3	5	0	1	0	0	0	0	0-0	0	1	.200	.200	.200	2	-1	0-0	1.000	0	146	0	O3(2/0/1)	0	-0.1
Total	2	25	40	2	6	1	0	0	5	2-0	0	8	.150	.190	.175	-4	-7	1-0	1.000	-0	106	0	O15(12/0/3),D2	0	-0.7
Coolbaugh, Mike	Michael Robert; B6.5.1972 Binghamton NY; BR/TR/6´1˝/185; [TorA90 16/447]; d7.16; b–Scott																								
2001	Mil N	39	70	10	14	6	0	2	7	5-0	2	16	.200	.273	.371	66	-4	0-0	.971	-1	92	189	3b27,S3	0	-0.4
2002	StL N	5	12	0	1	0	0	0	0	1-0	0	3	.083	.154	.083	-35	-2	0-0	1.000	1	143	530	3b4	0	-0.1
Total	2	44	82	10	15	6	0	2	7	6-0	2	19	.183	.256	.329	51	-6	0-0	.977	0	101	247	3b31,S3	0	-0.5
Coolbaugh, Scott	Scott Robert; B6.13.1966 Binghamton NY; BR/TR/5´11˝/(185–195); [TexA87 3/77]; d9.2; b–Mike; Col Texas																								
1989	Tex A	25	51	7	14	1	0	2	7	4-0	0	12	.275	.321	.412	105	0	0-0	.958	4	133	113	3b23,D2	0	0.4
1990	Tex A	67	180	21	36	6	0	2	13	15-0	1	47	.200	.264	.267	49	-12	1-0	.941	6	111	118	3b66	0	-0.6
1991	SD N	60	180	12	39	8	1	2	15	19-2	1	45	.217	.294	.306	67	-8	0-3	.952	0	105	101	3b54	0	-0.9
1994	StL N	15	21	4	4	0	0	2	6	1-0	0	4	.190	.217	.476	77	-1	0-0	1.000	-1	0	146	1b4,3b4	0	-0.2
Total	4	167	432	44	93	15	1	8	41	39-2	2	108	.215	.281	.310	65	-21	1-3	.949	11	112	108	3b147,1b4,D2	0	-1.3
Cooley, Duff	Duff Gordon "Dick"; B3.29.1873 Leavenworth KS; D8.9.1937 Dallas TX; BL/TR/5´11˝/158; d7.27; OF(549/479/69)																								
1893	StL N	29	107	20	37	2	3	0	21	8	0	9	.346	.391	.421	115	2	8	.947	-5	50	0	O15R,C10,S5	—	-0.2
1894	StL N	54	206	35	61	3	1	1	21	12	0	16	.296	.335	.335	62	-13	7	.833	-11	15	63	O39(8/4/28),3b13/S1	—	-2.0
1895	StL N	133	567	108	194	9	20	7	75	37	3	29	.342	.386	.466	121	14	27	.934	8	86	21	O125(116/8/1),3b5,S3/C	—	0.9
1896	StL N	40	166	29	51	5	3	0	13	7	0	3	.307	.335	.373	90	-3	12	.959	-2	33	0	O40L	—	-0.7
	Phi N	64	287	63	88	6	4	2	22	18	0	16	.307	.348	.376	92	-4	18	.901	-4	71	86	O64(22/40/2)	—	-1.0
	Year	104	453	92	139	11	7	2	35	25	0	19	.307	.343	.375	91	-7	30	.923	-6	55	50	O104(62/40/2)	—	-1.7
1897	Phi N	**133**	566	124	186	14	13	4	40	51	2	—	.329	.386	.420	116	13	31	.960	3	84	162	O131(0/108/23),1b2	—	0.7
1898	Phi N	149	629	123	196	24	12	4	55	48	4	—	.312	.364	.407	126	21	17	.943	1	73	40	O149C	—	1.1
1899	Phi N	94	406	75	112	15	8	1	31	29	4	—	.276	.330	.360	92	-5	15	.971	-6	88	126	1b79,O14C/2	—	-1.0
1900	Pit N	66	249	30	50	8	1	0	22	14	0	—	.201	.243	.241	34	-23	9	.989	-5	53	118	1b66	—	-2.7
1901	Bos N	63	240	27	62	13	3	0	27	14	1	—	.258	.302	.338	78	-7	5	.943	-1	68	59	O53(29/24/0),1b10	—	-1.1
1902	Bos N	135	548	73	162	26	8	0	58	34	2	—	.296	.339	.372	118	11	27	.952	-7	40	46	O127(94/33/0),1b7	—	-0.3
1903	Bos N	138	553	76	160	26	10	1	70	44	0	—	.289	.342	.378	109	6	27	.952	-5	62	88	O126(124/3/0),1b13	—	-0.6
1904	Bos N	122	467	41	127	18	7	5	70	24	3	—	.272	.312	.373	115	7	14	.976	-7	20	82	O116L,1b6	—	-0.7
1905	Det A	97	377	25	93	11	9	1	32	26	1	—	.247	.297	.332	99	-2	7	.959	5	113	192	O96C	—	-0.1
Total	13	1317	5368	849	1579	180	102	26	557	366	20	73	.294	.342	.380	104	17	224	.945	-34	63	78	O1095L,1b184,3b18,C11,S9/2	—	-7.7
Coombs, Cecil	Cecil Lysander; B3.18.1888 Moweaqua IL; D11.25.1975 Fort Worth TX; BR/TR/5´9˝/160; d8.7																								
1914	Chi A	7	23	1	4	1	0	0	1	1	0	7	.174	.208	.217	28	-2	0-1	1.000	1	93	245	O7C	—	-0.2
Coombs, Jack	John Wesley "Colby Jack"; B11.18.1882 LeGrand IA; D4.15.1957 Palestine TX; BB/TR/6´0˝/185; d7.5; M1/C1; Col Colby; ▲																								
1906	Phi A	24	67	9	16	2	0	0	3	1	1	—	.239	.261	.269	64	1	2	.967	-1	80	**288**	P23	—	0.0
1907	Phi A	24	48	4	8	0	0	1	4	0	0	—	.167	.167	.229	25	-1	1	.979	-0	89	185	P23	—	0.0
1908	Phi A	78	220	24	56	9	5	1	23	9	1	—	.255	.287	.355	101	-1	6	.990	5	106	194	O47(1/11/35),P26/1	—	0.3
1909	Phi A	37	83	4	14	4	0	0	10	4	1	—	.169	.216	.217	36	1	1	.973	-0	95	127	P30	—	0.0
1910	†Phi A	46	132	20	29	3	0	0	9	7	2	—	.220	.270	.242	61	3	3	**.990**	-5	68	74	P45	—	0.0
1911	†Phi A	52	141	31	45	6	1	2	23	8	0	—	.319	.356	.418	118	13	5	.913	-3	77	118	P47	—	0.0
1912	Phi A	56	110	10	28	2	0	0	13	14	1	—	.255	.344	.273	80	6	1	**1.000**	-1	87	188	P40	—	0.0
1913	Phi A	2	3	1	1	1	0	0	0	0	0	2	.333	.333	.667	195	1	0	.500	-0	0	0	P2	—	0.0
1914	Phi A	5	11	0	3	1	0	0	2	1	0	1	.273	.333	.364	114	0	0-1	1.000	-0	44	0	P2,O2C	—	0.0
1915	Bro N	29	75	8	21	1	1	0	5	2	0	17	.280	.299	.320	86	4	0-1	.980	-4	58	110	P29	—	0.0
1916	†Bro N	27	61	2	11	2	0	0	3	2	0	10	.180	.206	.213	28	0	0	**1.000**	-6	36	82	P27	—	0.0
1917	Bro N	32	44	4	10	0	1	0	2	4	0	9	.227	.292	.273	72	2	1	.971	-3	65	76	P31	—	0.0
1918	Bro N	46	113	6	19	3	2	0	3	7	1	5	.168	.223	.230	38	-9	1	.962	-4	75	0	P27,O13(0/3/11)	—	-0.5
1920	Det A	2	2	0	0	0	0	0	0	0	0	0	.000	.000	.000	-99	0	0-0	1.000	-0	65	0	P2	—	0.0
Total	14	460	1110	123	261	34	10	4	100	59	7	44	.235	.278	.295	74	20	21-2	.966	-23	75	118	P354,O62(1/16/46)/1	—	-0.2
Coomer, Ron	Ronald Bryan; B11.18.1966 Crest Hill IL; BR/TR/5´11˝/(195–225); [OakA87 14/355]; d8.1; Col Taft (CA) JC																								
1995	Min A	37	101	15	26	3	1	5	19	9-0	1	11	.257	.324	.455	100	1	0-1	.993	1	111	92	1b22,3b13/rfD	0	-0.1
1996	Min A	95	233	34	69	12	1	12	41	17-1	0	24	.296	.340	.511	110	3	3-0	.993	2	161	83	1b57,O23R,3b9,D3	0	0.1
1997	Min A	140	523	63	156	30	2	13	85	22-5	0	91	.298	.324	.438	95	-5	4-3	.966	-3	99	102	3b119,1b9,O7R,D7	0	-0.8
1998	Min A	137	529	54	146	22	1	15	72	18-1	0	72	.276	.295	.406	79	-18	2-2	.972	-4	90	83	3b75,1b54,D13,O3R	0	-2.5
1999	Min A★	127	467	53	123	25	1	16	65	30-1	1	69	.263	.307	.424	80	-15	2-1	.996	9	130	108	1b71,3b57/rfD	0	-1.1
2000	Min A	140	544	64	147	29	1	16	82	36-2	4	50	.270	.317	.415	79	-18	2-0	.995	2	92	94	1b124,3b5,D9	0	-2.5
2001	Chi N	111	349	25	91	19	1	8	53	29-1	2	70	.261	.316	.390	85	-8	0-0	.954	1	91	105	3b76,1b36/D	22	-0.8
2002	†NY A	55	148	14	39	7	0	3	17	6-1	0	23	.264	.290	.372	75	-6	0-0	.882	-4	78	58	3b26,D15,1b11	0	-1.1
2003	LA N	69	125	11	30	4	0	4	15	10-2	1	19	.240	.299	.368	75	-5	0-0	1.000	-0	115	96	1b24,3b11,D4	26	-0.6
Total	9	911	3019	333	827	151	8	92	449	177-14	9	429	.274	.313	.421	86	-73	13-7	.996	3	115	97	1b408,3b391,D63,O35R	48	-9.4

YEAR	TM LG	G	AB	R	H	2B	3B	HR	RBI	BB-IB	HP	SO	AVG	OBP	SLG	AOPS	ABR	SB-CS	FA	FR	RNG	THR	GAMES AT POSITION	DL	BFW
Coon, William	William K.; B3.21.1855 PA; D8.30.1915 Burlington NJ; d9.4																								
1875	Ath NA	4	12	1	2	0	0	0	1	0	—	0	.167	.167	.167	15	-1	1-0	.810	-0	—	—	C4/rf	—	-0.1
1876	Phi N	54	220	30	50	5	1	0	22	2	—	4	.227	.234	.259	65	-8	—	.761	-13	160	76	O29(0/2/29),C18,3b4,2b4,P2	—	-1.8
Cooney, Jimmy	James Edward "Scoops"; B8.24.1894 Cranston RI; D8.7.1991 Warwick RI; BR/TR/5´11˝/160; d9.22; Mil 1918; f–Jimmy b–Johnny																								
1917	Bos A	11	36	4	8	1	0	0	3	6	0	2	.222	.333	.250	79	-1	0	1.000	3	107	167	2b10/S	—	0.3
1919	NY N	5	14	3	3	0	0	0	1	0	0	0	.214	.214	.214	29	-1	0	1.000	0	100	170	S4/2	—	-0.1
1924	StL N	110	383	44	113	20	8	1	57	20	0	20	.295	.330	.397	96	-3	12-10	.969	4	97	102	S99,3b7/2	—	1.1
1925	StL N	54	187	27	51	11	2	0	18	4	1	5	.273	.292	.353	62	-11	1-3	.976	-4	87	110	S37,2b15/lf	—	-1.2
1926	Chi N	141	513	52	129	18	5	1	47	23	3	10	.251	.288	.312	61	-29	11	**.972**	18	102	**120**	S141	—	0.4
1927	Chi N	33	132	16	32	2	0	0	6	8	0	7	.242	.286	.258	46	-10	1	.973	-1	97	66	S33	—	-0.8
	Phi N	76	259	33	70	12	1	0	15	13	0	9	.270	.305	.324	68	-12	4	.980	15	110	114	S74	—	1.0
	Year	109	391	49	102	14	1	0	21	21	0	16	.261	.299	.302	61	-22	5	**.978**	13	106	98	S107	—	0.2
1928	Bos N	18	51	2	7	0	0	0	3	2	0	5	.137	.170	.137	-20	-9	1	.982	1	99	150	S11,2b4	—	-0.7
Total	7	448	1575	181	413	64	16	2	150	76	4	58	.262	.298	.327	67	-76	30-13	.974	34	100	110	S400,2b31,3b7/lf	—	0.0
Cooney, Jimmy	James Joseph; B7.9.1865 Cranston RI; D7.1.1903 Cranston RI; BB/TR/5´9˝/155; d4.19; s–Jimmy s–Johnny																								
1890	Chi N	135	574	114	156	19	10	4	52	73	6	23	.272	.360	.361	106	5	45	**.936**	-1	98	114	S135/C	—	0.8
1891	Chi N	118	465	84	114	15	3	0	42	48	2	17	.245	.318	.290	78	-12	21	**.917**	9	**113**	102	S118	—	0.0
1892	Chi N	65	238	18	41	1	0	0	20	23	1	5	.172	.248	.176	29	-20	10	.912	-3	101	72	S65	—	-1.9
	Was N	6	25	5	4	0	1	0	4	4	0	3	.160	.276	.240	58	-1	1	.862	-2	72	49	S6	—	-0.3
	Year	71	263	23	45	1	1	0	24	27	1	8	.171	.251	.183	31	-22	11	.908	-5	99	70	S71	—	-2.2
Total	3	324	1302	221	315	35	14	4	118	148	9	48	.242	.324	.300	82	-28	77	.923	3	104	100	S324/C	—	-1.4
Cooney, Johnny	John Walter; B3.18.1901 Cranston RI; D7.8.1986 Sarasota FL; BR/TL/5´10˝/165; d4.19; M1/C21; f–Jimmy b–Jimmy; ▲																								
1921	Bos N	8	5	0	1	0	0	0	0	0	0	1	.200	.200	.200	7	0	0-0	1.000	0	91	0	P8	—	0.0
1922	Bos N	4	8	0	0	0	0	0	0	0	0	1	.000	.000	.000	-99	-1	0-0	1.000	0	103	392	P4	—	0.0
1923	Bos N	42	66	7	25	1	0	0	3	4	0	2	.379	.414	.394	119	2	0-1	1.000	0	61	79	P23,O11(2/8/1)/1	—	0.1
1924	Bos N	55	130	10	33	2	1	0	4	9	0	5	.254	.302	.285	61	-7	0-4	.962	-1	72	132	P34,O16(0/15/1)/1	—	-0.5
1925	Bos N	54	103	17	33	7	0	0	13	3	1	6	.320	.346	.388	96	-1	1-0	.949	1	104	167	P31,1b3/lf	—	0.0
1926	Bos N	64	126	17	38	3	2	0	18	13	0	7	.302	.367	.357	105	1	6	.996	4	160	121	1b31,P19/rf	—	0.3
1927	Bos N	10	1	3	0	0	0	0	0	0	0	0	.000	.000	.000	-99	0	0	ø	0	—	—	/H	—	0.0
1928	Bos N	33	41	2	7	0	0	0	2	4	0	3	.171	.244	.171	11	-5	0	1.000	3	153	231	P24,1b3,O2(0/1/1)	—	0.0
1929	Bos N	41	72	10	23	4	1	0	6	3	1	3	.319	.355	.403	91	-1	1	1.000	2	121	0	O16(4/10/2),P14	—	0.0
1930	Bos N	4	3	0	0	0	0	0	0	0	0	0	.000	.000	.000	-99	-1	0	1.000	1	283	0	P2	—	0.0
1935	Bro N	10	29	3	9	0	1	0	1	3	0	2	.310	.375	.379	106	0	0	1.000	-0	109	0	O10C	—	0.0
1936	Bro N	130	507	71	143	17	5	0	30	24	0	15	.282	.315	.335	74	-19	3	**.994**	9	108	131	O130C	—	-1.3
1937	Bro N	120	430	61	126	18	5	0	37	22	0	10	.293	.327	.358	85	-10	5	.976	5	108	105	O111(5/104/3),1b2	—	-0.7
1938	Bos N	120	432	45	117	25	5	0	17	22	1	12	.271	.308	.352	90	-7	2	.982	-2	101	68	O110(17/15/84),1b13	—	-1.6
1939	Bos N	118	368	39	101	8	1	2	27	21	2	8	.274	.317	.318	77	-13	2	.992	2	99	128	O116(0/112/5),1b2	—	-1.4
1940	Bos N	108	365	40	116	14	3	0	21	25	1	9	.318	.363	.373	109	5	4	.992	1	106	67	O99(0/98/1),1b7	—	0.2
1941	Bos N	123	442	52	141	25	2	0	29	27	0	15	.319	.358	.385	114	8	3	**.996**	3	104	106	O111C,1b4	0	0.8
1942	Bos N	74	198	23	41	6	0	0	7	23	0	5	.207	.290	.237	56	-10	2	.984	-2	96	77	O54(5/16/34),1b23	0	-1.7
1943	Bro N	37	34	7	7	0	0	0	2	4	0	3	.206	.289	.206	44	-2	1	1.000	0	0	89	1b3,O2C	0	-0.3
1944	Bro N	7	4	0	3	0	0	0	1	0	0	0	.750	.750	.750	329	1	0	1.000	0	120	0	O2(1/1/0)	0	0.1
	NY A	10	8	1	1	0	0	0	1	1	0	0	.125	.222	.125	1	-1	0-0	1.000	0	173	0	O2L	0	-0.1
Total	20	1172	3372	408	965	130	26	2	219	208	6	107	.286	.329	.342	87	-61	30-5	.988	25	105	98	O794(37/633/133),P159,1b93	0	-6.1
Cooney, Phil	Philip Clarence (b Philip Clarence Cohen); B9.14.1882 New York NY; D10.6.1957 New York NY; BL/TR/5´8˝/155; d9.27																								
1905	NY A	1	3	0	0	0	0	0	0	0	0	—	.000	.000	.000	-90	-1	0	1.000	-0	74	0	/3	—	-0.1
Cooney, Bill	William Ambrose "Cush"; B4.7.1883 Boston MA; D11.6.1928 Roxbury MA; TR; d9.22; Col Princeton																								
1909	Bos N	5	10	0	3	0	0	0	0	0	0	—	.300	.300	.300	82	0	0	.500	-0	60	0	P3/2S	—	0.0
1910	Bos N	8	12	2	3	0	0	0	1	2	0	0	.250	.357	.250	74	0	0	ø	-0	0	0	O2R	—	0.0
Total	2	13	22	2	6	0	0	0	1	2	0	0	.273	.333	.273	78	0	0	.500	-0	60	0	P3,O2R/S2	—	0.0
Cooper, Cecil	Cecil Celester; B12.20.1949 Brenham TX; BL/TL/6´2˝/(165–190); [BosA68 6/128]; d9.8; C3																								
1971	Bos A	14	42	9	13	4	1	0	3	5-1	1	4	.310	.388	.452	130	2	1-0	.988	-2	43	62	1b11	0	0.0
1972	Bos A	12	17	0	4	1	0	0	2	2-1	0	5	.235	.316	.294	78	0	0-0	1.000	-1	0	94	1b3	0	-0.1
1973	Bos A	30	101	12	24	2	0	3	11	7-1	0	12	.238	.284	.347	73	-4	1-2	.984	-0	99	103	1b29	0	-0.7
1974	Bos A	121	414	55	114	24	1	8	43	32-3	1	74	.275	.327	.396	101	1	2-5	.983	-2	96	112	1b74,D41	0	-1.0
1975	†Bos A	106	305	49	95	17	6	14	44	19-6	3	33	.311	.355	.544	140	15	1-4	.995	2	126	105	D54,1b35	0	1.2
1976	Bos A	123	451	66	127	22	6	15	78	16-6	1	62	.282	.304	.457	109	3	7-1	.994	-2	91	96	1b66,D53	0	-0.5
1977	Mil A	160	643	86	193	31	7	20	78	28-4	0	110	.300	.326	.463	113	9	13-8	.992	7	116	104	1b148,D10	0	0.6
1978	Mil A	107	407	60	127	23	2	13	54	32-3	0	72	.312	.359	.474	133	17	3-4	.988	4	125	108	1b84,D19	42	1.5
1979	Mil A★	150	590	83	182	**44**	1	24	106	56-10	0	77	.308	.364	.508	133	28	15-3	.993	-8	84	103	1b135,D15	0	1.4
1980	Mil A★	153	622	96	219	33	4	25	**122**	39-15	2	42	.352	.387	.539	156	46	17-6	**.997**	5	115	**125**	1b142,D11	0	4.3
1981	†Mil A	106	416	70	133	**35**	1	12	60	28-2	3	30	.320	.363	.495	153	28	5-4	.992	1	109	**123**	1b101,D5	0	2.3
1982	†Mil A★	155	654	104	205	38	3	32	121	32-7	0	53	.313	.342	.528	143	35	2-3	.997	1	100	117	1b154/D	0	2.5
1983	Mil A★	160	661	106	203	37	3	30	**126**	37-7	1	63	.307	.341	.508	141	34	2-1	.993	-10	79	100	1b158,D2	0	1.4
1984	Mil A	148	603	63	166	28	3	11	67	27-6	2	59	.275	.307	.386	94	-6	8-2	.991	3	108	100	1b122,D26	0	-1.1
1985	Mil A★	154	631	82	185	39	8	16	99	30-3	2	77	.293	.322	.456	112	9	10-3	.986	-2	100	93	1b123,D30	0	-0.1
1986	Mil A	134	542	46	140	24	1	12	75	41-2	1	87	.258	.310	.373	83	-13	1-2	.988	-3	90	102	1b90,D44	11	-2.3
1987	Mil A	63	250	25	62	13	0	6	36	17-2	0	51	.248	.293	.372	73	-10	1-1	ø	0	0	0	D62	3	-1.1
Total	17	1896	7349	1012	2192	415	47	241	1125	448-79	17	911	.298	.337	.466	121	194	89-49	.992	-8	101	107	1b1475,D373	56	8.3
Cooper, Claude	Claude William; B4.1.1892 Troup TX; D1.21.1974 Plainview TX; BL/TL/5´9˝/158; d4.14; Mil 1918; Col TCU																								
1913	†NY N	27	30	11	9	4	0	0	4	4	0	6	.300	.382	.433	132	2	3-3	.895	-0	106	108	O15(6/10/0)	—	0.1
1914	Bro F	113	399	56	96	14	11	2	25	26	4	60	.241	.294	.346	74	-23	25	.926	-2	106	76	O101(45/21/38)	—	-3.2
1915	Bro F	**153**	527	75	155	26	12	2	63	77	4	78	.294	.388	.400	123	12	31	.958	13	111	150	O121(112/7/2),1b32	—	2.0
1916	Phi N	56	104	9	20	2	0	0	11	7	1	15	.192	.250	.212	41	-7	1	.945	-1	107	39	O29(15/13/1)/1	—	-1.0
1917	Phi N	24	29	5	3	1	0	0	1	5	0	4	.103	.235	.138	15	-3	0	.923	-1	98	0	O12(9/3/2)	—	-0.4
Total	5	373	1089	156	283	47	23	4	104	119	9	163	.260	.338	.356	95	-19	60-3	.943	10	108	108	O278(187/54/43),1b33	—	-2.5
Cooper, Gary	Gary Clifton; B8.13.1964 Lynwood CA; BR/TR/6´1˝/200; [HouN86 7/172]; d9.15; Col Brigham Young																								
1991	Hou N	9	16	1	4	1	0	0	2	3-0	0	6	.250	.368	.313	99	0	0-0	.833	-2	32	0	3b4	0	-0.2
Cooper, Gary	Gary Nathaniel; B12.22.1956 Savannah GA; BB/TR/6´3˝/175; [AtlN75 3/66]; d8.25																								
1980	Atl N	21	2	3	0	0	0	0	0	0-0	0	1	.000	.000	.000	-99	-1	2-1	1.000	1	89	511	O13(11/2/0)	0	0.0
Cooper, Pat	Orge Patterson; B11.26.1917 Albemarle NC; D3.15.1993 Charlotte NC; BR/TR/6´3˝/180; d5.11																								
1946	Phi A	1	0	0	0	0	0	0	0	0	0	0	ø	ø	ø	ø	0	0-0	ø	-0	0	0	/P	0	0.0
1947	Phi A	13	16	0	4	2	0	0	3	0	0	5	.250	.250	.375	71	-1	0-0	1.000	-0	0	125	/1	0	-0.1
Total	2	14	16	0	4	2	0	0	3	0	0	5	.250	.250	.375	71	-1	0-0	1.000	-0	0	125	/1P	0	-0.1
Cooper, Scott	Scott Kendrick; B10.13.1967 St.Louis MO; BL/TR/6´3˝/(200–215); [BosA86 3/69]; d9.5																								
1990	Bos A	2	1	0	0	0	0	0	0	0-0	0	1	.000	.000	.000	-95	0	0-0	ø	0	—	—	/H	0	0.0
1991	Bos A	14	35	6	16	4	2	0	7	2-0	0	2	.457	.486	.686	209	5	0-0	.933	1	112	56	3b13	0	0.6
1992	Bos A	123	337	34	93	21	0	5	33	37-0	0	33	.276	.346	.383	97	0	1-1	.990	6	101	107	1b62,3b47/2SD	0	0.2
1993	Bos A★	156	526	67	147	29	3	9	63	58-15	5	81	.279	.355	.397	96	-2	5-2	.937	-11	89	87	3b154,1b2/S	0	-1.1
1994	Bos A★	104	369	49	104	16	4	13	53	30-2	1	65	.282	.333	.453	97	-3	0-3	.944	10	**116**	125	3b104	8	0.6
1995	StL N	118	374	29	86	18	2	3	40	49-3	3	85	.230	.321	.313	68	-16	0-3	.945	9	**111**	141	3b110	0	-0.8
1997	KC A	75	159	12	32	6	1	3	15	17-0	2	32	.201	.283	.308	54	-11	1-1	1.000	-2	94	80	3b39,1b8,D5	40	-1.3
Total	7	592	1801	197	478	94	12	33	211	193-20	11	299	.265	.337	.386	89	-27	7-10	.948	12	104	106	3b467,1b72,D7,S2/2	48	-1.8

YEAR	TM LG	G	AB	R	H	2B	3B	HR	RBI	BB-IB	HP	SO	AVG	OBP	SLG	AOPS	ABR	SB-CS	FA	FR	RNG	THR	GAMES AT POSITION	DL	BFW
COOPER, WALKER	William Walker "Walk"; B1.8.1915 Atherton MO; D4.11.1991 Scottsdale AZ; BR/TR/6´3˝/(195–215); d9.25; Mil 1945; C2; b–Mort																								
1940	StL N	6	19	3	6	1	0	0	2	2	0	2	.316	.381	.368	102	0	1	1.000	-0	86	144	C6	—	0.0
1941	StL N	68	200	19	49	9	1	1	20	13	0	14	.245	.291	.315	66	-9	1	.966	3	123	122	C63	0	-0.3
1942	†StL N★	125	438	58	123	32	7	7	65	29	1	29	.281	.327	.434	113	6	4	.972	7	**158**	103	C115	0	2.1
1943	†StL N★	122	449	52	143	30	4	9	81	19	2	19	.318	.349	.463	128	14	1	.975	1	**169**	75	C112	0	2.3
1944	†StL N★	112	397	56	126	25	5	13	72	20	1	19	.317	.352	.504	136	17	4	.980	5	146	74	C97	0	2.8
1945	StL N	4	18	3	7	0	0	0	1	0	0	1	.389	.389	.389	114	0	0	.966	0	115	66	C4	0	0.1
1946	NY N★	87	280	29	75	10	1	8	46	17	0	12	.268	.310	.396	99	-2	0	.972	-7	87	103	C73	0	-0.6
1947	NY N★	140	515	79	157	24	8	35	122	24	3	43	.305	.339	.586	141	24	2	.979	-6	**163**	67	C132	0	2.5
1948	NY N★	91	290	40	77	12	0	16	54	28	1	29	.266	.332	.472	115	5	1	.979	-7	118	44	C79	0	0.2
1949	NY N	42	147	14	31	4	2	4	21	7	3	8	.211	.261	.347	62	-9	0	.982	-1	91	83	C40	0	-0.7
	Cin N☆	82	307	34	86	9	2	16	62	21	2	24	.280	.330	.479	113	4	0	.978	-3	118	105	C77	0	0.6
	Year	124	454	48	117	13	4	20	83	28	5	32	.258	.308	.436	97	-5	0	.979	-3	109	98	C117	0	-0.1
1950	Cin N	15	47	3	9	3	0	0	4	0	0	5	.191	.191	.255	16	-6	0	.972	-0	73	104	C13	0	-0.6
	Bos N☆	102	337	52	111	19	3	14	60	30	3	26	.329	.389	.528	148	23	1	.973	-3	82	114	C88	0	2.4
	Year	117	384	55	120	22	3	14	64	30	3	31	.313	.367	.495	132	17	1	.973	-4	81	113	C101	0	1.8
1951	Bos N	109	342	42	107	14	1	18	59	28	1	18	.313	.367	.518	145	20	1-1	.981	-2	78	**138**	C90	0	2.3
1952	Bos N	102	349	33	82	12	1	10	55	22	1	32	.235	.282	.361	80	-11	1-0	.983	-5	93	114	C89	0	-1.1
1953	Mil N	53	137	12	30	6	0	3	16	12	1	15	.219	.287	.328	64	-7	1-0	.983	-3	86	54	C35	0	-0.8
1954	Pit N	14	15	0	3	2	0	0	1	2	0	1	.200	.294	.333	64	-1	0-0	1.000	-0	36	0	C2	0	-0.1
	Chi N	57	158	21	49	10	2	7	32	21	2	23	.310	.398	.532	138	9	0-0	.978	-3	59	132	C48	0	0.8
	Year	71	173	21	52	12	2	7	33	23	2	24	.301	.389	.514	132	9	0-0	.978	-3	58	128	C50	0	0.7
1955	Chi N	54	111	11	31	8	1	7	15	6-1	1	19	.279	.322	.559	128	4	0-0	.961	-7	58	96	C31	0	-0.2
1956	StL N	40	68	5	18	5	1	2	14	3-1	0	8	.265	.296	.456	98	0	0-0	.984	-2	87	46	C16	0	-0.2
1957	StL N	48	78	7	21	5	1	3	10	5-1	0	10	.269	.310	.474	106	0	0-0	.957	-0	178	44	C13	0	0.1
Total	18	1473	4702	573	1341	240	40	173	812	309-3	22	357	.285	.332	.464	116	81	18-1	.977	-31	119	93	C1223	0	11.6
COQUILLETTE, TRACE	Trace Robert; B6.4.1974 Carmichael CA; BR/TR/6´0˝/185; [MonN93 10/286]; d9.7; Col Sacramento (CA) City																								
1999	Mon N	17	49	2	13	3	0	0	4	4-0	1	7	.265	.333	.327	71	-2	1-0	.944	-1	81	59	3b11,2b6	0	-0.2
2000	Mon N	34	59	6	12	4	0	1	8	7-0	0	19	.203	.284	.322	53	-4	0-0	.958	-1	105	93	3b19,2b8,O2(2/0/1)	0	-0.5
Total	2	51	108	8	25	7	0	1	12	11-0	1	26	.231	.306	.324	61	-6	1-0	.952	-2	94	77	3b30,2b14,O2(2/0/1)	0	-0.7
CORA, ALEX	Jose Alexander; B10.18.1975 Caguas, PR; BL/TR/6´0˝/(180–200); [LAN96 3/88]; d6.7; b–Joey; Col Miami																								
1998	LA N	29	33	1	4	0	1	0	0	2-0	1	8	.121	.194	.182	-0	-5	0-0	.956	3	83	117	S21,2b4	0	-0.2
1999	LA N	11	30	2	5	1	0	0	3	0-0	1	4	.167	.194	.200	-0	-5	0-0	1.000	0	94	80	S8,2b3	83	-0.4
2000	LA N	109	353	39	84	18	6	4	32	26-4	7	53	.238	.302	.357	69	-18	4-1	.972	3	99	123	S101,2b8	0	-0.7
2001	LA N	134	405	38	88	18	3	4	29	31-6	8	58	.217	.285	.306	57	-27	0-2	.962	-5	97	88	S132/2	0	-2.3
2002	LA N	115	258	37	75	14	4	5	28	26-4	7	38	.291	.371	.434	118	7	7-2	.977	-3	94	105	S61,2b40	0	0.9
2003	LA N	148	477	39	119	24	3	4	34	16-3	10	59	.249	.287	.338	64	-26	4-2	.978	31	106	**146**	2b141,S15	0	1.1
2004	†LA N	138	405	47	107	9	4	10	47	47-10	18	41	.264	.364	.380	95	-2	3-4	.987	3	101	**124**	2b138	0	0.6
2005	Cle A	49	146	11	30	5	2	1	8	5-0	4	18	.205	.250	.288	45	-12	6-0	.974	9	127	85	S24,2b15/lf	0	0.1
	†Bos A	47	104	14	28	3	2	2	16	6-0	1	12	.269	.310	.394	84	-3	1-2	.983	3	90	108	2b35,S11,3b5	0	0.1
	Year	96	250	25	58	8	4	3	24	11-0	5	30	.232	.275	.332	61	-15	7-2	.989	12	101	118	2b50,S35,3b5/lf	0	0.2
2006	Bos A	96	235	31	56	7	2	1	18	19-1	6	29	.238	.312	.298	58	-15	6-2	.975	7	119	143	S63,2b18,3b11,D2	0	-0.3
Total	9	876	2446	259	596	99	27	31	215	178-28	63	320	.244	.310	.344	72	-106	31-15	.971	50	102	109	S436,2b403,3b16,D2/lf	83	-1.1
CORA, JOEY	Jose Manuel (Amaro); B5.14.1965 Caguas, PR; BB/TR/5´8˝/(150–162); [SDN85 1/23]; d4.6; C3; b–Alex; Col Vanderbilt																								
1987	SD N	77	241	23	57	7	2	0	13	28-1	1	26	.237	.317	.282	63	-12	15-11	.975	1	109	82	2b66,S6	0	-0.9
1989	SD N	12	19	5	6	1	0	0	1	1-0	0	0	.316	.350	.368	105	0	1-0	.960	1	110	93	S7,3b2/2	0	0.2
1990	SD N	51	100	12	27	3	0	0	2	6-1	0	9	.270	.311	.300	68	-4	8-3	.833	-7	50	49	S21,2b15/C	0	-1.0
1991	Chi A	100	228	37	55	2	3	0	18	20-0	5	21	.241	.313	.276	67	-10	11-6	.970	-13	95	82	2b80,S5,D2	19	-2.2
1992	Chi A	68	122	27	30	7	1	0	9	22-1	4	13	.246	.371	.320	98	1	10-3	.984	-2	99	118	2b28,D18,S6,3b5	0	0.1
1993	†Chi A	153	579	95	155	15	13	2	51	67-0	9	63	.268	.351	.349	91	-7	20-8	.974	-17	93	89	2b151,3b3	0	-1.4
1994	Chi A	90	312	55	86	13	4	2	30	38-0	2	32	.276	.353	.362	87	-5	8-4	.978	-9	84	106	2b84/D	15	-0.9
1995	†Sea A	120	427	64	127	19	2	3	39	37-0	6	31	.297	.359	.372	90	-5	18-7	.955	-16	84	72	2b112/SD	0	-1.3
1996	Sea A	144	530	90	154	37	6	6	45	35-1	7	32	.291	.340	.417	90	-8	5-5	.979	-2	90	102	2b140/3	0	-0.4
1997	†Sea A★	149	574	105	172	40	4	11	54	53-2	5	49	.300	.359	.441	109	9	6-7	.973	-7	86	91	2b142	0	0.7
1998	Sea A	131	519	95	147	23	6	6	26	62-0	4	50	.283	.362	.385	94	-3	13-5	.962	-24	82	87	2b130	0	-1.9
	†Cle A	24	83	16	19	4	0	0	6	11-0	1	9	.229	.326	.277	57	-5	2-1	.986	-11	65	60	2b21	0	-1.5
	Year	155	602	111	166	27	6	6	32	73-0	5	59	.276	.357	.370	89	-8	15-6	.965	-35	80	83	2b151	0	-3.4
Total	11	1119	3734	624	1035	171	41	30	294	380-6	44	335	.277	.348	.369	90	-49	117-60	.971	-105	89	91	2b970,S46,D22,3b11/C	34	-10.5
CORBETT, GENE	Eugene Louis; B10.25.1913 Winona MN; BL/TR/6´1.5˝/190; d9.19																								
1936	Phi N	6	21	1	3	0	0	0	2	2	0	3	.143	.217	.143	-1	-3	0	1.000	-1	54	149	1b6	—	-0.4
1937	Phi N	7	12	4	4	2	0	0	1	0	0	0	.333	.333	.500	114	0	0	.800	-1	92	0	3b3/2	—	0.0
1938	Phi N	24	75	7	6	1	0	2	7	6	0	11	.080	.148	.173	-12	-12	0	.995	-1	86	88	1b22	—	-1.5
Total	3	37	108	12	13	3	0	2	10	8	0	14	.120	.181	.204	5	-15	0	.996	-2	79	101	1b28,3b3/2	—	-1.9
CORBITT, CLAUDE	Claude Elliott; B7.21.1915 Sunbury NC; D5.1.1978 Cincinnati OH; BR/TR/5´10˝/170; d9.23; Col Duke																								
1945	Bro N	2	4	1	2	0	0	0	0	1	0	0	.500	.600	.500	209	1	0	1.000	0	118	433	3b2	0	0.1
1946	Cin N	82	274	25	68	10	1	1	16	23	1	13	.248	.309	.303	77	-9	3	.947	-6	101	109	S77	0	-1.1
1948	Cin N	87	258	24	66	11	0	0	18	14	1	16	.256	.297	.298	64	-13	4	.973	-4	96	68	2b52,3b16,S11	0	-1.4
1949	Cin N	44	94	10	17	1	0	0	3	9	0	1	.181	.252	.191	20	-11	1	.984	-5	77	127	S18,2b17/3	0	-1.5
Total	4	215	630	60	153	22	1	1	37	47	2	30	.243	.297	.286	63	-32	8	.956	-15	96	106	S106,2b69,3b19	0	-3.9
CORCORAN, ART	Arthur Andrew "Bunny"; B11.23.1894 Roxbury MA; D7.27.1958 Chelsea MA; TR/5´11˝/185; d9.9; Col Georgetown																								
1915	Phi A	1	4	0	0	0	0	0	0	0	0	2	.000	.000	.000	-99	-1	0	1.000	-0	59	0	/3	—	-0.1
CORCORAN, JOHN	John A.; B1873 Cincinnati OH; D11.2.1901 Cincinnati OH; TL; d9.17																								
1895	Pit N	6	20	0	3	0	0	0	1	0	0	2	.150	.150	.150	-24	-4	0	.895	-1	100	0	S4,3b2	—	-0.4
CORCORAN, JACK	John H.; B5.15.1858 Lowell MA; D12.28.1935 Jersey City NJ; d5.1																								
1884	Bro AA	52	185	17	39	4	3	0	—	8	2	—	.211	.251	.265	68	-6	—	.873	-7	—	—	C38,O9(4/2/3),2b4,S2/P	—	-1.0
CORCORAN, LARRY	Lawrence J.; B8.10.1859 Brooklyn NY; D10.14.1891 Newark NJ; BL/TR (TB 1884p)/5´3˝/127; d5.1; b–Mike; ▲																								
1880	Chi N	72	286	41	66	11	1	0	25	10	—	33	.231	.257	.276	76	-7	—	.957	5	114	117	P63,O8(0/5/3),S8	—	0.1
1881	Chi N	47	189	25	42	8	0	0	9	5	—	22	.222	.242	.265	57	-9	—	.893	-1	83	0	P45,S2/lf	—	-0.1
1882	Chi N	40	169	23	35	10	2	1	24	6	—	18	.207	.234	.308	69	-6	—	.915	-0	95	55	P39/3	—	0.0
1883	Chi N	68	263	40	55	12	7	0	25	6	—	62	.209	.227	.308	56	-15	—	.906	-2	94	113	P56,O13(8/4/1),S3/2	—	-0.4
1884	Chi N	64	251	43	61	3	4	1	19	10	—	33	.243	.272	.299	73	-9	—	.882	7	125	145	P60,O4R,S2	—	0.3
1885	Chi N	7	22	6	6	1	0	0	4	6	—	1	.273	.429	.318	127	1	—	.905	-0	98	0	P7/S	—	0.0
	NY N	3	14	3	5	0	0	0	2	0	—	1	.357	.357	.357	133	1	—	1.000	1	177	1558	P3	—	0.0
	Year	10	36	9	11	1	0	0	6	6	—	2	.306	.405	.333	129	1	—	.935	1	122	464	P10/S	—	0.0
1886	NY N	1	4	0	0	0	0	0	0	0	—	2	.000	.000	.000	-99	-1	0	.000	-1	0	0	/rf	—	-0.1
	Was N	21	81	9	15	2	1	0	3	7	—	14	.185	.250	.235	52	-4	3	.619	-3	178	256	O11R,S9,P2	—	-0.6
	Year	22	85	9	15	2	1	0	3	7	—	16	.176	.239	.224	44	-5	3	.591	-4	166	239	O12R,S9,P2	—	-0.7
1887	Ind N	3	10	2	2	0	0	0	0	2	0	1	.200	.333	.200	53	-1	2	1.000	0	0	0	O2(0/1/1),P2	—	0.0
Total	8	326	1289	192	287	47	15	2	111	52	0	187	.223	.253	.287	67	-50	5	.910	6	105	104	P277,O40(9/10/21),S25/23	—	-0.8
CORCORAN, MICKEY	Michael Joseph; B8.26.1882 Buffalo NY; D12.9.1950 Buffalo NY; BR/TR/5´8˝/165; d9.15																								
1910	Cin N	14	46	3	10	3	0	0	7	5	1	9	.217	.308	.283	76	-1	0	.911	-2	108	86	2b14	—	-0.3

YEAR	TM LG	G	AB	R	H	2B	3B	HR	RBI	BB-IB	HP	SO	AVG	OBP	SLG	AOPS	ABR	SB-CS	FA	FR	RNG	THR	GAMES AT POSITION	DL	BFW
CORCORAN, TOMMY	Thomas William "Corky"; B1.4.1869 New Haven CT; D6.25.1960 Plainfield CT; BR/TR/5´9˝/164; d4.19; U1																								
1890	Pit P	123	503	80	117	14	13	1	61	38	2	45	.233	.289	.318	68	-24	43	.884	6	**106**	76	S123	—	-1.2
1891	Phi AA	133	511	84	130	11	15	7	71	29	10	56	.254	.307	.376	95	-8	30	**.911**	12	104	11	S133	—	0.7
1892	Bro N	151	613	77	145	11	6	1	74	34	4	51	.237	.281	.279	72	-22	39	**.925**	-6	96	93	S151	—	-1.9
1893	Bro N	115	459	61	126	11	10	2	58	27	2	12	.275	.318	.355	82	-14	14	.907	13	**111**	93	S115	—	0.5
1894	Bro N	129	576	123	173	21	20	5	92	25	0	17	.300	.329	.432	88	-15	33	.904	-4	99	79	S129	—	-1.0
1895	Bro N	128	540	83	145	17	10	2	69	23	3	11	.269	.302	.348	73	-23	17	.925	17	111	100	S128	—	0.0
1896	Bro N	132	532	63	154	15	7	3	73	15	1	13	.289	.310	.361	81	-17	16	.926	26	108	126	S132	—	1.3
1897	Cin N	109	445	76	128	30	5	3	57	13	2	—	.288	.311	.398	81	-14	15	.913	4	97	142	S63,2b47	—	-0.5
1898	Cin N	153	619	80	155	28	15	2	87	26	2	—	.250	.283	.354	77	-23	19	.932	10	**108**	119	S153	—	-0.5
1899	Cin N	138	540	93	150	11	8	0	81	29	2	—	.278	.317	.328	76	-20	32	.930	0	98	115	S124,2b14	—	-1.1
1900	Cin N	127	523	64	128	21	9	1	54	22	2	—	.245	.278	.325	68	-25	27	.921	-7	97	114	S124,2b5	—	-2.3
1901	Cin N	31	115	14	24	3	3	0	15	11	0	—	.209	.278	.287	68	-5	6	.919	1	102	150	S30	—	-0.2
1902	Cin N	138	538	54	136	18	4	0	54	11	0	—	.253	.268	.301	69	-21	20	.926	-11	92	101	S137/2	—	-3.0
1903	Cin N	115	459	61	113	18	7	2	73	12	1	—	.246	.267	.329	63	-25	12	.943	9	100	105	S115	—	-1.2
1904	Cin N	150	578	55	133	17	9	2	74	19	2	—	.230	.257	.301	66	-25	19	**.936**	0	100	109	S150	—	-2.1
1905	Cin N	151	605	70	150	21	11	2	85	23	1	—	.248	.277	.329	72	-23	28	**.952**	20	107	105	S151	—	0.2
1906	Cin N	117	430	29	89	13	1	1	33	19	1	—	.207	.242	.249	51	-25	8	.941	2	99	124	S117	—	-2.2
1907	NY N	62	226	21	60	9	2	0	24	7	0	—	.265	.288	.323	88	-4	9	.939	-8	98	71	2b62	—	-1.3
Total	18	2202	8812	1188	2256	289	155	34	1135	383	35	205	.256	.290	.336	74	-333	387	.924	84	102	100	S2075,2b129	—	-15.8
CORCORAN, TIM	Timothy Michael; B3.19.1953 Glendale CA; BL/TL/5´11˝/175; d5.18; Col Cal St.–Los Angeles																								
1977	Det A	55	103	13	29	3	0	3	15	6-1	0	9	.282	.315	.398	90	-2	0-1	1.000	-1	101	0	O18(4/6/8),D3	0	-0.3
1978	Det A	116	324	37	86	13	1	1	27	24-2	5	27	.265	.322	.321	80	-8	3-2	.985	-4	93	84	O109(0/2/107)/D	0	-1.7
1979	Det A	18	22	4	5	1	0	0	6	4-1	0	2	.227	.333	.273	67	-1	1-1	1.000	1	142	391	O9(3/0/6),1b5,D2	0	0.0
1980	Det A	84	153	20	44	7	1	3	18	22-2	1	10	.288	.379	.405	113	4	0-2	.985	-1	90	116	1b48,O18(7/0/11),D5	0	-0.1
1981	Min A	22	51	4	9	3	0	0	4	6-0	0	7	.176	.259	.235	42	-4	0-0	1.000	0	103	84	1b16,D3	0	-0.4
1983	Phi N	3	0	0	0	0	0	0	0	0-0	0	0	ø	ø	ø	ø	0	0-0	1.000	-0	0	0	1b3	0	0.0
1984	Phi N	102	208	30	71	13	1	5	36	37-5	1	27	.341	.440	.486	158	19	0-1	.997	-2	91	70	1b51,O17(4/0/13)	15	1.4
1985	Phi N	103	182	11	39	6	1	0	22	29-4	0	20	.214	.312	.258	63	-8	0-0	.993	-1	88	73	1b59,O3(2/0/2)	0	-1.3
1986	NY N	6	7	1	0	0	0	0	0	2-1	0	0	.000	.222	.000	-34	-1	0-0	1.000	0	134	136	/1	0	-0.1
Total	9	509	1050	120	283	46	4	12	128	130-16	7	102	.270	.349	.355	96	-1	4-7	.993	-7	90	84	1b183,O174(20/8/147),D14	15	-2.5
CORDERO, WIL	Wilfredo (Nieva); B10.3.1971 Mayaguez, PR; BR/TR/6´2˝/(185–230); d7.24; OF(400/0/17)																								
1992	Mon N	45	126	17	38	4	1	2	8	9-0	1	31	.302	.353	.397	113	2	0-0	.949	-8	85	72	S35,2b9	0	-0.4
1993	Mon N	138	475	56	118	32	2	10	58	34-8	7	60	.248	.308	.387	81	-13	12-3	.941	-20	96	83	S134,3b2	0	-2.1
1994	Mon N★	110	415	65	122	30	3	15	63	41-3	6	62	.294	.363	.489	119	12	16-3	.952	-13	95	93	S109	0	1.0
1995	Mon N	131	514	64	147	35	2	10	49	36-4	9	88	.286	.341	.420	96	-2	9-5	.960	-25	87	78	S105,O26L	0	-2.0
1996	Bos A	59	198	29	57	14	0	3	37	11-4	2	31	.288	.330	.404	83	-5	2-1	.949	-2	97	66	2b37,D13/1	83	-0.5
1997	Bos A	140	570	82	160	26	3	18	72	31-7	4	122	.281	.320	.432	92	-8	1-3	.992	-5	89	90	O137L/2D	0	-1.8
1998	Chi A	96	341	58	91	18	2	13	49	22-0	3	66	.267	.314	.446	97	-3	2-1	.992	4	131	115	1b83,O11(4/0/8)	0	-0.5
1999	†Cle A	54	194	35	58	15	0	8	32	15-0	6	37	.299	.364	.500	113	4	2-0	.981	-2	90	0	O29L,D23	91	0.0
2000	Pit N	89	348	46	98	24	3	16	51	25-1	4	58	.282	.336	.506	109	3	1-2	.983	-10	69	57	O85L/D	0	-1.0
	Cle A	38	148	18	39	11	2	0	17	7-0	3	18	.264	.310	.365	68	-7	0-0	1.000	2	110	96	O38L	0	-0.6
2001	†Cle A	89	268	30	67	11	1	4	21	22-2	4	50	.250	.313	.343	71	-11	0-0	.985	-5	81	41	O51(49/0/4),1b22,D12	15	-1.9
2002	Cle A	6	18	1	4	0	0	0	1	0-0	0	3	.222	.222	.222	18	-2	0-0	1.000	2	107	916	O4L/1	0	-0.1
	Mon N	66	143	21	39	9	0	6	29	17-0	2	26	.273	.349	.462	108	2	2-0	.958	1	109	73	O28(24/0/5),1b10,D2	15	0.1
2003	Mon N	130	436	57	121	27	0	16	71	49-5	4	90	.278	.354	.450	106	5	1-1	.996	-6	81	96	1b123/lfD	0	-1.2
2004	Fla N	27	66	6	13	3	0	1	6	3-0	2	19	.197	.250	.288	42	-6	1-0	.991	-1	54	116	1b13,O3L	113	-0.8
2005	Was N	29	51	2	6	2	0	0	2	3-1	0	14	.118	.161	.157	-15	-9	0-0	1.000	-1	38	73	1b12,D3	52	-1.1
Total	14	1247	4311	587	1178	261	19	122	566	325-35	57	775	.273	.330	.428	94	-38	49-19	.980	-90	88	74	O413L,S383,1b265,D58,2b47,3b2	369	-12.9
CORDOVA, MARTY	Martin Keevin; B7.10.1969 Las Vegas NV; BR/TR/6´0˝/(193–206); [MinA89 10/269]; d4.26; Col Orange Coast (CA) JC; [DL 2004 Bal A 183]																								
1995	Min A	137	512	81	142	27	4	24	84	52-1	10	111	.277	.352	.486	116	11	20-7	.986	14	117	127	O137(132/11/0)	0	2.1
1996	Min A	145	569	97	176	46	1	16	111	53-4	8	96	.309	.371	.478	112	12	11-5	.991	5	107	87	O145L	0	1.1
1997	Min A	103	378	44	93	18	4	15	51	30-2	3	92	.246	.305	.434	89	-8	5-3	.991	9	109	186	O101L,D2	46	-0.3
1998	Min A	119	438	52	111	20	2	10	69	50-3	5	103	.253	.333	.377	83	-10	3-6	.978	4	114	73	O115L,D4	15	-1.1
1999	Min A	124	425	62	121	28	3	14	70	48-2	9	96	.285	.365	.464	105	4	13-4	.927	-4	80	0	D85,O29(6/0/25)	0	-0.3
2000	Tor A	62	200	23	49	7	0	4	18	18-0	3	35	.245	.317	.340	64	-11	3-2	.982	-6	67	39	O41(23/0/18),D15	0	-1.8
2001	†Cle A	122	409	61	123	20	2	20	69	23-0	8	81	.301	.348	.506	117	9	0-3	.990	6	109	138	O106(83/2/30),D7	0	1.0
2002	Bal A	131	458	55	116	25	2	18	64	47-3	3	111	.253	.325	.434	106	3	1-6	.971	-5	86	46	O72L,D56	12	-0.9
2003	Bal A	9	30	5	7	1	0	1	4	8-1	1	5	.233	.410	.367	108	1	1-0	1.000	1	85	815	O4L,D5	159	0.2
Total	9	952	3419	480	938	192	18	122	540	329-16	50	730	.274	.344	.448	102	11	57-36	.984	24	105	107	O750(681/13/73),D174	415	-0.0
COREY, FRED	Frederick Harrison; B1855 Coventry RI; D11.27.1912 Providence RI; BR/TR/5´7˝/160; d5.1; OF(8/29/46); ▲																								
1878	Pro N	7	21	3	3	0	0	0	1	0	—	2	.143	.143	.143	-6	-2	—	1.000	0	42	0	P5,2b2/1	—	-0.1
1880	Wor N	41	138	11	24	8	1	0	6	4	—	27	.174	.197	.246	45	-8	—	.759	-7	68	135	O29(2/6/21),P25,S3/31	—	-1.0
1881	Wor N	51	203	22	45	8	4	0	10	5	—	10	.222	.240	.300	65	-9	—	.827	1	96	96	O25(1/0/24),P23,S7	—	-0.4
1882	Wor N	64	255	33	63	7	12	0	29	5	—	31	.247	.262	.369	97	-2	—	.847	-5	100	58	S26,P21,O15(5/10/0),3b6,1b5	—	-0.6
1883	Phi AA	71	298	45	77	16	2	1	40	12	—	—	.258	.287	.336	91	-3	—	.799	-1	116	109	3b34,P18,O14(0/13/1),2b9/SC	—	-0.3
1884	Phi AA	104	439	64	121	17	16	5	—	17	2	—	.276	.306	.421	127	10	—	**.887**	12	110	91	3b104	—	2.2
1885	Phi AA	94	384	61	94	14	8	1	38	17	3	—	.245	.282	.331	88	-7	—	.872	7	106	103	3b92/SP	—	0.2
Total	7	432	1738	239	427	70	43	7	124	60	5	70	.246	.273	.348	93	-21	—	.863	7	108	96	3b237,P93,O83R,S38,2b11,1b7/C	—	0.0
COREY, MARK	Mark Mundell; B11.3.1955 Tucumcari NM; BR/TR/6´2˝/(200–205); [BalA76*2/43]; d9.1; Col Central Arizona JC																								
1979	Bal A	13	13	1	2	0	0	0	1	0-0	0	4	.154	.154	.154	-17	-2	1-0	1.000	0	116	0	O11R/D	0	-0.2
1980	Bal A	36	36	7	10	2	0	1	2	5-0	0	7	.278	.366	.417	116	1	0-1	1.000	-2	72	0	O34(15/0/19)	0	-0.2
1981	Bal A	10	8	2	0	0	0	0	0	2-0	0	2	.000	.200	.000	-38	-1	0-0	1.000	0	78	388	O9(7/0/2)	0	-0.1
Total	3	59	57	10	12	2	0	1	3	7-0	0	13	.211	.297	.298	65	-2	1-1	1.000	-2	82	65	O54(22/0/32)/D	0	-0.5
CORGAN, CHUCK	Charles Howard; B12.4.1902 Wagoner OK; D6.13.1928 Wagoner OK; BB/TR/5´11˝/180; d9.19; Col Arkansas																								
1925	Bro N	14	47	4	8	1	1	0	0	3	0	9	.170	.220	.234	16	-6	0-0	.908	1	115	56	S14	—	-0.3
1927	Bro N	19	57	3	15	1	0	0	1	4	0	4	.263	.311	.281	59	-3	0	.969	0	116	65	2b13,S3	—	-0.3
Total	2	33	104	7	23	2	1	0	1	7	0	13	.221	.270	.260	40	-9	0-0	.900	1	108	58	S17,2b13	—	-0.6
CORHAN, ROY	Roy George "Irish"; B10.21.1887 Indianapolis IN; D11.24.1958 San Francisco CA; BR/TR/5´9.5˝/165; d4.20																								
1911	Chi A	43	131	14	28	6	2	0	8	15	2	—	.214	.304	.290	68	-5	2	.924	10	112	137	S43	—	0.7
1916	StL N	92	295	30	62	6	3	0	18	20	2	31	.210	.265	.251	59	-14	15	.917	1	106	92	S84	—	-0.9
Total	2	135	426	44	90	12	5	0	26	35	4	31	.211	.277	.263	62	-19	17	.920	10	108	107	S127	—	-0.2
CORIDAN, PHIL	Philip F.; B8.19.1858 Walpole (now Fortville) IN; D7.1.1915 Indianapolis IN; BL; d7.16																								
1884	CP U	2	7	1	1	0	0	0	—	0	—	—	.143	.143	.143	-13	-1	—	.800	-1	81	0	2b2/lf	—	-0.2
CORKHILL, POP	John Stewart; B4.11.1858 Parkesburg PA; D4.3.1921 Pennsauken NJ; BL/TR/5´10˝/180; d5.1; OF(6/615/420); ▲																								
1883	Cin AA	88	375	53	81	10	8	2	46	3	—	—	.216	.222	.301	63	-17	—	**.930**	0	60	0	O85(0/15/70),S2,2b2,1b2	—	-1.5
1884	Cin AA	110	452	85	124	13	11	4	70	6	4	—	.274	.290	.378	111	3	—	**.934**	7	162	181	O92R,S11,1b6,3b3/P	—	0.9
1885	Cin AA	**112**	440	64	111	10	8	1	53	7	7	—	.252	.275	.318	85	-9	—	.938	17	**189**	139	O110R,P8,1b3	—	0.6
1886	Cin AA	129	540	81	143	9	7	5	97	23	6	—	.265	.302	.335	96	-5	24	.918	-0	136	166	O112R,3b12,1b7,S3/P	—	-0.5
1887	Cin AA	128	541	79	168	19	11	5	97	14	4	—	.311	.333	.414	105	0	30	**.952**	12	136	164	O128(0/121/7),P5	—	0.6
1888	Cin AA	118	490	68	133	11	9	1	74	15	4	—	.271	.299	.337	98	-4	27	.958	1	86	123	O116(4/112/0),P2/12	—	-0.7
	Bro AA	19	71	17	27	4	3	1	19	4	2	—	.380	.429	.563	217	9	3	.980	0	60	0	O19C	—	0.8
	Year	137	561	85	160	15	12	2	93	19	6	—	.285	.316	.365	113	5	30	**.961**	1	82	105	O135(4/131/0),P2/12	—	0.1
1889	†Bro AA	**138**	537	91	134	21	9	8	78	42	3	24	.250	.308	.367	91	-8	22	**.949**	9	131	146	O138C/S1	—	-0.4
1890	Bro N	51	204	23	46	4	2	1	21	15	0	11	.225	.279	.279	62	-10	6	.977	2	71	62	O48C,1b6	—	-0.9
1891	Phi AA	83	349	50	73	7	7	0	31	26	2	15	.209	.268	.269	54	-23	12	.956	4	94	97	O83(0/73/10)	—	-1.8

YEAR	TM LG	G	AB	R	H	2B	3B	HR	RBI	BB-IB	HP	SO	AVG	OBP	SLG	AOPS	ABR	SB-CS	FA	FR	RNG	THR	GAMES AT POSITION	DL	BFW
	Cin N	1	4	0	0	0	0	0	0	0	0	1	.000	.000	.000	-99	-1	0	1.000	0	0	0	/cf	—	-0.1
	Pit N	41	145	16	33	1	1	3	20	7	1	10	.228	.268	.310	70	-6	7	.935	3	160	316	O41(1/40/0)	—	-0.4
	Year	42	149	16	33	1	1	3	20	7	1	11	.221	.261	.302	65	-7	7	.939	3	150	296	O42(1/41/0)	—	-0.5
1892	Pit N	68	256	23	47	1	4	0	25	12	3	19	.184	.229	.219	35	-21	6	.953	5	114	163	O68(1/48/19)	—	-2.0
Total	10	1086	4404	650	1120	110	80	31	631	174	36	80	.254	.288	.337	87	-92	137	.947	59	122	134	O1041C,1b26,P17,S17,3b15,2b3	—	-5.4
Corrales, Pat	Patrick; B3.20.1941 Los Angeles CA; BR/TR/6´0˝/(190–195); d8.2; M9/C22; Col Fresno (CA) City																								
1964	Phi N	2	1	1	0	0	0	0	0	1-0	0	0	.000	.500	.000	55	0	0-0	ø	0	—	—	/H	0	0.0
1965	Phi N	63	174	16	39	8	1	2	15	25-5	1	42	.224	.323	.316	83	-3	0-0	.982	-8	99	76	C62	0	-0.8
1966	StL N	28	72	5	13	2	0	0	3	2-0	2	17	.181	.221	.208	21	-8	1-0	.975	6	223	199	C27	0	-0.1
1968	Cin N	20	56	3	15	4	0	0	6	6-0	1	16	.268	.349	.339	101	1	0-0	.991	-2	64	68	C20	0	-0.1
1969	Cin N	29	72	10	19	5	0	1	5	8-0	1	17	.264	.346	.375	97	0	0-1	.986	1	87	52	C29	0	0.2
1970	†Cin N	43	106	9	25	5	1	1	10	8-1	0	22	.236	.289	.330	65	-5	0-0	.983	1	196	103	C42	0	-0.3
1971	Cin N	40	94	6	17	2	0	0	6	6-1	0	17	.181	.230	.202	24	-10	0-0	.980	-3	107	14	C39	0	-1.2
1972	Cin N	2	1	0	0	0	0	0	0	2-1	0	0	.000	.667	.000	109	0	0-0	1.000	1	0	341	C2	0	0.1
	SD N	44	119	6	23	0	0	0	6	11-1	1	26	.193	.267	.193	35	-10	0-0	.993	-1	93	81	C43	0	-1.0
	Year	46	120	6	23	0	0	0	6	13-2	1	26	.192	.276	.192	38	-10	0-0	.993	-0	91	88	C45	0	-0.9
1973	SD N	29	72	7	15	2	1	0	3	6-1	1	10	.208	.275	.264	55	-5	0-0	.986	-5	71	76	C28	0	-0.9
Total	9	300	767	63	166	28	3	4	54	75-10	7	167	.216	.291	.276	61	-40	1-1	.984	-11	117	83	C292	0	-4.1
Correia, Rod	Ronald Douglas; B9.13.1967 Providence RI; BR/TR/5´11˝/185; [OakA88 15/385]; d6.20; Col Massachusetts–Dartmouth																								
1993	Cal A	64	128	12	34	5	0	0	9	6-0	4	20	.266	.319	.305	66	-6	2-4	.981	1	105	79	S40,2b11,3b3,D6	0	-0.3
1994	Cal A	6	17	4	4	1	0	0	0	0-0	2	0	.235	.316	.294	58	-1	0-0	1.000	-2	52	69	2b5/S	0	-0.3
1995	Cal A	14	21	3	5	1	1	0	3	0-0	0	5	.238	.238	.381	58	-1	0-0	.850	-0	81	143	S7,2b3,3b2/D	0	-0.1
Total	3	84	166	19	43	7	1	0	12	6-0	6	25	.259	.309	.313	65	-8	2-4	.968	-1	102	89	S48,2b19,D7,3b5	0	-0.7
Correll, Vic	Victor Crosby; B2.5.1946 Washington DC; BR/TR/5´10˝/(175–185); [CleA67 9/171]; d10.4; Col Georgia Southern																								
1972	Bos A	1	4	1	2	0	0	0	1	0-0	0	1	.500	.500	.500	187	0	0-0	1.000	1	0	0	/C	0	0.1
1974	Atl N	73	202	20	48	15	1	4	29	21-3	4	38	.238	.317	.381	93	-2	0-0	.988	5	94	61	C59	0	0.6
1975	Atl N	103	325	37	70	12	1	11	39	42-5	1	66	.215	.305	.360	82	-8	0-2	.973	-5	84	99	C97	0	-1.0
1976	Atl N	69	200	26	45	6	2	5	16	21-5	1	37	.225	.302	.350	80	-6	0-1	.981	-3	76	110	C65	0	-0.7
1977	Atl N	54	144	16	30	7	0	7	16	22-1	1	33	.208	.314	.403	82	-3	2-3	.973	-6	60	120	C49	0	-0.8
1978	Cin N	52	105	9	25	7	0	1	6	8-3	0	17	.238	.292	.333	74	-4	0-2	.980	-3	118	110	C52	0	-0.6
1979	Cin N	48	133	14	31	12	0	1	15	14-2	1	26	.233	.309	.346	79	-3	0-0	.992	-1	77	62	C47	0	-0.2
1980	Cin N	10	19	1	8	1	0	0	3	0-0	0	2	.421	.421	.474	152	1	0-0	.919	-3	48	41	C10	145	-0.1
Total	8	410	1132	124	259	60	4	29	125	128-19	8	220	.229	.310	.366	84	-25	2-8	.979	-15	83	92	C380	145	-2.7
Corriden, John	John Michael Jr.; B1.6.1918 Logansport IN; D6.4.2001 Indianapolis IN; BB/TR/5´6˝/160; d4.20; f–Red; Col Indiana																								
1946	Bro N	1	0	1	0	0	0	0	0	0	0	0	ø	ø	ø	ø	0	0	ø	0	—	—	/R	0	0.0
Corriden, Red	John Michael Sr.; B9.4.1887 Logansport IN; D9.28.1959 Indianapolis IN; BR/TR/5´9˝/165; d9.8; M1/C18; s–John																								
1910	StL A	26	84	19	13	3	0	1	4	13	4	—	.155	.297	.226	68	-2	5	.902	2	115	49	S14,3b12	—	0.1
1912	Det A	38	138	22	28	6	0	0	5	15	1	—	.203	.286	.246	54	-8	4	.929	-2	102	138	3b25,2b7,S3	—	-0.9
1913	Chi N	46	97	13	17	3	0	2	9	10	0	14	.175	.252	.268	49	-7	4-3	.907	-2	102	127	S37,2b2/3	—	-0.7
1914	Chi N	107	318	42	73	9	5	3	29	35	9	33	.230	.323	.318	91	-3	13	.894	-27	78	95	S91,3b8,2b3	—	-2.6
1915	Chi N	6	3	1	0	0	0	0	0	2	2	1	.000	.571	.000	79	1	0	.667	-1	56	0	/3cf	—	0.0
Total	5	223	640	97	131	21	5	6	47	75	16	48	.205	.304	.281	74	-19	26-3	.896	-29	88	94	S145,3b47,2b12/cf	—	-4.1
Cortazzo, Jess	John Francis; B9.26.1904 Wilmerding PA; D3.4.1963 Pittsburgh PA; BR/TR/5´3.5˝/142; d9.1																								
1923	Chi A	1	1	0	0	0	0	0	0	0	0	0	.000	.000	.000	-99	0	0-0	ø	0	—	—	/H	—	0.0
Cortez, Fernando	Fernando; B8.10.1981 Stockton CA; BL/TR/6´1˝/175; [TBA01 9/259]; d7.5; Col Grossmont (CA) CC																								
2005	TB A	8	13	0	1	0	0	0	1	1-0	0	3	.077	.143	.077	-40	-3	0-0	1.000	-3	41	0	2b3,S2/3	0	-0.5
Coscarart, Joe	Joseph Marvin; B11.18.1909 Escondido CA; D4.5.1993 Sequim WA; BR/TR/6´0˝/185; d4.26; b–Pete																								
1935	Bos N	86	284	30	67	11	2	1	29	16	0	28	.236	.277	.299	59	-17	2	.962	-3	120	87	3b41,S27,2b15	—	-1.6
1936	Bos N	104	367	28	90	11	2	2	44	19	5	37	.245	.292	.302	64	-19	0	.935	1	109	136	3b97,S6/2	—	-1.5
Total	2	190	651	58	157	22	4	3	73	35	5	65	.241	.285	.301	62	-36	2	.943	-2	112	123	3b138,S33,2b16	—	-3.1
Coscarart, Pete	Peter Joseph; B6.16.1913 Escondido CA; D7.24.2002 Escondido CA; BR/TR/5´11.5˝/175; d4.26; b–Joe; Col San Diego St.																								
1938	Bro N	32	79	10	12	3	0	0	6	9	2	18	.152	.256	.190	24	-8	0	.955	1	97	115	2b27	—	-0.6
1939	Bro N	115	419	59	116	22	2	4	43	46	4	56	.277	.354	.368	91	-4	10	.960	-10	98	102	2b107,3b4,S2	—	-0.7
1940	Bro N★	143	506	55	120	24	4	9	58	53	1	59	.237	.311	.354	78	-15	5	.958	-34	85	73	2b140	—	-4.1
1941	†Bro N	43	62	13	8	1	0	0	5	7	0	12	.129	.217	.145	3	-8	1	.948	1	111	74	2b19/S	0	-0.7
1942	Pit N	133	487	57	111	12	4	3	29	38	3	56	.228	.288	.287	67	-21	2	.952	-19	97	80	S108,2b25	0	-3.3
1943	Pit N	133	491	57	119	19	6	0	48	46	0	48	.242	.307	.305	75	-16	4	.961	-3	103	105	2b85,S47/3	0	-1.2
1944	Pit N	139	554	89	146	30	4	4	42	41	1	57	.264	.315	.354	85	-11	10	.967	-3	99	91	2b136,S4/rf	0	-0.7
1945	Pit N	123	392	59	95	17	2	8	38	55	4	55	.242	.341	.357	91	-4	2	.978	21	**116**	**124**	2b122/S	0	2.3
1946	Pit N	3	2	0	1	1	0	0	0	0	0	0	.500	.500	1.000	312	1	0	ø	-0	0	0	/S	0	0.0
Total	9	864	2992	399	728	129	22	28	269	295	15	361	.243	.314	.329	78	-86	34	.963	-47	99	97	2b661,S164,3b5/rf	0	-9.0
Cosey, Ray	Donald Ray; B2.15.1956 San Rafael CA; BL/TL/5´10˝/185; d4.14																								
1980	Oak A	9	9	0	1	0	0	0	0	0-0	0	0	.111	.111	.111	-41	-2	0-0	ø	0	—	—	/H	0	-0.2
Costa, Shane	Shane Jeremy; B12.12.1981 Visalia CA; BL/TR/6´0˝/(200–220); [KCA03 2/42]; d6.2; Col Cal St.–Fullerton																								
2005	KC A	27	81	13	19	2	0	2	7	5-0	1	11	.235	.287	.333	67	-4	0-0	1.000	-1	81	100	O20L,D4	0	-0.6
2006	KC A	72	237	23	65	20	1	3	23	6-2	5	29	.274	.304	.405	84	-6	2-0	.959	-2	109	0	O65(5/21/39)/D	20	-0.8
Total	2	99	318	36	84	22	1	5	30	11-2	6	40	.264	.300	.387	79	-10	2-0	.966	-3	102	24	O85(34/21/39),D5	20	-1.4
Coste, Chris	Christopher Robert; B2.4.1973 Fargo ND; BR/TR/6´1˝/200; d5.26; Col Concordia–Moorhead (MN)																								
2006	Phi N	65	198	25	65	14	0	7	32	10-1	5	31	.328	.376	.505	117	5	0-0	.988	-10	116	53	C54,1b2	0	-0.1
Costello, Dan	Daniel Francis "Dashing Dan"; B9.9.1891 Jessup PA; D3.26.1936 Pittsburgh PA; BL/TR/6´0.5˝/185; d7.2; Col Mount St. Marys																								
1913	NY A	2	2	1	1	0	0	0	0	0	0	0	.500	.500	.500	192	0	0	ø	0	—	—	/H	—	0.0
1914	Pit N	21	64	7	19	1	0	0	5	8	0	16	.297	.375	.313	110	1	2	.970	0	100	107	O20R	—	0.1
1915	Pit N	71	125	16	27	4	1	0	11	7	0	23	.216	.258	.264	59	-6	7-1	.893	-3	70	52	O22(5/12/5)/1	—	-1.1
1916	Pit N	60	159	11	38	1	3	0	8	6	0	23	.239	.267	.283	68	-7	3	.976	-1	114	0	O41(33/1/7)	—	-1.1
Total	4	154	350	35	85	6	4	0	24	21	0	62	.243	.286	.283	73	-12	12-1	.959	-4	101	37	O83(38/13/32)/1	—	-2.1
Costo, Tim	Timothy Roger; B2.16.1969 Melrose Park IL; BR/TR/6´5˝/(220–230); [CleA90 1/8]; d9.18; Col Iowa																								
1992	Cin N	12	36	3	8	2	0	0	2	5-0	0	6	.222	.310	.278	68	-1	0-0	1.000	0	104	203	1b12	0	-0.2
1993	Cin N	31	98	13	22	5	0	3	12	4-0	0	17	.224	.250	.367	64	-5	0-0	.980	0	104	56	O26(11/0/16),1b2,3b2	0	-0.7
Total	2	43	134	16	30	7	0	3	14	9-0	0	23	.224	.267	.343	65	-6	0-0	.980	1	104	56	O26(11/0/16),1b14,3b2	0	-0.9
Cota, Humberto	Humberto Figueroa; B2.7.1979 San Luis Rio Colorado, Sonora, Mexico; BR/TR/6´0˝/(175–215); d9.9																								
2001	Pit N	7	9	0	2	0	0	0	1	0-0	0	5	.222	.222	.222	15	-1	0-0	1.000	1	0	0	C3	0	0.0
2002	Pit N	7	17	2	5	1	0	0	0	1-1	0	4	.294	.333	.353	79	0	0-0	1.000	1	262	83	C7	0	0.1
2003	Pit N	10	16	1	4	1	0	0	1	1-0	0	5	.250	.294	.313	58	-1	0-0	1.000	0	129	171	C4	0	-0.1
2004	Pit N	36	66	10	15	1	1	5	8	3-1	1	20	.227	.271	.500	93	-1	0-0	.991	-1	205	32	C24	66	-0.1
2005	Pit N	93	297	29	72	20	1	7	43	17-2	2	80	.242	.285	.387	75	-12	0-0	.992	0	119	79	C87	16	-0.6
2006	Pit N	38	100	5	19	1	0	0	5	8-0	0	26	.190	.248	.200	17	-13	0-0	1.000	1	91	143	C33	0	-1.0
Total	6	191	505	47	117	24	2	12	58	30-4	3	140	.232	.277	.358	64	-28	0-0	.994	2	127	88	C158	82	-1.7
Cote, Henry	Henry Joseph; B2.19.1864 Troy NY; D4.28.1940 Troy NY; TR/5´9.5˝/165; d9.16																								
1894	Lou N	10	31	7	9	2	2	0	3	5	0	6	.290	.389	.484	117	1	2	.918	3	*100*	*145*	C10	—	0.4
1895	Lou N	10	33	10	10	0	0	0	5	3	0	3	.303	.361	.303	77	-1	2	.872	-3	*90*	*53*	C10	—	-0.3
Total	2	20	64	17	19	2	2	0	8	8	0	9	.297	.375	.391	98	0	4	.900	-0	*95*	*102*	C20	—	0.1

YEAR	TM LG	G	AB	R	H	2B	3B	HR	RBI	BB-IB	HP	SO	AVG	OBP	SLG	AOPS	ABR	SB-CS	FA	FR	RNG	THR	GAMES AT POSITION	DL	BFW
COTE, PETE	Warren Peter; B8.30.1902 Cambridge MA; D10.17.1987 Middleton MA; BR/TR/5´6´´/148; d6.18; Col Holy Cross																								
1926	NY N	2	1	0	0	0	0	0	0	0	0	0	.000	.000	.000	-99	0	0	ø	0	—	—	/H	—	0.0
COTTER, ED	Edward Christopher; B7.4.1904 Hartford CT; D6.14.1959 Hartford CT; BR/TR/6´0´´/185; d6.12; Col Villanova																								
1926	Phi N	17	26	3	8	0	1	0	1	1	0	4	.308	.333	.385	88	-1	1	.833	-1	111	0	3b8,S5	—	-0.1
COTTER, HOOKS	Harvey Louis; B5.22.1900 Holden MO; D8.6.1955 Los Angeles CA; BL/TL/5´10´´/160; d4.15																								
1922	Chi N	1	1	0	1	1	0	0	0	0	0	0	1.000	1.000	2.000	644	1	0-0	ø	0	—	—	/H	—	0.1
1924	Chi N	98	310	39	81	16	4	4	33	36	0	31	.261	.338	.377	91	-3	3-5	.989	4	119	99	1b90	—	-0.7
Total	2	99	311	39	82	17	4	4	33	36	0	31	.264	.340	.383	92	-2	3-5	.989	4	119	99	1b90	—	-0.6
COTTER, DICK	Richard Raphael; B10.12.1889 Manchester NH; D4.4.1945 Brooklyn NY; BR/TR/5´11´´/172; d8.17; Col Manhattan																								
1911	Phi N	20	46	2	13	0	0	0	5	5	0	7	.283	.353	.283	78	-1	1	.975	-2	*81*	*133*	C17	—	-0.2
1912	Chi N	26	54	6	15	0	2	0	10	6	1	13	.278	.361	.352	96	0	1	.954	-1	*128*	*85*	C24	—	0.0
Total	2	46	100	8	28	0	2	0	15	11	1	20	.280	.357	.320	87	-1	2	.964	-3	*107*	*107*	C41	—	-0.2
COTTER, TOM	Thomas Benedict; B9.30.1866 Waltham MA; D11.22.1906 Brookline MA; BR/TR/5´10.5´´/149; d9.3																								
1891	Bos AA	6	12	1	3	0	0	0	4	1	0	2	.250	.308	.250	61	-1	0	.938	-0	*154*	*106*	C5/rf	—	0.0
COTTIER, CHUCK	Charles Keith; B1.8.1936 Delta CO; BR/TR/5´10.5´´/(175–178); d4.17; M3/C18																								
1959	Mil N	10	24	1	3	1	0	0	1	3-0	0	7	.125	.222	.167	6	-3	0-0	.976	-2	92	38	2b10	0	-0.5
1960	Mil N	95	229	29	52	8	0	3	19	14-3	2	21	.227	.273	.301	63	-12	1-0	.968	5	108	90	2b92	0	-0.2
1961	Det A	10	7	2	2	0	0	0	1	1-0	0	1	.286	.375	.286	77	0	0-0	.889	-0	19	96	S8,2b2	0	0.0
	Was A	101	337	37	79	14	4	2	34	30-1	1	51	.234	.296	.318	66	-17	9-1	.982	11	116	104	2b100	0	0.4
	Year	111	344	39	81	14	4	2	35	31-1	1	52	.235	.297	.317	66	-17	9-1	.982	11	117	106	2b102,S8	0	0.4
1962	Was A	136	443	50	107	14	6	6	40	44-0	2	57	.242	.310	.341	76	-15	14-8	.981	24	108	**123**	2b134	0	1.9
1963	Was A	113	337	30	69	16	4	5	21	24-6	0	63	.205	.257	.320	61	-18	2-1	.963	2	105	94	2b85,S24/3	0	-0.8
1964	Was A	73	137	16	23	6	2	3	10	19-1	0	33	.168	.268	.307	60	-7	2-0	.982	-2	96	113	2b53,3b3,S2	0	-0.5
1965	Was A	7	1	1	0	0	0	0	0	0-0	0	0	.000	.000	.000	-99	0	0-0	ø	0	—	—	/H	0	0.0
1968	Cal A	33	67	2	13	4	1	0	1	2-0	0	15	.194	.217	.284	52	-4	0-0	.963	-1	98	59	3b27,2b4	0	-0.6
1969	Cal A	2	2	0	0	0	0	0	0	0-0	0	0	.000	.000	.000	-99	-1	0-0	1.000	-0	79	0	2b2	22	-0.1
Total	9	580	1584	168	348	63	17	19	127	137-11	5	248	.220	.282	.317	65	-77	28-10	.976	37	108	105	2b482,S34,3b31	22	-0.4
COTTO, HENRY	Henry; B1.5.1961 New York NY; BR/TR/6´2´´/(178–180); d4.5																								
1984	†Chi N	105	146	24	40	5	0	0	8	10-2	1	23	.274	.325	.308	73	-5	9-3	.984	7	131	123	O88(47/34/10)	0	0.2
1985	NY A	34	56	4	17	1	0	1	6	3-0	0	12	.304	.339	.375	97	0	1-1	.977	1	100	185	O30(14/20/1)	41	0.0
1986	NY A	35	80	11	17	3	0	1	6	2-0	0	17	.213	.229	.287	41	-7	3-0	1.000	1	108	77	O29(11/19/0)/D	0	-0.6
1987	NY A	68	149	21	35	10	0	5	20	6-0	1	35	.235	.269	.403	75	-6	4-2	.989	-1	96	102	O57(15/41/2)	0	-0.7
1988	Sea A	133	386	50	100	18	1	8	33	23-0	2	53	.259	.302	.373	85	-8	27-3	.992	-3	93	130	O120C,D2	0	-0.7
1989	Sea A	100	295	44	78	11	2	9	33	12-3	3	44	.264	.300	.407	94	-3	10-4	.988	3	95	212	O90(57/30/14),D2	0	-0.1
1990	Sea A	127	355	40	92	14	3	4	33	22-2	4	52	.259	.307	.349	83	-9	21-3	.990	2	108	70	O118(41/18/67),D3	0	-0.6
1991	Sea A	66	177	35	54	6	2	6	23	10-0	2	27	.305	.347	.463	122	5	16-3	.981	3	116	88	O56(38/19/8),D6	65	0.9
1992	Sea A	108	294	42	76	11	1	5	27	14-3	1	49	.259	.294	.354	80	-9	23-2	1.000	1	112	45	O92(63/30/6),D3	0	-0.5
1993	Sea A	54	105	10	20	1	0	2	7	2-0	1	22	.190	.213	.257	25	-12	5-4	.983	1	117	0	O34(23/9/4),D15	0	-1.2
	Fla N	54	135	15	40	7	0	3	14	3-0	1	18	.296	.312	.415	89	-2	11-1	.977	2	120	46	O46(13/15/21)	0	0.1
Total	10	884	2178	296	569	87	9	44	210	107-10	16	352	.261	.299	.370	83	-56	130-26	.989	16	106	104	O760(322/355/133),D32	106	-3.2
COUGHLIN, DENNIS	Dennis H.; B1844 NY; D5.14.1913 Washington DC; d4.27																								
1872	Nat NA	8	37	5	11	1	0	0	7	0	—	0	.297	.297	.324	78	-1	0-0	.941	1	187	646	O5C/12S	—	-0.1
COUGHLIN, ED	Edward E.; B8.5.1861 Hartford CT; D12.25.1952 Hartford CT; d5.15																								
1884	Buf N	1	4	0	1	0	0	0	1	0	—	2	.250	.250	.250	56	0	—	.750	-0	0	0	/rfP	—	0.0
COUGHLIN, BILL	William Paul "Scranton Bill"; B7.12.1878 Scranton PA; D5.7.1943 Scranton PA; BR/TR/5´9´´/140; d8.9																								
1899	Was N	6	24	2	3	0	1	0	3	1	0	—	.125	.160	.208	1	-4	1	.818	-1	85	0	3b6	—	-0.4
1901	Was A	137	506	75	139	17	13	6	68	25	6	—	.275	.317	.395	98	-3	16	.922	3	92	85	3b137	—	0.3
1902	Was A	123	469	84	141	27	4	6	71	26	8	—	.301	.348	.414	110	6	29	.926	7	106	60	3b66,S31,2b26	—	1.5
1903	Was A	125	473	56	116	18	3	1	31	9	5	—	.245	.267	.302	69	-18	30	.952	3	98	96	3b119,S4,2b2	—	-1.2
1904	Was A	65	265	28	73	15	4	0	17	9	3	—	.275	.307	.362	113	3	10	.939	4	99	105	3b64	—	1.0
	Det A	56	206	22	47	6	0	0	17	5	3	—	.228	.257	.257	65	-8	1	.929	-5	99	38	3b56	—	-1.3
	Year	121	471	50	120	21	4	0	34	14	6	—	.255	.285	.316	92	-5	11	.935	-1	99	74	3b120	—	-0.3
1905	Det A	137	489	48	123	20	6	0	44	34	7	—	.252	.309	.317	98	-1	16	.914	-7	96	98	3b136	—	-0.5
1906	Det A	147	498	54	117	15	5	2	60	36	5	—	.235	.293	.297	83	-10	31	.940	-12	90	103	3b147	—	-1.9
1907	†Det A	134	519	80	126	10	2	0	46	35	8	—	.243	.301	.270	79	-11	15	.930	-9	89	66	3b133	—	-1.9
1908	†Det A	119	405	32	87	5	1	0	23	23	7	—	.215	.269	.232	61	-17	10	.941	-13	92	91	3b119	—	-3.2
Total	9	1049	3854	481	972	133	39	15	380	203	52	—	.252	.299	.319	86	-63	159	.931	-30	94	86	3b983,S35,2b28	—	-7.6
COUGHTRY, MARLAN	James Marlan; B9.11.1934 Hollywood CA; BL/TR/6´1´´/170; d9.2; Col Long Beach (CA) City																								
1960	Bos A	15	19	3	3	0	0	0	0	5-0	0	8	.158	.333	.158	36	-1	0-0	.909	-1	95	22	2b13/3	0	-0.2
1962	LA A	11	22	0	4	0	0	0	2	0-0	0	6	.182	.182	.182	-2	-3	0-0	.867	3	136	142	3b5,2b2	0	-0.1
	KC A	6	11	1	2	0	0	0	1	4-0	0	3	.182	.400	.182	60	0	0-0	.917	1	179	174	3b3	0	0.1
	Cle A	3	2	1	1	0	0	0	1	1-0	0	1	.500	.667	.500	226	1	0-0	ø	0	—	—	/H	0	0.1
	Year	20	35	2	7	0	0	0	4	5-0	0	10	.200	.300	.200	38	-3	0-0	.889	4	155	156	3b8,2b2	0	0.1
Total	2	35	54	5	10	0	0	0	4	10-0	0	18	.185	.313	.185	37	-3	0-0	.915	3	108	81	2b15,3b9	0	-0.1
COULSON, BOB	Robert Jackson; B6.17.1887 Courtney PA; D9.11.1953 Washington PA; BR/TR/5´10.5´´/175; d8.4; Col Penn St.																								
1908	Cin N	8	18	3	6	1	1	0	1	3	0	—	.333	.429	.500	202	2	0	1.000	1	126	0	O6(4/1/1)	—	0.3
1910	Bro N	25	89	14	22	3	4	1	13	6	1	14	.247	.302	.404	109	0	9	.922	0	101	111	O25R	—	-0.1
1911	Bro N	146	521	52	122	23	7	0	50	42	8	78	.234	.301	.305	73	-20	32	.968	0	101	102	O145(0/2/144)	—	-2.7
1914	Pit F	18	64	7	13	1	0	0	3	7	0	10	.203	.282	.219	38	-7	2	.931	-1	97	39	O18(11/0/7)	—	-0.9
Total	4	197	692	76	163	28	12	1	67	58	9	102	.236	.303	.315	77	-25	43	.960	-0	101	95	O194(15/3/177)	—	-3.4
COULTER, CHIP	Thomas Lee; B6.5.1945 Steubenville OH; BB/TR/5´10´´/170; d9.18																								
1969	StL N	6	19	3	6	1	1	0	4	2-0	0	6	.316	.381	.474	137	1	0-1	.960	-1	100	146	2b6	0	0.0
COUNSELL, CRAIG	Craig John; B8.21.1970 South Bend IN; BL/TR/6´0´´/(170–185); [ColN92 11/319]; d9.17; Col Notre Dame																								
1995	Col N	3	1	0	0	0	0	0	0	1-0	0	0	.000	.500	.000	36	0	0-0	1.000	-0	60	275	S3	0	0.0
1997	Col N	1	0	0	0	0	0	0	0	0-0	0	0	ø	ø	ø	ø	0	0-0	ø	0	—	—	/R	0	0.0
	†Fla N	51	164	20	49	9	2	1	16	18-2	3	17	.299	.376	.396	108	3	1-1	.989	13	107	121	2b51	0	1.7
	Year	52	164	20	49	9	2	1	16	18-2	3	17	.299	.376	.396	107	2	1-1	.989	13	107	121	2b51	0	1.7
1998	Fla N	107	335	43	84	19	5	4	40	51-7	4	47	.251	.355	.373	98	1	3-0	.991	5	104	94	2b104	55	1.1
1999	Fla N	37	66	4	10	1	0	0	2	5-0	0	10	.152	.211	.167	-3	-11	0-0	.980	-2	98	56	2b12	0	-1.1
	LA N	50	108	20	28	6	0	0	9	9-0	0	14	.259	.311	.315	63	-6	1-0	.993	3	114	79	2b38,S2	0	-0.1
	Year	87	174	24	38	7	0	0	11	14-0	0	24	.218	.274	.259	38	-17	1-0	.989	2	110	73	2b50,S2	0	-1.2
2000	Ari N	67	152	23	48	8	1	2	11	20-0	2	18	.316	.400	.421	105	2	3-3	.974	2	100	122	2b25,3b23,S6	0	0.5
2001	†Ari N	141	458	76	126	22	3	4	38	61-3	2	76	.275	.359	.362	83	-10	6-8	.975	14	90	121	S58,2b55,3b38,1b2	0	0.8
2002	Ari N	112	436	63	123	22	1	2	51	45-3	1	52	.282	.348	.351	78	-12	7-5	.974	16	109	84	3b94,S22,2b13	52	0.5
2003	Ari N	89	303	40	71	6	3	3	21	41-0	2	32	.234	.328	.304	62	-17	11-4	.986	11	110	104	3b57,S26,2b10,1b2	61	-0.3
2004	Mil N	140	473	59	114	19	5	2	23	59-9	5	88	.241	.330	.315	68	-22	17-4	.983	-10	96	91	S129/3	0	-1.9
2005	Ari N	150	578	85	148	34	4	9	42	78-4	8	69	.256	.350	.375	87	-9	26-7	.990	22	113	100	2b143/S	0	2.3
2006	Ari N	105	372	56	95	14	4	4	30	31-0	9	47	.255	.327	.347	69	-17	15-8	.979	32	127	143	S88,3b7,2b2	38	2.1
Total	11	1053	3446	489	896	160	28	31	283	419-28	36	470	.260	.344	.350	79	-98	90-40	.990	106	108	103	2b453,S335,3b220,1b4	206	5.6

YEAR	TM LG	G	AB	R	H	2B	3B	HR	RBI	BB-IB	HP	SO	AVG	OBP	SLG	AOPS	ABR	SB-CS	FA	FR	RNG	THR	GAMES AT POSITION	DL	BFW
COURTNEY, CLINT	Clinton Dawson "Scrap Iron"; B3.16.1927 Hall Summit LA; D6.16.1975 Rochester NY; BL/TR/5´8˝/180; d9.29; C1																								
1951	NY A	1	2	0	0	0	0	0	0	0	1	1	.000	.333	.000	-5	0	0-0	.800	-0	*0*	*511*	/C	0	0.0
1952	StL A	119	413	38	118	24	3	5	50	39	1	26	.286	.349	.395	104	2	0-2	**.996**	1	*97*	***113***	C113	0	0.9
1953	StL A	106	355	28	89	12	2	4	19	25	1	20	.251	.302	.330	69	-16	0-1	.980	-7	*91*	*126*	C103	0	-1.9
1954	Bal A	122	397	25	107	18	3	4	37	30	3	7	.270	.323	.360	95	-4	2-1	.990	-5	*82*	***125***	C111	0	-0.3
1955	Chi A	19	37	7	14	3	0	1	10	7-2	0	0	.378	.467	.541	168	4	0-0	1.000	0	*113*	*54*	C17	0	0.5
	Was A	75	238	26	71	8	4	2	30	19-4	1	9	.298	.349	.391	105	1	0-0	.983	-9	*78*	*128*	C67	0	-0.5
	Year	94	275	33	85	11	4	3	40	26-6	1	9	.309	.366	.411	114	5	0-0	.985	-9	*83*	*117*	C84	0	0.0
1956	Was A	101	283	31	85	20	3	5	44	20-4	9	10	.300	.362	.445	113	5	0-5	.979	-11	*75*	*134*	C76	0	-0.4
1957	Was A	91	232	23	62	14	1	6	27	16-5	12	11	.267	.346	.414	108	3	0-0	.994	-1	78	157	C59	0	0.5
1958	Was A	134	450	46	113	18	0	8	62	48-3	9	23	.251	.332	.344	89	-5	1-5	.991	-4	69	106	C128	0	-0.5
1959	Was A	72	189	19	44	4	1	2	18	20-1	1	19	.233	.308	.296	68	-8	0-1	.987	-12	55	19	C53	30	-1.9
1960	Bal A	83	154	14	35	3	0	1	12	30-3	8	14	.227	.374	.266	79	-2	0-1	.975	2	66	138	C58	0	0.1
1961	KC A	1	1	0	0	0	0	0	0	0-0	0	0	.000	.000	.000	-98	0	0-0	ø	0	—	—	/H	0	0.0
	Bal A	22	45	3	12	2	0	0	4	10-0	0	3	.267	.400	.311	96	0	0-0	1.000	1	116	79	C16	0	0.2
	Year	23	46	3	12	2	0	0	4	10-0	0	3	.261	.393	.304	92	0	0-0	1.000	1	116	79	C16	0	0.2
Total	11	946	2796	260	750	126	17	38	313	264-22	46	143	.268	.339	.366	94	-20	3-16	.987	-46	*80*	*116*	C802	30	-3.3
COURTNEY, ERNIE	Edward Ernest; B1.20.1875 Des Moines IA; D2.29.1920 Buffalo NY; BL/TR/5´8˝/168; d4.17; OF(40/1/6)																								
1902	Bos N	48	165	23	36	3	0	0	17	13	4	—	.218	.291	.236	62	-7	3	.974	-0	92	0	O39(36/1/3),S3	—	-1.0
	Bal A	1	4	3	2	0	1	0	1	1	0	—	.500	.600	1.000	324	1	0	1.000	0	66	0	/3	—	0.1
1903	NY A	25	79	7	21	3	3	1	8	7	2	—	.266	.341	.418	119	2	1	.916	1	116	122	S19,2b4/1	—	0.3
	Det A	23	74	7	17	0	0	0	6	5	3	—	.230	.305	.230	64	-3	1	.938	-2	59	80	3b13,S9	—	-0.5
	Year	48	153	14	38	3	3	1	14	12	5	—	.248	.324	.327	94	-1	2	.921	-1	116	94	S28,3b13,2b4/1	—	-0.2
1905	Phi N	**155**	601	77	165	14	7	2	77	47	7	—	.275	.334	.331	102	2	17	.923	-20	83	73	3b155	—	-1.4
1906	Phi N	116	398	53	94	12	2	0	42	45	1	—	.236	.315	.276	84	-6	6	.923	-9	90	86	3b96,1b13,O3R/S	—	-1.5
1907	Phi N	130	440	42	107	17	4	2	43	55	6	—	.243	.335	.314	105	5	6	.907	-5	93	118	3b75,1b48,O4L,2b2,S2	—	0.1
1908	Phi N	60	160	14	29	3	0	0	6	15	2	—	.181	.260	.200	46	-9	1	.915	-3	96	46	3b22,1b13,2b5,S2	—	-1.4
Total	6	558	1921	226	471	52	17	5	200	188	25	—	.245	.321	.298	91	-15	35	.920	-40	87	84	3b362,1b75,O46L,S36,2b11	—	-5.3
COUSINEAU, DEE	Edward Thomas; B12.16.1898 Watertown MA; D7.14.1951 Watertown MA; BR/TR/6´0˝/170; d10.6; Col Fordham																								
1923	Bos N	1	2	1	2	0	0	0	2	0	0	0	1.000	1.000	1.000	447	1	0-0	ø	0	*0*	*0*	/C	—	0.1
1924	Bos N	3	2	0	0	0	0	0	0	0	0	0	.000	.000	.000	-99	-1	0-0	.500	-0	*0*	*0*	C3	—	-0.1
1925	Bos N	1	0	0	0	0	0	0	0	0	0	0	ø	ø	ø	ø	0	0-0	ø	0	*0*	*0*	/C	—	0.0
Total	3	5	4	1	2	0	0	0	2	0	0	0	.500	.500	.500	174	0	0-0	.500	-0	*0*	*0*	C5	—	0.0
COVENEY, JACK	John Patrick; B6.10.1880 S.Natick MA; D3.28.1961 Wayland MA; BR/TR/5´9˝/175; d9.19; Col St. Anselm																								
1903	StL N	4	14	0	2	0	0	0	0	0	0	—	.143	.143	.143	-19	-2	0	.923	0	*94*	*172*	C4	—	-0.2
COVINGTON, SAM	Clarence Calvert; B11.18.1894 Denison TX; D1.4.1963 Denison TX; BL/TR/6´1˝/190; d8.25; Mil 1918; b–Tex																								
1913	StL A	20	60	3	9	0	1	0	4	4	0	6	.150	.203	.183	14	-7	3	.994	3	184	83	1b16	—	-0.4
1917	Bos N	17	66	8	13	2	0	1	10	5	1	5	.197	.264	.273	69	-2	1	.994	0	99	166	1b17	—	-0.3
1918	Bos N	3	3	0	1	0	0	0	0	0	0	0	.333	.333	.333	108	0	0	ø	0	—	—	/H	—	0.0
Total	3	40	129	11	23	2	1	1	14	9	1	11	.178	.237	.233	43	-9	4	.994	4	139	127	1b33	—	-0.7
COVINGTON, WES	John Wesley; B3.27.1932 Laurinburg NC; BL/TR/6´1˝/(205–211); d4.19																								
1956	Mil N	75	138	17	39	4	0	2	16	16-3	1	20	.283	.361	.355	100	0	1-0	.979	-1	85	115	O35(34/0/1)	0	-0.2
1957	†Mil N	96	328	51	93	4	8	21	65	29-7	2	44	.284	.339	.537	143	17	4-1	.981	-1	87	149	O89L	0	1.1
1958	†Mil N	90	294	43	97	12	1	24	74	20-7	5	35	.330	.380	.622	175	30	0-0	.953	-4	87	58	O82L	0	2.1
1959	Mil N	103	373	38	104	17	3	7	45	26-8	3	41	.279	.329	.397	101	0	0-1	.962	-7	80	78	O94L	0	-1.4
1960	Mil N	95	281	25	70	16	1	10	35	15-1	1	37	.249	.288	.420	99	-2	1-2	.964	-6	86	37	O72L	0	-1.2
1961	Mil N	9	21	3	4	1	0	0	0	2-0	0	4	.190	.261	.238	36	-2	0-0	1.000	-1	38	0	O5L	0	-0.3
	Chi A	22	59	5	17	1	0	4	15	4-1	0	5	.288	.333	.508	123	2	0-0	.900	-1	64	204	O14(11/0/3)	0	0.0
	KC A	17	44	3	7	0	0	1	6	4-0	2	7	.159	.260	.227	31	-4	0-0	1.000	-2	69	0	O12(11/0/1)	0	-0.7
	Year	39	103	8	24	1	0	5	21	8-1	2	12	.233	.301	.388	83	-3	0-0	.941	-3	75	115	O26(22/0/4)	0	-0.7
	Phi N	57	165	23	50	9	0	7	26	15-1	0	17	.303	.355	.485	124	6	0-0	.950	-3	75	115	O45(10/0/36)	0	0.0
1962	Phi N	116	304	36	86	12	1	9	44	19-1	2	44	.283	.324	.418	102	0	0-0	.944	-4	84	65	O88L	0	-0.8
1963	Phi N	119	353	46	107	24	1	17	64	26-7	2	56	.303	.354	.521	150	23	1-0	.937	-5	84	81	O101L	0	1.4
1964	Phi N	129	339	37	95	18	0	13	58	38-6	3	50	.280	.355	.448	127	13	0-0	.972	-5	78	84	O99(97/1/2)	0	0.5
1965	Phi N	101	235	27	58	10	1	15	45	26-8	1	47	.247	.322	.489	128	8	0-0	.968	0	102	71	O64L	0	0.6
1966	Chi N	9	11	0	1	0	0	0	0	1-1	0	2	.091	.167	.091	-26	-2	0-0	1.000	0	115	0	/lf	0	-0.2
	†LA N	37	33	1	4	0	1	1	6	6-0	2	5	.121	.293	.273	63	-2	0-0	1.000	-0	36	0	O2L	0	-0.2
	Year	46	44	1	5	0	1	1	6	7-1	2	7	.114	.264	.227	41	-4	0-0	1.000	-0	66	0	O3L	0	-0.4
Total	11	1075	2978	355	832	128	17	131	499	247-51	24	414	.279	.337	.466	123	87	7-4	.961	-41	84	84	O803(761/1/43)	0	0.7
COWAN, BILLY	Billy Rolland; B8.28.1938 Calhoun City MS; BR/TR/6´0˝/170; d9.9; Col Utah																								
1963	Chi N	14	36	1	9	1	1	1	2	0-0	0	11	.250	.250	.417	84	-1	0-1	.917	-1	58	183	O10(1/7/2)	0	-0.3
1964	Chi N	139	497	52	120	16	4	19	50	18-5	1	128	.241	.268	.404	83	-13	12-3	.968	-10	99	23	O134C	0	-2.7
1965	NY N	82	156	16	28	8	2	3	9	4-1	1	45	.179	.205	.314	45	-12	3-2	1.000	-2	90	87	O61(2/59/0),2b2/S	0	-1.6
	Mil N	19	27	4	5	1	0	0	0	0-0	0	9	.185	.185	.222	14	-3	0-0	1.000	-1	81	0	O10(7/3/0)	0	-0.4
	Year	101	183	20	33	9	2	3	9	4-1	1	54	.180	.202	.301	41	-15	3-2	1.000	-2	89	76	O71(9/62/0),2b2/S	0	-2.0
1967	Phi N	34	59	11	9	0	0	3	6	4-0	0	14	.153	.203	.305	44	-5	1-0	1.000	-2	80	0	O20(16/0/4)/23	0	-0.8
1969	NY A	32	48	5	8	0	0	1	3	3-0	0	9	.167	.216	.229	25	-5	0-0	1.000	-0	82	140	O14(8/4/2)	0	-0.6
	Cal A	28	56	10	17	1	0	4	10	3-1	1	9	.304	.350	.536	151	3	0-0	1.000	1	95	482	O13(3/2/8),1b6	0	0.4
	Year	60	104	15	25	1	0	5	13	6-1	1	18	.240	.288	.394	93	-2	0-0	1.000	1	88	301	O27(11/6/10),1b6	0	-0.2
1970	Cal A	68	134	20	37	9	1	5	25	11-2	1	29	.276	.336	.470	124	4	0-1	.929	-3	79	0	O27(3/1/23),1b14,3b2	0	-0.1
1971	Cal A	74	174	12	48	8	0	4	20	7-1	0	41	.276	.304	.391	103	0	1-1	1.000	-0	108	47	O40(38/0/2),1b5	0	-0.3
1972	Cal A	3	3	0	0	0	0	0	0	0-0	0	2	.000	.000	.000	-99	-1	0-0	ø	0	—	—	/H	0	-0.1
Total	8	493	1190	131	281	44	8	40	125	50-10	4	297	.236	.269	.387	83	-33	17-8	.977	-16	94	56	O329(78/210/41),1b25,3b3,2b3/S	0	-6.5
COWENS, AL	Alfred Edward; B10.25.1951 Los Angeles CA; D3.11.2002 Downey CA; BR/TR/6´2˝/(197–205); [KCA69 75/1026]; d4.6																								
1974	KC A	110	269	28	65	7	1	1	25	23-0	1	38	.242	.303	.286	67	-11	5-0	.988	2	89	219	O102(6/24/75);3b2,D4	0	-1.2
1975	KC A	120	328	44	91	13	8	4	42	28-1	4	36	.277	.340	.402	107	2	12-7	.978	-0	107	55	O113(22/35/65),D2	0	-0.2
1976	†KC A	152	581	71	154	23	6	3	59	26-0	3	50	.265	.298	.341	87	-11	23-16	.986	3	101	115	O148(0/12/142)/D	0	-1.8
1977	†KC A	**162**	606	98	189	32	14	23	112	41-4	8	64	.312	.361	.525	137	29	16-12	.982	0	96	127	O159(0/26/141)/D	0	2.1
1978	†KC A	132	485	63	133	24	8	5	63	31-3	6	54	.274	.319	.388	97	-3	14-6	.990	3	99	106	O127(0/16/119),3b5,D2	25	-0.5
1979	KC A	136	516	69	152	18	7	9	73	40-4	3	44	.295	.345	.409	101	0	10-8	.986	-7	99	29	O134(0/1/134)/D	21	-1.4
1980	Cal A	34	119	11	27	5	0	1	17	12-1	1	21	.227	.303	.294	65	-5	1-2	1.000	-0	95	133	O30(3/10/19)/D	0	-0.7
	Det A	108	403	58	113	15	3	5	42	37-4	1	40	.280	.339	.370	93	-4	5-6	.986	-3	92	97	O107R/D	0	-1.4
	Year	142	522	69	140	20	3	6	59	49-5	2	61	.268	.331	.352	87	-9	6-8	.989	-4	93	105	O137(3/10/126),D2	0	-2.1
1981	Det A	85	253	27	66	11	4	1	18	22-3	1	36	.261	.319	.348	90	-3	3-3	.994	-4	93	68	O83(0/65/18)	0	-0.9
1982	Sea A	146	560	72	151	39	8	20	78	46-3	1	81	.270	.325	.475	113	9	11-7	.987	-2	94	133	O145R/D	0	-0.1
1983	Sea A	110	356	39	73	19	2	7	35	23-0	2	38	.205	.255	.329	58	-21	10-2	.985	2	101	157	O70(2/4/65),D34	29	-2.2
1984	Sea A	139	524	60	145	34	2	15	78	27-2	2	83	.277	.312	.435	106	3	9-5	.987	-4	92	108	O130(0/2/130),D7	0	-0.7
1985	Sea A	122	452	59	120	32	5	14	69	30-3	1	56	.265	.310	.451	105	2	0-0	.967	-1	92	140	O110R,D5	0	-0.5
1986	Sea A	28	82	5	15	4	0	0	6	3-0	0	18	.183	.209	.232	20	-9	1-0	.971	-0	87	161	O19(1/0/18)/D	0	-1.0
Total	13	1584	5534	704	1494	276	68	108	717	389-28	34	659	.270	.319	.403	98	-22	120-74	.985	-12	96	111	O1477(34/195/1288),D61,3b7	75	-10.5
COX, STEVE	Charles Steven; B10.31.1974 Delano CA; BL/TL/6´4˝/222; [OakA92 5/144]; d9.19																								
1999	TB A	6	19	0	4	1	0	0	0	0-0	0	2	.211	.211	.263	20	-2	0-0	1.000	-1	52	157	1b4,O2L	0	-0.3
2000	TB A	116	318	44	90	19	1	11	35	45-2	5	47	.283	.379	.453	111	7	1-2	.948	-1	107	94	O56(26/0/30),1b24,D17	0	0.1
2001	TB A	108	342	37	88	22	0	12	51	24-0	10	75	.257	.323	.427	97	-1	2-2	.998	0	96	101	1b78,O8(6/0/2),D4	17	-0.8
2002	TB A	148	560	65	142	30	1	16	72	60-5	7	116	.254	.330	.396	95	-3	5-0	.993	5	**119**	101	1b110,D35	0	-0.9
Total	4	378	1239	146	324	72	2	39	158	129-7	22	240	.262	.340	.417	99	1	8-4	.994	3	106	99	1b216,O66(34/0/32),D56	17	-1.9

YEAR	TM LG	G	AB	R	H	2B	3B	HR	RBI	BB-IB	HP	SO	AVG	OBP	SLG	AOPS	ABR	SB-CS	FA	FR	RNG	THR	GAMES AT POSITION	DL	BFW
COX, DICK	Elmer Joseph; B9.30.1895 Pasadena CA; D6.1.1966 Morro Bay CA; BR/TR/5´7.5˝/158; d4.16																								
1925	Bro N	122	434	68	143	23	10	7	64	37	0	29	.329	.382	.477	121	14	4-3	.968	-3	93	96	O111(3/0/108)	—	0.2
1926	Bro N	124	398	53	118	17	4	1	45	46	4	20	.296	.375	.367	102	3	6	.964	-3	95	86	O117(0/1/116)	—	-0.8
Total	2	246	832	121	261	40	14	8	109	83	4	49	.314	.379	.424	112	17	10-3	.966	-6	94	91	O228(3/1/224)	—	-0.6
COX, FRANK	Francis Bernard "Runt"; B8.29.1857 Waltham MA; D6.24.1928 Hartford CT; 5´6˝/?; d8.13																								
1884	Det N	27	102	6	13	3	1	0	4	2	—	36	.127	.144	.176	0	-11	—	.812	-3	99	106	S27	—	-1.2
COX, JIM	James Charles; B5.28.1950 Bloomington IL; BR/TR/5´11˝/(175–180); [MonN72*S1/2]; d7.19; Col Iowa																								
1973	Mon N	9	15	1	2	1	0	0	0	1-0	0	4	.133	.188	.200	7	-2	0-0	.950	-2	75	33	2b7	0	-0.4
1974	Mon N	77	236	29	52	9	1	2	26	23-2	1	36	.220	.288	.292	60	-12	2-3	.968	5	104	106	2b72	27	-0.4
1975	Mon N	11	27	1	7	1	0	1	5	1-1	0	2	.259	.276	.407	86	-1	1-0	1.000	-1	103	145	2b8	0	-0.1
1976	Mon N	13	29	2	5	0	1	0	2	2-0	0	2	.172	.226	.241	31	-3	0-0	.958	-1	86	96	2b11	0	-0.3
Total	4	110	307	33	66	11	2	3	33	27-3	1	44	.215	.276	.293	58	-18	3-3	.969	1	101	104	2b98	27	-1.2
COX, DARRON	James Darron; B11.21.1967 Oklahoma City OK; BR/TR/6´1˝/205; [CinN89 5/134]; d4.6; Col Oklahoma																								
1999	Mon N	15	25	2	6	1	0	1	2	0-0	2	5	.240	.296	.400	77	-1	0-0	.963	3	227	55	C14	99	0.2
COX, JEFF	Jeffrey Lindon; B11.9.1955 Los Angeles CA; BR/TR/5´11˝/170; d7.1; C8																								
1980	Oak A	59	169	20	36	3	0	0	9	14-0	0	23	.213	.273	.231	42	-13	8-5	.979	-18	86	72	2b58	0	-2.8
1981	Oak A	2	0	0	0	0	0	0	0	0-0	0	0	ø	ø	ø	ø	0	0-0	1.000	0	264	0	/2	0	0.0
Total	2	61	169	20	36	3	0	0	9	14-0	0	23	.213	.273	.231	42	-13	8-5	.979	-17	86	72	2b59	0	-2.8
COX, LARRY	Larry Eugene; B9.11.1947 Bluffton OH; D2.17.1990 Bellefontaine OH; BR/TR/5´11˝/(178–190); d4.18; C2																								
1973	Phi N	1	0	0	0	0	0	0	0	0-0	0	0	ø	ø	ø	ø	0	0-0	1.000	0	0	0	/C	0	0.0
1974	Phi N	30	53	5	9	2	0	0	4	4-0	1	9	.170	.241	.208	25	-5	0-0	.990	-3	76	19	C29	28	-0.8
1975	Phi N	11	5	0	1	0	0	0	1	1-0	0	0	.200	.286	.200	48	0	1-0	1.000	-1	138	0	C10	0	-0.1
1977	Sea A	35	93	6	23	6	0	2	6	10-0	0	12	.247	.320	.376	90	-1	1-1	.970	-4	72	158	C35	13	-0.4
1978	Chi N	59	121	10	34	5	0	2	18	12-0	0	16	.281	.346	.372	90	-1	0-0	.967	-1	110	108	C58	39	-0.1
1979	Sea A	100	293	32	63	11	3	4	36	22-0	0	39	.215	.266	.314	56	-19	2-1	.981	-7	68	119	C99	0	-2.2
1980	Sea A	105	243	18	49	6	2	4	20	19-0	0	36	.202	.260	.292	50	-17	1-2	**.993**	8	102	108	C104	0	-0.7
1981	Tex A	5	13	0	3	1	0	0	0	0-0	0	4	.231	.231	.308	57	-1	0-0	1.000	1	43	0	C5	0	0.0
1982	Chi N	2	4	1	0	0	0	0	0	2-1	0	1	.000	.333	.000	1	0	0-0	1.000	1	48	306	C2	0	0.0
Total	9	348	825	72	182	31	5	12	85	70-1	1	117	.221	.280	.314	61	-44	5-4	.983	-7	86	110	C343	80	-4.3
COX, BOBBY	Robert Joseph; B5.21.1941 Tulsa OK; BR/TR/5´11˝/(180–190); d4.14; M25/C1																								
1968	NY A	135	437	33	100	15	1	7	41	41-7	5	85	.229	.300	.316	90	-5	3-2	.957	-5	105	97	3b132	0	-1.2
1969	NY A	85	191	17	41	7	1	2	17	34-7	1	41	.215	.332	.293	80	-4	0-1	.935	6	114	149	3b56,2b6	0	0.2
Total	2	220	628	50	141	22	2	9	58	75-14	6	126	.225	.310	.309	87	-9	3-3	.950	1	107	111	3b188,2b6	0	-1.0
COX, BILLY	William Richard; B8.29.1919 Newport PA; D3.30.1978 Harrisburg PA; BR/TR/5´10˝/150; d9.20; Mil 1942–45																								
1941	Pit N	10	37	4	10	3	1	0	2	3	0	2	.270	.325	.405	105	0	1	.943	1	118	142	S10	0	0.2
1946	Pit N	121	411	32	119	22	6	2	36	26	1	15	.290	.333	.387	101	0	4	.935	-13	94	83	S114	0	-0.7
1947	Pit N	132	529	75	145	30	7	15	54	29	1	28	.274	.313	.442	96	-6	5	.968	-11	99	78	S129	0	-0.8
1948	Bro N	88	237	36	59	13	2	3	15	38	0	19	.249	.353	.359	90	-2	3	.958	-5	93	75	3b70,S6/2	0	-0.7
1949	†Bro N	100	390	48	91	18	2	8	40	30	1	18	.233	.290	.351	68	-18	5	.964	7	100	145	3b100	0	-1.2
1950	Bro N	119	451	62	116	17	2	8	44	35	0	24	.257	.311	.357	74	-18	6	**.957**	12	**108**	**165**	3b107,2b13,S9	0	-0.5
1951	Bro N	142	455	62	127	25	4	9	51	37	2	30	.279	.336	.411	98	-2	5-5	.967	-5	95	87	3b139/S	0	-0.8
1952	†Bro N	116	455	56	118	12	3	6	34	25	2	32	.259	.301	.338	76	-16	10-12	.970	-7	88	175	3b100,S10,2b9	0	-2.5
1953	†Bro N	100	327	44	95	18	1	10	44	37	0	21	.291	.363	.443	106	4	2-2	.974	-2	90	123	3b89,S6/2	0	0.1
1954	Bro N	77	226	26	53	9	2	2	17	21	0	13	.235	.297	.319	59	-14	0-0	.961	1	98	85	3b58,2b11,S8	0	-1.2
1955	Bal A	53	194	25	41	7	2	3	14	17-0	0	16	.211	.275	.314	63	-11	1-2	.969	-5	100	71	3b37,2b18,S6	0	-1.7
Total	11	1058	3712	470	974	174	32	66	351	298-0	7	218	.262	.318	.380	85	-83	42-21	.965	-27	96	124	3b700,S299,2b53	0	-9.8
COX, TED	William Ted; B1.24.1955 Oklahoma City OK; BR/TR/6´3˝/(190–205); [BosA73 1/17]; d9.18																								
1977	Bos A	13	58	11	21	3	1	1	6	3-0	0	6	.362	.393	.500	127	2	0-0	ø	0	0	0	D13	0	0.2
1978	Cle A	82	227	14	53	7	0	1	19	16-1	1	30	.233	.286	.278	60	-12	0-1	.980	-4	78	156	O38(33/0/5),3b20,D12,1b7/S	0	-2.0
1979	Cle A	78	189	17	40	6	0	4	22	14-1	2	27	.212	.272	.307	56	-12	3-4	.964	-1	95	142	3b52,O16L,2b4/D	0	-1.5
1980	Sea A	83	247	17	60	9	0	2	23	19-3	0	25	.243	.295	.304	64	-12	0-0	.945	-4	95	135	3b80	0	-1.8
1981	Tor A	16	50	6	15	4	0	2	9	5-0	0	10	.300	.364	.500	138	3	0-1	.897	-4	75	40	3b14/1D	0	-0.2
Total	5	272	771	65	189	29	1	10	79	57-5	3	98	.245	.298	.324	71	-31	3-6	.947	-14	91	120	3b166,O54(49/0/5),D27,1b8,2b4/S	0	-5.3
COYNE, TOOTS	Martin Albert; B10.20.1894 St.Louis MO; D9.18.1939 St.Louis MO; TR; d9.28																								
1914	Phi A	1	2	0	0	0	0	0	0	0	0	2	.000	.000	.000	-99	-1	0	1.000	-0	112	0	/3	—	-0.1
CRABTREE, ESTEL	Estel Crayton "Crabby"; B8.19.1903 Crabtree OH; D1.4.1967 Logan OH; BL/TR/6´0˝/168; d4.18; C2																								
1929	Cin N	1	1	0	0	0	0	0	0	0	0	0	.000	.000	.000	-99	0	0	ø	0	—	—	/H	—	0.0
1931	Cin N	117	443	70	119	12	12	4	37	23	3	33	.269	.309	.377	89	-10	3	.974	10	107	172	O101(9/16/76),3b4,1b2	—	-0.5
1932	Cin N	108	402	38	110	14	9	2	35	23	2	26	.274	.316	.368	86	-9	2	.990	5	108	103	O95(14/73/9)	—	-0.7
1933	StL N	23	34	6	9	3	0	0	3	2	0	3	.265	.306	.353	83	-1	1	.947	0	128	0	O7(0/4/3)	—	-0.1
1941	StL N	77	167	27	57	6	3	5	28	26	3	24	.341	.439	.503	154	13	1	1.000	-2	91	71	O50(17/16/19)/3	0	1.0
1942	StL N	10	9	1	3	2	0	0	2	1	0	3	.333	.400	.556	166	1	0	ø	-0	—	—	/H	0	0.1
1943	Cin N	95	254	25	70	12	0	2	26	25	2	17	.276	.345	.346	101	1	1	.939	-6	89	66	O65(2/44/17)	0	-0.8
1944	Cin N	58	98	7	28	4	1	0	11	13	0	3	.286	.369	.347	106	1	0	1.000	-1	80	86	O19(15/3/1),1b2	0	-0.1
Total	8	489	1408	174	396	53	25	13	142	113	10	109	.281	.339	.382	100	-4	8	.976	6	101	111	O337(57/156/125),3b5,1b4	0	-1.1
CRADLE, RICKEY	Rickey Nelson; B6.20.1973 Norfolk VA; BR/TR/6´2˝/180; [TorA91 5/146]; d7.1																								
1998	Sea A	5	7	0	1	0	0	0	2	1-0	0	5	.143	.250	.143	6	-1	1-0	1.000	-0	57	0	O4(1/2/1)	27	-0.1
CRAFT, HARRY	Harry Francis "Wildfire"; B4.19.1915 Ellisville MS; D8.3.1995 Conroe TX; BR/TR/6´1˝/185; d9.19; M7/C5; Col Mississippi College																								
1937	Cin N	10	42	7	13	2	1	0	4	1	0	3	.310	.326	.405	102	0	0	1.000	0	94	131	O10C	—	0.0
1938	Cin N	**151**	612	70	165	28	9	15	83	29	2	46	.270	.305	.418	100	-4	3	.983	7	110	112	O151C	—	0.0
1939	†Cin N	134	502	58	129	20	7	13	67	27	3	54	.257	.299	.402	86	-12	5	.981	-3	91	122	O134C	—	-1.9
1940	†Cin N	115	422	47	103	18	5	6	48	17	2	46	.244	.277	.353	72	-18	2	**.997**	0	103	76	O109(0/106/3),1b2	—	-2.1
1941	Cin N	119	413	48	103	15	2	10	59	33	2	43	.249	.308	.368	90	-7	4	.983	-2	102	68	O115C	0	-1.2
1942	Cin N	37	113	7	20	2	1	0	6	3	1	11	.177	.205	.212	22	-12	0	.987	2	101	147	O33C	0	-1.2
Total	6	566	2104	237	533	85	25	44	267	110	10	203	.253	.294	.380	85	-53	14	.986	4	102	100	O552(0/549/3),1b2	0	-6.4
CRAIG, ROD	Rodney Paul; B1.12.1958 Los Angeles CA; BB/TR/6´1˝/195; d9.11; Col San Jacinto North (TX) JC																								
1979	Sea A	16	52	9	20	8	1	0	6	1-0	0	5	.385	.396	.577	155	4	1-1	.923	-2	87	0	O15R	0	0.1
1980	Sea A	70	240	30	57	15	1	3	20	17-3	2	35	.237	.293	.346	73	-9	3-6	.987	-5	90	45	O63(3/58/2)	15	-1.6
1982	Cle A	49	65	7	15	2	0	0	1	4-0	0	6	.231	.275	.262	48	-5	3-1	.966	-1	105	0	O22(11/4/7),D4	0	-0.5
1986	Chi A	10	10	3	2	0	0	0	0	2-0	0	2	.200	.333	.200	48	-1	0-0	ø	-0	0	0	O2(1/0/1)	0	-0.1
Total	4	145	367	49	94	25	2	3	27	24-3	2	48	.256	.305	.360	80	-11	7-8	.977	-8	91	32	O102(15/62/26),D4	15	-2.1
CRAMER, DOC	Roger Maxwell "Flit"; B7.22.1905 Beach Haven NJ; D9.9.1990 Manahawkin NJ; BL/TR/6´2˝/185; d9.18; C4																								
1929	Phi A	2	6	0	0	0	0	0	0	0	0	2	.000	.000	.000	-97	-2	0-0	1.000	0	167	0	/lf	—	-0.2
1930	Phi A	30	82	12	19	1	1	0	6	2	0	8	.232	.250	.268	30	-9	0-0	.927	-1	97	85	O21(6/13/2)/S	—	-1.0
1931	†Phi A	65	223	37	58	8	2	2	20	11	2	15	.260	.301	.341	64	-12	2-1	.979	0	97	118	O55(2/47/6)	—	-1.3
1932	Phi A	92	384	73	129	27	6	3	46	17	2	27	.336	.367	.461	109	5	3-1	.976	4	110	98	O86(0/45/42)	—	0.5
1933	Phi A	**152**	661	109	195	27	8	8	75	36	0	24	.295	.331	.396	91	-11	5-4	.971	-0	100	121	O152C	—	-1.4
1934	Phi A	**153**	649	99	202	29	9	6	46	40	2	35	.311	.353	.411	100	-2	1-5	.985	2	101	102	O152C	—	-0.5
1935	Phi A★	**149**	644	96	214	37	4	3	70	37	5	34	.332	.373	.416	105	4	6-7	.975	-1	104	51	O149C	—	-0.2
1936	Bos A	154	643	99	188	31	7	0	41	49	5	20	.292	.347	.362	71	-29	4-6	.975	11	106	149	O154C	—	-2.1
1937	Bos A☆	133	560	90	171	22	11	0	51	35	4	14	.305	.351	.384	82	-17	8-6	.969	2	103	98	O133C	—	-1.7
1938	Bos A★	148	658	116	198	36	8	0	71	51	3	19	.301	.354	.380	80	-20	4-9	.986	6	104	106	O148C/P	—	-1.9

YEAR	TM LG	G	AB	R	H	2B	3B	HR	RBI	BB-IB	HP	SO	AVG	OBP	SLG	AOPS	ABR	SB-CS	FA	FR	RNG	THR	GAMES AT POSITION	DL	BFW
1939	Bos A★	137	589	110	183	30	6	0	56	36	2	17	.311	.352	.382	85	-14	3-3	.984	-5	92	100	O135C	—	-2.1
1940	Bos A☆	150	661	94	**200**	27	12	1	51	36	1	29	.303	.340	.384	84	-17	3-5	.969	-7	91	98	O149(16/96/37)	—	-2.9
1941	Was A	154	660	93	180	25	6	2	66	37	6	15	.273	.317	.338	77	-24	4-1	.984	-11	90	71	O152C	0	-3.8
1942	Det A	151	630	71	166	26	4	0	43	43	3	18	.263	.314	.317	72	-24	4-4	.981	-4	90	139	O150C	0	-3.3
1943	Det A	140	606	79	182	18	4	1	43	31	1	13	.300	.335	.348	93	-7	4-3	.989	-5	95	86	O138C	0	-1.7
1944	Det A	143	578	69	169	20	9	2	42	37	2	21	.292	.337	.369	96	-4	6-5	.980	-12	86	95	O141C	0	-2.1
1945	†Det A	141	541	62	149	22	8	6	58	36	3	21	.275	.324	.379	97	-3	2-9	**.991**	-15	84	59	O140C	0	-2.7
1946	Det A	68	204	26	60	8	2	1	26	15	0	8	.294	.342	.368	93	-2	3-0	1.000	-4	83	73	O50C	0	-0.7
1947	Det A	73	157	21	42	2	2	2	30	20	0	5	.268	.350	.344	91	-2	0-4	.965	-1	93	149	O35C	0	-0.5
1948	Det A	4	4	1	0	0	0	0	1	3	0	0	.000	.429	.000	19	0	0-0	1.000	-0	69	0	/cf	0	0.0
Total	20	2239	9140	1357	2705	396	109	37	842	572	41	345	.296	.340	.375	87	-190	62-73	.979	-40	96	99	O2142(25/2031/87)/PS	0	-29.6
CRAMER, DICK	William B.; B Brooklyn NY; D8.11.1885 Camden NJ; d5.12																								
1883	NY N	2	6	0	0	0	0	0	0	1	—	5	.000	.143	.000	-52	-1	—	ø	-0	0	0	O2(0/1/1)	—	-0.1
CRANDALL, DEL	Delmar Wesley; B3.5.1930 Ontario CA; BR/TR/6´1˝/(185–205); d6.17; Mil 1951–52; M6/C1																								
1949	Bos N	67	228	21	60	10	1	4	34	9	0	18	.263	.291	.368	80	-8	2	.982	4	*99*	*117*	C63	0	0.0
1950	Bos N	79	255	21	56	11	0	4	37	13	0	24	.220	.257	.310	52	-19	0	.967	0	*82*	*132*	C75/1	0	-1.5
1953	Mil N✳	116	382	55	104	13	1	15	51	33	0	47	.272	.330	.429	102	0	2-1	.986	11	*90*	***140***	C108	0	1.6
1954	Mil N☆	138	463	60	112	18	2	21	64	40	3	56	.242	.305	.425	94	-6	0-3	.989	11	*97*	***117***	C136	0	1.0
1955	Mil N★	133	440	61	104	15	2	26	62	40-11	2	56	.236	.299	.457	103	0	2-1	.985	-2	***126***	*117*	C131	0	0.4
1956	Mil N✳	112	311	37	74	14	2	16	48	35-15	1	30	.238	.313	.450	110	4	1-2	**.996**	5	***147***	*100*	C109	0	1.3
1957	†Mil N	118	383	45	97	11	2	15	46	30-9	1	38	.253	.308	.410	98	-3	1-2	.987	-7	85	108	C102,O9(1/0/9)/1	0	-0.6
1958	†Mil N★	131	427	50	116	23	1	18	63	48-18	4	38	.272	.348	.457	122	14	4-1	**.990**	8	130	111	C124	0	2.8
1959	Mil N★	150	518	65	133	19	2	21	72	46-8	3	48	.257	.318	.423	105	2	5-1	**.994**	9	181	95	C146	0	1.9
1960	Mil N★	142	537	81	158	14	1	19	77	34-6	4	36	.294	.334	.430	118	12	4-6	.988	-8	**167**	68	C141	0	1.0
1961	Mil N	15	30	3	6	3	0	0	1	1-0	0	0	.200	.226	.300	40	-3	0-0	1.000	-1	89	91	C5	56	-0.3
1962	Mil N★	107	350	35	104	12	3	8	45	27-2	2	24	.297	.348	.417	108	4	3-4	**.994**	4	**174**	92	C90,1b5	0	1.1
1963	Mil N	86	259	18	52	4	0	3	28	18-5	0	22	.201	.251	.251	46	-18	1-4	.991	-4	89	103	C75,1b7	0	-2.2
1964	SF N	69	195	12	45	8	1	3	11	22-9	0	21	.231	.309	.328	78	-5	0-3	.993	6	107	80	C65	0	0.3
1965	Pit N	60	140	11	30	2	0	2	10	14-7	1	10	.214	.288	.271	59	-8	1-0	.996	3	207	112	C60	0	-0.2
1966	Cle A	50	108	10	25	2	0	4	8	14-5	0	9	.231	.320	.361	95	-1	0-0	.991	7	105	81	C49	20	0.9
Total	16	1573	5026	585	1276	179	18	179	657	424-95	21	477	.254	.312	.404	97	-35	26-28	.989	47	*128*	*105*	C1479,1b14,O9(1/0/9)	76	7.5
CRANDALL, DOC	James Otis; B10.8.1887 Wadena IN; D8.17.1951 Bell CA; BR/TR/5´10.5˝/180; d4.24; C4; ▲																								
1908	NY N	34	72	8	16	4	0	2	6	4	1	—	.222	.273	.361	97	0	0	.985	-2	85	131	P32/2	—	-0.1
1909	NY N	30	41	4	10	0	1	1	1	1	0	—	.244	.262	.366	93	2	0	.941	2	116	432	P30	—	0.0
1910	NY N	45	73	10	25	2	4	1	13	5	0	7	.342	.385	.521	163	5	0	.984	-2	84	164	P42/S	—	-0.1
1911	†NY N	61	113	12	27	1	4	2	21	8	1	16	.239	.295	.372	83	-4	2	.958	0	110	114	P41,S6,2b3	—	-0.1
1912	†NY N	50	80	9	25	6	2	0	19	6	0	7	.313	.360	.438	114	1	0	.957	-0	101	0	P37,2b2/1	—	0.0
1913	†NY N	31	25	4	7	2	1	0	2	1	0	5	.280	.308	.440	111	0	0	1.000	1	120	0	P24,2b2	—	0.1
	StL N	2	2	0	0	0	0	0	0	0	0	2	.000	.000	.000	-99	-1	0	ø	0	—	—	/H	—	-0.1
	†NY N	15	22	3	8	2	0	0	2	2	0	3	.364	.417	.455	148	3	0	1.000	1	120	0	P11	—	0.0
	Year	48	49	7	15	4	1	0	4	3	0	10	.306	.346	.429	120	1	0	1.000	1	124	0	P35,2b2	—	0.0
1914	StL F	118	278	40	86	16	5	2	41	58	0	32	.309	.429	.424	126	10	3	.926	-13	96	48	2b63,P27/Scf	—	-0.4
1915	StL F	84	141	18	40	2	2	1	19	27	2	15	.284	.406	.348	107	13	4	.958	1	103	105	P51	—	0.0
1916	StL A	16	12	0	1	0	0	0	0	2	0	4	.083	.214	.083	-11	0	0	.000	-0	0	0	P2	—	0.0
1918	Bos N	14	28	1	8	0	0	0	2	4	0	3	.286	.375	.286	107	0	0	1.000	-0	101	302	P5,O3R	—	0.0
Total	10	500	887	109	253	35	19	9	126	118	4	94	.285	.372	.398	114	29	9	.962	-13	99	129	P302,2b71,S8,O4(0/1/2)/1	—	-0.7
CRANE, ED	Edward Nicholas "Cannon-Ball"; B5.27.1862 Boston MA; D9.20.1896 Rochester NY; BR/TR/5´10.5˝/204; d4.17; ▲																								
1884	Bos U	101	428	83	122	23	6	12	—	14	—	—	.285	.308	.451	129	2	—	.826	-6	127	125	O57(18/0/39),C42,1b5,P4	—	-0.3
1885	Pro N	1	2	0	0	0	0	0	0	1	—	1	.000	.333	.000	15	0	—	.500	0	663	0	/lf	—	0.0
	Buf N	13	51	5	14	0	1	2	9	3	—	8	.275	.315	.431	135	2	—	.769	-3	0	0	O13(10/3/0)	—	-0.1
	Year	14	53	5	14	0	1	2	9	4	—	9	.264	.316	.415	131	2	—	.750	-2	38	0	O14(11/3/0)	—	-0.1
1886	Was N	80	292	20	50	11	3	0	20	13	—	54	.171	.207	.229	35	-22	8	.866	1	113	162	O68(8/9/51),P10,C4	—	-1.8
1888	†NY N	12	37	3	6	2	0	1	2	3	0	11	.162	.225	.297	66	1	1	.867	1	115	0	P12	—	0.0
1889	†NY N	29	103	16	21	1	0	2	11	13	0	21	.204	.293	.272	57	-6	6	.762	-4	51	57	P29/1	—	-0.2
1890	NY P	43	146	27	46	5	4	0	16	10	1	26	.315	.363	.404	96	7	5	.846	-4	83	0	P43	—	0.0
1891	Cin AA	34	110	13	17	0	0	1	7	8	0	28	.155	.212	.182	12	-13	4	.822	-3	92	0	P32,O3(0/1/2)	—	-0.3
	Cin N	15	46	3	5	0	0	0	2	3	0	12	.109	.163	.109	-20	-3	3	.906	0	108	239	P15	—	0.0
1892	NY N	48	163	20	40	1	1	0	14	11	1	30	.245	.297	.264	71	-6	2	.814	-2	85	140	P47/rf	—	-0.2
1893	NY N	12	26	8	12	1	0	0	3	7	0	0	.462	.576	.500	186	4	0	.889	-1	93	0	P10/1rf	—	0.0
	Bro N	3	5	1	2	1	0	0	0	0	0	0	.400	.400	.600	172	1	0	.500	-1	0	0	P2/rf	—	0.0
	Year	15	31	9	14	2	0	0	3	7	0	0	.452	.553	.516	186	5	0	.850	-1	81	0	P12,O2R/1	—	0.0
Total	9	391	1409	199	335	45	15	18	84	86	2	191	.238	.283	.329	81	-33	29	.840	-21	86	59	P204,O145(37/13/95),C46,1b7	—	-2.9
CRANE, FRED	Frederic William Hotchkiss; B11.4.1840 Old Saybrook CT; D4.27.1925 Brooklyn NY; 5´9˝/135; d5.26																								
1873	Res NA	1	4	0	1	0	0	0	1	0	—	0	.250	.250	.250	52	0	0-0	.667	-1	79	0	/2	—	-0.1
1875	Atl NA	21	81	7	17	1	0	0	4	0	—	4	.210	.210	.222	58	-3	0-0	.953	2	255	136	1b20/Srf	—	0.0
Total	2NA	22	85	7	18	1	0	0	5	0	—	4	.212	.212	.224	57	-3	0-0	.953	1	255	136	1b20/rfS2	—	-0.1
CRANE, SAM	Samuel Byren "Lucky","Red"; B9.13.1894 Harrisburg PA; D11.12.1955 Philadelphia PA; BR/TR/5´11.5˝/154; d10.2																								
1914	Phi A	2	6	0	0	0	0	0	0	2	0	3	.000	.250	.000	-25	-1	0	.929	0	111	0	S2	—	-0.1
1915	Phi A	8	23	3	2	2	0	0	1	0	0	4	.087	.087	.174	-23	-4	0	.900	0	106	66	S6/2	—	-0.3
1916	Phi A	2	4	1	1	0	0	0	0	2	0	1	.250	.500	.250	132	0	0	1.000	0	120	0	S2	—	0.1
1917	Was A	32	95	6	17	2	0	0	4	4	0	14	.179	.212	.200	26	-9	0	.889	-4	90	108	S32	—	-1.2
1920	Cin N	54	144	20	31	4	0	0	9	7	2	9	.215	.261	.243	46	-10	5-4	.945	-7	81	112	S25,3b10,2b4,O3R	—	-1.7
1921	Cin N	73	215	20	50	10	2	0	16	14	4	14	.233	.292	.298	59	-12	2-5	.953	-14	85	106	S63,3b2/rf	—	-2.1
1922	Bro N	3	8	1	2	1	0	0	0	0	1	1	.250	.333	.375	83	0	0-0	.875	1	115	103	S3	—	0.1
Total	7	174	495	51	103	19	2	0	30	29	7	46	.208	.262	.255	46	-36	7-9	.931	-23	88	102	S133,3b12,2b5,O4R	—	-5.2
CRANE, SAM	Samuel Newhall; B1.2.1854 Springfield MA; D6.26.1925 New York NY; BR/TR/6´0˝/190; d5.1; M2																								
1880	Buf N	10	31	4	4	0	0	0	2	1	—	8	.129	.156	.129	-2	-3	—	.866	-1	90	114	2b10/cfM	—	-0.4
1883	NY AA	96	349	57	82	8	5	0	—	13	—	—	.235	.262	.287	73	-11	—	.859	-12	86	84	2b96/cf	—	-1.7
1884	Cin U	80	309	56	72	9	3	1	—	11	—	—	.233	.259	.291	62	-24	—	.858	-12	97	124	2b80,M	—	-3.0
1885	Det N	68	245	23	47	4	6	1	20	13	—	45	.192	.233	.269	62	-11	—	.908	-4	93	72	2b68	—	-1.2
1886	Det N	47	185	24	26	2	2	1	12	8	—	34	.141	.176	.189	11	-20	8	.903	-1	96	134	2b38,S8,O4(1/0/3)	—	-1.8
	StL N	39	116	10	20	3	1	0	7	13	—	27	.172	.256	.216	48	-7	6	.897	-4	93	91	2b39	—	-0.8
	Year	86	301	34	46	5	3	1	19	21	—	61	.153	.208	.199	25	-27	14	.900	-5	95	113	2b77,S8,O4(1/0/3)	—	-2.6
1887	Was N	7	30	6	9	1	1	0	1	1	0	6	.300	.323	.400	106	0	5	.865	-0	98	139	S7	—	0.0
1890	NY N	2	6	0	0	0	0	0	0	0	0	0	.000	.000	.000	-99	-2	1	.778	-1	0	0	/1rf	—	-0.2
	Pit N	22	82	3	16	3	0	0	3	0	1	7	.195	.205	.232	31	-7	5	.880	2	117	53	2b15,S7/rf	—	-0.4
	NY N	2	6	0	0	0	0	0	0	0	0	0	.000	.000	.000	-99	-2	0	1.000	0	114	433	2b2	—	-0.1
	Year	26	94	3	16	3	0	0	3	0	1	7	.170	.179	.202	12	-11	6	.883	1	117	67	2b17,S7,O2R/1	—	-0.7
Total	7	373	1359	183	276	30	18	3	45	60	1	127	.203	.237	.258	53	-87	25	.878	-33	93	97	2b348,S22,O8(1/2/5)/1	—	-9.6
CRAVATH, GAVY	Clifford Carlton "Cactus"; B3.23.1881 Poway CA; D5.23.1963 Laguna Beach CA; BR/TR/5´10.5˝/186; d4.18; M2/C1																								
1908	Bos A	94	277	43	71	10	11	1	34	38	4	—	.256	.354	.383	136	12	6	.925	-1	80	127	O77(62/0/15),1b5	—	0.8
1909	Chi A	19	50	7	9	0	0	1	8	19	0	—	.180	.406	.240	109	2	3	.944	-2	0	0	O18C	—	-0.1
	Was A	4	6	0	0	0	0	0	1	1	0	—	.000	.143	.000	-57	-1	0	1.000	1	685	0	/rf	—	-0.1
	Year	23	56	7	9	0	0	1	9	20	0	—	.161	.382	.214	93	1	3	.947	-2	43	0	O19(0/18/1)	—	-0.2
1912	Phi N	130	436	63	124	30	9	11	70	47	3	77	.284	.358	.470	118	10	15	.966	6	94	**154**	O113(30/14/73)	—	0.9
1913	Phi N	147	525	78	**179**	34	14	**19**	**128**	55	3	63	.341	.407	**.568**	**169**	**47**	10-11	.958	-8	84	106	O141(3/7/133)	—	3.0
1914	Phi N	149	499	76	149	27	8	**19**	100	83	3	72	.299	.402	.499	**157**	38	14	.930	1	85	148	O143(1/0/142)	—	3.3

YEAR	TM LG	G	AB	R	H	2B	3B	HR	RBI	BB-IB	HP	SO	AVG	OBP	SLG	AOPS	ABR	SB-CS	FA	FR	RNG	THR	GAMES AT POSITION	DL	BFW
1915	†Phi N	150	522	**89**	149	31	7	**24**	**115**	**86**	6	77	.285	**.393**	**.510**	**170**	**47**	11-9	.946	9	101	**173**	O149R	—	**5.2**
1916	Phi N	137	448	70	127	21	8	11	70	64	5	89	.283	**.379**	.440	146	27	9	.966	-5	86	106	O130R	—	1.7
1917	Phi N	140	503	70	141	29	16	**12**	83	70	1	57	.280	.369	.473	151	32	6	.946	-7	89	94	O139R	—	2.0
1918	Phi N	121	426	43	99	27	5	**8**	54	54	1	46	.232	.320	.376	105	4	7	.931	-8	85	98	O118(7/0/110)	—	-1.2
1919	Phi N	83	214	34	73	18	5	**12**	45	35	2	21	.341	.438	.640	207	29	8	.914	-2	94	94	O56(2/1/53),M	—	2.7
1920	Phi N	46	45	2	13	5	0	1	11	9	0	12	.289	.407	.467	144	3	0-0	.667	-1	43	0	O5(3/0/2),M	—	0.2
Total	11	1220	3951	575	1134	232	83	119	719	561	28	514	.287	.380	.478	149	250	89-20	.944	-18	88	122	O1090(108/40/947),1b5	—	18.4

CRAVER, BILL William H.; B6.1844 Troy NY; D6.17.1901 Troy NY; BR/TR/5´9˝/160; d5.9; M4; OF NA(0/7/5)

YEAR	TM LG	G	AB	R	H	2B	3B	HR	RBI	BB-IB	HP	SO	AVG	OBP	SLG	AOPS	ABR	SB-CS	FA	FR	RNG	THR	GAMES AT POSITION	DL	BFW
1871	Tro NA	27	118	26	38	8	1	0	26	3	—	0	.322	.339	.407	112	2	6-3	.870	7	110	167	2b18,S4,C3,1b2/rfM	—	0.5
1872	Bal NA	35	178	55	50	3	3	0	24	5	—	2	.281	.301	.331	90	-3	9-1	.876	7	—	—	C27,2b5,O4R,3b2,M	—	0.3
1873	Bal NA	41	197	45	57	9	3	0	26	2	—	3	.289	.296	.365	95	-1	5-4	.933	6	—	—	C22,S15,O7C,1b3	—	0.3
1874	Phi NA	55	265	68	91	19	11	0	56	4	—	2	.343	.353	.498	164	18	11-3	.807	4	95	156	2b54,C5/1	—	1.5
1875	Cen NA	**14**	65	8	18	4	2	0	5	2	—	4	.277	.299	.400	153	4	1-0	.773	2	135	95	S9,3b4/1M	—	0.5
	Ath NA	54	260	71	83	11	11	2	40	4	—	5	.319	.330	.469	157	12	8-4	.856	-4	93	**174**	2b54,C2/3	—	0.4
	Year	68	325	79	101	15	**13**	2	45	6	—	9	.311	.323	.455	156	16	9-4	.856	-2	93	**174**	2b54,S9,3b5,C2/1	—	0.9
1876	NY N	56	246	24	55	4	0	0	22	2	—	7	.224	.230	.240	65	-7	—	.814	-24	69	41	2b42,C11,S6,M	—	-2.6
1877	Lou N	57	238	33	63	5	2	0	29	5	—	11	.265	.280	.303	71	-9	—	.904	-1	98	124	S57	—	-0.7
Total	5NA	226	1083	273	337	54	31	2	177	20	—	16	.311	.324	.424	130	32	40-15	.834	22	—	—	2b131,C59,S28,O12C,3b7,1b7	—	3.5
Total	2	113	484	57	118	9	2	0	51	7	—	18	.244	.255	.271	69	-16	—	.897	-26	—	—	S63,2b42,C11	—	-3.3

CRAWFORD, CARL Carl Demonte; B8.5.1981 Houston TX; BL/TL/6´2˝/(203–220); [TBA99 2/52]; d7.20

YEAR	TM LG	G	AB	R	H	2B	3B	HR	RBI	BB-IB	HP	SO	AVG	OBP	SLG	AOPS	ABR	SB-CS	FA	FR	RNG	THR	GAMES AT POSITION	DL	BFW
2002	TB A	63	259	23	67	11	6	2	30	9-0	3	41	.259	.290	.371	76	-10	9-5	.994	6	118	127	O63L	0	-0.6
2003	TB A	151	630	80	177	18	9	5	54	26-4	1	102	.281	.309	.362	78	-22	**55**-10	.992	11	112	112	O146(137/13/0)/D	0	-0.7
2004	TB A★	152	626	104	185	26	**19**	11	55	35-2	1	81	.296	.331	.450	104	1	**59**-15	.994	9	**119**	64	O145(122/30/0),D5	0	1.3
2005	TB A	156	644	101	194	33	**15**	15	81	27-1	5	84	.301	.331	.469	113	9	46-8	.995	9	**123**	37	O154(147/8/0)/D	0	1.9
2006	TB A	151	600	89	183	20	**16**	18	77	37-3	4	85	.305	.348	.482	113	9	**58**-9	.991	5	108	96	O148(148/2/0),D3	0	1.7
Total	5	673	2759	397	806	108	65	51	297	134-10	14	393	.292	.326	.434	100	-13	227-47	.993	40	116	82	O656(617/53/0),D10	0	3.6

CRAWFORD, PAT Clifford Rankin; B1.28.1902 Society Hill SC; D1.25.1994 Morehead City NC; BL/TR/5´11˝/170; d4.18; Col Davidson

YEAR	TM LG	G	AB	R	H	2B	3B	HR	RBI	BB-IB	HP	SO	AVG	OBP	SLG	AOPS	ABR	SB-CS	FA	FR	RNG	THR	GAMES AT POSITION	DL	BFW
1929	NY N	65	57	13	17	3	0	3	24	11	0	5	.298	.412	.509	127	3	1	1.000	-0	79	33	1b7/3	—	0.2
1930	NY N	25	76	11	21	3	2	3	17	7	1	2	.276	.345	.487	100	0	0	.966	-1	93	108	2b18/1	—	-0.1
	Cin N	76	224	24	65	7	1	3	26	23	1	10	.290	.359	.371	81	-7	2	.969	-4	99	73	2b54,1b13	—	-0.9
	Year	101	300	35	86	10	3	6	43	30	2	12	.287	.355	.400	86	-7	2	.968	-6	97	82	2b72,1b14	—	-1.0
1933	StL N	91	224	24	60	8	2	0	21	14	2	9	.268	.317	.321	78	-6	1	.986	1	117	87	1b29,2b15,3b7	—	-0.7
1934	†StL N	61	70	3	19	2	0	0	16	5	0	3	.271	.320	.300	63	-4	0	.900	1	100	0	3b9,2b4	—	-0.3
Total	4	318	651	75	182	23	5	9	104	60	4	29	.280	.344	.372	85	-14	4	.969	-4	99	87	2b91,1b50,3b17	—	-1.8

CRAWFORD, FORREST Forrest A.; B5.10.1881 Rockdale TX; D3.29.1908 Austin TX; BL/TR; d7.30

YEAR	TM LG	G	AB	R	H	2B	3B	HR	RBI	BB-IB	HP	SO	AVG	OBP	SLG	AOPS	ABR	SB-CS	FA	FR	RNG	THR	GAMES AT POSITION	DL	BFW
1906	StL N	45	145	8	30	3	1	0	11	7	1	—	.207	.248	.241	55	-8	1	.927	-6	97	57	S39,3b6	—	-1.5
1907	StL N	7	22	0	5	0	0	0	3	2	0	—	.227	.292	.227	65	-1	0	.912	-1	94	90	S7	—	-0.1
Total	2	52	167	8	35	3	1	0	14	9	1	—	.210	.254	.240	56	-9	1	.924	-7	97	62	S46,3b6	—	-1.6

CRAWFORD, GEORGE George; d10.8

YEAR	TM LG	G	AB	R	H	2B	3B	HR	RBI	BB-IB	HP	SO	AVG	OBP	SLG	AOPS	ABR	SB-CS	FA	FR	RNG	THR	GAMES AT POSITION	DL	BFW
1890	Phi AA	5	17	1	2	0	0	0	3	0	0	—	.118	.118	.118	-31	-3	1	1.000	1	0	0	O4R/S	—	-0.2

CRAWFORD, GLENN Glenn Martin "Shorty"; B12.2.1913 North Branch MI; D1.2.1972 Saginaw MI; BL/TR/5´9˝/165; d4.22

YEAR	TM LG	G	AB	R	H	2B	3B	HR	RBI	BB-IB	HP	SO	AVG	OBP	SLG	AOPS	ABR	SB-CS	FA	FR	RNG	THR	GAMES AT POSITION	DL	BFW
1945	StL N	4	3	0	0	0	0	0	0	1	0	0	.000	.250	.000	-26	0	0	ø	-0	0	0	/lf	0	-0.1
	Phi N	82	302	41	89	13	2	2	24	36	1	15	.295	.372	.371	110	5	5	.976	3	98	87	O38(6/0/32),S34,2b14	0	0.8
	Year	86	305	41	89	13	2	2	24	37	1	15	.292	.370	.367	108	5	5	.976	3	98	87	O39(7/0/32),S34,2b14	0	0.7
1946	Phi N	1	1	0	0	0	0	0	0	0	0	0	.000	.000	.000	-99	0	0	ø	0	—	—	/H	0	0.0
Total	2	87	306	41	89	13	2	2	24	37	1	15	.291	.369	.366	108	5	5	.976	3	98	87	O39(7/0/32),S34,2b14	0	0.7

CRAWFORD, KEN Kenneth Daniel; B10.31.1894 South Bend IN; D11.11.1976 Pittsburgh PA; BL/TR/5´9˝/145; d9.6; Col Pittsburgh

YEAR	TM LG	G	AB	R	H	2B	3B	HR	RBI	BB-IB	HP	SO	AVG	OBP	SLG	AOPS	ABR	SB-CS	FA	FR	RNG	THR	GAMES AT POSITION	DL	BFW
1915	Bal F	23	82	4	20	2	1	0	7	1	0	18	.244	.253	.293	52	-7	0	.978	-2	81	37	1b14,O4(1/0/3)	—	-1.0

CRAWFORD, JAKE Rufus; B3.20.1928 Campbell MO; BR/TR/6´1.5˝/185; d9.7; Col Missouri

YEAR	TM LG	G	AB	R	H	2B	3B	HR	RBI	BB-IB	HP	SO	AVG	OBP	SLG	AOPS	ABR	SB-CS	FA	FR	RNG	THR	GAMES AT POSITION	DL	BFW
1952	StL A	7	11	1	2	1	0	0	0	1	0	5	.182	.250	.273	44	-1	1-0	1.000	0	116	0	O3(0/2/1)	0	-0.1

CRAWFORD, SAM Samuel Earl "Wahoo Sam"; B4.18.1880 Wahoo NE; D6.15.1968 Hollywood CA; BL/TL/6´0˝/190; d9.10; HF1957

YEAR	TM LG	G	AB	R	H	2B	3B	HR	RBI	BB-IB	HP	SO	AVG	OBP	SLG	AOPS	ABR	SB-CS	FA	FR	RNG	THR	GAMES AT POSITION	DL	BFW
1899	Cin N	31	127	25	39	3	7	1	20	2	0	—	.307	.318	.465	111	0	6	.970	3	213	183	O31(9/22/0)	—	0.2
1900	Cin N	101	389	68	101	15	15	7	59	28	3	—	.260	.314	.429	107	1	14	.948	4	119	51	O95(70/12/12)	—	-0.4
1901	Cin N	131	515	91	170	20	16	**16**	104	37	3	—	.330	.378	.524	172	44	13	.923	2	124	134	O127(1/0/126)	—	3.9
1902	Cin N	140	555	92	185	18	**22**	3	78	47	1	—	.333	.386	.461	147	29	16	.932	3	130	105	O140(7/0/133)	—	2.7
1903	Det A	**137**	550	88	184	23	**25**	4	89	25	2	—	.335	.366	.489	159	36	18	.960	5	109	79	O137(45/0/92)	—	3.6
1904	Det A	150	562	49	143	22	16	2	73	44	0	—	.254	.309	.361	115	9	20	.973	5	110	177	O150(1/0/149)	—	0.7
1905	Det A	**154**	575	73	171	38	10	6	75	50	3	—	.297	.357	.430	148	31	22	**.988**	13	166	113	O103R,1b51	—	4.2
1906	Det A	145	563	65	166	25	16	2	72	38	1	—	.295	.341	.407	130	18	24	.984	5	136	60	O116(0/2/116),1b32	—	1.9
1907	†Det A	144	582	**102**	188	34	17	4	81	37	2	—	.323	.366	.460	157	35	18	.965	7	122	48	O144C,1b2	—	3.9
1908	†Det A	152	591	102	184	33	16	**7**	80	37	3	—	.311	.355	.457	157	35	15	.970	-10	61	47	O134C,1b17	—	2.1
1909	†Det A	156	589	83	185	**35**	14	6	97	47	1	—	.314	.366	.452	151	33	30	.965	-15	38	50	O139C,1b18	—	1.2
1910	Det A	154	588	83	170	26	**19**	5	**120**	37	1	—	.289	.332	.423	128	16	20	.963	-8	102	49	O153(0/26/127)/1	—	0.1
1911	Det A	146	574	109	217	36	14	7	115	61	0	—	.378	.438	.526	160	47	37	.975	-13	86	63	O146R	—	2.6
1912	Det A	149	581	81	189	30	21	4	109	42	2	—	.325	.373	.470	145	31	42	.984	-16	72	72	O149R	—	0.6
1913	Det A	**153**	609	78	193	32	**23**	9	83	52	0	28	.317	.371	.489	154	37	13	.964	-11	91	63	O140R,1b13	—	1.9
1914	Det A	**157**	582	74	183	22	**26**	8	**104**	69	1	31	.314	.388	.483	157	38	25-16	.977	-10	82	86	O157R	—	2.1
1915	Det A	**156**	612	81	183	31	**19**	4	**112**	66	0	29	.299	.367	.431	132	23	24-14	.974	-17	87	40	O156R	—	-0.3
1916	Det A	100	322	41	92	11	13	0	42	37	0	10	.286	.359	.401	124	9	10	.978	-8	75	69	O79(1/0/78),1b2	—	-0.4
1917	Det A	61	104	6	18	4	0	2	12	4	0	6	.173	.204	.269	44	-8	0	.988	-3	22	62	1b15,O3R	—	-1.3
Total	19	2517	9570	1391	2961	458	309	97	1525	760	23	104	.309	.362	.452	143	464	367-30	.965	-65	100	78	O2299(134/479/1687),1b151	—	29.3

CRAWFORD, WILLIE Willie Murphy; B9.7.1946 Los Angeles CA; D8.27.2004 Los Angeles CA; BL/TL/6´1˝/(197–205); d9.16

YEAR	TM LG	G	AB	R	H	2B	3B	HR	RBI	BB-IB	HP	SO	AVG	OBP	SLG	AOPS	ABR	SB-CS	FA	FR	RNG	THR	GAMES AT POSITION	DL	BFW
1964	LA N	10	16	3	5	1	0	0	0	1-0	0	7	.313	.353	.375	113	0	1-1	1.000	0	129	0	O4(1/0/3)	0	0.0
1965	†LA N	52	27	10	4	0	0	0	0	2-0	0	8	.148	.207	.148	2	-4	2-0	1.000	-0	86	0	O8(2/1/5)	0	-0.4
1966	LA N	6	0	1	0	0	0	0	0	0-0	0	0	ø	ø	ø	ø	0	0-0	ø	0	—	—	/R	0	0.0
1967	LA N	4	4	0	1	0	0	0	0	1-0	0	3	.250	.400	.250	98	0	0-0	.000	-0	0	0	/rf	0	0.0
1968	LA N	61	175	25	44	12	1	4	14	20-0	2	64	.251	.335	.400	129	7	1-3	.966	5	116	223	O48(45/1/4)	0	1.0
1969	LA N	129	389	64	96	17	5	11	41	49-3	0	85	.247	.331	.401	111	5	4-5	.973	-2	96	79	O113(56/22/38)	0	-0.3
1970	LA N	109	299	48	70	8	6	8	40	33-4	2	88	.234	.313	.381	89	-6	4-4	.960	4	105	157	O94(34/4/64)	0	-0.7
1971	LA N	114	342	64	96	16	6	9	40	28-2	1	49	.281	.334	.442	125	10	5-2	.981	-4	91	86	O97(63/5/35)	0	0.2
1972	LA N	96	243	28	61	7	3	8	27	35-3	2	55	.251	.349	.403	115	5	4-2	.983	-4	91	43	O74(51/0/28)	0	-0.3
1973	LA N	145	457	75	135	26	2	14	66	78-12	1	91	.295	.396	.453	140	29	12-5	.978	-1	94	109	O138(11/5/125)	0	2.2
1974	†LA N	139	468	73	138	23	4	11	61	64-9	0	88	.295	.376	.432	131	21	7-8	.966	-9	94	34	O133(0/2/132)	0	0.4
1975	LA N	124	373	46	98	15	2	9	46	49-11	0	43	.263	.345	.386	108	4	5-5	.990	-2	105	29	O113(25/0/93)	0	-0.4
1976	StL N	120	392	49	119	17	5	9	50	37-6	1	53	.304	.360	.441	126	13	2-1	.982	-1	103	70	O107(3/0/105)	0	0.7
1977	Hou N	42	114	14	29	3	0	2	18	16-1	0	10	.254	.341	.333	90	-2	0-0	.959	-2	91	0	O30L	0	-0.4
	Oak A	59	136	7	25	7	1	1	16	18-4	0	20	.184	.277	.272	52	-9	0-0	.978	2	108	219	O22(2/0/20),D18	0	-0.8
Total	14	1210	3435	507	921	152	35	86	419	431-55	9	664	.268	.349	.408	116	74	47-36	.975	-13	98	82	O982(323/40/653),D18	0	1.2

CREAMER, GEORGE George W. (b George W. Triebel); B1855 Philadelphia PA; D6.27.1886 Philadelphia PA; BR/TR/6´2˝/?; d5.1; M1

YEAR	TM LG	G	AB	R	H	2B	3B	HR	RBI	BB-IB	HP	SO	AVG	OBP	SLG	AOPS	ABR	SB-CS	FA	FR	RNG	THR	GAMES AT POSITION	DL	BFW
1878	Mil N	50	193	30	41	7	3	0	15	5	—	15	.212	.232	.280	63	-8	—	.839	-2	120	47	2b28,O17(0/16/4),3b6	—	-0.9
1879	Syr N	15	60	3	13	2	0	0	3	1	—	2	.217	.230	.250	65	-2	—	.825	-8	87	23	2b10,S3,O2(0/1/1)	—	-0.9
1880	Wor N	**85**	306	40	61	6	3	0	27	4	—	21	.199	.210	.239	47	-17	—	.883	-8	97	101	2b85	—	-2.1
1881	Wor N	80	309	42	64	9	2	0	25	11	—	27	.207	.234	.249	49	-18	—	.904	-9	96	87	2b80	—	-2.2
1882	Wor N	81	286	27	65	16	6	1	29	14	—	24	.227	.263	.336	88	-4	—	.907	11	**112**	107	2b81	—	0.9
1883	Pit AA	91	369	54	94	7	9	0	—	20	—	—	.255	.293	.322	102	1	—	.897	8	102	101	2b91	—	1.1

YEAR	TM LG	G	AB	R	H	2B	3B	HR	RBI	BB-IB	HP	SO	AVG	OBP	SLG	AOPS	ABR	SB-CS	FA	FR	RNG	THR	GAMES AT POSITION	DL	BFW
1884	Pit AA	98	339	38	62	8	5	0	—	16	2	—	.183	.224	.236	51	-18	—	**.937**	16	110	97	2b98,M	—	0.2
Total	7	500	1862	234	400	55	28	1	99	71	2	89	.215	.244	.276	67	-66	—	.901	8	104	94	2b473,O19(0/17/5),3b6,S3	—	-3.9
Crede, Joe	Joseph; B4.26.1978 Jefferson City MO; BR/TR/6´3˝/(195–220); [ChiA96 5/137]; d9.12																								
2000	Chi A	7	14	2	5	1	0	0	3	0-0	0	3	.357	.333	.429	94	0	0-0	.933	1	129	156	3b6/D	0	0.1
2001	Chi A	17	50	1	11	1	1	0	7	3-0	1	11	.220	.273	.280	45	-4	1-0	1.000	-1	71	136	3b15	0	-0.5
2002	Chi A	53	200	28	57	10	0	12	35	8-0	0	40	.285	.311	.515	110	2	0-2	.938	-5	89	138	3b53	0	-0.3
2003	Chi A	151	536	68	140	31	2	19	75	32-1	6	75	.261	.308	.433	89	-9	1-1	.964	-0	95	121	3b151	0	-0.8
2004	Chi A	144	490	67	117	25	0	21	69	34-0	10	81	.239	.299	.418	82	-14	1-2	.965	-8	93	102	3b144	0	-2.1
2005	†Chi A	132	432	54	109	21	0	22	62	25-3	8	66	.252	.303	.454	95	-4	1-1	.971	-0	98	135	3b130/SD	15	-0.4
2006	Chi A	150	544	76	154	31	0	30	94	28-1	7	58	.283	.323	.506	108	5	0-2	.978	22	**117**	119	3b149	0	2.5
Total	7	654	2266	296	593	120	3	104	345	130-5	32	334	.262	.308	.455	94	-24	4-8	.968	8	99	121	3b648,D2/S	15	-1.5
Cree, Birdie	William Franklin; B10.23.1882 Khedive PA; D11.8.1942 Sunbury PA; BR/TR/5´6˝/150; d9.17; Col Penn St.																								
1908	NY A	21	78	5	21	0	2	0	4	7	2	—	.269	.345	.321	115	1	1	1.000	1	186	302	O21C	—	0.2
1909	NY A	104	343	48	90	6	3	2	27	30	9	—	.262	.338	.315	105	3	10	.949	-1	100	93	O79(24/32/25),S6,2b4/3	—	-0.1
1910	NY A	134	467	58	134	19	16	4	73	40	8	—	.287	.353	.422	135	18	28	.955	-8	92	67	O134(49/85/0)	—	0.4
1911	NY A	137	520	90	181	30	22	4	88	56	3	—	.348	.415	.513	149	33	48	.964	-2	99	90	O132(122/7/3),S4,2b2	—	2.4
1912	NY A	50	190	25	63	11	6	0	22	20	5	—	.332	.409	.453	138	10	12	.948	4	124	77	O50L	—	1.1
1913	NY A	145	534	51	145	25	6	1	63	50	4	51	.272	.338	.346	100	1	22	**.988**	-4	91	89	O144L	—	-1.0
1914	NY A	77	275	45	85	18	5	0	40	30	6	24	.309	.389	.411	141	15	4-9	.976	4	109	98	O76C	—	1.2
1915	NY A	74	196	23	42	8	2	0	15	36	6	22	.214	.353	.276	88	0	7-8	.945	-4	89	84	O53(0/37/16)	—	-0.9
Total	8	742	2603	345	761	117	62	11	332	269	43	97	.292	.368	.398	124	81	132-17	.965	-10	101	91	O689(389/258/44),S10,2b6/3	—	3.3
Creeden, Connie	Cornelius Stephen; B7.21.1915 Danvers MA; D11.30.1969 Santa Ana CA; BL/TL/6´1˝/200; d4.28																								
1943	Bos N	5	4	0	1	0	0	0	1	1	0	0	.250	.400	.250	91	0	0	ø	0	—	—	/H	0	0.0
Creeden, Pat	Patrick Francis "Whoops"; B5.23.1906 Newburyport MA; D4.20.1992 Brockton MA; BL/TR/5´8˝/175; d4.14; Col Boston College																								
1931	Bos A	5	8	0	0	0	0	0	0	1	0	3	.000	.111	.000	-73	-2	0-0	.846	-1	83	87	2b2	—	-0.2
Creegan, Marty	Mark (b Marcus Kragen); B7.31.1864 San Francisco CA; D9.29.1920 San Francisco CA; ?/161; d4.17																								
1884	Was U	9	33	4	5	0	0	0	—	1	—	—	.152	.176	.152	0	-5	—	.667	-2	77	950	O6(0/5/1),C3,3b2/1	—	-0.6
Creely, Gus	August L.; B6.6.1870 Florissant MO; D4.22.1934 St.Louis MO; 5´6˝/150; d10.9																								
1890	StL AA	4	15	0	0	0	0	0	0	0	0	—	.000	.000	.000	-88	-4	1	.769	-2	76	0	S4	—	-0.5
Cregan, Pete	Peter James "Peekskill Pete"; B4.13.1875 Kingston NY; D5.18.1945 New York NY; BR/TR/5´7.5˝/150; d9.8																								
1899	NY N	1	2	0	0	0	0	0	0	0	0	—	.000	.000	.000	-99	-1	0	1.000	-0	0	0	/rf	—	-0.1
1903	Cin N	6	19	0	2	0	0	0	0	1	1	—	.105	.190	.105	-13	-3	0	.769	-1	0	0	O6(5/0/1)	—	-0.4
Total	2	7	21	0	2	0	0	0	0	1	1	—	.095	.174	.095	-21	-4	0	.786	-1	0	0	O7(5/0/2)	—	-0.5
Creger, Bernie	Bernard Odell; B3.21.1927 Wytheville VA; D11.30.1997 Lynchburg VA; BR/TR/6´0˝/175; d4.29																								
1947	StL N	15	16	3	3	1	0	0	0	1	0	3	.188	.235	.250	28	-2	1	.828	-2	96	58	S13	0	-0.4
Crespi, Creepy	Frank Angelo Joseph; B2.16.1918 St.Louis MO; D3.1.1990 Florissant MO; BR/TR/5´8.5˝/175; d9.14; Mil 1943–46																								
1938	StL N	7	19	2	5	2	0	0	1	2	0	7	.263	.333	.368	88	0	0	.813	-3	66	111	S7	—	-0.3
1939	StL N	15	29	3	5	1	0	0	6	3	0	6	.172	.250	.207	23	-3	0	.962	-0	114	34	2b6,S4	—	-0.3
1940	StL N	3	11	2	3	1	0	0	0	1	0	2	.273	.333	.364	87	0	1	1.000	-1	27	0	3b2/S	—	-0.1
1941	StL N	146	560	85	156	24	2	4	46	57	9	58	.279	.355	.350	93	-3	3	.962	-2	98	115	2b145	0	0.4
1942	†StL N	93	292	33	71	4	2	0	35	27	1	29	.243	.309	.271	65	-13	4	.967	-6	85	101	2b83,S5	0	-1.5
Total	5	264	911	125	240	32	4	4	88	90	10	102	.263	.336	.321	82	-19	8	.963	-13	94	109	2b234,S17,3b2	0	-1.8
Crespo, Cesar	Cesar Antonio (Claudio); B5.23.1979 Rio Piedras, PR; BB/TR/5´11˝/170; [NYN97 3/90]; d5.29; b–Felipe																								
2001	SD N	55	153	27	32	6	0	4	12	25-0	0	50	.209	.320	.327	73	-6	6-2	.970	-5	85	71	2b34,O18(6/11/2),3b2/S	0	-0.9
2002	SD N	25	29	5	5	2	0	0	0	3-0	0	6	.172	.250	.241	33	-3	3-2	1.000	-1	57	903	O7(6/1/1),2b4,3b4/S	0	-0.4
2004	Bos A	52	79	6	13	2	1	0	2	0-0	0	20	.165	.165	.215	-2	-12	2-0	.943	-0	98	121	S27,O19(10/7/2),2b11	0	-1.0
Total	3	132	261	38	50	10	1	4	14	28-0	0	76	.192	.270	.284	46	-21	11-4	.976	-6	86	69	2b49,O44(22/19/5),S29,3b6	0	-2.3
Crespo, Felipe	Felipe Javier (Clausio); B3.5.1973 Rio Piedras, PR; BB/TR/5´11˝/(200–210); [TorA90 3/95]; d4.28; b–Cesar																								
1996	Tor A	22	49	6	9	4	0	0	4	12-0	3	13	.184	.375	.265	66	-2	1-0	.982	3	95	117	2b10,3b6,1b2	22	0.2
1997	Tor A	12	28	3	8	0	1	1	5	2-0	0	4	.286	.333	.464	105	0	0-0	.933	-2	54	100	3b7/2D	0	-0.1
1998	Tor A	66	130	11	34	8	1	1	15	15-1	2	27	.262	.342	.362	84	-3	4-3	1.000	-1	102	54	O42(19/1/24),2b8,3b2/1D	0	-0.4
2000	†SF N	89	131	17	38	6	1	4	29	10-2	4	23	.290	.351	.443	108	1	3-2	.962	-2	83	0	O26(18/0/9),1b11,2b7/D	0	-0.2
2001	SF N	40	66	8	13	1	0	4	10	7-1	2	26	.197	.286	.394	80	-2	1-1	.972	-2	44	111	1b16,2b2/rfD	31	-0.6
	Phi N	33	41	1	7	3	1	0	5	4-0	0	8	.171	.234	.293	40	-4	0-0	1.000	1	160	718	O4L,1b2/2	0	-0.3
	Year	73	107	9	20	4	1	4	15	11-1	2	34	.187	.266	.355	65	-6	1-1	.977	-1	38	124	1b18,O5(4/0/1),2b3/D	0	-0.9
Total	5	262	445	46	109	22	4	10	68	50-4	11	101	.245	.330	.380	86	-10	9-6	.989	-3	99	65	O73(41/1/34),1b32,2b29,3b15,D6	53	-1.4
Criger, Lou	Louis; B2.3.1872 Elkhart IN; D5.14.1934 Tucson AZ; BR/TR/5´10˝/165; d9.21																								
1896	Cle N	2	5	0	0	0	0	0	0	1	0	0	.000	.167	.000	-51	-1	1	1.000	1	*138*	*123*	/C	—	0.0
1897	Cle N	39	138	15	31	4	1	0	22	23	1	—	.225	.340	.268	58	-8	5	.937	0	*113*	*86*	C37,1b2	—	-0.3
1898	Cle N	84	287	43	80	13	4	1	32	40	5	—	.279	.377	.362	113	7	2	.957	16	*114*	*101*	C82	—	2.9
1899	StL N	77	258	39	66	4	5	2	44	28	2	—	.256	.333	.333	81	-7	14	.949	7	*125*	*97*	C75	—	0.6
1900	StL N	80	288	31	78	8	6	2	38	4	2	—	.271	.286	.361	78	-10	5	.953	4	*94*	*104*	C75/3	—	0.0
1901	Bos A	76	268	26	62	6	3	0	24	11	3	—	.231	.270	.276	52	-18	7	.967	19	*113*	*109*	C68,1b8	—	0.7
1902	Bos A	83	266	32	68	16	6	0	28	27	0	—	.256	.324	.361	87	-4	7	.965	14	***133***	*104*	C80/lf	—	1.7
1903	†Bos A	96	317	41	61	7	10	3	31	26	1	—	.192	.256	.306	65	-15	5	.979	23	***125***	***114***	C96	—	1.8
1904	Bos A	98	299	34	63	10	5	2	34	27	3	—	.211	.283	.298	79	-7	1	.981	18	***142***	*91*	C95	—	2.3
1905	Bos A	109	313	33	62	6	7	1	36	54	3	—	.198	.322	.272	88	-2	5	.972	7	***127***	*104*	C109	—	1.7
1906	Bos A	7	17	0	3	1	0	0	1	1	0	—	.176	.222	.235	43	-1	1	.981	2	*112*	*70*	C6	—	0.2
1907	Bos A	75	226	12	41	4	0	0	14	19	2	—	.181	.251	.199	44	-14	2	.978	4	*112*	*100*	C75	—	-0.3
1908	Bos A	84	237	12	45	4	2	0	25	13	0	—	.190	.232	.224	47	-14	1	.980	13	*102*	*108*	C84	—	0.7
1909	StL A	74	212	15	36	1	1	0	9	25	1	—	.170	.261	.184	44	-13	2	.986	6	*98*	*96*	C73	—	0.0
1910	NY A	27	69	3	13	2	0	0	4	10	0	—	.188	.291	.217	56	-3	0	.993	-1	*101*	*87*	C27	—	-0.1
1912	StL A	1	2	1	0	0	0	0	0	0	0	—	.000	.000	.000	-99	-1	0	1.000	0	*120*	*104*	/C	—	0.0
Total	16	1012	3202	337	709	86	50	11	342	309	23	0	.221	.295	.290	72	-111	58	.971	133	*118*	*101*	C984,1b10/lf3	—	11.9
Cripe, Dave	David Gordon; B4.7.1951 Ramona CA; BR/TR/6´0˝/180; d9.10; Col William and Mary																								
1978	KC A	7	13	1	2	0	0	0	1	0-0	0	2	.154	.154	.154	-13	-2	0-0	1.000	-3	15	0	3b5	0	-0.5
Criscione, Dave	David Gerald; B9.2.1951 Dunkirk NY; BR/TR/5´8˝/185; [TexA69 5/95]; d7.17																								
1977	Bal A	7	9	1	3	0	0	1	1	0-0	0	1	.333	.333	.667	174	1	0-0	1.000	-1	88	0	C7	0	0.0
Criscola, Tony	Anthony Paul; B7.9.1915 Walla Walla WA; D7.10.2001 LaJolla CA; BL/TR/5´11.5˝/180; d4.15; Col Whitman																								
1942	StL A	91	158	17	47	9	2	1	13	8	0	13	.297	.331	.399	103	0	2-2	.955	-3	93	0	O52(37/13/2)	0	-0.5
1943	StL A	29	52	4	8	0	0	0	1	8	0	7	.154	.267	.154	24	-5	0-0	.960	-1	103	0	O13(10/2/1)	0	-0.7
1944	Cin N	64	157	14	36	3	2	0	14	14	1	12	.229	.297	.274	64	-8	0	.977	1	106	101	O35(3/0/32)	0	-1.0
Total	3	184	367	35	91	12	4	1	28	30	1	32	.248	.307	.311	75	-13	2-2	.966	-3	100	47	O100(50/15/35)	0	-2.2
Crisham, Pat	Patrick J.; B6.4.1877 Amesbury MA; D6.12.1915 Syracuse NY; 6´0˝/168; d5.5																								
1899	Bal N	53	172	23	50	5	3	0	20	4	1	—	.291	.311	.355	78	-6	4	.979	-1	94	37	1b26,C22	—	-0.5
Crisp, Coco	Covelli Loyce; B11.1.1979 Los Angeles CA; BB/TR/6´0˝/(180–185); [StLN99 7/222]; d8.15; Col Los Angeles Pierce (CA) JC																								
2002	Cle A	32	127	16	33	9	2	1	9	11-0	0	19	.260	.314	.386	85	-3	4-1	.988	0	103	61	O32(2/31/0)	0	-0.2
2003	Cle A	99	414	55	110	15	6	3	27	23-1	0	51	.266	.302	.353	73	-17	15-9	.995	-2	95	100	O90(39/53/0),D7	0	-2.0
2004	Cle A	139	491	78	146	24	2	15	71	36-4	0	69	.297	.344	.446	108	5	20-13	.986	-3	97	78	O128(37/94/0),D6	0	0.1
2005	Cle A	145	594	86	178	42	4	16	69	44-1	0	81	.300	.345	.465	118	15	15-6	.985	0	108	38	O145(138/10/0)	15	1.1

YEAR	TM LG	G	AB	R	H	2B	3B	HR	RBI	BB-IB	HP	SO	AVG	OBP	SLG	AOPS	ABR	SB-CS	FA	FR	RNG	THR	GAMES AT POSITION	DL	BFW
2006	Bos A	105	413	58	109	22	2	8	36	31-1	1	67	.264	.317	.385	79	-13	22-4	.996	-4	95	59	O103C	49	-1.2
Total	5	520	2039	293	576	112	16	43	212	145-7	1	287	.282	.329	.416	96	-13	76-33	.990	-10	100	65	O498(216/291/0),D13	64	-2.2
Crisp, Joe	Joseph Shelby; B7.8.1885 Higginsville MO; D2.5.1939 Kansas City MO; BR/TR/6´4˝/200; d9.2																								
1910	StL A	1	1	0	0	0	0	0	0	0	0	—	.000	.000	.000	-99	0	0	1.000	-0	*45*	*0*	/C	—	0.0
1911	StL A	1	1	0	1	0	0	0	0	0	0	—	1.000	1.000	1.000	477	0	0	ø	0	—	—	/H	—	0.0
Total	2	2	2	0	1	0	0	0	0	0	0	—	.500	.500	.500	206	0	0	1.000	-0	*45*	*0*	/C	—	0.0
Criss, Dode	Dode; B3.12.1885 Sherman MS; D9.8.1955 Sherman MS; BL/TR/6´2˝/200; d4.20; ▲																								
1908	StL A	64	82	15	28	6	0	0	14	9	0	—	.341	.407	.415	166	7	1	.933	-1	189	0	O11R,P9/1	—	0.6
1909	StL A	35	48	2	14	6	1	0	7	0	1	—	.292	.306	.458	152	6	0	1.000	-1	59	0	P11	—	0.0
1910	StL A	70	91	11	21	4	2	1	11	11	1	—	.231	.320	.352	118	2	2	.983	-1	66	90	1b11,P6	—	0.1
1911	StL A	58	83	10	21	3	1	2	15	11	1	—	.253	.347	.386	109	1	0	.956	-2	70	76	1b14,P4	—	-0.1
Total	4	227	304	38	84	19	4	3	47	31	3	—	.276	.349	.395	133	16	3	.964	-4	72	0	P30,1b26,O11R	—	0.6
Crist, Ches	Chester Arthur "Squak"; B2.10.1882 Cozaddale OH; D1.7.1957 Cincinnati OH; BR/TR/5´11˝/165; d5.18																								
1906	Phi N	6	11	1	0	0	0	0	0	0	1	—	.000	.083	.000	-74	-2	0	.800	-2	*71*	*43*	C6	—	-0.5
Critz, Hughie	Hugh Melville; B9.17.1900 Starkville MS; D1.10.1980 Greenwood MS; BR/TR/5´8˝/147; d5.31; Col Mississippi St.																								
1924	Cin N	102	413	67	133	15	14	3	35	19	0	18	.322	.352	.448	115	6	19-11	.956	2	102	101	2b96/S	—	1.1
1925	Cin N	144	541	74	150	14	8	2	51	34	1	17	.277	.321	.344	72	-24	13-13	.970	20	**110**	**126**	2b144	—	-0.2
1926	Cin N	155	607	96	164	24	14	3	79	39	2	25	.270	.316	.371	87	-14	7	**.981**	**23**	**110**	**128**	2b155	—	1.4
1927	Cin N	113	396	50	110	10	8	4	49	16	0	18	.278	.306	.374	84	-11	7	.969	-1	103	114	2b113	—	-0.9
1928	Cin N	**153**	641	95	190	21	11	5	52	37	0	24	.296	.335	.387	90	-12	18	.971	-15	98	124	2b153	—	-2.2
1929	Cin N	107	425	55	105	17	9	1	50	27	0	21	.247	.292	.336	58	-30	9	**.974**	7	**112**	**115**	2b106/S	—	-1.8
1930	Cin N	28	104	15	24	3	2	0	11	6	0	6	.231	.273	.298	40	-11	1	.987	-1	105	91	2b28	—	-0.9
	NY N	124	558	93	148	17	11	4	50	24	0	26	.265	.296	.357	58	-41	7	.972	8	98	106	2b124	—	-2.7
	Year	152	662	108	172	20	13	4	61	30	0	32	.260	.292	.347	55	-51	8	**.974**	7	99	103	2b152	—	-3.6
1931	NY N	66	238	33	69	7	2	4	17	8	0	17	.290	.313	.387	89	-5	4	.984	2	98	83	2b54	—	0.1
1932	NY N	151	659	90	182	32	7	2	50	34	1	27	.276	.313	.355	81	-18	3	.974	6	100	103	2b151	—	-0.3
1933	†NY N	133	558	68	137	18	5	2	33	23	3	24	.246	.279	.306	68	-24	4	**.982**	**45**	**126**	118	2b133	—	3.1
1934	NY N	137	571	77	138	17	1	6	40	19	2	24	.242	.269	.306	55	-38	3	**.978**	**27**	**114**	**125**	2b137	—	-0.2
1935	NY N	65	219	19	41	0	3	2	14	3	0	10	.187	.198	.242	18	-27	2	.966	0	100	112	2b59	—	-2.2
Total	12	1478	5930	832	1591	195	95	38	531	289	9	257	.268	.303	.352	74	-249	97-24	.974	124	107	115	2b1453,S2	—	-5.7
Crockett, Davey	Daniel Solomon; B10.5.1875 Roanoke VA; D2.23.1961 Charlottesville VA; BL/TR/6´1˝/175; d7.11																								
1901	Det A	28	102	10	29	2	2	0	14	6	2	—	.284	.336	.343	85	-2	1	.968	-1	100	121	1b27	—	-0.3
Croft, Art	Arthur F.; B1.23.1855 St.Louis MO; D3.16.1884 St.Louis MO; d5.4																								
1875	RS NA	**19**	75	5	15	3	0	0	2	0	—	2	.200	.200	.240	58	-2	5-1	.800	-3	0	0	O19(10/7/2)	—	-0.4
1877	StL N	54	220	23	51	5	2	0	27	1	—	15	.232	.235	.273	63	-9	—	.971	-3	79	81	1b28,O25(25/1/1)/2	—	-1.3
1878	Ind N	60	222	22	35	6	0	0	16	5	—	23	.158	.176	.185	22	-17	—	.963	-2	55	79	1b51,O9L	—	-2.1
Total	2	114	442	45	86	11	2	0	43	6	—	38	.195	.205	.229	43	-26	—	.965	-5	63	80	1b79,O34(34/1/1)/2	—	-3.4
Croft, Harry	Henry T.; B8.1.1875 Chicago IL; D12.11.1933 Oak Park IL; d5.19; Col Niagara																								
1899	Lou N	2	2	0	0	0	0	0	0	0	0	—	.000	.000	.000	-99	-1	0	ø	0	—	—	/H	—	-0.1
	Phi N	2	7	0	1	0	0	0	0	1	0	—	.143	.250	.143	9	-1	0	1.000	-0	111	0	2b2	—	-0.1
	Year	4	9	0	1	0	0	0	0	1	0	—	.111	.200	.111	-14	-1	0	1.000	-0	111	0	2b2	—	-0.2
1901	Chi N	3	12	1	4	0	0	0	4	0	0	—	.333	.333	.333	97	0	0	1.000	2	652	0	O3R	—	0.2
Total	2	7	21	1	5	0	0	0	4	1	0	—	.238	.273	.238	47	-2	0	1.000	2	652	0	O3R,2b2	—	0.0
Crolius, Fred	Frederick Joseph; B12.16.1876 Jersey City NJ; D8.25.1960 Ormond Beach FL; d4.19; Col Dartmouth																								
1901	Bos N	49	200	22	48	4	1	1	13	9	10	—	.240	.306	.285	66	-9	6	.850	-8	48	69	O49(0/3/46)	—	-1.8
1902	Pit N	9	38	4	10	2	1	0	7	0	0	—	.263	.263	.368	91	-1	0	1.000	-0	97	0	O9R	—	-0.1
Total	2	58	238	26	58	6	2	1	20	9	10	—	.244	.300	.298	69	-10	6	.868	-8	55	60	O58(0/3/55)	—	-1.9
Cromartie, Warren	Warren Livingston; B9.29.1953 Miami Beach FL; BL/TL/6´0˝/(180–200); [MonN73 S1/5]; d9.6; Col Miami–Dade North (FL) CC																								
1974	Mon N	8	17	2	3	0	0	0	0	3-0	0	3	.176	.300	.176	34	-1	1-0	1.000	-1	76	0	O6L	0	-0.2
1976	Mon N	33	81	8	17	1	0	0	2	1-0	0	5	.210	.220	.222	24	-8	1-2	.943	-1	98	74	O20(5/0/16)	0	-1.1
1977	Mon N	155	620	64	175	41	7	5	50	33-3	4	40	.282	.321	.395	93	-7	10-3	.976	5	102	95	O155(153/0/4)	0	-0.8
1978	Mon N	159	607	77	180	32	6	10	56	33-5	7	60	.297	.337	.418	111	8	8-8	.978	17	**114**	180	O158(157/0/1),1b4	0	1.8
1979	Mon N	158	659	84	181	46	5	8	46	38-19	1	78	.275	.313	.396	92	-7	8-7	.976	10	109	126	O158L	0	-0.6
1980	Mon N	**162**	597	74	172	33	5	14	70	51-**24**	2	64	.288	.345	.430	113	11	8-8	.991	-5	90	87	1b158,O2L	0	-0.6
1981	†Mon N	99	358	41	109	19	2	6	42	39-12	0	27	.304	.370	.419	120	11	2-3	.992	-4	75	90	1b62,O38R	0	0.1
1982	Mon N	144	497	59	126	24	3	14	62	69-15	3	60	.254	.346	.398	105	5	3-0	.979	6	114	107	O136(2/0/135),1b9	0	0.5
1983	Mon N	120	360	37	100	26	2	3	43	43-7	1	48	.278	.352	.386	106	4	8-3	.973	11	124	187	O101R/1	0	1.2
1991	KC A	69	131	13	41	7	2	1	20	15-0	0	18	.313	.381	.420	121	4	1-3	.996	-4	46	90	1b29,O6(4/1/1)/D	0	-0.2
Total	10	1107	3927	459	1104	229	32	61	391	325-85	18	403	.281	.336	.402	103	20	50-37	.977	36	111	127	O780(487/1/296),1b263/D	0	0.1
Cromer, D.T.	David Thomas; B3.19.1971 Lake City SC; BL/TL/6´2˝/220; [OakA92 11/312]; d4.5; b–Tripp; Col South Carolina																								
2000	Cin N	35	47	7	16	4	0	2	8	1-1	1	14	.340	.360	.553	124	2	0-0	.964	-1	65	145	1b13	0	0.0
2001	Cin N	50	57	7	16	3	0	5	12	3-0	0	19	.281	.302	.596	122	1	0-0	.973	0	128	76	1b8/D	0	0.1
Total	2	85	104	14	32	7	0	7	20	4-1	1	33	.308	.327	.577	123	3	0-0	.967	-1	91	117	1b21/D	0	0.1
Cromer, Tripp	Roy Bunyan; B11.21.1967 Lake City SC; BR/TR/6´2˝/(165–170); [StLN89 3/66]; d9.7; b–D.T.; Col South Carolina																								
1993	StL N	10	23	1	2	0	0	0	0	1-0	0	6	.087	.125	.087	-42	-5	0-0	.912	-0	101	88	S9	0	-0.5
1994	StL N	2	0	1	0	0	0	0	0	0-0	0	0	ø	ø	ø	ø	0	0-0	.000	-1	0	0	S2	0	-0.1
1995	StL N	105	345	36	78	19	0	5	18	14-2	4	66	.226	.261	.325	53	-24	0-0	.960	-1	106	113	S95,2b11	0	-1.8
1997	LA N	28	86	8	25	3	0	4	20	6-3	0	16	.291	.333	.465	115	1	0-1	.968	-3	84	85	2b17,S10/3	62	0.0
1998	LA N	6	6	1	1	0	0	1	1	0-0	0	2	.167	.167	.667	111	0	0-0	ø	0	—	—	/H	140	0.0
1999	LA N	33	52	5	10	0	0	2	8	5-0	0	10	.192	.263	.308	46	-5	0-0	1.000	4	134	169	2b9,S9,3b2,O2(1/0/1)/1	58	0.0
2000	Hou N	9	8	2	1	0	0	0	0	1-0	0	1	.125	.222	.125	-9	-1	0-0	.500	-1	124	0	3b2/2S	37	-0.2
2003	Hou N	3	4	0	1	0	1	0	1	0-0	0	0	.250	.250	.750	140	0	0-0	1.000	1	202	445	/2	0	0.1
Total	8	196	524	54	118	22	1	12	48	27-5	4	101	.225	.266	.340	58	-34	0-1	.959	-0	106	110	S126,2b39,3b5,O2(1/0/1)/1	297	-2.5
Crompton, Ned	Edward; B2.13.1889 Liverpool, England; D9.28.1950 Aspinwall PA; BL/TL/5´10.5˝/175; d9.13																								
1909	StL A	17	63	7	10	2	1	0	2	7	1	—	.159	.254	.222	54	-3	1	.909	1	178	191	O17L	—	-0.4
1910	Cin N	1	2	0	0	0	0	0	0	0	0	2	.000	.000	.000	-99	-1	0	ø	-0	0	0	/cf	—	-0.1
Total	2	18	65	7	10	2	1	0	2	7	1	2	.154	.247	.215	49	-4	1	.909	1	177	190	O18(17/1/0)	—	-0.5
Crompton, Herb	Herbert Bryan "Workhorse"; B11.7.1911 Taylor Ridge IL; D8.5.1963 Moline IL; BR/TR/6´0˝/185; d4.26																								
1937	Was A	2	3	0	1	0	0	0	0	0	0	0	.333	.333	.333	72	0	0-0	1.000	0	*0*	*449*	C2	—	0.0
1945	NY A	36	99	6	19	3	0	0	12	2	0	7	.192	.208	.222	24	-10	0-0	.984	-1	*80*	*136*	C33	0	-1.0
Total	2	38	102	6	20	3	0	0	12	2	0	7	.196	.212	.225	25	-10	0-0	.984	-1	*78*	*145*	C35	0	-1.0
Cron, Chris	Christopher John; B3.31.1964 Albuquerque NM; BR/TR/6´2˝/200; [AtlN84*S2/38]; d8.15; Col Santa Ana (CA) JC																								
1991	Cal A	6	15	0	2	0	0	0	0	2-0	0	5	.133	.235	.133	5	-2	0-0	1.000	1	202	26	1b5/D	0	-0.1
1992	Chi A	6	10	0	0	0	0	0	0	0-0	0	4	.000	.000	.000	-99	-3	0-0	.923	0	162	69	1b5/lf	0	-0.3
Total	2	12	25	0	2	0	0	0	0	2-0	0	9	.080	.148	.080	-35	-5	0-0	.980	1	191	37	1b10/lfD	0	-0.4
Cronin, Dan	Daniel T.; B4.1.1857 S.Boston MA; D11.30.1885 Boston MA; 5´8˝/170; d7.9																								
1884	CP U	1	4	1	1	0	0	0	—	0	—	—	.250	.250	.250	52	0	—	.200	-2	0	345	/2	—	-0.2
	StL U	1	5	0	0	0	0	0	—	0	—	—	.000	.000	.000	-96	-1	—	.000	-1	0	0	/lf	—	-0.2
	Year	2	9	1	1	0	0	0	—	0	—	—	.111	.111	.111	-32	-2	—	.000	-3	0	345	/2lf	—	-0.4
Cronin, Jim	James John; B8.7.1905 Richmond CA; D6.10.1983 Concord CA; BB/TR/5´10.5˝/150; d7.4																								
1929	Phi A	25	56	7	13	2	1	0	4	5	0	7	.232	.295	.304	52	-4	0-0	.966	2	126	130	2b10,S9,3b4	—	-0.1

Cronin, Joe
Joseph Edward; B10.12.1906 San Francisco CA; D9.7.1984 Barnstable MA; BR/TR/5´11.5˝/180; d4.29; M15; HF1956

YEAR	TM LG	G	AB	R	H	2B	3B	HR	RBI	BB-IB	HP	SO	AVG	OBP	SLG	AOPS	ABR	SB-CS	FA	FR	RNG	THR	GAMES AT POSITION	DL	BFW
1926	Pit N	38	83	9	22	2	2	0	11	6	0	15	.265	.315	.337	72	-3	0	.977	5	105	150	2b27,S7	—	0.2
1927	Pit N	12	22	2	5	1	0	0	3	2	0	3	.227	.292	.273	48	-2	0	1.000	-3	56	0	2b7,S4/1	—	-0.4
1928	Was A	63	227	23	55	10	4	0	25	22	0	27	.242	.309	.322	66	-11	4-0	.953	8	107	125	S63	—	0.4
1929	Was A	145	494	72	139	29	8	8	61	85	1	37	.281	.388	.421	107	9	5-9	.923	5	**104**	106	S143/2	—	2.6
1930	Was A	**154**	587	127	203	41	9	13	126	72	5	36	.346	.422	.513	135	34	17-10	.960	**27**	**110**	111	S154	—	6.9
1931	Was A	**156**	611	103	187	44	13	12	126	81	4	52	.306	.391	.480	127	26	10-9	.950	13	101	**114**	S155	—	4.5
1932	Was A	143	557	95	177	43	**18**	6	116	66	3	45	.318	.393	.492	129	25	7-5	**.959**	7	103	111	S141	—	3.8
1933	†Was A★	152	602	89	186	**45**	11	5	118	87	2	49	.309	.398	.445	124	25	5-4	**.960**	6	106	118	S152,M	—	3.9
1934	Was A★	127	504	68	143	30	9	7	101	53	1	28	.284	.353	.421	103	1	8-0	.951	13	**114**	102	S127,M	—	2.4
1935	Bos A★	144	556	70	164	37	14	9	95	63	3	40	.295	.370	.460	106	5	3-3	.949	-15	95	98	S139,1b2,M	—	-0.1
1936	Bos A	81	295	36	83	22	4	2	43	32	1	21	.281	.354	.403	82	-8	1-3	.930	-5	98	89	S60,3b21,M	—	-0.8
1937	Bos A★	148	570	102	175	40	4	18	110	84	6	73	.307	.402	.486	118	18	5-3	.958	-16	87	95	S148,M	—	1.2
1938	Bos A★	143	530	98	172	**51**	5	17	94	91	5	60	.325	.428	.536	134	32	7-5	.954	7	103	115	S142,M	—	4.4
1939	Bos A★	143	520	97	160	33	3	19	107	87	0	48	.308	.407	.492	124	22	6-6	.959	4	99	105	S142,M	—	3.2
1940	Bos A	149	548	104	156	35	6	24	111	83	1	65	.285	.380	.502	122	19	7-5	.948	-0	**105**	94	S146,3b2,M	—	2.7
1941	Bos A★	143	518	98	161	38	8	16	95	82	1	55	.311	.406	.508	137	30	1-4	.958	-1	99	85	S119,3b22/lfM	0	3.5
1942	Bos A	45	79	7	24	3	0	4	24	15	0	21	.304	.415	.494	150	6	0-1	.865	-1	103	200	3b11,1b5/SM	0	0.5
1943	Bos A	59	77	8	24	4	0	5	29	11	0	4	.312	.398	.558	176	7	0-0	.968	-0	98	55	3b10,M	0	0.8
1944	Bos A	76	191	24	46	7	0	5	28	34	1	19	.241	.358	.356	106	3	1-4	.981	-2	93	90	1b49,M	0	-0.3
1945	Bos A	3	8	1	3	0	0	0	1	3	0	2	.375	.545	.375	165	1	0-0	1.000	1	148	355	3b3,M	67	0.2
Total	20	2124	7579	1233	2285	515	118	170	1424	1059	34	700	.301	.390	.468	119	239	87-71	.951	53	102	105	S1843,3b69,1b57,2b35/lf	67	39.6

Cronin, Bill
William Patrick "Crungy"; B12.26.1902 W.Newton MA; D10.26.1966 Newton MA; BR/TR/5´9˝/167; d7.4

YEAR	TM LG	G	AB	R	H	2B	3B	HR	RBI	BB-IB	HP	SO	AVG	OBP	SLG	AOPS	ABR	SB-CS	FA	FR	RNG	THR	GAMES AT POSITION	DL	BFW
1928	Bos N	3	2	1	0	0	0	0	0	1	0	0	.000	.333	.000	-6	0	0	1.000	0	*0*	*0*	C3	—	0.0
1929	Bos N	6	9	0	1	0	0	0	0	0	0	0	.111	.111	.111	-47	-2	0	1.000	1	*157*	*88*	C6	—	-0.1
1930	Bos N	66	178	19	45	9	1	0	17	4	2	8	.253	.277	.315	44	-16	0	.983	4	*117*	*90*	C64	—	-0.7
1931	Bos N	51	107	8	22	6	1	0	10	7	2	5	.206	.267	.280	49	-8	0	.941	0	*105*	*94*	C50	—	-0.6
Total	4	126	296	28	68	15	2	0	27	12	4	13	.230	.269	.294	43	-26	0	.968	5	*113*	*91*	C123	—	-1.4

Crooke, Tom
Thomas Aloysius; B7.26.1884 Washington DC; D4.5.1929 Quantico VA; BR/TR/6´0˝/180; d9.29

YEAR	TM LG	G	AB	R	H	2B	3B	HR	RBI	BB-IB	HP	SO	AVG	OBP	SLG	AOPS	ABR	SB-CS	FA	FR	RNG	THR	GAMES AT POSITION	DL	BFW
1909	Was A	3	7	2	2	1	0	0	2	2	0	—	.286	.444	.429	184	1	1	.969	-1	0	207	1b3	—	0.0
1910	Was A	8	21	1	4	1	0	0	1	1	0	—	.190	.227	.238	48	-1	0	1.000	-0	75	97	1b5	—	-0.2
Total	2	11	28	3	6	2	0	0	3	3	0	—	.214	.290	.286	85	0	1	.988	-1	47	138	1b8	—	-0.2

Crooks, Jack
John Charles; B11.9.1865 St.Paul MN; D2.2.1918 St.Louis MO; BR/TR/5´10˝/170; d9.26; M1

YEAR	TM LG	G	AB	R	H	2B	3B	HR	RBI	BB-IB	HP	SO	AVG	OBP	SLG	AOPS	ABR	SB-CS	FA	FR	RNG	THR	GAMES AT POSITION	DL	BFW
1889	Col AA	12	43	13	14	2	3	0	7	10	1	4	.326	.463	.512	187	6	10	.987	4	123	64	2b12	—	0.8
1890	Col AA	135	485	86	107	5	4	1	62	96	7	—	.221	.357	.254	86	-1	57	.937	-1	93	121	2b134/3lf	—	0.3
1891	Col AA	**138**	519	110	127	19	13	0	46	103	9	47	.245	.379	.331	110	14	50	**.957**	18	98	129	2b138	—	3.2
1892	StL N	128	445	82	95	7	4	7	38	**136**	2	52	.213	.400	.294	116	22	23	.928	-5	94	96	2b100,3b26,O2R,M	—	2.0
1893	StL N	128	448	93	106	10	9	1	48	**121**	9	37	.237	.408	.306	91	2	31	.908	2	99	87	3b123,S4/C	—	0.6
1895	Was N	118	412	81	117	19	8	6	58	70	8	39	.284	.398	.413	111	10	36	**.956**	18	104	79	2b118	—	2.6
1896	Was N	25	84	20	24	3	0	3	20	16	1	8	.286	.406	.429	120	3	2	.916	-2	86	60	2b20,3b4	—	0.1
	Lou N	39	122	19	29	5	1	2	15	20	2	8	.238	.354	.344	88	-1	8	.925	1	92	130	2b39	—	0.1
	Year	64	206	39	53	8	1	5	35	36	3	16	.257	.376	.379	101	2	10	.922	-2	90	107	2b59,3b4	—	0.2
1898	StL N	72	225	33	52	4	2	1	20	40	5	—	.231	.359	.280	82	-3	3	.959	2	99	81	2b66,3b3,S2/O(1/1/0)	—	0.2
Total	8	795	2783	537	671	74	44	21	314	612	44	195	.241	.386	.322	102	52	220	.946	37	97	104	2b627,3b157,S6,O4(2/1/2)/C	—	9.9

Crosby, Ed
Edward Carlton; B5.26.1949 Long Beach CA; BL/TR/6´2˝/(170–180); [StLN69*2/43]; d7.12; s–Bobby; Col Long Beach (CA) City

YEAR	TM LG	G	AB	R	H	2B	3B	HR	RBI	BB-IB	HP	SO	AVG	OBP	SLG	AOPS	ABR	SB-CS	FA	FR	RNG	THR	GAMES AT POSITION	DL	BFW
1970	StL N	38	95	9	24	4	1	0	6	7-0	1	5	.253	.308	.316	66	-5	0-0	.954	2	109	94	S35,3b3,2b2	0	0.0
1972	StL N	101	276	27	60	9	1	0	19	18-1	2	27	.217	.269	.257	51	-18	1-1	.979	-4	94	112	S43,2b38,3b14	0	-1.7
1973	StL N	22	39	4	5	2	1	0	1	4-1	0	4	.128	.209	.231	22	-4	0-0	.938	-3	86	99	S7,2b5,3b4	0	-0.7
	†Cin N	36	51	4	11	1	1	0	5	7-1	2	12	.216	.333	.275	73	-2	0-1	.953	1	116	86	S29,2b5	0	0.1
	Year	58	90	8	16	3	2	0	6	11-2	2	16	.178	.282	.256	51	-6	0-1	.950	-2	111	88	S36,2b10,3b4	0	-0.6
1974	Cle A	37	86	11	18	3	0	0	6	6-0	0	12	.209	.258	.244	46	-6	0-1	.926	-3	71	99	3b18,S13,2b3	0	-0.9
1975	Cle A	61	128	12	30	3	0	0	7	13-0	0	14	.234	.305	.258	60	-6	0-4	.974	-1	100	84	S30,2b19,3b13	0	-0.5
1976	Cle A	2	2	0	1	0	0	0	0	0-0	0	0	.500	.500	.500	195	0	0-0	1.000	1	293	0	/3D	0	0.1
Total	6	297	677	67	149	22	4	0	44	55-3	5	74	.220	.282	.264	55	-41	1-7	.964	-7	104	92	S157,2b72,3b53/D	0	-3.6

Crosby, Bubba
Richard Stephen; B8.11.1976 Houston TX; BL/TL/5´11˝/(180–185); [LAN98 1/23]; d5.29; Col Rice

YEAR	TM LG	G	AB	R	H	2B	3B	HR	RBI	BB-IB	HP	SO	AVG	OBP	SLG	AOPS	ABR	SB-CS	FA	FR	RNG	THR	GAMES AT POSITION	DL	BFW
2003	LA N	9	12	0	1	0	0	0	1	0-0	0	3	.083	.083	.083	-58	-3	0-0	.667	-0	114	0	/lf	0	-0.3
2004	†NY A	55	53	8	8	2	0	2	7	2-0	1	13	.151	.196	.302	27	-6	2-0	.973	-1	98	0	O45(11/12/25),D2	0	-0.7
2005	†NY A	76	98	15	27	0	1	1	6	4-0	0	14	.276	.304	.327	68	-5	4-1	1.000	3	120	125	O67(4/41/23),D4	0	-0.1
2006	NY A	65	87	9	18	3	1	1	6	4-0	2	21	.207	.258	.299	44	-8	3-1	1.000	-1	98	59	O62(10/24/31)/D	27	-0.8
Total	4	205	250	32	54	5	2	4	20	10-0	3	51	.216	.255	.300	45	-22	9-2	.989	1	107	71	O175(26/77/79),D7	27	-1.9

Crosby, Bobby
Robert Edward; B1.12.1980 Lakewood CA; BR/TR/6´3˝/(195–215); [OakA01 1/25]; d9.2; f–Ed; Col Cal St.–Long Beach

YEAR	TM LG	G	AB	R	H	2B	3B	HR	RBI	BB-IB	HP	SO	AVG	OBP	SLG	AOPS	ABR	SB-CS	FA	FR	RNG	THR	GAMES AT POSITION	DL	BFW
2003	Oak A	11	12	1	0	0	0	0	0	1-0	1	5	.000	.143	.000	-57	-3	0-0	.889	2	165	144	S9,D2	0	-0.1
2004	Oak A	151	545	70	130	34	1	22	64	58-0	9	141	.239	.319	.426	93	-5	7-3	.975	16	110	111	S151	0	2.2
2005	Oak A	84	333	66	92	25	4	9	38	35-0	1	54	.276	.346	.456	112	6	0-0	.981	5	103	120	S84	77	1.7
2006	Oak A	96	358	42	82	12	0	9	40	36-1	0	76	.229	.298	.338	66	-19	8-1	.972	-4	99	95	S95	59	-1.3
Total	4	342	1248	179	304	71	5	40	142	130-1	11	276	.244	.318	.405	89	-21	15-4	.975	19	106	109	S339,D2	136	2.5

Crosetti, Frankie
Frank Peter Joseph "Crow"; B10.4.1910 San Francisco CA; D2.11.2002 Stockton CA; BR/TR/5´10˝/165; d4.12; Def 1944; C25

YEAR	TM LG	G	AB	R	H	2B	3B	HR	RBI	BB-IB	HP	SO	AVG	OBP	SLG	AOPS	ABR	SB-CS	FA	FR	RNG	THR	GAMES AT POSITION	DL	BFW
1932	†NY A	116	398	47	96	20	9	5	57	51	5	51	.241	.335	.374	88	-7	3-2	.937	-5	89	104	S84,3b33/2	—	-0.5
1933	NY A	136	451	71	114	20	5	9	60	55	2	40	.253	.337	.379	95	-3	4-1	.936	-8	91	75	S133	—	-0.1
1934	NY A	138	554	85	147	22	10	11	67	61	**5**	58	.265	.344	.401	98	-3	5-6	.945	-11	91	111	S119,3b23/2	—	-0.5
1935	NY A	87	305	49	78	17	6	8	50	41	4	27	.256	.351	.430	107	3	3-1	.963	-7	94	88	S87	—	0.2
1936	†NY A★	151	632	137	182	35	7	15	78	90	**12**	83	.288	.387	.437	107	9	18-7	.948	-13	94	96	S151	—	0.8
1937	†NY A	149	611	127	143	29	5	11	49	86	**12**	105	.234	.340	.352	74	-23	13-7	.948	0	98	101	S147	—	-1.1
1938	†NY A	**157**	631	113	166	35	3	9	55	106	**15**	97	.263	.382	.371	90	-5	**27**-12	.948	18	**106**	**119**	S157	—	2.4
1939	†NY A☆	**152**	656	109	153	25	5	10	56	65	**13**	81	.233	.315	.332	67	-34	11-7	**.968**	10	97	**148**	S152	—	-1.2
1940	NY A	145	546	84	106	23	4	4	31	72	**10**	77	.194	.299	.273	52	-39	14-8	.954	-13	97	91	S145	—	-3.9
1941	NY A	50	148	13	33	2	2	1	22	18	3	14	.223	.320	.284	61	-8	0-2	.944	5	100	107	S32,3b13	0	-0.1
1942	†NY A	74	285	50	69	5	5	4	23	31	**9**	31	.242	.335	.337	91	-3	1-1	.951	0	88	140	3b62,S8,2b2	0	-0.1
1943	†NY A	95	348	36	81	8	1	2	20	36	7	47	.233	.317	.279	74	-11	4-4	.946	-0	96	107	S90	0	-0.4
1944	NY A	55	197	20	47	4	2	5	30	11	6	21	.239	.299	.355	84	-5	3-0	.960	-5	88	96	S55	0	-0.5
1945	NY A	130	441	57	105	12	0	4	48	59	**10**	65	.238	.341	.293	81	-8	7-1	.946	-5	96	115	S126	0	-0.3
1946	NY A	28	59	4	17	3	0	0	3	8	1	2	.288	.382	.339	101	1	0-3	.940	5	124	146	S24	0	0.6
1947	NY A	3	1	0	0	0	0	0	0	0	0	0	.000	.000	.000	-99	0	0-0	ø	-0	0	0	/2S	0	-0.1
1948	NY A	17	14	4	4	0	1	0	0	2	0	0	.286	.375	.429	115	0	0-0	1.000	0	117	251	2b6,S5	0	0.0
Total	17	1683	6277	1006	1541	260	65	98	649	792	114	799	.245	.341	.354	84	-136	113-62	.949	-30	96	107	S1516,3b131,2b11	0	-4.8

Cross, Amos
Amos C.; B1861 , Czechoslovakia; D7.16.1888 Cleveland OH; d4.22; b–Frank b–Lave

YEAR	TM LG	G	AB	R	H	2B	3B	HR	RBI	BB-IB	HP	SO	AVG	OBP	SLG	AOPS	ABR	SB-CS	FA	FR	RNG	THR	GAMES AT POSITION	DL	BFW
1885	Lou AA	35	130	11	37	2	1	0	14	0	1	—	.285	.290	.315	91	-2	—	.936	-0	—	—	C35	—	0.1
1886	Lou AA	74	283	51	78	14	6	1	42	44	1	—	.276	.375	.378	129	11	13	.910	-7	—	—	C51,1b20,S2/lf	—	0.5
1887	Lou AA	8	28	0	3	0	0	0	0	1	0	—	.107	.138	.107	-31	-5	0	.808	-2	—	—	C5,1b2/rf	—	-0.6
Total	3	117	441	62	118	16	7	1	56	45	2	—	.268	.338	.342	108	4	13	.916	-10	—	—	C91,1b22,O2(1/0/1),S2	—	0.0

Cross, Clarence
Clarence (b Clarence Crause); B3.4.1856 St.Louis MO; D6.23.1931 Seattle WA; d5.5

YEAR	TM LG	G	AB	R	H	2B	3B	HR	RBI	BB-IB	HP	SO	AVG	OBP	SLG	AOPS	ABR	SB-CS	FA	FR	RNG	THR	GAMES AT POSITION	DL	BFW
1884	Alt U	2	7	1	4	1	0	0	—	2	—	—	.571	.667	.714	315	2	—	.500	-2	22	0	3b2	—	0.0
	Phi U	2	9	0	2	0	0	0	—	0	—	—	.222	.222	.222	38	-1	—	.545	-2	84	0	S2	—	-0.2
	KC U	25	93	13	20	1	0	0	—	6	—	—	.215	.263	.226	57	-7	—	.836	4	137	68	S24/3	—	-0.2
	Year	29	109	14	26	2	0	0	—	8	—	—	.239	.291	.257	76	-6	—	.813	1	133	62	S26,3b3	—	-0.4

YEAR	TM LG	G	AB	R	H	2B	3B	HR	RBI	BB-IB	HP	SO	AVG	OBP	SLG	AOPS	ABR	SB-CS	FA	FR	RNG	THR	GAMES AT POSITION	DL	BFW
1887	NY AA	16	55	9	11	2	1	0	5	2	3	—	.200	.267	.273	53	-3	0	.833	-2	105	34	S13,3b4	—	-0.4
Total	2	45	164	23	37	4	1	0	5	10	3	—	.226	.282	.262	67	-9	0	.818	-1	125	54	S39,3b7	—	-0.8
Cross, Frank	Frank Atwell "Mickey"; B1.20.1873 Cleveland OH; D11.2.1932 Geauga Lake OH; TR/5´9˝/161; d5.20; b–Amos b–Lave																								
1901	Cle A	1	5	0	3	0	0	0	0	0	0	—	.600	.600	.600	243	1	0	ø	-0	0	0	/rf	—	0.1
Cross, Jeff	Joffre James; B8.28.1918 Tulsa OK; D7.23.1997 Huntsville TX; BR/TR/5´11˝/160; d9.27; Mil 1943–45; Col Oklahoma																								
1942	StL N	1	4	0	1	0	0	0	1	0	0	0	.250	.250	.250	43	0	0	1.000	-0	123	0	/S	0	0.0
1946	StL N	49	69	17	15	3	0	0	6	10	0	8	.217	.316	.261	62	-3	4	.970	3	113	154	S17,2b8/3	0	0.0
1947	StL N	51	49	4	5	1	0	0	3	10	0	6	.102	.254	.122	3	-7	0	.947	2	129	118	3b15,S14,2b2	0	-0.4
1948	StL N	2	0	0	0	0	0	0	0	0	0	0	ø	ø	ø	ø	0	0	ø	0	—	—	/R	0	0.0
	Chi N	16	20	1	2	0	0	0	0	0	0	4	.100	.100	.100	-48	-4	0	.786	-3	79	0	S9/2	0	-0.7
	Year	18	20	1	2	0	0	0	0	0	0	4	.100	.100	.100	-47	-4	0	.786	-3	79	0	S9/2	0	-0.7
Total	4	119	142	22	23	4	0	0	10	20	0	18	.162	.265	.190	26	-14	4	.932	2	107	135	S41,3b16,2b11	0	-1.1
Cross, Lave	Lafayette Napoleon; B5.12.1866 Milwaukee WI; D9.6.1927 Toledo OH; BR/TR/5´8.5˝/155; d4.23; M1; b–Amos b–Frank; OF(13/34/72)																								
1887	Lou AA	54	203	32	54	8	3	0	26	15	1	—	.266	.320	.335	81	-5	15	.916	-2	—	—	C44,O10(3/1/6)	—	-0.3
1888	Lou AA	47	181	20	41	3	0	0	15	2	1	—	.227	.239	.243	56	-9	10	.929	2	—	—	C37,O12(2/0/10),S2	—	-0.4
1889	Phi AA	55	199	22	44	8	2	0	23	14	0	9	.221	.272	.281	58	-11	11	.934	14	—	—	C55	—	0.6
1890	Phi P	63	245	42	73	7	8	3	47	12	0	6	.298	.331	.429	100	-2	5	.885	3	*98*	*120*	C49,O15(0/5/10)	—	0.3
1891	Phi AA	110	402	66	121	20	14	5	52	38	3	23	.301	.366	.458	135	16	14	.971	1	145	279	O43R,C43,3b24/S2	—	1.8
1892	Phi N	140	541	84	149	15	10	4	69	39	3	16	.275	.328	.362	109	4	18	.921	6	107	55	3b65,C39,O25(8/17/0),2b14,S5	—	1.2
1893	Phi N	96	415	81	124	17	6	4	78	26	1	7	.299	.342	.398	96	-4	18	.974	15	*128*	*97*	C40,3b30,O10(0/9/1),S10,1b6	—	1.2
1894	Phi N	122	542	128	210	35	10	7	132	31	3	7	.387	.424	.528	131	27	23	.916	23	**120**	**148**	3b103,C16,S7/2	—	4.0
1895	Phi N	125	535	95	145	26	9	2	101	35	3	8	.271	.319	.364	76	-21	21	**.940**	32	**121**	121	3b125	—	1.1
1896	Phi N	106	406	63	104	23	5	1	73	32	1	14	.256	.312	.345	74	-16	8	.937	13	110	95	3b61,S37,2b6,O2C/C	—	0.0
1897	Phi N	88	344	37	89	17	5	3	51	10	1	—	.259	.282	.363	71	-16	10	.912	-1	98	81	3b47,2b38,O2R/S	—	-1.2
1898	StL N	151	602	71	191	28	8	3	79	28	0	—	.317	.348	.405	113	8	14	**.945**	20	**112**	90	3b149,S2	—	2.8
1899	Cle N	38	154	15	44	5	0	1	20	8	1	—	.286	.325	.338	88	-2	2	.955	5	98	99	3b38,M	—	0.3
	StL N	103	403	61	122	14	5	4	64	17	1	—	.303	.333	.392	96	-4	11	.960	31	122	178	3b103	—	2.5
	Year	141	557	76	166	19	5	5	84	25	2	—	.298	.330	.377	94	-6	13	**.959**	36	**116**	**157**	3b141	—	2.8
1900	StL N	16	61	6	18	1	0	0	6	1	0	—	.295	.306	.311	71	-3	1	.962	2	120	56	3b16	—	-0.1
	†Bro N	117	461	73	135	14	6	4	67	25	2	—	.293	.332	.375	90	-8	20	.943	3	101	61	3b117	—	-0.3
	Year	133	522	79	153	15	6	4	73	26	2	—	.293	.329	.368	88	-11	21	**.945**	5	103	60	3b133	—	-0.4
1901	Phi A	100	424	82	139	28	12	2	73	19	1	—	.328	.358	.465	121	11	23	.919	7	107	49	3b100	—	1.8
1902	Phi A	**137**	559	90	191	39	8	0	108	27	2	—	.342	.374	.440	120	15	25	.942	6	99	89	3b137	—	2.3
1903	Phi A	**137**	559	60	163	22	4	2	90	10	0	—	.292	.304	.356	93	-6	14	.950	-3	88	100	3b136/1	—	-0.5
1904	Phi A	**155**	607	73	176	31	10	1	71	13	5	—	.290	.310	.379	112	6	10	.936	-9	83	111	3b155	—	0.2
1905	†Phi A	147	587	69	156	29	5	0	77	26	2	—	.266	.299	.332	98	-2	8	.928	-12	85	49	3b147	—	-1.1
1906	Was A	130	494	55	130	14	6	1	46	28	0	—	.263	.303	.322	100	-1	19	**.952**	-4	93	65	3b130	—	-0.1
1907	Was A	41	161	13	32	8	0	0	10	10	0	—	.199	.246	.248	62	-7	3	.978	8	124	46	3b41	—	0.3
Total	21	2278	9085	1338	2651	412	136	47	1378	466	31	90	.292	.329	.383	100	-30	303	.938	160	103	92	3b1724,C324,O119R,S65,2b60,1b7	—	16.4
Cross, Monte	Montford Montgomery; B8.31.1869 Philadelphia PA; D6.21.1934 Philadelphia PA; BR/TR/5´8.5˝/148; d9.27; U1																								
1892	Bal N	15	50	5	8	0	0	0	2	4	0	10	.160	.222	.160	16	-5	2	.864	-2	100	41	S15	—	-0.6
1894	Pit N	13	43	14	19	1	5	2	13	5	2	4	.442	.520	.837	225	8	6	.924	-0	89	127	S13	—	0.7
1895	Pit N	109	397	67	101	14	13	3	54	38	3	38	.254	.324	.378	85	-10	39	.884	-17	87	95	S108/2	—	-1.7
1896	StL N	125	427	66	104	10	6	6	52	58	6	48	.244	.342	.337	83	-9	40	.892	-13	94	54	S125	—	-1.3
1897	StL N	132	465	60	133	17	11	4	55	62	7	—	.286	.378	.396	107	6	38	.918	30	**117**	81	S132	—	3.6
1898	Phi N	149	525	68	135	25	5	1	50	55	8	—	.257	.337	.330	95	-1	20	.907	16	103	103	S149	—	2.1
1899	Phi N	**154**	557	85	143	25	6	3	65	56	10	—	.257	.335	.339	88	-7	26	.909	2	101	98	S154	—	0.2
1900	Phi N	131	466	59	94	11	3	3	62	51	6	—	.202	.289	.258	52	-30	19	.928	-7	94	119	S131	—	-2.8
1901	Phi N	139	483	49	95	14	1	1	44	52	5	—	.197	.281	.236	50	-29	24	.924	-16	93	65	S139	—	-4.0
1902	Phi A	**137**	497	72	115	22	2	3	59	32	8	—	.231	.289	.302	61	-26	17	.927	9	99	62	S137	—	-1.2
1903	Phi A	**137**	470	44	116	21	2	3	45	49	6	—	.247	.326	.319	90	-3	31	.940	8	92	78	S137/2	—	0.9
1904	Phi A	153	503	33	95	23	4	1	38	46	7	—	.189	.266	.256	62	-20	19	.937	-15	86	58	S153	—	-3.3
1905	†Phi A	79	252	28	67	17	2	0	24	19	6	—	.266	.332	.349	114	5	8	.929	-10	84	97	S77,2b2	—	-0.3
1906	Phi A	134	445	32	89	23	3	1	40	50	7	—	.200	.291	.272	74	-11	22	.938	3	91	111	S134	—	-0.4
1907	Phi A	77	248	37	51	9	5	0	18	39	1	—	.206	.316	.282	89	-1	17	.954	8	97	84	S74	—	0.9
Total	15	1684	5828	719	1365	232	68	31	621	616	82	100	.234	.316	.313	80	-133	328	.920	-4	96	84	S1678,2b4	—	-7.2
Crossin, Frank	Frank Patrick; B6.15.1891 Avondale PA; D12.6.1965 Kingston PA; BR/TR/5´10˝/160; d9.24																								
1912	StL A	8	22	2	5	0	0	0	2	1	0	—	.227	.261	.227	41	-2	1	.920	-3	*70*	*81*	C8	—	-0.5
1913	StL A	4	4	1	1	0	0	0	0	1	1	1	.250	.500	.250	124	0	0	.857	-1	*85*	*73*	C2	—	0.0
1914	StL A	43	90	5	11	1	1	0	5	10	2	10	.122	.225	.156	15	-9	3	.934	-2	*101*	*90*	C41	—	-0.8
Total	3	55	116	8	17	1	1	0	7	12	3	11	.147	.244	.172	25	-11	4	.930	-5	*96*	*88*	C51	—	-1.3
Crotty, Joe	Joseph P.; B12.24.1860 Cincinnati OH; D6.22.1926 Minneapolis MN; BR/TR; d5.4																								
1882	Lou AA	5	20	1	2	0	0	0	—	0	—	—	.100	.100	.100	-34	-3	—	.882	0	—	—	C5	—	-0.2
	StL AA	8	28	2	4	1	0	0	—	3	—	—	.143	.226	.179	37	-2	—	.882	-1	—	—	C7/cf	—	-0.2
	Year	13	48	3	6	1	0	0	—	3	—	—	.125	.176	.146	10	-4	—	.882	-0	—	—	C12/cf	—	-0.4
1884	Cin U	21	84	11	22	4	2	1	—	1	—	—	.262	.271	.393	91	-4	—	.896	-3	—	—	C21	—	-0.5
1885	Lou AA	39	129	14	20	2	0	0	7	3	3	—	.155	.193	.171	15	-12	—	.931	0	—	—	C38/1	—	-0.8
1886	NY AA	14	47	6	8	0	1	0	2	4	1	—	.170	.250	.213	50	-3	3	.933	-0	—	—	C14	—	-0.2
Total	4	87	308	34	56	7	3	1	9	11	4	—	.182	.220	.234	43	-24	3	.915	-4	—	—	C85/1cf	—	-1.9
Crouch, Jack	Jack Albert "Roxy"; B10.12.1903 Cooleemee NC; D8.25.1972 Leesburg FL; BR/TR/5´9˝/165; d9.18																								
1930	StL A	6	14	1	2	1	0	0	1	1	0	3	.143	.200	.214	5	-2	0-0	1.000	1	*197*	*146*	C5	—	-0.1
1931	StL A	8	12	0	0	0	0	0	1	0	0	4	.000	.000	.000	-97	-3	0-0	.895	0	*171*	*87*	C7	—	-0.3
1933	StL A	19	30	1	5	0	0	1	5	2	0	6	.167	.219	.267	26	-3	0-0	1.000	-0	*88*	*206*	C9	—	-0.3
	Cin N	10	16	5	2	0	0	0	1	0	2	0	.125	.222	.125	1	-2	1	1.000	1	*84*	*70*	C6	—	-0.1
Total	3	43	72	7	9	1	0	1	8	3	2	13	.125	.182	.181	-3	-10	1-0	.976	1	*129*	*130*	C27	—	-0.8
Croucher, Frank	Frank Donald "Dingle"; B7.23.1914 San Antonio TX; D5.21.1980 Houston TX; BR/TR/5´11˝/165; d4.18; Mil 1943–45																								
1939	Det A	97	324	38	87	15	0	5	40	16	0	42	.269	.303	.361	64	-18	2-2	.934	-6	98	93	S93,2b3	—	-1.7
1940	†Det A	37	57	3	6	0	0	0	2	4	0	5	.105	.164	.105	-26	-11	0-0	.936	-2	100	35	S26,2b7/3	—	-1.1
1941	Det A	136	489	51	124	21	4	2	39	33	3	72	.254	.305	.325	61	-28	2-0	.935	-4	94	96	S136	0	-2.1
1942	Was A	26	65	2	18	1	1	0	5	3	0	9	.277	.309	.323	79	-2	0-0	.950	1	116	75	2b18	0	0.0
Total	4	296	935	94	235	37	5	7	86	56	3	128	.251	.296	.324	58	-59	4-2	.934	-10	96	92	S255,2b28/3	0	-4.9
Crouse, Buck	Clyde Ellsworth; B1.6.1897 Anderson IN; D10.23.1983 Muncie IN; BL/TR/5´8˝/158; d8.1																								
1923	Chi A	23	70	6	18	2	1	1	7	3	1	4	.257	.297	.357	73	-3	0-0	.955	-2	*73*	*107*	C22	—	-0.4
1924	Chi A	94	305	30	79	10	1	1	44	23	4	12	.259	.319	.308	64	-17	3-2	.945	-2	*80*	***127***	C90	—	-1.2
1925	Chi A	54	131	18	46	7	0	2	25	12	1	4	.351	.410	.450	125	5	1-2	.952	-0	*185*	*138*	C48	—	0.6
1926	Chi A	49	135	10	32	4	1	0	17	14	0	7	.237	.309	.281	57	-9	0-0	.985	2	*137*	*106*	C45	—	-0.4
1927	Chi A	85	222	22	53	11	0	0	20	21	1	10	.239	.307	.288	57	-14	4-1	.972	7	***117***	*142*	C81	—	-0.2
1928	Chi A	78	218	17	55	5	2	2	20	19	1	14	.252	.315	.321	68	-10	3-4	.959	2	*131*	*128*	C76	—	-0.5
1929	Chi A	45	107	11	29	7	0	2	12	5	2	7	.271	.316	.393	82	-3	2-0	.979	3	*115*	*104*	C40	—	0.3
1930	Chi A	42	118	14	30	8	1	0	15	17	0	10	.254	.348	.339	78	-3	1-1	.979	4	*107*	*120*	C38	—	0.2
Total	8	470	1306	128	342	54	6	8	160	114	10	68	.262	.326	.331	72	-54	14-10	.964	13	*116*	*125*	C440	—	-1.6
Crow, Don	Donald Le Roy; B8.18.1958 Yakima WA; BR/TR/6´4˝/195; [LAN79 3/76]; d7.25; Col Washington St.																								
1982	LA N	4	4	0	0	0	0	0	0	0-0	0	3	.000	.000	.000	-99	-1	0-0	1.000	-1	43	123	C4	0	-0.2

YEAR	TM LG	G	AB	R	H	2B	3B	HR	RBI	BB-IB	HP	SO	AVG	OBP	SLG	AOPS	ABR	SB-CS	FA	FR	RNG	THR	GAMES AT POSITION	DL	BFW
Crowe, George	George Daniel “Big George”; B3.22.1921 Whiteland IN; BL/TL/6´2˝/(210–212); d4.16; Col Indianapolis																								
1952	Bos N	73	217	25	56	13	1	4	20	18	5	25	.258	.329	.382	100	0	0-1	.985	1	112	82	1b55	0	-0.1
1953	Mil N	47	42	6	12	2	0	2	6	2	1	7	.286	.333	.476	115	1	0-0	1.000	0	161	65	1b9	0	0.1
1955	Mil N	104	303	41	85	12	4	15	55	45-8	1	44	.281	.374	.495	135	16	1-0	.989	2	111	88	1b79	0	1.3
1956	Cin N	77	144	22	36	2	1	10	23	11-1	2	28	.250	.312	.486	104	0	0-0	.988	2	128	69	1b32	0	0.1
1957	Cin N	133	494	71	134	20	1	31	92	32-3	1	62	.271	.314	.504	108	5	1-1	.989	-2	97	87	1b120	0	-0.4
1958	Cin N☆	111	345	31	95	12	5	7	61	41-3	0	51	.275	.348	.400	94	-3	1-0	.992	-1	94	87	1b93/2	0	-0.9
1959	StL N	77	103	14	31	6	0	8	29	5-2	0	12	.301	.330	.592	132	4	0-0	1.000	2	166	100	1b14	0	0.6
1960	StL N	73	72	5	17	3	0	4	13	5-1	0	16	.236	.278	.444	89	-1	0-0	1.000	0	112	51	1b5	0	-0.1
1961	StL N	7	7	0	1	0	0	0	0	0-0	0	1	.143	.143	.143	-22	-1	0-0	ø	0	—	—	/H	0	-0.1
Total	9	702	1727	215	467	70	12	81	299	159-18	10	246	.270	.333	.466	109	21	3-2	.990	5	106	85	1b407/2	0	0.5
Crowley, Ed	Edgar Jewel; B8.20.1906 Watkinsville GA; D4.14.1970 Birmingham AL; BR/TR/6´1˝/180; d6.21; Col Georgia Tech																								
1928	Was A	2	1	0	0	0	0	0	0	0	0	0	.000	.000	.000	-99	0	0-0	.000	-1	0	0	3b2	—	-0.1
Crowley, John	John A.; B1.12.1862 Lawrence MA; D9.23.1896 Lawrence MA; 5´10˝/164; d5.1																								
1884	Phi N	48	168	26	41	7	3	0	19	15	—	21	.244	.306	.321	102	1	—	.832	-20	—	—	C48	—	-1.3
Crowley, Terry	Terrence Michael; B2.16.1947 Staten Island NY; BL/TL/6´0˝/(170–182); [BalA66 11/216]; d9.4; C20; Col Long Island–Brooklyn																								
1969	Bal A	7	18	2	6	0	0	0	3	1-0	0	4	.333	.350	.333	96	0	0-0	1.000	0	135	179	1b3,O2L	0	0.0
1970	†Bal A	83	152	25	39	5	0	5	20	35-3	0	26	.257	.394	.388	115	5	2-0	.973	-4	85	0	O27(6/0/22),1b23	0	-0.1
1971	Bal A	18	23	2	4	0	0	0	1	3-0	0	4	.174	.269	.174	27	-2	0-0	1.000	-1	73	0	O6(1/0/5),1b2	0	-0.3
1972	Bal A	97	247	30	57	10	0	11	29	32-5	1	26	.231	.319	.405	111	4	0-0	.990	-3	87	49	O68(3/0/65),1b15	0	-0.4
1973	†Bal A	54	131	16	27	4	0	3	15	16-1	1	14	.206	.297	.305	70	-5	0-0	.867	0	76	184	D23,O10(2/0/8),1b7	0	-0.7
1974	Cin N	84	125	11	30	12	0	1	20	10-0	1	16	.240	.293	.360	86	-2	1-0	1.000	0	94	88	O22(1/0/21),1b7	0	-0.3
1975	†Cin N	66	71	8	19	6	0	1	11	7-1	0	6	.268	.333	.394	100	0	0-0	1.000	2	161	180	1b4,O4(3/0/1)	0	0.2
1976	Atl N	7	6	0	0	0	0	0	1	0-0	0	0	.000	.000	.000	-94	-2	0-0	ø	0	—	—	/H	0	-0.2
	Bal A	33	61	5	15	1	0	0	5	7-1	1	11	.246	.333	.262	80	-1	0-0	1.000	0	178	74	D17/1	0	-0.2
1977	Bal A	18	22	3	8	1	0	1	9	1-0	0	3	.364	.391	.545	161	2	0-0	1.000	0	0	0	/1D	0	0.2
1978	Bal A	62	95	9	24	2	0	0	12	8-0	1	12	.253	.314	.274	72	-3	0-0	1.000	1	143	4397	D17,O2L/1	0	-0.3
1979	†Bal A	61	63	8	20	5	1	1	8	14-2	1	13	.317	.449	.476	155	6	0-0	1.000	-0	0	188	D15,1b2	0	0.5
1980	Bal A	92	233	33	67	8	0	12	50	29-2	0	21	.288	.364	.476	131	10	0-0	1.000	2	357	52	D65,1b3	0	0.9
1981	Bal A	68	134	12	33	6	0	4	25	29-5	0	12	.246	.376	.381	120	5	0-0	1.000	0	105	79	D42,1b4	0	0.4
1982	Bal A	65	93	8	22	2	0	3	17	21-1	0	9	.237	.377	.355	103	1	0-0	.988	0	107	167	D14,1b10	0	0.0
1983	Mon N	50	44	2	8	0	0	0	3	9-0	1	4	.182	.327	.182	46	-3	0-0	1.000	-1	0	116	1b4	0	-0.4
Total	15	865	1518	174	379	62	1	42	229	222-21	7	181	.250	.345	.375	104	15	3-0	.980	-4	88	76	D195,O141(20/0/122),1b87	0	-0.7
Crowley, Bill	William Michael; B4.8.1857 Philadelphia PA; D7.14.1891 Gloucester NJ; BR/TR/5´7.5˝/159; d4.26; OF(82/150/254)																								
1875	Phi NA	9	37	4	3	0	0	0	3	1	—	0	.081	.105	.081	-33	-5	0-0	.800	-1	80	0	3b4,O4C/1	—	-0.5
1877	Lou N	**61**	238	30	67	9	3	1	23	4	—	13	.282	.293	.357	88	-5	—	.849	7	**185**	121	O58(0/57/2),S2,C2/32	—	0.0
1879	Buf N	60	261	41	75	9	5	0	30	6	—	14	.287	.303	.360	115	4	—	.809	-1	143	403	O43(3/1/39),C10,1b7,2b3	—	0.2
1880	Buf N	**85**	354	57	95	16	4	0	20	19	—	23	.268	.306	.336	115	6	—	.824	-2	126	80	O74(8/21/48),C22	—	0.3
1881	Bos N	72	279	33	71	12	0	0	31	14	—	15	.254	.290	.297	89	-2	—	.880	-3	88	170	O72(0/47/26)	—	-0.6
1883	Phi AA	23	96	16	24	4	3	0	16	3	—	—	.250	.273	.354	92	-1	—	.810	-2	78	0	O22(0/21/1)/1	—	-0.4
	Cle N	11	41	3	12	5	0	0	5	1	—	7	.293	.310	.415	119	1	—	.923	-2	0	0	O11R	—	-0.1
1884	Bos N	108	407	50	110	14	6	6	61	33	—	74	.270	.325	.378	121	10	—	.870	-7	96	168	O108(0/2/107)	—	0.2
1885	Buf N	92	344	29	83	14	1	1	36	21	—	32	.241	.285	.297	85	-5	—	.874	-4	47	37	O92(71/1/20)	—	-1.1
Total	7	512	2020	259	537	83	22	8	222	101	—	178	.266	.301	.341	103	8	—	.853	-13	103	136	O480R,C34,1b8,2b4,S2/3	—	-1.5
Crozier, Eric	Eric Le Roi; B8.11.1978 Columbus OH; BL/TL/6´4˝/200; [CleA00 41/1234]; d9.4; Col Norfolk St.																								
2004	Tor A	14	33	5	5	2	0	2	4	6-0	0	19	.152	.282	.394	70	-2	0-0	.972	-0	74	57	1b5,D8	0	-0.2
Cruise, Walton	Walton Edwin; B5.6.1890 Childersburg AL; D1.9.1975 Sylacauga AL; BL/TR/6´0˝/175; d4.14; Mil 1918																								
1914	StL N	95	256	20	58	9	3	4	28	25	3	42	.227	.303	.332	90	-3	3	.976	-1	102	66	O81(43/38/0)	—	-1.0
1916	StL N	3	3	0	2	0	0	0	0	1	0	0	.667	.750	.667	339	1	0	1.000	0	118	0	O2(1/1/0)	—	0.1
1917	StL N	153	529	70	156	20	10	5	59	38	1	73	.295	.343	.399	131	18	16	.965	-11	88	77	O152(49/85/26)	—	-0.1
1918	StL N	70	240	34	65	5	4	6	39	30	3	26	.271	.359	.400	136	11	2	.964	-8	83	51	O65(48/0/17)	—	0.0
1919	StL N	9	21	0	2	1	0	0	0	1	0	6	.095	.136	.143	-17	-3	0	.833	-1	70	0	O5(0/4/1),1b2	—	-0.4
	Bos N	73	241	23	52	7	0	1	21	17	0	29	.216	.267	.257	61	-11	8	.978	-2	96	87	O66(31/23/14)	—	-1.9
	Year	82	262	23	54	8	0	1	21	18	0	35	.206	.257	.248	55	-14	8	.971	-3	95	83	O71(31/27/15),1b2	—	-2.3
1920	Bos N	91	288	40	80	7	5	1	21	31	2	26	.278	.352	.347	106	3	5-3	.950	-6	81	99	O82R	—	-0.8
1921	Bos N	108	344	47	119	16	7	8	55	48	2	24	.346	.429	.503	154	29	10-8	.963	-1	115	18	O102(100/2/0),1b2	—	2.0
1922	Bos N	104	352	51	98	15	10	4	46	44	1	20	.278	.360	.412	103	2	4-4	.948	2	113	76	O100(37/0/64),1b2	—	-0.4
1923	Bos N	21	38	4	8	2	0	0	0	3	0	2	.211	.268	.263	42	-3	1-0	.952	-0	119	0	O9(8/0/1)	—	-0.3
1924	Bos N	9	9	4	4	1	0	1	3	0	0	2	.444	.444	.889	260	2	0-0	ø	0	—	—	/H	—	0.2
Total	10	736	2321	293	644	83	39	30	272	238	12	250	.277	.348	.386	114	46	49-15	.962	-27	97	66	O664(317/153/205),1b6	—	-2.6
Crumling, Gene	Eugene Leon; B4.5.1922 Wrightsville PA; BR/TR/6´0˝/180; d9.11																								
1945	StL N	6	12	0	1	0	0	0	1	0	0	1	.083	.083	.083	-52	-3	0	1.000	1	*83*	*183*	C6	0	-0.1
Crump, Buddy	Arthur Elliott; B11.29.1901 Norfolk VA; D9.26.1976 Raleigh NC; BL/TL/5´10˝/156; d9.28																								
1924	NY N	1	4	0	0	0	0	0	1	0	0	1	.000	.000	.000	-99	-1	0-0	.500	-1	47	0	/cf	—	-0.2
Cruthers, Press	Charles Preston; B9.8.1890 Marshallton DE; D12.27.1976 Kenosha WI; BR/TR/5´9˝/152; d9.29																								
1913	Phi A	3	12	0	3	1	0	0	0	0	0	0	.250	.250	.333	72	0	0	.923	-2	55	93	2b3	—	-0.2
1914	Phi A	4	15	1	3	0	1	0	0	0	0	4	.200	.200	.333	63	-1	0-1	1.000	1	91	74	2b4	—	-0.1
Total	2	7	27	1	6	1	1	0	0	0	0	4	.222	.222	.333	67	-1	0-1	.973	-1	76	82	2b7	—	-0.3
Cruz, Tommy	Cirilo (Dilan); B2.15.1951 Arroyo, PR; BL/TL/5´9˝/165; d9.4; b–Hector b–Jose																								
1973	StL N	3	0	1	0	0	0	0	0	0-0	0	0	ø	ø	ø	ø	0	0-0	ø	-0	0	0	/lf	0	0.0
1977	Chi A	4	2	1	0	0	0	0	0	0-0	0	0	.000	.000	.000	-99	-1	0-0	1.000	0	112	0	O2L	0	-0.1
Total	2	7	2	2	0	0	0	0	0	0-0	0	0	.000	.000	.000	-99	-1	0-0	1.000	-0	75	0	O3L	0	-0.1
Cruz, Deivi	Deivi (Garcia); B11.16.1972 Bani, D.R.; BR/TR/6´0˝/(175–205); d4.1																								
1997	Det A	147	436	35	105	26	0	2	40	14-0	0	55	.241	.263	.314	50	-32	3-6	.979	9	109	**112**	S147	0	-1.4
1998	Det A	135	454	52	118	22	3	5	45	13-0	3	55	.260	.284	.355	64	-25	3-4	.983	16	**115**	115	S135	27	0.1
1999	Det A	155	518	64	147	35	0	13	58	12-0	4	57	.284	.302	.427	83	-15	1-4	.983	7	104	103	S155	0	0.2
2000	Det A	156	583	68	176	46	5	10	82	13-2	4	43	.302	.318	.449	93	-8	1-4	.982	7	106	112	S156	0	0.9
2001	Det A	110	414	39	106	28	1	7	52	17-0	4	46	.256	.291	.379	77	-14	4-1	.964	-10	101	96	S109,3b7	40	-1.5
2002	SD N	151	514	49	135	28	2	7	47	22-2	3	58	.263	.294	.366	80	-17	2-3	.973	-8	98	91	S147/1	0	-1.6
2003	Bal A	152	548	61	137	24	2	14	65	13-1	2	49	.250	.269	.378	69	-27	1-2	.975	1	102	98	S147,D5	0	-1.5
2004	SF N	127	397	46	116	30	2	7	55	17-6	3	32	.292	.322	.431	90	-6	1-3	.980	-4	100	104	S104,2b2/3	0	-0.4
2005	SF N	81	209	26	56	10	1	5	19	10-1	0	31	.268	.301	.397	79	-7	0-1	.985	-1	93	110	2b33,S16,3b5	0	-0.6
	Was N	20	51	2	13	1	0	0	1	1-0	1	3	.255	.283	.275	49	-4	0-0	1.000	-1	91	165	2b16,S8	0	-0.4
	Year	101	260	28	69	11	1	5	20	11-1	1	34	.265	.298	.373	74	-11	0-1	.989	-2	93	123	2b49,S24,3b5	0	-1.0
Total	9	1234	4124	442	1109	250	16	70	464	132-12	24	429	.269	.293	.388	76	-155	16-28	.978	17	105	104	S1124,2b51,3b13,D5/1	67	-6.2
Cruz, Enrique	Enrique Michael; B11.21.1981 Santo Domingo, D.R.; BR/TR/6´1˝/180; d4.2																								
2003	Mil N	60	71	6	6	1	0	0	2	4-0	1	30	.085	.145	.099	-35	-14	0-0	1.000	-4	82	54	S13,2b6,3b2	0	-1.8
Cruz, Fausto	Fausto (Santiago); B5.1.1972 Monte Cristi, D.R.; BR/TR/5´10˝/165; d4.10																								
1994	Oak A	17	28	2	3	0	0	0	0	4-0	0	6	.107	.219	.107	-13	-5	0-0	.960	3	109	105	S10,3b4/2	0	-0.1
1995	Oak A	8	23	0	5	0	0	0	5	3-0	0	5	.217	.286	.217	42	-2	1-1	.971	-1	104	37	S8	0	-0.2
1996	Det A	14	38	5	9	2	0	0	0	1-0	0	11	.237	.256	.289	38	-4	0-0	.906	-2	104	56	2b8,S4/D	0	-0.5
Total	3	39	89	7	17	2	0	0	5	8-0	0	22	.191	.253	.213	23	-11	1-1	.934	1	107	66	S22,2b9,3b4/D	0	-0.8

YEAR	TM LG	G	AB	R	H	2B	3B	HR	RBI	BB-IB	HP	SO	AVG	OBP	SLG	AOPS	ABR	SB-CS	FA	FR	RNG	THR	GAMES AT POSITION	DL	BFW
CRUZ, HECTOR	Hector Louis (Dilan) "Heity"; B4.2.1953 Arroyo, PR; BR/TR/5´11˝/(173–180); d8.11; b–Tommy b–Jose																								
1973	StL N	11	11	1	0	0	0	0	0	1-0	0	3	.000	.083	.000	-75	-3	0-0	1.000	0	111	0	O5(1/4/0)	0	-0.3
1975	StL N	23	48	7	7	2	2	0	6	2-0	0	4	.146	.176	.271	23	-5	0-0	.800	-2	42	0	3b12,O6(4/0/2)	0	-0.9
1976	StL N	151	526	54	120	17	1	13	71	42-7	2	119	.228	.286	.338	76	-18	1-0	.934	-23	89	68	3b148	0	-4.5
1977	StL N	118	339	50	80	19	2	6	42	46-1	1	56	.236	.326	.357	85	-6	4-3	.964	-3	87	130	O106(27/0/85),3b2	0	-1.5
1978	Chi N	30	76	8	18	5	0	2	9	3-1	0	6	.237	.266	.382	70	-3	0-0	1.000	-2	93	0	O14(1/14/0),3b7	0	-0.5
	SF N	79	197	19	44	8	1	6	24	21-2	1	39	.223	.301	.365	88	-3	0-2	.978	-2	97	159	O53(31/17/14),3b14	0	-0.8
	Year	109	273	27	62	13	1	8	33	24-3	1	45	.227	.292	.370	83	-7	0-2	.983	-4	96	123	O67(32/31/14),3b21	0	-1.3
1979	SF N	16	25	2	3	0	0	0	1	3-0	0	7	.120	.214	.120	-7	-4	0-0	1.000	-1	94	0	O6(5/0/1),3b2	0	-0.5
	†Cin N	74	182	24	44	10	2	4	27	31-3	0	39	.242	.350	.385	101	1	0-1	.984	4	100	185	O69(13/23/49)	0	0.2
	Year	90	207	26	47	10	2	4	28	34-3	0	46	.227	.335	.353	89	-2	0-1	.985	3	100	176	O75(18/23/50),3b2	0	-0.3
1980	Cin N	52	75	5	16	4	1	1	5	8-1	0	16	.213	.289	.333	75	-3	0-0	.955	0	122	0	O29(15/1/15)	0	-0.4
1981	Chi N	53	109	15	25	5	0	7	15	17-0	0	24	.229	.331	.468	118	3	2-2	.925	-1	97	0	3b18,O16(8/0/10)	0	0.1
1982	Chi N	17	19	1	4	1	0	0	0	2-0	0	4	.211	.286	.263	52	-1	0-0	1.000	-1	30	0	O4(4/0/1)	0	-0.2
Total	9	624	1607	186	361	71	9	39	200	176-15	4	317	.225	.301	.353	81	-42	7-8	.975	-31	96	122	O308(109/59/177),3b203	0	-9.3
CRUZ, HENRY	Henry (Acosta); B2.27.1952 Christiansted, V.I.; BL/TL/6´0˝/(170–175); d4.18																								
1975	LA N	53	94	8	25	3	1	0	5	7-0	0	6	.266	.317	.319	80	-3	1-1	.960	-2	89	0	O41(17/23/4)	0	-0.7
1976	LA N	49	88	8	16	2	1	4	14	9-3	0	11	.182	.258	.364	76	-3	0-2	.976	-0	96	68	O23(5/5/17)	0	-0.6
1977	Chi A	16	21	3	6	0	0	2	5	1-1	0	3	.286	.318	.571	137	1	0-0	.833	-1	57	0	O9(1/2/6)	0	-0.1
1978	Chi A	53	77	13	17	2	1	2	10	8-0	1	11	.221	.292	.351	82	-2	0-1	1.000	3	96	270	O40(10/24/6)/D	0	0.0
Total	4	171	280	32	64	7	3	8	34	25-4	1	31	.229	.291	.361	84	-7	1-4	.974	-2	91	107	O113(33/54/33)/D	0	-1.4
CRUZ, JACOB	Jacob; B1.28.1973 Oxnard CA; BL/TL/6´0˝/(175–210); [SFN94 1/32]; d7.18; Col Arizona St.																								
1996	SF N	33	77	10	18	3	0	3	10	12-0	2	24	.234	.352	.390	97	0	0-1	.977	0	106	75	O23(6/0/17)	0	-0.1
1997	SF N	16	25	3	4	1	0	0	3	3-0	0	4	.160	.241	.200	20	-3	0-0	.933	2	124	535	O11(2/0/10)	0	-0.1
1998	SF N	3	3	0	0	0	0	0	0	0-0	0	2	.000	.000	.000	-99	-1	0-0	ø	0	—	—	/H	0	-0.1
	Cle A	1	1	0	0	0	0	0	0	0-0	0	1	.000	.000	.000	-96	0	0-0	ø	0	—	—	/H	0	0.0
1999	Cle A	32	88	14	29	5	1	3	17	5-0	1	13	.330	.368	.511	116	2	0-2	1.000	0	115	0	O24(11/15/2),D2	82	0.1
2000	Cle A	11	29	3	7	3	0	0	5	5-0	1	4	.241	.361	.345	80	-1	1-0	1.000	0	91	277	O9(1/8/0),D2	154	0.0
2001	Cle A	28	68	12	15	4	0	3	11	5-0	3	23	.221	.303	.412	83	-2	0-2	.976	0	116	0	O22(3/15/5)	0	-0.2
	Col N	44	76	7	16	1	0	1	7	10-0	1	27	.211	.303	.263	42	-6	0-2	.931	-2	80	85	O24(18/1/6)	31	-0.9
2002	Det A	35	88	12	24	3	1	2	6	13-0	3	20	.273	.377	.398	113	2	3-1	.929	-2	63	0	D14,O12(3/0/9),1b4	116	-0.1
2004	Cin N	96	147	22	33	8	0	3	28	16-2	4	43	.224	.317	.340	72	-6	0-0	1.000	-1	92	79	O29(4/0/26),1b6,D2	0	-0.8
2005	Cin N	110	127	12	30	10	0	4	18	16-1	1	46	.236	.324	.409	91	-1	0-0	1.000	-1	56	156	O20(8/0/12),1b5/D	0	-0.4
Total	9	409	729	95	176	38	2	19	105	85-3	16	207	.241	.331	.377	83	-16	4-8	.977	-3	95	88	O174(56/39/87),D21,1b15	383	-2.6
CRUZ, JOSE	Jose (Dilan); B8.8.1947 Arroyo, PR; BL/TL/6´0˝/(170–185); d9.19; C10; b–Tommy b–Hector s–Jose; [DL 1969 StL N 34]																								
1970	StL N	6	17	2	6	1	0	0	1	4-0	1	0	.353	.500	.412	143	2	0-0	1.000	1	195	0	O4(1/0/3)	0	0.3
1971	StL N	83	292	46	80	13	2	9	27	49-6	1	35	.274	.377	.425	122	10	6-3	.975	-4	97	43	O83(1/82/0)	0	0.4
1972	StL N	117	332	33	78	14	4	2	23	36-3	1	54	.235	.309	.319	80	-8	9-3	.979	4	104	162	O102(10/87/7)	0	-0.6
1973	StL N	132	406	51	92	22	5	10	57	51-4	1	66	.227	.310	.379	91	-5	10-4	.979	-2	112	24	O118(1/85/37)	0	-1.1
1974	StL N	107	161	24	42	4	3	5	20	20-5	0	27	.261	.341	.416	111	2	4-2	.975	1	110	84	O53(21/8/24)/1	0	0.1
1975	Hou N	120	315	44	81	15	2	9	49	52-6	1	44	.257	.358	.403	121	10	6-3	.980	5	116	102	O94(27/2/65)	0	1.2
1976	Hou N	133	439	49	133	21	5	4	61	53-5	0	46	.303	.377	.401	132	20	28-11	.972	7	108	118	O125(85/13/27)	0	2.4
1977	Hou N	157	579	87	173	31	10	17	87	69-13	0	67	.299	.368	.475	136	30	44-23	.973	-2	102	91	O155(0/6/155)	0	2.2
1978	Hou N	153	565	79	178	34	9	10	83	57-9	0	57	.315	.376	.460	142	32	37-9	.975	-2	112	33	O152R,1b2	0	2.8
1979	Hou N	157	558	73	161	33	7	9	72	72-16	0	66	.289	.367	.421	122	19	36-14	.959	1	104	59	O156L	0	1.7
1980	†Hou N☆	160	612	79	185	29	7	11	91	60-13	0	66	.302	.360	.426	131	25	36-11	.969	7	101	136	O158L	0	3.0
1981	†Hou N	107	409	53	109	16	5	13	55	35-4	0	49	.267	.319	.425	118	8	5-7	.984	4	116	54	O105L	0	0.6
1982	Hou N	155	570	62	157	27	2	9	68	60-12	1	67	.275	.342	.377	111	9	21-11	.964	6	111	72	O155L	0	0.9
1983	Hou N	160	594	85	**189**	28	8	14	92	65-10	1	86	.318	.385	.463	142	34	30-16	.979	-1	100	71	O160L	0	2.8
1984	Hou N	160	600	96	187	28	13	12	95	73-10	0	68	.312	.381	.462	147	38	22-8	.976	2	101	87	O160L	0	3.6
1985	Hou N★	141	544	69	163	34	4	9	79	43-10	0	74	.300	.349	.426	119	14	16-5	.971	4	100	122	O137(136/1/0)	0	1.3
1986	†Hou N	141	479	48	133	22	4	10	72	55-12	0	86	.278	.351	.403	111	7	3-4	.984	1	104	62	O134L	12	0.2
1987	Hou N	126	365	47	88	17	4	11	38	36-3	0	65	.241	.307	.400	89	-7	4-1	.984	4	108	85	O97L	0	-0.6
1988	NY A	38	80	9	16	2	0	1	7	8-1	0	8	.200	.273	.262	51	-5	0-1	.889	-1	74	0	D12,O8(4/0/4)	21	-0.7
Total	19	2353	7917	1036	2251	391	94	165	1077	898-142	7	1031	.284	.354	.420	121	235	317-136	.974	35	106	82	O2156(1411/284/474),D12,1b3	67	20.5
CRUZ, JOSE	Jose Luis; B4.19.1974 Arroyo, PR; BB/TR/6´0˝/(190–210); [SeaA95 1/3]; d5.31; f–Jose; Col Rice																								
1997	Sea A	49	183	28	49	12	1	12	34	13-0	0	45	.268	.315	.541	119	4	1-0	.966	-3	99	35	O49L	0	0.0
	Tor A	55	212	31	49	7	0	14	34	28-2	0	72	.231	.316	.462	101	0	6-2	.981	-2	89	89	O55(51/4/0)	0	-0.4
	Year	104	395	59	98	19	1	26	68	41-2	0	117	.248	.315	.499	109	3	7-2	.974	-5	94	64	O104(100/4/0)	0	-0.4
1998	Tor A	105	352	55	89	14	3	11	42	57-3	0	99	.253	.354	.403	97	-1	11-4	.984	-1	97	113	O105(6/103/0)	0	0.0
1999	Tor A	106	349	63	84	19	3	14	45	64-5	0	91	.241	.358	.433	99	0	14-4	.990	7	112	129	O106(9/97/0)	15	0.9
2000	Tor A	**162**	603	91	146	32	5	31	76	71-3	2	129	.242	.323	.466	94	-8	15-5	.993	-4	96	109	O162C	0	-0.8
2001	Tor A	146	577	92	158	38	4	34	88	45-4	1	138	.274	.326	.530	118	13	32-5	.990	-19	79	60	O143(14/133/0)	15	0.1
2002	Tor A	124	466	64	114	26	5	18	70	51-1	0	106	.245	.317	.438	95	-4	7-1	.992	3	101	127	O119(56/21/47),D2	36	-0.4
2003	†SF N	158	539	90	135	26	1	20	68	102-6	0	121	.250	.366	.414	103	5	5-8	.994	15	111	176	O158(0/3/157)	0	1.0
2004	TB A	153	545	76	132	25	8	21	78	76-8	2	117	.242	.333	.433	101	1	11-6	.970	-1	100	97	O152(0/1/151)	0	-0.7
2005	Bos A	4	12	0	3	1	0	0	0	1-0	0	4	.250	.308	.333	68	-1	0-0	1.000	-1	28	0	O4R	0	-0.2
	Ari N	64	202	23	43	9	0	12	28	42-2	0	54	.213	.347	.436	99	0	0-1	.980	-7	77	70	O58(3/53/6)	29	-0.7
	LA N	47	156	23	47	14	2	6	22	23-1	0	43	.301	.391	.532	138	9	0-1	.954	3	124	124	O45(1/0/45)	0	1.0
	Year	111	358	46	90	23	2	18	50	65-3	0	97	.251	.366	.478	115	9	0-2	.967	-4	98	94	O103(4/53/51)	0	0.3
2006	LA N	86	223	34	52	16	1	5	17	43-2	0	54	.233	.353	.381	89	-2	5-1	1.000	-1	106	0	O71(40/15/24)	0	-0.4
Total	10	1259	4419	670	1101	239	33	198	602	616-37	5	1073	.249	.339	.453	103	16	107-38	.986	-12	99	103	O1227(229/592/434),D2	95	-0.6
CRUZ, JULIO	Julio Luis; B12.2.1954 Brooklyn NY; BB/TR/5´9˝/(159–180); d7.4; Col San Bernardino Valley (CA) JC																								
1977	Sea A	60	199	25	51	3	1	1	7	24-1	0	29	.256	.336	.296	75	-6	15-6	.983	1	103	79	2b54/D	0	-0.1
1978	Sea A	147	550	77	129	14	1	1	25	69-0	1	66	.235	.319	.269	68	-22	59-10	**.987**	13	111	104	2b141,S5/D	0	0.9
1979	Sea A	107	414	70	112	16	2	1	29	62-0	0	61	.271	.363	.326	86	-5	49-9	.979	20	112	107	2b107	59	2.7
1980	Sea A	119	422	66	88	9	3	2	16	59-0	1	49	.209	.306	.258	56	-25	45-7	.983	10	**106**	102	2b115,D3	15	-0.1
1981	Sea A	94	352	57	90	12	3	2	24	39-0	3	40	.256	.332	.324	86	-5	43-8	.982	12	107	108	2b92/S	0	1.9
1982	Sea A	154	549	83	133	22	5	8	49	57-1	3	71	.242	.316	.344	79	-16	46-13	.987	3	98	97	2b151,S2/3D	0	0.2
1983	Sea A	61	181	24	46	10	1	2	12	20-1	2	22	.254	.332	.354	86	-3	33-6	.984	6	99	96	2b60/D	0	1.1
	†Chi A	99	334	47	84	9	4	1	40	29-0	2	44	.251	.311	.311	70	-14	24-6	.983	12	107	113	2b97	0	0.7
	Year	160	515	71	130	19	5	3	52	49-1	4	66	.252	.318	.326	76	-16	57-12	.983	19	104	107	2b157/D	0	1.8
1984	Chi A	143	415	42	92	14	4	5	43	45-0	0	58	.222	.295	.311	65	-19	14-6	.976	24	114	113	2b141	0	1.2
1985	Chi A	91	234	28	46	2	3	0	15	32-0	2	40	.197	.297	.231	45	-17	8-5	.982	9	101	116	2b87,D2	17	-0.4
1986	Chi A	81	209	38	45	2	0	0	19	42-0	0	28	.215	.343	.225	57	-11	7-2	.985	-8	96	97	2b78,D3	45	-1.3
Total	10	1156	3859	557	916	113	27	23	279	478-3	14	508	.237	.321	.299	71	-143	343-78	.983	103	106	104	2b1123,D13,S8/3	136	6.8
CRUZ, IVAN	Luis Ivan; B5.3.1968 Fajardo, PR; BL/TL/6´3˝/(210–225); [DetA89 28/733]; d7.18; Col Jacksonville																								
1997	NY A	11	20	0	5	1	0	0	3	2-0	0	4	.250	.318	.300	63	-1	0-0	1.000	-0	0	0	1b3/lfD	0	-0.1
1999	Pit N	5	10	3	4	0	0	1	2	0-0	0	2	.400	.400	.700	170	1	0-0	1.000	0	149	356	/1rf	92	0.1
2000	Pit N	8	11	0	1	0	0	0	0	0-0	0	8	.091	.091	.091	-54	-3	0-0	1.000	-0	0	0	/1	0	-0.3
2002	StL N	17	14	2	5	0	0	1	3	1-0	0	3	.357	.400	.571	151	1	0-0	1.000	0	95	0	1b7	0	0.1
Total	4	41	55	5	15	1	0	2	8	3-0	0	17	.273	.310	.400	82	-2	0-0	1.000	-0	67	80	1b12,D4,O2(1/0/1)	92	-0.2
CRUZ, NELSON	Nelson Ramon; B7.1.1980 Monte Cristi, D.R.; BR/TR/6´3˝/(175–225); d9.17																								
2005	Mil N	8	5	1	1	1	0	0	0	2-0	0	0	.200	.429	.400	118	0	0-0	1.000	0	104	0	O8(2/0/6)	0	0.0
2006	Tex A	41	130	15	29	3	0	6	22	7-0	0	32	.223	.261	.385	65	-8	1-0	1.000	1	94	177	O39(1/2/38)	0	-0.8
Total	2	49	135	16	30	4	0	6	22	9-0	0	32	.222	.269	.385	67	-8	1-0	1.000	1	95	167	O47(3/2/44)	0	-0.8

YEAR	TM LG	G	AB	R	H	2B	3B	HR	RBI	BB-IB	HP	SO	AVG	OBP	SLG	AOPS	ABR	SB-CS	FA	FR	RNG	THR	GAMES AT POSITION	DL	BFW
Cruz, Todd	Todd Ruben; B11.23.1955 Highland Park MI; BR/TR/6´0˝/(170–185); [PhiN73 2/26]; d9.4; [DL 1981 Chi A 56]																								
1978	Phi N	3	4	0	2	0	0	0	2	0-0	0	0	.500	.500	.500	177	0	0-1	1.000	1	183	0	S2	0	0.1
1979	KC A	55	118	9	24	7	0	2	15	3-0	1	19	.203	.224	.314	44	-10	0-1	.974	-6	95	58	S48,3b9	0	-1.2
1980	Cal A	18	40	5	11	3	0	1	5	5-1	0	8	.275	.356	.425	115	1	0-0	.860	-5	90	109	S12,3b4/2lf	0	-0.3
	Chi A	90	293	23	68	11	1	2	18	9-0	2	54	.232	.259	.297	52	-20	2-1	.956	4	105	86	S90	0	-0.7
	Year	108	333	28	79	14	1	3	23	14-1	2	62	.237	.271	.312	60	-19	2-1	.948	-1	104	88	S102,3b4/2lf	0	-1.0
1982	Sea A	136	492	44	113	20	2	16	57	12-1	0	95	.230	.246	.376	66	-25	2-10	.963	16	103	122	S136	15	0.2
1983	Sea A	65	216	21	41	4	2	7	21	7-2	2	56	.190	.221	.324	46	-17	1-3	.964	21	119	108	S63	0	0.9
	†Bal A	81	221	16	46	9	1	3	27	15-0	1	52	.208	.259	.299	54	-14	3-4	.942	3	108	134	3b79,2b2	0	-1.3
	Year	146	437	37	87	13	3	10	48	22-2	3	108	.199	.241	.311	51	-31	4-7	.942	**24**	108	134	3b79,S63,2b2	0	-0.4
1984	Bal A	96	142	15	31	4	0	3	9	8-0	1	33	.218	.263	.310	59	-8	1-4	.955	3	117	123	3b89/PD	0	-0.7
Total	6	544	1526	133	336	58	6	34	154	59-4	7	317	.220	.251	.333	58	-93	9-24	.960	37	106	103	S351,3b181,2b3/DPlf	71	-3.0
Cubbage, Mike	Michael Lee; B7.21.1950 Charlottesville VA; BL/TR/6´0˝/180; [TexA71 D2/25]; d4.7; M1/C14; Col Virginia																								
1974	Tex A	9	15	0	0	0	0	0	0	0-0	0	4	.000	.000	.000	-99	-4	0-0	1.000	2	129	0	3b3,2b2	0	-0.2
1975	Tex A	58	143	12	32	6	0	4	21	18-2	0	14	.224	.305	.350	87	-2	0-0	.962	1	112	105	2b37,3b3,D2	0	0.1
1976	Tex A	14	32	2	7	0	0	0	0	7-0	0	7	.219	.359	.219	70	-1	0-0	1.000	-1	75	118	2b5/3D	0	-0.2
	Min A	104	342	40	89	19	5	3	49	42-3	3	37	.260	.344	.371	108	5	1-1	.940	7	112	129	3b99,2b2,D2	0	1.2
	Year	118	374	42	96	19	5	3	49	49-3	3	44	.257	.346	.358	105	4	1-1	.940	6	112	129	3b100,D8,2b7	0	1.0
1977	Min A	129	417	60	110	16	5	9	55	37-6	0	49	.264	.321	.391	95	-4	1-4	.952	14	**118**	133	3b126/D	0	0.7
1978	Min A	125	394	40	111	12	7	7	57	40-3	1	44	.282	.348	.401	108	4	3-1	.971	7	113	**122**	3b115,2b5	0	1.0
1979	Min A	94	243	26	67	10	1	2	23	39-2	0	26	.276	.371	.350	93	-1	1-8	.928	-7	89	95	3b63,D21/12	18	-1.1
1980	Min A	103	285	29	70	9	0	8	42	23-4	1	37	.246	.301	.361	76	-10	0-1	.996	8	124	108	1b72,3b32/2D	15	-0.6
1981	NY N	67	80	9	17	2	2	1	4	9-1	0	15	.213	.289	.325	75	-3	0-0	.963	0	112	0	3b12	0	-0.3
Total	8	703	1951	218	503	74	20	34	251	215-21	5	233	.258	.330	.369	94	-16	6-15	.952	31	111	121	3b454,1b73,2b53,D33	33	0.6
Cuccinello, Al	Alfred Edward; B8.26.1914 Long Island City NY; D3.29.2004 Malverne NY; BR/TR/5´10˝/165; d5.17; b–Tony																								
1935	NY N	54	165	27	41	7	1	4	20	1	2	20	.248	.262	.376	70	-8	0	.951	1	102	119	2b48,3b2	—	-0.4
Cuccinello, Tony	Anthony Francis "Cooch","Chick"; B11.8.1907 Long Island City NY; D9.21.1995 Tampa FL; BR/TR/5´7˝/160; d4.15; C21; b–Al																								
1930	Cin N	125	443	64	138	22	5	10	78	47	2	44	.312	.380	.451	105	5	5	.920	-12	96	82	3b109,2b15,S4	—	0.0
1931	Cin N	**154**	575	67	181	39	11	2	93	54	0	28	.315	.374	.431	123	19	1	.969	7	103	**126**	2b154	—	3.5
1932	Bro N	**154**	597	76	168	32	6	12	77	46	4	47	.281	.337	.415	103	3	5	.973	21	**109**	**118**	2b154	—	3.2
1933	Bro N★	134	485	58	122	31	4	9	65	44	2	40	.252	.316	.388	105	3	4	.977	-17	88	87	2b120,3b14	—	-0.7
1934	Bro N	140	528	59	138	32	2	14	94	49	1	45	.261	.325	.409	100	0	0	.974	9	107	90	2b101,3b43	—	1.6
1935	Bro N	102	360	49	105	20	3	8	53	40	2	35	.292	.366	.431	116	9	3	.977	8	100	147	2b64,3b36	—	2.1
1936	Bos N	150	565	68	174	26	3	7	86	58	2	49	.308	.374	.402	116	15	1	.971	18	110	**141**	2b150	—	4.0
1937	Bos N	**152**	575	77	156	36	4	11	80	61	0	40	.271	.341	.405	112	10	2	.967	-13	104	110	2b151	—	0.7
1938	Bos N☆	147	555	62	147	25	2	9	76	52	3	32	.265	.331	.366	102	1	4	.974	-30	94	92	2b147	—	-1.9
1939	Bos N	81	310	42	95	17	1	2	40	26	0	26	.306	.360	.387	109	4	5	.970	-5	97	121	2b80	—	0.5
1940	Bos N	34	126	14	34	9	0	0	19	8	1	9	.270	.319	.341	87	-2	1	.978	2	110	164	3b33	—	0.1
	NY N	88	307	26	64	9	2	5	36	16	0	42	.208	.248	.300	50	-22	1	.987	7	105	69	2b47,3b37	—	-1.2
	Year	122	433	40	98	18	2	5	55	24	1	51	.226	.269	.312	60	-25	2	.971	9	108	144	3b70,2b47	—	-1.1
1942	Bos N	40	104	8	21	3	0	1	8	9	0	11	.202	.265	.260	55	-6	1	.907	-0	90	188	3b20,2b14	0	-0.6
1943	Bos N	13	19	0	0	0	0	0	2	3	0	1	.000	.136	.000	-60	-4	0	.929	0	118	346	3b4,2b2/S	0	-0.4
	Chi A	34	103	5	28	5	0	2	11	13	0	13	.272	.353	.379	114	2	3-1	.965	-1	92	100	3b30	0	0.2
1944	Chi A	38	130	5	34	3	0	0	17	8	0	16	.262	.304	.285	70	-5	0-0	.959	-1	98	97	3b30,2b6	0	-0.7
1945	Chi A✳	118	402	50	124	25	3	2	49	45	1	19	.308	.379	.400	130	17	6-2	.936	-6	101	109	3b112	0	1.3
Total	15	1704	6184	730	1729	334	46	94	884	579	18	497	.280	.343	.394	105	49	42-3	.973	-14	102	112	2b1205,3b468,S5	0	11.7
Cuddyer, Michael	Michael Brent; B3.27.1979 Norfolk VA; BR/TR/6´2˝/(202–220); [MinA97 1/9]; d9.23; OF(9/0/212)																								
2001	Min A	8	18	1	4	2	0	0	1	2-0	0	6	.222	.300	.333	63	-1	1-0	.975	-1	68	111	1b5,3b2/D	0	-0.2
2002	†Min A	41	112	12	29	7	0	4	13	8-0	1	30	.259	.311	.429	92	-1	2-0	.980	2	125	85	O25R,3b10,1b6,D3	0	0.0
2003	†Min A	35	102	14	25	1	3	4	8	12-0	0	19	.245	.325	.431	94	-1	1-1	1.000	-5	73	107	O18(1/0/17),3b7,1b5/2D	0	-0.7
2004	†Min A	115	339	49	89	22	1	12	45	37-2	3	74	.263	.339	.440	98	0	5-5	.982	-11	107	75	2b48,3b43,O15(7/0/8),1b10,D5	0	-1.0
2005	Min A	126	422	55	111	25	3	12	42	41-5	3	93	.263	.330	.422	97	-1	3-4	.942	-4	104	95	3b95,O20R,2b11,1b8	17	-0.6
2006	†Min A	150	557	102	158	41	5	24	109	62-5	10	130	.284	.362	.504	122	19	6-0	.981	-4	89	130	O143(1/0/142),1b6,D2	0	0.9
Total	6	475	1550	233	416	98	12	56	218	162-12	17	352	.268	.342	.455	105	15	18-10	.984	-23	91	106	O221R,3b157,2b60,1b40,D13	17	-1.6
Cudworth, Jim	James Alaric "Cuddy"; B8.22.1858 Fairhaven MA; D12.21.1943 Middleboro MA; BR/TR/6´0˝/165; d7.27; ▲																								
1884	KC U	32	116	7	17	3	1	0	—	2	—	—	.147	.161	.190	7	-17	—	.963	2	123	132	1b19,O12C,P2	—	-1.4
Cueto, Manuel	Manuel "Patato"; B2.8.1892 Guanajay, Cuba; D6.29.1942 Regla, Cuba; BR/TR/5´5˝/157; d6.25																								
1914	StL F	19	43	2	4	0	0	0	2	5	0	7	.093	.188	.093	-21	-8	0	.941	-2	89	0	3b10,S5,2b2	—	-1.0
1917	Cin N	56	140	10	28	3	0	1	11	16	1	17	.200	.287	.243	66	-5	4	.963	1	109	70	O38(32/4/3),2b6,C5	—	-0.6
1918	Cin N	47	108	14	32	5	1	0	14	19	1	5	.296	.406	.361	137	6	4	.929	-7	92	60	O19(12/1/4),2b10,S9,C6	—	0.0
1919	Cin N	29	88	10	22	2	0	0	4	10	2	4	.250	.340	.273	88	-1	5	.982	3	101	192	O25(7/0/18)/3	—	0.1
Total	4	151	379	36	86	10	1	1	31	50	4	33	.227	.323	.266	80	-8	13	.964	-4	103	111	O82(51/5/25),2b18,S14,C11,3b11	—	-1.5
Cuff, John	John Patrick; B6.1864 Jersey City NJ; D12.5.1916 Hoboken NJ; d9.11																								
1884	Bal U	3	11	1	1	1	0	0	—	1	—	—	.091	.167	.182	5	-2	—	.920	1	—	—	C3	—	-0.1
Culberson, Leon	Delbert Leon "Lee"; B8.6.1919 Halls GA; D9.17.1989 Rome GA; BR/TR/5´11˝/180; d5.16																								
1943	Bos A	81	312	36	85	16	6	3	34	31	0	35	.272	.338	.391	111	4	14-0	.978	2	98	150	O79(28/51/0)	0	0.6
1944	Bos A	75	282	41	67	11	5	2	21	20	0	20	.238	.288	.333	78	-9	6-4	.979	-1	99	94	O72C	0	-1.2
1945	Bos A	97	331	26	91	21	6	6	45	20	0	37	.275	.316	.429	113	4	4-3	.967	3	96	190	O91(1/89/1)	0	0.4
1946	†Bos A	59	179	34	56	10	1	3	18	16	0	19	.313	.369	.430	116	4	3-2	.967	-3	95	31	O49(6/18/26),3b4	0	-0.1
1947	Bos A	47	84	10	20	1	0	0	11	12	3	10	.238	.354	.250	65	-3	1-1	.974	-1	92	162	O25(5/4/16),3b4	0	-0.5
1948	Was A	12	29	1	5	0	0	0	2	8	0	5	.172	.351	.172	43	-2	0-0	1.000	-1	74	162	O11C	0	-0.3
Total	6	371	1217	148	324	59	18	14	131	107	3	126	.266	.327	.379	100	-2	28-10	.974	0	96	134	O327(40/245/43),3b8	0	-1.1
Cullen, John	John Joseph; B7.9.1854 New Orleans LA; D2.11.1921 Ukiah CA; 5´10.5˝/171; d8.18																								
1884	Wil U	9	31	2	6	0	0	0	—	1	—	—	.194	.219	.194	25	-4	—	.750	-2	63	0	O6(4/0/2),S3	—	-0.5
Cullen, Tim	Timothy Leo; B2.16.1942 San Francisco CA; BR/TR/6´1˝/185; d8.8; Col Santa Clara																								
1966	Was A	18	34	8	8	1	0	0	0	2-0	0	8	.235	.278	.265	57	-2	0-0	.889	-1	71	99	3b8,2b5	0	-0.3
1967	Was A	124	402	35	95	7	0	2	31	40-2	1	47	.236	.306	.269	74	-12	4-5	.951	15	121	114	S69,2b46,3b15/rf	0	1.1
1968	Chi A	72	155	16	31	7	0	2	13	15-5	1	23	.200	.275	.284	69	-6	0-0	.966	-2	109	113	2b71	0	-0.4
	Was A	47	114	8	31	4	2	1	16	7-1	2	12	.272	.323	.368	114	2	0-0	.968	-4	93	83	S33,2b16,3b3	0	0.0
	Year	119	269	24	62	11	2	3	29	22-6	3	35	.230	.295	.320	87	-4	0-0	.965	-7	109	107	2b87,S33,3b3	0	-0.4
1969	Was A	119	249	22	52	7	0	1	15	14-1	2	27	.209	.253	.249	44	-19	1-1	.981	4	103	102	2b105,S9/3	0	-1.1
1970	Was A	123	262	22	56	10	2	1	18	31-6	3	38	.214	.301	.279	65	-12	3-2	**.994**	12	111	119	2b112,S6	0	0.6
1971	Was A	125	403	34	77	13	4	2	26	33-4	0	47	.191	.252	.258	47	-29	2-1	.997	15	113	99	2b78,S62	0	-0.4
1972	†Oak A	72	142	10	37	8	1	0	15	5-0	0	17	.261	.286	.331	87	-3	0-1	.952	-4	100	93	2b65,3b4/S	0	-0.4
Total	7	700	1761	155	387	57	9	9	134	147-19	9	219	.220	.282	.278	65	-81	10-9	.979	35	108	106	2b498,S180,3b31/rf	0	-0.9
Cullenbine, Roy	Roy Joseph; B10.18.1913 Nashville TN; D5.28.1991 Mt.Clemens MI; BB/TR/6´1˝/190; d4.19																								
1938	Det A	25	67	12	19	1	3	0	9	12	0	9	.284	.392	.388	91	-1	2-0	1.000	0	104	88	O17L	—	-0.1
1939	Det A	75	179	31	43	9	2	6	23	34	0	29	.240	.362	.413	91	-2	0-1	.902	-2	96	70	O46(24/4/19),1b2	—	-0.7
1940	Bro N	22	61	8	11	1	0	1	9	23	0	11	.180	.405	.246	78	0	2	1.000	1	93	206	O19R	—	-0.1
	StL A	86	257	41	59	11	2	7	31	50	2	34	.230	.359	.370	87	-3	0-1	.975	-1	94	105	O57(11/0/49),1b6	—	-0.8
1941	StL A★	149	501	82	159	29	9	9	98	121	2	43	.317	.452	.465	138	36	6-4	.964	-1	94	113	O120(108/7/5),1b22	0	2.6
1942	StL A	38	109	15	21	7	1	2	14	30	0	20	.193	.367	.330	95	1	0-1	.930	1	81	228	O27L,1b5	0	-0.1
	Was A	64	241	30	69	19	0	2	35	44	0	18	.286	.396	.390	123	10	1-2	.966	6	108	222	O35L,3b28	0	1.5
	†NY A	21	77	16	28	7	0	2	17	18	0	2	.364	.484	.532	190	11	0-1	.980	1	111	128	O19R/1	0	1.0

YEAR	TM LG	G	AB	R	H	2B	3B	HR	RBI	BB-IB	HP	SO	AVG	OBP	SLG	AOPS	ABR	SB-CS	FA	FR	RNG	THR	GAMES AT POSITION	DL	BFW
	Year	123	427	61	118	33	1	6	66	92	0	40	.276	.405	.400	127	22	1-4	.959	8	100	199	O81(62/0/19),3b28,1b6	0	2.4
1943	Cle A	138	488	66	141	24	4	8	56	96	1	58	.289	.407	.404	146	34	3-4	.981	3	96	**157**	O121R,1b13	0	2.9
1944	Cle A☆	154	571	98	162	34	5	16	80	87	2	49	.284	.380	.445	141	33	4-4	.967	-3	89	142	O151(0/1/150)	0	2.0
1945	Cle A	8	13	3	1	1	0	0	0	11	0	0	.077	.500	.154	97	2	0-0	1.000	-1	105	0	O4R,3b3	0	0.0
	†Det A	146	523	80	145	27	5	18	93	102	3	36	.277	.398	.451	137	29	2-0	.980	9	105	152	O146(2/0/145)	0	3.1
	Year	154	536	83	146	28	5	18	93	**113**	3	36	.272	.402	.444	137	31	2-0	.980	8	105	**150**	O150(2/0/149),3b3	0	3.1
1946	Det A	113	328	63	110	21	0	15	56	88	1	39	.335	.477	.537	172	39	3-0	.965	2	86	191	O81(12/0/69),1b21	0	3.9
1947	Det A	142	464	82	104	18	1	24	78	137	0	51	.224	.401	.422	125	23	3-2	.989	18	**144**	90	1b138	0	3.6
Total	10	1181	3879	627	1072	209	32	110	599	853	11	399	.276	.408	.432	132	212	26-20	.969	32	96	146	O843(236/12/600),1b208,3b31	0	18.8
Culler, Dick	Richard Broadus; B1.15.1915 High Point NC; D6.16.1964 Chapel Hill NC; BR/TR/5´9.5˝/155; d9.19; Col High Point																								
1936	Phi A	9	38	3	9	0	0	0	1	1	0	3	.237	.256	.237	23	-5	0-0	.946	-2	71	86	2b7,S2	—	-0.6
1943	Chi A	53	148	9	32	5	1	0	11	16	1	11	.216	.297	.264	65	-6	4-5	.950	7	98	188	3b26,2b19,S3	0	0.1
1944	Bos N	8	28	2	2	0	0	0	0	4	0	2	.071	.188	.071	-24	-5	0	.904	1	120	117	S8	0	-0.3
1945	Bos N	136	527	87	138	12	1	2	30	50	2	35	.262	.328	.300	75	-17	7	.954	-9	99	103	S126,3b6	0	-1.7
1946	Bos N	134	482	70	123	15	3	0	33	62	2	18	.255	.342	.299	82	-10	7	.948	-4	95	92	S132	0	-0.6
1947	Bos N	77	214	20	53	5	1	0	19	19	0	15	.248	.309	.280	59	-13	1	.967	2	109	88	S77	0	-0.7
1948	Chi N	48	89	4	15	2	0	0	5	13	0	3	.169	.275	.191	29	-9	0	.968	10	120	99	S43,2b2	0	0.3
1949	NY N	7	1	0	0	0	0	0	0	1	0	0	.000	.500	.000	45	0	0	.889	1	141	307	S7	0	0.1
Total	8	472	1527	195	372	39	6	2	99	166	5	87	.244	.320	.281	68	-65	19-5	.954	4	102	96	S398,3b32,2b28	0	-3.4
Cullop, Nick	Henry Nicholas "Tomato Face" (b Heinrich Nicholas Kolop); B10.16.1900 St.Louis MO; D12.8.1978 Westerville OH; BR/TR/6´0˝/200; d4.14																								
1926	NY A	2	2	0	1	0	0	0	0	0	0	1	.500	.500	.500	164	0	0-0	ø	0	—	—	/H	—	0.0
1927	Was A	15	23	2	5	2	0	0	1	1	0	6	.217	.250	.304	44	-2	0-0	1.000	-0	102	0	O5(2/0/3)/1	—	-0.2
	Cle A	32	68	9	16	2	3	1	8	9	1	19	.235	.333	.397	88	-2	0-4	.982	2	110	199	O20(0/13/7)/P	—	-0.1
	Year	47	91	11	21	4	3	1	9	10	1	25	.231	.314	.374	78	-3	0-4	.984	2	109	172	O25(2/13/10)/1P	—	-0.3
1929	Bro N	13	41	7	8	2	2	1	5	8	0	7	.195	.327	.415	84	-1	0	1.000	1	92	222	O11(5/6/2)/1	—	-0.1
1930	Cin N	7	22	2	4	0	0	1	5	1	0	9	.182	.217	.318	29	-3	0	1.000	1	70	651	O5C	—	-0.2
1931	Cin N	104	334	29	88	23	7	8	48	21	1	86	.263	.309	.446	107	1	1	.968	1	101	115	O83L	—	-0.2
Total	5	173	490	49	122	29	12	11	67	40	2	128	.249	.308	.424	96	-7	1-4	.975	4	101	153	O124(90/24/12),1b2/P	—	-0.8
Culmer, Wil	Wilfred Hillard; B11.11.1957 Nassau, Bahamas; D10.14.2003 Nassau, Bahamas; BR/TR/6´4˝/210; d4.12; Col Chipola (FL) JC																								
1983	Cle A	7	19	0	2	0	0	0	1	0-0	0	4	.105	.100	.105	-40	-4	0-1	1.000	-1	32	0	O4R,D2	0	-0.5
Culp, Benny	Benjamin Baldy; B1.19.1914 Philadelphia PA; D10.23.2000 Philadelphia PA; BR/TR/5´9˝/175; d9.17; Mil 1944–45; C2																								
1942	Phi N	1	0	0	0	0	0	0	0	0	0	0	ø	ø	ø	ø	0	0	.500	-0	*0*	*0*	/C	0	0.0
1943	Phi N	10	24	4	5	1	0	0	2	3	0	3	.208	.296	.250	61	-1	0	.958	-1	*103*	*62*	C10	0	-0.2
1944	Phi N	4	2	1	0	0	0	0	0	0	0	0	.000	.000	.000	-99	-1	0	1.000	-0	*0*	*0*	/C	0	-0.1
Total	3	15	26	5	5	1	0	0	2	3	0	3	.192	.276	.231	49	-2	0	.926	-2	*95*	*57*	C12	0	-0.3
Cummings, Jack	John William; B4.1.1904 Pittsburgh PA; D10.5.1962 W.Mifflin PA; BR/TR/6´0˝/195; d9.11																								
1926	NY N	7	16	3	5	3	0	0	4	4	0	2	.313	.450	.500	157	2	0	.958	0	*87*	*149*	C6	—	0.2
1927	NY N	43	80	8	29	6	1	2	14	5	1	10	.363	.407	.538	151	6	0	.974	-3	*113*	*77*	C34	—	0.4
1928	NY N	33	27	4	9	2	0	2	9	3	0	4	.333	.400	.630	165	2	0	.833	-0	*0*	*0*	C4	—	0.2
1929	NY N	3	3	0	1	0	0	0	0	0	0	0	.333	.333	.333	66	0	0	1.000	-0	*0*	*0*	/C	—	0.0
	Bos N	3	6	0	1	0	0	0	1	0	0	2	.167	.167	.167	-18	-1	0	.667	-1	*85*	*0*	C3	—	-0.2
	Year	6	9	0	2	0	0	0	1	0	0	2	.222	.222	.222	11	-1	0	.714	-1	*74*	*0*	C4	—	-0.2
Total	4	89	132	15	45	11	1	4	28	12	1	18	.341	.400	.530	145	9	0	.947	-4	*101*	*84*	C48	—	0.6
Cummings, Midre	Midre Almeric; B10.14.1971 St.Croix, V.I.; BL/TR/6´0˝/(190–225); [MinA90 1/29]; d9.10																								
1993	Pit N	13	36	5	4	1	0	0	3	4-0	0	9	.111	.195	.139	-7	-6	0-0	1.000	-1	97	0	O11(5/5/1)	0	-0.6
1994	Pit N	24	86	11	21	4	0	1	12	4-0	1	18	.244	.283	.326	58	-5	0-0	.962	-0	104	67	O24(18/5/4)	0	-0.6
1995	Pit N	59	152	13	37	7	1	2	15	13-3	0	30	.243	.303	.342	68	-7	1-0	.988	2	110	98	O41(8/20/14)	0	-0.6
1996	Pit N	24	85	11	19	3	1	3	7	0-0	0	16	.224	.221	.388	55	-6	0-0	.980	-0	111	0	O21(0/11/10)	0	-0.6
1997	Pit N	52	106	11	20	6	2	3	8	8-0	1	26	.189	.252	.368	59	-7	0-0	1.000	-0	98	71	O25(14/0/11)	0	-0.8
	Phi N	63	208	24	63	16	4	1	23	23-0	0	30	.303	.369	.433	112	4	2-3	.991	-0	106	44	O54(0/53/2)	0	0.3
	Year	115	314	35	83	22	6	4	31	31-0	1	56	.264	.330	.411	93	-3	2-3	.993	-1	104	52	O79(14/53/13)	0	-0.5
1998	†Bos A	67	120	20	34	8	0	5	15	17-0	2	19	.283	.381	.475	118	4	3-3	.941	-1	85	0	D29,O17R	40	0.0
1999	Min A	16	38	1	10	0	0	1	9	3-0	0	7	.263	.310	.342	65	-2	2-0	1.000	-1	75	0	O5(1/0/5),D5	0	-0.2
2000	Min A	77	181	28	50	10	0	4	22	11-1	3	25	.276	.328	.398	77	-6	0-0	1.000	4	110	226	O40(7/0/33),D15	0	-0.4
	Bos A	21	25	1	7	0	0	0	2	6-0	0	3	.280	.419	.280	80	0	0-0	1.000	-0	106	0	O4(0/1/3)/D	0	-0.1
	Year	98	206	29	57	10	0	4	24	17-1	3	28	.277	.341	.383	78	-7	0-0	1.000	3	110	201	O44(7/1/36),D16	0	-0.5
2001	†Ari N	20	20	1	6	1	0	0	1	0-0	0	4	.300	.286	.350	63	-1	0-0	1.000	0	216	0	O4(3/0/1)	0	-0.1
2004	TB A	22	54	10	15	4	0	2	7	5-0	2	12	.278	.361	.463	115	1	1-0	1.000	-0	78	0	D12,O2L	0	0.1
2005	Bal A	2	2	0	0	0	0	0	0	0-0	0	1	.000	.000	.000	-99	-1	0-0	ø	-0	0	0	/lf	0	-0.1
Total	11	460	1113	136	286	60	8	22	124	94-4	9	200	.257	.318	.385	80	-32	9-6	.987	1	105	71	O249(59/95/101),D62	40	-3.7
Cunningham, Joe	Joseph Robert; B8.27.1931 Paterson NJ; BL/TL/6´1˝/(180–190); d6.30; C1																								
1954	StL N	85	310	40	88	11	3	11	50	43	2	40	.284	.375	.445	112	6	1-1	.989	1	107	119	1b85	0	0.2
1956	StL N	4	3	1	0	0	0	0	0	1-0	0	1	.000	.250	.000	-25	-1	0-0	1.000	-0	0	0	/1	0	-0.1
1957	StL N	122	261	50	83	15	0	9	52	56-6	5	29	.318	.439	.479	146	22	3-3	1.000	-3	72	68	1b57,O46R	0	1.5
1958	StL N	131	337	61	105	20	3	12	57	82-3	3	23	.312	.449	.496	144	28	4-4	.997	-5	85	51	1b67,O66(24/0/42)	0	1.7
1959	StL N★	144	458	65	158	28	6	7	60	88-9	5	47	.345	**.453**	.478	140	33	2-6	.972	-4	98	59	O121(20/0/109),1b35	0	2.2
1960	StL N	139	492	68	138	28	3	6	39	59-4	6	59	.280	.363	.386	97	1	1-7	.950	-5	97	63	O116(1/0/116),1b15	0	-1.2
1961	StL N	113	322	60	92	11	2	7	40	53-3	**11**	32	.286	.403	.398	104	5	1-0	.964	-6	98	30	O86(1/1/85),1b10	0	-0.7
1962	Chi A	149	526	91	155	32	7	8	70	101-3	7	59	.295	.410	.428	128	27	3-3	**.994**	-5	87	104	1b143,O5R	0	1.3
1963	Chi A	67	210	32	60	12	1	1	31	33-2	4	23	.286	.388	.367	116	7	1-0	.989	-6	63	95	1b58	90	-0.2
1964	Chi A	40	108	13	27	7	0	0	10	14-1	3	15	.250	.352	.315	90	-1	0-1	.996	-1	86	123	1b33	0	-0.4
	Was A	49	126	15	27	4	0	0	7	23-0	2	13	.214	.344	.246	68	-4	0-1	.997	-4	56	97	1b41	0	-1.2
	Year	89	234	28	54	11	0	0	17	37-1	5	28	.231	.348	.278	78	-5	0-2	.997	-5	70	109	1b74	0	-1.6
1965	Was A	95	201	29	46	9	1	3	20	46-0	1	27	.229	.375	.328	103	4	0-1	.986	-3	81	110	1b59	0	-0.3
1966	Was A	3	8	0	1	0	0	0	0	0-0	0	1	.125	.125	.125	-28	-1	0-0	1.000	1	264	56	1b3	0	0.0
Total	12	1141	3362	525	980	177	26	64	436	599-31	49	369	.291	.403	.417	119	126	16-27	.993	-40	84	101	1b607,O440(46/1/403)	90	2.8
Cunningham, Ray	Raymond Lee; B1.17.1905 Mesquite TX; D7.30.2005 Pearland TX; BR/TR/5´7.5˝/150; d9.16																								
1931	StL N	3	4	0	0	0	0	0	1	0	0	0	.000	.000	.000	-96	-1	0	1.000	1	184	0	3b3	—	0.0
1932	StL N	11	22	4	4	1	0	0	0	3	0	4	.182	.280	.227	37	-2	0	1.000	2	92	0	3b8,2b2	—	0.0
Total	2	14	26	4	4	1	0	0	1	3	0	4	.154	.241	.192	18	-3	0	1.000	2	109	0	3b11,2b2	—	0.0
Cunningham, Bill	William Aloysius; B7.30.1894 San Francisco CA; D9.26.1953 Colusa CA; BR/TR/5´8˝/155; d7.14; C1; Col St. Marys (CA)																								
1921	NY N	40	76	10	21	2	1	1	12	3	1	3	.276	.313	.368	79	-2	0-1	1.000	-1	97	49	O20(1/18/1)	—	-0.4
1922	†NY N	85	229	37	75	15	2	2	33	7	1	9	.328	.350	.437	101	0	4-5	.988	-1	96	93	O71(2/68/0)/3	—	-0.4
1923	†NY N	79	203	22	55	7	1	5	27	10	0	9	.271	.305	.389	83	-6	5-2	.992	-1	89	120	O68(10/58/0),2b4	—	-0.8
1924	Bos N	114	437	44	119	15	8	1	40	32	3	27	.272	.326	.350	85	-10	8-5	.970	5	102	141	O109(95/15/0)	—	-1.2
Total	4	318	945	113	270	39	12	9	112	52	5	48	.286	.326	.381	88	-18	17-13	.982	3	97	119	O268(108/159/1),2b4/3	—	-2.8
Cunningham, Bill	William James; B6.9.1886 Schenectady NY; D2.21.1946 Schenectady NY; BR/TR/5´9˝/170; d9.12																								
1910	Was A	21	74	3	22	5	1	0	14	12	1	—	.297	.402	.392	156	6	4	.957	-2	94	105	2b21	—	0.5
1911	Was A	94	331	34	63	10	5	3	37	19	2	—	.190	.239	.278	45	-26	10	.932	-9	98	59	2b93	—	-3.4
1912	Was A	8	27	5	5	1	0	1	8	3	0	—	.185	.267	.333	71	-1	2	.962	-2	95	47	2b7/S	—	-0.3
Total	3	123	432	42	90	16	6	4	59	34	3	—	.208	.271	.301	64	-21	16	.938	-12	97	66	2b121/S	—	-3.2
Curley, Doc	Walter James; B3.12.1874 Upton MA; D9.23.1920 Worcester MA; BR/TR; d9.12; Col Virginia																								
1899	Chi N	10	37	7	4	0	1	0	2	3	3	—	.108	.233	.162	9	-5	0	.907	-4	95	58	2b10	—	-0.7

YEAR	TM LG	G	AB	R	H	2B	3B	HR	RBI	BB-IB	HP	SO	AVG	OBP	SLG	AOPS	ABR	SB-CS	FA	FR	RNG	THR	GAMES AT POSITION	DL	BFW
Curren, Pete	Peter; B Baltimore MD; ?/175; d9.12																								
1876	Phi N	3	12	5	4	1	0	0	2	0	—	0	.333	.333	.417	150	1	—	.588	-2	—	—	C2/rf	—	-0.1
Currin, Perry	Perry Gilmore; B9.27.1928 Washington DC; BL/TR/6´0˝/175; d6.29																								
1947	StL A	3	2	0	0	0	0	0	0	1	0	0	.000	.333	.000	-3	0	0-0	1.000	1	115	477	/S	0	0.0
Curry, Tony	George Anthony; B12.22.1937 Nassau, Bahamas; D10.16.2006 Nassau, Bahamas; BL/TL/5´11˝/185; d4.12																								
1960	Phi N	95	245	26	64	14	2	6	34	16-2	1	53	.261	.308	.408	94	-2	0-2	.925	-5	90	43	O64(51/3/14)	0	-1.2
1961	Phi N	15	36	3	7	2	0	0	3	1-0	0	8	.194	.216	.250	24	-4	0-0	.833	0	64	367	O8L	0	-0.4
1966	Cle A	19	16	4	2	0	0	0	3	3-0	0	8	.125	.263	.125	16	-2	0-0	ø	0	—	—	/H	0	-0.2
Total	3	129	297	33	73	16	2	6	40	20-2	1	69	.246	.295	.374	82	-8	0-2	.915	-5	87	79	O72(59/3/14)	0	-1.8
Curry, Jim	James L.; B3.10.1886 Camden NJ; D8.2.1938 Grenloch NJ; BR/TR/5´11˝/160; d10.2																								
1909	Phi A	1	4	1	1	0	0	0	0	0	0	—	.250	.250	.250	57	0	0	1.000	-0	105	0	/2	—	-0.1
1911	NY A	4	11	3	2	0	0	0	0	1	0	—	.182	.250	.182	20	-1	0	.773	-2	56	78	2b4	—	-0.3
1918	Det A	5	20	1	5	1	0	0	0	0	1	0	.250	.286	.300	80	-1	0	.952	-2	92	0	2b5	—	-0.2
Total	3	10	35	5	8	1	0	0	0	1	1	0	.229	.270	.257	56	-2	0	.867	-4	78	32	2b10	—	-0.6
Curtis, Chad	Chad David; B11.6.1968 Marion IN; BR/TR/5´10˝/(175–185); [CalA89 45/1157]; d4.8; Col Grand Canyon																								
1992	Cal A	139	441	59	114	16	2	10	46	51-2	6	71	.259	.341	.372	99	0	43-18	.978	1	90	**199**	O135(48/35/62)/D	0	0.1
1993	Cal A	152	583	94	166	25	3	6	59	70-2	4	89	.285	.361	.369	95	-2	48-24	.980	7	105	155	O151C,2b3	0	0.9
1994	Cal A	114	453	67	116	23	4	11	50	37-0	5	69	.256	.317	.397	82	-13	25-11	.988	7	109	146	O114C	0	-0.2
1995	Det A	**144**	586	96	157	29	3	21	67	70-3	7	93	.268	.349	.435	104	3	27-15	.992	-8	93	66	O144C	0	-0.2
1996	Det A	104	400	65	105	20	1	10	37	53-0	1	73	.262	.346	.393	87	-7	16-10	.965	-2	98	92	O104(48/80/0)	0	-0.9
	†LA N	43	104	20	22	5	0	2	9	17-0	0	15	.212	.322	.317	74	-4	2-1	.985	1	102	150	O40C	0	-0.2
1997	Cle A	22	29	8	6	1	0	3	5	7-0	0	10	.207	.361	.552	129	1	0-0	1.000	-0	104	0	O19(3/12/4)	26	0.1
	†NY A	93	320	51	93	21	1	12	50	36-1	5	49	.291	.362	.475	120	10	12-6	.978	-5	87	117	O92(53/43/5)	0	0.4
	Year	115	349	59	99	22	1	15	55	43-1	5	59	.284	.362	.481	120	11	12-6	.980	-5	88	107	O111(56/55/9)	0	0.5
1998	†NY A	151	456	79	111	21	1	10	56	75-3	7	80	.243	.355	.360	92	-3	21-5	.984	4	108	99	O148(100/45/9),D2	0	0.1
1999	†NY A	96	195	37	51	6	0	5	24	43-0	3	35	.262	.398	.369	100	2	8-4	.990	-4	86	55	O81(72/6/3),D14	0	-0.4
2000	Tex A	108	335	48	91	25	1	8	48	37-0	1	71	.272	.343	.424	92	-3	3-3	.965	-2	96	91	O80(51/0/30),D16	0	-0.9
2001	Tex A	38	115	24	29	3	0	3	10	14-0	1	21	.252	.338	.357	81	-3	7-1	.988	3	120	112	O33(10/16/9),D2	98	0.1
Total	10	1204	4017	648	1061	195	16	101	461	510-11	40	676	.264	.349	.396	95	-19	212-98	.982	1	99	118	O1141(385/686/122),D35,2b3	124	-1.1
Curtis, Ervin	Ervin Duane; B12.27.1861 Coldwater MI; D2.14.1945 N.Adams MA; BL/TL/5´8.5˝/157; d7.15																								
1891	Cin N	27	108	11	29	3	3	1	13	9	1	19	.269	.331	.380	106	0	3	.862	-2	136	134	O27(0/24/3)	—	-0.2
	Was AA	29	103	17	26	3	2	0	12	13	2	16	.252	.347	.320	96	0	2	.797	-1	141	0	O29(0/20/9)	—	-0.2
Total	1	56	211	28	55	6	5	1	25	22	3	35	.261	.339	.351	101	0	5	.829	-3	138	68	O56(0/44/12)	—	-0.4
Curtis, Gene	Eugene Holmes "Eude"; B5.5.1883 Bethany WV; D1.1.1919 Steubenville OH; BR/TR/6´3˝/220; d9.21; Col West Virginia																								
1903	Pit N	5	19	2	8	1	0	0	3	1	0	—	.421	.450	.474	158	1	0	.833	-1	129	0	O5L	—	0.1
Curtis, Fred	Frederick Marion; B10.30.1880 Beaver Lake MI; D4.5.1939 Minneapolis MN; BR/TR/6´1˝/?; d7.24																								
1905	NY A	2	9	0	2	1	0	0	2	1	0	—	.222	.300	.333	90	0	1	1.000	-0	72	0	1b2	—	0.0
Curtis, Harry	Harry Albert; B2.19.1883 Portland ME; D8.1.1951 Evanston IL; TR/5´10.5˝/170; d8.28; Col Notre Dame																								
1907	NY N	6	9	2	2	0	0	0	1	2	0	—	.222	.364	.222	81	0	2	.909	-0	*112*	*107*	C6	—	0.0
Curtright, Guy	Guy Paxton; B10.18.1912 Holliday MO; D8.23.1997 Sun City Center FL; BR/TR/5´11˝/200; d4.21; Col Truman St.																								
1943	Chi A	138	488	67	142	20	7	3	48	69	3	60	.291	.382	.379	123	17	13-12	.972	-2	102	66	O128L	0	0.6
1944	Chi A	72	198	22	50	8	2	2	23	23	0	21	.253	.330	.343	94	-1	4-3	.948	3	98	207	O51(35/0/17)	0	-0.2
1945	Chi A	98	324	51	91	15	7	4	32	39	0	29	.281	.358	.407	125	10	3-4	.986	1	100	110	O84(26/46/13)	0	0.7
1946	Chi A	23	55	7	11	2	0	0	5	11	0	14	.200	.333	.236	63	-2	0-1	1.000	1	98	164	O15(2/2/11)	0	-0.2
Total	4	331	1065	147	294	45	16	9	108	142	3	124	.276	.363	.374	115	24	20-20	.973	2	101	109	O278(191/48/41)	0	0.9
Cusick, Tony	Andrew Daniel "Andy"; B12.1857 Fall River MA; D8.6.1929 Chicago IL; BR/TR/5´9.5˝/190; d8.21																								
1884	Wil U	11	34	0	5	0	0	0	—	1	—	—	.147	.171	.147	-3	-5	—	.871	0	—	—	C6,S3,O3(1/1/1)/23	—	-0.4
	Phi N	9	29	2	4	0	0	0	1	0	—	3	.138	.138	.138	-14	-4	—	.930	2	—	—	C9	—	-0.1
1885	Phi N	39	141	12	25	1	0	0	5	1	—	24	.177	.183	.184	19	-13	—	.808	-5	—	—	C38/cf	—	-1.4
1886	Phi N	29	104	10	23	5	1	0	4	3	—	14	.221	.243	.288	61	-5	1	.891	-3	—	—	C25,O3(1/0/2)/1	—	-0.6
1887	Phi N	7	24	3	7	1	0	0	5	3	1	1	.292	.393	.333	98	0	0	.643	-4	—	—	C4,1b3/2	—	-0.3
Total	4	95	332	27	64	7	1	0	15	8	1	42	.193	.214	.220	35	-27	1	.844	-10	—	—	C82,O7(2/2/3),1b4,S3,2b2/3	—	-2.8
Cusick, Jack	John Peter; B6.12.1928 Weehawken NJ; D11.17.1989 Englewood NJ; BR/TR/6´0˝/170; d4.24																								
1951	Chi N	65	164	16	29	3	2	2	16	17	0	29	.177	.254	.256	37	-15	2-1	.953	-2	104	78	S56	0	-1.4
1952	Bos N	49	78	5	13	1	0	0	6	6	0	9	.167	.226	.179	14	-9	0-1	.969	-3	89	31	S28,3b3	0	-1.1
Total	2	114	242	21	42	4	2	2	22	23	0	38	.174	.245	.231	30	-24	2-2	.958	-4	100	65	S84,3b3	0	-2.5
Cust, Jack	John Joseph; B1.16.1979 Flemington NJ; BL/TR/6´2˝/(205–230); [AriN97 1/30]; d9.26																								
2001	Ari N	3	2	0	1	0	0	0	0	1-0	0	0	.500	.667	.500	195	0	0-0	ø	-0	0	0	/lf	0	0.0
2002	Col N	35	65	8	11	2	0	1	8	12-0	0	32	.169	.295	.246	40	-5	0-1	.960	-1	93	0	O18L	0	-0.8
2003	Bal A	27	73	7	19	7	0	4	11	10-0	1	25	.260	.357	.521	128	3	0-0	1.000	0	254	0	D23/lf	0	0.2
2004	Bal A	1	1	0	0	0	0	0	0	0-0	0	1	.000	.000	.000	-99	0	0-0	ø	0	—	—	/H	0	0.0
2006	SD N	4	3	1	1	0	0	0	0	0-0	0	1	.333	.333	.333	76	0	0-0	ø	-0	0	0	/lf	0	0.0
Total	5	70	144	16	32	9	0	5	19	23-0	1	59	.222	.331	.389	84	-2	0-1	.964	-1	96	0	D23,O21L	0	-0.6
Cuthbert, Ned	Edgar Edward; B6.20.1845 Philadelphia PA; D2.6.1905 St.Louis MO; BR/TR/5´6˝/140; d5.20; M1/U1																								
1871	Ath NA	**28**	150	47	37	7	5	3	30	10	—	2	.247	.294	.420	103	1	16-2	.890	4	93	0	O27L/C	—	0.5
1872	Ath NA	**47**	260	83	88	10	0	1	47	6	—	10	.338	.353	.388	127	8	14-4	.858	-3	39	0	O47L	—	0.6
1873	Phi NA	51	279	78	77	5	3	2	34	2	—	4	.276	.281	.337	79	-8	14-2	.842	-6	27	76	O51L	—	-0.7
1874	Chi NA	58	295	65	79	6	1	2	24	5	—	5	.268	.280	.315	90	-3	8-0	.806	-1	121	66	O55(55/2/0),C4	—	0.0
1875	StL NA	68	319	68	78	9	2	0	17	3	—	8	.245	.252	.285	95	0	18-1	.860	-12	18	0	O67(65/2/0),C3/2	—	-0.5
1876	StL N	63	283	46	70	10	1	0	25	7	—	4	.247	.266	.290	90	-2	—	.843	-7	68	125	O63L	—	-1.1
1877	Cin N	12	56	6	10	5	0	0	2	1	—	2	.179	.193	.268	49	-3	—	.830	4	219	413	O12L	—	0.1
1882	StL AA	60	233	28	52	16	5	0	—	17	—	—	.223	.276	.335	101	1	—	.896	-3	90	0	O60L,M	—	-0.3
1883	StL AA	21	71	3	12	1	0	0	3	4	—	—	.169	.213	.183	27	-6	—	.794	-1	127	0	O20(18/1/1)/1	—	-0.7
1884	Bal U	44	168	29	34	5	0	0	—	10	—	—	.202	.247	.232	42	-17	—	.750	-5	104	0	O44C	—	-2.0
Total	5NA	252	1303	341	359	37	11	8	152	26	—	29	.276	.290	.339	98	-2	70-9	.845	-18	56	31	O247(245/4/0),C8/2	—	-0.1
Total	5	200	811	112	178	37	6	0	30	39	—	6	.219	.255	.280	73	-27	—	.833	-11	98	68	O199(153/45/1)/1	—	-4.0
Cutshaw, George	George William "Clancy"; B7.29.1886 Wilmington IL; D8.22.1973 San Diego CA; BR/TR/5´9˝/160; d4.25; Col Notre Dame																								
1912	Bro N	102	357	41	100	14	4	0	28	31	2	16	.280	.341	.342	91	-4	16	.958	4	108	80	2b91,3b5/S	—	0.1
1913	Bro N	147	592	72	158	23	13	7	80	39	3	22	.267	.315	.385	97	-5	39-17	.957	17	101	134	2b147	—	1.8
1914	Bro N	153	583	69	150	22	12	2	78	30	3	32	.257	.297	.346	89	-10	34	.959	28	99	127	2b153	—	2.1
1915	Bro N	**154**	566	68	139	18	9	0	62	34	4	35	.246	.293	.309	81	-14	28-23	**.971**	14	106	82	2b154	—	0.1
1916	†Bro N	154	581	58	151	21	4	2	63	25	1	32	.260	.292	.320	85	-11	27-20	.958	6	101	88	2b154	—	-0.4
1917	Bro N	135	487	42	126	17	7	4	49	21	2	26	.259	.292	.347	93	-5	22	.963	-11	94	71	2b134	—	-1.6
1918	Pit N	**126**	463	56	132	16	10	5	68	27	1	18	.285	.326	.395	116	7	25	.964	-3	93	119	2b126	—	0.7
1919	Pit N	**139**	512	49	124	15	8	3	51	30	2	22	.242	.287	.320	79	-14	36	**.980**	-9	89	107	2b139	—	-2.2
1920	Pit N	131	488	56	123	16	8	0	47	23	2	10	.252	.287	.318	71	-19	17-14	.968	1	97	105	2b129	—	-1.8
1921	Pit N	98	350	46	119	18	4	0	53	11	1	11	.340	.362	.414	102	1	14-5	.951	-23	85	92	2b84	—	-1.8
1922	Det A	132	499	57	133	14	8	2	61	20	4	13	.267	.300	.339	68	-25	11-5	.972	5	101	97	2b132	—	-1.6
1923	Det A	45	143	15	32	1	2	0	13	9	2	5	.224	.279	.259	43	-12	2-1	.988	8	116	86	2b43,3b2	—	-0.4
Total	12	1516	5621	629	1487	195	89	25	653	300	26	242	.265	.305	.344	86	-111	271-85	.965	37	98	101	2b1486,3b7/S	—	-5.0

CUYLER, KIKI Hazen Shirley; B8.30.1898 Harrisville MI; D2.11.1950 Ann Arbor MI; BR/TR/5´10.5˝/180; d9.29; C4; HF1968

YEAR	TM LG	G	AB	R	H	2B	3B	HR	RBI	BB-IB	HP	SO	AVG	OBP	SLG	AOPS	ABR	SB-CS	FA	FR	RNG	THR	GAMES AT POSITION	DL	BFW
1921	Pit N	1	3	0	0	0	0	0	0	0	0	1	.000	.000	.000	-97	-1	0-0	1.000	-0	90	0	/rf	—	-0.1
1922	Pit N	1	0	0	0	0	0	0	0	0	0	0	ø	ø	ø	ø	0	0-0	ø	0	—	—	/R	—	0.0
1923	Pit N	11	40	4	10	1	1	0	2	5	1	3	.250	.348	.325	77	-1	2-3	.931	-0	105	88	O11(10/3/0)	—	-0.3
1924	Pit N	117	466	94	165	27	16	9	85	30	7	62	.354	.402	.539	147	30	32-11	.943	3	98	145	O114(78/4/35)	—	2.7
1925	†Pit N	**153**	617	**144**	220	43	**26**	18	102	58	**13**	56	.357	.423	.598	148	44	41-13	.967	2	104	97	O153(0/25/129)	—	3.6
1926	Pit N	**157**	614	**113**	197	31	15	8	92	50	9	66	.321	.380	.459	119	16	**35**	.968	7	106	117	O157(62/79/18)	—	1.3
1927	Pit N	85	285	60	88	13	7	3	31	37	3	36	.309	.394	.435	114	7	20	.980	0	105	76	O73(12/49/13)	—	0.3
1928	Chi N	133	499	92	142	25	9	17	79	51	7	61	.285	.359	.473	117	12	**37**	.982	1	91	140	O127(13/7/108)	—	0.2
1929	†Chi N	139	509	111	183	29	7	15	102	66	5	56	.360	.438	.532	139	34	**43**	.974	1	98	110	O129(16/8/114)	—	2.2
1930	Chi N	**156**	642	155	228	50	17	13	134	72	**10**	49	.355	.428	.547	133	37	**37**	.980	6	104	108	O156(29/0/131)	—	2.6
1931	Chi N	154	613	110	202	37	12	9	88	72	5	54	.330	.404	.473	133	31	13	.970	-9	93	68	O153(0/66/84)	—	1.5
1932	†Chi N	110	446	58	130	19	9	10	77	29	4	43	.291	.340	.442	109	5	9	.969	-11	87	65	O109(0/49/60)	—	-1.1
1933	Chi N	70	262	37	83	13	3	5	35	21	4	29	.317	.376	.447	135	12	4	.978	-5	91	39	O69(35/15/19)	—	0.4
1934	Chi N★	142	559	80	189	**42**	8	6	69	31	4	62	.338	.377	.474	129	23	15	.971	-3	90	151	O142(0/136/6)	—	1.5
1935	Chi N	45	157	22	42	5	1	4	18	10	5	16	.268	.331	.389	92	-2	3	.981	-1	91	147	O42(0/41/2)	—	-0.3
	Cin N	62	223	36	56	8	3	2	22	27	2	18	.251	.337	.341	85	-4	5	.985	-4	85	109	O57(5/49/3)	—	-0.9
	Year	107	380	58	98	13	4	6	40	37	7	34	.258	.335	.361	88	-6	8	.983	-4	88	125	O99(5/90/5)	—	-1.2
1936	Cin N	144	567	96	185	29	11	7	74	47	2	67	.326	.380	.453	132	25	16	.974	-5	94	87	O140(22/105/14)	—	1.5
1937	Cin N	117	406	48	110	12	4	0	32	36	2	50	.271	.333	.320	82	-10	10	.973	-5	86	107	O106(41/47/16)	—	-1.9
1938	Bro N	82	253	45	69	10	8	2	23	34	2	23	.273	.363	.399	107	3	6	.993	3	98	171	O68(8/17/43)	—	0.3
Total	18	1879	7161	1305	2299	394	157	128	1065	676	85	752	.321	.386	.474	125	261	328-27	.972	-20	96	108	O1807(331/700/796)	—	13.5

CUYLER, MILT Milton; B10.7.1968 Macon GA; BB/TR/5´10˝/(175–185); [DetA86 2/46]; d9.6

YEAR	TM LG	G	AB	R	H	2B	3B	HR	RBI	BB-IB	HP	SO	AVG	OBP	SLG	AOPS	ABR	SB-CS	FA	FR	RNG	THR	GAMES AT POSITION	DL	BFW
1990	Det A	19	51	8	13	3	1	0	8	5-0	0	10	.255	.316	.353	87	-1	1-2	.976	0	91	245	O17(0/17/1)	0	-0.1
1991	Det A	154	475	77	122	15	7	3	33	52-0	5	92	.257	.335	.337	85	-9	41-10	.986	3	107	91	O151(1/150/0)	0	-0.1
1992	Det A	89	291	39	70	11	1	3	28	10-0	4	62	.241	.275	.316	64	-15	8-5	.983	-4	95	80	O89(0/88/1)	71	-2.0
1993	Det A	82	249	46	53	11	7	0	19	19-0	3	53	.213	.276	.313	58	-16	13-2	.968	1	110	50	O80C	56	-1.1
1994	Det A	48	116	20	28	3	1	1	11	13-0	1	21	.241	.318	.310	63	-6	5-3	.975	-3	85	47	O45(13/29/8)	60	-0.9
1995	Det A	41	88	15	18	1	4	0	5	8-0	0	16	.205	.271	.307	50	-7	2-1	.929	-1	92	111	O36(34/1/1),D2	0	-0.9
1996	Bos A	50	110	19	22	1	2	2	12	13-0	3	19	.200	.299	.300	52	-9	7-3	.972	2	128	0	O45(0/30/22),D2	109	-0.6
1998	Tex A	7	6	3	3	2	0	1	3	1-0	0	0	.500	.571	1.333	355	2	0-0	1.000	0	106	0	O3C,D3	0	0.2
Total	8	490	1386	227	329	47	23	10	119	121-0	16	273	.237	.305	.326	71	-61	77-26	.977	-1	103	77	O466(48/398/33),D7	296	-5.5

CYPERT, AL Alfred Boyd "Cy"; B8.8.1889 Little Rock AR; D1.9.1973 Washington DC; BR/TR/5´10.5˝/150; d6.27; Col Harvard

YEAR	TM LG	G	AB	R	H	2B	3B	HR	RBI	BB-IB	HP	SO	AVG	OBP	SLG	AOPS	ABR	SB-CS	FA	FR	RNG	THR	GAMES AT POSITION	DL	BFW
1914	Cle A	1	1	0	0	0	0	0	0	0	0	1	.000	.000	.000	-96	0	0	ø	-0	0	0	/3	—	0.0

DADE, PAUL Lonnie Paul; B12.7.1951 Seattle WA; BR/TR/6´0˝/(185–195); [AnaA70 1/10]; d9.12

YEAR	TM LG	G	AB	R	H	2B	3B	HR	RBI	BB-IB	HP	SO	AVG	OBP	SLG	AOPS	ABR	SB-CS	FA	FR	RNG	THR	GAMES AT POSITION	DL	BFW
1975	Cal A	11	30	5	6	4	0	0	1	6-0	0	7	.200	.333	.333	95	0	0-0	1.000	1	145	0	O3(1/0/2)/3D	0	0.1
1976	Cal A	13	9	2	1	0	0	0	1	3-0	0	3	.111	.333	.111	36	-1	0-0	.750	1	88	1254	O4(3/0/1),2b2/3D	0	0.1
1977	Cle A	134	461	65	134	15	3	3	45	32-4	2	58	.291	.333	.356	92	-5	16-8	.989	-2	87	156	O99(32/28/46),3b26/2D	0	-1.0
1978	Cle A	93	307	37	78	12	1	3	20	34-1	2	45	.254	.331	.329	87	-4	12-9	.962	3	109	111	O81(1/7/75),D9	0	-0.6
1979	Cle A	44	170	22	48	4	1	3	18	12-1	0	22	.282	.326	.371	88	-3	12-6	.962	1	100	151	O37(20/0/17),3b2,D4	0	-0.3
	SD N	76	283	38	78	19	2	1	19	14-0	2	48	.276	.311	.367	91	-4	13-5	.949	5	115	101	3b70,O4(1/3/0)	0	0.1
1980	SD N	68	53	17	10	0	0	0	3	12-0	0	10	.189	.338	.189	54	-3	4-5	.846	-1	97	80	3b21,O8(4/3/1)/2	22	-0.5
Total	6	439	1313	186	355	54	7	10	107	113-6	6	193	.270	.328	.345	89	-20	57-33	.970	6	97	150	0236(62/41/142),3b121,D28,2b4	22	-2.1

DAGRES, ANGELO Angelo George "Junior"; B8.22.1934 Newburyport MA; BL/TL/5´11˝/175; d9.11; Col Rhode Island

YEAR	TM LG	G	AB	R	H	2B	3B	HR	RBI	BB-IB	HP	SO	AVG	OBP	SLG	AOPS	ABR	SB-CS	FA	FR	RNG	THR	GAMES AT POSITION	DL	BFW
1955	Bal A	8	15	5	4	0	0	0	3	1-0	0	2	.267	.278	.267	61	-1	0-0	.818	-1	100	0	O5(1/0/4)	0	-0.2

DAHLEN, BILL William Frederick "Bad Bill"; B1.5.1870 Nelliston NY; D12.5.1950 Brooklyn NY; BR/TR/5´9˝/180; d4.22; M4

YEAR	TM LG	G	AB	R	H	2B	3B	HR	RBI	BB-IB	HP	SO	AVG	OBP	SLG	AOPS	ABR	SB-CS	FA	FR	RNG	THR	GAMES AT POSITION	DL	BFW
1891	Chi N	135	549	114	143	18	13	9	76	67	7	60	.260	.348	.390	115	10	21	.887	4	108	108	3b84,O37(30/0/7),S15	—	1.4
1892	Chi N	143	581	114	170	23	19	5	58	45	5	56	.293	.349	.423	132	19	60	.909	15	91	113	S72,3b68,O2C/2	—	3.6
1893	Chi N	116	485	113	146	28	15	5	64	58	5	30	.301	.381	.452	123	16	31	.892	6	101	86	S88,O17(5/8/4),2b10,3b3	—	2.1
1894	Chi N	122	507	150	182	32	14	15	108	76	3	33	.359	.445	.566	135	29	43	.900	26	107	129	S67,3b55	—	4.5
1895	Chi N	129	516	106	131	19	10	7	62	61	10	51	.254	.344	.370	79	-17	38	.904	35	**119**	128	S129/cf	—	1.9
1896	Chi N	125	474	137	167	30	19	9	74	64	8	36	.352	.438	.553	154	38	51	.915	22	107	120	S125	—	5.5
1897	Chi N	75	276	67	80	18	8	6	40	43	7	—	.290	.399	.478	126	11	15	.930	24	110	152	S75	—	3.3
1898	Chi N	142	521	96	151	35	8	1	79	58	23	—	.290	.385	.393	123	20	27	.921	20	**108**	**138**	S142	—	4.3
1899	Bro N	121	428	87	121	22	7	4	76	67	15	—	.283	.398	.395	115	13	29	.941	14	100	116	S110,3b11	—	2.9
1900	†Bro N	133	483	87	125	16	11	1	69	73	7	—	.259	.364	.344	90	-4	31	.938	21	107	110	S133	—	2.1
1901	Bro N	131	511	69	136	17	9	4	82	30	5	—	.266	.313	.358	92	-6	23	.929	14	103	97	S129,2b2	—	1.1
1902	Bro N	138	527	67	139	25	8	2	74	43	8	—	.264	.329	.353	110	6	20	.916	-6	98	76	S138	—	0.6
1903	Bro N	138	474	71	124	17	9	1	64	82	2	—	.262	.373	.342	107	9	34	**.948**	19	**109**	99	S138	—	3.1
1904	NY N	145	523	70	140	26	2	2	**80**	44	1	—	.268	.326	.337	100	1	47	.930	25	**108**	**139**	S145	—	3.2
1905	†NY N	148	520	67	126	20	4	7	81	62	12	—	.242	.337	.337	99	2	37	.948	20	102	114	S147/lf	—	2.7
1906	NY N	143	471	63	113	18	3	1	49	76	10	—	.240	.357	.297	102	6	16	.938	2	101	79	S143	—	1.4
1907	NY N	143	464	40	96	20	1	0	34	51	4	—	.207	.291	.254	69	-15	11	.941	6	100	88	S143	—	-0.4
1908	Bos N	144	524	50	125	23	2	3	48	35	8	—	.239	.296	.307	94	-3	10	.952	**38**	**120**	**131**	S144	—	4.5
1909	Bos N	69	197	22	46	6	1	2	16	29	0	—	.234	.332	.305	93	-1	4	.908	6	117	99	S49,2b6,3b2	—	0.8
1910	Bro N	3	2	0	0	0	0	0	0	0	0	0	.000	.000	.000	-99	-1	0	ø	0	—	—	/HM	—	-0.1
1911	Bro N	1	3	0	0	0	0	0	0	0	0	3	.000	.000	.000	-99	-1	0	1.000	1	159	246	/SM	—	0.0
Total	21	2444	9036	1590	2461	413	163	84	1234	1064	140	269	.272	.358	.382	109	132	548	.927	310	106	111	S2133,3b223,O58(36/11/11),2b19	—	48.5

DAHLGREN, BABE Ellsworth Tenney; B6.15.1912 San Francisco CA; D9.4.1996 Arcadia CA; BR/TR/6´0˝/190; d4.16; C1

YEAR	TM LG	G	AB	R	H	2B	3B	HR	RBI	BB-IB	HP	SO	AVG	OBP	SLG	AOPS	ABR	SB-CS	FA	FR	RNG	THR	GAMES AT POSITION	DL	BFW
1935	Bos A	149	525	77	138	27	7	9	63	56	3	67	.263	.337	.392	83	-14	6-5	.988	-6	86	89	1b149	—	-3.3
1936	Bos A	16	57	6	16	3	1	1	7	7	0	1	.281	.359	.421	87	-1	2-1	.980	-0	99	78	1b16	—	-0.3
1937	NY A	1	1	0	0	0	0	0	0	0	0	0	.000	.000	.000	-99	0	0-0	ø	0	—	—	/H	—	0.0
1938	NY A	27	43	8	8	1	0	0	1	1	0	7	.186	.205	.209	4	-7	0-0	.826	-2	58	0	3b8,1b6	—	-0.8
1939	†NY A	144	531	71	125	18	6	15	89	57	2	54	.235	.312	.377	76	-21	2-3	.991	-7	78	**133**	1b144	—	-4.0
1940	NY A	**155**	568	51	150	24	4	12	73	46	5	54	.264	.325	.384	86	-13	1-1	.990	-11	74	116	1b155	—	-3.7
1941	Bos N	44	166	20	39	8	1	7	30	16	1	13	.235	.306	.422	108	1	0	.993	2	116	136	1b39,3b5	0	-0.1
	Chi N	99	359	50	101	20	1	16	59	43	1	39	.281	.360	.476	139	18	2	.991	-8	64	105	1b98	0	0.1
	Year	143	525	70	140	28	2	23	89	59	2	52	.267	.343	.459	129	19	2	.992	-6	79	**114**	1b137,3b5	0	0.0
1942	Chi N	17	56	4	12	1	0	0	6	4	0	2	.214	.267	.232	48	-4	0	.986	0	116	63	1b14	0	-0.5
	StL A	2	2	0	0	0	0	0	0	0	0	0	.000	.000	.000	-99	-1	0-0	ø	0	—	—	/H	0	-0.1
	Bro N	17	19	2	1	0	0	0	0	4	0	5	.053	.217	.053	-19	-3	0	1.000	1	143	192	1b10	0	-0.3
1943	Phi N★	136	508	55	146	19	2	5	56	50	2	39	.287	.354	.362	111	8	2	.988	-17	97	104	1b73,3b35,S25/C	0	-1.2
1944	Pit N	**158**	599	67	173	28	7	12	101	47	6	56	.289	.347	.419	110	7	2	.987	9	126	85	1b158	0	0.8
1945	Pit N	144	531	57	133	24	8	5	75	51	2	51	.250	.318	.354	84	-12	1	**.996**	2	99	108	1b144	0	-1.8
1946	StL A	28	80	2	14	1	0	0	9	8	0	13	.175	.250	.188	22	-8	0-1	.981	1	126	81	1b24	0	-0.9
Total	12	1137	4045	470	1056	174	37	82	569	390	22	401	.261	.329	.383	92	-50	18-11	.990	-37	93	106	1b1030,3b48,S25/C	0	-16.1

DAILEY, JOHN John J.; B10.26.1853 Brooklyn NY; d4.29

YEAR	TM LG	G	AB	R	H	2B	3B	HR	RBI	BB-IB	HP	SO	AVG	OBP	SLG	AOPS	ABR	SB-CS	FA	FR	RNG	THR	GAMES AT POSITION	DL	BFW
1875	Was NA	27	110	16	20	5	4	0	13	0	—	1	.182	.182	.300	67	-3	3-2	.810	-2	114	39	S20,3b5,2b2	—	-0.5
	Atl NA	2	8	3	1	0	0	0	0	0	—	1	.125	.125	.125	-15	-1	0-0	1.000	-2	0	0	O2R/1S	—	-0.3
	Year	29	118	19	21	5	4	0	13	0	—	2	.178	.178	.288	62	-4	3-2	.797	-4	108	37	S21,3b5,2b2,O2R/1	—	-0.8

DAILEY, VINCE Vincent Perry; B12.25.1864 Osceola PA; D11.14.1919 Hornell NY; 6´0˝/200; d4.21

YEAR	TM LG	G	AB	R	H	2B	3B	HR	RBI	BB-IB	HP	SO	AVG	OBP	SLG	AOPS	ABR	SB-CS	FA	FR	RNG	THR	GAMES AT POSITION	DL	BFW
1890	Cle N	64	246	41	71	5	7	0	32	33	0	23	.289	.373	.366	118	6	17	.859	0	116	80	O64R,P2	—	0.5

DAILY, CON Cornelius F.; B9.11.1864 Blackstone MA; D6.14.1928 Brooklyn NY; BL/6´0˝/192; d6.9; b–Ed

YEAR	TM LG	G	AB	R	H	2B	3B	HR	RBI	BB-IB	HP	SO	AVG	OBP	SLG	AOPS	ABR	SB-CS	FA	FR	RNG	THR	GAMES AT POSITION	DL	BFW
1884	Phi U	2	8	0	0	0	0	0	—	0	—	—	.000	.000	.000	-99	-2	—	.857	-1	—	—	C2	—	-0.3
1885	Pro N	60	223	20	58	6	1	0	19	12	—	20	.260	.298	.296	95	-1	—	.876	1	—	—	C48,1b7,O6(1/3/2)	—	0.3
1886	Bos N	50	180	25	43	4	2	0	21	19	—	29	.239	.312	.283	84	-3	2	.911	-9	—	—	C49/lf	—	-0.7

YEAR	TM LG	G	AB	R	H	2B	3B	HR	RBI	BB-IB	HP	SO	AVG	OBP	SLG	AOPS	ABR	SB-CS	FA	FR	RNG	THR	GAMES AT POSITION	DL	BFW
1887	Bos N	36	120	12	19	5	0	0	13	9	2	8	.158	.229	.200	20	-13	7	.889	-2	—	—	C36	—	-1.1
1888	Ind N	57	202	14	44	6	1	0	14	10	0	28	.218	.255	.257	62	-8	15	.893	-4	—	—	C42,O5R,3b5,1b5/2	—	-0.9
1889	Ind N	62	219	35	55	6	2	0	26	28	4	21	.251	.347	.297	78	-5	14	.887	-11	—	—	C51,O6(1/3/2),1b6/3	—	-1.2
1890	Bro P	46	168	20	42	6	3	0	35	15	1	14	.250	.315	.321	66	-9	6	.879	-0	*129*	*80*	C40,1b6/rf	—	-0.5
1891	Bro N	60	206	25	66	10	1	0	30	15	4	13	.320	.378	.379	121	6	7	.925	1	*97*	*107*	C55,O3R,S2/1	—	1.0
1892	Bro N	80	278	38	65	10	1	0	28	38	1	21	.234	.328	.277	87	-2	18	.943	1	*104*	*108*	C68,O13(2/3/8)	—	0.4
1893	Bro N	61	215	33	57	4	2	1	32	20	5	12	.265	.342	.316	79	-6	13	.935	-1	*99*	*80*	C51,O9(2/0/7)	—	-0.2
1894	Bro N	67	234	40	60	14	7	0	32	31	3	22	.256	.351	.376	81	-7	8	.930	-5	*90*	*101*	C60,1b7	—	-0.5
1895	Bro N	40	142	17	30	3	2	1	11	10	1	18	.211	.268	.282	45	-12	3	.956	1	*132*	*64*	C39/lf	—	-0.6
1896	Chi N	9	27	1	2	0	0	0	1	1	0	2	.074	.107	.074	-50	-6	1	.969	-1	*93*	*104*	C9	—	-0.6
Total	13	630	2222	280	541	74	22	2	262	208	21	208	.243	.314	.299	75	-68	94	.912	-33	*105*	*93*	C550,O45(8/9/28),1b32,3b6,S2/2	—	-4.9

DAILY, ED Edward M.; B9.7.1862 Providence RI; D10.21.1891 Washington DC; BR/TR/5´10.5˝/174; d5.4; b–Con; ▲

YEAR	TM LG	G	AB	R	H	2B	3B	HR	RBI	BB-IB	HP	SO	AVG	OBP	SLG	AOPS	ABR	SB-CS	FA	FR	RNG	THR	GAMES AT POSITION	DL	BFW
1885	Phi N	50	184	22	38	8	2	1	13	0	—	25	.207	.207	.288	60	0	—	.891	-4	88	78	P50	—	0.0
1886	Phi N	79	309	40	70	17	1	4	50	7	—	34	.227	.244	.327	72	-11	23	.827	3	148	129	O56(13/11/32),P27	—	-0.5
1887	Phi N	26	106	18	30	11	1	1	17	3	0	9	.283	.303	.434	96	-1	8	.659	-4	64	0	O22(1/20/1),P6	—	-0.5
	Was N	78	311	39	78	6	10	2	36	14	1	27	.251	.285	.354	82	-9	26	.855	-5	61	42	O77R/P	—	-1.2
	Year	104	417	57	108	17	11	3	53	17	1	36	.259	.290	.374	86	-9	34	.812	-9	62	34	O99(1/20/78),P7	—	-1.7
1888	Was N	110	453	56	102	8	4	7	39	7	1	42	.225	.239	.307	78	-12	44	.912	4	114	113	O100R,P9/1	—	-0.8
1889	Col AA	136	578	105	148	22	8	3	70	38	1	65	.256	.303	.337	87	-11	60	.854	-3	105	65	O136L,P2	—	-1.5
1890	Bro AA	91	394	68	94	15	7	1	39	24	1	—	.239	.284	.320	81	-11	49	.892	3	147	100	O64R,P27	—	-0.5
	NY N	4	15	1	2	1	0	0	1	0	0	4	.133	.133	.200	-3	-2	0	.500	1	432	0	O3(1/0/2),P2	—	0.0
	†Lou AA	23	80	24	20	0	2	0	9	13	0	—	.250	.355	.300	95	0	13	.925	2	166	203	P12,O11(0/2/9)	—	0.0
1891	Lou AA	22	64	10	16	2	0	0	8	8	1	6	.250	.342	.281	80	-1	4	.884	-0	105	0	P15,O7(2/0/5)	—	-0.1
	Was AA	21	79	13	18	2	0	0	6	11	0	10	.228	.322	.253	68	-3	8	.719	-3	59	117	O21R	—	-0.5
	Year	43	143	23	34	4	0	0	14	19	1	16	.238	.331	.266	73	-4	12	.750	-4	63	182	O28(2/0/26),P15	—	-0.6
Total	7	640	2573	396	616	92	35	19	288	125	5	222	.239	.276	.325	80	-61	235	.857	-6	108	87	O497(153/33/311),P151/1	—	-5.6

DAISY, GEORGE George R.; B1857 Gloucester NJ; D4.27.1931 Cumberland MD; 5´11˝/190; d5.31

YEAR	TM LG	G	AB	R	H	2B	3B	HR	RBI	BB-IB	HP	SO	AVG	OBP	SLG	AOPS	ABR	SB-CS	FA	FR	RNG	THR	GAMES AT POSITION	DL	BFW
1884	Alt U	1	4	0	0	0	0	0	—	0	—	—	.000	.000	.000	-99	-1	—	.000	-1	0	0	/lf	—	-0.2

DALENA, PETE Peter Martin; B6.26.1960 Fresno CA; BL/TR/5´11˝/200; [NYA82 27/691]; d7.7; Col Cal St.–Fresno

YEAR	TM LG	G	AB	R	H	2B	3B	HR	RBI	BB-IB	HP	SO	AVG	OBP	SLG	AOPS	ABR	SB-CS	FA	FR	RNG	THR	GAMES AT POSITION	DL	BFW
1989	Cle A	5	7	0	1	1	0	0	0	0-0	0	3	.143	.143	.286	18	-1	0-0	ø	0	—	—	/D	0	-0.1

DALESANDRO, MARK Mark Anthony; B5.14.1968 Chicago IL; BR/TR/6´0˝/(185–195); [CalA90 18/503]; d6.6; Col Illinois

YEAR	TM LG	G	AB	R	H	2B	3B	HR	RBI	BB-IB	HP	SO	AVG	OBP	SLG	AOPS	ABR	SB-CS	FA	FR	RNG	THR	GAMES AT POSITION	DL	BFW
1994	Cal A	19	25	5	5	1	0	1	2	2-0	0	4	.200	.259	.360	57	-2	0-0	1.000	-2	223	0	C11,3b5,O2L	0	-0.3
1995	Cal A	11	10	1	1	1	0	0	0	0-0	0	2	.100	.100	.200	-25	-2	0-0	1.000	-1	48	161	C8/lfD	0	-0.3
1998	Tor A	32	67	8	20	5	0	2	14	1-0	0	6	.299	.304	.463	97	-1	0-0	.986	-6	97	75	C18,3b8,1b2/rf	0	-0.5
1999	Tor A	16	27	3	5	0	0	0	1	0-0	1	2	.185	.207	.185	3	-4	1-0	1.000	0	49	207	C8,3b2,D5	0	-0.3
2001	Chi A	1	0	0	0	0	0	0	0	0-0	0	0	ø	ø	ø	ø	0	0-0	ø	-0	0	0	/C	0	0.0
Total	5	79	129	17	31	7	0	3	17	3-0	1	14	.240	.259	.364	60	-9	1-0	.992	-9	103	91	C46,3b15,D6,O4(3/0/1),1b2	0	-1.4

DALEY, JOHN John Francis; B5.25.1887 Pittsburgh PA; D8.31.1988 Mansfield OH; BR/TR/5´7.5˝/155; d7.19; Col Fordham

YEAR	TM LG	G	AB	R	H	2B	3B	HR	RBI	BB-IB	HP	SO	AVG	OBP	SLG	AOPS	ABR	SB-CS	FA	FR	RNG	THR	GAMES AT POSITION	DL	BFW
1912	StL A	18	52	7	9	0	0	1	3	9	2	—	.173	.317	.231	60	-2	4	.833	-4	96	129	S17	—	-0.5

DALEY, JUD Judson Lawrence; B3.14.1884 S.Coventry CT; D1.26.1967 Gadsden AL; BL/TR/5´8˝/172; d9.19

YEAR	TM LG	G	AB	R	H	2B	3B	HR	RBI	BB-IB	HP	SO	AVG	OBP	SLG	AOPS	ABR	SB-CS	FA	FR	RNG	THR	GAMES AT POSITION	DL	BFW
1911	Bro N	19	65	8	15	2	1	0	7	2	3	8	.231	.286	.292	65	-3	2	.952	1	108	122	O16L	—	-0.3
1912	Bro N	61	199	22	51	9	1	1	13	24	2	17	.256	.342	.327	87	-3	2	.947	1	97	119	O55(24/24/7)	—	-0.5
Total	2	80	264	30	66	11	2	1	20	26	5	25	.250	.329	.318	82	-6	4	.949	2	100	120	O71(40/24/7)	—	-0.8

DALEY, PETE Peter Harvey; B1.14.1930 Grass Valley CA; BR/TR/6´0˝/195; d5.3

YEAR	TM LG	G	AB	R	H	2B	3B	HR	RBI	BB-IB	HP	SO	AVG	OBP	SLG	AOPS	ABR	SB-CS	FA	FR	RNG	THR	GAMES AT POSITION	DL	BFW
1955	Bos A	17	50	4	11	2	1	0	5	3-0	0	6	.220	.264	.300	47	-4	0-0	1.000	2	*83*	*71*	C14	0	-0.2
1956	Bos A	59	187	22	50	11	3	5	29	18-5	2	30	.267	.338	.439	92	-2	1-0	.992	-6	*108*	*49*	C57	0	-0.5
1957	Bos A	78	191	17	43	10	0	3	25	16-4	1	31	.225	.288	.325	64	-9	0-0	**1.000**	2	**170**	65	C77	0	-0.5
1958	Bos A	27	56	10	18	2	1	2	8	7-1	0	11	.321	.397	.500	136	3	0-0	.990	-0	92	41	C27	0	0.4
1959	Bos A	65	169	9	38	7	0	1	11	13-1	0	31	.225	.279	.284	53	-11	1-1	.996	7	282	97	C58	0	-0.2
1960	KC A	73	228	19	60	10	2	5	25	16-1	0	41	.263	.311	.390	88	-4	0-0	.990	-6	61	90	C61/lf	0	-0.7
1961	Was A	72	203	12	39	7	1	2	17	14-3	0	37	.192	.244	.266	37	-19	0-1	.988	1	64	132	C72	0	-1.6
Total	7	391	1084	93	259	49	8	18	120	87-15	3	187	.239	.297	.349	71	-46	2-2	.993	-1	*125*	*84*	C366/lf	0	-3.3

DALEY, TOM Thomas Francis "Pete"; B11.13.1884 DuBois PA; D12.2.1934 Los Angeles CA; BL/TR/5´5˝/168; d8.29

YEAR	TM LG	G	AB	R	H	2B	3B	HR	RBI	BB-IB	HP	SO	AVG	OBP	SLG	AOPS	ABR	SB-CS	FA	FR	RNG	THR	GAMES AT POSITION	DL	BFW
1908	Cin N	14	46	5	5	0	0	0	1	3	2	—	.109	.196	.109	-2	-5	1	1.000	1	143	295	O13R	—	-0.6
1913	Phi A	62	141	13	36	2	1	0	11	13	2	28	.255	.327	.284	81	-3	4	.963	0	99	95	O39C	—	-0.6
1914	Phi A	28	86	17	22	1	3	0	7	12	0	14	.256	.347	.337	110	1	4-7	1.000	2	106	130	O24(15/10/0)	—	0.0
	NY A	69	191	36	48	6	4	0	9	38	1	13	.251	.378	.325	112	5	8-8	.958	4	103	150	O58(28/29/0)	—	0.5
	Year	97	277	53	70	7	7	0	16	50	1	27	.253	.369	.329	111	6	12-15	.969	6	104	144	O82(43/39/0)	—	0.5
1915	NY A	10	8	2	2	0	0	0	1	2	0	2	.250	.400	.250	95	0	1	1.000	0	147	0	O2(1/0/1)	—	0.1
Total	4	183	472	73	113	9	8	0	29	68	5	57	.239	.341	.292	92	-2	18-15	.970	7	106	143	O136(44/77/14)	—	-0.6

DALLESSANDRO, DOM Nicholas Dominic "Dim Dom"; B10.3.1913 Reading PA; D4.29.1988 Indianapolis IN; BL/TL/5´6˝/168; d4.24; Mil 1945

YEAR	TM LG	G	AB	R	H	2B	3B	HR	RBI	BB-IB	HP	SO	AVG	OBP	SLG	AOPS	ABR	SB-CS	FA	FR	RNG	THR	GAMES AT POSITION	DL	BFW
1937	Bos A	68	147	18	34	7	1	0	11	27	0	16	.231	.351	.293	61	-8	2-1	.965	-2	91	44	O35(30/1/4)	—	-1.1
1940	Chi N	107	287	33	77	19	6	1	36	34	1	13	.268	.348	.387	104	2	4	.969	-0	108	20	O74L	—	-0.2
1941	Chi N	140	486	73	132	36	2	6	85	68	1	37	.272	.362	.391	116	13	3	.987	-5	98	42	O131(69/62/0)	0	0.3
1942	Chi N	96	264	30	69	12	4	4	43	36	0	18	.261	.350	.383	119	7	4	.986	-1	92	115	O66(31/32/4)	0	0.3
1943	Chi N	87	176	13	39	8	3	1	31	40	1	14	.222	.369	.318	101	2	1	.967	-3	92	51	O45(31/14/0)	0	-0.3
1944	Chi N	117	381	53	116	19	4	8	74	61	0	29	.304	.400	.438	137	21	1	.982	-3	91	112	O106(91/16/0)	0	1.3
1946	Chi N	65	89	4	20	2	2	1	9	23	0	12	.225	.384	.326	104	2	1	.971	-1	103	0	O20(16/0/4)	0	0.0
1947	Chi N	66	115	18	33	7	1	1	14	21	0	11	.287	.397	.391	115	4	0	1.000	-1	95	55	O28L	0	0.1
Total	8	746	1945	242	520	110	23	22	303	310	3	150	.267	.369	.381	112	43	16-1	.980	-16	96	64	O505(370/125/12)	0	0.4

DALLIMORE, BRIAN Brian Scott; B11.15.1973 Las Vegas NV; BR/TR/6´1˝/180; [HouN96 9/264]; d4.29; Col Stanford

YEAR	TM LG	G	AB	R	H	2B	3B	HR	RBI	BB-IB	HP	SO	AVG	OBP	SLG	AOPS	ABR	SB-CS	FA	FR	RNG	THR	GAMES AT POSITION	DL	BFW
2004	SF N	20	43	8	12	2	0	1	7	4-0	1	7	.279	.347	.395	90	-1	0-1	.963	0	113	83	2b9,3b6	0	0.0
2005	SF N	7	7	1	1	1	0	0	0	0-0	0	0	.143	.143	.286	8	-1	0-0	1.000	1	173	354	2b2/S	0	0.0
Total	2	27	50	9	13	3	0	1	7	4-0	1	7	.260	.321	.380	80	-2	0-1	.970	1	124	132	2b11,3b6/S	0	0.0

DALRYMPLE, ABNER Abner Frank; B9.9.1857 Gratiot WI; D1.25.1939 Warren IL; BL/TR/5´10.5˝/175; d5.1

YEAR	TM LG	G	AB	R	H	2B	3B	HR	RBI	BB-IB	HP	SO	AVG	OBP	SLG	AOPS	ABR	SB-CS	FA	FR	RNG	THR	GAMES AT POSITION	DL	BFW
1878	Mil N	**61**	271	52	96	10	4	0	15	6	—	29	**.354**	.368	.421	149	13	—	.832	7	69	120	O61L	—	1.5
1879	Chi N	71	333	47	97	25	1	0	23	4	—	29	.291	.300	.372	113	5	—	.728	-15	24	55	O71(66/1/4)	—	-1.4
1880	Chi N	**86**	382	**91**	**126**	25	12	0	36	3	—	18	.330	.335	.458	156	20	—	.859	4	92	125	O86L	—	1.8
1881	Chi N	82	362	72	117	22	4	1	37	15	—	22	.323	.350	.414	133	13	—	.835	-7	64	33	O82L	—	0.1
1882	Chi N	**84**	397	96	117	25	11	1	36	14	—	18	.295	.319	.421	129	12	—	.877	0	42	114	O84L	—	0.9
1883	Chi N	80	363	78	108	24	4	2	37	11	—	29	.298	.318	.402	108	3	—	.826	-2	65	99	O80L	—	-0.1
1884	Chi N	111	521	111	161	18	9	22	69	14	—	39	.309	.327	.505	146	23	—	.882	0	78	133	O111L	—	1.8
1885	†Chi N	**113**	492	109	135	27	12	**11**	61	46	—	42	.274	.336	.445	133	16	—	.879	-1	74	75	O113(112/1/0)	—	1.1
1886	†Chi N	82	331	62	77	7	12	3	26	33	—	44	.233	.302	.353	86	-7	16	.953	3	91	44	O82L	—	-0.6
1887	Pit N	92	358	45	76	18	5	2	31	45	6	43	.212	.311	.307	78	-8	29	.900	2	83	34	O92L	—	-0.6
1888	Pit N	57	227	19	50	9	2	0	14	6	2	28	.220	.247	.278	73	-7	7	.909	-2	98	0	O57(56/0/1)	—	-0.9
1891	Mil AA	32	135	31	42	7	5	1	22	7	0	18	.311	.345	.459	108	0	6	.909	-1	107	92	O32L	—	-0.2
Total	12	951	4172	813	1202	217	81	43	407	204	8	359	.288	.323	.410	120	83	58	.863	-10	72	79	O951(944/2/5)	—	3.4

DALRYMPLE, CLAY Clayton Errol; B12.3.1936 Chico CA; BL/TR/6´0˝/(190–199); d4.24; Col Cal St.–Chico

YEAR	TM LG	G	AB	R	H	2B	3B	HR	RBI	BB-IB	HP	SO	AVG	OBP	SLG	AOPS	ABR	SB-CS	FA	FR	RNG	THR	GAMES AT POSITION	DL	BFW
1960	Phi N	82	158	11	43	6	2	4	21	15-4	3	21	.272	.343	.411	106	1	0-0	.966	-3	73	129	C48	0	0.1
1961	Phi N	129	378	23	83	11	1	5	42	30-9	4	30	.220	.281	.294	54	-25	0-2	.978	2	112	**178**	C122	0	-1.9
1962	Phi N	123	370	40	102	13	3	11	54	70-7	4	32	.276	.393	.416	122	15	1-3	.987	-1	137	104	C119	0	1.8
1963	Phi N	142	452	40	114	15	3	10	40	45-15	5	55	.252	.327	.365	100	1	0-2	.981	-1	100	124	C142	0	0.6
1964	Phi N	127	382	36	91	16	3	6	46	39-6	0	40	.238	.303	.343	84	-7	0-1	.991	4	144	107	C124	0	0.1

YEAR	TM LG	G	AB	R	H	2B	3B	HR	RBI	BB-IB	HP	SO	AVG	OBP	SLG	AOPS	ABR	SB-CS	FA	FR	RNG	THR	GAMES AT POSITION	DL	BFW
1965	Phi N	103	301	14	64	5	5	4	23	34-7	0	37	.213	.292	.302	69	-13	0-1	.993	20	122	**154**	C102	0	1.2
1966	Phi N	114	331	30	81	13	3	4	39	60-10	3	57	.245	.365	.338	97	2	0-0	.993	1	**139**	95	C110	0	0.9
1967	Phi N	101	268	12	46	7	1	3	21	36-6	1	49	.172	.271	.239	47	-18	1-2	.994	19	155	132	C97	0	0.5
1968	Phi N	85	241	19	50	9	1	3	26	22-9	1	57	.207	.272	.290	70	-8	1-2	.990	-2	100	102	C80	0	-0.8
1969	†Bal A	37	80	8	19	1	1	3	6	13-1	0	8	.237	.340	.387	103	0	0-0	1.000	-0	123	175	C30	0	0.1
1970	Bal A	13	32	4	7	1	0	1	3	7-2	0	4	.219	.350	.344	93	0	0-0	1.000	4	87	241	C11	75	0.5
1971	Bal A	23	49	6	10	1	0	1	6	16-1	1	13	.204	.409	.286	99	1	0-0	.971	3	173	135	C18	0	0.5
Total	12	1079	3042	243	710	98	23	55	327	387-77	22	403	.233	.322	.335	85	-51	3-13	.987	45	124	128	C1003	75	3.6

DALRYMPLE, BILL William Dunn; B2.7.1891 Baltimore MD; D7.14.1967 San Diego CA; TR; d7.6

YEAR	TM LG	G	AB	R	H	2B	3B	HR	RBI	BB-IB	HP	SO	AVG	OBP	SLG	AOPS	ABR	SB-CS	FA	FR	RNG	THR	GAMES AT POSITION	DL	BFW
1915	StL A	3	2	0	0	0	0	0	0	0	0	0	.000	.000	.000	-99	-1	0	1.000	0	233	0	/3	—	0.0

DALTON, JACK Tolbert Percy; B7.3.1885 Henderson TN; BR/TR/5´8.5˝/145; d6.20; Col Virginia

YEAR	TM LG	G	AB	R	H	2B	3B	HR	RBI	BB-IB	HP	SO	AVG	OBP	SLG	AOPS	ABR	SB-CS	FA	FR	RNG	THR	GAMES AT POSITION	DL	BFW
1910	Bro N	77	273	33	62	9	4	1	21	26	4	30	.227	.304	.300	79	-8	5	.966	1	101	110	O72R	—	-1.0
1914	Bro N	128	442	65	141	13	8	1	45	53	3	39	.319	.396	.391	131	19	19	.965	-9	93	50	O116(5/109/2)	—	.2
1915	Buf F	132	437	68	128	17	3	2	46	50	2	38	.293	.368	.359	103	-3	28	.966	-4	99	71	O119(10/60/52)	—	-1.5
1916	Det A	8	11	1	2	0	0	0	0	0	0	5	.182	.182	.182	9	-1	0	1.000	-0	103	0	O4(1/0/3)	—	-0.2
Total	4	345	1163	167	333	39	15	4	112	129	9	112	.286	.362	.356	107	7	52	.966	-12	97	72	O311(16/169/129)	—	-2.5

DALY, BERT Albert Joseph; B4.8.1881 Bayonne NJ; D9.3.1952 Bayonne NJ; BR/TR/5´9˝/170; d8.7; Col Maryland

YEAR	TM LG	G	AB	R	H	2B	3B	HR	RBI	BB-IB	HP	SO	AVG	OBP	SLG	AOPS	ABR	SB-CS	FA	FR	RNG	THR	GAMES AT POSITION	DL	BFW
1903	Phi A	10	21	2	4	0	2	0	4	1	0	—	.190	.227	.381	76	-1	0	.700	-3	69	0	2b4,3b3/S	—	-0.4

DALY, SUN James J.; B1.6.1865 Port Henry NY; D4.30.1938 Albany NY; BL/?/184; d9.30

YEAR	TM LG	G	AB	R	H	2B	3B	HR	RBI	BB-IB	HP	SO	AVG	OBP	SLG	AOPS	ABR	SB-CS	FA	FR	RNG	THR	GAMES AT POSITION	DL	BFW
1892	Bal N	13	48	5	12	0	2	0	7	1	0	4	.250	.265	.333	79	-2	0	.923	1	106	211	O13(10/3/0)	—	-0.2

DALY, JOE Joseph John; B9.21.1868 Conshohocken PA; D3.21.1943 Philadelphia PA; TR/5´8˝/157; d9.19; b–Tom

YEAR	TM LG	G	AB	R	H	2B	3B	HR	RBI	BB-IB	HP	SO	AVG	OBP	SLG	AOPS	ABR	SB-CS	FA	FR	RNG	THR	GAMES AT POSITION	DL	BFW
1890	Phi AA	21	75	8	21	4	1	0	7	3	0	—	.280	.308	.360	97	-1	1	.900	-5	168	0	O14(3/8/3),C9	—	-0.4
1891	Cle N	1	3	0	0	0	0	0	0	0	0	2	.000	.000	.000	-96	-1	0	1.000	0	0	0	/rf	—	-0.1
1892	Bos N	1	0	0	0	0	0	0	0	0	0	0	ø	ø	ø	ø	0	0	1.000	0	*0*	*0*	/C	—	0.0
Total	3	23	78	8	21	4	1	0	7	3	0	<u>2</u>	.269	.296	.346	90	-2	1	.909	-4	153	0	O15(3/8/4),C10	—	-0.5

DALY, TOM Thomas Daniel; B12.12.1891 St.John NB, Can.; D11.7.1946 Medford MA; BR/TR/5´11.5˝/171; d9.23; C14

YEAR	TM LG	G	AB	R	H	2B	3B	HR	RBI	BB-IB	HP	SO	AVG	OBP	SLG	AOPS	ABR	SB-CS	FA	FR	RNG	THR	GAMES AT POSITION	DL	BFW
1913	Chi A	1	3	0	0	0	0	0	0	0	0	0	.000	.000	.000	-99	-1	0	1.000	0	*127*	*97*	/C	—	0.0
1914	Chi A	62	133	13	31	2	0	0	8	7	0	13	.233	.271	.248	57	-7	3-4	.909	-5	72	47	O23(14/0/10),3b5,C4,1b2	—	-1.5
1915	Chi A	29	47	5	9	1	0	0	3	5	0	9	.191	.269	.213	43	-3	0	.958	-1	*178*	*55*	C19/1	—	-0.3
1916	Cle A	31	73	3	16	1	1	0	8	1	0	2	.219	.230	.260	45	-5	0	.982	-1	108	107	C25/rf	—	-0.5
1918	Chi N	1	1	0	0	0	0	0	0	0	0	0	.000	.000	.000	-98	0	0	.667	-0	*0*	*0*	/C	—	-0.1
1919	Chi N	25	50	4	11	0	1	0	1	2	0	5	.220	.250	.260	53	-3	0	.956	-1	*95*	*61*	C18	—	-0.4
1920	Chi N	44	90	12	28	6	0	0	13	2	1	6	.311	.333	.378	102	0	1-1	.981	-1	*100*	*85*	C29	—	0.1
1921	Chi N	51	143	12	34	7	1	0	22	8	0	8	.238	.278	.301	53	-10	1-2	.973	2	*100*	*105*	C47	—	-0.5
Total	8	244	540	49	129	17	3	0	55	25	1	43	.239	.274	.281	59	-29	5-<u>7</u>	.972	-6	*109*	*89*	C144,O24(14/0/11),3b5,1b3	—	-3.2

DALY, TOM Thomas Peter "Tido"; B2.7.1866 Philadelphia PA; D10.29.1938 Brooklyn NY; BB/TR/5´7˝/170; d4.30; C1; b–Joe; OF(9/17/29)

YEAR	TM LG	G	AB	R	H	2B	3B	HR	RBI	BB-IB	HP	SO	AVG	OBP	SLG	AOPS	ABR	SB-CS	FA	FR	RNG	THR	GAMES AT POSITION	DL	BFW
1887	Chi N	74	256	45	53	10	4	2	17	22	0	25	.207	.270	.301	52	-18	29	**.935**	29	—	—	C64,O8(2/3/3),S2,2b2,1b2	—	1.4
1888	Chi N	65	219	34	42	2	6	0	29	10	1	26	.192	.230	.256	51	-13	10	.939	14	—	—	C62,O4(0/1/3)	—	0.6
1889	Was N	71	250	39	75	13	5	1	40	38	1	28	.300	.394	.404	130	12	18	.917	4	—	—	C57,1b8,2b4,O3(1/0/2)/S	—	1.8
1890	†Bro N	82	292	55	71	9	4	5	43	32	4	43	.243	.326	.353	97	-1	20	.953	2	*87*	*82*	C69,1b12/rf	—	0.5
1891	Bro N	58	200	29	50	11	5	2	27	21	2	34	.250	.327	.385	108	2	7	.881	-6	*97*	*48*	C26,1b15,S11,O7R	—	-0.3
1892	Bro N	124	446	76	114	15	6	4	51	64	5	62	.256	.355	.343	116	11	34	.897	-10	84	96	3b57,O30(5/13/12),C27,2b10	—	0.3
1893	Bro N	126	470	94	136	21	14	8	70	76	0	65	.289	.388	.445	127	20	32	.915	-26	96	55	2b82,3b45	—	-0.2
1894	Bro N	124	496	135	168	22	10	8	82	77	5	42	.339	.433	.472	127	27	51	.909	-21	91	87	2b124	—	0.9
1895	Bro N	121	460	90	129	17	8	2	68	52	3	52	.280	.357	.365	94	-2	28	.931	-22	92	85	2b121	—	-1.5
1896	Bro N	67	224	43	63	13	6	3	29	33	5	25	.281	.385	.433	122	9	19	.909	-7	93	115	2b66/C	—	0.4
1898	Bro N	23	73	11	24	3	1	0	11	14	1	—	.329	.443	.397	142	5	6	.993	3	107	127	2b23	—	0.8
1899	Bro N	141	498	95	156	24	9	5	88	69	12	—	.313	.409	.428	127	22	43	.929	16	104	**131**	2b141	—	3.9
1900	†Bro N	97	343	72	107	17	3	4	55	46	6	—	.312	.403	.414	118	11	27	.921	-7	91	105	2b93,1b3,O2(1/0/1)	—	0.7
1901	Bro N	133	520	88	164	**38**	10	3	90	42	4	—	.315	.371	.444	132	22	31	.944	10	94	98	2b133	—	3.2
1902	Chi A	137	489	57	110	22	3	1	54	55	0	—	.225	.303	.288	68	-20	19	.957	-15	90	129	2b137	—	-3.2
1903	Chi A	43	150	20	31	11	0	0	19	20	1	—	.207	.304	.280	80	-2	6	.948	-13	81	77	2b43	—	-1.6
	Cin N	80	307	42	90	14	9	1	38	16	2	—	.293	.332	.407	99	-2	5	.937	-7	97	86	2b79	—	-0.8
Total	16	1566	5693	1025	1583	262	103	49	811	687	52	<u>402</u>	.278	.361	.386	107	83	385	.931	-56	94	100	2b1058,C306,3b102,O55R,1b40,S14	—	6.9

DAM, BILL Elbridge Rust; B4.4.1885 Cambridge MA; D6.22.1930 Quincy MA; BL/TL; d8.23

YEAR	TM LG	G	AB	R	H	2B	3B	HR	RBI	BB-IB	HP	SO	AVG	OBP	SLG	AOPS	ABR	SB-CS	FA	FR	RNG	THR	GAMES AT POSITION	DL	BFW
1909	Bos N	1	2	1	1	1	0	0	0	1	0	—	.500	.667	1.000	398	1	0	1.000	-0	0	0	/lf	—	0.1

DAMASKA, JACK Jack Lloyd; B8.21.1937 Beaver Falls PA; BR/TR/5´11˝/168; d7.3

YEAR	TM LG	G	AB	R	H	2B	3B	HR	RBI	BB-IB	HP	SO	AVG	OBP	SLG	AOPS	ABR	SB-CS	FA	FR	RNG	THR	GAMES AT POSITION	DL	BFW
1963	StL N	5	5	1	1	0	0	0	1	0-0	0	4	.200	.200	.200	14	-1	0-0	ø	-0	0	0	/2lf	0	-0.1

DAMON, JOHNNY Johnny David; B11.5.1973 Fort Riley KS; BL/TL/6´2˝/(175–190); [KCA92 1/35]; d8.12

YEAR	TM LG	G	AB	R	H	2B	3B	HR	RBI	BB-IB	HP	SO	AVG	OBP	SLG	AOPS	ABR	SB-CS	FA	FR	RNG	THR	GAMES AT POSITION	DL	BFW
1995	KC A	47	188	32	53	11	5	3	23	12-0	1	22	.282	.324	.441	96	-2	7-0	.991	-4	92	0	O47(0/44/4)	0	-0.4
1996	KC A	145	517	61	140	22	5	6	50	31-3	3	64	.271	.313	.368	72	-24	25-5	.983	-0	106	54	O144(0/89/63)/D	0	-2.0
1997	KC A	146	472	70	130	12	8	8	48	42-2	3	70	.275	.338	.386	86	-11	16-10	.988	5	112	67	O136(48/65/47),D5	0	-0.8
1998	KC A	**161**	642	104	178	30	10	18	66	58-4	4	84	.277	.339	.439	97	-4	26-12	.990	-2	96	101	O158(14/130/24)	0	-0.4
1999	KC A	145	583	101	179	39	9	14	77	67-5	3	50	.307	.379	.477	113	12	36-6	.987	0	102	85	O140(132/8/3),D4	0	1.2
2000	KC A	159	655	**136**	214	42	10	16	88	65-4	1	60	.327	.382	.495	115	15	**46**-9	.986	2	105	80	O133(67/69/0),D25	0	2.0
2001	†Oak A	155	644	108	165	34	4	9	49	61-1	5	70	.256	.324	.363	81	-17	27-12	.991	-6	98	44	O154(67/86/5)	0	-2.2
2002	Bos A★	154	623	118	178	34	**11**	14	63	65-5	6	70	.286	.356	.443	110	9	31-6	.997	-5	93	92	O151C/D	0	1.0
2003	†Bos A	145	608	103	166	32	6	12	67	68-4	2	74	.273	.345	.405	94	-4	30-6	**.997**	-2	98	109	O144C/D	0	0.0
2004	†Bos A	150	621	123	189	35	6	20	94	76-1	2	71	.304	.380	.477	115	15	19-8	.986	-4	99	58	O148C/D	0	1.4
2005	†Bos A★	148	624	117	197	35	6	10	75	53-3	2	69	.316	.366	.439	110	10	18-1	.985	4	111	72	O147C/D	0	1.9
2006	†NY A	149	593	115	169	35	5	24	80	67-1	4	85	.285	.359	.482	116	14	25-10	.990	-6	96	48	O131C,D16/1	0	1.0
Total	12	1704	6770	1188	1958	361	85	154	780	665-33	36	789	.289	.353	.436	101	13	306-85	.989	-18	101	72	O1633(328/1212/146),D55/1	0	2.7

DAMRAU, HARRY Harry Robert; B9.11.1890 Newburgh NY; D8.21.1957 Staten Island NY; BR/TR/5´10˝/178; d9.17

YEAR	TM LG	G	AB	R	H	2B	3B	HR	RBI	BB-IB	HP	SO	AVG	OBP	SLG	AOPS	ABR	SB-CS	FA	FR	RNG	THR	GAMES AT POSITION	DL	BFW
1915	Phi A	16	56	4	11	1	0	0	3	5	0	17	.196	.262	.214	44	-4	1-1	.870	-2	90	36	3b16	—	-0.6

DANIEL, JAKE Handley Jacob; B4.22.1911 Roanoke AL; D4.23.1996 LaGrange GA; BL/TL/5´11˝/175; d7.24

YEAR	TM LG	G	AB	R	H	2B	3B	HR	RBI	BB-IB	HP	SO	AVG	OBP	SLG	AOPS	ABR	SB-CS	FA	FR	RNG	THR	GAMES AT POSITION	DL	BFW
1937	Bro N	12	27	3	5	1	0	0	3	3	0	4	.185	.267	.222	34	-2	0	1.000	-0	77	66	1b7	—	-0.3

DANIELS, BERT Bernard Elmer; B10.31.1882 Danville IL; D6.6.1958 Cedar Grove NJ; BR/TR/5´10˝/170; d6.25; Col Bucknell

YEAR	TM LG	G	AB	R	H	2B	3B	HR	RBI	BB-IB	HP	SO	AVG	OBP	SLG	AOPS	ABR	SB-CS	FA	FR	RNG	THR	GAMES AT POSITION	DL	BFW
1910	NY A	95	356	68	90	13	8	1	17	41	**16**	—	.253	.356	.343	112	7	41	.957	-1	107	73	O85(79/6/0),3b6,1b4	—	0.1
1911	NY A	131	462	74	132	16	9	2	31	48	18	—	.286	.375	.372	112	3	40	.941	-5	101	73	O120(8/86/26)	—	-1.0
1912	NY A	135	496	72	136	25	11	2	41	51	**18**	—	.274	.363	.381	106	5	37	.945	3	115	74	O131(92/0/39)	—	0.2
1913	NY A	94	320	52	69	13	5	0	22	44	**18**	36	.216	.343	.287	85	-3	27	.966	1	97	114	O87R	—	-0.7
1914	Cin N	71	269	29	59	9	7	0	19	19	2	40	.219	.276	.305	70	-11	14	.974	-2	100	66	O71(11/26/38)	—	-1.9
Total	5	526	1903	295	486	76	40	5	130	203	72	<u>76</u>	.255	.349	.345	98	1	159	.953	-4	105	79	O494(190/118/190),3b6,1b4	—	-3.3

DANIELS, TONY Frederick Clinton; B12.28.1924 Gastonia NC; BR/TR/5´9.5˝/185; d6.12

YEAR	TM LG	G	AB	R	H	2B	3B	HR	RBI	BB-IB	HP	SO	AVG	OBP	SLG	AOPS	ABR	SB-CS	FA	FR	RNG	THR	GAMES AT POSITION	DL	BFW
1945	Phi N	76	230	15	46	3	2	0	10	12	3	22	.200	.249	.230	35	-21	1	.955	4	107	94	2b75/3	0	-1.4

DANIELS, JACK Harold Jack "Sour Mash Jack"; B12.21.1927 Chester PA; BL/TL/5´10˝/165; d4.18

YEAR	TM LG	G	AB	R	H	2B	3B	HR	RBI	BB-IB	HP	SO	AVG	OBP	SLG	AOPS	ABR	SB-CS	FA	FR	RNG	THR	GAMES AT POSITION	DL	BFW
1952	Bos N	106	219	31	41	5	1	2	14	28	3	30	.187	.288	.247	51	-14	3-3	.977	-1	96	102	O87(13/0/75)	0	-1.9

DANIELS, KAL Kalvoski; B8.20.1963 Vienna GA; BL/TR/5´11˝/(185–205); [CinN82 S1/7]; d4.9; Col Middle Georgia JC

YEAR	TM LG	G	AB	R	H	2B	3B	HR	RBI	BB-IB	HP	SO	AVG	OBP	SLG	AOPS	ABR	SB-CS	FA	FR	RNG	THR	GAMES AT POSITION	DL	BFW
1986	Cin N	74	181	34	58	10	4	6	23	22-1	2	30	.320	.398	.519	146	12	15-2	.967	-0	113	0	O47L	0	1.3
1987	Cin N	108	368	73	123	24	1	26	64	60-11	1	62	.334	.429	.617	167	37	26-8	.968	-1	101	78	O94L	31	3.5
1988	Cin N	140	495	95	144	29	1	18	64	87-10	3	94	.291	**.397**	.463	142	32	27-6	.982	-1	100	119	O137L	0	3.3

YEAR	TM LG	G	AB	R	H	2B	3B	HR	RBI	BB-IB	HP	SO	AVG	OBP	SLG	AOPS	ABR	SB-CS	FA	FR	RNG	THR	GAMES AT POSITION	DL	BFW
1989	Cin N	44	133	26	29	11	0	2	9	36-1	2	28	.218	.390	.346	109	4	6-4	1.000	0	88	188	O38L	37	0.3
	LA N	11	38	7	13	2	0	2	8	7-0	0	5	.342	.435	.553	186	5	3-0	1.000	-0	102	0	O11L	56	0.5
	Year	55	171	33	42	13	0	4	17	43-1	2	33	.246	.399	.392	125	9	9-4	1.000	0	91	149	O49L	0	0.8
1990	LA N	130	450	81	133	23	1	27	94	68-1	3	104	.296	.389	.531	155	35	4-3	.987	1	87	161	O127L	0	3.3
1991	LA N	137	461	54	115	15	1	17	73	63-4	1	116	.249	.337	.397	109	6	6-1	.979	-2	88	132	O132L	0	0.1
1992	LA N	35	104	9	24	5	0	2	8	10-0	1	30	.231	.302	.337	82	-2	0-0	.964	-2	69	116	O21L,1b8	20	-0.6
	Chi N	48	108	12	27	6	0	4	17	12-0	1	24	.250	.328	.417	107	1	0-2	1.000	-1	70	277	O28L	0	-0.1
	Year	83	212	21	51	11	0	6	25	22-0	2	54	.241	.315	.377	95	-1	0-2	.984	-3	70	204	O49L,1b8	0	-0.7
Total	7	727	2338	391	666	125	8	104	360	365-28	14	493	.285	.382	.479	137	130	87-26	.980	-6	93	124	O635L,1b8	144	11.6
DANIELS, LAW	Lawrence Long; B7.14.1862 Newton MA; D1.7.1929 Waltham MA; BR/TR/5´10˝/170; d4.25																								
1887	Bal AA	48	165	23	41	5	1	0	32	8	1	—	.248	.287	.291	65	-7	7	.845	-8	—	—	C26,O15(10/5/0),1b4,2b2/S3	—	-1.2
1888	KC AA	61	218	32	45	2	0	2	28	14	3	—	.206	.264	.243	59	-10	20	.855	-3	174	253	O30(14/9/7),C29,3b2/S	—	-1.1
Total	2	109	383	55	86	7	1	2	60	22	4	—	.225	.274	.264	62	-17	27	.859	-12	—	—	C55,O45(24/14/7),1b4,3b3,S2,2b2	—	-2.3
DANNER, BUCK	Henry Frederick; B6.8.1891 Dedham MA; D9.19.1949 Dedham MA; BR/TR/5´11˝/140; d9.17																								
1915	Phi A	3	12	1	3	0	0	0	0	0	0	1	.250	.250	.250	51	-1	1	.750	-2	51	0	S3	—	-0.3
DANNING, HARRY	Harry "Harry the Horse"; B9.6.1911 Los Angeles CA; D11.29.2004 Valparaiso IN; BR/TR/6´1˝/190; d7.30; Mil 1943–45; b–Ike																								
1933	NY N	3	2	0	0	0	0	0	0	1	0	0	.000	.333	.000	2	0	0	1.000	0	*0*	*0*	/C	—	0.0
1934	NY N	53	97	8	32	7	0	1	7	1	0	9	.330	.337	.433	107	1	1	.989	1	*112*	*113*	C37	—	0.2
1935	NY N	65	152	16	37	11	1	2	20	9	0	16	.243	.286	.368	76	-5	0	.978	2	*124*	*102*	C44	—	-0.1
1936	†NY N	32	69	3	11	2	2	0	4	1	1	5	.159	.183	.246	15	-9	0	.988	2	*138*	*83*	C24	—	-0.6
1937	†NY N	93	292	30	84	12	4	8	51	18	1	20	.288	.331	.438	106	1	0	.982	1	*161*	*101*	C86	—	0.7
1938	NY N☆	120	448	59	137	26	3	9	60	23	4	40	.306	.345	.438	113	7	1	.984	-2	*121*	*60*	C114	—	1.2
1939	NY N☆	135	520	79	163	28	5	16	74	35	2	42	.313	.359	.479	122	15	4	.991	6	*82*	*105*	C132	—	2.9
1940	NY N★	140	524	65	157	34	4	13	91	35	5	31	.300	.349	.454	119	13	3	.980	9	***135***	*89*	C131	—	3.1
1941	NY N★	130	459	58	112	22	4	7	56	30	1	25	.244	.292	.355	80	-14	1	.993	7	*117*	*100*	C116/1	0	0.1
1942	NY N	119	408	45	114	20	3	1	34	34	0	29	.279	.335	.350	100	0	3	.979	-0	*126*	*73*	C116	0	0.7
Total	10	890	2971	363	847	162	26	57	397	187	14	217	.285	.330	.415	104	9	13	.985	25	*121*	*89*	C801/1	0	8.2
DANNING, IKE	Isaac; B1.20.1905 Los Angeles CA; D3.30.1983 Santa Monica CA; BR/TR/5´10˝/160; d9.21; b–Harry																								
1928	StL A	2	6	0	3	0	0	0	1	1	0	2	.500	.571	.500	178	1	0-0	.917	0	*123*	*220*	C2	—	0.1
DANTONIO, FATS	John James; B12.31.1918 New Orleans LA; D5.28.1993 New Orleans LA; BR/TR/5´8˝/165; d9.18																								
1944	Bro N	3	7	0	1	0	0	0	0	0	0	1	.143	.143	.143	-20	-1	0	.846	-1	*65*	*0*	C3	0	-0.2
1945	Bro N	47	128	12	32	6	1	0	12	11	0	6	.250	.309	.313	74	-5	3	.929	-5	*108*	*76*	C45	0	-0.7
Total	2	50	135	12	33	6	1	0	12	11	0	7	.244	.301	.304	69	-6	3	.923	-5	*105*	*72*	C48	0	-0.9
DANZIG, BABE	Harold Paul; B4.30.1887 Binghamton NY; D7.14.1931 San Francisco CA; BR/TR/6´2˝/205; d4.12																								
1909	Bos A	6	13	0	2	0	0	0	0	2	1	—	.154	.313	.154	47	-1	0	.960	-1	0	212	1b3	—	-0.2
DAPPER, CLIFF	Clifford Roland; B1.2.1920 Los Angeles CA; BR/TR/6´2˝/190; d4.19; Mil 1943–45																								
1942	Bro N	8	17	2	8	1	0	1	9	2	0	2	.471	.526	.706	255	3	0	1.000	0	*145*	*82*	C8	0	0.4
DARINGER, CLIFF	Clifford Clarence "Shanty"; B4.10.1885 Hayden IN; D12.26.1971 Sacramento CA; BL/TR/5´7.5˝/155; d4.20; b–Rolla																								
1914	KC F	64	160	12	42	2	1	0	16	11	3	7	.262	.322	.287	70	-9	9	.944	5	122	94	S24,3b19,2b14	—	-0.2
DARINGER, ROLLA	Rolla Harrison; B11.15.1888 N.Vernon IN; D5.23.1974 Seymour IN; BL/TR/5´10˝/155; d9.19; b–Cliff																								
1914	StL N	2	4	1	2	1	0	0	0	1	0	2	.500	.600	.750	304	1	0	.667	-1	81	373	/S	—	0.1
1915	StL N	10	23	3	2	0	0	0	0	9	0	5	.087	.344	.087	33	-1	0-1	.947	-2	91	151	S10	—	-0.3
Total	2	12	27	4	4	1	0	0	0	10	0	7	.148	.378	.185	72	0	0-1	.927	-2	90	171	S11	—	-0.2
DARK, ALVIN	Alvin Ralph "Blackie"; B1.7.1922 Comanche OK; BR/TR/5´11˝/(175–185); d7.14; M13/C2; Col Louisiana St.; OF(39/0/4)																								
1946	Bos N	15	13	0	3	3	0	0	1	0	0	3	.231	.231	.462	93	0	0	.905	1	143	110	S12/lf	0	0.1
1948	†Bos N	137	543	85	175	39	6	3	48	24	2	36	.322	.353	.433	114	9	4	.963	-14	95	95	S133	0	0.4
1949	Bos N	130	529	74	146	23	5	3	53	31	1	43	.276	.317	.355	85	-13	5	.961	-3	98	100	S125,3b4	0	-0.8
1950	NY N	**154**	587	79	164	36	5	16	67	39	6	60	.279	.331	.440	100	-1	9	.962	-11	97	**106**	S154	0	-0.3
1951	†NY N★	156	646	114	196	**41**	7	14	69	42	6	39	.303	.352	.454	114	12	12-7	.944	4	100	**123**	S156	0	2.6
1952	NY N☆	151	589	92	177	29	3	14	73	47	5	39	.301	.357	.431	117	13	6-6	.965	5	96	**120**	S150	0	2.7
1953	NY N	**155**	647	126	194	41	6	23	88	28	6	34	.300	.335	.488	109	7	7-2	.967	8	105	107	S110,2b26,O17(13/0/4),3b8/P	0	2.5
1954	†NY N★	**154**	644	98	189	26	6	20	70	27	5	40	.293	.325	.446	98	-4	5-3	.956	2	102	105	S154	0	1.1
1955	NY N	115	475	77	134	20	3	9	45	22-2	5	32	.282	.319	.394	88	-9	2-1	.962	-12	93	94	S115	0	-1.1
1956	NY N	48	206	19	52	12	0	2	17	8-0	1	13	.252	.279	.340	67	-10	0-0	.961	-7	89	86	S48	0	-1.3
	StL N	100	413	54	118	14	7	4	37	21-0	2	33	.286	.320	.383	89	-7	3-1	.959	-1	100	104	S99	0	0.0
	Year	148	619	73	170	26	7	6	54	29-0	3	46	.275	.307	.368	82	-17	3-1	.960	-8	96	98	S147	0	-1.3
1957	StL N	140	583	80	169	25	8	4	64	29-4	4	56	.290	.326	.381	88	-10	3-4	.965	17	106	122	S139/3	0	1.8
1958	StL N	18	64	7	19	0	0	1	5	2-0	0	6	.297	.318	.344	72	-3	0-0	.943	-1	104	114	S8,3b8	0	-0.3
	Chi N	114	464	54	137	16	4	3	43	29-1	5	23	.295	.339	.366	89	-7	1-1	.949	1	98	105	3b111	0	-0.7
	Year	132	528	61	156	16	4	4	48	31-1	5	29	.295	.337	.364	87	-10	1-1	.948	-0	98	100	3b119,S8	0	-1.0
1959	Chi N	136	477	60	126	22	9	6	45	55-9	3	50	.264	.342	.386	95	-3	1-1	.948	2	107	104	3b131,1b4/S	0	-0.2
1960	Phi N	55	198	29	48	5	1	3	14	19-2	2	14	.242	.315	.323	75	-7	1-1	.953	-2	93	81	3b53/1	0	-1.0
	Mil N	50	141	16	42	6	2	1	18	7-2	1	13	.298	.329	.390	106	1	0-0	.960	-2	103	102	O25L,1b10,3b4,2b3	0	-0.3
	Year	105	339	45	90	11	3	4	32	26-4	3	27	.265	.321	.351	88	-6	1-1	.954	-4	91	78	3b57,O25L,1b11,2b3	0	-1.3
Total	14	1828	7219	1064	2089	358	72	126	757	430-20	54	534	.289	.333	.411	98	-32	59-27	.960	-14	99	107	S1404,3b320,O43L,2b29,1b15/P	0	5.2
DARLING, DELL	Conrad; B12.21.1861 Erie PA; D11.20.1904 Erie PA; BR/TR/5´8˝/170; d7.3																								
1883	Buf N	6	18	1	3	0	0	0	1	2	—	5	.167	.250	.167	29	-1	—	.875	-2	—	—	C6	—	-0.3
1887	Chi N	38	141	28	45	7	4	3	20	22	0	18	.319	.411	.489	132	6	19	.786	2	132	189	O20R,C20	—	0.8
1888	Chi N	20	75	12	16	3	1	2	7	3	1	12	.213	.253	.360	87	-1	0	.932	1	—	—	C20	—	0.2
1889	Chi N	36	120	14	23	1	1	0	7	25	0	22	.192	.331	.217	51	-7	5	.960	2	—	—	C36	—	-0.2
1890	Chi P	58	221	45	57	12	4	2	39	29	3	28	.258	.352	.376	91	-3	5	.957	-8	88	99	1b29,S15,C9,O7R,2b3,3b2	—	-1.0
1891	StL AA	17	53	9	7	1	3	0	9	10	0	11	.132	.270	.264	46	-4	0	.894	-0	*117*	*117*	C17,2b2/S	—	-0.3
Total	6	175	628	109	151	24	13	7	83	91	4	96	.240	.340	.354	87	-10	29	.923	-4	*115*	*116*	C108,1b29,O27R,S16,2b5,3b2	—	-0.8
DARR, MIKE	Michael Curtis; B3.21.1976 Corona CA; D2.15.2002 Phoenix AZ; BL/TR/6´3˝/205; [DetA94 2/52]; d5.23																								
1999	SD N	25	48	6	13	1	0	2	3	5-0	0	18	.271	.340	.417	97	0	2-1	1.000	-0	110	0	O22(0/3/21)	0	-0.1
2000	SD N	58	205	21	55	14	4	1	30	23-1	0	45	.268	.342	.390	90	-3	9-1	1.000	5	107	203	O57(8/19/47)	0	0.1
2001	SD N	105	289	36	80	13	1	2	34	39-3	1	72	.277	.363	.349	93	-2	6-2	.990	5	112	123	O93(5/29/69)	21	0.2
Total	3	188	542	63	148	28	5	5	67	67-4	1	135	.273	.353	.371	92	-5	17-4	.994	10	110	142	O172(13/51/137)	21	0.2
DARRAGH, JIMMY	James S.; B7.17.1866 Ebensburg PA; D8.12.1939 Rochester PA; 6´2.5˝/180; d5.13; Col Penn																								
1891	Lou AA	1	2	0	1	0	0	0	0	0	0	0	.500	.500	.500	188	0	0	1.000	0	353	0	/1	—	0.0
DARWIN, BOBBY	Arthur Bobby Lee; B2.16.1943 Los Angeles CA; BR/TR/6´2˝/(190–200); d9.30																								
1962	LA A	1	1	0	0	0	0	0	0	0-0	0	1	.000	.000	.000	-99	0	0-0	.000	-0	0	0	/P	0	0.0
1969	LA N	6	0	1	0	0	0	0	0	0-0	0	0	ø	ø	ø	ø	0	0-0	ø	-0	0	0	P3	0	0.0
1971	LA N	11	20	2	5	1	0	1	4	2-0	0	9	.250	.318	.450	121	1	0-0	1.000	0	131	0	O4R	0	0.1
1972	Min A	145	513	48	137	20	2	22	80	38-4	8	145	.267	.326	.442	121	13	2-3	.980	-8	92	84	O142(9/86/47)	0	-0.1
1973	Min A	145	560	69	141	20	2	18	90	46-5	3	137	.252	.309	.391	93	-6	5-2	.980	-4	88	142	O140R/D	0	-1.8
1974	Min A	152	575	67	152	13	7	25	94	37-2	14	127	.264	.322	.442	115	9	1-3	.970	-7	93	75	O142R	0	-0.7
1975	Min A	48	169	26	37	6	0	5	18	18-1	4	44	.219	.307	.343	83	-4	2-0	.969	-4	56	140	O27R,D19	0	-0.9
	Mil A	55	186	19	46	6	2	8	23	11-0	3	54	.247	.300	.430	104	0	4-1	.978	3	103	165	O43(25/0/20),D9	34	0.1
	Year	103	355	45	83	12	2	13	41	29-1	7	98	.234	.304	.389	94	-4	6-1	.975	-1	84	155	O70(25/0/47),D28	0	-0.8
1976	Mil A	25	73	6	18	3	1	1	5	6-1	2	16	.247	.321	.356	100	0	0-0	.977	1	117	79	O21(0/1/21)/D	0	0.0
	Bos A	43	106	9	19	5	2	3	13	2-0	3	35	.179	.216	.349	57	-6	1-0	.964	0	103	111	O17(3/0/14),D16	0	-0.7

YEAR	TM LG	G	AB	R	H	2B	3B	HR	RBI	BB-IB	HP	SO	AVG	OBP	SLG	AOPS	ABR	SB-CS	FA	FR	RNG	THR	GAMES AT POSITION	DL	BFW
	Year	68	179	15	37	8	3	4	18	8-1	5	51	.207	.260	.352	73	-7	1-0	.972	1	111	92	O38(3/1/35),D17	0	-0.7
1977	Bos A	4	9	1	2	1	0	0	1	0-0	0	4	.222	.222	.333	44	-1	0-0	.500	-0	225	0	/rfD	0	-0.1
	Chi N	11	12	2	2	1	0	0	0	0-0	0	5	.167	.167	.250	9	-2	0-0	ø	-0	0	0	/rf	0	-0.2
Total	9	646	2224	250	559	76	16	83	328	160-13	37	577	.251	.311	.412	103	4	15-9	.976	-19	91	106	O538(37/87/417),D48,P4	34	-4.3
DASCENZO, DOUG	Douglas Craig; B6.30.1964 Cleveland OH; BB/TL/5´8˝/160; [ChiN85 12/312]; d9.2; Col Oklahoma St.																								
1988	Chi N	26	75	9	16	3	0	0	4	9-1	0	4	.213	.298	.253	57	-4	6-1	1.000	2	118	121	O20C	0	-0.1
1989	Chi N	47	139	20	23	1	0	1	12	13-0	0	13	.165	.234	.194	23	-14	6-3	1.000	-1	103	0	O45(8/37/1)	0	-1.6
1990	Chi N	113	241	27	61	9	5	1	26	21-2	1	18	.253	.312	.344	76	-8	15-6	1.000	2	108	44	O107(65/38/22)/P	0	-0.7
1991	Chi N	118	239	40	61	11	0	1	18	24-2	2	26	.255	.327	.314	78	-6	14-7	.985	-4	95	0	O86(32/59/16),P3	0	-1.1
1992	Chi N	139	376	37	96	13	4	0	20	27-2	0	32	.255	.304	.311	73	-14	6-8	.978	-6	93	36	O122(25/80/28)	0	-2.4
1993	Tex A	76	146	20	29	5	1	2	10	8-0	0	22	.199	.239	.288	43	-13	2-0	.990	3	100	216	O68(16/35/25),D2	0	-1.0
1996	SD N	21	9	3	1	0	0	0	0	1-0	0	2	.111	.200	.111	-16	-2	0-1	1.000	-1	58	0	O10(0/1/9)	0	-0.2
Total	7	540	1225	156	287	42	10	5	90	103-7	3	117	.234	.293	.297	64	-61	49-26	.990	-4	100	53	O458(146/270/101),P4,D2	0	-7.1
DASHIELL, WALLY	John Wallace; B5.9.1902 Jewett TX; D5.20.1972 Pensacola FL; BR/TR/5´9.5˝/170; d4.20; Col Lon Morris (TX) JC																								
1924	Chi A	1	2	0	0	0	0	0	0	0	0	0	.000	.000	.000	-99	-1	0-0	.667	-1	48	0	/S	—	-0.1
DATZ, JEFF	Jeffrey William; B11.28.1959 Camden NJ; BR/TR/6´4˝/220; [HouN82 19/485]; d9.5; C5; Col Rowan																								
1989	Det A	7	10	0	2	0	0	0	0	1-0	1	1	.200	.333	.200	55	-1	0-0	1.000	1	0	146	C6/D	0	0.1
DAUBACH, BRIAN	Brian Michael; B2.11.1972 Belleville IL; BL/TR/6´1˝/(201–230); [NYN90 17/469]; d9.10																								
1998	Fla N	10	15	0	3	1	0	0	3	1-0	1	5	.200	.294	.267	52	-1	0-0	1.000	-0	50	155	1b4	0	-0.2
1999	†Bos A	110	381	61	112	33	3	21	73	36-0	3	92	.294	.360	.562	126	15	0-1	.983	-0	101	80	1b61,D43,O2L/3	0	0.6
2000	Bos A	142	495	55	123	32	2	21	76	44-2	6	130	.248	.315	.448	89	-10	1-1	.996	2	102	79	1b83,D41,O8(7/0/1)/3	0	-1.6
2001	Bos A	122	407	54	107	28	3	22	71	53-7	5	108	.263	.350	.509	124	15	1-0	.988	0	101	83	1b106,O14(6/0/8)	17	0.5
2002	Bos A	137	444	62	118	24	2	20	78	51-4	7	126	.266	.348	.464	112	8	2-1	.990	-4	85	95	1b60,O48(35/0/13),D28	0	-0.3
2003	Chi A	95	183	26	42	11	0	6	21	34-1	1	54	.230	.352	.388	92	-1	1-0	.996	-1	99	84	1b45,D14,O12(3/0/9)	0	-0.6
2004	Bos A	30	75	9	17	8	0	2	8	10-0	1	21	.227	.326	.413	86	-1	0-0	.982	1	126	101	1b14,O7(6/0/1)	0	-0.2
2005	NY N	15	25	4	3	2	0	1	3	7-1	1	5	.120	.324	.320	74	-1	0-0	.977	-0	97	74	1b6,D2	0	-0.1
Total	8	661	2025	271	525	139	10	93	333	236-15	25	541	.259	.341	.476	107	24	5-3	.990	-2	99	85	1b379,D128,O91(59/0/32),3b2	17	-1.9
DAUBERT, HARRY	Harry "Jake"; B6.19.1892 Columbus OH; D1.8.1944 Detroit MI; BR/TR/6´0˝/160; d9.4																								
1915	Pit N	1	1	0	0	0	0	0	0	0	0	1	.000	.000	.000	-99	0	0	ø	0	—	—	/H	—	0.0
DAUBERT, JAKE	Jacob Ellsworth; B4.7.1884 Shamokin PA; D10.9.1924 Cincinnati OH; BL/TL/5´10.5˝/160; d4.14																								
1910	Bro N	144	552	67	146	15	15	8	50	47	5	53	.264	.328	.389	112	5	23	.989	-3	87	94	1b144	—	-0.1
1911	Bro N	149	573	89	176	17	8	5	45	51	2	56	.307	.366	.391	117	12	32	.989	2	104	**107**	1b149	—	1.0
1912	Bro N	145	559	81	172	19	16	3	66	48	6	45	.308	.369	.415	119	13	29	**.993**	1	97	87	1b143	—	1.0
1913	Bro N	139	508	76	178	17	7	2	52	44	3	40	**.350**	.405	.423	133	23	25-21	.991	3	105	**128**	1b139	—	2.1
1914	Bro N	126	474	89	156	17	7	6	45	30	5	34	**.329**	.375	.432	137	20	25	.993	-6	71	107	1b126	—	1.2
1915	Bro N	150	544	62	164	21	8	2	47	57	1	48	.301	.369	.381	125	17	11-13	.993	8	126	84	1b150	—	2.2
1916	†Bro N	127	478	75	151	16	7	3	33	38	4	39	.316	.371	.397	132	19	21-7	**.993**	3	106	85	1b126	—	2.4
1917	Bro N	125	468	59	122	4	4	2	30	51	6	30	.261	.341	.299	94	-1	11	.991	6	**121**	76	1b125	—	0.2
1918	Bro N	108	396	50	122	12	**15**	2	47	27	5	18	.308	.360	.429	141	18	10	.991	-0	94	71	1b105	—	1.7
1919	†Cin N	**140**	537	79	148	10	12	2	44	35	2	23	.276	.322	.350	105	2	11	.989	-1	95	109	1b140	—	-0.4
1920	Cin N	142	553	97	168	28	13	4	48	47	3	29	.304	.362	.423	127	19	11-13	.990	-8	75	101	1b140	—	0.6
1921	Cin N	136	516	69	158	18	12	2	64	24	3	16	.306	.341	.399	100	-2	12-6	.993	3	106	109	1b136	—	-0.7
1922	Cin N	**156**	610	114	205	15	**22**	12	66	56	3	21	.336	.395	.492	130	25	14-17	**.994**	-0	97	**124**	1b156	—	1.1
1923	Cin N	125	500	63	146	27	10	2	54	40	4	20	.292	.349	.398	99	-1	11-12	.993	6	**122**	104	1b121	—	-0.4
1924	Cin N	102	405	47	114	14	9	1	31	28	2	17	.281	.331	.368	88	-7	5-10	.990	7	130	104	1b102	—	-1.0
Total	15	2014	7673	1117	2326	250	165	56	722	623	54	489	.303	.360	.401	117	162	251-99	.991	20	102	100	1b2002	—	10.9
DAUER, RICH	Richard Fremont; B7.27.1952 San Bernardino CA; BR/TR/6´0˝/(177–190); [BalA74 1/24]; d9.11; C11; Col USC																								
1976	Bal A	11	39	0	4	0	0	0	3	1-0	1	3	.103	.143	.103	-28	-6	0-0	1.000	-2	82	118	2b10	0	-0.9
1977	Bal A	96	304	38	74	15	1	5	25	20-0	2	28	.243	.294	.349	79	-9	1-0	.982	11	109	126	2b83,3b9,D2	0	0.6
1978	Bal A	133	459	57	121	23	0	6	46	26-0	0	22	.264	.301	.353	89	-8	0-4	.998	5	95	115	2b87,3b52/D	0	-0.1
1979	†Bal A	142	479	63	123	20	0	9	61	36-2	1	36	.257	.305	.355	82	-13	0-1	.979	-11	91	115	2b103,3b44	0	-1.9
1980	Bal A	152	557	71	158	32	0	2	63	46-1	3	19	.284	.338	.352	92	-5	3-2	.991	3	94	**124**	2b137,3b35	0	0.4
1981	Bal A	96	369	41	97	27	0	4	38	27-0	3	18	.263	.317	.369	98	0	0-0	**.989**	-10	90	110	2b94,3b4	0	-0.6
1982	Bal A	158	558	75	156	24	2	8	57	50-1	1	34	.280	.337	.373	96	-2	0-1	.987	-29	84	91	2b123,3b61	0	-2.6
1983	†Bal A	140	459	49	108	19	0	5	41	47-2	2	29	.235	.306	.309	72	-17	1-1	.988	-22	89	94	2b131,3b17	0	-3.2
1984	Bal A	127	397	29	101	26	0	2	24	24-1	0	23	.254	.296	.335	76	-13	1-3	.980	-9	98	106	2b123,3b3	0	-1.6
1985	Bal A	85	208	25	42	7	0	2	14	20-0	1	7	.202	.275	.264	50	-14	0-1	.990	2	103	106	2b73,3b17/1	0	-0.9
Total	10	1140	3829	448	984	193	3	43	372	297-7	14	219	.257	.310	.343	83	-87	6-13	.987	-61	94	109	2b964,3b242,D3/1	0	-10.8
DAUGHERTY, DOC	Harold Ray; B10.12.1927 Paris PA; BR/TR/6´0˝/180; d4.22																								
1951	Det A	1	1	0	0	0	0	0	0	0	0	1	.000	.000	.000	-99	0	0-0	ø	0	—	—	/H	0	0.0
DAUGHERTY, JACK	John Michael; B7.3.1960 Hialeah FL; BB/TL/6´0˝/(185–195); d9.1; Col Arizona																								
1987	Mon N	11	10	1	1	1	0	0	1	0-0	0	3	.100	.100	.200	-22	-2	0-0	1.000	0	383	0	/1	0	-0.1
1989	Tex A	52	106	15	32	4	2	1	10	11-0	1	21	.302	.364	.406	117	3	2-1	1.000	1	116	81	1b23,O5(4/0/1),D8	0	0.3
1990	Tex A	125	310	36	93	20	2	6	47	22-0	2	49	.300	.347	.435	118	7	0-0	.982	-0	71	183	O42(39/0/4),1b30,D21	0	0.4
1991	Tex A	58	144	8	28	3	2	1	11	16-1	0	23	.194	.270	.264	51	-10	1-0	.981	-2	91	64	O37(34/0/3),1b11/D	86	-1.3
1992	Tex A	59	127	13	26	9	0	0	9	16-1	1	21	.205	.295	.276	64	-6	2-1	.939	0	94	98	O26(16/1/11),D13,1b8	91	-0.7
1993	Hou N	4	3	0	1	0	0	0	0	0-0	0	0	.333	.333	.333	82	0	0-0	ø	0	0	0	/1rf	0	0.0
	Cin N	46	59	7	13	2	0	2	9	11-0	0	15	.220	.338	.356	87	-1	0-0	.917	-2	67	0	O16(11/0/5),1b2	0	-0.3
	Year	50	62	7	14	2	0	2	9	11-0	0	15	.226	.338	.355	87	-1	0-0	.923	-1	72	0	O17(11/0/6),1b3	0	-0.3
Total	6	355	759	80	194	39	6	10	87	76-2	4	132	.256	.322	.362	92	-9	5-2	.969	-2	80	127	O127(104/1/25),1b76,D43	177	-1.7
DAUGHTERS, BOB	Robert Francis "Red"; B8.5.1914 Cincinnati OH; D8.22.1988 Southbury CT; BR/TR/6´2˝/185; d4.24; Col Holy Cross																								
1937	Bos A	1	0	1	0	0	0	0	0	0	0	0	ø	ø	ø	ø	0	0-0	ø	0	—	—	/R	—	0.0
DAULTON, DARREN	Darren Arthur; B1.3.1962 Arkansas City KS; BL/TR/6´2˝/(180–207); [PhiN80 25/629]; d9.25; C1																								
1983	Phi N	2	3	1	1	0	0	0	0	1-0	0	1	.333	.500	.333	136	0	0-0	1.000	-0	51	0	C2	0	0.0
1985	Phi N	36	103	14	21	3	1	4	11	16-0	0	37	.204	.311	.369	87	-2	3-0	.994	1	90	101	C28	84	0.1
1986	Phi N	49	138	18	31	4	0	8	21	38-3	1	41	.225	.391	.428	122	6	2-3	.985	-4	78	104	C48	106	0.3
1987	Phi N	53	129	10	25	6	0	3	13	16-1	0	37	.194	.281	.310	55	-8	0-0	.991	-1	99	68	C40/1	10	-0.7
1988	Phi N	58	144	13	30	6	0	1	12	17-1	0	26	.208	.288	.271	61	-7	2-1	.977	-8	93	65	C44/1	36	-1.4
1989	Phi N	131	368	29	74	12	2	8	44	52-8	2	58	.201	.303	.310	76	-11	2-1	.984	-3	109	98	C126	0	-0.8
1990	Phi N	143	459	62	123	30	1	12	57	72-9	2	72	.268	.367	.416	116	13	7-1	.989	7	**151**	87	C139	0	2.9
1991	Phi N	89	285	36	56	12	0	12	42	41-4	2	66	.196	.297	.365	87	-5	5-0	.985	-14	84	51	C88	66	-1.3
1992	Phi N★	145	485	80	131	32	5	27	**109**	88-11	6	103	.270	.385	.524	156	39	11-2	.987	-3	122	92	C141	0	4.9
1993	†Phi N★	147	510	90	131	35	4	24	105	117-12	2	111	.257	.392	.482	136	32	5-0	.991	-6	124	88	C146	0	3.7
1994	Phi N	69	257	43	77	17	1	15	56	33-2	1	43	.300	.380	.549	136	14	4-1	.994	7	78	99	C68	44	2.5
1995	Phi N★	98	342	44	85	19	3	9	55	55-2	5	52	.249	.359	.401	100	2	3-0	.994	-3	100	86	C95	37	0.5
1996	Phi N	5	12	3	2	0	0	0	0	7-0	1	5	.167	.500	.167	85	1	0-0	1.000	-1	80	0	O5L	176	0.0
1997	Phi N	84	269	46	71	13	6	11	42	54-4	1	57	.264	.381	.480	128	12	4-0	.979	5	121	137	O70R,1b3,D6	0	1.4
	†Fla N	52	126	22	33	8	2	3	21	22-1	1	17	.262	.371	.429	115	4	2-1	.984	-2	83	98	1b39,O3(1/0/3)/D	0	-0.1
	Year	136	395	68	104	21	8	14	63	76-5	2	74	.263	.378	.463	124	16	6-1	.979	3	118	134	O73(1/0/73),1b42,D7	0	1.3
Total	14	1161	3630	511	891	197	25	137	588	629-58	24	726	.245	.357	.427	114	90	50-10	.989	-25	111	86	C965,O78(6/0/73),1b44,D7	559	12.0
DAVALILLO, YO-YO	Pompeyo Antonio (Romero); B6.30.1931 Caracas, Distrito Capital, Venez.; BR/TR/5´3˝/154; d8.1; b-Vic																								
1953	Was A	19	58	10	17	1	0	0	2	1	0	7	.293	.305	.310	68	-3	1-0	.935	-2	90	96	S17	0	-0.3

YEAR	TM LG	G	AB	R	H	2B	3B	HR	RBI	BB-IB	HP	SO	AVG	OBP	SLG	AOPS	ABR	SB-CS	FA	FR	RNG	THR	GAMES AT POSITION	DL	BFW
Davalillo, Vic	Victor Jose (Romero); B7.31.1936 Cabimas, Zulia, Venez.; BL/TL/5´7˝/(150–155); d4.9; b–Yo–Yo																								
1963	Cle A	90	370	44	108	18	5	7	36	16-0	1	41	.292	.321	.424	108	3	3-3	.988	9	121	180	O89C	59	0.9
1964	Cle A	150	577	64	156	26	2	6	51	34-2	1	77	.270	.309	.354	85	-12	21-11	.986	4	105	110	O143C	0	-1.3
1965	Cle A★	142	505	67	152	19	1	5	40	35-9	0	50	.301	.344	.372	103	2	26-7	.988	8	**117**	96	O134C	0	1.0
1966	Cle A	121	344	42	86	6	4	3	19	24-6	0	37	.250	.297	.317	77	-11	8-6	.986	2	107	118	O108C	0	-1.2
1967	Cle A	139	359	47	103	17	5	2	22	10-0	1	30	.287	.307	.379	101	-1	6-7	.986	-0	104	97	O125(1/125/0)	0	-0.6
1968	Cle A	51	180	15	43	2	3	2	13	3-0	1	19	.239	.254	.317	74	-7	8-6	.967	2	108	156	O49(3/2/48)	0	-1.0
	Cal A	93	339	34	101	15	4	1	18	15-1	0	34	.298	.326	.375	116	5	17-10	.995	5	116	75	O86(0/70/17)	0	0.8
	Year	144	519	49	144	17	7	3	31	18-1	1	53	.277	.301	.355	101	-2	25-16	.987	7	**113**	105	O135(3/72/65)	0	-0.2
1969	Cal A	33	71	10	11	1	1	0	1	6-1	1	5	.155	.231	.197	22	-8	3-0	1.000	-0	108	0	O22(0/2/20),1b3	0	-0.9
	StL N	63	98	15	26	3	0	2	10	7-0	0	8	.265	.314	.357	87	-2	1-1	1.000	0	113	0	O23(2/10/11),P2	0	-0.3
1970	StL N	111	183	29	57	14	3	1	33	13-1	0	19	.311	.355	.437	108	2	4-1	.972	1	97	157	O54(12/33/13)	0	0.2
1971	†Pit N	99	295	48	84	14	6	1	33	11-1	2	31	.285	.312	.383	96	-3	10-2	.983	1	105	143	O61(11/20/31),1b16	0	-0.4
1972	†Pit N	117	368	59	117	19	2	4	28	26-6	3	44	.318	.367	.413	123	11	14-1	.979	1	105	65	O97(64/7/26),1b8	0	1.1
1973	Pit N	59	83	9	15	1	0	1	3	2-0	0	7	.181	.200	.229	19	-10	0-2	.977	2	165	108	1b10,O10(7/0/3)	0	-1.0
	†Oak A	38	64	5	12	1	0	0	4	3-1	0	4	.188	.224	.203	22	-7	0-0	.967	0	100	103	O19(8/1/10),1b8,D2	0	-0.8
1974	Oak A	17	23	0	4	0	0	0	1	2-1	0	2	.174	.231	.174	22	-2	0-0	1.000	-1	49	0	O6(2/2/2),D4	0	-0.4
1977	†LA N	24	48	3	15	2	0	0	4	0-0	0	6	.313	.313	.354	78	-2	0-0	1.000	-1	75	0	O12(2/4/8)	0	-0.3
1978	†LA N	75	77	15	24	1	1	1	11	3-0	0	7	.312	.333	.390	102	0	2-1	1.000	-1	91	0	O25(16/2/7)/1	0	-0.1
1979	LA N	29	27	2	7	1	0	0	2	2-0	0	0	.259	.310	.296	68	-1	2-0	1.000	-0	80	0	O3L	0	-0.1
1980	LA N	7	6	1	1	0	0	0	0	0-0	0	1	.167	.167	.167	-7	-1	0-0	1.000	0	0	1230	/1	0	-0.1
Total	16	1458	4017	509	1122	160	37	36	329	212-29	10	422	.279	.315	.364	94	-44	125-58	.986	30	109	106	O1066(131/752/196),1b47,D6,P2	59	-4.5
DaVanon, Jerry	Frank Gerald; B8.21.1945 Oceanside CA; BR/TR/5´11˝/175; [StLN66 S1/17]; d4.11; s–Jeff; Col San Diego Mesa (CA) JC/San Diego (CA) City																								
1969	SD N	24	59	4	8	1	0	0	3	3-0	0	12	.136	.177	.153	-7	-9	0-3	.932	1	93	53	2b15,S7	0	-0.9
	StL N	16	40	7	12	3	0	1	7	6-1	0	8	.300	.391	.450	134	2	0-0	.958	2	105	90	S16	0	0.6
	Year	40	99	11	20	4	0	1	10	9-1	0	20	.202	.269	.273	53	-6	0-3	.959	3	118	97	S23,2b15	0	-0.3
1970	StL N	11	18	2	2	1	0	0	0	2-0	0	5	.111	.200	.167	-1	-3	0-0	1.000	2	88	442	3b5,2b3	0	0.0
1971	Bal A	38	81	14	19	5	0	0	4	12-0	1	20	.235	.340	.296	81	-1	0-0	.970	-5	86	74	2b20,S11,3b3/1	0	-0.5
1973	Cal A	41	49	6	12	3	0	0	2	3-0	0	9	.245	.288	.306	73	-2	1-2	.927	-2	100	101	S14,2b12,3b7	0	-0.3
1974	StL N	30	40	4	6	1	0	0	4	4-0	2	5	.150	.255	.175	24	-4	0-1	.840	-3	70	87	S14,3b8,2b7/rf	0	-0.7
1975	Hou N	32	97	15	27	4	2	1	10	16-1	1	7	.278	.386	.392	125	4	2-0	.944	3	102	102	S21,2b9,3b3	0	1.0
1976	Hou N	61	107	19	31	3	3	1	20	21-1	1	12	.290	.408	.402	143	7	0-2	.980	2	134	63	2b17,S17,3b9	0	1.1
1977	StL N	9	8	2	0	0	0	0	0	1-0	0	2	.000	.111	.000	-68	-2	0-0	.923	0	129	0	2b5	0	-0.2
Total	8	262	499	73	117	21	5	3	50	68-3	5	80	.234	.331	.315	85	-8	3-8	.936	-1	99	107	S100,2b88,3b35/rf1	0	0.1
DaVanon, Jeff	Jeffrey Graham; B12.8.1973 San Diego CA; BB/TR/6´0˝/(185–200); [OakA95 26/708]; d9.7; f–Jerry; Col San Diego St.; [DL 2000 Ana A 181]																								
1999	Ana A	7	20	4	4	0	1	1	4	2-0	0	7	.200	.273	.450	80	-1	0-1	1.000	-1	60	0	O5(3/0/2),D2	0	-0.2
2001	Ana A	40	88	7	17	2	1	5	9	11-0	0	29	.193	.280	.409	78	-3	1-3	.980	-0	86	205	O29(0/13/17),D6	0	-0.5
2002	Ana A	16	30	3	5	3	0	1	4	2-0	0	6	.167	.219	.367	53	-2	1-0	1.000	-0	101	0	O10(2/4/4),D4	0	-0.2
2003	Ana A	123	330	56	93	16	1	12	43	42-0	1	59	.282	.360	.445	117	9	17-5	.983	4	118	41	O115(8/31/91)/D	0	1.2
2004	†Ana A	108	285	41	79	11	4	7	34	46-2	0	54	.277	.372	.418	112	6	18-3	.993	2	107	61	O81(24/39/29),D19	17	0.8
2005	†LA A	108	225	42	52	10	1	2	15	39-1	2	44	.231	.347	.311	80	-5	11-6	.991	3	120	47	O63(17/24/26),D30	0	-0.4
2006	Ari N	87	221	38	64	12	4	5	35	31-0	0	42	.290	.371	.448	104	2	10-4	.979	-5	88	0	O58(8/36/16),D3	57	-0.2
Total	7	489	1199	191	314	54	12	33	144	173-3	3	241	.262	.352	.410	101	6	58-22	.986	2	107	52	O361(62/147/185),D65	255	0.5
Davenport, Jim	James Houston; B8.17.1933 Siluria AL; BR/TR/5´11˝/(170–175); d4.15; M1/C15; Col Southern Mississippi																								
1958	SF N	134	434	70	111	22	3	12	41	33-0	7	64	.256	.317	.403	92	-6	1-3	.960	-12	96	89	3b130,S5	0	-1.9
1959	SF N	123	469	65	121	16	3	6	38	28-0	2	65	.258	.301	.343	73	-19	0-1	**.978**	-3	96	86	3b121/S	0	-2.3
1960	SF N	112	363	43	91	15	3	6	38	26-1	4	58	.251	.306	.358	87	-7	0-2	**.961**	-3	96	79	3b103,S7	0	-1.1
1961	SF N	137	436	64	121	28	4	12	65	45-1	2	65	.278	.342	.443	112	8	4-3	**.965**	7	101	114	3b132	0	1.4
1962	†SF N★	144	485	83	144	25	5	14	58	45-3	2	76	.297	.357	.456	119	13	2-5	.952	-2	97	**120**	3b141	0	0.9
1963	SF N	147	460	40	116	19	3	4	36	32-4	0	87	.252	.297	.333	83	-10	5-2	.962	-11	89	57	3b127,2b22/S	0	-2.2
1964	SF N	116	297	24	70	10	6	2	26	29-2	0	46	.236	.299	.330	77	-9	2-0	.979	-6	89	60	S64,3b41,2b30	0	-1.0
1965	SF N	106	271	29	68	14	3	4	31	21-2	1	47	.251	.304	.369	87	-5	0-0	.949	-16	101	76	3b39,S37,2b26	0	-1.8
1966	SF N	111	305	42	76	6	2	9	30	22-2	1	40	.249	.300	.370	83	-7	1-1	.961	-7	103	82	S58,3b36,2b21,1b2	0	-1.1
1967	SF N	124	295	42	81	10	3	5	30	39-6	4	50	.275	.366	.380	116	7	1-4	1.000	6	98	106	3b64,S28,2b12	0	1.5
1968	SF N	113	272	27	61	1	1	1	17	26-0	0	32	.224	.292	.246	63	-12	0-3	.960	-8	90	108	3b82,S17/2	0	-2.4
1969	SF N	112	303	20	73	10	1	2	42	29-1	0	37	.241	.304	.300	72	-11	0-1	.967	-2	96	111	3b104/1Srf	0	-1.5
1970	SF N	22	37	3	9	1	0	0	4	7-1	0	6	.243	.356	.270	73	-1	0-0	1.000	-4	46	0	3b10	0	-0.5
Total	13	1501	4427	552	1142	177	37	77	456	382-23	23	673	.258	.318	.367	90	-59	16-25	.964	-62	96	96	3b1130,S219,2b112,1b3/rf	0	-12.0
David, Andre	Andre Anter; B5.18.1958 Hollywood CA; BL/TL/6´0˝/(170–186); [MinA80 8/194]; d6.29; C2; Col Cal St.–Fullerton																								
1984	Min A	33	48	5	12	2	0	1	5	7-2	1	11	.250	.351	.354	93	0	0-0	1.000	-1	74	0	O14(10/0/4),D2	0	-0.2
1986	Min A	5	5	0	1	0	0	0	0	0-0	1	2	.200	.333	.200	48	0	0-0	ø	0	—	—	/D	0	0.0
Total	2	38	53	5	13	2	0	1	5	7-2	2	13	.245	.349	.340	88	0	0-0	1.000	-1	74	0	O14(10/0/4),D3	0	-0.2
Davidson, Claude	Claude Boucher "Davey"; B10.13.1896 Boston MA; D4.18.1956 Weymouth MA; BL/TR/5´11˝/155; d4.25; Col Brown																								
1918	Phi A	31	81	4	15	1	0	0	4	5	0	9	.185	.233	.198	29	-7	0	.943	-1	91	99	2b15,O8(1/0/7)/3	—	-1.0
1919	Was A	2	7	1	3	0	0	0	0	1	0	1	.429	.500	.429	163	1	0	1.000	-0	90	0	3b2	—	0.1
Total	2	33	88	5	18	1	0	0	4	6	0	10	.205	.255	.216	41	-6	0	.943	-1	91	99	2b15,O8(1/0/7),3b3	—	-0.9
Davidson, Cleatus	Cleatus La Von; B11.1.1976 Bartow FL; BB/TR/5´10˝/170; [MinA94 2/42]; d5.30																								
1999	Min A	12	22	3	3	0	0	0	3	0-0	0	4	.136	.136	.136	-29	-4	2-0	.973	4	162	221	2b6,S4	5	0.1
Davidson, Homer	Homer Hurd "Divvy"; B10.14.1884 Cleveland OH; D7.26.1948 Detroit MI; BR/TR/5´10.5˝/155; d4.25; Col Penn																								
1908	Cle A	9	4	2	0	0	0	0	0	0	0	—	.000	.000	.000	-99	-1	1	1.000	1	*0*	*124*	C5/rf	—	0.0
Davidson, Mark	John Mark; B2.15.1961 Knoxville TN; BR/TR/6´2˝/190; [MinA82 11/266]; d6.20; Col Clemson																								
1986	Min A	36	68	5	8	3	0	0	2	6-0	0	22	.118	.189	.162	-3	-10	2-3	.980	-0	111	0	O31(20/5/7),D3	0	-1.1
1987	†Min A	102	150	32	40	4	1	1	14	13-1	0	26	.267	.321	.327	71	-6	9-2	1.000	1	103	102	O86(36/20/33),D9	0	-0.6
1988	Min A	100	106	22	23	7	0	1	10	10-0	1	20	.217	.288	.311	67	-5	3-3	.955	5	132	137	O91(4/4/84)/3D	0	-0.1
1989	Hou N	33	65	7	13	2	1	1	5	7-0	0	14	.200	.278	.308	70	-3	1-0	1.000	-0	104	0	O23(7/3/15)	0	-0.4
1990	Hou N	57	130	12	38	5	1	1	11	10-1	0	18	.292	.340	.369	99	0	0-3	.981	4	131	37	O51(26/1/27)	28	0.1
1991	Hou N	85	142	10	27	6	0	2	15	12-0	2	28	.190	.263	.275	54	-9	0-0	1.000	1	108	47	O63(32/4/32)	0	-1.0
Total	6	413	661	88	149	27	3	6	57	58-2	3	128	.225	.289	.303	64	-33	15-11	.983	10	116	67	O345(125/37/198),D15/3	28	-3.1
Davidson, Bill	William Simpson; B5.10.1884 Lafayette IN; D5.23.1954 Lincoln NE; BR/TR/5´10˝/170; d9.29																								
1909	Chi N	2	7	2	1	0	0	0	0	1	0	—	.143	.250	.143	22	-1	1	1.000	-0	0	0	O2(1/1/0)	—	-0.1
1910	Bro N	136	509	48	121	13	7	0	34	24	4	54	.238	.277	.291	68	-23	27	.961	-11	92	60	O131(0/127/4)	—	-4.3
1911	Bro N	87	292	33	68	3	4	1	26	16	1	21	.233	.275	.281	58	-18	18	.956	-6	99	37	O74C	—	-3.0
Total	3	225	808	83	190	16	11	1	60	41	5	75	.235	.276	.286	64	-42	46	.959	-17	94	51	O207(1/202/4)	—	-7.4
Davies, Chick	Lloyd Garrison; B3.6.1892 Peabody MA; D9.5.1973 Middletown CT; BL/TL/5´8˝/145; d7.11; Col Massachusetts; ▲																								
1914	Phi A	19	46	6	11	3	1	0	5	5	0	13	.239	.314	.348	103	0	1	.926	-1	111	0	O10(9/0/1)/P	—	-0.1
1915	Phi A	56	132	13	24	5	3	0	11	14	2	31	.182	.270	.265	62	-6	2-4	.973	4	99	193	O32(7/21/4),P4	—	-0.6
1925	NY N	4	6	1	0	0	0	0	0	0	0	1	.000	.000	.000	-99	-2	0-0	1.000	0	182	0	P2/rf	—	-0.1
1926	NY N	38	18	4	4	0	0	0	1	3	0	5	.222	.333	.222	53	1	0	.938	1	118	174	P38	—	0.0
Total	4	117	202	24	39	8	4	0	17	22	2	50	.193	.279	.272	65	-7	3-4	.938	4	124	214	P45,O43(16/21/6)	—	-0.8
Davis, Lefty	Alphonzo De Ford; B2.4.1875 Nashville TN; D2.4.1919 Collins NY; BL/TL/5´10˝/170; d4.18																								
1901	Bro N	25	91	11	19	2	0	0	7	10	0	—	.209	.287	.231	50	-6	4	.822	-5	0	0	O24(12/2/10)/2	—	-1.1
	Pit N	87	335	87	105	8	11	2	33	56	2	—	.313	.415	.421	138	19	22	.975	5	158	273	O86R	—	2.0
	Year	112	426	98	124	10	11	2	40	66	2	—	.291	.389	.380	120	13	26	.942	1	126	**217**	O110(12/2/96)/2	—	0.9
1902	Pit N	59	232	52	65	7	3	0	20	35	1	—	.280	.377	.336	116	6	19	.945	-2	78	58	O59R	—	0.1

YEAR	TM LG	G	AB	R	H	2B	3B	HR	RBI	BB-IB	HP	SO	AVG	OBP	SLG	AOPS	ABR	SB-CS	FA	FR	RNG	THR	GAMES AT POSITION	DL	BFW
1903	NY A	104	372	54	88	10	0	0	25	43	2	—	.237	.319	.263	72	-11	11	.906	-8	60	35	O102(95/1/6)/S	—	-2.6
1907	Cin N	73	266	28	61	5	5	1	25	23	1	—	.229	.293	.297	82	-6	9	.972	3	113	124	O70(0/69/1)	—	-0.7
Total	4	348	1296	232	338	32	19	3	110	167	6	—	.261	.348	.322	98	2	65	.939	-6	95	116	O341(107/72/162)/S2	—	-2.3

DAVIS, ALVIN Alvin Glenn; B9.9.1960 Riverside CA; BL/TR/6´1˝/190; [SeaA82 6/138]; d4.11; Col Arizona St.

YEAR	TM LG	G	AB	R	H	2B	3B	HR	RBI	BB-IB	HP	SO	AVG	OBP	SLG	AOPS	ABR	SB-CS	FA	FR	RNG	THR	GAMES AT POSITION	DL	BFW
1984	Sea A★	152	567	80	161	34	3	27	116	97-16	7	78	.284	.391	.497	146	40	5-4	.992	-2	90	80	1b147,D7	0	2.8
1985	Sea A	155	578	78	166	33	1	18	78	90-7	2	71	.287	.381	.441	124	23	1-2	.992	-3	91	93	1b154	0	1.0
1986	Sea A	135	479	66	130	18	1	18	72	76-10	3	68	.271	.373	.426	116	13	0-3	.986	1	106	122	1b101,D32	22	0.6
1987	Sea A	157	580	86	171	37	2	29	100	72-6	2	84	.295	.370	.516	126	23	0-0	.994	-5	87	107	1b157	0	0.8
1988	Sea A	140	478	67	141	24	1	18	69	95-13	4	53	.295	.412	.462	139	30	1-1	.994	-5	80	**116**	1b115,D25	19	1.6
1989	Sea A	142	498	84	152	30	1	21	95	101-15	6	49	.305	.424	.496	155	43	0-1	.992	-4	90	107	1b125,D14	16	3.0
1990	Sea A	140	494	63	140	21	0	17	68	85-10	4	68	.283	.387	.429	128	23	0-2	.994	-1	89	94	D87,1b52	15	1.5
1991	Sea A	145	462	39	102	15	1	12	69	56-9	0	78	.221	.299	.335	77	-15	0-3	1.000	-0	85	134	D126,1b14	0	-2.1
1992	Cal A	40	104	5	26	8	0	0	16	13-2	0	9	.250	.331	.327	85	-2	0-0	.995	0	105	119	1b22,D9	0	-0.3
Total	9	1206	4240	568	1189	220	10	160	683	685-88	28	558	.280	.380	.450	126	178	7-16	.992	-19	90	103	1b887,D300	72	8.9

DAVIS, BILL Arthur Willard; B6.6.1942 Graceville MN; BL/TL/6´7˝/(215–226); d9.16; Col Minnesota

YEAR	TM LG	G	AB	R	H	2B	3B	HR	RBI	BB-IB	HP	SO	AVG	OBP	SLG	AOPS	ABR	SB-CS	FA	FR	RNG	THR	GAMES AT POSITION	DL	BFW
1965	Cle A	10	10	0	3	1	0	0	0	0-0	0	1	.300	.300	.400	96	0	0-0	ø	0	—	—	/H	0	0.0
1966	Cle A	23	38	2	6	1	0	1	4	6-0	0	9	.158	.267	.263	55	-2	0-0	.981	0	100	109	1b9	0	-0.3
1969	SD N	31	57	1	10	1	0	0	1	8-0	1	18	.175	.288	.193	38	-4	0-0	.992	-1	68	108	1b14	0	-0.7
Total	3	64	105	3	19	3	0	1	5	14-0	1	28	.181	.281	.238	50	-6	0-0	.988	-1	80	108	1b23	0	-1.0

DAVIS, BROCK Bryshear Barnett; B10.19.1943 Oakland CA; BL/TL/5´10˝/(160–168); d4.9; Col Cal St.–Los Angeles

YEAR	TM LG	G	AB	R	H	2B	3B	HR	RBI	BB-IB	HP	SO	AVG	OBP	SLG	AOPS	ABR	SB-CS	FA	FR	RNG	THR	GAMES AT POSITION	DL	BFW
1963	Hou N	34	55	7	11	2	0	1	2	4-1	0	10	.200	.254	.291	60	-3	0-0	.864	-0	95	155	O14(5/6/3)	0	-0.4
1964	Hou N	1	3	0	0	0	0	0	0	1-0	0	1	.000	.250	.000	-24	0	0-0	1.000	0	126	0	/lf	0	0.0
1966	Hou N	10	27	2	4	1	0	0	1	5-0	0	4	.148	.281	.185	35	-2	1-0	1.000	-0	101	0	O7C	0	-0.3
1970	Chi N	6	3	0	0	0	0	0	0	0-0	0	1	.000	.000	.000	-89	-1	0-0	ø	-0	0	0	/cf	0	-0.1
1971	Chi N	106	301	22	77	7	5	0	28	35-0	2	34	.256	.335	.312	74	-9	0-6	.982	2	104	104	O93(3/85/5)	0	-1.3
1972	Mil A	85	154	17	49	2	0	0	12	12-0	0	23	.318	.365	.331	111	2	6-4	.970	-1	95	89	O43(19/19/5)	0	-0.1
Total	6	242	543	48	141	12	5	1	43	57-1	2	73	.260	.331	.306	79	-13	7-10	.973	-1	101	98	O159(28/118/13)	0	-2.2

DAVIS, CHILI Charles Theodore; B1.17.1960 Kingston, Jamaica; BB/TR/6´3˝/(195–240); [SFN77 11/270]; d4.10

YEAR	TM LG	G	AB	R	H	2B	3B	HR	RBI	BB-IB	HP	SO	AVG	OBP	SLG	AOPS	ABR	SB-CS	FA	FR	RNG	THR	GAMES AT POSITION	DL	BFW
1981	SF N	8	15	1	2	0	0	0	0	1-0	0	2	.133	.188	.133	-8	-2	2-0	1.000	-0	92	0	O6(1/2/3)	0	-0.2
1982	SF N	154	641	86	167	27	6	19	76	45-2	2	115	.261	.308	.410	101	-1	24-13	.972	5	104	163	O153(13/142/1)	0	0.3
1983	SF N	137	486	54	113	21	2	11	59	55-6	0	108	.233	.305	.352	86	-10	10-12	.976	4	108	105	O133(0/121/12)	0	-1.0
1984	SF N★	137	499	87	157	21	6	21	81	42-6	1	74	.315	.368	.507	148	30	12-8	.971	3	106	121	O123(1/67/57)	0	3.1
1985	SF N	136	481	53	130	25	2	13	56	62-12	0	74	.270	.349	.412	119	13	15-7	.980	7	110	123	O126(0/36/91)	0	1.6
1986	SF N★	153	526	71	146	28	3	13	70	84-23	1	96	.278	.375	.416	125	21	16-13	.972	-1	104	83	O148(0/53/117)	0	1.3
1987	†SF N	149	500	80	125	22	1	24	76	72-15	2	109	.250	.344	.442	112	9	16-9	.975	-7	91	78	O135(18/114/36)	0	0.0
1988	Cal A	158	600	81	161	29	3	21	93	56-14	0	118	.268	.326	.432	114	11	9-10	.942	-10	89	103	O153(0/3/154),D3	0	-0.6
1989	Cal A	154	560	81	152	24	1	22	90	61-12	0	109	.271	.340	.436	120	15	3-0	.979	-11	87	56	O147L,D6	0	0.0
1990	Cal A	113	412	58	109	17	1	12	58	61-4	0	89	.265	.357	.398	114	9	1-2	.965	-3	79	159	D60,O52(46/0/7)	23	0.2
1991	†Min A	153	534	84	148	34	1	29	93	95-13	1	117	.277	.385	.507	139	31	5-6	1.000	0	280	0	D150,O2L	0	2.5
1992	Min A	138	444	63	128	27	2	12	66	73-11	3	76	.288	.386	.439	128	20	4-5	1.000	0	130	0	D125,O4(1/0/3)/1	0	1.5
1993	Cal A	153	573	74	139	32	0	27	112	71-12	1	135	.243	.327	.440	101	0	4-1	ø	-0	0	0	D150/P	0	-0.7
1994	Cal A★	108	392	72	122	18	1	26	84	69-11	1	84	.311	.410	.561	146	29	3-2	1.000	0	124	0	D106,O2L	0	2.1
1995	Cal A	119	424	81	135	23	0	20	86	89-12	0	79	.318	.429	.514	148	35	3-3	ø	0	0	0	D119	28	2.6
1996	Cal A	145	530	73	155	24	0	28	95	86-11	0	99	.292	.387	.496	121	19	5-2	ø	0	0	0	D143	0	1.0
1997	KC A	140	477	71	133	20	0	30	90	85-16	1	96	.279	.386	.509	128	21	6-3	ø	0	0	0	D133	13	1.4
1998	†NY A	35	103	11	30	7	0	3	9	14-1	0	18	.291	.373	.447	118	3	0-1	ø	0	0	0	D34	136	0.1
1999	†NY A	146	476	59	128	25	1	19	78	73-7	2	100	.269	.366	.445	108	7	4-1	ø	0	0	0	D132	0	0.1
Total	19	2436	8673	1240	2380	424	30	350	1372	1194-188	15	1698	.274	.360	.451	120	260	142-98	.971	-13	99	106	O1184(231/538/481),D1161/P1	200	15.3

DAVIS, DOUG Douglas Raymond; B9.24.1962 Bloomsburg PA; BR/TR/6´0˝/180; [CalA84 9/216]; d7.8; C2; Col North Carolina St.

YEAR	TM LG	G	AB	R	H	2B	3B	HR	RBI	BB-IB	HP	SO	AVG	OBP	SLG	AOPS	ABR	SB-CS	FA	FR	RNG	THR	GAMES AT POSITION	DL	BFW
1988	Cal A	6	12	1	0	0	0	0	0	0-0	1	3	.000	.077	.000	-78	-3	0-0	1.000	-2	99	226	C3,3b3	0	-0.6
1992	Tex A	1	1	0	1	0	0	0	0	0-0	0	0	1.000	1.000	1.000	476	0	0-0	ø	-0	0	0	/C	0	0.0
Total	2	7	13	1	1	0	0	0	0	0-0	1	3	.077	.143	.077	-38	-3	0-0	1.000	-3	92	210	C4,3b3	0	-0.6

DAVIS, ERIC Eric Keith; B5.29.1962 Los Angeles CA; BR/TR/6´3˝/(165–200); [CinN80 8/201]; d5.19

YEAR	TM LG	G	AB	R	H	2B	3B	HR	RBI	BB-IB	HP	SO	AVG	OBP	SLG	AOPS	ABR	SB-CS	FA	FR	RNG	THR	GAMES AT POSITION	DL	BFW
1984	Cin N	57	174	33	39	10	1	10	30	24-0	1	48	.224	.320	.466	113	3	10-2	.992	5	114	158	O51(2/46/10)	16	0.9
1985	Cin N	56	122	26	30	3	3	8	18	7-0	0	39	.246	.287	.516	114	1	16-3	.987	3	112	158	O47(24/28/5)	0	0.6
1986	Cin N	132	415	97	115	15	3	27	71	68-5	1	100	.277	.378	.523	141	24	80-11	.975	0	111	27	O121(72/71/16)	0	3.5
1987	Cin N★	129	474	120	139	23	4	37	100	84-8	1	134	.293	.399	.593	153	38	50-6	.990	16	**124**	136	O128(4/124/0)	0	**5.9**
1988	Cin N	135	472	81	129	18	3	26	93	65-10	3	124	.273	.363	.489	138	24	35-3	.981	-9	92	34	O130(0/125/5)	0	2.2
1989	Cin N★	131	462	74	130	14	2	34	101	68-12	1	116	.281	.367	.541	154	32	21-7	.984	-7	97	31	O125(4/118/3)	15	2.8
1990	†Cin N	127	453	84	118	26	2	24	86	60-6	2	100	.260	.347	.486	122	14	21-3	.993	-1	94	148	O122(56/66/0)	24	1.5
1991	Cin N	89	285	39	67	10	0	11	33	48-5	5	92	.235	.353	.386	104	3	14-2	.985	2	106	120	O81(7/77/0)	41	0.7
1992	LA N	76	267	21	61	8	1	5	32	36-2	3	71	.228	.325	.322	85	-4	19-1	.961	-7	84	0	O74(69/5/4)	50	-1.1
1993	LA N	108	376	57	88	17	0	14	53	41-6	1	88	.234	.308	.391	91	-5	33-5	.991	5	107	93	O103(101/3/0)	0	0.2
	Det A	23	75	14	19	1	1	6	15	14-1	0	18	.253	.371	.533	140	4	2-2	.981	0	111	0	O18C,D5	0	0.4
1994	Det A	37	120	19	22	4	0	3	13	18-0	0	45	.183	.290	.292	50	-9	5-0	.989	-2	96	56	O35C	73	-0.8
1996	Cin N	129	415	81	119	20	0	26	83	70-3	6	121	.287	.394	.523	138	25	23-9	.989	-1	105	51	O126(14/115/0)/1	15	2.6
1997	†Bal A	42	158	29	48	11	0	8	25	14-0	1	47	.304	.358	.525	132	7	6-0	.975	-5	68	0	O30R,D12	112	0.2
1998	Bal A	131	452	81	148	29	1	28	89	44-0	5	108	.327	.388	.582	152	35	7-6	.992	-3	90	88	O72(0/11/64),D53	0	2.4
1999	StL N	58	191	27	49	9	2	5	30	30-1	1	49	.257	.359	.403	91	-2	5-4	1.000	0	96	126	O51(0/3/50),D2	98	-0.4
2000	†StL N	92	254	38	77	14	0	6	40	36-0	1	60	.303	.389	.429	105	3	1-1	.968	-1	108	28	O69R,D4	0	0.0
2001	SF N	74	156	17	32	7	3	4	22	13-0	1	38	.205	.269	.365	66	-9	1-1	.962	-0	106	44	O48R/D	19	-1.1
Total	17	1626	5321	938	1430	239	26	282	934	740-59	33	1398	.269	.359	.482	124	184	349-66	.984	-5	102	74	O1431(353/845/304),D77/1	463	20.5

DAVIS, GEORGE George Stacey; B8.23.1870 Cohoes NY; D10.17.1940 Philadelphia PA; BB/TR/5´9˝/180; d4.19; M3; HF1998; OF(12/243/48)

YEAR	TM LG	G	AB	R	H	2B	3B	HR	RBI	BB-IB	HP	SO	AVG	OBP	SLG	AOPS	ABR	SB-CS	FA	FR	RNG	THR	GAMES AT POSITION	DL	BFW
1890	Cle N	**136**	526	98	139	22	9	6	73	53	4	34	.264	.336	.375	109	6	22	.946	12	**158**	182	O133(0/129/4),2b2/S	—	1.2
1891	Cle N	136	570	115	165	35	12	3	89	53	4	29	.289	.354	.409	117	11	42	.931	8	**154**	32	O116(4/111/1),3b22,P3	—	1.5
1892	†Cle N	144	597	95	144	27	12	5	82	58	3	51	.241	.312	.352	97	-4	36	.914	-8	95	76	3b79,O44(0/3/41),S20,2b3	—	-1.1
1893	NY N	133	549	112	195	22	27	11	119	42	9	20	.355	.410	.554	154	38	37	.884	-1	99	**114**	3b133/S	—	3.2
1894	†NY N	124	486	125	171	27	19	9	93	67	4	10	.352	.434	.541	135	28	42	.908	-1	99	104	3b124	—	2.2
1895	NY N	110	430	108	146	36	9	5	101	55	2	12	.340	.417	.500	139	27	48	.881	11	103	150	3b80,1b14,2b10,O7(5/0/2),M	—	3.2
1896	NY N	124	494	98	158	25	12	5	99	50	4	24	.320	.387	.449	124	17	48	.917	15	109	99	3b74,S45,O3L,1b3	—	3.0
1897	NY N	131	521	112	184	31	10	10	**135**	43	7	—	.353	.410	.509	146	34	65	.926	20	99	**139**	S130	—	5.1
1898	NY N	121	486	80	149	20	5	2	86	32	1	—	.307	.351	.381	113	8	26	.933	**30**	101	112	S121	—	4.0
1899	NY N	109	419	69	141	22	5	1	59	38	2	—	.337	.394	.420	128	17	35	**.946**	**46**	**112**	119	S109	—	**6.1**
1900	NY N	114	426	69	136	20	4	3	61	35	4	—	.319	.376	.406	121	14	29	**.944**	**29**	**111**	105	S114,M	—	4.3
1901	NY N	130	491	69	148	26	7	7	65	40	2	—	.301	.356	.426	131	20	27	.939	24	102	89	S113,3b17,M	—	4.6
1902	Chi A	132	485	76	145	27	7	3	93	65	4	—	.299	.386	.402	124	20	31	**.951**	-3	96	**134**	S129,1b3	—	2.0
1903	NY N	4	15	2	4	0	0	0	1	1	0	—	.267	.313	.267	63	-1	0	.870	-2	68	0	S4	—	-0.2
1904	Chi A	152	563	75	142	27	15	1	69	43	5	—	.252	.311	.359	116	10	32	.937	18	107	**149**	S152	—	3.7
1905	Chi A	151	550	74	153	29	1	1	55	60	4	—	.278	.353	.340	125	19	31	**.948**	16	110	**137**	S151	—	**4.4**
1906	†Chi A	133	484	63	134	26	6	0	80	41	4	—	.277	.338	.355	120	13	27	.946	13	110	121	S129/2	—	3.2
1907	Chi A	132	466	59	111	16	2	1	52	47	4	—	.238	.313	.288	95	-1	15	.949	7	**108**	138	S132	—	1.2
1908	Chi A	128	419	41	91	14	1	0	26	41	7	—	.217	.298	.255	81	-6	22	.960	2	109	97	2b95,S23,1b4	—	-0.4
1909	Chi A	28	68	5	9	1	0	0	2	10	1	—	.132	.253	.147	28	-5	4	.986	1	143	93	1b17,2b2	—	-0.5
Total	20	2372	9045	1545	2665	453	163	73	1440	874	75	180	.295	.362	.405	121	265	619	.940	236	104	122	S1374,3b529,O303C,2b113,1b41,P3	—	50.7

YEAR	TM LG	G	AB	R	H	2B	3B	HR	RBI	BB-IB	HP	SO	AVG	OBP	SLG	AOPS	ABR	SB-CS	FA	FR	RNG	THR	GAMES AT POSITION	DL	BFW
Davis, Kiddo	George Willis; B2.12.1902 Bridgeport CT; D3.4.1983 Bridgeport CT; BR/TR/5´11˝/178; d6.15; Col NYU																								
1926	NY A	1	0	0	0	0	0	0	0	0	0	0	ø	ø	ø	ø	0	0-0	ø	-0	0	0	/rf	—	0.0
1932	Phi N	137	576	100	178	39	6	5	57	44	1	56	.309	.359	.424	98	0	16	.975	8	108	122	O133(1/132/0)	—	0.4
1933	†NY N	126	434	61	112	20	4	7	37	25	0	30	.258	.298	.371	92	-6	10	.988	-9	85	92	O120C	—	-1.9
1934	StL N	16	33	6	10	3	0	1	4	3	0	1	.303	.361	.485	117	1	1	.960	1	110	174	O9C	—	0.1
	Phi N	100	393	50	115	25	5	3	48	27	0	28	.293	.338	.405	86	-7	1	.991	13	115	178	O100C	—	0.3
	Year	116	426	56	125	28	5	4	52	30	0	29	.293	.340	.411	89	-6	2	.988	14	**115**	178	O109C	—	0.4
1935	NY N	47	91	16	24	7	1	2	6	10	1	4	.264	.343	.429	108	1	2	.977	-1	97	49	O21(2/2/17)	—	-0.1
1936	†NY N	47	67	6	16	1	0	0	5	6	0	5	.239	.301	.254	51	-5	0	1.000	2	107	229	O22(6/11/6)	—	-0.3
1937	NY N	56	76	20	20	10	0	0	9	10	1	7	.263	.356	.395	103	1	1	.932	-2	93	0	O37(11/25/0)	—	-0.2
	Cin N	40	136	19	35	6	0	1	5	16	1	6	.257	.340	.324	85	-2	1	.959	-1	104	33	O35(9/26/0)	—	-0.5
	Year	96	212	39	55	16	0	1	14	26	2	13	.259	.346	.349	90	-1	2	.951	-3	100	22	O72(20/51/0)	—	-0.7
1938	Cin N	5	18	3	5	1	0	0	0	1	0	4	.278	.316	.333	81	0	0	1.000	0	92	265	O5(2/0/5)	—	0.0
Total	8	575	1824	281	515	112	16	19	171	142	4	141	.282	.336	.393	92	-17	32-0	.980	11	102	117	O483(31/425/29)	—	-2.2
Davis, Gerry	Gerald Edward; B12.25.1958 Trenton NJ; BR/TR/6´0˝/185; [SDN80 6/135]; d9.20; Col Howard																								
1983	SD N	5	15	3	5	2	0	0	1	3-0	0	4	.333	.444	.467	157	1	1-0	1.000	0	91	306	O5R	0	0.2
1985	SD N	44	58	10	17	3	1	0	2	5-0	0	7	.293	.349	.379	105	0	0-0	.952	0	87	263	O23(7/1/14)	0	0.0
Total	2	49	73	13	22	5	1	0	3	8-0	0	11	.301	.370	.397	116	1	1-0	.967	1	88	276	O28(7/1/19)	0	0.2
Davis, Glenn	Glenn Earle; B3.28.1961 Jacksonville FL; BR/TR/6´3˝/(200–212); [HouN81*S1/5]; d9.2; Col Georgia																								
1984	Hou N	18	61	6	13	5	0	2	8	4-0	0	12	.213	.258	.393	87	-1	0-0	.988	2	144	109	1b16	0	-0.1
1985	Hou N	100	350	51	95	11	0	20	64	27-6	7	68	.271	.332	.474	127	11	0-0	.985	-2	97	109	1b89,O9R	0	0.4
1986	†Hou N★	158	574	91	152	32	3	31	101	64-6	9	72	.265	.344	.493	133	25	3-1	.992	2	98	85	1b156	0	1.8
1987	Hou N	151	578	70	145	35	2	27	93	47-10	5	84	.251	.310	.458	105	2	4-1	.991	3	101	79	1b151	0	-0.4
1988	Hou N	152	561	78	152	26	0	30	99	53-20	11	77	.271	.341	.478	140	28	4-3	**.996**	1	96	99	1b151	0	1.9
1989	Hou N★	158	581	87	156	26	1	34	89	69-17	7	123	.269	.350	.492	144	33	4-2	.992	2	106	92	1b156	0	2.5
1990	Hou N	93	327	44	82	15	4	22	64	46-17	**8**	54	.251	.357	.523	143	19	8-3	.995	-5	82	93	1b91	65	0.8
1991	Bal A	49	176	29	40	9	1	10	28	16-0	5	29	.227	.307	.460	114	3	4-0	.976	4	152	116	1b36,D12	116	0.5
1992	Bal A	106	398	46	110	15	2	13	48	37-2	2	65	.276	.338	.422	109	4	1-0	1.000	-0	65	59	D103,1b2	28	0.1
1993	Bal A	30	113	8	20	3	0	1	9	7-0	1	29	.177	.230	.230	23	-13	0-1	.990	-1	86	112	1b22,D7	91	-1.6
Total	10	1015	3719	510	965	177	13	190	603	370-78	55	613	.259	.332	.467	124	111	28-11	.991	6	101	93	1b870,D122,O9R	300	5.9
Davis, Harry	Harry Albert "Stinky"; B5.7.1908 Shreveport LA; D3.3.1997 Shreveport LA; BL/TL/5´10.5˝/160; d4.13; Col Centenary Louisiana																								
1932	Det A	141	590	92	159	32	13	4	74	60	2	53	.269	.339	.388	84	-14	12-7	.989	-4	87	105	1b141	—	-3.0
1933	Det A	66	173	24	37	8	2	0	14	22	0	8	.214	.303	.283	55	-11	2-3	.978	-5	57	104	1b44	—	-2.0
1937	StL A	120	450	89	124	25	3	3	35	71	0	26	.276	.374	.364	86	-7	7-6	.991	-4	86	98	1b112/rf	—	-2.0
Total	3	327	1213	205	320	65	18	7	123	153	2	87	.264	.347	.364	81	-32	21-16	.988	-13	82	102	1b297/rf	—	-7.0
Davis, Harry	Harry H (b Harry Davis) "Jasper"; B7.19.1873 Philadelphia PA; D8.11.1947 Philadelphia PA; BR/TR/5´10˝/180; d9.21; M1/C6; OF(50/19/11)																								
1895	NY N	7	24	1	7	0	1	0	6	2	0	0	.292	.346	.375	88	-1	1	.957	0	118	108	1b7	—	-0.1
1896	NY N	64	233	43	64	11	10	2	50	31	5	20	.275	.372	.433	115	5	16	.883	-5	34	0	O40(39/1/0),1b23	—	-0.3
	Pit N	44	168	24	32	5	6	0	23	13	2	21	.190	.257	.292	46	-14	9	.966	0	98	82	1b35,O10(9/0/1)/S	—	-1.3
	Year	108	401	67	96	16	16	2	73	44	7	41	.239	.325	.374	87	-9	25	.973	-5	96	91	1b58,O50(48/1/1)/S	—	-1.6
1897	Pit N	111	429	70	131	10	**28**	2	63	26	10	—	.305	.359	.473	123	11	21	.965	-12	84	78	1b64,3b32,O14(0/7/9)/S	—	-0.1
1898	Pit N	58	222	31	65	9	13	1	24	12	1	—	.293	.332	.464	130	6	7	.980	-1	85	99	1b53,O6C	—	0.4
	Lou N	37	138	18	30	5	2	1	16	7	0	—	.217	.255	.304	61	-8	6	.967	-0	124	111	1b34,2b2/rf	—	-0.8
	Was N	1	3	0	0	0	0	0	0	0	0	—	.000	.000	.000	-99	-1	0	.875	-0	0	0	/1	—	-0.1
	Year	96	363	49	95	14	15	2	40	19	1	—	.262	.300	.399	102	-2	13	.974	-2	99	103	1b88,O7(0/6/1),2b2	—	-0.5
1899	Was N	18	64	3	12	2	3	0	8	8	1	—	.188	.288	.313	65	-3	2	.988	-1	48	53	1b18	—	-0.4
1901	Phi A	117	496	92	152	28	10	8	76	23	2	—	.306	.340	.452	113	7	21	.976	8	133	97	1b117	—	1.1
1902	Phi A	133	561	89	172	**43**	8	6	92	30	1	—	.307	.343	.444	112	8	28	.984	8	122	76	1b128,O5C	—	1.3
1903	Phi A	106	420	77	125	28	7	6	55	24	5	—	.298	.343	.440	128	14	24	.972	-1	98	77	1b104,O2L	—	1.2
1904	Phi A	102	404	54	125	21	11	**10**	62	23	2	—	.309	.350	.490	156	24	12	.983	-1	88	79	1b102	—	2.3
1905	†Phi A	150	607	**93**	173	**47**	6	**8**	**83**	43	2	—	.285	.334	.422	137	25	36	.985	0	92	71	1b150	—	2.4
1906	Phi A	145	551	94	161	42	7	**12**	**96**	49	5	—	.292	.355	.459	150	32	23	.975	0	100	109	1b145	—	3.2
1907	Phi A	149	582	84	155	**35**	8	**8**	87	42	2	—	.266	.318	.395	124	15	20	.977	4	109	79	1b149	—	1.7
1908	Phi A	147	513	65	127	23	9	5	62	61	4	—	.248	.332	.357	116	11	20	.986	1	96	68	1b147	—	1.0
1909	Phi A	149	530	73	142	22	11	4	75	51	5	—	.268	.338	.374	122	14	20	.988	-6	80	98	1b149	—	0.6
1910	†Phi A	139	492	61	122	19	4	1	41	53	9	—	.248	.332	.309	102	3	17	.986	-5	79	**126**	1b139	—	-0.5
1911	†Phi A	57	183	27	36	9	1	1	22	24	2	—	.197	.297	.273	60	-9	2	.977	2	113	94	1b53	—	-0.8
1912	Cle A	2	5	0	0	0	0	0	0	0	0	—	.000	.000	.000	-97	-1	0	.941	0	233	137	1b2,M	—	-0.1
1913	Phi A	7	17	2	6	2	0	0	4	1	0	4	.353	.389	.471	155	1	0	1.000	1	173	101	1b6	—	0.2
1914	Phi A	5	7	0	3	0	0	0	2	1	1	0	.429	.556	.429	204	1	0-2	1.000	-0	0	0	/1	—	0.0
1915	Phi A	5	3	0	1	0	0	0	4	0	0	0	.333	.333	.333	103	0	0	ø	0	0	0	/1	—	0.0
1916	Phi A	1	0	0	0	0	0	0	0	1	0	0	ø	1.000	ø	213	0	0	ø	0	—	—	/H	—	0.0
1917	Phi A	1	1	0	0	0	0	0	0	0	0	0	.000	.000	.000	-99	0	0	ø	0	—	—	/H	—	0.0
Total	22	1755	6653	1001	1841	361	145	75	951	525	59	45	.277	.335	.408	119	140	285-2	.980	-7	99	89	1b1628,O78L,3b32,2b2,S2	—	10.9
Davis, Tommy	Herman Thomas; B3.21.1939 Brooklyn NY; BR/TR/6´2˝/(195–205); d9.22; C1; OF(1101/122/56)																								
1959	LA N	1	1	0	0	0	0	0	0	0-0	0	1	.000	.000	.000	-93	0	0-0	ø	0	—	—	/H	0	0.0
1960	LA N	110	352	43	97	18	1	11	44	13-2	2	35	.276	.302	.426	92	-5	6-2	.975	-1	90	119	O87(24/55/10),3b5	0	-0.9
1961	LA N	132	460	60	128	13	2	15	58	32-4	2	53	.278	.325	.413	87	-9	10-4	.973	-3	113	59	O86(44/39/30),3b59	0	-1.4
1962	LA N★	163	665	120	**230**	27	9	27	**153**	33-6	2	65	**.346**	.374	.535	151	44	18-6	.961	0	105	100	O146(134/13/5),3b39	0	3.8
1963	†LA N★	146	556	69	181	19	3	16	88	29-5	4	59	**.326**	.359	.457	144	30	15-10	.969	-3	98	102	O129(120/14/3),3b40	0	2.1
1964	LA N	152	592	70	163	20	5	14	86	29-6	4	68	.275	.311	.397	106	2	11-8	.982	7	108	97	O148L	0	0.1
1965	LA N	17	60	3	15	1	1	0	9	2-1	0	4	.250	.270	.300	66	-3	2-1	1.000	0	93	129	O16L	143	-0.4
1966	†LA N	100	313	27	98	11	1	3	27	16-4	0	36	.313	.345	.383	111	4	3-3	.972	-0	86	109	O79L,3b2	0	0.0
1967	NY N	154	577	72	174	32	0	16	73	31-10	7	71	.302	.342	.440	125	18	9-3	.975	-3	99	59	O149L/1	0	0.9
1968	Chi A	132	456	30	122	5	3	8	50	16-3	0	48	.268	.289	.344	91	-7	4-2	.962	-4	87	112	O116(115/0/4),1b6	0	-2.1
1969	Sea A	123	454	52	123	29	1	6	80	30-5	4	46	.271	.318	.379	96	-3	19-4	.967	-9	85	36	O112L/1	0	-1.6
	Hou N	24	79	2	19	3	0	1	9	8-0	1	9	.241	.318	.316	79	-2	1-1	1.000	-0	88	102	O21(20/1/0)	0	-0.4
1970	Hou N	57	213	24	60	12	2	3	30	7-1	0	25	.282	.305	.399	90	-4	8-3	.949	-2	86	116	O53L	0	-0.8
	Oak A	66	200	17	58	9	1	1	27	8-1	1	18	.290	.318	.360	90	-3	2-4	.963	-5	74	43	O45(43/0/2),1b8	0	-1.2
	Chi N	11	42	4	11	2	0	2	8	1-0	0	1	.262	.279	.452	82	-1	0-0	.938	-1	98	0	O10L	0	-0.2
1971	†Oak A	79	219	26	71	8	1	3	42	15-1	0	19	.324	.363	.411	122	6	7-1	.989	4	150	102	1b35,O16L,2b3,3b2	15	0.8
1972	Chi N	15	26	3	7	1	0	0	6	2-0	0	3	.269	.321	.308	72	-1	0-1	1.000	-0	77	0	1b3,O2(1/0/1)	0	-0.2
	Bal A	26	82	9	21	3	0	0	6	6-0	0	18	.256	.307	.293	76	-2	2-0	1.000	1	104	0	O18(17/0/1),1b3	0	-0.3
1973	†Bal A	137	552	53	169	20	3	7	89	30-3	1	56	.306	.341	.391	106	3	11-3	.971	-0	107	127	D127,1b4	0	0.1
1974	†Bal A	158	626	67	181	20	1	11	84	34-9	3	49	.289	.325	.377	105	3	6-2	ø	0	0	0	D155	0	-0.1
1975	Bal A	116	460	43	130	14	1	6	57	23-2	0	52	.283	.315	.357	95	-5	2-0	ø	0	0	0	D111	0	-0.7
1976	Cal A	72	219	16	58	5	0	3	26	15-3	1	18	.265	.312	.329	94	-2	0-1	1.000	-0	0	0	D54/1	0	-0.4
	KC A	8	19	1	5	0	0	0	0	1-0	0	0	.263	.300	.263	65	-1	0-0	ø	0	—	—	D3	0	-0.1
	Year	80	238	17	63	5	0	3	26	16-3	1	18	.265	.311	.324	92	-3	0-1	1.000	-0	0	0	D57/1	0	-0.5
Total	18	1999	7223	811	2121	272	35	153	1052	381-66	32	754	.294	.329	.405	108	62	136-59	.970	-19	96	85	O1233L,D450,3b147,1b62,2b3	158	-3.0
Davis, Ike	Isaac Marion; B6.14.1895 Pueblo CO; D4.2.1984 Tucson AZ; BR/TR/5´7˝/140; d4.23																								
1919	Was A	8	14	0	0	0	0	0	0	0	0	6	.000	.000	.000	-99	-4	0	.857	-2	24	101	S4	—	-0.6
1924	Chi A	10	33	5	8	1	1	0	4	2	0	5	.242	.286	.333	61	-2	0-0	.940	1	120	63	S10	—	-0.1
1925	Chi A	146	562	105	135	31	9	0	61	71	7	58	.240	.333	.327	72	-23	19-14	.937	7	106	**113**	S144	—	-0.1
Total	3	164	609	110	143	32	10	0	65	73	7	69	.235	.324	.320	68	-29	19-14	.936	6	105	110	S158	—	-0.8
Davis, Ira	J. Ira "Slats"; B7.8.1870 Philadelphia PA; D12.21.1942 Brooklyn NY; ?/162; d4.22; Col Penn																								
1899	NY N	6	17	3	4	1	1	0	2	0	0	—	.235	.235	.412	79	-1	1	.750	-0	114	289	S3,1b2	—	-0.1

YEAR	TM LG	G	AB	R	H	2B	3B	HR	RBI	BB-IB	HP	SO	AVG	OBP	SLG	AOPS	ABR	SB-CS	FA	FR	RNG	THR	GAMES AT POSITION	DL	BFW
DAVIS, JACKE	Jacke Sylvesta; B3.5.1936 Carthage TX; BR/TR/5´11˝/185; d4.19; Col Baylor																								
1962	Phi N	48	75	9	16	0	1	1	6	4-0	0	20	.213	.253	.280	44	-6	1-0	.926	-2	86	0	O26(16/5/7)	0	-0.9
DAVIS, JUMBO	James J.; B9.5.1861 New York NY; D2.14.1921 St.Louis MO; BL/TR/5´11˝/195; d7.27; U1																								
1884	KC U	7	29	3	6	0	0	0	—	0	—	—	.207	.207	.207	30	-3	—	.633	-1	119	0	3b7	—	-0.4
1886	Bal AA	60	216	23	42	5	2	1	20	11	2	—	.194	.240	.250	55	-11	12	.848	4	96	71	3b60	—	-0.6
1887	Bal AA	130	485	81	150	23	**19**	8	109	28	5	—	.309	.353	.485	141	24	49	.826	1	116	56	3b87,S43	—	2.3
1888	KC AA	121	491	70	131	22	8	3	61	20	6	—	.267	.304	.363	107	1	42	.843	29	**139**	**141**	3b113,S8	—	2.9
1889	KC AA	62	241	40	64	4	3	0	30	17	2	35	.266	.319	.307	74	-9	25	.803	-3	103	111	3b62	—	-1.0
	StL AA	2	4	1	0	0	0	0	0	1	0	1	.000	.200	.000	-36	-1	0	1.000	-0	0	0	/Slf	—	-0.1
	Year	64	245	41	64	4	3	0	30	18	2	36	.261	.317	.302	72	-10	25	.803	-4	103	111	3b62/Slf	—	-1.1
1890	StL AA	21	71	8	18	3	1	0	13	9	0	—	.254	.338	.324	83	-2	5	.731	-3	105	60	3b21	—	-0.4
	Bro AA	38	142	33	43	9	2	2	28	15	4	—	.303	.385	.437	147	9	10	.845	-4	105	132	3b38	—	0.5
	Year	59	213	41	61	12	3	2	41	24	4	—	.286	.369	.399	123	6	15	.800	-6	105	105	3b59	—	0.1
1891	Was AA	12	44	7	14	3	2	0	9	7	0	5	.318	.412	.477	162	4	8	.820	-1	91	94	3b12	—	0.3
Total	7	453	1723	266	468	69	37	14	270	108	19	41	.272	.322	.379	107	12	151	.824	22	115	99	3b400,S52/lf	—	3.5
DAVIS, J.J.	Jerry C.; B10.25.1978 Glendora CA; BR/TR/6´4˝/250; [PitN97 1/8]; d9.4																								
2002	Pit N	9	10	1	1	0	0	0	0	0-0	1	4	.100	.182	.100	-23	-2	0-0	1.000	-0	68	0	O4R	0	-0.2
2003	Pit N	19	35	1	7	0	0	1	4	3-0	0	13	.200	.263	.286	43	-3	0-1	1.000	-0	85	191	O10R	0	-0.4
2004	Pit N	25	35	4	5	1	0	0	3	4-0	0	10	.143	.225	.171	6	-5	2-0	.895	-0	91	178	O17(5/0/12)	118	-0.5
2005	Was N	14	26	0	6	0	0	0	2	2-0	0	7	.231	.286	.231	39	-2	1-1	1.000	1	122	258	O10(9/0/1)	0	-0.2
Total	4	67	106	6	19	1	0	1	9	9-0	1	34	.179	.248	.217	23	-12	3-2	.962	0	95	187	O41(14/0/27)	118	-1.3
DAVIS, JODY	Jody Richard; B11.12.1956 Gainesville GA; BR/TR/6´3˝/(192–210); [NYN76*3/62]; d4.21; Col Middle Georgia JC																								
1981	Chi N	56	180	14	46	5	1	4	21	21-3	1	28	.256	.333	.361	93	-1	0-1	.972	2	118	130	C56	0	0.2
1982	Chi N	130	418	41	109	20	2	12	52	36-4	1	92	.261	.316	.404	98	-2	0-1	.984	6	115	114	C129	0	1.0
1983	Chi N	151	510	56	138	31	2	24	84	33-5	2	93	.271	.315	.480	113	7	0-2	.984	-12	101	78	C150	0	0.1
1984	†Chi N★	150	523	55	134	25	2	19	94	47-15	1	99	.256	.315	.421	98	-2	5-6	.984	7	101	105	C146	0	1.1
1985	Chi N	142	482	47	112	30	0	17	58	48-5	0	83	.232	.300	.400	86	-9	1-0	.990	3	86	**133**	C138	0	0.0
1986	Chi N★	148	528	61	132	27	2	21	74	41-4	0	110	.250	.300	.428	93	-7	0-1	.992	11	137	**142**	C145/1	0	1.0
1987	Chi N	125	428	57	106	12	2	19	51	52-2	2	91	.248	.331	.418	93	-5	1-2	.989	-1	95	113	C123	0	0.0
1988	Chi N	88	249	19	57	9	0	6	33	29-3	1	51	.229	.309	.337	82	-5	0-3	.995	-2	109	92	C74	16	-0.4
	Atl N	2	8	2	2	0	0	1	3	0-0	0	1	.250	.250	.625	138	0	0-0	1.000	1	95	135	C2	0	0.1
	Year	90	257	21	59	9	0	7	36	29-3	1	52	.230	.307	.346	84	-5	0-3	.995	-1	109	93	C76	0	-0.3
1989	Atl N	78	231	12	39	5	0	4	19	23-3	1	61	.169	.246	.242	40	-18	0-0	.985	1	131	117	C72,1b2	0	-1.5
1990	Atl N	12	28	0	2	0	0	0	1	3-0	0	3	.071	.161	.071	-32	-5	0-0	1.000	1	166	120	1b6,C4	0	-0.4
Total	10	1082	3585	364	877	164	11	127	490	333-44	9	712	.245	.307	.403	91	-47	7-16	.987	17	109	113	C1039,1b9	16	1.2
DAVIS, JOHN	John Humphrey "Red"; B7.15.1915 Wilkes–Barre PA; D4.26.2002 Laurel MS; BR/TR/5´11˝/172; d9.9; Mil 1942–45																								
1941	NY N	21	70	8	15	3	0	0	5	8	0	12	.214	.295	.257	55	-4	0	.970	1	108	108	3b21	0	-0.2
DAVIS, CRASH	Lawrence Columbus; B7.14.1919 Canon GA; D8.31.2001 Greensboro NC; BR/TR/6´0˝/173; d6.15; Mil 1943–45; Col Duke																								
1940	Phi A	23	67	4	18	1	1	0	9	3	1	10	.269	.310	.313	63	-4	1-0	.963	0	96	85	2b19/S	—	-0.2
1941	Phi A	39	105	8	23	3	0	0	8	11	0	16	.219	.293	.248	45	-8	0-0	.952	-2	108	94	2b20,1b12	0	-0.9
1942	Phi A	86	272	31	61	8	1	2	26	21	1	30	.224	.282	.283	60	-15	1-0	.965	-9	91	55	2b57,S26,1b3	0	-1.9
Total	3	148	444	43	102	12	2	2	43	35	2	56	.230	.289	.279	57	-27	2-0	.961	-10	96	70	2b96,S27,1b15	0	-3.0
DAVIS, MARK	Mark Anthony; B11.25.1964 San Diego CA; BR/TR/6´0˝/170; [ChiA86 12/309]; d7.2; b–Mike; Col Stanford																								
1991	Cal A	3	2	0	0	0	0	0	0	0-0	0	0	.000	.000	.000	-99	-1	0-0	.500	-0	71	0	O3R	0	-0.1
DAVIS, BEN	Mark Christopher; B3.10.1977 Chester PA; BB/TR/6´4˝/(205–225); [SDN95 1/2]; d9.25																								
1998	SD N	1	1	0	0	0	0	0	0	0-0	0	0	.000	.000	.000	-99	0	0-0	1.000	0	0	0	/C	0	0.0
1999	SD N	76	266	29	65	14	1	5	30	25-3	0	70	.244	.307	.361	74	-11	2-1	.986	-5	115	94	C74	0	-1.1
2000	SD N	43	130	12	29	6	0	3	14	14-1	0	35	.223	.297	.338	64	-7	1-1	.996	0	103	72	C38/D	19	-0.5
2001	SD N	138	448	56	107	20	0	11	57	66-5	4	112	.239	.337	.357	88	-7	4-4	.990	-5	94	115	C135,1b2	0	-0.4
2002	Sea A	80	228	24	59	10	1	7	43	18-1	2	58	.259	.313	.404	93	-3	1-1	.998	3	138	120	C77,1b2	0	0.5
2003	Sea A	80	246	25	58	18	0	6	42	18-2	0	61	.236	.284	.382	79	-8	0-0	.991	3	114	107	C73/D	0	-0.1
2004	Sea A	14	33	1	3	0	0	0	2	3-0	0	9	.091	.162	.091	-32	-7	0-0	1.000	1	277	76	C14	0	-0.5
	Chi A	54	160	21	37	9	0	6	16	9-0	1	40	.231	.276	.400	71	-7	1-1	.991	4	73	113	C53	0	0.0
	Year	68	193	22	40	9	0	6	18	12-0	1	49	.207	.256	.347	55	-14	1-1	.993	5	113	106	C67	0	-0.5
Total	7	486	1512	168	358	77	2	38	204	153-12	7	385	.237	.306	.366	78	-50	9-8	.992	1	111	106	C465,1b4,D2	19	-2.1
DAVIS, MIKE	Michael Dwayne; B6.11.1959 San Diego CA; BL/TL/6´3˝/(165–190); [OakA77 3/69]; d4.10; b–Mark																								
1980	Oak A	51	95	11	20	2	1	1	8	7-0	0	14	.211	.262	.284	54	-6	2-1	1.000	2	116	201	O18(5/0/13),1b7,D6	0	-0.5
1981	†Oak A	17	20	0	1	1	0	0	0	2-0	0	4	.050	.136	.100	-32	-3	0-0	1.000	0	160	0	O2L/1D	0	-0.4
1982	Oak A	23	75	12	30	4	0	1	10	2-0	0	8	.400	.416	.493	153	5	3-2	.946	1	141	0	O13(8/3/5),1b7	0	0.5
1983	Oak A	128	443	61	122	24	4	8	62	27-1	5	74	.275	.322	.402	104	2	32-15	.974	11	111	186	O121(0/21/110),D3	16	0.9
1984	Oak A	134	382	47	88	18	3	9	46	31-2	1	66	.230	.285	.364	85	-9	14-9	.961	7	121	85	O127(1/16/121),D4	0	-0.8
1985	Oak A	154	547	92	157	34	1	24	82	50-8	2	99	.287	.348	.484	134	26	24-10	.979	5	116	59	O151(0/31/138)	0	2.5
1986	Oak A	142	489	77	131	28	3	19	55	34-2	1	91	.268	.314	.454	115	8	27-4	.973	6	**113**	106	O139(0/34/120)	0	1.3
1987	Oak A	139	494	69	131	32	1	22	72	42-5	1	94	.265	.320	.468	114	9	19-7	.942	-8	97	38	O124R,D14	0	-0.3
1988	†LA N	108	281	29	55	11	2	2	17	25-0	0	59	.196	.260	.270	54	-17	7-3	.961	-4	89	94	O76(1/23/63)	0	-2.4
1989	LA N	67	173	21	43	7	1	5	19	16-1	0	28	.249	.309	.387	100	0	6-5	.987	-2	90	43	O48(16/0/34)	62	-0.5
Total	10	963	2999	419	778	161	16	91	371	236-19	10	537	.259	.313	.415	104	15	134-56	.968	18	109	91	O819(33/128/728),D30,1b15	78	0.3
DAVIS, ODIE	Odie Ernest; B8.13.1955 San Antonio TX; BR/TR/6´1˝/178; [TexA77 7/165]; d9.3; Col Prairie View A&M																								
1980	Tex A	17	8	0	1	0	0	0	0	0-0	0	2	.125	.125	.125	-32	-1	0-0	.880	1	124	109	S13/3	0	0.0
DAVIS, OTIS	Otis Allen "Scat"; B9.24.1920 Charleston AR; BL/TR/6´0˝/160; d4.22																								
1946	Bro N	1	0	1	0	0	0	0	0	0	0	0	ø	ø	ø	ø	0	0	ø	0	—	—	/R	0	0.0
DAVIS, RAJAI	Rajai Lavae; B10.19.1980 Norwich CT; BR/TR/5´11˝/195; [PitN01 38/1134]; d8.14; Col Avery Point (CT) JC																								
2006	Pit N	20	14	1	2	1	0	0	0	2-0	0	3	.143	.250	.214	20	-2	1-3	ø	-0	0	0	/rf	0	-0.3
DAVIS, DICK	Richard Earl; B9.25.1953 Long Beach CA; BR/TR/6´3˝/(185–195); d7.12; Col Snow (UT) JC																								
1977	Mil A	22	51	7	14	2	0	0	6	1-0	0	8	.275	.278	.314	64	-3	0-0	1.000	-2	67	0	O12L,D6	0	-0.5
1978	Mil A	69	218	28	54	10	1	5	26	7-0	2	23	.248	.273	.372	80	-6	2-5	1.000	1	108	123	D34,O28(18/4/8)	0	-0.9
1979	Mil A	91	335	51	89	13	1	12	41	16-0	0	46	.266	.298	.418	91	-6	3-3	.973	-1	103	39	D53,O35(32/0/3)	0	-1.0
1980	Mil A	106	365	50	99	26	2	4	30	11-0	3	43	.271	.297	.386	88	-7	5-3	.971	-1	87	112	D63,O38(13/0/27)	0	-1.1
1981	†Phi N	45	96	12	32	6	1	2	19	8-0	1	13	.333	.387	.479	138	5	1-2	.974	-2	86	55	O32(1/0/31)	0	0.2
1982	Phi N	28	68	5	19	3	1	2	7	2-0	0	9	.279	.296	.441	102	0	1-0	1.000	0	114	0	O16R	0	-0.1
	Tor A	3	7	0	2	0	0	0	2	0-0	0	1	.286	.250	.286	53	0	0-0	1.000	0	97	0	/lfD	0	-0.1
	Pit N	39	77	7	14	2	1	2	10	5-0	0	9	.182	.224	.312	48	-6	1-0	.971	-2	93	0	O28(1/0/27)	0	-0.9
Total	6	403	1217	160	323	62	7	27	141	50-0	6	152	.265	.294	.394	89	-23	13-13	.981	-6	95	58	O190(78/4/112),D157	0	-4.4
DAVIS, BRANDY	Robert Brandon; B9.10.1927 Newark DE; D6.12.2005 Newark DE; BR/TR/6´0˝/170; d4.15; C1; Col Duke																								
1952	Pit N	55	95	14	17	1	1	0	1	11	0	28	.179	.264	.211	32	-9	9-2	.932	-0	105	95	O29(9/9/12)	0	-0.9
1953	Pit N	12	39	5	8	2	0	0	2	0	0	3	.205	.205	.256	20	-5	0-2	.955	-0	114	0	O9L	0	-0.6
Total	2	67	134	19	25	3	1	0	3	11	0	31	.187	.248	.224	29	-14	9-4	.938	-1	107	69	O38(18/9/12)	0	-1.5
DAVIS, BOB	Robert John Eugene; B3.1.1952 Pryor OK; BR/TR/6´0˝/(180–190); [SDN70 6/124]; d4.6																								
1973	SD N	5	11	1	1	0	0	0	0	0-0	0	5	.091	.091	.091	-54	-2	0-0	.941	0	66	87	C5	0	-0.2
1975	SD N	43	128	6	30	3	2	0	7	11-3	3	31	.234	.310	.289	72	-5	0-0	.986	0	100	99	C43	0	-0.3
1976	SD N	51	83	7	17	0	1	0	5	5-1	0	13	.205	.244	.229	40	-7	0-0	.965	0	105	117	C47	0	-0.6
1977	SD N	48	94	9	17	2	0	1	10	5-2	2	24	.181	.235	.234	30	-10	0-0	.975	-6	194	124	C46	0	-1.5

YEAR	TM LG	G	AB	R	H	2B	3B	HR	RBI	BB-IB	HP	SO	AVG	OBP	SLG	AOPS	ABR	SB-CS	FA	FR	RNG	THR	GAMES AT POSITION	DL	BFW
1978	SD N	19	40	3	8	1	0	0	2	1-1	0	5	.200	.220	.225	26	-4	0-1	.960	-4	78	123	C16	0	-0.9
1979	Tor A	32	89	6	11	2	0	1	8	6-0	1	15	.124	.188	.180	-0	-13	0-0	.984	-2	118	87	C32	0	-1.4
1980	Tor A	91	218	18	47	11	0	4	19	12-0	1	25	.216	.260	.321	56	-14	0-0	.983	-2	101	87	C89	0	-1.3
1981	Cal A	1	2	0	0	0	0	0	0	0-0	0	0	.000	.000	.000	-99	-1	0-0	1.000	-1	21	0	/C	0	-0.1
Total	8	290	665	50	131	19	3	6	51	40-7	7	118	.197	.249	.262	42	-56	0-1	.978	-14	115	100	C279	0	-6.3
Davis, Ron	Ronald Everette; B10.21.1941 Roanoke Rapids NC; D9.5.1992 Houston TX; BR/TR/6´0˝/(175–180); d8.1; Col Duke																								
1962	Hou N	6	14	1	3	0	0	0	1	1-0	0	7	.214	.267	.214	33	-1	1-0	1.000	-0	102	0	O5C	0	-0.1
1966	Hou N	48	194	21	48	10	1	2	19	13-2	4	26	.247	.308	.340	86	-4	2-2	.982	3	94	284	O48C	0	-0.2
1967	Hou N	94	285	31	73	19	1	7	38	17-2	2	48	.256	.303	.404	104	1	5-3	.976	2	96	166	O80(63/11/8)	0	-0.1
1968	Hou N	52	217	22	46	10	1	1	12	13-0	4	48	.212	.268	.281	67	-9	0-4	.971	3	111	124	O52C	0	-1.1
	†StL N	33	79	11	14	4	2	0	5	5-0	0	17	.177	.221	.278	51	-5	1-0	.979	1	97	178	O25(2/10/14)	0	-0.6
	Year	85	296	33	60	14	3	1	17	18-0	4	65	.203	.255	.280	63	-14	1-4	.973	4	107	140	O77(2/62/14)	0	-1.7
1969	Pit N	62	64	10	15	1	1	0	4	7-0	0	14	.234	.310	.281	68	-3	0-0	.933	-2	76	78	O51(22/12/20)	0	-0.6
Total	5	295	853	96	199	44	6	10	79	56-4	10	160	.233	.287	.334	82	-21	9-9	.974	6	98	171	O261(87/138/42)	0	-2.7
Davis, Russ	Russell Stuart; B9.13.1969 Birmingham AL; BR/TR/6´0˝/(170–200); [NYA88 29/755]; d7.6; Col Shelton St. (AL) CC																								
1994	NY A	4	14	0	2	0	0	0	1	0-0	0	4	.143	.143	.143	-27	-3	0-0	1.000	-1	82	0	3b4	0	-0.3
1995	†NY A	40	98	14	27	5	2	2	12	10-0	1	26	.276	.349	.429	102	0	0-0	.968	-2	92	23	3b34,1b2,D4	0	-0.2
1996	Sea A	51	167	24	39	9	0	5	18	17-1	2	50	.234	.312	.377	73	-7	2-0	.933	-10	75	57	3b51	114	-1.6
1997	Sea A	119	420	57	114	29	1	20	63	27-2	2	100	.271	.317	.488	107	3	6-2	.939	-3	95	**122**	3b117/D	32	0.1
1998	Sea A	141	502	68	130	30	1	20	82	34-1	3	134	.259	.305	.442	92	-7	4-3	.906	-3	101	131	3b137,O3L	0	-0.9
1999	Sea A	124	432	55	106	17	1	21	59	32-1	5	111	.245	.304	.435	87	-11	3-3	.959	-15	87	78	3b124,S2	0	-2.3
2000	†SF N	80	180	27	47	5	0	9	24	9-0	2	29	.261	.302	.439	90	-4	0-3	.933	-11	68	52	3b43,1b6,D3	0	-1.5
2001	SF N	53	167	16	43	13	1	7	17	17-2	1	49	.257	.326	.473	111	2	1-0	.890	-12	74	122	3b46/D	0	-0.9
Total	8	612	1980	261	508	108	6	84	276	146-7	16	503	.257	.310	.444	93	-27	16-11	.932	-56	89	98	3b556,D9,1b8,O3L,S2	146	-7.6
Davis, Steve	Steven Michael; B12.30.1953 Oakland CA; BR/TR/6´1˝/200; [ChiN76 14/319]; d9.23; Col Stanford																								
1979	Chi N	3	4	0	0	0	0	0	1	0-0	0	0	.000	.000	.000	-91	-1	0-0	1.000	-0	143	0	2b2/3	0	-0.1
Davis, Tommy	Thomas James; B5.21.1973 Mobile AL; BR/TR/6´1˝/210; [BalA94 2/54]; d5.14; Col Southern Mississippi																								
1999	Bal A	5	6	0	1	0	0	0	0	0-0	0	2	.167	.167	.167	-15	-1	0-0	.909	-0	40	253	C4/1	0	-0.1
Davis, Tod	Thomas Oscar; B7.24.1924 Los Angeles CA; D12.31.1978 W.Covina CA; BR/TR/6´2˝/190; d4.27																								
1949	Phi A	31	75	7	20	0	1	1	6	9	0	16	.267	.345	.333	83	-2	0-0	.912	-1	84	114	S14,3b12/2	0	-0.2
1951	Phi A	11	15	0	1	0	0	0	0	1	0	3	.067	.125	.067	-46	-3	0-0	1.000	-0	0	0	2b2/3	0	-0.3
Total	2	42	90	7	21	0	1	1	6	10	0	19	.233	.310	.289	61	-5	0-0	.912	-1	84	114	S14,3b13,2b3	0	-0.5
Davis, Trench	Trench Neal; B9.12.1960 Baltimore MD; BL/TL/6´3˝/171; d6.4																								
1985	Pit N	2	7	1	1	0	0	0	0	0-0	0	0	.143	.143	.143	-20	-1	1-0	.667	-1	52	0	O2C	0	-0.2
1986	Pit N	15	23	2	3	0	0	0	1	0-0	0	4	.130	.125	.130	-27	-4	0-0	.917	0	87	350	O7C	0	-0.4
1987	Atl N	6	3	0	0	0	0	0	0	0-0	0	1	.000	.000	.000	-96	-1	0-0	ø	0	—	—	/H	0	-0.1
Total	3	23	33	3	4	0	0	0	1	0-0	0	5	.121	.118	.121	-32	-6	1-0	.867	-1	78	263	O9C	0	-0.7
Davis, Spud	Virgil Lawrence; B12.20.1904 Birmingham AL; D8.14.1984 Birmingham AL; BR/TR/6´1˝/197; d4.30; M1/C9																								
1928	StL N	2	5	1	1	0	0	0	1	1	0	0	.200	.333	.200	42	0	0	.750	-1	*86*	*0*	C2	—	-0.1
	Phi N	67	163	16	46	2	0	3	18	15	0	11	.282	.343	.350	79	-5	0	.980	-1	*75*	*152*	C49	—	-0.3
	Year	69	168	17	47	2	0	3	19	16	0	11	.280	.342	.345	78	-5	0	.971	-2	*75*	*145*	C51	—	-0.4
1929	Phi N	98	263	31	90	18	0	7	48	19	2	17	.342	.391	.490	110	4	1	.961	-10	*92*	*103*	C89	—	-0.1
1930	Phi N	106	329	41	103	16	1	14	65	17	1	20	.313	.349	.495	94	-4	1	.986	-9	*73*	*110*	C96	—	-0.6
1931	Phi N	120	393	30	128	32	1	4	51	36	0	28	.326	.382	.443	112	9	0	.994	-1	*75*	*118*	C114	—	1.4
1932	Phi N	125	402	44	135	23	5	14	70	40	2	39	.336	.399	.522	130	18	1	.987	-3	*88*	*82*	C120	—	2.2
1933	Phi N	141	495	51	173	28	3	9	65	32	5	24	.349	.395	.473	130	21	2	.983	-10	*74*	*106*	C132	—	1.9
1934	†StL N	107	347	45	104	22	4	9	65	34	2	27	.300	.366	.464	113	7	0	.988	3	*106*	*87*	C94	—	1.5
1935	StL N	102	315	28	100	24	2	1	60	33	2	30	.317	.386	.416	111	7	0	**.992**	-2	*114*	*33*	C81,1b5	—	0.9
1936	StL N	112	363	24	99	26	2	4	59	35	3	34	.273	.342	.388	97	-1	0	.985	-7	*116*	*99*	C103,3b2	—	-0.2
1937	Cin N	76	209	19	56	10	1	3	33	23	0	15	.268	.341	.368	97	0	0	.980	4	*74*	*102*	C59	—	0.7
1938	Cin N	12	36	3	6	1	0	0	1	5	1	6	.167	.286	.194	35	-3	0	.962	0	*154*	*119*	C11	—	-0.2
	Phi N	70	215	11	53	7	0	2	23	14	0	14	.247	.293	.307	67	-10	1	.980	-10	*60*	*94*	C63	—	-1.7
	Year	82	251	14	59	8	0	2	24	19	1	20	.235	.292	.291	62	-13	1	.977	-10	*75*	*98*	C74	—	-1.9
1939	Phi N	87	202	10	62	8	1	0	23	24	1	20	.307	.383	.356	103	2	0	**1.000**	-6	*54*	*124*	C85	—	0.0
1940	Pit N	99	285	23	93	14	1	5	39	35	2	20	.326	.404	.435	132	14	0	.967	-5	*73*	***139***	C87	—	1.4
1941	Pit N	57	107	3	27	4	1	0	6	11	0	11	.252	.322	.308	78	-3	0	1.000	-0	*101*	*90*	C49	0	-0.1
1944	Pit N	54	93	6	28	7	0	2	14	10	0	8	.301	.369	.441	122	3	0	.966	0	*95*	*94*	C35	0	0.5
1945	Pit N	23	33	2	8	2	0	0	6	2	1	2	.242	.306	.303	67	-1	0	.968	-0	*91*	*111*	C13	0	-0.1
Total	16	1458	4255	388	1312	244	22	77	647	386	22	326	.308	.369	.430	108	58	6	.984	-58	*85*	*102*	C1282,1b5,3b2	0	7.1
Davis, Butch	Wallace McArthur; B6.19.1958 Martin Co. NC; BR/TR/6´0˝/(185–193); [KCA80 12/302]; d8.23; Col East Carolina																								
1983	KC A	33	122	13	42	2	6	2	18	4-0	0	19	.344	.359	.508	136	5	4-3	.977	0	112	36	O33L	0	0.4
1984	KC A	41	116	11	17	3	0	2	12	10-0	0	19	.147	.211	.224	21	-13	4-3	.959	-0	104	90	O35(34/1/1),D2	0	-1.5
1987	Pit N	7	7	3	1	1	0	0	0	1-0	0	3	.143	.250	.286	41	-1	0-0	1.000	0	218	0	/lf	0	0.0
1988	Bal A	13	25	2	6	1	0	0	0	0-0	0	8	.240	.240	.280	46	-2	1-0	1.000	1	119	256	O10(2/0/8)/D	0	-0.1
1989	Bal A	5	6	1	1	1	0	0	0	0-0	0	3	.167	.167	.333	39	0	0-0	1.000	-0	91	0	O3(2/0/1)/D	0	-0.1
1991	LA N	1	1	0	0	0	0	0	0	0-0	0	0	.000	.000	.000	-99	0	0-0	ø	0	—	—	/H	0	0.0
1993	Tex A	62	159	24	39	10	4	3	20	5-1	1	28	.245	.273	.415	85	-5	3-1	.960	2	118	85	O44(23/10/17),D11	15	-0.4
1994	Tex A	4	17	2	4	3	0	0	0	0-0	0	3	.235	.235	.412	62	-1	1-0	1.000	0	75	343	O4R	0	0.0
Total	8	166	453	56	110	21	10	7	50	20-1	1	83	.243	.274	.380	77	-17	13-7	.969	4	111	89	O130(95/11/31),D15	15	-1.7
Davis, Willie	William Henry; B4.15.1940 Mineral Springs AR; BL/TL/6´2˝/(180–185); d9.8																								
1960	LA N	22	88	12	28	6	1	2	10	4-2	0	12	.318	.348	.477	116	2	3-5	.981	-0	103	67	O22C	0	-0.1
1961	LA N	128	339	56	86	19	6	12	45	27-4	5	46	.254	.316	.451	93	-4	12-5	.983	1	**111**	65	O114C	0	-0.4
1962	LA N	157	600	103	171	18	**10**	21	85	42-10	6	72	.285	.334	.453	117	12	32-7	.963	5	108	132	O156(1/155/0)	0	1.7
1963	†LA N	156	515	60	126	19	8	9	60	25-6	3	61	.245	.281	.365	92	-8	25-11	.978	10	109	182	O153C	0	-0.1
1964	LA N	157	613	91	180	23	7	12	77	22-1	1	59	.294	.316	.413	112	7	42-13	.983	15	**119**	164	O155C	0	2.3
1965	†LA N	142	558	52	133	24	3	10	57	14-3	7	81	.238	.263	.346	76	-20	25-9	.967	-1	105	77	O141C	0	-2.5
1966	†LA N	153	624	74	177	31	6	11	61	15-2	4	68	.284	.302	.405	104	0	21-10	.970	1	107	91	O152C	0	-0.3
1967	LA N	143	569	65	146	27	9	6	41	29-5	3	65	.257	.295	.367	97	-5	20-6	.971	-4	96	78	O138C	0	-1.2
1968	LA N	160	643	86	161	24	10	7	31	31-4	1	88	.250	.284	.351	98	-5	36-10	.973	-2	99	95	O158C	0	-0.9
1969	LA N	129	498	66	155	23	8	11	59	33-5	4	39	.311	.356	.456	135	21	24-10	.979	-2	99	106	O125C	21	1.9
1970	LA N	146	593	92	181	23	**16**	8	93	29-2	1	54	.305	.335	.438	111	5	38-14	.992	6	105	144	O143(0/139/4)	0	1.1
1971	LA N★	158	641	84	198	33	10	10	74	23-3	0	47	.309	.330	.438	123	15	20-8	.981	1	106	80	O157C	0	1.5
1972	LA N	149	615	81	178	22	7	19	79	27-4	1	61	.289	.317	.441	116	9	20-3	.987	0	101	110	O146C	0	0.9
1973	LA N★	152	599	82	171	29	9	16	77	29-12	5	62	.285	.320	.444	115	8	17-5	.980	-9	97	64	O146C	0	-0.2
1974	Mon N	153	611	86	180	27	9	12	89	27-9	3	69	.295	.322	.427	104	1	25-7	.969	-4	102	90	O151C	0	-0.4
1975	Tex A	42	169	16	42	8	2	5	17	4-0	1	25	.249	.270	.408	90	-3	13-5	.990	-3	94	35	O42C	0	-0.7
	StL N	98	350	41	102	19	6	6	50	14-1	4	27	.291	.319	.431	104	0	10-1	.970	3	112	88	O89(8/15/71)	0	0.1
1976	SD N	141	493	61	132	18	10	5	46	19-2	2	34	.268	.295	.375	98	-5	14-2	.992	3	110	77	O128C	0	-0.4
1979	†Cal A	43	56	9	14	2	1	0	2	4-0	0	7	.250	.300	.321	70	-3	1-0	1.000	-0	100	0	O7(1/0/6),D6	0	-0.3
Total	18	2429	9174	1217	2561	395	138	182	1053	418-75	51	977	.279	.311	.412	106	27	398-131	.978	20	105	103	O2323(10/2237/81),D6	21	2.0
Dawkins, Gookie	Travis Sentell; B5.12.1979 Newberry SC; BR/TR/6´1˝/180; [CinN97 2/66]; d9.3																								
1999	Cin N	7	7	1	1	0	0	0	0	0-0	1	4	.143	.250	.143	3	-1	0-0	1.000	-1	69	88	S7	0	-0.2
2000	Cin N	14	41	5	9	2	0	0	3	2-1	0	7	.220	.256	.268	32	-4	0-0	.965	2	102	179	S14	0	-0.2
2002	Cin N	31	48	2	6	2	0	0	0	6-0	0	21	.125	.222	.167	4	-7	2-1	.944	-7	82	64	S21,2b3	0	-1.3
2003	KC A	3	2	0	0	0	0	0	0	1-0	0	2	.000	.333	.000	-1	0	0-0	1.000	0	113	0	2b3	0	0.0
Total	4	55	98	8	16	4	0	0	3	9-1	1	34	.163	.241	.204	16	-12	2-1	.957	-6	89	114	S42,2b6	0	-1.7

YEAR	TM LG	G	AB	R	H	2B	3B	HR	RBI	BB-IB	HP	SO	AVG	OBP	SLG	AOPS	ABR	SB-CS	FA	FR	RNG	THR	GAMES AT POSITION	DL	BFW
Dawson, Andre	Andre Nolan; B7.10.1954 Miami FL; BR/TR/6´3˝/(180–197); [MonN75 11/250]; d9.11; Col Florida A&M																								
1976	Mon N	24	85	9	20	4	1	0	7	5-1	0	13	.235	.278	.306	62	-4	1-2	.969	1	112	64	O24(8/14/2)	0	-0.5
1977	Mon N	139	525	64	148	26	9	19	65	34-4	2	93	.282	.326	.474	115	8	21-7	.989	1	102	98	O136(13/129/3)	0	0.9
1978	Mon N	157	609	84	154	24	8	25	72	30-3	**12**	128	.253	.299	.442	105	1	28-11	.988	4	99	189	O153C	0	0.6
1979	Mon N	155	639	90	176	24	12	25	92	27-5	6	115	.275	.309	.468	109	4	35-10	.988	-9	96	60	O153C	0	-0.3
1980	Mon N	151	577	96	178	41	7	17	87	44-7	**6**	69	.308	.358	.492	134	26	34-9	.986	7	106	140	O147C	0	3.8
1981	†Mon N★	103	394	71	119	21	3	24	64	35-14	**7**	50	.302	.365	.553	154	27	26-4	.980	12	**121**	140	O103C	0	4.4
1982	Mon N★	148	608	107	183	37	7	23	83	34-4	8	96	.301	.343	.498	129	22	39-10	.982	8	116	91	O147C	0	3.5
1983	Mon N★	159	633	104	**189**	36	10	32	113	38-12	**9**	81	.299	.338	.539	142	32	25-11	.980	-0	104	76	O157C	0	3.4
1984	Mon N	138	533	73	132	23	6	17	86	41-2	2	80	.248	.301	.409	103	0	13-5	.975	8	116	121	O134R	0	0.2
1985	Mon N	139	529	65	135	27	2	23	91	29-8	4	92	.255	.295	.444	111	5	13-4	.973	-2	97	103	O131(0/24/123)	0	-0.2
1986	Mon N	130	496	65	141	32	2	20	78	37-11	6	79	.284	.338	.478	124	15	18-12	.986	-4	89	110	O127R	25	0.4
1987	Chi N★	153	621	90	178	24	2	**49**	**137**	32-7	7	103	.287	.328	.568	127	20	11-3	.986	1	98	119	O152R	0	1.4
1988	Chi N★	157	591	78	179	31	8	24	79	37-12	4	73	.303	.344	.504	136	25	12-4	.989	-2	95	98	O147R	0	2.1
1989	†Chi N★	118	416	62	105	18	6	21	77	35-13	1	62	.252	.307	.476	114	6	8-5	.987	1	107	67	O112R	36	0.4
1990	Chi N★	147	529	72	164	28	5	27	100	42-**21**	2	65	.310	.358	.535	134	24	16-2	.981	-4	90	103	O139R	0	1.8
1991	Chi N★	149	563	69	153	21	4	31	104	22-3	5	80	.272	.302	.488	114	7	4-5	.988	-7	90	66	O137R	0	-0.6
1992	Chi N	143	542	60	150	27	2	22	90	30-8	4	70	.277	.316	.456	114	8	6-2	.992	-8	81	115	O139R	0	-0.4
1993	Bos A	121	461	44	126	29	1	13	67	17-4	13	49	.273	.313	.425	92	-6	2-1	1.000	-0	112	0	D97,O20R	19	-1.2
1994	Bos A	75	292	34	70	18	0	16	48	9-3	4	53	.240	.271	.466	82	-10	2-2	ø	0	0	0	D74	31	-1.3
1995	Fla N	79	226	30	58	10	3	8	37	9-1	8	45	.257	.305	.434	92	-4	0-0	.908	-4	84	89	O59(12/0/47)	29	-1.0
1996	Fla N	42	58	6	16	2	0	2	14	2-0	1	13	.276	.311	.414	92	-1	0-0	.833	-1	52	0	O6L	79	-0.2
Total	21	2627	9927	1373	2774	503	98	438	1591	589-143	111	1509	.279	.323	.482	118	205	314-109	.983	1	100	104	O2323(39/1027/1284),D171	219	17.2
Day, Boots	Charles Frederick; B8.31.1947 Ilion NY; BL/TL/5´9˝/160; d6.15; Col Mohawk Valley (NY) CC																								
1969	StL N	11	6	1	0	0	0	0	0	1-0	0	1	.000	.143	.000	-56	-1	0-0	ø	-0	0	0	/cf	0	-0.1
1970	Chi N	11	8	2	2	0	0	0	0	0-0	0	3	.250	.250	.250	31	-1	0-0	.875	1	116	763	O7C	0	0.0
	Mon N	41	108	14	29	4	0	0	5	6-2	0	18	.269	.307	.306	65	-5	3-2	.987	3	125	65	O35(5/30/0)	0	-0.4
	Year	52	116	16	31	4	0	0	5	6-2	0	21	.267	.303	.302	61	-6	3-2	.976	3	124	121	O42(5/37/0)	0	-0.4
1971	Mon N	127	371	53	105	10	2	4	33	33-5	1	39	.283	.342	.353	96	-2	9-4	.982	7	107	**176**	O120(3/118/0)	0	0.4
1972	Mon N	128	386	32	90	7	4	0	30	29-3	1	44	.233	.288	.272	59	-21	3-6	.979	-4	93	109	O117(0/103/15)	0	-3.2
1973	Mon N	101	207	36	57	7	0	4	28	21-1	0	28	.275	.342	.367	93	-2	0-3	1.000	-2	78	68	O51(12/45/6)	0	-0.7
1974	Mon N	52	65	8	12	0	0	0	2	5-0	0	8	.185	.239	.185	20	-7	0-0	1.000	-1	91	0	O16(14/0/2)	0	-0.9
Total	6	471	1151	146	295	28	6	8	98	95-11	2	141	.256	.314	.312	75	-39	15-15	.983	4	99	124	O347(34/304/23)	0	-4.9
Dayett, Brian	Brian Kelly; B1.22.1957 New London CT; BR/TR/5´10˝/(180–185); [NYA78 16/416]; d9.11; Col St. Leo																								
1983	NY A	11	29	3	6	0	1	0	5	2-0	0	4	.207	.258	.276	48	-2	0-0	1.000	2	142	167	O9L	0	-0.1
1984	NY A	64	127	14	31	8	0	4	23	9-0	1	14	.244	.295	.402	95	-1	0-0	.988	1	102	115	O62(55/0/10)/D	0	-0.2
1985	Chi N	22	26	1	6	0	0	1	4	0-0	1	6	.231	.259	.346	62	-1	0-0	1.000	-0	106	0	O10L	109	-0.2
1986	Chi N	24	67	7	18	4	0	4	11	6-0	0	10	.269	.316	.507	118	1	0-1	1.000	-1	88	72	O24(15/1/12)	0	-0.1
1987	Chi N	97	177	20	49	14	1	5	25	20-0	0	37	.277	.348	.452	106	2	0-0	1.000	-2	88	68	O78(68/0/12)	0	-0.2
Total	5	218	426	45	110	26	2	14	68	37-0	2	71	.258	.316	.427	99	-1	0-1	.995	-1	97	89	O183(158/1/34)/D	109	-0.8
Deal, Charlie	Charles Albert; B10.30.1891 Wilkinsburg PA; D9.16.1979 Covina CA; BR/TR/6´0˝/160; d7.19																								
1912	Det A	42	142	13	32	4	2	0	11	9	0	—	.225	.272	.282	60	-8	4	.942	6	129	46	3b41	—	0.0
1913	Det A	16	50	3	11	0	2	0	3	1	0	7	.220	.235	.300	57	-3	2	.862	1	124	135	3b15	—	-0.2
	Bos N	10	36	6	11	1	0	0	3	2	1	1	.306	.359	.333	96	0	1-2	.935	-3	83	34	2b10	—	-0.3
1914	†Bos N	79	257	17	54	13	2	0	23	20	1	23	.210	.270	.276	63	-12	4	.948	-2	95	85	3b74/S	—	-1.3
1915	StL F	65	223	21	72	12	4	1	27	12	0	16	.323	.357	.426	114	1	10	.951	7	111	110	3b65	—	1.0
1916	StL A	23	74	7	10	1	0	0	10	6	0	8	.135	.200	.149	5	-9	4	.970	-2	91	136	3b22/2	—	-1.1
	Chi N	2	8	2	2	1	0	0	3	0	0	0	.250	.250	.375	82	0	0	1.000	1	167	296	3b2	—	0.1
1917	Chi N	135	449	46	114	11	3	0	47	19	0	18	.254	.284	.292	71	-16	10	.957	8	99	102	3b130	—	-0.5
1918	†Chi N	119	414	43	99	9	3	2	34	21	2	13	.239	.279	.290	72	-15	11	.942	-6	92	112	3b118	—	-1.9
1919	Chi N	116	405	37	117	23	5	2	52	12	4	12	.289	.316	.385	110	4	11	**.973**	6	97	93	3b116	—	1.4
1920	Chi N	129	450	48	108	10	5	3	39	20	8	14	.240	.285	.304	68	-19	5-8	**.973**	11	109	101	3b128	—	-0.7
1921	Chi N	115	422	52	122	19	8	3	66	13	0	9	.289	.310	.393	85	-10	3-5	**.973**	13	109	89	3b112	—	0.8
Total	10	851	2930	295	752	104	34	11	318	135	16	121	.257	.293	.327	79	-87	65-15	.958	40	103	99	3b823,2b11/S	—	-2.7
Deal, Lindsay	Fred Lindsay; B9.3.1911 Lenoir NC; D4.18.1979 Little Rock AR; BL/TR/6´0˝/175; d9.13																								
1939	Bro N	4	7	0	0	0	0	0	0	0	0	2	.000	.000	.000	-97	-2	0	1.000	-0	91	0	/cf	—	-0.2
Deal, Snake	John Wesley; B1.21.1879 Lancaster PA; D5.9.1944 Harrisburg PA; BR/TR/6´0˝/164; d7.9; Col Villanova																								
1906	Cin N	65	231	13	48	4	3	0	21	6	0	—	.208	.228	.251	47	-15	15	.985	2	113	80	1b65	—	-1.6
Dealy, Pat	Patrick E.; B11.12.1861 Underhill VT; D12.16.1924 Buffalo NY; BR/TR/5´8˝/145; d9.30																								
1884	StP U	5	15	2	2	0	0	0	—	0	—	—	.133	.133	.133	-35	-3	—	.871	2	—	—	C4/rf	—	-0.1
1885	Bos N	35	130	18	29	4	1	1	9	2	—	14	.223	.235	.292	72	-4	—	.903	0	—	—	C29,3b3,O2(1/1/0),S2/1	—	-0.1
1886	Bos N	15	46	9	15	1	1	0	3	4	—	4	.326	.380	.391	139	2	5	.929	-2	—	—	C14/lf	—	0.1
1887	Was N	58	212	33	55	8	2	1	18	8	2	8	.259	.293	.330	78	-6	36	.931	-4	—	—	C28,S23,O5(4/1/0),3b5	—	-0.7
1890	Syr AA	18	66	9	12	1	0	0	4	5	1	—	.182	.250	.197	36	-5	4	.900	-5	77	*94*	C10,3b6,O2(0/1/1)	—	-0.9
Total	5	131	469	71	113	14	4	2	34	19	3	26	.241	.275	.301	75	-16	45	.914	-10	*77*	*94*	C85,S25,3b14,O11(6/3/2)/1	—	-1.7
Dean, Chubby	Alfred Lovell; B8.24.1915 Mt.Airy NC; D12.21.1970 Riverside NJ; BL/TL/5´11˝/181; d4.14; Mil 1943–46; ▲																								
1936	Phi A	111	342	41	98	21	3	1	48	24	2	24	.287	.337	.374	77	-13	3-2	.989	-1	97	93	1b77	—	-1.8
1937	Phi A	104	309	36	81	14	4	2	31	42	0	10	.262	.350	.353	79	-9	2-1	.991	-2	89	81	1b78,P2	—	-1.7
1938	Phi A	16	20	3	6	2	0	0	1	1	0	4	.300	.333	.400	85	2	0-0	1.000	1	184	0	P6	—	0.0
1939	Phi A	80	77	12	27	4	0	0	19	8	0	4	.351	.412	.403	111	9	0-0	.935	1	131	258	P54	—	0.0
1940	Phi A	67	90	6	26	2	0	0	6	16	0	9	.289	.396	.311	88	-1	0-0	.976	1	125	54	P30/1	—	0.0
1941	Phi A	27	37	0	9	2	0	0	9	4	0	3	.243	.317	.297	65	-2	0-0	1.000	0	93	96	P18/1	0	0.0
	Cle A	17	25	2	4	1	0	0	2	3	0	2	.160	.250	.200	21	1	0-0	1.000	1	155	0	P8	0	0.0
	Year	44	62	2	13	3	0	0	11	7	0	5	.210	.290	.258	47	-5	0-0	1.000	1	118	57	P26/1	0	0.0
1942	Cle A	70	101	4	27	1	0	0	7	11	0	7	.267	.339	.277	79	8	0-0	.939	-3	69	0	P27	0	0.0
1943	Cle A	41	46	2	9	0	0	0	5	6	0	2	.196	.288	.196	45	1	0-0	.929	-1	71	106	P17	0	0.0
Total	8	533	1047	106	287	47	7	3	128	115	2	65	.274	.347	.341	79	-4	5-3	.964	-4	107	79	P162,1b157	0	-3.5
Dean, Tommy	Tommy Douglas; B8.30.1945 Iuka MS; BR/TR/6´0˝/(165–170); d9.17																								
1967	LA N	12	28	1	4	1	0	0	2	0-0	0	9	.143	.143	.179	-9	-4	0-0	.981	2	101	169	S12	0	-0.2
1969	SD N	101	273	14	48	9	2	2	9	27-4	1	54	.176	.251	.245	41	-22	0-3	.978	-6	100	77	S97,2b2	0	-2.0
1970	SD N	61	158	18	35	5	1	2	13	11-3	0	29	.222	.271	.304	56	-10	2-0	.974	-4	93	97	S55	0	-0.8
1971	SD N	41	70	2	8	0	0	0	1	4-0	0	13	.114	.162	.114	-22	-11	1-0	.969	-1	94	95	S28,3b11/2	0	-1.1
Total	4	215	529	35	95	15	3	4	25	42-7	1	105	.180	.240	.242	36	-47	3-3	.976	-10	97	91	S192,3b11,2b3	0	-4.1
Deane, Harry	John Henry; B5.6.1846 Trenton NJ; D5.31.1925 Indianapolis IN; 5´7˝/150; d7.12; M1																								
1871	Kek NA	6	22	3	4	0	1	0	2	2	—	0	.182	.250	.273	49	-2	0-0	1.000	2	0	0	O6L,M	—	0.0
1874	Bal NA	**47**	203	29	50	8	1	0	13	4	—	3	.246	.261	.296	79	-4	2-1	.818	-5	94	143	O46C,2b2/S	—	-0.7
Total	2NA	53	225	32	54	8	2	0	15	6	—	3	.240	.260	.293	75	-6	2-1	.850	-3	83	126	O52(6/46/0),2b2/S	—	-0.7
Dear, Buddy	Paul Stanford; B12.1.1905 Norfolk VA; D8.29.1989 Radford VA; BR/TR/5´8˝/143; d9.9; Col VPI																								
1927	Was A	2	1	1	0	0	0	0	0	0	0	0	.000	.000	.000	-99	0	0-0	ø	-0	0	0	/2	—	0.0
DeArmond, Charlie	Charles Hommer "Hummer"; B2.13.1877 Okeana OH; D12.17.1933 Morning Sun OH; BR/TR/5´10˝/165; d9.19																								
1903	Cin N	11	39	10	11	2	1	0	7	3	1	—	.282	.349	.385	98	0	1	.878	-1	74	92	3b11	—	-0.1

YEAR	TM LG	G	AB	R	H	2B	3B	HR	RBI	BB-IB	HP	SO	AVG	OBP	SLG	AOPS	ABR	SB-CS	FA	FR	RNG	THR	GAMES AT POSITION	DL	BFW
DEASLEY, JOHN	John; B1.1861 Philadelphia PA; D12.25.1910 Philadelphia PA; d6.17; b–Pat																								
1884	Was U	31	134	20	29	1	1	0	—	3	—	—	.216	.234	.239	45	-13	—	.836	1	99	141	S31	—	-1.0
	KC U	13	40	3	7	2	0	0	—	2	—	—	.175	.214	.225	38	-4	—	.833	1	109	207	S13	—	-0.2
	Year	44	174	23	36	3	1	0	—	5	—	—	.207	.229	.236	44	-17	—	.835	3	102	158	S44	—	-1.2
DEASLEY, PAT	Thomas H.; B11.17.1857 , Ireland; D4.1.1943 Philadelphia PA; BR/TR/5´8.5˝/154; d5.18; b–John																								
1881	Bos N	43	147	13	35	5	2	0	8	5	—	10	.238	.263	.299	80	-3	—	.914	-1	—	—	C28,O7(0/2/6),S7,1b2	—	-0.3
1882	Bos N	67	264	36	70	8	0	0	29	7	—	22	.265	.284	.295	86	-4	—	**.958**	2	—	—	C56,O14(1/0/13)/S	—	0.2
1883	StL AA	58	206	27	53	2	1	0	15	6	—	—	.257	.278	.277	75	-6	—	**.930**	8	—	—	C56,O2C	—	0.6
1884	StL AA	75	254	27	52	5	4	0	—	7	3	—	.205	.235	.256	58	-12	—	.919	9	—	—	C75,O2(1/0/1)/1	—	0.3
1885	NY N	54	207	22	53	5	1	0	24	9	—	20	.256	.287	.290	88	-3	—	.935	7	—	—	C54,O2C/S	—	0.8
1886	NY N	41	143	18	38	6	1	0	17	4	—	12	.266	.286	.322	84	-3	2	.925	4	—	—	C30,O15(1/6/8)	—	0.2
1887	NY N	30	118	12	37	5	0	0	23	9	1	7	.314	.367	.356	107	2	3	.867	-10	—	—	C24,3b7/S	—	-0.5
1888	Was N	34	127	6	20	1	0	0	4	2	0	18	.157	.171	.165	8	-13	2	.922	6	—	—	C31/rfS2	—	-0.4
Total	8	402	1466	161	358	37	9	0	120	49	4	89	.244	.271	.282	75	-42	7	.927	25	—	—	C354,O43(3/12/29),S11,3b7,1b3/2	—	0.9
DEBERRY, HANK	John Herman; B12.29.1894 Savannah TN; D9.10.1951 Savannah TN; BR/TR/5´11˝/195; d9.12; Mil 1918; Col Tennessee																								
1916	Cle A	15	33	7	9	4	0	0	4	6	0	9	.273	.385	.394	126	1	0	1.000	-1	94	91	C14	—	0.1
1917	Cle A	25	33	3	9	2	0	0	1	2	1	7	.273	.333	.333	96	0	0	.968	1	*110*	*113*	C9	—	0.1
1922	Bro N	85	259	29	78	10	1	3	35	20	1	9	.301	.354	.382	91	-3	4-1	.971	-5	*75*	*94*	C81	—	-0.3
1923	Bro N	78	235	21	67	11	6	1	48	20	2	12	.285	.346	.396	98	-1	2-1	.971	4	*84*	*106*	C60	—	0.7
1924	Bro N	77	218	20	53	10	3	3	26	20	0	21	.243	.307	.358	80	-6	0-1	.993	12	*108*	*92*	C63	—	1.0
1925	Bro N	67	193	26	50	8	1	2	24	16	2	8	.259	.322	.342	72	-8	2-2	.981	8	*86*	*118*	C55	—	0.3
1926	Bro N	48	115	6	33	11	0	0	13	8	0	5	.287	.333	.383	94	-1	0	.976	3	*79*	*82*	C37	—	0.5
1927	Bro N	68	201	15	47	3	2	1	21	17	0	8	.234	.294	.284	55	-13	1	.988	15	*79*	*133*	C67	—	0.6
1928	Bro N	82	258	19	65	8	2	0	23	18	0	15	.252	.301	.298	58	-16	3	.977	9	*75*	***114***	C80	—	-0.2
1929	Bro N	68	210	13	55	11	1	1	25	17	0	15	.262	.317	.338	64	-12	1	.991	-3	*59*	*94*	C68	—	-0.9
1930	Bro N	35	95	11	28	3	0	0	14	4	0	10	.295	.323	.326	58	-6	0	.978	7	*101*	*74*	C35	—	0.2
Total	11	648	1850	170	494	81	16	11	234	148	6	119	.267	.323	.346	76	-65	13-5	.982	51	*82*	*103*	C569	—	2.1
DEBUS, ADAM	Adam Joseph; B10.7.1892 Chicago IL; D5.13.1977 Chicago IL; BR/TR/5´10.5˝/150; d7.14; Mil 1918																								
1917	Pit N	38	131	9	30	5	4	0	7	7	2	14	.229	.279	.328	83	-3	2	.898	-7	91	60	S21,3b18	—	-1.0
DECASTER, YURENDELL	Yurendell Eithel; B9.26.1979 Brevengat, Curacao, Netherlands Antilles; BR/TR/6´1˝/205; d5.21																								
2006	Pit N	3	2	0	0	0	0	0	0	0-0	0	2	.000	.000	.000	-98	-1	0-0	ø	0	—	—	/H	0	-0.1
DECINCES, DOUG	Douglas Vernon; B8.29.1950 Burbank CA; BR/TR/6´2˝/(190–195); [BalA70*S3/65]; d9.9; Col Los Angeles Pierce (CA) JC																								
1973	Bal A	10	18	2	2	0	0	0	3	1-0	0	5	.111	.158	.111	-23	-3	0-0	.895	1	121	224	3b8,2b2/S	0	-0.2
1974	Bal A	1	1	0	0	0	0	0	0	1-0	0	0	.000	.500	.000	55	0	0-0	1.000	0	121	0	/3	0	0.0
1975	Bal A	61	167	20	42	6	3	4	23	13-2	1	32	.251	.306	.395	104	0	0-1	.947	6	122	153	3b34,S13,2b11,1b2	0	0.7
1976	Bal A	129	440	36	103	17	2	11	42	29-1	2	68	.234	.284	.357	92	-6	8-4	.941	-5	93	53	3b109,2b17,1b11,S2/D	0	-1.1
1977	Bal A	150	522	63	135	28	3	19	69	64-6	2	86	.259	.339	.433	116	12	8-8	.958	-3	99	128	3b148/12D	0	0.6
1978	Bal A	142	511	72	146	37	1	28	80	46-2	2	81	.286	.346	.526	151	33	7-7	.975	11	103	117	3b130,2b12	0	4.2
1979	†Bal A	120	422	67	97	27	1	16	61	54-5	3	68	.230	.318	.412	100	0	5-3	.964	-3	95	105	3b120	39	-0.5
1980	Bal A	145	489	64	122	23	2	16	64	49-5	3	83	.249	.319	.403	99	-1	11-6	.960	26	**117**	**154**	3b142/1	0	2.3
1981	Bal A	100	346	49	91	23	2	13	55	41-2	1	32	.263	.341	.454	128	13	0-3	.942	-2	92	**173**	3b100/1lf	0	0.9
1982	†Cal A	153	575	94	173	42	5	30	97	66-7	1	80	.301	.369	.548	148	38	7-5	.961	23	122	132	3b153,S2	0	5.7
1983	Cal A★	95	370	49	104	19	3	18	65	32-2	0	56	.281	.332	.495	126	12	2-0	.955	8	113	129	3b84,D10	36	1.9
1984	Cal A	146	547	77	147	23	3	20	82	53-4	0	79	.269	.327	.431	110	7	4-1	.964	0	103	87	3b140,D5	0	0.5
1985	Cal A	120	427	50	104	22	1	20	78	47-11	2	71	.244	.317	.440	106	3	1-4	.958	-2	98	**132**	3b111,D3	19	-0.1
1986	†Cal A	140	512	69	131	20	3	26	96	52-4	2	74	.256	.325	.459	112	7	2-2	.965	-3	93	93	3b132/SD	0	0.2
1987	Cal A	133	453	65	106	23	0	16	63	70-6	2	87	.234	.337	.391	96	-1	3-4	.948	-6	99	109	3b128,1b4/SD	0	-0.9
	StL N	4	9	1	2	2	0	0	1	0-0	0	2	.222	.222	.444	69	0	0-0	.833	1	158	0	3b3	0	0.0
Total	15	1649	5809	778	1505	312	29	237	879	618-57	21	904	.259	.329	.445	115	114	58-48	.958	54	103	118	3b1543,2b43,D24,1b20,S20/lf	94	14.2
DECKER, HARRY	Earle Harry; B9.3.1864 Lockport IL; BR/TR/5´11˝/180; d8.23; OF(12/4/8)																								
1884	Ind AA	4	15	1	4	1	0	0	—	1	0	—	.267	.313	.333	114	0	—	.870	-2	—	—	C4	—	-0.2
	KC U	23	75	8	10	2	0	0	—	5	—	—	.133	.188	.160	7	-11	—	.813	2	182	162	O16(6/4/6),C11	—	-0.7
1886	Det N	14	54	2	12	1	0	0	6	2	—	9	.222	.250	.241	48	-3	0	.871	2	—	—	C14/lf	—	0.0
	Was N	7	23	0	5	1	1	0	1	1	—	5	.217	.250	.348	87	0	0	.946	0	—	—	C4,3b2/S	—	0.0
	Year	21	77	2	17	2	1	0	7	3	—	14	.221	.250	.273	59	-4	0	.886	2	—	—	C18,3b2/lfS	—	0.0
1889	Phi N	11	30	4	3	0	0	0	2	2	0	5	.100	.156	.100	-26	-5	1	.857	-1	98	119	2b7,C3/lf	—	-0.5
1890	Phi N	5	19	5	7	1	0	0	2	4	0	1	.368	.478	.421	159	2	4	.938	-2	158	205	1b2,O2L/C	—	0.0
	Pit N	92	354	52	97	14	3	5	38	26	0	36	.274	.324	.373	116	7	8	.909	-37	*65*	*93*	C70,1b16,O4(2/0/2)/2S	—	-2.3
	Year	97	373	57	104	15	3	5	40	30	0	37	.279	.333	.375	119	9	12	.909	-39	*65*	92	C71,1b18,O6(4/0/2)/2S	—	-2.3
Total	4	156	570	72	138	20	4	5	49	41	0	56	.242	.293	.318	87	-10	13	.903	-38	*65*	*92*	C107,O24L,1b18,2b8,S2,3b2	—	-3.7
DECKER, FRANK	Frank; B2.26.1856 St.Louis MO; D2.5.1940 St.Louis MO; BR/TR; d6.25																								
1879	Syr N	3	10	0	1	0	0	0	0	0	—	3	.100	.100	.100	-38	-1	—	.714	-2	—	—	C2/rf1	—	-0.3
1882	StL AA	2	8	0	2	0	0	0	1	0	—	—	.250	.250	.250	66	0	—	.813	-1	98	94	2b2	—	-0.1
Total	2	5	18	0	3	0	0	0	1	0	—	3	.167	.167	.167	12	-1	—	.813	-2	—	—	2b2,C2/1rf	—	-0.4
DECKER, GEORGE	George A "Gentleman George"; B6.1.1869 York PA; D6.7.1909 Patton CA; BL/TL/6´1˝/180; d7.11; OF(189/34/111)																								
1892	Chi N	78	291	32	66	6	7	1	28	20	0	49	.227	.277	.306	75	-10	9	.876	-7	126	156	O62R,2b16	—	-1.8
1893	Chi N	81	328	57	89	9	8	2	48	24	2	22	.271	.325	.366	85	-9	22	.878	-6	182	161	O33(23/0/10),1b27,2b20,S2	—	-1.4
1894	Chi N	93	393	76	122	17	7	8	93	24	5	20	.310	.358	.450	89	-10	23	.974	-7	56	86	1b49,O29(0/23/6),3b8,2b2/S	—	-1.4
1895	Chi N	73	297	51	82	9	7	2	41	17	4	22	.276	.324	.374	75	-13	11	.910	-7	36	0	O57(25/8/24),1b11,3b3/S2	—	-1.9
1896	Chi N	107	421	68	118	23	11	5	61	23	0	14	.280	.318	.423	91	-9	20	.928	-1	106	0	O71(67/3/1),1b36	—	-1.4
1897	Chi N	111	428	72	124	12	7	5	63	24	4	—	.290	.333	.386	86	-11	11	.925	-2	120	48	O75(74/0/1),1b38/2	—	-1.6
1898	StL N	76	286	26	74	10	0	1	45	20	3	—	.259	.314	.304	76	-9	4	.980	-7	48	67	1b75	—	-1.5
	Lou N	42	148	27	44	4	3	0	19	9	1	—	.297	.342	.365	104	0	9	.993	-0	82	96	1b32,O6R	—	0.0
	Year	118	434	53	118	14	3	1	64	29	4	—	.272	.323	.325	85	-9	13	**.984**	-7	58	75	1b107,O6R	—	-1.5
1899	Lou N	39	138	14	37	8	1	1	18	12	2	—	.268	.336	.362	92	-1	3	.968	-3	77	102	1b39	—	-0.4
	Was N	4	9	0	0	0	0	0	0	0	0	—	.000	.000	.000	-99	-3	0	.955	-0	97	72	1b2/rf	—	-0.3
	Year	43	147	14	37	8	1	1	18	12	2	—	.252	.317	.340	80	-4	3	.968	-3	78	100	1b41/rf	—	-0.7
Total	8	704	2739	423	756	98	51	25	416	173	21	127	.276	.324	.376	84	-75	112	.900	-40	117	57	O334L,1b309,2b40,3b11,S4	—	-11.7
DECKER, STEVE	Steven Michael; B10.25.1965 Rock Island IL; BR/TR/6´3˝/(205–220); [SFN88 21/542]; d9.18; Col Lewis–Clark St.																								
1990	SF N	15	54	5	16	2	0	3	8	1-0	0	10	.296	.309	.500	123	1	0-0	.989	2	109	134	C15	0	0.4
1991	SF N	79	233	11	48	7	1	5	24	16-1	3	44	.206	.262	.309	63	-12	0-1	.984	1	115	103	C78	0	-0.8
1992	SF N	15	43	3	7	1	0	0	1	6-0	1	7	.163	.280	.186	36	-3	0-0	1.000	3	537	40	C15	0	0.0
1993	Fla N	8	15	0	0	0	0	0	1	3-0	0	3	.000	.158	.000	-48	-3	0-0	.968	1	70	78	C5	139	-0.2
1995	Fla N	51	133	12	30	2	1	3	13	19-1	0	22	.226	.318	.323	70	-6	1-0	.985	5	117	94	C46,1b2	0	0.2
1996	SF N	57	122	16	28	1	0	1	12	15-4	0	26	.230	.309	.262	55	-8	0-0	1.000	2	90	110	C30,1b3,3b2	0	-0.4
	Col N	10	25	8	8	2	0	1	8	3-0	0	3	.320	.393	.520	112	1	1-0	1.000	2	188	88	C10	0	0.4
	Year	67	147	24	36	3	0	2	20	18-4	0	29	.245	.323	.306	67	-7	1-0	1.000	4	112	105	C40,1b3,3b2	0	0.0
1999	Ana A	28	63	5	15	6	0	0	5	13-0	1	9	.238	.372	.333	83	-1	0-0	.987	-2	101	91	C17,1b6,D3	0	-0.2
Total	7	263	688	60	152	21	2	13	72	76-6	5	124	.221	.299	.314	68	-31	2-1	.988	14	143	98	C216,1b11,D3,3b2	139	-0.6
DEDE, ARTIE	Arthur Richard; B7.12.1895 Brooklyn NY; D9.6.1971 Keene NH; BR/TR/5´9˝/155; d10.4																								
1916	Bro N	1	1	0	0	0	0	0	0	0	0	0	.000	.000	.000	-97	0	0	1.000	-0	0	0	/C	—	-0.1
DEDEAUX, ROD	Raoul Martial; B2.17.1914 New Orleans LA; D1.5.2006 Glendale CA; BR/TR/5´11˝/160; d9.28; Col USC																								
1935	Bro N	2	4	0	1	0	0	0	1	0	0	0	.250	.250	.250	36	0	0	.857	0	116	159	S2	—	0.0

YEAR	TM LG	G	AB	R	H	2B	3B	HR	RBI	BB-IB	HP	SO	AVG	OBP	SLG	AOPS	ABR	SB-CS	FA	FR	RNG	THR	GAMES AT POSITION	DL	BFW
DEE, JIM	James D.; B Buffalo NY; d7.30																								
1884	Pit AA	12	40	0	5	0	0	0	—	1	0	—	.125	.146	.125	-11	-5	—	.860	1	106	193	S12	—	-0.3
DEE, SHORTY	Maurice Leo; B10.4.1889 Halifax NS, Can.; D8.12.1971 Jamaica Plain MA; BR/TR/5´6˝/155; d9.14																								
1915	StL A	1	3	1	0	0	0	0	0	1	0	0	.000	.250	.000	-26	0	0-1	.500	-1	36	0	/S	—	-0.2
DEER, ROB	Robert George; B9.29.1960 Orange CA; BR/TR/6´3˝/(210–230); [SFN78 4/85]; d9.4																								
1984	SF N	13	24	5	4	0	0	3	3	7-0	1	10	.167	.375	.542	159	2	1-1	.905	-0	111	0	O9L	0	0.1
1985	SF N	78	162	22	30	5	1	8	20	23-0	0	71	.185	.283	.377	88	-3	0-1	.982	-3	94	46	O37(21/0/17),1b10	0	-0.9
1986	Mil A	134	466	75	108	17	3	33	86	72-3	3	179	.232	.336	.494	119	12	5-2	.974	4	110	90	O131(1/0/131),1b4	0	0.8
1987	Mil A	134	474	71	113	15	2	28	80	86-6	5	186	.238	.360	.456	111	9	12-4	.974	6	110	124	O123(98/0/29),1b12,D4	0	1.0
1988	Mil A	135	492	71	124	24	0	23	85	51-4	7	153	.252	.328	.441	113	8	9-5	.990	3	100	124	O133(54/2/79)/D	23	0.7
1989	Mil A	130	466	72	98	18	2	26	65	60-5	4	158	.210	.305	.425	104	2	4-8	.972	1	102	105	O125(2/1/123),D5	16	-0.3
1990	Mil A	134	440	57	92	15	1	27	69	64-6	4	147	.209	.313	.432	107	4	2-3	.970	8	107	176	O117R,1b21/D	0	0.7
1991	Det A	134	448	64	80	14	2	25	64	89-1	0	175	.179	.314	.386	91	-5	1-3	.978	4	108	78	O132R,D2	0	-0.6
1992	Det A	110	393	66	97	20	1	32	64	51-1	3	131	.247	.337	.547	142	21	4-2	.983	0	100	106	O106R,D2	45	1.8
1993	Det A	90	323	48	70	11	0	14	39	38-1	3	120	.217	.302	.381	83	-8	3-2	.975	2	108	79	O86(0/2/84),D4	15	-1.0
	Bos A	38	143	18	28	6	1	7	16	20-0	2	49	.196	.303	.399	82	-4	2-0	.970	3	127	75	O36R,D2	0	-0.2
	Year	128	466	66	98	17	1	21	55	58-1	5	169	.210	.303	.386	83	-12	5-2	.973	5	114	78	O122(0/2/120),D6	0	-1.2
1996	SD N	25	50	9	9	3	0	4	9	14-0	0	30	.180	.359	.480	124	2	0-0	1.000	-0	106	0	O18(1/0/17)	0	0.1
Total	11	1155	3881	578	853	148	13	230	600	575-27	32	1409	.220	.324	.442	108	40	43-31	.977	27	106	104	O1053(186/5/871),1b47,D21	99	2.2
DEES, CHARLIE	Charles Henry; B6.24.1935 Birmingham AL; BL/TL/6´1˝/(173–174); d5.26																								
1963	LA A	60	202	23	62	11	1	3	27	11-1	8	31	.307	.362	.416	126	7	3-3	.986	-4	80	92	1b56	0	0.0
1964	LA A	26	26	3	2	1	0	0	1	1-0	1	4	.077	.143	.115	-30	-5	1-2	.981	-1	71	142	1b12	0	-0.7
1965	Cal A	12	32	1	5	0	0	0	1	1-1	0	8	.156	.182	.156	-3	-4	1-2	.986	-1	43	86	1b8	0	-0.7
Total	3	98	260	27	69	12	1	3	29	13-2	9	43	.265	.319	.354	95	-2	5-7	.986	-6	75	96	1b76	0	-1.4
DEFATE, TONY	Clyde Herbert; B2.22.1895 Kansas City MO; D9.3.1963 New Orleans LA; BR/TR/5´8.5˝/158; d4.18																								
1917	StL N	14	14	0	2	0	0	0	1	4	0	5	.143	.333	.143	50	-1	0	1.000	0	101	0	3b5/2	—	-0.1
	Det A	3	2	1	0	0	0	0	0	0	0	1	.000	.000	.000	-99	0	0	1.000	-0	102	0	/2	—	-0.1
Total	1	17	16	1	2	0	0	0	1	4	0	6	.125	.300	.125	33	-1	0	1.000	-0	101	0	3b5,2b2	—	-0.2
DEFREITES, ARTURO	Arturo Marcelino (Simon); B4.26.1953 San Pedro de Macoris, D.R.; BR/TR/6´2˝/195; d9.7																								
1978	Cin N	9	19	1	4	1	0	1	2	1-0	0	4	.211	.238	.421	84	-1	0-0	1.000	0	97	131	1b6	0	-0.1
1979	Cin N	23	34	2	7	2	0	0	4	0-0	0	16	.206	.200	.265	27	-3	0-0	.974	-1	0	154	1b6/rf	0	-0.5
Total	2	32	53	3	11	3	0	1	6	1-0	0	20	.208	.214	.321	48	-4	0-0	.988	-1	52	142	1b12/rf	0	-0.6
DEGROFF, RUBE	Edward Arthur; B9.2.1879 Hyde Park NY; D12.17.1955 Poughkeepsie NY; BL/TL/5´11˝/?; d9.22																								
1905	StL N	15	56	3	14	2	1	0	5	5	0	—	.250	.311	.321	91	-1	1	.909	0	149	197	O15(0/8/7)	—	-0.1
1906	StL N	1	4	1	0	0	0	0	0	0	0	—	.000	.000	.000	-99	-1	0	ø	-0	0	0	/rf	—	-0.1
Total	2	16	60	4	14	2	1	0	5	5	0	—	.233	.292	.300	80	-2	1	.909	-0	148	196	O16(0/8/8)	—	-0.2
DEHAAN, KORY	Korwin Jay; B7.16.1976 Pella IA; BL/TR/6´2˝/187; [PitN97 7/212]; d4.25; Col Morningside																								
2000	SD N	90	103	19	21	7	0	2	13	5-0	0	39	.204	.239	.330	45	-9	4-2	1.000	1	99	188	O60(10/4/49)/D	20	-0.8
2002	SD N	12	11	1	1	0	0	0	0	0-0	0	6	.091	.091	.091	-57	-3	0-0	1.000	-0	108	0	O9(6/2/1)	0	-0.3
Total	2	102	114	20	22	7	0	2	13	5-0	0	45	.193	.225	.307	36	-12	4-2	1.000	1	100	168	O69(16/6/50)/D	20	-1.1
DEHLMAN, HERMAN	Herman J. "Dutch"; B1852 Brooklyn NY; D3.13.1885 Wilkes–Barre PA; d5.2; U1																								
1872	Atl NA	**37**	164	30	37	4	1	0	15	3	—	1	.226	.240	.262	46	-13	4-2	.928	-1	89	49	1b37	—	-0.9
1873	Atl NA	54	219	50	52	5	1	0	18	11	—	9	.237	.274	.269	69	-5	5-0	.926	-3	72	87	1b54/S	—	-0.4
1874	Atl NA	53	218	40	49	3	1	0	18	7	—	5	.225	.249	.248	68	-5	2-0	.944	-1	89	45	1b53	—	-0.4
1875	StL NA	67	254	42	57	12	2	0	14	**11**	—	21	.224	.257	.287	98	2	23-9	**.955**	1	92	113	1b67,O2R	—	0.6
1876	StL N	**64**	245	40	45	6	0	0	9	9	—	10	.184	.213	.208	43	-13	—	.958	0	71	138	1b64	—	-1.4
1877	StL N	32	119	24	22	4	0	0	11	7	—	21	.185	.230	.218	44	-7	—	.931	-4	41	102	1b31/lf	—	-1.0
Total	4NA	211	855	162	195	24	5	0	65	32	—	36	.228	.256	.268	71	-21	34-11	.940	-4	86	78	1b211,O2R/S	—	-1.1
Total	2	96	364	64	67	10	0	0	20	16	—	31	.184	.218	.212	43	-20	—	.950	-3	61	126	1b95/lf	—	-2.4
DEIDEL, JIM	James Lawrence; B6.6.1949 Denver CO; BR/TR/6´2˝/195; d5.31																								
1974	NY A	2	2	0	0	0	0	0	0	0-0	0	0	.000	.000	.000	-99	-1	0-0	1.000	1	0	316	C2	0	0.0
DEININGER, PEP	Otto Charles; B10.10.1877 Wasseralfingen, Germany; D9.25.1950 Boston MA; BL/TL/5´8.5˝/180; d4.26; ▲																								
1902	Bos A	2	6	0	2	1	1	0	0	0	0	—	.333	.333	.833	210	1	0	1.000	-1	29	882	P2	—	0.0
1908	Phi N	1	0	0	0	0	0	0	0	0	0	—	ø	ø	ø	ø	0	0	ø	-0	0	0	/cf	—	0.0
1909	Phi N	55	169	22	44	9	0	0	16	11	1	—	.260	.309	.314	93	-1	5	.989	-1	87	0	O45(1/38/6)/2	—	-0.5
Total	3	58	175	22	46	10	1	0	16	11	1	—	.263	.310	.331	97	0	5	.989	-2	87	0	O46(1/39/6),P2/2	—	-0.5
DEISEL, PAT	Edward; B4.29.1876 Ripley OH; D4.17.1948 Cincinnati OH; BR/TR/5´5˝/145; d8.21																								
1902	Bro N	1	3	0	2	0	0	0	1	1	1	—	.667	.800	.667	351	1	0	1.000	0	*70*	*0*	/C	—	0.1
1903	Cin N	2	0	0	0	0	0	0	0	1	0	—	ø	1.000	ø	174	0	0	ø	0	*0*	*0*	/C	—	0.0
Total	2	3	3	0	2	0	0	0	1	2	1	—	.667	.833	.667	352	1	0	1.000	0	*64*	*0*	C2	—	0.1
DEITRICK, BILL	William Alexander; B4.30.1902 Hanover Co. VA; D5.6.1946 Bethesda MD; BR/TR/5´10˝/160; d9.19; Col Virginia																								
1927	Phi N	5	6	1	1	0	0	0	0	0	0	0	.167	.167	.167	-10	-1	0	.750	-1	46	220	S5	—	-0.2
1928	Phi N	52	100	13	20	6	0	0	7	17	1	10	.200	.322	.260	52	-6	1	1.000	0	101	208	O21(17/1/3),S8	—	-0.7
Total	2	57	106	14	21	6	0	0	7	17	1	10	.198	.315	.255	49	-7	1	1.000	-1	101	208	O21(17/1/3),S13	—	-0.9
DEJAN, MIKE	Michael Dan; B1.13.1915 Cleveland OH; D2.2.1953 W.Los Angeles CA; BL/TL/6´1˝/185; d7.13																								
1940	Cin N	12	16	1	3	0	1	0	2	3	0	3	.188	.316	.313	73	-1	0	1.000	-0	90	0	O2L	—	-0.1
DEJESUS, DAVID	David Christopher; B12.20.1979 Brooklyn NY; BL/TL/6´0˝/(170–185); [KCA00 4/104]; d9.2; Col Rutgers																								
2003	KC A	12	7	0	2	0	1	0	0	1-0	1	2	.286	.444	.571	155	1	0-0	1.000	-1	30	0	O9(0/8/1)	0	0.0
2004	KC A	96	363	58	104	15	3	7	39	33-0	9	53	.287	.360	.402	99	0	8-11	.984	1	107	64	O94(4/85/6)	0	0.0
2005	KC A	122	461	69	135	31	6	9	56	42-1	9	76	.293	.359	.445	117	13	5-5	.987	4	105	124	O119C	0	1.6
2006	KC A	119	491	83	145	36	7	8	56	43-4	12	70	.295	.364	.446	111	9	6-3	.990	8	107	161	O119(73/61/0)	40	1.4
Total	4	349	1322	210	386	82	17	24	151	119-5	31	201	.292	.362	.434	110	23	19-19	.987	11	106	120	O341(77/273/7)	40	3.0
DEJESUS, IVAN	Ivan (Alvarez); B1.9.1953 Santurce, PR; BR/TR/5´11˝/(160–185); d9.13																								
1974	LA N	3	3	1	1	0	0	0	0	0-0	0	2	.333	.333	.333	90	0	0-0	1.000	-1	0	0	S2	0	-0.1
1975	LA N	63	87	10	16	2	1	0	2	11-0	0	15	.184	.276	.230	43	-7	1-2	.974	1	104	112	S63	0	-0.2
1976	LA N	22	41	4	7	2	1	0	2	4-0	0	9	.171	.244	.268	46	-3	0-1	.950	3	119	124	S13,3b7	0	0.1
1977	Chi N	155	624	91	166	31	7	3	40	56-4	4	90	.266	.328	.353	75	-21	24-12	.962	**46**	**125**	108	S154	0	4.2
1978	Chi N	160	619	**104**	172	24	7	3	35	74-5	2	78	.278	.356	.354	88	-7	41-12	.967	15	**113**	103	S160	0	3.1
1979	Chi N	160	636	92	180	26	10	5	52	59-1	2	82	.283	.345	.379	89	-9	24-20	.959	8	103	100	S160	0	1.4
1980	Chi N	157	618	78	160	26	3	3	33	60-2	4	81	.259	.327	.325	77	-17	44-16	.969	10	106	99	S156	0	1.3
1981	Chi N	**106**	403	49	78	8	4	0	13	46-2	0	61	.194	.276	.233	43	-30	21-9	.959	9	101	112	S106	0	-0.8
1982	Phi N	161	536	53	128	21	5	3	59	54-9	2	70	.239	.309	.313	73	-19	14-4	.973	-3	95	94	S154,3b7	0	-0.5
1983	†Phi N	158	497	60	126	15	7	4	45	53-18	0	77	.254	.323	.336	84	-11	11-4	.966	-17	91	71	S158	0	-1.1
1984	Phi N	144	435	40	112	15	3	0	35	43-7	2	76	.257	.325	.306	77	-12	12-5	.951	-18	98	78	S141	0	-1.6
1985	†StL N	59	72	11	16	5	0	0	7	4-0	0	16	.222	.260	.292	55	-4	2-2	1.000	-2	121	128	3b20,S13	0	-0.6
1986	NY A	7	4	1	0	0	0	0	0	1-0	0	1	.000	.200	.000	-40	-1	0-0	.900	-2	53	0	S7	0	-0.2
1987	SF N	9	10	0	2	0	0	0	1	0-0	0	2	.200	.200	.200	7	-1	0-1	.840	1	132	100	S9	0	0.0
1988	Det A	7	17	1	3	0	0	0	0	1-0	0	4	.176	.222	.176	14	-2	0-0	.893	-2	88	100	S7	0	-0.4
Total	15	1371	4602	595	1167	175	48	21	324	466-48	16	664	.254	.323	.326	76	-144	194-88	.963	48	104	95	S1303,3b34	0	4.6

DEJOHN, MARK Mark Stephen; B9.18.1953 Middletown CT; BB/TR/5´11˝/175; [NYN71 23/540]; d4.28; C6

YEAR	TM LG	G	AB	R	H	2B	3B	HR	RBI	BB-IB	HP	SO	AVG	OBP	SLG	AOPS	ABR	SB-CS	FA	FR	RNG	THR	GAMES AT POSITION	DL	BFW
1982	Det A	24	21	1	4	2	0	0	1	4-0	0	4	.190	.320	.286	67	-1	1-0	.978	3	98	140	S20,3b4/2	0	0.3

DEKONING, BILL William Callahan; B12.19.1918 Brooklyn NY; D7.26.1979 Palm Harbor FL; BR/TR/5´11˝/185; d5.27; Col Boston College

YEAR	TM LG	G	AB	R	H	2B	3B	HR	RBI	BB-IB	HP	SO	AVG	OBP	SLG	AOPS	ABR	SB-CS	FA	FR	RNG	THR	GAMES AT POSITION	DL	BFW
1945	NY N	3	1	0	0	0	0	0	0	0	0	1	.000	.000	.000	-99	0	0	1.000	-0	*0*	*0*	C2	0	0.0

DELAHANTY, ED Edward James "Big Ed"; B10.30.1867 Cleveland OH; D7.2.1903 Niagara Falls ON, Can.; BR/TR/6´1˝/170; d5.22; HF1945; b–Frank b–Jim b–Joe b–Tom; OF(1056/250/40)

YEAR	TM LG	G	AB	R	H	2B	3B	HR	RBI	BB-IB	HP	SO	AVG	OBP	SLG	AOPS	ABR	SB-CS	FA	FR	RNG	THR	GAMES AT POSITION	DL	BFW
1888	Phi N	74	290	40	66	12	2	1	31	12	1	26	.228	.261	.293	72	-9	38	.872	-9	94	101	2b56,O17(10/1/6)	—	-1.7
1889	Phi N	56	246	37	72	13	3	0	27	14	1	17	.293	.333	.370	88	-5	19	.956	-8	80	0	O31(30/0/1),2b24/S	—	-1.1
1890	Cle P	115	517	107	153	26	13	3	64	24	8	30	.296	.337	.414	109	5	25	.830	-6	99	98	S76,2b20,O18(4/11/3),3b3/1	—	0.1
1891	Phi N	128	543	92	132	19	9	5	86	33	8	50	.243	.296	.339	83	-14	25	.909	-4	139	108	O99(2/95/2),1b27,2b3	—	-2.2
1892	Phi N	123	477	79	146	30	**21**	6	91	31	9	32	.306	.360	**.495**	158	30	29	.944	7	126	150	O121(1/120/0),3b4	—	2.7
1893	Phi N	132	595	145	219	35	18	**19**	**146**	47	10	20	.368	.423	**.583**	167	**53**	37	.948	24	149	181	O117(100/17/0),2b15,1b6	—	**5.4**
1894	Phi N	116	495	148	200	39	19	4	133	60	7	16	.404	.475	.584	158	50	21	.927	12	147	106	O90(84/0/6),1b12,3b9,S8,2b6	—	4.2
1895	Phi N	116	480	149	194	**49**	10	11	106	86	6	31	.404	**.500**	.617	**186**	**69**	46	.944	-2	100	105	O103(98/5/0),S9,2b6/3	—	4.6
1896	Phi N	123	499	131	198	**44**	17	**13**	**126**	62	9	22	.397	.472	**.631**	**192**	**68**	37	.952	13	127	103	O99L,1b22/2	—	6.0
1897	Phi N	129	530	109	200	40	15	5	96	60	3	—	.377	.444	.538	163	50	26	.970	9	125	56	O129(128/0/1)/1	—	4.0
1898	Phi N	144	548	115	183	36	9	4	92	77	11	—	.334	.426	.454	159	**48**	**58**	.964	7	100	103	O144L	—	3.9
1899	Phi N	146	581	135	**238**	**55**	9	9	**137**	55	4	—	**.410**	.464	**.582**	**193**	**76**	30	.968	-2	97	72	O143L	—	5.6
1900	Phi N	131	539	82	174	32	10	2	109	41	7	—	.323	.378	.430	124	18	16	.981	-4	88	109	1b130	—	1.3
1901	Phi N	139	542	106	192	**38**	16	8	108	65	4	—	.354	.427	.528	173	52	29	.949	-3	85	83	O84(82/1/1),1b58	—	4.1
1902	Was A	123	473	103	178	**43**	14	10	93	62	4	—	**.376**	**.453**	**.590**	**186**	**58**	16	.961	2	76	0	O111L,1b13	—	5.0
1903	Was A	42	156	22	52	11	1	1	21	12	2	—	.333	.388	.436	144	9	3	.962	2	139	86	O40(20/0/20)/1	—	0.9
Total	16	1837	7511	1600	2597	522	186	101	1466	741	94	244	.346	.411	.505	152	558	455	.951	37	115	96	O1346L,1b271,2b131,S94,3b17	—	42.8

DELAHANTY, FRANK Frank George "Pudgie"; B12.29.1882 Cleveland OH; D7.22.1966 Cleveland OH; BR/TR/5´9˝/160; d8.23; b–Ed b–Jim b–Joe b–Tom

YEAR	TM LG	G	AB	R	H	2B	3B	HR	RBI	BB-IB	HP	SO	AVG	OBP	SLG	AOPS	ABR	SB-CS	FA	FR	RNG	THR	GAMES AT POSITION	DL	BFW
1905	NY A	9	27	0	6	1	0	0	2	1	0	—	.222	.250	.259	55	-1	0	.932	-1	68	0	1b5,O3L	—	-0.3
1906	NY A	92	307	37	73	11	8	2	41	16	3	—	.238	.282	.345	87	-6	11	.954	3	62	42	O86L	—	-0.9
1907	Cle A	15	52	3	9	0	1	0	4	4	0	—	.173	.232	.212	41	-4	2	.917	0	166	0	O15(9/0/6)	—	-0.5
1908	NY A	37	125	12	32	1	2	0	10	10	1	—	.256	.316	.296	98	0	9	.957	-0	49	0	O36L	—	-0.3
1914	Buf F	79	274	29	55	4	7	2	27	23	1	19	.201	.265	.288	50	-25	21	.976	-4	91	73	O78L	—	-3.4
	Pit F	41	159	25	38	4	4	1	7	11	2	11	.239	.297	.333	72	-9	7	.984	-2	102	90	O36(13/1/23),2b4	—	-1.3
	Year	120	433	54	93	8	11	3	34	34	3	30	.215	.277	.305	58	-35	28	**.979**	-5	94	78	O114(91/1/23),2b4	—	-4.7
1915	Pit F	14	42	3	10	1	0	0	3	1	0	0	.238	.256	.262	46	-4	0	1.000	1	108	154	O11L	—	-0.3
Total	6	287	986	109	223	22	22	5	94	66	7	30	.226	.280	.308	70	-49	50	.964	-3	81	53	O265(236/1/29),1b5,2b4	—	-7.0

DELAHANTY, JIM James Christopher; B6.20.1879 Cleveland OH; D10.17.1953 Cleveland OH; BR/TR/5´10.5˝/170; d4.19; b–Ed b–Frank b–Joe b–Tom; OF(176/1/12)

YEAR	TM LG	G	AB	R	H	2B	3B	HR	RBI	BB-IB	HP	SO	AVG	OBP	SLG	AOPS	ABR	SB-CS	FA	FR	RNG	THR	GAMES AT POSITION	DL	BFW
1901	Chi N	17	63	4	12	2	0	0	4	3	1	—	.190	.239	.222	35	-5	5	.877	-2	88	108	3b17/2	—	-0.6
1902	NY N	7	26	3	6	1	0	0	3	1	0	—	.231	.259	.269	64	-1	0	.917	-1	0	0	O7R	—	-0.2
1904	Bos N	142	499	56	142	27	8	3	60	27	9	—	.285	.333	.389	127	15	16	.888	2	102	88	3b113,2b18,O9(8/1/0)/P	—	2.0
1905	Bos N	125	461	50	119	11	8	5	55	28	10	—	.258	.315	.349	100	-1	12	.962	-7	98	24	O124(123/0/1)/P	—	-1.6
1906	Cin N	115	379	63	106	21	4	1	39	45	10	—	.280	.371	.364	124	13	21	.903	-15	85	34	3b105,S5,O2L	—	0.1
1907	StL A	33	95	8	21	3	0	0	6	5	2	—	.221	.275	.253	68	-3	6	.889	-2	86	50	3b21,O4R,2b2	—	-0.5
	Was A	108	404	44	118	18	7	2	54	36	12	—	.292	.367	.386	152	25	18	.941	-10	88	75	2b68,3b27,O9L,1b4	—	1.8
	Year	141	499	52	139	21	7	2	60	41	14	—	.279	.350	.361	135	21	24	.942	-11	89	74	2b70,3b48,O13(10/0/4),1b4	—	1.3
1908	Was A	83	287	33	91	11	4	1	30	24	3	—	.317	.376	.394	164	20	16	.963	-0	96	103	2b80	—	2.4
1909	Was A	90	302	18	67	13	5	1	21	23	6	—	.222	.290	.308	93	-2	4	.956	-1	94	89	2b85	—	-0.3
	†Det A	46	150	29	38	10	1	0	20	17	9	—	.253	.364	.333	115	4	9	.943	-5	101	88	2b46	—	0.0
	Year	136	452	47	105	23	6	1	41	40	15	—	.232	.316	.316	101	2	13	.951	-6	97	89	2b131	—	-0.3
1910	Det A	106	378	67	111	16	2	3	45	43	9	—	.294	.379	.370	126	14	15	.940	-15	91	95	2b106	—	0.0
1911	Det A	144	542	83	184	30	14	3	94	56	10	—	.339	.411	.463	137	28	15	.978	-13	45	48	1b71,2b59,3b13	—	1.5
1912	Det A	79	266	34	76	14	1	0	41	42	7	—	.286	.397	.346	117	9	9	.930	-3	107	130	2b44,O33L	—	0.6
1914	Bro F	74	214	28	62	13	5	0	15	25	3	21	.290	.372	.397	110	1	4	.957	-12	83	76	2b55,1b5	—	-1.1
1915	Bro F	17	25	0	6	1	0	0	2	3	1	3	.240	.345	.280	77	-1	1	.857	-1	102	0	2b4	—	-0.2
Total	13	1186	4091	520	1159	191	59	19	489	378	92	24	.283	.357	.373	122	116	151	.946	-83	95	89	2b568,3b296,O188L,1b80,S5,P2	—	3.9

DELAHANTY, JOE Joseph Nicholas; B10.18.1875 Cleveland OH; D1.29.1936 Cleveland OH; BR/TR/5´9˝/168; d9.30; b–Ed b–Frank b–Jim b–Tom

YEAR	TM LG	G	AB	R	H	2B	3B	HR	RBI	BB-IB	HP	SO	AVG	OBP	SLG	AOPS	ABR	SB-CS	FA	FR	RNG	THR	GAMES AT POSITION	DL	BFW
1907	StL N	7	22	3	7	0	0	1	2	0	0	—	.318	.318	.455	147	1	3	.933	-0	0	0	O7L	—	0.0
1908	StL N	140	499	37	127	14	11	1	44	32	7	—	.255	.309	.333	110	4	11	.977	-3	64	23	O138L	—	-0.8
1909	StL N	123	411	28	88	16	4	2	54	42	3	—	.214	.292	.287	85	-7	10	.985	-11	90	90	O63(14/45/7),2b48	—	-2.4
Total	3	270	932	68	222	30	15	4	100	74	10	—	.238	.301	.315	100	-2	24	.978	-15	70	43	O208(159/45/7),2b48	—	-3.2

DELAHANTY, TOM Thomas James; B3.9.1872 Cleveland OH; D1.10.1951 Sanford FL; BL/TR/5´8˝/175; d9.29; b–Ed b–Frank b–Jim b–Joe

YEAR	TM LG	G	AB	R	H	2B	3B	HR	RBI	BB-IB	HP	SO	AVG	OBP	SLG	AOPS	ABR	SB-CS	FA	FR	RNG	THR	GAMES AT POSITION	DL	BFW
1894	Phi N	1	4	0	1	0	0	0	0	0	0	1	.250	.250	.250	21	-1	0	.875	-1	55	0	/2	—	-0.1
1896	Cle N	16	56	11	13	4	0	0	4	8	1	4	.232	.338	.304	66	-2	4	.823	-3	96	44	3b16	—	-0.4
	Pit N	1	3	1	1	0	0	0	0	0	0	0	.333	.333	.333	79	0	0	.750	-0	73	295	/S	—	0.0
	Year	17	59	12	14	4	0	0	4	8	1	4	.237	.338	.305	67	-3	4	.823	-3	96	44	3b16/S	—	-0.4
1897	Lou N	1	4	1	1	1	0	0	2	0	0	—	.250	.250	.500	99	0	0	.333	-1	0	0	/2	—	-0.1
Total	3	19	67	13	16	5	0	0	6	8	1	5	.239	.329	.313	66	-3	4	.823	-5	96	44	3b16,2b2/S	—	-0.6

DE LA HOZ, MIKE Miguel Angel (Piloto); B10.2.1938 Havana, Cuba; BR/TR/5´11˝/(170–175); d7.22

YEAR	TM LG	G	AB	R	H	2B	3B	HR	RBI	BB-IB	HP	SO	AVG	OBP	SLG	AOPS	ABR	SB-CS	FA	FR	RNG	THR	GAMES AT POSITION	DL	BFW
1960	Cle A	49	160	20	41	6	2	6	23	9-0	1	12	.256	.290	.431	98	-1	0-0	.950	-12	85	55	S38,3b8	0	-1.1
1961	Cle A	61	173	20	45	10	0	3	23	7-0	2	10	.260	.295	.370	79	-6	0-0	.969	0	105	22	2b17,S17,3b16	0	-0.3
1962	Cle A	12	12	0	1	0	0	0	0	0-0	0	3	.083	.083	.083	-57	-3	0-0	1.000	-0	123	0	2b2	0	-0.3
1963	Cle A	67	150	15	40	10	0	5	25	9-0	1	29	.267	.313	.433	107	1	0-0	.962	7	116	121	2b34,3b6,S2,O2L	0	1.1
1964	Mil N	78	189	25	55	7	1	4	12	14-4	2	22	.291	.346	.402	109	2	1-1	.968	2	113	80	2b25,3b25,S8	0	0.6
1965	Mil N	81	176	15	45	3	2	2	11	8-1	2	21	.256	.293	.330	75	-6	0-1	.963	-0	91	111	S41,3b22,2b10/1	0	-0.5
1966	Atl N	71	110	11	24	3	0	2	7	5-1	0	18	.218	.250	.300	52	-7	0-1	.950	-5	88	78	3b30,2b8/S	0	-1.3
1967	Atl N	74	143	10	29	3	0	3	14	4-3	0	14	.203	.224	.287	46	-11	1-0	1.000	-4	72	112	2b23,3b22/S	0	-1.4
1969	Cin N	1	1	0	0	0	0	0	0	0-0	0	1	.000	.000	.000	-95	0	0-0	ø	0	—	—	/H	0	0.0
Total	9	494	1114	116	280	42	5	25	115	56-9	8	130	.251	.290	.365	82	-31	2-3	.936	-12	97	98	3b129,2b119,S108,O2L/1	0	-3.2

DELANCEY, BILL William Pinkney; B11.28.1911 Greensboro NC; D11.28.1946 Phoenix AZ; BL/TR/5´11.5˝/185; d9.11

YEAR	TM LG	G	AB	R	H	2B	3B	HR	RBI	BB-IB	HP	SO	AVG	OBP	SLG	AOPS	ABR	SB-CS	FA	FR	RNG	THR	GAMES AT POSITION	DL	BFW
1932	StL N	8	26	1	5	0	2	0	2	2	0	1	.192	.250	.346	57	-2	0	.930	0	*76*	*217*	C8	—	-0.1
1934	†StL N	93	253	41	80	18	3	13	40	41	1	37	.316	.414	.565	150	19	1	.980	3	*105*	*92*	C77	—	2.6
1935	StL N	103	301	37	84	14	5	6	41	42	1	34	.279	.369	.419	107	4	0	.971	-2	*110*	*31*	C83	—	0.7
1940	StL N	15	18	0	4	0	0	0	2	0	0	2	.222	.222	.222	22	-2	0	.929	0	*82*	*75*	C12	—	-0.2
Total	4	219	598	79	173	32	10	19	85	85	2	74	.289	.380	.472	121	19	1	.972	2	*106*	*67*	C180	—	3.0

DELANEY, BILL William L.; B3.4.1863 Cincinnati OH; D3.1.1942 Canton OH; BR/TR/5´10˝/170; d8.21

YEAR	TM LG	G	AB	R	H	2B	3B	HR	RBI	BB-IB	HP	SO	AVG	OBP	SLG	AOPS	ABR	SB-CS	FA	FR	RNG	THR	GAMES AT POSITION	DL	BFW
1890	Cle N	36	116	16	22	1	1	1	7	21	0	19	.190	.314	.241	64	-5	5	.926	-6	88	125	2b36	—	-0.8

DE LA ROSA, JESUS Jesus (b Jesus De Los Santos (De La Rosa)); B8.5.1953 Santo Domingo, D.R.; BR/TR/6´1˝/153; d8.2

YEAR	TM LG	G	AB	R	H	2B	3B	HR	RBI	BB-IB	HP	SO	AVG	OBP	SLG	AOPS	ABR	SB-CS	FA	FR	RNG	THR	GAMES AT POSITION	DL	BFW
1975	Hou N	3	3	1	1	1	0	0	0	0-0	0	0	.333	.333	.667	186	0	0-0	ø	0	—	—	/H	0	0.0

DE LA ROSA, TOMAS Tomas Agramonte; B1.28.1978 LaVictoria, D.R.; BR/TR/5´10˝/(165–180); d7.17

YEAR	TM LG	G	AB	R	H	2B	3B	HR	RBI	BB-IB	HP	SO	AVG	OBP	SLG	AOPS	ABR	SB-CS	FA	FR	RNG	THR	GAMES AT POSITION	DL	BFW
2000	Mon N	32	66	7	19	3	1	2	9	7-0	1	11	.288	.365	.455	105	0	2-1	.980	2	107	55	S29	0	0.4
2001	Mon N	1	1	0	0	0	0	0	0	0-0	0	0	.000	.000	.000	-99	0	0-0	ø	0	—	—	/H	0	0.0
2006	SF N	16	16	1	5	0	0	0	1	1-0	0	3	.313	.353	.313	72	-1	0-0	.933	-2	65	0	S8,2b2,3b2	0	-0.2
Total	3	49	83	8	24	3	1	2	10	8-0	1	14	.289	.359	.422	96	-1	2-1	.974	0	100	46	S37,3b2,2b2	0	0.2

DELGADO, ALEX Alexander; B1.11.1971 Palmerejo, Zulia, Venez.; BR/TR/6´0˝/160; d4.4

YEAR	TM LG	G	AB	R	H	2B	3B	HR	RBI	BB-IB	HP	SO	AVG	OBP	SLG	AOPS	ABR	SB-CS	FA	FR	RNG	THR	GAMES AT POSITION	DL	BFW
1996	Bos A	26	20	5	5	0	0	0	1	3-0	0	3	.250	.348	.250	54	-1	0-0	.889	-0	51	0	C14,O6(5/0/2),3b4/12	0	-0.2

YEAR	TM LG	G	AB	R	H	2B	3B	HR	RBI	BB-IB	HP	SO	AVG	OBP	SLG	AOPS	ABR	SB-CS	FA	FR	RNG	THR	GAMES AT POSITION	DL	BFW
Delgado, Carlos	Carlos Juan (Hernandez); B6.25.1972 Aguadilla, PR; BL/TR/6´3˝/(215–240); d10.1																								
1993	Tor A	2	1	0	0	0	0	0	0	1-0	0	0	.000	.500	.000	46	0	0-0	1.000	0	0	0	/CD	0	0.0
1994	Tor A	43	130	17	28	2	0	9	24	25-4	3	46	.215	.352	.438	102	0	1-1	.966	-4	75	79	O41L/C	0	-0.5
1995	Tor A	37	91	7	15	3	0	3	11	6-0	0	26	.165	.212	.297	32	-10	0-0	1.000	1	113	101	O17L,1b4,D7	0	-0.9
1996	Tor A	138	488	68	132	28	2	25	92	58-2	9	139	.270	.353	.490	112	9	0-0	.983	-3	71	95	D108,1b27	0	-0.1
1997	Tor A	153	519	79	136	42	3	30	91	64-9	8	133	.262	.350	.528	125	19	0-3	.988	-6	80	105	1b119,D32	0	0.0
1998	Tor A	142	530	94	155	43	1	38	115	73-13	11	139	.292	.385	.592	150	41	3-0	.992	-6	83	95	1b141/D	24	2.1
1999	Tor A	152	573	113	156	39	0	44	134	86-7	15	141	.272	.377	.571	136	33	1-1	.990	-2	96	100	1b147,D5	0	1.6
2000	Tor A★	**162**	569	115	196	**57**	1	41	137	123-18	**15**	104	.344	.470	.664	178	**77**	0-1	.991	-10	78	105	1b162	0	4.7
2001	Tor A	**162**	574	102	160	31	1	39	102	111-22	16	136	.279	.408	.540	144	42	3-0	.994	-5	90	121	1b161	0	2.2
2002	Tor A	143	505	103	140	34	2	33	108	102-18	13	126	.277	.406	.549	147	39	1-0	.991	-1	99	99	1b140,D3	16	2.5
2003	Tor A★	161	570	117	172	38	1	42	**145**	109-23	19	137	.302	.426	.593	**160**	**56**	0-0	.993	1	102	109	1b147,D14	0	4.1
2004	Tor A	128	458	74	123	26	0	32	99	69-12	13	115	.269	.372	.535	127	20	0-1	.996	4	110	95	1b120,D8	37	1.2
2005	Fla N	144	521	81	157	41	3	33	115	72-20	17	121	.301	.399	.582	162	50	0-0	.989	-1	99	108	1b141/D	16	3.6
2006	†NY N	144	524	89	139	30	2	38	114	74-11	10	120	.265	.361	.548	133	26	0-0	.994	-6	82	85	1b141/D	0	0.8
Total	14	1711	6053	1059	1709	414	16	407	1287	973-159	149	1483	.282	.390	.558	141	402	9-7	.992	-37	91	103	1b1450,D181,O58L,C2	93	21.3
Delgado, Puchy	Luis Felipe (Robles); B2.2.1954 Hatillo, PR; BB/TL/5´11˝/170; d9.6																								
1977	Sea A	13	22	4	4	0	0	0	2	1-0	0	8	.182	.217	.182	10	-3	0-0	1.000	1	105	219	O13(1/2/10)	0	-0.2
Delgado, Wilson	Wilson (Duran); B7.15.1972 San Cristobal, D.R.; BB/TR/5´11˝/(155–165); d9.24																								
1996	SF N	6	22	3	8	0	0	0	2	1-0	2	5	.364	.440	.364	118	1	1-0	.960	-2	68	79	S6	0	-0.1
1997	SF N	8	7	1	1	1	0	0	0	0-0	0	2	.143	.143	.286	9	-1	0-0	1.000	-1	96	137	2b3/S	0	-0.1
1998	SF N	10	12	1	2	1	0	0	1	1-0	0	3	.167	.231	.250	28	-1	0-0	1.000	0	105	174	S6	0	-0.1
1999	SF N	35	71	7	18	2	1	0	3	5-0	1	9	.254	.312	.310	62	-4	1-0	.932	-4	102	142	S20,2b15	0	-0.7
2000	NY A	31	45	6	11	1	0	1	4	5-0	0	9	.244	.314	.333	67	-2	1-0	.950	-3	91	53	2b14,S11,3b5	0	-0.4
	KC A	33	83	15	22	1	0	0	7	6-0	0	17	.265	.311	.277	49	-7	1-1	1.000	12	151	138	2b19,S12,3b3	0	0.6
	Year	64	128	21	33	2	0	1	11	11-0	0	26	.258	.312	.297	55	-9	2-1	.986	9	130	108	2b33,S23,3b8	0	0.2
2001	KC A	14	25	1	3	0	0	0	1	3-0	0	10	.120	.214	.120	-8	-4	0-0	1.000	1	134	113	S6,3b3,2b2	0	-0.3
2002	StL N	12	20	2	4	2	0	2	5	0-0	0	6	.200	.200	.600	100	0	0-0	1.000	-3	63	32	S8	0	-0.2
2003	StL N	43	77	8	13	3	0	0	3	3-0	1	10	.169	.207	.208	10	-10	0-0	1.000	-3	117	78	2b12,3b11,S11	0	-1.3
	Ana A	19	50	4	16	0	0	0	4	8-0	0	8	.320	.414	.320	101	1	0-0	.867	0	98	212	3b9,S9/2	0	0.1
2004	NY N	42	130	11	38	4	1	2	13	15-3	0	29	.292	.366	.385	97	0	1-0	.957	2	112	113	S39	0	0.5
Total	9	253	542	59	136	15	2	5	43	47-3	4	108	.251	.314	.314	64	-27	5-1	.962	1	102	108	S129,2b66,3b31	0	-2.0
Del Greco, Bobby	Robert George; B4.7.1933 Pittsburgh PA; BR/TR/5´11˝/(175–190); d4.16																								
1952	Pit N	99	341	34	74	14	2	1	20	38	3	70	.217	.301	.279	60	-18	6-5	.977	2	102	119	O93(1/88/4)	0	-2.0
1956	Pit N	14	20	4	4	0	0	2	3	3-0	0	3	.200	.304	.500	114	0	0-0	1.000	0	112	0	O7C,3b3	0	0.0
	StL N	102	270	29	58	16	2	5	18	32-3	6	50	.215	.308	.344	76	-8	1-1	.987	-6	94	46	O99C	0	-1.9
	Year	116	290	33	62	16	2	7	21	35-3	6	53	.214	.307	.355	79	-8	1-1	.987	-6	95	44	O106C,3b3	0	-1.9
1957	Chi N	20	40	2	8	2	0	0	3	10-0	0	17	.200	.360	.250	69	-1	1-0	.967	1	96	260	O16C	0	-0.1
	NY A	8	7	3	3	0	0	0	0	2-0	0	2	.429	.556	.429	175	1	1-0	1.000	-1	65	0	O6C	0	0.0
1958	NY A	12	5	1	1	0	0	0	0	1-0	0	1	.200	.333	.200	52	0	0-1	1.000	-0	94	0	O12(11/1/0)	0	-0.1
1960	Phi N	100	300	48	71	16	4	10	26	54-0	1	64	.237	.355	.417	110	6	1-5	.970	10	119	160	O89(0/87/2)	0	1.1
1961	Phi N	41	112	14	29	5	0	2	11	12-1	3	17	.259	.344	.357	88	-1	0-0	1.000	0	112	46	O32(1/31/0)/23	0	-0.2
	KC A	74	239	34	55	14	1	5	21	30-2	1	31	.230	.317	.360	79	-7	1-0	.983	3	102	224	O73C	0	-0.5
1962	KC A	132	338	61	86	21	1	9	38	49-0	**13**	62	.254	.370	.402	103	4	4-1	.984	9	116	**190**	O124(33/95/4)	0	1.0
1963	KC A	121	306	40	65	7	1	8	29	40-1	5	52	.212	.311	.320	74	-10	1-2	.981	-1	105	87	O110(24/85/6),3b2	0	-1.5
1965	Phi N	8	4	1	0	0	0	0	0	0-0	0	3	.000	.000	.000	-99	-1	0-0	ø	-0	0	0	O4L	0	-0.2
Total	9	731	1982	271	454	95	11	42	169	271-7	32	372	.229	.330	.352	84	-35	16-15	.981	17	106	130	O665(74/588/16),3b6/2	0	-4.4
Delis, Juan	Juan Francisco; B2.27.1928 Santiago de Cuba, Cuba; D7.23.2003 Havana, Cuba; BR/TR/5´11˝/170; d4.16																								
1955	Was A	54	132	12	25	3	1	0	11	3-0	2	15	.189	.219	.227	21	-15	1-2	.918	-1	112	144	3b24,O8(2/0/6)/2	0	-1.7
Delker, Eddie	Edward Alberts; B4.17.1906 Palo Alto PA; D5.14.1997 Pottsville PA; BR/TR/5´10.5˝/170; d4.28																								
1929	StL N	22	40	5	6	0	1	0	3	2	2	12	.150	.227	.200	7	-6	0	.750	-3	68	0	S9,2b7,3b3	—	-0.8
1931	StL N	1	2	0	1	1	0	0	2	0	0	0	.500	.500	1.000	283	1	0	1.000	-0	0	0	/3	—	0.0
1932	StL N	20	42	1	5	4	0	0	2	8	0	7	.119	.260	.214	28	-4	0	1.000	3	111	155	2b10,3b5,S4	—	-0.1
	Phi N	30	62	7	10	1	1	1	7	6	0	14	.161	.235	.258	29	-6	0	.925	-4	89	52	2b27	—	-1.0
	Year	50	104	8	15	5	1	1	9	14	0	21	.144	.246	.240	29	-10	0	.946	-2	95	78	2b37,3b5,S4	—	-1.1
1933	Phi N	25	41	6	7	3	1	0	1	0	0	12	.171	.171	.293	27	-4	0	.968	3	121	64	2b17,3b4	—	0.0
Total	4	98	187	19	29	9	3	1	15	16	2	45	.155	.229	.251	26	-19	0	.952	-2	100	76	2b61,3b13,S13	—	-1.9
Dellaero, Jason	Jason Christopher; B12.17.1976 Mount Kisco NY; BB/TR/6´2˝/195; [ChiA97 1/15]; d9.7; Col South Florida																								
1999	Chi A	11	33	1	3	0	0	0	2	1-0	0	13	.091	.114	.091	-45	-7	0-0	.917	-2	96	71	S11	0	-0.8
Dellucci, David	David Michael; B10.31.1973 Baton Rouge LA; BL/TL/5´10˝/(180–198); [BalA95 10/276]; d6.3; Col U. of Mississippi																								
1997	Bal A	17	27	3	6	1	0	1	3	4-1	1	7	.222	.344	.370	89	0	0-0	1.000	2	168	281	O9(3/0/6),D5	0	0.1
1998	Ari N	124	416	43	108	19	**12**	5	51	33-2	3	103	.260	.318	.399	87	-9	3-5	.987	2	109	42	O117(95/19/15)	0	-1.2
1999	Ari N	63	109	27	43	7	1	1	15	11-0	3	24	.394	.463	.505	144	8	2-0	1.000	-1	93	81	O31(13/4/19)/D	71	0.7
2000	Ari N	34	50	2	15	3	0	0	2	4-0	0	9	.300	.352	.360	78	-2	0-2	1.000	0	107	0	O12(1/0/11)	0	-0.2
2001	†Ari N	115	217	28	60	10	2	10	40	22-4	2	52	.276	.349	.479	104	1	2-1	.989	-2	100	0	O58(8/18/35)	0	-0.2
2002	†Ari N	97	229	34	56	11	2	7	29	28-5	1	55	.245	.326	.402	83	-6	2-4	.967	-4	86	60	O64(20/2/45),D3	22	-1.2
2003	Ari N	70	165	18	40	11	3	2	19	19-1	3	45	.242	.328	.382	79	-5	9-0	.976	-1	103	40	O53(4/9/43)	15	-0.6
	†NY A	21	51	8	9	1	0	1	4	4-0	2	13	.176	.263	.255	38	-5	3-0	1.000	1	103	117	O18(2/1/16),D2	30	-0.4
2004	Tex A	107	331	59	80	13	1	17	61	47-3	5	88	.242	.342	.441	99	0	9-4	.989	-2	104	0	O94(84/7/6),D9	0	-0.5
2005	Tex A	128	435	97	109	17	5	29	65	76-0	5	121	.251	.367	.513	128	18	5-3	.970	-0	94	150	D67,O52(47/3/3)	0	1.2
2006	Phi N	132	264	41	77	14	5	13	39	28-0	6	62	.292	.369	.530	122	8	1-3	.990	-3	92	36	O67(45/0/31),D2	0	0.3
Total	10	908	2294	360	603	107	31	86	328	276-16	31	579	.263	.348	.449	103	8	36-22	.985	-8	101	49	O575(322/63/230),D89	138	-2.0
Delmas, Bert	Albert Charles; B5.20.1911 San Francisco CA; D12.4.1979 Huntington Beach CA; BL/TR/5´11˝/165; d9.10; Col Stanford																								
1933	Bro N	12	28	4	7	0	0	0	0	1	0	7	.250	.276	.250	53	-2	0	.912	-3	82	75	2b10	—	-0.4
de los Santos, Luis	Luis Manuel (Martinez); B12.29.1966 San Cristobal, D.R.; BR/TR/6´5˝/(190–225); [KCA84 2/44]; d9.7																								
1988	KC A	11	22	1	2	1	1	0	1	4-0	0	4	.091	.231	.227	28	-2	0-0	1.000	-0	50	125	1b5,D3	0	-0.3
1989	KC A	28	87	6	22	3	1	0	6	5-0	0	14	.253	.293	.310	70	-4	0-0	.986	-0	97	121	1b27	0	-0.6
1991	Det A	16	30	1	5	2	0	0	0	2-0	0	4	.167	.219	.233	25	-3	0-0	1.000	-1	155	0	O3L,1b2,3b2,D9	0	-0.4
Total	3	55	139	8	29	6	2	0	7	11-0	0	22	.209	.267	.281	53	-9	0-0	.988	-1	91	121	1b34,D12,O3L,3b2	0	-1.3
Del Savio, Garton	Garton Orville; B11.26.1913 New York NY; D11.9.2006 Blauvelt NY; BR/TR/5´9.5˝/165; d4.24																								
1943	Phi N	4	11	0	1	0	0	0	0	1	0	0	.091	.167	.091	-26	-2	0	.857	-1	98	44	S4	0	-0.3
Delsing, Jim	James Henry; B11.13.1925 Rudolph WI; D5.4.2006 Chesterfield MO; BL/TR/5´10˝/175; d4.21																								
1948	Chi A	20	63	5	12	0	0	0	5	5	1	12	.190	.261	.190	22	-7	0-0	1.000	-1	93	90	O15C	0	-0.8
1949	NY A	9	20	5	7	1	0	1	3	1	0	2	.350	.381	.550	145	1	0-0	1.000	-1	71	0	O5C	0	0.0
1950	NY A	12	10	2	4	0	0	0	2	2	0	0	.400	.500	.400	137	1	0-0	ø	0	—	—	/H	0	0.1
	StL A	69	209	25	55	5	2	0	15	20	0	23	.263	.328	.306	61	-12	1-4	.994	2	106	91	O53C	0	-1.2
	Year	81	219	27	59	5	2	0	17	22	0	23	.269	.336	.311	65	-12	1-4	.994	2	106	91	O53C	0	-1.1
1951	StL A	131	449	59	112	20	2	8	45	56	4	39	.249	.338	.356	85	-9	2-9	.983	8	108	128	O124(4/118/4)	0	-0.7
1952	StL A	93	298	34	76	13	6	1	34	25	5	29	.255	.323	.349	85	-7	3-3	.986	3	109	71	O85(34/44/10)	0	-0.8
	Det A	33	113	14	31	2	1	3	15	11	1	8	.274	.344	.389	103	0	1-0	.958	-0	104	52	O32L	0	-0.2
	Year	126	411	48	107	15	7	4	49	36	6	37	.260	.329	.360	90	-6	4-3	.979	2	108	65	O117(66/44/10)	0	-1.0
1953	Det A	138	479	77	138	26	6	11	62	66	5	39	.288	.380	.436	121	16	1-3	.992	-6	96	60	O133C	0	0.3
1954	Det A	122	371	39	92	24	2	6	38	49	1	38	.248	.336	.372	96	-1	4-4	**.996**	3	107	75	O108(90/5/16)	0	-0.5
1955	Det A	114	356	49	85	15	2	10	60	48-2	1	40	.239	.328	.376	92	-4	2-0	.995	-6	91	39	O101(98/3/0)	0	-1.5

YEAR	TM LG	G	AB	R	H	2B	3B	HR	RBI	BB-IB	HP	SO	AVG	OBP	SLG	AOPS	ABR	SB-CS	FA	FR	RNG	THR	GAMES AT POSITION	DL	BFW
1956	Det A	10	12	0	0	0	0	0	0	3-0	1	3	.000	.250	.000	-29	-2	0-0	1.000	-0	88	0	O3L	0	-0.2
	Chi A	55	41	11	5	3	0	0	2	10-0	0	13	.122	.294	.195	31	-4	1-0	.957	1	119	164	O29(13/7/9)	0	-0.3
	Year	65	53	11	5	3	0	0	2	13-0	1	16	.094	.284	.151	17	-6	1-0	.962	1	114	135	O32(16/7/9)	0	-0.5
1960	KC A	16	40	2	10	3	0	0	5	3-0	0	5	.250	.302	.325	69	-2	0-0	1.000	1	120	0	O10L	0	-0.2
Total	10	822	2461	322	627	112	21	40	286	299-2	19	251	.255	.339	.366	91	-30	15-23	.989	3	102	76	O698(284/383/39)	0	-6.0
DeMaestri, Joe	Joseph Paul "Oats"; B12.9.1928 San Francisco CA; BR/TR/6´0˝/(174–180); d4.19																								
1951	Chi A	56	74	8	15	0	2	1	3	5	0	11	.203	.253	.297	49	-6	0-4	.959	2	121	141	S27,2b11,3b8	0	-0.4
1952	StL A	81	186	13	42	9	1	1	18	8	0	25	.226	.258	.301	54	-12	0-1	.939	-5	98	81	S77/23	0	-1.5
1953	Phi A	111	420	53	107	17	3	6	35	24	1	39	.255	.297	.352	72	-18	0-1	.964	-17	92	74	S108	0	-2.7
1954	Phi A	146	539	49	124	16	3	8	40	20	3	63	.230	.258	.315	57	-34	1-4	.965	-6	96	85	S142/23	0	-3.1
1955	KC A	123	457	42	114	14	1	6	37	20-1	3	47	.249	.284	.324	63	-26	3-5	.964	-12	97	93	S122	0	-2.9
1956	KC A	133	434	41	101	16	1	6	39	25-2	3	73	.233	.277	.316	57	-29	3-3	.964	9	**109**	110	S132,2b2	0	-1.0
1957	KC A☆	135	461	44	113	14	6	9	33	22-1	2	82	.245	.280	.360	73	-19	6-1	**.980**	-5	95	97	S134	0	-1.3
1958	KC A	139	442	32	97	11	1	6	38	16-1	1	84	.219	.247	.290	47	-33	1-0	**.980**	8	107	111	S137	0	-1.5
1959	KC A	118	352	31	86	16	5	6	34	28-8	4	65	.244	.305	.369	83	-9	1-0	.957	-2	**101**	92	S115	0	-0.1
1960	†NY A	49	35	8	8	1	0	0	2	0-0	0	9	.229	.229	.257	33	-3	0-0	.952	-1	74	107	2b19,S17	0	-0.3
1961	NY A	30	41	1	6	0	0	0	2	0-0	0	13	.146	.146	.146	-23	-7	0-0	.981	2	109	135	S18,2b5,3b4	0	-0.4
Total	11	1121	3441	322	813	114	23	49	281	168-13	17	511	.236	.274	.325	62	-196	15-19	.967	-26	100	95	S1029,2b39,3b14	0	-15.2
Demaree, Frank	Joseph Franklin; B6.10.1910 Winters CA; D8.30.1958 Los Angeles CA; BR/TR/5´11.5˝/185; d7.22; Col St. Marys (CA)																								
1932	†Chi N	23	56	4	14	3	0	0	6	2	1	7	.250	.288	.304	60	-3	0	1.000	1	92	173	O17(4/9/4)	—	-0.3
1933	Chi N	134	515	68	140	24	6	6	51	22	2	42	.272	.304	.377	94	-6	4	.965	-4	94	130	O133(10/123/0)	—	-1.4
1935	†Chi N	107	385	60	125	19	4	2	66	26	1	23	.325	.369	.410	108	5	6	.973	-2	88	157	O98(0/69/29)	—	0.0
1936	Chi N★	**154**	605	93	212	34	3	16	96	49	1	30	.350	.400	.496	137	32	4	.968	-2	97	107	O154(36/0/118)	—	2.0
1937	Chi N★	**154**	615	104	199	36	6	17	115	57	1	31	.324	.382	.485	129	25	6	.980	-0	97	107	O154R	—	1.5
1938	†Chi N	129	476	63	130	15	7	8	62	45	4	34	.273	.341	.384	96	-2	1	.972	-6	85	112	O125(9/0/119)	—	-1.6
1939	NY N	150	560	68	170	27	2	11	79	66	4	40	.304	.381	.418	114	13	2	.986	-8	90	86	O150(1/116/36)	—	0.0
1940	NY N	121	460	68	139	18	6	7	61	45	0	39	.302	.364	.413	113	8	5	.980	-8	89	65	O119(9/74/37)	—	-0.4
1941	NY N	16	35	3	6	0	0	0	1	4	0	1	.171	.256	.171	22	-4	0	1.000	0	98	156	O10(1/8/1)	0	-0.4
	Bos N	48	113	20	26	5	2	2	15	12	0	5	.230	.304	.363	91	-2	2	1.000	-2	88	58	O28(9/7/12)	0	-0.4
	Year	64	148	23	32	5	2	2	16	16	0	6	.216	.293	.318	74	-5	2	1.000	-1	91	85	O38(10/15/13)	0	-0.8
1942	Bos N	64	187	18	42	5	0	3	24	17	0	10	.225	.289	.299	74	-6	2	1.000	3	109	101	O49(27/0/22)	0	-0.8
1943	†StL N	39	86	5	25	2	0	0	9	8	0	4	.291	.351	.314	89	-1	1	1.000	-1	99	58	O23(12/0/12)	0	-0.3
1944	StL A	16	51	4	13	2	0	0	6	6	0	3	.255	.333	.294	76	-1	0-0	.969	-0	101	88	O16(15/0/1)	0	-0.2
Total	12	1155	4144	578	1241	190	36	72	591	359	14	269	.299	.357	.415	110	58	33-0	.978	-29	93	106	O1076(133/406/545)	0	-2.3
DeMars, Billy	William Lester "Kid"; B8.26.1925 Brooklyn NY; BR/TR/5´10˝/160; d5.18; C19																								
1948	Phi A	18	29	3	5	0	0	0	1	5	0	3	.172	.294	.172	26	-3	0-0	.927	2	110	144	S9/23	0	-0.1
1950	StL A	61	178	25	44	5	1	0	13	22	0	13	.247	.330	.287	57	-11	0-1	.933	-9	88	81	S54,3b5	0	-1.7
1951	StL A	1	4	1	1	0	0	0	0	1	0	0	.250	.400	.250	76	0	0-0	1.000	-0	109	93	/S	0	0.0
Total	3	80	211	29	50	5	1	0	14	28	0	16	.237	.326	.270	53	-14	0-1	.933	-8	91	89	S64,3b6/2	0	-1.8
DeMerit, John	John Stephen "Thumper"; B1.8.1936 West Bend WI; BR/TR/6´1.5˝/(180–198); d6.18; Col Wisconsin–Madison																								
1957	†Mil N	33	34	8	5	0	0	0	1	0-0	0	8	.147	.147	.147	-22	-6	1-0	1.000	-0	104	0	O13(2/11/0)	0	-0.7
1958	Mil N	3	3	1	2	0	0	0	0	0-0	0	0	.667	.667	.667	278	1	0-0	1.000	-0	72	0	O2(0/1/1)	0	0.0
1959	Mil N	11	5	4	1	0	0	0	0	1-0	0	2	.200	.333	.200	51	0	0-0	1.000	1	182	0	O4(3/1/0)	0	0.0
1961	Mil N	32	74	5	12	3	0	2	5	5-0	1	19	.162	.225	.284	36	-7	0-0	1.000	0	102	114	O21(2/5/15)	0	-0.8
1962	NY N	14	16	3	3	0	0	1	1	2-0	0	4	.188	.278	.375	72	-1	0-0	1.000	-2	38	0	O9(3/2/4)	0	-0.3
Total	5	93	132	21	23	3	0	3	7	8-0	1	33	.174	.227	.265	32	-13	1-0	1.000	-1	96	61	O49(10/20/20)	0	-1.8
Demeter, Don	Donald Lee; B6.25.1935 Oklahoma City OK; BR/TR/6´4˝/(189–190); d9.18																								
1956	Bro N	3	3	1	1	0	0	1	1	0-0	0	1	.333	.333	1.333	297	1	0-0	1.000	0	114	0	/cf	0	0.1
1958	LA N	43	106	11	20	2	0	5	8	5-0	0	32	.189	.225	.349	48	-9	2-3	1.000	-2	101	0	O39(11/25/4)	0	-1.3
1959	†LA N	139	371	55	95	11	1	18	70	16-1	6	87	.256	.294	.437	86	-9	5-6	.983	-2	101	95	O124C	0	-1.7
1960	LA N	64	168	23	46	7	1	9	29	8-1	1	34	.274	.306	.488	108	1	0-1	.989	-3	89	65	O62(0/61/1)	0	-0.4
1961	LA N	15	29	3	5	0	0	1	2	3-0	0	6	.172	.250	.276	36	-3	0-0	.950	1	126	154	O14(0/3/12)	0	-0.2
	Phi N	106	382	54	98	18	4	20	68	19-2	5	74	.257	.300	.482	105	0	2-1	.995	5	106	148	O79(23/44/17),1b22	0	0.1
	Year	121	411	57	103	18	4	21	70	22-2	5	80	.251	.297	.467	99	-3	2-1	.990	6	108	149	O93(23/47/29),1b22	0	-0.1
1962	Phi N	153	550	85	169	24	3	29	107	41-6	10	93	.307	.359	.520	139	29	2-7	.937	-5	99	100	3b105,O63(23/42/4)/1	0	1.9
1963	Phi N	154	515	63	133	20	2	22	83	31-10	6	93	.258	.306	.433	112	7	1-4	**1.000**	1	98	116	O119(41/80/0),3b43,1b26	0	0.2
1964	Det A	134	441	57	113	22	1	22	80	17-6	5	85	.256	.290	.460	104	0	4-1	1.000	-4	96	58	O88(24/52/13),1b23	0	-0.8
1965	Det A	122	389	50	108	16	4	16	58	23-3	6	65	.278	.325	.463	121	9	4-2	.988	-3	108	29	O82(1/56/25),1b34	0	0.2
1966	Det A	32	99	12	21	5	0	5	12	3-0	0	19	.212	.235	.414	81	-3	1-0	.985	5	136	152	O27(4/20/3),1b4	0	0.2
	Bos A	73	226	31	66	13	1	9	29	5-1	1	42	.292	.305	.478	111	3	1-0	.982	-4	89	93	O57(0/55/3),1b2	0	-0.2
	Year	105	325	43	87	18	1	14	41	8-1	1	61	.268	.284	.458	102	0	2-0	.984	2	103	110	O84(4/75/6),1b6	0	0.0
1967	Bos A	20	43	7	12	5	0	1	4	3-0	0	11	.279	.326	.465	122	1	0-0	1.000	1	97	175	O12(3/1/9)/3	0	0.2
	Cle A	51	121	15	25	4	0	5	12	6-1	2	16	.207	.256	.364	80	-3	0-0	.985	2	109	116	O35(13/28/1)/3	0	-0.3
	Year	71	164	22	37	9	0	6	16	9-1	2	27	.226	.274	.390	92	-2	0-0	.988	2	106	130	O47(16/29/10),3b2	0	-0.1
Total	11	1109	3443	467	912	147	17	163	563	180-31	42	658	.265	.307	.459	108	24	22-25	.990	-8	101	82	O802(143/592/92),3b150,1b112	0	-2.0
Demeter, Steve	Stephen; B1.27.1935 Homer City PA; BR/TR/5´9.5˝/(185–190); d7.29; C1																								
1959	Det A	11	18	1	2	1	0	0	1	0-0	0	1	.111	.111	.167	-24	-3	0-0	.909	1	118	243	3b4	0	-0.2
1960	Cle A	4	5	0	0	0	0	0	0	0-0	0	1	.000	.000	.000	-99	-1	0-0	1.000	0	55	513	3b3	0	-0.1
Total	2	15	23	1	2	1	0	0	1	0-0	0	2	.087	.087	.130	-40	-4	0-0	.933	1	101	317	3b7	0	-0.3
Demmitt, Ray	Charles Raymond; B2.2.1884 Illiopolis IL; D2.19.1956 Glen Ellyn IL; BL/TR/5´8˝/170; d4.12; Col Illinois																								
1909	NY A	123	427	68	105	12	12	4	30	55	6	—	.246	.340	.358	120	11	16	.908	-2	145	193	O109(0/70/39)	—	0.3
1910	StL A	10	23	4	4	1	0	0	2	3	1	—	.174	.296	.217	65	-1	0	1.000	1	108	198	O8R	—	0.0
1914	Det A	1	0	0	0	0	0	0	0	0	0	0	ø	ø	ø	ø	0	0	ø	0	—	—	/R	—	0.0
	Chi A	146	515	63	133	13	12	2	46	61	6	48	.258	.344	.342	108	5	12-20	.953	-6	81	119	O142(127/4/12)	—	-1.3
	Year	147	515	63	133	13	12	2	46	61	6	48	.258	.344	.342	108	5	12-20	.953	-6	81	119	O142(127/4/12)	—	-1.3
1915	Chi A	9	6	0	0	0	0	0	0	1	0	2	.000	.143	.000	-55	-1	0	1.000	0	107	0	O3(1/0/2)	—	-0.1
1917	StL A	14	53	6	15	1	2	0	7	0	1	8	.283	.296	.377	109	0	1	1.000	-2	86	0	O14R	—	-0.2
1918	StL A	116	405	45	114	23	5	1	61	38	2	35	.281	.346	.370	120	10	10	.951	9	104	**164**	O114R	—	1.4
1919	StL A	79	202	19	48	11	2	1	19	14	1	27	.238	.290	.327	71	-8	3	.868	-4	80	103	O49R	—	-1.5
Total	7	498	1631	205	419	61	33	8	165	172	17	120	.257	.334	.349	108	16	42-20	.934	-4	105	147	O439(128/74/238)	—	-1.4
DeMontreville, Gene	Eugene Napoleon; B3.10.1873 St.Paul MN; D2.18.1935 Memphis TN; BR/TR/5´8˝/165; d8.20; b–Lee																								
1894	Pit N	2	8	0	2	0	0	0	0	1	0	4	.250	.333	.250	43	-1	0	.889	-0	116	0	S2	—	-0.1
1895	Was N	12	46	7	10	1	3	0	9	3	0	4	.217	.265	.370	63	-3	5	.929	4	105	138	S12	—	0.1
1896	Was N	**133**	533	94	183	24	5	8	77	29	3	27	.343	.381	.452	119	13	28	.890	19	**110**	88	S133	—	3.3
1897	Was N	**133**	566	92	193	27	8	3	93	21	1	—	.341	.366	.433	111	7	30	.886	10	104	118	S99,2b33	—	1.9
1898	Bal N	151	567	93	186	19	2	0	86	52	10	—	.328	.394	.369	117	15	49	.944	3	101	81	2b123,S28	—	2.3
1899	Chi N	82	310	43	87	6	3	0	40	17	5	—	.281	.328	.319	80	-9	26	.902	7	108	123	S82	—	0.2
	Bal N	60	240	40	67	13	4	1	36	10	2	—	.279	.313	.379	85	-6	21	.961	4	101	70	2b60	—	0.1
	Year	142	550	83	154	19	7	1	76	27	7	—	.280	.322	.345	82	-14	47	.902	11	108	123	S82,2b60	—	0.3
1900	Bro N	69	234	34	57	8	1	0	28	10	3	—	.244	.283	.286	54	-15	21	.952	-1	97	83	2b48,S12,3b7/cf1	—	-1.3
1901	Bos N	**140**	577	83	173	14	4	5	72	17	1	—	.300	.321	.364	90	-9	25	**.954**	1	99	93	2b120,3b20	—	-0.7
1902	Bos N	124	481	51	125	16	5	0	53	12	0	—	.260	.278	.314	82	-12	23	.940	-17	88	59	2b112,S10	—	-3.0
1903	Was A	12	44	0	12	2	0	0	3	0	0	—	.273	.273	.318	75	-1	0	.931	-3	79	24	2b11/S	—	-0.5
1904	StL A	4	9	0	1	0	0	0	0	2	0	—	.111	.273	.111	25	-1	0	1.000	-0	95	0	2b3	—	-0.1
Total	11	922	3615	537	1096	130	35	17	497	174	25	35	.303	.340	.373	97	-22	228	.948	24	97	74	2b510,S379,3b27/1cf	—	2.2
DeMontreville, Lee	Leon; B9.23.1874 Washington Co. MN; D3.22.1962 Pelham Manor NY; BR/TR/5´7˝/140; d7.10; b–Gene																								
1903	StL N	26	70	8	17	3	1	0	7	8	2	—	.243	.338	.314	89	-1	3	.901	-2	104	152	S15,2b4/rf	—	-0.2

YEAR TM LG	G	AB	R	H	2B	3B	HR	RBI	BB-IB	HP	SO	AVG	OBP	SLG	AOPS	ABR	SB-CS	FA	FR	RNG	THR	GAMES AT POSITION	DL	BFW
Dempsey, Rick	John Rikard; B9.13.1949 Fayetteville TN; BR/TR (BB 1982p)/6´0˝/(178–195); [MinA67 12/237]; d9.23; C7																							
1969 Min A	5	6	1	3	1	0	0	0	1-0	0	0	.500	.571	.667	239	1	0-0	.833	-1	63	0	C3	0	0.0
1970 Min A	5	7	1	0	0	0	0	0	1-0	0	1	.000	.125	.000	-62	-2	0-0	.923	-1	40	0	C3	0	-0.2
1971 Min A	6	13	2	4	1	0	0	0	1-0	0	1	.308	.357	.385	107	0	0-0	.944	1	46	170	C6	0	0.1
1972 Min A	25	40	0	8	1	0	0	0	6-0	0	8	.200	.304	.225	56	-2	0-0	.986	-2	118	109	C23	0	-0.4
1973 NY A	6	11	0	2	0	0	0	0	1-0	0	3	.182	.250	.182	24	-1	0-0	.818	-3	65	0	C5	0	-0.4
1974 NY A	43	109	12	26	3	0	2	12	8-0	0	7	.239	.288	.321	77	-3	1-0	.978	6	291	150	C31,O2(1/0/1)/D	0	0.4
1975 NY A	71	145	18	38	8	0	1	11	21-1	0	15	.262	.353	.338	98	1	0-0	.977	2	83	72	C19,D18,O8(1/0/7)/3	0	0.2
1976 NY A	21	42	1	5	0	0	0	2	5-0	0	4	.119	.213	.119	-1	-5	0-0	1.000	3	160	119	C9,O4R	0	-0.3
Bal A	59	174	11	37	2	0	0	10	13-0	2	17	.213	.275	.224	50	-11	1-1	.987	11	197	114	C58,O3(1/0/2)	0	0.2
Year	80	216	12	42	2	0	0	12	18-0	2	21	.194	.263	.204	39	-16	1-1	.988	13	192	115	C67,O7(1/0/6)	0	-0.1
1977 Bal A	91	270	27	61	7	4	3	34	34-1	2	34	.226	.314	.315	77	-8	2-3	.977	7	181	117	C91	43	0.2
1978 Bal A	136	441	41	114	25	0	6	32	48-2	0	54	.259	.327	.356	99	1	7-3	.985	4	138	108	C135	0	1.1
1979 †Bal A	124	368	48	88	23	0	6	41	38-1	0	37	.239	.307	.351	81	-9	0-1	.990	27	159	105	C124	0	2.2
1980 Bal A	119	362	51	95	26	3	9	40	36-1	3	45	.262	.333	.425	108	5	3-1	.987	11	118	**131**	C112,O6(3/0/3),1b2/D	0	2.0
1981 Bal A	92	251	24	54	10	1	6	15	32-1	1	36	.215	.306	.335	85	-4	0-1	**.998**	5	**154**	87	C90/D	0	0.4
1982 Bal A	125	344	35	88	15	1	5	36	46-1	0	37	.256	.339	.349	91	-3	0-3	.991	1	143	71	C124/D	0	0.2
1983 †Bal A	128	347	33	80	16	2	4	32	40-1	3	54	.231	.311	.323	77	-10	1-1	**.997**	19	129	93	C128	0	1.4
1984 Bal A	109	330	37	76	11	0	11	34	40-0	1	58	.230	.312	.364	89	-5	1-2	.992	-6	102	68	C108	0	-0.7
1985 Bal A	132	362	54	92	19	0	12	52	50-0	1	87	.254	.345	.406	107	5	0-1	.987	-10	95	83	C131	0	-0.1
1986 Bal A	122	327	42	68	15	1	13	29	45-0	3	78	.208	.309	.379	87	-6	1-0	.990	4	102	95	C121	0	0.3
1987 Cle A	60	141	16	25	10	0	1	9	23-0	1	29	.177	.295	.270	51	-9	0-0	.984	1	102	112	C59	51	-0.6
1988 †LA N	77	167	25	42	13	0	7	30	25-0	0	44	.251	.338	.455	133	8	1-0	.989	2	99	99	C74	0	1.4
1989 LA N	79	151	16	27	7	0	4	16	30-3	1	37	.179	.319	.305	80	-3	1-0	.984	4	131	160	C62	0	0.4
1990 LA N	62	128	13	25	5	0	2	15	23-0	0	29	.195	.318	.281	68	-5	1-0	.992	-1	96	130	C53	17	-0.4
1991 Mil A	61	147	15	34	5	0	4	21	23-1	0	20	.231	.329	.347	91	-1	0-2	.993	-2	101	81	C56,P2/1	0	-0.1
1992 Bal A	8	9	2	1	0	0	0	0	2-0	0	1	.111	.273	.111	11	-1	0-0	1.000	-2	64	0	C8	0	-0.3
Total 24	1766	4692	525	1093	223	12	96	471	592-13	18	736	.233	.319	.347	87	-67	20-19	.988	81	131	100	C1633,O23(6/0/17),D22,1b3,P2/3	111	7.0
Denneheу, Tod	Thomas Francis; B5.12.1899 Philadelphia PA; D8.8.1977 Philadelphia PA; BL/TL/5´10˝/180; d4.21																							
1923 Phi N	9	24	4	7	2	0	0	2	1	0	3	.292	.320	.375	74	-1	0-1	1.000	0	121	0	O9(7/0/2)	—	-0.1
Denning, Otto	Otto George "Dutch"; B12.28.1912 Hays KS; D5.25.1992 Chicago IL; BR/TR/6´0˝/180; d4.15																							
1942 Cle A	92	214	15	45	14	0	1	19	18	1	14	.210	.275	.290	62	-11	0-0	**.992**	1	*108*	*89*	C78,O2L	0	-0.7
1943 Cle A	37	129	8	31	6	0	0	13	5	0	1	.240	.269	.287	67	-6	3-1	.966	-4	78	135	1b34	0	-1.2
Total 2	129	343	23	76	20	0	1	32	23	1	15	.222	.272	.289	64	-17	3-1	.992	-3	*108*	*89*	C78,1b34,O2L	0	-1.9
Denny, Jerry	Jeremiah Dennis (b Jeremiah Dennis Eldridge); B3.16.1859 New York NY; D8.16.1927 Houston TX; BR/TR/5´11.5˝/180; d5.2; Col St. Marys (CA); OF(1/2/7)																							
1881 Pro N	**85**	320	38	77	16	2	1	24	5	—	44	.241	.252	.313	78	-8	—	.840	6	106	92	3b85	—	0.0
1882 Pro N	**84**	329	54	81	10	9	2	42	4	—	46	.246	.255	.350	92	-4	—	.861	11	114	72	3b84	—	0.8
1883 Pro N	**98**	393	73	108	26	8	8	55	9	—	48	.275	.291	.443	116	7	—	**.876**	10	96	115	3b98	—	1.6
1884 †Pro N	110	439	57	109	22	9	6	59	14	—	58	.248	.272	.380	105	2	—	.874	-5	86	52	3b99,1b9,2b3/C	—	-0.2
1885 Pro N	83	318	40	71	14	4	3	24	12	—	53	.223	.252	.321	87	-5	—	.869	1	96	96	3b83	—	-0.3
1886 StL N	119	475	58	122	24	6	9	62	14	—	68	.257	.278	.389	108	4	16	.895	**25**	**116**	**161**	3b117,S3	—	2.8
1887 Ind N	122	510	86	165	34	12	11	97	13	3	22	.324	.344	.502	137	23	29	.889	21	113	102	3b116,S4/rf2	—	3.9
1888 Ind N	126	524	92	137	27	7	12	63	9	2	79	.261	.277	.408	114	6	32	.894	16	109	95	3b96,S25,2b5/cfP	—	2.4
1889 Ind N	133	578	96	163	24	0	18	112	27	0	63	.282	.314	.417	100	-3	22	**.913**	13	**107**	53	3b123,2b7,S5	—	1.0
1890 NY N	114	437	50	93	18	7	3	42	28	6	62	.213	.270	.307	68	-20	11	.889	7	95	89	3b106,S7/2	—	-1.0
1891 NY N	4	16	0	4	1	0	0	1	0	0	3	.250	.250	.313	66	-1	2	.700	-2	24	190	3b4	—	-0.3
Cle N	36	138	17	31	5	0	0	21	12	1	23	.225	.291	.261	59	-7	3	.884	-0	105	26	3b29,O7(1/1/6)	—	-0.6
Phi N	19	73	5	21	1	1	0	11	4	0	6	.288	.325	.329	88	-1	1	.977	-1	36	75	1b12,3b7	—	-0.3
Year	59	227	22	56	7	1	0	33	16	1	32	.247	.299	.286	69	-9	6	.876	-4	98	59	3b40,1b12,O7(1/1/6)	—	-1.2
1893 Lou N	44	175	22	43	5	4	1	22	9	0	15	.246	.283	.337	70	-9	4	.920	2	99	87	S42,3b2	—	-0.4
1894 Lou N	60	221	26	61	11	7	0	32	13	3	12	.276	.325	.389	77	-9	10	.874	3	104	121	3b60	—	-0.4
Total 13	1237	4946	714	1286	238	76	74	667	173	15	602	.260	.287	.384	98	-25	130	.882	106	104	93	3b1109,S86,1b21,2b17,O9R/PC	—	9.0
Denorfia, Chris	Christopher Anthony; B7.15.1980 Bristol CT; BR/TR/6´1˝/195; [CinN02 19/555]; d9.7; Col Wheaton (MA)																							
2005 Cin N	18	38	8	10	3	0	1	2	6-0	0	9	.263	.364	.421	104	0	1-0	.962	1	143	0	O12(2/10/2)	0	0.1
2006 Cin N	49	106	14	30	6	0	1	7	11-1	1	21	.283	.356	.368	81	-3	1-1	1.000	1	102	153	O37(11/12/15)	0	-0.2
Total 2	67	144	22	40	9	0	2	9	17-1	1	30	.278	.358	.382	87	-3	2-1	.988	2	111	118	O49(13/22/17)	0	-0.1
Denson, Drew	Andrew; B11.16.1965 Cincinnati OH; BB/TR/6´5˝/(210–220); [AtlN84 1/19]; d9.13																							
1989 Atl N	12	36	1	9	1	0	0	5	3-0	0	9	.250	.308	.278	67	-1	1-0	.988	2	170	46	1b12	0	0.0
1993 Chi A	4	5	0	1	0	0	0	0	0-0	0	2	.200	.200	.200	8	-1	0-0	.800	-0	0	176	1b3	0	-0.1
Total 2	16	41	1	10	1	0	0	5	3-0	0	11	.244	.295	.268	60	-2	1-0	.977	1	159	55	1b15	0	-0.1
Dent, Bucky	Russell Earl (b Russell Earl O'Dey); B11.25.1951 Savannah GA; BR/TR/5´11˝/(170–190); [ChiA70 S1/6]; d6.1; M2/C12; Col Miami–Dade North (FL) CC																							
1973 Chi A	40	117	17	29	2	0	0	10	10-0	1	18	.248	.308	.265	62	-6	2-3	.963	7	118	96	S36,2b3/3	0	0.4
1974 Chi A	154	496	55	136	15	3	5	45	28-0	3	48	.274	.316	.347	88	-8	3-4	.972	6	100	112	S154	0	1.6
1975 Chi A★	157	602	52	159	29	4	3	58	36-3	0	48	.264	.301	.341	81	-16	2-4	**.981**	18	106	101	S157	0	2.1
1976 Chi A	158	562	44	138	18	4	2	52	43-3	2	45	.246	.300	.302	77	-17	3-5	.976	-4	94	96	S158	0	-0.4
1977 †NY A	158	477	54	118	18	4	8	49	39-0	1	28	.247	.300	.352	79	-14	1-1	.974	-10	95	108	S158	0	-0.8
1978 †NY A	123	379	40	92	11	1	5	40	23-1	2	24	.243	.286	.317	72	-15	3-1	.981	-5	97	91	S123	22	-0.7
1979 NY A	141	431	47	99	14	2	2	32	37-1	1	30	.230	.287	.285	57	-26	0-0	.977	32	**116**	122	S141	0	2.0
1980 †NY A★	141	489	57	128	26	2	5	52	48-1	2	37	.262	.327	.354	89	-6	0-3	**.982**	12	105	84	S141	15	1.9
1981 NY A★	73	227	20	54	11	0	7	27	19-0	2	17	.238	.300	.379	96	-1	0-1	.970	-2	91	117	S73	35	0.4
1982 NY A	59	160	11	27	1	1	0	9	8-0	0	11	.169	.207	.188	10	-20	0-0	.962	6	108	89	S58	0	-0.9
Tex A	46	146	16	32	9	0	1	14	13-0	0	10	.219	.280	.301	63	-7	0-0	.980	0	105	107	S45	0	-0.2
Year	105	306	27	59	10	1	1	23	21-0	0	21	.193	.242	.242	35	-28	0-0	.970	7	107	97	S103	0	-1.1
1983 Tex A	131	417	36	99	15	2	2	34	23-0	1	31	.237	.278	.297	59	-24	3-7	**.979**	-12	97	98	S129/D	0	-2.4
1984 KC A	11	9	2	3	0	0	0	1	1-0	0	2	.333	.400	.333	104	0	0-0	1.000	-3	53	0	S9,3b2	0	-0.3
Total 12	1392	4512	451	1114	169	23	40	423	328-9	15	349	.247	.297	.321	74	-160	17-29	.976	46	101	102	S1382,3b3,2b3/D	72	2.7
Dente, Sam	Samuel Joseph "Blackie"; B4.26.1922 Harrison NJ; D4.21.2002 Montclair NJ; BR/TR/5´11˝/(172–175); d7.10																							
1947 Bos A	46	168	14	39	4	2	0	11	19	0	15	.232	.310	.280	60	-9	0-1	.939	-3	96	138	3b46	0	-1.2
1948 StL A	98	267	26	72	11	2	0	22	22	1	8	.270	.328	.326	72	-11	1-3	.958	1	102	86	S76,3b6	0	-0.7
1949 Was A	153	590	48	161	24	4	1	53	31	0	24	.273	.309	.332	71	-27	4-4	.957	-7	101	82	S153	0	-2.5
1950 Was A	**155**	603	56	144	20	5	2	59	39	1	19	.239	.286	.299	52	-46	1-1	.952	-1	104	87	S128,2b29	0	-3.6
1951 Was A	88	273	21	65	8	1	0	29	25	0	10	.238	.302	.275	58	-16	3-0	.962	-1	102	97	S65,2b10,3b5	0	-1.2
1952 Chi A	62	145	12	32	0	1	0	11	5	2	8	.221	.257	.234	37	-13	0-0	.942	2	89	109	S27,3b18,2b6,O6(4/0/2),1b2	0	-1.0
1953 Chi A	2	0	0	0	0	0	0	0	0	0	0	ø	ø	ø	ø	0	0-0	ø	-0	0	0	/S	0	0.0
1954 †Cle A	68	169	18	45	7	1	1	19	14	0	4	.266	.319	.337	79	-5	0-0	.971	-2	100	131	S60,2b7	0	-0.3
1955 Cle A	73	105	10	27	4	0	0	10	12-1	0	8	.257	.331	.295	68	-4	0-0	.976	6	113	100	S53,3b13,2b4	0	0.3
Total 9	745	2320	205	585	78	16	4	214	167-1	4	96	.252	.303	.305	62	-131	9-9	.958	-6	102	92	S563,3b88,2b56,O6(4/0/2),1b2	0	-10.2
DePangher, Mike	Michael Anthony; B9.11.1858 Marysville CA; D7.7.1915 San Francisco CA; BL/5´8˝/190; d8.8																							
1884 Phi N	4	10	0	2	0	0	0	0	1	—	3	.200	.273	.200	54	0	—	.920	0	—	—	C4	—	0.0
DePastino, Joe	Joseph Bernard; B9.4.1973 Philadelphia PA; BR/TR/6´2˝/210; [BosA92 7/198]; d8.5																							
2003 NY N	2	2	0	0	0	0	0	0	0-0	0	1	.000	.000	.000	-99	-1	0-0	1.000	0	0	0	/C	0	-0.1
DePhillips, Tony	Anthony Andrew; B9.20.1912 New York NY; D5.5.1994 Port Jefferson NY; BR/TR/6´2˝/185; d4.25; Col Fordham																							
1943 Cin N	35	20	0	2	1	0	0	2	1	0	5	.100	.143	.150	-16	-3	0	.981	3	*126*	*100*	C35	0	0.1

YEAR TM LG	G	AB	R	H	2B	3B	HR	RBI	BB-IB	HP	SO	AVG	OBP	SLG	AOPS	ABR	SB-CS	FA	FR	RNG	THR	GAMES AT POSITION	DL	BFW
DERBY, GENE Eugene A.; B2.3.1860 Fitchburg MA; D9.13.1917 Waterbury CT; 5´7˝/160; d9.3																								
1885 Bal AA	10	31	4	4	0	0	0	2	1	1	—	.129	.182	.129	-1	-3	—	.952	1	—	—	C9/lf	—	-0.2
DERNIER, BOB Robert Eugene; B1.5.1957 Kansas City MO; BR/TR/6´0˝/(160–165); d9.7; Col Longview (MO) CC																								
1980 Phi N	10	7	5	4	0	0	0	1	1-0	0	0	.571	.625	.571	221	1	3-0	1.000	1	185	0	O3C	0	0.3
1981 Phi N	10	4	0	3	0	0	0	0	0-0	0	0	.750	.750	.750	309	1	2-1	1.000	-0	62	0	O5C	0	0.1
1982 Phi N	122	370	56	92	10	2	4	21	36-0	1	69	.249	.315	.319	76	-12	42-12	.981	8	**124**	83	O119(0/70/62)	0	-0.2
1983 †Phi N	122	221	41	51	10	0	1	15	18-0	0	21	.231	.287	.290	61	-12	35-7	.988	5	120	91	O107(12/68/31)	0	-0.3
1984 †Chi N	143	536	94	149	26	5	3	32	63-0	2	60	.278	.356	.362	94	-2	45-17	.986	-1	104	67	O140(1/139/0)	0	0.0
1985 Chi N	121	469	63	119	20	3	1	21	40-1	3	44	.254	.315	.316	70	-18	31-8	.972	1	112	58	O116C	22	-1.4
1986 Chi N	108	324	32	73	14	1	4	18	22-1	0	41	.225	.275	.312	57	-19	27-2	.987	-1	107	58	O105C	38	-1.6
1987 Chi N	93	199	38	63	4	4	8	21	19-0	1	19	.317	.379	.497	125	7	16-7	.989	-4	85	83	O71C	0	0.3
1988 Phi N	68	166	19	48	3	1	1	10	9-0	1	19	.289	.330	.337	90	-2	13-6	.980	0	101	116	O54(0/53/1)	39	-0.2
1989 Phi N	107	187	26	32	5	0	1	13	14-0	0	28	.171	.225	.214	27	-18	4-3	.970	0	108	48	O74(28/29/20)	0	-2.0
Total 10	904	2483	374	634	92	16	23	152	222-2	8	301	.255	.318	.333	78	-74	218-63	.982	10	110	72	O794(41/660/114)	99	-5.0
DEROSA, MARK Mark Thomas; B2.26.1975 Passaic NJ; BR/TR/6´1˝/(190–205); [AtlN96 7/212]; d9.2; Col Penn; OF(13/0/90)																								
1998 Atl N	5	3	2	1	0	0	0	0	0-0	0	1	.333	.333	.333	77	0	0-0	1.000	-1	37	0	S4	0	-0.1
1999 Atl N	7	8	0	0	0	0	0	0	0-0	0	2	.000	.000	.000	-99	-2	0-0	1.000	0	87	0	S2	0	-0.2
2000 Atl N	22	13	9	4	1	0	0	3	2-0	0	1	.308	.400	.385	100	0	0-0	1.000	-2	59	85	S10	0	-0.1
2001 †Atl N	66	164	27	47	8	0	3	20	12-6	5	19	.287	.350	.390	91	-2	2-1	.960	-0	100	91	S48,2b5/3lfD	0	0.1
2002 †Atl N	72	212	24	63	9	2	5	23	12-3	3	24	.297	.339	.429	102	0	2-3	.974	6	116	131	2b32,S19,O7(2/0/5),3b4	60	0.8
2003 †Atl N	103	266	40	70	14	0	6	22	16-0	5	49	.263	.316	.383	82	-7	1-0	.984	4	105	119	2b29,3b25,S20,O2L/1D	0	0.0
2004 Atl N	118	309	33	74	16	0	3	31	23-3	3	53	.239	.293	.320	60	-19	1-3	.939	-5	103	61	3b72,S11,2b5,O3L	0	-2.3
2005 Tex A	66	148	26	36	5	0	8	20	16-0	2	35	.243	.325	.439	98	-1	1-0	1.000	-1	106	79	O25R,2b17,S16,3b5/1D	0	-0.1
2006 Tex A	136	520	78	154	40	2	13	74	44-1	6	102	.296	.357	.456	109	8	4-4	.993	8	103	124	O64(5/0/60),3b40,2b26,S7/1D	15	1.3
Total 9	595	1643	239	449	93	4	38	193	125-13	24	286	.273	.331	.404	90	-23	11-11	.947	10	102	72	3b147,S137,2b114,O102R,D12,1b3	75	-0.6
DERRICK, CLAUD Claud Lester "Deek"; B6.11.1886 Burton GA; D7.15.1974 Clayton GA; BR/TR/6´0˝/175; d9.8; Col Georgia																								
1910 Phi A	2	1	0	0	0	0	0	0	0	0	—	.000	.000	.000	-99	0	0	.500	-1	0	0	/S	—	-0.1
1911 Phi A	36	100	14	23	1	2	0	5	7	2	—	.230	.294	.280	61	-5	7	.960	-0	99	113	2b21,S6,1b3,3b2	—	-0.5
1912 Phi A	21	58	7	14	0	1	0	7	5	1	—	.241	.313	.276	71	-2	1	.884	-1	109	93	S18	—	-0.2
1913 NY A	23	65	7	19	1	0	1	7	5	1	8	.292	.352	.354	106	0	2	.874	-2	102	108	S17,3b4/2	—	0.0
1914 Cin N	3	6	2	2	1	0	0	1	0	0	0	.333	.333	.500	142	0	1	.889	0	94	203	S2	—	0.1
Chi N	28	96	5	21	3	1	0	13	5	0	13	.219	.257	.271	57	-5	2	.895	-3	94	85	S28	—	-0.7
Year	31	102	7	23	4	1	0	14	5	0	13	.225	.262	.284	62	-5	3	.894	-3	94	90	S30	—	-0.6
Total 5	113	326	35	79	6	4	1	33	22	4	21	.242	.298	.294	72	-12	13	.892	-6	99	88	S72,2b22,3b6,1b3	—	-1.4
DERRICK, MIKE James Michael; B9.19.1943 Columbia SC; BL/TR/6´0˝/190; d4.9																								
1970 Bos A	24	33	3	7	1	0	0	5	0-0	0	11	.212	.206	.242	23	-3	0-1	1.000	0	140	0	O2L/1	0	-0.4
DERRY, RUSS Alva Russell; B10.7.1916 Princeton MO; D10.26.2004 Kansas City MO; BL/TR/6´1˝/180; d7.4																								
1944 NY A	38	114	14	29	3	0	4	14	20	0	19	.254	.366	.386	111	2	1-0	.949	-1	92	93	O28(16/0/12)	0	-0.1
1945 NY A	78	253	37	57	6	2	13	45	31	1	49	.225	.312	.419	107	1	1-0	.978	-0	105	68	O68(10/44/15)	0	-0.2
1946 Phi A	69	184	17	38	8	5	0	14	27	1	54	.207	.311	.304	73	-7	0-0	.985	4	116	87	O50(45/2/5)	0	-0.6
1949 StL N	2	2	0	0	0	0	0	0	0	0	2	.000	.000	.000	-96	-1	0	ø	0	—	—	/H	0	-0.1
Total 4	187	553	68	124	17	7	17	73	78	2	124	.224	.322	.373	95	-5	2-0	.976	3	106	80	O146(71/46/32)	0	-1.0
DESA, JOE Joseph; B7.27.1959 Honolulu HI; D12.20.1986 San Juan, PR; BL/TL/5´11˝/170; [StLN77 3/58]; d9.6																								
1980 StL N	7	11	0	3	0	0	0	0	0-0	0	2	.273	.273	.273	50	-1	0-0	1.000	-0	0	0	/1rf	0	-0.1
1985 Chi A	28	44	5	8	2	0	2	7	3-1	0	6	.182	.234	.364	58	-3	0-0	1.000	1	149	71	1b9/lfD	0	-0.2
Total 2	35	55	5	11	2	0	2	7	3-1	0	8	.200	.241	.345	57	-4	0-0	1.000	1	137	65	1b10,D4,O2(1/0/1)	0	-0.3
DESAUTELS, GENE Eugene Abraham "Red"; B6.13.1907 Worcester MA; D11.5.1994 Flint MI; BR/TR/5´11˝/170; d6.22; Mil 1944–45; Col Holy Cross																								
1930 Det A	42	126	13	24	4	2	0	9	7	1	9	.190	.239	.254	25	-15	2-0	.996	3	74	115	C42	—	-0.8
1931 Det A	3	11	1	1	0	0	0	1	0	0	1	.091	.091	.091	-50	-2	0-0	1.000	-0	58	233	C3	—	-0.3
1932 Det A	28	72	8	17	2	0	0	2	13	1	11	.236	.360	.264	62	-3	0-0	.984	2	103	93	C24	—	0.0
1933 Det A	30	42	5	6	1	0	0	4	4	1	6	.143	.234	.167	8	-6	0-0	.976	0	73	69	C30	—	-0.4
1937 Bos A	96	305	33	74	10	3	0	27	36	1	26	.243	.325	.295	55	-21	1-2	**.993**	4	111	70	C94	—	-1.1
1938 Bos A	108	333	47	97	16	2	2	48	57	1	31	.291	.396	.369	89	-3	1-1	.985	4	110	106	C108	—	0.7
1939 Bos A	76	226	26	55	14	0	0	21	33	0	13	.243	.340	.305	64	-11	3-1	.994	7	95	118	C73	—	0.0
1940 Bos A	71	222	19	50	7	1	0	17	32	2	13	.225	.328	.266	54	-14	0-1	.992	-6	97	79	C70	—	-1.6
1941 Cle A	66	189	20	38	5	1	1	17	14	1	12	.201	.260	.254	38	-18	1-0	.997	5	122	94	C66	0	-0.8
1942 Cle A	62	162	14	40	5	0	0	9	12	1	13	.247	.303	.278	68	-7	1-0	.975	-5	102	51	C61	71	-0.9
1943 Cle A	68	185	14	38	6	1	0	19	11	0	16	.205	.250	.249	49	-13	2-0	.982	3	147	78	C66	0	-0.7
1945 Cle A	10	9	1	1	0	0	0	0	1	0	1	.111	.200	.111	-9	-1	0-0	1.000	0	95	135	C10	0	-0.1
1946 Phi A	52	130	10	28	3	1	0	13	12	0	16	.215	.282	.254	51	-9	1-1	.989	3	118	160	C52	0	-0.4
Total 13	712	2012	211	469	73	11	3	187	232	9	168	.233	.315	.285	57	-123	12-6	.989	20	107	94	C699	71	-6.4
DESHIELDS, DELINO Delino Lamont; B1.15.1969 Seaford DE; BL/TR/6´1˝/(170–175); [MonN87 1/12]; d4.9; OF(118/3/1)																								
1990 Mon N	129	499	69	144	28	6	4	45	66-3	4	96	.289	.375	.393	116	13	42-22	.981	-5	99	101	2b128	26	1.4
1991 Mon N	151	563	83	134	15	4	10	51	95-2	2	151	.238	.347	.332	94	-1	56-23	.962	-21	95	91	2b148	0	-1.5
1992 Mon N	135	530	82	155	19	8	7	56	54-4	3	108	.292	.359	.398	115	11	46-15	.976	-22	89	91	2b134	0	-0.3
1993 Mon N	123	481	75	142	17	7	2	29	72-3	3	64	.295	.389	.372	101	4	43-10	.983	7	**108**	101	2b123	30	2.2
1994 LA N	89	320	51	80	11	3	2	33	54-0	0	53	.250	.357	.322	84	-6	27-7	.986	5	105	99	2b88,S10	25	0.7
1995 †LA N	127	425	66	109	18	3	8	37	63-4	1	83	.256	.353	.369	98	0	39-14	.980	-5	98	83	2b113	0	0.4
1996 †LA N	154	581	75	130	12	8	5	41	53-7	1	124	.224	.287	.298	59	-37	48-11	.975	-20	91	87	2b154	0	-4.2
1997 StL N	150	572	92	169	26	**14**	11	58	55-1	3	72	.295	.357	.448	110	7	55-14	.972	-8	96	108	2b147	0	1.3
1998 StL N	117	420	74	122	21	8	7	44	56-2	0	61	.290	.371	.429	111	8	26-10	.983	-10	93	97	2b111/1	36	0.5
1999 Bal A	96	330	46	87	11	2	6	34	37-0	1	52	.264	.339	.364	82	-9	11-8	.977	-5	94	93	2b93	42	-1.0
2000 Bal A	151	561	84	166	43	5	10	86	69-2	1	82	.296	.369	.444	111	12	37-10	.975	-16	90	69	2b96,O41(39/2/0),D10	0	0.3
2001 Bal A	58	188	29	37	8	2	3	21	31-1	1	42	.197	.312	.309	69	-8	11-1	.967	-3	88	68	O47(46/1/0),D8	0	-1.0
Chi N	68	163	26	45	9	3	2	16	28-0	0	35	.276	.380	.405	107	3	12-1	.976	-3	89	63	O33L,2b16,3b5/1	0	0.1
2002 Chi N	67	146	20	28	6	1	3	10	21-2	0	38	.192	.292	.308	59	-9	10-1	.970	2	99	67	2b41/rf	15	-0.3
Total 13	1615	5779	872	1548	244	74	80	561	754-31	20	1061	.268	.352	.377	97	-12	463-147	.977	-104	96	92	2b1392,O122L,D18,S10,3b5,1b2	174	-1.4
DESTRADE, ORESTES Orestes (Cucuas); B5.8.1962 Santiago de Cuba, Cuba; BB/TR/6´4˝/(210–230); d9.11; Col Florida JC																								
1987 NY A	9	19	5	5	0	0	0	1	5-0	0	5	.263	.417	.263	86	0	0-0	1.000	-0	62	103	1b3,D2	0	0.0
1988 Pit N	36	47	2	7	1	0	1	3	5-0	0	17	.149	.226	.234	34	-4	0-0	1.000	-1	47	73	1b8	0	-0.6
1993 Fla N	153	569	61	145	20	3	20	87	58-8	3	130	.255	.324	.406	89	-9	0-2	.987	-9	82	93	1b152	0	-3.2
1994 Fla N	39	130	12	27	4	0	5	15	19-1	2	32	.208	.316	.354	72	-5	1-0	.983	-3	75	100	1b37	0	-1.1
Total 4	237	765	80	184	25	3	26	106	87-9	5	184	.241	.319	.383	83	-18	1-2	.987	-13	79	94	1b200,D2	0	-4.9
DETHERAGE, BOB Robert Wayne; B9.20.1954 Springfield MO; BR/TR/6´0˝/180; [LAN72 3/65]; d4.11																								
1980 KC A	20	26	2	8	2	0	1	7	1-0	0	4	.308	.333	.500	123	1	1-1	1.000	-2	75	0	O20(12/0/11)	0	-0.2
DETORE, GEORGE George Francis; B11.11.1906 Utica NY; D2.7.1991 Utica NY; BR/TR/5´8˝/170; d9.14; C1; Col Colgate																								
1930 Cle A	3	12	0	2	1	0	0	2	0	0	2	.167	.167	.250	4	-2	0-0	.750	-1	50	243	3b3	—	-0.3
1931 Cle A	30	56	3	15	6	0	0	7	8	0	2	.268	.359	.375	88	-1	0-2	.958	2	156	0	3b13,S10,2b3	—	0.2
Total 2	33	68	3	17	7	0	0	9	8	0	4	.250	.329	.353	74	-3	0-2	.929	1	131	58	3b16,S10,2b3	—	-0.1
DETWEILER, DUCKY Robert Sterling; B2.15.1919 Trumbauersville PA; BR/TR/5´11˝/178; d9.12; Mil 1943–45																								
1942 Bos N	12	44	3	14	2	1	0	5	2	0	7	.318	.348	.409	123	1	0	.929	-2	80	104	3b12	0	-0.1
1946 Bos N	1	1	0	0	0	0	0	0	0	0	0	.000	.000	.000	-99	0	0	ø	0	—	—	/H	0	0.0
Total 2	13	45	3	14	2	1	0	5	2	0	7	.311	.340	.400	118	1	0	.929	-2	80	104	3b12	0	-0.1

YEAR TM LG	G	AB	R	H	2B	3B	HR	RBI	BB-IB	HP	SO	AVG	OBP	SLG	AOPS	ABR	SB-CS	FA	FR	RNG	THR	GAMES AT POSITION	DL	BFW
DEVAREZ, CESAR	Cesar Salvatore (Santana); B9.22.1969 San Francisco de Macoris, D.R.; BR/TR/5´10˝/175; d6.3																							
1995 Bal A	6	4	0	0	0	0	0	0	0-0	0	0	.000	.000	.000	-98	-1	0-0	1.000	0	32	0	C6	0	-0.1
1996 Bal A	10	18	3	2	0	1	0	0	1-0	0	3	.111	.158	.222	-5	-3	0-0	1.000	-0	67	69	C10	0	-0.3
Total 2	16	22	3	2	0	1	0	0	1-0	0	3	.091	.130	.182	-22	-4	0-0	1.000	0	59	54	C16	0	-0.4
DEVEREAUX, MIKE	Michael; B4.10.1963 Casper WY; BR/TR/6´0˝/(191–195); [LAN85 5/116]; d9.2; Col Arizona St.																							
1987 LA N	19	54	7	12	3	0	0	4	3-0	0	10	.222	.263	.278	45	-4	3-1	1.000	-1	81	111	O18(11/2/5)	0	-0.5
1988 LA N	30	43	4	5	1	0	0	2	2-0	0	10	.116	.156	.140	-15	-7	0-1	1.000	-0	102	0	O26(0/17/8)	0	-0.8
1989 Bal A	122	391	55	104	14	3	8	46	36-0	2	60	.266	.329	.379	102	1	22-11	.983	0	109	16	O112(4/80/35),D5	0	0.0
1990 Bal A	108	367	48	88	18	1	12	49	28-0	0	48	.240	.291	.392	93	-5	13-12	.983	2	108	78	O104C,D3	29	-0.5
1991 Bal A	149	608	82	158	27	10	19	59	47-2	2	115	.260	.313	.431	108	4	16-9	.993	4	104	131	O149(1/148/0)	0	0.7
1992 Bal A	156	653	76	180	29	11	24	107	44-1	4	94	.276	.321	.464	115	10	10-8	.989	-8	96	54	O155C	0	0.0
1993 Bal A	131	527	72	132	31	3	14	75	43-0	1	99	.250	.306	.400	85	-12	3-3	.988	-6	90	111	O130C	24	-1.7
1994 Bal A	85	301	35	61	8	2	9	33	22-0	1	72	.203	.256	.332	48	-25	1-2	.995	-2	97	71	O84C/D	15	-2.5
1995 Chi A	92	333	48	102	21	1	10	55	25-3	0	51	.306	.352	.465	116	7	6-6	.985	4	114	75	O90(0/9/87)	0	0.6
†Atl N	29	55	7	14	3	0	1	8	2-0	0	11	.255	.281	.364	65	-3	2-0	1.000	2	138	0	O27(14/9/4)	0	-0.1
1996 †Bal A	127	323	49	74	11	2	8	34	34-0	2	53	.229	.305	.350	66	-18	8-2	.983	2	99	131	O112(35/30/62),D10	0	-1.7
1997 Tex A	29	72	8	15	3	0	0	7	7-0	0	10	.208	.275	.250	37	-7	1-0	1.000	-2	92	0	O28(5/3/24)	0	-0.9
1998 LA N	9	13	0	4	1	0	0	1	3-0	0	2	.308	.438	.385	125	1	0-1	1.000	1	128	489	O5(1/3/1)	0	0.1
Total 12	1086	3740	491	949	170	33	105	480	296-6	12	635	.254	.308	.401	91	-58	85-56	.988	-5	102	82	O1040(71/774/226),D19	68	-7.3
DEVINE, MICKEY	William Patrick; B5.9.1892 Albany NY; D10.1.1937 Albany NY; BR/TR/5´10˝/165; d8.2																							
1918 Phi N	4	8	0	1	1	0	0	0	0	0	1	.125	.125	.250	13	-1	0	.909	-0	110	58	C3	—	-0.1
1920 Bos A	8	12	1	2	0	0	0	0	1	0	2	.167	.231	.167	7	-2	1-0	.955	0	102	53	C5	—	-0.1
1925 NY N	21	33	6	9	3	0	0	4	2	0	3	.273	.314	.364	76	-1	0-0	.933	0	113	116	C11/3	—	0.0
Total 3	33	53	7	12	4	0	0	4	3	0	6	.226	.268	.302	51	-4	1-0	.936	0	110	91	C19/3	—	-0.2
DEVIVEIROS, BERNIE	Bernard John; B4.19.1901 Oakland CA; D7.5.1994 Oakland CA; BR/TR/5´7˝/160; d9.13																							
1924 Chi A	1	1	0	0	0	0	0	0	0	0	0	.000	.000	.000	-99	0	0-0	.333	-1	0	0	/S	—	-0.1
1927 Det A	24	22	4	5	1	0	0	2	2	0	8	.227	.292	.273	46	-2	1-0	.913	-0	107	160	S14/3	—	-0.1
Total 2	25	23	4	5	1	0	0	2	2	0	8	.217	.280	.261	40	-2	1-0	.846	-1	97	144	S15/3	—	-0.2
DEVLIN, ART	Arthur McArthur; B10.16.1879 Washington DC; D9.18.1948 Jersey City NJ; BR/TR/6´0˝/175; d4.14; C2; Col Georgetown																							
1904 NY N	130	474	81	133	16	8	1	66	62	6	—	.281	.371	.354	119	13	33	.907	5	108	81	3b130	—	2.3
1905 †NY N	153	525	74	129	14	7	2	61	66	13	—	.246	.344	.310	94	-1	**59**	.932	6	103	91	3b153	—	0.9
1906 NY N	148	498	76	149	23	8	2	65	74	6	—	.299	.396	.390	142	28	54	.944	**29**	**122**	136	3b148	—	6.6
1907 NY N	143	491	61	136	16	2	1	54	63	**15**	—	.277	.376	.324	116	14	38	.940	-2	96	69	3b140,S3	—	1.8
1908 NY N	**157**	534	59	135	18	4	2	45	62	14	—	.253	.346	.313	106	7	19	**.947**	12	105	110	3b157	—	2.6
1909 NY N	143	491	61	130	19	8	0	56	65	10	—	.265	.362	.336	115	12	26	.934	17	110	**125**	3b143	—	3.5
1910 NY N	147	493	71	128	17	5	2	67	62	9	32	.260	.353	.327	98	1	28	.933	6	101	102	3b147	—	1.1
1911 NY N	95	260	42	71	16	2	0	25	42	6	19	.273	.386	.350	103	4	9	.944	4	111	34	3b79,1b6,2b6,S6	—	1.0
1912 Bos N	124	436	59	126	18	8	0	54	51	3	37	.289	.367	.367	99	1	11	.992	-1	95	79	1b69,S26,3b26/lf	—	0.0
1913 Bos N	73	210	19	48	7	5	0	12	29	2	17	.229	.328	.310	81	-5	8-8	.973	5	106	45	3b69	—	0.2
Total 10	1313	4412	603	1185	164	57	10	505	576	84	105	.269	.364	.338	109	74	285-8	.938	81	107	97	3b1192,1b75,S35,2b6/lf	—	20.0
DEVLIN, JIM	James Alexander; B6.6.1849 Philadelphia PA; D10.10.1883 Philadelphia PA; BR/TR/5´11˝/175; d4.21; ▲																							
1873 Phi NA	23	99	18	24	4	4	0	10	2	—	4	.242	.257	.364	79	-3	0-0	.938	-2	150	171	1b12,3b6,S4,O2R	—	-0.4
1874 Chi NA	45	203	26	58	5	0	0	26	2	—	9	.286	.293	.310	93	-2	2-1	.930	-2	63	57	1b24,O17R,3b5	—	-0.2
1875 Chi NA	**69**	318	60	92	17	6	0	40	4	—	4	.289	.298	.381	133	10	6-1	.934	1	134	71	1b42,P28,O4(0/3/1)	—	0.7
1876 Lou N	68	298	38	94	14	1	0	28	1	—	11	.315	.318	.369	109	1	—	.941	2	102	147	P68/1	—	0.1
1877 Lou N	**61**	268	38	72	6	3	1	27	7	—	27	.269	.287	.325	78	-1	—	.933	2	111	158	P61	—	0.0
Total 3NA	137	620	104	174	26	10	0	76	8	—	17	.281	.290	.355	110	5	8-2	.933	-3	114	81	1b78,P28,O23(0/3/20),3b11,S4	—	0.1
Total 2	129	566	76	166	20	4	1	55	8	—	38	.293	.303	.348	94	0	—	.937	4	106	152	P129/1	—	0.1
DEVLIN, JIM	James Raymond; B8.25.1922 Plains PA; D1.15.2004 Danville PA; BL/TR/5´11.5˝/165; d4.27																							
1944 Cle A	1	1	0	0	0	0	0	0	0	0	0	.000	.000	.000	-99	0	0-0	1.000	0	0	0	/C	0	0.0
DEVOGT, REX	Rex Eugene; B1.4.1888 Clare MI; D11.9.1935 Alma MI; BR/TR/5´9˝/170; d4.17																							
1913 Bos N	3	6	0	0	0	0	0	0	0	0	3	.000	.000	.000	-98	-2	0	.941	1	137	142	C3	—	-0.1
DEVORE, DOUG	Douglas Rinehart; B12.14.1977 Columbus OH; BL/TL/6´4˝/215; [AriN99 12/358]; d5.6; Col Indiana																							
2004 Ari N	50	107	5	24	3	2	3	13	7-0	0	31	.224	.272	.374	61	-7	1-1	1.000	3	123	146	O31(18/1/15)	0	-0.5
DEVORE, JOSH	Joshua M.; B11.13.1887 Murray City OH; D10.6.1954 Chillicothe OH; BL/TL/5´6˝/160; d9.25																							
1908 NY N	5	6	1	1	0	0	0	2	1	0	—	.167	.286	.167	43	0	1	1.000	-0	0	0	O2R	—	-0.1
1909 NY N	22	28	6	4	1	0	0	1	2	2	—	.143	.250	.179	33	-2	3	.824	-1	103	0	O12(3/10/1)	—	-0.3
1910 NY N	133	490	92	149	11	10	2	27	46	6	67	.304	.371	.380	119	11	43	.929	-7	81	116	O130(106/2/22)	—	-0.3
1911 †NY N	149	565	96	158	19	10	3	50	81	6	69	.280	.376	.365	104	6	61	.934	0	89	143	O149(104/0/48)	—	-0.1
1912 †NY N	106	327	66	90	14	6	2	37	51	5	43	.275	.381	.373	104	4	27	.918	-5	86	106	O96(76/1/19)	—	-0.5
1913 NY N	16	21	4	4	0	1	0	1	3	1	4	.190	.320	.286	73	-1	6-2	1.000	0	68	214	O8(1/5/2)	—	0.0
Cin N	66	217	30	58	6	4	3	14	12	1	21	.267	.309	.373	95	-3	17-7	.920	-2	88	126	O57(0/57/1)	—	-0.7
Phi N	23	39	9	11	1	0	0	5	4	1	7	.282	.364	.308	89	0	0	.889	-0	81	185	O14(8/6/0)	—	-0.1
Year	105	277	43	73	7	5	3	20	19	3	32	.264	.318	.357	92	-4	23-9	.919	-2	86	138	O79(9/68/3)	—	-0.8
1914 Phi N	30	53	5	16	2	0	0	7	4	0	5	.302	.351	.340	99	0	0	.947	3	86	399	O9(7/2/0)	—	0.2
†Bos N	51	128	22	29	4	0	1	5	18	1	14	.227	.327	.281	82	-2	2	.915	-4	79	79	O42(23/20/0)	—	-0.8
Year	81	181	27	45	6	0	1	12	22	1	19	.249	.333	.298	87	-2	2	.923	-1	80	147	O51(30/22/0)	—	-0.6
Total 7	601	1874	331	520	58	31	11	149	222	23	230	.277	.361	.359	103	13	160-9	.925	-16	85	126	O519(328/103/95)	—	-2.7
DEVORMER, AL	Albert E.; B8.19.1891 Grand Rapids MI; D8.29.1966 Grand Rapids MI; BR/TR/6´0.5˝/175; d8.4																							
1918 Chi A	8	19	2	5	2	0	0	0	0	0	4	.263	.263	.368	90	0	1	1.000	-1	106	79	C6/rf	—	-0.1
1921 †NY A	22	49	6	17	4	0	0	7	2	0	4	.347	.373	.429	102	0	2-0	.950	-1	109	91	C17	—	0.1
1922 NY A	24	59	8	12	4	1	0	11	1	0	6	.203	.217	.305	34	-6	0-0	.968	-1	128	104	C17/1	—	-0.6
1923 Bos A	74	209	20	54	7	3	0	18	6	1	21	.258	.282	.321	58	-14	3-0	.979	-1	81	107	C55,1b2	—	-1.0
1927 NY N	68	141	14	35	3	1	2	21	11	2	11	.248	.312	.326	71	-6	1	.953	-3	122	103	C54,1b3	—	-0.7
Total 5	196	477	50	123	20	5	2	57	20	3	46	.258	.292	.333	65	-26	7-0	.967	-6	103	103	C149,1b6/rf	—	-2.3
DEVOY, WALT	Walter Joseph; B3.14.1886 St.Louis MO; D12.17.1953 St.Louis MO; BR/TR/5´11˝/165; d9.13																							
1909 StL A	19	69	7	17	3	1	0	8	3	0	—	.246	.278	.319	95	-1	4	.944	-0	127	0	O16R,1b3	—	-0.2
DEWILLIS, JEFF	Jeffrey Allen; B4.13.1965 Houston TX; BR/TR/6´2˝/190; [TorA83 3/63]; d4.19																							
1987 Tor A	13	25	2	3	1	0	1	2	2-0	0	12	.120	.185	.280	20	-3	0-0	.964	-1	174	160	C13	0	-0.3
DEXTER, CHARLIE	Charles Dana; B6.15.1876 Evansville IN; D6.9.1934 Cedar Rapids IA; BR/TR/5´7˝/155; d4.17; Col Univ. of the South; OF(8/159/236)																							
1896 Lou N	107	402	65	112	18	7	3	37	17	6	34	.279	.318	.381	87	-9	21	.903	-9	79	120	C55,O47(0/46/1)	—	-1.4
1897 Lou N	76	257	43	72	12	5	2	46	21	3	—	.280	.342	.389	96	-2	12	.907	-1	252	404	O32(3/14/16),C23,3b14,S2	—	-0.2
1898 Lou N	112	421	76	132	13	5	1	66	26	7	—	.314	.363	.375	113	7	44	.958	-3	99	62	O95R,2b8,C7	—	0.1
1899 Lou N	81	298	47	76	7	1	1	34	21	5	—	.255	.315	.295	68	-13	21	.943	2	142	68	O72(1/0/71),S6	—	-1.3
1900 Chi N	40	125	7	25	5	0	2	20	1	1	—	.200	.213	.288	39	-11	2	.943	4	95	136	C22,O13R/2	—	-0.5
1901 Chi N	116	460	46	123	9	5	1	66	16	7	—	.267	.302	.315	82	-11	22	.982	2	131	106	1b54,3b25,O21(1/9/11),2b13,C3	—	-1.0
1902 Chi N	71	273	31	62	13	0	2	26	19	5	—	.227	.290	.297	83	-5	13	.846	-14	70	99	3b41,1b22,O10(1/4/5)	—	-2.0
Bos N	48	183	33	47	3	0	1	18	16	2	—	.257	.323	.290	88	-2	16	.901	-3	100	78	S22,2b19,O7(0/4/3)/3	—	-0.5
Year	119	456	64	109	16	0	3	44	35	7	—	.239	.303	.294	85	-7	29	.847	-17	70	98	3b42,1b22,S22,2b19,O17(1/8/8)	—	-2.5
1903 Bos N	123	457	82	102	15	1	3	34	61	6	—	.223	.323	.280	75	-12	32	.941	-9	91	165	O106(2/82/21),S9,C6	—	-2.4
Total 8	774	2876	430	751	95	24	16	347	198	42	34	.261	.318	.328	85	-58	183	.942	-30	115	138	O403R,C116,3b81,1b76,2b41,S39	—	-9.2

YEAR	TM LG	G	AB	R	H	2B	3B	HR	RBI	BB-IB	HP	SO	AVG	OBP	SLG	AOPS	ABR	SB-CS	FA	FR	RNG	THR	GAMES AT POSITION	DL	BFW
DIAZ, ALEX Alexis; B10.5.1968 Brooklyn NY; BB/TR/5´11˝/(175–180); d7.25																									
1992	Mil A	22	9	5	1	0	0	0	1	0-0	0	0	.111	.111	.111	-38	-2	3-2	1.000	0	109	0	O11(2/10/0),D2	0	-0.2
1993	Mil A	32	69	9	22	2	0	0	1	0-0	0	12	.319	.319	.348	80	-2	5-3	.979	-0	99	77	O28(4/12/13)/D	119	-0.3
1994	Mil A	79	187	17	47	5	7	1	17	10-1	0	19	.251	.285	.369	65	-11	5-5	.993	1	96	150	O73(0/58/20),2b2/D	12	-1.0
1995	†Sea A	103	270	44	67	14	0	3	27	13-2	2	27	.248	.286	.333	60	-16	18-8	.987	-1	94	122	O88(17/69/4)	0	-1.5
1996	Sea A	38	79	11	19	2	0	1	5	2-0	2	8	.241	.274	.304	47	-7	6-3	.982	3	139	77	O28(19/5/5)/D	81	-0.4
1997	Tex A	28	90	8	20	4	0	2	12	5-0	1	13	.222	.268	.333	53	-6	1-1	.980	1	104	137	O23(3/0/20)/12	0	-0.6
1998	SF N	34	62	5	8	2	0	0	5	0-0	0	15	.129	.129	.161	-26	-12	1-1	1.000	1	105	268	O21(4/15/3)	0	-1.0
1999	Hou N	30	50	3	11	2	0	1	7	3-0	0	13	.220	.264	.320	47	-4	2-2	.900	-0	64	258	O8(7/0/1)	71	-0.5
Total	8	366	816	102	195	31	7	8	75	33-3	5	107	.239	.271	.324	53	-60	41-25	.986	5	100	133	O280(56/169/66),D5,2b3/1	283	-5.5
DIAZ, BO Baudilio Jose (Seijas); B3.23.1953 Cua, Miranda, Venezuela; D11.23.1990 Caracas, Distrito Capital, Venez.; BR/TR/5´11˝/(190–205); d9.6																									
1977	Bos A	2	1	0	0	0	0	0	0	0-0	0	1	.000	.000	.000	-90	0	0-0	1.000	1	0	0	C2	0	0.0
1978	Cle A	44	127	12	30	4	0	2	11	4-0	0	17	.236	.260	.315	61	-7	0-0	.971	-5	112	92	C44	61	-1.0
1979	Cle A	15	32	0	5	2	0	0	1	2-0	0	6	.156	.206	.219	15	-4	0-0	.958	-0	72	76	C15	55	-0.4
1980	Cle A	76	207	15	47	11	2	3	32	7-3	0	27	.227	.250	.343	61	-12	1-0	.989	2	78	83	C75	0	-0.7
1981	Cle A★	63	182	25	57	19	0	7	38	13-2	1	23	.313	.359	.533	156	13	2-2	.975	-3	122	84	C51,D3	0	1.2
1982	Phi N	144	525	69	151	29	1	18	85	36-5	3	87	.288	.333	.450	115	9	3-6	.989	-4	103	101	C144	0	1.1
1983	†Phi N	136	471	49	111	17	0	15	64	38-4	2	57	.236	.295	.367	83	-12	1-4	.986	18	106	114	C134	0	1.1
1984	Phi N	27	75	5	16	4	0	1	9	5-0	0	13	.213	.256	.307	58	-4	0-0	.992	-1	89	89	C23	97	-0.5
1985	Phi N	26	76	9	16	5	1	2	16	6-0	0	7	.211	.268	.382	78	-2	0-0	.972	2	86	125	C24	43	0.1
	Cin N	51	161	12	42	8	0	3	15	15-0	1	18	.261	.324	.366	89	-2	0-0	.988	13	116	98	C51	0	1.3
	Year	77	237	21	58	13	1	5	31	21-0	1	25	.245	.307	.371	86	-4	0-0	.983	15	107	106	C75	0	1.4
1986	Cin N	134	474	50	129	21	0	10	56	40-0	0	52	.272	.327	.380	91	-6	1-1	.984	2	115	98	C134	0	0.2
1987	Cin N★	140	496	49	134	28	1	15	82	19-1	5	73	.270	.300	.421	86	-11	1-0	.992	2	116	117	C137	0	-0.3
1988	Cin N	92	315	26	69	9	0	10	35	7-4	1	41	.219	.236	.343	63	-17	0-2	.990	5	126	127	C88	15	-0.8
1989	Cin N	43	132	6	27	5	0	1	8	6-3	0	7	.205	.239	.265	43	-10	0-2	.984	-1	96	55	C43	65	-1.0
Total	13	993	3274	327	834	162	5	87	452	198-22	13	429	.255	.297	.387	87	-65	9-17	.986	30	108	103	C965,D3	336	0.3
DIAZ, CARLOS Carlos Francisco; B12.24.1964 Elizabeth NJ; BR/TR/6´3˝/190; [TorA86 14/367]; d5.8; Col Oklahoma St.																									
1990	Tor A	9	3	1	1	0	0	0	0	0-0	0	2	.333	.333	.333	85	0	0-0	1.000	2	97	197	C9	0	0.2
DIAZ, EDDY Eddy Javier; B9.29.1971 Barquisimeto, Lara, Venez.; BR/TR/5´10˝/160; d4.17																									
1997	Mil A	16	50	4	11	2	1	0	7	1-0	0	5	.220	.235	.300	38	-5	0-0	1.000	1	100	132	2b14/3S	0	-0.3
DIAZ, EDGAR Edgar (Serrano); B2.8.1964 Santurce, PR; BR/TR/6´0˝/160; d9.16; [DL 1987 Mil A 58]																									
1986	Mil A	5	13	0	3	0	0	0	0	1-0	0	3	.231	.286	.231	41	-1	0-0	.875	-3	62	70	S5	0	-0.3
1990	Mil A	86	218	27	59	2	2	0	14	21-0	1	32	.271	.338	.298	79	-6	3-2	.950	-5	96	93	S65,2b15,3b7/D	0	-0.7
Total	2	91	231	27	62	2	2	0	14	22-0	1	35	.268	.335	.294	77	-7	3-2	.946	-8	93	91	S70,2b15,3b7/D	58	-1.0
DIAZ, EDWIN Edwin (Rosario); B1.15.1975 Bayamon, PR; BR/TR/5´11˝/170; [TexA93 2/52]; d3.31																									
1998	Ari N	3	7	0	0	0	0	0	0	0-0	0	2	.000	.000	.000	-99	-2	0-0	.938	1	125	141	2b3	0	-0.1
1999	Ari N	4	5	2	2	2	0	0	1	3-1	0	1	.400	.625	.800	255	2	0-0	1.000	-0	250	0	2b2,S2	27	0.1
Total	2	7	12	2	2	2	0	0	1	3-1	0	3	.167	.333	.333	72	0	0-0	.947	1	146	118	2b5,S2	27	0.0
DIAZ, EINAR Einar Antonio; B12.28.1972 Chiriqui, Pan; BR/TR/5´10˝/(165–200); d9.9																									
1996	Cle A	4	1	0	0	0	0	0	0	0-0	0	0	.000	.000	.000	-99	0	0-0	1.000	0	0	0	C4	0	0.0
1997	Cle A	5	7	1	1	1	0	0	1	0-0	0	2	.143	.143	.286	8	-1	0-0	.955	0	26	262	C5	0	-0.1
1998	†Cle A	17	48	8	11	1	0	2	9	3-0	2	2	.229	.286	.375	72	-2	0-0	.973	2	105	124	C17	0	0.0
1999	†Cle A	119	392	43	110	21	1	3	32	23-0	5	41	.281	.328	.362	72	-16	11-4	.988	4	96	112	C119	0	-0.4
2000	Cle A	75	250	29	68	14	2	4	25	11-0	8	29	.272	.323	.392	77	-9	4-2	.994	17	120	104	C74/3	0	1.2
2001	†Cle A	134	437	54	121	34	1	4	56	17-0	16	44	.277	.328	.387	84	-9	1-2	.992	15	111	**133**	C134/2	0	1.3
2002	Cle A	102	320	34	66	19	0	2	16	17-1	6	27	.206	.258	.284	44	-26	0-1	.989	3	65	**149**	C100	38	-1.6
2003	Tex A	101	334	30	86	14	1	4	35	9-0	10	32	.257	.294	.341	64	-18	3-1	.989	5	110	99	C101	0	-0.6
2004	Mon N	55	139	9	31	6	1	1	11	11-3	4	10	.223	.293	.302	54	-10	2-0	.990	5	90	64	C44/3	0	-0.2
2005	StL N	58	130	14	27	6	0	1	17	5-0	2	12	.208	.248	.277	37	-12	0-0	.995	1	160	112	C50,1b3	0	-0.9
2006	LA N	3	3	0	2	0	0	0	0	0-0	0	0	.667	.667	.667	243	1	0-0	ø	-0	0	0	/C	0	0.0
Total	11	673	2061	222	523	116	6	21	202	96-4	53	199	.254	.302	.346	66	-102	21-10	.990	52	103	117	C649,1b3,3b2/2	38	-1.3
DIAZ, JUAN Juan Carlos; B2.19.1974 San Jose de las Lajas, Cuba; BR/TR/6´2˝/228; d6.12																									
2002	Bos A	4	7	2	2	1	0	1	2	1-0	0	2	.286	.375	.857	210	1	0-0	1.000	-0	0	0	/1D	0	0.1
DIAZ, MARIO Mario Rafael (Torres); B1.10.1962 Humacao, PR; BR/TR/5´10˝/160; d9.12; [DL 1990 Sea A 25]																									
1987	Sea A	11	23	4	7	0	1	0	3	0-0	0	4	.304	.304	.391	78	-1	0-0	.972	3	130	155	S10	0	-0.2
1988	Sea A	28	72	6	22	5	0	0	9	3-0	0	5	.306	.329	.375	94	-1	0-0	.985	-6	73	75	S21,2b4/13	17	-0.5
1989	Sea A	52	74	9	10	0	0	1	7	7-0	0	7	.135	.210	.176	9	-9	0-0	.930	-15	64	36	S37,2b14,3b3	0	-2.3
1990	NY N	16	22	0	3	1	0	0	1	0-0	0	3	.136	.130	.182	-13	-3	0-0	.958	1	131	42	S10/2	0	-0.2
1991	Tex A	96	182	24	48	7	0	1	22	15-0	0	18	.264	.318	.319	78	-5	0-1	.962	-3	91	91	S65,2b20,3b8/D	17	-0.5
1992	Tex A	19	31	2	7	1	0	0	1	1-1	0	2	.226	.250	.258	44	-2	0-1	.975	-2	83	30	S16,2b3/3	0	-0.5
1993	Tex A	71	205	24	56	10	1	2	24	8-0	1	13	.273	.297	.361	80	-6	1-0	.986	-3	93	88	S57,3b12/1	0	-0.5
1994	Fla N	32	77	10	25	4	2	0	11	6-0	1	6	.325	.376	.429	106	1	0-0	.964	1	105	211	3b11,2b7,S7	0	0.2
1995	Fla N	49	87	5	20	3	0	1	6	1-0	0	12	.230	.239	.299	40	-8	0-0	.944	-1	97	179	2b9,S5,3b3	0	-0.8
Total	9	374	773	84	198	31	4	5	84	41-1	2	70	.256	.292	.326	69	-34	1-2	.972	-24	88	81	S228,2b58,3b39,1b2/D	59	-4.9
DIAZ, MATT Matthew Edward; B3.3.1978 Portland OR; BR/TR/6´1˝/(200–206); [TBA99 17/505]; d7.19; Col Florida St.																									
2003	TB A	4	9	2	1	0	0	0	0	1-0	0	3	.111	.200	.111	-15	-2	0-0	.857	1	274	0	/lfD	0	-0.1
2004	TB A	10	21	3	4	1	1	1	3	1-0	2	6	.190	.292	.476	98	0	0-0	1.000	1	165	0	O4(3/0/1),D4	0	0.0
2005	KC A	34	89	7	25	4	2	1	9	4-0	2	15	.281	.323	.404	96	-1	0-1	.950	-0	114	0	O21(19/0/2),D7	37	-0.2
2006	Atl N	124	297	37	97	15	4	7	32	11-3	9	49	.327	.364	.475	113	5	5-5	.977	8	124	136	O99(95/0/6)	0	1.0
Total	4	172	416	49	127	20	7	9	44	17-3	13	73	.305	.348	.452	106	2	5-6	.970	9	125	104	O125(118/0/9),D13	37	0.7
DIAZ, MIKE Michael Anthony; B4.15.1960 San Francisco CA; BR/TR/6´2˝/(195–220); [ChiN78 30/685]; d9.15																									
1983	Chi N	6	7	2	2	1	0	0	1	0-0	0	0	.286	.286	.429	91	0	0-0	1.000	-1	37	0	C3	0	-0.1
1986	Pit N	97	209	22	56	9	0	12	36	19-0	2	43	.268	.330	.483	120	5	0-1	.966	-3	96	50	O38(37/0/1),1b20,3b5/C	0	0.0
1987	Pit N	103	241	28	58	8	2	16	48	31-3	3	42	.241	.326	.490	114	4	1-0	.960	-1	86	105	O37(27/0/10),1b32,C8	0	0.0
1988	Pit N	47	74	6	17	3	0	0	5	16-1	0	13	.230	.367	.270	86	0	0-0	1.000	-2	66	0	O19(9/0/9),1b6/C	33	-0.3
	Chi A	40	152	12	36	6	0	3	12	5-0	1	30	.237	.266	.336	67	-7	0-1	.987	-1	95	92	1b39/D	0	-1.2
Total	4	293	683	70	169	27	2	31	102	71-4	6	128	.247	.319	.429	103	2	1-2	.988	-8	91	88	1b97,O94(73/0/20),C13,3b5/D	33	-1.6
DIAZ, VICTOR Victor Israel; B12.10.1981 Santo Domingo, D.R.; BR/TR/6´0˝/200; [LAN00 37/1107]; d9.11; Col Grayson Co. (TX) JC																									
2004	NY N	15	51	8	15	3	0	3	8	1-0	1	15	.294	.321	.529	117	1	0-0	.935	-0	115	0	O14R	0	0.0
2005	NY N	89	280	41	72	17	3	12	38	30-7	1	82	.257	.329	.468	109	3	6-2	.981	-0	103	67	O81(3/0/78)	0	-0.1
2006	NY N	6	11	0	2	1	0	0	2	0-0	0	5	.182	.182	.273	15	-1	0-0	.800	-0	93	0	O4L	0	-0.2
Total	3	110	342	49	89	21	3	15	48	31-7	2	102	.260	.324	.471	107	3	6-2	.970	-1	104	56	O99(7/0/92)	0	-0.3
DICKEN, PAUL Paul Franklin; B10.2.1943 DeLand FL; BR/TR/6´5˝/195; d6.7; Col Manatee (FL) CC/Palm Beach (FL) CC																									
1964	Cle A	11	11	0	0	0	0	0	0	0-0	0	5	.000	.000	.000	-99	-3	0-0	ø	0	—	—	/H	0	-0.3
1966	Cle A	2	2	0	0	0	0	0	0	0-0	0	1	.000	.000	.000	-99	-1	0-0	ø	0	—	—	/H	0	-0.1
Total	2	13	13	0	0	0	0	0	0	0-0	0	6	.000	.000	.000	-99	-4	0-0	ø	0	—	—	0	—	-0.4
DICKERSON, BUTTERCUP Lewis Pessano; B10.11.1858 Tyaskin MD; D7.23.1920 Baltimore MD; BL/TR/5´6˝/140; d7.15																									
1878	Cin N	29	123	17	38	5	1	0	9	0	—	7	.309	.309	.366	134	4	—	.877	-2	13	0	O29(10/19/0)	—	0.1
1879	Cin N	**81**	350	73	102	18	**14**	2	57	3	—	27	.291	.297	.440	147	17	—	.801	-4	50	48	O81L	—	0.7
1880	Tro N	30	119	15	23	2	2	0	10	2	—	3	.193	.207	.244	49	-6	—	.903	4	91	207	O30(0/29/1)/S	—	-0.4
	Wor N	31	133	22	39	8	6	0	20	1	—	2	.293	.299	.444	136	4	—	.852	-4	53	155	O31C	—	-0.1
	Year	61	252	37	62	10	8	0	30	3	—	5	.246	.255	.349	96	-2	—	.883	0	72	181	O61(0/60/1)/S	—	-0.5

YEAR	TM LG	G	AB	R	H	2B	3B	HR	RBI	BB-IB	HP	SO	AVG	OBP	SLG	AOPS	ABR	SB-CS	FA	FR	RNG	THR	GAMES AT POSITION	DL	BFW
1881	Wor N	80	367	48	116	18	6	1	31	8	—	8	.316	.331	.406	123	9	—	.892	9	131	169	O80(79/0/1)	—	1.2
1883	Pit AA	85	354	62	88	15	1	0	—	18	—	—	.249	.285	.297	91	-2	—	.798	-1	184	97	O78(1/30/47),S8,2b2	—	-0.3
1884	StL U	46	211	49	77	15	1	0	—	8	—	—	.365	.388	.445	146	6	—	.895	4	113	145	O42L,3b4	—	0.8
	Bal AA	13	56	9	12	2	1	0	—	4	2	—	.214	.290	.286	85	-1	—	.941	-2	47	0	O12R/3	—	-0.2
	Lou AA	8	28	6	4	0	2	1	—	3	0	—	.143	.226	.393	103	0	—	.813	0	149	0	O8(1/5/3)	—	0.0
	Year	21	84	15	16	2	3	1	—	7	2	—	.190	.269	.321	91	-1	—	.879	-2	86	0	O20(1/5/15)/3	—	-0.2
1885	Buf N	5	21	1	1	1	0	0	0	1	—	4	.048	.091	.095	-38	-3	—	1.000	1	226	0	O5(2/3/0)	—	-0.3
Total	7	408	1762	302	500	84	34	4	127	48	—	51	.284	.304	.377	118	28	—	.854	6	104	108	O396(216/117/64),S9,3b5,2b2	—	1.5
Dickey, George	George Willard "Skeets"; B7.10.1915 Kensett AR; D6.16.1976 DeWitt AR; BB/TR/6´2˝/180; d9.21; Mil 1943–45; b–Bill																								
1935	Bos A	5	11	1	0	0	0	0	1	1	0	3	.000	.083	.000	-72	-3	0-0	1.000	-1	*74*	*0*	C4	—	-0.3
1936	Bos A	10	23	0	1	1	0	0	0	2	0	3	.043	.120	.087	-46	-5	0-0	.912	0	*95*	*193*	C10	—	-0.4
1941	Chi A	32	55	6	11	1	0	2	8	5	0	7	.200	.267	.327	57	-4	0-0	1.000	1	*102*	*68*	C17	0	-0.2
1942	Chi A	59	116	6	27	3	0	1	17	9	0	11	.233	.288	.284	63	-6	0-0	.918	-3	*98*	*54*	C29	0	-0.8
1946	Chi A	37	78	8	15	1	0	0	1	12	0	13	.192	.300	.205	45	-5	0-2	1.000	2	*84*	*106*	C30	0	-0.3
1947	Chi A	83	211	15	47	6	0	1	27	34	0	25	.223	.331	.265	69	-8	4-2	.985	-1	*79*	*105*	C80	0	-0.5
Total	6	226	494	36	101	12	0	4	54	63	0	62	.204	.294	.253	53	-31	4-4	.974	-2	*86*	*95*	C170	0	-2.5
Dickey, Bill	William Malcolm; B6.6.1907 Bastrop LA; D11.12.1993 Little Rock AR; BL/TR/6´1.5˝/185; d8.15; Mil 1944–45; M1/C10; HF1954; b–George																								
1928	NY A	10	15	1	3	1	1	0	2	0	0	2	.200	.200	.400	56	-1	0-0	1.000	-1	*71*	*102*	C6	—	-0.2
1929	NY A	130	447	60	145	30	6	10	65	14	1	16	.324	.346	.485	120	10	4-6	.979	2	*108*	*86*	C127	—	1.8
1930	NY A	109	366	55	124	25	7	5	65	21	0	14	.339	.375	.486	122	11	7-1	.977	-10	*85*	*92*	C101	—	0.8
1931	NY A	130	477	65	156	17	10	6	78	39	0	20	.327	.378	.442	122	14	2-1	**.996**	-1	*101*	*110*	C125	—	2.0
1932	†NY A	108	423	66	131	20	4	15	84	34	0	13	.310	.361	.482	123	13	2-4	.987	-2	*105*	*74*	C108	—	1.6
1933	NY A☆	130	478	58	152	24	8	14	97	47	2	14	.318	.381	.490	138	25	3-4	.993	5	*152*	*97*	C127	—	3.5
1934	NY A★	104	395	56	127	24	4	12	72	38	2	18	.322	.384	.494	134	19	0-3	.986	-0	*99*	*85*	C104	—	2.3
1935	NY A	120	448	54	125	26	6	14	81	35	6	11	.279	.339	.458	111	5	1-1	**.995**	3	*128*	*90*	C118	—	1.4
1936	†NY A★	112	423	99	153	26	8	22	107	46	3	16	.362	.428	.617	161	39	0-2	.976	3	***149***	*101*	C107	—	4.2
1937	†NY A★	140	530	87	176	35	2	29	133	73	4	22	.332	.417	.570	145	38	3-2	.991	16	***139***	*86*	C137	—	5.6
1938	†NY A★	132	454	84	142	27	4	27	115	75	2	22	.313	.412	.568	144	32	3-0	.987	6	*128*	*85*	C126	—	4.1
1939	†NY A★	128	480	98	145	23	3	24	105	77	4	37	.302	.403	.512	135	27	5-0	**.989**	14	***145***	*75*	C126	—	4.5
1940	NY A★	106	372	45	92	11	1	9	54	48	2	32	.247	.336	.355	83	-9	0-3	.994	2	*139*	*104*	C102	—	-0.2
1941	†NY A★	109	348	35	99	15	5	7	71	45	3	17	.284	.371	.417	110	5	2-1	**.994**	3	***139***	*88*	C104	0	1.3
1942	†NY A✳	82	268	28	79	13	1	2	37	26	1	11	.295	.359	.373	108	3	2-2	.976	7	***184***	*105*	C80	0	1.4
1943	†NY A☆	85	242	29	85	18	2	4	33	41	0	12	.351	.445	.492	173	25	2-1	.994	4	*170*	*83*	C71	0	3.4
1946	NY A★	54	134	10	35	8	0	2	10	19	1	12	.261	.357	.366	101	1	0-1	.987	7	*125*	*131*	C39,M	0	1.0
Total	17	1789	6300	930	1969	343	72	202	1209	678	31	289	.313	.382	.486	128	257	36-32	.988	57	*130*	*91*	C1708	0	38.5
Dickshot, Johnny	John Oscar "Ugly" (b John Oscar Dicksus); B1.24.1910 Waukegan IL; D11.4.1997 Waukegan IL; BR/TR/6´0˝/195; d4.16																								
1936	Pit N	9	9	2	2	0	0	0	1	1	0	2	.222	.300	.222	42	-1	0	ø	-0	0	0	/cf	—	-0.1
1937	Pit N	82	264	42	67	8	4	3	33	26	1	36	.254	.323	.348	82	-7	0	.950	-1	94	115	O64(58/0/6)	—	-1.1
1938	Pit N	29	35	3	8	0	0	0	4	8	0	5	.229	.372	.229	68	-1	3	1.000	-0	103	0	O10(5/0/5)	—	-0.2
1939	NY N	10	34	3	8	0	0	0	5	5	0	3	.235	.333	.235	55	-2	0	1.000	-0	78	130	O10R	—	-0.3
1944	Chi A	62	162	18	41	8	5	0	15	13	1	10	.253	.313	.364	94	-2	2-0	.974	-0	95	103	O40(35/0/5)	0	-0.4
1945	Chi A	130	486	74	147	19	10	4	58	48	1	41	.302	.366	.407	128	16	18-3	.971	0	97	115	O124L	0	1.3
Total	6	322	990	142	273	35	19	7	116	101	3	97	.276	.345	.371	104	3	23-3	.968	-2	95	110	O249(222/1/26)	0	-0.8
Didier, Bob	Robert Daniel; B2.16.1949 Hattiesburg MS; BB/TR/6´0˝/(180–190); d4.7; C5																								
1969	†Atl N	114	352	30	90	16	1	0	32	34-5	0	39	.256	.321	.307	76	-10	1-3	.994	-3	86	78	C114	0	-1.0
1970	Atl N	57	168	9	25	2	1	0	7	12-4	1	11	.149	.210	.173	3	-23	1-0	.988	-5	63	101	C57	0	-2.6
1971	Atl N	51	155	9	34	4	1	0	5	6-5	0	17	.219	.248	.258	41	-12	0-0	1.000	-0	126	47	C50	0	-1.1
1972	Atl N	13	40	5	12	2	1	0	5	2-0	1	4	.300	.341	.400	103	0	0-0	1.000	1	67	96	C11	0	0.1
1973	Det A	7	22	3	10	1	0	0	1	3-0	0	0	.455	.520	.500	177	3	0-0	1.000	2	85	96	C7	0	0.4
1974	Bos A	5	14	0	1	0	0	0	1	2-2	0	1	.071	.176	.071	-22	-2	0-0	.968	-1	44	104	C5	0	-0.3
Total	6	247	751	56	172	25	4	0	51	59-16	2	72	.229	.286	.273	54	-44	2-3	.994	-7	87	79	C244	0	-4.5
Diehl, Ernie	Ernest Guy; B10.2.1877 Cincinnati OH; D11.6.1958 Miami FL; BR/TR/6´1˝/190; d5.31																								
1903	Pit N	1	3	0	1	0	0	0	0	0	0	—	.333	.333	.333	87	0	0	ø	-0	0	0	/lf	—	0.0
1904	Pit N	12	37	6	6	0	0	0	4	6	2	—	.162	.311	.162	46	-2	3	1.000	1	158	0	O7(2/0/5),S4	—	-0.1
1906	Bos N	3	11	1	5	0	1	0	0	0	0	—	.455	.455	.636	247	2	0	1.000	-0	0	0	O2L/S	—	0.1
1909	Bos N	1	4	1	2	1	0	0	0	0	0	—	.500	.500	.750	275	1	0	.800	1	485	0	/lf	—	0.1
Total	4	17	55	8	14	1	1	0	4	6	2	—	.255	.349	.309	101	1	3	.944	1	170	0	O11(6/0/5),S5	—	0.1
Diering, Chuck	Charles Edward Allen; B2.5.1923 St.Louis MO; BR/TR/5´10˝/165; d4.15																								
1947	StL N	105	74	22	16	3	1	2	11	19	1	22	.216	.383	.365	95	0	3	1.000	3	118	190	O75(13/31/31)	0	0.3
1948	StL N	7	7	2	0	0	0	0	0	2	0	2	.000	.222	.000	-33	-1	1	1.000	1	102	672	O5L	0	-0.1
1949	StL N	131	369	60	97	21	8	3	38	35	1	49	.263	.328	.388	87	-7	1	.987	6	**112**	100	O124(0/123/1)	0	-0.3
1950	StL N	89	204	34	51	12	0	3	18	35	0	38	.250	.360	.353	84	-3	1	.989	7	111	157	O81(0/78/3)	0	0.2
1951	StL N	64	85	9	22	5	1	0	8	6	0	15	.259	.308	.341	74	-3	0-1	1.000	3	116	149	O44(6/33/5)	0	-0.2
1952	NY N	41	23	2	4	1	1	0	2	4	0	3	.174	.296	.304	66	-1	0-2	1.000	2	135	137	O36(27/4/5)	0	-0.1
1954	Bal A	128	418	35	108	14	1	2	29	56	4	57	.258	.349	.311	89	-4	3-7	.983	10	107	**159**	O119C	0	-0.2
1955	Bal A✳	137	371	38	95	16	2	3	31	57-1	0	45	.256	.355	.334	93	-2	5-8	.976	6	**110**	121	O107(2/105/0),3b34,S12	0	-0.1
1956	Bal A	50	97	15	18	4	0	1	4	23-0	0	19	.186	.342	.258	65	-4	2-5	1.000	2	107	210	O40(7/34/2),3b2	0	-0.5
Total	9	752	1648	217	411	76	14	14	141	237-1	6	250	.249	.345	.338	86	-25	16-23	.987	38	111	145	O631(60/527/47),3b36,S12	0	-1.0
Dietz, Dick	Richard Allen; B9.18.1941 Crawfordsville IN; D6.27.2005 Clayton GA; BR/TR/6´1˝/(175–185); d6.18																								
1966	SF N	13	23	1	1	0	0	0	0	0-0	1	9	.043	.083	.043	-62	-5	0-0	1.000	-1	65	235	C6	0	-0.6
1967	SF N	56	120	10	27	3	0	4	19	25-0	1	44	.225	.358	.350	106	2	0-1	.983	-3	85	109	C43	0	0.1
1968	SF N	98	301	21	82	14	2	6	38	34-3	1	68	.272	.347	.392	122	9	1-1	.976	-9	61	87	C90	0	0.5
1969	SF N	79	244	28	56	8	1	11	35	53-3	3	53	.230	.372	.406	120	9	0-0	.973	-1	107	96	C73	0	1.2
1970	SF N★	148	493	82	148	36	2	22	107	109-10	3	106	.300	.426	.515	153	44	0-1	.984	-22	80	56	C139	0	2.9
1971	†SF N	142	453	58	114	19	0	19	72	97-8	4	86	.252	.387	.419	130	23	1-3	.982	-9	102	45	C135	0	2.1
1972	LA N	27	56	4	9	1	0	1	6	14-2	0	11	.161	.329	.232	63	-2	2-0	1.000	4	142	136	C22	33	0.3
1973	Atl N	83	139	22	41	8	1	3	24	49-4	0	25	.295	.474	.432	143	13	0-0	.989	-2	121	76	1b36,C20	0	1.0
Total	8	646	1829	226	478	89	6	66	301	381-30	13	402	.261	.390	.425	129	93	4-6	.980	-41	88	72	C528,1b36	33	7.5
Dietzel, Roy	Leroy Louis; B1.9.1931 Baltimore MD; BR/TR/6´0˝/190; d9.2																								
1954	Was A	9	21	1	5	0	0	0	1	5	0	4	.238	.385	.238	78	0	0-0	.960	-1	110	104	2b7,3b2	0	0.0
Difani, Jay	Clarence Joseph; B12.21.1922 Crystal City MO; D12.3.2003 Crystal City MO; BR/TR/6´0˝/170; d4.23; Col Missouri																								
1948	Was A	2	2	0	0	0	0	0	0	0	0	2	.000	.000	.000	-99	-1	0-0	ø	0	—	—	/H	0	-0.1
1949	Was A	2	1	0	1	1	0	0	0	0	0	0	1.000	1.000	2.000	699	1	0-0	1.000	0	149	0	/2	0	0.1
Total	2	4	3	0	1	1	0	0	0	0	0	2	.333	.333	.667	166	0	0-0	1.000	0	149	0	/2	0	0.0
Difelice, Mike	Michael William; B5.28.1969 Philadelphia PA; BR/TR/6´2˝/(200–205); [StLN91 11/285]; d9.1; Col Tennessee																								
1996	StL N	4	7	0	2	1	0	0	2	0-0	0	1	.286	.286	.429	85	0	0-0	1.000	0	52	161	C4	0	0.0
1997	StL N	93	260	16	62	10	1	4	30	19-0	3	61	.238	.297	.331	64	-14	1-1	.991	16	95	122	C91/1	0	0.7
1998	TB A	84	248	17	57	12	3	3	23	15-0	1	56	.230	.274	.339	57	-16	0-0	.993	13	111	**132**	C84	0	0.1
1999	TB A	51	179	21	55	11	0	6	27	8-0	3	23	.307	.346	.469	104	1	0-0	.987	5	143	108	C51	0	0.8
2000	TB A	60	204	23	49	13	1	6	19	12-0	0	40	.240	.280	.402	72	-10	0-0	.980	6	94	119	C59	0	0.0
2001	TB A	48	149	13	31	5	1	2	9	8-0	3	39	.208	.259	.295	48	-12	1-1	.982	5	113	123	C48	0	-0.4
	Ari N	12	21	1	1	0	0	0	1	0-0	1	10	.048	.091	.048	-59	-5	0-0	.982	1	383	158	C12	0	-0.4
2002	†StL N	70	174	17	40	11	0	4	19	17-3	1	42	.230	.297	.362	73	-7	0-0	.991	5	124	68	C61	0	0.1
2003	KC A	62	189	29	48	16	1	3	25	9-0	4	30	.254	.299	.397	77	-6	1-0	.994	3	78	127	C58,D2	0	0.1
2004	Det A	13	22	3	3	0	1	0	2	3-0	0	3	.136	.240	.227	24	-3	0-0	1.000	1	344	63	C12/D	0	-0.1
	Chi N	4	3	0	0	0	0	0	0	0-0	0	1	.000	.000	.000	-97	-1	0-0	1.000	-0	0	0	C4	0	-0.1

YEAR	TM LG	G	AB	R	H	2B	3B	HR	RBI	BB-IB	HP	SO	AVG	OBP	SLG	AOPS	ABR	SB-CS	FA	FR	RNG	THR	GAMES AT POSITION	DL	BFW
2005	NY N	11	17	0	2	0	0	0	0	2-0	0	5	.118	.211	.118	-11	-3	0-0	.976	1	278	84	C11	0	-0.2
2006	NY N	15	25	3	2	1	0	0	1	5-0	0	10	.080	.233	.120	-5	-4	0-0	.974	-1	77	47	C15	0	-0.4
Total	11	527	1498	143	352	80	8	28	158	98-3	16	321	.235	.287	.355	65	-80	3-2	.988	53	116	114	C510,D3/1	0	0.2
DIGNAN, STEVE	Stephen E.; B4.16.1859 Boston MA; D7.11.1881 Boston MA; d6.1; Col Boston College																								
1880	Bos N	8	34	4	11	1	0	0	4	0	—	3	.324	.324	.353	133	1	—	.684	-0	148	501	O8(1/0/7)	—	0.1
	Wor N	3	10	1	3	0	1	0	2	0	—	1	.300	.300	.500	153	0	—	.750	-1	0	0	O3C	—	0.0
	Year	11	44	5	14	1	1	0	6	0	—	4	.318	.318	.386	137	1	—	.696	-1	116	393	O11(1/3/7)	—	0.1
DILLARD, DON	David Donald; B1.8.1937 Greenville SC; BL/TR/6´1˝/200; d4.24																								
1959	Cle A	10	10	0	4	0	0	0	1	0-0	0	2	.400	.400	.400	125	0	0-0	ø	0	—	—	/H	0	0.0
1960	Cle A	6	7	0	1	0	0	0	0	1-0	0	3	.143	.250	.143	9	-1	0-0	ø	-0	0	0	/rf	0	-0.1
1961	Cle A	74	147	27	40	5	0	7	17	15-1	0	28	.272	.340	.449	112	2	0-0	1.000	-1	101	0	O39(14/24/1)	0	0.0
1962	Cle A	95	174	22	40	5	1	5	14	11-1	0	25	.230	.276	.356	71	-8	0-1	.965	-4	74	54	O50(28/20/4)	0	-1.5
1963	Mil N	67	119	9	28	6	4	1	12	5-0	1	21	.235	.270	.378	86	-3	0-2	.951	1	83	337	O30(24/5/1)	0	-0.3
1965	Mil N	20	19	1	3	0	0	1	3	0-0	0	6	.158	.158	.316	30	-2	0-0	ø	0	0	0	/lf	0	-0.2
Total	6	272	476	59	116	16	5	14	47	32-2	1	85	.244	.292	.387	86	-12	0-3	.976	-5	85	110	O121(67/49/7)	0	-2.1
DILLARD, PAT	Robert Lee; B6.12.1873 Chattanooga TN; D7.22.1907 Denver CO; BL/TR/6´0˝/180; d4.21																								
1900	StL N	57	183	24	42	5	2	0	12	13	1	—	.230	.284	.279	56	-11	7	.942	-3	136	0	O26(0/20/6),3b21,S3	—	-1.4
DILLARD, STEVE	Stephen Bradley; B2.8.1951 Memphis TN; BR/TR/6´1˝/(170–180); [BosA72 2/40]; d9.28; Col U. of Mississippi																								
1975	Bos A	1	5	2	2	0	0	0	0	0-0	0	0	.400	.400	.400	117	0	1-0	1.000	1	136	147	/2	0	0.1
1976	Bos A	57	167	22	46	14	0	1	15	17-1	0	20	.275	.341	.377	99	1	6-4	.918	-7	102	168	3b18,2b17,S12,D7	0	-0.5
1977	Bos A	66	141	22	34	7	0	1	13	7-0	0	13	.241	.270	.312	54	-9	4-3	.967	-1	99	97	2b45,S9,D6	0	-0.7
1978	Det A	56	130	21	29	5	2	0	7	6-0	0	11	.223	.257	.292	53	-9	1-2	.958	-0	98	128	2b41,D4	0	-0.8
1979	Chi N	89	166	31	47	6	1	5	24	17-4	1	24	.283	.351	.422	101	0	1-0	.988	5	98	104	2b60,3b9	0	0.8
1980	Chi N	100	244	31	55	8	1	4	27	20-2	1	54	.225	.285	.316	63	-12	2-2	.908	-2	111	95	3b51,2b38,S2	0	-1.4
1981	Chi N	53	119	18	26	7	1	2	11	8-0	0	20	.218	.268	.345	69	-5	0-0	.974	4	118	122	2b32,3b7,S2	0	0.0
1982	Chi A	16	41	1	7	3	1	0	5	1-0	0	5	.171	.190	.293	30	-4	0-1	.959	2	118	57	2b16	0	-0.2
Total	8	438	1013	148	246	50	6	13	102	76-7	2	147	.243	.295	.343	72	-38	15-12	.973	2	101	100	2b250,3b85,S25,D17	0	-2.7
DILLHOEFER, PICKLES	William Martin; B10.13.1893 Cleveland OH; D2.23.1922 St.Louis MO; BR/TR/5´7˝/154; d4.16; Mil 1918																								
1917	Chi N	42	95	3	12	1	1	0	8	2	0	9	.126	.144	.158	-7	-12	1	.985	6	*101*	*132*	C37	—	-0.4
1918	Phi N	8	11	0	1	0	0	0	0	1	0	1	.091	.167	.091	-19	-2	2	.923	-1	*93*	*92*	C6	—	-0.2
1919	StL N	45	108	11	23	3	2	0	12	8	0	6	.213	.267	.278	68	-4	5	.967	-2	*99*	*92*	C39	—	-0.5
1920	StL N	76	224	26	59	8	3	0	13	13	0	7	.263	.304	.326	84	-5	2-1	.953	-5	*90*	*86*	C74	—	-0.4
1921	StL N	76	162	19	39	4	4	0	15	11	0	7	.241	.289	.315	61	-10	2-1	.953	-0	*100*	*105*	C69	—	-0.6
Total	5	247	600	59	134	16	10	0	48	35	0	30	.223	.266	.283	58	-33	12-2	.961	-2	*96*	*100*	C225	—	-2.1
DILLINGER, BOB	Robert Bernard "Duke"; B9.17.1918 Glendale CA; BR/TR/5´11.5˝/170; d4.16; Col Idaho																								
1946	StL A	83	225	33	63	6	3	0	11	19	2	32	.280	.341	.333	85	-4	8-1	.922	-3	94	93	3b54/S	0	-0.7
1947	StL A	137	571	70	168	23	6	3	37	56	4	38	.294	.361	.371	102	2	**34**-13	.958	5	102	83	3b137	0	1.0
1948	StL A	153	644	110	**207**	34	10	2	44	65	1	34	.321	.385	.415	110	9	**28**-11	.955	-16	83	96	3b153	0	-0.5
1949	StL A★	137	544	68	176	22	13	1	51	51	3	40	.324	.385	.417	108	5	**20**-14	.938	-18	83	65	3b133	0	-1.3
1950	Phi A	84	356	55	110	21	9	3	41	31	1	20	.309	.366	.444	109	3	5-3	.957	-1	100	95	3b84	0	0.2
	Pit N	58	222	23	64	8	2	1	9	13	0	22	.288	.328	.356	77	-8	4	.957	1	101	110	3b51	0	-0.7
1951	Pit N	12	43	3	10	3	0	0	0	1	0	0	.233	.250	.302	47	-3	2-0	.963	-1	85	0	3b10	0	-0.4
	Chi A	89	299	39	90	6	4	0	20	15	1	17	.301	.337	.348	87	-7	5-5	.930	-6	94	82	3b70	0	-1.4
Total	6	753	2904	401	888	123	47	10	213	251	12	203	.306	.363	.391	100	-3	106-47	.948	-40	92	86	3b692/S	0	-3.8
DILLON, POP	Frank Edward; B10.17.1873 Normal IL; D9.12.1931 Pasadena CA; BL/TR/6´1˝/185; d9.8																								
1899	Pit N	30	121	21	31	5	0	0	20	5	0	—	.256	.286	.298	60	-7	5	.988	1	111	89	1b30	—	-0.5
1900	Pit N	5	18	3	2	1	0	0	1	0	0	—	.111	.111	.167	-24	-3	0	.981	1	189	86	1b5	—	-0.2
1901	Det A	74	281	40	81	14	6	1	42	15	0	—	.288	.324	.391	94	-3	14	.979	3	114	135	1b74	—	-0.2
1902	Det A	66	243	21	50	6	3	0	22	16	0	—	.206	.255	.255	41	-20	2	.976	5	140	111	1b66	—	-1.6
	Bal A	2	7	1	2	0	1	0	0	2	0	—	.286	.444	.571	173	1	0	.960	0	159	0	1b2	—	0.1
	Year	68	250	22	52	6	4	0	22	18	0	—	.208	.261	.264	45	-19	2	.975	5	141	107	1b68	—	-1.5
1904	Bro N	135	511	60	132	18	6	0	31	40	1	—	.258	.313	.317	97	-1	13	.982	4	112	96	1b134	—	0.0
Total	5	312	1181	146	298	44	16	1	116	78	1	—	.252	.299	.319	79	-33	34	.980	14	120	107	1b311	—	-2.4
DILLON, JOHN	John; d5.8; b–Packy																								
1875	RS NA	1	1	0	0	0	0	0	0	0	—	0	.000	.000	.000	-99	0	0-0	ø	-0	0	0	/S	—	0.0
DILLON, JOE	Joseph William; B8.2.1975 Modesto CA; BR/TR/6´2˝/200; [KCA97 7/211]; d5.18; Col Texas Tech																								
2005	Fla N	27	36	6	6	1	0	1	1	1-0	1	8	.167	.211	.278	28	-4	0-0	.923	-1	84	98	2b4,O3L,3b2/1	0	-0.5
DILLON, PACKY	Patrick; B St.Louis MO; d5.4; b–John																								
1875	RS NA	3	13	1	3	1	0	0	1	0	—	0	.231	.231	.308	94	0	0-0	.923	-2	—	—	C3	—	-0.2
DILONE, MIGUEL	Miguel Angel (Reyes); B11.1.1954 Santiago, D.R.; BB/TR/6´0˝/(150–175); d9.2																								
1974	Pit N	12	2	3	0	0	0	0	0	1-0	0	0	.000	.333	.000	-1	0	2-0	1.000	0	188	0	O2(0/1/1)	0	0.0
1975	Pit N	18	6	8	0	0	0	0	0	0-0	0	1	.000	.000	.000	-99	-2	2-2	1.000	-0	103	0	O2C	0	-0.2
1976	Pit N	16	17	7	4	0	0	0	0	0-0	0	0	.235	.235	.235	33	-2	5-1	1.000	1	146	0	O3(1/2/0)	0	0.0
1977	Pit N	29	44	5	6	0	0	0	0	2-0	0	3	.136	.174	.136	-15	-7	12-0	1.000	0	95	152	O17(9/7/2)	40	-0.5
1978	Oak A	135	258	34	59	8	0	1	14	23-0	1	30	.229	.294	.271	63	-12	50-23	.985	4	117	59	O99(47/25/36),D11,3b3	0	-0.9
1979	Oak A	30	91	15	17	1	2	1	6	6-0	0	7	.187	.237	.275	40	-8	6-5	.959	-2	99	0	O25(5/0/20)	0	-1.2
	Chi N	43	36	14	11	0	0	0	1	2-0	0	5	.306	.342	.306	71	-1	15-5	1.000	-0	102	0	O22(4/18/0)	0	0.0
1980	Cle A	132	528	82	180	30	9	0	40	28-1	2	45	.341	.375	.432	119	14	61-18	.973	-1	102	85	O118(90/23/13),D11	0	1.6
1981	Cle A	72	269	33	78	5	5	0	19	18-1	0	28	.290	.334	.346	97	-2	29-10	.971	4	107	184	O56L,D11	0	0.3
1982	Cle A	104	379	50	89	12	3	3	25	25-0	2	36	.235	.286	.306	62	-20	33-5	.964	-3	95	55	O97(96/1/0)/D	0	-2.2
1983	Cle A	32	68	15	13	3	1	0	7	10-0	0	5	.191	.295	.265	53	-4	5-1	1.000	1	116	0	O19L	0	-0.4
	Chi A	4	3	1	0	0	0	0	0	0-0	0	0	.000	.000	.000	-96	-1	1-0	1.000	0	108	0	O2C,D2	0	-0.1
	Year	36	71	16	13	3	1	0	7	10-0	0	5	.183	.284	.254	47	-5	6-1	1.000	1	116	0	O21(19/2/0),D2	0	-0.5
	Pit N	7	0	1	0	0	0	0	0	0-0	0	0	ø	ø	ø	ø	0	2-0	ø	0	—	—	/R	0	0.0
1984	Mon N	88	169	28	47	8	2	1	10	17-0	1	18	.278	.346	.367	105	1	27-2	.987	1	113	37	O41L	0	0.7
1985	Mon N	51	84	10	16	0	2	0	6	6-0	0	11	.190	.242	.238	37	-8	7-3	.974	-0	101	96	O22(8/13/2)	0	-0.8
	SD N	27	46	8	10	0	1	0	1	4-0	0	8	.217	.280	.261	53	-3	10-3	.917	-1	86	145	O14(4/9/1)	0	-0.3
	Year	78	130	18	26	0	3	0	7	10-0	0	19	.200	.255	.246	43	-11	17-6	.952	-1	95	115	O36(12/22/3)	0	-1.1
Total	12	800	2000	314	530	67	25	6	129	142-2	6	197	.265	.315	.333	81	-55	267-78	.975	4	105	76	O539(380/103/75),D36,3b3	40	-4.0
DIMAGGIO, DOM	Dominic Paul "The Little Professor"; B2.12.1917 San Francisco CA; BR/TR/5´9˝/(160–168); d4.16; Mil 1943–45; b–Joe b–Vince																								
1940	Bos A	108	418	81	126	32	6	8	46	41	2	46	.301	.367	.464	109	6	7-6	.977	6	96	208	O94(11/59/26)	—	0.7
1941	Bos A★	144	584	117	165	37	6	8	58	90	**7**	57	.283	.385	.408	107	10	13-6	.964	4	102	137	O144C	0	1.0
1942	Bos A☆	151	622	110	178	36	8	14	48	70	6	52	.286	.364	.437	121	17	16-10	.987	13	107	**169**	O151C	0	2.7
1946	†Bos A★	142	534	85	169	24	7	7	73	66	1	58	.316	.393	.427	122	18	10-6	.985	2	105	94	O142C	0	1.7
1947	Bos A	136	513	75	145	21	5	8	71	74	3	62	.283	.376	.390	105	6	10-6	.977	15	109	**213**	O134C	0	1.8
1948	Bos A	**155**	648	127	185	40	4	9	87	101	2	58	.285	.383	.401	104	7	10-2	.981	9	109	98	O155C	0	1.2
1949	Bos A★	145	605	126	186	34	5	8	60	96	2	55	.307	.404	.420	110	12	9-7	.977	6	106	130	O144C	0	1.3
1950	Bos A★	141	588	**131**	193	30	**11**	7	70	82	4	68	.328	.414	.452	111	12	**15**-4	.983	3	101	126	O140C	0	1.3
1951	Bos A★	146	639	**113**	189	34	4	12	72	73	2	53	.296	.370	.418	103	3	4-7	.973	-8	92	99	O146C	0	-1.0
1952	Bos A★	128	486	81	143	20	1	6	33	57	2	61	.294	.371	.377	100	2	6-8	.975	-4	91	130	O123C	0	-0.6
1953	Bos A	3	3	0	1	0	0	0	0	0	0	1	.333	.333	.333	76	0	0-0	ø	0	—	—	/H	0	0.0
Total	11	1399	5640	1046	1680	308	57	87	618	750	31	571	.298	.383	.419	109	93	100-62	.978	46	102	138	O1373(11/1338/26)	0	10.1

YEAR	TM LG	G	AB	R	H	2B	3B	HR	RBI	BB-IB	HP	SO	AVG	OBP	SLG	AOPS	ABR	SB-CS	FA	FR	RNG	THR	GAMES AT POSITION	DL	BFW
DiMaggio, Joe	Joseph Paul "Joltin' Joe","The Yankee Clipper"; B11.25.1914 Martinez CA; D3.8.1999 Hollywood FL; BR/TR/6´2˝/193; d5.3; Mil 1943–45; C2; HF1955; b–Dom b–Vince																								
1936	†NY A★	138	637	132	206	44	**15**	29	125	24	4	39	.323	.352	.576	130	23	4-0	.978	8	100	**171**	O138(66/55/18)	—	2.2
1937	†NY A★	151	621	**151**	215	35	15	**46**	167	64	5	37	.346	.412	**.673**	168	60	3-0	.962	6	102	148	O150C	—	5.7
1938	†NY A★	145	599	129	194	32	13	32	140	59	2	21	.324	.386	.581	140	33	6-1	.963	-2	92	143	O145C	—	2.6
1939	†NY A★	120	462	108	176	32	6	30	126	52	4	20	**.381**	.448	.671	**185**	59	3-0	.986	5	102	129	O117C	—	**5.5**
1940	NY A★	132	508	93	179	28	9	31	133	61	3	30	**.352**	.425	.626	**176**	56	1-2	.978	-4	101	51	O130C	—	**4.5**
1941	†NY A★	139	541	122	193	43	11	30	**125**	76	4	13	.357	.440	.643	186	68	4-2	.978	6	102	138	O139C	0	6.6
1942	†NY A★	**154**	610	123	186	29	13	21	114	68	2	36	.305	.376	.498	148	37	4-2	.981	-3	98	88	O154C	0	3.1
1946	NY A☆	132	503	81	146	20	8	25	95	59	2	24	.290	.367	.511	142	26	1-0	.982	2	96	**179**	O131(3/128/0)	0	2.6
1947	†NY A★	141	534	97	168	31	10	20	97	64	3	32	.315	.391	.522	154	38	3-0	**.997**	-14	87	23	O139C	0	2.2
1948	NY A★	153	594	110	190	26	11	**39**	**155**	67	**8**	30	.320	.396	.598	164	50	1-1	.972	1	107	67	O152C	0	4.5
1949	†NY A★	76	272	58	94	14	6	14	67	55	2	18	.346	.459	.596	178	32	0-1	.985	-4	99	20	O76C	0	2.5
1950	†NY A★	139	525	114	158	33	10	32	122	80	1	33	.301	.394	**.585**	152	39	0-0	.976	-4	99	79	O137C/1	0	3.0
1951	†NY A☆	116	415	72	109	22	4	12	71	61	6	36	.263	.365	.422	117	11	0-0	.990	1	100	103	O113C	0	0.8
Total	13	1736	6821	1390	2214	389	131	361	1537	790	46	369	.325	.398	.579	156	532	30-9	.978	-0	99	106	O1721(69/1635/18)/1	0	45.8
DiMaggio, Vince	Vincent Paul; B9.6.1912 Martinez CA; D10.3.1986 N.Hollywood CA; BR/TR/5´11˝/183; d4.19; b–Dom b–Joe																								
1937	Bos N	132	493	56	126	18	4	13	69	39	1	111	.256	.311	.387	98	-4	8	.982	8	99	**180**	O130(0/129/1)	—	0.1
1938	Bos N	150	540	71	123	28	3	14	61	65	2	134	.228	.313	.369	96	-3	11	.973	10	109	148	O149C/2	—	0.4
1939	Cin N	8	14	1	1	1	0	0	2	2	0	10	.071	.188	.143	-10	-2	0	1.000	1	100	275	O7(3/3/1)	—	-0.2
1940	Cin N	2	4	2	1	0	0	0	0	1	0	0	.250	.400	.250	82	0	0	1.000	-0	103	0	/rf	—	0.0
	Pit N	110	356	59	103	26	0	19	54	37	5	83	.289	.364	.522	143	21	11	.979	1	94	166	O108(1/103/4)	—	1.9
	Year	112	360	61	104	26	0	19	54	38	5	83	.289	.365	.519	142	21	11	.979	1	94	**164**	O109(1/103/5)	—	1.9
1941	Pit N	151	528	73	141	27	5	21	100	68	3	100	.267	.354	.456	128	19	10	.976	2	104	91	O151C	0	1.7
1942	Pit N	143	496	57	118	22	3	15	75	52	1	87	.238	.311	.385	101	-1	10	.978	12	111	151	O138C	0	0.9
1943	Pit N★	**157**	580	64	144	41	2	15	88	70	0	126	.248	.329	.403	107	6	11	.985	12	**113**	110	O156C/S	0	1.4
1944	Pit N★	109	342	41	82	20	4	9	50	33	0	83	.240	.307	.401	94	-3	6	.984	-1	97	100	O101C/3	0	-0.7
1945	Phi N	127	452	64	116	25	3	19	84	43	0	91	.257	.321	.451	117	8	12	.994	9	105	165	O121C	0	1.3
1946	Phi N	6	19	1	4	1	0	0	1	0	0	7	.211	.211	.263	35	-2	0	1.000	-0	96	0	O6C	0	-0.2
	NY N	15	25	2	0	0	0	0	0	2	0	5	.000	.074	.000	-78	-6	0	.967	0	125	0	O13C	0	-0.6
	Year	21	44	3	4	1	0	0	1	2	0	12	.091	.130	.114	-31	-8	0	.975	-0	116	0	O19C	0	-0.8
Total	10	1110	3849	491	959	209	24	125	584	412	12	837	.249	.324	.413	108	33	79	.981	52	105	137	O1081(4/1070/7)/3S2	0	6.0
Dimmel, Mike	Michael Wayne; B10.16.1954 Albert Lea MN; BR/TR/6´0˝/180; [LAN73 6/138]; d9.2																								
1977	Bal A	25	5	8	0	0	0	0	0	0-0	0	1	.000	.000	.000	-99	-1	1-0	1.000	2	151	314	O23(0/1/22)	0	0.0
1978	Bal A	8	0	2	0	0	0	0	0	0-0	0	0	ø	ø	ø	ø	0	0-1	.667	-0	89	0	O7(1/1/5)	0	-0.1
1979	StL N	6	3	1	1	0	0	0	0	0-0	0	0	.333	.333	.333	81	0	0-1	1.000	-0	105	0	O5(5/1/0)	0	-0.1
Total	3	39	8	11	1	0	0	0	0	0-0	0	1	.125	.125	.125	-33	-1	1-2	.952	1	132	202	O35(6/3/27)	0	-0.2
Dineen, Kerry	Kerry Michael; B7.1.1952 Englewood NJ; BL/TL/5´11˝/165; [NYA73 4/85]; d6.14; Col San Diego																								
1975	NY A	7	22	3	8	1	0	0	1	2-0	0	1	.364	.417	.409	135	1	0-0	1.000	1	128	0	O7C	0	0.1
1976	NY A	4	7	0	2	0	0	0	1	1-0	0	2	.286	.375	.286	96	0	1-1	.900	0	128	0	O4(0/2/2)	0	0.0
1978	Phi N	5	8	0	2	1	0	0	0	1-0	0	0	.250	.333	.375	96	0	0-0	1.000	-0	58	0	/lf	0	0.0
Total	3	16	37	3	12	2	0	0	2	4-0	0	3	.324	.390	.378	119	1	1-1	.967	1	121	0	O12(1/9/2)	0	0.1
Dinges, Vance	Vance George; B5.29.1915 Elizabeth NJ; D10.4.1990 Harrisonburg VA; BL/TL/6´2˝/175; d4.17																								
1945	Phi N	109	397	46	114	15	4	1	36	35	1	17	.287	.346	.353	97	-1	5	.986	2	98	195	O65(16/18/33),1b42	0	-0.5
1946	Phi N	50	104	7	32	5	1	1	10	9	0	12	.308	.363	.404	121	3	2	.985	1	115	89	1b26/lf	0	0.3
Total	2	159	501	53	146	20	5	2	46	44	1	29	.291	.350	.363	102	2	7	.986	3	94	96	1b68,O66(17/18/33)	0	-0.2
DiPietro, Bob	Robert Louis Paul; B9.1.1927 San Francisco CA; BR/TR/5´11˝/185; d9.23; Col San Jose St.																								
1951	Bos A	4	11	0	1	0	0	0	0	1	0	1	.091	.167	.091	-26	-2	0-0	.833	0	71	501	O3R	0	-0.2
DiSarcina, Gary	Gary Thomas; B11.19.1967 Malden MA; BR/TR/6´1˝/(170–205); [CalA88 6/143]; d9.23; Col Massachusetts; [DL 2001 Ana A 190]																								
1989	Cal A	2	0	0	0	0	0	0	0	0-0	0	0	ø	ø	ø	ø	0	0-0	ø	-0	0	0	/S	-0	0.0
1990	Cal A	18	57	8	8	1	1	0	0	3-0	0	10	.140	.183	.193	5	-8	1-0	.940	0	113	82	S14,2b3	0	-0.6
1991	Cal A	18	57	5	12	2	0	0	3	3-0	2	4	.211	.274	.246	45	-4	0-0	.915	-4	89	33	S10,2b7,3b2	0	-0.8
1992	Cal A	157	518	48	128	19	0	3	42	20-0	7	50	.247	.283	.301	63	-26	9-7	.967	3	99	108	S157	0	-1.2
1993	Cal A	126	416	44	99	20	1	3	45	15-0	6	38	.238	.273	.313	56	-27	5-7	.975	-8	96	98	S126	38	-2.6
1994	Cal A	112	389	53	101	14	2	3	33	18-0	2	28	.260	.294	.329	60	-24	3-7	.983	3	104	96	S110	0	-1.4
1995	Cal A★	99	362	61	111	28	6	5	41	20-0	2	25	.307	.344	.459	108	4	7-4	.986	-11	92	79	S98	44	0.0
1996	Cal A	150	536	62	137	26	4	5	48	21-0	2	36	.256	.286	.347	58	-36	2-1	.971	7	106	91	S150	0	-1.6
1997	Ana A	154	549	52	135	28	2	4	47	17-0	4	29	.246	.271	.326	55	-37	7-8	.977	-13	95	87	S153	0	-3.8
1998	Ana A	157	551	73	158	39	3	3	56	21-0	8	51	.287	.321	.385	81	-15	11-7	.980	-6	94	101	S157	0	-0.8
1999	Ana A	81	271	32	62	7	1	1	29	15-0	2	32	.229	.273	.273	40	-25	2-2	.963	2	104	111	S81	78	-1.7
2000	Ana A	12	38	6	15	2	0	1	11	1-0	1	3	.395	.425	.526	135	2	0-1	.934	6	139	154	S12	159	0.7
Total	12	1086	3744	444	966	186	20	28	355	154-0	36	306	.258	.292	.341	65	-196	47-44	.973	-21	99	96	S1069,2b10,3b2	509	-13.8
DiStefano, Benny	Benito James; B1.23.1962 Brooklyn NY; BL/TL/6´1˝/(195–210); [PitN82*S2/29]; d5.18; Col Alvin (TX) CC																								
1984	Pit N	45	78	10	13	1	2	3	9	5-1	1	13	.167	.226	.346	59	-5	0-1	.946	4	135	224	O20(7/0/15),1b17	0	-0.3
1986	Pit N	31	39	3	7	1	0	1	5	1-0	0	5	.179	.190	.282	31	-4	0-0	1.000	0	136	0	O9R/1	0	-0.4
1988	Pit N	16	29	6	10	3	1	1	6	3-1	0	4	.345	.394	.621	193	3	0-0	1.000	0	100	34	1b5,O2R	0	0.3
1989	Pit N	96	154	12	38	8	0	2	15	17-3	3	30	.247	.333	.338	95	0	1-0	.981	-4	73	93	1b48,C3/rf	15	-0.7
1992	Hou N	52	60	4	14	0	2	0	7	5-1	1	14	.233	.303	.300	74	-2	0-0	1.000	2	141	318	O12(7/0/5),1b6	0	-0.1
Total	5	240	360	35	82	13	5	7	42	31-6	5	66	.228	.296	.350	85	-8	1-1	.985	1	91	95	1b77,O44(14/0/32),C3	15	-1.2
Distel, Dutch	George Adam; B4.15.1896 Madison IN; D2.12.1967 Madison IN; BR/TR/5´9˝/165; d6.21																								
1918	StL N	8	17	3	3	1	1	0	1	2	0	3	.176	.263	.353	90	0	0	.900	-1	118	63	2b5,S2/rf	—	-0.2
Dittmer, Jack	John Douglas; B1.10.1928 Elkader IA; BL/TR/6´1˝/(175–180); d6.17; Col Iowa																								
1952	Bos N	93	326	26	63	7	2	7	41	26	1	26	.193	.255	.291	53	-22	1-0	.982	-1	100	94	2b90	0	-1.8
1953	Mil N	138	504	54	134	22	1	9	63	18	1	35	.266	.293	.367	75	-20	1-0	.965	-23	88	105	2b138	0	-3.2
1954	Mil N	66	192	22	47	8	0	6	20	19	3	17	.245	.319	.380	88	-4	0-1	.977	-2	100	89	2b55	0	-0.3
1955	Mil N	38	72	4	9	1	1	1	4	4-1	0	15	.125	.171	.208	0	-11	0-0	.977	-1	96	80	2b28	0	-1.0
1956	Mil N	44	102	8	25	4	0	1	6	8-0	0	8	.245	.300	.314	69	-4	0-0	.979	0	106	91	2b42	0	-0.2
1957	Det A	16	22	3	5	1	0	0	2	2-1	0	1	.227	.292	.273	54	-1	0-0	1.000	-1	79	0	3b3/2	0	-0.2
Total	6	395	1218	117	283	43	4	24	136	77-2	5	102	.232	.280	.333	66	-62	2-1	.974	-26	95	97	2b354,3b3	0	-6.7
Divis, Moxie	Edward George; B1.16.1894 Cleveland OH; D12.19.1955 Lakewood OH; 5´6˝/?; d8.4																								
1916	Phi A	3	6	0	1	0	0	0	1	0	0	2	.167	.167	.167	0	-1	0	1.000	1	46	720	/lf	—	0.0
Dixon, Leo	Leo Moses; B9.4.1894 Chicago IL; D4.11.1984 Chicago IL; BR/TR/5´11˝/170; d4.14																								
1925	StL A	76	205	27	46	11	1	1	19	24	4	42	.224	.318	.302	55	-14	3-2	.981	4	*91*	*153*	C75	—	-0.6
1926	StL A	33	89	7	17	3	1	0	8	11	2	14	.191	.294	.247	40	-8	1-4	.977	3	*135*	*137*	C33	—	-0.4
1927	StL A	36	103	6	20	3	1	0	12	7	0	6	.194	.245	.243	26	-12	0-1	.937	1	*118*	*142*	C35	—	-0.9
1929	Cin N	14	30	0	5	2	0	0	2	3	0	7	.167	.242	.233	19	-4	0	1.000	2	*113*	*121*	C14	—	-0.1
Total	4	159	427	40	88	19	3	1	41	45	6	69	.206	.291	.272	43	-38	4-7	.971	9	*109*	*144*	C157	—	-2.0
Dobbek, Dan	Daniel John; B12.6.1934 Ontonagon MI; BL/TR/6´0˝/(190–195); d9.9; Col Western Michigan																								
1959	Was A	16	60	8	15	1	2	1	5	5-1	0	13	.250	.308	.383	89	-1	0-0	1.000	-0	99	109	O16R	0	-0.2
1960	Was A	110	248	32	54	8	2	10	30	35-7	1	41	.218	.316	.387	90	-4	4-3	.973	0	101	130	O78(12/58/17)	0	-0.7
1961	Min A	72	125	12	21	3	1	4	14	13-1	2	18	.168	.255	.304	47	-10	1-2	.985	1	110	48	O48(32/10/13)	0	-1.2
Total	3	198	433	52	90	12	5	15	49	53-9	3	72	.208	.297	.363	77	-15	5-5	.980	1	103	104	O142(44/68/46)	0	-2.1

YEAR	TM LG	G	AB	R	H	2B	3B	HR	RBI	BB-IB	HP	SO	AVG	OBP	SLG	AOPS	ABR	SB-CS	FA	FR	RNG	THR	GAMES AT POSITION	DL	BFW
DOBBS, GREG	Gregory Stuart; B7.2.1978 Los Angeles CA; BL/TR/6´1˝/205; d9.8; Col Oklahoma																								
2004	Sea A	18	53	4	12	1	0	1	9	1-0	1	14	.226	.250	.302	46	-4	0-0	.929	-2	90	147	3b14/D	0	-0.6
2005	Sea A	59	142	8	35	7	1	1	20	9-3	0	25	.246	.288	.331	70	-6	1-0	1.000	3	295	0	D24,1b5,O4L,3b2	0	-0.4
2006	Sea A	23	27	4	10	3	1	0	3	0-0	1	4	.370	.393	.556	151	2	0-1	1.000	-0	0	369	1b3,O3R,3b2,D5	0	0.1
Total	3	100	222	16	57	11	2	2	32	10-3	2	43	.257	.291	.351	74	-8	1-1	.947	1	99	171	D30,3b18,1b8,O7(4/0/3)	0	-0.9
DOBBS, JOHN	John Gordon; B6.3.1875 Chattanooga TN; D9.9.1934 Charlotte NC; BL/TR/5´9.5˝/170; d4.20																								
1901	Cin N	109	435	71	119	17	4	2	27	36	6	—	.274	.338	.345	105	4	19	.948	-6	89	117	O100C,3b8	—	-0.6
1902	Cin N	63	256	39	76	7	3	1	16	19	1	—	.297	.348	.359	108	2	7	.963	6	121	86	O63L	—	0.5
	Chi N	59	235	31	71	8	2	0	35	18	0	—	.302	.352	.353	121	6	3	.977	2	106	332	O59C	—	0.5
	Year	122	491	70	147	15	5	1	51	37	1	—	.299	.350	.356	114	8	10	.970	8	114	198	O122(63/59/0)	—	1.0
1903	Chi N	16	61	8	14	1	1	0	4	7	2	—	.230	.329	.279	76	-2	0	1.000	0	46	0	O16C	—	-0.2
	Bro N	111	414	61	98	15	7	2	59	48	5	—	.237	.323	.321	86	-6	23	.966	2	72	109	O110C	—	-1.0
	Year	127	475	69	112	16	8	2	63	55	7	—	.236	.324	.316	85	-8	23	.970	2	69	95	O126C	—	-1.2
1904	Bro N	101	363	36	90	16	2	0	30	28	1	—	.248	.304	.303	90	-4	11	.936	-2	54	0	O92(2/86/3),2b2,S2	—	-1.0
1905	Bro N	123	460	59	117	21	4	2	36	31	2	—	.254	.304	.330	96	-2	15	.938	-5	72	24	O123C	—	-1.3
Total	5	582	2224	305	585	85	23	7	207	187	17	—	.263	.325	.331	98	-2	78	.954	-3	81	92	O563(65/494/3),3b8,S2,2b2	—	-3.1
DOBY, LARRY	Lawrence Eugene; B12.13.1923 Camden SC; D6.18.2003 Montclair NJ; BL/TR/6´1˝/(182–185); d7.5; M1/C7; HF1998; Negro Lg 1942–47 Mil 1944–45; Col Long Island–Brooklyn																								
1947	Cle A	29	32	3	5	1	0	0	2	1	0	11	.156	.182	.188	3	-4	0-0	1.000	-1	111	0	2b4/1S	0	-0.5
1948	†Cle A	121	439	83	132	23	9	14	66	54	5	77	.301	.384	.490	135	21	9-9	.955	-3	94	128	O114(0/68/46)	0	1.3
1949	Cle A★	147	547	106	153	25	3	24	85	91	**7**	90	.280	.389	.468	129	23	10-9	.976	-11	92	61	O147(0/117/39)	0	0.7
1950	Cle A★	142	503	110	164	25	5	25	102	98	6	71	.326	**.442**	.545	**156**	**47**	8-6	.987	-9	99	17	O140C	0	3.2
1951	Cle A★	134	447	84	132	27	5	20	69	101	3	81	.295	.428	.512	**163**	45	4-1	.977	-2	98	99	O132C	0	3.8
1952	Cle A★	140	519	**104**	143	26	8	**32**	104	90	0	111	.276	.383	**.541**	**166**	46	5-2	.986	1	101	100	O136C	0	4.4
1953	Cle A★	149	513	92	135	18	5	29	102	96	6	121	.263	.385	.487	138	29	3-2	.984	-10	90	81	O146C	0	1.2
1954	†Cle A★	153	577	94	157	18	4	**32**	**126**	85	3	94	.272	.364	.484	130	23	3-1	.995	1	100	98	O153C	0	1.8
1955	Cle A☆	131	491	91	143	17	5	26	75	61-8	2	100	.291	.369	.505	129	19	2-0	.994	-6	93	80	O129C	0	0.8
1956	Chi A	140	504	89	135	22	3	24	102	102-6	4	105	.268	.392	.466	125	21	0-1	.987	-3	103	43	O137C	0	1.1
1957	Chi A	119	416	57	120	27	2	14	79	56-3	2	79	.288	.373	.464	127	17	2-3	.985	-11	91	39	O110C	0	0.1
1958	Cle A	89	247	41	70	10	1	13	45	26-2	0	49	.283	.348	.490	132	10	0-2	1.000	0	99	146	O68(8/59/1)	0	0.7
1959	Det A	18	55	5	12	3	1	0	4	8-0	0	9	.218	.313	.309	69	-2	0-0	.960	-0	86	117	O16(11/0/5)	0	-0.3
	Chi A	21	58	1	14	1	1	0	9	2-0	0	13	.241	.267	.293	54	-4	1-0	.955	-0	95	156	O12(1/2/10),1b2	0	-0.5
	Year	39	113	6	26	4	2	0	13	10-0	0	22	.230	.290	.301	62	-6	1-0	.957	-1	90	134	O28(12/2/15),1b2	0	-0.8
Total	13	1533	5348	960	1515	243	52	253	970	871-19	38	1011	.283	.386	.490	137	291	47-36	.983	-53	96	78	O1440(20/1329/101),2b4,1b3/S	0	17.8
DODD, ONA	Ona Melvin.; B10.14.1886 Springtown TX; D12.17.1956 Carter OK; BR/TR/5´8˝/150; d7.26; Col TCU																								
1912	Pit N	5	9	0	0	0	0	0	1	1	0	3	.000	.100	.000	-73	-2	0	1.000	0	109	0	3b4/2	—	-0.2
DODD, TOM	Thomas Marion; B8.15.1958 Portland OR; BR/TR/6´0˝/190; [NYA80*S1/7]; d7.25; Col Oregon																								
1986	Bal A	8	13	1	3	0	0	1	2	2-0	1	2	.231	.375	.462	128	1	0-0	ø	-0	0	0	/3D	0	0.0
DODGE, JOHN	John Lewis; B4.27.1889 Bolivar TN; D6.19.1916 Mobile AL; BR/TR/5´11.5˝/165; d8.29																								
1912	Phi N	30	92	3	11	1	0	0	3	4	0	11	.120	.156	.130	-20	-15	2	1.000	4	119	177	3b23,2b5/S	—	-1.1
1913	Phi N	3	3	0	1	0	0	0	0	2	0	0	.333	.600	.333	164	1	0	1.000	-0	85	0	S3	—	0.0
	Cin N	94	323	35	78	8	8	4	45	10	2	34	.241	.269	.353	77	-12	11-7	.908	3	108	86	3b91	—	-0.7
	Year	97	326	35	79	8	8	4	45	12	2	34	.242	.274	.353	78	-11	11-7	.908	2	108	86	3b91,S3	—	-0.7
Total	2	127	418	38	90	9	8	4	48	16	2	45	.215	.248	.304	55	-26	13-7	.926	6	110	104	3b114,2b5,S4	—	-1.8
DODSON, PAT	Patrick Neal; B10.11.1959 Santa Monica CA; BL/TL/6´4˝/(210–220); [BosA80 6/154]; d9.5; Col UCLA																								
1986	Bos A	9	12	3	5	2	0	1	3	3-0	0	3	.417	.533	.833	263	3	0-0	1.000	-1	38	230	1b7	0	0.2
1987	Bos A	26	42	4	7	3	0	2	6	8-1	0	13	.167	.288	.381	77	-1	0-0	1.000	-2	43	115	1b21/D	0	-0.4
1988	Bos A	17	45	5	8	3	1	1	1	6-0	0	17	.178	.275	.356	72	-2	0-0	1.000	1	119	64	1b17	0	-0.1
Total	3	52	99	12	20	8	1	4	10	17-1	0	33	.202	.314	.424	97	0	0-0	1.000	-1	77	104	1b45/D	0	-0.3
DOERR, BOBBY	Robert Pershing; B4.7.1918 Los Angeles CA; BR/TR/5´11˝/175; d4.20; Mil 1944–45; C8; HF1986																								
1937	Bos A	55	147	22	33	5	1	2	14	18	1	25	.224	.313	.313	56	-10	2-4	.973	2	103	104	2b47	—	-0.6
1938	Bos A	145	509	70	147	26	7	5	80	59	0	39	.289	.363	.397	86	-11	5-10	.968	9	103	**121**	2b145	—	0.4
1939	Bos A	127	525	75	167	28	2	12	73	38	1	32	.318	.365	.448	103	2	1-10	.976	**27**	**115**	110	2b126	—	3.0
1940	Bos A	151	595	87	173	37	10	22	105	57	0	53	.291	.353	.497	113	10	10-5	.977	13	103	103	2b151	—	3.1
1941	Bos A★	132	500	74	141	28	4	16	93	43	0	43	.282	.339	.450	105	2	1-3	.971	-1	101	95	2b132	0	0.8
1942	Bos A☆	144	545	71	158	35	5	15	102	67	1	55	.290	.369	.455	127	20	4-4	**.975**	12	103	117	2b142	0	4.1
1943	Bos A★	**155**	604	78	163	32	3	16	75	62	1	59	.270	.339	.412	117	12	8-8	**.990**	9	104	115	2b155	0	3.2
1944	Bos A★	125	468	95	152	30	10	15	81	58	0	31	.325	.399	**.528**	166	40	5-2	.976	2	98	101	2b125	0	5.1
1946	†Bos A★	151	583	95	158	34	9	18	116	66	1	67	.271	.346	.453	115	11	5-6	**.986**	**27**	108	**126**	2b151	0	4.8
1947	Bos A★	146	561	79	145	23	10	17	95	59	0	47	.258	.329	.426	101	-1	3-3	.981	**25**	**111**	**115**	2b146	0	3.3
1948	Bos A★	140	527	94	150	23	6	27	111	83	4	49	.285	.386	.505	129	22	3-2	.993	9	102	**116**	2b138	0	3.7
1949	Bos A	139	541	91	167	30	9	18	109	75	0	33	.309	.393	.497	126	19	2-2	.980	**27**	109	**119**	2b139	0	5.1
1950	Bos A★	149	586	103	172	29	**11**	27	120	67	1	42	.294	.367	.519	114	9	3-4	**.988**	9	99	99	2b149	0	2.4
1951	Bos A★	106	402	60	116	21	2	13	73	57	1	33	.289	.378	.448	112	8	2-1	.981	6	99	118	2b106	0	1.9
Total	14	1865	7093	1094	2042	381	89	223	1247	809	11	608	.288	.362	.461	114	133	54-64	.980	178	104	112	2b1852	0	40.3
DOHERTY, JOHN	John Michael; B8.22.1951 Woburn MA; BL/TL/5´11˝/185; [AnaA70*S1/7]; d6.1																								
1974	Cal A	74	223	20	57	14	1	3	15	8-1	0	13	.256	.280	.368	90	-4	2-1	.991	-2	83	100	1b70,D2	0	-1.0
1975	Cal A	30	94	7	19	3	0	1	12	8-1	0	12	.202	.262	.266	54	-6	1-1	.983	-1	83	93	1b26/D	0	-1.0
Total	2	104	317	27	76	17	1	4	27	16-2	0	25	.240	.275	.338	79	-10	3-2	.989	-3	83	98	1b96,D3	0	-2.0
DOLAN, COZY	Albert J. (b James Alberts); B12.23.1889 Chicago IL; D12.10.1958 Chicago IL; BR/TR/5´10˝/160; d8.15; C3; OF(126/48/33)																								
1909	Cin N	3	6	2	1	0	0	0	0	2	0	—	.167	.375	.167	69	0	0	.750	-1	85	334	3b3	—	-0.1
1911	NY A	19	69	19	21	1	2	0	6	8	1	—	.304	.385	.377	106	1	12	.947	-1	90	159	3b19	—	0.0
1912	NY A	18	60	15	12	1	3	0	11	5	1	—	.200	.273	.317	64	-3	5	.768	-4	88	43	3b17	—	-0.7
	Phi N	11	50	8	14	2	2	0	7	1	0	10	.280	.294	.400	83	-2	3	.872	-1	94	64	3b11	—	-0.2
1913	Phi N	55	126	15	33	4	0	0	8	1	1	21	.262	.273	.294	59	-7	9-4	.905	-6	87	0	O12(8/0/4),S10,2b9,3b4/1	—	-1.3
	Pit N	35	133	22	27	5	2	0	9	15	1	14	.203	.289	.271	63	-6	14-7	.937	-1	97	171	3b35	—	-0.6
	Year	90	259	37	60	9	2	0	17	16	2	35	.232	.282	.282	61	-13	23-11	.932	-7	97	161	3b39,O12(8/0/4),S10,2b9/1	—	-1.9
1914	StL N	126	421	76	101	16	3	4	32	55	5	74	.240	.335	.321	96	0	42	.955	-11	93	77	O96(90/1/5),3b27	—	-1.6
1915	StL N	111	322	53	90	14	9	2	38	34	4	37	.280	.356	.398	127	11	17-11	.929	-8	98	38	O98(28/47/24)	—	-0.2
1922	NY N	1	0	0	0	0	0	0	0	0	0	0	ø	ø	ø	ø	0	0-0	ø	0	—	—	/R	—	0.0
Total	7	379	1187	210	299	43	21	6	111	121	13	156	.252	.328	.339	95	-6	102-22	.940	-33	95	55	O206L,3b116,S10,2b9/1	—	-4.7
DOLAN, JOE	Joseph; B2.24.1873 Baltimore MD; D3.24.1938 Omaha NE; TR/5´10˝/155; d8.11																								
1896	Lou N	44	165	14	35	2	1	3	18	9	0	12	.212	.253	.291	45	-14	6	.940	7	108	118	S44	—	-0.4
1897	Lou N	36	133	10	28	2	2	0	7	8	3	—	.211	.271	.256	41	-12	6	.849	-5	83	72	S18,2b18	—	-1.3
1899	Phi N	61	222	27	57	6	3	1	30	11	2	—	.257	.298	.324	73	-9	3	.915	-6	107	47	2b61	—	-1.2
1900	Phi N	74	257	39	51	7	3	1	27	16	5	—	.198	.259	.261	44	-20	10	.931	0	111	81	3b31,2b29,S12	—	-1.7
1901	Phi N	10	37	0	3	0	0	0	2	2	0	—	.081	.128	.081	-38	-7	0	.973	-1	96	157	2b10	—	-0.8
	Phi A	98	338	50	73	21	2	1	38	26	5	—	.216	.282	.299	58	-19	3	.881	12	116	132	S61,3b35/2rf	—	-0.3
Total	5	323	1152	140	247	38	11	6	122	72	15	12	.214	.270	.282	51	-81	28	.902	8	107	118	S135,2b119,3b66/rf	—	-5.7
DOLAN, BIDDY	Leon Mark; B7.9.1881 Onalaska WI; D7.15.1950 Indianapolis IN; BR/TR/6´0˝/?; d4.16																								
1914	Ind F	32	103	13	23	4	2	1	15	12	2	13	.223	.316	.330	69	-6	5	.979	1	113	82	1b31	—	-0.7

YEAR	TM LG	G	AB	R	H	2B	3B	HR	RBI	BB-IB	HP	SO	AVG	OBP	SLG	AOPS	ABR	SB-CS	FA	FR	RNG	THR	GAMES AT POSITION	DL	BFW
DOLAN, COZY	Patrick Henry; B12.3.1872 Cambridge MA; D3.29.1907 Louisville KY; BL/TL/5´10˝/160; d4.26; ▲																								
1895	Bos N	26	83	12	20	4	1	0	7	6	1	7	.241	.300	.313	54	-6	3	.949	3	138	145	P25/cf	—	0.1
1896	Bos N	6	14	4	2	0	0	0	0	0	0	1	.143	.143	.143	-23	-2	0	.765	-0	79	0	P6	—	0.0
1900	Chi N	13	48	5	13	1	0	0	2	2	0	—	.271	.300	.292	66	-2	2	.826	-1	63	0	O13R	—	-0.4
1901	Chi N	43	171	29	45	1	2	0	16	7	1	—	.263	.296	.292	74	-6	3	.878	1	163	209	O41R	—	-0.7
	Bro N	66	253	33	66	11	1	0	29	17	2	—	.261	.313	.312	79	-6	7	.967	0	123	104	O64(2/57/5)	—	-0.9
	Year	109	424	62	111	12	3	0	45	24	3	—	.262	.306	.304	77	-12	10	.931	1	140	149	O105(2/57/46)	—	-1.6
1902	Bro N	**141**	592	72	166	16	7	1	54	33	5	—	.280	.324	.336	103	1	24	.936	-11	53	45	O141(1/140/0)	—	-1.7
1903	Chi A	27	104	16	27	5	1	0	7	6	2	—	.260	.313	.327	96	0	5	.971	0	125	68	1b19,O4(2/2/0)	—	-0.1
	Cin N	93	385	64	111	20	3	0	58	28	2	—	.288	.340	.356	88	-6	11	.937	-3	97	73	O93R	—	-1.2
1904	Cin N	129	465	88	132	8	10	6	51	39	2	—	.284	.342	.383	113	6	19	.939	-2	105	0	O102(0/7/95),1b24	—	-0.1
1905	Cin N	22	77	7	18	2	1	0	4	7	1	—	.234	.306	.286	69	-3	2	.965	-3	86	87	1b13,O9(1/0/8)	—	-0.7
	Bos N	112	433	44	119	11	7	3	48	27	3	—	.275	.322	.353	103	1	21	.946	3	129	54	O111R,P2,1b2	—	-0.1
	Year	134	510	51	137	13	8	3	52	34	4	—	.269	.319	.343	97	-3	23	.931	-0	121	51	O120(1/0/119),1b15,P2	—	-0.8
1906	Bos N	**152**	549	54	136	20	4	0	39	55	2	—	.248	.318	.299	95	-2	17	.928	-1	**146**	87	O144(2/0/143),2b7,P2/1	—	-1.0
Total	9	830	3174	428	855	99	37	10	315	227	21	8	.269	.322	.333	94	-25	114	.931	-15	108	65	O723(8/207/509),1b59,P35,2b7	—	-6.8
DOLAN, TOM	Thomas J.; B1.10.1855 New York NY; D1.16.1913 St.Louis MO; BR/TR/5´11˝/185; d9.30																								
1879	Chi N	1	4	0	0	0	0	0	0	0	—	2	.000	.000	.000	-94	-1	—	1.000	1	—	—	/C	—	0.0
1882	Buf N	22	89	12	14	0	1	0	8	2	—	11	.157	.176	.180	14	-9	—	.941	-4	—	—	C18,O4(1/2/1),3b2	—	-1.0
1883	StL AA	81	295	32	63	9	2	1	18	9	—	—	.214	.237	.268	59	-14	—	.957	11	—	—	C42,O40(19/19/2)/P	—	-0.1
1884	StL AA	35	137	19	36	6	2	0	—	6	1	—	.263	.299	.336	103	0	—	.873	-6	—	—	C34,O2(1/1/0)	—	-0.3
	StL U	19	69	9	13	3	0	0	—	4	—	—	.188	.233	.232	40	-7	—	.897	7	—	—	C14,3b3,O2(0/1/1)	—	0.1
1885	StL N	3	9	1	2	0	0	0	0	2	—	1	.222	.364	.222	99	0	—	.810	-1	—	—	C3	—	-0.1
1886	StL N	15	44	8	11	3	0	0	1	7	—	9	.250	.353	.318	113	1	2	.928	5	—	—	C15	—	0.7
	Bal AA	38	125	13	19	3	2	0	12	8	0	—	.152	.203	.208	30	-10	8	.918	-4	—	—	C35,O3L	—	-1.0
1888	StL AA	11	36	1	7	1	0	0	1	1	0	—	.194	.216	.222	37	-3	1	.914	0	—	—	C11	—	-0.2
Total	7	225	808	95	165	25	7	1	40	39	1	23	.204	.242	.256	57	-43	11	.916	9	—	—	C173,O51(24/23/4),3b5/P	—	-1.9
DOLE, LESTER	Lester Carrington; B7.8.1855 Meriden CT; D12.10.1918 Concord NH; 5´11˝/?; d5.27																								
1875	NH NA	1	4	1	2	0	0	0	0	0	—	0	.500	.500	.500	285	1	0-0	.750	-0	0	0	/cf	—	0.0
DOLJACK, FRANK	Frank Joseph "Dolie"; B10.5.1907 Cleveland OH; D1.23.1948 Cleveland OH; BR/TR/5´11˝/175; d9.4																								
1930	Det A	20	74	10	19	5	1	3	17	2	1	11	.257	.286	.473	87	-2	0-1	.930	1	106	130	O20(0/4/16)	—	-0.3
1931	Det A	63	187	20	52	13	3	4	20	15	1	17	.278	.335	.444	100	-1	3-2	.925	2	101	183	O54(3/44/8)	—	-0.1
1932	Det A	8	26	5	10	1	0	1	7	2	0	2	.385	.429	.538	143	2	1-0	1.000	-1	67	0	O6L	—	0.1
1933	Det A	42	147	18	42	5	2	0	22	14	0	13	.286	.348	.347	83	-4	2-6	.941	1	92	160	O37(32/0/5)	—	-0.6
1934	†Det A	56	120	15	28	7	1	1	19	13	1	15	.233	.313	.333	67	-6	2-1	.943	0	98	174	O30(6/12/12),1b3	—	-0.6
1943	Cle A	3	7	0	0	0	0	0	0	1	0	2	.000	.125	.000	-66	-1	0-0	1.000	-0	75	0	O2(1/0/1)	0	-0.2
Total	6	192	561	68	151	31	7	9	85	47	3	60	.269	.329	.398	87	-12	8-10	.934	2	97	161	O149(48/60/42),1b3	0	-1.7
DOMINIQUE, ANDY	Andrew John; B10.30.1975 Tarzana CA; BR/TR/6´0˝/220; [PhiN97 26/776]; d5.25; Col Nevada–Reno																								
2004	Bos A	7	11	0	2	0	0	0	1	0-0	0	3	.182	.182	.182	-5	-2	0-0	.963	-1	67	118	1b5/C	0	-0.2
2005	Tor A	2	2	0	0	0	0	0	0	0-0	1	0	.000	.333	.000	0	0	0-0	1.000	-1	18	0	/C	0	-0.1
Total	2	9	13	0	2	0	0	0	1	0-0	1	3	.154	.214	.154	-1	-2	0-0	.963	-1	67	118	1b5,C2	0	-0.3
DONAHUE, SHE	Charles Michael; B6.29.1877 Oswego NY; D8.28.1947 New York NY; BR/TR/5´9˝/?; d4.29																								
1904	StL N	4	15	1	4	0	0	0	2	0	0	—	.267	.267	.267	68	-1	3	.846	-2	70	125	2b3/S	—	-0.3
	Phi N	58	200	21	43	4	0	0	14	3	0	—	.215	.227	.235	44	-14	7	.857	-14	85	92	S29,3b24,1b3,2b2	—	-2.9
	Year	62	215	22	47	4	0	0	16	3	0	—	.219	.229	.237	46	-14	10	.852	-16	84	91	S30,3b24,2b5,1b3	—	-3.2
DONAHUE, JIM	James Augustus; B1.8.1862 Lockport IL; D4.19.1935 Lockport IL; BR/TR/6´0˝/175; d4.19																								
1886	NY AA	49	186	14	37	0	0	0	9	10	3	—	.199	.251	.199	45	-11	1	.803	-2	56	0	O32(12/21/1),C19	—	-1.1
1887	NY AA	60	220	33	62	4	1	1	29	21	2	—	.282	.350	.323	92	-1	6	.890	-6	—	—	C51,O5(0/2/3),1b4/32	—	-0.3
1888	KC AA	88	337	29	79	11	3	1	28	21	1	—	.234	.281	.294	79	-9	12	.902	-8	—	—	C67,O18(12/5/1),3b5/2	—	-1.1
1889	KC AA	67	252	30	59	5	4	0	32	21	0	20	.234	.293	.286	61	-14	12	.887	-6	—	—	C46,O14L,3b10	—	-1.4
1891	Col AA	77	280	27	61	4	3	0	35	31	1	18	.218	.298	.254	62	-13	2	.942	-9	*74*	*115*	C75/rf1	—	-1.5
Total	5	341	1275	133	298	24	11	2	133	104	7	38	.234	.295	.275	70	-48	33	.911	-31	*74*	*115*	C258,O70(38/28/6),3b16,1b5,2b2	—	-5.4
DONAHUE, JIGGS	John Augustus; B7.13.1879 Springfield OH; D7.19.1913 Columbus OH; BL/TL/6´1˝/178; d9.10; b–Pat																								
1900	Pit N	3	10	1	2	0	1	0	3	0	0	—	.200	.200	.400	63	-1	1	.889	-1	*148*	*42*	C2/rf	—	-0.1
1901	Pit N	2	0	0	0	0	0	0	0	0	0	—	ø	ø	ø	ø	0	0	ø	-0	*0*	*0*	/Clf	—	0.0
	Mil A	37	107	10	34	5	4	0	16	10	2	—	.318	.387	.439	135	5	4	.933	-4	*77*	*105*	C19,1b13	—	0.3
1902	StL A	30	89	11	21	1	1	1	7	12	0	—	.236	.327	.303	76	-3	2	.956	-1	*116*	*104*	C23,1b5	—	-0.2
1904	Chi A	102	367	46	91	9	7	1	48	25	1	—	.248	.298	.319	99	-1	18	.979	7	133	126	1b101	—	0.5
1905	Chi A	149	533	71	153	22	4	1	76	44	4	—	.287	.346	.349	126	17	32	**.988**	7	116	**142**	1b149	—	2.3
1906	†Chi A	**154**	556	70	143	17	7	1	57	48	3	—	.257	.320	.318	103	2	36	**.988**	9	119	107	1b154	—	0.9
1907	Chi A	**157**	609	75	158	16	4	0	68	28	3	—	.259	.295	.299	93	-6	27	**.994**	21	**141**	118	1b157	—	1.2
1908	Chi A	93	304	22	62	8	2	0	22	25	3	—	.204	.271	.243	69	-10	14	.994	4	114	95	1b83	—	-0.8
1909	Chi A	2	4	0	0	0	0	0	2	1	0	—	.000	.200	.000	-38	-1	0	1.000	-0	0	0	1b2	—	-0.1
	Was A	84	283	13	67	12	1	0	28	22	1	—	.237	.294	.286	87	-4	9	.984	-4	79	73	1b81	—	-1.0
	Year	86	287	13	67	12	1	0	30	23	1	—	.233	.293	.282	86	-4	9	.984	-4	78	72	1b83	—	-1.1
Total	9	813	2862	319	731	90	31	4	327	215	17	—	.255	.311	.313	99	-2	143	.987	38	119	115	1b745,C45,O2(1/0/1)	—	3.0
DONAHUE, JOHN	John Frederick "Jiggs"; B4.19.1894 Roxbury MA; D10.3.1949 Boston MA; BB/TR/5´8˝/170; d9.25																								
1923	Bos A	10	36	5	10	4	0	0	1	4	0	5	.278	.350	.389	94	0	0-1	1.000	3	105	294	O9R	—	0.1
DONAHUE, PAT	Patrick William; B11.8.1884 Springfield OH; D1.31.1966 Springfield OH; BR/TR/6´0˝/175; d5.29; b–Jiggs																								
1908	Bos A	35	86	8	17	2	0	1	6	9	2	—	.198	.289	.256	75	-2	0	.959	1	*99*	*91*	C32,1b3	—	0.2
1909	Bos A	65	177	14	42	4	1	2	25	17	1	—	.237	.308	.305	92	-2	2	.982	-1	*113*	*97*	C58	—	0.4
1910	Bos A	2	4	0	0	0	0	0	0	0	0	—	.000	.000	.000	-98	-1	0	1.000	0	*120*	*0*	/C	—	-0.1
	Phi A	14	34	2	5	0	0	0	4	3	1	—	.147	.237	.147	21	-3	1	1.000	3	*114*	*118*	C13	—	0.1
	Cle A	2	6	0	1	0	0	0	0	0	0	—	.167	.167	.167	4	-1	0	1.000	-0	*83*	*75*	C2/1	—	-0.1
	Phi A	1	1	0	0	0	0	0	0	0	0	—	.000	.000	.000	-99	0	0	1.000	0	*114*	*118*	/C	—	0.0
	Year	19	45	2	6	0	0	0	4	3	1	—	.133	.204	.133	6	-5	1	1.000	3	*109*	*110*	C17/1	—	-0.1
Total	3	119	308	24	65	6	1	3	35	29	4	—	.211	.287	.266	75	-9	3	.978	4	*108*	*97*	C107,1b4	—	0.5
DONAHUE, TIM	Timothy Cornelius "Bridget"; B6.8.1870 Raynham MA; D6.12.1902 Taunton MA; BL/TR/5´11˝/180; d7.28																								
1891	Bos AA	4	7	0	0	0	0	0	0	0	0	5	.000	.000	.000	-99	-2	0	.833	-1	*111*	*74*	C4	—	-0.2
1895	Chi N	63	219	29	59	9	1	2	36	20	3	25	.269	.339	.347	72	-9	5	.915	-5	*94*	*70*	C63	—	-0.7
1896	Chi N	57	188	27	41	10	1	0	20	11	4	15	.218	.276	.282	45	-15	11	.934	-1	*93*	*104*	C57	—	-0.9
1897	Chi N	58	188	28	45	7	3	0	21	9	2	—	.239	.281	.309	54	-13	3	.949	1	*87*	*121*	C55,S2/1	—	-0.6
1898	Chi N	122	396	52	87	12	3	0	39	49	8	—	.220	.318	.265	68	-15	17	.962	16	*154*	*86*	C122	—	1.2
1899	Chi N	92	278	39	69	9	3	0	29	34	7	—	.248	.345	.302	80	-6	10	.951	4	*107*	*97*	C91/1	—	0.6
1900	Chi N	67	216	21	51	10	1	0	17	19	5	—	.236	.313	.292	70	-8	8	.928	-7	*95*	*79*	C66/2	—	-0.8
1902	Was A	3	8	0	2	0	0	0	1	0	0	—	.250	.250	.250	39	-1	0	1.000	-0	*89*	*142*	C3	—	-0.1
Total	8	466	1500	196	354	57	12	2	163	142	29	45	.236	.314	.294	66	-69	54	.943	9	*112*	*92*	C461,1b2,S2/2	—	-1.5
DONALDSON, JOHN	John David; B5.5.1943 Charlotte NC; BL/TR/5´11˝/165; d8.26																								
1966	KC A	15	30	4	4	0	0	0	1	3-0	0	4	.133	.212	.133	2	-4	1-0	1.000	-2	64	44	2b9	0	-0.5
1967	KC A	105	377	27	104	16	5	0	28	37-3	2	39	.276	.343	.345	107	4	6-3	.982	-15	88	70	2b101/S	0	-0.2
1968	Oak A	127	363	37	80	9	2	2	27	45-0	2	44	.220	.307	.273	81	-7	5-5	.971	-2	102	95	2b98,3b5/S	0	-0.2
1969	Oak A	12	13	1	1	0	0	0	0	2-1	0	4	.077	.200	.077	-21	-2	0-0	.857	0	136	155	/2	0	-0.2
	Sea A	95	338	22	79	8	3	1	19	36-5	0	36	.234	.307	.284	67	-15	6-1	.974	-6	94	87	2b90,3b2/S	0	-1.4
	Year	107	351	23	80	8	3	1	19	38-6	0	40	.228	.303	.276	64	-17	6-1	.972	-5	94	88	2b91,3b2/S	0	-1.6

YEAR	TM LG	G	AB	R	H	2B	3B	HR	RBI	BB-IB	HP	SO	AVG	OBP	SLG	AOPS	ABR	SB-CS	FA	FR	RNG	THR	GAMES AT POSITION	DL	BFW
1970	Oak A	41	89	4	22	2	1	1	11	9-3	0	6	.247	.316	.326	80	-3	1-0	.986	-5	95	68	2b21,S6/3	0	-0.5
1974	Oak A	10	15	1	2	0	0	0	0	0-0	0	0	.133	.133	.133	-25	-2	0-0	.962	2	152	207	2b7,3b3	0	-0.1
Total	6	405	1225	96	292	35	11	4	86	132-12	4	133	.238	.313	.295	80	-29	19-9	.976	-27	95	83	2b327,3b11,S9	0	-3.1
DONDERO, LEN	Leonard Peter "Mike"; B9.12.1903 Newark CA; D1.1.1999 Fremont CA; BR/TR/5´11˝/178; d4.21; Col St. Marys (CA)																								
1929	StL A	19	31	2	6	0	0	1	8	0	0	4	.194	.194	.290	22	-4	0-0	.857	-2	59	0	3b10,2b5	—	-0.5
DONLIN, MIKE	Michael Joseph "Turkey Mike"; B5.30.1878 Peoria IL; D9.24.1933 Hollywood CA; BL/TL/5´9˝/170; d7.19; ▲																								
1899	StL N	66	266	49	86	9	6	6	27	17	1	—	.323	.366	.470	126	8	20	.873	-8	92	102	O51(1/50/0),1b13,S3,P3	—	-0.4
1900	StL N	78	276	40	90	8	6	10	48	14	1	—	.326	.361	.507	139	12	14	.922	-4	110	311	O47(2/35/10),1b21	—	0.5
1901	Bal A	121	476	107	162	23	13	5	67	53	2	—	.340	.409	.475	138	25	33	.918	8	118	83	O74(73/1/0),1b47	—	2.5
1902	Cin N	34	143	30	41	5	4	0	9	9	1	—	.287	.333	.378	109	1	9	.877	-2	107	83	O32(30/0/2)/PS	—	-0.3
1903	Cin N	126	496	110	174	25	18	7	67	56	3	—	.351	.420	.516	150	31	26	.900	-5	86	96	O118(70/0/48),1b7	—	1.9
1904	Cin N	60	236	42	84	11	7	1	38	18	2	—	.356	.406	.475	158	16	21	.872	-1	126	58	O53(52/0/1),1b6	—	1.2
	NY N	42	132	17	37	7	3	2	14	10	2	—	.280	.340	.424	130	4	1	.918	-4	26	104	O37(23/11/3)	—	-0.1
	Year	102	368	59	121	18	10	3	52	28	4	—	.329	.382	.457	148	20	22	.886	-5	88	75	O90(75/11/4),1b6	—	1.1
1905	†NY N	150	606	**124**	216	31	16	7	80	56	2	—	.356	.413	.495	166	49	33	.934	-13	87	97	O150(4/147/0)	—	3.0
1906	NY N	37	121	15	38	5	1	1	14	11	0	—	.314	.371	.397	136	5	9	.929	-5	0	0	O29C/1	—	-0.1
1908	NY N	155	593	71	198	26	13	6	106	23	5	—	.334	.364	.452	153	32	30	.977	-0	106	23	O155(29/0/127)	—	2.8
1911	NY N	12	12	3	4	0	0	1	1	0	0	1	.333	.333	.583	150	1	2	1.000	-0	74	0	O3(0/2/1)	—	0.0
	Bos N	56	222	33	70	16	1	2	34	22	0	17	.315	.377	.423	115	5	7	.912	-3	93	100	O56C	—	-0.2
	Year	68	234	36	74	16	1	3	35	22	0	18	.316	.375	.432	117	6	9	.913	-3	93	99	O59(0/58/1)	—	-0.2
1912	Pit N	77	244	27	77	9	8	2	35	20	1	16	.316	.370	.443	124	7	8	.982	-0	100	94	O62(2/10/51)	—	0.3
1914	NY N	35	31	1	5	1	1	1	3	3	0	5	.161	.235	.355	77	-1	0	ø	0	—	—	/H	—	-0.1
Total	12	1049	3854	669	1282	176	97	51	543	312	20	39	.333	.386	.468	142	195	213	.924	-37	94	88	O867(286/341/243),1b95,P4,S4	—	11.0
DONNELLY, JIM	James B.; B7.19.1865 New Haven CT; D3.5.1915 Meriden CT; BR/TR/5´10.5˝/155; d8.11																								
1884	Ind AA	40	134	22	34	2	2	0	—	5	4	—	.254	.301	.299	99	0	—	.850	-4	72	78	3b24,S8,O6(2/2/2),2b2	—	-0.3
1885	Det N	56	211	24	49	4	3	1	22	10	—	29	.232	.267	.294	81	-5	—	.850	-2	94	56	3b56	—	-0.6
1886	KC N	113	438	51	88	11	3	0	38	36	—	57	.201	.262	.240	50	-26	16	.845	1	107	87	3b113	—	-2.2
1887	Was N	117	425	51	85	9	6	1	46	16	3	26	.200	.234	.256	39	-35	42	.867	16	**120**	115	3b115,S2	—	-1.5
1888	Was N	122	428	43	86	9	4	0	23	20	3	16	.201	.242	.241	58	-20	44	.875	-1	103	92	3b117,S5	—	-1.9
1889	Was N	4	13	3	2	0	0	0	0	2	0	0	.154	.267	.154	20	-1	1	.667	-1	89	153	3b4	—	-0.2
1890	StL AA	11	42	11	14	0	0	0	3	8	1	—	.333	.451	.333	115	1	5	.795	-2	71	270	3b11	—	0.0
1891	Col AA	17	54	6	13	0	0	0	9	13	0	5	.241	.388	.241	85	0	7	.855	2	119	179	3b17	—	0.2
1896	Bal N	106	396	70	130	14	10	0	71	34	4	11	.328	.387	.414	110	5	38	.884	-4	99	106	3b106	—	0.3
1897	Pit N	44	161	22	31	4	0	0	14	16	1	—	.193	.270	.217	31	-16	14	.920	2	106	19	3b44	—	-1.2
	NY N	23	85	19	16	3	0	0	11	9	0	—	.188	.266	.224	31	-8	6	.869	-3	89	82	3b23	—	-1.0
	Year	67	246	41	47	7	0	0	25	25	1	—	.191	.268	.220	31	-24	20	.905	-1	100	39	3b67	—	-2.2
1898	StL N	1	1	0	1	0	0	0	0	0	0	—	1.000	1.000	1.000	463	0	0	.500	-0	135	0	/3	—	0.0
Total	11	654	2388	322	549	56	28	2	237	169	16	144	.230	.285	.279	66	-105	173	.865	3	104	94	3b631,S15,O6(2/2/2),2b2	—	-8.4
DONNELLY, JIM	James J.; 5´10.5˝/155; d7.11																								
1884	KC U	6	23	2	3	1	0	0	—	1	—	—	.130	.167	.174	4	-3	—	.536	-4	73	0	3b5/C	—	-0.6
DONNELLY, JOHN	John; B Elizabeth NJ; d4.14; b–Pete																								
1873	Was NA	30	137	15	35	2	0	0	19	1	—	0	.255	.261	.270	59	-6	0-0	.750	0	83	119	S13,2b12,O6C/3	—	-0.5
1874	Phi NA	6	22	2	5	0	0	0	2	0	—	0	.227	.227	.227	45	-1	0-0	.667	-2	0	0	O3R,S2/2	—	-0.3
Total	2NA	36	159	17	40	2	0	0	21	1	—	0	.252	.256	.264	57	-7	0-0	.734	-2	81	107	S15,2b13,O9(0/6/3)/3	—	-0.8
DONNELLY, PETE	Peter J.; B10.8.1849 Philadelphia PA; D10.1.1890 Jersey City NJ; d5.13; b–John																								
1871	Kek NA	9	34	7	7	1	1	0	3	1	—	2	.206	.229	.294	48	-2	0-0	.714	-4	0	0	O9(2/1/6),3b2	—	-0.4
DONNELS, CHRIS	Chris Barton; B4.21.1966 Los Angeles CA; BL/TR/6´0˝/185; [NYN87 1/24]; d5.7; Col Loyola Marymount																								
1991	NY N	37	89	7	20	2	0	0	5	14-1	0	19	.225	.330	.247	65	-4	1-1	1.000	4	114	106	1b15,3b11	0	-0.1
1992	NY N	45	121	8	21	4	0	0	6	17-0	0	25	.174	.275	.207	39	-9	1-0	.941	2	109	78	3b29,2b12	0	-0.8
1993	Hou N	88	179	18	46	14	2	2	24	19-0	0	33	.257	.327	.391	95	-1	2-0	.898	-1	108	152	3b31,1b23/2	0	-0.3
1994	Hou N	54	86	12	23	5	0	3	5	13-0	0	18	.267	.364	.430	111	2	1-0	1.000	-0	89	0	3b14,1b4,2b4	0	0.2
1995	Hou N	19	30	4	9	0	0	0	2	3-2	0	6	.300	.364	.300	83	-1	0-0	.818	-3	57	232	3b9/2	17	-0.3
	Bos A	40	91	13	23	2	2	2	11	9-0	0	18	.253	.317	.385	80	-3	0-0	.927	-0	92	58	3b27,1b8,2b3	0	-0.3
2000	LA N	27	34	8	10	3	0	4	9	6-1	0	7	.294	.390	.735	187	5	0-0	1.000	-1	143	0	O6L,1b4,3b2/2	29	0.3
2001	LA N	66	88	8	15	2	0	3	8	12-2	1	25	.170	.277	.295	51	-7	0-0	.897	0	110	115	3b14,1b7/P	16	-0.7
2002	†Ari N	74	80	5	19	4	1	3	16	10-1	0	14	.237	.312	.425	86	-2	0-0	1.000	-2	67	0	3b26/1	32	-0.4
Total	8	450	798	83	186	36	5	17	86	103-7	1	165	.233	.319	.355	82	-20	5-1	.932	-2	98	94	3b163,1b62,2b22,O6L/P	94	-2.4
DONOHUE, ALEX	Alexander; B1869 Altoona PA; d8.24																								
1891	Phi N	6	22	2	7	1	0	0	2	1	1	3	.318	.375	.364	113	0	0	1.000	-1	0	0	O4C,S2	—	-0.1
DONOHUE, TOM	Thomas James; B11.15.1952 Mineola NY; BR/TR/6´0˝/195; [AnaA72*1/9]; d4.6; Col Nassau (NY) CC																								
1979	Cal A	38	107	13	24	3	1	3	14	3-0	2	29	.224	.259	.355	66	-6	2-0	.981	-8	86	122	C38	0	-1.2
1980	Cal A	84	218	18	41	4	1	2	14	7-0	1	63	.188	.216	.243	26	-23	5-1	.986	-13	67	98	C84	15	-3.3
Total	2	122	325	31	65	7	2	5	28	10-0	3	92	.200	.230	.280	39	-29	7-1	.985	-21	73	105	C122	15	-4.5
DONOVAN, FRED	Frederick Maurice; B7.4.1864 Epping NH; D3.7.1916 Bloomington IL; BR/TR; d6.23																								
1895	Cle N	3	12	1	1	0	0	0	1	1	0	2	.083	.154	.083	-36	-3	0	.938	-0	*124*	*55*	C3	—	-0.2
DONOVAN, JERRY	Jeremiah Francis; B9.3.1876 Lock Haven PA; D6.27.1938 St.Petersburg FL; BR/TR; d4.12; b–Tom																								
1906	Phi N	61	166	11	33	4	0	0	15	6	2	—	.199	.236	.223	43	-11	2	.955	-4	*90*	*80*	C53/Slf	—	-1.2
DONOVAN, MIKE	Michael Berchman; B10.18.1881 Brooklyn NY; D2.3.1938 New York NY; BR/TR/5´8˝/155; d5.29																								
1904	Cle A	2	2	0	0	0	0	0	0	0	0	—	.000	.000	.000	-99	0	0	ø	-0	0	0	/S	—	-0.1
1908	NY A	5	19	2	5	1	0	0	2	0	0	—	.263	.263	.316	87	0	0	1.000	1	86	0	3b5	—	0.1
Total	2	7	21	2	5	1	0	0	2	0	0	—	.238	.238	.286	69	0	0	1.000	1	86	0	3b5/S	—	0.0
DONOVAN, PATSY	Patrick Joseph; B3.16.1865 Co. Cork, Ireland; D12.25.1953 Lawrence MA; BL/TL/5´11.5˝/175; d4.19; M11																								
1890	Bos N	32	140	17	36	0	0	0	9	8	2	17	.257	.307	.257	60	-8	10	.891	-4	80	108	O32C	—	-1.1
	†Bro N	28	105	17	23	5	1	0	8	5	2	5	.219	.268	.286	61	-5	3	1.000	1	63	109	O28(1/24/3)	—	-0.5
	Year	60	245	34	59	5	1	0	17	13	4	22	.241	.290	.269	61	-13	13	.952	-3	72	108	O60(1/56/3)	—	-1.6
1891	Lou AA	105	439	73	141	10	3	2	53	30	8	18	.321	.375	.371	115	8	27	.912	3	79	0	O105L	—	0.7
	Was AA	17	70	9	14	1	0	0	3	4	0	5	.200	.243	.214	33	-6	1	.857	-2	78	154	O17(0/13/4)	—	-0.7
	Year	122	509	82	155	11	3	2	56	34	8	23	.305	.358	.350	104	2	28	.907	1	79	18	O122(105/13/4)	—	0.0
1892	Was N	40	163	29	39	3	3	0	12	11	2	13	.239	.295	.294	81	-4	16	.844	1	144	213	O40(14/0/26)	—	-0.5
	Pit N	90	388	77	114	15	3	2	26	20	3	16	.294	.333	.363	110	4	40	.872	-2	131	135	O90(1/1/90)	—	-0.2
	Year	130	551	106	153	18	6	2	38	31	5	29	.278	.322	.343	102	0	56	.862	-1	135	159	O130(15/1/116)	—	-0.7
1893	Pit N	113	499	114	158	5	8	2	56	42	3	8	.317	.373	.371	100	0	46	.937	-2	86	133	O112R	—	-0.6
1894	Pit N	**133**	577	147	175	21	10	4	76	36	5	12	.303	.350	.395	80	-20	41	.933	6	101	91	O133R	—	-1.6
1895	Pit N	126	522	115	162	18	6	1	59	48	8	19	.310	.377	.374	99	2	36	.961	-6	59	49	O126(0/1/125)	—	-0.8
1896	Pit N	**131**	573	113	183	20	5	3	59	35	11	18	.319	.370	.387	104	4	48	.954	6	129	171	O131R	—	0.3
1897	Pit N	120	479	82	154	16	7	0	57	25	4	—	.322	.360	.384	100	0	34	.949	1	101	154	O120R,M	—	-0.5
1898	Pit N	147	610	112	184	16	9	0	37	34	7	—	.302	.346	.357	103	2	41	.928	-2	101	87	O147R	—	-0.7
1899	Pit N	122	536	82	156	11	7	1	56	17	5	—	.291	.319	.343	82	-15	26	.942	-13	49	61	O122(0/1/121),M	—	-3.1
1900	StL N	126	503	78	159	11	1	0	61	38	3	—	.316	.368	.342	97	-1	**45**	.951	-4	78	95	O124R	—	-1.0
1901	StL N	130	531	92	161	23	5	1	73	27	6	—	.303	.344	.371	113	9	28	.979	2	114	193	O129R,M	—	0.5
1902	StL N	126	502	70	158	12	4	0	35	28	10	—	.315	.363	.355	127	16	34	.959	9	**177**	126	O126R,M	—	2.0
1903	StL N	105	410	63	134	15	3	0	39	25	3	—	.327	.370	.378	117	9	25	.952	0	115	138	O105R,M	—	0.5
1904	Was A	125	436	30	100	6	0	0	19	24	1	—	.229	.271	.243	64	-18	17	.963	9	111	99	O122(0/2/120),M	—	-1.6

YEAR	TM LG	G	AB	R	H	2B	3B	HR	RBI	BB-IB	HP	SO	AVG	OBP	SLG	AOPS	ABR	SB-CS	FA	FR	RNG	THR	GAMES AT POSITION	DL	BFW
1906	Bro N	7	21	1	5	0	0	0	0	0	0	—	.238	.238	.238	53	-1	0	1.000	-0	0	0	O6R,M	—	-0.2
1907	Bro N	1	1	0	0	0	0	0	0	0	0	—	.000	.000	.000	-99	0	0	1.000	0	0	0	/rfM	—	0.0
Total	17	1824	7505	1321	2256	208	75	16	738	457	83	131	.301	.348	.355	98	-24	518	.941	5	102	112	O1816(121/74/1623)	—	-9.1
DONOVAN, TOM	Thomas Joseph; B1.1.1873 West Troy NY; D3.25.1933 Watervliet NY; BR/TR/6´2˝/168; d9.10; b–Jerry																								
1901	Cle A	18	71	9	18	3	1	0	5	0	0	—	.254	.254	.324	62	-4	1	.862	0	209	0	O18R/P	—	-0.4
DONOVAN, BILL	William Edward "Wild Bill"; B10.13.1876 Lawrence MA; D12.9.1923 Forsyth NY; BR/TR/5´11˝/190; d4.22; M4/C1; ▲																								
1898	Was N	39	103	11	17	2	2	2	8	4	2	—	.165	.211	.282	41	-9	2	.933	1	156	444	O20(6/6/8),P17/S2	—	-0.5
1899	Bro N	5	13	2	3	1	0	0	0	0	0	—	.231	.231	.308	46	0	0	.857	-0	79	0	P5	—	0.0
1900	Bro N	5	13	0	0	0	0	0	2	0	0	—	.000	.000	.000	-94	-2	0	1.000	1	154	0	P5	—	0.0
1901	Bro N	46	135	16	23	3	0	2	13	8	0	—	.170	.217	.237	31	-1	1	.927	-1	84	176	P45	—	0.0
1902	Bro N	48	161	16	28	3	2	1	16	9	2	—	.174	.227	.236	43	-11	7	.948	1	94	97	P35,1b8,O4(2/0/2)/2	—	-0.3
1903	Det A	40	124	11	30	3	2	0	12	4	0	—	.242	.266	.298	71	-5	3	.938	-3	70	92	P35,S2/2cf	—	-0.1
1904	Det A	46	140	12	38	2	1	1	6	3	0	—	.271	.287	.321	95	-1	2	.967	-2	93	67	P34,1b8/rf	—	-0.3
1905	Det A	44	130	16	25	4	0	0	5	12	1	—	.192	.266	.223	55	-6	8	.933	-1	78	118	P34,O8(7/0/1),2b2	—	-0.1
1906	Det A	28	91	5	11	0	1	0	0	1	0	—	.121	.130	.143	-14	-12	6	.961	-2	97	53	P25,2b3/cf	—	-0.3
1907	†Det A	37	109	20	29	7	2	0	19	6	0	—	.266	.304	.367	110	7	4	.945	-6	66	0	P32	—	0.0
1908	†Det A	30	82	5	13	1	0	0	2	10	0	—	.159	.250	.171	36	0	2	.917	-6	53	0	P29	—	0.0
1909	†Det A	22	45	6	9	0	0	0	1	2	1	—	.200	.250	.200	41	0	0	.974	-2	67	88	P21	—	0.0
1910	Det A	26	69	6	10	1	0	0	2	5	0	—	.145	.203	.159	13	-2	0	.955	-6	50	112	P26	—	0.0
1911	Det A	24	60	11	12	3	1	1	6	11	0	—	.200	.324	.333	79	3	1	.935	-5	54	0	P20	—	0.0
1912	Det A	6	13	3	1	0	0	0	0	1	0	—	.077	.143	.077	-38	-2	0	1.000	-1	35	0	P3,1b2,O2R	—	-0.2
1915	NY A	10	12	1	1	0	0	0	0	1	0	6	.083	.154	.083	-29	-1	0	1.000	-1	70	0	P9,M	—	0.0
1916	NY A	1	0	0	0	0	0	0	0	0	0	0	ø	ø	ø	ø	0	0	ø	-0	0	0	/PM	—	0.0
1918	Det A	2	2	1	1	0	0	0	1	0	0	0	.500	.500	.500	210	0	0	1.000	-0	62	0	P2	—	0.0
Total	18	459	1302	142	251	30	11	7	93	77	6	6	.193	.241	.249	49	-42	36	.944	-32	76	81	P378,O37(15/8/14),1b18,2b8,S3	—	-1.8
DOOIN, RED	Charles Sebastian; B6.12.1879 Cincinnati OH; D5.14.1952 Rochester NY; BR/TR/5´9.5˝/165; d4.18; M5; Col Xavier																								
1902	Phi N	94	333	20	77	7	3	0	35	10	4	—	.231	.262	.270	64	-15	8	.950	-6	83	110	C84,O6L	—	-1.4
1903	Phi N	62	188	18	41	5	1	0	14	8	1	—	.218	.254	.255	47	-14	9	.940	-7	85	114	C51/1rf	—	-1.5
1904	Phi N	108	355	41	86	11	4	6	36	8	1	—	.242	.261	.346	90	-6	15	.938	-3	85	113	C96,1b4,O3(1/2/0)/3	—	0.0
1905	Phi N	113	380	45	95	13	5	0	36	10	0	—	.250	.269	.311	75	-13	12	.965	11	120	96	C107/3	—	0.9
1906	Phi N	113	351	25	86	19	1	0	32	13	1	—	.245	.274	.305	80	-9	15	.948	-9	90	80	C107	—	-0.9
1907	Phi N	101	313	18	66	8	4	0	14	15	2	—	.211	.252	.262	62	-15	10	.959	8	124	92	C94/2lf	—	0.3
1908	Phi N	133	435	28	108	17	4	0	41	17	4	—	.248	.283	.306	85	-8	20	.966	19	**130**	**110**	C132	—	2.8
1909	Phi N	141	468	42	105	14	1	2	38	21	4	—	.224	.264	.271	66	-20	14	.958	6	102	97	C140	—	0.0
1910	Phi N	103	331	30	80	13	4	0	30	22	0	17	.242	.289	.305	71	-13	10	.956	-6	96	97	C91,O3(1/1/1),M	—	-1.0
1911	Phi N	74	247	18	81	15	1	1	16	14	1	12	.328	.366	.409	115	5	6	.967	-2	91	91	C74,M	—	1.0
1912	Phi N	69	184	20	43	9	0	0	22	5	2	12	.234	.262	.283	46	-14	8	.958	-1	90	98	C58,M	—	-1.1
1913	Phi N	55	129	6	33	4	1	0	13	3	0	9	.256	.273	.302	62	-7	1-4	.962	1	112	93	C50,M	—	-0.3
1914	Phi N	53	118	10	21	2	0	1	8	4	0	14	.178	.205	.220	25	-11	4	.967	-3	73	114	C40,O2L,M	—	-1.2
1915	Cin N	10	31	2	10	0	0	0	0	2	0	5	.323	.364	.323	106	0	1	.915	-3	87	62	C10	—	-0.2
	NY N	46	124	9	27	2	2	0	9	3	0	15	.218	.236	.266	55	-8	0-2	.964	-3	90	112	C46	—	-0.8
	Year	56	155	11	37	2	2	0	9	5	0	20	.239	.262	.277	66	-7	1-2	.956	-5	89	103	C56	—	-1.0
1916	NY N	15	17	1	2	0	0	0	0	0	0	3	.118	.118	.118	-29	-3	0	.972	0	131	25	C15	—	-0.2
Total	15	1290	4004	333	961	139	31	10	344	155	20	87	.240	.272	.298	72	-151	133-6	.957	5	102	99	C1195,O16(11/3/2),1b5,3b2/2	—	-3.6
DOOLAN, MICKEY	Michael Joseph "Doc" (b Michael Joseph Doolittle); B5.7.1880 Ashland PA; D11.1.1951 Orlando FL; BR/TR/5´10.5˝/170; d4.14; C7; Col Villanova																								
1905	Phi N	136	492	53	125	27	11	1	48	24	2	—	.254	.292	.360	97	-4	17	.935	-16	96	86	S135	—	-1.5
1906	Phi N	**154**	535	41	123	19	7	1	55	27	2	—	.230	.270	.297	77	-17	16	.930	8	100	100	S154	—	-0.4
1907	Phi N	145	509	33	104	19	7	1	47	25	1	—	.204	.243	.275	63	-24	18	.929	15	105	125	S145	—	-0.5
1908	Phi N	129	445	29	104	25	4	2	49	17	3	—	.234	.267	.321	85	-9	5	.939	-2	100	86	S129	—	-0.7
1909	Phi N	147	493	39	108	12	10	1	35	37	2	—	.219	.276	.290	75	-16	10	.939	24	**105**	114	S147	—	1.4
1910	Phi N	148	536	58	141	31	6	2	57	35	6	56	.263	.315	.354	92	-6	16	**.948**	18	**108**	116	S148	—	1.7
1911	Phi N	146	512	51	122	23	6	1	49	44	2	65	.238	.301	.313	71	-21	14	.936	17	104	**116**	S145	—	0.6
1912	Phi N	146	532	47	137	26	6	1	62	34	2	59	.258	.305	.335	70	-23	6	.950	10	104	83	S146	—	-0.2
1913	Phi N	151	518	32	113	12	6	1	43	29	2	68	.218	.262	.270	50	-35	17-8	.941	9	103	113	S148,2b3	—	-1.5
1914	Bal F	145	486	58	119	23	6	1	53	40	7	47	.245	.311	.323	71	-27	30	**.949**	**34**	**112**	109	S145	—	1.7
1915	Bal F	119	404	41	75	13	7	2	21	24	4	39	.186	.238	.267	41	-40	10	.946	32	111	132	S119	—	0.1
	Chi F	24	86	9	23	1	1	0	9	2	1	7	.267	.292	.302	72	-5	5	.914	-1	107	56	S24	—	-0.5
	Year	143	490	50	98	14	8	2	30	26	5	46	.200	.248	.273	46	-45	15	.941	**31**	**110**	**119**	S143	—	-0.4
1916	Chi N	28	70	4	15	2	1	0	5	8	0	7	.214	.295	.271	67	-2	0	.918	0	105	86	S24	—	-0.1
	NY N	18	51	4	12	3	1	1	3	2	0	4	.235	.264	.392	106	0	1	.975	2	105	112	S16,2b2	—	0.3
	Year	46	121	8	27	5	2	1	8	10	0	11	.223	.282	.322	82	-3	1	.939	2	105	96	S40,2b2	—	0.2
1918	Bro N	92	308	14	55	8	2	0	18	22	0	24	.179	.233	.218	38	-23	8	**.968**	10	101	99	2b91	—	-1.3
Total	13	1728	5977	513	1376	244	81	15	554	370	34	376	.230	.279	.306	71	-252	173-8	.940	160	104	106	S1625,2b96	—	-0.9
DOOMS, HARRY	Henry E. "Jack"; B1.30.1867 St.Louis MO; D12.14.1899 St.Louis MO; d8.7																								
1892	Lou N	1	4	0	0	0	0	0	0	1	0	3	.000	.200	.000	-42	-1	0	.000	-1	0	0	/rf	—	-0.1
DORAN, TOM	Thomas J. "Long Tom"; B12.2.1880 Westchester Co. NY; D6.22.1910 New York NY; BL/TR/5´11˝/152; d4.19																								
1904	Bos A	12	32	1	4	0	1	0	0	4	1	—	.125	.243	.188	35	-2	1	.898	-3	131	41	C11	—	-0.5
1905	Bos A	3	3	0	0	0	0	0	0	0	0	—	.000	.000	.000	-99	-1	0	1.000	0	0	330	/C	—	0.0
	Det A	34	94	8	15	3	0	0	4	8	3	—	.160	.248	.191	40	-6	2	.963	-6	69	103	C32	—	-1.0
	Year	37	97	8	15	3	0	0	4	8	3	—	.155	.241	.186	35	-7	2	.964	-5	68	106	C33	—	-1.0
1906	Bos A	2	3	1	0	0	0	0	0	0	0	—	.000	.000	.000	-99	-1	0	1.000	0	91	137	C2	—	-0.1
Total	3	51	132	10	19	3	1	0	4	12	4	—	.144	.236	.182	33	-10	3	.950	-8	84	91	C46	—	-1.6
DORAN, BILL	William Donald; B5.28.1958 Cincinnati OH; BB/TR/5´11˝/(175–180); [HouN79 6/138]; d9.6; C3; Col Miami–Ohio																								
1982	Hou N	26	97	11	27	3	0	0	6	4-0	0	11	.278	.304	.309	79	-3	5-0	.975	-4	94	111	2b26	0	-0.4
1983	Hou N	154	535	70	145	12	7	8	39	86-11	0	67	.271	.371	.364	111	10	12-12	.979	3	99	117	2b153	0	2.1
1984	Hou N	147	548	92	143	18	11	4	41	66-7	2	69	.261	.341	.356	103	2	21-12	.986	8	106	104	2b139,S13	0	2.0
1985	Hou N	148	578	84	166	31	6	14	59	71-6	0	69	.287	.362	.434	126	21	23-15	.980	6	100	112	2b147	0	3.6
1986	†Hou N	145	550	92	152	29	3	6	37	81-7	2	57	.276	.368	.373	109	10	42-19	.974	-34	78	81	2b144	0	-1.4
1987	Hou N	**162**	625	82	177	23	3	16	79	82-3	3	64	.283	.365	.406	109	10	31-11	**.992**	-13	91	72	2b162,S3	0	0.8
1988	Hou N	132	480	66	119	18	1	7	53	65-3	1	60	.248	.338	.333	97	0	17-4	**.987**	2	99	101	2b130	0	0.9
1989	Hou N	142	507	65	111	25	2	8	58	59-2	2	63	.219	.301	.323	82	-11	22-3	.980	-25	90	84	2b138	0	-3.1
1990	Hou N	109	344	49	99	21	2	6	32	71-1	0	53	.288	.405	.413	130	19	18-9	.989	-12	96	87	2b99	15	1.0
	Cin N	17	59	10	22	8	0	1	5	8-1	0	5	.373	.448	.559	168	6	5-0	.985	1	111	97	2b12,3b4	0	0.9
	Year	126	403	59	121	29	2	7	37	79-2	0	58	.300	.411	.434	136	25	23-9	.988	-11	98	88	2b111,3b4	0	1.9
1991	Cin N	111	361	51	101	12	2	6	35	46-1	0	39	.280	.359	.374	103	3	5-4	.981	-9	91	108	2b88,O6L,1b4	22	-0.5
1992	Cin N	132	387	48	91	16	2	8	47	64-9	0	40	.235	.342	.349	94	-1	7-4	.988	-6	92	106	2b104,1b25	0	-0.6
1993	Mil A	28	60	7	13	4	0	0	6	6-1	0	3	.217	.284	.283	55	-4	1-0	.964	-3	79	67	2b17,1b4	45	-0.6
Total	12	1453	5131	727	1366	220	39	84	497	709-52	10	600	.266	.354	.373	106	62	209-93	.983	-85	94	97	2b1359,1b33,S16,O6L,3b4	82	4.7
DORAN, BILL	William James; B6.14.1898 San Francisco CA; D3.9.1978 Santa Monica CA; BL/TR/5´11.5˝/175; d6.23; Col St. Marys (CA)																								
1922	Cle A	3	2	0	1	0	0	0	0	1	0	0	.500	.667	.500	206	0	0-0	ø	-0	0	0	3b2	—	0.0
DORGAN, JERRY	Jeremiah F.; B1856 Meriden CT; D6.10.1891 New Haven CT; BL/TR/?/165; d7.8; b–Mike																								
1880	Wor N	10	35	2	7	1	0	0	1	0	—	1	.200	.200	.229	41	-2	—	.750	-2	0	0	O9R/C	—	-0.4
1882	Phi AA	44	181	25	51	9	1	0	24	4	—	—	.282	.297	.343	108	1	—	.880	-2	—	—	C25,O22(1/1/20)/3	—	0.0
1884	Ind AA	34	141	22	42	6	1	0	—	2	2	—	.298	.317	.355	122	3	—	.793	-3	156	102	O29R,C5	—	0.1
	Bro AA	4	13	2	4	0	0	0	—	0	0	—	.308	.308	.308	101	0	—	.921	1	—	—	C4	—	0.1
	Year	38	154	24	46	6	1	0	—	2	2	—	.299	.316	.351	120	3	—	.793	-1	156	102	O29R,C9	—	0.2

YEAR	TM LG	G	AB	R	H	2B	3B	HR	RBI	BB-IB	HP	SO	AVG	OBP	SLG	AOPS	ABR	SB-CS	FA	FR	RNG	THR	GAMES AT POSITION	DL	BFW
1885	Det N	39	161	23	46	6	2	0	24	8	—	10	.286	.320	.348	115	3	—	.857	-3	71	200	O39(0/1/38)	—	0.0
Total	4	131	531	74	150	22	4	0	49	14	—	11	.282	.303	.339	109	5	—	.817	-9	—	—	O99(1/2/96),C35/3	—	-0.2
DORGAN, MIKE	Michael Cornelius; B10.2.1853 Middletown CT; D4.26.1909 Hartford CT; BR/TR/5´9˝/180; d5.8; M3; b–Jerry; OF(29/17/556); ▲																								
1877	StL N	**60**	266	45	82	9	7	0	23	9	—	13	.308	.331	.395	135	11	—	.824	-7	54	198	O50(20/1/29),C12,3b2/S2	—	0.2
1879	Syr N	59	270	38	72	11	5	1	17	4	—	13	.267	.277	.356	120	7	—	.954	-6	143	46	1b21,O16R,3b11,S6,C4,P2/2M	—	0.1
1880	Pro N	79	321	45	79	10	1	0	31	10	—	18	.246	.269	.283	90	-3	—	.858	-1	135	146	O77R,3b2/PM	—	-0.3
1881	Wor N	51	220	36	61	5	0	0	18	8	—	4	.277	.303	.300	85	-4	—	.953	-0	82	72	1b26,O23R,S2,M	—	-0.5
	Det N	8	34	5	8	1	0	0	5	1	—	0	.235	.257	.265	62	-1	—	1.000	-1	70	0	O5(0/4/1),3b2/1	—	-0.2
	Year	59	254	41	69	6	0	0	23	9	—	4	.272	.297	.295	82	-5	—	.897	-1	101	76	O28(0/4/24),1b27,S2,3b2	—	-0.7
1883	NY N	64	261	32	61	11	3	0	27	2	—	23	.234	.240	.299	63	-12	—	.847	-8	50	45	O59(0/9/51),C6/P	—	-1.7
1884	NY N	83	341	61	94	11	6	1	48	13	—	27	.276	.302	.352	103	0	—	.851	-2	93	124	O64(2/2/60),P14,C6,2b3	—	-0.2
1885	NY N	89	347	60	113	17	8	0	46	11	—	24	.326	.346	.421	149	18	—	.905	-4	66	212	O88R/1	—	1.3
1886	NY N	118	442	61	129	19	4	2	79	29	—	37	.292	.335	.367	112	7	9	.888	-10	57	122	O116(6/1/110),1b3	—	-0.4
1887	NY N	71	283	41	73	10	0	0	34	15	3	20	.258	.302	.293	69	-11	22	.870	-3	47	0	O69(1/0/68),1b2	—	-1.2
1890	Syr AA	33	139	19	30	8	0	0	18	16	1	—	.216	.301	.273	77	-3	8	.900	-2	92	77	O33R	—	-0.4
Total	10	715	2924	443	802	112	34	4	346	118	4	179	.274	.303	.340	102	9	39	.867	-43	77	126	O600R,1b54,C28,P18,3b17,S9,2b5	—	-3.3
DORMAN, RED	Charles Dwight "Curlie"; B10.3.1900 Jacksonville IL; D12.7.1974 Anaheim CA; BR/TR/5´10.5˝/180; d8.21																								
1928	Cle A	25	77	12	28	6	0	0	11	9	0	6	.364	.430	.442	128	4	1-0	.915	-2	97	43	O24(5/19/0)	—	0.1
DORMAN, CHARLIE	Charles William "Slats"; B4.23.1898 San Francisco CA; D11.15.1928 San Francisco CA; BR/TR/6´2˝/185; d5.14																								
1923	Chi A	1	2	0	1	0	0	0	0	0	0	0	.500	.500	.500	166	0	0-0	1.000	-0	*0*	*391*	/C	—	0.0
DORSETT, BRIAN	Brian Richard; B4.9.1961 Terre Haute IN; BR/TR/6´3˝/(215–222); [OakA83 10/241]; d9.8; Col Indiana St.; [DL 1988 Cle A 64]																								
1987	Cle A	5	11	2	3	0	0	1	3	0-0	1	3	.273	.333	.545	126	0	0-0	1.000	-1	45	0	C4	0	-0.1
1988	Cal A	7	11	0	1	0	0	0	2	1-0	0	5	.091	.167	.091	-26	-2	0-0	1.000	0	126	178	C7	0	-0.1
1989	NY A	8	22	3	8	1	0	0	4	1-0	0	3	.364	.391	.409	127	1	0-0	1.000	-0	209	104	C8	0	0.1
1990	NY A	14	35	2	5	2	0	0	0	2-0	0	4	.143	.189	.200	9	-4	0-0	1.000	-1	71	0	C9,D5	0	-0.6
1991	SD N	11	12	0	1	0	0	0	1	0-0	0	3	.083	.083	.083	-51	-2	0-0	1.000	0	244	0	1b2	0	-0.2
1993	Cin N	25	63	7	16	4	0	2	12	3-0	0	14	.254	.288	.413	84	-2	0-0	1.000	2	118	61	C18,1b3	0	0.2
1994	Cin N	76	216	21	53	8	0	5	26	21-7	1	33	.245	.313	.352	74	-8	0-0	.991	3	133	104	C73/1	0	-0.1
1996	Chi N	17	41	3	5	0	0	1	3	4-0	0	8	.122	.196	.195	5	-6	0-0	1.000	4	405	94	C15	0	-0.1
Total	8	163	411	38	92	15	0	9	51	32-7	2	73	.224	.281	.326	61	-23	0-0	.995	7	157	92	C134,1b6,D5	64	-0.9
DORSEY, JERRY	Jeremiah; B1885 Oakland CA; BL/TL/5´11˝/175; d9.23																								
1911	Pit N	2	6	0	0	0	0	0	0	0	0	1	.000	.000	.000	-96	-2	0	1.000	0	118	0	/cf	—	-0.2
DORTA, MELVIN	Melvin A.; B1.15.1982 Valencia, Venezuela; BR/TR/5´11˝/160; d7.21																								
2006	Was N	15	19	3	4	1	0	0	0	1-0	0	2	.211	.250	.263	33	-2	0-2	1.000	0	82	0	3b3,S3	0	-0.2
DOSCHER, HERM	John Henry Sr.; B12.20.1852 New York NY; D3.20.1934 Buffalo NY; BR/TR/5´10˝/182; d9.5; U4; s–Jack																								
1872	Atl NA	6	24	4	9	0	0	0	5	0	—	1	.375	.375	.375	112	0	0-1	.714	0	142	0	O6R	—	0.0
1873	Atl NA	1	6	1	1	0	0	0	1	0	—	0	.167	.167	.167	-1	-1	0-0	.500	-1	0	0	/cf	—	-0.1
1875	Was NA	22	81	5	15	4	0	0	5	0	—	6	.185	.185	.235	46	-4	1-0	.752	0	114	31	3b22	—	-0.4
1879	Tro N	47	191	16	42	8	0	0	18	2	—	10	.220	.228	.262	65	-6	—	.806	-3	100	111	3b47	—	-0.7
	Chi N	3	11	1	2	0	0	0	1	0	—	3	.182	.182	.182	19	-1	—	.700	-1	90	0	3b3	—	-0.2
	Year	50	202	17	44	8	0	0	19	2	—	13	.218	.225	.257	62	-7	—	.800	-4	99	105	3b50	—	-0.9
1881	Cle N	5	19	2	4	0	0	0	0	0	—	2	.211	.211	.211	35	-1	—	.895	-0	91	126	3b5	—	-0.2
1882	Cle N	25	104	7	25	2	0	0	10	0	—	11	.240	.240	.260	63	-4	—	.857	-1	96	73	3b22,O2L/S	—	-0.4
Total	3NA	29	111	10	25	4	0	0	11	0	—	7	.225	.225	.261	62	-5	1-1	.752	-1	114	31	3b22,O7(0/1/6)	—	-0.5
Total	3	80	325	26	73	10	0	0	29	2	—	26	.225	.229	.255	61	-12	—	.823	-5	98	97	3b77,O2L/S	—	-1.5
DOSTER, DAVID	David Eric; B10.8.1970 Ft.Wayne IN; BR/TR/5´10˝/(181–185); [PhiN93 27/748]; d6.16; Col Indiana St.																								
1996	Phi N	39	105	14	28	8	0	1	8	7-0	0	21	.267	.313	.371	79	-3	0-0	.973	-2	90	85	2b24/3	0	-0.4
1999	Phi N	99	97	9	19	2	0	3	10	12-1	0	23	.196	.282	.309	49	-8	1-0	.993	7	104	132	2b77,3b6,S5	0	0.1
Total	2	138	202	23	47	10	0	4	18	19-1	0	44	.233	.297	.342	64	-11	1-0	.984	6	97	110	2b101,3b7,S5	0	-0.3
DOTTERER, DUTCH	Henry John; B11.11.1931 Syracuse NY; D10.9.1999 Syracuse NY; BR/TR/6´0˝/(198–209); d9.25; Col Syracuse																								
1957	Cin N	4	12	0	1	0	0	0	2	1-0	0	2	.083	.154	.083	-32	-2	0-0	1.000	-1	0	0	C4	0	-0.3
1958	Cin N	11	28	1	7	1	0	1	2	2-0	0	4	.250	.300	.393	77	-1	0-0	.981	3	33	162	C8	0	0.2
1959	Cin N	52	161	21	43	7	0	2	17	16-1	0	23	.267	.328	.348	79	-4	0-0	.992	-1	76	81	C51	0	-0.3
1960	Cin N	33	79	4	18	5	0	2	11	13-0	0	10	.228	.337	.367	91	0	0-1	.979	-1	60	142	C31	0	-0.1
1961	Was A	7	19	1	5	2	0	0	1	3-0	0	5	.263	.364	.368	98	0	0-0	1.000	1	70	170	C7	0	0.2
Total	5	107	299	27	74	15	0	5	33	35-1	0	44	.247	.323	.348	79	-7	0-1	.988	1	65	108	C101	0	-0.3
DOUGHERTY, CHARLIE	Charles William; B2.7.1862 Darlington WI; D2.18.1925 Milwaukee WI; d4.17																								
1884	Alt U	23	85	6	22	5	0	0	—	2	—	—	.259	.276	.318	79	-5	—	.854	-3	90	30	2b16,O8(2/2/4)/S	—	-0.6
DOUGHERTY, PATSY	Patrick Henry; B10.27.1876 Andover NY; D4.30.1940 Bolivar NY; BL/TR/6´2˝/190; d4.19																								
1902	Bos A	108	438	77	150	12	6	0	34	42	6	—	.342	.407	.397	120	14	20	.899	-10	61	41	O102L/3	—	-0.1
1903	†Bos A	139	590	**107**	**195**	19	12	4	59	33	6	—	.331	.372	.424	131	22	35	.952	4	103	84	O139L	—	1.8
1904	Bos A	49	195	33	53	5	4	0	4	25	0	—	.272	.355	.338	113	4	10	.925	-0	72	240	O49L	—	0.1
	NY A	106	452	80	128	13	10	6	22	19	3	—	.283	.316	.396	119	8	11	.925	-7	120	36	O106L	—	-0.6
	Year	155	647	**113**	181	18	14	6	26	44	3	—	.280	.329	.379	117	12	21	.925	-7	104	102	O155L	—	-0.5
1905	NY A	116	418	56	110	9	6	3	29	28	6	—	.263	.319	.335	96	-2	17	.898	-3	97	75	O108L/3	—	-1.2
1906	NY A	12	52	3	10	2	0	0	4	0	0	—	.192	.192	.231	29	-4	0	1.000	2	197	315	O12L	—	-0.3
	†Chi A	75	253	30	59	9	4	1	27	19	3	—	.233	.295	.312	92	-2	11	.985	-2	105	55	O74L	—	-0.9
	Year	87	305	33	69	11	4	1	31	19	3	—	.226	.278	.298	81	-7	11	.987	1	118	91	O86L	—	-1.2
1907	Chi A	148	533	69	144	17	2	1	59	36	5	—	.270	.322	.315	107	5	33	.946	-7	98	98	O148L	—	-1.2
1908	Chi A	138	482	68	134	11	6	0	45	58	10	—	.278	.367	.326	128	18	**47**	.947	-15	47	28	O128L	—	-0.5
1909	Chi A	139	491	71	140	23	13	1	55	51	6	—	.285	.359	.391	143	25	36	.942	-14	57	0	O138L	—	0.4
1910	Chi A	127	443	45	110	8	6	1	43	41	4	—	.248	.318	.300	98	-1	22	.923	-12	81	59	O121L	—	-2.3
1911	Chi A	76	211	39	61	10	9	0	32	26	5	—	.289	.380	.422	128	8	19	.933	-6	80	72	O56L	—	0.0
Total	10	1233	4558	678	1294	138	78	17	413	378	54	—	.284	.346	.360	117	95	261	.935	-69	85	65	O1181L,3b2	—	-4.8
DOUGLAS, JOHN	John Franklin; B9.14.1917 Thayer WV; D2.11.1984 Miami FL; BL/TL/6´2.5˝/195; d4.21; Col Miami–Ohio																								
1945	Bro N	5	9	0	0	0	0	0	0	2	0	4	.000	.182	.000	-47	-2	0	.971	-1	0	44	1b4	0	-0.3
DOUGLASS, ASTYANAX	Astyanax Saunders; B9.19.1897 Covington TX; D1.26.1975 El Paso TX; BL/TR/6´1˝/190; d7.30; Col TCU																								
1921	Cin N	4	7	1	1	0	0	0	0	0	0	1	.143	.143	.143	-25	-1	0-0	1.000	0	*114*	*185*	C4	—	-0.1
1925	Cin N	7	17	1	3	0	0	0	1	1	0	3	.176	.222	.176	3	-3	0-0	.889	-1	*79*	*172*	C7	—	-0.3
Total	2	11	24	2	4	0	0	0	1	1	0	4	.167	.200	.167	-4	-4	0-0	.926	-1	*89*	*176*	C11	—	-0.4
DOUGLASS, KLONDIKE	William Bingham; B5.10.1872 Boston PA; D12.13.1953 Bend OR; BL/TR/6´0˝/200; d4.23; OF(68/9/55)																								
1896	StL N	81	296	42	78	6	4	1	28	35	5	15	.264	.351	.321	81	-7	18	.894	-3	136	113	O74(29/5/41),C6,S2	—	-1.2
1897	StL N	126	519	77	170	15	3	6	50	52	13	—	.328	.402	.403	115	14	12	.948	-22	*68*	*108*	C61,O44(28/2/14),1b17,3b7/S	—	-0.4
1898	Phi N	146	582	105	150	26	4	2	48	55	11	—	.258	.333	.326	93	-3	18	.976	2	105	83	1b146	—	-0.1
1899	Phi N	77	275	26	70	6	6	0	27	10	6	—	.255	.296	.320	71	-12	7	.970	2	*109*	*95*	C66,3b4,1b4/cf	—	-0.4
1900	Phi N	50	160	23	48	9	4	0	25	13	2	—	.300	.360	.406	112	3	7	.934	-9	*78*	*101*	C47,3b2	—	-0.2
1901	Phi N	51	173	14	56	6	1	0	23	11	2	—	.324	.371	.370	113	3	10	.979	2	*103*	*62*	C41,1b6,O2(1/1/0)	—	0.8
1902	Phi N	109	408	37	95	12	3	0	37	23	0	—	.233	.274	.277	70	-15	6	.986	-6	84	68	1b69,C29,O10L	—	-2.2
1903	Phi N	105	377	43	96	5	4	1	36	28	1	—	.255	.308	.297	75	-13	6	.985	-1	91	80	1b97	—	-1.5
1904	Phi N	3	10	1	3	0	0	0	1	0	1	—	.300	.364	.300	109	0	0	.970	-1	52	72	1b3	—	0.0
Total	9	748	2800	368	766	85	29	10	275	227	41	15	.274	.337	.335	91	-30	84	.981	-35	94	78	1b342,C250,O131L,3b13,S3	—	-5.2

YEAR	TM LG	G	AB	R	H	2B	3B	HR	RBI	BB-IB	HP	SO	AVG	OBP	SLG	AOPS	ABR	SB-CS	FA	FR	RNG	THR	GAMES AT POSITION	DL	BFW
DOUMIT, RYAN	Ryan Matthew; B4.3.1981 Moses Lake WA; BB/TR/6´0˝/(200–215); [PitN99 2/59]; d6.5																								
2005	Pit N	75	231	25	59	13	1	6	35	11-1	13	48	.255	.324	.398	88	-4	2-1	.975	-1	119	137	C50,O3R,D6	0	-0.1
2006	Pit N	61	149	15	31	9	0	6	17	15-1	11	42	.208	.322	.389	81	-4	0-0	.987	0	91	102	1b28,C11,D3	100	-0.5
Total	2	136	380	40	90	22	1	12	52	26-2	24	90	.237	.323	.395	85	-8	2-1	.978	-0	108	142	C61,1b28,D9,O3R	100	-0.6
DOUTHIT, TAYLOR	Taylor Lee; B4.22.1901 Little Rock AR; D5.28.1986 Fremont CA; BR/TR/5´11.5˝/175; d9.14; Col California																								
1923	StL N	9	27	3	5	0	2	0	0	0	0	4	.185	.185	.333	35	-3	1-0	1.000	1	104	168	O7(3/0/4)	—	-0.3
1924	StL N	53	173	24	48	13	1	0	13	16	3	19	.277	.349	.364	93	-1	4-3	.976	3	113	99	O50(9/22/19)	—	-0.1
1925	StL N	30	73	13	20	3	1	1	8	2	2	6	.274	.312	.384	75	-3	0-0	.981	1	113	61	O21(4/16/1)	—	-0.3
1926	†StL N	139	530	96	163	20	4	3	52	55	2	46	.308	.375	.377	99	1	23	.958	7	**111**	100	O138(1/137/0)	—	0.2
1927	StL N	130	488	81	128	29	6	5	50	52	2	45	.262	.336	.377	88	-8	6	.964	-1	107	55	O125(1/122/1)	—	-1.4
1928	†StL N	**154**	648	111	191	35	3	3	43	84	**10**	36	.295	.384	.372	97	2	11	.984	13	**120**	66	O154C	—	0.8
1929	StL N	150	613	128	206	42	7	9	62	79	5	49	.336	.416	.471	118	21	8	.974	-1	107	55	O150C	—	1.3
1930	†StL N	**154**	664	109	201	41	10	7	93	60	4	38	.303	.364	.426	87	-13	4	.964	0	106	65	O154C	—	-1.7
1931	StL N	36	133	21	44	11	2	1	21	11	1	9	.331	.386	.466	123	5	1	.972	-1	106	0	O36(0/35/1)	—	0.2
	Cin N	95	374	42	98	9	1	0	24	42	2	24	.262	.340	.291	76	-12	4	.983	1	104	72	O95C	—	-1.3
	Year	131	507	63	142	20	3	1	45	53	3	33	.280	.352	.337	89	-6	5	.980	-0	105	52	O131(0/130/1)	—	-1.1
1932	Cin N	96	333	28	81	12	1	0	25	31	2	29	.243	.311	.285	64	-16	3	.985	2	106	79	O88(2/86/0)	—	-1.6
1933	Cin N	1	0	1	0	0	0	0	0	0	0	0	ø	ø	ø	ø	0	0	ø	0	—	—	/R	—	0.0
	Chi N	27	71	8	16	5	0	0	5	11	0	7	.225	.329	.296	80	-1	2	.930	-1	84	238	O18(5/13/0)	—	-0.2
	Year	28	71	9	16	5	0	0	5	11	0	7	.225	.329	.296	80	-1	2	.930	-1	84	238	O18(5/13/0)	—	-0.2
Total	11	1074	4127	665	1201	220	38	29	396	443	33	312	.291	.364	.384	93	-28	67-3	.972	24	109	72	O1036(25/984/26)	—	-4.4
DOW, CLARENCE	Clarence G.; B10.2.1854 Charlestown MA; D3.11.1893 West Somerville MA; d9.22																								
1884	Bos U	1	6	1	2	0	0	0	—	0	—	—	.333	.333	.333	104	0	—	1.000	1	545	0	/cf	—	0.1
DOWD, JOHN	John Leo (b John Leo O'Dowd); B1.3.1891 Weymouth MA; D1.31.1981 Ft.Lauderdale FL; BR/TR/5´8˝/170; d7.3; Col Vermont																								
1912	NY A	10	31	1	6	1	0	0	0	6	1	—	.194	.342	.226	60	-1	0	.840	-3	96	31	S10	—	-0.3
DOWD, SNOOKS	Raymond Bernard; B12.20.1897 Springfield MA; D4.4.1962 Northampton MA; BR/TR/5´8˝/163; d4.27; Col Lehigh																								
1919	Det A	1	0	0	0	0	0	0	0	0	0	0	ø	ø	ø	ø	0	0	ø	0	—	—	/R	—	0.0
	Phi A	13	18	4	3	0	0	0	6	0	0	5	.167	.167	.167	-6	-3	2	.800	0	138	129	2b3,S2/3cf	—	-0.2
	Year	14	18	4	3	0	0	0	6	0	0	5	.167	.167	.167	-6	-3	2	.800	0	138	129	2b3,S2/3cf	—	-0.2
1926	Bro N	2	8	0	0	0	0	0	0	0	0	0	.000	.000	.000	-99	-2	0	1.000	-1	39	0	2b2	—	-0.4
Total	2	16	26	4	3	0	0	0	6	0	0	5	.115	.115	.115	-36	-5	2	.875	-1	92	69	2b5,S2/cf3	—	-0.6
DOWD, TOMMY	Thomas Jefferson "Buttermilk Tommy"; B4.20.1869 Holyoke MA; D7.2.1933 Holyoke MA; BR/TR/5´8˝/173; d4.8; M2; Col Brown; OF(284/331/350)																								
1891	Bos AA	4	11	1	1	0	0	0	0	0	0	1	.091	.091	.091	-49	-2	0	ø	-0	0	0	O4R	—	-0.2
	Was AA	112	464	66	120	9	10	1	44	19	2	44	.259	.291	.328	81	-15	39	.885	-13	94	75	2b107,O5L	—	-2.1
	Year	116	475	67	121	9	10	1	44	19	2	45	.255	.286	.322	78	-17	39	.885	-13	94	75	2b107,O9(5/0/4)	—	-2.3
1892	Was N	144	584	94	142	9	10	1	50	34	1	49	.243	.286	.298	79	-17	49	.891	-19	95	83	2b98,O23(7/0/16),3b18,S6	—	-3.1
1893	StL N	132	581	114	164	18	7	1	54	49	2	23	.282	.340	.343	81	-16	59	.944	3	121	196	O132(64/5/63)/2	—	-1.9
1894	StL N	123	524	92	142	16	8	4	62	54	2	33	.271	.341	.355	68	-28	31	.930	-7	73	89	O117(48/0/69),2b7/3	—	-3.2
1895	StL N	130	508	95	164	19	17	7	74	31	3	31	.323	.365	.469	116	9	32	.928	-4	67	76	O116(14/36/66),3b17,2b2	—	-0.1
1896	StL N	126	521	93	138	17	11	5	46	42	2	19	.265	.322	.369	85	-13	40	.920	-13	92	63	2b78,O48C,M	—	-2.2
1897	StL N	35	145	25	38	9	1	0	9	6	0	—	.262	.291	.338	67	-7	11	.915	-7	0	0	O30C,2b5,M	—	-1.3
	Phi N	91	391	68	114	14	4	0	43	19	0	—	.292	.324	.348	80	-12	30	.919	-5	98	169	O73(0/23/50),2b19	—	-1.7
	Year	126	536	93	152	23	5	0	52	25	0	—	.284	.316	.345	76	-19	41	.918	-12	68	117	O103(0/53/50),2b24	—	-3.0
1898	StL N	139	586	70	143	17	7	0	32	30	5	—	.244	.287	.297	66	-28	16	.920	-13	64	69	O129(9/42/82),2b11	—	-4.5
1899	Cle N	147	605	81	168	17	6	2	35	48	2	—	.278	.333	.336	90	-8	28	.954	-2	47	26	O147C	—	-1.7
1901	Bos A	**138**	594	104	159	18	7	3	52	38	3	—	.268	.315	.337	82	-15	33	.937	1	61	85	O137L,1b2/3	—	-1.9
Total	10	1321	5514	903	1493	163	88	24	501	370	22	200	.271	.319	.345	82	-152	368	.933	-78	71	98	O961R,2b328,3b37,S6,1b2	—	-23.9
DOWELL, KEN	Kenneth Allen; B1.19.1961 Sacramento CA; BR/TR/5´9˝/160; [PhiN80 S3/61]; d6.24; Col Sacramento (CA) City																								
1987	Phi N	15	39	4	5	0	0	0	1	2-0	0	5	.128	.171	.128	-19	-7	0-0	1.000	-1	98	99	S15	0	-0.6
DOWIE, JOE	Joseph E.; B7.15.1865 New Orleans LA; D3.4.1917 New Orleans LA; 5´8˝/150; d7.10																								
1889	Bal AA	20	75	12	17	5	0	0	8	2	2	10	.227	.266	.293	58	-4	5	.947	0	54	0	O20R	—	-0.4
DOWNEY, RED	Alexander Cummings; B2.6.1889 Aurora IN; D7.10.1949 Detroit MI; BL/TL/5´11˝/174; d9.14; Col Georgetown																								
1909	Bro N	19	78	7	20	1	0	0	8	2	0	—	.256	.275	.269	71	-3	4	1.000	-1	83	0	O19(0/3/16)	—	-0.5
DOWNEY, TOM	Thomas Edward; B1.1.1884 Lewiston ME; D8.3.1961 Passaic NJ; BR/TR/5´10˝/178; d5.7																								
1909	Cin N	119	416	39	96	9	6	1	32	32	1	—	.231	.287	.288	79	-11	16	.909	-6	98	124	S119/C	—	-1.4
1910	Cin N	111	378	43	102	9	3	2	32	34	3	28	.270	.335	.325	97	-2	12	.879	-8	95	64	S68,3b41	—	-0.6
1911	Cin N	111	360	50	94	16	7	0	36	44	2	38	.261	.345	.344	97	-1	10	.906	-11	94	72	S93,2b6,3b5,1b2/rf	—	-0.5
1912	Phi N	54	171	27	50	6	3	1	23	21	0	20	.292	.370	.380	99	0	3	.893	-5	87	49	3b46,S3	—	-0.4
	Chi N	13	22	4	4	0	2	0	4	1	0	5	.182	.217	.364	58	-2	0	.792	-0	108	0	S5,3b3/2	—	-0.2
	Year	67	193	31	54	6	5	1	27	22	0	25	.280	.353	.378	95	-2	3	.892	-6	88	47	3b49,S8/2	—	-0.6
1914	Buf F	151	541	69	118	20	3	2	42	40	1	55	.218	.273	.277	49	-47	35	**.962**	10	**109**	110	2b129,S16,3b5	—	-3.6
1915	Buf F	92	282	24	56	9	1	1	19	26	1	26	.199	.269	.248	45	-25	11	.930	-1	89	106	2b48,3b35,S2/1	—	-2.7
Total	6	651	2170	256	520	69	25	7	188	198	8	172	.240	.306	.304	74	-88	87	.901	-20	96	91	S306,2b184,3b135,1b3/rfC	—	-9.4
DOWNING, BRIAN	Brian Jay; B10.9.1950 Los Angeles CA; BR/TR/5´10˝/(170–205); d5.31; Col Cypress (CA) JC																								
1973	Chi A	34	73	5	13	1	0	2	4	10-1	0	17	.178	.277	.274	54	-5	0-0	1.000	5	95	144	O13(8/0/6),C11,3b8/D	38	0.0
1974	Chi A	108	293	41	66	12	1	10	39	51-3	2	72	.225	.344	.375	104	3	0-1	.994	-1	79	105	C63,O39(5/0/34),D9	0	0.3
1975	Chi A	138	420	58	101	12	1	7	41	76-5	3	75	.240	.356	.324	93	0	13-4	.990	5	106	114	C137/D	0	1.3
1976	Chi A	104	317	38	81	14	0	3	30	40-0	1	55	.256	.338	.328	96	0	7-3	.988	-7	91	101	C93,D11	16	-0.4
1977	Chi A	69	169	28	48	4	2	4	25	34-0	2	21	.284	.402	.402	122	7	1-2	.983	2	67	102	C61,O3(2/0/1),D2	0	1.0
1978	Cal A	133	412	42	105	15	0	7	46	52-2	6	47	.255	.345	.342	97	1	3-2	.993	-7	71	138	C128,D2	0	-0.1
1979	†Cal A★	148	509	87	166	27	3	12	75	77-4	5	57	.326	.418	.462	142	34	3-3	.985	-19	81	75	C129,D18	0	2.0
1980	Cal A	30	93	5	27	6	0	2	25	12-1	0	12	.290	.364	.419	118	3	0-2	1.000	-3	43	22	C16,D13	134	0.0
1981	Cal A	93	317	47	79	14	0	9	41	46-1	4	35	.249	.351	.379	109	6	1-1	.990	-4	87	28	O56L,C37,D5	0	0.0
1982	†Cal A	158	623	109	175	37	2	28	84	86-1	5	58	.281	.368	.482	131	29	2-1	**1.000**	-1	95	94	O158L	0	2.1
1983	Cal A	113	403	68	99	15	1	19	53	62-4	5	59	.246	.352	.429	114	9	1-2	.994	-2	88	133	O84L,D26	41	0.3
1984	Cal A	156	539	65	148	28	2	23	91	70-3	7	66	.275	.360	.462	127	22	0-4	**1.000**	-4	95	54	O131L,D21	0	1.0
1985	Cal A	150	520	80	137	23	1	20	85	78-3	13	61	.263	.371	.427	119	17	5-3	.992	-4	93	64	O121L,D25	0	0.7
1986	†Cal A	152	513	90	137	27	4	20	95	90-2	17	84	.267	.389	.452	131	27	4-4	.989	-4	94	57	O138L,D10	0	1.6
1987	Cal A	155	567	110	154	29	3	29	77	**106**-6	17	85	.272	.400	.487	138	37	5-5	1.000	-3	76	96	D118,O34L	0	2.8
1988	Cal A	135	484	80	117	18	2	25	64	81-5	14	63	.242	.362	.442	128	21	3-4	ø	0	0	0	D132	16	1.6
1989	Cal A	142	544	59	154	25	2	14	59	56-3	6	87	.283	.354	.414	118	14	0-2	ø	0	0	0	D141	0	0.9
1990	Cal A	96	330	47	90	18	2	14	51	50-2	6	45	.273	.374	.467	137	18	0-0	ø	0	0	0	D87	0	1.6
1991	Tex A	123	407	76	113	17	2	17	49	58-7	8	70	.278	.377	.455	131	19	1-1	ø	0	0	0	D109	0	1.5
1992	Tex A	107	320	53	89	18	0	10	39	62-2	8	58	.278	.407	.428	138	21	1-0	ø	0	0	0	D93	0	1.8
Total	20	2344	7853	1188	2099	360	28	275	1073	1197-55	129	1127	.267	.370	.425	122	283	50-44	.995	-48	92	75	D824,O777(737/0/41),C675,3b8	245	20.0
DOWNS, RED	Jerome Willis; B8.23.1883 Neola IA; D10.19.1939 Council Bluffs IA; BR/TR/5´11˝/155; d5.2																								
1907	Det A	105	374	28	82	13	5	1	42	13	2	—	.219	.249	.289	69	-14	3	.930	-21	91	40	2b80,O20(12/8/0)/S3	—	-4.0
1908	†Det A	84	289	28	64	10	3	1	35	5	1	—	.221	.237	.287	67	-11	2	.925	-4	104	88	2b82/3	—	-1.7
1912	Bro N	9	32	2	8	3	0	0	3	1	0	5	.250	.273	.344	71	-1	3	.881	-2	100	61	2b9	—	-0.3
	Chi N	43	95	9	25	4	3	1	14	9	0	17	.263	.327	.400	99	-1	5	.907	2	101	147	2b16,S9,3b5	—	0.2
	Year	52	127	11	33	7	3	1	17	10	0	22	.260	.314	.386	92	-2	8	.896	0	101	110	2b25,S9,3b5	—	-0.1
Total	3	241	790	67	179	30	11	3	94	28	3	22	.227	.256	.304	72	-27	13	.924	-25	98	70	2b187,O20(12/8/0),S10,3b7	—	-5.8

YEAR	TM LG	G	AB	R	H	2B	3B	HR	RBI	BB-IB	HP	SO	AVG	OBP	SLG	AOPS	ABR	SB-CS	FA	FR	RNG	THR	GAMES AT POSITION	DL	BFW
Dowse, Tom	Thomas Joseph; B8.12.1866 Mohill, Ireland; D12.14.1946 Riverside CA; BR/TR/5´11˝/175; d4.21																								
1890	Cle N	40	159	20	33	2	1	0	9	12	1	22	.208	.267	.233	47	-11	3	.870	0	177	226	O26(6/3/19),1b10,C3/P	—	-1.1
1891	Col AA	55	201	24	45	7	0	0	22	13	2	22	.224	.278	.259	57	-11	2	.919	-14	*74*	*81*	C51,O5(2/0/3)	—	-1.8
1892	Lou N	41	145	10	21	2	0	0	7	2	3	15	.145	.173	.159	1	-18	1	.918	-1	*90*	*120*	C29,1b11,O3R/2	—	-1.6
	Cin N	1	4	0	0	0	0	0	0	0	0	0	.000	.000	.000	-99	-1	0	1.000	-0	*139*	*0*	/C	—	-0.1
	Phi N	16	54	3	10	0	0	0	6	2	1	4	.185	.228	.185	25	-5	1	.973	2	*133*	*68*	C15	—	-0.2
	Was N	7	27	5	7	1	0	0	2	0	0	3	.259	.259	.296	70	-1	0	.800	-1	0	0	O4L,C3	—	-0.1
	Year	65	230	18	38	3	0	0	15	4	4	22	.165	.193	.178	13	-25	2	.931	-0	*102*	*104*	C48,1b11,O7(4/0/3)/2	—	-2.0
Total	3	160	590	62	116	12	1	0	46	29	7	66	.197	.243	.220	38	-47	7	.921	-15	*88*	*91*	C102,O38(12/3/25),1b21/2P	—	-4.9
Doyle, Brian	Brian Reed; B1.26.1955 Glasgow KY; BL/TR/5´10˝/(160–162); [TexA72 4/76]; d4.30; b–Denny																								
1978	†NY A	39	52	6	10	0	0	0	0	0-0	0	3	.192	.192	.192	9	-7	0-3	.989	4	109	131	2b29,S7,3b5	0	-0.2
1979	NY A	20	32	2	4	2	0	0	5	3-0	0	1	.125	.200	.188	5	-4	0-0	.944	-2	116	107	2b13,3b6	0	-0.6
1980	NY A	34	75	8	13	1	0	1	5	6-0	0	7	.173	.235	.227	27	-8	1-1	.953	0	93	59	2b20,S12,3b2	0	-0.6
1981	Oak A	17	40	2	5	0	0	0	3	1-0	0	2	.125	.146	.125	-22	-6	0-1	1.000	-3	86	65	2b17	17	-1.0
Total	4	110	199	18	32	3	0	1	13	10-0	0	13	.161	.201	.191	10	-25	1-5	.977	-1	99	91	2b79,S19,3b13	17	-2.4
Doyle, Conny	Cornelius J.; B1862 , Ireland; D7.29.1921 El Paso TX; 5´10˝/185; d6.23																								
1883	Phi N	16	68	3	15	3	2	0	3	0	—	15	.221	.221	.324	69	-3	—	.788	-1	85	0	O16L	—	-0.4
1884	Pit AA	15	58	8	17	3	2	0	—	2	0	—	.293	.317	.414	138	2	—	.818	-1	41	0	O14L/S	—	0.1
Total	2	31	126	11	32	6	4	0	3	2	0	15	.254	.266	.365	101	-1	—	.800	-2	65	0	O30L/S	—	-0.3
Doyle, Danny	Howard James; B1.24.1917 McLoud OK; D12.14.2004 Stillwater OK; BB/TR/6´1˝/195; d9.14; Mil 1944–45; Col Oklahoma St.																								
1943	Bos A	13	43	2	9	1	0	0	6	7	0	9	.209	.320	.233	62	-2	0-1	.964	-2	*87*	*91*	C13	0	-0.4
Doyle, Jacob	Jacob Dixon; B11.26.1855 Leesburg VA; D8.15.1941 Waukegan IL; d4.20																								
1872	Nat NA	9	41	6	11	1	0	0	9	0	—	0	.268	.268	.293	62	-2	0-0	.667	-4	86	0	S8/2	—	-0.5
Doyle, Jim	James Francis; B12.25.1881 Detroit MI; D2.1.1912 Syracuse NY; BR/TR/5´10˝/168; d5.4; Col Niagara																								
1910	Cin N	7	13	1	2	2	0	0	1	0	0	2	.154	.154	.308	36	-1	0	.875	-1	44	0	3b3/cf	—	-0.2
1911	Chi N	130	472	69	133	23	12	5	62	40	2	54	.282	.340	.413	110	5	19	.922	8	**116**	**145**	3b127	—	1.6
Total	2	137	485	70	135	25	12	5	63	40	2	56	.278	.336	.410	109	4	19	.921	7	115	142	3b130/cf	—	1.4
Doyle, Jeff	Jeffrey Donald; B10.2.1956 Havre MT; BB/TR/5´9˝/160; [StLN77 6/136]; d9.13; Col Oregon St.																								
1983	StL N	13	37	4	11	1	2	0	2	1-1	0	3	.297	.316	.432	105	0	0-0	.966	-0	91	164	2b12	0	0.0
Doyle, Jack	John Joseph "Dirty Jack"; B10.25.1869 Killorglin, Ireland; D12.31.1958 Holyoke MA; BR/TR/5´9˝/155; d8.27; M2/U1; Col Fordham; OF(13/45/76)																								
1889	Col AA	11	36	6	10	1	1	0	3	6	0	6	.278	.381	.361	118	1	9	.897	-2	—	—	C7,O3R,2b2	—	0.0
1890	Col AA	77	298	47	80	17	7	2	44	13	0	—	.268	.299	.393	111	2	27	.887	-4	*105*	*97*	C38,S25,O9(2/6/1),2b6,3b3	—	0.1
1891	Cle N	69	250	43	69	14	4	0	43	26	3	44	.276	.351	.364	104	2	24	.897	-5	*92*	*113*	C29,O21(4/8/10),3b20/S	—	-0.1
1892	Cle N	24	88	17	26	4	1	1	14	6	0	10	.295	.340	.398	118	2	5	.875	0	145	261	O12(1/0/11),C9/1S	—	0.2
	NY N	90	366	61	109	22	1	5	55	18	3	30	.298	.336	.404	126	10	42	.864	-20	91	62	2b31,C26,O17(0/10/7),3b13,S7	—	-0.6
	Year	114	454	78	135	26	2	6	69	24	3	40	.297	.337	.403	124	12	47	.890	-20	*86*	*150*	C35,2b31,O29(1/10/18),3b13,S8/1	—	-0.4
1893	NY N	82	318	56	102	17	5	1	51	27	5	12	.321	.383	.415	111	5	40	.919	-1	*98*	*130*	C48,O29(0/21/8),S4,3b3/1	—	0.6
1894	†NY N	107	427	94	157	30	8	3	103	37	3	3	.368	.422	.496	121	16	44	.965	-1	106	90	1b101,C6	—	1.2
1895	NY N	82	319	52	100	21	3	1	66	24	2	12	.313	.365	.408	101	1	35	.968	-3	108	78	1b58,2b13,3b6,C4,M	—	0.0
1896	†Bal N	118	487	116	165	29	4	1	101	42	8	15	.339	.400	.421	115	13	73	.974	-12	64	126	1b118/2	—	0.0
1897	†Bal N	114	460	91	163	29	4	2	87	29	1	—	.354	.394	.448	122	15	62	.979	4	118	**126**	1b114	—	1.6
1898	Was N	43	177	26	54	2	2	2	26	7	1	—	.305	.335	.373	103	0	9	.963	-1	96	93	1b38,2b5,M	—	-0.2
	NY N	82	297	42	84	15	3	1	43	12	3	—	.283	.317	.364	98	-2	14	.860	2	189	152	O38(6/0/32),1b24,S15,3b5,C2	—	-0.1
	Year	125	474	68	138	17	5	3	69	19	4	—	.291	.324	.367	100	-2	23	.970	0	102	85	1b62,O38(6/0/32),S15,2b5,3b5,C2	—	-0.3
1899	NY N	119	452	56	135	16	7	3	77	33	4	—	.299	.352	.385	106	3	35	.976	6	129	102	1b114,C5	—	0.9
1900	NY N	133	505	69	135	24	1	1	66	34	3	—	.267	.317	.325	81	-12	34	.971	7	130	112	1b133	—	-0.5
1901	Chi N	75	285	21	66	9	2	0	39	7	5	—	.232	.263	.277	59	-15	8	.973	7	145	87	1b75	—	-1.0
1902	NY N	51	193	22	58	13	0	0	18	11	1	—	.301	.341	.368	120	5	12	.991	5	134	108	1b51	—	0.9
	Was A	78	312	52	77	15	2	1	20	29	0	—	.247	.311	.317	74	-11	6	.929	-7	100	60	2b68,1b7,O4R,C2	—	-1.7
1903	Bro N	**139**	524	84	164	27	6	0	91	54	5	—	.313	.383	.387	123	18	34	.981	2	103	107	1b139	—	1.7
1904	Bro N	8	22	2	5	1	0	0	2	6	1	—	.227	.414	.273	116	1	1	1.000	1	138	30	1b8	—	0.2
	Phi N	66	236	20	52	10	3	1	22	19	1	—	.220	.281	.301	83	-5	4	.977	4	124	89	1b65/2	—	-0.3
	Year	74	258	22	57	11	3	1	24	25	2	—	.221	.295	.298	86	-4	5	.980	5	126	83	1b73/2	—	-0.1
1905	NY A	1	3	0	0	0	0	0	0	0	0	—	.000	.000	.000	-90	-1	0	.833	-1	0	0	/1	—	-0.2
Total	17	1569	6055	977	1811	316	64	25	971	440	49	132	.299	.351	.385	106	48	518	.975	-18	113	104	1b1048,C176,O133R,2b127,S53,3b50	—	2.7
Doyle, Larry	Lawrence Joseph "Laughing Larry"; B7.31.1886 Caseyville IL; D3.1.1974 Saranac Lake NY; BL/TR/5´10˝/165; d7.22																								
1907	NY N	69	227	16	59	3	0	0	16	20	0	—	.260	.320	.273	83	-4	3	.917	-21	81	32	2b69	—	-2.9
1908	NY N	104	377	65	116	16	9	0	33	22	5	—	.308	.354	.398	134	13	17	.935	-8	96	108	2b102	—	0.7
1909	NY N	147	570	86	**172**	27	11	6	49	45	7	—	.302	.360	.419	140	25	31	.940	-17	84	**116**	2b144	—	1.0
1910	NY N	151	575	97	164	21	14	8	69	71	5	26	.285	.369	.412	128	20	39	.930	-18	91	100	2b151	—	0.3
1911	†NY N	143	526	102	163	25	**25**	13	77	71	5	39	.310	.397	.527	153	35	38	.944	-21	85	88	2b141	—	1.6
1912	†NY N	143	558	98	184	33	8	10	90	56	2	20	.330	.393	.471	132	25	36	.948	-3	93	**131**	2b143	—	2.3
1913	†NY N	132	482	67	135	25	6	5	73	59	5	29	.280	.364	.388	114	11	38-14	.955	-14	87	118	2b130	—	0.2
1914	NY N	145	539	87	140	19	8	5	63	58	10	25	.260	.343	.353	111	8	17	.959	-17	89	119	2b145	—	-0.7
1915	NY N	150	591	86	**189**	**40**	10	4	70	32	3	28	**.320**	.358	.442	150	34	22-18	.947	-9	94	**112**	2b147	—	2.8
1916	NY N	113	441	55	118	24	10	2	47	27	4	23	.268	.316	.381	120	9	17	.960	14	103	123	2b113	—	2.8
	Chi N	9	38	6	15	5	1	1	7	1	0	1	.395	.410	.658	203	4	2	.982	4	122	265	2b9	—	0.9
	Year	122	479	61	133	29	11	3	54	28	4	24	.278	.323	.403	127	14	19	.962	18	104	**134**	2b122	—	3.7
1917	Chi N	135	476	48	121	19	5	6	61	48	0	28	.254	.323	.353	99	0	5	.952	2	94	96	2b128	—	0.5
1918	NY N	75	257	38	67	7	4	3	36	37	0	10	.261	.354	.354	118	7	10	.969	-7	101	90	2b73	—	0.1
1919	NY N	113	381	61	110	14	10	7	52	31	5	17	.289	.350	.433	136	16	12	.956	7	**106**	**130**	2b100	—	2.7
1920	NY N	137	471	48	134	21	2	4	50	47	2	28	.285	.352	.363	107	6	11-9	.967	-23	91	106	2b133	—	-1.7
Total	14	1766	6509	960	1887	299	123	74	793	625	53	274	.290	.357	.408	126	209	298-41	.949	-133	92	109	2b1728	—	10.6
Doyle, Denny	Robert Dennis; B1.17.1944 Glasgow KY; BL/TR/5´9˝/(170–174); d4.7; b–Brian; Col Morehead St.																								
1970	Phi N	112	413	43	86	10	7	2	16	33-3	0	64	.208	.266	.281	48	-32	6-5	.978	-17	83	83	2b103	0	-4.4
1971	Phi N	95	342	34	79	12	1	3	24	19-0	5	31	.231	.280	.298	64	-16	4-2	.967	8	106	106	2b91	15	-0.2
1972	Phi N	123	442	33	110	14	2	1	26	31-2	0	33	.249	.295	.296	68	-19	6-7	.982	-11	92	90	2b119	0	-2.5
1973	Phi N	116	370	45	101	9	3	3	26	31-8	0	32	.273	.327	.338	83	-9	1-3	.974	3	103	100	2b114	0	0.0
1974	Cal A	147	511	47	133	19	2	1	34	25-2	1	49	.260	.295	.311	79	-15	6-7	.983	18	105	91	2b146,S2	0	1.1
1975	Cal A	8	15	0	1	0	0	0	0	1-0	0	1	.067	.125	.067	-48	-3	0-0	.926	1	112	70	2b6/3	0	-0.2
	†Bos A	89	310	50	96	21	2	4	36	14-0	1	11	.310	.339	.429	108	3	5-7	.974	-22	90	70	2b84,3b6,S2	0	-1.6
	Year	97	325	50	97	21	2	4	36	15-0	1	12	.298	.329	.412	102	0	5-7	.970	-21	91	70	2b90,3b7,S2	0	-1.8
1976	Bos A	117	432	51	108	15	5	0	26	22-0	0	39	.250	.285	.308	66	-19	8-5	.977	-13	97	100	2b112	0	-2.7
1977	Bos A	137	455	54	109	13	6	2	49	29-3	4	50	.240	.289	.308	57	-27	2-4	.979	-7	100	110	2b137	0	-2.8
Total	8	944	3290	357	823	113	28	16	237	205-18	11	310	.250	.295	.316	70	-137	38-40	.977	-40	97	95	2b912,3b7,S4	15	-13.3
Dozier, D. J.	William Henry; B9.21.1965 Norfolk VA; BR/TR/6´0˝/202; d5.6; Col Penn St.																								
1992	NY N	25	47	4	9	2	0	0	2	4-0	1	19	.191	.264	.234	44	-3	4-0	.971	1	122	0	O17L	0	-0.3
Drake, Delos	Delos Daniel; B12.3.1886 Girard OH; D10.3.1965 Findlay OH; BR/TL/5´11.5˝/170; d4.30																								
1911	Det A	95	315	37	88	9	9	1	36	17	4	—	.279	.324	.375	90	-6	20	.942	-6	102	33	O83(74/5/5),1b2	—	-1.5
1914	StL F	138	514	51	129	18	8	3	42	31	1	57	.251	.295	.335	68	-32	17	.957	-0	103	98	O116(69/36/11),1b18	—	-4.1
1915	StL F	102	343	32	91	23	4	1	41	23	1	27	.265	.313	.364	86	-11	6	.974	-1	103	83	O97(7/62/33)/1	—	-1.9
Total	3	335	1172	120	308	50	21	5	119	71	6	84	.263	.308	.354	79	-49	43	.959	-7	103	76	O296(150/103/49),1b21	—	-7.5

YEAR	TM LG	G	AB	R	H	2B	3B	HR	RBI	BB-IB	HP	SO	AVG	OBP	SLG	AOPS	ABR	SB-CS	FA	FR	RNG	THR	GAMES AT POSITION	DL	BFW
Drake, Larry	Larry Francis; B5.4.1921 McKinney TX; D7.14.1985 Houston TX; BL/TR/6´1.5˝/195; d7.20; Col Baylor																								
1945	Phi A	1	2	0	0	0	0	0	0	0	0	2	.000	.000	.000	-99	-1	0-0	1.000	0	116	0	/lf	0	-0.1
1948	Was A	4	7	0	2	0	0	0	1	1	0	3	.286	.375	.286	79	0	0-0	1.000	-0	95	0	O2R	0	0.0
Total	2	5	9	0	2	0	0	0	1	1	0	5	.222	.300	.222	44	-1	0-0	1.000	-0	102	0	O3(1/0/2)	0	-0.1
Drake, Lyman	Lyman Daniel; B2.9.1852 Berea OH; D2.6.1932 Muskegon MI; 6´0˝/?; d6.29																								
1884	Was AA	2	7	0	2	1	0	0	2	0	0	—	.286	.286	.429	147	0	—	.000	-1	0	0	O2R	—	0.0
Drake, Sammy	Samuel Harrison; B10.7.1934 Little Rock AR; BB/TR/5´11˝/175; d4.17; b–Solly; Col Philander Smith																								
1960	Chi N	15	15	5	1	0	0	0	0	1-0	0	4	.067	.125	.067	-46	-3	0-0	1.000	-2	58	0	3b6,2b2	0	-0.6
1961	Chi N	13	5	1	0	0	0	0	0	1-0	0	1	.000	.167	.000	-50	-1	0-0	1.000	-0	79	0	/rf	0	-0.1
1962	NY N	25	52	2	10	0	0	0	7	6-1	0	12	.192	.276	.192	28	-5	0-0	.977	-3	100	111	2b10,3b6	0	-0.7
Total	3	53	72	8	11	0	0	0	7	8-1	0	17	.153	.237	.153	8	-9	0-0	.978	-5	89	94	2b12,3b12/rf	0	-1.4
Drake, Solly	Solomon Louis; B10.23.1930 Little Rock AR; BB/TR/6´0˝/170; d4.17; b–Sammy; Col Philander Smith; [DL 1955 Chi N 109]																								
1956	Chi N	65	215	29	55	9	1	2	15	23-0	1	35	.256	.331	.335	81	-5	9-5	.993	0	103	78	O53C	0	-0.7
1959	LA N	9	8	2	2	0	0	0	0	1-0	0	3	.250	.333	.250	54	0	1-0	.667	-0	70	0	O4R	0	-0.1
	Phi N	67	62	10	9	1	0	0	3	8-0	0	15	.145	.243	.161	10	-8	5-5	1.000	-0	110	0	O37(22/11/9)	0	-1.0
	Year	76	70	12	11	1	0	0	3	9-0	0	18	.157	.253	.171	15	-8	6-5	.974	-1	106	0	O41(22/11/13)	0	-1.1
Total	2	141	285	41	66	10	1	2	18	32-0	1	53	.232	.311	.295	64	-13	15-10	.989	-0	104	59	O94(22/64/13)	109	-1.8
Dransfeldt, Kelly	Kelly Daniel; B4.16.1975 Joliet IL; BR/TR/6´2˝/(190–200); [TexA96 4/113]; d5.1; Col Michigan																								
1999	Tex A	16	53	3	10	1	0	1	5	3-0	0	12	.189	.232	.264	25	-6	0-0	.966	4	118	118	S16	0	-0.1
2000	Tex A	16	26	2	3	2	0	0	2	1-0	0	14	.115	.148	.192	-14	-5	0-0	1.000	3	125	143	S14,2b2	0	-0.1
2001	Tex A	4	3	0	0	0	0	0	0	0-0	0	0	.000	.000	.000	-97	-1	0-0	1.000	0	176	0	S3/3	0	-0.1
2004	Chi A	15	30	5	10	0	0	0	4	0-0	0	6	.333	.333	.333	72	-1	0-0	.947	-2	106	35	S8,3b3/D	0	-0.2
Total	4	51	112	10	23	3	0	1	11	4-0	0	32	.205	.233	.259	25	-13	0-0	.974	6	120	108	S41,3b4,2b2/D	0	-0.5
Drauby, Jake	Jacob C.; B1865 Harrisburg PA; 5´10˝/163; d10.3																								
1892	Was N	10	34	3	7	0	1	0	3	2	0	12	.206	.250	.265	57	-2	0	.763	-2	88	135	3b10	—	-0.3
Dreesen, Bill	William Richard; B7.26.1904 New York NY; D11.9.1971 Mt.Vernon NY; BL/TR/5´7.5˝/160; d5.1																								
1931	Bos N	48	180	38	40	10	4	1	10	23	0	23	.222	.310	.339	77	-6	1	.910	-4	102	14	3b47	—	-0.9
Drescher, Bill	William Clayton "Dutch"; B5.23.1921 Congers NY; D5.15.1968 Haverstraw NY; BL/TR/6´2˝/190; d4.19																								
1944	NY A	4	7	0	1	0	0	0	0	0	0	0	.143	.143	.143	-18	-1	0-0	.875	-0	*0*	*0*	/C	0	-0.1
1945	NY A	48	126	10	34	3	1	0	15	8	0	5	.270	.313	.310	77	-4	0-2	.991	-6	*68*	*93*	C33	0	-0.9
1946	NY A	5	6	0	2	1	0	0	1	0	0	0	.333	.333	.500	129	0	0-0	1.000	1	*0*	*0*	C3	0	0.1
Total	3	57	139	10	37	4	1	0	16	8	0	5	.266	.306	.309	75	-5	0-2	.985	-5	*63*	*86*	C37	0	-0.9
Dressen, Chuck	Charles Walter; B9.20.1898 Decatur IL; D8.10.1966 Detroit MI; BR/TR/5´5.5˝/146; d4.17; M16/C12																								
1925	Cin N	76	215	35	59	8	2	3	19	12	2	4	.274	.319	.372	78	-8	5-3	.951	4	118	115	3b47,2b5,O4(3/0/1)	—	-0.1
1926	Cin N	127	474	76	126	27	11	4	48	49	3	31	.266	.338	.395	99	-1	0	.966	16	**122**	101	3b123/Slf	—	2.2
1927	Cin N	144	548	78	160	36	10	2	55	71	3	32	.292	.376	.405	113	13	7	**.967**	12	116	96	3b142,S2	—	3.3
1928	Cin N	135	498	72	145	26	3	1	59	43	6	22	.291	.355	.361	89	-7	10	.938	-2	103	110	3b135	—	0.0
1929	Cin N	110	401	49	98	22	3	1	36	41	4	21	.244	.321	.322	63	-23	8	.932	-13	89	70	3b98,2b8	—	-2.7
1930	Cin N	33	19	0	4	0	0	0	1	1	0	3	.211	.250	.211	14	-3	0	1.000	1	197	0	3b10,2b3	—	-0.1
1931	Cin N	5	15	0	1	0	0	0	0	1	0	1	.067	.125	.067	-50	-3	0	.846	-0	99	144	3b4	—	-0.4
1933	NY N	16	45	3	10	4	0	0	3	1	0	4	.222	.239	.311	57	-3	0	.972	-0	87	129	3b16	—	-0.3
Total	8	646	2215	313	603	123	29	11	221	219	18	118	.272	.343	.369	89	-35	30-3	.953	18	109	98	3b575,2b16,O5(4/0/1),S3	—	1.9
Dressen, Lee	Leo August; B7.23.1889 Ellinwood KS; D6.30.1931 Diller NE; BL/TL/6´0˝/165; d4.21																								
1914	StL N	46	103	16	24	2	1	0	7	11	0	20	.233	.307	.272	73	-3	2	.982	-1	89	116	1b38	—	-0.5
1918	Det A	31	107	10	19	1	2	0	3	21	2	10	.178	.323	.224	68	-3	2	.988	-4	55	62	1b30	—	-0.8
Total	2	77	210	26	43	3	3	0	10	32	2	30	.205	.316	.248	71	-6	4	.985	-5	71	87	1b68	—	-1.3
Drew, Cameron	Cameron Steward; B2.12.1964 Boston MA; BL/TR/6´5˝/215; [HouN85 1/12]; d9.9; Col New Haven																								
1988	Hou N	7	16	1	3	0	1	0	1	0-0	0	1	.188	.188	.313	43	-1	0-0	1.000	0	123	0	O5(3/0/2)	0	-0.1
Drew, Dave	David; d5.14																								
1884	Phi U	2	9	1	4	0	0	0	—	0	—	—	.444	.444	.444	184	1	—	ø	0	0	0	/P2S	—	0.0
	Was U	13	53	8	16	1	2	0	—	1	—	—	.302	.315	.396	118	-1	—	.806	1	91	0	S8,1b5/cf	—	0.0
	Year	15	62	9	20	1	2	0	—	1	—	—	.323	.333	.403	127	0	—	.813	1	88	0	S9,1b5/P2cf	—	0.0
Drew, J.D.	David Jonathan; B11.20.1975 Tallahassee FL; BL/TR/6´1˝/(195–200); [StLN98 1/5]; d9.8; b–Stephen b–Tim; Col Florida St.																								
1998	StL N	14	36	9	15	3	1	5	13	4-0	0	10	.417	.463	.972	270	9	0-0	1.000	1	111	168	O11(6/2/5)	0	0.9
1999	StL N	104	368	72	89	16	6	13	39	50-0	6	77	.242	.340	.424	91	-6	19-3	.972	2	101	174	O98(1/97/0)	32	0.1
2000	†StL N	135	407	73	120	17	2	18	57	67-4	6	99	.295	.401	.479	119	14	17-9	.966	2	108	85	O127(24/26/98)	18	1.2
2001	†StL N	109	375	80	121	18	5	27	73	57-4	4	75	.323	.414	.613	158	34	13-3	.973	-1	99	104	O107(1/20/97)	43	2.9
2002	†StL N	135	424	61	107	19	1	18	56	57-4	8	104	.252	.349	.429	104	3	8-2	.987	-2	103	54	O120(0/6/119)	15	-0.3
2003	StL N	100	287	60	83	13	3	15	42	36-0	3	48	.289	.374	.512	130	12	2-2	.994	4	106	161	O75(1/26/53)	44	1.4
2004	†Atl N	145	518	118	158	28	8	31	93	118-2	5	116	.305	.436	.569	157	50	12-3	.990	5	105	132	O142(0/8/138)/D	0	4.8
2005	LA N	72	252	48	72	12	1	15	36	51-3	5	50	.286	.412	.520	142	18	1-1	.987	-2	98	76	O72(0/30/44)	91	1.4
2006	†LA N	146	494	84	140	34	6	20	100	89-8	4	106	.283	.393	.498	127	23	2-3	.983	3	111	47	O135R,D4	0	1.8
Total	9	960	3161	605	905	160	33	162	509	529-25	41	685	.286	.393	.512	130	157	74-26	.981	12	104	102	O887(33/215/689),D5	243	14.2
Drew, Stephen	Stephen Oris; B3.16.1983 Hahira GA; BL/TR/6´1˝/185; [AriN04 1/15]; d7.15; b–J.D. b–Tim; Col Florida St.																								
2006	Ari N	59	209	27	66	13	7	5	23	14-4	0	50	.316	.357	.517	114	4	2-0	.978	-2	98	103	S56	0	0.6
Drews, Frank	Frank John; B5.25.1916 Buffalo NY; D4.22.1972 Buffalo NY; BR/TR/5´10˝/175; d8.13																								
1944	Bos N	46	141	14	29	9	1	0	10	25	1	14	.206	.329	.284	71	-4	0	.959	1	98	102	2b46	0	-0.1
1945	Bos N	49	147	13	30	4	1	0	19	16	0	18	.204	.282	.245	47	-10	0	.976	2	111	111	2b48	0	-0.6
Total	2	95	288	27	59	13	2	0	29	41	1	32	.205	.306	.264	59	-14	0	.967	3	104	106	2b94	0	-0.7
Driessen, Dan	Daniel; B7.29.1951 Hilton Head Island SC; BL/TR/5´11˝/(187–200); d6.9																								
1973	†Cin N	102	366	49	110	15	2	4	47	24-4	2	37	.301	.346	.385	107	3	8-3	.946	-4	93	139	3b87,1b35/rf	0	-0.2
1974	Cin N	150	470	63	132	23	6	7	56	48-5	1	62	.281	.347	.400	111	7	10-5	.915	-15	86	101	3b126,1b47,O3R	0	-1.0
1975	†Cin N	88	210	38	59	8	1	7	38	35-2	2	30	.281	.386	.429	125	8	10-3	.986	-3	101	144	1b41,O29(10/0/19)	8	0.3
1976	†Cin N	98	219	32	54	11	1	7	44	43-2	0	32	.247	.362	.402	116	6	14-1	.997	-2	93	124	1b40,O20L	0	0.4
1977	Cin N	151	536	75	161	31	4	17	91	64-8	3	85	.300	.375	.468	123	19	31-13	.994	-3	86	106	1b148	0	0.9
1978	Cin N	153	524	68	131	23	3	16	70	75-7	4	79	.250	.345	.397	107	7	28-9	**.996**	1	98	79	1b151	0	0.2
1979	†Cin N	150	515	72	129	24	3	18	75	62-11	3	77	.250	.330	.414	103	2	11-5	.993	-5	87	105	1b143	0	-1.1
1980	Cin N	154	524	81	139	36	1	14	74	**93**-17	**6**	68	.265	.377	.418	125	23	19-6	.995	-5	85	102	1b151	0	1.2
1981	Cin N	82	233	35	55	14	0	7	33	40-3	2	31	.236	.349	.386	110	5	2-4	.995	-7	60	104	1b74	0	-0.8
1982	Cin N	149	516	64	139	25	1	17	57	82-8	2	62	.269	.368	.421	121	17	11-6	**.998**	-8	73	109	1b144	0	0.0
1983	Cin N	122	386	57	107	17	1	12	57	75-10	0	51	.277	.390	.420	121	15	6-4	**.996**	-4	84	82	1b112	20	0.4
1984	Cin N	81	218	27	61	13	0	7	28	37-2	0	25	.280	.378	.436	124	9	2-1	.991	-4	72	64	1b70	0	0.1
	Mon N	51	169	20	43	11	0	9	32	17-6	0	15	.254	.321	.479	128	6	0-1	.995	-3	75	117	1b45	0	0.0
	Year	132	387	47	104	24	0	16	60	54-8	0	40	.269	.354	.455	125	14	2-2	.992	-7	73	86	1b115	0	0.1
1985	Mon N	91	312	31	78	18	0	6	25	33-9	2	29	.250	.324	.365	98	0	2-2	.997	2	109	118	1b88	0	-0.4
	SF N	54	181	22	42	8	0	3	22	17-3	1	22	.232	.297	.326	79	-5	0-0	.998	-1	89	83	1b49	0	-0.9
	Year	145	493	53	120	26	0	9	47	50-12	3	51	.243	.314	.351	91	-5	2-2	.997	2	102	106	1b137	0	-1.3
1986	SF N	15	16	2	3	2	0	0	0	4-1	0	4	.188	.350	.313	88	0	0-0	1.000	0	143	0	1b4	0	0.0
	Hou N	17	24	5	7	1	0	1	3	5-1	0	2	.292	.414	.458	144	2	0-0	1.000	-1	60	106	1b12	0	0.1
	Year	32	40	7	10	3	0	1	3	9-2	0	6	.250	.388	.400	122	2	0-0	1.000	-0	84	76	1b16	0	0.1

YEAR	TM LG	G	AB	R	H	2B	3B	HR	RBI	BB-IB	HP	SO	AVG	OBP	SLG	AOPS	ABR	SB-CS	FA	FR	RNG	THR	GAMES AT POSITION	DL	BFW
1987	†StL N	24	60	5	14	2	0	1	11	7-1	0	8	.233	.309	.317	66	-3	0-0	.993	-0	95	104	1b21	0	-0.4
Total	15	1732	5479	746	1464	282	23	153	763	761-100	28	719	.267	.356	.411	114	121	154-63	.995	-59	87	101	1b1375,3b213,O53(30/0/23)	28	-1.2
DRILL, LEW	Lewis L; B5.9.1877 Browerville MN; D7.4.1969 St.Paul MN; BR/TR/5´6˝/186; d4.23; Col Georgetown																								
1902	Was A	38	123	21	34	7	2	1	16	16	2	—	.276	.369	.390	110	2	0	.919	-10	*94*	*78*	C28,2b4,O4(1/0/3)/3	—	-0.5
	Bal A	2	8	2	2	0	0	0	0	0	0	—	.250	.250	.250	37	-1	0	1.000	0	*93*	*272*	/C1	—	0.0
	Was A	33	98	12	24	3	2	0	13	10	2	—	.245	.327	.316	78	-3	5	.926	-4	*94*	*78*	C25,O4R/2	—	-0.4
	Year	73	229	35	60	10	4	1	29	26	4	—	.262	.347	.354	94	-1	5	.924	-13	*97*	*86*	C54,O8(1/0/7),2b5/31	—	-0.9
1903	Was A	51	154	11	39	9	3	0	23	15	3	—	.253	.331	.351	103	1	4	.966	-7	*76*	*90*	C47,1b3	—	-0.1
1904	Was A	46	142	17	38	7	2	1	11	21	6	—	.268	.385	.366	140	8	3	.934	-6	*73*	*102*	C29,O14(0/3/11)	—	0.6
	Det A	51	160	7	39	6	1	0	13	20	2	—	.244	.335	.294	103	2	2	.950	-6	*83*	*96*	C49,1b2	—	0.0
	Year	97	302	24	77	13	3	1	24	41	8	—	.255	.359	.328	121	10	5	.944	-12	*79*	*98*	C78,O14(0/3/11),1b2	—	0.6
1905	Det A	72	211	17	55	9	0	0	24	32	3	—	.261	.366	.303	112	5	7	.970	-6	*72*	*92*	C71	—	0.7
Total	4	293	896	87	231	41	10	2	100	114	18	—	.258	.353	.333	108	14	21	.953	-39	*80*	*92*	C250,O22(1/3/18),1b6,2b5/3	—	0.3
DRISCOLL, DENNIS	Dennis F.; B10.10.1862 Providence RI; D2.21.1901 Providence RI; d7.25																								
1885	Buf N	7	19	2	3	0	0	0	0	2	—	5	.158	.238	.158	29	-1	—	.719	-4	70	41	2b7	—	-0.5
DRISCOLL, JIM	James Bernard; B5.14.1944 Medford MA; BL/TR/5´11˝/175; d6.17																								
1970	Oak A	21	52	2	10	0	0	1	2	2-0	1	15	.192	.236	.250	35	-5	0-0	.967	-3	94	143	2b7,S7	0	-0.7
1972	Tex A	15	18	0	0	0	0	0	0	2-1	0	3	.000	.100	.000	-71	-4	0-0	.900	1	107	203	2b4,3b2	0	-0.3
Total	2	36	70	2	10	0	0	1	2	4-1	1	18	.143	.200	.186	9	-9	0-0	.950	-2	97	155	2b11,S7,3b2	0	-1.0
DRISCOLL, DENNY	John F.; B11.19.1855 Lowell MA; D7.11.1886 Lowell MA; BL/TL/5´10.5˝/160; d7.1; ▲																								
1880	Buf N	18	65	1	10	1	0	0	4	1	—	7	.154	.167	.169	14	-6	—	.895	0	96	466	O14C,P6	—	-0.4
1882	Pit AA	23	80	12	11	2	0	1	—	3	—	—	.138	.169	.200	25	-2	—	.885	-4	75	111	P23	—	0.0
1883	Pit AA	41	148	19	27	2	1	0	—	4	—	—	.182	.204	.209	35	-10	—	.890	5	**146**	97	P41,O4(0/2/2)/3	—	0.2
1884	Lou AA	13	48	5	9	1	0	0	1	2	0	—	.188	.220	.208	42	-3	—	.816	2	181	561	P13,O2(1/1/0)	—	0.1
Total	4	95	341	37	57	6	1	1	5	10	0	7	.167	.191	.199	30	-21	—	.872	3	127	165	P83,O20(1/17/2)/3	—	-0.1
DRISCOLL, PADDY	John Leo; B1.11.1895 Evanston IL; D6.28.1968 Chicago IL; BR/TR/5´8.5˝/155; d6.12; Mil 1918; Col Northwestern																								
1917	Chi N	13	28	2	3	1	0	0	3	2	0	6	.107	.167	.143	-4	-3	2	.882	0	114	166	2b8,3b2/S	—	-0.4
DRISSEL, MIKE	Michael F.; B12.19.1864 St.Louis MO; D2.26.1913 St.Louis MO; BR/TR/5´11˝/?; d9.5																								
1885	StL AA	6	20	0	1	0	0	0	0	0	0	—	.050	.050	.050	-65	-4	—	.971	0	—	—	C6	—	-0.3
DROPO, WALT	Walter "Moose"; B1.30.1923 Moosup CT; BR/TR/6´5˝/(220–225); d4.19; Col Connecticut																								
1949	Bos A	11	41	3	6	2	0	0	1	3	0	7	.146	.205	.195	6	-6	0-0	1.000	-1	54	118	1b11	0	-0.7
1950	Bos A★	136	559	101	180	28	8	34	**144**	45	5	75	.322	.378	.583	130	22	0-0	.988	-3	90	104	1b134	0	1.3
1951	Bos A	99	360	37	86	14	0	11	57	38	0	52	.239	.312	.369	76	-13	0-0	.987	-0	100	98	1b93	0	-1.6
1952	Bos A	37	132	13	35	7	1	6	27	11	2	22	.265	.331	.470	112	2	0-0	.994	-1	85	95	1b35	0	0.0
	Det A	115	459	56	128	17	3	23	70	26	2	63	.279	.320	.479	120	8	2-2	.989	1	99	95	1b115	0	0.5
	Year	152	591	69	163	24	4	29	97	37	4	85	.276	.323	.477	118	10	2-2	.990	-0	96	95	1b150	0	0.5
1953	Det A	152	606	61	150	30	3	13	96	29	6	69	.248	.289	.371	78	-21	2-0	.990	13	**131**	77	1b150	0	-1.7
1954	Det A	107	320	27	90	14	2	4	44	24	0	41	.281	.328	.375	95	-3	0-1	.996	2	104	88	1b95	0	-0.7
1955	Chi A	141	453	55	127	15	2	19	79	42-8	2	71	.280	.343	.448	109	4	0-1	.995	-5	79	**103**	1b140	0	-0.9
1956	Chi A	125	361	42	96	13	1	8	52	37-2	3	51	.266	.334	.374	87	-7	1-0	**.993**	-4	83	111	1b117	0	-1.6
1957	Chi A	93	223	24	57	2	0	13	49	16-2	0	40	.256	.300	.439	101	-1	0-1	.987	2	121	108	1b69	0	-0.3
1958	Chi A	28	52	3	10	1	0	2	8	5-0	1	11	.192	.271	.327	67	-3	0-0	1.000	1	113	80	1b16	0	-0.3
	Cin N	63	162	18	47	7	2	7	31	12-0	1	31	.290	.335	.488	111	2	0-0	1.000	2	110	96	1b43	0	0.1
1959	Cin N	26	39	4	4	1	0	1	2	4-0	1	7	.103	.205	.205	9	-5	0-0	1.000	1	130	111	1b23	0	-0.5
	Bal A	62	151	17	42	9	0	6	21	12-0	0	20	.278	.329	.457	117	3	0-0	.990	-3	70	130	1b54,3b2	0	-0.2
1960	Bal A	79	179	16	48	8	0	4	21	20-1	1	19	.268	.343	.380	97	0	0-1	.993	-2	84	122	1b67/3	0	-0.5
1961	Bal A	14	27	1	7	0	0	1	2	4-0	0	3	.259	.355	.370	97	0	0-0	1.000	0	104	174	1b12	0	0.0
Total	13	1288	4124	478	1113	168	22	152	704	328-12	24	582	.270	.326	.432	100	-18	5-6	.992	1	98	100	1b1174,3b3	0	-7.1
DRUMRIGHT, KEITH	Keith Alan; B10.21.1954 Springfield MO; BL/TR/5´10˝/(165–170); [ChiN76 4/79]; d9.1; Col Oklahoma																								
1978	Hou N	17	55	5	9	0	0	0	2	3-0	0	4	.164	.207	.164	5	-7	0-1	.944	-2	94	102	2b17	0	-0.9
1981	†Oak A	31	86	8	25	1	1	0	11	4-0	0	4	.291	.319	.326	90	-1	0-0	.989	-4	88	61	2b19,D5	15	-0.4
Total	2	48	141	13	34	1	1	0	13	7-0	0	8	.241	.275	.262	57	-8	0-1	.969	-5	91	80	2b36,D5	15	-1.3
DUBOIS, JASON	Jason Bradford; B3.26.1979 Virginia Beach VA; BR/TR/6´5˝/220; [ChiN00 14/403]; d5.19; Col Virginia Commonwealth																								
2004	Chi N	20	23	2	5	0	1	1	5	1-0	0	7	.217	.240	.435	70	-1	0-0	1.000	0	111	0	O5(1/0/4)/1	0	-0.1
2005	Chi N	52	142	15	34	12	0	7	22	7-1	3	49	.239	.289	.472	92	-2	0-1	.980	-2	81	114	O38L,D3	0	-0.5
	Cle A	14	45	6	10	0	0	2	2	5-0	0	25	.222	.300	.356	76	-2	0-0	1.000	0	110	0	O7(3/0/4),D7	0	-0.2
Total	2	86	210	23	49	12	1	10	29	13-1	3	81	.233	.286	.443	86	-5	0-1	.986	-2	87	90	O50(42/0/8),D10/1	0	-0.8
DUCEY, ROB	Robert Thomas; B5.24.1965 Toronto ON, Can.; BL/TR/6´2˝/(173–183); d5.1; Col Seminole (FL) CC																								
1987	Tor A	34	48	12	9	1	0	1	6	8-0	0	10	.188	.298	.271	53	-3	2-0	1.000	-1	97	0	O28(17/11/3)/D	0	-0.4
1988	Tor A	27	54	15	17	4	1	0	6	5-0	0	7	.315	.361	.426	122	2	1-0	1.000	-3	70	116	O26(1/25/0)/D	0	-0.1
1989	Tor A	41	76	5	16	4	0	0	7	9-1	0	25	.211	.294	.263	59	-4	2-1	1.000	2	102	170	O35(16/2/18)/D	85	-0.3
1990	Tor A	19	53	7	16	5	0	0	7	7-0	1	15	.302	.387	.396	119	2	1-1	1.000	-1	104	0	O19L	0	0.1
1991	†Tor A	39	68	8	16	2	2	1	4	6-0	0	26	.235	.297	.368	80	-2	2-0	.892	-2	89	95	O24(18/1/6),D2	0	-0.4
1992	Tor A	23	21	3	1	1	0	0	0	0-0	0	10	.048	.048	.095	-58	-4	0-1	1.000	-1	85	0	O13(3/2/8),D4	0	-0.6
	Cal A	31	59	4	14	3	0	0	2	5-0	0	12	.237	.292	.288	64	-3	2-3	.944	-0	94	176	O20(17/1/2)/D	0	-0.4
	Year	54	80	7	15	4	0	0	2	5-0	0	22	.188	.233	.237	32	-7	2-4	.957	-1	92	129	O33(20/3/10),D5	0	-1.0
1993	Tex A	27	85	15	24	6	3	2	9	10-2	0	17	.282	.351	.494	131	3	2-3	1.000	-1	91	65	O26(1/14/13)	0	0.1
1994	Tex A	11	29	1	5	1	0	0	1	2-0	0	1	.172	.226	.207	12	-4	0-0	.882	-1	87	0	O10R	0	-0.5
1997	†Sea A	76	143	25	41	15	2	5	10	6-0	0	31	.287	.311	.524	114	3	3-3	.986	-2	88	130	O69(43/12/19)	18	-0.1
1998	Sea A	97	217	30	52	18	2	5	23	23-2	9	61	.240	.336	.410	92	-2	4-3	.970	2	111	102	O83(23/6/61)	20	-0.2
1999	Phi N	104	188	29	49	10	2	8	33	38-1	0	57	.261	.383	.463	112	4	2-1	1.000	1	110	41	O58(39/9/11),D2	0	0.4
2000	Phi N	70	106	16	20	3	1	6	20	20-0	0	36	.189	.317	.406	81	-3	1-0	.919	-2	82	76	O26(24/1/1),D5	0	-0.6
	Tor A	5	13	2	2	1	0	0	1	2-0	0	2	.154	.267	.231	27	-1	0-0	.889	0	135	0	O3(2/0/1)	0	-0.1
	Phi N	42	46	8	10	1	0	0	5	9-1	0	11	.217	.333	.239	52	-3	0-0	1.000	-7	82	76	O7(4/1/2)	0	-1.1
2001	Phi N	30	27	4	6	1	0	1	4	6-0	0	11	.222	.364	.370	95	0	0-0	1.000	0	134	0	O3(1/1/1)	15	0.0
	Mon N	27	46	6	11	2	0	2	8	10-0	1	14	.239	.379	.413	108	1	0-1	1.000	1	117	160	O14(9/3/3),D3	77	0.1
	Year	57	73	10	17	3	0	3	12	16-0	1	25	.233	.374	.397	104	1	0-1	1.000	1	120	136	O17(10/4/4),D3	0	0.1
Total	13	703	1279	190	309	78	13	31	146	166-7	11	346	.242	.331	.396	91	-14	22-17	.976	-13	93	83	O464(237/89/159),D20	215	-4.1
DUDRA, JOHN	John Joseph; B5.27.1916 Assumption IL; D10.24.1965 Pana IL; BR/TR/5´11.5˝/175; d9.7; Mil 1942–45																								
1941	Bos N	14	25	3	9	3	1	0	3	3	0	4	.360	.429	.560	185	3	0	.933	0	116	182	2b5,3b5/1S	0	0.3
DUFF, PAT	Patrick Henry; B5.6.1875 Providence RI; D9.11.1925 Providence RI; TR/5´10˝/?; d4.16; Col Manhattan																								
1906	Was A	1	1	0	0	0	0	0	0	0	0	—	.000	.000	.000	-99	0	0	ø	0	—	—	/H	—	0.0
DUFFEE, CHARLIE	Charles Edward "Home Run"; B1.27.1866 Mobile AL; D12.24.1894 Mobile AL; BR/TR/5´5.5˝/151; d4.17; OF(152/257/48)																								
1889	StL AA	137	509	93	124	15	11	16	86	60	3	81	.244	.327	.411	97	-7	21	.936	14	**167**	136	O132(1/132/0),3b5,2b2	—	0.3
1890	StL AA	98	378	68	104	11	7	3	54	37	3	—	.275	.344	.365	96	-5	20	.951	8	144	324	O66(1/65/0),3b33/S	—	0.1
1891	Col AA	137	552	86	166	28	4	10	90	42	3	36	.301	.353	.420	129	19	41	.927	6	138	142	O128(73/55/0),3b7,S2	—	1.8
1892	Was N	132	492	64	122	12	11	6	51	36	2	33	.248	.302	.354	101	-2	28	.913	18	**168**	**176**	O125(73/5/48),3b6,1b4	—	0.7
1893	Cin N	4	12	3	2	1	0	0	0	5	0	0	.167	.412	.250	76	0	0	.400	-2	0	0	O4L	—	-0.2
Total	5	508	1943	314	518	67	33	35	281	180	11	150	.267	.332	.389	106	5	110	.927	44	154	175	O455C,3b51,1b4,S3,2b2	—	2.7

DUFFY, CHRIS Christopher Ellis; B4.20.1980 Brattleboro VT; BL/TL/5´10˝/(185–190); [PitN01 8/234]; d4.7; Col Arizona St.

YEAR	TM LG	G	AB	R	H	2B	3B	HR	RBI	BB-IB	HP	SO	AVG	OBP	SLG	AOPS	ABR	SB-CS	FA	FR	RNG	THR	GAMES AT POSITION	DL	BFW
2005	Pit N	39	126	22	43	4	2	1	9	7-0	2	22	.341	.385	.429	113	2	2-2	.988	1	115	66	O34(0/33/1)	38	0.4
2006	Pit N	84	314	46	80	14	3	2	18	19-1	10	71	.255	.317	.338	67	-16	26-1	.983	-5	89	108	O77C	0	-1.4
Total	2	123	440	68	123	18	5	3	27	26-1	12	93	.280	.336	.364	80	-14	28-3	.984	-3	96	97	O111(0/110/1)	38	-1.0

DUFFY, ED Edward Charles; B1844 , Ireland; D10.16.1888 Brooklyn NY; TR/5´7.5˝/152; d5.8

YEAR	TM LG	G	AB	R	H	2B	3B	HR	RBI	BB-IB	HP	SO	AVG	OBP	SLG	AOPS	ABR	SB-CS	FA	FR	RNG	THR	GAMES AT POSITION	DL	BFW
1871	Chi NA	26	121	30	28	5	0	0	15	3	—	2	.231	.250	.273	45	-10	11-4	.750	-4	95	95	S26/3	—	-0.8

DUFFY, FRANK Frank Thomas; B10.14.1946 Oakland CA; BR/TR/6´1˝/180; [CinN67 S1/6]; d9.4; Col Stanford

YEAR	TM LG	G	AB	R	H	2B	3B	HR	RBI	BB-IB	HP	SO	AVG	OBP	SLG	AOPS	ABR	SB-CS	FA	FR	RNG	THR	GAMES AT POSITION	DL	BFW
1970	Cin N	6	11	1	2	2	0	0	0	1-0	0	2	.182	.250	.364	62	-1	1-0	1.000	1	127	221	S5	0	0.1
1971	Cin N	13	16	0	3	1	0	0	1	1-0	0	2	.188	.235	.250	38	-1	0-0	.944	3	144	165	S10	0	0.3
	†SF N	21	28	4	5	0	0	0	2	0-0	0	10	.179	.179	.179	1	-4	0-0	.968	2	104	164	S6/23	0	-0.1
	Year	34	44	4	8	1	0	0	3	1-0	0	12	.182	.200	.205	15	-5	0-0	.955	5	124	165	S16/23	0	0.2
1972	Cle A	130	385	23	92	16	4	3	27	31-5	1	54	.239	.297	.325	82	-9	6-2	.977	-3	98	106	S126	0	0.3
1973	Cle A	116	361	34	95	16	4	8	50	25-0	2	41	.263	.312	.396	97	-2	6-6	**.986**	16	106	109	S115	25	2.6
1974	Cle A	158	549	62	128	18	0	8	48	30-0	0	64	.233	.272	.310	68	-24	7-8	.980	-8	102	90	S158	0	-1.6
1975	Cle A	146	482	44	117	22	2	1	47	27-0	2	60	.243	.283	.303	66	-22	10-10	.977	15	109	101	S145	0	0.9
1976	Cle A	133	392	38	83	11	2	2	30	29-2	2	50	.212	.268	.265	57	-21	10-0	**.983**	3	91	**114**	S132	0	-0.2
1977	Cle A	122	334	30	67	13	2	4	31	21-0	0	47	.201	.247	.287	47	-25	8-3	.967	-10	96	99	S121	0	-2.3
1978	Bos A	64	104	12	27	5	0	0	4	6-0	1	11	.260	.306	.308	66	-5	1-1	.960	-2	86	64	3b22,S21,2b12,D6	0	-0.5
1979	Bos A	6	3	0	0	0	0	0	0	0-0	0	1	.000	.000	.000	-95	-1	0-0	1.000	-1	55	0	2b3/1	0	-0.1
Total	10	915	2665	248	619	104	14	26	240	171-7	8	342	.232	.279	.311	68	-115	49-30	.977	17	101	104	S839,3b23,2b16,D6/1	25	-0.6

DUFFY, HUGH Hugh; B11.26.1866 Cranston RI; D10.19.1954 Boston MA; BR/TR/5´7˝/168; d6.23; M8/C1; HF1945; OF(574/677/437)

YEAR	TM LG	G	AB	R	H	2B	3B	HR	RBI	BB-IB	HP	SO	AVG	OBP	SLG	AOPS	ABR	SB-CS	FA	FR	RNG	THR	GAMES AT POSITION	DL	BFW
1888	Chi N	71	298	60	84	10	4	7	41	9	1	32	.282	.305	.413	118	5	13	.910	3	162	210	O67(3/0/64),S3/3	—	0.7
1889	Chi N	**136**	584	144	182	21	7	12	89	46	2	30	.312	.364	.433	115	10	52	.894	-16	76	46	O126R,S10	—	-0.6
1890	Chi P	**138**	596	**161**	**191**	36	16	7	82	59	2	20	.320	.384	.470	122	17	78	.917	9	130	103	O137(0/17/120)	—	1.9
1891	Bos AA	127	536	134	180	20	8	9	**110**	61	4	29	.336	.408	.453	149	34	85	.917	-2	104	70	O124(7/2/118),3b3/S	—	2.7
1892	†Bos N	147	612	125	184	28	12	5	81	60	1	37	.301	.364	.410	123	15	51	.942	-10	75	93	O146C,3b2	—	-0.4
1893	Bos N	**131**	560	147	203	23	7	6	118	50	1	13	**.363**	.416	.461	123	17	44	.953	-5	67	138	O131(0/128/3)	—	0.3
1894	Bos N	125	539	160	**237**	**51**	16	**18**	145	66	1	15	**.440**	.502	.694	172	64	48	.927	3	131	105	O124(4/121/0),S2	—	4.5
1895	Bos N	131	533	112	188	30	6	9	100	65	5	17	.353	.428	.482	125	21	42	.946	3	106	194	O131C	—	1.2
1896	Bos N	131	527	97	158	16	8	5	113	52	2	19	.300	.365	.389	93	-6	39	.957	-2	86	48	O120(114/6/0),2b9,S2	—	-1.6
1897	†Bos N	134	550	130	187	25	10	**11**	129	52	6	—	.340	.403	.482	125	19	41	.975	-2	64	62	O129L,2b6,S2	—	0.5
1898	Bos N	**152**	568	97	169	13	3	8	108	59	1	—	.298	.365	.373	106	4	29	.956	1	83	45	O152(115/39/0)/31C	—	-0.6
1899	Bos N	147	588	103	164	29	7	5	102	39	3	—	.279	.327	.378	85	-14	26	.970	-6	38	18	O147(138/8/1)	—	-3.1
1900	Bos N	55	181	27	55	5	4	2	31	16	0	—	.304	.360	.409	100	-1	11	.957	-1	74	118	O49(44/5/0)/2	—	-0.5
1901	Mil A	79	285	40	86	15	9	2	45	16	1	—	.302	.341	.439	121	7	12	.967	-4	54	0	O77(12/65/0),M	—	-0.1
1904	Phi N	18	46	10	13	1	1	0	5	13	0	—	.283	.441	.348	150	4	3	.850	-2	73	0	O14(8/6/0),M	—	0.2
1905	Phi N	15	40	7	12	2	1	0	3	1	0	—	.300	.317	.400	117	1	0	.909	-0	76	0	O8(0/3/5),M	—	0.0
1906	Phi N	1	1	0	0	0	0	0	0	0	0	—	.000	.000	.000	-99	0	0	ø	0	—	—	/HM	—	0.0
Total	17	1738	7044	1554	2293	325	119	106	1302	664	30	212	.326	.386	.451	121	197	574	.943	-31	88	85	O1682C,S20,2b16,3b7/C1	—	5.1

DUGAN, JOE Joseph Anthony "Jumping Joe"; B5.12.1897 Mahanoy City PA; D7.7.1982 Norwood MA; BR/TR/5´11˝/160; d7.5; Col Holy Cross

YEAR	TM LG	G	AB	R	H	2B	3B	HR	RBI	BB-IB	HP	SO	AVG	OBP	SLG	AOPS	ABR	SB-CS	FA	FR	RNG	THR	GAMES AT POSITION	DL	BFW
1917	Phi A	43	134	9	26	8	0	0	16	3	3	16	.194	.229	.254	48	-9	0	.917	1	108	76	S39,2b2	—	-0.6
1918	Phi A	121	411	26	80	11	3	3	34	16	3	55	.195	.230	.258	47	-29	4	.930	17	106	126	S86,2b34	—	-0.6
1919	Phi A	104	387	25	105	17	2	1	30	11	5	30	.271	.300	.333	77	-13	9	.929	1	99	96	S98,2b4,3b2	—	-0.5
1920	Phi A	123	491	65	158	40	5	3	60	19	3	51	.322	.351	.442	108	5	5-8	.948	3	94	129	3b60,S32,2b31	—	1.0
1921	Phi A	119	461	54	136	22	6	10	58	28	5	45	.295	.342	.434	96	-4	5-1	.953	-22	84	85	3b119	—	-1.7
1922	Bos A	84	341	45	98	22	3	3	38	9	1	28	.287	.308	.396	83	-10	2-3	.943	-7	102	101	3b64,S21	—	-1.2
	†NY A	60	252	44	72	9	1	3	25	13	4	21	.286	.331	.365	79	-8	1-0	.967	-8	89	96	3b60	—	-1.2
	Year	144	593	89	170	31	4	6	63	22	5	49	.287	.318	.383	81	-18	3-3	.954	-16	96	**99**	3b124,S21	—	-2.4
1923	†NY A	146	644	111	182	30	7	7	67	25	2	41	.283	.311	.384	81	-21	4-2	**.974**	-13	91	113	3b146	—	-2.4
1924	NY A	148	610	105	184	31	7	3	56	31	5	33	.302	.341	.390	88	-13	1-2	.962	-12	86	94	3b148,2b2	—	-1.5
1925	NY A	102	404	50	118	19	4	0	31	19	4	20	.292	.330	.359	76	-16	2-4	.970	6	102	101	3b96	—	-0.5
1926	†NY A	123	434	39	125	19	5	1	64	25	1	16	.288	.328	.362	81	-13	2-4	.955	-13	89	53	3b122	—	-2.0
1927	†NY A	112	387	44	104	24	3	2	43	27	3	37	.269	.321	.362	79	-12	1-4	.938	-18	91	78	3b111	—	-2.4
1928	†NY A	94	312	33	86	15	0	6	34	16	3	15	.276	.317	.381	85	-7	1-0	.952	-16	79	91	3b91/2	—	-1.7
1929	Bos N	60	125	14	38	10	0	0	15	8	0	8	.304	.346	.384	84	-3	0	.918	-7	81	96	3b24,S5,2b2,O2L	—	-0.7
1931	Det A	8	17	1	4	0	0	0	0	0	0	3	.235	.235	.235	23	-2	0-0	.900	-1	81	0	3b5	—	-0.2
Total	14	1447	5410	665	1516	277	46	42	571	250	42	419	.280	.317	.372	82	-155	37-28	.957	-88	90	92	3b1048,S281,2b76,O2L	—	-16.2

DUGAN, BILL William H.; B1864 New York NY; D7.24.1921 New York NY; d8.5; b–Ed

YEAR	TM LG	G	AB	R	H	2B	3B	HR	RBI	BB-IB	HP	SO	AVG	OBP	SLG	AOPS	ABR	SB-CS	FA	FR	RNG	THR	GAMES AT POSITION	DL	BFW
1884	Ric AA	9	28	4	3	1	0	0	—	0	1	—	.107	.138	.143	-8	-3	—	.889	-3	—	—	C9	—	-0.5
	KC U	3	6	0	0	0	0	0	—	0	—	—	.000	.000	.000	-99	-2	—	.400	-1	0	0	O3(1/2/0)	—	-0.2
Total	1	12	34	4	3	1	0	0	—	0	—	—	.088	.114	.118	-26	-5	—	.889	-3	—	—	C9,O3(1/2/0)	—	-0.7

DUGAS, GUS Augustin Joseph; B3.24.1907 St.Jean de Matha QC, Can.; D4.14.1997 Colchester CT; BL/TL/5´9˝/165; d9.17

YEAR	TM LG	G	AB	R	H	2B	3B	HR	RBI	BB-IB	HP	SO	AVG	OBP	SLG	AOPS	ABR	SB-CS	FA	FR	RNG	THR	GAMES AT POSITION	DL	BFW
1930	Pit N	9	31	8	9	2	0	0	1	7	0	4	.290	.421	.355	90	0	0	.864	-1	93	90	O9R	—	-0.1
1932	Pit N	55	97	13	23	3	3	3	12	7	0	11	.237	.288	.423	90	-2	0	.952	-1	110	0	O20(6/1/13)	—	-0.4
1933	Phi N	37	71	4	12	3	0	0	9	1	0	9	.169	.181	.211	10	-8	0	.984	0	111	70	1b11/cf	—	-1.0
1934	Was A	24	19	2	1	1	0	0	1	3	0	3	.053	.182	.105	-25	-4	0-0	1.000	0	124	0	O2(0/1/1)	—	-0.3
Total	4	125	218	27	45	9	3	3	23	18	0	27	.206	.267	.317	54	-14	0-0	.926	-1	105	29	O32(6/3/23),1b11	—	-1.8

DUGDALE, DAN Daniel Edward; B10.28.1864 Peoria IL; D3.9.1934 Seattle WA; BR/5´8˝/180; d5.20

YEAR	TM LG	G	AB	R	H	2B	3B	HR	RBI	BB-IB	HP	SO	AVG	OBP	SLG	AOPS	ABR	SB-CS	FA	FR	RNG	THR	GAMES AT POSITION	DL	BFW
1886	KC N	12	40	4	7	0	0	0	2	2	—	13	.175	.214	.175	18	-4	1	.884	-2	—	—	C7,O6(0/1/5)	—	-0.5
1894	Was N	38	134	19	32	4	2	0	16	13	0	14	.239	.306	.299	48	-12	7	.874	-8	*71*	*112*	C33,3b3,O2L	—	-1.3
Total	2	50	174	23	39	4	2	0	18	15	0	27	.224	.286	.270	42	-16	8	.877	-10	*71*	*112*	C40,O8(2/1/5),3b3	—	-1.8

DUGEY, OSCAR Oscar Joseph "Jake"; B10.25.1887 Palestine TX; D1.1.1966 Dallas TX; BR/TR/5´8˝/160; d9.13; C5

YEAR	TM LG	G	AB	R	H	2B	3B	HR	RBI	BB-IB	HP	SO	AVG	OBP	SLG	AOPS	ABR	SB-CS	FA	FR	RNG	THR	GAMES AT POSITION	DL	BFW
1913	Bos N	5	8	1	2	0	0	0	0	1	0	1	.250	.333	.250	67	0	0	.500	-1	67	0	3b2/2S	—	-0.1
1914	Bos N	58	109	17	21	2	0	1	10	10	1	15	.193	.267	.239	51	-7	10	.933	-2	96	77	O16R,2b16/3	—	-1.0
1915	†Phi N	42	39	4	6	1	0	0	0	7	0	5	.154	.283	.179	41	-2	2-1	.941	2	134	49	2b14	—	-0.1
1916	Phi N	41	50	9	11	3	0	0	1	9	0	8	.220	.339	.280	88	0	3	.967	2	113	75	2b12	—	0.2
1917	Phi N	44	72	12	14	4	1	0	9	4	0	9	.194	.237	.278	55	-4	2	.871	-1	84	43	2b15,O4(1/2/0)	—	-0.6
1920	Bos N	5	0	2	0	0	0	0	0	0	0	0	ø	ø	ø	ø	0	0-0	ø	0	—	—	/R	—	0.0
Total	6	195	278	45	54	10	1	1	20	31	1	38	.194	.277	.248	58	-13	17-1	.915	-2	100	64	2b58,O20(1/2/16),3b3/S	—	-1.6

DUGGAN, JIM James Elmer "Mer"; B6.1.1885 Whiteland IN; D12.5.1951 Indianapolis IN; BL/TL/5´10˝/165; d6.29; Col Franklin

YEAR	TM LG	G	AB	R	H	2B	3B	HR	RBI	BB-IB	HP	SO	AVG	OBP	SLG	AOPS	ABR	SB-CS	FA	FR	RNG	THR	GAMES AT POSITION	DL	BFW
1911	StL A	1	4	1	0	0	0	0	1	1	0	—	.000	.200	.000	-44	-1	0	1.000	0	125	324	/1	—	-0.1

DUNBAR, TOM Thomas Jerome; B11.24.1959 Graniteville SC; BL/TL/6´2˝/192; [TexA80*S1/25]; d9.7; Col Middle Georgia JC

YEAR	TM LG	G	AB	R	H	2B	3B	HR	RBI	BB-IB	HP	SO	AVG	OBP	SLG	AOPS	ABR	SB-CS	FA	FR	RNG	THR	GAMES AT POSITION	DL	BFW
1983	Tex A	12	24	3	6	0	0	0	3	5-0	0	7	.250	.379	.250	78	0	3-1	.875	-2	51	0	O9(2/0/7)/D	0	-0.2
1984	Tex A	34	97	9	25	2	0	2	10	6-1	0	16	.258	.301	.340	74	-4	1-0	.939	-2	85	0	O20(9/0/11),D6	0	-0.7
1985	Tex A	45	104	7	21	4	0	1	5	12-3	1	9	.202	.291	.269	53	-6	0-3	.933	-3	57	0	D18,O14(12/0/3)	16	-1.1
Total	3	91	225	19	52	6	0	3	18	23-4	1	32	.231	.305	.298	65	-10	4-4	.929	-7	70	0	O43(23/0/21),D25	16	-2.0

DUNCAN, CHRIS Christopher Edward; B5.5.1981 Tucson AZ; BL/TR/6´5˝/210; [StLN99 1/46]; d9.10; f–Dave

YEAR	TM LG	G	AB	R	H	2B	3B	HR	RBI	BB-IB	HP	SO	AVG	OBP	SLG	AOPS	ABR	SB-CS	FA	FR	RNG	THR	GAMES AT POSITION	DL	BFW
2005	StL N	9	10	2	2	1	0	1	3	0-0	0	5	.200	.200	.600	97	0	0-0	1.000	-0	0	0	1b2/rf	0	0.0
2006	†StL N	90	280	60	82	11	3	22	43	30-0	2	69	.293	.363	.589	138	15	0-0	.948	-2	98	69	O70(49/0/24),1b11/D	0	0.9
Total	2	99	290	62	84	12	3	23	46	30-0	2	74	.290	.358	.590	136	15	0-0	.948	-2	98	69	O71(49/0/25),1b13/D	0	0.9

DUNCAN, DAVE David Edwin; B9.26.1945 Dallas TX; BR/TR/6´2˝/(195–200); d5.6; C29; s–Chris

YEAR	TM LG	G	AB	R	H	2B	3B	HR	RBI	BB-IB	HP	SO	AVG	OBP	SLG	AOPS	ABR	SB-CS	FA	FR	RNG	THR	GAMES AT POSITION	DL	BFW
1964	KC A	25	53	2	9	0	1	1	5	2-0	0	20	.170	.200	.264	27	-6	0-0	.981	-2	35	162	C22	0	-0.8
1967	KC A	34	101	9	19	4	0	5	11	4-0	0	50	.188	.219	.376	75	-4	0-1	.979	-4	55	53	C32	0	-0.8
1968	Oak A	82	246	15	47	4	0	7	28	25-3	1	68	.191	.266	.293	73	-8	1-2	.987	-1	88	104	C79	0	-0.7

YEAR	TM LG	G	AB	R	H	2B	3B	HR	RBI	BB-IB	HP	SO	AVG	OBP	SLG	AOPS	ABR	SB-CS	FA	FR	RNG	THR	GAMES AT POSITION	DL	BFW
1969	Oak A	58	127	11	16	3	0	3	22	19-4	0	41	.126	.236	.220	31	-12	0-0	.982	-12	81	100	C56	0	-2.4
1970	Oak A	86	232	21	60	7	0	10	29	22-2	0	38	.259	.320	.418	106	1	0-0	.978	1	100	97	C73	0	0.6
1971	†Oak A☆	103	363	39	92	13	1	15	40	28-2	1	77	.253	.307	.419	106	1	1-1	.984	-2	88	67	C102	0	0.4
1972	†Oak A	121	403	39	88	13	0	19	59	34-5	5	68	.218	.283	.392	106	1	0-2	.993	-5	97	90	C113	0	0.1
1973	Cle A	95	344	43	80	11	1	17	43	35-1	3	86	.233	.309	.419	101	0	3-3	.988	-6	70	84	C86,D9	47	-0.3
1974	Cle A	136	425	45	85	10	1	16	46	42-3	2	91	.200	.274	.341	77	-14	0-4	.976	-7	124	73	C134,1b3/D	0	-1.7
1975	Bal A	96	307	30	63	7	0	12	41	16-0	1	82	.205	.245	.345	70	-14	0-0	.982	-3	**152**	78	C95	0	-1.3
1976	Bal A	93	284	20	58	7	0	4	17	25-0	1	56	.204	.271	.271	62	-14	0-0	.985	-11	103	77	C93	0	-2.2
Total	11	929	2885	274	617	79	4	109	341	252-20	14	677	.214	.279	.357	85	-69	5-13	.984	-52	100	84	C885,D10,1b3	47	-9.1

DUNCAN, JIM James William; B7.1.1871 Saltsburg PA; D10.16.1901 Foxburg PA; BR/TR/5´8˝/140; d7.18

YEAR	TM LG	G	AB	R	H	2B	3B	HR	RBI	BB-IB	HP	SO	AVG	OBP	SLG	AOPS	ABR	SB-CS	FA	FR	RNG	THR	GAMES AT POSITION	DL	BFW
1899	Was N	15	47	5	11	2	0	0	5	4	0	—	.234	.294	.277	57	-3	1	.940	-2	*77*	*117*	C14	—	-0.4
	Cle N	31	105	9	24	2	3	2	9	4	0	—	.229	.257	.362	74	-5	0	.971	-6	76	104	1b17,C14	—	-0.9
	Year	46	152	14	35	4	3	2	14	8	0	—	.230	.269	.336	69	-7	1	.904	-9	*70*	*117*	C28,1b17	—	-1.3

DUNCAN, JEFF Jeffrey Matthew; B12.9.1978 Harvey IL; BL/TL/6´2˝/(180–190); [NYN00 7/215]; d5.20; Col Arizona St.

YEAR	TM LG	G	AB	R	H	2B	3B	HR	RBI	BB-IB	HP	SO	AVG	OBP	SLG	AOPS	ABR	SB-CS	FA	FR	RNG	THR	GAMES AT POSITION	DL	BFW
2003	NY N	56	139	13	27	0	2	1	10	17-3	2	41	.194	.291	.245	44	-12	4-2	1.000	5	134	0	O52(1/52/0)	0	-0.6
2004	NY N	13	15	2	1	0	0	0	1	1-0	0	5	.067	.125	.067	-50	-3	3-0	1.000	0	120	0	O4(2/2/0)	0	-0.3
Total	2	69	154	15	28	0	2	1	11	18-3	2	46	.182	.276	.227	35	-15	7-2	1.000	5	133	0	O56(3/54/0)	0	-0.9

DUNCAN, PAT Louis Baird; B10.6.1893 Coalton OH; D7.17.1960 Columbus OH; BR/TR/5´9˝/170; d7.16; Mil 1918–19

YEAR	TM LG	G	AB	R	H	2B	3B	HR	RBI	BB-IB	HP	SO	AVG	OBP	SLG	AOPS	ABR	SB-CS	FA	FR	RNG	THR	GAMES AT POSITION	DL	BFW
1915	Pit N	3	5	0	1	0	0	0	0	0	0	1	.200	.200	.200	22	0	0	1.000	-0	74	0	/cf	—	-0.1
1919	†Cin N	31	90	9	22	3	3	2	17	8	0	7	.244	.306	.411	118	2	2	.982	0	103	94	O27L	—	0.1
1920	Cin N	**154**	576	75	170	16	11	2	83	42	7	42	.295	.350	.372	109	7	18-18	.964	2	106	87	O154L	—	-0.1
1921	Cin N	145	532	57	164	27	10	2	60	44	5	33	.308	.367	.408	110	8	7-18	.971	5	106	101	O145(129/16/1)	—	-0.3
1922	Cin N	151	607	94	199	44	12	8	94	40	1	31	.328	.370	.479	120	17	12-28	.971	1	100	100	O151L	—	-0.1
1923	Cin N	147	566	92	185	26	8	7	83	30	2	27	.327	.363	.438	113	9	15-13	**.993**	-5	93	78	O146(144/3/0)	—	-0.8
1924	Cin N	96	319	34	86	21	6	2	37	20	0	23	.270	.313	.392	89	-5	1-7	.927	-10	83	41	O83(82/0/1)	—	-2.3
Total	7	727	2695	361	827	137	50	23	374	184	15	164	.307	.355	.420	110	38	55-84	.970	-6	100	86	O707(687/20/2)	—	-3.6

DUNCAN, MARIANO Mariano (Nalasco); B3.13.1963 San Pedro de Macoris, D.R.; BR/TR (BB 1985–87)/6´0˝/(160–200); d4.9; C1; OF(88/2/6)

YEAR	TM LG	G	AB	R	H	2B	3B	HR	RBI	BB-IB	HP	SO	AVG	OBP	SLG	AOPS	ABR	SB-CS	FA	FR	RNG	THR	GAMES AT POSITION	DL	BFW
1985	†LA N	142	562	74	137	24	6	6	39	38-4	3	113	.244	.293	.340	79	-17	38-8	.954	-7	99	86	S123,2b19	0	-0.5
1986	LA N	109	407	47	93	7	0	8	30	30-1	2	78	.229	.284	.305	67	-20	48-13	.951	-1	98	75	S106	29	-0.4
1987	LA N	76	261	31	56	8	1	6	18	17-1	2	62	.215	.267	.322	57	-17	11-1	.930	5	104	102	S67,2b7,O2(1/0/1)	64	-0.4
1989	LA N	49	84	9	21	5	1	0	8	0-0	2	15	.250	.267	.333	72	-3	3-3	.943	0	107	161	S16,2b8,O7(4/0/4)	30	-0.3
	Cin N	45	174	23	43	10	1	3	13	8-0	3	36	.247	.292	.368	85	-4	6-2	.955	-6	87	80	S44,2b5	0	-0.6
	Year	94	258	32	64	15	2	3	21	8-0	5	51	.248	.284	.357	81	-7	9-5	.952	-5	91	96	S60,2b13,O7(4/0/4)	0	-0.9
1990	†Cin N	125	435	67	133	22	**11**	10	55	24-4	4	67	.306	.345	.476	119	10	13-7	.973	4	98	93	2b115,S12/lf	0	1.8
1991	Cin N	100	333	46	86	7	4	12	40	12-0	3	57	.258	.288	.411	91	-6	5-4	.974	-4	90	95	2b62,S32,O7(6/2/0)	15	-0.7
1992	Phi N	142	574	71	153	40	3	8	50	17-0	5	108	.267	.292	.389	92	-8	23-3	.976	-10	103	36	O65L,2b52,S42,3b4	0	-1.3
1993	†Phi N	124	496	68	140	26	4	11	73	12-0	4	88	.282	.304	.417	92	-7	6-5	.969	-18	95	76	2b65,S59	15	-1.9
1994	Phi N★	88	347	49	93	22	1	8	48	17-1	4	72	.268	.306	.406	83	-9	10-2	.972	-8	100	107	2b37,3b28,S19,1b6	15	-1.2
1995	Phi N	52	196	20	56	12	1	3	23	0-0	1	43	.286	.285	.403	80	-6	1-2	.957	9	102	131	2b24,S14,1b12/3	0	0.3
	†Cin N	29	69	16	20	2	1	3	13	5-0	0	19	.290	.329	.478	111	1	0-1	.963	-3	76	81	2b7,1b6,S6,O3L	0	-0.2
	Year	81	265	36	76	14	2	6	36	5-0	1	62	.287	.297	.423	88	-6	1-3	.958	6	96	119	2b31,S20,1b18,O3L/3	0	0.1
1996	†NY A	109	400	62	136	34	3	8	56	9-1	1	77	.340	.352	.500	113	7	4-3	.975	-1	96	93	2b104,3b3,O3(2/0/1),D2	18	1.1
1997	NY A	50	172	16	42	8	0	1	13	6-0	0	39	.244	.270	.308	51	-13	2-1	.976	1	106	93	2b41,O6L,D2	0	-0.9
	Tor A	39	167	20	38	6	0	0	12	6-0	3	39	.228	.267	.263	39	-15	4-2	.984	3	98	106	2b39	0	-1.0
	Year	89	339	36	80	14	0	1	25	12-0	3	78	.236	.268	.286	45	-28	6-3	.980	4	102	100	2b80,O6L,D2	0	-1.9
Total	12	1279	4677	619	1247	233	37	87	491	201-12	37	913	.267	.300	.388	86	-107	174-57	.972	-34	96	94	2b585,S540,O94L,3b36,1b24,D4	186	-6.2

DUNCAN, TAYLOR Taylor McDowell; B5.12.1953 Memphis TN; D1.3.2004 Asheville NC; BR/TR/6´0˝/(165–180); [AtlN71 1/10]; d9.15

YEAR	TM LG	G	AB	R	H	2B	3B	HR	RBI	BB-IB	HP	SO	AVG	OBP	SLG	AOPS	ABR	SB-CS	FA	FR	RNG	THR	GAMES AT POSITION	DL	BFW
1977	StL N	8	12	2	4	0	0	1	2	2-0	0	1	.333	.400	.583	170	1	0-0	1.000	-2	35	0	3b5	0	-0.1
1978	Oak A	104	319	25	82	15	2	2	37	19-0	0	38	.257	.296	.335	82	-8	1-2	.953	-11	83	28	3b84,2b11/SD	0	-2.2
Total	2	112	331	27	86	15	2	3	39	21-0	0	39	.260	.301	.344	86	-7	1-2	.953	-13	81	27	3b89,2b11,D7/S	0	-2.3

DUNCAN, VERN Vernon Van Duke; B1.6.1890 Clayton NC; D6.1.1954 Daytona Beach FL; BL/TR/5´9˝/155; d9.11; Col North Carolina

YEAR	TM LG	G	AB	R	H	2B	3B	HR	RBI	BB-IB	HP	SO	AVG	OBP	SLG	AOPS	ABR	SB-CS	FA	FR	RNG	THR	GAMES AT POSITION	DL	BFW
1913	Phi N	8	12	3	5	1	0	0	1	0	0	3	.417	.417	.500	155	1	0	1.000	0	61	418	O3(1/0/2)	—	0.1
1914	Bal F	157	557	99	160	20	8	2	53	67	**11**	55	.287	.375	.363	98	-7	13	.914	-6	93	99	O148(36/101/11),3b8/2	—	-2.3
1915	Bal F	146	531	68	142	18	4	2	43	54	2	40	.267	.337	.328	85	-17	19	.965	-4	103	113	O124(60/64/0),3b21/2	—	-3.0
Total	3	311	1100	170	307	39	12	4	97	121	13	98	.279	.357	.347	93	-23	32	.939	-9	97	108	O275(97/165/13),3b29,2b2	—	-5.2

DUNDON, GUS Augustus Joseph; B7.10.1874 Columbus OH; D9.1.1940 Pittsburgh PA; BR/TR/5´10˝/165; d4.14

YEAR	TM LG	G	AB	R	H	2B	3B	HR	RBI	BB-IB	HP	SO	AVG	OBP	SLG	AOPS	ABR	SB-CS	FA	FR	RNG	THR	GAMES AT POSITION	DL	BFW
1904	Chi A	108	373	40	85	9	3	0	36	30	4	—	.228	.292	.268	81	-7	19	**.973**	-13	95	95	2b103,3b3,S2	—	-2.2
1905	Chi A	106	364	30	70	7	3	0	22	23	4	—	.192	.248	.228	53	-19	14	.983	4	106	95	2b100,S6	—	-1.6
1906	Chi A	33	96	7	13	1	0	0	4	11	0	—	.135	.224	.146	17	-9	4	.921	1	96	90	2b18,S14	—	-0.8
Total	3	247	833	77	168	17	6	0	62	64	8	—	.202	.265	.236	61	-35	37	.972	-8	100	95	2b221,S22,3b3	—	-4.6

DUNDON, ED Edward Joseph "Dummy"; B7.10.1859 Columbus OH; D8.18.1893 Columbus OH; TR/6´0˝/170; d6.2; ▲

YEAR	TM LG	G	AB	R	H	2B	3B	HR	RBI	BB-IB	HP	SO	AVG	OBP	SLG	AOPS	ABR	SB-CS	FA	FR	RNG	THR	GAMES AT POSITION	DL	BFW
1883	Col AA	26	93	8	15	1	0	0	—	3	—	—	.161	.188	.172	18	-8	—	.804	1	104	**299**	P20,O9(6/2/1)/2	—	-0.1
1884	Col AA	26	86	6	12	2	2	0	—	5	1	—	.140	.196	.209	35	-6	—	.966	3	125	460	O16(14/1/1),P11,1b3	—	-0.2
Total	2	52	179	14	27	3	2	0	—	8	1	—	.151	.191	.190	26	-14	—	.857	4	106	309	P31,O25(20/3/2),1b3/2	—	-0.3

DUNGAN, SAM Samuel Morrison; B7.29.1866 Ferndale CA; D3.16.1939 Santa Ana CA; BR/5´11˝/180; d4.12

YEAR	TM LG	G	AB	R	H	2B	3B	HR	RBI	BB-IB	HP	SO	AVG	OBP	SLG	AOPS	ABR	SB-CS	FA	FR	RNG	THR	GAMES AT POSITION	DL	BFW
1892	Chi N	113	433	46	123	19	7	0	53	35	6	19	.284	.346	.360	112	6	15	.905	-9	43	53	O113(37/0/76)	—	-0.9
1893	Chi N	107	465	86	138	23	7	2	64	29	9	8	.297	.350	.389	98	-2	11	.920	3	112	74	O107(1/0/106)	—	-0.4
1894	Chi N	10	39	5	9	2	0	0	3	7	0	1	.231	.348	.282	50	-3	1	1.000	1	140	267	O10R	—	-0.2
	Lou N	8	32	6	11	1	0	0	3	4	0	1	.344	.417	.375	99	0	2	.941	-0	69	274	O8R	—	0.0
	Year	18	71	11	20	3	0	0	6	11	0	2	.282	.378	.324	70	-3	3	.971	1	104	271	O18R	—	-0.2
1900	Chi N	6	15	1	4	0	0	0	1	1	0	—	.267	.313	.267	63	-1	0	.800	-1	0	0	O3C	—	-0.2
1901	Was A	**138**	559	70	179	26	12	1	73	40	2	—	.320	.368	.415	118	14	9	.947	-4	117	136	O104(1/0/103),1b35	—	0.5
Total	5	382	1543	214	464	71	26	3	197	116	17	29	.301	.356	.386	107	14	38	.924	-9	89	94	O345(39/3/303),1b35	—	-1.2

DUNHAM, LEE Leland Huffield; B6.9.1902 Atlanta IL; D5.11.1961 Atlanta IL; BL/TL/5´11˝/185; d4.17; Col Illinois Wesleyan

YEAR	TM LG	G	AB	R	H	2B	3B	HR	RBI	BB-IB	HP	SO	AVG	OBP	SLG	AOPS	ABR	SB-CS	FA	FR	RNG	THR	GAMES AT POSITION	DL	BFW
926	Phi N	5	4	0	1	0	0	0	1	0	0	1	.250	.250	.250	33	0	0	1.000	-0	0	0	1b2	—	0.0

DUNLAP, FRED Frederick C. "Sure Shot"; B5.21.1859 Philadelphia PA; D12.1.1902 Philadelphia PA; BR/TR/5´8˝/165; d5.1; M4

YEAR	TM LG	G	AB	R	H	2B	3B	HR	RBI	BB-IB	HP	SO	AVG	OBP	SLG	AOPS	ABR	SB-CS	FA	FR	RNG	THR	GAMES AT POSITION	DL	BFW
1880	Cle N	**85**	373	61	103	**27**	9	4	30	7	—	32	.276	.289	.429	143	17	—	.911	7	**103**	**134**	2b85	—	2.6
1881	Cle N	80	351	60	114	25	4	3	24	18	—	24	.325	.358	.444	159	25	—	.909	7	101	111	2b79/3	—	3.2
1882	Cle N	**84**	364	68	102	19	4	0	28	23	—	26	.280	.323	.354	121	10	—	.900	18	**112**	**165**	2b84,M	—	2.8
1883	Cle N	93	396	81	129	34	2	4	37	22	—	21	.326	.361	.452	147	24	—	.911	7	95	126	2b93/rf	—	2.9
1884	StL U	101	449	**160**	**185**	39	8	**13**	—	29	—	—	**.412**	**.448**	**.621**	**213**	**50**	—	**.926**	**30**	**111**	**214**	2b100/rfPM	—	**7.1**
1885	StL N	106	423	70	114	11	5	2	25	41	—	24	.270	.334	.333	124	14	—	**.934**	**27**	**113**	119	2b106,M	—	4.1
1886	StL N	71	285	53	76	15	2	3	32	28	—	30	.267	.332	.365	119	8	7	.931	14	105	133	2b71/cf	—	2.2
	Det N	51	196	32	56	8	3	4	37	16	—	21	.286	.340	.418	125	6	13	.918	4	107	119	2b51	—	1.0
	Year	122	481	85	132	23	5	7	69	44	—	51	.274	.335	.387	122	14	20	.926	17	106	127	2b122/cf	—	3.2
1887	†Det N	65	272	60	72	13	10	5	45	25	0	12	.265	.327	.441	107	2	15	.948	23	107	168	2b65/P	—	2.2
1888	Pit N	82	321	41	84	12	4	1	36	16	3	30	.262	.303	.333	112	5	24	.940	11	104	143	2b82	—	1.8
1889	Pit N	121	451	59	106	19	0	2	65	46	2	33	.235	.309	.290	74	-13	21	**.950**	-4	98	95	2b121,M	—	-1.2
1890	Pit N	17	64	9	11	1	1	0	3	7	1	6	.172	.264	.219	46	-4	2	.873	-2	105	48	2b17	—	-0.5
	NY P	1	4	1	2	0	0	0	0	0	0	0	.500	.500	.500	154	0	0	1.000	-1	47	0	/2	—	0.0
1891	Was AA	8	25	4	5	1	1	0	4	5	1	4	.200	.355	.320	98	0	3	.818	-2	98	93	2b8	—	-0.1
Total	12	965	3974	759	1159	224	53	41	366	283	7	263	.292	.340	.406	132	144	85	.924	137	105	136	2b963,O3(0/1/2),P2/3	—	28.1

YEAR	TM LG	G	AB	R	H	2B	3B	HR	RBI	BB-IB	HP	SO	AVG	OBP	SLG	AOPS	ABR	SB-CS	FA	FR	RNG	THR	GAMES AT POSITION	DL	BFW
Dunlap, Grant	Grant Lester "Snap"; B12.20.1923 Stockton CA; BR/TR/6´2˝/180; d4.21; Col Pacific (CA)																								
1953	StL N	16	17	2	6	0	1	1	3	0	0	2	.353	.353	.647	154	1	0-0	ø	-0	0	0	/rf	0	0.1
Dunlap, Bill	William James; B5.1.1909 Palmer MA; D11.29.1980 Reading PA; BR/TR/5´11˝/170; d9.2																								
1929	Bos N	10	29	6	12	0	1	1	4	4	0	4	.414	.485	.586	171	3	0	.889	-1	103	0	O9(8/0/1)	—	0.2
1930	Bos N	16	29	3	2	1	0	0	0	0	0	6	.069	.069	.103	-61	-8	0	1.000	0	129	0	O7(0/2/5)	—	-0.7
Total	2	26	58	9	14	1	1	1	4	4	0	10	.241	.290	.345	57	-5	0	.939	-0	113	0	O16(8/2/6)	—	-0.5
Dunleavy, Jack	John Francis; B9.14.1879 Harrison NJ; D4.11.1944 S.Norwalk CT; BL/TL/5´6˝/167; d5.30; Col Amherst; ▲																								
1903	StL N	61	193	23	48	3	3	0	10	13	3	—	.249	.306	.295	74	-7	10	.972	5	200	349	O38(6/0/32),P14	—	-0.2
1904	StL N	51	172	23	40	7	3	1	14	16	2	—	.233	.305	.326	99	0	8	.987	2	120	145	O44(5/3/36),P7	—	0.0
1905	StL N	119	435	52	105	8	8	1	25	55	1	—	.241	.328	.303	91	-3	15	.962	7	**165**	184	O118(13/0/115)/2	—	-0.1
Total	3	231	800	98	193	18	14	2	49	84	6	—	.241	.318	.306	89	-10	33	.969	15	163	210	O200(24/3/183),P21/2	—	-0.3
Dunlop, George	George Henry; B7.19.1888 Meriden CT; D12.12.1971 Meriden CT; BR/TR/5´10˝/170; d9.9																								
1913	Cle A	7	17	3	4	1	0	0	0	0	0	5	.235	.235	.294	53	-1	0	.923	1	83	0	S4,3b3	—	0.0
1914	Cle A	1	3	0	0	0	0	0	0	1	0	1	.000	.250	.000	-23	0	0	1.000	-1	49	0	/S	—	-0.1
Total	2	8	20	3	4	1	0	0	0	1	0	6	.200	.238	.250	42	-1	0	.929	-0	75	0	S5,3b3	—	-0.1
Dunn, Adam	Adam Troy; B11.9.1979 Houston TX; BL/TR/6´6˝/(240–275); [CinN98 2/50]; d7.20																								
2001	Cin N	66	244	54	64	18	1	19	43	38-2	4	74	.262	.371	.578	132	12	4-2	.986	2	108	69	O63(30/0/38)	0	1.1
2002	Cin N★	158	535	84	133	28	2	26	71	128-13	9	170	.249	.400	.454	121	22	19-9	.959	-4	91	136	O118(112/0/17),1b44/D	0	1.1
2003	Cin N	116	381	70	82	12	1	27	57	74-8	10	126	.215	.354	.465	118	11	8-2	.955	3	110	80	O102(99/0/4),1b19,D2	44	1.0
2004	Cin N	161	568	105	151	34	0	46	102	108-11	5	195	.266	.388	.569	146	41	6-1	.970	-5	89	117	O156L,1b10/D	0	3.0
2005	Cin N	160	543	107	134	35	2	40	101	114-14	12	168	.247	.387	.540	139	35	4-2	.981	-2	104	82	O133L,1b33	0	2.6
2006	Cin N	160	561	99	131	24	0	40	92	112-12	6	194	.234	.365	.490	110	11	7-0	.960	-3	96	86	O156L,1b2/D	0	0.3
Total	6	821	2832	519	695	151	6	198	466	574-60	46	927	.245	.380	.513	128	132	48-16	.967	-10	98	98	O728(686/0/59),1b108,D5	44	9.1
Dunn, Jack	John Joseph; B10.6.1872 Meadville PA; D10.22.1928 Towson MD; BR/TR/5´9˝/?; d5.6; OF(8/10/41); ▲																								
1897	Bro N	36	131	20	29	4	0	0	17	4	0	—	.221	.244	.252	33	-13	2	.911	-2	111	119	P25,2b4,O3L,3b3/S	—	-0.4
1898	Bro N	51	167	21	41	0	1	0	19	7	1	—	.246	.280	.257	54	-10	3	.939	-1	88	75	P41,O4(1/2/1),S4,3b2	—	-0.3
1899	Bro N	43	122	21	30	2	1	0	16	3	1	—	.246	.270	.279	49	-9	3	.963	2	110	47	P41/S	—	0.1
1900	Bro N	10	26	2	6	0	0	0	1	1	0	—	.231	.259	.231	34	-1	0	.960	1	139	0	P10	—	0.0
	Phi N	10	33	3	10	1	0	0	5	0	0	—	.303	.303	.333	76	1	1	.920	-1	90	0	P10	—	0.0
	Year	20	59	5	16	1	0	0	6	1	0	—	.271	.283	.288	56	1	1	.940	0	112	0	P20	—	0.0
1901	Phi N	2	1	1	1	0	0	0	0	1	0	—	1.000	1.000	1.000	471	1	0	1.000	-0	79	0	P2	—	0.0
	Bal A	96	362	41	90	9	4	0	36	21	6	—	.249	.301	.296	63	-18	10	.872	-12	88	61	3b67,S19,P9/2cf	—	-2.5
1902	NY N	100	342	26	72	11	1	0	14	20	1	—	.211	.256	.249	56	-18	13	.962	-5	90	178	O43(0/3/40),S36,3b18,P3,2b2	—	-2.3
1903	NY N	78	257	35	62	15	1	0	37	15	3	—	.241	.291	.307	68	-11	12	.907	-3	94	207	S27,3b25,2b19/lf	—	-1.2
1904	NY N	64	181	27	56	12	2	1	19	11	2	—	.309	.356	.414	132	7	11	.914	-4	97	296	3b28,S10,2b9,O7(3/4/0)/P	—	0.4
Total	8	490	1622	197	397	54	10	1	164	83	14	—	.245	.287	.292	66	-71	55	.890	-25	91	114	3b143,P142,S98,O59R,2b35	—	-6.2
Dunn, Joe	Joseph Edward; B3.11.1885 Springfield OH; D3.19.1944 Springfield OH; BR/TR/5´9˝/160; d9.12																								
1908	Bro N	20	64	3	11	3	0	0	5	0	0	—	.172	.172	.219	26	-6	0	.957	4	*92*	*149*	C20	—	0.0
1909	Bro N	10	25	1	4	1	0	0	2	0	1	—	.160	.192	.200	23	-2	0	.952	-1	*89*	*75*	C7	—	-0.3
Total	2	30	89	4	15	4	0	0	7	0	1	—	.169	.178	.213	25	-8	0	.956	3	*91*	*131*	C27	—	-0.3
Dunn, Ron	Ronald Ray; B1.24.1950 Oklahoma City OK; BR/TR/5´11˝/(175–180); [BalA68 5/94]; d9.3																								
1974	Chi N	23	68	6	20	7	0	2	15	12-3	0	8	.294	.400	.485	141	4	0-0	.917	-6	86	57	2b21,3b6	0	-0.1
1975	Chi N	32	44	2	7	3	0	1	6	6-0	0	17	.159	.250	.295	51	-3	0-0	.957	-1	105	0	3b11,O2L/2	0	-0.4
Total	2	55	112	8	27	10	0	3	21	18-3	0	25	.241	.341	.411	106	1	0-0	.918	-7	86	56	2b22,3b17,O2L	0	-0.5
Dunn, Steve	Stephen B.; B12.21.1858 London ON, Can.; D5.5.1933 London ON, Can.; BL/5´9.5˝/173; d9.27																								
1884	StP U	**9**	32	2	8	2	0	0	—	0	—	—	.250	.250	.313	128	0	—	.972	1	241	70	1b9/3	—	0.1
Dunn, Steve	Steven Robert; B4.18.1970 Champaign IL; BL/TL/6´4˝/(219–225); [MinA88 4/103]; d5.3																								
1994	Min A	14	35	2	8	5	0	0	4	1-0	0	12	.229	.250	.371	57	-2	0-0	.990	1	134	134	1b12	0	-0.2
1995	Min A	5	6	0	0	0	0	0	0	1-0	0	3	.000	.143	.000	-58	-1	0-0	1.000	-0	0	322	1b3	0	-0.2
Total	2	19	41	2	8	5	0	0	4	2-0	0	15	.195	.233	.317	40	-3	0-0	.990	1	125	147	1b15	0	-0.4
Dunn, Todd	Todd Kent; B7.29.1970 Tulsa OK; BR/TR/6´5˝/220; [MilA93 1/35]; d9.8; Col North Florida; [DL 1998 Mil N 69]																								
1996	Mil A	6	10	2	3	1	0	0	1	0-0	0	3	.300	.300	.400	72	0	0-0	1.000	-0	105	0	O6(1/1/4)	0	-0.1
1997	Mil A	44	118	17	27	5	0	3	9	2-0	0	39	.229	.242	.347	51	-9	3-0	.909	-0	108	87	O27(19/2/7),D14	0	-1.0
Total	2	50	128	19	30	6	0	3	10	2-0	0	42	.234	.246	.352	52	-9	3-0	.920	-1	108	76	O33(20/3/11),D14	69	-1.1
Dunston, Shawon	Shawon Donnell; B3.21.1963 Brooklyn NY; BR/TR/6´1˝/(175–180); [ChiN82 1/1]; d4.9; OF(107/75/70)																								
1985	Chi N	74	250	40	65	12	4	4	18	19-3	0	42	.260	.310	.388	86	-5	11-3	.958	18	116	92	S73	0	2.2
1986	Chi N	150	581	66	145	37	3	17	68	21-5	3	114	.250	.278	.411	82	-16	13-11	.961	21	**104**	104	S149	0	2.1
1987	Chi N	95	346	40	85	18	3	5	22	10-1	1	68	.246	.267	.358	62	-20	12-3	.969	4	99	93	S94	66	-0.5
1988	Chi N☆	155	575	69	143	23	6	9	56	16-8	2	108	.249	.271	.357	75	-20	30-9	.973	14	106	90	S151	0	0.8
1989	†Chi N	138	471	52	131	20	6	9	60	30-15	1	86	.278	.320	.403	99	-1	19-11	.972	5	102	114	S138	0	1.5
1990	Chi N★	146	545	73	143	22	8	17	66	15-1	3	87	.262	.283	.426	87	-12	25-5	.970	-1	99	95	S144	0	0.2
1991	Chi N	142	492	59	128	22	7	12	50	23-5	4	64	.260	.292	.407	92	-7	21-6	.968	-0	98	100	S142	0	0.6
1992	Chi N	18	73	8	23	3	1	0	2	3-0	0	13	.315	.342	.384	102	0	2-3	.986	-2	90	101	S18	153	-0.1
1993	Chi N	7	10	3	4	2	0	0	2	0-0	0	1	.400	.400	.600	165	1	0-0	1.000	-0	0	0	S2	149	0.1
1994	Chi N	88	331	38	92	19	0	11	35	16-3	2	48	.278	.313	.435	93	-4	3-8	.966	-7	94	98	S84	0	-0.7
1995	Chi N	127	477	58	141	30	6	14	69	10-3	6	75	.296	.317	.472	105	1	10-5	.969	-8	97	73	S125	0	0.2
1996	SF N	82	287	27	86	12	2	5	25	13-0	1	40	.300	.331	.408	96	-3	8-0	.957	-1	99	108	S78	75	0.3
1997	Chi N	114	419	57	119	18	4	9	41	8-0	3	64	.284	.300	.411	82	-13	29-7	.970	-16	82	81	S108,O7L	15	-1.8
	Pit N	18	71	14	28	4	1	5	16	0-0	0	11	.394	.389	.690	174	7	3-1	.965	2	109	74	S18	0	1.0
	Year	132	490	71	147	22	5	14	57	8-0	3	75	.300	.312	.451	95	-6	32-8	.969	-15	86	80	S126,O7L	0	-0.8
1998	Cle A	62	156	26	37	11	3	3	12	6-0	1	18	.237	.265	.404	70	-8	9-2	.978	-3	100	76	2b24,S14,O12(11/1/0),D7	0	-0.7
	SF N	36	51	10	9	2	0	3	8	0-0	3	10	.176	.222	.392	60	-3	0-2	.938	-4	32	0	S9,O6C/2	0	-0.7
1999	StL N	62	150	23	46	5	2	5	25	2-0	3	23	.307	.327	.467	97	-2	6-3	1.000	-0	103	100	O23(9/11/4),1b8,S7,3b5,D2	16	-0.2
	†NY N	42	93	12	32	6	1	0	16	0-0	2	16	.344	.354	.430	103	0	4-1	.978	1	102	97	O27(9/16/5)/3	0	0.1
	Year	104	243	35	78	11	3	5	41	2-0	5	39	.321	.337	.453	99	-1	10-4	.988	0	102	98	O50(18/27/9),1b8,S7,3b6,D2	0	-0.1
2000	†StL N	98	216	28	54	11	2	12	43	6-0	3	47	.250	.278	.486	87	-6	3-1	.989	1	115	44	O58(41/9/13),S8,1b6,3b5/D	0	-0.6
2001	SF N	88	186	26	52	10	3	9	25	2-0	2	32	.280	.293	.511	109	1	3-1	.966	2	102	178	O60(12/23/26)/1D	15	0.2
2002	†SF N	72	147	7	34	5	0	1	9	3-0	1	33	.231	.250	.286	43	-13	1-0	1.000	-4	79	0	O49(18/9/22)/1SD	38	-1.8
Total	18	1814	5927	736	1597	292	62	150	668	203-44	41	1000	.269	.296	.416	88	-123	212-82	.967	21	99	95	S1363,O242L,2b25,1b16,D14,3b11	527	2.2
Dunwoody, Todd	Todd Franklin; B4.11.1975 Lafayette IN; BL/TL/6´1˝/(195–210); [FlaN93 7/211]; d5.10																								
1997	Fla N	19	50	7	13	2	2	2	7	7-0	1	21	.260	.362	.500	129	2	2-0	.929	-1	101	0	O14(6/8/0)	0	0.1
1998	Fla N	116	434	53	109	27	7	5	28	21-0	4	113	.251	.292	.380	80	-15	5-1	.989	7	113	141	O111C	0	-0.5
1999	Fla N	64	186	20	41	6	3	2	20	12-0	1	41	.220	.270	.317	51	-15	3-4	.981	-3	89	110	O55(8/44/5)	0	-1.8
2000	KC A	61	178	12	37	9	0	1	23	8-0	1	42	.208	.238	.275	30	-19	3-0	.976	-2	101	0	O40(14/19/9),D11	60	-2.0
2001	Chi N	33	61	6	13	4	0	1	3	3-0	0	14	.213	.250	.328	49	-5	0-1	.973	1	120	112	O26(15/6/7)	0	-0.4
2002	Cle A	2	6	0	0	0	0	0	0	0-0	0	3	.000	.000	.000	-98	-2	0-0	1.000	-1	32	0	O2(1/0/1)	38	-0.2
Total	6	295	915	98	213	48	12	11	81	51-0	7	234	.233	.277	.348	63	-54	13-6	.982	3	105	100	O248(44/188/22),D11	98	-4.8
Duran, Dan	Daniel James; B3.16.1954 Palo Alto CA; BL/TL/5´11˝/190; [TexA73 30/646]; d4.17; Col Foothill (CA) JC																								
1981	Tex A	13	16	1	4	0	0	0	0	1-0	0	1	.250	.294	.250	61	-1	0-0	1.000	0	65	335	O7L/1	0	-0.1
Durant, Mike	Michael Joseph; B9.14.1969 Columbus OH; BR/TR/6´2˝/200; [MinA91 2/47]; d4.3; Col Ohio St.																								
1996	Min A	40	81	15	17	3	0	0	5	10-0	0	15	.210	.293	.247	39	-8	3-0	.975	5	151	81	C37	0	0.0

YEAR	TM LG	G	AB	R	H	2B	3B	HR	RBI	BB-IB	HP	SO	AVG	OBP	SLG	AOPS	ABR	SB-CS	FA	FR	RNG	THR	GAMES AT POSITION	DL	BFW
Durazo, Erubiel	Erubiel (Cardenas); B1.23.1974 Hermosillo, Sonora, Mexico; BL/TL/6´3˝/(225–240); d7.26; Col Pima (AZ) CC																								
1999	†Ari N	52	155	31	51	4	2	11	30	26-1	1	43	.329	.422	.594	154	13	1-1	1.000	-1	83	84	1b44	0	0.8
2000	Ari N	67	196	35	52	11	0	8	33	34-2	1	43	.265	.373	.444	102	2	1-0	.989	-4	70	90	1b60	81	-0.6
2001	†Ari N	92	175	34	47	11	0	12	38	28-1	2	49	.269	.372	.537	124	7	0-0	.993	1	94	105	1b38,O2R,D7	17	0.5
2002	†Ari N	76	222	46	58	12	2	16	48	49-2	2	60	.261	.395	.550	133	12	0-1	.984	-3	79	73	1b56,O2R,D6	73	0.4
2003	†Oak A	154	537	92	139	29	0	21	77	100-12	2	105	.259	.374	.430	112	13	1-1	.981	-5	46	103	D121,1b33	0	-0.1
2004	Oak A	142	511	80	164	35	1	22	88	56-9	9	104	.321	.396	.523	138	31	3-2	.882	-1	79	114	D132,1b4	0	2.2
2005	Oak A	41	152	15	36	6	1	4	16	14-0	1	24	.237	.305	.368	79	-5	1-0	1.000	-0	0	277	D39/1	131	-0.7
Total	7	624	1948	333	547	108	6	94	330	307-27	18	428	.281	.381	.487	122	73	7-5	.988	-12	74	90	D305,1b236,O4R	302	2.5
Durbin, Kid	Blaine Alphonsus; B9.10.1886 Lamar MO; D9.11.1943 Kirkwood MO; BL/TL/5´8˝/155; d4.24; ▲																								
1907	Chi N	11	18	2	6	0	0	0	0	1	0	—	.333	.368	.333	113	0	0	1.000	1	106	0	P5,O5(1/0/4)	—	0.1
1908	Chi N	14	28	3	7	1	0	0	0	2	1	—	.250	.323	.286	91	0	0	1.000	-1	0	0	O11C	—	-0.1
1909	Cin N	6	5	1	1	0	0	0	0	1	0	—	.200	.333	.200	66	0	0	ø	0	—	—	/H	—	0.0
	Pit N	1	0	0	0	0	0	0	0	0	0	—	ø	ø	ø	ø	0	0	ø	0	—	—	/R	—	0.0
	Year	7	5	1	1	0	0	0	0	1	0	—	.200	.333	.200	65	0	0	ø	0	—	—	—	—	0.0
Total	3	32	51	6	14	1	0	0	0	4	1	—	.275	.339	.294	96	0	0	1.000	1	151	0	O16(1/11/4),P5	—	0.0
Durham, Joe	Joseph Vann "Pop"; B7.31.1931 Newport News VA; BR/TR/6´1˝/(186–192); d9.10; Mil 1955–56; Negro Lg 1952; Col Shaw																								
1954	Bal A	10	40	4	9	0	0	1	3	4	0	7	.225	.295	.300	68	-2	0-0	.917	-1	90	0	O10(10/1/0)	0	-0.4
1957	Bal A	77	157	19	29	2	0	4	17	16-1	0	42	.185	.259	.274	49	-12	1-1	1.000	-4	82	37	O59(36/5/25)	0	-1.9
1959	StL N	6	5	2	0	0	0	0	0	0-0	0	1	.000	.000	.000	-94	-1	0-0	1.000	0	119	0	/rf	0	-0.1
Total	3	93	202	25	38	2	0	5	20	20-1	0	50	.188	.260	.272	49	-15	1-1	.979	-5	84	29	O70(46/6/26)	0	-2.4
Durham, Leon	Leon; B7.31.1957 Cincinnati OH; BL/TL/6´2˝/(185–215); [StLN76 1/15]; d5.27																								
1980	StL N	96	303	42	82	15	4	8	42	18-1	1	55	.271	.309	.426	100	-1	8-5	.987	10	103	255	O78(35/2/43),1b8	0	0.5
1981	Chi N	87	328	42	95	14	6	10	35	27-6	0	53	.290	.344	.460	119	7	25-11	.970	-3	100	58	O83R,1b3	68	0.2
1982	Chi N☆	148	539	84	168	33	7	22	90	66-14	2	77	.312	.388	.521	147	35	28-14	.963	-3	98	116	O143(0/74/89)/1	0	2.9
1983	Chi N★	100	337	58	87	18	8	12	55	66-12	3	83	.258	.381	.466	128	15	12-6	.966	-11	82	34	O95(51/40/4),1b6	15	0.2
1984	†Chi N	137	473	86	132	30	4	23	96	69-11	1	86	.279	.369	.505	133	22	16-8	.994	3	107	96	1b130	18	1.9
1985	Chi N	153	542	58	153	32	2	21	75	64-**24**	0	99	.282	.357	.465	117	13	7-6	.995	3	106	98	1b151	0	0.7
1986	Chi N	141	484	66	127	18	7	20	65	67-16	1	98	.262	.350	.452	112	8	8-7	.995	-7	80	90	1b141	0	-0.9
1987	Chi N	131	439	70	120	22	1	27	63	51-9	0	92	.273	.348	.513	120	12	2-2	.990	-10	68	92	1b123	0	-0.6
1988	Chi N	24	73	10	16	6	1	3	6	9-2	0	20	.219	.305	.452	109	1	0-1	.995	1	110	114	1b20	21	0.0
	Cin N	21	51	4	11	3	0	1	2	5-1	0	12	.216	.286	.333	75	-2	0-0	.993	-1	69	86	1b17	67	-0.4
	Year	45	124	14	27	9	1	4	8	14-3	0	32	.218	.297	.403	95	-1	0-1	.994	-0	93	102	1b37	0	-0.4
1989	StL N	29	18	2	1	1	0	0	1	2-0	1	4	.056	.182	.111	-11	-3	0-1	.961	0	145	209	1b18	23	-0.3
Total	10	1067	3587	522	992	192	40	147	530	444-96	9	679	.277	.356	.475	122	107	106-61	.994	-19	93	95	1b618,O399(86/116/219)	212	4.2
Durham, Ray	Ray; B11.30.1971 Charlotte NC; BB/TR/5´8˝/(170–195); [ChiA90 5/132]; d4.26																								
1995	Chi A	125	471	68	121	27	6	7	51	31-2	6	83	.257	.309	.384	83	-13	18-5	.973	-22	86	78	2b122/D	0	-2.5
1996	Chi A	156	557	79	153	33	5	10	65	58-4	10	95	.275	.350	.406	95	-3	30-4	.984	-21	96	84	2b150,D3	0	-1.1
1997	Chi A	155	634	106	172	27	5	11	53	61-0	6	96	.271	.337	.382	91	-8	33-16	.974	-29	91	77	2b153/D	0	-2.7
1998	Chi A★	158	635	126	181	35	8	19	67	73-3	6	105	.285	.363	.455	113	13	36-9	.976	1	103	**128**	2b158	0	2.5
1999	Chi A	153	612	109	181	30	8	13	60	73-1	4	105	.296	.373	.435	104	5	34-11	.974	-6	98	97	2b148,D4	0	0.9
2000	†Chi A★	151	614	121	172	35	9	17	75	75-0	7	105	.280	.361	.450	101	2	25-13	.980	4	99	**122**	2b151	0	1.2
2001	Chi A	152	611	104	163	42	10	20	65	64-3	4	110	.267	.337	.466	103	3	23-10	.986	6	107	94	2b150/D	0	1.6
2002	Chi A	96	345	71	103	20	2	9	48	49-0	5	59	.299	.390	.446	118	11	20-5	.968	6	103	107	2b92	0	2.3
	†Oak A	54	219	43	60	14	4	6	22	24-1	2	34	.274	.350	.457	113	4	6-2	.967	3	121	175	D43,2b11	0	0.6
	Year	150	564	114	163	34	6	15	70	73-1	7	93	.289	.374	.450	116	15	26-7	.968	9	105	115	2b103,D43	0	2.9
2003	†SF N	110	410	61	117	30	5	8	33	50-2	3	82	.285	.366	.441	108	6	7-7	.990	3	108	103	2b105	40	1.3
2004	SF N	120	471	95	133	28	8	17	65	57-3	6	60	.282	.364	.484	114	10	10-4	.972	-4	100	103	2b118	38	1.2
2005	SF N	142	497	67	144	33	0	12	62	48-2	7	59	.290	.356	.429	103	4	6-3	.982	-19	94	93	2b133/cf	0	-0.8
2006	SF N	137	498	79	146	30	7	26	93	51-6	2	61	.293	.360	.538	126	18	7-2	.982	-16	92	94	2b133	15	0.9
Total	12	1709	6574	1129	1846	384	77	175	759	714-27	68	1054	.281	.354	.443	105	52	255-91	.978	-95	98	99	2b1624,D53/cf	93	5.4
Durnbaugh, Bobby	Robert Eugene "Scroggy"; B1.15.1933 Dayton OH; BR/TR/5´8˝/170; d9.22																								
1957	Cin N	2	1	0	0	0	0	0	0	0-0	0	0	.000	.000	.000	-93	0	0-0	.500	-1	60	0	S2	0	-0.1
Durning, George	George Dewey; B5.9.1898 Philadelphia PA; D4.18.1986 Tampa FL; BR/TR/5´11˝/175; d9.12																								
1925	Phi N	5	14	3	5	0	0	0	1	2	0	1	.357	.438	.357	97	0	0-0	1.000	2	121	315	O4R	—	0.1
Durocher, Leo	Leo Ernest "The Lip"; B7.27.1905 W.Springfield MA; D10.7.1991 Palm Springs CA; BR/TR (BB 1928–29)/5´10˝/160; d10.2; M24/C4; HF1994																								
1925	NY A	2	1	1	0	0	0	0	0	0	0	0	.000	.000	.000	-99	0	0-0	ø	0	—	—	/H	—	0.0
1928	†NY A	102	296	46	80	8	6	0	31	22	3	52	.270	.327	.338	77	-10	1-4	.948	5	108	106	2b66,S29	—	-0.2
1929	NY A	106	341	53	84	4	5	0	32	34	3	33	.246	.320	.287	62	-20	3-1	.958	20	111	114	S93,2b12	—	1.0
1930	Cin N	119	354	31	86	15	3	3	32	20	2	45	.243	.287	.328	51	-29	0	.959	11	107	111	S103,2b13	—	-0.7
1931	Cin N	121	361	26	82	11	5	1	29	18	0	32	.227	.264	.294	53	-26	0	.965	0	102	**121**	S120	—	-1.8
1932	Cin N	143	457	43	99	22	5	1	33	36	1	40	.217	.275	.293	55	-29	3	.960	-12	97	99	S142	—	-3.1
1933	Cin N	16	51	6	11	1	0	1	3	4	0	5	.216	.273	.294	63	-3	0	.953	3	115	95	S16	—	0.1
	StL N	123	395	45	102	18	4	2	41	26	1	32	.258	.306	.339	80	-10	3	.961	-5	93	86	S123	—	-0.7
	Year	139	446	51	113	19	4	3	44	30	1	37	.253	.302	.334	78	-13	3	**.960**	-3	96	87	S139	—	-0.6
1934	†StL N	146	500	62	130	26	5	3	70	33	2	40	.260	.308	.350	71	-20	2	.957	-4	90	111	S146	—	-1.3
1935	StL N	143	513	62	136	23	5	8	78	29	0	46	.265	.304	.376	79	-16	4	.963	6	99	113	S142	—	0.0
1936	StL N★	136	510	57	146	22	3	1	58	29	2	47	.286	.327	.347	82	-13	3	**.971**	-11	92	92	S136	—	-1.4
1937	StL N	135	477	46	97	11	3	1	47	38	0	36	.203	.262	.245	38	-42	6	.959	-14	92	90	S134	—	-4.6
1938	Bro N★	141	479	41	105	18	5	1	56	47	3	30	.219	.293	.284	58	-27	3	**.966**	-3	95	105	S141	—	-2.1
1939	Bro N	116	390	42	108	21	6	1	34	27	1	24	.277	.325	.369	83	-9	2	.957	-11	93	110	S113/3M	—	-1.3
1940	Bro N☆	62	160	10	37	9	1	1	14	12	0	13	.231	.285	.319	62	-8	1	.959	-3	92	91	S53,2b4,M	—	-0.8
1941	Bro N	18	42	2	12	1	0	0	6	1	0	3	.286	.302	.310	70	-2	0	.917	-0	110	70	S12/2M	0	-0.1
1943	Bro N	6	18	1	4	0	0	0	1	1	0	2	.222	.263	.222	41	-1	0	1.000	1	62	141	S6,M	0	-0.1
1945	Bro N	2	5	1	1	0	0	0	2	0	0	0	.200	.200	.200	11	-1	0	1.000	0	119	156	2b2,M	0	0.0
Total	17	1637	5350	575	1320	210	56	24	567	377	18	480	.247	.299	.320	66	-266	31-5	.961	-15	97	103	S1509,2b98/3	0	-17.1
Durrett, Red	Elmer Cable; B2.3.1921 Sherman TX; D1.17.1992 Waxahachie TX; BL/TL/5´10˝/170; d9.14																								
1944	Bro N	11	32	3	5	1	0	1	1	7	0	10	.156	.308	.281	68	-1	0	.933	1	124	111	O9(0/5/4)	0	-0.1
1945	Bro N	8	16	2	2	0	0	0	0	3	0	3	.125	.263	.125	10	-2	0	1.000	-0	93	0	O4C	0	-0.2
Total	2	19	48	5	7	1	0	1	1	10	0	13	.146	.293	.229	48	-3	0	.947	1	116	82	O13(0/9/4)	0	-0.3
Durrington, Trent	Trent John; B8.27.1975 Sydney, New South Wales, Australia; BR/TR/5´10˝/(172–198); d8.6																								
1999	Ana A	43	122	14	22	2	0	0	2	9-0	0	28	.180	.237	.197	12	-17	4-3	.966	-4	96	80	2b41	0	-1.8
2000	Ana A	4	3	0	0	0	0	0	0	0-0	0	0	.000	.000	.000	-97	-1	0-0	1.000	-1	67	0	/2	0	-0.2
2003	Ana A	12	14	5	2	0	0	0	1	3-0	0	0	.143	.294	.143	22	-2	1-1	1.000	-2	70	0	2b5,3b4/lfD	0	-0.3
2004	Mil N	53	82	13	19	2	3	2	4	4-0	0	23	.232	.267	.402	69	-4	4-0	.789	-2	82	0	3b11,2b6/PD	0	-0.6
2005	Mil N	28	14	3	3	1	0	0	2	1-0	0	3	.214	.267	.286	45	-1	5-2	.000	-1	0	0	/3	0	-0.2
Total	5	140	235	35	46	5	3	2	9	17-0	0	54	.196	.250	.268	33	-25	14-6	.971	-10	94	69	2b53,3b16,D3/Plf	0	-3.1
Durst, Cedric	Cedric Montgomery; B8.23.1896 Austin TX; D2.16.1971 San Diego CA; BL/TL/5´11˝/160; d5.30																								
1922	StL A	15	12	5	4	1	0	0	0	0	0	1	.333	.333	.417	91	0	0-0	.857	-0	133	0	O6(1/4/1)	—	0.0
1923	StL A	45	85	11	18	2	0	5	11	8	0	14	.212	.280	.412	76	-4	0-0	1.000	-2	98	0	O10(4/5/1),1b8	—	-0.7
1926	StL A	80	219	32	52	7	5	3	16	22	1	19	.237	.310	.356	70	-11	0-5	.980	2	108	90	O57(5/42/10),1b4	—	-1.3
1927	†NY A	65	129	18	32	4	3	0	25	6	0	7	.248	.281	.326	59	-9	0-3	.980	-1	95	41	O36(13/6/17),1b2	—	-1.2
1928	†NY A	74	135	18	34	2	1	2	10	7	0	9	.252	.289	.326	63	-8	1-0	.983	1	105	79	O33(13/5/15),1b3	—	-0.9
1929	NY A	92	202	32	52	3	3	4	31	15	0	25	.257	.309	.361	77	-8	3-2	.987	6	128	89	O72(46/6/20)/1	—	-0.6
1930	NY A	8	19	0	3	1	0	0	5	0	0	1	.158	.158	.211	-8	-3	0-0	1.000	0	128	0	O6L	—	-0.3

YEAR	TM LG	G	AB	R	H	2B	3B	HR	RBI	BB-IB	HP	SO	AVG	OBP	SLG	AOPS	ABR	SB-CS	FA	FR	RNG	THR	GAMES AT POSITION	DL	BFW
	Bos A	102	302	29	74	19	5	1	24	17	2	24	.245	.290	.351	64	-17	3-1	.968	-2	98	65	O75(46/0/29)	—	-2.3
	Year	110	321	29	77	20	5	1	29	17	2	25	.240	.282	.343	60	-20	3-1	.970	-2	100	61	O81(52/0/29)	—	-2.6
Total	7	481	1103	145	269	39	17	15	122	75	3	100	.244	.294	.351	67	-60	7-11	.979	4	108	71	O295(134/68/93),1b18	—	-7.3
DUSAK, ERV	Ervin Frank "Four Sack"; B7.29.1920 Chicago IL; D11.6.1994 Glendale Heights IL; BR/TR/6´2˝/(183–185); d9.18; Mil 1943–45; OF(105/106/67); ▲																								
1941	StL N	6	14	1	2	0	0	0	3	2	0	6	.143	.250	.143	12	-2	1	1.000	1	152	0	O4(1/2/1)	0	-0.1
1942	StL N	12	27	4	5	3	0	0	3	3	0	7	.185	.267	.296	60	-1	0	1.000	1	124	0	O8(5/0/3)/3	0	0.0
1946	†StL N	100	275	38	66	9	1	9	42	33	0	63	.240	.321	.378	94	-3	7	.993	7	100	203	O77(72/5/0),3b11,2b2	0	-0.1
1947	StL N	111	328	56	93	7	3	6	28	50	0	34	.284	.378	.378	97	0	1	.970	4	95	195	O89(22/28/47),3b7	0	0.0
1948	StL N	114	311	60	65	9	2	6	19	49	0	55	.209	.317	.309	66	-14	3	.992	-2	94	76	O68(2/55/12),2b29,3b9/PS	0	-1.6
1949	StL N	1	0	1	0	0	0	0	0	0	0	0	ø	ø	ø	ø	0	0	ø	0	—	—	/R	0	0.0
1950	StL N	23	12	0	1	1	0	0	0	0	0	3	.083	.083	.167	-34	-2	0	1.000	1	108	211	P14,O2C	0	0.0
1951	StL N	5	2	1	1	0	0	1	1	0	0	1	.500	.500	2.000	537	1	0-0	1.000	0	169	0	P5	0	0.0
	Pit N	21	39	6	12	3	0	1	7	3	0	11	.308	.357	.462	115	1	0-0	1.000	-3	70	0	O12(1/10/1),P3,2b2,3b2	70	-0.2
	Year	26	41	7	13	3	0	2	8	3	0	12	.317	.364	.537	136	2	0-0	1.000	-3	70	0	O12(1/10/1),P8,2b2,3b2	0	-0.2
1952	Pit N	20	27	1	6	0	0	1	3	2	0	8	.222	.276	.333	66	-1	0-0	.818	0	65	453	O11(2/4/3)	0	-0.1
Total	9	413	1035	168	251	32	6	24	106	142	0	188	.243	.334	.355	84	-21	12-0	.981	9	97	159	O271C,2b33,3b30,P23/S	70	-2.1
DWIGHT, AL	Albert Ward; B1.4.1856 New York NY; D2.20.1903 San Francisco CA; d6.19																								
1884	KC U	12	43	8	10	2	0	0	—	2	—	—	.233	.267	.279	75	-2	—	.953	0	—	—	C10/cf2	—	-0.2
DWYER, JIM	James Edward "Pig Pen"; B1.3.1950 Evergreen Park IL; BL/TL/5´10˝/(165–195); [StLN71 11/253]; d6.10; Col Southern Illinois																								
1973	StL N	28	57	7	11	1	1	0	0	1-0	0	5	.193	.207	.246	25	-6	0-0	1.000	-1	97	0	O20(9/10/1)	0	-0.8
1974	StL N	74	86	13	24	1	0	2	11	11-2	1	16	.279	.360	.360	104	1	0-0	1.000	1	102	103	O25(8/1/16),1b3	0	0.1
1975	StL N	21	31	4	6	1	0	0	1	4-0	0	6	.194	.286	.226	41	-2	0-0	1.000	1	126	0	O9(5/3/2)	0	-0.2
	Mon N	60	175	22	50	7	1	3	20	23-0	0	30	.286	.365	.389	105	2	4-1	.959	1	90	214	O52(46/3/3)	0	0.1
	Year	81	206	26	56	8	1	3	21	27-0	0	36	.272	.353	.364	95	-1	4-1	.966	2	94	188	O61(51/6/5)	0	-0.1
1976	Mon N	50	92	7	17	3	1	0	5	11-1	0	10	.185	.269	.239	44	-7	0-0	.970	-1	92	0	O19(15/0/5)	0	-1.0
	NY N	11	13	2	2	0	0	0	0	2-1	0	1	.154	.267	.154	23	-1	0-0	1.000	0	107	0	O2R	0	-0.2
	Year	61	105	9	19	3	1	0	5	13-2	0	11	.181	.269	.229	42	-8	0-0	.972	-1	93	0	O21(15/0/7)	0	-1.2
1977	StL N	13	31	3	7	1	0	0	2	4-0	2	5	.226	.351	.258	67	-1	0-0	1.000	-1	89	0	O12(3/0/10)	0	-0.3
1978	StL N	34	65	8	14	3	0	1	4	9-1	1	3	.215	.320	.308	76	-2	1-0	.952	-3	59	73	O22(18/0/5)	0	-0.5
	SF N	73	173	22	39	9	2	5	22	28-3	0	29	.225	.327	.387	104	1	6-0	.987	3	98	330	O36(3/26/9),1b29	0	0.4
	Year	107	238	30	53	12	2	6	26	37-4	1	32	.223	.325	.366	96	0	7-0	.979	0	84	235	O58(21/26/14),1b29	0	-0.1
1979	Bos A	76	113	19	30	7	0	2	14	17-1	1	9	.265	.361	.381	96	0	3-1	.981	1	128	111	1b25,O19(6/1/12),D4	0	0.0
1980	Bos A	93	260	41	74	11	1	9	38	28-5	2	23	.285	.357	.438	111	4	3-2	.975	-0	83	170	O65(11/29/27),D12,1b9	0	0.2
1981	Bal A	68	134	16	30	0	1	3	10	20-0	0	19	.224	.318	.306	83	-3	0-2	.977	-0	105	75	O59(43/2/19),1b3/D	0	-0.6
1982	Bal A	71	148	28	45	4	3	6	15	27-4	0	24	.304	.407	.493	148	11	2-0	.976	-3	100	0	O49(16/0/37)/1D	0	0.7
1983	†Bal A	100	196	37	56	17	1	8	38	31-3	0	29	.286	.382	.505	144	13	1-1	.966	-1	111	35	O56(7/0/49),D10,1b4	0	1.0
1984	Bal A	76	161	22	41	9	1	2	21	23-0	0	24	.255	.337	.360	98	0	0-2	.966	0	99	119	O52(1/0/51),D3	41	-0.2
1985	Bal A	101	233	35	58	8	3	7	36	37-2	1	31	.249	.353	.399	108	3	0-3	.993	3	109	105	O78(46/0/33),D3	0	0.2
1986	Bal A	94	160	18	39	13	1	8	31	23-1	2	31	.244	.339	.488	125	6	0-2	1.000	3	110	300	O24(8/0/16),D24/1	0	0.7
1987	Bal A	92	241	54	66	7	1	15	33	37-4	1	57	.274	.371	.498	131	11	4-1	1.000	-0	104	51	D41,O30(3/0/29)	0	0.8
1988	Bal A	35	53	3	12	0	0	0	3	12-3	0	11	.226	.364	.226	73	-1	0-0	1.000	0	240	0	D17,O2(1/0/1)	50	-0.1
	Min A	20	41	6	12	1	0	2	15	13-1	1	8	.293	.464	.463	158	4	0-0	ø	0	0	0	D13	0	0.4
	Year	55	94	9	24	1	0	2	18	25-4	1	19	.255	.410	.330	112	3	0-0	1.000	0	240	0	D30,O2(1/0/1)	0	0.3
1989	Min A	88	225	34	71	11	0	3	23	28-1	0	23	.316	.390	.404	117	6	2-0	ø	-0	0	0	D74/rf	0	0.4
	Mon N	13	10	1	3	1	0	0	2	1-0	0	1	.300	.364	.400	116	0	0-0	ø	0	—	—	/H	0	0.0
1990	Min A	37	63	7	12	0	0	1	5	12-1	0	7	.190	.320	.238	55	-4	0-0	1.000	0	279	0	D23,O2(1/0/1)	0	-0.4
Total	18	1328	2761	409	719	115	17	77	349	402-34	12	402	.260	.353	.398	107	35	26-15	.979	3	99	113	O634(250/75/329),D226,1b75	91	0.7
DWYER, JOHN	John E.; d5.16																								
1882	Cle N	1	3	0	0	0	0	0	1	0	—	0	.000	.000	.000	-99	-1	—	ø	-1	0	0	/lfC	—	-0.1
DWYER, DOUBLE JOE	Joseph Michael; B3.27.1903 Orange NJ; D10.21.1992 Glen Ridge NJ; BL/TL/5´9˝/186; d4.20																								
1937	Cin N	12	11	2	3	0	0	0	1	1	0	0	.273	.333	.273	70	0	0	ø	0	—	—	/H	—	0.0
DYBZINSKI, JERRY	Jerome Matthew; B7.7.1955 Cleveland OH; BR/TR/6´2˝/(180–186); [CleA77 15/375]; d4.11; Col Cleveland St.																								
1980	Cle A	114	248	32	57	11	1	1	23	13-0	2	35	.230	.273	.294	55	-15	4-1	.971	14	110	93	S73,2b29,3b4,D2	0	0.6
1981	Cle A	48	57	10	17	0	0	0	6	5-0	0	8	.298	.355	.298	90	-1	7-1	.970	2	104	73	S34,2b3,3b3/D	0	0.5
1982	Cle A	80	212	19	49	6	2	0	22	21-0	3	25	.231	.305	.278	63	-11	3-5	.957	16	117	95	S77,3b3	0	1.1
1983	†Chi A	127	256	30	59	10	1	1	32	18-0	2	29	.230	.283	.289	56	-15	11-4	.966	-2	93	96	S118,3b9	0	-0.7
1984	Chi A	94	132	17	31	5	1	1	10	13-0	2	12	.235	.311	.311	70	-5	7-2	.974	6	114	121	S76,3b14/2D	0	0.7
1985	Pit N	5	4	0	0	0	0	0	0	0-0	0	0	.000	.000	.000	-99	-1	0-0	.900	0	118	0	S5	0	-0.1
Total	6	468	909	108	213	32	5	3	93	70-0	9	109	.234	.293	.290	61	-48	32-13	.966	36	107	97	S383,3b33,2b33,D4	0	2.1
DYCK, JIM	James Robert; B2.3.1922 Omaha NE; D1.11.1999 Cheney WA; BR/TR/6´2˝/(190–205); d9.27																								
1951	StL A	4	15	1	1	0	0	0	0	1	0	1	.067	.125	.067	-46	-3	0-0	1.000	0	80	107	3b4	0	-0.3
1952	StL A	122	402	60	108	22	3	15	64	50	3	68	.269	.354	.450	119	10	0-4	.962	7	110	91	3b74,O48(39/8/2)	0	1.3
1953	StL A	112	334	38	71	15	1	9	27	38	3	40	.213	.299	.344	72	-14	3-2	.981	-1	105	148	O55(32/19/8),3b51	0	-1.7
1954	Cle A	2	1	0	1	0	0	0	1	1	0	0	1.000	1.000	1.000	441	1	0-0	ø	0	—	—	/H	0	0.1
1955	Bal A	61	197	32	55	13	1	2	22	28-1	1	21	.279	.372	.386	112	4	1-0	.989	-0	100	116	O45L,3b17	0	0.2
1956	Bal A	11	23	3	5	2	0	0	0	10-0	0	5	.217	.455	.304	112	2	0-0	.923	1	77	410	O9L	0	0.2
	Cin N	18	11	5	1	0	0	0	0	3-0	0	5	.091	.286	.091	7	-1	0-0	1.000	-0	0	0	/13	0	-0.1
Total	6	330	983	139	242	52	5	26	114	131-1	7	140	.246	.339	.389	98	-1	4-6	.982	6	104	121	O157(125/27/10),3b147/1	0	-0.3
DYE, JERMAINE	Jermaine Terrell; B1.28.1974 Oakland CA; BR/TR/6´4˝/(210–235); [AtlN93 17/488]; d5.17; Col Cosumnes River (CA) JC																								
1996	†Atl N	98	292	32	82	16	0	12	37	8-0	3	67	.281	.304	.459	93	-4	1-4	.950	-0	110	43	O92(25/4/71)	0	-0.8
1997	KC A	75	263	26	62	14	0	7	22	17-0	1	51	.236	.284	.369	67	-13	2-1	.966	6	111	152	O75(1/0/75)	57	-1.0
1998	KC A	60	214	24	50	5	1	5	23	11-2	1	46	.234	.270	.336	55	-15	2-2	.987	7	128	93	O59R	65	-1.0
1999	KC A	158	608	96	179	44	8	27	119	58-4	1	119	.294	.354	.526	117	14	2-3	.984	14	113	151	O157R/D	0	1.9
2000	KC A★	157	601	107	193	41	2	33	118	69-6	3	99	.321	.390	.561	130	29	0-1	.976	-3	95	108	O146R,D10	0	1.6
2001	KC A	97	367	50	100	14	0	13	47	30-3	6	68	.272	.333	.417	88	-6	7-1	.984	-3	96	79	O93(0/2/92),D4	0	-1.2
	†Oak A	61	232	41	69	17	1	13	59	27-3	1	44	.297	.366	.547	138	13	2-0	.972	-2	80	174	O61R	0	0.8
	Year	158	599	91	169	31	1	26	106	57-6	7	112	.282	.346	.467	106	6	9-1	.979	-6	90	117	O154(0/2/153),D4	0	-0.4
2002	†Oak A	131	488	74	123	27	1	24	86	52-2	10	108	.252	.333	.459	109	7	2-0	.972	-14	77	29	O111R,D19	26	-1.3
2003	†Oak A	65	221	28	38	6	0	4	20	25-2	3	42	.172	.261	.253	38	-20	1-0	1.000	-4	88	30	O61(1/3/60),D3	91	-2.6
2004	Oak A	137	532	87	141	29	4	23	80	49-4	4	128	.265	.329	.464	105	3	4-2	.992	-10	89	32	O134R,D2	0	-1.2
2005	†Chi A	145	529	74	145	29	2	31	86	39-3	9	99	.274	.333	.512	116	11	11-4	.971	-6	90	107	O140R/1SD	0	0.0
2006	Chi A★	146	539	103	170	27	3	44	120	59-4	6	118	.315	.385	.622	152	41	7-3	.981	-1	105	55	O146R	0	3.1
Total	11	1330	4886	742	1352	269	22	236	817	444-33	48	989	.277	.339	.486	109	60	41-21	.979	-15	98	87	O1275(27/9/1252),D40/S1	239	-1.7
DYER, BEN	Benjamin Franklin; B2.13.1893 Chicago IL; D8.7.1959 Kenosha WI; BR/TR/5´11˝/170; d5.23; Mil 1918																								
1914	NY N	7	4	1	1	0	0	0	0	0	0	1	.250	.250	.250	50	0	1	1.000	0	142	331	S6/2	—	0.0
1915	NY N	7	19	4	4	0	1	0	0	4	1	3	.211	.375	.316	117	1	0	.889	-1	93	0	3b6/S	—	0.0
1916	Det A	4	14	4	4	1	0	0	1	1	0	1	.286	.333	.357	104	0	0	1.000	-1	80	0	S4	—	-0.1
1917	Det A	30	67	6	14	5	0	0	0	2	0	17	.209	.232	.284	57	-4	3	.846	-1	95	106	S14,3b8	—	-0.4
1918	Det A	13	18	1	5	0	0	0	2	0	0	6	.278	.278	.278	71	-1	0	1.000	1	185	0	P2,1b2,O2(1/0/1)/2	—	0.0
1919	Det A	44	85	11	21	4	0	0	15	8	0	19	.247	.312	.294	72	-3	0	.953	1	110	0	3b23,S11/rf	—	-0.1
Total	6	105	207	27	49	10	1	0	18	15	1	47	.237	.291	.295	74	-7	4	.937	-0	110	0	3b37,S36,O3(1/0/2),1b2,P2,2b2	—	-0.6
DYER, DUFFY	Don Robert; B8.15.1945 Dayton OH; BR/TR/6´0˝/(190–200); [NYN66 S1/9]; d9.21; C11; Col Arizona St.																								
1968	NY N	1	3	0	1	0	0	0	0	1-0	0	1	.333	.500	.333	153	0	0-0	1.000	0	0	0	/C	0	0.1
1969	†NY N	29	74	5	19	3	1	3	12	4-0	0	22	.257	.295	.446	102	0	0-0	.991	-2	97	58	C19	0	-0.2
1970	NY N	59	148	8	31	1	0	2	12	21-4	0	32	.209	.308	.257	52	-10	1-1	.991	1	96	140	C57	0	-0.7
1971	NY N	59	169	13	39	7	1	2	18	14-4	1	45	.231	.292	.320	74	-6	1-0	.992	-2	80	105	C53	0	-0.6

YEAR	TM LG	G	AB	R	H	2B	3B	HR	RBI	BB-IB	HP	SO	AVG	OBP	SLG	AOPS	ABR	SB-CS	FA	FR	RNG	THR	GAMES AT POSITION	DL	BFW
1972	NY N	94	325	33	75	17	3	8	36	28-9	5	71	.231	.299	.375	93	-3	0-1	.993	18	123	**144**	C91/rf	0	1.9
1973	NY N	70	189	9	35	6	1	1	9	13-1	2	40	.185	.245	.243	36	-17	0-1	.994	-2	109	117	C60	0	-1.7
1974	NY N	63	142	14	30	1	1	0	10	18-2	1	15	.211	.302	.232	52	-9	0-0	.982	-7	87	96	C45	0	-1.5
1975	†Pit N	48	132	8	30	5	2	3	16	6-0	1	22	.227	.266	.364	73	-6	0-0	.990	5	194	100	C36	0	0.1
1976	Pit N	69	184	12	41	8	0	3	9	29-10	3	35	.223	.336	.315	85	-2	0-0	.994	6	120	125	C58	0	0.7
1977	Pit N	94	270	27	65	11	1	3	19	54-11	3	49	.241	.370	.322	85	-3	6-0	**.996**	0	100	98	C93	0	0.3
1978	Pit N	58	175	7	37	8	1	0	13	18-3	3	32	.211	.294	.269	56	-10	2-1	.991	-1	72	96	C55	17	-0.8
1979	Mon N	28	74	4	18	6	0	1	8	9-4	0	17	.243	.325	.365	88	-1	0-0	.993	4	79	115	C27	0	0.4
1980	Det A	48	108	11	20	1	0	4	11	13-1	0	34	.185	.273	.306	57	-7	0-0	.986	-4	71	44	C37,D10	0	-1.0
1981	Det A	2	0	0	0	0	0	0	0	0-0	0	0	ø	ø	ø	ø	0	0-0	ø	-0	0	0	C2	0	0.0
Total	14	722	1993	151	441	74	11	30	173	228-49	19	415	.221	.306	.315	72	-74	10-4	.992	15	104	110	C634,D10/rf	17	-3.0
Dyer, Eddie	Edwin Hawley; B10.11.1899 Morgan City LA; D4.20.1964 Houston TX; BL/TL/5´11.5˝/168; d7.8; M5; Col Rice; ▲																								
1922	StL N	6	3	1	1	1	0	0	0	0	0	0	.333	.333	.667	159	1	0-0	1.000	0	0	0	P2	—	0.0
1923	StL N	35	45	17	12	3	0	2	5	3	0	5	.267	.313	.467	105	0	1-0	1.000	-0	114	0	O8(7/2/0),P4	—	0.0
1924	StL N	50	76	8	18	2	3	0	8	3	0	8	.237	.266	.342	63	-5	1-0	.909	1	119	57	P29/cf	—	0.0
1925	StL N	31	31	4	3	1	0	0	0	3	0	1	.097	.176	.129	-20	-2	1-1	.917	0	114	85	P27	—	0.0
1926	StL N	6	2	1	1	0	0	0	0	0	0	0	.500	.500	.500	164	0	0	1.000	0	134	0	P6	—	0.0
1927	StL N	1	0	0	0	0	0	0	0	1	0	0	ø	1.000	ø	181	0	0	ø	-0	0	0	/P	—	0.0
Total	6	129	157	31	35	7	3	2	13	10	0	14	.223	.269	.344	61	-6	3-1	.921	1	112	58	P69,O9(7/3/0)	—	0.0
Dykes, Jimmy	James Joseph; B11.10.1896 Philadelphia PA; D6.15.1976 Philadelphia PA; BR/TR/5´9˝/185; d5.6; Mil 1918; M21/C10; OF(2/4/1)																								
1918	Phi A	59	186	13	35	3	3	0	13	19	1	32	.188	.267	.237	51	-11	3	.940	9	111	127	2b56/3	—	-0.2
1919	Phi A	17	49	4	9	1	0	0	1	7	0	11	.184	.286	.204	38	-4	0	.945	3	129	73	2b16	—	0.0
1920	Phi A	142	546	81	140	25	4	8	35	55	9	73	.256	.334	.361	83	-13	6-9	.957	16	**110**	71	2b108,3b34	—	0.4
1921	Phi A	**155**	613	88	168	32	13	16	77	60	15	75	.274	.353	.447	102	1	6-5	.954	21	109	104	2b155	—	2.4
1922	Phi A	145	501	66	138	23	7	12	68	55	10	98	.275	.359	.421	100	0	6-2	.945	-5	96	75	3b141,2b5	—	0.4
1923	Phi A	124	416	50	105	28	1	4	43	35	5	40	.252	.318	.353	76	-15	6-4	.964	2	106	95	2b102,S20,3b2	—	-0.8
1924	Phi A	110	410	68	128	26	6	3	50	38	1	60	.312	.372	.427	105	3	1-3	.961	10	109	103	2b77,3b27,S4	—	1.5
1925	Phi A	122	465	93	150	32	11	5	55	46	8	49	.323	.393	.471	111	8	3-2	.944	6	94	62	3b64,2b58,S2	—	1.8
1926	Phi A	124	429	54	123	32	5	1	44	49	8	34	.287	.370	.392	94	-2	6-2	.950	16	107	128	3b82,2b44/S	—	2.0
1927	Phi A	121	417	61	135	33	6	3	60	44	4	23	.324	.394	.453	113	9	2-3	.989	-3	90	100	1b82,3b25,S5,O5(0/4/1),2b3,P2	—	0.2
1928	Phi A	85	242	39	67	11	0	5	30	27	5	21	.277	.361	.384	93	-1	2-1	.982	-2	95	92	2b32,S22,3b20,1b8/lf	—	0.0
1929	†Phi A	119	401	76	131	34	6	13	79	51	**7**	25	.327	.412	.539	138	24	8-3	.928	-17	80	79	S60,3b48,2b12	—	1.7
1930	†Phi A	125	435	69	131	28	4	6	73	74	**10**	53	.301	.414	.425	109	10	3-3	.960	-13	82	90	3b123/lf	—	0.4
1931	†Phi A	101	355	48	97	28	2	3	46	49	6	47	.273	.371	.389	94	-1	1-2	.974	-2	93	149	3b87,S15	—	0.1
1932	Phi A	153	558	71	148	29	5	7	90	77	4	65	.265	.358	.373	87	-9	8-2	**.980**	-9	89	89	3b141,S10/2	—	-1.1
1933	Chi A★	**151**	554	49	144	22	6	1	68	69	**12**	37	.260	.354	.327	85	-9	3-7	.953	-1	**109**	83	3b151	—	-0.6
1934	Chi A☆	127	456	52	122	17	4	7	82	64	4	28	.268	.363	.368	86	-8	1-1	.944	-5	113	59	3b74,1b27,2b27,M	—	-1.0
1935	Chi A	117	403	45	116	24	2	4	61	59	2	28	.288	.381	.387	97	0	4-3	.953	-6	96	96	3b98,1b16,2b3,M	—	-0.4
1936	Chi A	127	435	62	116	16	3	7	60	61	4	36	.267	.362	.366	77	-15	1-3	.951	-6	104	71	3b125,M	—	-1.6
1937	Chi A	30	85	10	26	5	0	1	23	9	0	7	.306	.372	.400	95	0	0-0	.993	0	65	108	1b15,3b11,M	—	-0.1
1938	Chi A	26	89	9	27	4	2	2	13	10	0	8	.303	.374	.461	105	1	0-0	.941	-3	92	76	2b23/S3M	—	-0.1
1939	Chi A	2	1	0	0	0	0	0	0	0	0	0	.000	.000	.000	-97	0	0-0	.667	-0	0	0	3b2,M	—	-0.1
Total	22	2282	8046	1108	2256	453	90	108	1071	958	115	850	.280	.365	.399	96	-32	70-55	.952	11	98	95	3b1257,2b722,1b148,S140,O7C,P2	—	4.9
Dykstra, Lenny	Leonard Kyle "Nails"; B2.10.1963 Santa Ana CA; BL/TL/5´10˝/(160–195); [NYN81 13/315]; d5.3; [DL 1997 Phi N 181, 1998 Phi N 181]																								
1985	NY N	83	236	40	60	9	3	1	19	30-0	1	24	.254	.338	.331	90	-2	15-2	.994	6	114	167	O74C	0	0.6
1986	†NY N	147	431	77	127	27	7	8	45	58-1	0	55	.295	.377	.445	129	18	31-7	.990	4	110	125	O139(1/138/0)	0	2.7
1987	NY N	132	431	86	123	37	3	10	43	40-3	4	67	.285	.352	.455	116	11	27-7	.988	-1	103	73	O118C	0	1.2
1988	†NY N	126	429	57	116	19	3	8	33	30-2	3	43	.270	.321	.385	106	3	30-8	.996	5	**114**	71	O112C	0	1.2
1989	NY N	56	159	27	43	12	1	3	13	23-0	2	15	.270	.362	.415	129	7	13-1	.984	2	118	46	O51C	0	1.2
	Phi N	90	352	39	78	20	3	4	19	37-1	1	38	.222	.297	.330	79	-9	17-11	.991	2	98	207	O88C	0	-0.9
	Year	146	511	66	121	32	4	7	32	60-1	3	53	.237	.318	.356	95	-2	30-12	.988	4	105	152	O139C	0	0.3
1990	Phi N★	149	590	106	**192**	35	3	9	60	89-14	7	48	.325	**.418**	.441	137	36	33-5	.987	7	**113**	84	O149C	0	4.8
1991	Phi N	63	246	48	73	13	5	3	12	37-1	1	20	.297	.391	.427	131	12	24-4	.977	1	111	87	O63C	111	1.7
1992	Phi N	85	345	53	104	18	0	6	39	40-4	3	32	.301	.375	.406	122	12	30-5	.989	6	113	123	O85C	83	2.3
1993	†Phi N	161	637	**143**	**194**	44	6	19	66	**129**-9	2	64	.305	.420	.482	144	48	37-12	.979	4	113	24	O160C	0	5.6
1994	Phi N✳	84	315	68	86	26	5	5	24	68-11	2	44	.273	.404	.435	117	12	15-4	.984	4	114	88	O82C	35	1.9
1995	Phi N★	62	254	37	67	15	1	2	18	33-2	3	28	.264	.353	.354	88	-3	10-5	.987	1	109	59	O61(9/52/0)	86	-0.1
1996	Phi N	40	134	21	35	6	3	3	13	26-2	2	25	.261	.387	.418	112	3	3-1	1.000	6	127	170	O39C	134	0.9
Total	12	1278	4559	802	1298	281	43	81	404	640-50	31	503	.285	.375	.419	119	148	285-72	.987	46	111	94	O1221(10/1213/0)	811	23.1
Dyler, John	John F.; B6.5.1852 Louisville KY; D8.15.1916 Fort Myers FL; d7.22; U1																								
1882	Lou AA	1	4	0	0	0	0	0	—	0	—	—	.000	.000	.000	-99	-1	—	ø	-0	0	0	/lf	—	-0.1
Eaddy, Don	Donald Johnson; B2.16.1934 Grand Rapids MI; BR/TR/5´11˝/170; d4.24; Col Michigan																								
1959	Chi N	15	1	3	0	0	0	0	0	0-0	0	1	.000	.000	.000	-99	0	0-0	.500	-0	114	0	/3	0	-0.1
Eagan, Truck	Charles Eugene; B8.10.1877 San Francisco CA; D3.19.1949 San Francisco CA; BR/TR/5´11˝/190; d5.1																								
1901	Pit N	4	12	0	1	0	0	0	2	0	0	—	.083	.083	.083	-50	-2	1	.923	-1	105	0	S3	—	-0.3
	Cle A	5	18	2	3	0	1	0	2	1	0	—	.167	.211	.278	36	-2	0	1.000	1	139	0	2b5/3	—	-0.1
Total	1	9	30	2	4	0	1	0	4	1	0	—	.133	.161	.200	2	-4	1	1.000	0	139	0	2b5,S3/3	—	-0.4
Eagan, Bill	William "Bad Bill"; B6.1.1869 Camden NJ; D2.13.1905 Denver CO; d4.8																								
1891	StL AA	82	297	49	65	11	4	4	43	44	3	53	.219	.326	.323	75	-11	21	.929	18	116	93	2b82	—	0.8
1893	Chi N	6	19	3	5	0	0	0	2	5	0	5	.263	.417	.263	83	0	4	.912	0	106	144	2b6	—	0.0
1898	Pit N	19	61	14	20	2	3	0	5	8	6	—	.328	.453	.459	165	6	1	.914	1	106	147	2b17	—	0.7
Total	3	107	377	66	90	13	7	4	50	57	9	58	.239	.352	.342	88	-5	26	.926	19	114	105	2b105	—	1.5
Eagle, Bill	William Lycurgus; B7.25.1877 Rockville MD; D4.27.1951 Churchton MD; d8.20																								
1898	Was N	4	13	0	4	1	0	0	2	0	0	—	.308	.308	.385	98	0	0	.750	-0	281	0	O4(1/0/1)	—	0.0
Eakle, Charlie	Charles Emory; B9.27.1887 MD; D6.15.1959 Baltimore MD; d8.20																								
1915	Bal F	2	7	0	2	1	0	0	0	0	0	0	.286	.286	.429	97	0	1	.600	-2	47	0	2b2	—	-0.2
Earl, Howard	Howard J. "Slim Jim"; B2.27.1869 MA; D12.22.1916 North Bay NY; 6´2˝/180; d4.19																								
1890	Chi N	92	384	57	95	10	3	7	51	18	2	47	.247	.285	.344	80	-13	17	.861	-6	107	71	O49R,2b39,S4,1b3	—	-1.5
1891	Mil AA	31	129	21	32	5	2	1	17	5	1	13	.248	.281	.341	65	-7	3	.978	-2	38	98	O30R,1b2	—	-0.8
Total	2	123	513	78	127	15	5	8	68	23	3	60	.248	.284	.343	76	-20	20	.904	-7	79	82	O79R,2b39,1b5,S4	—	-2.3
Earl, Scott	William Scott; B9.18.1960 Seymour IN; BR/TR/5´11˝/165; [DetA81 14/354]; d9.10; Col Eastern Kentucky																								
1984	Det A	14	35	3	4	0	1	0	1	0-0	0	9	.114	.114	.171	-22	-6	1-0	.959	0	85	166	2b14	0	-0.5
Earle, Billy	William Moffat "The Little Globetrotter"; B11.10.1867 Philadelphia PA; D5.30.1946 Omaha NE; BR/TR/5´10.5˝/170; d4.27																								
1889	Cin AA	53	169	37	45	4	7	4	31	30	3	24	.266	.386	.444	132	7	26	.776	-4	133	175	O26(2/1/23),C23,1b5	—	0.3
1890	StL AA	22	73	16	17	3	1	0	12	7	2	—	.233	.317	.301	72	-3	6	.955	3	*100*	*105*	C18,O3R/S32	—	0.1
1892	Pit N	5	13	5	7	2	0	0	3	4	0	1	.538	.647	.692	304	4	2	.909	-0	*108*	*106*	C5	—	0.4
1893	Pit N	27	95	21	24	4	4	2	15	7	0	6	.253	.304	.442	99	-1	1	.959	0	*98*	*71*	C27	—	0.1
1894	Lou N	21	65	10	23	1	0	0	7	9	0	3	.354	.432	.369	102	1	2	.954	3	*98*	*169*	C18/123lf	—	0.4
	Bro N	14	50	13	17	6	0	0	6	6	1	2	.340	.421	.460	121	2	4	.930	-2	*90*	*139*	C12/2	—	0.1
	Year	35	115	23	40	7	0	0	13	15	1	5	.348	.427	.409	110	4	6	.944	1	*95*	*157*	C30,2b2/13lf	—	0.5
Total	5	142	465	102	133	20	12	6	74	63	6	36	.286	.378	.419	114	10	41	.929	-1	*98*	*113*	C103,O30(3/1/26),1b6,2b3,3b2/S	—	1.4

EARLY, JAKE Jacob Willard; B5.19.1915 Kings Mountain NC; D5.31.1985 Melbourne FL; BL/TR/5´11˝/168; d5.4; Mil 1944–45

YEAR	TM LG	G	AB	R	H	2B	3B	HR	RBI	BB-IB	HP	SO	AVG	OBP	SLG	AOPS	ABR	SB-CS	FA	FR	RNG	THR	GAMES AT POSITION	DL	BFW
1939	Was A	32	84	8	22	7	2	0	14	5	0	14	.262	.303	.393	83	-3	0-0	.963	-1	*165*	*50*	C24	—	-0.2
1940	Was A	80	206	26	53	8	4	5	14	23	1	22	.257	.335	.408	98	-1	0-1	.969	2	*88*	*135*	C56	—	0.3
1941	Was A	104	355	42	102	20	7	10	54	24	3	38	.287	.338	.468	117	6	0-1	.965	-10	*93*	*114*	C100	0	0.2
1942	Was A	104	353	31	72	14	2	3	46	37	1	37	.204	.281	.280	59	-20	0-0	.981	-4	*94*	***133***	C98	0	-1.8
1943	Was A★	126	423	37	109	23	3	5	60	53	4	43	.258	.346	.362	111	7	5-3	.980	-4	*113*	*94*	C122	0	1.1
1946	Was A	64	189	13	38	6	0	4	18	23	0	27	.201	.288	.296	67	-9	0-0	.960	-2	*96*	*146*	C64	0	-0.7
1947	StL A	87	214	25	48	9	3	3	19	54	0	34	.224	.381	.336	98	2	0-1	.989	-5	*73*	*125*	C85	0	0.1
1948	Was A	97	246	22	54	7	2	1	28	36	1	33	.220	.322	.276	62	-13	2-1	.991	1	*115*	***185***	C92	0	-0.7
1949	Was A	53	138	12	34	4	0	1	11	26	1	11	.246	.370	.297	79	-3	0-1	.973	-5	*82*	*101*	C53	0	-0.6
Total	9	747	2208	216	532	98	23	32	264	281	11	259	.241	.330	.350	89	-34	7-8	.976	-28	*99*	*124*	C694	0	-2.3

EASLER, MIKE Michael Anthony; B11.29.1950 Cleveland OH; BL/TR/6´1˝/(190–196); [HouN69 14/312]; d9.5; C6

YEAR	TM LG	G	AB	R	H	2B	3B	HR	RBI	BB-IB	HP	SO	AVG	OBP	SLG	AOPS	ABR	SB-CS	FA	FR	RNG	THR	GAMES AT POSITION	DL	BFW
1973	Hou N	6	7	1	0	0	0	0	0	2-1	0	4	.000	.222	.000	-34	-1	0-0	.500	-1	27	0	O2(1/0/1)	0	-0.2
1974	Hou N	15	15	0	1	0	0	0	0	0-0	0	5	.067	.067	.067	-66	-3	0-0	ø	0	—	—	/H	0	-0.4
1975	Hou N	5	5	0	0	0	0	0	0	0-0	0	1	.000	.000	.000	-99	-1	0-0	ø	0	—	—	/H	0	-0.2
1976	Cal A	21	54	6	13	1	1	0	4	2-1	0	11	.241	.259	.296	69	-2	1-1	ø	0	0	0	D16	0	-0.3
1977	Pit N	10	18	3	8	2	0	1	5	0-0	0	1	.444	.421	.722	200	2	0-0	1.000	-0	103	0	O4(1/0/3)	0	0.2
1979	†Pit N	55	54	8	15	1	1	2	11	8-0	0	13	.278	.371	.444	115	1	0-1	ø	-1	0	0	O4(2/0/2)	0	0.0
1980	Pit N	132	393	66	133	27	3	21	74	43-6	0	65	.338	.396	.583	166	35	5-9	.986	-1	100	74	O119(91/0/42)	0	2.9
1981	Pit N★	95	339	43	97	18	5	7	42	24-7	0	45	.286	.328	.431	110	4	4-7	.980	6	104	163	O90(72/0/25)	0	0.5
1982	Pit N	142	475	52	131	27	2	15	58	40-12	6	85	.276	.337	.436	110	7	1-1	.973	-1	98	78	O138(137/0/3)	0	0.0
1983	Pit N	115	381	44	117	17	2	10	54	22-1	3	64	.307	.349	.441	114	7	4-2	.965	-5	88	84	O105L	22	-0.2
1984	Bos A	156	601	87	188	31	5	27	91	58-4	4	134	.313	.376	.516	137	31	1-1	.976	3	138	82	D126,1b29	0	2.8
1985	Bos A	155	568	71	149	29	4	16	74	53-1	3	129	.262	.325	.412	97	-2	0-1	.914	-2	88	0	D130,O20(18/0/2)	0	-0.9
1986	NY A	146	490	64	148	26	2	14	78	49-13	0	87	.302	.362	.449	121	15	3-2	.958	0	122	0	D129,O11(8/0/3)	0	1.0
1987	Phi N	33	110	7	31	4	0	1	10	6-0	0	20	.282	.316	.345	73	-4	0-1	.981	2	101	222	O30L	15	-0.4
	NY A	65	167	13	47	6	0	4	21	14-0	1	32	.281	.337	.389	94	-1	1-0	1.000	-1	89	106	D32,O15(14/0/1)	0	-0.3
Total	14	1151	3677	465	1078	189	25	118	522	321-46	17	696	.293	.349	.454	117	88	20-26	.974	0	97	97	O538(479/0/82),D433,1b29	37	4.5

EASLEY, DAMION Jacinto Damion; B11.11.1969 New York NY; BR/TR/5´11˝/(155–190); [CalA88 30/767]; d8.13; Col Long Beach (CA) City; OF(0/2/6)

YEAR	TM LG	G	AB	R	H	2B	3B	HR	RBI	BB-IB	HP	SO	AVG	OBP	SLG	AOPS	ABR	SB-CS	FA	FR	RNG	THR	GAMES AT POSITION	DL	BFW
1992	Cal A	47	151	14	39	5	0	1	12	8-0	3	26	.258	.307	.311	73	-5	9-5	.970	5	108	175	3b45,S3	0	0.0
1993	Cal A	73	230	33	72	13	2	2	22	28-2	3	35	.313	.392	.413	114	6	6-6	.978	-11	88	74	2b54,3b14/D	83	-0.3
1994	Cal A	88	316	41	68	16	1	6	30	29-0	4	48	.215	.288	.329	58	-20	4-5	.953	-4	92	54	3b47,2b40	18	-2.2
1995	Cal A	114	357	35	77	14	2	4	35	32-1	6	47	.216	.288	.300	55	-24	5-2	.981	-8	93	79	2b88,S25	0	-2.5
1996	Cal A	28	45	4	7	1	0	2	7	6-0	0	12	.156	.255	.311	42	-4	0-0	.943	-1	103	182	S13,2b9,3b3,O2C,D2	39	-0.4
	Det A	21	67	10	23	1	0	2	10	4-0	1	13	.343	.384	.448	111	1	3-1	.974	1	111	67	2b8,S8,3b2/D	0	0.2
	Year	49	112	14	30	2	0	4	17	10-0	1	25	.268	.331	.393	82	-3	3-1	.951	-0	103	154	S21,2b17,3b5,D3,O2C	0	-0.2
1997	Det A	151	527	97	139	37	3	22	72	68-3	16	102	.264	.362	.471	116	15	28-13	.981	-9	102	100	2b137,S21,D4	0	1.4
1998	Det A★	153	594	84	161	38	2	27	100	39-2	16	112	.271	.332	.478	106	4	15-5	**.985**	**26**	**113**	118	2b140,S30,D2	0	3.7
1999	Det A	151	549	83	146	30	1	20	65	51-2	19	124	.266	.346	.434	97	-2	11-3	.989	7	99	115	2b147,S19	0	1.2
2000	Det A	126	464	76	120	27	2	14	58	55-1	11	79	.259	.350	.416	94	-3	13-4	**.990**	11	110	118	2b125	37	1.3
2001	Det A	154	585	77	146	27	7	11	65	52-3	13	90	.250	.323	.376	86	-12	10-5	.982	13	**112**	106	2b153	0	0.8
2002	Det A	85	304	29	68	14	1	8	30	27-3	11	43	.224	.307	.355	79	-9	1-3	.980	4	108	93	2b84	45	-0.1
2003	TB A	36	107	8	20	3	1	1	7	2-0	0	18	.187	.202	.262	21	-13	0-0	.922	-5	91	51	3b23,2b4,D8	0	-1.7
2004	Fla N	98	223	26	53	20	1	9	43	24-1	8	36	.238	.331	.457	107	3	4-1	.965	-1	104	101	2b25,1b18,S15,3b6,O5R,D3	0	0.2
2005	Fla N	102	267	37	64	19	1	9	30	26-3	4	47	.240	.312	.419	96	-2	4-1	.978	4	95	102	2b46,S30,3b10	0	0.7
2006	Ari N	90	189	24	44	6	1	9	28	21-0	5	30	.233	.323	.418	84	-5	1-1	.976	-7	89	62	S27,3b20,2b9,1b3/rfD	0	-1.0
Total	15	1517	4975	678	1247	271	25	147	614	472-21	120	862	.251	.328	.404	90	-70	114-55	.984	24	104	105	2b1069,S191,3b170,D22,1b21,O8R	222	1.3

EAST, CARL Carlton William; B8.27.1894 Marietta GA; D1.15.1953 Whitesburg GA; BL/TR/6´2˝/178; d8.24

YEAR	TM LG	G	AB	R	H	2B	3B	HR	RBI	BB-IB	HP	SO	AVG	OBP	SLG	AOPS	ABR	SB-CS	FA	FR	RNG	THR	GAMES AT POSITION	DL	BFW
1915	StL A	1	1	0	0	0	0	0	0	0	0	0	.000	.000	.000	-99	0	0	ø	-0	0	0	/P	—	0.0
1924	Was A	2	6	1	2	1	0	0	2	2	0	1	.333	.500	.500	163	1	0-0	.800	-0	107	0	O2R	—	0.0
Total	2	3	7	1	2	1	0	0	2	2	0	1	.286	.444	.429	134	1	0-0	.800	-1	107	0	O2R/P	—	0.0

EAST, HARRY Henry H.; B4.1863 St.Louis MO; D6.12.1905 St.Louis MO; d6.17

YEAR	TM LG	G	AB	R	H	2B	3B	HR	RBI	BB-IB	HP	SO	AVG	OBP	SLG	AOPS	ABR	SB-CS	FA	FR	RNG	THR	GAMES AT POSITION	DL	BFW
1882	Bal AA	1	4	0	0	0	0	0	—	0	—	—	.000	.000	.000	-99	-1	—	.600	-1	88	0	/3	—	-0.1

EASTER, LUKE Luscious Luke; B8.4.1915 Jonestown MS; D3.29.1979 Euclid OH; BL/TR/6´4.5˝/(235–240); d8.11; C1; Negro Lg 1946–48

YEAR	TM LG	G	AB	R	H	2B	3B	HR	RBI	BB-IB	HP	SO	AVG	OBP	SLG	AOPS	ABR	SB-CS	FA	FR	RNG	THR	GAMES AT POSITION	DL	BFW
1949	Cle A	21	45	6	10	3	0	0	2	8	0	6	.222	.340	.289	68	-2	0-1	1.000	-2	61	0	O12R	0	-0.4
1950	Cle A	141	540	96	151	20	4	28	107	70	**10**	95	.280	.373	.487	123	17	0-3	.991	-3	91	94	1b128,O13R	0	0.8
1951	Cle A	128	486	65	131	12	5	27	103	37	9	71	.270	.333	.481	125	13	0-1	.988	-9	75	98	1b125	0	-0.1
1952	Cle A	127	437	63	115	10	3	31	97	44	5	84	.263	.337	.513	144	22	1-1	.983	1	107	91	1b118	0	2.0
1953	Cle A	68	211	26	64	9	0	7	31	15	4	35	.303	.361	.445	120	5	0-2	.981	-2	88	123	1b56	56	0.0
1954	Cle A	6	6	0	1	0	0	0	0	0	0	2	.167	.167	.167	-8	-1	0-0	ø	0	—	—	/H	0	-0.1
Total	6	491	1725	256	472	54	12	93	340	174	28	293	.274	.350	.481	126	54	1-8	.986	-14	90	98	1b427,O25R	56	2.2

EASTERDAY, HENRY Henry P.; B9.16.1864 Philadelphia PA; D3.30.1895 Philadelphia PA; BR/TR/5´6˝/145; d6.23

YEAR	TM LG	G	AB	R	H	2B	3B	HR	RBI	BB-IB	HP	SO	AVG	OBP	SLG	AOPS	ABR	SB-CS	FA	FR	RNG	THR	GAMES AT POSITION	DL	BFW
1884	Phi U	28	115	12	28	5	0	0	—	5	—	—	.243	.275	.287	76	-6	—	.875	7	123	111	S28	—	0.1
1888	KC AA	115	401	42	76	7	6	3	37	31	5	—	.190	.256	.259	62	-18	23	**.888**	26	**125**	92	S115	—	1.0
1889	Col AA	95	324	43	56	5	8	4	34	41	2	57	.173	.270	.275	58	-18	10	.890	15	109	81	S89,2b5/3	—	-0.1
1890	Col AA	58	197	25	31	5	1	1	17	23	1	—	.157	.249	.208	37	-15	5	.879	5	107	133	S58	—	-0.7
	Phi AA	19	68	17	10	1	0	1	3	10	0	—	.147	.256	.206	37	-5	4	.876	-1	97	104	S19	—	-0.5
	Lou AA	7	24	2	2	0	0	0	1	2	1	—	.083	.185	.083	-21	-4	1	.886	0	123	66	S6/3	—	-0.3
	Year	84	289	44	43	6	1	2	21	35	2	—	.149	.245	.197	32	-24	10	.879	5	106	122	S83/3	—	-1.5
Total	4	322	1129	141	203	23	15	9	92	112	9	57	.180	.259	.251	54	-66	43	.885	52	115	98	S315,2b5,3b2	—	-0.5

EASTERLING, PAUL Paul; B9.28.1905 Reidsville GA; D3.15.1993 Reidsville GA; BR/TR/5´11˝/180; d4.11

YEAR	TM LG	G	AB	R	H	2B	3B	HR	RBI	BB-IB	HP	SO	AVG	OBP	SLG	AOPS	ABR	SB-CS	FA	FR	RNG	THR	GAMES AT POSITION	DL	BFW
1928	Det A	43	114	17	37	7	1	3	12	8	1	24	.325	.374	.482	122	3	2-1	.921	-1	101	67	O34(32/0/2)	—	0.0
1930	Det A	29	79	7	16	6	0	1	14	6	0	18	.203	.259	.316	44	-7	0-1	1.000	1	91	216	O25(8/1/16)	—	-0.7
1938	Phi A	4	7	1	2	0	0	0	0	1	0	2	.286	.375	.286	70	0	0-0	.750	-0	81	0	/cf	—	-0.1
Total	3	76	200	25	55	13	1	4	26	15	1	44	.275	.329	.410	88	-4	2-2	.938	-0	97	116	O60(40/2/18)	—	-0.8

EASTERLY, TED Theodore Harrison; B4.20.1885 Lincoln NE; D7.6.1951 Clearlake Highlands CA; BL/TR/5´8˝/165; d4.17

YEAR	TM LG	G	AB	R	H	2B	3B	HR	RBI	BB-IB	HP	SO	AVG	OBP	SLG	AOPS	ABR	SB-CS	FA	FR	RNG	THR	GAMES AT POSITION	DL	BFW
1909	Cle A	98	287	32	75	14	10	1	27	13	0	—	.261	.293	.390	111	2	8	.965	3	*105*	*110*	C76	—	1.3
1910	Cle A	110	363	34	111	16	6	0	55	21	0	—	.306	.344	.383	126	10	10	.964	-9	*82*	*103*	C65,O32R	—	0.7
1911	Cle A	99	287	34	93	19	5	1	37	8	1	—	.324	.345	.436	116	5	6	.910	-6	100	94	O54(0/2/52),C22	—	-0.2
1912	Cle A	65	186	17	55	4	0	2	21	7	2	—	.296	.328	.349	91	-3	3	.958	-1	*91*	*92*	C51	—	0.0
	Chi A	30	55	5	20	2	0	0	14	2	0	—	.364	.386	.400	129	2	2	.964	-2	*87*	*86*	C10/lf	—	0.1
	Year	95	241	22	75	6	0	2	35	9	2	—	.311	.341	.361	100	-1	5	.959	-3	*90*	*91*	C61/lf	—	0.1
1913	Chi A	60	97	3	23	1	0	0	8	4	0	9	.237	.267	.247	51	-6	2	.976	3	*140*	*84*	C19	—	-0.2
1914	KC F	134	436	58	146	20	12	1	67	31	4	25	.335	.384	.443	130	11	10	.969	-16	*92*	*93*	C128	—	0.5
1915	KC F	110	309	32	84	12	5	3	32	21	1	15	.272	.320	.372	99	-7	2	.969	3	*98*	*96*	C88	—	0.4
Total	7	706	2020	215	607	88	38	8	261	107	8	49	.300	.338	.394	112	14	43	.965	-27	*95*	*97*	C459,O87(1/2/84)	—	2.6

EASTERWOOD, ROY Roy Charles "Shag"; B1.12.1915 Waxahachie TX; D8.24.1984 Graham TX; BR/TR/6´0.5˝/196; d4.21

YEAR	TM LG	G	AB	R	H	2B	3B	HR	RBI	BB-IB	HP	SO	AVG	OBP	SLG	AOPS	ABR	SB-CS	FA	FR	RNG	THR	GAMES AT POSITION	DL	BFW
1944	Chi N	17	33	1	7	2	0	1	2	1	0	11	.212	.235	.364	67	-2	0	1.000	-0	*108*	*125*	C12	0	-0.1

EASTON, JOHN John David "Goose"; B3.4.1933 Trenton NJ; D7.28.2001 Princeton NJ; BR/TR/6´2˝/185; d6.19; Col Princeton

YEAR	TM LG	G	AB	R	H	2B	3B	HR	RBI	BB-IB	HP	SO	AVG	OBP	SLG	AOPS	ABR	SB-CS	FA	FR	RNG	THR	GAMES AT POSITION	DL	BFW
1955	Phi N	1	0	0	0	0	0	0	0	0-0	0	0	ø	ø	ø	ø	0	0-0	ø	0	—	—	/R	0	0.0
1959	Phi N	3	3	0	0	0	0	0	0	0-0	0	3	.000	.000	.000	-98	-1	0-0	ø	0	—	—	/H	0	-0.1
Total	2	4	3	0	0	0	0	0	0	0-0	0	3	.000	.000	.000	-98	-1	0-0	ø	0	—	—	0	—	-0.1

YEAR	TM LG	G	AB	R	H	2B	3B	HR	RBI	BB-IB	HP	SO	AVG	OBP	SLG	AOPS	ABR	SB-CS	FA	FR	RNG	THR	GAMES AT POSITION	DL	BFW
EAYRS, EDDIE	Edwin; B11.10.1890 Blackstone MA; D11.30.1969 Warwick RI; BL/TL/5´7˝/160; d6.30; Col Brown; ▲																								
1913	Pit N	4	6	0	1	0	0	0	0	0	0	1	.167	.167	.167	-5	0	0	.667	-0	97	0	P2	—	0.0
1920	Bos N	87	244	31	80	5	2	1	24	30	4	18	.328	.410	.377	133	12	4-3	.950	-3	87	85	O63(43/7/13),P7	—	0.5
1921	Bos N	15	15	0	1	0	0	0	1	0	0	4	.067	.067	.067	-68	-2	0-0	ø	-0	0	0	P2	—	0.0
	Bro N	8	6	1	1	0	0	0	1	2	0	0	.167	.375	.167	47	0	0-0	ø	-0	0	0	/rf	—	0.0
	Year	23	21	1	2	0	0	0	2	2	0	4	.095	.174	.095	-27	-4	0-0	ø	-0	0	0	P2/rf	—	0.0
Total	3	114	271	32	83	5	2	1	26	32	4	23	.306	.388	.351	116	10	4-3	.950	-4	87	85	O64(43/7/14),P11	—	0.5
EBRIGHT, HI	Hiram C. "Buck"; B6.12.1859 Lancaster Co. PA; D10.24.1916 Milwaukee WI; BR/TR/5´9˝/180; d4.24																								
1889	Was N	16	59	7	15	2	2	1	6	3	1	8	.254	.302	.407	102	0	1	.875	3	—	—	C9,O4R,S3	—	0.3
ECHEVARRIA, ANGEL	Angel Santos; B5.25.1971 Bridgeport CT; BR/TR/6´3˝/(214–230); [ColN92 17/487]; d7.15; Col Rutgers																								
1996	Col N	26	21	2	6	0	0	0	6	2-0	1	5	.286	.346	.286	63	-1	0-0	1.000	-1	19	0	O11(4/0/7)	0	-0.2
1997	Col N	15	20	4	5	2	0	0	0	2-0	0	5	.250	.318	.350	61	-1	0-0	1.000	0	58	481	O7(2/2/3)	0	-0.1
1998	Col N	19	29	7	11	3	0	1	9	2-0	2	3	.379	.455	.586	141	2	0-0	1.000	-1	89	116	1b4,O4(3/0/1)	0	0.1
1999	Col N	102	191	28	56	7	0	11	35	17-0	3	34	.293	.360	.503	92	-2	1-3	.985	2	107	151	O49(20/0/31),1b10	0	-0.3
2000	Col N	10	9	0	1	0	0	0	2	0-0	0	2	.111	.111	.111	-36	-2	0-0	1.000	-0	0	262	1b2/lf	0	-0.2
	Mil N	31	42	3	9	2	0	1	4	7-0	0	9	.214	.327	.333	68	-2	0-0	1.000	0	109	119	1b9,O5(2/0/3)	0	-0.2
	Year	41	51	3	10	2	0	1	6	7-0	0	11	.196	.293	.294	47	-4	0-0	1.000	-0	98	134	1b11,O6(3/0/3)	0	-0.4
2001	Mil N	75	133	12	34	11	0	5	13	8-0	3	29	.256	.310	.451	96	-1	0-1	.931	-3	75	0	O23(19/0/5),1b10/D	0	-0.6
2002	Chi N	50	98	14	30	7	0	3	21	8-0	1	17	.306	.351	.469	118	3	0-0	.971	1	138	123	O19(8/0/11),1b13	0	0.3
Total	7	328	543	70	152	32	0	21	90	46-0	10	104	.280	.343	.455	93	-4	1-4	.972	-2	94	125	O119(59/2/61),1b48/D	0	-1.2
ECHOLS, JOHNNY	John Gresham; B1.9.1917 Atlanta GA; D11.13.1972 Atlanta GA; BR/TR/5´10.5˝/175; d5.24																								
1939	StL N	2	0	0	0	0	0	0	0	0	0	0	ø	ø	ø	ø	0	0	ø	0	—	—	/R	—	0.0
ECKHARDT, OX	Oscar George; B12.23.1901 Yorktown TX; D4.22.1951 Yorktown TX; BL/TR/6´1˝/185; d4.16; Col Texas																								
1932	Bos N	8	8	1	2	0	0	0	1	0	0	1	.250	.250	.250	36	-1	0	ø	0	—	—	/H	—	-0.1
1936	Bro N	16	44	5	8	1	0	1	6	5	0	2	.182	.265	.273	45	-3	0	1.000	0	111	87	O10R	—	-0.4
Total	2	24	52	6	10	1	0	1	7	5	0	3	.192	.263	.269	43	-4	0	1.000	0	111	87	O10R	—	-0.5
ECKSTEIN, DAVID	David Mark; B1.20.1975 Sanford FL; BR/TR/5´6.5˝/(165–170); [BosA97 19/581]; d4.3; Col Florida																								
2001	Ana A	153	582	82	166	26	2	4	41	43-0	**21**	60	.285	.355	.357	87	-9	29-4	.971	-12	98	90	S126,2b14,D14	0	-0.7
2002	†Ana A	152	608	107	178	22	6	8	63	45-0	**27**	44	.293	.363	.388	103	4	21-13	.977	-13	96	106	S147,D3	0	0.2
2003	Ana A	120	452	59	114	22	1	3	31	36-0	15	45	.252	.325	.325	76	-14	16-5	.984	-3	94	94	S116,D3	22	-0.7
2004	†Ana A	142	566	92	156	24	1	2	35	42-1	13	49	.276	.339	.332	80	-16	16-5	**.988**	-25	81	90	S138/D	0	-2.7
2005	†StL N★	158	630	90	185	26	7	8	61	58-0	13	44	.294	.363	.395	97	-1	11-8	.981	**33**	**118**	**134**	S156	0	4.2
2006	†StL N★	123	500	68	146	18	1	2	23	31-0	15	41	.292	.350	.344	79	-15	7-6	.989	15	110	121	S120	27	0.8
Total	6	848	3338	498	945	138	18	27	254	255-1	104	283	.283	.351	.359	88	-51	100-41	.982	-5	100	107	S803,D21,2b14	49	1.1
EDEN, CHARLIE	Charles M.; B1.18.1855 Lexington KY; D9.17.1920 Cincinnati OH; BL/TL/?/168; d8.17; ▲																								
1877	Chi N	15	55	9	12	0	1	0	5	3	—	6	.218	.259	.255	56	-3	—	.679	-2	78	229	O15R	—	-0.4
1879	Cle N	81	353	40	96	**31**	7	3	34	6	—	20	.272	.284	.425	131	13	—	.808	-4	118	138	O80(0/1/79),1b3/C	—	0.8
1884	Pit AA	32	122	12	33	7	4	1	—	7	6	—	.270	.341	.418	148	7	—	.759	-4	72	0	O31C,P2	—	0.2
1885	Pit AA	98	405	57	103	18	6	0	38	17	8	—	.254	.298	.328	99	0	—	.814	-16	43	71	O96L,P4,3b2	—	-1.6
Total	4	226	935	118	244	56	18	4	77	33	14	26	.261	.296	.372	115	17	—	.793	-26	77	97	O222(96/32/94),P6,1b3,3b2/C	—	-1.0
EDEN, MIKE	Edward Michael; B5.22.1949 Fort Clayton, Canal Zone; BB/TR/5´10˝/170; d8.2; Col Southern Illinois																								
1976	Atl N	5	8	0	0	0	0	0	1	0-0	0	0	.000	.000	.000	-94	-2	0-0	1.000	0	128	114	2b2	0	-0.2
1978	Chi A	10	17	1	2	0	0	0	0	4-0	0	0	.118	.286	.118	17	-2	0-0	.905	-0	91	136	S5,2b4	0	-0.2
Total	2	15	25	1	2	0	0	0	1	4-0	0	0	.080	.207	.080	-16	-4	0-0	1.000	0	85	141	2b6,S5	0	-0.4
EDINGTON, STUMP	Jacob Frank; B7.4.1891 Koleen IN; D11.11.1969 Bastrop LA; BL/TL/5´8˝/170; d6.20																								
1912	Pit N	15	53	4	16	0	2	0	12	3	0	1	.302	.339	.377	97	-1	0	1.000	1	101	155	O14R	—	0.0
EDLER, DAVE	David Delmar; B8.5.1956 Sioux City IA; BR/TR/6´0˝/(185–190); [SeaA78 21/520]; d9.4; Col Washington St.																								
1980	Sea A	28	89	11	20	1	0	3	9	8-1	0	16	.225	.289	.337	70	-4	2-3	.965	1	107	101	3b28	0	-0.4
1981	Sea A	29	78	7	11	3	0	0	5	11-0	1	13	.141	.250	.179	26	-7	3-3	.884	-4	89	90	3b26/S	0	-1.3
1982	Sea A	40	104	14	29	2	2	2	18	11-1	0	13	.279	.345	.394	100	0	4-2	.922	1	93	78	3b31,O2(1/0/1),D2	0	0.0
1983	Sea A	29	63	2	12	1	1	1	4	5-0	1	11	.190	.257	.286	48	-5	3-3	.875	-3	75	39	3b13,1b5/rfD	0	-0.9
Total	4	126	334	34	72	7	3	6	36	35-2	2	53	.216	.291	.308	65	-16	12-11	.922	-6	94	84	3b98,D8,1b5,O3(1/0/2)/S	0	-2.6
EDMONDS, JIM	James Patrick; B6.27.1970 Fullerton CA; BL/TL/6´1˝/(190–218); [CalA88 7/169]; d9.9																								
1993	Cal A	18	61	5	15	4	1	0	4	2-1	0	16	.246	.270	.344	62	-3	0-2	.981	5	140	354	O17(1/1/15)	0	0.1
1994	Cal A	94	289	35	79	13	1	5	37	30-3	1	72	.273	.343	.377	84	-7	4-2	.981	9	**122**	215	O77(59/5/19),1b22	0	-0.1
1995	Cal A★	141	558	120	162	30	4	33	107	51-4	5	130	.290	.352	.536	129	22	1-4	.998	12	116	119	O139C	0	3.2
1996	Cal A	114	431	73	131	28	3	27	66	46-2	4	101	.304	.375	.571	133	21	4-0	.997	1	104	94	O111C/D	51	2.2
1997	Ana A	133	502	82	146	27	0	26	80	60-5	4	80	.291	.368	.500	124	18	5-7	.985	8	111	159	O115C,1b11,D8	16	2.4
1998	Ana A	154	599	115	184	42	1	25	91	57-7	1	114	.307	.368	.506	122	20	7-5	.988	2	103	109	O153C	0	2.2
1999	Ana A	55	204	34	51	17	2	5	23	28-0	0	45	.250	.339	.426	94	-1	5-4	.992	2	105	144	O42C,1b2,D9	119	0.0
2000	†StL N★	152	525	129	155	25	0	42	108	103-3	6	167	.295	.411	.583	146	40	10-3	.989	3	105	120	O146C,1b6	0	4.2
2001	†StL N	150	500	95	152	38	1	30	110	93-12	4	136	.304	.410	.564	147	39	5-5	.982	-5	93	156	O147C,1b2	0	3.5
2002	†StL N	144	476	96	148	31	2	28	83	86-14	8	134	.311	.420	.561	156	43	4-3	.986	6	107	147	O139C	15	4.9
2003	StL N★	137	447	89	123	32	2	39	89	77-6	4	127	.275	.385	.617	158	39	1-3	.986	13	**116**	178	O129(1/128/0),D2	0	5.1
2004	†StL N	153	498	102	150	38	3	42	111	101-12	5	150	.301	.418	.643	168	55	8-3	.988	-4	91	152	O146C/1D	0	5.1
2005	†StL N★	142	467	88	123	37	1	29	89	91-10	4	139	.263	.385	.533	136	27	5-5	.994	-3	98	86	O139C	0	2.5
2006	†StL N	110	350	52	90	18	0	19	70	53-7	0	101	.257	.350	.471	108	5	4-0	.987	-3	99	89	O99C,1b6	0	0.3
Total	14	1697	5907	1115	1709	380	21	350	1068	878-86	46	1512	.289	.382	.539	134	318	63-46	.989	45	105	135	O1599(61/1510/34),1b50,D21	201	35.6
EDMONDSON, BOB	Robert E.; B4.30.1879 Paris KY; D8.14.1931 Lawrence KS; BR/TR/5´11˝/185; d9.15; ▲																								
1906	Was A	3	3	1	1	0	0	0	0	0	0	—	.333	.333	.333	114	0	0	1.000	0	166	0	P2/rf	—	0.0
1908	Was A	26	80	5	15	4	1	0	2	7	1	—	.188	.261	.262	77	-2	0	.878	-2	75	140	O24(1/9/14)	—	-0.6
Total	2	29	83	6	16	4	1	0	2	7	1	—	.193	.264	.265	78	-2	0	.878	-2	74	139	O25(1/9/15),P2	—	-0.6
EDMONSON, EDDIE	Earl Edward; B11.20.1889 Hopewell PA; D5.10.1971 Leesburg FL; BL/TR/6´0˝/175; d10.4																								
1913	Cle A	2	5	0	0	0	0	0	0	0	0	0	.000	.000	.000	-97	-1	0	1.000	-0	0	0	/1O	—	-0.2
EDWARDS, BRUCE	Charles Bruce "Bull"; B7.15.1923 Quincy IL; D4.25.1975 Sacramento CA; BR/TR/5´7˝/(185–194); d6.23																								
1946	Bro N	92	292	24	78	13	5	1	25	34	2	20	.267	.348	.356	99	0	1	.982	8	***152***	*108*	C91	0	1.3
1947	†Bro N★	130	471	53	139	15	8	9	80	49	2	55	.295	.364	.418	103	2	2	.983	6	*93*	*106*	C128	0	1.4
1948	Bro N	96	286	36	79	17	2	8	54	26	2	28	.276	.341	.434	105	2	4	.984	-3	*138*	*119*	C48,O21L,3b14/1	0	0.0
1949	†Bro N	64	148	24	31	3	0	8	25	25	0	15	.209	.324	.392	87	-3	0	.990	-1	*153*	*101*	C41,O4L/3	0	-0.2
1950	Bro N	50	142	16	26	4	1	8	16	13	1	22	.183	.256	.394	67	-8	1	.980	-2	*128*	*126*	C38,1b2	0	-0.8
1951	Bro N	17	36	6	9	2	0	1	8	1	0	3	.250	.270	.389	74	-1	0-0	1.000	1	*232*	*70*	C9	0	-0.1
	Chi N☆	51	141	19	33	9	2	3	17	16	1	14	.234	.316	.390	87	-2	1-2	.962	-4	*57*	*92*	C28,1b9	0	-0.5
	Year	68	177	25	42	11	2	4	25	17	1	17	.237	.308	.390	85	-4	1-2	.971	-3	*93*	*88*	C37,1b9	0	-0.6
1952	Chi N	50	94	7	23	2	2	1	12	8	0	12	.245	.304	.340	77	-3	0-0	.989	-2	*56*	*69*	C22/2	0	-0.5
1954	Chi N	4	3	1	0	0	0	0	1	2	0	2	.000	.400	.000	15	0	0-0	ø	0	—	—	/H	0	0.0
1955	Was A	30	57	5	10	2	0	0	3	16-0	0	6	.175	.356	.211	58	-2	0-1	.980	3	*112*	*179*	C22,3b5	0	0.1
1956	Cin N	7	5	0	1	0	0	0	0	0-0	0	2	.200	.200	.200	8	-1	0-0	.000	-1	*0*	*0*	C2/23	0	-0.1
Total	10	591	1675	191	429	67	20	39	241	190-0	8	179	.256	.335	.390	93	-16	9-3	.982	3	*118*	*109*	C429,O25L,3b21,1b12,2b2	0	0.6
EDWARDS, DAVE	David Leonard; B2.24.1954 Los Angeles CA; BR/TR/6´0˝/(166–177); [MinA71 7/167]; d9.11; b–Marshall b–Mike																								
1978	Min A	15	44	7	11	3	0	1	3	7-0	2	13	.250	.377	.386	112	1	1-1	.950	3	114	352	O15(10/8/0)	0	0.3
1979	Min A	96	229	42	57	8	0	8	35	24-1	1	45	.249	.323	.389	87	-4	6-3	.983	3	104	142	O86(37/31/23),D3	0	-0.3
1980	Min A	81	200	26	50	9	1	2	20	12-1	1	51	.250	.294	.335	68	-9	2-1	.932	-1	96	164	O72(27/47/2),D3	20	-1.1

YEAR	TM LG	G	AB	R	H	2B	3B	HR	RBI	BB-IB	HP	SO	AVG	OBP	SLG	AOPS	ABR	SB-CS	FA	FR	RNG	THR	GAMES AT POSITION	DL	BFW
1981	SD N	58	112	13	24	4	1	2	13	11-0	0	24	.214	.282	.321	78	-4	3-1	.970	3	99	236	O49(11/2/40)	0	-0.2
1982	SD N	71	55	7	10	2	0	1	2	1-0	0	14	.182	.196	.273	32	-5	0-0	.944	-1	108	0	O45(18/25/2)/1	0	-0.7
Total	5	321	640	95	152	26	2	14	73	55-2	4	147	.237	.301	.350	77	-21	12-6	.958	7	102	169	O267(103/113/67),D6/1	20	-2.0
EDWARDS, HANK	Henry Albert; B1.29.1919 Elmwood Place OH; D6.22.1988 Anaheim CA; BL/TL/6´0˝/(190–192); d9.10; Mil 1944–45																								
1941	Cle A	16	68	10	15	1	1	1	6	2	0	4	.221	.243	.309	47	-6	0-0	.929	-1	72	203	O16(2/0/14)	0	-0.8
1942	Cle A	13	48	6	12	2	1	0	7	5	0	8	.250	.321	.333	89	-1	2-1	.968	-1	99	0	O12C	0	-0.2
1943	Cle A	92	297	38	82	18	6	3	28	30	0	34	.276	.343	.407	127	9	4-8	.983	-3	95	76	O74C	0	0.2
1946	Cle A	124	458	62	138	33	**16**	10	54	43	0	48	.301	.361	.509	151	28	1-3	.968	2	102	128	O123(0/1/122)	0	2.7
1947	Cle A	108	393	54	102	12	3	15	59	31	1	55	.260	.315	.420	106	0	1-3	.990	-3	99	44	O100(39/0/67)	0	-0.9
1948	Cle A	55	160	27	43	9	2	3	18	18	1	18	.269	.346	.406	102	0	1-1	.987	-2	98	36	O41R	61	-0.3
1949	Cle A	5	15	3	4	0	0	1	1	1	0	2	.267	.313	.467	107	0	0-0	1.000	-0	91	0	O5R	0	-0.1
	Chi N	58	176	25	51	8	4	7	21	19	0	22	.290	.359	.500	131	7	0	.988	-1	89	103	O51(18/0/34)	0	0.4
1950	Chi N	41	110	13	40	11	1	2	21	10	0	13	.364	.417	.536	150	8	0	.976	-2	85	108	O29R	0	0.6
1951	Bro N	35	31	1	7	3	0	0	3	4	0	9	.226	.314	.323	70	-1	0-0	ø	0	—	—	/H	0	-0.1
	Cin N	41	127	14	40	9	1	3	20	13	0	17	.315	.379	.472	126	5	0-2	.985	-2	102	0	O34(26/0/8)	0	0.1
	Year	76	158	15	47	12	1	3	23	17	0	26	.297	.366	.443	115	4	0-2	.985	-2	102	0	O34(26/0/8)	0	0.0
1952	Cin N	74	184	24	52	7	6	6	28	19	0	22	.283	.350	.484	129	6	0-3	.988	0	105	63	O51(33/0/18)	0	0.3
	Chi A	8	18	2	6	0	0	0	1	0	0	2	.333	.333	.333	85	0	0-0	1.000	0	115	0	O3L	0	-0.1
1953	StL A	65	106	6	21	3	0	0	9	13	0	10	.198	.286	.226	39	-9	0-1	1.000	0	97	142	O21(11/4/7)	0	-1.0
Total	11	735	2191	285	613	116	41	51	276	208	2	264	.280	.343	.440	119	46	9-22	.981	-12	97	81	O560(132/91/345)	61	0.8
EDWARDS, DOC	Howard Rodney; B12.10.1936 Red Jacket WV; BR/TR/6´2˝/(200–215); d4.21; M3/C8; Col Mira Costa (CA) JC																								
1962	Cle A	53	143	13	39	6	0	3	9	9-0	2	14	.273	.325	.378	91	-2	0-0	.992	7	159	122	C39	0	0.7
1963	Cle A	10	31	6	8	2	0	0	0	2-2	0	6	.258	.303	.323	76	-1	0-0	.988	3	159	67	C10	0	0.3
	KC A	71	240	16	60	12	0	6	35	11-6	2	23	.250	.287	.375	80	-7	0-1	.987	-6	63	100	C63	0	-1.0
	Year	81	271	22	68	14	0	6	35	13-8	2	29	.251	.289	.369	79	-7	0-1	.987	-3	76	96	C73	0	-0.7
1964	KC A	97	294	25	66	10	0	5	28	13-0	3	40	.224	.265	.310	57	-17	0-1	.986	0	62	111	C79,1b7	0	-1.5
1965	KC A	6	20	1	3	0	0	0	0	1-0	0	2	.150	.190	.150	-2	-3	0-0	1.000	-0	225	86	C6	0	-0.3
	NY A	45	100	3	19	3	0	1	9	13-6	1	14	.190	.289	.250	55	-6	1-2	.986	-2	121	68	C43	0	-0.6
	Year	51	120	4	22	3	0	1	9	14-6	1	16	.183	.274	.233	46	-8	1-2	.988	-2	137	71	C49	0	-0.9
1970	Phi N	35	78	5	21	0	0	0	6	4-3	1	10	.269	.313	.269	59	-5	0-0	.970	1	47	191	C34	0	-0.3
Total	5	317	906	69	216	33	0	15	87	53-17	9	109	.238	.287	.325	68	-41	1-4	.986	4	91	110	C274,1b7	0	-2.7
EDWARDS, JOHNNY	John Alban; B6.10.1938 Columbus OH; BL/TR/6´4˝/(195–216); d6.27; Col Ohio St.																								
1961	†Cin N	52	145	14	27	5	0	2	14	18-4	1	28	.186	.279	.262	45	-11	1-0	.982	-2	88	78	C52	0	-1.1
1962	Cin N	133	452	47	115	28	5	8	50	45-9	1	70	.254	.322	.392	88	-7	1-1	.987	13	121	98	C130	0	1.2
1963	Cin N★	148	495	46	128	19	4	11	67	45-5	4	93	.259	.322	.380	99	0	1-5	**.995**	15	110	107	C148	0	2.2
1964	Cin N★	126	423	47	119	23	1	7	55	34-9	1	65	.281	.331	.390	100	1	1-2	.992	22	91	104	C120	0	2.9
1965	Cin N☆	114	371	47	99	22	2	17	51	50-16	1	45	.267	.353	.474	123	13	0-0	.990	8	98	129	C110	0	2.7
1966	Cin N	98	282	24	54	8	0	6	39	31-8	0	42	.191	.269	.284	50	-19	1-3	.992	2	75	100	C98	0	-1.4
1967	Cin N	80	209	10	43	6	0	2	20	16-8	0	28	.206	.261	.263	46	-14	1-4	.990	13	95	111	C73	0	0.0
1968	†StL N	85	230	14	55	9	1	3	29	16-0	1	20	.239	.287	.326	86	-4	1-1	.992	3	199	92	C54	0	0.2
1969	Hou N	151	496	52	115	20	6	6	50	53-12	2	69	.232	.306	.333	81	-13	2-1	**.994**	10	105	129	C151	0	0.4
1970	Hou N	140	458	46	101	16	4	7	49	51-16	1	63	.221	.299	.319	69	-21	1-0	**.995**	13	117	**140**	C139	0	-0.1
1971	Hou N	106	317	18	74	13	4	1	23	26-9	0	38	.233	.291	.309	72	-12	1-1	**.995**	8	120	111	C104	0	0.1
1972	Hou N	108	332	33	89	16	2	5	40	50-12	1	39	.268	.358	.373	114	8	2-4	.988	-9	78	85	C105	0	0.3
1973	Hou N	79	250	24	61	10	2	5	27	19-7	2	23	.244	.301	.360	84	-6	1-0	.989	-3	70	84	C76	33	-0.6
1974	Hou N	50	117	8	26	7	1	1	10	11-3	1	12	.222	.292	.325	76	-4	1-1	.989	3	64	71	C32	0	0.1
Total	14	1470	4577	430	1106	202	32	81	524	465-118	16	635	.242	.311	.353	85	-89	15-23	.992	96	104	108	C1392	33	6.9
EDWARDS, MARSHALL	Marshall Lynn; B8.27.1952 Fort Lewis WA; BL/TL/5´9˝/157; d4.11; b–David twb–Mike; Col UCLA																								
1981	†Mil A	40	58	10	14	1	1	0	4	0-0	0	2	.241	.241	.293	56	-4	6-2	.979	-1	92	79	O36(2/21/14)/D	0	-0.5
1982	†Mil A	69	178	24	44	4	1	2	14	4-0	0	8	.247	.261	.315	61	-10	10-4	.984	1	109	57	O54(4/13/41),D6	0	-1.1
1983	Mil A	51	74	14	22	1	1	0	5	1-0	0	9	.297	.303	.338	83	-2	5-5	1.000	2	102	225	O35(12/12/13),D4	0	-0.1
Total	3	160	310	48	80	6	3	2	23	5-0	0	19	.258	.267	.316	65	-16	21-11	.987	2	104	105	O125(18/46/68),D11	0	-1.7
EDWARDS, MIKE	Michael Donald; B11.24.1976 Goshen NY; BR/TR/6´1˝/(180–200); [CleA95 9/250]; d9.20																								
2003	Oak A	4	4	0	1	0	0	0	0	2-0	0	1	.250	.500	.250	106	0	0-0	ø	-0	0	0	O2L,D2	0	0.0
2005	LA N	88	239	23	59	9	2	3	15	16-0	2	34	.247	.300	.339	67	-12	1-1	.918	-5	89	82	3b39,O34(32/0/3)/SD	0	-1.8
2006	Pit N	14	16	1	3	0	0	0	0	1-0	0	5	.188	.235	.188	10	-2	0-0	1.000	-1	66	0	3b3	0	-0.3
Total	3	106	259	24	63	9	2	3	15	19-0	2	40	.243	.300	.328	64	-14	1-1	.922	-5	88	77	3b42,O36(34/0/3),D4/S	0	-2.1
EDWARDS, MIKE	Michael Lewis; B8.27.1952 Fort Lewis WA; BR/TR/5´10˝/(152–160); [PitN74 7/155]; d9.10; b–Dave twb–Marshall; Col UCLA																								
1977	Pit N	7	6	1	0	0	0	0	0	0-0	1	3	.000	.143	.000	-56	-1	0-2	1.000	1	120	143	2b4	0	-0.1
1978	Oak A	142	414	48	113	16	2	1	23	16-0	2	32	.273	.303	.329	81	-11	27-21	.964	-23	87	92	2b133,S9,D4	0	-3.0
1979	Oak A	122	400	35	93	12	2	1	23	15-0	2	37	.233	.263	.280	49	-30	10-6	.962	-13	95	61	2b113,S3,D2	0	-3.6
1980	Oak A	46	59	10	14	0	0	0	3	1-0	0	5	.237	.250	.237	36	-5	1-1	.971	-3	101	74	2b23/rfD	0	-0.8
Total	4	317	879	94	220	28	4	2	49	32-0	5	77	.250	.280	.298	62	-47	38-30	.964	-38	92	77	2b273,S12,D11/rf	0	-7.5
EDWARDS, RALPH	Ralph Strunk; B12.14.1882 Brewster NY; D1.5.1949 White Plains NY; BR/TR/5´9˝/165; d9.17																								
1915	Phi A	2	5	0	0	0	0	0	0	0	0	3	.000	.000	.000	-99	-1	0	1.000	-1	50	0	/2	—	-0.2
EENHOORN, ROBERT	Robert Franciscus; B2.9.1968 Rotterdam, Netherlands; BR/TR/6´3˝/185; [NYA90 2/45]; d4.27; Col Davidson																								
1994	NY A	3	4	1	2	1	0	0	0	0-0	0	0	.500	.500	.750	224	1	0-0	1.000	-1	41	206	S3	0	0.0
1995	NY A	5	14	1	2	1	0	0	2	1-0	0	3	.143	.200	.214	8	-2	0-0	1.000	-1	82	123	2b3,S2	0	-0.2
1996	NY A	12	14	2	1	0	0	0	2	2-0	0	3	.071	.167	.071	-31	-3	0-0	1.000	1	75	138	2b10,3b2	0	-0.2
	Cal A	6	15	1	4	0	0	0	0	0-0	0	2	.267	.267	.267	35	-2	0-0	.875	-1	74	52	S4,2b2	0	-0.2
	Year	18	29	3	5	0	0	0	2	2-0	0	5	.172	.212	.172	3	-4	0-0	.971	-1	85	137	2b12,S4,3b2	0	-0.4
1997	Ana A	11	20	2	7	1	0	1	6	0-0	0	2	.350	.333	.550	130	1	0-0	.833	-3	59	0	3b5,2b3,S2	0	-0.2
Total	4	37	67	7	16	3	0	1	10	3-0	0	10	.239	.260	.328	53	-5	0-0	.963	-5	78	117	2b18,S11,3b7	0	-0.8
EGAN, BEN	Arthur Augustus; B11.20.1883 Augusta NY; D2.18.1968 Sherrill NY; BR/TR/6´0˝/195; d9.29; C2																								
1908	Phi A	2	6	1	1	1	0	0	0	1	0	—	.167	.286	.333	95	0	0	.933	-0	*76*	*105*	C2	—	0.0
1912	Phi A	49	138	9	24	3	4	0	13	6	0	—	.174	.208	.254	33	-13	3	.958	4	*135*	*122*	C46	—	-0.6
1914	Cle A	29	88	7	20	2	1	0	11	3	3	20	.227	.277	.273	63	-4	0-1	.975	2	*91*	*116*	C27	—	0.0
1915	Cle A	42	120	4	13	3	0	0	6	8	0	14	.108	.164	.133	-11	-17	0	.970	6	*115*	*107*	C40	—	-0.8
Total	4	122	352	21	58	9	5	0	30	18	3	34	.165	.212	.219	27	-34	3-1	.966	11	*116*	*115*	C115	—	-1.4
EGAN, JIM	James K. "Troy Terrier"; B1858 Derby CT; D9.26.1884 New Haven CT; TL; d5.15; ▲																								
1882	Tro N	30	115	15	23	3	2	0	10	1	—	21	.200	.207	.261	51	-6	—	.625	-6	62	132	O18(2/16/0),P12,C2	—	-0.8
EGAN, DICK	Richard Joseph; B6.23.1884 Portland OR; D7.7.1947 Oakland CA; BR/TR/5´11˝/162; d9.15; Col Fordham; OF(11/2/14)																								
1908	Cin N	18	68	8	14	3	1	0	5	2	0	—	.206	.229	.279	64	-3	7	.891	-2	92	202	2b18	—	-0.6
1909	Cin N	127	480	59	132	14	3	2	53	37	2	—	.275	.329	.329	105	3	39	.950	**24**	**117**	112	2b116,S10	—	3.0
1910	Cin N	135	474	70	116	11	5	0	46	53	1	38	.245	.322	.289	82	-10	41	.961	-10	101	80	2b131,S3	—	-2.0
1911	Cin N	153	558	80	139	11	5	1	56	59	1	50	.249	.322	.292	75	-18	37	.949	10	109	103	2b152	—	-0.6
1912	Cin N	149	507	69	125	14	5	0	52	56	2	26	.247	.324	.294	72	-19	24	**.973**	1	101	85	2b149	—	-1.5
1913	Cin N	60	195	15	55	7	3	0	22	15	0	13	.282	.333	.349	95	-1	6-10	.972	-1	96	113	2b37,S17,3b2	—	-0.2
1914	Bro N	106	337	30	76	10	3	1	21	22	0	25	.226	.273	.282	64	-16	8	.914	-10	94	74	S83,3b10,O3(0/2/1),2b2/1	—	-2.2
1915	Bro N	3	3	0	0	0	0	0	0	0	0	0	.000	.000	.000	-98	-1	0	ø	0	—	—	/H	—	-0.1
	Bos N	83	220	20	57	9	1	0	21	28	0	18	.259	.343	.309	102	2	3-4	.974	1	101	86	O24(11/0/13),2b22,S10,1b9,3b4	—	0.2
	Year	86	223	20	57	9	1	0	21	28	0	18	.256	.339	.305	100	1	3-4	.974	1	101	86	O24(11/0/13),2b22,S10,1b9,3b4	—	0.1
1916	Bos N	83	238	23	53	8	3	0	16	19	0	21	.223	.280	.282	76	-7	2	.949	-18	83	60	2b59,S12,3b8	—	-2.7
Total	9	917	3080	374	767	87	29	4	292	291	6	191	.249	.315	.300	82	-70	167-14	.956	-5	104	98	2b686,S135,O27R,3b24,1b10	—	-6.7

EGAN, TOM Thomas Patrick; B6.9.1946 Los Angeles CA; BR/TR (BB 1974p, 75)/6´4˝/(215–218); d5.27

YEAR	TM LG	G	AB	R	H	2B	3B	HR	RBI	BB-IB	HP	SO	AVG	OBP	SLG	AOPS	ABR	SB-CS	FA	FR	RNG	THR	GAMES AT POSITION	DL	BFW
1965	Cal A	18	38	3	10	0	1	0	1	3-0	0	12	.263	.317	.316	82	-1	0-0	1.000	-2	115	0	C16	32	-0.3
1966	Cal A	7	11	0	0	0	0	0	0	1-0	0	5	.000	.083	.000	-76	-3	0-0	1.000	2	0	0	C6	0	-0.1
1967	Cal A	1	1	0	0	0	0	0	0	0-0	0	0	.000	.000	.000	-99	0	0-0	1.000	0	0	0	/C	0	0.0
1968	Cal A	16	43	2	5	1	0	1	4	2-0	0	15	.116	.156	.209	10	-5	0-0	1.000	0	53	91	C14	0	-0.5
1969	Cal A	46	120	7	17	1	0	5	16	17-2	1	41	.142	.248	.275	50	-9	0-1	.985	4	96	147	C46	36	-0.3
1970	Cal A	79	210	14	50	6	0	4	20	14-1	1	67	.238	.286	.324	71	-9	0-0	.988	-5	81	97	C79	0	-1.1
1971	Chi A	85	251	29	60	11	1	10	34	26-1	4	94	.239	.320	.410	103	1	1-0	.986	3	59	82	C77/1	0	0.7
1972	Chi A	50	141	8	27	3	0	2	9	4-0	2	48	.191	.224	.255	42	-11	0-0	.986	4	65	109	C46	0	-0.6
1974	Cal A	43	94	4	11	0	0	0	4	8-0	1	40	.117	.194	.117	-9	-13	1-0	.996	5	59	125	C41	0	-0.7
1975	Cal A	28	70	7	16	3	1	0	3	5-0	0	14	.229	.280	.300	69	-3	0-0	.965	-2	46	158	C28	0	-0.4
Total	10	373	979	74	196	25	3	22	91	80-4	9	336	.200	.266	.299	62	-53	2-1	.987	9	70	105	C354/1	68	-3.3

EGGERT, ELMER Elmer Albert "Mose"; B1.29.1902 Rochester NY; D4.9.1971 Rochester NY; BR/TR/5´9˝/160; d4.27

YEAR	TM LG	G	AB	R	H	2B	3B	HR	RBI	BB-IB	HP	SO	AVG	OBP	SLG	AOPS	ABR	SB-CS	FA	FR	RNG	THR	GAMES AT POSITION	DL	BFW
1927	Bos A	5	3	0	0	0	0	0	0	1	0	1	.000	.250	.000	-31	-1	0-0	ø	-0	0	0	/2	—	-0.1

EGGLER, DAVE David Daniel; B4.30.1849 Brooklyn NY; D4.5.1902 Buffalo NY; BR/TR/5´9˝/165; d5.18

YEAR	TM LG	G	AB	R	H	2B	3B	HR	RBI	BB-IB	HP	SO	AVG	OBP	SLG	AOPS	ABR	SB-CS	FA	FR	RNG	THR	GAMES AT POSITION	DL	BFW
1871	Mut NA	**33**	147	37	47	7	3	0	18	4	—	3	.320	.338	.408	124	6	14-3	.910	5	78	158	O33C	—	0.8
1872	Mut NA	**56**	290	**94**	97	20	0	0	19	8	—	9	.334	.352	.403	141	17	**18**-6	**.917**	14	**194**	181	O56(1/55/0)	—	2.2
1873	Mut NA	**53**	266	82	90	13	4	0	35	6	—	2	.338	.353	.417	128	9	3-2	.856	4	81	79	O53C/3	—	0.9
1874	Phi NA	**58**	299	70	95	13	8	0	31	5	—	1	.318	.329	.415	132	9	5-6	**.906**	7	111	198	O57(7/50/0),2b2	—	1.2
1875	Ath NA	66	295	66	89	13	7	0	33	1	—	10	.302	.304	.393	126	6	6-5	**.921**	4	68	**162**	O66(2/65/0)	—	0.7
1876	Phi N	39	174	28	52	4	0	0	19	2	—	4	.299	.307	.322	111	2	—	.913	3	87	55	O39(1/37/1)	—	0.3
1877	Chi N	33	136	20	36	3	0	0	20	1	—	5	.265	.270	.287	67	-5	—	.861	2	132	290	O33C	—	-0.4
1879	Buf N	78	317	41	66	5	7	0	27	11	—	41	.208	.235	.268	64	-13	—	.919	-7	63	113	O78C	—	-2.2
1883	Bal AA	53	202	15	38	2	0	0	7	1	—	—	.188	.192	.198	25	-17	—	.916	-0	61	76	O53C	—	-1.7
	Buf N	38	153	13	38	2	1	0	13	2	—	29	.248	.258	.275	61	-8	—	.845	-4	43	70	O38(1/37/0)	—	-1.1
1884	Buf N	63	241	25	47	3	1	0	20	6	—	54	.195	.215	.216	35	-18	—	.887	0	111	51	O63(2/61/0)	—	-1.9
1885	Buf N	6	24	0	2	0	0	0	0	2	—	4	.083	.154	.083	-21	-3	—	.938	0	79	0	O6C	—	-0.3
Total	5NA	266	1297	349	418	66	22	0	136	24	—	25	.322	.335	.407	130	47	46-22	.902	33	109	157	O265(10/256/0),2b2/3	—	5.8
Total	6	310	1247	142	279	19	9	0	106	25	—	137	.224	.239	.253	56	-62	—	.894	-5	80	98	O310(4/305/1)	—	-7.3

EHRET, RED Philip Sydney; B8.31.1868 Louisville KY; D7.28.1940 Cincinnati OH; BR/TR/6´0˝/175; d7.7; ▲

YEAR	TM LG	G	AB	R	H	2B	3B	HR	RBI	BB-IB	HP	SO	AVG	OBP	SLG	AOPS	ABR	SB-CS	FA	FR	RNG	THR	GAMES AT POSITION	DL	BFW
1888	KC AA	17	63	4	12	4	0	0	4	1	0	—	.190	.203	.254	43	-4	1	.750	-2	0	0	O10(5/2/3),P7/21	—	-0.4
1889	Lou AA	67	258	27	65	6	6	1	31	4	0	23	.252	.263	.333	71	-12	4	.891	-2	123	121	P45,O22(6/1/15)/S32	—	-0.6
1890	†Lou AA	43	146	11	31	2	1	0	10	1	0	—	.212	.218	.240	36	-3	1	.859	-3	89	105	P43	—	0.0
1891	Lou AA	26	91	9	22	2	1	0	9	5	0	15	.242	.281	.286	63	1	3	.871	-0	108	235	P26	—	0.0
1892	Pit N	40	132	12	34	2	0	0	19	7	0	22	.258	.295	.273	72	3	1	.855	-4	81	41	P39	—	0.0
1893	Pit N	40	136	16	24	3	0	1	17	10	0	18	.176	.233	.221	21	-6	1	.893	1	115	0	P39	—	0.0
1894	Pit N	46	135	6	23	4	1	0	11	8	0	22	.170	.217	.215	4	-11	0	.859	-2	93	86	P46	—	0.0
1895	StL N	37	96	13	21	2	1	1	9	6	0	12	.219	.265	.292	44	-2	0	.848	-0	106	0	P37	—	0.0
1896	Cin N	34	102	10	20	2	0	1	20	10	0	12	.196	.268	.245	33	-10	2	.923	0	100	138	P34/1	—	0.0
1897	Cin N	34	66	6	13	2	0	0	6	4	1	—	.197	.254	.227	26	-3	2	.957	-1	79	292	P34	—	0.0
1898	Cin N	13	40	3	9	3	1	0	4	1	1	—	.225	.262	.350	76	1	0	.800	-2	77	0	P12	—	0.0
Total	11	397	1265	117	274	32	11	4	140	57	2	124	.217	.252	.269	44	-46	15	.882	-15	100	97	P362,O32(11/3/18),1b2,2b2/3S	—	-1.0

EIBEL, HACK Henry Hack; B12.6.1893 Brooklyn NY; D10.16.1945 Macon GA; BL/TL/5´11˝/220; d6.13; ▲

YEAR	TM LG	G	AB	R	H	2B	3B	HR	RBI	BB-IB	HP	SO	AVG	OBP	SLG	AOPS	ABR	SB-CS	FA	FR	RNG	THR	GAMES AT POSITION	DL	BFW
1912	Cle A	1	3	0	0	0	0	0	0	0	0	—	.000	.000	.000	-97	-1	0	ø	-0	0	0	/rf	—	-0.1
1920	Bos A	29	43	4	8	2	0	0	6	3	0	6	.186	.239	.233	26	-5	1-1	.800	-1	54	0	O5(3/0/2),P3/1	—	-0.5
Total	2	30	46	4	8	2	0	0	6	3	0	6	.174	.224	.217	19	-6	1-1	.800	-2	52	0	O6(3/0/3),P3/1	—	-0.6

EICHRODT, IKE Frederick George; B1.6.1903 Chicago IL; D7.14.1965 Indianapolis IN; BR/TR/5´11.5˝/167; d9.7

YEAR	TM LG	G	AB	R	H	2B	3B	HR	RBI	BB-IB	HP	SO	AVG	OBP	SLG	AOPS	ABR	SB-CS	FA	FR	RNG	THR	GAMES AT POSITION	DL	BFW
1925	Cle A	15	52	4	12	3	1	0	4	2	0	7	.231	.259	.327	48	-4	0-0	.938	-2	96	0	O13C	—	-0.6
1926	Cle A	37	80	14	25	7	1	0	7	2	0	11	.313	.329	.425	95	-1	1-0	.976	1	100	173	O27(19/6/2)	—	-0.1
1927	Cle A	85	267	24	59	19	2	0	25	16	0	25	.221	.265	.307	48	-21	2-3	.979	5	98	183	O81(13/64/5)	—	-1.9
1931	Chi A	34	117	9	25	5	1	0	15	1	0	8	.214	.220	.274	31	-12	0-0	1.000	-1	104	0	O32(0/30/3)	—	-1.3
Total	4	171	516	51	121	34	5	0	51	21	0	51	.234	.264	.320	52	-38	3-3	.979	4	99	128	O153(32/113/10)	—	-3.9

EISENREICH, JIM James Michael; B4.18.1959 St.Cloud MN; BL/TL/5´11˝/(175–200); [MinA80 16/402]; d4.6; Col St. Cloud St.

YEAR	TM LG	G	AB	R	H	2B	3B	HR	RBI	BB-IB	HP	SO	AVG	OBP	SLG	AOPS	ABR	SB-CS	FA	FR	RNG	THR	GAMES AT POSITION	DL	BFW
1982	Min A	34	99	10	30	6	0	2	9	11-0	1	13	.303	.378	.424	116	3	0-0	.973	0	113	0	O30C	97	0.3
1983	Min A	2	7	1	2	1	0	0	0	1-0	0	1	.286	.375	.429	116	0	0-0	1.000	1	105	771	O2C	50	0.1
1984	Min A	12	32	1	7	1	0	0	3	2-1	0	4	.219	.250	.250	41	-3	2-0	1.000	-1	61	0	O3(0/2/1),D6	22	-0.3
1987	KC A	44	105	10	25	8	2	4	21	7-2	0	13	.238	.278	.467	92	-2	1-1	ø	0	0	0	D26	15	-0.2
1988	KC A	82	202	26	44	8	1	1	19	6-1	0	31	.218	.236	.282	45	-15	9-3	.965	1	117	0	O64(30/15/21),D13	0	-1.6
1989	KC A	134	475	64	139	33	7	9	59	37-9	0	44	.293	.341	.448	122	13	27-8	.989	-1	103	56	O123(26/67/58),D10	15	1.3
1990	KC A	142	496	61	139	29	7	5	51	42-2	1	51	.280	.335	.397	106	4	12-14	**.996**	-1	98	73	O138(70/19/78),D2	0	-0.3
1991	KC A	135	375	47	113	22	3	2	47	20-1	1	35	.301	.333	.392	101	0	5-3	.973	-6	87	21	O105(59/13/42),1b15/D	0	-0.9
1992	KC A	113	353	31	95	13	3	2	28	24-4	0	36	.269	.313	.340	81	-9	11-6	.995	-2	105	18	O88(24/1/66),D8	26	-1.4
1993	†Phi N	153	362	51	115	17	4	7	54	26-5	1	36	.318	.363	.445	117	8	5-0	.996	7	118	86	O137(1/3/133)/1	0	1.1
1994	Phi N	104	290	42	87	15	4	4	43	33-3	1	31	.300	.371	.421	105	3	6-2	.989	4	115	69	O93(0/5/90)	0	0.4
1995	Phi N	129	377	46	119	22	2	10	55	38-4	1	44	.316	.375	.464	121	12	10-0	**1.000**	3	**115**	32	O111(39/6/68)	0	1.3
1996	Phi N	113	338	45	122	24	3	3	41	31-9	1	32	.361	.413	.476	134	18	11-1	.977	2	111	59	O91(43/3/50)	0	1.8
1997	†Fla N	120	293	36	82	19	1	2	34	30-4	1	28	.280	.345	.372	93	-2	0-0	.987	-2	94	68	O55(43/0/13),1b29,D4	0	-0.7
1998	Fla N	30	64	9	16	1	0	1	7	4-1	0	14	.250	.294	.313	64	-4	2-0	.965	-2	38	102	1b10,O8(5/0/3)	0	-0.6
	LA N	75	127	12	25	2	1	2	6	12-1	0	22	.197	.266	.244	37	-12	4-0	.971	0	104	90	O24(22/0/2),1b9,D2	0	-1.2
	Year	105	191	21	41	3	2	1	13	16-2	0	36	.215	.275	.267	46	-16	6-0	.977	-2	103	71	O32(27/0/5),1b19,D2	0	-1.8
Total	15	1422	3995	492	1160	221	39	52	477	324-47	8	435	.290	.341	.404	103	14	105-38	.988	2	106	52	O1072(362/166/625),D72,1b64	225	-0.9

ELAND ; d4.14

YEAR	TM LG	G	AB	R	H	2B	3B	HR	RBI	BB-IB	HP	SO	AVG	OBP	SLG	AOPS	ABR	SB-CS	FA	FR	RNG	THR	GAMES AT POSITION	DL	BFW
1873	Mar NA	1	3	0	0	0	0	0	0	0	—	0	.000	.000	.000	-99	-1	0-0	.667	-0	0	0	/rf	—	-0.1

ELBERFELD, KID Norman Arthur "The Tabasco Kid"; B4.13.1875 Pomeroy OH; D1.13.1944 Chattanooga TN; BR/TR/5´7˝/158; d5.30; M1

YEAR	TM LG	G	AB	R	H	2B	3B	HR	RBI	BB-IB	HP	SO	AVG	OBP	SLG	AOPS	ABR	SB-CS	FA	FR	RNG	THR	GAMES AT POSITION	DL	BFW
1898	Phi N	14	38	1	9	4	0	0	7	5	7	—	.237	.420	.342	124	3	0	.795	-5	70	57	3b14	—	-0.2
1899	Cin N	41	138	23	36	4	2	0	22	15	11	—	.261	.378	.319	90	0	5	.878	-6	90	75	S24,3b18	—	-0.4
1901	Det A	121	432	76	133	21	11	3	76	57	7	—	.308	.397	.428	123	16	23	.907	19	104	**134**	S121	—	3.5
1902	Det A	130	488	70	127	17	6	1	64	55	11	—	.260	.348	.326	86	-7	19	.921	12	**105**	111	S130	—	0.8
1903	Det A	35	132	29	45	5	3	0	19	11	5	—	.341	.412	.424	156	10	6	.932	5	107	89	S34/3	—	1.6
	NY A	90	349	49	100	18	5	0	45	22	10	—	.287	.346	.367	107	4	16	.914	4	100	130	S90	—	1.1
	Year	125	481	78	145	23	8	0	64	33	**15**	—	.301	.365	.383	120	13	22	.919	9	102	**119**	S124/3	—	2.7
1904	NY A	122	445	55	117	13	5	2	46	37	13	—	.263	.337	.328	106	5	18	.933	11	**108**	125	S122	—	2.2
1905	NY A	111	390	48	102	18	2	0	53	23	16	—	.262	.329	.318	95	-1	18	.908	-4	98	104	S108	—	-0.1
1906	NY A	99	346	59	106	11	5	2	31	30	16	—	.306	.378	.384	126	12	19	.925	-1	100	61	S98	—	1.5
1907	NY A	120	447	61	121	17	6	0	51	36	13	—	.271	.343	.336	108	5	22	.930	13	104	78	S118	—	2.4
1908	NY A	19	56	11	11	3	0	0	5	6	5	—	.196	.328	.250	87	0	1	.916	-2	92	35	S17,M	—	-0.1
1909	NY A	106	379	47	90	9	5	0	26	28	14	—	.237	.314	.288	89	-4	23	.943	4	93	112	S61,3b44	—	0.4
1910	Was A	127	455	53	114	9	2	2	42	35	13	—	.251	.322	.292	97	-1	19	**.943**	-5	94	100	3b113,2b10,S3	—	-0.3
1911	Was A	127	404	58	110	19	4	0	47	65	**25**	—	.272	.405	.339	110	13	24	.957	7	98	99	2b68,3b52	—	2.2
1914	Bro N	30	62	7	14	1	0	0	1	2	5	4	.226	.304	.242	62	-3	0	.901	-3	77	122	S18/2	—	-0.6
Total	14	1292	4561	647	1235	169	56	10	535	427	165	4	.271	.355	.339	105	52	213	.920	51	102	105	S944,3b242,2b79	—	14.0

ELDER, GEORGE George Rezin; B3.10.1921 Lebanon KY; BL/TR/5´11˝/180; d7.22; Col UCLA

YEAR	TM LG	G	AB	R	H	2B	3B	HR	RBI	BB-IB	HP	SO	AVG	OBP	SLG	AOPS	ABR	SB-CS	FA	FR	RNG	THR	GAMES AT POSITION	DL	BFW
1949	StL A	41	44	9	11	3	0	0	2	4	0	11	.250	.313	.318	64	-2	0-0	1.000	1	129	0	O10L	0	-0.2

ELDRED, BRAD Bradley Ross; B7.12.1980 Ft.Lauderdale FL; BR/TR/6´6˝/270; [PitN02 6/163]; d7.22; Col Florida International

YEAR	TM LG	G	AB	R	H	2B	3B	HR	RBI	BB-IB	HP	SO	AVG	OBP	SLG	AOPS	ABR	SB-CS	FA	FR	RNG	THR	GAMES AT POSITION	DL	BFW
2005	Pit N	55	190	23	42	9	0	12	27	13-0	3	77	.221	.279	.458	89	-4	1-1	.985	-6	56	110	1b50	0	-1.4

YEAR	TM LG	G	AB	R	H	2B	3B	HR	RBI	BB-IB	HP	SO	AVG	OBP	SLG	AOPS	ABR	SB-CS	FA	FR	RNG	THR	GAMES AT POSITION	DL	BFW
Elia, Lee	Lee Constantine; B7.16.1937 Philadelphia PA; BR/TR/5´11˝/(175–180); d4.23; M4/C16; Col Delaware																								
1966	Chi A	80	195	16	40	5	2	3	22	15-3	2	39	.205	.265	.297	67	-9	0-1	.954	-3	100	117	S75	0	-0.7
1968	Chi N	15	17	1	3	0	0	0	3	0-0	1	6	.176	.222	.176	20	-2	0-0	1.000	-1	45	0	S2/23	0	-0.3
Total	2	95	212	17	43	5	2	3	25	15-3	3	45	.203	.262	.288	63	-11	0-1	.954	-4	99	116	S77/32	0	-1.0
Elko, Pete	Peter "Piccolo Pete"; B6.17.1918 Wilkes–Barre PA; D9.17.1993 Wilkes–Barre PA; BR/TR/5´11˝/185; d9.17																								
1943	Chi N	9	30	1	4	0	0	0	0	4	0	5	.133	.235	.133	8	-4	0	.852	-2	87	69	3b9	0	-0.6
1944	Chi N	7	22	2	5	1	0	0	0	0	0	1	.227	.227	.273	40	-2	0	1.000	0	94	140	3b6	0	-0.2
Total	2	16	52	3	9	1	0	0	0	4	0	6	.173	.232	.192	22	-6	0	.902	-2	89	92	3b15	0	-0.8
Ellam, Roy	Roy "Whitey","Slippery"; B2.8.1886 W.Conshohocken PA; D10.28.1948 Conshohocken PA; BR/TR/5´10.5˝/203; d9.18																								
1909	Cin N	10	21	4	4	0	1	1	4	7	0	—	.190	.393	.429	156	2	1	.895	-1	93	158	S9	—	0.1
1918	Pit N	26	77	9	10	1	1	0	2	17	2	17	.130	.302	.169	43	-4	2	.924	-6	87	69	S26	—	-1.0
Total	2	36	98	13	14	1	2	1	6	24	2	17	.143	.323	.224	67	-2	3	.917	-7	88	90	S35	—	-0.9
Ellerbe, Frank	Francis Rogers "Governor"; B12.25.1895 Marion Co. SC; D7.8.1988 Latta SC; BR/TR/5´10.5˝/165; d8.28; Col Wofford																								
1919	Was A	28	105	13	29	4	1	0	16	2	0	15	.276	.290	.333	75	-4	5	.945	-3	89	50	S28	—	-0.5
1920	Was A	101	336	38	98	14	2	0	36	19	1	23	.292	.331	.345	82	-9	5-4	.934	-6	100	65	3b75,S19/rf	—	-1.2
1921	Was A	10	10	1	2	0	1	0	1	0	0	2	.200	.200	.400	52	-1	0-0	ø	0	—	—	/H	—	-0.1
	StL A	105	430	65	124	20	12	2	49	22	3	42	.288	.327	.405	81	-14	1-6	.953	1	97	44	3b105	—	-0.8
	Year	115	440	66	126	20	13	2	50	22	3	44	.286	.325	.405	81	-15	1-6	.953	1	97	44	3b105	—	-0.9
1922	StL A	91	342	42	84	16	3	1	33	25	3	36	.246	.303	.319	60	-20	1-1	.955	12	107	117	3b91	—	-0.3
1923	StL A	18	49	6	9	0	0	0	1	1	0	5	.184	.200	.184	1	-7	0-1	.967	-2	81	111	3b14	—	-0.8
1924	StL A	21	61	7	12	3	0	0	2	2	0	3	.197	.222	.246	19	-8	0-1	.953	1	91	231	3b21	—	-0.6
	Cle A	46	120	7	31	1	3	1	14	1	1	10	.258	.270	.342	56	-9	0-0	.975	5	120	38	3b39,2b2	—	-0.2
	Year	67	181	14	43	4	3	1	16	3	1	13	.238	.254	.309	44	-17	0-1	.967	5	109	111	3b60,2b2	—	-0.8
Total	6	420	1453	179	389	58	22	4	152	72	8	136	.268	.306	.346	68	-72	12-13	.952	8	102	81	3b345,S47,2b2/rf	—	-4.5
Ellick, Joe	Joseph J.; B4.3.1854 Cincinnati OH; D4.21.1923 Kansas City KS; 5´10˝/162; d5.13; M1/U1																								
1875	RS NA	7	27	1	6	1	0	0	1	0	—	1	.222	.222	.259	74	0	1-0	.471	-4	60	0	3b5,O2C	—	-0.4
1878	Mil N	3	13	2	2	0	0	0	1	0	—	1	.154	.154	.154	1	-1	—	.769	-2	—	—	C2/3P	—	-0.3
1880	Wor N	5	18	1	1	0	0	0	0	1	—	2	.056	.105	.056	-40	-3	—	.882	0	116	0	3b5	—	-0.2
1884	CP U	**92**	394	71	93	11	0	0	—	16	—	—	.236	.266	.264	62	-30	—	.903	-0	98	52	O57(3/0/54),S33,2b4,M	—	-2.6
	KC U	2	8	0	0	0	0	0	—	0	—	—	.000	.000	.000	-99	-2	—	.778	-1	88	0	/2rf	—	-0.3
	Bal U	7	27	2	4	0	0	0	—	2	—	—	.148	.207	.148	8	-4	—	.714	-1	107	0	S6/rf	—	-0.4
	Year	101	429	73	97	11	0	0	—	18	—	—	.226	.257	.252	55	-36	—	.894	-2	101	94	O59(3/0/56),S39,2b5	—	-3.3
Total	3	109	460	76	100	11	0	0	1	19	—	3	.217	.248	.241	50	-40	—	.894	-3	101	94	O59(3/0/56),S39,3b6,2b5,C2/P	—	-3.8
Elliot, Larry	Lawrence Lee; B3.5.1938 San Diego CA; BL/TL/6´2˝/200; d4.19; Col San Diego (CA) City																								
1962	Pit N	8	10	2	3	0	0	1	2	0-0	0	1	.300	.300	.600	135	0	0-0	1.000	0	127	0	O3R	0	0.0
1963	Pit N	4	4	0	0	0	0	0	0	0-0	0	3	.000	.000	.000	-99	-1	0-0	ø	0	—	—	/H	0	-0.1
1964	NY N	80	224	27	51	8	0	9	22	28-2	3	55	.228	.320	.384	100	1	1-2	.985	-2	100	52	O63(4/57/4)	0	-0.4
1966	NY N	65	199	24	49	14	2	5	32	17-1	0	46	.246	.306	.412	100	0	0-1	.912	1	83	288	O54(25/0/31)	0	-0.2
Total	4	157	437	53	103	22	2	15	56	45-3	3	105	.236	.311	.398	99	0	1-3	.956	-1	93	158	O120(29/57/38)	0	-0.7
Elliott, Allen	Allen Clifford "Ace"; B12.25.1897 St.Louis MO; D5.6.1979 St.Louis MO; BL/TR/6´0˝/170; d6.14																								
1923	Chi N	53	168	21	42	8	2	2	29	2	2	12	.250	.267	.357	63	-10	3-3	.992	-2	80	106	1b52	—	-1.4
1924	Chi N	10	14	0	2	0	0	0	0	0	0	1	.143	.143	.143	-23	-2	0-0	1.000	-0	43	88	1b10	—	-0.3
Total	2	63	182	21	44	8	2	2	29	2	2	13	.242	.258	.341	57	-12	3-3	.992	-2	77	104	1b62	—	-1.7
Elliott, Carter	Carter Ward; B11.29.1893 Atchison KS; D5.21.1959 Palm Springs CA; BL/TR/5´11˝/165; d9.10																								
1921	Chi N	12	28	5	7	2	0	0	0	5	0	3	.250	.364	.321	83	0	0-0	.964	2	104	85	S10	—	0.2
Elliott, Gene	Eugene Birminghouse; B2.8.1889 Fayette Co. PA; D1.5.1976 Huntingdon PA; BL/TR/5´7˝/150; d4.13																								
1911	NY A	5	13	1	1	1	0	0	1	2	0	—	.077	.200	.154	-1	-2	0	ø	-1	0	0	O2R/3	—	-0.2
Elliott, Rowdy	Harold Bell; B7.8.1890 Kokomo IN; D2.12.1934 San Francisco CA; BR/TR/5´9˝/160; d9.24; Mil 1918																								
1910	Bos N	3	2	0	0	0	0	0	0	0	0	0	.000	.000	.000	-96	0	0	1.000	-0	*0*	*0*	/C	—	-0.1
1916	Chi N	23	55	5	14	3	0	0	3	3	0	5	.255	.293	.309	77	-1	1	.969	-1	97	78	C18	—	-0.1
1917	Chi N	85	223	18	56	8	5	0	28	11	2	11	.251	.292	.332	84	-4	4	.969	4	*97*	*115*	C73	—	0.6
1918	Chi N	5	10	0	0	0	0	0	0	2	0	1	.000	.167	.000	-47	-2	0	.952	0	*113*	*114*	C5	—	-0.1
1920	Bro N	41	112	13	27	4	0	1	13	3	1	6	.241	.267	.304	62	-6	0-0	.964	1	*102*	*117*	C39	—	-0.1
Total	5	157	402	36	97	15	5	1	44	19	3	23	.241	.281	.311	73	-13	5-0	.967	5	*99*	*110*	C136	—	0.2
Elliott, Harry	Harry Lewis; B12.30.1923 San Francisco CA; BR/TR/5´9˝/(175–180); d8.1; Col Minnesota																								
1953	StL N	24	59	6	15	6	1	1	6	3	1	8	.254	.302	.441	91	-1	0-0	1.000	0	111	75	O17(15/0/2)	0	-0.1
1955	StL N	68	117	9	30	4	0	1	12	11-3	1	9	.256	.321	.316	71	-5	0-2	.978	-1	103	56	O28(8/0/20)	0	-0.7
Total	2	92	176	15	45	10	1	2	18	14-3	2	17	.256	.314	.358	78	-6	0-2	.988	-0	106	64	O45(23/0/22)	0	-0.8
Elliott, Randy	Randy Lee; B6.5.1951 Oxnard CA; BR/TR/6´2˝/190; [SDN69 1/24]; d9.10																								
1972	SD N	14	49	5	10	3	1	0	6	2-0	0	11	.204	.235	.306	57	-3	0-0	1.000	1	131	0	O13R	0	-0.3
1974	SD N	13	33	5	7	1	0	1	2	7-1	0	9	.212	.350	.333	96	0	0-1	1.000	-2	49	0	O11(7/0/4)/1	0	-0.3
1977	SF N	73	167	17	40	5	1	7	26	8-1	1	24	.240	.275	.407	81	-5	0-2	.973	2	93	200	O46L	0	-0.6
1980	Oak A	14	39	4	5	3	0	0	1	1-0	0	13	.128	.150	.205	-4	-6	0-0	ø	0	0	0	D11	0	-0.6
Total	4	114	288	31	62	12	2	8	35	18-2	1	57	.215	.262	.354	69	-14	0-3	.982	0	94	127	O70(53/0/17),D11/1	0	-1.8
Elliott, Bob	Robert Irving "Mr. Team"; B11.26.1916 San Francisco CA; D5.4.1966 San Diego CA; BR/TR/6´0˝/185; d9.2; M1/C1; Col El Centro (CA) JC																								
1939	Pit N	32	129	18	43	10	3	3	19	9	0	4	.333	.377	.527	143	7	0	.978	0	110	39	O30C	—	0.7
1940	Pit N	148	551	88	161	34	11	5	64	45	2	28	.292	.348	.421	112	9	13	.978	2	104	107	O147(4/31/113)	—	0.3
1941	Pit N★	141	527	74	144	24	10	3	76	64	1	52	.273	.353	.374	105	4	6	.970	-0	106	76	O139(4/2/134)	0	-0.4
1942	Pit N★	143	560	75	166	26	7	9	89	52	2	35	.296	.358	.416	123	16	2	.927	-1	102	82	3b142/lf	0	2.1
1943	Pit N	156	581	82	183	30	12	7	101	56	1	24	.315	.376	.444	132	23	4	.949	-4	101	**137**	3b151,2b2/S	0	2.3
1944	Pit N★	143	538	85	160	28	16	10	108	75	0	42	.297	.383	.465	132	24	9	.944	-4	97	96	3b140/S	0	2.2
1945	Pit N✳	144	541	80	157	36	6	8	108	64	1	38	.290	.366	.423	115	12	5	.928	7	108	126	3b81,O61R	0	1.6
1946	Pit N	140	486	50	128	25	3	5	68	64	2	44	.263	.351	.358	99	1	6	.995	6	108	89	O92R,3b43	0	0.4
1947	Bos N✳	150	555	93	176	35	5	22	113	87	0	60	.317	.410	.517	148	41	3	**.956**	-2	105	103	3b148	0	3.8
1948	†Bos N★	151	540	99	153	24	5	23	100	**131**	0	57	.283	.423	.474	145	41	6	.945	-12	97	78	3b150	0	2.9
1949	Bos N	139	482	77	135	29	5	17	76	90	2	38	.280	.395	.467	138	29	0	.963	11	**108**	**99**	3b130	0	4.0
1950	Bos N	142	531	94	162	28	5	24	107	68	2	67	.305	.386	.512	143	34	2	.952	-17	87	89	3b137	0	1.6
1951	Bos N★	136	480	73	137	29	2	15	70	65	0	56	.285	.371	.448	128	20	2-0	.941	-8	93	103	3b127	0	1.3
1952	NY N	98	272	33	62	6	2	10	35	36	2	20	.228	.323	.375	92	-3	1-0	.978	-1	85	151	O65(52/0/15),3b13	0	-0.8
1953	StL A	48	160	19	40	7	1	5	29	30	0	18	.250	.368	.400	105	2	0-1	.954	-1	96	103	3b45	0	0.0
	Chi A	67	208	24	54	11	1	4	32	31	1	21	.260	.358	.380	96	0	1-1	.963	-5	91	74	3b58,O2L	0	-0.6
	Year	115	368	43	94	18	2	9	61	61	1	39	.255	.363	.389	100	2	1-2	.959	-7	93	87	3b103,O2L	0	-0.6
Total	15	1978	7141	1064	2061	382	94	170	1195	967	16	604	.289	.375	.440	124	260	60-2	.947	-28	99	99	3b1365,O537(63/63/415),S2,2b2	0	21.4
Ellis, Ben	Alfred Benjamin; B7.1870 New York NY; D7.26.1931 Schenectady NY; 5´10˝/165; d7.16																								
1896	Phi N	4	16	0	1	0	0	0	0	3	0	6	.063	.211	.063	-26	-3	0	.800	-1	69	126	S2,3b2	—	-0.3
Ellis, Rube	George William; B11.17.1885 Downey CA; D3.13.1938 Rivera CA; BL/TL/6´0˝/170; d4.15																								
1909	StL N	149	575	76	154	10	9	3	46	54	3	—	.268	.334	.332	114	8	18	.955	13	135	175	O145(144/0/1)	—	1.4
1910	StL N	142	550	87	142	18	8	4	54	62	5	70	.258	.339	.342	102	2	25	.942	2	93	**139**	O141L	—	-0.5
1911	StL N	155	555	69	139	20	11	2	66	66	2	64	.250	.332	.337	90	-7	9	.938	0	101	100	O148L	—	-1.4
1912	StL N	109	305	47	82	18	2	4	33	34	0	36	.269	.342	.380	100	0	6	.929	-1	103	83	O76(65/4/7)	—	-0.4
Total	4	555	1985	279	517	66	30	13	199	216	10	170	.260	.336	.344	101	3	58	.943	14	109	130	O510(498/4/8)	—	-0.9

YEAR	TM LG	G	AB	R	H	2B	3B	HR	RBI	BB-IB	HP	SO	AVG	OBP	SLG	AOPS	ABR	SB-CS	FA	FR	RNG	THR	GAMES AT POSITION	DL	BFW
Ellis, John	John Charles; B8.21.1948 New London CT; BR/TR/6´2.5˝/(210–220); d5.17; Col Mitchell (CT) JC																								
1969	NY A	22	62	2	18	4	0	1	8	1-0	1	11	.290	.308	.403	102	0	0-2	.978	-3	33	96	C15	0	-0.3
1970	NY A	78	226	24	56	12	1	7	29	18-0	2	47	.248	.305	.403	99	-1	0-1	.992	-2	123	100	1b53,3b5,C2	0	-0.7
1971	NY A	83	238	16	58	12	1	3	34	23-5	6	42	.244	.322	.340	93	-2	0-0	.990	-3	89	134	1b65,C2	0	-1.0
1972	NY A	52	136	13	40	5	1	5	25	8-0	0	22	.294	.333	.456	136	5	0-0	.965	2	109	72	C25,1b8	0	0.8
1973	Cle A	127	437	59	118	12	2	14	68	46-2	3	57	.270	.339	.403	107	4	0-0	.980	-17	105	96	C72,D38,1b12	0	-1.2
1974	Cle A	128	477	58	136	23	6	10	64	32-3	1	53	.285	.330	.421	116	9	1-2	.992	-4	86	100	1b69,C42,D21	29	0.0
1975	Cle A	92	296	22	68	11	1	7	32	14-2	2	33	.230	.266	.345	72	-12	0-1	.976	-5	97	114	C84,1b2,D3	17	-1.5
1976	Tex A	11	31	4	13	2	0	1	8	0-0	0	4	.419	.419	.581	187	3	0-0	1.000	-0	195	100	C7,D3	148	0.3
1977	Tex A	49	119	7	28	7	0	4	15	8-2	0	26	.235	.283	.395	82	-3	0-0	1.000	-2	59	32	C16,D15,1b8	0	-0.6
1978	Tex A	34	94	7	23	4	0	3	17	6-0	0	20	.245	.282	.383	87	-2	0-1	.958	-2	120	59	C22,D7	0	-0.3
1979	Tex A	111	316	33	90	12	0	12	61	15-1	2	55	.285	.318	.437	103	0	2-2	.978	-3	71	94	D62,1b30,C7	0	-0.6
1980	Tex A	73	182	12	43	9	1	1	23	14-1	1	23	.236	.290	.313	68	-8	3-0	.992	-2	65	83	1b39,D20,C3	21	-1.2
1981	Tex A	23	58	2	8	3	0	1	7	5-1	1	10	.138	.219	.241	34	-5	0-1	.993	-1	86	144	1b18/D	0	-0.7
Total	13	883	2672	259	699	116	13	69	391	190-17	19	403	.262	.312	.392	99	-12	6-10	.989	-42	86	103	1b304,C297,D170,3b5	215	-7.0
Ellis, Mark	Mark William; B6.6.1977 Rapid City SD; BR/TR/5´11˝/(180–195); [KCA99 9/271]; d4.9; Col Florida; [DL 2004 Oak A 183]																								
2002	†Oak A	98	345	58	94	16	4	6	35	44-1	4	54	.272	.359	.394	101	2	4-2	.978	6	101	93	2b85,S8,3b7/D	0	1.1
2003	†Oak A	154	553	78	137	31	5	9	52	48-4	7	94	.248	.313	.371	80	-16	6-2	.982	30	113	105	2b153	0	2.1
2005	Oak A	122	434	76	137	21	5	13	52	44-1	4	51	.316	.384	.477	128	18	1-3	.989	8	102	**120**	2b115,S7,1b2/D	0	3.0
2006	†Oak A	124	441	64	110	25	1	11	52	40-1	8	76	.249	.319	.385	84	-10	4-0	**.997**	8	102	106	2b123/1	29	0.4
Total	4	498	1773	276	478	93	15	39	191	176-7	23	275	.270	.341	.405	97	-6	15-7	.987	52	105	107	2b476,S15,3b7,1b3,D2	212	6.6
Ellis, Rob	Robert Walter; B7.3.1950 Grand Rapids MI; BR/TR/5´11˝/180; [MilA71 D1/3]; d6.18; Col Michigan St.																								
1971	Mil A	36	111	9	22	2	0	0	6	12-0	1	24	.198	.278	.216	43	-8	0-2	.923	-6	70	144	3b19,O15(1/1/13)	0	-1.7
1974	Mil A	22	48	4	14	2	0	0	4	4-0	0	11	.292	.346	.333	97	0	0-0	1.000	1	78	493	O11(4/0/8)/3D	0	0.1
1975	Mil A	6	7	3	2	0	0	0	0	0-0	0	0	.286	.286	.286	61	0	0-0	1.000	-1	17	0	O5L/D	0	-0.2
Total	3	64	166	16	38	4	0	0	10	16-0	1	35	.229	.297	.253	59	-8	0-2	.976	-5	80	160	O31(10/1/21),3b20,D10	0	-1.8
Ellison, Babe	Herbert Spencer "Bert"; B11.15.1896 Ola AR; D8.11.1955 San Francisco CA; BR/TR/5´11˝/170; d9.18; Mil 1918; Col Arkansas																								
1916	Det A	2	7	0	1	0	0	0	1	0	0	1	.143	.143	.143	-14	-1	0	1.000	-1	26	0	3b2	—	-0.2
1917	Det A	9	29	2	5	1	2	1	4	6	1	3	.172	.333	.448	139	1	0	.980	-2	17	96	1b9	—	-0.1
1918	Det A	7	23	1	6	1	0	0	2	3	0	1	.261	.346	.304	100	0	1	1.000	1	104	0	O4R,2b3	—	0.1
1919	Det A	56	134	18	29	4	0	0	11	13	1	24	.216	.291	.246	53	-8	4	.966	-2	99	80	2b25,O10(1/1/8)/S	—	-1.1
1920	Det A	61	155	11	34	7	2	0	21	8	0	26	.219	.258	.290	46	-13	4-1	.997	3	114	61	1b38,O4(0/2/2)/3	—	-1.0
Total	5	135	348	32	75	13	4	1	39	30	2	55	.216	.282	.284	58	-21	9-1	.994	-2	94	68	1b47,2b28,O18(1/3/14),3b3/S	—	-2.3
Ellison, Jason	Jason Jerome; B4.4.1978 Quincy CA; BR/TR/5´10˝/180; [NYA95 47/1307]; d5.9; Col Lewis–Clark St.																								
2003	SF N	7	10	1	1	0	0	0	0	0-0	0	1	.100	.100	.100	-47	-2	0-0	1.000	-0	77	0	O4(3/1/0)	0	-0.3
2004	SF N	13	4	4	2	0	0	0	1	3	0-0	1	.500	.500	1.250	320	1	2-0	1.000	0	178	0	O4C	0	0.2
2005	SF N	131	352	49	93	18	2	4	24	24-1	3	44	.264	.316	.361	75	-13	14-6	.968	5	112	103	O122(15/78/32)	0	-0.8
2006	SF N	84	81	14	18	5	1	2	4	5-0	1	14	.222	.273	.383	66	-4	2-2	.960	1	100	167	O64(44/4/17)	0	-0.5
Total	4	235	447	68	114	23	3	7	31	29-1	4	60	.255	.305	.367	73	-18	18-8	.967	6	110	113	O194(62/87/49)	0	-1.4
Elmore, Verdo	Verdo Wilson "Ellie"; B12.10.1899 Gordo AL; D8.5.1969 Birmingham AL; BL/TR/5´11˝/185; d9.11; Col Alabama																								
1924	StL A	7	17	2	3	3	0	0	0	1	0	3	.176	.222	.353	44	-1	0-0	.000	-1	0	0	O3R	—	-0.2
Elsh, Roy	Eugene Raybold; B3.1.1891 Penns Grove NJ; D11.12.1978 Philadelphia PA; BR/TR/5´9˝/165; d4.19																								
1923	Chi A	81	209	28	52	7	2	0	24	16	1	23	.249	.305	.301	61	-12	16-8	.957	2	109	108	O57(50/6/1)	—	-1.3
1924	Chi A	60	147	21	45	9	1	0	11	10	0	14	.306	.350	.381	91	-2	6-1	.953	-1	104	79	O38(2/5/31),1b2	—	-0.4
1925	Chi A	32	48	6	9	1	0	0	4	5	0	7	.188	.264	.208	22	-6	2-0	.964	2	117	183	O16(2/3/11),1b3	—	-0.4
Total	3	173	404	55	106	17	3	0	39	31	1	44	.262	.317	.319	67	-20	24-9	.957	2	108	107	O111(54/14/43),1b5	—	-2.1
Elster, Kevin	Kevin Daniel; B8.3.1964 San Pedro CA; BR/TR/6´2˝/(180–205); [NYN84*2/28]; d9.2; Col Golden West (CA) JC																								
1986	†NY N	19	30	3	5	1	0	0	0	3-1	0	8	.167	.242	.200	24	-3	0-0	.962	2	112	108	S19	0	0.0
1987	NY N	5	10	1	4	2	0	0	1	0-0	0	1	.400	.400	.600	167	1	0-0	.909	-0	98	0	S3	0	0.1
1988	†NY N	149	406	41	87	11	1	9	37	35-12	3	47	.214	.282	.313	73	-15	2-0	.977	2	93	98	S148	0	-0.3
1989	NY N	151	458	52	106	25	2	10	55	34-11	2	77	.231	.283	.360	88	-8	4-3	.976	7	95	96	S150	0	1.0
1990	NY N	92	314	36	65	20	1	9	45	30-2	1	54	.207	.274	.363	75	-11	2-0	.960	10	96	94	S92	61	0.6
1991	NY N	115	348	33	84	16	2	6	36	40-6	1	53	.241	.318	.351	89	-5	2-3	.970	5	104	82	S107	15	0.8
1992	NY N	6	18	0	4	0	0	0	0	0-0	0	2	.222	.222	.222	26	-2	0-0	1.000	-1	76	121	S5	175	-0.2
1994	NY A	7	20	0	0	0	0	0	0	1-0	0	6	.000	.048	.000	-89	-6	0-0	1.000	2	130	171	S7	36	-0.3
1995	NY A	10	17	1	2	1	0	0	0	1-0	0	5	.118	.167	.176	-11	-3	0-0	1.000	-1	88	59	S10/2	0	-0.3
	Phi N	26	53	10	11	4	1	1	9	7-1	1	14	.208	.302	.377	80	-1	0-0	.982	-1	90	139	S19,1b4,3b2	0	-0.2
1996	†Tex A	157	515	79	130	32	2	24	99	52-1	2	138	.252	.317	.462	90	-10	4-1	.981	5	99	99	S157	0	0.7
1997	Pit N	39	138	14	31	6	2	7	25	21-0	1	39	.225	.327	.449	100	0	0-2	.994	4	109	91	S39	135	0.5
1998	Tex A	84	297	33	69	10	1	8	37	33-0	2	66	.232	.311	.354	69	-14	0-2	.976	-2	105	87	S84	15	-1.0
2000	LA N	80	220	29	50	8	0	14	32	38-5	0	52	.227	.341	.455	104	1	0-0	.946	-9	92	80	S55,3b8/1	30	-0.4
Total	13	940	2844	332	648	136	12	88	376	295-39	13	562	.228	.300	.377	82	-76	14-11	.974	23	98	94	S895,3b10,1b5/2	467	1.0
Ely, Bones	William Frederick; B6.7.1863 N.Girard PA; D1.10.1952 Berkeley CA; BR/TR/6´1˝/155; d6.19; OF(74/9/1); ▲																								
1884	Buf N	1	4	0	0	0	0	0	0	0	—	2	.000	.000	.000	-97	-1	—	.000	-0	0	0	/rfP	—	-0.1
1886	Lou AA	10	32	5	5	0	0	0	6	2	0	—	.156	.206	.156	13	-3	1	1.000	-0	106	0	P6,O5(4/1/0)	—	-0.2
1890	Syr AA	119	496	72	130	16	6	0	64	31	2	—	.262	.308	.319	95	-4	44	.914	10	87	28	O78(70/8/0),S36,1b4,2b2/3P	—	0.4
1891	Bro N	31	111	9	17	0	1	0	11	7	0	9	.153	.203	.171	9	-13	4	.870	5	116	93	S28,3b2/2	—	-0.7
1893	StL N	44	178	25	45	1	6	0	16	17	0	13	.253	.318	.326	71	-8	2	.905	-5	91	90	S44	—	-0.9
1894	StL N	127	510	85	156	20	12	12	89	30	0	34	.306	.344	.463	93	-10	23	.901	1	101	95	S126/2P	—	-0.2
1895	StL N	118	471	68	122	16	2	1	47	19	0	18	.259	.288	.308	54	-33	29	.925	5	101	100	S118	—	-1.8
1896	Pit N	128	537	85	153	15	9	3	77	33	0	33	.285	.326	.363	85	-13	18	.918	-6	98	95	S128	—	-1.0
1897	Pit N	133	516	63	146	20	8	2	74	25	1	—	.283	.317	.364	83	-14	10	.927	5	100	81	S133	—	-0.3
1898	Pit N	148	519	49	110	14	5	2	44	24	0	—	.212	.247	.270	49	-36	6	**.943**	8	106	100	S148	—	-1.9
1899	Pit N	139	526	67	146	18	6	3	72	22	5	—	.278	.313	.352	82	-14	8	.928	-5	102	90	S133,2b6	—	-1.1
1900	†Pit N	130	475	60	116	6	6	0	51	17	1	—	.244	.272	.282	53	-33	6	.935	11	106	**133**	S130	—	-1.3
1901	Pit N	65	240	18	50	6	3	0	28	6	2	—	.208	.234	.258	41	-19	5	.916	-3	104	112	S64/3	—	-1.9
	Phi A	45	171	11	37	6	2	0	16	3	0	—	.216	.230	.275	38	-15	6	.913	2	106	108	S45	—	-1.1
1902	Was A	105	381	39	100	11	2	1	62	21	0	—	.262	.301	.310	69	-16	3	.923	-7	99	67	S105	—	-1.9
Total	14	1343	5167	656	1333	149	68	24	657	257	11	109	.258	.295	.327	70	-232	165	.923	21	102	97	S1238,O84L,2b10,P9,3b4,1b4	—	-14.0
Emerson, Chester	Chester Arthur "Chuck"; B10.27.1889 Stow ME; D7.2.1971 Augusta ME; BL/TR/5´8˝/165; d9.27; Col Dartmouth																								
1911	Phi A	7	18	2	4	0	0	0	0	6	0	—	.222	.417	.222	82	0	1	1.000	-0	132	0	O7(0/1/6)	—	-0.1
1912	Phi A	1	1	0	0	0	0	0	0	0	0	—	.000	.000	.000	-99	0	0	ø	0	—	—	/H	—	0.0
Total	2	8	19	2	4	0	0	0	0	6	0	—	.211	.400	.211	74	0	1	1.000	-0	132	0	O7(0/1/6)	—	-0.1
Emery, Cal	Calvin Wayne; B6.28.1937 Centre Hall PA; BL/TL/6´2˝/205; d7.15; C1; Col Penn St.																								
1963	Phi N	16	19	0	3	1	0	0	0	0-0	0	2	.158	.158	.211	5	-2	0-0	1.000	-0	0	0	1b2	0	-0.3
Emery, Spoke	Herrick Smith; B12.10.1898 Bay City MI; D6.2.1975 Cape Canaveral FL; BR/TR/5´9˝/165; d7.18																								
1924	Phi N	5	3	3	2	0	0	0	0	0	0	0	.667	.667	.667	230	1	0-1	1.000	0	165	0	/lf	—	0.0
Emmer, Frank	Frank William; B2.17.1896 Crestline OH; D10.18.1963 Homestead FL; BR/TR/5´8˝/150; d4.25																								
1916	Cin N	42	89	8	13	3	1	0	2	7	0	27	.146	.208	.202	27	-8	1	.899	-0	109	63	S29,O2L/23	—	-0.7
1926	Cin N	80	224	22	44	7	6	0	18	13	1	30	.196	.244	.281	42	-19	1	.918	-9	101	99	S79	—	-2.1
Total	2	122	313	30	57	10	7	0	20	20	1	57	.182	.234	.259	38	-27	2	.913	-9	103	90	S108,O2L/32	—	-2.8
Emmerich, Bob	Robert George; B8.1.1897 New York NY; D11.22.1948 Bridgeport CT; BR/TR/5´3˝/155; d9.22																								
1923	Bos N	13	24	3	2	0	0	0	0	2	0	3	.083	.154	.083	-37	-5	1-1	1.000	0	101	148	O8C	—	-0.5

YEAR	TM LG	G	AB	R	H	2B	3B	HR	RBI	BB-IB	HP	SO	AVG	OBP	SLG	AOPS	ABR	SB-CS	FA	FR	RNG	THR	GAMES AT POSITION	DL	BFW
ENCARNACION, ANGELO	Angelo Benjamin; B4.18.1969 Santo Domingo, D.R.; BR/TR/5´8˝/(177–180); d5.2; [DL 1998 Ana A 107]																								
1995	Pit N	58	159	18	36	7	2	2	10	13-5	0	28	.226	.285	.333	61	-9	1-1	.979	6	95	143	C55	0	0.0
1996	Pit N	7	22	3	7	2	0	0	1	0-0	0	5	.318	.318	.409	87	0	0-0	.951	-2	79	53	C7	0	-0.2
1997	Ana A	11	17	2	7	1	0	1	4	0-0	0	1	.412	.412	.647	170	2	2-0	.940	1	49	61	C11	0	0.3
Total	3	76	198	23	50	10	2	3	15	13-5	0	34	.253	.299	.369	73	-7	3-1	.971	5	89	126	C73	107	0.1
ENCARNACION, EDWIN	Edwin Elpidio; B1.7.1983 LaRomana, D.R.; BR/TR/6´1˝/195; [TexA00 9/274]; d6.24																								
2005	Cin N	69	211	25	49	16	0	9	31	20-2	3	60	.232	.308	.436	92	-3	3-0	.944	3	105	91	3b56	0	0.2
2006	Cin N	117	406	60	112	33	1	15	72	41-3	13	78	.276	.359	.473	105	5	6-3	.916	-8	94	85	3b111,1b2	29	-0.3
Total	2	186	617	85	161	49	1	24	103	61-5	16	138	.261	.341	.460	101	2	9-3	.926	-5	98	87	3b167,1b2	29	-0.1
ENCARNACION, JUAN	Juan De Dios; B3.8.1976 Las Matas de Farfan, D.R.; BR/TR/6´2˝/(160–215); d9.2																								
1997	Det A	11	33	3	7	1	1	1	5	3-0	2	12	.212	.316	.394	84	-1	3-1	1.000	-0	106	0	O10(0/2/10)	0	-0.1
1998	Det A	40	164	30	54	9	4	7	21	7-0	1	31	.329	.354	.561	133	7	7-4	.985	-5	68	145	O39(8/13/21)/D	29	0.1
1999	Det A	132	509	62	130	30	6	19	74	14-1	9	113	.255	.287	.450	83	-16	33-12	.968	1	100	123	O131(118/22/1)	0	-1.5
2000	Det A	141	547	75	158	25	6	14	72	29-1	7	90	.289	.330	.433	93	-8	16-4	.987	-5	100	43	O141C	0	-0.8
2001	Det A	120	417	52	101	19	7	12	52	25-1	6	93	.242	.292	.408	84	-11	9-5	.977	-7	94	68	O116(0/56/63)/D	0	-1.9
2002	Cin N	83	321	43	89	11	2	16	51	26-0	1	63	.277	.330	.474	106	1	9-4	.977	4	112	102	O82(0/59/31)	0	0.5
	Fla N	69	263	34	69	11	3	8	34	20-0	3	50	.262	.317	.418	97	-2	12-5	.993	-0	99	91	O67(0/12/61)	0	-0.4
	Year	152	584	77	158	22	5	24	85	46-0	4	113	.271	.324	.449	102	-1	21-9	.983	4	106	97	O149(0/71/92)	0	0.1
2003	†Fla N	156	601	80	162	37	6	19	94	37-0	4	82	.270	.313	.446	100	-3	19-8	**1.000**	6	110	70	O155R	0	-0.3
2004	LA N	86	324	42	76	18	1	13	43	21-0	4	53	.235	.289	.417	81	-11	3-3	.976	-3	95	55	O85(9/0/77)	15	-1.8
	Fla N	49	160	21	38	12	1	3	19	17-2	3	33	.237	.320	.381	85	-3	2-1	.980	1	110	71	O48R	0	-0.4
	Year	135	484	63	114	30	2	16	62	38-2	7	86	.236	.299	.405	82	-14	5-4	.978	-2	100	61	O133(9/0/125)	0	-2.2
2005	Fla N	141	506	59	145	27	3	16	76	41-2	9	104	.287	.349	.447	113	9	6-5	.983	-9	88	54	O139(0/11/135)	0	-0.7
2006	†StL N	153	557	74	155	25	5	19	79	30-6	4	86	.278	.317	.443	92	-9	6-5	.978	-9	91	57	O148(1/32/125)	0	-2.3
Total	10	1181	4402	575	1184	225	45	147	620	270-13	53	810	.269	.316	.441	95	-47	125-57	.983	-27	98	73	O1161(136/348/727),D2	44	-9.6
ENCARNACION, MARIO	Mario (Gonzalez); B9.24.1975 Bani, D.R.; D10.3.2005 Danshuei, Taiwan; BR/TR/6´2˝/210; d8.26																								
2001	Col N	20	62	3	14	1	0	0	3	5-0	0	14	.226	.284	.242	32	-6	2-1	1.000	1	109	87	O20(14/0/6)	0	-0.6
2002	Chi N	3	7	0	0	0	0	0	0	2-0	0	3	.000	.222	.000	-35	-1	0-0	1.000	0	194	0	O2L	0	-0.1
Total	2	23	69	3	14	1	0	0	3	7-0	0	17	.203	.276	.217	26	-7	2-1	1.000	1	116	80	O22(16/0/6)	0	-0.7
ENDICOTT, BILL	William Franklin; B9.4.1918 Acorn MO; BL/TL/5´11.5˝/175; d4.21																								
1946	StL N	20	20	2	4	3	0	0	3	4	0	4	.200	.333	.350	90	0	0	1.000	0	120	0	O2L	0	0.0
ENGLE, CLYDE	Arthur Clyde "Hack"; B3.19.1884 Dayton OH; D12.26.1939 Boston MA; BR/TR/5´10˝/190; d4.12; OF(142/111/26)																								
1909	NY A	135	492	66	137	20	5	3	71	47	5	—	.278	.347	.358	122	13	18	.946	15	99	122	O134(119/16/0)	—	2.3
1910	NY A	5	13	0	3	0	0	0	0	2	0	—	.231	.333	.231	73	0	1	.857	-0	105	0	O3L	—	-0.1
	Bos A	106	363	59	96	18	7	2	38	31	2	—	.264	.326	.369	115	6	12	.915	-2	108	100	3b51,2b27,O15(0/13/2),S7	—	0.6
	Year	111	376	59	99	18	7	2	38	33	2	—	.263	.326	.364	113	5	13	.915	-2	108	100	3b51,2b27,O18(3/13/2),S7	—	0.5
1911	Bos A	146	514	58	139	13	3	2	48	51	6	—	.270	.343	.319	86	-8	24	.975	-1	107	86	1b65,3b51,2b13,O10(3/7/0)	—	-1.0
1912	†Bos A	58	171	32	40	5	3	0	18	28	2	—	.234	.348	.298	81	-3	12	.977	-7	60	114	1b25,2b15,3b11,S2/rf	—	-1.0
1913	Bos A	143	498	75	144	17	12	2	50	53	5	41	.289	.363	.384	116	10	28	.987	-7	69	75	1b133,O2(0/1/1)	—	-0.1
1914	Bos A	59	134	14	26	2	0	0	9	14	1	11	.194	.275	.209	46	-9	4-9	.976	-4	56	106	1b29,2b5,3b3/rf	—	-1.8
	Buf F	32	110	12	28	4	1	0	12	11	1	18	.255	.328	.309	73	-6	5	.889	-5	63	65	3b23,O9(3/0/7)	—	-1.1
1915	Buf F	141	501	56	131	22	8	3	71	34	3	43	.261	.312	.355	86	-18	24	.969	-7	100	56	O100(14/74/13),2b21,3b17/1	—	-3.3
1916	Cle A	11	26	1	4	0	0	0	1	0	0	6	.154	.154	.154	-7	-3	0	.810	-2	98	0	3b7,1b2/rf	—	-0.6
Total	8	836	2822	373	748	101	39	12	318	271	25	119	.265	.335	.341	97	-18	128-9	.959	-20	99	102	O276L,1b255,3b163,2b81,S9	—	-6.1
ENGLE, CHARLIE	Charlie August "Cholly"; B8.27.1903 New York NY; D10.12.1983 San Antonio TX; BR/TR/5´8˝/145; d9.14																								
1925	Phi A	1	0	0	0	0	0	0	0	0	0	0	ø	ø	ø	ø	0	0-0	ø	-0	0	0	/S	—	0.0
1926	Phi A	19	19	7	2	0	0	0	0	10	1	6	.105	.433	.105	43	-1	0-0	.930	1	111	147	S16	—	0.1
1930	Pit N	67	216	34	57	10	1	0	15	22	1	20	.264	.335	.319	59	-14	1	.975	-1	113	65	3b24,S23,2b10	—	-1.0
Total	3	87	235	41	59	10	1	0	15	32	2	26	.251	.346	.302	59	-15	1-0	.937	-0	105	89	S40,3b24,2b10	—	-0.9
ENGLE, DAVE	Ralph David; B11.30.1956 San Diego CA; BR/TR/6´3˝/(210–220); [CalA78 3/66]; d4.14; C3; Col USC; OF(17/1/119)																								
1981	Min A	82	248	29	64	14	4	5	32	13-1	1	37	.258	.295	.407	95	-2	0-1	.980	1	106	83	O76R/3D	0	-0.6
1982	Min A	58	186	20	42	7	2	4	16	10-0	1	22	.226	.269	.349	66	-9	0-0	.985	3	115	158	O34(2/1/32),D20	0	-0.9
1983	Min A	120	374	46	114	22	4	8	43	28-1	1	39	.305	.350	.449	115	8	2-1	.973	-12	96	76	C73,D29,O4R	0	-0.2
1984	Min A☆	109	391	56	104	20	1	4	38	26-3	0	22	.266	.308	.353	79	-11	0-1	.981	-0	92	94	C86,D22	0	-0.8
1985	Min A	70	172	28	44	8	2	7	25	21-1	0	28	.256	.333	.448	106	1	2-2	.984	2	184	28	D38,C17,O3L	0	0.2
1986	Det A	35	86	6	22	7	0	0	4	7-0	0	13	.256	.312	.337	76	-3	0-0	1.000	-1	83	123	1b23,O4(2/0/2),C3,D5	38	-0.4
1987	Mon N	59	84	7	19	4	0	1	14	6-1	0	11	.226	.278	.310	53	-6	1-0	1.000	1	122	182	O11(9/0/2),C6,1b2/3	0	-0.5
1988	Mon N	34	37	4	8	3	0	0	1	5-0	0	5	.216	.310	.297	71	-1	0-0	1.000	0	65	96	C9,O4(1/0/3)/3	0	-0.1
1989	Mil A	27	65	5	14	3	0	2	8	4-0	0	13	.215	.261	.354	72	-3	0-0	.973	0	125	94	1b18,C3,D3	0	-0.4
Total	9	594	1643	201	431	88	13	31	181	120-7	3	190	.262	.311	.388	89	-26	5-5	.979	-7	99	83	C197,O136R,D118,1b43,3b3	38	-3.7
ENGLISH, CHARLIE	Charles Dewie; B4.8.1910 Darlington SC; D6.25.1999 Pasadena CA; BR/TR/5´9.5˝/160; d7.23																								
1932	Chi A	24	63	7	20	3	1	1	8	3	0	7	.317	.348	.444	111	1	0-0	.821	-3	100	89	3b13/S	—	-0.1
1933	Chi A	3	9	2	4	2	0	0	1	1	0	1	.444	.500	.667	216	2	0-0	.923	-1	82	148	2b3	—	0.1
1936	NY N	6	1	0	0	0	0	0	0	0	0	0	.000	.000	.000	-99	0	0	ø	-0	0	0	/2	—	0.0
1937	Cin N	17	63	1	15	3	1	0	4	0	0	2	.238	.238	.317	52	-5	0	.958	2	112	106	3b15,2b2	—	-0.2
Total	4	50	136	10	39	8	2	1	13	4	0	10	.287	.307	.397	90	-2	0-0	.897	-2	106	98	3b28,2b6/S	—	-0.2
ENGLISH, WOODY	Elwood George; B3.2.1906 Fredonia OH; D9.26.1997 Newark OH; BR/TR/5´10˝/155; d4.26																								
1927	Chi N	87	334	46	97	14	4	1	28	16	1	26	.290	.325	.365	84	-8	1	.940	2	105	94	S84/3	—	0.3
1928	Chi N	116	475	68	142	22	4	2	34	30	2	28	.299	.343	.375	89	-8	4	.946	7	101	119	S114,3b2	—	1.1
1929	†Chi N	144	608	131	168	29	3	1	52	68	3	50	.276	.352	.339	72	-25	13	.955	14	102	116	S144	—	0.5
1930	Chi N	**156**	638	152	214	36	17	14	59	100	6	72	.335	.430	.511	125	31	3	.973	-11	88	126	3b83,S78	—	2.9
1931	Chi N	**156**	634	117	202	38	8	2	53	68	7	80	.319	.391	.413	114	16	12	.965	1	96	78	S138,3b18	—	2.7
1932	†Chi N	127	522	70	142	23	7	3	47	55	2	73	.272	.344	.360	90	-6	5	.957	1	98	79	3b93,S38	—	0.1
1933	Chi N★	105	398	54	104	19	2	3	41	53	0	44	.261	.348	.342	98	1	5	**.973**	-8	92	68	3b103/S	—	-0.3
1934	Chi N	109	421	65	117	26	5	3	31	48	1	65	.278	.353	.385	99	1	6	.971	-1	76	89	S56,3b46,2b7	—	0.5
1935	Chi N	34	84	11	17	2	0	2	8	20	2	4	.202	.368	.298	81	-1	1	.868	-3	94	97	3b16,S12	—	-0.2
1936	Chi N	64	182	33	45	9	0	0	20	40	4	28	.247	.394	.297	86	0	1	.976	4	105	121	S42,3b17/2	—	0.7
1937	Bro N	129	378	45	90	16	2	1	42	65	0	55	.238	.350	.299	77	-9	4	.956	-14	90	76	S116,2b11	—	-1.5
1938	Bro N	34	72	9	18	2	0	0	7	8	1	11	.250	.333	.278	68	-3	2	.958	0	99	147	3b21,2b3,S3	—	-0.2
Total	12	1261	4746	801	1356	236	52	32	422	571	29	536	.286	.366	.378	95	-11	57	.957	-8	97	98	S826,3b400,2b22	—	6.6
ENGLISH, GIL	Gilbert Raymond; B7.2.1909 Glenola NC; D8.31.1996 Trinity NC; BR/TR/5´11˝/180; d9.20																								
1931	NY N	3	8	0	0	0	0	0	0	1	0	3	.000	.111	.000	-69	-2	0	1.000	-0	86	0	3b3	—	-0.2
1932	NY N	59	204	22	46	7	5	2	19	5	0	20	.225	.244	.338	56	-14	0	.931	2	106	157	3b39,S23	—	-0.9
1936	Det A	1	1	0	0	0	0	0	0	0	0	1	.000	.000	.000	-99	0	0-0	1.000	0	111	0	/3	—	0.0
1937	Det A	18	65	6	17	1	0	1	6	6	1	4	.262	.333	.323	65	-4	1-1	.962	-5	82	66	2b12,3b6	—	-0.7
	Bos N	79	269	25	78	5	2	2	37	23	1	27	.290	.348	.346	98	-1	3	.958	-5	101	114	3b71	—	-0.4
1938	Bos N	53	165	17	41	6	0	2	21	15	1	16	.248	.315	.321	84	-4	1	.956	-3	103	48	3b43,O3L,2b2,S2	—	-0.5
1944	Bro N	27	79	4	12	3	0	1	7	6	0	7	.152	.212	.228	24	-8	0	.918	-3	106	94	S13,3b11,2b2	0	-1.1
Total	6	240	791	74	194	22	7	8	90	56	3	78	.245	.298	.321	72	-33	5-1	.950	-14	101	104	3b174,S38,2b16,O3L	0	-3.8
ENNIS, DEL	Delmer; B6.8.1925 Philadelphia PA; D2.8.1996 Huntingdon Valley PA; BR/TR/6´0˝/195; d4.28																								
1946	Phi N★	141	540	70	169	30	6	17	73	39	4	65	.313	.364	.485	144	28	5	.975	10	111	126	O138(138/0/1)	0	2.9
1947	Phi N	139	541	71	149	25	6	12	81	37	3	51	.275	.325	.410	98	-4	9	.979	4	103	112	O135(135/0/2)	0	-1.0
1948	Phi N	152	589	86	171	40	4	30	95	47	2	58	.290	.345	.525	135	26	2	.957	3	101	134	O151R	0	2.3
1949	Phi N	**154**	610	92	184	39	11	25	110	59	4	61	.302	.367	.525	140	33	2	.966	-1	97	114	O154L	0	2.0

YEAR	TM LG	G	AB	R	H	2B	3B	HR	RBI	BB-IB	HP	SO	AVG	OBP	SLG	AOPS	ABR	SB-CS	FA	FR	RNG	THR	GAMES AT POSITION	DL	BFW
1950	†Phi N	153	595	92	185	34	8	31	**126**	56	2	59	.311	.372	.551	142	34	2	.970	-3	99	87	O149(14/1/140)	0	2.5
1951	Phi N★	144	532	76	142	20	5	15	73	68	2	42	.267	.352	.408	105	5	4-2	.969	-2	97	109	O135(26/0/116)	0	-0.2
1952	Phi N	151	592	90	171	30	10	20	107	47	0	65	.289	.341	.475	125	18	6-4	.970	-5	93	92	O149(120/0/31)	0	0.3
1953	Phi N	152	578	79	165	22	3	29	125	57	5	53	.285	.355	.484	117	13	1-3	.980	-3	94	108	O150L	0	0.0
1954	Phi N	145	556	73	145	23	2	25	119	50	2	60	.261	.318	.444	98	-3	2-1	.957	-2	103	79	O142(72/0/71)/1	0	-1.3
1955	Phi N★	146	564	82	167	24	7	29	120	46-8	2	46	.296	.346	.518	129	22	4-2	.987	1	102	84	O145(143/0/3)	0	1.4
1956	Phi N	153	630	80	164	23	3	26	95	33-8	3	62	.260	.299	.430	95	-7	7-3	.962	-8	89	80	O153L	0	-2.5
1957	StL N	136	490	61	140	24	3	24	105	37-3	1	50	.286	.332	.494	117	11	1-3	.943	-17	76	35	O127(74/0/53)	0	-1.3
1958	StL N	106	329	22	86	18	1	3	47	15-3	1	35	.261	.290	.350	67	-15	0-1	.993	2	84	198	O84L	0	-1.9
1959	Cin N	5	12	1	4	0	0	0	1	2-1	0	2	.333	.429	.333	103	0	0-0	1.000	-0	94	0	O3L	0	0.0
	Chi A	26	96	10	21	6	0	2	7	4-0	0	10	.219	.250	.344	62	-5	0-0	.909	-3	65	145	O25L	0	-0.9
Total	14	1903	7254	985	2063	358	69	288	1284	597-23	31	719	.284	.340	.472	117	156	45-19	.969	-23	96	102	O1840(1291/1/568)/1	0	2.3
Ennis, Russ	Russell Elwood "Hack"; B3.10.1897 Superior WI; D1.21.1949 Superior WI; BR/TR/5´11.5˝/160; d9.19																								
1926	Was A	1	0	0	0	0	0	0	0	0	0	0	ø	ø	ø	ø	0	0-0	ø	-0	*0*	*0*	/C	—	0.0
Enright, George	George Albert; B5.9.1954 New Britain CT; BR/TR/5´11˝/175; [ChiA72 6/132]; d8.8																								
1976	Chi A	2	1	0	0	0	0	0	0	0-0	0	0	.000	.000	.000	-99	0	0-0	1.000	-1	17	282	C2	0	-0.1
Ens, Mutz	Anton; B11.8.1884 St.Louis MO; D6.28.1950 St.Louis MO; BL/TL/6´1˝/180; d9.2; b–Jewel																								
1912	Chi A	3	6	0	0	0	0	0	0	0	0	—	.000	.000	.000	-99	-2	0	.857	-1	0	162	1b3	—	-0.2
Ens, Jewel	Jewel Winklemeyer; B8.24.1889 St.Louis MO; D1.17.1950 Syracuse NY; BR/TR/5´10.5˝/165; d4.29; M3/C13; b–Mutz																								
1922	Pit N	47	142	18	42	7	3	0	17	7	2	9	.296	.338	.387	85	-3	3-0	.951	-13	74	52	2b29,3b3,1b2/S	—	-1.4
1923	Pit N	12	29	3	8	1	1	0	5	0	0	3	.276	.276	.379	70	-1	2-0	.975	-0	0	135	1b4,3b3	—	-0.1
1924	Pit N	5	10	2	3	0	0	0	0	0	0	3	.300	.300	.300	60	-1	0-0	1.000	-0	71	51	1b5	—	-0.1
1925	Pit N	3	5	2	1	0	0	1	2	0	0	1	.200	.200	.800	133	0	0-0	1.000	-0	0	0	1b3	—	0.0
Total	4	67	186	25	54	8	4	1	24	7	2	16	.290	.323	.392	83	-5	5-0	.951	-14	74	52	2b29,1b14,3b6/S	—	-1.6
Ensberg, Morgan	Morgan Paul; B8.26.1975 Redondo Beach CA; BR/TR/6´2˝/(210–220); [HouN98 9/272]; d9.20; Col USC																								
2000	Hou N	4	7	0	2	0	0	0	0	0-0	0	1	.286	.286	.286	42	-1	0-0	.667	-1	55	0	/3	0	-0.1
2002	Hou N	49	132	14	32	7	2	3	19	18-0	3	25	.242	.346	.394	87	-2	2-0	.929	3	108	68	3b43	0	0.1
2003	Hou N	127	385	69	112	15	1	25	60	48-1	6	60	.291	.377	.530	127	15	7-2	.967	4	98	109	3b111/D	0	2.0
2004	†Hou N	131	411	51	113	20	3	10	66	36-1	0	46	.275	.330	.411	88	-8	6-4	.949	-6	83	**123**	3b118/S	0	-1.3
2005	†Hou N★	150	526	86	149	30	3	36	101	85-9	8	119	.283	.388	.557	142	34	6-7	.964	8	102	126	3b148	0	4.2
2006	Hou N	127	387	67	91	17	1	23	58	101-7	4	96	.235	.396	.463	117	14	1-4	.963	8	106	**131**	3b117	22	2.1
Total	6	588	1848	287	499	89	10	97	304	288-18	21	347	.270	.372	.486	117	52	22-17	.958	16	98	119	3b538/SD	22	7.0
Enwright, Charlie	Charles Massey; B10.6.1887 Sacramento CA; D1.19.1917 Sacramento CA; BL/TR/5´10˝/?; d4.19; Col St. Marys (CA)																								
1909	StL N	3	7	1	1	0	0	0	1	2	0	—	.143	.333	.143	51	0	0	.444	-3	34	0	S2	—	-0.4
Enzenroth, Jack	Clarence Herman; B11.4.1885 Mineral Point WI; D2.21.1944 Detroit MI; BR/TR/5´7˝/160; d5.1; Col Michigan																								
1914	StL A	3	6	0	1	0	0	0	0	2	1	3	.167	.444	.167	88	0	0-1	.923	-1	*96*	*41*	C3	—	0.0
	KC F	26	67	7	12	4	1	0	5	5	0	19	.179	.236	.269	39	-7	0	.965	-2	*91*	*105*	C24	—	-0.8
1915	KC F	14	19	3	3	0	0	0	3	6	0	0	.158	.360	.158	50	-1	0	.973	1	*112*	*130*	C8	—	0.1
Total	2	43	92	10	16	4	1	0	8	13	1	22	.174	.283	.239	47	-8	0-1	.963	-1	*96*	*105*	C35	—	-0.7
Eppard, Jim	James Gerhard; B4.27.1960 South Bend IN; BL/TL/6´2˝/(180–181); [OakA82 13/340]; d9.8; Col California																								
1987	Cal A	8	9	2	3	0	0	0	0	2-0	0	0	.333	.455	.333	117	0	0-0	1.000	-0	55	0	/rf	0	0.0
1988	Cal A	56	113	7	32	3	1	0	14	11-0	0	15	.283	.347	.327	92	-1	0-0	.971	1	116	0	O17L,D10,1b6	0	-0.1
1989	Cal A	12	12	0	3	0	0	0	2	1-0	0	4	.250	.308	.250	60	-1	0-0	1.000	-0	0	154	1b4	0	-0.1
1990	Tor A	6	5	0	1	0	0	0	0	0-0	1	2	.200	.333	.200	51	0	0-0	ø	0	—	—	/H	0	0.0
Total	4	82	139	9	39	3	1	0	16	14-0	1	21	.281	.351	.317	90	-2	0-0	.972	0	112	0	O18(17/0/1),1b10,D10	0	-0.2
Epps, Aubrey	Aubrey Lee "Yo-Yo"; B3.3.1912 Memphis TN; D11.13.1984 Ackerman MS; BR/TR/5´10˝/170; d9.29																								
1935	Pit N	1	4	1	3	0	1	0	3	0	0	0	.750	.750	1.250	414	2	0	.750	-1	*43*	*0*	/C	—	0.1
Epps, Hal	Harold Franklin; B3.26.1914 Athens GA; D8.25.2004 Houston TX; BL/TL/6´0˝/175; d9.9; Mil 1945–46																								
1938	StL N	17	50	8	15	0	0	1	3	2	0	4	.300	.327	.360	84	-1	2	.963	-1	103	0	O10C	—	-0.2
1940	StL N	11	15	6	3	0	0	0	1	0	0	3	.200	.200	.200	10	-2	0	.800	-0	99	0	O3C	—	-0.2
1943	StL A	8	35	2	10	4	0	0	1	3	0	4	.286	.342	.400	114	1	1-1	1.000	-1	91	0	O8C	0	0.0
1944	StL A	22	62	15	11	1	1	0	3	14	1	14	.177	.338	.226	59	-3	0-1	.962	1	96	176	O18C	0	-0.3
	Phi A	67	229	27	60	8	8	0	13	18	0	18	.262	.316	.367	96	-2	2-1	.973	-2	96	79	O60(0/44/16)	0	-0.7
	Year	89	291	42	71	9	9	0	16	32	1	32	.244	.321	.337	88	-5	2-2	.970	-1	96	102	O78(0/62/16)	0	-1.0
Total	4	125	391	58	99	13	9	1	21	37	1	43	.253	.319	.340	86	-7	5-3	.968	-3	96	81	O99(0/83/16)	0	-1.4
Epstein, Mike	Michael Peter "Superjew"; B4.4.1943 Bronx NY; BL/TL/6´3.5˝/(225–230); d9.16; Col California																								
1966	Bal A	6	11	1	2	0	1	0	3	1-0	0	3	.182	.250	.364	75	0	0-0	1.000	0	105	140	1b4	0	-0.1
1967	Bal A	9	13	0	2	0	0	0	0	3-0	0	5	.154	.313	.154	42	-1	0-0	1.000	-0	55	108	1b3	0	-0.1
	Was A	96	284	32	65	7	4	9	29	38-5	6	74	.229	.331	.377	114	5	1-4	.987	-1	104	127	1b80	0	-0.2
	Year	105	297	32	67	7	4	9	29	41-5	6	79	.226	.330	.367	110	4	1-4	.988	-1	102	126	1b83	0	-0.3
1968	Was A	123	385	40	90	8	2	13	33	48-5	13	91	.234	.338	.366	118	9	1-1	.987	-1	103	97	1b110	0	0.2
1969	Was A	131	403	73	112	18	1	30	85	85-10	10	99	.278	.414	.551	177	46	2-5	.990	-4	91	105	1b118	0	3.3
1970	Was A	140	430	55	110	15	3	20	56	73-6	9	117	.256	.371	.444	131	20	2-3	.992	-5	88	105	1b122	0	0.5
1971	Was A	24	85	6	21	1	1	1	9	12-1	4	31	.247	.366	.318	100	1	1-0	.992	-2	77	142	1b24	0	-0.3
	†Oak A	104	329	43	77	13	0	18	51	62-5	8	71	.234	.368	.438	130	15	0-3	.995	-2	89	137	1b96	0	0.6
	Year	128	414	49	98	14	1	19	60	74-6	**12**	102	.237	.367	.413	124	16	1-3	.994	-3	86	**138**	1b120	0	0.3
1972	†Oak A	138	455	63	123	18	2	26	70	68-9	11	68	.270	.376	.490	165	38	0-1	.990	-0	102	108	1b137	0	3.1
1973	Tex A	27	85	9	16	3	0	1	6	14-0	3	19	.188	.317	.259	68	-3	0-0	.991	-1	77	79	1b25	0	-0.6
	Cal A	91	312	30	67	8	2	8	32	34-2	5	54	.215	.300	.330	84	-7	0-0	.993	1	97	82	1b86	0	-1.4
	Year	118	397	39	83	11	2	9	38	48-2	8	73	.209	.304	.315	80	-10	0-0	.993	-1	93	81	1b111	0	-2.0
1974	Cal A	18	62	10	10	2	0	4	6	10-0	1	13	.161	.288	.387	98	0	0-0	.993	1	119	91	1b18	0	0.0
Total	9	907	2854	362	695	93	16	130	380	448-43	70	645	.244	.358	.424	130	123	7-17	.991	-13	95	108	1b823	0	5.0
Erautt, Joe	Joseph Michael "Stubby"; B9.1.1921 Vibank SK, Can.; D10.6.1976 Portland OR; BR/TR/5´9˝/175; d5.9; b–Eddie; Col Portland																								
1950	Chi A	16	18	0	4	0	0	0	1	1	0	3	.222	.263	.222	26	-2	0-0	1.000	1	*57*	*220*	C5	0	-0.1
1951	Chi A	16	25	3	4	1	0	0	0	3	1	2	.160	.276	.200	31	-2	0-0	.977	2	*112*	*116*	C12	0	0.0
Total	2	32	43	3	8	1	0	0	1	4	1	5	.186	.271	.209	29	-4	0-0	.983	2	*99*	*140*	C17	0	-0.1
Erickson, Hank	Henry Nels "Popeye"; B11.11.1907 Chicago IL; D12.13.1964 Louisville KY; BR/TR/6´1˝/185; d4.17																								
1935	Cin N	37	88	9	23	3	2	1	4	6	2	4	.261	.323	.375	90	-1	0	.972	2	*93*	*155*	C25	—	0.2
Erickson, Matt	Matt; B7.30.1975 Appleton WI; BL/TR/5´11˝/190; [FlaN97 7/216]; d7.9; Col Arkansas																								
2004	Mil N	4	6	0	1	0	0	0	0	0-0	0	1	.167	.167	.167	-13	-1	0-0	1.000	1	116	.179	/2S	0	0.0
Ermer, Cal	Calvin Coolidge; B11.10.1923 Baltimore MD; BR/TR/6´0.5˝/175; d9.26; M2/C4																								
1947	Was A	1	3	0	0	0	0	0	0	0	0	0	.000	.000	.000	-99	-1	0-0	1.000	0	101	0	/2	0	-0.1
Ernaga, Frank	Frank John; B8.22.1930 Susanville CA; BR/TR/6´1˝/(190–195); d5.24; Col UCLA																								
1957	Chi N	20	35	9	11	3	2	2	7	9-0	0	14	.314	.455	.686	204	6	0-0	.950	0	124	0	O10(3/0/7)	0	0.5
1958	Chi N	9	8	0	1	0	0	0	0	0-0	0	2	.125	.125	.125	-34	-2	0-0	ø	0	—	—	/H	0	-0.2
Total	2	29	43	9	12	3	2	2	7	9-0	0	16	.279	.404	.581	163	4	0-0	.950	0	124	0	O10(3/0/7)	0	0.3
Erstad, Darin	Darin Charles; B6.4.1974 Jamestown ND; BL/TL/6´2˝/(210–220); [CalA95 1/1]; d6.14; Col Nebraska																								
1996	Cal A	57	208	34	59	5	1	4	20	17-1	0	29	.284	.333	.375	79	-7	3-3	.976	-1	106	67	O48(11/36/1)	0	-0.7
1997	Ana A	139	539	99	161	34	4	16	77	51-4	4	86	.299	.360	.466	114	11	23-8	.990	-6	82	88	1b126/cfD	0	-0.3
1998	Ana A★	133	537	84	159	39	3	19	82	43-7	6	77	.296	.353	.486	114	11	20-6	.992	-2	87	99	O72(70/3/0),1b70,D2	15	0.3

YEAR	TM LG	G	AB	R	H	2B	3B	HR	RBI	BB-IB	HP	SO	AVG	OBP	SLG	AOPS	ABR	SB-CS	FA	FR	RNG	THR	GAMES AT POSITION	DL	BFW
1999	Ana A	142	585	84	148	22	5	13	53	47-3	1	101	.253	.308	.374	73	-25	13-7	.999	12	96	91	1b78,O69(67/2/0),D2	15	-2.1
2000	Ana A★	157	676	121	**240**	39	6	25	100	64-9	1	82	.355	.409	.541	135	37	28-8	.992	9	**113**	107	O136(112/30/0),D20,1b3	0	4.0
2001	Ana A	157	631	89	163	35	1	9	63	62-7	10	113	.258	.331	.360	81	-15	24-10	**.998**	6	106	119	O146C,1b12,D4	0	-0.6
2002	†Ana A	150	625	99	177	28	4	10	73	27-4	2	67	.283	.313	.389	87	-13	23-3	.998	19	**122**	147	O143C,1b5,D4	0	1.1
2003	Ana A	67	258	35	65	7	1	4	17	18-1	4	40	.252	.309	.333	73	-11	9-1	1.000	4	114	69	O66C	103	-0.4
2004	†Ana A	125	495	79	146	29	1	7	69	37-1	4	74	.295	.346	.400	99	0	16-1	.996	-6	79	86	1b124	36	-1.3
2005	†LA A	153	609	86	166	33	3	7	66	47-3	1	109	.273	.325	.371	87	-11	10-3	.997	-6	81	94	1b147,D5	0	-2.8
2006	LA A	40	95	8	21	8	1	0	5	6-0	2	18	.221	.279	.326	59	-6	1-1	1.000	1	114	82	O27C,1b13	117	-0.5
Total	11	1320	5258	818	1505	279	30	114	625	419-40	35	796	.286	.341	.416	97	-29	170-51	.995	30	112	114	O708(260/454/1),1b578,D46	286	-3.3
Erwin, Tex	Ross Emil; B12.22.1885 Forney TX; D4.5.1953 Rochester NY; BL/TR/6´0˝/185; d8.26																								
1907	Det A	4	5	0	1	0	0	0	1	1	0	—	.200	.333	.200	68	0	0	.909	-0	*94*	*134*	C4	—	0.0
1910	Bro N	81	202	15	38	3	1	1	10	24	1	12	.188	.278	.228	49	-13	3	.949	-1	*94*	*111*	C68	—	-0.8
1911	Bro N	91	218	30	59	13	2	7	34	31	2	23	.271	.367	.445	132	10	5	.971	-7	*79*	*109*	C74	—	0.8
1912	Bro N	59	133	14	28	3	0	2	14	18	0	16	.211	.305	.278	62	-7	1	.949	-2	*92*	*94*	C41	—	-0.6
1913	Bro N	20	31	6	8	1	0	0	3	4	0	5	.258	.343	.290	80	-1	0-1	.950	-2	*90*	57	C13	—	-0.2
1914	Bro N	9	11	0	5	0	0	0	1	2	0	1	.455	.538	.455	192	1	1	1.000	-1	*69*	*121*	C4	—	0.1
	Cin N	12	35	5	11	3	0	1	7	2	0	3	.314	.351	.486	144	2	0	.962	0	*107*	*74*	C12	—	0.3
	Year	21	46	5	16	3	0	1	8	4	0	4	.348	.400	.478	157	3	1	.966	-0	*102*	*81*	C16	—	0.4
Total	6	276	635	70	150	23	3	11	70	82	3	60	.236	.326	.334	90	-8	10-1	.957	-13	*89*	*103*	C216	—	-0.4
Esasky, Nick	Nicholas Andrew; B2.24.1960 Hialeah FL; BR/TR/6´3˝/(200–215); [CinN78 1/17]; d6.19; [DL 1991 Atl N 182, 1992 Atl N 85]																								
1983	Cin N	85	302	41	80	10	5	12	46	27-1	3	99	.265	.328	.450	111	3	6-2	.935	-9	87	81	3b84	0	-0.7
1984	Cin N	113	322	30	62	10	5	10	45	52-3	0	103	.193	.301	.348	79	-9	1-2	.910	-8	94	67	3b82,1b25	0	-2.1
1985	Cin N	125	413	61	108	21	0	21	66	41-3	4	102	.262	.332	.465	115	8	3-4	.946	-1	91	147	3b62,O54L,1b12	0	0.3
1986	Cin N	102	330	35	76	17	2	12	41	47-0	1	97	.230	.325	.403	97	-1	0-2	.991	-2	74	96	1b70,O42L/3	32	-0.9
1987	Cin N	100	346	48	94	19	2	22	59	29-3	0	76	.272	.327	.529	118	7	0-0	.994	-9	63	102	1b93/3lf	43	-0.7
1988	Cin N	122	391	40	95	17	2	15	62	48-4	4	104	.243	.327	.412	108	5	7-2	.994	-6	76	95	1b116	23	-0.9
1989	Bos A	154	564	79	156	26	5	30	108	66-9	3	117	.277	.355	.500	130	22	1-2	.996	0	94	97	1b153/lf	0	1.1
1990	Atl N	9	35	2	6	0	0	0	0	4-0	0	14	.171	.256	.171	19	-4	0-0	.944	-1	81	102	1b9	165	-0.6
Total	8	810	2703	336	677	120	21	122	427	314-23	15	712	.250	.329	.446	110	31	18-14	.993	-36	78	96	1b478,3b230,O98L	530	-4.5
Escalera, Nino	Saturnino Cuadrado; B12.1.1929 Santurce, PR; BL/TR/5´10˝/165; d4.17																								
1954	Cin N	73	69	15	11	1	1	0	3	7	0	11	.159	.234	.203	15	-9	1-0	.962	2	125	422	O14(1/3/10),1b8/S	0	-0.7
Escalona, Felix	Felix Eduardo; B3.12.1979 Puerto Cabello, Carabobo, Venezuela; BR/TR/6´0˝/(185–190); d4.4																								
2002	TB A	59	157	17	34	8	2	0	9	3-0	7	44	.217	.262	.293	49	-12	7-2	.945	-2	106	118	S26,2b25,3b4/D	0	-1.0
2003	TB A	10	27	2	5	2	0	0	2	2-0	0	6	.185	.241	.259	33	-3	1-0	1.000	2	96	147	S8/23	0	0.0
2004	NY A	5	8	1	0	0	0	0	0	0-0	1	2	.000	.111	.000	-68	-2	0-0	1.000	-0	100	64	S4/3	0	-0.2
2005	NY A	10	14	0	4	1	0	0	2	1-0	1	4	.286	.375	.357	97	0	0-0	1.000	0	84	139	S5,3b3/12	0	0.1
Total	4	84	206	20	43	11	2	0	13	6-0	9	56	.209	.261	.282	45	-17	8-2	.967	-1	101	123	S43,2b27,3b9/1D	0	-1.1
Eschen, Jim	James Godrich; B8.21.1891 Brooklyn NY; D9.27.1960 Sloatsburg NY; BR/TR/5´10.5˝/160; d7.10; s–Larry																								
1915	Cle A	15	42	11	10	1	0	0	2	5	0	9	.238	.319	.262	73	-1	0-1	.968	0	115	64	O10C	—	-0.2
Eschen, Larry	Lawrence Edward; B9.22.1920 Suffern NY; BR/TR/6´0˝/180; d6.16; f–Jim; Col St. Lawrence																								
1942	Phi A	12	11	0	0	0	0	0	0	4	0	6	.000	.267	.000	-22	-2	0-0	.824	-2	48	0	S7/2	0	-0.4
Escobar, Alex	Alexander Jose; B9.6.1978 Valencia, Carabobo, Venez.; BR/TR/6´1˝/(180–190); d5.8; [DL 2002 Cle A 183, 2004 Chi A 48, 2005 Was N 183]																								
2001	NY N	18	50	3	10	1	0	3	8	3-0	0	19	.200	.245	.400	67	-3	1-0	.935	1	88	375	O15(0/9/7)	0	-0.2
2003	Cle A	28	99	16	27	2	0	5	14	7-1	1	33	.273	.324	.444	101	0	1-0	.969	3	111	201	O25R	0	0.2
2004	Cle A	46	152	20	32	8	2	1	12	23-0	1	42	.211	.318	.309	67	-7	1-1	.991	7	103	364	O42(8/21/15),D3	0	-0.1
2006	Was N	33	87	14	31	3	2	4	18	8-0	0	18	.356	.394	.575	156	7	2-0	.984	2	123	99	O23(0/23/1)	82	0.9
Total	4	125	388	53	100	14	4	13	52	41-1	2	112	.258	.328	.415	96	-3	5-1	.978	12	107	273	O105(8/53/48),D3	496	0.8
Escobar, Angel	Angel Rubenque (Rivas); B5.12.1965 LaSabana, Vargas, Venez.; BB/TR/6´0˝/160; d5.17																								
1988	SF N	3	3	1	1	0	0	0	0	0-0	0	0	.333	.333	.333	96	0	0-0	1.000	0	0	0	/S3	0	0.0
Escobar, Jose	Jose Elias (Sanchez); B10.30.1960 Las Flores, Venezuela; BR/TR/5´10˝/140; d4.13																								
1991	Cle A	10	15	0	3	0	0	0	1	1-0	0	4	.200	.250	.200	26	-2	0-0	1.000	-1	51	0	S5,2b4/3	0	-0.2
Esmond, Jimmy	James Joseph; B10.8.1889 Albany NY; D6.26.1948 Troy NY; BR/TR/5´11˝/167; d4.20																								
1911	Cin N	73	198	27	54	4	6	1	11	17	0	30	.273	.330	.369	99	-1	7	.918	-3	85	121	S44,3b14,2b2	—	-0.1
1912	Cin N	82	231	24	45	5	3	1	40	20	0	31	.195	.259	.255	42	-19	11	.930	-8	87	82	S74	—	-2.2
1914	Ind F	151	542	74	160	23	**15**	2	49	40	0	48	.295	.344	.404	93	-13	25	.919	-8	98	96	S151	—	-1.2
1915	New F	**155**	569	79	147	20	11	4	62	59	1	54	.258	.329	.353	98	-12	18	.939	1	101	109	S155	—	0.1
Total	4	461	1540	204	406	52	35	8	162	136	1	163	.264	.324	.358	88	-45	61	.929	-18	96	101	S424,3b14,2b2	—	-3.4
Espino, Juan	Juan (Reyes); B3.16.1956 Bonao, D.R.; BR/TR/6´1˝/190; d6.25																								
1982	NY A	3	2	0	0	0	0	0	0	0-0	0	1	.000	.000	.000	-99	-1	0-0	1.000	-0	0	0	C3	0	-0.1
1983	NY A	10	23	1	6	0	0	1	3	1-0	0	5	.261	.280	.391	89	-1	0-0	1.000	-1	96	43	C10	0	-0.2
1985	NY A	9	11	0	4	0	0	0	0	0-0	0	0	.364	.364	.364	102	0	0-0	1.000	0	108	0	C9	0	0.0
1986	NY A	27	37	1	6	2	0	0	5	2-0	0	9	.162	.200	.216	15	-4	0-0	.987	0	84	50	C27	0	-0.4
Total	4	49	73	2	16	2	0	1	8	3-0	0	15	.219	.244	.288	47	-6	0-0	.993	-1	89	39	C49	0	-0.7
Espinoza, Alvaro	Alvaro Alberto; B2.19.1962 Valencia, Carabobo, Venez.; BR/TR/6´0˝/(170–190); d9.14																								
1984	Min A	1	0	0	0	0	0	0	0	0-0	0	0	ø	ø	ø	ø	0	0-0	ø	0	0	0	/S	0	0.0
1985	Min A	32	57	5	15	2	0	0	9	1-0	1	9	.263	.288	.298	57	-3	0-1	.949	1	112	113	S31	0	-0.1
1986	Min A	37	42	4	9	1	0	0	1	1-0	0	10	.214	.233	.238	28	-4	0-1	.941	-1	130	105	2b19,S18	0	-0.4
1988	NY A	3	3	0	0	0	0	0	0	0-0	0	0	.000	.000	.000	-99	-1	0-0	1.000	-0	31	0	2b2/S	0	-0.1
1989	NY A	146	503	51	142	23	1	0	41	14-1	1	60	.282	.301	.332	79	-15	3-3	.970	19	108	118	S146	0	1.4
1990	NY A	150	438	31	98	12	2	2	20	16-0	5	54	.224	.258	.274	49	-31	1-2	.977	**23**	**108**	107	S150	0	0.2
1991	NY A	148	480	51	123	23	2	5	33	16-0	2	57	.256	.282	.344	72	-20	4-1	.969	21	107	**129**	S147,3b2/P	0	1.2
1993	Cle A	129	263	34	73	15	0	4	27	8-0	1	36	.278	.298	.380	82	-8	2-2	.937	-6	96	81	3b99,S35,2b2	0	-1.2
1994	Cle A	90	231	27	55	13	0	1	19	6-0	1	33	.238	.258	.307	45	-19	1-3	.915	16	101	68	3b37,S36,2b20,1b3	0	-0.1
1995	†Cle A	66	143	15	36	4	0	2	17	2-0	1	16	.252	.264	.322	51	-11	0-2	.966	-4	108	97	2b22,3b22,S19,1b2,D3	0	-1.3
1996	Cle A	59	112	12	25	4	2	4	11	6-0	3	18	.223	.279	.402	70	-6	1-1	.947	1	79	73	3b20,1b18,S16,2b5/D	0	-0.5
	NY N	48	134	19	41	7	2	4	16	4-0	0	19	.306	.324	.478	114	2	0-2	.900	-3	93	40	3b38,S7,2b2/1	0	-0.1
1997	Sea A	33	72	3	13	1	0	0	7	2-0	1	12	.181	.213	.194	7	-10	1-1	.965	2	84	57	S17,2b14/3	15	-0.6
Total	12	942	2478	252	630	105	9	22	201	76-1	16	324	.254	.279	.331	65	-126	13-19	.971	68	107	117	S624,3b219,2b86,1b24,D4/P	15	-1.6
Esposito, Sammy	Samuel; B12.15.1931 Chicago IL; BR/TR/5´9˝/165; d9.28; Mil 1952–55; Col Indiana																								
1952	Chi A	1	4	0	1	0	0	0	0	0	0	2	.250	.250	.250	39	0	0-1	.500	-1	38	0	/S	0	-0.2
1955	Chi A	3	4	3	0	0	0	0	0	1-0	0	0	.000	.200	.000	-41	-1	0-0	1.000	-1	0	0	3b2	0	-0.1
1956	Chi A	81	184	30	42	8	2	3	25	41-0	2	19	.228	.371	.342	89	-1	1-2	.962	2	105	181	3b61,S19,2b3	0	0.0
1957	Chi A	94	176	26	36	3	0	2	15	38-0	0	27	.205	.344	.256	66	-7	5-1	.960	10	108	142	3b53,S22,2b4/cf	0	0.6
1958	Chi A	98	81	16	20	3	0	0	3	12-1	2	6	.247	.358	.284	81	-1	1-1	.979	-5	88	52	3b63,S22,2b2/lf	0	-0.6
1959	†Chi A	69	66	12	11	1	0	1	5	11-1	0	16	.167	.282	.227	43	-5	0-1	.979	-1	82	39	3b45,S14,2b2	0	-0.6
1960	Chi A	57	77	14	14	5	0	1	11	10-1	0	20	.182	.273	.286	53	-5	0-0	.929	-8	94	96	3b37,S11,2b5	0	-1.3
1961	Chi A	63	94	12	16	5	0	1	8	12-0	0	21	.170	.259	.255	40	-8	0-0	.976	-0	123	225	3b28,S20,2b11	0	-0.6
1962	Chi A	75	81	14	19	1	0	0	4	17-1	0	13	.235	.367	.247	69	-3	0-1	.846	-8	65	46	3b41,S20,2b7	0	-1.0
1963	Chi A	1	0	0	0	0	0	0	0	0-0	0	0	ø	ø	ø	ø	0	0-0	ø	0	—	—	/R	0	0.0
	KC A	18	25	3	5	1	0	0	2	3-0	0	3	.200	.276	.240	47	-2	0-0	1.000	-6	54	41	2b7,S4,3b3	0	-0.7
	Year	19	25	3	5	1	0	0	2	3-0	0	3	.200	.276	.240	47	-2	0-0	1.000	-6	54	41	2b7,S4,3b3	0	-0.7
Total	10	560	792	130	164	27	2	8	73	145-4	4	127	.207	.330	.277	66	-33	7-7	.957	-19	98	124	3b333,S133,2b41,O2(1/1/0)	0	-4.5

YEAR	TM LG	G	AB	R	H	2B	3B	HR	RBI	BB-IB	HP	SO	AVG	OBP	SLG	AOPS	ABR	SB-CS	FA	FR	RNG	THR	GAMES AT POSITION	DL	BFW
ESPY, CECIL	Cecil Edward; B1.20.1963 San Diego CA; BB/TR/6´3˝/(178–195); [ChiA80 1/8]; d9.2																								
1983	LA N	20	11	4	3	1	0	0	1	1-0	0	2	.273	.333	.364	93	0	0-0	1.000	0	123	0	O15C	0	0.0
1987	Tex A	14	8	1	0	0	0	0	0	1-0	0	3	.000	.111	.000	-67	-2	2-0	1.000	1	122	439	O8(5/0/3)	0	-0.1
1988	Tex A	123	347	46	86	17	6	2	39	20-1	1	83	.248	.288	.349	76	-12	33-10	.972	2	99	223	O98(52/46/8),D12,S3,C2/12	15	-0.8
1989	Tex A	142	475	65	122	12	7	3	31	38-2	2	99	.257	.313	.331	80	-13	45-20	.990	-1	100	87	O133(3/131/1),D3	0	-1.2
1990	Tex A	52	71	10	9	0	0	0	1	10-0	0	20	.127	.235	.127	4	-9	11-5	1.000	2	117	93	O39(4/28/9)/2D	0	-0.7
1991	†Pit N	43	82	7	20	4	0	1	11	5-0	0	17	.244	.281	.329	74	-3	4-0	.966	2	106	219	O35(2/25/11)	0	-0.1
1992	†Pit N	112	194	21	50	7	3	1	20	15-2	0	40	.258	.310	.340	85	-4	6-3	.955	-3	91	38	O82(11/18/56)	0	-0.9
1993	Cin N	40	60	6	14	2	0	0	5	14-0	0	13	.233	.368	.267	76	-1	2-2	.931	1	101	214	O18(18/0/1)	0	-0.1
Total	8	546	1248	160	304	43	16	7	108	104-5	3	277	.244	.301	.321	74	-44	103-40	.977	4	101	136	O428(95/263/89),D19,S3,2b2,C2/1	15	-3.9
ESSEGIAN, CHUCK	Charles Abraham; B8.9.1931 Boston MA; BR/TR/5´11˝/(200–202); d4.15; Col Stanford																								
1958	Phi N	39	114	15	28	5	2	5	16	12-0	0	34	.246	.317	.456	103	0	0-0	.952	-1	101	46	O30(28/2/0)	0	-0.2
1959	StL N	17	39	2	7	2	1	0	5	1-0	0	13	.179	.200	.282	25	-4	0-0	1.000	-1	57	172	O9L	0	-0.6
	†LA N	24	46	6	14	6	0	1	5	4-1	0	11	.304	.360	.500	118	1	0-0	1.000	-1	69	0	O10(4/0/6)	0	0.0
	Year	41	85	8	21	8	1	1	10	5-1	0	24	.247	.289	.400	76	-3	0-0	1.000	-2	64	78	O19(13/0/6)	0	-0.6
1960	LA N	52	79	8	17	3	0	3	11	8-1	0	24	.215	.284	.367	73	-3	0-0	.968	1	133	100	O18(13/0/5)	0	-0.2
1961	Bal A	1	1	0	0	0	0	0	0	0-0	0	0	.000	.000	.000	-99	0	0-0	ø	0	—	—	/H	0	0.0
	KC A	4	6	1	2	1	0	0	1	1-0	0	2	.333	.429	.500	145	0	0-0	1.000	0	199	0	/lf	0	0.1
	Cle A	60	166	25	48	7	1	12	35	10-0	1	33	.289	.328	.560	138	8	0-0	.968	1	97	181	O49(16/19/16)	0	0.6
	Year	65	173	26	50	8	1	12	36	11-0	1	35	.289	.330	.555	137	8	0-0	.969	1	100	177	O50(17/19/16)	0	0.7
1962	Cle A	106	336	59	92	12	0	21	50	42-2	7	68	.274	.363	.497	134	16	0-0	.994	-4	90	21	O90(88/1/1)	0	0.8
1963	KC A	101	231	23	52	9	0	5	27	19-0	1	48	.225	.285	.329	68	-10	0-0	.990	0	99	59	O53L	0	-1.3
Total	6	404	1018	139	260	45	4	47	150	97-4	9	233	.255	.323	.446	106	8	0-0	.981	-4	96	69	O260(212/22/28)	0	-0.8
ESSIAN, JIM	James Sarkis; B1.2.1951 Detroit MI; BR/TR/6´2˝/(187–205); d9.15; M1																								
1973	Phi N	2	3	0	0	0	0	0	0	0-0	0	1	.000	.000	.000	-97	-1	0-0	ø	-0	0	0	/C	0	-0.1
1974	Phi N	17	20	1	2	0	0	0	0	2-0	0	1	.100	.182	.100	-19	-3	0-0	.976	-2	50	90	C15/13	0	-0.5
1975	Phi N	2	1	1	1	0	0	0	1	1-0	0	0	1.000	1.000	1.000	434	1	0-0	1.000	0	0	798	C2	0	0.1
1976	Chi A	78	199	20	49	7	0	0	21	23-0	1	28	.246	.326	.281	79	-4	2-1	.974	0	124	128	C77,1b2/3	0	-0.1
1977	Chi A	114	322	50	88	18	2	10	44	52-1	1	35	.273	.374	.435	120	11	1-4	.986	0	98	121	C111,3b2	0	1.4
1978	Oak A	126	278	21	62	9	1	3	26	44-1	0	22	.223	.326	.295	81	-6	2-1	.981	9	92	**158**	C119,1b3/2D	0	0.8
1979	Oak A	98	313	34	76	16	0	8	40	25-1	2	29	.243	.295	.371	85	-7	0-1	.981	7	70	163	C70,3b10,1b4,O4(3/0/1),D3	15	0.2
1980	Oak A	87	285	19	66	11	0	5	29	30-0	0	18	.232	.302	.323	77	-9	1-3	.987	6	102	172	C68,D11/1	0	-0.2
1981	Chi A	27	52	6	16	3	0	0	5	4-0	0	5	.308	.357	.365	110	1	0-1	.990	1	96	100	C25,3b2	0	0.2
1982	Sea A	48	153	14	42	8	0	3	20	11-0	1	7	.275	.327	.386	92	-2	2-0	.994	-0	50	62	C48	101	0.1
1983	Cle A	48	93	11	19	4	0	2	11	16-0	0	8	.204	.315	.312	72	-3	0-1	.989	-1	96	125	C47/3	0	-0.3
1984	Oak A	63	136	17	32	9	0	2	10	23-0	1	17	.235	.348	.346	99	1	1-1	.985	3	79	176	C59/3D	34	0.6
Total	12	710	1855	194	453	85	3	33	207	231-3	6	171	.244	.327	.347	89	-21	9-13	.984	23	91	139	C642,3b18,D16,1b11,O4(3/0/1)/2	150	2.2
ESTALELLA, BOBBY	Robert M; B8.23.1974 Hialeah FL; BR/TR/6´1˝/(195–225); [PhiN92 23/641]; d9.17; gf–Bobby; Col Miami–Dade Kendall (FL) CC																								
1996	Phi N	7	17	5	6	0	0	2	4	1-0	0	6	.353	.389	.706	180	2	1-0	1.000	-0	309	81	C4	0	0.2
1997	Phi N	13	29	9	10	1	0	4	9	7-0	0	7	.345	.472	.793	227	6	0-0	1.000	-3	214	34	C11	0	0.3
1998	Phi N	47	165	16	31	6	1	8	20	13-0	1	49	.188	.247	.382	63	-10	0-0	.988	-10	77	55	C47	0	-1.7
1999	Phi N	9	18	2	3	0	0	0	1	4-0	0	7	.167	.318	.167	27	-2	0-1	.976	-1	56	61	C7	24	-0.2
2000	†SF N	106	299	45	70	22	3	14	53	57-9	2	92	.234	.357	.468	114	8	3-0	.993	14	106	101	C106	0	2.6
2001	SF N	29	93	11	19	5	1	3	10	11-2	1	28	.204	.295	.376	76	-4	0-0	1.000	2	107	82	C28	0	0.0
	NY A	3	4	1	0	0	0	0	0	1-0	1	2	.000	.333	.000	-1	-1	0-0	1.000	1	111	0	C3	0	0.0
2002	Col N	38	112	17	23	8	0	8	25	14-0	0	33	.205	.285	.491	90	-2	0-1	.995	-3	99	58	C38	84	-0.3
2003	Col N	46	140	17	28	7	0	7	21	19-0	1	55	.200	.294	.400	71	-6	2-0	.985	0	86	127	C46	49	-0.3
2004	Ari N	7	14	2	2	0	0	2	4	0-0	0	6	.143	.143	.571	68	-1	0-0	1.000	-1	0	0	C6	0	-0.2
	Tor A	5	13	1	3	0	0	0	0	3-0	1	5	.231	.412	.231	70	0	0-0	1.000	-0	37	0	C3,D2	108	0.0
Total	9	310	904	126	195	49	5	48	147	130-11	7	290	.216	.315	.440	92	-10	6-2	.992	-1	100	84	C299,D2	265	0.4
ESTALELLA, BOBBY	Roberto (Ventoza); B4.25.1911 Cardenas, Cuba; D1.6.1991 Hialeah FL; BR/TR/5´8˝/180; d9,7; gs–Bobby																								
1935	Was A	15	51	7	16	2	0	2	10	17	0	7	.314	.485	.471	153	6	1-0	.895	1	126	44	3b15	—	0.7
1936	Was A	13	9	2	2	0	2	0	0	4	0	5	.222	.462	.667	186	1	0-0	ø	0	—	—	/H	—	0.1
1939	Was A	82	280	51	77	18	6	8	41	40	1	27	.275	.368	.468	121	9	2-3	.964	-3	97	59	O74(70/0/4)	—	0.1
1941	StL A	46	83	7	20	6	1	0	14	18	0	13	.241	.376	.337	87	-1	0-0	1.000	-2	78	0	O17(15/0/2)	0	-0.3
1942	Was A	133	429	68	119	24	5	8	65	85	3	42	.277	.400	.413	130	22	5-2	.941	-5	94	26	3b78,O36(17/2/17)	0	1.9
1943	Phi A	117	367	43	95	14	4	11	63	52	1	44	.259	.352	.409	123	11	1-3	.975	1	106	67	O97(95/1/1)	0	0.6
1944	Phi A	140	506	54	151	17	9	7	60	59	2	60	.298	.374	.409	125	17	3-3	.988	-1	96	104	O128(5/103/25),1b6	0	1.2
1945	Phi A	126	451	45	135	25	6	8	52	74	1	46	.299	.399	.435	142	27	1-6	.988	-6	92	91	O124(9/118/0)	0	1.7
1949	Phi A	8	20	2	5	0	0	0	3	1	0	2	.250	.286	.250	44	-2	0-0	1.000	1	99	230	O6R	0	-0.1
Total	9	680	2196	279	620	106	33	44	308	350	8	246	.282	.383	.421	127	90	13-17	.982	-12	97	83	O482(211/224/55),3b93,1b6	0	5.9
ESTERBROOK, DUDE	Thomas John; B6.20.1857 Staten Is. NY; D4.30.1901 Middletown NY; BR/TR/5´11˝/167; d5.1; M1; OF(40/24/12)																								
1880	Buf N	64	253	20	61	12	1	0	35	0	—	15	.241	.241	.296	80	-5	—	.939	-2	147	86	1b47,O15(1/14/0),2b6/SC	—	-0.9
1882	Cle N	45	179	13	44	4	3	0	19	5	—	12	.246	.266	.302	85	-3	—	.893	7	133	263	O45(38/7/0)/1	—	0.3
1883	NY AA	**97**	407	55	103	9	7	0	—	15	—	—	.253	.280	.310	86	-7	—	.871	-6	84	92	3b97	—	-1.0
1884	†NY AA	**112**	477	110	150	29	11	1	—	12	10	—	.314	.345	.428	154	29	—	.886	9	102	109	3b112	—	3.5
1885	NY N	88	359	48	92	14	5	2	44	4	—	28	.256	.264	.340	96	-3	—	.885	-1	92	**153**	3b84,O4(1/0/3)	—	-0.3
1886	NY N	123	473	62	125	20	6	3	43	8	—	43	.264	.277	.351	89	-8	13	**.895**	-6	89	69	3b123	—	-1.1
1887	NY AA	26	101	11	17	1	0	0	7	6	1	—	.168	.222	.178	13	-12	8	.950	-6	121	93	1b9,O7(0/3/5),S5,2b5	—	-1.5
1888	Ind N	64	246	21	54	8	0	0	17	2	2	20	.220	.232	.252	53	-13	11	.976	-3	89	97	1b61,3b3	—	-2.1
	Lou AA	23	93	9	21	6	0	0	7	3	2	—	.226	.265	.290	80	-2	5	.962	0	120	74	1b23	—	-0.4
1889	Lou AA	11	44	8	14	3	0	0	9	5	1	2	.318	.400	.386	127	2	6	.931	-0	140	58	1b8,O2R/SM	—	0.1
1890	NY N	45	197	29	57	14	1	0	29	10	3	8	.289	.333	.371	105	1	12	.984	0	86	101	1b45	—	-0.2
1891	Bro N	3	8	1	3	0	0	0	0	0	1	1	.375	.444	.375	140	0	0	1.000	-1	0	0	O2R/2	—	0.0
Total	11	701	2837	387	741	120	34	6	210	70	20	129	.261	.284	.334	94	-21	55	.884	-8	92	102	3b419,1b194,O75L,2b12,S7/C	—	-3.6
ESTRADA, FRANK	Francisco (Soto); B2.12.1948 Navojoa, Sonora, Mexico; BR/TR/5´8˝/180; [NYN71*5/85]; d9.14; Col Cuesta (CA) JC																								
1971	NY N	1	2	0	1	0	0	0	0	0-0	0	0	.500	.500	.500	184	0	0-0	1.000	-1	0	0	/C	0	0.0
ESTRADA, JOHNNY	Johnny Pulado; B6.27.1976 Hayward CA; BB/TR/5´11˝/(209–215); [PhiN97 17/506]; d5.15; Col Sequoias (CA) [JC]																								
2001	Phi N	89	298	26	68	15	0	8	37	16-6	4	32	.228	.273	.359	66	-16	0-0	.993	-4	138	76	C89	0	-1.4
2002	Phi N	10	17	0	2	1	0	0	2	2-1	0	2	.118	.211	.176	3	-2	0-0	1.000	-1	53	0	C10	0	-0.3
2003	Atl N	16	36	2	11	0	0	0	2	0-0	3	3	.306	.359	.306	76	-1	0-0	1.000	-3	72	0	C14	0	-0.4
2004	†Atl N★	134	462	56	145	36	0	9	76	39-7	11	66	.314	.378	.450	113	11	0-0	.989	-0	90	65	C133	0	1.8
2005	†Atl N	105	357	31	93	26	0	4	39	20-6	3	38	.261	.303	.367	75	-13	0-0	.997	8	83	131	C104	16	0.1
2006	Ari N	115	414	43	125	26	0	11	71	13-7	7	40	.302	.328	.444	92	-5	0-0	.996	-7	95	113	C108	0	-0.5
Total	6	469	1584	158	444	104	0	32	227	90-27	28	181	.280	.327	.407	88	-26	0-0	.994	-6	98	92	C458	16	-0.7
ETCHEBARREN, ANDY	Andrew Auguste; B6.20.1943 Whittier CA; BR/TR/6´1˝/(195–197); d9.26; C10																								
1962	Bal A	2	6	0	2	0	0	0	1	0-0	0	2	.333	.333	.333	85	0	0-0	.875	-2	67	0	C2	0	-0.2
1965	Bal A	5	6	1	1	0	0	1	4	0-0	0	2	.167	.167	.667	123	0	0-0	1.000	2	31	0	C5	0	0.2
1966	†Bal A☆	121	412	49	91	14	6	11	50	38-12	5	106	.221	.293	.364	89	-6	0-1	.989	-7	89	**123**	C121	0	-0.9
1967	Bal A☆	112	330	29	71	13	0	7	35	38-9	2	80	.215	.298	.318	83	-6	1-0	.989	-3	80	73	C110	0	-0.4
1968	Bal A	74	189	20	44	11	2	5	20	19-4	3	46	.233	.311	.392	112	3	0-0	.998	6	119	81	C70	36	1.4
1969	†Bal A	73	217	29	54	9	2	3	26	28-2	7	42	.249	.350	.350	96	0	1-2	.990	8	300	87	C72	0	1.1
1970	†Bal A	78	230	19	56	10	1	4	28	21-2	3	41	.243	.313	.348	81	-6	4-1	.984	-0	124	58	C76	0	-0.3
1971	†Bal A	70	222	21	60	8	0	9	29	16-2	1	40	.270	.321	.428	110	2	1-4	.986	2	152	126	C70	0	0.7
1972	Bal A	71	188	11	38	6	1	2	21	17-2	3	43	.202	.276	.277	63	-8	0-2	.992	8	196	98	C70	0	0.2
1973	†Bal A	54	152	16	39	9	1	2	23	12-1	2	21	.257	.317	.368	93	-1	1-1	.991	1	139	90	C51	0	0.1
1974	†Bal A	62	180	13	40	8	0	2	15	6-0	1	26	.222	.249	.300	59	-10	1-0	.976	5	167	79	C60	0	-0.3

YEAR	TM LG	G	AB	R	H	2B	3B	HR	RBI	BB-IB	HP	SO	AVG	OBP	SLG	AOPS	ABR	SB-CS	FA	FR	RNG	THR	GAMES AT POSITION	DL	BFW
1975	Bal A	8	20	0	4	1	0	0	3	0-0	0	3	.200	.200	.250	28	-2	0-0	1.000	-1	79	125	C7	35	-0.2
	Cal A	31	100	10	28	0	1	3	17	14-1	0	19	.280	.365	.390	123	3	1-0	.981	-2	93	94	C31	56	0.2
	Year	39	120	10	32	1	1	3	20	14-1	0	22	.267	.341	.367	108	1	1-0	.983	-3	91	99	C38	0	0.0
1976	Cal A	103	247	15	56	9	1	0	21	24-0	4	37	.227	.305	.271	74	-7	0-2	.980	-2	82	**128**	C102	0	-0.7
1977	Cal A	80	114	11	29	2	2	0	14	12-0	0	19	.254	.320	.307	76	-4	3-1	.987	-4	74	86	C80	0	-0.5
1978	Mil A	4	5	1	2	1	0	0	2	1-0	0	2	.400	.500	.600	207	1	0-0	1.000	2	0	112	C4	106	0.2
Total	15	948	2618	245	615	101	17	49	309	246-41	31	529	.235	.306	.343	88	-41	13-14	.987	11	129	96	C931	233	0.6
Etchison, Buck	Clarence Hampton; B1.27.1915 Baltimore MD; D1.24.1980 Cambridge MD; BL/TL/6´1˝/190; d9.22																								
1943	Bos N	10	19	2	6	3	0	0	2	2	0	2	.316	.381	.474	148	1	0	.956	-1	72	211	1b6	0	0.0
1944	Bos N	109	308	30	66	16	0	8	33	33	1	50	.214	.292	.344	76	-10	1	.993	-2	89	102	1b85	0	-1.7
Total	2	119	327	32	72	19	0	8	35	35	1	52	.220	.298	.352	79	-9	1	.991	-3	88	107	1b91	0	-1.7
Etheridge, Bobby	Bobby Lamar "Luke"; B11.25.1942 Greenville MS; BR/TR/5´9˝/178; d7.16; Col Mississippi St.; [DL 1970 SD N 21]																								
1967	SF N	40	115	13	26	7	2	1	15	7-0	5	12	.226	.297	.348	86	-2	0-0	.925	-5	83	149	3b37	0	-0.8
1969	SF N	56	131	13	34	9	0	1	10	19-0	1	26	.260	.358	.351	100	1	0-0	.899	-3	99	91	3b39/S	0	-0.2
Total	2	96	246	26	60	16	2	2	25	26-0	6	38	.244	.330	.350	94	-1	0-0	.911	-8	91	119	3b76/S	21	-1.0
Ethier, Andre	Andre Everett; B4.10.1982 Phoenix AZ; BL/TL/6´1˝/210; [OakA03 2/62]; d5.2; Col Arizona St.																								
2006	†LA N	126	396	50	122	20	7	11	55	34-2	5	77	.308	.365	.477	115	8	5-5	.968	-3	85	144	O109L	0	0.1
Etten, Nick	Nicholas Raymond Thomas; B9.19.1913 Spring Grove IL; D10.18.1990 Hinsdale IL; BL/TL/6´2˝/198; d9.8; Col Villanova																								
1938	Phi A	22	81	6	21	6	2	0	11	9	0	7	.259	.333	.383	81	-3	1-0	.987	-2	69	96	1b22	—	-0.6
1939	Phi A	43	155	20	39	11	2	3	29	16	0	11	.252	.322	.406	87	-3	0-0	.990	-3	77	79	1b41	—	-0.9
1941	Phi N	151	540	78	168	27	4	14	79	82	3	33	.311	.405	.454	147	37	9	.984	-3	96	92	1b150	0	2.1
1942	Phi N	139	459	37	121	21	3	8	41	67	0	26	.264	.357	.375	120	14	3	.985	0	105	93	1b135	0	0.2
1943	†NY A	154	583	78	158	35	5	14	107	76	0	31	.271	.355	.420	126	20	3-7	.989	-12	72	**119**	1b154	0	-0.3
1944	NY A	**154**	573	88	168	25	4	**22**	91	**97**	4	29	.293	.399	.466	142	35	4-2	.989	3	108	106	1b154	0	3.1
1945	NY A✻	**152**	565	77	161	24	4	18	**111**	90	4	23	.285	.387	.437	133	26	2-3	.989	-11	79	**121**	1b152	0	0.8
1946	NY A	108	323	37	75	14	1	9	49	38	1	35	.232	.315	.365	88	-5	0-1	.991	-0	98	116	1b84	0	-0.9
1947	Phi N	14	41	5	10	4	0	1	8	5	0	4	.244	.326	.415	99	0	0	.990	1	141	46	1b11	0	0.1
Total	9	937	3320	426	921	167	25	89	526	480	12	199	.277	.371	.423	125	121	22-13	.988	-25	91	105	1b903	0	3.6
Eunick, Fred	Fernandas Bowen; B4.22.1892 Baltimore MD; D12.9.1959 Baltimore MD; BR/TR/5´6˝/148; d8.29																								
1917	Cle A	1	2	0	0	0	0	0	0	0	0	0	.000	.000	.000	-93	0	0	1.000	-0	107	0	/3	—	-0.1
Eusebio, Tony	Raul Antonio Bare (b Raul Antonio Bare (Eusebio)); B4.27.1967 San Jose de los Llanos, D.R.; BR/TR/6´2˝/(180–210); d8.8																								
1991	Hou N	10	19	4	2	1	0	0	0	6-0	0	8	.105	.320	.158	41	-1	0-0	.981	1	139	74	C9	0	0.0
1994	Hou N	55	159	18	47	9	1	5	30	8-0	0	33	.296	.320	.459	108	1	0-1	.993	-3	90	152	C52	0	0.1
1995	Hou N	113	368	46	110	21	1	6	58	31-1	3	59	.299	.354	.410	109	5	0-2	.993	-9	106	97	C103	0	0.1
1996	Hou N	58	152	15	41	7	2	1	19	18-2	0	20	.270	.343	.362	94	-1	0-1	.996	-4	95	79	C47	86	-0.3
1997	†Hou N	60	164	12	45	2	0	1	18	19-1	4	27	.274	.364	.305	80	-4	0-1	.987	-2	86	62	C43	0	-0.4
1998	†Hou N	66	182	13	46	6	1	1	36	18-2	1	31	.253	.320	.313	70	-8	1-0	.992	5	147	83	C54	0	0.0
1999	†Hou N	103	323	31	88	15	0	4	33	40-4	0	67	.272	.353	.356	81	-8	0-0	.994	8	162	78	C98	16	0.5
2000	Hou N	74	218	24	61	18	0	7	33	25-2	4	45	.280	.361	.459	98	0	0-0	.988	-9	99	58	C68	0	-0.4
2001	†Hou N	59	154	16	39	8	0	5	14	17-3	3	34	.253	.339	.403	84	-3	0-0	.991	-2	117	70	C48	0	-0.2
Total	9	598	1739	179	479	87	5	30	241	182-15	15	324	.275	.346	.383	91	-19	1-5	.992	-15	117	85	C522	102	-0.6
Eustace, Frank	Frank John; B11.7.1873 New York NY; D10.16.1932 Pottsville PA; 5´9˝/160; d4.16																								
1896	Lou N	25	100	18	17	2	2	1	11	6	0	14	.170	.217	.260	26	-11	4	.841	-6	89	54	S22,2b3	—	-1.4
Evans	; d6.1																								
1875	NH NA	1	4	1	2	0	0	0	1	0	—	0	.500	.500	.500	285	1	0-0	ø	-0	0	0	/lf	—	0.1
Evans, Al	Alfred Hubert; B9.28.1916 Kenly NC; D4.6.1979 Wilson NC; BR/TR/5´11˝/190; d9.13; Mil 1943–44																								
1939	Was A	7	21	2	7	0	0	0	1	5	0	2	.333	.462	.333	115	1	0-0	.964	0	*137*	*120*	C6	—	0.1
1940	Was A	14	25	1	8	2	0	0	7	6	0	7	.320	.452	.400	131	2	1-0	1.000	-1	*76*	*57*	C9	—	0.2
1941	Was A	53	159	16	44	8	4	1	19	9	0	18	.277	.315	.396	91	-3	0-3	.969	-1	*97*	*113*	C51	0	-0.2
1942	Was A	74	223	22	51	4	1	0	10	25	1	36	.229	.309	.256	60	-11	3-0	.961	-5	*96*	*126*	C67	0	-1.3
1944	Was A	14	22	5	2	0	0	0	0	2	0	6	.091	.167	.091	-27	-4	0-0	.933	-1	*73*	*101*	C8	0	-0.5
1945	Was A	51	150	19	39	11	2	2	19	17	1	22	.260	.339	.400	125	5	2-1	.973	-4	*105*	*54*	C41	0	0.3
1946	Was A	88	272	30	69	10	4	2	30	30	2	28	.254	.332	.342	94	-2	1-2	.966	-10	*91*	*72*	C81	0	-0.9
1947	Was A	99	319	17	77	8	3	2	23	28	0	25	.241	.303	.304	71	-13	2-1	.989	-1	*94*	*117*	C94	0	-1.0
1948	Was A	93	228	19	59	6	3	2	28	38	1	20	.259	.367	.338	91	-2	1-1	.983	-2	*112*	*154*	C85	0	0.0
1949	Was A	109	321	32	87	12	3	2	42	50	0	19	.271	.369	.346	92	-3	4-1	**.992**	-14	*79*	*105*	C107	0	-1.1
1950	Was A	90	289	24	68	8	3	2	30	29	2	21	.235	.309	.304	61	-18	0-0	.987	-10	*65*	*68*	C88	0	-2.2
1951	Bos A	12	24	1	3	1	0	0	2	4	0	2	.125	.250	.167	13	-3	0-0	1.000	0	*130*	*0*	C10	0	-0.2
Total	12	704	2053	188	514	70	23	13	211	243	7	206	.250	.332	.326	82	-51	14-9	.979	-49	*91*	*101*	C647	0	-6.8
Evans, Barry	Barry Steven; B11.30.1956 Atlanta GA; BR/TR/6´1˝/180; [SDN77 2/34]; d9.4; Col West Georgia																								
1978	SD N	24	90	7	24	1	1	0	4	4-1	0	10	.267	.295	.300	73	-4	0-0	.947	2	116	103	3b24	0	-0.3
1979	SD N	56	162	9	35	5	0	1	14	5-0	0	16	.216	.237	.265	40	-14	0-2	.952	4	114	151	3b53,S2/2	0	-1.2
1980	SD N	73	125	11	29	3	2	1	14	17-1	0	21	.232	.317	.312	84	-3	1-1	.983	-5	79	54	3b43,2b19,S4/1	0	-0.8
1981	SD N	54	93	11	30	5	0	0	7	9-2	0	9	.323	.371	.376	126	4	2-2	.969	-4	76	45	3b24,1b10,2b6,S2	18	-0.1
1982	NY A	17	31	2	8	3	0	0	2	6-0	1	6	.258	.395	.355	109	1	0-0	1.000	-1	87	73	2b8,3b6,S4	0	0.0
Total	5	224	501	40	126	17	3	2	41	41-4	1	62	.251	.304	.309	77	-16	3-5	.960	-4	103	102	3b150,2b34,S12,1b11	18	-2.4
Evans, Darrell	Darrell Wayne; B5.26.1947 Pasadena CA; BL/TR/6´2˝/(200–205); [OakA67 S7/132]; d4.20; C1; Col Pasadena (CA) City																								
1969	Atl N	12	26	3	6	0	0	0	1	1-0	0	8	.231	.250	.231	38	-2	0-0	.917	-2	70	0	3b6	0	-0.4
1970	Atl N	12	44	4	14	1	1	0	9	7-0	1	5	.318	.423	.386	112	1	0-0	.941	1	120	0	3b12	0	0.2
1971	Atl N	89	260	42	63	11	1	12	38	39-4	1	54	.242	.338	.431	111	4	2-3	.937	7	111	115	3b72,O3L	0	1.1
1972	Atl N	125	418	67	106	12	0	19	71	90-4	4	58	.254	.384	.419	119	15	4-2	.941	14	114	92	3b123	0	3.0
1973	Atl N★	161	595	114	167	25	8	41	104	**124**-8	3	104	.281	.403	.556	153	46	6-3	.953	17	**118**	111	3b146,1b20	0	6.3
1974	Atl N	160	571	99	137	21	3	25	79	**126**-9	6	88	.240	.381	.419	120	20	4-2	.955	27	114	**154**	3b160	0	4.7
1975	Atl N	156	567	82	138	22	2	22	73	105-5	2	106	.243	.361	.406	110	10	12-3	.938	**31**	**123**	**141**	3b156,1b3	0	4.4
1976	Atl N	44	139	11	24	0	0	1	10	30-0	0	33	.173	.320	.194	46	-9	3-0	.994	1	96	84	1b36,3b7	0	-1.1
	SF N	92	257	42	57	9	1	10	36	42-4	0	38	.222	.329	.381	99	0	6-1	.991	8	138	88	1b83,3b5	0	0.4
	Year	136	396	53	81	9	1	11	46	72-4	0	71	.205	.326	.316	80	-9	9-1	.992	10	124	87	1b119,3b12	0	-0.7
1977	SF N	144	461	64	117	18	3	17	72	69-3	3	50	.254	.351	.416	106	5	9-6	.937	1	104	63	O81L,1b41,3b35	0	0.0
1978	SF N	159	547	82	133	24	2	20	78	105-12	0	64	.243	.360	.404	119	17	4-5	.952	5	101	99	3b155	0	2.0
1979	SF N	160	562	68	142	23	2	17	70	91-14	2	80	.253	.356	.391	112	12	6-7	.943	14	107	94	3b159	0	2.4
1980	SF N	154	556	69	147	23	0	20	78	83-6	2	65	.264	.359	.414	120	17	17-5	.946	12	107	118	3b140,1b14	0	3.0
1981	SF N	102	357	51	92	13	4	12	48	54-8	2	33	.258	.356	.417	123	12	2-3	.953	8	105	70	3b87,1b12	0	1.8
1982	SF N	141	465	64	119	20	4	16	61	77-7	2	64	.256	.360	.419	120	15	5-4	.933	4	94	93	3b84,1b49,S13	0	1.6
1983	SF N★	142	523	94	145	29	3	30	82	84-12	2	81	.277	.378	.516	150	37	6-6	.993	5	109	68	1b113,3b32,S9	0	3.6
1984	†Det A	131	401	60	93	11	1	16	63	77-10	0	70	.232	.353	.384	105	5	2-2	.997	3	135	102	D62,1b47,3b19	0	0.3
1985	Det A	151	505	81	125	17	0	**40**	94	85-12	1	85	.248	.356	.519	137	26	0-4	.984	13	143	95	1b113,D33,3b7	0	3.0
1986	Det A	151	507	78	122	15	0	29	85	91-5	1	105	.241	.356	.442	116	13	3-2	.998	13	141	108	1b105,D42,3b2	0	1.8
1987	†Det A	150	499	90	128	20	0	34	99	100-8	2	84	.257	.379	.501	137	30	6-5	.997	13	136	110	1b105,D44,3b7	0	3.3
1988	Det A	144	437	48	91	9	0	22	64	84-4	1	89	.208	.337	.380	104	4	1-4	.993	5	125	86	D72,1b65	0	0.1
1989	Atl N	107	276	31	57	6	1	11	39	41-6	0	46	.207	.303	.355	88	-4	0-1	.985	7	162	104	1b50,3b28	0	-0.1
Total	21	2687	8973	1344	2223	329	36	414	1354	1605-141	35	1410	.248	.361	.431	119	274	98-68	.946	207	110	110	3b1442,1b856,D253,O84L,S22	0	41.4

EVANS, DWIGHT Dwight Michael "Dewey"; B11.3.1951 Santa Monica CA; BR/TR/6´2˝/(180–208); [BosA69 5/107]; d9.16; C2

YEAR	TM LG	G	AB	R	H	2B	3B	HR	RBI	BB-IB	HP	SO	AVG	OBP	SLG	AOPS	ABR	SB-CS	FA	FR	RNG	THR	GAMES AT POSITION	DL	BFW
1972	Bos A	18	57	2	15	3	1	1	6	7-0	0	13	.263	.344	.404	115	1	0-0	1.000	1	82	241	O17(16/0/1)	0	0.1
1973	Bos A	119	282	46	63	13	1	10	32	40-2	1	52	.223	.320	.383	92	-2	5-0	.995	-0	101	67	O113(17/2/95),D2	0	-0.7
1974	Bos A	133	463	60	130	19	8	10	70	38-2	2	77	.281	.335	.421	110	5	4-4	.990	12	**126**	89	O122(1/3/120),D7	0	1.1
1975	†Bos A	128	412	61	113	24	6	13	56	47-3	4	60	.274	.353	.456	118	10	3-4	.987	19	**130**	164	O115R,D7	0	2.3
1976	Bos A	146	501	61	121	34	5	17	62	57-4	6	92	.242	.324	.431	108	6	6-7	**.994**	7	105	138	O145(0/8/140)/D	0	0.5
1977	Bos A	73	230	39	66	9	2	14	36	28-0	0	58	.287	.363	.526	125	8	4-2	.992	-1	105	48	O63(0/14/54),D6	44	0.5
1978	Bos A★	147	497	75	123	24	2	24	63	65-2	2	119	.247	.336	.449	108	6	8-5	.982	1	100	127	O142(0/3/140),D4	0	-0.1
1979	Bos A	152	489	69	134	24	1	21	58	69-7	1	76	.274	.364	.456	114	11	6-9	.988	5	103	136	O149R	0	0.5
1980	Bos A	148	463	72	123	37	5	18	60	64-6	5	98	.266	.358	.484	123	16	3-1	.982	-2	96	102	O144(0/1/144),D2	0	0.7
1981	Bos A★	**108**	412	84	122	19	4	**22**	71	**85**-1	1	85	.296	.415	.522	159	**35**	3-2	.993	6	109	108	O108(1/0/107)	0	3.6
1982	Bos A	**162**	609	122	178	37	7	32	98	112-1	1	125	.292	**.402**	.534	146	42	3-2	.973	-1	104	77	O161R/D	0	3.2
1983	Bos A	126	470	74	112	19	4	22	58	70-5	2	97	.238	.338	.436	104	3	3-0	.987	1	105	77	O99R,D21	19	-0.1
1984	Bos A	**162**	630	**121**	186	37	8	32	104	96-2	4	115	.295	.388	.532	145	42	3-1	.994	-4	97	72	O161R/D	0	2.9
1985	Bos A	159	617	110	162	29	1	29	78	**114**-4	5	105	.263	.378	.454	122	23	7-2	.990	-4	94	87	O152R,D7	0	1.2
1986	†Bos A	152	529	86	137	33	2	26	97	97-4	6	117	.259	.376	.476	130	26	3-3	.983	0	101	102	O149R/D	0	1.8
1987	Bos A★	154	541	109	165	37	2	34	123	**106**-6	3	98	.305	.417	.569	155	48	4-6	.982	-8	71	111	1b79,O77R,D4	0	2.8
1988	†Bos A	149	559	96	164	31	7	21	111	76-3	1	99	.293	.375	.487	134	27	5-1	.987	-6	101	91	O85(0/1/84),1b64,D6	0	1.6
1989	Bos A	146	520	82	148	27	3	20	100	99-1	3	84	.285	.397	.463	135	28	3-3	.981	-1	100	88	O77R,D69	0	2.3
1990	†Bos A	123	445	66	111	18	3	13	63	67-5	4	73	.249	.349	.391	103	3	3-4	ø	0	0	0	D122	16	-0.2
1991	Bal A	101	270	35	73	9	1	6	38	54-2	2	54	.270	.393	.378	119	10	2-3	.984	-0	92	133	O67R,D21	27	0.7
Total	20	2606	8996	1470	2446	483	73	385	1384	1391-60	53	1697	.272	.370	.470	125	348	78-59	.987	24	103	103	O2146(35/32/2092),D282,1b143	106	24.7

EVANS, JOE Joseph Patton "Doc"; B5.15.1895 Meridian MS; D8.9.1953 Gulfport MS; BR/TR/5´9˝/160; d7.3; Mil 1918; Col U. of Mississippi; OF(172/85/54)

YEAR	TM LG	G	AB	R	H	2B	3B	HR	RBI	BB-IB	HP	SO	AVG	OBP	SLG	AOPS	ABR	SB-CS	FA	FR	RNG	THR	GAMES AT POSITION	DL	BFW
1915	Cle A	42	109	17	28	4	2	0	11	22	0	18	.257	.382	.330	111	3	6-1	.885	-0	118	21	3b30,2b2	—	0.4
1916	Cle A	33	82	4	12	1	0	0	1	7	0	12	.146	.213	.159	11	-9	4	.915	3	120	67	3b28	—	-0.7
1917	Cle A	132	385	36	73	4	5	2	33	42	1	44	.190	.271	.242	53	-22	12	.939	1	**107**	111	3b127	—	-2.0
1918	Cle A	79	243	38	64	6	7	1	22	30	0	29	.263	.344	.358	102	1	7	.932	1	102	123	3b74	—	0.4
1919	Cle A	21	14	9	1	0	0	0	0	2	0	1	.071	.188	.071	-24	-2	1	.923	2	221	0	S6	—	0.0
1920	†Cle A	56	172	32	60	9	9	0	23	15	1	3	.349	.404	.506	136	8	6-2	.966	1	107	129	O43L,S6	—	0.8
1921	Cle A	57	153	36	51	11	0	0	21	19	1	5	.333	.410	.405	107	3	4-1	.933	3	105	162	O47L	—	0.3
1922	Cle A	75	145	35	39	6	2	0	22	8	0	4	.269	.307	.338	67	-7	11-2	.969	0	117	24	O49(30/17/3)	—	-0.8
1923	Was A	106	372	42	98	15	3	0	38	27	0	18	.263	.313	.320	70	-17	6-4	.982	-5	93	63	O72(2/65/5),3b21,1b5	—	-2.3
1924	StL A	77	209	30	53	3	3	0	19	24	0	12	.254	.330	.297	59	-13	4-4	.969	1	113	53	O49(38/1/10)	—	-1.6
1925	StL A	55	159	27	50	12	0	0	20	16	0	6	.314	.377	.390	90	-2	6-2	1.000	2	115	67	O47(12/2/36)	—	-0.2
Total	11	733	2043	306	529	71	31	3	210	212	3	152	.259	.329	.328	79	-57	67-16	.971	8	107	80	O307L,3b280,S12,1b5,2b2	—	-5.7

EVANS, STEVE Louis Richard; B2.17.1885 Cleveland OH; D12.28.1943 Cleveland OH; BL/TL/5´10˝/175; d4.16

YEAR	TM LG	G	AB	R	H	2B	3B	HR	RBI	BB-IB	HP	SO	AVG	OBP	SLG	AOPS	ABR	SB-CS	FA	FR	RNG	THR	GAMES AT POSITION	DL	BFW
1908	NY N	2	2	0	1	0	0	0	0	0	0	—	.500	.500	.500	209	0	0	ø	-0	0	0	/cf	—	0.0
1909	StL N	143	498	67	129	17	6	2	56	66	14	—	.259	.362	.329	122	17	14	.947	-3	99	**209**	O141R,1b2	—	0.9
1910	StL N	151	506	73	122	21	8	2	73	78	**31**	63	.241	.376	.326	109	12	10	.968	-3	101	84	O141R,1b10	—	0.3
1911	StL N	154	547	74	161	24	13	5	71	46	**19**	52	.294	.369	.413	122	16	13	.972	-3	101	81	O150R	—	0.5
1912	StL N	135	491	59	139	23	9	6	72	36	**17**	51	.283	.353	.403	109	6	11	.942	1	98	121	O134R	—	-0.1
1913	StL N	97	245	18	61	15	6	1	31	20	6	28	.249	.321	.371	99	0	5-5	.983	-1	109	63	O74(2/1/71)/1	—	-0.6
1914	Bro F	145	514	93	179	41	**15**	12	96	50	10	49	.348	.416	**.556**	**165**	**39**	18	.941	-1	101	80	O112(36/1/76),1b27	—	3.3
1915	Bro F	63	216	44	64	14	4	3	30	35	7	22	.296	.411	.440	140	11	7	.960	-1	93	103	O61R/1	—	0.7
	Bal F	88	340	50	107	20	6	1	37	28	7	34	.315	.379	.418	120	5	8	.925	-3	85	115	O88R,1b4	—	-0.2
	Year	151	556	94	171	**34**	10	4	67	63	**14**	56	.308	.392	.426	128	16	15	.940	-5	88	110	O149R,1b5	—	0.5
Total	8	978	3359	478	963	175	67	32	466	359	111	299	.287	.374	.407	125	106	86-5	.955	-16	99	112	O902(38/3/862),1b45	—	4.8

EVANS, TOM Thomas John; B7.9.1974 Kirkland WA; BR/TR/6´1˝/(180–200); [TorA92 4/121]; d9.2

YEAR	TM LG	G	AB	R	H	2B	3B	HR	RBI	BB-IB	HP	SO	AVG	OBP	SLG	AOPS	ABR	SB-CS	FA	FR	RNG	THR	GAMES AT POSITION	DL	BFW
1997	Tor A	12	38	7	11	2	0	1	2	2-0	1	10	.289	.341	.421	97	0	0-1	.917	2	122	56	3b12	0	0.1
1998	Tor A	7	10	0	0	0	0	0	0	1-0	0	2	.000	.091	.000	-73	-3	0-0	.889	-1	48	0	3b7	0	-0.3
2000	Tex A	23	54	10	15	4	0	0	5	10-0	1	13	.278	.394	.352	91	0	0-3	.909	1	108	140	3b21/1D	143	0.0
Total	3	42	102	17	26	6	0	1	7	13-0	2	25	.255	.347	.343	78	-3	0-4	.910	2	106	95	3b40/D1	143	-0.2

EVANS, JAKE Uriah L. P. "Bloody Jake"; B9.1856 Baltimore MD; D1.16.1907 Baltimore MD; TR/5´8˝/154; d5.1; ▲

YEAR	TM LG	G	AB	R	H	2B	3B	HR	RBI	BB-IB	HP	SO	AVG	OBP	SLG	AOPS	ABR	SB-CS	FA	FR	RNG	THR	GAMES AT POSITION	DL	BFW
1879	Tro N	72	280	30	65	9	5	0	17	5	—	18	.232	.246	.300	84	-4	—	.884	18	187	**197**	O72(2/7/64)	—	1.2
1880	Tro N	47	180	31	46	8	1	0	22	7	—	15	.256	.283	.311	96	-1	—	.906	-0	87	205	O47(0/6/41)/P	—	-0.1
1881	Tro N	83	315	35	76	11	5	0	28	14	—	30	.241	.274	.308	78	-8	—	.926	11	140	150	O83R	—	0.3
1882	Wor N	80	334	33	71	10	4	0	25	7	—	22	.213	.229	.266	57	-16	—	.910	17	**195**	47	O68(0/4/64),S11/32P	—	0.0
1883	Cle N	90	332	36	79	13	2	0	31	8	—	38	.238	.256	.289	66	-13	—	.902	3	144	34	O86R,S3,3b3/2P	—	-1.0
1884	Cle N	80	313	32	81	18	3	1	38	15	—	49	.259	.293	.345	97	-1	—	**.917**	8	125	115	O76(23/0/53),2b4,S2	—	0.5
1885	Bal AA	20	77	18	17	1	1	0	7	7	4	—	.221	.318	.260	85	-1	—	.894	1	140	277	O20R	—	0.0
Total	7	472	1831	215	435	70	21	1	168	63	4	172	.238	.264	.300	78	-44	—	.907	58	149	124	O452(25/17/411),S16,2b6,3b4,P3	—	0.9

EVERETT, CARL Carl Edward; B6.3.1971 Tampa FL; BB/TR/6´0˝/(181–220); [NYA90 1/10]; d7.1

YEAR	TM LG	G	AB	R	H	2B	3B	HR	RBI	BB-IB	HP	SO	AVG	OBP	SLG	AOPS	ABR	SB-CS	FA	FR	RNG	THR	GAMES AT POSITION	DL	BFW
1993	Fla N	11	19	0	2	0	0	0	0	1-0	0	9	.105	.150	.105	-29	-4	1-0	.857	-1	58	0	O8C	0	-0.5
1994	Fla N	16	51	7	11	1	0	2	6	3-0	0	15	.216	.259	.353	55	-4	4-0	1.000	1	102	234	O16(1/8/8)	18	-0.2
1995	NY N	79	289	48	75	13	1	12	54	39-2	2	67	.260	.352	.436	110	4	2-5	.981	2	96	165	O77(0/10/68)	0	0.2
1996	NY N	101	192	29	46	8	1	1	16	21-2	4	53	.240	.326	.307	72	-7	6-0	.935	4	126	162	O55(8/15/37)	15	-0.3
1997	NY N	142	443	58	110	28	3	14	57	32-3	7	102	.248	.308	.420	93	-6	17-9	.971	-1	98	120	O128(9/71/65)	0	-0.8
1998	†Hou N	133	467	72	138	34	4	15	76	44-2	3	102	.296	.359	.482	122	15	14-12	.987	6	106	162	O123(0/121/5)	0	2.0
1999	†Hou N	123	464	86	151	33	3	25	108	50-5	11	94	.325	.398	.571	145	33	27-7	.978	-4	89	167	O121(2/118/16),D2	21	3.1
2000	Bos A★	137	496	82	149	32	4	34	108	52-5	8	113	.300	.373	.587	135	25	11-4	.980	-3	90	184	O126C,D5	0	2.2
2001	Bos A	102	409	61	105	24	4	14	58	27-3	13	104	.257	.323	.438	98	-2	9-2	.974	-9	85	79	O93(0/84/9),D7	36	-0.9
2002	Tex A	105	374	47	100	16	0	16	62	33-4	6	77	.267	.333	.439	101	0	2-3	.969	-8	91	0	O83(18/33/39),D18	45	-1.1
2003	Tex A★	74	270	53	74	13	3	18	51	31-2	5	48	.274	.356	.544	125	10	4-1	.986	1	97	157	O72(40/15/33)/D	0	0.9
	Chi A	73	256	40	77	14	0	10	41	22-4	10	36	.301	.377	.473	118	7	4-3	.987	-1	98	112	O68(8/66/1),D3	0	0.7
	Year	147	526	93	151	27	3	28	92	53-6	15	84	.287	.366	.510	122	17	8-4	.986	1	97	136	O140(48/81/34),D4	0	1.6
2004	Mon N	39	127	8	32	10	0	2	14	8-2	5	19	.252	.319	.378	77	-4	0-0	.955	1	107	112	O33(19/0/14),D3	49	-0.5
	Chi A	43	154	21	41	7	1	5	21	8-1	5	26	.266	.320	.422	89	-3	1-0	1.000	1	65	2275	D41/lf	0	-0.4
2005	†Chi A	135	490	58	123	17	2	23	87	42-2	5	99	.251	.311	.435	94	-6	4-5	1.000	-2	78	82	D107,O22(14/0/8)	0	-1.4
2006	Sea A	92	308	37	70	8	0	11	33	29-2	3	57	.227	.297	.360	75	-13	1-3	1.000	-0	74	0	D80,O2(1/0/1)	0	-1.7
Total	14	1405	4809	707	1304	258	26	202	792	442-39	87	1021	.271	.341	.462	107	45	107-54	.977	-14	96	134	O1028(121/675/304),D267	184	1.3

EVERETT, ADAM Jeffrey Adam; B2.2.1977 Austell GA; BR/TR/6´0˝/(156–170); [BosA98 1/12]; d8.30; Col South Carolina

YEAR	TM LG	G	AB	R	H	2B	3B	HR	RBI	BB-IB	HP	SO	AVG	OBP	SLG	AOPS	ABR	SB-CS	FA	FR	RNG	THR	GAMES AT POSITION	DL	BFW
2001	Hou N	9	3	1	0	0	0	0	0	0-0	0	1	.000	.000	.000	-93	-1	1-0	.667	-0	89	214	S6	0	-0.1
2002	Hou N	40	88	11	17	3	0	0	4	12-1	1	19	.193	.297	.227	38	-8	3-0	.962	5	113	120	S34	0	0.0
2003	Hou N	128	387	51	99	18	3	8	51	28-6	9	66	.256	.320	.380	78	-13	8-1	.970	14	103	102	S128	0	1.1
2004	†Hou N	104	384	66	105	15	2	8	31	17-0	9	56	.273	.317	.385	79	-13	13-2	.977	11	102	97	S99	53	0.8
2005	†Hou N	152	549	58	136	27	2	11	54	26-1	8	103	.248	.290	.364	69	-26	21-7	.978	6	99	113	S150	0	-0.6
2006	Hou N	150	514	52	123	28	6	6	59	34-5	4	71	.239	.290	.352	62	-30	9-6	.990	28	**113**	**126**	S149	0	0.9
Total	6	583	1925	239	480	91	13	33	199	117-13	31	316	.249	.301	.362	69	-91	55-16	.978	64	105	112	S566	53	2.1

EVERITT, BILL William Lee "Wild Bill"; B12.13.1868 Ft.Wayne IN; D1.19.1938 Denver CO; BL/TR/6´0.5˝/185; d4.18

YEAR	TM LG	G	AB	R	H	2B	3B	HR	RBI	BB-IB	HP	SO	AVG	OBP	SLG	AOPS	ABR	SB-CS	FA	FR	RNG	THR	GAMES AT POSITION	DL	BFW
1895	Chi N	**133**	550	129	197	16	10	3	88	33	4	42	.358	.399	.440	109	6	47	.854	-8	97	61	3b130,2b3	—	0.0
1896	Chi N	**132**	575	130	184	16	13	2	46	41	2	43	.320	.367	.403	99	-2	46	.882	-13	86	65	3b97,O35(27/6/2)	—	-1.4
1897	Chi N	92	379	63	119	14	7	5	39	36	0	—	.314	.373	.427	107	3	26	.864	-6	92	83	3b83,O8(4/4/0)	—	-0.2
1898	Chi N	149	596	102	190	15	6	0	69	53	3	—	.319	.377	.364	113	11	28	.974	-3	96	**144**	1b149	—	0.7
1899	Chi N	136	536	87	166	17	5	1	74	31	3	—	.310	.351	.366	99	-1	30	.971	8	**140**	130	1b136	—	0.6
1900	Chi N	23	91	10	24	4	0	0	17	3	0	—	.264	.287	.308	67	-4	2	.979	-2	72	104	1b23	—	-0.6
1901	Was A	33	115	14	22	3	2	0	8	15	3	—	.191	.301	.252	55	-6	7	.967	-4	49	68	1b33	—	-1.0
Total	7	698	2842	535	902	85	43	11	341	212	15	85	.317	.368	.389	102	7	186	.973	-26	108	129	1b341,3b310,O43(31/10/2),2b3	—	-1.9

EVERS, JOHNNY John Joseph "Crab","Trojan"; B7.21.1881 Troy NY; D3.28.1947 Albany NY; BL/TR/5´9˝/125; d9.1; M3/C7; HF1946; b–Joe

YEAR	TM LG	G	AB	R	H	2B	3B	HR	RBI	BB-IB	HP	SO	AVG	OBP	SLG	AOPS	ABR	SB-CS	FA	FR	RNG	THR	GAMES AT POSITION	DL	BFW
1902	Chi N	26	90	7	20	0	0	0	2	3	2	—	.222	.263	.222	51	-5	1	.990	1	112	81	2b18,S8	—	-0.4
1903	Chi N	124	464	70	136	27	7	0	52	19	3	—	.293	.325	.381	104	1	25	.937	-14	95	116	2b110,S11,3b2	—	-1.2
1904	Chi N	152	532	49	141	14	7	0	47	28	4	—	.265	.307	.318	93	-6	26	.943	28	**109**	125	2b152	—	2.5
1905	Chi N	99	340	44	94	11	2	1	37	27	2	—	.276	.333	.329	94	-2	19	.937	-1	94	137	2b99	—	-0.2
1906	†Chi N	**154**	533	65	136	17	6	1	51	36	2	—	.255	.305	.315	88	-8	49	.947	2	97	118	2b153/3	—	-0.6
1907	†Chi N	151	508	66	127	18	4	2	51	38	5	—	.250	.309	.313	89	-6	46	.964	**27**	**113**	126	2b151	—	2.5
1908	†Chi N	126	416	83	125	19	6	0	37	66	5	—	.300	.402	.375	143	25	36	.960	-1	99	122	2b122/rf	—	2.8
1909	Chi N	127	463	88	122	19	6	1	24	73	4	—	.263	.369	.337	116	13	28	.942	1	100	79	2b126	—	1.7
1910	Chi N	125	433	87	114	11	7	0	28	108	2	18	.263	.413	.321	115	17	28	.950	-3	97	108	2b125	—	1.6
1911	Chi N	46	155	29	35	4	3	0	7	34	2	10	.226	.372	.290	86	-1	6	.975	-2	99	132	2b33,3b11	—	-0.3
1912	Chi N	143	478	73	163	23	11	1	63	74	2	18	.341	**.431**	.441	139	30	16	.959	6	**104**	122	2b143	—	3.7
1913	Chi N	136	446	81	127	20	5	3	49	50	3	14	.285	.361	.372	109	7	11-18	.960	**28**	**113**	**135**	2b136,M	—	3.4
1914	†Bos N	139	491	81	137	20	3	1	40	87	2	26	.279	.390	.338	118	17	12	**.976**	6	99	**145**	2b139	—	2.7
1915	Bos N	83	278	38	73	4	1	1	22	50	0	16	.263	.375	.295	109	6	7-8	.959	-2	95	112	2b82	—	0.5
1916	Bos N	71	241	33	52	4	1	0	15	40	1	19	.216	.330	.241	80	-3	5	.951	-15	88	120	2b71	—	-2.0
1917	Bos N	24	83	5	16	0	0	0	0	13	0	8	.193	.302	.193	56	-4	1	.950	-4	97	129	2b24	—	-0.8
	Phi N	56	183	20	41	5	1	1	12	30	0	13	.224	.333	.279	85	-2	8	.983	1	108	78	2b49,3b7	—	0.1
	Year	80	266	25	57	5	1	1	12	43	0	21	.214	.324	.252	77	-5	9	.973	-3	104	95	2b73,3b7	—	-0.7
1922	Chi A	1	3	0	0	0	0	0	1	2	0	0	.000	.400	.000	12	0	0-0	1.000	-0	85	0	/2	—	0.0
1929	Bos N	1	0	0	0	0	0	0	0	0	0	0	ø	ø	ø	ø	0	0	.000	-1	0	0	/2	—	-0.1
Total	18	1784	6137	919	1659	216	70	12	538	778	39	142	.270	.356	.334	106	79	324-26	.955	58	101	119	2b1735,3b21,S19/rf	—	15.9

EVERS, JOE Joseph Francis; B9.10.1891 Troy NY; D1.4.1949 Albany NY; BR/TR/5´9˝/135; d4.24; b–Johnny

YEAR	TM LG	G	AB	R	H	2B	3B	HR	RBI	BB-IB	HP	SO	AVG	OBP	SLG	AOPS	ABR	SB-CS	FA	FR	RNG	THR	GAMES AT POSITION	DL	BFW
1913	NY N	1	0	0	0	0	0	0	0	0	0	0	ø	ø	ø	ø	0	0	ø	0	—	—	/R	—	0.0

EVERS, TOM Thomas Francis; B3.31.1852 Troy NY; D3.23.1925 Washington DC; TL; d5.25

YEAR	TM LG	G	AB	R	H	2B	3B	HR	RBI	BB-IB	HP	SO	AVG	OBP	SLG	AOPS	ABR	SB-CS	FA	FR	RNG	THR	GAMES AT POSITION	DL	BFW
1882	Bal AA	1	4	0	0	0	0	0	—	0	—	—	.000	.000	.000	-99	-1	—	.500	-2	0	0	/2	—	-0.3
1884	Was U	109	427	54	99	6	1	0	—	7	—	—	.232	.244	.251	52	-38	—	.869	15	103	83	2b109	—	-1.7
Total	2	110	431	54	99	6	1	0	—	7	—	—	.230	.242	.248	51	-39	—	.866	13	102	82	2b110	—	-2.0

EVERS, HOOT Walter Arthur; B2.8.1921 St.Louis MO; D1.25.1991 Houston TX; BR/TR/6´2˝/185; d9.16; Mil 1943–45; C1; Col Illinois

YEAR	TM LG	G	AB	R	H	2B	3B	HR	RBI	BB-IB	HP	SO	AVG	OBP	SLG	AOPS	ABR	SB-CS	FA	FR	RNG	THR	GAMES AT POSITION	DL	BFW
1941	Det A	1	4	0	0	0	0	0	0	0	0	2	.000	.000	.000	-91	-1	0-0	ø	-0	0	0	/rf	0	-0.1
1946	Det A	81	304	42	81	8	4	4	33	34	2	43	.266	.344	.359	91	-3	7-1	.975	-5	97	38	O76(1/76/0)	0	-1.0
1947	Det A	126	460	67	136	24	5	10	67	45	6	49	.296	.366	.435	119	11	8-7	.978	3	103	123	O123C	0	1.1
1948	Det A★	139	538	81	169	33	6	10	103	51	4	31	.314	.378	.454	117	13	3-4	.973	-4	99	70	O138C	0	0.4
1949	Det A	132	432	68	131	21	6	7	72	70	2	38	.303	.403	.428	120	14	6-7	.994	8	108	133	O123(81/42/2)	0	1.3
1950	Det A★	143	526	100	170	35	**11**	21	103	71	4	40	.323	.408	.551	139	31	5-9	**.997**	3	96	129	O139(139/3/0)	0	1.9
1951	Det A	116	393	47	88	15	2	11	46	40	1	47	.224	.297	.356	76	-15	5-3	.976	-4	93	99	O108(66/45/1)	0	-2.4
1952	Det A	1	1	0	1	0	0	0	0	0	0	0	1.000	1.000	1.000	454	0	0-0	ø	0	—	—	/H	0	0.0
	Bos A	106	401	53	105	17	4	14	59	29	4	55	.262	.318	.429	99	-2	5-2	.974	1	98	114	O105(90/12/20)	0	-0.8
	Year	107	402	53	106	17	4	14	59	29	4	55	.264	.320	.430	100	-2	5-2	.974	1	98	114	O105(90/12/20)	0	-0.8
1953	Bos A	99	300	39	72	10	1	11	31	23	3	41	.240	.301	.390	81	-9	2-1	.988	-3	97	52	O93(78/16/0)	0	-1.6
1954	Bos A	6	8	1	0	0	0	0	0	0	0	2	.000	.000	.000	-90	-2	0-0	1.000	-0	83	0	/lf	0	-0.2
	NY N	12	11	1	1	0	0	1	3	0	0	6	.091	.091	.364	12	-2	0-0	1.000	0	149	0	O4(2/2/0)	0	-0.1
	Det A	30	60	5	11	4	0	0	5	5	1	8	.183	.258	.250	40	-5	1-0	1.000	1	108	99	O24(17/2/6)	0	-0.5
1955	Bal A	60	185	21	44	10	1	6	30	19-0	0	28	.238	.307	.400	96	-2	2-1	.991	-2	103	28	O55(10/16/31)	0	-0.5
	Cle A	39	66	10	19	7	1	2	9	3-0	0	12	.288	.314	.515	117	1	0-1	1.000	1	105	96	O25(15/9/2)	0	0.1
	Year	99	251	31	63	17	2	8	39	22-0	0	40	.251	.309	.430	101	-1	2-2	.993	-1	103	44	O80(25/25/33)	0	-0.4
1956	Cle A	3	0	1	0	0	0	0	0	1-0	0	0	ø	1.000	ø	180	0	0-0	ø	0	—	—	/H	0	0.0
	Bal A	48	112	20	27	3	0	1	4	24-0	0	18	.241	.375	.295	85	-1	1-0	.985	0	109	46	O36(3/2/34)	0	-0.2
	Year	51	112	21	27	3	0	1	4	25-0	0	18	.241	.380	.295	86	-1	1-0	.985	0	109	46	O36(3/2/34)	0	-0.2
Total	12	1142	3801	556	1055	187	41	98	565	415-0	27	420	.278	.353	.426	106	28	45-36	.983	-1	100	94	O1051(503/486/97)	0	-2.6

EWELL, GEORGE George W.; B2.1850 Philadelphia PA; D10.20.1910 Philadelphia PA; d6.26

YEAR	TM LG	G	AB	R	H	2B	3B	HR	RBI	BB-IB	HP	SO	AVG	OBP	SLG	AOPS	ABR	SB-CS	FA	FR	RNG	THR	GAMES AT POSITION	DL	BFW
1871	Cle NA	1	3	0	0	0	0	0	0	0	—	0	.000	.000	.000	-99	-1	0-0	1.000	0	0	0	/rf	—	0.0

EWING, REUBEN Reuben (b Reuben Cohen); B11.30.1899 Odessa, Russia; D10.5.1970 W.Hartford CT; BR/TR/5´4.5˝/150; d6.21; Col Lebanon Valley

YEAR	TM LG	G	AB	R	H	2B	3B	HR	RBI	BB-IB	HP	SO	AVG	OBP	SLG	AOPS	ABR	SB-CS	FA	FR	RNG	THR	GAMES AT POSITION	DL	BFW
1921	StL N	3	1	0	0	0	0	0	0	0	0	1	.000	.000	.000	-99	0	0-0	1.000	0	258	0	/S	—	0.0

EWING, SAM Samuel James; B4.9.1949 Lewisburg TN; BL/TL/6´3˝/(195–200); [ChiA71*A1/5]; d9.11; Col Tennessee

YEAR	TM LG	G	AB	R	H	2B	3B	HR	RBI	BB-IB	HP	SO	AVG	OBP	SLG	AOPS	ABR	SB-CS	FA	FR	RNG	THR	GAMES AT POSITION	DL	BFW
1973	Chi A	11	20	1	3	1	0	0	2	2-0	0	6	.150	.227	.200	20	-2	0-0	1.000	1	163	190	1b4	0	-0.2
1976	Chi A	19	41	3	9	2	1	0	2	2-0	0	8	.220	.256	.317	67	-2	0-0	1.000	-0	0	0	D12/1	0	-0.2
1977	Tor A	97	244	24	70	8	2	4	34	19-4	0	42	.287	.338	.385	95	-2	1-1	.957	-4	85	36	O46(15/0/31),D27,1b2	0	-0.9
1978	Tor A	40	56	3	10	0	0	2	9	5-2	0	9	.179	.242	.286	48	-4	0-0	1.000	0	118	0	O3R,D9	0	-0.4
Total	4	167	361	31	92	11	3	6	47	28-6	0	65	.255	.308	.352	81	-10	1-1	.959	-3	86	35	O49(15/0/34),D48,1b7	0	-1.7

EWING, BUCK William; B10.17.1859 Hoagland OH; D10.20.1906 Cincinnati OH; BR/TR/5´10˝/188; d9.9; M7; HF1939; b–John; OF(9/34/193); ▲

YEAR	TM LG	G	AB	R	H	2B	3B	HR	RBI	BB-IB	HP	SO	AVG	OBP	SLG	AOPS	ABR	SB-CS	FA	FR	RNG	THR	GAMES AT POSITION	DL	BFW
1880	Tro N	13	45	1	8	1	0	0	5	1	—	3	.178	.196	.200	33	-3	—	.864	-3	—	—	C10,O4R	—	-0.6
1881	Tro N	67	272	40	68	14	7	0	25	7	—	8	.250	.269	.353	89	-4	—	.915	19	—	—	C44,S22,O2L/3	—	1.6
1882	Tro N	74	328	67	89	16	11	2	29	10	—	15	.271	.293	.405	127	10	—	.887	14	119	171	3b44,C25,2b4/cf1P	—	2.4
1883	NY N	88	376	90	114	11	13	**10**	41	20	—	14	.303	.338	.481	147	20	—	.922	7	—	—	C63,O14(0/10/4),2b11,S4/3	—	2.8
1884	NY N	94	382	90	106	15	**20**	3	41	28	—	22	.277	.327	.445	137	15	—	.933	14	—	—	C80,O12(3/1/8),S3/3P	—	3.1
1885	NY N	81	342	81	104	15	12	6	63	13	—	17	.304	.330	.471	159	20	—	.918	6	—	—	C63,O14(1/3/10),3b8/S1P	—	2.9
1886	NY N	73	275	59	85	11	7	4	31	16	—	17	.309	.347	.444	138	11	18	.921	7	—	—	C50,O23(2/18/3),1b2	—	1.9
1887	NY N	77	318	83	97	17	13	6	44	30	3	33	.305	.370	.497	146	20	26	.863	-1	95	75	3b51,2b19,C8	—	1.7
1888	†NY N	103	415	83	127	18	15	6	58	24	3	28	.306	.348	.465	159	27	53	.947	6	—	—	C78,3b21,S4,P2	—	3.8
1889	†NY N	99	407	91	133	23	13	4	87	37	0	32	.327	.383	.477	138	20	34	.937	16	—	—	C97,P3/lf	—	3.7
1890	NY P	83	352	98	119	19	15	8	72	39	1	12	.338	.406	.545	141	17	36	**.949**	8	*100*	*111*	C81/2PM	—	2.5
1891	NY N	14	49	8	17	2	1	0	18	5	0	5	.347	.407	.429	150	3	5	.881	-1	121	107	2b8,C6	—	0.2
1892	NY N	105	393	58	122	10	15	8	76	38	0	26	.310	.371	.473	157	25	42	.974	3	132	86	1b73,C30,2b2	—	2.8
1893	Cle N	116	500	117	172	28	15	6	122	41	0	18	.344	.394	.496	128	17	47	.927	-1	73	77	O112(0/1/112),2b5/1C	—	0.8
1894	Cle N	53	211	32	53	12	4	2	39	24	0	9	.251	.328	.374	66	-13	18	.912	-2	83	105	O52R/2	—	-1.3
1895	Cin N	105	434	90	138	24	13	5	94	30	1	22	.318	.363	.468	109	3	34	.976	8	139	110	1b105,M	—	0.9
1896	Cin N	69	263	41	73	14	4	1	38	29	0	13	.278	.349	.373	85	-6	41	.980	5	133	108	1b69,M	—	-0.1
1897	Cin N	1	1	0	0	0	0	0	0	0	1	—	.000	.500	.000	36	0	0	.800	-0	0	0	/1M	—	0.0
Total	18	1315	5363	1129	1625	250	178	71	883	392	9	294	.303	.351	.456	129	182	354	.931	104	*91*	*116*	C636,1b253,O235R,3b127,2b51,S34,P9	—	29.1

EWOLDT, ART Arthur Lee "Sheriff"; B1.8.1894 Paullina IA; D12.8.1977 Des Moines IA; BR/TR/5´10˝/165; d9.17

YEAR	TM LG	G	AB	R	H	2B	3B	HR	RBI	BB-IB	HP	SO	AVG	OBP	SLG	AOPS	ABR	SB-CS	FA	FR	RNG	THR	GAMES AT POSITION	DL	BFW
1919	Phi A	9	32	2	7	1	0	0	2	1	0	5	.219	.242	.250	38	-3	0	1.000	0	99	0	3b9	—	-0.2

EZZELL, HOMER Homer Estell; B2.28.1896 Victoria TX; D8.3.1976 San Antonio TX; BR/TR/5´10˝/158; d4.22

YEAR	TM LG	G	AB	R	H	2B	3B	HR	RBI	BB-IB	HP	SO	AVG	OBP	SLG	AOPS	ABR	SB-CS	FA	FR	RNG	THR	GAMES AT POSITION	DL	BFW
1923	StL A	88	279	31	68	6	0	0	14	15	2	20	.244	.287	.265	44	-23	4-3	.961	3	98	100	3b73,2b8	—	-1.5
1924	Bos A	90	277	35	75	8	4	0	32	14	2	21	.271	.311	.329	65	-16	12-5	.984	8	125	68	3b64,S21/C	—	-0.1
1925	Bos A	58	186	40	53	6	4	0	15	19	0	18	.285	.351	.360	81	-6	9-7	.916	-6	99	62	3b47,2b9	—	-0.9
Total	3	236	742	106	196	20	8	0	61	48	4	59	.264	.312	.313	61	-45	25-15	.957	5	106	80	3b184,S21,2b17/C	—	-2.5

FAATZ, JAY Jayson S.; B10.24.1860 Weedsport NY; D4.10.1923 Syracuse NY; BR/TR/6´4˝/196; d8.22; M1

YEAR	TM LG	G	AB	R	H	2B	3B	HR	RBI	BB-IB	HP	SO	AVG	OBP	SLG	AOPS	ABR	SB-CS	FA	FR	RNG	THR	GAMES AT POSITION	DL	BFW
1884	Pit AA	29	112	18	27	2	3	0	—	1	4	—	.241	.274	.313	92	-1	—	.963	-1	64	108	1b29	—	-0.4
1888	Cle AA	120	470	73	124	10	2	0	51	12	21	—	.264	.312	.294	97	-1	64	**.989**	2	90	86	1b120	—	-0.9
1889	Cle N	117	442	50	102	12	5	2	38	17	10	28	.231	.275	.294	59	-26	27	.981	6	120	105	1b117	—	-2.7
1890	Buf P	32	111	18	21	0	2	1	16	9	8	5	.189	.297	.252	52	-7	2	.982	-2	48	89	1b32,M	—	-1.0
Total	4	298	1135	159	274	24	12	3	105	39	43	33	.241	.293	.292	76	-35	93	.982	5	95	96	1b298	—	-5.0

YEAR	TM LG	G	AB	R	H	2B	3B	HR	RBI	BB-IB	HP	SO	AVG	OBP	SLG	AOPS	ABR	SB-CS	FA	FR	RNG	THR	GAMES AT POSITION	DL	BFW
FABREGAS, JORGE	Jorge; B3.13.1970 Miami FL; BL/TR/6´3˝/(205–220); [CalA91 1/34]; d4.24; Col Miami																								
1994	Cal A	43	127	12	36	3	0	0	16	7-1	0	18	.283	.321	.307	62	-7	2-1	.987	-1	85	88	C41	0	-0.6
1995	Cal A	73	227	24	56	10	0	1	22	17-0	0	28	.247	.298	.304	58	-14	0-2	.986	3	122	120	C73	0	-0.7
1996	Cal A	90	254	18	73	6	0	2	26	17-3	0	27	.287	.326	.335	68	-12	0-1	.989	0	81	105	C89/D	0	-0.7
1997	Ana A	21	38	2	3	1	0	0	3	3-0	0	3	.079	.146	.105	-33	-8	0-0	.989	1	196	54	C21	0	-0.5
	Chi A	100	322	31	90	10	1	7	48	11-0	1	43	.280	.302	.382	81	-11	1-1	.988	2	94	124	C92/1	0	-0.3
	Year	121	360	33	93	11	1	7	51	14-0	1	46	.258	.285	.353	68	-18	1-1	.988	3	107	115	C113/1	0	-0.8
1998	Ari N	50	151	8	30	4	0	1	15	13-1	1	26	.199	.263	.245	36	-14	0-0	.996	7	114	201	C41	30	-0.5
	NY N	20	32	3	6	0	0	1	5	1-0	0	6	.188	.212	.281	29	-4	0-0	.971	3	57	147	C12	0	0.0
	Year	70	183	11	36	4	0	2	20	14-1	1	32	.197	.255	.251	35	-18	0-0	.991	10	105	192	C53	0	-0.5
1999	Fla N	82	223	20	46	10	2	3	21	26-6	2	27	.206	.289	.309	56	-15	0-0	.989	7	139	144	C78	0	-0.4
	†Atl N	6	8	0	0	0	0	0	0	0-0	0	0	.000	.000	.000	-99	-2	0-0	1.000	2	0	0	C4/1	0	-0.1
	Year	88	231	20	46	10	2	3	21	26-6	2	27	.199	.280	.299	51	-18	0-0	.990	9	135	140	C82/1	0	-0.5
2000	KC A	43	142	13	40	4	0	3	17	8-1	0	11	.282	.320	.373	71	-7	1-0	.992	2	142	104	C39/D	43	-0.1
2001	Ana A	53	148	9	33	4	2	2	16	3-0	0	15	.223	.235	.318	44	-13	0-0	.990	6	105	120	C53	16	-0.4
2002	Ana A	35	88	8	17	1	0	0	8	6-1	0	6	.193	.245	.205	22	-10	0-0	.994	0	71	82	C32	0	-0.8
	Mil N	30	67	5	11	3	0	3	14	2-0	0	7	.164	.178	.343	36	-7	0-0	.992	1	139	112	C20	0	-0.4
Total	9	646	1827	153	441	56	5	23	211	114-13	4	217	.241	.284	.315	56	-124	4-5	.989	33	109	121	C595,1b2,D2	89	-5.5
FABRIQUE, BUNNY	Albert La Verne; B12.23.1887 Clinton MI; D1.10.1960 Ann Arbor MI; BB/TR/5´8.5˝/150; d10.4																								
1916	Bro N	2	2	0	0	0	0	0	0	0	0	1	.000	.000	.000	-97	0	0	1.000	0	91	374	S2	—	0.0
1917	Bro N	25	88	8	18	3	0	1	3	8	0	9	.205	.271	.273	65	-3	0	.874	-5	85	80	S21	—	-0.8
Total	2	27	90	8	18	3	0	1	3	8	0	10	.200	.265	.267	62	-3	0	.878	-5	85	89	S23	—	-0.8
FAEDO, LENNY	Leonardo Lago; B5.13.1960 Tampa FL; BR/TR/6´0˝/(170–180); [MinA78 1/16]; d9.6																								
1980	Min A	5	8	1	2	1	0	0	0	0-0	0	0	.250	.250	.375	64	0	0-0	.818	-3	49	0	S5	0	-0.3
1981	Min A	12	41	3	8	0	1	0	6	1-0	0	5	.195	.209	.244	30	-4	0-0	.971	2	107	113	S12	0	-0.1
1982	Min A	90	255	16	62	8	0	3	22	16-0	1	22	.243	.288	.310	63	-13	1-0	.967	-10	87	103	S88/D	0	-1.4
1983	Min A	51	173	16	48	7	0	1	18	4-1	0	19	.277	.291	.335	70	-7	0-0	.954	-17	85	66	S51	89	-1.9
1984	Min A	16	52	6	13	1	0	1	6	4-0	0	3	.250	.304	.327	71	-2	0-0	.968	-5	86	45	S15/D	0	-0.5
Total	5	174	529	42	133	17	1	5	52	25-1	1	49	.251	.284	.316	63	-26	1-0	.961	-32	87	85	S171,D2	89	-4.2
FAGIN, FRED	Frederick H.; B Cincinnati OH; d6.25																								
1895	StL N	1	3	0	1	0	0	0	2	0	0	0	.333	.333	.333	73	0	0	.636	-1	*74*	*172*	/C	—	-0.1
FAHEY, BRANDON	Brandon Michael; B1.18.1981 Dallas TX; BL/TR/6´2˝/160; [BalA02 12/346]; d4.30; f–Bill; Col Texas																								
2006	Bal A	91	251	36	59	8	2	2	23	23-0	3	48	.235	.307	.307	61	-15	3-3	.954	4	122	65	O54(53/0/1),S17,2b13/3	0	-1.1
FAHEY, FRANK	Francis Raymond; B1.22.1896 Milford MA; D3.19.1954 Boston MA; BB/TR/6´1˝/190; d4.25; Col Catholic America; ▲																								
1918	Phi A	10	17	2	3	1	0	0	1	0	0	3	.176	.176	.235	24	-2	0	1.000	-1	81	0	O5(4/1/0),P3	—	-0.2
FAHEY, HOWARD	Howard Simpson "Cap","Kid"; B6.24.1892 Medford MA; D10.24.1971 Clearwater FL; BR/TR/5´7.5˝/145; d7.23; Col Dartmouth																								
1912	Phi A	5	8	0	0	0	0	0	0	0	0	—	.000	.000	.000	-99	-2	0	1.000	-1	0	1059	3b2/2S	—	-0.3
FAHEY, BILL	William Roger; B6.14.1950 Detroit MI; BL/TR/6´0˝/(190–200); [TexA70*S1/1]; d9.26; C6; s–Brandon; Col Detroit Mercy; [DL 1978 Tex A 41]																								
1971	Was A	2	8	0	0	0	0	0	0	0-0	0	0	.000	.000	.000	-99	-2	0-0	.909	-0	85	186	C2	0	-0.3
1972	Tex A	39	119	8	20	2	0	1	10	12-0	1	23	.168	.250	.210	39	-9	4-0	.992	5	75	166	C39	0	-0.2
1974	Tex A	6	16	1	4	0	0	0	0	0-0	0	1	.250	.250	.250	45	-1	0-0	1.000	-1	0	59	C6	0	-0.2
1975	Tex A	21	37	3	11	1	1	0	3	1-0	0	10	.297	.316	.378	96	0	0-0	.983	-2	71	63	C21	53	-0.2
1976	Tex A	38	80	12	20	2	0	1	9	11-0	1	6	.250	.348	.313	92	0	1-0	.993	1	99	94	C38	0	0.2
1977	Tex A	37	68	3	15	4	0	0	5	1-0	0	8	.221	.232	.279	38	-6	0-0	1.000	-6	72	47	C34	0	-1.0
1979	SD N	73	209	14	60	8	1	3	19	21-5	0	17	.287	.348	.378	106	2	1-1	.994	-6	110	100	C68	0	-0.1
1980	SD N	93	241	18	62	4	0	1	22	21-6	0	16	.257	.314	.286	74	-8	2-0	.977	-7	92	102	C85	0	-1.3
1981	Det A	27	67	5	17	2	0	1	9	2-0	0	4	.254	.271	.328	71	-3	0-1	.981	1	93	95	C27	30	-0.2
1982	Det A	28	67	7	10	2	0	0	4	0-0	0	5	.149	.147	.179	-10	-10	1-0	1.000	3	103	158	C28	29	-0.7
1983	Det A	19	22	4	6	1	0	0	2	5-1	0	3	.273	.407	.318	105	1	0-0	1.000	-3	630	0	C18	42	-0.2
Total	11	383	934	75	225	26	2	7	83	74-12	2	93	.241	.296	.296	69	-36	9-2	.989	-15	109	103	C366	195	-4.2
FAIN, FERRIS	Ferris Roy "Burrhead"; B3.29.1921 San Antonio TX; D10.18.2001 Georgetown CA; BL/TL/5´11˝/186; d4.15																								
1947	Phi A	136	461	70	134	28	6	7	71	95	2	34	.291	.414	.423	130	24	4-5	.985	-1	104	104	1b132	0	1.9
1948	Phi A	145	520	81	146	27	6	7	88	113	3	37	.281	.412	.396	115	18	10-5	.989	8	**122**	105	1b145	0	2.0
1949	Phi A	150	525	81	138	21	5	3	78	136	0	51	.263	.415	.339	104	12	8-1	.984	5	115	119	1b150	0	1.3
1950	Phi A★	151	522	83	147	25	4	10	83	133	3	26	.282	.430	.402	116	22	8-5	.987	11	**132**	113	1b151	0	2.5
1951	Phi A★	117	425	63	146	30	3	6	57	80	3	20	**.344**	.451	.471	146	33	0-3	.990	16	**159**	**119**	1b108,O11(1/0/10)	0	**4.3**
1952	Phi A☆	145	538	82	176	**43**	3	2	59	105	1	26	**.327**	**.438**	.429	133	32	3-5	.984	18	**148**	92	1b144	0	**4.5**
1953	Chi A★	128	446	73	114	18	2	6	52	108	4	28	.256	.405	.345	101	8	3-2	.989	9	125	86	1b127	0	0.9
1954	Chi A✳	65	235	30	71	10	1	5	51	40	1	14	.302	.399	.417	121	9	5-1	.987	-4	75	105	1b64	66	0.2
1955	Det A	58	140	23	37	8	0	2	23	52-2	0	12	.264	.459	.364	128	11	2-1	.988	-0	104	113	1b44	0	0.8
	Cle A	56	118	9	30	3	0	0	8	42-1	1	13	.254	.451	.280	97	3	3-0	.992	3	120	91	1b51	0	0.4
	Year	114	258	32	67	11	0	2	31	94-3	1	25	.260	.455	.326	113	14	5-1	.990	3	112	102	1b95	0	1.2
Total	9	1151	3930	595	1139	213	30	48	570	904-3	18	261	.290	.424	.396	120	172	46-28	.987	63	124	105	1b1116,O11(1/0/10)	66	18.8
FAIR, BOBBY	George T.; B1.13.1856 Boston MA; D2.12.1939 Roslindale MA; 5´7.5˝/140; d7.29																								
1876	NY N	1	4	0	0	0	0	0	0	0	—	0	.000	.000	.000	-99	-1	—	.750	-0	105	187	/2	—	-0.1
FAIREY, JIM	James Burke; B9.22.1944 Orangeburg SC; BL/TL/5´10˝/(179–190); d4.14; Col Erskine																								
1968	LA N	99	156	17	31	3	3	1	10	9-0	0	32	.199	.241	.276	60	-9	1-1	.944	1	110	122	O63(40/2/23)	0	-1.1
1969	Mon N	20	49	6	14	1	0	1	6	1-0	0	7	.286	.300	.367	86	-1	0-2	.913	-1	90	163	O13(1/12/0)	0	-0.3
1970	Mon N	92	211	35	51	9	3	3	25	14-4	2	38	.242	.293	.355	73	-9	1-3	.978	-2	95	34	O59(33/30/4)	10	-1.4
1971	Mon N	92	200	19	49	8	1	1	19	12-5	0	23	.245	.285	.310	68	-9	3-3	.968	3	96	231	O58(56/2/1)	0	-0.9
1972	Mon N	86	141	9	33	7	0	1	15	10-2	0	21	.234	.285	.305	66	-6	1-3	.932	-2	85	56	O37(20/1/18)	0	-1.2
1973	LA N	10	9	0	2	0	0	0	0	1-0	0	1	.222	.300	.222	48	-1	0-0	ø	0	—	—	/H	0	-0.1
Total	6	399	766	86	180	28	7	7	75	47-11	2	122	.235	.279	.317	69	-35	6-12	.957	-1	97	121	O230(150/47/46)	10	-5.0
FAIRLY, RON	Ronald Ray; B7.12.1938 Macon GA; BL/TL/5´10˝/(175–181); d9.9; Col USC																								
1958	LA N	15	53	6	15	1	0	2	8	6-0	0	7	.283	.350	.415	100	0	0-0	.971	-1	105	0	O15(4/11/1)	0	-0.1
1959	†LA N	118	244	27	58	12	1	4	23	31-2	1	29	.238	.324	.344	73	-8	0-4	.963	-2	81	184	O88(7/23/62)	0	-1.5
1960	LA N	14	37	6	4	0	3	1	3	7-0	0	12	.108	.250	.351	59	-2	0-0	1.000	-1	75	105	O13(5/0/8)	0	-0.4
1961	LA N	111	245	42	79	15	2	10	48	48-0	1	22	.322	.434	.522	140	17	0-0	.989	1	96	177	O71(6/15/53),1b23	0	1.4
1962	LA N	147	460	80	128	15	7	14	71	75-6	3	59	.278	.379	.433	126	19	1-1	.989	-10	57	79	1b120,O48(4/5/42)	0	0.1
1963	†LA N	152	490	62	133	21	0	12	77	58-7	1	69	.271	.347	.388	120	14	5-2	**.995**	-6	71	99	1b119,O45(16/22/10)	0	0.1
1964	LA N	150	454	62	116	19	5	10	74	65-6	2	59	.256	.349	.385	116	11	4-0	.987	-0	99	95	1b141	0	0.4
1965	†LA N	158	555	73	152	28	1	9	70	76-11	3	72	.274	.361	.377	117	16	2-0	.982	-5	95	72	O148(0/17/133),1b13	0	0.1
1966	†LA N	117	351	53	101	20	0	14	61	52-4	2	38	.288	.380	.464	146	24	3-2	.974	-9	77	36	O98(0/6/95),1b25	0	0.9
1967	LA N	153	486	45	107	19	0	10	55	54-9	1	51	.220	.295	.321	85	-9	1-4	.986	5	96	151	O97(1/0/97),1b68	0	-1.6
1968	LA N	141	441	32	103	15	1	4	43	41-10	4	61	.234	.301	.299	88	-6	0-2	.989	2	96	172	O105R,1b36	0	-1.5
1969	LA N	30	64	3	14	3	2	0	8	9-1	0	6	.219	.315	.328	86	-1	0-0	.981	1	137	65	1b12,O10(1/0/10)	0	-0.2
	Mon N	70	253	35	73	13	4	12	39	28-2	0	22	.289	.358	.514	141	13	1-0	.991	1	117	121	1b52,O21(3/18/0)	32	1.0
	Year	100	317	38	87	16	6	12	47	37-3	0	28	.274	.349	.476	132	13	1-0	.989	1	121	111	1b64,O31(4/18/10)	0	0.8
1970	Mon N	119	385	54	111	19	0	15	61	72-9	4	64	.288	.402	.455	130	20	10-2	.995	5	114	**117**	1b118,O4(2/2/0)	31	1.7
1971	Mon N	146	447	58	115	23	0	13	71	81-10	5	65	.257	.373	.396	118	15	1-3	.992	4	115	97	1b135,O10(10/1/0)	0	0.9
1972	Mon N	140	446	51	124	15	1	17	68	46-7	3	45	.278	.348	.430	118	11	3-4	.985	5	104	165	O70R,1b68	0	0.7
1973	Mon N★	142	413	70	123	13	1	17	49	86-11	3	33	.298	.422	.458	139	27	2-2	.974	-4	84	56	O121L,1b5	0	1.7
1974	Mon N	101	282	35	69	9	1	12	43	57-6	1	28	.245	.372	.411	113	7	2-1	.989	0	99	85	1b67,O20(19/0/1)	0	0.1
1975	StL N	107	229	32	69	13	2	7	37	45-9	3	22	.301	.421	.467	140	15	0-1	.980	1	114	92	1b56,O20(4/0/16)	0	1.2

YEAR	TM LG	G	AB	R	H	2B	3B	HR	RBI	BB-IB	HP	SO	AVG	OBP	SLG	AOPS	ABR	SB-CS	FA	FR	RNG	THR	GAMES AT POSITION	DL	BFW
1976	StL N	73	110	13	29	4	0	0	21	23-3	0	12	.264	.385	.300	96	1	0-0	.995	3	159	109	1b27	0	0.3
	Oak A	15	46	9	11	1	0	3	10	9-3	0	12	.239	.364	.457	145	3	0-0	1.000	0	97	88	1b15	0	0.2
1977	Tor A★	132	458	60	128	24	2	19	64	58-11	2	58	.279	.362	.465	122	15	0-4	.986	4	116	84	D58,1b40,O33(9/0/24)	0	1.2
1978	Cal A	91	235	23	51	5	0	10	40	25-2	1	31	.217	.289	.366	88	-5	0-1	.998	-3	72	91	1b78,D5	0	-1.3
Total	21	2442	7184	931	1913	307	33	215	1044	1052-129	40	877	.266	.360	.408	117	197	35-33	.991	-10	98	97	1b1218,O1037(212/120/727),D63	63	5.4

FALCH, ANTON Anton C.; B12.4.1860 Milwaukee WI; D3.31.1936 Wauwatosa WI; 6´6˝/220; d9.30

YEAR	TM LG	G	AB	R	H	2B	3B	HR	RBI	BB-IB	HP	SO	AVG	OBP	SLG	AOPS	ABR	SB-CS	FA	FR	RNG	THR	GAMES AT POSITION	DL	BFW
1884	Mil U	5	18	0	2	0	0	0	—	0	—	—	.111	.111	.111	-60	-4	—	.600	-0	101	0	O3L,C2	—	-0.4

FALK, BIBB Bibb August "Jockey"; B1.27.1899 Austin TX; D6.8.1989 Austin TX; BL/TL/6´0˝/175; d9.17; M1/C2; b–Chet; Col Texas

YEAR	TM LG	G	AB	R	H	2B	3B	HR	RBI	BB-IB	HP	SO	AVG	OBP	SLG	AOPS	ABR	SB-CS	FA	FR	RNG	THR	GAMES AT POSITION	DL	BFW
1920	Chi A	7	17	1	5	1	1	0	2	0	0	5	.294	.294	.471	100	0	0-0	1.000	-0	93	0	O4R	—	-0.1
1921	Chi A	152	585	62	167	31	11	5	82	37	2	69	.285	.330	.402	87	-14	4-4	.958	-13	89	48	O149(148/1/0)	—	-3.7
1922	Chi A	131	483	58	144	27	1	12	79	27	0	55	.298	.335	.433	99	-2	2-6	.963	-9	91	62	O129(126/2/1)	—	-2.2
1923	Chi A	87	274	44	84	18	6	5	38	25	1	12	.307	.367	.471	121	7	5-5	.951	-3	97	69	O80L	—	-0.2
1924	Chi A	138	526	77	185	37	8	6	99	47	1	21	.352	.406	.487	134	26	6-6	.970	8	96	**178**	O134L	—	2.1
1925	Chi A	**154**	602	80	181	35	9	4	99	51	2	25	.301	.357	.409	99	-2	4-5	.959	-6	90	102	O153L	—	-1.9
1926	Chi A	**155**	566	86	195	43	4	8	108	66	2	22	.345	.415	.477	137	33	9-10	**.992**	8	107	109	O155L	—	2.7
1927	Chi A	145	535	76	175	35	6	9	83	52	4	19	.327	.391	.465	125	20	5-7	.978	**18**	**115**	146	O145L	—	2.4
1928	Chi A	98	286	42	83	18	4	1	37	25	0	16	.290	.347	.392	95	-2	5-1	.972	2	100	125	O78L	—	-0.5
1929	Cle A	125	426	65	133	30	7	13	93	42	0	14	.312	.374	.507	120	12	4-4	.943	-4	89	123	O120(61/0/61)	—	-0.2
1930	Cle A	82	191	34	62	12	1	4	36	23	0	8	.325	.397	.461	113	4	2-0	.967	0	98	111	O42(25/0/18)	—	0.2
1931	Cle A	79	161	30	49	13	1	2	28	17	0	13	.304	.371	.435	105	2	1-1	.949	-2	95	36	O33(2/0/31)	—	-0.2
Total	12	1353	4652	655	1463	300	59	69	784	412	12	279	.314	.372	.449	113	84	47-49	.967	-1	97	106	O1222(1107/3/115)	—	-1.6

FALLON, CHARLIE Charles Augustus; B3.7.1881 New York NY; D6.10.1960 Kings Park NY; BR/TR/5´6˝/?; d6.30

YEAR	TM LG	G	AB	R	H	2B	3B	HR	RBI	BB-IB	HP	SO	AVG	OBP	SLG	AOPS	ABR	SB-CS	FA	FR	RNG	THR	GAMES AT POSITION	DL	BFW
1905	NY A	1	0	0	0	0	0	0	0	0	0	—	ø	ø	ø	ø	0	0	ø	0	—	—	/R	—	0.0

FALLON, GEORGE George Decatur "Flash"; B7.8.1914 Jersey City NJ; D10.25.1994 Lake Worth FL; BR/TR/5´9˝/155; d9.27; Mil 1945

YEAR	TM LG	G	AB	R	H	2B	3B	HR	RBI	BB-IB	HP	SO	AVG	OBP	SLG	AOPS	ABR	SB-CS	FA	FR	RNG	THR	GAMES AT POSITION	DL	BFW
1937	Bro N	4	8	0	2	1	0	0	0	1	0	0	.250	.333	.375	91	0	0	.895	-0	87	56	2b4	—	0.0
1943	StL N	36	78	6	18	1	0	0	5	2	1	9	.231	.259	.244	44	-6	0	.968	9	122	133	2b36	0	0.4
1944	†StL N	69	141	16	28	6	0	1	9	16	1	11	.199	.285	.262	54	-8	1	.973	1	86	104	2b38,S24,3b6	0	-0.5
1945	StL N	24	55	4	13	2	1	0	7	6	0	6	.236	.311	.309	71	-2	1	.948	-3	84	108	S20,2b4	0	-0.4
Total	4	133	282	26	61	10	1	1	21	25	2	26	.216	.285	.270	56	-16	2	.966	6	103	112	2b82,S44,3b6	0	-0.5

FALSEY, PETE Peter James; B4.24.1891 New Haven CT; D5.23.1976 Los Angeles CA; BL/TL/5´6.5˝/132; d7.16; Col Yale

YEAR	TM LG	G	AB	R	H	2B	3B	HR	RBI	BB-IB	HP	SO	AVG	OBP	SLG	AOPS	ABR	SB-CS	FA	FR	RNG	THR	GAMES AT POSITION	DL	BFW
1914	Pit N	3	1	0	0	0	0	0	0	0	0	1	.000	.000	.000	-99	0	0	ø	0	—	—	/H	—	0.0

FANEYTE, RIKKERT Rikkert; B5.31.1969 Amsterdam, Netherlands; BR/TR/6´1˝/170; [SFN90 16/446]; d8.29; Col Miami–Dade Kendall (FL) CC

YEAR	TM LG	G	AB	R	H	2B	3B	HR	RBI	BB-IB	HP	SO	AVG	OBP	SLG	AOPS	ABR	SB-CS	FA	FR	RNG	THR	GAMES AT POSITION	DL	BFW
1993	SF N	7	15	2	2	0	0	0	0	2-0	0	4	.133	.235	.133	2	-2	0-0	1.000	0	112	0	O6(1/5/0)	0	-0.2
1994	SF N	19	26	1	3	3	0	0	4	3-0	0	11	.115	.207	.231	14	-3	0-0	.900	0	122	0	O6(0/2/4)	0	-0.3
1995	SF N	46	86	7	17	4	1	0	4	11-0	0	27	.198	.289	.267	49	-6	1-0	.981	1	97	239	O34(3/22/11)	0	-0.5
1996	Tex A	8	5	0	1	0	0	0	1	0-0	0	0	.200	.200	.200	1	-1	0-0	1.000	1	182	0	O6(2/4/0),D2	0	0.0
Total	4	80	132	10	23	7	1	0	9	16-0	0	42	.174	.264	.242	35	-12	1-0	.976	2	108	167	O52(6/33/15),D2	0	-1.0

FANNING, JIM William James; B9.14.1927 Chicago IL; BR/TR/5´11˝/180; d9.11; M3/C1; Col Buena Vista

YEAR	TM LG	G	AB	R	H	2B	3B	HR	RBI	BB-IB	HP	SO	AVG	OBP	SLG	AOPS	ABR	SB-CS	FA	FR	RNG	THR	GAMES AT POSITION	DL	BFW
1954	Chi N	11	38	2	7	0	0	0	1	1	0	7	.184	.205	.184	2	-6	0-0	1.000	-1	*51*	*111*	C11	0	-0.7
1955	Chi N	5	10	0	0	0	0	0	0	1-0	0	2	.000	.091	.000	-73	-3	0-0	1.000	1	*137*	*97*	C5	0	-0.1
1956	Chi N	1	4	0	1	0	0	0	0	0-0	0	0	.250	.250	.250	36	0	0-0	.800	0	*0*	*398*	/C	0	0.0
1957	Chi N	47	89	3	16	2	0	0	4	4-1	1	17	.180	.223	.202	16	-11	0-0	.981	-1	102	192	C35	0	-1.1
Total	4	64	141	5	24	2	0	0	5	6-1	1	26	.170	.209	.184	6	-20	0-0	.979	-1	*90*	*169*	C52	0	-1.9

FANZONE, CARMEN Carmen Ronald; B8.30.1943 Detroit MI; BR/TR/6´0˝/200; d7.21; Col Central Michigan

YEAR	TM LG	G	AB	R	H	2B	3B	HR	RBI	BB-IB	HP	SO	AVG	OBP	SLG	AOPS	ABR	SB-CS	FA	FR	RNG	THR	GAMES AT POSITION	DL	BFW
1970	Bos A	10	15	0	3	1	0	0	3	2-0	1	2	.200	.316	.267	63	-1	0-0	.750	-0	109	134	3b5	0	-0.1
1971	Chi N	12	43	5	8	2	0	2	5	2-0	0	7	.186	.222	.372	57	-3	0-0	1.000	0	84	0	O6(5/0/1),3b3,1b2	0	-0.3
1972	Chi N	86	222	26	50	11	0	8	42	35-6	3	45	.225	.333	.383	94	0	2-3	.923	2	112	137	3b36,1b21,2b13/Slf	0	0.0
1973	Chi N	64	150	22	41	7	0	6	22	20-1	0	38	.273	.357	.440	112	3	1-2	.922	-2	89	0	3b25,1b24,O6L	0	-0.1
1974	Chi N	65	158	13	30	6	0	4	22	15-1	2	27	.190	.264	.304	57	-9	0-1	.885	-0	99	127	3b35,2b10,1b7/lf	0	-1.1
Total	5	237	588	66	132	27	0	20	94	74-8	6	119	.224	.313	.372	86	-10	3-6	.896	0	104	101	3b104,1b54,2b23,O14(13/0/1)/S	0	-1.6

FARIES, PAUL Paul Tyrrell; B2.20.1965 Berkeley CA; BR/TR/5´10˝/(165–170); [SDN87 23/588]; d9.6; Col Pepperdine

YEAR	TM LG	G	AB	R	H	2B	3B	HR	RBI	BB-IB	HP	SO	AVG	OBP	SLG	AOPS	ABR	SB-CS	FA	FR	RNG	THR	GAMES AT POSITION	DL	BFW
1990	SD N	14	37	4	7	1	0	0	2	4-0	1	7	.189	.279	.216	40	-3	0-1	1.000	2	94	83	2b7,S4/3	0	-0.1
1991	SD N	57	130	13	23	3	1	0	7	14-0	1	21	.177	.262	.215	35	-11	3-1	.988	6	115	129	2b36,3b12,S8	25	-0.4
1992	SD N	10	11	3	5	1	0	0	1	1-0	0	2	.455	.500	.545	192	1	0-0	1.000	-1	94	115	2b4,3b2/S	0	0.0
1993	SF N	15	36	6	8	2	1	0	4	1-0	0	4	.222	.237	.333	54	-3	2-0	1.000	-1	107	94	2b7,S4/3	0	-0.3
Total	4	96	214	26	43	7	2	0	14	20-0	2	34	.201	.273	.252	47	-16	5-2	.992	6	110	116	2b54,S17,3b16	25	-0.8

FARISS, MONTY Monty Ted; B10.13.1967 Cordell OK; BR/TR/6´4˝/(200–205); [TexA88 1/6]; d9.6; Col Oklahoma St.

YEAR	TM LG	G	AB	R	H	2B	3B	HR	RBI	BB-IB	HP	SO	AVG	OBP	SLG	AOPS	ABR	SB-CS	FA	FR	RNG	THR	GAMES AT POSITION	DL	BFW
1991	Tex A	19	31	6	8	1	0	1	6	7-0	0	11	.258	.395	.387	119	1	0-0	1.000	3	190	0	O8L,2b4,D4	0	0.4
1992	Tex A	67	166	13	36	7	1	3	21	17-0	2	51	.217	.297	.325	77	-5	0-2	1.000	-7	73	0	O49(28/10/12),2b17/1D	19	-1.4
1993	Fla N	18	29	3	5	2	1	0	2	5-0	0	13	.172	.294	.310	58	-2	0-0	1.000	-0	110	0	O8(1/0/7)	0	-0.2
Total	3	104	226	22	49	10	2	4	29	29-0	2	75	.217	.311	.332	80	-6	0-2	1.000	-4	91	0	O65(37/10/19),2b21,D8/1	19	-1.2

FARLEY, BOB Robert Jacob; B11.15.1937 Watsontown PA; BL/TL/6´2˝/200; d4.15

YEAR	TM LG	G	AB	R	H	2B	3B	HR	RBI	BB-IB	HP	SO	AVG	OBP	SLG	AOPS	ABR	SB-CS	FA	FR	RNG	THR	GAMES AT POSITION	DL	BFW
1961	SF N	13	20	3	2	0	0	0	1	3-0	0	5	.100	.217	.100	-13	-3	0-0	1.000	-1	60	0	O3L/1	0	-0.4
1962	Chi A	35	53	7	10	1	1	1	4	13-0	0	13	.189	.348	.302	77	-1	0-1	.989	-1	70	102	1b14	0	-0.3
	Det A	36	50	9	8	2	0	1	4	14-0	0	10	.160	.338	.260	63	-2	0-0	.857	-3	35	0	O11R,1b6	0	-0.6
	Year	71	103	16	18	3	1	2	8	27-0	0	23	.175	.344	.282	70	-3	0-1	.974	-4	76	107	1b20,O11R	0	-0.9
Total	2	84	123	19	20	3	1	2	9	30-0	0	28	.163	.325	.252	58	-6	0-1	.975	-5	73	113	1b21,O14(3/0/11)	0	-1.3

FARLEY, TOM Thomas T.; B Chicago IL; d6.24

YEAR	TM LG	G	AB	R	H	2B	3B	HR	RBI	BB-IB	HP	SO	AVG	OBP	SLG	AOPS	ABR	SB-CS	FA	FR	RNG	THR	GAMES AT POSITION	DL	BFW
1884	Was AA	14	52	5	11	4	0	0	—	1	1	—	.212	.241	.288	81	-1	—	.867	1	74	193	O14L	—	0.0

FARMER, ALEX Alexander Johnson; B5.9.1877 New York NY; D3.5.1920 Bronx NY; BR/TR/6´0˝/175; d9.1

YEAR	TM LG	G	AB	R	H	2B	3B	HR	RBI	BB-IB	HP	SO	AVG	OBP	SLG	AOPS	ABR	SB-CS	FA	FR	RNG	THR	GAMES AT POSITION	DL	BFW
1908	Bro N	12	30	1	5	1	0	0	2	1	0	—	.167	.194	.200	27	-3	0	.966	-0	*85*	*58*	C11	—	-0.2

FARMER, JACK Floyd Haskell; B7.14.1892 Granville TN; D5.21.1970 Columbia LA; BR/TR/6´0˝/180; d7.8; Col Cumberland

YEAR	TM LG	G	AB	R	H	2B	3B	HR	RBI	BB-IB	HP	SO	AVG	OBP	SLG	AOPS	ABR	SB-CS	FA	FR	RNG	THR	GAMES AT POSITION	DL	BFW
1916	Pit N	55	166	10	45	6	4	0	14	7	2	24	.271	.309	.355	103	0	1	.929	-9	88	50	2b31,O15(8/0/7),S4/3	—	-1.1
1918	Cle A	7	9	1	2	0	0	0	1	0	1	3	.222	.300	.222	53	0	2	.429	-1	63	0	O3(2/0/1)	—	-0.2
Total	2	62	175	11	47	6	4	0	15	7	3	27	.269	.308	.349	100	0	3	.929	-11	88	50	2b31,O18(10/0/8),S4/3	—	-1.3

FARMER, BILL William; B12.27.1870; BR/TR/5´11.5˝/187; d5.1

YEAR	TM LG	G	AB	R	H	2B	3B	HR	RBI	BB-IB	HP	SO	AVG	OBP	SLG	AOPS	ABR	SB-CS	FA	FR	RNG	THR	GAMES AT POSITION	DL	BFW
1888	Pit N	2	4	0	0	0	0	0	0	0	0	1	.000	.000	.000	-99	-1	0	.667	-0	—	—	/Crf	—	-0.1
	Phi AA	3	12	0	2	0	0	0	1	0	0	—	.167	.167	.167	7	-1	0	.960	0	—	—	C3	—	-0.1
Total	1	5	16	0	2	0	0	0	1	0	0	1	.125	.125	.125	-20	-2	0	.903	0	—	—	C4/rf	—	-0.2

FARRAR, SID Sidney Douglas; B8.10.1859 Paris Hill ME; D5.7.1935 New York NY; TR/5´10˝/185; d5.1

YEAR	TM LG	G	AB	R	H	2B	3B	HR	RBI	BB-IB	HP	SO	AVG	OBP	SLG	AOPS	ABR	SB-CS	FA	FR	RNG	THR	GAMES AT POSITION	DL	BFW
1883	Phi N	**99**	377	41	88	19	8	0	29	4	—	37	.233	.241	.326	77	-9	—	.965	-0	96	69	1b99	—	-1.6
1884	Phi N	111	428	62	105	16	6	1	45	9	—	25	.245	.261	.318	85	-7	—	.966	5	**131**	74	1b111	—	-1.1
1885	Phi N	**111**	420	49	103	20	3	3	36	28	—	34	.245	.292	.329	103	2	—	.975	2	108	94	1b111	—	-0.5
1886	Phi N	118	439	55	109	19	7	5	50	16	—	47	.248	.275	.358	90	-6	10	**.980**	3	99	75	1b118	—	-1.3
1887	Phi N	116	443	83	125	20	9	4	72	42	10	29	.282	.358	.395	103	2	24	.977	3	108	90	1b116	—	-0.5
1888	Phi N	**131**	508	53	124	24	7	1	53	31	**13**	38	.244	.304	.325	95	-2	21	.979	3	110	94	1b131	—	-1.1
1889	Phi N	**130**	477	70	128	22	2	3	58	52	6	36	.268	.348	.342	85	-10	28	.978	-5	72	87	1b130	—	-2.3
1890	Phi P	127	481	84	123	17	11	1	69	51	5	23	.256	.333	.343	79	-15	9	.973	-2	93	106	1b127	—	-2.3
Total	8	943	3573	497	905	157	53	18	412	233	34	269	.253	.305	.342	90	-45	92	.974	8	102	87	1b943	—	-10.7

YEAR	TM LG	G	AB	R	H	2B	3B	HR	RBI	BB-IB	HP	SO	AVG	OBP	SLG	AOPS	ABR	SB-CS	FA	FR	RNG	THR	GAMES AT POSITION	DL	BFW
FARRELL, DUKE	Charles Andrew; B8.31.1866 Oakdale MA; D2.15.1925 Boston MA; BB/TR/6´1˝/208; d4.21; C6; OF(48/22/39)																								
1888	Chi N	64	241	34	56	6	3	3	19	4	0	41	.232	.245	.320	73	-8	8	.874	-8	—	—	C33,O31(10/2/19)/1	—	-1.4
1889	Chi N	101	407	66	107	19	7	11	75	41	1	21	.263	.332	.425	105	0	13	.910	-2	—	—	C76,O25(7/15/3)	—	0.4
1890	Chi P	117	451	79	131	21	12	2	84	42	1	28	.290	.352	.404	98	-3	8	.929	**30**	***115***	***127***	C90,1b22,O10(0/2/8)	—	2.6
1891	Bos AA	122	473	108	143	19	13	**12**	**110**	59	4	48	.302	.384	.474	148	28	21	.918	21	115	85	3b66,C37,O23(20/0/3),1b4	—	**4.4**
1892	Pit N	**152**	605	96	130	10	13	8	77	46	5	53	.215	.276	.314	78	-19	20	.879	-9	96	97	3b133,O20(11/3/6)	—	-2.6
1893	Was N	124	511	84	144	13	13	4	75	47	5	12	.282	.348	.382	96	-4	11	.923	2	*77*	***161***	C81,3b41,1b3	—	0.5
1894	†NY N	116	404	50	116	20	12	5	70	38	3	15	.287	.353	.433	89	-9	9	.925	26	*107*	***130***	C105,3b5,1b4	—	2.0
1895	NY N	90	312	38	90	16	9	1	58	38	3	18	.288	.371	.407	103	2	11	.941	2	*96*	*112*	C62,3b24,1b2	—	0.8
1896	NY N	58	191	23	54	7	3	1	37	19	1	7	.283	.351	.366	92	-2	2	.954	-5	*94*	*107*	C34,S13,3b7	—	-0.3
	Was N	37	130	18	39	7	3	1	30	7	2	3	.300	.345	.423	102	0	2	1.000	-0	*88*	*130*	C18,3b14	—	0.1
	Year	95	321	41	93	14	6	2	67	26	3	10	.290	.349	.389	96	-2	4	.970	-5	*92*	*115*	C52,3b21,S13	—	-0.2
1897	Was N	78	261	41	84	9	6	0	53	17	1	—	.322	.366	.402	103	1	8	.945	3	*80*	*149*	C63/1	—	0.8
1898	Was N	99	338	47	106	12	6	1	53	34	4	—	.314	.383	.393	123	11	12	.929	-13	*65*	*145*	C61,1b28	—	0.3
1899	Was N	5	12	2	4	1	0	0	1	2	0	—	.333	.429	.417	134	1	1	1.000	-0	*74*	*142*	C4	—	0.1
	Bro N	80	254	40	76	10	7	2	55	35	7	—	.299	.399	.417	121	9	6	.948	6	*91*	*115*	C78	—	1.9
	Year	85	266	42	80	11	7	2	56	37	7	—	.301	.400	.417	122	10	7	.949	5	*90*	*116*	C82	—	2.0
1900	†Bro N	76	273	33	75	11	5	0	39	11	3	—	.275	.310	.352	78	-9	3	.944	-4	*94*	*97*	C74	—	-0.6
1901	Bro N	80	284	38	84	10	6	1	31	7	3	—	.296	.320	.384	101	-1	7	.979	-1	*80*	*129*	C59,1b17	—	0.4
1902	Bro N	74	264	14	64	5	2	0	24	12	2	—	.242	.281	.277	71	-9	6	.976	-1	*84*	*124*	C49,1b24	—	-0.6
1903	†Bos A	17	52	5	21	5	1	0	8	5	1	—	.404	.466	.538	190	6	1	.960	1	*118*	*114*	C17	—	0.9
1904	Bos A	68	198	11	42	9	2	0	15	15	4	—	.212	.281	.278	73	-5	1	.958	-1	*128*	*91*	C56	—	-0.1
1905	Bos A	7	21	2	6	1	0	0	2	1	0	—	.286	.318	.333	105	0	0	1.000	1	*146*	*119*	C7	—	0.2
Total	18	1565	5682	829	1572	211	123	52	916	480	50	246	.277	.338	.385	100	-11	150	.938	49	*96*	*127*	C1004,3b290,O109L,1b106,S13	—	9.8
FARRELL, DOC	Edward Stephen; B12.26.1901 Johnson City NY; D12.20.1966 Livingston NJ; BR/TR/5´8˝/160; d6.15; Col Penn																								
1925	NY N	27	56	6	12	1	0	0	4	4	0	6	.214	.267	.232	30	-6	0-1	.900	1	130	50	S13,3b7/2	—	-0.4
1926	NY N	67	171	19	49	10	1	2	23	12	2	17	.287	.341	.392	98	0	4	.950	-8	86	86	S53,2b3	—	-0.4
1927	NY N	42	142	13	55	10	1	3	34	12	2	11	.387	.442	.535	161	13	0	.919	-0	105	93	S36,3b2	—	1.6
	Bos N	110	424	44	124	13	2	1	58	14	0	21	.292	.315	.340	82	-12	4	.931	-8	103	70	S57,2b40,3b18	—	-1.2
	Year	152	566	57	179	23	3	4	92	26	2	32	.316	.348	.389	103	1	4	.926	-8	104	79	S93,2b40,3b20	—	0.4
1928	Bos N	134	483	36	104	14	2	3	43	26	5	26	.215	.263	.271	42	-43	3	.933	-17	96	79	S132/2	—	-4.5
1929	Bos N	5	8	0	1	0	0	0	2	0	0	1	.125	.125	.125	-39	-2	0	ø	-0	0	0	/2S	—	-0.2
	NY N	63	178	18	38	6	0	0	16	9	0	17	.213	.251	.247	24	-22	2	.925	2	109	193	3b28,2b25,S4	—	-1.5
	Year	68	186	18	39	6	0	0	18	9	0	18	.210	.246	.242	22	-23	2	.925	2	109	193	3b28,2b26,S5	—	-1.7
1930	StL N	23	61	3	13	1	1	0	6	4	0	2	.213	.262	.262	26	-8	1	.944	1	88	118	S15,2b6/1	—	-0.5
	Chi N	46	113	21	33	6	0	1	16	9	0	5	.292	.344	.372	73	-5	0	.937	-1	101	87	S38/2	—	-0.2
	Year	69	174	24	46	7	1	1	22	13	0	7	.264	.316	.333	56	-12	1	.938	-1	97	95	S53,2b7/1	—	-0.7
1932	NY A	26	63	4	11	1	1	0	4	2	1	8	.175	.212	.222	13	-9	0-0	.963	-1	90	120	2b16,S5,1b2/3	—	-0.8
1933	NY A	44	93	16	25	0	0	0	6	16	0	6	.269	.376	.269	78	-2	0-0	.947	-4	77	94	S22,2b20	—	-0.4
1935	Bos A	4	7	1	2	1	0	0	1	1	0	0	.286	.375	.429	101	0	0-0	.917	-1	81	78	2b4	—	0.0
Total	9	591	1799	181	467	63	8	10	213	109	10	120	.260	.306	.320	66	-96	14-1	.934	-36	97	82	S376,2b118,3b56,1b3	—	-8.5
FARRELL, JACK	John "Hartford Jack"; B1.2.1856 Hartford CT; D11.15.1916 Hartford CT; d10.27																								
1874	Har NA	3	13	3	5	0	0	0	0	1	—	0	.385	.429	.385	155	1	0-0	1.000	-0	0	0	O3C	—	0.1
FARRELL, JACK	John A. "Moose"; B7.5.1857 Newark NJ; D2.10.1914 Cedar Grove NJ; BR/TR/5´9˝/165; d5.1; M1																								
1879	Syr N	54	241	40	73	6	2	1	21	3	—	13	.303	.311	.357	135	9	—	.870	-19	93	65	2b54	—	-0.7
	Pro N	12	51	5	13	2	0	0	5	0	—	0	.255	.255	.294	82	-1	—	.915	5	117	169	2b12	—	0.4
	Year	66	292	45	86	8	2	1	26	3	—	13	.295	.302	.346	125	8	—	.879	-14	98	85	2b66	—	-0.3
1880	Pro N	80	339	46	92	12	5	3	36	10	—	6	.271	.292	.363	125	9	—	.887	-13	101	91	2b80	—	0.0
1881	Pro N	84	345	69	82	16	5	5	36	29	—	23	.238	.297	.357	106	4	—	.881	-5	**103**	98	2b82,O3C,M	—	0.2
1882	Pro N	**84**	366	67	93	21	6	2	31	16	—	23	.254	.285	.361	106	3	—	.875	-6	105	118	2b84	—	0.0
1883	Pro N	95	420	92	128	24	11	3	61	15	—	21	.305	.329	.436	126	12	—	**.924**	**25**	**117**	136	2b95	—	**3.5**
1884	†Pro N	111	469	70	102	13	6	1	37	35	—	44	.217	.272	.277	74	-13	—	.922	-8	98	104	2b109,3b3	—	-1.5
1885	Pro N	68	257	27	53	7	1	1	19	10	—	25	.206	.236	.253	60	-11	—	.900	-13	92	57	2b68	—	-2.1
1886	Phi N	17	60	7	11	0	1	0	3	3	—	11	.183	.222	.217	34	-5	1	.825	-5	112	32	2b17	—	-0.8
	Was N	47	171	24	41	11	4	2	18	15	—	12	.240	.301	.386	116	4	12	.913	-2	100	59	2b47	—	0.3
	Year	64	231	31	52	11	5	2	21	18	—	23	.225	.281	.342	94	-1	13	.888	-7	103	51	2b64	—	-0.5
1887	Was N	87	339	40	75	14	9	0	41	20	1	12	.221	.267	.316	65	-16	31	.876	-4	97	91	S48,2b40	—	-1.4
1888	Bal AA	103	398	72	81	19	5	4	36	26	2	—	.204	.256	.307	82	-8	29	.902	9	101	80	S54,2b52	—	0.4
1889	Bal AA	42	157	25	33	3	0	1	26	15	2	15	.210	.287	.248	52	-10	14	.891	-6	88	85	S42	—	-1.2
Total	11	884	3613	584	877	148	55	23	370	197	5	205	.243	.283	.333	94	-23	87	.899	-42	104	95	2b740,S144,3b3,O3C	—	-2.9
FARRELL, JACK	John Joseph; B6.16.1892 Chicago IL; D3.24.1918 Chicago IL; BB/TR/5´8˝/145; d4.16																								
1914	Chi F	156	524	58	123	23	4	0	35	52	3	65	.235	.307	.294	68	-32	12	.954	-4	102	107	2b155,S3	—	-3.5
1915	Chi F	70	222	27	48	10	1	0	14	25	1	18	.216	.298	.270	64	-14	8	.941	-3	98	112	2b70/S	—	-1.7
Total	2	226	746	85	171	33	5	0	49	77	4	83	.229	.305	.287	67	-46	20	.950	-7	101	108	2b225,S4	—	-5.2
FARRELL, JOHN	John Sebastian; B12.4.1876 Covington KY; D5.13.1921 Kansas City MO; BR/TR/5´10˝/160; d4.26																								
1901	Was A	135	555	100	151	32	11	3	63	52	1	—	.272	.336	.386	101	1	25	.915	9	106	134	2b72,O62C/3	—	0.7
1902	StL N	138	565	68	141	13	5	0	25	43	5	—	.250	.308	.290	88	-7	9	.947	**32**	**119**	**146**	2b118,S21	—	2.7
1903	StL N	130	519	83	141	25	8	1	32	48	2	—	.272	.336	.356	100	1	17	.927	24	**115**	**124**	2b118,O12(2/10/0)	—	2.4
1904	StL N	131	509	72	130	23	3	0	20	46	2	—	.255	.320	.312	100	1	16	.934	15	**109**	**143**	2b130	—	1.8
1905	StL N	7	24	6	4	0	1	0	1	4	0	—	.167	.286	.250	62	-1	1	.892	-3	66	0	2b7	—	-0.5
Total	5	541	2172	329	567	93	28	4	141	193	10	—	.261	.324	.335	97	-5	68	.932	77	112	135	2b445,O74(2/72/0),S21/3	—	7.1
FARRELL, JOE	Joseph F.; B1857 Brooklyn NY; D4.17.1893 Brooklyn NY; BR/5´6˝/160; d5.1																								
1882	Det N	69	283	34	70	12	2	1	24	4	—	20	.247	.258	.314	83	-6	—	.816	-15	75	153	3b42,2b18,S9	—	-1.7
1883	Det N	**101**	444	58	108	13	5	0	36	5	—	29	.243	.252	.295	69	-17	—	.845	13	123	92	3b101	—	-0.2
1884	Det N	110	461	59	104	10	5	3	41	14	—	66	.226	.248	.289	73	-14	—	.842	-4	97	83	3b110/lf	—	-1.5
1886	Bal AA	73	301	36	63	8	3	1	31	12	0	—	.209	.240	.266	60	-15	5	.870	-8	94	36	2b45,3b27/cf	—	-1.8
Total	4	353	1489	187	345	43	15	5	132	35	0	115	.232	.249	.291	71	-52	5	.840	-14	104	94	3b280,2b63,S9,O2(1/1/0)	—	-5.2
FARRELL, KERBY	Major Kerby; B9.3.1913 Leapwood TN; D12.17.1975 Nashville TN; BL/TL/5´11˝/172; d4.24; M1/C6; Col Freed–Hardeman; ▲																								
1943	Bos N	85	280	11	75	14	1	0	21	16	0	15	.268	.307	.325	84	-6	1	.996	1	104	107	1b69,P5	0	-1.0
1945	Chi A	103	396	44	102	11	3	0	34	24	0	18	.258	.300	.301	76	-13	4-9	.989	2	106	90	1b97	0	-2.0
Total	2	188	676	55	177	25	4	0	55	40	0	33	.262	.303	.311	80	-19	5-9	.992	2	105	97	1b166,P5	0	-3.0
FARRELL, BILL	William; d5.3																								
1882	Phi AA	2	7	2	2	1	0	0	1	1	—	—	.286	.375	.429	160	1	—	ø	-0	0	0	O2(0/1/1)/C	—	0.0
1883	Bal AA	2	7	0	0	0	0	0	—	1	—	—	.000	.125	.000	-55	-1	—	.750	-1	88	203	S2	—	-0.1
Total	2	4	14	2	2	1	0	0	1	2	—	—	.143	.250	.214	52	0	—	.750	-1	88	203	S2,O2(0/1/1)/C	—	-0.1
FARROW, JOHN	John Jacob; B11.8.1853 Verplanck NY; D12.31.1914 Perth Amboy NJ; BL/TR; d4.28																								
1873	Res NA	12	48	2	8	1	0	0	3	0	—	3	.167	.167	.188	5	-5	0-0	.686	-3	—	—	C9,O4R/1S	—	-0.6
1874	Atl NA	27	122	16	26	3	0	0	10	1	—	1	.213	.220	.238	53	-5	0-0	.694	-1	—	—	C16,2b12,O3(0/2/1)	—	-0.6
1884	Bro AA	16	58	7	11	2	0	0	—	3	0	—	.190	.230	.224	48	-3	—	.915	-0	—	—	C16	—	-0.2
Total	2NA	39	170	18	34	4	0	0	13	1	—	4	.200	.205	.224	38	-10	0-0	.691	-4	—	—	C25,2b12,O7(0/2/5)/S1	—	-1.2
FASANO, SAL	Salvatore Frank; B8.10.1971 Chicago IL; BR/TR/6´2˝/(220–245); [KCA93 37/1029]; d4.3; Col Evansville																								
1996	KC A	51	143	20	29	2	0	6	19	14-0	2	25	.203	.283	.343	57	-10	1-1	.984	7	138	87	C51	0	0.0
1997	KC A	13	38	4	8	2	0	1	1	1-0	0	12	.211	.231	.342	45	-3	0-0	.982	-1	675	93	C12/D	0	-0.4
1998	KC A	74	216	21	49	10	0	8	31	10-1	16	56	.227	.307	.384	76	-8	1-0	.996	1	203	83	C70,1b5/3	48	-0.2
1999	KC A	23	60	11	14	2	0	5	16	7-0	7	17	.233	.373	.517	121	2	0-1	1.000	7	181	47	C23	0	0.9

YEAR	TM LG	G	AB	R	H	2B	3B	HR	RBI	BB-IB	HP	SO	AVG	OBP	SLG	AOPS	ABR	SB-CS	FA	FR	RNG	THR	GAMES AT POSITION	DL	BFW
2000	†Oak A	52	126	21	27	6	0	7	19	14-0	3	47	.214	.306	.429	85	-3	0-0	.981	-1	106	103	C52	0	-0.1
2001	Oak A	11	21	2	1	0	0	0	0	1-0	1	12	.048	.130	.048	-50	-5	0-0	.952	-1	158	102	C9/D	0	-0.5
	KC A	3	1	0	0	0	0	0	0	0-0	0	0	.000	.000	.000	-91	0	0-0	1.000	-0	0	0	C3	0	-0.1
	Year	14	22	2	1	0	0	0	0	1-0	1	12	.045	.125	.045	-51	-5	0-0	.955	-1	179	110	C12/D	0	-0.6
	Col N	25	63	10	16	5	0	3	9	4-0	3	19	.254	.329	.476	87	-1	0-0	.982	7	179	110	C25	0	0.7
2002	Ana A	2	1	0	0	0	0	0	0	0-0	0	1	.000	.000	.000	-99	0	0-0	1.000	2	42	1009	C2	0	0.1
2005	Bal A	64	160	25	40	3	0	11	20	9-0	5	41	.250	.310	.475	105	0	0-0	.987	-8	68	66	C60/1D	0	-0.5
2006	Phi N	50	140	9	34	8	0	4	10	5-0	3	47	.243	.284	.386	66	-7	0-1	.990	-5	84	84	C50	19	-1.0
	NY A	28	49	3	7	4	0	1	5	2-0	3	14	.143	.222	.286	30	-5	0-0	.991	-1	149	75	C27/D	0	-0.4
Total	9	396	1018	126	225	42	0	46	130	67-1	43	291	.221	.296	.398	75	-40	2-3	.988	7	153	86	C384,1b6,D6/3	67	-1.5
Fausett, Buck	Robert Shaw "Leaky"; B4.8.1908 Sheridan AR; D5.2.1994 College Station TX; BL/TR/5´10˝/170; d4.18; Col Texas A&M–Commerce; ▲																								
1944	Cin N	13	31	2	3	0	1	0	1	1	0	2	.097	.125	.161	-21	-5	0	1.000	2	136	96	3b6,P2	0	-0.3
Fautsch, Joe	Joseph Roamon; B2.28.1887 Minneapolis MN; D3.16.1971 New Hope MN; BR/TR/5´10˝/162; d4.24																								
1916	Chi A	1	1	0	0	0	0	0	0	0	0	0	.000	.000	.000	-99	0	0	ø	0	—	—	/H	—	0.0
Fazio, Ernie	Ernest Joseph; B1.25.1942 Oakland CA; BR/TR/5´7˝/165; d7.3; Col Santa Clara																								
1962	Hou N	12	12	3	1	0	0	0	1	2-0	0	5	.083	.214	.083	-18	-2	0-0	.783	-1	101	38	S10	0	-0.3
1963	Hou N	102	228	31	42	10	3	2	5	27-1	1	70	.184	.273	.281	64	-10	4-4	.972	-19	81	51	2b84/S3	0	-2.7
1966	KC A	27	34	3	7	0	1	0	2	4-2	0	10	.206	.289	.265	62	-2	1-0	1.000	-1	103	84	2b10,S4	0	-0.2
Total	3	141	274	37	50	10	4	2	8	33-3	1	85	.182	.273	.270	60	-14	5-4	.974	-21	83	54	2b94,S15/3	0	-3.2
Febles, Carlos	Carlos Manuel; B5.24.1976 Santa Cruz de El Seibo, D.R.; BR/TR/5´11˝/(170–185); d9.14																								
1998	KC A	11	25	5	10	1	2	0	2	4-0	0	7	.400	.483	.600	172	3	2-1	1.000	-1	89	42	2b11	0	0.2
1999	KC A	123	453	71	116	22	9	10	53	47-0	9	91	.256	.336	.411	86	-10	20-4	.979	3	103	112	2b122	27	0.2
2000	KC A	100	339	59	87	12	1	2	29	36-1	10	48	.257	.345	.316	65	-17	17-6	.978	-7	98	111	2b99	60	-1.6
2001	KC A	79	292	45	69	9	2	8	25	22-0	1	58	.236	.291	.363	65	-16	5-2	.981	-2	101	127	2b78	50	-1.3
2002	KC A	119	351	44	86	16	4	4	26	41-0	7	63	.245	.336	.348	73	-13	16-5	.971	-2	103	105	2b116/S	0	-0.8
2003	KC A	74	196	31	46	5	0	0	11	13-0	5	30	.235	.299	.260	46	-15	8-2	.989	-10	97	82	2b67/SD	18	-2.1
Total	6	506	1656	255	414	65	18	24	146	163-1	32	297	.250	.328	.354	72	-68	68-20	.979	-19	101	108	2b493,D4,S2	155	-5.4
Federoff, Al	Alfred "Whitey"; B7.11.1924 Bairdford PA; BR/TR/5´10.5˝/(165–168); d9.27																								
1951	Det A	2	4	0	0	0	0	0	0	0	0	0	.000	.000	.000	-99	-1	0-0	.889	0	148	0	/2	0	-0.1
1952	Det A	74	231	14	56	4	2	0	14	16	1	13	.242	.294	.277	59	-13	1-0	.976	3	108	90	2b70,S7	0	-0.6
Total	2	76	235	14	56	4	2	0	14	16	1	13	.238	.290	.272	56	-14	1-0	.973	4	109	88	2b71,S7	0	-0.7
Fehring, Dutch	William Paul "Bill"; B5.31.1912 Columbus IN; D4.13.2006 Palo Alto CA; BB/TR/6´0˝/195; d6.25; Col Purdue																								
1934	Chi A	1	1	0	0	0	0	0	0	0	0	1	.000	.000	.000	-97	0	0-0	1.000	0	*0*	*0*	/C	—	0.0
Feinberg, Eddie	Edward Isadore "Itzzy"; B9.29.1917 Philadelphia PA; D4.20.1986 Hollywood FL; BB/TR/5´9˝/165; d9.11																								
1938	Phi N	10	20	0	3	0	0	0	0	0	0	1	.150	.150	.150	-18	-3	0	.957	2	124	128	S4,O2(1/0/2)	—	-0.1
1939	Phi N	6	18	2	4	1	0	0	0	2	0	0	.222	.300	.278	58	-1	0	.909	-3	64	92	2b4/S	—	-0.3
Total	2	16	38	2	7	1	0	0	0	2	0	1	.184	.225	.211	20	-4	0	.957	-1	116	120	S5,2b4,O2(1/0/2)	—	-0.4
Felder, Mike	Michael Otis; B11.18.1961 Vallejo CA; BB/TR/5´8˝/(160–175); [MilA81*3/74]; d9.11; Col Contra Costa (CA) JC																								
1985	Mil A	15	56	8	11	1	0	0	0	5-0	0	6	.196	.262	.214	32	-5	4-1	1.000	-1	84	111	O14C	0	-0.6
1986	Mil A	44	155	24	37	2	4	1	13	13-1	0	16	.239	.289	.323	67	-8	16-2	1.000	1	115	0	O42(30/7/6)/D	33	-0.6
1987	Mil A	108	289	48	77	5	7	2	31	28-0	0	23	.266	.329	.353	79	-9	34-8	.975	9	120	149	O99(80/22/0)/2D	0	0.1
1988	Mil A	50	81	14	14	1	0	0	5	0-0	1	11	.173	.183	.185	3	-11	8-2	.976	-1	104	0	O28(12/11/5),D16/2	63	-1.2
1989	Mil A	117	315	50	76	11	3	3	23	23-2	0	38	.241	.293	.324	74	-11	26-5	.985	6	108	158	O93(30/34/38),D11,2b10	0	-0.4
1990	Mil A	121	237	38	65	7	2	3	27	22-0	0	17	.274	.330	.359	95	-2	20-9	.972	7	111	173	O109(61/15/44)/23D	0	0.4
1991	SF N	132	348	51	92	10	6	0	18	30-2	1	31	.264	.325	.328	86	-7	21-6	.985	5	112	60	O107(45/38/44),3b3/2	15	-0.1
1992	SF N	145	322	44	92	13	3	4	23	21-1	2	29	.286	.330	.382	107	2	14-4	.994	-4	94	52	O105(53/58/11),2b3	0	-0.1
1993	Sea A	109	342	31	72	7	5	1	20	22-2	2	34	.211	.262	.269	42	-29	15-9	.987	0	89	190	O95(89/7/0),3b2,D6	20	-3.1
1994	Hou N	58	117	10	28	2	2	0	13	4-0	0	12	.239	.264	.291	47	-10	3-0	.974	-1	83	136	O32(8/6/21)	0	-1.1
Total	10	899	2262	318	564	59	32	14	173	168-8	6	217	.249	.301	.322	73	-90	161-46	.984	20	105	117	O724(408/212/169),D38,2b17,3b6	131	-6.7
Felderman, Marv	Marvin Wilfred "Coonie"; B12.20.1915 Bellevue IA; D8.6.2000 Riverside CA; BR/TR/6´1˝/187; d4.19; Mil 1943–45																								
1942	Chi N	3	6	0	1	0	0	0	0	1	0	4	.167	.286	.167	35	0	0	1.000	0	*60*	*198*	C2	0	0.0
Felix, Gus	August Guenther; B5.24.1895 Cincinnati OH; D5.12.1960 Montgomery AL; BR/TR/6´0˝/180; d4.19																								
1923	Bos N	139	506	64	138	17	2	6	44	51	7	65	.273	.348	.350	88	-7	8-13	.950	-1	104	92	O123(121/6/0),2b5,3b4	—	-2.0
1924	Bos N	59	204	25	43	7	1	1	10	18	0	16	.211	.275	.270	48	-15	0-3	.950	2	110	106	O51(11/38/2)	—	-1.7
1925	Bos N	121	459	60	141	25	7	2	66	30	5	34	.307	.356	.405	103	2	5-5	.972	10	111	134	O114(42/74/3)	—	0.4
1926	Bro N	134	432	64	121	21	7	3	53	51	3	32	.280	.360	.382	101	2	9	.956	-0	100	104	O125(53/74/0)	—	-0.5
1927	Bro N	130	445	43	118	21	8	0	57	39	2	47	.265	.327	.348	81	-12	6	.947	-5	90	117	O119(117/4/0)	—	-2.6
Total	5	583	2046	256	561	91	25	12	230	189	17	194	.274	.341	.361	89	-30	28-21	.957	5	102	111	O532(344/196/5),2b5,3b4	—	-6.4
Felix, Junior	Junior Francisco (Sanchez); B10.3.1967 Laguna Salada, D.R.; BB/TR/5´11˝/(165–170); d5.3																								
1989	†Tor A	110	415	62	107	14	8	9	46	33-2	3	101	.258	.315	.395	101	-1	18-12	.966	0	100	116	O107(0/24/86),D2	0	-0.4
1990	Tor A	127	463	73	122	28	7	15	65	45-0	2	99	.263	.328	.441	112	6	13-8	.966	-6	87	126	O125(0/28/99)/D	27	-0.3
1991	Cal A	66	230	32	65	10	2	2	26	11-0	3	55	.283	.321	.370	91	-3	7-5	.977	-9	81	32	O65(0/63/2)	81	-1.3
1992	Cal A	139	509	63	125	22	5	9	72	33-5	2	128	.246	.289	.361	82	-14	8-8	.983	1	99	128	O128(0/125/4),D8	15	-1.6
1993	Fla N	57	214	25	51	11	1	7	22	10-1	1	50	.238	.276	.397	73	-9	2-1	.940	-4	90	79	O52(0/3/50)	0	-1.5
1994	Det A	86	301	54	92	25	1	13	49	26-2	8	76	.306	.372	.525	127	13	1-6	.980	2	112	65	O81(5/2/75),D2	18	0.8
Total	6	585	2132	309	562	105	24	55	280	158-10	19	509	.264	.317	.413	99	-8	49-40	.972	-15	95	101	O558(5/245/316),D13	141	-4.3
Feliz, Pedro	Pedro Julio; B4.27.1975 Azua, D.R.; BR/TR/6´1˝/(195–210); d9.5																								
2000	SF N	8	7	1	2	0	0	0	0	0-0	0	1	.286	.286	.286	48	-1	0-0	ø	-1	0	0	3b4	0	-0.1
2001	SF N	94	220	23	50	9	1	7	22	10-2	2	50	.227	.264	.373	67	-12	2-1	.908	-17	70	59	3b86/D	0	-2.8
2002	†SF N	67	146	14	37	4	1	2	13	6-1	0	27	.253	.281	.336	64	-8	0-0	.966	-1	93	150	3b44/Slf	0	-0.9
2003	†SF N	95	235	31	58	9	3	16	48	10-0	1	53	.247	.278	.515	100	-2	2-2	.972	5	123	136	3b49,O15(14/0/1),1b12	0	0.2
2004	SF N	144	503	72	139	33	3	22	84	23-1	0	85	.276	.305	.485	97	-4	5-2	.991	5	105	117	1b70,3b51,S20,O4(2/0/2)	0	-0.3
2005	SF N	156	569	69	142	30	4	20	81	38-1	1	102	.250	.295	.422	84	-15	0-2	.969	-1	104	131	3b79,O75L,1b15	0	-2.1
2006	SF N	160	603	75	147	35	5	22	98	33-4	1	112	.244	.281	.428	79	-22	1-1	.955	11	111	103	3b159,O3L,S2	0	-0.9
Total	7	724	2283	285	575	120	17	89	346	120-9	5	430	.252	.288	.436	84	-64	10-8	.957	2	103	107	3b472,O98(95/0/3),1b97,S23/D	0	-6.9
Feller, Jack	Jack Leland; B12.10.1936 Adrian MI; BR/TR/5´10.5˝/185; d9.13																								
1958	Det A	1	0	0	0	0	0	0	0	0-0	0	0	ø	ø	ø	ø	0	0-0	1.000	0	0	0	/C	0	0.0
Felsch, Happy	Oscar Emil; B8.22.1891 Milwaukee WI; D8.17.1964 Milwaukee WI; BR/TR/5´11˝/175; d4.14; Def 1918																								
1915	Chi A	121	427	65	106	18	11	3	53	51	4	59	.248	.334	.363	105	2	16-18	.959	-6	99	56	O118(34/73/10)	—	-1.4
1916	Chi A	146	546	73	164	24	12	7	70	31	3	67	.300	.341	.427	129	16	13	**.981**	1	102	94	O141C	—	0.7
1917	†Chi A	152	575	75	177	17	10	6	102	33	6	52	.308	.352	.403	128	16	26	.985	15	**117**	107	O152C	—	2.2
1918	Chi A	53	206	16	52	2	5	1	20	15	1	13	.252	.306	.325	90	-4	6	.957	5	120	94	O53C	—	-0.3
1919	†Chi A	135	502	68	138	34	11	7	86	40	6	35	.275	.336	.428	113	8	19	.968	17	107	**166**	O135C	—	1.6
1920	Chi A	142	556	88	188	40	15	14	115	37	4	25	.338	.384	.540	143	31	8-13	.981	12	109	**136**	O142C	—	3.0
Total	6	749	2812	385	825	135	64	38	446	207	24	251	.293	.347	.427	123	69	88-31	.975	44	108	112	O741(34/696/10)	—	5.8
Felske, John	John Frederick; B5.30.1942 Chicago IL; BR/TR/6´3˝/(190–195); d7.26; M3/C3; Col Illinois																								
1968	Chi N	4	2	0	0	0	0	0	0	0-0	0	1	.000	.000	.000	-94	0	0-0	.833	0	0	0	C3	0	0.0
1972	Mil A	37	80	6	11	3	0	1	5	8-0	0	23	.138	.216	.213	28	-7	0-0	.972	-2	143	38	C23,1b8	0	-1.0
1973	Mil A	13	22	1	3	0	1	0	4	1-0	0	11	.136	.167	.227	12	-3	0-0	1.000	-1	107	75	C7,1b6	0	-0.4
Total	3	54	104	7	14	3	1	1	9	9-0	0	35	.135	.202	.212	23	-10	0-0	.969	-3	133	44	C33,1b14	0	-1.4

YEAR	TM LG	G	AB	R	H	2B	3B	HR	RBI	BB-IB	HP	SO	AVG	OBP	SLG	AOPS	ABR	SB-CS	FA	FR	RNG	THR	GAMES AT POSITION	DL	BFW
FENNELLY, FRANK	Francis John; B2.18.1860 Fall River MA; D8.4.1920 Fall River MA; BR/TR/5´8˝/168; d5.1																								
1884	Was AA	62	257	52	75	17	7	2	—	20	0	—	.292	.343	.436	172	22	—	.863	13	117	78	S60,2b4	—	3.3
	Cin AA	28	122	42	43	5	8	2	—	11	2	—	.352	.415	.574	209	14	—	.813	-6	95	172	S28	—	0.8
	Year	90	379	94	118	22	15	4	—	31	2	—	.311	.367	.480	186	37	—	.849	7	110	109	S88,2b4	—	4.1
1885	Cin AA	**112**	454	82	124	14	17	10	**89**	38	3	—	.273	.333	.445	142	20	—	.873	-12	95	**135**	S112	—	1.0
1886	Cin AA	132	497	113	124	13	17	6	72	60	**18**	—	.249	.351	.380	125	15	32	.848	11	**113**	**130**	S132	—	2.6
1887	Cin AA	134	526	133	140	15	16	8	97	82	4	—	.266	.369	.401	112	9	74	.855	-11	101	96	S134	—	0.2
1888	Cin AA	120	448	64	88	8	7	2	56	63	1	—	.196	.297	.259	75	-12	43	.858	11	112	140	S112,2b4,O4(2/2/0)	—	0.3
	Phi AA	15	47	13	11	2	2	1	12	9	0	—	.234	.357	.426	151	3	5	.912	-1	91	121	S15	—	0.3
	Year	135	495	77	99	10	9	3	68	72	1	—	.200	.303	.275	82	-9	48	.863	10	110	**138**	S127,2b4,O4(2/2/0)	—	0.6
1889	Phi AA	**138**	513	70	132	20	5	1	64	65	3	78	.257	.344	.322	91	-3	15	.872	-20	95	106	S138	—	-1.6
1890	Bro AA	45	178	40	44	8	3	2	18	30	0	—	.247	.356	.360	115	4	6	.858	-5	103	56	S38,3b7	—	0.1
Total	7	786	3042	609	781	102	82	34	408	378	31	78	.257	.345	.378	118	72	175	.860	-19	104	116	S769,2b8,3b7,O4(2/2/0)	—	7.0
FENWICK, BOBBY	Robert Richard; B12.10.1946 Naha, Okinawa; BR/TR/5´9˝/165; [SFN67 S1/16]; d4.26; Col Minnesota																								
1972	Hou N	36	50	7	9	3	0	0	4	3-1	0	13	.180	.226	.240	34	-4	0-1	.945	-1	100	174	2b17,S4,3b2	0	-0.5
1973	StL N	5	6	0	1	0	0	0	1	0-0	0	2	.167	.167	.167	-7	-1	0-0	.750	-2	23	227	2b3	0	-0.2
Total	2	41	56	7	10	3	0	0	5	3-1	0	15	.179	.220	.232	29	-5	0-1	.932	-2	91	180	2b20,S4,3b2	0	-0.7
FERGUSON, JOE	Joseph Vance; B9.19.1946 San Francisco CA; BR/TR/6´2˝/(195–215); [LAN68 8/161]; d9.12; C6; Col Pacific (CA)																								
1970	LA N	5	4	0	1	0	0	0	1	2-0	0	2	.250	.429	.250	112	0	0-0	1.000	0	63	0	C3	0	0.0
1971	LA N	36	102	13	22	3	0	2	7	12-1	1	15	.216	.304	.304	77	-3	1-0	.983	-2	110	84	C35	0	-0.4
1972	LA N	8	24	2	7	3	0	1	5	2-0	0	4	.292	.346	.542	151	2	0-0	1.000	1	141	176	C7,O2R	0	0.3
1973	LA N	136	487	84	128	26	0	25	88	87-9	1	81	.263	.369	.470	137	28	1-1	**.996**	6	113	84	C122,O20(5/1/14)	19	4.0
1974	†LA N	111	349	54	88	14	1	16	57	75-10	0	73	.252	.380	.436	134	19	2-2	.988	-1	125	103	C82,O32R	0	2.1
1975	LA N	66	202	15	42	2	1	5	23	35-5	1	47	.208	.325	.302	79	-5	2-1	.994	2	133	107	C35,O34(2/0/32)	89	-0.4
1976	LA N	54	185	24	41	7	0	6	18	25-1	1	41	.222	.318	.357	92	-2	2-0	.966	-0	108	63	O39R,C17	0	-0.3
	StL N	71	189	22	38	8	4	4	21	32-3	1	40	.201	.317	.349	88	-3	4-2	.978	9	169	131	C48,O14R	0	0.9
	Year	125	374	46	79	15	4	10	39	57-4	2	81	.211	.317	.353	90	-4	6-2	.975	9	142	123	C65,O53R	0	0.6
1977	Hou N	132	421	59	108	21	3	16	61	85-7	0	79	.257	.379	.435	128	20	6-2	.985	-6	94	122	C122/1	0	2.0
1978	Hou N	51	150	20	31	5	0	7	22	37-6	1	30	.207	.363	.380	117	5	0-0	.994	0	98	104	C51	0	0.8
	†LA N	67	198	20	47	11	0	7	28	34-5	1	41	.237	.350	.399	109	4	1-2	.984	-2	129	64	C62,O3(2/0/1)	0	0.4
	Year	118	348	40	78	16	0	14	50	71-11	2	71	.224	.356	.391	112	9	1-2	.989	-2	115	82	C113,O3(2/0/1)	0	1.2
1979	LA N	122	363	54	95	14	0	20	69	70-6	2	68	.262	.380	.466	133	19	1-0	.981	-4	90	75	C67,O52(5/0/47)	0	1.6
1980	LA N	77	172	20	41	3	2	9	29	38-11	0	46	.238	.371	.436	129	8	2-2	.982	-2	83	56	C66/rf	23	0.8
1981	LA N	17	14	2	2	1	0	0	1	2-0	0	5	.143	.250	.214	34	-1	0-0	ø	-0	0	0	/rf	0	-0.1
	Cal A	12	30	5	7	1	0	1	5	9-0	0	8	.233	.400	.367	124	2	0-0	.976	-0	99	168	C8,O4(3/0/1)	0	0.2
1982	Cal A	36	84	10	19	2	0	3	8	12-0	0	19	.226	.323	.357	86	-2	0-0	.993	4	76	154	C32,O2R	0	0.4
1983	Cal A	12	27	3	2	0	0	0	2	5-0	0	8	.074	.219	.074	-15	-4	0-0	.968	-1	72	98	C9,O3(1/0/2)	15	-0.6
Total	14	1013	3001	407	719	121	11	122	445	562-64	9	607	.240	.358	.409	117	87	22-12	.987	3	109	98	C766,O207(18/1/188)/1	146	11.7
FERGUSON, BOB	Robert Vavasour; B1.31.1845 Brooklyn NY; D5.3.1894 Brooklyn NY; BB/TR/5´9.5˝/149; d5.18; M16/U10; OF(0/1/5); ▲																								
1871	Mut NA	**33**	158	30	38	6	1	0	25	3	—	2	.241	.255	.291	62	-6	4-4	.774	4	**145**	148	3b20,2b11,C5/PM	—	-0.2
1872	Atl NA	**37**	164	33	46	3	0	0	19	3	—	0	.280	.293	.299	70	-8	4-2	.807	**34**	**195**	141	3b37/CM	—	1.7
1873	Atl NA	51	228	36	59	3	5	0	25	4	—	8	.259	.272	.316	82	-3	1-2	.746	**28**	**164**	123	3b50,P4,M	—	1.6
1874	Atl NA	**56**	245	34	64	4	0	0	19	2	—	7	.261	.267	.278	85	-2	5-3	.760	2	120	13	3b55,C2/PM	—	-0.1
1875	Har NA	85	366	65	88	10	4	0	43	3	—	5	.240	.247	.290	82	-8	2-1	**.827**	9	91	106	3b85/PM	—	-0.1
1876	Har N	**69**	310	48	82	8	5	0	32	2	—	11	.265	.269	.323	89	-5	—	.826	2	96	105	3b69,M	—	0.0
1877	Har N	58	254	40	65	7	2	0	35	3	—	10	.256	.265	.299	86	-3	—	.841	17	**139**	102	3b56,P3,M	—	1.4
1878	Chi N	**61**	259	44	91	10	2	0	39	10	—	12	.351	**.375**	.405	147	13	—	.881	15	**124**	137	S57,2b4/CM	—	2.8
1879	Tro N	30	123	18	31	5	2	0	4	4	—	3	.252	.276	.325	104	1	—	.808	2	105	145	3b24,2b6,M	—	0.3
1880	Tro N	82	332	55	87	9	0	0	22	**24**	—	24	.262	.312	.289	100	0	—	.904	-5	94	105	2b82,M	—	0.0
1881	Tro N	**85**	339	56	96	13	5	1	35	29	—	12	.283	.340	.360	114	6	—	.904	-13	91	108	2b85,M	—	-0.3
1882	Tro N	81	319	44	82	15	2	0	32	23	—	21	.257	.307	.317	106	4	—	.914	-12	90	94	2b79,S2,M	—	-0.5
1883	Phi N	86	329	39	85	9	2	0	27	18	—	21	.258	.297	.298	89	-3	—	.862	-11	101	74	2b86/PM	—	-1.0
1884	Pit AA	10	41	2	6	0	0	0	—	0	0	—	.146	.146	.146	-4	-5	—	.714	-3	0	0	O6(0/1/5),1b3/3M	—	-0.7
Total	5NA	262	1161	198	295	26	10	0	131	15	—	22	.254	.264	.294	77	-27	16-12	.784	76	132	97	3b247,2b11,C8,P7	—	2.9
Total	9	562	2306	346	625	76	20	1	226	113	0	114	.271	.305	.323	102	8	—	.895	-7	94	95	2b342,3b150,S59,O6R,P4,1b3/C	—	2.0
FERMIN, FELIX	Felix Jose (Minaya); B10.9.1963 Mao Valverde, D.R.; BR/TR/5´11˝/(166–185); d7.8																								
1987	Pit N	23	68	6	17	0	0	0	4	4-1	1	9	.250	.301	.250	47	-5	0-0	.980	2	103	113	S23	36	-0.2
1988	Pit N	43	87	9	24	0	2	0	2	8-1	3	10	.276	.354	.322	97	0	3-1	.955	-7	86	86	S43	0	-0.4
1989	Cle A	156	484	50	115	9	1	0	21	41-0	4	27	.238	.302	.260	59	-26	6-4	.967	12	110	91	S153,2b2	0	-0.2
1990	Cle A	148	414	47	106	13	2	1	40	26-0	0	22	.256	.297	.304	69	-18	3-3	.975	5	105	90	S147/2	0	-0.3
1991	Cle A	129	424	30	111	13	2	0	31	26-0	3	27	.262	.307	.302	69	-18	5-4	.980	2	100	91	S129	19	-0.7
1992	Cle A	79	215	27	58	7	2	0	13	18-1	1	10	.270	.326	.321	84	-5	0-0	.971	-6	93	114	S55,3b17,2b7,1b2	0	-0.7
1993	Cle A	140	480	48	126	16	2	2	45	24-1	4	14	.262	.303	.317	67	-23	4-5	.960	-28	86	95	S140	0	-4.2
1994	Sea A	101	379	52	120	21	0	1	35	11-0	4	22	.317	.338	.380	84	-9	4-4	.974	-6	80	86	S77,2b25	0	-0.8
1995	†Sea A	73	200	21	39	6	0	0	15	6-0	4	6	.195	.232	.225	20	-24	2-0	.971	5	89	128	S46,2b29	21	-1.4
1996	Chi N	11	16	4	2	1	0	0	1	2-0	0	0	.125	.222	.188	9	-2	0-0	.875	-3	59	57	2b6,S2	0	-0.5
Total	10	903	2767	294	718	86	11	4	207	166-4	24	147	.259	.305	.303	66	-130	27-21	.971	-24	97	95	S815,2b70,3b17,1b2	76	-9.4
FERNANDES, ED	Edward Paul; B3.11.1918 Oakland CA; D11.27.1968 Hayward CA; BB/TR/5´9˝/185; d6.9; Mil 1945																								
1940	Pit N	28	33	1	4	1	0	0	2	7	0	6	.121	.275	.152	21	-3	0	.981	-0	*77*	*96*	C27	—	-0.3
1946	Chi A	14	32	4	8	2	0	0	4	8	0	7	.250	.400	.313	105	1	0-0	.922	-1	*77*	*117*	C12	0	0.0
Total	2	42	65	5	12	3	0	0	6	15	0	13	.185	.338	.231	61	-2	0-0	.952	-1	*77*	*106*	C39	0	-0.3
FERNANDEZ, FRANK	Frank; B4.16.1943 Staten Island NY; BR/TR/6´1˝/(192–195); d9.12; Mil 1967																								
1967	NY A	9	28	1	6	2	0	1	4	2-0	1	7	.214	.281	.393	104	0	1-1	1.000	1	0	49	C7,O2R	0	0.1
1968	NY A	51	135	15	23	6	1	7	30	35-2	0	50	.170	.341	.385	124	5	1-0	.989	4	104	123	C45,O4R	0	1.3
1969	NY A	89	229	34	51	6	1	12	29	65-3	3	68	.223	.399	.415	133	14	1-3	.994	1	106	123	C65,O14R	0	1.7
1970	Oak A	94	252	30	54	5	0	15	44	40-4	2	76	.214	.327	.413	106	2	1-0	.993	2	127	74	C76/lf	0	0.8
1971	Oak A	2	4	0	0	0	0	0	0	1-0	0	2	.000	.200	.000	-40	-1	0-0	1.000	-2	0	145	C2	24	-0.3
	Was A	18	30	0	3	0	0	0	4	4-0	0	10	.100	.194	.100	-12	-4	0-0	1.000	-1	73	311	O6(3/1/2)/C	0	-0.6
	Oak A	2	5	1	1	1	0	0	1	0-0	0	1	.200	.200	.400	68	0	0-0	1.000	-2	0	145	/C	0	-0.3
	Year	22	39	1	4	1	0	0	5	5-0	0	13	.103	.196	.128	-4	-5	0-0	1.000	-5	73	311	O6(3/1/2),C4	0	-1.2
	Chi N	17	41	11	7	1	0	4	4	17-0	0	15	.171	.414	.488	135	3	0-0	.980	1	112	168	C16	0	0.4
1972	Chi N	3	3	0	0	0	0	0	0	0-0	0	2	.000	.000	.000	-90	-1	0-0	1.000	0	0	0	/C	0	-0.1
Total	6	285	727	92	145	21	2	39	116	164-9	6	231	.199	.350	.395	113	18	4-4	.992	3	106	106	C214,O27(4/1/22)	24	3.0
FERNANDEZ, NANNY	Froilan; B10.25.1918 Wilmington CA; D9.19.1996 Harbor City CA; BR/TR/5´9˝/170; d4.14; Mil 1943–45																								
1942	Bos N	145	577	63	147	29	3	6	55	38	2	61	.255	.303	.347	92	-8	15	.914	2	102	83	3b98,O44(42/3/0)	0	-0.5
1946	Bos N	115	372	37	95	15	2	2	42	30	1	44	.255	.313	.323	79	-10	1	.940	1	104	92	3b81,S18,O14L	0	-1.1
1947	Bos N	83	209	16	43	4	0	2	21	22	0	20	.206	.281	.254	44	-17	2	.933	-9	95	79	S62,O8R,3b6	0	-2.3
1950	Pit N	65	198	23	51	11	0	6	27	19	1	17	.258	.326	.404	88	-4	2	.925	-3	99	57	3b52	0	-0.7
Total	4	408	1356	139	336	59	5	16	145	109	4	142	.248	.306	.334	80	-39	20	.925	-10	101	79	3b237,S80,O66(56/3/8)	0	-4.6
FERNANDEZ, CHICO	Humberto (Perez); B3.2.1932 Havana, Cuba; BR/TR/6´0˝/(165–172); d7.14																								
1956	Bro N	34	66	11	15	2	0	1	9	3-1	0	10	.227	.261	.303	47	-5	2-3	.978	4	114	114	S25	0	0.0
1957	Phi N	149	500	42	131	14	4	5	51	31-5	1	64	.262	.302	.336	75	-19	18-5	.960	-17	89	81	S149	0	-2.2
1958	Phi N	148	522	38	120	18	5	6	51	37-3	2	48	.230	.280	.318	60	-31	12-6	.975	-13	94	88	S148	0	-3.2
1959	Phi N	45	123	15	26	5	1	0	3	10-0	0	11	.211	.269	.268	43	-10	2-1	.958	-3	82	113	S40,2b2	0	-1.1
1960	Det A	133	435	44	105	13	3	4	35	39-4	1	50	.241	.303	.313	66	-21	13-4	.947	-7	98	86	S130	0	-1.7
1961	Det A	133	435	41	108	15	4	3	40	36-4	0	45	.248	.305	.322	66	-21	8-5	.958	-9	94	91	S121,3b8	0	-2.1
1962	Det A	141	503	64	125	17	2	20	59	42-2	0	69	.249	.305	.410	88	-10	10-3	.960	-28	86	65	S138,3b2/1	0	-2.5

YEAR	TM LG	G	AB	R	H	2B	3B	HR	RBI	BB-IB	HP	SO	AVG	OBP	SLG	AOPS	ABR	SB-CS	FA	FR	RNG	THR	GAMES AT POSITION	DL	BFW
1963	Det A	15	49	3	7	1	0	0	2	6-0	0	11	.143	.236	.163	14	-6	0-1	.947	0	98	97	S14	0	-0.5
	NY N	58	145	12	29	6	0	1	9	9-2	0	30	.200	.244	.262	46	-10	3-0	.944	-9	87	80	S45,3b5,2b3	0	-1.7
Total	8	856	2778	270	666	91	19	40	259	213-21	4	338	.240	.292	.329	67	-133	68-28	.960	-82	92	84	S810,3b15,2b5/1	0	-15.0

FERNANDEZ, JOSE Jose Mayobanex (Rojas); B11.2.1974 LaVega, D.R.; BR/TR/6´2˝/220; d7.3

YEAR	TM LG	G	AB	R	H	2B	3B	HR	RBI	BB-IB	HP	SO	AVG	OBP	SLG	AOPS	ABR	SB-CS	FA	FR	RNG	THR	GAMES AT POSITION	DL	BFW
1999	Mon N	8	24	0	5	2	0	0	1	1-0	0	7	.208	.240	.292	35	-2	0-0	.889	0	101	0	3b6	0	-0.2
2001	Ana A	13	25	1	2	1	0	0	0	2-0	0	10	.080	.148	.120	-27	-5	0-1	.000	-0	0	0	1b2/3D	0	-0.5
Total	2	21	49	1	7	3	0	0	1	3-0	0	17	.143	.192	.204	3	-7	0-1	.889	-0	99	0	D7,3b7,1b2	0	-0.7

FERNANDEZ, CHICO Lorenzo Marto (Mosquera); B4.23.1939 Havana, Cuba; BR/TR/5´10˝/160; d4.20

YEAR	TM LG	G	AB	R	H	2B	3B	HR	RBI	BB-IB	HP	SO	AVG	OBP	SLG	AOPS	ABR	SB-CS	FA	FR	RNG	THR	GAMES AT POSITION	DL	BFW
1968	Bal A	24	18	0	2	0	0	0	0	1-0	0	2	.111	.158	.111	-17	-3	0-0	.923	-1	94	161	S7,2b4	0	-0.3

FERNANDEZ, TONY Octavio Antonio (Castro) (b Octavio Antonio Fernando (Castro)); B6.30.1962 San Pedro de Macoris, D.R.; BB/TR/6´2˝/(165–195); d9.2; [DL 1996 NY A 182]

YEAR	TM LG	G	AB	R	H	2B	3B	HR	RBI	BB-IB	HP	SO	AVG	OBP	SLG	AOPS	ABR	SB-CS	FA	FR	RNG	THR	GAMES AT POSITION	DL	BFW
1983	Tor A	15	34	5	9	1	1	0	2	2-0	1	2	.265	.324	.353	81	-1	0-1	1.000	-3	65	111	S13/D	0	-0.3
1984	Tor A	88	233	29	63	5	3	3	19	17-0	0	15	.270	.317	.356	83	-6	5-7	.974	14	107	115	S73,3b10/D	0	1.3
1985	†Tor A	**161**	564	71	163	31	10	2	51	43-2	2	41	.289	.340	.390	97	-2	13-6	.962	9	104	118	S160	0	2.4
1986	Tor A★	**163**	687	91	213	33	9	10	65	27-0	4	52	.310	.338	.428	104	3	25-12	**.983**	3	98	105	S163	0	2.4
1987	Tor A★	146	578	90	186	29	8	5	67	51-3	5	48	.322	.379	.426	111	10	32-12	.979	16	98	115	S146	0	4.1
1988	Tor A	154	648	76	186	41	4	5	70	45-3	4	65	.287	.335	.386	101	1	15-5	.981	10	103	109	S154	0	2.4
1989	†Tor A★	140	573	64	147	25	9	11	64	29-1	3	51	.257	.291	.389	93	-8	22-6	**.992**	16	107	104	S140	24	2.1
1990	Tor A	161	635	84	175	27	**17**	4	66	71-4	7	70	.276	.352	.391	106	6	26-13	.989	9	101	96	S161	0	2.7
1991	SD N	145	558	81	152	27	5	4	38	55-0	0	74	.272	.337	.360	93	-4	23-9	.972	10	104	**115**	S145	0	1.9
1992	SD N★	155	622	84	171	32	4	4	37	56-4	4	62	.275	.337	.359	96	-2	20-20	.983	-18	90	80	S154	0	-1.2
1993	NY N	48	173	20	39	5	2	1	14	25-0	1	19	.225	.323	.295	69	-7	6-2	.975	3	104	100	S48	0	0.0
	†Tor A	94	353	45	108	18	9	4	50	31-3	0	26	.306	.361	.442	113	6	15-8	.985	10	95	102	S94	0	2.2
1994	Cin N	104	366	50	102	18	6	8	50	44-8	5	40	.279	.361	.426	105	3	12-7	**.991**	0	98	92	3b93,S9,2b5	0	0.5
1995	†NY A	108	384	57	94	20	2	5	45	42-4	4	40	.245	.322	.346	76	-13	6-6	.976	-14	91	99	S103,2b4	18	-1.9
1997	†Cle A	120	409	55	117	21	1	11	44	22-0	2	47	.286	.323	.423	90	-7	6-6	.980	14	**105**	94	2b109,S10/D	0	1.1
1998	Tor A	138	486	71	156	36	2	9	72	45-5	11	53	.321	.387	.459	120	16	13-8	.975	-12	94	90	2b82,3b54/D	0	0.8
1999	Tor A★	142	485	73	159	41	0	6	75	77-11	10	62	.328	.427	.449	123	23	6-7	.939	-14	90	99	3b132,D9/2	0	0.8
2001	Mil N	28	64	6	18	0	0	1	3	7-0	0	9	.281	.352	.328	79	-2	1-2	.966	0	114	172	3b13	0	-0.2
	Tor A	48	59	5	18	4	0	1	12	1-0	1	8	.305	.323	.424	94	-1	0-1	ø	0	0	0	D13	0	-0.2
Total	17	2158	7911	1057	2276	414	92	94	844	690-48	64	784	.288	.347	.399	101	15	246-138	.980	51	100	105	S1573,3b302,2b201,D26	224	20.9

FERRARA, AL Alfred John "The Bull"; B12.22.1939 Brooklyn NY; BR/TR/6´1˝/(200–203); d7.30; Col Long Island–Brooklyn

YEAR	TM LG	G	AB	R	H	2B	3B	HR	RBI	BB-IB	HP	SO	AVG	OBP	SLG	AOPS	ABR	SB-CS	FA	FR	RNG	THR	GAMES AT POSITION	DL	BFW
1963	LA N	21	44	2	7	0	0	1	1	6-0	1	9	.159	.275	.227	50	-3	0-0	.950	0	105	145	O11(7/0/4)	0	-0.3
1965	LA N	41	81	5	17	2	1	1	10	9-0	1	20	.210	.297	.296	72	-3	0-0	.927	-1	102	0	O27(10/0/19)	0	-0.6
1966	†LA N	63	115	15	31	4	0	5	23	9-0	3	35	.270	.333	.435	123	3	0-0	.956	-1	109	0	O32(4/1/27)	0	0.1
1967	LA N	122	347	41	96	16	1	16	50	33-4	3	73	.277	.345	.467	142	18	0-1	.978	-7	89	17	O94(27/0/71)	0	0.5
1968	LA N	2	7	0	1	0	0	0	0	0-0	0	2	.143	.143	.143	-15	-1	0-0	.500	-1	35	0	O2L	144	-0.2
1969	SD N	138	366	39	95	22	1	14	56	45-5	7	69	.260	.349	.440	124	13	0-0	.958	-4	85	100	O96(95/1/0)	0	0.4
1970	SD N	138	372	44	103	15	4	13	51	46-2	11	63	.277	.372	.444	122	13	0-0	.968	-8	83	33	O96L	0	0.0
1971	SD N	17	17	0	2	1	0	0	2	5-1	0	5	.118	.318	.176	46	-1	0-0	1.000	-1	29	0	O2L	0	-0.2
	Cin N	32	33	2	6	0	0	1	5	3-0	1	10	.182	.270	.273	55	-2	0-0	1.000	0	137	0	O5L	0	-0.2
	Year	49	50	2	8	1	0	1	7	8-1	1	15	.160	.288	.240	52	-3	0-0	1.000	-0	92	0	O7L	0	-0.4
Total	8	574	1382	148	358	60	7	51	198	156-12	27	286	.259	.344	.423	119	37	0-1	.962	-22	89	46	O365(248/2/121)	144	-0.5

FERRARO, MIKE Michael Dennis; B8.18.1944 Kingston NY; BR/TR/5´11˝/175; d9.6; M2/C13

YEAR	TM LG	G	AB	R	H	2B	3B	HR	RBI	BB-IB	HP	SO	AVG	OBP	SLG	AOPS	ABR	SB-CS	FA	FR	RNG	THR	GAMES AT POSITION	DL	BFW
1966	NY A	10	28	4	5	0	0	0	0	3-0	1	3	.179	.281	.179	37	-2	0-0	.926	1	117	198	3b10	0	-0.2
1968	NY A	23	87	5	14	0	1	0	1	2-1	0	17	.161	.180	.184	11	-10	0-0	.975	4	134	77	3b22	0	-0.7
1969	Sea A	5	4	0	0	0	0	0	0	1-0	0	0	.000	.200	.000	-40	-1	0-0	ø	0	—	—	/H	0	-0.1
1972	Mil A	124	381	19	97	18	1	2	29	17-1	0	41	.255	.284	.323	82	-9	0-5	.950	-17	83	77	3b115/S	0	-3.3
Total	4	162	500	28	116	18	2	2	30	23-2	1	61	.232	.265	.288	67	-22	0-5	.953	-12	94	85	3b147/S	0	-4.3

FERRELL, RICK Richard Benjamin; B10.12.1905 Durham NC; D7.27.1995 Bloomfield Hills MI; BR/TR/5´10˝/160; d4.19; C8; HF1984; b–Wes; Col Guilford

YEAR	TM LG	G	AB	R	H	2B	3B	HR	RBI	BB-IB	HP	SO	AVG	OBP	SLG	AOPS	ABR	SB-CS	FA	FR	RNG	THR	GAMES AT POSITION	DL	BFW
1929	StL A	64	144	21	33	6	1	0	20	32	1	10	.229	.373	.285	69	-5	1-2	.962	1	*136*	*108*	C45	—	-0.2
1930	StL A	101	314	43	84	18	4	1	41	46	1	10	.268	.363	.360	81	-8	1-4	.983	-4	*117*	***123***	C101	—	-0.6
1931	StL A	117	386	47	118	30	4	3	57	56	0	12	.306	.394	.427	112	9	2-3	.973	7	*114*	*98*	C108	—	2.0
1932	StL A	126	438	67	138	30	5	2	65	66	1	18	.315	.406	.420	108	9	5-5	.986	2	*110*	*104*	C120	—	1.6
1933	StL A	22	72	8	18	2	0	1	5	12	0	4	.250	.357	.319	76	-2	2-0	.991	2	*131*	*108*	C21	—	0.2
	Bos A★	118	421	50	125	19	4	3	72	58	2	19	.297	.385	.382	105	5	2-2	.990	2	*81*	*118*	C116	—	1.4
	Year	140	493	58	143	21	4	4	77	70	2	23	.290	.381	.373	100	3	4-2	.990	5	*89*	*116*	C137	—	1.6
1934	Bos A☆	132	437	50	130	29	4	1	48	66	0	20	.297	.390	.389	95	-1	0-0	**.990**	5	*100*	*79*	C128	—	1.1
1935	Bos A☆	133	458	54	138	34	4	3	61	65	0	15	.301	.388	.413	100	3	5-8	.979	13	*116*	***142***	C131	—	2.1
1936	Bos A★	121	410	59	128	27	5	8	55	65	0	17	.312	.406	.461	108	7	0-1	.987	9	*88*	*93*	C121	—	2.0
1937	Bos A	18	65	8	20	2	0	1	4	15	0	4	.308	.438	.385	105	1	0-0	.990	1	*113*	*88*	C18	—	0.3
	Was A☆	86	279	31	64	6	0	1	32	50	1	18	.229	.348	.262	59	-16	1-1	.987	-5	*96*	*97*	C84	—	-1.4
	Year	104	344	39	84	8	0	2	36	65	1	22	.244	.366	.285	68	-14	1-1	.988	-4	*99*	*95*	C102	—	-1.1
1938	Was A☆	135	411	55	120	24	5	1	58	75	0	17	.292	.401	.382	104	7	1-0	.981	-7	*109*	*93*	C131	—	0.8
1939	Was A	87	274	32	77	13	1	0	31	41	1	12	.281	.377	.336	90	-2	1-1	.976	-2	***145***	*81*	C83	—	0.1
1940	Was A	103	326	35	89	18	2	0	28	47	0	15	.273	.365	.340	90	-3	1-1	.980	-5	*80*	*130*	C99	—	-0.2
1941	Was A	21	66	8	18	5	0	0	13	15	0	4	.273	.407	.348	107	2	1-0	.980	-1	*91*	*131*	C21	0	0.2
	StL A	100	321	30	81	14	3	2	23	52	0	22	.252	.357	.333	81	-7	2-1	.995	-4	*93*	*92*	C98	0	-0.5
	Year	121	387	38	99	19	3	2	36	67	0	26	.256	.366	.336	85	-6	3-1	.992	-5	*93*	*99*	C119	0	-0.3
1942	StL A	99	273	20	61	6	1	0	26	33	0	13	.223	.307	.253	57	-15	0-1	.986	3	*87*	*91*	C95	0	-0.7
1943	StL A	74	209	12	50	7	0	0	20	34	1	14	.239	.348	.273	81	-3	0-0	.987	3	*72*	*113*	C70	0	0.5
1944	Was A☆	99	339	14	94	11	1	0	25	46	0	13	.277	.364	.316	99	2	2-1	.981	2	*87*	*93*	C96	0	1.0
1945	Was A✳	91	286	33	76	12	1	1	38	43	2	13	.266	.366	.325	110	6	2-4	.990	-1	*110*	*81*	C83	0	1.0
1947	Was A	37	99	10	30	11	0	0	12	14	0	7	.303	.389	.414	127	5	0-0	.994	2	*97*	*151*	C37	0	0.8
Total	18	1884	6028	687	1692	324	45	28	734	931	10	277	.281	.378	.363	95	-6	29-35	.984	24	*102*	*104*	C1806	0	11.5

FERRELL, WES Wesley Cheek; B2.2.1908 Greensboro NC; D12.9.1976 Sarasota FL; BR/TR/6´2˝/195; d9.9; b–Rick; ▲

YEAR	TM LG	G	AB	R	H	2B	3B	HR	RBI	BB-IB	HP	SO	AVG	OBP	SLG	AOPS	ABR	SB-CS	FA	FR	RNG	THR	GAMES AT POSITION	DL	BFW
1927	Cle A	1	0	0	0	0	0	0	0	0	0	0	ø	ø	ø	ø	0	0-0	ø	-0	0	0	/P	—	0.0
1928	Cle A	2	4	0	1	0	1	0	0	0	0	0	.250	.250	.750	152	1	0-0	1.000	0	110	0	P2	—	0.0
1929	Cle A	47	93	12	22	5	3	1	12	6	0	28	.237	.283	.387	68	4	1-0	.973	3	121	106	P43	—	0.0
1930	Cle A	53	118	19	35	8	3	0	14	12	0	15	.297	.362	.415	93	8	0-0	.967	-3	65	0	P43	—	0.0
1931	Cle A	48	116	24	37	6	1	9	30	10	0	21	.319	.373	.621	149	17	0-0	.969	5	132	96	P40	—	0.0
1932	Cle A	55	128	14	31	5	2	2	18	6	0	21	.242	.276	.359	59	4	0-0	.986	0	101	148	P38	—	0.0
1933	Cle A☆	61	140	26	38	7	0	7	26	20	0	22	.271	.363	.471	114	3	0-0	**1.000**	2	111	183	P28,O13L	—	0.1
1934	Bos A	34	78	12	22	4	0	4	17	7	0	15	.282	.341	.487	104	8	1-0	.969	-3	64	104	P26	—	0.0
1935	Bos A	75	150	25	52	5	1	7	32	21	0	16	.347	.427	.533	138	20	0-0	.977	2	119	29	P41	—	0.0
1936	Bos A	61	135	20	36	6	1	5	24	14	0	10	.267	.336	.437	84	11	0-0	.962	-3	76	67	P39	—	0.0
1937	Bos A	18	33	7	12	2	0	1	9	7	0	3	.364	.475	.515	144	6	0-0	.964	2	152	570	P12	—	0.0
	Was A☆	53	106	7	27	5	0	0	16	9	0	18	.255	.313	.302	58	6	0-0	.975	-1	86	0	P25	—	0.0
	Year	71	139	14	39	7	0	1	25	16	0	21	.281	.355	.353	81	12	0-0	.971	1	103	148	P37	—	0.0
1938	Was A	26	49	6	11	2	0	1	6	15	0	7	.224	.406	.327	92	7	0-0	.976	1	114	163	P23	—	0.0
	NY A	5	12	1	2	1	0	0	1	1	0	4	.167	.231	.250	20	0	0-0	.917	1	159	884	P5	—	0.0
	Year	31	61	7	13	3	0	1	7	16	0	11	.213	.377	.311	79	7	0-0	.962	1	122	284	P28	—	0.0
1939	NY A	3	8	0	1	1	0	0	1	0	0	2	.125	.125	.250	-6	0	0-0	1.000	0	124	0	P3	—	0.0
1940	Bro N	2	2	0	0	0	0	0	0	0	0	2	.000	.000	.000	-94	0	0	1.000	1	372	0	/P	—	0.0
1941	Bos N	4	4	2	2	0	0	1	2	1	0	1	.500	.600	1.250	430	2	0	1.000	-0	35	0	P4	0	0.0
Total	15	548	1176	175	329	57	12	38	208	129	0	185	.280	.351	.446	99	97	2-0	.975	5	101	104	P374,O13L	0	0.1

YEAR	TM LG	G	AB	R	H	2B	3B	HR	RBI	BB-IB	HP	SO	AVG	OBP	SLG	AOPS	ABR	SB-CS	FA	FR	RNG	THR	GAMES AT POSITION	DL	BFW
FERRER, SERGIO	Sergio (Marrero); B1.29.1951 Santurce, PR; BB/TR/5´7˝/(140–145); d4.5																								
1974	Min A	24	57	12	16	0	2	0	0	8-0	1	6	.281	.379	.351	107	1	3-2	.855	-7	79	68	S20/2	0	-0.4
1975	Min A	32	81	14	20	3	1	0	2	3-0	1	11	.247	.279	.309	66	-4	3-4	.924	-1	119	133	S18,2b10,D2	0	-0.4
1978	NY N	37	33	8	7	0	1	0	1	4-0	1	7	.212	.316	.273	68	-1	1-0	.971	3	114	98	S29,2b3,3b2	0	0.3
1979	NY N	32	7	7	0	0	0	0	0	2-0	0	3	.000	.222	.000	-35	-1	0-2	.833	-0	48	0	3b12,S5,2b4	0	-0.2
Total	4	125	178	41	43	3	4	0	3	17-0	3	27	.242	.317	.303	76	-5	7-8	.922	-5	103	103	S72,2b18,3b14,D2	0	-0.7
FERRIS, HOBE	Albert Sayles; B12.7.1877 Providence RI; D3.18.1938 Detroit MI; BR/TR/5´8˝/162; d4.26																								
1901	Bos A	**138**	523	68	131	16	15	2	63	23	6	—	.250	.290	.350	78	-18	13	.930	7	103	**130**	2b138/S	—	-0.8
1902	Bos A	134	499	57	122	16	14	8	63	21	1	—	.244	.276	.381	79	-18	11	.952	**24**	**114**	115	2b134	—	.7
1903	†Bos A	**141**	525	69	132	19	7	9	66	25	1	—	.251	.287	.366	90	-8	11	.950	14	105	111	2b139,S2	—	0.8
1904	Bos A	156	563	50	120	23	10	3	63	23	1	—	.213	.245	.306	70	-20	7	.962	-0	98	107	2b156	—	-2.2
1905	Bos A	142	523	51	115	24	16	6	59	23	0	—	.220	.253	.361	93	-8	11	.960	15	**108**	111	2b142	—	0.9
1906	Bos A	130	495	47	121	25	13	2	44	10	2	—	.244	.262	.360	94	-6	8	.960	8	104	97	2b126,3b4	—	0.3
1907	Bos A	150	561	41	135	25	2	4	60	10	0	—	.241	.254	.314	82	-14	11	.967	8	102	94	2b150	—	-0.6
1908	StL A	148	555	54	150	26	7	2	74	14	2	—	.270	.291	.353	108	3	6	**.952**	14	103	**168**	3b148	—	2.3
1909	StL A	148	556	36	120	18	5	4	58	12	0	—	.216	.232	.288	69	-23	11	.937	7	103	103	3b114,2b34	—	-1.5
Total	9	1287	4800	473	1146	192	89	40	550	161	13	—	.239	.265	.341	84	-112	89	.954	96	104	109	2b1019,3b266,S3	—	-0.1
FETZER, WILLY	William McKinnon; B6.24.1884 Concord NC; D5.3.1959 Franklin NC; BL/TR/5´10.5˝/180; d9.4; Col Davidson																								
1906	Phi A	1	1	0	0	0	0	0	0	0	0	—	.000	.000	.000	-97	0	0	ø	0	—	—	/H	—	0.0
FEWSTER, CHICK	Wilson Lloyd; B11.10.1895 Baltimore MD; D4.16.1945 Baltimore MD; BR/TR/5´11˝/160; d9.19																								
1917	NY A	11	36	2	8	0	0	0	1	5	0	5	.222	.317	.222	64	-1	1	.919	-0	98	114	2b11	—	-0.1
1918	NY A	5	2	1	1	0	0	0	0	0	0	0	.500	.500	.500	197	0	0	ø	-0	0	0	2b2	—	0.0
1919	NY A	81	244	38	69	9	3	1	15	34	7	36	.283	.386	.357	108	5	8	.946	4	81	236	O41(0/13/28),S24,2b4,3b2	—	0.8
1920	NY A	21	21	8	6	1	0	0	1	7	0	2	.286	.464	.333	110	1	0-1	.840	-1	91	66	S6,2b3	—	0.0
1921	†NY A	66	207	44	58	19	0	1	19	28	6	43	.280	.382	.386	94	0	4-4	.974	-1	88	118	O43(7/35/1),2b15	—	-0.2
1922	NY A	44	132	20	32	4	1	1	9	16	0	23	.242	.324	.311	65	-7	2-4	.975	2	86	198	O38(35/4/0),2b2	—	-0.8
	Bos A	23	83	8	24	4	1	0	9	6	1	10	.289	.344	.361	85	-2	8-3	.959	2	113	78	3b23	—	0.2
	Year	67	215	28	56	8	2	1	18	22	1	33	.260	.332	.330	72	-9	10-7	.975	4	86	198	O38(35/4/0),3b23,2b2	—	-0.6
1923	Bos A	90	284	32	67	10	1	0	15	39	3	35	.236	.334	.278	62	-14	7-14	.938	-10	99	74	2b49,S37,3b3	—	-2.3
1924	Cle A	101	322	36	86	12	2	0	36	24	3	36	.267	.324	.317	65	-17	12-12	.961	-20	91	73	2b94,3b5	—	-3.5
1925	Cle A	93	294	39	73	16	1	1	38	36	0	25	.248	.330	.320	65	-15	6-9	.939	-11	93	83	2b83,3b10/rf	—	-2.4
1926	Bro N	105	337	53	82	16	3	2	24	45	5	49	.243	.341	.326	82	-7	9	.953	-12	90	66	2b103	—	-1.6
1927	Bro N	4	1	1	0	0	0	0	0	0	0	0	.000	.000	.000	-99	0	0	ø	0	—	—	/H	—	0.0
Total	11	644	1963	282	506	91	12	6	167	240	25	264	.258	.346	.326	77	-57	57-47	.945	-47	93	78	2b366,O123(42/52/30),S67,3b43	—	-9.9
FIALA, NEIL	Neil Stephen; B8.24.1956 St.Louis MO; BL/TR/6´1˝/185; [StLN77 32/720]; d9.3; Col Southern Illinois																								
1981	StL N	3	3	0	0	0	0	0	0	0-0	0	1	.000	.000	.000	-96	-1	0-0	ø	0	—	—	/H	0	-0.1
	Cin N	2	2	1	1	0	0	0	1	0-0	0	1	.500	.500	.500	185	0	0-0	ø	0	—	—	/H	0	0.0
	Year	5	5	1	1	0	0	0	1	0-0	0	2	.200	.200	.200	13	-1	0-0	ø	0	—	—	0	—	-0.1
FICK, ROBERT	Robert Charles John; B3.15.1974 Torrance CA; BL/TR/6´1˝/(189–205); [DetA96 5/131]; d9.19; Col Cal St.–Northridge; OF(17/0/171)																								
1998	Det A	7	22	6	8	1	0	3	7	2-0	0	7	.364	.417	.818	208	3	1-0	.950	0	89	124	C3/1D	0	0.3
1999	Det A	15	41	6	9	0	0	3	10	7-0	0	6	.220	.327	.439	93	-1	1-0	1.000	1	98	0	C4,D8	155	0.0
2000	Det A	66	163	18	41	7	2	3	22	22-2	1	39	.252	.340	.374	83	-4	2-1	.984	-3	114	95	1b34,C16,D12	56	-0.8
2001	Det A	124	401	62	109	21	2	19	61	39-3	4	62	.272	.339	.476	115	8	0-3	.986	-3	80	61	C78,1b26,O8R,D8	0	0.7
2002	Det A★	148	556	66	150	36	2	17	63	46-4	7	90	.270	.331	.433	106	4	0-1	.963	9	101	**234**	O140R,D6	0	0.6
2003	†Atl N	126	409	52	110	26	1	11	80	42-4	2	47	.269	.335	.418	97	-2	1-0	.987	-8	78	102	1b115	16	-1.9
2004	TB A	76	214	12	43	5	2	6	26	20-2	2	32	.201	.273	.327	57	-14	0-0	.976	-1	121	0	D34,O21(13/0/8),1b10,C3	0	-1.8
	SD N	13	12	2	2	0	0	0	0	2-0	1	4	.167	.333	.167	37	-1	0-0	1.000	-0	0	143	/1	0	-0.1
2005	†SD N	93	230	25	61	10	2	3	30	26-2	1	33	.265	.340	.365	90	-3	0-2	.992	-2	80	121	1b29,C28,O13(4/0/9)/3D	0	-0.7
2006	Was N	60	128	14	34	4	0	2	9	10-1	1	24	.266	.324	.344	75	-5	1-1	.991	-6	63	25	C26,1b13,O6R	64	-1.1
Total	9	728	2176	263	567	110	11	67	308	216-18	19	344	.261	.329	.414	96	-15	6-8	.988	-13	83	98	1b229,O188R,C158,D72/3	291	-4.8
FIELD, JIM	James C.; B4.24.1863 Philadelphia PA; D5.13.1953 Atlantic City NJ; 6´1˝/170; d6.2; ▲																								
1883	Col AA	75	291	31	75	10	6	1	—	7	—	—	.258	.275	.344	107	3	—	.938	-7	47	115	1b75	—	-0.9
1884	Col AA	105	417	74	97	9	7	4	—	23	12	—	.233	.292	.317	107	5	—	.958	-4	75	134	1b105	—	-0.7
1885	Pit AA	56	209	28	50	9	1	1	15	13	7	—	.239	.306	.306	95	0	—	.965	-0	99	123	1b56	—	-0.5
	Bal AA	38	144	16	30	3	2	0	10	13	1	—	.208	.278	.257	71	-4	—	.963	1	129	71	1b38	—	-0.6
	Year	94	353	44	80	12	3	1	25	26	8	—	.227	.295	.286	85	-4	—	.964	1	111	102	1b94	—	-1.1
1890	Roc AA	52	188	30	38	7	5	4	25	21	8	—	.202	.309	.356	104	1	8	.964	-4	61	92	1b51,P2	—	-0.7
1898	Was N	5	21	1	2	0	0	0	0	0	0	—	.095	.095	.095	-46	-4	1	.979	-0	86	0	1b5	—	-0.4
Total	5	331	1270	180	292	38	21	10	50	77	28	—	.230	.289	.317	97	1	9	.956	-15	77	112	1b330,P2	—	-3.8
FIELD, SAM	Samuel Jay; B10.12.1848 Philadelphia PA; D10.28.1904 Sinking Spring PA; BR/TR/5´9.5˝/182; d5.19																								
1875	Cen NA	3	11	2	1	0	0	0	0	0	—	0	.091	.091	.091	-40	-1	0-0	.714	-1	—	—	C2/rf	—	-0.2
	Was NA	5	16	0	5	0	0	0	1	0	—	1	.313	.313	.313	122	0	1-0	.731	-2	—	—	C4/rf	—	-0.1
	Year	8	27	2	6	0	0	0	1	0	—	1	.222	.222	.222	58	-1	1-0	.723	-3	—	—	C6,O2R	—	-0.3
1876	Cin N	4	14	2	0	0	0	0	0	1	—	3	.000	.067	.000	-89	-3	—	.667	-3	—	—	C3,2b2	—	-0.5
FIELDER, CECIL	Cecil Grant; B9.21.1963 Los Angeles CA; BR/TR/6´3˝/(220–261); [KCA82 S4/67]; d7.20; s–Prince; Col Nevada–Las Vegas																								
1985	†Tor A	30	74	6	23	4	0	4	16	6-0	0	16	.311	.358	.527	136	4	0-0	.979	0	117	144	1b25	0	0.3
1986	Tor A	34	83	7	13	2	0	4	13	6-0	1	27	.157	.222	.325	45	-7	0-0	1.000	-0	83	82	D22,1b7,3b2/lf	0	-0.8
1987	Tor A	82	175	30	47	7	1	14	32	20-2	1	48	.269	.345	.560	132	7	0-1	1.000	-1	74	136	D55,1b16,3b2	0	0.4
1988	Tor A	74	174	24	40	6	1	9	23	14-0	1	53	.230	.289	.431	98	-1	0-1	.991	0	113	92	D50,1b17,3b3,2b2	0	-0.4
1990	Det A★	159	573	104	159	25	1	**51**	**132**	90-11	5	182	.277	.377	**.592**	166	51	0-1	.989	5	114	107	1b143,D15	0	4.4
1991	Det A★	**162**	624	102	163	25	0	**44**	**133**	78-12	6	151	.261	.347	.513	133	27	0-0	.993	0	105	101	1b122,D42	0	1.7
1992	Det A	155	594	80	145	22	0	35	**124**	73-8	2	151	.244	.325	.458	117	12	0-0	.991	4	118	100	1b114,D43	0	0.7
1993	Det A★	154	573	80	153	23	0	30	117	90-15	4	125	.267	.368	.464	123	20	0-1	.991	-0	103	88	1b119,D36	0	0.7
1994	Det A	109	425	67	110	16	2	28	90	50-4	2	110	.259	.337	.504	112	6	0-0	.993	16	**162**	85	1b102,D7	0	1.2
1995	Det A	136	494	70	120	18	1	31	82	75-8	5	116	.243	.346	.472	111	7	0-1	.993	7	139	95	1b77,D58	0	0.5
1996	Det A	107	391	55	97	12	0	26	80	63-8	3	91	.248	.354	.478	108	5	2-0	.989	4	123	71	1b71,D36	0	0.1
	†NY A	53	200	30	52	8	0	13	37	24-4	2	48	.260	.342	.495	109	2	0-0	1.000	-0	71	103	D43,1b9	0	-0.1
	Year	160	591	85	149	20	0	39	117	87-12	5	139	.252	.350	.484	109	7	2-0	.990	4	117	75	1b80,D79	0	0.0
1997	†NY A	98	361	40	94	15	0	13	61	51-3	7	87	.260	.358	.410	102	2	0-0	1.000	1	130	129	D87,1b8	62	-0.2
1998	Ana A	103	381	48	92	16	1	17	68	52-1	3	98	.241	.335	.423	94	-3	0-1	.997	-2	84	101	1b72,D31	0	-1.3
	Cle A	14	35	1	5	1	0	0	0	1-0	1	13	.143	.189	.171	-5	-6	0-0	.933	0	121	51	D10,1b3	0	-0.6
	Year	117	416	49	97	17	1	17	68	53-1	4	111	.233	.324	.401	86	-9	0-1	.995	-2	85	99	1b75,D41	0	-1.9
Total	13	1470	5157	744	1313	200	7	319	1008	693-76	43	1316	.255	.345	.482	118	126	2-6	.992	33	117	97	1b905,D535,3b7,2b2/lf	62	6.6
FIELDER, PRINCE	Prince Semien; B5.9.1984 Ontario CA; BL/TR/6´0˝/260; [MilN02 1/7]; d6.13; f–Cecil																								
2005	Mil N	39	59	2	17	4	0	2	10	2-0	0	17	.288	.306	.458	98	0	0-0	1.000	1	172	61	1b7,D5	0	0.0
2006	Mil N	157	569	82	154	35	1	28	81	59-5	12	125	.271	.347	.483	110	9	7-2	.992	1	100	91	1b152/D	0	-0.3
Total	2	196	628	84	171	39	1	30	91	61-5	12	142	.272	.344	.481	109	9	7-2	.992	2	102	90	1b159,D6	0	-0.3
FIELDS, BRUCE	Bruce Alan; B10.6.1960 Cleveland OH; BL/TR/6´0˝/185; [DetA78 7/168]; d9.3; C3																								
1986	Det A	16	43	4	12	1	1	0	6	1-0	0	6	.279	.283	.349	74	-2	1-1	.962	-1	102	0	O14L/D	0	-0.3
1988	Sea A	39	67	8	18	5	0	1	5	4-0	0	11	.269	.310	.388	90	-1	0-1	1.000	-2	79	0	O23(14/1/8),D6	0	-0.3
1989	Sea A	3	3	2	1	1	0	0	0	0-0	0	1	.333	.333	.667	170	0	0-0	ø	-0	0	0	/rf	0	0.0
Total	3	58	113	14	31	7	1	1	11	5-0	0	18	.274	.300	.381	86	-3	1-2	.980	-2	89	0	O38(28/1/9),D7	0	-0.6
FIELDS, GEORGE	George W.; B7.1853 Waterbury CT; D9.22.1933 Waterbury CT; d5.2																								
1872	Man NA	18	86	17	19	3	1	0	14	0	—	2	.221	.221	.279	56	-4	0-0	.629	-7	72	0	3b12,O5(1/0/4)/S	—	-0.8

YEAR	TM LG	G	AB	R	H	2B	3B	HR	RBI	BB-IB	HP	SO	AVG	OBP	SLG	AOPS	ABR	SB-CS	FA	FR	RNG	THR	GAMES AT POSITION	DL	BFW
Fields, Jocko	John Joseph; B10.20.1864 Cork, Ireland; D10.14.1950 Jersey City NJ; BR/TR/5´10˝/160; d5.31; OF(160/20/27)																								
1887	Pit N	43	164	26	44	9	2	0	17	7	2	13	.268	.306	.348	88	-2	7	.933	-0	100	0	O27(7/13/7),C14,1b3/3P	—	-0.2
1888	Pit N	45	169	22	33	7	2	1	15	8	0	19	.195	.232	.278	68	-6	9	.887	-4	118	0	O29(23/2/4),C14,3b3	—	-0.9
1889	Pit N	75	289	41	90	22	5	2	43	29	1	30	.311	.376	.443	141	17	7	.860	-5	64	103	O60(54/2/4),C16	—	1.1
1890	Pit P	126	526	101	148	18	20	9	86	57	3	52	.281	.355	.443	123	16	24	.879	-11	137	104	O80(76/3/1),2b30,C15,S4	—	0.4
1891	Pit N	23	75	10	18	3	0	0	5	10	1	13	.240	.337	.280	82	-1	1	.897	-2	*103*	*104*	C15,S8	—	-0.2
	Phi N	8	30	4	7	2	1	0	5	4	0	2	.233	.324	.367	98	0	0	.769	-4	*90*	*76*	C8	—	-0.3
	Year	31	105	14	25	5	1	0	10	14	1	15	.238	.333	.305	87	-1	1	.857	-6	*98*	*94*	C23,S8	—	-0.5
1892	NY N	21	66	8	18	4	2	0	5	9	1	10	.273	.368	.394	133	3	2	.917	-2	252	0	O11R,C10	—	0.1
Total	6	341	1319	212	358	65	32	12	176	124	8	139	.271	.338	.397	114	27	50	.883	-29	113	72	O207L,C92,2b30,S12,3b4,1b3/P	—	-0.0
Fields, Josh	Joshua Dean; B12.14.1982 Ada OK; BR/TR/6´1˝/215; [ChiA04 1/18]; d9.13; Col Oklahoma St.																								
2006	Chi A	11	20	4	3	2	0	1	2	5-0	0	8	.150	.320	.400	83	0	0-0	1.000	2	145	0	3b6/lfD	0	0.1
Figga, Mike	Michael Anthony; B7.31.1970 Tampa FL; BR/TR/6´0˝/200; [NYA89 44/1140]; d9.16; Col Central Florida CC; [DL 1996 NY A 30]																								
1997	NY A	2	4	0	0	0	0	0	0	0-0	0	3	.000	.000	.000	-99	-1	0-0	1.000	-0	0	0	/CD	0	-0.1
1998	NY A	1	4	1	1	0	0	0	0	0-0	0	1	.250	.250	.250	32	0	0-0	1.000	-0	0	0	/C	0	-0.1
1999	NY A	2	0	0	0	0	0	0	0	0-0	0	0	ø	ø	ø	ø	0	0-0	1.000	0	0	0	C2	0	0.0
	Bal A	41	86	12	19	4	0	1	5	2-0	0	27	.221	.236	.302	38	-8	0-2	.973	-4	81	79	C41	0	-1.1
	Year	43	86	12	19	4	0	1	5	2-0	0	27	.221	.236	.302	38	-8	0-2	.973	-4	80	78	C43	0	-1.1
Total	3	46	94	13	20	4	0	1	5	2-0	0	31	.213	.227	.287	32	-9	0-2	.975	-5	75	73	C45/D	30	-1.3
Figgins, Chone	Desmond Dechone; B1.22.1978 Leary GA; BB/TR/5´8˝/(155–180); [ColN97 4/132]; d8.25; OF(35/244/16)																								
2002	†Ana A	15	12	6	2	1	0	0	1	0-0	0	5	.167	.167	.250	9	-2	2-1	.941	-0	95	102	2b8	0	-0.1
2003	Ana A	71	240	34	71	9	4	0	27	20-0	0	38	.296	.345	.367	93	-2	13-7	1.000	-3	104	52	O47(3/44/0),2b14,S8,D3	0	-0.4
2004	†Ana A	148	577	83	171	22	17	5	60	49-0	0	94	.296	.350	.419	104	2	34-13	.944	-6	94	71	3b92,O57(1/54/2),2b20,S13/D	0	0.1
2005	†LA A	158	642	113	186	25	10	8	57	64-1	0	101	.290	.352	.397	102	2	**62**-17	.989	1	110	90	O72(15/50/8),3b56,2b42,S4,D7	0	1.2
2006	LA A	155	604	93	161	23	8	9	62	65-1	2	100	.267	.336	.376	88	-11	52-16	.982	-4	101	143	O112(16/96/6),3b34,2b9,S2,D6	0	-0.8
Total	5	547	2075	329	591	80	39	22	207	198-2	2	338	.285	.345	.393	97	-11	163-54	.988	-13	104	100	O288C,3b182,2b93,S27,D17	0	0.0
Figueroa, Bien	Bienvenido; B2.7.1964 Santo Domingo, D.R.; BR/TR/5´10˝/170; [StLN86 5/130]; d5.17; Col Florida St.																								
1992	StL N	12	11	1	2	1	0	0	4	1-0	0	2	.182	.250	.273	49	-1	0-0	.938	-1	81	0	S9,2b3	0	-0.1
Figueroa, Jesus	Jesus Maria (Figueroa); B2.20.1957 Santo Domingo, D.R.; BL/TL/5´10˝/160; d4.22																								
1980	Chi N	115	198	20	50	5	0	1	11	14-0	2	16	.253	.308	.293	63	-9	2-1	.979	2	92	222	O57(22/36/1)	0	-0.8
Figueroa, Luis	Luis R.; B2.16.1974 Bayamon, D.R.; BB/TR/5´9˝/(152–165); d6.27																								
2001	Pit N	4	2	0	0	0	0	0	0	0-0	0	0	.000	.000	.000	-98	-1	0-0	1.000	1	224	222	2b3	0	0.0
2006	Tor A	8	9	1	1	1	0	0	0	0-0	0	2	.111	.111	.222	-16	-2	0-0	.900	-1	104	173	2b5,S2	0	-0.2
Total	2	12	11	1	1	1	0	0	0	0-0	0	2	.091	.091	.182	-31	-3	0-0	.933	0	138	187	2b8,S2	0	-0.2
File, Sam	Samuel Lawrence; B5.18.1922 Chester PA; BR/TR/5´11˝/160; d9.10																								
1940	Phi N	7	13	0	1	0	0	0	1	0	0	2	.077	.077	.077	-60	-3	0	.850	0	126	99	S6/3	—	-0.3
Filipowicz, Steve	Stephen Charles "Flip"; B6.28.1921 Donora PA; D2.21.1975 Wilkes–Barre PA; BR/TR/5´8˝/195; d9.3; Col Fordham																								
1944	NY N	15	41	10	8	2	1	0	7	3	0	7	.195	.250	.293	52	-3	0	1.000	-1	94	0	O10(6/4/0)/C	0	-0.4
1945	NY N	35	112	14	23	5	0	2	16	4	1	13	.205	.239	.304	50	-8	0	.935	-3	80	57	O31(27/2/2)	0	-1.3
1948	Cin N	7	26	0	9	0	1	0	3	2	0	1	.346	.393	.423	125	1	0	1.000	0	83	220	O7L	0	0.0
Total	3	57	179	24	40	7	2	2	26	9	1	21	.223	.265	.318	61	-10	0	.961	-4	84	67	O48(40/6/2)/C	0	-1.7
Fimple, Jack	John Joseph; B2.10.1959 Darby PA; BR/TR/6´2˝/(185–195); [CleA80 29/702]; d7.30; Col Humboldt St.																								
1983	†LA N	54	148	16	37	8	1	2	22	11-0	0	39	.250	.300	.358	82	-4	1-0	.989	11	116	136	C54	0	1.0
1984	LA N	12	26	2	5	1	0	0	3	1-0	0	6	.192	.214	.231	27	-3	0-0	.983	-1	83	153	C12	0	-0.3
1986	LA N	13	13	2	1	0	0	0	2	6-1	0	6	.077	.350	.077	32	-1	0-0	1.000	0	133	107	C7/12	0	0.0
1987	Cal A	13	10	1	2	0	0	0	1	1-0	0	2	.200	.273	.200	29	-1	0-0	.913	-1	92	161	C13	0	-0.1
Total	4	92	197	21	45	9	1	2	28	19-1	0	53	.228	.292	.315	70	-9	1-0	.986	10	111	138	C86/21	0	0.6
Finigan, Jim	James Leroy; B8.19.1928 Quincy IL; D5.16.1981 Quincy IL; BR/TR/5´11˝/(170–175); d4.25; Col St. Ambrose																								
1954	Phi A☆	136	487	57	147	25	6	7	51	64	0	66	.302	.381	.421	120	15	2-8	.948	6	107	114	3b136	0	1.8
1955	KC A★	150	545	72	139	30	7	9	68	61-6	3	49	.255	.333	.385	92	-7	1-3	.975	-5	95	93	2b90,3b59	0	-0.6
1956	KC A	91	250	29	54	7	2	2	21	30-1	1	28	.216	.298	.284	55	-16	3-1	.969	1	94	108	2b52,3b32	0	-1.2
1957	Det A	64	174	20	47	4	2	0	17	23-2	1	18	.270	.357	.316	84	-3	1-1	.954	1	103	98	3b59,2b3	0	-0.3
1958	SF N	23	25	3	5	2	0	0	1	3-1	1	5	.200	.310	.280	59	-1	0-0	.917	-2	86	93	2b8,3b4	0	-0.3
1959	Bal A	48	119	14	30	6	0	1	10	9-0	0	10	.252	.300	.328	75	-4	1-0	.959	2	99	75	3b42,2b6,S2	0	-0.2
Total	6	512	1600	195	422	74	17	19	168	190-10	6	176	.264	.342	.367	92	-16	8-13	.948	2	108	105	3b332,2b159,S2	0	-0.8
Finley, Bob	Robert Edward; B11.25.1915 Ennis TX; D1.2.1986 W.Covina CA; BR/TR/6´1˝/200; d7.4; Col SMU																								
1943	Phi N	28	81	9	21	2	0	1	7	4	0	10	.259	.294	.321	81	-2	0	.962	2	*89*	*160*	C24	0	0.1
1944	Phi N	94	281	18	70	11	1	1	21	12	5	25	.249	.292	.306	71	-11	1	.967	-2	*103*	*89*	C74	0	-0.9
Total	2	122	362	27	91	13	1	2	28	16	5	35	.251	.292	.309	73	-13	1	.966	-1	*100*	*106*	C98	0	-0.8
Finley, Steve	Steven Allen; B3.12.1965 Union City TN; BL/TL/6´2˝/(175–195); [BalA87 13/325]; d4.3; Col Southern Illinois																								
1989	Bal A	81	217	35	54	5	2	2	25	15-1	1	30	.249	.298	.318	76	-7	17-3	.986	-2	102	24	O76(14/23/41),D3	52	-0.8
1990	Bal A	142	464	46	119	16	4	3	37	32-3	2	53	.256	.304	.328	80	-13	22-9	.977	2	112	52	O133(21/44/73),D2	0	-1.3
1991	Hou N	159	596	84	170	28	10	8	54	42-5	2	65	.285	.331	.406	113	9	34-18	.985	2	99	151	O153(1/124/69)	0	1.0
1992	Hou N	**162**	607	84	177	29	13	5	55	58-6	3	63	.292	.355	.407	120	16	44-9	.993	1	104	92	O160C	0	2.4
1993	Hou N	142	545	69	145	15	**13**	8	44	28-1	3	65	.266	.304	.385	86	-14	19-6	.988	3	98	**178**	O140C	19	-0.7
1994	Hou N	94	373	64	103	16	5	11	33	28-0	2	52	.276	.329	.434	102	0	13-7	.982	1	96	184	O92C	20	0.2
1995	SD N	139	562	104	167	23	8	10	44	59-5	3	62	.297	.366	.420	110	8	36-12	.977	-5	93	113	O138C	0	0.9
1996	†SD N	161	655	126	195	45	9	30	95	56-5	4	87	.298	.354	.531	136	32	22-8	.982	-2	101	84	O160C	0	3.3
1997	SD N★	143	560	101	146	26	5	28	92	43-2	3	92	.261	.313	.475	111	5	15-3	.989	6	108	152	O140C	16	1.5
1998	†SD N	159	619	92	154	40	6	14	67	45-0	3	103	.249	.301	.401	89	-12	12-3	.981	1	101	130	O157C	0	-0.7
1999	†Ari N	156	590	100	156	32	10	34	103	63-7	3	94	.264	.336	.525	113	9	8-4	.995	-0	106	60	O155C/D	0	1.0
2000	Ari N★	152	539	100	151	27	5	35	96	65-7	8	87	.280	.361	.544	121	16	12-6	.992	-2	99	117	O148C,D2	0	1.6
2001	†Ari N	140	495	66	136	27	4	14	73	47-9	1	67	.275	.337	.430	91	-7	11-7	.994	-1	103	89	O131C/P	0	-0.6
2002	†Ari N	150	505	82	145	24	4	25	89	65-7	3	73	.287	.370	.499	115	12	16-4	.994	0	107	58	O144C	0	1.6
2003	Ari N	147	516	82	148	24	**10**	22	70	57-4	6	94	.287	.363	.500	113	10	15-8	.982	-7	87	131	O140C	0	0.4
2004	Ari N	104	404	61	111	16	1	23	48	40-1	1	52	.275	.338	.490	104	2	8-4	.991	-5	90	101	O103C	0	-0.1
	†LA N	58	224	31	59	12	0	13	46	21-0	0	30	.263	.324	.491	109	2	1-3	.993	-0	108	0	O55C/D	0	0.2
	Year	162	628	92	170	28	1	36	94	61-1	1	82	.271	.333	.490	106	4	9-7	.992	-5	96	66	O158C/D	0	0.1
2005	†LA A	112	406	41	90	20	3	12	54	26-3	3	71	.222	.271	.374	72	-18	8-4	.985	1	104	101	O104C,D5	23	-1.4
2006	SF N	139	426	66	105	21	12	6	40	46-2	2	55	.246	.320	.394	82	-12	7-0	.997	1	104	91	O130C	0	-0.8
Total	18	2540	9303	1434	2531	446	124	303	1165	836-68	53	1295	.272	.333	.444	105	38	320-118	.988	-7	101	105	O2459(36/2288/183),D14/P	130	7.7
Finley, Bill	William James; B10.4.1863 New York NY; D10.6.1912 Asbury Park NJ; 5´3˝/170; d7.12; Col Columbia/Manhattan																								
1886	NY N	13	44	2	8	0	0	0	5	1	—	8	.182	.200	.182	17	-4	2	.800	-2	0	0	O8(0/7/1),C8	—	-0.5
Finn, Neal	Cornelius Francis "Mickey"; B1.24.1904 Brooklyn NY; D7.7.1933 Allentown PA; BR/TR/5´11˝/168; d4.21																								
1930	Bro N	87	273	42	76	13	0	3	30	26	4	18	.278	.350	.359	73	-11	3	.948	-5	92	138	2b81	—	-1.2
1931	Bro N	118	413	46	113	22	2	0	45	21	3	42	.274	.314	.337	75	-14	2	.975	0	97	93	2b112	—	-0.7
1932	Bro N	65	189	22	45	5	2	0	14	11	1	15	.238	.284	.286	55	-12	2	.933	4	118	95	3b50,2b2/S	—	-0.7
1933	Phi N	51	169	15	40	4	1	0	13	10	2	14	.237	.287	.272	54	-10	2	.964	1	108	107	2b51	—	-0.7
Total	4	321	1044	125	274	44	5	3	102	68	10	89	.262	.314	.323	67	-47	9	.964	-1	98	111	2b246,3b50/S	—	-3.3

YEAR	TM LG	G	AB	R	H	2B	3B	HR	RBI	BB-IB	HP	SO	AVG	OBP	SLG	AOPS	ABR	SB-CS	FA	FR	RNG	THR	GAMES AT POSITION	DL	BFW
FINNEY, HAL	Harold Wilson; B7.30.1905 Lafayette AL; D12.20.1991 Lafayette AL; BR/TR/5´11˝/170; d6.24; b–Lou																								
1931	Pit N	10	26	2	8	1	0	0	2	0	1	1	.308	.333	.346	84	-1	1	1.000	0	*109*	*54*	C6	—	0.0
1932	Pit N	31	33	14	7	3	0	0	4	3	1	4	.212	.297	.303	63	-2	0	.971	1	*77*	*54*	C11	—	0.0
1933	Pit N	56	133	17	31	4	1	1	18	3	0	19	.233	.250	.301	57	-8	0	.993	-2	*75*	*62*	C47	—	-0.8
1934	Pit N	5	0	3	0	0	0	0	0	0	1	0	ø	1.000	ø	188	0	0	ø	0	*0*	*0*	/C	—	0.0
1936	Pit N	21	35	3	0	0	0	0	3	0	0	8	.000	.000	.000	-98	-10	0	.956	0	*87*	*88*	C14	—	-0.9
Total	5	123	227	39	46	8	1	1	27	6	3	32	.203	.233	.260	37	-21	1	.983	-0	*81*	*64*	C79	—	-1.7
FINNEY, LOU	Louis Klopsche; B8.13.1910 Buffalo AL; D4.22.1966 Lafayette AL; BL/TR/6´0˝/180; d9.12; Def 1943–45; b–Hal																								
1931	Phi A	9	24	7	9	0	1	0	3	6	1	1	.375	.516	.458	149	2	0-0	1.000	1	124	134	O8R	—	0.3
1933	Phi A	74	240	26	64	12	2	3	32	13	1	17	.267	.307	.371	78	-8	1-3	.947	2	112	106	O63(17/1/46)	—	-1.0
1934	Phi A	92	272	32	76	11	4	1	28	14	0	17	.279	.315	.360	77	-11	4-3	.943	-0	104	70	O54(12/4/40),1b15	—	-1.4
1935	Phi A	109	410	45	112	11	6	0	31	18	2	18	.273	.307	.329	65	-23	7-2	.943	-1	102	82	O76(5/0/72),1b18	—	-2.8
1936	Phi A	151	653	100	197	26	10	1	41	47	3	22	.302	.351	.377	81	-20	7-9	.990	-5	80	95	1b78,O73(22/21/32)	—	-3.4
1937	Phi A	92	379	53	95	14	9	1	20	20	0	16	.251	.288	.343	59	-26	2-5	.989	-4	104	89	1b50,O39(2/37/0)/2	—	-3.4
1938	Phi A	122	454	61	125	21	12	10	48	39	0	25	.275	.333	.441	94	-7	5-8	.990	-5	59	59	1b64,O46(19/21/6)	—	-2.0
1939	Phi A	9	22	1	3	0	0	0	1	2	0	0	.136	.208	.136	-10	-4	0-0	1.000	0	112	0	O4(0/3/1)	—	-0.4
	Bos A	95	249	43	81	18	3	1	46	24	0	11	.325	.385	.434	105	2	2-5	.986	-5	60	101	1b32,O24(3/16/5)	—	-0.7
	Year	104	271	44	84	18	3	1	47	26	0	11	.310	.370	.410	96	-1	2-5	.986	-5	60	101	1b32,O28(3/19/6)	—	-1.1
1940	Bos A★	130	534	73	171	31	15	5	73	33	0	13	.320	.360	.463	107	4	5-2	.975	-1	100	167	O69R,1b51	—	-0.5
1941	Bos A	127	497	83	143	24	10	4	53	38	1	17	.288	.340	.400	93	-6	2-5	.945	-4	98	80	O92(1/0/91),1b24	0	-1.9
1942	Bos A	113	397	58	113	16	7	3	61	29	1	11	.285	.335	.383	98	-2	3-3	.976	-1	99	108	O95(3/1/92),1b2	0	-1.0
1944	Bos A	68	251	37	72	11	2	0	32	23	0	7	.287	.347	.347	100	0	1-0	.987	-5	65	101	1b59,O2(1/0/1)	0	-0.8
1945	Bos A	2	2	0	0	0	0	0	0	0	0	1	.000	.000	.000	-98	-1	0-0	ø	0	—	—	/H	0	-0.1
	StL A	57	213	24	59	8	4	2	22	21	1	6	.277	.345	.380	105	1	0-0	.986	0	100	131	O36(24/0/13),1b22/3	0	-0.2
	Year	59	215	24	59	8	4	2	22	21	1	7	.274	.342	.377	103	1	0-0	.986	0	100	131	O36(24/0/13),1b22/3	0	-0.3
1946	StL A	16	30	0	9	0	0	0	3	2	0	4	.300	.344	.300	77	-1	0-0	.938	0	106	205	O7(4/0/3)	0	-0.1
1947	Phi N	4	4	0	0	0	0	0	0	0	0	0	.000	.000	.000	-99	-1	0	ø	0	—	—	/H	0	-0.1
Total	15	1270	4631	643	1329	203	85	31	494	329	10	186	.287	.336	.388	88	-101	39-45	.961	-26	102	95	O688(113/104/479),1b415/32	0	-19.5
FIORE, MIKE	Michael Gary Joseph; B10.11.1944 Brooklyn NY; BL/TL/6´0˝/(180–185); d9.21																								
1968	Bal A	6	17	2	1	0	0	0	0	4-0	1	4	.059	.273	.059	5	-2	0-0	.943	-0	110	238	1b5/lf	0	-0.3
1969	KC A	107	339	53	93	14	1	12	35	84-4	2	63	.274	.420	.428	136	22	4-4	.988	12	159	75	1b91,O13(3/8/2)	0	2.7
1970	KC A	25	72	6	13	2	0	0	4	13-0	0	24	.181	.306	.208	44	-5	1-1	.986	1	118	70	1b20	0	-0.6
	Bos A	41	50	5	7	0	0	0	4	8-1	0	4	.140	.254	.140	12	-6	0-0	1.000	0	133	45	1b17,O2(1/0/1)	0	-0.7
	Year	66	122	11	20	2	0	0	8	21-1	0	28	.164	.285	.180	30	-11	1-1	.991	1	122	63	1b37,O2(1/0/1)	0	-1.3
1971	Bos A	51	62	9	11	2	0	1	6	12-1	0	14	.177	.311	.258	58	-3	0-3	1.000	-0	91	105	1b12	0	-0.5
1972	StL N	17	10	0	1	0	0	0	1	2-0	0	3	.100	.250	.100	3	-1	0-0	1.000	-0	0	270	1b6/rf	0	-0.2
	SD N	7	6	0	0	0	0	0	0	1-1	0	3	.000	.143	.000	-61	-1	0-0	ø	0	—	—	/H	0	-0.1
	Year	24	16	0	1	0	0	0	1	3-1	0	6	.063	.211	.063	-20	-2	0-0	1.000	-0	0	270	1b6/rf	0	-0.3
Total	5	254	556	75	126	18	1	13	50	124-7	3	115	.227	.369	.333	96	4	5-8	.988	12	144	81	1b151,O17(5/8/4)	0	0.3
FIORENTINO, JEFF	Jeffrey Philip; B4.14.1983 Pembrroke Pines FL; BL/TR/6´1˝/(180–190); [BalA04 3/79]; d5.12; Col Florida Atlantic																								
2005	Bal A	13	44	7	11	2	0	1	5	2-0	0	10	.250	.277	.364	71	-2	1-0	1.000	-0	107	0	O12C	0	-0.2
2006	Bal A	19	39	8	10	2	0	0	7	7-0	1	3	.256	.375	.308	85	0	1-0	1.000	3	119	346	O17(15/1/1),D2	0	0.2
Total	2	32	83	15	21	4	0	1	12	9-0	1	13	.253	.326	.337	78	-2	2-0	1.000	3	113	182	O29(15/13/1),D2	0	0.0
FIROVA, DAN	Daniel Michael; B10.16.1956 Refugio TX; BR/TR/6´0˝/185; [SeaA80*S2/39]; d9.1; Col Texas–Pan American																								
1981	Sea A	13	2	0	0	0	0	0	0	0-0	0	1	.000	.000	.000	-96	-1	0-0	1.000	-1	0	123	C13	0	-0.1
1982	Sea A	3	5	0	0	0	0	0	0	0-0	0	0	.000	.000	.000	-97	-1	0-0	.900	0	0	0	C3	0	-0.1
1988	Cle A	1	0	0	0	0	0	0	0	0-0	0	0	ø	ø	ø	ø	0	0-0	ø	-0	0	0	/C	0	0.0
Total	3	17	7	0	0	0	0	0	0	0-0	0	1	.000	.000	.000	-96	-2	0-0	.944	-1	0	75	C17	0	-0.2
FISCHER, WILLIAM	William Charles; B3.2.1891 New York NY; D9.4.1945 Richmond VA; BL/TR/6´0˝/174; d6.9																								
1913	Bro N	62	165	16	44	9	4	1	12	10	1	5	.267	.313	.388	97	-1	0-1	.974	-2	96	100	C51	—	0.1
1914	Bro N	43	105	12	27	1	2	0	8	8	0	12	.257	.310	.305	81	-3	1	.958	0	*90*	*115*	C30	—	0.0
1915	Chi F	105	292	30	96	15	4	4	50	24	2	19	.329	.384	.449	142	12	5	.972	-4	*115*	*94*	C80	—	1.5
1916	Chi N	65	179	15	35	9	2	1	14	11	1	8	.196	.246	.285	57	-9	2	.973	0	101	111	C56	—	-0.5
	Pit N	42	113	11	29	7	1	1	6	10	1	3	.257	.323	.363	109	2	1	.974	1	91	109	C35	—	0.7
	Year	107	292	26	64	16	3	2	20	21	2	11	.219	.276	.315	76	-8	3	.973	1	97	110	C91	—	0.2
1917	Pit N	95	245	25	70	9	2	3	25	27	1	19	.286	.359	.376	121	7	11	.961	-11	*71*	*99*	C69,1b2	—	0.2
Total	5	412	1099	109	301	50	15	10	115	90	6	66	.274	.332	.374	107	8	20-1	.969	-15	*95*	*103*	C321,1b2	—	2.0
FISCHLIN, MIKE	Michael Thomas; B9.13.1955 Sacramento CA; BR/TR/6´1˝/165; [NYA75 7/163]; d9.3; Col Cal St.–Sacramento																								
1977	Hou N	13	15	0	3	0	0	0	0	0-0	0	2	.200	.200	.200	8	-2	0-0	1.000	-1	111	37	S12	0	-0.2
1978	Hou N	44	86	3	10	1	0	0	0	4-1	1	9	.116	.165	.128	-18	-14	1-0	.928	-9	75	66	S41	0	-2.2
1980	Hou N	1	1	0	0	0	0	0	0	0-0	0	1	.000	.000	.000	-99	0	0-0	1.000	-0	0	0	/S	0	0.0
1981	Cle A	22	43	3	10	1	0	0	5	3-0	0	6	.233	.277	.256	56	-2	3-2	.955	-2	81	73	S19/2	0	-0.3
1982	Cle A	112	276	34	74	12	1	0	21	34-0	2	36	.268	.351	.319	86	-4	9-5	.970	-8	97	80	S101,3b8,2b6/C	0	-0.2
1983	Cle A	95	225	31	47	5	2	2	23	26-0	2	32	.209	.294	.276	56	-13	9-2	.965	6	100	106	2b71,S15,3b4/D	0	-0.2
1984	Cle A	85	133	17	30	4	2	1	14	12-0	0	20	.226	.290	.308	64	-7	2-2	.981	2	100	99	2b55,3b17,S15	0	-0.2
1985	Cle A	73	60	12	12	4	1	0	2	5-0	0	7	.200	.262	.300	54	-4	0-1	.990	10	120	120	2b31,S22,1b6,3b3,D5	0	0.7
1986	NY A	71	102	9	21	2	0	0	3	8-0	0	29	.206	.261	.225	35	-9	0-1	.955	-4	103	87	S42,2b27	0	-1.1
1987	Atl N	1	0	0	0	0	0	0	0	0-0	0	0	ø	ø	ø	ø	0	0-0	ø	0	—	—	/R	0	0.0
Total	10	517	941	109	207	29	6	3	68	92-1	5	142	.220	.291	.273	57	-55	24-13	.959	-7	95	83	S268,2b191,3b32,1b6,D6/C	0	-3.7
FISHBURN, SAM	Samuel E.; B5.15.1893 Haverhill MA; D4.11.1965 Bethlehem PA; BR/TR/5´9˝/157; d5.30; Col Lehigh																								
1919	StL N	9	6	0	2	1	0	0	2	0	0	0	.333	.333	.500	158	0	0	1.000	0	0	0	/12	—	0.1
FISHEL, JOHN	John Alan; B11.8.1962 Fullerton CA; BR/TR/5´11˝/185; [HouN85 9/222]; d7.14; Col Cal St.–Fullerton																								
1988	Hou N	19	26	1	6	0	0	1	2	3-0	0	6	.231	.310	.346	92	0	0-0	1.000	-1	29	0	O6(5/0/2)	0	-0.2
FISHER, GUS	August Harris; B10.21.1885 Pottsboro TX; D4.8.1972 Portland OR; BL/TR/5´10˝/175; d4.18																								
1911	Cle A	70	203	20	53	6	3	0	12	7	5	—	.261	.302	.320	73	-8	6	.956	2	*92*	*118*	C58/1	—	-0.1
1912	NY A	4	10	1	1	0	0	0	0	0	0	—	.100	.100	.100	-40	-2	0	1.000	1	*98*	*95*	C4	—	-0.1
Total	2	74	213	21	54	6	3	0	12	7	5	—	.254	.293	.310	68	-10	6	.958	2	*92*	*117*	C62/1	—	-0.2
FISHER, CHARLES	Charles; d6.15																								
1889	Lou AA	1	2	0	1	0	0	0	0	0	0	0	.500	.500	.500	189	0	0	ø	-0	0	0	/lf	—	0.0
FISHER, CHARLES	Charles G. (b Charles G. Fish); B3.10.1852 Boxford MA; D2.18.1917 Eagle AK; BL/TR/5´8˝/143; d6.7																								
1884	KC U	10	40	3	8	2	0	0	—	0	—	—	.200	.200	.250	41	-4	—	.711	0	134	0	3b9/S	—	-0.3
	CP U	1	3	1	2	0	0	0	—	1	—	—	.667	.750	.667	336	1	—	.500	-1	0	0	/3	—	0.0
	Year	11	43	4	10	2	0	0	—	1	—	—	.233	.250	.279	68	-3	—	.702	-1	123	0	3b10/S	—	-0.3
FISHER, SHOWBOAT	George Aloys; B1.16.1899 Wesley IA; D5.15.1994 St.Cloud MN; BL/TR/5´10˝/170; d4.24																								
1923	Was A	13	23	4	6	2	0	0	2	4	0	3	.261	.370	.348	95	0	0-0	.750	0	75	318	O5R	—	0.0
1924	Was A	15	41	7	9	1	0	0	6	6	0	6	.220	.319	.244	48	-3	2-0	.933	-1	94	0	O11R	—	-0.4
1930	†StL N	92	254	49	95	18	6	8	61	25	1	21	.374	.432	.587	139	16	4	.962	-2	95	94	O67(24/0/42)	—	0.9
1932	StL A	18	22	2	4	0	0	0	2	2	0	5	.182	.250	.182	13	-3	0-0	1.000	0	112	0	O5L	—	-0.3
Total	4	138	340	62	114	21	6	8	71	37	1	35	.335	.402	.503	119	10	6-0	.946	-3	94	95	O88(29/0/58)	—	0.2
FISHER, GEORGE	George Cresse; B8.20.1855 Wilmington DE; D1.29.1937 Oakland CA; BL; d8.9																								
1884	Cle N	6	24	2	3	0	0	0	0	0	—	3	.125	.125	.125	-20	-3	—	.897	-2	76	88	2b6/C	—	-0.5
	Wil U	8	29	0	2	0	0	0	—	0	—	—	.069	.069	.069	-56	-6	—	.818	-1	0	0	O6(0/6/1),S2	—	-0.7
Total	1	14	53	2	5	0	0	0	0	0	—	3	.094	.094	.094	-40	-9	—	.818	-3	0	0	O6(0/6/1),2b6,S2/C	—	-1.2

YEAR	TM LG	G	AB	R	H	2B	3B	HR	RBI	BB-IB	HP	SO	AVG	OBP	SLG	AOPS	ABR	SB-CS	FA	FR	RNG	THR	GAMES AT POSITION	DL	BFW
FISHER, HARRY	Harry Devereux; B1.3.1926 Newbury ON, Can.; D9.20.1981 Waterloo ON, Can.; BL/TR/6´0˝/180; d9.16; ▲																								
1951	Pit N	3	3	0	0	0	0	0	0	0	0	0	.000	.000	.000	-97	-1	0-0	ø	0	—	—	/H	0	-0.1
1952	Pit N	15	15	0	5	1	0	0	1	0	0	3	.333	.333	.400	100	1	0-0	1.000	-1	31	0	P8	0	0.0
Total	2	18	18	0	5	1	0	0	1	0	0	3	.278	.278	.333	66	0	0-0	1.000	-1	31	0	P8	0	-0.1
FISHER, RED	John Gus; B6.22.1887 Pittsburgh PA; D1.31.1940 Louisville KY; BL/TR/5´9˝/176; d4.25																								
1910	StL A	23	72	5	9	2	1	0	3	8	1	—	.125	.222	.181	28	-6	5	.935	-1	91	82	O19(14/0/5)	—	-0.9
FISHER, NEWT	Newton "Ike"; B6.28.1871 Nashville TN; D2.28.1947 Norwood Park IL; BR/TR/5´9.5˝/171; d5.17; b–Bob																								
1898	Phi N	9	26	0	3	1	0	0	0	0	1	—	.115	.148	.154	-14	-4	1	.844	-1	*114*	37	C8/3	—	-0.4
FISHER, BOB	Robert Taylor; B11.3.1886 Nashville TN; D8.4.1963 Jacksonville FL; BR/TR/5´9.5˝/170; d6.3; b–Newt																								
1912	Bro N	82	257	27	60	10	3	0	26	14	0	32	.233	.273	.296	58	-16	7	.917	-11	94	83	S74/23	—	-2.2
1913	Bro N	132	474	42	124	11	10	4	54	10	1	43	.262	.278	.352	77	-17	16-16	.923	-20	90	**128**	S131	—	-3.1
1914	Chi N	15	50	5	15	2	2	0	5	3	0	4	.300	.340	.420	126	1	2	.943	-1	105	61	S15	—	0.2
1915	Chi N	147	568	70	163	22	5	5	53	30	3	51	.287	.326	.370	110	6	9-20	.933	-19	95	56	S145	—	-1.0
1916	Cin N	61	136	9	37	4	3	0	11	8	0	14	.272	.313	.346	104	0	7	.905	-8	91	72	S29,2b6/lf	—	-0.7
1918	StL N	63	246	36	78	11	3	2	20	15	0	11	.317	.356	.411	138	11	7	.979	16	119	121	2b63	—	3.0
1919	StL N	3	11	0	3	1	0	0	1	0	0	2	.273	.273	.364	96	0	0	.900	0	91	144	2b3	—	0.0
Total	7	503	1742	189	480	61	26	11	170	80	4	157	.276	.309	.359	96	-15	48-36	.925	-42	93	86	S394,2b73/lf3	—	-3.8
FISHER, WILBUR	Wilbur McCullough; B7.18.1894 Green Bottom WV; D10.24.1960 Welch WV; BL/TR/6´0˝/174; d6.13; Col Marshall																								
1916	Pit N	1	1	0	0	0	0	0	0	0	0	0	.000	.000	.000	-99	0	0	ø	0	—	—	/H	—	0.0
FISHER, CHEROKEE	William Charles; B12.1845 Philadelphia PA; D9.26.1912 New York NY; BR/TR/5´9˝/164; d5.6; OF NA(5/14/66); ▲																								
1871	Rok NA	**25**	123	24	28	3	3	1	22	3	—	1	.228	.246	.325	65	-5	1-2	**.927**	4	**147**	**181**	P24,1b2/2	—	0.1
1872	Bal NA	46	225	39	52	10	3	1	36	2	—	5	.231	.238	.316	66	-10	1-1	.761	-5	113	176	P19,O19(0/3/17),3b18	—	-0.9
1873	Ath NA	51	253	50	66	4	3	1	37	4	—	5	.261	.272	.312	67	-12	2-2	.743	4	192	285	O46(1/2/43),P13,2b3/1	—	-0.2
1874	Har NA	52	241	28	54	7	0	0	31	2	—	7	.224	.230	.253	52	-13	2-3	.833	-4	76	154	P39,O12(0/8/6),3b7,S2	—	-0.6
1875	Phi NA	41	177	26	41	3	1	0	11	1	—	6	.232	.236	.260	69	-6	4-3	.896	-3	71	34	P41,O5(4/1/0)	—	-0.1
1876	Cin N	35	129	12	32	1	0	0	4	0	—	8	.248	.248	.256	80	-2	—	.793	-3	75	0	P28,O11(0/7/4)/S1	—	-0.2
1877	Chi N	1	4	0	0	0	0	0	0	0	—	2	.000	.000	.000	-89	-1	—	.667	-0	127	0	/3	—	-0.1
1878	Pro N	1	3	0	0	0	0	0	0	0	—	0	.000	.000	.000	-99	0	—	1.000	-0	54	0	/P	—	0.0
Total	5NA	215	1019	167	241	27	10	3	137	12	—	24	.237	.245	.291	64	-46	10-11	.862	-4	91	110	P136,O82R,3b25,2b4,1b3,S2	—	-1.7
Total	3	37	136	12	32	1	0	0	4	0	—	10	.235	.235	.243	68	-3	—	.803	-3	74	0	P29,O11(0/7/4)/31S	—	-0.3
FISK, CARLTON	Carlton Ernest "Pudge"; B12.26.1947 Bellows Falls VT; BR/TR/6´2˝/(200–235); [BosA67*1/4]; d9.18; HF2000; Col New Hampshire																								
1969	Bos A	2	5	0	0	0	0	0	0	0-0	0	2	.000	.000	.000	-96	-1	0-0	1.000	-1	0	0	/C	0	-0.3
1971	Bos A	14	48	7	15	2	1	2	6	1-0	0	10	.313	.327	.521	127	1	0-0	.975	-1	147	134	C14	0	0.1
1972	Bos A★	131	457	74	134	28	**9**	22	61	52-6	4	83	.293	.370	.538	159	33	5-2	.984	6	105	95	C131	0	5.1
1973	Bos A★	135	508	65	125	21	0	26	71	37-2	10	99	.246	.309	.441	103	1	7-2	.983	11	134	72	C131,D3	0	1.9
1974	Bos A✱	52	187	36	56	12	1	11	26	24-2	2	23	.299	.383	.551	156	14	5-1	.980	6	128	79	C50,D2	119	2.3
1975	†Bos A	79	263	47	87	14	4	10	52	27-4	2	32	.331	.395	.529	147	16	4-3	.979	5	138	76	C71,D6	77	2.4
1976	Bos A★	134	487	76	124	17	5	17	58	56-3	6	71	.255	.336	.415	107	5	12-5	.984	19	**129**	86	C133/D	0	3.3
1977	Bos A★	152	536	106	169	26	3	26	102	75-3	9	85	.315	.402	.521	136	29	7-6	.987	12	163	80	C151	0	4.6
1978	Bos A★	157	571	94	162	39	5	20	88	71-6	7	83	.284	.366	.475	123	19	7-2	.980	11	98	80	C154/lfD	0	3.9
1979	Bos A	91	320	49	87	23	2	10	42	10-0	6	38	.272	.304	.450	96	-3	3-0	.982	-5	94	40	D42,C39/lf	37	-0.6
1980	Bos A★	131	478	73	138	25	3	18	62	36-6	**13**	62	.289	.353	.467	117	11	11-5	.983	-4	99	78	C115,O5L,1b3,3b3,D5	0	1.2
1981	Chi A★	96	338	44	89	12	0	7	45	38-3	12	37	.263	.354	.361	109	6	3-2	.990	3	79	95	C92/13lf	0	1.3
1982	Chi A★	135	476	66	127	17	3	14	65	46-7	6	60	.267	.336	.403	102	2	17-2	.994	4	93	100	C133,1b2	0	1.5
1983	†Chi A	138	488	85	141	26	4	26	86	46-3	6	88	.289	.355	.518	132	21	9-6	.991	5	102	78	C133,D2	0	3.1
1984	Chi A	102	359	54	83	20	1	21	43	26-4	5	60	.231	.289	.468	101	0	6-0	.987	-7	90	79	C90,D5	22	-0.2
1985	Chi A★	153	543	85	129	23	1	37	107	52-12	17	81	.238	.320	.488	113	9	17-9	.989	7	92	117	C130,D28	0	2.1
1986	Chi A	125	457	42	101	11	0	14	63	22-2	6	92	.221	.263	.337	61	-27	2-4	.991	9	73	108	C71,O31L,D22	0	-1.8
1987	Chi A	135	454	68	116	22	1	23	71	39-8	8	72	.256	.321	.460	102	1	1-4	.990	12	116	89	C122,1b9,O2L,D7	0	1.5
1988	Chi A	76	253	37	70	8	1	19	50	37-9	5	40	.277	.377	.542	155	19	0-0	.995	-1	83	90	C74	78	2.2
1989	Chi A	103	375	47	110	25	2	13	68	36-8	3	60	.293	.356	.475	136	18	1-0	**.993**	-6	103	98	C90,D13	51	1.7
1990	Chi A	137	452	65	129	21	0	18	65	61-8	7	73	.285	.378	.451	134	22	7-2	.994	12	99	117	C116,D14	0	4.1
1991	Chi A★	134	460	42	111	25	0	18	74	32-4	7	86	.241	.299	.413	97	-3	1-2	.993	9	104	**132**	C106,D13,1b12	0	0.9
1992	Chi A	62	188	12	43	4	1	3	21	23-5	1	38	.229	.313	.309	76	-6	3-0	.993	-1	86	109	C54,D2	59	-0.4
1993	Chi A	25	53	2	10	0	0	1	4	2-0	1	11	.189	.228	.245	29	-6	0-1	1.000	-6	44	37	C25	0	-1.1
Total	24	2499	8756	1276	2356	421	47	376	1330	849-105	143	1386	.269	.341	.457	116	181	128-58	.988	98	107	91	C2226,D166,O41L,1b27,3b4	443	38.8
FISLER, WES	Weston Dickson "Icicle"; B7.5.1841 Camden NJ; D12.25.1922 Philadelphia PA; TR/5´6˝/137; d5.20																								
1871	Ath NA	**28**	147	43	41	8	2	0	16	3	—	2	.279	.293	.361	88	-2	6-3	**.972**	1	24	80	1b26,2b2	—	0.0
1872	Ath NA	**47**	244	49	85	13	3	0	48	4	—	4	.348	.359	.426	140	11	3-0	.889	7	108	92	2b47	—	1.1
1873	Ath NA	44	218	44	75	11	4	1	41	2	—	2	.344	.350	.445	124	5	3-1	.855	2	107	136	2b36,1b10	—	0.3
1874	Ath NA	37	180	26	59	12	1	0	22	0	—	1	.328	.328	.406	123	4	2-0	.953	5	194	210	1b28,2b9/rf	—	0.7
1875	Ath NA	58	268	54	74	13	3	0	31	4	—	4	.276	.287	.347	107	1	1-4	.958	2	66	145	1b46,O10(0/1/9),2b5	—	0.2
1876	Phi N	59	278	42	80	15	1	1	30	2	—	4	.288	.293	.360	117	5	—	.911	2	133	100	O24(0/15/9),2b21,1b14/S	—	0.6
Total	5NA	214	1057	216	334	57	13	1	158	13	—	13	.316	.324	.397	118	19	15-8	.951	16	92	142	1b110,2b99,O11(0/1/10)	—	2.3
FITZBERGER, CHARLIE	Charles Casper; B2.13.1904 Baltimore MD; D1.25.1965 Baltimore MD; BL/TL/6´1.5˝/170; d9.11																								
1928	Bos N	7	7	0	2	0	0	0	0	0	0	3	.286	.286	.286	52	-1	0	ø	0	—	—	/H	—	-0.1
FITZGERALD, DENNIS	Dennis S.; B3.1865 , England; D10.16.1936 New Haven CT; 5´10˝/160; d4.17																								
1890	Phi AA	2	8	0	2	0	0	0	0	0	0	—	.250	.250	.250	48	-1	0	.667	-2	67	0	S2	—	-0.2
FITZ GERALD, ED	Edward Raymond; B5.21.1924 Santa Ynez CA; BR/TR/6´0˝/(175–185); d4.19; C5; Col St. Marys (CA)																								
1948	Pit N	102	262	31	70	9	3	1	35	32	1	37	.267	.349	.336	84	-5	3	.961	-3	*104*	*100*	C96	0	-0.3
1949	Pit N	75	160	16	42	7	0	2	18	8	1	27	.262	.302	.344	71	-7	1	.974	-2	*125*	*115*	C56	0	-0.6
1950	Pit N	6	15	1	1	1	0	0	0	0	0	3	.067	.067	.133	-47	-3	0	.950	-0	*119*	*106*	C5	0	-0.3
1951	Pit N	55	97	8	22	6	0	0	13	7	1	10	.227	.286	.289	53	-6	1-1	.965	-1	*106*	*94*	C38	0	-0.7
1952	Pit N	51	73	4	17	1	0	1	7	7	0	15	.233	.300	.288	62	-4	0-2	1.000	-1	*80*	*82*	C18,3b2	0	-0.5
1953	Pit N	6	17	2	2	1	0	0	1	0	0	2	.118	.118	.176	-25	-3	0-0	1.000	-1	*49*	173	C5	0	-0.4
	Was A	88	288	23	72	13	0	3	39	19	1	34	.250	.299	.326	70	-13	2-1	.989	0	*103*	*79*	C85	0	-0.8
1954	Was A	115	360	33	104	13	5	4	40	33	2	22	.289	.349	.386	108	3	0-1	.973	-14	*86*	*68*	C107	0	-0.6
1955	Was A	74	236	28	56	3	1	4	19	25-0	3	23	.237	.317	.309	73	-9	0-1	.982	-7	*83*	*115*	C72	0	-1.3
1956	Was A	64	148	15	45	8	0	2	12	20-1	0	16	.304	.387	.399	108	3	0-0	.974	-2	*85*	*116*	C50	0	0.3
1957	Was A	45	125	14	34	8	0	1	13	10-1	1	9	.272	.331	.360	90	-2	2-0	.963	-8	53	49	C37	0	-0.8
1958	Was A	58	114	7	30	3	0	0	11	8-0	0	15	.263	.309	.289	68	-5	0-0	.970	-6	33	47	C21,1b5	0	-1.1
1959	Was A	19	62	5	12	3	0	0	5	4-0	0	8	.194	.242	.242	34	-6	0-0	1.000	1	100	178	C16	0	-0.4
	Cle A	49	129	12	35	6	1	1	4	12-1	2	14	.271	.343	.357	96	0	0-0	.978	-2	101	179	C45	30	0.0
	Year	68	191	17	47	9	1	1	9	16-1	2	22	.246	.311	.319	76	-6	0-0	.984	-1	101	179	C61	0	-0.4
Total	12	807	2086	199	542	82	10	19	217	185-3	12	235	.260	.323	.336	80	-57	9-6	.975	-45	*92*	*98*	C651,1b5,3b2	30	-7.5
FITZGERALD, HOWIE	Howard Chumney "Lefty"; B5.16.1902 Eagle Lake TX; D2.27.1959 Matthews TX; BL/TL/5´11.5˝/163; d9.17; Col Texas																								
1922	Chi N	10	24	3	8	1	0	0	4	3	0	2	.333	.407	.375	101	0	1-0	.818	-1	81	0	O6R	—	-0.1
1924	Chi N	7	19	1	3	0	0	0	2	0	0	2	.158	.158	.158	-15	-3	0-0	1.000	-1	64	0	O5(0/1/4)	—	-0.4
1926	Bos A	31	97	11	25	2	0	0	8	5	0	7	.258	.294	.278	52	-7	1-4	.882	-3	66	99	O23(21/0/2)	—	-1.3
Total	3	48	140	15	36	3	0	0	14	8	0	11	.257	.297	.279	52	-10	2-4	.878	-5	69	70	O34(21/1/12)	—	-1.8

THE BATTER REGISTER

YEAR	TM LG	G	AB	R	H	2B	3B	HR	RBI	BB-IB	HP	SO	AVG	OBP	SLG	AOPS	ABR	SB-CS	FA	FR	RNG	THR	GAMES AT POSITION	DL	BFW
FITZGERALD, JUSTIN	Justin Howard; B6.26.1891 San Mateo CA; D1.18.1945 San Mateo CA; BL/TR/5´8˝/160; d6.20; Col Santa Clara																								
1911	NY A	16	37	6	10	1	0	0	6	4	0	—	.270	.341	.297	74	-1	4	1.000	-1	73	94	O9L	—	-0.2
1918	Phi N	66	133	21	39	8	0	0	6	13	1	6	.293	.361	.353	110	2	3	.966	-4	84	48	O59(34/2/19)	—	-0.3
Total	2	82	170	27	49	9	0	0	12	17	1	6	.288	.356	.341	102	1	7	.971	-4	82	56	O68(43/2/19)	—	-0.5
FITZGERALD, MATTY	Matthew William; B8.31.1880 Albany NY; D9.22.1949 Albany NY; BR/TR/6´0˝/185; d9.15																								
1906	NY N	4	6	2	4	0	0	0	2	0	0	—	.667	.667	.667	309	1	1	1.000	0	*161*	*0*	C3	—	0.2
1907	NY N	7	15	1	2	1	0	0	1	0	0	—	.133	.133	.200	4	-2	0	.952	-1	*129*	*93*	C6	—	-0.2
Total	2	11	21	3	6	1	0	0	3	0	0	—	.286	.286	.333	91	-1	1	.967	-1	*138*	*66*	C9	—	0.0
FITZGERALD, MIKE	Michael Patrick; B3.28.1964 Savannah GA; BR/TR/6´1˝/200; [StLN84 S1/20]; d6.23; Col Middle Georgia JC																								
1988	StL N	13	46	4	9	1	0	0	1	0-0	1	9	.196	.213	.217	23	-5	0-0	.990	-1	54	128	1b12	0	-0.8
FITZGERALD, MIKE	Michael Roy; B7.13.1960 Long Beach CA; BR/TR/5´11˝/(185–198); [NYN78 6/133]; d9.13; OF(15/0/15)																								
1983	NY N	8	20	1	2	0	0	1	2	3-1	0	6	.100	.217	.250	29	-2	0-0	.957	1	52	195	C8	0	-0.1
1984	NY N	112	360	20	87	15	1	2	33	24-7	1	71	.242	.288	.306	69	-15	1-0	**.995**	7	100	99	C107	0	-0.4
1985	Mon N	108	295	25	61	7	1	5	34	38-12	2	55	.207	.297	.288	69	-12	5-3	.987	-7	75	81	C108	0	-1.5
1986	Mon N	73	209	20	59	13	1	6	37	27-6	1	34	.282	.364	.440	122	7	3-2	.993	-4	69	78	C71	65	0.6
1987	Mon N	107	287	32	69	11	0	3	36	42-7	1	54	.240	.338	.310	71	-11	3-4	.981	-7	70	67	C104/12	14	-1.5
1988	Mon N	63	155	17	42	6	1	5	23	19-0	0	22	.271	.347	.419	114	3	2-2	.979	2	57	81	C47,O4(3/0/1)	0	0.7
1989	Mon N	100	290	33	69	18	2	7	42	35-3	2	61	.238	.322	.386	100	1	3-4	.984	-7	72	103	C77,3b8,O6L	0	-0.3
1990	Mon N	111	313	36	76	18	1	9	41	60-2	2	60	.243	.365	.393	113	9	8-1	.990	-4	74	85	C98,O6(1/0/5)	0	1.2
1991	Mon N	71	198	17	40	5	2	4	28	22-4	0	35	.202	.278	.308	67	-9	4-2	.994	2	62	112	C54,1b3,O3R	49	-0.5
1992	Cal A	95	189	19	40	2	0	6	17	22-0	0	34	.212	.294	.317	70	-8	2-2	.990	-6	93	96	C74,O11(5/0/6),3b3,1b2/2D	0	-1.2
Total	10	848	2316	220	545	95	9	48	293	292-42	9	432	.235	.321	.346	87	-37	31-20	.988	-24	76	89	C748,O30L,3b11,1b6,2b2/D	128	-3.0
FITZGERALD, RAY	Raymond Francis; B12.5.1904 Chicopee MA; D9.6.1977 Westfield MA; BR/TR/5´9˝/168; d4.18																								
1931	Cin N	1	1	0	0	0	0	0	0	0	0	0	.000	.000	.000	-99	0	0	ø	0	—	—	/H	—	0.0
FITZMAURICE, SHAUN	Shaun Earle; B8.25.1942 Worcester MA; BR/TR/6´0˝/180; d9.9; Col Notre Dame																								
1966	NY N	9	13	2	2	0	0	0	0	2-0	0	6	.154	.267	.154	21	-1	1-0	1.000	1	126	417	O5(2/3/0)	0	0.0
FITZPATRICK, ED	Edward Henry; B12.9.1889 Lewistown PA; D10.23.1965 Bethlehem PA; BR/TR/5´8˝/165; d4.17; Mil 1918																								
1915	Bos N	105	303	54	67	19	3	0	24	43	14	36	.221	.344	.304	101	4	13-8	.967	-1	94	102	2b71,O29(0/7/22)	—	0.3
1916	Bos N	83	216	17	46	8	0	1	18	15	5	26	.213	.280	.264	70	-7	5	.950	-10	81	97	2b46,O28(2/3/23)	—	-2.0
1917	Bos N	63	178	20	45	8	4	0	17	12	5	22	.253	.318	.343	109	2	4	.929	-11	86	25	2b22,O19(4/6/7),3b15	—	-1.0
Total	3	251	697	91	158	35	7	1	59	70	24	84	.227	.319	.301	94	-1	22-8	.956	-22	88	88	2b139,O76(6/16/52),3b15	—	-2.7
FITZSIMMONS, TOM	Thomas William; B4.6.1890 Oakland CA; D12.20.1971 Oakland CA; BR/TR/6´1˝/190; d6.12; Col St. Marys (CA)																								
1919	Bro N	4	4	1	0	0	0	0	0	1	0	2	.000	.200	.000	-36	-1	0	.500	-1	36	0	3b4	—	-0.2
FLACK, MAX	Max John; B2.5.1890 Belleville IL; D7.31.1975 Belleville IL; BL/TL/5´7˝/148; d4.16																								
1914	Chi F	134	502	66	124	15	3	2	39	51	6	48	.247	.324	.301	75	-25	37	.973	-2	98	85	O133(112/0/23)	—	-3.5
1915	Chi F	141	523	88	164	20	14	3	45	40	2	21	.314	.365	.423	129	10	37	.969	5	97	137	O138(61/0/81)	—	0.9
1916	Chi N	141	465	65	120	14	3	3	20	42	0	43	.258	.320	.320	87	-6	24-19	**.991**	3	91	138	O136R	—	-1.3
1917	Chi N	131	447	65	111	18	7	0	21	51	0	34	.248	.325	.320	91	-3	17	.947	-2	97	97	O117(40/6/77)	—	-1.3
1918	†Chi N	123	478	74	123	17	10	4	41	56	6	19	.257	.343	.360	111	8	17	.978	-1	94	102	O121R	—	0.0
1919	Chi N	116	469	71	138	20	4	6	35	34	3	13	.294	.346	.392	121	12	18	.986	-0	94	109	O116R	—	0.6
1920	Chi N	135	520	85	157	30	6	4	49	52	7	15	.302	.373	.406	121	17	13-19	.967	-5	90	99	O132(0/1/131)	—	0.1
1921	Chi N	133	572	80	172	31	4	6	37	32	4	15	.301	.342	.400	96	-3	17-11	**.989**	-0	97	106	O130R	—	-1.4
1922	Chi N	17	54	7	12	1	0	0	6	2	0	4	.222	.250	.241	27	-6	2-1	.933	-2	101	0	O15R	—	-0.8
	StL N	66	267	46	78	12	1	2	21	31	1	11	.292	.368	.367	95	-1	3-5	.968	-3	94	62	O66(0/1/65)	—	-1.0
	Year	83	321	53	90	13	1	2	27	33	1	15	.280	.349	.346	83	-7	5-6	.961	-5	95	51	O81(0/1/80)	—	-1.8
1923	StL N	128	505	82	147	16	9	3	28	41	3	16	.291	.348	.376	93	-5	7-8	.951	-5	100	58	O121R	—	-2.0
1924	StL N	67	209	31	55	11	3	2	21	21	0	5	.263	.330	.373	90	-3	3-5	.971	2	99	162	O52R	—	-0.5
1925	StL N	79	241	23	60	7	8	0	28	21	0	9	.249	.309	.344	65	-13	5-3	.991	1	100	116	O59(5/0/54)	—	-1.5
Total	12	1411	5252	783	1461	212	72	35	391	474	32	253	.278	.342	.366	99	-18	200-71	.972	-10	96	103	O1336(218/8/1122)	—	-11.7
FLAGER, WALLY	Walter Leonard; B11.3.1921 Chicago Heights IL; D12.16.1990 Keizer OR; BL/TR/5´11˝/160; d4.17																								
1945	Cin N	21	52	5	11	1	0	0	6	8	0	5	.212	.317	.231	55	-3	0	.933	-4	85	58	S15	0	-0.6
	Phi N	49	168	21	42	4	1	2	15	17	1	15	.250	.323	.321	82	-4	1	.946	5	105	91	S48/2	0	0.4
	Year	70	220	26	53	5	1	2	21	25	1	20	.241	.321	.300	75	-7	1	.943	0	101	84	S63/2	0	-0.2
FLAGSTEAD, IRA	Ira James "Pete"; B9.22.1893 Montague MI; D3.13.1940 Olympia WA; BR/TR/5´9˝/165; d7.20; Mil 1918																								
1917	Det A	4	4	0	0	0	0	0	0	0	0	1	.000	.000	.000	-99	-1	0	ø	-0	0	0	O2R	—	-0.1
1919	Det A	97	287	43	95	22	3	5	41	35	7	39	.331	.416	.481	155	23	6	.951	1	93	127	O83R	—	2.0
1920	Det A	110	311	40	73	13	5	3	35	37	1	27	.235	.318	.338	76	-11	3-4	.967	3	105	113	O82(1/6/75)	—	-1.3
1921	Det A	85	259	40	79	16	2	0	31	21	6	21	.305	.371	.382	93	-2	8-4	.903	-7	90	33	S55,O12(6/2/5),2b8/3	—	-0.3
1922	Det A	44	91	21	28	5	3	3	8	14	2	16	.308	.411	.527	148	7	0-1	.967	0	96	132	O32(8/9/15)	—	0.5
1923	Det A	1	1	0	0	0	0	0	0	0	0	0	.000	.000	.000	-99	0	0-0	ø	0	—	—	/H	—	0.0
	Bos A	109	382	55	119	23	4	8	53	37	5	26	.312	.380	.455	119	10	7-10	.965	14	101	213	O102(0/3/99)/S	—	1.3
	Year	110	383	55	119	23	4	8	53	37	5	26	.311	.379	.454	118	10	7-10	.965	14	101	213	O102(0/3/99)/S	—	1.3
1924	Bos A	149	560	106	172	35	7	5	43	77	11	41	.307	.401	.421	112	14	10-13	.975	-10	94	64	O144(0/143/1)	—	-0.4
1925	Bos A	148	572	84	160	38	2	6	61	63	5	30	.280	.356	.385	88	-9	5-6	.976	14	108	154	O144C	—	-0.2
1926	Bos A	98	415	65	124	31	7	3	31	36	6	22	.299	.363	.429	110	6	4-6	.982	2	96	133	O98C	—	0.2
1927	Bos A	131	466	63	133	26	8	4	69	57	9	25	.285	.374	.401	103	4	12-2	**.986**	4	97	145	O129(0/128/1)	—	0.4
1928	Bos A	140	510	84	148	41	4	1	39	60	1	23	.290	.366	.392	101	3	12-9	.973	2	99	123	O135C	—	-0.1
1929	Bos A	14	36	9	11	2	0	0	3	5	0	1	.306	.390	.361	97	0	1-3	.955	-1	97	0	O13(13/1/0)	—	-0.2
	Was A	18	39	5	7	1	0	0	9	4	0	5	.179	.256	.205	20	-5	1-0	.971	3	103	353	O11(1/10/0)	—	-0.2
	Year	32	75	14	18	3	0	0	12	9	0	6	.240	.321	.280	57	-5	2-3	.965	2	103	0	O24(14/11/0)	—	-0.4
	Pit N	26	50	8	14	2	1	0	6	4	0	2	.280	.333	.360	70	-2	1	1.000	-0	103	0	O9(6/1/2)	—	-0.3
1930	Pit N	44	156	21	39	7	4	2	21	17	0	9	.250	.324	.385	70	-8	1	.961	-1	89	141	O40(21/15/5)	—	-1.0
Total	13	1218	4139	644	1202	262	50	40	450	467	53	288	.290	.370	.407	103	29	71-58	.974	25	99	134	O1036(56/695/288),S56,2b8/3	—	0.3
FLAHERTY, JOHN	John Timothy; B10.21.1967 New York NY; BR/TR/6´1˝/(195–205); [BosA88 25/641]; d4.12; Col George Washington																								
1992	Bos A	35	66	3	13	2	0	0	2	3-0	0	7	.197	.229	.227	27	-7	0-0	.982	-6	107	83	C34	0	-1.2
1993	Bos A	13	25	3	3	2	0	0	2	2-0	1	6	.120	.214	.200	11	-3	0-0	1.000	-2	67	146	C13	0	-0.5
1994	Det A	34	40	2	6	1	0	0	4	1-0	0	11	.150	.167	.175	-10	-7	0-1	1.000	0	69	111	C33/D	0	-0.5
1995	Det A	112	354	39	86	22	1	11	40	18-0	3	47	.243	.284	.404	77	-13	0-0	.982	-11	88	80	C112	0	-1.6
1996	Det A	47	152	18	38	12	0	4	23	8-1	1	25	.250	.290	.408	74	-6	1-0	.981	-9	122	79	C46	0	-1.1
	†SD N	72	264	22	80	12	0	9	41	9-1	2	36	.303	.327	.451	108	2	2-3	.990	-7	96	111	C72	0	-0.1
1997	SD N	129	439	38	120	21	1	9	46	33-7	0	62	.273	.323	.387	91	-7	4-4	.987	-26	71	120	C124	0	-2.5
1998	TB A	91	304	21	63	11	0	3	24	22-0	1	46	.207	.261	.273	39	-28	0-5	.993	8	129	105	C91	25	-1.5
1999	TB A	117	446	53	124	19	0	14	71	19-0	6	64	.278	.310	.415	83	-13	0-2	.993	9	95	**147**	C115/D	0	0.3
2000	TB A	109	394	36	103	15	0	10	39	20-2	0	57	.261	.296	.376	70	-20	0-0	.993	-2	76	111	C108	0	-1.3
2001	TB A	78	248	20	59	17	1	4	29	10-1	1	33	.238	.269	.363	66	-13	1-0	.986	-6	89	77	C78	0	-1.4
2002	TB A	76	281	27	73	20	0	4	33	15-0	1	50	.260	.296	.374	79	-8	2-2	.992	-6	85	136	C75	0	-0.9
2003	†NY A	40	105	16	28	8	0	4	14	4-1	1	19	.267	.297	.457	97	-1	0-0	.991	-6	93	116	C40	0	-0.5
2004	NY A	47	127	11	32	9	0	6	16	5-2	1	25	.252	.286	.465	91	-2	0-2	.989	1	83	77	C46	0	0.1
2005	†NY A	47	127	10	21	5	0	2	11	6-0	1	26	.165	.206	.252	22	-15	0-0	.994	7	59	122	C45/1	0	-0.5
Total	14	1047	3372	319	849	176	3	80	395	175-15	19	514	.252	.290	.377	73	-141	10-19	.989	-57	90	109	C1032,D2/1	25	-13.2
FLAHERTY, MARTIN	Martin John; B9.24.1853 Worcester MA; D6.10.1920 Providence RI; BL/TL; d8.18																								
1881	Wor N	1	2	0	0	0	0	0	0	0	—	2	.000	.000	.000	-95	0	—	.000	-1	0	0	/O(1/1/0)	—	-0.1

YEAR	TM LG	G	AB	R	H	2B	3B	HR	RBI	BB-IB	HP	SO	AVG	OBP	SLG	AOPS	ABR	SB-CS	FA	FR	RNG	THR	GAMES AT POSITION	DL	BFW
FLAHERTY, PAT	Patrick Henry; B1.31.1866 St.Louis MO; D1.28.1946 Chicago IL; BR/5´9˝/166; d7.11																								
1894	Lou N	39	150	15	43	5	3	0	15	9	1	7	.287	.331	.360	71	-7	2	.852	-2	99	117	3b39	—	-0.6
FLAHERTY, PATSY	Patrick Joseph; B6.29.1876 Mansfield PA; D1.23.1968 Alexandria LA; BL/TL/5´8˝/165; d9.8; ▲																								
1899	Lou N	7	24	3	5	1	1	0	6	3	0	—	.208	.296	.333	73	-1	0	.692	-1	71	0	P5,O2R	—	-0.1
1900	Pit N	4	9	0	1	0	0	0	0	1	0	—	.111	.200	.111	-13	-1	0	1.000	1	181	0	P4	—	0.0
1903	Chi A	40	102	7	14	4	0	0	5	5	0	—	.137	.178	.176	7	-3	4	.914	2	121	241	P40	—	0.0
1904	Chi A	5	12	1	4	1	0	0	0	4	0	—	.333	.500	.417	199	3	0	.880	1	129	0	P5	—	0.0
	Pit N	36	104	9	22	3	4	2	19	8	0	—	.212	.268	.375	95	-1	0	.965	4	132	146	P29,O2C	—	0.2
1905	Pit N	30	76	7	15	4	2	0	4	3	0	—	.197	.228	.303	56	-4	0	.894	2	133	69	P27,O2(0/1/1)	—	0.0
1907	Bos N	41	115	9	22	3	2	2	11	2	1	—	.191	.212	.304	62	-6	1	.907	3	126	**316**	P27,O8(6/0/2)	—	-0.1
1908	Bos N	32	86	8	12	0	2	0	5	6	0	—	.140	.196	.186	22	0	2	.961	2	114	152	P31	—	0.0
1910	Phi N	2	2	0	1	0	0	0	0	0	0	0	.500	.500	.500	186	0	0	ø	0	0	0	/Pcf	—	0.0
1911	Bos N	38	94	9	27	3	2	2	20	8	0	11	.287	.343	.426	106	0	2	.933	-3	74	82	O19(1/11/7),P4	—	-0.3
Total	9	235	624	53	123	19	13	6	70	40	1	<u>11</u>	.197	.247	.298	63	-13	9	.921	10	124	173	P173,O34(7/15/12)	—	-0.3
FLAIR, AL	Albert Dell "Broadway"; B7.24.1916 New Orleans LA; D7.26.1988 New Orleans LA; BL/TL/6´4˝/195; d9.6; Mil 1942–45; Col Louisiana St.																								
1941	Bos A	10	30	3	6	2	1	0	2	1	0	1	.200	.226	.333	45	-3	1-1	1.000	-0	85	86	1b8	0	-0.3
FLANAGAN, ED	Edward J. "Sleepy"; B9.15.1861 Lowell MA; D11.10.1926 Lowell MA; TR/6´1˝/190; d4.16																								
1887	Phi AA	19	80	12	20	5	0	1	10	3	1	—	.250	.286	.350	77	-3	3	.948	-1	82	100	1b19	—	-0.4
1889	Lou AA	23	88	11	22	7	3	0	8	7	0	11	.250	.305	.398	101	0	1	.953	-1	116	71	1b23	—	-0.3
Total	2	42	168	23	42	12	3	1	18	10	1	<u>11</u>	.250	.296	.375	89	-3	4	.951	-2	101	84	1b42	—	-0.7
FLANAGAN, STEAMER	James Paul; B4.20.1881 Kingston PA; D4.21.1947 Wilkes–Barre PA; BL/TL/6´1˝/185; d9.25; Col Notre Dame																								
1905	Pit N	7	25	7	7	1	1	0	3	1	0	—	.280	.308	.400	108	0	3	1.000	0	0	0	O5C	—	0.0
FLANNERY, JOHN	John Michael; B1.25.1957 Long Beach CA; BR/TR/6´3˝/173; [AnaA75 9/193]; d9.2																								
1977	Chi A	7	2	1	0	0	0	0	0	1-0	0	1	.000	.333	.000	0	0	0-0	1.000	0	117	140	S4/3D	0	0.0
FLANNERY, TIM	Timothy Earl; B9.29.1957 Tulsa OK; BL/TR/5´11˝/(170–181); [SDN78 6/135]; d9.3; C7; Col Chapman																								
1979	SD N	22	65	2	10	0	1	0	4	4-1	2	5	.154	.222	.185	14	-8	0-0	.991	3	113	132	2b21	0	-0.4
1980	SD N	95	292	15	70	12	0	0	25	18-4	0	30	.240	.283	.281	62	-15	2-2	.988	3	105	110	2b53,3b41	0	-1.2
1981	SD N	37	67	4	17	4	1	0	6	2-1	0	4	.254	.268	.343	81	-2	1-0	.967	-4	78	196	3b15,2b7	0	-0.6
1982	SD N	122	379	40	100	11	7	0	30	30-10	2	32	.264	.317	.330	88	-7	1-0	.974	-19	92	83	2b104,3b5,S2	0	-2.1
1983	SD N	92	214	24	50	7	3	3	19	20-8	5	23	.234	.309	.336	83	-5	2-2	.969	6	114	197	3b52,2b21,S7	0	0.1
1984	†SD N	86	128	24	35	3	3	2	10	12-1	3	17	.273	.347	.391	107	1	4-1	.944	-6	99	55	2b22,3b14,S14	0	-0.4
1985	SD N	126	384	50	108	14	3	1	40	58-1	9	39	.281	.386	.341	107	7	2-5	.977	-19	89	106	2b121/3	0	-0.8
1986	SD N	134	368	48	103	11	2	3	28	54-4	5	61	.280	.378	.345	103	4	3-6	.993	3	96	96	2b108,3b23,S8	0	1.1
1987	SD N	106	276	23	63	5	1	0	20	42-4	2	30	.228	.332	.254	61	-14	2-4	.986	-0	100	90	2b84,3b8,S2	25	-1.2
1988	SD N	79	170	16	45	5	4	0	19	24-1	4	32	.265	.365	.341	107	3	3-2	.972	-5	93	121	3b51,2b2/S	24	-0.2
1989	SD N	73	130	9	30	5	0	0	8	13-0	0	20	.231	.299	.269	64	-6	2-0	.920	1	110	77	3b33/2	15	-0.5
Total	11	972	2473	255	631	77	25	9	209	277-35	32	293	.255	.335	.317	86	-42	22-22	.982	-38	96	95	2b544,3b243,S34	64	-6.2
FLANNIGAN, CHARLIE	Charles Joseph; B12.31.1891 Oakland CA; D1.8.1930 San Francisco CA; BR/TR/6´0˝/175; d7.9																								
1913	StL A	4	3	0	0	0	0	0	0	1	0	0	.000	.250	.000	-26	0	0	ø	-0	0	0	/3lf	—	-0.1
FLASKAMPER, ROY	Raymond Harold "Flash"; B10.31.1901 St.Louis MO; D2.3.1978 San Antonio TX; BB/TR/5´7˝/140; d8.16																								
1927	Chi A	26	95	12	21	5	0	0	6	3	2	8	.221	.260	.274	40	-9	0-0	.962	-1	96	80	S25	—	-0.7
FLEET, FRANK	Frank H.; B1848 New York NY; D6.13.1900 New York NY; d10.18; ▲																								
1871	Mut NA	1	6	1	2	0	0	0	1	0	—	0	.333	.333	.333	101	0	0-0	1.000	1	322	0	/P	—	0.0
1872	Eck NA	13	53	9	12	1	0	0	6	0	—	2	.226	.226	.245	53	-2	1-0	.800	2	107	56	3b10,2b2,O2(0/1/1)	—	0.0
1873	Res NA	22	89	11	23	3	0	0	10	1	—	3	.258	.267	.292	71	-2	0-2	.808	3	105	88	S9,2b8,P3,3b3/1	—	-0.1
1874	Atl NA	22	97	18	22	0	0	0	10	1	—	1	.227	.235	.227	55	-4	1-0	.759	-5	—	—	C13,2b11/lf	—	-0.7
1875	StL NA	4	16	1	1	0	0	0	1	0	—	0	.063	.063	.063	-62	-2	0-0	.900	0	124	479	P3/3cf	—	-0.1
	Atl NA	26	111	13	25	2	0	0	9	1	—	1	.225	.232	.243	75	-2	0-0	.719	-9	—	—	C11,2b10,S9,P2/3	—	-1.0
	Year	30	127	14	26	2	0	0	10	1	—	1	.205	.211	.220	57	-4	0-0	.719	-8	—	—	C11,2b10,S9,P5,3b2/cf	—	-1.1
Total	5NA	88	372	53	85	6	0	0	37	3	—	7	.228	.235	.245	60	-12	2-2	.772	-7	—	—	2b31,C24,S18,3b15,P9,O4(1/2/1)/1	—	-1.9
FLEITAS, ANGEL	Angel Felix Husta; B11.10.1914 Los Abreus, Cuba; D7.10.2006 Miami FL; BR/TR/5´9˝/160; d7.5																								
1948	Was A	15	13	1	1	0	0	0	1	3	0	5	.077	.250	.077	-11	-2	0-2	.952	1	132	0	S7	0	-0.2
FLEMING, LES	Leslie Harvey "Moe"; B8.7.1915 Singleton TX; D3.5.1980 Cleveland TX; BL/TL/5´10˝/185; d4.22; Col St. Marys (TX)																								
1939	Det A	8	16	0	0	0	0	0	1	0	0	4	.000	.000	.000	-93	-5	0-0	1.000	0	113	0	O3(1/0/2)	—	-0.5
1941	Cle A	2	8	0	2	1	0	0	2	0	0	0	.250	.250	.375	67	0	0-0	1.000	-0	70	171	1b2	0	-0.1
1942	Cle A	**156**	548	71	160	27	4	14	82	106	6	57	.292	.412	.432	146	40	6-8	**.993**	-7	84	116	1b156	0	1.7
1945	Cle A	42	140	18	46	10	2	3	22	11	1	5	.329	.382	.493	160	10	0-0	.938	-1	102	68	O33R,1b5	0	0.8
1946	Cle A	99	306	40	85	17	5	8	42	50	2	42	.278	.383	.444	140	18	1-0	.984	3	113	87	1b80/rf	0	1.8
1947	Cle A	103	281	39	68	14	2	4	43	53	0	42	.242	.362	.349	101	2	0-0	.989	3	115	123	1b77	0	0.3
1949	Pit N	24	31	0	8	0	2	0	7	6	1	2	.258	.395	.387	108	0	0	1.000	-1	0	105	1b5	0	-0.1
Total	7	434	1330	168	369	69	15	29	199	226	10	152	.277	.386	.417	131	65	7-<u>8</u>	.990	-3	98	110	1b325,O37(1/0/36)	0	3.9
FLEMING, TOM	Thomas Vincent "Sleuth"; B11.20.1873 Philadelphia PA; D12.26.1957 Boston MA; BL/TL/5´11˝/155; d9.19																								
1899	NY N	22	77	9	16	1	1	0	4	1	0	—	.208	.218	.247	28	-8	1	.909	1	178	0	O22C	—	-0.8
1902	Phi N	5	16	2	6	0	0	0	2	1	0	—	.375	.412	.375	143	1	0	1.000	1	396	0	O5R	—	0.1
1904	Phi N	3	6	0	0	0	0	0	0	0	0	—	.000	.000	.000	-99	-1	0	1.000	1	994	0	/rf	—	-0.1
Total	3	30	99	11	22	1	1	0	6	2	0	—	.222	.238	.253	39	-8	1	.920	2	243	0	O28(0/22/6)	—	-0.8
FLETCHER, ART	Arthur; B1.5.1885 Collinsville IL; D2.6.1950 Los Angeles CA; BR/TR/5´10.5˝/170; d4.15; M5/C19																								
1909	NY N	33	98	7	21	0	1	0	6	1	2	—	.214	.238	.235	46	-7	1	.893	-1	93	116	S22,2b7,3b6	—	-0.7
1910	NY N	51	125	12	28	2	1	0	13	4	0	9	.224	.248	.256	47	-9	9	.895	-5	82	90	S22,2b11,3b11	—	-1.4
1911	†NY N	112	326	73	104	17	8	1	37	30	14	27	.319	.400	.429	128	13	20	.926	5	102	88	S74,3b21,2b13	—	2.4
1912	†NY N	129	419	64	118	17	9	1	57	16	14	29	.282	.330	.372	89	-8	16	.927	15	108	131	S126,2b2/3	—	1.5
1913	†NY N	136	538	76	160	20	9	4	71	24	**15**	35	.297	.345	.390	109	5	32-18	.932	-6	102	96	S136	—	1.0
1914	NY N	135	514	62	147	26	8	2	79	22	**13**	37	.286	.332	.379	115	8	15	.922	6	105	101	S135	—	2.5
1915	NY N	149	562	59	143	17	7	3	74	6	14	36	.254	.280	.326	88	-11	12-18	.936	**35**	**118**	127	S149	—	3.3
1916	NY N	133	500	53	143	23	8	3	66	13	**14**	36	.286	.323	.382	122	11	15	.940	22	**114**	105	S133	—	4.7
1917	†NY N	151	557	70	145	24	5	4	56	23	**19**	28	.260	.312	.343	104	3	12	**.956**	28	**114**	119	S151	—	4.5
1918	NY N	**124**	468	51	123	20	2	0	47	18	**15**	26	.263	.311	.314	93	-4	12	**.959**	**25**	**113**	116	S124	—	3.3
1919	NY N	127	488	54	135	20	5	3	54	9	7	28	.277	.300	.357	98	-3	6	.944	25	**119**	95	S127	—	3.4
1920	NY N	41	171	21	44	7	2	0	24	1	5	15	.257	.282	.322	74	-6	3-2	.914	1	112	94	S41	—	-0.3
	Phi N	102	379	36	112	25	7	4	38	15	4	28	.296	.329	.430	112	5	4-6	.958	14	109	93	S102	—	2.6
	Year	143	550	57	156	32	9	4	62	16	9	43	.284	.315	.396	100	-1	7-8	.945	14	110	93	S143	—	2.3
1922	Phi N	110	396	46	111	20	5	7	53	21	5	14	.280	.325	.409	80	-12	3-2	.939	6	**111**	102	S106	—	0.4
Total	13	1533	5541	684	1534	238	77	32	675	203	141	<u>348</u>	.277	.319	.365	100	-15	160-<u>46</u>	.939	169	110	108	S1448,3b39,2b33	—	27.2
FLETCHER, DARRIN	Darrin Glen; B10.3.1966 Elmhurst IL; BL/TR/6´1˝/(195–205); [LAN87 6/144]; d9.10; f–Tom; Col Illinois																								
1989	LA N	5	8	1	4	0	0	1	2	1-0	0	0	.500	.556	.875	307	2	0-0	1.000	0	0	0	C5	0	0.3
1990	LA N	2	1	0	0	0	0	0	0	0-0	0	1	.000	.000	.000	-99	0	0-0	ø	-0	0	0	/C	0	-0.1
	Phi N	9	22	3	3	1	0	0	1	1-0	0	5	.136	.174	.182	-2	-3	0-0	1.000	-1	59	0	C6	0	-0.4
	Year	11	23	3	3	1	0	0	1	1-0	0	6	.130	.167	.174	-6	-3	0-0	1.000	-2	58	0	C7	0	-0.5
1991	Phi N	46	136	5	31	8	0	1	12	5-0	0	15	.228	.255	.309	58	-8	0-1	.992	0	99	80	C45	0	-0.6
1992	Mon N	83	222	13	54	10	2	2	26	14-3	2	28	.243	.289	.333	78	-7	0-2	.995	-7	63	109	C69	34	-1.2
1993	Mon N	133	396	33	101	20	1	9	60	34-2	6	40	.255	.320	.379	83	-9	0-0	.988	-6	73	73	C127	0	-0.7
1994	Mon N★	94	285	28	74	18	1	10	57	25-4	3	23	.260	.314	.435	95	-2	0-0	.996	-8	79	79	C81	0	-0.5

YEAR	TM LG	G	AB	R	H	2B	3B	HR	RBI	BB-IB	HP	SO	AVG	OBP	SLG	AOPS	ABR	SB-CS	FA	FR	RNG	THR	GAMES AT POSITION	DL	BFW
1995	Mon N	110	350	42	100	21	1	11	45	32-1	4	23	.286	.351	.446	105	3	0-1	.994	7	82	127	C98	0	1.5
1996	Mon N	127	394	41	105	22	0	12	57	27-4	6	42	.266	.321	.414	91	-6	0-0	.992	-11	70	88	C112	0	-1.0
1997	Mon N	96	310	39	86	20	1	17	55	17-3	5	35	.277	.323	.513	117	6	1-1	.994	0	87	56	C83	15	1.1
1998	Tor A	124	407	37	115	23	1	9	52	25-7	6	39	.283	.328	.410	92	-5	0-0	.991	6	75	92	C121/D	15	0.8
1999	Tor A	115	412	48	120	26	0	18	80	26-0	6	47	.291	.339	.485	106	3	0-0	.997	-15	85	87	C113	31	-0.4
2000	Tor A	122	416	43	133	19	1	20	58	20-3	5	45	.320	.355	.514	114	7	1-0	.994	-9	83	79	C117,D2	22	0.5
2001	Tor A	134	416	36	94	20	0	11	56	24-4	6	43	.226	.274	.353	63	-23	0-1	.995	-8	109	90	C129/D	0	-2.2
2002	Tor A	45	127	8	28	6	0	3	22	4-0	0	13	.220	.239	.339	51	-9	0-0	.995	-2	69	92	C36,D4	15	-0.9
Total	14	1245	3902	377	1048	214	8	124	583	255-31	49	399	.269	.318	.423	92	-51	2-6	.993	-53	82	87	C1143,D8	132	-3.8
FLETCHER, ELBIE	Elburt Preston; B3.18.1916 Milton MA; D3.9.1994 Milton MA; BL/TL/6´0˝/180; d9.16; Mil 1944–45																								
1934	Bos N	8	4	4	2	0	0	0	0	0	0	2	.500	.500	.500	182	0	1	.875	-0	0	287	/1	—	0.0
1935	Bos N	39	148	12	35	7	1	1	9	7	0	13	.236	.271	.318	63	-8	1	.997	2	117	75	1b39	—	-0.9
1937	Bos N	148	539	56	133	22	4	1	38	56	3	64	.247	.321	.308	79	-15	3	.993	-1	101	110	1b148	—	-3.0
1938	Bos N	147	529	71	144	24	7	6	48	60	4	40	.272	.351	.378	112	9	5	.990	8	**127**	93	1b146	—	0.4
1939	Bos N	35	106	14	26	2	0	0	6	19	1	5	.245	.365	.264	77	-2	1	.986	-6	39	123	1b31	—	-1.1
	Pit N	102	370	49	112	23	4	12	71	48	2	28	.303	.386	.484	134	19	3	.993	-5	82	104	1b101	—	0.5
	Year	137	476	63	138	25	4	12	77	67	3	33	.290	.381	.435	122	17	4	.991	-10	72	108	1b132	—	-0.6
1940	Pit N	147	510	94	139	22	7	16	104	**119**	**9**	54	.273	**.418**	.437	137	34	5	.993	5	**111**	97	1b147	—	2.5
1941	Pit N	151	521	95	150	29	13	11	74	**118**	2	54	.288	**.421**	.457	148	40	5	.991	10	**128**	93	1b151	0	3.6
1942	Pit N	145	506	86	146	22	5	7	57	105	6	60	.289	**.417**	.393	134	29	0	.992	11	**131**	92	1b144	0	2.8
1943	Pit N★	154	544	91	154	24	5	9	70	95	6	49	.283	.395	.395	124	22	1	**.996**	3	107	109	1b154	0	1.8
1946	Pit N	148	532	72	136	25	8	4	66	111	0	37	.256	.384	.355	108	11	4	.995	2	104	78	1b147	0	0.9
1947	Pit N	69	157	22	38	9	1	1	22	29	1	24	.242	.364	.331	83	-2	2	.986	-1	99	86	1b50	0	-0.4
1949	Bos N	122	413	57	108	19	3	11	51	84	8	65	.262	.396	.402	121	17	1	.991	1	**102**	99	1b121	0	1.4
Total	12	1415	4879	723	1323	228	58	79	616	851	42	495	.271	.384	.390	118	154	32	.993	30	110	97	1b1380	0	8.5
FLETCHER, GEORGE	George Horace Elliott; B4.21.1845 Brooklyn NY; D6.18.1879 Brooklyn NY; d6.21																								
1872	Eck NA	2	8	1	2	0	0	0	1	0	—	1	.250	.250	.250	64	0	0-0	.600	-0	0	0	O2R	—	0.0
FLETCHER, FRANK	Oliver Frank; B3.6.1891 Hildreth IL; D10.7.1974 St.Petersburg FL; BR/TR/5´10˝/165; d7.14																								
1914	Phi N	1	1	0	0	0	0	0	0	0	0	1	.000	.000	.000	-94	0	0	ø	0	—	—	/H	—	0.0
FLETCHER, SCOTT	Scott Brian; B7.30.1958 Fort Walton Beach FL; BR/TR/5´11˝/(150–173); [ChiN79 S1/6]; d4.25; Col Georgia Southern																								
1981	Chi N	19	46	6	10	4	0	0	1	2-0	0	4	.217	.250	.304	53	-3	0-0	.972	4	108	131	2b13,S4/3	0	0.2
1982	Chi N	11	24	4	4	0	0	0	1	4-0	0	5	.167	.286	.167	28	-2	1-0	1.000	-1	100	70	S11	0	-0.2
1983	†Chi A	114	262	42	62	16	5	3	31	29-0	2	22	.237	.315	.370	85	-5	5-1	.965	23	116	122	S100,2b12,3b7/D	0	2.7
1984	Chi A	149	456	46	114	13	3	3	35	46-2	8	46	.250	.328	.311	75	-15	10-4	.973	14	107	108	S134,2b28,3b3	0	1.4
1985	Chi A	119	301	38	77	8	1	2	31	35-0	0	47	.256	.332	.309	74	-10	5-5	.934	3	89	97	3b55,S44,2b37,D2	0	-0.4
1986	Tex A	147	530	82	159	34	5	3	50	47-0	4	59	.300	.360	.400	104	4	12-11	.973	6	101	102	S136,3b12,2b11/D	0	2.3
1987	Tex A	156	588	82	169	28	4	5	63	61-3	5	66	.287	.358	.374	94	-3	13-12	.966	12	100	105	S155	0	2.2
1988	Tex A	140	515	59	142	19	4	0	47	62-1	12	34	.276	.364	.328	94	-1	8-5	.983	10	104	101	S139	0	1.9
1989	Tex A	83	314	47	75	14	1	0	22	38-1	2	41	.239	.323	.290	73	-10	1-0	.960	-14	78	86	S81/D	15	-1.8
	Chi A	59	232	30	63	11	1	1	21	26-0	1	19	.272	.344	.341	96	0	1-1	1.000	-5	102	103	2b53,S8	0	-0.3
	Year	142	546	77	138	25	2	1	43	64-1	3	60	.253	.332	.311	83	-10	2-1	.957	-18	76	88	S89,2b53/D	0	-2.1
1990	Chi A	151	509	54	123	18	3	4	56	45-3	3	63	.242	.304	.312	75	-17	1-3	.988	-6	96	**115**	2b151	0	-2.1
1991	Chi A	90	248	14	51	10	1	1	28	17-0	3	26	.206	.262	.266	48	-18	0-2	.992	-9	86	105	2b86,3b4	0	-2.5
1992	Mil A	123	386	53	106	18	3	3	51	30-1	7	33	.275	.335	.360	97	-1	17-10	.992	10	107	119	2b106,S22/3	0	1.3
1993	Bos A	121	480	81	137	31	5	5	45	37-1	5	35	.285	.341	.402	93	-4	16-3	.982	13	111	95	2b116,S2/3D	15	1.6
1994	Bos A	63	185	31	42	9	1	3	11	16-1	2	14	.227	.296	.335	59	-11	8-1	.996	11	107	120	2b53,D4	29	0.3
1995	Det A	67	182	19	42	10	1	1	17	19-0	3	27	.231	.312	.313	64	-9	1-0	1.000	5	107	131	2b63,S3/1D	21	-0.2
Total	15	1612	5258	688	1376	243	38	34	510	514-13	57	541	.262	.332	.342	84	-105	99-58	.971	78	101	104	S839,2b729,3b84,D11/1	80	6.4
FLICK, ELMER	Elmer Harrison; B1.11.1876 Bedford OH; D1.9.1971 Bedford OH; BL/TR/5´9˝/168; d4.26; HF1963																								
1898	Phi N	134	453	84	137	16	13	8	81	86	15	—	.302	.430	.448	158	41	23	.931	6	114	89	O133R	—	3.7
1899	Phi N	127	485	98	166	22	11	2	98	42	11	—	.342	.407	.445	138	27	31	.931	7	124	139	O125R	—	2.5
1900	Phi N	138	545	106	200	32	16	11	**110**	56	16	—	.367	.441	.545	173	**56**	35	.914	1	119	110	O138R	—	**4.5**
1901	Phi N	138	540	112	180	32	17	8	88	52	7	—	.333	.399	.500	157	39	30	.962	14	130	175	O138(1/0/137)	—	4.5
1902	Phi A	11	37	15	11	2	1	0	3	6	3	—	.297	.435	.405	128	2	4	.947	-0	70	0	O11R	—	0.1
	Cle A	110	424	70	126	19	11	2	61	47	3	—	.297	.371	.408	121	13	20	.929	-5	90	69	O110R	—	0.3
	Year	121	461	85	137	21	12	2	64	53	6	—	.297	.377	.408	121	15	24	.930	-5	88	63	O121R	—	0.4
1903	Cle A	**140**	523	81	155	23	16	2	51	51	8	—	.296	.368	.413	136	25	24	.955	-1	96	78	O140(6/0/134)	—	1.7
1904	Cle A	150	579	97	177	31	17	6	56	51	9	—	.306	.371	.449	160	40	**38**	.955	7	116	120	O145(0/6/139),2b6	—	4.5
1905	Cle A	132	500	72	154	29	**18**	4	64	53	8	—	**.308**	.383	**.462**	**165**	**38**	35	.939	-2	121	91	O131R/2	—	3.3
1906	Cle A	**157**	624	**98**	194	34	**22**	1	62	54	7	—	.311	.372	.441	156	40	**39**	.981	-11	70	111	O150(0/86/65),2b8	—	2.4
1907	Cle A	147	549	80	166	15	**18**	3	58	64	11	—	.302	.386	.412	153	35	41	.956	-1	115	162	O147(1/23/122)	—	3.0
1908	Cle A	9	35	4	8	1	1	0	2	3	0	—	.229	.289	.314	96	0	0	1.000	-0	103	416	O9R	—	-0.1
1909	Cle A	66	235	28	60	10	2	0	15	22	1	—	.255	.322	.315	97	0	9	.958	-2	56	63	O61(1/12/48)	—	-0.6
1910	Cle A	24	68	5	18	2	1	1	7	10	0	—	.265	.359	.368	126	2	1	.955	-2	94	0	O18R	—	-0.1
Total	13	1483	5597	950	1752	268	164	48	756	597	99	—	.313	.389	.445	149	358	330	.947	11	107	113	O1456(9/127/1320),2b15	—	29.7
FLICK, LEW	Lewis Miller "Noisy"; B2.18.1915 Bristol TN; D12.7.1990 Weber City VA; BL/TL/5´9˝/155; d9.28																								
1943	Phi A	1	5	2	3	0	0	0	0	0	0	0	.600	.600	.600	253	1	0-0	1.000	0	117	0	/rf	0	0.1
1944	Phi A	19	35	1	4	0	0	0	2	1	0	2	.114	.139	.114	-28	-6	1-0	1.000	-1	89	0	O6(0/1/5)	0	-0.7
Total	2	20	40	3	7	0	0	0	2	1	0	2	.175	.195	.175	6	-5	1-0	1.000	-1	95	0	O7(0/1/6)	0	-0.6
FLINN, DON	Don Raphael; B11.17.1892 Bluff Dale TX; D3.9.1959 Waco TX; BR/TR/6´1˝/185; d9.2																								
1917	Pit N	14	37	1	11	1	1	0	1	1	0	6	.297	.316	.378	109	0	1	1.000	1	122	77	O12(7/1/4)	—	0.1
FLINT, SILVER	Frank Sylvester; B8.3.1855 Philadelphia PA; D1.14.1892 Chicago IL; BR/TR/6´0˝/180; d5.4; M1																								
1875	RS NA	17	61	4	5	0	0	0	1	1	—	10	.082	.097	.082	-41	-8	2-0	.820	-3	—	—	C16,O2(1/0/1)/3	—	-0.9
1878	Ind N	**63**	254	23	57	7	0	0	18	2	—	15	.224	.230	.252	67	-8	—	.908	-3	—	—	C59,O9(5/0/4)	—	-0.9
1879	Chi N	79	324	46	92	22	6	1	41	6	—	44	.284	.297	.398	120	6	—	.915	5	—	—	C78/rfM	—	1.2
1880	Chi N	74	284	30	46	10	4	0	17	5	—	32	.162	.176	.225	33	-20	—	**.934**	7	—	—	C67,O13(0/4/10)	—	-1.1
1881	Chi N	80	306	46	95	18	0	1	34	6	—	39	.310	.324	.379	115	5	—	.938	-6	—	—	C80,O8R/1	—	0.1
1882	Chi N	81	331	48	83	18	8	4	44	2	—	50	.251	.255	.390	99	-2	—	.935	-1	—	—	C81,O10R	—	0.4
1883	Chi N	85	332	57	88	23	4	0	32	3	—	69	.265	.272	.358	83	-8	—	.877	-2	—	—	C83,O23R	—	-0.3
1884	Chi N	73	279	35	57	5	2	9	45	7	—	57	.204	.224	.333	67	-12	—	.884	-5	—	—	C73	—	-0.9
1885	†Chi N	68	249	27	52	8	2	1	17	2	—	52	.209	.215	.269	49	-15	—	**.927**	8	—	—	C68/rf	—	-0.2
1886	†Chi N	54	173	30	35	6	2	1	13	12	—	36	.202	.254	.277	54	-10	1	.893	9	—	—	C54,1b3	—	0.3
1887	Chi N	49	187	22	50	8	6	3	21	4	0	28	.267	.283	.422	83	-6	7	.909	5	—	—	C47,1b2	—	0.2
1888	Chi N	22	77	6	14	3	0	0	3	1	1	21	.182	.203	.221	33	-6	1	.926	1	—	—	C22	—	-0.3
1889	Chi N	15	56	6	13	1	0	1	9	3	0	18	.232	.271	.304	57	-4	1	.903	-2	—	—	C15	—	-0.4
Total	12	743	2852	376	682	129	34	21	294	53	1	461	.239	.253	.330	78	-80	10	.913	16	—	—	C727,O65(5/4/57),1b6	—	-1.9
FLOOD, CURT	Curtis Charles; B1.18.1938 Houston TX; D1.20.1997 Los Angeles CA; BR/TR/5´9˝/(160–170); d9.9																								
1956	Cin N	5	1	0	0	0	0	0	0	0-0	0	1	.000	.000	.000	-94	0	0-0	ø	0	—	—	/H	0	0.0
1957	Cin N	3	3	2	1	0	0	1	1	0-0	0	0	.333	.333	1.333	299	1	0-0	ø	-0	0	0	3b2/2	0	0.0
1958	StL N	121	422	50	110	17	2	10	41	31-1	4	56	.261	.317	.382	81	-12	2-12	.978	16	118	**199**	O120C/3	0	-0.5
1959	StL N	121	208	24	53	7	3	7	26	16-0	0	35	.255	.305	.418	86	-5	2-1	.967	-4	102	29	O106(2/103/1)/2	0	-1.2
1960	StL N	140	396	37	94	20	1	8	38	35-7	4	54	.237	.303	.354	73	-14	0-3	**.993**	1	104	84	O134(1/133/0)/3	0	-2.0
1961	StL N	132	335	53	108	15	5	2	21	35-2	3	33	.322	.391	.415	104	3	6-2	.984	8	110	196	O119C	0	1.0
1962	StL N	151	635	99	188	30	5	12	70	42-0	10	57	.296	.346	.416	95	-3	8-6	.990	6	107	118	O151C	0	-0.2
1963	StL N	158	662	112	200	34	9	5	63	42-3	2	57	.302	.345	.403	105	5	17-12	.988	8	110	116	O158C	0	0.9
1964	†StL N★	**162**	679	97	**211**	25	3	5	46	43-1	5	53	.311	.356	.378	98	0	8-11	.988	3	108	96	O162C	0	-0.4
1965	StL N	156	617	90	191	30	3	11	83	51-4	6	50	.310	.366	.421	111	11	9-3	.986	-1	102	79	O151C	0	0.7

YEAR	TM LG	G	AB	R	H	2B	3B	HR	RBI	BB-IB	HP	SO	AVG	OBP	SLG	AOPS	ABR	SB-CS	FA	FR	RNG	THR	GAMES AT POSITION	DL	BFW
1966	StL N★	160	626	64	167	21	5	10	78	26-0	4	50	.267	.298	.364	83	-15	14-7	**1.000**	0	108	45	O159C	0	-2.0
1967	†StL N	134	514	68	172	24	1	5	50	37-1	2	46	.335	.378	.414	129	20	2-2	.988	5	**112**	58	O126C	22	2.3
1968	†StL N★	150	618	71	186	17	4	5	60	33-2	5	58	.301	.339	.366	114	9	11-6	.983	9	111	116	O149C	0	1.6
1969	StL N	153	606	80	173	31	3	4	57	48-1	7	57	.285	.344	.366	99	0	9-7	.989	7	107	150	O152C	0	0.3
1971	Was A	13	35	4	7	0	0	0	2	5-0	0	2	.200	.300	.200	46	-2	0-1	.941	-2	76	0	O10C	0	-0.5
Total	15	1759	6357	851	1861	271	44	85	636	444-22	52	609	.293	.342	.389	99	-2	88-73	.987	57	108	107	O1697(3/1693/1),3b4,2b2	22	-0.0
Flood, Tim	Thomas Timothy; B3.13.1877 Montgomery City MO; D6.15.1929 St.Louis MO; BR/TR/5´9˝/160; d9.24																								
1899	StL N	10	31	0	9	0	0	0	3	4	0	—	.290	.371	.290	81	-1	1	.878	-1	107	97	2b10	—	-0.1
1902	Bro N	132	476	43	104	11	4	3	51	23	9	—	.218	.268	.277	68	-19	8	.942	-15	94	72	2b132/lf	—	-3.5
1903	Bro N	89	309	27	77	15	2	0	32	15	3	—	.249	.291	.311	73	-11	14	.924	-11	88	133	2b84,S2/cf	—	-2.0
Total	3	231	816	70	190	26	6	3	86	42	12	—	.233	.280	.290	70	-31	23	.933	-27	92	96	2b226,S2,O2(1/1/0)	—	-5.6
Flora, Kevin	Kevin Scot; B6.10.1969 Fontana CA; BR/TR/6´0˝/(180–185); [CalA87 2/57]; d9.27																								
1991	Cal A	3	8	1	1	0	0	0	0	1-0	0	5	.125	.222	.125	-1	-1	1-0	.846	-2	40	56	2b3	0	-0.3
1995	Cal A	2	1	1	0	0	0	0	0	0-0	0	1	.000	.000	.000	-99	0	0-0	ø	0	—	—	/D	0	0.0
	Phi N	24	75	12	16	3	0	2	7	4-0	0	22	.213	.253	.333	53	-5	1-0	1.000	-1	85	105	O20(5/15/0)	0	-0.6
Total	2	29	84	14	17	3	0	2	7	5-0	0	28	.202	.247	.310	46	-6	2-0	1.000	-3	85	105	O20(5/15/0),2b3/D	0	-0.9
Florence, Paul	Paul Robert "Pep"; B4.22.1900 Chicago IL; D5.28.1986 Gainesville FL; BB/TR/6´1˝/185; d5.22; Col Georgetown																								
1926	NY N	76	188	19	43	4	3	2	14	23	3	12	.229	.322	.314	73	-7	2	.937	-8	*85*	*90*	C76	—	-1.1
Flores, Gil	Gilberto (Garcia); B10.27.1952 Ponce, PR; BR/TR/6´0˝/180; d5.8																								
1977	Cal A	104	342	41	95	19	4	1	26	23-2	1	39	.278	.325	.365	91	-4	12-10	.978	0	101	92	O85(41/45/9),D8	0	-0.7
1978	NY N	11	29	8	8	0	1	0	1	3-0	0	5	.276	.344	.345	95	0	1-0	.944	-1	97	0	O8(1/6/2)	0	-0.1
1979	NY N	70	93	9	18	1	1	1	10	8-0	1	17	.194	.262	.258	44	-7	2-0	.976	1	117	75	O32(0/6/28)	0	-0.7
Total	3	185	464	58	121	20	6	2	37	34-2	2	61	.261	.313	.343	82	-11	15-10	.976	0	103	83	O125(42/57/39),D8	0	-1.5
Flores, Jose	Jose Carlos; B6.28.1973 New York NY; BR/TR/5´11˝/180; [PhiN94 34/954]; d9.7; Col Texas																								
2002	Oak A	7	3	2	0	0	0	0	0	1-0	1	0	.000	.400	.000	20	0	1-1	ø	-1	0	0	2b2/S	0	-0.1
2004	LA N	9	4	0	1	0	0	0	0	1-0	0	2	.250	.400	.250	75	0	0-0	ø	-1	0	0	/23	0	-0.1
Total	2	16	7	2	1	0	0	0	0	2-0	1	2	.143	.400	.143	52	0	1-1	.000	-2	0	0	2b3/3S	0	-0.2
Flowers, Dickie	Charles Richard; B1850 Philadelphia PA; D10.5.1892 Philadelphia PA; d6.3																								
1871	Tro NA	21	105	39	33	5	4	0	18	4	—	0	.314	.339	.438	120	2	8-2	.769	-2	95	**142**	S20/P2	—	0.1
1872	Ath NA	3	15	1	4	0	0	0	4	2	—	2	.267	.353	.267	93	0	0-0	.643	-1	85	0	S3	—	-0.1
Total	2NA	24	120	40	37	5	4	0	22	6	—	2	.308	.341	.417	117	2	8-2	.757	-3	94	125	S23/2P	—	0.0
Flowers, Jake	D'Arcy Raymond; B3.16.1902 Cambridge MD; D12.27.1962 Clearwater FL; BR/TR/5´11.5˝/170; d9.7; C9; Col Washington College																								
1923	StL N	13	32	0	3	1	0	0	2	2	0	7	.094	.147	.125	-28	-6	1-2	.971	-1	118	28	S7,2b2,3b2	—	-0.6
1926	†StL N	40	74	13	20	1	0	3	9	5	1	9	.270	.325	.405	92	-1	1	.984	-1	115	67	2b11,1b3/S	—	-0.2
1927	Bro N	67	231	26	54	5	5	2	20	21	1	25	.234	.300	.325	67	-11	3	.944	-7	89	81	S65/2	—	-1.1
1928	Bro N	103	339	51	93	11	6	2	44	47	2	30	.274	.366	.360	92	-3	10	.971	-2	91	81	2b94,S6	—	-0.3
1929	Bro N	46	130	16	26	6	0	1	16	22	0	6	.200	.316	.269	47	-10	9	.962	-7	84	69	2b39	—	-1.5
1930	Bro N	89	253	37	81	18	3	2	50	21	0	18	.320	.372	.439	96	-1	5	.949	-6	93	108	2b65/rf	—	-0.5
1931	Bro N	22	31	3	7	0	0	0	1	7	0	4	.226	.368	.226	64	-1	1	1.000	0	83	62	2b6/S	—	0.0
	†StL N	45	137	19	34	11	1	2	19	9	0	6	.248	.295	.387	79	-4	7	.971	3	103	109	S24,2b21/3	—	0.1
	Year	67	168	22	41	11	1	2	20	16	0	10	.244	.310	.357	77	-5	8	.991	4	100	117	2b27,S25/3	—	0.1
1932	StL N	67	247	35	63	11	1	2	18	31	1	18	.255	.341	.332	79	-6	7	.980	-0	89	99	3b54,S7,2b2	—	-0.4
1933	Bro N	78	210	28	49	11	2	2	22	24	0	15	.233	.312	.333	88	-3	13	.955	-9	85	61	S36,2b19,3b8/rf	—	-0.8
1934	Cin N	13	9	1	3	0	0	0	0	1	1	1	.333	.455	.333	117	0	1	ø	0	—	—	/H	—	0.0
Total	10	583	1693	229	433	75	18	16	201	190	6	139	.256	.333	.350	80	-46	58-2	.967	-29	93	85	2b260,S147,3b65,1b3,O2R	—	-5.3
Floyd, Cliff	Cornelius Clifford; B12.5.1972 Chicago IL; BL/TL/6´4˝/(220–250); [MonN91 1/14]; d9.18																								
1993	Mon N	10	31	3	7	0	0	1	2	0-0	0	9	.226	.226	.323	43	-3	0-0	1.000	-1	73	85	1b10	0	-0.4
1994	Mon N	100	334	43	94	19	4	4	41	24-0	3	63	.281	.332	.398	89	-5	10-3	.991	-1	90	93	1b77,O26(17/0/9)	0	-1.2
1995	Mon N	29	69	6	9	1	0	1	8	7-0	1	22	.130	.221	.188	9	-9	3-0	.987	-0	118	111	1b18,O4(2/1/1)	118	-1.0
1996	Mon N	117	227	29	55	15	4	6	26	30-1	5	52	.242	.340	.423	99	0	7-1	.960	-3	95	66	O85(69/16/7),1b2	0	-0.4
1997	†Fla N	61	137	23	32	9	1	6	19	24-0	2	33	.234	.354	.445	113	3	6-2	.970	2	106	222	O38(24/9/6),1b9	87	0.4
1998	Fla N	153	588	85	166	45	3	22	90	47-7	3	112	.282	.337	.481	120	16	27-14	.974	-2	92	103	O146(146/2/0),D3	0	0.9
1999	Fla N	69	251	37	76	19	1	11	49	30-5	2	47	.303	.379	.518	132	13	5-6	.952	-0	95	106	O62L,D3	101	0.9
2000	Fla N	121	420	75	126	30	0	22	91	50-5	8	82	.300	.378	.529	135	23	24-3	.951	-4	87	112	O108L/D	30	1.9
2001	Fla N★	149	555	123	176	44	4	31	103	59-19	10	101	.317	.390	.578	151	43	18-3	.972	3	104	87	O142L,D3	0	4.2
2002	Fla N	84	296	49	85	20	0	18	57	58-18	7	68	.287	.414	.537	154	26	10-5	.983	4	111	94	O80(20/0/60)/D	0	2.6
	Mon N	15	53	7	11	2	0	3	4	3-1	1	10	.208	.263	.415	71	-2	1-0	.941	-1	57	248	O13L	0	-0.4
	Year	99	349	56	96	22	0	21	61	61-19	8	78	.275	.394	.519	141	23	11-5	.980	3	84	70	O93(33/0/60)/D	0	2.2
	Bos A	47	171	30	54	21	0	7	18	15-0	2	28	.316	.374	.561	143	11	4-0	.977	-2	84	70	O26(21/0/6),D19	0	0.8
2003	NY N	108	365	57	106	25	2	18	68	51-2	3	66	.290	.376	.518	137	21	3-0	.971	4	104	153	O95L,D9	41	2.2
2004	NY N	113	396	55	103	26	0	18	63	47-6	11	103	.260	.352	.462	111	8	11-4	.988	-4	92	89	O106L/D	31	0.1
2005	NY N	150	550	85	150	22	2	34	98	63-13	11	98	.273	.358	.505	126	20	12-2	.993	8	103	**178**	O150L	0	2.5
2006	†NY N	97	332	45	81	19	1	11	44	29-3	12	58	.244	.324	.407	88	-6	6-0	.987	-4	90	65	O92L	47	-1.2
Total	14	1423	4775	752	1331	317	22	213	781	537-80	81	952	.279	.359	.488	121	159	147-43	.974	-1	97	112	O1173(1067/28/89),1b116,D40	455	11.9
Floyd, Bubba	Leslie Roe; B6.23.1917 Dallas TX; D12.15.2000 Dallas TX; BR/TR/5´11˝/160; d6.16; Col SMU																								
1944	Det A	3	9	1	4	1	0	0	0	1	0	0	.444	.500	.556	191	1	0-0	1.000	-0	119	0	S3	0	0.1
Floyd, Bobby	Robert Nathan; B10.20.1943 Hawthorne CA; BR/TR/6´0˝/(175–181); d9.18; C2; Col UCLA																								
1968	Bal A	5	9	0	1	1	0	0	1	0-0	0	3	.111	.100	.222	-1	-1	0-0	1.000	1	105	190	S4	0	0.0
1969	Bal A	39	84	7	17	4	0	0	1	6-1	0	17	.202	.253	.250	41	-7	0-0	.984	5	123	152	2b15,S15,3b9	0	0.1
1970	Bal A	3	2	0	0	0	0	0	0	0-0	0	2	.000	.000	.000	-98	-1	0-0	1.000	-2	0	0	S2/2	0	-0.2
	KC A	14	43	5	14	4	0	0	9	4-0	0	9	.326	.375	.419	121	1	0-1	.880	0	111	104	S8,3b6	0	0.2
	Year	17	45	5	14	4	0	0	9	4-0	0	11	.311	.360	.400	111	1	0-1	.882	-1	106	100	S10,3b6/2	0	0.0
1971	KC A	31	66	8	10	3	0	0	2	7-0	0	21	.152	.233	.197	23	-7	0-0	.970	2	107	142	S15,2b8/3	0	-0.3
1972	KC A	61	134	9	24	3	0	0	5	5-0	0	29	.179	.209	.201	23	-13	1-0	.967	-11	68	64	3b30,S29,2b2	0	-2.6
1973	KC A	51	78	10	26	3	1	0	8	4-0	0	14	.333	.357	.397	107	1	1-1	1.000	-1	84	71	2b25,S24	0	0.2
1974	KC A	10	9	1	1	0	0	0	0	2-0	0	4	.111	.273	.111	13	-1	0-0	1.000	1	138	0	2b5,3b2/S	0	0.0
Total	7	214	425	40	93	18	1	0	26	28-1	0	99	.219	.264	.266	52	-28	2-2	.940	-5	100	111	S98,2b56,3b48	0	-2.6
Fluhrer, John	John Lester (aka Wm. G. Morris 1 Game in 1915); B1.3.1894 Adrian MI; D7.17.1946 Columbus OH; BR/TR/5´9˝/165; d9.5; Col Penn																								
1915	Chi N	6	6	0	2	0	0	0	0	1	0	0	.333	.429	.333	132	0	1	.500	-0	65	0	O2L	—	0.0
Flynn, Ed	Edward J.; B1.25.1864 Chicago IL; D8.28.1929 Chicago IL; BL/5´9˝/165; d5.5; b–George																								
1887	Cle AA	7	27	0	5	1	0	0	4	1	0	—	.185	.214	.222	22	-3	3	.786	-1	73	0	3b6/rf	—	-0.3
Flynn, George	George A. "Dibby"; B5.24.1871 Chicago IL; D12.28.1901 Chicago IL; 5´9˝/150; d4.17; b–Ed																								
1896	Chi N	29	106	15	27	1	2	0	4	11	2	9	.255	.336	.302	66	-5	12	.878	1	130	250	O29L	—	-0.7
Flynn, John	John Anthony; B9.7.1883 Providence RI; D3.23.1935 Providence RI; BR/TR/6´0.5˝/175; d4.22; f–Joe; Col Holy Cross																								
1910	Pit N	96	332	32	91	10	2	6	52	30	1	47	.274	.336	.370	100	-1	6	.977	-3	93	107	1b93	—	-0.6
1911	Pit N	33	59	5	12	0	1	0	3	9	0	8	.203	.309	.237	52	-4	0	1.000	1	121	123	1b13/rf	—	-0.3
1912	Was A	20	71	9	12	4	1	0	5	7	1	—	.169	.253	.254	45	-5	2	.974	1	131	102	1b20	—	-0.4
Total	3	149	462	46	115	14	4	6	60	46	2	55	.249	.320	.335	85	-10	8	.978	-1	102	108	1b126/rf	—	-1.3

YEAR	TM LG	G	AB	R	H	2B	3B	HR	RBI	BB-IB	HP	SO	AVG	OBP	SLG	AOPS	ABR	SB-CS	FA	FR	RNG	THR	GAMES AT POSITION	DL	BFW
FLYNN, JOE	Joseph Nicholas; B12.29.1861 Providence RI; D12.22.1933 Providence RI; d4.18; s–John																								
1884	Phi U	52	209	38	52	9	4	4	—	11	—	—	.249	.286	.388	111	-4	—	.778	-12	90	176	O43(2/0/41),C10/1S	—	-1.3
	Bos U	9	31	4	7	2	0	0	—	2	—	—	.226	.273	.290	72	-2	—	.864	3	—	—	C7,O4(1/2/2)/1	—	0.1
	Year	61	240	42	59	11	4	4	—	13	—	—	.246	.285	.375	106	-6	—	.764	-9	111	158	O47(3/2/43),C17,1b2/S	—	-1.2
FLYNN, MIKE	Michael J.; B3.15.1872 Co. Kildare, Ireland; D6.16.1941 Los Angeles CA; d8.31																								
1891	Bos AA	1	2	0	0	0	0	0	0	0	0	1	.000	.000	.000	-99	-1	0	1.000	1	*121*	*272*	/C	—	0.0
FLYNN, DOUG	Robert Douglas; B4.18.1951 Lexington KY; BR/TR/5´11˝/(160–172); d4.9; Col Kentucky																								
1975	Cin N	89	127	17	34	7	0	1	20	11-2	0	13	.268	.324	.346	85	-2	3-0	.962	-4	80	53	3b40,2b30,S17	0	-0.3
1976	†Cin N	93	219	20	62	5	2	1	20	10-1	0	24	.283	.312	.338	83	-6	2-0	.988	-19	77	84	2b55,3b23,S20	0	-2.1
1977	Cin N	36	32	0	8	1	1	0	5	0-0	0	6	.250	.242	.344	56	-2	0-0	1.000	1	116	0	3b25,2b9,S4	0	-0.1
	NY N	90	282	14	54	6	1	0	14	11-2	0	23	.191	.220	.220	20	-33	1-3	.954	-16	78	75	S65,2b29,3b2	0	-4.4
	Year	126	314	14	62	7	2	0	19	11-2	0	29	.197	.223	.232	23	-35	1-3	.956	-15	80	78	S69,2b38,3b27	0	-4.5
1978	NY N	156	532	37	126	12	8	0	36	30-10	1	50	.237	.277	.289	61	-30	3-5	.986	-16	98	109	2b128,S60	0	-3.9
1979	NY N	157	555	35	135	19	5	4	61	17-7	0	46	.243	.265	.317	60	-33	0-3	.983	-8	93	104	2b148,S20	0	-3.5
1980	NY N	128	443	46	113	9	8	0	24	22-14	0	20	.255	.288	.312	69	-20	2-2	**.991**	-6	93	86	2b128,S3	17	-2.0
1981	NY N	**105**	325	24	72	12	4	1	20	11-8	0	19	.222	.247	.292	53	-22	1-2	.987	14	104	100	2b100,S5	0	-0.3
1982	Tex A	88	270	13	57	6	2	0	19	4-0	0	14	.211	.221	.248	30	-27	6-2	.989	-2	97	81	2b55,S35	0	-2.2
	Mon N	58	193	13	47	6	2	0	20	4-0	0	23	.244	.256	.295	53	-13	0-2	.983	-2	87	126	2b58	0	-1.3
1983	Mon N	143	452	44	107	18	4	0	26	19-8	0	38	.237	.267	.294	55	-28	2-1	.986	-13	93	94	2b107,S37	0	-3.5
1984	Mon N	124	366	23	89	12	1	0	17	12-6	0	41	.243	.267	.281	57	-22	0-0	.979	-19	93	102	2b88,S34	0	-3.6
1985	Mon N	9	6	0	1	0	0	0	0	0-0	0	0	.167	.167	.167	-7	-1	0-0	1.000	-1	64	0	2b6/S	0	-0.2
	Det A	32	51	2	13	2	1	0	2	0-0	0	3	.255	.250	.333	60	-3	0-0	.984	-0	90	186	2b20,S8,3b4	0	-0.2
Total	11	1308	3853	288	918	115	39	7	284	151-58	1	320	.238	.266	.294	56	-242	20-20	.986	-92	94	100	2b961,S309,3b94	17	-27.6
FLYNN, CLIPPER	William; B4.29.1849 Lansingburg NY; D11.11.1881 Lansingburg NY; TR/5´7˝/140; d5.9																								
1871	Tro NA	**29**	142	43	48	6	1	0	27	4	—	2	.338	.356	.394	114	2	3-3	.955	4	268	120	1b19,O8R/23	—	0.5
1872	Oly NA	**9**	40	4	9	1	0	0	2	0	—	0	.225	.225	.250	48	-2	0-0	.900	-1	95	103	1b9	—	-0.2
Total	2NA	38	182	47	57	7	1	0	29	4	—	2	.313	.328	.363	101	0	3-3	.934	3	212	114	1b28,O8R/32	—	0.3
FOGARTY, JIM	James G.; B2.12.1864 San Francisco CA; D5.20.1891 Philadelphia PA; BR/TR/5´10.5˝/180; d5.1; M1; b–Joe; Col St. Marys (CA); OF(0/312/373); ▲																								
1884	Phi N	97	378	42	80	12	6	1	37	20	—	54	.212	.251	.283	71	-12	—	.915	3	75	105	O78(0/72/6),3b14,2b4,S3/P	—	-1.0
1885	Phi N	**111**	427	49	99	13	3	0	39	30	—	37	.232	.282	.276	83	-7	—	.941	19	154	233	O88C,2b10,S8,3b5	—	0.9
1886	Phi N	77	280	54	82	13	5	3	47	42	—	16	.293	.385	.407	140	15	30	.953	-5	74	181	O60(0/1/59),2b13,S3,3b3/P	—	0.9
1887	Phi N	126	495	113	129	26	12	8	50	**82**	10	44	.261	.376	.410	112	10	102	.920	29	**176**	**240**	O123R,S2,3b2/2P	—	3.2
1888	Phi N	121	454	72	107	14	6	1	35	53	7	66	.236	.325	.300	95	-1	58	.930	12	130	**241**	O117R,3b5/S	—	1.0
1889	Phi N	128	499	107	129	15	17	3	54	65	7	60	.259	.352	.375	94	-6	**99**	**.961**	18	**171**	129	O128C,P4	—	0.7
1890	Phi P	91	347	71	83	17	6	4	58	59	9	50	.239	.364	.357	91	-3	36	.963	5	97	85	O91(0/23/68)/3M	—	0.1
Total	7	751	2880	508	709	110	55	20	320	351	33	327	.246	.335	.343	98	-4	325	.940	81	133	177	O685R,3b30,2b28,S17,P7	—	5.8
FOGARTY, JOE	Joseph J.; B San Francisco CA; 5´9˝/158; d9.18; b–Jim																								
1885	StL N	2	8	1	1	0	0	0	0	0	—	1	.125	.125	.125	-20	-1	—	1.000	-0	0	0	O2L	—	-0.1
FOHL, LEE	Leo Alexander; B11.28.1876 Lowell OH; D10.30.1965 Cleveland OH; BL/TR/5´10˝/175; d8.29; M11/C1																								
1902	Pit N	1	3	0	0	0	0	0	1	0	0	—	.000	.000	.000	-97	-1	0	.875	0	*118*	*105*	/C	—	0.0
1903	Cin N	4	14	3	5	1	1	0	2	0	1	—	.357	.400	.571	158	1	0	.955	-0	*132*	*115*	C4	—	0.1
Total	2	5	17	3	5	1	1	0	3	0	1	—	.294	.333	.471	120	0	0	.933	-0	*129*	*113*	C5	—	0.1
FOILES, HANK	Henry Lee; B6.10.1929 Richmond VA; BR/TR/6´0˝/(190–200); d4.21; Col Virginia																								
1953	Cin N	5	13	1	2	0	0	0	0	1	0	2	.154	.214	.154	-2	-2	0-0	.909	-0	*79*	*202*	C3	0	-0.2
	Cle A	7	7	2	1	0	0	0	0	1	0	1	.143	.250	.143	9	-1	0-0	.933	0	*72*	*297*	C7	0	-0.1
1955	Cle A	62	111	13	29	9	0	1	7	17-3	0	18	.261	.354	.369	93	0	0-0	.988	9	*123*	*133*	C41	0	1.0
1956	Cle A	1	0	0	0	0	0	0	0	0-0	0	0	ø	ø	ø	ø	0	0-0	ø	-0	*0*	*0*	/C	0	0.0
	Pit N	79	222	24	47	10	2	7	25	17-4	0	56	.212	.266	.369	71	-10	0-1	.988	1	*100*	*123*	C73	0	-0.6
1957	Pit N★	109	281	32	76	10	4	9	36	37-5	0	53	.270	.352	.431	113	6	1-3	.981	-1	142	66	C109	0	0.8
1958	Pit N	104	264	31	54	10	2	8	30	45-10	1	53	.205	.322	.348	80	-7	0-1	.990	12	168	93	C103	0	0.9
1959	Pit N	53	80	10	18	3	0	3	4	7-2	0	16	.225	.287	.375	75	-3	0-0	1.000	3	248	51	C51	31	0.1
1960	KC A	6	7	1	4	0	0	0	1	3-0	0	2	.571	.700	.571	246	2	0-0	.900	0	0	0	C2	0	0.2
	Cle A	24	68	9	19	1	0	1	6	7-0	0	5	.279	.347	.338	89	-1	0-0	.982	0	89	158	C22	0	0.0
	Det A	26	56	5	14	3	0	0	3	1-1	0	8	.250	.263	.304	51	-4	1-0	1.000	4	163	144	C22	0	0.1
	Year	56	131	15	37	4	0	1	10	11-1	0	15	.282	.338	.336	83	-3	1-0	.987	5	117	145	C46	0	0.3
1961	Bal A	43	124	18	34	6	0	6	19	12-1	0	27	.274	.336	.468	117	3	0-2	.995	-2	63	102	C38	61	0.2
1962	Cin N	43	131	17	36	6	1	7	25	13-3	0	39	.275	.340	.496	118	3	0-0	.981	-1	85	65	C41	0	0.4
1963	Cin N	1	3	0	0	0	0	0	0	1-1	0	0	.000	.250	.000	-21	0	1-0	1.000	-1	45	0	/C	0	-0.1
	LA A	41	84	8	18	1	1	4	10	8-1	1	13	.214	.290	.393	95	-1	0-0	.974	2	75	171	C30	0	0.2
1964	LA A	4	4	0	1	0	0	0	0	0-0	0	2	.250	.250	.250	44	0	0-0	ø	0	—	—	/H	0	0.0
Total	11	608	1455	171	353	59	10	46	166	170-31	2	295	.243	.321	.392	92	-15	3-7	.986	27	*129*	*100*	C544	92	2.9
FOLEY, CURRY	Charles Joseph; B1.14.1856 Milltown, Ireland; D10.20.1898 Boston MA; TL/5´10˝/160; d5.13; ▲																								
1879	Bos N	35	146	16	46	3	1	0	17	3	—	4	.315	.329	.349	121	3	—	.857	-5	77	0	P21,O17(0/2/15),1b2	—	-0.2
1880	Bos N	80	332	44	97	13	2	2	31	8	—	14	.292	.309	.361	130	10	—	.953	-0	103	0	P36,O35R,1b25	—	0.5
1881	Buf N	**83**	375	58	96	20	2	1	25	7	—	27	.256	.270	.328	88	-5	—	.795	-4	99	215	O55(3/4/50),1b27,P10	—	-0.9
1882	Buf N	**84**	341	51	104	16	4	3	49	12	—	26	.305	.329	.402	131	11	—	.833	1	120	184	O84(0/1/84)/P	—	1.0
1883	Buf N	23	111	23	30	5	3	0	6	4	—	12	.270	.296	.369	98	0	—	.885	-2	39	0	O23(1/21/1)/P	—	-0.3
Total	5	305	1305	192	373	57	12	6	128	34	—	83	.286	.304	.362	114	19	—	.819	-10	101	148	O214(4/28/185),P69,1b54	—	0.1
FOLEY, MARV	Marvis Edwin; B8.29.1953 Stanford KY; BL/TR/6´0˝/195; [ChiA75 17/395]; d9.11; C2; Col Kentucky																								
1978	Chi A	11	34	3	12	0	0	0	6	4-0	0	6	.353	.421	.353	118	1	0-1	.938	-3	45	86	C10	0	-0.2
1979	Chi A	34	97	6	24	3	0	2	10	7-1	0	5	.247	.292	.340	71	-4	0-0	.993	-3	76	96	C33	0	-0.6
1980	Chi A	68	137	14	29	5	0	4	15	9-3	2	22	.212	.263	.336	65	-7	0-0	.991	3	76	127	C64,1b3	0	-0.2
1982	Chi A	27	36	1	4	0	0	0	1	6-1	0	4	.111	.238	.111	-0	-5	0-0	.980	1	78	183	C15,3b2/1D	15	-0.4
1984	Tex A	63	115	13	25	2	0	6	19	15-1	1	24	.217	.306	.391	90	-2	0-0	.988	1	47	66	C36/13D	0	0.0
Total	5	203	419	37	94	10	0	12	51	41-6	3	61	.224	.292	.334	72	-17	0-1	.986	-2	67	106	C158,D5,1b5,3b3	15	-1.4
FOLEY, RAY	Raymond Kirwin; B6.23.1906 Naugatuck CT; D3.22.1980 Vero Beach FL; BL/TR/5´11˝/173; d7.4; Col Catholic America																								
1928	NY N	2	1	1	0	0	0	0	0	1	0	1	.000	.500	.000	41	0	0	ø	0	—	—	/H	—	0.0
FOLEY, TOM	Thomas J.; B1847 Chicago IL; D1.4.1896 LaGrange IL; 5´9.5˝/157; d5.8																								
1871	Chi NA	18	84	18	22	3	1	0	13	3	—	2	.262	.287	.321	67	-4	1-4	.633	-5	58	0	O16(2/9/5),C4/3	—	-0.7
FOLEY, TOM	Thomas Michael; B9.9.1959 Columbus GA; BL/TR/6´1˝/(160–185); [CinN77 7/180]; d4.9; C5																								
1983	Cin N	68	98	7	20	4	1	0	9	13-2	0	17	.204	.297	.265	55	-6	1-0	.983	1	94	102	S37,2b5	0	-0.2
1984	Cin N	106	277	26	70	8	3	5	27	24-7	0	36	.253	.310	.357	84	-6	3-2	.965	-9	91	73	S83,2b10/3	0	-0.8
1985	Cin N	43	92	7	18	5	1	0	6	6-1	0	16	.196	.245	.272	42	-7	1-0	.983	3	91	119	2b18,S15/3	0	-0.2
	Phi N	46	158	17	42	8	0	3	17	13-7	0	18	.266	.322	.373	91	-2	1-3	.981	0	95	97	S45	0	0.2
	Year	89	250	24	60	13	1	3	23	19-8	0	34	.240	.294	.336	73	-9	2-3	.978	3	99	113	S60,2b18/3	0	0.0
1986	Phi N	39	61	8	18	2	1	0	5	10-1	0	11	.295	.389	.361	106	1	2-0	.975	0	89	109	S24/23	22	0.3
	Mon N	64	202	18	52	13	2	1	18	20-5	0	26	.257	.320	.356	88	-3	8-3	.965	-1	78	61	S29,2b25,3b15	0	0.0
	Year	103	263	26	70	15	3	1	23	30-6	0	37	.266	.337	.357	92	-2	10-3	.970	-1	82	80	S53,2b26,3b16	0	0.3
1987	Mon N	106	280	35	82	18	3	5	28	11-0	1	40	.293	.322	.432	94	-3	6-10	.963	-1	95	115	S49,2b39,3b9	16	-0.1
1988	Mon N	127	377	33	100	21	3	5	43	30-10	1	49	.265	.319	.377	95	-2	2-7	.972	3	106	107	2b89,S32,3b9	0	0.3
1989	Mon N	122	375	34	86	19	2	7	39	45-4	3	53	.229	.314	.347	88	-5	2-3	.988	16	109	105	2b108,3b16,S14/P	17	1.3
1990	Mon N	73	164	11	35	2	1	0	12	12-2	0	22	.213	.266	.238	41	-14	0-1	.987	-2	107	148	S45,2b20,3b7/1	0	-1.4
1991	Mon N	86	168	12	35	11	1	0	15	14-4	1	30	.208	.269	.286	58	-9	2-0	.967	-2	91	90	S43,1b31,3b6,2b2	0	-1.1
1992	Mon N	72	115	7	20	3	1	0	5	8-2	1	21	.174	.230	.217	29	-11	3-0	.967	1	106	99	S33,2b13,1b12,3b4/lf	0	-0.9

YEAR	TM LG	G	AB	R	H	2B	3B	HR	RBI	BB-IB	HP	SO	AVG	OBP	SLG	AOPS	ABR	SB-CS	FA	FR	RNG	THR	GAMES AT POSITION	DL	BFW
1993	Pit N	86	194	18	49	11	1	3	22	11-1	0	26	.253	.287	.366	75	-7	0-0	.993	3	82	109	2b35,1b12,3b7,S6	16	-0.3
1994	Pit N	59	123	13	29	7	0	3	15	13-2	0	18	.236	.307	.366	74	-5	0-0	.986	8	113	172	2b17,3b14,S8,1b3	18	0.4
1995	Mon N	11	24	2	5	2	0	0	2	2-0	0	4	.208	.269	.292	46	-2	1-0	1.000	1	109	47	1b4,2b3	18	-0.1
Total	13	1108	2708	248	661	134	20	32	263	232-48	7	387	.244	.303	.344	78	-81	32-29	.972	18	96	104	S463,2b385,3b90,1b63/lfP	107	-2.6

FOLEY, WILL William Brown; B11.15.1855 Chicago IL; D11.12.1916 Chicago IL; BR/TR/5´9.5˝/150; d8.23

YEAR	TM LG	G	AB	R	H	2B	3B	HR	RBI	BB-IB	HP	SO	AVG	OBP	SLG	AOPS	ABR	SB-CS	FA	FR	RNG	THR	GAMES AT POSITION	DL	BFW
1875	Chi NA	3	12	0	3	1	0	0	1	0	—	2	.250	.250	.333	100	0	0-0	.813	1	142	339	3b3	—	0.1
1876	Cin N	58	221	19	50	3	2	0	9	0	—	14	.226	.226	.258	71	-5	—	.804	-1	113	85	3b46,C20	—	-0.4
1877	Cin N	56	216	23	41	5	1	0	18	4	—	13	.190	.205	.222	39	-14	—	.836	7	117	113	3b56	—	-0.5
1878	Mil N	56	229	33	62	8	5	0	22	7	—	14	.271	.292	.349	103	0	—	.812	-8	84	131	3b53,C7	—	-0.6
1879	Cin N	56	218	22	46	5	1	0	25	2	—	16	.211	.218	.243	55	-10	—	.820	3	97	239	3b29,O25R,2b3	—	-0.6
1881	Det N	5	15	0	2	0	0	0	1	2	—	3	.133	.235	.133	18	-1	—	.769	-1	66	508	3b5	—	-0.2
1884	CP U	19	71	15	20	1	1	0	—	5	—	—	.282	.329	.324	99	-2	—	.804	-1	77	129	3b19	—	-0.3
Total	6	250	970	112	221	22	10	0	75	20	—	60	.228	.243	.271	70	-32	—	.817	-2	101	137	3b208,C27,O25R,2b3	—	-2.6

FOLI, TIM Timothy John; B12.8.1950 Culver City CA; BR/TR/6´0˝/(170–176); [NYN68 1/1]; d9.11; C10

YEAR	TM LG	G	AB	R	H	2B	3B	HR	RBI	BB-IB	HP	SO	AVG	OBP	SLG	AOPS	ABR	SB-CS	FA	FR	RNG	THR	GAMES AT POSITION	DL	BFW
1970	NY N	5	11	0	4	0	0	0	1	0-0	0	2	.364	.364	.364	94	0	0-0	1.000	2	191	0	S2,3b2	0	0.2
1971	NY N	97	288	32	65	12	2	0	24	18-4	1	50	.226	.272	.281	57	-16	5-0	.964	5	91	111	2b58,3b36,S12/cf	0	-0.7
1972	Mon N	149	540	45	130	12	2	2	35	25-2	6	43	.241	.280	.281	59	-29	11-7	.966	18	106	104	S148/2	0	0.7
1973	Mon N	126	458	37	110	11	0	2	36	28-11	1	40	.240	.284	.277	54	-28	6-3	.960	18	107	108	S123,2b2/cf	29	0.5
1974	Mon N	121	441	41	112	10	3	0	39	28-0	3	27	.254	.300	.290	63	-22	8-2	.971	**35**	**116**	128	S120/3	16	2.8
1975	Mon N	152	572	64	136	25	2	1	29	36-5	2	49	.238	.284	.294	58	-33	13-3	.973	11	104	110	S151/2	0	-0.3
1976	Mon N	149	546	41	144	36	1	6	54	16-1	0	33	.264	.281	.366	80	-15	6-5	.975	17	105	108	S146/3	0	1.8
1977	Mon N	13	57	2	10	5	1	0	3	0-0	0	4	.175	.172	.298	25	-6	0-0	1.000	1	98	77	S13	0	-0.4
	SF N	104	368	30	84	17	3	4	27	11-1	0	16	.228	.247	.323	53	-26	2-4	.974	7	100	127	S102/23lf	30	-1.0
	Year	117	425	32	94	22	4	4	30	11-1	0	20	.221	.238	.320	49	-32	2-4	.977	8	100	121	S115/23lf	0	-1.4
1978	NY N	113	413	37	106	21	1	1	27	14-1	2	30	.257	.283	.320	70	-17	2-5	.966	-1	97	**130**	S112	26	-0.9
1979	NY N	3	7	0	0	0	0	0	0	0-0	0	0	.000	.000	.000	-99	-2	0-0	1.000	0	103	89	S3	0	-0.2
	†Pit N	133	525	70	153	23	1	1	65	28-0	9	14	.291	.335	.345	82	-12	6-5	.978	7	97	132	S132	0	0.8
	Year	136	532	70	153	23	1	1	65	28-0	9	14	.288	.330	.340	80	-14	6-5	.978	7	97	**131**	S135	0	0.6
1980	Pit N	127	495	61	131	22	0	3	38	19-1	**6**	23	.265	.296	.327	72	-18	11-7	**.981**	11	102	**125**	S125	15	0.6
1981	Pit N	86	316	32	78	12	2	0	20	17-0	1	10	.247	.285	.297	63	-16	7-7	.965	-4	99	103	S81	0	-1.4
1982	†Cal A	150	480	46	121	14	2	3	56	14-1	2	22	.252	.273	.308	60	-28	2-4	**.985**	14	108	115	S139,2b8,3b2	0	0.0
1983	Cal A	88	330	29	83	10	0	2	29	5-1	1	18	.252	.263	.300	55	-21	2-3	.975	13	123	108	S74,3b13	0	-0.1
1984	NY A	61	163	8	41	11	0	0	16	2-0	1	16	.252	.265	.319	63	-8	0-0	.950	7	92	132	S28,2b21,3b10,1b2	0	0.1
1985	Pit N	19	37	1	7	0	0	0	2	4-1	0	2	.189	.268	.189	30	-3	0-0	.980	4	128	111	S13	24	0.1
Total	16	1696	6047	576	1515	241	20	25	501	265-29	35	399	.251	.283	.309	64	-300	81-55	.973	165	105	116	S1524,2b92,3b66,O3(1/2/0),1b2	140	2.6

FONDY, DEE Dee Virgil; B10.31.1924 Slaton TX; D8.19.1999 Redlands CA; BL/TL/6´3˝/196; d4.17

YEAR	TM LG	G	AB	R	H	2B	3B	HR	RBI	BB-IB	HP	SO	AVG	OBP	SLG	AOPS	ABR	SB-CS	FA	FR	RNG	THR	GAMES AT POSITION	DL	BFW
1951	Chi N	49	170	23	46	7	2	3	20	11	1	20	.271	.319	.388	88	-3	5-6	.976	-3	89	95	1b44	0	-0.8
1952	Chi N	145	554	69	166	21	9	10	67	28	1	60	.300	.334	.424	108	3	13-11	.990	1	103	75	1b143	0	-0.2
1953	Chi N	150	595	79	184	24	11	18	78	44	1	106	.309	.358	.477	113	10	10-7	.987	4	111	75	1b149	0	0.4
1954	Chi N	141	568	77	162	30	4	9	49	35	1	84	.285	.326	.400	87	-11	20-5	.993	8	**120**	100	1b138	0	-0.8
1955	Chi N	150	574	69	152	23	8	17	65	35-6	2	87	.265	.307	.422	92	-9	8-9	.991	1	103	102	1b147	0	-1.8
1956	Chi N	137	543	52	146	22	9	9	46	20-5	0	74	.269	.290	.392	84	-14	9-7	.985	-4	92	88	1b133	0	-2.7
1957	Chi N	11	51	3	16	3	1	0	2	0-0	0	9	.314	.314	.412	94	-1	1-2	.991	-1	69	103	1b11	0	-0.3
	Pit N	95	323	42	101	13	2	2	35	25-0	1	59	.313	.360	.384	104	2	11-5	.982	-3	95	102	1b73	0	-0.4
	Year	106	374	45	117	16	3	2	37	25-0	1	68	.313	.354	.388	103	2	12-7	.983	-4	92	102	1b84	0	-0.7
1958	Cin N	89	124	23	27	1	1	1	11	5-0	0	27	.218	.246	.266	34	-12	7-1	.987	1	148	106	1b36,O22(7/0/15)	0	-1.1
Total	8	967	3502	437	1000	144	47	69	373	203-11	7	526	.286	.324	.413	95	-35	84-53	.988	5	104	90	1b874,O22(7/0/15)	0	-7.7

FONSECA, LEW Lewis Albert; B1.21.1899 Oakland CA; D11.26.1989 Ely IA; BR/TR/5´10.5˝/180; d4.13; M3; Col St. Marys (CA); OF(99/15/5)

YEAR	TM LG	G	AB	R	H	2B	3B	HR	RBI	BB-IB	HP	SO	AVG	OBP	SLG	AOPS	ABR	SB-CS	FA	FR	RNG	THR	GAMES AT POSITION	DL	BFW
1921	Cin N	82	297	38	82	10	3	1	41	8	4	13	.276	.304	.340	74	-12	2-3	.961	-3	95	92	2b50,1b16,O16(14/0/2)	—	-1.6
1922	Cin N	81	291	55	105	20	3	4	45	14	0	18	.361	.390	.491	128	12	7-8	.970	9	103	117	2b71	—	2.0
1923	Cin N	65	237	33	66	11	4	3	28	9	2	16	.278	.310	.397	87	-5	4-0	.957	6	107	102	2b45,1b14	—	0.2
1924	Cin N	20	57	5	13	2	1	0	9	4	0	4	.228	.279	.298	55	-4	1-0	1.000	-1	107	72	2b10,1b6	—	-0.4
1925	Phi N	126	467	78	149	30	5	7	60	21	3	42	.319	.352	.450	95	-4	6-2	.956	-7	98	76	2b69,1b55	—	-1.1
1927	Cle A	112	428	60	133	20	7	2	40	12	2	17	.311	.333	.404	90	-9	12-4	.973	-2	101	89	2b96,1b13	—	-0.7
1928	Cle A	75	263	38	86	19	4	3	36	13	1	17	.327	.361	.464	114	5	4-2	1.000	5	122	143	1b56,3b15,S4/2	—	0.7
1929	Cle A	148	566	97	209	44	15	6	103	50	**7**	23	**.369**	.427	.532	140	35	19-11	.995	7	**118**	**109**	1b147	—	3.0
1930	Cle A	40	129	20	36	9	2	0	17	7	0	7	.279	.316	.380	73	-5	1-0	.980	1	154	64	1b28,3b6	—	-0.5
1931	Cle A	26	108	21	40	9	1	1	14	8	1	7	.370	.419	.500	133	5	3-2	.993	0	98	80	1b26	—	0.3
	Chi A	121	465	65	139	26	5	2	71	32	3	22	.299	.348	.389	99	-1	4-4	.974	-9	96	62	O95(80/15/0),2b21,1b2/3	—	-1.3
	Year	147	573	86	179	35	6	3	85	40	4	29	.312	.361	.410	106	5	7-6	.974	-9	96	62	O95(80/15/0),1b28,2b21/3	—	-1.0
1932	Chi A	18	37	0	5	1	0	0	6	1	0	7	.135	.158	.162	-18	-7	0-0	1.000	1	92	362	O8(5/0/3)/PM	—	-0.5
1933	Chi A	23	59	8	12	2	0	2	15	7	0	6	.203	.288	.339	68	-3	1-0	1.000	2	172	149	1b12,M	—	-0.2
Total	12	937	3404	518	1075	203	50	31	485	186	23	199	.316	.355	.432	103	7	64-36	.994	10	112	104	1b375,2b363,O119L,3b22,S4/P	—	-0.1

FONTENOT, MIKE Michael Eugene; B6.9.1980 Slidell LA; BL/TR/5´8˝/165; [BalA01 1/19]; d4.13; Col Louisiana St.

YEAR	TM LG	G	AB	R	H	2B	3B	HR	RBI	BB-IB	HP	SO	AVG	OBP	SLG	AOPS	ABR	SB-CS	FA	FR	RNG	THR	GAMES AT POSITION	DL	BFW
2005	Chi N	7	2	4	0	0	0	0	0	2-0	1	0	.000	.600	.000	73	0	0-0	ø	0	—	—	/H	0	0.0

FONVILLE, CHAD Chad Everette; B3.5.1971 Jacksonville NC; BB/TR/5´6˝/155; [SFN92 11/299]; d4.28; Col Louisburg (NC) JC

YEAR	TM LG	G	AB	R	H	2B	3B	HR	RBI	BB-IB	HP	SO	AVG	OBP	SLG	AOPS	ABR	SB-CS	FA	FR	RNG	THR	GAMES AT POSITION	DL	BFW
1995	Mon N	14	12	2	4	0	0	0	0	0-0	0	3	.333	.333	.333	74	0	0-2	ø	-0	0	0	2b2	0	-0.2
	†LA N	88	308	41	85	6	1	0	16	23-1	1	39	.276	.328	.302	73	-12	20-5	.971	-1	102	74	S38,2b36,O11(10/2/0)	0	-0.7
	Year	102	320	43	89	6	1	0	16	23-1	1	42	.278	.328	.303	72	-13	20-7	.971	-2	95	70	2b38,S38,O11(10/2/0)	0	-0.9
1996	LA N	103	201	34	41	4	1	0	13	17-1	0	31	.204	.266	.234	35	-19	7-2	.964	-4	103	159	O35(19/18/0),2b23,S20,3b2	0	-2.1
1997	LA N	9	14	1	2	0	0	0	1	2-0	0	3	.143	.250	.143	7	-2	0-1	.833	-4	47	0	2b3	0	-0.6
	Chi A	9	9	1	1	0	0	0	1	1-0	0	1	.111	.200	.111	-16	-2	2-0	1.000	-1	245	0	O3(1/2/0),2b2,S2/D	0	-0.1
1999	Bos A	3	2	1	0	0	0	0	0	2-0	0	0	.000	.500	.000	41	0	1-0	.900	1	85	142	2b2	0	0.1
Total	4	226	546	80	133	10	2	0	31	45-2	1	77	.244	.302	.269	56	-35	30-10	.964	-10	92	75	2b68,S60,O49(30/22/0),3b2/D	0	-3.6

FOOTE, BARRY Barry Clifton; B2.16.1952 Smithfield NC; BR/TR/6´3˝/(205–220); [MonN70 1/3]; d9.14; C3

YEAR	TM LG	G	AB	R	H	2B	3B	HR	RBI	BB-IB	HP	SO	AVG	OBP	SLG	AOPS	ABR	SB-CS	FA	FR	RNG	THR	GAMES AT POSITION	DL	BFW
1973	Mon N	6	6	0	4	0	1	0	1	0-0	0	0	.667	.667	1.000	343	2	0-0	ø	0	—	—	/H	0	0.2
1974	Mon N	125	420	44	110	23	4	11	60	35-11	3	74	.262	.315	.414	100	-1	2-1	.984	11	109	113	C122	0	1.6
1975	Mon N	118	387	25	75	16	1	7	30	17-6	1	48	.194	.229	.295	42	-31	0-1	.985	5	121	83	C115	0	-2.3
1976	Mon N	105	350	32	82	12	2	7	27	17-3	1	32	.234	.272	.340	69	-15	2-1	.989	7	112	123	C96,3b2/1	16	-0.4
1977	Mon N	15	49	4	12	3	1	2	8	4-0	0	10	.245	.302	.469	105	0	0-0	.988	2	258	107	C13	0	0.2
	Phi N	18	32	3	7	1	0	1	3	3-0	0	6	.219	.286	.344	65	-2	0-0	.980	-1	113	54	C17	0	-0.2
	Year	33	81	7	19	4	1	3	11	7-0	0	16	.235	.295	.420	88	-2	0-0	.985	1	199	86	C30	0	0.0
1978	†Phi N	39	57	4	9	0	0	1	4	1-0	0	11	.158	.172	.211	6	-7	0-0	1.000	1	362	57	C31	0	-0.6
1979	Chi N	132	429	47	109	26	0	16	56	34-7	5	49	.254	.316	.427	92	-5	5-2	.979	4	115	104	C129	0	0.4
1980	Chi N	63	202	16	48	13	1	6	28	13-2	0	18	.238	.282	.401	82	-5	1-1	.992	5	121	114	C55	34	0.3
1981	Chi N	9	22	0	0	0	0	0	1	3-0	0	7	.000	.115	.000	-60	-5	0-0	1.000	-0	267	116	C8	0	-0.5
	†NY A	40	125	12	26	4	0	6	10	8-0	0	21	.208	.256	.384	83	-3	0-0	.996	8	82	117	C34/1D	0	0.6
1982	NY A	17	48	4	7	5	0	0	2	1-0	0	11	.146	.160	.250	12	-6	0-0	.973	-4	117	64	C17	31	-0.9
Total	10	687	2127	191	489	103	10	57	230	136-29	10	287	.230	.277	.368	75	-78	10-6	.985	39	124	104	C637,D4,1b2,3b2	81	-1.6

FORAN, JIM James H.; B1848 NY; D1.30.1928 Los Angeles CA; 5´6.5˝/159; d5.4

YEAR	TM LG	G	AB	R	H	2B	3B	HR	RBI	BB-IB	HP	SO	AVG	OBP	SLG	AOPS	ABR	SB-CS	FA	FR	RNG	THR	GAMES AT POSITION	DL	BFW
1871	Kek NA	**19**	89	21	31	1	3	1	18	2	—	1	.348	.363	.461	132	3	1-0	.878	0	163	27	1b16,O4(3/1/0)	—	0.2

FORBES, P.J. Patrick Joseph; B9.22.1967 Pittsburg KS; BR/TR/5´10˝/160; [CalA90 20/556]; d7.21; Col Wichita St.

YEAR	TM LG	G	AB	R	H	2B	3B	HR	RBI	BB-IB	HP	SO	AVG	OBP	SLG	AOPS	ABR	SB-CS	FA	FR	RNG	THR	GAMES AT POSITION	DL	BFW
1998	Bal A	9	10	0	1	0	0	0	2	0-0	0	0	.100	.100	.100	-49	-2	0-0	1.000	1	131	135	2b7/3S	0	-0.1
2001	Phi N	3	7	1	2	0	0	0	1	0-0	0	2	.286	.286	.286	51	-1	0-0	1.000	-0	74	0	/2	0	-0.1
Total	2	12	17	1	3	0	0	0	3	0-0	0	2	.176	.176	.176	-8	-3	0-0	1.000	0	114	95	2b8/S3	0	-0.2

Force, Davy David W. "Wee Davy","Tom Thumb"; B7.27.1849 New York NY; D6.21.1918 Englewood NJ; BR/TR/5´4˝/130; d5.5; ▲

YEAR	TM LG	G	AB	R	H	2B	3B	HR	RBI	BB-IB	HP	SO	AVG	OBP	SLG	AOPS	ABR	SB-CS	FA	FR	RNG	THR	GAMES AT POSITION	DL	BFW
1871	Oly NA	**32**	162	45	45	9	4	0	29	4	—	0	.278	.295	.383	98	1	8-0	**.844**	**18**	**136**	104	S31/3	—	1.2
1872	Tro NA	**25**	130	40	53	11	0	0	19	1	—	0	.408	.412	.492	175	11	2-2	.871	4	105	227	3b16,S9	—	0.9
	Bal NA	19	95	29	41	2	2	0	14	1	—	0	.432	.438	.495	178	8	5-0	.846	4	100	0	3b19	—	0.8
	Year	44	225	69	94	13	2	0	33	2	—	0	.418	.423	.493	176	19	7-2	**.857**	7	102	107	3b35,S9	—	1.7
1873	Bal NA	49	233	77	85	10	1	0	30	9	—	1	.365	.388	.416	139	12	1-0	**.830**	7	101	26	3b34,S17,P3	—	1.2
1874	Chi NA	**59**	294	61	92	9	0	0	26	3	—	1	.313	.320	.344	112	4	4-0	.802	9	111	100	3b42,S18/P	—	0.9
1875	Ath NA	**77**	386	78	120	22	5	0	49	7	—	5	.311	.323	.394	133	11	6-3	**.887**	11	100	**162**	S77,3b2	—	1.7
1876	Phi N	**60**	284	48	66	6	0	0	17	5	—	3	.232	.246	.254	67	-9	—	.898	20	122	75	S60,3b2	—	1.1
	NY N	1	3	0	0	0	0	0	0	0	—	0	.000	.000	.000	-99	-1	—	.833	0	105	0	/S	—	0.0
	Year	**61**	287	48	66	6	0	0	17	5	—	3	.230	.243	.251	66	-10	—	.897	20	**122**	74	S61,3b2	—	1.1
1877	StL N	58	225	24	59	5	3	0	22	11	—	15	.262	.297	.311	97	0	—	**.914**	6	102	80	S50,3b8	—	0.7
1879	Buf N	**79**	316	36	66	5	2	0	8	13	—	37	.209	.240	.237	57	-15	—	**.929**	2	101	**164**	S78/3	—	-0.8
1880	Buf N	81	290	22	49	10	0	0	17	10	—	35	.169	.197	.203	35	-19	—	.939	26	121	108	2b53,S30	—	1.1
1881	Buf N	75	278	21	50	9	1	0	15	11	—	29	.180	.211	.219	36	-20	—	.937	**25**	130	66	2b51,S21,O3R/3	—	0.8
1882	Buf N	73	278	39	67	10	1	1	28	12	—	17	.241	.272	.295	81	-6	—	**.908**	7	106	74	S61,3b11/2	—	0.3
1883	Buf N	96	378	40	82	11	3	0	35	12	—	39	.217	.241	.262	52	-22	—	.884	-9	96	103	S78,3b13,2b7	—	-2.5
1884	Buf N	106	403	47	83	13	3	0	36	27	—	41	.206	.256	.253	59	-19	—	**.898**	-4	97	91	S105/2	—	-1.8
1885	Buf N	71	253	20	57	6	1	0	15	13	—	19	.225	.263	.257	66	-10	—	.882	0	105	115	2b42,S24,3b6	—	-0.6
1886	Was N	68	242	26	44	5	1	0	16	17	—	26	.182	.236	.211	39	-17	9	.909	18	124	119	S56,2b8,3b4	—	0.3
Total	5NA	261	1300	330	436	63	12	0	167	25	—	7	.335	.348	.402	132	47	26-5	.865	52	107	133	S152,3b114,P4	—	6.7
Total	10	768	2950	323	623	80	15	1	209	131	—	261	.211	.245	.249	58	-138	9	.908	92	106	100	S564,2b163,3b46,O3R	—	-1.4

Ford, Curt Curtis Glenn; B10.11.1960 Jackson MS; BL/TR/5´10˝/(150–165); [StLN81 4/85]; d6.22; Col Jackson St.

YEAR	TM LG	G	AB	R	H	2B	3B	HR	RBI	BB-IB	HP	SO	AVG	OBP	SLG	AOPS	ABR	SB-CS	FA	FR	RNG	THR	GAMES AT POSITION	DL	BFW
1985	StL N	11	12	2	6	2	0	0	3	4-0	0	1	.500	.625	.667	263	3	1-0	.750	-1	71	0	O4(1/0/4)	0	0.3
1986	StL N	85	214	30	53	15	2	2	29	23-2	0	29	.248	.318	.364	89	-3	13-5	.975	4	105	169	O64(24/0/40)	0	0.0
1987	†StL N	89	228	32	65	9	5	3	26	14-0	1	32	.285	.325	.408	91	-3	11-8	.981	7	136	48	O75(15/2/61)	39	0.0
1988	StL N	91	128	11	25	6	0	1	18	8-1	0	26	.195	.239	.266	45	-9	6-1	.965	3	119	78	O40(24/3/13),1b7	0	-0.7
1989	Phi N	108	142	13	31	5	1	1	13	16-0	1	33	.218	.298	.289	70	-5	5-3	1.000	1	95	225	O52(26/2/25)/12	0	-0.5
1990	Phi N	22	18	0	2	0	0	0	0	1-0	0	5	.111	.158	.111	-25	-3	0-0	1.000	0	162	0	O3R	0	-0.3
Total	6	406	742	88	182	37	8	7	89	66-3	2	126	.245	.305	.345	79	-20	36-17	.977	14	116	118	O238(90/7/146),1b8/2	39	-1.2

Ford, Dan Darnell Glenn; B5.19.1952 Los Angeles CA; BR/TR/6´1˝/(185–197); [OakA70 1/18]; d4.12

YEAR	TM LG	G	AB	R	H	2B	3B	HR	RBI	BB-IB	HP	SO	AVG	OBP	SLG	AOPS	ABR	SB-CS	FA	FR	RNG	THR	GAMES AT POSITION	DL	BFW
1975	Min A	130	440	72	123	21	1	15	59	30-2	5	79	.280	.333	.434	114	7	6-7	.988	-11	88	40	O120(0/118/2),D3	0	-0.8
1976	Min A	145	514	87	137	24	7	20	86	36-2	10	118	.267	.323	.457	126	15	17-6	.968	-7	95	59	O139(1/0/139),D3	0	0.2
1977	Min A	144	453	66	121	25	7	11	60	41-3	10	79	.267	.338	.426	109	6	6-4	.964	-7	85	104	O137(1/3/135),D3	0	-0.7
1978	Min A	151	592	78	162	36	10	11	82	48-6	5	88	.274	.332	.424	109	6	7-7	.977	-15	88	59	O149(0/145/4)/D	0	-1.1
1979	†Cal A	142	569	100	165	26	5	21	101	40-0	3	86	.290	.333	.464	118	12	8-5	.977	6	113	99	O141(0/29/124)	0	1.1
1980	Cal A	65	226	22	63	11	0	7	26	19-1	2	45	.279	.339	.420	109	3	0-1	.940	-2	93	98	O45R,D15	63	-0.2
1981	Cal A	97	375	53	104	14	1	15	48	23-3	5	71	.277	.327	.440	118	8	2-2	.960	-7	94	42	O97R	0	-0.5
1982	Bal A	123	421	46	99	21	3	10	43	23-1	4	71	.235	.279	.371	78	-14	5-2	.975	5	116	76	O119R/D	0	-1.4
1983	†Bal A	103	407	63	114	30	4	9	55	29-1	3	55	.280	.328	.440	112	7	9-2	.987	-2	107	26	O103R	28	0.0
1984	Bal A	25	91	7	21	4	0	1	5	7-0	0	13	.231	.286	.308	65	-4	1-0	1.000	1	120	111	O15R,D8	125	-0.4
1985	Bal A	28	75	4	14	2	0	1	7	7-0	0	17	.187	.256	.253	41	-6	0-1	ø	0	0	0	D28	121	-0.7
Total	11	1153	4163	598	1123	214	38	121	566	303-19	47	722	.270	.324	.427	108	40	61-37	.974	-38	98	67	O1065(2/295/783),D62	337	-4.5

Ford, Ed Edgar Lee; B4.10.1862 Richmond VA; D6.8.1931 Richmond VA; 5´9.5˝/160; d10.9

YEAR	TM LG	G	AB	R	H	2B	3B	HR	RBI	BB-IB	HP	SO	AVG	OBP	SLG	AOPS	ABR	SB-CS	FA	FR	RNG	THR	GAMES AT POSITION	DL	BFW
1884	Ric AA	2	5	0	0	0	0	0	—	0	0	—	.000	.000	.000	-99	-1	—	.556	1	116	0	/S1	—	-0.1

Ford, Hod Horace Hills; B7.23.1897 New Haven CT; D1.29.1977 Winchester MA; BR/TR/5´10˝/165; d9.8; Col Tufts

YEAR	TM LG	G	AB	R	H	2B	3B	HR	RBI	BB-IB	HP	SO	AVG	OBP	SLG	AOPS	ABR	SB-CS	FA	FR	RNG	THR	GAMES AT POSITION	DL	BFW
1919	Bos N	10	28	4	6	0	1	0	3	2	1	6	.214	.290	.286	77	-1	0	.946	2	133	122	S8,3b2	—	0.2
1920	Bos N	88	257	16	62	12	5	1	30	18	2	25	.241	.296	.339	86	-5	3-3	.972	11	117	73	2b59,S18,1b4	—	0.8
1921	Bos N	152	555	50	155	29	5	2	61	36	4	49	.279	.328	.360	87	-10	2-11	**.973**	4	103	84	2b119,S33	—	-0.3
1922	Bos N	143	515	58	140	23	9	2	60	30	4	36	.272	.317	.363	78	-18	2-1	.953	-0	99	84	S115,2b28	—	-0.4
1923	Bos N	111	380	27	103	16	7	2	50	31	0	30	.271	.326	.366	86	-8	1-1	.970	-8	97	106	2b95,S19	—	-1.1
1924	Phi N	145	530	58	144	27	5	3	53	27	1	40	.272	.308	.358	70	-22	1-9	.970	9	**106**	95	2b145	—	-1.2
1925	Bro N	66	216	32	59	11	0	1	15	26	2	15	.273	.357	.338	81	-5	0-3	.966	2	97	88	S66	—	0.2
1926	Cin N	57	197	14	55	6	1	0	18	14	3	12	.279	.336	.320	79	-5	1	.963	2	94	168	S57	—	0.3
1927	Cin N	115	409	45	112	16	2	1	46	33	2	34	.274	.331	.330	80	-11	0	.952	-6	96	**129**	S104,2b12	—	-0.5
1928	Cin N	149	506	49	122	17	4	0	54	47	2	31	.241	.308	.291	58	-31	1	**.972**	15	102	**134**	S149	—	0.0
1929	Cin N	148	529	68	146	14	6	3	50	41	1	25	.276	.329	.342	70	-26	8	.953	8	100	**128**	S108,2b42	—	-0.5
1930	Cin N	132	424	36	98	16	7	1	34	24	0	28	.231	.272	.309	42	-41	2	.974	5	99	107	S74,2b66	—	-2.5
1931	Cin N	84	175	18	40	8	1	0	13	13	1	13	.229	.286	.286	57	-11	0	.954	0	101	121	S73,2b3/3	—	-0.7
1932	StL N	1	2	0	0	0	0	0	0	0	0	0	.000	.000	.000	-97	-1	0	.750	-0	45	235	/S	—	-0.1
	Bos N	40	95	9	26	5	2	0	6	6	1	9	.274	.324	.368	89	-2	0	.984	-1	96	118	2b20,S16,3b2	—	-0.1
	Year	41	97	9	26	5	2	0	6	6	1	9	.268	.317	.361	85	-2	0	.984	-1	96	118	2b20,S17,3b2	—	-0.2
1933	Bos N	5	15	0	1	0	0	0	1	3	0	1	.067	.222	.067	-16	-2	0	1.000	3	120	117	S5	—	0.1
Total	15	1446	4833	484	1269	200	55	16	494	351	24	354	.263	.316	.337	72	-199	21-28	.960	45	100	116	S846,2b589,3b5,1b4	—	-5.8

Ford, Lew Jon Lewis; B8.12.1976 Beaumont TX; BR/TR/6´0˝/(190–200); [BosA99 12/379]; d5.29; Col Dallas Baptist

YEAR	TM LG	G	AB	R	H	2B	3B	HR	RBI	BB-IB	HP	SO	AVG	OBP	SLG	AOPS	ABR	SB-CS	FA	FR	RNG	THR	GAMES AT POSITION	DL	BFW
2003	†Min A	34	73	16	24	7	1	3	15	8-0	1	9	.329	.402	.575	148	5	2-0	.923	-2	86	108	O25(8/13/6),D4	50	0.4
2004	†Min A	154	569	89	170	31	4	15	72	67-3	13	75	.299	.381	.446	113	13	20-2	.986	-1	100	101	O126(81/46/10),D26	0	1.1
2005	Min A	147	522	70	138	30	4	7	53	45-2	16	85	.264	.338	.377	90	-6	13-6	.972	-3	87	182	O95(18/63/16),D44	0	-1.2
2006	†Min A	104	234	40	53	6	1	4	18	16-0	4	43	.226	.287	.312	55	-16	9-1	.986	3	112	102	O92(64/13/22),D5	28	-1.3
Total	4	439	1398	215	385	74	10	29	158	136-5	34	212	.275	.351	.405	97	-4	44-9	.978	-3	98	127	O338(171/135/54),D79	78	-1.0

Ford, Ted Theodore Henry; B2.7.1947 Vineland NJ; BR/TR/5´10˝/(170–180); [CleA66*1/11]; d4.7

YEAR	TM LG	G	AB	R	H	2B	3B	HR	RBI	BB-IB	HP	SO	AVG	OBP	SLG	AOPS	ABR	SB-CS	FA	FR	RNG	THR	GAMES AT POSITION	DL	BFW
1970	Cle A	26	46	5	8	1	0	1	1	3-0	0	13	.174	.224	.261	32	-4	0-0	1.000	2	143	171	O12(2/1/10)	0	-0.3
1971	Cle A	74	196	15	38	6	0	2	14	9-0	0	34	.194	.229	.255	34	-17	2-2	1.000	5	116	144	O55(12/20/29)	0	-1.6
1972	Tex A	129	429	43	101	19	1	14	50	37-2	3	80	.235	.297	.382	106	2	4-3	.977	7	**113**	133	O119(16/0/104)	0	0.4
1973	Cle A	11	40	3	9	0	1	0	3	2-0	0	7	.225	.250	.275	50	-3	1-0	1.000	-4	27	0	O10(0/6/5)	0	-0.7
Total	4	240	711	66	156	26	2	17	68	51-2	3	134	.219	.272	.333	76	-22	7-5	.985	10	110	130	O196(30/27/148)	0	-2.2

Fordyce, Brook Brook Alexander; B5.7.1970 New London CT; BR/TR/6´1˝/(185–195); [NYN89 3/84]; d4.26

YEAR	TM LG	G	AB	R	H	2B	3B	HR	RBI	BB-IB	HP	SO	AVG	OBP	SLG	AOPS	ABR	SB-CS	FA	FR	RNG	THR	GAMES AT POSITION	DL	BFW
1995	NY N	4	2	1	1	1	0	0	0	1-0	0	0	.500	.667	1.000	344	1	0-0	ø	0	—	—	/H	0	0.1
1996	Cin N	4	7	0	2	1	0	0	1	3-0	0	1	.286	.500	.429	146	1	0-0	1.000	-1	223	112	C4	0	0.0
1997	Cin N	47	96	7	20	5	0	1	8	8-1	0	15	.208	.267	.292	46	-8	2-0	.983	-5	59	73	C30/D	20	-1.1
1998	Cin N	57	146	8	37	9	0	3	14	11-3	0	28	.253	.306	.377	77	-5	0-1	.978	-1	90	133	C54	30	-0.3
1999	Chi A	105	333	36	99	25	1	9	49	21-0	3	48	.297	.343	.459	101	0	2-0	.987	-9	96	93	C103	0	-0.2
2000	Chi A	40	125	18	34	7	1	5	21	6-0	2	23	.272	.313	.464	91	-2	0-0	1.000	8	139	116	C40	49	0.7
	Bal A	53	177	23	57	11	0	9	28	11-0	2	27	.322	.361	.537	132	8	0-0	.988	-8	68	50	C52	0	0.3
	Year	93	302	41	91	18	1	14	49	17-0	4	50	.301	.341	.507	114	5	0-0	.993	0	97	77	C92	0	1.0
2001	Bal A	95	292	30	61	18	0	5	19	21-1	3	56	.209	.268	.322	58	-18	1-2	.983	-13	64	93	C95	0	-2.5
2002	Bal A	56	130	7	30	8	0	1	8	9-0	4	19	.231	.301	.315	68	-6	1-0	.986	-8	54	76	C55	0	-1.0
2003	Bal A	108	348	28	95	12	2	6	31	19-1	1	44	.273	.311	.371	80	-11	2-3	.996	-6	79	83	C107	0	-1.0
2004	TB A	54	151	14	31	6	0	2	9	9-0	2	34	.205	.259	.285	43	-13	0-0	.990	-2	97	83	C51/D	0	-1.2
Total	10	623	1807	172	467	103	4	41	188	119-6	17	295	.258	.309	.388	81	-53	8-6	.988	-45	83	89	C591,D2	99	-6.2

Forster, Tom Thomas W.; B5.1.1859 New York NY; D7.17.1946 New York NY; BR/TR/5´9˝/153; d8.4

YEAR	TM LG	G	AB	R	H	2B	3B	HR	RBI	BB-IB	HP	SO	AVG	OBP	SLG	AOPS	ABR	SB-CS	FA	FR	RNG	THR	GAMES AT POSITION	DL	BFW
1882	Det N	21	76	5	7	0	0	0	2	5	—	12	.092	.148	.092	-21	-10	—	.830	-8	81	51	2b21	—	-1.7
1884	Pit AA	35	126	10	28	5	0	0	—	7	0	—	.222	.263	.262	73	-3	—	.897	4	110	93	S28,3b6/2	—	0.2
	†NY AA	0	0	0	0	0	0	0	—	0	0	—	ø	ø	ø	ø	0	—	.000	0	—	—	/H	—	0.0
1885	NY AA	57	213	28	47	7	2	0	18	17	1	—	.221	.281	.272	79	-4	—	.903	-5	95	95	2b52,O5(3/2/0)	—	-0.7
1886	NY AA	67	251	33	49	3	2	1	20	20	3	—	.195	.263	.235	61	-10	9	.891	-4	101	97	2b62,O4(2/2/0)/S	—	-1.0
Total	4	180	666	76	131	15	4	1	40	49	4	12	.197	.256	.236	59	-27	9	.885	-13	96	88	2b136,S29,O9(5/4/0),3b6	—	-3.2

YEAR	TM LG	G	AB	R	H	2B	3B	HR	RBI	BB-IB	HP	SO	AVG	OBP	SLG	AOPS	ABR	SB-CS	FA	FR	RNG	THR	GAMES AT POSITION	DL	BFW
Forsythe, Ed	Edward James; B4.30.1887 Kingston NY; D6.22.1956 Hoboken NJ; BR/TR/5´10˝/155; d10.2																								
1915	Bal F	1	3	0	0	0	0	0	0	1	0	0	.000	.250	.000	-26	-1	0	.667	-0	112	0	/3	—	-0.1
Foss, George	George Dueward "Deeby"; B6.13.1897 Register GA; D11.10.1969 Brandon FL; BR/TR/5´10.5˝/170; d4.16																								
1921	Was A	4	7	0	0	0	0	0	0	0	0	1	.000	.000	.000	-99	-2	0-0	.750	-0	89	536	/3	—	-0.2
Fosse, Ray	Raymond Earl; B4.4.1947 Marion IL; BR/TR/6´2˝/(205–215); [CleA65 1/7]; d9.8; [DL 1978 Mil A 179]																								
1967	Cle A	7	16	0	1	0	0	0	0	0-0	0	5	.063	.063	.063	-62	-3	0-0	1.000	2	75	275	C7	0	-0.1
1968	Cle A	1	0	0	0	0	0	0	0	0-0	0	0	ø	ø	ø	ø	0	0-0	1.000	-0	0	0	/C	0	0.0
1969	Cle A	37	116	11	20	3	0	2	9	8-1	1	29	.172	.230	.250	34	-11	1-0	.977	-2	48	142	C37	80	-1.2
1970	Cle A★	120	450	62	138	17	1	18	61	39-5	1	55	.307	.361	.469	122	13	1-5	.989	9	139	137	C120	0	2.6
1971	Cle A★	133	486	53	134	21	1	12	62	36-6	4	62	.276	.329	.397	96	-2	4-1	.988	4	96	112	C126,1b4	0	0.8
1972	Cle A	134	457	42	110	20	1	10	41	45-15	3	46	.241	.312	.354	95	-2	5-1	.985	8	108	90	C124,1b3	0	1.3
1973	†Oak A	143	492	37	126	23	2	7	52	25-4	1	62	.256	.291	.354	85	-11	2-2	.987	7	**171**	114	C141,D2	0	0.2
1974	†Oak A	69	204	20	40	8	3	4	23	11-1	2	31	.196	.241	.324	66	-10	1-1	.973	1	101	86	C68/D	77	-0.7
1975	†Oak A	82	136	14	19	3	2	0	12	8-0	1	19	.140	.192	.191	9	-17	0-1	.981	-3	85	69	C82/12	0	-1.9
1976	Cle A	90	276	26	83	9	1	2	30	20-1	0	20	.301	.347	.362	109	3	1-2	.987	2	103	88	C85,1b3/D	33	0.8
1977	Cle A	78	238	25	63	7	1	6	27	7-2	3	26	.265	.293	.378	84	-6	0-5	.983	3	66	128	C77/1D	0	-0.2
	Sea A	11	34	3	12	3	0	0	5	2-0	0	2	.353	.389	.441	126	1	0-1	.968	-2	205	0	C8,D2	0	-0.1
	Year	89	272	28	75	10	1	6	32	9-2	3	28	.276	.305	.386	90	-5	0-6	.982	1	78	117	C85,D3/1	0	-0.3
1979	Mil A	19	52	6	12	3	1	0	2	2-0	2	6	.231	.286	.327	65	-3	0-0	1.000	2	221	81	C13/1D	0	-0.1
Total	12	924	2957	299	758	117	13	61	324	203-35	18	363	.256	.306	.367	89	-48	15-19	.985	29	115	109	C889,1b13,D12/2	369	1.4
Foster, Pop	Clarence Francis; B4.8.1878 New Haven CT; D4.16.1944 Princeton NJ; BR/TR/5´8.5˝/?; d9.13; Col NYU																								
1898	NY N	32	112	10	30	6	1	0	9	0	0	—	.268	.268	.339	76	-4	0	.967	-3	39	0	O21(17/0/4),3b10,S2	—	-0.8
1899	NY N	84	301	48	89	9	7	3	57	20	4	—	.296	.348	.402	109	3	7	.949	-9	65	77	O84(1/0/84)/S3	—	-0.9
1900	NY N	31	84	19	22	3	1	0	11	11	0	—	.262	.347	.321	89	-1	0	1.000	1	65	218	O12(1/0/11),S7,2b5	—	0.0
1901	Was A	103	392	65	109	16	9	6	54	41	4	—	.278	.352	.411	113	7	10	.925	0	69	34	O102L,S2	—	0.1
	Chi A	12	35	4	10	2	1	1	6	4	0	—	.286	.359	.543	152	2	0	.909	-1	111	0	O9R	—	0.1
	Year	115	427	69	119	18	11	7	60	45	4	—	.279	.353	.422	116	9	10	.924	-0	72	32	O111(102/0/9),S2	—	0.2
Total	4	262	924	146	260	36	20	10	137	76	8	—	.281	.341	.396	107	7	17	.938	-11	66	55	O228(121/0/108),S12,3b11,2b5	—	-1.5
Foster, Eddie	Edward Cunningham "Kid"; B2.13.1887 Chicago IL; D1.15.1937 Washington DC; BR/TR/5´6.5˝/145; d4.14																								
1910	NY A	30	83	5	11	2	0	0	1	8	1	—	.133	.217	.157	16	-8	2	.909	-2	99	88	S22	—	-1.0
1912	Was A	**154**	618	98	176	34	9	2	70	53	4	—	.285	.345	.379	106	5	27	.920	10	**108**	105	3b154	—	1.9
1913	Was A	106	409	56	101	11	5	1	41	36	1	31	.247	.309	.306	78	-12	22	.901	2	**106**	**146**	3b105	—	-0.7
1914	Was A	**157**	616	82	174	16	10	2	50	60	2	47	.282	.348	.351	106	4	31-18	.929	-19	80	123	3b157	—	-1.1
1915	Was A	154	618	75	170	25	10	0	52	48	2	30	.275	.329	.348	101	-1	20-6	.919	-7	98	124	3b79,2b75	—	-0.2
1916	Was A	158	606	75	153	18	9	1	44	68	4	26	.252	.332	.317	96	-3	23-16	.929	-17	78	88	3b84,2b72	—	-1.8
1917	Was A	143	554	66	130	16	8	0	43	46	0	23	.235	.293	.292	80	-15	11	.935	-6	98	116	3b86,2b57	—	-2.0
1918	Was A	129	519	70	147	13	3	0	29	41	3	20	.283	.339	.320	101	0	12	.936	-3	100	**133**	3b127,2b2	—	0.1
1919	Was A	120	478	57	126	12	5	0	26	33	2	21	.264	.314	.310	76	-16	20	.946	7	109	85	3b115	—	-0.7
1920	Bos A	117	386	48	100	17	6	0	41	42	3	17	.259	.336	.334	82	-10	10-4	.957	9	110	138	3b88,2b21	—	0.2
1921	Bos A	120	412	51	117	18	6	0	35	57	0	15	.284	.371	.357	89	-5	13-7	.943	-10	99	115	3b94,2b22	—	-0.8
1922	Bos A	48	109	11	23	3	0	0	3	9	1	10	.211	.277	.239	36	-10	1-1	.886	-7	83	44	3b28,S3	—	-1.6
	StL A	37	144	29	44	4	0	0	12	20	1	8	.306	.394	.333	88	-1	3-1	.916	0	100	187	3b37	—	0.1
	Year	85	253	40	67	7	0	0	15	29	2	18	.265	.345	.292	67	-11	4-2	.905	-7	93	132	3b65,S3	—	-1.5
1923	StL A	27	100	9	18	2	0	0	4	7	1	7	.180	.241	.200	16	-12	0-0	.961	-4	81	125	2b20,3b7	—	-1.6
Total	13	1500	5652	732	1490	191	71	6	451	528	25	255	.264	.329	.326	89	-84	195-53	.930	-48	98	119	3b1161,2b269,S25	—	-9.2
Foster, Elmer	Elmer Ellsworth; B8.15.1861 Minneapolis MN; D7.22.1946 Deephaven MN; BR/TL/5´10˝/178; d4.17																								
1886	NY AA	35	125	16	23	0	1	0	7	7	2	—	.184	.239	.200	41	-8	3	.853	-4	108	41	2b21,O14(9/5/0)	—	-1.0
1888	NY N	37	136	15	20	3	2	0	10	9	3	20	.147	.216	.199	33	-10	13	.852	-3	78	0	O37(16/21/0)/3	—	-1.4
1889	NY N	2	4	2	0	0	0	0	0	3	0	1	.000	.429	.000	24	0	2	1.000	0	0	0	O2C	—	0.0
1890	Chi N	27	105	20	26	4	2	5	23	9	3	21	.248	.325	.467	125	2	18	.986	2	46	0	O27C	—	0.3
1891	Chi N	4	16	3	3	0	0	1	1	1	0	2	.188	.235	.375	77	-1	1	.875	0	189	0	O4C	—	-0.1
Total	5	105	386	56	72	7	5	6	41	29	8	44	.187	.258	.277	66	-17	37	.883	-5	73	0	O84(25/59/0),2b21/3	—	-2.2
Foster, George	George Arthur; B12.1.1948 Tuscaloosa AL; BR/TR/6´1˝/(175–198); [SFN68*3/55]; d9.10; Col El Camino (CA) JC																								
1969	SF N	9	5	1	2	0	0	0	1	0-0	0	1	.400	.400	.400	126	0	0-0	1.000	-0	87	0	O8R	0	0.0
1970	SF N	9	19	2	6	1	1	1	4	2-1	0	5	.316	.381	.632	168	2	0-0	1.000	-0	107	0	O7(6/0/1)	0	0.1
1971	SF N	36	105	11	28	5	0	3	8	6-1	0	27	.267	.304	.400	100	0	0-1	.980	-1	93	54	O30(24/0/7)	0	-0.4
	Cin N	104	368	39	86	18	4	10	50	23-2	7	93	.234	.289	.386	91	-5	7-6	.986	5	103	133	O102(1/101/1)	0	-0.4
	Year	140	473	50	114	23	4	13	58	29-3	7	120	.241	.292	.389	93	-6	7-7	.985	4	101	116	O132(25/101/8)	0	-0.8
1972	†Cin N	59	145	15	29	4	1	2	12	5-1	1	44	.200	.230	.283	48	-11	2-1	.973	-2	100	36	O47(2/1/44)	0	-1.5
1973	Cin N	17	39	6	11	3	0	4	9	4-0	0	7	.282	.349	.667	183	4	0-1	1.000	-0	81	148	O13(1/11/5)	0	0.3
1974	Cin N	106	276	31	73	18	0	7	41	30-5	4	52	.264	.343	.406	111	5	3-2	.989	-1	102	39	O98(6/45/69)	0	0.0
1975	†Cin N	134	463	71	139	24	4	23	78	40-11	3	73	.300	.356	.518	139	23	2-1	.990	10	112	118	O125(95/30/18)/1	0	2.7
1976	†Cin N★	144	562	86	172	21	9	29	**121**	52-4	4	89	.306	.364	.530	149	34	17-3	**.994**	5	106	89	O142(116/36/24)/1	0	3.6
1977	Cin N★	158	615	**124**	197	31	2	**52**	**149**	61-10	5	107	.320	.382	**.631**	164	**54**	6-4	.992	11	112	117	O158(136/32/1)	0	5.8
1978	Cin N★	158	604	97	170	26	7	**40**	**120**	70-16	7	138	.281	.360	.546	150	39	4-4	.971	-0	100	76	O157(154/11/0)	0	3.3
1979	†Cin N★	121	440	68	133	18	3	30	98	59-7	3	105	.302	.386	.561	156	34	0-2	.982	-2	93	78	O116L	21	2.7
1980	Cin N	144	528	79	144	21	5	25	93	75-14	1	99	.273	.362	.473	135	25	1-0	.997	3	107	58	O141L	0	2.3
1981	Cin N★	**108**	414	64	122	23	2	22	90	51-5	3	75	.295	.373	.519	153	29	4-0	.991	3	103	84	O108L	0	2.9
1982	NY N	151	550	64	136	23	2	13	70	50-9	2	123	.247	.309	.367	89	-8	1-1	.974	6	105	106	O138L	0	-0.9
1983	NY N	157	601	74	145	19	2	28	90	38-5	4	111	.241	.289	.419	95	-7	1-1	.988	3	98	97	O153L	0	-1.2
1984	NY N	146	553	67	149	22	1	24	86	30-9	6	122	.269	.311	.443	112	6	2-2	.976	2	105	56	O141L	0	0.1
1985	NY N	129	452	57	119	24	1	21	77	46-5	2	87	.263	.331	.460	122	13	0-1	.976	-5	87	81	O123L	0	0.2
1986	NY N	72	233	28	53	6	1	13	38	21-1	0	53	.227	.289	.429	98	-2	1-1	.962	-2	87	102	O62L	0	-0.7
	Chi A	15	51	2	11	0	2	1	4	3-0	0	8	.216	.259	.353	62	-3	0-0	1.000	1	90	307	O11L,D3	0	-0.3
Total	18	1977	7023	986	1925	307	47	348	1239	666-106	52	1419	.274	.338	.480	127	232	51-31	.984	33	102	88	O1880(1534/267/178),D3,1b2	21	18.6
Foster, Leo	Leonard Norris; B2.2.1951 Covington KY; BR/TR/5´11˝/(160–165); [AtlN69 2/36]; d7.9																								
1971	Atl N	9	10	1	0	0	0	0	0	0-0	0	1	.000	.000	.000	-94	-3	0-0	.900	-0	114	141	S3	0	-0.3
1973	Atl N	3	6	1	1	1	0	0	0	0-0	0	2	.167	.167	.333	33	-1	0-0	1.000	-1	24	115	/S	0	-0.1
1974	Atl N	72	112	16	22	2	0	1	5	9-0	0	22	.196	.254	.241	38	-9	1-2	.977	-3	98	91	S43,2b10,3b3/rf	0	-1.0
1976	NY N	24	59	11	12	2	0	1	15	8-1	0	5	.203	.299	.288	70	-2	3-0	.920	-1	101	82	3b9,S7,2b3	0	-0.2
1977	NY N	36	75	6	17	3	0	0	6	5-0	1	14	.227	.284	.267	50	-5	3-1	.968	-3	79	83	2b20,S8,3b2	0	-0.7
Total	5	144	262	35	52	8	0	2	26	22-1	1	44	.198	.262	.252	43	-20	7-3	.964	-9	97	90	S62,2b33,3b14/rf	0	-2.3
Foster, Reddy	Oscar E.; B8.1864 Richmond VA; D12.19.1908 Richmond VA; d6.3																								
1896	NY N	1	1	0	0	0	0	0	0	0	0	0	.000	.000	.000	-99	0	0	ø	0	—	—	/H	—	0.0
Foster, Bob	Robert; d6.18																								
1884	Phi U	1	3	0	1	0	1	0	—	0	—	—	.333	.333	1.000	314	1	—	.625	-1	—	—	/C	—	-0.1
	Phi AA	4	11	4	2	0	0	0	—	3	0	—	.182	.357	.182	76	0	—	.885	-1	—	—	C4/rf	—	-0.1
Total	1	5	14	4	3	0	1	0	—	3	0	—	.214	.353	.357	124	1	—	.824	-2	—	—	C5/rf	—	-0.2
Foster, Roy	Roy; B7.29.1945 Bixby OK; BR/TR/6´0˝/(185–195); d4.7																								
1970	Cle A	139	477	66	128	26	0	23	60	54-4	**12**	75	.268	.357	.468	120	14	3-3	.965	-6	88	79	O131(114/0/17)	0	0.1
1971	Cle A	125	396	51	97	21	1	18	45	35-2	6	48	.245	.314	.439	102	1	6-1	.968	0	94	142	O107(46/0/64)	0	-0.4
1972	Cle A	73	143	19	32	4	0	4	13	21-2	2	23	.224	.325	.336	95	0	0-2	.966	-2	87	82	O45(15/0/31)	0	-0.5
Total	3	337	1016	136	257	51	1	45	118	110-8	20	146	.253	.336	.438	110	15	9-6	.967	-8	90	104	O283(175/0/112)	0	-0.8

YEAR	TM LG	G	AB	R	H	2B	3B	HR	RBI	BB-IB		HP	SO	AVG	OBP	SLG	AOPS	ABR	SB-CS	FA	FR	RNG	THR	GAMES AT POSITION	DL	BFW
Fothergill, Bob	Robert Roy "Fats"; B8.16.1897 Massillon OH; D3.20.1938 Detroit MI; BR/TR/5´10.5˝/230; d4.18																									
1922	Det A	42	152	20	49	12	4	0	29	8		0	9	.322	.356	.454	113	3	1-5	.945	-5	73	53	O38(2/10/26)	—	-0.7
1923	Det A	101	241	34	76	18	2	1	49	12		4	19	.315	.358	.419	106	2	5-4	.977	-2	99	61	O68(45/20/3)	—	-0.4
1924	Det A	54	166	28	50	8	3	0	15	5		1	13	.301	.326	.386	84	-5	2-3	.968	-2	101	46	O45(43/0/2)	—	-1.0
1925	Det A	71	204	38	72	14	0	2	28	6		2	3	.353	.377	.451	111	3	3-2	.977	3	109	112	O59(40/16/4)	—	0.3
1926	Det A	110	387	63	142	31	7	3	73	33		3	23	.367	.421	.506	139	23	4-12	.961	-2	**110**	29	O103(76/19/9)	—	1.0
1927	Det A	143	527	93	189	38	9	9	114	47		2	31	.359	.413	.516	138	30	9-15	.961	-7	103	21	O137L	—	0.8
1928	Det A	111	347	49	110	28	10	3	63	24		3	19	.317	.366	.481	119	9	8-3	.959	-4	96	69	O90(70/0/20)	—	-0.1
1929	Det A	115	277	42	98	24	9	6	62	11		0	11	.354	.378	.570	140	15	3-1	.967	-1	109	38	O59(39/0/20)	—	1.0
1930	Det A	55	143	14	37	9	3	2	14	6		0	10	.259	.289	.406	72	-7	1-1	.947	-2	92	45	O38(32/0/6)	—	-1.0
	Chi A	52	135	10	40	9	0	0	24	4		2	8	.296	.326	.363	77	-5	0-0	.879	-2	95	85	O31(8/0/22)	—	-0.8
	Year	107	278	24	77	18	3	2	38	10		2	18	.277	.307	.385	75	-11	1-1	.913	-4	93	64	O69(40/0/28)	—	-1.8
1931	Chi A	108	312	25	88	9	4	3	56	17		2	17	.282	.323	.365	86	-8	2-2	.972	-1	109	33	O74(48/0/26)	—	-1.2
1932	Chi A	116	346	36	102	24	1	7	50	27		1	10	.295	.348	.431	107	4	4-4	.952	-6	87	70	O86(53/0/34)	—	-0.6
1933	Bos A	28	32	1	11	1	0	0	5	2		0	4	.344	.382	.375	102	0	0-0	1.000	-0	97	0	O4(1/0/3)	—	0.0
Total	12	1106	3269	453	1064	225	52	36	582	202		20	177	.325	.368	.459	115	64	42-52	.961	-30	101	49	O832(594/65/175)	—	-2.7
Fournier, Jack	John Frank; B9.28.1889 AuSable MI; D9.5.1973 Tacoma WA; BL/TR/6´0˝/195; d4.13																									
1912	Chi A	35	73	6	14	5	2	0	2	4		3	—	.192	.262	.315	67	-3	2	.988	3	172	55	1b17	—	-0.1
1913	Chi A	68	172	20	40	8	5	1	23	21		2	23	.233	.323	.355	99	0	9	.990	3	105	72	1b29,O23(11/0/12)	—	0.1
1914	Chi A	109	379	44	118	14	9	6	44	31		3	44	.311	.368	.443	146	19	10-13	.978	4	127	69	1b97,O6(3/1/2)	—	2.0
1915	Chi A	126	422	86	136	20	18	5	77	64		**15**	37	.322	.429	**.491**	170	38	21-16	.986	1	104	105	1b65,O57(38/13/6)	—	3.6
1916	Chi A	105	313	36	75	13	9	3	44	36		5	40	.240	.328	.367	108	2	19	.976	-3	95	109	1b85/lf	—	-0.3
1917	Chi A	1	1	0	0	0	0	0	0	0		0	1	.000	.000	.000	-98	0	0	ø	0	—	—	/H	—	0.0
1918	NY A	27	100	9	35	6	1	0	12	7		0	7	.350	.393	.430	145	5	7	.976	-3	74	137	1b27	—	0.2
1920	StL N	141	530	77	162	33	14	3	61	42		**12**	42	.306	.370	.438	136	26	26-20	.983	0	106	101	1b138	—	2.2
1921	StL N	149	574	103	197	27	9	16	86	56		**8**	48	.343	.409	.505	144	38	20-22	.987	-4	89	89	1b149	—	2.0
1922	StL N	128	404	64	119	23	9	10	61	40		7	21	.295	.368	.470	120	12	6-8	.982	2	115	82	1b109/P	—	0.6
1923	Bro N	133	515	91	181	30	13	22	102	43		9	28	.351	.411	.588	165	47	11-4	.985	4	118	83	1b133	—	**4.2**
1924	Bro N	**154**	563	93	188	25	4	**27**	116	83		10	46	.334	.428	.536	162	54	7-5	.985	7	117	83	1b153	—	4.9
1925	Bro N	145	545	99	191	21	16	22	130	**86**		8	39	.350	.446	.569	162	54	4-6	.989	3	105	85	1b145	—	4.2
1926	Bro N	87	243	39	69	9	2	11	48	30		1	16	.284	.365	.473	126	9	0	.986	-2	84	40	1b64	—	0.3
1927	Bos N	122	374	55	106	18	2	10	53	44		6	16	.283	.368	.422	121	12	4	.989	-0	100	73	1b102	—	0.5
Total	15	1530	5208	822	1631	252	113	136	859	587		89	408	.313	.392	.483	143	313	146-94	.984	16	107	85	1b1313,O87(53/14/20)/P	—	24.4
Fouser, Bill	William C.; B10.1855 Philadelphia PA; D3.1.1919 Philadelphia PA; d4.22																									
1876	Phi N	21	89	11	12	0	1	0	2	0		—	0	.135	.135	.157	-3	-10	—	.827	1	124	49	2b14,O7(0/1/6)/1	—	-0.7
Foutz, Dave	David Luther "Scissors"; B9.7.1856 Carroll Co. MD; D3.5.1897 Waverly MD; BR/TR/6´2˝/161; d7.29; M4; b–Frank; ▲																									
1884	StL AA	33	119	17	27	4	0	0	—	8		0	—	.227	.276	.261	73	-3	—	.940	1	108	**728**	P25,O14(0/3/11)	—	-0.1
1885	†StL AA	65	238	42	59	6	4	0	34	11		0	—	.248	.281	.307	82	-6	—	.899	6	**150**	207	P47,1b15,O4L	—	0.0
1886	†StL AA	102	414	66	116	18	9	3	59	9		1	—	.280	.297	.389	109	1	17	.949	2	86	86	P59,O34R,1b11	—	0.0
1887	†StL AA	102	423	79	151	26	13	4	108	23		2	—	.357	.393	.508	136	17	22	.899	-4	49	0	O50R,P40,1b15	—	0.4
1888	Bro AA	140	563	91	156	20	13	3	99	28		2	—	.277	.314	.375	121	11	35	.895	2	103	125	O78(0/1/77),1b42,P23	—	0.5
1889	†Bro AA	**138**	553	118	152	19	8	6	113	64		3	23	.275	.353	.371	106	5	43	.979	-3	70	95	1b134,P12	—	-0.9
1890	†Bro N	**129**	509	106	154	25	13	5	98	52		1	25	.303	.368	.432	133	20	42	.978	-1	98	114	1b113,O13(4/9/1),P5	—	0.7
1891	Bro N	130	521	87	134	26	8	2	73	40		2	25	.257	.313	.349	93	-5	48	.976	-3	85	75	1b124,P6/S	—	-1.7
1892	Bro N	61	220	33	41	5	3	1	26	14		0	14	.186	.235	.250	48	-14	19	.850	1	137	0	O29(11/7/11),P27,1b6	—	-1.0
1893	Bro N	**130**	557	91	137	20	10	7	67	32		0	34	.246	.287	.355	74	-25	39	.913	-7	75	36	O77(66/11/0),1b54,P6,M	—	-3.1
1894	Bro N	73	297	40	90	12	9	0	52	14		1	13	.303	.337	.404	84	-9	14	.976	-3	81	78	1b73/PM	—	-0.9
1895	Bro N	31	115	14	34	4	1	0	21	4		0	2	.296	.319	.348	78	-4	1	.879	-3	120	188	O20(7/2/11),1b8,M	—	-0.7
1896	Bro N	2	8	0	2	1	0	0	0	1		0	0	.250	.333	.375	92	0	0	1.000	1	1032	0	/rf1M	—	0.0
Total	13	1136	4537	784	1253	186	91	31	750	300		12	136	.276	.323	.378	101	-12	280	.977	-13	81	94	1b596,O320(92/33/196),P251/S	—	-6.8
Foutz, Frank	Frank Hayes; B4.8.1877 Baltimore MD; D12.25.1961 Lima OH; BR/TR/5´11˝/165; d4.26; b–Dave																									
1901	Bal A	20	72	13	17	4	1	2	14	8		1	—	.236	.321	.403	96	0	0	.959	-0	107	69	1b20	—	-0.1
Fowler, Boob	Joseph Chester "Gink"; B11.11.1900 Waco TX; D10.8.1988 Dallas TX; BL/TR/5´11.5˝/180; d5.6; Col TCU																									
1923	Cin N	11	33	9	11	0	1	1	6	1		0	3	.333	.353	.485	121	1	1-0	.847	-2	88	115	S10	—	0.0
1924	Cin N	59	129	20	43	6	1	0	9	5		0	15	.333	.358	.395	103	1	2-2	.936	-4	96	87	S32,2b4,3b2	—	-0.1
1925	Cin N	6	5	0	2	1	0	0	2	0		0	1	.400	.400	.600	155	0	0-0	ø	0	—	—	/H	—	0.0
1926	Bos A	2	8	1	1	0	0	0	1	0		0	0	.125	.125	.125	-36	-2	0-0	.800	-0	117	0	3b2	—	-0.2
Total	4	78	175	30	57	7	2	1	18	6		0	19	.326	.348	.406	102	0	3-2	.910	-6	94	94	S42,3b4,2b4	—	-0.3
Fox, Andy	Andrew Junipero; B1.12.1971 Sacramento CA; BL/TR/6´4˝/(200–205); [NYA89 2/45]; d4.7; OF(24/10/47)																									
1996	†NY A	113	189	26	37	4	0	3	13	20-0		1	28	.196	.276	.265	38	-19	11-3	.958	-3	87	71	2b72,3b31,S9/rfD	0	-1.6
1997	†NY A	22	31	13	7	1	0	0	1	7-0		0	9	.226	.368	.258	68	-1	2-1	1.000	4	132	124	3b11,2b5,S2,O2R,D2	0	0.3
1998	Ari N	139	502	67	139	21	6	9	44	43-0		18	97	.277	.355	.396	97	-2	14-7	.982	-13	83	73	2b60,O48(10/8/33),3b26,1b12	0	-1.3
1999	†Ari N	99	274	34	70	12	2	6	33	33-10		9	61	.255	.351	.380	85	-6	4-1	.958	-12	88	84	S82,3b12	15	-1.1
2000	Ari N	31	86	10	18	4	0	1	10	4-1		0	16	.209	.244	.291	33	-9	2-1	.952	-3	81	101	3b20,O6(1/1/4)/1	13	-1.1
	Fla N	69	164	19	40	4	2	3	10	18-3		3	37	.244	.330	.348	75	-7	8-3	.932	3	111	68	S33,O14(9/0/5),3b12,2b2	0	-0.1
	Year	100	250	29	58	8	2	4	20	22-4		3	53	.232	.302	.328	60	-16	10-4	.932	1	111	68	S33,3b32,O20(10/1/9),2b2/1	0	-1.2
2001	Fla N	54	81	8	15	0	1	3	7	15-1		2	17	.185	.327	.321	71	-4	1-0	.938	-2	94	122	S12,3b9,2b2,O2(1/1/0)	92	-0.4
2002	Fla N	133	435	55	109	14	5	4	41	49-6		10	94	.251	.338	.333	81	-11	31-7	.965	-6	90	101	S112,2b7,3b4/rf	0	-0.4
2003	Fla N	70	108	12	21	5	1	0	8	7-0		4	29	.194	.269	.259	40	-10	1-2	.923	-6	80	92	2b15,S9,3b5,1b2,O2L	0	-1.5
2004	Mon N	34	43	2	4	0	0	1	1	0-0		0	16	.093	.093	.163	-34	-9	0-0	1.000	-1	74	0	S5,2b3,3b3/1	0	-0.9
	Tex A	12	12	2	1	0	0	0	0	1-0		0	3	.083	.154	.083	-34	-2	0-0	1.000	1	137	131	2b3,3b2,O2(1/0/1)/D	0	-0.1
Total	9	776	1925	248	461	65	17	30	168	197-21		47	407	.239	.324	.338	73	-80	74-25	.956	-36	92	93	S264,2b169,3b135,O78R,1b16,D6	120	-8.2
Fox, Charlie	Charles Francis "Irish"; B10.7.1921 New York NY; D2.16.2004 Stanford CA; BR/TR/5´11˝/180; d9.24; Mil 1943–45; M7/C5																									
1942	NY N	3	7	1	3	0	0	0	1	1		0	2	.429	.500	.429	172	1	0	1.000	-1	*67*	*0*	C3	0	0.0
Fox, Eric	Eric Hollis; B8.15.1963 Lemoore CA; BB/TL/5´10˝/180; [SeaA86*S1/5]; d7.7; Col Cal St.–Fresno																									
1992	†Oak A	51	143	24	34	5	2	3	13	13-0		0	29	.238	.299	.364	90	-3	3-4	.990	2	104	127	O43(20/19/16),D4	0	-0.2
1993	Oak A	29	56	5	8	1	0	1	5	2-0		0	7	.143	.172	.214	3	-8	0-2	1.000	1	112	0	O26(5/18/3),D2	0	-0.8
1994	Oak A	26	44	7	9	2	0	1	1	3-0		0	8	.205	.255	.318	51	-3	2-0	1.000	1	110	142	O24(0/16/8)	0	-0.2
1995	Tex A	10	15	2	0	0	0	0	0	3-0		0	4	.000	.167	.000	-50	-3	0-0	1.000	0	117	0	O8(3/2/3)/D	0	-0.3
Total	4	116	258	38	51	8	2	5	19	21-0		0	48	.198	.257	.302	55	-17	5-6	.995	4	108	91	O101(28/55/30),D7	0	-1.5
Fox, Pete	Ervin; B3.8.1909 Evansville IN; D7.5.1966 Detroit MI; BR/TR/5´11˝/165; d4.12																									
1933	Det A	128	535	82	154	26	13	7	57	23		2	38	.288	.320	.424	94	-8	9-6	.978	-5	100	56	O124(0/116/8)	—	-1.6
1934	†Det A	128	516	101	147	31	2	2	45	49		4	53	.285	.351	.364	85	-11	25-10	.974	4	101	137	O121(0/11/110)	—	-1.1
1935	†Det A	131	517	116	166	38	8	15	73	45		6	52	.321	.382	.513	134	25	14-4	.988	-1	100	87	O125(0/6/123)	—	1.7
1936	Det A	73	220	46	67	12	1	4	26	34		3	23	.305	.405	.423	104	3	1-3	.968	-1	107	59	O55(5/0/50)	—	-0.2
1937	Det A	148	628	116	208	39	8	12	82	41		0	43	.331	.372	.476	110	8	12-8	.976	-5	102	43	O143(11/27/106)	—	-0.4
1938	Det A	**155**	634	91	186	35	10	7	96	31		2	39	.293	.328	.413	80	-22	16-7	**.994**	-3	96	90	O155(1/0/154)	—	-3.0
1939	Det A	141	519	69	153	24	6	7	66	35		2	41	.295	.342	.405	84	-14	23-12	.970	8	**113**	126	O126R	—	-1.1
1940	†Det A	93	350	49	101	17	4	5	48	21		0	30	.289	.329	.403	81	-10	7-7	.967	0	103	90	O85(2/1/82)	—	-1.6
1941	Bos A	73	268	38	81	12	7	0	31	21		2	32	.302	.357	.399	97	-1	9-2	.977	-0	100	91	O62(8/5/49)	0	-0.4
1942	Bos A	77	256	42	67	15	5	3	42	20		3	28	.262	.323	.395	98	-1	8-7	.966	-5	90	44	O71(7/0/64)	0	-1.1
1943	Bos A	127	489	54	141	24	4	2	44	34		2	40	.288	.337	.366	104	2	22-8	.961	-4	95	104	O125(3/0/122)	0	-0.9
1944	Bos A☆	121	496	70	156	37	6	1	64	27		3	34	.315	.354	.419	122	13	10-5	.987	-1	98	88	O119R	0	0.5
1945	Bos A	66	208	21	51	4	1	0	20	11		4	18	.245	.296	.274	64	-10	2-2	.989	-3	84	99	O57R	0	-1.8
Total	13	1461	5636	895	1678	314	75	65	694	392		33	471	.298	.347	.415	98	-26	158-81	.977	-15	100	87	O1368(37/166/1170)	0	-11.0

Fox, Paddy George B.; B12.1.1868 Pottstown PA; D5.8.1914 Philadelphia PA; d7.13

YEAR	TM LG	G	AB	R	H	2B	3B	HR	RBI	BB-IB	HP	SO	AVG	OBP	SLG	AOPS	ABR	SB-CS	FA	FR	RNG	THR	GAMES AT POSITION	DL	BFW
1891	Lou AA	6	19	1	2	0	1	0	2	2	2	3	.105	.261	.211	36	-2	0	.929	-1	69	0	3b6	—	-0.3
1899	Pit N	13	41	4	10	0	1	1	3	3	1	—	.244	.311	.366	86	-1	2	.971	2	153	204	1b9,C3	—	0.1
Total	2	19	60	5	12	0	2	1	5	5	3	3	.200	.294	.317	70	-3	2	.971	0	153	204	1b9,3b6,C3	—	-0.2

Fox, Nellie Jacob Nelson; B12.25.1927 St.Thomas PA; D12.1.1975 Baltimore MD; BL/TR/5´9˝/(150–162); d6.8; C8; HF1997

YEAR	TM LG	G	AB	R	H	2B	3B	HR	RBI	BB-IB	HP	SO	AVG	OBP	SLG	AOPS	ABR	SB-CS	FA	FR	RNG	THR	GAMES AT POSITION	DL	BFW
1947	Phi A	7	3	2	0	0	0	0	0	1	0	0	.000	.250	.000	-26	0	0-0	1.000	-0	0	0	/2	0	-0.1
1948	Phi A	3	13	0	2	0	0	0	0	1	0	0	.154	.214	.154	-1	-2	1-0	.950	-2	53	36	2b3	0	-0.3
1949	Phi A	88	247	42	63	6	2	0	21	32	6	9	.255	.354	.296	75	-8	2-2	.982	-1	97	117	2b77	0	-0.5
1950	Chi A	130	457	45	113	12	7	0	30	35	2	17	.247	.304	.304	58	-31	4-3	.974	4	102	97	2b121	0	-2.0
1951	Chi A★	147	604	93	189	32	12	4	55	43	14	11	.313	.372	.425	118	14	9-12	.981	-9	96	103	2b147	0	1.2
1952	Chi A☆	152	648	76	**192**	25	10	0	39	34	3	14	.296	.334	.366	94	-7	5-5	**.985**	9	98	105	2b151	0	0.9
1953	Chi A★	154	624	92	178	31	8	3	72	49	7	18	.285	.344	.375	91	-7	4-5	.983	3	95	87	2b154	0	0.6
1954	Chi A★	**155**	631	111	**201**	24	8	2	47	51	5	12	.319	.372	.391	106	6	16-9	**.989**	-2	96	99	2b155	0	1.6
1955	Chi A★	154	636	100	198	28	7	6	59	38-1	**17**	15	.311	.364	.406	104	4	7-9	.974	**31**	**117**	100	2b154	0	4.4
1956	Chi A★	**154**	649	109	192	20	10	4	52	44-1	10	14	.296	.347	.376	90	-10	8-4	**.986**	4	95	110	2b154	0	0.6
1957	Chi A★	**155**	619	110	**196**	27	8	6	61	75-2	16	13	.317	.403	.415	124	24	5-6	.986	25	**109**	**131**	2b155	0	6.0
1958	Chi A★	**155**	623	82	**187**	21	6	0	49	47-5	11	11	.300	.357	.353	99	0	5-6	.985	1	94	101	2b155	0	1.2
1959	†Chi A★	**156**	624	84	191	34	6	2	70	71-8	7	13	.306	.380	.389	114	15	5-6	**.988**	-8	102	89	2b156	0	1.9
1960	Chi A★	150	605	85	175	24	**10**	2	59	50-2	10	13	.289	.351	.372	97	-2	2-4	.985	19	**109**	**113**	2b149	0	2.8
1961	Chi A★	159	606	67	152	11	5	2	51	59-3	9	12	.251	.323	.295	69	-27	2-3	.982	2	100	92	2b159	0	-1.2
1962	Chi A	157	621	79	166	27	7	2	54	38-0	7	12	.267	.314	.343	78	-20	1-2	**.990**	5	102	96	2b154	0	-0.2
1963	Chi A★	137	539	54	140	19	0	2	42	24-1	7	17	.260	.299	.306	72	-21	0-2	**.988**	-3	98	94	2b134	0	-1.4
1964	Hou N	133	442	45	117	12	6	0	28	27-1	10	13	.265	.320	.319	86	-8	0-2	.977	-8	96	80	2b115	0	-0.8
1965	Hou N	21	41	3	11	2	0	0	1	0-0	1	2	.268	.286	.317	75	-1	0-0	1.000	1	119	120	3b6,1b2/2	0	-0.1
Total	19	2367	9232	1279	2663	355	112	35	790	719-24	142	216	.288	.348	.363	94	-81	76-80	.984	71	100	101	2b2295,3b6,1b2	0	14.6

Fox, Jack John Paul; B5.21.1885 Reading PA; D6.28.1963 Reading PA; BR/TR/5´10˝/185; d6.2

YEAR	TM LG	G	AB	R	H	2B	3B	HR	RBI	BB-IB	HP	SO	AVG	OBP	SLG	AOPS	ABR	SB-CS	FA	FR	RNG	THR	GAMES AT POSITION	DL	BFW
1908	Phi A	9	30	2	6	0	0	0	0	0	0	—	.200	.200	.200	28	-2	2	.923	-1	0	0	O8(0/1/7)	—	-0.4

Fox, Bill William Henry; B1.15.1872 Sturbridge MA; D5.7.1946 Minneapolis MN; BB/TR/5´10˝/160; d8.20; Col Holy Cross

YEAR	TM LG	G	AB	R	H	2B	3B	HR	RBI	BB-IB	HP	SO	AVG	OBP	SLG	AOPS	ABR	SB-CS	FA	FR	RNG	THR	GAMES AT POSITION	DL	BFW
1897	Was N	4	14	4	4	0	0	0	0	1	0	—	.286	.333	.286	65	-1	0	.700	-1	127	0	S2,2b2	—	-0.1
1901	Cin N	43	159	9	28	2	1	0	7	4	1	—	.176	.201	.201	18	-17	9	.948	4	106	115	2b43	—	-1.2
Total	2	47	173	13	32	2	1	0	7	5	1	—	.185	.212	.208	22	-18	9	.944	4	103	125	2b45,S2	—	-1.3

Foxx, Jimmie James Emory "Beast","Double X"; B10.22.1907 Sudlersville MD; D7.21.1967 Miami FL; BR/TR/6´0˝/195; d5.1; C1; HF1951; OF(12/0/9); ▲

YEAR	TM LG	G	AB	R	H	2B	3B	HR	RBI	BB-IB	HP	SO	AVG	OBP	SLG	AOPS	ABR	SB-CS	FA	FR	RNG	THR	GAMES AT POSITION	DL	BFW
1925	Phi A	10	9	2	6	1	0	0	0	0	0	1	.667	.667	.778	249	2	0-0	ø	0	*0*	*0*	/C	—	0.2
1926	Phi A	26	32	8	10	2	1	0	5	1	0	6	.313	.333	.438	95	0	1-0	1.000	1	*105*	*128*	C12,O3R	—	0.1
1927	Phi A	61	130	23	42	6	5	3	20	14	1	11	.323	.393	.515	127	5	2-1	.975	-2	86	53	1b32,C5	—	0.2
1928	Phi A	118	400	85	131	29	10	13	79	60	1	43	.327	.416	.548	147	29	3-9	.940	0	104	92	3b60,1b30,C19	—	2.8
1929	†Phi A	149	517	123	183	23	9	33	118	103	2	70	.354	**.463**	.625	171	59	9-7	.995	-3	85	89	1b142,3b8	—	4.3
1930	†Phi A	153	562	127	188	33	13	37	156	93	0	66	.335	.429	.637	159	51	7-7	.990	-1	91	87	1b153	—	3.5
1931	†Phi A	139	515	93	150	32	10	30	120	73	1	84	.291	.380	.567	138	27	4-3	.993	-3	83	120	1b112,3b26/lf	—	1.3
1932	Phi A	**154**	585	**151**	213	33	9	**58**	**169**	116	0	96	.364	.469	**.749**	203	**91**	3-7	**.994**	-3	94	104	1b141,3b13	—	**6.7**
1933	Phi A☆	149	573	125	204	37	9	**48**	**163**	96	1	93	**.356**	.449	**.703**	**199**	**82**	2-2	.990	7	**122**	78	1b149/S	—	**6.9**
1934	Phi A★	150	539	120	180	28	6	44	130	**111**	1	75	.334	.449	.653	188	73	11-2	.993	4	**112**	107	1b140,3b9	—	6.1
1935	Phi A★	147	535	118	185	33	7	**36**	115	114	0	99	.346	.461	**.636**	**182**	70	6-4	**.997**	4	113	97	1b121,C26,3b2	—	**5.9**
1936	Bos A★	**155**	585	130	198	32	8	41	143	105	1	119	.338	.440	.631	153	49	13-4	.991	1	106	95	1b139,O16(11/0/5)/3	—	3.3
1937	Bos A★	150	569	111	162	24	6	36	127	99	1	96	.285	.392	.538	127	23	10-8	**.994**	11	**129**	91	1b150/C	—	1.8
1938	Bos A★	149	565	139	197	33	9	50	**175**	**119**	0	76	**.349**	**.462**	**.704**	**180**	**72**	5-4	.987	7	**123**	115	1b149	—	**5.8**
1939	Bos A☆	124	467	130	168	31	10	**35**	105	89	2	72	.360	**.464**	**.694**	185	**62**	4-3	.992	8	125	98	1b123/P	—	5.2
1940	Bos A★	144	515	106	153	30	4	36	119	101	0	87	.297	.412	.581	148	39	4-7	.990	0	132	101	1b95,C42/3	—	3.0
1941	Bos A★	135	487	87	146	27	8	19	105	93	0	103	.300	.412	.505	138	30	2-5	.992	8	**125**	95	1b124,3b5/rf	0	2.3
1942	Bos A	30	100	18	27	4	0	5	14	18	2	15	.270	.392	.460	134	5	0-0	.996	6	174	127	1b27	0	0.9
	Chi N	70	205	25	42	8	0	3	19	22	0	55	.205	.282	.288	69	-8	1	.983	-4	78	80	1b52/C	0	-1.8
1944	Chi N	15	20	0	1	1	0	0	2	2	0	5	.050	.136	.100	-33	-4	0	1.000	1	163	0	3b2/C	0	-0.2
1945	Phi N	89	224	30	60	11	1	7	38	23	0	39	.268	.336	.420	112	3	0	.988	-1	113	63	1b40,3b14,P9	0	0.0
Total	20	2317	8134	1751	2646	458	125	534	1922	1452	13	1311	.325	.428	.609	161	760	87-73	.992	41	109	96	1b1919,3b141,C108,O21L,P10/S	0	58.3

Foy, Joe Joseph Anthony; B2.21.1943 New York NY; D10.12.1989 Bronx NY; BR/TR/6´0˝/(210–215); d4.13

YEAR	TM LG	G	AB	R	H	2B	3B	HR	RBI	BB-IB	HP	SO	AVG	OBP	SLG	AOPS	ABR	SB-CS	FA	FR	RNG	THR	GAMES AT POSITION	DL	BFW
1966	Bos A	151	554	97	145	23	8	15	63	91-2	2	80	.262	.364	.413	112	12	2-5	.953	4	103	104	3b139,S13	0	1.6
1967	†Bos A	130	446	70	112	22	4	16	49	46-1	3	87	.251	.325	.426	111	7	8-6	.921	-11	90	71	3b118/rf	0	-0.6
1968	Bos A	150	515	65	116	18	2	10	60	84-5	4	91	.225	.336	.326	96	1	26-8	.935	2	105	**132**	3b147,O3L	0	0.6
1969	KC A	145	519	72	136	19	2	11	71	74-4	5	75	.262	.354	.370	103	4	37-15	.964	-12	89	89	3b113,1b16,O16(2/13/1),S5,2b3	0	-0.6
1970	NY N	99	322	39	76	12	0	6	37	68-5	4	58	.236	.373	.329	89	-1	22-13	.937	-1	94	123	3b97	0	-0.2
1971	Was A	41	128	12	30	8	0	0	11	27-0	0	14	.234	.363	.297	94	1	4-1	.960	4	105	158	3b37,2b3/S	0	0.5
Total	6	716	2484	355	615	102	16	58	291	390-17	18	405	.248	.351	.372	103	24	99-48	.943	-14	98	108	3b651,O20(5/13/2),S19,1b16,2b6	0	1.3

Franco, Julio Julio Cesar (b Julio Cesar Robles (Franco)); B8.23.1958 Hato Mayor, D.R.; BR/TR/6´0˝/(155–210); d4.23; OF(4/0/1)

YEAR	TM LG	G	AB	R	H	2B	3B	HR	RBI	BB-IB	HP	SO	AVG	OBP	SLG	AOPS	ABR	SB-CS	FA	FR	RNG	THR	GAMES AT POSITION	DL	BFW
1982	Phi N	16	29	3	8	1	0	0	3	2-1	0	4	.276	.323	.310	75	-1	0-2	1.000	-3	84	42	S11,3b2	0	-0.4
1983	Cle A	149	560	68	153	24	8	8	80	27-1	2	50	.273	.306	.387	87	-12	32-12	.961	-3	97	95	S149	0	0.4
1984	Cle A	160	658	82	188	22	5	3	79	43-1	6	68	.286	.331	.348	88	-11	19-10	.955	3	101	114	S159/D	0	1.0
1985	Cle A	160	636	97	183	33	4	6	90	54-2	4	74	.288	.343	.381	100	1	13-9	.949	-15	98	94	S151,2b8/D	0	0.1
1986	Cle A	149	599	80	183	30	5	10	74	32-1	0	66	.306	.338	.422	108	5	10-7	.971	-3	104	90	S134,2b13,D3	0	1.6
1987	Cle A	128	495	86	158	24	3	8	52	57-2	3	56	.319	.389	.428	117	14	32-9	.963	-18	92	76	S111,2b9,D8	26	1.1
1988	Cle A	152	613	88	186	23	6	10	54	56-4	2	72	.303	.361	.409	113	11	25-11	.982	-2	102	87	2b151/D	0	1.4
1989	Tex A★	150	548	80	173	31	5	13	92	66-11	1	69	.316	.386	.462	137	28	21-3	.980	-5	92	76	2b140,D10	0	3.1
1990	Tex A★	157	582	96	172	27	1	11	69	82-3	2	83	.296	.383	.402	120	19	31-10	.975	0	98	96	2b152,D3	0	2.7
1991	Tex A☆	146	589	108	201	27	3	15	78	65-8	3	78	**.341**	.408	.474	146	39	36-9	.979	-33	84	76	2b146	0	1.4
1992	Tex A	35	107	19	25	7	0	2	8	15-2	0	17	.234	.328	.355	94	0	1-1	.906	-4	70	35	D15,2b9,O4(4/0/1)	129	-0.5
1993	Tex A	144	532	85	154	31	3	14	84	62-4	1	95	.289	.360	.438	118	15	9-3	ø	0	0	0	D140	0	0.8
1994	Chi A	112	433	72	138	19	2	20	98	62-4	5	75	.319	.406	.510	137	26	8-1	.969	-1	79	91	D99,1b14	0	1.8
1996	†Cle A	112	432	72	139	20	1	14	76	61-2	3	82	.322	.407	.470	122	17	8-8	.990	3	114	113	1b97,D13	44	0.9
1997	Cle A	78	289	46	82	13	1	3	25	38-2	0	75	.284	.367	.367	89	-3	8-5	.983	6	111	106	D42,2b35/1	0	0.2
	Mil A	42	141	22	34	3	0	4	19	31-2	1	41	.241	.373	.348	91	-1	7-1	.992	1	119	178	D28,1b13	0	-0.1
	Year	120	430	68	116	16	1	7	44	69-4	1	116	.270	.369	.360	90	-4	15-6	.983	7	111	106	D70,2b35,1b14	0	0.1
1999	TB A	1	1	0	0	0	0	0	0	0-0	0	1	.000	.000	.000	-98	0	0-0	1.000	0	0	0	/1	0	0.0
2001	†Atl N	25	90	13	27	4	0	3	11	10-1	1	20	.300	.376	.444	110	2	0-0	.995	1	121	127	1b23	0	0.1
2002	†Atl N	125	338	51	96	13	1	6	30	39-3	1	75	.284	.357	.382	96	-1	5-1	.990	3	123	127	1b95,D2	0	-0.5
2003	†Atl N	103	197	28	58	12	2	5	31	25-5	0	43	.294	.372	.452	115	5	0-1	.998	1	107	120	1b75	15	0.1
2004	†Atl N	125	320	37	99	18	3	6	57	36-4	1	68	.309	.378	.441	111	6	4-2	.997	-0	98	116	1b84/D	0	0.0
2005	†Atl N	108	233	30	64	12	1	9	42	27-1	1	57	.275	.348	.451	108	3	4-0	.990	2	121	114	1b62,D4	0	0.1
2006	†NY N	95	165	14	45	10	0	2	26	13-2	1	49	.273	.330	.370	81	-5	6-1	.995	-3	38	127	1b27,3b3,D3	0	-0.8
Total	22	2472	8587	1277	2566	404	54	172	1178	903-66	38	1318	.299	.365	.419	111	157	279-106	.960	-69	98	95	S715,2b663,1b492,D374,3b5,O4L	214	14.5

Franco, Matt Matthew Neil; B8.19.1969 Santa Monica CA; BL/TR/6´1˝/(200–210); [ChiN87 7/166]; d9.6; OF(34/0/8)

YEAR	TM LG	G	AB	R	H	2B	3B	HR	RBI	BB-IB	HP	SO	AVG	OBP	SLG	AOPS	ABR	SB-CS	FA	FR	RNG	THR	GAMES AT POSITION	DL	BFW
1995	Chi N	16	17	3	5	1	0	0	1	0-0	0	4	.294	.294	.353	70	-1	0-0	1.000	-1	64	0	2b3/13	0	-0.2
1996	NY N	14	31	3	6	1	0	1	2	1-0	1	5	.194	.235	.323	50	-2	0-0	.824	-0	116	0	3b8,1b2	0	-0.3
1997	NY N	112	163	21	45	5	0	5	21	13-4	0	23	.276	.330	.399	94	-2	1-0	.937	1	118	165	3b39,1b13/lfD	0	-0.1
1998	NY N	103	161	20	44	7	2	1	13	23-6	1	26	.273	.366	.360	95	0	0-1	1.000	-2	95	122	3b13,O13(12/0/1),1b11,D2	15	-0.3
1999	†NY N	122	132	18	31	5	0	4	21	28-3	0	21	.235	.366	.364	90	-1	0-0	1.000	2	157	212	1b19,O19(15/0/3),3b12,P2,D4	0	0.0
2000	†NY N	101	134	9	32	4	0	2	14	21-3	0	22	.239	.340	.313	71	-6	0-0	.990	-1	109	104	1b28,3b22,O3L/2D	0	-0.7
2002	†Atl N	81	205	25	65	15	4	6	30	27-2	0	31	.317	.395	.517	138	12	1-0	.990	0	113	91	1b51,O4(2/0/2)	0	0.8
2003	†Atl N	112	134	11	33	5	0	3	15	11-0	0	26	.246	.299	.351	70	-6	0-1	.977	-2	82	135	1b15,O3(1/0/2),D3	0	-0.9
Total	8	661	977	110	261	43	6	22	117	124-18	2	158	.267	.349	.391	95	-6	2-2	.990	-2	105	103	1b140,3b95,O43L,D12,2b4,P2	15	-1.7

YEAR	TM LG	G	AB	R	H	2B	3B	HR	RBI	BB-IB	HP	SO	AVG	OBP	SLG	AOPS	ABR	SB-CS	FA	FR	RNG	THR	GAMES AT POSITION	DL	BFW
FRANCOEUR, JEFF	Jeffrey Braden; B1.8.1984 Atlanta GA; BR/TR/6´4˝/220; [AtlN02 1/23]; d7.7																								
2005	†Atl N	70	257	41	77	20	1	14	45	11-3	4	58	.300	.336	.549	126	9	3-2	.966	6	97	324	O67R	0	1.1
2006	Atl N	**162**	651	83	169	24	6	29	103	23-6	9	132	.260	.293	.449	85	-18	1-6	.973	3	99	162	O162(0/2/162)	0	-2.5
Total	2	232	908	124	246	44	7	43	148	34-9	13	190	.271	.305	.477	97	-9	4-8	.971	9	98	209	O229(0/2/229)	0	-1.4
FRANCONA, TITO	John Patsy; B11.4.1933 Aliquippa PA; BL/TL/5´11˝/(180–193); d4.17; s–Terry																								
1956	Bal A	139	445	62	115	16	4	9	57	51-4	1	60	.258	.334	.373	94	-5	11-5	.977	2	103	127	O122(1/41/97),1b21	0	-0.7
1957	Bal A	97	279	35	65	8	3	7	38	29-4	3	48	.233	.307	.358	88	-5	7-3	.992	-5	94	0	O73(28/2/55),1b4	0	-1.3
1958	Chi A	41	128	10	33	3	2	1	10	14-1	0	24	.258	.331	.336	86	-3	2-3	1.000	-2	80	113	O35(7/0/32)	0	-0.6
	Det A	45	69	11	17	5	0	0	10	15-3	0	16	.246	.381	.319	88	0	0-0	1.000	-2	79	0	O18(11/0/9)/1	0	-0.3
	Year	86	197	21	50	8	2	1	20	29-4	0	40	.254	.350	.330	86	-3	2-3	1.000	-4	80	78	O53(18/0/41)/1	0	-0.9
1959	Cle A	122	399	68	145	17	2	20	79	35-3	3	42	.363	.414	.566	174	40	2-0	.972	-7	88	48	O64(4/61/0),1b35	0	2.9
1960	Cle A	147	544	84	159	**36**	2	17	79	67-7	5	67	.292	.372	.460	128	23	4-1	.989	-1	97	41	O138(138/0/1),1b13	0	1.4
1961	Cle A☆	155	592	87	178	30	8	16	85	56-3	4	52	.301	.363	.459	122	18	2-1	.987	-0	106	48	O138L,1b14	0	0.9
1962	Cle A	158	621	82	169	28	5	14	70	47-3	7	74	.272	.327	.401	99	-2	3-2	.986	0	105	119	1b158	0	-1.2
1963	Cle A	142	500	57	114	29	0	10	41	47-7	2	77	.228	.296	.346	80	-13	9-1	.986	-3	97	25	O122(121/0/1),1b11	0	-2.3
1964	Cle A	111	270	35	67	13	2	8	24	44-9	4	46	.248	.361	.400	113	6	1-3	.985	-8	67	60	O69(1/1/68),1b17	0	-0.8
1965	StL N	81	174	15	45	6	2	5	19	17-0	0	30	.259	.323	.402	95	-1	0-0	.972	-6	73	0	O34(1/0/34),1b13	0	-1.0
1966	StL N	83	156	14	33	4	1	4	17	7-1	1	27	.212	.250	.327	59	-9	0-0	.987	2	127	110	1b30,O9L	0	-1.0
1967	Phi N	27	73	7	15	1	0	0	3	7-1	0	10	.205	.272	.219	43	-5	0-1	1.000	2	123	106	1b24/rf	0	-0.6
	Atl N	82	254	28	63	5	1	6	25	20-2	1	34	.248	.304	.346	87	-5	1-0	.991	-0	97	87	1b56,O6(5/0/1)	0	-0.9
	Year	109	327	35	78	6	1	6	28	27-3	1	44	.239	.297	.318	77	-10	1-1	.993	1	104	92	1b80,O7(5/0/2)	0	-1.5
1968	Atl N	122	346	32	99	13	1	2	47	51-5	0	45	.286	.376	.347	118	11	3-0	.978	-6	93	54	O65L,1b33	0	0.0
1969	Atl N	51	88	5	26	1	0	2	22	13-2	0	10	.295	.371	.375	113	2	0-1	.957	0	101	152	O15L,1b7	30	0.1
	Oak A	32	85	12	29	6	1	3	20	12-2	0	11	.341	.418	.541	174	9	0-0	.988	-3	47	76	1b19/lf	0	0.5
1970	Oak A	32	33	2	8	0	0	1	6	6-1	1	6	.242	.375	.333	100	0	0-0	1.000	1	141	131	1b6/lf	0	0.1
	Mil A	52	65	4	15	3	0	0	4	6-1	0	15	.231	.296	.277	59	-4	1-0	1.000	1	125	149	1b13	0	-0.3
	Year	84	98	6	23	3	0	1	10	12-2	1	21	.235	.324	.296	73	-3	1-0	1.000	1	129	144	1b19/lf	0	-0.2
Total	15	1719	5121	650	1395	224	34	125	656	544-59	32	694	.272	.343	.403	108	57	46-21	.984	-37	94	57	O911(546/105/299),1b475	30	-5.1
FRANCONA, TERRY	Terry Jon; B4.22.1959 Aberdeen SD; BL/TL/6´1˝/(175–190); [MonN80 1/22]; d8.19; M7/C3; f–Tito; Col Arizona																								
1981	†Mon N	34	95	11	26	0	1	1	8	5-1	1	6	.274	.317	.326	80	-3	1-0	1.000	1	86	243	O26(24/0/2)/1	0	-0.2
1982	Mon N	46	131	14	42	3	0	0	9	8-0	0	11	.321	.360	.344	94	-1	2-3	.936	-5	77	0	O33(30/1/3),1b16	102	-0.8
1983	Mon N	120	230	21	59	11	1	3	22	6-2	0	20	.257	.273	.352	73	-9	0-2	.978	0	106	102	O51(13/3/37),1b47	0	-1.3
1984	Mon N	58	214	18	74	19	2	1	18	5-3	1	12	.346	.360	.467	138	10	0-0	.994	6	142	117	1b50,O6(5/0/2)	82	1.3
1985	Mon N	107	281	19	75	15	1	2	31	12-4	1	12	.267	.299	.349	85	-6	5-5	.988	4	119	95	1b57,O28(5/0/24)/3	0	-0.7
1986	Chi N	86	124	13	31	3	0	2	8	6-0	1	8	.250	.286	.323	64	-6	0-1	1.000	-1	110	0	O30(20/2/10),1b23	0	-0.9
1987	Cin N	102	207	16	47	5	0	3	12	10-1	1	12	.227	.266	.295	47	-16	2-0	.995	6	153	116	1b57,O8(2/0/6)	0	-1.3
1988	Cle A	62	212	24	66	8	0	1	12	5-1	0	18	.311	.324	.363	90	-3	0-0	.977	1	109	90	D38,1b5,O5L	0	-0.4
1989	Mil A	90	233	26	54	10	1	3	23	8-3	0	20	.232	.255	.322	63	-12	2-1	.989	1	98	103	1b46,D23,O16R/P	0	-1.6
1990	Mil A	3	4	1	0	0	0	0	0	0-0	0	0	.000	.000	.000	-99	-1	0-0	1.000	-0	0	121	1b2/D	0	-0.1
Total	10	708	1731	163	474	74	6	16	143	65-15	5	119	.274	.300	.351	81	-47	12-12	.992	13	121	107	1b304,O203(104/6/100),D62/P3	184	-6.0
FRANDSEN, KEVIN	Kevin Vincent; B5.24.1982 San Jose CA; BR/TR/6´0˝/175; [SFN04 12/370]; d4.28; Col San Jose St.																								
2006	SF N	41	93	12	20	4	0	2	7	3-0	6	14	.215	.284	.323	55	-6	0-1	.977	-6	89	51	2b28,S3	15	-1.2
FRANK, CHARLIE	Charles; B5.30.1870 Mobile AL; D5.24.1922 Memphis TN; BL/TL/5´10˝/170; d8.18																								
1893	StL N	40	164	29	55	6	3	1	17	18	2	8	.335	.408	.427	122	5	8	.930	2	123	67	O40L	—	0.3
1894	StL N	80	319	52	89	12	7	4	42	44	3	13	.279	.372	.398	86	-7	14	.869	-4	80	124	O77(77/0/1),1b3,P2	—	-1.4
Total	2	120	483	81	144	18	10	5	59	62	5	21	.298	.384	.408	97	-2	22	.889	-2	95	104	O117(117/0/1),1b3,P2	—	-1.1
FRANK, FRED	John Frederick; B3.11.1873 Louisa KY; D3.27.1950 Ashland KY; 5´9˝/162; d9.27																								
1898	Cle N	17	53	3	11	1	1	0	3	4	1	—	.208	.276	.264	56	-3	1	.915	2	121	374	O17(0/6/11)	—	-0.2
FRANK, MIKE	Stephen Michael; B1.14.1974 Pomona CA; BL/TL/6´2˝/190; [CinN97 7/218]; d6.19; Col Santa Clara																								
1998	Cin N	28	89	14	20	6	0	0	7	7-0	0	12	.225	.278	.292	51	-6	0-0	1.000	1	112	70	O28(1/25/2)	29	-0.5
FRANKLIN	; d9.27																								
1884	Was U	1	3	0	0	0	0	0	—	0	—	—	.000	.000	.000	-99	-1	—	1.000	0	0	0	/cf	—	-0.1
FRANKLIN, MICAH	Micah Ishanti; B4.25.1972 San Francisco CA; BB/TR/6´0˝/205; [NYN90 3/90]; d5.13																								
1997	StL N	17	34	6	11	0	0	2	2	3-0	0	10	.324	.378	.500	127	1	0-0	1.000	-1	92	0	O13(4/0/9)	0	0.0
FRANKLIN, MOE	Murray Asher; B4.1.1914 Chicago IL; D3.16.1978 Harbor City CA; BR/TR/6´0˝/175; d8.12; Mil 1943–45; Col Illinois																								
1941	Det A	13	10	1	3	1	0	0	0	2	0	2	.300	.417	.400	106	0	0-0	.750	-1	77	167	S4/3	0	0.0
1942	Det A	48	154	24	40	7	0	2	16	7	2	5	.260	.301	.344	75	-5	0-0	.967	-3	88	73	S32,2b7	0	-0.6
Total	2	61	164	25	43	8	0	2	16	9	2	7	.262	.309	.348	77	-5	0-0	.961	-4	88	76	S36,2b7/3	0	-0.6
FRANKS, HERMAN	Herman Louis; B1.4.1914 Price UT; BL/TR/5´10.5˝/187; d4.27; Mil 1942–45; M7/C10																								
1939	StL N	17	17	1	1	0	0	0	3	3	0	3	.059	.200	.059	-26	-3	0	.973	2	*165*	72	C13	—	-0.1
1940	Bro N	65	131	11	24	4	0	1	14	20	1	6	.183	.296	.237	46	-9	2	.990	6	*120*	*84*	C43	—	-0.1
1941	†Bro N	57	139	10	28	7	0	1	11	14	0	13	.201	.275	.273	52	-9	0	.986	3	*152*	*85*	C54/rf	0	-0.3
1947	Phi A	8	15	2	3	0	1	0	1	4	0	4	.200	.368	.333	94	0	0-0	1.000	-0	*108*	*111*	C4	0	0.0
1948	Phi A	40	98	10	22	7	1	1	14	16	2	11	.224	.345	.347	84	-2	0-0	.977	1	*119*	*122*	C27	0	0.1
1949	NY N	1	3	1	2	0	0	0	0	0	0	0	.667	.667	.667	259	1	0	1.000	0	*0*	*0*	/C	0	0.1
Total	6	188	403	35	80	18	2	3	43	57	3	37	.199	.302	.275	57	-22	2-0	.985	11	*132*	*93*	C142/rf	0	-0.3
FRAZIER, LOU	Arthur Louis; B1.26.1965 St.Louis MO; BB/TR/6´2˝/(175–180); [HouN86 S1/5]; d4.8; Col Scottsdale (AZ) CC																								
1993	Mon N	112	189	27	54	7	1	1	16	16-0	0	24	.286	.340	.349	82	-5	17-2	.986	-0	96	110	O60(52/7/2),1b8/2	0	-0.3
1994	Mon N	76	140	25	38	3	1	0	14	18-0	1	23	.271	.358	.307	75	-5	20-4	1.000	1	105	123	O36(31/5/0),2b6/1	0	-0.2
1995	Mon N	35	63	6	12	2	0	0	3	8-0	2	12	.190	.297	.222	39	-5	4-0	.973	1	123	0	O25(10/11/5)/2	0	-0.4
	Tex A	49	99	19	21	2	0	0	8	7-0	2	20	.212	.278	.232	33	-10	9-1	.973	2	114	106	O47(43/6/0),D2	0	-0.7
1996	Tex A	30	50	5	13	2	1	0	5	8-0	1	10	.260	.373	.340	77	-2	4-2	.971	2	112	349	O15(12/3/0),D13/2	0	-0.1
1998	Chi A	7	7	0	0	0	0	0	0	2-0	0	6	.000	.222	.000	-36	-1	4-0	1.000	0	111	0	O3C	0	0.0
Total	5	309	548	82	138	16	3	1	46	59-0	6	95	.252	.330	.297	64	-28	58-9	.982	5	107	122	O186(148/35/7),D15,2b9,1b9	0	-1.7
FRAZIER, JOE	Joseph Filmore; B10.6.1922 Liberty NC; BL/TR/6´0˝/(195–200); d8.31; M2																								
1947	Cle A	9	14	1	1	1	0	0	0	1	0	1	.071	.133	.143	-24	-2	0-0	.857	-0	105	0	O5R	0	-0.3
1954	StL N	81	88	8	26	5	2	3	18	13	1	17	.295	.388	.500	129	4	0-0	.938	-1	96	0	O11(2/0/8)/1	0	0.3
1955	StL N	58	70	12	14	1	0	4	9	6-0	1	12	.200	.269	.386	72	-3	0-0	1.000	-1	102	0	O14(1/0/13)	0	-0.4
1956	StL N	14	19	1	4	2	0	1	4	3-0	0	3	.211	.318	.474	109	0	0-1	.800	-1	78	0	O3R	0	-0.1
	Cin N	10	17	2	4	0	0	1	2	1-0	0	7	.235	.278	.412	77	-1	0-0	ø	-0	0	0	O4L	0	-0.1
	Year	24	36	3	8	2	0	2	6	4-0	0	10	.222	.300	.444	94	0	0-1	.800	-1	108	183	O7(4/0/3)	0	-0.2
	Bal A	45	74	7	19	6	0	1	12	11-2	1	6	.257	.356	.378	103	1	0-0	1.000	1	108	183	O19R	0	0.2
Total	4	217	282	31	68	15	2	10	45	35-2	3	46	.241	.328	.415	97	-1	0-1	.961	-1	101	73	O56(7/0/48)/1	0	-0.4
FREDERICK, JOHNNY	John Henry; B1.26.1902 Denver CO; D6.18.1977 Tigard OR; BL/TL/5´11˝/165; d4.18																								
1929	Bro N	148	628	127	206	**52**	6	24	75	39	5	34	.328	.372	.545	126	24	6	.975	1	103	93	O143C	—	1.7
1930	Bro N	142	616	120	206	44	11	17	76	46	3	34	.334	.383	.524	118	18	1	.990	4	103	103	O142C	—	1.4
1931	Bro N	146	611	81	165	34	8	17	71	31	6	46	.270	.312	.435	99	-3	2	.965	-2	101	84	O145C	—	-0.8
1932	Bro N	118	384	54	115	28	2	16	56	25	4	35	.299	.349	.508	130	16	1	.976	-4	94	74	O88(1/47/39)	—	0.8
1933	Bro N	147	556	65	171	22	7	7	64	36	5	14	.308	.355	.410	123	16	9	.971	-5	97	67	O138(10/26/102)	—	0.4
1934	Bro N	104	307	51	91	20	1	4	35	33	3	13	.296	.370	.407	114	7	4	.957	2	88	193	O77(22/0/55)/1	—	0.5
Total	6	805	3102	498	954	200	35	85	377	210	26	176	.308	.357	.477	118	78	23	.974	-4	99	95	O733(33/503/196)/1	—	4.0

YEAR	TM LG	G	AB	R	H	2B	3B	HR	RBI	BB-IB	HP	SO	AVG	OBP	SLG	AOPS	ABR	SB-CS	FA	FR	RNG	THR	GAMES AT POSITION	DL	BFW
FREED, ED	Edwin Charles; B8.22.1919 Centre Valley PA; D11.15.2002 Rock Hill SC; BR/TR/5´6˝/165; d9.11; Mil 1943–45																								
1942	Phi N	13	33	3	10	3	1	0	1	4	0	3	.303	.378	.455	151	2	1	1.000	0	75	308	O11(3/7/1)	0	0.2
FREED, ROGER	Roger Vernon; B6.2.1946 Los Angeles CA; D1.9.1996 Chino CA; BR/TR/6´0˝/(190–205); d9.18; Col Mt. San Antonio (CA) JC																								
1970	Bal A	4	13	0	2	0	0	0	1	3-0	0	4	.154	.294	.154	32	-1	0-0	1.000	-0	52	264	1b3/rf	0	-0.2
1971	Phi N	118	348	23	77	12	1	6	37	44-3	3	86	.221	.312	.313	78	-9	0-3	.989	-4	97	57	O106(7/0/99)/C	0	-2.0
1972	Phi N	73	129	10	29	4	0	6	18	23-2	1	39	.225	.344	.395	107	2	0-1	.971	3	110	178	O46(1/0/45)	0	0.3
1974	Cin N	6	6	1	2	0	0	1	3	1-0	0	1	.333	.429	.833	251	1	0-0	1.000	-0	0	0	/1	0	0.1
1976	Mon N	8	15	0	3	1	0	0	1	0-0	0	3	.200	.200	.267	30	-1	0-0	1.000	-0	54	40	1b3/rf	0	-0.2
1977	StL N	49	83	10	33	2	1	5	21	11-0	0	9	.398	.463	.627	192	11	0-0	1.000	-1	99	150	1b18,O6R	0	0.9
1978	StL N	52	92	3	22	6	0	2	20	8-0	0	17	.239	.297	.370	87	-2	1-0	.992	-1	121	134	1b15,O6(3/0/3)	0	-0.3
1979	StL N	34	31	2	8	2	0	2	8	5-0	0	7	.258	.361	.516	134	2	0-0	.889	0	166	0	/1	0	0.1
Total	8	344	717	49	176	27	2	22	109	95-5	4	166	.245	.334	.381	100	3	1-4	.982	-3	97	80	O166(11/0/156),1b41/C	0	-1.3
FREEHAN, BILL	William Ashley; B11.29.1941 Detroit MI; BR/TR/6´2˝/(202–210); d9.26; Col Michigan																								
1961	Det A	4	10	1	4	0	0	0	4	1-0	0	0	.400	.455	.400	127	0	0-0	1.000	1	41	0	C3	0	0.2
1963	Det A	100	300	37	73	12	2	9	36	39-4	2	56	.243	.331	.387	98	0	2-0	.995	3	149	107	C73,1b19	0	0.6
1964	Det A☆	144	520	69	156	14	8	18	80	36-3	**8**	68	.300	.350	.462	123	15	5-1	.993	9	**194**	96	C141/1	0	3.2
1965	Det A★	130	431	45	101	15	0	10	43	39-5	7	63	.234	.306	.339	83	-9	4-2	.996	5	137	84	C129	0	0.3
1966	Det A★	136	492	47	115	22	0	12	46	40-9	3	72	.234	.294	.352	83	-10	5-2	**.996**	4	136	68	C132,1b5	0	0.0
1967	Det A★	155	517	66	146	23	1	20	74	73-**15**	**20**	71	.282	.389	.447	143	32	1-2	.992	-4	101	79	C147,1b11	0	3.8
1968	†Det A★	155	540	73	142	24	2	25	84	65-4	**24**	64	.263	.366	.454	144	31	0-1	.994	10	107	96	C138,1b21/rf	0	5.2
1969	Det A★	143	489	61	128	16	3	16	49	53-6	8	55	.262	.342	.405	104	3	1-2	.992	4	92	92	C120,1b20	0	1.1
1970	Det A★	117	395	44	95	17	3	16	52	52-5	4	48	.241	.332	.420	106	3	0-3	**.997**	-10	125	110	C114	32	-0.2
1971	Det A★	148	516	57	143	26	4	21	71	54-9	9	48	.277	.353	.465	125	18	2-7	.996	-12	99	89	C144/lf	0	1.2
1972	†Det A★	111	374	51	98	18	2	10	56	48-0	6	51	.262	.354	.401	120	11	0-1	.989	4	85	114	C105/1	0	2.2
1973	Det A☆	110	380	33	89	10	1	6	29	40-2	11	30	.234	.323	.313	75	-11	0-0	**.995**	6	94	**128**	C98,1b7,D3	0	-0.1
1974	Det A	130	445	58	132	17	5	18	60	42-2	5	44	.297	.361	.479	136	20	2-0	.994	-7	97	81	1b65,C63/D	0	1.1
1975	Det A☆	120	427	42	105	17	3	14	47	32-3	6	56	.246	.306	.398	94	-4	2-0	.991	-1	100	102	C113,1b5	0	-0.1
1976	Det A	71	237	22	64	10	1	5	27	12-0	1	27	.270	.303	.384	98	-1	0-0	.983	2	90	62	C61,1b2,D3	0	0.3
Total	15	1774	6073	706	1591	241	35	200	758	626-67	114	753	.262	.340	.412	111	98	24-21	.993	14	115	96	C1581,1b157,D7,O2(1/0/1)	32	18.8
FREEL, RYAN	Ryan Paul; B3.8.1976 Jacksonville FL; BR/TR/5´10˝/(180–185); [TorA95 10/272]; d4.4; Col Tallahassee (FL) CC																								
2001	Tor A	9	22	1	6	1	0	0	3	1-0	1	4	.273	.333	.318	71	-1	2-1	.969	1	123	112	2b7/lf	0	-0.1
2003	Cin N	43	137	23	39	6	1	4	12	9-1	4	13	.285	.344	.431	106	1	9-4	1.000	-3	111	157	O24(5/20/0),2b11,3b2	36	-0.1
2004	Cin N	143	505	74	140	21	8	3	28	67-0	12	88	.277	.375	.368	95	-1	37-10	.985	15	120	196	O89(12/42/46),3b56,2b15	0	1.8
2005	Cin N	103	369	69	100	19	3	4	21	51-0	8	59	.271	.371	.371	95	0	36-10	1.000	12	137	322	O51(25/18/13),2b48,3b10	51	1.7
2006	Cin N	132	454	67	123	30	2	8	27	57-0	9	98	.271	.363	.399	90	-5	37-11	.980	12	117	265	O105(13/54/42),2b13,3b13	0	1.1
Total	5	430	1487	234	408	77	14	19	91	185-1	34	262	.274	.367	.383	94	-6	121-36	.987	38	121	242	O270(56/134/101),2b94,3b81	87	4.6
FREEMAN, JERRY	Frank Ellsworth "Buck"; B12.26.1879 Placerville CA; D9.30.1952 Los Angeles CA; BL/TR/6´2˝/220; d4.14																								
1908	Was A	154	531	45	134	15	5	1	45	36	3	—	.252	.304	.305	107	3	6	.975	-13	71	105	1b154	—	-1.4
1909	Was A	19	48	2	8	0	1	0	3	4	1	—	.167	.245	.208	46	-3	3	.956	-2	86	159	1b14/lf	—	-0.6
Total	2	173	579	47	142	15	6	1	48	40	4	—	.245	.299	.297	101	0	9	.974	-15	72	109	1b168/lf	—	-2.0
FREEMAN, JOHN	John Edward; B1.24.1901 Boston MA; D4.14.1958 Washington DC; BR/TR/5´8˝/160; d6.17; Col Holy Cross																								
1927	Bos A	4	2	0	0	0	0	0	0	0	0	0	.000	.000	.000	-99	-1	0-0	ø	-0	0	0	O3(1/2/0)	—	-0.1
FREEMAN, BUCK	John Frank; B10.30.1871 Catasauqua PA; D6.25.1949 Wilkes-Barre PA; BL/TL/5´9˝/169; d6.27; ▲																								
1891	Was AA	5	18	1	4	1	0	0	1	2	0	2	.222	.300	.278	69	1	0	.769	-0	95	0	P5	—	0.0
1898	Was N	29	107	19	39	2	3	3	21	7	4	—	.364	.424	.523	171	9	2	.978	2	143	216	O29R	—	0.9
1899	Was N	**155**	588	107	187	19	25	**25**	122	23	18	—	.318	.362	.563	154	36	21	.944	-10	63	44	O155R,P2	—	1.7
1900	Bos N	117	418	58	126	19	13	6	65	25	10	—	.301	.355	.452	109	3	10	.950	-6	28	38	O91(16/3/72),1b19	—	-0.7
1901	Bos A	129	490	88	166	23	15	12	114	44	6	—	.339	.400	.520	157	37	17	.974	-5	84	**115**	1b128/2rf	—	2.7
1902	Bos A	**138**	564	75	174	38	19	11	**121**	32	6	—	.309	.352	.502	131	21	17	.944	-2	82	89	O138R	—	1.2
1903	†Bos A	**141**	567	74	163	39	20	**13**	**104**	30	4	—	.287	.328	.496	137	23	5	.933	-7	83	56	O141R	—	1.0
1904	Bos A	**157**	597	64	167	20	**19**	7	84	32	12	—	.280	.329	.412	126	16	7	.954	-7	80	102	O157R	—	0.2
1905	Bos A	130	455	59	109	20	8	3	49	46	5	—	.240	.316	.338	106	4	8	.973	-11	72	82	1b66,O57(0/1/56),3b2	—	-1.1
1906	Bos A	121	392	42	98	18	9	1	30	28	1	—	.250	.302	.349	104	1	5	.989	4	157	121	O65(0/3/62),1b43,3b4	—	0.2
1907	Bos A	4	12	1	2	0	0	1	2	3	0	—	.167	.333	.417	140	1	0	1.000	-0	0	0	O3R	—	0.0
Total	11	1126	4208	588	1235	199	131	82	713	272	66	2	.293	.346	.462	131	152	92	.950	-42	75	73	O837(16/7/814),1b256,P7,3b6/2	—	6.1
FREEMAN, LA VEL	La Vel Maurice; B2.18.1963 Oakland CA; BL/TL/5´9˝/170; [MilA83*1/26]; d4.7; Col Sacramento (CA) City																								
1989	Mil A	2	3	1	0	0	0	0	0	0-0	0	2	.000	.000	.000	-99	-1	0-0	ø	0	—	—	D2	0	-0.1
FREEMAN, CHOO	Raphael; B10.20.1979 Pine Bluff AR; BR/TR/6´2˝/200; [ColN98 1/36]; d6.4																								
2004	Col N	45	90	15	17	3	2	1	11	14-1	0	21	.189	.298	.300	49	-7	1-1	.986	-1	100	69	O41C	0	-0.7
2005	Col N	18	22	6	6	1	1	0	0	0-0	0	5	.273	.273	.409	68	-1	0-0	1.000	2	107	825	O6C	0	0.1
2006	Col N	88	173	24	41	6	3	2	18	14-2	1	42	.237	.298	.341	58	-11	5-6	.991	0	110	0	O51(5/44/2)	0	-1.2
Total	3	151	285	45	64	10	6	3	29	28-3	1	68	.225	.296	.333	56	-19	6-7	.990	1	106	81	O98(5/91/2)	0	-1.8
FREESE, GENE	Eugene Lewis "Augie"; B1.8.1934 Wheeling WV; BR/TR/5´11˝/(160–185); d4.13; b-George; Col West Liberty St.																								
1955	Pit N	134	455	69	115	21	8	14	44	34-4	4	57	.253	.310	.426	94	-5	5-1	.943	-0	101	121	3b65,2b57	0	-0.1
1956	Pit N	65	207	17	43	9	0	3	14	16-3	3	45	.208	.273	.295	54	-13	2-1	.963	-3	95	32	3b47,2b26	0	-1.6
1957	Pit N	114	346	44	98	18	2	6	31	17-0	2	42	.283	.319	.399	95	-3	9-4	.924	-2	103	127	3b74,2b10,O10L	0	-0.4
1958	Pit N	17	18	1	3	0	0	1	2	1-0	0	2	.167	.211	.333	42	-2	0-0	.800	1	219	0	/3	0	-0.1
	StL N	62	191	28	49	11	1	6	16	10-0	0	32	.257	.294	.419	83	-5	1-1	.924	-16	71	57	S28,2b14,3b3	0	-1.8
	Year	79	209	29	52	11	1	7	18	11-0	0	34	.249	.286	.411	80	-7	1-1	.924	-15	71	57	S28,2b14,3b4	0	-1.9
1959	Phi N	132	400	60	107	14	5	23	70	43-4	5	61	.268	.343	.500	120	11	8-4	.916	-18	83	94	3b109,2b6	0	-0.8
1960	Chi A	127	455	60	124	32	6	17	79	29-2	1	65	.273	.312	.481	114	7	10-6	.946	-3	105	**118**	3b122	0	0.4
1961	†Cin N	152	575	78	159	27	2	26	87	27-5	0	78	.277	.307	.466	101	-2	8-2	.950	-14	90	84	3b151/2	0	-1.5
1962	Cin N	18	42	2	6	1	0	0	1	6-2	0	8	.143	.250	.167	14	-5	0-0	1.000	-3	53	56	3b10	126	-0.8
1963	Cin N	66	217	20	53	9	1	6	26	17-2	2	42	.244	.303	.378	93	-2	4-2	.930	-7	86	93	3b62/rf	0	-1.0
1964	Pit N	99	289	33	65	13	2	9	40	19-4	0	45	.225	.269	.377	81	-8	1-2	.920	-10	85	108	3b72	0	-1.9
1965	Pit N	43	80	6	21	4	0	0	8	6-1	2	18	.262	.326	.313	82	-2	0-2	.951	-2	94	42	3b19	0	-0.4
	Chi A	17	32	2	9	0	1	1	4	5-0	0	9	.281	.368	.438	140	2	0-0	.824	-4	65	76	3b8	0	-0.2
1966	Chi A	48	106	8	22	2	0	3	10	8-1	1	20	.208	.270	.311	71	-4	2-1	.894	1	121	121	3b34	0	-0.4
	Hou N	21	33	1	3	0	0	0	0	5-0	0	11	.091	.211	.091	-13	-5	1-0	.800	0	136	0	3b4,2b3/lf	0	-0.5
Total	12	1115	3446	429	877	161	28	115	432	243-28	20	535	.254	.305	.418	94	-36	51-26	.934	-79	94	98	3b781,2b117,S28,O12(11/0/1)	126	-11.1
FREESE, GEORGE	George Walter "Bud"; B9.12.1926 Wheeling WV; BR/TR/6´0˝/190; d4.29; C2; b-Gene; Col West Virginia																								
1953	Det A	1	1	0	0	0	0	0	0	0	0	0	.000	.000	.000	-99	0	0-0	ø	0	—	—	/H	0	0.0
1955	Pit N	51	179	17	46	8	2	3	22	17-2	2	18	.257	.327	.374	87	-3	1-1	.936	-7	88	31	3b50	0	-1.0
1961	Chi N	9	7	0	2	0	0	0	1	1-0	0	4	.286	.375	.286	78	0	0-0	ø	0	—	—	/H	0	0.0
Total	3	61	187	17	48	8	2	3	23	18-2	2	22	.257	.327	.369	86	-3	1-1	.936	-7	88	31	3b50	0	-1.0
FREGOSI, JIM	James Louis; B4.4.1942 San Francisco CA; BR/TR/6´1˝/(187–205); d9.14; M15																								
1961	LA A	11	27	7	6	0	0	0	3	1-0	0	4	.222	.250	.222	25	-3	0-0	.944	-1	98	59	S11	0	-0.3
1962	LA A	58	175	15	51	3	4	3	23	18-1	0	27	.291	.356	.406	108	2	2-1	.943	1	103	107	S52	0	0.7
1963	LA A	154	592	83	170	29	12	9	50	36-3	0	104	.287	.325	.422	115	10	2-2	.964	5	105	100	S151	0	2.8
1964	LA A★	147	505	86	140	22	9	18	72	72-2	4	87	.277	.369	.463	145	32	8-3	.966	10	**108**	111	S137	0	**5.6**
1965	Cal A	161	602	66	167	19	7	15	64	54-4	4	107	.277	.337	.407	114	10	13-5	.968	10	104	103	S160	0	3.7
1966	Cal A★	**162**	611	78	154	32	7	13	67	67-1	2	89	.252	.325	.391	109	8	17-8	.959	19	**111**	**128**	S162/1	0	4.4
1967	Cal A★	151	590	75	171	23	6	9	56	49-2	5	77	.290	.349	.395	124	17	9-6	.965	-2	100	89	S151	0	3.1
1968	Cal A★	159	614	77	150	21	**13**	9	49	60-4	5	101	.244	.315	.365	109	6	9-4	.962	-12	95	108	S159	0	1.0

YEAR	TM LG	G	AB	R	H	2B	3B	HR	RBI	BB-IB	HP	SO	AVG	OBP	SLG	AOPS	ABR	SB-CS	FA	FR	RNG	THR	GAMES AT POSITION	DL	BFW
1969	Cal A★	161	580	78	151	22	6	12	47	93-7	1	86	.260	.361	.381	113	13	9-2	.972	-6	97	100	S160	0	2.8
1970	Cal A★	158	601	95	167	33	5	22	82	69-3	3	92	.278	.353	.459	127	22	0-2	.973	7	101	**117**	S150,1b6	0	4.6
1971	Cal A	107	347	31	81	15	1	5	33	39-6	5	61	.233	.317	.326	89	-4	2-1	.938	-3	108	76	S74,1b18,O7L	24	0.0
1972	NY N	101	340	31	79	15	4	5	32	38-2	1	71	.232	.311	.344	87	-6	0-1	.935	-7	82	68	3b85,S6,1b3	0	-1.4
1973	NY N	45	124	7	29	4	1	0	11	20-3	0	25	.234	.340	.282	75	-3	1-2	.906	-7	73	111	S17,3b17,1b3/lf	0	-1.0
	Tex A	45	157	25	42	6	2	6	16	12-0	1	31	.268	.318	.446	119	3	0-1	.937	-7	73	108	3b34,1b10,S6	0	-0.5
1974	Tex A	78	230	31	60	5	0	12	34	22-4	0	41	.261	.324	.439	121	5	0-1	1.000	0	103	104	1b47,3b32	0	0.2
1975	Tex A	77	191	25	50	5	0	7	33	20-4	1	39	.262	.329	.398	107	2	0-1	.985	1	123	96	1b54,D13,3b4	0	-0.1
1976	Tex A	58	133	17	31	7	0	2	12	23-1	0	33	.233	.342	.331	97	1	2-0	.995	-1	88	113	1b26,D18,3b5	0	-0.2
1977	Tex A	13	28	4	7	1	0	1	5	3-0	0	4	.250	.313	.393	93	0	0-0	1.000	1	164	78	1b5,D3	20	0.0
	Pit N	36	56	10	16	1	1	3	16	13-1	0	10	.286	.408	.500	141	4	2-0	.981	-1	70	98	1b15/3	0	0.2
1978	Pit N	20	20	3	4	1	0	0	1	6-0	0	8	.200	.385	.250	77	0	0-0	.667	-1	87	0	3b5,1b2/2	0	-0.1
Total	18	1902	6523	844	1726	264	78	151	706	715-48	32	1097	.265	.338	.398	113	119	76-40	.963	6	102	106	S1396,1b190,3b183,D34,O8L/2	44	25.5

FREIBURGER, VERN Vern Donald; B12.19.1923 Detroit MI; D2.27.1990 Palm Springs CA; BR/TL/6´1˝/170; d9.6

YEAR	TM LG	G	AB	R	H	2B	3B	HR	RBI	BB-IB	HP	SO	AVG	OBP	SLG	AOPS	ABR	SB-CS	FA	FR	RNG	THR	GAMES AT POSITION	DL	BFW
1941	Cle A	2	8	0	1	0	0	0	1	0	0	2	.125	.125	.125	-35	-2	0-0	.947	1	223	120	1b2	0	-0.1

FREIGAU, HOWARD Howard Earl "Ty"; B8.1.1902 Dayton OH; D7.18.1932 Chattanooga TN; BR/TR/5´10.5˝/160; d9.13; Col Ohio Wesleyan

YEAR	TM LG	G	AB	R	H	2B	3B	HR	RBI	BB-IB	HP	SO	AVG	OBP	SLG	AOPS	ABR	SB-CS	FA	FR	RNG	THR	GAMES AT POSITION	DL	BFW
1922	StL N	3	1	0	0	0	0	0	0	0	0	0	.000	.000	.000	-99	0	0-0	1.000	1	154	290	S2/3	—	0.0
1923	StL N	113	358	30	94	18	1	1	35	25	2	36	.263	.314	.327	71	-15	5-4	.929	-6	100	82	S87,2b16,1b9/3lf	—	-1.2
1924	StL N	98	376	35	101	17	6	2	39	19	1	24	.269	.306	.362	80	-12	10-3	.958	-2	92	132	3b98,S2	—	-0.6
1925	StL N	9	26	2	4	0	0	0	0	2	0	1	.154	.214	.154	-4	-4	0-0	.936	1	111	133	S7/2	—	-0.2
	Chi N	117	476	77	146	22	10	8	71	30	1	31	.307	.349	.445	100	-1	10-6	.913	-4	103	114	3b96,S17,1b7	—	0.2
	Year	126	502	79	150	22	10	8	71	32	1	32	.299	.342	.430	94	-6	10-6	.913	-3	103	114	3b96,S24,1b7/2	—	0.0
1926	Chi N	140	508	51	137	27	7	3	51	43	0	42	.270	.327	.368	86	-10	6	**.966**	-2	95	97	3b135,S2/cf	—	-0.4
1927	Chi N	30	86	12	20	5	0	0	10	9	1	10	.233	.313	.291	62	-4	0	.883	-1	107	82	3b30	—	-0.3
1928	Bro N	17	34	6	7	2	0	0	3	1	0	3	.206	.229	.265	29	-4	0	.810	-3	61	0	3b10/S	—	-0.6
	Bos N	52	109	11	28	8	1	1	17	9	1	14	.257	.319	.376	86	-2	1	.938	-8	82	58	S14,2b11	—	-0.9
	Year	69	143	17	35	10	1	1	20	10	1	17	.245	.299	.350	72	-6	1	.938	-11	81	57	S15,2b11,3b10	—	-1.5
Total	7	579	1974	224	537	99	25	15	226	138	6	161	.272	.322	.370	82	-52	32-13	.940	-24	96	108	3b371,S132,2b28,1b16,O2(1/1/0)	—	-4.0

FREIRE, ALEJANDRO Alejandro; B8.23.1974 Caracas, Distrito Capital, Venezuela; BR/TR/6´2˝/225; d8.9

YEAR	TM LG	G	AB	R	H	2B	3B	HR	RBI	BB-IB	HP	SO	AVG	OBP	SLG	AOPS	ABR	SB-CS	FA	FR	RNG	THR	GAMES AT POSITION	DL	BFW
2005	Bal A	25	65	7	16	3	0	1	4	6-0	1	17	.246	.319	.338	76	-2	0-0	.991	-1	68	95	1b16/lfD	0	-0.4

FRENCH, CHARLIE Charles Calvin; B10.12.1883 Indianapolis IN; D3.30.1962 Indianapolis IN; BL/TR/5´6˝/140; d5.23

YEAR	TM LG	G	AB	R	H	2B	3B	HR	RBI	BB-IB	HP	SO	AVG	OBP	SLG	AOPS	ABR	SB-CS	FA	FR	RNG	THR	GAMES AT POSITION	DL	BFW
1909	Bos A	51	167	15	42	3	1	0	13	15	3	—	.251	.324	.281	90	-1	8	.921	-5	103	106	2b28,S23	—	-0.7
1910	Bos A	9	40	4	8	1	0	0	3	1	0	—	.200	.220	.225	38	-3	0	.889	-0	115	106	2b8	—	-0.4
	Chi A	45	170	17	28	1	1	0	4	10	3	—	.165	.224	.182	29	-14	5	.930	-9	77	76	2b28,O16R	—	-2.7
	Year	54	210	21	36	2	1	0	7	11	3	—	.171	.223	.190	31	-17	5	.919	-9	87	84	2b36,O16R	—	-3.1
Total	2	105	377	36	78	5	2	0	20	26	6	—	.207	.269	.231	58	-18	13	.920	-15	93	93	2b64,S23,O16R	—	-3.8

FRENCH, PAT Frank Alexander; B9.22.1893 Dover NH; D7.13.1969 Bath ME; BR/TR/6´1˝/180; d7.2; Col Maine

YEAR	TM LG	G	AB	R	H	2B	3B	HR	RBI	BB-IB	HP	SO	AVG	OBP	SLG	AOPS	ABR	SB-CS	FA	FR	RNG	THR	GAMES AT POSITION	DL	BFW
1917	Phi A	3	2	0	0	0	0	0	0	0	0	0	.000	.000	.000	-99	0	0	1.000	0	133	0	/rf	—	-0.1

FRENCH, RAY Raymond Edward; B1.9.1895 Alameda CA; D4.3.1978 Alameda CA; BR/TR/5´9.5˝/158; d9.17

YEAR	TM LG	G	AB	R	H	2B	3B	HR	RBI	BB-IB	HP	SO	AVG	OBP	SLG	AOPS	ABR	SB-CS	FA	FR	RNG	THR	GAMES AT POSITION	DL	BFW
1920	NY A	2	2	2	0	0	0	0	1	0	0	1	.000	.000	.000	-97	-1	0-0	.500	-1	0	0	/S	—	-0.1
1923	Bro N	43	73	14	16	2	1	0	7	4	1	7	.219	.269	.274	45	-6	0-0	.874	1	109	127	S30	—	-0.2
1924	Chi A	37	112	13	20	4	0	0	11	10	0	13	.179	.246	.214	20	-14	3-1	.927	-2	113	64	S28,2b3	—	-1.2
Total	3	82	187	29	36	6	1	0	19	14	1	21	.193	.252	.235	28	-21	3-1	.897	-1	110	92	S59,2b3	—	-1.5

FRENCH, JIM Richard James; B8.13.1941 Warren OH; BL/TR/5´7˝/182; d9.12; Col Ohio U.

YEAR	TM LG	G	AB	R	H	2B	3B	HR	RBI	BB-IB	HP	SO	AVG	OBP	SLG	AOPS	ABR	SB-CS	FA	FR	RNG	THR	GAMES AT POSITION	DL	BFW
1965	Was A	13	37	4	11	0	0	1	7	9-1	0	5	.297	.435	.378	135	2	1-0	.974	-0	140	142	C13	0	0.3
1966	Was A	10	24	0	5	1	0	0	3	4-0	0	5	.208	.321	.250	67	-1	0-1	.979	-2	58	143	C10	35	-0.3
1967	Was A	6	16	0	1	0	0	0	1	3-1	0	4	.063	.211	.063	-16	-2	0-0	.968	-2	35	69	C6	0	-0.4
1968	Was A	59	165	9	32	5	0	1	10	19-0	1	19	.194	.277	.242	62	-7	1-2	.984	-1	84	146	C53	0	-0.7
1969	Was A	63	158	14	29	6	3	2	13	41-6	0	15	.184	.348	.297	88	-1	1-0	.989	8	96	190	C63	0	1.1
1970	Was A	69	166	20	35	3	1	1	13	38-2	0	23	.211	.358	.259	76	-3	0-1	.973	-4	137	139	C62/lf	0	-0.6
1971	Was A	14	41	6	6	2	0	0	4	7-0	0	7	.146	.271	.195	35	-3	0-2	.985	-1	144	110	C14	0	-0.5
Total	7	234	607	53	119	17	4	5	51	121-10	1	78	.196	.328	.262	74	-15	3-6	.982	-2	107	152	C221/lf	35	-1.1

FRENCH, WALTER Walter Edward "Piggy","Fitz"; B7.12.1899 Moorestown NJ; D5.13.1984 Mountain Home AR; BL/TR/5´7.5˝/155; d9.15; Col Army

YEAR	TM LG	G	AB	R	H	2B	3B	HR	RBI	BB-IB	HP	SO	AVG	OBP	SLG	AOPS	ABR	SB-CS	FA	FR	RNG	THR	GAMES AT POSITION	DL	BFW
1923	Phi A	16	39	7	9	3	0	0	2	5	0	7	.231	.318	.308	64	-2	0-1	1.000	-1	83	108	O10C	—	-0.3
1925	Phi A	67	100	20	37	9	0	0	14	1	0	9	.370	.376	.460	104	1	1-1	.971	1	101	179	O19(3/0/16)	—	0.0
1926	Phi A	112	397	51	121	18	7	1	36	18	3	24	.305	.340	.393	86	-10	2-3	.971	0	98	107	O99(0/1/98)	—	-1.8
1927	Phi A	109	326	48	99	10	5	0	41	16	1	14	.304	.338	.365	78	-11	9-1	.956	2	115	66	O94(8/5/81)	—	-1.4
1928	Phi A	48	74	9	19	4	0	0	7	2	1	5	.257	.286	.311	55	-5	1-1	1.000	1	128	77	O19(8/0/11)	—	-0.5
1929	†Phi A	45	45	7	12	1	0	1	9	2	0	3	.267	.298	.356	65	-3	0-0	1.000	0	120	0	O10(6/1/3)	—	-0.3
Total	6	397	981	142	297	45	12	2	109	44	5	62	.303	.336	.379	81	-30	13-7	.968	4	106	93	O251(25/17/209)	—	-4.3

FRENCH, BILL William; B Baltimore MD; d4.14; ▲

YEAR	TM LG	G	AB	R	H	2B	3B	HR	RBI	BB-IB	HP	SO	AVG	OBP	SLG	AOPS	ABR	SB-CS	FA	FR	RNG	THR	GAMES AT POSITION	DL	BFW
1873	Mar NA	5	18	3	4	0	0	0	1	0	—	0	.222	.222	.222	42	-1	0-0	.905	-0	0	0	1b2,O2R/P3	—	-0.1

FREY, LONNY Linus Reinhard "Junior"; B8.23.1910 St.Louis MO; BL/TR (BB 1933–38)/5´10˝/160; d8.29; Mil 1944–45

YEAR	TM LG	G	AB	R	H	2B	3B	HR	RBI	BB-IB	HP	SO	AVG	OBP	SLG	AOPS	ABR	SB-CS	FA	FR	RNG	THR	GAMES AT POSITION	DL	BFW
1933	Bro N	34	135	25	43	5	3	0	12	13	0	13	.319	.378	.400	128	5	4	.896	-11	85	52	S34	—	-0.3
1934	Bro N	125	490	77	139	24	5	8	57	52	5	54	.284	.358	.402	109	7	11	.945	10	107	**121**	S109,3b13	—	2.4
1935	Bro N	131	515	88	135	35	11	11	77	66	5	68	.262	.352	.437	113	11	6	.937	-1	101	103	S127,2b4	—	1.9
1936	Bro N	148	524	63	146	29	4	4	60	71	4	56	.279	.369	.372	99	3	7	.918	-32	89	70	S117,2b30/cf	—	-1.8
1937	Chi N	78	198	33	55	9	3	1	22	33	0	15	.278	.381	.369	100	2	6	.938	-13	75	65	S30,2b13,3b9,O5(4/1/0)	—	-0.9
1938	Cin N	124	501	76	133	26	6	4	36	49	0	50	.265	.331	.365	94	-4	4	.964	-7	98	110	2b121,S3	—	-0.3
1939	†Cin N★	125	484	95	141	27	9	11	55	72	4	46	.291	.387	.452	124	19	5	.976	14	**105**	**106**	2b124	—	4.0
1940	†Cin N	150	563	102	150	23	6	8	54	80	3	48	.266	.361	.371	101	4	**22**	.977	15	105	**132**	2b150	—	2.8
1941	Cin N★	146	543	78	138	29	5	6	59	72	3	37	.254	.345	.359	98	0	16	**.970**	-4	98	111	2b145	0	0.6
1942	Cin N	141	523	66	139	23	6	2	39	87	2	38	.266	.373	.344	111	11	9	.977	5	103	**119**	2b140	0	2.7
1943	Cin N★	144	586	78	154	20	8	2	43	76	0	56	.263	.347	.334	99	1	7	**.985**	13	103	122	2b144	0	2.3
1946	Cin N	111	333	46	82	10	3	3	24	63	1	31	.246	.368	.321	100	3	5	.963	1	103	107	2b65,O28(3/13/12)	0	0.7
1947	Chi N	24	43	4	9	0	0	0	3	4	0	6	.209	.277	.209	32	-4	0	1.000	-1	95	77	2b9	0	-0.5
	†NY A	24	28	10	5	2	0	0	2	10	1	1	.179	.410	.250	87	1	3-0	.923	1	114	158	2b8	0	0.3
1948	NY A	1	0	1	0	0	0	0	0	0	0	0	ø	ø	ø	ø	0	0-0	ø	0	—	—	/R	0	0.0
	NY N	29	51	6	13	1	0	1	6	4	0	6	.255	.309	.333	73	-2	0	.920	-2	90	76	2b13	0	-0.3
Total	14	1535	5517	848	1482	263	69	61	549	752	28	525	.269	.359	.374	104	57	105-0	.973	-10	101	115	2b966,S420,O34(7/15/12),3b22	0	13.6

FRIAS, HANLEY Hanley (Acevedo); B12.5.1973 Villa Altagracia, D.R.; BB/TR/6´0˝/(160–173); d6.21

YEAR	TM LG	G	AB	R	H	2B	3B	HR	RBI	BB-IB	HP	SO	AVG	OBP	SLG	AOPS	ABR	SB-CS	FA	FR	RNG	THR	GAMES AT POSITION	DL	BFW
1997	Tex A	14	26	4	5	1	0	0	1	1-0	0	4	.192	.222	.231	17	-3	0-0	1.000	-5	50	38	S12/2	0	-0.7
1998	Ari N	15	23	4	3	0	1	1	2	0-0	0	5	.130	.130	.348	20	-3	0-0	1.000	0	82	149	2b3,3b2,S2	105	-0.3
1999	†Ari N	69	150	27	41	3	2	1	16	29-2	0	18	.273	.391	.340	87	-2	4-3	.965	-9	83	73	S53,2b8	0	-0.8
2000	Ari N	75	112	18	23	5	0	2	6	17-0	0	18	.205	.310	.304	54	-8	2-2	.938	-3	94	135	S21,2b15,3b7	0	-0.9
Total	4	173	311	53	72	9	3	4	25	47-2	0	45	.232	.332	.318	65	-16	6-5	.962	-17	82	83	S88,2b27,3b9	105	-2.7

FRIAS, PEPE Jesus Maria (Andujar); B7.14.1948 San Pedro de Macoris, D.R.; BR/TR (BB 1976p, 1977–7)/5´10˝/(150–165); d4.6

YEAR	TM LG	G	AB	R	H	2B	3B	HR	RBI	BB-IB	HP	SO	AVG	OBP	SLG	AOPS	ABR	SB-CS	FA	FR	RNG	THR	GAMES AT POSITION	DL	BFW
1973	Mon N	100	225	19	52	10	1	0	22	10-2	1	24	.231	.266	.284	51	-15	1-3	.950	2	111	101	S46,2b44,3b6/rf	0	-0.8
1974	Mon N	75	112	12	24	4	1	0	7	7-3	0	10	.214	.258	.268	45	-8	1-0	.962	7	107	98	S30,3b27,2b15,O3(1/0/2)	0	0.2
1975	Mon N	51	64	4	8	2	0	0	4	3-0	0	13	.125	.162	.156	-10	-10	0-1	.938	-0	90	107	S29,3b11,2b7	0	-0.8
1976	Mon N	76	113	7	28	5	0	0	8	4-3	0	14	.248	.271	.292	58	-6	1-1	.957	-2	95	105	2b35,S35,3b4/cf	0	-0.5
1977	Mon N	53	70	10	18	1	0	0	5	0-0	0	10	.257	.257	.271	43	-6	1-0	.978	0	110	138	2b16,S14/3	0	-0.5
1978	Mon N	73	15	5	4	2	1	0	5	0-0	0	3	.267	.250	.533	119	0	0-0	1.000	-5	79	91	2b61,S3	0	-0.4
1979	Atl N	140	475	41	123	18	4	1	44	20-5	2	36	.259	.290	.320	63	-25	3-2	.954	8	104	96	S137	0	-0.3

YEAR	TM LG	G	AB	R	H	2B	3B	HR	RBI	BB-IB	HP	SO	AVG	OBP	SLG	AOPS	ABR	SB-CS	FA	FR	RNG	THR	GAMES AT POSITION	DL	BFW
1980	Tex A	116	227	27	55	5	1	0	10	4-0	1	23	.242	.256	.273	47	-17	5-1	.947	-16	77	77	S106,3b7,2b2	0	-2.6
	LA N	14	9	1	2	1	0	0	0	0-0	0	0	.222	.222	.333	55	-1	0-0	.933	-1	82	106	S11	0	-0.1
1981	LA N	25	36	6	9	1	0	0	3	1-1	1	3	.250	.282	.278	64	-2	0-0	.906	-8	63	41	S15,2b6/3	0	-0.9
Total	9	723	1346	132	323	49	8	1	108	49-14	5	136	.240	.267	.290	53	-90	12-8	.951	-14	96	91	S426,2b186,3b57,O5(1/1/3)	0	-6.7
FRIBERG, BERNIE	Bernard Albert (b Gustaf Bernhard Friberg); B8.18.1899 Manchester NH; D12.8.1958 Lynn MA; BR/TR/5´11˝/178; d8.20; OF(84/52/62)																								
1919	Chi N	8	20	0	4	1	0	0	1	0	0	2	.200	.200	.250	35	-2	0	1.000	-0	110	0	O7(2/5/0)	—	-0.2
1920	Chi N	50	114	11	24	5	1	0	7	6	0	20	.211	.250	.272	49	-8	2-2	.963	4	105	84	2b24,O24(15/8/3)	—	-0.5
1922	Chi N	97	296	51	92	8	2	0	23	37	2	37	.311	.391	.351	91	-2	8-10	.972	0	87	147	O74(8/11/55),1b6,3b5,2b3	—	-0.8
1923	Chi N	146	547	91	174	27	11	12	88	45	2	49	.318	.372	.473	122	16	13-19	.955	10	105	**136**	3b146	—	3.0
1924	Chi N	142	495	67	138	19	3	5	82	66	5	53	.279	.369	.360	95	0	19-27	.954	5	105	90	3b142	—	0.9
1925	Chi N	44	152	12	39	5	3	1	16	14	2	22	.257	.327	.349	72	-7	0-1	.889	-3	93	119	3b26,O12L,1b6,S2	—	-0.9
	Phi N	91	304	41	82	12	1	5	22	39	0	35	.270	.353	.365	77	-10	1-1	.965	-1	102	78	2b77,3b14/PC	—	-0.7
	Year	135	456	53	121	17	4	6	38	53	2	57	.265	.344	.360	75	-16	1-2	.965	-3	102	78	2b77,3b40,O12L,1b6,S2/PC	—	-1.6
1926	Phi N	144	478	38	128	21	3	1	51	57	0	77	.268	.346	.331	79	-12	2	.976	22	107	94	2b144	—	1.3
1927	Phi N	111	335	31	78	8	2	1	28	41	3	49	.233	.322	.278	61	-17	3	.959	20	**118**	**129**	3b103,2b5	—	0.9
1928	Phi N	52	94	11	19	3	0	1	7	12	0	16	.202	.292	.266	45	-7	0	.908	0	95	109	S31,3b5,2b3,O3(2/1/0),1b2	—	-0.5
1929	Phi N	128	455	74	137	21	10	7	55	49	1	54	.301	.370	.437	93	-5	1	.923	-18	86	65	S73,O40(18/19/4),2b8,1b2	—	-1.7
1930	Phi N	105	331	62	113	21	1	4	42	47	1	35	.341	.425	.447	104	5	1	.953	-1	102	77	2b44,O35(27/8/0),S12,3b8	—	0.3
1931	Phi N	103	353	33	92	19	5	1	26	33	0	25	.261	.324	.351	75	-12	1	.955	6	103	95	2b64,3b25,1b5,S3	—	-0.1
1932	Phi N	61	154	17	37	8	2	0	14	19	0	23	.240	.324	.318	66	-7	0	.957	-5	98	77	2b56	—	-0.9
1933	Bos A	17	41	5	13	3	0	0	9	6	0	1	.317	.404	.390	112	1	0-0	.950	1	113	123	2b6,3b5,S2	—	0.2
Total	14	1299	4169	544	1170	181	44	38	471	471	16	498	.281	.356	.373	87	-67	51-60	.953	41	107	109	3b479,2b434,O195L,S123,1b21/CP	—	0.3
FRIDLEY, JIM	James Riley "Big Jim"; B9.6.1924 Philippi WV; D2.28.2003 Port Charlotte FL; BR/TR/6´2˝/205; d4.15; Col West Virginia																								
1952	Cle A	62	175	23	44	2	0	4	16	14	1	40	.251	.311	.331	84	-5	3-3	.978	-1	97	98	O54(37/0/20)	0	-0.9
1954	Bal A	85	240	25	59	8	5	4	36	21	2	41	.246	.311	.371	93	-4	0-1	.985	-2	99	25	O67(64/0/3)	0	-1.0
1958	Cin N	5	9	2	2	2	0	0	1	0-0	0	2	.222	.222	.444	67	0	0-0	1.000	-0	44	0	O2L	0	-0.1
Total	3	152	424	50	105	12	5	8	53	35-0	3	83	.248	.309	.356	89	-9	3-4	.982	-3	98	54	O123(103/0/23)	0	-2.0
FRIEL, PAT	Patrick Henry; B6.11.1860 Lewisburg VA (now West Virginia); D1.15.1924 Providence RI; BB/5´11˝/170; d7.13; b–Bill																								
1890	Syr AA	62	261	51	65	8	2	3	21	17	3	—	.249	.302	.330	96	-1	34	.913	-4	72	87	O62(13/0/49)	—	-0.5
1891	Phi AA	2	8	2	2	1	0	0	0	0	0	0	.250	.250	.375	78	0	0	1.000	-0	0	0	O2R	—	0.0
Total	2	64	269	53	67	9	2	3	21	17	3	0	.249	.301	.331	96	-1	34	.914	-4	71	85	O64(13/0/51)	—	-0.5
FRIEL, BILL	William Edward; B4.1.1876 Renovo PA; D12.24.1959 St.Louis MO; BL/TR/5´10˝/165; d5.3; C1/U1; b–Pat; Col Niagara; OF(6/27/39)																								
1901	Mil A	106	376	51	100	13	7	4	35	23	1	—	.266	.310	.370	92	-5	15	.866	-6	107	119	3b61,O29(5/23/1),2b9,S6	—	-0.9
1902	StL A	80	267	26	64	9	2	2	20	14	2	—	.240	.283	.311	65	-13	4	.921	-6	97	168	O33(1/0/32),2b25,1b10,3b8,S3/PC	—	-1.9
1903	StL A	97	351	46	80	11	8	0	25	23	2	—	.228	.279	.305	77	-10	4	.915	-11	92	69	2b63,3b24,O9(0/4/6)	—	-2.1
Total	3	283	994	123	244	33	17	6	80	60	5	—	.245	.292	.331	80	-28	23	.924	-24	91	70	2b97,3b93,O71R,1b10,S9/CP	—	-4.9
FRIEND, FRANK	Frank B. (b Lawrence Joseph Freund); B7.5.1875 Jeffersonville IN; D11.5.1933 Jeffersonville IN; TR/5´10˝/180; d8.2																								
1896	Lou N	2	5	1	1	0	0	0	0	1	0	1	.200	.333	.200	44	0	0	1.000	0	*76*	*149*	C2	—	0.0
FRIEND, OWEN	Owen Lacey "Red"; B3.21.1927 Granite City IL; BR/TR/6´1˝/(175–180); d10.2; Mil 1951–52; C1																								
1949	StL A	2	8	1	3	0	0	0	1	0	0	0	.375	.375	.375	95	0	0-0	1.000	1	140	57	2b2	0	0.1
1950	StL A	119	372	48	88	15	2	8	50	40	1	68	.237	.312	.352	67	-19	2-1	.961	-3	112	74	2b93,3b24,S3	0	-1.6
1953	Det A	31	96	10	17	4	0	3	10	6	1	9	.177	.233	.313	47	-8	0-1	.947	-0	98	101	2b26	0	-0.6
	Cle A	34	68	7	16	2	0	2	13	5	0	16	.235	.288	.353	74	-3	0-0	1.000	5	115	152	2b19,S8/3	0	0.3
	Year	65	164	17	33	6	0	5	23	11	1	25	.201	.256	.329	58	-11	0-1	.964	5	104	118	2b45,S8/3	0	-0.3
1955	Bos A	14	42	3	11	3	0	0	2	4-0	0	11	.262	.326	.333	71	-2	0-0	.951	1	114	73	S14/2	0	0.0
	Chi N	6	10	0	1	0	0	0	0	0-0	0	3	.100	.100	.100	-47	-2	0-0	1.000	-1	67	0	3b2/S	0	-0.3
1956	Chi N	2	2	0	0	0	0	0	0	0-0	0	2	.000	.000	.000	-99	-1	0-0	ø	0	—	—	/H	0	-0.1
Total	5	208	598	69	136	24	2	13	76	55-0	2	109	.227	.295	.339	63	-35	2-2	.963	3	110	86	2b141,3b27,S26	0	-2.2
FRIERSON, BUCK	Robert Lawrence; B7.29.1917 Chicota TX; D6.26.1996 Paris TX; BR/TR/6´3˝/195; d9.9																								
1941	Cle A	5	11	2	3	1	0	0	2	1	0	1	.273	.333	.364	89	0	0-0	1.000	-0	57	0	O3(2/0/1)	0	-0.1
FRINK, FRED	Frederick Ferdinand; B8.25.1911 Macon GA; D5.19.1995 Miami Springs FL; BR/TR/6´1˝/180; d7.1; Col Illinois																								
1934	Phi N	2	0	0	0	0	0	0	0	0	0	0	ø	ø	ø	ø	0	0	ø	-0	0	0	/cf	—	0.0
FRISBEE, CHARLIE	Charles Augustus "Bunt"; B2.2.1874 Dows IA; D11.7.1954 Iowa Falls IA; BB/TR/5´9˝/175; d6.22; Col Grinnell																								
1899	Bos N	42	152	22	50	4	2	0	20	9	2	—	.329	.374	.382	98	-1	10	.875	-2	156	73	O40(0/36/4)	—	-0.4
1900	NY N	4	13	2	2	1	0	0	3	2	0	—	.154	.267	.231	40	-1	0	.400	-2	0	0	O4R	—	-0.3
Total	2	46	165	24	52	5	2	0	23	11	2	—	.315	.365	.370	94	-2	10	.849	-3	142	66	O44(0/36/8)	—	-0.7
FRISCH, FRANKIE	Frank Francis "The Fordham Flash"; B9.9.1898 Bronx NY; D3.12.1973 Wilmington DE; BB/TR/5´11˝/165; d6.14; M16/C1; HF1947; Col Fordham																								
1919	NY N	54	190	21	43	3	2	2	24	4	0	14	.226	.242	.295	62	-10	15	.972	3	101	61	2b29,3b20/S	—	-0.7
1920	NY N	110	440	57	123	10	10	4	77	20	0	18	.280	.311	.375	97	-4	34-11	.967	10	**116**	**134**	3b109,S2	—	1.4
1921	†NY N	**153**	618	121	211	31	17	8	100	42	1	28	.341	.384	.485	128	24	**49**-13	.936	8	112	105	3b93,2b61	—	4.5
1922	†NY N	132	514	101	168	16	13	5	51	47	3	13	.327	.387	.438	111	9	31-17	.975	8	105	104	2b85,3b53/S	—	2.1
1923	†NY N	151	641	116	**223**	32	10	12	111	46	4	12	.348	.395	.485	133	30	29-12	**.973**	0	98	106	2b135,3b17	—	3.5
1924	†NY N	145	603	**121**	198	33	15	7	69	56	2	24	.328	.387	.468	132	28	22-9	.972	**28**	**106**	117	2b143,S10,3b2	—	6.0
1925	NY N	120	502	89	166	26	6	11	48	32	3	14	.331	.374	.472	119	14	21-12	.931	4	111	49	3b46,2b42,S39	—	2.4
1926	NY N	135	545	75	171	29	4	5	44	33	0	16	.314	.353	.409	106	4	23	.975	10	108	99	2b127,3b7	—	1.7
1927	StL N	**153**	617	112	208	31	11	10	78	43	7	10	.337	.387	.472	125	22	**48**	**.979**	**49**	**120**	**124**	2b153/S	—	**7.2**
1928	†StL N	141	547	107	164	29	9	10	86	64	1	17	.300	.374	.441	110	9	29	**.976**	-5	100	92	2b139	—	0.8
1929	StL N	138	527	93	176	40	12	5	74	53	2	12	.334	.397	.484	116	14	24	.970	-6	94	89	2b121,3b13/S	—	1.1
1930	†StL N	133	540	121	187	46	9	10	114	55	0	16	.346	.407	.520	118	18	15	.969	**22**	**108**	**106**	2b123,3b10	—	3.9
1931	†StL N	131	518	96	161	24	4	4	82	45	2	13	.311	.368	.396	101	2	**28**	.974	11	103	113	2b129	—	2.1
1932	StL N	115	486	59	142	26	2	3	60	25	0	13	.292	.327	.372	85	-10	18	.971	16	103	111	2b75,3b37,S4	—	1.2
1933	StL N★	147	585	74	177	32	6	4	66	48	3	16	.303	.358	.398	110	9	18	.982	-6	90	88	2b132,S15,M	—	1.4
1934	†StL N★	140	550	74	168	30	6	3	75	45	1	10	.305	.359	.398	96	-2	11	.977	3	95	117	2b115,3b25,M	—	0.9
1935	StL N☆	103	354	52	104	16	2	1	55	33	1	16	.294	.356	.359	89	-4	2	.982	-5	95	112	2b88,3b5,M	—	-0.4
1936	StL N	93	303	40	83	10	0	1	26	36	1	10	.274	.353	.317	82	-6	2	.965	-13	94	79	2b60,3b22/SM	—	-1.5
1937	StL N	17	32	3	7	2	0	0	4	1	0	0	.219	.242	.281	41	-3	0	1.000	-1	89	0	2b5,M	—	-0.3
Total	19	2311	9112	1532	2880	466	138	105	1244	728	31	272	.316	.369	.432	110	144	419-74	.974	135	102	104	2b1762,3b459,S75	—	37.3
FRISK, EMIL	John Emil; B10.15.1874 Kalkaska MI; D1.27.1922 Seattle WA; BL/TR/6´1˝/190; d9.2; ▲																								
1899	Cin N	9	25	5	7	1	0	0	2	2	1	—	.280	.357	.320	85	1	0	.950	-0	87	0	P9	—	0.0
1901	Det A	20	48	10	15	3	0	1	7	3	1	—	.313	.365	.438	117	1	0	.851	2	168	0	P11,O2(0/1/1)	—	0.1
1905	StL A	124	429	58	112	11	6	3	36	42	11	—	.261	.342	.336	122	12	7	.923	-7	121	70	O115R	—	0.0
1907	StL A	5	4	0	1	0	0	0	0	1	0	—	.250	.400	.250	108	0	0	ø	0	—	—	/H	—	0.0
Total	4	158	506	73	135	15	6	4	45	48	13	—	.267	.346	.344	119	14	7	.918	-5	119	69	O117(0/1/116),P20	—	0.1
FRITZ, HARRY	Harry Koch "Dutchman"; B9.30.1890 Philadelphia PA; D11.4.1974 Columbus OH; BR/TR/5´8˝/170; d9.29																								
1913	Phi A	5	13	1	0	0	0	0	0	2	1	4	.000	.188	.000	-45	-2	0	.846	-1	71	0	3b5	—	-0.3
1914	Chi F	65	174	16	37	5	1	0	13	18	3	18	.213	.297	.253	54	-14	2	.912	-6	89	152	3b46,S9/2	—	-1.9
1915	Chi F	79	236	27	59	8	4	3	26	13	3	27	.250	.298	.356	89	-9	4	.964	-5	90	101	3b70,2b6/S	—	-1.3
Total	3	149	423	44	96	13	5	3	39	33	7	49	.227	.294	.303	70	-25	6	.941	-12	89	116	3b121,S10,2b7	—	-3.5
FRITZ, LARRY	Lawrence Joseph; B2.14.1949 E.Chicago IN; BL/TL/6´2˝/225; [NYN69 S3/57]; d5.30; Col Arizona St.																								
1975	Phi N	1	1	0	0	0	0	0	0	0-0	0	0	.000	.000	.000	-95	0	0-0	ø	0	—	—	/H	0	0.0

YEAR	TM LG	G	AB	R	H	2B	3B	HR	RBI	BB-IB	HP	SO	AVG	OBP	SLG	AOPS	ABR	SB-CS	FA	FR	RNG	THR	GAMES AT POSITION	DL	BFW
Frobel, Doug	Douglas Steven; B6.6.1959 Ottawa ON, Can.; BL/TR/6´4˝/(193–205); d9.5																								
1982	Pit N	16	34	5	7	2	0	2	3	1-0	0	11	.206	.229	.441	80	-1	1-1	1.000	0	117	0	O12R	0	-0.2
1983	Pit N	32	60	10	17	4	1	3	11	4-0	0	17	.283	.328	.533	131	2	1-1	.964	-2	91	0	O24(18/0/6)	0	0.0
1984	Pit N	126	276	33	56	9	3	12	28	24-2	2	84	.203	.271	.388	83	-8	7-5	.956	9	121	168	O112R	0	-0.4
1985	Pit N	53	109	14	22	5	0	0	7	19-5	0	24	.202	.320	.248	61	-5	4-3	.941	-1	86	101	O36(20/0/16)	0	-0.8
	Mon N	12	23	3	3	1	0	1	4	2-0	0	6	.130	.200	.304	41	-2	0-0	.923	-0	114	0	O6(1/2/3)	0	-0.2
	Year	65	132	17	25	6	0	1	11	21-5	0	30	.189	.301	.258	58	-7	4-3	.938	-2	90	86	O42(21/2/19)	0	-1.0
1987	Cle A	29	40	5	4	0	0	2	5	5-1	0	13	.100	.196	.250	18	-5	0-0	1.000	-1	63	0	O12(2/2/7),D5	0	-0.6
Total	5	268	542	70	109	21	4	20	58	55-8	2	155	.201	.276	.365	77	-19	13-10	.957	5	108	115	O202(41/4/156),D5	0	-2.2
Froelich, Ben	William Palmer; B11.12.1887 Pittsburgh PA; D9.1.1916 Pittsburgh PA; BR/TR; d7.2																								
1909	Phi N	1	1	0	0	0	0	0	0	0	0	—	.000	.000	.000	-99	0	0	ø	0	*0*	*0*	/C	—	0.0
Fry, Jerry	Jerry Ray; B2.29.1956 Salinas CA; BR/TR/6´0˝/185; [MonN74 2/33]; d9.4																								
1978	Mon N	4	9	0	0	0	0	0	0	1-0	0	5	.000	.100	.000	-70	-2	0-0	1.000	-1	27	0	C4	0	-0.3
Frye, Jeff	Jeffrey Dustin; B8.31.1966 Oakland CA; BR/TR/5´9˝/(160–170); [TexA88 30/765]; d7.9; Col Southeastern Oklahoma; OF(9/8/18); [DL 1993 Tex A 182, 1998 Bos A 181]																								
1992	Tex A	67	199	24	51	9	1	1	12	16-0	3	27	.256	.320	.327	84	-4	1-3	.978	2	101	94	2b67	0	-0.1
1994	Tex A	57	205	37	67	20	3	0	18	29-0	1	23	.327	.408	.454	122	9	6-1	.983	-6	95	87	2b54/3D	15	0.5
1995	Tex A	90	313	38	87	15	2	4	29	24-0	5	45	.278	.335	.377	83	-8	3-3	.975	7	106	102	2b83	30	0.2
1996	Bos A	105	419	74	120	27	2	4	41	54-0	5	57	.286	.372	.389	92	-3	18-4	.983	14	106	92	2b100,O5(2/1/2),S3/D	0	1.7
1997	Bos A	127	404	56	126	36	2	3	51	27-1	2	44	.312	.352	.433	103	3	19-8	.991	8	99	114	2b80,3b18,O13(5/5/3),D11,S3/1	0	1.5
1999	Bos A	41	114	14	32	3	0	1	12	14-1	1	11	.281	.362	.333	77	-4	2-2	.980	-6	77	63	2b26,3b7,S2,D2	77	-0.8
2000	Bos A	69	239	35	69	13	0	1	13	28-0	1	38	.289	.364	.356	82	-6	1-3	.991	-5	91	69	2b52,O15(1/2/13),3b3,D3	0	-0.9
	Col N	37	87	14	31	6	0	0	3	8-0	1	16	.356	.412	.425	92	0	4-0	.989	2	106	118	2b27/3	0	0.3
2001	Tor A	74	175	24	43	6	1	2	15	12-0	3	18	.246	.305	.326	65	-9	2-1	.995	3	104	117	2b47,3b27,S2/lf	8	-0.4
Total	8	667	2155	316	626	135	11	16	194	212-2	22	279	.290	.357	.386	91	-22	56-25	.984	18	100	96	2b536,3b57,O34R,D18,S10/1	493	2.0
Fryman, Travis	David Travis; B3.25.1969 Lexington KY; BR/TR/6´1˝/(180–195); [DetA87 1/30]; d7.7																								
1990	Det A	66	232	32	69	11	1	9	27	17-0	1	51	.297	.348	.470	125	7	3-3	.915	1	109	142	3b48,S17/D	0	0.9
1991	Det A	149	557	65	144	36	3	21	91	40-0	3	149	.259	.309	.447	105	2	12-5	.946	-20	86	77	3b85,S71	0	-1.2
1992	Det A★	161	659	87	175	31	4	20	96	45-1	6	144	.266	.316	.416	103	0	8-4	.970	-1	107	98	S137,3b26	0	1.0
1993	Det A★	151	607	98	182	37	5	22	97	77-1	4	128	.300	.379	.486	131	28	9-4	.953	-5	106	112	S81,3b69/D	0	3.0
1994	Det A★	114	464	66	122	34	5	18	85	45-1	5	128	.263	.326	.474	104	2	2-2	.955	-1	105	67	3b114	0	0.1
1995	Det A	**144**	567	79	156	21	5	15	81	63-4	3	100	.275	.347	.409	97	-3	4-2	.969	**27**	**127**	137	3b144	0	2.4
1996	Det A★	157	616	90	165	32	3	22	100	57-2	4	118	.268	.329	.437	93	-8	4-3	**.979**	23	**122**	94	3b128,S29	0	1.6
1997	Det A	154	595	90	163	27	3	22	102	46-5	5	113	.274	.326	.440	100	-2	16-3	**.978**	14	111	84	3b153	0	1.5
1998	†Cle A	146	557	74	160	33	2	28	96	44-0	3	125	.287	.340	.504	112	9	10-8	.963	-3	98	94	3b144,S3,D2	0	0.6
1999	†Cle A	85	322	45	82	16	2	10	48	25-1	1	57	.255	.309	.410	78	-12	2-1	.969	-1	99	88	3b85	79	-1.2
2000	Cle A★	155	574	93	184	38	4	22	106	73-2	1	111	.321	.392	.516	125	23	1-1	**.978**	-1	97	71	3b154/1D	0	2.1
2001	†Cle A	98	334	34	88	15	0	3	38	30-1	3	63	.263	.327	.335	73	-12	1-2	.944	-10	78	88	3b96/SD	62	-2.2
2002	Cle A	118	397	42	86	14	3	11	55	40-1	2	82	.217	.292	.350	68	-19	0-0	.960	-6	93	**139**	3b113	15	-2.3
Total	13	1698	6481	895	1776	345	40	223	1022	602-19	41	1369	.274	.336	.443	103	15	72-38	.965	17	103	95	3b1359,S339,D7/1	156	6.3
Fuentes, Mike	Michael Jay; B7.11.1958 Miami FL; BR/TR/6´3˝/190; [MonN81 2/44]; d9.2; Col Florida St.																								
1983	Mon N	6	4	1	1	0	0	0	0	0-0	0	2	.250	.250	.250	39	0	0-0	ø	0	—	—	/H	0	-0.1
1984	Mon N	3	4	0	1	0	0	0	0	1-0	0	2	.250	.400	.250	90	0	0-0	1.000	0	221	0	/lf	0	0.0
Total	2	9	8	1	2	0	0	0	0	1-0	0	4	.250	.333	.250	66	0	0-0	1.000	0	221	0	/lf	0	-0.1
Fuentes, Tito	Rigoberto (Peat); B1.4.1944 Havana, Cuba; BB/TR (BR 1965–67, 70p)/5´11˝/175; d8.18																								
1965	SF N	26	72	12	15	1	0	0	1	5-1	1	14	.208	.269	.222	39	-6	0-1	.919	-6	82	54	S18,2b7/3	0	-1.2
1966	SF N	133	541	63	141	21	3	9	40	9-1	3	57	.261	.276	.360	73	-21	6-3	.957	2	100	106	S76,2b60	0	-0.8
1967	SF N	133	344	27	72	12	1	5	29	27-9	0	61	.209	.266	.294	61	-18	4-3	.980	17	108	**128**	2b130,S5	0	0.9
1969	SF N	67	183	28	54	4	3	1	14	15-1	1	25	.295	.350	.366	103	0	2-4	.925	-4	109	145	3b36,S30	24	-0.2
1970	SF N	123	435	49	116	13	7	2	32	36-3	3	52	.267	.323	.343	80	-13	4-5	.966	-0	105	87	2b78,S36,3b24	0	-0.7
1971	†SF N	152	630	63	172	28	6	4	52	18-2	6	46	.273	.299	.356	86	-14	12-2	.973	2	101	108	2b152	0	0.0
1972	SF N	152	572	64	151	33	6	7	53	39-3	3	56	.264	.310	.379	95	-5	16-5	.964	-16	95	92	2b152	0	-1.0
1973	SF N	160	656	78	182	25	5	6	63	45-0	7	62	.277	.328	.358	87	-11	12-6	**.993**	-6	98	97	2b160/3	0	-0.6
1974	SF N	108	390	33	97	15	2	0	22	22-0	3	32	.249	.293	.297	63	-20	7-3	.979	2	100	111	2b103	0	-1.1
1975	SD N	146	565	57	158	21	3	4	43	25-2	3	51	.280	.309	.349	89	-11	8-8	.970	9	107	107	2b142	0	0.8
1976	SD N	135	520	48	137	18	0	2	36	18-0	1	38	.263	.287	.310	76	-19	5-3	.971	11	108	108	2b127	0	0.1
1977	Det A	151	615	83	190	19	10	5	51	38-1	2	61	.309	.348	.397	98	-2	4-4	.970	8	101	118	2b151/D	0	1.3
1978	Oak A	13	43	5	6	1	0	0	2	1-0	0	6	.140	.159	.163	-10	-6	0-0	.944	-6	57	61	2b13	0	-1.3
Total	13	1499	5566	610	1491	211	46	45	438	298-23	33	561	.268	.307	.347	82	-146	80-47	.974	13	102	105	2b1275,S165,3b62/D	24	-3.8
Fuhrman, Ollie	Alfred George; B7.20.1896 Jordan MN; D1.11.1969 Peoria IL; BB/TR/5´11˝/185; d4.13																								
1922	Phi A	6	6	1	2	1	0	0	0	0	0	0	.333	.333	.500	112	0	0-0	1.000	0	*59*	*0*	C4	—	0.0
Fulghum, Dot	James Lavoisier; B7.4.1900 Valdosta GA; D11.2.1967 Miami FL; BR/TR/5´8.5˝/165; d9.15																								
1921	Phi A	2	2	0	0	0	0	0	0	1	0	1	.000	.333	.000	-9	0	0-0	ø	-0	0	0	/S	—	0.0
Fuller, Nig	Charles F. (b Charles F. Furrer); B3.30.1879 Toledo OH; D3.1.1937 Toledo OH; BR/TR/5´11˝/165; d7.1																								
1902	Bro N	3	9	0	0	0	0	0	1	0	0	—	.000	.000	.000	-99	-2	0	1.000	-1	*66*	*47*	C3	—	-0.3
Fuller, Frank	Frank Edward "Rabbit"; B1.1.1893 Detroit MI; D10.29.1965 Warren MI; BB/TR/5´7˝/150; d4.14																								
1915	Det A	14	32	6	5	0	0	0	2	9	0	7	.156	.341	.156	47	-2	2-3	.962	-3	93	41	2b9/S	—	-0.6
1916	Det A	20	10	2	1	0	0	0	1	1	0	4	.100	.182	.100	-15	-1	3	.846	1	166	323	2b8/S	—	-0.1
1923	Bos A	6	21	3	5	0	0	0	0	1	0	1	.238	.273	.238	35	-2	1-1	.952	0	100	50	2b6	—	-0.2
Total	3	40	63	11	11	0	0	0	3	11	0	12	.175	.297	.175	35	-5	6-4	.938	-2	104	73	2b23,S2	—	-0.9
Fuller, Harry	Henry W.; B12.5.1862 Cincinnati OH; D12.12.1895 Cincinnati OH; 5´8˝/160; d9.19; b–Shorty																								
1891	StL AA	1	2	0	0	0	0	0	0	0	0	1	.000	.000	.000	-87	0	0	.000	-1	0	0	/3	—	-0.1
Fuller, Jim	James Hardy; B11.28.1950 Bethesda MD; BR/TR/6´3˝/(210–215); [BalA70*S2/41]; d9.10; Col San Diego Mesa (CA) JC																								
1973	Bal A	9	26	2	3	0	0	2	4	1-0	0	17	.115	.148	.346	35	-3	0-0	1.000	2	161	396	O5R,1b2/D	0	-0.1
1974	Bal A	64	189	17	42	11	0	7	28	8-2	3	68	.222	.265	.392	89	-3	1-0	.960	1	109	75	O59(4/0/56),1b4,D2	0	-0.5
1977	Hou N	34	100	5	16	6	0	2	9	10-1	1	45	.160	.243	.280	43	-8	0-1	.983	4	102	285	O27(26/0/1)/1	0	-0.6
Total	3	107	315	24	61	17	0	11	41	19-3	4	130	.194	.249	.352	70	-14	1-1	.969	7	109	160	O91(30/0/62),1b7,D3	0	-1.2
Fuller, John	John Edward; B1.29.1950 Lynwood CA; BL/TL/6´2˝/180; [AtlN68 11/235]; d5.9																								
1974	Atl N	3	3	1	1	0	0	0	0	0-0	0	0	.333	.333	.333	84	0	0-0	1.000	0	337	0	/cf	0	0.0
Fuller, Vern	Vernon Gordon; B3.1.1944 Menomonie WI; BR/TR/6´1˝/(160–190); d9.5																								
1964	Cle A	2	1	0	0	0	0	0	0	0-0	0	0	.000	.000	.000	-99	0	0-0	ø	0	—	—	/H	141	0.0
1966	Cle A	16	47	7	11	2	1	2	2	7-0	2	6	.234	.357	.447	129	2	0-0	1.000	-3	70	141	2b16	0	0.0
1967	Cle A	73	206	18	46	10	0	7	21	19-0	4	55	.223	.300	.374	98	0	2-3	.986	-3	92	114	2b64,S2	0	0.2
1968	Cle A	97	244	14	59	8	2	0	18	24-2	4	49	.242	.316	.291	88	-3	2-2	.988	-18	83	79	2b73,3b23,S4	0	-1.9
1969	Cle A	108	254	25	60	11	1	4	22	20-2	2	53	.236	.295	.335	74	-9	2-1	.978	6	94	101	2b102,3b7	0	0.3
1970	Cle A	29	33	3	6	2	0	1	2	3-0	0	9	.182	.250	.333	57	-2	0-0	.919	-1	78	80	2b16,3b4/1	0	-0.3
Total	6	325	785	67	182	33	4	14	65	73-4	12	172	.232	.305	.338	87	-12	6-6	.982	-19	88	101	2b271,3b34,S6/1	141	-1.7
Fuller, Shorty	William Benjamin; B10.10.1867 Cincinnati OH; D4.11.1904 Cincinnati OH; BR/TR/5´6˝/157; d7.19; b–Harry																								
1888	Was N	49	170	11	31	5	2	0	12	10	1	14	.182	.232	.235	53	-9	6	.845	-2	103	101	S47,2b2	—	-0.9
1889	StL AA	**140**	517	91	117	18	6	0	51	52	5	56	.226	.303	.284	60	-29	38	**.913**	-2	93	101	S140	—	-2.3
1890	StL AA	130	526	118	146	9	9	1	40	73	11	—	.278	.377	.335	96	-3	60	.870	-0	92	105	S130	—	0.1
1891	StL AA	135	576	105	122	14	7	2	61	67	4	28	.212	.298	.271	55	-37	42	.857	-4	96	111	S102,2b38	—	-3.2

YEAR	TM LG	G	AB	R	H	2B	3B	HR	RBI	BB-IB	HP	SO	AVG	OBP	SLG	AOPS	ABR	SB-CS	FA	FR	RNG	THR	GAMES AT POSITION	DL	BFW
1892	NY N	141	508	74	116	11	4	1	48	52	0	24	.228	.300	.272	74	-15	37	.888	3	94	88	S141	—	-0.5
1893	NY N	130	474	78	112	14	8	0	51	60	2	21	.236	.325	.300	66	-23	26	.911	9	103	91	S130	—	-0.6
1894	†NY N	95	377	82	104	14	4	2	47	52	2	16	.276	.367	.350	74	-15	32	.881	-11	91	108	S91,O2R,3b2/2	—	-1.6
1895	NY N	126	458	82	103	11	3	0	32	64	2	34	.225	.323	.262	53	-30	15	.913	33	114	114	S126	—	0.8
1896	NY N	18	72	10	12	0	0	0	7	14	1	5	.167	.310	.167	28	-7	4	.874	0	100	103	S18	—	-0.5
Total	9	964	3678	651	863	96	43	6	349	444	28	198	.235	.322	.289	67	-168	260	.890	26	98	102	S925,2b41,3b2,O2R	—	-8.7
Fullis, Chick	Charles Philip; B2.27.1904 Girardville PA; D3.28.1946 Ashland PA; BR/TR/5´9˝/170; d4.13																								
1928	NY N	11	1	5	0	0	0	0	0	1	0	1	.000	.500	.000	41	0	0	ø	0	—	—	/H	—	0.0
1929	NY N	86	274	67	79	11	1	7	29	30	3	26	.288	.365	.412	92	-3	7	.962	-9	84	48	O78(33/46/1)	—	-1.5
1930	NY N	13	6	2	0	0	0	0	0	0	0	1	.000	.000	.000	-99	-2	1	ø	-0	0	0	O2(1/1/0)	—	-0.2
1931	NY N	89	302	61	99	15	2	3	28	23	4	13	.328	.383	.421	119	9	13	.988	-4	90	97	O68(1/65/0),2b9	—	0.3
1932	NY N	96	235	35	70	14	3	1	21	11	1	12	.298	.332	.396	97	-1	1	.990	-4	91	31	O55(36/19/0)/2	—	-0.7
1933	Phi N	151	647	91	200	31	6	1	45	36	5	34	.309	.350	.380	96	-2	18	.977	2	100	140	O151C/3	—	-0.3
1934	Phi N	28	102	8	23	6	0	0	12	10	1	4	.225	.301	.284	51	-7	2	.956	-2	89	65	O27(24/3/0)	—	-0.9
	†StL N	69	199	21	52	9	1	0	26	14	0	11	.261	.310	.317	64	-10	4	.969	-2	99	57	O56(8/48/0)	—	-1.3
	Year	97	301	29	75	15	1	0	38	24	1	15	.249	.307	.306	59	-17	6	.966	-3	96	59	O83(32/51/0)	—	-2.2
1936	StL N	47	89	15	25	6	1	0	6	7	0	11	.281	.333	.371	90	-1	0	1.000	2	109	115	O26(2/15/9)	—	0.0
Total	8	590	1855	305	548	92	14	12	167	132	14	113	.295	.347	.380	92	-17	46	.977	-16	95	91	O463(105/348/10),2b10/3	—	-4.6
Fullmer, Brad	Bradley Ryan; B1.17.1975 Chatsworth CA; BL/TR/6´0˝/(190–220); [MonN93 2/60]; d9.2																								
1997	Mon N	19	40	4	12	2	0	3	8	2-1	1	7	.300	.349	.575	138	2	0-0	.982	0	138	116	1b8,O2L	0	0.2
1998	Mon N	140	505	58	138	44	2	13	73	39-4	2	70	.273	.327	.446	104	3	6-6	.985	-7	86	79	1b137	0	-1.6
1999	Mon N	100	347	38	96	34	2	9	47	22-6	2	35	.277	.321	.464	100	-1	2-3	.991	-8	67	66	1b94	0	-1.7
2000	Tor A	133	482	76	142	29	1	32	104	30-3	6	68	.295	.340	.558	119	12	3-1	1.000	0	683	0	D129/1	0	0.5
2001	Tor A	146	522	71	143	31	2	18	83	38-8	6	88	.274	.326	.444	99	-1	5-2	1.000	0	158	131	D135/1	0	-0.7
2002	†Ana A	130	429	75	124	35	6	19	59	32-6	15	44	.289	.357	.531	135	21	10-3	.995	-3	51	122	D94,1b29	0	1.2
2003	Ana A	63	206	32	63	9	2	9	35	26-4	2	31	.306	.387	.500	137	12	5-4	1.000	-0	92	123	D41,1b19	94	0.7
2004	Tex A	76	258	41	60	19	1	11	33	27-1	3	30	.233	.310	.442	90	-4	1-2	1.000	-1	0	282	D66,1b4	71	-0.8
Total	8	807	2789	395	778	203	16	114	442	216-33	37	373	.279	.336	.486	111	44	32-21	.989	-19	78	84	D465,1b293,O2L	165	-2.2
Fulmer, Chick	Charles John; B2.12.1851 Philadelphia PA; D2.15.1940 Philadelphia PA; BR/TR/6´0˝/158; d6.5; U1; b–Washington																								
1871	Rok NA	16	63	11	17	1	3	0	3	5	—	1	.270	.324	.381	106	1	0-0	.770	2	110	107	S16/1	—	0.1
1872	Mut NA	36	165	29	50	1	1	1	15	3	—	3	.303	.315	.339	108	2	1-1	.752	-5	75	81	3b22,S14	—	-0.3
1873	Phi NA	49	236	42	66	11	3	1	38	2	—	4	.280	.286	.364	88	-4	3-1	.801	18	**123**	**144**	S49,P2/C1	—	0.9
1874	Phi NA	57	258	49	72	3	2	0	37	2	—	5	.279	.285	.306	86	-5	0-2	.793	3	109	127	S32,3b25	—	-0.3
1875	Phi NA	69	295	50	65	6	1	0	24	0	—	6	.220	.220	.247	60	-12	10-4	.835	-2	99	74	S53,3b17	—	-1.3
1876	Lou N	66	267	28	73	9	5	1	29	1	—	10	.273	.276	.356	93	-4	—	.861	-5	95	104	S66	—	-0.6
1879	Buf N	76	306	30	82	11	5	0	28	5	—	34	.268	.280	.337	100	-1	—	.905	18	110	**171**	2b76	—	1.9
1880	Buf N	11	44	3	7	0	0	0	1	2	—	4	.159	.196	.159	21	-4	—	.882	-1	96	40	2b11	—	-0.4
1882	Cin AA	79	324	54	91	13	4	0	27	10	—	—	.281	.302	.346	112	3	—	**.897**	-16	85	81	S79	—	-0.9
1883	Cin AA	92	362	52	92	13	5	5	52	12	—	—	.254	.278	.359	98	-2	—	.863	-0	94	**155**	S92	—	0.1
1884	Cin AA	31	114	13	20	2	1	0	8	1	0	—	.175	.183	.211	27	-9	—	.786	-8	85	115	S29,O2(0/1/1)/3	—	-1.6
	StL AA	1	5	0	0	0	0	0	—	0	0	—	.000	.000	.000	-97	-1	—	.778	-1	69	0	/2	—	-0.2
	Year	32	119	13	20	2	1	0	8	1	0	—	.168	.175	.202	22	-10	—	.786	-9	85	115	S29,O2(0/1/1)/32	—	-1.8
Total	5NA	227	1017	181	270	22	10	2	117	12	—	19	.265	.274	.313	84	-18	14-8	.807	16	109	118	S164,3b64,P2,1b2/C	—	-0.9
Total	6	356	1422	180	365	48	20	6	145	31	0	48	.257	.273	.331	92	-18	—	.867	-13	91	116	S266,2b88,O2(0/1/1)/3	—	-1.7
Fulmer, Chris	Christopher; B7.4.1858 Tamaqua PA; D11.9.1931 Tamaqua PA; BR/TR/5´8˝/165; d8.4																								
1884	Was U	48	181	39	50	9	0	0	—	11	—	—	.276	.318	.326	99	-5	—	.937	2	—	—	C34,O16(0/7/9),1b5	—	-0.1
1886	Bal AA	80	270	54	66	9	3	1	30	48	2	—	.244	.363	.311	115	8	29	.949	-5	—	—	C68,O12(6/5/1)/P	—	0.8
1887	Bal AA	56	201	52	54	11	4	0	32	36	1	—	.269	.382	.363	115	7	35	.913	-7	—	—	C48,O8L	—	0.3
1888	Bal AA	52	166	20	31	5	1	0	10	21	2	—	.187	.286	.229	67	-5	10	.903	-14	—	—	C45,O7(2/1/4)	—	-1.4
1889	Bal AA	16	58	11	15	3	1	0	13	6	1	12	.259	.338	.345	93	0	2	.938	-3	0	0	O14(0/11/3),C2	—	-0.3
Total	5	252	876	176	216	37	9	1	85	122	6	12	.247	.343	.313	102	5	76	.929	-25	—	—	C197,O57(16/24/17),1b5/P	—	-0.7
Fulmer, Washington	Washington Fayette; B6.15.1840 Philadelphia PA; D12.8.1907 Philadelphia PA; 5´9˝/180; d7.19; b–Chick																								
1875	Atl NA	1	4	1	2	0	0	0	1	0	—	0	.500	.500	.500	285	1	0-0	.750	-0	0	0	/cf	—	0.0
Fultz, Dave	David Lewis; B5.29.1875 Staunton VA; D10.29.1959 DeLand FL; BR/TR/5´11˝/170; d7.1; Col Brown; OF(34/510/10)																								
1898	Phi N	19	55	7	10	2	2	0	5	6	0	—	.182	.262	.291	61	-3	1	.871	-1	59	244	O14(8/3/3),2b3/S	—	-0.5
1899	Phi N	2	5	0	2	0	0	0	0	0	0	—	.400	.400	.400	124	0	1	.750	-1	79	0	/2S	—	-0.1
	Bal N	57	210	31	62	3	2	0	18	13	2	—	.295	.342	.329	80	-6	17	.940	-7	0	0	O31(14/14/3),3b20,2b2/1	—	-1.4
	Year	59	215	31	64	3	2	0	18	13	2	—	.298	.343	.330	81	-6	18	.940	-8	0	0	O31(14/14/3),3b20,2b3/S1	—	-1.5
1901	Phi A	132	561	95	164	17	9	0	52	32	3	—	.292	.334	.355	87	-11	36	.935	-8	93	0	O106(11/95/0),2b18,S9	—	-2.1
1902	Phi A	129	506	**109**	153	20	5	1	49	62	2	—	.302	.381	.368	104	5	44	.961	-9	120	33	O114C,2b16	—	-0.9
1903	NY A	79	295	39	66	12	1	0	25	25	5	—	.224	.295	.271	67	-11	29	.933	-2	131	97	O77(1/73/3),3b2	—	-1.7
1904	NY A	97	339	39	93	17	4	2	32	24	1	—	.274	.324	.366	113	5	17	.976	1	80	84	O90C	—	0.2
1905	NY A	129	422	49	98	13	3	0	42	39	7	—	.232	.308	.277	77	-10	44	.966	-7	30	65	O122(0/121/1)	—	-2.5
Total	7	644	2393	369	648	84	26	3	223	201	20	—	.271	.332	.331	89	-31	189	.952	-35	82	53	O554C,2b40,3b22,S11/1	—	-9.0
Funderburk, Mark	Mark Clifford; B5.16.1957 Charlotte NC; BR/TR/6´4˝/226; [MinA76 16/370]; d9.4; Col Louisburg (NC) JC																								
1981	Min A	8	15	2	3	1	0	0	2	2-0	0	1	.200	.278	.267	59	-1	0-0	1.000	-1	39	302	O6L/D	0	-0.2
1985	Min A	23	70	7	22	7	1	2	13	5-0	0	12	.314	.351	.529	131	3	0-1	1.000	-0	102	0	D15,O5L/1	0	0.2
Total	2	31	85	9	25	8	1	2	15	7-0	0	13	.294	.337	.482	119	2	0-1	1.000	-1	65	178	D16,O11L/1	0	0.0
Funk, Liz	Elias Calvin; B10.28.1904 LaCygne KS; D1.16.1968 Norman OK; BL/TL/5´8.5˝/160; d4.26; Col Oklahoma																								
1929	NY A	1	0	0	0	0	0	0	0	0	0	0	ø	ø	ø	ø	0	0-0	ø	0	—	—	/R	—	0.0
1930	Det A	140	527	74	145	26	11	4	65	29	5	39	.275	.319	.389	77	-20	12-6	.965	1	102	86	O129(0/128/1)	—	-2.2
1932	Chi A	122	440	59	114	21	5	2	40	43	0	19	.259	.325	.343	78	-14	17-15	.979	6	101	**156**	O120(4/115/1)	—	-1.2
1933	Chi A	10	9	1	2	0	0	0	0	1	0	0	.222	.300	.222	42	-1	0-0	ø	-0	0	0	O2(1/1/0)	—	-0.1
Total	4	273	976	134	261	47	16	6	105	73	5	58	.267	.322	.367	77	-35	29-21	.972	7	101	119	O251(5/244/2)	—	-3.5
Furcal, Rafael	Rafael; B8.24.1980 Loma de Cabrera, D.R.; BB/TR/5´10˝/(165–175); d4.4																								
2000	†Atl N	131	455	87	134	20	4	4	37	73-0	3	80	.295	.394	.382	99	2	40-14	.950	5	104	98	S110,2b31	15	1.9
2001	Atl N	79	324	39	89	19	0	4	30	24-1	1	56	.275	.321	.370	79	-10	22-6	.970	0	98	108	S79	93	-0.1
2002	†Atl N	154	636	95	175	31	8	8	47	43-0	3	114	.275	.323	.387	86	-14	27-15	.963	10	105	**123**	S150,2b4	0	0.8
2003	†Atl N★	156	664	130	194	35	**10**	15	61	60-2	3	76	.292	.352	.443	107	6	25-2	.959	4	106	112	S155	0	2.6
2004	†Atl N	143	563	103	157	24	5	14	59	58-4	1	71	.279	.344	.414	95	-4	29-6	.962	15	**111**	127	S131/2	0	2.4
2005	†Atl N	154	616	100	175	31	11	12	58	62-3	1	78	.284	.348	.429	102	1	46-10	.981	31	117	124	S152	0	5.0
2006	†LA N	159	654	113	196	32	9	15	63	73-3	1	98	.300	.369	.445	107	8	37-13	.966	26	110	122	S156	0	4.7
Total	7	976	3912	667	1120	192	47	72	355	393-13	13	573	.286	.351	.415	98	-11	226-66	.965	92	108	118	S933,2b36	108	17.3
Furillo, Carl	Carl Anthony "Skoonj","The Reading Rifle"; B3.8.1922 Stony Creek Mills PA; D1.21.1989 Stony Creek Mills PA; BR/TR/6´0˝/(190–203); d4.16																								
1946	Bro N	117	335	29	95	18	6	3	35	31	1	20	.284	.346	.400	110	4	6	.984	9	**117**	102	O112(5/103/4)	0	1.0
1947	†Bro N	124	437	61	129	24	7	8	88	34	1	24	.295	.347	.437	103	1	7	.977	1	101	111	O121(28/93/2)	0	-0.2
1948	Bro N	108	364	55	108	20	4	4	44	43	2	32	.297	.374	.407	108	5	6	.983	7	106	**178**	O104(0/96/12)	0	0.9
1949	†Bro N	142	549	95	177	27	10	18	106	37	3	29	.322	.368	.506	127	19	4	.965	2	105	102	O142R	0	1.6
1950	Bro N	153	620	99	189	30	6	18	106	41	5	40	.305	.353	.460	110	7	8	.971	0	93	**164**	O153R	0	0.3
1951	Bro N	**158**	667	93	197	32	4	16	91	43	7	33	.295	.344	.427	104	3	8-7	.986	12	107	**165**	O157R	0	1.0
1952	†Bro N☆	134	425	52	105	18	1	8	59	31	4	33	.247	.304	.351	80	-12	1-4	.988	2	103	111	O131R	0	-1.5
1953	†Bro N☆	132	479	82	165	38	6	21	92	34	4	32	**.344**	.393	.580	146	32	1-1	.988	1	97	117	O131R	0	2.7
1954	Bro N	150	547	56	161	23	1	19	96	49	5	35	.294	.356	.444	104	4	2-4	.972	4	111	79	O149(3/5/145)	0	0.1
1955	†Bro N	140	523	83	164	24	3	26	95	43-5	7	43	.314	.371	.520	130	23	4-5	.981	-3	96	87	O140(6/1/139)	0	1.3
1956	†Bro N	149	523	66	151	30	0	21	83	57-15	1	41	.289	.357	.467	111	10	1-1	.984	-7	89	82	O146(9/3/143)	0	-0.3
1957	Bro N	119	395	61	121	17	4	12	66	29-4	5	33	.306	.358	.461	108	5	0-2	.988	-7	81	94	O107(1/0/106)	0	-0.7

YEAR	TM LG	G	AB	R	H	2B	3B	HR	RBI	BB-IB	HP	SO	AVG	OBP	SLG	AOPS	ABR	SB-CS	FA	FR	RNG	THR	GAMES AT POSITION	DL	BFW
1958	LA N	122	411	54	119	19	3	18	83	35-2	2	28	.290	.343	.482	113	7	0-2	.975	-7	93	57	O119(1/7/116)	0	-0.5
1959	†LA N	50	93	8	27	4	0	0	13	7-2	0	11	.290	.333	.333	75	-3	0-0	.920	-3	77	0	O25R	32	-0.6
1960	LA N	8	10	1	2	0	1	0	1	0-0	0	2	.200	.200	.400	56	-1	0-0	1.000	-0	103	0	O2R	0	-0.1
Total	15	1806	6378	895	1910	324	56	192	1058	514-28	47	436	.299	.355	.458	112	104	48-26	.979	11	100	111	O1739(53/308/1408)	32	5.0
FURMANIAK, J.J.	Jason Joseph; B7.31.1979 Naperville IL; BR/TR/6´3˝/190; [SDN00 22/649]; d9.13; Col Lewis																								
2005	Pit N	13	26	3	5	1	1	0	1	4-0	0	4	.192	.300	.308	60	-2	0-0	.960	-3	61	24	2b9,S2	0	-0.4
FUSSELBACK, EDDIE	Edward L.; B7.17.1856 Philadelphia PA; D4.14.1926 Philadelphia PA; BR/5´6˝/156; d5.3; ▲																								
1882	StL AA	35	136	13	31	2	0	0	—	5	—	—	.228	.255	.243	66	-5	—	.853	2	—	—	C19,O15(4/0/11),P4	—	-0.1
1884	Bal U	68	303	60	86	16	3	1	—	3	—	—	.284	.291	.366	89	-13	—	.912	14	—	—	C54,3b6,S5,O4(1/2/1)	—	0.5
1885	Phi AA	5	19	2	6	1	0	0	2	0	0	—	.316	.316	.368	109	0	—	.911	0	—	—	C5	—	0.1
1888	Lou AA	1	4	0	1	0	0	0	1	0	0	—	.250	.250	.250	62	0	0	1.000	1	769	0	/rf	—	0.0
Total	4	109	462	75	124	19	3	1	3	8	0	—	.268	.281	.329	84	-18	0	.901	16	—	—	C78,O20(5/2/13),3b6,S5,P4	—	0.5
FUSSELMAN, LES	Lester Leroy; B3.7.1921 Pryor OK; D5.21.1970 Cleveland OH; BR/TR/6´1˝/195; d4.16; Col Western Illinois																								
1952	StL N	32	63	5	10	3	0	1	3	0	0	9	.159	.159	.254	13	-8	0-0	.991	2	*145*	*90*	C32	0	-0.5
1953	StL N	11	8	1	2	1	0	0	0	0	0	0	.250	.250	.375	60	0	0-0	1.000	1	*91*	*181*	C11	0	0.1
Total	2	43	71	6	12	4	0	1	3	0	0	9	.169	.169	.268	18	-8	0-0	.992	3	*137*	*104*	C43	0	-0.4
GABLER, BILL	William Louis "Gabe"; B8.4.1930 St.Louis MO; BL/TR/6´1˝/190; d9.16																								
1958	Chi N	3	3	0	0	0	0	0	0	0-0	0	3	.000	.000	.000	-99	-1	0-0	ø	0	—	—	/H	0	-0.1
GABRIELSON, LEN	Leonard Gary; B2.14.1940 Oakland CA; BL/TR/6´4˝/(205–220); d9.9; f–Len; Col USC																								
1960	Mil N	4	3	1	0	0	0	0	0	1-0	0	0	.000	.250	.000	-27	-1	0-0	ø	-0	0	0	/lf	0	-0.1
1963	Mil N	46	120	14	26	5	0	3	15	8-1	0	23	.217	.264	.333	72	-4	1-1	1.000	-0	114	0	O22(18/6/1),1b16,3b3	0	-0.7
1964	Mil N	24	38	0	7	2	0	0	1	1-0	0	8	.184	.205	.237	24	-4	1-0	1.000	-1	52	197	1b12,O2R	0	-0.5
	Chi N	89	272	22	67	11	2	5	23	19-1	1	37	.246	.298	.357	80	-7	9-4	.984	-1	96	105	O68(1/12/58),1b8	0	-1.2
	Year	113	310	22	74	13	2	5	24	20-1	1	45	.239	.287	.342	74	-11	10-4	.984	-1	96	103	O70(1/12/60),1b20	0	-1.7
1965	Chi N	28	48	4	12	0	0	3	5	7-2	0	16	.250	.345	.438	116	1	0-2	1.000	-2	74	0	O14(0/2/12)/1	0	-0.2
	SF N	88	269	36	81	6	5	4	26	26-5	2	48	.301	.365	.405	114	5	4-0	.975	1	96	79	O77(70/0/9),1b5	0	0.3
	Year	116	317	40	93	6	5	7	31	33-7	2	64	.293	.362	.410	114	6	4-2	.977	-1	93	69	O91(70/2/21),1b6	0	0.1
1966	SF N	94	240	27	52	7	0	4	16	21-3	0	51	.217	.278	.296	58	-13	0-1	.948	-7	73	26	O67(61/0/9),1b6	0	-2.5
1967	Cal A	11	12	2	1	0	0	0	2	2-0	0	4	.083	.214	.083	-9	-2	0-0	ø	-0	0	0	/lf	0	-0.2
	LA N	90	238	20	62	10	3	7	29	15-3	1	41	.261	.307	.416	114	3	3-1	.980	0	89	179	O68(47/1/26)	0	0.0
1968	LA N	108	304	38	82	16	1	10	35	32-4	0	47	.270	.337	.428	139	14	1-1	.976	-1	92	116	O86(57/0/30)	0	1.0
1969	LA N	83	178	13	48	5	1	1	18	12-1	0	25	.270	.313	.326	85	-4	1-2	.981	-4	78	40	O47(13/0/34),1b2	0	-1.1
1970	LA N	43	42	1	8	2	0	0	6	1-0	0	15	.190	.205	.238	20	-5	0-0	1.000	0	82	0	O2R/1	0	-0.5
Total	9	708	1764	178	446	64	12	37	176	145-20	4	315	.253	.309	.366	94	-17	20-12	.977	-14	89	89	O455(269/21/183),1b51,3b3	0	-5.7
GABRIELSON, LEN	Leonard Hilbourne; B9.8.1915 Oakland CA; D11.14.2000 Stanford CA; BL/TL/6´3˝/210; d4.21; s–Len																								
1939	Phi N	5	18	3	4	0	0	0	1	2	0	3	.222	.300	.222	43	-1	0	.977	2	289	66	1b5	—	0.0
GAEDEL, EDDIE	Edward Carl (b Edward Carl Gaedele); B6.8.1925 Chicago IL; D6.18.1961 Chicago IL; BR/TL/3–7/ 65; d8.19																								
1951	StL A	1	0	0	0	0	0	0	0	1	0	0	ø	1.000	ø	182	0	0-0	ø	0	—	—	/H	0	0.0
GAETTI, GARY	Gary Joseph; B8.19.1958 Centralia IL; BR/TR/6´0˝/(180–205); [MinA79 S1/11]; d9.20; C3; Col Northwest Missouri; OF(13/0/1)																								
1981	Min A	9	26	4	5	0	0	2	3	0-0	0	6	.192	.192	.423	69	-1	0-0	1.000	2	125	76	3b8/D	0	0.0
1982	Min A	145	508	59	117	25	4	25	84	37-2	3	107	.230	.280	.443	94	-6	0-4	.963	-6	93	115	3b142,S2/D	0	-1.6
1983	Min A	157	584	81	143	30	3	21	78	54-2	4	121	.245	.309	.414	94	-5	7-1	.967	9	103	**124**	3b154,S3/D	0	0.3
1984	Min A	**162**	588	55	154	29	4	5	65	44-1	4	81	.262	.315	.350	80	-15	11-5	.960	15	111	95	3b154,O8L,S2	0	-0.2
1985	Min A	160	560	71	138	31	0	20	63	37-3	7	89	.246	.301	.409	87	-11	13-5	.962	18	**110**	113	3b156,O4L/1D	0	0.6
1986	Min A	157	596	91	171	34	1	34	108	52-4	6	108	.287	.347	.518	129	23	14-15	.956	17	**112**	**128**	3b156,S2/2lf	0	3.4
1987	†Min A	154	584	95	150	36	2	31	109	37-7	3	92	.257	.303	.485	101	-1	10-7	.973	1	93	99	3b150,D2	0	-0.2
1988	Min A★	133	468	66	141	29	2	28	88	36-5	5	85	.301	.353	.551	146	28	7-4	.977	-1	88	132	3b115,S2,D5	15	2.7
1989	Min A★	130	498	63	125	11	4	19	75	25-5	3	87	.251	.286	.404	88	-10	6-2	.973	9	102	110	3b125,1b2,D3	18	-0.1
1990	Min A	154	577	61	132	27	5	16	85	36-1	3	101	.229	.274	.376	76	-20	6-1	.959	9	**107**	**133**	3b151,1b2,S2	0	-1.0
1991	Cal A	152	586	58	144	22	1	18	66	33-3	8	104	.246	.293	.379	85	-14	5-5	.965	16	105	139	3b152	0	0.1
1992	Cal A	130	456	41	103	13	2	12	48	21-4	6	79	.226	.267	.342	69	-21	3-1	.927	14	117	161	3b67,1b44,D17	0	-1.1
1993	Cal A	20	50	3	9	2	0	0	4	5-0	0	12	.180	.250	.220	28	-5	1-0	.857	-1	92	213	3b7,1b6,D5	0	-0.6
	KC A	82	281	37	72	18	1	14	46	16-0	8	75	.256	.309	.477	103	0	0-3	.974	10	113	132	3b72,1b18/D	0	0.8
	Year	102	331	40	81	20	1	14	50	21-0	8	87	.245	.300	.438	92	-5	1-3	.970	9	112	135	3b79,1b24,D6	0	0.2
1994	KC A	90	327	53	94	15	3	12	57	19-3	2	63	.287	.328	.462	97	-3	0-2	**.982**	10	113	121	3b85,1b9	15	0.6
1995	KC A	137	514	76	134	27	0	35	96	47-6	8	91	.261	.329	.518	115	9	3-3	.954	-1	101	104	3b123,1b11,D6	0	0.7
1996	†StL N	141	522	71	143	27	4	23	80	35-6	8	97	.274	.326	.473	108	4	2-2	.970	-15	90	83	3b133,1b14	16	-1.1
1997	StL N	148	502	63	126	24	1	17	69	36-3	6	88	.251	.305	.404	85	-13	7-3	**.978**	6	107	115	3b132,1b20/P	0	-0.6
1998	StL N	91	306	39	81	23	1	11	43	31-1	5	39	.265	.339	.454	108	4	1-1	.985	-3	102	105	3b83,1b3/P2rf	0	0.1
	†Chi N	37	128	21	41	11	0	8	27	12-1	5	23	.320	.397	.594	152	10	0-0	.979	2	109	33	3b36	0	1.2
	Year	128	434	60	122	34	1	19	70	43-2	10	62	.281	.356	.495	121	14	1-1	**.983**	-1	104	83	3b119,1b3/P2rf	0	1.3
1999	Chi N	113	280	22	57	9	1	9	46	21-0	2	51	.204	.260	.339	51	-22	0-1	.962	3	112	72	3b81,1b8/SP	0	-1.9
2000	Bos A	5	10	0	0	0	0	0	1	0-0	0	3	.000	.000	.000	-97	-3	0-0	ø	0	—	—	D5	0	-0.3
Total	20	2507	8951	1130	2280	443	39	360	1341	634-57	96	1602	.255	.308	.434	96	-72	96-65	.965	114	104	114	3b2282,1b138,D48,O14L,S14,P3,2b2	64	1.8
GAFFKE, FABIAN	Fabian Sebastian; B8.5.1913 Milwaukee WI; D2.8.1992 Milwaukee WI; BR/TR/5´10˝/185; d9.9																								
1936	Bos A	15	55	5	7	2	0	1	3	4	1	5	.127	.200	.218	3	-9	0-0	1.000	-0	94	87	O15(5/0/10)	—	-0.9
1937	Bos A	54	184	32	53	10	4	6	34	15	0	25	.288	.342	.484	102	-1	1-2	.965	-1	96	81	O50(16/1/33)	—	-0.5
1938	Bos A	15	10	2	1	0	0	0	1	3	0	2	.100	.308	.100	6	-1	0-0	ø	0	0	0	O2R/C	—	-0.1
1939	Bos A	1	1	0	0	0	0	0	1	0	0	0	.000	.000	.000	-96	0	0-0	ø	0	—	—	/H	—	0.0
1941	Cle A	4	4	0	1	0	0	0	0	2	0	2	.250	.500	.250	109	0	0-0	1.000	-0	84	0	O2C	0	0.0
1942	Cle A	40	67	4	11	2	0	0	3	6	1	13	.164	.243	.194	25	-7	1-0	1.000	-0	111	0	O16(5/1/10)	0	-0.8
Total	6	129	321	43	73	14	4	7	42	30	2	47	.227	.297	.361	67	-18	2-2	.979	-2	98	66	O85(26/4/55)/C	0	-2.3
GAGLIANO, PHIL	Philip Joseph; B12.27.1941 Memphis TN; BR/TR/6´1˝/(179–188); d4.16; b–Ralph; OF(34/0/31)																								
1963	StL N	10	5	1	2	0	0	0	1	1-0	0	1	.400	.500	.400	149	0	0-0	1.000	1	80	0	2b3/3	0	0.1
1964	StL N	40	58	5	15	4	0	1	9	3-0	0	10	.259	.290	.379	81	-1	0-1	.918	0	116	98	2b12,O2(1/0/1)/13	0	-0.1
1965	StL N	122	363	46	87	14	2	8	53	40-0	1	45	.240	.312	.355	81	-8	2-1	.960	2	96	104	2b57,O25(4/0/23),3b19	0	-0.4
1966	StL N	90	213	23	54	8	2	2	15	24-1	1	29	.254	.329	.338	86	-3	2-1	.982	-2	91	96	3b41,1b8,O5L/2	0	-0.6
1967	†StL N	73	217	20	48	7	0	2	21	19-3	1	26	.221	.283	.281	64	-10	0-0	.972	-12	81	65	2b27,3b25,1b4,S2	0	-2.2
1968	†StL N	53	105	13	24	4	2	0	13	7-0	1	12	.229	.281	.305	77	-3	0-0	.982	1	103	97	2b17,3b10,O5(4/0/1)	0	-0.2
1969	StL N	62	128	7	29	2	0	1	10	14-0	0	12	.227	.303	.266	60	-7	0-0	.989	-0	82	104	2b20,1b9,3b9,O2R	0	-0.7
1970	StL N	18	32	0	6	0	0	0	2	1-0	0	3	.188	.212	.188	8	-4	0-1	1.000	-2	47	119	3b6,1b3,2b2	0	-0.6
	Chi N	26	40	5	6	0	0	0	5	5-0	0	5	.150	.244	.150	7	-5	0-0	1.000	-1	106	39	2b16/13	0	-0.6
	Year	44	72	5	12	0	0	0	7	6-0	0	8	.167	.231	.167	8	-9	0-1	.980	-3	108	50	2b18,3b7,1b4	0	-1.2
1971	Bos A	47	68	11	22	5	0	0	13	11-0	0	5	.324	.412	.397	123	3	0-0	1.000	-3	78	0	O11(7/0/4),2b7,3b4	0	0.0
1972	Bos A	52	82	9	21	4	1	0	10	10-0	0	13	.256	.333	.329	93	0	1-0	.962	1	144	478	O12L,3b5,2b4,1b2	0	0.1
1973	†Cin N	63	69	8	20	2	0	0	7	13-2	0	16	.290	.402	.319	107	2	0-0	.824	-2	79	103	3b7,2b4/1lf	0	0.0
1974	Cin N	46	31	2	2	0	0	0	0	15-1	0	7	.065	.370	.065	27	-2	0-0	1.000	-0	0	0	2b2/13	0	-0.2
Total	12	702	1411	150	336	50	7	14	159	163-7	4	184	.238	.316	.313	77	-38	5-4	.969	-17	94	85	2b172,3b130,O63L,1b30,S2	0	-5.4
GAGLIANO, RALPH	Ralph Michael; B10.8.1946 Memphis TN; BL/TR/5´11˝/170; d9.21; b–Phil																								
1965	Cle A	1	0	0	0	0	0	0	0	0-0	0	0	ø	ø	ø	ø	0	0-0	ø	0	—	—	/R	142	0.0
GAGNE, GREG	Gregory Carpenter; B11.12.1961 Fall River MA; BR/TR/5´11˝/(172–185); [NYA79 5/129]; d6.5																								
1983	Min A	10	27	2	3	1	0	0	3	0-0	0	6	.111	.103	.148	-28	-5	0-0	.923	-8	49	33	S10	0	-1.2
1984	Min A	2	1	0	0	0	0	0	0	0-0	0	0	.000	.000	.000	-95	0	0-0	ø	0	—	—	/H	0	0.0
1985	Min A	114	293	37	66	15	3	2	23	20-0	3	57	.225	.279	.317	60	-16	10-4	.968	3	104	86	S106,D5	22	-0.3

YEAR	TM LG	G	AB	R	H	2B	3B	HR	RBI	BB-IB	HP	SO	AVG	OBP	SLG	AOPS	ABR	SB-CS	FA	FR	RNG	THR	GAMES AT POSITION	DL	BFW
1986	Min A	156	472	63	118	22	6	12	54	30-0	6	108	.250	.301	.398	86	-10	12-10	.959	-14	92	101	S155,2b4	0	-1.0
1987	†Min A	137	437	68	116	28	7	10	40	25-0	4	84	.265	.310	.430	90	-7	6-6	.970	19	111	102	S136,O4(0/3/1)/2D	0	2.3
1988	Min A	149	461	70	109	20	6	14	48	27-2	7	110	.236	.288	.397	87	-10	15-7	.970	-12	93	94	S146,O2C/23	0	-1.0
1989	Min A	149	460	69	125	29	7	9	48	17-0	2	80	.272	.298	.424	96	-4	11-4	.971	-9	95	76	S146/cf	0	-0.2
1990	Min A	138	388	38	91	22	3	7	38	24-0	1	76	.235	.280	.361	73	-15	8-8	.976	-4	102	77	S135/cfD	0	-1.1
1991	†Min A	139	408	52	108	23	3	8	42	26-0	3	72	.265	.310	.395	90	-6	11-9	.984	4	105	96	S137/D	0	0.6
1992	Min A	146	439	53	108	23	0	7	39	19-0	2	83	.246	.280	.346	72	-17	6-7	.973	19	**109**	106	S141	0	1.1
1993	KC A	159	540	66	151	32	3	10	57	33-1	0	93	.280	.319	.406	88	-10	10-12	**.986**	12	101	99	S159	0	1.1
1994	KC A	107	375	39	97	23	3	7	51	27-0	4	79	.259	.314	.392	77	-13	10-17	.977	13	106	102	S106	0	0.4
1995	KC A	120	430	58	110	25	4	6	49	38-2	2	60	.256	.316	.374	78	-14	3-5	.969	12	**115**	**119**	S118,D2	21	0.5
1996	†LA N	128	428	48	109	13	2	10	55	50-11	2	93	.255	.333	.364	90	-6	4-2	.966	14	**106**	**113**	S127	33	1.7
1997	LA N	144	514	49	129	20	3	9	57	31-4	4	120	.251	.298	.354	75	-21	2-5	.971	-25	89	71	S143	0	-3.6
Total	15	1798	5673	712	1440	296	50	111	604	367-20	40	1121	.254	.302	.382	82	-154	108-96	.972	26	101	95	S1765,D11,O8(0/7/1),2b6/3	76	-0.7

GAGNIER, ED Edward John; B4.16.1882 Paris, France; D9.13.1946 Detroit MI; BR/TR/5´9˝/170; d4.14

YEAR	TM LG	G	AB	R	H	2B	3B	HR	RBI	BB-IB	HP	SO	AVG	OBP	SLG	AOPS	ABR	SB-CS	FA	FR	RNG	THR	GAMES AT POSITION	DL	BFW
1914	Bro F	94	337	22	63	12	2	0	25	13	1	24	.187	.219	.234	24	-43	8	.933	-1	93	108	S88,3b6	—	-3.9
1915	Bro F	20	50	8	13	1	0	0	4	10	1	5	.260	.393	.280	92	0	2	.930	2	117	114	S13,2b6	—	0.2
	Buf F	1	2	0	0	0	0	0	0	0	0	0	.000	.000	.000	-98	-1	0	.800	-1	44	0	/2	—	-0.1
	Year	21	52	8	13	1	0	0	4	10	1	5	.250	.381	.269	85	-1	2	.930	1	117	114	S13,2b7	—	0.1
Total	2	115	389	30	76	13	2	0	29	23	2	29	.195	.244	.239	33	-44	10	.933	1	96	109	S101,2b7,3b6	—	-3.8

GAGNON, CHICK Harold Dennis; B9.27.1897 Millbury MA; D4.30.1970 Wilmington DE; BR/TR/5´7.5˝/158; d6.27; Col Holy Cross

YEAR	TM LG	G	AB	R	H	2B	3B	HR	RBI	BB-IB	HP	SO	AVG	OBP	SLG	AOPS	ABR	SB-CS	FA	FR	RNG	THR	GAMES AT POSITION	DL	BFW
1922	Det A	10	4	2	1	0	0	0	0	0	0	2	.250	.250	.250	32	0	0-0	ø	-1	0	0	/S3	—	-0.1
1924	Was A	4	5	1	1	0	0	0	1	0	0	0	.200	.200	.200	3	-1	0-0	1.000	0	116	0	S2	—	0.0
Total	2	14	9	3	2	0	0	0	1	0	0	2	.222	.222	.222	16	-1	0-0	1.000	-1	97	0	S3/3	—	-0.1

GAINER, DEL Dellos Clinton "Sheriff"; B11.10.1886 Montrose WV; D1.29.1947 Elkins WV; BR/TR/6´0˝/180; d10.2; Mil 1918

YEAR	TM LG	G	AB	R	H	2B	3B	HR	RBI	BB-IB	HP	SO	AVG	OBP	SLG	AOPS	ABR	SB-CS	FA	FR	RNG	THR	GAMES AT POSITION	DL	BFW
1909	Det A	2	5	0	1	0	0	0	0	0	0	—	.200	.200	.200	25	0	0	.929	-0	132	0	1b2	—	-0.1
1911	Det A	70	248	32	75	11	4	2	25	20	5	—	.302	.366	.403	109	3	10	.975	-4	85	107	1b69	—	-0.2
1912	Det A	52	179	28	43	5	6	0	20	18	3	—	.240	.320	.335	90	-3	15	.986	-3	76	99	1b50/cf	—	-0.7
1913	Det A	105	363	47	97	16	8	2	25	30	6	45	.267	.333	.372	108	3	10	.988	-5	82	95	1b103	—	-0.5
1914	Det A	1	0	0	0	0	0	0	0	0	0	0	ø	ø	ø	ø	0	0	1.000	-0	0	0	/1	—	0.0
	Bos A	38	84	11	20	9	2	2	13	8	1	14	.238	.312	.464	133	3	2-2	.981	-2	91	44	1b18,2b11/cf	—	0.1
	Year	39	84	11	20	9	2	2	13	8	1	14	.238	.312	.464	133	3	2-2	.982	-2	88	43	1b19,2b11/cf	—	0.1
1915	†Bos A	82	200	30	59	5	8	1	29	21	3	31	.295	.371	.415	139	9	7-2	.988	2	114	99	1b56,O6(0/5/1)	—	1.1
1916	†Bos A	56	142	14	36	6	0	3	18	10	0	24	.254	.303	.359	98	-1	5	.997	1	107	94	1b48,2b2	—	-0.1
1917	Bos A	52	172	28	53	10	2	2	19	15	3	21	.308	.374	.424	145	9	1	.989	-1	96	123	1b50	—	0.8
1919	Bos A	47	118	9	28	6	2	0	13	13	1	15	.237	.318	.322	85	-2	5	.978	-0	98	67	1b21,O18L	—	-0.4
1922	StL N	43	97	19	26	7	4	2	23	14	0	6	.268	.360	.485	122	3	0-2	.979	0	91	48	1b26,O10(6/4/0)	—	0.1
Total	10	548	1608	218	438	75	36	14	185	149	22	156	.272	.342	.390	113	24	55-6	.985	-11	91	96	1b444,O36(24/11/1),2b13	—	0.1

GAINER, JAY Johnathan Keith; B10.8.1966 Panama City FL; BL/TL/6´0˝/190; [SDN90 24/655]; d5.14; Col South Alabama

YEAR	TM LG	G	AB	R	H	2B	3B	HR	RBI	BB-IB	HP	SO	AVG	OBP	SLG	AOPS	ABR	SB-CS	FA	FR	RNG	THR	GAMES AT POSITION	DL	BFW
1993	Col N	23	41	4	7	0	0	3	6	4-0	0	12	.171	.244	.390	57	-3	1-1	.982	-1	40	49	1b7	0	-0.5

GAINES, JOE Arnesta Joe; B11.22.1936 Bryan TX; BR/TR/6´1˝/(185–190); d6.29

YEAR	TM LG	G	AB	R	H	2B	3B	HR	RBI	BB-IB	HP	SO	AVG	OBP	SLG	AOPS	ABR	SB-CS	FA	FR	RNG	THR	GAMES AT POSITION	DL	BFW
1960	Cin N	11	15	2	3	0	0	0	1	0-0	0	1	.200	.200	.200	10	-2	0-0	1.000	-0	97	0	O3(1/1/2)	0	-0.2
1961	Cin N	5	3	2	0	0	0	0	0	2-0	0	1	.000	.400	.000	18	0	0-0	.500	-1	44	0	O3(1/2/0)	0	-0.1
1962	Cin N	64	52	12	12	3	0	1	7	8-0	0	16	.231	.333	.346	80	-1	0-0	1.000	-0	96	0	O13(11/0/2)	0	-0.2
1963	Bal A	66	126	24	36	4	1	6	20	20-0	0	39	.286	.381	.476	145	8	2-1	.945	-2	94	0	O39(34/4/2)	0	0.5
1964	Bal A	16	26	2	4	0	0	1	2	3-0	0	7	.154	.241	.269	42	-2	0-0	.846	0	149	0	O5L	0	-0.2
	Hou N	89	307	37	78	9	7	7	34	27-0	2	69	.254	.318	.397	106	2	8-2	.957	-3	96	69	O81(1/0/81)	0	-0.6
1965	Hou N	100	229	21	52	8	1	6	31	18-0	3	59	.227	.290	.349	86	-5	4-1	.913	-6	86	29	O65(26/0/39)	0	-1.4
1966	Hou N	11	13	4	1	1	0	0	0	3-0	0	5	.077	.250	.154	17	-1	0-0	.500	-1	27	0	O3(1/0/2)	0	-0.3
Total	7	362	771	104	186	25	9	21	95	81-0	5	197	.241	.316	.379	99	-1	14-4	.934	-13	93	39	O212(80/7/128)	0	-2.5

GAINEY, TY Telmanch; B12.25.1960 Cheraw SC; BL/TR/6´1˝/190; [HouN79 2/34]; d4.24; [DL 1988 Hou N 182]

YEAR	TM LG	G	AB	R	H	2B	3B	HR	RBI	BB-IB	HP	SO	AVG	OBP	SLG	AOPS	ABR	SB-CS	FA	FR	RNG	THR	GAMES AT POSITION	DL	BFW
1985	Hou N	13	37	5	6	0	0	0	0	2-0	2	9	.162	.244	.162	16	-4	0-0	.913	-1	97	0	O9(0/8/1)	0	-0.6
1986	Hou N	26	50	6	15	3	1	1	6	6-0	0	19	.300	.375	.460	133	2	3-1	1.000	0	115	0	O19(7/14/3)	0	0.3
1987	Hou N	18	24	1	3	0	0	0	1	2-0	0	9	.125	.192	.125	-14	-4	1-0	1.000	1	145	0	O6L	0	-0.4
Total	3	57	111	12	24	3	1	1	7	10-0	2	37	.216	.293	.288	62	-6	4-1	.968	-0	113	0	O34(13/22/4)	182	-0.7

GALAN, AUGIE August John; B5.23.1912 Berkeley CA; D12.28.1993 Fairfield CA; BB/TR (BL 1943p, 44–49)/6´0˝/175; d4.29; C1; OF(1000/335/38)

YEAR	TM LG	G	AB	R	H	2B	3B	HR	RBI	BB-IB	HP	SO	AVG	OBP	SLG	AOPS	ABR	SB-CS	FA	FR	RNG	THR	GAMES AT POSITION	DL	BFW
1934	Chi N	66	192	31	50	6	2	5	22	16	0	15	.260	.317	.391	90	-3	4	.961	-5	86	79	2b43,3b3/S	—	-0.6
1935	†Chi N	**154**	646	**133**	203	41	11	12	79	87	4	53	.314	.399	.467	131	32	**22**	.978	4	102	106	O154L	—	2.6
1936	Chi N★	145	575	74	152	26	4	8	81	67	3	50	.264	.344	.365	89	-7	16	.987	-0	99	86	O145(8/139/0)	—	-1.1
1937	Chi N	147	611	104	154	24	10	18	78	79	1	48	.252	.339	.412	99	-1	**23**	.980	8	110	84	O140(133/6/1),2b8,S2	—	-0.1
1938	†Chi N	110	395	52	113	16	9	6	69	49	2	17	.286	.368	.418	112	7	8	.987	3	98	127	O103L	—	0.5
1939	Chi N	148	549	104	167	36	8	6	71	75	4	26	.304	.392	.432	119	18	8	.970	-3	98	68	O145L	—	0.7
1940	Chi N	68	209	33	48	14	2	3	22	37	0	23	.230	.346	.359	96	0	9	.984	-0	95	149	O54(31/24/0),2b2	—	-0.2
1941	Chi N	65	120	18	25	3	0	1	13	22	0	10	.208	.331	.258	70	-4	0	.959	-2	85	113	O31(17/11/4)	0	-0.7
	†Bro N	17	27	3	7	3	0	0	4	3	0	1	.259	.333	.370	94	0	0	1.000	1	99	279	O6C	0	0.0
	Year	82	147	21	32	6	0	1	17	25	0	11	.218	.331	.279	74	-4	0	.967	-1	87	139	O37(17/17/4)	0	-0.7
1942	Bro N	69	209	24	55	16	0	0	22	24	0	12	.263	.339	.340	97	0	2	.990	-2	97	51	O55(20/26/10),1b4,2b3	0	-0.4
1943	Bro N★	139	495	83	142	26	3	9	67	**103**	2	39	.287	.412	.406	136	30	6	.981	10	111	101	O124(28/97/0),1b13	0	3.6
1944	Bro N★	151	547	96	174	43	9	12	93	**101**	2	23	.318	.426	.495	162	51	4	.988	1	103	91	O147(126/25/2),2b2	0	4.5
1945	Bro N	152	576	114	177	36	7	9	92	114	2	27	.307	.423	.441	142	40	13	.988	-7	78	108	1b66,O49L,3b40	0	2.6
1946	Bro N	99	274	53	85	22	5	3	38	68	2	21	.310	.451	.460	157	26	8	.935	-5	96	94	O60L,3b19,1b12	0	1.8
1947	Cin N	124	392	60	123	18	2	6	61	94	2	19	.314	**.449**	.416	132	26	0	.988	-3	102	24	O118(118/1/1)	0	1.4
1948	Cin N	54	77	18	22	3	2	2	16	26	1	4	.286	.471	.455	157	9	0	.967	-1	96	0	O18(1/0/17)	0	0.7
1949	NY N	22	17	0	1	1	0	0	2	5	0	3	.059	.273	.118	8	-2	0	1.000	-0	0	156	1b3/rf	0	-0.2
	Phi A	12	26	4	8	2	0	0	0	9	0	2	.308	.486	.385	136	2	0	1.000	-0	107	0	O9(7/0/2)	0	0.2
Total	16	1742	5937	1004	1706	336	74	100	830	979	25	393	.287	.390	.419	122	224	123-0	.981	-4	102	87	O1359L,1b98,3b62,2b58,S3	0	15.3

GALARRAGA, ANDRES Andres Jose "The Big Cat" (b Andres Jose Padovani (Galarraga)); B6.18.1961 Caracas, Distrito Capital, Venez.; BR/TR/6´3˝/(209–265); d8.23; [DL 1999 Atl N 182]

YEAR	TM LG	G	AB	R	H	2B	3B	HR	RBI	BB-IB	HP	SO	AVG	OBP	SLG	AOPS	ABR	SB-CS	FA	FR	RNG	THR	GAMES AT POSITION	DL	BFW
1985	Mon N	24	75	9	14	1	0	2	4	3-0	1	18	.187	.228	.280	44	-6	1-2	.995	4	166	93	1b23	0	-0.5
1986	Mon N	105	321	39	87	13	0	10	42	30-5	3	79	.271	.338	.405	105	2	6-5	.995	-11	57	88	1b102	55	-1.6
1987	Mon N	147	551	72	168	40	3	13	90	41-13	**10**	127	.305	.361	.459	112	11	7-10	.993	-2	93	89	1b146	0	-0.3
1988	Mon N★	157	609	99	**184**	**42**	8	29	92	39-9	10	153	.302	.352	.540	146	35	13-4	.991	-7	87	118	1b156	0	1.9
1989	Mon N	152	572	76	147	30	1	23	85	48-10	**13**	158	.257	.327	.434	114	10	12-5	.992	-4	88	98	1b147	0	-0.4
1990	Mon N	155	579	65	148	29	0	20	87	40-8	4	169	.256	.306	.409	99	-2	10-1	.993	-8	82	95	1b154	0	-2.1
1991	Mon N	107	375	34	82	13	2	9	33	23-5	2	86	.219	.268	.336	69	-17	5-6	.991	3	112	101	1b105	39	-2.3
1992	StL N	95	325	38	79	14	2	10	39	11-0	8	69	.243	.282	.391	92	-5	5-4	.991	-3	96	124	1b90	44	-1.6
1993	Col N★	120	470	71	174	35	4	22	98	24-12	6	73	**.370**	.403	.602	143	29	2-4	.990	7	122	85	1b119	44	2.4
1994	Col N	103	417	77	133	21	0	31	85	19-8	8	93	.319	.356	.592	122	13	8-3	.992	-5	83	94	1b103	14	-0.1
1995	†Col N	143	554	89	155	29	3	31	106	32-6	13	146	.280	.331	.511	93	-6	12-2	.991	3	111	107	1b142	0	-1.3
1996	Col N	159	626	119	190	39	3	**47**	**150**	40-3	17	157	.304	.357	.601	120	17	18-8	.992	-2	99	108	1b159/3	0	0.2
1997	Col N★	154	600	120	191	31	3	41	**140**	54-2	17	141	.318	.389	.585	123	21	15-8	.991	-5	98	**131**	1b154	0	0.3
1998	†Atl N★	153	555	103	169	27	1	44	121	63-11	25	146	.305	.397	.595	158	48	7-6	.992	-7	79	108	1b149,D2	0	2.7
2000	†Atl N★	141	494	67	149	25	1	28	100	36-5	17	126	.302	.369	.526	124	17	3-5	.988	-8	79	106	1b132/D	0	-0.2
2001	Tex A	72	243	33	57	16	0	10	34	18-1	9	68	.235	.310	.424	89	-4	1-0	.995	0	101	112	D39,1b25	0	-0.8
	SF N	49	156	17	45	12	1	7	35	13-1	3	49	.288	.351	.513	128	6	0-3	.984	-5	58	130	1b41	0	-0.2
2002	Mon N	104	292	30	76	12	0	9	40	30-6	9	81	.260	.344	.394	90	-4	2-2	.981	2	116	87	1b89	24	-0.9
2003	†SF N	110	272	36	82	15	0	12	42	19-1	2	61	.301	.352	.489	115	5	1-3	.994	-4	74	116	1b69,D2	0	-0.5
2004	Ana A	7	10	1	3	0	0	1	2	0-0	1	3	.300	.364	.600	151	1	0-0	1.000	0	141	245	/1D	0	0.1
Total	19	2257	8096	1195	2333	444	32	399	1425	583-106	178	2003	.288	.347	.499	116	171	128-81	.991	-52	93	105	1b2106,D48/3	402	-5.2

YEAR	TM LG	G	AB	R	H	2B	3B	HR	RBI	BB-IB	HP	SO	AVG	OBP	SLG	AOPS	ABR	SB-CS	FA	FR	RNG	THR	GAMES AT POSITION	DL	BFW
GALATZER, MILT	Milton; B5.4.1907 Chicago IL; D1.29.1976 San Francisco CA; BL/TL/5´10˝/168; d6.25																								
1933	Cle A	57	160	19	38	2	1	1	17	23	0	21	.237	.333	.281	61	-9	2-3	.975	0	95	116	O40(11/4/25),1b5	—	-1.1
1934	Cle A	49	196	29	53	10	2	0	15	21	1	8	.270	.344	.342	76	-7	3-2	.980	1	93	179	O49(3/0/46)	—	-0.8
1935	Cle A	93	259	45	78	9	3	0	19	35	2	8	.301	.389	.359	93	-1	4-5	.934	-4	88	118	O81(8/18/56)	—	-1.0
1936	Cle A	49	97	12	23	4	1	0	6	13	1	8	.237	.333	.299	57	-7	1-2	.964	-0	98	92	O42(6/9/27)/P1	—	-0.7
1939	Cin N	3	5	0	0	0	0	0	0	0	0	1	.000	.000	.000	-99	-1	0	1.000	-0	0	0	1b2	—	-0.2
Total	5	251	717	105	192	25	7	1	57	92	4	46	.268	.354	.326	75	-25	10-12	.959	-3	92	131	O212(28/31/154),1b8/P	—	-3.8
GALL, JOHN	John Christopher; B4.2.1978 Stanford CA; BR/TR/6´0˝/195; [StLN00 11/323]; d7.26; Col Stanford																								
2005	†StL N	22	37	5	10	3	0	2	10	1-0	0	8	.270	.282	.514	103	0	0-0	1.000	-0	64	301	O10L	0	0.0
2006	StL N	8	12	1	3	0	0	0	1	0-0	0	5	.250	.250	.250	29	-1	0-0	1.000	-0	97	0	O2L/1	0	-0.1
Total	2	30	49	6	13	3	0	2	11	1-0	0	13	.265	.275	.449	84	-1	0-0	1.000	-0	69	254	O12L/1	0	-0.1
GALLAGHER, AL	Alan Mitchell Edward George Patrick Henry; B10.19.1945 San Francisco CA; BR/TR/6´0˝/180; [SFN65 1/14]; d4.7; Col Santa Clara																								
1970	SF N	109	282	31	75	15	2	4	28	30-4	0	37	.266	.335	.376	91	-3	2-1	.971	-4	92	83	3b91	0	-0.7
1971	†SF N	136	429	47	119	18	5	5	57	40-10	2	57	.277	.340	.378	105	3	2-1	.951	-7	93	99	3b128	0	-0.5
1972	SF N	82	233	19	52	3	1	2	18	33-4	1	39	.223	.317	.270	69	-9	2-1	.974	-3	92	64	3b69	0	-1.3
1973	SF N	5	9	1	2	0	0	0	1	0-0	1	0	.222	.300	.222	45	-1	0-0	.833	-1	20	0	3b5	0	-0.2
	Cal A	110	311	16	85	6	1	0	26	35-3	1	31	.273	.345	.299	90	-3	1-3	.961	1	99	77	3b98/2S	0	-0.3
Total	4	442	1264	114	333	42	9	11	130	138-21	5	164	.263	.335	.337	91	-13	7-6	.961	-15	94	83	3b391/S2	0	-3.0
GALLAGHER, SHORTY	Charles William; B4.30.1872 Detroit MI; D6.23.1924 Detroit MI; d8.13																								
1901	Cle A	2	4	0	0	0	0	0	0	0	0	—	.000	.000	.000	-99	-1	0	.667	-0	0	0	O2R	—	-0.1
GALLAGHER, DAVE	David Thomas; B9.20.1960 Trenton NJ; BR/TR/6´0˝/(165–185); [CleA80 S1/8]; d4.12; Col Mercer Co. (NJ) CC																								
1987	Cle A	15	36	2	4	1	1	0	1	2-0	0	5	.111	.158	.194	-7	-6	2-0	.972	1	106	180	O14C	0	-0.4
1988	Chi A	101	347	59	105	15	3	5	31	29-3	0	40	.303	.354	.406	113	6	5-4	1.000	-2	94	109	O95(5/78/17),D2	0	0.3
1989	Chi A	**161**	601	74	160	22	2	1	46	46-1	2	79	.266	.320	.314	81	-15	5-6	.993	-1	99	93	O160(1/138/27)/D	0	-1.9
1990	Chi A	45	75	5	21	3	1	0	5	3-0	1	9	.280	.316	.347	87	-1	0-1	.981	-1	93	84	O37(14/22/1),D4	29	-0.3
	Bal A	23	51	7	11	1	0	0	2	4-0	0	3	.216	.268	.235	44	-4	1-1	.980	4	136	202	O20(17/2/1),D2	0	-0.1
	Year	68	126	12	32	4	1	0	7	7-0	1	12	.254	.296	.302	70	-5	1-2	.980	3	111	132	O57(31/24/2),D6	0	-0.4
1991	Cal A	90	270	32	79	17	0	1	30	24-0	2	43	.293	.355	.367	100	1	2-4	1.000	3	98	185	O87(7/61/23),D2	0	0.1
1992	NY N	98	175	20	42	11	1	1	21	19-0	1	16	.240	.307	.331	85	-3	4-5	.982	4	111	149	O76(22/13/48)	44	-0.1
1993	NY N	99	201	34	55	12	2	6	28	20-1	0	18	.274	.338	.443	109	2	1-1	1.000	2	99	180	O72(19/39/20),1b9	0	0.3
1994	Atl N	89	152	27	34	5	0	2	14	22-2	1	17	.224	.326	.296	61	-8	0-2	.989	3	120	41	O77(71/5/7)/1	0	-0.8
1995	Phi N	62	157	12	50	12	0	1	12	16-0	0	20	.318	.379	.414	109	3	0-0	1.000	-1	102	37	O55(8/21/28)	0	0.1
	Cal A	11	16	1	3	1	0	0	0	2-0	0	1	.188	.278	.250	39	-1	0-0	1.000	1	113	483	O6(2/3/1)/D	20	0.0
Total	9	794	2081	273	564	100	10	17	190	187-7	7	251	.271	.331	.353	90	-26	20-24	.993	13	102	120	O699(166/396/173),D12,1b10	93	-2.8
GALLAGHER, JIM	James E.; B Findlay OH; D3.29.1894 Scranton PA; d9.4																								
1886	Was N	1	5	1	1	0	0	0	0	0	—	2	.200	.200	.200	24	0	0	.875	0	140	0	/S	—	0.0
GALLAGHER, JOHN	John Carroll; B2.18.1892 Pittsburgh PA; D3.30.1952 Norfolk VA; BR/TR/5´10.5˝/156; d8.20; Col Georgetown																								
1915	Bal F	40	126	11	25	4	0	0	4	5	0	22	.198	.229	.230	28	-14	1	.945	-1	104	70	2b37,S5/3	—	-1.6
GALLAGHER, JACKIE	John Laurence; B1.28.1902 Providence RI; D9.10.1984 Gladwyne PA; BL/TR/5´10˝/175; d8.24																								
1923	Cle A	1	1	0	1	0	0	0	0	0	0	0	1.000	1.000	1.000	428	0	0-0	ø	-0	0	0	/lf	—	0.0
GALLAGHER, JOE	Joseph Emmett "Muscles"; B3.7.1914 Buffalo NY; D2.25.1998 Houston TX; BR/TR/6´2˝/210; d4.20; Mil 1941–45; Col Manhattan																								
1939	NY A	14	41	8	10	0	1	2	9	3	1	8	.244	.311	.439	91	-1	1-0	1.000	0	97	138	O12R	—	-0.1
	StL A	71	266	41	75	17	2	9	40	17	1	42	.282	.327	.462	98	-2	0-1	.944	1	96	170	O67(56/0/11)	—	-0.5
	Year	85	307	49	85	17	3	11	49	20	2	50	.277	.325	.459	97	-3	1-1	.950	1	96	166	O79(56/0/23)	—	-0.6
1940	StL A	23	70	14	19	3	1	2	8	4	0	12	.271	.311	.429	88	-2	2-0	.966	-1	85	95	O15L	—	-0.3
	Bro N	57	110	10	29	6	1	3	16	2	1	14	.264	.283	.418	86	-3	1	.941	-1	93	75	O20(3/0/17)	—	-0.5
Total	2	165	487	73	133	26	5	16	73	26	3	76	.273	.314	.446	93	-8	4-1	.950	-1	94	142	O114(74/0/40)	—	-1.4
GALLAGHER, GIL	Lawrence Kirby; B9.5.1896 Washington DC; D1.6.1957 Washington DC; BB/TR/5´8˝/155; d9.13																								
1922	Bos N	7	22	1	1	1	0	0	2	1	0	7	.045	.087	.091	-57	-5	0-0	.893	-1	120	0	S6	—	-0.6
GALLAGHER, BOB	Robert Collins; B7.7.1948 Newton MA; BL/TL/6´3˝/185; [LAN68 17/377]; d5.17; gf–Shano Collins; Col Stanford																								
1972	Bos A	7	5	0	0	0	0	0	0	0-0	0	3	.000	.000	.000	-94	-1	0-0	ø	0	—	—	/H	0	-0.1
1973	Hou N	71	148	16	39	3	1	2	10	3-1	0	27	.264	.275	.338	70	-7	0-1	1.000	2	125	44	O42(15/12/16)/1	0	-0.6
1974	Hou N	102	87	13	15	2	0	0	3	12-1	1	23	.172	.280	.195	36	-7	1-0	.978	-1	102	0	O62(5/4/53),1b4	0	-0.9
1975	NY N	33	15	5	2	1	0	0	0	1-0	0	3	.133	.188	.200	8	-2	0-0	.900	0	151	0	O16(10/1/5)	0	-0.2
Total	4	213	255	34	56	6	1	2	13	16-2	1	56	.220	.266	.275	52	-17	1-1	.985	2	118	24	O120(30/17/74),1b5	0	-1.8
GALLAGHER, WILLIAM	William Howard; B2.4.1874 Boston MA; D3.11.1950 Worcester MA; d8.19																								
1896	Phi N	14	49	9	15	2	0	0	6	10	1	0	.306	.433	.347	108	2	0	.894	-2	99	87	S14	—	0.0
GALLAGHER, BILL	William John; B Philadelphia PA; TL; d5.2; ▲																								
1883	Bal AA	16	61	9	10	3	1	0	—	3	—	—	.164	.203	.246	43	-4	—	.824	-1	135	508	O9(1/0/8),P7,S4	—	-0.3
	Phi N	2	8	1	0	0	0	0	0	0	—	4	.000	.000	.000	-99	-2	—	1.000	-0	0	0	O2C	—	-0.2
1884	Phi U	3	11	1	1	0	0	0	—	0	—	—	.091	.091	.091	-48	-2	—	.800	-0	107	0	P3	—	0.0
Total	2	21	80	11	11	3	1	0	0	3	—	4	.138	.169	.200	16	-8	—	.850	-2	113	425	O11(1/2/8),P10,S4	—	-0.5
GALLE, STAN	Stanley Joseph (b Stanley Joseph Galazewski); B2.7.1919 Milwaukee WI; D1.28.2006 Mobile AL; BR/TR/5´7˝/165; d4.14; Mil 1942–45																								
1942	Was A	13	18	3	2	0	0	0	1	1	0	0	.111	.158	.111	-24	-3	0-0	.857	-0	76	0	3b3	0	-0.4
GALLEGO, MIKE	Michael Anthony; B10.31.1960 Whittier CA; BR/TR/5´8˝/(160–175); [OakA81 2/33]; d4.11; C3; Col UCLA																								
1985	Oak A	76	77	13	16	5	1	1	9	12-0	1	14	.208	.319	.338	87	-1	1-1	.991	-2	93	133	2b42,S21,3b12	0	-0.1
1986	Oak A	20	37	2	10	2	0	0	4	1-0	0	6	.270	.289	.324	72	-2	0-2	.986	5	135	72	2b19,3b2/S	0	0.3
1987	Oak A	72	124	18	31	6	0	2	14	12-0	1	21	.250	.319	.347	82	-3	0-1	.968	7	116	160	2b31,3b24,S17	46	0.6
1988	†Oak A	129	277	38	58	8	0	2	20	34-0	1	53	.209	.298	.260	60	-14	2-3	.993	-12	92	85	2b83,S42,3b16	0	-2.3
1989	†Oak A	133	357	45	90	14	2	3	30	35-0	6	43	.252	.327	.328	88	-5	7-5	.967	10	102	136	S94,2b41,3b3/D	0	1.2
1990	†Oak A	140	389	36	80	13	2	3	34	35-0	4	50	.206	.277	.272	57	-23	5-5	.990	-2	109	104	2b83,S38,3b27/rfD	0	-2.1
1991	Oak A	159	482	67	119	15	4	12	49	67-3	5	84	.247	.343	.369	103	3	6-9	.989	-15	99	81	2b135,S55	0	-0.7
1992	NY A	53	173	24	44	7	1	3	14	20-0	4	22	.254	.343	.358	98	0	0-1	.990	1	98	101	2b40,S14	113	0.3
1993	NY A	119	403	63	114	20	1	10	54	50-0	4	65	.283	.364	.412	112	8	3-2	.976	**26**	124	123	S55,2b52,3b27/D	15	3.8
1994	NY A	89	306	39	73	17	1	6	41	38-1	4	46	.239	.327	.359	81	-8	0-1	.970	16	114	125	S72,2b26	20	1.2
1995	Oak A	43	120	11	28	0	0	0	8	9-0	1	24	.233	.292	.233	41	-11	0-1	.960	-1	107	91	2b18,S14,3b12	84	-1.0
1996	†StL N	51	143	12	30	2	0	0	4	12-1	1	31	.210	.276	.224	34	-14	0-0	.985	1	101	126	2b43,3b7/S	102	-1.0
1997	StL N	27	43	6	7	2	0	0	1	1-0	0	6	.163	.178	.209	2	-6	0-0	.962	3	110	99	2b11,S10,3b7	0	-0.3
Total	13	1111	2931	374	700	111	12	42	282	326-5	32	465	.239	.320	.328	80	-76	24-31	.986	38	105	103	2b624,S434,3b137,D3/rf	380	-0.1
GALLIGAN, JOHN	John T.; B6.1865 Easton PA; D8.22.1937 Bronx NY; 5´10˝/160; d9.2																								
1889	Lou AA	31	120	6	20	0	2	0	7	6	1	17	.167	.213	.200	18	-13	1	.915	1	112	62	O31L	—	-1.2
GALLOWAY, CHICK	Clarence Edward; B8.4.1896 Clinton SC; D11.7.1969 Clinton SC; BR/TR/5´8˝/160; d9.9; Col Presbyterian																								
1919	Phi A	17	63	2	9	0	0	0	4	1	0	8	.143	.156	.143	-16	-10	0	.969	2	93	153	S17	—	-0.8
1920	Phi A	98	298	28	60	9	3	0	18	22	1	22	.201	.259	.252	35	-29	2-2	.928	3	101	67	S84,2b4,3b3	—	-2.0
1921	Phi A	131	465	42	123	28	5	3	47	29	2	43	.265	.310	.366	72	-21	12-7	.922	-25	91	98	S110,3b20/2	—	-3.1
1922	Phi A	**155**	571	83	185	26	9	6	69	39	1	39	.324	.368	.433	105	4	10-19	.952	6	100	95	S155	—	2.1
1923	Phi A	134	504	64	140	18	9	2	62	37	0	30	.278	.327	.361	80	-16	12-10	.944	2	99	105	S134	—	0.0
1924	Phi A	129	464	41	128	16	4	2	48	23	1	23	.276	.311	.341	67	-24	11-12	.952	-4	96	103	S129	—	-1.4
1925	Phi A	149	481	52	116	11	4	3	71	59	0	28	.241	.324	.299	55	-33	16-9	.954	-4	96	105	S148	—	-1.9
1926	Phi A	133	408	37	98	13	6	0	49	31	1	20	.240	.295	.301	53	-29	8-7	.935	-16	85	78	S133	—	-3.2

YEAR	TM LG	G	AB	R	H	2B	3B	HR	RBI	BB-IB	HP	SO	AVG	OBP	SLG	AOPS	ABR	SB-CS	FA	FR	RNG	THR	GAMES AT POSITION	DL	BFW
1927	Phi A	77	181	25	48	10	4	0	22	18	0	9	.265	.332	.365	76	-7	1-3	.946	-1	94	74	S61,3b7	—	-0.3
1928	Det A	53	148	17	39	5	2	1	17	15	0	3	.264	.331	.345	77	-5	7-3	.914	-2	84	94	S22,3b21/1lf	—	-0.4
Total	10	1076	3583	391	946	136	46	17	407	274	6	225	.264	.317	.342	69	-170	79-72	.943	-39	95	95	S993,3b51,2b5/lf1	—	-11.0
Galloway, Jim	James Cato "Bad News"; B9.16.1887 Iredell TX; D5.3.1950 Fort Worth TX; BB/TR/6´3˝/187; d8.24																								
1912	StL N	21	54	4	10	2	0	0	4	5	0	8	.185	.254	.222	32	-5	2	.971	2	116	91	2b16/S	—	-0.3
Galvin, Jim	James Joseph; B8.11.1907 Somerville MA; D9.30.1969 Marietta GA; BR/TR/5´11.5˝/180; d9.27																								
1930	Bos A	2	2	0	0	0	0	0	0	0	0	0	.000	.000	.000	-99	-1	0-0	ø	0	—	—	/H	—	-0.1
Galvin, John	John A.; B8.1842 Brooklyn NY; D4.20.1904 Brooklyn NY; 5´7˝/178; d5.7																								
1872	Atl NA	1	4	0	0	0	0	0	0	0	—	0	.000	.000	.000	-85	-1	0-0	.200	-2	0	0	/2	—	-0.2
Gamble, John	John Robert; B2.10.1948 Reno NV; BR/TR/5´10˝/165; [LAN66 2/39]; d9.7																								
1972	Det A	6	3	0	0	0	0	0	0	0-0	0	0	.000	.000	.000	-97	-1	0-0	1.000	0	77	0	/S	0	-0.1
1973	Det A	7	0	1	0	0	0	0	0	0-0	0	0	ø	ø	ø	ø	0	0-0	ø	0	—	—	/R	0	0.0
Total	2	13	3	1	0	0	0	0	0	0-0	0	0	.000	.000	.000	-97	-1	0-0	1.000	0	77	0	/S	0	-0.1
Gamble, Lee	Lee Jesse; B6.28.1910 Renovo PA; D10.5.1994 Punxsutawney PA; BL/TR/6´1˝/170; d9.15																								
1935	Cin N	2	4	2	2	1	0	0	2	1	0	0	.500	.600	.750	269	1	1	1.000	-0	101	0	O2L	—	0.1
1938	Cin N	53	75	13	24	3	1	0	5	0	0	6	.320	.320	.387	96	-1	0	1.000	0	114	0	O9L	—	-0.1
1939	†Cin N	72	221	24	59	7	2	0	14	9	0	14	.267	.296	.317	64	-12	5	.989	-3	78	150	O56(55/1/0)	—	-1.8
1940	Cin N	38	42	12	6	1	0	0	0	0	0	1	.143	.143	.167	-15	-7	0	1.000	1	135	190	O10(2/0/8)	—	-0.6
Total	4	165	342	51	91	12	3	0	21	10	0	21	.266	.287	.319	64	-19	6	.993	-2	88	134	O77(68/1/8)	—	-2.4
Gamble, Oscar	Oscar Charles; B12.20.1949 Ramer AL; BL/TR/5´11˝/(160–187); [ChiN68 16/363]; d8.27																								
1969	Chi N	24	71	6	16	1	1	1	5	10-1	0	12	.225	.321	.310	69	-3	0-2	.913	-2	86	76	O24(1/23/0)	0	-0.7
1970	Phi N	88	275	31	72	12	4	1	19	27-3	1	37	.262	.330	.345	83	-7	5-4	.956	-1	103	96	O74(0/47/28)	0	-1.0
1971	Phi N	92	280	24	62	11	1	6	23	21-2	1	35	.221	.275	.332	72	-11	5-2	.970	-3	91	80	O80(54/1/26)	0	-1.9
1972	Phi N	74	135	17	32	5	2	1	13	19-0	1	16	.237	.331	.326	86	-2	0-1	1.000	-0	98	93	O35R/1	0	-0.4
1973	Cle A	113	390	56	104	11	3	20	44	34-1	3	37	.267	.329	.464	119	8	3-4	.971	-1	107	46	D70,O37(2/1/35)	0	0.4
1974	Cle A	135	454	74	132	16	4	19	59	48-10	5	51	.291	.363	.469	139	23	5-6	1.000	0	89	138	D115,O13(12/0/1)	0	1.9
1975	Cle A	121	348	60	91	16	3	15	45	53-4	2	39	.261	.361	.454	129	14	11-5	.987	1	93	144	O82(81/0/1),D29	0	1.1
1976	†NY A	110	340	43	79	13	1	17	57	38-4	4	38	.232	.317	.426	117	7	5-3	.981	2	98	139	O104R/D	0	0.4
1977	Chi A	137	408	75	121	22	2	31	83	54-2	6	54	.297	.386	.588	161	35	1-2	.987	-4	87	35	D79,O49(5/7/38)	0	2.7
1978	SD N	126	375	46	103	15	3	7	47	51-11	6	45	.275	.366	.387	120	12	1-2	.979	2	95	154	O107(39/0/70)	0	0.9
1979	Tex A	64	161	27	54	6	0	8	32	37-11	1	15	.335	.458	.522	166	18	2-1	1.000	2	115	153	D37,O21R	27	1.7
	NY A	36	113	21	44	4	1	11	32	13-1	0	13	.389	.452	.735	217	18	0-0	.943	0	96	164	O27(25/2/0),D6	0	1.7
	Year	100	274	48	98	10	1	19	64	50-12	1	28	.358	.456	.609	187	36	2-1	.969	2	104	159	O48(25/2/21),D43	0	3.4
1980	†NY A	78	194	40	54	10	2	14	50	28-4	4	21	.278	.376	.567	158	16	2-0	1.000	-2	89	74	O49(36/0/14),D20	40	1.2
1981	†NY A	80	189	24	45	8	0	10	27	35-2	1	23	.238	.357	.439	131	9	0-2	1.000	1	121	0	O43(16/0/27),D33	0	0.7
1982	NY A	108	316	49	86	21	2	18	57	58-2	4	47	.272	.387	.522	150	24	6-3	1.000	5	111	332	D74,O29(1/0/28)	0	2.6
1983	NY A	74	180	26	47	10	2	7	26	25-1	3	23	.261	.361	.456	127	7	0-0	.942	0	113	49	O32(2/0/30),D21	0	0.5
1984	NY A	54	125	17	23	2	0	10	27	25-0	0	18	.184	.318	.440	112	2	1-0	1.000	-1	73	164	D28,O12R	48	0.0
1985	Chi A	70	148	20	30	5	0	4	20	34-3	1	22	.203	.353	.318	82	-2	0-0	ø	0	0	0	D48	0	-0.4
Total	17	1584	4502	656	1195	188	31	200	666	610-62	43	546	.265	.356	.454	126	168	47-37	.977	1	98	113	O818(274/81/469),D561/1	115	11.4
Gammons, Daff	John Ashley; B3.17.1876 New Bedford MA; D9:24.1963 E.Greenwich RI; BR/TR/5´11˝/170; d4.23; Col Harvard																								
1901	Bos N	28	93	10	18	0	1	0	10	3	3	—	.194	.242	.215	30	-8	5	.880	-3	203	0	O23(20/0/3),2b2/3	—	-1.2
Gandil, Chick	Arnold; B1.19.1887 St.Paul MN; D12.13.1970 Calistoga CA; BR/TR/6´1.5˝/190; d4.14																								
1910	Chi A	77	275	21	53	7	3	2	21	24	4	—	.193	.267	.262	69	-10	12	.989	6	130	107	1b74,O2L	—	-0.6
1912	Was A	117	443	59	135	20	15	2	81	27	4	—	.305	.350	.431	122	10	19	**.990**	2	98	91	1b117	—	0.9
1913	Was A	148	550	61	175	25	8	1	72	36	3	33	.318	.363	.398	120	13	22	.990	8	**115**	**123**	1b145	—	1.8
1914	Was A	145	526	48	136	24	10	3	75	44	7	44	.259	.324	.359	101	0	30-19	.991	23	**156**	**126**	1b145	—	2.1
1915	Was A	136	485	53	141	20	15	2	64	29	7	33	.291	.340	.406	121	9	20-13	.986	-1	96	105	1b134	—	0.5
1916	Cle A	146	533	51	138	26	9	0	72	36	5	48	.259	.312	.341	91	-7	13	**.995**	8	**118**	99	1b145	—	-0.3
1917	†Chi A	149	553	53	151	9	7	0	57	30	5	36	.273	.316	.315	91	-8	16	**.995**	-6	81	103	1b149	—	-2.0
1918	Chi A	114	439	49	119	18	4	0	55	27	4	19	.271	.319	.330	95	-4	9	.992	-3	86	107	1b114	—	-1.0
1919	†Chi A	115	441	54	128	24	7	1	60	20	3	20	.290	.325	.383	98	-3	10	**.997**	-4	79	124	1b115	—	-1.0
Total	9	1147	4245	449	1176	173	78	11	557	273	42	233	.277	.327	.362	103	0	151-32	.992	35	107	110	1b1138,O2L	—	0.4
Gandy, Bob	Robert Brinkley "String"; B8.25.1893 Jacksonville FL; D6.19.1945 Jacksonville FL; BL/TR/6´3˝/180; d10.5																								
1916	Phi N	1	2	0	0	0	0	0	0	0	0	1	.000	.000	.000	-97	0	0	1.000	0	124	0	/cf	—	-0.1
Ganley, Bob	Robert Stephen; B4.23.1875 Lowell MA; D10.9.1945 Lowell MA; BL/TL/5´7˝/156; d9.1																								
1905	Pit N	32	127	12	40	1	2	0	7	8	0	—	.315	.356	.354	109	1	3	1.000	-2	76	0	O32(0/6/27)	—	-0.2
1906	Pit N	137	511	63	132	7	6	0	31	41	2	—	.258	.316	.295	87	-8	19	.965	-3	96	137	O134(0/12/122)	—	-1.9
1907	Was A	**154**	605	73	167	10	5	1	35	54	2	—	.276	.337	.314	117	13	40	.940	7	112	98	O154(62/13/78)	—	1.2
1908	Was A	150	549	61	131	19	9	1	36	45	2	—	.239	.299	.311	107	4	30	.964	4	74	21	O150L	—	0.0
1909	Was A	19	63	5	16	3	0	0	5	1	0	—	.254	.266	.302	83	-1	4	1.000	-2	0	0	O17(11/5/1)	—	-0.5
	Phi A	80	274	32	54	4	2	0	9	28	0	—	.197	.272	.226	56	-13	16	.980	4	90	98	O77C	—	-1.5
	Year	99	337	37	70	7	2	0	14	29	0	—	.208	.270	.240	61	-15	20	.982	2	77	84	O94(11/82/1)	—	-2.0
Total	5	572	2129	246	540	44	24	2	123	177	6	—	.254	.313	.300	97	-4	112	.962	9	90	79	O564(223/113/228)	—	-2.9
Gannon, Billy	William Patrick; B3.17.1873 New Haven CT; D4.26.1927 Fort Worth TX; 5´9˝/170; d9.9																								
1901	Chi N	15	61	2	9	0	0	0	0	1	0	—	.148	.161	.148	-11	-9	5	1.000	-0	128	0	O15R	—	-1.0
Gant, Ron	Ronald Edwin; B3.2.1965 Victoria TX; BR/TR/6´0˝/(172–200); [AtlN83 4/100]; d9.6; OF(1184/299/9); [DL 1994 Cin N 52]																								
1987	Atl N	21	83	9	22	4	0	2	9	1-0	0	11	.265	.271	.386	70	-4	4-2	.972	2	104	131	2b20	0	-0.1
1988	Atl N	146	563	85	146	28	8	19	60	46-4	3	118	.259	.317	.439	111	7	19-10	.963	4	105	104	2b122,3b22	0	1.5
1989	Atl N	75	260	26	46	8	3	9	25	20-0	1	63	.177	.237	.335	61	-15	9-6	.887	-1	102	99	3b53,O14(2/14/0)	0	-1.7
1990	Atl N	152	575	107	174	34	3	32	84	50-0	1	86	.303	.357	.539	136	27	33-16	.978	-0	104	84	O146(38/113/3)	0	2.7
1991	†Atl N	154	561	101	141	35	3	32	105	71-8	5	104	.251	.338	.496	125	19	34-15	.983	-8	95	86	O148C	0	1.2
1992	†Atl N★	153	544	74	141	22	6	17	80	45-5	7	101	.259	.321	.415	102	0	32-10	.986	-6	95	73	O147(138/23/0)	0	-0.6
1993	†Atl N	157	606	113	166	27	4	36	117	67-2	2	117	.274	.345	.510	123	19	26-9	.962	-13	89	42	O155L	0	0.2
1995	†Cin N★	119	410	79	113	19	4	29	88	74-5	3	108	.276	.386	.554	144	27	23-8	.985	1	103	106	O117L	0	2.5
1996	†StL N	122	419	74	103	14	2	30	82	73-5	3	98	.246	.359	.504	125	15	13-4	.978	1	106	61	O116L	34	1.3
1997	StL N	139	502	68	115	21	4	17	62	58-3	1	162	.229	.310	.388	81	-15	14-6	.977	1	105	49	O128L/D	0	-1.7
1998	StL N	121	383	60	92	17	1	26	67	51-2	2	92	.240	.331	.493	114	7	8-0	.971	-4	89	63	O104L	20	0.1
1999	Phi N	138	516	107	134	27	5	17	77	85-0	1	112	.260	.364	.430	99	1	13-3	.993	4	102	87	O133L,D2	0	0.1
2000	Phi N	89	343	54	87	16	2	20	38	36-1	1	73	.254	.324	.487	102	0	5-4	.968	4	116	80	O84L	0	0.0
	Ana A	34	82	15	19	3	1	6	16	20-0	0	18	.232	.379	.512	120	3	1-2	.977	2	127	103	O21L,D12	0	0.3
2001	Col N	59	171	31	44	8	2	8	22	24-2	0	56	.257	.345	.468	90	-2	3-1	.965	-1	102	67	O51L	0	-0.5
	†Oak A	34	81	15	21	5	1	2	13	11-0	0	24	.259	.344	.420	101	0	2-0	1.000	-3	24	0	D20,O11L	0	-0.3
2002	SD N	102	309	58	81	14	1	18	59	36-1	2	59	.262	.338	.489	127	11	4-6	.980	4	108	137	O80(78/1/5),D4	27	1.1
2003	Oak A	17	41	4	6	0	0	1	4	2-0	0	9	.146	.182	.220	6	-6	0-0	1.000	-1	81	0	O9(8/0/1),D6	0	-0.7
Total	16	1832	6449	1080	1651	302	50	321	1008	770-38	32	1411	.256	.336	.468	111	94	243-102	.978	-15	100	74	O1464L,2b142,3b75,D45	133	5.4
Gantenbein, Joe	Joseph Steven "Sep"; B8.25.1916 San Francisco CA; D8.2.1993 Novato CA; BL/TR/5´9˝/168; d4.20																								
1939	Phi A	111	348	47	101	14	4	4	36	32	2	22	.290	.353	.388	91	-5	1-5	.948	-28	84	51	2b76,3b14;S5	—	-2.7
1940	Phi A	75	197	21	47	6	2	4	23	11	1	21	.239	.282	.350	64	-11	1-0	.930	-4	95	144	3b45,1b6,S3/lf	—	-1.3
Total	2	186	545	68	148	20	6	8	59	43	3	43	.272	.328	.374	82	-16	2-5	.948	-32	84	51	2b76,3b59,S8,1b6/lf	—	-4.0

YEAR	TM LG	G	AB	R	H	2B	3B	HR	RBI	BB-IB	HP	SO	AVG	OBP	SLG	AOPS	ABR	SB-CS	FA	FR	RNG	THR	GAMES AT POSITION	DL	BFW
GANTNER, JIM	James Elmer; B1.5.1953 Fond Du Lac WI; BL/TR/6´0˝/175; [MilA74 12/270]; d9.3; C2; Col Wisconsin–Oshkosh																								
1976	Mil A	26	69	6	17	1	0	0	7	6-0	1	11	.246	.316	.261	71	-2	1-0	.982	-4	82	77	3b24,D2	0	-0.6
1977	Mil A	14	47	4	14	1	0	1	2	2-0	0	5	.298	.327	.383	92	-1	2-1	.902	1	116	129	3b14	0	0.0
1978	Mil A	43	97	14	21	1	0	1	8	5-0	2	10	.216	.269	.258	49	-7	2-0	.980	2	114	96	2b21,3b15/1S	0	-0.4
1979	Mil A	70	208	29	59	10	3	2	22	16-1	2	17	.284	.336	.389	96	-1	3-5	.952	1	93	125	3b42,2b22,S3/P	0	0.0
1980	Mil A	132	415	47	117	21	3	4	40	30-5	1	29	.282	.330	.376	96	-2	11-10	.938	-3	107	135	3b69,2b66/S	0	-0.3
1981	†Mil A	107	352	35	94	14	1	2	33	29-5	3	29	.267	.325	.330	94	-2	3-6	.984	15	111	**127**	2b107	0	1.7
1982	†Mil A	132	447	48	132	17	2	4	43	26-3	2	36	.295	.335	.369	99	-1	6-3	.982	10	108	116	2b131	0	1.6
1983	Mil A	161	603	85	170	23	8	11	74	38-5	6	46	.282	.329	.401	108	5	5-6	.984	8	106	110	2b158	0	2.0
1984	Mil A	153	613	61	173	27	1	3	56	30-0	3	51	.282	.314	.344	86	-12	6-5	.985	10	100	107	2b153	0	0.7
1985	Mil A	143	523	63	133	15	4	5	44	33-7	3	42	.254	.300	.327	72	-21	11-8	.988	6	107	103	2b124,3b24/S	0	-0.9
1986	Mil A	139	497	58	136	25	1	7	38	26-2	6	50	.274	.313	.370	84	-11	13-7	.985	-2	94	100	2b135,3b3/SD	0	-0.5
1987	Mil A	81	265	37	72	14	0	4	30	19-2	5	22	.272	.331	.370	83	-6	6-2	.984	2	113	112	2b57,3b38/D	38	-0.2
1988	Mil A	155	539	67	149	28	2	0	47	34-1	3	50	.276	.322	.336	84	-11	20-8	.986	-5	98	100	2b154/3	0	-1.0
1989	Mil A	116	409	51	112	18	3	0	34	21-2	**10**	33	.274	.321	.333	86	-7	20-6	.987	18	110	**122**	2b114,D2	47	1.6
1990	Mil A	88	323	36	85	8	5	0	25	29-0	2	19	.263	.328	.319	82	-8	18-3	.982	-9	97	97	2b80,3b9	66	-1.2
1991	Mil A	140	526	63	149	27	4	2	47	27-5	3	34	.283	.320	.361	90	-8	4-6	.976	0	92	88	3b90,2b59	0	-0.7
1992	Mil A	101	256	22	63	12	1	1	18	12-2	0	17	.246	.278	.313	67	-12	6-2	.994	2	101	119	2b68,3b31,1b2,D2	15	-0.8
Total	17	1801	6189	726	1696	262	38	47	568	383-40	52	501	.274	.319	.351	87	-107	137-78	.985	52	105	109	2b1449,3b360,D8,S7,1b3/P	166	1.0
GANZEL, CHARLIE	Charles William; B6.18.1862 Waterford WI; D4.7.1914 Quincy MA; BR/TR/6´0˝/161; d9.27; b–John s–Babe; OF(25/5/71)																								
1884	StP U	7	23	2	5	0	0	0	—	0	—	—	.217	.217	.217	59	-2	—	.956	0	—	—	C6/cf	—	-0.1
1885	Phi N	34	125	15	21	3	1	0	6	4	—	13	.168	.194	.208	31	-10	—	.888	0	—	—	C33/cf	—	-0.6
1886	Phi N	1	3	0	0	0	0	0	0	0	—	1	.000	.000	.000	-99	-1	0	.600	-1	—	—	/C	—	-0.2
	Det N	57	213	28	58	7	2	1	31	7	—	22	.272	.295	.338	89	-3	5	.911	3	—	—	C45,O7L,1b5	—	0.3
	Year	58	216	28	58	7	2	1	31	7	—	23	.269	.291	.333	87	-4	5	.903	2	—	—	C46,O7L,1b5	—	0.1
1887	†Det N	57	227	40	59	6	5	0	20	8	1	2	.260	.288	.330	69	-10	3	.913	7	—	—	C51,O4L,1b2/3	—	0.1
1888	Det N	95	386	45	96	13	5	1	46	14	1	15	.249	.277	.316	88	-6	12	.900	-1	102	62	2b49,C28,3b9,O5R,S3/1	—	-0.2
1889	Bos N	73	275	30	73	3	5	1	43	15	2	11	.265	.308	.324	71	-12	13	.927	7	—	—	C39,O26(0/1/25),1b7,S6/3	—	-0.2
1890	Bos N	38	163	21	44	7	3	0	24	5	2	6	.270	.300	.350	83	-5	1	.958	8	*127*	*92*	C22,O15(1/0/14),S3/2	—	0.4
1891	Bos N	70	263	33	68	18	5	1	29	12	5	13	.259	.304	.376	87	-6	7	.956	12	*128*	*90*	C59,O13(5/1/7)	—	0.9
1892	†Bos N	54	198	25	53	9	3	0	25	18	1	12	.268	.332	.343	95	-1	7	.933	2	*133*	*86*	C51,O2(1/1/0)/1	—	0.4
1893	Bos N	73	281	50	75	10	2	1	48	22	2	9	.267	.325	.327	68	-14	6	.952	3	*130*	*92*	C40,O23(6/0/18),1b10	—	-0.7
1894	Bos N	70	266	51	74	7	6	3	56	19	0	6	.278	.326	.383	65	-17	1	.897	0	*120*	*91*	C59,1b7,O3(1/0/2),S2/2	—	-0.9
1895	Bos N	81	280	38	73	2	5	1	52	25	1	6	.261	.324	.314	60	-18	1	.963	20	*129*	*83*	C77,S2,1b2	—	0.7
1896	Bos N	47	179	28	47	2	0	1	18	9	2	5	.263	.305	.291	54	-12	2	.989	9	*113*	*118*	C41,1b3,S2	—	0.0
1897	Bos N	30	105	15	28	4	3	0	14	4	1	—	.267	.300	.362	70	-5	2	.942	5	*153*	*89*	C27,1b2	—	0.2
Total	14	787	2987	421	774	91	45	10	412	162	18	121	.259	.301	.330	73	-122	60	.935	74	*128*	*91*	C579,O100R,2b51,1b40,S18,3b11	—	0.1
GANZEL, BABE	Foster Pirie; B5.22.1901 Malden MA; D2.6.1978 Jacksonville FL; BR/TR/5´10.5˝/172; d9.19; f–Charlie																								
1927	Was A	13	48	7	21	4	2	1	13	7	0	3	.438	.509	.667	206	8	0-0	.944	-1	101	74	O13(4/9/0)	—	0.6
1928	Was A	10	26	2	2	1	0	0	4	1	0	4	.077	.111	.115	-41	-5	0-0	1.000	0	92	200	O7(4/2/2)	—	-0.5
Total	2	23	74	9	23	5	2	1	17	8	0	7	.311	.378	.473	122	3	0-0	.957	-0	99	108	O20(8/11/2)	—	0.1
GANZEL, JOHN	John Henry; B4.7.1874 Kalamazoo MI; D1.14.1959 Orlando FL; BR/TR/6´0.5˝/195; d4.21; M2; b–Charlie																								
1898	Pit N	15	45	5	6	0	0	0	2	4	1	—	.133	.220	.133	2	-6	0	.963	-1	59	84	1b12	—	-0.7
1900	Chi N	78	284	29	78	14	4	4	32	10	7	—	.275	.316	.394	99	-1	5	.980	-4	77	94	1b78	—	-0.5
1901	NY N	138	526	42	113	13	3	2	66	20	9	—	.215	.256	.262	52	-33	6	**.986**	2	99	80	1b138	—	-3.2
1903	NY A	129	476	62	132	25	7	3	71	30	12	—	.277	.336	.378	107	5	9	**.988**	7	117	110	1b129	—	1.0
1904	NY A	130	465	50	121	16	10	6	48	24	9	—	.260	.309	.376	111	5	13	.988	-1	87	108	1b118,2b9/S	—	0.2
1907	Cin N	145	531	61	135	20	**16**	2	64	29	3	—	.254	.297	.363	102	-1	9	.990	1	97	123	1b143	—	-0.3
1908	Cin N	112	388	32	97	16	10	1	53	19	2	—	.250	.289	.351	107	1	6	**.990**	-2	91	109	1b108,M	—	-0.3
Total	7	747	2715	281	682	104	50	18	336	136	43	—	.251	.298	.346	93	-30	48	.987	2	96	104	1b726,2b9/S	—	-3.8
GARABITO, EDDY	Eddy Jorge; B12.2.1976 Manrreza, D.R.; BB/TR/5´8˝/190; d5.27																								
2005	Col N	42	88	15	27	5	0	1	8	8-0	3	12	.307	.384	.398	94	0	3-2	.986	-2	86	106	2b18,S2	0	-0.2
GARAGIOLA, JOE	Joseph Henry; B2.12.1926 St.Louis MO; BL/TR/6´0˝/(190–195); d5.26																								
1946	†StL N	74	211	21	50	4	1	3	22	23	0	25	.237	.312	.308	73	-8	0	.990	0	*148*	*71*	C70	0	-0.4
1947	StL N	77	183	20	47	10	2	5	25	40	3	14	.257	.398	.415	111	5	0	.987	2	*127*	*64*	C74	0	1.0
1948	StL N	24	56	9	6	1	0	2	7	12	1	9	.107	.275	.232	36	-5	0	.990	3	*352*	*107*	C23	0	-0.1
1949	StL N	81	241	25	63	14	0	3	26	31	1	19	.261	.348	.357	85	-4	0	.984	4	*128*	*85*	C80	0	0.5
1950	StL N	34	88	8	28	6	1	2	20	10	0	7	.318	.388	.477	120	3	0	1.000	-1	*142*	*71*	C30	74	0.3
1951	StL N	27	72	9	14	3	2	2	9	9	0	7	.194	.284	.375	75	-3	0-0	1.000	-1	*121*	*44*	C23	0	-0.3
	Pit N	72	212	24	54	8	2	9	35	32	2	20	.255	.358	.439	110	3	4-1	.986	-5	*96*	*79*	C61	0	0.2
	Year	99	284	33	68	11	4	11	44	41	2	27	.239	.339	.423	101	1	4-1	**.989**	-6	*102*	*70*	C84	0	-0.1
1952	Pit N	118	344	35	94	15	4	8	54	50	2	24	.273	.369	.410	113	7	0-1	.978	-1	*78*	**126**	C105	0	1.1
1953	Pit N	27	73	9	17	5	0	2	14	10	2	11	.233	.341	.384	89	-1	1-0	.989	-3	*66*	*97*	C22	0	-0.2
	Chi N	74	228	21	62	9	4	1	21	21	1	23	.272	.336	.360	80	-7	0-0	.988	-1	*88*	*116*	C68	0	-0.4
	Year	101	301	30	79	14	4	3	35	31	3	34	.262	.337	.365	82	-7	1-0	.988	-3	*83*	*112*	C90	0	-0.6
1954	Chi N	63	153	16	43	5	0	5	21	28	4	12	.281	.403	.412	112	4	0-0	.982	-7	*56*	*95*	C55	36	0.0
	NY N	5	11	1	3	2	0	0	1	1	0	2	.273	.308	.455	102	0	0-0	1.000	-0	*86*	*0*	C3	0	0.0
	Year	68	164	17	46	7	0	5	22	29	4	14	.280	.397	.415	112	5	0-0	.983	-7	*58*	*89*	C58	0	0.0
Total	9	676	1872	198	481	82	16	42	255	267	16	173	.257	.354	.385	96	-6	5-2	.986	-9	*112*	*91*	C614	110	1.7
GARBARK, MIKE	Nathaniel Michael; B2.3.1916 Houston TX; D8.31.1994 Charlotte NC; BR/TR/6´0˝/200; d4.18; b–Bob; Col Villanova																								
1944	NY A	89	299	23	78	9	4	1	33	25	1	27	.261	.320	.328	82	-7	0-1	.988	6	*116*	*92*	C85	0	0.4
1945	NY A	60	176	23	38	5	3	1	26	23	1	12	.216	.310	.295	73	-6	0-1	.972	-1	*76*	*156*	C59	0	-0.4
Total	2	149	475	46	116	14	7	2	59	48	2	39	.244	.316	.316	79	-13	0-2	.982	6	*100*	*117*	C144	0	0.0
GARBARK, BOB	Robert Michael; B11.13.1909 Houston TX; D8.15.1990 Meadville PA; BR/TR/5´11˝/178; d9.3; b–Mike																								
1934	Cle A	5	11	1	0	0	0	0	0	1	0	3	.000	.083	.000	-76	-3	0-0	1.000	-1	*103*	*0*	C5	—	-0.4
1935	Cle A	6	18	4	6	1	0	0	4	5	0	1	.333	.478	.389	124	1	0-0	1.000	1	*138*	*109*	C6	—	0.2
1937	Chi N	1	1	0	0	0	0	0	0	0	0	0	.000	.000	.000	-96	0	0	ø	0	—	—	/H	—	0.0
1938	Chi N	23	54	2	14	0	0	0	5	1	0	0	.259	.273	.259	46	-4	0	1.000	1	*125*	*97*	C20/1	—	-0.3
1939	Chi N	24	21	1	3	0	0	0	0	0	0	3	.143	.143	.143	-23	-4	0	1.000	0	*134*	*88*	C21	—	-0.3
1944	Phi A	18	23	2	6	2	0	0	2	1	0	0	.261	.292	.348	83	-1	0-0	1.000	-0	*74*	*73*	C15	0	-0.1
1945	Bos A	68	199	21	52	6	0	0	17	18	2	10	.261	.329	.291	79	-5	0-1	.993	-2	*108*	*83*	C67	0	-0.4
Total	7	145	327	31	81	9	0	0	28	26	2	17	.248	.307	.275	64	-16	0-1	.996	-2	*112*	*85*	C134/1	0	-1.3
GARBEY, BARBARO	Barbaro (Garbey); B12.4.1956 Santiago de Cuba, Cuba; BR/TR/5´10˝/170; d4.3; OF(25/2/16)																								
1984	†Det A	110	327	45	94	17	1	5	52	17-2	2	35	.287	.325	.391	98	-1	6-7	.989	-3	112	134	1b65,3b20,D17,O10(8/1/1),2b3	0	-0.9
1985	Det A	86	237	27	61	9	1	6	29	15-1	3	37	.257	.305	.380	88	-4	3-2	.991	-2	114	130	1b37,O24(10/1/14),D21/3	0	-0.9
1988	Tex A	30	62	4	12	2	0	0	5	4-0	0	11	.194	.239	.226	31	-6	0-0	.900	1	90	0	O8(7/0/1),1b7,3b3,D7	34	-0.5
Total	3	226	626	76	167	28	2	11	86	36-3	5	83	.267	.309	.371	87	-11	9-9	.990	-4	119	129	1b109,D45,O42L,3b24,2b3	34	-2.3
GARBOWSKI, ALEX	Alexander; B6.25.1925 Yonkers NY; BR/TR/6´1˝/185; d4.16																								
1952	Det A	2	0	0	0	0	0	0	0	0	0	0	ø	ø	ø	ø	0	0-0	ø	0	—	—	/R	0	0.0
GARCIA, KIKO	Alfonso Rafael; B10.14.1953 Martinez CA; BR/TR/5´11˝/(170–180); [BalA71 3/69]; d9.11																								
1976	Bal A	11	32	2	7	1	1	1	4	0-0	0	4	.219	.219	.406	85	-1	2-1	1.000	-0	94	137	S11	0	0.0
1977	Bal A	65	131	20	29	6	0	2	10	6-0	0	31	.221	.255	.313	57	-8	2-3	.966	14	121	189	S61,2b2	0	1.0
1978	Bal A	79	186	17	49	6	4	0	13	7-0	0	43	.263	.287	.339	81	-6	7-1	.945	8	111	122	S74,2b3	0	0.9
1979	†Bal A	126	417	54	103	15	9	5	24	32-0	2	87	.247	.303	.362	82	-12	11-9	.955	-10	88	117	S113,2b25,3b2,O2L	0	-1.1
1980	Bal A	111	311	27	62	8	0	1	27	24-0	0	57	.199	.255	.235	36	-28	8-4	.974	5	97	105	S96,2b27/lf	15	-1.3

YEAR	TM LG	G	AB	R	H	2B	3B	HR	RBI	BB-IB	HP	SO	AVG	OBP	SLG	AOPS	ABR	SB-CS	FA	FR	RNG	THR	GAMES AT POSITION	DL	BFW
1981	†Hou N	48	136	9	37	6	1	0	15	10-3	1	16	.272	.324	.331	92	-1	2-2	.950	3	105	89	S28,3b13,2b9	11	0.4
1982	Hou N	34	76	5	16	5	0	1	5	3-1	0	15	.211	.241	.316	59	-4	1-0	.946	3	110	137	S21,3b2/2	15	0.1
1983	Phi N	84	118	22	34	7	1	2	9	9-2	1	20	.288	.344	.415	110	2	1-2	.970	8	102	86	2b52,S22,3b10	0	1.1
1984	Phi N	57	60	6	14	2	0	0	5	4-1	0	11	.233	.281	.267	54	-4	0-0	.965	-1	102	30	S30,3b23/2	0	-0.4
1985	Phi N	4	3	0	0	0	0	0	0	0-0	0	1	.000	.000	.000	-98	-1	0-0	1.000	-1	69	0	S3/3	0	-0.2
Total	10	619	1470	162	351	56	16	12	112	95-7	4	285	.239	.286	.323	70	-63	34-22	.961	29	101	119	S459,2b120,3b51,O3L	41	0.5
Garcia, Amaury	Amaury Miguel (Paula); B5.20.1975 Santo Domingo, D.R.; BR/TR/5´10˝/160; d7.5																								
1999	Fla N	10	24	6	6	0	1	2	2	3-0	0	11	.250	.333	.583	133	1	0-0	.932	3	142	114	2b8	0	0.4
Garcia, Carlos	Carlos Jesus (Guerrero); B10.15.1967 Tachira, Venezuela; BR/TR/6´1˝/(185–205); d9.20; C2																								
1990	Pit N	4	4	1	2	0	0	0	0	0-0	0	2	.500	.500	.500	182	0	0-0	1.000	0	136	201	S3	0	0.1
1991	Pit N	12	24	2	6	0	2	0	1	1-0	0	8	.250	.280	.417	94	-1	0-0	.947	0	105	155	S9,3b2/2	0	0.0
1992	†Pit N	22	39	4	8	1	0	0	4	0-0	0	9	.205	.195	.231	23	-4	0-0	.977	0	101	169	2b14,S8	0	-0.4
1993	Pit N	141	546	77	147	25	5	12	47	31-2	9	67	.269	.316	.399	91	-8	18-11	.983	-20	90	99	2b140,S3	0	-2.2
1994	Pit N★	98	412	49	114	15	2	6	28	16-2	4	67	.277	.309	.367	74	-16	18-9	.978	18	**114**	**122**	2b98	0	0.7
1995	Pit N	104	367	41	108	24	2	6	50	25-5	2	55	.294	.340	.420	97	-1	8-4	.982	7	104	114	2b92,S15	17	1.1
1996	Pit N	101	390	66	111	18	4	6	44	23-3	4	58	.285	.329	.397	88	-7	16-6	.985	7	110	81	2b77,S19,3b14	51	0.5
1997	Tor A	103	350	29	77	18	2	3	23	15-0	2	60	.220	.253	.309	46	-28	11-3	.981	-10	91	89	2b96,S5,3b4	0	-3.1
1998	Ana A	19	35	4	5	1	0	0	0	3-0	1	11	.143	.231	.171	7	-5	2-0	.978	2	109	133	2b11,S5,D3	31	-0.1
1999	SD N	6	11	1	2	0	0	0	0	1-0	0	3	.182	.250	.182	13	-2	0-0	.778	-1	67	0	3b4/1	0	-0.2
Total	10	610	2178	274	580	102	17	33	197	115-12	22	340	.266	.307	.374	79	-72	73-33	.982	5	100	104	2b529,S67,3b24,D3/1	99	-3.6
Garcia, Damaso	Damaso Domingo (Sanchez); B2.7.1955 Moca, D.R.; BR/TR/6´0˝/(155–185); d6.24; [DL 1987 Atl N 148]																								
1978	NY A	18	41	5	8	0	0	0	1	2-0	0	6	.195	.227	.195	22	-4	1-0	.959	-1	88	129	2b16,S3	0	-0.5
1979	NY A	11	38	3	10	1	0	0	4	0-0	0	2	.263	.263	.289	50	-3	2-0	.902	-4	90	65	S10/3	0	-0.5
1980	Tor A	140	543	50	151	30	7	4	46	12-2	3	55	.278	.296	.381	81	-15	13-13	.980	7	105	104	2b138/D	0	-0.3
1981	Tor A	64	250	24	63	8	1	1	13	9-1	0	32	.252	.277	.304	64	-12	13-3	.972	-19	85	68	2b62/D	44	-2.8
1982	Tor A	147	597	89	185	32	3	5	42	21-1	5	44	.310	.338	.399	93	-5	54-20	.980	6	105	100	2b141,D4	0	1.3
1983	Tor A	131	525	84	161	23	6	3	38	24-3	2	34	.307	.336	.390	94	-5	31-17	.981	-14	90	85	2b130	0	-1.1
1984	Tor A★	152	633	79	180	32	5	5	46	16-1	9	46	.284	.310	.374	85	-13	46-12	.980	-16	92	102	2b149/D	0	-1.5
1985	†Tor A★	146	600	70	169	25	4	8	65	15-2	4	41	.282	.302	.377	83	-16	28-15	.981	-15	89	105	2b143	0	-2.3
1986	Tor A	122	424	57	119	22	0	6	46	13-0	4	32	.281	.306	.375	83	-11	9-6	.985	-0	97	104	2b106,D11/1	0	-0.6
1988	Atl N	21	60	3	7	1	0	1	4	3-0	0	10	.117	.159	.183	-2	-8	1-0	.984	-3	91	59	2b13	0	-1.2
1989	Mon N	80	203	26	55	9	1	3	18	15-1	0	20	.271	.317	.369	95	-1	5-4	.972	7	113	97	2b62/3	19	0.7
Total	11	1032	3914	490	1108	183	27	36	323	130-11	27	322	.283	.309	.371	83	-93	203-90	.980	-54	96	97	2b960,D18,S13,3b2/1	211	-8.8
Garcia, Daniel	Daniel Joseph; B4.12.1980 Riverside CA; BR/TR/6´0˝/(175–180); [NYN01 5/162]; d9.2; Col Pepperdine																								
2003	NY N	19	56	5	12	2	0	2	6	2-0	3	11	.214	.274	.357	67	-3	0-0	.950	-2	96	83	2b17/lf	0	-0.4
2004	NY N	58	138	23	32	7	1	3	17	22-2	9	34	.232	.371	.362	93	0	3-0	.969	-7	86	75	2b44	0	-0.4
Total	2	77	194	28	44	9	1	5	23	24-2	12	45	.227	.345	.361	87	-3	3-0	.964	-9	89	77	2b61/lf	0	-0.8
Garcia, Danny	Daniel Raphael; B4.29.1954 Brooklyn NY; BL/TL/6´1˝/182; [KCA75 11/249]; d4.26; Col Baruch																								
1981	KC A	12	14	4	2	0	0	0	0	0-0	0	2	.143	.143	.143	-17	-2	0-0	1.000	-1	70	0	O6(1/0/5),1b2	0	-0.3
Garcia, Freddy	Freddy Adrian (Felix); B8.1.1972 LaRomana, D.R.; BR/TR/6´2˝/(190–224); d5.2; [DL 2000 Sea A 75]																								
1995	Pit N	42	57	5	8	1	1	0	1	8-0	0	17	.140	.246	.193	17	-7	0-1	1.000	3	97	0	O10L,3b8	0	-0.4
1997	Pit N	20	40	4	6	1	0	3	5	2-0	0	17	.150	.190	.400	49	-3	0-0	.842	-3	60	70	3b10,1b2	0	-0.6
1998	Pit N	56	172	27	44	11	1	9	26	18-3	2	45	.256	.332	.488	112	3	0-2	.949	5	116	113	3b47,1b4	0	0.7
1999	Pit N	55	130	16	30	5	0	6	23	4-0	0	41	.231	.252	.408	63	-8	0-0	.977	-0	113	0	O24(17/0/7),3b9,D2	0	-0.9
	Atl N	2	2	1	1	0	0	1	1	1-0	0	1	.500	.667	2.000	544	1	0-0	ø	-0	0	0	/1lf	0	0.1
	Year	57	132	17	31	5	0	7	24	5-0	0	42	.235	.261	.432	71	-7	0-0	.977	-1	110	0	O25(18/0/7),3b9,D2/1	0	-0.8
Total	4	175	401	53	89	18	2	19	56	33-3	2	121	.222	.283	.419	79	-14	0-3	.938	5	112	132	3b74,O35(28/0/7),1b7,D2	75	-1.1
Garcia, Guillermo	Guillermo Antonio (Morel); B4.4.1972 Santiago, D.R.; BR/TR/6´3˝/215; d7.19																								
1998	Cin N	12	36	3	7	2	0	2	4	2-0	0	13	.194	.237	.417	67	-2	0-0	.988	2	65	258	C11	0	0.1
1999	Fla N	4	4	0	1	0	0	0	0	0-0	0	2	.250	.250	.250	29	0	0-0	1.000	0	0	0	C3	0	0.0
Total	2	16	40	3	8	2	0	2	4	2-0	0	15	.200	.238	.400	63	-2	0-0	.988	2	62	246	C14	0	0.1
Garcia, Karim	Gustavo Karim; B10.29.1975 Ciudad Obregon, Sonora, Mexico; BL/TL/6´0˝/(172–210); d9.2																								
1995	LA N	13	20	1	4	0	0	0	0	0-0	0	4	.200	.200	.200	6	-3	0-0	1.000	2	92	1007	O5(2/0/3)	0	-0.1
1996	LA N	1	1	0	0	0	0	0	0	0-0	0	1	.000	.000	.000	-99	0	0-0	ø	0	—	—	/H	0	0.0
1997	LA N	15	39	5	5	0	0	1	8	6-1	0	14	.128	.239	.205	21	-5	0-0	1.000	-1	72	0	O12(12/0/2)	10	-0.6
1998	Ari N	113	333	39	74	10	8	9	43	18-1	0	78	.222	.260	.381	66	-19	5-4	.975	3	109	98	O103(0/7/100)	0	-2.0
1999	Det A	96	288	38	69	10	3	14	32	20-1	0	67	.240	.288	.441	81	-10	2-4	.958	2	102	137	O81(35/0/55),D6	0	-1.2
2000	Det A	8	17	1	3	0	0	0	0	0-0	0	4	.176	.176	.176	-10	-3	0-0	1.000	-1	74	0	O7R/D	0	-0.4
	Bal A	8	16	0	0	0	0	0	0	0-0	0	6	.000	.000	.000	-99	-5	0-0	1.000	0	208	0	O2L,D4	0	-0.5
	Year	16	33	1	3	0	0	0	0	0-0	0	10	.091	.091	.091	-55	-8	0-0	1.000	-1	85	0	O9(2/0/7),D5	0	-0.9
2001	Cle A	20	45	8	14	3	0	5	9	3-0	1	13	.311	.360	.711	168	4	0-0	.905	0	59	485	O18(6/0/13),1b2	0	0.3
2002	NY A	2	5	1	1	0	0	0	0	0-0	0	1	.200	.200	.200	7	-1	0-0	1.000	-0	44	0	O2(1/0/1)	0	-0.1
	Cle A	51	197	29	59	8	0	16	52	6-0	0	40	.299	.317	.584	131	7	0-3	.990	-1	99	66	O51(1/3/48)	0	0.3
	Year	53	202	30	60	8	0	16	52	6-0	0	41	.297	.314	.574	128	7	0-3	.990	-1	98	65	O53(2/3/49)	0	0.2
2003	Cle A	24	93	8	18	1	0	5	14	5-1	1	20	.194	.238	.366	58	-6	0-0	.905	-3	71	158	O23(0/7/17)/D	46	-1.0
	†NY A	52	151	17	46	5	0	6	21	9-1	0	32	.305	.342	.457	110	2	0-2	.981	4	112	202	O50(13/3/37)/D	0	0.3
	Year	76	244	25	64	6	0	11	35	14-2	1	52	.262	.302	.422	90	-5	0-2	.959	1	98	187	O73(13/10/54),D2	0	-0.7
2004	NY N	62	192	24	45	7	2	7	22	10-0	0	35	.234	.272	.401	73	-9	3-0	.968	-2	101	0	O51R	15	-1.3
	Bal A	23	66	9	14	0	0	3	11	4-1	0	15	.212	.247	.348	56	-5	0-0	1.000	-2	84	0	O19(0/15/7)/1	0	-0.6
Total	10	488	1463	180	352	44	13	66	212	81-6	2	330	.241	.279	.424	81	-53	10-13	.970	-0	99	118	O424(72/35/341),D13,1b3	71	-6.9
Garcia, Jesse	Jesus Jesse; B9.24.1973 Corpus Christi TX; BR/TR/5´10˝/(170–171); [BalA93 26/735]; d4.5																								
1999	Bal A	17	29	6	6	0	0	2	2	2-0	0	3	.207	.258	.414	70	-2	0-0	1.000	-1	96	156	S7,2b6,3b2/D	0	-0.2
2000	Bal A	14	17	2	1	0	0	0	0	2-0	0	2	.059	.158	.059	-44	-4	0-0	1.000	2	162	114	2b6,S5	0	-0.1
2001	Atl N	22	5	3	1	0	0	0	0	0-0	0	1	.200	.200	.200	4	-1	6-2	1.000	-0	82	192	2b4,S2	0	0.0
2002	Atl N	39	61	6	12	1	0	0	5	0-0	0	14	.197	.197	.213	8	-8	0-1	.986	5	118	123	2b21,S5,O4(2/0/2)	0	-0.3
2003	†Atl N	13	10	6	4	0	1	0	2	0-0	0	1	.400	.400	.600	157	1	0-1	1.000	-0	95	100	2b6,S3,3b2	0	0.0
2004	Atl N	50	115	14	29	4	1	1	10	1-0	1	16	.252	.265	.330	52	-9	1-2	.963	4	115	104	S25,2b11,3b3	0	-0.3
2005	SD N	16	36	4	6	0	0	2	4	3-1	0	11	.167	.231	.333	48	-3	0-0	1.000	-2	72	68	S13,2b2	0	-0.5
Total	7	171	273	41	59	5	2	5	23	8-1	1	48	.216	.241	.304	41	-26	7-6	.978	6	100	113	S60,2b56,3b7,O4(2/0/2)/D	0	-1.4
Garcia, Leo	Leonardo Antonio (Peralta); B11.6.1962 Santiago, D.R.; BL/TL/5´8˝/165; d4.6																								
1987	Cin N	31	30	8	6	0	0	1	2	4-0	0	8	.200	.286	.300	56	-2	3-1	1.000	0	121	0	O14(0/13/1)	0	-0.1
1988	Cin N	23	28	2	4	1	0	0	0	4-1	0	5	.143	.250	.179	24	-3	0-1	1.000	0	103	0	O9(2/4/3)	0	-0.3
Total	2	54	58	10	10	1	0	1	2	8-1	0	13	.172	.269	.241	41	-5	3-2	1.000	0	113	0	O23(2/17/4)	0	-0.4
Garcia, Luis	Luis Carlos; B9.22.1975 Hermosillo, Sonora, Mexico; BR/TR/6´3˝/200; [ChiA94 19/537]; d4.10																								
2002	Bal A	6	3	0	1	0	0	0	0	0-0	0	1	.333	.333	.333	82	0	0-0	1.000	0	132	0	O2(0/1/1)	0	0.0
Garcia, Luis	Luis Rafael; B5.20.1975 San Francisco de Macoris, D.R.; BR/TR/6´0˝/175; d4.5																								
1999	Det A	8	9	0	1	1	0	0	0	0-0	0	2	.111	.111	.222	-18	-2	0-0	1.000	-2	37	0	S7/2	0	-0.3
Garcia, Pedro	Pedro Modesto (Delfi); B4.17.1950 Guayama, PR; BR/TR/5´10˝/175; d4.6																								
1973	Mil A	160	580	67	142	**32**	5	15	54	40-4	5	119	.245	.296	.395	95	-5	11-10	.970	-21	96	91	2b160	0	-1.7
1974	Mil A	141	452	46	90	15	4	12	54	26-4	5	67	.199	.248	.330	66	-22	8-5	.970	-9	96	101	2b140	0	-2.3
1975	Mil A	98	302	40	68	15	2	6	38	18-1	2	59	.225	.271	.348	74	-11	12-6	.985	10	109	99	2b94/D	23	0.6
1976	Mil A	41	106	12	23	7	1	1	9	4-0	2	23	.217	.257	.330	73	-4	2-2	.971	-3	96	113	2b39	0	-0.5
	Det A	77	227	21	45	10	2	3	20	9-0	4	40	.198	.239	.300	56	-13	2-3	.958	8	108	110	2b77	0	-0.2

YEAR	TM LG	G	AB	R	H	2B	3B	HR	RBI	BB-IB	HP	SO	AVG	OBP	SLG	AOPS	ABR	SB-CS	FA	FR	RNG	THR	GAMES AT POSITION	DL	BFW
	Year	118	333	33	68	17	3	4	29	13-0	6	63	.204	.244	.309	61	-17	4-5	.962	5	104	111	2b116	0	-0.7
1977	Tor A	41	130	10	27	10	1	0	9	5-0	3	21	.208	.254	.300	50	-9	0-0	.971	-3	94	91	2b34,D4	0	-1.0
Total	5	558	1797	196	395	89	15	37	184	102-9	21	329	.220	.267	.348	75	-64	35-26	.971	-18	100	99	2b544,D5	23	-5.1
GARCIA, CHICO	Vinicio Uzcanga; B12.24.1924 Veracruz, Veracruz, Mexico; BR/TR/5´8˝/170; d4.24																								
1954	Bal A	39	62	6	7	0	2	0	5	8	0	3	.113	.211	.177	9	-8	0-0	.962	2	93	115	2b24	0	-0.5
GARCIAPARRA, NOMAR	Anthony Nomar; B7.23.1973 Whittier CA; BR/TR/6´0˝/(167–190); [BosA94 1/12]; d8.31; Col Georgia Tech																								
1996	Bos A	24	87	11	21	2	3	4	16	4-0	0	14	.241	.272	.471	82	-3	5-0	.988	-4	80	69	S22/2D	0	-0.4
1997	Bos A★	153	684	122	**209**	44	**11**	30	98	35-2	6	92	.306	.342	.534	122	19	22-9	.971	3	103	106	S153	0	3.4
1998	†Bos A	143	604	111	195	37	8	35	122	33-1	8	62	.323	.362	.584	139	32	12-6	.962	-11	96	80	S143	19	3.0
1999	†Bos A★	135	532	103	190	42	4	27	104	51-7	8	39	**.357**	.418	.603	152	43	14-3	.972	-4	92	87	S134	0	4.7
2000	Bos A★	140	529	104	197	51	3	21	96	61-**20**	2	50	**.372**	.434	.599	155	47	5-2	.971	-3	100	77	S136/D	14	5.0
2001	Bos A	21	83	13	24	3	0	4	8	7-0	1	9	.289	.352	.470	114	2	0-1	.968	1	98	100	S21	161	0.4
2002	Bos A★	156	635	101	197	**56**	5	24	120	41-4	6	63	.310	.352	.528	129	26	5-2	.965	19	109	103	S154	0	5.4
2003	†Bos A★	156	658	120	198	37	13	28	105	39-1	11	61	.301	.345	.524	121	18	19-5	.971	7	**106**	82	S156	0	3.7
2004	Bos A	38	156	24	50	7	3	5	21	8-2	4	16	.321	.367	.500	116	3	2-0	.957	-8	82	79	S37/D	66	-0.1
	Chi N	43	165	28	49	14	0	4	20	16-0	2	14	.297	.364	.455	107	2	2-1	.982	-5	79	70	S42	0	0.0
2005	Chi N	62	230	28	65	12	0	9	30	12-0	2	24	.283	.320	.452	97	-1	0-0	.934	-4	100	16	3b34,S26	106	-0.4
2006	†LA N☆	122	469	82	142	31	2	20	93	42-9	8	30	.303	.367	.505	121	15	3-0	.996	-5	84	118	1b118	29	0.1
Total	11	1193	4832	847	1537	336	52	211	833	349-46	58	474	.318	.367	.540	129	203	89-29	.968	-13	99	89	S1024,1b118,3b34,D3/2	395	24.8
GARDELLA, AL	Alfred Stephan; B1.11.1918 New York NY; D9.10.2006 Coral Springs FL; BL/TL/5´10˝/172; d5.17; b–Danny																								
1945	NY N	16	26	2	2	0	0	0	1	4	1	3	.077	.226	.077	-14	-4	0	.961	-1	82	39	1b9/cf	0	-0.5
GARDELLA, DANNY	Daniel Lewis; B2.26.1920 New York NY; D3.6.2005 Yonkers NY; BL/TL/5´7.5˝/160; d5.14; b–Al																								
1944	NY N	47	112	20	28	2	2	6	14	11	1	13	.250	.323	.464	120	2	0	.912	1	101	167	O25(11/4/10)	0	0.1
1945	NY N	121	430	54	117	10	1	18	71	46	5	55	.272	.349	.426	113	7	2	.954	-4	89	87	O94(85/0/9),1b15	0	-0.3
1950	StL N	1	1	0	0	0	0	0	0	0	0	0	.000	.000	.000	-95	0	0	ø	0	—	—	/H	0	0.0
Total	3	169	543	74	145	12	3	24	85	57	6	68	.267	.343	.433	114	9	2	.943	-3	92	105	O119(96/4/19),1b15	0	-0.2
GARDENHIRE, RON	Ronald Clyde; B10.24.1957 Butzbach, West Germany; BR/TR/6´0˝/(174–175); [NYN79 6/132]; d9.1; M5/C11; Col Texas																								
1981	NY N	27	48	2	13	1	0	0	3	5-2	0	9	.271	.340	.292	81	-1	2-2	.969	0	99	84	S18,2b6/3	0	0.1
1982	NY N	141	384	29	92	17	1	3	33	23-2	0	55	.240	.279	.313	66	-18	5-6	.956	7	105	92	S135/23	0	0.0
1983	NY N	17	32	1	2	0	0	0	1	1-0	0	4	.063	.091	.063	-57	-7	0-0	1.000	-1	101	66	S15	0	-0.8
1984	NY N	74	207	20	51	7	1	1	10	9-1	0	43	.246	.276	.304	64	-10	6-1	.947	-1	88	67	S49,2b18,3b7	41	-0.6
1985	NY N	26	39	5	7	2	1	0	2	8-0	0	11	.179	.319	.282	71	-1	0-0	.911	-1	110	71	S13,2b5,3b2	86	-0.1
Total	5	285	710	57	165	27	3	4	49	46-5	0	122	.232	.277	.296	61	-37	13-9	.955	4	101	84	S230,2b30,3b11	127	-1.4
GARDNER, ALEX	Alexander; B4.28.1861 Toronto ON, Can.; D6.18.1926 Danvers MA; BR; d5.10																								
1884	Was AA	1	3	0	0	0	0	0	—	0	0	—	.000	.000	.000	-99	-1	—	.600	-2	—	—	/C	—	-0.2
GARDNER, ART	Arthur Junior; B9.21.1952 Madden MS; BL/TL/5´11˝/(165–180); [HouN71 2/36]; d9.2																								
1975	Hou N	13	31	3	6	0	0	0	2	1-1	1	8	.194	.242	.194	24	-3	1-0	1.000	-0	98	0	O8(3/1/4)	0	-0.4
1977	Hou N	66	65	7	10	0	0	0	3	3-1	1	15	.154	.203	.154	-3	-10	0-0	1.000	1	102	110	O26(14/9/4)	0	-1.0
1978	SF N	7	3	2	0	0	0	0	0	0-0	0	2	.000	.000	.000	-99	-1	0-1	ø	0	—	—	/H	0	-0.1
Total	3	86	99	12	16	0	0	0	5	4-2	2	25	.162	.210	.162	2	-14	1-1	1.000	1	101	72	O34(17/10/8)	0	-1.5
GARDNER, EARLE	Earle McClurkin; B1.24.1884 Sparta IL; D3.2.1943 Sparta IL; BR/TR/5´11˝/160; d9.18																								
1908	NY A	20	75	7	16	2	0	0	4	1	1	—	.213	.234	.240	53	-4	0	.947	1	96	184	2b20	—	-0.3
1909	NY A	22	85	12	28	4	0	0	15	3	0	—	.329	.352	.376	129	3	4	.945	-6	85	39	2b22	—	-0.4
1910	NY A	86	271	36	66	4	2	1	24	21	2	—	.244	.303	.284	79	-7	9	.936	0	97	145	2b70	—	-0.6
1911	NY A	102	357	36	94	13	2	0	39	20	5	—	.263	.312	.311	69	-15	14	.959	3	105	134	2b101	—	-1.1
1912	NY A	43	160	14	45	3	1	0	26	5	0	—	.281	.303	.313	72	-6	11	.922	-7	90	70	2b43	—	-1.3
Total	5	273	948	105	249	26	5	1	108	50	8	—	.263	.305	.304	76	-29	38	.944	-8	98	122	2b256	—	-3.7
GARDNER, GID	Franklin Washington; B5.6.1859 Boston MA; D8.1.1914 Cambridge MA; ?/165; d8.23; OF(16/36/69); ▲																								
1879	Tro N	2	6	1	1	0	0	0	0	0	—	0	.167	.167	.167	11	0	—	.429	-1	68	0	P2	—	0.0
1880	Cle N	10	32	0	6	1	1	0	4	2	—	4	.188	.235	.281	76	-1	—	.850	-0	111	0	P9/cf	—	0.0
1883	Bal AA	42	161	28	44	10	3	1	—	18	—	—	.273	.346	.391	133	7	—	.837	-3	72	0	O35C,2b4,3b3,P2	—	0.2
1884	Bal AA	41	173	32	37	6	8	2	—	14	2	—	.214	.280	.376	108	1	—	.860	0	131	0	O40(1/0/39),1b2	—	0.1
	CP U	38	149	22	38	10	2	0	—	10	—	—	.255	.302	.349	98	-4	—	.872	-1	28	0	O29(15/0/14),3b8/P2	—	-0.6
	Bal U	1	4	0	1	0	0	0	—	0	—	—	.250	.250	.250	47	0	—	.714	-0	55	476	/S	—	-0.1
	Year	39	153	22	39	10	2	0	—	10	—	—	.255	.301	.346	96	-5	—	.872	-2	28	0	O29(15/0/14),3b8/P2S	—	-0.7
1885	Bal AA	44	170	22	37	5	4	0	17	12	0	—	.218	.269	.294	79	-4	—	.891	-1	105	85	2b39,O5R/1P	—	-0.3
1887	Ind N	18	63	8	11	1	0	1	8	12	0	11	.175	.307	.238	55	-3	7	1.000	-2	67	0	O11R,2b7	—	-0.4
1888	Was N	1	3	0	1	0	0	0	0	1	0	1	.333	.500	.333	182	0	0	.750	0	107	263	/S	—	0.0
	Phi N	1	3	0	2	0	0	0	1	0	0	0	.667	.667	.667	309	1	0	1.000	-0	45	0	/2	—	0.0
	Was N	1	1	0	0	0	0	0	0	0	0	0	.000	.000	.000	-99	0	0	1.000	-0	0	0	/2	—	-0.1
	Year	3	7	0	3	0	0	0	1	1	0	1	.429	.500	.429	204	1	0	1.000	-1	27	0	2b2/S	—	-0.1
Total	7	199	765	113	178	33	18	4	30	69	2	16	.233	.298	.339	99	-3	7	.855	-8	85	0	O121R,2b53,P15,3b11,1b3,S2	—	-1.2
GARDNER, JEFF	Jeffrey Scott; B2.4.1964 Newport Beach CA; BL/TR/5´11˝/(165–175); d9.10																								
1991	NY N	13	37	3	6	0	0	0	1	4-0	0	6	.162	.238	.162	16	-4	0-0	.818	-3	91	55	S8,2b3	0	-0.7
1992	SD N	15	19	0	2	0	0	0	0	1-0	0	8	.105	.150	.105	-26	-3	0-0	1.000	2	136	100	2b11	0	-0.1
1993	SD N	140	404	53	106	21	7	1	24	45-0	1	69	.262	.337	.356	85	-8	2-6	.983	-11	92	73	2b133/3S	0	-1.5
1994	Mon N	18	32	4	7	0	1	0	1	3-0	0	5	.219	.286	.281	48	-3	0-0	.714	-5	22	0	3b9,2b4	0	-0.7
Total	4	186	492	60	121	21	8	1	26	53-0	1	88	.246	.319	.327	74	-18	2-6	.984	-16	94	73	2b151,3b10,S9	0	-3.0
GARDNER, RAY	Raymond Vincent; B10.25.1901 Frederick MD; D5.3.1968 Frederick MD; BR/TR/5´8˝/145; d4.16																								
1929	Cle A	82	256	28	67	3	2	1	24	29	0	16	.262	.337	.301	63	-14	10-13	.952	11	108	107	S82	—	0.3
1930	Cle A	33	13	7	1	0	0	0	1	0	0	0	.077	.077	.077	-59	-3	0-1	.861	3	165	39	S22,2b5/3	—	0.0
Total	2	115	269	35	68	3	2	1	25	29	0	16	.253	.326	.290	57	-17	10-14	.945	15	111	104	S104,2b5/3	—	0.3
GARDNER, BILLY	William Frederick "Shotgun"; B7.19.1927 Waterford CT; BR/TR/6´0˝/(170–180); d4.22; M6/C5																								
1954	NY N	62	108	10	23	5	0	1	7	6	1	19	.213	.261	.287	42	-9	0-1	.987	5	127	52	3b30,2b13,S5	0	-0.4
1955	NY N	59	187	26	38	10	1	3	17	13-0	2	19	.203	.261	.316	52	-13	0-0	.940	-2	102	109	S38,3b10,2b4	0	-1.2
1956	Bal A	144	515	53	119	16	2	11	50	29-1	7	53	.231	.281	.334	67	-28	5-5	.974	-10	**99**	84	2b132,S25,3b6	0	-2.8
1957	Bal A	**154**	644	79	169	**36**	3	6	55	53-2	8	67	.262	.325	.356	92	-7	10-7	**.987**	7	105	92	2b148,S9	0	1.2
1958	Bal A	151	560	32	126	28	2	3	33	34-4	3	53	.225	.271	.298	60	-31	2-3	.985	-19	91	106	2b151,S13	0	-4.1
1959	Bal A	140	401	34	87	13	2	6	27	38-9	1	61	.217	.284	.304	64	-20	2-1	.976	**22**	**112**	**126**	2b139/S3	0	1.1
1960	Was A	145	592	71	152	26	5	9	56	43-0	6	76	.257	.313	.363	83	-15	0-4	.973	-1	104	92	2b145,S13	0	-0.7
1961	Min A	45	154	13	36	9	0	1	11	10-1	0	14	.234	.280	.312	55	-10	0-0	.973	-7	89	110	2b41,3b2	0	-1.4
	†NY A	41	99	11	21	5	0	1	2	6-0	3	18	.212	.278	.293	56	-6	0-0	.952	1	105	136	3b33,2b6	0	-0.5
	Year	86	253	24	57	14	0	2	13	16-1	3	32	.225	.279	.304	56	-16	0-0	.975	-6	88	108	2b47,3b35	0	-1.9
1962	NY A	4	1	1	0	0	0	0	0	0-0	0	1	.000	.000	.000	-99	0	0-0	1.000	1	0	0	/23	0	0.0
	Bos A	53	199	22	54	9	2	0	12	10-0	1	39	.271	.310	.337	72	-8	0-1	.963	-6	86	83	2b38,3b7,S4	0	-1.1
	Year	57	200	23	54	9	2	0	12	10-0	1	40	.270	.308	.335	71	-8	0-1	.963	-5	85	82	2b39,3b8,S4	0	-1.1
1963	Bos A	36	84	4	16	2	1	0	1	4-1	1	19	.190	.236	.238	32	-8	0-0	.989	3	104	113	2b21,3b2	0	-0.3
Total	10	1034	3544	356	841	159	18	41	271	246-18	33	439	.237	.292	.327	70	-155	19-22	.978	-6	100	99	2b839,S108,3b92	0	-10.2
GARDNER, LARRY	William Lawrence; B5.13.1886 Enosburg Falls VT; D3.11.1976 St.George VT; BL/TR/5´8˝/165; d6.25; Col Vermont																								
1908	Bos A	3	10	0	3	1	0	0	1	0	0	—	.300	.300	.400	124	0	0	.571	-2	44	0	3b3	—	-0.2
1909	Bos A	19	37	7	11	1	2	0	5	4	1	—	.297	.381	.432	153	2	1	.800	-3	94	0	3b8,S5	—	0.0
1910	Bos A	113	413	56	117	12	10	2	36	41	4	—	.283	.354	.375	125	12	8	.944	-9	101	73	2b113	—	0.4
1911	Bos A	138	492	80	140	17	8	4	44	64	5	—	.285	.373	.376	110	9	27	.962	23	113	31	3b72,2b62	—	3.3

YEAR	TM LG	G	AB	R	H	2B	3B	HR	RBI	BB-IB	HP	SO	AVG	OBP	SLG	AOPS	ABR	SB-CS	FA	FR	RNG	THR	GAMES AT POSITION	DL	BFW
1912	†Bos A	143	517	88	163	24	18	3	86	56	1	—	.315	.383	.449	131	20	25	.930	-1	99	88	3b143	—	2.2
1913	Bos A	131	473	64	133	17	10	0	63	47	1	34	.281	.347	.359	104	2	18	.943	-15	89	72	3b130	—	-0.9
1914	Bos A	155	553	50	143	23	19	3	68	35	0	39	.259	.303	.385	107	0	16-23	.942	-1	103	96	3b153	—	-0.1
1915	†Bos A	127	430	51	111	14	6	1	55	39	5	24	.258	.327	.326	98	-1	11-12	.933	-7	96	91	3b127	—	-0.7
1916	†Bos A	148	493	47	152	19	7	2	62	48	2	27	.308	.372	.387	128	17	12	.953	-12	93	97	3b147	—	0.9
1917	Bos A	146	501	53	133	23	7	1	61	54	3	37	.265	.341	.345	110	7	16	.937	-7	101	91	3b146	—	0.5
1918	Phi A	127	463	50	132	22	6	1	52	43	0	22	.285	.346	.365	113	7	9	.964	13	**110**	126	3b127	—	2.6
1919	Cle A	**139**	524	67	157	29	7	2	79	39	3	29	.300	.352	.393	103	2	7	.946	-5	101	106	3b139	—	0.1
1920	†Cle A	**154**	597	72	185	31	11	3	118	53	1	25	.310	.367	.414	103	3	3-20	**.976**	-1	101	**133**	3b154	—	0.0
1921	Cle A	153	586	101	187	32	14	3	120	65	4	16	.319	.391	.437	109	9	3-3	.950	1	101	84	3b152	—	1.8
1922	Cle A	137	470	74	134	31	3	2	68	49	2	21	.285	.355	.377	90	-5	9-8	.951	-6	96	96	3b128	—	-0.4
1923	Cle A	52	79	4	20	5	1	0	12	12	0	7	.253	.352	.342	83	-2	0-1	.962	3	135	79	3b19	—	0.2
1924	Cle A	38	50	3	10	0	0	0	4	5	0	1	.200	.273	.200	23	-6	0-1	.875	-2	127	248	3b8,2b6	—	-0.8
Total	17	1923	6688	867	1931	301	129	27	934	654	32	282	.289	.355	.384	109	76	165-68	.948	-31	100	95	3b1656,2b181,S5	—	8.9
GARIBALDI, ART	Arthur Edward; B8.21.1907 San Francisco CA; D10.19.1967 Sacramento CA; BR/TR/5´8˝/165; d6.20																								
1936	StL N	71	232	30	64	12	0	1	20	16	0	30	.276	.323	.341	79	-7	3	.925	-7	83	42	3b46,2b24	—	-1.0
GARKO, RYAN	Ryan F.; B1.2.1981 Pittsburgh PA; BR/TR/6´2˝/225; [CleA03 3/78]; d9.18; Col Stanford																								
2005	Cle A	1	1	0	0	0	0	0	0	0-0	0	1	.000	.000	.000	-99	0	0-0	ø	0	—	—	/D	0	0.0
2006	Cle A	50	185	28	54	12	0	7	45	14-0	7	37	.292	.359	.470	119	5	0-0	.986	1	116	123	1b45,D2	0	0.2
Total	2	51	186	28	54	12	0	7	45	14-0	7	38	.290	.357	.468	117	5	0-0	.986	1	116	123	1b45,D3	0	0.2
GARMS, DEBS	Debs C. "Tex"; B6.26.1907 Bangs TX; D12.16.1984 Glen Rose TX; BL/TR/5´8.5˝/165; d8.10; Col Howard Payne																								
1932	StL A	34	134	20	38	7	1	1	8	17	0	7	.284	.364	.373	86	-2	4-3	.953	-1	92	114	O33(0/32/1)	—	-0.4
1933	StL A	78	189	35	60	10	2	4	24	30	2	21	.317	.416	.455	123	8	2-5	.960	-0	93	131	O47(28/17/3)	—	0.4
1934	StL A	91	232	25	68	14	4	0	31	27	2	19	.293	.372	.388	89	-3	0-0	.942	-3	99	44	O56(42/1/13)	—	-0.9
1935	StL A	10	15	1	4	0	0	0	0	2	0	2	.267	.353	.267	59	-1	0-0	.800	-0	90	0	O2R	—	-0.1
1937	Bos N	125	478	60	124	15	8	2	37	37	3	33	.259	.317	.337	85	-11	2	.977	-6	99	17	O81(64/15/2),3b36	—	-2.0
1938	Bos N	117	428	62	135	19	1	0	47	34	4	22	.315	.371	.364	114	10	4	.985	-3	91	114	O63(51/2/12),3b54/2	—	0.5
1939	Bos N	132	513	68	153	24	9	2	37	39	2	20	.298	.350	.392	107	4	2	.964	1	96	75	O96(25/0/73),3b37	—	0.1
1940	Pit N	103	358	76	127	23	7	5	57	23	1	6	**.355**	.395	.500	147	22	3	.964	3	104	144	3b64,O19(8/4/8)	—	2.6
1941	Pit N	83	220	25	58	9	3	3	42	22	0	12	.264	.331	.373	98	-1	0	.911	-6	86	22	3b29,O24(23/0/1)	0	-0.8
1943	†StL N	90	249	26	64	10	2	0	22	13	2	8	.257	.299	.313	74	-9	1	.980	-4	106	69	O47(18/0/29),3b23/S	0	-1.6
1944	†StL N	73	149	17	30	3	0	0	5	13	0	8	.201	.265	.221	37	-12	0	1.000	-4	96	0	O23(3/2/18),3b21	0	-1.8
1945	StL N	74	146	23	49	7	2	0	18	31	0	3	.336	.452	.411	137	10	0	.956	-4	83	96	3b32,O10(1/0/9)	0	0.6
Total	12	1010	3111	438	910	141	39	17	328	288	16	161	.293	.355	.379	103	15	18-8	.966	-28	96	75	O501(263/73/171),3b296/S2	0	-3.4
GARNER, PHIL	Philip Mason; B4.30.1949 Jefferson City TN; BR/TR/5´10˝/(175–180); [OakA71*A1/3]; d9.10; M14/C3; Col Tennessee																								
1973	Oak A	9	5	0	0	0	0	0	0	0-0	0	3	.000	.000	.000	-99	-1	0-0	1.000	-1	45	198	3b9	0	-0.3
1974	Oak A	30	28	4	5	1	0	0	1	1-0	0	5	.179	.207	.214	23	-3	1-1	.955	-2	83	65	3b19,S8,2b3,D2	0	-0.5
1975	†Oak A	160	488	46	120	21	5	6	54	30-1	5	65	.246	.295	.346	83	-12	4-6	.968	-2	102	98	2b160/S	0	-0.6
1976	Oak A★	159	555	54	145	29	12	8	74	36-1	2	71	.261	.307	.400	111	5	35-13	.975	-10	98	92	2b159	0	0.9
1977	Pit N	153	585	99	152	35	10	17	77	55-4	2	65	.260	.325	.441	100	-1	32-9	.971	-3	103	185	3b107,2b50,S12	0	0.1
1978	Pit N	154	528	66	138	25	9	10	66	66-12	5	71	.261	.345	.400	103	3	27-14	.976	7	98	110	2b81,3b81,S4	0	1.5
1979	†Pit N	150	549	76	161	32	8	11	59	55-15	3	74	.293	.359	.441	111	9	17-8	.981	1	102	122	2b83,3b78,S14	0	1.6
1980	Pit N★	151	548	62	142	27	6	5	58	46-12	2	53	.259	.315	.358	85	-10	32-7	.976	16	106	124	2b151/S	0	1.9
1981	Pit N★	56	181	22	46	6	2	1	20	21-1	0	21	.254	.327	.326	83	-4	4-6	.968	-8	89	94	2b50	15	-1.1
	†Hou N	31	113	13	27	3	1	0	6	15-1	0	11	.239	.326	.283	79	-3	6-2	.982	4	108	104	2b31	0	0.4
	Year	87	294	35	73	9	3	1	26	36-2	0	32	.248	.326	.310	81	-6	10-8	.973	-4	96	98	2b81	0	-0.7
1982	Hou N	155	588	65	161	33	8	13	83	40-4	3	92	.274	.320	.423	116	10	24-13	.980	1	98	112	2b136,3b18	0	2.1
1983	Hou N	154	567	76	135	24	2	14	79	63-8	5	84	.238	.317	.362	94	-5	18-12	.945	3	106	93	3b154	0	-0.5
1984	Hou N	128	374	60	104	17	6	4	45	43-2	4	63	.278	.355	.388	117	9	3-2	.979	19	115	140	3b82,2b35	0	3.0
1985	Hou N	135	463	65	124	23	10	6	51	34-3	2	72	.268	.317	.400	103	0	4-4	.932	-10	90	74	3b123,2b15	0	-1.2
1986	†Hou N	107	313	43	83	14	3	9	41	30-2	1	45	.265	.329	.415	108	3	12-6	.896	-1	97	120	3b84,2b7	0	0.2
1987	Hou N	43	112	15	25	5	0	3	15	8-1	0	20	.223	.268	.348	66	-6	1-0	.976	1	92	63	3b36,2b2	0	-0.5
	LA N	70	126	14	24	4	0	2	8	20-7	0	24	.190	.299	.270	54	-8	5-1	.923	3	109	95	3b46,2b12,S2	0	-0.4
	Year	113	238	29	49	9	0	5	23	28-8	0	44	.206	.285	.307	60	-14	6-1	.947	4	101	79	3b82,2b14,S2	0	-0.9
1988	SF N	15	13	0	2	0	0	0	1	1-0	0	3	.154	.214	.154	8	-2	0-1	ø	-0	0	0	3b2	142	-0.3
Total	16	1860	6136	780	1594	299	82	109	738	564-74	34	842	.260	.323	.389	99	-16	225-105	.974	17	99	107	2b975,3b839,S42,D2	157	6.3
GARR, RALPH	Ralph Allen "Road Runner"; B12.12.1945 Monroe LA; BL/TR/5´11˝/(185–197); [AtlN67 3/52]; d9.3; Col Grambling St.																								
1968	Atl N	11	7	3	2	0	0	0	0	1-0	0	0	.286	.375	.286	100	0	1-0	ø	0	—	—	/H	0	0.0
1969	Atl N	22	27	6	6	1	0	0	2	2-1	0	4	.222	.276	.259	50	-2	1-1	.857	-1	57	0	O7L	0	-0.4
1970	Atl N	37	96	18	27	3	0	0	8	5-1	0	12	.281	.314	.313	65	-5	5-2	1.000	0	111	0	O21(1/8/12)	0	-0.5
1971	Atl N	154	639	101	219	24	6	9	44	30-1	2	68	.343	.372	.441	122	18	30-14	.968	9	96	130	O153L	0	2.0
1972	Atl N	134	554	87	180	22	0	12	53	25-2	6	41	.325	.359	.430	114	10	25-9	.962	-3	92	82	O131(70/13/59)	0	0.2
1973	Atl N	148	668	94	200	32	6	11	55	22-5	2	64	.299	.323	.415	96	-5	35-11	.968	-4	95	63	O148(21/0/127)	0	-1.4
1974	Atl N★	143	606	87	**214**	24	**17**	11	54	28-10	2	52	**.353**	.383	.503	142	30	26-16	.967	-5	92	79	O139(107/0/80)	0	1.7
1975	Atl N	151	625	74	174	26	**11**	6	31	44-**17**	3	50	.278	.327	.384	94	-6	14-9	.966	-1	96	100	O148L	0	-1.7
1976	Chi A	136	527	63	158	22	6	4	36	17-2	2	41	.300	.322	.387	107	2	14-5	.978	-5	93	80	O125(35/41/57),D6	0	-0.8
1977	Chi A	134	543	78	163	29	7	10	54	27-4	0	44	.300	.333	.435	107	4	12-7	.987	0	96	115	O126(125/0/1),D2	0	-0.1
1978	Chi A	118	443	67	122	18	9	3	29	24-1	1	41	.275	.314	.377	92	-6	7-5	.959	-2	101	75	O109L,D9	0	-1.3
1979	Chi A	102	307	34	86	10	2	9	39	17-0	1	19	.280	.318	.414	96	-3	2-4	.951	-4	91	76	O67L,D17	0	-1.0
	Cal A	6	24	0	3	0	0	0	0	0-0	0	3	.125	.125	.125	-33	-5	0-0	ø	0	—	—	D6	0	-0.5
	Year	108	331	34	89	10	2	9	39	17-0	1	22	.269	.305	.393	87	-7	2-4	.951	-4	91	76	O67L,D23	0	-1.5
1980	Cal A	21	42	5	8	1	0	0	3	4-2	0	6	.190	.261	.214	32	-4	0-0	.750	-0	129	0	O2(1/0/1),D8	0	-0.4
Total	13	1317	5108	717	1562	212	64	75	408	246-46	19	445	.306	.339	.416	106	28	172-83	.968	-16	95	88	O1176(844/62/337),D48	0	-4.2
GARRETT, ADRIAN	Henry Adrian "Pat"; B1.3.1943 Brooksville FL; BL/TR/6´3˝/185; d4.13; Mil 1971; C5; b–Wayne																								
1966	Atl N	4	3	0	0	0	0	0	0	0-0	0	2	.000	.000	.000	-99	-1	0-0	ø	-0	0	0	/rf	0	-0.1
1970	Chi N	3	3	0	0	0	0	0	0	0-0	0	3	.000	.000	.000	-89	-1	0-0	ø	0	—	—	/H	0	-0.1
1971	Oak A	14	21	1	3	0	0	1	2	5-1	0	7	.143	.308	.286	70	-1	0-0	1.000	0	121	0	O5(4/0/1)	0	-0.1
1972	Oak A	14	11	0	0	0	0	0	0	1-0	0	4	.000	.083	.000	-77	-2	0-0	1.000	0	117	0	O2L	0	-0.3
1973	Chi N	36	54	7	12	0	0	3	8	4-1	0	18	.222	.267	.389	76	-2	1-0	1.000	0	94	0	O7(3/0/4),C6	0	-0.2
1974	Chi N	10	8	0	0	0	0	0	0	1-0	0	1	.000	.111	.000	-64	-2	0-0	1.000	1	0	0	C3/1lf	0	-0.1
1975	Chi N	16	21	1	2	0	0	1	6	1-0	0	8	.095	.130	.238	2	-3	0-0	1.000	1	211	163	1b4	0	-0.2
	Cal A	37	107	17	28	5	0	6	18	14-0	0	28	.262	.344	.477	140	6	3-0	1.000	0	130	126	D23,1b10,O2R/C	0	0.5
1976	Cal A	29	48	4	6	3	0	0	3	5-0	0	16	.125	.204	.188	17	-5	0-0	.974	-3	84	34	C15/1D	0	-0.9
Total	8	163	276	30	51	8	0	11	37	31-2	0	87	.185	.263	.333	71	-11	4-0	.959	-2	70	112	D27,C25,O18(10/0/8),1b16	0	-1.5
GARRETT, WAYNE	Ronald Wayne; B12.3.1947 Brooksville FL; BL/TR/5´11˝/(160–185); [AtlN65 6/104]; d4.12; Mil 1971; b–Adrian																								
1969	†NY N	124	400	38	87	11	3	1	39	40-3	3	75	.218	.290	.268	57	-23	4-2	.951	-11	85	97	3b72,2b47,S9	0	-3.3
1970	NY N	114	366	74	93	17	4	12	45	81-6	2	60	.254	.390	.421	116	12	5-1	.944	-12	82	51	3b70,2b45/S	0	0.3
1971	NY N	56	202	20	43	2	0	1	11	28-2	1	31	.213	.310	.238	58	-10	1-3	.967	-2	94	94	3b53,2b9	0	-1.4
1972	NY N	111	298	41	69	13	3	2	29	70-3	0	58	.232	.374	.315	100	4	3-2	.960	1	98	113	3b82,2b22	0	0.6
1973	†NY N	140	504	76	129	20	3	16	58	72-4	1	74	.256	.348	.403	109	7	6-5	.942	4	103	**165**	3b130,S9,2b6	0	1.2
1974	NY N	151	522	55	117	14	3	13	53	89-7	2	96	.224	.337	.337	90	-5	4-6	.955	2	97	115	3b144,S9	0	-0.4
1975	NY N	107	274	49	73	8	3	6	34	50-4	1	45	.266	.379	.383	116	8	3-2	.966	8	101	193	3b94,S3/2	15	1.6
1976	NY N	80	251	36	56	8	1	4	26	52-5	1	26	.223	.359	.311	95	1	7-5	.948	5	105	127	3b64,2b10/S	0	0.6
	Mon N	59	177	15	43	4	1	2	11	30-7	0	20	.243	.353	.311	85	-2	2-2	.982	6	108	91	2b54,3b2	0	0.7
	Year	139	428	51	99	12	2	6	37	82-12	1	46	.231	.356	.311	91	-1	9-7	.949	11	104	125	3b66,2b64/S	0	1.3
1977	Mon N	68	159	17	43	6	1	2	22	30-7	1	18	.270	.385	.358	104	3	2-2	1.000	3	112	28	3b49/2	52	0.4
1978	Mon N	49	69	6	12	0	0	1	2	8-1	0	10	.174	.260	.217	35	-6	0-0	.969	-1	97	104	3b13	0	-0.8
	StL N	33	63	11	21	4	0	1	10	11-1	0	16	.333	.432	.444	146	5	1-0	.927	-1	91	202	3b19	0	0.4

YEAR	TM LG	G	AB	R	H	2B	3B	HR	RBI	BB-IB	HP	SO	AVG	OBP	SLG	AOPS	ABR	SB-CS	FA	FR	RNG	THR	GAMES AT POSITION	DL	BFW
	Year	82	132	17	33	4	0	2	12	19-2	0	26	.250	.344	.326	88	-1	1-0	.945	-2	94	159	3b32	0	-0.4
Total	10	1092	3285	438	786	107	22	61	340	561-50	12	529	.239	.350	.341	94	-6	38-30	.956	2	97	119	3b792,2b195,S32	67	-0.1

GARRIDO, GIL Gil Gonzalo; B6.26.1941 Panama City, Pan; BR/TR/5´8˝/(150–160); d4.24

YEAR	TM LG	G	AB	R	H	2B	3B	HR	RBI	BB-IB	HP	SO	AVG	OBP	SLG	AOPS	ABR	SB-CS	FA	FR	RNG	THR	GAMES AT POSITION	DL	BFW
1964	SF N	14	25	1	2	0	0	0	1	2-0	0	7	.080	.148	.080	-33	-4	1-0	.969	-3	97	60	S14	0	-0.7
1968	Atl N	18	53	5	11	0	0	0	2	2-1	0	2	.208	.228	.208	34	-4	0-0	.987	2	107	152	S17	0	-0.1
1969	†Atl N	82	227	18	50	5	1	0	10	16-3	0	11	.220	.272	.251	47	-16	0-0	.973	-19	87	83	S81	0	-2.9
1970	Atl N	101	367	38	97	5	4	1	19	15-3	0	16	.264	.290	.308	58	-23	0-2	.975	-4	100	84	S80,2b26	0	-1.7
1971	Atl N	79	125	8	27	3	0	0	12	15-1	0	12	.216	.300	.240	51	-8	0-1	.961	-5	91	114	S32,3b28,2b18	0	-0.9
1972	Atl N	40	75	11	20	1	0	0	7	11-1	1	6	.267	.368	.280	79	-1	1-1	.989	-1	108	81	2b21,S10,3b3	0	-0.1
Total	6	334	872	81	207	14	5	1	51	61-9	1	54	.237	.286	.268	53	-56	2-4	.974	-29	94	92	S234,2b65,3b31	0	-6.4

GARRIOTT, CECIL Virgil Cecil; B8.15.1916 Harristown IL; D2.20.1990 Lake Elsinore CA; BL/TR/5´8˝/165; d9.4; Col Millikin

YEAR	TM LG	G	AB	R	H	2B	3B	HR	RBI	BB-IB	HP	SO	AVG	OBP	SLG	AOPS	ABR	SB-CS	FA	FR	RNG	THR	GAMES AT POSITION	DL	BFW
1946	Chi N	6	5	1	0	0	0	0	0	0	1	2	.000	.167	.000	-52	-1	0	ø	0	—	—	/H	0	-0.1

GARRISON, FORD Robert Ford "Rocky","Snapper"; B8.29.1915 Greenville SC; D6.6.2001 Largo FL; BR/TR/5´10.5˝/180; d4.22; Mil 1945; C1

YEAR	TM LG	G	AB	R	H	2B	3B	HR	RBI	BB-IB	HP	SO	AVG	OBP	SLG	AOPS	ABR	SB-CS	FA	FR	RNG	THR	GAMES AT POSITION	DL	BFW
1943	Bos A	36	129	13	36	5	1	1	11	5	0	14	.279	.306	.357	92	-2	0-1	.988	-0	100	76	O32(26/6/0)	0	-0.5
1944	Bos A	13	49	5	12	3	0	0	2	6	0	4	.245	.327	.306	82	-1	0-0	.969	-0	114	0	O12R	0	-0.2
	Phi A	121	449	58	121	13	2	4	37	22	2	40	.269	.307	.334	84	-11	10-4	.987	5	114	63	O119(95/0/24)	0	-1.3
	Year	134	498	63	133	16	2	4	39	28	2	44	.267	.309	.331	84	-12	10-4	.985	5	114	56	O131(95/0/36)	0	-1.5
1945	Phi A	6	23	3	7	1	0	1	6	4	0	3	.304	.407	.478	157	2	1-0	1.000	0	93	202	O5L	0	0.2
1946	Phi A	9	37	1	4	0	0	0	0	0	0	6	.108	.108	.108	-40	-7	0-0	1.000	-1	65	0	O8L	0	-1.0
Total	4	185	687	80	180	22	3	6	56	37	2	67	.262	.302	.329	81	-19	11-5	.986	4	109	63	O176(134/6/36)	0	-2.8

GARRISON, WEBSTER Webster Leotis; B8.24.1965 Marrero LA; BR/TR/5´11˝/170; [TorA83 2/37]; d8.2

YEAR	TM LG	G	AB	R	H	2B	3B	HR	RBI	BB-IB	HP	SO	AVG	OBP	SLG	AOPS	ABR	SB-CS	FA	FR	RNG	THR	GAMES AT POSITION	DL	BFW
1996	Oak A	5	9	0	0	0	0	0	0	1-0	0	0	.000	.100	.000	-73	-2	0-0	.875	-1	67	66	2b3/1	0	-0.3

GARRITY, HANK Francis Joseph; B2.4.1908 Boston MA; D9.1.1962 Boston MA; BR/TR/6´1˝/185; d7.26; Col Holy Cross

YEAR	TM LG	G	AB	R	H	2B	3B	HR	RBI	BB-IB	HP	SO	AVG	OBP	SLG	AOPS	ABR	SB-CS	FA	FR	RNG	THR	GAMES AT POSITION	DL	BFW
1931	Chi A	8	14	0	3	1	0	0	2	1	0	2	.214	.267	.286	48	-1	0-0	.941	-1	*61*	*142*	C7	—	-0.1

GARVEY, STEVE Steven Patrick; B12.22.1948 Tampa FL; BR/TR/5´10˝/190; [LAN68 S1/13]; d9.1; Col Michigan St.

YEAR	TM LG	G	AB	R	H	2B	3B	HR	RBI	BB-IB	HP	SO	AVG	OBP	SLG	AOPS	ABR	SB-CS	FA	FR	RNG	THR	GAMES AT POSITION	DL	BFW
1969	LA N	3	3	0	1	0	0	0	0	0-0	0	1	.333	.333	.333	93	0	0-0	ø	0	—	—	/H	0	0.0
1970	LA N	34	93	8	25	5	0	1	6	6-0	0	17	.269	.310	.355	82	-3	1-1	.943	5	130	100	3b27/2	0	0.2
1971	LA N	81	225	27	51	12	1	7	26	21-2	0	33	.227	.290	.382	94	-2	1-2	.939	12	123	110	3b79	33	1.0
1972	LA N	96	294	36	79	14	2	9	30	19-3	1	36	.269	.312	.422	109	3	4-2	.902	8	112	155	3b85,1b3	0	1.1
1973	LA N	114	349	37	106	17	3	8	50	11-4	3	42	.304	.328	.438	115	5	0-2	.993	-7	62	108	1b76,O10(8/0/2)	0	-0.9
1974	†LA N★	156	642	95	200	32	3	21	111	31-4	3	66	.312	.342	.469	131	23	5-4	.995	-12	64	95	1b156	0	-0.3
1975	LA N★	160	659	85	210	38	6	18	95	33-6	3	66	.319	.351	.476	134	27	11-2	**.995**	-11	70	85	1b160	0	0.4
1976	LA N★	**162**	631	85	200	37	4	13	80	50-11	1	69	.317	.363	.450	133	26	19-8	**.998**	-15	62	**110**	1b162	0	-0.1
1977	†LA N★	**162**	646	91	192	25	3	33	115	38-10	1	90	.297	.335	.498	120	15	9-6	**.995**	-16	57	122	1b160	0	-1.1
1978	†LA N★	**162**	639	89	**202**	36	9	21	113	40-9	1	70	.316	.353	.499	137	29	10-5	.994	-8	77	103	1b161	0	1.1
1979	LA N★	**162**	648	92	204	32	1	28	110	37-16	2	59	.315	.351	.497	132	26	3-6	.995	-3	89	78	1b162	0	1.2
1980	LA N★	**163**	658	78	**200**	27	1	26	106	36-6	3	67	.304	.341	.467	127	21	6-11	.996	3	103	103	1b162	0	1.1
1981	†LA N★	**110**	431	63	122	23	1	10	64	25-6	1	49	.283	.322	.411	112	5	3-5	**.999**	-4	78	106	1b110	0	-0.7
1982	LA N	**162**	625	66	176	35	1	16	86	20-10	1	86	.282	.301	.418	103	-0	5-3	.995	5	109	93	1b158	0	-0.6
1983	SD N	100	388	76	114	22	0	14	59	29-11	3	39	.294	.344	.459	125	13	4-1	.994	-8	72	91	1b100	65	-0.1
1984	†SD N★	161	617	72	175	27	2	8	86	24-3	1	64	.284	.307	.373	91	-9	1-2	**1.000**	-2	92	101	1b159	0	-2.2
1985	SD N★	**162**	654	80	184	34	6	17	81	35-7	3	67	.281	.318	.430	109	5	0-0	.997	-8	83	109	1b162	0	-1.4
1986	SD N	155	557	58	142	22	0	21	81	23-5	1	72	.255	.284	.408	91	-10	1-2	.994	-18	54	87	1b148	0	-3.9
1987	SD N	27	76	5	16	2	0	1	9	1-0	1	10	.211	.231	.276	35	-7	0-0	1.000	-0	89	76	1b20	134	-0.9
Total	19	2332	8835	1143	2599	440	43	272	1308	479-113	29	1003	.294	.329	.446	117	167	83-62	.996	-79	78	99	1b2059,3b191,O10(8/0/2)/2	232	-6.1

GASPAR, ROD Rodney Earl; B4.3.1946 Long Beach CA; BB/TL/5´11˝/(160–170); d4.8; Col Cal St.–Long Beach

YEAR	TM LG	G	AB	R	H	2B	3B	HR	RBI	BB-IB	HP	SO	AVG	OBP	SLG	AOPS	ABR	SB-CS	FA	FR	RNG	THR	GAMES AT POSITION	DL	BFW
1969	†NY N	118	215	26	49	6	1	1	14	25-2	2	19	.228	.313	.279	66	-9	7-3	.983	8	99	308	O91(22/16/64)	0	-0.4
1970	NY N	11	14	4	0	0	0	0	0	1-0	0	4	.000	.067	.000	-80	-4	1-0	1.000	1	138	0	O8(0/4/5)	0	-0.3
1971	SD N	16	17	1	2	0	0	0	2	3-0	0	3	.118	.250	.118	8	-2	0-1	1.000	0	42	0	O2L	0	-0.3
1974	SD N	33	14	4	3	0	0	0	1	4-0	0	3	.214	.389	.214	76	0	0-0	1.000	1	143	0	O8(2/5/1),1b2	0	0.0
Total	4	178	260	35	54	6	1	1	17	33-2	2	29	.208	.301	.250	55	-15	8-4	.986	9	101	271	O109(26/25/70),1b2	0	-1.0

GASTALL, TOM Thomas Everett; B6.13.1932 Fall River MA; D9.20.1956 Riviera Beach MD; BR/TR/6´2˝/187; d6.21; Col Boston U.

YEAR	TM LG	G	AB	R	H	2B	3B	HR	RBI	BB-IB	HP	SO	AVG	OBP	SLG	AOPS	ABR	SB-CS	FA	FR	RNG	THR	GAMES AT POSITION	DL	BFW
1955	Bal A	20	27	4	4	1	0	0	0	3-0	0	5	.148	.233	.185	15	-3	0-0	.967	-1	*77*	*0*	C15	0	-0.4
1956	Bal A	32	56	3	11	2	0	0	4	3-0	1	8	.196	.246	.232	30	-6	0-0	1.000	1	*84*	*87*	C20	0	-0.4
Total	2	52	83	7	15	3	0	0	4	6-0	1	13	.181	.242	.217	25	-9	0-0	.990	-0	*82*	*58*	C35	0	-0.8

GASTFIELD, ED Edward; B8.1.1865 Chicago IL; D12.1.1899 Chicago IL; BR/5´9.5˝/155; d8.13

YEAR	TM LG	G	AB	R	H	2B	3B	HR	RBI	BB-IB	HP	SO	AVG	OBP	SLG	AOPS	ABR	SB-CS	FA	FR	RNG	THR	GAMES AT POSITION	DL	BFW
1884	Det N	23	82	6	6	1	0	0	2	2	—	34	.073	.095	.085	-45	-13	—	.827	4	—	—	C19,O2R,1b2	—	-0.7
1885	Det N	1	3	0	0	0	0	0	0	0	—	2	.000	.000	.000	-99	-1	—	.714	-1	—	—	/C	—	-0.1
	Chi N	1	3	0	0	0	0	0	0	0	—	1	.000	.000	.000	-88	-1	—	1.000	1	—	—	/C	—	0.0
	Year	2	6	0	0	0	0	0	0	0	—	3	.000	.000	.000	-93	-1	—	.889	0	—	—	C2	—	-0.1
Total	2	25	88	6	6	1	0	0	2	2	—	37	.068	.089	.080	-49	-15	—	.832	4	—	—	C21,1b2,O2R	—	-0.8

GASTON, ALEX Alexander Nathaniel; B3.12.1893 New York NY; D2.8.1979 Marina Del Ray CA; BR/TR/5´9˝/170; d9.26; b–Milt

YEAR	TM LG	G	AB	R	H	2B	3B	HR	RBI	BB-IB	HP	SO	AVG	OBP	SLG	AOPS	ABR	SB-CS	FA	FR	RNG	THR	GAMES AT POSITION	DL	BFW
1920	NY N	4	10	2	1	0	0	0	1	1	0	2	.100	.182	.100	-18	-2	0-0	.917	-1	*107*	*52*	C3	—	-0.2
1921	NY N	20	22	1	5	1	1	0	3	1	0	9	.227	.261	.364	63	-1	0-0	.950	-0	*125*	*0*	C11	—	-0.1
1922	NY N	16	26	1	5	0	0	0	1	0	0	3	.192	.192	.192	-1	-4	1-0	1.000	0	*119*	*32*	C13	—	-0.3
1923	NY N	22	39	3	8	2	0	1	5	0	1	6	.205	.225	.333	46	-3	0-0	.957	0	*160*	*115*	C21	—	-0.2
1926	Bos A	98	301	37	67	5	3	0	21	21	4	28	.223	.282	.259	43	-26	3-0	.981	-15	*62*	*86*	C98	—	-3.4
1929	Bos A	55	116	14	26	5	2	2	9	6	0	8	.224	.262	.353	58	-8	1-0	.986	1	*103*	*126*	C49	—	-0.5
Total	6	215	514	58	112	13	6	3	40	29	5	56	.218	.266	.284	45	-44	5-0	.979	-15	*83*	*91*	C195	—	-4.7

GASTON, CITO Clarence Edwin; B3.17.1944 San Antonio TX; BR/TR/6´4˝/(200–210); d9.14; M9/C10

YEAR	TM LG	G	AB	R	H	2B	3B	HR	RBI	BB-IB	HP	SO	AVG	OBP	SLG	AOPS	ABR	SB-CS	FA	FR	RNG	THR	GAMES AT POSITION	DL	BFW
1967	Atl N	9	25	1	3	0	1	0	1	0-0	0	5	.120	.120	.200	-10	-4	1-0	.800	-2	45	239	O7(0/6/1)	0	-0.6
1969	SD N	129	391	20	90	11	7	2	28	24-0	1	117	.230	.275	.309	66	-19	4-4	.959	2	100	**179**	O113C	0	-2.2
1970	SD N★	146	584	92	186	26	9	29	93	41-2	2	142	.318	.364	.543	145	34	4-1	.975	-5	97	87	O142(1/142/0)	0	2.5
1971	SD N	141	518	57	118	13	9	17	61	24-1	2	121	.228	.264	.386	88	-13	1-0	.982	-7	81	101	O133(6/126/1)	0	-2.5
1972	SD N	111	379	30	102	14	0	7	44	22-2	2	76	.269	.313	.361	98	-2	0-2	.977	-1	90	149	O94(18/7/73)	16	-1.0
1973	SD N	133	476	51	119	18	4	16	57	20-3	1	88	.250	.281	.405	96	-7	0-0	.947	0	89	153	O119(1/0/118)	0	-1.3
1974	SD N	106	267	19	57	11	0	6	33	16-2	1	51	.213	.259	.322	65	-14	0-0	.992	4	107	170	O63(18/0/50)	0	-1.3
1975	Atl N	64	141	17	34	4	0	6	15	17-3	0	33	.241	.321	.397	96	-1	1-0	.974	-0	102	96	O35(2/17/17)/1	0	-0.3
1976	Atl N	69	134	15	39	4	0	4	25	13-1	0	21	.291	.354	.410	110	2	1-0	.977	-2	85	58	O28(25/0/3),1b2	0	-0.1
1977	Atl N	56	85	6	23	4	0	3	21	5-0	0	19	.271	.301	.424	85	-2	1-0	1.000	0	90	0	O9(7/0/2),1b5	0	-0.2
1978	Atl N	60	118	5	27	1	0	1	9	3-0	0	20	.229	.244	.263	39	-10	0-0	.957	-1	114	0	O29(13/1/17),1b4	0	-1.3
	Pit N	2	2	1	1	0	0	0	0	0-0	0	0	.500	.500	.500	171	0	0-0	ø	-0	0	0	/lf	0	0.0
	Year	62	120	6	28	1	0	1	9	3-0	0	20	.233	.248	.267	41	-10	0-0	.957	-1	112	0	O30(14/1/17),1b4	0	-1.3
Total	11	1026	3120	314	799	106	30	91	387	185-14	9	693	.256	.298	.397	95	-36	13-7	.970	-11	93	125	O773(92/412/282),1b12	16	-8.3

GATES, BRENT Brent Robert; B3.14.1970 Grand Rapids MI; BB/TR/6´1˝/(180–191); [OakA91 1/26]; d5.5; Col Minnesota

YEAR	TM LG	G	AB	R	H	2B	3B	HR	RBI	BB-IB	HP	SO	AVG	OBP	SLG	AOPS	ABR	SB-CS	FA	FR	RNG	THR	GAMES AT POSITION	DL	BFW
1993	Oak A	139	535	64	155	29	2	7	69	56-4	4	75	.290	.357	.391	108	7	7-3	.981	-5	102	88	2b139	0	0.9
1994	Oak A	64	233	29	66	11	1	2	24	21-1	1	32	.283	.337	.365	90	-3	3-0	.974	-11	86	72	2b63/1	51	-0.9
1995	Oak A	136	524	60	133	24	4	5	56	46-2	0	84	.254	.308	.344	75	-20	3-3	.982	11	107	91	2b132/1D	0	-0.3
1996	Oak A	64	247	26	65	19	2	2	30	18-0	2	35	.263	.316	.381	77	-9	1-1	.973	-1	100	105	2b63	106	-0.7
1997	†Sea A	65	151	18	36	8	0	3	20	14-0	0	21	.238	.298	.351	70	-7	0-0	.934	-4	90	90	3b32,2b21,S5/1lfD	0	-0.9
1998	Min A	107	333	31	83	15	0	3	42	36-0	2	46	.249	.324	.321	68	-15	3-3	.961	-7	90	48	3b77,2b21/1SD	0	-2.0
1999	Min A	110	306	40	78	13	2	3	38	34-1	1	56	.255	.328	.340	68	-15	1-3	.972	-3	98	146	3b61,2b47,1b5/SD	0	-1.6
Total	7	685	2329	268	616	119	11	25	279	225-8	10	349	.264	.327	.357	81	-62	18-13	.980	-19	102	89	2b486,3b170,1b9,S7,D7/lf	157	-5.5

YEAR	TM LG	G	AB	R	H	2B	3B	HR	RBI	BB-IB	HP	SO	AVG	OBP	SLG	AOPS	ABR	SB-CS	FA	FR	RNG	THR	GAMES AT POSITION	DL	BFW
Gates, Joe	Joseph Daniel; B10.3.1954 Gary IN; BL/TR/5´7˝/175; d9.12; Col Manatee (FL) CC																								
1978	Chi A	8	24	6	6	0	0	0	1	4-0	1	6	.250	.379	.250	79	0	1-0	.972	-1	109	73	2b8	0	-0.1
1979	Chi A	16	16	5	1	0	1	0	1	2-0	0	3	.063	.167	.188	-5	-3	1-1	.966	1	126	88	2b8/3D	0	-0.1
Total	2	24	40	11	7	0	1	0	2	6-0	1	9	.175	.298	.225	46	-3	2-1	.969	0	115	78	2b16/D3	0	-0.2
Gates, Mike	Michael Grant; B9.20.1956 Culver City CA; BL/TR/6´0˝/165; [MonN79 7/166]; d5.6; Col Pepperdine																								
1981	Mon N	1	2	1	1	0	1	0	1	0-0	0	1	.500	.500	1.500	436	1	0-0	1.000	0	135	0	/2	0	0.1
1982	Mon N	36	121	16	28	2	3	0	8	9-0	0	19	.231	.280	.298	61	-7	0-0	1.000	-2	94	106	2b36	0	-0.8
Total	2	37	123	17	29	2	4	0	9	9-0	0	20	.236	.284	.317	67	-6	0-0	1.000	-2	94	105	2b37	0	-0.7
Gathright, Joey	Joey Renard; B4.22.1982 Hattiesburg MS; BL/TR/5´10˝/(170–175); [TBA01 32/949]; d6.25																								
2004	TB A	19	52	11	13	0	0	0	1	2-0	3	14	.250	.316	.250	51	-4	6-1	1.000	-1	86	0	O16(4/11/1)/D	0	-0.4
2005	TB A	76	203	29	56	7	3	0	13	10-0	2	39	.276	.316	.340	76	-7	20-5	.984	6	123	106	O70C	0	0.2
2006	TB A	55	154	25	31	6	0	0	13	20-0	3	30	.201	.305	.240	44	-12	12-3	.994	5	122	80	O54C	0	-0.5
	KC A	79	229	34	60	6	3	1	28	22-0	4	45	.262	.332	.328	75	-9	10-6	.990	2	108	88	O76C/D	0	-0.5
	Year	134	383	59	91	12	3	1	41	42-0	7	75	.238	.321	.292	62	-21	22-9	.991	7	114	85	O130C/D	0	-1.0
Total	3	229	638	99	160	19	6	1	55	54-0	12	128	.251	.319	.304	66	-32	48-15	.989	12	115	85	O216(4/211/1),D2	0	-1.2
Gatins, Frank	Frank Anthony; B3.6.1871 Johnstown PA; D11.8.1911 Johnstown PA; d9.21																								
1898	Was N	17	58	6	13	2	0	0	5	3	1	—	.224	.274	.259	53	-4	2	.790	-5	91	94	S17	—	-0.7
1901	Bro N	50	197	21	45	7	2	1	21	5	2	—	.228	.255	.299	59	-11	6	.919	-8	69	104	3b46,S5	—	-1.7
Total	2	67	255	27	58	9	2	1	26	8	3	—	.227	.259	.290	58	-15	8	.919	-12	69	104	3b46,S22	—	-2.4
Gaudet, Jim	James Jennings; B6.3.1955 New Orleans LA; BR/TR/6´0˝/185; [KCA76 6/138]; d9.10; Col Tulane																								
1978	KC A	3	8	0	0	0	0	0	0	0-0	0	3	.000	.000	.000	-97	-2	0-0	.938	1	0	0	C3	0	-0.1
1979	KC A	3	6	0	1	0	0	0	0	0-0	0	0	.167	.167	.167	-10	-1	0-0	1.000	1	32	0	C3	0	0.0
Total	2	6	14	0	1	0	0	0	0	0-0	0	3	.071	.071	.071	-59	-3	0-0	.966	1	13	0	C6	0	-0.1
Gaule, Mike	Michael John; B8.4.1869 Baltimore MD; D1.24.1918 Baltimore MD; BL/TL/6´2˝/?; d6.15																								
1889	Lou AA	1	2	0	0	0	0	0	0	0	0	1	.000	.000	.000	-99	-1	0	.000	-1	0	0	/cf	—	-0.1
Gautreau, Doc	Walter Paul "Punk"; B7.26.1901 Cambridge MA; D8.23.1970 Salt Lake City UT; BR/TR/5´4˝/129; d6.22; Col Holy Cross																								
1925	Phi A	4	7	0	0	0	0	0	0	0	0	3	.000	.000	.000	-94	-2	0-0	.933	1	109	85	2b4	—	-0.1
	Bos N	68	279	45	73	13	3	0	23	35	1	13	.262	.346	.330	81	-7	11-7	.976	-9	94	93	2b68	—	-1.3
1926	Bos N	79	266	36	71	9	4	0	8	35	2	24	.267	.356	.331	94	-1	17	.942	-19	83	94	2b74	—	-1.8
1927	Bos N	87	236	38	58	12	2	0	20	25	1	20	.246	.321	.314	76	-7	11	.965	-6	98	61	2b57	—	-1.1
1928	Bos N	23	18	3	5	0	1	0	1	4	0	3	.278	.409	.389	116	1	1	.750	-1	89	206	2b4/S	—	0.0
Total	4	261	806	122	207	34	10	0	52	99	4	63	.257	.341	.324	83	-16	40-7	.960	-34	91	85	2b207/S	—	-4.3
Gautreaux, Sid	Sidney Allen "Pudge"; B5.4.1912 Schriever LA; D4.19.1980 Morgan City LA; BB/TR/5´8˝/190; d4.15																								
1936	Bro N	75	71	8	19	3	0	0	16	9	1	7	.268	.358	.310	80	-1	0	.963	-0	78	73	C15	—	-0.1
1937	Bro N	11	10	0	1	1	0	0	2	1	0	1	.100	.182	.200	4	-1	0	ø	0	—	—	/H	—	-0.1
Total	2	86	81	8	20	4	0	0	18	10	1	8	.247	.337	.296	71	-2	0	.963	-0	78	73	C15	—	-0.2
Gavern	; d6.15																								
1874	Atl NA	1	4	1	0	0	0	0	0	0	—	0	.000	.000	.000	-99	-1	0-0	.750	1	237	0	/2	—	0.0
Gazella, Mike	Michael; B10.13.1895 Olyphant PA; D9.11.1978 Odessa TX; BR/TR/5´7.5˝/165; d7.2; Col Lafayette																								
1923	NY A	8	13	2	1	0	0	0	1	2	0	3	.077	.200	.077	-25	-2	0-0	1.000	-0	121	0	S4,2b2,3b2	—	-0.3
1926	†NY A	66	168	21	39	6	0	0	20	25	1	24	.232	.335	.268	60	-9	2-2	.913	-6	93	79	3b45,S11	—	-1.1
1927	NY A	54	115	17	32	8	4	0	9	23	1	16	.278	.403	.417	117	4	4-1	.961	-6	82	95	3b44,S6	—	0.0
1928	NY A	32	56	11	13	0	0	0	2	6	1	7	.232	.317	.232	48	-4	2-1	.969	-2	95	52	3b16,2b4,S3	—	-0.5
Total	4	160	352	51	85	14	4	0	32	56	3	50	.241	.350	.304	73	-11	8-4	.940	-14	89	81	3b107,S24,2b6	—	-1.9
Gear, Dale	Dale Dudley; B2.2.1872 Lone Elm KS; D9.23.1951 Topeka KS; BR/TR/5´11˝/165; d8.15; Col Kansas; ▲																								
1896	Cle N	4	15	5	6	1	1	0	3	1	0	1	.400	.438	.600	163	1	0	.857	-1	70	0	P3/1	—	0.0
1897	Cle N	7	24	3	4	1	0	0	2	3	1	—	.167	.286	.208	30	-2	2	.750	0	342	0	O6C	—	-0.2
1901	Was A	58	199	17	47	9	2	0	20	4	0	—	.236	.251	.302	54	-13	2	.944	3	159	350	O35(12/1/22),P24	—	-0.7
Total	3	69	238	25	57	11	3	0	25	8	1	1	.239	.267	.311	59	-14	4	.900	2	191	290	O41(12/7/22),P27/1	—	-0.9
Gearhart, Gary	Lloyd William; B8.10.1923 New Lebanon OH; D4.2.2001 Dayton OH; BR/TL/5´11˝/180; d4.18																								
1947	NY N	73	179	26	44	9	0	6	17	17	1	30	.246	.315	.397	87	-4	1	.961	-1	91	133	O44(17/28/0)	0	-0.7
Geary, Huck	Eugene Francis Joseph; B1.22.1917 Buffalo NY; D1.27.1981 Cuba NY; BL/TR/5´10.5˝/170; d7.17; Mil 1944–45; [DL 1946 Pit N 115]																								
1942	Pit N	9	22	3	5	0	0	0	2	2	0	3	.227	.292	.227	52	-1	0	.939	-1	77	142	S8	0	-0.2
1943	Pit N	46	166	17	25	4	0	1	13	18	0	6	.151	.234	.193	23	-16	3	.956	-3	94	102	S46	0	-1.7
Total	2	55	188	20	30	4	0	1	15	20	0	9	.160	.240	.197	26	-17	3	.954	-3	92	107	S54	115	-1.9
Gedeon, Elmer	Elmer John; B4.15.1917 Cleveland OH; D4.20.1944 St.Pol, France; BR/TR/6´4˝/196; d9.18; Col Michigan																								
1939	Was A	5	15	1	3	0	0	0	1	2	0	5	.200	.294	.200	31	-2	0-0	1.000	0	127	0	O5(0/4/1)	—	-0.1
Gedeon, Joe	Elmer Joseph; B12.5.1893 Sacramento CA; D5.19.1941 San Francisco CA; BR/TR/6´0˝/167; d5.13																								
1913	Was A	29	71	3	13	1	3	0	6	1	1	6	.183	.205	.282	41	-6	3	.929	1	95	167	O15(14/0/1),3b7,2b2,S2/P	—	-0.5
1914	Was A	4	2	0	0	0	0	0	0	1	0	1	.000	.333	.000	1	0	0	.667	-0	100	0	O4(0/1/3)	—	-0.1
1916	NY A	122	435	50	92	14	4	0	27	40	3	61	.211	.282	.262	62	-20	14	.955	-13	95	114	2b122	—	-3.5
1917	NY A	33	117	15	28	7	0	0	8	7	1	13	.239	.288	.299	78	-3	4	.983	1	93	93	2b31	—	-0.2
1918	StL A	**123**	441	39	94	14	3	1	41	27	**8**	29	.213	.271	.265	64	-20	8	**.977**	16	**107**	86	2b123	—	-0.3
1919	StL A	120	437	57	111	13	4	0	27	50	7	35	.254	.340	.302	79	-11	4	**.975**	-3	96	90	2b118	—	-1.2
1920	StL A	153	606	95	177	33	6	0	61	55	4	36	.292	.355	.366	89	-9	1-3	.964	-27	88	102	2b153	—	-3.3
Total	7	584	2109	259	515	82	20	1	171	180	25	181	.244	.311	.303	75	-69	34-3	.969	-26	96	98	2b549,O19(14/1/4),3b7,S2/P	—	-9.1
Gedman, Rich	Richard Leo; B9.26.1959 Worcester MA; BL/TR/6´0˝/(205–222); d9.7																								
1980	Bos A	9	24	2	5	0	0	0	1	0-0	0	5	.208	.208	.208	14	-3	0-0	.867	-0	66	0	C2,D4	0	-0.3
1981	Bos A	62	205	22	59	15	0	5	26	9-1	1	31	.288	.317	.434	109	2	0-0	.990	-7	72	105	C59	0	-0.2
1982	Bos A	92	289	30	72	17	2	4	26	10-2	2	37	.249	.279	.363	71	-12	0-1	.977	-7	80	82	C86	0	-1.6
1983	Bos A	81	204	21	60	16	1	2	18	15-6	1	37	.294	.345	.412	100	0	0-1	.980	-5	60	66	C68	0	-0.2
1984	Bos A	133	449	54	121	26	4	24	72	29-8	1	72	.269	.312	.506	117	9	0-0	.977	-4	91	**136**	C125	0	1.0
1985	Bos A★	144	498	66	147	30	5	18	80	50-11	3	79	.295	.362	.484	124	17	2-0	.983	13	125	**125**	C139	0	3.5
1986	†Bos A★	135	462	49	119	29	0	16	65	37-13	4	61	.258	.315	.424	99	-1	1-0	.994	18	153	**126**	C134	0	2.3
1987	Bos A	52	151	11	31	8	0	1	13	10-2	0	24	.205	.250	.278	40	-13	0-0	.976	1	147	94	C51	82	-1.0
1988	†Bos A	95	299	33	69	14	0	9	39	18-2	3	49	.231	.279	.368	77	-10	0-0	.992	4	118	117	C93/D	24	-0.1
1989	Bos A	93	260	24	55	9	0	4	16	23-1	0	47	.212	.273	.292	56	-15	0-1	.981	-8	74	99	C91	0	-1.9
1990	Bos A	10	15	3	3	0	0	0	0	5-0	1	6	.200	.429	.200	77	0	0-0	.970	-2	44	201	C9	0	-0.2
	Hou N	40	104	4	21	7	0	1	10	15-6	0	24	.202	.300	.298	68	-4	0-0	1.000	3	73	114	C39	0	0.1
1991	StL N	46	94	7	10	1	0	3	8	4-0	0	15	.106	.140	.213	-1	-13	0-1	.976	6	76	91	C43	0	-0.6
1992	StL N	41	105	5	23	4	0	1	8	11-1	0	22	.219	.291	.286	66	-5	0-0	.988	4	66	27	C40	0	0.2
Total	13	1033	3159	331	795	176	12	88	382	236-53	16	509	.252	.304	.399	90	-48	3-4	.984	17	103	108	C979,D5	106	1.0
Gedney, Count	Alfred W.; B5.10.1849 Brooklyn NY; D3.26.1922 Hackensack NJ; 5´9˝/140; d4.27; ▲																								
1872	Tro NA	9	47	14	20	3	0	3	18	0	—	0	.426	.426	.681	232	7	1-0	.933	-1	0	0	O9C	—	0.4
	Eck NA	18	71	5	13	1	0	0	6	0	—	3	.183	.183	.197	20	-5	2-2	.881	1	0	0	O18L	—	-0.3
	Year	27	118	19	33	4	0	3	24	0	—	3	.280	.280	.390	115	3	3-2	.892	0	0	0	O27(18/9/0)	—	0.1
1873	Mut NA	**53**	225	41	60	5	5	1	24	6	—	4	.267	.286	.347	87	-4	1-0	.852	14	134	313	O53L	—	0.9
1874	Ath NA	54	222	49	61	4	1	1	34	7	—	11	.275	.297	.315	89	-4	2-2	.822	0	44	188	O51L,1b4	—	-0.2
1875	Mut NA	68	267	30	55	12	2	0	17	0	—	8	.206	.206	.266	60	-11	2-3	.843	11	70	91	O67(67/0/1),P2	—	0.2
Total	4NA	202	832	139	209	25	8	5	99	13	—	26	.251	.263	.319	82	-17	8-7	.846	26	72	162	O198(189/9/1),1b4,P2	—	1.0

YEAR	TM LG	G	AB	R	H	2B	3B	HR	RBI	BB-IB	HP	SO	AVG	OBP	SLG	AOPS	ABR	SB-CS	FA	FR	RNG	THR	GAMES AT POSITION	DL	BFW
GEER, BILLY	William Henry Harrison (b George Harrison Geer); TR/5´8˝/160; d10.15																								
1874	Mut NA	2	8	0	2	0	0	0	1	0	—	0	.250	.250	.250	59	0	0-0	.889	2	482	1500	O2(1/1/0)	—	0.1
1875	NH NA	37	164	20	40	4	1	0	9	1	—	4	.244	.248	.280	96	1	2-2	.765	1	205	476	O17(4/11/3),2b13,S6/13	—	0.0
1878	Cin N	**61**	237	31	52	13	2	0	20	10	—	18	.219	.251	.291	86	-2	—	.867	-4	93	118	S60,2b2	—	-0.3
1880	Wor N	2	6	0	0	0	0	0	0	0	—	0	.000	.000	.000	-92	-1	—	1.000	-0	0	0	/rfS	—	-0.1
1884	Phi U	9	36	7	9	2	1	0	—	4	—	—	.250	.325	.361	117	0	—	.772	0	121	52	S9	—	0.0
	Bro AA	107	391	68	82	15	7	0	—	38	1	—	.210	.281	.284	84	-5	—	.870	17	109	122	S107,P2,2b2	—	1.3
1885	Lou AA	14	51	2	6	2	0	0	3	2	1	—	.118	.167	.157	3	-5	—	.872	-0	96	47	S14	—	-0.5
Total	2NA	39	172	20	42	4	1	0	10	1	—	4	.244	.249	.279	93	1	2-2	.791	2	244	620	O19(5/12/3),2b13,S6/31	—	0.1
Total	4	193	721	108	149	32	10	0	23	54	2	18	.207	.264	.279	79	-13	—	.864	13	104	111	S191,2b4,P2/rf	—	0.4
GEHRIG, LOU	Henry Louis "The Iron Horse"; B6.19.1903 New York NY; D6.2.1941 Riverdale NY; BL/TL/6´0˝/200; d6.15; HF1939; Col Columbia																								
1923	NY A	13	26	6	11	4	1	1	9	2	0	5	.423	.464	.769	217	4	0-0	.933	-1	82	104	1b9	—	0.3
1924	NY A	10	12	2	6	1	0	0	5	1	0	3	.500	.538	.583	190	2	0-0	1.000	0	138	0	1b2/rf	—	0.2
1925	NY A	126	437	73	129	23	10	20	68	46	2	49	.295	.365	.531	127	15	6-3	.989	-9	70	82	1b114,O6(2/0/4)	—	-0.2
1926	†NY A	**155**	572	135	179	47	**20**	16	112	105	1	73	.313	.420	.549	154	48	6-5	.991	-8	76	79	1b155	—	2.7
1927	†NY A	**155**	584	149	218	**52**	18	47	**175**	109	3	84	.373	.474	.765	224	**109**	10-8	.992	-7	83	99	1b155	—	8.4
1928	†NY A	**154**	562	139	210	**47**	13	27	**142**	95	4	69	.374	**.467**	.648	197	83	4-11	.989	-9	80	96	1b154	—	5.9
1929	NY A	**154**	553	127	166	32	10	35	126	122	5	68	.300	.431	.584	170	63	4-3	.994	-4	87	108	1b154	—	4.5
1930	NY A	**154**	581	143	220	42	17	41	**174**	101	3	63	.379	.473	.721	207	99	12-14	.989	2	102	86	1b153/lf	—	**7.7**
1931	NY A	**155**	619	**163**	**211**	31	15	**46**	**184**	117	0	56	.341	.446	.662	199	91	17-12	.991	-10	68	101	1b154/rf	—	6.0
1932	†NY A	**156**	596	138	208	42	9	34	151	108	3	38	.349	.451	.621	184	79	4-11	.987	-6	80	83	1b156	—	5.1
1933	NY A★	**152**	593	**138**	198	41	12	32	139	92	1	42	.334	.424	.605	181	70	9-13	.993	-3	81	85	1b152	—	4.7
1934	NY A★	**154**	579	128	210	40	6	**49**	**165**	109	2	31	**.363**	**.465**	**.706**	**213**	**100**	9-5	.994	1	99	107	1b153/S	—	**7.9**
1935	NY A★	**149**	535	**125**	176	26	10	30	119	**132**	5	38	.329	**.466**	.583	180	**72**	8-7	.990	0	100	89	1b149	—	5.3
1936	†NY A★	**155**	579	**167**	205	37	7	**49**	152	**130**	7	46	.354	**.478**	**.696**	**193**	**91**	3-4	.994	1	98	99	1b155	—	**6.6**
1937	†NY A★	**157**	569	138	200	37	9	37	159	**127**	4	49	.351	**.473**	.643	**177**	**74**	4-3	.989	-6	84	92	1b157	—	4.8
1938	†NY A★	**157**	576	115	170	32	6	29	114	107	5	75	.295	.410	.523	133	32	6-1	.991	-1	97	**117**	1b157	—	1.5
1939	NY A✳	8	28	2	4	0	0	0	1	5	0	1	.143	.273	.143	9	-4	0-0	.971	-1	86	90	1b8	—	-0.5
Total	17	2164	8001	1888	2721	534	163	493	1995	1508	45	790	.340	.447	.632	182	1028	102-100	.991	-59	86	95	1b2137,O9(3/0/6)/S	—	70.9
GEHRINGER, CHARLIE	Charles Leonard "The Mechanical Man"; B5.11.1903 Fowlerville MI; D1.21.1993 Bloomfield Hills MI; BL/TR/5´11˝/180; d9.22; Mil 1942–45; C1; HF1949; Col Michigan																								
1924	Det A	5	13	2	6	0	0	0	1	0	0	2	.462	.462	.462	141	1	1-1	.967	2	139	90	2b5	—	0.3
1925	Det A	8	18	3	3	0	0	0	0	2	0	0	.167	.250	.167	7	-3	0-1	1.000	3	151	199	2b6	—	0.0
1926	Det A	123	459	62	127	19	17	1	48	30	1	42	.277	.322	.399	86	-12	9-7	.973	-6	94	89	2b112,3b6	—	-1.5
1927	Det A	133	508	110	161	29	11	4	61	52	2	31	.317	.383	.441	112	9	17-8	.965	17	108	**110**	2b121	—	2.9
1928	Det A	**154**	603	108	193	29	16	6	74	69	6	22	.320	.395	.451	120	19	15-9	.962	-0	99	103	2b154	—	2.2
1929	Det A	**155**	634	**131**	**215**	**45**	**19**	13	106	64	6	19	.339	.405	.532	139	36	**27**-10	**.975**	-8	96	82	2b154	—	3.3
1930	Det A	**154**	610	144	201	47	15	16	98	69	7	17	.330	.404	.534	133	32	19-15	**.979**	5	97	94	2b154	—	3.6
1931	Det A	101	383	67	119	24	5	4	53	29	0	15	.311	.359	.431	103	1	13-4	.979	-4	91	102	2b78,1b9	—	0.3
1932	Det A	152	618	112	184	44	11	19	107	68	3	34	.298	.370	.497	118	16	9-8	.967	2	97	110	2b152	—	2.4
1933	Det A★	**155**	628	103	204	42	6	12	105	68	3	27	.325	.393	.468	125	24	5-4	.981	5	102	117	2b155	—	3.6
1934	†Det A★	**154**	601	**134**	**214**	50	7	11	127	99	3	25	.356	.450	.517	149	50	11-8	.981	7	103	101	2b154	—	6.0
1935	†Det A★	150	610	123	201	32	8	19	108	79	3	16	.330	.409	.502	139	37	11-4	**.985**	2	99	104	2b149	—	4.6
1936	Det A★	**154**	641	144	227	**60**	12	15	116	83	4	13	.354	.431	.555	141	44	4-1	**.974**	16	103	**116**	2b154	—	6.1
1937	Det A★	144	564	133	209	40	1	14	96	90	1	25	**.371**	.458	.520	143	43	11-4	**.986**	-0	106	100	2b142	—	4.8
1938	Det A★	152	568	133	174	32	5	20	107	113	4	21	.306	.425	.486	121	23	14-1	.976	1	100	107	2b152	—	3.2
1939	Det A	118	406	86	132	29	6	16	86	68	1	16	.325	.423	.544	135	23	4-3	**.977**	4	100	101	2b107	—	3.1
1940	†Det A	139	515	108	161	33	3	10	81	101	3	17	.313	.428	.447	116	18	10-0	.972	-19	89	77	2b138	—	1.0
1941	Det A	127	436	65	96	19	4	3	46	95	3	26	.220	.363	.303	71	-15	1-2	**.982**	0	95	77	2b116	0	-0.8
1942	Det A	45	45	6	12	0	0	1	7	7	0	4	.267	.365	.333	90	0	0-0	1.000	1	113	59	2b3	0	0.0
Total	19	2323	8860	1774	2839	574	146	184	1427	1186	50	372	.320	.404	.480	123	346	181-90	.976	27	99	100	2b2206,1b9,3b6	0	45.1
GEIER, PHIL	Philip Louis "Little Phil"; B11.3.1875 Washington DC; D9.25.1967 Spokane WA; BL/TR/5´7˝/145; d8.17; OF(14/167/98)																								
1896	Phi N	17	56	12	13	0	1	0	6	6	1	7	.232	.317	.268	56	-4	3	.813	-1	85	0	O12(2/0/10),2b3,C2	—	-0.4
1897	Phi N	92	316	51	88	6	2	1	35	56	3	—	.278	.392	.320	91	0	19	.932	-5	185	87	O45(2/3/40),2b37,S6,3b2	—	-0.4
1900	Cin N	30	113	18	29	1	4	0	10	7	1	—	.257	.306	.336	79	-4	3	.941	0	128	0	O27(0/9/18),3b2	—	-0.5
1901	Phi A	50	211	42	49	5	2	0	23	24	1	—	.232	.314	.275	61	-11	7	.934	-5	76	65	O50(6/14/30),S2/3	—	-1.7
	Mil A	11	39	4	7	1	1	0	1	5	0	—	.179	.273	.256	50	-3	4	1.000	0	276	574	O8C,3b3	—	-0.3
	Year	61	250	46	56	6	3	0	24	29	1	—	.224	.307	.272	60	-13	11	.941	-5	96	116	O58(6/22/30),3b4,S2	—	-2.0
1904	Bos N	149	580	70	141	17	2	1	27	56	4	—	.243	.314	.284	88	-6	18	.933	-4	120	198	O137(4/133/0),3b7,2b5/S	—	-1.7
Total	5	349	1315	197	327	30	12	2	102	154	10	7	.249	.332	.294	81	-28	54	.932	-15	125	136	O279C,2b45,3b15,S9,C2	—	-5.0
GEIGER, GARY	Gary Merle; B4.4.1937 Sand Ridge IL; D4.24.1996 Murphysboro IL; BL/TR/6´0˝/(162–170); d4.15																								
1958	Cle A	91	195	28	45	3	1	1	6	27-0	3	43	.231	.330	.272	70	-7	2-2	.986	5	124	108	O53(1/44/8),3b2/P	0	-0.5
1959	Bos A	120	335	45	82	10	4	11	48	21-0	0	55	.245	.289	.397	83	-9	9-3	.989	-2	95	95	O95(46/61/1)	0	-1.5
1960	Bos A	77	245	32	74	13	3	9	33	23-0	3	38	.302	.369	.490	126	9	2-2	1.000	5	104	230	O66(5/7/59)	67	1.1
1961	Bos A	140	499	82	116	21	6	18	64	87-4	4	91	.232	.349	.407	99	1	16-4	.988	3	102	**173**	O137C	0	0.2
1962	Bos A	131	466	67	116	18	4	16	54	67-3	2	66	.249	.344	.408	99	0	18-11	.987	-1	100	137	O129C	0	-0.4
1963	Bos A	121	399	67	105	13	5	16	44	36-2	3	63	.263	.327	.441	110	5	9-4	.984	8	115	196	O95(2/89/4),1b6	0	1.0
1964	Bos A	5	13	3	5	0	1	0	1	2-0	0	2	.385	.467	.538	170	1	0-0	1.000	0	111	0	O4(0/1/3)	0	0.1
1965	Bos A	24	45	5	9	3	0	1	2	13-1	0	10	.200	.379	.333	98	1	3-0	.970	0	117	0	O16(5/10/1)	94	0.1
1966	Atl N	78	126	23	33	5	3	4	10	21-1	1	29	.262	.367	.444	124	5	0-1	.982	-1	74	226	O49(5/33/15)	0	0.2
1967	Atl N	69	117	17	19	1	1	1	5	20-0	0	35	.162	.285	.214	45	-8	1-1	.980	-2	81	120	O38(6/26/7)	0	-1.2
1969	Hou N	93	125	19	28	4	1	0	16	24-2	1	34	.224	.351	.272	78	-2	2-1	.968	1	103	153	O65(47/5/14)	0	-0.3
1970	Hou N	5	4	0	1	0	0	0	0	0-0	0	0	.250	.250	.250	36	0	0-0	1.000	0	101	0	O2R	0	0.0
Total	12	954	2569	388	633	91	29	77	283	341-13	17	466	.246	.337	.394	98	-4	62-29	.986	17	102	155	O749(117/542/114),1b6,3b2/P	161	-1.2
GEIS, BILL	William J. (b William J. Geiss); B7.15.1858 Chicago IL; D9.18.1924 Chicago IL; 5´10˝/164; d7.19; b–Emil; ▲																								
1882	Bal AA	13	41	2	6	0	1	0	2	1	—	—	.146	.167	.195	23	-3	—	.738	-3	73	0	P13,O4(0/3/2)	—	-0.1
1884	Det N	75	283	22	50	11	4	2	16	6	—	60	.177	.194	.265	46	-17	—	.862	-7	95	86	2b73/rf1P	—	-2.0
Total	2	88	324	24	56	11	5	2	18	7	—	60	.173	.190	.256	43	-20	—	.862	-10	95	86	2b73,P14,O5(0/3/3)/1	—	-2.1
GEISS, EMIL	Emil August; B3.20.1867 Chicago IL; D10.4.1911 Chicago IL; BR/TR/5´11˝/170; d5.18; b–Bill; ▲																								
1887	Chi N	3	12	0	1	0	0	0	0	0	0	7	.083	.083	.083	-47	-2	0	.571	-1	58	0	/21P	—	-0.3
GELBERT, CHARLIE	Charles Magnus; B1.26.1906 Scranton PA; D1.13.1967 Easton PA; BR/TR/5´11˝/170; d4.16; Col Lebanon Valley																								
1929	StL N	146	512	60	134	29	8	3	65	51	0	46	.262	.329	.367	71	-23	8	.948	8	101	100	S146	—	0.0
1930	†StL N	139	513	92	156	39	11	3	72	43	2	41	.304	.360	.441	89	-8	6	.947	5	97	104	S139	—	1.0
1931	†StL N	131	447	61	129	29	5	1	62	54	0	31	.289	.365	.383	97	1	7	.959	9	101	105	S130	—	1.9
1932	StL N	122	455	60	122	28	9	1	45	39	3	30	.268	.330	.376	87	-8	8	.945	-3	94	87	S122	—	-0.1
1935	StL N	62	168	24	49	7	2	2	21	17	0	18	.292	.357	.393	97	0	0	.978	3	103	187	3b37,S21,2b3	—	0.5
1936	StL N	93	280	33	64	15	2	3	27	25	0	26	.229	.292	.329	67	-13	2	.965	4	110	153	3b60,S28,2b8	—	-0.5
1937	Cin N	43	114	12	22	4	0	1	13	15	0	12	.193	.287	.254	51	-8	1	.968	-0	93	85	S37,2b9/3	—	-0.5
	Det A	20	47	4	4	2	0	0	1	4	0	11	.085	.157	.128	-27	-9	0-0	.934	-1	102	101	S16	—	-0.5
1939	Was A	68	188	36	48	7	5	3	29	30	1	11	.255	.361	.394	100	0	2-0	.970	-2	104	100	S28,3b20/2	—	-0.9
1940	Was A	22	54	7	20	7	1	0	7	4	1	3	.370	.424	.537	157	5	0-0	.920	-4	81	42	S12,P2/2	—	0.1
	Bos A	30	91	9	18	2	0	0	8	8	0	16	.198	.263	.220	25	-10	0-0	.926	3	122	97	3b29/S	—	0.1
	Year	52	145	16	38	9	1	0	15	12	1	19	.262	.323	.338	72	-6	0-0	.926	-1	122	97	3b29,S13,P2/2	—	-0.6
																								—	-0.5
Total	9	876	2869	398	766	169	43	17	350	290	7	245	.267	.336	.374	82	-73	34-0	.951	22	98	98	S680,3b147,2b22,P2	—	1.0

YEAR	TM LG	G	AB	R	H	2B	3B	HR	RBI	BB-IB	HP	SO	AVG	OBP	SLG	AOPS	ABR	SB-CS	FA	FR	RNG	THR	GAMES AT POSITION	DL	BFW
Genins, Frank	C. Frank "Frenchy"; B11.2.1866 St.Louis MO; D9.30.1922 St.Louis MO; TR; d7.5																								
1892	Cin N	35	110	12	20	4	0	0	7	12	0	12	.182	.262	.218	46	-7	7	.901	3	115	119	S17,O14(7/7/0),3b4	—	-0.4
	StL N	15	51	5	10	1	0	0	4	1	0	11	.196	.212	.216	31	-4	3	.821	-6	75	94	S14/rf	—	-0.9
	Year	50	161	17	30	5	0	0	11	13	0	23	.186	.247	.217	42	-11	10	.868	-3	97	108	S31,O15(7/7/1),3b4	—	-1.3
1895	Pit N	73	252	43	63	8	0	2	24	22	2	14	.250	.315	.306	64	-13	19	.931	-7	24	0	O29(14/3/12),3b16,2b16,S8,1b2	—	-1.7
1901	Cle A	26	101	15	23	5	0	0	9	8	0	—	.228	.284	.277	58	-5	3	.940	1	94	125	O26C	—	-0.5
Total	3	149	514	75	116	18	0	2	44	43	2	37	.226	.288	.272	56	-29	32	.934	-9	66	48	O70(21/36/13),S39,3b20,2b16,1b2	—	-3.5
Genovese, George	George Michael; B2.22.1922 Staten Island NY; BL/TR/5´6.5˝/160; d4.29																								
1950	Was A	3	1	1	0	0	0	0	0	1	0	0	.000	.500	.000	39	0	0-0	ø	0	—	—	/H	0	0.0
Gentile, Jim	James Edward "Diamond Jim"; B6.3.1934 San Francisco CA; BL/TL/6´4˝/(205–215); d9.10																								
1957	Bro N	4	6	1	1	0	0	1	1	1-0	0	1	.167	.286	.667	133	0	0-0	1.000	-0	0	351	1b2	0	0.0
1958	LA N	12	30	0	4	1	0	0	4	4-1	0	6	.133	.235	.167	9	-4	0-0	.981	-1	48	145	1b8	0	-0.5
1960	Bal A★	138	384	67	112	17	0	21	98	68-5	7	72	.292	.403	.500	146	28	0-0	.993	-6	75	110	1b124	0	1.6
1961	Bal A★	148	486	96	147	25	2	46	141	96-5	11	106	.302	.423	.646	189	65	1-1	.989	-0	99	116	1b144	0	5.5
1962	Bal A★	152	545	80	137	21	1	33	87	77-**16**	7	100	.251	.346	.475	128	22	1-0	.988	4	110	103	1b150	0	1.7
1963	Bal A	145	496	65	123	16	1	24	72	76-9	6	101	.248	.353	.429	123	17	1-0	**.995**	8	**118**	**114**	1b143	0	1.8
1964	KC A	136	439	71	110	10	0	28	71	84-6	4	122	.251	.372	.465	128	20	0-0	.988	-1	100	82	1b128	0	1.2
1965	KC A	38	118	14	29	5	0	10	22	9-1	1	26	.246	.305	.542	138	5	0-0	.981	-2	86	98	1b35	0	0.2
	Hou N	81	227	22	55	11	1	7	31	34-7	5	72	.242	.352	.392	118	7	0-0	.993	-0	98	85	1b68	0	0.3
1966	Hou N	49	144	16	35	6	1	7	18	21-3	4	39	.243	.355	.444	129	6	0-0	.989	2	113	86	1b43	0	0.6
	Cle A	33	47	2	6	1	0	2	4	5-1	0	18	.128	.212	.277	39	-4	0-0	.944	-0	105	76	1b9	0	-0.5
Total	9	936	2922	434	759	113	6	179	549	475-54	45	663	.260	.368	.486	137	162	3-1	.990	4	101	103	1b854	0	11.9
Gentile, Sam	Samuel Christopher; B10.12.1916 Charlestown MA; D5.4.1998 Everett MA; BL/TR/5´11˝/180; d4.24; Mil 1944–45; Col St. Johns																								
1943	Bos N	8	4	1	1	1	0	0	0	1	0	0	.250	.400	.500	162	0	0	ø	0	—	—	/H	0	0.0
Gentry, Harvey	Harvey William; B5.27.1926 Winston–Salem NC; BL/TR/6´0˝/170; d4,14; b–Rufe																								
1954	NY N	5	4	0	1	0	0	0	1	1	0	0	.250	.400	.250	73	0	0-0	ø	0	—	—	/H	0	0.0
George, Alex	Alex Thomas M.; B9.27.1938 Kansas City MO; BL/TR/5´11.5˝/170; d9.16																								
1955	KC A	5	10	0	1	0	0	0	0	1-0	0	7	.100	.182	.100	-22	-2	0-0	.917	-1	62	55	S5	0	-0.3
George, Greek	Charles Peter; B12.25.1912 Waycross GA; D8.15.1999 Metairie LA; BR/TR/6´2˝/200; d6.30; Col Oglethorpe																								
1935	Cle A	2	0	0	0	0	0	0	0	0	0	0	ø	ø	ø	ø	0	0-0	1.000	0	*0*	*0*	/C	—	0.0
1936	Cle A	23	77	3	15	3	0	0	5	9	0	16	.195	.279	.234	28	-9	0-0	.994	8	*122*	*122*	C22	—	0.1
1938	Bro N	7	20	0	4	0	1	0	2	0	0	4	.200	.200	.300	35	-2	0	1.000	1	*72*	*170*	C7	—	-0.1
1941	Chi N	35	64	4	10	2	0	0	6	2	0	10	.156	.182	.188	4	-8	0	.973	1	*91*	*102*	C18	0	-0.7
1945	Phi A	51	138	8	24	4	1	0	11	17	0	29	.174	.265	.217	41	-10	0-0	.972	-5	*87*	62	C46	0	-1.4
Total	5	118	299	15	53	9	2	0	24	28	0	59	.177	.248	.221	29	-29	0-0	.983	5	*97*	*94*	C94	0	-2.1
Geraghty, Ben	Benjamin Raymond; B7.19.1912 Jersey City NJ; D6.18.1963 Jacksonville FL; BR/TR/5´11˝/175; d4.17; Col Villanova																								
1936	Bro N	51	129	11	25	4	0	0	9	8	0	16	.194	.241	.225	26	-14	4	.922	-7	83	60	S31,2b9,3b5	—	-1.8
1943	Bos N	8	1	2	0	0	0	0	0	0	0	0	.000	.000	.000	-99	0	0	1.000	0	139	0	/2S3	0	0.0
1944	Bos N	11	16	3	4	0	0	0	0	1	0	2	.250	.294	.250	52	-1	0	1.000	-1	131	0	2b4,3b3	0	-0.2
Total	3	70	146	16	29	4	0	0	9	9	0	18	.199	.245	.226	28	-15	4	.922	-8	82	59	S32,2b14,3b9	0	-2.0
Gerber, Craig	Craig Stuart; B1.8.1959 Chicago IL; BL/TR/6´0˝/175; [AnaA81 20/496]; d4.11; Col Cal Poly–San Luis Obispo																								
1985	Cal A	65	91	8	24	1	2	0	6	2-0	0	3	.264	.277	.319	63	-5	0-3	.970	9	128	145	S53,3b9/2D	0	0.6
Gerber, Wally	Walter "Spooks"; B8.18.1891 Columbus OH; D6.19.1951 Columbus OH; BR/TR/5´10˝/152; d9.23; Mil 1918																								
1914	Pit N	17	54	5	13	1	1	0	5	2	1	8	.241	.281	.296	75	-2	0	.921	1	115	122	S17	—	0.0
1915	Pit N	56	144	8	28	2	0	0	7	9	2	16	.194	.252	.208	40	-10	6-1	.930	1	97	72	3b23,S21,2b2	—	-0.7
1917	StL A	14	39	2	12	1	1	0	2	3	0	2	.308	.357	.385	131	1	1	.939	0	115	45	S12,2b2	—	0.2
1918	StL A	56	171	10	41	4	0	0	10	19	0	11	.240	.316	.263	77	-4	2	.922	-10	95	88	S56	—	-1.1
1919	StL A	**140**	462	43	105	14	6	1	37	49	5	36	.227	.308	.290	67	-20	1	.940	-9	99	82	S140	—	-2.0
1920	StL A	**154**	584	70	163	26	2	2	60	58	2	32	.279	.346	.341	80	-15	4-13	.939	7	**106**	104	S154	—	-0.1
1921	StL A	114	436	55	121	12	9	2	48	34	5	19	.278	.337	.360	73	-18	4-7	.943	-1	94	111	S113	—	-0.8
1922	StL A	153	604	81	161	22	8	1	51	52	1	34	.267	.326	.334	70	-27	6-4	.944	-1	94	**127**	S153	—	-1.1
1923	StL A	**154**	605	85	170	26	3	1	62	54	2	50	.281	.342	.339	75	-21	4-6	.950	7	97	111	S154	—	0.2
1924	StL A	148	496	61	135	20	4	0	55	43	9	34	.272	.341	.329	69	-22	4-5	.946	-6	94	107	S147	—	-1.3
1925	StL A	72	246	29	67	13	1	0	19	26	1	15	.272	.344	.333	69	-11	1-2	.949	5	104	94	S71	—	0.0
1926	StL A	131	411	37	111	8	0	0	42	40	3	29	.270	.339	.290	62	-22	0-2	.944	2	99	**127**	S129	—	-0.8
1927	StL A	142	438	44	98	13	9	0	45	35	2	25	.224	.284	.295	49	-35	3-6	.946	9	102	110	S141/3	—	-1.2
1928	StL A	6	18	1	5	1	0	0	0	1	0	3	.278	.316	.333	69	-1	0-0	.783	-2	91	158	S6	—	-0.2
	Bos A	104	300	21	64	6	1	0	28	32	0	31	.213	.289	.240	41	-26	6-1	.955	27	124	94	S103	—	1.2
	Year	110	318	22	69	7	1	0	28	33	0	34	.217	.291	.245	43	-26	6-1	.948	**26**	**122**	97	S109	—	1.0
1929	Bos A	61	91	6	15	3	1	0	5	8	0	12	.165	.232	.220	17	-12	1-0	.937	5	102	38	S30,2b22	—	-0.4
Total	15	1522	5099	558	1309	172	46	7	476	465	33	357	.257	.323	.313	67	-245	43-47	.943	36	100	106	S1447,2b26,3b24	—	-8.1
Geren, Bob	Robert Peter; B9.22.1961 San Diego CA; BR/TR/6´3˝/(200–228); [SDN79 1/24]; d5.17; C4																								
1988	NY A	10	10	0	1	0	0	0	0	2-0	0	3	.100	.250	.100	2	-1	0-0	1.000	-0	124	0	C10	0	-0.1
1989	NY A	65	205	26	59	5	1	9	27	12-0	1	44	.288	.329	.454	120	4	0-0	.991	5	189	81	C60,D2	0	1.2
1990	NY A	110	277	21	59	7	0	8	31	13-1	5	73	.213	.259	.325	62	-15	0-0	.993	1	101	**142**	C107/D	0	-0.9
1991	NY A	64	128	7	28	3	0	2	12	9-0	0	31	.219	.270	.289	54	-8	0-1	.989	-3	87	98	C63	0	-0.9
1993	SD N	58	145	8	31	6	0	3	6	13-4	0	28	.214	.278	.317	59	-9	0-0	.993	1	80	133	C49/13	0	-0.5
Total	5	307	765	62	178	21	1	22	76	49-5	6	179	.233	.283	.349	74	-29	0-1	.992	4	116	115	C289,D3/31	0	-1.2
Gerhardt, Joe	John Joseph "Move Up Joe"; B2.14.1855 Washington DC; D3.11.1922 Middletown NY; BR/TR/6´0˝/160; d9.1; M2																								
1873	Was NA	13	57	6	12	3	0	0	9	0	—	6	.211	.211	.263	40	-4	0-1	.710	-4	91	123	S13	—	-0.6
1874	Bal NA	14	61	10	19	0	1	0	6	0	—	0	.311	.311	.344	111	1	0-0	.750	1	125	94	S14	—	0.1
1875	Mut NA	58	252	29	54	7	3	0	20	0	—	2	.214	.214	.266	62	-10	0-5	.753	0	109	67	3b47,2b13/Slf	—	-1.2
1876	Lou N	65	292	33	76	10	3	2	18	3	—	5	.260	.268	.336	85	-7	—	.944	4	**133**	83	1b54,2b5,S3,O2L,3b2	—	-0.5
1877	Lou N	59	250	41	76	6	5	1	35	5	—	8	.304	.318	.380	101	-2	—	.888	19	**121**	**150**	2b57/cfS1	—	1.7
1878	Cin N	60	259	46	77	7	2	0	28	7	—	14	.297	.316	.340	127	8	—	.906	6	102	118	2b60	—	1.6
1879	Cin N	79	313	22	62	12	3	1	39	3	—	19	.198	.206	.265	57	-14	—	.908	4	94	100	2b55,3b16,1b8/S	—	-0.7
1881	Det N	80	297	35	72	13	6	0	36	7	—	31	.242	.260	.327	80	-7	—	.908	6	94	**153**	2b79/3	—	0.2
1883	Lou AA	78	319	56	84	11	9	0	—	14	—	—	.263	.294	.354	116	7	—	.906	18	112	133	2b78,M	—	2.4
1884	Lou AA	106	404	39	89	7	8	0	40	13	5	—	.220	.254	.277	76	-10	—	.920	23	113	**164**	2b106	—	1.5
1885	NY N	**112**	399	43	62	12	2	0	33	24	—	47	.155	.203	.195	30	-30	—	.911	9	98	151	2b112	—	-1.6
1886	NY N	123	426	44	81	11	7	0	40	22	—	63	.190	.230	.249	45	-29	8	.924	9	96	105	2b123	—	-1.4
1887	NY N	1	4	0	0	0	0	0	0	0	0	0	.000	.000	.000	-99	-1	0	1.000	0	108	0	/3	—	-0.1
	NY AA	85	307	40	68	13	2	0	27	24	1	—	.221	.280	.277	58	-16	15	.896	9	104	116	2b84/3	—	-0.4
1890	Bro AA	99	369	34	75	10	4	2	40	30	4	—	.203	.270	.268	61	-19	9	.938	33	122	133	2b99	—	1.5
	StL AA	37	125	15	32	0	0	1	11	9	3	—	.256	.321	.280	68	-6	5	.955	6	101	64	2b20,3b17,M	—	0.1
	Year	136	494	49	107	10	4	3	51	39	7	—	.217	.283	.271	63	-25	14	**.940**	**38**	**119**	**122**	2b119,3b17	—	1.6
1891	Lou AA	2	6	0	0	0	0	0	0	1	0	0	.000	.143	.000	-59	-1	0	.833	-1	98	0	2b2	—	-0.2
Total	3NA	85	370	45	85	10	4	0	35	0	—	8	.230	.230	.278	67	-13	0-6	.753	-2	109	67	3b47,S28,2b13/lf	—	-1.7
Total	12	986	3770	448	854	112	51	7	347	162	13	187	.227	.261	.289	72	-127	37	.913	144	105	131	2b880,1b63,3b38,S5,O3(2/1/0)	—	4.1

YEAR	TM LG	G	AB	R	H	2B	3B	HR	RBI	BB-IB	HP	SO	AVG	OBP	SLG	AOPS	ABR	SB-CS	FA	FR	RNG	THR	GAMES AT POSITION	DL	BFW
Gerhart, Ken	Harold Kenneth; B5.19.1961 Charleston SC; BR/TR/6´0˝/(185–195); [BalA82 5/130]; d9.14; Col Middle Tennessee																								
1986	Bal A	20	69	4	16	2	0	1	7	4-0	0	18	.232	.267	.304	58	-4	0-1	.971	-2	84	0	O20(6/14/0)	0	-0.7
1987	Bal A	92	284	41	69	10	2	14	34	17-0	1	53	.243	.286	.440	91	-5	9-2	.973	-4	93	64	O91(53/42/0)	53	-1.0
1988	Bal A	103	262	27	51	10	1	9	23	21-0	2	57	.195	.256	.344	69	-12	7-3	.975	-2	97	75	O93(30/57/10),D3	12	-1.5
Total	3	215	615	72	136	22	3	24	64	42-0	3	128	.221	.271	.384	78	-21	16-6	.974	-8	94	63	O204(89/113/10),D3	65	-3.2
Gerken, George	George Herbert "Pickles"; B7.28.1903 Chicago IL; D10.23.1977 Arcadia CA; BR/TR/5´11.5˝/175; d4.19																								
1927	Cle A	6	14	1	3	0	0	0	2	1	0	3	.214	.267	.214	26	-2	0-0	.917	0	105	250	O5(2/3/0)	—	-0.1
1928	Cle A	38	115	16	26	7	2	0	9	12	1	22	.226	.305	.322	64	-6	3-4	.940	-1	99	89	O34(14/16/4)	—	-1.0
Total	2	44	129	17	29	7	2	0	11	13	1	25	.225	.301	.310	60	-8	3-4	.937	-1	100	106	O39(16/19/4)	—	-1.1
Gerlach, Johnny	John Glenn; B5.11.1917 Shullsburg WI; D8.28.1999 Madison WI; BR/TR/5´9˝/165; d9.3; Col Wisconsin–Madison																								
1938	Chi A	9	25	2	7	0	0	0	1	4	0	2	.280	.379	.280	66	-1	0-0	.949	1	97	197	S8	—	0.0
1939	Chi A	3	2	0	2	0	0	0	0	0	0	0	1.000	1.000	1.000	402	1	0-0	1.000	0	140	0	/3	—	0.1
Total	2	12	27	2	9	0	0	0	1	4	0	2	.333	.419	.333	89	0	0-0	.949	1	97	197	S8/3	—	0.1
German, Esteban	Esteban (Guridi); B1.26.1978 Haina, D.R.; BR/TR/5´10˝/(165–180); d5.21																								
2002	Oak A	9	35	4	7	0	0	0	0	4-0	1	11	.200	.300	.200	37	-3	1-0	.978	1	95	111	2b8	0	-0.2
2003	Oak A	5	4	0	1	0	0	0	1	0-0	0	1	.250	.250	.250	32	0	0-0	1.000	1	149	110	2b5	0	0.1
2004	Oak A	31	60	9	15	1	1	0	7	4-0	0	13	.250	.297	.300	57	-4	0-1	.935	2	91	159	3b15,2b10,D2	27	-0.2
2005	Tex A	5	4	3	3	1	0	0	1	0-0	0	1	.750	.750	1.000	351	1	2-0	.917	2	267	268	/23	0	0.4
2006	KC A	106	279	44	91	18	5	3	34	40-0	6	49	.326	.422	.459	130	15	7-3	.987	-10	78	81	2b26,O25(14/11/0),D25,3b24/1S	0	0.5
Total	5	156	382	60	117	20	6	3	43	48-0	7	75	.306	.394	.414	112	9	10-4	.983	-4	102	111	2b50,3b40,D27,O25(14/11/0)/S1	27	0.6
Gernert, Dick	Richard Edward; B9.28.1928 Reading PA; BR/TR/6´3˝/(205–210); d4.16; C2; Col Temple																								
1952	Bos A	102	367	58	89	20	2	19	67	35	5	83	.243	.317	.463	107	2	4-1	.987	-1	97	113	1b99	0	-0.2
1953	Bos A	139	494	73	125	15	1	21	71	88	5	82	.253	.371	.415	106	7	0-7	.986	-2	97	107	1b136	0	-0.6
1954	Bos A	14	23	2	6	2	0	0	1	6	0	4	.261	.414	.348	99	0	0-0	1.000	-1	31	110	1b6	0	-0.1
1955	Bos A	7	20	6	4	2	0	0	1	1-0	0	5	.200	.238	.300	40	-2	0-0	.974	-0	105	54	1b5	0	-0.2
1956	Bos A	106	306	53	89	11	0	16	68	56-1	2	57	.291	.399	.484	119	10	1-0	.985	4	81	146	O50L,1b37	0	0.9
1957	Bos A	99	316	45	75	13	3	14	58	39-3	3	62	.237	.324	.430	99	-1	1-1	.989	-1	107	123	1b71,O16L	0	-0.6
1958	Bos A	122	431	59	102	19	1	20	69	59-4	2	78	.237	.330	.425	100	0	2-0	.991	8	**129**	104	1b114	0	0.2
1959	Bos A	117	298	41	78	14	1	11	42	52-3	0	49	.262	.369	.426	113	7	1-2	.995	6	129	100	1b75,O25(21/0/7)	0	0.8
1960	Chi N	52	96	8	24	3	0	0	11	10-0	0	19	.250	.321	.281	67	-4	1-0	.987	3	144	103	1b18,O5L	0	-0.2
	Det A	21	50	6	15	4	0	1	5	4-0	0	5	.300	.352	.440	110	1	0-0	1.000	-1	65	160	1b13,O6L	0	-0.1
1961	Det A	6	5	1	1	0	0	1	1	1-0	0	2	.200	.333	.800	187	1	0-0	ø	0	—	—	/H	0	0.1
	†Cin N	40	63	4	19	1	0	0	7	7-1	0	9	.302	.361	.317	84	-1	0-0	.993	3	156	74	1b21	0	0.1
1962	Hou N	10	24	1	5	0	0	0	1	5-0	0	7	.208	.345	.208	57	-1	0-0	1.000	-1	39	151	1b9	0	-0.3
Total	11	835	2493	357	632	104	8	103	402	363-12	17	462	.254	.351	.426	104	19	10-11	.990	16	113	108	1b604,O102(98/0/7)	0	-0.2
Geronimo, Cesar	Cesar Francisco (Zorrilla); B3.11.1948 Santa Cruz de El Seibo, D.R.; BL/TL/6´2˝/(164–175); d4.16																								
1969	Hou N	28	8	8	2	1	0	0	0	0-0	0	3	.250	.250	.375	74	0	0-0	1.000	-0	45	0	O9(4/1/4)	0	-0.1
1970	Hou N	47	37	5	9	0	0	0	2	2-0	1	5	.243	.293	.243	49	-3	0-0	.920	0	129	0	O26(12/5/10)	0	-0.3
1971	Hou N	94	82	13	18	2	2	1	6	5-0	0	31	.220	.264	.329	69	-4	2-2	.977	-1	76	50	O64(47/3/15)	0	-0.7
1972	†Cin N	120	255	32	70	9	7	4	29	24-7	3	64	.275	.344	.412	120	6	2-7	.982	3	102	179	O106(0/21/91)	0	0.3
1973	†Cin N	139	324	35	68	14	3	4	33	23-3	3	74	.210	.266	.309	62	-18	5-5	.992	4	106	135	O130(0/104/26)	0	-1.8
1974	Cin N	150	474	73	133	17	8	7	54	46-11	2	96	.281	.345	.395	109	5	9-5	.987	11	113	169	O145C	0	1.3
1975	†Cin N	148	501	69	129	25	5	6	53	48-8	4	97	.257	.327	.363	90	-7	13-5	.993	11	113	134	O148C	0	0.2
1976	†Cin N	149	486	59	149	24	11	2	49	56-13	6	95	.307	.382	.414	123	17	22-5	.985	-2	107	45	O146C	0	1.5
1977	Cin N	149	492	54	131	22	4	10	52	35-13	5	89	.266	.321	.388	87	-9	10-4	.992	7	113	102	O147C	0	-0.3
1978	Cin N	122	296	28	67	15	1	5	27	43-10	3	67	.226	.329	.334	86	-4	8-3	.981	2	108	77	O115C	0	-0.3
1979	†Cin N	123	356	38	85	17	4	4	38	37-11	2	56	.239	.312	.343	79	-10	1-1	.993	6	109	144	O118C	0	-0.5
1980	Cin N	103	145	16	37	5	0	2	9	14-3	0	24	.255	.319	.331	84	-3	2-1	1.000	0	102	72	O86C	0	-0.4
1981	†KC A	59	118	14	29	0	2	2	13	11-2	0	16	.246	.305	.331	85	-3	6-1	.980	2	120	37	O57(5/4/50)	0	-0.2
1982	KC A	53	119	14	32	6	3	4	23	8-2	0	16	.269	.305	.471	111	1	2-0	1.000	3	114	141	O44(10/32/3)/D	24	0.4
1983	KC A	38	87	2	18	4	0	0	4	2-0	2	13	.207	.242	.253	36	-8	0-1	.986	3	132	106	O35(9/3/26)	18	-0.6
Total	15	1522	3780	460	977	161	50	51	392	354-83	31	746	.258	.325	.368	93	-40	82-40	.988	48	109	113	O1376(87/1079/225)/D	42	-1.5
Gertenrich, Lou	Louis Wilhelm; B5.4.1875 Chicago IL; D10.20.1933 Chicago IL; BR/TR/5´8˝/175; d9.15																								
1901	Mil A	2	3	1	1	0	0	0	0	0	0	—	.333	.333	.333	90	0	0	ø	-0	0	0	/rf	—	0.0
1903	Pit N	1	3	0	0	0	0	0	0	0	0	—	.000	.000	.000	-97	-1	0	1.000	0	0	0	/rf	—	-0.1
Total	2	3	6	1	1	0	0	0	0	0	0	—	.167	.167	.167	-6	-1	0	1.000	-0	0	0	O2R	—	-0.1
Gerut, Jody	Joseph Diego; B9.18.1977 Elmhurst IL; BL/TL/6´0˝/190; [ColN98 2/71]; d4.26; Col Stanford; [DL 2006 Pit N 134]																								
2003	Cle A	127	480	66	134	33	2	22	75	35-4	7	70	.279	.336	.494	116	10	4-5	.984	2	98	138	O113(36/14/63),D11	0	0.6
2004	Cle A	134	481	72	121	31	5	11	51	54-4	7	59	.252	.334	.405	95	-3	13-6	.986	-1	100	83	O131(2/12/118)/D	16	-0.8
2005	Cle A	44	138	12	38	9	1	1	12	18-1	0	14	.275	.357	.377	100	1	1-1	1.000	-4	80	49	O38(17/0/21),D3	40	-0.5
	Chi N	11	14	1	1	1	0	0	0	2-0	0	3	.071	.188	.143	-11	-2	0-0	1.000	1	219	0	O5(4/0/1)	0	-0.1
	Pit N	4	18	2	4	1	0	0	2	0-0	0	3	.222	.222	.278	30	-2	0-0	1.000	-1	39	0	O4R	53	-0.3
	Year	15	32	3	5	2	0	0	2	2-0	0	6	.156	.206	.219	11	-4	0-0	1.000	-0	107	0	O9(4/0/5)	0	-0.4
Total	3	320	1131	153	298	75	8	34	140	109-9	14	149	.263	.334	.434	102	4	18-12	.987	-3	97	98	O291(59/26/207),D15	243	-1.1
Gessler, Doc	Henry Homer "Brownie"; B12.23.1880 Greensburg PA; D12.24.1924 Greensburg PA; BL/TL/5´10˝/180; d4.23; M1; Col Ohio U.																								
1903	Det A	29	105	9	25	5	4	0	12	3	2	—	.238	.273	.362	92	-1	1	.974	-1	40	153	O28R	—	-0.3
	Bro N	49	154	20	38	8	3	0	18	17	12	—	.247	.366	.338	104	2	9	.984	-2	71	74	O43(0/2/41)	—	-0.1
1904	Bro N	104	341	41	99	18	4	2	28	30	4	—	.290	.355	.384	131	13	13	.920	3	144	64	O88(14/72/2)/12	—	1.3
1905	Bro N	126	431	44	125	17	4	3	46	38	14	—	.290	.366	.369	129	18	26	.973	2	115	89	1b107,O12(1/1/10)	—	1.8
1906	Bro N	9	33	3	8	1	2	0	4	3	1	—	.242	.324	.394	134	1	3	.946	1	153	89	1b9	—	0.2
	†Chi N	34	83	8	21	3	0	0	10	12	1	—	.253	.354	.289	95	0	4	1.000	1	193	0	O21(0/19/2)/1	—	0.0
	Year	43	116	11	29	4	2	0	14	15	2	—	.250	.346	.319	104	1	7	1.000	1	193	0	O21(0/19/2),1b10	—	0.2
1908	Bos A	128	435	55	134	13	14	3	63	51	11	—	.308	**.394**	.423	161	31	19	.950	-4	60	111	O126R	—	2.4
1909	Bos A	111	396	57	115	24	1	0	46	31	8	—	.290	.354	.356	122	11	16	.933	1	138	34	O109R	—	0.9
	Was A	17	54	10	13	2	1	0	8	12	3	—	.241	.406	.315	134	4	4	1.000	-0	54	226	O16R/1	—	0.3
	Year	128	450	67	128	26	2	0	54	43	11	—	.284	.361	.351	123	15	20	.940	1	128	58	O125R/1	—	1.2
1910	Was A	145	487	58	126	17	12	2	50	62	**16**	—	.259	.361	.355	131	20	18	.953	-1	87	126	O144R	—	1.4
1911	Was A	128	450	65	127	19	5	4	78	74	20	—	.282	.406	.373	120	19	29	.943	-8	78	96	O126(2/0/124)/1	—	0.4
Total	8	880	2969	370	831	127	50	14	363	333	92	—	.280	.370	.370	128	118	142	.945	-9	95	91	O713(17/94/602),1b120/2	—	8.3
Gettig, Charlie	Charles Henry; B12.1870 Baltimore MD; D4.11.1935 Baltimore MD; BR/5´10˝/172; d8.5; OF(3/1/21); ▲																								
1896	NY N	6	9	3	3	1	0	0	0	0	0	0	.333	.333	.444	107	1	0	1.000	0	144	0	P4	—	0.0
1897	NY N	22	75	8	15	6	0	0	12	6	2	—	.200	.277	.280	49	-5	3	.556	-6	37	0	3b7,2b6,O3L,S3,P3	—	-1.0
1898	NY N	64	196	30	49	6	2	0	26	15	2	—	.250	.310	.301	78	-6	5	.833	-4	56	0	O21(0/1/20),P17,2b12,S9,3b4,1b2/C	—	-0.8
1899	NY N	34	97	7	24	3	0	0	9	7	1	—	.247	.305	.278	63	-5	4	.833	-3	99	0	P18,3b8,2b3,1b3/rf	—	-0.4
Total	4	126	377	48	91	16	2	0	47	28	5	0	.241	.302	.294	68	-15	12	.879	-13	116	43	P42,O25R,2b21,3b19,S12,1b5/C	—	-2.2
Gettinger, Tom	Lewis Thomas Leyton (b Lewis Thomas Leyton Gittinger); B12.11.1868 Frederick MD; D7.26.1943 Pensacola FL; BL/TL/5´10˝/180; d9.21																								
1889	StL AA	4	16	2	7	0	0	1	2	2	0	1	.438	.500	.625	194	2	0	.750	-1	0	0	O4(1/3/0)	—	0.0
1890	StL AA	58	227	31	54	7	5	3	30	20	1	—	.238	.302	.352	81	-7	8	.886	-4	88	52	O58L	—	-1.1
1895	Lou N	63	260	28	70	11	5	2	32	8	2	15	.269	.296	.373	77	-10	6	.910	-4	54	42	O63(0/34/29),P2	—	-1.4
Total	3	125	503	61	131	18	10	6	64	30	3	16	.260	.306	.372	82	-15	14	.897	-9	68	45	O125(59/37/29),P2	—	-2.5
Gettis, Byron	Byron Earl; B3.13.1980 Centreville IL; BR/TR/6´0˝/240; d5.27																								
2004	KC A	21	39	7	7	1	1	0	1	8-1	1	14	.179	.327	.256	57	-2	0-1	.930	2	123	211	O21(11/0/10)	0	-0.1

YEAR	TM LG	G	AB	R	H	2B	3B	HR	RBI	BB-IB	HP	SO	AVG	OBP	SLG	AOPS	ABR	SB-CS	FA	FR	RNG	THR	GAMES AT POSITION	DL	BFW
GETTMAN, JAKE	Jacob John; B10.25.1875 Frank, Russia; D10.4.1956 Denver CO; BB/TL/5´11˝/185; d8.20																								
1897	Was N	36	143	28	45	7	3	3	29	7	3	—	.315	.359	.469	118	3	8	.981	-2	63	0	O36R	—	0.0
1898	Was N	142	567	75	157	16	5	5	47	29	6	—	.277	.319	.349	92	-8	32	.926	2	96	80	O139(6/19/114),1b3	—	-1.2
1899	Was N	19	62	5	13	1	0	0	2	4	0	—	.210	.258	.226	33	-6	4	1.000	0	54	0	O16(6/10/0),1b2	—	-0.6
Total	3	197	772	108	215	24	8	8	78	40	9	—	.278	.322	.361	92	-11	44	.941	1	87	60	O191(12/29/150),1b5	—	-1.8
GETZ, GUS	Gustave "Gee-Gee"; B8.3.1889 Pittsburgh PA; D5.28.1969 Red Bank NJ; BR/TR/5´11˝/165; d8.15																								
1909	Bos N	40	148	6	33	2	0	0	9	1	0	—	.223	.228	.236	42	-11	2	.934	3	122	65	3b36,2b2,S2	—	-0.8
1910	Bos N	54	144	14	28	0	1	0	7	6	1	10	.194	.232	.208	27	-14	2	.915	5	117	141	3b22,2b13,O8(4/1/3),S4	—	-1.0
1914	Bro N	55	210	13	52	8	1	0	20	2	0	15	.248	.255	.295	62	-11	9	.949	12	123	159	3b55	—	0.3
1915	Bro N	130	477	39	123	10	5	2	46	8	3	14	.258	.275	.312	76	-16	19-15	.951	6	**113**	77	3b128,S2	—	-0.8
1916	†Bro N	40	96	9	21	1	2	0	8	0	0	5	.219	.219	.271	49	-6	9	.913	-3	81	0	3b20,S7,1b3	—	-1.0
1917	Cin N	7	14	2	4	0	0	0	3	3	0	0	.286	.412	.286	121	1	0	.875	-2	40	124	2b4,3b3	—	-0.2
1918	Cle A	6	15	2	2	1	0	0	0	4	1	1	.133	.350	.200	60	0	0	.941	-0	98	0	3b5	—	-0.1
	Pit N	7	10	0	2	0	0	0	0	0	0	1	.200	.200	.200	21	-1	0	.875	0	96	334	3b2	—	-0.1
Total	7	339	1114	85	265	22	9	2	93	24	5	46	.238	.257	.279	60	-58	41-15	.942	21	114	93	3b271,2b19,S15,O8(4/1/3),1b3	—	-3.7
GEYGAN, CHAPPIE	James Edward; B6.3.1903 Ironton OH; D3.15.1966 Columbus OH; BR/TR/5´11˝/170; d7.16																								
1924	Bos A	33	82	7	21	5	2	0	4	4	2	16	.256	.307	.366	73	-4	0-2	.952	2	99	94	S32	—	0.0
1925	Bos A	3	11	0	2	0	0	0	0	0	0	2	.182	.182	.182	-8	-2	0-0	.813	-2	69	55	S3	—	-0.3
1926	Bos A	4	10	0	3	0	0	0	0	1	0	1	.300	.364	.300	77	0	0-0	.800	-1	89	0	3b3	—	-0.1
Total	3	40	103	7	26	5	2	0	4	5	2	19	.252	.300	.340	65	-6	0-2	.938	-0	96	90	S35,3b3	—	-0.4
GHARRITY, PATSY	Edward Patrick; B3.13.1892 Parnell IA; D10.10.1966 Beloit WI; BR/TR/5´10˝/170; d5.16; C7																								
1916	Was A	39	92	8	21	5	1	0	9	8	1	18	.228	.297	.304	81	-2	2	1.000	-2	103	107	C16,1b16	—	-0.4
1917	Was A	76	176	15	50	5	0	0	18	14	0	18	.284	.337	.313	99	0	7	.980	1	116	84	1b46,C5/rf	—	0.0
1918	Was A	4	4	0	1	1	0	0	2	0	0	1	.250	.250	.500	129	0	0	ø	0	—	—	/H	—	0.0
1919	Was A	111	347	35	94	19	4	2	43	25	3	39	.271	.325	.366	95	-3	4	.969	-0	*88*	*98*	C60,O33(30/2/1),1b7	—	0.0
1920	Was A	131	428	51	105	18	3	3	44	37	1	52	.245	.307	.322	69	-20	6-5	.965	-2	*89*	*126*	C121,1b7/lf	—	-1.2
1921	Was A	121	387	62	120	19	8	7	55	45	3	44	.310	.386	.455	120	12	4-3	.977	6	***137***	*104*	C115	—	2.3
1922	Was A	96	273	40	70	16	6	5	45	36	4	30	.256	.351	.414	104	2	3-3	.981	5	*97*	***122***	C87	—	1.1
1923	Was A	93	251	26	52	9	4	3	33	22	2	27	.207	.276	.311	57	-17	6-2	.986	1	*97*	*114*	C35,1b33	—	-1.5
1929	Was A	3	2	0	0	0	0	0	0	1	0	2	.000	.333	.000	-7	0	0-0	ø	0	—	—	/H	—	0.0
1930	Was A	2	1	0	0	0	0	0	0	0	0	0	.000	.000	.000	-99	0	0-0	1.000	-0	0	0	/1	—	0.0
Total	10	676	1961	237	513	92	26	20	249	188	14	231	.262	.331	.366	90	-28	32-13	.974	8	*105*	*114*	C439,1b110,O35(31/2/2)	—	0.3
GIAMBI, JASON	Jason Gilbert; B1.8.1971 W.Covina CA; BL/TR/6´3˝/(200–235); [OakA92 2/58]; d5.8; b–Jeremy; Col Cal St.–Long Beach																								
1995	Oak A	54	176	27	45	7	0	6	25	28-0	3	31	.256	.364	.398	104	2	2-1	.960	0	100	88	3b30,1b26,D2	0	0.0
1996	Oak A	140	536	84	156	40	1	20	79	51-3	5	95	.291	.355	.481	111	9	0-1	.993	5	110	95	1b45,O45(44/0/1),3b39,D12	0	0.7
1997	Oak A	142	519	66	152	41	2	20	81	55-3	6	89	.293	.362	.495	123	18	0-1	.982	-2	80	124	O68L,1b51,D25	0	0.7
1998	Oak A	153	562	92	166	28	0	27	110	81-7	5	102	.295	.384	.489	128	25	2-2	.990	-11	76	100	1b146,D7	0	0.1
1999	Oak A	158	575	115	181	36	1	33	123	105-6	7	106	.315	.422	.553	152	50	1-1	.995	-16	53	103	1b142,D15/3	0	1.9
2000	†Oak A★	152	510	108	170	29	1	43	137	**137**-6	9	96	.333	**.476**	.647	**185**	77	2-0	.995	-8	74	101	1b124,D24	0	5.1
2001	†Oak A★	154	520	109	178	**47**	2	38	120	**129**-24	13	83	.342	**.477**	**.660**	**196**	**84**	2-0	.992	-4	89	107	1b136,D17	0	6.3
2002	†NY A★	155	560	120	176	34	1	41	122	109-4	15	112	.314	.435	.598	173	66	2-2	.995	-7	64	77	1b92,D63	0	4.5
2003	†NY A★	156	535	97	134	25	0	41	107	**129**-9	**21**	140	.250	.412	.527	148	45	2-1	.995	-13	35	94	1b85,D69	0	1.9
2004	NY A★	80	264	33	55	9	0	12	40	47-1	8	62	.208	.342	.379	89	-3	0-1	.990	-7	47	87	1b47,D28	65	-1.5
2005	†NY A	139	417	74	113	14	0	32	87	**108**-5	19	109	.271	**.440**	.535	159	43	0-0	.988	-9	46	90	1b78,D60	0	2.4
2006	†NY A	139	446	92	113	25	0	37	113	110-12	16	106	.253	.413	.558	150	39	2-0	.985	-10	33	91	D70,1b68	0	2.0
Total	12	1622	5620	1017	1639	335	8	350	1144	1089-80	127	1131	.292	.413	.541	148	455	15-10	.992	-83	67	97	1b1040,D392,O113(112/0/1),3b70	65	24.1
GIAMBI, JEREMY	Jeremy Dean; B9.30.1974 San Jose CA; BL/TL/6´0˝/(185–218); [KCA96 6/169]; d9.1; b–Jason; Col Cal St.–Fullerton																								
1998	KC A	18	58	6	13	4	0	2	8	11-0	0	9	.224	.343	.397	89	-1	0-1	1.000	-0	82	191	O9L,D7	0	-0.1
1999	KC A	90	288	34	82	13	1	3	34	40-5	3	67	.285	.373	.368	88	-4	0-0	.991	-4	54	92	D48,1b26,O5L	40	-1.1
2000	†Oak A	104	260	42	66	10	2	10	50	32-2	3	61	.254	.338	.423	94	-3	0-0	.966	-2	91	99	O55(6/0/49),D21,1b15	16	-0.8
2001	†Oak A	124	371	64	105	26	0	12	57	63-1	4	83	.283	.391	.450	121	15	0-1	.943	-9	62	38	D60,O47(11/0/37),1b10	24	-0.1
2002	Oak A	42	157	26	43	7	0	8	17	27-0	3	40	.274	.390	.471	129	8	0-0	.984	-4	84	0	O40L,D2	0	0.2
	Phi N	82	156	32	38	10	0	12	28	52-2	1	54	.244	.435	.538	165	18	0-1	.989	-4	76	119	1b21,O20(2/0/18),D8	0	1.2
2003	Bos A	50	127	15	25	5	0	5	15	26-0	2	42	.197	.342	.354	81	-3	1-0	.944	0	113	0	D30,O11(9/0/2)	83	-0.4
Total	6	510	1417	219	372	75	3	52	209	251-10	16	356	.263	.377	.430	110	30	1-3	.963	-23	81	48	O187(82/0/106),D176,1b72	163	-1.1
GIANNELLI, RAY	Raymond John; B2.5.1966 Brooklyn NY; BL/TR/6´0˝/195; [TorA88 38/992]; d5.4; Col New York Tech																								
1991	Tor A	9	24	2	4	1	0	0	0	5-0	0	9	.167	.310	.208	45	-2	1-0	.923	-2	78	149	3b9	0	-0.4
1995	StL N	9	11	0	1	0	0	0	0	3-0	0	4	.091	.286	.091	5	-1	0-0	1.000	-0	0	123	1b2,O2(1/0/1)	0	-0.2
Total	2	18	35	2	5	1	0	0	0	8-0	0	13	.143	.302	.171	32	-3	1-0	.923	-3	78	149	3b9,O2(1/0/1),1b2	0	-0.6
GIANNINI, JOE	Joseph Francis; B9.8.1888 Drytown CA; D9.26.1942 San Francisco CA; BL/TR/5´8˝/155; d8.7; Col San Francisco																								
1911	Bos A	1	2	0	1	1	0	0	0	0	0	—	.500	.500	1.000	317	1	0	.500	-1	108	0	/S	—	0.0
GIARRATANO, TONY	Anthony James; B11.29.1982 Queens NY; BB/TR/6´0˝/180; [DetA03 3/70]; d6.1; Col Tulane; [DL 2006 Det A 34]																								
2005	Det A	15	42	4	6	0	0	1	4	5-0	0	7	.143	.234	.214	21	-5	1-0	.949	-1	109	63	S13	0	-0.4
GIBBONS, JAY	Jay Jonathan; B3.2.1977 Rochester MI; BL/TL/6´0˝/(195–205); [TorA98 14/411]; d4.6; Col Cal St.–Los Angeles																								
2001	Bal A	73	225	27	53	10	0	15	36	17-0	4	39	.236	.301	.480	107	1	0-1	1.000	2	114	183	O28L,D28,1b7	64	0.0
2002	Bal A	136	490	71	121	29	1	28	69	45-3	2	66	.247	.311	.482	113	8	1-3	.994	-2	97	105	O92R,1b30,D12	0	-0.3
2003	Bal A	160	625	80	173	39	2	23	100	49-11	3	89	.277	.330	.456	106	5	0-1	.983	-2	97	95	O144R,1b13,D5	0	-0.6
2004	Bal A	97	346	36	85	14	1	10	47	29-0	1	64	.246	.303	.379	78	-12	1-1	.984	1	89	140	O66R,D16,1b14	61	-1.6
2005	Bal A	139	488	72	135	33	3	26	79	28-3	1	56	.277	.317	.516	117	10	0-0	.986	3	106	165	O71R,D42,1b22	0	0.5
2006	Bal A	90	343	34	95	23	0	13	46	32-2	2	48	.277	.341	.458	108	4	0-0	.980	2	121	41	D46,O44R	61	0.2
Total	6	695	2517	320	662	148	7	115	377	200-19	13	362	.263	.319	.464	106	16	2-6	.987	3	100	114	O445(28/0/417),D149,1b86	186	-1.8
GIBBONS, JOHN	John Michael; B6.8.1962 Great Falls MT; BR/TR/5´11˝/187; [NYN80 1/24]; d4.11; M3/C3																								
1984	NY N	10	31	1	2	0	0	0	1	3-1	1	11	.065	.171	.065	-32	-6	0-0	.983	-1	85	144	C9	33	-0.7
1986	NY N	8	19	4	9	4	0	1	1	3-1	0	5	.474	.545	.842	283	5	0-0	1.000	-0	110	39	C8	0	0.5
Total	2	18	50	5	11	4	0	1	2	6-2	1	16	.220	.316	.360	89	-1	0-0	.990	-1	95	102	C17	33	-0.2
GIBBS, JAKE	Jerry Dean; B11.7.1938 Grenada MS; BL/TR/6´0˝/(180–188); d9.11; Col U. of Mississippi																								
1962	NY A	2	0	2	0	0	0	0	0	0-0	0	0	ø	ø	ø	ø	0	0-0	ø	-0	0	0	/3	0	0.0
1963	NY A	4	8	1	2	0	0	0	0	0-0	0	1	.250	.250	.250	41	-1	0-0	1.000	-1	0	0	/C	0	-0.2
1964	NY A	3	6	1	1	0	0	0	0	0-0	0	2	.167	.167	.167	-7	-1	0-0	1.000	0	0	0	C2	0	-0.1
1965	NY A	37	68	6	15	1	0	2	7	4-0	1	20	.221	.267	.324	70	-3	0-0	.991	0	94	131	C21	0	-0.2
1966	NY A	62	182	19	47	6	0	3	20	19-2	0	16	.258	.327	.341	96	-1	5-2	.988	6	172	96	C54	35	0.9
1967	NY A	116	374	33	87	7	1	4	25	28-1	4	57	.233	.291	.289	75	-12	7-6	.975	-1	97	**129**	C99	0	-0.9
1968	NY A	124	423	31	90	12	3	3	29	27-5	6	68	.213	.270	.277	68	-17	9-8	.991	6	165	91	C121	0	-0.7
1969	NY A	71	219	18	49	9	2	0	18	23-9	0	30	.224	.294	.283	65	-10	3-4	.990	8	170	68	C66	0	0.0
1970	NY A	49	153	23	46	9	2	8	26	7-1	1	14	.301	.331	.542	144	8	2-0	.987	2	171	62	C44	0	1.2
1971	NY A	70	206	23	45	9	0	5	21	12-1	3	23	.218	.270	.335	74	-8	2-2	.988	-4	143	37	C51	0	-1.1
Total	10	538	1639	157	382	53	8	25	146	120-19	15	231	.233	.289	.321	80	-45	28-22	.986	16	146	89	C459/3	35	-1.1
GIBRALTER, STEVE	Stephan Benson; B10.9.1972 Dallas TX; BR/TR/6´0˝/190; [CinN90 6/162]; d6.1; [DL 1997 Cin N 181]																								
1995	Cin N	4	3	0	1	0	0	0	0	0-0	0	0	.333	.333	.333	76	0	0-0	1.000	0	91	0	O2C	1	0.0
1996	Cin N	2	2	0	0	0	0	0	0	0-0	0	2	.000	.000	.000	-98	-1	0-0	.000	-1	0	0	O2(1/1/0)	0	-0.1
Total	2	6	5	0	1	0	0	0	0	0-0	0	2	.200	.200	.200	6	-1	0-0	.500	-1	40	0	O4(1/3/0)	182	-0.1
GIBSON, CHARLIE	Charles Ellsworth "Gibby"; B11.17.1879 Sharon PA; D11.22.1954 Sharon PA; BR/TR/6´0˝/160; d9.23																								
1905	StL A	1	3	0	0	0	0	0	0	0	0	—	.000	.000	.000	-99	-1	0	1.000	-0	*75*	*166*	/C	—	-0.1

YEAR	TM LG	G	AB	R	H	2B	3B	HR	RBI	BB-IB	HP	SO	AVG	OBP	SLG	AOPS	ABR	SB-CS	FA	FR	RNG	THR	GAMES AT POSITION	DL	BFW
Gibson, Charlie	Charles Griffin; B11.21.1899 LaGrange GA; D12.18.1990 LaGrange GA; BR/TR/5´8˝/160; d5.30; Col Auburn																								
1924	Phi A	12	15	1	2	0	0	0	1	2	0	0	.133	.235	.133	-3	-2	0-0	.870	-1	100	128	C12	—	-0.3
Gibson, Derrick	Derrick Lamont; B2.5.1975 Winter Haven FL; BR/TR/6´2˝/244; [ColN93 13/380]; d9.8																								
1998	Col N	7	21	4	9	1	0	0	2	1-0	1	4	.429	.478	.476	126	1	0-0	.929	1	100	523	O7L	0	0.2
1999	Col N	10	28	2	5	1	0	2	6	0-0	1	7	.179	.207	.429	44	-3	0-0	.944	2	112	447	O10R	0	-0.1
Total	2	17	49	6	14	2	0	2	8	1-0	2	11	.286	.327	.449	78	-2	0-0	.938	3	106	482	O17(7/0/10)	0	0.1
Gibson, Frank	Frank Gilbert; B9.27.1890 Omaha NE; D4.27.1961 Austin TX; BB/TR (BL 1913)/6´0.5˝/172; d4.22																								
1913	Det A	23	57	8	8	1	0	0	2	3	1	9	.140	.197	.158	4	-7	2	.914	-6	78	82	C19,O2R	—	-1.2
1921	Bos N	63	125	14	33	5	4	2	13	3	2	17	.264	.292	.416	90	-3	0-0	.979	1	113	104	C41	—	0.0
1922	Bos N	66	164	15	49	7	2	3	20	10	0	27	.299	.339	.421	99	-1	4-1	.981	-0	98	99	C29,1b20	—	0.0
1923	Bos N	41	50	13	15	1	0	0	5	7	0	7	.300	.386	.320	92	0	0-2	.923	-1	89	64	C20	—	-0.2
1924	Bos N	90	229	25	71	15	6	1	30	10	1	23	.310	.342	.441	113	3	1-1	.972	-2	83	118	C46,1b10,3b2	—	0.4
1925	Bos N	104	316	36	88	23	5	2	50	15	1	28	.278	.313	.402	89	-6	3-3	.968	-2	113	85	C86,1b2	—	-0.2
1926	Bos N	24	47	3	16	4	0	0	7	4	0	6	.340	.392	.426	132	2	0	1.000	1	85	151	C13	—	0.4
1927	Bos N	60	167	7	37	1	2	0	19	3	0	10	.222	.235	.251	33	-17	2	.965	-2	100	125	C47	—	-1.7
Total	8	471	1155	121	317	57	19	8	146	55	5	127	.274	.310	.377	86	-29	12-7	.967	-11	100	102	C301,1b32,3b2,O2R	—	-2.5
Gibson, George	George C. "Moon"; B7.22.1880 London ON, Can.; D1.25.1967 London ON, Can.; BR/TR/5´11.5˝/190; d7.2; M7/C3																								
1905	Pit N	46	135	14	24	2	2	2	14	15	2	—	.178	.270	.267	59	-7	2	.966	4	129	90	C44	—	0.1
1906	Pit N	81	259	8	46	6	1	0	20	16	0	—	.178	.225	.208	34	-20	1	.971	-1	118	94	C81	—	-1.5
1907	Pit N	113	382	28	84	8	7	3	35	18	3	—	.220	.261	.301	75	-13	2	.972	7	**132**	91	C109/1	—	0.5
1908	Pit N	143	486	37	111	19	4	2	45	19	2	—	.228	.260	.296	78	-14	4	.973	-2	124	71	C140	—	-0.2
1909	†Pit N	150	510	42	135	25	9	2	52	44	2	—	.265	.326	.361	104	2	9	**.983**	17	**148**	91	C150	—	3.7
1910	Pit N	143	482	53	125	22	6	3	44	47	6	31	.259	.333	.349	93	-4	7	**.984**	10	123	90	C143	—	2.1
1911	Pit N	100	311	32	65	12	2	0	19	29	2	16	.209	.281	.260	50	-21	3	.979	6	116	92	C98	—	-0.7
1912	Pit N	95	300	23	72	14	3	2	35	20	1	16	.240	.290	.327	69	-14	0	**.990**	2	**132**	86	C94	—	-0.3
1913	Pit N	48	118	6	33	4	2	0	12	10	1	8	.280	.341	.347	101	0	2-1	.986	-5	84	58	C48	—	-0.2
1914	Pit N	102	274	19	78	9	5	0	30	27	5	27	.285	.359	.354	117	7	4	.974	-4	108	94	C101	—	1.1
1915	Pit N	120	351	28	88	15	6	1	30	31	1	25	.251	.313	.336	98	-1	5-2	.965	2	90	95	C118	—	1.3
1916	Pit N	33	84	4	17	2	2	0	4	3	1	7	.202	.239	.274	57	-5	0	.989	3	94	118	C29	—	0.1
1917	NY N	35	82	1	14	3	0	0	5	7	0	2	.171	.236	.207	38	-6	1	.986	1	107	69	C35	—	-0.3
1918	NY N	4	2	0	1	1	0	0	0	0	0	0	.500	.500	1.000	360	1	0	1.000	-0	56	230	C4	—	0.1
Total	14	1213	3776	295	893	142	49	15	345	286	26	132	.236	.295	.312	81	-95	40-3	.977	39	121	88	C1194/1	—	5.8
Gibson, Russ	John Russell; B5.6.1939 Fall River MA; BR/TR/6´1˝/195; d4.14																								
1967	†Bos A	49	138	8	28	7	0	1	15	12-3	0	31	.203	.263	.275	56	-7	0-0	1.000	-3	168	88	C48	0	-0.9
1968	Bos A	76	231	15	52	11	1	3	20	8-1	0	38	.225	.247	.320	68	-9	1-2	.983	-2	82	104	C74/1	22	-1.0
1969	Bos A	85	287	21	72	9	1	3	27	15-1	1	25	.251	.289	.321	68	-13	1-1	.979	-7	108	**122**	C83	0	-1.7
1970	SF N	24	69	3	16	6	0	0	6	7-1	0	12	.232	.303	.319	67	-3	0-0	.971	-1	67	139	C23	0	-0.4
1971	SF N	25	57	2	11	1	1	1	7	2-0	0	13	.193	.220	.298	46	-4	0-0	.965	-3	170	78	C22	0	-0.7
1972	SF N	5	12	0	2	0	1	0	3	0-0	0	4	.167	.167	.333	38	-1	0-0	1.000	-2	30	87	C5	0	-0.3
Total	6	264	794	49	181	34	4	8	78	44-6	1	123	.228	.267	.311	64	-37	2-3	.983	-18	111	108	C255/1	22	-5.0
Gibson, Kirk	Kirk Harold; B5.28.1957 Pontiac MI; BL/TL/6´3˝/(210–225); [DetA78 1/12]; d9.8; C3; Col Michigan St.																								
1979	Det A	12	38	3	9	3	0	1	4	1-0	0	3	.237	.256	.395	70	-2	3-3	1.000	-2	75	0	O10(7/1/2)	0	-0.4
1980	Det A	51	175	23	46	2	1	9	16	10-0	1	45	.263	.303	.440	99	-1	4-7	.992	-2	100	32	O49C/D	110	-0.5
1981	Det A	83	290	41	95	11	3	9	40	18-1	2	64	.328	.369	.479	138	13	17-5	.973	-4	97	23	O67(8/26/37),D9	0	0.9
1982	Det A	69	266	34	74	16	2	8	35	25-2	1	41	.278	.341	.444	113	5	9-7	.994	-2	94	91	O64C,D4	85	0.2
1983	Det A	128	401	60	91	12	9	15	51	53-3	4	96	.227	.320	.414	103	1	14-3	.975	-1	101	58	D66,O54(29/22/4)	0	-0.1
1984	†Det A	149	531	92	150	23	10	27	91	63-6	8	103	.282	.363	.516	141	30	29-9	.954	-11	90	48	O139(0/1/140),D6	0	1.5
1985	Det A	154	581	96	167	37	5	29	97	71-16	5	137	.287	.364	.518	140	33	30-4	.963	-12	95	10	O144(0/20/127),D8	0	2.0
1986	Det A	119	441	84	118	11	2	28	86	68-4	7	107	.268	.371	.492	133	21	34-6	.990	-12	83	25	O114(0/1/114),D4	40	0.8
1987	†Det A	128	487	95	135	25	3	24	79	71-8	5	117	.277	.372	.489	132	24	26-7	.974	1	104	74	O121(119/2/0),D4	29	2.2
1988	†LA N	150	542	106	157	28	1	25	76	73-14	7	120	.290	.377	.483	151	38	31-4	.964	3	107	67	O148(148/1/0)	0	4.4
1989	LA N	71	253	35	54	8	2	9	28	35-5	2	55	.213	.312	.368	95	-1	12-3	.980	1	102	82	O70(62/15/0)	98	-0.1
1990	LA N	89	315	59	82	20	0	8	38	39-0	3	65	.260	.345	.400	107	4	26-2	.995	0	103	94	O81(11/70/0)	54	0.9
1991	KC A	132	462	81	109	17	6	16	55	69-3	6	103	.236	.341	.403	105	4	18-4	.976	-5	87	61	O94(91/0/3),D30	0	-0.3
1992	Pit N	16	56	6	11	0	0	2	5	3-0	0	12	.196	.237	.304	52	-4	3-1	1.000	-0	92	108	O13R	0	-0.4
1993	Det A	116	403	62	105	18	6	13	62	44-4	4	87	.261	.337	.432	106	2	15-6	.987	-1	103	0	D76,O32(2/30/0)	0	-0.1
1994	Det A	98	330	71	91	17	2	23	72	42-3	3	69	.276	.358	.548	129	14	4-5	.988	-1	93	145	D56,O38(0/23/15)	0	0.8
1995	Det A	70	227	37	59	12	2	9	35	33-3	3	61	.260	.358	.449	109	4	9-2	ø	-0	0	0	D63/rf	0	0.1
Total	17	1635	5798	985	1553	260	54	255	870	718-72	61	1285	.268	.352	.463	123	185	284-78	.976	-47	96	55	O1239(477/325/456),D327	416	11.9
Gibson, Whitey	Leighton P.; B10.6.1868 Lancaster PA; D10.12.1907 Talmage PA; TR/5´9˝/178; d5.2																								
1888	Phi AA	1	3	0	0	0	0	0	0	0	0	—	.000	.000	.000	-99	-1	0	1.000	1	—	—	/C	—	0.0
Giebel, Joe	Joseph Henry; B11.30.1891 Washington DC; D3.17.1981 Silver Spring MD; BR/TR/5´10.5˝/175; d9.30																								
1913	Phi A	1	3	0	1	0	0	0	0	0	0	1	.333	.333	.333	97	0	0	1.000	-0	107	0	/C	—	0.0
Gigon, Norm	Norman Phillip; B5.12.1938 Teaneck NJ; BR/TR/6´0˝/195; d4.12; Col Colby																								
1967	Chi N	34	70	8	12	3	1	1	6	4-0	2	14	.171	.234	.286	47	-5	0-0	.982	1	128	104	2b12,O4R/3	0	-0.4
Gil, Geronimo	Geronimo; B8.7.1975 Estacion Lagunas, Oaxaca, Mexico; BR/TR/6´2˝/(195–234); d9.8																								
2001	Bal A	17	58	3	17	2	0	0	6	5-0	2	7	.293	.369	.328	91	0	0-0	.985	3	93	99	C17	0	0.4
2002	Bal A	125	422	33	98	19	0	12	45	21-1	1	88	.232	.270	.363	70	-20	2-2	.995	1	106	115	C125	0	-1.0
2003	Bal A	54	169	22	40	4	0	3	16	12-0	3	34	.237	.299	.314	62	-9	0-0	.984	5	72	85	C53	0	-0.1
2004	Bal A	12	32	1	9	2	0	0	4	3-1	0	5	.281	.343	.344	81	-1	0-0	1.000	1	112	188	C11	0	0.1
2005	Bal A	64	125	7	24	3	0	4	17	5-0	0	23	.192	.220	.312	40	-11	0-0	.993	3	91	112	C62	61	-0.5
Total	5	272	806	66	188	30	0	19	88	46-2	6	157	.233	.279	.341	66	-41	2-2	.992	14	96	110	C268	61	-1.1
Gil, Jerry	Jerry Bienvenido; B10.14.1982 San Pedro de Macoris, D.R.; BR/TR/6´3˝/185; d8.22; [DL 2005 Ari N 62, 2005 Ari N 24]																								
2004	Ari N	29	86	3	15	2	1	0	8	0-0	1	33	.174	.182	.221	4	-12	2-0	.955	2	102	110	S28	0	-0.8
Gil, Benji	Romar Benjamin (Aguilar); B10.6.1972 Tijuana, Baja California, Mexico; BR/TR/6´2˝/(182–210); [TexA91 1/19]; d4.5																								
1993	Tex A	22	57	3	7	0	0	0	2	5-0	0	22	.123	.194	.123	-13	-9	1-2	.954	4	123	76	S22	0	-0.4
1995	Tex A	130	415	36	91	20	3	9	46	26-0	1	147	.219	.266	.347	56	-28	2-4	.974	18	110	113	S130	0	-0.1
1996	Tex A	5	5	0	2	0	0	0	1	1-0	0	1	.400	.500	.400	124	0	0-1	.923	0	107	0	S5	51	0.0
1997	Tex A	110	317	35	71	13	2	5	31	17-0	1	96	.224	.263	.325	50	-24	1-2	.963	18	117	108	S106,D4	0	0.1
2000	Ana A	110	301	28	72	14	1	6	23	30-0	5	59	.239	.317	.352	68	-15	10-6	.957	-1	102	101	S94,2b7,1b3,D6	0	-0.9
2001	Ana A	104	260	33	77	15	4	8	39	14-0	0	57	.296	.330	.477	108	2	3-4	.945	5	101	101	S44,2b21,1b18,D14/cf	0	0.8
2002	†Ana A	61	130	11	37	8	1	3	20	5-0	0	33	.285	.307	.431	96	-1	2-1	.990	3	98	90	2b26,S14,1b10,D10	54	0.3
2003	Ana A	62	125	12	24	5	1	1	9	4-1	0	33	.192	.214	.272	29	-13	5-1	.979	1	107	114	2b28,S20,1b5,3b4,D2	0	-0.9
Total	8	604	1610	158	381	75	12	32	171	102-1	7	448	.237	.283	.358	64	-88	24-21	.962	48	110	106	S435,2b82,1b36,D36,3b4/cf	105	-1.1
Gil, Gus	Tomas Gustavo (Guillen); B4.19.1939 Caracas, Distrito Capital, Venez.; BR/TR/5´10˝/180; d4.11																								
1967	Cle A	51	96	11	11	4	0	0	5	9-0	1	18	.115	.198	.156	6	-11	0-0	1.000	-3	83	74	2b49/1	0	-1.3
1969	Sea A	92	221	20	49	7	0	0	17	16-0	0	28	.222	.272	.253	49	-15	2-0	.942	1	121	116	3b38,2b18,S12	0	-1.3
1970	Mil A	64	119	12	22	4	0	1	12	21-4	0	12	.185	.303	.244	54	-7	2-0	.978	-5	71	66	2b38,3b14	0	-1.0
1971	Mil A	14	32	3	5	1	0	0	3	10-1	0	5	.156	.357	.188	59	-1	1-0	.977	1	109	58	2b8,3b6	36	0.0
Total	4	221	468	46	87	16	0	1	37	56-5	1	63	.186	.272	.226	43	-34	5-0	.987	-6	84	69	2b113,3b58,S12/1	36	-3.6
Gilbert, Shawn	Albert Shawn; B3.12.1965 Camden NJ; BR/TR/5´9˝/185; [MinA87 12/295]; d6.2; Col Cal St.–Fresno																								
1997	NY N	29	22	3	3	0	0	1	1	1-0	0	8	.136	.174	.273	15	-3	1-0	.875	-2	20	97	2b8,S6,3b3/lf	18	-0.4
1998	NY N	3	3	1	0	0	0	0	0	0-0	0	1	.000	.000	.000	-99	-1	0-0	ø	-0	0	0	/3	0	-0.1
	StL N	4	2	0	1	0	0	0	0	0-0	0	1	.500	.500	.500	165	0	1-0	1.000	-0	0	0	2b2	0	0.0
	Year	7	5	1	1	0	0	0	0	0-0	0	2	.200	.200	.200	6	-1	1-0	1.000	-1	0	0	2b2/3	0	-0.1
2000	LA N	15	20	5	3	1	0	1	3	2-0	0	7	.150	.227	.350	45	-2	0-0	.941	1	123	297	O14(8/4/2)	0	-0.1
Total	3	51	47	9	7	1	0	2	4	3-0	0	17	.149	.200	.298	27	-6	2-0	.941	-1	118	285	O15(9/4/2),2b10,S6,3b4	18	-0.6

YEAR	TM LG	G	AB	R	H	2B	3B	HR	RBI	BB-IB	HP	SO	AVG	OBP	SLG	AOPS	ABR	SB-CS	FA	FR	RNG	THR	GAMES AT POSITION	DL	BFW
GILBERT, ANDY	Andrew; B7.18.1914 Bradenville PA; D8.29.1992 Davis CA; BR/TR/6´0˝/203; d9.14; Mil 1943–45; C4																								
1942	Bos A	6	11	0	1	0	0	0	1	1	0	3	.091	.167	.091	-26	-2	0-0	1.000	-0	93	0	O5C	0	-0.2
1946	Bos A	2	1	1	0	0	0	0	0	0	0	0	.000	.000	.000	-95	0	0-0	ø	-0	0	0	/cf	0	0.0
Total	2	8	12	1	1	0	0	0	1	1	0	3	.083	.154	.083	-31	-2	0-0	1.000	-0	89	0	O6C	0	-0.2
GILBERT, CHARLIE	Charles Mader; B7.8.1919 New Orleans LA; D8.13.1983 New Orleans LA; BL/TL/5´9˝/165; d4.16; Mil 1944–45; b–Tookie f–Larry																								
1940	Bro N	57	142	23	35	9	1	2	8	8	0	13	.246	.287	.366	74	-5	0	.960	1	101	135	O43C	—	-0.6
1941	Chi N	39	86	11	24	2	1	0	12	11	0	6	.279	.361	.326	98	0	1	1.000	-1	106	0	O22(0/21/1)	0	-0.1
1942	Chi N	74	179	18	33	6	3	0	7	25	0	24	.184	.284	.251	60	-9	1	.981	0	93	149	O47(3/44/0)	0	-1.1
1943	Chi N	8	20	1	3	0	0	0	0	3	0	3	.150	.261	.150	20	-2	1	1.000	0	84	230	O6(3/3/0)	0	-0.2
1946	Chi N	15	13	2	1	0	0	0	1	1	0	4	.077	.143	.077	-38	-2	0	1.000	1	82	2356	O2C	0	-0.2
	Phi N	88	260	34	63	5	2	1	17	25	2	18	.242	.314	.288	73	-9	3	1.000	5	108	138	O69(8/16/46)	0	-0.7
	Year	103	273	36	64	5	2	1	18	26	2	22	.234	.306	.278	68	-12	3	1.000	6	108	153	O71(8/18/46)	0	-0.9
1947	Phi N	83	152	20	36	5	2	2	10	13	1	14	.237	.301	.336	72	-7	1	.961	2	104	168	O37(18/7/12)	0	-0.6
Total	6	364	852	109	195	27	9	5	55	86	3	82	.229	.302	.299	70	-34	7	.982	8	102	138	O226(32/136/59)	0	-3.5
GILBERT, BUDDY	Drew Edward; B7.26.1935 Knoxville TN; BL/TR/6´3˝/200; d9.9; Col Tennessee																								
1959	Cin N	7	20	4	3	0	0	2	2	3-0	0	4	.150	.261	.450	82	-1	0-0	1.000	1	146	0	O6R	0	0.0
GILBERT, TOOKIE	Harold Joseph; B4.4.1929 New Orleans LA; D6.23.1967 New Orleans LA; BL/TR/6´2.5˝/185; d5.5; b–Charlie f–Larry																								
1950	NY N	113	322	40	71	12	2	4	32	43	1	36	.220	.314	.307	64	-16	3	.988	0	102	105	1b111	0	-1.9
1953	NY N	70	160	12	27	3	0	3	16	22	0	21	.169	.269	.244	34	-16	1-0	.995	-1	92	96	1b44	0	-1.8
Total	2	183	482	52	98	15	2	7	48	65	1	57	.203	.299	.286	54	-32	4-0	.991	-1	99	102	1b155	0	-3.7
GILBERT, HARRY	Harry H.; B7.7.1868 Pottstown PA; D12.23.1909 Pottstown PA; d6.23; b–John																								
1890	Pit N	2	8	1	2	0	0	0	0	0	0	3	.250	.250	.250	52	-1	0	1.000	-0	109	132	2b2	—	-0.1
GILBERT, JOHN	John G.; B1.8.1864 Pottstown PA; D11.12.1903 Pottstown PA; d6.23; b–Harry																								
1890	Pit N	2	8	0	0	0	0	0	0	0	0	2	.000	.000	.000	-99	-2	0	1.000	-0	81	118	S2	—	-0.2
GILBERT, JACK	John Robert "Jackrabbit"; B9.4.1875 Rhinecliff NY; D7.7.1941 Albany NY; d9.11																								
1898	Was N	2	5	0	1	0	0	0	1	1	1	—	.200	.429	.200	82	0	1	.500	0	514	0	O2(0/1/1)	—	0.0
	NY N	1	4	0	1	0	0	0	0	0	1	—	.250	.250	.250	45	0	1	.500	-1	0	0	/rf	—	-0.1
	Year	3	9	0	2	0	0	0	1	1	1	—	.222	.364	.222	70	0	2	.500	-1	280	0	O3(0/1/2)	—	-0.1
1904	Pit N	25	87	13	21	0	0	0	3	12	3	—	.241	.353	.241	82	-1	3	.857	-4	0	0	O25L	—	-0.7
Total	2	28	96	13	23	0	0	0	4	13	4	—	.240	.354	.240	81	-1	5	.821	-5	29	0	O28(25/1/2)	—	-0.8
GILBERT, LARRY	Lawrence William; B12.3.1891 New Orleans LA; D2.17.1965 New Orleans LA; BL/TL/5´9˝/158; d4.14; s–Charlie s–Tookie																								
1914	†Bos N	72	224	32	60	6	1	5	25	26	1	34	.268	.347	.371	114	4	3	.979	1	79	158	O60(3/6/51)	—	0.2
1915	Bos N	45	106	11	16	4	0	0	4	11	0	13	.151	.231	.189	29	-9	4-1	.941	0	83	171	O27(2/0/26)	—	-1.0
Total	2	117	330	43	76	10	1	5	29	37	1	47	.230	.310	.312	88	-5	7-1	.969	1	80	162	O87(5/6/77)	—	-0.8
GILBERT, MARK	Mark David; B8.22.1956 Atlanta GA; BB/TR/6´0˝/175; [ChiN78 14/351]; d7.21; Col Florida St.																								
1985	Chi A	7	22	3	6	1	0	0	3	4-0	0	5	.273	.385	.318	91	0	0-0	1.000	-1	92	0	O7(2/5/1)	0	-0.1
GILBERT, PETE	Peter; B9.6.1867 Baltic CT; D1.1.1912 Springfield MA; TR/5´8˝/180; d9.6																								
1890	Bal AA	29	100	25	28	2	1	1	18	10	3	—	.280	.363	.350	105	1	12	.899	0	96	126	3b29	—	0.1
1891	Bal AA	**139**	513	81	118	15	7	3	72	37	28	77	.230	.317	.304	77	-16	31	.862	2	**105**	**151**	3b139	—	-1.0
1892	Bal N	4	15	0	3	0	0	0	0	1	0	3	.200	.250	.200	35	-1	1	.889	1	147	0	3b4	—	0.0
1894	Bro N	6	25	1	2	0	0	0	1	1	1	3	.080	.148	.080	-47	-6	2	.938	1	126	0	2b3,3b3	—	-0.4
	Lou N	28	108	13	33	3	1	1	14	5	3	4	.306	.353	.380	82	-3	2	.742	-7	83	100	3b28	—	-0.7
	Year	34	133	14	35	3	1	1	15	6	4	7	.263	.315	.323	58	-9	4	.766	-6	86	126	3b31,2b3	—	-1.1
Total	4	206	761	120	184	20	9	5	105	54	35	87	.242	.321	.311	76	-25	48	.851	-3	101	141	3b203,2b3	—	-2.0
GILBERT, WALLY	Walter John; B12.19.1900 Oscoda MI; D9.7.1958 Duluth MN; BR/TR/6´0˝/180; d8.18; Col Valparaiso																								
1928	Bro N	39	153	26	31	4	0	0	3	14	1	8	.203	.274	.229	33	-15	2	.965	0	101	103	3b39	—	-1.2
1929	Bro N	143	569	88	173	31	4	3	58	42	7	29	.304	.359	.388	87	-11	7	.956	9	104	77	3b142	—	0.6
1930	Bro N	150	623	92	183	34	5	3	67	47	2	33	.294	.345	.379	76	-24	7	.944	9	110	**112**	3b150	—	-0.5
1931	Bro N	145	552	60	147	25	6	0	46	39	6	38	.266	.322	.333	77	-18	3	.948	8	**107**	95	3b145	—	-0.5
1932	Cin N	114	420	35	90	18	2	1	40	20	1	23	.214	.252	.274	43	-35	2	.929	-7	102	92	3b111	—	-3.7
Total	5	591	2317	301	624	112	17	7	214	162	17	131	.269	.322	.341	71	-103	21	.947	19	106	95	3b587	—	-5.3
GILBERT, BILLY	William Oliver; B6.21.1876 Tullytown PA; D8.8.1927 New York NY; BR/TR/5´4˝/153; d4.25																								
1901	Mil A	127	492	77	133	14	7	0	43	31	5	—	.270	.320	.327	84	-10	19	.936	-3	98	113	2b127	—	-1.1
1902	Bal A	129	445	74	109	12	3	2	38	45	9	—	.245	.327	.299	71	-16	38	.907	-3	94	114	S129	—	-1.4
1903	NY N	128	413	62	104	9	0	1	40	41	20	—	.252	.348	.281	77	-10	37	.935	6	98	107	2b128	—	-0.2
1904	NY N	146	478	57	121	13	3	1	54	46	17	—	.253	.340	.299	94	-1	33	.946	6	101	122	2b146	—	0.6
1905	†NY N	115	376	45	93	11	3	0	24	41	6	—	.247	.331	.293	84	-5	11	.947	20	105	**128**	2b115	—	1.6
1906	NY N	104	307	44	71	6	1	0	27	42	9	—	.231	.341	.257	85	-3	22	.940	22	113	105	2b98	—	2.2
1908	StL N	89	276	12	59	7	0	0	10	20	3	—	.214	.274	.239	67	-10	6	.952	5	96	86	2b89	—	-0.4
1909	StL N	12	29	4	5	0	0	0	1	4	3	—	.172	.333	.172	61	-1	1	.922	-1	107	29	2b12	—	-0.1
Total	8	850	2816	375	695	72	17	4	237	270	72	—	.247	.328	.289	81	-56	167	.942	53	102	111	2b715,S129	—	1.2
GILBREATH, ROD	Rodney Joe; B9.24.1952 Laurel MS; BR/TR (BB 1975p)/6´2˝/(170–185); [AtlN70 3/69]; d6.17																								
1972	Atl N	18	38	2	9	1	0	0	1	2-0	1	10	.237	.293	.263	54	-2	1-1	1.000	1	84	86	2b7,3b4	0	-0.1
1973	Atl N	29	74	10	21	2	1	0	2	6-1	1	10	.284	.341	.338	84	-1	2-1	.960	-0	97	112	3b22	0	-0.2
1974	Atl N	3	6	2	2	0	0	0	0	2-0	0	0	.333	.500	.333	132	0	0-0	1.000	-0	95	83	2b2	0	0.0
1975	Atl N	90	202	24	49	3	1	2	16	24-0	1	26	.243	.323	.297	72	-7	5-5	.980	0	97	97	2b52,3b10/S	0	-0.6
1976	Atl N	116	383	57	96	11	8	1	32	42-1	4	36	.251	.329	.329	83	-8	7-7	.975	6	101	110	2b104,3b7/S	0	0.4
1977	Atl N	128	407	47	99	15	2	8	43	45-6	2	79	.243	.320	.349	72	-16	3-9	.978	-6	90	77	2b122/3	0	-1.8
1978	Atl N	116	326	22	80	13	3	3	31	26-3	0	51	.245	.300	.331	69	-13	7-6	.968	-7	106	94	3b62,2b39	0	-2.1
Total	7	500	1436	164	356	45	15	14	125	147-11	9	212	.248	.320	.329	75	-47	25-29	.978	-6	94	89	2b326,3b106,S2	0	-4.4
GILE, DON	Donald Loren "Bear"; B4.19.1935 Modesto CA; BR/TR/6´6˝/(220–225); d9.25; Col Arizona																								
1959	Bos A	3	10	1	2	1	0	0	1	0-0	1	2	.200	.250	.300	55	-1	0-0	1.000	0	45	0	C3	0	0.0
1960	Bos A	29	51	6	9	1	1	1	4	1-0	0	13	.176	.189	.294	29	-5	0-0	1.000	-2	75	201	C15,1b11	0	-0.8
1961	Bos A	8	18	2	5	0	0	1	1	1-0	0	5	.278	.316	.444	98	0	0-0	.958	-1	55	68	1b6/C	0	-0.1
1962	Bos A	18	41	3	2	0	0	1	3	3-0	1	15	.049	.133	.122	-30	-8	0-0	.990	-1	61	120	1b14	0	-1.0
Total	4	58	120	12	18	2	1	3	9	5-0	2	35	.150	.194	.258	21	-14	0-0	.982	-4	59	92	1b31,C19	0	-1.9
GILES, BRIAN	Brian Jeffrey; B4.27.1960 Manhattan KS; BR/TR/6´1˝/(162–175); [NYN78 3/55]; d9.12																								
1981	NY N	9	7	0	0	0	0	0	0	0-0	0	3	.000	.000	.000	-99	-2	0-0	1.000	1	110	277	2b2,S2	0	0.0
1982	NY N	45	138	14	29	5	0	3	10	12-1	0	29	.210	.270	.312	63	-7	6-1	.992	8	102	99	2b45,S2	0	0.4
1983	NY N	145	400	39	98	15	0	2	27	36-1	2	77	.245	.308	.298	70	-16	17-10	.980	8	104	111	2b140,S12	0	-0.1
1985	Mil A	34	58	6	10	1	0	1	1	7-0	0	16	.172	.262	.241	39	-5	2-1	.963	1	98	70	S20,2b13,D2	0	-0.3
1986	Chi A	9	11	0	3	0	0	0	1	0-0	0	2	.273	.273	.273	47	-1	0-0	1.000	2	120	304	2b7/S	42	0.2
1990	Sea A	45	95	15	22	6	0	4	11	15-0	0	24	.232	.336	.421	109	1	2-1	.978	3	92	134	S37,2b2/3D	0	0.7
Total	6	287	709	74	162	27	0	10	50	70-2	2	151	.228	.298	.309	69	-30	27-13	.985	23	103	111	2b209,S74,D3/3	42	0.9
GILES, BRIAN	Brian Stephen; B1.20.1971 El Cajon CA; BL/TL/5´11˝/(195–205); [CleA89 17/437]; d9.16; b–Marcus																								
1995	Cle A	6	9	6	5	0	0	1	3	0-0	0	1	.556	.556	.889	263	2	0-0	1.000	1	91	1304	O3R/D	0	0.2
1996	†Cle A	51	121	26	43	14	1	5	27	19-4	0	13	.355	.434	.612	163	13	3-0	1.000	1	128	0	D21,O16(11/0/5)	0	1.1
1997	†Cle A	130	377	62	101	15	3	17	61	63-2	1	50	.268	.368	.459	112	7	13-3	.972	-1	96	113	O115(82/20/25),D9	0	0.5
1998	†Cle A	112	350	56	94	19	0	16	66	73-8	3	75	.269	.396	.460	118	13	10-5	.978	5	107	119	O101(95/3/6),D6	36	1.3
1999	Pit N	141	521	109	164	33	3	39	115	95-7	3	80	.315	.418	.614	157	48	6-2	.990	-6	93	104	O138(8/108/25),D3	0	4.0
2000	Pit N★	156	559	111	176	37	7	35	123	114-13	7	69	.315	.432	.594	157	54	6-0	.982	-2	93	145	O155(46/72/39)	0	4.7

YEAR	TM LG	G	AB	R	H	2B	3B	HR	RBI	BB-IB	HP	SO	AVG	OBP	SLG	AOPS	ABR	SB-CS	FA	FR	RNG	THR	GAMES AT POSITION	DL	BFW
2001	Pit N★	160	576	116	178	37	7	37	95	90-14	4	67	.309	.404	.590	149	44	13-6	.969	-7	96	69	O159(124/61/0)	0	3.3
2002	Pit N	153	497	95	148	37	5	38	103	135-24	7	74	.298	.450	.622	176	63	15-6	.973	-3	88	138	O151(151/3/0)	0	5.5
2003	Pit N	105	388	70	116	30	4	16	70	85-11	6	48	.299	.430	.521	145	31	0-3	.992	3	108	60	O105(99/16/0)	26	2.9
	SD N	29	104	23	31	4	2	4	18	20-1	2	10	.298	.414	.490	150	9	4-0	.966	1	105	116	O29L	0	0.9
	Year	134	492	93	147	34	6	20	88	105-12	8	58	.299	.427	.514	146	40	4-3	.987	4	107	72	O134(128/16/0)	0	3.8
2004	SD N	159	609	97	173	33	7	23	94	89-6	4	80	.284	.374	.475	125	24	10-3	.979	2	106	81	O159R	0	1.9
2005	†SD N	158	545	92	164	38	8	15	83	**119**-9	2	64	.301	.423	.483	145	43	13-5	.988	3	109	69	O155(1/17/143)	0	4.0
2006	†SD N	158	604	87	159	37	1	14	83	104-6	5	60	.263	.374	.397	104	8	9-4	.978	-5	96	88	O158R	0	-0.4
Total	12	1518	5260	950	1552	334	48	260	941	1006-105	44	691	.295	.408	.525	141	359	102-37	.980	-9	99	99	O1444(646/300/563),D40	62	29.9
GILES, MARCUS	Marcus William; B5.18.1978 San Diego CA; BR/TR/5´8˝/(175–180); [AtlN96 53/1512]; d4.17; b–Brian; Col Grossmont (CA) JC																								
2001	†Atl N	68	244	36	64	10	2	9	31	28-0	0	37	.262	.338	.430	96	-2	2-5	.978	-1	105	92	2b62	0	-0.1
2002	†Atl N	68	213	27	49	10	1	8	23	25-3	2	41	.230	.315	.399	87	-4	1-1	.977	4	107	117	2b52,3b8	48	0.2
2003	†Atl N✱	145	551	101	174	49	2	21	69	59-2	11	80	.316	.390	.526	138	33	14-4	.982	18	**120**	91	2b139	0	5.7
2004	†Atl N	102	379	61	118	22	2	8	48	36-0	9	70	.311	.378	.443	112	8	17-4	.975	12	113	122	2b97	60	2.6
2005	†Atl N	152	577	104	168	45	4	15	63	64-1	5	108	.291	.365	.461	114	14	16-3	.984	8	112	101	2b149/3	0	3.1
2006	Atl N	141	550	87	144	32	2	11	60	62-0	6	105	.262	.341	.387	86	-11	10-5	.983	-8	98	90	2b134	0	-1.2
Total	6	676	2514	416	717	168	13	72	294	274-6	33	441	.285	.361	.448	109	38	60-22	.981	33	110	100	2b633,3b9	108	10.3
GILHAM, GEORGE	George Louis; B9.17.1899 Shamokin PA; D4.25.1937 Lansdowne PA; BR/TR/5´11˝/164; d9.24																								
1920	StL N	1	3	0	0	0	0	0	0	0	0	1	.000	.000	.000	-99	-1	0-0	.750	-1	*60*	*187*	/C	—	-0.2
1921	StL N	1	1	0	0	0	0	0	0	0	0	0	.000	.000	.000	-99	0	0-0	ø	0	—	—	/H	—	0.0
Total	2	2	4	0	0	0	0	0	0	0	0	1	.000	.000	.000	-99	-1	0-0	.750	-1	*60*	*187*	/C	—	-0.2
GILHOOLEY, FRANK	Frank Patrick "Flash"; B6.10.1892 Toledo OH; D7.11.1959 Toledo OH; BL/TR/5´8˝/155; d9.18; Col St. Johns																								
1911	StL N	1	0	0	0	0	0	0	0	0	0	0	ø	ø	ø	ø	0	0	ø	-0	0	0	/rf	—	0.0
1912	StL N	13	49	5	11	0	0	0	2	3	0	8	.224	.269	.224	37	-4	0	1.000	-1	76	72	O11C	—	-0.6
1913	NY A	24	85	10	29	2	1	0	14	4	1	9	.341	.378	.388	124	2	6	.977	-0	112	56	O24R	—	0.1
1914	NY A	1	3	0	2	0	0	0	0	1	0	0	.667	.750	.667	327	1	0	ø	0	0	0	/rf	—	0.1
1915	NY A	1	4	0	0	0	0	0	0	0	0	1	.000	.000	.000	-99	-1	0	1.000	-0	81	0	/rf	—	-0.1
1916	NY A	58	223	40	62	5	3	1	10	37	1	17	.278	.383	.341	115	6	16	.971	0	95	121	O57(0/2/55)	—	0.3
1917	NY A	54	165	14	40	6	1	0	8	30	1	13	.242	.362	.291	99	2	6	.933	-1	102	81	O46R	—	-0.2
1918	NY A	112	427	59	118	13	5	1	23	53	1	24	.276	.358	.337	107	5	7	.961	1	101	98	O111(0/4/107)	—	0.0
1919	Bos A	48	112	14	27	4	0	0	1	12	0	8	.241	.315	.277	71	-4	2	.922	-1	92	120	O33(30/2/1)	—	-0.6
Total	9	312	1068	142	289	30	10	2	58	140	4	80	.271	.357	.323	102	7	37	.957	-3	99	97	O285(30/19/236)	—	-1.0
GILKEY, BERNARD	Otis Bernard; B9.24.1966 St.Louis MO; BR/TR/6´0˝/(170–200); d9.4																								
1990	StL N	18	64	11	19	5	2	1	3	8-0	0	5	.297	.375	.484	134	3	6-1	.961	2	128	157	O18(18/1/0)	0	0.6
1991	StL N	81	268	28	58	7	2	5	20	39-0	1	33	.216	.316	.313	77	-7	14-8	.994	6	109	146	O74L	27	-0.3
1992	StL N	131	384	56	116	19	4	7	43	39-1	1	52	.302	.364	.427	128	14	18-12	.978	7	108	192	O111(110/0/1)	0	2.0
1993	StL N	137	557	99	170	40	5	16	70	56-2	4	66	.305	.370	.481	127	23	15-10	.969	-3	84	**178**	O134(133/0/2),1b3	15	1.4
1994	StL N	105	380	52	96	22	1	6	45	39-2	10	65	.253	.336	.363	83	-8	15-8	.983	-1	90	146	O102L	0	-1.2
1995	StL N	121	480	73	143	33	4	17	69	42-3	5	70	.298	.358	.490	119	13	12-6	.986	3	100	138	O118L	19	1.2
1996	NY N	153	571	108	181	44	3	30	117	73-7	4	125	.317	.393	.562	158	49	17-9	.982	18	112	**209**	O151L	0	5.9
1997	NY N	145	518	85	129	31	1	18	78	70-1	6	111	.249	.338	.417	103	4	7-11	.989	6	94	181	O136(136/1/0),D2	0	0.2
1998	NY N	82	264	33	60	15	0	4	28	32-1	4	66	.227	.317	.330	74	-10	5-1	.992	4	95	201	O77(76/1/4)	16	-0.7
	Ari N	29	101	8	25	0	0	1	5	11-0	1	14	.248	.327	.277	61	-6	4-2	.981	1	98	169	O27L	0	-0.5
	Year	111	365	41	85	15	0	5	33	43-1	5	80	.233	.320	.315	70	-15	9-3	.989	5	96	192	O104(103/1/4)	0	-1.2
1999	†Ari N	94	204	28	60	16	1	8	39	29-2	2	42	.294	.379	.500	121	8	2-2	.969	1	104	105	O53(15/0/40)	0	0.6
2000	Ari N	38	73	6	8	1	0	2	6	7-2	0	16	.110	.185	.205	-1	-12	0-0	1.000	0	101	112	O17(2/0/16)	0	-1.2
	Bos A	36	91	11	21	5	1	1	9	10-0	3	12	.231	.327	.341	68	-4	0-0	1.000	1	117	97	O22(7/0/16),D8	0	-0.4
2001	†Atl N	69	106	8	29	6	0	2	14	11-0	1	31	.274	.339	.387	89	-2	0-1	1.000	-1	104	0	O36(28/0/8)/D	18	-0.3
Total	12	1239	4061	606	1115	244	24	118	546	466-21	42	708	.275	.352	.434	110	65	115-71	.983	45	100	166	O1076(997/3/87),D11,1b3	95	7.3
GILKS, BOB	Robert James; B7.2.1864 Cincinnati OH; D8.21.1944 Brunswick GA; BR/TR/5´8˝/178; d8.25; OF(181/56/21); ▲																								
1887	Cle AA	22	83	12	26	2	0	0	13	3	2	—	.313	.352	.337	96	0	5	.881	3	132	337	P13,1b6,O3(0/2/1)/2	—	0.1
1888	Cle AA	119	484	59	111	14	4	1	63	7	3	—	.229	.245	.281	70	-17	16	.899	1	75	63	O87(57/27/3),3b28,S4,P4/2	—	-1.7
1889	Cle N	53	210	17	50	5	2	0	18	7	3	20	.238	.273	.281	55	-13	6	1.000	1	104	0	O29(2/26/1),S13,1b10/2	—	-1.2
1890	Cle N	130	544	65	116	10	3	0	41	32	6	38	.213	.265	.243	49	-36	17	.941	3	97	43	O123(121/1/1),P4,S3,2b2	—	-3.1
1893	Bal N	15	64	10	17	2	0	0	7	0	1	3	.266	.277	.297	52	-5	3	.969	3	203	182	O15(1/0/15)	—	-0.2
Total	5	339	1385	163	320	33	9	1	142	49	15	61	.231	.265	.270	60	-71	47	.937	11	98	63	O257L,3b28,P21,S20,1b16,2b5	—	-6.1
GILL, JIM	James Clifford; B7.1866; D4.10.1923 Beaver Falls PA; d6.27																								
1889	StL AA	2	8	2	2	1	0	0	1	1	0	2	.250	.333	.375	90	0	1	1.000	-1	0	0	/cf2	—	-0.1
GILL, JOHNNY	John Wesley "Patcheye"; B3.27.1905 Nashville TN; D12.26.1984 Nashville TN; BL/TR/6´2˝/190; d8.28																								
1927	Cle A	21	60	8	13	3	0	1	4	7	2	13	.217	.319	.317	65	-3	1-1	1.000	0	84	153	O17(14/3/0)	—	-0.4
1928	Cle A	2	2	0	0	0	0	0	0	0	0	1	.000	.000	.000	-99	-1	0-0	ø	0	—	—	/H	—	-0.1
1931	Was A	8	30	2	8	2	1	0	5	1	1	6	.267	.313	.400	86	-1	0-1	1.000	2	128	220	O8R	—	0.1
1934	Was A	13	53	7	13	3	0	2	7	2	1	3	.245	.286	.415	82	-2	0-0	1.000	-1	103	0	O13(2/0/11)	—	-0.3
1935	Chi N	3	3	2	1	1	0	0	1	0	0	1	.333	.333	.667	161	0	0	ø	0	—	—	/H	—	0.0
1936	Chi N	71	174	20	44	8	0	7	28	13	1	19	.253	.309	.420	92	-2	0	.938	-1	95	104	O41(35/1/5)	—	-0.6
Total	6	118	322	39	79	17	1	10	45	23	5	43	.245	.306	.398	84	-9	1-2	.968	1	99	111	O79(51/4/24)	—	-1.3
GILL, WARREN	Warren Darst "Doc"; B12.21.1878 Ladoga IN; D11.26.1952 Laguna Beach CA; BR/TR/6´1˝/175; d8.26; Col Washington–St. Louis																								
1908	Pit N	27	76	10	17	0	1	0	14	11	6	—	.224	.366	.250	97	1	3	1.000	-3	47	103	1b25	—	-0.2
GILLEN, SAM	Samuel (b Samuel Gilleland); B11.14.1867 Pittsburgh PA; D5.13.1905 Pittsburgh PA; 5´8˝/?; d8.19																								
1893	Pit N	3	6	0	0	0	0	0	0	0	0	1	.000	.000	.000	-99	-2	0	.750	-0	106	189	S3	—	-0.2
1897	Phi N	75	270	32	70	10	3	0	27	35	4	—	.259	.353	.319	80	-6	2	.896	-23	88	24	S69,3b6	—	-2.2
Total	2	78	276	32	70	10	3	0	27	35	4	1	.254	.346	.312	76	-8	2	.892	-23	88	27	S72,3b6	—	-2.4
GILLEN, TOM	Thomas J.; B5.18.1862 Philadelphia PA; D1.26.1889 Philadelphia PA; 5´8˝/160; d4.18																								
1884	Phi U	29	116	5	18	2	0	0	—	1	—	—	.155	.162	.172	2	-18	—	.895	-5	—	—	C27,O3L	—	-1.8
1886	Det N	2	10	2	4	0	0	0	4	0	—	1	.400	.400	.400	139	0	0	.889	-1	—	—	C2	—	0.0
Total	2	31	126	7	22	2	0	0	4	1	—	1	.175	.181	.190	14	-18	0	.895	-6	—	—	C29,O3L	—	-1.8
GILLENWATER, CARDEN	Carden Edison; B5.13.1917 Riceville TN; D5.10.2000 Largo FL; BR/TR/6´1˝/178; d9.22																								
1940	StL N	7	25	1	4	1	0	0	5	0	0	2	.160	.160	.200	-1	-3	0	1.000	-0	99	0	O7(5/2/0)	—	-0.4
1943	Bro N	8	17	1	3	0	0	0	2	2	0	3	.176	.263	.176	28	-2	0	1.000	0	73	328	O4(2/1/1)	0	-0.2
1945	Bos N	144	517	74	149	20	2	7	72	73	3	70	.288	.379	.375	110	10	13	.979	17	110	**194**	O140C	0	2.2
1946	Bos N	99	224	30	51	10	1	1	14	39	0	27	.228	.342	.295	81	-4	3	.979	4	111	104	O78(11/67/0)	0	-0.3
1948	Was A	77	221	23	54	10	4	3	21	39	0	36	.244	.358	.367	96	-1	4-2	.974	-1	101	75	O67(1/65/1)	0	-0.3
Total	5	335	1004	129	261	41	7	11	114	153	3	138	.260	.359	.348	96	0	20-2	.979	19	108	145	O296(19/275/2)	0	1.0
GILLESPIE, JOHN	John William Linden; B1862 NY; BL/TR; d10.1																								
1890	Buf P	1	3	0	0	0	0	0	0	0	0	2	.000	.000	.000	-99	-1	0	.250	-0	391	0	/rf	—	-0.1
GILLESPIE, PAUL	Paul Allen; B9.18.1920 Sugar Valley GA; D8.11.1970 Anniston AL; BL/TR/6´3˝/195; d9.11																								
1942	Chi N	5	16	3	4	0	0	2	4	1	0	2	.250	.294	.625	172	1	0	1.000	-1	*119*	*99*	C4	0	0.1
1944	Chi N	9	26	2	7	1	0	1	2	3	0	3	.269	.345	.423	116	1	0	.903	-1	*101*	*200*	C7	0	0.0
1945	†Chi N	75	163	12	47	6	0	3	25	18	2	9	.288	.366	.380	110	3	2	.989	3	*145*	*86*	C45/rf	0	0.8
Total	3	89	205	17	58	7	0	6	31	22	2	14	.283	.358	.405	115	5	2	.978	1	*137*	*103*	C56/rf	0	0.9

YEAR	TM LG	G	AB	R	H	2B	3B	HR	RBI	BB-IB	HP	SO	AVG	OBP	SLG	AOPS	ABR	SB-CS	FA	FR	RNG	THR	GAMES AT POSITION	DL	BFW
Gillespie, Pete	Peter Patrick; B11.30.1851 Carbondale PA; D5.4.1910 Carbondale PA; BL/TR/6´1.5˝/178; d5.1																								
1880	Tro N	82	346	50	84	20	5	2	24	17	—	35	.243	.278	.347	105	2	—	.905	6	72	136	O82L	—	0.3
1881	Tro N	84	348	43	96	14	3	0	41	9	—	24	.276	.294	.333	92	-4	—	.933	3	70	145	O84L	—	-0.6
1882	Tro N	74	298	46	82	5	4	2	33	9	—	14	.275	.296	.339	108	3	—	.827	-6	53	25	O74L	—	-0.4
1883	NY N	**98**	411	64	129	23	12	1	62	9	—	27	.314	.329	.436	131	14	—	.897	6	50	169	O98(97/1/0)	—	1.6
1884	NY N	101	413	75	109	7	4	2	44	19	—	35	.264	.296	.315	90	-5	—	.893	-3	39	28	O101(100/0/1)	—	-1.0
1885	NY N	102	420	67	123	17	6	0	52	15	—	32	.293	.317	.362	121	9	—	**.942**	-4	63	93	O102L	—	0.2
1886	NY N	97	396	65	108	13	8	0	58	16	—	30	.273	.301	.346	95	-3	17	.901	-12	31	0	O97(95/1/1)	—	-1.6
1887	NY N	76	295	40	78	9	3	3	37	12	5	21	.264	.304	.346	84	-6	37	.946	2	119	49	O76L/3	—	-0.5
Total	8	714	2927	450	809	108	45	10	351	106	5	218	.276	.303	.354	104	10	54	.903	-7	60	82	O714(710/2/2)/3	—	-2.0
Gilliam, Jim	James William "Junior"; B10.17.1928 Nashville TN; D10.8.1978 Inglewood CA; BB/TR/5´10.5˝/175; d4.14; C14; Negro Lg 1945–51; OF(207/5/26)																								
1953	†Bro N	151	605	125	168	31	**17**	6	63	100	3	38	.278	.383	.415	106	8	21-14	.976	1	97	106	2b149	0	1.9
1954	Bro N	146	607	107	171	28	8	13	52	76	2	30	.282	.361	.418	100	1	8-7	.977	-14	92	97	2b143,O4(4/0/2)	0	-0.3
1955	†Bro N	147	538	110	134	20	8	7	40	70-4	6	37	.249	.341	.355	83	-12	15-15	.968	-6	98	102	2b99,O46(41/4/7)	0	-1.6
1956	†Bro N☆	153	594	102	178	23	8	6	43	95-6	4	39	.300	.399	.396	107	11	21-9	.981	11	107	103	2b102,O56(53/0/7)	0	2.7
1957	Bro N	149	617	89	154	26	4	2	37	64-0	4	31	.250	.323	.314	66	-27	26-10	**.986**	6	92	101	2b148,O2L	0	-0.8
1958	LA N	147	555	81	145	25	5	2	43	78-1	0	22	.261	.352	.335	81	-13	18-11	.987	10	108	97	O75(71/1/5),3b44,2b32	0	-0.5
1959	†LA N★	145	553	91	156	18	4	3	34	**96**-4	0	25	.282	.387	.345	91	-2	23-10	.958	-3	92	86	3b132,2b8,O3(3/0/1)	0	-0.4
1960	LA N	151	557	96	138	20	2	5	40	96-1	3	28	.248	.359	.318	82	-9	12-9	.960	15	**110**	106	3b130,2b30	0	0.8
1961	LA N	144	439	74	107	26	3	4	32	79-2	0	34	.244	.358	.344	81	-9	8-4	.956	14	114	101	3b74,2b71,O11L	0	1.0
1962	LA N	160	588	83	159	24	1	4	43	93-0	2	35	.270	.370	.335	97	3	17-7	.981	5	103	100	2b113,3b90/O(1/0/1)	0	1.7
1963	†LA N	148	525	77	148	27	4	6	49	60-2	2	28	.282	.354	.383	122	17	19-5	.985	7	99	102	2b119,3b55	0	3.7
1964	LA N	116	334	44	76	8	3	2	27	42-2	3	21	.228	.318	.287	78	-9	4-4	.936	-12	86	67	3b86,2b25,O2R	0	-2.1
1965	†LA N	111	372	54	104	19	4	4	39	53-5	4	31	.280	.374	.384	123	14	9-5	.960	-1	96	138	3b80,O22(21/0/1),2b5	0	1.2
1966	†LA N	88	235	30	51	9	0	1	16	34-3	0	17	.217	.315	.268	70	-8	2-1	.953	-5	87	84	3b70,1b2,2b2	0	-1.4
Total	14	1956	7119	1163	1889	304	71	65	558	1036-30	33	416	.265	.360	.355	92	-35	203-111	.979	28	97	99	2b1046,3b761,O222L,1b2	0	5.9
Gilligan, Barney	Andrew Bernard; B1.3.1856 Cambridge MA; D4.1.1934 Lynn MA; BR/TR/5´6.5˝/130; d9.25																								
1875	Atl NA	2	8	2	2	0	0	0	0	0	—	0	.250	.250	.250	85	0	0-0	1.000	-0	—	—	/Crf	—	0.0
1879	Cle N	52	205	20	35	6	2	0	11	0	—	13	.171	.171	.220	28	-16	—	.870	-0	—	—	C27,O23(21/2/0),S2	—	-1.5
1880	Cle N	30	99	9	17	4	3	1	13	6	—	12	.172	.219	.303	77	-2	—	.969	6	—	—	C23,O4C,S4	—	0.4
1881	Pro N	46	183	19	40	7	2	0	20	9	—	24	.219	.255	.279	69	-6	—	.930	-1	—	—	C36,S10/cf	—	-0.6
1882	Pro N	56	201	32	45	7	6	0	26	4	—	26	.224	.239	.318	77	-5	—	.932	6	—	—	C54,S2	—	0.5
1883	Pro N	74	263	34	52	13	3	0	24	26	—	32	.198	.270	.270	63	-11	—	.900	9	—	—	C74	—	0.3
1884	†Pro N	82	294	47	72	13	2	1	38	35	—	41	.245	.325	.313	104	3	—	.928	13	—	—	C81/31	—	2.0
1885	Pro N	71	252	23	54	7	3	0	12	23	—	33	.214	.280	.266	80	-5	—	.872	-2	—	—	C65,S5/lf2	—	-0.1
1886	Was N	81	273	23	52	9	2	0	17	39	—	35	.190	.292	.238	68	-8	6	.925	-6	—	—	C71,O14(1/6/7)/S3	—	-0.8
1887	Was N	28	90	7	18	2	0	1	6	5	0	18	.200	.242	.256	41	-7	2	.874	-3	—	—	C26,S3/cf	—	-0.7
1888	Det N	1	5	1	1	0	0	0	0	0	0	1	.200	.200	.200	28	0	0	.875	0	—	—	/C	—	0.0
Total	10	521	1865	215	386	68	23	3	167	147	0	235	.207	.265	.273	71	-57	8	.912	21	—	—	C458,O44(23/14/7),S27,3b2/21	—	-0.5
Gillis, Grant	Grant; B1.24.1901 Grove Hill AL; D2.4.1981 Thomasville AL; BR/TR/5´10˝/165; d9.19; Col Alabama																								
1927	Was A	10	36	8	8	3	1	0	2	2	0	0	.222	.263	.361	61	-2	0-0	1.000	-1	82	131	S10	—	-0.2
1928	Was A	24	87	13	22	5	1	0	10	4	3	5	.253	.309	.333	69	-4	0-1	.910	-7	79	52	S16,2b5,3b3	—	-0.9
1929	Bos A	28	73	5	18	4	0	0	11	6	0	8	.247	.304	.301	58	-5	0-1	.956	-3	98	81	2b25	—	-0.7
Total	3	62	196	26	48	12	2	0	23	12	3	13	.245	.299	.327	63	-11	0-2	.948	-11	94	82	2b30,S26,3b3	—	-1.8
Gilman, Jimmy	James Joseph; B6.14.1870; D12.21.1912 Cleveland OH; TR; d7.10																								
1893	Cle N	2	7	1	2	0	0	0	1	0	0	2	.286	.286	.286	49	-1	0	.667	-1	88	0	3b2	—	-0.1
Gilman, Pit	Pitkin Clark; B3.14.1864 Laporte OH; D8.17.1950 Elyria OH; BL/TL/?/170; d9.18																								
1884	Cle N	2	10	0	1	0	0	0	0	0	—	3	.100	.100	.100	-36	-2	—	1.000	0	0	0	O2L	—	-0.1
Gilmore, Grover	Ernest Grover; B11.1.1888 Chicago IL; D11.25.1919 Sioux City IA; BL/TL/5´9.5˝/170; d4.18																								
1914	KC F	139	530	91	152	25	5	1	32	37	3	108	.287	.337	.358	93	-14	23	.973	-1	92	107	O132(0/10/122)	—	-2.3
1915	KC F	119	411	53	117	22	15	1	47	26	13	50	.285	.347	.418	120	3	19	.979	5	109	107	O119R	—	0.2
Total	2	258	941	144	269	47	20	2	79	63	16	158	.286	.341	.385	105	-11	42	.976	4	100	107	O251(0/10/241)	—	-2.1
Gilmore, Jim	James; B5.1853 Baltimore MD; D11.18.1928 Baltimore MD; d4.26																								
1875	Was NA	3	12	2	3	0	0	0	0	0	—	3	.250	.250	.250	77	0	0-0	.667	-1	—	—	C2/3rf	—	-0.1
Gilroy	; d9.7																								
1874	Chi NA	8	38	4	8	1	0	0	7	1	—	3	.211	.231	.237	50	-2	0-0	.816	-1	—	—	C8	—	-0.2
1875	Ath NA	2	6	0	1	0	0	0	0	0	—	0	.167	.167	.167	15	-1	0-0	.800	1	—	—	/Crf	—	0.0
Total	2NA	10	44	4	9	1	0	0	7	1	—	3	.205	.222	.227	45	-3	0-0	.814	0	—	—	C9/rf	—	-0.2
Gimenez, Hector	Hector C.; B9.28.1982 San Felipe, Venezuela; BB/TR/5´10˝/180; d9.25																								
2006	Hou N	2	2	0	0	0	0	0	0	0-0	0	1	.000	.000	.000	-97	-1	0-0	ø	0	—	—	/H	0	-0.1
Ginn, Tinsley	Tinsley Rucker; B9.26.1891 Royston GA; D8.30.1931 Atlanta GA; BL/TR/5´9˝/180; d6.27; Col Georgia																								
1914	Cle A	2	1	0	0	0	0	0	0	0	0	0	.000	.000	.000	-96	0	0	ø	0	0	0	O2	—	0.0
Ginsberg, Joe	Myron Nathan; B10.11.1926 New York NY; BL/TR/5´11˝/(178–182); d9.15																								
1948	Det A	11	36	7	13	0	0	0	1	3	0	1	.361	.410	.361	103	0	0-0	.943	-1	*104*	*43*	C11	0	0.0
1950	Det A	36	95	12	22	6	0	0	12	11	1	6	.232	.318	.295	56	-6	1-0	.981	-2	*147*	*68*	C31	0	-0.6
1951	Det A	102	304	44	79	10	2	8	37	43	2	21	.260	.355	.385	100	0	0-2	.978	-4	*76*	*108*	C95	0	0.1
1952	Det A	113	307	29	68	13	2	6	36	51	3	21	.221	.338	.336	87	-4	1-1	.984	-8	*97*	*86*	C101	0	-0.7
1953	Det A	18	53	6	16	2	0	0	3	10	1	1	.302	.422	.340	109	2	0-0	.988	-1	*83*	*187*	C15	0	0.1
	Cle A	46	109	10	31	4	0	0	10	14	1	4	.284	.371	.321	91	-1	0-0	.966	-3	*91*	*52*	C39	0	-0.2
	Year	64	162	16	47	6	0	0	13	24	2	5	.290	.388	.327	97	1	0-0	.974	-4	*88*	*97*	C54	0	-0.1
1954	Cle A	3	2	0	1	0	1	0	1	0	0	0	.500	.667	1.500	473	1	0-0	1.000	0	*0*	*0*	/C	0	0.1
1956	KC A	71	195	15	48	8	1	1	12	23-3	0	17	.246	.323	.313	69	-8	1-1	.989	-1	*81*	*120*	C57	0	-0.7
	Bal A	15	28	0	2	0	0	0	2	2-0	0	4	.071	.129	.071	-48	-6	0-0	1.000	-0	*83*	*89*	C8	0	-0.6
	Year	86	223	15	50	8	1	1	14	25-3	0	21	.224	.299	.283	56	-14	1-1	.990	-2	*81*	*117*	C65	0	-1.3
1957	Bal A	85	175	15	48	8	2	1	18	18-1	2	19	.274	.342	.360	100	0	2-1	.986	-5	80	102	C66	0	-0.3
1958	Bal A	61	109	4	23	1	0	3	16	13-1	2	14	.211	.302	.303	72	-4	0-0	.994	1	133	73	C39	0	-0.2
1959	Bal A	65	166	14	30	2	0	1	14	21-3	0	13	.181	.268	.211	35	-15	1-0	.993	0	242	114	C62	0	-1.2
1960	Bal A	14	30	3	8	1	0	0	6	6-1	0	1	.267	.389	.300	90	0	0-0	.940	-1	71	42	C14	0	-0.1
	Chi A	28	75	8	19	4	0	0	9	10-0	1	8	.253	.345	.307	80	-2	1-0	.993	4	74	64	C25	0	0.3
	Year	42	105	11	27	5	0	0	15	16-1	1	9	.257	.358	.305	83	-2	1-0	.976	2	73	57	C39	0	0.2
1961	Chi A	6	3	0	0	0	0	0	0	1-0	0	2	.000	.250	.000	-27	-1	0-0	1.000	0	0	0	C2	0	0.0
	Bos A	19	24	1	6	0	0	0	5	0-0	0	2	.250	.250	.250	33	-2	0-0	1.000	-2	35	173	C6	0	-0.4
	Year	25	27	1	6	0	0	0	5	1-0	0	4	.222	.250	.222	27	-3	0-0	1.000	-2	31	155	C8	0	-0.4
1962	NY N	2	5	0	0	0	0	0	0	0-0	0	1	.000	.000	.000	-98	-1	0-0	1.000	1	0	0	C2	0	0.0
Total	13	695	1716	168	414	59	8	20	182	226-9	14	135	.241	.332	.320	79	-47	7-5	.983	-22	*106*	*95*	C574	0	-4.4
Ginter, Keith	Keith Michael; B5.5.1976 Norwalk CA; BR/TR/5´10˝/(190–195); [HouN98 10/302]; d9.20; Col Texas Tech																								
2000	Hou N	5	8	3	2	0	0	1	3	1-0	0	3	.250	.300	.625	125	0	0-0	1.000	-0	84	145	2b2	0	0.0
2001	Hou N	1	1	0	0	0	0	0	0	0-0	0	0	.000	.000	.000	-93	0	0-0	ø	0	—	—	/H	0	0.0
2002	Hou N	7	5	1	1	1	0	0	0	2-0	1	1	.200	.500	.400	130	1	0-0	.875	1	144	345	3b4/S	0	0.2
	Mil N	21	76	6	18	8	0	1	8	15-0	0	14	.237	.363	.382	97	0	0-0	.961	-4	75	67	3b21	0	-0.3
	Year	28	81	7	19	9	0	1	8	17-0	1	15	.235	.374	.383	98	1	0-0	.949	-3	80	85	3b25/S	0	-0.1
2003	Mil N	127	358	51	92	15	2	14	44	37-1	17	87	.257	.352	.427	103	2	1-1	.991	-19	89	95	2b53,3b40,S2,O2L	0	-1.4
2004	Mil N	113	386	47	101	23	2	19	60	37-2	6	100	.262	.333	.479	106	3	8-1	.973	-17	85	59	2b54,3b47,O2R,D2	34	-1.0

YEAR	TM LG	G	AB	R	H	2B	3B	HR	RBI	BB-IB	HP	SO	AVG	OBP	SLG	AOPS	ABR	SB-CS	FA	FR	RNG	THR	GAMES AT POSITION	DL	BFW
2005	Oak A	51	137	12	22	5	0	3	25	13-0	1	25	.161	.234	.263	34	-13	0-0	.975	2	101	118	2b25,3b12,O2L,D9	0	-1.0
Total	6	325	971	120	236	52	4	38	140	105-3	25	230	.243	.329	.422	95	-7	9-2	.981	-37	89	85	2b134,3b124,D11,O6(4/0/2),S3	34	-3.5
Gionfriddo, Al	Albert Francis; B3.8.1922 Dysart PA; D3.14.2003 Solvang CA; BL/TL/5´6˝/165; d9.23																								
1944	Pit N	4	6	0	1	0	0	0	0	1	0	1	.167	.286	.167	28	-1	0	1.000	-0	94	0	/cf	0	-0.1
1945	Pit N	122	409	74	116	18	9	2	42	60	1	22	.284	.377	.386	108	6	12	.964	-7	91	73	O106(13/82/11)	0	-0.5
1946	Pit N	64	102	11	26	2	2	0	10	14	0	5	.255	.345	.314	85	-2	1	.944	-0	101	99	O33(8/13/12)	0	-0.3
1947	Pit N	1	1	0	0	0	0	0	0	0	0	0	.000	.000	.000	-97	0	0	ø	0	—	—	/H	0	0.0
	†Bro N	37	62	10	11	2	1	0	6	16	0	11	.177	.346	.242	57	-3	2	.938	-1	96	89	O17(11/0/6)	0	-0.5
	Year	38	63	10	11	2	1	0	6	16	0	11	.175	.342	.238	54	-4	2	.938	-1	96	89	O17(11/0/6)	0	-0.5
Total	4	228	580	95	154	22	12	2	58	91	1	39	.266	.366	.355	97	0	15	.959	-8	93	78	O157(32/96/29)	0	-1.4
Giordano, Tommy	Thomas Arthur "T-Bone" (b Carmine Arthur Giordano); B10.9.1925 Newark NJ; BR/TR/6´0˝/175; d9.11																								
1953	Phi A	11	40	6	7	2	0	2	5	5	0	6	.175	.267	.375	69	-2	0-1	.984	0	101	117	2b11	0	-0.1
Giovanola, Ed	Edward Thomas; B3.4.1969 Los Gatos CA; BL/TR/5´10˝/(170–188); [AtlN90 7/183]; d9.10; Col Santa Clara																								
1995	Atl N	13	14	2	1	0	0	0	0	3-0	0	5	.071	.235	.071	-14	-2	0-0	1.000	-1	61	57	2b7,3b3/S	0	-0.3
1996	Atl N	43	82	10	19	2	0	0	7	8-0	1	13	.232	.304	.256	48	-6	1-0	.983	1	89	112	S25,3b6,2b5	0	-0.4
1997	Atl N	14	8	0	2	0	0	0	0	2-1	0	1	.250	.400	.250	74	0	0-0	1.000	-0	94	0	3b8/2S	0	0.0
1998	SD N	92	139	19	32	3	3	1	9	22-0	0	22	.230	.335	.317	78	-4	1-2	.965	12	127	66	3b37,2b36/S	0	0.8
1999	SD N	56	58	10	11	0	1	0	3	9-0	0	8	.190	.294	.224	38	-6	2-0	.938	4	124	0	3b25,2b19,S7/P	0	-0.1
Total	5	218	301	41	65	5	4	1	19	44-1	1	49	.216	.316	.269	57	-18	4-2	.964	15	119	66	3b79,2b68,S35/P	0	-0.0
Gipson, Charles	Charles Wells; B12.16.1972 Orange CA; BR/TR/6´2˝/(180–195); [SeaA91 63/1493]; d3.31; Col Cypress (CA) JC; OF(142/62/82)																								
1998	Sea A	44	51	11	12	1	0	0	2	5-1	1	9	.235	.316	.255	51	-4	2-1	.973	2	121	229	O36(14/11/13),3b4	0	-0.2
1999	Sea A	55	80	16	18	5	2	0	9	6-0	1	13	.225	.287	.338	59	-5	3-4	.960	9	105	895	O28(8/9/15),3b17,2b3,S3,D4	52	0.3
2000	†Sea A	59	29	7	9	1	1	0	3	4-0	0	9	.310	.394	.414	107	0	2-3	1.000	1	86	136	O48(14/8/29),3b5,S5/D	0	0.0
2001	†Sea A	94	64	16	14	2	2	0	5	4-0	2	20	.219	.282	.313	61	-4	1-1	1.000	-1	94	82	O65(41/14/11),D11,3b9,S6/2	0	-0.6
2002	Sea A	79	72	22	17	5	2	0	8	9-0	1	14	.236	.329	.361	86	-1	4-0	.971	2	114	121	O73(57/5/13),3b4	0	0.0
2003	NY A	18	10	3	2	0	0	0	2	1-0	0	2	.200	.273	.200	28	-1	2-1	1.000	-0	88	0	O8C,D3	0	-0.1
2004	TB A	5	4	1	2	0	0	0	0	0-0	0	1	.500	.500	.500	166	0	1-0	1.000	0	122	265	S2,O2(1/2/0)/D	0	0.1
2005	Hou N	19	11	2	2	1	0	0	1	1-0	0	3	.182	.250	.273	36	-1	1-1	1.000	-1	74	0	O13(7/5/1)	0	-0.2
Total	8	373	321	78	76	15	7	0	30	30-1	5	71	.237	.311	.327	68	-16	16-11	.981	11	104	193	O273L,3b39,D20,S16,2b4	52	-0.7
Girardi, Joe	Joseph Elliott; B10.14.1964 Peoria IL; BR/TR/5´11˝/(195–200); [ChiN86 5/116]; d4.4; M1/C1; Col Northwestern																								
1989	†Chi N	59	157	15	39	10	0	1	14	11-5	2	26	.248	.304	.331	77	-4	2-1	.981	9	107	121	C59	0	0.8
1990	Chi N	133	419	36	113	24	2	1	38	17-11	3	50	.270	.300	.344	72	-16	8-3	.985	-8	137	103	C133	0	-1.6
1991	Chi N	21	47	3	9	2	0	0	6	6-1	0	6	.191	.283	.234	45	-3	0-0	.972	1	92	96	C21	111	-0.2
1992	Chi N	91	270	19	73	3	1	1	12	19-3	1	38	.270	.320	.300	75	-9	0-2	.991	-3	131	114	C86	0	-0.9
1993	Col N	86	310	35	90	14	5	3	31	24-0	3	41	.290	.346	.397	84	-6	6-6	.989	-3	92	111	C84	67	-0.4
1994	Col N	93	330	47	91	9	4	4	34	21-1	2	48	.276	.321	.364	67	-16	3-3	.992	8	98	118	C93	15	-0.2
1995	†Col N	125	462	63	121	17	2	8	55	29-0	2	76	.262	.308	.359	59	-27	3-3	.988	-1	104	87	C122	0	-2.0
1996	†NY A	124	422	55	124	22	3	2	45	30-1	5	55	.294	.346	.374	83	-11	13-4	.996	2	78	99	C120,D2	0	0.0
1997	†NY A	112	398	38	105	23	1	1	50	26-1	2	53	.264	.311	.334	69	-18	2-3	.994	12	106	104	C111/D	0	0.1
1998	†NY A	78	254	31	70	11	4	3	31	14-1	2	38	.276	.317	.386	86	-6	2-4	.995	11	97	79	C78	0	0.9
1999	†NY A	65	209	23	50	16	1	2	27	10-0	0	26	.239	.271	.354	60	-13	3-1	.984	3	72	98	C65	0	-0.5
2000	Chi N☆	106	363	47	101	15	1	6	40	32-3	3	61	.278	.339	.375	82	-10	1-0	.993	-10	96	134	C103	0	-1.3
2001	Chi N	78	229	22	58	10	1	3	25	21-4	0	50	.253	.315	.345	73	-9	0-1	1.000	-1	131	114	C71	0	-0.6
2002	Chi N	90	234	19	53	10	1	1	13	16-3	0	35	.226	.275	.291	49	-18	1-0	.990	-6	91	103	C88	15	-1.9
2003	StL N	16	23	1	3	0	0	0	1	3-0	0	4	.130	.231	.130	-2	-4	0-0	.958	-4	98	0	C13	135	-0.8
Total	15	1277	4127	454	1100	186	26	36	422	279-34	25	607	.267	.315	.350	71	-170	44-31	.991	12	103	105	C1247,D3	343	-8.6
Giuliani, Tony	Angelo John; B11.24.1912 St.Paul MN; D10.8.2004 St.Paul MN; BR/TR/5´11˝/175; d4.18																								
1936	StL A	71	198	17	43	3	0	0	13	11	0	13	.217	.258	.232	21	-25	0-0	.966	2	*109*	*47*	C66	—	-1.8
1937	StL A	19	53	6	16	1	0	0	3	3	0	3	.302	.339	.321	67	-3	0-0	.986	-1	*90*	*95*	C19	—	-0.3
1938	Was A	46	115	10	25	4	0	0	15	8	0	3	.217	.268	.252	33	-12	1-0	1.000	-1	*109*	*92*	C46	—	-1.0
1939	Was A	54	172	20	43	6	2	0	18	4	0	7	.250	.267	.308	50	-14	0-1	.979	2	*151*	*85*	C50	—	-0.9
1940	Bro N	1	1	0	0	0	0	0	0	0	0	1	.000	.000	.000	-94	0	0	1.000	-0	*0*	*0*	/C	—	0.0
1941	Bro N	3	2	0	0	0	0	0	0	0	0	0	.000	.000	.000	-96	-1	0	1.000	1	*0*	*0*	C3	0	0.0
1943	Was A	49	133	5	30	4	1	0	20	12	0	14	.226	.290	.271	67	-6	0-1	.962	-1	*119*	*81*	C49	0	-0.6
Total	7	243	674	58	157	18	3	0	69	38	0	41	.233	.274	.269	42	-61	1-2	.976	1	*119*	*75*	C234	0	-4.6
Gladd, Jim	James Walter; B10.2.1922 Ft.Gibson OK; D11.8.1977 Long Beach CA; BR/TR/6´2˝/190; d9.9																								
1946	NY N	4	11	0	1	0	0	0	0	1	0	4	.091	.167	.091	-26	-2	0	1.000	2	*89*	*74*	C4	0	0.0
Gladden, Dan	Clinton Daniel; B7.7.1957 San Jose CA; BR/TR/5´11˝/(175–184); d9.5; Col Cal St.–Fresno																								
1983	SF N	18	63	6	14	2	0	1	9	5-0	0	11	.222	.275	.302	63	-3	4-3	1.000	2	125	0	O18(0/17/1)	0	-0.2
1984	SF N	86	342	71	120	17	2	4	31	33-2	2	37	.351	.410	.447	145	22	31-16	.988	4	105	164	O85C	0	2.7
1985	SF N	142	502	64	122	15	8	7	41	40-1	7	78	.243	.307	.347	86	-11	32-15	.975	-7	97	41	O124(14/111/1)	0	-1.9
1986	SF N	102	351	55	97	16	1	4	29	39-3	5	59	.276	.357	.362	104	3	27-10	.987	5	113	141	O89C	49	1.0
1987	†Min A	121	438	69	109	21	2	8	38	38-2	3	72	.249	.312	.361	75	-16	25-9	.987	7	110	136	O111(105/8/2),D4	0	-1.0
1988	Min A	141	576	91	155	32	6	11	62	46-4	4	74	.269	.325	.403	100	0	28-8	.991	12	113	151	O140L/23P	0	1.1
1989	Min A	121	461	69	136	23	3	8	46	23-3	5	53	.295	.331	.410	102	1	23-7	.966	4	110	122	O117(116/2/0)/PD	36	0.4
1990	Min A	136	534	64	147	27	6	5	40	26-2	6	67	.275	.314	.376	87	-10	25-9	.980	9	110	146	O133(133/1/0),D2	0	-0.3
1991	†Min A	126	461	65	114	14	9	6	52	36-1	5	60	.247	.306	.356	79	-14	15-9	.988	0	102	63	O126L	25	-1.7
1992	Det A	113	417	57	106	20	1	7	42	30-0	2	64	.254	.304	.357	84	-9	4-2	.987	1	98	130	O108(95/17/0),D2	31	-1.1
1993	Det A	91	356	52	95	16	2	13	56	21-0	3	50	.267	.312	.433	98	-3	8-5	.986	4	104	173	O86(69/18/0),D5	50	-0.1
Total	11	1197	4501	663	1215	203	40	74	446	337-18	42	625	.270	.324	.382	94	-40	222-93	.984	40	107	122	O1137(798/349/4),D15,P2/32	191	-1.1
Gladmon, Buck	James Henry; B11.1863 Washington DC; D1.13.1890 Washington DC; d7.7																								
1883	Phi N	1	4	1	0	0	0	0	0	0	—	2	.000	.000	.000	-99	-1	—	1.000	-0	74	0	/3	—	-0.1
1884	Was AA	56	224	17	35	5	3	1	—	3	3	—	.156	.178	.219	33	-15	—	.796	-5	94	70	3b53,O2R/S	—	-1.8
1886	Was N	44	152	17	21	5	3	1	15	12	—	30	.138	.201	.230	33	-12	5	.830	-2	92	154	3b44	—	-1.2
Total	3	101	380	35	56	10	6	2	15	15	—	32	.147	.186	.221	31	-28	5	.812	-7	93	105	3b98,O2R/S	—	-3.1
Gladu, Roland	Roland Edouard; B5.10.1911 Montreal QC, Can.; D7.26.1994 Montreal QC, Can.; BL/TR/5´8.5˝/185; d4.18																								
1944	Bos N	21	66	5	16	2	1	1	7	3	0	8	.242	.275	.348	72	-3	0	.891	-2	74	244	3b15,O3L	0	-0.5
Glanville, Doug	Douglas Metunwa; B8.25.1970 Hackensack NJ; BR/TR/6´2˝/(170–180); [ChiN91 1/12]; d6.9; Col Penn																								
1996	Chi N	49	83	10	20	5	1	1	10	3-0	0	11	.241	.264	.361	62	-5	2-0	.973	-0	97	95	O35(19/9/8)	0	-0.5
1997	Chi N	146	474	79	142	22	5	4	35	24-0	1	46	.300	.333	.392	87	-10	19-11	.989	9	108	166	O138(120/30/1)	0	-0.4
1998	Phi N	158	678	106	189	28	7	8	49	42-1	6	89	.279	.325	.376	84	-17	23-6	.995	-1	97	142	O158C	0	-1.3
1999	Phi N	150	628	101	204	38	6	11	73	48-1	6	82	.325	.376	.457	109	9	34-2	.980	6	107	163	O148C	0	2.2
2000	Phi N	154	637	89	175	27	6	8	52	31-1	2	76	.275	.307	.374	72	-29	31-8	.990	4	108	103	O150C	0	-1.9
2001	Phi N	153	634	74	166	24	3	14	55	19-1	4	91	.262	.285	.375	73	-29	28-6	.991	6	114	96	O150C	0	-1.6
2002	Phi N	138	422	49	105	16	3	6	29	25-4	2	57	.249	.292	.344	72	-19	19-2	**1.000**	-5	89	123	O117C	0	-1.9
2003	Tex A	52	195	22	53	5	0	4	14	6-1	0	25	.272	.294	.359	66	-10	4-0	1.000	-3	94	46	O52C	53	-1.1
	†Chi N	28	51	2	12	0	0	1	2	2-0	0	4	.235	.259	.294	44	-4	0-1	1.000	2	136	188	O18(3/15/1)	0	-0.2
2004	Phi N	87	162	21	34	1	1	2	14	8-1	0	21	.210	.244	.265	32	-17	8-0	1.000	2	121	0	O68(13/56/0)	0	-1.3
Total	9	1115	3964	553	1100	166	32	59	333	208-10	21	502	.277	.315	.380	80	-131	168-36	.991	21	105	121	O1034(155/885/10)	53	-8.0
Glasscock, Jack	John Wesley "Pebbly Jack"; B7.22.1857 Wheeling VA (now West Virgina); D2.24.1947 Wheeling WV; BR/TR/5´8˝/160; d5.1; M2																								
1879	Cle N	80	325	31	68	9	3	0	29	6	—	24	.209	.224	.255	58	-14	—	.919	-9	86	63	2b66,3b14	—	-1.8
1880	Cle N	77	296	37	72	13	3	0	27	2	—	21	.243	.248	.307	89	-3	—	.891	5	100	114	S77	—	0.5
1881	Cle N	**85**	335	49	86	9	5	0	33	15	—	8	.257	.289	.313	94	-2	—	**.911**	9	**105**	123	S79,2b6	—	1.0
1882	Cle N	**84**	358	66	104	27	9	4	46	13	—	9	.291	.315	.450	147	19	—	.900	**24**	**118**	**174**	S83/3	—	**4.1**

YEAR	TM LG	G	AB	R	H	2B	3B	HR	RBI	BB-IB	HP	SO	AVG	OBP	SLG	AOPS	ABR	SB-CS	FA	FR	RNG	THR	GAMES AT POSITION	DL	BFW
1883	Cle N	96	383	67	110	19	6	0	46	13	—	23	.287	.311	.368	107	3	—	**.922**	18	**107**	119	S93,2b3	—	2.0
1884	Cle N	72	281	45	70	4	4	1	22	25	—	16	.249	.310	.302	91	-3	—	.893	26	125	96	S69,2b3,P2	—	2.2
	Cin U	38	172	48	72	9	5	2	—	8	—	—	.419	.444	.564	189	14	—	.889	1	104	81	S36,2b2	—	1.4
1885	StL N	**111**	446	66	125	18	3	1	40	29	—	10	.280	.324	.341	123	13	—	**.917**	21	**112**	98	S110/2	—	3.5
1886	StL N	121	486	96	158	29	7	3	40	38	—	13	.325	.374	.432	154	34	38	**.906**	15	**107**	**124**	S120/rf	—	4.6
1887	Ind N	122	483	91	142	18	7	0	40	41	10	8	.294	.361	.360	105	6	62	.906	**39**	**122**	135	S122/P	—	4.0
1888	Ind N	113	442	63	119	17	3	1	45	14	7	17	.269	.302	.328	99	-1	48	**.901**	14	**106**	110	S110,2b3/P	—	1.6
1889	Ind N	134	582	128	**205**	40	3	7	85	31	5	10	.352	.390	.467	135	27	57	**.915**	**38**	**118**	**129**	S132,2b2/PM	—	**5.8**
1890	NY N	124	512	91	**172**	32	9	1	66	41	9	8	**.336**	.395	.439	143	28	54	.910	23	101	102	S124	—	**4.8**
1891	NY N	97	369	46	89	12	6	0	55	36	5	11	.241	.317	.306	85	-6	29	.913	1	91	126	S97	—	-0.2
1892	StL N	139	566	83	151	27	5	3	72	44	7	19	.267	.327	.348	110	7	26	.916	6	102	87	S139,M	—	1.9
1893	StL N	48	195	32	56	8	1	1	26	25	5	3	.287	.382	.354	96	0	20	.907	-5	96	100	S48	—	-0.2
	Pit N	66	293	49	100	7	11	1	74	17	4	4	.341	.385	.451	124	8	16	.934	10	103	153	S66	—	1.8
	Year	114	488	81	156	15	12	2	100	42	9	7	.320	.384	.412	113	9	36	.923	5	100	131	S114	—	1.6
1894	Pit N	87	335	47	94	10	7	1	65	32	4	4	.281	.350	.361	73	-15	18	.933	3	99	121	S86	—	-0.6
1895	Lou N	18	74	9	25	3	1	1	6	3	3	1	.338	.387	.446	122	3	1	.900	1	102	91	S13,1b5	—	0.3
	Was N	25	100	20	23	2	0	0	10	7	3	3	.230	.300	.250	43	-8	3	.895	6	118	84	S25	—	-0.1
	Year	43	174	29	48	5	1	1	16	10	6	4	.276	.337	.333	76	-6	4	.897	7	112	86	S38,1b5	—	0.2
Total	17	1737	7033	1164	2041	313	98	27	827	440	62	212	.290	.337	.374	112	110	372	.910	246	108	117	S1629,2b86,3b15,1b5,P5/rf	—	36.6
GLAUS, TROY	Troy; B8.3.1976 Tarzana CA; BR/TR/6´5˝/(225–245); [CalA97 1/3]; d7.31; Col UCLA																								
1998	Ana A	48	165	19	36	9	0	1	23	15-0	0	51	.218	.280	.291	49	-12	1-0	.941	0	102	99	3b48	0	-1.1
1999	Ana A	154	551	85	132	29	0	29	79	71-1	6	143	.240	.331	.450	97	-3	5-1	.954	-6	97	99	3b153/D	0	-0.7
2000	Ana A★	159	563	120	160	37	1	**47**	102	112-6	2	163	.284	.404	.604	147	43	14-11	.933	12	**117**	115	3b156,S6,D4	0	4.9
2001	Ana A★	161	588	100	147	38	2	41	108	107-7	6	158	.250	.367	.531	131	29	10-3	.953	-16	92	79	3b159,S2,D2	0	1.4
2002	†Ana A	156	569	99	142	24	1	30	111	88-4	6	144	.250	.352	.453	115	14	10-3	.950	-2	100	128	3b156,S2	0	1.3
2003	Ana A★	91	319	53	79	17	2	16	50	46-4	1	73	.248	.343	.464	115	7	7-2	.923	-8	91	79	3b87,D4	69	0.1
2004	†Ana A	58	207	47	52	11	1	18	42	31-3	3	52	.251	.355	.575	143	13	2-3	.950	-2	84	68	D39,3b19	109	0.8
2005	Ari N	149	538	78	139	29	1	37	97	84-2	7	145	.258	.363	.522	123	19	4-2	.946	8	**110**	92	3b145/D	0	2.8
2006	Tor A★	153	540	105	136	27	0	38	104	86-6	3	134	.252	.355	.513	117	14	3-2	.963	-1	95	136	3b145,S8,D4	0	1.4
Total	9	1129	4040	706	1023	221	8	257	716	640-33	34	1063	.253	.357	.503	120	124	56-27	.947	-14	101	104	3b1068,D55,S18	178	10.9
GLAVIANO, TOMMY	Thomas Giatano "Rabbit"; B10.26.1923 Sacramento CA; D1.19.2004 Sacramento CA; BR/TR/5´9˝/(175–185); d4.19																								
1949	StL N	87	258	32	69	16	1	6	36	41	6	35	.267	.380	.407	106	4	0	.929	7	113	106	3b73,2b7	0	1.1
1950	StL N	115	410	92	117	29	2	11	44	90	6	74	.285	.421	.446	122	19	6	.935	2	106	71	3b106,2b5/S	0	2.1
1951	StL N	54	104	20	19	4	0	1	4	26	2	18	.183	.356	.250	66	-4	3-0	.972	-2	87	0	O17(2/14/1),2b9	0	-0.5
1952	StL N	80	162	30	39	5	1	3	19	27	5	26	.241	.366	.340	97	1	0-0	.934	2	105	70	3b52/2	0	0.2
1953	Phi N	53	74	17	15	1	2	3	5	24	2	20	.203	.410	.392	111	3	2-0	.892	-2	82	82	3b14,2b12/S	0	0.1
Total	5	389	1008	191	259	55	6	24	108	208	21	173	.257	.395	.395	108	23	11-0	.931	6	107	82	3b245,2b34,O17(2/14/1),S2	0	3.0
GLAVINE, MIKE	Michael Patrick; B1.24.1973 Concord MA; BL/TL/6´3˝/210; [CleA95 22/614]; d9.14; b–Tom; Col Northeastern																								
2003	NY N	6	7	0	1	0	0	0	0	0-0	0	2	.143	.143	.143	-26	-1	0-0	1.000	0	157	109	1b3	0	-0.1
GLEASON, HARRY	Harry Gilbert; B3.28.1875 Camden NJ; D10.21.1961 Camden NJ; BR/TR/5´6˝/160; d9.27; b–Kid																								
1901	Bos A	1	1	0	1	0	0	0	0	0	0	—	1.000	1.000	1.000	464	0	1	.667	0	195	1796	/3	—	0.1
1902	Bos A	71	240	30	54	5	5	2	25	10	3	—	.225	.265	.313	58	-15	6	.930	-3	98	174	3b35,O23(8/15/0),2b4	—	-1.7
1903	Bos A	6	13	3	2	1	0	0	2	0	0	—	.154	.154	.231	13	-1	0	.750	-1	92	0	3b2	—	-0.2
1904	StL A	46	155	10	33	7	1	0	6	4	3	—	.213	.247	.271	68	-6	1	.908	-4	109	132	S20,3b20,2b5/cf	—	-1.0
1905	StL A	150	535	45	116	11	5	1	57	34	4	—	.217	.269	.262	72	-18	23	.911	-15	95	64	3b144,2b7	—	-3.2
Total	5	274	944	88	206	24	11	3	90	48	10	—	.218	.263	.276	67	-40	31	.914	-22	95	99	3b202,O24(8/16/0),S20,2b16	—	-6.0
GLEASON, JACK	John Day; B7.14.1854 St.Louis MO; D9.4.1944 St.Louis MO; BR/TR/?/170; d10.2; b–Bill																								
1877	StL N	1	4	0	1	0	0	0	0	0	—	1	.250	.250	.250	61	0	—	ø	-0	0	0	/cf	—	0.0
1882	StL AA	78	331	53	84	10	1	2	—	**27**	—	—	.254	.310	.308	105	2	—	.768	3	**105**	**134**	3b73,O6R/2	—	0.6
1883	StL AA	9	34	2	8	0	0	0	—	4	—	—	.235	.316	.235	76	-1	—	.833	1	186	0	O9L/3	—	0.0
	Lou AA	84	355	69	106	11	4	2	—	25	—	—	.299	.345	.369	140	18	—	.795	-32	62	66	3b83/S	—	-1.1
	Year	93	389	71	114	11	4	2	—	29	—	—	.293	.342	.357	134	17	—	.798	-31	64	65	3b84,O9L/S	—	-1.1
1884	StL U	92	395	90	128	30	2	4	—	23	—	—	.324	.361	.441	137	7	—	.768	-4	**105**	**146**	3b92	—	0.4
1885	StL N	2	7	0	1	0	0	0	0	0	—	1	.143	.143	.143	-8	-1	—	.857	-0	77	0	3b2	—	-0.1
1886	Phi AA	77	299	39	56	8	7	1	31	16	11	—	.187	.255	.271	64	-13	8	.797	-6	98	162	3b77	—	-1.6
Total	6	343	1425	253	384	59	14	9	31	95	11	2	.269	.320	.349	112	12	8	.781	-39	93	125	3b328,O16(9/1/6)/S2	—	-1.8
GLEASON, ROY	Roy William; B4.9.1943 Melrose Park IL; BB/TR/6´5.5˝/225; d9.3																								
1963	LA N	8	1	3	1	1	0	0	0	0-0	0	0	1.000	1.000	2.000	795	1	0-0	ø	0	—	—	/H	0	0.1
GLEASON, BILL	William G. "Will"; B11.12.1858 St.Louis MO; D7.21.1932 St.Louis MO; BR/TR/5´8˝/170; d5.2; U1; b–Jack																								
1882	StL AA	**79**	347	63	100	11	6	1	—	6	—	—	.288	.300	.363	118	5	—	.833	10	106	112	S79	—	1.6
1883	StL AA	**98**	425	81	122	21	9	2	42	15	—	—	.287	.311	.393	119	8	—	.871	-2	93	129	S98	—	0.7
1884	StL AA	**110**	472	97	127	21	7	1	—	27	12	—	.269	.325	.350	116	9	—	.867	-21	89	87	S110/3	—	-0.8
1885	†StL AA	**112**	472	79	119	9	5	3	53	29	**15**	—	.252	.316	.311	94	-3	—	.869	-42	80	63	S112	—	-3.8
1886	†StL AA	125	524	97	141	18	5	0	61	43	7	—	.269	.333	.323	101	1	19	.853	-30	86	113	S125	—	-2.2
1887	†StL AA	135	598	135	172	19	1	0	76	41	8	—	.288	.342	.323	78	-20	23	.875	-11	98	85	S135	—	-2.2
1888	Phi AA	123	499	55	112	10	2	0	61	12	9	—	.224	.256	.253	63	-21	27	.858	-14	94	118	S121/31	—	-2.9
1889	Lou AA	16	58	6	14	2	0	0	5	4	1	1	.241	.302	.276	66	-2	1	.822	-1	107	63	S16	—	-0.3
Total	8	798	3395	613	907	111	35	7	298	177	52	1	.267	.313	.327	95	-23	70	.860	-110	92	99	S796,3b2/1	—	-9.9
GLEASON, KID	William J.; B10.26.1866 Camden NJ; D1.2.1933 Philadelphia PA; BB/TR/5´7˝/158; d4.20; M5/C16; b–Harry; OF(14/15/13); ▲																								
1888	Phi N	24	83	4	17	2	0	0	5	3	0	16	.205	.233	.229	45	-5	3	.841	-3	72	112	P24/rf	—	-0.2
1889	Phi N	30	99	11	25	5	0	0	8	8	0	12	.253	.308	.303	65	-5	4	.862	-1	109	61	P29,O3C,2b2	—	-0.1
1890	Phi N	63	224	22	47	3	0	0	17	12	0	21	.210	.250	.223	37	-18	10	.937	-2	93	118	P60,2b2	—	-0.2
1891	Phi N	65	214	31	53	5	2	0	17	20	2	17	.248	.318	.290	75	-7	6	.896	-6	85	64	P53,O9(1/8/0),S4	—	-0.5
1892	StL N	66	233	35	50	4	2	3	25	34	0	23	.215	.315	.288	87	-3	7	.934	4	112	122	P47,O10(3/2/6),2b9/1	—	0.1
1893	StL N	59	199	25	51	6	4	0	20	19	2	8	.256	.327	.327	74	-8	2	.907	-1	103	112	P48,O11(5/0/6)/S	—	-0.3
1894	StL N	9	28	3	7	0	1	0	1	2	0	1	.250	.300	.321	50	-3	0	.885	1	146	0	P8/1	—	0.0
	†Bal N	26	86	22	30	5	1	0	17	7	0	2	.349	.398	.430	95	-1	1	.900	-2	65	91	P21/1	—	-0.1
	Year	35	114	25	37	5	2	0	18	9	0	3	.325	.374	.404	85	-3	1	.894	-1	85	68	P29,1b2	—	-0.1
1895	†Bal N	112	421	90	130	14	12	0	74	33	5	18	.309	.366	.399	95	-5	19	.899	-16	96	99	2b85,3b12,P9,O4L	—	-1.3
1896	NY N	**133**	541	79	162	17	5	4	89	42	2	13	.299	.352	.372	93	-5	46	.938	7	101	72	2b130,3b3/cf	—	0.6
1897	NY N	132	543	86	172	16	4	1	106	27	3	—	.317	.353	.366	93	-6	44	.930	-3	95	98	2b130,S3	—	-0.2
1898	NY N	150	570	78	126	8	5	0	62	39	6	—	.221	.278	.253	54	-34	21	.938	18	104	94	2b144,S6	—	-0.9
1899	NY N	147	580	73	154	14	5	0	60	24	0	—	.266	.295	.307	67	-27	29	.946	28	**105**	93	2b147	—	0.7
1900	NY N	111	420	60	104	11	3	1	29	17	2	—	.248	.280	.295	62	-23	23	.931	13	104	101	2b111/S	—	-0.5
1901	Det A	**135**	547	82	150	16	12	3	75	41	2	—	.274	.327	.364	87	-11	32	.925	4	**107**	113	2b135	—	-0.5
1902	Det A	118	441	42	109	11	4	1	38	25	3	—	.247	.292	.297	62	-23	17	.941	6	99	132	2b118	—	-1.5
1903	Phi N	106	412	65	117	19	6	1	49	23	3	—	.284	.326	.367	101	-1	12	.959	-3	97	85	2b102,O4C	—	-0.3
1904	Phi N	153	587	61	161	23	6	0	42	37	2	—	.274	.319	.334	106	4	17	.942	4	99	84	2b152/3	—	1.0
1905	Phi N	**155**	608	95	150	17	7	1	50	45	3	—	.247	.302	.303	83	-13	16	.947	-11	95	99	2b155	—	-2.3
1906	Phi N	135	494	47	112	17	2	0	34	36	1	—	.227	.281	.269	71	-17	17	.947	-26	92	90	2b135	—	-4.8
1907	Phi N	36	126	11	18	3	0	0	6	7	2	—	.143	.200	.167	15	-12	3	.979	-2	88	90	2b26,1b4,S4/cf	—	-1.6
1908	Phi N	2	1	0	0	0	0	0	0	0	0	—	.000	.000	.000	-97	0	0	1.000	0	99	0	/2lf	—	0.0
1912	Chi A	1	2	0	1	0	0	0	0	0	0	—	.500	.500	.500	192	0	0	1.000	-0	83	0	/2	—	0.0
Total	22	1968	7459	1022	1946	216	81	15	824	501	38	131	.261	.311	.318	78	-223	329	.938	10	99	96	2b1585,P299,O45C,S19,3b16,1b7	—	-12.9

YEAR	TM LG	G	AB	R	H	2B	3B	HR	RBI	BB-IB	HP	SO	AVG	OBP	SLG	AOPS	ABR	SB-CS	FA	FR	RNG	THR	GAMES AT POSITION	DL	BFW
Gleason, Billy	William Patrick; B9.6.1894 Chicago IL; D1.9.1957 Holyoke MA; BR/TR/5´6.5˝/157; d9.25																								
1916	Pit N	1	2	0	0	0	0	0	0	0	0	0	.000	.000	.000	-99	0	0	1.000	-0	75	0	/2	—	-0.1
1917	Pit N	13	42	3	7	1	0	0	0	5	0	5	.167	.255	.190	36	-3	1	.978	-3	88	62	2b13	—	-0.7
1921	StL A	26	74	6	19	0	1	0	8	6	2	6	.257	.329	.284	54	-5	0-1	.960	-3	94	96	2b25	—	-0.8
Total	3	40	118	9	26	1	1	0	8	11	2	11	.220	.298	.246	47	-8	1-1	.966	-6	92	83	2b39	—	-1.6
Gleeson, Jim	James Joseph "Gee Gee"; B3.5.1912 Kansas City MO; D5.1.1996 Kansas City MO; BB/TR/6´1˝/191; d4.25; C2; Col Rockhurst																								
1936	Cle A	41	139	26	36	9	2	4	12	18	0	17	.259	.344	.439	91	-2	2-1	.958	-2	100	32	O33(4/0/30)	—	-0.6
1939	Chi N	111	332	43	74	19	6	4	45	39	2	46	.223	.308	.352	76	-11	7	.957	-3	98	68	O91(13/12/66)	—	-2.0
1940	Chi N	129	485	76	152	39	11	5	61	54	6	52	.313	.389	.470	139	27	4	.983	-1	92	139	O123(32/82/13)	—	2.1
1941	Cin N	102	301	47	70	10	0	3	34	45	4	30	.233	.340	.296	80	-6	7	.981	-5	98	16	O84(22/15/50)	0	-1.6
1942	Cin N	9	20	3	4	0	0	0	2	2	1	2	.200	.304	.200	49	-1	0	.889	-0	77	238	O5R	0	-0.2
Total	5	392	1277	195	336	77	19	16	154	158	13	147	.263	.350	.391	101	7	20-1	.972	-12	96	82	O336(71/109/164)	0	-2.3
Gleich, Frank	Frank Elmer "Inch"; B3.7.1894 Columbus OH; D3.27.1949 Columbus OH; BL/TR/5´11˝/175; d9.17																								
1919	NY A	5	4	0	1	0	0	0	1	1	0	0	.250	.400	.250	84	0	0	.000	-1	0	0	O4(3/1/0)	—	-0.1
1920	NY A	24	41	6	5	0	0	0	3	6	0	10	.122	.234	.122	-4	-6	0-0	.864	-2	93	0	O15(9/4/2)	—	-0.8
Total	2	29	45	6	6	0	0	0	4	7	0	10	.133	.250	.133	4	-6	0-0	.826	-3	85	0	O19(12/5/2)	—	-0.9
Glenalvin, Bob	Robert J. (b Edward A. Dowling); B1.17.1867 Indianapolis IN; D3.24.1944 Detroit MI; BB/TR/5´9˝/160; d7.12																								
1890	Chi N	66	250	43	67	10	3	4	26	19	7	31	.268	.337	.380	105	1	30	.928	-8	96	86	2b66	—	-0.4
1893	Chi N	16	61	11	21	3	1	0	12	7	0	3	.344	.412	.426	125	2	7	.928	-3	89	55	2b16	—	0.0
Total	2	82	311	54	88	13	4	4	38	26	7	34	.283	.352	.389	109	3	37	.928	-11	95	80	2b82	—	-0.4
Glenn, Ed	Edward C. "Mouse"; B9.19.1860 Richmond VA; D2.10.1892 Richmond VA; BR/TR/5´10˝/160; d8.5																								
1884	Ric AA	43	175	26	43	2	4	1	—	5	1	—	.246	.271	.320	93	-2	—	.833	5	63	150	O43L	—	0.2
1886	Pit AA	71	277	32	53	6	5	0	26	17	1	—	.191	.241	.249	54	-15	19	.865	-0	82	101	O71L	—	-1.6
1888	KC AA	3	8	0	0	0	0	0	0	0	2	—	.000	.200	.000	-32	-1	1	.857	-0	0	0	O3L	—	-0.1
	Bos N	20	65	8	10	0	2	0	3	2	2	8	.154	.203	.215	33	-5	0	.957	1	55	283	O19L/3	—	-0.5
Total	3	137	525	66	106	8	11	1	29	24	6	8	.202	.245	.265	62	-23	20	.867	6	70	142	O136L/3	—	-2.0
Glenn, Ed	Edward D.; B10.1875 Cincinnati OH; D12.6.1911 Ludlow KY; BR/TR; d9.7																								
1898	Was N	1	4	0	0	0	0	0	0	0	0	—	.000	.000	.000	-99	-1	0	1.000	-0	86	0	/S	—	-0.1
	NY N	2	4	1	1	0	0	0	0	3	0	—	.250	.571	.250	142	1	1	.750	-1	47	0	S2	—	-0.1
	Year	3	8	1	1	0	0	0	0	3	0	—	.125	.364	.125	42	0	1	.857	-2	61	0	S3	—	-0.2
1902	Chi N	2	7	0	0	0	0	0	0	1	0	—	.000	.125	.000	-63	-1	0	1.000	-0	115	0	S2	—	-0.2
Total	2	5	15	1	1	0	0	0	0	4	0	—	.067	.263	.067	-2	-1	1	.923	-2	85	0	S5	—	-0.4
Glenn, Harry	Harry Melville "Husky"; B6.9.1890 Shelburn IN; D10.12.1918 St.Paul MN; BR/TR/6´1˝/200; d4.14																								
1915	StL N	6	16	1	5	0	0	0	1	3	0	0	.313	.421	.313	123	1	0	.929	-1	*109*	*55*	C5	—	0.0
Glenn, John	John; B7.10.1928 Moultrie GA; BR/TR/6´3˝/180; d6.16																								
1960	StL N	32	31	4	8	0	1	0	5	0-0	0	9	.258	.250	.323	53	-2	0-0	1.000	-1	90	0	O28(19/5/4)	0	-0.4
Glenn, John	John W.; B1.1850 Rochester NY; D11.10.1888 Sandy Hill (now Hudson Falls) NY; BR/TR/5´8.5˝/169; d5.13																								
1871	Oly NA	26	120	25	37	3	2	0	21	3	—	1	.308	.325	.367	104	1	1-1	.860	1	112	**443**	O26(1/0/25)	—	0.3
1872	Oly NA	**9**	39	6	6	0	0	0	3	1	—	0	.154	.175	.154	2	-4	0-1	.800	3	313	725	O9L	—	-0.1
	Nat NA	1	4	0	2	0	0	0	0	0	—	0	.500	.500	.500	179	0	0-0	.667	-0	0	0	/cf	—	0.0
	Year	10	43	6	8	0	0	0	3	1	—	0	.186	.205	.186	22	-4	0-1	.791	3	281	651	O10(9/1/0)	—	-0.1
1873	Was NA	**39**	186	39	49	9	2	1	22	3	—	0	.263	.275	.349	86	-2	3-1	.915	-2	45	81	1b39	—	-0.3
1874	Chi NA	55	237	33	67	9	0	0	32	5	—	4	.283	.298	.321	97	0	2-2	.918	0	135	81	1b37,O19(2/1/17)	—	0.1
1875	Chi NA	**69**	308	46	75	8	0	0	27	3	—	6	.244	.251	.269	80	-6	10-2	.898	-3	37	69	O44(39/7/1),1b29	—	-0.5
1876	Chi N	**66**	276	55	84	9	2	0	32	12	—	6	.304	.333	.351	115	3	—	.881	-1	54	60	O56L,1b15	—	-0.1
1877	Chi N	50	202	31	46	6	1	0	20	8	—	16	.228	.257	.267	58	-10	—	.948	1	99	83	O36(36/0/1),1b14	—	-1.1
Total	5NA	199	894	149	236	29	4	1	105	15	—	11	.264	.276	.309	86	-11	16-7	.918	-1	65	87	1b105,O99(51/9/43)	—	-0.5
Total	2	116	478	86	130	15	3	0	52	20	—	22	.272	.301	.316	90	-7	—	.904	0	72	69	O92(92/0/1),1b29	—	-1.2
Glenn, Joe	Joseph Charles "Gabby" (b Joseph Charles Gurzensky); B11.19.1908 Dickson City PA; D5.6.1985 Tunkhannock PA; BR/TR/5´11˝/175; d9.15																								
1932	NY A	6	16	0	2	0	0	0	0	1	1	5	.125	.222	.125	-8	-3	0-0	1.000	-1	*72*	*0*	C5	—	-0.3
1933	NY A	5	21	1	3	0	0	0	1	0	0	3	.143	.143	.143	-26	-4	0-0	1.000	-1	*155*	*0*	C5	—	-0.4
1935	NY A	17	43	7	10	4	0	0	6	4	0	1	.233	.298	.326	65	-2	0-0	.984	0	*146*	*99*	C16	—	-0.1
1936	NY A	44	129	21	35	7	0	1	20	20	1	10	.271	.373	.349	82	-3	1-1	.970	2	*159*	*120*	C44	—	0.2
1937	NY A	25	53	6	15	2	2	0	4	10	0	11	.283	.397	.396	100	0	0-0	.978	3	*143*	*116*	C24	—	0.4
1938	NY A	41	123	10	32	7	2	0	25	10	0	14	.260	.316	.350	67	-7	1-0	.974	1	*129*	*69*	C40	—	-0.4
1939	StL A	88	286	29	78	13	1	4	29	31	0	40	.273	.344	.367	80	-8	4-4	.968	-13	*75*	***140***	C82	—	-1.6
1940	Bos A	22	47	3	6	1	0	0	4	5	0	7	.128	.212	.149	-5	-7	0-0	.961	-2	*107*	*83*	C19	—	-0.8
Total	8	248	718	77	181	34	5	5	89	81	2	91	.252	.330	.334	69	-34	6-5	.972	-10	*114*	*110*	C235	—	-3.0
Gload, Ross	Ross Peter; B4.5.1976 Brooklyn NY; BL/TL/6´2˝/(185–210); [FlaN97 13/396]; d8.31; Col South Florida																								
2000	Chi N	18	31	4	6	0	1	1	3	3-0	0	10	.194	.257	.355	55	-2	0-0	1.000	-1	95	0	O8(7/0/1),1b2	0	-0.3
2002	Col N	26	31	4	8	1	0	1	4	3-0	0	7	.258	.324	.387	76	-1	0-0	1.000	1	202	47	1b4,O2L	0	0.0
2004	Chi A	110	234	28	75	16	0	7	44	20-1	2	37	.321	.375	.479	118	7	0-3	1.000	-1	77	74	1b42,O39(17/1/22),D13	0	0.0
2005	Chi A	28	42	2	7	2	0	0	5	2-0	0	9	.167	.205	.214	11	-5	0-0	.987	-1	61	113	1b24,O3(2/0/1)	83	-0.7
2006	Chi A	77	156	22	51	8	2	3	18	6-0	1	15	.327	.354	.462	107	1	6-0	.986	-3	76	101	1b49,O19(4/0/15)/D	0	-0.4
Total	5	259	494	60	147	27	3	12	74	34-1	3	78	.298	.343	.437	99	0	6-3	.992	-5	77	93	1b121,O71(32/1/39),D14	83	-1.4
Glockson, Norm	Norman Stanley; B6.15.1894 Blue Island IL; D8.5.1955 Maywood IL; BR/TR/6´2˝/200; d9.16																								
1914	Cin N	7	12	0	0	0	0	0	0	1	0	6	.000	.077	.000	-74	-3	0	.923	-1	*102*	*92*	C7	—	-0.3
Glossop, Al	Alban; B7.12.1914 Christopher IL; D7.2.1991 Walnut Creek CA; BB/TR/6´0˝/170; d9.23; Mil 1944–45																								
1939	NY N	10	32	3	6	0	0	1	3	4	0	2	.188	.278	.281	50	-2	0	.980	2	128	121	2b10	—	0.0
1940	NY N	27	91	16	19	3	0	4	8	10	1	16	.209	.294	.374	82	-2	1	.952	2	113	53	2b24	—	0.1
	Bos N	60	148	17	35	2	1	3	14	17	0	22	.236	.315	.324	81	-4	1	.938	4	120	112	2b18,3b18/S	—	0.2
	Year	87	239	33	54	5	1	7	22	27	1	38	.226	.307	.343	82	-6	2	.947	6	116	76	2b42,3b18/S	—	0.3
1942	Phi N	121	454	33	102	15	1	4	40	29	1	35	.225	.273	.289	68	-20	3	.961	10	103	104	2b118/3	0	-0.3
1943	Bro N	87	217	28	37	9	0	3	21	28	1	27	.171	.268	.253	51	-13	0	.927	-9	103	92	S33,2b24,3b17/rf	0	-2.0
1946	Chi N	4	10	2	0	0	0	0	0	1	2	3	.000	.231	.000	-32	-2	0	1.000	-2	61	0	2b2,S2	0	-0.3
Total	5	309	952	99	199	29	2	15	86	89	5	105	.209	.280	.291	66	-43	5	.954	8	105	93	2b196,S36,3b36/rf	0	-2.3
Glynn, Bill	William Vincent; B7.30.1925 Sussex NJ; BL/TL/6´0˝/(190–195); d9.16																								
1949	Phi N	8	10	0	2	0	0	0	1	0	0	3	.200	.200	.200	8	-1	0	1.000	0	159	0	/1	0	-0.1
1952	Cle A	44	92	15	25	5	0	2	7	5	0	16	.272	.309	.391	101	0	1-0	.973	-0	106	105	1b32	0	-0.1
1953	Cle A	147	411	60	100	14	2	3	30	44	5	65	.243	.324	.309	74	-15	1-3	**.993**	3	108	**138**	1b135,O2(1/0/1)	0	-1.9
1954	†Cle A	111	171	19	43	3	2	5	18	12	0	21	.251	.297	.380	84	-5	3-2	.987	1	113	111	1b96/rf	0	-0.7
Total	4	310	684	94	170	22	4	10	56	61	5	105	.249	.314	.336	79	-21	5-5	.989	4	109	126	1b264,O3(1/0/2)	0	-2.8
Gochnaur, John	John Peter; B9.12.1875 Altoona PA; D9.27.1929 Altoona PA; BR/TR/5´9˝/160; d9.29																								
1901	Bro N	3	11	1	4	0	0	0	2	1	0	—	.364	.417	.364	124	0	1	1.000	0	105	0	S3	—	0.0
1902	Cle A	127	459	45	85	16	4	0	37	38	0	—	.185	.247	.237	36	-40	7	.933	-5	103	109	S127	—	-3.9
1903	Cle A	134	438	48	81	16	4	0	48	48	0	—	.185	.265	.240	53	-23	10	.869	-23	97	101	S134	—	-4.4
Total	3	264	908	94	170	32	8	0	87	87	0	—	.187	.258	.240	45	-63	18	.901	-28	100	104	S264	—	-8.3
Godar, John	John Michael; B10.25.1864 Cincinnati OH; D6.23.1949 Park Ridge IL; BR/TR/5´9˝/170; d7.8																								
1892	Bal N	5	14	2	3	0	0	0	1	2	1	1	.214	.353	.214	70	0	1	1.000	0	188	0	O5R	—	0.0

YEAR	TM LG	G	AB	R	H	2B	3B	HR	RBI	BB-IB	HP	SO	AVG	OBP	SLG	AOPS	ABR	SB-CS	FA	FR	RNG	THR	GAMES AT POSITION	DL	BFW
Godby, Danny	Danny Ray; B11.4.1946 Logan WV; BR/TR/6´0˝/185; d8.10; Col Bowling Green																								
1974	StL N	13	13	2	2	0	0	0	1	3-1	0	4	.154	.294	.154	33	-1	0-0	1.000	1	152	520	O4(2/0/2)	0	0.0
Goddard, Joe	Joseph Harold; B7.23.1950 Beckley WV; BR/TR/5´11˝/190; [SDN71 8/173]; d7.31; Col Marshall																								
1972	SD N	12	35	0	7	2	0	0	2	5-0	0	9	.200	.300	.257	64	-1	0-0	.973	-5	38	88	C12	0	-0.6
Godwin, Tyrell	Carlton Tyrell; B7.10.1979 Wilmington NC; BL/TR/6´0˝/200; [TorA01 3/91]; d5.27; Col North Carolina																								
2005	Was N	3	3	0	0	0	0	0	0	0-0	0	1	.000	.000	.000	-99	-1	0-0	ø	0	—	—	/H	0	-0.1
Godwin, John	John Henry "Bunny"; B3.10.1877 E.Liverpool OH; D5.5.1956 E.Liverpool OH; BR/TR/6´0˝/190; d8.14																								
1905	Bos A	15	43	4	14	1	0	0	10	3	3	—	.326	.408	.349	139	2	3	.950	-0	0	0	O7(5/2/0),2b5	—	0.2
1906	Bos A	66	193	11	36	2	1	0	15	6	1	—	.187	.215	.207	32	-15	6	.907	1	107	218	3b27,S14,O10(0/1/9),2b3/1	—	-1.5
Total	2	81	236	15	50	3	1	0	25	9	4	—	.212	.253	.233	53	-13	9	.907	0	107	218	3b27,O17(5/3/9),S14,2b8/1	—	-1.3
Goebel, Ed	Wilbur Edwin; B9.1.1898 Brooklyn NY; D8.12.1959 Brooklyn NY; BR/TR/5´11˝/170; d5.13																								
1922	Was A	37	59	13	16	1	0	1	3	8	0	16	.271	.358	.339	87	-1	1-1	1.000	1	120	70	O16(2/1/13)	—	-0.1
Goeckel, Billy	William John; B9.3.1871 Wilkes–Barre PA; D11.1.1922 Philadelphia PA; BR/TL/5´11˝/162; d8.10; Col Penn																								
1899	Phi N	37	141	17	37	3	1	0	16	1	3	—	.262	.283	.298	61	-8	6	.978	-3	61	57	1b36	—	-1.0
Goff, Jerry	Jerry Leroy; B4.12.1964 San Rafael CA; BL/TR/6´3˝/(200–210); [SeaA86 3/63]; d5.15; Col California																								
1990	Mon N	52	119	14	27	1	0	3	7	21-4	0	36	.227	.343	.311	84	-2	0-2	.963	-7	82	62	C38,1b3,3b3	0	-0.8
1992	Mon N	3	3	0	0	0	0	0	0	0-0	0	3	.000	.000	.000	-99	-1	0-0	ø	0	—	—	/H	0	-0.1
1993	Pit N	14	37	5	11	2	0	2	6	8-1	0	9	.297	.422	.514	150	3	0-0	.984	-2	129	98	C14	0	0.2
1994	Pit N	8	25	0	2	0	0	0	1	0-0	0	11	.080	.080	.080	-57	-6	0-0	.950	-1	124	87	C7	0	-0.7
1995	Hou N	12	26	2	4	2	0	1	3	4-0	0	13	.154	.267	.346	64	-1	0-0	1.000	4	49	159	C11	0	0.3
1996	Hou N	1	4	1	2	0	0	1	2	0-0	0	1	.500	.500	1.250	370	1	0-0	1.000	0	68	0	/C	0	0.2
Total	6	90	214	22	46	5	0	7	19	33-5	0	73	.215	.320	.336	80	-6	0-2	.974	-6	92	84	C71,3b3,1b3	0	-0.9
Goggin, Chuck	Charles Francis; B7.7.1945 Pompano Beach FL; BB/TR/5´11˝/175; d9.8; Col Broward (FL) CC																								
1972	Pit N	5	7	0	2	0	0	0	0	1-0	0	1	.286	.375	.286	91	0	0-0	1.000	-0	129	0	/2	0	0.0
1973	Pit N	1	1	1	1	0	0	0	0	0-0	0	0	1.000	1.000	1.000	465	0	0-0	1.000	0	0	0	/C	0	0.0
	Atl N	64	90	18	26	5	0	0	7	9-0	0	19	.289	.350	.344	88	-1	0-1	.938	-7	93	88	2b19,O6(5/0/1),S5/C	0	-0.7
	Year	65	91	19	27	5	0	0	7	9-0	0	19	.297	.356	.352	91	-1	0-1	.938	-7	93	88	2b19,O6(5/0/1),S5,C2	0	-0.7
1974	Bos A	2	1	0	0	0	0	0	0	0-0	0	1	.000	.000	.000	-93	0	0-0	.667	0	158	601	2b2	19	0.0
Total	3	72	99	19	29	5	0	0	7	10-0	0	21	.293	.355	.343	89	-1	0-1	.927	-7	99	101	2b22,O6(5/0/1),S5,C2	19	-0.7
Golden, Mike	Michael Henry; B9.11.1851 Shirley MA; D1.11.1929 Rockford IL; BR/TR/5´8˝/168; d5.4; ▲																								
1875	Wes NA	**13**	46	6	6	0	0	0	1	0	—	3	.130	.130	.130	-9	-4	0-0	.844	-1	76	0	P13	—	0.0
	Chi NA	39	155	16	40	3	0	0	14	2	—	10	.258	.268	.277	89	-2	3-2	.833	0	120	133	O27(25/0/2),P14	—	0.0
	Year	52	201	22	46	3	0	0	15	2	—	13	.229	.236	.244	66	-7	3-2	.833	-1	81	0	P27,O27(25/0/2)	—	0.0
1878	Mil N	55	214	16	44	6	3	0	20	3	—	35	.206	.217	.262	53	-11	—	.831	-3	96	135	O39(0/25/14),P22/1	—	-1.1
Goldman, Jonah	Jonah John; B8.29.1906 New York NY; D8.17.1980 Palm Beach FL; BR/TR/5´7˝/170; d9.22; Col Syracuse																								
1928	Cle A	7	21	1	5	1	0	0	2	3	0	0	.238	.333	.286	63	-1	0-0	.878	-1	111	45	S7	—	-0.1
1930	Cle A	111	306	32	74	18	0	1	44	28	3	25	.242	.312	.310	56	-20	3-5	.945	15	108	102	S93,3b20	—	0.3
1931	Cle A	30	62	0	8	1	0	0	3	4	0	6	.129	.182	.145	-12	-10	1-1	.947	10	140	100	S30	—	0.1
Total	3	148	389	33	87	20	0	1	49	35	3	31	.224	.293	.283	46	-31	4-6	.941	25	114	98	S130,3b20	—	0.3
Goldsberry, Gordon	Gordon Frederick; B8.30.1927 Sacramento CA; D2.23.1996 Laguna Hills CA; BL/TL/6´0˝/170; d4.20																								
1949	Chi A	39	145	25	36	3	2	1	13	18	0	9	.248	.331	.317	74	-6	2-0	.990	-1	93	95	1b38	0	-0.7
1950	Chi A	82	127	19	34	8	2	2	25	26	0	18	.268	.392	.409	108	3	0-2	.989	5	167	128	1b40,O3(1/0/2)	0	0.5
1951	Chi A	10	11	4	1	0	0	0	1	2	0	2	.091	.231	.091	-11	-2	0-0	1.000	1	225	144	1b8	0	-0.1
1952	StL A	86	227	30	52	9	3	3	17	34	0	37	.229	.330	.335	83	-5	0-2	.983	-2	93	96	1b72,O2L	0	-1.0
Total	4	217	510	78	123	20	7	6	56	80	0	66	.241	.344	.343	85	-10	2-4	.987	3	112	104	1b158,O5(3/0/2)	0	-1.3
Goldsby, Walt	Walton Hugh; B12.31.1861 Marion LA; D1,11.1914 Dallas TX; BL/?/197; d5.28																								
1884	StL AA	5	20	2	4	0	0	0	1	0	0	—	.200	.200	.200	30	-2	—	.800	-1	0	0	O5(1/4/0)	—	-0.3
	Was AA	6	24	4	9	0	0	0	3	1	0	—	.375	.400	.375	174	2	—	.909	1	182	0	O6(1/3/2)	—	0.2
	Ric AA	11	40	4	9	1	0	0	4	1	1	—	.225	.262	.250	69	-1	—	.737	0	117	687	O11(2/6/3)	—	-0.1
	Year	22	84	10	22	1	0	0	8	2	1	—	.262	.287	.274	87	-1	—	.800	-0	104	306	O22(4/13/5)	—	-0.2
1886	Was N	6	18	0	4	1	0	0	1	2	—	3	.222	.300	.278	83	0	0	.818	-1	0	0	O6(0/5/1)	—	-0.1
1888	Bal AA	45	165	13	39	1	1	0	14	8	4	—	.236	.288	.255	76	-4	17	.903	-3	47	0	O45L	—	-0.8
Total	3	73	267	23	65	3	1	0	23	12	5	3	.243	.289	.262	80	-5	17	.858	-4	62	96	O73(49/18/6)	—	-1.1
Goldsmith, Wally	Warren M.; B10.1848 Baltimore MD; D9.16.1915 Washington DC; 5´7˝/146; d5.4																								
1871	Kek NA	**19**	88	8	18	1	0	0	12	4	—	2	.205	.239	.216	31	-8	0-0	.767	-10	70	36	S14,3b8,C2	—	-1.2
1872	Oly NA	**9**	41	4	10	2	0	0	5	0	—	0	.244	.244	.293	68	-1	0-0	.679	-2	80	72	S5,2b4	—	-0.2
1873	Mar NA	1	4	0	0	0	0	0	0	0	—	0	.000	.000	.000	-99	-1	0-0	.667	-1	118	0	/2	—	-0.1
1875	Wes NA	**13**	51	3	6	0	0	0	1	0	—	2	.118	.118	.118	-17	-6	0-0	.814	-1	90	172	3b13	—	-0.6
Total	4NA	42	184	15	34	3	0	0	18	4	—	4	.185	.202	.201	24	-16	0-0	.694	-13	73	117	3b21,S19,2b5,C2	—	-2.1
Goldstein, Lonnie	Leslie Elmer; B5.13.1918 Austin TX; BL/TL/6´2.5˝/190; d9.11; Mil 1945–46																								
1943	Cin N	5	5	1	1	0	0	0	0	2	0	1	.200	.429	.200	85	0	0	1.000	-0	0	0	1b2	0	0.0
1946	Cin N	6	5	1	0	0	0	0	0	1-0	0	1	.000	.167	.000	-53	-1	0	ø	0	—	—	/H	0	-0.1
Total	2	11	10	2	1	0	0	0	0	3	0	2	.100	.308	.100	20	-1	0	1.000	-0	0	0	1b2	0	-0.1
Goldy, Purnal	Purnal William; B11.28.1937 Camden NJ; BR/TR/6´5˝/205; d4.12; Col Temple																								
1962	Det A	20	70	8	16	1	1	3	12	0-0	1	12	.229	.236	.400	66	-4	0-0	.964	-1	86	107	O15R	0	-0.6
1963	Det A	9	8	1	2	0	0	0	0	0-0	0	4	.250	.250	.250	39	-1	0-0	ø	0	—	—	/H	0	-0.1
Total	2	29	78	9	18	1	1	3	12	0-0	1	16	.231	.237	.385	64	-5	0-0	.964	-1	86	107	O15R	0	-0.7
Goletz, Stan	Stanley "Stash"; B5.21.1918 Crescent OH; D6.7.1997 Temple TX; BL/TL/6´3˝/200; d9.9; Mil 1942–45; Col Ohio St.																								
1941	Chi A	5	5	0	3	0	0	0	0	0	0	2	.600	.600	.600	221	1	0-0	ø	0	—	—	/H	0	0.1
Goliat, Mike	Mike Mitchel; B11.5.1921 Yatesboro PA; D1.13.2004 Seven Hills OH; BR/TR/6´0˝/180; d8.3																								
1949	Phi N	55	189	24	40	6	3	3	19	20	1	32	.212	.290	.323	66	-10	0	.969	-5	99	91	2b50,1b5	0	-1.2
1950	†Phi N	145	483	49	113	13	6	13	64	53	3	75	.234	.314	.366	80	-16	3	.972	-15	98	89	2b145	0	-2.2
1951	Phi N	41	138	14	31	2	1	4	15	9	1	18	.225	.277	.341	66	-7	0-1	.968	-8	89	87	2b37,3b2	0	-1.4
	StL A	5	11	0	2	0	0	0	0	1	0	1	.182	.182	.182	-1	-2	0-0	1.000	0	101	97	2b2	0	-0.1
1952	StL A	3	4	0	0	0	0	0	0	1	0	1	.000	.200	.000	-40	-1	0-0	1.000	1	103	287	2b3	0	0.0
Total	4	249	825	87	186	21	10	20	99	83	5	127	.225	.300	.348	73	-36	3-1	.971	-27	97	90	2b237,1b5,3b2	0	-4.9
Golvin, Walt	Walter George; B2.1.1894 Hershey NE; D6.11.1973 Gardena CA; BL/TL/6´0˝/165; d4.15																								
1922	Chi N	2	2	0	0	0	0	0	1	0	0	0	.000	.000	.000	-98	-1	0-0	1.000	-0	0	0	1b2	—	-0.1
Gomes, Jonny	Jonny Johnson; B11.22.1980 Petaluma CA; BR/TR/6´1˝/(200–205); [TBA01 18/529]; d9.12; Col Santa Rosa (CA) JC																								
2003	TB A	8	15	1	2	1	0	0	0	0-0	1	6	.133	.188	.200	2	-2	0-0	ø	0	—	—	D8	0	-0.2
2004	TB A	5	14	0	1	0	0	0	1	0-0	0	6	.071	.133	.071	-46	-3	0-0	ø	0	—	—	D4	0	-0.3
2005	TB A	101	348	61	98	13	6	21	54	39-1	14	113	.282	.372	.534	141	21	9-5	.963	5	107	267	O50(14/0/36),D49	0	2.0
2006	TB A	117	385	53	83	21	1	20	59	61-2	6	116	.216	.325	.431	96	-2	1-5	1.000	1	137	0	D101,O8R	41	-0.8
Total	4	231	762	115	184	35	7	41	114	101-3	21	241	.241	.341	.467	112	14	10-10	.969	5	111	232	D162,O58(14/0/44)	41	0.7
Gomez, Alexis	Alexis De Jesus; B8.6.1978 Loma de Cabrera, D.R.; BL/TL/6´2˝/180; d6.16																								
2002	KC A	5	10	0	2	0	0	0	0	0-0	0	2	.200	.200	.200	6	-1	0-0	1.000	1	115	909	O2R	0	0.0
2004	KC A	13	29	1	8	1	0	0	4	2-0	0	8	.276	.323	.310	66	-1	0-0	.955	0	124	0	O12(6/2/5)	0	-0.2
2005	Det A	9	16	2	3	0	0	0	1	2-0	0	2	.188	.278	.188	28	-2	0-0	1.000	-0	94	0	O9(6/3/0)	0	-0.2

YEAR	TM LG	G	AB	R	H	2B	3B	HR	RBI	BB-IB	HP	SO	AVG	OBP	SLG	AOPS	ABR	SB-CS	FA	FR	RNG	THR	GAMES AT POSITION	DL	BFW
2006	†Det A	62	103	17	28	5	2	1	6	6-0	1	21	.272	.318	.388	83	-3	4-0	1.000	-1	88	119	O52(32/0/21),D7	0	-0.4
Total	4	89	158	20	41	6	2	1	11	10-0	1	33	.259	.308	.342	69	-7	4-0	.988	0	98	115	O75(44/5/28),D7	0	-0.8
GOMEZ, CHRIS	Christopher Cory; B6.16.1971 Los Angeles CA; BR/TR/6´1˝/(183–195); [DetA92 3/84]; d7.19; Col Cal St.–Long Beach																								
1993	Det A	46	128	11	32	7	1	0	11	9-0	1	17	.250	.304	.320	68	-6	2-2	.963	-1	104	105	S29,2b17/D	0	-0.5
1994	Det A	84	296	32	76	19	0	8	53	33-0	3	64	.257	.336	.402	88	-5	5-3	.981	-24	84	58	S57,2b30	0	-2.1
1995	Det A	123	431	49	96	20	2	11	50	41-0	3	96	.223	.292	.355	68	-21	4-1	.973	-2	104	92	S97,2b31,D2	0	-1.3
1996	Det A	48	128	21	31	5	0	1	16	18-0	1	20	.242	.340	.305	65	-6	1-1	.970	4	101	111	S47	0	0.0
	†SD N	89	328	32	86	16	1	3	29	39-1	6	64	.262	.349	.345	88	-4	2-2	.967	-7	96	101	S89	0	-0.4
1997	SD N	150	522	62	132	19	2	5	54	53-1	5	114	.253	.326	.326	76	-18	5-8	.978	-4	101	84	S150	0	-1.2
1998	†SD N	145	449	55	120	32	3	4	39	51-7	5	87	.267	.346	.379	98	0	1-3	**.980**	9	101	120	S143	0	1.8
1999	SD N	76	234	20	59	8	1	1	15	27-3	1	49	.252	.331	.308	68	-11	1-2	.961	1	98	115	S75	59	-0.5
2000	SD N	33	54	4	12	0	0	0	3	7-0	0	5	.222	.306	.222	41	-5	0-0	.928	2	109	122	S17,2b3	101	-0.2
2001	SD N	40	112	6	21	3	0	0	7	9-0	0	14	.188	.244	.214	23	-13	1-0	.937	-11	74	82	S36,2b8	0	-2.2
	TB A	58	189	31	57	16	0	8	36	8-0	2	24	.302	.332	.513	122	6	3-0	.968	-11	85	80	S58	0	0.0
2002	TB A	130	461	51	122	31	3	10	46	21-0	7	58	.265	.305	.410	90	-7	1-3	.980	-1	98	104	S130	0	0.0
2003	†Min A	58	175	14	44	9	3	1	15	7-1	0	13	.251	.279	.354	64	-10	2-1	.989	-7	96	89	2b23,3b18,S17	28	-1.5
2004	Tor A	109	341	41	96	11	1	3	37	28-0	2	41	.282	.337	.346	75	-12	3-2	.969	-3	100	94	S77,1b19,3b5,2b3,D5	0	-1.0
2005	Bal A	89	219	27	61	11	0	1	18	27-1	1	17	.279	.359	.342	89	-2	2-1	.993	-1	87	118	1b42,2b18,3b17,S10,D6	0	-0.5
2006	Bal A	55	132	14	45	7	0	2	17	7-1	3	11	.341	.387	.439	117	4	1-2	1.000	-1	77	93	1b27,2b15,S6,3b5,D2	61	0.2
Total	14	1333	4199	470	1090	214	17	58	446	385-15	40	694	.260	.326	.360	81	-110	34-31	.972	-59	97	97	S1038,2b148,1b88,3b45,D16	249	-9.4
GOMEZ, CHILE	Jose Luis (Gonzales); B5.23.1909 Mazatlan, Sinaloa, Mexico; D12.1.1992 Nuevo Laredo, Tamaulipas, Mexico; BR/TR/5´10˝/165; d7.27																								
1935	Phi N	67	222	24	51	3	0	0	16	17	0	34	.230	.285	.243	39	-19	2	.948	9	104	44	S36,2b32	—	-0.5
1936	Phi N	108	332	24	77	4	1	0	28	14	1	32	.232	.265	.250	36	-30	0	.948	11	116	84	2b71,S40	—	-1.3
1942	Was A	25	73	8	14	2	2	0	6	9	0	7	.192	.280	.274	57	-4	1-0	.973	-2	97	88	2b23/3	0	-0.5
Total	3	200	627	56	142	9	3	0	50	40	1	73	.226	.274	.250	39	-53	3-0	.954	18	114	103	2b126,S76/3	0	-2.3
GOMEZ, LEO	Leonardo (Velez); B3.2.1966 Canovanas, PR; BR/TR/6´0˝/(180–208); d9.17																								
1990	Bal A	12	39	3	9	0	0	0	1	8-0	0	7	.231	.362	.231	71	-1	0-0	.886	-2	88	92	3b12	0	-0.3
1991	Bal A	118	391	40	91	17	2	16	45	40-0	2	82	.233	.302	.409	100	-1	1-1	.972	-13	89	99	3b105,D10,1b3	0	-1.4
1992	Bal A	137	468	62	124	24	0	17	64	63-4	8	78	.265	.356	.425	116	12	2-3	.951	-10	93	82	3b137	0	0.2
1993	Bal A	71	244	30	48	7	0	10	25	32-1	3	60	.197	.295	.348	70	-11	0-1	.951	6	110	137	3b70/D	55	-0.5
1994	Bal A	84	285	46	78	20	0	15	56	41-0	3	55	.274	.366	.502	116	7	0-0	.975	-1	94	108	3b78/1D	0	0.6
1995	Bal A	53	127	16	30	5	0	4	12	18-1	2	23	.236	.336	.370	83	-3	0-1	.978	2	105	54	3b44,1b3,D5	63	-0.1
1996	Chi N	136	362	44	86	19	0	17	56	53-0	7	94	.238	.344	.431	100	1	1-4	**.972**	-1	97	110	3b124,1b8/S	0	-0.1
Total	7	611	1916	241	466	92	2	79	259	255-6	25	399	.243	.336	.417	101	4	4-10	.962	-18	96	100	3b570,D21,1b15/S	118	-1.6
GOMEZ, LUIS	Luis (Sanchez); B8.19.1951 Guadalajara, Jalisco, Mexico; BR/TR/5´9˝/(150–151); [MinA73 7/155]; d4.28; Col UCLA																								
1974	Min A	82	168	18	35	1	0	0	3	12-0	0	16	.208	.261	.214	37	-14	2-3	.960	6	103	103	S74,2b2/D	0	-0.1
1975	Min A	89	72	7	10	0	0	0	5	4-0	0	12	.139	.182	.139	-8	-10	0-2	.975	-4	77	99	S70,2b6,D7	0	-1.2
1976	Min A	38	57	5	11	1	0	0	3	3-0	0	3	.193	.233	.211	30	-5	1-0	.988	1	96	146	S24,2b8,3b4/cfD	0	-0.2
1977	Min A	32	65	6	16	4	2	0	11	4-0	0	9	.246	.290	.369	79	-2	0-2	.983	2	102	70	2b19,S7,3b4/cfD	0	0.0
1978	Tor A	153	413	39	92	7	3	0	32	34-1	0	41	.223	.280	.254	51	-27	2-10	.976	-7	92	105	S153	0	-2.3
1979	Tor A	59	163	11	39	7	0	0	11	6-0	0	17	.239	.266	.282	47	-12	1-0	1.000	-1	82	202	3b22,2b20,S15	0	-1.1
1980	Atl N	121	278	18	53	6	0	0	24	17-2	1	27	.191	.239	.212	27	-27	0-4	.968	0	105	101	S119	0	-2.0
1981	Atl N	35	35	4	7	0	0	0	1	6-0	0	4	.200	.317	.200	49	-2	0-1	.895	-7	77	42	S21,3b9,2b3/P	0	-0.9
Total	8	609	1251	108	263	26	5	0	90	86-3	1	129	.210	.261	.239	41	-99	6-22	.970	-10	97	105	S483,2b58,3b39,D11,O2C/P	0	-7.8
GOMEZ, PRESTON	Pedro (Martinez); B4.20.1923 Preston, Cuba; BR/TR/5´11˝/170; d5.5; M7/C13																								
1944	Was A	8	7	2	2	1	0	0	2	0	0	4	.286	.286	.429	107	0	0-0	1.000	-1	0	0	2b2,S2	0	-0.1
GOMEZ, RANDY	Randell Scott; B2.4.1957 San Mateo CA; BR/TR/5´10˝/185; [SFN80 25/624]; d8.21; Col Utah																								
1984	SF N	14	30	0	5	1	0	0	0	8-0	0	3	.167	.342	.200	57	-1	0-0	.951	-2	42	49	C14	0	-0.2
GONDER, JESSE	Jesse Lemar; B1.20.1936 Monticello AR; D11.14.2004 Oakland CA; BL/TR/5´10˝/190; d9.23																								
1960	NY A	7	7	1	2	0	0	1	3	1-0	0	1	.286	.333	.714	199	1	0-0	1.000	0	36	0	/C	0	0.1
1961	NY A	15	12	2	4	1	0	0	3	3-1	0	1	.333	.467	.417	146	1	0-0	ø	0	—	—	/H	0	0.1
1962	Cin N	4	4	0	0	0	0	0	0	0-0	0	3	.000	.000	.000	-97	-1	0-0	ø	0	—	—	/H	0	-0.1
1963	Cin N	31	32	5	10	2	0	3	5	1-0	0	12	.313	.333	.656	172	3	0-0	1.000	0	38	0	C7	0	0.3
	NY N	42	126	12	38	4	0	3	15	6-0	0	25	.302	.328	.405	110	1	1-2	.978	-9	121	60	C31	0	-0.7
	Year	73	158	17	48	6	0	6	20	7-0	0	37	.304	.329	.456	122	4	1-2	.981	-9	113	55	C38	0	-0.4
1964	NY N	131	341	28	92	11	1	7	35	29-5	2	65	.270	.329	.370	99	0	0-0	.979	0	75	**157**	C97	0	0.4
1965	NY N	53	105	6	25	4	0	4	9	11-4	0	20	.238	.308	.390	100	0	0-0	.992	1	41	217	C31	0	0.2
	Mil N	31	53	2	8	2	0	1	5	4-0	0	9	.151	.211	.245	28	-5	0-0	.989	6	138	254	C13	0	0.1
	Year	84	158	8	33	6	0	5	14	15-4	0	29	.209	.276	.342	75	-5	0-0	.991	7	72	229	C44	0	0.3
1966	Pit N	59	160	13	36	3	1	7	16	12-7	2	39	.225	.287	.387	85	-4	0-0	.978	-2	96	105	C52	0	-0.4
1967	Pit N	22	36	4	5	1	0	0	3	5-3	2	9	.139	.279	.167	30	-3	0-0	.971	-1	41	32	C18	0	-0.4
Total	8	395	876	73	220	28	2	26	94	72-20	6	184	.251	.310	.377	94	-7	1-2	.981	-5	83	132	C250	0	-0.4
GONZALES, DAN	Daniel David; B9.30.1953 Whittier CA; BL/TR/6´1˝/(180–195); [DetA72*2/43]; d4.7; Col Fullerton (CA) JC																								
1979	Det A	7	18	1	4	1	0	0	2	0-0	0	2	.222	.222	.278	33	-2	1-0	1.000	-1	50	0	O3R/D	0	-0.2
1980	Det A	2	7	1	1	0	0	0	0	0-0	0	1	.143	.143	.143	-21	-1	0-0	.750	-0	148	0	/lfD	0	-0.1
Total	2	9	25	2	5	1	0	0	2	0-0	0	3	.200	.200	.240	18	-3	1-0	.857	-1	73	0	O4(1/0/3),D2	0	-0.3
GONZALES, LARRY	Lawrence Christopher; B3.28.1967 West Covina CA; BR/TR/6´3˝/200; [CalA88 22/559]; d6.13; Col Hawaii–Manoa																								
1993	Cal A	2	2	0	1	0	0	0	1	1-0	0	0	.500	.667	.500	212	0	0-0	1.000	0	0	0	C2	0	0.1
GONZALES, RENE	Rene Adrian; B9.3.1960 Austin TX; BR/TR/6´3˝/(180–220); [MonN82 5/123]; d7.27; Col Cal St.–Los Angeles; OF(1/0/2)																								
1984	Mon N	29	30	5	7	1	0	0	2	2-0	1	5	.233	.303	.267	64	-1	0-0	.957	-4	77	76	S27	0	-0.5
1986	Mon N	11	26	1	3	0	0	0	0	2-0	0	7	.115	.179	.115	-17	-4	0-2	1.000	-0	97	91	S6,3b5	0	-0.5
1987	Bal A	37	60	14	16	2	1	1	7	3-0	0	11	.267	.302	.383	82	-2	1-0	.963	3	105	62	3b29,2b6/S	0	0.1
1988	Bal A	92	237	13	51	6	0	2	15	13-0	3	32	.215	.263	.266	50	-16	2-0	.966	13	129	164	3b80,2b14,S2/1rf	0	-0.2
1989	Bal A	71	166	16	36	4	0	1	11	12-0	0	30	.217	.268	.259	51	-11	5-3	.978	-4	98	126	2b54,3b17/S	0	-1.5
1990	Bal A	67	103	13	22	3	1	1	12	12-0	0	14	.214	.296	.291	66	-5	1-2	.994	1	105	98	2b43,3b16,S9/rf	0	-0.3
1991	†Tor A	71	118	16	23	3	0	1	6	12-0	4	22	.195	.289	.246	48	-8	0-0	.973	0	84	88	S36,3b26,2b11,1b2	0	-0.6
1992	Cal A	104	329	47	91	17	1	7	38	41-1	4	46	.277	.363	.398	112	7	7-4	.954	2	103	102	3b53,2b42,1b13,S8	54	0.9
1993	Cal A	118	335	34	84	17	0	2	31	49-2	1	45	.251	.346	.319	78	-8	5-5	.956	0	102	151	3b79,1b31,S5,2b4/P	0	-1.0
1994	Cle A	22	23	6	8	1	1	1	5	5-0	0	3	.348	.448	.609	172	3	2-0	.952	2	157	0	3b13,1b4,S4/2	0	0.5
1995	Cal A	30	18	1	6	1	0	1	3	0-0	0	4	.333	.333	.556	127	1	0-0	1.000	-1	65	0	3b18,2b6/SD	0	0.0
1996	†Tex A	51	92	19	20	4	0	2	5	10-0	0	11	.217	.288	.326	53	-7	0-0	.989	4	74	106	1b23,3b15,S10,2b5/lf	0	-0.3
1997	Col N	2	2	0	1	0	0	0	1	0-0	0	0	.500	.500	.500	133	0	0-0	ø	-0	0	0	/3	0	0.0
Total	13	705	1539	185	368	59	4	19	136	161-3	13	230	.239	.315	.320	74	-51	23-16	.957	16	113	129	3b352,2b186,S110,1b74,O3R/DP	54	-3.4
GONZALEZ, ADRIAN	Adrian; B5.8.1982 San Diego CA; BL/TL/6´2˝/220; [FlaN00 1/1]; d4.18																								
2004	Tex A	16	42	7	10	3	0	1	7	2-0	0	6	.238	.273	.381	65	-2	0-0	.990	-0	92	148	1b11/D	0	-0.3
2005	Tex A	43	150	17	34	7	1	6	17	10-2	0	37	.227	.272	.407	76	-6	0-0	.978	0	115	93	D32,1b10/rf	0	-0.8
2006	†SD N	156	570	83	173	38	1	24	82	52-9	3	113	.304	.362	.500	125	21	0-1	.995	6	114	103	1b155	0	1.2
Total	3	215	762	107	217	48	2	31	106	64-11	3	156	.285	.340	.475	112	13	0-1	.994	5	113	105	1b176,D33/rf	0	0.1
GONZALEZ, ALEX	Alexander; B2.15.1977 Cagua, Aragua, Venez.; BR/TR/6´0˝/(170–200); d8.25																								
1998	Fla N	25	86	11	13	2	0	3	7	9-0	1	30	.151	.240	.279	38	-8	0-0	.978	-7	83	101	S25	0	-1.3
1999	Fla N★	136	560	81	155	28	8	14	59	15-0	12	113	.277	.308	.430	90	-12	3-5	.955	-8	95	99	S135	0	-1.1
2000	Fla N	109	385	35	77	17	4	7	42	13-0	2	77	.200	.229	.319	39	-39	7-1	.957	1	104	100	S104	34	-2.8
2001	Fla N	145	515	57	129	36	1	9	48	30-6	10	107	.250	.303	.377	77	-18	2-2	.960	5	101	114	S142	0	-0.2
2002	Fla N	42	151	15	34	7	1	2	18	12-1	4	32	.225	.296	.325	67	-8	3-1	.984	3	99	120	S42	134	-0.1

YEAR	TM LG	G	AB	R	H	2B	3B	HR	RBI	BB-IB	HP	SO	AVG	OBP	SLG	AOPS	ABR	SB-CS	FA	FR	RNG	THR	GAMES AT POSITION	DL	BFW
2003	†Fla N	150	528	52	135	33	6	18	77	33-13	13	106	.256	.313	.443	99	-3	0-4	.976	4	96	**117**	S150	0	1.1
2004	Fla N	159	561	67	130	30	3	23	79	27-9	4	126	.232	.270	.419	79	-21	3-1	.976	-1	95	109	S158	0	-1.0
2005	Fla N	130	435	45	115	30	0	5	45	31-10	5	81	.264	.319	.368	84	-10	5-3	.974	16	101	122	S124	0	1.5
2006	Bos A	111	388	48	99	24	2	9	50	22-1	5	67	.255	.299	.397	78	-13	1-0	**.985**	-1	98	93	S111	15	-0.6
Total	9	1007	3609	411	887	207	25	90	425	192-40	56	739	.246	.292	.392	78	-132	24-17	.970	12	98	109	S991	183	-4.5
GONZALEZ, ALEX	Alexander Scott; B4.8.1973 Miami FL; BR/TR/6´0˝/(170–200); [TorA91 14/380]; d4.4																								
1994	Tor A	15	53	7	8	3	1	0	1	4-0	1	17	.151	.224	.245	21	-6	3-0	.918	1	113	62	S15	28	-0.3
1995	Tor A	111	367	51	89	19	4	10	42	44-1	1	114	.243	.322	.398	87	-8	4-4	.957	-29	77	68	S97,3b9,D3	0	-2.9
1996	Tor A	147	527	64	124	30	5	14	64	45-0	5	127	.235	.300	.391	74	-23	16-6	.973	**28**	**109**	126	S147	0	1.7
1997	Tor A	126	426	46	102	23	2	12	35	34-1	5	94	.239	.302	.387	78	-14	15-6	**.986**	7	97	102	S125	31	0.3
1998	Tor A	158	568	70	136	28	1	13	51	28-1	6	121	.239	.281	.361	66	-30	21-6	.976	-7	93	99	S158	0	-2.2
1999	Tor A	38	154	22	45	13	0	2	12	16-0	3	23	.292	.370	.416	98	0	4-2	.980	12	120	130	S37/D	140	1.4
2000	Tor A	141	527	68	133	31	2	15	69	43-0	4	113	.252	.313	.404	77	-19	4-4	.975	-8	97	102	S141	14	-1.5
2001	Tor A	154	636	79	161	25	5	17	76	43-0	7	149	.253	.303	.388	80	-20	18-11	.987	**33**	**118**	**122**	S154	0	2.4
2002	Chi N	142	513	58	127	27	5	18	61	46-7	3	136	.248	.312	.425	92	-8	5-3	.965	1	90	93	S142	15	0.4
2003	†Chi N	152	536	71	122	37	0	20	59	47-1	6	123	.228	.295	.409	80	-17	3-3	**.984**	26	104	109	S150	0	1.9
2004	Chi N	37	129	15	28	10	0	3	8	4-0	0	26	.217	.241	.364	52	-9	1-1	.967	0	85	91	S37	74	-0.7
	Mon N	35	133	19	32	7	0	4	16	8-0	1	32	.241	.289	.383	69	-6	1-1	.960	-2	93	113	S33	0	-0.6
	SD N	11	23	2	4	1	1	0	3	2-0	0	6	.174	.240	.304	41	-2	0-0	1.000	-2	81	89	S11	0	-0.3
	Year	83	285	36	64	18	1	7	27	14-0	1	64	.225	.263	.368	59	-18	2-2	.967	-4	88	101	S81	0	-1.6
2005	TB A	109	349	47	94	20	1	9	38	26-1	3	74	.269	.323	.410	96	-2	2-1	.945	-10	95	56	3b98,S12	20	-1.1
2006	Phi N	20	36	4	4	0	0	0	1	2-0	0	10	.111	.158	.111	-28	-7	0-0	1.000	-2	252	92	1b3,S3,3b2/lf	0	-0.9
Total	13	1396	4977	623	1209	274	27	137	536	392-12	45	1165	.243	.302	.391	78	-171	97-48	.975	49	99	104	S1262,3b109,D4,1b3/lf	322	-2.4
GONZALEZ, TONY	Andres Antonio (Gonzalez); B8.28.1936 Central Cunagua, Cuba; BL/TR/5´9˝/(168–175); d4.12																								
1960	Cin N	39	99	10	21	5	1	3	14	4-0	1	27	.212	.248	.374	67	-5	1-0	.957	-1	94	87	O31(1/0/30)	0	-0.7
	Phi N	78	241	27	72	17	5	6	33	11-0	3	47	.299	.337	.485	122	7	2-2	.981	2	105	137	O67(3/61/5)	0	0.6
	Year	117	340	37	93	22	6	9	47	15-0	4	74	.274	.311	.453	106	2	3-2	.975	1	102	122	O98(4/61/35)	0	-0.1
1961	Phi N	126	426	58	118	16	8	12	58	49-7	6	66	.277	.358	.437	112	7	15-5	.984	-5	95	77	O118(1/86/34)	0	-0.1
1962	Phi N	118	437	76	132	16	4	20	63	40-5	9	82	.302	.371	.494	134	21	17-8	**1.000**	2	103	109	O114(0/114/1)	0	2.1
1963	Phi N	155	555	78	170	36	12	4	66	53-5	8	68	.306	.372	.436	134	26	13-8	.986	-5	88	118	O151(56/107/9)	0	1.6
1964	Phi N	131	421	55	117	25	3	4	40	44-7	6	74	.278	.352	.380	108	7	0-5	**.996**	0	105	74	O119(6/114/0)	0	0.2
1965	Phi N	108	370	48	109	19	1	13	41	31-3	3	52	.295	.351	.457	129	14	3-4	.983	-5	91	57	O104(53/60/2)	0	0.5
1966	Phi N	132	384	53	110	20	4	6	40	26-1	3	60	.286	.335	.406	105	3	2-6	.986	4	108	104	O121(73/47/4)	0	0.1
1967	Phi N	149	508	74	172	23	9	9	59	47-14	5	58	.339	.396	.472	147	32	10-9	**.993**	8	**112**	125	O143(105/29/16)	0	3.4
1968	Phi N	121	416	45	110	13	4	3	38	40-3	7	42	.264	.335	.337	104	3	6-5	.979	-4	97	58	O117(19/98/4)	0	-0.6
1969	SD N	53	182	17	41	4	0	2	8	19-2	3	24	.225	.309	.280	68	-7	1-0	.975	4	127	71	O49(40/11/3)	0	-0.6
	†Atl N	89	320	51	94	15	2	10	50	27-1	5	22	.294	.354	.447	123	10	3-1	.989	-1	105	21	O82(35/49/0)	0	0.7
	Year	142	502	68	135	19	2	12	58	46-3	8	46	.269	.338	.386	104	3	4-1	.983	4	113	40	O131(75/60/3)	0	0.1
1970	Atl N	123	430	57	114	18	2	7	55	46-10	8	45	.265	.345	.365	86	-7	3-5	.987	-8	94	16	O119(3/116/0)	0	-2.0
	Cal A	26	92	9	28	2	0	1	12	2-0	1	11	.304	.326	.359	91	-1	3-2	.960	-2	86	137	O24(0/23/1)	0	-0.4
1971	Cal A	111	314	32	77	9	2	3	38	28-5	3	28	.245	.310	.315	84	-7	0-1	.987	-3	94	81	O88(67/18/9)	0	-1.6
Total	12	1559	5195	690	1485	238	57	103	615	467-63	71	706	.286	.350	.413	114	103	79-61	.987	-12	100	83	O1447(462/933/118)	0	3.2
GONZALEZ, DENNY	Denio Mariano (Manzueta); B7.22.1963 Sabana Grande de Boya, D.R.; BR/TR/5´11˝/(175–185); d8.6																								
1984	Pit N	26	82	9	15	3	1	0	4	7-1	0	21	.183	.247	.244	38	-7	1-1	1.000	-1	113	183	3b11,S10,O3L	0	-0.8
1985	Pit N	35	124	11	28	4	0	4	12	13-2	0	27	.226	.299	.355	83	-3	2-4	.894	-5	72	85	3b21,O13L,2b6	0	-1.0
1987	Pit N	5	7	1	0	0	0	0	0	1-0	0	2	.000	.125	.000	-63	-2	0-0	1.000	-1	33	0	/S	0	-0.2
1988	Pit N	24	32	5	6	1	0	0	1	6-0	0	10	.188	.316	.219	57	-2	0-0	1.000	0	68	105	S14,2b4,3b2	0	-0.1
1989	Cle A	8	17	3	5	1	0	0	1	0-0	1	4	.294	.333	.353	92	0	0-0	.000	-0	0	0	/3D	0	0.0
Total	5	98	262	29	54	9	1	4	18	27-3	1	64	.206	.283	.294	62	-14	3-5	.925	-7	87	118	3b35,S25,O16L,2b10,D6	0	-2.1
GONZALEZ, EUSEBIO	Eusebio Miguel (Lopez) "Papo"; B7.13.1892 Havana, Cuba; D2.14.1976 Havana, Cuba; BR/TR/5´10˝/165; d7.26																								
1918	Bos A	3	5	2	2	0	1	0	0	1	1	1	.400	.571	.800	319	1	0	1.000	-0	95	0	S2/3	—	0.1
GONZALEZ, FERNANDO	Jose Fernando (Quinones); B6.19.1950 Arecibo, PR; BR/TR/5´10˝/(165–178); d9.15																								
1972	Pit N	3	2	0	0	0	0	0	0	0-0	0	2	.000	.000	.000	-99	-1	0-0	.500	0	468	0	/3	0	0.0
1973	Pit N	37	49	5	11	0	1	1	5	1-0	1	11	.224	.255	.327	61	-3	0-0	.923	-1	77	0	3b5	0	-0.4
1974	KC A	9	21	1	3	1	0	0	2	0-0	0	4	.143	.143	.190	-5	-3	1-0	1.000	0	71	97	3b8/D	0	-0.3
	NY A	51	121	11	26	5	1	1	7	7-0	0	7	.215	.258	.298	60	-7	0-0	.982	-0	90	92	2b42,3b7,S3	0	-0.5
	Year	60	142	12	29	6	1	1	9	7-0	0	11	.204	.242	.282	50	-9	1-0	.982	-0	90	92	2b42,3b15,S3/D	0	-0.8
1977	Pit N	80	181	17	50	10	0	4	27	13-6	0	21	.276	.320	.398	89	-3	3-3	.972	-5	92	79	3b37,O16(15/0/1),2b6,S2	0	-0.9
1978	Pit N	9	21	2	4	1	0	0	0	1-0	0	3	.190	.227	.238	29	-2	0-0	.923	-4	65	0	2b4,3b3	0	-0.7
	SD N	101	320	27	80	10	2	2	29	18-3	0	32	.250	.286	.313	74	-13	4-4	.982	7	108	132	2b94	0	-0.2
	Year	110	341	29	84	11	2	2	29	19-3	0	35	.246	.282	.308	70	-15	4-4	.981	2	106	127	2b98,3b3	0	-0.9
1979	SD N	114	323	22	70	13	3	9	34	18-11	0	34	.217	.258	.359	71	-15	0-0	.976	-9	93	94	2b103,3b3	0	-2.0
Total	6	404	1038	85	244	40	7	17	104	58-20	1	114	.235	.274	.336	71	-47	8-7	.979	-13	98	107	2b249,3b64,O16(15/0/1),S5/D	0	-5.0
GONZALEZ, JOSE	Jose Rafael (Gutierrez); B11.23.1964 Puerto Plata, D.R.; BR/TR/6´2˝/(190–200); d9.2																								
1985	LA N	23	11	6	3	2	0	0	0	1-0	0	3	.273	.333	.455	121	0	1-1	1.000	-0	99	0	O18(5/6/8)	0	0.0
1986	LA N	57	93	15	20	5	1	2	6	7-0	0	29	.215	.270	.355	76	-4	4-3	.924	-3	102	0	O57(0/49/8)	0	-0.7
1987	LA N	19	16	2	3	2	0	0	1	1-0	0	2	.188	.222	.313	45	-1	5-0	1.000	2	153	278	O16(8/5/3)	0	0.2
1988	†LA N	37	24	7	2	1	0	0	0	2-0	0	10	.083	.154	.125	-20	-4	3-0	.938	-0	104	0	O24(9/9/9)	0	-0.4
1989	LA N	95	261	31	70	11	2	3	18	23-5	0	53	.268	.326	.360	98	-1	9-3	.968	5	105	216	O87(4/55/34)	0	0.4
1990	LA N	106	99	15	23	5	3	2	8	6-1	1	27	.232	.280	.404	89	-2	3-1	1.000	-0	99	53	O81(43/18/25)	0	-0.3
1991	LA N	42	28	3	0	0	0	0	0	2-0	0	9	.000	.067	.000	-81	-7	0-0	1.000	1	127	0	O27(12/1/15)	0	-0.7
	Pit N	16	20	2	2	0	0	1	3	0-0	0	6	.100	.095	.250	-5	-3	0-0	1.000	2	146	307	O14(3/6/5)	0	-0.1
	Year	58	48	5	2	0	0	1	3	2-0	0	15	.042	.078	.104	-49	-10	0-0	1.000	2	103	66	O41(15/7/20)	0	-0.8
	Cle A	33	69	10	11	2	1	1	4	11-0	1	27	.159	.284	.261	51	-5	8-0	.981	-0	103	66	O32(5/10/17)	0	-0.4
1992	Cal A	33	55	4	10	2	0	0	2	7-1	0	20	.182	.270	.218	39	-4	0-1	1.000	-0	96	101	O22(11/5/8)/D	0	-0.6
Total	8	461	676	95	144	30	7	9	42	60-7	2	186	.213	.277	.318	68	-31	33-9	.972	5	106	116	O378(100/164/132)/D	0	-2.6
GONZALEZ, JUAN	Juan Alberto (Vazquez); B10.20.1969 Arecibo, PR; BR/TR/6´3˝/(175–220); d9.1																								
1989	Tex A	24	60	6	9	3	0	1	7	6-0	0	17	.150	.227	.250	34	-5	0-0	.964	0	112	0	O24(1/24/0)	0	-0.6
1990	Tex A	25	90	11	26	7	1	4	12	2-0	2	18	.289	.316	.522	131	3	0-1	1.000	-1	93	0	O16(1/12/4),D9	0	0.2
1991	Tex A	142	545	78	144	34	1	27	102	42-7	5	118	.264	.321	.479	121	14	4-4	.981	-2	97	82	O136(92/93/8),D4	18	0.8
1992	Tex A	155	584	77	152	24	2	**43**	109	35-1	5	143	.260	.304	.529	134	21	0-1	.975	2	103	111	O148(31/123/1),D4	0	2.2
1993	Tex A★	140	536	105	166	33	1	**46**	118	37-7	13	99	.310	.368	**.632**	169	49	4-1	.985	-1	105	66	O129L,D10	0	4.2
1994	Tex A	107	422	57	116	18	4	19	85	30-10	7	66	.275	.330	.472	103	0	6-4	.991	3	103	117	O107L	0	-0.1
1995	Tex A	90	352	57	104	20	2	27	82	17-3	0	66	.295	.324	.594	129	12	0-0	1.000	0	70	347	D83,O5L	57	0.7
1996	†Tex A	134	541	89	170	33	2	47	144	45-12	3	82	.314	.368	.643	141	31	2-0	.988	-8	81	85	O102R,D32	24	1.6
1997	Tex A	133	533	87	158	24	3	42	131	33-7	3	107	.296	.335	.589	128	19	0-0	.971	1	96	143	D69,O64R	31	1.2
1998	†Tex A★	154	606	110	193	**50**	2	45	**157**	46-9	6	126	.318	.366	.630	146	40	2-1	.982	-4	94	96	O116R,D38	0	2.7
1999	†Tex A	144	562	114	183	36	1	39	128	51-7	4	105	.326	.378	.601	138	32	3-3	.983	-7	89	78	O131R,D14	0	1.6
2000	Det A	115	461	69	133	30	2	22	67	32-3	2	84	.289	.337	.505	110	6	1-2	.992	-3	95	46	O66R,D48	0	-0.3
2001	†Cle A★	140	532	97	173	34	1	35	140	41-5	6	94	.325	.370	.590	145	34	1-0	.987	4	103	143	O119R,D21	0	3.0
2002	Tex A	70	277	38	78	21	1	8	35	17-1	1	56	.282	.324	.451	101	0	2-0	.992	5	100	247	O62R,D8	98	0.2
2003	Tex A	82	327	49	96	17	1	24	70	14-1	4	73	.294	.329	.572	123	10	1-1	1.000	5	93	329	O57R,D24	71	1.0
2004	KC A	33	127	17	35	4	1	5	17	9-1	1	19	.276	.326	.441	98	-1	0-1	.948	-0	89	160	O29R,D4	135	-0.3
2005	Cle A	1	1	0	0	0	0	0	0	0-0	0	0	.000	.000	.000	-99	0	0-0	ø	0	—	—	/H	181	0.0
Total	17	1689	6556	1061	1936	388	25	434	1404	457-74	62	1273	.295	.343	.561	131	265	26-19	.983	-5	97	113	O1311(366/252/759),D368	615	18.1

YEAR	TM LG	G	AB	R	H	2B	3B	HR	RBI	BB-IB	HP	SO	AVG	OBP	SLG	AOPS	ABR	SB-CS	FA	FR	RNG	THR	GAMES AT POSITION	DL	BFW
GONZALEZ, JULIO	Julio Cesar (Hernandez); B12.25.1952 Caguas, PR; BR/TR/5´11˝/(162–167); d4.8																								
1977	Hou N	110	383	34	94	18	3	1	27	19-1	4	45	.245	.287	.316	67	-19	3-3	.921	-15	86	90	S63,2b45	0	-2.6
1978	Hou N	78	223	24	52	3	1	1	16	8-1	1	31	.233	.263	.269	52	-15	6-1	.983	-13	89	83	2b54,S17,3b4	0	-2.6
1979	Hou N	68	181	16	45	5	2	0	10	5-0	3	14	.249	.280	.298	62	-10	2-1	.987	4	104	97	2b32,S21,3b9	0	-0.3
1980	Hou N	40	52	5	6	1	0	0	1	1-1	0	8	.115	.132	.135	-28	-9	1-0	1.000	1	89	152	S16,3b11,2b2	0	-0.8
1981	StL N	20	22	2	7	1	0	1	3	1-0	0	3	.318	.348	.500	132	1	0-0	1.000	0	147	115	S5,2b4,3b2	0	0.1
1982	StL N	42	87	9	21	3	2	1	7	1-0	1	24	.241	.258	.356	68	-4	1-1	.907	-2	93	39	3b21,2b9/S	0	-0.7
1983	Det A	12	21	0	3	1	0	0	2	1-0	0	7	.143	.182	.190	3	-3	0-0	.889	0	129	36	S6,2b5/3	0	-0.2
Total	7	370	969	90	228	32	8	4	66	36-3	9	132	.235	.269	.297	58	-59	13-6	.976	-25	100	98	2b151,S129,3b48	0	-7.1
GONZALEZ, LUIS	Luis Alberto; B6.26.1979 Maracay, Aragua, Venezuela; BR/TR/5´11˝/(170–205); d4.6; OF(22/0/24)																								
2004	Col N	102	322	42	94	17	2	12	40	15-1	4	67	.292	.330	.469	92	-4	1-5	.994	0	107	109	2b40,O29(20/0/11),3b18,S10/D	0	-0.4
2005	Col N	128	404	51	118	25	0	9	44	20-0	6	63	.292	.333	.421	86	-8	3-4	1.000	-3	104	80	2b83,S17,3b12,1b10,O8(1/0/7)	0	-0.8
2006	Col N	61	149	7	36	9	1	2	14	4-0	2	27	.242	.269	.356	54	-10	1-1	.984	-5	100	41	2b32,1b7,O7(1/0/6),3b3	15	-1.5
Total	3	291	875	100	248	51	3	23	98	39-1	12	157	.283	.321	.427	83	-22	5-10	.995	-9	104	80	2b155,O44R,3b33,S27,1b17/D	15	-2.7
GONZALEZ, LUIS	Luis Emilio; B9.3.1967 Tampa FL; BL/TR/6´2˝/(180–200); [HouN88 4/90]; d9.4; Col South Alabama																								
1990	Hou N	12	21	1	4	2	0	0	0	2-1	0	5	.190	.261	.286	52	-1	0-0	1.000	2	170	218	3b4,1b2	0	0.1
1991	Hou N	137	473	51	120	28	9	13	69	40-4	8	101	.254	.320	.433	117	9	10-7	.984	9	**114**	85	O133L	15	1.5
1992	Hou N	122	387	40	94	19	3	10	55	24-3	2	52	.243	.289	.385	93	-5	7-7	.993	14	**129**	108	O111L	15	0.5
1993	Hou N	154	540	82	162	34	3	15	72	47-7	10	83	.300	.361	.457	123	18	20-9	.978	15	**124**	95	O149L	0	2.9
1994	Hou N	112	392	57	107	29	4	8	67	49-6	3	57	.273	.353	.429	109	7	15-13	.991	6	112	77	O111L	0	0.7
1995	Hou N	56	209	35	54	10	4	6	35	18-3	3	30	.258	.322	.431	104	0	1-3	.980	-1	101	62	O55L	0	-0.3
	Chi N	77	262	34	76	19	4	7	34	39-5	3	33	.290	.384	.473	126	11	5-5	.978	8	126	111	O76(74/6/0)	0	1.6
	Year	133	471	69	130	29	8	13	69	57-8	6	63	.276	.357	.454	117	12	6-8	.978	7	**115**	90	O131(129/6/0)	0	1.3
1996	Chi N	146	483	70	131	30	4	15	79	61-8	4	49	.271	.354	.443	106	5	9-6	.988	-0	96	79	O139L,1b2	0	0.0
1997	†Hou N	152	550	78	142	31	2	10	68	71-7	5	67	.258	.345	.376	93	-4	10-7	.982	1	98	105	O146L/1	0	-0.9
1998	Det A	154	547	84	146	35	5	23	71	57-7	8	62	.267	.340	.475	109	7	12-7	.988	-7	86	99	O132(132/3/0),D19	0	-0.5
1999	†Ari N★	153	614	112	**206**	45	4	26	111	66-6	7	63	.336	.403	.549	138	37	9-5	.983	-1	97	107	O148L,D4	0	2.9
2000	Ari N	**162**	618	106	192	47	2	31	114	78-6	12	85	.311	.392	.544	130	31	2-4	.990	-2	103	42	O162L	0	2.1
2001	†Ari N★	**162**	609	128	198	36	7	57	142	100-24	14	83	.325	.429	.688	171	67	1-1	**1.000**	-0	100	77	O161L	0	5.8
2002	Ari N★	148	524	90	151	19	3	28	103	97-8	5	76	.288	.400	.496	123	21	9-2	.985	-1	105	48	O146L	0	1.6
2003	Ari N★	156	579	92	176	46	4	26	104	94-17	3	67	.304	.402	.532	131	30	5-3	.989	-2	92	100	O154L	0	2.1
2004	Ari N	105	379	69	98	28	5	17	48	68-11	2	58	.259	.373	.493	114	10	2-2	.965	-6	93	36	O104L/D	63	-0.1
2005	Ari N★	155	579	90	157	37	0	24	79	78-12	11	90	.271	.366	.459	110	11	4-1	.989	-4	93	79	O152L	0	0.2
2006	Ari N	153	586	93	159	52	2	15	73	69-10	7	58	.271	.352	.444	97	0	0-1	.996	-8	85	37	O150L/D	0	-1.4
Total	17	2316	8352	1312	2373	547	65	331	1324	1058-145	107	1119	.284	.368	.484	119	254	121-83	.986	22	102	79	O2229(2227/9/0),D25,1b5,3b4	93	18.8
GONZALEZ, MIKE	Miguel Angel (Cordero); B9.24.1890 Havana, Cuba; D2.19.1977 Havana, Cuba; BR/TR/6´1˝/200; d9.28; M2/C13																								
1912	Bos N	1	2	0	0	0	0	0	0	1	0	1	.000	.333	.000	-5	0	0	.875	0	*135*	*278*	/C	—	0.0
1914	Cin N	95	176	19	41	6	0	0	10	13	2	16	.233	.293	.267	65	-7	2	.954	6	*100*	***130***	C83	—	0.4
1915	StL N	51	97	12	22	2	2	0	10	8	3	9	.227	.306	.289	80	-2	4-2	.992	4	*118*	*88*	C32,1b8	—	0.4
1916	StL N	118	331	33	79	15	4	0	29	28	3	18	.239	.304	.308	89	-4	5	.981	4	82	119	C93,1b13	—	0.8
1917	StL N	106	290	28	76	8	1	1	28	22	1	24	.262	.316	.307	94	-2	12	.977	2	*119*	*118*	C68,1b18/rf	—	0.6
1918	StL N	117	349	33	88	13	4	3	20	39	0	30	.252	.327	.338	107	4	14	.978	-6	*82*	*109*	C100,O5(1/1/3),1b2	—	0.7
1919	NY N	58	158	18	30	6	0	0	8	20	3	9	.190	.293	.228	58	-7	3	.962	-3	*102*	*76*	C52,1b4	—	-0.6
1920	NY N	11	13	1	3	0	0	0	0	3	0	1	.231	.375	.231	77	0	1-0	1.000	-0	*120*	*94*	C8	—	0.0
1921	NY N	13	24	3	9	1	0	0	0	1	0	0	.375	.400	.417	116	1	0-0	.981	-1	80	171	1b6,C2	—	0.0
1924	StL N	120	402	34	119	27	1	3	53	24	1	22	.296	.337	.391	96	-2	1-5	.986	-3	*98*	*86*	C119	—	0.1
1925	StL N	22	71	9	22	3	0	0	4	6	2	2	.310	.380	.352	86	-1	1-2	.982	3	*134*	*75*	C22	—	0.3
	Chi N	70	197	26	52	13	1	3	18	13	2	15	.264	.316	.386	77	-7	2-1	.989	3	*136*	*94*	C50,1b9	—	-0.1
	Year	92	268	35	74	16	1	3	22	19	4	17	.276	.333	.377	80	-8	3-3	.987	7	*135*	*87*	C72,1b9	—	0.2
1926	Chi N	80	253	24	63	13	3	1	23	13	1	17	.249	.288	.336	67	-12	3	**.989**	9	*173*	*82*	C78	—	0.2
1927	Chi N	39	108	15	26	4	1	1	15	10	1	8	.241	.311	.324	70	-5	1	.994	7	*156*	*109*	C36	—	0.5
1928	Chi N	49	158	12	43	9	2	1	21	12	0	7	.272	.324	.373	83	-4	2	.983	8	*178*	*95*	C45	—	0.7
1929	†Chi N	60	167	15	40	3	0	0	18	18	1	14	.240	.317	.257	44	-14	1	.992	6	*127*	*103*	C60	—	-0.5
1931	StL N	15	19	1	2	0	0	0	3	0	0	3	.105	.105	.105	-42	-4	0	1.000	0	*120*	*196*	C12	—	-0.4
1932	StL N	17	14	0	2	0	0	0	3	0	0	2	.143	.143	.143	-22	-2	0	1.000	1	*51*	*244*	C7	—	-0.2
Total	17	1042	2829	283	717	123	19	13	263	231	20	198	.253	.314	.324	81	-68	52-10	.980	40	*117*	*101*	C868,1b60,O6(1/1/4)	—	2.9
GONZALEZ, ORLANDO	Orlando Eugene; B11.15.1951 Havana, Cuba; BL/TL/6´2˝/180; [CleA74 18/410]; d6.7; Col Miami																								
1976	Cle A	28	68	5	17	2	0	0	4	5-0	0	7	.250	.301	.279	71	-2	1-2	.992	-1	89	68	1b15,O7(3/0/4),D2	0	-0.5
1978	†Phi N	26	26	1	5	0	0	0	0	1-0	0	1	.192	.222	.192	16	-3	0-0	1.000	0	135	0	O11(1/0/10),1b3	0	-0.3
1980	Oak A	25	70	10	17	0	0	0	1	9-0	0	8	.243	.329	.243	63	-3	0-2	.990	1	113	85	1b11,O2L,D8	0	-0.4
Total	3	79	164	16	39	2	0	0	5	15-0	0	16	.238	.302	.250	59	-8	1-4	.991	1	98	74	1b29,O20(6/0/14),D10	0	-1.2
GONZALEZ, PEDRO	Pedro (Olivares); B12.12.1937 San Pedro de Macoris, D.R.; BR/TR/6´0˝/(173–180); d4.11																								
1963	NY A	14	26	3	5	1	0	0	1	0-0	0	5	.192	.192	.231	18	-3	0-1	.963	-2	59	62	2b7	0	-0.5
1964	†NY A	80	112	18	31	8	1	0	5	7-0	2	22	.277	.331	.366	92	-1	3-4	.992	1	157	122	1b31,O20(5/0/15),3b9,2b6	0	-0.1
1965	NY A	7	5	0	2	1	0	0	0	0-0	0	2	.400	.400	.600	181	1	0-0	ø	0	—	—	/H	0	0.1
	Cle A	116	400	38	101	14	3	5	39	18-7	3	57	.253	.288	.340	78	-13	7-4	.980	8	98	91	2b112,O3R,3b2	0	0.5
	Year	123	405	38	103	15	3	5	39	18-7	3	59	.254	.289	.343	79	-12	7-4	.980	8	98	91	2b112,O3R,3b2	0	0.6
1966	Cle A	110	352	21	82	9	2	2	17	15-1	2	54	.233	.268	.287	60	-19	8-5	.984	9	98	107	2b104/3rf	0	-0.2
1967	Cle A	80	189	19	43	6	0	1	8	12-0	1	36	.228	.275	.275	63	-9	4-6	.971	-5	91	101	2b64,1b4,3b4,S3	0	-1.2
Total	5	407	1084	99	264	39	6	8	70	52-8	8	176	.244	.282	.313	70	-44	22-20	.980	11	95	98	2b293,1b35,O24(5/0/19),3b16,S3	0	-1.4
GONZALEZ, RAUL	Victor Raul; B12.27.1973 Santurce, PR; BR/TR/5´8˝/190; [KCA90 17/477]; d5.25																								
2000	Chi N	3	2	0	0	0	0	0	0	0-0	0	2	.000	.000	.000	-99	-1	0-0	ø	-0	0	0	O2L	0	-0.1
2001	Cin N	11	14	0	3	0	0	0	0	1-0	0	3	.214	.267	.214	25	-2	0-0	1.000	0	105	0	O2L	0	-0.2
2002	Cin N	10	23	4	6	1	0	0	1	2-0	0	5	.261	.320	.304	63	-1	2-0	1.000	0	93	360	O6(1/5/0)	0	-0.0
	NY N	30	81	9	21	2	0	3	11	4-0	0	17	.259	.291	.395	84	-2	2-2	1.000	1	112	92	O24(11/13/4)	0	-0.2
	Year	40	104	13	27	3	0	3	12	6-0	0	22	.260	.297	.375	79	-4	4-2	1.000	1	108	147	O30(12/18/4)	0	-0.2
2003	NY N	107	217	28	50	12	2	2	21	27-1	1	34	.230	.317	.332	73	-8	3-0	.993	5	120	116	O88(45/25/40)	0	-0.4
2004	Cle A	7	11	0	1	0	0	0	0	0-0	0	4	.091	.091	.091	-54	-3	0-0	1.000	1	166	0	O4(1/0/3)	0	-0.2
Total	5	168	348	41	81	15	2	5	33	34-1	1	65	.233	.301	.330	68	-17	7-2	.995	7	117	119	O126(62/43/47)	0	-1.1
GONZALEZ, WIKI	Wiklenman Vicente; B5.17.1974 Aragua, Venezuela; BR/TR/5´11˝/(203–205); d8.14																								
1999	SD N	30	83	7	21	2	1	3	12	1-0	1	8	.253	.271	.410	74	-4	0-0	.992	3	417	155	C17	0	0.0
2000	SD N	95	284	25	66	15	1	5	30	30-4	3	31	.232	.311	.345	70	-13	1-2	.991	3	102	115	C87	0	-0.5
2001	SD N	64	160	16	44	6	0	8	27	11-1	4	28	.275	.335	.463	112	2	2-0	.989	-4	92	126	C47/D	30	0.2
2002	SD N	56	164	16	36	8	1	1	20	27-3	1	24	.220	.330	.299	74	-5	0-0	.985	1	134	112	C54	76	-0.1
2003	SD N	24	65	1	13	5	0	0	10	5-1	1	13	.200	.264	.277	47	-5	0-0	.993	-1	61	105	C23/P	0	-0.5
2005	Sea A	14	45	7	12	5	0	0	2	2-0	0	3	.267	.298	.378	84	-1	0-0	1.000	3	226	104	C14	47	0.3
2006	Was N	12	35	3	8	0	0	0	2	2-0	0	5	.229	.263	.229	31	-4	0-0	.972	0	98	137	C12	0	-0.3
Total	7	295	836	75	200	41	3	17	103	78-9	10	112	.239	.310	.356	77	-30	3-2	.989	6	136	119	C254/PD	153	-0.9
GOOCH, CHARLIE	Charles Furman; B6.5.1902 Smyrna TN; D5.30.1982 Lanham MD; BR/TR/5´9˝/170; d4.18																								
1929	Was A	39	57	6	16	2	1	0	5	7	0	8	.281	.359	.351	83	-1	0-1	.970	-1	218	65	1b7,3b7/S	—	-0.2
GOOCH, JOHNNY	John Beverley; B11.9.1897 Smyrna TN; D5.15.1975 Nashville TN; BB/TR/5´11˝/175; d9.9; C3																								
1921	Pit N	13	38	2	9	0	0	0	3	3	0	3	.237	.293	.237	41	-3	1-0	.985	2	*149*	*106*	C13	—	0.0
1922	Pit N	105	353	45	116	15	3	1	42	39	5	15	.329	.403	.397	106	5	1-1	.970	-3	*95*	*87*	C103	—	0.9
1923	Pit N	66	202	16	56	10	2	1	20	17	1	13	.277	.336	.361	82	-5	2-1	.975	4	*133*	*81*	C66	—	0.3
1924	Pit N	70	224	26	65	6	5	0	25	16	2	12	.290	.343	.362	88	-4	1-3	.988	1	*142*	*71*	C69	—	0.0
1925	†Pit N	79	215	24	64	8	4	0	30	20	0	16	.298	.357	.372	81	-6	1-0	.968	1	*125*	*73*	C76	—	-0.1

YEAR	TM LG	G	AB	R	H	2B	3B	HR	RBI	BB-IB	HP	SO	AVG	OBP	SLG	AOPS	ABR	SB-CS	FA	FR	RNG	THR	GAMES AT POSITION	DL	BFW
1926	Pit N	86	218	19	59	15	1	1	42	20	3	14	.271	.340	.362	85	-4	1	.980	0	*119*	*72*	C80	—	0.1
1927	†Pit N	101	291	22	75	17	2	2	48	19	1	21	.258	.305	.351	70	-12	0	.974	5	*133*	*74*	C91	—	-0.2
1928	Pit N	31	80	7	19	2	1	0	5	3	0	6	.237	.265	.287	43	-7	0	.957	1	*81*	*119*	C31	—	-0.4
	Bro N	42	101	9	32	1	2	0	12	7	0	9	.317	.361	.366	92	-1	0	.969	-1	*77*	*85*	C38	—	0.0
	Year	73	181	16	51	3	3	0	17	10	0	15	.282	.319	.331	70	-9	0	.964	0	*79*	*102*	C69	—	-0.4
1929	Bro N	1	1	0	0	0	0	0	0	0	0	0	.000	.000	.000	-99	0	0	ø	0	—	—	/H	—	0.0
	Cin N	92	287	22	86	13	5	0	34	24	1	10	.300	.356	.380	86	-6	4	.975	5	*108*	*117*	C86	—	0.4
	Year	93	288	22	86	13	5	0	34	24	1	10	.299	.355	.378	86	-6	4	.975	5	*108*	*117*	C86	—	0.4
1930	Cin N	82	276	29	67	10	3	2	30	27	2	15	.243	.315	.322	57	-19	0	.955	-5	*91*	*101*	C79	—	-1.7
1933	Bos A	37	77	6	14	1	1	0	2	11	0	7	.182	.284	.221	36	-7	0-0	.991	2	*82*	*176*	C26	—	-0.4
Total	11	805	2363	227	662	98	29	7	293	206	15	141	.280	.342	.355	79	-69	11-5	.973	12	*113*	*90*	C758	—	-1.1

GOOCH, LEE Lee Currin; B2.23.1890 Oxford NC; D5.18.1966 Raleigh NC; BR/TR/6´0˝/190; d8.17; Col Wake Forest

YEAR	TM LG	G	AB	R	H	2B	3B	HR	RBI	BB-IB	HP	SO	AVG	OBP	SLG	AOPS	ABR	SB-CS	FA	FR	RNG	THR	GAMES AT POSITION	DL	BFW
1915	Cle A	2	2	0	1	0	0	0	0	0	0	0	.500	.500	.500	196	0	0	ø	0	—	—	/H	—	0.0
1917	Phi A	17	59	4	17	2	0	1	8	4	0	10	.288	.333	.373	117	1	0	.893	-2	87	45	O16R	—	-0.2
Total	2	19	61	4	18	2	0	1	8	4	0	10	.295	.338	.377	120	1	0	.893	-2	87	45	O16R	—	-0.2

GOOD, GENE Eugene Joseph; B12.13.1882 Roxbury MA; D8.6.1947 Boston MA; BL/TR/5´6˝/130; d4.12

YEAR	TM LG	G	AB	R	H	2B	3B	HR	RBI	BB-IB	HP	SO	AVG	OBP	SLG	AOPS	ABR	SB-CS	FA	FR	RNG	THR	GAMES AT POSITION	DL	BFW
1906	Bos N	34	119	4	18	0	0	0	0	13	2	—	.151	.246	.151	25	-10	2	.873	-3	114	88	O34(24/10/0)	—	-1.7

GOOD, WILBUR Wilbur David "Lefty"; B9.28.1885 Punxsutawney PA; D12.30.1963 Brooksville FL; BL/TL/5´11.5˝/180; d8.18; ▲

YEAR	TM LG	G	AB	R	H	2B	3B	HR	RBI	BB-IB	HP	SO	AVG	OBP	SLG	AOPS	ABR	SB-CS	FA	FR	RNG	THR	GAMES AT POSITION	DL	BFW
1905	NY A	5	8	2	3	0	0	0	0	0	0	—	.375	.375	.375	124	1	0	.889	0	120	0	P5	—	0.0
1908	Cle A	46	154	23	43	1	3	1	14	13	4	—	.279	.351	.344	126	4	7	.845	-8	0	0	O42(2/17/23)	—	-0.7
1909	Cle A	94	318	33	68	6	5	0	17	28	9	—	.214	.296	.264	74	-9	13	.953	2	119	90	O80R	—	-1.2
1910	Bos N	23	86	15	29	5	4	0	11	6	2	13	.337	.394	.488	150	5	5	.969	3	100	207	O23(0/22/1)	—	0.7
1911	Bos N	43	165	21	44	9	3	0	15	12	0	22	.267	.316	.358	82	-4	3	.945	5	102	192	O43(0/41/2)	—	-0.3
	Chi N	58	145	27	39	5	4	2	21	11	2	17	.269	.329	.400	103	0	10	.928	-4	90	56	O40(3/34/3)	—	-0.7
	Year	101	310	48	83	14	7	2	36	23	2	39	.268	.322	.377	92	-4	13	.938	1	97	132	O83(3/75/5)	—	-1.0
1912	Chi N	39	35	7	5	0	0	0	1	3	0	7	.143	.211	.143	-2	-5	3	1.000	1	112	229	O10(5/4/1)	—	-0.4
1913	Chi N	49	91	11	23	3	2	1	12	11	1	16	.253	.340	.363	100	0	5-2	.974	-1	107	39	O26(3/1/22)	—	-0.1
1914	Chi N	154	580	70	158	24	7	2	43	53	7	74	.272	.341	.348	105	5	31	.930	-0	99	106	O154R	—	-0.4
1915	Chi N	128	498	66	126	18	9	2	27	34	5	65	.253	.307	.337	95	-4	19-17	.936	-1	101	98	O125(0/1/125)	—	-1.4
1916	Phi N	75	136	25	34	4	3	1	15	8	3	13	.250	.306	.346	96	-1	7	.983	0	98	101	O46(9/1/36)	—	-0.3
1918	Chi A	35	148	24	37	9	4	0	11	11	3	16	.250	.315	.365	104	0	1	.982	3	120	77	O35(1/33/1)	—	0.1
Total	11	749	2364	324	609	84	44	9	187	190	36	243	.258	.322	.342	98	-8	104-19	.942	-1	96	99	O624(23/154/448),P5	—	-4.7

GOODENOUGH, BILL William B.; B1863 NY; D5.24.1905 St.Louis MO; BL/6´1˝/170; d8.31

YEAR	TM LG	G	AB	R	H	2B	3B	HR	RBI	BB-IB	HP	SO	AVG	OBP	SLG	AOPS	ABR	SB-CS	FA	FR	RNG	THR	GAMES AT POSITION	DL	BFW
1893	StL N	10	31	4	5	1	0	0	2	3	3	4	.161	.297	.194	31	-3	2	.880	-1	69	0	O10C	—	-0.3

GOODFELLOW, MIKE Michael J.; B10.3.1866 Port Jervis NY; D2.12.1920 Newark NJ; BR/TR/6´0˝/180; d6.13

YEAR	TM LG	G	AB	R	H	2B	3B	HR	RBI	BB-IB	HP	SO	AVG	OBP	SLG	AOPS	ABR	SB-CS	FA	FR	RNG	THR	GAMES AT POSITION	DL	BFW
1887	StL AA	1	4	0	0	0	0	0	0	0	0	—	.000	.000	.000	-90	-1	0	.800	-0	—	—	/C	—	-0.1
1888	Cle AA	68	269	24	66	7	0	0	29	11	3	—	.245	.283	.271	80	-6	7	.863	-4	75	39	O62(11/0/52),C4,1b3/S	—	-0.9
Total	2	69	273	24	66	7	0	0	29	11	3	—	.242	.279	.267	77	-7	7	.863	-4	—	—	O62(11/0/52),C5,1b3/S	—	-1.0

GOODMAN, IVAL Ival Richard "Goodie"; B7.23.1908 Northview MO; D11.25.1984 Cincinnati OH; BL/TR/5´11˝/170; d4.16

YEAR	TM LG	G	AB	R	H	2B	3B	HR	RBI	BB-IB	HP	SO	AVG	OBP	SLG	AOPS	ABR	SB-CS	FA	FR	RNG	THR	GAMES AT POSITION	DL	BFW
1935	Cin N	148	592	86	159	23	**18**	12	72	35	4	50	.269	.314	.429	101	-3	14	.960	5	108	111	O146(2/0/144)	—	-0.7
1936	Cin N	136	489	81	139	15	**14**	17	71	38	**9**	53	.284	.347	.476	128	16	6	.972	-2	110	44	O120(1/1/118)	—	0.7
1937	Cin N	147	549	86	150	25	12	12	55	55	7	58	.273	.347	.428	115	11	10	.974	3	109	92	O141(7/1/133)	—	0.5
1938	Cin N★	145	568	103	166	27	10	30	92	53	**15**	51	.292	.368	.533	149	37	3	.988	3	108	77	O142R	—	3.0
1939	†Cin N★	124	470	85	152	37	16	7	84	54	**7**	32	.323	.401	.515	144	30	2	.981	7	105	148	O123R	—	2.9
1940	†Cin N	136	519	78	134	20	6	12	63	60	0	54	.258	.335	.389	98	-1	9	.970	-7	97	56	O135R	—	-1.7
1941	Cin N	42	149	14	40	5	2	1	12	16	1	15	.268	.343	.349	95	-1	1	.966	-1	110	29	O40R	0	-0.5
1942	Cin N	87	226	21	55	18	1	0	15	24	1	32	.243	.319	.332	91	-2	0	.991	1	95	142	O57R	0	-0.5
1943	Chi N	80	225	31	72	10	5	3	45	24	2	20	.320	.390	.449	144	13	4	.968	-4	95	36	O61(55/10/0)	0	0.6
1944	Chi N	62	141	24	37	8	1	1	16	23	3	15	.262	.377	.355	107	3	0	1.000	-3	89	0	O35(23/14/0)	0	-0.2
Total	10	1107	3928	609	1104	188	85	95	525	382	49	380	.281	.352	.445	120	103	49	.975	1	105	82	O1000(88/26/892)	0	4.1

GOODMAN, JAKE Jacob; B9.14.1853 Lancaster PA; D3.9.1890 Reading PA; 6´1.5˝/?; d5.2

YEAR	TM LG	G	AB	R	H	2B	3B	HR	RBI	BB-IB	HP	SO	AVG	OBP	SLG	AOPS	ABR	SB-CS	FA	FR	RNG	THR	GAMES AT POSITION	DL	BFW
1878	Mil N	60	252	28	62	4	3	1	27	7	—	33	.246	.266	.298	80	-6	—	.944	-4	71	52	1b60	—	-1.2
1882	Pit AA	10	41	5	13	2	2	0	—	2	—	—	.317	.349	.463	180	3	—	.962	1	177	0	1b10	—	0.3
Total	2	70	293	33	75	6	5	1	27	9	—	33	.256	.278	.321	92	-3	—	.946	-3	85	45	1b70	—	-0.9

GOODMAN, BILLY William Dale; B3.22.1926 Concord NC; D10.1.1984 Sarasota FL; BL/TR/5´11˝/(158–165); d4.19; C3; OF(68/0/43)

YEAR	TM LG	G	AB	R	H	2B	3B	HR	RBI	BB-IB	HP	SO	AVG	OBP	SLG	AOPS	ABR	SB-CS	FA	FR	RNG	THR	GAMES AT POSITION	DL	BFW
1947	Bos A	12	11	1	2	0	0	0	1	1	0	2	.182	.250	.182	20	-1	0-0	1.000	0	146	0	/rf	0	-0.1
1948	Bos A	127	445	65	138	27	2	1	66	74	5	44	.310	.414	.387	108	10	5-3	.993	-3	91	107	1b117,2b2,3b2	0	0.3
1949	Bos A★	122	443	54	132	23	3	0	56	58	2	21	.298	.382	.363	91	-4	2-0	**.992**	-1	95	**121**	1b117	0	-0.7
1950	Bos A	110	424	91	150	25	3	4	68	52	2	25	**.354**	.427	.455	115	12	2-4	.991	-2	99	55	O45L,3b27,1b21,2b5/S	0	0.5
1951	Bos A	141	546	92	162	34	4	0	50	79	2	37	.297	.388	.374	97	1	7-4	.995	-2	72	102	1b62,2b44,O38(2/0/36)/3	0	-0.1
1952	Bos A	138	513	79	157	27	3	4	56	48	4	23	.306	.370	.394	104	4	8-2	.975	**23**	**113**	118	2b103,1b23,3b5,O4L	0	3.4
1953	Bos A★	128	514	73	161	33	5	2	41	57	2	11	.313	.384	.409	108	8	1-4	.974	-1	102	104	2b112,1b20	0	1.3
1954	Bos A	127	489	71	148	25	4	1	36	51	2	15	.303	.370	.376	95	-2	3-3	.979	6	110	108	2b72,1b27,O13L,3b12	0	0.7
1955	Bos A	149	599	100	176	31	2	0	52	99-1	3	44	.294	.394	.352	94	1	5-5	.969	-21	93	84	2b143,1b5/rf	0	-1.0
1956	Bos A	105	399	61	117	22	8	2	38	40-1	0	22	.293	.356	.404	90	-6	0-3	.966	-8	100	94	2b95	0	-0.8
1957	Bos A	18	16	1	1	1	0	0	0	2-0	0	1	.063	.167	.125	-18	-3	0-0	ø	0	—	—	/H	0	-0.3
	Bal A	73	263	36	81	10	3	3	33	21-1	3	18	.308	.362	.403	117	6	0-2	.961	-4	93	106	3b54,O9(4/0/5),1b8,2b5,S5	0	0.1
	Year	91	279	37	82	11	3	3	33	23-1	3	19	.294	.351	.387	106	2	0-2	.961	-4	93	106	3b54,O9(4/0/5),1b8,2b5,S5	0	-0.2
1958	Chi A	116	425	41	127	15	5	0	40	37-1	2	21	.299	.355	.358	100	0	1-0	.954	-4	103	84	3b111,1b3/2S	0	-0.4
1959	†Chi A	104	268	21	67	14	1	1	28	19-0	2	20	.250	.304	.321	73	-10	3-0	.950	4	114	102	3b74,2b3	0	-0.5
1960	Chi A	30	77	5	18	4	0	0	6	12-1	0	8	.234	.337	.286	71	-3	0-0	.982	4	136	73	3b20,2b7	0	0.2
1961	Chi A	41	51	4	13	4	0	1	10	7-0	0	6	.255	.339	.392	98	0	0-0	.944	-0	106	89	3b7,1b2/2	0	0.0
1962	Hou N	82	161	12	41	4	1	0	10	12-2	0	11	.255	.306	.292	66	-8	0-0	.972	-4	93	56	2b31,3b17/1	0	-1.1
Total	16	1623	5644	807	1691	299	44	19	591	669-7	29	329	.300	.376	.378	98	5	37-30	.972	-12	102	99	2b624,1b406,3b330,O111L,S7	0	1.5

GOODSON, ED James Edward; B1.25.1948 Pulaski VA; BL/TR (BB 1975p)/6´3˝/(175–185); [SFN68 S1/3]; d9.5; Col East Tennessee

YEAR	TM LG	G	AB	R	H	2B	3B	HR	RBI	BB-IB	HP	SO	AVG	OBP	SLG	AOPS	ABR	SB-CS	FA	FR	RNG	THR	GAMES AT POSITION	DL	BFW
1970	SF N	7	11	1	3	0	0	0	0	0-0	0	2	.273	.273	.273	47	-1	0-0	.941	0	163	67	1b2	0	-0.1
1971	SF N	20	42	4	8	1	0	0	1	2-0	0	4	.190	.227	.214	26	-4	0-0	1.000	0	106	39	1b14	0	-0.5
1972	SF N	58	150	15	42	1	1	6	30	8-2	1	12	.280	.319	.420	107	1	0-0	.991	2	132	32	1b42	43	0.0
1973	SF N	102	384	37	116	20	1	12	53	15-4	2	44	.302	.331	.453	111	4	0-1	.911	-8	97	76	3b93	0	-0.4
1974	SF N	98	298	25	81	15	0	6	48	18-6	3	22	.272	.320	.383	92	-4	1-0	.997	-2	73	100	1b73,3b8	20	-1.1
1975	SF N	39	121	10	25	7	0	1	8	7-2	0	14	.207	.248	.289	48	-9	0-1	.993	2	125	95	1b16,3b13	0	-0.9
	Atl N	47	76	5	16	2	0	1	8	2-0	0	8	.211	.228	.276	39	-7	0-0	.990	-0	100	88	1b13/3	0	-0.8
	Year	86	197	15	41	9	0	2	16	9-2	0	22	.208	.240	.284	44	-15	0-1	.992	2	115	92	1b29,3b14	0	-1.7
1976	LA N	83	118	8	27	4	0	3	17	8-2	0	19	.229	.273	.339	75	-4	0-0	.833	-4	93	85	3b16,1b3,O2L/2	0	-0.9
1977	†LA N	61	66	3	11	1	0	1	5	3-2	0	10	.167	.203	.227	15	-8	0-1	1.000	0	94	203	1b13,3b4	15	-0.9
Total	8	515	1266	108	329	51	2	30	170	63-18	6	135	.260	.297	.374	84	-32	1-3	.994	-9	99	79	1b176,3b135,O2L/2	78	-5.6

GOODWIN, PEP Claire Vernon; B12.19.1891 Pocatello ID; D2.15.1972 Oakland CA; BL/TR/5´10.5˝/160; d4.16; Col California

YEAR	TM LG	G	AB	R	H	2B	3B	HR	RBI	BB-IB	HP	SO	AVG	OBP	SLG	AOPS	ABR	SB-CS	FA	FR	RNG	THR	GAMES AT POSITION	DL	BFW
1914	KC F	112	374	38	88	15	6	1	32	27	2	23	.235	.290	.316	68	-24	4	.907	-7	111	89	S67,3b40/1	—	-2.7
1915	KC F	81	229	22	54	5	1	0	16	15	3	23	.236	.291	.266	60	-16	6	.906	-5	97	82	S42,2b23	—	-2.0
Total	2	193	603	60	142	20	7	1	48	42	5	46	.235	.291	.297	65	-40	10	.907	-12	106	86	S109,3b40,2b23/1	—	-4.7

GOODWIN, CURTIS Curtis La Mar; B9.30.1972 Oakland CA; BL/TL/5´11˝/180; [BalA91 12/316]; d6.2

YEAR	TM LG	G	AB	R	H	2B	3B	HR	RBI	BB-IB	HP	SO	AVG	OBP	SLG	AOPS	ABR	SB-CS	FA	FR	RNG	THR	GAMES AT POSITION	DL	BFW
1995	Bal A	87	289	40	76	11	3	1	24	15-0	2	53	.263	.301	.332	64	-16	22-4	.990	-1	104	26	O84C,D3	15	-1.2
1996	Cin N	49	136	20	31	3	0	0	5	19-0	0	34	.228	.323	.250	53	-9	15-6	.970	-4	85	0	O42(9/28/6)	0	-1.1
1997	Cin N	85	265	27	67	11	0	1	12	24-0	1	53	.253	.316	.306	63	-14	22-13	1.000	4	116	82	O71(32/41/1)	0	-1.0
1998	Col N	119	159	27	39	7	0	1	6	16-0	0	40	.245	.313	.308	53	-10	5-1	.983	1	112	35	O91(14/74/7)	0	-0.9

YEAR	TM LG	G	AB	R	H	2B	3B	HR	RBI	BB-IB	HP	SO	AVG	OBP	SLG	AOPS	ABR	SB-CS	FA	FR	RNG	THR	GAMES AT POSITION	DL	BFW
1999	Chi N	89	157	15	38	6	1	0	9	13-1	0	38	.242	.298	.293	51	-12	2-4	.983	4	112	123	O76(36/42/0)	0	-0.9
	Tor A	2	8	0	0	0	0	0	0	0-0	0	3	.000	.000	.000	-98	-2	0-0	1.000	1	142	821	O2C	0	-0.1
Total	5	431	1014	129	251	38	4	3	56	87-1	3	221	.248	.307	.302	57	-63	66-28	.988	5	107	59	O366(91/271/14),D3	15	-5.2
GOODWIN, DANNY	Danny Kay; B9.2.1953 St.Louis MO; BL/TR/6´1˝/(195–205); [AnaA75 1/1]; d9.3; Col Southern A&M																								
1975	Cal A	4	10	0	1	0	0	0	0	0-0	0	5	.100	.100	.100	-47	-2	0-0	ø	0	—	—	D3	0	-0.2
1977	Cal A	35	91	5	19	6	1	1	8	5-1	0	19	.209	.250	.330	58	-5	0-0	ø	0	0	0	D23	0	-0.6
1978	Cal A	24	58	9	16	5	0	2	10	10-0	0	13	.276	.377	.466	142	4	0-0	ø	0	0	0	D15	0	0.3
1979	Min A	58	159	22	46	8	5	5	27	11-1	0	23	.289	.335	.497	116	3	0-0	1.000	-1	55	104	D51,1b8	0	0.0
1980	Min A	55	115	12	23	5	0	1	11	17-0	0	32	.200	.301	.270	54	-7	0-0	1.000	0	109	74	D38,1b13	0	-0.8
1981	Min A	59	151	18	34	6	1	2	17	16-2	0	32	.225	.298	.318	73	-5	3-1	.992	-2	76	76	1b40/lfD	0	-1.0
1982	Oak A	17	52	6	11	2	1	2	8	2-0	0	13	.212	.236	.404	76	-2	0-0	ø	0	0	0	D15	0	-0.3
Total	7	252	636	72	150	32	8	13	81	61-4	0	137	.236	.301	.373	83	-14	3-1	.994	-3	80	79	D150,1b61/lf	0	-2.6
GOODWIN, TOM	Thomas Jones; B7.27.1968 Fresno CA; BL/TR/6´1˝/(165–195); [LAN89 1/22]; d9.1; Col Cal St.–Fresno																								
1991	LA N	16	7	3	1	0	0	0	0	0-0	0	0	.143	.143	.143	-20	-1	1-1	1.000	1	167	0	O5(2/4/0)	0	-0.1
1992	LA N	57	73	15	17	1	1	0	3	6-0	0	10	.233	.291	.274	62	-4	7-3	1.000	-1	92	0	O45(35/9/2)	0	-0.6
1993	LA N	30	17	6	5	1	0	0	1	1-0	0	4	.294	.333	.353	89	0	1-2	1.000	-0	93	0	O12(6/4/2)	0	-0.1
1994	KC A	2	2	0	0	0	0	0	0	0-0	0	1	.000	.000	.000	-95	-1	0-0	1.000	0	146	0	/rfD	0	-0.1
1995	KC A	133	480	72	138	16	3	4	28	38-0	5	72	.287	.346	.358	82	-13	50-18	.990	-7	90	82	O130(37/95/1),D2	0	-1.4
1996	KC A	143	524	80	148	14	4	1	35	39-0	2	79	.282	.334	.330	69	-25	66-22	.984	-6	94	77	O136(75/81/0),D5	0	-2.4
1997	KC A	97	367	51	100	13	4	2	22	19-0	2	51	.272	.311	.346	69	-17	34-10	.996	-4	96	61	O96C	0	-1.6
	Tex A	53	207	39	49	13	2	0	17	25-1	1	37	.237	.319	.319	64	-11	16-6	.986	3	110	118	O51(5/49/0)	0	-0.6
	Year	150	574	90	149	26	6	2	39	44-1	3	88	.260	.314	.336	67	-28	50-16	.992	-2	101	81	O147(5/145/0)	0	-2.2
1998	†Tex A	154	520	102	151	13	3	2	33	73-0	2	90	.290	.378	.338	84	-9	38-20	.992	4	109	61	O150C/D	0	-0.3
1999	†Tex A	109	405	63	105	12	6	3	33	40-0	0	61	.259	.324	.341	66	-21	39-11	.989	-5	96	61	O107C	54	-1.9
2000	Col N	91	317	65	86	8	8	5	47	50-2	1	76	.271	.368	.394	76	-11	39-7	.986	-1	107	62	O88C	0	-0.4
	LA N	56	211	29	53	3	1	1	11	18-0	0	41	.251	.310	.289	55	-15	16-3	1.000	3	114	65	O55(10/48/0)	0	-0.9
	Year	147	528	94	139	11	9	6	58	68-2	1	117	.263	.346	.352	69	-25	55-10	.992	2	110	63	O143(10/136/0)	0	-1.3
2001	LA N	105	286	51	66	8	5	4	22	23-0	0	58	.231	.286	.336	64	-17	22-8	.994	-5	94	26	O78(8/70/0)	19	-1.9
2002	†SF N	78	154	23	40	5	2	1	17	14-0	0	25	.260	.321	.338	76	-6	16-2	.990	3	129	0	O53(28/22/7)	0	-0.1
2003	†Chi N	87	171	26	49	10	0	1	12	11-0	0	33	.287	.328	.363	79	-5	19-5	1.000	-3	92	0	O57(17/27/15)	27	-0.6
2004	Chi N	77	105	11	21	8	0	0	3	8-0	0	22	.200	.254	.276	37	-10	5-0	1.000	-0	102	0	O28(14/8/7)	18	-0.9
Total	14	1288	3846	636	1029	125	39	24	284	365-3	13	660	.268	.332	.339	71	-166	369-118	.991	-20	100	59	O1092(237/858/35),D9	118	-13.9
GOOLSBY, RAY	Raymond Daniel "Ox"; B9.5.1919 Florala AL; D11.13.1999 Apopka FL; BR/TR/6´1˝/185; d4.18																								
1946	Was A	3	4	0	0	0	0	0	0	1	0	1	.000	.200	.000	-43	-1	0-0	1.000	-0	65	0	/lf	0	-0.1
GOOSSEN, GREG	Gregory Bryant; B12.14.1945 Los Angeles CA; BR/TR/6´1.5˝/(205–210); d9.3																								
1965	NY N	11	31	2	9	0	0	1	2	1-0	0	5	.290	.313	.387	99	0	0-0	.979	-1	90	52	C8	0	-0.1
1966	NY N	13	32	1	6	2	0	1	5	1-0	1	11	.188	.235	.344	60	-2	0-0	1.000	-5	55	119	C11	0	-0.7
1967	NY N	37	69	2	11	1	0	0	3	4-0	1	26	.159	.216	.174	13	-8	0-0	.973	-0	38	97	C23	0	-0.8
1968	NY N	38	106	4	22	7	0	0	6	10-0	2	21	.208	.288	.274	69	-3	0-0	.992	2	131	94	1b31/C	0	-0.4
1969	Sea A	52	139	19	43	8	1	10	24	14-0	3	29	.309	.385	.597	172	13	1-1	.993	1	111	55	1b31,O2L	0	1.2
1970	Mil A	21	47	3	12	3	0	1	3	10-0	2	12	.255	.407	.383	119	2	0-0	.990	-2	57	77	1b15	0	0.0
	Was A	21	36	2	8	3	0	0	1	2-0	0	8	.222	.256	.306	59	-2	0-0	1.000	-0	51	0	O5L,1b2	0	-0.3
	Year	42	83	5	20	6	0	1	4	12-0	2	20	.241	.347	.349	96	0	0-0	.992	-2	81	101	1b17,O5L	0	-0.3
Total	6	193	460	33	111	24	1	13	44	42-0	9	112	.241	.316	.383	99	0	1-1	.992	-4	113	79	1b79,C43,O7L	0	-1.1
GORBOUS, GLEN	Glen Edward; B7.8.1930 Drumheller AL, Can.; D6.12.1990 Calgary AL, Can.; BL/TR/6´2˝/175; d4.11																								
1955	Cin N	8	18	2	6	3	0	0	4	3-0	0	1	.333	.429	.500	137	1	0-0	.857	-0	115	0	O5L	0	0.1
	Phi N	91	224	25	53	9	1	4	23	21-3	0	17	.237	.301	.339	71	-9	0-3	.984	7	111	226	O57(0/4/53)	0	-0.6
	Year	99	242	27	59	12	1	4	27	24-3	0	18	.244	.311	.351	77	-8	0-3	.971	6	111	207	O62(5/4/53)	0	-0.5
1956	Phi N	15	33	1	6	0	0	0	1	0-0	0	1	.182	.182	.182	-2	-5	0-0	1.000	-1	84	0	O8R	0	-0.6
1957	Phi N	3	2	1	1	1	0	0	1	1-0	0	0	.500	.667	1.000	351	1	0-0	ø	0	—	—	/H	0	0.1
Total	3	117	277	29	66	13	1	4	29	25-3	0	19	.238	.300	.336	70	-12	0-3	.973	6	109	190	O70(5/4/61)	0	-1.0
GORDON, JOE	Joseph Lowell "Flash"; B2.18.1915 Los Angeles CA; D4.14.1978 Sacramento CA; BR/TR/5´10˝/180; d4.18; Mil 1944–45; M5/C1; Col Oregon																								
1938	†NY A	127	458	83	117	24	7	25	97	56	3	72	.255	.340	.502	109	3	11-3	.960	**21**	**116**	115	2b126	—	3.0
1939	†NY A★	151	567	92	161	32	5	28	111	75	2	57	.284	.370	.506	124	19	11-10	.967	8	102	**135**	2b151	—	3.3
1940	NY A★	**155**	616	112	173	32	10	30	103	52	3	57	.281	.340	.511	122	16	18-8	.975	14	105	116	2b155	—	3.8
1941	†NY A★	**156**	588	104	162	26	7	24	87	72	4	80	.276	.358	.466	118	14	10-9	.958	9	102	**134**	2b131,1b30	0	2.7
1942	†NY A★	147	538	88	173	29	4	18	103	79	1	95	.322	.409	.491	156	42	12-6	.966	6	98	**146**	2b147	0	5.8
1943	†NY A☆	152	543	82	135	28	5	17	69	98	2	75	.249	.365	.413	126	21	4-7	.969	25	**107**	**117**	2b152	0	5.6
1946	NY A★	112	376	35	79	15	0	11	47	49	4	72	.210	.308	.338	79	-10	2-5	.974	18	**109**	120	2b108	0	1.3
1947	Cle A★	155	562	89	153	27	6	29	93	62	1	49	.272	.346	.496	136	24	7-3	.978	-6	101	106	2b155	0	2.8
1948	†Cle A★	144	550	96	154	21	4	32	124	77	3	68	.280	.371	.507	136	26	5-2	.971	-8	100	103	2b144,S2	0	2.5
1949	Cle A★	148	541	74	136	18	3	20	84	83	4	33	.251	.355	.407	103	2	5-6	.980	-17	97	115	2b145	0	-0.7
1950	Cle A	119	368	59	87	12	1	19	57	56	2	44	.236	.340	.429	99	-2	4-1	.969	-18	91	88	2b105	0	-1.3
Total	11	1566	5707	914	1530	264	52	253	975	759	29	702	.268	.357	.466	121	155	89-60	.970	51	103	118	2b1519,1b30,S2	0	28.8
GORDON, KEITH	Keith Bradley; B1.22.1969 Bethesda MD; BR/TR/6´1˝/205; [CinN90 2/47]; d7.9; Col Wright St.																								
1993	Cin N	3	6	0	1	0	0	0	0	0-0	0	2	.167	.167	.167	-10	-1	0-0	1.000	-0	89	0	O2L	0	-0.1
GORDON, MIKE	Michael William; B9.11.1953 Leominster MA; BB/TR/6´3˝/(210–215); [ChiN72 3/63]; d4.7																								
1977	Chi N	8	23	0	1	0	0	0	2	2-0	0	8	.043	.120	.043	-49	-5	0-0	.970	-3	55	38	C8	0	-0.8
1978	Chi N	4	5	0	1	0	0	0	0	3-1	1	2	.200	.556	.200	106	1	0-0	1.000	0	81	0	C4	0	0.1
Total	2	12	28	0	2	0	0	0	2	5-1	1	10	.071	.235	.071	-11	-4	0-0	.979	-3	62	28	C12	0	-0.7
GORDON, SID	Sidney; B8.13.1917 Brooklyn NY; D6.17.1975 New York NY; BR/TR/5´10˝/(180–185); d9.11; Mil 1944–45; Col Long Island–Brooklyn																								
1941	NY N	9	31	4	8	1	1	0	4	6	0	1	.258	.378	.355	105	0	0	1.000	-1	97	0	O9(3/6/0)	0	0.0
1942	NY N	6	19	4	6	0	1	0	2	3	0	2	.316	.409	.421	142	1	0	.913	1	109	0	3b6	0	0.2
1943	NY N	131	474	50	119	9	11	9	63	43	1	32	.251	.315	.373	98	-4	2	.941	2	106	117	3b53,1b41,O28L,2b3	0	-0.6
1946	NY N	135	450	64	132	15	4	5	45	60	3	27	.293	.380	.378	115	11	1	.995	1	95	91	O101L,3b30	0	0.4
1947	NY N	130	437	57	119	19	8	13	57	50	0	21	.272	.347	.442	107	4	2	.971	-1	96	142	O124L,3b2	0	-0.6
1948	NY N☆	142	521	100	156	26	4	30	107	74	3	39	.299	.390	.537	148	35	8	**.948**	-3	97	99	3b115,O23(18/0/2)	0	3.0
1949	NY N★	141	489	87	139	26	2	26	90	95	3	37	.284	.404	.505	142	33	1	.958	-18	84	79	3b123,O15(3/0/12)/1	0	1.4
1950	Bos N	134	481	78	146	33	4	27	103	78	2	31	.304	.403	.557	160	44	2	.990	3	105	87	O123L,3b10	0	3.6
1951	Bos N	150	550	96	158	28	1	29	109	80	5	32	.287	.383	.500	146	37	2-0	.984	-5	101	38	O122(103/0/23),3b34	0	2.4
1952	Bos N	144	522	69	151	22	2	25	75	77	3	49	.289	.384	.483	144	33	0-4	**.996**	-1	98	88	O142L,3b2	0	2.1
1953	Mil N	140	464	67	127	22	4	19	75	71	2	40	.274	.372	.461	123	18	1-1	.977	2	106	99	O137L	0	1.2
1954	Pit N	131	363	38	111	12	0	12	49	67	0	24	.306	.405	.438	124	16	0-0	.977	2	100	165	O73(8/0/66),3b40	0	1.5
1955	Pit N	16	47	2	8	1	0	0	1	2-0	0	6	.170	.204	.191	6	-6	0-0	1.000	2	132	238	3b8,O4L	0	-0.5
	NY N	66	144	19	35	6	1	7	25	25-2	0	15	.243	.349	.444	110	3	0-0	1.000	6	110	121	3b31,O17(12/0/5)	0	0.7
	Year	82	191	21	43	7	1	7	26	27-2	0	21	.225	.317	.382	86	-4	0-0	1.000	7	115	149	3b39,O21(16/0/5)	0	0.2
Total	13	1475	4992	735	1415	220	43	202	805	731-2	22	356	.283	.377	.466	130	225	19-5	.985	-10	100	98	O918(806/6/108),3b454,1b42,2b3	0	14.8
GORE, GEORGE	George F. "Piano Legs"; B5.3.1857 Saccarappa ME; D9.16.1933 Utica NY; BL/TR/5´11˝/195; d5.1; M1																								
1879	Chi N	63	266	43	70	17	4	0	32	8	—	30	.263	.285	.357	104	1	—	.872	-3	73	0	O54(0/48/6),1b9	—	-0.4
1880	Chi N	77	322	70	116	23	2	2	47	21	—	10	**.360**	**.399**	**.463**	**180**	**27**	—	.879	2	100	142	O74(0/73/1),1b7	—	2.5
1881	Chi N	73	309	**86**	92	18	9	1	44	27	—	23	.298	.354	.424	137	13	—	.874	1	110	114	O72C/31	—	1.0
1882	Chi N	**84**	367	**99**	117	15	7	3	51	**29**	—	19	.319	.369	.422	146	19	—	.842	3	122	143	O84C	—	1.7
1883	Chi N	92	392	105	131	30	9	2	52	27	—	13	.334	.377	.472	144	20	—	.867	9	130	117	O92C	—	2.2
1884	Chi N	103	422	104	134	18	4	5	34	**61**	—	26	.318	.404	.415	146	24	—	.868	-1	116	141	O103(0/103/1)	—	1.8
1885	†Chi N	109	441	115	138	21	13	5	57	68	—	25	.313	.405	.454	156	28	—	.884	-5	83	80	O109(1/108/0)	—	1.8
1886	†Chi N	118	444	150	135	20	12	6	63	**102**	—	30	.304	.434	.444	146	28	23	.876	-6	85	124	O118(0/115/3)	—	1.6

YEAR	TM LG	G	AB	R	H	2B	3B	HR	RBI	BB-IB	HP	SO	AVG	OBP	SLG	AOPS	ABR	SB-CS	FA	FR	RNG	THR	GAMES AT POSITION	DL	BFW
1887	NY N	111	459	95	133	16	5	1	49	42	7	18	.290	.358	.353	103	5	39	.889	0	103	210	O111C	—	0.1
1888	†NY N	64	254	37	56	4	4	2	17	30	2	31	.220	.308	.291	93	-1	11	.836	-10	37	0	O64(42/21/1)	—	-1.2
1889	†NY N	120	488	132	149	21	7	7	54	84	8	28	.305	.416	.420	132	26	28	.864	-8	92	122	O120(0/118/3)	—	1.2
1890	NY P	93	399	132	127	26	8	10	55	77	3	23	.318	.432	.499	136	22	28	.877	-13	62	87	O93(52/33/10)	—	0.5
1891	NY N	130	528	103	150	22	7	2	48	74	7	34	.284	.379	.364	122	19	19	.909	-11	78	86	O130(1/127/3)	—	0.3
1892	NY N	53	193	47	49	11	2	0	11	49	3	16	.254	.412	.332	127	11	20	.932	0	93	107	O53(0/50/3)	—	0.7
	StL N	20	73	9	15	0	1	0	4	18	0	6	.205	.363	.233	85	0	2	.844	-2	99	0	O20C,M	—	-0.3
	Year	73	266	56	64	11	3	0	15	67	3	22	.241	.399	.305	116	11	22	.908	-1	95	79	O73(0/70/3)	—	0.4
Total	14	1310	5357	1327	1612	262	94	46	618	717	30	332	.301	.386	.411	134	242	170	.876	-42	93	109	O1297(96/1175/31),1b17/3	—	13.5
GORINSKI, BOB	Robert John; B1.7.1952 Latrobe PA; BR/TR/6´3˝/210; [MinA70 1/22]; d4.10																								
1977	Min A	54	118	14	23	4	1	3	22	5-0	0	29	.195	.226	.322	48	-9	1-0	.936	-3	87	0	O37(30/0/7),D9	0	-1.3
GORMAN, HERB	Herbert Allen; B12.19.1924 San Francisco CA; D4.5.1953 San Diego CA; BL/TL/5´11˝/180; d4.19																								
1952	StL N	1	1	0	0	0	0	0	0	0	0	0	.000	.000	.000	-99	0	0-0	ø	0	—	—	/H	0	0.0
GORMAN, HOWIE	Howard Paul "Lefty"; B5.14.1913 Pittsburgh PA; D4.29.1984 Harrisburg PA; BL/TL/6´2˝/160; d8.7																								
1937	Phi N	13	19	3	4	1	0	0	1	1	0	1	.211	.250	.263	37	-2	1	.500	-1	26	0	O7R	—	-0.3
1938	Phi N	1	1	0	0	0	0	0	0	0	0	0	.000	.000	.000	-99	0	0	ø	0	—	—	/H	—	0.0
Total	2	14	20	3	4	1	0	0	1	1	0	1	.200	.238	.250	30	-2	1	.500	-1	26	0	O7R	—	-0.3
GORMAN, JACK	John F. "Stooping Jack"; B1859 St.Louis MO; D9.9.1889 St.Louis MO; d7.1; ▲																								
1883	StL AA	1	4	0	0	0	0	0	—	0	—	—	.000	.000	.000	-95	-1	—	.667	0	349	0	/lf	—	-0.1
1884	KC U	8	31	3	4	1	0	0	—	0	—	—	.129	.129	.161	-14	-5	—	.579	-1	60	0	3b4,O4L	—	-0.6
	Pit AA	8	27	3	4	0	1	0	—	1	0	—	.148	.179	.222	30	-2	—	.750	-1	120	0	P3,O3(0/1/2),3b2	—	-0.2
Total	2	17	62	6	8	1	1	0	—	1	0	—	.129	.143	.177	0	-8	—	.933	-2	128	302	O8(5/1/2),3b6,P3	—	-0.9
GORMAN, TOM	Thomas; B St.Louis MO; BL/TL; d6.10																								
1884	KC U	25	106	22	34	4	2	0	—	4	—	—	.321	.345	.396	143	3	—	.954	-1	56	70	1b24/lf	—	-0.1
GORYL, JOHNNY	John Albert; B10.21.1933 Cumberland RI; BR/TR/5´10˝/(170–175); d9.20; M2/C13																								
1957	Chi N	9	38	7	8	2	0	0	1	5-0	1	9	.211	.318	.263	59	-2	0-1	.952	-1	88	237	3b9	0	-0.3
1958	Chi N	83	219	27	53	9	3	4	14	27-2	2	34	.242	.331	.365	85	-4	0-1	.931	6	108	160	3b44,2b35	0	0.2
1959	Chi N	25	48	1	9	3	1	1	6	5-0	0	3	.188	.264	.354	63	-3	1-1	.973	-3	99	18	2b11,3b4	0	-0.5
1962	Min A	37	26	6	5	0	1	2	2	2-0	0	6	.192	.250	.500	93	-1	0-0	.923	1	177	75	2b4/S	0	0.0
1963	Min A	64	150	29	43	5	3	9	24	15-4	1	29	.287	.353	.540	144	8	0-0	.958	-8	87	87	2b34,3b11,S7	0	0.4
1964	Min A	58	114	9	16	0	2	0	1	10-2	1	25	.140	.216	.175	10	-14	1-0	.975	4	109	64	2b28,3b13	0	-0.9
Total	6	276	595	79	134	19	10	16	48	64-8	5	106	.225	.305	.371	83	-16	2-3	.960	-1	101	72	2b112,3b81,S8	0	-1.1
GOSGER, JIM	James Charles; B11.6.1942 Port Huron MI; BL/TL/5´11˝/(178–185); d5.4; Col St. Clair Co. (MI) CC																								
1963	Bos A	19	16	3	1	0	0	0	0	3-0	0	5	.063	.211	.063	-19	-3	0-0	.818	0	168	0	O4(0/2/2)	0	-0.3
1965	Bos A	81	324	45	83	15	4	9	35	29-1	2	61	.256	.318	.410	100	0	3-1	.975	5	116	104	O81(0/61/22)	0	0.2
1966	Bos A	40	126	16	32	4	0	5	17	15-0	0	20	.254	.333	.405	101	0	0-1	.985	-3	95	0	O32(0/29/4)	0	-0.4
	KC A	88	272	34	61	14	1	5	27	37-1	2	53	.224	.321	.338	93	-1	5-3	.994	1	107	67	O77(47/33/1)	0	-0.4
	Year	128	398	50	93	18	1	10	44	52-1	2	73	.234	.325	.359	96	-1	5-4	.991	-2	103	47	O109(47/62/5)	0	-0.8
1967	KC A	134	356	31	86	14	5	5	36	53-8	0	69	.242	.337	.351	108	5	5-7	.981	4	112	97	O113(54/30/40)	0	0.3
1968	Oak A	88	150	7	27	1	1	0	5	17-8	0	21	.180	.262	.200	44	-10	4-0	1.000	5	111	176	O64(39/26/4)	0	-0.8
1969	Sea A	39	55	4	6	2	1	1	1	6-0	0	11	.109	.197	.236	21	-6	2-1	1.000	1	113	112	O26(1/24/1)	0	-0.6
	NY N	10	15	0	2	2	0	0	1	1-1	0	6	.133	.188	.267	25	-1	0-0	1.000	-0	78	0	O5(4/1/0)	0	-0.2
1970	Mon N	91	274	38	72	11	2	5	37	35-3	1	35	.263	.348	.372	93	-2	5-3	1.000	1	104	149	O71(21/50/4),1b19	0	-0.4
1971	Mon N	51	102	7	16	2	2	0	8	9-0	1	17	.157	.230	.216	27	-10	1-1	.952	1	96	79	O23(20/6/1),1b6	30	-1.1
1973	NY N	38	92	9	22	2	0	0	10	9-2	0	16	.239	.304	.261	59	-5	0-1	1.000	-3	85	0	O35(21/18/0)	0	-0.9
1974	NY N	26	33	3	3	0	0	0	0	3-1	0	2	.091	.167	.091	-27	-6	0-0	1.000	-2	68	0	O24(9/11/4)	0	-0.8
Total	10	705	1815	197	411	67	16	30	177	217-25	6	316	.226	.309	.331	83	-39	25-18	.985	10	107	92	O555(216/291/83),1b25	30	-5.4
GOSLIN, GOOSE	Leon Allen; B10.16.1900 Salem NJ; D5.15.1971 Bridgeton NJ; BL/TR/5´11.5˝/185; d9.16; HF1968																								
1921	Was A	14	50	8	13	1	1	1	6	6	1	5	.260	.351	.380	91	-1	0-0	1.000	1	123	55	O14(1/0/14)	—	-0.1
1922	Was A	101	358	44	116	19	7	3	53	25	3	26	.324	.373	.441	117	8	4-4	.932	-3	103	70	O92(88/0/5)	—	-0.2
1923	Was A	150	600	86	180	29	**18**	9	99	40	3	53	.300	.347	.453	115	9	7-2	.957	4	97	141	O149L	—	0.1
1924	†Was A	154	579	100	199	30	17	12	**129**	68	9	29	.344	.421	.516	145	39	15-14	.960	4	111	74	O154L	—	2.8
1925	†Was A	150	601	116	201	34	**20**	18	113	53	6	50	.334	.394	.547	140	33	27-8	.971	14	**112**	139	O150(140/20/0)	—	3.5
1926	Was A	147	568	105	201	26	15	17	108	63	7	38	.354	.425	.542	155	45	8-8	.964	14	107	**168**	O147(86/61/0)	—	4.6
1927	Was A	148	581	96	194	37	15	13	120	50	5	28	.334	.392	.516	136	29	21-6	.955	-2	106	51	O148(146/2/0)	—	1.6
1928	Was A	135	456	80	173	36	10	17	102	48	3	19	**.379**	.442	.614	176	51	16-3	.962	8	109	128	O125(125/0/2)	—	4.9
1929	Was A	145	553	82	159	28	7	18	91	66	2	33	.288	.366	.461	111	9	11-3	.968	-6	98	50	O142L	—	-0.7
1930	Was A	47	188	34	51	11	5	7	38	19	2	19	.271	.344	.495	110	2	3-2	.937	-4	83	61	O47L	—	-0.5
	StL A	101	396	81	129	25	7	30	100	48	1	35	.326	.400	.652	156	32	14-9	.973	9	111	163	O101L	—	2.9
	Year	148	584	115	180	36	12	37	138	67	3	54	.308	.382	.601	142	35	17-11	.964	5	103	133	O148L	—	2.4
1931	StL A	151	591	114	194	42	10	24	105	80	4	41	.328	.412	.555	147	41	9-6	.960	2	101	127	O151L	—	3.2
1932	StL A	150	572	88	171	28	9	17	104	92	2	35	.299	.398	.469	117	16	12-9	.951	5	102	139	O149(148/1/0)/3	—	1.1
1933	†Was A	132	549	97	163	35	10	10	64	42	1	32	.297	.348	.452	112	7	5-2	.965	5	100	140	O128(3/0/125)	—	0.4
1934	†Det A	151	614	106	187	38	7	13	100	65	2	38	.305	.373	.453	112	11	5-4	.953	0	98	124	O149(145/0/4)	—	0.2
1935	†Det A	147	590	88	172	34	6	9	109	56	2	31	.292	.355	.415	102	1	5-4	.965	0	108	51	O144(128/0/18)	—	-0.6
1936	Det A★	147	572	122	180	33	8	24	125	85	0	50	.315	.403	.526	127	25	14-4	.955	-4	95	93	O144L	—	1.3
1937	Det A	79	181	30	43	11	1	4	35	35	2	18	.238	.367	.376	86	-3	0-1	.954	-2	97	65	O40(39/0/1)/1	—	-0.7
1938	Was A	38	57	6	9	3	0	2	8	8	0	5	.158	.262	.316	47	-5	0-0	1.000	0	114	0	O13(12/0/1)	—	-0.5
Total	18	2287	8656	1483	2735	500	173	248	1609	949	55	585	.316	.387	.500	128	349	176-89	.960	44	103	108	O2187(1949/84/170)/13	—	23.3
GOSS, HOWIE	Howard Wayne; B11.1.1934 Wewoka OK; D7.31.1996 Reno NV; BR/TR/6´4˝/(202–204); d4.10; Col Bakersfield (CA) JC																								
1962	Pit N	89	111	19	27	6	0	2	10	9-0	1	36	.243	.306	.351	76	-4	5-2	.985	0	99	87	O66(47/18/6)	0	-0.5
1963	Hou N	133	411	37	86	18	2	9	44	31-2	0	128	.209	.264	.328	74	-14	4-6	.993	4	109	97	O123C	0	-1.6
Total	2	222	522	56	113	24	2	11	54	40-2	1	164	.216	.273	.333	75	-18	9-8	.991	5	107	95	O189(47/141/6)	0	-2.1
GOSSETT, DICK	John Star; B8.21.1890 Dennison OH; D10.6.1962 Massillon OH; BR/TR/5´11˝/185; d4.30																								
1913	NY A	39	105	9	17	2	0	0	9	10	3	22	.162	.254	.181	28	-9	1	.972	-6	*66*	*116*	C38	—	-1.4
1914	NY A	10	21	3	3	0	0	0	1	5	1	5	.143	.333	.143	44	-1	0	.977	-1	*87*	*54*	C10	—	-0.1
Total	2	49	126	12	20	2	0	0	10	15	4	27	.159	.269	.175	31	-10	1	.973	-7	*70*	*104*	C48	—	-1.5
GOTAY, JULIO	Julio Enrique (Sanchez); B6.9.1939 Fajardo, PR; BR/TR/6´0˝/180; d8.6																								
1960	StL N	3	8	1	3	0	0	0	0	0-0	0	2	.375	.375	.375	98	0	1-0	.750	-1	60	0	S2/3	0	-0.1
1961	StL N	10	45	5	11	4	0	0	5	3-1	0	5	.244	.292	.333	59	-2	0-0	.804	-4	83	90	S10	0	-0.6
1962	StL N	127	369	47	94	12	1	2	27	27-6	6	47	.255	.316	.309	62	-19	7-3	.956	11	109	108	S120,2b8,O2L/3	0	0.2
1963	Pit N	4	2	0	1	0	0	0	0	0-0	0	0	.500	.500	.500	188	0	0-0	.667	-0	0	0	/2	0	0.0
1964	Pit N	3	2	1	1	0	0	0	0	1-0	0	0	.500	.667	.500	235	1	0-0	ø	0	—	—	/H	0	0.1
1965	Cal A	40	77	6	19	4	0	1	3	4-2	0	9	.247	.284	.338	78	-2	0-0	.961	2	122	85	2b23,3b9/S	0	-0.1
1966	Hou N	4	5	0	0	0	0	0	0	0-0	0	0	.000	.000	.000	-99	-1	0-0	1.000	0	221	0	/3	0	-0.1
1967	Hou N	77	234	30	66	10	2	2	15	15-1	2	30	.282	.329	.368	103	1	1-1	.971	-2	90	90	2b30,S20,3b3	0	0.3
1968	Hou N	75	165	9	41	3	0	1	11	4-0	1	21	.248	.271	.285	68	-7	1-2	.982	6	95	113	2b48/3	0	0.3
1969	Hou N	46	81	7	21	5	0	0	9	7-1	0	13	.259	.318	.321	81	-2	2-1	.987	5	108	138	2b16/3	0	0.4
Total	10	389	988	106	257	38	3	6	70	61-11	9	127	.260	.309	.323	75	-31	12-7	.944	17	106	101	S153,2b126,3b17,O2L	0	0.6
GOTAY, RUBEN	Ruben A.; B12.25.1982 Rio Piedras, PR; BB/TR/5´11˝/(160–175); [KCA00 31/914]; d8.3; Col Indian Hills (IA) CC																								
2004	KC A	44	152	17	41	7	3	1	16	9-0	2	36	.270	.315	.375	80	-5	0-1	.983	-9	86	100	2b42	0	-1.2
2005	KC A	86	282	32	64	14	2	5	29	22-0	4	51	.227	.288	.344	71	-12	2-2	.980	4	103	84	2b81,D2	0	-0.5
Total	2	130	434	49	105	21	5	6	45	31-0	6	87	.242	.297	.355	74	-17	2-3	.981	-5	97	90	2b123,D2	0	-1.7

YEAR	TM LG	G	AB	R	H	2B	3B	HR	RBI	BB-IB	HP	SO	AVG	OBP	SLG	AOPS	ABR	SB-CS	FA	FR	RNG	THR	GAMES AT POSITION	DL	BFW
GOULD, CHARLIE	Charles Harvey; B8.21.1847 Cincinnati OH; D4.9.1917 Flushing NY; BR/TR/6´0˝/172; d5.5; M2																								
1871	Bos NA	**31**	151	38	43	9	2	2	32	3	—	1	.285	.299	.411	98	-1	6-2	.906	-4	62	**160**	1b30/rf	—	-0.2
1872	Bos NA	45	212	40	54	9	**8**	0	32	2	—	3	.255	.262	.373	88	-5	0-0	.933	-0	**116**	**251**	1b44,O2R	—	-0.3
1874	Bal NA	33	143	19	32	6	0	0	14	2	—	2	.224	.234	.266	60	-6	1-0	.951	0	68	86	1b32/C	—	-0.4
1875	NH NA	27	109	9	29	4	1	0	8	1	—	2	.266	.273	.321	121	3	0-1	.946	-4	58	69	1b26/CrfM	—	0.0
1876	Cin N	61	258	27	65	7	0	0	11	6	—	11	.252	.269	.279	97	2	—	.939	1	122	114	1b61,P2,M	—	0.0
1877	Cin N	24	91	5	25	2	1	0	13	5	—	5	.275	.313	.319	112	2	—	.922	-1	124	99	1b24/lf	—	0.0
Total	4NA	136	615	106	158	28	11	2	86	8	—	8	.257	.266	.348	90	-9	7-3	.934	-7	81	154	1b132,O4R,C2	—	-0.9
Total	2	85	349	32	90	9	1	0	24	11	—	16	.258	.281	.289	101	4	—	.934	0	123	110	1b85,P2/lf	—	0.0
GOULISH, NICK	Nicholas Edward; B11.13.1916 Punxsutawney PA; D5.15.1984 Youngstown OH; BL/TL/6´1˝/179; d4.19																								
1944	Phi N	1	1	0	0	0	0	0	0	0	0	0	.000	.000	.000	-99	0	0	ø	0	—	—	/H		
1945	Phi N	13	11	4	3	0	0	0	2	1	0	3	.273	.333	.273	72	0	0	1.000	-0	69	0	O2(1/0/1)	0	0.0
Total	2	14	12	4	3	0	0	0	2	1	0	3	.250	.308	.250	58	0	0	1.000	-0	69	0	O2(1/0/1)	0	-0.1
GOUZZIE, CLAUDE	Claude; B1873 , France; D9.21.1907 Denver CO; BR/TR/5´9˝/170; d7.22																								
1903	StL A	1	1	0	0	0	0	0	0	0	0	—	.000	.000	.000	-99	0	0	1.000	0	149	0	/2	—	0.0
GOWDY, HANK	Henry Morgan; B8.24.1889 Columbus OH; D8.1.1966 Columbus OH; BR/TR/6´2˝/182; d9.13; Mil 1917–19; M1/C18																								
1910	NY N	7	14	1	3	1	0	0	2	2	0	3	.214	.313	.286	75	0	1	.943	0	152	52	1b5	—	0.0
1911	NY N	4	4	1	1	1	0	0	0	2	0	0	.250	.500	.500	175	1	0	1.000	-0	0	0	1b2	—	0.0
	Bos N	29	97	9	28	4	2	0	16	4	1	19	.289	.324	.371	87	-2	2	.966	-2	88	56	1b26/C	—	-0.4
	Year	33	101	10	29	5	2	0	16	6	1	19	.287	.333	.376	92	-1	2	.969	-2	83	53	1b28/C	—	-0.4
1912	Bos N	44	96	16	26	6	1	3	10	16	2	13	.271	.386	.448	126	4	3	.926	-3	*91*	*108*	C22,1b7	—	0.3
1913	Bos N	3	5	0	3	1	0	0	2	3	0	2	.600	.750	.800	336	2	0	1.000	-1	108	0	C2	—	0.2
1914	†Bos N	128	366	42	89	17	6	3	46	48	4	40	.243	.337	.347	104	3	14	.968	3	***133***	*93*	C115,1b9	—	1.6
1915	Bos N	118	316	27	78	15	3	2	30	41	3	34	.247	.339	.332	108	5	10-4	.974	6	***138***	*104*	C114	—	2.3
1916	Bos N	118	349	32	88	14	1	1	34	24	6	33	.252	.311	.307	94	-2	8	.980	15	**171**	93	C116	—	2.6
1917	Bos N	49	154	12	33	7	0	0	14	15	1	13	.214	.288	.260	73	-4	2	.969	1	*110*	*120*	C49	—	0.1
1919	Bos N	78	219	18	61	8	1	1	22	19	1	16	.279	.339	.338	108	3	5	.977	4	*101*	*113*	C74/1	—	1.3
1920	Bos N	80	214	14	52	11	2	0	18	20	2	15	.243	.314	.313	84	-4	6-1	.980	10	*114*	*130*	C74	—	1.3
1921	Bos N	64	164	17	49	7	2	2	17	16	2	11	.299	.368	.402	110	3	2-0	.981	-0	*110*	*107*	C53	—	0.6
1922	Bos N	92	221	23	70	11	1	1	27	24	3	13	.317	.391	.389	107	4	2-1	.971	-0	*99*	*131*	C72/1	—	0.7
1923	Bos N	23	48	5	6	1	1	0	5	15	2	5	.125	.354	.188	48	-3	1-1	.982	-1	*80*	*98*	C15	—	-0.3
	†NY N	53	122	13	40	6	3	1	18	21	0	9	.328	.427	.451	133	7	2-0	.986	-3	*149*	*59*	C43	—	0.7
	Year	76	170	18	46	7	4	1	23	36	2	14	.271	.404	.376	109	5	3-1	.985	-4	*128*	*71*	C58	—	0.4
1924	†NY N	87	191	25	62	9	1	4	37	26	2	11	.325	.411	.445	133	10	1-0	.982	1	*110*	*89*	C78	—	1.6
1925	NY N	47	114	14	37	4	3	3	19	12	0	7	.325	.389	.491	128	5	0-0	1.000	1	*92*	*112*	C41	—	0.7
1929	Bos N	10	16	1	7	0	0	0	3	0	0	2	.438	.438	.438	122	1	0	1.000	0	*101*	*68*	C9	—	0.1
1930	Bos N	16	25	0	5	1	0	0	2	3	1	1	.200	.310	.240	37	-2	0	.972	0	*100*	*85*	C15	—	-0.2
Total	17	1050	2735	270	738	124	27	21	322	311	30	247	.270	.351	.358	105	31	59-7	.975	31	*124*	*104*	C893,1b51	—	13.2
GRABARKEWITZ, BILLY	Billy Cordell; B1.18.1946 Lockhart TX; BR/TR/5´10˝/170; [LAN66 12/239]; d4.22; Col St. Marys (TX)																								
1969	LA N	34	65	4	6	1	1	0	5	4-1	0	19	.092	.145	.138	-22	-11	1-0	.954	-6	87	46	S18,3b6,2b3	0	-1.6
1970	LA N★	156	529	92	153	20	8	17	84	95-8	6	149	.289	.399	.454	134	30	19-9	.959	-10	103	116	3b97,S50,2b20	0	2.6
1971	LA N	44	71	9	16	5	0	0	6	19-0	0	16	.225	.389	.296	101	2	1-2	1.000	4	110	127	2b13,3b10/S	72	0.7
1972	LA N	53	144	17	24	4	0	4	16	18-1	2	53	.167	.265	.278	56	-8	3-0	.902	-3	88	32	3b24,2b19,S2	15	-1.0
1973	Cal A	61	129	27	21	6	1	3	9	28-0	1	27	.163	.316	.295	78	-3	2-2	.965	-3	94	95	2b18,3b12/SlfD	0	-0.5
	Phi N	25	66	12	19	2	0	2	7	12-0	0	18	.288	.397	.409	120	2	3-1	.960	3	105	134	2b20,3b3/rf	0	0.6
1974	Phi N	34	30	7	4	0	0	1	2	5-0	0	10	.133	.257	.233	36	-3	3-1	1.000	-0	93	0	O5L/3	0	-0.3
	Chi N	53	125	21	31	3	2	1	12	21-2	1	28	.248	.358	.328	90	-1	1-2	.954	-2	100	34	2b45,S7,3b6	0	-0.1
	Year	87	155	28	35	3	2	2	14	26-2	1	38	.226	.339	.310	79	-4	4-3	.954	-3	100	34	2b45,3b7,S7,O5L	0	-0.4
1975	Oak A	6	2	0	0	0	0	0	0	0-0	0	1	.000	.000	.000	-99	-1	0-0	.833	0	106	0	2b4/D	0	0.0
Total	7	466	1161	189	274	41	12	28	141	202-12	10	321	.236	.351	.364	100	7	33-17	.952	-17	101	105	3b159,2b142,S79,O7(6/0/1),D6	87	0.4
GRABER, ROD	Rodney Blaine; B6.20.1930 Massillon OH; BL/TL/5´11˝/175; d9.9																								
1958	Cle A	4	8	0	1	0	0	0	0	1-0	0	2	.125	.222	.125	-2	-1	0-0	1.000	-0	95	0	O2C	0	-0.1
GRABOWSKI, JASON	Jason William; B5.24.1976 New Haven CT; BL/TR/6´3˝/200; [TexA97 2/75]; d9.22; Col Connecticut																								
2002	Oak A	4	8	3	3	1	1	0	1	3-0	0	1	.375	.545	.750	241	2	0-0	1.000	-0	96	0	O4L	0	0.2
2003	Oak A	8	8	0	0	0	0	0	0	1-0	0	5	.000	.111	.000	-67	-2	0-0	1.000	0	185	0	O3R/3D	0	-0.2
2004	†LA N	113	173	18	38	7	0	7	20	19-0	0	50	.220	.297	.382	75	-7	0-0	.977	-2	90	0	O31(30/0/3),1b3,D3	0	-1.0
2005	LA N	65	112	14	18	0	0	4	12	10-1	0	29	.161	.228	.268	30	-12	1-0	.974	-2	85	78	O32(28/0/4),1b3	20	-1.5
Total	4	190	301	35	59	8	1	11	33	33-1	0	85	.196	.275	.339	59	-19	1-0	.978	-4	90	33	O70(62/0/10),1b6,D4/3	20	-2.5
GRABOWSKI, JOHNNY	John Patrick "Nig"; B1.7.1900 Ware MA; D5.23.1946 Albany NY; BR/TR/5´10˝/185; d7.11																								
1924	Chi A	20	56	10	14	3	0	0	3	2	0	4	.250	.276	.304	51	-4	0-0	.972	1	*77*	*158*	C19	—	-0.3
1925	Chi A	21	46	5	14	4	1	0	10	2	0	4	.304	.333	.435	99	0	0-1	.983	0	*172*	*85*	C21	—	0.1
1926	Chi A	48	122	6	32	1	1	1	11	4	0	15	.262	.286	.311	58	-8	0-1	.973	-1	*129*	*91*	C38/1	—	-0.8
1927	†NY A	70	195	29	54	2	4	0	25	20	2	15	.277	.350	.328	79	-6	0-0	.984	2	*104*	*67*	C68	—	-0.1
1928	NY A	75	202	21	48	7	1	1	21	10	0	21	.238	.274	.297	51	-15	0-0	.987	0	*94*	*81*	C75	—	-1.0
1929	NY A	22	59	4	12	1	0	0	2	3	0	6	.203	.242	.220	21	-7	1-0	.943	-1	*112*	*71*	C22	—	-0.6
1931	Det A	40	136	9	32	7	1	1	14	6	0	19	.235	.268	.324	53	-10	0-0	.984	0	*76*	*123*	C39	—	-0.7
Total	7	296	816	84	206	25	8	3	86	47	2	84	.252	.295	.314	60	-50	1-2	.979	1	*103*	*91*	C282/1	—	-3.4
GRACE, JOE	Joseph Laverne; B1.5.1914 Gorham IL; D9.18.1969 Murphysboro IL; BL/TR/6´1˝/180; d9.24; Mil 1942–45																								
1938	StL A	12	47	7	16	1	0	0	4	2	0	3	.340	.367	.362	83	-1	0-1	.933	-1	75	126	O12R	—	-0.3
1939	StL A	74	207	35	63	11	2	3	22	19	0	24	.304	.363	.420	98	-1	3-2	.968	1	82	265	O53(10/22/21)	—	-0.2
1940	StL A	80	229	45	59	14	2	5	25	26	1	23	.258	.336	.402	88	-4	2-2	.958	-2	89	153	O51(3/0/48),C12	—	-0.8
1941	StL A	115	362	53	112	17	4	6	60	57	5	31	.309	.410	.428	118	12	1-3	.983	0	95	157	O88R,C9	0	0.6
1946	StL A	48	161	21	37	7	2	1	13	16	2	20	.230	.307	.317	71	-6	1-3	.967	1	99	159	O43R	0	-0.7
	Was A	77	321	39	97	17	4	2	31	24	4	19	.302	.358	.399	118	7	1-4	.959	-1	101	65	O74(60/0/14)	0	-0.1
	Year	125	482	60	134	24	6	3	44	40	6	39	.278	.341	.371	101	0	2-7	.962	0	100	96	O117(60/0/57)	0	-0.8
1947	Was A	78	234	25	58	9	4	3	17	35	1	15	.248	.348	.359	99	0	1-2	.976	2	109	87	O67(56/3/8)	0	-0.2
Total	6	484	1561	225	442	76	18	20	172	179	13	135	.283	.362	.393	102	7	9-17	.969	1	97	135	O388(129/25/234),C21	0	-1.7
GRACE, MARK	Mark Eugene; B6.28.1964 Winston–Salem NC; BL/TL/6´2˝/(190–200); [ChiN85 24/624]; d5.2; Col San Diego St.																								
1988	Chi N	134	486	65	144	23	4	7	57	60-5	0	43	.296	.371	.403	117	13	3-3	.987	-4	92	93	1b133	0	-0.1
1989	†Chi N	142	510	74	160	28	3	13	79	80-13	0	42	.314	.405	.457	137	28	14-7	.996	12	**128**	95	1b142	18	3.2
1990	Chi N	157	589	72	182	32	1	9	82	59-5	5	54	.309	.372	.413	109	10	15-6	.992	**25**	**156**	103	1b153	0	2.6
1991	Chi N	**160**	619	87	169	28	5	8	58	70-7	3	53	.273	.346	.373	99	1	3-4	.995	17	**134**	95	1b160	0	0.5
1992	Chi N	158	603	72	185	37	5	9	79	72-8	4	36	.307	.380	.430	126	24	6-1	.998	6	112	102	1b157	0	2.1
1993	Chi N★	155	594	86	193	39	4	14	98	71-14	1	32	.325	.393	.475	133	31	8-4	.997	1	101	112	1b154	0	1.9
1994	Chi N	106	403	55	120	23	3	6	44	48-5	0	41	.298	.370	.414	105	4	0-1	.993	-1	98	108	1b103	0	-0.6
1995	Chi N★	143	552	97	180	**51**	3	16	92	65-9	2	46	.326	.395	.516	139	34	6-2	.995	1	102	81	1b143	0	2.2
1996	Chi N	142	547	88	181	39	1	9	75	62-8	1	41	.331	.396	.455	121	19	2-3	.997	0	100	110	1b141	17	0.6
1997	Chi N★	151	555	87	177	32	5	13	78	88-3	2	45	.319	.409	.465	125	25	2-4	.995	5	108	79	1b148	15	1.5
1998	†Chi N	158	595	92	184	39	3	17	89	93-8	3	56	.309	.401	.471	125	26	4-7	.994	0	99	63	1b156	0	1.1
1999	Chi N	161	593	107	183	44	5	16	91	83-4	2	44	.309	.390	.481	121	22	3-4	.994	-4	91	90	1b160	0	0.3
2000	Chi N	143	510	75	143	41	1	11	82	95-11	6	28	.280	.394	.429	111	14	1-2	**.997**	5	109	87	1b140	19	0.6
2001	†Ari N	145	476	66	142	31	2	15	78	67-6	4	36	.298	.386	.466	112	11	1-0	.995	-4	81	112	1b135	0	-0.3
2002	†Ari N	124	298	43	75	19	0	7	48	46-6	1	30	.252	.351	.386	86	-4	2-0	.990	-5	71	101	1b98/P	0	-1.6
2003	Ari N	66	135	13	27	5	0	3	16	16-2	0	15	.200	.279	.304	49	-10	0-0	.993	-0	92	97	1b39/D	26	-1.3
Total	16	2245	8065	1179	2445	511	45	173	1146	1075-114	34	642	.303	.383	.442	118	248	70-48	.995	54	107	95	1b2162/DP	95	12.7

GRACE, MIKE Michael Lee; B6.14.1956 Pontiac MI; BR/TR/6´0˝/170; [CinN74 2/47]; d4.18

YEAR	TM LG	G	AB	R	H	2B	3B	HR	RBI	BB-IB	HP	SO	AVG	OBP	SLG	AOPS	ABR	SB-CS	FA	FR	RNG	THR	GAMES AT POSITION	DL	BFW
1978	Cin N	5	3	0	0	0	0	0	0	0-0	0	2	.000	.000	.000	-99	-1	0-0	1.000	0	219	0	3b2	0	0.0

GRACE, EARL Robert Earl; B2.24.1907 Barlow KY; D12.22.1980 Phoenix AZ; BL/TR/6´0˝/175; d4.23

YEAR	TM LG	G	AB	R	H	2B	3B	HR	RBI	BB-IB	HP	SO	AVG	OBP	SLG	AOPS	ABR	SB-CS	FA	FR	RNG	THR	GAMES AT POSITION	DL	BFW
1929	Chi N	27	80	7	20	1	0	2	17	9	1	7	.250	.333	.338	67	-4	0	1.000	3	133	113	C27	—	0.0
1931	Chi N	7	9	2	1	0	0	0	1	4	0	1	.111	.385	.111	39	0	0	1.000	0	78	0	C2	—	0.0
	Pit N	47	150	8	42	6	1	1	20	13	0	5	.280	.337	.353	87	-3	0	.974	-1	99	82	C45	—	-0.1
	Year	54	159	10	43	6	1	1	21	17	0	6	.270	.341	.340	84	-3	0	.976	-1	98	78	C47	—	-0.1
1932	Pit N	115	390	41	107	17	5	8	55	14	3	23	.274	.305	.405	91	-7	0	**.998**	-3	83	68	C114	—	-0.3
1933	Pit N	93	291	22	84	13	1	3	44	26	1	23	.289	.349	.371	106	3	0	.980	-1	78	72	C88	—	0.8
1934	Pit N	95	289	27	78	17	1	4	24	20	0	19	.270	.317	.377	83	-7	0	.982	-8	67	56	C83/1	—	-1.0
1935	Pit N	77	224	19	59	8	1	3	29	32	0	17	.263	.355	.348	87	-3	1	.990	4	83	103	C69	—	0.5
1936	Phi N	86	221	24	55	11	0	4	32	34	1	20	.249	.352	.353	82	-4	0	.976	-3	94	71	C65	—	-0.4
1937	Phi N	80	223	19	47	10	1	6	29	33	0	15	.211	.313	.345	73	-8	0	.990	-2	136	69	C64	—	-0.6
Total	8	627	1877	169	493	83	10	31	251	185	6	130	.263	.331	.367	86	-33	1	.987	-11	91	75	C557/1	—	-1.1

GRADY, JOHN John J.; B6.18.1860 Lowell MA; D7.15.1893 Lowell MA; 5´7˝/150; d5.10

YEAR	TM LG	G	AB	R	H	2B	3B	HR	RBI	BB-IB	HP	SO	AVG	OBP	SLG	AOPS	ABR	SB-CS	FA	FR	RNG	THR	GAMES AT POSITION	DL	BFW
1884	Alt U	9	36	5	11	3	0	0	—	2	—	—	.306	.342	.389	120	0	—	.909	-1	121	27	1b8/cf	—	-0.2

GRADY, MIKE Michael William; B12.23.1869 Kennett Square PA; D12.3.1943 Kennett Square PA; BR/TR/5´11˝/190; d4.24; OF(14/7/29)

YEAR	TM LG	G	AB	R	H	2B	3B	HR	RBI	BB-IB	HP	SO	AVG	OBP	SLG	AOPS	ABR	SB-CS	FA	FR	RNG	THR	GAMES AT POSITION	DL	BFW
1894	Phi N	61	190	45	69	13	8	0	40	14	7	13	.363	.427	.516	129	9	3	.878	-11	91	82	C45,1b11,O2(1/0/1)	—	0.1
1895	Phi N	46	123	21	40	3	1	1	23	14	3	8	.325	.407	.390	106	2	5	.926	-9	93	37	C38,O5(3/0/2)/31	—	-0.4
1896	Phi N	72	242	49	77	20	7	1	44	16	9	19	.318	.382	.471	126	9	10	.942	-6	104	104	C61,3b7	—	0.7
1897	Phi N	4	13	1	2	0	0	0	0	1	0	—	.154	.214	.154	-2	-2	0	1.000	0	111	124	C3	—	-0.1
	StL N	84	326	49	91	11	3	8	57	26	10	—	.279	.351	.405	101	0	7	.974	-1	105	106	1b84/rf	—	0.0
	Year	88	339	50	93	11	3	8	57	27	10	—	.274	.346	.395	97	-2	7	.974	-0	105	106	1b84,C3/rf	—	-0.1
1898	NY N	93	287	64	85	19	5	3	49	38	11	—	.296	.399	.429	142	18	20	.944	-6	91	109	C57,O30(7/7/16),1b7,S3	—	1.4
1899	NY N	87	315	49	106	18	8	2	54	29	7	—	.337	.405	.463	143	19	20	.940	-8	86	116	C44,3b35,O4R,1b4	—	1.4
1900	NY N	83	251	36	55	8	4	0	27	34	8	—	.219	.331	.283	74	-7	9	.932	-4	110	82	C41,1b12,S11,3b7,O5R,2b2	—	-0.7
1901	Was A	94	347	57	99	17	10	9	56	27	8	—	.285	.351	.470	128	12	14	.975	8	173	104	1b59,C30,O3L	—	1.9
1904	StL N	101	323	44	101	15	11	5	43	31	2	—	.313	.376	.474	169	26	6	.955	-18	81	65	C77,1b11,2b3/3	—	1.6
1905	StL N	100	311	41	89	20	7	4	41	33	3	—	.286	.360	.434	141	16	15	.956	-11	84	85	C71,1b20	—	1.2
1906	StL N	97	280	33	70	11	3	2	27	48	5	—	.250	.369	.332	124	11	5	.983	-11	72	97	C60,1b38	—	0.5
Total	11	922	3008	489	884	155	67	35	461	311	73	40	.294	.374	.425	126	113	114	.946	-74	91	87	C527,1b247,3b51,O50R,S14,2b5	—	7.6

GRAF, FRED Frederick Gottleib; B8.25.1889 Canton OH; D10.4.1979 Chattanooga TN; BR/TR/5´10.5˝/164; d5.14

YEAR	TM LG	G	AB	R	H	2B	3B	HR	RBI	BB-IB	HP	SO	AVG	OBP	SLG	AOPS	ABR	SB-CS	FA	FR	RNG	THR	GAMES AT POSITION	DL	BFW
1913	StL A	4	5	1	2	1	0	0	2	3	0	3	.400	.625	.600	266	2	0	1.000	-0	109	363	3b4	—	0.2

GRAFF, LOUIS Louis George "Chappie"; B7.25.1866 Philadelphia PA; D4.16.1955 Bryn Mawr PA; TR; d6.23

YEAR	TM LG	G	AB	R	H	2B	3B	HR	RBI	BB-IB	HP	SO	AVG	OBP	SLG	AOPS	ABR	SB-CS	FA	FR	RNG	THR	GAMES AT POSITION	DL	BFW
1890	Syr AA	1	5	0	2	1	0	0	3	0	0	—	.400	.400	.600	217	1	0	.333	-2	75	0	/C	—	-0.1

GRAFF, MILT Milton Edward; B12.30.1930 Jefferson Center PA; D8.2.2005 Rockdale TX; BL/TR/5´7.5˝/(158–165); d4.16; C1; Col Penn St.

YEAR	TM LG	G	AB	R	H	2B	3B	HR	RBI	BB-IB	HP	SO	AVG	OBP	SLG	AOPS	ABR	SB-CS	FA	FR	RNG	THR	GAMES AT POSITION	DL	BFW
1957	KC A	56	155	16	28	4	3	0	10	15-0	2	10	.181	.260	.245	39	-13	2-5	.988	1	104	107	2b53	0	-1.1
1958	KC A	5	1	0	0	0	0	0	0	0-0	0	0	.000	.000	.000	-98	0	0-0	1.000	0	0	0	/2	0	0.0
Total	2	61	156	16	28	4	3	0	10	15-0	2	10	.179	.259	.244	38	-13	2-5	.988	1	104	107	2b54	0	-1.1

GRAFFANINO, TONY Anthony Joseph; B6.6.1972 Amityville NY; BR/TR/6´1˝/(175–195); [AtlN90 10/264]; d4.19

YEAR	TM LG	G	AB	R	H	2B	3B	HR	RBI	BB-IB	HP	SO	AVG	OBP	SLG	AOPS	ABR	SB-CS	FA	FR	RNG	THR	GAMES AT POSITION	DL	BFW
1996	Atl N	22	46	7	8	1	1	0	2	4-0	1	13	.174	.250	.239	29	-5	0-0	.969	1	110	121	2b18	0	-0.3
1997	†Atl N	104	186	33	48	9	1	8	20	26-1	1	46	.258	.344	.446	106	2	6-4	.982	7	118	97	2b75,3b2,S2/1	0	1.1
1998	†Atl N	105	289	32	61	14	1	5	22	24-0	2	68	.211	.275	.318	56	-19	1-4	.971	13	114	99	2b93,S2/3	0	-0.4
1999	TB A	39	130	20	41	9	4	2	19	9-0	1	22	.315	.364	.492	114	2	3-2	.990	8	129	108	2b17,S17/3	0	1.1
2000	TB A	13	20	8	6	1	0	0	1	1-0	1	2	.300	.364	.350	83	0	0-0	1.000	2	114	127	2b6,3b3/S	0	0.2
	†Chi A	57	148	25	40	5	1	2	16	21-0	1	25	.270	.363	.358	81	-4	7-4	.966	6	108	127	S21,2b19,3b12,D3	0	0.4
	Year	70	168	33	46	6	1	2	17	22-0	2	27	.274	.363	.357	82	-4	7-4	.973	8	124	119	2b25,S22,3b15,D3	0	0.6
2001	Chi A	74	145	23	44	9	0	2	15	16-0	1	29	.303	.370	.407	100	1	4-1	.923	4	106	28	3b38,2b20,S5,O3L/1D	0	0.6
2002	Chi A	70	229	35	60	12	4	6	31	22-1	2	38	.262	.329	.428	96	-1	2-1	.952	2	101	93	3b35,2b25,S8	35	0.2
2003	Chi A	90	250	51	65	15	3	7	23	24-1	3	37	.260	.331	.428	95	-2	8-0	.968	9	106	105	S36,2b29,3b20,1b2,D3	0	1.1
2004	KC A	75	278	37	73	11	0	3	26	27-0	3	38	.263	.332	.335	75	-10	10-2	.988	19	114	136	2b75	91	1.4
2005	KC A	59	191	29	57	5	2	3	18	22-1	2	28	.298	.377	.393	109	3	3-1	.987	-7	84	55	2b22,1b22,3b17/SD	0	-0.4
	†Bos A	51	188	39	60	12	1	4	20	9-1	2	23	.319	.355	.457	110	3	4-1	.987	-2	98	86	2b51	0	0.3
	Year	110	379	68	117	17	3	7	38	31-2	4	51	.309	.366	.425	110	6	7-2	.987	-9	94	77	2b73,1b22,3b17/SD	0	-0.1
2006	KC A	69	220	34	59	16	0	5	32	25-1	1	31	.268	.346	.409	96	-1	3-4	.975	-3	122	35	3b27,1b16,2b10,S9,D6	0	-0.4
	Mil N	60	236	34	66	17	3	2	27	20-0	4	37	.280	.345	.403	90	-3	2-0	.987	-12	79	55	2b57,S4	0	-1.1
Total	11	888	2556	407	688	136	21	49	272	250-6	25	437	.269	.338	.396	90	-34	53-24	.981	46	107	104	2b517,3b156,S106,1b42,D16,O3L	126	3.8

GRAHAM, MOONLIGHT Archibald Wright; B11.12.1877 Fayetteville NC; D8.25.1965 Chisholm MN; BL/TR/5´10.5˝/170; d6.29; Col Maryland

YEAR	TM LG	G	AB	R	H	2B	3B	HR	RBI	BB-IB	HP	SO	AVG	OBP	SLG	AOPS	ABR	SB-CS	FA	FR	RNG	THR	GAMES AT POSITION	DL	BFW
1905	NY N	1	0	0	0	0	0	0	0	0	0	—	ø	ø	ø	ø	0	0	ø	0	0	0	/rf	—	0.0

GRAHAM, SKINNY Arthur William; B8.12.1909 Somerville MA; D7.10.1967 Cambridge MA; BL/TR/5´7˝/162; d9.14

YEAR	TM LG	G	AB	R	H	2B	3B	HR	RBI	BB-IB	HP	SO	AVG	OBP	SLG	AOPS	ABR	SB-CS	FA	FR	RNG	THR	GAMES AT POSITION	DL	BFW
1934	Bos A	13	47	7	11	2	1	0	3	6	0	13	.234	.321	.319	61	-3	2-2	1.000	-1	83	113	O13(0/4/9)	—	-0.4
1935	Bos A	8	10	1	3	0	0	0	1	1	0	3	.300	.364	.300	69	0	1-0	1.000	-0	89	0	O2R	—	0.0
Total	2	21	57	8	14	2	1	0	4	7	0	16	.246	.328	.316	62	-3	3-2	1.000	-1	84	103	O15(0/4/11)	—	-0.4

GRAHAM, BERNIE Bernard W.; B1860 Beloit WI; D10.30.1886 Mobile AL; BL; d7.11

YEAR	TM LG	G	AB	R	H	2B	3B	HR	RBI	BB-IB	HP	SO	AVG	OBP	SLG	AOPS	ABR	SB-CS	FA	FR	RNG	THR	GAMES AT POSITION	DL	BFW
1884	CP U	1	5	2	1	0	0	0	—	0	—	—	.200	.200	.200	22	-1	—	1.000	-0	0	0	/lf	—	-0.1
	Bal U	41	167	21	45	11	0	0	—	2	—	—	.269	.278	.335	77	-9	—	.814	-1	94	115	O40(0/25/15)/1	—	-1.1
	Year	42	172	23	46	11	0	0	—	2	—	—	.267	.276	.331	76	-10	—	.816	-2	92	112	O41(1/25/15)/1	—	-1.2

GRAHAM, BERT Bert "B.G."; B4.3.1886 Tilton IL; D6.19.1971 Cottonwood AZ; BB/TR/5´11.5˝/187; d9.9

YEAR	TM LG	G	AB	R	H	2B	3B	HR	RBI	BB-IB	HP	SO	AVG	OBP	SLG	AOPS	ABR	SB-CS	FA	FR	RNG	THR	GAMES AT POSITION	DL	BFW
1910	StL A	8	26	1	3	2	1	0	5	1	0	—	.115	.148	.269	32	-2	0	.964	1	146	0	1b5,2b2	—	-0.1

GRAHAM, CHARLIE Charles Henry; B4.24.1878 Santa Clara CA; D8.29.1948 San Francisco CA; BR/TR/6´0˝/190; d4.16; Col Santa Clara

YEAR	TM LG	G	AB	R	H	2B	3B	HR	RBI	BB-IB	HP	SO	AVG	OBP	SLG	AOPS	ABR	SB-CS	FA	FR	RNG	THR	GAMES AT POSITION	DL	BFW
1906	Bos A	30	90	10	21	1	0	1	12	10	3	—	.233	.330	.278	91	0	1	.963	2	88	128	C27	—	0.5

GRAHAM, DAN Daniel Jay; B7.19.1954 Ray AZ; BL/TR/6´1˝/212; [MinA75 5/109]; d6.8; Col La Verne

YEAR	TM LG	G	AB	R	H	2B	3B	HR	RBI	BB-IB	HP	SO	AVG	OBP	SLG	AOPS	ABR	SB-CS	FA	FR	RNG	THR	GAMES AT POSITION	DL	BFW
1979	Min A	2	4	0	0	0	0	0	0	0-0	0	0	.000	.000	.000	-96	-1	0-0	ø	0	—	—	/D	0	-0.1
1980	Bal A	86	266	32	74	7	1	15	54	14-0	0	40	.278	.310	.481	116	4	0-0	.981	1	106	99	C73,3b9/rfD	0	0.8
1981	Bal A	55	142	7	25	3	0	2	11	13-1	0	32	.176	.244	.239	40	-11	0-0	.975	-3	93	153	C40,3b4,D6	0	-1.4
Total	3	143	412	39	99	10	1	17	65	27-1	0	72	.240	.284	.393	89	-8	0-0	.979	-2	102	116	C113,3b13,D9/rf	0	-0.7

GRAHAM, TINY Dawson Francis; B9.9.1892 Nashville TN; D12.29.1962 Nashville TN; BR/TR/6´2˝/185; d8.30

YEAR	TM LG	G	AB	R	H	2B	3B	HR	RBI	BB-IB	HP	SO	AVG	OBP	SLG	AOPS	ABR	SB-CS	FA	FR	RNG	THR	GAMES AT POSITION	DL	BFW
1914	Cin N	25	61	5	14	1	0	0	3	3	0	10	.230	.266	.246	51	-4	1	.961	-2	87	142	1b25	—	-0.6

GRAHAM, PEACHES George Frederick; B3.23.1877 Aledo IL; D7.25.1939 Long Beach CA; BR/TR/5´9˝/180; d9.14; s–Jack

YEAR	TM LG	G	AB	R	H	2B	3B	HR	RBI	BB-IB	HP	SO	AVG	OBP	SLG	AOPS	ABR	SB-CS	FA	FR	RNG	THR	GAMES AT POSITION	DL	BFW
1902	Cle A	2	6	0	2	0	0	0	1	1	0	—	.333	.429	.333	118	0	0	1.000	0	123	0	/2	—	0.0
1903	Chi N	1	2	0	0	0	0	0	0	0	0	—	.000	.000	.000	-99	0	0	1.000	0	220	0	/P	—	0.0
1908	Bos N	75	215	22	59	5	0	0	22	23	6	—	.274	.361	.298	112	5	4	.955	-5	91	99	C62,2b5	—	0.6
1909	Bos N	92	267	27	64	6	3	0	17	24	0	—	.240	.302	.285	79	-7	7	.948	-5	83	113	C76,O6(1/0/3)/S3	—	-0.5
1910	Bos N	110	291	31	82	13	2	0	21	33	2	15	.282	.359	.340	100	1	5	.966	-10	82	111	C87,3b2/1rf	—	-0.1
1911	Bos N	33	88	7	24	6	1	0	12	14	0	5	.273	.373	.364	98	0	2	.912	-7	75	97	C26	—	-0.4
	Chi N	36	71	6	17	3	0	0	8	11	3	8	.239	.365	.282	82	-1	2	.972	0	149	89	C28	—	0.1
	Year	69	159	13	41	9	1	0	20	25	3	13	.258	.369	.327	92	0	4	.937	-7	108	93	C54	—	-0.3
1912	Phi N	24	59	6	17	1	0	1	4	8	0	5	.288	.373	.356	94	0	1	.944	-2	88	107	C19	—	-0.1
Total	7	373	999	99	265	34	6	1	85	114	11	33	.265	.347	.314	95	-2	21	.953	-29	89	106	C298,O7(1/0/4),2b6,3b3/1SP	—	-0.4

THE BATTER REGISTER

YEAR	TM LG	G	AB	R	H	2B	3B	HR	RBI	BB-IB	HP	SO	AVG	OBP	SLG	AOPS	ABR	SB-CS	FA	FR	RNG	THR	GAMES AT POSITION	DL	BFW
GRAHAM, BARNEY	James; B Philadelphia PA; d9.4																								
1889	Phi AA	4	18	0	3	0	0	0	0	0	0	0	.167	.167	.167	-5	-3	0	.933	1	155	151	3b4	—	-0.1
GRAHAM, JACK	John Bernard; B12.24.1916 Minneapolis MN; D12.30.1998 Los Alamitos CA; BL/TL/6´2˝/200; d4.16; f–Peaches																								
1946	Bro N	2	5	0	1	0	0	0	0	0	0	0	.200	.200	.200	14	-1	0	1.000	0	104	0	1b2	0	-0.1
	NY N	100	270	34	59	6	4	14	47	23	1	37	.219	.282	.426	99	-3	1	.949	-1	97	125	O62(1/0/60),1b7	0	-0.6
	Year	102	275	34	60	6	4	14	47	23	1	37	.218	.281	.422	97	-4	1	.949	-1	97	125	O62(1/0/60),1b9	0	-0.7
1949	StL A	137	500	71	119	22	1	24	79	61	4	62	.238	.326	.430	95	-6	0-1	.984	-6	88	77	1b136	0	-1.7
Total	2	239	775	105	179	28	5	38	126	84	5	99	.231	.310	.427	96	-10	1-1	.985	-6	88	75	1b145,O62(1/0/60)	0	-2.4
GRAHAM, LEE	Lee Willard; B9.22.1959 Summerfield FL; BL/TL/5´10˝/170; [BosA77 26/641]; d9.3																								
1983	Bos A	5	6	2	0	0	0	0	1	0-0	0	0	.000	.000	.000	-93	-2	0-1	1.000	1	125	923	O3(0/2/1)	0	-0.1
GRAHAM, ROY	Roy Vincent; B2.22.1895 San Francisco CA; D4.26.1933 Manila, Philippines; BR/TR/5´10.5˝/175; d5.28																								
1922	Chi A	5	3	0	0	0	0	0	0	0	2	0	.000	.400	.000	12	0	0-0	1.000	-0	*0*	*0*	C3	—	0.0
1923	Chi A	36	82	3	16	2	0	0	6	9	2	6	.195	.290	.220	36	-7	0-0	.949	-5	*71*	*79*	C33	—	-1.1
Total	2	41	85	3	16	2	0	0	6	9	4	6	.188	.296	.212	35	-7	0-0	.950	-5	*69*	*77*	C36	—	-1.1
GRAHAM, WAYNE	Wayne Leon; B4.6.1936 Yoakum TX; BR/TR/6´0˝/200; d4.10; Col Texas																								
1963	Phi N	10	22	1	4	0	0	0	0	3-0	0	1	.182	.280	.182	36	-2	0-0	.857	-1	71	0	O6L	0	-0.3
1964	NY N	20	33	1	3	1	0	0	0	0-0	0	5	.091	.091	.121	-42	-6	0-0	1.000	-3	58	0	3b11	0	-1.0
Total	2	30	55	2	7	1	0	0	0	3-0	0	6	.127	.172	.145	-9	-8	0-0	1.000	-4	58	0	3b11,O6L	0	-1.3
GRAMMAS, ALEX	Alexander Peter; B4.3.1926 Birmingham AL; BR/TR/6´0˝/(175–178); d4.13; M3/C26; Col Mississippi St.																								
1954	StL N	142	401	57	106	17	4	2	29	40	5	29	.264	.335	.342	77	-13	6-1	.966	22	**113**	118	S142/3	0	2.1
1955	StL N	128	366	32	88	19	2	3	25	33-9	3	36	.240	.308	.328	69	-16	4-1	.968	4	98	102	S126	0	-0.1
1956	StL N	6	12	1	3	0	0	0	1	1-0	0	2	.250	.308	.250	52	-1	0-0	1.000	0	117	60	S5	0	0.0
	Cin N	77	140	17	34	11	0	0	16	16-1	1	18	.243	.323	.321	70	-5	0-1	.968	-0	101	117	3b58,S12,2b5	0	-0.5
	Year	83	152	18	37	11	0	0	17	17-1	1	20	.243	.322	.316	69	-6	0-1	.968	0	101	117	3b58,S17,2b5	0	-0.5
1957	Cin N	73	99	14	30	4	0	0	8	10-0	0	6	.303	.364	.343	86	-1	1-3	.966	-7	89	38	S42,2b20,3b9	0	-0.7
1958	Cin N	105	216	25	47	8	0	0	12	34-1	2	24	.218	.329	.255	54	-13	2-2	.993	-5	98	114	S61,3b38,2b14	0	-1.5
1959	StL N	131	368	43	99	14	2	3	30	38-6	1	26	.269	.337	.342	77	-11	3-3	.964	11	105	107	S130	0	0.9
1960	StL N	102	196	20	48	4	1	4	17	12-1	1	15	.245	.290	.337	66	-9	0-1	.972	7	99	74	S46,2b38,3b13	0	0.1
1961	StL N	89	170	23	36	10	1	0	21	19-3	1	21	.212	.293	.282	49	-12	0-1	.960	13	113	109	S65,2b18,3b3	0	0.5
1962	StL N	21	18	0	2	0	0	0	1	1-1	0	6	.111	.158	.111	-24	-3	0-0	.933	-2	90	54	S16,2b2	0	-0.4
	Chi N	23	60	3	14	3	0	0	3	2-0	1	7	.233	.270	.283	47	-4	1-1	1.000	1	108	127	S13,2b3/3	0	-0.3
	Year	44	78	3	16	3	0	0	4	3-1	1	13	.205	.244	.244	29	-8	1-1	.978	-1	102	103	S29,2b5/3	0	-0.7
1963	Chi N	16	27	1	5	0	0	0	0	0-0	0	3	.185	.185	.185	7	-3	0-0	.955	-4	66	27	S13	0	-0.8
Total	10	913	2073	236	512	90	10	12	163	206-22	15	193	.247	.318	.317	67	-91	17-14	.968	41	104	104	S671,3b123,2b100	0	-0.7
GRANDERSON, CURTIS	Curtis; B3.16.1981 Blue Island IL; BL/TR/6´1˝/185; [DetA02 3/80]; d9.13; Col Illinois–Chicago																								
2004	Det A	9	25	2	6	1	1	0	0	3-0	0	8	.240	.321	.360	80	-1	0-0	1.000	0	90	287	O8C	0	0.0
2005	Det A	47	162	18	44	6	3	8	20	10-0	0	43	.272	.314	.494	112	2	1-1	1.000	5	120	91	O45(20/41/0)	0	0.6
2006	†Det A	159	596	90	155	31	9	19	68	66-0	4	174	.260	.335	.438	100	0	8-5	**.997**	-5	100	39	O157C	0	-0.3
Total	3	215	783	110	205	38	13	27	88	79-0	4	225	.262	.330	.447	102	1	9-6	.998	0	104	59	O210(20/206/0)	0	0.3
GRANEY, JACK	John Gladstone; B6.10.1886 St.Thomas ON, Can.; D4.20.1978 Louisiana MO; BL/TL/5´9˝/180; d4.30																								
1908	Cle A	2	0	0	0	0	0	0	0	0	0	—	ø	ø	ø	ø	0	0	ø	-0	0	0	P2	—	0.0
1910	Cle A	116	454	62	107	13	9	1	31	37	0	—	.236	.293	.311	88	-7	18	.949	-2	99	85	O114(53/43/18)	—	-1.8
1911	Cle A	146	527	84	142	25	5	1	45	66	11	—	.269	.363	.342	96	0	21	.927	3	105	104	O142(139/1/2)	—	-0.3
1912	Cle A	78	264	44	64	13	2	0	20	50	2	—	.242	.367	.307	90	0	9	.958	4	105	118	O75L	—	0.1
1913	Cle A	148	517	56	138	18	12	3	68	48	5	55	.267	.335	.366	102	0	27	.970	0	103	81	O148(144/0/4)	—	-0.7
1914	Cle A	130	460	63	122	17	10	1	39	67	3	46	.265	.362	.352	111	8	20-18	.935	5	118	86	O127L	—	0.6
1915	Cle A	116	404	42	105	20	7	1	56	59	2	29	.260	.357	.351	110	7	12-15	.972	5	105	117	O115(107/1/8)	—	0.3
1916	Cle A	155	589	106	142	**41**	14	5	54	102	2	72	.241	.355	.384	115	14	10	.959	1	97	109	O154L	—	0.9
1917	Cle A	146	535	87	122	29	7	3	35	**94**	4	49	.228	.348	.325	98	3	16	.959	-11	92	65	O145L	—	-1.6
1918	Cle A	70	177	27	42	7	4	0	9	28	3	13	.237	.351	.322	94	0	3	.975	-4	94	37	O45(44/0/1)	—	-0.6
1919	Cle A	128	461	79	108	22	8	1	30	**105**	3	39	.234	.380	.323	93	1	7	.961	3	108	98	O125L	—	-0.1
1920	†Cle A	62	152	31	45	11	1	0	13	27	3	21	.296	.412	.382	108	4	4-2	.941	-1	97	82	O47(44/2/1)	—	0.1
1921	Cle A	68	107	19	32	3	0	2	18	20	1	9	.299	.414	.383	103	2	1-1	.933	-3	98	0	O32(17/11/5)	—	-0.2
1922	Cle A	37	58	6	9	0	0	0	2	9	1	12	.155	.279	.155	16	-7	0-0	.862	-1	96	75	O13(2/4/7)	—	-0.9
Total	14	1402	4705	706	1178	219	79	18	420	712	40	345	.250	.354	.342	100	25	148-36	.953	-0	103	90	O1282(1176/62/46),P2	—	-4.2
GRANT, EDDIE	Edward Leslie "Harvard Eddie"; B5.21.1883 Franklin MA; D10.5.1918 Argonne Forest, France; BL/TR/5´11.5˝/168; d8.4; Col Harvard																								
1905	Cle A	2	8	1	3	0	0	0	0	0	0	—	.375	.375	.375	136	0	0	.833	-1	92	0	2b2	—	-0.1
1907	Phi N	74	268	26	65	4	3	0	19	10	1	—	.243	.272	.280	74	-9	10	.916	-4	93	63	3b74	—	-1.2
1908	Phi N	147	598	69	146	13	8	0	32	35	3	—	.244	.289	.293	83	-12	27	.930	-2	99	**138**	3b134,S13	—	-1.2
1909	Phi N	**154**	631	75	170	18	4	1	37	35	3	—	.269	.311	.315	94	-6	28	.957	3	101	98	3b154	—	0.1
1910	Phi N	152	579	70	155	15	5	1	67	39	1	54	.268	.315	.316	81	-15	25	.935	-12	87	101	3b152	—	-2.4
1911	Cin N	136	458	49	102	12	7	1	53	51	0	47	.223	.301	.286	67	-21	28	.953	-5	97	129	3b122,S11	—	-2.2
1912	Cin N	96	255	37	61	6	1	2	20	18	1	27	.239	.292	.294	62	-14	11	.948	0	103	92	S56,3b15	—	-0.9
1913	Cin N	27	94	12	20	1	0	0	9	11	0	10	.213	.295	.223	49	-6	7-4	.929	-1	98	126	3b26	—	-0.6
	†NY N	27	20	8	4	1	0	0	1	2	0	2	.200	.273	.250	49	-1	1-1	1.000	3	269	0	3b5,2b3/S	—	0.2
	Year	54	114	20	24	2	0	0	10	13	0	12	.211	.291	.228	49	-7	8-5	.940	2	114	114	3b31,2b3/S	—	-0.4
1914	NY N	88	282	34	78	7	1	0	29	23	1	21	.277	.333	.309	94	-2	11	.948	-3	108	115	3b52,S21,2b16	—	-0.2
1915	NY N	87	192	18	40	2	1	0	10	9	1	20	.208	.248	.229	47	-13	5-6	.970	-2	90	70	3b35,2b9/1S	—	-1.7
Total	10	990	3385	399	844	79	30	5	277	233	11	181	.249	.300	.295	78	-99	153-11	.942	-21	97	108	3b769,S103,2b30/1	—	-10.2
GRANT, JIMMY	James Charles; B10.6.1918 Racine WI; D7.8.1970 Rochester MN; BL/TR/5´8˝/166; d9.8																								
1942	Chi A	12	36	0	6	1	1	0	1	5	0	6	.167	.268	.250	47	-3	0-0	.944	0	93	164	3b10	0	-0.2
1943	Chi A	58	197	23	51	9	2	4	22	18	0	34	.259	.321	.386	106	1	4-3	.893	-2	109	113	3b51	0	-0.1
	Cle A	15	22	3	3	2	0	0	1	4	0	7	.136	.269	.227	49	-1	0-0	.941	1	142	0	3b5	0	0.0
	Year	73	219	26	54	11	2	4	23	22	0	41	.247	.315	.370	101	0	4-3	.897	-1	112	104	3b56	0	-0.1
1944	Cle A	61	99	12	27	4	3	1	12	11	2	20	.273	.357	.404	122	3	1-0	.926	-4	98	47	2b20,3b4	0	0.0
Total	3	146	354	38	87	16	6	5	36	38	2	67	.246	.322	.367	101	0	5-3	.907	-4	108	110	3b70,2b20	0	-0.3
GRANT, TOM	Thomas Raymond; B5.28.1957 Worcester MA; BL/TR/6´2˝/190; [ChiN79 16/402]; d6.17; Col New Haven																								
1983	Chi N	16	20	2	3	1	0	0	2	3-0	0	4	.150	.261	.200	28	-2	0-0	1.000	0	72	316	O10(5/0/5)	0	-0.2
GRANTHAM, GEORGE	George Farley "Boots"; B5.20.1900 Galena KS; D3.16.1954 Kingman AZ; BL/TR/5´10˝/170; d9.20; Col Northern Arizona																								
1922	Chi N	7	23	3	4	1	1	0	3	1	0	3	.174	.208	.304	30	-3	2-0	1.000	-1	52	149	3b5	—	-0.3
1923	Chi N	152	570	81	160	36	8	8	70	71	0	92	.281	.360	.414	104	5	43-28	.942	4	101	106	2b150	—	1.2
1924	Chi N	127	469	85	148	19	6	12	60	55	2	63	.316	.390	.458	125	18	21-21	.941	-1	101	108	2b118,3b6	—	1.8
1925	†Pit N	114	359	74	117	24	6	8	52	50	3	29	.326	.413	.493	122	14	14-4	.989	-4	82	123	1b102	—	0.5
1926	Pit N	141	449	66	143	27	13	8	70	60	1	42	.318	.400	.490	131	21	6	.990	-2	92	106	1b132	—	1.1
1927	†Pit N	151	531	96	162	33	11	8	66	74	6	39	.305	.396	.454	119	17	9	.953	-22	88	101	2b124,1b29	—	-0.4
1928	Pit N	124	440	93	142	24	9	10	85	59	4	37	.323	.408	.486	128	19	9	.986	1	109	86	1b119/23	—	1.3
1929	Pit N	110	349	85	107	23	10	12	90	93	1	38	.307	.454	.533	140	27	10	.967	0	96	125	2b76,O19L,1b12	—	2.5
1930	Pit N	146	552	120	179	34	14	18	99	81	2	66	.324	.413	.534	126	25	5	.958	-12	101	82	2b141,1b4	—	1.5
1931	Pit N	127	465	91	142	26	6	10	46	71	2	50	.305	.400	.452	130	23	5	.985	-22	63	100	1b78,2b51	—	-0.4
1932	Cin N	126	493	81	144	29	6	6	39	56	0	40	.292	.364	.412	112	10	4	.959	-25	95	70	2b115,1b10	—	-0.9
1933	Cin N	87	260	32	53	14	3	4	28	38	2	21	.204	.310	.327	83	-5	4	.948	-8	95	93	2b72,1b12	—	-1.0
1934	NY N	32	29	5	7	2	0	1	4	8	0	6	.241	.405	.414	123	1	0	1.000	0	82	71	1b4,3b2	—	0.1
Total	13	1444	4989	912	1508	292	93	105	712	717	23	526	.302	.392	.461	121	172	132-53	.949	-92	97	97	2b848,1b502,O19L,3b14	—	7.0

YEAR	TM LG	G	AB	R	H	2B	3B	HR	RBI	BB-IB	HP	SO	AVG	OBP	SLG	AOPS	ABR	SB-CS	FA	FR	RNG	THR	GAMES AT POSITION	DL	BFW
GRASSO, MICKEY	Newton Michael; B5.10.1920 Newark NJ; D10.15.1975 Miami FL; BR/TR/6´0˝/195; d9.18; [DL 1954 Was A 141]																								
1946	NY N	7	22	1	3	0	0	0	1	0	0	3	.136	.136	.136	-22	-4	0	.967	0	*106*	*184*	C7	0	-0.3
1950	Was A	75	195	25	56	4	1	1	22	25	2	31	.287	.374	.333	86	-3	1-1	.942	-1	*74*	*138*	C69	0	-0.1
1951	Was A	52	175	16	36	3	0	1	14	14	1	17	.206	.268	.240	39	-15	0-0	.967	-3	*102*	*108*	C49	0	-1.6
1952	Was A	115	361	22	78	9	0	0	27	29	1	36	.216	.276	.241	46	-27	1-0	.970	4	*116*	*75*	C114	0	-1.7
1953	Was A	61	196	13	41	7	0	2	22	9	2	20	.209	.251	.276	43	-16	0-0	.984	2	*105*	*85*	C59	0	-1.2
1954	†Cle A	4	6	1	2	0	0	1	1	1	1	1	.333	.500	.833	256	1	0-0	.833	-1	*68*	*191*	C4	0	0.1
1955	NY N	8	2	0	0	0	0	0	0	3-0	0	0	.000	.600	.000	77	0	0-0	.900	-0	*0*	*0*	C8	0	0.0
Total	7	322	957	78	216	23	1	5	87	81-0	7	108	.226	.291	.268	53	-64	2-1	.964	-0	*101*	*99*	C310	141	-4.8
GRAULICH, LEW	Lewis; B1862 Philadelphia PA; d9.17																								
1891	Phi N	7	26	2	8	0	0	0	3	1	0	2	.308	.333	.308	85	-1	0	.640	-3	*94*	*46*	C4,1b3	—	-0.3
GRAVES, FRANK	Frank Norris; B11.2.1860 Cincinnati OH; BR/6´0˝/163; d5.10																								
1886	StL N	43	138	7	21	2	0	0	9	7	—	48	.152	.193	.167	11	-14	11	.885	0	—	—	C41,O3C/P	—	-1.0
GRAVES, JOE	Joseph Ebenezer; B2.26.1906 Marblehead MA; D12.22.1980 Salem MA; BR/TR/5´10˝/160; d9.26; b–Sid																								
1926	Chi N	2	5	0	0	0	0	0	0	0	0	1	.000	.000	.000	-99	-1	0	.250	-1	42	470	3b2	—	-0.3
GRAVES, SID	Samuel Sidney "Whitey"; B11.30.1901 Marblehead MA; D12.26.1983 Biddeford ME; BR/TR/6´0˝/170; d7.23; b–Joe; Col Bowdoin																								
1927	Bos N	7	20	5	5	1	1	0	2	0	0	1	.250	.250	.400	78	-1	1	.857	0	78	405	O5C	—	-0.1
GRAY, GARY	Gary George; B9.21.1952 New Orleans LA; BR/TR/6´0˝/(180–215); [TexA74 18/408]; d6.23; Col Southeastern Oklahoma																								
1977	Tex A	1	2	0	0	0	0	0	0	0-0	0	1	.000	.000	.000	-99	-1	0-0	ø	-0	0	0	/lf	0	-0.1
1978	Tex A	17	50	4	12	1	0	2	6	1-0	0	12	.240	.255	.380	76	-2	1-0	ø	0	0	0	D11	0	-0.2
1979	Tex A	16	42	4	10	0	0	0	1	2-0	0	8	.238	.273	.238	39	-4	1-1	ø	0	0	0	D13	0	-0.4
1980	Cle A	28	54	4	8	1	0	2	4	3-1	0	13	.148	.193	.278	27	-6	0-0	1.000	-0	148	50	1b6,O6L,D9	0	-0.6
1981	Sea A	69	208	27	51	7	1	13	31	4-1	0	44	.245	.257	.476	103	-1	2-0	.993	-2	78	119	1b34,D15,O4L	0	-0.6
1982	Sea A	80	269	26	69	14	2	7	29	24-0	2	59	.257	.322	.401	94	-2	1-1	.984	-3	82	77	1b60,D14	0	-0.9
Total	6	211	625	65	150	23	3	24	71	34-2	2	137	.240	.281	.402	86	-16	5-2	.988	-6	82	91	1b100,D62,O11L	0	-2.8
GRAY, REDDY	James W.; B8.1863 Allegheny (now part of Pittsburgh) PA; D1.31.1938 Pittsburgh PA; TR; d10.9																								
1884	Pit AA	1	2	0	1	0	0	0	—	0	0	—	.500	.500	.500	230	0	—	.500	-0	138	0	/3	—	0.0
1890	Pit P	2	9	3	2	0	0	1	3	0	0	2	.222	.222	.556	114	0	0	.813	-1	67	0	2b2	—	-0.1
	Pit N	1	3	0	0	0	0	0	0	0	0	1	.000	.000	.000	-99	-1	0	.571	-1	57	210	/S	—	-0.2
1893	Pit N	2	9	0	4	1	0	0	2	0	0	1	.444	.444	.556	168	1	0	.800	-2	20	0	S2	—	-0.1
Total	3	6	23	3	7	1	0	1	5	0	0	4	.304	.304	.478	119	0	0	.667	-4	35	86	S3,2b2/3	—	-0.4
GRAY, LORENZO	Lorenzo; B3.4.1958 Mound Bayou MS; BR/TR/6´1˝/180; [ChiA76 8/176]; d7.8																								
1982	Chi A	17	28	4	8	1	0	0	0	2-0	0	4	.286	.333	.321	80	-1	1-0	.864	-3	59	122	3b16	0	-0.3
1983	Chi A	41	78	18	14	3	0	1	4	8-0	0	16	.179	.256	.256	40	-6	1-0	.940	-2	89	65	3b31,D7	0	-0.9
Total	2	58	106	22	22	4	0	1	4	10-0	0	20	.208	.276	.274	50	-7	2-0	.921	-5	81	79	3b47,D7	0	-1.2
GRAY, MILT	Milton Marshall; B2.21.1914 Louisville KY; D6.30.1969 Quincy FL; BR/TR/6´1˝/170; d5.27																								
1937	Was A	2	6	0	0	0	0	0	0	0	0	1	.000	.000	.000	-99	-2	0-0	1.000	0	*84*	*0*	C2	—	-0.2
GRAY, PETE	Peter J. (b Peter Wyshner); B3.6.1915 Nanticoke PA; D6.30.2002 Nanticoke PA; BL/TL/6´1˝/169; d4.17																								
1945	StL A	77	234	26	51	6	2	0	13	13	0	11	.218	.259	.261	49	-16	5-6	.959	2	117	59	O61(35/29/0)	0	-1.9
GRAY, DICK	Richard Benjamin; B7.11.1931 Jefferson PA; BR/TR/5´11˝/165; d4.15; Col Waynesburg																								
1958	LA N	58	197	25	49	5	6	9	30	19-0	4	30	.249	.327	.472	105	1	1-1	.929	11	119	159	3b55	0	1.2
1959	LA N	21	52	8	8	1	0	2	4	6-0	0	12	.154	.241	.288	38	-5	0-0	1.000	-1	89	113	3b11	0	-0.6
	StL N	36	51	9	16	1	0	1	6	6-1	0	8	.314	.386	.392	101	0	3-0	.958	-5	64	71	S13,3b6,2b2/lf	0	-0.4
	Year	57	103	17	24	2	0	3	10	12-1	0	20	.233	.313	.340	69	-4	3-0	.935	-7	84	89	3b17,S13,2b2/lf	0	-1.0
1960	StL N	9	5	1	0	0	0	0	1	2-0	0	2	.000	.250	.000	-13	-1	0-0	1.000	1	143	320	2b4/3	0	0.0
Total	3	124	305	43	73	7	6	12	41	33-1	4	52	.239	.321	.420	91	-5	4-1	.930	6	112	144	3b73,S13,2b6/lf	0	0.2
GRAY, STAN	Stanley Oscar; B12.10.1888 Ladonia TX; D10.11.1964 Snyder TX; BR/TR/6´0.5˝/184; d9.17																								
1912	Pit N	6	20	4	5	0	1	0	2	0	0	3	.250	.250	.350	64	-1	0	1.000	-1	0	94	1b4	—	-0.2
GRAY, BILL	William Tolan; B4.15.1871 Philadelphia PA; D12.8.1932 Philadelphia PA; 5´11˝/175; d5.14; OF(8/7/9)																								
1890	Phi N	34	128	20	31	8	4	0	21	6	2	3	.242	.287	.367	88	-3	5	1.000	-6	170	0	O10(6/3/1),3b8,2b8,C7/1	—	-0.7
1891	Phi N	23	75	11	18	0	0	0	7	3	3	10	.240	.296	.240	55	-4	3	.804	-5	*92*	*66*	C11,O10(0/4/6),S3/3	—	-0.8
1895	Cin N	52	181	24	55	17	4	1	29	15	2	8	.304	.364	.459	107	2	4	.906	-3	97	162	3b27,2b16,S5,C5/lf	—	0.0
1896	Cin N	46	121	15	25	2	1	0	17	19	0	11	.207	.314	.240	44	-10	6	.927	1	126	123	2b12,C11,S8,O3(1/0/2),1b2/3	—	-0.6
1898	Pit N	137	528	56	121	17	5	0	67	28	12	—	.229	.283	.280	63	-26	5	.879	-21	88	86	3b137	—	-4.2
Total	5	292	1033	126	250	44	14	1	141	71	19	32	.242	.303	.315	72	-41	23	.879	-34	87	97	3b174,2b36,C34,O24R,S16,1b3	—	-6.3
GREBECK, CRAIG	Craig Allen; B12.29.1964 Johnstown PA; BR/TR/5´7˝/(148–160); d4.13; Col Cal St.–Dominguez Hills																								
1990	Chi A	59	119	7	20	3	1	1	9	8-0	2	24	.168	.227	.235	32	-11	0-0	.987	1	112	65	3b35,S16,2b6/D	0	-1.0
1991	Chi A	107	224	37	63	16	3	6	31	38-0	1	40	.281	.386	.460	136	13	1-3	.933	-3	108	151	3b49,2b36,S26	0	1.1
1992	Chi A	88	287	24	77	21	2	3	35	30-0	3	34	.268	.341	.387	105	3	0-3	.980	2	111	89	S85,3b7,O2(1/0/1)	57	1.0
1993	†Chi A	72	190	25	43	5	0	1	12	26-0	0	26	.226	.319	.268	61	-10	1-2	.983	10	106	111	S46,2b16,3b14	0	0.3
1994	Chi A	35	97	17	30	5	0	0	5	12-0	1	5	.309	.391	.361	97	0	0-0	.982	-5	78	50	2b14,S14,3b7	40	-0.3
1995	Chi A	53	154	19	40	12	0	1	18	21-0	3	23	.260	.360	.357	91	-1	0-0	.961	4	118	106	S31,3b18,2b8	0	0.5
1996	Fla N	50	95	8	20	1	0	1	9	4-1	1	14	.211	.245	.253	34	-9	0-0	.985	5	100	160	2b29,S2/3	40	-0.3
1997	Ana A	63	126	12	34	9	0	1	6	18-1	0	11	.270	.359	.365	90	-1	0-1	1.000	-5	94	124	2b26,S20,3b15,O3L,D2	0	-0.4
1998	Tor A	102	301	33	77	17	2	2	27	29-0	4	42	.256	.327	.346	76	-10	2-2	.975	1	101	76	2b91,S6,3b4	15	-0.5
1999	Tor A	34	113	18	41	7	0	0	10	15-0	2	13	.363	.443	.425	122	5	0-0	.959	-6	85	65	2b17,D10,S4,3b2	93	0.0
2000	Tor A	66	241	38	71	19	0	3	23	25-0	2	33	.295	.364	.411	93	-2	0-0	.968	4	109	87	2b56,S8	0	0.5
2001	Bos A	23	41	1	2	1	0	0	2	2-0	0	9	.049	.093	.073	-55	-9	0-0	1.000	-3	87	47	S23	143	-1.1
Total	12	752	1988	239	518	116	8	19	187	228-2	19	274	.261	.340	.356	86	-32	4-11	.981	7	101	93	2b299,S281,3b152,D13,O5(4/0/1)	388	-0.2
GREEN, ANDY	Andrew Mulligan; B7.7.1977 Lexington KY; BR/TR/5´9˝/(165–180); [AriN00 24/729]; d6.12; Col Kentucky																								
2004	Ari N	46	109	13	22	2	1	1	4	5-0	1	17	.202	.241	.266	30	-12	1-1	.918	3	121	38	3b18,2b14,O9L	0	-0.8
2005	Ari N	17	31	5	7	1	0	0	2	7-0	0	3	.226	.359	.258	65	-1	0-0	1.000	0	94	131	2b5,S2,O2L	0	-0.1
2006	Ari N	73	86	15	16	4	0	1	6	13-0	0	20	.186	.293	.267	43	-7	1-0	1.000	-0	124	0	3b7,O7L,2b6,S2/D	29	-0.7
Total	3	136	226	33	45	7	1	2	12	25-0	1	40	.199	.280	.265	40	-20	2-1	.984	3	93	110	2b25,3b25,O18L,S4/D	29	-1.6
GREEN, SCARBOROUGH	Bertrum Scarborough; B6.9.1974 Creve Coeur MO; BB/TR/5´10˝/170; [StLN92 10/279]; d8.2																								
1997	StL N	20	31	5	3	0	0	0	1	2-0	0	5	.097	.152	.097	-33	-6	0-0	.952	0	101	209	O19(7/12/0)	0	-0.6
1999	Tex A	18	13	4	4	0	0	0	0	1-0	0	2	.308	.357	.308	68	-1	0-1	1.000	-0	84	0	O9(3/4/3),D4	0	-0.1
2000	Tex A	79	124	21	29	1	1	0	9	10-0	0	26	.234	.291	.258	40	-12	10-6	1.000	8	114	393	O65(3/41/23),D6	0	-0.4
Total	3	117	168	30	36	1	1	0	10	13-0	0	33	.214	.271	.232	29	-19	10-7	.993	8	110	333	O93(13/57/26),D10	0	-1.1
GREEN, DAVID	David Alejandro (Casaya); B12.4.1960 Managua, Nicaragua; BR/TR/6´3˝/(165–170); d9.4																								
1981	StL N	21	34	6	5	1	0	0	2	6-1	0	5	.147	.275	.176	29	-3	0-1	.970	0	103	126	O18C	0	-0.4
1982	†StL N	76	166	21	47	7	1	2	23	8-2	1	29	.283	.315	.373	91	-2	11-3	.991	1	102	134	O68(7/46/19)	15	-0.1
1983	StL N	146	422	52	120	14	10	8	69	26-1	1	76	.284	.325	.422	106	1	34-16	.970	-1	94	130	O136(20/19/100)	0	-0.4
1984	StL N	126	452	49	121	14	4	15	65	20-4	1	105	.268	.297	.416	102	-2	17-9	.991	-2	96	114	1b117,O14(0/6/8)	22	-1.1
1985	SF N	106	294	36	73	10	2	5	20	22-3	1	58	.248	.301	.347	85	-7	6-5	.987	-2	93	94	1b78,O12(1/0/11)	0	-1.4
1987	StL N	14	30	4	8	2	1	1	1	2-0	0	5	.267	.313	.500	108	0	0-1	.882	0	104	206	O10(1/0/9),1b3	0	0.0
Total	6	489	1398	168	374	48	18	31	180	84-11	4	278	.268	.308	.394	96	-13	68-35	.972	-3	98	131	O258(29/89/147),1b198	37	-3.4

YEAR	TM LG	G	AB	R	H	2B	3B	HR	RBI	BB-IB	HP	SO	AVG	OBP	SLG	AOPS	ABR	SB-CS	FA	FR	RNG	THR	GAMES AT POSITION	DL	BFW
GREEN, DANNY	Edward; B11.6.1876 Burlington NJ; D11.9.1914 Camden NJ; BL/TR; d8.17																								
1898	Chi N	47	188	26	59	4	3	4	27	7	1	—	.314	.342	.431	121	4	12	.970	4	148	331	O47(8/2/37)	—	0.5
1899	Chi N	117	475	90	140	12	11	6	56	35	7	—	.295	.352	.404	110	5	18	.947	1	126	**261**	O115(9/0/106)	—	0.0
1900	Chi N	103	389	63	116	21	5	5	49	17	7	—	.298	.339	.416	112	5	28	.938	-0	73	56	O102(3/60/39)	—	-0.1
1901	Chi N	133	537	82	168	16	12	6	61	40	3	—	.313	.364	.421	132	21	31	.932	7	96	161	O133C	—	2.1
1902	Chi A	129	481	77	150	16	11	0	62	53	7	—	.312	.388	.391	122	17	35	.942	-3	66	124	O129(18/2/110)	—	0.7
1903	Chi A	135	499	75	154	26	7	6	62	47	6	—	.309	.375	.425	146	30	29	.933	2	111	**216**	O133R	—	2.7
1904	Chi A	147	536	83	142	16	10	2	62	63	9	—	.265	.352	.343	125	18	28	.964	1	81	133	O146R	—	1.4
1905	Chi A	112	379	56	92	13	6	0	44	53	6	—	.243	.345	.309	112	8	11	.914	-8	83	138	O107(0/7/100)	—	-0.4
Total	8	923	3484	552	1021	124	65	29	423	315	46	—	.293	.359	.391	124	108	192	.941	3	94	167	O912(38/204/671)	—	6.9
GREEN, PUMPSIE	Elijah Jerry; B10.27.1933 Oakland CA; BB/TR/6´0˝/175; d7.21																								
1959	Bos A	50	172	30	40	6	3	1	10	29-0	2	22	.233	.350	.320	81	-3	4-2	.972	5	107	117	2b45/S	0	0.5
1960	Bos A	133	260	36	63	10	3	3	21	44-2	1	47	.242	.350	.338	85	-4	3-4	.982	-13	87	62	2b69,S41	0	-1.3
1961	Bos A	88	219	33	57	12	3	6	27	42-3	0	32	.260	.376	.425	112	5	4-2	.940	-3	107	98	S57,2b7	38	0.8
1962	Bos A	56	91	12	21	2	1	2	11	11-0	0	18	.231	.308	.341	74	-3	1-0	.953	-6	77	77	2b18,S5	0	-0.8
1963	NY N	17	54	8	15	1	2	1	5	12-0	0	13	.278	.409	.426	139	3	0-2	.857	1	126	82	3b16	0	0.4
Total	5	344	796	119	196	31	12	13	74	138-5	3	132	.246	.357	.364	94	-2	12-10	.975	-16	94	89	2b139,S104,3b16	38	-0.4
GREEN, GARY	Gary Allan; B1.14.1962 Pittsburgh PA; BR/TR/6´3˝/(170–180); [SDN84 1/27]; d9.14; f–Fred; Col Oklahoma St.																								
1986	SD N	13	33	2	7	1	0	0	2	1-0	0	11	.212	.235	.242	33	-3	0-0	1.000	2	109	141	S13	0	0.0
1989	SD N	15	27	4	7	3	0	0	0	1-0	0	1	.259	.286	.370	86	0	0-1	.921	2	133	189	S11/3	0	0.2
1990	Tex A	62	88	10	19	3	0	0	8	6-0	0	18	.216	.263	.250	45	-7	1-1	.972	7	111	119	S58	0	0.3
1991	Tex A	8	20	0	3	1	0	0	1	1-0	0	6	.150	.190	.200	8	-3	0-0	.968	1	112	124	S8	39	-0.1
1992	Cin N	8	12	3	4	1	0	0	0	0-0	0	2	.333	.333	.417	108	0	0-0	1.000	-3	32	0	S6/3	0	-0.3
Total	5	106	180	19	40	9	0	0	11	9-0	0	38	.222	.258	.272	49	-13	1-2	.970	9	109	126	S96,3b2	39	0.1
GREEN, GENE	Gene Leroy; B6.26.1933 Los Angeles CA; D5.23.1981 St.Louis MO; BR/TR/6´2˝/(200–207); d9.10																								
1957	StL N	6	15	0	3	1	0	0	2	0-0	0	3	.200	.188	.267	23	-2	0-0	1.000	-1	34	0	O3R	0	-0.3
1958	StL N	137	442	47	124	18	3	13	55	37-4	1	48	.281	.333	.423	96	-3	2-1	.956	9	108	206	O75(0/1/75),C48	0	0.6
1959	StL N	30	74	8	14	6	0	1	3	5-1	0	18	.189	.241	.311	43	-6	0-0	.944	6	97	495	O19R,C11	0	0.0
1960	Bal A	1	4	0	1	0	0	0	0	0-0	0	0	.250	.250	.250	36	0	0-0	1.000	0	0	1763	/rf	0	0.0
1961	Was A	110	364	52	102	16	3	18	62	35-5	1	65	.280	.341	.489	122	10	0-2	.986	-17	69	72	C79,O21R	0	-0.5
1962	Cle A	66	143	16	40	4	1	11	28	8-0	0	21	.280	.316	.552	133	5	0-0	.964	1	107	135	O33(3/0/30),1b2	0	0.4
1963	Cle A	43	78	4	16	3	0	2	7	4-0	2	22	.205	.259	.321	63	-4	0-0	1.000	-2	65	115	O18(1/0/17)	0	-0.7
	Cin N	15	31	3	7	1	0	1	3	0-0	1	8	.226	.250	.355	70	-1	0-0	.932	-3	44	51	C8	0	-0.4
Total	7	408	1151	130	307	49	7	46	160	89-10	5	185	.267	.318	.441	101	-1	2-3	.963	-6	96	195	O170(4/1/166),C146,1b2	0	-0.9
GREEN, JIM	James F.; B5.22.1854 Windham Co. CT; D12.12.1912 Cleveland OH; d7.19																								
1884	Was U	10	36	4	5	1	0	0	—	0	—	—	.139	.139	.167	-8	-6	—	.818	0	119	0	3b9/rf	—	-0.5
GREEN, JOE	Joseph Henry (aka Joseph Henry Greene); B9.17.1897 Philadelphia PA; D2.4.1972 Bryn Mawr PA; BR/TR/6´2˝/170; d7.2																								
1924	Phi A	1	1	0	0	0	0	0	0	0	0	0	.000	.000	.000	-99	0	0-0	ø	0	—	—	/H	—	0.0
GREEN, LENNY	Leonard Charles; B1.6.1933 Detroit MI; BL/TL/5´11˝/(161–177); d8.25																								
1957	Bal A	19	33	2	6	1	1	1	5	1-0	0	4	.182	.206	.364	56	-2	0-1	.950	-1	86	0	O15(3/12/2)	0	-0.5
1958	Bal A	69	91	10	21	4	0	0	4	9-0	0	10	.231	.297	.275	63	-4	0-2	.965	3	130	57	O53(28/30/6)	0	-0.4
1959	Bal A	27	24	3	7	0	0	1	2	1-0	1	3	.292	.346	.417	111	0	0-0	1.000	-0	52	362	O23(20/0/5)	0	-0.1
	Was A	88	190	29	46	6	1	2	15	20-0	0	15	.242	.314	.316	74	-7	9-5	.979	1	102	151	O58(21/13/27)	0	-0.7
	Year	115	214	32	53	6	1	3	17	21-0	1	18	.248	.318	.327	78	-6	9-5	.981	1	94	186	O81(41/13/32)	0	-0.8
1960	Was A	127	330	62	97	16	7	5	33	43-4	6	25	.294	.383	.430	121	11	21-8	.991	2	110	76	O100(20/92/0)	0	1.1
1961	Min A	156	600	92	171	28	7	9	50	81-2	6	50	.285	.374	.400	102	4	17-11	.978	-4	105	34	O153(56/141/4)	0	-0.5
1962	Min A	158	619	97	168	33	3	14	63	88-2	8	36	.271	.367	.402	104	7	8-4	.995	6	108	102	O156(88/146/0)	0	0.7
1963	Min A	145	280	41	67	10	1	4	27	31-1	2	21	.239	.315	.325	80	-7	11-5	.988	-4	101	22	O119(15/118/0)	0	-1.4
1964	Min A	26	15	3	0	0	0	0	0	4-0	0	6	.000	.211	.000	-35	-3	0-1	1.000	-0	72	0	O7(6/1/0)	0	-0.3
	LA A	39	92	13	23	2	0	2	4	10-0	1	8	.250	.327	.337	96	-1	2-0	.977	-1	94	78	O23(11/13/0)	0	-0.2
	Bal A	14	21	0	4	0	0	0	1	7-1	0	3	.190	.393	.190	69	0	1-0	1.000	2	195	0	O8(2/6/0)	0	0.2
	Year	79	128	16	27	2	0	2	5	21-1	1	17	.211	.325	.273	72	-4	3-1	.985	1	113	61	O38(19/20/0)	0	-0.3
1965	Bos A	119	373	69	103	24	6	7	24	48-0	3	43	.276	.361	.429	117	10	8-2	.980	-0	106	52	O95(12/86/0)	0	0.9
1966	Bos A	85	133	18	32	6	0	1	12	15-1	2	19	.241	.325	.308	76	-3	0-1	.978	-1	84	227	O27(4/23/0)	0	-0.5
1967	Det A	58	151	22	42	8	1	1	13	9-0	0	17	.278	.317	.364	99	0	1-1	.983	-2	93	0	O44(43/2/0)	0	-0.5
1968	Det A	6	4	0	1	0	0	0	0	1-1	0	0	.250	.400	.250	98	0	0-0	ø	-0	0	0	O2L	0	0.0
Total	12	1136	2956	461	788	138	27	47	253	368-12	29	260	.267	.351	.379	99	5	78-41	.984	1	105	71	O883(331/683/44)	0	-2.2
GREEN, NICK	Nicholas Anthony; B9.10.1978 Pensacola FL; BR/TR/6´0˝/(175–180); [AtlN98 32/971]; d5.15; Col Georgia Perimeter JC; [DL 2002 Atl N 23]																								
2004	†Atl N	95	264	40	72	15	3	3	26	12-1	4	63	.273	.312	.386	79	-9	1-2	.977	5	109	107	2b75,3b5/rf	0	-0.1
2005	TB A	111	318	53	76	15	2	5	29	33-0	11	86	.239	.329	.346	82	-7	3-1	.988	-25	84	70	2b91,3b13/rf	0	-2.7
2006	TB A	17	39	4	3	0	0	0	0	6-0	0	11	.077	.200	.077	-24	-7	0-3	1.000	-1	95	109	S10,2b4/rfD	0	-0.9
	NY A	46	75	8	18	5	0	2	4	5-0	1	29	.240	.296	.387	75	-3	1-1	.985	1	85	75	2b19,3b17,S10/1D	0	-0.1
	Year	63	114	12	21	5	0	2	4	11-0	1	40	.184	.262	.281	41	-10	1-4	.988	-0	83	82	2b23,S20,3b17,D2/rf1	0	-1.0
Total	3	269	696	105	169	35	5	10	59	56-1	16	189	.243	.312	.351	74	-26	5-7	.983	-20	94	86	2b189,3b35,S20,O3R,D2/1	23	-3.8
GREEN, DICK	Richard Larry; B4.21.1941 Sioux City IA; BR/TR/5´10˝/(175–180); d9.9																								
1963	KC A	13	37	5	10	2	0	1	4	2-0	1	10	.270	.317	.405	98	0	0-0	.941	3	138	85	S6,2b4	0	0.3
1964	KC A	130	435	48	115	14	5	11	37	27-3	3	87	.264	.311	.395	92	-5	3-3	.990	13	112	82	2b120	0	1.8
1965	KC A	133	474	64	110	15	1	15	55	50-1	3	110	.232	.308	.363	92	-5	0-2	.980	-7	101	87	2b126	0	-0.3
1966	KC A	140	507	58	127	24	3	9	62	27-4	7	101	.250	.297	.363	92	-6	6-1	.979	-6	101	92	2b137,3b2	0	0.1
1967	KC A	122	349	26	69	12	4	5	37	30-1	0	68	.198	.260	.298	67	-15	6-3	.946	-4	88	61	3b59,2b50/1S	0	-1.7
1968	Oak A	76	202	19	47	6	0	6	18	21-3	1	41	.233	.307	.351	104	1	3-1	.974	7	107	113	2b61/C3	0	1.4
1969	Oak A	136	483	61	133	25	6	12	64	53-3	8	94	.275	.353	.427	123	15	2-3	**.986**	-4	99	111	2b131	0	2.0
1970	Oak A	135	384	34	73	7	0	4	29	38-5	3	73	.190	.267	.240	42	-31	3-0	.978	-3	99	96	2b127,3b5/C	0	-2.7
1971	†Oak A	144	475	58	116	14	1	12	49	51-14	3	83	.244	.320	.354	93	-5	1-1	.986	3	97	114	2b143/S	0	0.9
1972	†Oak A	26	42	1	12	1	1	0	3	3-0	1	5	.286	.348	.357	115	1	0-1	.964	-1	105	95	2b26	117	0.1
1973	†Oak A	133	332	33	87	17	0	3	42	21-0	2	63	.262	.308	.340	87	-6	0-2	.988	-0	102	123	2b133/S3	0	0.0
1974	†Oak A	100	287	20	61	8	2	2	22	22-0	0	50	.213	.269	.275	60	-15	2-3	.983	8	105	111	2b100	66	-0.2
Total	12	1288	4007	427	960	145	23	80	422	345-34	32	785	.240	.303	.347	87	-71	26-20	.983	8	101	102	2b1158,3b68,S9,C2/1	183	1.7
GREEN, SHAWN	Shawn David; B11.10.1972 Des Plaines IL; BL/TL/6´4˝/(190–210); [TorA91 1/16]; d9.28																								
1993	Tor A	3	6	0	0	0	0	0	0	0-0	0	1	.000	.000	.000	-98	-2	0-0	1.000	-0	62	0	O2R/D	0	-0.2
1994	Tor A	14	33	1	3	1	0	0	1	1-0	0	8	.091	.118	.121	-38	-7	1-0	1.000	0	68	325	O14(10/0/5)	0	-0.7
1995	Tor A	121	379	52	109	31	4	15	54	20-3	3	68	.288	.326	.509	114	6	1-2	.973	5	107	135	O109R	0	0.5
1996	Tor A	132	422	52	118	32	3	11	45	33-3	8	75	.280	.342	.448	99	-1	5-1	.992	8	111	124	O127(0/2/127)/D	0	0.2
1997	Tor A	135	429	57	123	22	4	16	53	36-4	1	99	.287	.340	.469	109	5	14-3	.984	4	106	116	O91(45/0/46),D35	0	0.4
1998	Tor A	158	630	106	175	33	4	35	100	50-2	5	142	.278	.334	.510	115	12	35-12	.979	1	100	132	O157(0/32/128)	0	1.0
1999	Tor A★	153	614	134	190	**45**	0	42	123	66-4	11	117	.309	.384	.588	141	39	20-7	.997	5	112	47	O152R	0	3.4
2000	LA N	**162**	610	98	164	44	4	24	99	90-9	8	121	.269	.367	.472	116	17	24-5	.980	-9	88	88	O161(0/1/161)	0	0.4
2001	LA N	161	619	121	184	31	4	49	125	72-10	5	107	.297	.372	.598	155	49	20-4	.982	-2	100	77	O159(0/2/159)/1	0	4.0
2002	LA N★	158	582	110	166	31	1	42	114	93-22	5	112	.285	.385	.558	154	47	8-5	.994	3	106	66	O156R/D	0	4.2
2003	LA N	160	611	84	171	49	2	19	85	68-2	6	112	.280	.355	.460	114	14	6-2	.982	-7	88	91	O157R,D2	0	0.0
2004	†LA N	157	590	92	157	28	1	28	86	71-6	8	114	.266	.352	.459	109	8	5-2	.995	-9	79	101	1b111,O52R,D3	0	-1.2
2005	Ari N	158	581	87	166	37	4	22	73	62-6	5	95	.286	.355	.477	111	10	8-4	**1.000**	-5	98	46	O155(0/41/135)	0	0.0
2006	Ari N	115	417	59	118	22	3	11	51	37-4	6	64	.283	.348	.429	93	-4	4-4	.988	-9	87	21	O100R,1b12	0	-1.9
	†NY N	34	113	14	29	9	0	4	15	8-1	4	18	.257	.325	.442	97	0	0-0	.949	-2	95	0	O31R/1D	0	-0.4
	Year	149	530	73	147	31	3	15	66	45-5	10	82	.277	.344	.432	94	-5	4-4	.978	-11	89	16	O131R,1b13/D	0	-2.3
Total	14	1821	6636	1067	1873	415	34	318	1024	707-76	75	1253	.282	.355	.499	119	193	151-51	.986	-19	99	83	O1623(55/78/1520),1b125,D44	0	9.7

YEAR	TM LG	G	AB	R	H	2B	3B	HR	RBI	BB-IB	HP	SO	AVG	OBP	SLG	AOPS	ABR	SB-CS	FA	FR	RNG	THR	GAMES AT POSITION	DL	BFW
GREENBERG, ADAM	Adam Daniel; B2.21.1981 New Haven CT; BL/TL/5´9˝/180; [ChiN02 9/273]; d7.9; Col North Carolina																								
2005	Chi N	1	0	0	0	0	0	0	0	0-0	1	0	ø	1.000	ø	187	0	0-0	ø	0	—	—	/H	18	0.0
GREENBERG, HANK	Henry Benjamin "Hammerin' Hank"; B1.1.1911 New York NY; D9.4.1986 Beverly Hills CA; BR/TR/6´3.5˝/210; d9.14; Mil 1941–45; HF1956																								
1930	Det A	1	1	0	0	0	0	0	0	0	0	0	.000	.000	.000	-98	0	0-0	ø	0	—	—	/H	—	0.0
1933	Det A	117	449	59	135	33	3	12	87	46	1	78	.301	.367	.468	118	11	6-2	.988	1	103	**129**	1b117	—	0.2
1934	†Det A	153	593	118	201	**63**	7	26	139	63	2	93	.339	.404	.600	156	49	9-5	.990	1	101	102	1b153	—	3.3
1935	†Det A	**152**	619	121	203	46	16	**36**	**170**	87	0	91	.328	.411	.628	171	64	4-3	.992	6	**114**	**118**	1b152	—	5.0
1936	Det A	12	46	10	16	6	2	1	16	9	0	6	.348	.455	.630	165	5	1-0	.992	1	136	135	1b12	—	0.4
1937	Det A☆	154	594	137	200	49	14	40	**183**	102	3	101	.337	.436	.668	171	65	8-3	.992	5	115	98	1b154	—	5.1
1938	Det A✳	**155**	556	**144**	175	23	4	**58**	146	**119**	3	92	.315	.438	.683	167	58	7-5	.991	7	118	103	1b155	—	4.5
1939	Det A★	138	500	112	156	42	7	33	112	91	2	95	.312	.420	.622	152	40	8-3	**.993**	-2	90	97	1b136	—	2.4
1940	†Det A★	148	573	129	195	**50**	8	**41**	**150**	93	1	75	.340	.433	**.670**	166	**57**	6-3	.954	-1	95	133	O148L	—	4.5
1941	Det A	19	67	12	18	5	1	2	12	16	0	12	.269	.410	.463	118	2	1-0	.914	-3	86	0	O19L	0	-0.1
1945	†Det A✳	78	270	47	84	20	2	13	60	42	0	40	.311	.404	.544	164	23	3-1	1.000	-5	89	48	O72L	0	1.5
1946	Det A	142	523	91	145	29	5	**44**	**127**	80	0	88	.277	.373	.604	160	41	5-1	.989	2	100	99	1b140	0	3.9
1947	Pit N	125	402	71	100	13	2	25	74	**104**	4	73	.249	.408	.478	131	22	0	.992	1	104	86	1b119	0	1.9
Total	13	1394	5193	1051	1628	379	71	331	1276	852	16	844	.313	.412	.605	157	437	58-<u>26</u>	.991	11	106	104	1b1138,O239L	0	32.6
GREENE, ALTAR	Altar Alphonse; B11.9.1954 Detroit MI; BL/TR/5´11˝/190; d7.23; Col Northwood																								
1979	Det A	29	59	9	8	1	0	3	6	10-1	0	15	.136	.257	.305	50	-4	0-1	1.000	1	203	0	D15,O6(4/0/2)	0	-0.4
GREENE, CHARLIE	Charles Patrick; B1.23.1971 Miami FL; BR/TR/6´2˝/(170–190); [SDN91 19/497]; d9.15; Col Miami–Dade Kendall (FL) CC																								
1996	NY N	2	1	0	0	0	0	0	0	0-0	0	0	.000	.000	.000	-99	0	0-0	1.000	0	0	0	/C	0	0.0
1997	Bal A	5	2	0	0	0	0	0	1	0-0	0	1	.000	.000	.000	-99	-1	0-0	1.000	0	0	0	C4	0	-0.1
1998	Bal A	13	21	1	4	1	0	0	0	0-0	0	8	.190	.190	.238	11	-3	0-0	1.000	3	499	45	C13	0	0.1
1999	Mil N	32	42	4	8	1	0	0	1	5-0	0	11	.190	.271	.214	26	-5	0-0	.991	-1	70	82	C31	0	-0.4
2000	Tor A	3	9	0	1	0	0	0	0	0-0	0	5	.111	.111	.111	-42	-2	0-0	1.000	-0	0	0	C3	0	-0.2
Total	5	55	75	5	13	2	0	0	2	5-0	0	25	.173	.222	.200	10	-11	0-0	.995	2	177	62	C52	0	-0.6
GREENE, JUNE	Julius Foust; B6.25.1899 Ramseur NC; D3.19.1974 Glendora CA; BL/TR/6´2.5˝/185; d4.20; ▲																								
1928	Phi N	11	6	0	3	0	0	0	0	3	0	1	.500	.667	.500	202	2	0	1.000	0	429	0	/P	—	0.0
1929	Phi N	21	19	1	4	1	0	0	0	2	0	4	.211	.286	.263	35	0	0	1.000	0	128	0	P5	—	0.0
Total	2	32	25	1	7	1	0	0	0	5	0	5	.280	.400	.320	79	2	0	1.000	1	166	0	P6	—	0.0
GREENE, KHALIL	Khalil Thabit; B10.21.1979 Butler PA; BR/TR/5´11˝/210; [SDN02 1/13]; d9.3; Col Clemson																								
2003	SD N	20	65	8	14	4	1	2	6	4-0	1	19	.215	.271	.400	79	-2	0-1	.963	0	100	96	S20	0	-0.1
2004	SD N	139	484	67	132	31	4	15	65	53-10	8	94	.273	.349	.446	111	8	4-2	.965	-6	98	103	S136	0	1.2
2005	†SD N	121	436	51	109	30	2	15	70	25-3	6	93	.250	.296	.431	93	-6	5-0	.971	-12	94	86	S121	37	-0.9
2006	†SD N	121	412	56	101	26	2	15	55	39-0	7	87	.245	.320	.427	94	-4	5-1	.980	-10	97	95	S113	16	-0.5
Total	4	401	1397	182	356	91	9	47	196	121-13	22	293	.255	.321	.434	99	-4	14-4	.971	-28	97	95	S390	53	-0.3
GREENE, PADDY	Patrick Joseph "Patsy" (aka Patrick Foley in 1902); B3.20.1875 Providence RI; D10.20.1934 Providence RI; BR/TR/5´8˝/150; d9.10; Col Villanova																								
1902	Phi N	19	65	6	11	1	0	0	1	2	1	—	.169	.206	.185	21	-6	2	.912	0	104	78	3b19	—	-0.6
1903	NY A	4	13	1	4	1	0	0	0	0	0	—	.308	.308	.385	100	0	0	1.000	1	191	0	3b2/S	—	0.1
	Det A	1	3	0	0	0	0	0	0	0	0	—	.000	.000	.000	-99	-1	0	.750	-1	0	0	/3	—	-0.2
	Year	5	16	1	4	1	0	0	0	0	0	—	.250	.250	.313	65	-1	0	.933	0	135	0	3b3/S	—	-0.1
Total	2	24	81	7	15	2	0	0	1	2	1	—	.185	.214	.210	30	-7	2	.916	1	109	64	3b22/S	—	-0.7
GREENE, TODD	Todd Anthony; B5.8.1971 Augusta GA; BR/TR/5´10˝/(200–210); [CalA93 12/327]; d7.30; Col Georgia Southern																								
1996	Cal A	29	79	9	15	1	0	2	9	4-0	1	11	.190	.238	.278	30	-9	2-0	1.000	0	83	142	C26/D	0	-0.6
1997	Ana A	34	124	24	36	6	0	9	24	7-1	0	25	.290	.328	.556	125	4	2-0	1.000	-3	108	78	C26,D8	39	0.3
1998	Ana A	29	71	3	18	4	0	1	7	2-0	0	20	.254	.274	.352	60	-4	0-0	1.000	-2	68	0	O12L,1b3,D4	127	-0.6
1999	Ana A	97	321	36	78	20	0	14	42	12-0	3	63	.243	.275	.436	78	-12	1-4	.974	-5	67	54	D44,O30(5/0/25),C12	0	-2.0
2000	Tor A	34	85	11	20	2	0	5	10	5-0	0	18	.235	.278	.435	74	-4	0-0	1.000	-1	27	0	D23,C2/lf	14	-0.5
2001	†NY A	35	96	9	20	4	0	1	11	3-0	1	21	.208	.240	.281	36	-9	0-0	1.000	-6	46	78	C34,D2	0	-1.3
2002	Tex A	42	112	15	30	5	0	10	19	2-0	1	23	.268	.282	.580	119	2	0-0	.989	3	55	98	C15,1b15/lfD	0	0.5
2003	Tex A	62	205	25	47	10	1	10	20	2-0	2	47	.229	.243	.434	69	-10	0-0	.987	-8	72	160	C51,1b2,D3	15	-1.4
2004	Col N	75	195	23	55	14	0	10	35	13-4	0	38	.282	.325	.508	99	0	0-0	.989	-14	91	70	C53	24	-1.1
2005	Col N	38	126	10	32	4	0	7	23	7-0	1	21	.254	.299	.452	83	-3	0-0	.975	-15	60	63	C33	72	-1.6
2006	SF N	61	159	16	46	12	2	2	17	10-3	1	45	.289	.335	.428	93	-2	0-0	.995	-9	111	130	C42,1b5/D	0	-0.8
Total	11	536	1573	181	397	82	3	71	217	67-8	10	332	.252	.286	.444	82	-47	5-4	.991	-58	82	108	C294,D90,O44(19/0/25),1b25	291	-9.1
GREENE, WILLIE	Willie Louis; B9.23.1971 Milledgeville GA; BL/TR/5´11˝/(160–192); [PitN89 1/18]; d9.1																								
1992	Cin N	29	93	10	25	5	2	2	13	10-0	0	23	.269	.337	.430	114	2	0-2	.948	-2	83	155	3b25	0	-0.1
1993	Cin N	15	50	7	8	1	1	2	5	2-0	0	19	.160	.189	.340	39	-5	0-0	.978	2	105	145	S10,3b5	44	-0.2
1994	Cin N	16	37	5	8	2	0	0	3	6-1	0	14	.216	.318	.270	58	-2	0-0	.958	-1	104	64	3b13/lf	0	-0.3
1995	Cin N	8	19	1	2	0	0	0	0	3-0	0	7	.105	.227	.105	-9	-3	0-0	1.000	-0	106	113	3b7	0	-0.3
1996	Cin N	115	287	48	70	5	5	19	63	36-6	0	88	.244	.327	.495	111	3	0-1	.927	10	121	129	3b74,O10(9/0/1),1b2/S	15	1.3
1997	Cin N	151	495	62	125	22	1	26	91	78-5	1	111	.253	.354	.459	109	7	6-0	.934	-11	90	43	3b103,O39(6/0/33),1b7,S3	0	-0.3
1998	Cin N	111	356	57	96	18	1	14	49	56-2	3	80	.270	.372	.444	113	8	6-3	.936	-2	93	161	3b76,O28(9/0/22),S2/D	0	0.6
	Bal A	24	40	8	6	1	0	1	5	13-0	0	10	.150	.358	.250	63	-2	1-0	.941	-1	72	132	O14(1/0/13)/D	0	-0.3
1999	Tor A	81	226	22	46	7	0	12	41	20-0	0	56	.204	.266	.394	65	-13	0-0	.917	-2	62	0	D51,3b7,O3R	0	-1.7
2000	Chi N	105	299	34	60	15	2	10	37	36-2	2	69	.201	.289	.365	65	-17	4-0	.967	5	108	124	3b90	27	-1.0
Total	9	655	1902	254	446	76	12	86	307	260-16	6	477	.234	.326	.423	93	-22	17-6	.943	-1	100	107	3b400,O95(26/0/72),D53,S16,1b9	86	-2.3
GREENGRASS, JIM	James Raymond; B10.24.1927 Addison NY; BR/TR/6´1˝/200; d9.9																								
1952	Cin N	18	68	10	21	2	1	5	24	7	0	12	.309	.373	.588	163	5	0-0	.965	-1	110	0	O17(4/13/0)	0	0.4
1953	Cin N	154	606	86	173	22	7	20	100	47	3	83	.285	.340	.444	102	0	6-4	.983	3	110	80	O153L	0	-0.6
1954	Cin N	139	542	79	152	27	4	27	95	41	0	81	.280	.329	.494	109	5	0-3	.968	3	105	101	O137L	0	-0.2
1955	Cin N	13	39	1	4	2	0	0	1	9-0	0	9	.103	.271	.154	16	-5	0-0	1.000	1	125	111	O11L	0	-0.4
	Phi N	94	323	43	88	20	2	12	37	33-2	1	43	.272	.339	.458	112	6	0-2	.988	3	106	151	O83(5/0/79),3b2	0	0.4
	Year	107	362	44	92	22	2	12	38	42-2	1	52	.254	.331	.425	100	1	0-2	.990	4	108	146	O94(16/0/79),3b2	0	0.0
1956	Phi N	86	215	24	44	9	2	5	25	28-3	0	43	.205	.294	.335	71	-9	0-0	.991	-0	105	63	O62R	0	-1.1
Total	5	504	1793	243	482	82	16	69	282	165-<u>5</u>	4	271	.269	.330	.448	102	2	6-9	.980	8	108	94	O463(310/13/141),3b2	0	-1.5
GREENWELL, MIKE	Michael Lewis; B7.18.1963 Louisville KY; BL/TR/6´0˝/(170–205); [BosA82 3/72]; d9.5; C1																								
1985	Bos A	17	31	7	10	1	0	4	8	3-1	0	4	.323	.382	.742	191	4	1-0	1.000	-1	74	0	O17(16/0/3)	0	0.2
1986	†Bos A	31	35	4	11	2	0	0	4	5-0	0	7	.314	.400	.371	111	1	0-0	1.000	2	153	257	O15(8/0/7),D3	0	0.3
1987	Bos A	125	412	71	135	31	6	19	89	35-1	6	40	.328	.386	.570	146	27	5-4	.971	1	98	141	O91(64/0/28),D15/C	0	2.2
1988	†Bos A★	158	590	86	192	39	8	22	119	87-**18**	9	38	.325	.416	.531	157	49	16-8	.981	3	104	75	O147(143/0/8),D11	0	4.7
1989	Bos A★	145	578	87	178	36	0	14	95	56-15	3	44	.308	.370	.443	121	18	13-5	.967	-10	76	136	O139L,D5	15	0.5
1990	†Bos A	159	610	71	181	30	6	14	73	65-12	4	43	.297	.367	.434	118	15	8-7	.977	-3	87	130	O159L	0	0.6
1991	Bos A	147	544	76	163	26	6	9	83	43-6	3	35	.300	.350	.419	107	5	15-5	.989	0	96	120	O143L/D	0	0.2
1992	Bos A	49	180	16	42	2	0	2	18	18-1	2	19	.233	.307	.278	61	-9	2-3	1.000	-1	102	36	O41L,D6	120	-1.3
1993	Bos A	146	540	77	170	38	6	13	72	54-12	4	46	.315	.379	.480	122	18	5-4	.993	-1	98	77	O134L,D10	15	1.0
1994	Bos A	95	327	60	88	25	1	11	45	38-6	4	26	.269	.348	.453	101	1	2-2	.993	0	86	175	O84L,D6	8	-0.2
1995	†Bos A	120	481	67	143	25	4	15	76	38-4	2	35	.297	.349	.459	106	3	9-5	.972	-7	81	133	O118L,D2	21	-0.8
1996	Bos A	77	295	35	87	20	1	7	44	18-3	2	27	.295	.336	.441	94	-3	4-0	.973	3	96	188	O76(75/1/1)	82	-0.2
Total	12	1269	4623	657	1400	275	38	130	726	460-79	39	364	.303	.368	.463	119	129	80-43	.981	-15	92	121	O1164(1124/1/47),D59/C	261	7.2
GREENWOOD, BILL	William F.; B1857 Philadelphia PA; D5.2.1902 Philadelphia PA; BB/TL/5´7.5˝/180; d9.16																								
1882	Phi AA	7	30	8	9	1	0	0	1	1	—	—	.300	.323	.333	114	0	—	.909	-1	0	0	O7R,2b2	—	-0.1
1884	Bro AA	92	385	52	83	8	3	3	—	10	1	—	.216	.237	.275	66	-15	—	.900	-9	103	96	2b92/S	—	-1.9
1887	Bal AA	118	495	114	130	16	6	0	65	54	1	—	.263	.336	.319	88	-5	71	**.928**	10	102	69	2b117/lf	—	0.7

YEAR	TM LG	G	AB	R	H	2B	3B	HR	RBI	BB-IB	HP	SO	AVG	OBP	SLG	AOPS	ABR	SB-CS	FA	FR	RNG	THR	GAMES AT POSITION	DL	BFW
1888	Bal AA	115	409	69	78	13	1	0	29	30	6	—	.191	.256	.227	57	-18	46	.913	-17	102	54	2b86,S28/rf	—	-3.0
1889	Col AA	118	414	62	93	7	10	3	49	58	5	71	.225	.327	.312	86	-6	37	.914	-2	95	84	2b118	—	-0.3
1890	Roc AA	124	437	76	97	11	6	2	41	48	8	—	.222	.310	.288	83	-8	40	.921	1	100	114	2b123/S	—	-0.2
Total	6	574	2170	381	490	56	26	8	185	201	21	71	.226	.298	.287	78	-52	194	.916	-18	100	85	2b538,S30,O9(1/0/8)	—	-4.8
GREER, BRIAN	Brian Keith; B5.14.1959 Lynwood CA; BR/TR/6´3˝/210; [SDN77 1/8]; d9.13																								
1977	SD N	1	1	0	0	0	0	0	0	0-0	0	1	.000	.000	.000	-99	0	0-0	ø	0	—	—	/H	0	0.0
1979	SD N	4	3	0	0	0	0	0	0	0-0	0	1	.000	.000	.000	-99	-1	0-0	1.000	-0	102	0	O4C	0	-0.1
Total	2	5	4	0	0	0	0	0	0	0-0	0	2	.000	.000	.000	-99	-1	0-0	1.000	-0	102	0	O4C	0	-0.1
GREER, ED	Edward C.; B1865 Philadelphia PA; D2.4.1890 Philadelphia PA; BR; d6.24																								
1885	Bal AA	56	211	32	42	7	0	0	21	8	2	—	.199	.235	.232	49	-12	—	.908	-1	74	61	O47(2/38/7),C12	—	-1.2
1886	Bal AA	11	38	2	5	1	0	0	4	2	0	—	.132	.175	.158	5	-4	4	.875	-1	207	0	O9L,C2	—	-0.4
	Phi AA	71	264	33	51	5	3	1	20	8	2	—	.193	.223	.246	46	-17	12	.921	6	86	145	O70(0/66/4)/C	—	-1.2
	Year	82	302	35	56	6	3	1	24	10	2	—	.185	.217	.235	41	-21	16	.919	6	96	133	O79(9/66/4),C3	—	-1.6
1887	Phi AA	3	11	1	2	0	0	0	0	0	0	—	.182	.182	.182	2	-1	2	.857	0	238	0	O3C	—	-0.1
	Bro AA	91	327	49	83	13	2	2	48	25	6	—	.254	.318	.324	79	-9	33	.921	2	64	35	O76L,C16	—	-0.6
	Year	94	338	50	85	13	2	2	48	25	6	—	.251	.314	.320	76	-11	35	.918	3	70	34	O79(76/3/0),C16	—	-0.7
Total	3	232	851	117	183	26	5	3	93	43	10	—	.215	.261	.268	58	-43	51	.916	7	80	76	O205(87/107/11),C31	—	-3.5
GREER, RUSTY	Thurman Clyde; B1.21.1969 Fort Rucker AL; BL/TL/6´0˝/(190–195); [TexA90 10/279]; d5.16; Col Montevallo; [DL 2003 Tex A 183, 2004 Tex A 183]																								
1994	Tex A	80	277	36	87	16	1	10	46	46-2	2	46	.314	.410	.487	130	15	0-0	.976	-4	101	41	O73(11/23/53),1b9	0	0.7
1995	Tex A	131	417	58	113	21	2	13	61	55-1	1	66	.271	.355	.424	99	0	3-1	.982	-2	95	121	O125(51/4/101),1b3	0	-0.7
1996	†Tex A	139	542	96	180	41	6	18	100	62-4	3	86	.332	.397	.530	125	23	9-0	.984	2	105	62	O137(136/1/0)/1D	0	1.9
1997	Tex A	157	601	112	193	42	3	26	87	83-4	3	87	.321	.405	.531	133	32	9-5	.965	-1	101	93	O153(148/19/1),D2	0	2.4
1998	†Tex A	155	598	107	183	31	5	16	108	80-1	4	93	.306	.386	.455	113	14	2-4	.990	-1	100	66	O154(154/2/0)	0	0.6
1999	†Tex A	147	556	107	167	41	3	20	101	96-2	5	67	.300	.405	.493	121	22	2-2	.983	-6	97	32	O145L/D	0	1.0
2000	Tex A	105	394	65	117	34	3	8	65	51-1	3	61	.297	.377	.459	110	8	4-1	.985	-4	99	51	O97L,D2	43	0.1
2001	Tex A	62	245	38	67	23	0	7	29	27-1	1	32	.273	.342	.453	106	3	1-2	.962	-1	106	54	O60L/D	118	0.0
2002	Tex A	51	199	24	59	9	2	1	17	19-0	0	17	.296	.356	.377	93	-2	1-0	.947	-5	71	0	O26(22/0/6),D22/1	117	-0.8
Total	9	1027	3829	643	1166	258	25	119	614	519-16	22	555	.305	.387	.478	117	115	31-15	.979	-21	99	65	O970(824/49/161),D29,1b14	644	5.2
GREGG, TOMMY	William Thomas; B7.29.1963 Boone NC; BL/TL/6´1˝/190; [PitN85 7/164]; d9.14; Col Wake Forest																								
1987	Pit N	10	8	3	2	1	0	0	0	0-0	0	2	.250	.250	.375	62	0	0-0	1.000	-0	83	0	O4(1/2/2)	0	-0.1
1988	Pit N	14	15	4	3	1	0	1	3	1-0	0	4	.200	.235	.467	102	0	0-1	1.000	-0	71	0	O6(5/0/1)	0	-0.1
	Atl N	11	29	1	10	3	0	0	4	2-1	0	2	.345	.387	.448	134	1	0-0	1.000	2	142	242	O7(5/3/0)	0	0.3
	Year	25	44	5	13	4	0	1	7	3-1	0	6	.295	.333	.455	125	1	0-1	1.000	2	122	174	O13(10/3/1)	0	0.2
1989	Atl N	102	276	24	67	8	0	6	23	18-2	0	45	.243	.288	.337	77	-9	3-4	.967	-4	81	51	O48(7/2/41),1b37	43	-1.9
1990	Atl N	124	239	18	63	13	1	5	32	20-4	1	39	.264	.322	.389	90	-3	4-3	.987	1	123	101	1b50,O20(7/0/12)	0	-0.6
1991	†Atl N	72	107	13	20	8	1	1	4	12-2	1	24	.187	.275	.308	60	-5	2-2	1.000	0	91	0	O14(9/0/5),1b13	42	-0.7
1992	Atl N	18	19	1	5	0	0	1	1	1-0	0	7	.263	.300	.421	96	0	1-0	1.000	1	188	0	O9(2/4/4)	106	0.1
1993	Cin N	10	12	1	2	0	0	0	1	0-0	0	0	.167	.154	.167	-10	-2	0-0	1.000	-1	50	0	O4(3/0/1)	0	-0.3
1995	Fla N	72	156	20	37	5	0	6	20	16-1	2	33	.237	.313	.385	82	-4	3-1	.984	-2	97	0	O38(6/4/30),1b2	21	-0.8
1997	†Atl N	13	19	1	5	2	0	0	0	1-0	0	2	.263	.300	.368	73	-1	1-1	1.000	-1	37	0	O6(5/0/1)/1	0	-0.2
Total	9	446	880	86	214	41	2	20	88	71-10	4	158	.243	.301	.363	81	-23	14-12	.981	-4	92	32	O156(50/15/97),1b103	212	-4.3
GREGORIO, TOM	Thomas Andrew; B5.5.1977 Brooklyn NY; BR/TR/6´2˝/200; [AnaA99 27/821]; d9.5; Col Troy St.																								
2003	Ana A	12	19	1	3	0	0	0	2	1-0	1	8	.158	.238	.158	8	-3	0-0	.979	-0	121	129	C12	0	-0.2
GREMMINGER, ED	Lorenzo Edward "Battleship"; B3.30.1874 Canton OH; D5.26.1942 Canton OH; BR/TR/6´1˝/200; d4.21																								
1895	Cle N	20	78	10	21	1	0	0	15	5	0	13	.269	.313	.282	51	-6	0	.873	-1	95	119	3b20	—	-0.5
1902	Bos N	140	522	55	134	20	12	1	65	39	5	—	.257	.314	.347	103	1	7	**.951**	2	94	83	3b140	—	0.7
1903	Bos N	**140**	511	57	135	24	9	5	56	31	5	—	.264	.313	.376	100	-2	12	.935	16	106	132	3b140	—	1.7
1904	Det A	83	309	18	66	13	3	1	28	14	4	—	.214	.257	.285	73	-9	3	.950	-13	78	38	3b83	—	-2.4
Total	4	383	1420	140	356	58	24	7	164	89	14	13	.251	.301	.340	92	-16	22	.940	4	95	93	3b383	—	-0.5
GREMP, BUDDY	Lewis Edward; B8.5.1919 Denver CO; D1.30.1995 Manteca CA; BR/TR/6´1˝/175; d9.13; Mil 1942–45																								
1940	Bos N	4	9	0	2	0	0	0	2	0	0	0	.222	.222	.222	24	-1	0	1.000	-0	80	117	1b3	—	-0.1
1941	Bos N	37	75	7	18	3	0	0	10	5	0	3	.240	.287	.280	63	-4	0	.977	-3	59	115	1b21,2b6,C3	0	-0.9
1942	Bos N	72	207	12	45	11	0	3	19	13	1	21	.217	.267	.314	71	-8	1	.991	1	108	10	1b62/3	0	-1.3
Total	3	113	291	19	65	14	0	3	31	18	1	24	.223	.271	.302	67	-13	1	.988	-3	96	38	1b86,2b6,C3/3	0	-2.3
GREY, REDDY	Romer Carl (b Romer Carl Gray); B4.8.1875 Zanesville OH; D11.9.1934 Altadena CA; BL/TL/5´11˝/175; d5.28																								
1903	Pit N	1	3	1	1	0	0	0	1	1	0	—	.333	.500	.333	135	0	0	1.000	-0	0	0	/lf	—	0.0
GRICH, BOBBY	Robert Anthony; B1.15.1949 Muskegon MI; BR/TR/6´2˝/(180–190); [BalA67 1/19]; d6.29																								
1970	Bal A	30	95	11	20	1	3	0	8	9-0	0	21	.211	.279	.284	55	-6	1-1	.915	2	101	49	S20,2b9/3	0	-0.2
1971	Bal A	7	30	7	9	0	0	1	6	5-0	0	8	.300	.400	.400	126	1	1-0	1.000	3	149	73	S5,2b2	0	0.5
1972	Bal A★	133	460	66	128	21	3	12	50	53-3	7	96	.278	.358	.415	126	16	13-6	.950	-6	97	126	S81,2b45,1b16,3b8	0	2.4
1973	†Bal A	**162**	581	82	146	29	7	12	50	107-3	7	91	.251	.373	.387	114	16	17-9	**.995**	27	**114**	**129**	2b162	0	5.4
1974	†Bal A★	160	582	92	153	29	6	19	82	90-6	**20**	117	.263	.376	.431	136	32	17-11	.979	16	**108**	**114**	2b160	0	6.0
1975	Bal A	150	524	81	136	26	4	13	57	107-4	8	88	.260	.389	.399	131	29	14-10	.977	26	**111**	**133**	2b150	0	6.4
1976	Bal A★	144	518	93	138	31	4	13	54	86-1	3	99	.266	.373	.417	139	30	14-6	.985	6	101	103	2b140,3b2,D2	0	**4.8**
1977	Cal A	52	181	24	44	6	0	7	23	37-4	1	40	.243	.369	.392	113	5	6-6	.983	-3	89	74	S52	116	0.6
1978	Cal A	144	487	68	122	16	2	6	42	75-1	7	83	.251	.357	.329	97	2	4-3	.983	0	96	82	2b144	0	1.0
1979	†Cal A★	153	534	78	157	30	5	30	101	59-10	2	84	.294	.365	.537	144	33	1-0	.984	-1	93	102	2b153	0	3.9
1980	Cal A★	150	498	60	135	22	2	14	62	84-2	4	108	.271	.377	.408	118	16	3-7	.989	4	102	91	2b146,1b3	0	2.6
1981	Cal A	100	352	56	107	14	2	**22**	61	40-4	4	71	.304	.378	**.543**	**162**	28	2-4	.983	18	**113**	122	2b100	59	**5.2**
1982	†Cal A★	145	506	74	132	28	5	19	65	82-3	8	109	.261	.371	.449	123	19	3-3	.986	17	108	120	2b142/D	0	4.2
1983	Cal A	120	387	65	113	17	0	16	62	76-2	7	62	.292	.414	.460	142	27	2-4	.969	18	**122**	106	2b118/S	34	4.9
1984	Cal A	116	363	60	93	15	1	18	58	57-3	2	70	.256	.357	.452	123	13	2-5	.982	-3	99	120	2b91,1b25,3b21	0	1.2
1985	Cal A	144	479	74	116	17	3	13	53	81-3	3	77	.242	.355	.372	99	2	3-5	**.997**	12	110	**135**	2b116,1b16,3b15,D6	0	1.8
1986	†Cal A	98	313	42	84	18	0	9	30	39-1	3	50	.268	.354	.412	109	5	1-3	.980	-9	95	106	2b87,1b11,3b2	0	-0.1
Total	17	2008	6890	1033	1833	320	47	224	864	1087-50	86	1278	.266	.371	.424	124	268	104-83	.984	126	106	112	2b1765,S159,1b71,3b49,D9	209	50.6
GRIESENBECK, TIM	Carlos Phillipe Timothy; B12.10.1897 San Antonio TX; D3.25.1953 San Antonio TX; BR/TR/5´10.5˝/190; d9.11; Col Texas A&M																								
1920	StL N	5	3	1	1	0	0	0	0	0	0	0	.333	.333	.333	95	0	0-0	1.000	0	*0*	*0*	C3	—	0.0
GRIEVE, BEN	Benjamin; B5.4.1976 Arlington TX; BL/TR/6´4˝/(200–230); [OakA94 1/2]; d9.3; f–Tom																								
1997	Oak A	24	93	12	29	6	0	3	24	13-1	1	25	.312	.402	.473	127	4	0-0	1.000	-2	78	63	O24R	0	0.1
1998	Oak A★	155	583	94	168	41	2	18	89	85-3	9	123	.288	.386	.458	120	21	2-2	.993	-10	88	64	O151R,D3	0	0.3
1999	Oak A	148	486	80	129	21	0	28	86	63-2	8	108	.265	.358	.481	115	11	4-0	.988	-2	96	77	O137(131/0/8),D4	0	0.5
2000	†Oak A	158	594	92	166	40	1	27	104	73-2	3	130	.279	.359	.487	114	13	3-0	.988	-10	84	73	O144L,D12	0	-0.2
2001	TB A	154	542	72	143	30	2	11	72	87-2	8	159	.264	.372	.387	103	6	7-1	.984	0	106	55	O120(56/0/64),D32	0	0.1
2002	TB A	136	482	62	121	30	0	19	64	69-5	8	121	.251	.353	.432	110	9	8-2	.988	0	103	79	O118R,D16	0	0.3
2003	TB A	55	165	28	38	7	0	4	17	32-1	6	41	.230	.371	.345	94	0	0-0	.947	-0	86	175	D37,O10R	107	-0.2
2004	Mil N	108	234	28	61	15	0	7	29	39-5	0	65	.261	.364	.415	100	1	0-0	.964	-3	102	0	O65R	0	-0.4
	Chi N	15	16	2	4	2	0	1	6	0-0	2	5	.250	.316	.563	122	1	0-0	1.000	0	104	0	O4(1/0/3)/D	0	0.0
	Year	123	250	30	65	17	0	8	35	39-5	2	70	.260	.361	.424	102	2	0-0	.965	-3	102	0	O69(1/0/68)/D	0	-0.4
2005	Chi N	23	20	1	5	0	0	0	1	5-1	0	7	.250	.400	.250	73	-1	0-0	ø	-0	0	0	/lf	0	-0.1
Total	9	976	3215	471	864	192	5	118	492	466-22	45	784	.269	.367	.442	111	65	24-5	.986	-27	95	65	O774(333/0/443),D105	107	0.4
GRIEVE, TOM	Thomas Alan; B3.4.1948 Pittsfield MA; BR/TR/6´2˝/190; [TexA66 1/6]; d7.5; s–Ben																								
1970	Was A	47	116	12	23	5	1	3	10	14-0	1	38	.198	.290	.336	75	-4	0-0	.939	-4	82	0	O39(15/1/24)	0	-1.0
1972	Tex A	64	142	12	29	2	1	3	11	11-1	2	39	.204	.271	.296	71	-6	1-3	.985	1	89	218	O49(45/3/5)	0	-0.8
1973	Tex A	66	123	22	38	6	0	7	21	7-0	1	25	.309	.348	.528	150	7	1-0	1.000	-3	92	0	O59(34/10/19)/D	0	0.3

YEAR	TM LG	G	AB	R	H	2B	3B	HR	RBI	BB-IB	HP	SO	AVG	OBP	SLG	AOPS	ABR	SB-CS	FA	FR	RNG	THR	GAMES AT POSITION	DL	BFW
1974	Tex A	84	259	30	66	10	4	9	32	20-1	2	48	.255	.311	.429	114	4	0-0	1.000	3	99	232	D40,O38(31/0/7)/1	0	0.4
1975	Tex A	118	369	46	102	17	1	14	61	22-0	0	74	.276	.316	.442	114	5	0-2	.990	-4	83	73	O63(46/2/16),D45	0	-0.4
1976	Tex A	149	546	57	139	23	3	20	81	35-5	4	119	.255	.301	.418	108	3	4-1	.983	2	107	110	D96,O52(45/0/8)	0	0.1
1977	Tex A	79	236	24	53	9	0	7	30	13-1	3	57	.225	.273	.352	68	-11	1-0	.976	-3	76	136	O60(30/0/32),D13	41	-1.7
1978	NY N	54	101	5	21	3	0	2	8	9-0	0	23	.208	.273	.297	61	-6	0-1	.979	3	120	195	O26(2/0/24),1b2	0	-0.4
1979	StL N	9	15	1	3	1	0	0	0	4-1	0	1	.200	.368	.267	75	0	0-0	.875	-1	89	0	O5L	0	-0.1
Total	9	670	1907	209	474	76	10	65	254	135-9	13	424	.249	.301	.401	100	-8	7-7	.982	-4	91	113	O391(253/16/135),D195,1b3	41	-3.6
GRIFFEY, KEN	George Kenneth Jr. "Junior"; B11.21.1969 Donora PA; BL/TL/6´3˝/(195–220); [SeaA87 1/1]; d4.3; f–Ken																								
1989	Sea A	127	455	61	120	23	0	16	61	44-8	2	83	.264	.329	.420	107	4	16-7	.969	0	95	**184**	O127C	27	0.4
1990	Sea A★	155	597	91	179	28	7	22	80	63-12	2	81	.300	.366	.481	134	27	16-11	.980	-11	87	108	O151C,D2	0	1.4
1991	Sea A★	154	548	76	179	42	1	22	100	71-21	1	82	.327	.399	.527	155	44	18-6	.989	3	96	202	O152C/D	0	4.6
1992	Sea A★	142	565	83	174	39	4	27	103	44-15	5	67	.308	.361	.535	147	34	10-5	.997	-2	97	105	O137C,D3	16	3.1
1993	Sea A★	156	582	113	180	38	3	45	109	96-25	6	91	.309	.408	.617	169	59	17-9	.991	-7	89	109	O139C,D19/1	0	5.1
1994	Sea A★	111	433	94	140	24	4	**40**	90	56-19	2	73	.323	.402	.674	167	43	11-3	.983	1	91	**239**	O103(0/103/1),D9	0	4.2
1995	†Sea A✱	72	260	52	67	7	0	17	42	52-6	0	53	.258	.379	.481	121	9	4-2	.990	6	115	157	O70C,D2	80	1.5
1996	Sea A✱	140	545	125	165	26	2	49	140	78-13	7	104	.303	.392	.628	153	44	16-1	.990	5	109	122	O137C,D5	23	4.8
1997	†Sea A★	157	608	**125**	185	34	3	**56**	**147**	76-**23**	8	121	.304	.382	**.646**	164	56	15-4	.985	4	106	122	O153(1/153/0),D4	0	**6.0**
1998	Sea A★	**161**	633	120	180	33	3	**56**	146	76-11	7	121	.284	.365	.611	147	42	20-5	.988	8	108	120	O158(1/158/1)/1D	0	5.0
1999	Sea A★	160	606	123	173	26	3	**48**	134	91-**17**	7	108	.285	.384	.576	142	38	24-7	.978	-1	101	106	O158C,D6	0	3.9
2000	Cin N✱	145	520	100	141	22	3	40	118	94-17	9	117	.271	.387	.556	132	26	6-4	.987	2	106	103	O141C	0	2.8
2001	Cin N	111	364	57	104	20	2	22	65	44-6	4	72	.286	.365	.533	122	12	2-0	.985	-10	89	20	O90C,D2	47	0.3
2002	Cin N	70	197	17	52	8	0	8	23	28-6	3	39	.264	.358	.426	104	2	1-2	.971	-5	78	139	O55(1/54/1)	74	-0.4
2003	Cin N	53	166	34	41	12	1	13	26	27-5	6	44	.247	.370	.566	147	12	1-0	.989	-2	89	129	O43C,D3	110	1.0
2004	Cin N✱	83	300	49	76	18	0	20	60	44-3	2	67	.253	.351	.513	123	10	1-0	.994	-2	94	104	O77(0/76/1)/D	76	0.9
2005	Cin N	128	491	85	148	30	0	35	92	54-3	3	93	.301	.369	.576	144	31	0-1	.990	-4	96	94	O124C,D2	0	2.8
2006	Cin N	109	428	62	108	19	0	27	72	39-6	2	78	.252	.316	.486	96	-4	0-0	.979	-4	94	124	O100C,D3	28	-0.6
Total	18	2234	8298	1467	2412	449	36	563	1608	1077-216	76	1494	.291	.374	.557	141	489	178-67	.986	-20	98	126	O2115(3/2113/4),D65,1b2	481	46.8
GRIFFEY, KEN	George Kenneth Sr.; B4.10.1950 Donora PA; BL/TL/6´0˝/(185–210); [CinN69 29/680]; d8.25; C7; s–Ken																								
1973	†Cin N	25	86	19	33	5	1	3	14	6-0	0	10	.384	.424	.570	180	9	4-2	1.000	-4	62	53	O21R	0	0.5
1974	Cin N	88	227	24	57	9	5	2	19	27-2	1	43	.251	.333	.361	96	-1	9-4	1.000	1	102	120	O70(2/0/68)	0	-0.3
1975	†Cin N	132	463	95	141	15	9	4	46	67-2	1	67	.305	.391	.402	119	14	16-7	.967	-8	87	73	O119R	0	0.1
1976	†Cin N★	148	562	111	189	28	9	6	74	62-0	1	65	.336	.401	.450	138	30	34-11	.979	-3	98	86	O144R	0	2.5
1977	Cin N☆	154	585	117	186	35	8	12	57	69-2	0	84	.318	.389	.467	126	23	17-8	.990	4	108	91	O147R	0	2.1
1978	Cin N	158	614	90	177	33	8	10	63	54-1	0	70	.288	.344	.417	112	9	23-5	.969	-1	101	108	O154(0/13/142)	0	0.4
1979	Cin N	95	380	62	120	27	4	8	32	36-3	1	39	.316	.374	.471	130	16	12-5	.984	-3	94	103	O93(0/8/92)	24	1.0
1980	Cin N★	146	544	89	160	28	10	13	85	62-4	1	77	.294	.364	.454	130	23	23-1	.978	-3	106	43	O138(0/2/138)	0	1.8
1981	Cin N	101	396	65	123	21	6	2	34	39-6	1	42	.311	.370	.409	123	12	12-4	.989	5	109	123	O99C	0	1.9
1982	NY A	127	484	70	134	23	2	12	54	39-1	0	58	.277	.329	.407	103	2	10-4	.983	4	108	96	O125(0/26/102)	0	0.1
1983	NY A	118	458	60	140	21	3	11	46	34-3	2	45	.306	.355	.437	120	12	6-1	.992	1	98	99	1b101,O14(2/12/1),D2	31	0.8
1984	NY A	120	399	44	109	20	1	7	56	29-2	1	32	.273	.321	.381	97	-1	2-2	.974	-0	105	124	O82(38/35/9),1b27,D2	0	-0.6
1985	NY A	127	438	68	120	28	4	10	69	41-4	0	51	.274	.331	.425	109	5	7-7	.970	5	109	128	O110(106/5/1)/1D	15	0.5
1986	NY A	59	198	33	60	7	0	9	26	15-0	1	24	.303	.349	.475	124	6	2-2	.971	2	103	167	O51(50/2/1),D2	0	0.6
	Atl N	80	292	36	90	15	3	12	32	20-4	0	43	.308	.351	.503	127	10	12-7	.986	-2	96	20	O77L/1	0	0.5
1987	Atl N	122	399	65	114	24	1	14	64	46-11	1	54	.286	.358	.456	110	7	4-7	.995	-3	90	97	O107(107/1/0),1b3	5	-0.2
1988	Atl N	69	193	21	48	5	0	2	19	17-2	0	26	.249	.307	.306	74	-6	1-3	.969	-3	79	83	O42(41/0/2),1b11	0	-1.3
	Cin N	25	50	5	14	1	0	2	4	2-1	0	5	.280	.308	.420	103	0	0-0	.986	0	106	16	1b10	0	-0.1
	Year	94	243	26	62	6	0	4	23	19-3	0	31	.255	.307	.329	80	-6	1-3	.969	-3	79	83	O42(41/0/2),1b21	0	-1.4
1989	Cin N	106	236	26	62	8	3	8	30	29-3	1	42	.263	.346	.424	115	5	4-2	.987	-6	79	74	O58(58/0/1),1b9	0	-0.3
1990	Cin N	46	63	6	13	2	0	1	8	2-0	1	5	.206	.235	.286	43	-5	2-1	.979	1	113	60	1b9,O6(5/0/1)	0	-0.5
	Sea A	21	77	13	29	2	0	3	18	10-0	0	3	.377	.443	.519	168	7	0-0	.963	-2	73	93	O20L	0	0.5
1991	Sea A	30	85	10	24	7	0	1	9	13-0	1	13	.282	.380	.400	117	3	0-0	1.000	-3	75	0	O26L/D	136	-0.1
Total	19	2097	7229	1129	2143	364	77	152	859	719-51	14	898	.296	.359	.431	118	180	200-83	.981	-17	99	91	O1703(532/203/989),1b172,D14	211	9.9
GRIFFIN, ALFREDO	Alfredo Claudino (b Alfredo Claudino Baptist (Griffin)); B10.6.1957 Santo Domingo, D.R.; BB/TR/5´11˝/(151–167); d9.4; C9																								
1976	Cle A	12	4	0	1	0	0	0	0	0-0	0	2	.250	.250	.250	47	0	0-1	.750	-1	51	0	S6,D4	0	-0.2
1977	Cle A	14	41	5	6	1	0	0	3	3-0	0	5	.146	.205	.171	4	-6	2-2	.940	-3	86	86	S13/D	0	-0.8
1978	Cle A	5	4	1	2	1	0	0	0	2-0	0	1	.500	.667	.750	300	1	0-0	.917	1	123	439	S2	0	0.3
1979	Tor A	153	624	81	179	22	10	2	31	40-0	5	59	.287	.333	.364	87	-12	21-16	.956	11	105	112	S153	0	1.3
1980	Tor A	155	653	63	166	26	**15**	2	41	24-2	4	58	.254	.283	.349	70	-29	18-23	.955	4	101	113	S155	0	-1.3
1981	Tor A	101	388	30	81	19	6	0	21	17-1	1	38	.209	.243	.289	50	-26	8-12	.937	-12	92	96	S97,3b4/2	0	-3.2
1982	Tor A	**162**	539	57	130	20	8	1	48	22-0	0	48	.241	.269	.314	55	-34	10-8	.968	12	100	98	S162	0	-0.6
1983	Tor A	**162**	528	62	132	22	9	4	47	27-0	3	44	.250	.289	.348	70	-23	8-11	.965	-5	93	92	S157,2b5/D	0	-1.4
1984	Tor A★	140	419	53	101	8	2	4	30	4-0	1	33	.241	.248	.298	49	-30	11-3	.962	-17	86	99	S115,2b21,D5	0	-3.4
1985	Oak A	**162**	614	75	166	18	7	2	64	20-1	0	50	.270	.290	.332	76	-23	24-9	.960	-10	97	85	S162	0	-1.4
1986	Oak A	**162**	594	74	169	23	6	4	51	35-6	2	52	.285	.323	.364	94	-6	33-16	.966	-8	95	83	S162	0	0.4
1987	Oak A	144	494	69	130	23	5	3	60	28-2	4	41	.263	.306	.348	79	-16	26-13	.963	9	100	91	S137/2	0	0.8
1988	†LA N	95	316	39	63	8	3	1	27	24-7	2	30	.199	.259	.253	49	-21	7-5	.965	5	101	94	S93	64	-1.1
1989	LA N	136	506	49	125	27	2	0	29	29-2	0	57	.247	.287	.308	71	-19	10-7	.975	-3	93	113	S131	20	-1.4
1990	LA N	141	461	38	97	11	3	1	35	29-11	2	65	.210	.258	.254	43	-37	6-3	.959	12	104	95	S139	0	-1.6
1991	LA N	109	350	27	85	6	2	0	27	22-5	1	49	.243	.286	.271	60	-19	5-4	.961	21	**115**	89	S109	41	0.9
1992	†Tor A	63	150	21	35	7	0	0	10	9-0	0	19	.233	.273	.280	54	-9	3-1	.981	-4	93	55	S48,2b16	0	-1.0
1993	†Tor A	46	95	15	20	3	0	0	3	3-0	0	13	.211	.235	.242	28	-10	0-0	.960	-2	70	74	S20,2b11,3b6	25	-1.0
Total	18	1962	6780	759	1688	245	78	24	527	338-37	25	664	.249	.285	.319	67	-319	192-134	.961	9	98	96	S1861,2b55,D11,3b10	150	-14.7
GRIFFIN, DOUG	Douglas Lee; B6.4.1947 South Gate CA; BR/TR/6´0˝/(150–170); [AnaA65 14/538]; d9.11																								
1970	Cal A	18	55	2	7	1	0	0	4	6-1	0	5	.127	.213	.145	1	-8	0-0	.964	-1	115	141	2b11,3b8	0	-0.9
1971	Bos A	125	483	51	118	23	2	3	27	31-3	2	45	.244	.291	.319	68	-20	11-5	.986	6	102	104	2b124	27	-0.5
1972	Bos A	129	470	43	122	12	1	2	35	45-6	2	48	.260	.325	.302	83	-9	9-2	.978	-3	92	91	2b129	23	-0.2
1973	Bos A	113	396	43	101	14	5	1	33	21-0	3	42	.255	.293	.323	70	-16	7-5	.990	-6	92	100	2b113	50	-1.5
1974	Bos A	93	312	35	83	12	4	0	33	28-3	2	21	.266	.329	.330	85	-6	2-8	.979	-13	98	82	2b91/S	62	-1.6
1975	†Bos A	100	287	21	69	6	0	1	29	18-0	2	29	.240	.288	.272	55	-17	2-2	.967	-14	91	83	2b99/S	0	-2.7
1976	Bos A	49	127	14	24	2	0	0	4	9-0	1	14	.189	.248	.205	30	-11	2-1	.989	-12	84	62	2b44,D2	0	-2.2
1977	Bos A	5	6	0	0	0	0	0	0	0-0	0	0	.000	.000	.000	-90	-2	0-0	1.000	-0	99	125	2b3	0	-0.2
Total	8	632	2136	209	524	70	12	7	165	158-13	12	204	.245	.299	.299	68	-89	33-23	.981	-43	95	92	2b614,3b8,D2,S2	162	-9.8
GRIFFIN, PUG	Francis Arthur; B4.24.1896 Lincoln NE; D10.12.1951 Colorado Springs CO; BR/TR/5´11.5˝/187; d7.27																								
1917	Phi A	18	25	4	5	1	0	1	3	1	0	9	.200	.231	.360	81	-1	1	1.000	1	161	55	1b3	—	0.0
1920	NY N	5	4	0	1	0	0	0	0	1	0	2	.250	.400	.250	90	0	0-0	1.000	-0	56	0	O2(0/1/1)	—	0.0
Total	2	23	29	4	6	1	0	1	3	2	0	11	.207	.258	.345	83	-1	1-0	1.000	0	161	55	1b3,O2(0/1/1)	—	0.0
GRIFFIN, IVY	Ivy Moore; B11.16.1896 Thomasville AL; D8.25.1957 Gainesville GA; BL/TR/5´11˝/180; d9.9; Col Auburn																								
1919	Phi A	17	68	5	20	2	2	0	6	3	1	10	.294	.333	.382	99	0	0	.989	4	182	106	1b17	—	0.3
1920	Phi A	129	467	46	111	15	1	0	20	17	11	49	.238	.281	.274	47	-36	3-3	.990	5	118	101	1b127,2b2	—	-3.4
1921	Phi A	39	103	14	33	4	2	0	13	5	3	6	.320	.369	.398	95	-1	1-2	.973	-2	82	69	1b27	—	-0.5
Total	3	185	638	65	164	21	5	0	39	25	15	65	.257	.301	.306	60	-37	4-5	.988	7	119	97	1b171,2b2	—	-3.6
GRIFFIN, JOHN-FORD	John-Ford David; B11.19.1979 Sarasota FL; BL/TL/6´2˝/215; [NYA01 1/23]; d9.6; Col Florida St.																								
2005	Tor A	7	13	3	4	2	0	1	6	0-0	0	4	.308	.308	.692	148	1	0-0	ø	0	—	—	D4	0	0.1
GRIFFIN, MIKE	Michael Joseph; B3.20.1865 Utica NY; D4.10.1908 Utica NY; BL/TR/5´7˝/160; d4.16; M1																								
1887	Bal AA	136	532	142	160	32	13	3	94	55	8	—	.301	.375	.427	131	25	94	.924	-15	58	21	O136(1/135/0)	—	0.4
1888	Bal AA	**137**	542	103	139	21	11	0	46	55	5	—	.256	.331	.336	117	12	46	.938	5	123	117	O137C	—	1.2
1889	Bal AA	137	531	**152**	148	21	14	4	48	91	3	29	.279	.387	.394	120	17	39	.910	-12	81	108	O109C,S25,2b5	—	0.2

YEAR	TM LG	G	AB	R	H	2B	3B	HR	RBI	BB-IB	HP	SO	AVG	OBP	SLG	AOPS	ABR	SB-CS	FA	FR	RNG	THR	GAMES AT POSITION	DL	BFW
1890	Phi P	115	489	127	140	29	6	6	54	64	7	19	.286	.377	.407	107	6	30	**.954**	13	**148**	**223**	O115(4/100/13)	—	1.2
1891	Bro N	134	521	106	139	**36**	9	3	65	57	1	31	.267	.340	.388	113	9	65	**.960**	20	147	191	O134(2/132/0)	—	2.2
1892	Bro N	129	452	103	125	17	11	3	66	68	4	36	.277	.376	.383	134	22	49	**.986**	9	122	166	O127(0/126/1),S2	—	2.1
1893	Bro N	95	362	85	103	21	7	6	59	59	8	23	.285	.396	.431	126	16	30	**.965**	7	122	243	O93C,2b2	—	1.4
1894	Bro N	108	406	123	145	29	4	5	76	78	4	14	.357	.465	.485	139	35	39	.966	4	77	113	O107C	—	2.4
1895	Bro N	132	524	140	174	38	7	4	65	93	10	30	.332	.442	.454	143	44	27	**.969**	12	117	**287**	O132C/S	—	3.8
1896	Bro N	122	493	101	152	27	9	4	51	48	9	25	.308	.380	.424	118	15	23	.961	1	47	23	O122C	—	0.7
1897	Bro N	134	534	136	169	25	11	2	56	81	10	—	.316	.416	.416	127	27	16	.956	3	68	161	O134C	—	1.8
1898	Bro N	134	537	88	161	18	6	2	40	60	8	—	.300	.379	.367	114	12	15	**.974**	6	107	154	O134C,M	—	0.9
Total	12	1513	5923	1406	1755	314	108	42	720	809	77	207	.296	.388	.407	124	240	473	.956	52	102	149	O1480(7/1461/14),S28,2b7	—	18.3
GRIFFIN, THOMAS	Thomas William; B1.1857 Titusville PA; D4.17.1933 Rockford IL; d9.27																								
1884	Mil U	11	41	5	9	2	0	0	—	3	—	—	.220	.273	.268	118	0	—	.918	-2	31	0	1b11	—	-0.2
GRIFFIN, SANDY	Tobias Charles; B10.24.1858 Fayetteville NY; D6.4.1926 Syracuse NY; BR/TR/5´10˝/160; d5.26; M1																								
1884	NY N	16	62	7	11	2	0	0	6	1	—	19	.177	.190	.210	25	-5	—	.842	-2	78	227	O16(0/5/11)	—	-0.6
1890	Roc AA	107	407	85	125	28	4	5	53	50	4	—	.307	.388	.432	153	30	21	.856	-21	38	25	O107C/2	—	0.5
1891	Was AA	20	69	15	19	4	2	0	10	10	4	3	.275	.398	.391	132	4	2	.939	-2	35	138	O20C,M	—	0.1
1893	StL N	23	92	9	18	1	1	0	9	16	0	2	.196	.315	.228	45	-7	2	.906	-2	50	0	O23L	—	-0.9
Total	4	166	630	116	173	35	7	5	78	77	8	24	.275	.361	.376	120	22	25	.873	-26	43	49	O166(23/132/11)/2	—	-0.9
GRIFFITH, BERT	Bartholomew Joseph "Buck"; B3.3.1896 St.Louis MO; D5.5.1973 Bishop CA; BR/TR/5´11˝/185; d4.13; gs–Matt Williams																								
1922	Bro N	106	325	45	100	22	8	2	35	5	2	11	.308	.322	.443	96	-3	5-7	.981	0	102	77	O77(0/8/69),1b6	—	-1.0
1923	Bro N	79	248	23	73	8	4	2	37	13	1	16	.294	.332	.383	91	-4	1-2	.949	-5	96	19	O62(51/9/3)	—	-1.3
1924	Was A	6	8	1	1	0	0	0	0	0	0	1	.125	.125	.125	-37	-2	0-0	1.000	0	165	0	O2C	—	-0.1
Total	3	191	581	69	174	30	12	4	72	18	3	28	.299	.324	.413	92	-9	6-9	.968	-4	100	51	O141(51/19/72),1b6	—	-2.4
GRIFFITH, DERRELL	Robert Derrell; B12.12.1943 Anadarko OK; BL/TR/6´0˝/168; d9.26																								
1963	LA N	1	2	0	0	0	0	0	0	0-0	0	0	.000	.000	.000	-99	-1	0-0	ø	-1	0	0	/2	0	-0.1
1964	LA N	78	238	27	69	16	2	4	23	5-0	1	21	.290	.307	.424	112	3	5-1	.769	-8	95	70	3b35,O29(6/0/23)	0	-0.6
1965	LA N	22	41	3	7	0	0	1	2	0-0	0	9	.171	.171	.244	16	-5	0-0	1.000	0	114	0	O11(10/0/1)	0	-0.6
1966	LA N	23	15	3	1	0	0	0	2	2-2	0	3	.067	.176	.067	-32	-3	0-0	1.000	0	107	0	O7(5/1/2)	0	-0.3
Total	4	124	296	33	77	16	2	5	27	7-2	1	33	.260	.280	.378	90	-6	5-1	.970	-8	100	37	O47(21/1/26),3b35/2	0	-1.6
GRIFFITH, TOMMY	Thomas Herman; B10.26.1889 Prospect OH; D4.13.1967 Cincinnati OH; BL/TR/5´10˝/175; d8.25																								
1913	Bos N	37	127	16	32	4	1	1	12	9	0	8	.252	.301	.323	77	-4	1-7	.886	-0	93	152	O35R	—	-0.9
1914	Bos N	16	48	3	5	0	0	0	1	2	0	6	.104	.140	.104	-27	-8	0	.931	3	82	307	O14(1/0/14)	—	-0.6
1915	Cin N	**160**	583	59	179	31	16	4	85	41	2	34	.307	.355	.436	136	24	6-24	.952	-14	85	60	O160(2/0/160)	—	-0.7
1916	Cin N	**155**	595	50	158	28	7	2	61	36	2	37	.266	.310	.346	104	2	16	.967	2	90	140	O155R	—	-0.6
1917	Cin N	115	363	45	98	18	7	1	45	19	1	23	.270	.308	.366	111	4	5	.974	7	103	155	O100R	—	0.6
1918	Cin N	118	427	47	113	10	4	2	48	39	0	30	.265	.326	.321	99	0	10	.969	3	107	104	O118R	—	-0.3
1919	Bro N	125	484	65	136	18	4	6	57	23	1	32	.281	.315	.372	104	1	8	.954	-2	93	111	O125R	—	-0.8
1920	†Bro N	93	334	41	87	9	4	2	30	15	0	18	.260	.292	.329	76	-11	3-3	.972	-7	86	68	O92R	—	-2.5
1921	Bro N	129	455	66	142	21	6	12	71	36	1	13	.312	.364	.464	113	9	3-3	.972	7	95	**169**	O124R	—	0.6
1922	Bro N	99	329	44	104	17	8	4	49	23	0	10	.316	.361	.453	110	4	7-1	.952	2	101	120	O82R	—	0.0
1923	Bro N	131	481	70	141	21	9	8	66	50	1	19	.293	.361	.424	109	7	8-2	.927	-7	87	100	O127R	—	-0.9
1924	Bro N	140	482	43	121	19	5	3	67	34	0	19	.251	.300	.330	71	-20	0-5	.965	-7	94	65	O139R	—	-3.9
1925	Bro N	7	4	2	0	0	0	0	0	3	0	2	.000	.429	.000	20	0	1-0	1.000	0	145	0	O2R	—	0.0
	Chi N	76	235	38	67	12	1	7	27	21	1	11	.285	.346	.434	97	-1	2-4	.937	-2	92	117	O60(4/4/53)	—	-0.8
	Year	83	239	40	67	12	1	7	27	24	1	13	.280	.348	.427	96	-1	3-4	.938	-2	93	116	O62(4/4/55)	—	-0.8
Total	13	1401	4947	589	1383	208	72	52	619	351	9	262	.280	.328	.382	102	7	70-49	.956	-15	93	112	O1333(7/4/1326)	—	-10.8
GRIGGS, ART	Arthur Carle; B12.10.1884 Topeka KS; D12.19.1938 Los Angeles CA; BR/TR/5´11˝/185; d5.2; Col Pittsburgh																								
1909	StL A	108	364	38	102	17	5	0	43	24	3	—	.280	.330	.354	125	10	11	.982	-2	110	84	1b49,O41(36/2/3),2b8/S	—	0.5
1910	StL A	123	416	28	98	22	5	2	30	25	1	—	.236	.281	.327	96	-3	11	.878	-1	98	60	O49(6/0/43),2b41,1b17,S3,3b3	—	-0.7
1911	Cle A	27	68	7	17	3	2	1	7	5	0	—	.250	.301	.397	93	-1	1	.949	-1	104	76	2b11,O4(1/0/3),3b3/1	—	-0.1
1912	Cle A	89	273	29	83	16	7	0	39	33	1	—	.304	.381	.414	123	9	10	.986	1	102	93	1b71	—	0.8
1914	Bro F	40	112	10	32	6	1	1	15	5	2	11	.286	.328	.384	94	-3	1	.980	-3	61	71	1b27/lf	—	-0.6
1915	Bro F	27	38	4	11	1	0	1	2	3	2	7	.289	.372	.395	117	0	0	1.000	1	146	104	1b5/rf	—	0.1
1918	Det A	28	99	11	36	8	0	0	16	10	0	5	.364	.422	.444	168	9	2	.986	-3	55	64	1b25	—	0.6
Total	7	442	1370	127	379	73	20	5	152	105	9	23	.277	.332	.370	115	21	36	.983	-8	94	85	1b195,O96(44/2/50),2b60,3b6,S4	—	0.6
GRIGSBY, DENVER	Denver Clarence; B3.25.1901 Jackson KY; D11.10.1973 Sapulpa OK; BL/TR/5´9˝/155; d8.29																								
1923	Chi N	24	72	8	21	5	2	0	5	7	1	5	.292	.363	.417	105	1	1-3	1.000	-1	102	47	O22(6/1/16)	—	-0.2
1924	Chi N	124	411	58	123	18	2	3	48	31	6	47	.299	.357	.375	95	-1	10-19	.974	5	100	134	O121(108/5/8)	—	-1.0
1925	Chi N	51	137	20	35	5	0	0	20	19	0	12	.255	.346	.292	64	-7	1-1	.966	-0	96	115	O39(21/15/3)	—	-0.9
Total	3	199	620	86	179	28	4	3	73	57	7	64	.289	.355	.361	89	-7	12-23	.975	4	99	120	O182(135/21/27)	—	-2.1
GRIM, JOHN	John Helm; B8.9.1867 Lebanon KY; D7.28.1961 Indianapolis IN; BR/TR/6´2˝/175; d9.29; OF(2/0/12)																								
1888	Phi N	2	7	0	1	0	0	0	0	0	0	0	.143	.143	.143	-8	-1	0	ø	-1	0	0	/rf2	—	-0.2
1890	Roc AA	50	192	30	51	6	9	2	34	7	2	—	.266	.299	.422	121	3	14	.851	-5	78	122	S21,C15,3b8,2b4,O3R,1b2/P	—	0.0
1891	Mil AA	29	119	14	28	5	1	1	14	2	0	5	.235	.248	.319	52	-9	1	.926	4	*120*	*76*	C16,3b10,2b3	—	-0.3
1892	Lou N	97	370	40	90	16	4	1	36	13	6	24	.243	.280	.316	87	-7	18	.940	-9	*90*	*102*	C69,1b11,2b10,O8(1/0/7)/S3	—	-0.9
1893	Lou N	99	415	68	111	19	8	3	54	12	9	10	.267	.303	.373	86	-10	15	.952	-5	*105*	*112*	C92,1b3,2b2/rfS	—	-0.5
1894	Lou N	109	412	66	123	27	7	7	71	18	10	15	.299	.343	.449	96	-4	14	.927	10	*99*	*126*	C78,2b24,1b7/3	—	1.1
1895	Bro N	94	333	55	93	17	5	0	45	13	7	9	.279	.320	.360	82	-9	10	.947	8	*132*	*114*	C92/lf1	—	0.6
1896	Bro N	81	281	32	75	13	1	2	35	12	6	14	.267	.311	.342	76	-10	7	.939	-1	*105*	*103*	C77,1b5	—	-0.3
1897	Bro N	80	290	26	72	10	1	0	25	1	3	—	.248	.259	.290	47	-23	3	.947	-1	*89*	***129***	C77	—	-1.5
1898	Bro N	52	178	17	50	5	1	0	11	8	3	—	.281	.323	.320	85	-4	1	.950	-4	*93*	*102*	C52	—	-0.3
1899	Bro N	15	47	3	13	1	0	0	7	1	2	—	.277	.320	.298	68	-2	-0	.966	1	*89*	*112*	C12	—	0.0
Total	11	708	2644	351	707	119	37	16	332	87	48	77	.267	.303	.359	82	-76	83	.943	-3	*104*	*112*	C580,2b44,1b29,S23,3b20,O14R/P	—	-2.3
GRIMES, ROY	Austin Roy "Bummer"; B9.11.1893 Bergholz OH; D9.13.1954 Hanover Twp. OH; BR/TR/6´1˝/176; d7.5; twb–Ray																								
1920	NY N	26	57	5	9	1	0	0	3	3	0	8	.158	.200	.175	8	-7	1-1	.948	-2	106	48	2b21	—	-0.9
GRIMES, ED	Edward Adelbert; B9.8.1905 Chicago IL; D10.5.1974 Chicago IL; BR/TR/5´10˝/165; d4.19																								
1931	StL A	43	57	9	15	1	2	0	5	9	0	3	.263	.364	.351	86	-1	1-0	.892	-2	91	0	3b22,2b4,S3	—	-0.2
1932	StL A	31	68	7	16	0	1	0	13	6	0	12	.235	.297	.265	44	-6	0-1	.891	1	119	148	3b18,2b2/S	—	-0.4
Total	2	74	125	16	31	1	3	0	18	15	0	15	.248	.329	.304	63	-7	1-1	.891	-1	107	86	3b40,2b6,S4	—	-0.6
GRIMES, OSCAR	Oscar Ray Jr.; B4.13.1915 Minerva OH; D5.19.1993 Westlake OH; BR/TR/5´11˝/178; d9.28; f–Ray																								
1938	Cle A	4	10	2	2	0	1	0	2	2	0	0	.200	.333	.400	85	0	0-0	1.000	-1	58	123	2b2/1	—	-0.1
1939	Cle A	119	364	51	98	20	5	4	56	56	1	61	.269	.368	.385	96	-1	8-3	.968	-10	91	81	2b48,1b43,S37,3b3	—	-0.8
1940	Cle A	11	13	3	0	0	0	0	0	0	0	5	.000	.000	.000	-99	-4	0-0	.958	1	164	132	1b4/3	—	-0.3
1941	Cle A	77	244	28	58	9	3	4	24	39	1	47	.238	.345	.348	88	-4	4-0	.995	-4	75	104	1b62,2b13/3	0	-1.2
1942	Cle A	51	84	10	15	2	0	0	2	13	0	17	.179	.289	.202	42	-6	3-2	.944	-4	83	98	2b24,3b8/1S	0	-0.9
1943	NY A	9	20	4	3	0	0	0	1	3	0	7	.150	.261	.150	21	-2	0-0	1.000	0	105	224	S3/1	0	-0.2
1944	NY A	116	387	44	108	17	8	5	46	59	2	57	.279	.377	.403	119	11	6-0	.945	-11	90	79	3b97,S20	0	0.4
1945	NY A✱	142	480	64	127	19	7	4	45	97	6	73	.265	.395	.358	114	14	7-6	.937	7	105	**136**	3b141/1	0	2.3
1946	NY A	14	39	1	8	1	0	0	4	1	0	7	.205	.225	.231	27	-4	0-1	.895	-1	72	75	S7,2b5	0	-0.5
	Phi A	59	191	28	50	5	0	1	20	27	1	29	.262	.356	.304	86	-2	2-0	.958	-9	85	99	2b43,3b6,S4	0	-0.9
	Year	73	230	29	58	6	0	1	24	28	1	36	.252	.336	.291	76	-6	2-1	.957	-10	86	97	2b48,S11,3b6	0	-1.4
Total	9	602	1832	235	469	73	24	18	200	297	11	303	.256	.363	.352	98	2	30-12	.940	-32	100	109	3b257,2b135,1b113,S72	0	-2.2

GRIMES, RAY Oscar Ray Sr.; B9.11.1893 Bergholz OH; D5.25.1953 Minerva OH; BR/TR/5´11˝/168; d9.24; twb–Roy s–Oscar

YEAR	TM LG	G	AB	R	H	2B	3B	HR	RBI	BB-IB	HP	SO	AVG	OBP	SLG	AOPS	ABR	SB-CS	FA	FR	RNG	THR	GAMES AT POSITION	DL	BFW
1920	Bos A	1	4	1	1	0	0	0	0	1	0	0	.250	.400	.250	78	0	0-0	1.000	-0	0	283	/1	—	0.0
1921	Chi N	147	530	91	170	38	6	6	79	70	6	55	.321	.406	.449	126	24	5-8	.993	-5	83	86	1b147	—	0.8
1922	Chi N	138	509	99	180	45	12	14	99	75	6	33	.354	.442	.572	157	47	7-7	.987	-2	96	106	1b138	—	3.2
1923	Chi N	64	216	32	71	7	2	2	36	24	2	17	.329	.401	.407	114	5	5-0	.991	-1	91	99	1b62	—	0.1
1924	Chi N	51	177	33	53	6	5	5	34	28	2	15	.299	.401	.475	132	9	4-2	.982	-8	42	95	1b50	—	-0.2
1926	Phi N	32	101	13	30	5	0	0	15	6	1	13	.297	.343	.347	82	-2	0	.981	0	112	121	1b28	—	-0.4
Total	6	433	1537	269	505	101	25	27	263	204	17	133	.329	.413	.480	132	83	21-17	.989	-16	85	98	1b426	—	3.5

GRIMM, CHARLIE Charles John "Jolly Cholly"; B8.28.1898 St.Louis MO; D11.15.1983 Scottsdale AZ; BL/TL/5´11.5˝/173; d7.30; M19/C4

YEAR	TM LG	G	AB	R	H	2B	3B	HR	RBI	BB-IB	HP	SO	AVG	OBP	SLG	AOPS	ABR	SB-CS	FA	FR	RNG	THR	GAMES AT POSITION	DL	BFW
1916	Phi A	12	22	0	2	0	0	0	0	2	0	4	.091	.167	.091	-24	-3	0	.875	-1	91	0	O7(3/1/3)	—	-0.5
1918	StL N	50	141	11	31	7	0	0	12	6	2	15	.220	.262	.270	64	-6	2	.971	-3	65	115	1b42,O2R/3	—	-1.2
1919	Pit N	14	44	6	14	1	3	0	6	2	0	4	.318	.348	.477	141	2	1	.968	-3	29	17	1b13	—	-0.1
1920	Pit N	148	533	38	121	13	7	2	54	30	4	40	.227	.273	.289	60	-28	7-8	**.995**	4	108	106	1b148	—	-3.1
1921	Pit N	151	562	62	154	21	17	7	71	31	2	38	.274	.314	.409	88	-12	6-8	.994	-7	78	94	1b150	—	-3.0
1922	Pit N	154	593	64	173	28	13	0	76	43	3	15	.292	.343	.383	86	-13	6-10	.994	-3	84	94	1b154	—	-2.7
1923	Pit N	152	563	78	194	29	13	7	99	41	0	43	.345	.389	.480	125	20	6-9	**.995**	3	103	**111**	1b152	—	1.0
1924	Pit N	151	542	53	156	25	12	2	63	37	2	22	.288	.336	.389	92	-6	3-6	**.995**	-3	87	**121**	1b151	—	-2.1
1925	Chi N	141	519	73	159	29	5	10	76	38	0	25	.306	.354	.439	100	0	4-3	.989	-0	99	**112**	1b139	—	-0.9
1926	Chi N	147	524	58	145	30	6	8	82	49	3	25	.277	.342	.403	99	-1	3	.988	-6	81	119	1b147	—	-1.6
1927	Chi N	147	543	68	169	29	6	2	74	45	3	21	.311	.367	.398	105	5	3	.990	2	105	96	1b147	—	-0.3
1928	Chi N	147	547	67	161	25	5	5	62	39	1	20	.294	.342	.386	91	-8	7	**.993**	-2	86	122	1b147	—	-1.9
1929	†Chi N	120	463	66	138	28	3	10	91	42	1	25	.298	.358	.436	95	-3	3	.992	-1	94	116	1b120	—	-1.1
1930	Chi N	114	429	58	124	27	2	6	65	41	6	26	.289	.359	.403	83	-10	1	**.995**	0	96	99	1b113	—	-1.6
1931	Chi N	146	531	65	176	33	11	4	66	53	1	29	.331	.393	.458	126	21	1	**.993**	1	99	85	1b144	—	0.8
1932	†Chi N	149	570	66	175	42	2	7	80	35	2	22	.307	.349	.425	108	7	2	.993	9	119	**108**	1b149,M	—	0.2
1933	Chi N	107	384	38	95	15	2	3	37	23	0	15	.247	.290	.320	74	-13	1	**.996**	9	125	119	1b104,M	—	-1.5
1934	Chi N	75	267	24	79	8	1	5	47	16	1	12	.296	.338	.390	96	-2	1	.995	1	98	75	1b74,M	—	-0.8
1935	Chi N	2	8	0	0	0	0	0	0	0	0	1	.000	.000	.000	-99	-2	0	1.000	-0	65	236	1b2,M	—	-0.3
1936	Chi N	39	132	13	33	4	0	1	16	5	0	8	.250	.277	.303	55	-9	0	1.000	5	150	128	1b35,M	—	-0.6
Total	20	2166	7917	908	2299	394	108	79	1077	578	31	410	.290	.341	.397	95	-61	57-44	.993	5	97	106	1b2131,O9(3/1/5)/3	—	-21.3

GRIMSHAW, MYRON Myron Frederick; B11.30.1875 St.Johnsville NY; D12.11.1936 Canajoharie NY; BB/TR/6´1˝/173; d4.25

YEAR	TM LG	G	AB	R	H	2B	3B	HR	RBI	BB-IB	HP	SO	AVG	OBP	SLG	AOPS	ABR	SB-CS	FA	FR	RNG	THR	GAMES AT POSITION	DL	BFW
1905	Bos A	85	285	39	68	8	2	4	35	21	1	—	.239	.293	.323	94	-2	4	.980	-5	74	126	1b74	—	-1.0
1906	Bos A	110	428	46	124	16	12	0	48	23	4	—	.290	.332	.383	124	10	5	.987	-2	90	83	1b110	—	0.7
1907	Bos A	64	181	19	37	7	2	0	33	16	1	—	.204	.273	.265	72	-5	6	.980	-4	84	127	1b20,O18(1/0/17),S2	—	-1.1
Total	3	259	894	104	229	31	16	4	116	60	6	—	.256	.307	.340	104	3	15	.984	-11	84	103	1b204,O18(1/0/17),S2	—	-1.4

GRISSOM, MARQUIS Marquis Deon; B4.17.1967 Atlanta GA; BR/TR/5´11˝/(188–210); [MonN88 3/76]; d8.22; Col Florida A&M

YEAR	TM LG	G	AB	R	H	2B	3B	HR	RBI	BB-IB	HP	SO	AVG	OBP	SLG	AOPS	ABR	SB-CS	FA	FR	RNG	THR	GAMES AT POSITION	DL	BFW
1989	Mon N	26	74	16	19	2	0	1	2	12-0	0	21	.257	.360	.324	95	0	1-0	.943	-3	69	104	O23(1/22/1)	0	-0.3
1990	Mon N	98	288	42	74	14	2	3	29	27-2	0	40	.257	.320	.351	88	-5	22-2	.988	0	100	106	O87(18/35/40)	32	-0.2
1991	Mon N	148	558	73	149	23	9	6	39	34-0	1	89	.267	.310	.373	92	-8	**76**-17	.984	8	108	**194**	O138(3/125/11)	0	1.0
1992	Mon N	159	653	99	180	39	6	14	66	42-6	5	81	.276	.322	.418	109	7	**78**-13	.983	-7	97	78	O157C	0	1.2
1993	Mon N★	157	630	104	188	27	2	19	95	52-6	3	76	.298	.351	.438	106	5	53-10	.984	0	102	97	O157C	0	1.6
1994	Mon N★	110	475	96	137	25	4	11	45	41-4	1	66	.288	.344	.427	99	-1	36-6	.985	9	118	117	O109C	0	1.5
1995	†Atl N	139	551	80	142	23	3	12	42	47-4	3	61	.258	.317	.376	79	-17	29-9	.994	3	104	132	O136C	0	-0.9
1996	†Atl N	158	671	106	207	32	10	23	74	41-6	3	73	.308	.349	.489	112	9	28-11	.997	-3	94	127	O158C	0	1.1
1997	†Cle A	144	558	74	146	27	6	12	66	43-1	6	89	.262	.317	.396	83	-15	22-13	.992	-2	99	97	O144C	15	-1.4
1998	Mil N	142	542	57	147	28	1	10	60	24-2	2	78	.271	.304	.382	78	-19	13-8	.991	-2	100	95	O137C	0	-1.9
1999	Mil N	154	603	92	161	27	1	20	83	49-4	0	109	.267	.320	.415	84	-16	24-6	.987	-8	100	12	O149C	0	-1.8
2000	Mil N	146	595	67	145	18	2	14	62	39-2	0	99	.244	.288	.351	61	-38	20-10	.992	-12	95	33	O142C	0	-4.5
2001	LA N	135	448	56	99	17	1	21	60	16-0	2	107	.221	.250	.404	70	-24	7-5	**1.000**	-3	94	100	O123(26/95/3),D2	0	-2.7
2002	LA N	111	343	57	95	21	4	17	60	22-2	2	68	.277	.321	.510	122	9	5-1	.978	-4	92	103	O102(36/72/2)	0	0.5
2003	†SF N	149	587	82	176	33	3	20	79	20-0	2	82	.300	.322	.468	102	0	11-3	.977	-6	101	38	O148C	0	-0.3
2004	SF N	145	562	78	157	26	2	22	90	37-5	1	83	.279	.323	.450	94	-6	3-1	.994	-4	100	42	O142C	0	-0.8
2005	SF N	44	137	8	29	4	0	2	15	7-0	0	18	.212	.248	.285	39	-13	1-1	.986	-5	82	0	O36(1/34/1)	56	-1.8
Total	17	2165	8275	1187	2251	386	56	227	967	553-44	31	1240	.272	.318	.415	91	-132	429-116	.988	-38	100	88	O2088(85/1962/58),D2	103	-9.7

GROAT, DICK Richard Morrow; B11.4.1930 Wilkinsburg PA; BR/TR/5´11.5˝/(170–180); d6.19; Mil 1953–54; Col Duke

YEAR	TM LG	G	AB	R	H	2B	3B	HR	RBI	BB-IB	HP	SO	AVG	OBP	SLG	AOPS	ABR	SB-CS	FA	FR	RNG	THR	GAMES AT POSITION	DL	BFW
1952	Pit N	95	384	38	109	6	1	1	29	19	1	27	.284	.319	.313	74	-14	2-4	.952	5	99	91	S94	0	-0.5
1955	Pit N	151	521	45	139	28	2	4	51	38-11	1	26	.267	.317	.351	78	-16	0-2	.961	17	105	106	S149	0	1.2
1956	Pit N	142	520	40	142	19	3	0	37	35-3	0	25	.273	.317	.321	74	-19	0-3	.954	7	104	82	S141,3b2	0	-0.1
1957	Pit N	125	501	58	158	30	5	7	54	27-1	3	28	.315	.350	.437	114	10	0-1	.968	6	107	95	S123,3b2	0	2.6
1958	Pit N	151	584	67	175	36	9	3	66	23-7	4	32	.300	.328	.408	97	-4	2-2	.975	9	102	**126**	S149	0	1.7
1959	Pit N★	147	593	74	163	22	7	5	51	32-2	2	35	.275	.312	.361	80	-18	0-2	.964	1	103	**110**	S145	0	-0.5
1960	†Pit N★	138	573	85	186	26	4	2	50	39-0	4	35	**.325**	.371	.394	109	8	0-2	.966	14	**109**	**123**	S136	0	3.3
1961	Pit N	148	596	71	164	25	6	6	55	40-0	1	44	.275	.320	.367	82	-16	0-4	.957	12	108	**126**	S144/3	0	0.8
1962	Pit N★	**161**	678	76	199	34	3	2	61	31-1	3	61	.294	.325	.361	85	-15	2-1	.956	16	104	**125**	S161	0	1.5
1963	StL N★	158	631	85	201	**43**	11	6	73	56-2	6	58	.319	.377	.450	126	24	3-1	.964	-8	97	103	S158	0	3.2
1964	†StL N★	161	636	70	186	35	6	1	70	44-3	0	42	.292	.335	.371	92	-5	2-3	.949	-6	103	102	S160	0	0.1
1965	StL N	153	587	55	149	26	5	0	52	56-2	1	50	.254	.316	.315	73	-19	1-1	.962	-7	100	99	S148,3b2	0	-1.4
1966	Phi N	155	584	58	152	21	4	2	53	40-6	5	38	.260	.311	.320	77	-18	2-1	.974	21	108	99	S139,3b20/1	0	1.5
1967	Phi N	10	26	3	3	0	0	0	1	4-0	0	4	.115	.233	.115	3	-3	0-0	.947	3	125	149	S6	31	0.0
	SF N	34	70	4	12	1	1	0	4	6-1	0	7	.171	.237	.214	30	-6	0-0	.912	-5	84	113	S24/2	0	-1.2
	Year	44	96	7	15	1	1	0	5	10-1	0	11	.156	.236	.188	23	-10	0-0	.925	-3	95	122	S30/2	0	-1.2
Total	14	1929	7484	829	2138	352	67	39	707	490-39	31	512	.286	.330	.366	89	-111	14-27	.961	84	104	108	S1877,3b27/21	31	12.2

GROH, HEINIE Henry Knight; B9.18.1889 Rochester NY; D8.22.1968 Cincinnati OH; BR/TR/5´8˝/158; d4.12; M1; b–Lew

YEAR	TM LG	G	AB	R	H	2B	3B	HR	RBI	BB-IB	HP	SO	AVG	OBP	SLG	AOPS	ABR	SB-CS	FA	FR	RNG	THR	GAMES AT POSITION	DL	BFW
1912	NY N	27	48	8	13	2	1	0	3	8	0	7	.271	.375	.354	97	0	6	.887	0	103	124	2b12,S7,3b6	—	0.1
1913	NY N	4	2	0	0	0	0	0	0	0	0	1	.000	.000	.000	-99	-1	0	1.000	0	0	0	3b2/S	—	0.0
	Cin N	117	397	51	112	19	5	3	48	38	4	36	.282	.351	.378	109	5	24-17	.963	11	108	91	2b113,S4	—	1.8
	Year	121	399	51	112	19	5	3	48	38	4	37	.281	.349	.376	107	5	24-17	.963	11	108	91	2b113,S5,3b2	—	1.8
1914	Cin N	139	455	59	131	18	4	2	32	64	**13**	28	.288	.391	.358	120	15	24	.936	-5	100	108	2b134,S2	—	1.4
1915	Cin N	**160**	587	72	170	32	9	3	50	50	9	33	.290	.354	.390	123	17	12-17	.969	12	106	**183**	3b131,2b29	—	3.3
1916	Cin N	149	553	85	149	24	14	2	28	**84**	4	34	.269	.370	.374	132	25	13	.957	14	109	**179**	3b110,2b33,S5	—	**4.8**
1917	Cin N	156	599	91	**182**	**39**	11	1	53	71	8	30	.304	**.385**	.411	150	40	15	**.966**	9	104	104	3b154,2b2	—	5.8
1918	Cin N	126	493	**86**	158	**28**	3	1	37	54	7	24	.320	**.395**	.396	144	**30**	11	**.969**	5	93	**164**	3b126,M	—	**4.1**
1919	†Cin N	122	448	79	139	17	11	5	63	56	4	26	.310	.392	.431	151	30	21	.971	-2	90	**147**	3b121	—	3.4
1920	Cin N	145	550	86	164	28	12	0	49	60	8	29	.298	.375	.393	122	19	16-19	.969	-4	91	129	3b144/S	—	1.7
1921	Cin N	97	357	54	118	19	6	0	48	36	4	17	.331	.398	.417	122	13	22-14	.950	3	100	164	3b97	—	2.1
1922	†NY N	115	426	63	113	21	3	3	51	53	5	21	.265	.353	.350	81	-10	5-6	**.965**	4	107	**169**	3b110	—	0.0
1923	†NY N	123	465	91	135	22	5	4	48	60	6	22	.290	.379	.385	103	5	3-4	**.975**	4	105	96	3b118	—	1.5
1924	†NY N	145	559	82	157	32	3	2	46	52	**11**	29	.281	.354	.360	94	-2	8-6	**.983**	7	112	103	3b145	—	1.4
1925	NY N	25	65	7	15	4	0	0	4	6	0	3	.231	.296	.292	53	-4	0-0	.909	-4	68	46	3b16,2b2	—	-0.7
1926	NY N	12	35	2	8	2	0	0	3	2	0	3	.229	.270	.286	50	-2	0	.950	-0	99	88	3b7	—	-0.2
1927	†Pit N	14	35	2	10	1	0	0	3	2	0	2	.286	.324	.314	67	-2	0	.958	0	100	0	3b12	—	-0.1
Total	16	1676	6074	918	1774	308	87	26	566	696	83	345	.292	.373	.384	119	178	180-83	.967	55	101	139	3b1299,2b325,S20	—	30.4

GROH, LEW Lewis Carl "Silver"; B10.16.1883 Rochester NY; D10.20.1960 Rochester NY; BR/TR; d8.2; b–Heinie

YEAR	TM LG	G	AB	R	H	2B	3B	HR	RBI	BB-IB	HP	SO	AVG	OBP	SLG	AOPS	ABR	SB-CS	FA	FR	RNG	THR	GAMES AT POSITION	DL	BFW
1919	Phi A	2	4	0	0	0	0	0	0	0	0	2	.000	.000	.000	-99	-1	0	1.000	-0	85	0	/3	—	-0.1

GROSKLOSS, HOWDY Howard Hoffman; B4.10.1906 Pittsburgh PA; D7.15.2006 Vero Beach FL; BR/TR/5´9˝/176; d6.23; Col Amherst

YEAR	TM LG	G	AB	R	H	2B	3B	HR	RBI	BB-IB	HP	SO	AVG	OBP	SLG	AOPS	ABR	SB-CS	FA	FR	RNG	THR	GAMES AT POSITION	DL	BFW
1930	Pit N	2	3	0	1	0	0	0	1	0	0	0	.333	.333	.333	62	0	0	.000	-1	0	0	/S	—	-0.1
1931	Pit N	53	161	13	45	7	2	0	20	11	0	16	.280	.326	.348	82	-4	1	.981	-2	97	145	2b39,S3	—	-0.4
1932	Pit N	17	20	1	2	0	0	0	0	0	0	3	.100	.100	.100	-47	-4	0	.800	-1	60	0	/S	—	-0.5
Total	3	72	184	14	48	7	2	0	21	11	0	19	.261	.303	.321	68	-8	1	.981	-4	97	145	2b39,S5	—	-1.0

GROSS, EMIL Emil Michael; B3.3.1858 Chicago IL; D8.24.1921 Eagle River WI; BR/TR/6´0˝/190; d8.13

YEAR	TM LG	G	AB	R	H	2B	3B	HR	RBI	BB-IB	HP	SO	AVG	OBP	SLG	AOPS	ABR	SB-CS	FA	FR	RNG	THR	GAMES AT POSITION	DL	BFW
1879	Pro N	30	132	31	46	9	5	0	24	4	—	8	.348	.368	.492	183	12	—	.897	-3	—	—	C30	—	0.9
1880	Pro N	**87**	347	43	90	18	3	1	34	16	—	15	.259	.292	.337	116	7	—	.866	-18	—	—	C87	—	-0.8
1881	Pro N	51	182	15	50	9	4	1	24	13	—	11	.275	.323	.385	124	5	—	.893	-5	—	—	C50/rf	—	0.2
1883	Phi N	57	231	39	71	25	7	1	25	12	—	18	.307	.342	.489	163	19	—	.789	-23	—	—	C55,O2(1/1/0)	—	0.0
1884	CP U	23	95	13	34	6	2	4	—	6	—	—	.358	.396	.589	197	8	—	.860	-3	—	—	C15,O9(6/0/3)	—	0.6
Total	5	248	987	141	291	67	21	7	107	51	—	52	.295	.329	.427	146	51	—	.859	-50	—	—	C237,O12(7/1/4)	—	0.9

GROSS, TURKEY Ewell; B2.21.1896 Mesquite TX; D1.11.1936 Dallas TX; BR/TR/6´0˝/165; d4.14

YEAR	TM LG	G	AB	R	H	2B	3B	HR	RBI	BB-IB	HP	SO	AVG	OBP	SLG	AOPS	ABR	SB-CS	FA	FR	RNG	THR	GAMES AT POSITION	DL	BFW
1925	Bos A	9	32	2	3	0	1	0	2	2	1	2	.094	.171	.156	-16	-6	0-0	.976	1	119	78	S9	—	-0.4

GROSS, GABE Gabriel Jordan; B10.21.1979 Baltimore MD; BL/TR/6´3˝/210; [TorA01 1/15]; d8.7; Col Auburn

YEAR	TM LG	G	AB	R	H	2B	3B	HR	RBI	BB-IB	HP	SO	AVG	OBP	SLG	AOPS	ABR	SB-CS	FA	FR	RNG	THR	GAMES AT POSITION	DL	BFW
2004	Tor A	44	129	18	27	4	0	3	16	19-0	0	31	.209	.311	.310	59	-8	2-2	1.000	5	110	271	O38L,D7	0	-0.4
2005	Tor A	40	92	11	23	4	1	1	7	10-0	0	21	.250	.324	.348	75	-3	1-1	.981	-0	92	127	O37(19/0/20),D2	0	-0.5
2006	Mil N	117	208	42	57	15	0	9	38	36-3	2	60	.274	.382	.476	118	7	1-0	.984	7	119	263	O59(20/33/8)	0	1.3
Total	3	201	429	71	107	23	1	13	61	65-3	2	112	.249	.349	.399	91	-4	4-3	.989	11	109	231	O134(77/33/28),D9	0	0.4

GROSS, GREG Gregory Eugene; B8.1.1952 York PA; BL/TL/5´11˝/(160–180); [HouN70 4/80]; d9.5; C4

YEAR	TM LG	G	AB	R	H	2B	3B	HR	RBI	BB-IB	HP	SO	AVG	OBP	SLG	AOPS	ABR	SB-CS	FA	FR	RNG	THR	GAMES AT POSITION	DL	BFW
1973	Hou N	14	39	5	9	2	1	0	1	4-0	0	4	.231	.302	.333	77	-1	2-1	1.000	0	52	199	O9(4/2/3)	0	-0.2
1974	Hou N	156	589	78	185	21	8	0	36	76-4	1	39	.314	.393	.377	122	20	12-20	.994	5	101	139	O151(56/0/143)	0	1.3
1975	Hou N	132	483	67	142	14	10	0	41	63-1	0	37	.294	.373	.364	114	10	2-2	.958	-0	91	158	O121(60/0/61)	17	0.3
1976	Hou N	128	426	52	122	12	3	0	27	64-3	0	39	.286	.375	.329	111	9	2-6	.978	0	95	138	O115R	0	0.2
1977	Chi N	115	239	43	77	10	4	5	32	33-4	0	19	.322	.397	.460	118	7	0-1	.991	-1	92	82	O71(45/25/9)	0	0.4
1978	Chi N	124	347	34	92	12	7	1	39	33-5	0	19	.265	.323	.349	80	-9	3-1	.979	-5	87	104	O111(40/70/12)	0	-1.6
1979	Phi N	111	174	21	58	6	3	0	15	29-4	0	5	.333	.422	.402	123	7	5-2	.978	2	95	163	O73(49/19/11)	0	0.8
1980	†Phi N	127	154	19	37	7	2	0	12	24-1	1	7	.240	.346	.312	80	-3	1-1	.973	-1	84	166	O91(58/14/26)/1	0	-0.6
1981	†Phi N	83	102	14	23	6	1	0	7	15-4	0	5	.225	.319	.304	75	-3	2-2	.982	5	106	376	O55(13/5/38)	0	0.1
1982	Phi N	119	134	14	40	4	0	0	10	19-3	0	8	.299	.386	.328	98	1	4-3	.983	2	108	172	O71(50/12/19)	0	0.2
1983	†Phi N	136	245	25	74	12	3	0	29	34-4	1	16	.302	.385	.376	114	6	3-5	.991	-5	87	26	O110(77/27/25)/1	0	-0.2
1984	Phi N	112	202	19	65	9	1	0	16	24-3	1	11	.322	.393	.376	116	6	1-0	.986	4	130	101	O48(30/1/20),1b28	0	0.8
1985	Phi N	93	169	21	44	5	2	0	14	32-1	0	9	.260	.374	.314	93	0	1-0	1.000	-0	77	166	O52(46/0/9),1b8	31	-0.2
1986	Phi N	87	101	11	25	5	0	0	8	21-7	1	11	.248	.379	.297	87	0	1-0	1.000	2	122	102	O27(21/1/6),1b5/P	0	0.1
1987	Phi N	114	133	14	38	4	1	1	12	25-4	1	12	.286	.395	.353	99	1	0-0	1.000	-3	75	61	O50(49/0/1),1b11	0	-0.3
1988	Phi N	98	133	10	27	1	0	0	5	16-1	1	3	.203	.291	.211	46	-9	0-0	1.000	-1	87	138	O37(20/0/19),1b14	0	-1.2
1989	Hou N	60	75	2	15	0	0	0	4	11-2	1	6	.200	.310	.200	50	-4	0-0	.929	-1	84	0	O12(5/0/7),1b6/P	0	-0.7
Total	17	1809	3745	449	1073	130	46	7	308	523-51	8	250	.287	.372	.351	103	38	39-44	.982	3	94	133	O1204(623/176/524),1b74,P2	48	-0.8

GROSS, WAYNE Wayne Dale; B1.14.1952 Riverside CA; BL/TR/6´2˝/(205–221); [OakA73 9/215]; d8.21; Col Cal Poly–Pomona

YEAR	TM LG	G	AB	R	H	2B	3B	HR	RBI	BB-IB	HP	SO	AVG	OBP	SLG	AOPS	ABR	SB-CS	FA	FR	RNG	THR	GAMES AT POSITION	DL	BFW
1976	Oak A	10	18	0	4	0	0	0	1	2-0	0	1	.222	.300	.222	57	-1	0-0	.966	-1	54	99	1b3,O2R,D3	0	-0.2
1977	Oak A☆	146	485	66	113	21	1	22	63	86-6	5	84	.233	.352	.416	111	10	5-4	.932	-26	80	93	3b145/1	0	-1.8
1978	Oak A	118	285	18	57	10	2	7	23	40-2	5	63	.200	.308	.323	82	-6	0-2	.917	-8	88	131	3b106,1b15	0	-1.8
1979	Oak A	138	442	54	99	19	1	14	50	72-9	1	62	.224	.332	.367	93	-2	4-3	.943	-6	88	74	3b120,1b18,O2L	0	-1.1
1980	Oak A	113	366	45	103	20	3	14	61	44-9	1	39	.281	.355	.467	133	17	5-3	.948	-17	78	79	3b99,1b10/D	0	-0.1
1981	†Oak A	82	243	29	50	7	1	10	31	34-0	2	28	.206	.304	.366	97	-1	2-1	.946	-2	97	59	3b73,1b2/D	0	-0.4
1982	Oak A	129	386	43	97	14	0	9	41	53-0	2	50	.251	.342	.358	96	0	3-1	.970	-1	93	117	3b108,1b16/D	0	-0.3
1983	Oak A	137	339	34	79	18	0	12	44	36-4	3	52	.233	.311	.392	98	-1	3-5	.996	-10	64	88	1b74,3b67/PD	0	-1.6
1984	Bal A	127	342	53	74	9	1	22	64	68-4	1	69	.216	.346	.442	119	10	1-2	.937	-0	108	75	3b117,1b3/D	0	0.8
1985	Bal A	103	217	31	51	8	0	11	18	46-0	0	48	.235	.369	.424	119	7	1-1	.933	-0	98	137	3b67,D10,1b9	0	0.5
1986	Oak A	3	2	0	0	0	0	0	0	1-0	0	0	.000	.333	.000	0	0	0-0	.000	-0	0	0	/3	0	-0.1
Total	11	1106	3125	373	727	126	9	121	396	482-34	20	496	.233	.337	.395	105	33	24-22	.941	-71	90	93	3b903,1b151,D18,O4(2/0/2)/P	0	-6.1

GROSSART, GEORGE George Albert; B4.11.1880 Meadville PA; D4.18.1902 Pittsburgh PA; d6.7

YEAR	TM LG	G	AB	R	H	2B	3B	HR	RBI	BB-IB	HP	SO	AVG	OBP	SLG	AOPS	ABR	SB-CS	FA	FR	RNG	THR	GAMES AT POSITION	DL	BFW
1901	Bos N	7	26	4	3	0	0	0	1	0	0	—	.115	.115	.115	-30	-4	0	1.000	0	0	0	O7L	—	-0.5

GROTE, JERRY Gerald Wayne; B10.6.1942 San Antonio TX; BR/TR/5´10˝/(180–190); d9.21; Col Trinity (TX)

YEAR	TM LG	G	AB	R	H	2B	3B	HR	RBI	BB-IB	HP	SO	AVG	OBP	SLG	AOPS	ABR	SB-CS	FA	FR	RNG	THR	GAMES AT POSITION	DL	BFW
1963	Hou N	3	5	0	1	0	0	0	1	1-0	0	3	.200	.286	.200	61	0	0-0	1.000	-1	93	0	C3	0	-0.1
1964	Hou N	100	298	26	54	9	3	3	24	20-5	4	75	.181	.240	.262	44	-23	0-2	.985	-1	71	121	C98	0	-2.1
1966	NY N	120	317	26	75	12	2	3	31	40-8	3	81	.237	.327	.315	82	-6	4-3	.981	-2	117	85	C115,3b2	0	-0.4
1967	NY N	120	344	25	67	8	0	4	23	14-8	1	65	.195	.226	.253	38	-28	2-2	.990	1	115	126	C119	0	-2.4
1968	NY N★	124	404	29	114	18	0	3	31	44-11	3	81	.282	.357	.349	112	8	1-5	.994	7	124	95	C115	0	2.2
1969	†NY N	113	365	38	92	12	3	6	40	32-5	1	59	.252	.313	.351	84	-8	2-1	.991	19	140	**138**	C112	0	1.6
1970	NY N	126	415	38	106	14	1	2	34	36-8	1	39	.255	.313	.308	67	-19	2-1	.991	15	155	85	C125	0	0.2
1971	NY N	125	403	35	109	25	0	2	35	40-4	2	47	.270	.339	.347	95	-1	1-4	.990	4	101	64	C122	0	0.7
1972	NY N	64	205	15	43	5	1	3	21	26-8	3	27	.210	.304	.288	71	-7	1-0	.998	5	174	111	C59,3b3/rf	0	0.0
1973	†NY N	84	285	17	73	10	2	1	32	13-1	1	23	.256	.290	.316	68	-13	0-0	.995	10	130	76	C81,3b2	60	0.0
1974	NY N★	97	319	25	82	8	1	5	36	33-4	2	33	.257	.326	.335	87	-5	0-1	.988	0	117	94	C94	0	-0.1
1975	NY N	119	386	28	114	14	5	2	39	38-8	1	23	.295	.357	.373	107	4	0-1	**.995**	6	101	111	C111	0	1.5
1976	NY N	101	323	30	88	14	2	4	28	38-4	1	19	.272	.350	.365	108	4	1-2	.993	11	104	99	C95,O2(1/0/1)	0	2.0
1977	NY N	42	115	8	31	3	1	0	7	9-1	2	12	.270	.333	.313	77	-4	0-0	1.000	-2	87	87	C28,3b11	0	-0.5
	†LA N	18	27	3	7	0	0	0	4	2-1	0	5	.259	.310	.259	54	-2	0-1	1.000	3	64	96	C16,3b2	0	0.1
	Year	60	142	11	38	3	1	0	11	11-2	2	17	.268	.329	.303	72	-5	0-1	1.000	0	81	89	C44,3b13	0	-0.4
1978	†LA N	41	70	5	19	5	0	0	9	10-1	0	5	.271	.354	.343	98	0	0-0	.985	4	80	28	C32,3b7	38	0.6
1981	KC A	22	56	4	17	3	1	1	9	3-0	1	2	.304	.344	.446	128	2	1-0	1.000	-1	79	58	C22	0	0.2
	LA N	2	2	0	0	0	0	0	0	0-0	0	1	.000	.000	.000	-99	-1	0-0	1.000	0	0	0	/C	0	0.0
Total	16	1421	4339	352	1092	160	22	39	404	399-77	26	600	.252	.316	.326	82	-99	15-23	.991	77	117	98	C1348,3b27,O3(1/0/2)	98	3.5

GROTEWOLD, JEFF Jeffrey Scott; B12.8.1965 Madera CA; BL/TR/6´0˝/215; d4.12; Col San Diego

YEAR	TM LG	G	AB	R	H	2B	3B	HR	RBI	BB-IB	HP	SO	AVG	OBP	SLG	AOPS	ABR	SB-CS	FA	FR	RNG	THR	GAMES AT POSITION	DL	BFW
1992	Phi N	72	65	7	13	2	0	3	5	9-0	1	16	.200	.307	.369	91	-1	0-0	1.000	-0	0	0	C2,O2L/1	0	-0.1
1995	KC A	15	36	4	10	1	0	1	6	9-0	0	7	.278	.422	.389	110	1	0-0	.750	-0	0	257	D11/1	0	0.0
Total	2	87	101	11	23	3	0	4	11	18-0	1	23	.228	.350	.376	98	0	0-0	.833	-0	0	171	D11,1b2,O2L,C2	0	-0.1

GROTH, JOHNNY John Thomas; B7.23.1926 Chicago IL; BR/TR/6´0˝/(182–185); d9.5

YEAR	TM LG	G	AB	R	H	2B	3B	HR	RBI	BB-IB	HP	SO	AVG	OBP	SLG	AOPS	ABR	SB-CS	FA	FR	RNG	THR	GAMES AT POSITION	DL	BFW
1946	Det A	4	9	1	0	0	0	0	0	0	0	3	.000	.000	.000	-94	-2	0-0	1.000	-0	105	0	O4C	0	-0.3
1947	Det A	2	4	1	1	0	0	0	0	2	0	1	.250	.500	.250	109	0	0-0	1.000	0	133	0	/lf	0	0.0
1948	Det A	6	17	3	8	3	0	1	5	1	0	1	.471	.500	.824	242	3	0-0	.900	0	78	341	O4C	0	0.3
1949	Det A	103	348	60	102	19	5	11	73	65	2	27	.293	.407	.471	132	18	3-7	.966	-2	95	122	O99C	0	1.0
1950	Det A	**157**	566	95	173	30	8	12	85	95	2	27	.306	.407	.451	116	16	1-5	.985	-18	84	65	O157C	0	-0.7
1951	Det A	118	428	41	128	29	1	3	49	31	2	32	.299	.349	.393	100	0	1-1	**.993**	-5	90	109	O112C	0	-0.8
1952	Det A	141	524	56	149	22	2	4	51	51	0	39	.284	.348	.357	96	-3	2-10	.986	-5	88	135	O139(2/137/0)	0	-1.5
1953	StL A	141	557	65	141	27	4	10	57	42	2	53	.253	.308	.370	81	-16	5-6	.991	12	109	146	O141C	0	-1.2
1954	Chi A	125	422	41	116	20	0	7	60	42	2	37	.275	.341	.372	93	-4	3-9	.988	-1	102	66	O125(9/116/2)	0	-1.3
1955	Chi A	32	77	13	26	7	0	2	11	6-1	0	13	.338	.376	.506	135	4	1-0	1.000	1	107	79	O26C	0	0.4
	Was A	63	183	22	40	4	5	2	17	18-0	0	18	.219	.286	.328	69	-9	2-0	.984	-0	102	64	O48(12/40/1)	0	-1.2
	Year	95	260	35	66	11	5	4	28	24-1	0	31	.254	.313	.381	89	-5	3-0	.989	0	104	69	O74(12/66/1)	0	-0.8
1956	KC A	95	244	22	63	13	3	5	37	30-2	0	31	.258	.335	.398	94	-2	1-2	1.000	-1	86	168	O84(13/56/18)	0	-0.7
1957	KC A	55	59	10	15	0	0	0	2	7-0	0	6	.254	.333	.254	62	-3	0-0	.974	-2	89	0	O50(9/3/38)	0	-0.6
	Det A	38	103	11	30	10	0	0	16	6-0	1	7	.291	.333	.388	95	0	0-0	1.000	0	112	0	O36(12/25/0)	0	-0.2
	Year	93	162	21	45	10	0	0	18	13-0	1	13	.278	.333	.340	83	-3	0-0	.991	-2	102	0	O86(21/28/38)	0	-0.8
1958	Det A	88	146	24	41	5	2	2	11	13-0	0	19	.281	.340	.384	92	-2	0-1	.990	3	116	81	O80(52/19/10)	0	-0.2

YEAR	TM LG	G	AB	R	H	2B	3B	HR	RBI	BB-IB	HP	SO	AVG	OBP	SLG	AOPS	ABR	SB-CS	FA	FR	RNG	THR	GAMES AT POSITION	DL	BFW
1959	Det A	55	102	12	24	7	1	1	10	7-0	0	14	.235	.284	.353	70	-4	0-0	.983	-0	110	0	O41(11/18/13)	0	-0.6
1960	Det A	25	19	3	7	1	0	0	2	3-0	0	1	.368	.455	.421	135	1	0-1	1.000	-1	67	0	O8(0/7/1)	0	0.0
Total	15	1248	3808	480	1064	197	31	60	486	419-3	11	329	.279	.352	.395	99	-3	19-42	.987	-20	96	99	O1155(121/964/83)	0	-7.6

GROVER, ROY Roy Arthur; B1.17.1892 Snohomish WA; D2.7.1978 Milwaukie OR; BR/TR/5´8˝/150; d9.13

YEAR	TM LG	G	AB	R	H	2B	3B	HR	RBI	BB-IB	HP	SO	AVG	OBP	SLG	AOPS	ABR	SB-CS	FA	FR	RNG	THR	GAMES AT POSITION	DL	BFW
1916	Phi A	20	77	8	21	1	2	0	7	6	0	10	.273	.325	.338	104	0	5	.952	-3	78	81	2b20	—	-0.3
1917	Phi A	141	482	45	108	15	7	0	34	43	3	53	.224	.292	.284	77	-14	12	.960	6	105	81	2b139	—	-0.6
1919	Phi A	22	56	8	13	1	0	0	2	5	0	6	.232	.295	.250	53	-3	0	.915	-5	83	58	2b12,3b3	—	-0.9
	Was A	24	75	6	14	0	0	0	7	6	1	10	.187	.256	.187	25	-7	2	.947	-5	75	66	2b24	—	-1.3
	Year	46	131	14	27	1	0	0	9	11	1	16	.206	.273	.214	37	-11	2	.936	-10	78	63	2b36,3b3	—	-2.2
Total	3	207	690	67	156	17	9	0	50	60	4	79	.226	.292	.277	72	-24	19	.956	-7	98	78	2b195,3b3	—	-3.1

GRUBB, HARVEY Harvey Harrison; B9.18.1890 Lexington NC; D1.25.1970 Corpus Christi TX; BR/TR/6´0˝/165; d9.27

YEAR	TM LG	G	AB	R	H	2B	3B	HR	RBI	BB-IB	HP	SO	AVG	OBP	SLG	AOPS	ABR	SB-CS	FA	FR	RNG	THR	GAMES AT POSITION	DL	BFW
1912	Cle A	1	0	0	0	0	0	0	0	0	1	—	ø	1.000	ø	187	0	0	1.000	0	0	0	/3	—	0.0

GRUBB, JOHNNY John Maywood; B8.4.1948 Richmond VA; BL/TR/6´3˝/(175–188); [SDN71*A1/24]; d9.10; Col Florida St.; OF(389/408/280)

YEAR	TM LG	G	AB	R	H	2B	3B	HR	RBI	BB-IB	HP	SO	AVG	OBP	SLG	AOPS	ABR	SB-CS	FA	FR	RNG	THR	GAMES AT POSITION	DL	BFW
1972	SD N	7	21	4	7	1	1	0	1	1-0	0	3	.333	.364	.476	147	1	0-1	1.000	0	124	0	O6C	0	0.1
1973	SD N	113	389	52	121	22	3	8	37	37-2	2	50	.311	.373	.445	137	20	9-3	.988	1	98	181	O102(1/102/0),3b2	0	1.9
1974	SD N★	140	444	53	127	20	4	8	42	46-2	4	47	.286	.355	.403	118	11	4-0	.976	5	113	112	O122(8/114/0),3b2	0	1.4
1975	SD N	144	553	72	149	36	2	4	38	59-4	5	59	.269	.342	.363	104	4	2-7	.991	-13	90	33	O139C	0	-1.6
1976	SD N	109	384	54	109	22	1	5	27	65-10	4	53	.284	.391	.385	132	20	1-2	.974	-7	95	44	O98(63/15/30),1b9,3b3	32	0.9
1977	Cle A	34	93	8	28	3	3	2	14	19-2	1	18	.301	.425	.462	146	7	0-3	1.000	0	94	109	O28(27/0/1),D4	104	0.5
1978	Cle A	113	378	54	100	16	6	14	61	59-5	2	60	.265	.365	.450	130	16	5-1	.973	4	96	204	O110(108/0/6)	0	1.7
	Tex A	21	33	8	13	3	0	1	6	11-0	0	5	.394	.545	.576	214	6	1-1	1.000	1	88	382	O13(8/0/5),D3	0	0.7
	Year	134	411	62	113	19	6	15	67	70-5	2	65	.275	.381	.460	137	22	6-2	.974	5	95	**216**	O123(116/0/11),D3	0	2.4
1979	Tex A	102	289	42	79	14	0	10	37	34-3	1	44	.273	.350	.426	109	4	2-4	.986	-0	89	164	O82(38/29/25),D6	26	0.1
1980	Tex A	110	274	40	76	12	1	9	32	42-5	2	35	.277	.374	.427	123	10	2-3	.952	-4	86	124	O77(19/3/60),D8	0	0.3
1981	Tex A	67	199	26	46	9	1	3	26	23-0	2	25	.231	.316	.332	91	-2	0-3	.990	-5	83	50	O58(2/0/56)	0	-1.2
1982	Tex A	103	308	35	86	13	3	3	26	39-2	6	37	.279	.368	.370	109	6	0-3	.965	-4	90	85	O77(41/0/40),D18	21	-0.3
1983	Det A	57	134	20	34	5	2	4	22	28-1	2	17	.254	.388	.410	123	6	0-0	1.000	-2	85	66	O26(2/0/24),D18	48	0.2
1984	†Det A	86	176	25	47	5	0	8	17	36-5	2	36	.267	.395	.432	129	9	1-0	1.000	-1	96	0	O36(27/0/9),D33	0	0.6
1985	Det A	78	155	19	38	7	1	5	25	24-0	1	25	.245	.342	.400	105	2	0-1	1.000	-1	95	0	D33,O18(14/0/4)	15	-0.1
1986	Det A	81	210	32	70	13	1	13	51	28-0	2	28	.333	.412	.590	170	21	0-1	1.000	1	106	122	D52,O19(10/0/10)	38	1.9
1987	†Det A	59	114	9	23	6	0	2	13	15-0	0	16	.202	.290	.307	62	-6	0-0	1.000	0	108	75	O31(21/0/10),D16/3	26	-0.7
Total	16	1424	4154	553	1153	207	29	99	475	566-41	36	558	.278	.366	.413	121	135	27-33	.981	-24	95	106	O1042C,D191,1b9,3b8	310	6.4

GRUBE, FRANK Franklin Thomas "Hans"; B1.7.1905 Easton PA; D7.2.1945 New York NY; BR/TR/5´9˝/190; d5.12; Col Lafayette

YEAR	TM LG	G	AB	R	H	2B	3B	HR	RBI	BB-IB	HP	SO	AVG	OBP	SLG	AOPS	ABR	SB-CS	FA	FR	RNG	THR	GAMES AT POSITION	DL	BFW
1931	Chi A	88	265	29	58	13	2	1	24	22	2	22	.219	.284	.294	55	-18	2-2	.977	-10	*65*	*87*	C81	—	-2.2
1932	Chi A	93	277	36	78	16	2	0	31	33	2	13	.282	.362	.354	92	-2	6-1	.957	-5	*84*	*125*	C92	—	0.0
1933	Chi A	85	256	23	59	13	0	0	23	38	2	20	.230	.334	.281	67	-10	1-1	.984	-9	*85*	*82*	C83	—	-1.4
1934	StL A	65	170	22	49	10	0	0	11	24	1	11	.288	.379	.347	82	-3	2-1	.963	2	*99*	*81*	C55	—	0.1
1935	StL A	3	6	3	2	1	0	0	0	0	0	1	.333	.333	.500	108	0	0-0	1.000	0	*64*	*0*	C3	—	0.0
	Chi A	9	19	1	7	2	0	0	6	3	0	2	.368	.455	.474	137	1	0-0	.944	1	*132*	*109*	C9	—	0.3
	Year	12	25	4	9	3	0	0	6	3	0	3	.360	.429	.480	131	1	0-0	.955	1	*119*	*88*	C12	—	0.3
1936	Chi A	33	93	6	15	2	1	0	11	9	0	15	.161	.235	.204	9	-14	1-0	.991	3	*125*	*121*	C32	—	-0.9
1941	StL A	18	39	1	6	2	0	0	1	2	0	4	.154	.195	.205	6	-5	0-0	.951	1	*121*	*183*	C18	0	-0.4
Total	7	394	1125	121	274	59	5	1	107	131	7	88	.244	.326	.308	67	-51	12-5	.970	-18	*88*	*102*	C373	0	-4.5

GRUBER, KELLY Kelly Wayne; B2.26.1962 Houston TX; BR/TR/6´0˝/(175–185); [CleA80 1/10]; d4.20

YEAR	TM LG	G	AB	R	H	2B	3B	HR	RBI	BB-IB	HP	SO	AVG	OBP	SLG	AOPS	ABR	SB-CS	FA	FR	RNG	THR	GAMES AT POSITION	DL	BFW
1984	Tor A	15	16	1	1	0	0	1	2	0-0	0	5	.063	.063	.250	-17	-3	0-0	.933	2	180	0	3b12,O2R/S	0	0.0
1985	Tor A	5	13	0	3	0	0	0	1	0-0	0	3	.231	.231	.231	26	-1	0-0	1.000	-0	101	0	3b5/2	0	-0.2
1986	Tor A	87	143	20	28	4	1	5	15	5-0	0	27	.196	.220	.343	50	-11	2-5	.940	-2	112	64	3b42,2b14,D14,O9(4/2/3),S5	0	-1.4
1987	Tor A	138	341	50	80	14	3	12	36	17-2	7	70	.235	.283	.399	77	-13	12-2	.948	-3	102	75	3b119,S21,2b7,O2C/D	0	-1.3
1988	Tor A	158	569	75	158	33	5	16	81	38-1	7	92	.278	.328	.438	112	8	23-5	.971	26	**118**	125	3b156,2b7,O2C/SD	0	3.8
1989	†Tor A☆	135	545	83	158	24	4	18	73	30-0	3	60	.290	.328	.448	119	11	10-5	.945	16	119	76	3b119,O16(3/0/14)/SD	15	2.8
1990	Tor A★	150	592	92	162	36	6	31	118	48-2	8	94	.274	.330	.512	131	23	14-2	.955	-3	97	86	3b145,O6R/D	0	2.2
1991	†Tor A	113	429	58	108	18	2	20	65	31-5	6	70	.252	.308	.443	102	0	12-7	.962	5	101	80	3b111,D2	41	0.5
1992	†Tor A	120	446	42	102	16	3	11	43	26-3	4	72	.229	.275	.352	72	-18	7-7	.949	-1	93	52	3b120	25	-2.1
1993	Cal A	18	65	10	18	3	0	3	9	2-0	1	11	.277	.309	.462	101	0	0-0	.938	5	128	106	3b17/lfD	125	0.5
Total	10	939	3159	431	818	148	24	117	443	197-13	36	504	.259	.307	.432	101	-4	80-33	.955	46	106	84	3b846,O38(8/6/25),2b29,S29,D21	206	4.8

GRUDZIELANEK, MARK Mark James; B6.30.1970 Milwaukee WI; BR/TR/6´1˝/(185–190); [MonN91 11/295]; d4.28; Col Trinidad St. (CO) JC

YEAR	TM LG	G	AB	R	H	2B	3B	HR	RBI	BB-IB	HP	SO	AVG	OBP	SLG	AOPS	ABR	SB-CS	FA	FR	RNG	THR	GAMES AT POSITION	DL	BFW
1995	Mon N	78	269	27	66	12	2	1	20	14-4	7	47	.245	.300	.316	60	-15	8-3	.987	5	105	92	S34,3b31,2b13	0	-0.6
1996	Mon N★	153	657	99	201	34	4	6	49	26-3	9	83	.306	.340	.397	92	-8	33-7	.959	-6	97	89	S153	0	0.2
1997	Mon N	156	649	76	177	**54**	3	4	51	23-0	10	76	.273	.307	.384	81	-19	25-9	.955	-3	98	110	S156	0	-0.7
1998	Mon N	105	396	51	109	15	1	8	41	21-1	9	50	.275	.323	.379	87	-8	11-5	.950	-8	96	89	S105	0	-0.8
	LA N	51	193	11	51	6	0	2	21	5-1	2	23	.264	.286	.326	65	-11	7-0	.962	13	116	113	S51	0	0.7
	Year	156	589	62	160	21	1	10	62	26-2	11	73	.272	.311	.362	80	-19	18-5	.954	4	103	97	S156	0	-0.1
1999	LA N	123	488	72	159	23	5	7	46	31-1	10	65	.326	.376	.436	111	8	6-6	.973	-10	94	95	S119	33	0.6
2000	LA N	148	617	101	172	35	6	7	49	45-0	9	81	.279	.335	.389	87	-13	12-3	.976	2	99	106	2b148/S	0	-0.2
2001	LA N	133	539	83	146	21	3	13	55	28-0	11	83	.271	.317	.393	88	-11	4-4	.984	-6	95	96	2b133	16	-1.0
2002	LA N	150	536	56	145	23	0	9	50	22-4	3	89	.271	.301	.364	79	-19	4-1	.989	-11	99	90	2b147/D	0	-2.2
2003	†Chi N	121	481	73	151	38	1	3	38	30-0	11	64	.314	.366	.416	102	3	6-2	.986	17	97	123	2b121	30	2.5
2004	Chi N	81	257	32	79	12	1	6	23	15-0	1	32	.307	.347	.432	97	-1	1-1	.985	6	99	77	2b76	70	0.8
2005	†StL N	137	528	64	155	30	3	8	59	26-3	7	81	.294	.334	.407	92	-7	8-6	**.990**	21	**116**	**133**	2b137	0	2.0
2006	KC A	134	548	85	163	32	4	7	52	28-4	2	69	.297	.331	.409	93	-7	3-2	.994	4	104	111	2b132,S4	0	0.3
Total	12	1570	6158	830	1774	335	33	81	554	314-21	91	843	.288	.330	.393	89	-108	128-49	.986	24	101	106	2b907,S623,3b31/D	149	1.6

GRYSKA, SIG Sigmund Stanley; B11.4.1914 Chicago IL; D8.27.1994 Hines IL; BR/TR/5´11.5˝/173; d9.28

YEAR	TM LG	G	AB	R	H	2B	3B	HR	RBI	BB-IB	HP	SO	AVG	OBP	SLG	AOPS	ABR	SB-CS	FA	FR	RNG	THR	GAMES AT POSITION	DL	BFW
1938	StL A	7	21	3	10	2	1	0	4	3	0	3	.476	.542	.667	202	4	0-0	.912	-0	90	108	S7	—	0.3
1939	StL A	18	49	4	13	2	0	0	8	6	0	10	.265	.345	.306	66	-2	3-1	.873	-3	97	47	S14	—	-0.4
Total	2	25	70	7	23	4	1	0	12	9	0	13	.329	.405	.414	107	2	3-1	.887	-3	95	68	S21	—	-0.1

GUBANICH, CREIGHTON Creighton Wade; B3.27.1972 Belleville NJ; BR/TR/6´3˝/200; [OakA90 6/181]; d4.16

YEAR	TM LG	G	AB	R	H	2B	3B	HR	RBI	BB-IB	HP	SO	AVG	OBP	SLG	AOPS	ABR	SB-CS	FA	FR	RNG	THR	GAMES AT POSITION	DL	BFW
1999	Bos A	18	47	4	13	2	1	1	11	3-0	2	13	.277	.346	.426	92	-1	0-0	.979	-3	78	100	C14/3D	0	-0.3

GUDAT, MARV Marvin John; B8.27.1903 Goliad TX; D3.1.1954 Los Angeles CA; BL/TL/5´11˝/162; d5.21; Col UCLA; ▲

YEAR	TM LG	G	AB	R	H	2B	3B	HR	RBI	BB-IB	HP	SO	AVG	OBP	SLG	AOPS	ABR	SB-CS	FA	FR	RNG	THR	GAMES AT POSITION	DL	BFW
1929	Cin N	9	10	0	2	0	0	0	0	0	0	0	.200	.200	.200	-1	0	0	.800	-1	66	0	P7	—	0.0
1932	†Chi N	60	94	15	24	4	1	1	15	16	1	10	.255	.369	.351	96	0	0	.933	-2	77	0	O14(5/1/9),1b8/P	—	-0.3
Total	2	69	104	15	26	4	1	1	15	16	1	10	.250	.355	.337	87	0	0	.933	-3	77	0	O14(5/1/9),1b8,P8	—	-0.3

GUERRA, MIKE Fermin (Romero); B10.11.1912 Havana, Cuba; D10.9.1992 Miami Beach FL; BR/TR/5´9˝/162; d9.19

YEAR	TM LG	G	AB	R	H	2B	3B	HR	RBI	BB-IB	HP	SO	AVG	OBP	SLG	AOPS	ABR	SB-CS	FA	FR	RNG	THR	GAMES AT POSITION	DL	BFW
1937	Was A	1	3	0	0	0	0	0	0	0	0	2	.000	.000	.000	-99	-1	0-0	.750	-0	*0*	*0*	/C	—	-0.1
1944	Was A	75	210	29	59	7	2	1	29	13	0	14	.281	.323	.348	96	-2	8-2	.960	-3	*82*	*75*	C58/lf	0	-0.1
1945	Was A	56	138	11	29	1	1	1	15	10	1	12	.210	.268	.254	57	-8	4-1	.990	3	*119*	*76*	C38	0	-0.3
1946	Was A	41	83	3	21	2	1	0	4	5	0	6	.253	.295	.301	71	-4	1-0	.938	-2	*94*	*150*	C27	0	-0.4
1947	Phi A	72	209	20	45	2	2	0	18	10	0	15	.215	.251	.244	37	-19	1-2	.964	3	*145*	*130*	C62	0	-1.4
1948	Phi A	53	142	18	30	4	2	1	23	18	0	13	.211	.300	.289	57	-9	2-3	.973	-1	*120*	*95*	C47	0	-0.8
1949	Phi A	98	298	41	79	14	1	3	31	37	0	26	.265	.346	.349	87	-5	3-0	.982	-3	*101*	***111***	C95	0	-0.3
1950	Phi A	87	252	25	71	10	4	2	26	16	0	12	.282	.325	.377	81	-9	1-0	.990	-5	*87*	*78*	C78	0	-0.9
1951	Bos A	10	32	1	5	0	0	0	2	6	0	5	.156	.289	.156	21	-3	1-0	1.000	-0	*116*	*39*	C10	0	-0.3
	Was A	72	214	20	43	2	1	1	20	16	0	18	.201	.257	.234	34	-21	4-4	.977	-8	*95*	*89*	C66	0	-2.6
	Year	82	246	21	48	2	1	1	22	22	0	23	.195	.261	.224	32	-24	5-4	.982	-8	*98*	*81*	C76	0	-2.9
Total	9	565	1581	168	382	42	14	9	168	131	1	123	.242	.300	.303	65	-81	25-12	.975	-16	*104*	*96*	C482/lf	0	-7.2

GUERRERO, JUAN Juan Antonio; B2.1.1967 Los Llanos, D.R.; BR/TR/5´11˝/160; d4.9

YEAR	TM LG	G	AB	R	H	2B	3B	HR	RBI	BB-IB	HP	SO	AVG	OBP	SLG	AOPS	ABR	SB-CS	FA	FR	RNG	THR	GAMES AT POSITION	DL	BFW
1992	Hou N	79	125	8	25	4	2	1	14	10-2	1	32	.200	.261	.288	59	-7	1-0	.980	-6	82	61	S19,3b12,O3L,2b2	0	-1.3

GUERRERO, MARIO Mario Miguel (Abud); B9.28.1949 Santo Domingo, D.R.; BR/TR/5´10˝/(154–155); d4.8

YEAR	TM LG	G	AB	R	H	2B	3B	HR	RBI	BB-IB	HP	SO	AVG	OBP	SLG	AOPS	ABR	SB-CS	FA	FR	RNG	THR	GAMES AT POSITION	DL	BFW
1973	Bos A	66	219	19	51	5	2	0	11	10-0	2	21	.233	.272	.274	51	-15	2-2	.974	0	100	126	S46,2b24	0	-0.9
1974	Bos A	93	284	18	70	6	2	0	23	13-0	2	22	.246	.282	.282	59	-15	3-1	.969	-3	99	99	S93	0	-0.9
1975	StL N	64	184	17	44	9	0	0	11	10-1	2	7	.239	.281	.288	57	-11	0-0	.955	7	115	86	S64	0	0.3
1976	Cal A	83	268	24	76	12	0	1	18	7-2	3	12	.284	.304	.340	96	-2	0-0	.973	-9	91	83	2b41,S41,D7	0	-0.5
1977	Cal A	86	244	17	69	8	2	1	28	4-1	0	16	.283	.292	.344	76	-9	0-0	.985	-1	95	91	S31,D19,2b12	36	-0.7
1978	Oak A	143	505	27	139	18	4	3	38	15-2	6	35	.275	.302	.345	86	-11	0-5	.958	-24	82	80	S142	0	-2.4
1979	Oak A	46	166	12	38	5	0	0	18	6-0	0	7	.229	.253	.259	41	-14	0-1	.952	-2	98	100	S43	0	-1.1
1980	Oak A	116	381	32	91	16	2	2	23	19-2	1	32	.239	.273	.307	64	-20	3-3	.962	-36	80	71	S116	0	-4.5
Total	8	697	2251	166	578	79	12	7	170	84-8	16	152	.257	.285	.312	69	-97	8-12	.961	-67	91	87	S576,2b77,D26	36	-10.7

GUERRERO, PEDRO Pedro; B6.29.1956 San Pedro de Macoris, D.R.; BR/TR/6´0˝/(176–199); d9.22; OF(216/108/239)

YEAR	TM LG	G	AB	R	H	2B	3B	HR	RBI	BB-IB	HP	SO	AVG	OBP	SLG	AOPS	ABR	SB-CS	FA	FR	RNG	THR	GAMES AT POSITION	DL	BFW
1978	LA N	5	8	3	5	0	1	0	1	0-0	0	0	.625	.625	.875	314	2	0-0	1.000	-0	77	0	1b4	0	0.2
1979	LA N	25	62	7	15	2	0	2	9	1-1	0	14	.242	.250	.371	70	-3	2-0	1.000	-1	92	0	O12(4/1/9),1b8,3b3	0	-0.4
1980	LA N	75	183	27	59	9	1	7	31	12-3	0	31	.322	.359	.497	142	10	2-1	.987	-4	97	44	O40(3/25/15),2b12,3b3,1b2	23	0.5
1981	†LA N★	98	347	46	104	17	2	12	48	34-3	2	57	.300	.365	.464	140	18	5-9	.974	1	97	66	O75(0/8/70),3b21/1	0	1.4
1982	LA N	150	575	87	175	27	5	32	100	65-16	5	89	.304	.378	.536	158	44	22-5	.976	0	95	119	O137(0/44/105),3b24	0	4.3
1983	†LA N★	160	584	87	174	28	6	32	103	72-12	2	110	.298	.373	.531	149	38	23-7	.934	3	98	93	3b157,1b2	0	4.2
1984	LA N	144	535	85	162	29	4	16	72	49-7	1	105	.303	.358	.462	130	21	9-8	.917	-7	93	100	3b76,O58(1/20/38),1b16	15	1.0
1985	†LA N✳	137	487	99	156	22	2	33	87	83-14	6	68	.320	**.422**	**.577**	**182**	**56**	12-4	.974	4	98	129	O81(71/10/1),3b44,1b12	0	**5.8**
1986	LA N	31	61	7	15	3	0	5	10	2-0	1	19	.246	.281	.541	130	2	0-0	1.000	-1	78	240	O10L,1b4	137	0.1
1987	LA N★	152	545	89	184	25	2	27	89	74-18	4	85	.338	.416	.539	156	46	9-7	.971	-2	85	87	O109L,1b40	0	3.6
1988	LA N	59	215	24	64	7	1	5	35	25-2	3	33	.298	.374	.409	130	9	2-1	.895	-6	84	32	3b45,1b15,O2(1/0/1)	54	0.2
	StL N	44	149	16	40	7	1	5	30	21-7	2	26	.268	.358	.430	125	6	2-0	1.000	-1	95	74	1b37,O7L	0	0.3
	Year	103	364	40	104	14	2	10	65	46-9	5	59	.286	.367	.418	128	15	4-1	.998	-7	104	71	1b52,3b45,O9(8/0/1)	0	0.5
1989	StL N★	162	570	60	177	**42**	1	17	117	79-13	4	84	.311	.391	.477	144	37	2-0	.990	-13	71	101	1b160	0	1.4
1990	StL N	136	498	42	140	31	1	13	80	44-14	1	70	.281	.334	.426	109	6	1-1	.989	-8	83	86	1b132	15	-1.1
1991	StL N	115	427	41	116	12	1	8	70	37-2	1	46	.272	.326	.361	93	-4	4-2	.985	-9	80	105	1b112	42	-2.2
1992	StL N	43	146	10	32	6	1	1	16	11-3	0	25	.219	.270	.295	62	-7	2-2	.988	-7	29	93	1b28,O10L	121	-1.9
Total	15	1536	5392	730	1618	267	29	215	898	609-115	32	862	.300	.370	.480	138	281	97-47	.988	-51	82	94	1b573,O541R,3b373,2b12	407	17.4

GUERRERO, VLADIMIR Vladimir; B2.9.1976 Nizao Bani, D.R.; BR/TR/6´3˝/(165–235); d9.19; b–Wilton

YEAR	TM LG	G	AB	R	H	2B	3B	HR	RBI	BB-IB	HP	SO	AVG	OBP	SLG	AOPS	ABR	SB-CS	FA	FR	RNG	THR	GAMES AT POSITION	DL	BFW
1996	Mon N	9	27	2	5	0	0	1	1	0-0	0	3	.185	.185	.296	24	-3	0-0	1.000	-0	94	0	O8(0/1/7)	0	-0.4
1997	Mon N	90	325	44	98	22	2	11	40	19-2	7	39	.302	.350	.483	118	8	3-4	.929	1	97	165	O85(0/1/84)	61	0.4
1998	Mon N	159	623	108	202	37	7	38	109	42-13	7	95	.324	.371	.589	152	44	11-9	.951	2	109	86	O157R	0	3.7
1999	Mon N★	160	610	102	193	37	5	42	131	55-14	7	62	.316	.378	.600	148	43	14-7	.948	5	108	143	O160R	0	3.8
2000	Mon N★	154	571	101	197	28	11	44	123	58-**23**	8	74	.345	.410	.664	165	55	9-10	.969	3	103	129	O151R,D2	0	4.6
2001	Mon N★	159	599	107	184	45	4	34	108	60-24	9	88	.307	.377	.566	141	37	37-16	.965	5	103	136	O158R	0	3.5
2002	Mon N★	161	614	106	**206**	37	2	39	111	84-32	6	70	.336	.417	.593	155	51	40-20	.969	-1	95	130	O161R	0	4.3
2003	Mon N	112	394	71	130	20	3	25	79	63-22	6	53	.330	.426	.586	158	36	9-5	.970	3	104	140	O112R	46	3.2
2004	†Ana A★	156	612	**124**	206	39	2	39	126	52-14	8	74	.337	.391	.598	161	**54**	15-3	.973	8	111	140	O143R,D13	0	5.2
2005	†LA A★	141	520	95	165	29	2	32	108	61-**26**	8	48	.317	.394	.565	156	43	13-1	.988	3	104	117	O120R,D19	20	4.0
2006	LA A★	156	607	92	200	34	1	33	116	50-**25**	4	68	.329	.382	.552	143	39	15-5	.959	-1	104	92	O126R,D30	0	2.9
Total	11	1457	5502	952	1786	328	39	338	1052	544-195	70	674	.325	.390	.583	150	407	166-80	.963	27	104	126	O1381(0/2/1379),D64	127	35.2

GUERRERO, WILTON Wilton; B10.24.1974 Don Gregorio, D.R.; BB/TR (BR 1996)/6´0˝/(145–175); d9.3; b–Vladimir; OF(81/21/27)

YEAR	TM LG	G	AB	R	H	2B	3B	HR	RBI	BB-IB	HP	SO	AVG	OBP	SLG	AOPS	ABR	SB-CS	FA	FR	RNG	THR	GAMES AT POSITION	DL	BFW
1996	LA N	5	2	1	0	0	0	0	0	0-0	0	2	.000	.000	.000	-99	-1	0-0	ø	0	—	—	/H	0	-0.1
1997	LA N	111	357	39	104	10	9	4	32	8-1	0	52	.291	.305	.403	90	-8	6-5	.989	-18	88	50	2b90,S5	0	-2.2
1998	LA N	64	180	21	51	4	3	0	7	4-0	1	33	.283	.299	.339	72	-8	5-2	.968	-5	84	91	2b32,S14,O7(6/1/0)	0	-1.1
	Mon N	52	222	29	63	10	6	2	20	10-0	0	30	.284	.313	.410	91	-4	3-0	.975	-10	88	74	2b52	0	-1.1
	Year	116	402	50	114	14	9	2	27	14-0	1	63	.284	.307	.378	83	-12	8-2	.972	-15	87	80	2b84,S14,O7(6/1/0)	0	-2.2
1999	Mon N	132	315	42	92	15	7	2	31	13-0	2	38	.292	.324	.403	86	-8	7-6	.931	-14	87	66	2b54,O22L,D5	0	-2.1
2000	Mon N	127	288	30	77	7	2	2	23	19-0	0	41	.267	.312	.326	61	-18	8-1	.967	3	111	126	O75(42/13/24)/2D	0	-1.4
2001	Cin N	60	142	16	48	5	1	1	8	3-0	0	17	.338	.352	.408	91	-2	5-2	.927	-5	84	108	S16,2b11,O6L,3b4/D	0	-0.5
2002	Cin N	59	78	9	19	1	1	0	4	6-0	0	13	.244	.298	.282	52	-6	2-1	1.000	0	121	118	2b10,S7,3b3	0	-0.5
	Mon N	44	62	3	12	1	0	0	1	1-1	0	19	.194	.206	.210	9	-8	5-0	1.000	-2	100	362	O12(4/5/3),2b7,3b2	0	-0.9
	Year	103	140	12	31	2	1	0	5	7-1	0	32	.221	.259	.250	33	-14	7-1	1.000	-2	100	89	2b17,O12(4/5/3),S7,3b5	0	-1.4
2004	KC A	24	32	7	7	0	1	0	1	0-0	0	4	.219	.219	.281	29	-4	1-0	.960	-2	107	52	2b8,S3,O3(1/2/0),1b2,3b2,D2	0	-0.4
Total	8	678	1678	197	473	53	30	11	127	64-2	3	249	.282	.308	.369	76	-67	42-17	.974	-52	89	66	2b265,O125L,S45,D14,3b11,1b2	0	-10.3

GUEVARA, GIOMAR Giomar Antonio (Diaz); B10.23.1972 Miranda, Venezuela; BB/TR/5´8˝/150; d9.19

YEAR	TM LG	G	AB	R	H	2B	3B	HR	RBI	BB-IB	HP	SO	AVG	OBP	SLG	AOPS	ABR	SB-CS	FA	FR	RNG	THR	GAMES AT POSITION	DL	BFW
1997	Sea A	5	4	0	0	0	0	0	0	0-0	0	2	.000	.000	.000	-99	-1	1-0	.875	1	166	0	2b2/SD	0	0.0
1998	Sea A	11	13	4	3	2	0	0	0	4-0	1	4	.231	.444	.385	118	1	0-0	1.000	-0	124	116	2b5,S5	154	0.1
1999	Sea A	10	12	2	3	2	0	0	2	0-0	0	2	.250	.250	.417	67	-1	0-0	.870	-1	96	55	S9	0	-0.1
Total	3	26	29	6	6	4	0	0	2	4-0	1	8	.207	.324	.345	73	-1	1-0	.900	-1	85	57	S15,2b7,D2	154	0.0

GUIEL, AARON Aaron Colin; B10.5.1972 Vancouver BC, Can.; BL/TR/5´10˝/(190–200); [AnaA92 21/580]; d6.22

YEAR	TM LG	G	AB	R	H	2B	3B	HR	RBI	BB-IB	HP	SO	AVG	OBP	SLG	AOPS	ABR	SB-CS	FA	FR	RNG	THR	GAMES AT POSITION	DL	BFW
2002	KC A	70	240	30	56	13	0	4	38	19-1	4	61	.233	.296	.338	62	-13	1-5	.952	0	99	139	O61(0/1/61),D2	0	-1.7
2003	KC A	99	354	63	98	30	0	15	52	27-0	13	63	.277	.346	.489	110	6	3-5	.985	6	105	177	O89(1/1/87),D2	0	0.6
2004	KC A	42	135	15	21	4	0	5	13	17-0	3	42	.156	.263	.296	46	-11	1-1	.966	3	122	151	O39(38/0/1),D2	65	-0.9
2005	KC A	33	109	18	32	5	0	4	7	6-1	5	21	.294	.355	.450	117	3	1-0	.985	-1	99	74	O30(0/24/7)	0	0.2
2006	KC A	19	50	9	11	3	0	3	7	7-0	2	11	.220	.339	.460	106	1	0-0	1.000	1	109	122	O14(3/2/9),D3	0	0.1
	NY A	44	82	16	21	3	0	4	11	7-0	3	20	.256	.337	.439	99	0	2-1	1.000	-1	102	102	O27(4/3/21),1b15/D	0	-0.3
	Year	63	132	25	32	6	0	7	18	14-0	5	31	.242	.338	.447	101	0	2-1	1.000	-1	105	111	O41(7/5/30),1b15,D4	0	-0.2
Total	5	307	970	151	239	58	0	35	128	83-2	30	218	.246	.322	.414	88	-14	8-12	.976	7	105	144	O260(46/31/186),1b15,D10	65	-2.0

GUILLEN, CARLOS Carlos Alfonso; B9.30.1975 Maracay, Aragua, Venez.; BB/TR/6´1˝/(180–215); d9.6

YEAR	TM LG	G	AB	R	H	2B	3B	HR	RBI	BB-IB	HP	SO	AVG	OBP	SLG	AOPS	ABR	SB-CS	FA	FR	RNG	THR	GAMES AT POSITION	DL	BFW
1998	Sea A	10	39	9	13	1	1	0	5	3-0	0	9	.333	.381	.410	105	0	2-0	1.000	2	118	86	2b10	0	0.3
1999	Sea A	5	19	2	3	0	0	1	3	1-0	0	6	.158	.200	.316	29	-2	0-0	.938	2	130	58	S3,2b2	176	0.0
2000	†Sea A	90	288	45	74	15	2	7	42	28-0	2	53	.257	.324	.396	83	-8	1-3	.911	-5	96	63	3b68,S23	14	-1.0
2001	†Sea A	140	456	72	118	21	4	5	53	53-0	1	89	.259	.333	.355	88	-7	4-1	.980	-21	87	110	S137/D	0	-1.8
2002	Sea A	134	475	73	124	24	6	9	56	46-4	1	91	.261	.326	.394	94	-5	4-5	.966	-23	83	91	S130,D3	0	-1.9
2003	Sea A	109	388	63	107	19	3	7	52	52-2	1	64	.276	.359	.394	105	5	4-4	.963	-11	82	137	S76,3b32/D	25	-0.1
2004	Det A☆	136	522	97	166	37	10	20	97	52-3	2	87	.318	.379	.542	142	32	12-5	.974	17	109	105	S135	0	5.6
2005	Det A	87	334	48	107	15	4	5	23	24-3	2	45	.320	.368	.434	115	7	2-3	.978	0	109	97	S75,D10	61	1.1
2006	†Det A	153	543	100	174	41	5	19	85	71-10	4	87	.320	.400	.519	139	34	20-9	.956	-4	104	102	S145,1b8,D4	0	3.8
Total	9	864	3064	509	886	173	35	73	416	330-22	13	531	.289	.358	.440	112	56	49-30	.968	-43	96	106	S724,3b100,D19,2b12,1b8	276	6.0

GUILLEN, JOSE Jose Manuel; B5.17.1976 San Cristobal, D.R.; BR/TR/5´11˝/(185–196); d4.1

YEAR	TM LG	G	AB	R	H	2B	3B	HR	RBI	BB-IB	HP	SO	AVG	OBP	SLG	AOPS	ABR	SB-CS	FA	FR	RNG	THR	GAMES AT POSITION	DL	BFW
1997	Pit N	143	498	58	133	20	5	14	70	17-0	8	88	.267	.300	.412	83	-15	1-2	.963	-4	93	95	O136(0/4/134)	0	-2.5
1998	Pit N	153	573	60	153	38	2	14	84	21-0	6	100	.267	.298	.414	85	-14	3-5	.968	7	103	166	O151(0/2/149)	0	-1.6
1999	Pit N	40	120	18	32	6	0	1	18	10-1	0	21	.267	.321	.342	68	-6	1-0	.952	-1	98	51	O37R	0	-0.8
	TB A	47	168	24	41	10	0	2	13	10-1	7	36	.244	.312	.339	65	-9	0-0	.966	-1	88	156	O47R	0	-1.1
2000	TB A	105	316	40	80	16	5	10	41	18-1	13	65	.253	.320	.430	89	-7	3-1	.978	0	99	117	O99(0/1/98)	8	-0.9
2001	TB A	41	135	14	37	5	0	3	11	6-2	3	26	.274	.317	.378	84	-3	2-3	.969	8	129	309	O36R,D4	72	0.2
2002	Ari N	54	131	13	30	4	0	4	15	7-1	2	25	.229	.277	.351	59	-8	3-4	1.000	-0	94	106	O37(2/2/34)	0	-1.1
	Cin N	31	109	12	27	3	0	4	16	7-0	1	18	.248	.299	.385	76	-4	1-1	.980	-0	87	169	O27(4/0/26)/D	0	-0.6
	Year	85	240	25	57	7	0	8	31	14-1	3	43	.237	.287	.367	66	-12	4-5	.990	-1	91	135	O64(6/2/60)/D	0	-1.7
2003	Cin N	91	315	52	106	21	1	23	63	17-1	9	63	.337	.385	.629	167	30	1-3	.957	7	114	181	O78(22/1/63)	0	3.1
	†Oak A	45	170	25	45	7	1	8	23	7-1	5	32	.265	.311	.459	100	-1	0-0	.942	-7	75	0	O44(10/4/33)/D	0	-0.9
2004	Ana A	148	565	88	166	28	3	27	104	37-5	15	92	.294	.352	.497	123	18	5-4	.979	4	103	124	O136(135/0/4),D10	0	1.6
2005	Was N	148	551	81	156	32	2	24	76	31-6	**19**	102	.283	.338	.479	118	13	1-1	.978	7	111	122	O142(2/0/140),D2	0	1.2

YEAR	TM LG	G	AB	R	H	2B	3B	HR	RBI	BB-IB	HP	SO	AVG	OBP	SLG	AOPS	ABR	SB-CS	FA	FR	RNG	THR	GAMES AT POSITION	DL	BFW
2006	Was N	69	241	28	52	15	1	9	40	15-4	7	48	.216	.276	.398	75	-10	1-0	.988	8	132	97	O68R	90	-0.5
Total	10	1115	3892	513	1058	205	20	143	574	203-23	95	716	.272	.321	.445	99	-16	22-24	.972	26	103	129	O1038(175/14/869),D18	170	-3.9
GUILLEN, OZZIE	Oswaldo Jose (Barrios); B1.20.1964 Ocumare Del Tuy, Miranda, Venezuela; BL/TR/5´11˝/(150–165); d4.9; M3/C3																								
1985	Chi A	150	491	71	134	21	9	1	33	12-1	1	36	.273	.291	.358	74	-19	7-4	**.980**	4	95	93	S150	0	-0.1
1986	Chi A	159	547	58	137	19	4	2	47	12-1	1	52	.250	.265	.311	55	-36	8-4	.970	18	111	102	S157/D	0	-0.1
1987	Chi A	149	560	64	156	22	7	2	51	22-2	1	52	.279	.303	.354	72	-23	25-8	.975	19	112	**124**	S149	0	1.3
1988	Chi A✳	156	566	58	148	16	7	0	39	25-3	2	40	.261	.294	.314	71	-24	25-13	.977	**41**	**123**	111	S156	0	3.0
1989	Chi A	155	597	63	151	20	8	1	54	15-3	0	48	.253	.270	.318	67	-29	36-17	.973	18	109	102	S155	0	0.2
1990	Chi A★	160	516	61	144	21	4	1	58	26-8	1	37	.279	.312	.341	85	-11	13-17	.977	6	103	103	S159	0	0.3
1991	Chi A★	154	524	52	143	20	3	3	49	11-1	0	38	.273	.284	.340	74	-20	21-15	.970	0	101	103	S149	0	-1.0
1992	Chi A	12	40	5	8	4	0	0	7	1-0	0	5	.200	.214	.300	45	-3	1-0	1.000	1	106	90	S12	166	-0.1
1993	†Chi A	134	457	44	128	23	4	4	50	10-0	0	41	.280	.292	.374	80	-15	5-4	.972	-10	95	103	S133	0	-1.5
1994	Chi A	100	365	46	105	9	5	1	39	14-2	0	35	.288	.311	.348	71	-17	5-4	.959	-22	82	82	S99	0	-3.0
1995	Chi A	122	415	50	103	20	3	1	41	13-1	0	25	.248	.270	.318	55	-29	6-7	.976	-8	96	75	S120/D	0	-2.9
1996	Chi A	150	499	62	131	24	8	4	45	10-0	0	27	.263	.273	.367	64	-30	6-5	.981	-22	88	76	S146,O2L	0	-4.0
1997	Chi A	142	490	59	120	21	6	4	52	22-1	0	24	.245	.275	.337	61	-30	5-3	.974	-21	89	88	S139	0	-3.9
1998	Bal A	12	16	2	1	0	0	0	0	1-0	0	2	.063	.118	.063	-52	-4	0-1	.933	-0	113	48	S6/3	0	-0.4
	†Atl N	83	264	35	73	15	1	1	22	24-0	1	25	.277	.337	.352	83	-6	1-4	.977	-6	86	74	S71,2b2/13	0	-0.8
1999	†Atl N	92	232	21	56	16	0	1	20	15-2	0	17	.241	.284	.323	55	-16	4-2	.965	-1	100	110	S53,3b6/2	0	-1.3
2000	TB A	63	107	22	26	4	0	2	12	6-0	0	7	.243	.283	.336	57	-7	1-0	.948	1	108	85	S42,3b11,1b5,2b2	0	-0.4
Total	16	1993	6686	773	1764	275	69	28	619	239-25	7	511	.264	.287	.338	68	-319	169-108	.974	17	101	97	S1896,3b19,1b6,2b5,O2L,D2	166	-14.7
GUINDON, BOBBY	Robert Joseph; B9.4.1943 Brookline MA; BL/TL/6´2˝/185; d9.19																								
1964	Bos A	5	8	0	1	1	0	0	0	1-0	0	4	.125	.222	.250	30	-1	0-0	1.000	-0	0	0	/1lf	0	-0.1
GUINEY, BEN	Benjamin Franklin; B11.16.1858 Detroit MI; D12.5.1930 Detroit MI; BB/TR/6´0˝/170; d9.4																								
1883	Det N	1	5	1	1	0	0	0	0	0	—	1	.200	.200	.200	23	0	—	.000	-1	0	0	/cf	—	-0.1
1884	Det N	2	7	0	0	0	0	0	0	0	—	3	.000	.000	.000	-99	-2	—	.750	-1	—	—	C2	—	-0.2
Total	2	3	12	1	1	0	0	0	0	0	—	4	.083	.083	.083	-51	-2	—	.750	-2	—	—	C2/cf	—	-0.3
GUINTINI, BEN	Benjamin John (b Beniamino John Guintini); B1.13.1919 Los Banos CA; D12.2.1998 Roseville CA; BR/TR/6´1.5˝/190; d4.21																								
1946	Pit N	2	3	0	0	0	0	0	0	0	0	0	.000	.000	.000	-98	-1	0	1.000	0	112	0	/rf	0	-0.1
1950	Phi A	3	4	0	0	0	0	0	0	0	0	1	.000	.000	.000	-99	-1	0-0	1.000	1	0	2754	/lf	0	-0.1
Total	2	5	7	0	0	0	0	0	0	0	0	1	.000	.000	.000	-99	-2	0-0	1.000	1	56	1377	O2(1/0/1)	0	-0.2
GUISTO, LOU	Louis Joseph; B1.16.1895 Napa CA; D10.15.1989 Napa CA; BR/TR/5´11˝/193; d9.10; Mil 1917–18; Col St. Marys (CA)																								
1916	Cle A	6	19	2	3	0	0	0	2	4	0	3	.158	.304	.158	37	-1	1	1.000	-0	85	88	1b6	—	-0.2
1917	Cle A	73	200	9	37	4	2	0	29	25	2	18	.185	.282	.225	51	-11	3	.989	-1	93	144	1b59	—	-1.6
1921	Cle A	2	2	0	1	0	0	0	1	0	0	1	.500	.500	.500	153	0	0-0	1.000	0	337	0	/1	—	0.0
1922	Cle A	35	84	7	21	10	1	0	9	2	1	7	.250	.276	.393	72	-4	0-0	.995	1	108	103	1b24	—	-0.4
1923	Cle A	40	144	17	26	5	0	0	18	15	1	15	.181	.262	.215	27	-15	1-1	.988	1	116	104	1b40	—	-1.7
Total	5	156	449	35	88	19	3	0	59	46	4	44	.196	.277	.252	47	-31	5-1	.990	1	103	121	1b130	—	-3.9
GULAN, MIKE	Michael Watts; B12.18.1970 Steubenville OH; BR/TR/6´1˝/(192–211); [StLN92 2/53]; d5.14; Col Kent St.																								
1997	StL N	5	9	2	0	0	0	0	1	1-0	0	5	.000	.100	.000	-71	-2	0-0	1.000	-0	39	428	3b3	0	-0.3
2001	Fla N	6	6	1	0	0	0	0	0	2-0	0	2	.000	.250	.000	-28	-1	0-0	1.000	0	110	0	/3	0	-0.1
Total	2	11	15	3	0	0	0	0	1	3-0	0	7	.000	.167	.000	-52	-3	0-0	1.000	-0	69	245	3b4	0	-0.4
GULDEN, BRAD	Bradley Lee; B6.10.1956 New Ulm MN; BL/TR/5´11˝/(175–182); [LAN75 17/408]; d9.22																								
1978	LA N	3	4	0	0	0	0	0	0	0-0	0	2	.000	.000	.000	-99	-1	0-0	1.000	1	0	0	C3	0	0.0
1979	NY A	40	92	10	15	4	0	0	6	9-0	0	16	.163	.238	.207	21	-10	0-1	.995	8	102	138	C40	0	-0.1
1980	NY A	2	3	1	1	0	0	1	2	0-0	0	0	.333	.333	1.333	339	1	0-0	1.000	-0	0	0	C2	0	0.1
1981	Sea A	8	16	0	3	2	0	0	1	0-0	0	2	.188	.188	.313	40	-1	0-0	1.000	2	95	85	C6	0	0.1
1982	Mon N	5	6	1	0	0	0	0	0	1-0	0	1	.000	.143	.000	-55	-1	0-0	1.000	-0	23	233	C2	0	-0.1
1984	Cin N	107	292	31	66	8	2	4	33	33-2	2	35	.226	.307	.308	70	-11	2-2	.975	-2	87	111	C100	0	-1.0
1986	SF N	17	22	2	2	0	0	0	1	2-2	0	5	.091	.167	.091	-28	-4	0-0	1.000	0	120	62	C10	0	-0.4
Total	7	182	435	45	87	14	2	5	43	45-4	2	61	.200	.277	.276	53	-27	2-3	.982	8	90	115	C163	0	-1.4
GULLEY, TOM	Thomas Jefferson; B12.25.1899 Garner NC; D11.24.1966 St.Charles AR; BL/TR/5´11˝/178; d8.24; Col Mississippi College																								
1923	Cle A	2	3	1	1	1	0	0	0	0	0	0	.333	.333	.667	159	0	0-0	1.000	-0	85	0	/cf	—	0.0
1924	Cle A	8	20	4	3	0	1	0	1	3	0	2	.150	.261	.250	32	-2	0-0	.933	-0	118	0	O5(0/2/3)	—	-0.3
1926	Chi A	16	35	5	8	3	1	0	8	5	0	2	.229	.325	.371	84	-1	0-0	1.000	-0	113	0	O12R	—	-0.2
Total	3	26	58	10	12	4	2	0	9	8	0	4	.207	.303	.345	69	-3	0-0	.971	-1	114	0	O18(0/3/15)	—	-0.5
GULLIC, TED	Tedd Jasper; B1.2.1907 Koshkonong MO; D1.28.2000 West Plains MO; BR/TR/6´2˝/175; d4.15																								
1930	StL A	92	308	39	77	7	5	4	44	27	0	43	.250	.310	.344	64	-18	4-0	.967	0	85	153	O82R,1b3	—	-2.2
1933	StL A	104	304	34	74	18	3	5	35	15	1	38	.243	.281	.372	67	-15	3-1	.988	10	100	249	O36(14/16/7),3b33,1b14	—	-0.6
Total	2	196	612	73	151	25	8	9	79	42	1	81	.247	.296	.358	65	-33	7-1	.975	10	89	180	O118(14/16/89),3b33,1b17	—	-2.8
GULLIVER, GLENN	Glenn James; B10.15.1954 Detroit MI; BL/TR/5´11˝/175; [DetA76 8/170]; d7.17; Col Eastern Michigan																								
1982	Bal A	50	145	24	29	7	0	1	5	37-0	0	18	.200	.363	.269	77	-2	0-0	.970	2	106	74	3b50	0	-0.1
1983	Bal A	23	47	5	10	3	0	0	2	9-0	0	5	.213	.333	.277	73	-1	0-1	1.000	3	116	119	3b21	0	0.1
Total	2	73	192	29	39	10	0	1	7	46-0	0	23	.203	.356	.271	76	-3	0-1	.978	5	108	84	3b71	0	0.0
GUNKLE, FRED	Frederick William; B10.26.1857 Reading PA; D12.21.1936 Long Beach CA; d5.17																								
1879	Cle N	1	3	1	0	0	0	0	0	0	—	1	.000	.000	.000	-99	-1	—	1.000	-2	0	0	/rfC	—	-0.2
GUNNING, HY	Hyland; B8.6.1888 Maplewood NJ; D3.28.1975 Togus ME; BL/TR/6´1.5˝/189; d8.8; Col Princeton																								
1911	Bos A	4	9	0	1	0	0	0	2	2	0	—	.111	.273	.111	9	-1	0	1.000	-1	0	0	1b4	—	-0.2
GUNNING, TOM	Thomas Francis; B3.4.1862 Newmarket NH; D3.17.1931 Fall River MA; BR/TR/5´10˝/160; d7.26; U2; Col Boston College																								
1884	Bos N	12	45	4	5	1	1	0	2	1	—	12	.111	.130	.178	-4	-5	—	.914	-3	—	—	C12	—	-0.7
1885	Bos N	48	174	17	32	3	0	0	15	5	—	29	.184	.207	.201	34	-13	—	.877	-5	—	—	C48	—	-1.3
1886	Bos N	27	98	15	22	2	1	0	7	3	—	19	.224	.248	.265	58	-5	3	.892	-7	—	—	C27	—	-0.9
1887	Phi N	28	104	22	27	6	1	1	16	5	2	6	.260	.306	.365	81	-3	18	.895	5	—	—	C28	—	0.4
1888	Phi AA	23	92	18	18	0	0	0	5	2	3	—	.196	.237	.196	40	-6	14	.894	-1	—	—	C23	—	-0.5
1889	Phi AA	8	24	3	6	0	1	1	1	0	0	4	.250	.250	.458	101	0	3	.838	-1	—	—	C8	—	-0.1
Total	6	146	537	79	110	12	4	2	46	16	5	70	.205	.235	.253	50	-32	38	.887	-11	—	—	C146	—	-3.1
GUNSON, JOE	Joseph Brook; B3.23.1863 Philadelphia PA; D11.15.1942 Philadelphia PA; BR/TR/5´6˝/160; d6.14																								
1884	Was U	45	166	15	23	2	0	0	—	3	—	—	.139	.154	.151	-8	-27	—	.915	6	—	—	C33,O18(0/10/9)	—	-1.7
1889	KC AA	34	122	15	24	3	1	0	12	3	2	17	.197	.228	.238	31	-12	2	.862	-6	—	—	C32/lf3	—	-1.3
1892	Bal N	89	314	35	67	10	5	0	32	16	7	17	.213	.267	.277	63	-15	2	.921	-4	*95*	*109*	C67,O20(10/3/7),1b2/2	—	-1.3
1893	StL N	40	151	20	41	5	0	0	15	6	5	6	.272	.321	.305	66	-7	0	.927	2	*87*	*101*	C35,O5(1/0/4)	—	-0.2
	Cle N	21	73	11	19	1	0	0	9	6	0	0	.260	.316	.274	54	-5	0	.942	3	*114*	*111*	C20	—	-0.1
	Year	61	224	31	60	6	0	0	24	12	5	6	.268	.320	.295	62	-12	0	.932	4	*96*	*105*	C55,O5(1/0/4)	—	-0.3
Total	4	229	826	96	174	21	6	0	68	34	14	40	.211	.254	.251	45	-66	4	.912	1	*96*	*107*	C187,O44(12/13/20),1b2/23	—	-4.6
GUST, ERNIE	Ernest Herman Frank "Red"; B1.24.1888 Bay City MI; D10.26.1945 Maupin OR; BR/TR/6´0˝/170; d8.17																								
1911	StL A	3	12	0	0	0	0	0	0	0	0	—	.000	.000	.000	-99	-3	0	.974	-0	94	123	1b3	—	-0.4
GUSTINE, FRANKIE	Frank William; B2.20.1920 Hoopeston IL; D4.1.1991 Davenport IA; BR/TR/6´0˝/180; d9.13; C1																								
1939	Pit N	22	70	5	13	3	0	0	3	9	0	4	.186	.278	.229	38	-6	0	.896	2	125	74	3b22	—	-0.3
1940	Pit N	133	524	59	147	32	7	1	55	35	2	39	.281	.328	.374	94	-4	7	.941	-8	100	103	2b130	—	-0.4
1941	Pit N	121	463	46	125	24	7	1	46	28	1	38	.270	.313	.359	89	-8	5	.954	-2	105	73	2b104,3b15	0	-0.3
1942	Pit N	115	388	34	89	11	4	2	35	29	2	27	.229	.286	.294	68	-16	5	.954	-14	101	84	2b108,S2,3b2/C	0	-2.5

YEAR	TM LG	G	AB	R	H	2B	3B	HR	RBI	BB-IB	HP	SO	AVG	OBP	SLG	AOPS	ABR	SB-CS	FA	FR	RNG	THR	GAMES AT POSITION	DL	BFW
1943	Pit N	112	414	40	120	21	3	0	43	32	0	36	.290	.341	.355	98	-1	12	.938	-4	103	101	S68,2b40/1	0	0.3
1944	Pit N	127	405	42	93	18	3	2	42	33	0	41	.230	.288	.304	64	-20	8	.938	-23	94	85	S116,2b11/3	0	-3.5
1945	Pit N	128	478	67	134	27	5	2	66	37	2	33	.280	.335	.370	92	-5	8	.930	-14	93	98	S104,2b29/C	0	-1.0
1946	Pit N★	131	495	60	128	23	6	8	52	40	3	52	.259	.318	.378	95	-5	2	.967	8	**108**	92	2b113,S13,3b7	0	1.0
1947	Pit N★	**156**	616	102	183	30	6	9	67	63	2	65	.297	.364	.409	102	3	5	.944	16	**110**	122	3b156	0	1.8
1948	Pit N★	131	449	68	120	19	2	9	42	42	2	62	.267	.333	.379	90	-6	5	.947	**13**	**115**	114	3b118	0	0.6
1949	Chi N	76	261	29	59	13	4	4	27	18	1	22	.226	.279	.352	70	-12	3	.931	0	98	106	3b55,2b16	0	-1.1
1950	StL A	9	19	1	3	1	0	0	2	3	0	8	.158	.273	.211	24	-2	0-1	.857	-1	70	219	3b6	0	-0.3
Total	12	1261	4582	553	1214	222	47	38	480	369	15	427	.265	.322	.359	87	-82	60-1	.955	-27	103	90	2b551,3b382,S303,C2/1	0	-5.7
Guth, Bucky	Charles Henry; B8.18.1947 Baltimore MD; BR/TR/6´1˝/180; [AtlN69 20/466]; d9.12; Col West Virginia																								
1972	Min A	3	3	1	0	0	0	0	0	0-0	0	0	.000	.000	.000	-95	-1	0-0	1.000	-0	125	0	/S	0	-0.1
Gutierrez, Cesar	Cesar Dario "Cocoa"; B1.26.1943 Coro, Falcon, Venez.; D1.22.2005 Maracaibo, Zulia, Venez.; BR/TR/5´9˝/155; d4.16																								
1967	SF N	18	21	4	3	0	0	0	0	1-0	1	4	.143	.217	.143	5	-3	1-0	.946	1	105	124	S15/2	0	-0.1
1969	SF N	15	23	4	5	1	0	0	0	6-1	0	2	.217	.379	.261	83	0	1-0	.882	-2	105	0	3b7,S4	0	-0.1
	Det A	17	49	5	12	1	0	0	0	5-0	0	3	.245	.315	.265	61	-2	1-2	.946	0	100	75	S16	0	-0.1
1970	Det A	135	415	40	101	11	6	0	22	18-6	1	39	.243	.275	.299	58	-25	4-3	.957	-22	86	77	S135	0	-3.5
1971	Det A	38	37	8	7	0	0	0	4	0-0	1	3	.189	.211	.189	13	-4	0-0	.971	0	103	49	S14,3b5,2b2	41	-0.3
Total	4	223	545	61	128	13	6	0	26	30-7	3	51	.235	.277	.281	55	-34	7-5	.955	-22	89	77	S184,3b12,2b3	41	-4.1
Gutierrez, Franklin	Franklin Rafael; B2.21.1983 Caracas, Distrito Capital, Venezuela; BR/TR/6´2˝/180; d8.31																								
2005	Cle A	7	1	2	0	0	0	0	0	1-0	0	0	.000	.500	.000	52	0	0-0	1.000	0	115	0	O2C,D3	0	0.0
2006	Cle A	43	136	21	37	9	0	1	8	3-0	0	28	.272	.288	.360	69	-6	0-0	.966	-0	111	42	O42(10/7/28)	0	-0.8
Total	2	50	137	23	37	9	0	1	8	4-0	0	28	.270	.291	.358	69	-6	0-0	.967	-0	111	42	O44(10/9/28),D3	0	-0.8
Gutierrez, Jackie	Joaquin Fernando; B6.27.1960 Cartagena, Colombia; BR/TR/5´11˝/(145–180); d9.6																								
1983	Bos A	5	10	2	3	0	0	0	0	1-0	0	1	.300	.364	.300	79	0	0-1	.938	-1	61	50	S4	0	-0.1
1984	Bos A	151	449	55	118	12	3	2	29	15-0	0	49	.263	.284	.316	63	-23	12-5	.949	-25	84	68	S150	0	-3.4
1985	Bos A	103	275	33	60	5	2	2	21	12-0	0	37	.218	.250	.273	42	-23	10-2	.943	-3	98	85	S99	0	-1.6
1986	Bal A	61	145	8	27	3	0	0	4	3-0	1	27	.186	.207	.207	14	-18	3-1	.990	-5	85	107	2b53,3b6/D	74	-2.0
1987	Bal A	3	1	0	0	0	0	0	0	0-0	0	0	.000	.000	.000	-99	0	0-0	ø	-0	0	0	/23	0	-0.1
1988	Phi N	33	77	8	19	4	0	0	9	2-0	0	9	.247	.259	.299	60	-4	0-0	.919	-3	104	76	S22,3b13	0	-0.6
Total	6	356	957	106	227	24	5	4	63	33-0	1	123	.237	.261	.285	50	-68	25-9	.945	-38	90	74	S275,2b54,3b20/D	74	-7.8
Gutierrez, Ricky	Ricardo; B5.23.1970 Miami FL; BR/TR/6´1˝/(175–195); [BalA88 1/28]; d4.13																								
1993	SD N	133	438	76	110	10	5	5	26	50-2	5	97	.251	.334	.331	78	-13	4-3	.971	-3	92	83	S117,2b6,O5(3/0/2),3b4	0	-0.8
1994	SD N	90	275	27	66	11	2	1	28	32-1	2	54	.240	.321	.305	67	-13	2-6	.925	-11	91	77	S78,2b7	0	-2.0
1995	Hou N	52	156	22	43	6	0	0	12	10-3	1	33	.276	.321	.314	74	-6	5-0	.956	-6	88	70	S44,3b2	0	-0.8
1996	Hou N	89	218	28	62	8	1	1	15	23-3	3	42	.284	.359	.344	94	-1	6-1	.953	-9	85	90	S74,3b6,2b5	0	-0.5
1997	†Hou N	102	303	33	79	14	4	3	34	21-2	3	50	.261	.315	.363	79	-10	5-2	.967	-3	97	116	S64,3b22,2b9	35	-0.8
1998	†Hou N	141	491	55	128	24	3	2	46	54-5	6	84	.261	.337	.334	81	-12	13-7	.976	14	103	111	S141	0	1.2
1999	†Hou N	85	268	33	70	7	5	1	25	37-4	2	45	.261	.354	.336	77	-9	2-5	.971	-6	94	83	S80/3	70	-1.0
2000	Chi N	125	449	73	124	19	2	11	56	66-0	7	58	.276	.375	.401	98	1	8-2	**.986**	-13	88	82	S121	28	-0.2
2001	Chi N	147	528	76	153	23	3	10	66	40-0	10	56	.290	.345	.402	97	-2	4-3	.971	-8	91	81	S144	0	0.1
2002	Cle A	94	353	38	97	13	0	4	38	20-0	7	48	.275	.325	.346	77	-11	0-1	.976	12	109	103	2b93/D	64	0.4
2003	Cle A	16	50	2	13	3	0	0	3	3-0	1	5	.260	.309	.320	68	-2	0-0	.929	-3	102	71	S9,3b7	164	-0.5
2004	NY N	24	63	2	11	2	0	0	5	6-0	1	8	.175	.257	.206	23	-7	0-0	1.000	0	111	115	2b18,3b2	0	-0.6
	Bos A	21	40	6	11	1	0	0	3	2-0	0	6	.275	.310	.300	57	-3	1-0	1.000	0	102	127	2b14,S6	0	-0.1
Total	12	1119	3632	471	967	141	25	38	357	364-20	48	586	.266	.338	.350	82	-88	50-30	.967	-35	93	89	S878,2b152,3b44,O5(3/0/2)/D	361	-5.6
Gutteridge, Don	Donald Joseph; B6.19.1912 Pittsburg KS; BR/TR/5´10.5˝/165; d9.7; M2/C14; Col Pittsburg St. (KS)																								
1936	StL N	23	91	13	29	3	4	3	16	1	0	14	.319	.326	.538	130	3	3	.967	0	94	109	3b23	—	0.3
1937	StL N	119	447	66	121	26	10	7	61	25	1	66	.271	.311	.421	95	-5	12	.978	0	93	**133**	3b105,S8	—	0.0
1938	StL N	142	552	61	141	21	15	9	64	29	0	49	.255	.293	.397	83	-15	14	.945	-7	98	132	3b73,S68	—	-1.5
1939	StL N	148	524	71	141	27	4	7	54	27	3	70	.269	.309	.376	78	-17	5	.934	-19	79	107	3b143,S2	—	-3.2
1940	StL N	69	108	19	29	5	0	3	14	5	0	15	.269	.301	.398	86	-2	3	.877	-4	79	90	3b39	—	-0.6
1942	StL A	147	616	90	157	27	11	1	50	59	0	54	.255	.320	.339	84	-14	16-13	.973	2	102	98	2b145,3b2	0	-0.3
1943	StL A	132	538	77	147	35	6	1	36	50	0	46	.273	.335	.366	103	2	10-9	.958	-29	85	69	2b132	0	-2.2
1944	†StL A	148	603	89	148	27	11	3	36	51	0	63	.245	.304	.342	80	-17	20-8	.957	-10	96	94	2b146	0	-1.8
1945	StL A	143	543	72	129	24	3	2	49	43	1	46	.238	.295	.304	70	-21	9-6	.970	-17	91	83	2b128,O14L	0	-3.4
1946	†Bos A	22	47	8	11	3	0	1	6	2	0	7	.234	.265	.362	70	-2	0-0	1.000	-1	125	136	2b9,3b8	0	-0.3
1947	Bos A	54	131	20	22	2	0	2	5	17	0	13	.168	.264	.229	35	-12	3-1	.938	-2	96	85	2b20,3b19	0	-1.3
1948	Pit N	4	2	0	0	0	0	0	0	0	0	1	.000	.000	.000	-98	-1	0	ø	0	—	—	/H	0	-0.1
Total	12	1151	4202	586	1075	200	64	39	391	309	5	444	.256	.308	.362	84	-101	95-37	.964	-86	94	87	2b580,3b412,S78,O14L	0	-14.4
Guzman, Cristian	Cristian; B3.21.1978 Santo Domingo, D.R.; BB/TR/6´0˝/(188–205); d4.6; [DL 2006 Was N 182]																								
1999	Min A	131	420	47	95	12	3	1	26	22-0	3	90	.226	.267	.276	38	-41	9-7	.959	-5	100	101	S131	15	-3.5
2000	Min A	156	631	89	156	25	**20**	8	54	46-1	2	101	.247	.299	.388	68	-34	28-10	.967	-17	90	94	S151/D	0	-3.4
2001	Min A★	118	493	80	149	28	**14**	10	51	21-0	5	78	.302	.337	.477	105	2	25-8	.959	-10	100	85	S118	35	0.3
2002	†Min A	148	623	80	170	31	6	9	59	17-2	2	79	.273	.292	.385	76	-23	12-13	.981	-17	87	98	S147/D	0	-3.1
2003	†Min A	143	534	78	143	15	**14**	3	53	30-0	5	79	.268	.311	.365	75	-21	18-9	.980	-30	88	78	S141	0	-3.8
2004	†Min A	145	576	84	158	31	4	8	46	30-4	1	64	.274	.309	.384	78	-20	10-5	.983	9	102	115	S145	0	0.0
2005	Was N	142	456	39	100	19	6	4	31	25-6	1	76	.219	.260	.314	52	-34	7-4	.973	-23	88	99	S142	0	-4.8
Total	7	983	3733	497	971	161	67	43	320	191-13	19	567	.260	.298	.374	72	-171	109-56	.972	-93	93	96	S975,D2	232	-18.3
Guzman, Edwards	Edwards; B9.11.1976 Bayamon, PR; BL/TR/5´11˝/(204–205); [SFN95 50/1363]; d4.6																								
1999	SF N	14	15	0	0	0	0	0	0	0-0	0	4	.000	.000	.000	-99	-5	0-0	1.000	1	150	0	3b5/C	0	-0.4
2001	SF N	61	115	8	28	6	0	3	7	5-2	0	16	.243	.273	.374	70	-6	0-0	.990	-4	149	91	C26,1b7,3b7,2b3,O2L	0	-0.8
2003	Mon N	52	146	15	35	5	0	1	14	5-2	0	17	.240	.263	.295	45	-12	0-0	.956	-5	95	81	3b28,1b13,C4,D3	0	-1.7
Total	3	127	276	23	63	11	0	4	21	10-4	0	37	.228	.253	.312	47	-23	0-0	.969	-7	100	84	3b40,C31,1b20,D3,2b3,O2L	0	-2.9
Guzman, Freddy	Freddy Antonio; B1.20.1981 Santo Domingo, D.R.; BB/TR/5´10˝/165; d8.17; [DL 2005 SD N 183]																								
2004	SD N	20	76	8	16	3	0	0	5	3-0	1	13	.211	.250	.250	31	-8	5-2	.960	2	122	254	O17C	0	-0.5
2006	Tex A	9	7	1	2	0	0	0	0	1-0	1	1	.286	.444	.286	95	0	0-0	1.000	-0	94	0	O4(1/2/1)	0	0.0
Total	2	29	83	9	18	3	0	0	5	4-0	2	14	.217	.270	.253	38	-8	5-2	.964	2	118	222	O21(1/19/1)	183	-0.5
Guzman, Joel	Irvin Joel; B11.24.1984 Quisqueya, D.R.; BR/TR/6´6˝/250; d6.1																								
2006	LA N	8	19	2	4	0	0	0	3	3-0	1	2	.211	.348	.211	48	-1	0-0	1.000	-2	73	106	3b6/1lf	0	-0.3
Gwosdz, Doug	Douglas Wayne "Eye Chart"; B6.20.1960 Houston TX; BR/TR/5´11˝/180; [SDN78 2/40]; d8.17																								
1981	SD N	16	24	1	4	2	0	0	3	3-2	0	6	.167	.241	.250	49	-2	0-0	1.000	2	328	130	C13	0	0.1
1982	SD N	7	17	1	3	0	0	0	0	2-1	0	7	.176	.263	.176	27	-2	0-0	1.000	2	443	0	C7	0	0.1
1983	SD N	39	55	7	6	1	0	1	4	7-0	0	19	.109	.210	.182	10	-7	0-0	.971	-2	137	53	C32	0	-0.9
1984	SD N	7	8	0	2	0	0	0	1	2-0	0	5	.250	.400	.250	86	0	0-0	.963	2	114	98	C6	0	0.2
Total	4	69	104	9	15	3	0	1	8	14-3	0	37	.144	.242	.202	27	-11	0-0	.981	4	228	67	C58	0	-0.5
Gwynn, Tony	Anthony Keith Sr.; B5.9.1960 Los Angeles CA; BL/TL/5´11˝/(185–225); [SDN81 3/58]; d7.19; b–Chris s–Tony; Col San Diego St.; HF2006																								
1982	SD N	54	190	33	55	12	2	1	17	14-0	0	16	.289	.337	.389	110	2	8-3	.991	-2	100	29	O52(23/28/13)	15	0.0
1983	SD N	86	304	34	94	12	2	1	37	23-5	0	21	.309	.355	.372	106	2	7-4	.994	4	102	153	O81(26/6/54)	78	0.2
1984	†SD N★	158	606	88	**213**	21	10	5	71	59-13	2	23	**.351**	.410	.444	139	33	33-18	.989	9	112	103	O156(0/1/156)	0	3.6
1985	SD N★	154	622	90	197	29	5	6	46	45-4	2	33	.317	.364	.408	117	14	14-11	.989	11	112	129	O152R	0	1.6
1986	SD N★	160	642	**107**	**211**	33	7	14	59	52-11	3	35	.329	.381	.467	136	31	37-9	.989	14	113	147	O160R	0	4.2
1987	SD N★	157	589	119	**218**	36	13	7	54	82-26	3	35	**.370**	.447	.511	160	**55**	56-12	.981	4	104	123	O156R	0	5.8
1988	SD N	133	521	64	163	22	5	7	70	51-13	0	40	**.313**	.373	.415	129	20	26-11	.982	-3	94	122	O133(0/32/102)	21	1.7
1989	SD N★	158	604	82	**203**	27	7	4	62	56-16	1	30	**.336**	.389	.424	133	27	40-16	.984	1	97	153	O157(0/86/73)	0	3.0

YEAR	TM LG	G	AB	R	H	2B	3B	HR	RBI	BB-IB	HP	SO	AVG	OBP	SLG	AOPS	ABR	SB-CS	FA	FR	RNG	THR	GAMES AT POSITION	DL	BFW
1990	SD N★	141	573	79	177	29	10	4	72	44-20	1	23	.309	.357	.415	111	9	17-8	.985	6	107	104	O141R	0	1.1
1991	SD N★	134	530	69	168	27	11	4	62	34-8	0	19	.317	.355	.432	117	11	8-8	.990	5	108	78	O134R	0	1.1
1992	SD N★	128	520	77	165	27	3	6	41	46-12	0	16	.317	.371	.415	121	15	3-6	.982	4	104	102	O127R	0	1.4
1993	SD N★	122	489	70	175	41	3	7	59	36-11	1	19	.358	.398	.497	138	28	14-1	.981	2	107	90	O121(0/4/121)	0	2.6
1994	SD N★	110	419	79	**165**	35	1	12	64	48-16	2	19	**.394**	**.454**	.568	171	47	5-0	.985	-2	99	81	O106(0/1/105)	0	4.0
1995	SD N★	135	535	82	**197**	33	1	9	90	35-10	1	15	**.368**	.404	.484	138	30	17-5	.992	2	103	89	O133R	0	2.7
1996	†SD N✳	116	451	67	159	27	2	3	50	39-12	1	17	**.353**	.400	.441	129	20	11-4	.989	-10	87	27	O111R	35	0.6
1997	SD N★	149	592	97	**220**	49	2	17	119	43-12	3	28	**.372**	.409	.547	160	52	12-5	.983	-10	83	77	O143R,D3	0	3.5
1998	†SD N★	127	461	65	148	35	0	16	69	35-6	1	18	.321	.364	.501	136	24	3-1	.993	-11	75	74	O116R,D3	19	0.8
1999	SD N✳	111	411	59	139	27	0	10	62	29-5	2	14	.338	.381	.477	126	16	7-2	.993	-8	83	67	O104R,D2	50	0.4
2000	SD N	36	127	17	41	12	0	1	17	9-2	1	4	.323	.364	.441	111	3	0-1	1.000	-4	66	66	O26R,D6	114	-0.2
2001	SD N☆	71	102	5	33	9	1	1	17	10-1	0	9	.324	.384	.461	127	4	1-0	1.000	-0	72	254	O17R/D	71	0.4
Total	20	2440	9288	1383	3141	543	85	135	1138	790-203	24	434	.338	.388	.459	133	443	319-125	.987	12	100	102	O2326(49/158/2144),D15	403	38.5

GWYNN, TONY Anthony Keith Jr.; B10.4.1982 Long Beach CA; BL/TR/6´0˝/185; [MilN03 2/39]; d7.15; f–Tony; Col San Diego St.

YEAR	TM LG	G	AB	R	H	2B	3B	HR	RBI	BB-IB	HP	SO	AVG	OBP	SLG	AOPS	ABR	SB-CS	FA	FR	RNG	THR	GAMES AT POSITION	DL	BFW
2006	Mil N	32	77	5	20	2	1	0	4	2-0	0	15	.260	.275	.312	51	-6	3-1	1.000	2	121	145	O19C	0	-0.4

GWYNN, CHRIS Christopher Karlton; B10.13.1964 Los Angeles CA; BL/TL/6´0˝/(200–220); [LAN85 1/10]; d8.14; b–Tony; Col San Diego St.

YEAR	TM LG	G	AB	R	H	2B	3B	HR	RBI	BB-IB	HP	SO	AVG	OBP	SLG	AOPS	ABR	SB-CS	FA	FR	RNG	THR	GAMES AT POSITION	DL	BFW
1987	LA N	17	32	2	7	1	0	0	2	1-0	0	7	.219	.242	.250	32	-3	0-0	1.000	-1	83	0	O10L	0	-0.4
1988	LA N	12	11	1	2	0	0	0	0	1-0	0	2	.182	.250	.182	27	-1	0-0	ø	-0	0	0	O4L	0	-0.2
1989	LA N	32	68	8	16	4	1	0	7	2-0	0	9	.235	.254	.324	66	-3	1-0	1.000	-0	86	132	O19(14/5/2)	102	-0.4
1990	LA N	101	141	19	40	2	1	5	22	7-2	0	28	.284	.311	.418	103	0	0-1	1.000	-2	80	64	O44(32/5/8)	0	-0.3
1991	LA N	94	139	18	35	5	1	5	22	10-1	1	23	.252	.301	.410	101	0	1-0	1.000	-2	76	132	O41(31/2/14)	0	-0.2
1992	KC A	34	84	10	24	3	2	1	7	3-0	0	10	.286	.303	.405	96	-1	0-0	1.000	-2	91	0	O19(5/0/14),D2	118	-0.3
1993	KC A	103	287	36	86	14	4	1	25	24-5	1	34	.300	.354	.387	93	-3	0-1	.994	3	102	135	O83(66/0/19)/1D	0	-0.3
1994	LA N	58	71	9	19	0	0	3	13	7-0	0	7	.268	.333	.394	94	-1	0-2	1.000	-1	75	0	O20(19/0/1)	0	-0.3
1995	†LA N	67	84	8	18	3	2	1	10	6-1	1	23	.214	.272	.333	64	-5	0-0	1.000	0	109	0	O17(12/0/5),1b2	21	-0.5
1996	†SD N	81	90	8	16	4	0	1	10	10-0	0	28	.178	.260	.256	38	-8	0-0	1.000	-1	90	0	O29(5/0/24)/1	36	-0.9
Total	10	599	1007	119	263	36	11	17	118	71-9	3	171	.261	.308	.369	84	-25	2-4	.997	-5	91	84	O286(198/12/87),D7,1b4	277	-3.8

GYSELMAN, DICK Richard Renald; B4.6.1908 San Francisco CA; D9.20.1990 Seattle WA; BR/TR/6´2˝/170; d4.20

YEAR	TM LG	G	AB	R	H	2B	3B	HR	RBI	BB-IB	HP	SO	AVG	OBP	SLG	AOPS	ABR	SB-CS	FA	FR	RNG	THR	GAMES AT POSITION	DL	BFW
1933	Bos N	58	155	10	37	6	2	0	12	7	0	21	.239	.272	.303	70	-7	0	.926	2	110	72	3b42,2b5/S	—	-0.4
1934	Bos N	24	36	7	6	1	1	0	4	2	0	11	.167	.211	.250	25	-4	0	.739	-3	67	0	3b15,2b2	—	-0.7
Total	2	82	191	17	43	7	3	0	16	9	0	32	.225	.260	.293	61	-11	0	.901	-1	104	62	3b57,2b7/S	—	-1.1

HAAD, YAMID Yamid Salcedo; B9.2.1977 Cartagena, Colombia; BR/TR/6´2˝/(204–214); d7.5

YEAR	TM LG	G	AB	R	H	2B	3B	HR	RBI	BB-IB	HP	SO	AVG	OBP	SLG	AOPS	ABR	SB-CS	FA	FR	RNG	THR	GAMES AT POSITION	DL	BFW
1999	Pit N	1	1	0	0	0	0	0	0	0-0	0	0	.000	.000	.000	-99	0	0-0	ø	0	—	—	/H	0	0.0
2005	SF N	17	28	0	2	1	0	0	1	3-0	0	7	.071	.156	.107	-27	-5	0-0	.957	0	107	232	C16	0	-0.5
Total	2	18	29	0	2	1	0	0	1	3-0	0	7	.069	.152	.103	-29	-5	0-0	.957	0	107	232	C16	0	-0.5

HAAS, BERT Berthold John; B2.8.1914 Naperville IL; D6.23.1999 Tampa FL; BR/TR/5´11˝/180; d9.9; Mil 1944–45

YEAR	TM LG	G	AB	R	H	2B	3B	HR	RBI	BB-IB	HP	SO	AVG	OBP	SLG	AOPS	ABR	SB-CS	FA	FR	RNG	THR	GAMES AT POSITION	DL	BFW
1937	Bro N	16	25	2	10	3	0	0	2	1	0	1	.400	.423	.520	152	2	0	1.000	-0	109	0	O4R,1b3	—	0.1
1938	Bro N	1	0	0	0	0	0	0	0	0	0	0	ø	ø	ø	ø	0	0	ø	0	—	—	/H	—	0.0
1942	Cin N	**154**	585	59	140	21	6	6	54	59	1	54	.239	.310	.326	86	-10	6	.925	-14	91	**125**	3b146,1b6,O2L	0	-2.1
1943	Cin N	101	332	39	87	17	6	4	44	22	0	26	.262	.308	.386	101	-1	6	.993	6	169	142	1b44,3b23,O18C	0	0.3
1946	Cin N	140	535	57	141	24	7	3	50	33	3	42	.264	.310	.351	91	-9	22	.994	-2	93	**141**	1b140,3b6	0	-1.7
1947	Cin N★	135	482	58	138	17	7	3	67	42	2	27	.286	.346	.369	91	-7	9	.956	-6	108	47	O69(8/58/0),1b53	0	-1.7
1948	Phi N	95	333	35	94	9	2	4	34	36	1	25	.282	.354	.357	95	-2	8	.892	-7	85	101	3b54,1b35	0	-1.0
1949	Phi N	2	1	0	0	0	0	0	0	1	0	1	.000	.500	.000	47	0	0	ø	0	—	—	/H	0	0.0
	NY N	54	104	12	27	2	3	1	10	5	0	8	.260	.294	.365	76	-4	0	.983	-2	97	95	1b23,3b11	0	-0.7
	Year	56	105	12	27	2	3	1	10	6	0	9	.257	.297	.362	76	-4	0	.983	-2	97	95	1b23,3b11	0	-0.7
1951	Chi A	23	43	1	7	0	1	1	2	5	0	4	.163	.250	.279	44	-4	0-0	1.000	-0	99	80	1b7,O4(1/0/3)/3	0	-0.4
Total	9	721	2440	263	644	93	32	22	263	204	7	188	.264	.323	.355	91	-35	51-0	.991	-26	95	120	1b311,3b241,O97(11/76/7)	0	-7.2

HAAS, EDDIE George Edwin; B5.26.1935 Paducah KY; BL/TR/5´11˝/178; d9.8; M1/C5; [DL 1959 Mil N 145]

YEAR	TM LG	G	AB	R	H	2B	3B	HR	RBI	BB-IB	HP	SO	AVG	OBP	SLG	AOPS	ABR	SB-CS	FA	FR	RNG	THR	GAMES AT POSITION	DL	BFW
1957	Chi N	14	24	1	5	1	0	0	4	1-0	0	5	.208	.231	.250	32	-2	0-0	1.000	-1	49	0	O4(3/1/0)	0	-0.4
1958	Mil N	9	14	2	5	0	0	0	1	2-0	0	1	.357	.438	.357	124	1	0-0	1.000	-0	82	0	O3(0/2/1)	0	0.0
1960	Mil N	32	32	4	7	2	0	1	5	5-0	0	14	.219	.324	.375	98	0	0-0	1.000	-0	58	0	O2(1/0/1)	0	0.0
Total	3	55	70	7	17	3	0	1	10	8-0	0	20	.243	.316	.329	80	-1	0-0	1.000	-2	61	0	O9(4/3/2)	145	-0.4

HAAS, MULE George William; B10.15.1903 Montclair NJ; D6.30.1974 New Orleans LA; BL/TR/6´1˝/175; d8.15; C7

YEAR	TM LG	G	AB	R	H	2B	3B	HR	RBI	BB-IB	HP	SO	AVG	OBP	SLG	AOPS	ABR	SB-CS	FA	FR	RNG	THR	GAMES AT POSITION	DL	BFW
1925	Pit N	4	3	1	0	0	0	0	0	0	0	1	.000	.000	.000	-94	-1	0-0	1.000	0	142	0	O2(0/1/1)	—	-0.1
1928	Phi A	91	332	41	93	21	4	6	39	23	2	20	.280	.331	.422	94	-4	2-3	.974	-3	91	110	O82(10/69/4)	—	-1.1
1929	†Phi A	139	578	115	181	41	9	16	82	34	4	38	.313	.356	.498	113	9	0-4	.982	-4	97	68	O139(1/139/0)	—	-0.2
1930	†Phi A	132	532	91	159	33	7	2	68	43	1	33	.299	.352	.398	86	-11	2-2	.976	7	106	121	O131C	—	-0.8
1931	†Phi A	102	440	82	142	29	7	8	56	30	0	29	.323	.366	.475	113	7	0-0	.989	-1	98	75	O102C	—	0.3
1932	Phi A	143	558	91	170	28	5	6	65	62	2	49	.305	.376	.405	99	0	1-0	.987	1	106	54	O137(0/108/29)	—	-0.3
1933	Chi A	146	585	97	168	33	4	1	51	65	2	41	.287	.360	.362	96	-1	0-5	.983	-10	90	85	O146C	—	-1.5
1934	Chi A	106	351	54	94	16	3	2	22	47	0	22	.268	.354	.348	79	-10	1-0	.991	-5	92	72	O89(0/85/4)	—	-1.6
1935	Chi A	92	327	44	95	22	1	2	40	37	0	17	.291	.363	.382	90	-4	4-1	.989	-1	102	58	O84(0/22/64)	—	-0.8
1936	Chi A	119	408	75	116	26	2	0	46	64	1	29	.284	.383	.358	81	-10	1-1	.989	-5	91	79	O96(2/1/94),1b7	—	-1.8
1937	Chi A	54	111	8	23	3	3	0	15	16	1	10	.207	.313	.288	52	-8	1-0	.975	0	127	103	1b32,O2R	—	-1.0
1938	Phi A	40	78	7	16	2	0	0	12	12	0	10	.205	.311	.231	39	-7	0-0	1.000	-1	100	128	O12(0/5/7),1b6	—	-0.8
Total	12	1168	4303	706	1257	254	45	43	496	433	13	299	.292	.359	.402	93	-40	12-16	.984	-20	97	80	O1022(13/809/205),1b45	—	-9.7

HABERER, EMIL Emil Karl; B2.2.1878 Cincinnati OH; D10.19.1951 Louisville KY; BR/TR/6´1˝/204; d7.9

YEAR	TM LG	G	AB	R	H	2B	3B	HR	RBI	BB-IB	HP	SO	AVG	OBP	SLG	AOPS	ABR	SB-CS	FA	FR	RNG	THR	GAMES AT POSITION	DL	BFW
1901	Cin N	6	18	2	3	0	1	0	1	3	0	—	.167	.286	.278	68	-1	0	.545	-2	84	0	3b3,1b2	—	-0.2
1903	Cin N	5	13	1	1	0	0	0	0	2	0	—	.077	.200	.077	-18	-2	0	.933	-1	*92*	*53*	C4	—	-0.3
1909	Cin N	5	16	1	3	1	0	0	2	0	0	—	.188	.188	.250	36	-1	0	.895	-1	*81*	*59*	C4	—	-0.3
Total	3	16	47	4	7	1	1	0	3	5	0	—	.149	.231	.213	31	-4	0	.912	-4	*86*	*56*	C8,3b3,1b2	—	-0.8

HACH, IRV Irvin William "Major"; B6.5.1873 Louisville KY; D8.13.1936 Louisville KY; BR/TR; d7.1

YEAR	TM LG	G	AB	R	H	2B	3B	HR	RBI	BB-IB	HP	SO	AVG	OBP	SLG	AOPS	ABR	SB-CS	FA	FR	RNG	THR	GAMES AT POSITION	DL	BFW
1897	Lou N	16	51	5	11	2	0	0	3	5	3	—	.216	.322	.255	55	-3	1	.889	-2	97	88	2b9,3b7	—	-0.3

HACK, STAN Stanley Camfield "Smiling Stan"; B12.6.1909 Sacramento CA; D12.15.1979 Dixon IL; BL/TR/6´0˝/170; d4.12; M4/C3

YEAR	TM LG	G	AB	R	H	2B	3B	HR	RBI	BB-IB	HP	SO	AVG	OBP	SLG	AOPS	ABR	SB-CS	FA	FR	RNG	THR	GAMES AT POSITION	DL	BFW
1932	†Chi N	72	178	32	42	5	6	2	19	17	1	16	.236	.306	.365	80	-6	5	.913	-4	100	60	3b51	—	-0.8
1933	Chi N	20	60	10	21	3	1	1	2	8	3	3	.350	.451	.483	167	6	4	.983	4	113	320	3b17	—	1.1
1934	Chi N	111	402	54	116	16	6	1	21	45	2	42	.289	.363	.366	98	0	11	.949	8	107	77	3b109	—	1.1
1935	†Chi N	124	427	75	133	23	9	4	64	65	3	17	.311	.406	.436	125	19	14	.942	5	**112**	**128**	3b111,1b7	—	2.6
1936	Chi N	149	561	102	167	27	4	6	78	89	2	39	.298	.396	.392	110	13	17	.950	-13	87	82	3b140,1b11	—	0.4
1937	Chi N	**154**	582	106	173	27	6	2	63	83	3	42	.297	.388	.375	104	7	16	.968	-11	89	129	3b150,1b4	—	0.2
1938	†Chi N★	152	609	109	195	34	11	4	67	94	0	39	.320	.411	.432	128	29	**16**	.954	7	100	103	3b152	—	4.0
1939	Chi N★	**156**	641	112	191	28	6	8	56	65	2	35	.298	.364	.398	103	4	**17**	.956	-8	91	54	3b156	—	0.1
1940	Chi N	149	603	101	**191**	38	6	8	40	75	3	24	.317	.395	.439	132	30	21	.954	10	103	122	3b148/1	—	4.5
1941	Chi N★	151	586	111	**186**	33	5	7	45	99	1	40	.317	.417	.427	143	39	10	.954	-14	92	78	3b150/1	0	3.1
1942	Chi N	140	553	91	166	36	3	6	39	94	0	40	.300	.402	.409	143	36	9	**.965**	-12	92	75	3b139	0	3.1
1943	Chi N★	144	533	78	154	24	4	3	35	82	0	27	.289	.384	.366	119	17	5	.960	-5	98	48	3b136	0	1.4
1944	Chi N	98	383	65	108	16	1	3	32	53	0	21	.282	.369	.352	104	5	5	.939	5	108	55	3b75,1b18	0	1.0
1945	†Chi N✳	150	597	110	193	29	7	2	43	99	1	30	.323	.420	.405	133	33	12	**.975**	20	105	115	3b146,1b5	0	**5.3**
1946	Chi N	92	323	55	92	13	4	0	26	83	0	32	.285	.431	.350	125	18	3	.968	-2	97	45	3b90	0	1.6
1947	Chi N	76	240	28	65	11	2	0	12	41	0	19	.271	.377	.333	94	0	0	.962	8	115	97	3b66	0	0.7
Total	16	1938	7278	1239	2193	363	81	57	642	1092	21	466	.301	.394	.397	120	250	165	.957	-3	98	90	3b1836,1b47	0	29.4

HACKER, RICH Richard Warren; B10.6.1947 Belleville IL; BB/TR (BR 1971p)/6´0˝/155; [NYN67 S8/154]; d7.2; C9; Col Southern Illinois

YEAR	TM LG	G	AB	R	H	2B	3B	HR	RBI	BB-IB	HP	SO	AVG	OBP	SLG	AOPS	ABR	SB-CS	FA	FR	RNG	THR	GAMES AT POSITION	DL	BFW
1971	Mon N	16	33	2	4	1	0	0	2	3-0	0	12	.121	.194	.152	-1	-4	0-0	.984	4	129	119	S16	0	0.1

YEAR	TM LG	G	AB	R	H	2B	3B	HR	RBI	BB-IB	HP	SO	AVG	OBP	SLG	AOPS	ABR	SB-CS	FA	FR	RNG	THR	GAMES AT POSITION	DL	BFW
Hackett, Jim	James Joseph "Sunny Jim"; B10.1.1877 Jacksonville IL; D3.28.1961 Douglas MI; BR/TR/6´2˝/185; d9.14; ▲																								
1902	StL N	6	21	2	6	1	0	0	4	2	0	—	.286	.348	.333	115	0	1	.833	-1	92	0	P4,O2R	—	-0.1
1903	StL N	99	351	24	80	13	8	0	36	19	2	—	.228	.272	.311	68	-16	2	.972	-6	78	132	1b89,P7	—	-2.2
Total	2	105	372	26	86	14	8	0	40	21	2	—	.231	.276	.312	70	-16	3	.972	-7	78	132	1b89,P11,O2R	—	-2.3
Hackett, Mert	Mortimer Martin; B11.11.1859 Cambridge MA; D2.22.1938 Cambridge MA; BR/TR/5´10.5˝/175; d5.2; b–Walter																								
1883	Bos N	46	179	20	42	8	6	2	24	1	—	48	.235	.239	.380	82	-5	—	.909	-2	—	—	C44,O4(0/3/1)	—	-0.3
1884	Bos N	72	268	28	55	13	2	1	20	2	—	66	.205	.211	.280	53	-14	—	.928	7	—	—	C71/3	—	-0.1
1885	Bos N	34	115	9	21	7	1	0	4	2	—	28	.183	.197	.261	49	-6	—	.901	4	—	—	C34	—	0.1
1886	KC N	62	230	18	50	8	3	3	25	4	—	59	.217	.231	.317	61	-12	1	.926	-13	—	—	C52,O13(0/6/7)	—	-1.9
1887	Ind N	42	147	12	35	6	3	2	10	7	2	24	.238	.282	.361	80	-4	4	.938	-6	—	—	C40,O2(1/0/1)/1	—	-0.6
Total	5	256	939	87	203	42	15	8	83	16	2	225	.216	.231	.318	65	-41	5	.921	-10	—	—	C241,O19(1/9/9)/13	—	-2.8
Hackett, Walter	Walter Henry; B8.15.1857 Cambridge MA; D10.2.1920 Cambridge MA; d4.17; b–Mert																								
1884	Bos U	103	415	71	101	19	0	1	—	7	—	—	.243	.256	.296	68	-28	—	**.855**	12	99	79	S103	—	-1.2
1885	Bos N	35	125	8	23	3	0	0	9	3	—	22	.184	.203	.208	34	-9	—	.893	-7	85	61	2b20,S15	—	-1.5
Total	2	138	540	79	124	22	0	1	9	10	—	22	.230	.244	.276	61	-37	—	.852	4	97	81	S118,2b20	—	-2.7
Hadley, Kent	Kent William; B12.17.1934 Pocatello ID; D3.10.2005 Pocatello ID; BL/TL/6´3˝/190; d9.14; Col USC																								
1958	KC A	3	11	1	2	0	0	0	0	0-0	0	4	.182	.182	.182	0	-2	0-0	1.000	-1	0	56	1b2	0	-0.2
1959	KC A	113	288	40	73	11	1	10	39	24-0	1	74	.253	.310	.403	93	-3	1-2	.989	-2	89	97	1b95	0	-1.0
1960	NY A	55	64	8	13	2	0	4	11	6-0	0	19	.203	.271	.422	90	-1	0-0	.991	-1	77	95	1b24	0	-0.3
Total	3	171	363	49	88	13	1	14	50	30-0	1	97	.242	.300	.399	90	-6	1-2	.989	-3	85	96	1b121	0	-1.5
Haeffner, Bill	William Bernhard; B7.18.1894 Philadelphia PA; D1.27.1982 Springfield PA; BR/TR/5´9˝/165; d6.29																								
1915	Phi A	3	4	0	1	0	0	0	0	0	0	1	.250	.250	.250	51	0	0	1.000	-1	*34*	*199*	C3	—	-0.1
1920	Pit N	54	175	8	34	4	1	0	14	8	0	14	.194	.230	.229	31	-16	1-1	.972	-3	*96*	*78*	C52	—	-1.6
1928	NY N	2	1	0	0	0	0	0	0	0	0	0	.000	.000	.000	-99	0	0	.750	-0	*0*	*0*	C2	—	0.0
Total	3	59	180	8	35	4	1	0	14	8	0	15	.194	.229	.228	30	-16	1-1	.968	-4	*94*	*78*	C57	—	-1.7
Hafey, Chick	Charles James; B2.12.1903 Berkeley CA; D7.2.1973 Calistoga CA; BR/TR/6´0˝/185; d8.28; HF1971																								
1924	StL N	24	91	10	23	5	2	2	22	4	1	8	.253	.292	.418	90	-2	1-0	.927	0	99	133	O24(16/7/1)	—	-0.3
1925	StL N	93	358	36	108	25	2	5	57	10	0	29	.302	.321	.425	87	-8	3-7	.955	1	107	90	O88(25/5/58)	—	-1.4
1926	†StL N	78	225	30	61	19	2	4	38	11	2	36	.271	.311	.427	93	-2	2	.974	-0	99	96	O64(28/0/36)	—	-0.7
1927	StL N	103	346	62	114	26	5	18	63	36	5	41	.329	.401	**.590**	157	28	12	.980	5	89	199	O94(71/3/22)	—	2.5
1928	†StL N	138	520	101	175	46	6	27	111	40	2	53	.337	.386	.604	152	38	8	.965	-1	97	114	O133(117/0/16)	—	2.6
1929	StL N	134	517	101	175	47	9	29	125	45	2	42	.338	.394	.632	148	37	7	.966	2	105	93	O130L	—	2.6
1930	†StL N	120	446	108	150	39	12	26	107	46	7	51	.336	.407	.652	146	32	12	.976	-2	89	147	O116L	—	1.9
1931	†StL N	122	450	94	157	35	8	16	95	39	3	43	**.349**	**.404**	.569	153	34	11	.983	-5	93	66	O118L	—	2.2
1932	Cin N	83	253	34	87	19	3	2	36	22	3	20	.344	.403	.466	137	15	4	.965	-0	98	133	O65L	—	1.1
1933	Cin N★	144	568	77	172	34	6	7	62	40	2	44	.303	.351	.421	121	16	3	.987	6	102	149	O144(59/85/0)	—	1.7
1934	Cin N	140	535	75	157	29	6	18	67	52	3	63	.293	.359	.471	123	18	4	.967	-1	104	68	O140(18/122/0)	—	1.2
1935	Cin N	15	59	10	20	6	1	1	9	4	2	5	.339	.400	.525	151	4	1	.912	-3	82	0	O15C	—	0.1
1937	Cin N	89	257	39	67	11	5	9	41	23	1	42	.261	.324	.447	113	3	2	.971	-2	93	107	O64(20/44/0)	—	0.0
Total	13	1283	4625	777	1466	341	67	164	833	372	33	477	.317	.372	.526	133	213	70-7	.971	1	98	113	O1195(783/281/133)	—	13.5
Hafey, Bud	Daniel Albert; B8.6.1912 Berkeley CA; D7.27.1986 Sacramento CA; BR/TR/6´0˝/185; d4.21; b–Tom																								
1935	Chi A	2	0	1	0	0	0	0	0	0	0	0	ø	ø	ø	ø	0	0-0	ø	0	—	—	/R	—	0.0
	Pit N	58	184	29	42	11	2	6	16	16	0	48	.228	.290	.408	83	-5	0	.970	3	110	128	O47(1/36/10)	—	-0.3
1936	Pit N	39	118	19	25	6	1	4	13	10	0	27	.212	.273	.381	73	-5	0	.932	-1	97	126	O29(0/18/10)	—	-0.7
1939	Cin N	6	13	1	2	1	0	0	1	1	0	4	.154	.214	.231	19	-1	1	1.000	-0	97	0	O4L	—	-0.2
	Phi N	18	51	3	9	1	0	0	3	3	0	12	.176	.222	.196	14	-6	1	1.000	1	116	94	O13(3/1/9),P2	—	-0.6
	Year	24	64	4	11	2	0	0	4	4	0	16	.172	.221	.203	15	-8	2	1.000	1	112	73	O17(7/1/9),P2	—	-0.8
Total	3	123	366	53	78	19	3	10	33	30	0	91	.213	.273	.363	68	-17	2-0	.963	3	106	117	O93(8/55/29),P2	—	-1.8
Hafey, Tom	Thomas Francis "Heave-O","The Arm"; B7.12.1913 Berkeley CA; D10.2.1996 El Cerrito CA; BR/TR/6´1˝/180; d7.21; b–Bud																								
1939	NY N	70	256	37	62	10	1	6	26	10	0	44	.242	.271	.359	67	-13	1	.960	-0	99	84	3b70	—	-1.1
1944	StL A	8	14	1	5	2	0	0	2	1	0	4	.357	.400	.500	148	1	0-0	1.000	0	117	0	O4(3/0/1)/1	0	0.1
Total	2	78	270	38	67	12	1	6	28	11	0	48	.248	.278	.367	72	-12	1-0	.960	0	99	84	3b70,O4(3/0/1)/1	0	-1.0
Hafner, Travis	Travis Lee "Pronk"; B6.3.1977 Jamestown ND; BL/TR/6´3˝/240; [TexA96 31/923]; d8.6; Col Cowley Co. (KS) CC																								
2002	Tex A	23	62	6	15	4	1	1	6	8-1	0	15	.242	.329	.387	87	-1	0-1	.909	0	188	0	D13,1b3	0	-0.2
2003	Cle A	91	291	35	74	19	3	14	40	22-2	10	81	.254	.327	.485	111	4	2-1	.985	-3	77	152	D43,1b42	16	-0.4
2004	Cle A	140	482	96	150	41	3	28	109	68-7	**17**	111	.311	.410	.583	**162**	48	3-2	1.000	1	150	50	D128,1b11	0	3.9
2005	Cle A	137	486	94	148	42	0	33	108	79-7	9	123	.305	.408	.595	169	52	0-0	1.000	1	401	0	D130/1	18	4.4
2006	Cle A	129	454	100	140	31	1	42	117	100-16	7	111	.308	.439	**.659**	**187**	**64**	0-0	1.000	1	186	59	D122,1b4	0	**5.4**
Total	5	520	1775	331	527	137	8	118	380	277-33	43	441	.297	.402	.583	159	167	5-4	.987	0	107	119	D436,1b61	34	13.1
Hague, Joe	Joe Clarence; B4.25.1944 Huntington WV; D11.5.1994 San Antonio TX; BL/TL/6´0˝/(195–198); d9.19; Col Texas																								
1968	StL N	7	17	2	4	0	0	1	1	2-0	0	2	.235	.316	.412	119	0	0-0	.800	-1	76	0	O3R,1b2	0	-0.1
1969	StL N	40	100	8	17	2	1	2	8	12-1	0	23	.170	.259	.270	48	-7	0-2	.939	-1	110	0	O17(1/0/16),1b9	0	-1.1
1970	StL N	139	451	58	122	16	4	14	68	63-3	1	87	.271	.358	.417	105	4	2-1	.994	-3	97	103	1b82,O52(6/0/47)	0	-0.7
1971	StL N	129	380	46	86	9	3	16	54	58-10	2	69	.226	.330	.392	99	0	0-3	.996	-1	107	97	1b91,O36R	0	-1.0
1972	StL N	27	76	8	18	5	1	3	11	17-2	0	18	.237	.368	.447	134	4	0-1	1.000	-1	78	99	1b22,O3R	0	0.1
	†Cin N	69	138	17	34	7	1	4	20	20-5	0	18	.246	.340	.399	115	3	1-1	1.000	1	74	99	1b22,O19R	0	0.2
	Year	96	214	25	52	12	2	7	31	37-7	0	36	.243	.350	.416	123	7	1-2	1.000	-0	76	99	1b44,O22R	0	0.3
1973	Cin N	19	33	2	5	2	0	0	1	5-0	0	5	.152	.256	.212	35	-3	1-0	1.000	-1	65	0	O5R,1b4	62	-0.4
Total	6	430	1195	141	286	41	10	40	163	177-21	3	222	.239	.336	.391	100	1	4-8	.996	-6	97	98	1b232,O135(7/0/129)	62	-3.0
Hague, Bill	William L. (b William L. Haug); B1852 Philadelphia PA; BR/TR/5´9˝/164; d5.4																								
1875	StL NA	62	260	24	57	2	0	0	22	2	—	9	.219	.225	.227	63	-8	3-4	.781	2	107	58	3b62/1	—	-0.7
1876	Lou N	67	294	31	78	8	0	1	22	2	—	10	.265	.270	.303	77	-9	—	.754	-27	66	101	3b67/S	—	-3.0
1877	Lou N	59	263	38	70	7	1	1	24	7	—	18	.266	.285	.312	75	-9	—	.843	-19	65	65	3b59	—	-2.4
1878	Pro N	**62**	250	21	51	3	0	0	25	5	—	34	.204	.220	.216	44	-15	—	**.925**	19	**133**	64	3b62	—	0.6
1879	Pro N	51	209	20	47	3	1	0	21	3	—	19	.225	.236	.249	61	-9	—	.822	4	114	35	3b51	—	-0.3
Total	4	239	1016	110	246	21	2	2	92	17	—	81	.242	.255	.273	66	-42	—	.843	-23	93	69	3b239/S	—	-5.1
Hahn, Don	Donald Antone; B11.16.1948 San Francisco CA; BR/TR/6´1˝/(176–185); [SFN66 17/337]; d4.8																								
1969	Mon N	4	9	0	1	0	0	0	2	0-0	0	5	.111	.111	.111	-37	-2	0-0	1.000	0	60	728	O3C	0	-0.2
1970	Mon N	82	149	22	38	8	0	0	8	27-1	2	27	.255	.374	.309	86	-1	4-2	.986	1	91	195	O61(42/14/9)	0	-0.2
1971	NY N	98	178	16	42	5	1	1	11	21-1	1	32	.236	.317	.292	75	-5	2-3	.973	1	111	68	O80C	0	-0.7
1972	NY N	17	37	0	6	0	0	0	1	4-0	0	12	.162	.244	.162	18	-4	0-0	1.000	-2	49	0	O10(0/1/9)	0	-0.7
1973	†NY N	93	262	22	60	10	0	2	21	22-2	0	43	.229	.285	.290	61	-14	2-1	.989	-2	106	45	O87(4/83/2)	0	-1.8
1974	NY N	110	323	34	81	14	1	4	28	37-5	1	34	.251	.328	.337	87	-5	2-0	.987	-2	94	142	O106(0/104/2)	0	-1.0
1975	Phi N	9	5	0	0	0	0	0	0	0-0	0	2	.000	.000	.000	-95	-1	0-0	1.000	1	110	943	O7(1/4/2)	0	-0.1
	StL N	7	8	3	1	0	0	0	0	1-0	0	1	.125	.222	.125	-2	-1	0-0	1.000	-0	73	0	O4(1/2/1)	0	-0.2
	SD N	34	26	7	6	1	2	0	3	10-0	0	2	.231	.444	.423	152	3	1-0	1.000	1	104	142	O26(17/11/0)	0	0.3
	Year	50	39	10	7	1	2	0	3	11-0	0	5	.179	.360	.308	89	0	1-0	1,000	1	99	212	O37(19/17/3)	0	0.0
Total	7	454	997	104	235	38	4	7	74	122-9	4	158	.236	.319	.303	75	-30	11-6	.985	-2	99	113	O384(65/302/25)	0	-4.6
Hahn, Dick	Richard Frederick; B7.24.1916 Canton OH; D11.5.1992 Orlando FL; BR/TR/5´11˝/176; d9.7																								
1940	Was A	1	3	0	0	0	0	0	0	0	0	0	.000	.000	.000	-99	-1	0-0	1.000	0	*0*	*543*	/C	—	-0.1

YEAR	TM LG	G	AB	R	H	2B	3B	HR	RBI	BB-IB	HP	SO	AVG	OBP	SLG	AOPS	ABR	SB-CS	FA	FR	RNG	THR	GAMES AT POSITION	DL	BFW
HAHN, ED William Edgar; B8.27.1875 Nevada OH; D11.29.1941 Des Moines IA; BL/TR/?/160; d8.31																									
1905	NY A	43	160	32	51	5	0	0	11	25	5	—	.319	.426	.350	132	8	1	.957	1	99	85	O43(20/10/13)	—	0.7
1906	NY A	11	22	2	2	1	0	0	1	3	2	—	.091	.259	.136	23	-2	2	1.000	-0	0	0	O7(3/4/0)	—	-0.2
	†Chi A	130	484	80	110	7	5	0	27	69	9	—	.227	.335	.262	90	-1	21	.949	-5	128	97	O130(55/0/75)	—	-1.4
	Year	141	506	82	112	8	5	0	28	72	11	—	.221	.331	.257	86	-4	23	.952	-5	123	93	O137(58/4/75)	—	-1.6
1907	Chi A	156	592	87	151	9	7	0	45	84	12	—	.255	.359	.294	112	14	17	**.990**	-4	121	143	O156R	—	0.3
1908	Chi A	122	447	58	112	12	8	0	21	39	13	—	.251	.329	.313	111	7	11	.965	-12	29	62	O118(18/14/86)	—	-1.3
1909	Chi A	76	287	30	52	6	0	1	16	31	3	—	.181	.268	.213	54	-14	9	.990	-7	31	51	O76R	—	-2.8
1910	Chi A	15	53	2	6	2	0	0	1	7	0	—	.113	.217	.151	16	-5	0	.933	-2	83	0	O15R	—	-0.9
Total	6	553	2045	291	484	42	20	1	122	258	44	—	.237	.335	.278	97	7	61	.970	-29	86	92	O545(96/28/421)	—	-5.6
HAIGH, ED Edward E.; B2.7.1867 Philadelphia PA; D2.13.1953 Atlantic City NJ; d8.14																									
1892	StL N	1	4	0	1	0	0	0	0	0	0	2	.250	.250	.250	54	0	0	ø	-0	0	0	/rf	—	0.0
HAINES, HINKEY Henry Luther; B12.23.1898 Red Lion PA; D1.9.1979 Sharon Hill PA; BR/TR/5´10˝/170; d4.20; Col Penn St.																									
1923	†NY A	28	25	9	4	2	0	0	3	4	0	5	.160	.276	.240	36	-2	3-1	1.000	1	133	151	O14(2/8/4)	—	-0.1
HAIRSTON, JERRY Jerry Wayne Jr.; B5.29.1976 Des Moines IA; BR/TR/5´10˝/(172–185); [BalA97 11/345]; d9.11; b–Scott f–Jerry gf–Sammy; Col Southern Illinois; OF(68/75/40)																									
1998	Bal A	6	7	2	0	0	0	0	0	0-0	0	1	.000	.000	.000	-99	-2	0-0	.750	-2	38	89	2b4	0	-0.3
1999	Bal A	50	175	26	47	12	1	4	17	11-0	3	24	.269	.323	.417	90	-3	9-4	1.000	8	101	140	2b50	0	0.7
2000	Bal A	49	180	27	46	5	0	5	19	21-0	6	22	.256	.353	.367	87	-3	8-5	.981	6	104	126	2b49	0	0.5
2001	Bal A	159	532	63	124	25	5	8	47	44-0	13	73	.233	.305	.344	75	-19	29-11	.976	4	101	94	2b156	0	-0.5
2002	Bal A	122	426	55	114	25	3	5	32	34-0	7	55	.268	.329	.376	93	-4	21-6	.982	2	102	98	2b119	0	0.6
2003	Bal A	58	218	25	59	12	2	2	21	23-0	6	25	.271	.353	.372	93	-1	14-5	.980	1	96	104	2b48,D9	106	0.3
2004	Bal A	86	287	43	87	19	1	2	24	29-1	8	29	.303	.378	.397	105	4	13-8	.991	3	102	107	O52(10/15/27),D21,2b12/3	84	0.4
2005	Chi N	114	380	51	99	25	2	4	30	31-0	12	46	.261	.336	.368	82	-9	8-9	.983	3	96	109	O62(20/48/1),2b44/S	15	-0.6
2006	Chi N	38	82	8	17	3	0	0	4	4-2	1	14	.207	.253	.244	28	-9	3-0	1.000	-6	68	59	2b24,O8(3/0/5)/1	0	-1.4
	Tex A	63	88	17	18	3	1	0	6	9-0	1	20	.205	.286	.261	43	-8	2-2	1.000	6	97	470	O52(35/12/7),S3/23D	0	-0.2
Total	9	745	2375	317	611	129	15	30	200	206-3	57	309	.257	.330	.362	83	-54	107-50	.980	25	100	103	2b507,O174C,D33,S4,3b2/1	205	-0.5
HAIRSTON, JERRY Jerry Wayne Sr.; B2.16.1952 Birmingham AL; BB/TR/5´10˝/(170–196); [ChiA70 3/54]; d7.26; b–Johnny f–Sammy s–Jerry s–Scott																									
1973	Chi A	60	210	25	57	11	1	0	23	33-0	1	30	.271	.371	.333	97	1	0-0	.944	1	105	136	O33L,1b19,D8	0	-0.1
1974	Chi A	45	109	8	25	7	0	0	8	13-0	0	18	.229	.311	.294	73	-3	0-2	.926	-3	70	81	O22(19/0/3),D10	15	-0.8
1975	Chi A	69	219	26	62	8	0	0	23	46-3	1	23	.283	.407	.320	107	6	1-0	.951	-1	95	136	O59(57/0/3),D8	0	0.1
1976	Chi A	44	119	20	27	2	2	0	10	24-0	0	19	.227	.352	.277	87	-1	1-1	.973	-0	106	42	O40(1/0/39)	0	-0.3
1977	Chi A	13	26	3	8	2	0	0	4	5-0	0	7	.308	.419	.385	121	1	0-0	1.000	0	97	203	O11(6/6/0)	0	0.1
	Pit N	51	52	5	10	2	0	2	6	6-0	0	10	.192	.271	.346	63	-3	0-0	.923	-1	81	0	O14(6/0/8)/2	0	-0.4
1981	Chi A	9	25	5	7	1	0	1	6	2-0	1	4	.280	.345	.440	131	1	0-0	.933	-0	106	0	O7(4/2/1)	0	0.0
1982	Chi A	85	90	11	21	5	0	5	18	9-0	0	15	.233	.294	.456	104	0	0-0	1.000	1	104	208	O36(22/7/7),D2	0	0.1
1983	†Chi A	101	126	17	37	9	1	5	22	23-4	0	16	.294	.397	.500	141	8	0-1	.968	-2	84	88	O32(19/11/3),D4	0	0.6
1984	Chi A	115	227	41	59	13	2	5	19	41-3	1	29	.260	.373	.401	109	5	2-1	.967	-2	90	106	O37(22/13/3),D20	0	0.2
1985	Chi A	95	140	9	34	8	0	2	20	29-3	2	18	.243	.371	.343	96	1	0-0	1.000	-0	88	0	D29,O5L	0	0.0
1986	Chi A	101	225	32	61	15	0	5	26	26-3	1	26	.271	.348	.404	101	1	0-0	1.000	-2	61	83	D29,1b19,O11(9/0/2)	0	-0.3
1987	Chi A	66	126	14	29	8	0	5	20	25-2	1	25	.230	.357	.413	102	1	0-0	1.000	1	143	0	O13L,D13,1b7	0	0.1
1988	Chi A	2	2	0	0	0	0	0	0	0-0	0	0	.000	.000	.000	-99	-1	0-0	ø	0	—	—	/H	0	-0.1
1989	Chi A	3	3	0	1	0	0	0	0	0-0	0	0	.333	.333	.333	90	0	0-0	ø	0	—	—	D2	0	0.0
Total	14	859	1699	216	438	91	6	30	205	282-18	8	240	.258	.362	.371	102	17	4-5	.963	-6	97	107	O320(216/39/69),D125,1b45/2	15	-0.8
HAIRSTON, JOHNNY John Louis; B8.27.1944 Birmingham AL; BR/TR/6´2˝/190; [ChiN65 11/325]; d9.6; b–Jerry f–Sammy; Col Southern A&M																									
1969	Chi N	3	4	0	1	0	0	0	0	0-0	0	2	.250	.250	.250	36	0	0-0	1.000	0	0	0	/Clf	0	0.0
HAIRSTON, SAMMY Samuel Harding; B1.20.1920 Crawford MS; D10.31.1997 Birmingham AL; BR/TR/5´10.5˝/187; d7.21; C1; s–Jerry s–Johnny gs–Jerry gs–Scott; Negro Lg 1944–50																									
1951	Chi A	4	5	1	2	1	0	0	1	2	0	0	.400	.571	.600	222	1	0-0	1.000	-0	*0*	*0*	C2	0	0.1
HAIRSTON, SCOTT Scott Alexander; B5.25.1980 Fort Worth TX; BR/TR/6´0˝/(190–200); [AriN01 3/98]; d5.7; b–Jerry f–Jerry gf–Sammy; Col Central Arizona JC																									
2004	Ari N	101	339	39	84	15	6	13	29	21-0	1	88	.248	.293	.442	81	-11	3-3	.972	-2	95	85	2b85,O3(2/0/2)	0	-0.9
2005	Ari N	15	20	0	2	1	0	0	0	0-0	0	6	.100	.100	.150	-34	-4	0-0	1.000	-0	96	0	O4(4/1/0),D2	31	-0.4
2006	Ari N	9	15	2	6	2	0	0	2	1-0	0	5	.400	.438	.533	139	1	0-0	1.000	1	146	0	O5L	39	0.1
Total	3	125	374	41	92	18	6	13	31	22-0	1	99	.246	.289	.430	78	-14	3-3	.972	-2	95	85	2b85,O12(11/1/2),D2	70	-1.2
HAJDUK, CHET Chester; B7.21.1918 Chicago IL; D7.4.2006 Chicago IL; BR/TR/6´0˝/195; d4.16																									
1941	Chi A	1	1	0	0	0	0	0	0	0	0	0	.000	.000	.000	-99	0	0-0	ø	0	—	—	/H	0	0.0
HAJEK, DAVE David Vincent; B10.14.1967 Roseville CA; BR/TR/5´10˝/165; d9.15; Col Cal Poly–Pomona																									
1995	Hou N	5	2	0	0	0	0	0	0	1-0	0	1	.000	.333	.000	-3	0	1-0	ø	0	—	—	/H	0	0.0
1996	Hou N	8	10	3	3	1	0	0	0	2-0	0	0	.300	.417	.400	126	1	0-0	1.000	1	158	0	3b3,2b2	0	0.1
Total	2	13	12	3	3	1	0	0	0	3-0	0	1	.250	.400	.333	104	1	1-0	1.000	1	158	0	3b3,2b2	0	0.1
HALAS, GEORGE George Stanley; B2.2.1895 Chicago IL; D10.31.1983 Chicago IL; BB/TR/6´0˝/164; d5.6; Col Illinois																									
1919	NY A	12	22	0	2	0	0	0	0	0	0	8	.091	.091	.091	-49	-4	0	1.000	-0	101	0	O6(0/1/5)	—	-0.5
HALDEMAN, JOHN John Avery; B12.2.1855 Pewee Valley KY; D9.17.1899 Louisville KY; BL/TR/5´10˝/175; d7.3; Col Washington and Lee																									
1877	Lou N	1	4	0	0	0	0	0	0	0	—	0	.000	.000	.000	-85	-1	—	.571	-1	116	0	/2	—	-0.2
HALE, ODELL Arvel Odell "Bad News"; B8.10.1908 Hosston LA; D6.9.1980 El Dorado AR; BR/TR/5´10˝/175; d8.1																									
1931	Cle A	25	92	14	26	2	4	1	5	8	0	8	.283	.340	.424	94	-1	2-0	.918	-4	87	35	3b15,2b10/S	—	-0.3
1933	Cle A	98	351	49	97	19	8	10	64	30	0	37	.276	.333	.462	104	0	2-3	.954	-2	99	102	2b73,3b21	—	0.3
1934	Cle A	143	563	82	170	44	6	13	101	48	0	50	.302	.357	.471	110	7	8-12	.956	**26**	109	113	2b137,3b5	—	3.6
1935	Cle A	150	589	80	179	37	11	16	101	52	1	55	.304	.361	.486	115	11	15-13	.938	6	109	87	3b149/2	—	1.9
1936	Cle A	153	620	126	196	50	13	14	87	64	0	43	.316	.380	.506	116	14	8-5	.946	**17**	**108**	103	3b148,2b3	—	3.2
1937	Cle A	154	561	74	150	32	4	6	82	56	1	41	.267	.335	.371	77	-20	9-6	.964	22	109	130	3b90,2b64	—	0.9
1938	Cle A	130	496	69	138	32	2	8	69	44	1	39	.278	.338	.399	86	-12	8-1	.963	-11	90	81	2b127	—	-1.1
1939	Cle A	108	253	36	79	16	2	4	48	25	0	18	.312	.374	.439	111	4	4-5	.966	-11	85	83	2b73,3b2	—	-0.4
1940	Cle A	48	50	3	11	3	1	0	6	5	0	7	.220	.291	.320	60	-3	0-0	.700	-1	86	0	3b3	—	-0.4
1941	Bos A	12	24	5	5	2	0	1	1	3	0	4	.208	.296	.417	85	-1	0-0	.857	-3	43	0	3b6/2	0	-0.3
	NY N	41	102	13	20	3	0	0	9	18	0	13	.196	.317	.225	53	-6	1	.964	0	90	95	2b29	0	-0.4
Total	10	1062	3701	551	1071	240	51	73	573	353	3	315	.289	.352	.441	100	-7	57-45	.959	40	99	94	2b518,3b439/S	0	7.0
HALE, GEORGE George Wagner "Ducky"; B8.3.1894 Dexter KS; D11.1.1945 Wichita KS; BR/TR/5´10˝/160; d8.24																									
1914	StL A	6	11	1	2	0	0	0	0	0	0	3	.182	.182	.182	10	-1	0	.895	-1	*97*	*184*	C6	—	-0.2
1916	StL A	4	1	0	0	0	0	0	0	0	1	1	.000	.500	.000	54	0	0	1.000	0	0	0	C3	—	0.0
1917	StL A	38	61	4	12	2	1	0	8	10	0	12	.197	.310	.262	78	-1	0	.927	-0	*92*	*121*	C28	—	0.0
1918	StL A	12	30	0	4	1	0	0	1	1	0	5	.133	.161	.167	-1	-4	0	.981	1	*90*	*94*	C11	—	-0.2
Total	4	60	103	5	18	3	1	0	9	11	1	21	.175	.261	.223	49	-6	0	.940	0	*91*	*118*	C48	—	-0.4
HALE, JOHN John Steven; B8.5.1953 Fresno CA; BL/TR/6´2˝/195; [LAN71 14/337]; d9.8																									
1974	LA N	4	4	2	4	1	0	0	2	0-0	0	0	1.000	1.000	1.250	546	2	0-0	ø	-0	0	0	O3R	0	0.2
1975	LA N	71	204	20	43	7	0	6	22	26-4	2	51	.211	.303	.333	81	-5	1-2	.977	-2	99	53	O68(0/35/42)	0	-1.0
1976	LA N	44	91	4	14	2	1	0	8	16-1	2	14	.154	.291	.198	42	-6	4-1	.983	-1	86	132	O37(0/11/27)	0	-0.9
1977	LA N	79	108	10	26	4	1	2	11	15-1	0	28	.241	.331	.352	84	-2	2-1	.986	-2	92	38	O73(25/13/37)	0	-0.6
1978	Sea A	107	211	24	36	8	0	4	22	34-1	0	64	.171	.283	.265	56	-12	3-4	.988	-3	103	20	O98(27/24/47),D3	0	-1.8
1979	Sea A	54	63	6	14	3	0	2	7	12-4	0	26	.222	.342	.365	90	0	0-0	1.000	-3	80	0	O42(34/0/9),D2	0	-0.4
Total	6	359	681	66	137	25	2	14	72	103-11	4	183	.201	.307	.305	72	-23	10-8	.985	-11	95	45	O321(86/83/165),D5	0	-4.5

HALE, BOB Robert Houston; B11.7.1933 Sarasota FL; BL/TL/5´10˝/(190–195); d7.4

YEAR	TM LG	G	AB	R	H	2B	3B	HR	RBI	BB-IB	HP	SO	AVG	OBP	SLG	AOPS	ABR	SB-CS	FA	FR	RNG	THR	GAMES AT POSITION	DL	BFW
1955	Bal A	67	182	13	65	7	1	0	29	5-0	1	19	.357	.376	.407	119	4	0-2	.974	2	133	71	1b44	0	0.3
1956	Bal A	85	207	18	49	10	1	1	24	11-0	1	10	.237	.274	.309	60	-13	0-2	.975	-1	106	84	1b51	0	-1.6
1957	Bal A	42	44	2	11	0	0	0	7	2-1	0	2	.250	.265	.250	50	-3	0-0	1.000	-0	65	46	1b5	0	-0.4
1958	Bal A	19	20	2	7	2	0	0	3	2-0	0	1	.350	.409	.450	144	1	0-0	1.000	1	497	337	1b2	0	0.2
1959	Bal A	40	54	2	10	3	0	0	7	2-1	0	6	.185	.214	.241	25	-6	0-0	1.000	-0	62	122	1b8	0	-0.6
1960	Cle A	70	70	2	21	7	0	0	12	3-1	0	6	.300	.312	.400	99	0	0-0	.944	1	279	68	1b5	0	0.0
1961	Cle A	42	36	0	6	0	0	0	6	1-0	1	7	.167	.200	.167	2	-5	0-0	ø	0	—	—	/H	0	-0.5
	NY A	11	13	2	2	0	0	1	1	0-0	0	0	.154	.154	.385	41	-1	0-0	1.000	0	84	74	1b5	0	-0.1
	Year	53	49	2	8	0	0	1	7	1-0	1	7	.163	.189	.224	12	-6	0-0	1.000	0	84	74	1b5	0	-0.6
Total	7	376	626	41	171	29	2	2	89	26-3	3	51	.273	.299	.335	76	-23	0-4	.977	2	120	82	1b120	0	-2.7

HALE, SAMMY Samuel Douglas; B9.10.1896 Glen Rose TX; D9.6.1974 Wheeler TX; BR/TR/5´8.5˝/160; d4.20

YEAR	TM LG	G	AB	R	H	2B	3B	HR	RBI	BB-IB	HP	SO	AVG	OBP	SLG	AOPS	ABR	SB-CS	FA	FR	RNG	THR	GAMES AT POSITION	DL	BFW
1920	Det A	76	116	13	34	3	3	1	14	5	0	15	.293	.322	.397	92	-2	2-0	.886	-1	110	97	3b16,O4C/2	—	-0.2
1921	Det A	9	2	2	0	0	0	0	0	0	0	1	.000	.000	.000	-99	-1	0-1	ø	0	—	—	/H	—	-0.1
1923	Phi A	115	434	68	125	22	8	3	51	17	8	31	.288	.327	.396	89	-9	8-3	.916	-14	96	88	3b107	—	-1.6
1924	Phi A	80	261	41	83	14	2	2	17	17	3	19	.318	.367	.410	99	-1	3-2	.948	-2	103	112	3b55,O5(4/0/1)/S	—	0.0
1925	Phi A	110	391	62	135	30	11	8	63	17	2	27	.345	.376	.540	122	11	7-4	.919	-4	97	113	3b96/2	—	1.2
1926	Phi A	111	327	49	92	22	9	4	43	13	1	36	.281	.311	.440	89	-7	1-4	.947	0	96	142	3b77/rf	—	-0.4
1927	Phi A	131	501	77	157	24	8	5	81	32	3	32	.313	.358	.423	97	-4	11-3	.961	1	94	**189**	3b128	—	0.6
1928	Phi A	88	314	38	97	20	9	4	58	9	3	21	.309	.334	.468	106	1	2-0	.932	8	111	126	3b79	—	1.4
1929	Phi A	101	379	51	105	14	3	1	40	12	2	18	.277	.303	.338	62	-22	6-2	.956	-6	94	79	3b99/2	—	-2.1
1930	StL A	62	190	21	52	8	1	2	25	8	0	18	.274	.303	.358	65	-11	1-1	.947	-1	101	68	3b47	—	-0.9
Total	10	883	2915	422	880	157	54	30	392	130	22	218	.302	.336	.424	93	-45	41-20	.939	-19	98	120	3b704,O10(4/4/2),2b3/S	—	-2.1

HALE, CHIP Walter William; B12.2.1964 San Jose CA; BL/TR/5´11˝/(180–191); [MinA87 17/425]; d8.27; Col Arizona

YEAR	TM LG	G	AB	R	H	2B	3B	HR	RBI	BB-IB	HP	SO	AVG	OBP	SLG	AOPS	ABR	SB-CS	FA	FR	RNG	THR	GAMES AT POSITION	DL	BFW
1989	Min A	28	67	6	14	3	0	0	4	1-0	0	6	.209	.214	.254	31	-6	0-0	.980	-2	115	108	2b16,3b9,D2	0	-0.8
1990	Min A	1	2	0	0	0	0	0	2	0-0	0	1	.000	.000	.000	-94	-1	0-0	1.000	1	200	279	/2	0	0.1
1993	Min A	69	186	25	62	6	1	3	27	18-0	6	17	.333	.408	.425	123	7	2-1	.952	-1	104	98	2b21,3b19,D19/1S	0	0.6
1994	Min A	67	118	13	31	9	0	1	11	16-1	1	14	.263	.350	.364	86	-2	0-2	.964	4	139	70	3b21,D10,1b7,2b5/rf	0	0.1
1995	Min A	69	103	10	27	4	0	2	18	11-1	0	20	.262	.333	.359	80	-3	0-0	1.000	-1	102	89	D27,2b7,3b5,1b3	0	-0.5
1996	Min A	85	87	8	24	5	0	1	16	10-2	0	6	.276	.347	.368	81	-2	0-0	1.000	0	101	66	2b14,D10,1b6,3b3,O3R	0	-0.2
1997	LA N	14	12	0	1	0	0	0	0	2-0	0	4	.083	.214	.083	-20	-2	0-0	1.000	-0	0	0	3b2	0	-0.2
Total	7	333	575	62	159	27	1	7	78	58-4	7	68	.277	.346	.363	87	-9	2-3	.969	2	110	106	D68,2b64,3b59,1b17,O4R/S	0	-0.9

HALEY, J. J.; TR; d6.22

YEAR	TM LG	G	AB	R	H	2B	3B	HR	RBI	BB-IB	HP	SO	AVG	OBP	SLG	AOPS	ABR	SB-CS	FA	FR	RNG	THR	GAMES AT POSITION	DL	BFW
1880	Tro N	2	7	0	0	0	0	0	0	1	—	2	.000	.125	.000	-51	-1	—	.750	-2	—	—	C2	—	-0.3

HALEY, RAY Raymond Timothy "Pat"; B1.23.1891 Danbury IA; D10.8.1973 Bradenton FL; BR/TR/5´11˝/180; d4.21; Mil 1918–19; Col Western Illinois

YEAR	TM LG	G	AB	R	H	2B	3B	HR	RBI	BB-IB	HP	SO	AVG	OBP	SLG	AOPS	ABR	SB-CS	FA	FR	RNG	THR	GAMES AT POSITION	DL	BFW
1915	Bos A	5	7	2	1	1	0	0	0	1	0	0	.143	.250	.286	62	0	0	1.000	0	*123*	*113*	C4	—	0.0
1916	Bos A	1	1	0	0	0	0	0	0	0	0	1	.000	.000	.000	-99	0	0	ø	0	—	—	/H	—	0.0
	Phi A	34	108	8	25	5	0	0	4	6	1	19	.231	.278	.278	70	-4	0	.982	-1	60	171	C33	—	-0.2
	Year	35	109	8	25	5	0	0	4	6	1	20	.229	.276	.275	69	-4	0	.982	-1	60	171	C33	—	-0.2
1917	Phi A	41	98	7	27	2	1	0	11	4	1	12	.276	.311	.316	93	-1	2	.947	-5	*72*	*91*	C34	—	-0.5
Total	3	81	214	17	53	8	1	0	15	11	2	32	.248	.291	.294	80	-5	2	.970	-6	*67*	*136*	C71	—	-0.7

HALL, ALBERT Albert; B3.7.1958 Birmingham AL; BB/TR/5´11˝/(155–158); [AtlN77 6/134]; d9.12

YEAR	TM LG	G	AB	R	H	2B	3B	HR	RBI	BB-IB	HP	SO	AVG	OBP	SLG	AOPS	ABR	SB-CS	FA	FR	RNG	THR	GAMES AT POSITION	DL	BFW
1981	Atl N	6	2	1	0	0	0	0	0	1-0	0	1	.000	.333	.000	1	0	0-0	ø	-0	0	0	O2(1/0/1)	0	0.0
1982	Atl N	5	0	1	0	0	0	0	0	0-0	0	0	ø	ø	ø	ø	0	0-0	ø	0	—	—	/R	0	0.0
1983	Atl N	10	8	2	0	0	0	0	0	2-0	0	2	.000	.200	.000	-37	-1	1-1	.750	-1	62	0	O4(4/1/0)	0	-0.3
1984	Atl N	87	142	25	37	6	1	1	9	10-0	0	18	.261	.309	.338	76	-4	6-4	.932	-0	92	148	O66(48/2/17)	0	-0.7
1985	Atl N	54	47	5	7	0	1	0	3	9-1	0	12	.149	.286	.191	34	-4	1-1	.900	0	63	621	O13(6/6/3)	0	-0.4
1986	Atl N	16	50	6	12	2	0	0	1	5-0	0	6	.240	.309	.280	61	-3	8-3	.900	-0	109	95	O14R	0	-0.3
1987	Atl N	92	292	54	83	20	4	3	24	38-3	2	36	.284	.369	.411	103	3	33-10	.981	-2	93	132	O69(0/68/1)	16	0.3
1988	Atl N	85	231	27	57	7	1	1	15	21-1	2	35	.247	.314	.299	74	-7	15-10	.973	2	97	278	O63(1/63/0)	59	-0.6
1989	Pit N	20	33	4	6	2	1	0	1	3-0	0	5	.182	.250	.303	59	-2	3-0	.909	-1	71	0	O12(5/1/6)	0	-0.3
Total	9	375	805	125	202	37	8	5	53	89-5	4	115	.251	.328	.335	80	-18	67-29	.958	-3	93	182	O243(65/141/42)	75	-2.3

HALL, AL Archibald W.; B Worcester MA; D2.10.1885 Warren PA; d5.1

YEAR	TM LG	G	AB	R	H	2B	3B	HR	RBI	BB-IB	HP	SO	AVG	OBP	SLG	AOPS	ABR	SB-CS	FA	FR	RNG	THR	GAMES AT POSITION	DL	BFW
1879	Tro N	67	306	30	79	7	3	0	14	3	—	13	.258	.265	.301	92	-2	—	.842	2	114	150	O67(2/63/2)	—	-0.3
1880	Cle N	3	8	1	1	0	0	0	0	0	—	0	.125	.125	.125	-15	-1	—	1.000	-1	0	0	O3L	—	-0.2
Total	2	70	314	31	80	7	3	0	14	3	—	13	.255	.262	.296	90	-3	—	.843	1	111	146	O70(5/63/2)	—	-0.5

HALL, CHARLIE Charles Walter "Doc"; B8.24.1863 Toulon IL; D6.24.1921 Tacoma WA; 5´10˝/158; d5.3

YEAR	TM LG	G	AB	R	H	2B	3B	HR	RBI	BB-IB	HP	SO	AVG	OBP	SLG	AOPS	ABR	SB-CS	FA	FR	RNG	THR	GAMES AT POSITION	DL	BFW
1887	NY AA	3	12	1	1	0	0	0	0	2	0	—	.083	.214	.083	-16	-2	1	1.000	-0	0	0	O3C	—	-0.2

HALL, GEORGE George William; B3.29.1849 Stepney, England; D6.11.1923 Ridgewood NY; BL/5´7˝/142; d5.5

YEAR	TM LG	G	AB	R	H	2B	3B	HR	RBI	BB-IB	HP	SO	AVG	OBP	SLG	AOPS	ABR	SB-CS	FA	FR	RNG	THR	GAMES AT POSITION	DL	BFW
1871	Oly NA	**32**	136	31	40	3	3	2	17	8	—	0	.294	.333	.404	117	4	2-1	.913	6	81	0	O32(1/31/0)	—	0.6
1872	Bal NA	53	250	69	84	17	6	1	37	3	—	1	.336	.344	.464	140	10	8-1	.836	-3	71	191	O52(3/51/0)/1	—	0.6
1873	Bal NA	35	168	44	58	6	4	0	31	2	—	1	.345	.353	.429	131	6	0-0	.865	2	59	0	O35C	—	0.6
1874	Bos NA	47	222	58	64	10	8	1	34	1	—	0	.288	.291	.419	118	3	2-0	.811	-3	73	174	O47(20/21/7)	—	0.1
1875	Ath NA	**77**	358	71	107	10	12	4	62	3	—	4	.299	.305	.427	136	10	8-5	.887	4	63	87	O77(74/0/3)/1	—	1.4
1876	Phi N	**60**	268	51	98	7	13	**5**	45	8	—	4	.366	.384	.545	208	29	—	.801	-2	68	109	O60(59/0/1)	—	2.0
1877	Lou N	**61**	269	53	87	15	8	0	26	12	—	19	.323	.352	.439	125	6	—	**.900**	-5	60	56	O61L	—	-0.3
Total	5NA	244	1134	273	353	46	33	8	181	17	—	6	.311	.321	.431	130	33	20-7	.865	6	68	102	O243(98/138/10),1b2	—	3.3
Total	2	121	537	104	185	22	21	5	71	20	—	23	.345	.368	.492	162	35	—	.837	-7	64	82	O121(120/0/1)	—	1.7

HALL, IRV Irvin Gladstone; B10.7.1918 Alberton (now Daniels) MD; BR/TR/5´10.5˝/160; d4.20

YEAR	TM LG	G	AB	R	H	2B	3B	HR	RBI	BB-IB	HP	SO	AVG	OBP	SLG	AOPS	ABR	SB-CS	FA	FR	RNG	THR	GAMES AT POSITION	DL	BFW
1943	Phi A	151	544	37	139	15	4	0	54	22	6	42	.256	.292	.298	73	-21	10-7	.948	-9	98	88	S148/23	0	-1.9
1944	Phi A	143	559	60	150	20	8	0	45	31	2	46	.268	.309	.333	85	-13	2-5	.980	-8	99	62	2b97,S40,1b4	0	-1.4
1945	Phi A	151	616	62	161	17	5	0	50	35	6	42	.261	.307	.305	78	-18	3-10	.978	20	110	103	2b151	0	0.8
1946	Phi A	63	185	19	46	6	2	0	19	9	1	18	.249	.287	.303	65	-9	1-1	.973	-5	92	66	2b40,S7	0	-1.3
Total	4	508	1904	178	496	58	19	0	168	97	15	148	.261	.302	.311	77	-61	16-23	.977	-1	104	85	2b289,S195,1b4/3	0	-3.8

HALL, JIM James; D1.30.1886 Brooklyn NY; d5.20

YEAR	TM LG	G	AB	R	H	2B	3B	HR	RBI	BB-IB	HP	SO	AVG	OBP	SLG	AOPS	ABR	SB-CS	FA	FR	RNG	THR	GAMES AT POSITION	DL	BFW
1872	Atl NA	13	57	9	18	0	1	0	6	1	—	1	.316	.328	.351	93	-1	0-0	.750	-4	90	105	2b13	—	-0.4
1874	Atl NA	2	9	0	1	0	0	0	0	0	—	0	.111	.111	.111	-32	-1	0-0	.857	-1	50	0	2b2/rf	—	-0.2
1875	Wes NA	1	3	0	1	0	1	0	1	0	—	0	.333	.333	1.000	327	1	0-0	.000	-1	0	0	/lf	—	0.0
Total	3NA	16	69	9	20	0	2	0	7	1	—	1	.290	.300	.348	89	-1	0-0	.758	-5	86	95	2b15,O2(1/0/1)	—	-0.6

HALL, JIMMIE Jimmie Randolph; B3.17.1938 Mt.Holly NC; BL/TR/6´0˝/(175–180); d4.9

YEAR	TM LG	G	AB	R	H	2B	3B	HR	RBI	BB-IB	HP	SO	AVG	OBP	SLG	AOPS	ABR	SB-CS	FA	FR	RNG	THR	GAMES AT POSITION	DL	BFW
1963	Min A	156	497	88	129	21	5	33	80	63-4	0	101	.260	.342	.521	136	23	3-3	.982	11	113	151	O143(87/93/16)	0	2.8
1964	Min A★	149	510	61	144	20	3	25	75	44-3	1	112	.282	.338	.480	125	16	5-2	.985	6	107	143	O137C	0	1.9
1965	†Min A★	148	522	81	149	25	4	20	86	51-6	1	79	.285	.347	.464	124	16	14-7	.976	-5	93	116	O141(6/140/6)	0	0.8
1966	Min A	120	356	52	85	7	4	20	47	33-5	0	66	.239	.302	.449	106	2	1-2	.978	2	104	111	O103(69/27/12)	0	-0.2
1967	Cal A	129	401	54	100	8	3	16	55	42-7	0	65	.249	.318	.404	117	8	4-1	.990	0	104	86	O120(2/6/116)	0	0.1
1968	Cal A	46	126	15	27	3	0	1	8	16-3	0	19	.214	.303	.262	75	-3	1-0	.981	-3	89	0	O39(4/2/33)	0	-1.0
	Cle A	53	111	4	22	4	0	1	8	10-3	0	19	.198	.264	.261	61	-5	1-0	.983	3	139	72	O29(20/6/4)	0	-0.3
	Year	99	237	19	49	7	0	2	16	26-6	0	38	.207	.285	.262	68	-9	2-0	.982	0	109	29	O68(24/8/37)	0	-1.3
1969	Cle A	4	10	1	0	0	0	0	0	2-1	0	3	.000	.167	.000	-49	-2	1-0	1.000	-0	86	0	O3(2/1/0)	0	-0.2
	NY A	80	212	21	50	8	5	3	26	19-1	0	34	.236	.296	.363	87	-5	8-3	.963	-6	84	29	O50(9/19/22),1b7	0	-1.3
	Year	84	222	22	50	8	5	3	26	21-2	0	37	.225	.290	.347	81	-7	9-3	.966	-6	55	0	O63(11/20/22),1b7	0	-1.5
	Chi N	11	24	1	5	1	0	0	1	1-0	0	5	.208	.240	.250	33	-2	0-0	1.000	-1	55	0	O5(1/4/0)	0	-0.4
1970	Chi N	28	32	2	3	1	0	0	1	4-1	0	12	.094	.194	.125	-11	-5	0-0	1.000	-0	100	0	O8(2/7/0)	0	-0.5
	Atl N	39	47	7	10	2	0	2	4	2-1	0	14	.213	.245	.383	62	-3	0-0	1.000	-0	85	128	O28(19/1/8)	0	-0.4

YEAR	TM LG	G	AB	R	H	2B	3B	HR	RBI	BB-IB	HP	SO	AVG	OBP	SLG	AOPS	ABR	SB-CS	FA	FR	RNG	THR	GAMES AT POSITION	DL	BFW
	Year	67	79	9	13	3	0	2	5	6-2	0	26	.165	.224	.278	31	-8	0-0	1.000	-1	89	91	O36(21/8/8)	0	-0.9
Total	8	963	2848	387	724	100	24	121	391	287-35	2	529	.254	.321	.434	112	40	38-18	.982	6	103	108	O806(221/443/217),1b7	0	1.3

HALL, JOE Joseph Geroy; B3.6.1966 Paducah KY; BR/TR/6´0˝/180; [StLN88 10/262]; d4.5; Col Southern Illinois

YEAR	TM LG	G	AB	R	H	2B	3B	HR	RBI	BB-IB	HP	SO	AVG	OBP	SLG	AOPS	ABR	SB-CS	FA	FR	RNG	THR	GAMES AT POSITION	DL	BFW
1994	Chi A	17	28	6	11	3	0	1	5	2-0	1	4	.393	.452	.607	172	3	0-0	.917	-1	93	0	O9(7/0/2),D2	68	0.2
1995	Det A	7	15	2	2	0	0	0	0	2-0	0	3	.133	.235	.133	-1	-2	0-0	1.000	1	135	369	O5L,D2	0	-0.1
1997	Det A	2	4	1	2	1	0	0	3	0-0	0	0	.500	.500	.750	221	1	0-0	1.000	-0	60	0	/rf	0	0.0
Total	3	26	47	9	15	4	0	1	8	4-0	1	7	.319	.385	.468	120	2	0-0	.960	0	106	132	O15(12/0/3),D4	68	0.1

HALL, MEL Melvin; B9.16.1960 Lyons NY; BL/TL/6´1˝/(185–223); [ChiN78 2/39]; d9.3

YEAR	TM LG	G	AB	R	H	2B	3B	HR	RBI	BB-IB	HP	SO	AVG	OBP	SLG	AOPS	ABR	SB-CS	FA	FR	RNG	THR	GAMES AT POSITION	DL	BFW
1981	Chi N	10	11	1	1	0	0	1	2	1-0	0	4	.091	.167	.364	45	-1	0-0	ø	-1	0	0	O3(1/2/0)	0	-0.2
1982	Chi N	24	80	6	21	3	2	0	4	5-1	2	17	.262	.318	.350	85	-2	0-1	.939	-0	82	322	O22(0/21/1)	0	-0.3
1983	Chi N	112	410	60	116	23	5	17	56	42-6	3	101	.283	.352	.488	125	14	6-6	.988	-4	89	153	O112(5/108/0)	46	0.8
1984	Chi N	48	150	25	42	11	3	4	22	12-3	0	23	.280	.329	.473	115	3	2-1	.961	0	94	190	O46(5/5/40)	0	0.1
	Cle A	83	257	43	66	13	1	7	30	35-5	2	55	.257	.344	.397	104	3	1-1	.993	2	105	69	O69(64/1/6),D9	0	0.1
1985	Cle A	23	66	7	21	6	0	0	12	8-0	0	12	.318	.387	.409	120	2	0-1	1.000	-3	65	0	O15(15/0/1),D5	150	-0.1
1986	Cle A	140	442	68	131	29	2	18	77	33-8	2	65	.296	.346	.493	128	16	6-2	.972	-1	97	93	O126(123/0/14),D7	0	1.1
1987	Cle A	142	485	57	136	21	1	18	76	20-6	1	68	.280	.309	.439	95	-5	5-4	.989	6	118	40	O122L,D14	0	-0.5
1988	Cle A	150	515	69	144	32	4	6	71	28-12	0	50	.280	.312	.392	94	-4	7-3	.967	-2	105	39	O141(135/7/3),D6	0	-1.0
1989	NY A	113	361	54	94	9	0	17	58	21-4	0	37	.260	.295	.427	104	0	0-0	.993	1	105	70	O75(46/0/31),D34	30	-0.3
1990	NY A	113	360	41	93	23	2	12	46	6-2	2	46	.258	.272	.433	94	-5	0-0	.973	-5	77	67	D54,O50(36/0/15)	16	-1.3
1991	NY A	141	492	67	140	23	2	19	80	26-6	3	40	.285	.321	.455	112	6	0-1	.987	0	97	111	O120(62/1/65),D10	0	0.2
1992	NY A	152	583	67	163	36	3	15	81	29-4	1	53	.280	.310	.429	107	3	4-2	.990	1	99	109	O136(99/0/37),D11	0	0.0
1996	SF N	25	25	3	3	0	0	0	5	1-0	0	4	.120	.148	.120	-27	-5	0-0	ø	-1	0	0	O4(3/0/1)	0	-0.5
Total	13	1276	4237	568	1171	229	25	134	620	267-57	16	575	.276	.318	.437	106	25	31-22	.981	-6	99	94	O1041(716/145/214),D150	242	-1.9

HALL, DICK Richard Wallace; B9.27.1930 St.Louis MO; BR/TR/6´6˝/(199–220); d4.15; Col Swarthmore; ▲

YEAR	TM LG	G	AB	R	H	2B	3B	HR	RBI	BB-IB	HP	SO	AVG	OBP	SLG	AOPS	ABR	SB-CS	FA	FR	RNG	THR	GAMES AT POSITION	DL	BFW
1952	Pit N	26	80	6	11	1	0	0	2	2	0	17	.138	.159	.150	-14	-12	0-1	.972	0	105	79	O14(0/12/2),3b5	0	-1.4
1953	Pit N	7	24	2	4	0	0	0	1	1	0	3	.167	.200	.167	-3	-4	1-1	.978	2	112	113	2b7	0	-0.1
1954	Pit N	112	310	38	74	8	4	2	27	33	0	46	.239	.304	.310	64	-17	3-0	.956	3	113	75	O102(42/44/18)	0	-1.8
1955	Pit N	21	40	3	7	1	0	1	3	6-0	0	5	.175	.283	.275	50	-3	0-0	1.000	-2	39	0	P15,O3(1/3/0)	0	-0.1
1956	Pit N	33	29	5	10	0	0	0	1	5-0	0	7	.345	.441	.345	118	1	0-0	1.000	-1	58	0	P19/1	41	0.0
1957	Pit N	10	1	0	0	0	0	0	0	0-0	0	1	.000	.000	.000	-99	0	0-0	ø	-0	0	0	P8	30	0.0
1959	Pit N	2	2	0	0	0	0	0	0	0-0	0	0	.000	.000	.000	-99	0	0-0	1.000	-0	69	0	P2	0	0.0
1960	KC A	32	56	5	6	0	0	0	4	4-0	0	15	.107	.167	.107	-24	-2	1-0	.925	-1	97	46	P29	0	0.0
1961	Bal A	30	36	4	5	0	0	0	1	3-0	0	13	.139	.205	.139	-6	0	0-0	.970	1	118	74	P29	0	0.0
1962	Bal A	44	24	3	4	1	0	0	1	4-0	0	9	.167	.286	.208	38	1	0-0	1.000	-0	91	73	P43	0	0.0
1963	Bal A	48	28	7	13	1	0	1	4	0-0	0	8	.464	.464	.607	205	6	0-0	1.000	1	121	99	P47	0	0.0
1964	Bal A	45	16	1	2	0	0	0	3	1-0	0	3	.125	.176	.125	-14	0	0-0	1.000	-0	90	105	P45	0	0.0
1965	Bal A	49	15	1	5	2	0	0	4	1-0	1	4	.333	.412	.467	146	3	0-0	.923	-1	51	217	P48	0	0.0
1966	Bal A	32	12	0	2	0	0	0	2	0-0	1	5	.167	.231	.167	17	0	0-0	1.000	-0	95	0	P32	0	0.0
1967	Phi N	48	14	1	1	0	0	0	0	0-0	0	5	.071	.071	.071	-58	-1	0-0	1.000	1	147	121	P48	0	0.0
1968	Phi N	32	3	0	1	0	0	0	0	0-0	0	1	.333	.333	.333	101	0	0-0	1.000	-0	80	0	P32	0	0.0
1969	†Bal A	39	7	1	2	0	0	0	2	1-0	0	1	.286	.375	.286	86	1	1-0	1.000	-1	61	296	P39	0	0.0
1970	†Bal A	32	12	2	1	0	0	0	1	0-0	0	3	.083	.083	.083	-53	-1	0-0	1.000	-2	34	0	P32	0	0.0
1971	†Bal A	27	5	0	2	1	0	0	0	0-0	0	1	.400	.400	.600	179	1	0-0	.800	-1	44	0	P27	0	0.0
Total	19	669	714	79	150	15	4	4	56	61-0	2	147	.210	.271	.259	44	-27	6-2	.976	-3	85	77	P495,O119(43/59/20),2b7,3b5/1	71	-3.4

HALL, BOB Robert Prill; B12.20.1878 Baltimore MD; D12.1.1950 Wellesley MA; TR/5´10˝/158; d4.18

YEAR	TM LG	G	AB	R	H	2B	3B	HR	RBI	BB-IB	HP	SO	AVG	OBP	SLG	AOPS	ABR	SB-CS	FA	FR	RNG	THR	GAMES AT POSITION	DL	BFW
1904	Phi N	46	163	11	26	4	0	0	17	14	0	—	.160	.226	.184	28	-13	5	.843	-9	92	98	3b20,S15,1b11	—	-2.4
1905	NY N	1	3	1	1	0	0	0	0	0	0	—	.333	.333	.333	97	0	0	ø	0	0	0	/rf	—	0.0
	Bro N	56	203	21	48	4	1	2	15	11	1	—	.236	.279	.296	77	-6	8	.939	2	97	117	O42(24/12/7),2b7,1b3	—	-0.7
	Year	57	206	22	49	4	1	2	15	11	1	—	.238	.280	.296	77	-6	8	.939	2	97	117	O43(24/12/8),2b7,1b3	—	-0.7
Total	2	103	369	33	75	8	1	2	32	25	1	—	.203	.256	.247	55	-19	13	.939	-7	97	117	O43(24/12/8),3b20,S15,1b14,2b7	—	-3.1

HALL, RUSS Robert Russell; B9.29.1871 Shelbyville KY; D7.1.1937 Los Angeles CA; BL/TL/5´10˝/170; d4.15

YEAR	TM LG	G	AB	R	H	2B	3B	HR	RBI	BB-IB	HP	SO	AVG	OBP	SLG	AOPS	ABR	SB-CS	FA	FR	RNG	THR	GAMES AT POSITION	DL	BFW
1898	StL N	39	143	13	35	2	1	0	10	7	1	—	.245	.285	.273	59	-8	1	.835	-12	91	81	S35,3b3/rf	—	-1.7
1901	Cle A	1	4	2	2	0	0	0	0	0	0	—	.500	.500	.500	185	0	0	.500	-1	60	0	/S	—	-0.1
Total	2	40	147	15	37	2	1	0	10	7	1	—	.252	.290	.279	62	-8	1	.824	-13	90	79	S36,3b3/rf	—	-1.8

HALL, TOBY Toby Jason; B10.21.1975 Tacoma WA; BR/TR/6´3˝/(205–240); [TBA97 9/294]; d9.15; Col Nevada–Las Vegas

YEAR	TM LG	G	AB	R	H	2B	3B	HR	RBI	BB-IB	HP	SO	AVG	OBP	SLG	AOPS	ABR	SB-CS	FA	FR	RNG	THR	GAMES AT POSITION	DL	BFW
2000	TB A	4	12	1	2	0	0	1	1	1-0	0	0	.167	.231	.417	60	-1	0-0	1.000	1	0	0	C4	0	0.0
2001	TB A	49	188	28	56	16	0	4	30	4-0	3	16	.298	.321	.447	102	0	2-2	.986	4	124	87	C46	0	0.7
2002	TB A	85	330	37	85	19	1	6	42	17-3	1	27	.258	.293	.376	79	-11	0-1	.989	-4	112	114	C83	0	-0.9
2003	TB A	130	463	50	117	23	0	12	47	23-4	7	40	.253	.295	.380	79	-15	0-1	.988	1	151	115	C130	0	-0.6
2004	TB A	119	404	35	103	21	0	8	60	24-1	5	41	.255	.300	.366	76	-15	0-2	.992	-1	128	84	C119	0	-0.8
2005	TB A	135	432	28	124	20	0	5	48	16-1	5	39	.287	.315	.368	84	-10	0-0	.989	1	130	125	C135,1b2	0	-0.1
2006	TB A	64	221	15	51	13	0	8	23	8-2	2	17	.231	.261	.398	69	-11	0-2	.991	-11	88	89	C61/3D	0	-1.8
	LA N	21	57	2	21	4	0	0	8	2-2	0	5	.368	.383	.439	111	1	0-0	.989	-2	97	150	C21	0	0.0
Total	7	607	2107	196	559	116	1	44	259	95-13	23	185	.265	.301	.384	81	-62	2-8	.989	-12	125	106	C599,D2,1b2/3	0	-3.5

HALL, BILL William; B12.28.1979 Tupelo MS; BR/TR/6´0˝/(175–210); [MilN98 6/176]; d9.1

YEAR	TM LG	G	AB	R	H	2B	3B	HR	RBI	BB-IB	HP	SO	AVG	OBP	SLG	AOPS	ABR	SB-CS	FA	FR	RNG	THR	GAMES AT POSITION	DL	BFW
2002	Mil N	19	36	3	7	1	1	1	5	3-0	0	13	.194	.256	.361	61	-2	0-1	.949	-3	77	74	S13,3b2	0	-0.5
2003	Mil N	52	142	23	37	9	2	5	20	7-0	1	28	.261	.298	.458	94	-2	1-2	.956	-0	105	126	2b18,S18/3	0	0.0
2004	Mil N	126	390	43	93	20	3	9	53	20-1	1	119	.238	.276	.374	66	-21	12-6	.959	1	84	100	2b50,S37,3b11	0	-1.5
2005	Mil N	146	501	69	146	39	6	17	62	39-2	1	103	.291	.342	.495	116	11	18-6	.976	-8	94	86	S66,3b59,2b23	0	1.0
2006	Mil N	148	537	101	145	39	4	35	85	63-6	1	162	.270	.345	.553	125	19	8-9	.967	-16	88	73	S127,3b11,O7C,2b4	0	1.1
Total	5	491	1606	239	428	108	16	67	225	132-9	4	425	.267	.322	.479	104	5	39-24	.965	-27	93	82	S261,2b95,3b84,O7C	0	0.1

HALL, BILL William Lemuel; B7.30.1928 Moultrie GA; D1.1.1986 Moultrie GA; BL/TR/5´11˝/165; d4.18

YEAR	TM LG	G	AB	R	H	2B	3B	HR	RBI	BB-IB	HP	SO	AVG	OBP	SLG	AOPS	ABR	SB-CS	FA	FR	RNG	THR	GAMES AT POSITION	DL	BFW
1954	Pit N	5	7	0	0	0	0	0	0	0	0	0	.000	.000	.000	-99	-2	0-0	1.000	-0	*0*	*0*	/C	0	-0.2
1956	Pit N	1	3	0	0	0	0	0	0	0-0	0	1	.000	.000	.000	-99	-1	0-0	1.000	1	*0*	*0*	/C	0	0.0
1958	Pit N	51	116	15	33	6	0	1	15	15-8	0	13	.284	.366	.362	96	0	0-0	.982	4	65	126	C51	0	0.6
Total	3	57	126	15	33	6	0	1	15	15-8	0	14	.262	.340	.333	81	-3	0-0	.983	4	*62*	*120*	C53	0	0.4

HALLER, TOM Thomas Frank; B6.23.1937 Lockport IL; D11.26.2004 Los Angeles CA; BL/TR/6´4˝/(195–210); d4.11; C3; Col Illinois

YEAR	TM LG	G	AB	R	H	2B	3B	HR	RBI	BB-IB	HP	SO	AVG	OBP	SLG	AOPS	ABR	SB-CS	FA	FR	RNG	THR	GAMES AT POSITION	DL	BFW
1961	SF N	30	62	5	9	1	0	2	8	9-0	1	23	.145	.260	.258	41	-5	0-1	1.000	-1	61	74	C25	0	-0.6
1962	†SF N	99	272	53	71	13	1	18	55	51-1	4	59	.261	.384	.515	142	18	1-4	.992	-0	145	76	C91	0	2.0
1963	SF N	98	298	32	76	8	1	14	44	34-5	2	45	.255	.332	.430	120	8	4-6	.994	-4	130	97	C85,O7(1/0/6)	0	0.7
1964	SF N	117	388	43	98	14	3	16	48	55-10	2	51	.253	.345	.428	115	9	4-2	.989	1	86	85	C113,O3(1/0/2)	0	1.6
1965	SF N	134	422	40	106	4	3	16	49	47-15	8	67	.251	.335	.389	101	1	0-0	.987	2	140	56	C133	0	0.9
1966	SF N☆	142	471	74	113	19	2	27	67	53-11	6	74	.240	.323	.461	112	8	1-3	.991	-5	100	63	C136,1b4	0	0.9
1967	SF N★	141	455	54	114	23	5	14	49	62-9	4	61	.251	.344	.415	118	12	0-4	.997	0	101	89	C136/rf	0	1.9
1968	LA N★	144	474	37	135	27	5	4	53	46-13	2	76	.285	.345	.388	131	19	1-4	.994	12	113	133	C139	0	4.1
1969	LA N	134	445	46	117	18	3	6	39	48-13	2	58	.263	.337	.357	101	1	0-3	.992	-2	83	90	C132	0	0.4
1970	LA N	112	325	47	93	16	6	10	47	32-7	2	35	.286	.351	.465	122	9	3-0	.993	-6	76	77	C106	0	0.8
1971	LA N	84	202	23	54	5	0	5	32	25-8	2	30	.267	.346	.366	110	3	0-2	.978	2	75	104	C67	0	0.8
1972	†Det A	59	121	7	25	5	2	2	13	15-4	0	14	.207	.292	.331	83	-3	0-1	1.000	3	120	93	C36	0	0.2
Total	12	1294	3935	461	1011	153	31	134	504	477-96	35	593	.257	.340	.414	114	80	14-30	.992	3	105	86	C1199,O11(2/0/9),1b4	0	13.7

HALLIDAY, NEWT Newton Schurz; B6.18.1896 Chicago IL; D4.6.1918 Great Lakes IL; BR/TR/6´1˝/175; d8.19

YEAR	TM LG	G	AB	R	H	2B	3B	HR	RBI	BB-IB	HP	SO	AVG	OBP	SLG	AOPS	ABR	SB-CS	FA	FR	RNG	THR	GAMES AT POSITION	DL	BFW
1916	Pit N	1	1	0	0	0	0	0	0	0	0	1	.000	.000	.000	-99	0	0	1.000	0	603	0	/1	—	0.0

YEAR	TM LG	G	AB	R	H	2B	3B	HR	RBI	BB-IB	HP	SO	AVG	OBP	SLG	AOPS	ABR	SB-CS	FA	FR	RNG	THR	GAMES AT POSITION	DL	BFW
Halligan, Jocko	William E.; B12.8.1868 Avon NY; D2.13.1945 Buffalo NY; BL/5´9˝/166; d5.13																								
1890	Buf P	57	211	28	53	9	2	3	33	20	1	19	.251	.319	.355	87	-3	7	.824	-7	137	52	O43(1/5/37),C16	—	-0.8
1891	Cin N	61	247	43	77	13	6	3	44	24	1	25	.312	.375	.449	139	12	5	.856	-5	59	58	O61R	—	0.5
1892	Cin N	26	101	14	29	4	0	2	12	12	0	9	.287	.363	.386	128	4	3	.875	-1	95	115	O26R	—	0.1
	Bal N	46	178	38	48	4	7	2	43	30	2	24	.270	.381	.404	134	8	8	.861	-6	118	117	O22(1/0/21),1b19,C5	—	0.1
	Year	72	279	52	77	8	7	4	55	42	2	33	.276	.375	.398	132	12	11	.869	-7	105	116	O48(1/0/47),1b19,C5	—	0.2
Total	3	190	737	123	207	30	15	10	132	86	4	77	.281	.359	.403	121	21	23	.848	-20	94	74	O152(2/5/145),C21,1b19	—	-0.1
Hallinan, Ed	Edward S.; B8.23.1888 San Francisco CA; D8.24.1940 San Francisco CA; BR/TR/5´9˝/168; d5.13; Col Santa Clara																								
1911	StL A	52	169	13	35	3	1	0	14	14	0	—	.207	.268	.237	43	-13	4	.902	-5	94	164	S34,2b15,3b3	—	-1.6
1912	StL A	28	86	11	19	2	0	0	1	5	1	—	.221	.272	.244	50	-6	3	.866	-5	87	166	S26	—	-0.9
Total	2	80	255	24	54	5	1	0	15	19	1	—	.212	.269	.239	45	-19	7	.887	-10	91	165	S60,2b15,3b3	—	-2.5
Hallinan, Jimmy	James H.; B5.27.1849 , Ireland; D10.28.1879 Chicago IL; BL/TL/5´9˝/172; d7.26																								
1871	Kek NA	5	25	7	5	0	0	0	2	2	—	0	.200	.259	.200	34	-2	1-1	.475	-7	54	0	S5	—	-0.6
1875	Wes NA	**13**	51	12	14	2	1	0	3	0	—	1	.275	.275	.353	110	0	2-2	.742	-4	74	91	S13	—	-0.4
	Mut NA	44	203	29	58	6	3	3	21	1	—	2	.286	.289	.389	127	4	2-2	.765	-11	89	36	S43/3rf	—	-0.7
	Year	57	254	41	72	8	4	3	24	1	—	3	.283	.286	.382	123	5	4-4	.761	-15	86	48	S56/3rf	—	-1.1
1876	NY N	54	240	45	67	7	6	2	36	2	—	4	.279	.285	.383	139	11	—	.764	-17	102	57	S50,2b4,O2R	—	-0.3
1877	Cin N	16	73	18	27	1	1	0	7	1	—	1	.370	.378	.411	167	6	—	.854	-5	69	111	2b16	—	0.1
	Chi N	19	89	17	25	4	1	0	11	4	—	2	.281	.312	.348	96	-1	—	.800	-1	30	177	O19R	—	-0.2
	Year	35	162	35	52	5	2	0	18	5	—	3	.321	.341	.377	124	4	—	.800	-7	30	177	O19R,2b16	—	-0.1
1878	Chi N	16	67	14	19	3	0	0	2	5	—	6	.284	.333	.328	111	1	—	.789	-5	67	0	O11L,2b5	—	-0.4
	Ind N	3	12	0	3	2	0	0	1	0	—	2	.250	.250	.417	134	1	—	.667	-1	0	0	O3(2/1/0)	—	0.0
	Year	19	79	14	22	5	0	0	3	5	—	8	.278	.321	.342	114	2	—	.760	-5	53	0	O14(13/1/0),2b5	—	-0.4
Total	2NA	62	279	48	77	8	4	3	26	3	—	3	.276	.284	.366	114	2	5-5	.728	-22	83	44	S61/rf3	—	-1.7
Total	3	108	481	94	141	17	8	2	57	12	—	15	.293	.310	.374	129	18	—	.764	-29	102	57	S50,O35(13/1/21),2b25	—	-0.8
Hallman, Bill	William Harry; B3.15.1876 Philadelphia PA; D4.23.1950 Philadelphia PA; BL/TL/5´8˝/165; d4.25																								
1901	Mil A	**139**	549	70	135	27	6	2	47	41	2	—	.246	.301	.328	78	-16	12	.905	-1	121	144	O139(49/15/75)	—	-2.1
1903	Chi A	63	207	29	43	7	4	0	18	31	3	—	.208	.320	.280	85	-2	11	.953	2	111	0	O57(51/0/6)	—	-0.3
1906	Pit N	23	89	12	24	3	1	1	6	15	0	—	.270	.375	.360	124	3	3	.935	-1	107	0	O23(8/15/0)	—	0.1
1907	Pit N	94	302	39	67	6	2	0	15	33	3	—	.222	.305	.255	74	-8	21	.966	-1	87	41	O84(14/28/45)	—	-1.4
Total	4	319	1147	150	269	43	13	3	86	120	8	—	.235	.311	.303	82	-23	47	.933	-1	109	78	O303(122/58/126)	—	-3.7
Hallman, Bill	William Wilson; B3.31.1867 Pittsburgh PA; D9.11.1920 Philadelphia PA; BR/TR/5´8˝/160; d4.23; M1; OF(3/4/35)																								
1888	Phi N	18	63	5	13	4	1	0	6	1	0	12	.206	.219	.302	61	-3	1	.898	-4	—	—	C10,2b4,O3L/S3	—	-0.6
1889	Phi N	119	462	67	117	21	8	2	60	36	4	54	.253	.313	.346	76	-17	20	.895	3	98	98	S106,2b13/C	—	-0.9
1890	Phi P	84	356	59	95	16	7	1	37	33	5	24	.267	.338	.360	84	-9	6	.885	-3	100	397	O34(0/3/32),C26,2b14,3b10,S2	—	-0.8
1891	Phi AA	141	587	112	166	21	13	6	69	38	5	56	.283	.332	.394	107	2	18	.930	-4	96	93	2b141	—	0.2
1892	Phi N	138	586	106	171	27	10	2	84	32	6	52	.292	.335	.382	117	10	19	.936	-28	87	108	2b138	—	-1.1
1893	Phi N	132	596	119	183	28	7	5	76	51	5	27	.307	.367	.403	104	3	22	.950	-13	97	97	2b120,1b12	—	-0.4
1894	Phi N	122	519	111	162	19	9	0	69	37	5	15	.312	.364	.383	82	-15	37	.932	-19	87	114	2b122	—	-2.2
1895	Phi N	124	539	94	169	26	5	1	91	34	4	20	.314	.359	.386	92	-7	16	.943	4	105	105	2b122,S3	—	0.2
1896	Phi N	120	469	82	150	21	3	2	83	45	2	23	.320	.382	.390	105	5	16	.945	4	100	116	2b120/P	—	1.2
1897	Phi N	31	126	16	33	3	0	0	15	8	4	—	.262	.326	.286	64	-6	1	.958	-8	80	91	2b31	—	-1.1
	StL N	80	302	32	67	7	2	0	26	24	4	—	.222	.288	.258	46	-24	12	.940	5	104	117	2b78,1b3,M	—	-1.3
	Year	111	428	48	100	10	2	0	41	32	8	—	.234	.299	.266	51	-30	13	.945	-3	97	109	2b109,1b3	—	-2.4
1898	Bro N	134	509	57	124	10	7	2	63	29	5	—	.244	.291	.303	70	-21	9	.944	-4	108	90	2b124,3b10	—	-1.8
1901	Cle A	5	19	2	4	0	0	0	3	2	0	—	.211	.286	.211	41	-1	0	.815	-3	66	47	S5	—	-0.4
	Phi N	123	445	46	82	13	5	0	38	26	4	—	.184	.236	.236	36	-37	13	.971	-4	100	72	2b90,3b33	—	-3.9
1902	Phi N	73	254	14	63	8	4	0	35	14	0	—	.248	.287	.311	85	-5	9	.932	-1	104	32	3b72	—	-0.5
1903	Phi N	63	198	20	42	11	2	0	17	16	0	—	.212	.271	.288	61	-10	2	.932	-3	103	65	2b22,3b19,1b9,O4(0/1/3),S3	—	-1.2
Total	14	1507	6030	942	1641	235	83	21	772	426	53	283	.272	.326	.349	85	-135	201	.941	-79	—	—	2b1139,3b145,S120,O41R,C37,1b24/P	—	-14.6
Halpin, Jim	James Nathaniel; B10.4.1863 , England; D1.4.1893 Boston MA; d6.15																								
1882	Wor N	2	8	0	0	0	0	0	0	0	—	2	.000	.000	.000	-98	-2	—	.625	-1	53	0	3b2	—	-0.3
1884	Was U	46	168	24	31	3	0	0	—	2	—	—	.185	.194	.202	21	-21	—	.809	-5	88	65	S39,3b7	—	-2.3
1885	Det N	15	54	3	7	2	0	0	1	1	—	12	.130	.145	.167	1	-6	—	.846	-1	106	61	S15	—	-0.6
Total	3	63	230	27	38	5	0	0	1	3	—	14	.165	.176	.187	12	-29	—	.821	-7	93	64	S54,3b9	—	-3.2
Halt, Al	Alva William; B11.23.1890 Sandusky OH; D1.22.1973 Sandusky OH; BR/TR/6´0˝/180; d5.29																								
1914	Bro F	80	261	26	61	6	2	3	25	13	0	39	.234	.270	.307	57	-21	11	.890	-10	88	110	S71,2b3/cf	—	-2.8
1915	Bro F	151	524	41	131	22	7	3	64	39	4	79	.250	.307	.336	81	-22	20	.930	6	**106**	**138**	3b111,S40	—	-1.1
1918	Cle A	26	69	9	12	2	0	0	1	9	0	12	.174	.269	.203	39	-5	4	.971	1	97	49	3b14,2b4,S4,1b2	—	-0.4
Total	3	257	854	76	204	30	9	6	90	61	4	130	.239	.293	.316	70	-48	35	.933	-4	105	130	3b125,S115,2b7,1b2/cf	—	-4.3
Halter, Shane	Shane David; B11.8.1969 LaPlata MD; BR/TR/6´0˝/(160–195); [KCA91 5/132]; d4.6; Col Texas; OF(28/15/24)																								
1997	KC A	74	123	16	34	5	1	2	10	10-0	2	28	.276	.341	.382	86	-3	4-3	1.000	-4	92	96	O32(10/9/17),2b18,3b12,S5,D4	0	-0.7
1998	KC A	86	204	17	45	12	0	2	13	12-0	1	38	.221	.265	.309	47	-16	2-5	.964	5	116	90	S66,O9(6/0/3),3b8,2b6/1P	0	-0.8
1999	NY N	7	0	0	0	0	0	0	0	0-0	0	0	ø	ø	ø	ø	0	0-0	ø	-0	0	0	O2(0/1/1)/S	0	0.0
2000	Det A	105	238	26	62	12	2	3	27	14-0	1	49	.261	.302	.366	69	-12	5-2	.937	8	104	184	3b55,1b29,S17,2b10,O8(2/5/3),C2/P	0	-0.4
2001	Det A	136	450	53	128	32	7	12	65	37-2	7	100	.284	.344	.467	115	10	3-3	.924	14	129	102	3b74,S62,1b8/D	0	2.6
2002	Det A	122	410	46	98	22	6	10	39	39-1	4	92	.239	.309	.395	89	-7	0-4	.962	4	113	69	S81,3b30,O8L,2b4/1D	0	0.2
2003	Det A	114	360	33	78	5	2	12	30	27-0	0	77	.217	.269	.342	63	-21	2-3	.985	8	125	154	3b50,S27,2b24,1b12,O2L,D4	0	-1.1
2004	Ana A	46	114	10	23	5	0	4	13	7-0	0	30	.202	.248	.351	56	-8	1-1	.878	1	111	52	3b33,2b6,1b4,S3,D3	22	-0.7
Total	8	690	1899	201	468	93	18	45	197	146-3	15	414	.246	.303	.385	81	-57	17-21	.964	36	111	92	S262,3b262,2b68,O61L,1b55,D14,C2,P2	22	-0.9
Ham, Ralph	Ralph A.; B3.1849 Troy NY; D2.13.1905 Troy NY; 5´8˝/158; d5.6																								
1871	Rok NA	**25**	113	25	28	4	0	0	12	1	—	7	.248	.254	.283	57	-5	6-2	.723	-6	215	232	O19L,3b7,S2	—	-0.7
Hamburg, Charlie	Charles M. (b Charles M. Hambrick); B11.22.1863 Louisville KY; D5.18.1931 Union NJ; 6´0˝/175; d4.18																								
1890	†Lou AA	133	485	93	132	22	2	3	77	69	6	—	.272	.370	.344	113	12	46	.946	-3	72	69	O133L	—	0.4
Hamby, Jim	James Sanford "Cracker"; B7.29.1897 Wilkesboro NC; D10.21.1991 Springfield IL; BR/TR/6´0˝/170; d9.20																								
1926	NY N	1	3	0	0	0	0	0	0	0	0	0	.000	.000	.000	-99	-1	0	.600	-1	*48*	*0*	/C	—	-0.2
1927	NY N	21	52	6	10	0	1	0	5	7	0	7	.192	.288	.231	40	-4	1	.904	-1	*119*	*151*	C19	—	-0.4
Total	2	22	55	6	10	0	1	0	5	7	0	7	.182	.274	.218	33	-5	1	.885	-2	*115*	*142*	C20	—	-0.6
Hamelin, Bob	Robert James; B11.29.1967 Elizabeth NJ; BL/TL/6´0˝/235; [KCA88 2/48]; d9.12; Col UCLA																								
1993	KC A	16	49	2	11	3	0	2	5	6-0	0	15	.224	.309	.408	85	-1	0-0	.986	-1	90	88	1b15	0	-0.3
1994	KC A	101	312	64	88	25	1	24	65	56-3	1	62	.282	.388	.599	144	21	4-3	.992	0	106	57	D70,1b24	0	1.4
1995	KC A	72	208	20	35	7	1	7	25	26-1	6	56	.168	.278	.313	53	-15	0-1	1.000	2	171	180	D56,1b8	0	-1.7
1996	KC A	89	239	31	61	14	1	9	40	54-2	2	58	.255	.391	.435	110	6	5-2	.984	0	109	108	D47,1b33	28	0.1
1997	Det A	110	318	47	86	15	0	18	52	48-3	1	72	.270	.366	.487	121	11	2-1	1.000	-1	38	31	D95,1b7	0	0.4
1998	Mil N	109	146	15	32	6	0	7	22	16-1	1	30	.219	.295	.404	82	-4	0-1	.992	-5	35	93	1b51/D	0	-1.2
Total	6	497	1272	179	313	70	3	67	209	206-10	11	293	.246	.352	.464	108	18	11-8	.990	-5	87	92	D269,1b138	28	-1.3
Hamilton, Darryl	Darryl Quinn; B12.3.1964 Baton Rouge LA; BL/TR/6´1˝/(180–192); [MilA86 11/269]; d6.3; Col Nicholls St.																								
1988	Mil A	44	103	14	19	4	0	1	11	12-0	1	9	.184	.274	.252	48	-7	7-3	1.000	1	109	54	O37(8/6/23),D3	0	-0.7
1990	Mil A	89	156	27	46	5	0	1	18	9-0	0	12	.295	.333	.346	91	-2	10-3	.992	3	123	32	O72(41/6/25),D9	0	0.1
1991	Mil A	122	405	64	126	15	6	1	57	33-2	0	38	.311	.361	.385	109	5	16-6	.996	-5	95	45	O117(25/55/49)	24	-0.1
1992	Mil A	128	470	67	140	19	7	5	62	45-0	1	42	.298	.356	.400	114	9	41-14	**1.000**	2	100	121	O124(30/32/74)	18	1.2
1993	Mil A	135	520	74	161	21	1	9	48	45-5	3	62	.310	.367	.406	109	7	21-13	.992	11	**117**	117	O129(31/49/70)/D	15	1.4
1994	Mil A	36	141	23	37	10	1	1	13	15-1	0	17	.262	.331	.369	77	-5	3-0	1.000	-4	74	122	O32C,D4	78	-0.7
1995	Mil A	112	398	54	108	20	6	5	44	47-3	3	35	.271	.350	.389	88	-7	11-1	.989	-2	99	78	O109C,D2	0	-0.5

YEAR	TM LG	G	AB	R	H	2B	3B	HR	RBI	BB-IB	HP	SO	AVG	OBP	SLG	AOPS	ABR	SB-CS	FA	FR	RNG	THR	GAMES AT POSITION	DL	BFW
1996	†Tex A	148	627	94	184	29	4	6	51	54-4	2	66	.293	.348	.381	80	-19	15-5	**1.000**	-6	103	22	O147C	0	-1.9
1997	†SF N	125	460	78	124	23	3	5	43	61-1	0	61	.270	.354	.365	91	-5	15-10	.980	-8	96	19	O118C	22	-1.1
1998	SF N	97	367	65	108	19	2	1	26	59-0	2	53	.294	.393	.365	107	7	9-8	1.000	-9	87	67	O96C	0	-0.1
	Col N	51	194	30	65	9	1	5	25	23-1	1	20	.335	.406	.469	107	3	4-1	.990	-4	91	33	O48C	0	0.0
	Year	148	561	95	173	28	3	6	51	82-1	3	73	.308	.398	.401	107	10	13-9	**.997**	-13	88	56	O144C	0	-0.1
1999	Col N	91	337	63	102	11	3	4	24	38-0	1	21	.303	.374	.389	75	-12	4-5	1.000	-2	105	23	O82C	0	-1.3
	†NY N	55	168	19	57	8	1	5	21	19-0	1	18	.339	.410	.488	132	9	2-3	1.000	-3	92	83	O52C	0	0.6
	Year	146	505	82	159	19	4	9	45	57-0	2	39	.315	.386	.422	91	-5	6-8	**1.000**	-4	100	45	O134C	0	-0.7
2000	†NY N	43	105	20	29	4	1	1	6	14-0	0	20	.276	.358	.362	88	-2	2-0	1.000	-2	81	66	O33(17/11/8)	123	-0.3
2001	NY N	52	126	15	27	7	1	1	5	19-3	2	20	.214	.322	.310	71	-5	3-1	1.000	1	103	99	O37(24/11/3)	18	-0.5
Total	13	1328	4577	707	1333	204	37	51	454	493-20	17	494	.291	.360	.385	95	-24	163-73	.995	-27	100	63	O1233(176/854/252),D19	298	-3.9
HAMILTON, JEFF	Jeffrey Robert; B3.19.1964 Flint MI; BR/TR/6´3˝/(205–207); [LAN82 29/733]; d6.28																								
1986	LA N	71	147	22	33	5	0	5	19	2-1	0	43	.224	.232	.361	66	-8	0-0	.968	5	105	90	3b66,S2	0	-0.4
1987	LA N	35	83	5	18	3	0	0	1	7-2	1	22	.217	.286	.253	45	-7	0-1	.935	6	122	119	3b31/S	52	-0.1
1988	†LA N	111	309	34	73	14	2	6	33	10-1	4	51	.236	.268	.353	79	-10	0-2	.941	0	96	60	3b105,S2/1	36	-1.0
1989	LA N	151	548	45	134	35	1	12	56	20-5	3	71	.245	.272	.378	86	-12	0-0	.951	-1	88	**133**	3b147/P2S	0	-1.4
1990	LA N	7	24	1	3	0	0	0	1	0-0	0	3	.125	.125	.125	-32	-4	0-0	1.000	1	108	234	3b7	166	-0.4
1991	LA N	41	94	4	21	4	0	1	14	4-0	0	21	.223	.255	.298	56	-6	0-0	.928	0	101	56	3b33/S	79	-0.6
Total	6	416	1205	111	282	61	3	24	124	43-9	8	211	.234	.263	.349	74	-47	0-3	.948	11	96	104	3b389,S7/2P1	333	-3.9
HAMILTON, TOM	Thomas Ball "Ham"; B9.29.1925 Altoona KS; D11.29.1973 Tyler TX; BL/TR/6´4˝/213; d9.4; Col Texas																								
1952	Phi A	9	10	1	2	1	0	0	1	1	0	1	.200	.273	.300	56	-1	0-0	1.000	-0	0	79	1b5	0	-0.1
1953	Phi A	58	56	8	11	2	0	0	5	7	0	11	.196	.286	.232	40	-5	0-0	1.000	0	105	0	1b7,O2R	0	-0.5
Total	2	67	66	9	13	3	0	0	6	8	0	12	.197	.284	.242	42	-6	0-0	1.000	-0	72	25	1b12,O2R	0	-0.6
HAMILTON, BILLY	William Robert "Sliding Billy"; B2.16.1866 Newark NJ; D12.16.1940 Worcester MA; BL/TR/5´6˝/165; d7.31; HF1961																								
1888	KC AA	35	129	21	34	4	4	0	11	4	4	—	.264	.307	.357	106	0	19	.961	-0	82	0	O35(3/0/32)	—	0.0
1889	KC AA	137	534	144	161	17	12	3	77	87	14	41	.301	.413	.395	123	19	**111**	.857	-8	75	93	O137(7/0/130)	—	0.8
1890	Phi N	123	496	133	161	13	9	2	49	83	9	37	.325	.430	.399	139	29	**102**	.882	3	107	88	O123L	—	2.6
1891	Phi N	133	527	**141**	**179**	23	7	2	60	**102**	7	28	**.340**	**.453**	.421	151	42	**111**	.907	7	81	191	O133L	—	**4.0**
1892	Phi N	139	554	132	183	21	7	3	53	81	8	29	.330	.423	.410	152	40	57	.919	12	113	151	O139(138/1/0)	—	3.7
1893	Phi N	82	355	110	135	22	7	5	44	63	13	7	.380	**.490**	.524	**169**	41	43	.937	1	55	196	O82(19/63/0)	—	3.0
1894	Phi N	**132**	558	**198**	225	25	15	4	90	**128**	10	19	.403	**.522**	.523	156	**66**	**100**	.962	2	67	74	O132C	—	**4.5**
1895	Phi N	123	517	**166**	201	22	6	7	74	**96**	7	30	.389	.490	.495	154	50	**97**	.913	-4	60	114	O123(3/120/0)	—	3.1
1896	Bos N	131	524	153	192	24	10	3	55	**110**	2	29	.366	**.478**	.468	141	39	83	.934	-12	45	47	O131(6/125/0)	—	1.6
1897	†Bos N	127	507	**152**	174	17	5	3	61	**105**	6	—	.343	.461	.414	124	26	66	.962	-6	55	0	O126C	—	1.0
1898	Bos N	110	417	110	154	16	5	3	50	87	2	—	.369	**.480**	.453	**159**	39	54	.904	-17	53	64	O110C	—	1.4
1899	Bos N	84	297	63	92	7	1	1	33	72	1	—	.310	.446	.350	109	9	19	.952	-4	89	68	O81(2/78/1)	—	0.0
1900	Bos N	136	520	103	173	20	5	1	47	107	3	—	.333	.449	.396	119	21	32	.947	-0	76	130	O136C	—	1.1
1901	Bos N	102	348	71	100	11	2	3	38	64	4	—	.287	.404	.356	111	9	20	.945	-0	56	138	O99(0/98/1)	—	0.4
Total	14	1594	6283	1697	2164	242	95	40	742	1189	90	220	.344	.455	.432	139	430	914	.926	-28	73	102	O1587(434/989/164)	—	27.2
HAMLIN, KEN	Kenneth Lee; B5.18.1935 Detroit MI; BR/TR/5´10˝/(168–170); d6.17; Col Western Michigan																								
1957	Pit N	2	1	0	0	0	0	0	0	0-0	0	0	.000	.000	.000	-99	0	0-0	1.000	0	0	0	/S	0	0.0
1959	Pit N	3	8	1	1	0	0	0	0	2-0	0	1	.125	.300	.125	19	-1	0-0	1.000	0	100	173	S3	0	-0.1
1960	KC A	140	428	51	96	10	2	2	24	44-1	1	48	.224	.297	.271	55	-27	1-1	.955	-40	85	70	S139	0	-5.8
1961	LA A	42	91	4	19	3	0	1	5	11-2	1	9	.209	.298	.275	49	-6	0-1	.963	8	109	129	S39	0	0.4
1962	Was A	98	292	29	74	12	0	3	22	22-0	0	22	.253	.303	.325	70	-12	7-7	.963	-10	94	100	S87,2b2	0	-1.7
1965	Was A	117	362	45	99	21	1	4	22	33-1	1	45	.273	.333	.370	102	2	8-2	.976	-21	86	74	2b77,S47/3	0	-1.1
1966	Was A	66	158	13	34	7	1	1	16	13-1	0	21	.215	.267	.291	63	-7	1-0	.963	4	112	115	2b50/3	0	0.0
Total	7	468	1340	143	323	53	4	11	89	125-5	3	146	.241	.304	.311	71	-51	17-11	.959	-58	90	87	S316,2b129,3b2	0	-8.3
HAMMOCK, ROB	Robert Wade; B3.13.1977 Macon GA; BR/TR/5´11˝/(180–185); [AriN98 23/703]; d4.11; Col Georgia																								
2003	Ari N	65	195	30	55	10	2	8	28	17-3	2	44	.282	.343	.477	103	1	3-2	.993	15	83	105	C36,O17(5/0/12),3b16/D	0	1.7
2004	Ari N	62	195	22	47	16	2	4	18	13-6	0	39	.241	.287	.405	72	-8	3-3	.997	1	87	134	C46,O12L/3	73	-0.5
2006	Ari N	1	2	1	1	1	0	0	0	0-0	0	0	.500	.500	1.000	256	1	0-0	1.000	0	0	0	/1	0	0.0
Total	3	128	392	53	103	27	4	12	46	30-9	2	83	.263	.316	.444	88	-6	6-5	.995	16	85	122	C82,O29(17/0/12),3b17/1D	73	1.2
HAMMOND, STEVE	Steven Benjamin; B5.9.1957 Atlanta GA; BL/TR/6´2˝/190; d6.28; b–Chris; Col Florida St.																								
1982	KC A	46	126	14	29	5	1	1	11	4-0	0	18	.230	.252	.310	53	-8	0-1	1.000	4	121	130	O37R/D	0	-0.7
HAMMOND, JACK	Walter Charles "Wobby"; B2.26.1891 Amsterdam NY; D3.4.1942 Kenosha WI; BR/TR/5´11˝/170; d4.15; Col Colgate																								
1915	Cle A	35	84	9	18	2	1	0	4	1	0	19	.214	.224	.262	44	-6	0-1	.957	-5	87	80	2b19	—	-1.2
1922	Cle A	1	4	1	1	0	0	0	0	0	0	0	.250	.250	.250	30	0	0-0	.333	-1	41	0	/2	—	-0.2
	Pit N	9	11	3	3	0	0	0	0	1	0	0	.273	.333	.273	57	-1	0-0	1.000	0	83	156	2b4	—	0.0
Total	2	45	99	13	22	2	1	0	4	2	0	19	.222	.238	.263	45	-7	0-1	.943	-6	85	86	2b24	—	-1.4
HAMMONDS, JEFFREY	Jeffrey Bryan; B3.5.1971 Plainfield NJ; BR/TR/6´0˝/(195–220); [BalA92 1/4]; d6.25; Col Stanford																								
1993	Bal A	33	105	10	32	8	0	3	19	2-1	0	16	.305	.312	.467	103	0	4-0	.961	1	104	138	O23(14/0/10),D8	30	0.1
1994	Bal A	68	250	45	74	18	2	8	31	17-1	2	39	.296	.339	.480	104	1	5-0	.962	2	110	103	O66(9/0/58)	43	0.1
1995	Bal A	57	178	18	43	9	1	4	23	9-0	1	30	.242	.279	.371	67	-9	4-2	.989	0	109	36	O46R,D5	47	-1.1
1996	Bal A	71	248	38	56	10	1	9	27	23-1	4	53	.226	.301	.383	72	-11	3-3	.980	-0	105	63	O70(64/1/11)/D	37	-1.3
1997	†Bal A	118	397	71	105	19	3	21	55	32-1	3	73	.264	.323	.486	111	4	15-1	.980	1	107	66	O114(31/40/54),D4	0	0.6
1998	Bal A	63	171	36	46	12	1	6	28	26-1	3	38	.269	.369	.456	117	5	7-2	.980	-2	95	67	O53(7/24/29),D7	38	0.3
	Cin N	26	86	14	26	4	1	0	11	13-0	0	18	.302	.390	.372	102	1	1-1	.985	3	117	207	O25C	0	0.4
1999	Cin N	123	262	43	73	13	0	17	41	27-0	1	64	.279	.347	.523	113	4	3-6	1.000	5	111	118	O106(46/21/53)	0	0.6
2000	Col N★	122	454	94	152	24	2	20	106	44-4	5	83	.335	.395	.529	107	6	14-7	.991	-4	89	109	O118(32/9/85)	17	-0.2
2001	Mil N	49	174	20	43	11	1	6	21	14-1	4	42	.247	.314	.425	92	-2	5-3	.982	-3	95	78	O46C	123	-0.5
2002	Mil N	128	448	47	115	26	5	9	41	52-0	2	86	.257	.332	.397	93	-4	4-5	.992	-7	94	42	O125(2/78/55)	0	-1.4
2003	Mil N	10	38	2	6	2	0	1	3	3-0	0	7	.158	.220	.289	31	-4	0-0	1.000	-1	91	0	O10R	50	-0.5
	†SF N	36	94	20	26	10	0	3	10	13-0	1	21	.277	.370	.479	118	3	1-0	1.000	-1	95	70	O30(17/14/4)	0	0.2
	Year	46	132	22	32	12	0	4	13	16-0	1	28	.242	.329	.424	94	-1	1-0	1.000	-1	94	50	O40(17/14/14)	0	-0.3
2004	SF N	40	95	14	20	5	0	3	6	15-0	3	22	.211	.336	.358	77	-3	1-0	1.000	2	106	207	O28(7/1/20)	6	-0.2
2005	Was N	13	32	3	7	1	0	0	1	2-1	1	4	.219	.286	.250	44	-3	0-0	1.000	0	117	0	O11(10/0/1)/D	17	-0.3
Total	13	957	3032	475	824	172	17	110	423	292-11	30	596	.272	.338	.449	98	-12	67-30	.985	-3	101	84	O871(239/259/436),D26	408	-3.2
HAMNER, GRANNY	Granville Wilbur; B4.26.1927 Richmond VA; D9.12.1993 Philadelphia PA; BR/TR/5´10˝/(160–185); d9.14; Mil 1945; b–Garvin; ▲																								
1944	Phi N	21	77	6	19	1	0	0	5	3	0	7	.247	.275	.260	53	-5	0	.933	5	132	131	S21	0	0.2
1945	Phi N	14	41	3	7	2	0	0	6	1	0	3	.171	.190	.220	14	-5	0	.861	0	103	97	S13	0	-0.4
1946	Phi N	2	7	0	1	0	0	0	0	0	0	3	.143	.143	.143	-19	-1	0	.857	-1	101	98	S2	0	-0.2
1947	Phi N	2	7	1	2	0	0	0	0	1	0	0	.286	.375	.286	81	0	0	1.000	0	94	80	S2	0	0.0
1948	Phi N	129	446	42	116	21	5	3	48	22	2	39	.260	.298	.350	76	-16	2	.967	-10	98	92	2b87,S37,3b3	0	-2.0
1949	Phi N	**154**	662	83	174	32	5	6	53	25	0	47	.263	.290	.353	74	-27	6	.961	-3	104	**111**	S154	0	-2.0
1950	†Phi N	**157**	637	78	172	27	5	11	82	39	2	35	.270	.314	.380	83	-18	2	.944	-4	103	101	S157	0	-1.2
1951	Phi N	150	589	61	150	23	7	9	72	29	0	32	.255	.290	.363	76	-23	10-5	.958	-2	102	99	S150	0	-1.5
1952	Phi N★	151	596	74	164	30	5	17	87	27	0	51	.275	.307	.428	103	-1	7-3	.951	-2	106	113	S151	0	0.8
1953	Phi N★	154	609	90	168	30	8	21	92	32	1	28	.276	.313	.455	98	-5	2-1	.970	-6	108	108	2b93,S71	0	0.1
1954	Phi N★	152	596	83	178	39	11	13	89	53	0	44	.299	.351	.466	112	10	1-2	.978	-20	94	95	2b152/S	0	0.1
1955	Phi N	104	405	57	104	12	4	5	43	41-1	1	30	.257	.323	.343	79	-12	0-1	.960	-27	87	82	2b82,S32	0	-3.2
1956	Phi N	122	401	42	90	24	3	4	42	30-5	0	42	.224	.276	.329	64	-21	2-0	.937	-13	95	102	S110,2b11,P3	0	-2.5
1957	Phi N	133	502	59	114	19	5	10	62	34-3	0	42	.227	.274	.345	68	-24	3-1	.963	-27	84	75	2b125,S5/P	0	-4.4
1958	Phi N	35	133	18	40	7	3	2	18	8-0	0	16	.301	.340	.444	107	1	0-0	.984	-3	95	153	3b22,2b11,S3	118	-0.1
1959	Phi N	21	64	10	19	4	0	2	6	5-1	0	5	.297	.348	.453	109	1	0-1	.947	-3	101	50	S15/3	0	-0.1
	Cle A	27	67	4	11	1	1	1	3	1-0	0	8	.164	.174	.254	17	-8	0-0	.960	0	72	55	S10,2b7,3b5	33	-0.7

YEAR	TM LG	G	AB	R	H	2B	3B	HR	RBI	BB-IB	HP	SO	AVG	OBP	SLG	AOPS	ABR	SB-CS	FA	FR	RNG	THR	GAMES AT POSITION	DL	BFW
1962	KC A	3	0	0	0	0	0	0	0	0-0	0	0	ø	ø	ø	ø	0	0-0	1.000	0	157	0	P3	0	0.0
Total	17	1531	5839	711	1529	272	62	104	708	351-10	6	432	.262	.303	.383	84	-154	35-14	.946	-115	101	103	S934,2b568,3b31,P7	151	-17.1

HAMNER, GARVIN Wesley Garvin; B3.18.1924 Richmond VA; D12.15.2003 Richmond VA; BR/TR/5´11˝/172; d4.17; b-Granny

YEAR	TM LG	G	AB	R	H	2B	3B	HR	RBI	BB-IB	HP	SO	AVG	OBP	SLG	AOPS	ABR	SB-CS	FA	FR	RNG	THR	GAMES AT POSITION	DL	BFW
1945	Phi N	32	101	12	20	3	0	0	5	7	0	9	.198	.250	.228	34	-9	2	.962	-4	103	75	2b21,S9/3	0	-1.1

HAMPTON, IKE Isaac Bernard; B8.22.1951 Camden SC; BB/TR (BR 1978–79)/6´1˝/(165–185); d9.12

YEAR	TM LG	G	AB	R	H	2B	3B	HR	RBI	BB-IB	HP	SO	AVG	OBP	SLG	AOPS	ABR	SB-CS	FA	FR	RNG	THR	GAMES AT POSITION	DL	BFW
1974	NY N	4	4	0	0	0	0	0	1	0-0	0	1	.000	.000	.000	-99	-1	0-0	1.000	-0	30	0	/C	0	-0.1
1975	Cal A	31	66	8	10	3	0	0	4	7-0	1	19	.152	.243	.197	27	-6	0-0	.947	-9	100	125	C28,S2/3	0	-1.5
1976	Cal A	3	2	0	0	0	0	0	0	0-0	0	0	.000	.000	.000	-99	-1	0-0	1.000	0	0	0	C2/S	0	0.0
1977	Cal A	52	44	5	13	1	0	3	9	2-0	1	10	.295	.340	.523	136	2	0-0	.968	-4	85	98	C47,D2	0	-0.1
1978	Cal A	19	14	2	3	0	1	1	4	2-0	0	7	.214	.313	.571	148	1	1-0	.905	-1	52	81	C13/1D	0	0.0
1979	Cal A	4	5	0	2	0	0	0	0	0-0	0	1	.400	.400	.400	120	0	0-0	1.000	0	211	-0	1b2	0	0.0
Total	6	113	135	15	28	4	1	4	18	11-0	2	38	.207	.275	.341	75	-5	1-0	.953	-14	89	110	C91,D6,1b3,S3/3	0	-1.7

HAMRIC, BERT Odbert Herman; B3.1.1928 Clarksburg WV; D8.8.1984 Springboro OH; BL/TR/6´0˝/(165–180); d4.24

YEAR	TM LG	G	AB	R	H	2B	3B	HR	RBI	BB-IB	HP	SO	AVG	OBP	SLG	AOPS	ABR	SB-CS	FA	FR	RNG	THR	GAMES AT POSITION	DL	BFW
1955	Bro N	2	1	0	0	0	0	0	0	0-0	0	1	.000	.000	.000	-97	0	0-0	ø	0	—	—	/H	0	0.0
1958	Bal A	8	8	0	1	0	0	0	0	0-0	0	6	.125	.125	.125	-33	-1	0-0	ø	0	—	—	/H	0	-0.2
Total	2	10	9	0	1	0	0	0	0	0-0	0	7	.111	.111	.111	-41	-1	0-0	ø	0	—	—	0	—	-0.2

HAMRICK, RAY Raymond Bernard; B8.1.1921 Nashville TN; BR/TR/5´11.5˝/160; d8.14; Mil 1944–46

YEAR	TM LG	G	AB	R	H	2B	3B	HR	RBI	BB-IB	HP	SO	AVG	OBP	SLG	AOPS	ABR	SB-CS	FA	FR	RNG	THR	GAMES AT POSITION	DL	BFW
1943	Phi N	44	160	12	32	3	1	0	9	8	0	28	.200	.238	.231	37	-14	0	.960	-8	96	53	2b31,S12	0	-2.0
1944	Phi N	74	292	22	60	10	1	1	23	23	2	34	.205	.268	.257	50	-20	1	.948	13	114	122	S74	0	0.0
Total	2	118	452	34	92	13	2	1	32	31	2	62	.204	.258	.248	46	-34	1	.946	6	111	111	S86,2b31	0	-2.0

HANCKEN, BUDDY Morris Medlock; B8.30.1914 Birmingham AL; BR/TR/6´1˝/175; d5.14; C5; Col Birmingham–Southern

YEAR	TM LG	G	AB	R	H	2B	3B	HR	RBI	BB-IB	HP	SO	AVG	OBP	SLG	AOPS	ABR	SB-CS	FA	FR	RNG	THR	GAMES AT POSITION	DL	BFW
1940	Phi A	1	0	0	0	0	0	0	0	0	0	0	ø	ø	ø	ø	0	0-0	1.000	-0	*0*	*0*	/C	—	0.0

HANCOCK, FRED Fred James; B3.28.1920 Allenport PA; D3.12.1986 Clearwater FL; BR/TR/5´8˝/170; d4.26

YEAR	TM LG	G	AB	R	H	2B	3B	HR	RBI	BB-IB	HP	SO	AVG	OBP	SLG	AOPS	ABR	SB-CS	FA	FR	RNG	THR	GAMES AT POSITION	DL	BFW
1949	Chi A	39	52	7	7	2	1	0	9	8	1	9	.135	.262	.212	27	-6	0-1	.978	-2	83	140	S27,3b3/rf	0	-0.7

HANCOCK, GARRY Ronald Garry; B1.23.1954 Tampa FL; BL/TL/6´0˝/(175–190); [CleA76*S1/17]; d7.16; Col South Carolina

YEAR	TM LG	G	AB	R	H	2B	3B	HR	RBI	BB-IB	HP	SO	AVG	OBP	SLG	AOPS	ABR	SB-CS	FA	FR	RNG	THR	GAMES AT POSITION	DL	BFW
1978	Bos A	38	80	10	18	3	0	0	4	1-0	0	12	.225	.232	.262	36	-7	0-0	1.000	2	105	355	O19(4/5/10),D13	0	-0.5
1980	Bos A	46	115	9	33	6	0	4	19	3-0	0	11	.287	.300	.443	97	-1	0-3	.963	-1	81	185	O27(6/20/1),D12	0	-0.4
1981	Bos A	26	45	4	7	3	0	0	3	2-1	0	4	.156	.191	.222	18	-5	0-0	1.000	1	74	566	O8(0/5/3),D4	0	-0.4
1982	Bos A	11	14	3	0	0	0	0	0	1-0	0	1	.000	.067	.000	-75	-3	0-0	1.000	-1	58	0	O7R	0	-0.4
1983	Oak A	101	256	29	70	7	3	8	30	5-4	1	13	.273	.289	.418	97	-3	2-0	.981	-1	107	115	O67(26/1/40),1b27,D9	0	-0.6
1984	Oak A	51	60	2	13	2	0	0	8	0-0	0	1	.217	.217	.250	31	-6	0-0	1.000	0	131	0	O18(9/2/9),1b4/PD	31	-0.6
Total	6	273	570	57	141	21	3	12	64	12-5	1	42	.247	.262	.358	70	-25	2-3	.982	1	98	177	O146(45/33/70),D43,1b31/P	31	-2.9

HANDIBOE, MIKE Aloysius James "Coalyard Mike"; B7.21.1887 Washington DC; D1.31.1953 Savannah GA; BL/TL/5´10˝/155; d9.8

YEAR	TM LG	G	AB	R	H	2B	3B	HR	RBI	BB-IB	HP	SO	AVG	OBP	SLG	AOPS	ABR	SB-CS	FA	FR	RNG	THR	GAMES AT POSITION	DL	BFW
1911	NY A	5	15	0	1	0	0	0	0	2	0	—	.067	.176	.067	-29	-3	0	1.000	-0	108	0	O4(2/0/2)	—	-0.3

HANDLEY, GENE Eugene Louis; B11.25.1914 Kennett MO; BR/TR/5´10.5˝/165; d4.16; b-Lee; Col Bradley

YEAR	TM LG	G	AB	R	H	2B	3B	HR	RBI	BB-IB	HP	SO	AVG	OBP	SLG	AOPS	ABR	SB-CS	FA	FR	RNG	THR	GAMES AT POSITION	DL	BFW
1946	Phi A	89	251	31	63	8	5	0	21	22	0	25	.251	.311	.323	78	-8	8-3	.947	-16	80	71	2b68,3b4/S	0	-2.1
1947	Phi A	36	90	10	23	2	1	0	8	10	0	2	.256	.330	.300	74	-3	1-0	.973	-6	92	98	2b17,3b10/S	0	-0.8
Total	2	125	341	41	86	10	6	0	29	32	0	27	.252	.316	.317	77	-11	9-3	.952	-21	82	76	2b85,3b14,S2	0	-2.9

HANDLEY, LEE Lee Elmer "Jeep"; B7.31.1913 Clarion IA; D4.8.1970 Pittsburgh PA; BR/TR/5´7˝/160; d4.15; b-Gene; Col Bradley

YEAR	TM LG	G	AB	R	H	2B	3B	HR	RBI	BB-IB	HP	SO	AVG	OBP	SLG	AOPS	ABR	SB-CS	FA	FR	RNG	THR	GAMES AT POSITION	DL	BFW
1936	Cin N	24	78	10	24	1	0	2	8	7	0	16	.308	.365	.397	112	1	3	.926	-1	95	67	2b16,3b7	—	0.2
1937	Pit N	127	480	59	120	21	12	3	37	37	1	40	.250	.305	.363	81	-14	5	.950	-14	91	91	2b126/3	—	-2.0
1938	Pit N	139	570	91	153	25	8	6	51	53	1	31	.268	.332	.372	93	-6	7	.948	11	**115**	115	3b136	—	1.0
1939	Pit N	101	376	43	107	14	5	1	42	32	0	20	.285	.341	.356	89	-6	**17**	.936	-3	102	82	3b100	—	-0.6
1940	Pit N	98	302	50	85	7	4	1	19	27	0	16	.281	.340	.341	89	-4	7	.925	0	101	99	3b80,2b2	—	-0.1
1941	Pit N	124	459	59	132	18	4	0	33	35	0	22	.288	.338	.344	93	-5	16	.947	1	105	92	3b114	0	0.1
1944	Pit N	40	86	7	19	2	0	0	5	3	0	5	.221	.247	.244	37	-7	1	.947	1	92	101	2b19,3b11,S3	0	-0.6
1945	Pit N	98	312	39	93	16	2	1	32	20	0	16	.298	.340	.372	94	-3	7	.947	11	116	95	3b79	0	0.9
1946	Pit N	116	416	43	99	8	7	1	28	29	1	20	.238	.289	.298	65	-21	4	.958	12	122	82	3b102,2b3	0	-0.9
1947	Phi N	101	277	17	70	10	3	0	42	24	0	18	.253	.312	.310	68	-13	1	.975	0	101	62	3b83,2b3/S	0	-1.3
Total	10	968	3356	418	902	122	45	15	297	267	3	204	.269	.323	.345	84	-78	68	.949	18	110	92	3b713,2b169,S4	0	-3.3

HANEBRINK, HARRY Harry Aloysius; B11.12.1927 St.Louis MO; D9.9.1996 Bridgeton MO; BL/TR/6´0˝/(165–185); d5.3

YEAR	TM LG	G	AB	R	H	2B	3B	HR	RBI	BB-IB	HP	SO	AVG	OBP	SLG	AOPS	ABR	SB-CS	FA	FR	RNG	THR	GAMES AT POSITION	DL	BFW
1953	Mil N	51	80	8	19	1	1	1	8	6	0	8	.237	.291	.313	61	-5	1-0	.979	2	106	149	2b21/3	0	-0.2
1957	Mil N	6	7	0	2	0	0	0	0	1-0	0	2	.286	.375	.286	87	0	0-0	1.000	0	164	0	3b2	0	0.0
1958	†Mil N	63	133	14	25	3	0	4	10	13-2	2	9	.188	.270	.301	56	-9	0-1	.982	-0	94	135	O33(24/0/9),3b7	0	-1.1
1959	Phi N	57	97	10	25	3	1	1	7	2-0	0	12	.258	.273	.340	61	-6	0-0	.889	-3	78	167	2b15,3b9/rf	0	-0.8
Total	4	177	317	32	71	7	2	6	25	22-2	2	31	.224	.279	.315	60	-20	1-1	.959	-1	99	153	2b36,O34(24/0/10),3b19	0	-2.1

HANEY, FRED Fred Girard "Pudge"; B4.25.1898 Albuquerque NM; D11.9.1977 Beverly Hills CA; BR/TR/5´6˝/170; d4.18; M10/C1

YEAR	TM LG	G	AB	R	H	2B	3B	HR	RBI	BB-IB	HP	SO	AVG	OBP	SLG	AOPS	ABR	SB-CS	FA	FR	RNG	THR	GAMES AT POSITION	DL	BFW
1922	Det A	81	213	41	75	7	4	0	25	32	1	14	.352	.439	.423	129	11	3-8	.937	3	114	130	3b53,1b11,S2	—	1.3
1923	Det A	142	503	85	142	13	4	4	67	45	5	23	.282	.347	.348	85	-11	13-5	.955	-2	94	74	2b69,3b55,S16	—	-0.5
1924	Det A	86	256	54	79	11	1	1	30	39	0	13	.309	.400	.371	101	2	7-4	.933	1	117	90	3b59,S4,2b3	—	0.8
1925	Det A	114	398	84	111	15	3	0	40	66	2	29	.279	.384	.332	84	-6	11-1	.953	-1	99	107	3b106	—	0.1
1926	Bos A	138	462	47	102	15	7	0	52	74	1	28	.221	.330	.284	63	-24	13-6	.957	8	**110**	113	3b137	—	-0.7
1927	Bos A	47	116	23	32	4	1	3	12	25	0	14	.276	.404	.405	113	3	4-1	.936	-3	81	66	3b34/cf	—	0.3
	Chi N	4	3	0	0	0	0	0	0	0	0	0	.000	.000	.000	-99	-1	0	ø	0	—	—	/H	—	-0.1
1929	StL N	10	26	4	3	1	1	0	2	1	1	2	.115	.179	.231	1	-4	0	.958	1	110	191	3b6	—	-0.3
Total	7	622	1977	338	544	66	21	8	228	282	10	123	.275	.368	.342	87	-30	51-25	.949	7	106	110	3b450,2b72,S22,1b11/cf	—	0.9

HANEY, TODD Todd Michael; B7.30.1965 Waco TX; BR/TR/5´9˝/165; [SeaA87 38/958]; d9.9; Col Texas

YEAR	TM LG	G	AB	R	H	2B	3B	HR	RBI	BB-IB	HP	SO	AVG	OBP	SLG	AOPS	ABR	SB-CS	FA	FR	RNG	THR	GAMES AT POSITION	DL	BFW
1992	Mon N	7	10	0	3	1	0	0	1	0-0	0	0	.300	.300	.400	97	0	0-0	1.000	-1	93	80	2b5	0	-0.1
1994	Chi N	17	37	6	6	0	0	1	2	3-0	1	3	.162	.238	.243	28	-4	2-1	.979	-0	95	139	2b11,3b3	0	-0.4
1995	Chi N	25	73	11	30	8	0	2	6	7-0	0	11	.411	.463	.603	178	9	0-0	.978	4	125	124	2b17,3b4	0	1.3
1996	Chi N	49	82	11	11	1	0	0	3	7-0	0	15	.134	.200	.146	-6	-13	1-0	.978	4	129	124	2b23,3b4,S3	0	-0.7
1998	NY N	3	3	0	0	0	0	0	0	1-0	0	0	.000	.250	.000	-28	-1	0-0	ø	-1	0	0	/2lf	0	-0.1
Total	5	101	205	28	50	10	0	3	12	18-0	1	29	.244	.305	.337	69	-9	3-1	.979	7	118	124	2b57,3b11,S3/lf	0	-0.0

HANEY, LARRY Wallace Larry; B11.19.1942 Charlottesville VA; BR/TR/6´2˝/(165–195); d7.27; C14; s-Chris

YEAR	TM LG	G	AB	R	H	2B	3B	HR	RBI	BB-IB	HP	SO	AVG	OBP	SLG	AOPS	ABR	SB-CS	FA	FR	RNG	THR	GAMES AT POSITION	DL	BFW
1966	Bal A	20	56	3	9	1	0	1	3	1-0	1	15	.161	.190	.232	21	-6	0-0	.985	1	147	92	C20	0	-0.4
1967	Bal A	58	164	13	44	11	0	3	20	6-0	0	28	.268	.294	.390	101	0	1-0	.991	-1	103	139	C57	0	0.2
1968	Bal A	38	89	5	21	3	1	1	5	0-0	0	19	.236	.236	.326	69	-4	0-0	.994	1	89	186	C32	0	-0.3
1969	Sea A	22	59	3	15	3	0	2	7	6-0	0	12	.254	.323	.407	104	0	1-1	.956	-3	50	89	C20	0	-0.2
	Oak A	53	86	8	13	4	0	2	12	7-1	1	19	.151	.221	.267	38	-7	0-0	.994	-5	102	114	C53	0	-1.1
	Year	75	145	11	28	7	0	4	19	13-1	1	31	.193	.262	.324	66	-7	1-1	.979	-8	84	105	C73	0	-1.3
1970	Oak A	2	2	2	0	0	0	0	0	2-0	0	1	.000	.500	.000	51	0	0-0	1.000	-0	37	0	/C	0	0.0
1972	Oak A	5	4	0	0	0	0	0	0	0-0	0	1	.000	.000	.000	-99	-1	0-0	.800	-1	0	0	C4/2	0	-0.2
1973	Oak A	2	2	0	1	0	0	0	0	0-0	0	0	.500	.500	.500	191	0	0-0	1.000	0	0	0	C2	0	0.0
	StL N	2	1	0	0	0	0	0	0	0-0	0	1	.000	.000	.000	-99	0	0-0	1.000	-0	0	0	C2	0	0.0
1974	†Oak A	76	121	12	20	4	0	2	3	3-0	0	18	.165	.185	.248	25	-12	1-0	.992	2	152	94	C73,3b3,1b2	0	-0.9
1975	Oak A	47	26	3	5	0	0	1	2	1-0	0	4	.192	.222	.308	49	-2	0-0	1.000	0	115	59	C43,3b4	0	-0.1
1976	Oak A	88	177	12	40	2	0	0	10	13-0	1	26	.226	.280	.237	55	-10	0-1	.974	1	82	106	C87	0	-0.7
1977	Mil A	63	127	7	29	2	0	0	10	5-0	0	30	.228	.254	.244	38	-11	0-0	.985	5	118	84	C63	0	-0.4
1978	Mil A	4	5	0	1	0	0	0	1	0-0	0	1	.200	.200	.200	13	-1	0-0	1.000	-0	0	0	C4	0	-0.1
Total	12	480	919	68	198	30	1	12	73	44-1	3	175	.215	.252	.289	57	-54	3-2	.985	-1	105	108	C461,3b7,1b2/2	0	-4.2

YEAR	TM LG	G	AB	R	H	2B	3B	HR	RBI	BB-IB	HP	SO	AVG	OBP	SLG	AOPS	ABR	SB-CS	FA	FR	RNG	THR	GAMES AT POSITION	DL	BFW
HANFORD, CHARLIE	Charles Joseph; B6.3.1882 Tunstall, England; D7.19.1963 Trenton NJ; BR/TR/5´6.5˝/145; d4.13																								
1914	Buf F	**155**	597	83	174	28	13	12	90	32	4	81	.291	.332	.442	107	-6	37	.973	7	104	114	O155C	—	-1.0
1915	Chi F	77	179	27	43	4	5	0	22	12	2	28	.240	.295	.318	77	-9	10	.971	-2	105	41	O43(10/1/32)	—	-1.4
Total	2	232	776	110	217	32	18	12	112	44	6	109	.280	.323	.414	101	-15	47	.972	5	104	100	O198(10/156/32)	—	-2.4
HANKINS, JAY	Jay Nelson; B11.7.1935 St.Louis Co. MO; BL/TR/5´7˝/170; d4.15; Col Missouri																								
1961	KC A	76	173	23	32	0	3	3	6	8-0	1	17	.185	.225	.272	32	-18	2-0	.970	-3	95	32	O65(23/31/14)	0	-2.3
1963	KC A	10	34	2	6	0	1	1	4	0-0	0	3	.176	.176	.324	35	-3	0-1	.952	0	102	199	O9C	0	-0.4
Total	2	86	207	25	38	0	4	4	10	8-0	1	20	.184	.218	.280	32	-21	2-1	.967	-3	96	56	O74(23/40/14)	0	-2.7
HANKINSON, FRANK	Frank Edward; B4.29.1856 New York NY; D4.5.1911 Palisades Park NJ; BR/TR/5´11˝/168; d5.1; OF(26/8/1); ▲																								
1878	Chi N	58	240	38	64	8	3	1	27	5	—	36	.267	.282	.338	96	-2	—	.875	8	110	**135**	3b57/P	—	0.7
1879	Chi N	44	171	14	31	4	0	0	8	2	—	14	.181	.191	.205	29	-13	—	.933	7	139	105	P26,O14(10/4/0),3b5	—	-0.1
1880	Cle N	69	263	32	55	7	4	1	19	1	—	23	.209	.212	.278	66	-9	—	.844	-10	77	127	3b56,O12(10/2/0),P4	—	-1.8
1881	Tro N	**85**	321	34	62	15	0	1	19	10	—	41	.193	.218	.249	44	-20	—	.907	5	99	**161**	3b84/S	—	-1.1
1883	NY N	94	337	40	74	13	6	2	30	19	—	38	.220	.261	.312	74	-10	—	.870	-2	93	75	3b93/rf	—	-0.9
1884	NY N	105	389	44	90	16	7	2	43	23	—	59	.231	.274	.324	85	-7	—	.871	1	94	61	3b105/cf	—	-0.4
1885	NY AA	94	362	43	81	12	2	2	44	12	1	—	.224	.251	.285	72	-11	—	**.906**	21	**123**	67	3b94/P	—	1.0
1886	NY AA	136	522	66	126	14	5	2	63	49	0	—	.241	.306	.299	98	2	10	.873	27	**118**	**139**	3b136	—	2.7
1887	NY AA	127	512	79	137	29	11	1	71	38	0	—	.268	.318	.373	97	-2	19	.864	9	**109**	120	3b127	—	0.7
1888	KC AA	37	155	20	27	4	1	1	20	11	0	—	.174	.229	.232	45	-10	2	.947	-2	105	54	2b13,S9,O7(6/1/0),3b7,1b2	—	-1.0
Total	10	849	3272	410	747	122	39	13	344	170	1	211	.228	.267	.301	77	-82	31	.875	63	105	109	3b764,O35L,P32,2b13,S10,1b2	—	-0.2
HANLON, NED	Edward Hugh; B8.22.1857 Montville CT; D4.14.1937 Baltimore MD; BL/TR/5´9.5˝/170; d5.1; M19; HF1996																								
1880	Cle N	73	280	30	69	10	3	0	32	11	—	30	.246	.275	.304	98	0	—	.804	-6	50	135	O69(67/2/0),S4	—	-1.0
1881	Det N	76	305	63	85	14	8	2	28	22	—	11	.279	.327	.397	122	7	—	.897	-6	77	134	O74(2/72/0),S2	—	-0.1
1882	Det N	82	347	68	80	18	6	5	38	26	—	25	.231	.284	.360	105	3	—	.887	10	100	**201**	O82C/2	—	0.9
1883	Det N	100	413	65	100	13	2	1	40	34	—	44	.242	.300	.291	84	-6	—	.884	-2	63	172	O90(2/88/0),2b11	—	-0.9
1884	Det N	**114**	450	86	119	18	6	5	39	40	—	52	.264	.324	.364	124	15	—	.874	12	132	123	O114C	—	2.1
1885	Det N	105	424	93	128	18	8	1	29	47	—	18	.302	.372	.389	146	23	—	.863	1	95	71	O105C	—	2.0
1886	Det N	**126**	494	105	116	6	6	4	60	57	—	39	.235	.314	.296	83	-9	50	.929	-7	72	118	O126C/2	—	-1.9
1887	†Det N	118	471	79	129	13	7	4	69	30	2	24	.274	.320	.357	84	-11	69	.904	1	86	110	O118(1/117/0)	—	-1.2
1888	Det N	109	459	64	122	6	8	5	39	15	4	32	.266	.295	.346	103	0	38	.919	-8	38	87	O109C	—	-1.2
1889	Pit N	116	461	81	110	14	10	2	37	58	2	25	.239	.326	.325	90	-4	53	.919	-3	82	52	O116C,M	—	-1.0
1890	Pit P	118	472	106	131	16	6	1	44	80	6	24	.278	.389	.343	105	10	65	.911	-4	70	98	O118C,M	—	0.2
1891	Pit N	119	455	87	121	12	8	0	60	48	4	30	.266	.341	.327	97	-1	54	.881	-1	137	32	O119(39/80/0)/SM	—	-0.5
1892	Bal N	11	43	3	7	1	1	0	2	3	0	3	.163	.217	.233	35	-4	0	.786	-1	106	0	O11(8/2/1),M	—	-0.5
Total	13	1267	5074	930	1317	159	79	30	517	471	18	357	.260	.325	.340	102	23	329	.891	-13	85	106	O1251(119/1130/1),2b13,S7	—	-3.1
HANLON, BILL	William Joseph "Big Bill"; B6.24.1876 Los Angeles CA; D11.23.1905 Los Angeles CA; BR/6´0˝/175; d4.16; Col St. Marys (CA)																								
1903	Chi N	8	21	4	2	0	0	0	2	6	0	—	.095	.296	.095	14	-2	1	.980	-0	86	54	1b8	—	-0.2
HANNA, JOHN	John; B11.3.1863 Philadelphia PA; D11.7.1930 Philadelphia PA; d5.23																								
1884	Was AA	23	76	8	5	0	0	0	—	6	0	—	.066	.134	.066	-37	-11	—	.874	-0	—	—	C18,O6(1/1/4)	—	-0.9
	Ric AA	22	67	6	13	2	1	0	—	0	1	—	.194	.206	.254	50	-4	—	.924	3	—	—	C21/S	—	0.1
	Year	45	143	14	18	2	1	0	—	6	1	—	.126	.167	.154	6	-14	—	.900	2	—	—	C39,O6(1/1/4)/S	—	-0.8
HANNAH, TRUCK	James Harrison; B6.5.1889 Larimore ND; D4.27.1982 Fountain Valley CA; BR/TR/6´1˝/190; d4.15																								
1918	NY A	90	250	24	55	6	0	2	21	51	4	25	.220	.361	.268	88	0	5	.974	4	*121*	*99*	C88	—	1.2
1919	NY A	75	227	14	54	8	3	1	20	22	3	19	.238	.313	.313	76	-7	0	**.984**	-6	*103*	*82*	C73/1	—	-0.8
1920	NY A	79	259	24	64	11	1	2	25	24	1	35	.247	.313	.320	66	-13	2-0	.961	-2	*113*	*67*	C78	—	-0.7
Total	3	244	736	62	173	25	4	5	66	97	8	79	.235	.331	.300	76	-20	7-0	.973	-5	*113*	*83*	C239/1	—	-0.3
HANNAHAN, JACK	John Joseph; B3.4.1980 St.Paul MN; BL/TR/6´2˝/205; [DetA01 3/87]; d5.25; Col Minnesota																								
2006	Det A	3	9	0	0	0	0	0	0	1-0	0	1	.000	.100	.000	-72	-2	0-0	1.000	-0	0	0	/1D	0	-0.3
HANNIFIN, JACK	John Joseph; B2.25.1883 Holyoke MA; D10.27.1945 Northampton MA; BR/TR/5´11˝/167; d4.19																								
1906	Phi A	1	1	0	1	0	0	0	0	0	0	—	1.000	1.000	1.000	511	0	0	ø	0	—	—	/H	—	0.0
	NY N	10	30	4	6	0	1	0	3	2	0	—	.200	.250	.267	60	-2	1	.903	-0	98	107	S6,3b3/2	—	-0.2
1907	NY N	56	149	16	34	7	3	1	15	15	1	—	.228	.303	.336	97	-1	6	.996	-2	80	40	1b29,3b10,S9,O2(0/1/1)	—	-0.3
1908	NY N	1	2	0	0	0	0	0	0	0	0	—	.000	.000	.000	-95	0	0	ø	-0	0	0	/rf	—	-0.1
	Bos N	90	257	30	53	6	2	2	22	28	0	—	.206	.284	.268	78	-6	7	.930	5	113	342	3b35,2b22,S15,O7(2/1/2)	—	0.0
	Year	91	259	30	53	6	2	2	22	28	0	—	.205	.282	.266	77	-6	7	.930	5	113	342	3b35,2b22,S15,O8(2/1/3)	—	-0.1
Total	3	158	439	50	94	13	6	3	40	45	1	—	.214	.289	.292	84	-9	14	.937	2	106	302	3b48,S30,1b29,2b23,O10(2/2/4)	—	-0.6
HANNIVAN, PAT	Patrick James; B4.20.1866 Halifax NS, Can.; D11.5.1908 Springfield MA; BB/TL; d4.29																								
1897	Bro N	10	20	4	5	0	0	0	2	1	3	—	.250	.375	.250	71	-1	4	.867	0	302	774	O3(1/2/0),2b2	—	0.0
HANSEN, DAVE	David Andrew; B11.24.1968 Long Beach CA; BL/TR/6´0˝/(180–195); [LAN86 2/47]; d9.16																								
1990	LA N	5	7	0	1	0	0	0	1	0-0	0	3	.143	.143	.143	-22	-1	0-0	.500	-1	48	0	3b2	0	-0.2
1991	LA N	53	56	3	15	4	0	1	5	2-0	0	12	.268	.293	.393	93	-1	1-0	1.000	2	124	81	3b21/S	0	0.2
1992	LA N	132	341	30	73	11	0	6	22	34-3	1	49	.214	.286	.299	67	-15	0-2	**.968**	6	**107**	78	3b108	0	-1.0
1993	LA N	84	105	13	38	3	0	4	30	21-3	0	13	.362	.465	.505	170	12	0-1	.927	0	106	42	3b18	0	1.2
1994	LA N	40	44	3	15	3	0	0	5	5-0	0	5	.341	.408	.409	121	2	0-0	.857	-1	84	0	3b7	19	0.0
1995	†LA N	100	181	19	52	10	0	1	14	28-4	1	28	.287	.384	.359	105	3	0-0	.933	-4	85	91	3b58	0	-0.1
1996	†LA N	80	104	7	23	1	0	0	6	11-1	0	22	.221	.293	.231	44	-8	0-0	.962	0	103	67	3b19,1b8	0	-0.9
1997	Chi N	90	151	19	47	8	2	3	21	31-1	1	32	.311	.429	.450	127	8	1-2	.922	-5	78	94	3b51,1b4/2	0	0.2
1999	LA N	100	107	14	27	8	1	2	17	26-0	2	20	.252	.404	.402	111	4	0-0	.982	-2	100	129	1b20,3b13,O2R,D2	0	0.1
2000	LA N	102	121	18	35	6	2	8	26	26-0	0	32	.289	.415	.570	153	11	0-1	.980	0	136	121	1b16,3b16,O3L,D5	0	0.9
2001	LA N	92	140	13	33	10	0	2	20	32-5	0	29	.236	.371	.350	96	1	0-1	.984	4	105	86	1b25,3b21/D	26	0.3
2002	LA N	96	120	15	35	6	0	2	17	14-3	0	22	.292	.363	.392	105	1	1-0	1.000	-0	85	40	1b27,3b11,D4	0	0.0
2003	SD N	110	135	13	33	4	1	2	15	23-3	1	25	.244	.358	.333	90	-1	1-0	1.000	1	136	149	1b20,3b11/2D	0	-0.1
2004	Sea A	57	78	14	22	5	0	2	12	18-3	0	16	.282	.412	.423	126	4	0-0	1.000	2	167	31	1b7,3b6,D8	0	0.6
	SD N	29	28	1	4	0	0	0	0	3-0	0	5	.143	.226	.143	-2	-4	0-0	1.000	-2	75	135	1b7,3b2	0	-0.6
2005	Sea A	60	75	5	13	0	0	2	11	9-1	0	19	.173	.256	.253	41	-7	1-0	1.000	-1	101	113	1b9,3b7,D5	23	-0.7
Total	15	1230	1793	187	466	79	6	35	222	283-27	6	332	.260	.360	.369	99	9	5-7	.947	-0	99	78	3b371,1b143,D28,O5(3/0/2),2b2/S	68	-0.1
HANSEN, DOUG	Douglas William; B12.16.1928 Los Angeles CA; D9.16.1999 Orem UT; BR/TR/6´0˝/180; d9.4																								
1951	Cle A	3	0	2	0	0	0	0	0	0	0	0	ø	ø	ø	ø	0	0-0	ø	0	—	—	/R	0	0.0
HANSEN, JED	Jed Ramon; B8.19.1972 Tacoma WA; BR/TR/6´1˝/(180–195); [KCA94 2/50]; d7.29; Col Stanford																								
1997	KC A	34	94	11	29	6	1	1	14	13-0	1	29	.309	.394	.426	112	2	3-2	.993	-2	99	90	2b31	0	0.2
1998	KC A	4	3	0	0	0	0	0	0	0-0	0	3	.000	.000	.000	-96	-1	0-0	1.000	-1	0	0	2b2	0	-0.2
1999	KC A	49	79	16	16	1	0	3	5	10-0	0	32	.203	.289	.329	56	-6	0-1	.989	-1	79	130	2b21,S10,3b4,O2C/1D	0	-0.5
Total	3	87	176	27	45	7	1	4	19	23-0	1	64	.256	.342	.375	83	-5	3-3	.991	-3	90	105	2b54,S10,3b4,D3,O2C/1	0	-0.5
HANSEN, BOB	Robert Joseph; B5.26.1948 Boston MA; BL/TL/6´0˝/(195–200); [MilA69 21/499]; d5.10; Col Massachusetts																								
1974	Mil A	58	88	8	26	4	1	2	9	3-0	0	16	.295	.319	.432	115	1	2-1	1.000	-0	0	0	D18,1b3	0	0.0
1976	Mil A	24	61	4	10	1	0	0	4	6-0	0	8	.164	.239	.180	24	-6	0-0	ø	0	0	0	D14/1	0	-0.7
Total	2	82	149	12	36	5	1	2	13	9-0	0	24	.242	.285	.329	78	-5	2-1	1.000	-0	0	0	D32,1b4	0	-0.7
HANSEN, RON	Ronald Lavern; B4.5.1938 Oxford NE; BR/TR/6´3˝/(190–200); d4.15; C9																								
1958	Bal A	12	19	1	0	0	0	0	1	0-0	1	7	.000	.048	.000	-90	-5	0-0	.943	-1	101	87	S12	0	-0.6
1959	Bal A	2	4	0	0	0	0	0	0	1-0	0	1	.000	.200	.000	-41	-1	0-0	.889	0	133	115	S2	0	0.0
1960	Bal A★	153	530	72	135	22	5	22	86	69-5	2	94	.255	.342	.440	111	8	3-3	.964	12	98	117	S153	0	3.2
1961	Bal A★	155	533	51	132	13	2	12	51	66-2	1	96	.248	.329	.347	85	-11	1-3	.959	12	102	131	S149,2b7	0	1.3

YEAR	TM LG	G	AB	R	H	2B	3B	HR	RBI	BB-IB	HP	SO	AVG	OBP	SLG	AOPS	ABR	SB-CS	FA	FR	RNG	THR	GAMES AT POSITION	DL	BFW
1962	Bal A	71	196	12	34	7	0	3	17	30-3	2	36	.173	.289	.255	51	-13	0-1	.965	-3	93	105	S64	30	-1.2
1963	Chi A	144	482	55	109	17	2	13	67	78-2	0	74	.226	.330	.351	94	-2	1-1	.983	**28**	**115**	**122**	S144	0	3.9
1964	Chi A	158	575	85	150	25	3	20	68	73-7	6	73	.261	.347	.419	116	14	1-0	.975	18	**108**	**129**	S158	0	4.7
1965	Chi A	**162**	587	61	138	23	4	11	66	60-8	2	73	.235	.304	.344	91	-8	1-1	.969	13	**110**	114	S161/2	0	2.1
1966	Chi A	23	74	3	13	1	0	0	4	15-3	1	10	.176	.322	.189	55	-4	0-1	.946	-0	98	127	S23	130	-0.2
1967	Chi A	157	498	35	116	20	0	8	51	64-11	0	51	.233	.317	.321	94	-2	0-3	.964	2	106	**116**	S157	0	1.3
1968	Was A	86	275	28	51	12	0	8	28	35-5	2	49	.185	.281	.316	84	-5	0-0	.963	10	114	100	S81,3b5	0	1.4
	Chi A	40	87	7	20	3	0	1	4	11-0	0	12	.230	.316	.299	86	-1	0-0	.959	2	125	114	3b29,S7,2b2	0	0.2
	Year	126	362	35	71	15	0	9	32	46-5	2	61	.196	.290	.312	84	-6	0-0	.963	13	115	99	S88,3b34,2b2	0	1.6
1969	Chi A	85	185	15	48	6	1	2	22	18-0	1	25	.259	.327	.335	82	-4	2-0	.967	1	101	106	2b26,1b21,S8,3b7	0	-0.2
1970	NY A	59	91	13	27	4	0	4	14	19-0	1	9	.297	.420	.473	153	8	0-1	.983	0	106	88	S15,3b11/2	25	0.9
1971	NY A	61	145	6	30	3	0	2	20	9-2	0	27	.207	.245	.269	50	-10	0-0	.918	-3	97	190	3b30,2b9,S3	0	-1.3
1972	KC A	16	30	2	4	0	0	0	2	3-1	0	6	.133	.212	.133	4	-4	0-0	.944	4	134	54	S6,3b4/2	0	0.0
Total	15	1384	4311	446	1007	156	17	106	501	551-49	19	643	.234	.320	.351	92	-40	9-14	.968	95	106	117	S1143,3b86,2b47,1b21	185	15.5

HANSKI, DON Donald Thomas (b Donald Thomas Hanyzewski); B2.27.1916 LaPorte IN; D9.2.1957 Worth IL; BL/TL/5´11˝/180; d5.6; Mil 1945

YEAR	TM LG	G	AB	R	H	2B	3B	HR	RBI	BB-IB	HP	SO	AVG	OBP	SLG	AOPS	ABR	SB-CS	FA	FR	RNG	THR	GAMES AT POSITION	DL	BFW
1943	Chi A	9	21	1	5	1	0	0	2	0	0	5	.238	.238	.286	53	-1	0-1	.952	-0	105	135	1b5/P	0	-0.2
1944	Chi A	2	1	0	0	0	0	0	0	0	0	0	.000	.000	.000	-99	0	0-0	ø	-0	0	0	P2	0	0.0
Total	2	11	22	1	5	1	0	0	2	0	0	5	.227	.227	.273	46	-1	0-1	.952	-0	105	135	1b5,P3	0	-0.2

HANSON, HARRY Harry Francis; B1.17.1896 Elgin IL; D10.5.1966 Savannah GA; BR/TR/5´11˝/?; d7.14

YEAR	TM LG	G	AB	R	H	2B	3B	HR	RBI	BB-IB	HP	SO	AVG	OBP	SLG	AOPS	ABR	SB-CS	FA	FR	RNG	THR	GAMES AT POSITION	DL	BFW
1913	NY A	1	2	0	0	0	0	0	0	0	0	0	.000	.000	.000	-99	-1	0	1.000	-0	*62*	*201*	/C	—	-0.1

HAPPENNY, CLIFF John Clifford; B5.18.1901 Waltham MA; D12.29.1988 Coral Springs FL; BR/TR/5´11˝/165; d7.2; Col Illinois

YEAR	TM LG	G	AB	R	H	2B	3B	HR	RBI	BB-IB	HP	SO	AVG	OBP	SLG	AOPS	ABR	SB-CS	FA	FR	RNG	THR	GAMES AT POSITION	DL	BFW
1923	Chi A	32	86	7	19	5	0	0	10	3	1	13	.221	.256	.279	41	-8	0-0	.947	-1	124	133	2b19,S9,3b2	—	-0.7

HARBRIDGE, BILL William Arthur "Yaller Bill"; B3.29.1855 Philadelphia PA; D3.17.1924 Philadelphia PA; BL/TL/?/162; d5.15; OF(13/112/47)

YEAR	TM LG	G	AB	R	H	2B	3B	HR	RBI	BB-IB	HP	SO	AVG	OBP	SLG	AOPS	ABR	SB-CS	FA	FR	RNG	THR	GAMES AT POSITION	DL	BFW
1875	Har NA	53	208	32	50	3	3	0	26	9	—	3	.240	.272	.284	89	-3	2-4	.871	2	—	—	C31,O13R,2b11,1b3/S	—	-0.2
1876	Har N	30	106	11	23	2	1	0	6	3	—	2	.217	.239	.255	59	-5	—	.799	1	—	—	C24,O6(0/2/4),1b2	—	-0.3
1877	Har N	41	167	18	37	5	2	0	8	3	—	6	.222	.235	.275	68	-5	—	.881	-6	—	—	C32,O5(0/3/2),2b4/3	—	-0.9
1878	Chi N	54	240	32	71	12	0	0	37	6	—	13	.296	.313	.346	109	2	—	.878	-6	—	—	C53,O8(4/3/1)	—	-0.3
1879	Chi N	4	18	2	2	0	0	0	1	0	—	5	.111	.111	.111	-25	-2	—	.571	-1	125	0	O4(1/3/0)	—	-0.3
1880	Tro N	9	27	3	10	0	1	0	2	0	—	3	.370	.370	.444	166	2	—	.887	0	—	—	C9/O(0/1/1)	—	0.2
1882	Tro N	32	123	11	23	1	1	0	13	10	—	17	.187	.248	.211	52	-6	—	.836	-5	57	81	O23C,1b6,C3	—	-1.1
1883	Phi N	73	280	32	62	12	3	0	21	24	—	20	.221	.283	.286	81	-4	—	.796	-12	72	50	O44(8/36/0),S11,2b9,C7,3b5	—	-1.5
1884	Cin U	82	341	59	95	12	5	2	—	25	—	—	.279	.328	.361	100	-10	—	.906	4	**129**	79	O80(0/41/39),S3,1b2	—	-0.6
Total	8	325	1302	168	323	44	13	2	<u>88</u>	71	—	<u>66</u>	.248	.287	.306	86	-28	—	.849	-24	—	—	O171C,C128,S14,2b13,1b10,3b6	—	-4.8

HARDESTY, SCOTT Scott Durbin; B1.26.1870 Bellville OH; D10.29.1944 Fostoria OH; d8.17

YEAR	TM LG	G	AB	R	H	2B	3B	HR	RBI	BB-IB	HP	SO	AVG	OBP	SLG	AOPS	ABR	SB-CS	FA	FR	RNG	THR	GAMES AT POSITION	DL	BFW
1899	NY N	22	72	4	16	0	0	0	4	1	1	—	.222	.243	.222	29	-7	2	.895	4	117	118	S20,1b2	—	-0.2

HARDGROVE, PAT William Henry; B5.10.1895 Palmyra KS; D1.26.1973 Jackson MS; BR/TR/5´10˝/158; d6.8; Mil 1918

YEAR	TM LG	G	AB	R	H	2B	3B	HR	RBI	BB-IB	HP	SO	AVG	OBP	SLG	AOPS	ABR	SB-CS	FA	FR	RNG	THR	GAMES AT POSITION	DL	BFW
1918	Chi A	2	2	0	0	0	0	0	0	0	0	0	.000	.000	.000	-99	0	0	ø	0	—	—	/H	—	-0.1

HARDIE, LOU Louis W.; B8.24.1864 New York NY; D3.5.1929 Oakland CA; BR/5´11˝/180; d5.22

YEAR	TM LG	G	AB	R	H	2B	3B	HR	RBI	BB-IB	HP	SO	AVG	OBP	SLG	AOPS	ABR	SB-CS	FA	FR	RNG	THR	GAMES AT POSITION	DL	BFW
1884	Phi N	3	8	0	3	2	0	0	0	0	—	2	.375	.375	.625	219	1	—	.857	-2	—	—	C3	—	-0.1
1886	Chi N	16	51	4	9	0	0	0	3	4	—	10	.176	.236	.176	24	-5	1	.964	0	—	—	C13,O2R/3	—	-0.3
1890	Bos N	47	185	17	42	8	0	3	17	18	0	36	.227	.296	.319	73	-7	4	.886	1	*127*	*103*	C25,O15(6/4/6),3b7/S1	—	-0.4
1891	Bal AA	15	56	7	13	0	3	0	1	8	0	8	.232	.328	.339	90	-1	3	1.000	1	36	0	O15(0/3/12)	—	0.0
Total	4	81	300	28	67	10	3	3	21	30	0	56	.223	.294	.307	71	-12	8	.910	-0	<u>*127*</u>	<u>*103*</u>	C41,O32(6/7/20),3b8/1S	—	-0.8

HARDIN, BUD William Edgar; B6.14.1922 Shelby NC; D7.28.1997 Rancho Santa Fe CA; BR/TR/5´10˝/165; d4.15

YEAR	TM LG	G	AB	R	H	2B	3B	HR	RBI	BB-IB	HP	SO	AVG	OBP	SLG	AOPS	ABR	SB-CS	FA	FR	RNG	THR	GAMES AT POSITION	DL	BFW
1952	Chi N	3	7	1	1	0	0	0	0	0	0	0	.143	.143	.143	-20	-1	0-0	1.000	-0	100	153	S2/2	47	-0.1

HARDTKE, JASON Jason Robert; B9.15.1971 Milwaukee WI; BB/TR/5´10˝/175; [CleA90 3/81]; d9.8

YEAR	TM LG	G	AB	R	H	2B	3B	HR	RBI	BB-IB	HP	SO	AVG	OBP	SLG	AOPS	ABR	SB-CS	FA	FR	RNG	THR	GAMES AT POSITION	DL	BFW
1996	NY N	19	57	3	11	5	0	0	6	2-0	1	12	.193	.233	.281	37	-5	0-0	1.000	-3	85	102	2b18	0	-0.7
1997	NY N	30	56	9	15	2	0	2	8	4-1	1	6	.268	.323	.411	97	0	1-1	.981	-6	70	93	2b21/3	0	-0.6
1998	Chi N	18	21	2	5	0	0	0	2	2-0	0	6	.238	.304	.238	44	-2	0-0	1.000	-0	101	0	3b7/rfD	0	-0.2
Total	3	67	134	14	31	7	0	2	16	8-1	2	24	.231	.283	.328	63	-7	1-1	.991	-9	78	98	2b39,3b8/Drf	0	-1.5

HARDY, CARROLL Carroll William; B5.18.1933 Sturgis SD; BR/TR/6´0˝/185; d4.15; Col Colorado

YEAR	TM LG	G	AB	R	H	2B	3B	HR	RBI	BB-IB	HP	SO	AVG	OBP	SLG	AOPS	ABR	SB-CS	FA	FR	RNG	THR	GAMES AT POSITION	DL	BFW
1958	Cle A	27	49	10	10	3	0	1	6	6-0	1	14	.204	.298	.327	75	-1	1-2	1.000	2	112	265	O17(0/16/1)	30	-0.1
1959	Cle A	32	53	12	11	1	0	0	2	3-0	0	7	.208	.250	.226	33	-5	1-1	1.000	3	163	0	O15(1/14/0)	0	-0.3
1960	Cle A	29	18	7	2	1	0	0	1	2-0	0	2	.111	.200	.167	0	-3	0-0	1.000	0	117	0	O17(4/9/5)	0	-0.3
	Bos A	73	145	26	34	5	2	2	15	17-0	0	40	.234	.313	.338	74	-5	3-2	.968	2	110	115	O59(44/8/14)	0	-0.5
	Year	102	163	33	36	6	2	2	16	19-0	0	42	.221	.301	.319	67	-8	3-2	.973	2	111	98	O76(48/17/19)	0	-0.8
1961	Bos A	85	281	46	74	20	2	3	36	26-0	2	53	.263	.330	.381	87	-5	4-2	.961	0	95	157	O76(20/38/21)	0	-0.8
1962	Bos A	115	362	52	78	13	5	8	36	54-1	2	68	.215	.318	.345	77	-11	3-7	.991	0	100	130	O105(3/45/64)	0	-1.8
1963	Hou N	15	44	5	10	3	0	0	3	3-0	0	7	.227	.277	.295	69	-2	1-0	.947	0	95	154	O10L	0	-0.2
1964	Hou N	46	157	13	29	1	1	2	12	8-0	2	30	.185	.232	.242	36	-14	0-0	.990	4	122	119	O41(5/33/4)	0	-1.3
1967	Min A	11	8	1	3	0	0	1	2	1-0	0	1	.375	.444	.750	229	1	0-0	ø	-0	0	0	O4(1/0/3)	0	0.1
Total	8	433	1117	172	251	47	10	17	113	120-1	7	222	.225	.302	.330	72	-45	13-14	.981	10	106	132	O344(88/163/112)	30	-5.2

HARDY, J.J. James Jerry; B8.19.1982 Tucson AZ; BR/TR/6´2˝/(180–190); [MilN01 2/56]; d4.4

YEAR	TM LG	G	AB	R	H	2B	3B	HR	RBI	BB-IB	HP	SO	AVG	OBP	SLG	AOPS	ABR	SB-CS	FA	FR	RNG	THR	GAMES AT POSITION	DL	BFW
2005	Mil N	124	372	46	92	22	1	9	50	44-7	1	48	.247	.327	.384	86	-7	0-0	.975	-24	82	77	S119	0	-2.3
2006	Mil N	35	128	13	31	5	0	5	14	10-0	0	23	.242	.295	.398	75	-5	1-1	.986	7	106	137	S32	138	0.4
Total	2	159	500	59	123	27	1	14	64	54-7	1	71	.246	.319	.388	83	-12	1-1	.978	-16	87	90	S151	138	-1.9

HARDY, JACK John Doolittle; B6.23.1877 Cleveland OH; D10.20.1921 Cleveland OH; BR/TR/6´0˝/185; d8.29

YEAR	TM LG	G	AB	R	H	2B	3B	HR	RBI	BB-IB	HP	SO	AVG	OBP	SLG	AOPS	ABR	SB-CS	FA	FR	RNG	THR	GAMES AT POSITION	DL	BFW
1903	Cle A	5	19	1	3	1	0	0	1	1	0	—	.158	.200	.211	24	-2	1	1.000	-1	0	0	O5R	—	-0.3
1907	Chi N	1	4	0	1	0	0	0	0	0	0	—	.250	.250	.250	53	0	0	.909	-0	*158*	*76*	/C	—	0.0
1909	Was A	10	24	3	4	0	0	0	4	1	0	—	.167	.200	.167	17	-2	0	.974	-1	*83*	*32*	C9/2	—	-0.4
1910	Was A	7	8	1	2	0	0	0	0	0	0	—	.250	.250	.250	59	0	0	.933	0	*119*	*104*	C4/lf	—	0.0
Total	4	23	55	5	10	1	0	0	5	2	0	—	.182	.211	.200	28	-4	1	.953	-2	*102*	*54*	C14,O6(1/0/5)/2	—	-0.7

HARE, SHAWN Shawn Robert; B3.26.1967 St.Louis MO; BL/TL/6´2˝/(190–200); d9.6; Col Central Michigan

YEAR	TM LG	G	AB	R	H	2B	3B	HR	RBI	BB-IB	HP	SO	AVG	OBP	SLG	AOPS	ABR	SB-CS	FA	FR	RNG	THR	GAMES AT POSITION	DL	BFW
1991	Det A	9	19	0	1	1	0	0	0	2-0	0	1	.053	.143	.105	-30	-3	0-0	1.000	1	124	387	O6R,D2	0	-0.3
1992	Det A	15	26	0	3	1	0	0	5	2-0	0	4	.115	.172	.154	-6	-4	0-0	1.000	0	104	0	O9(3/0/7),1b4	63	-0.4
1994	NY N	22	40	7	9	1	1	0	2	4-0	0	11	.225	.295	.300	56	-3	0-0	1.000	0	119	0	O14L	0	-0.3
1995	Tex A	18	24	2	6	1	0	0	2	4-0	0	6	.250	.357	.292	69	-1	0-0	1.000	0	86	283	O9(4/0/5)/1D	0	-0.1
Total	4	64	109	9	19	4	1	0	9	12-0	0	22	.174	.254	.229	31	-11	0-0	1.000	2	109	117	O38(21/0/18),1b5,D5	63	-1.1

HARGIS, GARY Gary Lynn; B11.2.1956 Minneapolis MN; BR/TR/5´11˝/160; [PitN74 2/35]; d9.29

YEAR	TM LG	G	AB	R	H	2B	3B	HR	RBI	BB-IB	HP	SO	AVG	OBP	SLG	AOPS	ABR	SB-CS	FA	FR	RNG	THR	GAMES AT POSITION	DL	BFW
1979	Pit N	1	0	0	0	0	0	0	0	0-0	0	0	ø	ø	ø	ø	0	0-0	ø	0	—	—	/R	0	0.0

HARGRAVE, BUBBLES Eugene Franklin; B7.15.1892 New Haven IN; D2.23.1969 Cincinnati OH; BR/TR/5´10.5˝/174; d9.18; b–Pinky

YEAR	TM LG	G	AB	R	H	2B	3B	HR	RBI	BB-IB	HP	SO	AVG	OBP	SLG	AOPS	ABR	SB-CS	FA	FR	RNG	THR	GAMES AT POSITION	DL	BFW
1913	Chi N	3	3	0	1	0	0	0	1	0	0	0	.333	.333	.333	91	0	0	1.000	0	86	151	C2	—	0.0
1914	Chi N	23	36	3	8	2	0	0	2	0	0	4	.222	.222	.278	48	-2	2	.930	-3	*82*	*61*	C16	—	-0.5
1915	Chi N	15	19	2	3	0	1	0	2	1	0	5	.158	.200	.263	40	-2	0	1.000	-0	*79*	*147*	C9	—	-0.2
1921	Cin N	93	263	28	76	17	8	1	38	12	3	15	.289	.327	.426	102	0	4-2	.973	-1	*109*	*62*	C73	—	0.4
1922	Cin N	98	320	49	101	22	10	7	57	26	2	18	.316	.371	.512	128	12	7-4	.982	-2	*114*	*76*	C87	—	1.5
1923	Cin N	118	378	54	126	23	9	10	78	44	**12**	22	.333	.419	.521	150	29	4-5	.988	4	*106*	*110*	C109	—	3.8
1924	Cin N	98	312	42	94	19	10	3	33	30	4	20	.301	.370	.455	122	10	2-2	.983	0	*96*	*99*	C91	—	1.5
1925	Cin N	87	273	28	82	13	6	2	33	25	1	23	.300	.361	.414	100	0	4-3	.979	-7	*75*	*73*	C84	—	-0.2
1926	Cin N	105	326	42	115	22	8	6	62	25	4	17	**.353**	.406	.525	153	24	2	.988	-7	*109*	*62*	C93	—	2.2
1927	Cin N	102	305	36	94	18	3	0	35	31	2	18	.308	.376	.387	108	5	0	**.988**	-7	*83*	*63*	C92	—	0.4
1928	Cin N	65	190	19	56	12	3	0	23	13	4	14	.295	.353	.389	95	-1	4	.991	2	*103*	*99*	C57	—	0.4

YEAR	TM LG	G	AB	R	H	2B	3B	HR	RBI	BB-IB	HP	SO	AVG	OBP	SLG	AOPS	ABR	SB-CS	FA	FR	RNG	THR	GAMES AT POSITION	DL	BFW
1930	NY A	45	108	11	30	7	0	0	12	10	0	9	.278	.339	.343	77	-3	0-0	.992	-3	83	84	C34	—	-0.5
Total	12	852	2533	314	786	155	58	29	376	217	32	165	.310	.372	.452	119	72	29-16	.983	-25	99	82	C747	—	8.8
HARGRAVE, PINKY	William McKinley; B1.31.1896 New Haven IN; D10.3.1942 Ft.Wayne IN; BB/TR (BR 1923–26)/5´8.5˝/180; d5.18; b–Bubbles																								
1923	Was A	33	59	4	17	2	0	0	8	2	0	6	.288	.311	.322	70	-3	0-0	.917	-2	56	131	3b8,C5/lf	—	-0.4
1924	Was A	24	33	3	5	1	1	0	5	1	0	4	.152	.176	.242	8	-5	0-0	1.000	-0	122	51	C8	—	-0.5
1925	Was A	5	6	0	3	0	0	0	0	1	0	2	.500	.571	.500	177	1	0-0	1.000	1	0	194	/C	—	0.1
	StL A	67	225	34	64	15	2	8	43	13	1	13	.284	.326	.476	97	-3	2-0	.981	-5	83	106	C62	—	-0.3
	Year	72	231	34	67	15	2	8	43	14	1	15	.290	.333	.476	99	-2	2-0	.981	-5	81	108	C63	—	-0.2
1926	StL A	92	235	20	66	16	3	7	37	10	3	38	.281	.319	.464	98	-2	3-0	.977	1	128	132	C58	—	0.3
1928	Det A	121	320	38	88	13	5	10	63	32	1	28	.275	.343	.441	103	0	4-1	.977	-9	92	80	C88	—	-0.3
1929	Det A	76	185	26	61	12	0	3	26	20	2	24	.330	.401	.443	117	6	2-2	.973	-4	72	129	C48	—	0.4
1930	Det A	55	137	18	39	8	0	5	18	20	1	12	.285	.380	.453	108	2	2-0	.984	-4	67	74	C40	—	0.1
	Was A	10	31	3	6	2	2	1	7	3	0	1	.194	.265	.484	85	-1	1-0	1.000	1	131	107	C9	—	0.1
	Year	65	168	21	45	10	2	6	25	23	1	13	.268	.359	.458	104	1	3-0	.987	-3	79	80	C49	—	0.2
1931	Was A	40	80	6	26	8	0	1	19	9	0	12	.325	.393	.463	124	3	1-0	.978	-1	112	80	C25	—	0.3
1932	Bos N	82	217	20	57	14	3	4	33	24	0	18	.263	.336	.410	103	1	1	.968	-0	139	100	C73	—	0.5
1933	Bos N	45	73	5	13	0	0	0	6	5	1	7	.178	.241	.178	23	-7	1	.957	0	201	59	C25	—	-0.7
Total	10	650	1601	177	445	91	16	39	265	140	9	165	.278	.339	.428	98	-8	17-3	.976	-24	105	99	C442,3b8/lf	—	-0.4
HARGREAVES, CHARLIE	Charles Russell; B12.14.1896 Trenton NJ; D5.9.1979 Neptune NJ; BR/TR/6´0˝/170; d6.27																								
1923	Bro N	20	57	5	16	0	0	0	4	1	0	2	.281	.293	.281	54	-4	0-0	.921	-3	75	75	C15	—	-0.6
1924	Bro N	15	27	4	11	2	0	0	5	1	0	1	.407	.429	.481	148	2	0-1	1.000	-1	84	70	C9	—	0.1
1925	Bro N	45	83	9	23	3	1	0	13	6	0	1	.277	.326	.337	72	-4	1-1	.986	1	72	196	C18,1b2	—	-0.2
1926	Bro N	85	208	14	52	13	2	2	23	19	1	10	.250	.316	.361	83	-5	1	.986	3	78	148	C70	—	0.2
1927	Bro N	46	133	9	38	3	1	0	11	14	2	7	.286	.362	.323	85	-2	1	.985	1	78	125	C44	—	0.2
1928	Bro N	20	61	3	12	2	0	0	5	6	0	6	.197	.269	.230	32	-6	1	.979	1	73	109	C20	—	-0.4
	Pit N	79	260	15	74	8	2	1	32	12	1	9	.285	.319	.342	70	-12	1	.962	-5	80	105	C77	—	-1.1
	Year	99	321	18	86	10	2	1	37	18	1	15	.268	.309	.321	63	-18	2	.966	-4	79	106	C97	—	-1.5
1929	Pit N	102	328	33	88	12	5	1	44	16	2	12	.268	.306	.345	60	-22	1	.981	4	99	101	C101	—	-1.1
1930	Pit N	11	31	4	7	1	0	0	2	2	0	1	.226	.273	.258	29	-4	0	1.000	4	103	156	C11	—	0.1
Total	8	423	1188	96	321	44	11	4	139	77	6	49	.270	.318	.336	69	-57	6-2	.977	5	85	119	C365,1b2	—	-2.8
HARGROVE, MIKE	Dudley Michael "The Human Rain Delay"; B10.26.1949 Perryton TX; BL/TL/6´0˝/(195–200); [TexA72 25/572]; d4.7; M15/C2; Col Northwestern Oklahoma																								
1974	Tex A	131	415	57	134	18	6	4	66	49-4	4	42	.323	.395	.424	140	24	0-0	.987	8	140	84	1b91,D32,O6L	0	2.5
1975	Tex A★	145	519	82	157	22	2	11	62	79-10	4	66	.303	.395	.416	132	26	4-3	.964	1	94	29	O96L,1b48,D12	0	1.8
1976	Tex A	151	541	80	155	30	1	7	58	**97**-13	6	64	.287	.397	.384	128	26	2-3	.984	0	106	89	1b141,D5	0	1.5
1977	Tex A	153	525	98	160	28	4	18	69	103-7	6	59	.305	.420	.476	143	38	2-5	.993	-3	92	117	1b152	0	2.4
1978	Tex A	146	494	63	124	24	1	7	40	**107**-8	7	47	.251	.388	.346	108	13	2-5	.987	10	**132**	90	1b140,D4	0	1.4
1979	SD N	52	125	15	24	5	0	0	8	25-3	0	15	.192	.325	.232	59	-6	0-2	.986	-1	92	97	1b37	0	-1.0
	Cle A	100	338	60	110	21	4	10	56	63-2	5	40	.325	.433	.500	152	29	2-3	.993	-0	109	67	O65L,1b28,D7	0	2.3
1980	Cle A	**160**	589	86	179	22	2	11	85	111-10	8	36	.304	.415	.404	126	29	4-2	.993	-5	84	83	1b160	0	1.4
1981	Cle A	94	322	43	102	21	0	2	49	60-5	5	16	.317	**.424**	.401	142	23	5-4	.989	5	121	81	1b88,D4	0	2.3
1982	Cle A	160	591	67	160	26	1	4	65	101-3	3	58	.271	.377	.338	99	5	2-2	.996	8	115	83	1b153,D5	0	0.3
1983	Cle A	134	469	57	134	21	4	3	57	78-5	5	40	.286	.388	.367	106	8	0-6	.994	11	127	111	1b131/D	0	0.9
1984	Cle A	133	352	44	94	14	2	2	44	53-3	0	38	.267	.361	.335	93	-1	0-2	.991	4	117	104	1b124	0	-0.3
1985	Cle A	107	284	31	81	14	1	1	27	39-2	0	29	.285	.370	.352	100	2	1-0	.991	5	126	98	1b85	0	0.3
Total	12	1666	5564	783	1614	266	28	80	686	965-75	53	550	.290	.396	.391	121	216	24-37	.991	44	113	94	1b1378,O167L,D70	0	15.8
HARKNESS, TIM	Thomas William; B12.23.1937 Lachine QC, Can.; BL/TL/6´2˝/(180–182); d9.12																								
1961	LA N	5	8	4	4	2	0	0	0	3-0	0	1	.500	.636	.750	245	2	1-0	1.000	0	87	142	1b2	0	0.2
1962	LA N	92	62	9	16	2	0	2	7	10-1	1	20	.258	.370	.387	110	1	1-0	1.000	-1	75	103	1b59	0	0.0
1963	NY N	123	375	35	79	12	3	10	41	36-5	7	79	.211	.290	.339	80	-10	4-3	.986	16	164	85	1b106	0	0.0
1964	NY N	39	117	11	33	2	1	2	13	9-1	1	18	.282	.336	.368	101	0	1-1	.993	3	147	139	1b32	44	0.2
Total	4	259	562	59	132	18	4	14	61	58-7	9	118	.235	.315	.356	90	-7	7-4	.989	19	150	98	1b199	44	0.4
HARLEY, DICK	Richard Joseph; B9.25.1872 Philadelphia PA; D4.3.1952 Philadelphia PA; BL/TR/5´10.5˝/165; d6.2; Col Georgetown																								
1897	StL N	90	333	43	96	6	4	3	35	36	12	—	.288	.378	.357	97	0	23	.901	1	158	139	O90(1/89/0)	—	-0.4
1898	StL N	142	549	74	135	6	5	0	42	34	22	—	.246	.316	.275	68	-22	13	.926	8	129	60	O141(135/5/1)	—	-2.5
1899	Cle N	142	567	70	142	15	7	1	50	40	13	—	.250	.315	.307	76	-18	15	.924	8	128	94	O142(140/0/2)	—	-2.0
1900	Cin N	5	21	2	9	1	0	0	5	1	0	—	.429	.455	.476	161	2	4	1.000	-1	0	0	O5L	—	0.1
1901	Cin N	133	535	69	146	13	2	4	27	31	9	—	.273	.323	.327	95	-3	37	.898	-4	118	43	O133L	—	-1.5
1902	Det A	125	491	59	138	9	8	2	44	36	**12**	—	.281	.345	.344	90	-7	20	.930	1	96	31	O125L	—	-1.2
1903	Chi N	104	386	72	89	9	1	0	33	45	11	—	.231	.328	.259	70	-13	27	.923	2	124	62	O103R	—	-1.5
Total	7	741	2882	389	755	59	27	10	236	223	79	—	.262	.332	.312	83	-61	139	.918	14	123	68	O739(539/94/106)	—	-9.0
HARLOW, LARRY	Larry Duane; B11.13.1951 Colorado Springs CO; BL/TL/6´2˝/(175–176); d9.20; Col Mesa (AZ) CC																								
1975	Bal A	4	3	1	1	0	0	0	0	0-0	0	1	.333	.333	.333	94	0	0-0	1.000	-0	67	0	O4(2/2/0)	0	0.0
1977	Bal A	46	48	4	10	0	1	0	0	5-0	0	8	.208	.283	.250	49	-3	6-1	.887	-3	95	0	O38(0/37/1)	0	-0.5
1978	Bal A	147	460	67	112	25	1	8	26	55-3	1	72	.243	.324	.354	97	-1	14-11	.979	-4	97	91	O138(0/135/3)/P	0	-0.7
1979	Bal A	38	41	5	11	1	0	0	1	7-0	0	4	.268	.375	.293	86	0	1-3	.970	-1	94	0	O31(0/12/22)/D	0	-0.3
	†Cal A	62	159	22	37	8	2	0	14	25-0	2	34	.233	.344	.308	80	-3	1-3	.975	2	102	128	O58(11/33/15)	0	-0.4
	Year	100	200	27	48	9	2	0	15	32-0	2	38	.240	.350	.305	81	-4	2-6	.974	1	100	98	O89(11/45/37)/D	0	-0.7
1980	Cal A	109	301	47	83	13	4	4	27	48-1	1	61	.276	.376	.385	111	7	3-2	.976	13	123	179	O94(5/32/59)/1D	0	1.6
1981	Cal A	43	82	13	17	1	0	0	4	16-0	0	25	.207	.337	.220	63	-3	1-1	.981	-2	91	56	O39(21/7/13)	0	-0.6
Total	6	449	1094	159	271	48	8	12	72	156-4	4	205	.248	.343	.339	93	-3	26-21	.971	5	104	108	O402(39/258/113),D2/1P	0	-0.9
HARMAN, BILL	William Bell; B1.2.1919 Bridgewater VA; BR/TR/6´4˝/200; d6.17; Mil 1942; Col Virginia; ▲																								
1941	Phi N	15	14	1	1	0	0	0	0	0	0	3	.071	.071	.071	-62	-3	0	1.000	-1	75	0	P5,C5	0	-0.2
HARMON, CHUCK	Charles Byron; B4.23.1924 Washington IN; BR/TR/6´2˝/(170–175); d4.17; Negro Lg 1947; Col Toledo																								
1954	Cin N	94	286	39	68	7	3	2	25	17	1	27	.238	.277	.304	52	-21	7-3	.961	4	103	164	3b67,1b3	0	-1.7
1955	Cin N	96	198	31	50	6	3	5	28	26-0	3	24	.253	.345	.389	90	-2	9-9	.935	2	91	63	3b39,O32(32/2/0),1b4	0	-0.3
1956	Cin N	13	4	2	0	0	0	0	0	0-0	0	0	.000	.000	.000	-94	-1	1-0	1.000	0	155	0	O6(1/1/4),1b2	0	-0.1
	StL N	20	15	2	0	0	0	0	0	2-0	0	2	.000	.118	.000	-65	-4	0-0	1.000	-1	102	0	O11(3/4/5),1b2/3	0	-0.4
	Year	33	19	4	0	0	0	0	0	2-0	0	2	.000	.095	.000	-70	-5	1-0	1.000	-0	117	0	O17(4/5/9),1b4/3	0	-0.5
1957	StL N	9	3	2	1	0	1	0	1	0-0	0	0	.333	.333	1.000	236	0	1-0	1.000	0	110	0	O8(0/1/7)	0	0.1
	Phi N	57	86	14	22	2	1	0	5	1-0	0	4	.256	.264	.302	53	-6	7-2	1.000	0	133	0	O25(21/2/2),3b5,1b2	0	-0.6
	Year	66	89	16	23	2	2	0	6	1-0	0	4	.258	.267	.326	60	-6	8-2	1.000	0	130	0	O33(21/3/9),3b5,1b2	0	-0.5
Total	4	289	592	90	141	15	8	7	59	46-0	4	57	.238	.294	.326	62	-34	25-14	.952	7	98	132	3b112,O82(57/10/18),1b13	0	-3.0
HARMON, TERRY	Terry Walter; B4.12.1944 Toledo OH; BR/TR/6´2˝/(180–185); [PhiN65 5/85]; d7.23; Col Ohio U.																								
1967	Phi N	2	0	0	0	0	0	0	0	0-0	0	0	ø	ø	ø	ø	0	0-0	ø	0	—	—	/R	0	0.0
1969	Phi N	87	201	25	48	8	1	0	16	22-1	3	31	.239	.323	.289	74	-6	1-2	.968	7	105	130	S38,2b19,3b2	0	0.6
1970	Phi N	71	129	16	32	2	4	0	7	12-1	1	22	.248	.315	.326	74	-5	6-3	.989	-10	76	72	S35,2b14,3b2	0	-1.2
1971	Phi N	79	221	27	45	4	2	0	12	20-0	4	45	.204	.279	.240	49	-15	3-2	.986	4	111	111	2b58,S9,3b3,1b2	0	-0.7
1972	Phi N	73	218	35	62	8	2	2	13	29-0	2	28	.284	.372	.367	108	4	3-2	.996	6	114	112	2b50,S15,3b5	0	1.5
1973	Phi N	72	148	17	31	3	0	0	8	13-3	1	14	.209	.278	.230	41	-12	1-0	.988	-1	84	92	2b43,S19/3	0	-1.0
1974	Phi N	27	15	5	2	0	0	0	0	3-0	0	3	.133	.278	.133	17	-2	0-0	1.000	-1	41	71	S7,2b5	0	-0.2
1975	Phi N	48	72	14	13	1	2	0	5	9-0	1	13	.181	.280	.250	46	-5	0-0	.989	-5	86	68	S25,2b7/3	23	-0.8
1976	†Phi N	42	61	12	18	4	1	0	6	3-0	0	10	.295	.328	.393	100	0	3-0	.960	-3	85	64	S19,2b13,3b5	0	-0.1
1977	Phi N	46	60	13	11	1	0	2	5	6-0	1	9	.183	.265	.300	50	-4	0-2	.982	3	132	175	2b28,S16,3b3	0	-0.1
Total	10	547	1125	164	262	31	12	4	72	117-5	13	175	.233	.311	.292	69	-45	17-11	.989	1	106	107	2b237,S183,3b22,1b2	23	-2.0
HARPER, BRANDON	Brandon Scott; B4.29.1976 Odessa TX; BR/TR/6´4˝/200; [FlaN97 4/126]; d8.9; Col Dallas Bapist																								
2006	Was N	18	41	6	12	3	0	2	6	4-0	1	4	.293	.362	.512	128	2	0-0	.987	-3	75	0	C14	0	0.0

HARPER, BRIAN Brian David; B10.16.1959 Los Angeles CA; BR/TR/6´2˝/(195–208); [CalA77 4/85]; d9.29; OF(78/0/38)

YEAR	TM LG	G	AB	R	H	2B	3B	HR	RBI	BB-IB	HP	SO	AVG	OBP	SLG	AOPS	ABR	SB-CS	FA	FR	RNG	THR	GAMES AT POSITION	DL	BFW
1979	Cal A	1	2	0	0	0	0	0	0	0-0	0	1	.000	.000	.000	-99	-1	0-0	ø	0	—	—	/D	0	-0.1
1981	Cal A	4	11	1	3	0	0	0	1	0-0	0	0	.273	.250	.273	57	-1	1-0	.833	-0	125	0	O2(1/0/1)/D	0	-0.1
1982	Pit N	20	29	4	8	1	0	2	4	1-1	0	4	.276	.300	.517	119	1	0-0	1.000	-0	104	0	O8R	0	0.0
1983	Pit N	61	131	16	29	4	1	7	20	2-0	1	15	.221	.232	.427	79	-5	0-0	1.000	-3	82	0	O35(33/0/2)/1	0	-0.9
1984	Pit N	46	112	4	29	4	0	2	11	5-0	2	11	.259	.300	.348	82	-3	0-0	.981	1	101	150	O37(34/0/4),C2	47	-0.3
1985	†StL N	43	52	5	13	4	0	0	8	2-0	0	3	.250	.273	.327	69	-2	0-0	1.000	-1	109	0	O13(7/0/6),3b6,C2/1	0	-0.3
1986	Det A	19	36	2	5	1	0	0	3	3-0	0	3	.139	.200	.167	3	-5	0-0	.929	0	100	0	O11R,C2,1b2,D6	0	-0.5
1987	Oak A	11	17	1	4	1	0	0	3	0-0	0	4	.235	.222	.294	42	-1	0-0	ø	-0	0	0	/IfD	0	-0.1
1988	Min A	60	166	15	49	11	1	3	20	10-1	3	12	.295	.344	.428	112	3	0-3	.991	-5	123	100	C48,3b2,D5	0	-0.1
1989	Min A	126	385	43	125	24	0	8	57	13-3	6	16	.325	.353	.449	118	9	2-4	.978	-4	112	96	C101,D19,O3R,1b2,3b2	0	0.8
1990	Min A	134	479	61	141	42	3	6	54	19-2	7	27	.294	.328	.432	105	3	3-2	.985	9	86	130	C120,D11,3b3,1b2	0	1.9
1991	†Min A	123	441	54	137	28	1	10	69	14-3	6	22	.311	.336	.447	111	6	1-2	.988	-5	73	78	C119/1IfD	0	0.7
1992	Min A	140	502	58	154	25	0	9	73	26-7	7	22	.307	.343	.410	108	5	0-1	.984	-2	79	108	C133,D2	0	1.0
1993	Min A	147	530	52	161	26	1	12	73	29-9	9	29	.304	.347	.425	106	4	1-3	.988	-11	77	113	C134,D7	0	0.0
1994	Mil A	64	251	23	73	15	0	4	32	9-1	3	18	.291	.318	.398	81	-7	0-2	.981	1	58	118	D36,C25,O3(1/0/3)	58	-0.7
1995	Oak A	2	7	0	0	0	0	0	0	0-0	0	1	.000	.000	.000	-99	-2	0-0	1.000	-1	0	0	C2	0	-0.3
Total	16	1001	3151	339	931	186	7	63	428	133-27	44	188	.295	.329	.419	102	4	8-17	.985	-20	85	106	C688,O114L,D97,3b13,1b9	105	1.0

HARPER, GEORGE George Washington; B6.24.1892 Arlington KY; D8.18.1978 Magnolia AR; BL/TR/5´8˝/167; d4.15

YEAR	TM LG	G	AB	R	H	2B	3B	HR	RBI	BB-IB	HP	SO	AVG	OBP	SLG	AOPS	ABR	SB-CS	FA	FR	RNG	THR	GAMES AT POSITION	DL	BFW
1916	Det A	44	56	4	9	1	0	0	3	5	0	8	.161	.230	.179	22	-5	0	.938	-2	86	0	O14(2/4/8)	—	-0.8
1917	Det A	47	117	6	24	3	0	0	12	11	3	15	.205	.290	.231	59	-5	2	.980	-2	97	51	O31(0/3/28)	—	-1.0
1918	Det A	69	227	19	55	5	2	0	16	18	1	14	.242	.301	.282	79	-6	3	.956	-3	104	54	O64(0/1/63)	—	-1.4
1922	Cin N	128	430	67	146	22	8	2	68	35	6	22	.340	.397	.442	118	13	11-10	.955	-1	98	105	O109(1/5/103)	—	0.2
1923	Cin N	61	125	14	32	4	2	3	16	11	0	9	.256	.316	.392	88	-3	0-2	.967	-1	91	100	O29(9/17/3)	—	-0.6
1924	Cin N	28	74	7	20	3	0	0	3	13	2	5	.270	.393	.311	92	0	1-3	.964	0	98	129	O22(12/10/0)	—	-0.2
	Phi N	109	411	68	121	26	6	16	55	38	5	23	.294	.361	.504	115	9	10-11	.991	3	103	101	O109(0/3/107)	—	0.2
	Year	137	485	75	141	29	6	16	58	51	7	28	.291	.366	.474	113	10	11-14	**.986**	3	102	106	O131(12/13/107)	—	0.0
1925	Phi N	132	495	86	173	35	7	18	97	28	6	32	.349	.391	.558	128	20	10-8	.971	4	103	117	O126(36/61/33)	—	1.5
1926	Phi N	56	194	32	61	6	5	7	38	16	0	7	.314	.367	.505	126	6	6	.942	-3	102	39	O55(44/8/8)	—	0.0
1927	NY N	145	483	85	160	19	6	16	87	84	5	27	.331	.435	.495	149	38	7	.975	-2	101	75	O142R	—	2.5
1928	NY N	19	57	11	13	1	0	2	7	10	1	4	.228	.353	.351	84	-1	1	.957	2	100	210	O18R	—	-0.1
	†StL N	99	272	41	83	8	2	17	58	51	2	15	.305	.418	.537	145	19	2	.988	2	90	157	O84R	—	1.5
	Year	118	329	52	96	9	2	19	65	61	3	19	.292	.407	.505	135	18	3	.982	4	92	167	O102R	—	1.4
1929	Bos N	136	457	65	133	25	5	10	68	69	4	27	.291	.389	.433	108	8	5	.972	2	106	82	O130(119/1/10)	—	0.0
Total	11	1073	3398	505	1030	158	43	91	528	389	35	208	.303	.380	.455	118	93	58-34	.970	0	100	95	O933(223/113/607)	—	1.8

HARPER, TERRY Terry Joe; B8.19.1955 Douglasville GA; BR/TR/6´4˝/(195–205); [AtlN73 16/370]; d9.12

YEAR	TM LG	G	AB	R	H	2B	3B	HR	RBI	BB-IB	HP	SO	AVG	OBP	SLG	AOPS	ABR	SB-CS	FA	FR	RNG	THR	GAMES AT POSITION	DL	BFW
1980	Atl N	21	54	3	10	2	1	0	3	6-0	1	5	.185	.279	.259	50	-4	2-1	.968	-1	104	0	O18(15/1/3)	0	-0.5
1981	Atl N	40	73	9	19	1	0	2	8	11-0	0	17	.260	.353	.356	103	1	5-1	.976	1	107	129	O27(9/0/18)	0	0.2
1982	†Atl N	48	150	16	43	3	0	2	16	14-0	1	28	.287	.347	.347	94	-1	7-4	.987	1	98	133	O41(29/1/16)	53	-0.2
1983	Atl N	80	201	19	53	13	1	3	26	20-0	1	43	.264	.332	.383	91	-2	6-5	.952	1	101	140	O60(28/2/32)	0	-0.4
1984	Atl N	40	102	4	16	3	1	0	8	4-0	1	21	.157	.194	.206	12	-12	4-1	1.000	4	121	150	O29(28/0/1)	22	-1.0
1985	Atl N	138	492	58	130	15	2	17	72	44-4	3	76	.264	.327	.407	99	-1	9-9	.978	-4	87	107	O131(129/0/2)	0	-1.2
1986	Atl N	106	265	26	68	12	0	8	30	29-2	1	39	.257	.330	.392	95	-2	3-6	.970	-5	74	110	O83(66/0/25)	0	-1.2
1987	Det A	31	64	4	13	3	0	3	10	9-0	0	8	.203	.301	.391	85	-1	1-0	.952	-1	104	0	D15,O14(1/0/13)	0	-0.3
	Pit N	36	66	8	19	3	0	1	7	7-1	0	11	.288	.356	.379	94	0	0-1	1.000	-1	94	0	O20(10/0/11)	0	-0.2
Total	8	540	1467	147	371	55	5	36	180	144-7	8	248	.253	.321	.371	88	-22	37-28	.976	-4	92	108	O423(315/4/121),D15	75	-4.8

HARPER, TOMMY Tommy; B10.14.1940 Oak Grove LA; BR/TR/5´10˝/(160–168); d4.9; C18; Col San Francisco St.; OF(683/258/348)

YEAR	TM LG	G	AB	R	H	2B	3B	HR	RBI	BB-IB	HP	SO	AVG	OBP	SLG	AOPS	ABR	SB-CS	FA	FR	RNG	THR	GAMES AT POSITION	DL	BFW
1962	Cin N	6	23	1	4	0	0	0	1	2-0	0	6	.174	.240	.174	13	-3	1-0	.929	-2	64	97	3b6	0	-0.4
1963	Cin N	129	408	67	106	12	3	10	37	44-1	3	72	.260	.335	.377	102	2	12-1	.983	5	**117**	91	O118(1/23/94)/3	0	0.3
1964	Cin N	102	317	42	77	5	2	4	22	39-1	1	56	.243	.326	.309	78	-8	24-3	.994	5	109	71	O92(88/4/0),3b2	0	-0.4
1965	Cin N	159	646	**126**	166	28	3	18	64	78-0	5	127	.257	.340	.393	99	2	35-6	.983	4	109	72	O159(156/5/0),3b2/2	0	0.3
1966	Cin N	149	553	85	154	22	5	5	31	57-4	3	85	.278	.348	.363	91	-5	29-10	.996	0	105	53	O147(73/25/95)	0	-1.0
1967	Cin N	103	365	55	82	17	3	7	22	43-1	0	51	.225	.306	.345	77	-10	23-8	.995	7	123	89	O100(2/4/97)	59	-0.7
1968	Cle A	130	235	26	51	15	2	6	26	26-2	1	56	.217	.295	.374	104	1	11-7	.984	-4	99	0	O115(67/7/46),2b2	0	-0.8
1969	Sea A	148	537	78	126	10	2	9	41	95-2	1	90	.235	.349	.311	87	-6	**73**-18	.959	-6	92	83	2b59,3b59,O26(3/22/1)	0	0.0
1970	Mil A★	154	604	104	179	35	4	31	82	77-5	4	107	.296	.377	.522	146	39	38-16	.943	13	113	87	3b128,2b22,O13(8/5/2)	0	**5.6**
1971	Mil A	152	585	79	151	26	3	14	52	65-4	1	92	.258	.333	.385	104	3	25-3	.975	-6	97	40	O90(77/13/2),3b70/2	0	-0.3
1972	Bos A	144	556	92	141	29	2	14	49	67-1	9	104	.254	.341	.388	111	10	25-7	.985	-6	99	46	O144C	0	0.4
1973	Bos A	147	566	92	159	23	3	17	71	61-2	1	93	.281	.351	.422	110	8	**54**-14	.985	1	96	136	O143(139/5/0)/D	0	0.8
1974	Bos A	118	443	66	105	15	3	5	24	46-2	3	65	.237	.312	.318	77	-13	28-12	.982	-4	88	48	O61L,D51	0	-2.0
1975	Cal A	89	285	40	68	10	3	3	31	38-5	2	51	.239	.329	.312	89	-3	19-8	.992	-1	65	127	D57,1b19,O9(2/0/7)	0	-0.5
	†Oak A	34	69	11	22	4	0	2	7	5-0	1	9	.319	.373	.464	138	3	7-0	.963	-2	36	81	1b16,O9(5/1/4),3b2,D3	0	0.2
	Year	123	354	51	90	14	1	5	38	43-5	3	60	.254	.337	.342	98	0	26-8	.978	-3	51	105	D60,1b35,O18(7/1/11),3b2	0	-0.3
1976	Bal A	46	77	8	18	5	0	1	7	10-0	0	16	.234	.318	.338	99	0	4-3	1.000	-0	0	0	D27/1If	0	-0.1
Total	15	1810	6269	972	1609	256	36	146	567	753-30	35	1080	.257	.338	.379	100	20	408-116	.986	6	105	70	O1227L,3b270,D139,2b85,1b36	59	1.4

HARRAH, TOBY Colbert Dale; B10.26.1948 Sissonville WV; BR/TR/6´0˝/(165–190); d9.5; M1/C8

YEAR	TM LG	G	AB	R	H	2B	3B	HR	RBI	BB-IB	HP	SO	AVG	OBP	SLG	AOPS	ABR	SB-CS	FA	FR	RNG	THR	GAMES AT POSITION	DL	BFW
1969	Was A	8	1	4	0	0	0	0	0	0-0	0	0	.000	.000	.000	-99	0	0-0	ø	-0	0	0	/S	0	0.0
1971	Was A	127	383	45	88	11	3	2	22	40-3	0	48	.230	.300	.290	72	-14	10-9	.955	-4	98	108	S116,3b7	0	-0.8
1972	Tex A✳	116	374	47	97	14	3	1	31	34-1	0	31	.259	.316	.321	94	-3	16-7	.960	-8	95	91	S106	23	0.3
1973	Tex A	118	461	64	120	16	1	10	50	46-2	2	49	.260	.328	.364	99	-1	10-3	.951	3	112	81	S76,3b52	36	1.2
1974	Tex A	**161**	573	79	149	23	2	21	74	50-2	2	65	.260	.319	.417	114	9	15-14	.963	6	96	105	S158,3b3	0	3.3
1975	Tex A☆	151	522	81	153	24	1	20	93	98-3	1	71	.293	.403	.458	145	36	23-9	.963	16	112	101	S118,3b28,2b21	0	**6.9**
1976	Tex A★	155	584	64	152	21	1	15	67	91-5	3	59	.260	.360	.377	114	14	8-5	.955	2	101	92	S146,3b5,D4	0	3.6
1977	Tex A	159	539	90	142	25	5	27	87	**109**-7	10	73	.263	.393	.479	135	32	27-5	.963	-21	89	72	3b159/S	0	1.2
1978	Tex A	139	450	56	103	17	3	12	59	83-3	2	66	.229	.349	.360	100	3	31-8	.965	-2	91	93	3b91,S49	0	0.9
1979	Cle A	149	527	99	147	25	1	20	77	89-2	8	60	.279	.389	.444	124	22	20-9	.940	-42	64	81	3b127,S33,D9	0	-1.8
1980	Cle A	**160**	561	100	150	22	4	11	72	98-3	7	60	.267	.379	.380	109	12	17-2	.971	5	99	83	3b156,S2,D3	0	1.7
1981	Cle A	**103**	361	64	105	12	4	5	44	57-8	1	44	.291	.382	.388	125	14	12-1	.949	-11	90	63	3b101,S3/D	0	0.5
1982	Cle A☆	**162**	602	100	183	29	4	25	78	84-7	12	52	.304	.398	.490	142	38	17-3	.971	-15	89	76	3b159,2b3,S2	0	2.4
1983	Cle A	138	526	81	140	23	1	9	53	75-1	7	49	.266	.363	.365	98	2	16-10	**.971**	-5	95	100	3b137/2D	27	-0.5
1984	NY A	88	253	40	55	9	4	1	26	42-2	2	28	.217	.331	.296	78	-6	3-0	.968	1	97	140	3b74,2b4/rfD	17	-0.5
1985	Tex A	126	396	65	107	18	1	9	44	113-2	4	60	.270	.432	.389	126	23	11-4	.989	-6	97	86	2b122,S2/D	0	2.4
1986	Tex A	95	289	36	63	18	2	7	41	44-0	2	53	.218	.322	.367	86	-5	2-5	.982	-14	84	83	2b93	15	-1.6
Total	17	2155	7402	1115	1954	307	40	195	918	1153-51	63	868	.264	.365	.395	114	176	238-94	.963	-95	90	83	3b1099,S813,2b244,D21/rf	118	19.2

HARRELL, JOHN John Robert; B11.27.1947 Long Beach CA; BR/TR/6´2˝/190; [SFN66 31/605]; d10.1; Col West Valley (CA) CC

YEAR	TM LG	G	AB	R	H	2B	3B	HR	RBI	BB-IB	HP	SO	AVG	OBP	SLG	AOPS	ABR	SB-CS	FA	FR	RNG	THR	GAMES AT POSITION	DL	BFW
1969	SF N	2	6	0	3	0	0	0	2	2-0	0	1	.500	.625	.500	221	1	0-0	1.000	-0	0	0	C2	0	0.1

HARRELL, BILLY William; B7.18.1928 Norristown PA; BR/TR/6´1.5˝/180; d9.2; Negro Lg 1951; Col Siena

YEAR	TM LG	G	AB	R	H	2B	3B	HR	RBI	BB-IB	HP	SO	AVG	OBP	SLG	AOPS	ABR	SB-CS	FA	FR	RNG	THR	GAMES AT POSITION	DL	BFW
1955	Cle A	13	19	2	8	0	0	0	1	3-0	0	3	.421	.500	.421	144	1	1-0	.926	-0	106	30	S11	0	0.2
1957	Cle A	22	57	6	15	1	1	1	5	4-0	0	7	.263	.311	.368	86	-1	3-1	.893	-4	86	67	S14,3b6/2	0	-0.4
1958	Cle A	101	229	36	50	4	0	7	19	15-2	2	36	.218	.271	.328	66	-12	12-2	.986	-6	105	144	3b46,S45,2b7/rf	0	-1.3
1961	Bos A	37	37	10	6	2	0	0	1	1-0	0	8	.162	.184	.216	6	-5	1-0	1.000	2	109	250	3b10,S7,1b3	0	-0.3
Total	4	173	342	54	79	7	1	8	26	23-2	2	54	.231	.283	.327	68	-17	17-3	.933	-9	93	72	S77,3b62,2b8,1b3/rf	0	-1.8

HARRELSON, BUD Derrel McKinley; B6.6.1944 Niles CA; BB/TR (BR 1965, 1975p)/5´11˝/(150–160); d9.2; M2/C7; Col San Francisco St.

YEAR	TM LG	G	AB	R	H	2B	3B	HR	RBI	BB-IB	HP	SO	AVG	OBP	SLG	AOPS	ABR	SB-CS	FA	FR	RNG	THR	GAMES AT POSITION	DL	BFW
1965	NY N	19	37	3	4	1	1	0	0	2-0	0	11	.108	.154	.189	-4	-5	0-0	.955	-1	92	74	S18	0	-0.6
1966	NY N	33	99	20	22	2	4	0	4	13-1	0	23	.222	.313	.323	79	-3	7-3	.993	6	111	152	S29	0	0.7
1967	NY N	151	540	59	137	16	4	1	28	48-0	4	64	.254	.317	.304	80	-13	12-13	.958	15	107	102	S149	0	1.4
1968	NY N	111	402	38	88	7	3	0	14	29-2	1	68	.219	.273	.251	58	-21	4-5	.972	-0	94	105	S106	0	-1.5
1969	†NY N	123	395	42	98	11	6	0	24	54-7	2	54	.248	.341	.306	81	-9	1-3	.969	1	94	113	S119	0	0.6

YEAR	TM LG	G	AB	R	H	2B	3B	HR	RBI	BB-IB	HP	SO	AVG	OBP	SLG	AOPS	ABR	SB-CS	FA	FR	RNG	THR	GAMES AT POSITION	DL	BFW
1970	NY N★	157	564	72	137	18	8	1	42	95-4	3	74	.243	.351	.309	78	-14	23-4	.971	-26	80	97	S156	0	-1.8
1971	NY N★	142	547	55	138	16	6	0	32	53-0	2	59	.252	.319	.303	78	-15	28-7	.978	15	96	104	S140	0	2.1
1972	NY N	115	418	54	90	10	4	1	24	58-4	3	57	.215	.313	.266	68	-16	12-4	.970	-9	90	79	S115	22	-1.1
1973	†NY N	106	356	35	92	12	3	0	20	48-4	1	49	.258	.348	.309	84	-6	5-1	.979	-10	91	82	S103	48	-0.3
1974	NY N	106	331	48	75	10	0	1	13	71-1	2	39	.227	.366	.266	79	-5	9-4	.968	20	106	121	S97	0	2.8
1975	NY N	34	73	5	16	2	0	0	3	12-2	0	13	.219	.329	.247	64	-3	0-0	.941	-2	86	129	S34	97	-0.2
1976	NY N	118	359	34	84	12	4	1	26	63-5	2	56	.234	.351	.298	90	-2	9-3	.962	-11	87	73	S117	0	0.2
1977	NY N	107	269	25	48	6	2	1	12	27-1	1	28	.178	.255	.227	32	-27	5-4	.984	-2	92	92	S98	0	-2.1
1978	Phi N	71	103	16	22	1	0	0	9	18-0	0	21	.214	.331	.223	56	-5	5-2	.972	12	127	199	2b43,S15	0	0.9
1979	Phi N	53	71	7	20	6	0	0	7	13-0	1	14	.282	.395	.366	106	2	3-3	.990	1	97	103	2b25,S17,3b9/lf	0	0.4
1980	Tex A	87	180	26	49	6	0	1	9	29-0	0	23	.272	.373	.322	95	0	4-4	.952	11	104	119	S87,2b2	46	1.7
Total	16	1533	4744	539	1120	136	45	7	267	633-31	22	653	.236	.327	.288	75	-142	127-60	.969	21	94	100	S1400,2b70,3b9/lf	213	3.2
Harrelson, Ken	Kenneth Smith "Hawk"; B9.4.1941 Woodruff SC; BR/TR/6´2˝/(185–195); d6.9																								
1963	KC A	79	226	16	52	10	1	6	23	23-3	0	58	.230	.299	.363	81	-6	1-1	.980	-6	65	90	1b34,O28L	0	-1.7
1964	KC A	49	139	15	27	5	0	7	12	13-0	0	34	.194	.263	.381	74	-5	0-1	.977	4	110	193	O24L,1b15	0	-0.4
1965	KC A	150	483	61	115	17	3	23	66	66-3	1	112	.238	.329	.429	116	10	9-7	.992	-4	87	93	1b125,O4(3/0/1)	0	-0.2
1966	KC A	63	210	24	47	5	0	5	22	27-3	0	59	.224	.312	.319	85	-4	9-2	.985	2	119	87	1b58,O3(3/0/1)	0	-0.5
	Was A	71	250	25	62	8	1	7	28	26-2	1	53	.248	.321	.372	100	0	4-1	.991	-3	86	102	1b70	0	-0.7
	Year	134	460	49	109	13	1	12	50	53-5	1	112	.237	.317	.348	93	-4	13-3	.989	-1	101	95	1b128,O3(3/0/1)	0	-1.2
1967	Was A	26	79	10	16	0	0	3	10	7-1	0	15	.203	.261	.316	75	-3	1-0	.996	0	110	108	1b23	0	-0.4
	KC A	61	174	23	53	11	0	6	30	17-1	0	17	.305	.361	.471	151	11	8-2	.992	-2	84	68	1b45	0	0.9
	†Bos A	23	80	9	16	4	1	3	14	5-2	0	12	.200	.247	.387	79	-2	1-1	.929	-3	74	77	O23R/1	0	-0.7
	Year	110	333	42	85	15	1	12	54	29-4	0	44	.255	.311	.414	115	6	10-3	.993	-4	93	81	1b69,O23R	0	-0.2
1968	Bos A★	150	535	79	147	17	4	35	**109**	69-9	2	90	.275	.356	.518	154	35	2-6	**1.000**	4	110	111	O132R,1b19	0	3.1
1969	Bos A	10	46	6	10	1	0	3	8	4-0	0	6	.217	.275	.435	93	-1	0-1	.991	1	138	145	1b10	0	-0.1
	Cle A	149	519	83	115	13	4	27	84	95-6	2	96	.222	.341	.418	109	7	17-8	.985	1	105	66	O144(7/0/137),1b16	0	0.1
	Year	159	565	89	125	14	4	30	92	99-6	2	102	.221	.336	.419	108	7	17-9	.985	2	105	66	O144(7/0/137),1b26	0	0.0
1970	Cle A	17	39	3	11	1	0	1	1	6-0	0	4	.282	.378	.385	106	1	0-0	1.000	1	111	179	1b13	148	0.0
1971	Cle A	52	161	20	32	2	0	5	14	24-3	0	21	.199	.301	.304	66	-7	1-0	.988	-1	92	81	1b40,O7(5/0/2)	0	-1.2
Total	9	900	2941	374	703	94	14	131	421	382-33	6	577	.239	.325	.414	109	36	53-30	.990	-6	95	95	1b469,O365(70/0/296)	148	-1.8
Harrington, Andy	Andrew Matthew; B2.12.1903 Mountain View CA; D1.26.1979 Boise ID; BR/TR/5´11˝/170; d4.18; Col St. Marys (CA)																								
1925	Det A	1	1	0	0	0	0	0	0	0	0	0	.000	.000	.000	-99	0	0-0	ø	0	—	—	/H	—	0.0
Harrington, Mickey	Charles Michael; B10.8.1934 Hattiesburg MS; BR/TR/6´4˝/205; d7.10; Col Southern Mississippi																								
1963	Phi N	1	0	0	0	0	0	0	0	0-0	0	0	ø	ø	ø	ø	0	0-0	ø	0	—	—	/R	0	0.0
Harrington, Jerry	Jeremiah Peter; B8.12.1868 Hamden IA; D4.16.1913 Keokuk IA; BR/TR/5´11˝/220; d4.30																								
1890	Cin N	65	236	25	58	7	1	1	23	15	3	29	.246	.299	.297	74	-8	4	.957	11	*123*	*90*	C65	—	0.7
1891	Cin N	92	333	25	76	10	5	2	41	19	1	34	.228	.272	.306	68	-15	4	.908	-8	*90*	*96*	C92/3	—	-1.4
1892	Cin N	22	61	6	13	1	0	0	3	6	0	1	.213	.284	.230	56	-3	0	.989	2	*115*	*91*	C22/1	—	0.0
1893	Lou N	10	36	4	4	1	0	0	6	3	0	9	.111	.179	.139	-16	-6	0	.853	-3	*101*	*72*	C10	—	-0.7
Total	4	189	666	60	151	19	6	3	73	43	4	73	.227	.278	.287	64	-32	8	.932	1	*105*	*92*	C189/13	—	-1.4
Harrington, Joe	Joseph C.; B12.21.1869 Fall River MA; D9.13.1933 Fall River MA; BR/TR/5´8.5˝/162; d9.10																								
1895	Bos N	18	65	21	18	0	2	2	13	7	1	5	.277	.356	.431	95	-1	3	.912	-1	99	96	2b18	—	-0.1
1896	Bos N	54	199	26	40	5	3	1	25	19	1	17	.201	.274	.271	42	-18	2	.819	-6	104	107	3b49,S4/2	—	-2.0
Total	2	72	264	47	58	5	5	3	38	26	2	22	.220	.295	.311	55	-19	5	.819	-8	104	107	3b49,2b19,S4	—	-2.1
Harris, Candy	Alonzo; B9.17.1947 Selma AL; BB/TR/6´0˝/160; d4.13																								
1967	Hou N	6	1	0	0	0	0	0	0	0-0	0	1	.000	.000	.000	-99	0	0-0	ø	0	—	—	/H	25	0.0
Harris, Spencer	Anthony Spencer; B8.12.1900 Duluth MN; D7.3.1982 Minneapolis MN; BL/TL/5´9˝/145; d4.14																								
1925	Chi A	56	92	12	26	2	0	1	13	14	1	13	.283	.383	.337	89	-1	1-3	.957	-0	94	141	O27(1/12/17)	—	-0.3
1926	Chi A	80	222	36	56	11	3	2	27	20	1	15	.252	.317	.356	78	-8	8-3	.949	-1	95	101	O63(7/11/48)	—	-1.2
1929	Was A	6	14	1	3	1	0	0	1	0	0	3	.214	.214	.286	27	-2	1-0	1.000	-0	94	0	O4C	—	-0.2
1930	Phi A	22	49	4	9	1	0	0	5	5	0	2	.184	.259	.204	18	-6	0-0	.958	1	97	242	O13(10/1/2)	—	-0.6
Total	4	164	377	53	94	15	3	3	46	39	2	33	.249	.323	.329	70	-17	10-6	.954	-1	95	124	O107(18/28/67)	—	-2.3
Harris, Gail	Boyd Gail; B10.15.1931 Abingdon VA; BL/TL/6´0˝/(195–200); d6.3																								
1955	NY N	79	263	27	61	9	0	12	36	20-3	2	46	.232	.289	.403	82	-8	0-0	.982	-0	105	106	1b75	0	-1.2
1956	NY N	12	38	2	5	0	1	1	1	3-1	2	10	.132	.233	.263	33	-4	0-0	.975	0	113	128	1b11	0	-0.5
1957	NY N	90	225	28	54	7	3	9	31	16-2	6	28	.240	.305	.418	93	-3	1-0	.985	-2	92	115	1b61	0	-0.8
1958	Det A	134	451	63	123	18	8	20	83	36-3	4	60	.273	.328	.481	113	6	1-2	.986	2	108	88	1b122	0	0.1
1959	Det A	114	349	39	77	4	3	9	39	29-3	6	49	.221	.290	.327	66	-17	0-1	.992	3	106	87	1b93	0	-2.0
1960	Det A	8	5	0	0	0	0	0	0	2-1	0	1	.000	.286	.000	-15	-1	0-0	1.000	0	134	101	1b5	0	-0.1
Total	6	437	1331	159	320	38	15	51	190	106-13	20	194	.240	.304	.406	88	-27	2-3	.986	2	105	97	1b367	0	-4.5
Harris, Brendan	Brendan Michael; B8.26.1980 Albany NY; BR/TR/6´1˝/200; [ChiN01 5/138]; d7.6; Col William and Mary																								
2004	Chi N	3	9	0	2	1	0	0	1	1-0	0	1	.222	.300	.333	62	0	0-0	.889	0	84	0	3b3	0	0.0
	Mon N	20	50	4	8	2	0	1	2	2-0	1	11	.160	.208	.260	19	-6	0-0	.972	-6	73	49	2b11,3b4	0	-1.2
	Year	23	59	4	10	3	0	1	3	3-0	1	12	.169	.222	.271	26	-7	0-0	.972	-6	73	49	2b11,3b7	0	-1.2
2005	Was N	4	9	1	3	1	0	1	3	0-0	1	0	.333	.400	.778	208	1	0-0	1.000	1	112	101	2b2/3	0	0.2
2006	Was N	17	32	3	8	2	0	0	2	3-0	1	3	.250	.333	.313	70	-1	0-0	.923	-3	83	51	S5,2b4,3b3	0	-0.3
	Cin N	8	10	2	2	0	0	1	1	1-0	0	4	.200	.273	.500	87	0	0-0	1.000	0	79	221	2b3	0	0.0
	Year	25	42	5	10	2	0	1	3	4-0	1	7	.238	.319	.357	74	-2	0-0	1.000	-2	63	78	2b7,S5,3b3	0	-0.3
Total	3	52	110	10	23	6	0	3	9	7-0	3	19	.209	.275	.345	58	-6	0-0	.983	-7	74	62	2b20,3b11,S5	0	-1.3
Harris, Charlie	Charles Jenkins; B10.21.1877 Macon GA; D3.14.1963 Gainesville FL; BR/TR/5´8˝/200; d5.26; Col Mercer																								
1899	Bal N	30	68	16	19	3	0	0	1	3	1	—	.279	.319	.324	73	-3	4	.872	-3	92	106	3b21,O3(2/0/1),2b2/S	—	-0.5
Harris, Dave	David Stanley "Sheriff"; B7.14.1900 Summerfield NC; D9.18.1973 Atlanta GA; BR/TR/5´11˝/170; d4.14																								
1925	Bos N	92	340	49	90	8	7	5	36	27	1	44	.265	.321	.374	84	-10	6-4	.962	7	110	142	O90(87/4/0)	—	-0.9
1928	Bos N	7	17	2	2	1	0	0	0	2	0	6	.118	.211	.176	2	-2	0	.833	-1	105	0	O6L	—	-0.3
1930	Chi A	33	86	16	21	2	1	5	13	7	1	22	.244	.309	.465	96	-1	0-0	1.000	-0	107	62	O23L/2	—	-0.3
	Was A	73	205	40	65	19	8	4	44	28	0	35	.317	.399	.546	137	12	6-3	.983	4	99	190	O59(19/12/28)	—	1.1
	Year	106	291	56	86	21	9	9	57	35	1	57	.296	.373	.522	125	11	6-3	.988	4	101	152	O82(42/12/28)/2	—	0.8
1931	Was A	77	231	49	72	14	8	5	50	49	1	38	.312	.434	.506	146	18	7-6	.950	-1	100	76	O60(3/0/57)	—	1.2
1932	Was A	81	156	26	51	7	4	6	29	19	0	34	.327	.400	.538	143	10	4-4	.932	-0	100	127	O34(7/8/20)	—	0.7
1933	†Was A	82	177	33	46	9	2	5	38	25	2	26	.260	.358	.418	106	2	3-1	.964	-3	103	31	O45(4/11/32),1b6,3b2	—	-0.2
1934	Was A	97	235	28	59	14	3	2	37	39	0	40	.251	.358	.362	89	-3	2-3	.973	2	99	169	O64(15/1/49),3b5	—	-0.4
Total	7	542	1447	243	406	74	33	32	247	196	5	245	.281	.368	.444	112	26	28-21	.963	8	103	122	O381(164/36/186),3b7,1b6/2	—	0.9
Harris, Donald	Donald; B11.12.1967 Waco TX; BR/TR/6´1˝/185; [TexA89 1/5]; d9.4; Col Texas Tech																								
1991	Tex A	18	8	4	3	0	0	1	2	1-0	0	3	.375	.444	.750	228	1	1-0	1.000	-0	88	0	O12(2/7/5),D3	0	0.1
1992	Tex A	24	33	3	6	1	0	0	1	0-0	0	15	.182	.182	.212	10	-4	1-0	.974	2	125	150	O24(5/15/5)	0	-0.2
1993	Tex A	40	76	10	15	2	0	1	8	5-0	1	18	.197	.253	.263	41	-7	0-1	.943	-2	78	213	O38(1/27/11),D3	0	-0.9
Total	3	82	117	17	24	3	0	2	11	6-0	1	36	.205	.248	.282	46	-10	2-1	.959	-0	93	176	O74(8/49/21),D6	0	-1.0
Harris, Frank	Frank W.; B11.2.1858 Pittsburgh PA; D11.26.1939 E.Moline IL; BR/TR; d4.17																								
1884	Alt U	24	95	10	25	2	1	0	—	3	—	—	.263	.286	.305	78	-5	—	.941	1	160	13	1b17,O8(4/3/1)	—	-0.6

HARRIS, BILLY James William; B11.24.1943 Hamlet NC; BL/TR/6´0˝/176; [CleA66 27/531]; d6.16; Col North Carolina–Wilmington

YEAR	TM LG	G	AB	R	H	2B	3B	HR	RBI	BB-IB	HP	SO	AVG	OBP	SLG	AOPS	ABR	SB-CS	FA	FR	RNG	THR	GAMES AT POSITION	DL	BFW
1968	Cle A	38	94	10	20	5	1	0	3	8-0	0	22	.213	.275	.287	72	-3	2-0	.970	2	119	90	2b27,3b10/S	0	0.1
1969	KC A	5	7	1	2	1	0	0	0	0-0	0	1	.286	.286	.429	96	0	0-0	1.000	0	213	0	/2	53	0.0
Total	2	43	101	11	22	6	1	0	3	8-0	0	23	.218	.275	.297	74	-3	2-0	.971	2	121	88	2b28,3b10/S	53	0.1

HARRIS, JOHN John Thomas; B9.13.1954 Portland OR; BL/TL/6´3˝/(205–215); [AnaA76 29/638]; d9.26; Col Lubbock Christian

YEAR	TM LG	G	AB	R	H	2B	3B	HR	RBI	BB-IB	HP	SO	AVG	OBP	SLG	AOPS	ABR	SB-CS	FA	FR	RNG	THR	GAMES AT POSITION	DL	BFW
1979	Cal A	1	2	0	0	0	0	0	0	0-0	0	0	.000	.000	.000	-99	-1	0-0	1.000	-0	0	0	/1	0	-0.1
1980	Cal A	19	41	8	12	5	0	2	7	7-0	0	4	.293	.388	.561	161	4	0-1	1.000	-0	38	51	1b10,O3L	0	0.3
1981	Cal A	36	77	5	19	3	0	3	9	3-0	0	11	.247	.275	.403	92	-1	0-0	.976	-3	88	124	1b11,O10L/D	0	-0.5
Total	3	56	120	13	31	8	0	5	16	10-0	0	15	.258	.313	.450	114	2	0-1	.987	-3	61	85	1b22,O13L/D	0	-0.3

HARRIS, JOE Joseph "Moon"; B5.20.1891 Plum Borough PA; D12.10.1959 Renton PA; BR/TR/5´9˝/170; d6.9; Mil 1918

YEAR	TM LG	G	AB	R	H	2B	3B	HR	RBI	BB-IB	HP	SO	AVG	OBP	SLG	AOPS	ABR	SB-CS	FA	FR	RNG	THR	GAMES AT POSITION	DL	BFW
1914	NY A	2	1	0	0	0	0	0	0	3	1	1	.000	.800	.000	143	1	0	1.000	-0	0	0	/1lf	—	0.1
1917	Cle A	112	369	40	112	22	4	0	65	55	3	32	.304	.398	.385	129	16	11	.985	9	140	107	1b95,O5R,3b2	—	2.5
1919	Cle A	62	184	30	69	16	1	1	46	33	1	21	.375	.472	.489	160	18	2	.988	2	122	92	1b46,S4	—	2.0
1922	Bos A	119	408	53	129	30	9	6	54	30	1	15	.316	.364	.478	119	10	2-6	.953	6	102	139	O83(71/0/12),1b21	—	0.6
1923	Bos A	142	483	82	162	28	11	13	76	52	5	27	.335	.406	.520	142	29	7-3	.968	-1	106	71	O132L,1b9	—	1.7
1924	Bos A	133	491	82	148	36	9	3	77	81	5	25	.301	.406	.430	115	15	6-1	.993	5	111	104	1b128,O3L	—	1.2
1925	Bos A	8	19	4	3	0	1	1	2	5	0	5	.158	.333	.421	90	0	0-0	1.000	-1	31	48	1b6	—	-0.1
	†Was A	100	300	60	97	21	9	12	59	51	5	28	.323	.430	.573	156	27	6-3	.989	4	121	106	1b58,O41(16/0/25)	—	2.3
	Year	108	319	64	100	21	10	13	61	56	5	33	.313	.424	.564	152	26	6-3	.990	3	113	101	1b64,O41(16/0/25)	—	2.2
1926	Was A	92	257	43	79	13	9	5	55	37	5	9	.307	.405	.486	135	14	2-3	.994	-0	84	80	1b36,O35(3/0/32)	—	0.8
1927	†Pit N	129	411	57	134	27	9	5	73	48	4	19	.326	.402	.472	125	16	0	.990	2	105	96	1b116,O3L	—	1.0
1928	Pit N	16	23	2	9	2	1	0	2	4	1	2	.391	.500	.565	171	3	0	1.000	1	218	206	1b6	—	0.4
	Bro N	55	89	8	21	6	1	1	8	14	0	4	.236	.340	.360	84	-2	0	.958	-1	76	164	O16(6/0/10)	—	-0.3
	Year	71	112	10	30	8	2	1	10	18	1	6	.268	.374	.402	103	1	0	.958	1	76	164	O16(6/0/10),1b6	—	0.1
Total	10	970	3035	461	963	201	64	47	517	413	31	188	.317	.404	.472	131	147	36-16	.989	28	117	100	1b522,O319(235/0/84),S4,3b2	—	12.2

HARRIS, LENNY Leonard Anthony; B10.28.1964 Miami FL; BL/TR/5´10˝/(195–235); [CinN83 5/108]; d9.7; Col Miami–Dade North (FL) CC; OF(157/3/161)

YEAR	TM LG	G	AB	R	H	2B	3B	HR	RBI	BB-IB	HP	SO	AVG	OBP	SLG	AOPS	ABR	SB-CS	FA	FR	RNG	THR	GAMES AT POSITION	DL	BFW
1988	Cin N	16	43	7	16	1	0	0	8	5-0	0	4	.372	.420	.395	136	2	4-1	1.000	1	127	0	3b10,2b6	0	0.4
1989	Cin N	61	188	17	42	4	0	2	11	9-0	1	20	.223	.263	.277	53	-12	10-6	.980	5	91	112	2b32,S17,3b16	0	-0.6
	LA N	54	147	19	37	6	1	1	15	11-0	1	13	.252	.308	.327	83	-3	4-3	1.000	-5	76	94	O21(20/0/1),2b14,3b8/S	0	-1.0
	Year	115	335	36	79	10	1	3	26	20-0	2	33	.236	.283	.299	66	-16	14-9	.975	-1	87	115	2b46,3b24,O21(20/0/1),S18	0	-1.6
1990	LA N	137	431	61	131	16	4	2	29	29-2	1	31	.304	.348	.374	101	0	15-10	.959	-0	101	109	3b94,2b44,O2(0/1/1)/S	0	0.1
1991	LA N	145	429	59	123	16	1	3	38	37-5	5	32	.287	.349	.350	99	0	12-3	.943	7	95	116	3b113,2b27,S20/lf	0	1.1
1992	LA N	135	347	28	94	11	0	0	30	24-3	1	24	.271	.318	.303	78	-10	19-7	.963	17	108	99	2b81,3b33,O15(7/0/8),S10	0	1.1
1993	LA N	107	160	20	38	6	1	2	11	15-4	0	15	.237	.303	.325	72	-7	3-1	.987	-0	107	65	2b35,3b17,S3,O2R	0	-0.5
1994	Cin N	66	100	13	31	3	1	0	14	5-0	0	13	.310	.340	.360	84	-3	7-2	.846	1	128	132	3b15,1b4,O3R,2b2	0	-0.1
1995	†Cin N	101	197	32	41	8	3	2	16	14-0	0	20	.208	.259	.310	49	-15	10-1	.939	7	145	114	3b24,1b23,O8(4/0/4)/2	0	-0.8
1996	Cin N	125	302	33	86	17	2	5	32	21-1	1	31	.285	.330	.404	92	-4	14-6	1.000	3	102	138	O37(23/1/18),3b24,1b16,2b8	0	-0.2
1997	Cin N	120	238	32	65	13	1	3	28	18-1	2	18	.273	.327	.374	82	-6	4-3	.977	-2	88	58	O42(26/0/17),2b20,3b13,1b11	0	-0.9
1998	Cin N	57	122	12	36	8	0	0	10	8-2	1	9	.295	.338	.361	85	-2	1-3	.929	0	100	153	O32(13/0/20)/P	0	-0.4
	NY N	75	168	18	39	7	0	6	17	9-1	1	12	.232	.272	.381	73	-8	5-2	.988	2	112	119	O65(21/1/53),3b10,2b2/1D	0	-0.7
	Year	132	290	30	75	15	0	6	27	17-3	2	21	.259	.300	.372	78	-10	6-5	.968	2	108	131	O97(34/1/73),3b10,2b2/P1D	0	-1.1
1999	Col N	91	158	15	47	12	0	0	13	6-0	0	6	.297	.323	.373	60	-9	1-1	.924	5	114	157	2b24,O14(3/0/11),3b2,D2	0	-0.3
	†Ari N	19	29	2	11	1	0	1	7	0-0	0	1	.379	.367	.517	123	1	1-0	1.000	-0	65	352	3b5,O2R	0	0.1
	Year	110	187	17	58	13	0	1	20	6-0	0	7	.310	.330	.396	68	-8	2-1	.924	5	114	157	2b24,O16(3/0/13),3b7,D2	0	-0.2
2000	Ari N	36	85	9	16	1	1	1	13	3-1	0	5	.188	.209	.259	18	-11	5-0	.909	-3	80	33	3b20,O3R	0	-1.3
	†NY N	76	138	22	42	6	3	3	13	17-1	0	17	.304	.381	.457	117	3	8-1	.854	1	100	92	3b16,O11(6/0/5),1b10,2b3/D	0	0.5
	Year	112	223	31	58	7	4	4	26	20-2	0	22	.260	.317	.381	78	-8	13-1	.880	-2	88	57	3b36,O14(6/0/8),1b10,2b3/D	0	-0.8
2001	NY N	110	135	12	30	5	1	0	9	8-0	0	9	.222	.266	.274	43	-12	3-2	.875	-2	55	0	3b11,O8(5/0/3),1b7/2D	0	-1.4
2002	Mil N	122	197	23	60	8	2	3	17	14-1	2	17	.305	.355	.411	102	0	4-1	1.000	0	112	0	O16L,3b14,1b12,D2	0	0.0
2003	Chi N	75	131	11	24	3	0	1	7	13-3	0	20	.183	.255	.229	27	-14	1-0	.948	-1	90	86	3b35,1b2,O2(1/0/1)	0	-1.5
	†Fla N	13	14	3	4	0	0	0	1	3-0	0	1	.286	.412	.286	90	0	0-0	1.000	0	130	0	O4(2/0/2)	0	0.0
	Year	88	145	14	28	3	0	1	8	16-3	0	21	.193	.272	.234	34	-14	1-0	.948	-1	90	86	3b35,O6(3/0/3),1b2	0	-1.5
2004	Fla N	79	95	7	20	5	0	1	17	3-0	0	8	.211	.232	.295	38	-9	0-0	1.000	-1	91	0	O14(8/0/6),3b3,D2	0	-1.0
2005	Fla N	83	70	5	22	4	0	1	13	7-1	1	11	.314	.385	.414	115	2	0-1	ø	-0	0	0	3b2,O2(1/0/1)/1D	0	0.1
Total	18	1903	3924	460	1055	161	21	37	369	279-26	17	337	.269	.318	.349	80	-117	131-54	.937	32	99	103	3b485,O304R,2b300,1b87,S52,D12/P	0	-7.3

HARRIS, NED Robert Ned; B7.9.1916 Ames IA; D12.18.1976 W.Palm Beach FL; BL/TL/5´11˝/175; d4.20; Mil 1944–45; Col Brewton–Parker

YEAR	TM LG	G	AB	R	H	2B	3B	HR	RBI	BB-IB	HP	SO	AVG	OBP	SLG	AOPS	ABR	SB-CS	FA	FR	RNG	THR	GAMES AT POSITION	DL	BFW
1941	Det A	26	61	11	13	3	1	1	4	6	0	13	.213	.284	.344	59	-4	1-0	1.000	-1	78	0	O12L	0	-0.5
1942	Det A	121	398	53	108	16	10	9	45	49	0	35	.271	.351	.430	110	5	5-4	.944	-7	88	73	O104R	0	-0.9
1943	Det A	114	354	43	90	14	3	6	32	47	1	29	.254	.343	.362	99	0	6-8	.961	-3	96	87	O96(4/6/86)	0	-1.2
1946	Det A	1	1	0	0	0	0	0	0	0	0	0	.000	.000	.000	-94	0	0-0	ø	0	—	—	/H	0	0.0
Total	4	262	814	107	211	33	14	16	81	102	1	77	.259	.342	.393	101	1	12-12	.955	-12	91	76	O212(16/6/190)	0	-2.6

HARRIS, BUCKY Stanley Raymond; B11.8.1896 Port Jervis NY; D11.8.1977 Bethesda MD; BR/TR/5´9.5˝/156; d8.28; M29; HF1975

YEAR	TM LG	G	AB	R	H	2B	3B	HR	RBI	BB-IB	HP	SO	AVG	OBP	SLG	AOPS	ABR	SB-CS	FA	FR	RNG	THR	GAMES AT POSITION	DL	BFW
1919	Was A	8	28	0	6	2	0	0	4	1	1	3	.214	.267	.286	56	-2	0	.925	-0	100	105	2b8	—	-0.2
1920	Was A	136	506	76	152	26	6	1	68	41	**21**	36	.300	.377	.381	104	5	16-17	.958	-12	95	91	2b134	—	-0.7
1921	Was A	**154**	584	82	169	22	8	0	54	54	**18**	39	.289	.367	.354	89	-8	29-9	.959	12	103	116	2b154	—	1.2
1922	Was A	**154**	602	95	162	24	8	2	40	52	**14**	38	.269	.341	.346	84	-14	25-11	.970	**31**	**104**	**134**	2b154	—	2.2
1923	Was A	145	532	60	150	21	13	2	70	50	13	29	.282	.358	.382	100	0	23-16	.961	19	103	**136**	2b144/S	—	2.1
1924	†Was A	143	544	88	146	28	9	1	58	56	7	41	.268	.344	.358	84	-13	20-10	.968	-12	86	**136**	2b143,M	—	-1.9
1925	†Was A	144	551	91	158	30	3	1	66	64	9	21	.287	.370	.358	87	-8	14-12	.970	5	94	**129**	2b144,M	—	-0.1
1926	Was A	141	537	94	152	39	9	1	63	58	9	41	.283	.363	.395	100	1	16-11	.963	-11	93	90	2b141,M	—	-0.6
1927	Was A	128	475	98	127	20	3	1	55	66	5	33	.267	.363	.328	81	-10	18-3	**.972**	2	97	94	2b128,M	—	-0.2
1928	Was A	99	358	34	73	11	5	0	28	27	2	26	.204	.264	.263	39	-33	5-2	.970	11	104	110	2b96/3rfM	—	-1.9
1929	Det A	7	11	3	1	0	0	0	0	2	0	2	.091	.231	.091	-14	-2	1-0	.900	-0	131	0	2b4/SM	—	-0.2
1931	Det A	4	8	1	1	1	0	0	0	1	0	1	.125	.222	.250	23	-1	0-0	1.000	-0	96	79	2b3,M	—	-0.1
Total	12	1263	4736	722	1297	224	64	9	506	472	99	310	.274	.352	.354	86	-85	167-91	.965	44	98	116	2b1253,S2/rf3	—	-0.4

HARRIS, VIC Victor Lanier; B3.27.1950 Los Angeles CA; BB/TR/6´0˝/(165–175); [OakA70*S1/9]; d7.21; Col Los Angeles Valley (CA) JC

YEAR	TM LG	G	AB	R	H	2B	3B	HR	RBI	BB-IB	HP	SO	AVG	OBP	SLG	AOPS	ABR	SB-CS	FA	FR	RNG	THR	GAMES AT POSITION	DL	BFW
1972	Tex A	61	186	8	26	5	1	0	10	12-1	0	39	.140	.192	.177	11	-21	7-3	.960	-9	91	76	2b58/S	0	-3.1
1973	Tex A	152	555	71	138	14	7	8	44	55-1	2	81	.249	.317	.342	89	-9	13-12	.977	-4	108	63	O113(2/111/7),3b25,2b18	0	-1.7
1974	Chi N	62	200	18	39	6	3	0	11	29-3	0	26	.195	.294	.255	53	-12	9-3	.943	-9	92	54	2b56	88	-1.8
1975	Chi N	51	56	6	10	0	0	0	5	6-0	0	7	.179	.254	.179	22	-6	0-0	.900	-0	76	0	O11(9/2/0),3b7,2b5	0	-0.7
1976	StL N	97	259	21	59	12	3	1	19	16-0	1	55	.228	.275	.309	64	-13	1-2	.945	-1	99	91	2b37,O35(9/25/1),3b12/S	0	-1.3
1977	SF N	69	165	28	43	12	0	2	14	19-1	0	36	.261	.332	.370	89	-2	2-1	.973	-6	88	104	2b27,S11,3b9,O3(0/2/1)	0	-0.6
1978	SF N	53	100	8	15	4	0	1	11	11-1	0	24	.150	.230	.220	28	-10	0-0	.934	-4	96	59	S22,2b10,O6(4/2/1)	0	-1.3
1980	Mil A	34	89	8	19	4	1	1	7	12-0	0	13	.213	.304	.315	72	-3	4-1	.967	-1	106	52	O31(4/5/22),3b2/2	0	-0.5
Total	8	579	1610	168	349	57	15	13	121	160-7	3	281	.217	.287	.295	65	-76	36-22	.954	-33	93	77	2b212,O199(28/147/32),3b55,S35	88	-11.0

HARRIS, WILLIE William Charles; B6.22.1978 Cairo GA; BL/TR/5´9˝/(170–175); [BalA99 24/727]; d9.2; Col Kennesaw St.

YEAR	TM LG	G	AB	R	H	2B	3B	HR	RBI	BB-IB	HP	SO	AVG	OBP	SLG	AOPS	ABR	SB-CS	FA	FR	RNG	THR	GAMES AT POSITION	DL	BFW
2001	Bal A	9	24	3	3	1	0	0	0	0-0	0	7	.125	.125	.167	-25	-4	0-0	1.000	1	97	271	O8C	0	-0.4
2002	Chi A	49	163	14	38	4	0	2	12	9-0	0	21	.233	.270	.294	49	-12	8-0	.985	5	100	90	2b38,O6C	0	-0.4
2003	Chi A	79	137	19	28	3	1	0	5	10-0	0	28	.204	.259	.241	32	-14	12-2	.977	3	110	229	O61C,2b12	25	-0.8
2004	Chi A	129	409	68	107	15	2	2	27	51-0	1	79	.262	.343	.323	73	-15	19-7	.990	4	103	95	2b92,O30(1/29/0),D2	0	-0.5
2005	†Chi A	56	121	17	31	2	1	1	8	13-0	1	25	.256	.333	.314	71	-5	10-3	.986	-2	94	116	2b32,S5,D9	0	-0.4
2006	Bos A	47	45	17	7	2	0	0	1	4-0	2	11	.156	.250	.200	20	-5	6-3	1.000	0	106	117	O36(11/24/1)/2	0	-0.5
Total	6	369	899	138	214	27	4	5	53	87-0	4	171	.238	.306	.294	57	-55	55-15	.988	10	100	98	2b175,O141(12/128/1),D11,S5	25	-3.0

HARRISON, CHUCK Charles William; B4.25.1941 Abilene TX; BR/TR/5´10˝/(185–190); d9.15; Col Texas Tech

YEAR	TM LG	G	AB	R	H	2B	3B	HR	RBI	BB-IB	HP	SO	AVG	OBP	SLG	AOPS	ABR	SB-CS	FA	FR	RNG	THR	GAMES AT POSITION	DL	BFW
1965	Hou N	15	45	2	9	4	0	1	9	8-0	0	9	.200	.321	.356	97	0	0-0	.983	-0	94	96	1b12	0	-0.1
1966	Hou N	119	434	52	111	23	2	9	52	37-4	2	69	.256	.316	.380	100	0	2-0	.992	3	105	74	1b114	0	-0.4
1967	Hou N	70	177	13	43	7	3	2	26	13-0	0	30	.243	.292	.350	87	-4	0-0	.987	-1	95	61	1b59	0	-0.8

YEAR	TM LG	G	AB	R	H	2B	3B	HR	RBI	BB-IB	HP	SO	AVG	OBP	SLG	AOPS	ABR	SB-CS	FA	FR	RNG	THR	GAMES AT POSITION	DL	BFW
1969	KC A	75	213	18	47	5	1	3	18	16-2	1	20	.221	.276	.296	60	-12	1-2	.993	1	104	64	1b55	0	-1.7
1971	KC A	49	143	9	31	4	0	2	21	11-2	0	19	.217	.266	.287	59	-8	0-0	.992	-0	99	100	1b39	0	-1.2
Total	5	328	1012	94	241	43	6	17	126	85-8	3	147	.238	.297	.343	83	-24	3-2	.991	2	102	74	1b279	0	-4.2
Harrison, Ben	Ben; d9.27																								
1901	Was A	1	2	0	0	0	0	0	0	1	0	—	.000	.333	.000	-2	0	0	ø	-0	0	0	/lf	—	0.0
Harrison, Rit	Washington Ritter; B9.16.1849 Waterbury CT; D11.7.1888 Bridgeport CT; d5.20																								
1875	NH NA	1	4	0	2	1	0	0	1	0	—	0	.500	.500	.750	376	1	0-1	.333	-2	—	—	/CS	—	-0.1
Harshaney, Sam	Samuel; B4.24.1910 Madison IL; D2.1.2001 San Antonio TX; BR/TR/6´0˝/180; d9.28																								
1937	StL A	5	11	0	1	1	0	0	0	3	0	0	.091	.286	.182	20	-1	0-0	.905	-0	94	181	C4	—	-0.1
1938	StL A	11	24	2	7	0	0	0	0	3	0	2	.292	.370	.292	68	-1	0-0	.975	-1	78	109	C10	—	-0.1
1939	StL A	42	145	15	35	2	0	0	15	9	1	8	.241	.290	.255	40	-13	0-1	.994	-3	78	135	C36	—	-1.4
1940	StL A	3	1	0	0	0	0	0	0	1	0	0	.000	.500	.000	41	0	0-0	ø	0	0	0	C2	—	0.0
Total	4	61	181	17	43	3	0	0	15	16	1	10	.238	.303	.254	43	-15	0-1	.983	-4	79	135	C52	—	-1.6
Hart, Bo	Bodhi J.; B9.27.1976 Creswell OR; BR/TR/5´11˝/(170–175); [StLN99 33/1002]; d6.19; Col Gonzaga																								
2003	StL N	77	296	46	82	13	5	4	28	12-0	6	64	.277	.317	.395	86	-7	3-1	.989	-9	90	78	2b69,S3	0	-1.2
2004	StL N	11	13	0	2	0	0	0	2	1-0	0	3	.154	.214	.154	-2	-2	0-0	1.000	1	112	255	2b4/S	0	-0.1
Total	2	88	309	46	84	13	5	4	30	13-0	6	67	.272	.313	.385	82	-9	3-1	.989	-8	91	85	2b73,S4	0	-1.3
Hart, Burt	James Burton; B6.28.1870 Brown Co. MN; D1.29.1921 Sacramento CA; BB/6´3˝/200; d6.6																								
1901	Bal A	58	206	33	64	3	5	0	23	20	4	—	.311	.383	.374	106	2	7	.976	-8	30	83	1b58	—	-0.6
Hart, Hub	James Henry; B2.2.1878 Everett MA; D10.10.1960 Fort Wayne IN; BL/TR/5´11˝/170; d7.16; Col Georgetown																								
1905	Chi A	11	20	3	2	0	0	0	4	3	0	—	.100	.217	.100	2	-2	0	1.000	-1	120	26	C7	—	-0.3
1906	Chi A	17	37	1	6	0	0	0	0	2	0	—	.162	.205	.162	16	-4	0	.935	-2	125	55	C15	—	-0.5
1907	Chi A	29	70	6	19	1	0	0	7	5	1	—	.271	.329	.286	100	0	1	.956	-3	110	92	C25	—	-0.1
Total	3	57	127	10	27	1	0	0	11	10	1	—	.213	.275	.220	59	-6	1	.957	-5	116	73	C47	—	-0.9
Hart, Mike	James Michael; B12.20.1951 Kalamazoo MI; BB/TR/6´3˝/185; [MonN72 11/245]; d6.12; Col Alma																								
1980	Tex A	5	4	1	1	0	0	0	0	1-0	0	1	.250	.400	.250	85	0	0-0	1.000	-1	33	0	O2C	0	0.0
Hart, Jim Ray	James Ray; B10.30.1941 Hookerton NC; BR/TR/5´11˝/(185–195); d7.7																								
1963	SF N	7	20	1	4	1	0	0	2	3-1	2	6	.200	.360	.250	80	0	0-0	1.000	-0	74	107	3b7	70	0.0
1964	SF N	153	566	71	162	15	6	31	81	47-4	4	94	.286	.342	.498	132	22	5-2	.937	2	100	108	3b149,O6(1/0/5)	0	2.5
1965	SF N	160	591	91	177	30	6	23	96	47-3	2	75	.299	.349	.487	130	23	6-4	.919	-9	91	76	3b144,O15(14/0/1)	0	1.4
1966	SF N★	156	578	88	165	23	4	33	93	48-6	4	75	.285	.342	.510	130	23	2-5	.941	-2	104	98	3b139,O17(16/0/1)	0	1.8
1967	SF N	158	578	98	167	26	7	29	99	77-11	4	100	.289	.373	.509	153	41	1-1	.937	-13	98	75	3b89,O72L	0	2.5
1968	SF N	136	480	67	124	14	3	23	78	46-10	3	74	.258	.323	.444	130	16	3-1	.925	-11	80	97	3b72,O65L	0	0.3
1969	SF N	95	236	27	60	9	0	3	26	28-1	5	49	.254	.343	.331	91	-2	0-0	.943	-3	86	67	O68L,3b3	0	-0.9
1970	SF N	76	255	30	72	12	1	8	37	30-6	3	29	.282	.360	.431	113	5	0-0	.908	-13	76	22	3b56,O18L	0	-0.9
1971	†SF N	31	39	5	10	0	0	2	5	6-0	0	8	.256	.356	.410	118	1	0-1	.833	0	76	610	3b3,O3L	23	0.0
1972	SF N	24	79	10	24	5	0	5	8	6-0	1	10	.304	.360	.557	155	5	0-1	.886	-8	56	61	3b20	0	-0.3
1973	SF N	5	3	0	0	0	0	0	1	3-0	0	1	.000	.429	.000	48	0	0-0	.600	0	269	0	/3	0	0.0
	NY A	114	339	29	86	13	2	13	52	36-7	0	45	.254	.324	.419	111	4	0-2	ø	0	0	0	D106	0	0.1
1974	NY A	10	19	1	1	0	0	0	0	3-0	0	7	.053	.182	.053	-30	-3	0-0	ø	0	—	—	D4	0	-0.4
Total	12	1125	3783	518	1052	148	29	170	578	380-49	28	573	.278	.345	.467	128	135	17-17	.929	-56	93	87	3b683,O264(257/0/7),D110	93	6.1
Hart, Jason	Jason Wyatt; B9.5.1977 Walnut Creek CA; BR/TR/6´4˝/237; [OakA98 5/135]; d8.18; Col Missouri St.																								
2002	Tex A	10	15	2	4	3	0	0	0	2-0	0	7	.267	.353	.467	112	0	0-0	1.000	-0	97	0	O7L,1b2	0	0.0
Hart, Corey	Jon Corey; B3.24.1982 Bowling Green KY; BR/TR/6´6˝/(200–215); [MilN00 11/321]; d5.25																								
2004	Mil N	1	1	0	0	0	0	0	0	0-0	0	1	.000	.000	.000	-99	0	0-0	ø	0	—	—	/H	0	0.0
2005	Mil N	21	57	9	11	2	1	2	7	6-0	0	11	.193	.270	.368	65	-3	2-0	.966	-1	84	133	O16(2/11/3)	0	-0.4
2006	Mil N	87	237	32	67	13	2	9	33	17-1	0	58	.283	.328	.468	101	0	5-8	.991	1	105	119	O61(26/6/37),1b2	0	-0.3
Total	3	109	295	41	78	15	3	11	40	23-1	0	70	.264	.316	.447	93	-3	7-8	.985	0	100	122	O77(28/17/40),1b2	0	-0.7
Hart, Mike	Michael Lawrence; B2.17.1958 Milwaukee WI; BL/TL/5´11˝/185; [SeaA79 13/313]; d5.8; Col Wisconsin–Madison																								
1984	Min A	13	29	0	5	0	0	0	5	1-0	0	2	.172	.194	.172	4	-4	0-1	1.000	1	127	166	O11(8/0/3)	0	-0.3
1987	Bal A	34	76	7	12	2	0	4	12	6-0	0	19	.158	.217	.342	47	-6	1-4	1.000	1	113	0	O32(4/29/1)	0	-0.6
Total	2	47	105	7	17	2	0	4	17	7-0	0	21	.162	.211	.295	35	-10	1-5	1.000	3	117	42	O43(12/29/4)	0	-0.9
Hart, Tom	Thomas Henry "Bushy"; B6.15.1869 Canaan NY; D9.17.1939 Gardner MA; 5´7˝/160; d4.15																								
1891	Was AA	8	24	1	3	0	0	0	2	2	0	1	.125	.192	.125	-9	-3	1	1.000	1	81	203	C5,O3C	—	-0.2
Hart, Bill	William Woodrow; B3.4.1913 Wiconisco PA; D7.29.1968 Lykens PA; BR/TR/6´0˝/175; d9.18																								
1943	Bro N	8	19	0	3	0	0	0	1	1	0	2	.158	.200	.158	4	-2	0	1.000	2	127	112	3b6/S	0	0.0
1944	Bro N	29	90	8	16	4	2	0	4	9	0	7	.178	.253	.267	47	-7	1	.941	-6	95	44	S25,3b2	0	-1.1
1945	Bro N	58	161	27	37	6	2	3	27	14	0	21	.230	.291	.348	78	-6	7	.913	-5	78	111	3b39,S8	0	-1.0
Total	3	95	270	35	56	10	4	3	32	24	0	30	.207	.272	.307	63	-15	8	.924	-9	83	111	3b47,S34	0	-2.1
Hartford, Bruce	Bruce Daniel; B5.14.1892 Chicago IL; D5.25.1975 Los Angeles CA; BR/TR/6´0.5˝/190; d6.3																								
1914	Cle A	8	22	5	4	1	0	0	0	4	0	9	.182	.308	.227	59	-1	0	.913	-2	99	0	S8	—	-0.3
Harting, Ed	Edward "Jumbo"; B3.1864 St.Louis MO; D6.18.1947 St.Louis MO; 5´9.5˝/213; d10.5																								
1886	StL AA	1	3	0	1	1	0	0	1	0	0	—	.333	.333	.667	201	0	0	.889	1	—	—	/C	—	0.1
Hartje, Chris	Christian Henry; B3.25.1915 San Francisco CA; D6.26.1946 Seattle WA; BR/TR/5´10.5˝/165; d9.9																								
1939	Bro N	9	16	2	5	1	0	0	5	1	0	0	.313	.353	.375	92	0	0	.909	-1	90	0	C8	—	-0.1
Hartley, Grover	Grover Allen "Slick"; B7.2.1888 Osgood IN; D10.19.1964 Daytona Beach FL; BR/TR/5´11˝/175; d5.13; C10																								
1911	NY N	11	18	1	4	2	0	0	1	1	0	1	.222	.263	.333	64	-1	1	.962	2	149	84	C10	—	0.2
1912	NY N	25	34	3	8	2	1	0	7	0	1	4	.235	.257	.353	64	-2	2	.960	2	146	75	C25	—	0.1
1913	NY N	23	19	4	6	0	0	0	0	1	0	2	.316	.350	.316	90	0	4-1	.978	2	138	54	C21/1	—	0.2
1914	StL F	86	212	24	61	13	2	1	25	12	1	26	.288	.329	.382	89	-6	4	.956	-8	81	93	C32,2b13,1b9,3b3,O2C	—	-1.2
1915	StL F	120	394	47	108	21	6	1	50	42	8	21	.274	.356	.365	98	-5	10	.972	-4	102	91	C113/1	—	0.1
1916	StL A	89	222	19	50	8	0	0	12	30	3	24	.225	.325	.261	80	-4	4	.968	-3	85	84	C75	—	-0.1
1917	StL A	19	13	2	3	0	0	0	0	2	0	1	.231	.333	.231	75	0	0	.875	0	102	244	C4/S3	—	0.0
1924	NY N	4	7	1	2	1	0	0	1	1	0	0	.286	.375	.429	118	0	1-0	1.000	-0	112	100	C3	—	0.1
1925	NY N	46	95	9	30	1	1	0	8	8	1	3	.316	.375	.347	89	-1	2-0	.974	3	93	140	C37,1b8	—	0.3
1926	NY N	13	21	0	1	0	0	0	0	5	0	0	.048	.231	.048	-22	-4	0	1.000	0	90	72	C13	—	-0.3
1927	Bos A	103	244	23	67	11	0	1	31	22	1	14	.275	.337	.332	76	-8	1-0	.967	-14	60	70	C86	—	-1.7
1929	Cle A	24	33	2	9	0	1	0	8	2	0	1	.273	.314	.333	64	-2	0-0	1.000	-1	85	0	C13	—	-0.3
1930	Cle A	1	4	0	3	0	0	0	1	0	0	0	.750	.750	.750	271	1	0-0	.750	-1	46	0	/C	—	0.1
1934	StL A	5	3	0	1	1	0	0	0	1	0	0	.333	.500	.667	183	0	0-0	1.000	0	0	0	C2	—	0.1
Total	14	569	1319	135	353	60	11	3	144	127	15	97	.268	.339	.337	85	-32	29-1	.968	-23	90	86	C435,1b19,2b13,3b4,O2C/S	—	-2.4
Hartley, Chick	Walter Scott; B8.22.1880 Philadelphia PA; D7.18.1948 Philadelphia PA; BR/TR/5´8˝/180; d6.4																								
1902	NY N	1	4	0	0	0	0	0	0	0	0	—	.000	.000	.000	-99	-1	0	1.000	-0	0	0	/lf	—	-0.1
Hartman, Fred	Frederick Orrin "Dutch"; B4.25.1868 Allegheny (now part of Pittsburgh) PA; D11.11.1938 McKeesport PA; BR/TR/5´8˝/170; d7.26																								
1894	Pit N	49	182	41	58	4	7	2	20	16	5	11	.319	.389	.451	103	0	12	.876	-2	99	77	3b49	—	-0.1
1897	StL N	125	519	67	158	21	8	2	67	26	10	—	.304	.350	.387	96	-4	18	.867	-1	106	83	3b125	—	-0.2
1898	NY N	123	475	57	129	16	11	2	88	25	4	—	.272	.313	.364	97	-4	11	.882	8	107	87	3b123	—	0.5
1899	NY N	51	177	25	42	3	5	1	17	12	10	—	.237	.322	.328	81	-5	2	.883	-2	94	132	3b51	—	-0.5

YEAR	TM LG	G	AB	R	H	2B	3B	HR	RBI	BB-IB	HP	SO	AVG	OBP	SLG	AOPS	ABR	SB-CS	FA	FR	RNG	THR	GAMES AT POSITION	DL	BFW
1901	Chi A	120	473	77	146	23	13	3	89	25	9	—	.309	.355	.431	120	12	31	.894	-6	98	96	3b119	—	0.8
1902	StL N	114	416	30	90	10	3	0	52	14	5	—	.216	.251	.255	58	-21	14	.908	-4	102	59	3b105,S4,1b3	—	-2.4
Total	6	582	2242	297	623	77	47	10	333	118	43	11	.278	.326	.368	95	-22	88	.886	-7	102	86	3b572,S4,1b3	—	-1.9

HARTMAN, J C J C; B4.15.1934 Cottonton AL; BR/TR/6´0˝/175; d7.21; Negro Lg 1952–55

YEAR	TM LG	G	AB	R	H	2B	3B	HR	RBI	BB-IB	HP	SO	AVG	OBP	SLG	AOPS	ABR	SB-CS	FA	FR	RNG	THR	GAMES AT POSITION	DL	BFW
1962	Hou N	51	148	11	33	5	0	0	5	4-0	1	16	.223	.248	.257	39	-13	1-1	.972	5	97	122	S48	0	-0.5
1963	Hou N	39	90	2	11	1	0	0	3	2-1	1	13	.122	.151	.133	-19	-14	1-0	.950	-0	99	104	S32	0	-1.3
Total	2	90	238	13	44	6	0	0	8	6-1	2	29	.185	.211	.210	18	-27	2-1	.964	5	98	115	S80	0	-1.8

HARTNETT, GABBY Charles Leo; B12.20.1900 Woonsocket RI; D12.20.1972 Park Ridge IL; BR/TR/6´1˝/195; d4.12; M3/C3; HF1955; Col Dean (MA) JC

YEAR	TM LG	G	AB	R	H	2B	3B	HR	RBI	BB-IB	HP	SO	AVG	OBP	SLG	AOPS	ABR	SB-CS	FA	FR	RNG	THR	GAMES AT POSITION	DL	BFW
1922	Chi N	31	72	4	14	1	1	0	4	6	0	8	.194	.256	.236	27	-8	1-0	.982	4	128	167	C27	—	-0.2
1923	Chi N	85	231	28	62	12	2	8	39	25	3	22	.268	.347	.442	107	2	4-0	.994	5	118	75	C39,1b31	—	0.8
1924	Chi N	111	354	56	106	17	7	16	67	39	5	37	.299	.377	.523	137	19	10-2	.963	-1	**116**	118	C105	—	2.6
1925	Chi N	117	398	61	115	28	3	24	67	36	2	77	.289	.351	.555	126	14	1-5	.958	10	**143**	124	C110	—	2.8
1926	Chi N	93	284	35	78	25	3	8	41	32	2	37	.275	.352	.468	118	8	0	.978	9	**180**	121	C88	—	2.2
1927	Chi N	127	449	56	132	32	5	10	80	44	3	42	.294	.361	.454	117	11	2	.973	9	**163**	101	C126	—	2.9
1928	Chi N	120	388	61	117	26	9	14	57	65	2	32	.302	.404	.523	143	26	3	**.989**	15	**184**	112	C118	—	4.7
1929	†Chi N	25	22	2	6	2	1	1	9	5	0	5	.273	.407	.591	144	2	1	1.000	0	0	0	/C	—	0.2
1930	Chi N	141	508	84	172	31	3	37	122	55	1	62	.339	.404	.630	144	35	0	**.989**	3	**131**	89	C136	—	4.1
1931	Chi N	116	380	53	107	32	1	8	70	52	1	48	.282	.370	.434	113	9	3	.981	4	120	98	C105	—	2.0
1932	†Chi N	121	406	52	110	25	3	12	52	51	1	59	.271	.354	.436	112	8	0	.982	10	**194**	104	C117/1	—	2.4
1933	Chi N★	140	490	55	135	21	4	16	88	37	0	51	.276	.326	.433	115	9	1	.989	11	145	95	C140	—	2.9
1934	Chi N★	130	438	58	131	21	1	22	90	37	3	46	.299	.358	.502	130	18	0	**.996**	12	**120**	**129**	C129	—	3.6
1935	†Chi N★	116	413	67	142	32	6	13	91	41	1	46	.344	.404	.545	152	31	1	.984	11	109	**135**	C110	—	4.7
1936	Chi N★	121	424	49	130	25	6	7	64	30	6	36	.307	.361	.443	113	8	0	**.991**	9	121	106	C114	—	2.2
1937	Chi N★	110	356	47	126	21	6	12	82	43	0	19	.354	.424	.548	156	28	0	**.996**	0	121	102	C103	—	3.4
1938	†Chi N☆	88	299	40	82	19	1	10	59	48	3	17	.274	.380	.445	123	11	1	**.995**	-0	109	80	C83,M	—	1.6
1939	Chi N	97	306	36	85	18	2	12	59	37	1	32	.278	.358	.467	118	8	0	.992	-3	134	109	C86,M	—	1.0
1940	Chi N	37	64	3	17	3	0	1	12	8	0	7	.266	.347	.359	97	0	0	.951	-0	98	84	C22/1M	—	0.1
1941	NY N	64	150	20	45	5	0	5	26	12	1	14	.300	.356	.433	119	3	0	.994	-1	114	68	C34	0	0.4
Total	20	1990	6432	867	1912	396	64	236	1179	703	35	697	.297	.370	.489	126	242	28-7	.984	107	138	107	C1793,1b33	0	44.4

HARTNETT, PAT Patrick J. "Happy"; B10.20.1863 Boston MA; D4.10.1935 Boston MA; 6´1˝/175; d4.18

YEAR	TM LG	G	AB	R	H	2B	3B	HR	RBI	BB-IB	HP	SO	AVG	OBP	SLG	AOPS	ABR	SB-CS	FA	FR	RNG	THR	GAMES AT POSITION	DL	BFW
1890	StL AA	14	53	6	10	2	1	0	4	6	1	—	.189	.283	.264	54	-3	1	.954	-1	89	28	1b14	—	-0.5

HARTS, GREG Gregory Rudolph; B4.21.1950 Atlanta GA; BL/TL/6´0˝/161; d9.15

YEAR	TM LG	G	AB	R	H	2B	3B	HR	RBI	BB-IB	HP	SO	AVG	OBP	SLG	AOPS	ABR	SB-CS	FA	FR	RNG	THR	GAMES AT POSITION	DL	BFW
1973	NY N	3	2	0	1	0	0	0	0	0-0	0	0	.500	.500	.500	179	0	0-0	ø	0	—	—	/H	0	0.0

HARTSEL, TOPSY Tully Frederick; B6.26.1874 Polk OH; D10.14.1944 Toledo OH; BL/TL/5´5˝/155; d9.14

YEAR	TM LG	G	AB	R	H	2B	3B	HR	RBI	BB-IB	HP	SO	AVG	OBP	SLG	AOPS	ABR	SB-CS	FA	FR	RNG	THR	GAMES AT POSITION	DL	BFW
1898	Lou N	22	71	11	23	0	0	0	9	11	1	—	.324	.422	.324	116	2	2	.931	-1	78	159	O21R	—	0.0
1899	Lou N	30	75	8	18	1	1	1	7	11	1	—	.240	.345	.320	83	-1	1	.927	-1	70	135	O22(7/0/15)	—	-0.3
1900	Cin N	18	64	10	21	2	1	2	5	8	0	—	.328	.403	.484	148	4	7	.957	-4	0	0	O18L	—	0.0
1901	Chi N	**140**	558	111	187	25	16	7	54	74	1	—	.335	.414	.475	163	48	41	.951	-2	88	63	O140(131/0/9)	—	3.6
1902	Phi A	**137**	545	**109**	154	20	12	5	58	**87**	2	—	.283	.383	.391	110	11	**47**	.955	-1	100	55	O137L	—	0.1
1903	Phi A	98	373	65	116	19	14	5	26	49	0	—	.311	.391	.477	152	25	13	.968	-4	59	0	O96(94/2/0)	—	1.7
1904	Phi A	147	534	79	135	17	12	2	25	75	2	—	.253	.347	.341	112	10	19	.959	-3	94	50	O147(122/25/0)	—	0.0
1905	†Phi A	150	538	88	148	22	8	0	28	**121**	1	—	.275	**.409**	.346	138	33	37	.939	-9	35	27	O149(134/15/0)	—	1.6
1906	Phi A	144	533	96	136	21	9	1	30	**88**	2	—	.255	.363	.334	115	14	31	.969	1	82	127	O144L	—	0.7
1907	Phi A	143	507	93	142	23	6	3	29	**106**	0	—	.280	**.405**	.367	143	33	20	.967	-11	60	50	O143L	—	1.5
1908	Phi A	129	460	73	112	16	6	4	29	**93**	0	—	.243	.371	.330	120	16	15	.960	-4	41	50	O129L	—	0.6
1909	Phi A	83	267	30	72	4	4	1	18	48	0	—	.270	.381	.326	121	9	3	.966	-3	0	0	O74(72/0/2)	—	0.2
1910	†Phi A	90	285	45	63	10	3	0	22	58	0	—	.221	.353	.277	99	3	11	.945	-2	94	86	O83L	—	-0.3
1911	Phi A	25	38	8	9	2	0	0	1	8	2	—	.237	.396	.289	94	1	0	.941	1	92	248	O9L	—	0.1
Total	14	1356	4848	826	1336	182	92	31	341	837	12	—	.276	.384	.370	128	208	247	.956	-41	67	57	O1312(1223/42/47)	—	9.5

HARTSFIELD, ROY Roy Thomas "Spec"; B10.25.1925 Chattahoochee GA; BR/TR/5´9˝/165; d4.28; M3/C5

YEAR	TM LG	G	AB	R	H	2B	3B	HR	RBI	BB-IB	HP	SO	AVG	OBP	SLG	AOPS	ABR	SB-CS	FA	FR	RNG	THR	GAMES AT POSITION	DL	BFW
1950	Bos N	107	419	62	116	15	2	7	24	27	1	61	.277	.322	.372	88	-9	7	.949	-18	93	73	2b96	0	-2.1
1951	Bos N	120	450	63	122	11	2	6	31	41	1	73	.271	.333	.344	89	-7	7-2	.969	-5	92	97	2b114	0	-0.6
1952	Bos N	38	107	13	28	4	3	0	4	5	0	12	.262	.295	.355	82	-3	0-0	.950	-6	94	54	2b29	0	-0.8
Total	3	265	976	138	266	30	7	13	59	73	2	146	.273	.324	.358	88	-19	14-2	.959	-28	93	82	2b239	0	-3.5

HARTUNG, CLINT Clinton Clarence "Floppy","The Hondo Hurricane"; B8.10.1922 Hondo TX; BR/TR/6´4˝/(200–215); d4.15; ▲

YEAR	TM LG	G	AB	R	H	2B	3B	HR	RBI	BB-IB	HP	SO	AVG	OBP	SLG	AOPS	ABR	SB-CS	FA	FR	RNG	THR	GAMES AT POSITION	DL	BFW
1947	NY N	34	94	13	29	4	3	4	13	3	0	21	.309	.330	.543	127	3	0	1.000	-2	85	126	P23,O7L	0	-0.1
1948	NY N	43	56	5	10	1	1	0	3	7	0	24	.179	.270	.232	37	2	0	1.000	-0	102	60	P36	0	0.0
1949	NY N	38	63	7	12	0	0	4	7	4	0	21	.190	.239	.381	64	4	0	.957	2	130	55	P33	0	0.0
1950	NY N	32	43	7	13	2	1	3	10	1	0	13	.302	.318	.605	136	2	0	.939	2	197	0	P20,O2(1/0/1)/1	0	0.1
1951	†NY N	21	44	4	9	1	0	0	2	1	0	9	.205	.222	.227	21	-5	0-0	1.000	-0	82	157	O12R	0	-0.5
1952	NY N	28	78	6	17	2	1	3	8	9	0	24	.218	.299	.385	88	-2	0-0	.932	0	94	156	O24(3/0/22)	0	-0.2
Total	6	196	378	42	90	10	6	14	43	25	0	112	.238	.285	.407	84	4	0-0	.972	1	118	69	P112,O45(11/0/35)/1	0	-0.7

HARTZELL, ROY Roy Allen; B7.6.1881 Golden CO; D11.6.1961 Golden CO; BL/TR/5´8.5˝/155; d4.17; OF(213/32/307)

YEAR	TM LG	G	AB	R	H	2B	3B	HR	RBI	BB-IB	HP	SO	AVG	OBP	SLG	AOPS	ABR	SB-CS	FA	FR	RNG	THR	GAMES AT POSITION	DL	BFW
1906	StL A	113	404	43	86	7	0	0	24	19	10	—	.213	.266	.230	58	-19	21	.889	-3	**101**	**122**	3b103,S6,2b2	—	-2.2
1907	StL A	60	220	20	52	3	5	0	13	11	4	—	.236	.285	.295	85	-4	7	.911	-1	96	130	3b38,2b12,S2,O2R	—	-0.4
1908	StL A	115	422	41	112	5	6	2	32	19	3	—	.265	.302	.320	101	-1	24	.943	-2	164	208	O82(0/4/78),S18,3b7,2b4	—	-0.7
1909	StL A	152	595	64	161	12	5	0	32	29	7	—	.271	.312	.308	103	0	14	.940	6	188	193	O85R,S65/2	—	0.5
1910	StL A	151	542	52	118	13	5	2	30	49	6	—	.218	.290	.271	81	-12	18	.929	7	107	132	3b89,S38,O23R	—	-0.2
1911	NY A	144	527	67	156	17	11	3	91	63	4	—	.296	.375	.387	106	5	22	.936	-12	87	103	3b124,S12,O8(2/0/8)	—	-0.3
1912	NY A	125	416	50	113	10	11	1	38	64	1	—	.272	.370	.356	102	2	20	.906	-2	91	50	3b56,O56(0/13/43),S10,2b2	—	0.0
1913	NY A	141	490	60	127	18	1	0	38	67	4	40	.259	.353	.300	91	-2	26	.942	3	101	100	2b81,O31(4/11/16),3b21,S4	—	0.2
1914	NY A	137	481	55	112	15	9	1	32	68	6	38	.233	.335	.308	94	-2	22-25	.973	-2	100	80	O128(91/3/34),2b5	—	-1.6
1915	NY A	119	387	39	97	11	2	3	60	57	3	37	.251	.351	.313	99	2	7-19	.963	-4	96	72	O107(105/0/2),2b5,3b2	—	-1.3
1916	NY A	33	64	12	12	1	0	0	7	9	1	3	.188	.297	.203	49	-4	1	1.000	-1	95	50	O28(11/1/16)	—	-0.6
Total	11	1290	4548	503	1146	112	55	12	397	455	49	118	.252	.327	.309	93	-35	182-44	.959	-10	123	126	O550R,3b440,S155,2b112	—	-6.6

HARVEL, LUTHER Luther Raymond "Red"; B9.30.1905 Cambria IL; D4.10.1986 Kansas City MO; BR/TR/5´11˝/180; d7.31

YEAR	TM LG	G	AB	R	H	2B	3B	HR	RBI	BB-IB	HP	SO	AVG	OBP	SLG	AOPS	ABR	SB-CS	FA	FR	RNG	THR	GAMES AT POSITION	DL	BFW
1928	Cle A	40	136	12	30	6	1	0	12	4	4	17	.221	.264	.279	42	-12	1-1	.948	-1	92	153	O39C	—	-1.4

HARVEY, ZAZA Ervin King; B1.5.1879 Saratoga CA; D6.3.1954 Santa Monica CA; BL/TL/6´0˝/190; d5.3; ▲

YEAR	TM LG	G	AB	R	H	2B	3B	HR	RBI	BB-IB	HP	SO	AVG	OBP	SLG	AOPS	ABR	SB-CS	FA	FR	RNG	THR	GAMES AT POSITION	DL	BFW
1900	Chi N	2	3	0	0	0	0	0	0	0	0	—	.000	.000	.000	-99	-1	0	1.000	-0	0	0	/P	—	0.0
1901	Chi A	17	40	11	10	3	1	0	3	2	1	—	.250	.302	.375	89	2	1	.930	2	133	248	P16	—	0.0
	Cle A	45	170	21	60	5	5	1	24	9	2	—	.353	.392	.459	141	9	15	.890	2	121	276	O45(21/0/24)	—	0.8
	Year	62	210	32	70	8	6	1	27	11	3	—	.333	.375	.443	131	8	16	.890	3	121	276	O45(21/0/24),P16	—	0.8
1902	Cle A	12	46	5	16	2	0	0	5	3	0	—	.348	.388	.391	121	1	1	1.000	1	136	340	O12R	—	0.1
Total	3	76	259	37	86	10	6	1	32	14	3	—	.332	.373	.429	127	11	17	.907	4	124	289	O57(21/0/36),P17	—	0.9

HARVEY, KEN Kenneth Eugene; B3.1.1978 Los Angeles CA; BR/TR/6´2˝/(240–250); [KCA99 5/151]; d9.18; Col Nebraska

YEAR	TM LG	G	AB	R	H	2B	3B	HR	RBI	BB-IB	HP	SO	AVG	OBP	SLG	AOPS	ABR	SB-CS	FA	FR	RNG	THR	GAMES AT POSITION	DL	BFW
2001	KC A	4	12	1	3	1	0	0	2	0-0	0	4	.250	.250	.333	47	-1	0-1	1.000	-0	72	60	1b3/D	0	-0.2
2003	KC A	135	485	50	129	30	0	13	64	29-4	5	94	.266	.313	.408	83	-12	2-3	.988	6	132	94	1b99,D32	0	-1.6
2004	KC A★	120	456	47	131	20	1	13	55	28-2	8	89	.287	.338	.421	97	-3	1-1	.994	3	125	114	1b73,D41,O4L	15	-0.8
2005	KC A	12	45	4	10	3	0	1	5	3-0	0	13	.222	.271	.356	67	-2	0-0	1.000	-1	0	47	1b5,D7	137	-0.4
Total	4	271	998	102	273	54	1	27	126	60-6	13	200	.274	.322	.411	88	-18	3-5	.991	8	125	101	1b180,D81,O4L	152	-3.0

HASBROOK, ZIGGY Robert Lyndon "Ziggy" (b Robert Lyndon Hasbrouck); B11.21.1893 Grundy Center IA; D2.9.1976 Garland TX; BR/TR/6´1˝/180; d9.6

YEAR	TM LG	G	AB	R	H	2B	3B	HR	RBI	BB-IB	HP	SO	AVG	OBP	SLG	AOPS	ABR	SB-CS	FA	FR	RNG	THR	GAMES AT POSITION	DL	BFW
1916	Chi A	9	8	1	1	0	0	0	0	1	0	2	.125	.222	.125	4	-1	0	1.000	1	234	93	1b7	—	0.0
1917	Chi A	2	1	1	0	0	0	0	0	0	0	0	.000	.000	.000	-98	0	0	1.000	0	205	763	/2	—	0.0
Total	2	11	9	2	1	0	0	0	0	1	0	2	.111	.200	.111	-6	-1	0	1.000	1	234	93	1b7/2	—	0.0

YEAR	TM LG	G	AB	R	H	2B	3B	HR	RBI	BB-IB	HP	SO	AVG	OBP	SLG	AOPS	ABR	SB-CS	FA	FR	RNG	THR	GAMES AT POSITION	DL	BFW
HASELMAN, BILL	William Joseph; B5.25.1966 Long Branch NJ; BR/TR/6´3˝/(205–223); [TexA87 1/23]; d9.3; C2; Col UCLA; [DL 1992 Tex A 28]																								
1990	Tex A	7	13	0	2	0	0	0	3	1-0	0	5	.154	.214	.154	5	-2	0-0	1.000	1	0	0	/CD	0	-0.1
1992	Sea A	8	19	1	5	0	0	0	0	0-0	0	7	.263	.263	.263	47	-1	0-0	1.000	-1	280	142	C5,O2L	0	-0.2
1993	Sea A	58	137	21	35	8	0	5	16	12-0	1	19	.255	.316	.423	96	-1	2-1	.992	-2	67	77	C49,O2R,D4	0	-0.1
1994	Sea A	38	83	11	16	7	1	1	8	3-0	1	11	.193	.230	.337	43	-7	1-0	.982	-3	72	113	C33,O2R,D3	0	-0.8
1995	†Bos A	64	152	22	37	6	1	5	23	17-0	2	30	.243	.322	.395	84	-4	0-2	.989	4	103	101	C48,D11/13	0	0.2
1996	Bos A	77	237	33	65	13	1	8	34	19-3	1	52	.274	.331	.439	91	-4	4-2	.994	9	91	92	C69,1b2,D2	0	0.9
1997	Bos A	67	212	22	50	15	0	6	26	15-2	2	44	.236	.290	.392	75	-8	0-2	.983	-4	66	113	C66	39	-0.8
1998	Tex A	40	105	11	33	6	0	6	17	3-0	0	17	.314	.327	.543	116	2	0-0	.995	-2	75	68	C36,D2	0	0.2
1999	Det A	48	143	13	39	8	0	4	14	10-1	0	26	.273	.320	.413	84	-4	2-0	.996	-1	113	83	C39,D9	0	-0.2
2000	Tex A	62	193	23	53	18	0	6	26	15-0	1	36	.275	.329	.461	96	-1	0-1	.989	-0	95	95	C62	0	0.2
2001	Tex A	47	130	12	37	6	0	3	25	8-0	1	27	.285	.331	.400	89	-2	0-1	1.000	-6	82	128	C47	82	-0.5
2002	Tex A	69	179	16	44	7	0	3	18	11-1	2	25	.246	.297	.335	66	-9	0-0	.991	-10	87	76	C67,D2	0	-1.5
2003	Bos A	4	3	0	0	0	0	0	0	0-0	0	1	.000	.000	.000	-96	-1	0-0	1.000	-0	13	0	C2,D2	0	-0.1
Total	13	589	1606	185	416	94	3	47	210	114-7	11	300	.259	.311	.409	83	-42	9-9	.991	-15	87	95	C524,D38,O6(2/0/4),1b3/3	149	-2.8
HASENMAYER, DON	Donald Irvin; B4.4.1927 Roslyn PA; BR/TR/5´10.5˝/180; d5.2; Mil 1945																								
1945	Phi N	5	18	1	2	0	0	0	1	2	0	1	.111	.200	.111	-13	-3	0	.920	1	130	40	2b4/3	0	-0.1
1946	Phi N	6	12	0	1	1	0	0	0	0	0	2	.083	.083	.167	-31	-2	0	1.000	1	128	449	3b3	0	-0.1
Total	2	11	30	1	3	1	0	0	1	2	0	3	.100	.156	.133	-19	-5	0	1.000	3	142	295	3b4,2b4	0	-0.2
HASLIN, MICKEY	Michael Joseph (b Michael Joseph Haslinsky); B10.25.1909 Wilkes–Barre PA; D3.7.2002 Wilkes–Barre PA; BR/TR/5´8˝/165; d9.7																								
1933	Phi N	26	89	3	21	2	0	0	9	3	0	5	.236	.261	.258	43	-6	1	.956	-2	104	76	2b26	—	-0.8
1934	Phi N	72	166	28	44	8	2	1	11	16	0	13	.265	.330	.355	74	-6	1	.941	-3	100	115	3b26,2b21,S4	—	-0.7
1935	Phi N	110	407	53	108	17	3	3	52	19	1	25	.265	.300	.344	66	-20	5	.931	-2	96	98	S87,3b11,2b9	—	-1.4
1936	Phi N	16	64	6	22	1	1	0	6	3	0	5	.344	.373	.391	96	0	0	.938	-3	97	93	2b12,3b5	—	-0.3
	Bos N	36	104	14	29	1	2	2	11	5	0	9	.279	.312	.385	93	-2	0	.892	-3	65	0	3b17,2b7	—	-0.4
	Year	52	168	20	51	2	3	2	17	8	0	14	.304	.335	.387	95	-2	0	.854	-6	71	40	3b22,2b19	—	-0.7
1937	NY N	27	42	8	8	1	0	0	5	9	0	3	.190	.333	.214	51	-2	1	.920	5	148	96	S9,2b4,3b4	—	0.3
1938	NY N	31	102	13	33	3	0	3	15	4	2	4	.324	.361	.441	119	2	0	.902	-1	117	0	3b15,2b13	—	0.3
Total	6	318	974	125	265	33	8	9	109	59	3	64	.272	.316	.350	74	-34	8	.927	-9	100	99	S100,2b92,3b78	—	-3.0
HASNEY, PETE	Peter James; B5.26.1865 , England; D5.24.1908 Philadelphia PA; d9.13																								
1890	Phi AA	2	7	1	1	0	0	0	0	1	0	—	.143	.250	.143	16	-1	0	.000	-1	0	0	O2R	—	-0.2
HASSAMAER, BILL	William Louis "Roaring Bill"; B7.26.1864 St.Louis MO; D5.25.1910 St.Louis MO; 6´0˝/180; d4.19; OF(3/0/140)																								
1894	Was N	118	494	106	159	33	17	4	90	41	1	20	.322	.375	.482	108	5	16	.916	3	104	144	O68(3/0/65),3b31,2b14,S4	—	0.5
1895	Was N	86	363	42	101	18	4	1	60	26	0	13	.278	.326	.358	77	-13	8	.964	-6	40	39	O75R,1b10/S3	—	-1.7
	Lou N	23	96	7	20	2	2	0	14	3	0	4	.208	.232	.271	31	-10	0	.980	3	153	86	1b21/2S	—	-0.6
	Year	109	459	49	121	20	6	1	74	29	0	17	.264	.307	.340	68	-23	8	.964	-3	40	39	O75R,1b31,S2/32	—	-2.3
1896	Lou N	30	106	8	26	5	0	2	14	14	0	7	.245	.333	.349	83	-2	1	.976	6	195	116	1b29	—	0.3
Total	3	257	1059	163	306	58	23	7	178	84	1	44	.289	.342	.407	89	-20	25	.938	6	71	90	O143R,1b60,3b32,2b15,S6	—	-1.5
HASSETT, BUDDY	John Aloysius; B9.5.1911 New York NY; D8.23.1997 Westwood NJ; BL/TL/5´11˝/180; d4.14; Mil 1943–46; Col Manhattan																								
1936	Bro N	**156**	635	79	197	29	11	3	82	35	4	17	.310	.350	.405	102	0	5	.983	5	**114**	71	1b156	—	-0.9
1937	Bro N	137	556	71	169	31	6	1	53	20	5	19	.304	.334	.387	94	-5	13	.984	10	**129**	92	1b131,O7(1/6/1)	—	-0.8
1938	Bro N	115	335	49	98	11	6	0	40	32	1	19	.293	.356	.361	95	-2	3	.945	-2	102	0	O71(71/0/2),1b8	—	-0.8
1939	Bos N	147	590	72	182	15	3	2	60	29	1	14	.308	.342	.354	94	-7	13	.985	10	**139**	116	1b123,O23R	—	-0.9
1940	Bos N	124	458	59	107	19	4	0	27	25	0	16	.234	.273	.293	59	-27	4	.979	9	146	119	1b98,O13R	—	-2.8
1941	Bos N	118	405	59	120	9	4	1	33	36	0	15	.296	.354	.346	102	1	10	.991	7	129	111	1b99	0	-0.1
1942	†NY A	132	538	80	153	16	6	5	48	32	0	16	.284	.325	.364	95	-6	5-5	.991	11	126	**137**	1b132	0	-0.8
Total	7	929	3517	469	1026	130	40	12	343	209	11	116	.292	.333	.362	92	-46	53-5	.985	49	130	105	1b747,O114(72/6/39)	0	-7.1
HASSEY, RON	Ronald William; B2.27.1953 Tucson AZ; BL/TR/6´2˝/(195–200); [CleA76 18/422]; d4.23; C6; Col Arizona																								
1978	Cle A	25	74	5	15	0	0	2	9	5-0	1	7	.203	.256	.284	54	-5	2-0	.993	4	94	91	C24	0	0.0
1979	Cle A	75	223	20	64	14	0	4	32	19-2	0	19	.287	.339	.404	100	0	1-0	.992	3	76	82	C68,1b2/D	0	0.6
1980	Cle A	130	390	43	124	18	4	8	65	49-3	1	51	.318	.390	.446	129	17	0-2	.993	-9	86	114	C113,1b3,D7	0	1.2
1981	Cle A	61	190	8	44	4	0	1	25	17-0	2	11	.232	.297	.268	66	-8	0-1	.991	9	126	**155**	C56,1b5/D	0	0.2
1982	Cle A	113	323	33	81	18	0	5	34	53-5	1	32	.251	.356	.353	96	1	3-2	.993	2	67	116	C105,1b2,D2	0	0.6
1983	Cle A	117	341	48	92	21	0	6	42	38-2	2	35	.270	.342	.384	97	0	2-2	.995	2	106	95	C113/D	0	0.6
1984	Cle A	48	149	11	38	5	1	0	19	15-2	0	26	.255	.321	.302	73	-5	1-0	1.000	-3	80	83	C44/1D	0	-0.6
	Chi N	19	33	5	11	0	0	2	5	4-1	0	6	.333	.405	.515	145	2	0-1	1.000	1	108	69	C6,1b4	58	0.3
1985	NY A	92	267	31	79	16	1	13	42	28-4	3	21	.296	.369	.509	140	15	0-0	.984	-2	80	64	C69,1b2,D2	0	1.5
1986	NY A	64	191	23	57	14	0	6	29	24-1	2	16	.298	.381	.466	130	9	1-1	.985	-9	102	76	C51,D3	0	0.2
	Chi A	49	150	22	53	11	1	3	20	22-2	1	11	.353	.437	.500	150	12	0-0	1.000	5	178	107	D34,C11	0	1.6
	Year	113	341	45	110	25	1	9	49	46-3	3	27	.323	.406	.481	139	21	1-1	.988	-4	113	81	C62,D37	0	1.8
1987	Chi A	49	145	15	31	9	0	3	12	17-2	2	11	.214	.303	.338	68	-6	0-0	1.000	1	75	67	C24,D18	66	-0.5
1988	†Oak A	107	323	32	83	15	0	7	45	30-1	4	42	.257	.323	.368	98	-1	2-0	.994	-3	134	75	C91,D9	0	0.2
1989	†Oak A	97	268	29	61	12	0	5	23	24-2	1	45	.228	.290	.328	77	-8	1-0	.991	1	92	99	C78/1D	0	-0.3
1990	†Oak A	94	254	18	54	7	0	5	22	27-3	1	29	.213	.288	.299	68	-11	0-0	.997	5	178	63	C59,D15,1b3	0	-0.4
1991	Mon N	52	119	5	27	8	0	1	14	13-1	0	16	.227	.301	.319	76	-3	1-1	.989	-6	75	74	C34	0	-0.8
Total	14	1192	3440	348	914	172	7	71	438	385-31	21	378	.266	.340	.382	100	9	14-10	.993	-0	100	93	C946,D96,1b23	124	4.4
HASSLER, JOE	Joseph Frederick; B4.7.1905 Ft.Smith AR; D9.4.1971 Duncan OK; BR/TR/6´0˝/165; d5.26																								
1928	Phi A	28	34	5	9	2	0	0	3	2	0	4	.265	.306	.324	64	-2	0-1	.879	-2	89	79	S28	—	-0.3
1929	Phi A	4	4	1	0	0	0	0	0	0	0	2	.000	.000	.000	-97	-1	0-0	.600	-1	82	0	S2	—	-0.2
1930	StL A	5	8	3	2	0	0	0	1	0	0	1	.250	.250	.250	26	-1	0-0	1.000	1	126	312	S3	—	0.0
Total	3	37	46	9	11	2	0	0	4	2	0	7	.239	.271	.283	43	-4	0-1	.875	-2	93	100	S33	—	-0.5
HASSON, GENE	Charles Eugene; B7.20.1915 Connellsville PA; D7.30.2003 Pomona CA; BL/TL/6´0˝/197; d9.9																								
1937	Phi A	28	98	12	30	6	3	3	14	13	0	14	.306	.387	.520	129	4	0-0	1.000	-3	51	126	1b28	—	-0.1
1938	Phi A	19	69	10	19	6	2	1	12	12	0	7	.275	.383	.464	114	2	0-0	.958	-3	51	100	1b19	—	-0.3
Total	2	47	167	22	49	12	5	4	26	25	0	21	.293	.385	.497	123	6	0-0	.985	-6	51	116	1b47	—	-0.4
HASTINGS, SCOTT	Winfield Scott; B8.10.1847 Hillsboro OH; D8.14.1907 Sawtelle (now part of Los Angeles) CA; BR/TR/5´8˝/161; d5.6; M2																								
1871	Rok NA	**25**	118	27	30	6	4	0	20	2	—	4	.254	.267	.373	85	-2	11-2	.856	-1	—	—	C23,2b2,O2(2/1/0)/1M	—	0.0
1872	Cle NA	**22**	115	34	45	4	0	0	16	3	—	2	.391	.407	.426	165	10	5-1	.797	-7	—	—	C12,O8(0/3/5),2b6,M	—	0.2
	Bal NA	13	62	16	19	3	1	0	4	1	—	2	.306	.317	.387	111	0	0-1	.905	3	—	—	C13,2b2/cf	—	0.2
	Year	35	177	50	64	7	1	0	20	4	—	4	.362	.376	.412	145	10	5-2	.854	-4	—	—	C25,O9(0/4/5),2b8	—	0.4
1873	Bal NA	30	145	41	41	4	0	0	15	4	—	1	.283	.302	.310	82	-3	4-2	.901	0	—	—	C19,O12C/2	—	-0.2
1874	Har NA	52	247	60	80	11	2	0	30	4	—	3	.324	.335	.385	124	6	10-5	.753	-10	—	—	C39,O26(0/12/14)/2S	—	-0.3
1875	Chi NA	65	287	43	73	9	0	0	30	9	—	14	.254	.277	.286	95	-1	13-11	.815	4	—	—	C46,O29(1/15/15),2b3	—	0.3
1876	Lou N	67	283	36	73	6	1	0	21	5	—	11	.258	.271	.286	73	-10	—	.872	-9	102	203	O65C,C5	—	-1.9
1877	Cin N	20	71	7	10	1	0	0	3	3	—	6	.141	.176	.155	6	-7	—	.791	-7	—	—	C20/cf	—	-1.3
Total	5NA	207	974	221	288	37	7	0	115	23	—	26	.296	.312	.348	108	10	43-22	.824	-10	—	—	C152,O78(3/44/34),2b15/S1	—	0.2
Total	2	87	354	43	83	7	1	0	24	8	—	17	.234	.251	.260	61	-17	—	.872	-16	—	—	O66C,C25	—	-3.2
HATCHER, CHRIS	Christopher Kenneth; B1.7.1969 Anaheim CA; BR/TR/6´3˝/220; [HouN90 3/88]; d9.6; Col Iowa																								
1998	KC A	8	15	0	1	0	0	0	1	1-0	0	7	.067	.125	.067	-46	-3	0-0	1.000	-1	82	0	O5L	0	-0.4
HATCHER, MICKEY	Michael Vaughn; B3.15.1955 Cleveland OH; BR/TR/6´2˝/(184–200); [LAN77 5/124]; d8.3; C10; Col Oklahoma; OF(345/88/146)																								
1979	LA N	33	93	9	25	4	1	1	5	7-0	1	12	.269	.327	.366	90	-1	1-3	.974	1	109	72	O19(1/1/18),3b17	0	-0.2
1980	LA N	57	84	4	19	2	0	1	5	2-1	0	12	.226	.244	.286	49	-6	0-2	1.000	2	85	106	O25(4/0/21),3b18	0	-0.6
1981	Min A	99	377	36	96	23	2	3	37	15-2	2	29	.255	.285	.350	78	-11	3-1	.992	-2	100	55	O91(5/86/0),1b7,3b2/D	0	-1.5
1982	Min A	84	277	23	69	13	2	3	26	8-1	0	27	.249	.269	.343	65	-14	0-2	.988	2	87	250	O47(26/1/21),D29,3b5	0	-1.6

YEAR	TM LG	G	AB	R	H	2B	3B	HR	RBI	BB-IB	HP	SO	AVG	OBP	SLG	AOPS	ABR	SB-CS	FA	FR	RNG	THR	GAMES AT POSITION	DL	BFW
1983	Min A	106	375	50	119	15	3	9	47	14-0	1	19	.317	.342	.445	111	4	2-0	.979	7	130	102	O56(10/0/48),D39,1b7/3	39	0.7
1984	Min A	152	576	61	174	35	5	5	69	37-3	2	34	.302	.342	.406	102	2	0-1	.974	8	115	155	O100L,D37,1b17/3	0	0.4
1985	Min A	116	444	46	125	28	0	3	49	16-1	2	23	.282	.308	.365	79	-13	0-0	.991	5	112	102	O97(96/0/1),D11,1b4	15	-1.2
1986	Min A	115	317	40	88	13	3	3	32	19-2	0	26	.278	.315	.366	83	-8	2-1	.971	1	90	283	O46L,D28,1b22,3b3	0	-1.0
1987	LA N	101	287	27	81	19	1	7	42	20-4	1	19	.282	.328	.429	102	0	2-3	.929	4	104	105	3b49,1b37,O7(1/0/6)	0	0.1
1988	†LA N	88	191	22	56	8	0	1	25	7-3	2	7	.293	.322	.351	97	-1	0-0	1.000	1	90	189	O29(8/0/21),1b25,3b3	15	-0.2
1989	LA N	94	224	18	66	9	2	2	25	13-3	1	16	.295	.328	.379	106	1	1-2	.961	-0	93	252	O48(39/0/10),3b16,1b5/P	30	-0.1
1990	LA N	85	132	12	28	3	1	0	13	6-1	1	22	.212	.248	.250	39	-11	0-0	1.000	-2	79	120	1b25,3b10,O10L	0	-1.5
Total	12	1130	3377	348	946	172	20	38	375	164-21	13	246	.280	.313	.377	88	-58	11-15	.983	26	105	139	O575L,1b149,D145,3b125/P	99	-6.7

HATCHER, BILLY William Augustus; B10.4.1960 Williams AZ; BR/TR/5´9˝/(175–190); [ChiN81*6/131]; d9.10; C8; Col Yavapai (AZ) JC

YEAR	TM LG	G	AB	R	H	2B	3B	HR	RBI	BB-IB	HP	SO	AVG	OBP	SLG	AOPS	ABR	SB-CS	FA	FR	RNG	THR	GAMES AT POSITION	DL	BFW
1984	Chi N	8	9	1	1	0	0	0	0	1-1	0	0	.111	.200	.111	-10	-1	2-0	1.000	0	55	682	O4L	0	-0.1
1985	Chi N	53	163	24	40	12	1	2	10	8-0	3	12	.245	.290	.368	76	-5	2-4	.988	-3	86	79	O44(16/27/3)	15	-1.0
1986	†Hou N	127	419	55	108	15	4	6	36	22-1	5	52	.258	.302	.356	83	-11	38-14	.983	0	99	115	O121(39/95/9)	15	-1.2
1987	Hou N	141	564	96	167	28	3	11	63	42-1	9	70	.296	.352	.415	107	6	53-9	.986	5	96	**204**	O140(51/94/6)	15	1.6
1988	Hou N	145	530	79	142	25	4	7	52	37-4	8	56	.268	.321	.370	103	2	32-13	.983	-1	100	86	O142(124/25/0)	0	-0.1
1989	Hou N	108	395	49	90	15	3	3	44	30-2	1	53	.228	.281	.304	70	-16	22-6	.991	0	107	18	O104(96/11/0)	0	-1.7
	Pit N	27	86	10	21	4	0	1	7	0-0	1	9	.244	.253	.326	66	-4	2-1	1.000	-4	62	0	O20(2/10/9)	0	-0.9
	Year	135	481	59	111	19	3	4	51	30-2	2	62	.231	.277	.308	70	-20	24-7	.992	-4	100	15	O124(98/21/9)	0	-2.6
1990	†Cin N	139	504	68	139	28	5	5	25	33-5	6	42	.276	.327	.381	91	-6	30-10	**.997**	7	109	129	O131(76/69/0)	0	0.2
1991	Cin N	138	442	45	116	25	3	4	41	26-4	7	55	.262	.312	.360	85	-8	11-9	.981	0	107	66	O121(81/54/0)	0	-1.2
1992	Cin N	43	94	10	27	3	0	2	10	5-0	0	11	.287	.314	.383	97	-1	0-2	.967	-2	85	0	O23L	17	-0.4
	Bos A	75	315	37	75	16	2	1	23	17-1	3	41	.238	.283	.311	62	-16	4-6	.968	-4	91	103	O75(63/13/0)	0	-2.4
1993	Bos A	136	508	71	146	24	3	9	57	28-4	11	46	.287	.336	.400	92	-6	14-7	.993	-11	86	87	O130(0/129/2),2b2	0	-1.5
1994	Bos A	44	164	24	40	9	1	1	18	11-0	1	14	.244	.292	.329	58	-10	4-5	.968	0	104	98	O43R/D	0	-1.2
	Phi N	43	134	15	33	5	1	2	13	6-0	0	14	.246	.271	.343	60	-8	4-1	1.000	1	93	208	O40(7/26/11)	0	-0.7
1995	Tex A	6	12	2	1	1	0	0	0	1-0	0	1	.083	.154	.167	-16	-2	0-0	1.000	1	119	388	O5(1/0/4)/D	0	-0.1
Total	12	1233	4339	586	1146	210	30	54	399	267-23	55	476	.264	.312	.364	85	-86	218-87	.986	-8	98	105	O1143(583/553/87),D2,2b2	62	-10.5

HATFIELD, FRED Fred James; B3.18.1925 Lanett AL; D5.22.1998 Tallahassee FL; BL/TR/6´1˝/(171–176); d8.31; C2

YEAR	TM LG	G	AB	R	H	2B	3B	HR	RBI	BB-IB	HP	SO	AVG	OBP	SLG	AOPS	ABR	SB-CS	FA	FR	RNG	THR	GAMES AT POSITION	DL	BFW
1950	Bos A	10	12	3	3	0	0	0	2	3	0	1	.250	.400	.250	63	-1	0-0	1.000	2	152	320	3b3	0	0.1
1951	Bos A	80	163	23	28	4	2	2	14	22	1	27	.172	.274	.258	40	-14	1-0	.959	14	139	170	3b49	0	0.0
1952	Bos A	19	25	6	8	1	1	1	3	4	1	2	.320	.433	.560	162	2	0-3	1.000	2	137	0	3b17	0	0.3
	Det A	112	441	42	104	12	2	2	25	35	6	52	.236	.301	.286	63	-22	2-2	.968	10	107	124	3b107,S9	0	-1.3
	Year	131	466	48	112	13	3	3	28	39	7	54	.240	.309	.300	69	-20	2-5	**.971**	12	109	116	3b124,S9	0	-1.0
1953	Det A	109	311	41	79	11	1	3	19	40	1	34	.254	.341	.325	81	-7	3-5	.978	5	110	99	3b54,2b28/S	0	-0.1
1954	Det A	81	218	31	64	12	0	2	25	28	5	24	.294	.385	.376	112	5	4-2	.972	-6	98	84	2b54,3b15	0	0.3
1955	Det A	122	413	51	96	15	3	8	33	61-6	5	49	.232	.337	.341	85	-8	3-2	.975	-5	103	109	2b92,3b16,S14	0	-0.5
1956	Det A	8	12	2	3	0	0	0	2	2-0	1	1	.250	.400	.250	75	0	0-0	1.000	-1	83	48	2b4	0	-0.1
	Chi A	106	321	46	84	9	1	7	33	37-3	8	36	.262	.349	.361	88	-5	1-0	.961	-0	101	124	3b100,S3	0	-0.5
	Year	114	333	48	87	9	1	7	35	39-3	9	37	.261	.351	.357	87	-5	1-0	.961	-1	101	124	3b100,2b4,S3	0	-0.6
1957	Chi A	69	114	14	23	3	0	0	8	15-1	5	20	.202	.316	.228	52	-7	1-0	.951	3	118	193	3b44	0	-0.3
1958	Cle A	3	8	0	1	0	0	0	1	1-0	0	1	.125	.222	.125	-2	-1	0-0	1.000	0	140	0	3b2	0	-0.1
	Cin N	3	1	0	0	0	0	0	0	0-0	0	0	.000	.000	.000	-95	0	0-0	ø	-0	0	0	/23	0	-0.1
Total	9	722	2039	259	493	67	10	25	165	248-10	33	247	.242	.332	.321	78	-58	15-14	.962	25	111	129	3b408,2b179,S27	0	-2.3

HATFIELD, GIL Gilbert "Colonel"; B1.27.1855 Hoboken NJ; D5.26.1921 Hoboken NJ; TR/5´9.5˝/168; d9.24; b–John; ▲

YEAR	TM LG	G	AB	R	H	2B	3B	HR	RBI	BB-IB	HP	SO	AVG	OBP	SLG	AOPS	ABR	SB-CS	FA	FR	RNG	THR	GAMES AT POSITION	DL	BFW
1885	Buf N	11	30	1	4	0	1	0	0	0	—	11	.133	.133	.200	6	-3	—	.913	-0	112	0	3b8,2b3	—	-0.3
1887	NY N	2	7	2	3	1	0	0	3	0	0	1	.429	.429	.571	184	1	0	1.000	0	76	0	3b2	—	0.1
1888	†NY N	28	105	7	19	1	0	0	9	2	2	18	.181	.211	.190	29	-8	8	.813	-2	76	0	3b14,S13/cf2	—	-1.0
1889	NY N	32	125	21	23	2	0	1	12	9	2	15	.184	.250	.224	32	-12	9	.858	1	98	74	S24,P6,3b2	—	-0.7
1890	NY P	71	287	32	80	13	6	2	37	17	4	19	.279	.328	.387	83	-9	12	.836	-15	98	71	3b42,S27,P3/cf	—	-1.8
1891	Was AA	134	500	83	128	11	8	1	48	50	9	39	.256	.335	.316	90	-5	43	.869	13	104	99	S105,3b27,P4,O3(1/0/2)	—	0.9
1893	Bro N	34	120	24	35	3	3	2	19	17	2	5	.292	.388	.417	119	4	9	.875	-6	84	33	3b34	—	-0.2
1895	Lou N	5	16	3	3	0	0	0	1	1	1	1	.188	.278	.188	23	-2	0	.889	-0	94	0	3b3,S2	—	-0.2
Total	8	317	1190	173	295	31	18	6	129	96	20	109	.248	.315	.319	79	-34	81	.850	-10	100	93	S171,3b132,P13,O5(1/2/2),2b4	—	-3.2

HATFIELD, JOHN John Van Buskirk; B7.20.1847 NJ; D2.20.1909 Long Island City NY; 5´10˝/165; d5.18; M2; b–Gil

YEAR	TM LG	G	AB	R	H	2B	3B	HR	RBI	BB-IB	HP	SO	AVG	OBP	SLG	AOPS	ABR	SB-CS	FA	FR	RNG	THR	GAMES AT POSITION	DL	BFW
1871	Mut NA	**33**	168	41	43	3	2	0	22	4	—	0	.256	.273	.298	70	-5	10-3	.853	1	65	0	O24L,2b7,3b2	—	-0.1
1872	Mut NA	**56**	288	76	93	15	2	1	47	9	—	6	.323	.343	.399	136	15	12-5	.847	4	102	151	2b55/1M	—	1.1
1873	Mut NA	52	255	54	78	5	6	2	46	3	—	2	.306	.314	.396	109	2	2-0	.743	-9	79	91	3b45,2b12/rfM	—	-0.6
1874	Mut NA	63	292	47	66	12	1	0	29	7	—	12	.226	.244	.274	64	-11	4-0	.874	6	36	0	O58L,3b7,P3/1S	—	-0.2
1875	Mut NA	1	4	1	2	1	0	0	1	0	—	0	.500	.500	.750	312	1	0-0	1.000	0	0	0	/lf	—	0.1
1876	NY N	1	4	0	1	0	0	0	1	0	—	0	.250	.250	.250	77	0	—	.833	-0	126	0	/2	—	0.0
Total	5NA	205	1007	219	282	36	11	3	145	23	—	20	.280	.296	.347	98	2	28-8	.868	3	44	0	O84(83/0/1),2b74,3b54,P3,1b2/S	—	0.3

HATTEBERG, SCOTT Scott Allen; B12.14.1969 Salem OR; BL/TR/6´1˝/(192–210); [BosA91 1/43]; d9.8; Col Washington St.

YEAR	TM LG	G	AB	R	H	2B	3B	HR	RBI	BB-IB	HP	SO	AVG	OBP	SLG	AOPS	ABR	SB-CS	FA	FR	RNG	THR	GAMES AT POSITION	DL	BFW
1995	Bos A	2	2	1	1	0	0	0	0	0-0	0	0	.500	.500	.500	156	0	0-0	1.000	1	0	0	C2	0	0.1
1996	Bos A	10	11	3	2	1	0	0	0	3-0	0	2	.182	.357	.273	61	-1	0-0	1.000	-0	43	89	C10	0	0.0
1997	Bos A	114	350	46	97	23	1	10	44	40-2	2	70	.277	.354	.434	102	2	0-1	.983	-14	69	90	C106/D	0	-0.5
1998	†Bos A	112	359	46	99	23	1	12	43	43-3	5	58	.276	.359	.446	106	4	0-0	.993	8	94	114	C108	0	1.8
1999	†Bos A	30	80	12	22	5	0	1	11	18-0	1	14	.275	.410	.375	100	1	0-0	.993	1	51	105	C23,D6	112	0.3
2000	Bos A	92	230	21	61	15	0	8	36	38-3	0	39	.265	.367	.435	100	1	0-1	.981	-7	47	117	C48,D20/3	0	-0.4
2001	Bos A	94	278	34	68	19	0	3	25	33-0	4	26	.245	.332	.345	79	-7	1-1	.992	-23	43	60	C72,D8	0	-2.5
2002	†Oak A	136	492	58	138	22	4	15	61	68-1	6	56	.280	.374	.433	115	12	0-0	.994	9	147	120	1b91,D42	0	1.2
2003	†Oak A	147	541	63	137	34	0	12	61	66-0	9	53	.253	.342	.383	91	-5	0-1	.992	2	105	102	1b128,D15	0	-1.5
2004	Oak A	152	550	87	156	30	0	15	82	72-5	5	48	.284	.367	.420	107	8	0-0	.993	-1	101	114	1b148,D2	0	-0.6
2005	Oak A	134	464	52	119	19	0	7	59	51-4	4	54	.256	.334	.343	82	-11	0-1	.985	2	117	119	D79,1b53	0	-1.8
2006	Cin N	141	456	62	132	28	0	13	51	74-3	3	41	.289	.389	.436	106	7	2-2	.996	-2	92	83	1b131	0	-0.6
Total	12	1164	3813	485	1032	219	6	96	473	506-21	39	461	.271	.360	.407	99	11	3-7	.993	-23	109	105	1b551,C369,D173/3	112	-4.5

HATTIG, JOHN John Duane; B2.27.1980 Tamuning, Guam; BB/TR/6´2˝/230; [BosA98 25/745]; d8.19

YEAR	TM LG	G	AB	R	H	2B	3B	HR	RBI	BB-IB	HP	SO	AVG	OBP	SLG	AOPS	ABR	SB-CS	FA	FR	RNG	THR	GAMES AT POSITION	DL	BFW
2006	Tor A	13	24	2	8	1	0	0	3	5-0	0	8	.333	.448	.375	112	1	0-0	1.000	-0	92	69	3b10	0	0.0

HATTON, GRADY Grady Edgebert; B10.7.1922 Beaumont TX; BL/TR/5´9˝/175; d4.16; M3/C3; Col Texas

YEAR	TM LG	G	AB	R	H	2B	3B	HR	RBI	BB-IB	HP	SO	AVG	OBP	SLG	AOPS	ABR	SB-CS	FA	FR	RNG	THR	GAMES AT POSITION	DL	BFW
1946	Cin N	116	436	56	118	18	3	14	69	66	2	53	.271	.369	.422	129	18	6	.941	-16	92	**90**	3b116,O2L	0	0.1
1947	Cin N	146	524	91	147	24	8	16	77	81	0	50	.281	.377	.448	119	16	7	.938	-8	93	72	3b136	0	0.7
1948	Cin N	133	458	58	110	17	2	9	44	72	0	50	.240	.343	.345	90	-5	7	.932	4	100	103	3b123,2b3,S2/lf	0	-0.2
1949	Cin N	137	537	71	141	38	5	11	69	62	3	48	.263	.342	.413	101	1	4	**.975**	-3	98	98	3b136	0	-0.2
1950	Cin N	130	438	67	114	17	1	11	54	70	3	39	.260	.366	.379	96	0	6	.954	-1	93	76	3b126/2S	0	-0.2
1951	Cin N	96	331	41	84	9	3	4	37	33	0	32	.254	.321	.335	76	-11	4-2	.972	5	101	126	3b87,O2L	0	-0.7
1952	Cin N☆	128	433	48	92	14	1	9	57	66	2	60	.212	.319	.312	76	-13	5-4	**.990**	-9	91	86	2b120	0	-1.7
1953	Cin N	83	159	22	37	3	1	7	22	29	0	24	.233	.351	.396	94	-1	0-1	.991	-4	88	105	2b35,1b10,3b5	0	-0.4
1954	Cin N	1	1	0	0	0	0	0	0	0	0	0	.000	.000	.000	-97	0	0-0	ø	0	—	—	/H	0	0.0
	Chi A	13	30	3	5	1	0	0	3	5	0	3	.167	.278	.200	34	-3	1-0	1.000	-1	82	68	3b10,1b3	0	-0.3
	Bos A	99	302	40	85	12	3	5	33	58	2	25	.281	.399	.391	106	5	1-1	.966	6	111	116	3b93/1S	0	1.1
	Year	112	332	43	90	13	3	5	36	63	2	28	.271	.388	.373	100	3	2-1	**.969**	5	**108**	112	3b103,1b4/S	0	0.8
1955	Bos A	126	380	48	93	11	4	4	49	76-3	0	28	.245	.367	.326	81	-7	0-1	.976	4	**107**	106	3b111/2	0	-0.4
1956	Bos A	5	5	0	2	0	0	0	2	0-0	0	0	.400	.400	.400	100	0	0-0	ø.	0	—	—	/H	0	0.0
	StL N	44	73	10	18	1	2	0	7	13-0	0	7	.247	.360	.315	84	-1	1-0	.951	-2	100	100	2b13/3	0	-0.2
	Bal A	27	61	4	9	1	0	1	3	13-1	0	6	.148	.297	.213	40	-5	0-0	1.000	-2	99	42	2b15,3b12	0	-0.7
1960	Chi N	28	38	3	13	0	0	0	7	2-1	1	5	.342	.381	.342	104	0	0-0	.931	-1	108	58	2b8	0	0.0
Total	12	1312	4206	562	1068	166	33	91	533	646-5	13	430	.254	.354	.374	96	-6	42-9	.956	-28	98	95	3b956,2b196,1b14,O5L,S4	0	-3.1

YEAR	TM LG	G	AB	R	H	2B	3B	HR	RBI	BB-IB	HP	SO	AVG	OBP	SLG	AOPS	ABR	SB-CS	FA	FR	RNG	THR	GAMES AT POSITION	DL	BFW
HAUGER, ARTHUR	John Arthur; B11.18.1893 Delhi OH; D8.2.1944 Redwood City CA; BL/TR/5´11˝/168; d7.17																								
1912	Cle A	15	18	0	1	0	0	0	0	1	0	—	.056	.105	.056	-52	-4	0	1.000	-0	111	0	O5(1/2/2)	—	-0.4
HAUSER, ARNOLD	Arnold George "Peewee","Stub"; B9.25.1888 Chicago IL; D5.22.1966 Aurora IL; BR/TR/5´6˝/145; d4.21																								
1910	StL N	119	375	37	77	7	2	2	36	49	9	39	.205	.312	.251	67	-14	15	.931	-7	101	62	S117/3	—	-1.8
1911	StL N	136	515	61	124	11	8	3	46	26	7	67	.241	.286	.311	69	-24	24	.918	-13	98	93	S134,3b2	—	-2.9
1912	StL N	133	479	73	124	14	7	1	42	39	3	69	.259	.319	.324	78	-15	26	.934	8	**109**	96	S132	—	0.2
1913	StL N	22	45	3	13	0	3	0	9	2	2	2	.289	.347	.422	121	1	1-2	.848	-3	84	78	S8,2b4	—	-0.2
1915	Chi F	23	54	6	11	1	0	0	4	5	1	7	.204	.283	.222	46	-5	2	.851	-4	90	141	S16,3b6	—	-0.8
Total	5	433	1468	180	349	33	20	6	137	121	22	184	.238	.305	.300	72	-57	68-2	.924	-17	102	87	S407,3b9,2b4	—	-5.5
HAUSER, JOE	Joseph John "Unser Choe"; B1.12.1899 Milwaukee WI; D7.11.1997 Sheboygan WI; BL/TL/5´10.5˝/175; d4.18																								
1922	Phi A	111	368	61	119	21	5	9	43	30	2	37	.323	.378	.481	119	10	1-5	.986	-3	92	92	1b94	—	-0.1
1923	Phi A	146	537	93	165	21	9	17	94	69	12	52	.307	.398	.475	127	22	6-6	.990	-3	93	99	1b146	—	0.8
1924	Phi A	149	562	97	162	31	8	27	115	56	5	52	.288	.358	.516	123	15	7-5	.993	-3	92	116	1b146	—	0.3
1926	Phi A	91	229	31	44	10	0	8	36	39	1	35	.192	.312	.341	66	-11	1-1	.996	0	93	91	1b65	—	-1.5
1928	Phi A	95	300	61	78	19	5	16	59	52	0	45	.260	.369	.517	127	12	4-2	.986	-5	75	83	1b88	—	0.1
1929	Cle A	37	48	8	12	1	1	3	9	4	1	8	.250	.321	.500	104	0	0-0	.986	0	137	39	1b8	—	0.0
Total	6	629	2044	351	580	103	28	80	356	250	21	229	.284	.368	.479	117	48	19-19	.990	-13	90	98	1b547	—	-0.4
HAUSMANN, GEORGE	George John; B2.11.1916 St.Louis MO; D6.16.2004 Boerne TX; BR/TR/5´5˝/145; d4.18																								
1944	NY N	131	466	70	124	20	4	1	30	40	0	25	.266	.324	.333	85	-9	3	.960	-1	98	90	2b122	0	-0.4
1945	NY N	**154**	623	98	174	15	8	2	45	73	1	46	.279	.356	.339	92	-5	7	.968	2	103	76	2b154	0	0.6
1949	NY N	16	47	5	6	0	1	0	3	7	0	6	.128	.241	.170	12	-6	0	.984	1	114	104	2b13	0	-0.5
Total	3	301	1136	173	304	35	13	3	78	120	1	77	.268	.338	.329	86	-20	10	.965	2	101	83	2b289	0	-0.3
HAUTZ, CHARLIE	Charles A.; B2.5.1852 St.Louis MO; D1.24.1929 St.Louis MO; BR/5´7˝/150; d5.4; U3																								
1875	RS NA	**19**	83	5	25	3	0	0	4	0	—	9	.301	.301	.337	134	3	5-1	.921	-1	80	74	1b19	—	0.3
1884	Pit AA	7	24	0	5	0	0	0	—	3	0	—	.208	.296	.208	68	-1	—	.980	1	64	121	1b5,O2C	—	-0.1
HAWES, ROY	Roy Lee; B7.5.1926 Shiloh IL; BL/TL/6´2˝/190; d9.23																								
1951	Was A	3	6	0	1	0	0	0	0	0	0	1	.167	.167	.167	-10	-1	0-0	1.000	-0	0	0	/1	0	-0.1
HAWES, BILL	William Hildreth; B11.17.1853 Nashua NH; D6.16.1940 Lowell MA; BR/TR/5´10˝/155; d5.1																								
1879	Bos N	38	155	19	31	3	3	0	9	2	—	13	.200	.210	.258	52	-8	—	.828	-2	141	279	O34(1/7/26),C5	—	-0.9
1884	Cin U	79	349	80	97	7	4	4	—	5	—	—	.278	.288	.355	87	-17	—	.827	-7	51	0	O58(22/9/28),1b21	—	-2.4
Total	2	117	504	99	128	10	7	4	9	7	—	13	.254	.264	.325	77	-25	—	.827	-9	84	103	O92(23/16/54),1b21,C5	—	-3.3
HAWKES, THORNY	Thorndike Proctor; B10.15.1852 Danvers MA; D2.2.1929 Danvers MA; BR/TR/5´8˝/135; d5.1																								
1879	Tro N	64	250	24	52	6	1	0	20	4	—	14	.208	.220	.240	55	-11	—	.896	15	**116**	93	2b64	—	0.6
1884	Was AA	38	151	16	42	4	2	0	—	4	0	—	.278	.297	.331	118	3	—	.917	1	96	53	2b38,O2C	—	0.5
Total	2	102	401	40	94	10	3	0	20	8	0	14	.234	.249	.274	79	-8	—	.903	15	109	79	2b102,O2C	—	1.1
HAWKS, CHICKEN	Nelson Louis; B2.3.1896 San Francisco CA; D5.26.1973 San Rafael CA; BL/TL/5´11˝/167; d4.14; Col Santa Clara																								
1921	NY A	41	73	16	21	2	3	2	15	5	0	12	.288	.333	.479	103	0	0-1	.970	-1	105	0	O15(5/10/0)	—	-0.2
1925	Phi N	105	320	52	103	15	5	5	45	32	2	33	.322	.387	.447	103	2	3-6	.986	-0	102	90	1b90	—	-0.4
Total	2	146	393	68	124	17	8	7	60	37	2	45	.316	.377	.453	103	2	3-7	.986	-1	102	90	1b90,O15(5/10/0)	—	-0.6
HAWORTH, HOWIE	Homer Howard "Cully"; B8.27.1893 Newberg OR; D1.28.1953 Troutdale OR; BL/TR/5´10.5˝/165; d8.14																								
1915	Cle A	7	7	0	1	0	0	0	1	2	0	2	.143	.333	.143	42	0	0	.917	-1	*107*	*64*	C5	—	-0.1
HAWPE, BRAD	Bradley Bonte; B6.22.1979 Fort Worth TX; BL/TL/6´3˝/(200–205); [ColN00 11/317]; d5.1; Col Louisiana St.																								
2004	Col N	42	105	12	26	3	2	3	9	11-3	1	34	.248	.322	.400	76	-4	1-1	.982	-1	96	56	O34(2/0/32)	0	-0.6
2005	Col N	101	305	38	80	10	3	9	47	43-3	0	70	.262	.350	.403	87	-5	2-2	.981	3	96	220	O89R	52	-0.6
2006	Col N	150	499	67	146	33	6	22	84	74-11	0	123	.293	.383	.515	117	14	5-5	.987	8	100	229	O145R	0	1.4
Total	3	293	909	117	252	46	11	34	140	128-17	1	227	.277	.365	.464	102	5	8-8	.985	10	98	206	O268(2/0/266)	52	0.2
HAYDEN, JACK	John Francis; B10.21.1880 Bryn Mawr PA; D8.3.1942 Haverford PA; BL/TL/5´9˝/170; d4.26; Col Villanova																								
1901	Phi A	51	211	35	56	6	4	0	17	18	0	—	.265	.323	.332	78	-6	4	.841	-4	168	0	O50(30/4/16)	—	-1.2
1906	Bos A	85	322	22	80	6	4	1	14	17	3	—	.248	.292	.301	86	-6	6	.973	-3	61	41	O85R	—	-1.4
1908	Chi N	11	45	3	9	2	0	0	2	1	0	—	.200	.217	.244	45	-3	1	1.000	-1	0	0	O11R	—	-0.5
Total	3	147	578	60	145	14	8	1	33	36	3	—	.251	.298	.308	80	-15	11	.929	-8	91	24	O146(30/4/112)	—	-3.1
HAYES, CHARLIE	Charles Dewayne; B5.29.1965 Hattiesburg MS; BR/TR/6´0˝/(190–224); [SFN83 4/96]; d9.11; OF(4/0/1)																								
1988	SF N	7	11	0	1	0	0	0	0	0-0	0	3	.091	.091	.091	-50	-2	0-0	1.000	-1	98	0	O4(3/0/1),3b3	0	-0.3
1989	SF N	3	5	0	1	0	0	0	0	0-0	0	1	.200	.200	.200	15	-1	0-0	1.000	-1	39	0	3b3	0	-0.1
	Phi N	84	299	26	77	15	1	8	43	11-1	0	49	.258	.281	.395	92	-4	3-1	.910	4	109	109	3b82	0	0.0
	Year	87	304	26	78	15	1	8	43	11-1	0	50	.257	.280	.391	91	-5	3-1	.911	4	108	107	3b85	0	-0.1
1990	Phi N	152	561	56	145	20	0	10	57	28-3	2	91	.258	.293	.348	76	-19	4-4	.957	19	**114**	**139**	3b146,1b4/2	0	-0.1
1991	Phi N	142	460	34	106	23	1	12	53	16-3	1	75	.230	.257	.363	73	-18	3-3	.958	2	101	123	3b138,S2	0	-1.8
1992	NY A	142	509	52	131	19	2	18	66	28-0	3	100	.257	.297	.409	97	-5	3-5	.963	-9	93	117	3b139,1b4	0	-1.5
1993	Col N	157	573	89	175	**45**	2	25	98	43-6	5	82	.305	.355	.522	113	12	11-6	.954	8	105	79	3b154/S	0	2.0
1994	Col N	113	423	46	122	23	4	10	50	36-4	3	71	.288	.348	.433	87	-7	3-6	.944	6	109	95	3b110	0	-0.2
1995	Phi N	141	529	58	146	30	3	11	85	50-2	4	88	.276	.340	.406	96	-2	5-1	.963	-5	91	114	3b141	0	-0.6
1996	Pit N	128	459	51	114	21	2	10	62	36-4	0	78	.248	.301	.368	73	-18	6-0	.950	8	112	121	3b124	0	-0.8
	†NY A	20	67	7	19	3	0	2	13	1-0	0	12	.284	.294	.418	77	-3	0-0	1.000	2	101	144	3b19	0	0.0
1997	†NY A	100	353	39	91	16	0	11	53	40-2	1	66	.258	.332	.397	91	-5	3-2	.947	-5	91	126	3b98,2b5	0	-0.8
1998	SF N	111	329	39	94	8	0	12	62	34-0	0	61	.286	.351	.419	107	3	2-1	.989	-3	87	89	3b46,1b45,D2	0	-0.3
1999	SF N	95	264	33	54	9	1	6	48	33-0	1	41	.205	.292	.314	58	-18	3-1	.940	-9	85	36	3b55,1b20/lfD	19	-2.6
2000	Mil N	121	370	46	93	17	0	9	46	57-4	1	84	.251	.348	.370	84	-8	1-1	.976	-5	100	62	3b59,1b57/D	0	-1.7
2001	Hou N	31	50	4	10	2	0	0	4	7-1	0	16	.200	.293	.240	39	-4	0-0	1.000	-0	82	149	3b11,1b2/D	0	-0.5
Total	14	1547	5262	580	1379	251	16	144	740	420-30	21	918	.262	.316	.398	88	-99	47-31	.954	11	101	108	3b1328,1b132,D6,2b6,O5L,S3	19	-9.3
HAYES, FRANKIE	Franklin Witman "Blimp"; B10.13.1914 Jamesburg NJ; D6.22.1955 Point Pleasant NJ; BR/TR/6´0˝/185; d9.21																								
1933	Phi A	3	5	0	0	0	0	0	0	0	0	2	.000	.000	.000	-99	-1	0-0	.889	0	*0*	*0*	C3	—	-0.1
1934	Phi A	92	248	24	56	10	0	6	30	20	1	44	.226	.286	.339	63	-15	2-1	.955	-10	*85*	*94*	C89	—	-1.9
1936	Phi A	144	505	59	137	25	2	10	67	46	2	58	.271	.335	.388	79	-18	3-5	.972	-25	*69*	*101*	C143	—	-3.1
1937	Phi A	60	188	24	49	11	1	10	38	29	0	34	.261	.359	.489	114	4	0-0	.971	-5	*89*	*79*	C56	—	0.2
1938	Phi A	99	316	56	92	19	3	11	55	54	1	51	.291	.396	.475	120	11	2-3	.975	-14	*75*	*94*	C90	—	0.1
1939	Phi A☆	124	431	66	122	28	5	20	83	40	3	55	.283	.348	.510	119	10	4-1	.978	-16	*72*	*102*	C114	—	0.2
1940	Phi A★	136	465	73	143	23	4	16	70	61	1	59	.308	.389	.477	126	19	9-3	.971	-14	*64*	*78*	C134,1b2	—	1.3
1941	Phi A★	126	439	66	123	27	4	12	63	62	0	56	.280	.369	.442	117	11	2-0	.983	-10	*79*	*94*	C123	0	0.9
1942	Phi A	21	63	8	15	4	0	0	5	9	0	8	.238	.333	.302	80	-1	1-1	1.000	-3	*68*	*134*	C20	0	-0.4
	StL A	56	159	14	40	6	0	2	17	28	0	39	.252	.364	.327	94	0	0-0	.971	-6	*79*	*74*	C51	0	-0.4
	Year	77	222	22	55	10	0	2	22	37	0	47	.248	.355	.320	90	-1	1-1	.979	-9	*76*	*90*	C71	0	-0.8
1943	StL A	88	250	16	47	7	0	5	30	37	1	36	.188	.295	.276	66	-10	1-0	.983	-9	*64*	*83*	C76/1	0	-1.6
1944	Phi A★	**155**	581	62	144	18	6	13	78	57	0	59	.248	.315	.367	96	-5	2-1	.982	-3	*72*	*116*	C155/1	0	0.1
1945	Phi A	32	110	12	25	2	1	3	14	18	0	14	.227	.336	.345	98	0	1-0	.994	1	*91*	*134*	C32	0	0.3
	Cle A✳	119	385	39	91	15	6	6	43	53	4	52	.236	.335	.353	104	3	1-1	.988	5	*84*	*86*	C119	0	1.5
	Year	**151**	495	51	116	17	7	9	57	71	4	66	.234	.335	.352	103	3	2-1	.989	5	*86*	*97*	C151	0	1.8
1946	Cle A★	51	156	11	40	12	0	3	18	21	0	26	.256	.345	.391	112	3	1-3	.981	-1	*121*	*69*	C50	0	0.4
	Chi A	53	179	15	38	6	0	2	16	29	0	33	.212	.322	.279	72	-6	1-1	.979	-1	*83*	*111*	C52	0	-0.5
	Year	104	335	26	78	18	0	5	34	50	0	59	.233	.332	.331	90	-3	2-4	.980	-2	*102*	*90*	C102	0	-0.1
1947	Bos A	5	13	0	2	0	0	0	1	0	0	1	.154	.154	.154	-13	-2	0-0	.917	0	*129*	*92*	C4	0	-0.2
Total	14	1364	4493	545	1164	213	32	119	628	564	13	627	.259	.343	.400	100	3	30-20	.977	-112	*77*	*95*	C1311,1b4	0	-3.2

Hayes, Mike John Edward; B1.1855 New York NY; D5.25.1904 New York NY; 5´7.5˝/170; d9.9

YEAR	TM LG	G	AB	R	H	2B	3B	HR	RBI	BB-IB	HP	SO	AVG	OBP	SLG	AOPS	ABR	SB-CS	FA	FR	RNG	THR	GAMES AT POSITION	DL	BFW
1876	NY N	5	21	1	3	0	2	0	2	0	—	0	.143	.143	.333	63	-1	—	.882	0	0	0	O5L	—	-0.1

Hayes, Jackie John J.; B6.27.1861 Brooklyn NY; D4.25.1905 Brooklyn NY; TR/5´8˝/175; d5.2; OF(4/75/24)

YEAR	TM LG	G	AB	R	H	2B	3B	HR	RBI	BB-IB	HP	SO	AVG	OBP	SLG	AOPS	ABR	SB-CS	FA	FR	RNG	THR	GAMES AT POSITION	DL	BFW
1882	Wor N	78	326	27	88	22	4	4	54	6	—	26	.270	.283	.399	113	5	—	.855	-11	101	59	O58(0/55/3),C15,3b5/S	—	-0.6
1883	Pit AA	85	351	41	92	23	5	3	—	15	—	—	.262	.292	.382	120	9	—	.911	-16	—	—	C62,O18(0/15/3),S5,1b5/2	—	-0.2
1884	Pit AA	33	124	11	28	6	1	0	—	4	1	—	.226	.256	.290	79	-3	—	.912	-1	—	—	C24,1b5,O3R/2	—	-0.1
	Bro AA	16	51	4	12	3	0	0	—	3	0	—	.235	.278	.294	86	-1	—	.946	4	—	—	C14,O2(1/1/0)	—	0.4
	Year	49	175	15	40	9	1	0	—	7	1	—	.229	.262	.291	81	-3	—	.925	4	—	—	C38,1b5,O5(1/1/3)/2	—	0.3
1885	Bro AA	42	137	10	18	3	0	0	10	5	3	—	.131	.179	.153	6	-14	—	.900	-4	—	—	C42	—	-1.3
1886	Was N	26	89	8	17	3	0	3	9	4	—	23	.191	.226	.326	71	-3	0	.926	-2	—	—	C14,O12(1/4/7)/2	—	-0.4
1887	Bal AA	8	28	2	4	3	0	0	3	0	0	—	.143	.143	.250	9	-3	0	.250	-3	0	0	O4(2/0/2),3b3/C	—	-0.5
1890	Bro P	12	42	3	8	0	0	0	5	2	0	4	.190	.227	.190	11	-6	0	.867	-3	78	0	O6R,S3,C2/2	—	-0.7
Total	7	300	1148	106	267	63	10	10	81	39	4	53	.233	.260	.331	87	-16	0	.906	-34	—	—	C174,O103C,1b10,S9,3b8,2b4	—	-3.4

Hayes, Jackie Minter Carney; B7.19.1906 Clanton AL; D2.9.1983 Birmingham AL; BR/TR/5´10.5˝/165; d8.5; Col Alabama

YEAR	TM LG	G	AB	R	H	2B	3B	HR	RBI	BB-IB	HP	SO	AVG	OBP	SLG	AOPS	ABR	SB-CS	FA	FR	RNG	THR	GAMES AT POSITION	DL	BFW
1927	Was A	10	29	2	7	0	0	0	2	1	0	2	.241	.267	.241	33	-3	0-0	.969	-0	103	30	S8/3	—	-0.2
1928	Was A	60	210	30	54	7	3	0	22	5	0	10	.257	.274	.319	56	-14	3-0	.974	7	102	120	2b41,S15,3b2	—	-0.4
1929	Was A	123	424	52	117	20	3	2	57	24	1	29	.276	.316	.351	71	-19	4-5	.945	5	114	168	3b63,2b57,S2	—	-0.9
1930	Was A	51	166	25	47	7	2	1	20	7	0	8	.283	.312	.367	71	-8	2-3	.981	4	103	133	2b29,3b9,1b8	—	-0.3
1931	Was A	38	108	11	24	2	1	0	8	6	0	4	.222	.263	.259	38	-10	2-0	.962	-4	81	72	2b19,3b8,S3	—	-1.2
1932	Chi A	117	475	53	122	20	5	2	54	30	1	28	.257	.302	.333	69	-23	7-4	.967	2	106	114	2b97,S10,3b10	—	-1.3
1933	Chi A	138	535	65	138	23	5	2	47	55	3	36	.258	.331	.331	79	-16	2-3	.981	6	**107**	104	2b138	—	-0.1
1934	Chi A	62	226	19	58	9	1	1	31	23	0	20	.257	.325	.319	65	-12	3-2	.980	-10	93	77	2b61	—	-1.7
1935	Chi A	89	329	45	88	14	0	4	45	29	0	15	.267	.327	.347	72	-14	3-1	.966	-5	99	90	2b85	—	-1.2
1936	Chi A	108	417	53	130	34	3	5	84	35	1	25	.312	.366	.444	96	-3	4-2	.979	13	113	118	2b89,S13,3b2	—	1.5
1937	Chi A	143	573	63	131	27	4	2	79	41	2	37	.229	.282	.300	47	-48	1-6	.984	23	**109**	**123**	2b143	—	-1.6
1938	Chi A	62	238	40	78	21	2	1	20	24	0	6	.328	.389	.445	106	3	3-2	.976	-2	101	121	2b61	—	0.5
1939	Chi A	72	269	34	67	12	3	0	23	27	1	10	.249	.320	.316	62	-16	0-3	.974	3	101	125	2b69	—	-0.9
1940	Chi A	18	41	2	8	0	1	0	1	2	0	11	.195	.233	.244	23	-5	0-0	.981	-1	100	123	2b15	—	-0.5
Total	14	1091	4040	494	1069	196	33	20	493	309	9	241	.265	.318	.344	70	-188	34-31	.976	43	104	111	2b904,3b95,S51,1b8	—	-8.3

Hayes, Von Von Francis; B8.31.1958 Stockton CA; BL/TR/6´5˝/(180–190); [CleA79 7/163]; d4.14; Col St. Marys (CA); OF(207/398/555)

YEAR	TM LG	G	AB	R	H	2B	3B	HR	RBI	BB-IB	HP	SO	AVG	OBP	SLG	AOPS	ABR	SB-CS	FA	FR	RNG	THR	GAMES AT POSITION	DL	BFW
1981	Cle A	43	109	21	28	8	2	1	17	14-1	2	10	.257	.346	.394	115	3	8-1	.939	1	111	236	D21,O13(12/0/1),3b5	0	0.4
1982	Cle A	150	527	65	132	25	3	14	82	42-3	4	63	.250	.310	.389	90	-8	32-13	.981	5	111	95	O139(14/7/123),3b5,1b4	0	-0.7
1983	†Phi N	124	351	45	93	9	5	6	32	36-7	3	55	.265	.337	.370	97	-2	20-12	.972	-2	95	130	O103(3/39/77)	8	-0.7
1984	Phi N	152	561	85	164	27	6	16	67	59-4	0	84	.292	.359	.447	124	18	48-13	.988	-4	101	24	O148(14/116/36)	0	1.8
1985	Phi N	152	570	76	150	30	4	13	70	61-6	0	99	.263	.332	.398	102	2	21-8	.984	8	111	98	O146(66/123/14)	0	0.8
1986	Phi N	158	610	**107**	186	**46**	2	19	98	74-9	1	77	.305	.379	.480	131	28	24-12	.990	3	102	99	1b134,O31(24/6/3)	0	2.3
1987	Phi N	158	556	84	154	36	5	21	84	121-12	0	77	.277	.404	.473	128	28	16-7	.990	-5	88	94	1b144,O32(5/29/3)	0	1.5
1988	Phi N	104	367	43	100	28	2	6	45	49-5	1	59	.272	.355	.409	117	10	20-9	.990	1	97	98	1b85,O16(4/12/2),3b3	49	0.7
1989	Phi N★	154	540	93	140	27	2	26	78	101-14	4	103	.259	.376	.461	139	32	28-7	.980	5	99	140	O128(0/13/124),1b30,3b10	0	3.7
1990	Phi N	129	467	70	122	14	3	17	73	87-16	4	81	.261	.375	.413	119	15	16-7	.979	-1	100	85	O127(45/4/81)	15	1.2
1991	Phi N	77	284	43	64	15	1	0	21	31-1	3	42	.225	.303	.285	69	-11	9-2	.990	6	121	72	O72(20/49/6)	83	-0.5
1992	Cal A	94	307	35	69	17	1	4	29	37-4	0	54	.225	.305	.326	77	-9	11-6	.983	-2	101	19	O85R,1b4,D5	0	-1.4
Total	12	1495	5249	767	1402	282	36	143	696	712-82	22	804	.267	.354	.416	113	106	253-97	.983	14	105	90	O1040R,1b401,D26,3b23	155	9.1

Hayes, Bill William Ernest; B10.24.1957 Cheverly MD; BR/TR/6´0˝/195; [ChiN78 1/13]; d9.30; C1; Col Indiana St.

YEAR	TM LG	G	AB	R	H	2B	3B	HR	RBI	BB-IB	HP	SO	AVG	OBP	SLG	AOPS	ABR	SB-CS	FA	FR	RNG	THR	GAMES AT POSITION	DL	BFW
1980	Chi N	4	9	0	2	1	0	0	0	0-0	0	3	.222	.222	.333	49	-1	0-0	1.000	-1	69	329	C3	0	-0.1
1981	Chi N	1	0	0	0	0	0	0	0	0-0	0	0	ø	ø	ø	ø	0	0-0	ø	-0	0	0	/C	0	0.0
Total	2	5	9	0	2	1	0	0	0	0-0	0	3	.222	.222	.333	49	-1	0-0	1.000	-1	66	313	C4	0	-0.1

Hayworth, Red Myron Claude; B5.14.1916 High Point NC; D11.2.2006 High Point NC; BR/TR/6´1.5˝/200; d4.21; b–Ray; Col Oak Ridge Mil. Inst. [JC]

YEAR	TM LG	G	AB	R	H	2B	3B	HR	RBI	BB-IB	HP	SO	AVG	OBP	SLG	AOPS	ABR	SB-CS	FA	FR	RNG	THR	GAMES AT POSITION	DL	BFW
1944	†StL A	90	270	20	60	11	1	1	25	10	1	13	.222	.253	.281	50	-18	0-0	.967	-2	*94*	*77*	C87	0	-1.6
1945	StL A	56	160	7	31	4	0	0	17	7	0	6	.194	.228	.219	28	-15	0-2	.992	2	*108*	*69*	C55	0	-1.2
Total	2	146	430	27	91	15	1	1	42	17	1	19	.212	.243	.258	42	-33	0-2	.976	-0	*99*	*74*	C142	0	-2.8

Hayworth, Ray Raymond Hall; B1.29.1904 High Point NC; D9.25.2002 Salisbury NC; BR/TR/6´0˝/180; d6.27; C2; b–Red; Col Oak Ridge Mil. Inst. [JC]

YEAR	TM LG	G	AB	R	H	2B	3B	HR	RBI	BB-IB	HP	SO	AVG	OBP	SLG	AOPS	ABR	SB-CS	FA	FR	RNG	THR	GAMES AT POSITION	DL	BFW
1926	Det A	12	11	1	3	0	0	0	5	1	0	1	.273	.333	.273	59	-1	0-0	1.000	-1	*115*	*0*	C8	—	-0.1
1929	Det A	14	43	5	11	0	0	0	4	3	0	8	.256	.304	.256	45	-4	0-0	.951	-1	*75*	*146*	C14	—	-0.4
1930	Det A	77	227	24	63	15	4	0	22	20	0	19	.278	.336	.379	79	-7	0-2	.977	-11	*65*	*83*	C76	—	-1.3
1931	Det A	88	273	28	70	10	3	0	25	19	1	27	.256	.307	.315	62	-16	0-1	.973	-1	*78*	***125***	C88	—	-1.1
1932	Det A	109	338	41	99	20	2	2	44	31	1	22	.293	.354	.382	87	-6	1-1	.991	3	*92*	*102*	C106	—	0.2
1933	Det A	134	425	37	104	14	3	1	45	35	0	28	.245	.302	.299	59	-26	0-0	.994	-6	*61*	***121***	C133	—	-2.3
1934	†Det A	54	167	20	49	5	2	0	27	16	0	22	.293	.355	.347	82	-5	0-2	.984	4	*153*	*106*	C54	—	0.2
1935	Det A	51	175	22	54	14	2	0	22	9	0	14	.309	.342	.411	98	-1	0-0	.996	8	*138*	*148*	C48	—	0.9
1936	Det A	81	250	31	60	10	0	1	30	39	2	18	.240	.347	.292	59	-15	0-0	**.988**	-4	*123*	*73*	C81	—	-1.3
1937	Det A	30	78	9	21	2	0	1	8	14	2	15	.269	.394	.333	83	-1	0-0	.992	2	*101*	*87*	C28	—	0.2
1938	Det A	8	19	1	4	0	0	0	5	3	0	4	.211	.318	.211	33	-2	1-0	.971	1	*281*	*0*	C7	—	0.0
	Bro N	5	4	0	0	0	0	0	0	1	0	1	.000	.200	.000	-40	-1	0	1.000	0	*0*	*0*	C3	—	-0.1
1939	Bro N	21	26	0	4	2	0	0	1	4	0	7	.154	.267	.231	34	-2	0	1.000	1	*108*	*55*	C18	—	-0.1
	NY N	5	13	1	3	0	0	0	0	0	0	1	.231	.231	.231	24	-1	0	1.000	1	*113*	*210*	C5	—	0.0
	Year	26	39	1	7	2	0	0	1	4	0	8	.179	.256	.231	31	-4	0	1.000	2	*110*	*105*	C23	—	-0.1
1942	StL A	1	1	0	1	0	0	0	0	0	0	0	1.000	1.000	1.000	456	0	0-0	ø	0	—	—	/H	0	0.0
1944	Bro N	7	10	1	0	0	0	0	0	2	0	1	.000	.167	.000	-51	-2	0	1.000	1	*99*	*135*	C6	0	-0.1
1945	Bro N	2	2	0	0	0	0	0	0	1	0	0	.000	.333	.000	-3	0	0	1.000	0	*0*	*0*	C2	0	0.0
Total	15	699	2062	221	546	92	16	5	238	198	6	188	.265	.331	.332	71	-90	2-6	.987	-3	*95*	*106*	C677	0	-5.3

Hazewood, Drungo Drungo La Rue; B9.2.1959 Mobile AL; BR/TR/6´3˝/205; [BalA77 1/19]; d9.19

YEAR	TM LG	G	AB	R	H	2B	3B	HR	RBI	BB-IB	HP	SO	AVG	OBP	SLG	AOPS	ABR	SB-CS	FA	FR	RNG	THR	GAMES AT POSITION	DL	BFW
1980	Bal A	6	5	1	0	0	0	0	0	0-0	0	4	.000	.000	.000	-99	-1	0-0	1.000	-0	36	0	O3R	0	-0.2

Hazle, Bob Robert Sidney "Hurricane"; B12.9.1930 Laurens SC; D4.25.1992 Columbia SC; BL/TR/6´0˝/190; d9.8

YEAR	TM LG	G	AB	R	H	2B	3B	HR	RBI	BB-IB	HP	SO	AVG	OBP	SLG	AOPS	ABR	SB-CS	FA	FR	RNG	THR	GAMES AT POSITION	DL	BFW
1955	Cin N	6	13	0	3	0	0	0	0	0-0	0	3	.231	.231	.231	22	-1	0-0	1.000	1	149	333	O3L	0	0.0
1957	†Mil N	41	134	26	54	12	0	7	27	18-4	1	15	.403	.477	.649	214	23	1-3	.906	-6	79	35	O40R	0	1.5
1958	Mil N	20	56	6	10	0	0	0	5	9-0	1	4	.179	.303	.179	34	-5	0-0	1.000	-0	112	0	O20R	0	-0.6
	Det A	43	58	5	14	2	0	2	5	5-0	0	13	.241	.302	.379	80	-2	0-0	1.000	-1	72	0	O12(8/0/4)	0	-0.3
Total	3	110	261	37	81	14	0	9	37	32-4	2	35	.310	.390	.467	135	15	1-3	.951	-6	90	40	O75(11/0/64)	0	0.6

Hazleton, Doc Willard Carpenter; B8.28.1876 Strafford VT; D3.10.1941 Burlington VT; BR; d4.17; Col Tufts

YEAR	TM LG	G	AB	R	H	2B	3B	HR	RBI	BB-IB	HP	SO	AVG	OBP	SLG	AOPS	ABR	SB-CS	FA	FR	RNG	THR	GAMES AT POSITION	DL	BFW
1902	StL N	7	23	0	3	0	0	0	0	2	1	—	.130	.231	.130	12	-2	0	.973	0	109	209	1b7	—	-0.3

Healy, Fran Francis Xavier; B9.6.1946 Holyoke MA; BR/TR/6´5˝/210; d9.3; Col American International

YEAR	TM LG	G	AB	R	H	2B	3B	HR	RBI	BB-IB	HP	SO	AVG	OBP	SLG	AOPS	ABR	SB-CS	FA	FR	RNG	THR	GAMES AT POSITION	DL	BFW
1969	KC A	6	10	0	4	1	0	0	0	0-0	0	5	.400	.400	.500	148	1	0-0	1.000	0	124	0	C5	0	0.1
1971	SF N	47	93	10	26	3	0	2	11	15-0	0	24	.280	.380	.376	116	3	1-0	.966	-3	55	106	C22	0	0.1
1972	SF N	45	99	12	15	4	0	1	8	13-2	1	24	.152	.257	.222	36	-8	0-1	.995	4	114	172	C43	0	-0.3
1973	KC A	95	279	25	77	15	2	6	34	31-0	0	56	.276	.348	.409	105	2	3-4	.979	-1	117	112	C92/D	0	0.4
1974	KC A	139	445	59	112	24	2	9	53	62-1	1	73	.252	.343	.375	101	3	16-8	.977	-8	86	90	C138	0	0.2
1975	KC A	56	188	16	48	5	2	2	18	14-1	0	19	.255	.307	.335	79	-6	4-3	.982	-3	109	64	C51,D4	0	-0.6
1976	KC A	8	24	2	3	0	0	0	1	4-0	0	10	.125	.250	.125	12	-3	2-0	1.000	1	71	117	C6/D	0	-0.1
	NY A	46	120	10	32	3	0	0	9	9-0	0	17	.267	.318	.292	80	-3	3-1	.983	2	289	94	C31,D9	0	0.1
	Year	54	144	12	35	3	0	0	10	13-0	0	27	.243	.306	.264	68	-6	5-1	.987	3	245	99	C37,D10	0	0.0
1977	NY A	27	67	10	15	5	0	0	7	6-0	0	13	.224	.288	.299	60	-3	1-0	.971	-3	114	62	C26	0	-0.5
1978	NY A	1	1	0	1	0	0	0	0	0-0	0	0	1.000	1.000	1.000	-99	0	0-0	ø	-0	0	0	/C	0	-0.1
Total	9	470	1326	144	332	60	6	20	141	154-4	2	242	.250	.329	.350	90	-14	30-17	.980	-10	112	98	C415,D15	0	-0.7

YEAR	TM LG	G	AB	R	H	2B	3B	HR	RBI	BB-IB	HP	SO	AVG	OBP	SLG	AOPS	ABR	SB-CS	FA	FR	RNG	THR	GAMES AT POSITION	DL	BFW
HEALY, FRANCIS	Francis Xavier Paul; B6.29.1910 Holyoke MA; D2.12.1997 Springfield MA; BR/TR/5´9.5˝/175; d4.29																								
1930	NY N	7	2	2	0	0	0	0	0	0	0	0	.000	.000	.000	-99	-1	0	ø	0	*0*	*0*	/C	—	-0.1
1931	NY N	6	7	1	1	0	0	0	0	0	0	0	.143	.143	.143	-24	-1	0	1.000	0	*0*	*0*	C4	—	-0.1
1932	NY N	14	32	5	8	2	0	0	4	2	0	8	.250	.294	.313	65	-2	0	.960	1	*113*	*110*	C11	—	0.0
1934	StL N	15	13	1	4	1	0	0	1	0	0	2	.308	.308	.385	79	0	0	1.000	1	*0*	*0*	C2/3rf	—	0.0
Total	4	42	54	9	13	3	0	0	5	2	0	10	.241	.268	.296	51	-4	0	.969	1	*91*	*89*	C18/rf3	—	-0.2
HEALY, THOMAS	Thomas Fitzgerald; B10.30.1895 Altoona PA; D1.15.1974 Cleveland OH; BR/TR/6´0˝/172; d7.13; Col Pittsburgh																								
1915	Phi A	23	77	11	17	1	0	0	5	6	4	4	.221	.310	.234	65	-3	0-4	.933	4	116	107	3b17/S	—	0.0
1916	Phi A	6	23	4	6	1	1	0	2	1	1	2	.261	.320	.391	119	0	1	.947	0	100	77	3b6	—	0.1
Total	2	29	100	15	23	2	1	0	7	7	5	6	.230	.313	.270	77	-3	1-4	.936	4	112	100	3b23/S	—	0.1
HEARD, CHARLIE	Charles; B1.30.1872 Philadelphia PA; D2.20.1945 Philadelphia PA; BR/TR/6´2˝/190; d7.14; ▲																								
1890	Pit N	12	43	2	8	2	0	0	0	1	0	15	.186	.205	.233	31	-4	0	.600	-2	0	0	O6(1/0/5),P6	—	-0.3
HEARN, ED	Edward John; B8.23.1960 Stuart FL; BR/TR/6´3˝/(210–215); [PhiN78 4/101]; d5.17																								
1986	NY N	49	136	16	36	5	0	4	10	12-0	0	19	.265	.322	.390	98	-1	0-1	.987	-11	106	53	C45	0	-1.1
1987	KC A	6	17	2	5	2	0	0	3	4-0	0	2	.294	.429	.412	121	1	0-0	1.000	-1	126	59	C5	169	0.0
1988	KC A	7	18	1	4	2	0	0	1	0-0	0	1	.222	.222	.333	53	-1	0-0	1.000	-1	99	0	C4,D2	150	-0.2
Total	3	62	171	19	45	9	0	4	14	16-0	0	22	.263	.324	.386	96	-1	0-1	.989	-14	108	50	C54,D2	319	-1.3
HEARNE, ED	Edmund; B9.17.1887 Ventura CA; D9.8.1952 Los Angeles CA; BR/TR/5´9˝/160; d6.9																								
1910	Bos A	2	2	0	0	0	0	0	0	0	0	—	.000	.000	.000	-98	0	0	1.000	1	140	326	S2	—	0.0
HEARNE, HUGHIE	Hugh Joseph; B4.18.1873 Troy NY; D9.22.1932 Troy NY; BR/TR/5´8˝/182; d8.29																								
1901	Bro N	2	5	1	2	0	0	0	3	0	0	—	.400	.400	.400	129	0	0	1.000	-0	*70*	*179*	C2	—	0.0
1902	Bro N	66	231	22	65	10	0	0	28	16	3	—	.281	.336	.325	103	2	3	.966	-11	*78*	*89*	C65	—	-0.4
1903	Bro N	26	57	8	16	3	2	0	4	3	1	—	.281	.328	.404	111	1	2	.960	-1	*76*	*137*	C17,1b2	—	0.1
Total	3	94	293	31	83	13	2	0	35	19	4	—	.283	.335	.341	105	3	5	.965	-12	*77*	*100*	C84,1b2	—	-0.3
HEARRON, JEFF	Jeffrey Vernon; B11.19.1961 Long Beach CA; BR/TR/6´1˝/195; [TorA83 4/89]; d8.25; Col Texas																								
1985	†Tor A	4	7	0	1	0	0	0	0	0-0	0	2	.143	.143	.143	-21	-1	0-0	1.000	1	74	280	C4	0	0.0
1986	Tor A	12	23	2	5	1	0	0	4	3-0	0	7	.217	.308	.261	55	-1	0-0	.980	-1	102	38	C12	0	-0.2
Total	2	16	30	2	6	1	0	0	4	3-0	0	9	.200	.273	.233	38	-2	0-0	.985	-0	96	94	C16	0	-0.2
HEATH, JEFF	John Geoffrey; B4.1.1915 Ft.William ON, Can.; D12.9.1975 Seattle WA; BL/TR/5´11.5˝/200; d9.13																								
1936	Cle A	12	41	6	14	3	3	1	8	3	0	4	.341	.386	.634	147	2	1-0	1.000	-1	61	151	O12(10/2/0)	—	0.1
1937	Cle A	20	61	8	14	1	4	0	8	0	0	9	.230	.230	.377	50	-6	0-1	1.000	-1	105	0	O14(2/0/12)	—	-0.7
1938	Cle A	126	502	104	172	31	**18**	21	112	33	0	55	.343	.383	.602	146	31	3-1	.974	0	106	58	O122(113/0/9)	—	2.2
1939	Cle A	121	431	64	126	31	7	14	69	41	0	64	.292	.354	.494	119	11	8-4	.964	4	109	95	O108L	—	0.8
1940	Cle A	100	356	55	78	16	3	14	50	40	0	62	.219	.298	.399	81	-12	5-3	.971	2	104	93	O90L	—	-1.4
1941	Cle A★	151	585	89	199	32	**20**	24	123	50	4	69	.340	.396	.586	165	50	18-12	.949	-5	86	144	O151(25/0/126)	0	3.4
1942	Cle A	147	568	82	158	37	13	10	76	62	1	66	.278	.350	.442	130	21	9-9	.980	4	104	102	O146(145/0/2)	0	1.5
1943	Cle A★	118	424	58	116	22	6	18	79	63	1	58	.274	.369	.481	157	30	5-8	.968	-3	103	44	O111(107/3/4)	0	2.1
1944	Cle A✳	60	151	20	50	5	2	5	33	18	0	12	.331	.402	.490	160	12	0-1	.952	0	96	134	O37(31/5/1)	0	1.0
1945	Cle A✳	102	370	60	113	16	7	15	61	56	1	39	.305	.398	.508	169	33	3-1	.973	-6	97	32	O101L	0	2.2
1946	Was A	48	166	23	47	12	3	4	27	36	0	36	.283	.411	.464	153	14	0-4	.969	-1	92	97	O47L	0	0.8
	StL A	86	316	46	87	20	4	12	57	37	1	37	.275	.353	.478	124	10	0-2	.962	-2	94	103	O83L	0	0.3
	Year	134	482	69	134	32	7	16	84	73	1	73	.278	.374	.473	134	23	0-6	.965	-3	93	101	O130L	0	1.1
1947	StL A	141	491	81	123	20	7	27	85	88	1	87	.251	.366	.485	133	22	2-1	.987	0	99	76	O140L	0	1.2
1948	Bos N	115	364	64	116	26	5	20	76	51	1	46	.319	.404	.582	167	34	2	**.991**	1	103	76	O106(99/7/0)	0	2.8
1949	Bos N	36	111	17	34	7	0	9	23	15	0	26	.306	.389	.613	174	11	0	.983	-1	95	86	O31(26/0/5)	0	0.9
Total	14	1383	4937	777	1447	279	102	194	887	593	10	670	.293	.370	.509	140	263	56-47	.972	-7	100	85	O1299(1127/17/159)	0	17.2
HEATH, KELLY	Kelly Mark; B9.4.1957 Plattsburgh NY; BR/TR/5´7˝/155; [KCA77 7/177]; d4.20; Col Louisburg (NC) JC																								
1982	KC A	1	1	0	0	0	0	0	0	0-0	0	0	.000	.000	.000	-99	0	0-0	1.000	1	212	436	/2	0	0.0
HEATH, MIKE	Michael Thomas; B2.5.1955 Tampa FL; BR/TR/5´11˝/(175–200); [NYA73 2/37]; d6.3; OF(79/1/142)																								
1978	†NY A	33	92	6	21	3	1	0	8	4-0	1	9	.228	.265	.283	56	-6	0-0	.970	1	164	54	C33	0	-0.4
1979	Oak A	74	258	19	66	8	0	3	27	17-1	3	18	.256	.304	.322	74	-10	1-0	.978	-1	103	165	O46(23/0/23),C22,3b7,D3	0	-1.1
1980	Oak A	92	305	27	74	10	2	1	33	16-2	0	28	.243	.280	.298	62	-17	3-3	.986	15	191	96	C47,D31,O8(4/0/4)	0	-0.2
1981	†Oak A	84	301	26	71	7	1	8	30	13-1	1	36	.236	.269	.346	79	-10	3-3	.978	8	127	115	C78,O6(5/0/1)	0	0.2
1982	Oak A	101	318	43	77	18	4	3	39	27-3	0	36	.242	.298	.352	81	-8	8-3	.973	-6	114	117	C90,O10(9/0/2),3b5	15	-1.0
1983	Oak A	96	345	45	97	17	0	6	33	18-4	1	59	.281	.318	.383	97	-2	3-4	.973	-1	105	98	C80,O24(1/0/23),3b2,D2	30	-0.1
1984	Oak A	140	475	49	118	21	5	13	64	26-2	1	72	.248	.287	.396	93	-7	7-4	.986	-5	93	118	C108,O45(13/0/32),3b2/S	0	-0.9
1985	Oak A	138	436	71	109	18	6	13	55	41-0	1	63	.250	.313	.408	104	1	7-7	.981	2	129	97	C112,O35(16/0/24),3b13	0	0.5
1986	StL N	65	190	19	39	8	1	4	25	23-4	1	36	.205	.293	.321	70	-8	2-3	.967	0	139	73	C63,O2(1/0/1)	0	-0.6
	Det A	30	98	11	26	3	0	4	11	4-0	0	17	.265	.291	.418	91	-2	4-1	.987	-2	128	57	C29/3	0	-0.2
1987	†Det A	93	270	34	76	16	0	8	33	21-0	3	42	.281	.339	.430	106	3	1-5	.989	7	124	117	C67,O24(4/1/20),1b4,3b4,S2/2D	0	0.9
1988	Det A	86	219	24	54	7	2	5	18	18-0	1	32	.247	.307	.365	90	-3	1-0	.984	-1	141	63	C75,O9R	0	0.0
1989	Det A	122	396	38	104	16	2	10	43	24-2	4	71	.263	.308	.389	98	-2	7-1	.986	2	95	124	C117,3b4,O3L/D	0	0.7
1990	Det A	122	370	46	100	18	2	7	38	19-0	4	71	.270	.311	.386	93	-4	7-6	.980	-1	80	96	C117,O3R/SD	0	0.0
1991	Atl N	49	139	4	29	3	1	1	12	7-5	1	26	.209	.250	.266	43	-11	0-0	.991	-4	69	121	C45	86	-1.3
Total	14	1325	4212	462	1061	173	27	86	469	278-24	22	616	.252	.300	.367	87	-86	54-40	.981	14	115	103	C1083,O215R,D40,3b38,1b4,S4/2	131	-3.5
HEATH, MICKEY	Minor Wilson; B10.30.1903 Toledo OH; D7.30.1986 Dallas TX; BL/TL/6´0˝/175; d4.18																								
1931	Cin N	7	26	2	7	0	0	0	3	2	0	5	.269	.321	.269	64	-1	0	1.000	-0	87	128	1b7	—	-0.2
1932	Cin N	39	134	14	27	1	3	0	15	20	1	23	.201	.310	.254	55	-8	0	.991	1	114	94	1b39	—	-1.1
Total	2	46	160	16	34	1	3	0	18	22	1	28	.213	.311	.256	57	-9	0	.992	1	110	99	1b46	—	-1.3
HEATH, TOMMY	Thomas George; B8.18.1913 Akron CO; D2.26.1967 Los Gatos CA; BR/TR/5´10˝/185; d4.23																								
1935	StL A	47	93	10	22	3	0	0	9	20	0	13	.237	.372	.269	65	-4	0-0	.982	-0	*119*	*45*	C37	—	-0.3
1937	StL A	17	43	4	10	0	2	1	3	10	0	3	.233	.377	.395	94	0	0-0	1.000	-1	*88*	*55*	C14	—	0.0
1938	StL A	70	194	22	44	13	0	2	22	35	0	24	.227	.345	.325	69	-8	0-1	.986	3	*81*	*121*	C65	—	-0.2
Total	3	134	330	36	76	16	2	3	34	65	0	40	.230	.357	.318	71	-12	0-1	.987	2	*91*	*93*	C116	—	-0.5
HEATH, BILL	William Chris; B3.10.1939 Yuba City CA; BL/TR/5´8˝/175; d10.3; Col USC																								
1965	Chi A	1	1	0	0	0	0	0	0	0-0	0	0	.000	.000	.000	-99	0	0-0	ø	0	—	—	/H	0	0.0
1966	Hou N	55	123	12	37	6	0	0	8	9-1	1	11	.301	.353	.350	103	1	1-0	.995	-1	83	163	C37	0	0.2
1967	Hou N	9	11	0	1	0	0	0	0	4-0	0	3	.091	.333	.091	28	-1	0-0	1.000	1	23	303	C5	0	0.0
	Det A	20	32	0	4	0	0	0	4	1-0	0	4	.125	.152	.125	-17	-5	0-0	1.000	0	29	0	C7	0	-0.5
1969	Chi N	27	32	1	5	0	1	0	1	12-2	0	4	.156	.378	.219	65	-1	0-0	.979	-0	100	153	C9	23	-0.1
Total	4	112	199	13	47	6	1	0	13	26-3	1	22	.236	.326	.276	73	-6	1-0	.993	-0	77	151	C58	23	-0.4
HEATHCOTE, CLIFF	Clifton Earl; B1.24.1898 Glen Rock PA; D1.18.1939 York PA; BL/TL/5´10.5˝/160; d6.4; Col Penn St.																								
1918	StL N	88	348	37	90	12	3	4	32	20	1	40	.259	.301	.345	100	-1	12	.934	-8	97	50	O87(3/84/0)	—	-1.7
1919	StL N	114	401	53	112	13	4	1	29	20	1	41	.279	.315	.339	103	0	27	.967	-2	101	80	O101(1/85/17),1b2	—	-0.9
1920	StL N	133	489	55	139	18	8	3	56	25	1	31	.284	.320	.372	102	0	21-14	.964	10	105	**151**	O129(0/74/57)	—	0.2
1921	StL N	62	156	18	38	6	2	0	9	10	1	9	.244	.293	.308	61	-9	7-5	.926	-3	92	94	O51(1/40/10)	—	-1.4
1922	StL N	34	98	11	24	5	2	0	14	9	1	4	.245	.315	.337	71	-4	0-2	.950	2	123	58	O32C	—	-0.4
	Chi N	76	243	37	68	8	7	1	34	18	0	15	.280	.330	.383	82	-7	5-2	.986	-2	98	65	O60(0/21/40)	—	-1.2
	Year	110	341	48	92	13	9	1	48	27	1	19	.270	.325	.370	79	-11	5-4	.971	-0	106	63	O92(0/53/40)	—	-1.6
1923	Chi N	117	393	48	98	14	3	1	27	25	2	22	.249	.298	.308	60	-23	32-17	.980	4	105	111	O112(1/0/111)	—	-2.6
1924	Chi N	113	392	66	121	19	7	0	30	28	1	28	.309	.356	.393	100	0	26-24	.979	-2	104	57	O111(1/20/90)	—	-1.2
1925	Chi N	109	380	57	100	14	5	5	39	39	7	26	.263	.343	.366	80	-11	15-11	.970	8	105	141	O99(3/8/88)	—	-1.1
1926	Chi N	139	510	98	141	33	3	10	53	58	2	30	.276	.353	.412	104	4	18	**.985**	9	105	123	O133(13/13/110)	—	0.2

THE BATTER REGISTER

YEAR	TM LG	G	AB	R	H	2B	3B	HR	RBI	BB-IB	HP	SO	AVG	OBP	SLG	AOPS	ABR	SB-CS	FA	FR	RNG	THR	GAMES AT POSITION	DL	BFW
1927	Chi N	83	228	28	67	12	4	2	25	20	3	16	.294	.359	.408	105	2	6	.987	7	104	182	O57(0/9/49)	—	0.5
1928	Chi N	67	137	26	39	8	0	3	18	17	0	12	.285	.364	.409	103	1	6	.973	1	93	172	O39(7/13/20)	—	0.0
1929	†Chi N	82	224	45	70	17	0	2	31	25	1	17	.313	.384	.415	98	1	9	.985	1	107	70	O52(1/6/45)	—	-0.3
1930	Chi N	70	150	30	39	10	1	9	18	18	1	15	.260	.343	.520	104	0	4	.986	0	100	111	O35(0/3/32)	—	-0.1
1931	Cin N	90	252	24	65	15	6	0	28	32	0	16	.258	.342	.365	96	-1	3	.989	11	120	166	O59R	—	0.6
1932	Cin N	8	3	3	0	0	0	0	0	0	0	0	.000	.000	.000	-99	-1	0	ø	0	—	—	/H	—	-0.1
	Phi N	30	39	7	11	2	0	1	5	3	0	3	.282	.333	.410	88	-1	0	.962	-1	88	160	1b7	—	-0.2
	Year	38	42	10	11	2	0	1	5	3	0	3	.262	.311	.381	78	-1	0	.962	-1	88	160	1b7	—	-0.3
Total	15	1415	4443	643	1222	206	55	42	448	367	22	325	.275	.333	.375	92	-50	191-75	.971	35	104	109	O1157(31/408/728),1b9	—	-9.7
HEBNER, RICHIE	Richard Joseph; B11.26.1947 Boston MA; BL/TR/6´1˝/(188–210); [PitN66 1/15]; d9.23; C4; OF(5/0/27)																								
1968	Pit N	2	1	0	0	0	0	0	0	0-0	0	0	.000	.000	.000	-99	0	0-0	ø	0	—	—	/H	0	0.0
1969	Pit N	129	459	72	138	23	4	8	47	53-10	8	53	.301	.380	.420	128	19	4-1	.944	2	98	**147**	3b124/1	0	2.2
1970	†Pit N	120	420	60	122	24	8	11	46	42-5	7	48	.290	.362	.464	121	12	2-3	.940	1	107	112	3b117	0	1.2
1971	†Pit N	112	388	50	105	17	8	17	67	32-1	3	68	.271	.326	.487	128	13	2-2	.949	-4	93	126	3b108	0	0.8
1972	†Pit N	124	427	63	128	24	4	19	72	52-7	6	54	.300	.378	.508	154	31	0-0	.969	-11	94	92	3b121	0	2.1
1973	Pit N	144	509	73	138	28	1	25	74	56-12	4	60	.271	.346	.477	129	20	0-1	.939	-12	95	69	3b139	0	0.7
1974	†Pit N	146	550	97	160	21	6	18	68	60-5	6	53	.291	.363	.449	131	22	0-3	.937	-13	93	123	3b141	0	0.7
1975	†Pit N	128	472	65	116	16	4	15	57	43-6	10	48	.246	.319	.392	97	-3	0-1	.946	-16	88	83	3b126	0	-2.1
1976	Pit N	132	434	60	108	21	3	8	51	47-2	4	39	.249	.325	.366	95	-2	1-3	.953	-13	92	76	3b126	0	-1.8
1977	†Phi N	118	397	67	113	17	4	18	62	61-8	3	46	.285	.381	.484	124	15	7-8	.991	3	122	130	1b103,3b13/2	23	1.1
1978	†Phi N	137	435	61	123	22	3	17	71	53-16	9	58	.283	.369	.464	130	19	4-7	.994	-2	82	**120**	1b117,3b19/2	0	0.8
1979	NY N	136	473	54	127	25	2	10	79	59-6	8	59	.268	.354	.393	108	7	3-1	.940	-8	96	111	3b134,1b6	0	-0.2
1980	Det A	104	341	48	99	10	7	12	82	38-3	2	45	.290	.360	.466	123	10	0-3	.998	-2	98	71	1b61,3b32,D5	0	0.3
1981	Det A	78	226	19	51	8	2	5	28	27-5	2	28	.226	.311	.345	86	-4	1-2	.995	-4	76	81	1b61,D11	0	-1.2
1982	Det A	68	179	25	49	6	0	8	18	25-2	0	21	.274	.361	.441	119	5	1-1	.990	2	122	64	1b40,D20	0	0.4
	Pit N	25	70	6	21	2	0	2	12	5-0	0	3	.300	.347	.414	107	1	4-0	.964	-0	99	207	O21R,1b4/3	0	0.0
1983	Pit N	78	162	23	43	4	1	5	26	17-4	1	28	.265	.332	.395	100	0	8-3	.967	-9	68	20	3b40,1b7,O7(2/0/5)	0	-0.9
1984	†Chi N	44	81	12	27	3	0	2	8	10-2	0	15	.333	.407	.444	128	3	1-0	.963	0	115	109	3b14,1b3,O3(2/0/1)	50	0.4
1985	Chi N	83	120	10	26	2	0	3	22	7-1	1	15	.217	.266	.308	55	-7	0-1	.991	1	80	163	1b12,3b7/lf	0	-0.9
Total	18	1908	6144	865	1694	273	57	203	890	687-95	74	741	.276	.352	.438	119	161	38-40	.946	-86	95	103	3b1262,1b415,D36,O32R,2b2	73	3.6
HECHINGER, MIKE	Michael Vincent; B2.14.1890 Chicago IL; D8.13.1967 Chicago IL; BR/TR/6´0˝/175; d9.27																								
1912	Chi N	2	3	0	0	0	0	0	0	2	0	0	.000	.400	.000	14	0	0	1.000	0	*177*	*71*	C2	—	0.0
1913	Chi N	2	2	0	0	0	0	0	0	0	0	0	.000	.000	.000	-99	-1	0	ø	0	—	—	/H	—	-0.1
	Bro N	9	11	1	2	1	0	0	0	0	0	2	.182	.182	.273	28	-1	0	1.000	-1	78	81	C4	—	-0.2
	Year	11	13	1	2	1	0	0	0	0	0	2	.154	.154	.231	9	-2	0	1.000	-1	78	81	C4	—	-0.3
Total	2	13	16	1	2	1	0	0	0	2	0	2	.125	.222	.188	16	-2	0	1.000	-0	*130*	*76*	C6	—	-0.3
HECKER, GUY	Guy Jackson; B4.3.1856 Youngsville PA; D12.3.1938 Wooster OH; BR/TR/6´0˝/190; d5.2; M1/U1; ▲																								
1882	Lou AA	78	340	62	94	14	4	3	—	5	—	—	.276	.287	.368	126	9	—	.958	5	**132**	**163**	1b66,P13,O2C	—	0.5
1883	Lou AA	81	332	59	90	6	6	1	—	12	—	—	.271	.297	.334	111	5	—	.933	6	109	167	P53,O23(9/14/0),1b10	—	0.4
1884	Lou AA	78	316	53	94	14	8	4	42	10	2	—	.297	.323	.430	150	17	—	.951	5	108	128	P75,O5(4/1/0)	—	0.3
1885	Lou AA	70	297	48	81	9	2	2	35	5	1	—	.273	.287	.337	97	-2	—	.927	4	122	53	P53,1b17,O3L	—	0.0
1886	Lou AA	84	343	76	117	14	5	4	48	32	3	—	**.341**	.402	.446	157	22	25	.875	-3	101	229	P49,1b22,O17(6/0/11)	—	0.3
1887	Lou AA	91	370	89	118	21	6	4	50	31	6	—	.319	.381	.441	126	13	48	.954	-3	29	136	1b43,P34,O16L	—	-0.1
1888	Lou AA	56	211	32	48	9	2	0	29	11	6	—	.227	.285	.289	86	-3	20	.936	-4	46	79	1b30,P26/lf	—	-0.8
1889	Lou AA	81	327	42	93	17	5	1	36	18	6	27	.284	.333	.376	104	1	17	.969	0	103	106	1b65,P19/rf	—	-0.4
1890	Pit N	86	340	43	77	13	9	0	38	19	9	17	.226	.285	.318	86	-7	13	.962	2	136	58	1b69,P14,O7(5/1/1),M	—	-0.8
Total	9	705	2876	504	812	117	47	19	278	143	33	44	.282	.324	.376	118	55	123	.934	13	111	118	P336,1b322,O75(44/18/13)	—	-0.6
HEEP, DANNY	Daniel William; B7.3.1957 San Antonio TX; BL/TL/5´11˝/(176–185); [HouN78 2/37]; d8.31; Col St. Marys (TX)																								
1979	Hou N	14	14	0	2	0	0	0	2	1-1	0	4	.143	.176	.143	-5	-2	0-0	1.000	1	256	0	O2L	0	-0.1
1980	†Hou N	33	87	6	24	8	0	0	6	8-0	1	9	.276	.340	.368	107	1	0-0	.990	-2	58	55	1b22	0	-0.2
1981	Hou N	33	96	6	24	3	0	0	11	10-2	0	11	.250	.321	.281	76	-3	0-0	.990	-2	61	80	1b22/rf	15	-0.7
1982	Hou N	85	198	16	47	14	1	4	22	21-3	1	31	.237	.311	.379	101	0	0-2	1.000	-2	103	85	O39(1/0/39),1b16	0	-0.6
1983	NY N	115	253	30	64	12	0	8	21	29-6	1	40	.253	.326	.395	101	1	3-3	1.000	-3	82	118	O61(11/19/31),1b14	0	-0.6
1984	NY N	99	199	36	46	9	2	1	12	27-3	1	22	.231	.319	.312	81	-4	3-1	.967	2	118	36	O48(25/0/23),1b10	0	-0.5
1985	NY N	95	271	26	76	17	0	7	42	27-1	1	27	.280	.341	.421	116	6	2-2	.977	-3	96	21	O78(45/7/31),1b4	0	0.0
1986	†NY N	86	195	24	55	8	2	5	33	30-5	1	31	.282	.379	.421	123	7	1-4	.988	-1	95	61	O56(44/0/13)	0	0.3
1987	LA N	60	98	7	16	4	0	0	9	8-0	0	10	.163	.226	.204	15	-12	1-0	.962	1	91	219	O22(17/0/6),1b6	0	-1.2
1988	†LA N	95	149	14	36	2	0	0	11	22-0	1	13	.242	.341	.255	76	-4	2-0	1.000	2	122	97	O32(17/0/16),1b12/P	0	-0.2
1989	Bos A	113	320	36	96	17	0	5	49	29-4	1	26	.300	.356	.400	107	4	0-1	.989	-5	83	51	O75(17/0/59),1b19,D9	0	-0.4
1990	†Bos A	41	69	3	12	1	1	0	8	7-0	1	14	.174	.256	.217	33	-6	0-0	1.000	1	121	178	O14(1/0/13),1b5/PD	66	-0.5
1991	Atl N	14	12	4	5	1	0	0	3	1-0	0	4	.417	.462	.500	161	1	0-1	1.000	-0	0	0	/1lf	0	0.1
Total	13	883	1961	208	503	96	6	30	229	220-25	9	242	.257	.330	.357	94	-11	12-14	.986	-12	97	70	0429(181/26/232),1b131,D15,P2	81	-4.6
HEFFERNAN, BERT	Bertram Alexander; B3.3.1965 Centereach NY; BL/TR/5´10˝/185; [MilA88 9/237]; d5.13; Col Clemson																								
1992	Sea A	8	11	0	1	1	0	0	1	0-0	0	1	.091	.091	.182	-25	-2	0-0	1.000	-0	55	90	C5/D	0	-0.2
HEFFNER, DON	Donald Henry "Jeep"; B2.8.1911 Rouzerville PA; D8.1.1989 Pasadena CA; BR/TR/5´10˝/155; d4.17; M1/C8																								
1934	NY A	72	241	29	63	8	3	0	25	25	0	18	.261	.331	.320	73	-10	1-1	.971	-9	88	115	2b68	—	-1.4
1935	NY A	10	36	3	11	3	1	0	8	4	0	1	.306	.375	.444	118	1	0-0	.980	-1	93	89	2b10	—	0.1
1936	NY A	19	48	7	11	2	1	0	6	6	0	5	.229	.315	.313	57	-3	0-0	.971	2	123	138	3b8,2b5,S3	—	0.0
1937	NY A	60	201	23	50	6	5	0	21	19	0	19	.249	.314	.328	62	-13	1-4	.980	-6	78	116	2b38,S13,3b3/1rf	—	-1.6
1938	StL A	141	473	47	116	23	3	2	69	65	4	53	.245	.341	.319	67	-23	1-1	.971	-5	88	96	2b141	—	-1.7
1939	StL A	110	375	45	100	10	2	1	35	48	0	39	.267	.350	.312	69	-16	1-7	.944	-0	105	68	S73,2b32	—	-1.1
1940	StL A	126	487	52	115	23	2	3	53	39	2	37	.236	.295	.310	56	-32	5-5	**.977**	**16**	**111**	108	2b125	—	-0.9
1941	StL A	110	399	48	93	14	2	0	17	38	2	27	.233	.303	.278	53	-27	5-6	.974	-0	105	81	2b105	0	-2.1
1942	StL A	19	36	2	6	2	0	0	3	1	0	4	.167	.189	.222	15	-4	1-0	.906	0	108	31	2b6,1b4	0	-0.4
1943	StL A	18	33	2	4	1	0	0	2	2	0	2	.121	.171	.152	-5	-4	0-0	.974	-1	81	80	2b13/1	0	-0.5
	Phi A	52	178	17	37	6	0	0	8	18	1	12	.208	.284	.242	55	-10	3-2	.978	-7	94	82	2b47/1	0	-1.6
	Year	70	211	19	41	7	0	0	10	20	1	14	.194	.267	.227	45	-14	3-2	.978	-8	92	82	2b60,1b2	0	-2.1
1944	Det A	6	19	0	4	1	0	0	1	5	0	1	.211	.375	.263	80	0	0-0	.962	0	98	122	2b5	0	0.0
Total	11	743	2526	275	610	99	19	6	248	270	9	218	.241	.317	.303	61	-141	18-26	.973	-11	97	97	2b595,S89,3b11,1b7/rf	0	-11.2
HEGAN, JIM	James Edward; B8.3.1920 Lynn MA; D6.17.1984 Lynn MA; BR/TR/6´2˝/(190–195); d9.9; Mil 1943–45; C21; s–Mike																								
1941	Cle A	16	47	4	15	2	0	1	5	4	0	7	.319	.373	.426	116	1	0-0	.973	0	*104*	*113*	C16	0	0.2
1942	Cle A	68	170	10	33	5	0	0	11	11	0	31	.194	.243	.224	34	-15	1-3	.977	5	*118*	*88*	C66	0	-0.8
1946	Cle A	88	271	29	64	11	5	0	17	17	1	44	.236	.284	.314	71	-12	1-4	.991	5	*123*	***121***	C87	0	-0.3
1947	Cle A☆	135	378	38	94	14	5	4	42	41	1	49	.249	.324	.344	88	-7	3-1	.989	7	***174***	*86*	C133	0	0.8
1948	†Cle A	144	472	60	117	21	6	14	61	48	0	74	.248	.317	.407	94	-7	6-3	.990	22	***151***	*81*	C142	0	2.2
1949	Cle A☆	152	468	54	105	19	5	8	55	49	0	89	.224	.298	.338	69	-23	1-0	.990	13	***143***	*96*	C152	0	-0.2
1950	Cle A★	131	415	53	91	16	5	14	58	42	0	52	.219	.291	.383	74	-20	1-0	.993	21	***149***	*131*	C129	0	0.8
1951	Cle A★	133	416	60	99	17	5	6	43	38	0	72	.238	.302	.346	79	-14	0-3	.991	9	*97*	*82*	C129	0	0.1
1952	Cle A☆	112	333	39	75	17	2	4	41	29	0	47	.225	.287	.324	75	-12	0-2	.987	2	*97*	*96*	C107	0	-0.6
1953	Cle A	112	299	37	65	10	1	9	37	25	1	41	.217	.280	.348	71	-14	1-2	.976	-0	*95*	*76*	C106	0	-1.0
1954	†Cle A	139	423	56	99	12	7	11	40	34	0	48	.234	.289	.374	80	-14	0-1	**.994**	10	*114*	*90*	C137	0	0.2
1955	Cle A	116	304	30	67	5	2	9	40	34-5	0	33	.220	.293	.339	69	-15	0-1	**.997**	8	*114*	*69*	C111	0	-0.2
1956	Cle A	122	315	42	70	15	2	6	34	49-6	0	54	.222	.327	.340	75	-11	1-1	.985	9	*90*	*65*	C118	0	0.3
1957	Cle A	58	148	14	32	7	0	4	15	16-1	0	23	.216	.291	.345	74	-5	0-1	1.000	-2	118	58	C58	0	-0.6
1958	Det A	45	130	14	25	6	0	1	7	10-1	0	32	.192	.250	.262	38	-11	0-0	.996	-0	111	69	C45	0	-1.0
	Phi N	25	59	5	13	6	0	0	6	4-0	0	16	.220	.270	.322	57	-4	0-0	.991	-0	115	83	C25	0	-0.3
1959	Phi N	25	51	1	10	1	0	0	8	3-1	0	10	.196	.232	.216	22	-6	0-1	.990	-2	80	196	C25	0	-0.7
	SF N	21	30	0	4	1	0	0	0	1-0	0	10	.133	.161	.167	-13	-5	0-1	.975	1	92	83	C21	0	-0.4

YEAR	TM LG	G	AB	R	H	2B	3B	HR	RBI	BB-IB	HP	SO	AVG	OBP	SLG	AOPS	ABR	SB-CS	FA	FR	RNG	THR	GAMES AT POSITION	DL	BFW
	Year	46	81	1	14	2	0	0	8	4-1	0	20	.173	.207	.198	10	-11	0-2	.983	-0	85	152	C46	0	-1.1
1960	Chi N	24	43	4	9	2	1	1	5	1-0	1	10	.209	.244	.372	67	-2	0-0	.977	-1	55	162	C22	0	-0.3
Total	17	1666	4772	550	1087	187	46	92	525	456-14	4	742	.228	.295	.344	74	-196	15-24	.990	107	*122*	*91*	C1629	0	-1.8
HEGAN, MIKE	James Michael; B7.21.1942 Cleveland OH; BL/TL/6´1˝/(185–195); d9.13; Mil 1967; f–Jim; Col Holy Cross																								
1964	†NY A	5	5	0	0	0	0	0	0	1-0	0	2	.000	.167	.000	-48	-1	0-0	1.000	1	369	157	1b2	0	0.0
1966	NY A	13	39	7	8	0	1	0	2	7-0	0	11	.205	.326	.256	73	-1	1-1	.991	0	110	69	1b13	0	-0.2
1967	NY A	68	118	12	16	4	1	1	3	20-1	1	40	.136	.266	.212	44	-8	7-1	1.000	-1	95	123	1b54,O10R	0	-1.2
1969	Sea A✳	95	267	54	78	9	6	8	37	62-1	1	61	.292	.427	.461	149	21	6-5	.955	3	100	159	O64(2/1/61),1b19	0	2.0
1970	Mil A	148	476	70	116	21	2	11	52	67-3	1	116	.244	.336	.366	94	-2	9-7	.994	10	**127**	98	1b139,O8(2/0/6)	0	-0.3
1971	Mil A	46	122	19	27	4	1	4	11	26-2	0	19	.221	.356	.369	107	2	1-1	1.000	4	130	64	1b45	0	0.3
	†Oak A	65	55	5	13	3	0	0	3	5-0	0	13	.236	.300	.291	69	-2	1-0	1.000	0	113	112	1b47,O2(1/0/1)	0	-0.3
	Year	111	177	24	40	7	1	4	14	31-2	0	32	.226	.340	.345	96	0	2-1	1.000	4	125	79	1b92,O2(1/0/1)	0	0.0
1972	†Oak A	98	79	13	26	3	1	1	5	7-1	0	20	.329	.375	.430	149	5	1-0	1.000	1	90	150	1b64,O3R	0	0.4
1973	Oak A	75	71	8	13	2	0	1	5	5-1	0	17	.183	.237	.254	40	-6	0-0	.988	-3	37	87	1b56,O3(2/0/1),D3	0	-1.1
	NY A	37	131	12	36	3	2	6	14	7-1	0	34	.275	.309	.466	119	2	0-0	.992	1	114	82	1b37	0	0.0
	Year	112	202	20	49	5	2	7	19	12-2	0	51	.243	.284	.391	92	-3	0-0	.991	-2	88	84	1b93,O3(2/0/1),D3	0	-1.1
1974	NY A	18	53	3	12	2	0	2	9	5-0	2	9	.226	.317	.377	100	0	1-1	1.000	0	92	73	1b17	0	-0.1
	Mil A	89	190	21	45	7	1	7	32	33-4	0	34	.237	.347	.395	114	4	0-4	.991	-2	48	101	D37,1b17,O17(4/0/13)	0	-0.1
	Year	107	243	24	57	9	1	9	41	38-4	2	43	.235	.340	.391	111	4	1-5	.996	-2	70	87	D37,1b34,O17(4/0/13)	0	-0.2
1975	Mil A	93	203	19	51	11	0	5	22	31-3	0	42	.251	.347	.379	105	3	1-1	.984	1	95	44	O42(33/0/9),1b27,D5	0	0.0
1976	Mil A	80	218	30	54	4	3	5	31	25-1	1	54	.248	.324	.362	104	1	0-0	1.000	-0	103	0	D40,O20(5/0/15),1b10	0	-0.2
1977	Mil A	35	53	8	9	0	0	2	3	10-1	1	17	.170	.313	.283	64	-3	0-0	1.000	-0	68	0	O8L,1b6,D7	0	-0.3
Total	12	965	2080	281	504	73	18	53	229	311-19	7	489	.242	.341	.371	103	15	28-21	.995	15	112	97	1b553,O177(57/1/119),D92	0	-1.1
HEGMAN, BOB	Robert Hilmer; B2.26.1958 Springfield MN; BR/TR/6´1˝/180; [KCA80 15/380]; d8.8; Col St. Cloud St.																								
1985	KC A	1	0	0	0	0	0	0	0	0-0	0	0	ø	ø	ø	ø	0	0-0	ø	-0	0	0	/2	0	0.0
HEIDEMANN, JACK	Jack Seale; B7.11.1949 Brenham TX; BR/TR/6´0˝/(170–178); [CleA67 1/11]; d5.2																								
1969	Cle A	3	3	0	0	0	0	0	0	0-0	1	2	.000	.250	.000	-24	0	0-0	1.000	0	118	0	S3	0	0.0
1970	Cle A	133	445	44	94	14	2	6	37	34-8	2	88	.211	.265	.292	53	-29	2-4	.961	-8	90	98	S132	0	-2.4
1971	Cle A	81	240	16	50	7	0	0	9	12-0	2	46	.208	.251	.237	36	-20	1-3	.977	-14	85	70	S81	58	-2.9
1972	Cle A	10	20	0	3	0	0	0	0	2-0	1	3	.150	.261	.150	24	-2	0-0	.964	-2	80	73	S10	0	-0.4
1974	Cle A	12	11	2	1	0	0	0	0	0-0	0	2	.091	.091	.091	-48	-2	0-0	1.000	-2	30	0	3b6,S4/12	0	-0.4
	StL N	47	70	8	19	1	0	0	3	5-0	0	10	.271	.320	.286	70	-3	0-0	.967	-9	68	71	S45/3	0	-1.0
1975	NY N	61	145	12	31	4	2	1	16	17-3	0	28	.214	.291	.290	65	-7	1-0	.951	-9	75	70	S44,3b4/2	0	-1.2
1976	NY N	5	12	0	1	0	0	0	0	0-0	0	0	.083	.083	.083	-55	-2	0-0	1.000	-1	69	87	S3/2	0	-0.3
	Mil A	69	146	11	32	1	0	2	10	7-0	0	24	.219	.253	.267	54	-9	1-3	.962	-8	68	35	3b40,2b24/D	0	-1.8
1977	Mil A	5	1	1	0	0	0	0	0	1-0	0	0	.000	.500	.000	50	0	0-0	1.000	1	292	1287	/2D	0	0.1
Total	8	426	1093	94	231	27	4	9	75	78-11	6	203	.211	.264	.268	49	-74	5-10	.965	-52	85	83	S322,3b51,2b28,D4/1	58	-10.3
HEIDRICK, EMMET	R. Emmet “Snags”; B7.9.1876 Queenstown PA; D1.20.1916 Clarion PA; BL/TR/6´0˝/185; d9.14																								
1898	Cle N	19	76	10	23	2	2	0	8	3	0	—	.303	.329	.382	105	0	3	.850	-0	195	181	O19(1/12/7)	—	-0.1
1899	StL N	146	591	109	194	21	14	2	82	34	3	—	.328	.368	.421	114	9	55	.925	3	**154**	106	O145(0/2/143)	—	0.4
1900	StL N	85	339	51	102	6	8	2	45	18	1	—	.301	.338	.383	100	-2	22	.959	13	181	136	O83C	—	0.5
1901	StL N	118	502	94	170	24	12	6	67	21	1	—	.339	.366	.470	149	29	32	.945	-1	99	53	O118C	—	2.1
1902	StL A	110	447	75	129	19	10	3	56	34	0	—	.289	.339	.396	105	2	17	.940	-3	109	142	O109C/PS3	—	-0.6
1903	StL A	120	461	55	129	20	15	1	42	19	1	—	.280	.310	.395	113	6	19	.954	1	130	155	O119C/C	—	0.1
1904	StL A	133	538	66	147	14	10	1	36	16	0	—	.273	.294	.342	107	2	35	.963	6	149	155	O130C	—	0.2
1908	StL A	26	93	8	20	2	2	1	6	1	0	—	.215	.223	.312	73	-3	3	.957	-0	120	153	O25(2/23/0)	—	-0.5
Total	8	757	3047	468	914	108	73	16	342	146	6	—	.300	.333	.399	114	43	186	.946	18	137	126	O748(3/596/150)/C3SP	—	2.1
HEIFER, FRANK	Franklin “Heck”; B1.18.1854 Reading PA; D8.29.1893 Reading PA; 5´10.5˝/175; d6.3																								
1875	Bos NA	11	50	11	14	0	3	0	5	0	—	0	.280	.280	.400	129	1	0-0	.885	-2	0	56	1b9,O6(4/1/1),P2	—	-0.1
HEILEMAN, CHINK	John George; B8.10.1872 Cincinnati OH; D7.19.1940 Cincinnati OH; BR/TR/5´8˝/155; d7.8																								
1901	Cin N	5	15	1	2	1	0	0	1	0	0	—	.133	.133	.200	-4	-2	0	.667	-1	73	487	3b4/2	—	-0.3
HEILMANN, HARRY	Harry Edwin “Slug”; B8.3.1894 San Francisco CA; D7.9.1951 Southfield MI; BR/TR/6´1˝/195; d5.16; Mil 1918; C1; HF1952																								
1914	Det A	68	182	25	41	8	1	2	18	22	2	29	.225	.316	.313	86	-3	1-8	.870	-4	63	151	O31(2/29/0),1b16,2b6	—	-1.2
1916	Det A	136	451	57	127	30	11	2	73	42	5	40	.282	.349	.410	124	12	9	.952	-10	80	98	O77(5/6/66),1b30,2b9	—	-0.3
1917	Det A	150	556	57	156	22	11	5	86	41	3	54	.281	.333	.387	120	11	11	.960	-2	91	103	O123(0/28/95),1b27	—	0.2
1918	Det A	79	286	34	79	10	6	5	39	35	2	10	.276	.359	.406	136	12	13	.957	-3	88	115	O40R,1b37,2b2	—	0.7
1919	Det A	**140**	537	74	172	30	15	8	93	37	2	41	.320	.366	.477	139	25	7	.979	-10	82	80	1b140	—	1.2
1920	Det A	145	543	66	168	28	5	9	89	39	2	32	.309	.358	.429	111	7	3-7	.985	2	101	69	1b122,O22R	—	0.3
1921	Det A	149	602	114	**237**	43	14	19	139	53	2	37	**.394**	.444	.606	167	61	2-6	.962	-11	94	51	O147R,1b3	—	3.4
1922	Det A	118	455	92	162	27	10	21	92	58	3	28	.356	.432	.598	172	48	8-4	.948	-11	85	47	O115R,1b5	—	2.7
1923	Det A	144	524	121	211	44	11	18	115	74	5	40	**.403**	.481	.632	195	76	9-7	.960	-1	104	74	O130(6/0/124),1b12	—	6.0
1924	Det A	153	570	107	197	**45**	16	10	114	78	4	41	.346	.428	.533	149	43	13-5	.970	7	97	150	O147R,1b4	—	3.7
1925	Det A	150	573	97	225	40	11	13	134	67	1	27	**.393**	.457	.569	161	**55**	6-6	.970	-6	100	59	O148R	—	3.4
1926	Det A	141	502	90	184	41	8	9	103	67	4	19	.367	.445	.534	153	42	6-7	.972	-0	94	126	O134R	—	2.9
1927	Det A	141	505	106	201	50	9	14	120	72	2	16	**.398**	.475	.616	179	63	11-5	.966	-9	87	76	O135R	—	4.1
1928	Det A	151	558	83	183	38	10	14	107	57	0	45	.328	.390	.507	132	26	7-3	.971	-1	92	131	O125R,1b25	—	1.4
1929	Det A	125	453	86	156	41	7	15	120	50	2	39	.344	.412	.565	148	34	5-6	.966	-6	95	71	O114R,1b2	—	1.7
1930	Cin N	142	459	79	153	43	6	19	91	64	1	50	.333	.416	.577	144	35	2	.955	12	**120**	121	O106R,1b19	—	3.3
1932	Cin N	15	31	3	8	2	0	0	6	0	0	2	.258	.258	.323	57	-2	0	.981	-0	84	51	1b6	—	-0.3
Total	17	2147	7787	1291	2660	542	151	183	1539	856	40	550	.342	.410	.520	148	545	113-64	.962	-52	94	95	O1594(13/63/1518),1b448,2b17	—	33.2
HEIM, VAL	Val Raymond; B11.4.1920 Plymouth WI; BL/TR/5´11˝/170; d8.31; Mil 1942–45																								
1942	Chi A	13	45	6	9	1	1	0	7	5	1	3	.200	.294	.267	60	-2	1-0	.958	-1	94	0	O12(9/0/3)	0	-0.4
HEINE, BUD	William Henry; B9.22.1900 Elmira NY; D9.2.1976 Ft.Lauderdale FL; BL/TR/5´8˝/145; d10.1; Col St. Bonaventure																								
1921	NY N	1	2	0	0	0	0	0	0	0	0	0	.000	.000	.000	-99	-1	0-0	1.000	-0	106	0	/2	—	-0.1
HEINTZ, CHRIS	Christopher John; B8.6.1974 Syosset NY; BR/TR/6´1˝/210; [ChiA96 19/557]; d9.10; Col South Florida																								
2005	Min A	8	25	1	5	3	0	0	2	1-0	0	6	.200	.231	.320	44	-2	0-0	1.000	1	118	66	C8	0	0.0
2006	Min A	2	1	0	0	0	0	0	0	0-0	0	0	.000	.000	.000	-99	0	0-0	ø	-0	0	0	C2	0	-0.1
Total	2	10	26	1	5	3	0	0	2	1-0	0	6	.192	.222	.308	38	-2	0-0	1.000	1	114	64	C10	0	-0.1
HEINTZELMAN, TOM	Thomas Kenneth; B11.3.1946 St.Charles MO; BR/TR/6´1˝/180; [StLN68 7/151]; d8.12; f–Ken																								
1973	StL N	23	29	5	9	0	0	0	0	3-2	0	3	.310	.375	.310	91	0	0-0	1.000	0	107	120	2b6	0	0.0
1974	StL N	38	74	10	17	4	0	1	6	9-0	0	14	.230	.313	.324	79	-2	0-0	.978	-2	97	102	2b28,3b2/S	0	-0.3
1977	SF N	2	2	0	0	0	0	0	0	0-0	0	0	.000	.000	.000	-99	-1	0-0	ø	0	—	—	/H	0	-0.1
1978	SF N	27	35	2	8	1	0	2	6	2-0	0	5	.229	.270	.429	96	-1	0-0	1.000	2	152	73	2b5,3b3,1b2	0	0.2
Total	4	90	140	17	34	5	0	3	12	14-2	0	22	.243	.312	.343	83	-4	0-0	.984	0	104	102	2b39,3b5,1b2/S	0	-0.2
HEINZMAN, JACK	John Peter; B9.27.1863 New Albany IN; D11.10.1914 Louisville KY; BR/TR; d10.2																								
1886	Lou AA	1	5	1	0	0	0	0	0	0	0	—	.000	.000	.000	-95	-1	0	1.000	-0	0	0	/1	—	-0.1
HEISE, BOB	Robert Lowell; B5.12.1947 San Antonio TX; BR/TR/6´0˝/(165–175); d9.12; Col Solano (CA) CC																								
1967	NY N	16	62	7	20	4	0	0	3	3-0	0	1	.323	.354	.387	114	1	0-1	.973	3	102	84	2b12,S3,3b2	0	0.5
1968	NY N	6	23	3	5	0	0	0	1	1-0	0	1	.217	.250	.217	41	-2	0-0	.929	-5	36	126	S6/2	0	-0.8
1969	NY N	4	10	1	3	1	0	0	0	3-1	0	2	.300	.462	.400	140	1	0-0	1.000	-2	52	0	S3	0	-0.1
1970	SF N	67	154	15	36	5	1	1	22	5-0	0	13	.234	.256	.299	49	-12	0-1	.915	-3	112	107	S33,2b28,3b2	0	-1.1
1971	SF N	13	11	2	0	0	0	0	0	0-0	0	1	.000	.000	.000	-99	-3	0-0	.833	-1	67	120	S3,3b2/2	0	-0.4
	Mil A	68	189	10	48	7	0	0	7	7-1	0	15	.254	.279	.291	63	-10	1-1	.961	4	110	142	S51,3b11,2b3/lf	0	0.0

YEAR	TM LG	G	AB	R	H	2B	3B	HR	RBI	BB-IB	HP	SO	AVG	OBP	SLG	AOPS	ABR	SB-CS	FA	FR	RNG	THR	GAMES AT POSITION	DL	BFW
1972	Mil A	95	271	23	72	10	1	0	12	12-1	2	14	.266	.301	.310	84	-6	1-1	.990	-5	97	98	2b49,3b24,S9	0	-0.9
1973	Mil A	49	98	8	20	2	0	0	4	4-0	0	4	.204	.235	.224	30	-9	1-0	.956	-5	92	62	S29,3b9,1b4,2b4,D2	0	-1.2
1974	StL N	3	7	0	1	0	0	0	0	0-0	0	0	.143	.143	.143	-20	-1	0-0	1.000	2	141	159	2b3	0	0.0
	Cal A	29	75	7	20	7	0	0	6	5-0	0	10	.267	.313	.360	98	0	0-1	1.000	2	107	102	2b17,3b6,S3	0	0.3
1975	Bos A	63	126	12	27	3	0	0	21	4-0	2	6	.214	.246	.238	36	-11	0-0	.940	2	117	105	3b45,2b14,S4/1	0	-0.9
1976	Bos A	32	56	5	15	2	0	0	5	1-0	1	2	.268	.293	.304	67	-2	0-1	.968	-1	91	57	3b22,S9/2	26	-0.3
1977	KC A	54	62	11	16	2	1	0	5	2-0	1	8	.258	.292	.323	67	-3	0-1	1.000	2	94	132	2b21,S21,3b12/1	0	0.0
Total	11	499	1144	104	283	43	3	1	86	47-3	6	77	.247	.280	.293	63	-57	3-7	.945	-9	99	110	S174,2b154,3b135,1b6,D2/lf	26	-4.9

HEIST, AL Alfred Michael; B10.5.1927 Brooklyn NY; D10.2.2006 Tahlequah OK; BR/TR/6´2˝/(180–185); d7.17; C3

YEAR	TM LG	G	AB	R	H	2B	3B	HR	RBI	BB-IB	HP	SO	AVG	OBP	SLG	AOPS	ABR	SB-CS	FA	FR	RNG	THR	GAMES AT POSITION	DL	BFW
1960	Chi N	41	102	11	28	5	3	1	6	10-0	0	12	.275	.339	.412	106	1	3-1	.985	-0	98	100	O33(1/32/0)	0	-0.1
1961	Chi N	109	321	48	82	14	3	7	37	39-0	1	51	.255	.337	.383	90	-4	3-3	.978	2	104	146	O99C	0	-0.5
1962	Hou N	27	72	4	16	1	0	0	3	3-0	1	9	.222	.263	.236	38	-6	0-0	.974	-1	89	88	O23C	32	-0.8
Total	3	177	495	63	126	20	6	8	46	52-0	2	72	.255	.327	.368	86	-9	6-4	.979	0	101	128	O155(1/154/0)	32	-1.4

HEITMULLER, HEINIE William Frederick; B5.25.1883 San Francisco CA; D10.8.1912 Los Angeles CA; BR/TR/6´2˝/215; d4.26; Col California

YEAR	TM LG	G	AB	R	H	2B	3B	HR	RBI	BB-IB	HP	SO	AVG	OBP	SLG	AOPS	ABR	SB-CS	FA	FR	RNG	THR	GAMES AT POSITION	DL	BFW
1909	Phi A	64	210	36	60	9	8	0	15	18	3	—	.286	.351	.405	136	8	7	.927	-0	54	132	O61(54/7/0)	—	0.5
1910	Phi A	31	111	11	27	2	2	0	7	7	0	—	.243	.288	.297	84	-2	6	.981	-0	104	56	O28(15/11/2)	—	-0.5
Total	2	95	321	47	87	11	10	0	22	25	3	—	.271	.330	.368	118	6	13	.943	-0	70	108	O89(69/18/2)	—	0.0

HELD, WOODIE Woodson George; B3.25.1932 Sacramento CA; BR/TR/5´11˝/(170–185); d9.5; OF(113/276/111)

YEAR	TM LG	G	AB	R	H	2B	3B	HR	RBI	BB-IB	HP	SO	AVG	OBP	SLG	AOPS	ABR	SB-CS	FA	FR	RNG	THR	GAMES AT POSITION	DL	BFW
1954	NY A	4	3	2	0	0	0	0	0	2	0	1	.000	.400	.000	17	0	0-0	1.000	-0	86	140	S4/3	0	0.0
1957	NY A	1	1	0	0	0	0	0	0	0-0	0	0	.000	.000	.000	-99	0	0-0	ø	0	—	—	/H	0	0.0
	KC A	92	326	48	78	14	3	20	50	37-1	3	81	.239	.321	.485	116	6	4-0	.996	9	110	181	O92C	0	1.1
	Year	93	327	48	78	14	3	20	50	37-1	3	81	.239	.320	.483	115	5	4-0	.996	9	110	181	O92C	0	1.1
1958	KC A	47	131	13	28	2	0	4	16	10-0	2	28	.214	.276	.321	64	-7	0-1	1.000	-2	88	51	O41C,3b4/S	0	-1.1
	Cle A	67	144	12	28	4	1	3	17	15-0	4	36	.194	.285	.299	63	-7	1-2	.966	0	120	182	O43(7/37/0),S14,3b4	0	-0.9
	Year	114	275	25	56	6	1	7	33	25-0	6	64	.204	.281	.309	64	-14	1-3	.982	-2	103	111	O84(7/78/0),S15,3b8	0	-2.0
1959	Cle A	143	525	82	132	19	3	29	71	46-1	2	118	.251	.313	.465	115	8	1-2	.962	-9	91	71	S103,3b40,O6C,2b3	0	0.7
1960	Cle A	109	376	45	97	15	1	21	67	44-5	5	73	.258	.342	.471	122	11	0-1	.967	9	102	**120**	S109	45	2.8
1961	Cle A	146	509	67	136	23	5	23	78	69-11	3	111	.267	.354	.468	122	16	0-0	.960	-15	94	99	S144	0	1.3
1962	Cle A	139	466	55	116	12	2	19	58	73-5	11	107	.249	.362	.406	110	9	5-1	.956	-2	101	125	S133,3b5/cf	0	1.8
1963	Cle A	133	416	61	103	19	4	17	61	61-10	8	96	.248	.352	.435	121	13	2-2	.982	2	103	95	2b96,O35(12/12/12),S5,3b3	0	2.2
1964	Cle A	118	364	50	86	13	0	18	49	43-8	7	88	.236	.328	.420	107	4	1-0	.966	2	103	114	2b52,O41(5/19/18),3b30	0	0.8
1965	Was A	122	332	46	82	16	2	16	54	49-1	3	74	.247	.345	.452	128	13	0-0	.963	1	104	101	O106(57/43/50),3b5,2b4,S2	0	1.0
1966	Bal A	56	82	6	17	3	1	1	7	12-0	0	30	.207	.309	.305	78	-2	0-0	1.000	-3	77	219	O10L,2b5,S3,3b3	0	-0.5
1967	Bal A	26	41	4	6	3	0	1	6	6-0	2	12	.146	.286	.293	72	-1	0-0	.974	1	102	151	2b9,3b5,O2L	0	0.1
	Cal A	58	141	15	31	3	0	4	17	18-0	2	41	.220	.317	.326	94	-1	0-2	.979	0	117	123	3b19,O17(8/10/1),S13,2b3	0	-0.1
	Year	84	182	19	37	6	0	5	23	24-0	4	53	.203	.310	.319	88	-2	0-2	.962	1	118	114	3b24,O19(10/10/1),S13,2b12	0	0.0
1968	Cal A	33	45	4	5	1	0	0	0	5-0	2	15	.111	.231	.133	13	-5	0-0	1.000	-3	118	0	2b5,S5,3b5,O3(0/1/2)	0	-0.8
	Chi A	40	54	5	9	1	0	0	2	5-0	1	14	.167	.246	.185	33	-4	0-0	1.000	1	113	227	O33(9/3/23),3b5/2	0	-0.5
	Year	73	99	9	14	2	0	0	2	10-0	3	29	.141	.239	.162	24	-9	0-0	1.000	-2	112	212	O36(9/4/25),3b10,2b6,S5	0	-1.3
1969	Chi A	56	63	9	9	2	0	3	6	13-3	1	19	.143	.299	.317	69	-2	0-0	1.000	1	79	0	O18(3/11/5),S3,3b3/2	22	-0.2
Total	14	1390	4019	524	963	150	22	179	559	508-45	56	944	.240	.331	.421	109	51	14-11	.960	-8	97	104	S539,O448C,2b179,3b132	67	7.7

HELF, HANK Henry Hartz; B8.26.1913 Austin TX; D10.27.1984 Austin TX; BR/TR/6´1˝/196; d5.5; Mil 1944–45

YEAR	TM LG	G	AB	R	H	2B	3B	HR	RBI	BB-IB	HP	SO	AVG	OBP	SLG	AOPS	ABR	SB-CS	FA	FR	RNG	THR	GAMES AT POSITION	DL	BFW
1938	Cle A	6	13	1	1	0	0	0	1	1	0	1	.077	.143	.077	-44	-3	0-0	.947	0	*68*	*230*	C5	—	-0.2
1940	Cle A	1	1	0	0	0	0	0	0	0	0	0	.000	.000	.000	-99	0	0-0	1.000	-0	*0*	*0*	/C	—	0.0
1946	StL A	71	182	17	35	11	0	6	21	9	1	40	.192	.234	.352	59	-11	0-1	.965	3	*74*	*152*	C69	0	-0.5
Total	3	78	196	18	36	11	0	6	22	10	1	41	.184	.227	.332	51	-14	0-1	.964	3	*73*	*156*	C75	0	-0.7

HELFAND, ERIC Eric James; B3.25.1969 Erie PA; BL/TR/6´0˝/195; [OakA90 2/65]; d9.4; Col Arizona St.

YEAR	TM LG	G	AB	R	H	2B	3B	HR	RBI	BB-IB	HP	SO	AVG	OBP	SLG	AOPS	ABR	SB-CS	FA	FR	RNG	THR	GAMES AT POSITION	DL	BFW
1993	Oak A	8	13	1	3	0	0	0	1	0-0	0	1	.231	.231	.231	26	-1	0-0	1.000	3	63	185	C5	0	0.2
1994	Oak A	7	6	1	1	0	0	0	1	0-0	0	1	.167	.167	.167	-15	-1	0-0	1.000	2	0	0	C6	0	0.1
1995	Oak A	38	86	9	14	2	1	0	7	11-0	1	25	.163	.265	.209	27	-9	0-0	.994	-4	88	97	C36	0	-1.1
Total	3	53	105	11	18	2	1	0	9	11-0	1	27	.171	.256	.210	25	-11	0-0	.996	1	83	101	C47	0	-0.8

HELFRICH, TY Emory Wilbur; B10.9.1890 Pleasantville NJ; D3.18.1955 Pleasantville NJ; BR/TR/5´10˝/178; d6.30; Col Lafayette

YEAR	TM LG	G	AB	R	H	2B	3B	HR	RBI	BB-IB	HP	SO	AVG	OBP	SLG	AOPS	ABR	SB-CS	FA	FR	RNG	THR	GAMES AT POSITION	DL	BFW
1915	Bro F	43	104	12	25	6	0	0	5	15	0	21	.240	.336	.298	80	-4	2	.912	-2	113	38	2b34/rf	—	-0.5

HELLINGS B Philadelphia PA; d7.19

YEAR	TM LG	G	AB	R	H	2B	3B	HR	RBI	BB-IB	HP	SO	AVG	OBP	SLG	AOPS	ABR	SB-CS	FA	FR	RNG	THR	GAMES AT POSITION	DL	BFW
1875	Atl NA	1	4	0	1	0	0	0	0	0	—	0	.250	.250	.250	85	0	0-0	.750	-0	98	0	/2	—	0.0

HELLMAN, TONY Anthony Joseph; B1861 Cincinnati OH; D3.29.1898 Cincinnati OH; 5´9˝/175; d10.10

YEAR	TM LG	G	AB	R	H	2B	3B	HR	RBI	BB-IB	HP	SO	AVG	OBP	SLG	AOPS	ABR	SB-CS	FA	FR	RNG	THR	GAMES AT POSITION	DL	BFW
1886	Bal AA	1	3	0	0	0	0	0	0	0	0	—	.000	.000	.000	-99	-1	0	1.000	0	—	—	/C	—	0.0

HELMS, TOMMY Tommy Vann; B5.5.1941 Charlotte NC; BR/TR/5´10˝/(165–175); d9.23; M2/C9

YEAR	TM LG	G	AB	R	H	2B	3B	HR	RBI	BB-IB	HP	SO	AVG	OBP	SLG	AOPS	ABR	SB-CS	FA	FR	RNG	THR	GAMES AT POSITION	DL	BFW
1964	Cin N	2	1	0	0	0	0	0	0	0-0	0	1	.000	.000	.000	-97	0	0-0	ø	0	—	—	/H	0	0.0
1965	Cin N	21	42	4	16	2	2	0	6	3-1	1	7	.381	.435	.524	158	3	1-0	.973	-0	85	100	S8,3b2/2	0	0.4
1966	Cin N	138	542	72	154	23	1	9	49	24-2	2	31	.284	.315	.380	85	-10	3-4	.961	-7	87	71	3b113,2b20	0	-1.8
1967	Cin N★	137	497	40	136	27	4	2	35	24-8	0	41	.274	.305	.356	80	-12	5-10	.978	-20	86	90	2b88,S46	0	-2.5
1968	Cin N★	127	507	35	146	28	2	2	47	12-6	2	27	.288	.305	.363	94	-4	5-6	.979	5	100	99	2b127,S2/3	0	1.3
1969	Cin N	126	480	38	129	18	1	1	40	18-5	1	33	.269	.296	.317	68	-21	4-6	.975	-5	98	101	2b125,S4	21	-1.9
1970	†Cin N	150	575	42	136	21	1	1	45	21-4	0	33	.237	.262	.282	46	-45	2-2	**.983**	1	101	**116**	2b148,S12	0	-3.6
1971	Cin N	150	547	40	141	26	1	3	52	26-5	1	33	.258	.289	.325	76	-18	3-4	**.990**	**26**	**110**	**136**	2b149	0	1.8
1972	Hou N	139	518	45	134	20	5	5	60	24-8	4	27	.259	.291	.346	84	-12	4-3	.979	**29**	108	**126**	2b139	0	2.7
1973	Hou N	146	543	44	156	28	2	4	61	32-12	0	21	.287	.325	.368	93	-6	1-1	.988	2	103	105	2b145	0	0.6
1974	Hou N	137	452	32	126	21	1	5	50	23-7	1	27	.279	.313	.363	93	-6	5-4	**.985**	11	105	126	2b133	0	1.4
1975	Hou N	64	135	7	28	2	0	0	14	10-1	1	8	.207	.265	.222	40	-11	0-0	.988	4	119	89	2b42,3b3/S	23	-0.6
1976	Pit N	62	87	10	24	5	1	1	13	10-0	1	5	.276	.350	.391	110	1	0-0	.921	-1	103	188	3b22,2b11/S	0	0.1
1977	Pit N	15	12	0	0	0	0	0	0	0-0	0	3	.000	.000	.000	-97	-3	0-0	ø	0	—	—	/H	0	-0.4
	Bos A	21	59	5	16	2	0	1	5	4-1	1	4	.271	.328	.356	78	-2	0-0	1.000	-1	25	0	D13,3b2/2	0	-0.4
Total	14	1435	4997	414	1342	223	21	34	477	231-60	15	301	.269	.300	.342	79	-146	33-40	.983	42	102	112	2b1129,3b143,S74,D13	44	-2.9

HELMS, WES Wesley Ray; B5.12.1976 Gastonia NC; BR/TR/6´4˝/(225–230); [AtlN94 10/286]; d9.5; [DL 1999 Atl N 30]

YEAR	TM LG	G	AB	R	H	2B	3B	HR	RBI	BB-IB	HP	SO	AVG	OBP	SLG	AOPS	ABR	SB-CS	FA	FR	RNG	THR	GAMES AT POSITION	DL	BFW
1998	Atl N	7	13	2	4	1	0	1	2	0-0	0	4	.308	.308	.615	136	1	0-0	.750	-1	41	0	3b4	0	-0.1
2000	Atl N	6	5	0	1	0	0	0	0	0-0	0	2	.200	.200	.200	1	-1	0-0	.833	1	161	472	3b5	0	0.0
2001	Atl N	100	216	28	48	10	3	10	36	21-2	1	56	.222	.293	.435	84	-6	1-1	.991	0	94	105	1b77,3b17/lf	0	-1.1
2002	†Atl N	85	210	20	51	16	0	6	22	11-2	3	57	.243	.283	.405	81	-6	1-1	.987	-3	133	130	1b45,3b24,O9(5/0/4)	31	-1.2
2003	Mil N	134	476	56	124	21	0	23	67	43-3	10	131	.261	.330	.450	103	1	0-1	.945	-16	88	79	3b130	16	-1.4
2004	Mil N	92	274	24	72	13	1	4	28	24-1	5	60	.263	.331	.361	79	-8	0-1	.904	-9	87	91	3b66,1b10	40	-1.8
2005	Mil N	95	168	18	50	13	1	4	24	14-0	3	30	.298	.356	.458	113	3	0-1	.964	1	98	106	3b35,1b16,D3	0	0.3
2006	Fla N	140	240	30	79	19	5	10	47	21-1	6	55	.329	.390	.575	152	19	0-4	1.000	-1	86	110	1b88,3b24/lf	0	1.2
Total	8	659	1602	178	429	93	10	58	226	134-9	28	395	.268	.331	.447	101	3	2-9	.936	-29	88	78	3b305,1b236,O11(7/0/4),D3	117	-4.1

HELTON, TODD Todd Lynn; B8.20.1973 Knoxville TN; BL/TL/6´2˝/(190–220); [ColN95 1/8]; d8.2; Col Tennessee

YEAR	TM LG	G	AB	R	H	2B	3B	HR	RBI	BB-IB	HP	SO	AVG	OBP	SLG	AOPS	ABR	SB-CS	FA	FR	RNG	THR	GAMES AT POSITION	DL	BFW
1997	Col N	35	93	13	26	2	1	5	11	8-0	0	11	.280	.337	.484	91	-1	0-1	1.000	1	63	223	O15(13/0/2),1b8	0	-0.2
1998	Col N	152	530	78	167	37	1	25	97	53-5	6	54	.315	.380	.530	113	12	3-3	.995	16	**140**	**129**	1b146	0	1.5
1999	Col N	159	578	114	185	39	5	35	113	68-6	6	77	.320	.395	.587	115	14	7-6	.993	3	107	109	1b156	0	0.3
2000	Col N★	160	580	138	**216**	**59**	2	42	**147**	103-22	4	61	**.372**	**.463**	**.698**	154	53	5-3	.995	19	**145**	111	1b160	0	5.4
2001	Col N★	159	587	132	197	54	2	49	146	98-15	5	104	.336	.432	.685	152	50	7-5	**.999**	13	**133**	108	1b157	0	4.7
2002	Col N★	156	553	107	182	39	4	30	109	99-21	5	91	.329	.429	.577	144	40	5-1	.995	7	119	101	1b156	0	3.4
2003	Col N★	160	583	135	209	49	5	33	117	111-21	2	72	.358	.458	.630	159	57	0-4	.993	20	**153**	102	1b159	0	5.9
2004	Col N★	154	547	115	190	49	2	32	96	127-19	3	72	.347	.469	.620	159	57	3-0	**.997**	20	**154**	90	1b153	0	6.2
2005	Col N	144	509	92	163	45	2	20	79	106-22	9	80	.320	**.445**	.534	139	36	3-0	.996	14	**137**	99	1b144	15	3.8

YEAR	TM LG	G	AB	R	H	2B	3B	HR	RBI	BB-IB	HP	SO	AVG	OBP	SLG	AOPS	ABR	SB-CS	FA	FR	RNG	THR	GAMES AT POSITION	DL	BFW
2006	Col N	145	546	94	165	40	5	15	81	91-15	6	64	.302	.404	.476	115	17	3-2	**.997**	-1	98	123	1b145	15	0.3
Total	10	1424	5106	1018	1700	413	29	286	996	864-146	46	686	.333	.430	.593	139	335	36-25	.996	111	132	108	1b1384,O15(13/0/2)	30	31.3
Heltzel, Heinie	William Wade; B12.21.1913 York PA; D5.1.1998 York PA; BR/TR/5´10˝/150; d7.27																								
1943	Bos N	29	86	6	13	3	0	0	5	7	0	13	.151	.215	.186	17	-9	0	.880	-1	116	85	3b29	0	-1.1
1944	Phi N	11	22	1	4	1	0	0	0	2	1	3	.182	.280	.227	45	-2	0	.919	-2	80	27	S10	0	-0.3
Total	2	40	108	7	17	4	0	0	5	9	1	16	.157	.229	.194	23	-11	0	.880	-3	116	85	3b29,S10	0	-1.4
Hemingway, Ed	Edson Marshall; B5.8.1893 Sheridan MI; D7.5.1969 Grand Rapids MI; BB/TR/5´11.5˝/165; d9.17																								
1914	StL A	3	5	0	0	0	0	0	0	1	0	1	.000	.167	.000	-51	-1	1	1.000	-0	64	0	3b3	—	-0.1
1917	NY N	7	25	3	8	1	1	0	1	2	0	1	.320	.370	.440	153	1	2	.958	1	110	205	3b7	—	0.3
1918	Phi N	33	108	7	23	4	1	0	12	7	1	9	.213	.267	.269	59	-5	4	.955	-1	104	67	2b25,3b3/1	—	-0.6
Total	3	43	138	10	31	5	2	0	13	10	1	11	.225	.282	.290	71	-5	7	.955	0	104	67	2b25,3b13/1	—	-0.4
Hemond, Scott	Scott Mathew; B11.18.1965 Taunton MA; BR/TR/6´0˝/(205–215); [OakA86 1/12]; d9.9; Col South Florida; OF(8/1/3)																								
1989	Oak A	4	0	2	0	0	0	0	0	0-0	0	0	ø	ø	ø	ø	0	0-0	ø	0	—	—	R3	0	0.0
1990	Oak A	7	13	0	2	0	0	0	1	0-0	0	5	.154	.154	.154	-14	-2	0-0	1.000	-1	70	0	3b7/2	0	-0.4
1991	Oak A	23	23	4	5	0	0	0	0	1-0	0	7	.217	.250	.217	32	-2	1-2	.947	-1	216	88	C8,2b7,3b2/SD	0	-0.3
1992	Oak A	17	27	7	6	1	0	0	1	3-0	0	7	.222	.300	.259	61	-1	1-0	1.000	-1	65	150	C8,S3,3b2,O2(1/0/1)/D	88	-0.2
	Chi A	8	13	1	3	1	0	0	1	1-0	0	6	.231	.267	.308	67	-1	0-0	1.000	0	73	1133	O2L/C3D	0	0.0
	Year	25	40	8	9	2	0	0	2	4-0	0	13	.225	.289	.275	63	-2	1-0	1.000	-1	64	147	C9,D5,O4(3/0/1),S3,3b3	0	-0.2
1993	Oak A	91	215	31	55	16	0	6	26	32-0	1	55	.256	.353	.414	112	5	14-5	.991	-2	91	104	C75,O6(4/1/1)/12D	0	0.8
1994	Oak A	91	198	23	44	11	0	3	20	16-0	0	51	.222	.280	.323	60	-12	7-6	1.000	-6	169	84	C39,2b25,3b12,1b7,O2(1/0/1),D3	0	-1.5
1995	StL N	57	118	11	17	1	0	3	9	12-0	2	31	.144	.233	.229	22	-14	0-0	.985	1	98	186	C38,2b6	0	-1.1
Total	7	298	607	79	132	30	0	12	58	65-0	3	162	.217	.295	.326	68	-27	23-13	.991	-10	111	119	C169,2b40,3b24,D15,O12L,1b8,S4	88	-2.7
Hemp, Ducky	William H.; B12.27.1867 St.Louis MO; D3.3.1923 St.Louis MO; d10.6																								
1887	Lou AA	1	3	1	1	1	0	0	0	1	0	—	.333	.500	.667	219	1	0	.000	-1	0	0	/rf	—	0.0
1890	Pit N	21	81	9	19	0	2	0	4	8	1	12	.235	.311	.284	83	-2	3	.867	1	155	343	O21(2/14/5)	—	-0.1
	Syr AA	9	33	1	5	1	0	0	1	0	1	—	.152	.176	.182	6	-4	1	.947	3	302	635	O9(2/7/0)	—	-0.1
Total	2	31	117	11	25	2	2	0	5	9	2	12	.214	.281	.265	67	-5	4	.877	3	192	416	O31(4/21/6)	—	-0.2
Hemphill, Bret	Bret Ryan; B12.17.1971 Santa Clara CA; BB/TR/6´3˝/196; [AnaA94 14/377]; d6.28; Col Cal St.–Fullerton																								
1999	Ana A	12	21	3	3	0	0	0	2	4-0	0	4	.143	.269	.143	12	-3	0-0	.955	-1	103	202	C12	0	-0.3
Hemphill, Charlie	Charles Judson "Eagle Eye"; B4.20.1876 Greenville MI; D6.22.1953 Detroit MI; BL/TL/5´9˝/160; d6.27; b–Frank																								
1899	StL N	11	37	4	9	0	0	1	3	6	1	—	.243	.364	.324	87	0	0	.750	-2	141	274	O10C	—	-0.3
	Cle N	55	202	23	56	3	5	2	23	6	1	—	.277	.301	.371	91	-4	3	.859	-5	84	40	O54R	—	-1.1
	Year	66	239	27	65	3	5	3	26	12	2	—	.272	.312	.364	90	-5	3	.837	-7	93	79	O64(0/10/54)	—	-1.4
1901	Bos A	136	545	71	142	10	10	3	62	39	2	—	.261	.312	.332	80	-16	11	.925	-5	124	114	O136(0/2/134)	—	-2.4
1902	Cle A	25	94	14	25	2	0	0	11	5	0	—	.266	.303	.287	67	-4	4	.860	-2	108	0	O19(17/1/1)	—	-0.7
	StL A	103	416	67	132	14	11	6	58	44	0	—	.317	.383	.447	131	18	23	.952	-4	111	229	O101(1/31/71),2b2	—	0.9
	Year	128	510	81	157	16	11	6	69	49	0	—	.308	.369	.418	120	14	27	.935	-6	110	190	O120(18/32/72),2b2	—	0.2
1903	StL A	105	383	36	94	6	3	3	29	23	2	—	.245	.292	.300	80	-10	16	.961	2	150	144	O104(4/18/82)	—	-1.3
1904	StL A	114	438	47	112	13	2	2	45	35	0	—	.256	.311	.308	102	2	23	.926	-5	95	151	O108(6/26/76)/2	—	-1.0
1906	StL A	**154**	585	90	169	19	12	4	62	43	0	—	.289	.338	.383	131	19	33	.961	-5	84	25	O154(0/114/40)	—	0.8
1907	StL A	153	603	66	156	20	9	0	38	51	2	—	.259	.319	.322	105	3	14	.957	-7	60	44	O153(0/134/19)	—	-1.2
1908	NY A	142	505	62	150	12	9	0	44	59	3	—	.297	.374	.356	136	22	42	.937	-4	82	41	O142(4/130/8)	—	1.4
1909	NY A	73	181	23	44	5	1	0	10	32	0	—	.243	.357	.282	101	2	10	.976	1	117	82	O45(13/32/0)	—	0.1
1910	NY A	102	351	45	84	9	4	0	21	55	5	—	.239	.350	.288	95	1	19	.971	-4	96	77	O94(0/63/31)	—	-0.8
1911	NY A	69	201	32	57	4	2	1	15	37	1	—	.284	.397	.338	99	2	9	.952	-5	93	49	O55(0/46/9)	—	-0.6
Total	11	1242	4541	580	1230	117	68	22	421	435	17	—	.271	.337	.341	106	35	207	.944	-44	98	90	O1175(45/607/525),2b3	—	-6.2
Hemphill, Frank	Frank Vernon; B5.13.1878 Greenville MI; D11.16.1950 Chicago IL; BR/TR/5´11˝/165; d4.17; b–Charlie																								
1906	Chi A	13	40	0	3	0	0	0	2	9	2	—	.075	.275	.075	11	-3	1	.970	-0	48	0	O13L	—	-0.5
1909	Was A	1	3	0	0	0	0	0	0	0	0	—	.000	.000	.000	-99	-1	0	1.000	0	0	0	/lf	—	-0.1
Total	2	14	43	0	3	0	0	0	2	9	2	—	.070	.259	.070	5	-4	1	.971	-0	45	0	O14L	—	-0.6
Hemsley, Rollie	Ralston Burdett; B6.24.1907 Syracuse OH; D7.31.1972 Washington DC; BR/TR/5´10˝/170; d4.19; Mil 1944–45; C3																								
1928	Pit N	50	133	14	36	2	3	0	18	4	0	10	.271	.292	.331	60	-8	1	.962	-1	*79*	*105*	C49	—	-0.7
1929	Pit N	88	235	31	68	13	7	0	37	11	0	22	.289	.321	.404	77	-10	1	.954	5	*98*	*114*	C80	—	0.0
1930	Pit N	104	324	45	82	19	6	2	45	22	0	21	.253	.301	.367	60	-22	3	.979	4	*96*	*103*	C98	—	-1.0
1931	Pit N	10	35	3	6	3	0	0	1	3	0	3	.171	.237	.257	33	-3	0	1.000	0	*96*	*62*	C9	—	-0.3
	Chi N	66	204	28	63	17	4	3	31	17	0	30	.309	.362	.475	121	6	4	.975	4	*125*	*113*	C53	—	1.3
	Year	76	239	31	69	20	4	3	32	20	0	33	.289	.344	.444	109	3	4	.978	4	*120*	*105*	C62	—	1.0
1932	†Chi N	60	151	27	36	10	3	4	20	10	0	16	.238	.286	.424	89	-3	2	.974	3	*195*	*73*	C47/cf	—	0.2
1933	Cin N	49	116	9	22	8	0	0	7	6	0	8	.190	.230	.259	40	-9	0	.970	2	*98*	*101*	C41	—	-0.5
	StL A	32	95	7	23	2	1	1	15	11	0	12	.242	.321	.316	65	-5	0-0	.965	-1	*112*	*81*	C27	—	-0.4
1934	StL A	123	431	47	133	31	7	2	52	29	2	37	.309	.355	.427	93	-5	6-2	.973	23	*106*	***135***	C114,O6L	—	2.4
1935	StL A★	144	504	57	146	32	7	0	48	44	2	41	.290	.349	.381	85	-11	3-2	.979	11	*118*	*86*	C141	—	0.8
1936	StL A☆	116	377	43	99	24	2	2	39	46	0	30	.263	.343	.353	70	-17	2-3	.969	-5	*98*	*66*	C114	—	-1.5
1937	StL A	100	334	30	74	12	3	3	28	25	0	29	.222	.276	.302	45	-29	0-0	.969	-5	*91*	*116*	C94,1b2	—	-2.7
1938	Cle A	66	203	27	60	11	3	2	28	23	0	14	.296	.367	.409	96	-1	1-1	.980	6	*88*	*117*	C58	—	0.8
1939	Cle A☆	107	395	58	104	17	4	2	36	26	0	26	.263	.309	.342	69	-20	2-4	.984	7	*111*	*101*	C106	—	-0.7
1940	Cle A★	119	416	46	111	20	5	4	42	22	0	25	.267	.304	.368	75	-17	1-3	**.994**	12	***146***	*104*	C117	—	0.2
1941	Cle A	98	288	29	69	10	5	2	24	18	0	19	.240	.284	.330	65	-16	2-0	.980	1	*114*	*91*	C96	0	-1.0
1942	Cin N	36	115	7	13	1	2	0	7	4	0	11	.113	.143	.157	-12	-17	0	.982	5	*95*	*77*	C34	0	-1.0
	NY A	31	85	12	25	3	1	0	15	5	0	9	.294	.333	.353	95	-1	1-0	.991	3	*192*	*82*	C29	0	0.3
1943	NY A	62	180	12	43	6	3	2	24	13	0	9	.239	.290	.339	83	-5	0-1	.981	3	*176*	*97*	C52	0	0.1
1944	NY A★	81	284	23	76	12	5	2	26	9	0	13	.268	.290	.366	84	-7	0-2	.983	1	*107*	*91*	C76	0	-0.3
1946	Phi N	49	139	7	31	4	1	0	11	9	0	10	.223	.270	.266	54	-9	0	.977	7	*95*	*170*	C45	0	0.0
1947	Phi N	2	3	0	1	0	0	0	1	0	0	0	.333	.333	.333	80	0	0	1.000	0	*0*	*0*	C2	0	0.0
Total	19	1593	5047	562	1321	257	72	31	555	357	4	395	.262	.311	.360	74	-209	29-18	.978	82	*114*	*101*	C1482,O7(6/1/0),1b2	0	-4.0
Hemus, Solly	Solomon Joseph; B4.17.1923 Phoenix AZ; BL/TR/5´9˝/(170–175); d4.27; M3/C4																								
1949	StL N	20	33	8	11	1	0	0	2	7	0	3	.333	.450	.364	115	1	0	.981	1	105	72	2b16	0	0.3
1950	StL N	11	15	1	2	1	0	0	0	2	0	4	.133	.235	.200	15	-2	0	1.000	1	135	179	3b5	0	-0.1
1951	StL N	120	420	68	118	18	9	2	32	75	4	31	.281	.395	.381	109	9	7-7	.965	12	**111**	108	S105,2b12	0	2.7
1952	StL N	151	570	**105**	153	28	8	15	52	96	**20**	55	.268	.392	.425	126	26	1-5	.960	5	101	111	S148,3b2	0	3.9
1953	StL N	154	585	110	163	32	11	14	61	86	**12**	40	.279	.382	.443	114	16	2-1	.964	9	105	96	S150,2b3	0	3.5
1954	StL N	124	214	43	65	15	3	2	27	55	5	27	.304	.453	.430	131	15	5-1	.944	-9	95	76	S66,3b27,2b12	0	1.1
1955	StL N	96	206	36	50	10	2	5	21	27-0	2	22	.243	.335	.383	91	-2	1-1	.956	-3	95	100	3b43,2b10,S2	0	-0.5
1956	StL N	8	5	1	1	0	0	0	2	1-0	0	0	.200	.429	.200	77	0	0-0	ø	0	—	—	/H	0	0.0
	Phi N	78	187	24	54	10	4	5	24	28-2	7	21	.289	.397	.465	134	11	1-1	.974	-18	74	61	2b49/3	0	-0.4
	Year	86	192	25	55	10	4	5	26	29-2	8	21	.286	.398	.458	133	11	1-1	.974	-18	74	61	2b49/3	0	-0.4
1957	Phi N	70	108	8	20	6	1	0	5	20-4	2	8	.185	.323	.259	61	-5	1-1	.980	-3	82	84	2b24	0	-0.6
1958	Phi N	105	334	53	95	14	3	8	36	51-6	**8**	34	.284	.390	.416	116	10	3-1	.969	-10	95	89	2b85/3	0	0.7
1959	StL N	24	17	2	4	2	0	0	1	8-0	1	2	.235	.500	.353	124	2	0-0	1.000	-1	188	0	/23M	0	0.2
Total	11	961	2694	459	736	137	41	51	263	456-12	62	247	.273	.390	.411	115	81	21-18	.962	-12	104	102	S471,2b212,3b80	0	10.8
Henderson, Dave	David Lee; B7.21.1958 Merced CA; BR/TR/6´2˝/(210–220); [SeaA77 1/26]; d4.9																								
1981	Sea A	59	126	17	21	3	0	6	13	16-1	1	24	.167	.264	.333	68	-5	2-1	1.000	3	101	150	O58(2/33/31)	0	-0.4
1982	Sea A	104	324	47	82	17	1	14	48	36-2	0	67	.253	.327	.441	105	2	2-5	.985	5	100	179	O101(2/99/2)	15	0.5
1983	Sea A	137	484	50	130	24	5	17	55	28-3	1	93	.269	.306	.444	101	-1	9-3	.982	7	100	203	O133(0/80/56),D3	0	0.3
1984	Sea A	112	350	42	98	23	0	14	43	19-0	2	56	.280	.320	.466	115	7	5-5	.988	8	109	203	O97(0/88/11),D10	19	1.3
1985	Sea A	139	502	70	121	28	2	14	68	48-2	3	104	.241	.310	.388	89	-7	6-1	.986	-4	95	92	O138(1/126/27)	0	-1.3

YEAR	TM LG	G	AB	R	H	2B	3B	HR	RBI	BB-IB	HP	SO	AVG	OBP	SLG	AOPS	ABR	SB-CS	FA	FR	RNG	THR	GAMES AT POSITION	DL	BFW
1986	Sea A	103	337	51	93	19	4	14	44	37-4	2	95	.276	.350	.481	122	10	1-3	.979	5	105	208	O80(0/51/31),D22	0	1.2
	†Bos A	36	51	8	10	3	0	1	3	2-0	0	15	.196	.226	.314	45	-4	1-0	.981	3	126	256	O32C	0	-0.1
	Year	139	388	59	103	22	4	15	47	39-4	2	110	.265	.335	.459	112	6	2-3	.980	8	109	**216**	O112(0/83/31),D22	0	1.1
1987	Bos A	75	184	30	43	10	0	8	25	22-0	0	48	.234	.313	.418	90	-3	1-1	.958	-2	101	0	O64(5/29/30)/D	0	-0.7
	SF N	15	21	2	5	2	0	0	1	8-0	0	5	.238	.448	.333	116	1	2-0	1.000	0	78	319	O9(1/8/1)	0	0.2
1988	†Oak A	146	507	100	154	38	1	24	94	47-1	4	92	.304	.363	.525	151	35	2-4	.982	0	103	79	O143(1/142/0)	0	3.3
1989	†Oak A	152	579	77	145	24	3	15	80	54-1	3	131	.250	.315	.380	99	-1	8-5	.977	-5	99	63	O149C,D2	0	-0.8
1990	†Oak A	127	450	65	122	28	0	20	63	40-1	1	105	.271	.331	.467	125	14	3-1	.988	2	106	83	O116(1/110/5),D6	31	1.6
1991	Oak A★	150	572	86	158	33	0	25	85	58-3	4	113	.276	.346	.465	129	23	6-6	.997	2	101	139	O140(4/135/1)/2D	0	2.3
1992	Oak A	20	63	1	9	1	0	0	2	2-0	0	16	.143	.169	.159	-8	-9	0-0	.950	-2	73	0	O12(0/9/3),D4	142	-1.2
1993	Oak A	107	382	37	84	19	0	20	53	32-0	0	113	.220	.275	.427	92	-7	0-3	.991	7	112	164	O76(2/60/14),D28	24	-0.2
1994	KC A	56	198	27	49	14	1	5	31	16-1	1	28	.247	.304	.404	77	-7	2-0	.962	-1	91	154	O40(17/6/17),D16	13	-0.9
Total	14	1538	5130	710	1324	286	17	197	708	465-19	22	1105	.258	.320	.436	108	48	50-38	.984	28	102	129	O1388(36/1157/229),D99/2	244	5.1

HENDERSON, KEN Kenneth Joseph; B6.15.1946 Carroll IA; BB/TR/6´2˝/(180–190); d4.23

YEAR	TM LG	G	AB	R	H	2B	3B	HR	RBI	BB-IB	HP	SO	AVG	OBP	SLG	AOPS	ABR	SB-CS	FA	FR	RNG	THR	GAMES AT POSITION	DL	BFW
1965	SF N	63	73	10	14	1	1	0	7	9-4	0	19	.192	.277	.233	45	-5	1-1	.980	1	100	143	O48(5/31/16)	0	-0.6
1966	SF N	11	29	4	9	1	1	1	1	2-0	1	3	.310	.375	.517	141	2	0-0	.917	-2	67	0	O10(1/7/4)	0	-0.1
1967	SF N	65	179	15	34	3	0	4	14	19-0	2	52	.190	.274	.274	58	-10	0-1	.947	-1	94	108	O52(8/33/18)	0	-1.5
1968	SF N	3	3	1	1	0	0	0	0	2-0	0	1	.333	.600	.333	186	1	0-0	1.000	-0	83	0	O2(1/1/0)	0	0.1
1969	SF N	113	374	42	84	14	4	6	44	42-2	5	64	.225	.308	.332	81	-9	6-4	.969	0	95	145	O111(64/5/57),3b3	28	-1.5
1970	SF N	148	554	104	163	35	3	17	88	87-9	5	78	.294	.394	.460	130	27	20-3	.966	4	100	146	O146(113/25/35)	0	2.6
1971	†SF N	141	504	80	133	26	6	15	65	84-12	3	76	.264	.370	.429	128	21	18-3	.966	-3	104	33	O138(109/14/26)/1	0	1.5
1972	SF N	130	439	60	113	21	2	18	51	38-6	2	66	.257	.317	.437	111	6	14-7	.974	9	105	178	O123(95/26/2)	0	0.9
1973	Chi A	73	262	32	68	13	0	6	32	27-2	1	49	.260	.330	.378	96	-1	3-4	.972	-3	97	32	O44(8/36/0),D26	82	-0.7
1974	Chi A	162	602	76	176	35	5	20	95	66-9	2	112	.292	.360	.467	134	27	12-7	.987	-4	103	58	O162C	0	2.0
1975	Chi A	140	513	65	129	20	3	9	53	74-14	4	65	.251	.347	.355	98	1	5-3	.990	1	107	71	O137C/D	0	-0.1
1976	Atl N	133	435	52	114	19	0	13	61	62-7	1	68	.262	.352	.395	107	6	5-7	.987	-10	92	31	O122(0/20/115)	0	-1.3
1977	Tex A	75	244	23	63	14	0	5	23	18-4	3	37	.258	.317	.377	87	-4	2-1	.983	-6	91	0	O65(0/8/61),D3	54	-1.3
1978	NY N	7	22	2	5	2	0	1	4	4-1	0	4	.227	.346	.455	125	1	0-1	1.000	-0	113	0	O7R	28	0.0
	Cin N	64	144	10	24	6	1	3	19	23-3	0	32	.167	.278	.285	58	-8	0-0	1.000	-2	99	0	O38(0/30/9)	0	-1.1
	Year	71	166	12	29	8	1	4	23	27-4	0	36	.175	.287	.307	67	-7	0-1	1.000	-2	101	0	O45(0/30/16)	0	-1.1
1979	Cin N	10	13	1	3	1	0	0	2	0-0	0	2	.231	.231	.308	46	-1	0-0	1.000	-0	96	0	O2(1/0/1)	51	-0.1
	Chi N	62	81	11	19	2	0	2	8	15-1	1	16	.235	.361	.333	82	-1	0-0	.950	-2	83	0	O23(14/9/0)	0	-0.4
	Year	72	94	12	22	3	0	2	10	15-1	1	18	.234	.345	.330	78	-2	0-0	.955	-2	84	0	O25(15/9/1)	0	-0.5
1980	Chi N	44	82	7	16	3	0	2	9	17-3	0	19	.195	.333	.305	73	-2	0-0	.944	1	90	214	O22(15/0/9)	33	-0.3
Total	16	1444	4553	595	1168	216	26	122	576	589-77	30	763	.257	.343	.396	106	51	86-42	.977	-17	100	83	O1252(434/544/360),D30,3b3/1	276	-1.9

HENDERSON, RICKEY Rickey Henley; B12.25.1958 Chicago IL; BR/TL/5´10˝/(180–195); [OakA76 4/96]; d6.24

YEAR	TM LG	G	AB	R	H	2B	3B	HR	RBI	BB-IB	HP	SO	AVG	OBP	SLG	AOPS	ABR	SB-CS	FA	FR	RNG	THR	GAMES AT POSITION	DL	BFW
1979	Oak A	89	351	49	96	13	3	1	26	34-0	2	39	.274	.338	.336	88	-5	33-11	.973	1	106	78	O88(62/32/1)	0	-0.4
1980	Oak A★	158	591	111	179	22	4	9	53	117-7	5	54	.303	.420	.399	134	37	**100**-26	.984	14	111	121	O157(157/1/0)/D	0	5.5
1981	†Oak A	108	423	**89**	**135**	18	7	6	35	64-4	2	68	.319	.408	.437	150	30	**56**-22	.979	15	**128**	87	O107(107/1/0)	0	4.6
1982	Oak A★	149	536	119	143	24	4	10	51	**116**-1	2	94	.267	.398	.382	120	22	**130**-42	.977	4	112	21	O144(138/10/0),D4	0	3.3
1983	Oak A★	145	513	105	150	25	7	9	48	**103**-8	4	80	.292	.414	.421	138	34	**108**-19	.992	8	114	81	O142(138/10/0)/D	0	5.1
1984	Oak A★	142	502	113	147	27	4	16	58	86-1	5	81	.293	.399	.458	146	36	**66**-18	.969	8	116	74	O140(140/6/0)	0	4.6
1985	NY A★	143	547	**146**	172	28	5	24	72	99-1	3	65	.314	.419	.516	158	49	**80**-10	.980	10	**117**	79	O141(6/141/0)/D	14	**6.9**
1986	NY A★	153	608	**130**	160	31	5	28	74	89-2	2	81	.263	.358	.469	124	22	**87**-18	.986	4	110	50	O146(11/138/0),D5	0	3.6
1987	NY A★	95	358	78	104	17	3	17	37	80-1	2	52	.291	.423	.497	144	27	41-8	.980	5	120	79	O69(34/39/0),D24	61	3.4
1988	NY A★	140	554	118	169	30	2	6	50	82-1	3	54	.305	.394	.399	124	23	**93**-13	.965	4	110	86	O136(135/3/0),D3	0	3.8
1989	NY A	65	235	41	58	13	1	3	22	56-0	1	29	.247	.392	.349	112	8	25-8	.993	2	110	78	O65L	0	1.0
	†Oak A	85	306	72	90	13	2	9	35	70-5	2	39	.294	.425	.438	149	25	52-6	.985	4	112	62	O82L,D3	0	3.6
	Year	150	541	**113**	148	26	3	12	57	**126**-5	3	68	.274	.411	.399	133	33	**77**-14	.988	6	111	69	O147L,D3	0	**4.6**
1990	†Oak A★	136	489	**119**	159	33	3	28	61	97-2	4	60	.325	**.439**	.577	**189**	**64**	**65**-10	.983	7	115	65	O118L,D15	0	**7.7**
1991	Oak A★	134	470	105	126	17	1	18	57	98-7	7	73	.268	.400	.423	136	29	**58**-18	.970	7	105	160	O119L,D10	15	3.7
1992	†Oak A	117	396	77	112	18	3	15	46	95-5	6	56	.283	.426	.457	155	36	48-11	.984	5	104	130	O108L,D6	36	4.5
1993	Oak A	90	318	77	104	19	1	17	47	85-6	2	46	.327	.469	.553	184	45	31-6	.974	6	115	110	O74L,D16	0	4.9
	†Tor A	44	163	37	35	3	1	4	12	35-1	2	19	.215	.356	.319	83	-3	22-2	.975	-4	85	39	O44L	0	-0.4
	Year	134	481	114	139	22	2	21	59	120-7	4	65	.289	.432	.474	148	41	53-8	.974	2	104	83	O118L,D16	0	4.5
1994	Oak A	87	296	66	77	13	0	6	20	72-1	5	45	.260	.411	.365	111	11	22-7	.977	5	119	90	O71(66/10/0),D13	16	1.4
1995	Oak A	112	407	67	122	31	1	9	54	72-2	4	66	.300	.407	.447	129	22	32-10	.988	-2	92	87	O90L,D19	0	1.8
1996	†SD N	148	465	110	112	17	2	9	29	125-2	10	90	.241	.410	.344	107	14	37-15	.975	-5	96	40	O134(114/10/17)	0	0.7
1997	SD N	88	288	63	79	11	0	6	27	71-2	4	62	.274	.422	.375	119	13	29-4	.959	3	112	87	O78(55/17/8),D2	15	1.8
	Ana A	32	115	21	21	3	0	2	7	26-0	2	23	.183	.343	.261	60	-6	16-4	1.000	-0	111	0	D19,O13(11/2/0)	0	-0.5
1998	Oak A	152	542	101	128	16	1	14	57	**118**-0	5	114	.236	.376	.347	91	-2	**66**-13	.988	2	110	34	O151(142/24/0)	0	0.5
1999	†NY N	121	438	89	138	30	0	12	42	82-1	2	82	.315	.423	.466	131	26	37-14	.988	-8	88	0	O116L/D	19	1.6
2000	NY N	31	96	17	21	1	0	0	2	25-1	2	20	.219	.387	.229	65	-4	5-2	.946	-3	82	0	O29L	0	-0.7
	†Sea A	92	324	58	77	13	2	4	30	63-0	2	55	.238	.362	.327	79	-8	31-9	.984	-1	111	0	O88L	0	-0.8
2001	SD N	123	379	70	86	17	3	8	42	81-0	3	84	.227	.366	.351	94	0	25-7	.982	-3	90	80	O104L/D	0	-0.3
2002	Bos A	72	179	40	40	6	1	5	16	38-0	4	47	.223	.369	.352	92	0	8-2	.946	-2	88	152	O54(49/4/1),D5	0	-0.2
2003	LA N	30	72	7	15	1	0	2	5	11-0	1	16	.208	.321	.306	67	-3	3-0	.955	-1	73	108	O18L	0	-0.5
Total	25	3081	10961	2295	3055	510	66	297	1115	2190-61	98	1694	.279	.401	.419	127	542	1406-335	.979	84	108	73	O2826(2421/448/27),D149	176	70.2

HENDERSON, STEVE Stephen Curtis; B11.18.1952 Houston TX; BR/TR/6´2˝/(180–190); [CinN74 5/119]; d6.16; C5; Col Prairie View A&M

YEAR	TM LG	G	AB	R	H	2B	3B	HR	RBI	BB-IB	HP	SO	AVG	OBP	SLG	AOPS	ABR	SB-CS	FA	FR	RNG	THR	GAMES AT POSITION	DL	BFW
1977	NY N	99	350	67	104	16	6	12	65	43-2	1	79	.297	.372	.480	132	16	6-3	.980	4	111	68	O97L	0	1.6
1978	NY N	157	587	83	156	30	9	10	65	60-3	2	109	.266	.333	.399	107	5	13-7	.968	8	103	137	O155L	0	0.7
1979	NY N	98	350	42	107	16	8	5	39	38-6	4	58	.306	.380	.440	126	13	13-5	.990	4	106	80	O94L	48	1.4
1980	NY N	143	513	75	149	17	8	8	58	62-3	3	90	.290	.368	.402	117	13	23-12	.981	7	113	71	O136L	0	1.5
1981	Chi N	82	287	32	84	9	5	5	35	42-7	2	61	.293	.382	.411	119	9	5-7	.951	-3	98	58	O77L	74	0.1
1982	Chi N	92	257	23	60	12	4	2	29	22-3	0	64	.233	.293	.335	73	-10	6-5	.956	1	99	99	O70L	0	-1.3
1983	Sea A	121	436	50	128	32	3	10	54	44-2	0	82	.294	.356	.450	116	10	10-14	.970	0	85	192	O112L,D6	0	0.4
1984	Sea A	109	325	42	85	12	3	10	35	38-4	1	62	.262	.341	.409	107	3	2-4	.936	-2	91	131	O53L,D51	15	-0.3
1985	Oak A	85	193	25	58	8	3	3	31	18-0	0	34	.301	.358	.420	121	6	0-0	.953	-3	86	106	O58(47/0/11)/D	0	0.1
1986	Oak A	11	26	2	2	1	0	0	3	0-0	0	5	.077	.074	.115	-52	-6	0-0	.800	-1	67	0	O7L/D	0	-0.7
1987	Oak A	46	114	14	33	7	0	3	9	12-1	0	19	.289	.357	.430	115	3	0-0	.943	-4	72	0	O31(5/0/28),D9	0	-0.3
1988	Hou N	42	46	4	10	2	0	0	5	7-1	0	14	.217	.321	.261	72	-1	1-1	1.000	1	133	398	O8(4/0/4)/1	0	-0.1
Total	12	1085	3484	459	976	162	49	68	428	386-32	13	677	.280	.352	.413	112	61	79-58	.968	12	100	104	O898(856/0/43),D68/1	137	3.1

HENDRICK, GEORGE George Andrew; B10.18.1949 Los Angeles CA; BR/TR/6´3˝/(195–207); [OakA68*1/1]; d6.4; C6

YEAR	TM LG	G	AB	R	H	2B	3B	HR	RBI	BB-IB	HP	SO	AVG	OBP	SLG	AOPS	ABR	SB-CS	FA	FR	RNG	THR	GAMES AT POSITION	DL	BFW
1971	Oak A	42	114	8	27	4	1	0	8	3-0	0	20	.237	.254	.289	55	-7	0-1	.981	-2	86	56	O36(18/16/10)	0	-1.2
1972	†Oak A	58	121	10	22	1	1	4	15	3-0	1	22	.182	.205	.306	54	-8	3-2	1.000	-2	97	0	O41(5/28/12)	0	-1.3
1973	Cle A	113	440	64	118	18	0	21	61	25-1	2	71	.268	.308	.452	110	4	7-6	.988	-11	85	85	O110(0/107/3)	46	-1.1
1974	Cle A★	139	495	65	138	23	1	19	67	33-4	1	73	.279	.322	.444	120	11	6-4	.989	-5	96	91	O133(2/131/0)/D	0	0.3
1975	Cle A★	145	561	82	145	21	2	24	86	40-2	0	78	.258	.304	.431	107	2	6-7	.983	-9	97	36	O143(1/89/53)	0	-1.3
1976	Cle A	149	551	72	146	20	3	25	81	51-6	0	82	.265	.323	.448	126	16	4-4	.987	2	96	128	O146(136/13/3),D3	0	0.9
1977	SD N	152	541	75	168	25	2	23	81	61-8	2	74	.311	.381	.492	147	36	11-6	.983	8	109	115	O142(24/131/9)	0	4.2
1978	SD N	36	111	9	27	4	0	3	8	12-0	0	16	.243	.317	.360	96	-1	1-1	.986	-1	96	55	O33(1/26/6)	0	-0.3
	StL N	102	382	55	110	27	1	17	67	28-1	2	44	.288	.337	.497	132	15	1-0	.996	-2	98	85	O101(2/87/12)	0	1.3
	Year	138	493	64	137	31	1	20	75	40-1	2	60	.278	.332	.467	124	15	2-1	.994	-3	98	78	O134(3/113/18)	0	1.0
1979	StL N	140	493	67	148	27	1	16	75	49-5	0	62	.300	.359	.456	120	14	2-3	.993	3	92	**177**	O138(0/14/124)	0	1.0
1980	StL N★	150	572	73	173	33	2	25	109	32-9	4	67	.302	.342	.498	126	19	6-1	.994	-2	99	81	O149(0/54/121)	0	1.2
1981	StL N	101	394	67	112	19	3	18	61	41-7	4	44	.284	.356	.485	131	16	4-2	.983	-7	90	71	O101(0/51/59)	0	0.6
1982	†StL N	136	515	65	145	20	5	19	104	37-8	1	80	.282	.323	.450	113	7	3-2	.980	-8	93	61	O134R	0	-0.8
1983	StL N☆	144	529	73	168	33	3	18	97	51-15	2	76	.318	.373	.493	139	29	3-4	.992	-1	117	99	1b92,O51R	0	1.9
1984	StL N	120	441	57	122	28	1	9	69	32-2	1	75	.277	.324	.406	107	4	0-2	.990	-6	85	115	O116R/1	0	-0.9
1985	Pit N	69	256	23	59	15	0	2	25	18-1	0	42	.230	.278	.313	66	-12	1-0	.971	0	111	46	O65R	0	-1.6
	Cal A	16	41	5	5	1	0	2	6	4-1	0	8	.122	.196	.293	33	-4	0-0	1.000	-0	85	140	O12R/D	0	-0.5

YEAR	TM LG	G	AB	R	H	2B	3B	HR	RBI	BB-IB	HP	SO	AVG	OBP	SLG	AOPS	ABR	SB-CS	FA	FR	RNG	THR	GAMES AT POSITION	DL	BFW
1986	†Cal A	102	283	45	77	13	1	14	47	26-5	1	41	.272	.332	.473	118	7	1-1	.968	2	108	129	O93(0/2/92),1b7,D4	0	0.5
1987	Cal A	65	162	14	39	10	0	5	25	14-1	0	18	.241	.301	.395	85	-4	0-0	.967	-4	84	42	O45(37/0/11),1b9,D5	48	-0.9
1988	Cal A	69	127	12	31	1	0	3	19	7-1	1	20	.244	.283	.323	73	-5	0-1	.933	0	109	0	O24(20/0/4),1b12,D3	0	-0.7
Total	18	2048	7129	941	1980	343	27	267	1111	567-77	22	1013	.278	.329	.446	116	139	59-47	.985	-46	96	89	O1813(246/749/897),1b121,D17	94	1.3
Hendrick, Harvey	Harvey "Gink"; B11.9.1897 Mason TN; D10.29.1941 Covington TN; BL/TR/6´2˝/190; d4.20; Col Vanderbilt; OF(128/21/86)																								
1923	†NY A	37	66	9	18	3	1	3	12	2	0	8	.273	.294	.485	101	-1	3-0	.947	-0	78	179	O13(11/2/0)	—	-0.1
1924	NY A	40	76	7	20	0	0	1	11	2	1	7	.263	.291	.303	53	-6	1-0	.975	1	117	60	O17(15/0/2)	—	-0.6
1925	Cle A	25	28	2	8	1	2	0	9	3	0	5	.286	.355	.464	106	0	0-0	1.000	0	117	46	1b3	—	0.0
1927	Bro N	128	458	55	142	18	11	4	50	24	4	40	.310	.350	.424	106	2	29	.969	-3	88	88	O64(15/0/64),1b53/2	—	-0.8
1928	Bro N	126	425	83	135	15	10	11	59	54	2	34	.318	.397	.478	129	19	16	.913	0	103	115	3b91,O17(6/11/0)	—	2.3
1929	Bro N	110	384	69	136	25	6	14	82	31	1	20	.354	.404	.560	139	23	14	.975	1	98	107	O42(30/2/10),1b39,3b7,S4	—	1.7
1930	Bro N	68	167	29	43	10	1	5	28	20	2	19	.257	.344	.419	84	-4	2	.947	0	96	164	O42(36/6/0),1b7	—	-0.6
1931	Bro N	1	1	0	0	0	0	0	0	0	0	0	.000	.000	.000	-99	0	0	ø	0	—	—	/H	—	0.0
	Cin N	137	530	74	167	32	9	1	75	53	2	40	.315	.379	.415	121	17	3	.987	-6	87	**121**	1b137	—	-0.1
	Year	138	531	74	167	32	9	1	75	53	2	40	.315	.379	.414	120	16	3	.987	-6	87	**121**	1b137	—	-0.1
1932	StL N	28	72	8	18	2	0	1	5	5	0	9	.250	.299	.319	64	-4	0	.862	-1	82	147	3b12,O5R	—	-0.5
	Cin N	94	398	56	120	30	3	4	40	23	1	29	.302	.341	.422	107	4	3	.986	-4	91	100	1b94	—	-0.9
	Year	122	470	64	138	32	3	5	45	28	1	38	.294	.335	.406	100	0	3	.986	-5	91	100	1b94,3b12,O5R	—	-1.4
1933	Chi N	69	189	30	55	13	3	4	23	13	3	17	.291	.346	.455	128	7	4	.983	-1	99	114	1b38,O8(4/0/4)/3	—	0.2
1934	Phi N	59	116	12	34	8	0	0	19	9	0	15	.293	.344	.362	79	-3	0	.962	-2	98	121	O12(11/0/1),1b7,3b7	—	-0.6
Total	11	922	2910	434	896	157	46	48	413	239	16	243	.308	.364	.443	113	54	75-0	.986	-15	95	106	1b378,O220L,3b118,S4/2	—	-0.0
Hendricks, Elrod	Elrod Jerome; B12.22.1940 Charlotte Amalie, V.I.; D12.21.2005 Glen Burnie MD; BL/TR/6´1˝/(175–185); d4.13; C28																								
1968	Bal A	79	183	19	37	8	1	7	23	19-2	1	51	.202	.279	.372	96	-1	0-0	.991	-1	88	99	C53	0	0.0
1969	†Bal A	105	295	36	72	5	0	12	38	39-5	2	44	.244	.333	.383	100	0	0-1	**.998**	9	**156**	98	C87,1b4	0	1.2
1970	†Bal A	106	322	32	78	9	0	12	41	33-4	4	44	.242	.317	.382	91	-4	1-0	.986	-2	142	97	C95	0	-0.2
1971	†Bal A	101	316	33	79	14	1	9	42	39-5	2	38	.250	.334	.386	103	2	0-0	.985	-5	109	102	C90,1b3	0	0.1
1972	Bal A	33	84	6	13	4	0	0	4	12-2	0	19	.155	.258	.202	37	-6	0-1	.986	1	163	136	C28	0	-0.4
	Chi N	17	43	7	5	1	0	2	6	13-6	0	8	.116	.321	.279	65	-2	0-1	.978	2	75	101	C16	0	0.0
1973	Bal A	41	101	9	18	5	1	3	15	10-4	1	22	.178	.257	.337	66	-5	0-0	.994	1	93	82	C38/D	0	-0.2
1974	†Bal A	66	159	18	33	8	2	3	8	17-4	1	25	.208	.283	.340	82	-4	0-0	1.000	-6	95	82	C54/1D	0	-0.8
1975	Bal A	85	223	32	48	8	2	8	38	34-5	1	40	.215	.319	.377	102	1	0-1	**.995**	1	109	99	C83	0	0.5
1976	Bal A	28	79	2	11	1	0	1	4	7-1	0	13	.139	.209	.190	18	-8	0-1	.971	-7	66	77	C27	0	-1.6
	†NY A	26	53	6	12	1	0	3	5	3-0	0	10	.226	.263	.415	98	-1	0-0	1.000	-0	136	53	C18	0	0.0
	Year	54	132	8	23	2	0	4	9	10-1	0	23	.174	.231	.280	51	-9	0-1	.982	-7	91	68	C45	0	-1.6
1977	NY A	10	11	1	3	1	0	1	5	0-0	0	2	.273	.273	.636	140	1	0-0	1.000	-0	146	0	C6	0	0.0
1978	Bal A	13	18	4	6	1	0	1	1	3-2	0	3	.333	.429	.556	185	2	0-0	.955	0	104	81	C6/PD	0	0.3
1979	Bal A	1	1	0	0	0	0	0	0	0-0	0	0	.000	.000	.000	-99	0	0-0	.500	-1	11	0	/C	0	-0.1
Total	12	711	1888	205	415	66	7	62	230	229-40	12	319	.220	.306	.361	90	-25	1-5	.990	-8	118	96	C602,1b8,D3/P	0	-1.2
Hendricks, Jack	John Charles; B4.9.1875 Joliet IL; D5.13.1943 Chicago IL; BL/TL/5´11.5˝/160; d6.12; M7; Col Butler/North Central																								
1902	NY N	8	26	1	6	2	0	0	0	2	0	—	.231	.286	.308	84	0	2	.929	-0	92	0	O7R	—	-0.1
	Chi N	2	7	0	4	0	1	0	0	0	0	—	.571	.571	.857	350	2	0	1.000	0	0	0	O2R	—	0.2
	Year	10	33	1	10	2	1	0	0	2	0	—	.303	.343	.424	138	1	2	.950	-0	68	0	O9R	—	0.1
1903	Was A	32	112	10	20	1	3	0	4	13	0	—	.179	.264	.241	51	-7	3	.891	-3	33	122	O32R	—	-1.1
Total	2	42	145	11	30	3	4	0	4	15	0	—	.207	.281	.283	70	-5	5	.909	-3	43	87	O41R	—	-1.0
Hendryx, Tim	Timothy Green; B1.31.1891 LeRoy IL; D8.14.1957 Corpus Christi TX; BR/TR/5´9˝/170; d9.4																								
1911	Cle A	4	7	0	2	0	0	0	0	0	0	—	.286	.286	.286	59	0	0	1.000	0	84	0	3b3	—	0.0
1912	Cle A	23	70	9	17	2	4	1	14	8	1	—	.243	.329	.429	113	1	3	1.000	-1	99	34	O22C	—	-0.2
1915	NY A	13	40	4	8	2	0	0	1	4	1	2	.200	.289	.250	61	-2	0-3	.968	0	102	118	O12C	—	-0.3
1916	NY A	15	62	10	18	7	1	0	5	8	1	6	.290	.380	.435	142	4	4	1.000	-1	85	62	O15R	—	0.2
1917	NY A	125	393	43	98	14	7	5	44	62	5	45	.249	.359	.359	118	10	6	.955	2	104	111	O107(0/30/77)	—	0.6
1918	StL A	88	219	22	61	14	3	0	33	37	2	35	.279	.388	.370	133	11	5	.982	-4	94	52	O65(28/20/18)	—	0.5
1920	Bos A	99	363	54	119	21	5	0	73	42	2	27	.328	.400	.413	121	13	7-9	.964	-12	87	48	O98C	—	-0.8
1921	Bos A	49	137	10	33	8	2	0	22	24	2	13	.241	.362	.328	79	-3	1-1	.958	-3	100	41	O41(2/2/37)	—	-0.8
Total	8	416	1291	152	356	68	22	6	192	185	14	128	.276	.372	.376	115	34	26-13	.966	-19	96	70	O360(30/184/147),3b3	—	-0.8
Hengel, Dave	David Lee; B12.18.1961 Oakland CA; BR/TR/6´0˝/195; [SeaA83 3/61]; d9.3; Col California																								
1986	Sea A	21	63	3	12	1	0	1	6	1-0	1	13	.190	.215	.254	27	-7	0-0	1.000	-1	63	215	D11,O8(6/0/2)	0	-0.8
1987	Sea A	10	19	2	6	0	0	1	4	0-0	0	4	.316	.316	.474	100	0	0-0	.875	-1	81	0	O7(2/0/7)/D	0	-0.1
1988	Sea A	26	60	3	10	1	0	2	7	1-0	0	15	.167	.177	.283	26	-6	0-0	.952	-0	103	0	O12(4/0/8),D12	0	-0.7
1989	Cle A	12	25	2	3	1	0	0	1	2-0	0	4	.120	.185	.160	-2	-3	0-0	1.000	-1	71	199	O9L,D3	18	-0.4
Total	4	69	167	10	31	3	0	4	18	4-0	1	36	.186	.208	.275	31	-16	0-0	.962	-2	81	108	O36(21/0/17),D27	18	-2.0
Hengle, Moxie	Emery J.; B10.7.1857 Chicago IL; D12.11.1924 River Forest IL; BR/5´8˝/144; d4.20																								
1884	CP U	19	74	9	15	2	1	0	—	3	—	—	.203	.234	.257	49	-7	—	.840	-5	79	39	2b19	—	-1.0
	StP U	**9**	33	2	5	1	1	0	—	0	—	—	.152	.152	.242	32	-4	—	.923	3	106	106	2b9	—	-0.1
	Year	28	107	11	20	3	2	0	—	3	—	—	.187	.209	.252	46	-10	—	.870	-2	87	59	2b28	—	-1.1
1885	Buf N	7	26	2	4	0	0	0	0	1	—	2	.154	.185	.154	10	-3	—	.864	-2	49	52	2b5,O3(0/2/1)	—	-0.4
Total	2	35	133	13	24	3	2	0	0	4	—	2	.180	.204	.233	38	-14	—	.869	-4	82	58	2b33,O3(0/2/1)	—	-1.5
Henley, Gail	Gail Curtice; B10.15.1928 Wichita KS; BL/TR/5´9˝/175; d4.13; Col USC																								
1954	Pit N	14	30	7	9	1	0	1	2	4	0	4	.300	.382	.433	114	1	0-0	1.000	0	102	173	O9(1/0/8)	0	0.1
Henley, Bob	Robert Clifton; B1.30.1973 Mobile AL; BR/TR/6´2˝/205; [MonN91 26/685]; d7.19; [DL 1999 Mon N 182, 2000 Mon N 181]																								
1998	Mon N	41	115	16	35	8	1	3	18	11-0	3	26	.304	.377	.470	125	5	3-0	.995	-2	96	114	C35	35	0.5
Henline, Butch	Walter John; B12.20.1894 Ft.Wayne IN; D10.9.1957 Sarasota FL; BR/TR/5´10˝/175; d4.13; U4																								
1921	NY N	1	1	0	0	0	0	0	0	0	0	1	.000	.000	.000	-99	0	0-0	ø	0	—	—	/H	—	0.0
	Phi N	33	111	8	34	2	0	0	8	2	0	6	.306	.319	.324	65	-5	1-0	.987	3	*81*	*142*	C32	—	0.0
	Year	34	112	8	34	2	0	0	8	2	0	7	.304	.316	.321	64	-6	1-0	.987	3	*81*	*142*	C32	—	0.0
1922	Phi N	125	430	57	136	20	4	14	64	36	8	33	.316	.380	.479	110	6	2-2	**.983**	-3	*82*	*99*	C119	—	1.1
1923	Phi N	111	330	45	107	14	3	7	46	37	9	33	.324	.407	.448	112	8	7-5	.978	-16	*76*	*95*	C96/lf	—	-0.2
1924	Phi N	115	289	41	82	18	4	5	35	27	8	15	.284	.361	.426	98	0	1-2	.973	-2	*90*	*106*	C83,O2(1/1/0)	—	0.3
1925	Phi N	93	263	43	80	12	5	8	48	24	8	16	.304	.380	.479	108	3	3-1	.956	-3	*103*	*96*	C68/lf	—	0.5
1926	Phi N	99	283	32	80	14	1	2	30	21	3	18	.283	.339	.360	84	-6	1	.970	-7	*81*	*87*	C77,1b4,O2L	—	-0.9
1927	Bro N	67	177	12	47	10	3	1	18	17	2	10	.266	.337	.373	90	-2	1	.947	1	*78*	*146*	C60	—	0.2
1928	Bro N	55	132	12	28	3	1	2	8	17	0	8	.212	.302	.295	58	-8	2	.976	-1	*76*	*97*	C45	—	-0.7
1929	Bro N	27	62	5	15	2	0	1	7	9	0	9	.242	.338	.323	66	-3	0	.967	-1	*60*	*143*	C21	—	-0.3
1930	Chi A	3	8	1	1	0	0	0	2	0	0	3	.125	.125	.125	-38	-2	0-0	1.000	0	*121*	*113*	C3	—	-0.1
1931	Chi A	11	15	2	1	1	0	0	2	2	0	4	.067	.176	.133	-19	-3	0-0	.889	-1	*80*	*81*	C4	—	-0.3
Total	11	740	2101	258	611	96	21	40	268	192	38	156	.291	.361	.414	96	-12	18-10	.971	-30	*83*	*106*	C608,O6(5/1/0),1b4	—	-0.4
Hennessey, Les	Lester Baker; B12.12.1893 Lynn MA; D11.20.1976 New York NY; BR/TR/6´0˝/190; d6.4; Col Lafayette																								
1913	Det A	14	22	2	3	0	0	0	0	3	0	6	.136	.240	.136	11	-2	2	.880	-2	98	0	2b10	—	-0.4
Henrich, Fritz	Frank Wilde; B5.8.1899 Cincinnati OH; D5.1.1959 Philadelphia PA; BL/TL/5´10˝/160; d4.19; Col St. Josephs (PA)																								
1924	Phi N	36	90	4	19	4	0	0	4	2	0	12	.211	.228	.256	26	-9	0-0	.978	-1	92	92	O32(12/14/10)	—	-1.1
Henrich, Bobby	Robert Edward; B12.24.1938 Lawrence KS; BR/TR/6´1˝/(180–185); d5.3																								
1957	Cin N	29	10	8	2	0	0	0	1	1-0	0	4	.200	.250	.200	28	-1	0-0	.875	-1	84	0	S7,O6(4/2/0),3b2/2	0	-0.2
1958	Cin N	5	3	2	0	0	0	0	0	0-0	0	2	.000	.000	.000	-95	-1	0-0	1.000	-1	63	0	S2	0	-0.1
1959	Cin N	14	3	3	0	0	0	0	0	0-0	0	1	.000	.000	.000	-97	-1	0-0	1.000	-1	0	0	S5/3	0	-0.2
Total	3	48	16	13	2	0	0	0	1	1-0	0	7	.125	.167	.125	-17	-3	0-0	.929	-3	59	0	S14,O6(4/2/0),3b3/2	0	-0.5

THE BATTER REGISTER

YEAR	TM LG	G	AB	R	H	2B	3B	HR	RBI	BB-IB	HP	SO	AVG	OBP	SLG	AOPS	ABR	SB-CS	FA	FR	RNG	THR	GAMES AT POSITION	DL	BFW
Henrich, Tommy	Thomas David "The Clutch","Old Reliable"; B2.20.1913 Massillon OH; BL/TL/6´0˝/180; d5.11; Mil 1942–45; C4																								
1937	NY A	67	206	39	66	14	5	8	42	35	0	17	.320	.419	.553	142	14	4-0	.970	-1	87	137	O59(30/0/29)	—	1.0
1938	†NY A	131	471	109	127	24	7	22	91	92	2	32	.270	.391	.490	120	16	6-2	.984	-1	95	120	O130R	—	0.7
1939	NY A	99	347	64	96	18	4	9	57	51	1	23	.277	.371	.429	106	4	7-0	.991	1	102	99	O88(1/38/50)/1	—	0.2
1940	NY A	90	293	57	90	28	5	10	53	48	2	30	.307	.408	.539	149	23	1-2	.969	1	92	176	O76(1/24/52),1b2	—	1.9
1941	†NY A	144	538	106	149	27	5	31	85	81	5	40	.277	.377	.519	137	28	3-1	.980	-3	95	99	O139(0/19/121)	0	1.7
1942	NY A★	127	483	77	129	30	5	13	67	58	5	42	.267	.352	.431	122	14	4-4	.987	1	97	119	O119R,1b7	0	0.6
1946	NY A	150	565	92	142	25	4	19	83	87	**7**	63	.251	.358	.411	113	12	5-2	.992	-0	103	100	O111R,1b41	0	0.7
1947	†NY A★	142	550	109	158	35	**13**	16	98	71	3	54	.287	.372	.485	139	28	3-2	.983	3	105	138	O132(0/8/125),1b6	0	2.7
1948	NY A★	146	588	**138**	181	42	**14**	25	100	76	4	42	.308	.391	.554	151	41	2-3	.978	-1	102	108	O102(6/3/96),1b46	0	3.2
1949	†NY A☆	115	411	90	118	20	3	24	85	86	5	34	.287	.416	.526	148	31	2-2	.958	-5	94	89	O61R,1b52	0	2.1
1950	NY A★	73	151	20	41	6	8	6	34	27	0	6	.272	.382	.536	137	8	0-1	.987	-4	38	79	1b34	0	0.2
Total	11	1284	4603	901	1297	269	73	183	795	712	34	383	.282	.382	.491	132	219	37-19	.981	-9	98	117	O1017(38/92/894),1b189	0	15.0
Henriksen, Olaf	Olaf "Swede"; B4.26.1888 Kirkerup, Denmark; D10.17.1962 Norwood MA; BL/TL/5´7.5˝/158; d8.11																								
1911	Bos A	27	93	17	34	2	1	0	8	14	0	—	.366	.449	.409	141	6	4	.953	0	113	80	O25(5/0/20)	—	0.5
1912	†Bos A	44	56	20	18	3	1	0	8	14	0	—	.321	.457	.411	142	4	0	.909	-1	84	0	O11(0/1/10)	—	0.2
1913	Bos A	31	40	8	15	1	0	0	2	7	0	5	.375	.468	.400	151	3	3	1.000	-0	102	0	O7(6/1/0)	—	0.3
1914	Bos A	63	95	16	25	2	1	1	5	22	1	12	.263	.407	.337	124	4	5-4	.947	-1	100	40	O29(8/11/10)	—	0.2
1915	†Bos A	73	92	9	18	2	2	0	13	18	1	7	.196	.333	.261	80	-1	1-5	.967	1	101	105	O25(9/4/12)	—	-0.3
1916	†Bos A	68	99	13	20	2	2	0	11	19	0	15	.202	.331	.263	78	-2	2	1.000	0	106	74	O31(14/7/9)	—	-0.3
1917	Bos A	15	12	1	1	0	0	0	1	3	0	4	.083	.267	.083	7	-1	0	ø	0	—	—	/H	—	-0.1
Total	7	321	487	84	131	12	7	1	48	97	2	43	.269	.392	.329	112	13	15-9	.966	-2	104	64	O128(42/24/61)	—	0.5
Henry, Snake	Frederick Marshall; B7.19.1895 Waynesville NC; D10.12.1987 Wendell NC; BL/TL/6´0˝/170; d9.15																								
1922	Bos N	18	66	5	13	4	1	0	5	2	0	8	.197	.221	.288	32	-7	2-2	.995	1	130	52	1b18	—	-0.7
1923	Bos N	11	9	1	1	0	0	0	2	1	0	1	.111	.200	.111	-17	-2	0-0	ø	0	—	—	/H	—	-0.1
Total	2	29	75	6	14	4	1	0	7	3	0	9	.187	.218	.267	26	-9	2-2	.995	1	130	52	1b18	—	-0.8
Henry, George	George Washington; B8.10.1863 Philadelphia PA; D12.30.1934 Lynn MA; BR/TR/5´9˝/180; d4.27																								
1893	Cin N	21	83	11	23	3	0	0	13	11	2	12	.277	.375	.313	82	-2	2	.965	3	151	119	O21(10/0/11)	—	0.0
Henry, John	John Michael; B9.2.1863 Springfield MA; D6.11.1939 Hartford CT; TL; d8.13; ▲																								
1884	Cle N	9	26	2	4	0	0	0	0	0	—	12	.154	.154	.154	-3	-3	—	1.000	1	128	0	P5,O4R	—	0.0
1885	Bal AA	10	34	4	9	3	0	0	3	1	0	—	.265	.286	.353	102	0	—	.931	2	153	320	P9/lf	—	0.1
1886	Was N	4	14	3	5	0	0	0	0	0	—	3	.357	.357	.357	127	1	0	.833	-0	52	0	P4	—	0.0
1890	NY N	37	144	19	35	6	0	0	16	7	1	12	.243	.283	.285	65	-7	12	.870	-3	61	71	O37(34/1/3)	—	-0.9
Total	4	60	218	28	53	9	0	0	19	8	1	27	.243	.273	.284	66	-9	12	.867	-0	69	66	O42(35/1/7),P18	—	-0.8
Henry, John	John Park "Bull"; B12.26.1889 Amherst MA; D11.24.1941 Fort Huachuca AZ; BR/TR/6´0˝/180; d7.8; Col Amherst																								
1910	Was A	28	87	2	13	1	1	0	5	2	0	—	.149	.169	.184	11	-9	2	.989	3	*101*	*131*	C18,1b10	—	-0.6
1911	Was A	85	261	24	53	5	0	0	21	25	0	—	.203	.273	.222	39	-21	8	.969	9	*106*	*118*	C51,1b30	—	-0.9
1912	Was A	66	191	23	37	4	1	0	9	31	1	—	.194	.309	.225	53	-10	10	.977	13	*132*	*111*	C65	—	0.8
1913	Was A	96	273	26	61	8	4	1	26	30	4	43	.223	.309	.293	75	-8	5	**.982**	7	*114*	*103*	C96	—	0.6
1914	Was A	92	261	22	44	7	4	0	20	37	1	47	.169	.274	.226	49	-16	7-3	.980	5	*105*	*97*	C92	—	-0.3
1915	Was A	95	277	20	61	9	2	1	22	36	6	28	.220	.323	.278	78	-6	10-2	.972	8	*114*	*92*	C94	—	1.1
1916	Was A	117	305	28	76	12	3	0	46	49	6	40	.249	.364	.308	103	4	12	.981	-0	99	92	C116	—	1.4
1917	Was A	65	163	10	31	6	0	0	18	24	2	16	.190	.302	.227	62	-6	1	.988	1	*87*	*90*	C59	—	-0.1
1918	Bos N	43	102	6	21	2	0	0	4	10	1	15	.206	.283	.225	58	-5	0	.964	-2	*96*	*102*	C38	—	-0.4
Total	9	687	1920	161	397	54	15	2	171	244	21	189	.207	.303	.254	65	-77	55-5	.978	43	*107*	*100*	C629,1b40	—	1.6
Henry, Ron	Ronald Baxter; B8.7.1936 Chester PA; BR/TR/6´1˝/180; d4.15																								
1961	Min A	20	28	1	4	0	0	0	3	2-0	0	7	.143	.194	.143	-6	-4	0-0	1.000	-1	70	0	C5/1	0	-0.5
1964	Min A	22	41	4	5	1	1	2	5	2-0	0	17	.122	.163	.341	36	-4	0-0	.984	0	137	182	C13	0	-0.3
Total	2	42	69	5	9	1	1	2	8	4-0	0	24	.130	.176	.261	18	-8	0-0	.988	-0	116	124	C18/1	0	-0.8
Henson, Drew	Drew Daniel; B2.13.1980 San Diego CA; BR/TR/6´5˝/222; [NYA98 3/97]; d9.5																								
2002	NY A	3	1	1	0	0	0	0	0	0-0	0	1	.000	.000	.000	-99	0	0-0	ø	0	—	—	D2	0	0.0
2003	NY A	5	8	2	1	0	0	0	0	0-0	0	2	.125	.125	.125	-34	-2	0-0	1.000	0	80	0	3b3	0	-0.1
Total	2	8	9	3	1	0	0	0	0	0-0	0	3	.111	.111	.111	-42	-2	0-0	1.000	0	80	0	3b3,D2	0	-0.1
Herman, Babe	Floyd Caves; B6.26.1903 Buffalo NY; D11.27.1987 Glendale CA; BL/TL/6´4˝/190; d4.14; C1																								
1926	Bro N	137	496	64	158	35	11	11	81	44	1	53	.319	.375	.500	136	24	8	.986	1	107	69	1b101,O35(6/0/29)	—	1.7
1927	Bro N	130	412	65	112	26	9	14	73	39	1	41	.272	.336	.481	116	8	4	.980	1	107	81	1b105/lf	—	0.2
1928	Bro N	134	486	64	165	37	6	12	91	38	2	36	.340	.390	.514	136	26	1	.937	-8	86	97	O127R	—	0.8
1929	Bro N	146	569	105	217	42	13	21	113	55	0	45	.381	.436	.612	160	53	21	.941	-15	83	70	O141R,1b2	—	2.4
1930	Bro N	153	614	143	241	48	11	35	130	66	4	56	.393	.455	.678	171	72	18	.978	-21	78	52	O153R	—	3.4
1931	Bro N	151	610	93	191	43	16	18	97	50	0	65	.313	.365	.525	137	30	17	.960	-1	90	132	O150R	—	1.9
1932	Cin N	148	577	87	188	38	**19**	16	87	60	0	45	.326	.389	.541	152	42	7	.969	13	**117**	113	O146R	—	4.5
1933	Chi N	137	508	77	147	36	12	16	93	50	0	57	.289	.353	.502	142	27	6	.957	-6	92	96	O131R	—	1.4
1934	Chi N	125	467	65	142	34	5	14	84	35	0	71	.304	.353	.488	125	16	1	.971	-11	84	68	O113R,1b7	—	-0.2
1935	Pit N	26	81	8	19	8	1	0	7	3	1	10	.235	.271	.358	65	-4	0	.958	-2	79	110	O15L,1b3	—	-0.7
	Cin N	92	349	44	117	23	5	10	58	35	0	25	.335	.396	.516	147	24	5	.976	-0	98	95	O76L,1b14	—	1.7
	Year	118	430	52	136	31	6	10	65	38	1	35	.316	.373	.486	131	19	5	.974	-3	95	97	O91L,1b17	—	1.0
1936	Cin N	119	380	59	106	25	2	13	71	39	1	36	.279	.348	.458	123	12	4	.967	-3	99	47	O92(91/0/1),1b4	—	0.4
1937	Det A	17	20	2	6	3	0	0	3	1	1	6	.300	.364	.450	102	0	2-0	1.000	-0	93	0	O2L	—	0.0
1945	Bro N	37	34	6	9	1	0	1	9	5	0	7	.265	.359	.382	107	0	0	ø	-0	0	0	O3R	0	0.0
Total	13	1552	5603	882	1818	399	110	181	997	520	11	553	.324	.383	.532	141	330	94-0	.961	-52	91	88	O1185(191/0/994),1b236	0	17.5
Herman, Billy	William Jennings Bryan; B7.7.1909 New Albany IN; D9.5.1992 W.Palm Beach FL; BR/TR/5´11˝/180; d8.29; Mil 1944–45; M4/C16; HF1975																								
1931	Chi N	25	98	14	32	7	0	0	16	13	0	6	.327	.405	.398	115	3	2	.939	-2	90	93	2b25	—	0.3
1932	†Chi N	**154**	656	102	206	42	7	1	51	40	5	33	.314	.358	.404	105	6	14	.961	12	105	112	2b154	—	2.8
1933	Chi N	153	619	82	173	35	2	0	44	45	4	34	.279	.332	.342	93	-4	5	.956	29	103	**129**	2b153	—	3.7
1934	Chi N★	113	456	79	138	21	6	3	42	34	3	31	.303	.355	.395	102	2	6	.975	9	102	102	2b111	—	1.7
1935	†Chi N★	**154**	666	113	**227**	**57**	6	7	83	42	3	29	.341	.383	.476	128	28	6	**.964**	16	103	**135**	2b154	—	5.2
1936	Chi N★	153	632	101	211	57	7	5	93	59	1	30	.334	.392	.470	128	27	5	**.975**	17	97	128	2b153	—	5.2
1937	Chi N★	138	564	106	189	35	11	8	65	56	1	22	.335	.396	.479	131	26	2	.954	15	103	115	2b137	—	4.9
1938	†Chi N★	152	624	86	173	34	7	1	56	59	2	31	.277	.342	.359	90	-7	3	**.981**	22	103	120	2b151	—	2.4
1939	Chi N★	**156**	623	111	191	34	**18**	7	70	66	5	31	.307	.378	.453	120	18	9	.967	-4	99	92	2b156	—	2.4
1940	Chi N★	135	558	77	163	24	4	5	57	47	0	30	.292	.347	.376	101	1	1	.974	**20**	**107**	111	2b135	—	3.0
1941	Chi N	11	36	4	7	0	1	0	0	9	0	5	.194	.356	.250	75	-1	0	.898	-3	67	81	2b11	0	-0.4
	†Bro N★	133	536	77	156	30	4	3	41	58	1	38	.291	.361	.379	104	5	1	.970	-26	89	92	2b133	0	-1.4
	Year	144	572	81	163	30	5	3	41	67	1	43	.285	.361	.371	103	4	1	.964	-29	87	91	2b144	0	-1.8
1942	Bro N★	**155**	571	76	146	34	2	2	65	72	0	52	.256	.339	.333	95	-1	6	.973	-10	90	117	2b153,1b3	0	-0.2
1943	Bro N★	**153**	585	76	193	41	2	2	100	66	0	26	.330	.398	.417	135	30	4	.971	-17	88	88	2b117,3b37	0	2.0
1946	Bro N	47	184	24	53	8	4	0	28	26	0	10	.288	.376	.375	112	4	2	.945	-2	98	180	3b29,2b16	0	0.3
	Bos N	75	252	32	77	23	1	3	22	43	1	13	.306	.409	.440	139	16	1	.956	-12	85	99	2b44,1b22,3b5	0	0.5
	Year	122	436	56	130	31	5	3	50	69	1	23	.298	.395	.413	128	19	3	.968	-14	85	88	2b60,3b34,1b22	0	0.8
1947	Pit N	15	47	3	10	4	0	0	6	2	0	7	.213	.245	.298	42	-4	0	1.000	-5	60	38	2b10,1b2,M	0	-0.8
Total	15	1922	7707	1163	2345	486	82	47	839	737	26	428	.304	.367	.407	112	149	67	.967	59	98	111	2b1813,3b71,1b27	0	31.6
Hermann, Al	Albert Bartel; B3.28.1899 Milltown NJ; D8.20.1980 Lewes DE; BR/TR/6´0˝/180; d7.13; Col Colgate																								
1923	Bos N	31	93	2	22	4	0	0	11	0	0	7	.237	.237	.280	37	-9	3-2	.957	-4	100	49	2b15,3b5,1b4	—	-1.2
1924	Bos N	1	1	0	0	0	0	0	0	0	0	1	.000	.000	.000	-99	0	0-0	ø	0	—	—	/H	—	0.0
Total	2	32	94	2	22	4	0	0	11	0	0	8	.234	.234	.277	36	-9	3-2	.957	-4	100	49	2b15,3b5,1b4	—	-1.2

YEAR	TM LG	G	AB	R	H	2B	3B	HR	RBI	BB-IB	HP	SO	AVG	OBP	SLG	AOPS	ABR	SB-CS	FA	FR	RNG	THR	GAMES AT POSITION	DL	BFW
Hermansen, Chad	Chad Bruce; B9.10.1977 Salt Lake City UT; BR/TR/6´2˝/(185–190); [PitN95 1/10]; d9.7																								
1999	Pit N	19	60	5	14	3	0	1	1	7-1	1	19	.233	.324	.333	66	-3	2-2	1.000	-3	76	0	O18(3/9/6)	0	-0.6
2000	Pit N	33	108	12	20	4	1	2	8	6-0	0	37	.185	.226	.296	31	-12	0-0	.979	-6	63	112	O31(0/27/4)	0	-1.7
2001	Pit N	22	55	5	9	1	0	2	5	1-0	0	18	.164	.179	.291	18	-7	0-1	1.000	0	96	112	O20(0/6/15)	0	-0.8
2002	Pit N	65	194	22	40	11	1	7	15	17-0	1	68	.206	.272	.381	69	-9	7-5	.982	-0	94	187	O60(2/59/2)	41	-0.9
	Chi N	35	43	3	9	3	0	1	3	5-0	0	14	.209	.292	.349	68	-2	0-0	.895	-1	84	0	O21(4/9/9)	0	-0.4
	Year	100	237	25	49	14	1	8	18	22-0	1	82	.207	.276	.376	69	-11	7-5	.970	-1	92	154	O81(6/68/11)	0	-1.3
2003	LA N	11	25	2	4	1	0	0	2	2-0	0	9	.160	.222	.200	12	-3	0-0	1.000	-0	98	0	O6L	47	-0.4
2004	Tor A	4	7	0	0	0	0	0	0	0-0	0	3	.000	.000	.000	-95	-2	0-0	1.000	0	103	0	O4L	0	-0.2
Total	6	189	492	49	96	23	2	13	34	38-1	2	168	.195	.255	.329	49	-38	9-8	.980	-10	84	110	O160(19/110/36)	88	-5.0
Hermanski, Gene	Eugene Victor; B5.11.1920 Pittsfield MA; BL/TR/5´11.5˝/(185–188); d8.15; Mil 1943–45; Col Seton Hall																								
1943	Bro N	18	60	6	18	2	1	0	12	11	1	7	.300	.417	.367	127	3	1	.976	2	102	238	O17(11/0/6)	0	0.4
1946	Bro N	64	110	15	22	2	2	0	8	17	1	10	.200	.313	.255	61	-5	2	.938	-3	94	0	O34(12/4/17)	0	-1.0
1947	†Bro N	79	189	36	52	7	1	7	39	28	3	7	.275	.377	.434	111	4	5	.982	2	100	138	O66(64/1/3)	0	0.2
1948	Bro N	133	400	63	116	22	7	15	60	64	2	46	.290	.391	.493	133	20	15	.971	6	105	161	O119(6/0/113)	0	2.2
1949	†Bro N	87	224	48	67	12	3	8	42	47	5	21	.299	.431	.487	140	15	12	.980	2	102	128	O77(64/0/17)	0	1.3
1950	Bro N	94	289	36	86	17	3	7	34	36	3	26	.298	.381	.450	115	7	2	.989	5	116	97	O78(76/0/3)	0	0.7
1951	Bro N	31	80	8	20	4	0	1	5	10	0	12	.250	.333	.338	79	-2	0-2	.977	1	100	117	O19(18/0/1)	0	-0.4
	Chi N	75	231	28	65	12	1	3	20	35	4	30	.281	.385	.381	105	4	3-0	.966	2	103	147	O63(3/0/60)	0	0.4
	Year	106	311	36	85	16	1	4	25	45	4	42	.273	.372	.370	98	2	3-2	.969	3	102	140	O82(21/0/61)	0	0.0
1952	Chi N	99	275	28	70	6	0	4	34	29	2	32	.255	.330	.320	80	-7	2-0	.981	4	112	110	O76(3/0/73)	0	-0.5
1953	Chi N	18	40	1	6	1	0	0	1	4	0	7	.150	.227	.175	7	-6	1-0	1.000	-0	106	0	O13(3/0/10)	0	-0.6
	Pit N	41	62	7	11	0	0	1	4	8	1	14	.177	.282	.226	35	-6	0-0	1.000	0	121	0	O13(5/0/8)	0	-0.6
	Year	59	102	8	17	1	0	1	5	12	1	21	.167	.261	.206	24	-12	1-0	1.000	0	114	0	O26(8/0/18)	0	-1.2
Total	9	739	1960	276	533	85	18	46	259	289	22	212	.272	.372	.404	107	27	43-2	.977	21	106	124	O575(265/5/311)	0	2.1
Hermida, Jeremy	Jeremy Ryan; B1.30.1984 Atlanta GA; BL/TR/6´4˝/200; [FlaN02 1/11]; d8.31																								
2005	Fla N	23	41	9	12	2	0	4	11	6-1	0	12	.293	.383	.634	169	4	2-0	1.000	0	122	0	O14(4/0/10)	0	0.4
2006	Fla N	99	307	37	77	19	1	5	28	33-3	5	70	.251	.332	.368	84	-7	4-1	.957	-2	106	25	O89(0/9/85)	40	-1.2
Total	2	122	348	46	89	21	1	9	39	39-4	5	82	.256	.338	.399	93	-3	6-1	.961	-1	107	23	O103(4/9/95)	40	-0.8
Hermoso, Remy	Angel Remigio; B10.1.1946 Carabobo, Venezuela; BR/TR/5´8˝/(152–175); d9.14; [DL 1975 Cle A 35]																								
1967	Atl N	11	26	3	8	0	0	0	0	2-0	0	4	.308	.357	.308	93	0	1-0	.952	-2	95	86	S9,2b2	0	-0.1
1969	Mon N	28	74	6	12	0	0	0	3	5-0	1	10	.162	.225	.162	10	-9	3-1	.968	1	116	141	2b18,S6	0	-0.7
1970	Mon N	4	1	1	0	0	0	0	0	0-0	0	0	.000	.000	.000	-99	0	0-0	1.000	0	301	0	/23	0	0.0
1974	Cle A	48	122	15	27	3	1	0	5	7-0	0	7	.221	.262	.262	52	-8	2-2	.967	3	113	102	2b45	102	-0.3
Total	4	91	223	25	47	3	1	0	8	14-0	1	21	.211	.259	.233	42	-17	6-3	.968	3	113	113	2b66,S15/3	137	-1.1
Hernandez, Alex	Alexander (Vargas); B5.28.1977 San Juan, PR; BL/TL/6´4˝/(186–190); [PitN95 4/97]; d9.1																								
2000	Pit N	20	60	4	12	3	0	1	5	0-0	0	13	.200	.200	.300	24	-7	1-1	.992	-1	38	130	1b12,O5(3/0/2)	0	-0.9
2001	Pit N	7	11	0	1	0	0	0	0	0-0	0	2	.091	.091	.091	-51	-3	0-0	1.000	0	62	633	O4R,1b2	60	-0.2
Total	2	27	71	4	13	3	0	1	5	0-0	0	15	.183	.183	.268	12	-10	1-1	.992	-1	37	136	1b14,O9(3/0/6)	60	-1.1
Hernandez, Anderson	Anderson Mejia; B10.30.1982 Santo Domingo, D.R.; BB/TR/5´9˝/170; d9.18																								
2005	NY N	6	18	1	1	0	0	0	0	1-0	0	4	.056	.105	.056	-57	-4	0-1	1.000	-0	122	31	2b5,S2	0	-0.5
2006	†NY N	25	66	4	10	1	1	1	3	1-0	0	12	.152	.164	.242	2	-10	0-0	1.000	-8	77	38	2b13,S10	34	-1.7
Total	2	31	84	5	11	1	1	1	3	2-0	0	16	.131	.151	.202	-10	-14	0-1	1.000	-8	90	36	2b18,S12	34	-2.2
Hernandez, Carlos	Carlos Alberto (Almeida); B5.24.1967 San Felix, Venezuela; BR/TR/5´11˝/(185–218); d4.20; [DL 1999 SD N 181, 2001 StL N 190]																								
1990	LA N	10	20	2	4	1	0	0	1	0-0	0	2	.200	.200	.250	24	-2	0-0	1.000	0	537	185	C10	0	-0.2
1991	LA N	15	14	1	3	1	0	0	1	0-0	1	5	.214	.250	.286	56	-1	1-0	.966	-0	121	113	C13/3	0	0.0
1992	LA N	69	173	11	45	4	0	3	17	11-1	4	21	.260	.316	.335	86	-3	0-1	.979	-0	87	84	C63	0	-0.1
1993	LA N	50	99	6	25	5	0	2	7	2-0	0	11	.253	.267	.364	71	-5	0-0	.966	1	92	79	C43	0	-0.2
1994	LA N	32	64	6	14	2	0	2	6	1-0	0	14	.219	.231	.344	50	-5	0-0	1.000	1	80	136	C27	18	-0.3
1995	LA N	45	94	3	14	1	0	2	8	7-0	1	25	.149	.216	.223	17	-12	0-0	.983	8	177	133	C41	0	-0.2
1996	LA N	13	14	1	4	0	0	0	0	2-0	0	2	.286	.375	.286	82	0	0-0	1.000	1	282	88	C9	28	0.1
1997	SD N	50	134	15	42	7	1	3	14	3-0	0	27	.313	.328	.448	107	1	0-2	.989	1	83	192	C44,1b4	33	0.3
1998	†SD N	129	390	34	102	15	0	9	52	16-2	9	54	.262	.305	.369	82	-12	2-2	.992	7	112	80	C122/1	0	0.2
2000	SD N	58	191	16	48	11	0	2	25	16-1	3	26	.251	.316	.340	71	-8	1-3	.987	1	80	126	C54/1	35	-0.5
	†StL N	17	51	7	14	4	0	1	10	5-0	1	9	.275	.345	.412	90	-1	1-0	.963	-2	46	174	C16	0	-0.2
	Year	75	242	23	62	15	0	3	35	21-1	4	35	.256	.322	.355	75	-9	2-3	.982	-2	73	137	C70/1	0	-0.7
Total	10	488	1244	102	315	51	1	24	141	63-4	19	196	.253	.298	.354	76	-48	5-8	.985	17	109	112	C442,1b6/3	485	-1.1
Hernandez, Carlos	Carlos Eduardo; B12.12.1975 Caracas, Distrito Capital, Venez.; BR/TR/5´9˝/175; d5.26																								
1999	Hou N	16	14	4	2	0	0	0	1	0-0	0	0	.143	.143	.143	-28	-3	3-1	1.000	2	191	238	2b7,S2	0	0.0
2000	Sea A	2	1	0	0	0	0	0	0	0-0	0	1	.000	.000	.000	-99	0	0-1	1.000	-0	0	0	3b2	31	-0.1
Total	2	18	15	4	2	0	0	0	1	0-0	0	1	.133	.133	.133	-33	-3	3-2	1.000	2	191	238	2b7,3b2,S2	31	-0.1
Hernandez, Cesar	Cesar Dario (Perez); B9.28.1966 Yamasa, D.R.; BR/TR/6´0˝/(160–170); [MonN85 D1/1]; d7.19																								
1992	Cin N	34	51	6	14	4	0	0	4	0-0	0	10	.275	.275	.353	74	-2	3-1	.952	1	95	442	O18(12/6/1)	0	-0.1
1993	Cin N	27	24	3	2	0	0	0	1	1-0	0	8	.083	.120	.083	-44	-5	1-2	.970	4	155	394	O23(17/7/0)	0	-0.2
Total	2	61	75	9	16	4	0	0	5	1-0	0	18	.213	.224	.267	35	-7	4-3	.963	5	124	419	O41(29/13/1)	0	-0.3
Hernandez, Enzo	Enzo Octavio; B2.12.1949 Valle de Guanape, Anzoategui, Venez.; BR/TR/5´8˝/150; d4.17																								
1971	SD N	143	549	58	122	9	3	0	12	54-1	3	34	.222	.295	.250	59	-29	21-5	.955	-5	95	88	S143	0	-1.5
1972	SD N	114	329	33	64	11	2	1	15	22-6	0	25	.195	.243	.249	44	-25	24-3	.963	-7	97	88	S107,O3(2/0/1)	0	-1.7
1973	SD N	70	247	26	55	2	1	0	9	17-0	0	14	.223	.273	.239	47	-19	15-4	.977	1	97	106	S67	40	-0.9
1974	SD N	147	512	55	119	19	2	0	34	38-2	0	36	.232	.285	.277	61	-28	37-10	.966	-2	101	67	S145	0	-0.8
1975	SD N	116	344	37	75	12	2	0	19	26-0	2	25	.218	.275	.265	54	-22	20-4	.965	1	102	116	S111	0	-0.6
1976	SD N	113	340	31	87	13	3	1	24	32-4	0	16	.256	.319	.321	89	-5	12-7	.964	7	111	111	S101	0	1.4
1977	SD N	7	3	1	0	0	0	0	0	0-0	0	0	.000	.000	.000	-99	-1	0-0	1.000	0	101	0	S7	149	-0.1
1978	LA N	4	3	0	0	0	0	0	0	0-0	0	1	.000	.000	.000	-99	-1	0-0	ø	-1	0	0	S2	0	-0.2
Total	8	714	2327	241	522	66	13	2	113	189-13	5	151	.224	.283	.266	59	-130	129-33	.964	-5	100	92	S683,O3(2/0/1)	189	-4.4
Hernandez, Jackie	Jacinto (Zulueta); B9.11.1940 Central Tinguaro, Cuba; BR/TR/6´0˝/(163–175); d9.14																								
1965	Cal A	6	6	2	2	1	0	0	1	0-0	0	1	.333	.333	.500	137	0	1-0	1.000	-1	76	0	S2/3	0	0.0
1966	Cal A	58	23	19	1	0	0	0	2	1-0	0	4	.043	.080	.043	-64	-5	1-1	.857	1	100	0	3b11,2b8,S8,O3(0/1/2)	0	-0.4
1967	Min A	29	28	1	4	0	0	0	3	0-0	0	6	.143	.143	.143	-14	-4	0-0	.974	0	85	50	S15,3b13	0	-0.3
1968	Min A	83	199	13	35	3	0	2	17	9-2	2	52	.176	.218	.221	32	-17	5-2	.927	4	100	127	S79/1	0	-0.8
1969	KC A	145	504	54	112	14	2	4	40	38-1	2	111	.222	.278	.282	57	-30	17-7	.954	-13	89	76	S144	0	-2.7
1970	KC A	83	238	14	55	4	1	2	10	15-0	2	50	.231	.281	.282	56	-15	1-3	.951	-8	90	89	S77	0	-1.6
1971	†Pit N	88	233	30	48	7	3	3	26	17-2	0	45	.206	.257	.300	58	-14	0-2	.950	7	112	101	S75,3b9	0	0.1
1972	Pit N	72	176	12	33	7	1	1	14	9-1	0	43	.188	.227	.256	37	-15	0-0	.929	-1	102	106	S68,3b4	0	-1.0
1973	Pit N	54	73	8	18	1	2	0	8	4-2	0	12	.247	.286	.315	68	-4	0-0	.940	-0	99	114	S49	0	-0.1
Total	9	618	1480	153	308	37	9	12	121	93-8	6	324	.208	.256	.270	49	-104	25-15	.945	-11	96	95	S517,3b38,2b8,O3(0/1/2)/1	0	-6.8
Hernandez, Jose	Jose Antonio (Figueroa); B7.14.1969 Rio Piedras, PR; BR/TR/6´1˝/(180–190); d8.9; OF(62/50/16)																								
1991	Tex A	45	98	8	18	2	1	0	4	3-0	0	31	.184	.208	.224	20	-11	0-1	.975	3	110	75	S44/3	0	-0.6
1992	Cle A	3	4	0	0	0	0	0	0	0-0	0	2	.000	.000	.000	-99	-1	0-0	.857	0	108	0	S3	0	-0.1
1994	Chi N	56	132	18	32	2	3	1	9	8-0	1	29	.242	.291	.326	60	-8	2-2	.938	3	87	0	3b28,S21,2b8/cf	0	-0.5
1995	Chi N	93	245	37	60	11	4	13	40	13-3	0	69	.245	.281	.482	97	-3	1-0	.961	3	99	115	S43,2b29,3b20	0	0.4
1996	Chi N	131	331	52	80	14	1	10	41	24-4	1	97	.242	.293	.381	74	-13	4-0	.948	-6	95	109	S87,3b43/2cf	0	-1.2
1997	Chi N	121	183	33	50	8	5	7	26	14-2	0	42	.273	.323	.486	105	0	2-5	.922	-4	72	83	3b47,S21,2b20,O6L/1D	0	-0.3
1998	†Chi N	149	488	76	124	23	7	23	75	40-3	1	140	.254	.311	.471	99	-3	4-6	.958	7	106	38	3b72,O54(31/31/2),S45,1b3,2b2	0	0.5

YEAR	TM LG	G	AB	R	H	2B	3B	HR	RBI	BB-IB	HP	SO	AVG	OBP	SLG	AOPS	ABR	SB-CS	FA	FR	RNG	THR	GAMES AT POSITION	DL	BFW
1999	Chi N	99	342	57	93	12	2	15	43	40-3	5	101	.272	.357	.450	103	1	7-2	.971	6	110	103	S92,O20(6/14/2)/1	0	1.3
	†Atl N	48	166	22	42	8	0	4	19	12-3	0	44	.253	.302	.373	71	-8	4-1	.964	-1	100	110	S45/1lf	0	-0.5
	Year	147	508	79	135	20	2	19	62	52-6	5	145	.266	.339	.425	92	-7	11-3	.969	5	107	105	S137,O21(7/14/2),1b2	0	0.8
2000	Mil N	124	446	51	109	22	1	11	59	41-3	6	125	.244	.315	.372	74	-19	3-7	.950	8	107	137	3b95,S37,O2L	21	-0.9
2001	Mil N	152	542	67	135	26	2	25	78	39-8	2	185	.249	.300	.443	91	-10	5-4	.972	-1	104	93	S150,O2(1/1/0)	0	0.0
2002	Mil N★	152	525	72	151	24	2	24	73	52-5	4	188	.288	.356	.478	118	13	3-5	.973	17	107	108	S149	0	4.0
2003	Col N	69	257	33	61	6	1	8	27	27-0	0	95	.237	.308	.362	65	-13	1-1	.983	-5	93	104	S69/1	0	-1.3
	Chi N	23	69	6	13	3	1	2	9	3-0	0	26	.188	.222	.348	45	-6	0-0	.968	1	97	209	3b17,S5,O2C/2	0	-0.4
	Pit N	58	193	19	43	9	1	3	21	16-0	1	56	.223	.282	.326	59	-12	1-0	.955	13	138	146	3b58	0	0.1
	Year	150	519	58	117	18	3	13	57	46-0	1	177	.225	.287	.347	61	-31	2-1	.957	9	130	159	3b75,S74,O2C/12	0	-1.6
2004	†LA N	95	211	32	61	12	1	13	29	26-6	1	61	.289	.370	.540	133	10	3-1	.980	3	106	91	2b50,S13,3b12,O9L,1b8	0	1.5
2005	Cle A	84	234	28	54	7	0	6	31	14-0	2	60	.231	.277	.338	66	-12	1-3	.995	2	112	94	1b45,3b21,O6(3/0/3),2b4/SD	0	-1.4
2006	Pit N	67	120	8	32	2	1	2	12	11-0	0	29	.267	.328	.350	73	-5	0-0	.991	6	176	146	1b18,O10(3/0/7),S9,3b4,2b3	0	0.0
	Phi N	18	32	4	8	2	0	1	7	1-0	0	11	.250	.273	.406	67	-2	0-0	1.000	2	129	367	3b7,S2,O2R/1	0	0.0
	Year	85	152	12	40	4	1	3	19	12-0	0	40	.263	.317	.362	72	-7	0-0	.991	8	171	142	1b19,O12(3/0/9),S11,3b11,2b3	0	0.0
Total	15	1587	4618	623	1166	193	33	168	603	384-40	24	1391	.252	.312	.418	87	-102	41-38	.970	57	104	105	S836,3b425,2b118,O116L,1b79,D2	21	0.6
HERNANDEZ, KEITH	Keith; B10.20.1953 San Francisco CA; BL/TL/6´0˝/(175–205); [StLN71 42/783]; d8.30; [DL 1991 Cle A 182]																								
1974	StL N	14	34	3	10	1	2	0	2	7-0	0	8	.294	.415	.441	139	2	0-0	.973	-2	18	112	1b9	0	-0.1
1975	StL N	64	188	20	47	8	2	3	20	17-2	0	26	.250	.309	.362	83	-5	0-1	.996	1	105	80	1b56	0	-0.8
1976	StL N	129	374	54	108	21	5	7	46	49-5	3	53	.289	.376	.428	125	14	4-2	.990	16	**164**	101	1b110	0	2.3
1977	StL N	161	560	90	163	41	4	15	91	79-11	1	88	.291	.379	.459	125	22	7-7	.992	4	112	**127**	1b158	0	1.6
1978	StL N	159	542	90	138	32	4	11	64	82-11	2	68	.255	.351	.389	108	9	13-5	.994	-1	96	106	1b158	0	0.0
1979	StL N★	161	610	**116**	210	**48**	11	11	105	80-5	1	78	**.344**	.417	.513	151	46	11-6	.995	15	**137**	119	1b160	0	5.3
1980	StL N★	159	595	**111**	191	39	8	16	99	86-4	4	73	.321	**.408**	.494	144	39	14-8	.995	6	117	**120**	1b157	0	3.7
1981	StL N	**103**	376	65	115	27	4	8	48	61-6	2	45	.306	.401	.463	139	23	12-5	.997	6	126	**130**	1b98,O3L	0	2.5
1982	†StL N	160	579	79	173	33	6	7	94	100-**19**	2	67	.299	.397	.413	125	26	19-11	.994	5	117	121	1b158,O4(2/0/2)	0	2.2
1983	StL N	55	218	34	62	15	4	3	26	24-5	0	30	.284	.352	.431	116	5	1-1	.991	3	123	135	1b54	0	0.4
	NY N	95	320	43	98	8	3	9	37	64-9	2	42	.306	.424	.434	139	21	8-4	.993	10	139	115	1b90	0	2.6
	Year	150	538	77	160	23	7	12	63	88-14	2	72	.297	.396	.433	130	26	9-5	.992	12	133	123	1b144	0	3.0
1984	NY N★	154	550	83	171	31	0	15	94	97-12	1	89	.311	.409	.449	144	39	2-3	.994	17	**133**	104	1b153	0	4.6
1985	NY N	158	593	87	183	34	4	10	91	77-15	2	59	.309	.384	.430	132	28	3-3	**.997**	13	**124**	94	1b157	0	3.2
1986	†NY N★	149	551	94	171	34	1	13	83	**94**-9	4	69	.310	.413	.446	140	36	2-1	**.996**	18	138	108	1b149	0	4.6
1987	NY N★	154	587	87	170	28	2	18	89	81-8	4	104	.290	.377	.436	120	20	0-2	.993	16	**134**	96	1b154	0	2.5
1988	†NY N	95	348	43	96	16	0	11	55	31-3	1	57	.276	.333	.417	120	9	2-1	.998	9	125	110	1b93	57	1.2
1989	NY N	75	215	18	50	8	0	4	19	27-3	2	39	.233	.324	.326	90	-2	0-3	.991	-1	88	62	1b58	56	-0.9
1990	Cle A	43	130	7	26	2	0	1	8	14-3	1	17	.200	.283	.238	47	-9	0-0	.994	-2	80	87	1b42	107	-1.4
Total	17	2088	7370	1124	2182	426	60	162	1071	1070-130	32	1012	.296	.384	.436	128	323	98-63	.994	133	123	109	1b2014,O7(5/0/2)	402	33.5
HERNANDEZ, LEO	Leonardo Jesus; B11.6.1959 Santa Lucia, Venezuela; BR/TR/5´11˝/(170–200); d9.19																								
1982	Bal A	2	2	0	0	0	0	0	0	0-0	0	2	.000	.000	.000	-99	-1	0-0	ø	0	—	—	/H	0	-0.1
1983	Bal A	64	203	21	50	6	1	6	26	12-1	0	19	.246	.287	.374	82	-6	1-0	.922	-8	89	26	3b64	0	-1.5
1985	Bal A	12	21	0	1	0	0	0	0	0-0	0	4	.048	.048	.048	-75	-5	0-0	1.000	-0	0	0	/1lfD	0	-0.6
1986	NY A	7	22	2	5	2	0	1	4	1-0	0	8	.227	.261	.455	91	0	0-0	1.000	-1	95	0	3b7/2	0	-0.1
Total	4	85	248	23	56	8	1	7	30	13-1	0	33	.226	.263	.351	68	-12	1-0	.927	-9	90	24	3b71,D8/2lf1	0	-2.3
HERNANDEZ, MICHEL	Michel; B8.12.1978 LaHabana, Cuba; BR/TR/6´0˝/210; d9.6																								
2003	NY A	5	4	0	1	0	0	0	0	1-0	0	1	.250	.400	.250	78	0	0-0	1.000	-0	81	0	C5	0	0.0
HERNANDEZ, PEDRO	Pedro Julio (b Pedro Julio Montas (Hernandez)); B4.4.1959 LaRomana, D.R.; BR/TR/6´1˝/160; d9.8																								
1979	Tor A	3	0	1	0	0	0	0	0	0-0	0	0	ø	ø	ø	ø	0	0-0	ø	0	—	—	R2	0	0.0
1982	Tor A	8	9	1	0	0	0	0	0	0-0	0	3	.000	.000	.000	-92	-2	0-0	ø	-1	0	0	3b2/lfD	0	-0.3
Total	2	11	9	2	0	0	0	0	0	0-0	0	3	.000	.000	.000	-92	-2	0-0	.000	-1	0	0	D3,3b2/lf	0	-0.3
HERNANDEZ, TOBY	Rafael Tobias (Alvarado); B11.30.1958 Calabozo, Guarico, Venez.; BR/TR/6´1˝/160; d6.22																								
1984	Tor A	3	2	1	1	0	0	0	0	0-0	0	0	.500	.500	.500	171	0	0-0	1.000	-0	0	0	C3	0	0.0
HERNANDEZ, RAMON	Ramon Jose (Marin); B5.20.1976 Caracas, Distrito Capital, Venez.; BR/TR/6´0˝/(210–227); d6.29																								
1999	Oak A	40	136	13	38	7	0	3	21	18-0	1	11	.279	.363	.397	98	0	1-0	.980	5	79	89	C40	32	0.7
2000	†Oak A	143	419	52	101	19	0	14	62	38-1	7	64	.241	.311	.387	77	-15	1-0	.984	3	108	84	C142	0	-0.4
2001	†Oak A	136	453	55	115	25	0	15	60	37-3	6	68	.254	.316	.408	89	-7	1-1	.989	17	98	111	C135,1b2	0	1.7
2002	†Oak A	136	403	51	94	20	0	7	42	43-1	5	64	.233	.313	.335	73	-15	0-0	.992	12	156	91	C135	0	0.6
2003	†Oak A★	140	483	70	132	24	1	21	78	33-2	12	79	.273	.331	.458	106	4	0-0	.991	12	104	109	C139	0	2.3
2004	SD N	111	384	45	106	23	0	18	63	35-0	5	45	.276	.341	.477	115	8	1-0	.992	2	109	94	C108	35	1.6
2005	†SD N	99	369	36	107	19	2	12	58	18-0	1	40	.290	.322	.450	105	1	1-0	.988	-9	90	95	C97	58	-0.2
2006	Bal A	144	501	66	138	29	2	23	91	43-2	11	79	.275	.343	.479	114	10	1-0	.985	-5	118	**147**	C135,1b2,D6	0	1.3
Total	8	949	3148	388	831	166	5	113	475	265-9	48	450	.264	.328	.428	97	-14	6-1	.988	36	111	104	C931,D6,1b4	125	7.6
HERNANDEZ, RUDY	Rodolfo (Acosta); B10.18.1951 Empalme, Sonora, Mexico; BR/TR/5´9˝/150; d9.6																								
1972	Chi A	8	21	0	4	0	0	0	1	0-0	0	3	.190	.190	.190	13	-2	0-0	1.000	-0	91	92	S6	0	-0.2
HERNANDEZ, CHICO	Salvador Jose (Ramos); B1.3.1916 Havana, Cuba; D1.3.1986 Havana, Cuba; BR/TR/6´0˝/195; d4.16																								
1942	Chi N	47	118	6	27	5	0	0	7	11	0	13	.229	.295	.271	69	-5	0	.975	-2	*108*	*88*	C43	0	-0.5
1943	Chi N	43	126	10	34	4	0	0	9	9	1	9	.270	.324	.302	82	-3	0	.981	-2	*132*	*72*	C41	0	-0.3
Total	2	90	244	16	61	9	0	0	16	20	1	22	.250	.309	.287	76	-8	0	.978	-4	*120*	*80*	C84	0	-0.8
HERNDON, LARRY	Larry Darnell; B11.3.1953 Sunflower MS; BR/TR/6´3˝/(188–200); [StLN71 3/54]; d9.4; C7																								
1974	StL N	12	1	3	1	0	0	0	0	0-0	0	0	1.000	1.000	1.000	461	0	0-0	1.000	0	112	0	/cf	0	0.0
1976	SF N	115	337	42	97	11	3	2	23	23-0	2	45	.288	.337	.356	94	-3	12-10	.967	-1	99	144	O110C	0	-0.7
1977	SF N	49	109	13	26	4	3	1	5	5-1	1	20	.239	.278	.358	69	-5	4-2	.957	2	121	106	O44C	68	-0.4
1978	SF N	151	471	52	122	15	9	1	32	35-2	1	71	.259	.311	.335	84	-12	13-8	.974	-2	107	40	O149C	0	-1.5
1979	SF N	132	354	35	91	14	5	7	36	29-5	1	70	.257	.313	.384	97	-3	8-6	.963	-1	97	147	O122(40/84/12)	0	-0.7
1980	SF N	139	493	54	127	17	11	8	49	19-1	1	91	.258	.284	.385	89	-11	8-8	.959	-5	95	91	O122(53/53/28)	0	-2.2
1981	SF N	96	364	48	105	15	8	5	41	20-2	1	55	.288	.325	.415	113	4	15-6	.977	4	110	97	O93(82/7/10)	0	0.5
1982	Det A	157	614	92	179	21	13	23	88	38-3	1	92	.292	.332	.480	120	13	12-9	.983	0	94	113	O155L,D3	0	0.6
1983	Det A	153	603	88	182	28	9	20	92	46-6	3	95	.302	.351	.478	129	23	9-3	.951	-5	95	57	O133L,D19	0	1.2
1984	†Det A	125	407	52	114	18	5	7	43	32-1	2	63	.280	.333	.400	103	1	6-2	.986	-4	87	97	O117L,D4	0	-0.6
1985	Det A	137	442	45	108	12	7	12	37	33-1	1	79	.244	.298	.385	86	-11	2-1	.976	3	104	88	O136L	0	-1.3
1986	Det A	106	283	33	70	13	1	8	37	27-2	1	40	.247	.310	.385	89	-4	2-1	.988	-2	101	41	O83L,D18	0	-0.9
1987	†Det A	89	225	32	73	13	2	9	47	23-0	0	35	.324	.378	.520	143	14	1-0	.989	2	102	142	O57(32/0/26),D23	0	1.3
1988	Det A	76	174	16	39	5	0	4	20	23-0	1	37	.224	.313	.322	83	-4	0-1	1.000	0	108	0	D53,O15L	0	-0.6
Total	14	1537	4877	605	1334	186	76	107	550	353-24	16	793	.274	.322	.409	103	2	92-57	.972	-8	99	92	O1337(847/448/76),D120	68	-5.3
HERNON, TOM	Thomas H.; B11.4.1866 E.Bridgewater MA; D2.4.1902 New Bedford MA; BR/TR/5´7.5˝/156; d9.13																								
1897	Chi N	4	16	2	1	0	0	0	2	0	0	—	.063	.063	.063	-64	-4	1	1.000	-0	0	0	O4L	—	-0.4
HERR, JOE	Joseph; B3.1867 MO; BR/TR/5´9.5˝/179; d4.16																								
1887	Cle AA	11	44	6	12	2	0	0	6	6	0	—	.273	.360	.318	93	0	2	.729	-3	76	50	3b11	—	-0.2
1888	†StL AA	43	172	21	46	7	1	3	43	11	3	—	.267	.323	.372	110	1	9	.872	-6	80	75	S28,O11(4/4/3),3b4	—	-0.4
1890	StL AA	12	41	5	9	2	1	0	1	5	3	—	.220	.347	.317	84	-1	2	.793	-5	45	40	2b7,O4C/3	—	-0.5
Total	3	66	257	32	67	11	2	3	50	22	6	—	.261	.333	.354	102	0	13	.872	-14	80	75	S28,3b16,O15(4/8/3),2b7	—	-1.1
HERR, TOM	Thomas Mitchell; B4.4.1956 Lancaster PA; BB/TR/6´0˝/(175–196); d8.13																								
1979	StL N	14	10	4	2	0	0	0	1	2-0	0	2	.200	.333	.200	48	-1	1-0	1.000	1	108	147	2b6	0	0.1
1980	StL N	76	222	29	55	12	5	0	15	16-5	1	21	.248	.299	.347	77	-7	9-2	.984	3	102	131	2b58,S14	0	0.1
1981	StL N	**103**	411	50	110	14	9	0	46	39-3	1	30	.268	.329	.345	88	-6	23-7	**.992**	3	**113**	**118**	2b103	0	0.6

YEAR	TM LG	G	AB	R	H	2B	3B	HR	RBI	BB-IB	HP	SO	AVG	OBP	SLG	AOPS	ABR	SB-CS	FA	FR	RNG	THR	GAMES AT POSITION	DL	BFW
1982	†StL N	135	493	83	131	19	4	0	36	57-2	2	56	.266	.341	.320	85	-8	25-12	.987	9	**110**	**130**	2b128	0	0.9
1983	StL N	89	313	43	101	14	4	2	31	43-2	1	27	.323	.403	.412	127	13	6-8	.986	-2	103	115	2b86	80	1.4
1984	StL N	145	558	67	154	23	2	4	49	49-2	2	56	.276	.335	.346	94	-4	13-7	.992	9	105	**117**	2b144	0	1.4
1985	†StL N★	159	596	97	180	38	3	8	110	80-5	2	55	.302	.379	.416	125	24	31-3	.985	-25	93	121	2b158	0	1.4
1986	StL N	152	559	48	141	30	4	2	61	73-10	5	75	.252	.342	.331	87	-7	22-8	.988	-15	95	**141**	2b152	0	-1.2
1987	†StL N	141	510	73	134	29	0	2	83	68-3	3	62	.263	.346	.331	80	-11	19-4	.989	-11	94	120	2b137	18	-1.2
1988	StL N	15	50	4	13	0	0	1	3	11-3	0	4	.260	.393	.320	105	1	3-0	.984	-5	81	103	2b15	0	-0.3
	Min A	86	304	42	80	16	0	1	21	40-1	0	47	.263	.349	.326	87	-3	10-3	.988	-3	95	116	2b73,S2,D3	55	-0.3
1989	Phi N	151	561	65	161	25	6	2	37	54-2	3	63	.287	.352	.364	105	5	10-7	.990	11	107	94	2b144	0	2.1
1990	Phi N	119	447	39	118	21	3	4	50	36-4	2	47	.264	.320	.351	85	-9	7-1	.991	0	98	130	2b114	0	-0.5
	NY N	27	100	9	25	5	0	1	10	14-0	0	11	.250	.342	.330	86	-1	0-0	.979	-4	83	118	2b26	0	-0.5
	Year	146	547	48	143	26	3	5	60	50-4	2	58	.261	.324	.347	85	-11	7-1	.989	-4	95	**128**	2b140	0	-1.0
1991	NY N	70	155	17	30	7	0	1	14	32-4	0	21	.194	.328	.258	68	-5	7-2	1.000	4	96	130	2b57/cf	0	0.1
	SF N	32	60	6	15	1	1	0	7	13-1	0	7	.250	.384	.300	97	1	2-0	1.000	-4	83	66	2b15,3b3	0	-0.3
	Year	102	215	23	45	8	1	1	21	45-5	0	28	.209	.344	.270	76	-5	9-2	1.000	0	93	117	2b72,3b3/cf	0	-0.2
Total	13	1514	5349	676	1450	254	41	28	574	627-47	22	584	.271	.347	.350	94	-18	188-64	.989	-29	100	121	2b1416,S16,3b3,D3/cf	153	3.8
HERRERA, JOSE	Jose Concepcion (Ontiveros) "Loco"; B4.8.1942 San Lorenzo, Venezuela; BR/TR/5´8˝/(165–168); d6.3																								
1967	Hou N	5	4	0	1	0	0	0	1	0-0	0	1	.250	.250	.250	45	0	0-0	ø	0	—	—	/H	0	0.0
1968	Hou N	27	100	9	24	5	0	0	7	4-0	0	12	.240	.269	.290	69	-4	0-2	.958	-1	82	85	O17(5/0/12),2b7	0	-0.7
1969	Mon N	47	126	7	36	5	0	2	12	3-0	0	14	.286	.302	.373	88	-3	1-2	.980	-2	90	127	O31(20/13/0),2b2/3	0	-0.6
1970	Mon N	1	1	0	0	0	0	0	0	0-0	0	1	.000	.000	.000	-99	0	0-0	ø	0	—	—	/H	0	0.0
Total	4	80	231	16	61	10	0	2	20	7-0	0	28	.264	.286	.333	79	-7	1-4	.973	-3	87	112	O48(25/13/12),2b9/3	0	-1.3
HERRERA, JOSE	Jose Ramon (Catalino); B8.30.1972 Santo Domingo, D.R.; BL/TL/6´0˝/165; d8.12																								
1995	Oak A	33	70	9	17	1	2	0	2	6-0	0	11	.243	.299	.314	64	-4	1-3	.956	1	98	231	O25(0/22/5),D5	0	-0.4
1996	Oak A	108	320	44	86	15	1	6	30	20-1	3	59	.269	.318	.378	76	-12	8-2	.970	-0	110	35	O100(0/18/92)/D	0	-1.3
Total	2	141	390	53	103	16	3	6	32	26-1	3	70	.264	.314	.367	74	-16	9-5	.967	0	108	70	O125(0/40/97),D6	0	-1.7
HERRERA, PANCHO	Juan Francisco (Willavicencio); B6.16.1934 Santiago de Cuba, Cuba; D4.28.2005 Miami FL; BR/TR/6´3˝/(210–220); d4.15; Negro Lg 1954																								
1958	Phi N	29	63	5	17	3	0	1	6	7-0	1	15	.270	.347	.365	92	0	1-2	.980	-0	85	98	3b16,1b11	0	-0.2
1960	Phi N	145	512	61	144	26	6	17	71	51-6	5	136	.281	.348	.455	119	14	2-3	.988	8	**117**	89	1b134,2b17	0	1.5
1961	Phi N	126	400	56	103	17	2	13	51	55-4	4	120	.257	.351	.408	102	3	5-1	.993	5	**115**	103	1b115	0	0.2
Total	3	300	975	122	264	46	8	31	128	113-10	10	271	.271	.349	.430	110	17	8-6	.990	12	117	95	1b260,2b17,3b16	0	1.5
HERRERA, MIKE	Ramon; B12.19.1897 Havana, Cuba; D2.3.1978 Havana, Cuba; BR/TR/5´6˝/147; d9.22																								
1925	Bos A	10	39	2	15	0	0	0	8	2	0	2	.385	.415	.385	104	0	1-0	.958	2	128	45	2b10	—	0.3
1926	Bos A	74	237	20	61	14	1	0	19	15	1	13	.257	.304	.325	66	-12	0-5	.962	6	109	83	2b48,3b16,S4	—	-0.5
Total	2	84	276	22	76	14	1	0	27	17	1	15	.275	.320	.333	72	-12	1-5	.961	8	112	76	2b58,3b16,S4	—	-0.2
HERRING, LEFTY	Silas Clarke; B3.4.1880 Philadelphia PA; D2.11.1965 Massapequa NY; BL/TL/5´11˝/160; d5.16																								
1899	Was N	2	1	1	1	0	0	0	0	1	0	—	1.000	1.000	1.000	454	1	0	1.000	0	198	0	P2	—	0.0
1904	Was A	15	46	3	8	1	0	0	2	7	0	—	.174	.283	.196	54	-2	0	.991	1	162	125	1b10,O5C	—	-0.1
Total	2	17	47	4	9	1	0	0	2	8	0	—	.191	.309	.213	67	-1	0	.991	1	162	125	1b10,O5C,P2	—	-0.1
HERRMANN, ED	Edward Martin; B8.27.1946 San Diego CA; BL/TR/6´1˝/(200–210); d9.1; gf–Marty																								
1967	Chi A	2	3	1	2	1	0	0	1	1-1	0	0	.667	.750	1.000	429	1	0-0	1.000	1	0	337	C2	0	0.3
1969	Chi A	102	290	31	67	8	0	8	31	30-0	8	35	.231	.319	.341	81	-7	0-2	.983	-4	105	80	C92	0	-0.8
1970	Chi A	96	297	42	84	9	0	19	52	31-3	3	41	.283	.356	.505	130	12	0-1	.988	1	60	105	C88	0	1.6
1971	Chi A	101	294	32	63	6	0	11	35	44-12	2	48	.214	.317	.347	87	-5	2-0	.995	8	94	118	C97	24	0.9
1972	Chi A	116	354	23	88	9	0	10	40	43-**19**	4	37	.249	.333	.359	105	3	0-0	.989	2	108	**143**	C112	0	1.1
1973	Chi A	119	379	42	85	17	1	10	39	31-3	7	55	.224	.291	.354	79	-11	2-4	.984	4	74	96	C114,D2	0	-0.2
1974	Chi A✳	107	367	32	95	13	1	10	39	16-6	0	49	.259	.288	.381	89	-6	1-0	.987	1	105	105	C107	16	0.0
1975	NY A	80	200	16	51	9	2	6	30	16-5	0	23	.255	.309	.410	103	0	0-0	.979	8	138	83	D35,C24	0	0.8
1976	Cal A	29	46	5	8	3	0	2	8	7-2	0	8	.174	.278	.370	96	0	0-0	.954	-8	55	105	C27	0	-0.8
	Hou N	79	265	14	54	8	0	3	25	22-2	4	40	.204	.273	.268	59	-15	0-0	.987	-2	76	106	C79	0	-1.4
1977	Hou N	56	158	7	46	7	0	1	17	15-1	1	18	.291	.352	.354	99	0	1-1	.990	4	73	81	C49	0	0.6
1978	Hou N	16	36	1	4	1	0	0	0	3-1	0	3	.111	.179	.139	-11	-5	0-0	1.000	-3	76	73	C14	0	-0.8
	Mon N	19	40	1	7	1	0	0	3	1-0	0	4	.175	.195	.200	11	-5	0-0	.977	-4	45	88	C12	0	-0.9
	Year	35	76	2	11	2	0	0	3	4-1	0	7	.145	.188	.171	1	-10	0-0	.991	-6	62	80	C26	0	-1.7
Total	11	922	2729	247	654	92	4	80	320	260-55	29	361	.240	.310	.364	90	-38	6-8	.987	9	88	106	C817,D37	40	0.4
HERRNSTEIN, JOHN	John Ellett; B3.31.1938 Hampton VA; BL/TL/6´3˝/215; d9.15; Col Michigan																								
1962	Phi N	6	5	0	1	0	0	0	1	1-0	0	3	.200	.333	.200	48	0	0-0	ø	-0	0	0	/rf	0	0.0
1963	Phi N	15	12	1	2	0	0	1	1	1-0	0	5	.167	.231	.417	83	0	0-0	1.000	0	259	0	O2L/1	0	0.0
1964	Phi N	125	303	38	71	12	4	6	25	22-0	2	67	.234	.288	.360	83	-7	1-2	.977	-6	102	0	O69(63/4/3),1b68	0	-2.0
1965	Phi N	63	85	8	17	2	0	1	5	2-1	1	18	.200	.227	.259	37	-7	0-0	.984	0	94	127	1b18,O14(11/2/1)	0	-0.9
1966	Phi N	4	10	0	1	0	0	0	1	0-0	0	7	.100	.100	.100	-44	-2	0-0	1.000	-0	83	0	O2L	0	-0.2
	Chi N	9	17	3	3	0	0	0	0	3-0	0	8	.176	.300	.176	36	-1	0-0	.975	-1	0	109	1b4/lf	0	-0.3
	Atl N	17	18	2	4	0	0	0	1	0-0	0	7	.222	.222	.222	24	-2	0-0	1.000	0	131	0	O5L	0	-0.2
	Year	30	45	5	8	0	0	0	2	3-0	0	22	.178	.229	.178	15	-5	0-0	1.000	-1	105	0	O8L,1b4	0	-0.7
Total	5	239	450	52	99	14	4	8	34	29-1	3	115	.220	.270	.322	67	-19	1-2	.983	-7	101	55	O94(84/6/5),1b91	0	-3.6
HERRSCHER, RICK	Richard Franklin; B11.3.1936 St.Louis MO; BR/TR/6´2.5˝/187; d8.1; Col SMU																								
1962	NY N	35	50	5	11	3	0	1	6	5-0	0	11	.220	.291	.340	68	-2	0-0	1.000	1	133	110	1b10,3b6,O4(3/0/1),S3	0	-0.1
HERSH, EARL	Earl Walter; B5.21.1932 Ebbvale MD; BL/TL/6´0˝/205; d9.4; Col West Chester																								
1956	Mil N	7	13	0	3	3	0	0	0	0-0	0	5	.231	.231	.462	85	0	0-0	.000	-1	0	0	O2L	0	-0.1
HERSHBERGER, MIKE	Norman Michael; B10.9.1939 Massillon OH; BR/TR/5´10˝/(175–180); d9.5; Col Cincinnati																								
1961	Chi A	15	55	9	17	3	0	0	5	2-0	0	2	.309	.333	.364	88	-1	1-1	1.000	1	94	248	O13(1/9/3)	0	-0.1
1962	Chi A	148	427	54	112	14	2	4	46	37-0	3	36	.262	.324	.333	78	-13	10-6	.984	-1	100	112	O135(1/52/90)	0	-2.0
1963	Chi A	135	476	64	133	26	2	3	45	39-1	4	39	.279	.338	.361	98	0	9-3	.976	-1	94	**173**	O119(1/73/67)	0	-0.6
1964	Chi A	141	452	55	104	15	3	2	31	48-1	4	47	.230	.308	.290	70	-18	8-6	.984	-1	96	128	O134(0/64/85)	0	-2.7
1965	KC A	150	494	43	114	15	5	5	48	37-5	5	42	.231	.289	.312	72	-19	7-3	.988	5	100	167	O144(5/9/134)	0	-2.3
1966	KC A	146	538	55	136	27	7	2	57	47-3	3	37	.253	.313	.340	92	-5	13-5	.977	9	109	**168**	O143(12/3/130)	0	-0.5
1967	KC A	142	480	55	122	25	1	1	49	38-2	7	40	.254	.314	.317	91	-4	10-3	.982	8	101	218	O130(10/0/122)	0	-0.4
1968	Oak A	99	246	23	67	9	2	5	32	21-4	1	22	.272	.327	.386	122	6	8-3	.978	1	102	117	O90(71/6/27)	0	0.5
1969	Oak A	51	129	11	26	2	0	1	10	10-0	0	15	.202	.259	.240	42	-10	1-2	.980	-4	81	0	O35(16/8/13)	60	-1.8
1970	Mil A	49	98	7	23	5	0	1	6	10-0	0	8	.235	.306	.316	72	-4	1-2	.946	-2	81	65	O35R	78	-0.8
1971	Chi A	74	177	22	46	9	0	2	15	30-3	4	23	.260	.377	.345	103	3	6-2	.960	-6	84	34	O59(0/58/2)	0	-0.5
Total	11	1150	3572	398	900	150	22	26	344	319-19	31	311	.252	.316	.328	85	-65	74-36	.980	9	98	146	O1037(117/282/708)	138	-11.2
HERSHBERGER, WILLARD	Willard McKee "Bill"; B5.28.1910 Lemoncove CA; D8.3.1940 Boston MA; BR/TR/5´10.5˝/167; d4.19																								
1938	Cin N	49	105	12	29	3	1	0	12	5	1	6	.276	.315	.324	78	-3	1	.960	-1	*126*	*81*	C39/2	—	-0.3
1939	†Cin N	63	174	23	60	9	2	0	32	9	2	4	.345	.384	.420	115	4	1	.987	-1	*109*	*99*	C60	—	0.6
1940	Cin N	48	123	6	38	4	2	0	26	6	2	6	.309	.351	.374	99	0	0	.985	-1	*117*	*47*	C37	—	0.0
Total	3	160	402	41	127	16	5	0	70	20	5	16	.316	.356	.381	101	1	2	.980	-3	*116*	*79*	C136/2	—	0.3
HERTWECK, NEAL	Neal Charles; B11.22.1931 St.Louis MO; BL/TL/6´1.5˝/175; d9.27; Col Missouri																								
1952	StL N	2	6	0	0	0	0	0	0	1	0	1	.000	.143	.000	-57	-1	0-0	1.000	-0	78	241	1b2	0	-0.2
HERTZ, STEVE	Stephen Allan; B2.26.1945 Fairfield OH; BR/TR/6´1˝/195; d4.21																								
1964	Hou N	5	4	2	0	0	0	0	0	0-0	0	3	.000	.000	.000	-99	-1	0-0	1.000	0	0	0	3b2	0	-0.1

HERZOG, BUCK Charles Lincoln; B7.9.1885 Baltimore MD; D9.4.1953 Baltimore MD; BR/TR/5´11˝/160; d4.17; M3; Col Maryland; OF(28/0/4)

YEAR	TM LG	G	AB	R	H	2B	3B	HR	RBI	BB-IB	HP	SO	AVG	OBP	SLG	AOPS	ABR	SB-CS	FA	FR	RNG	THR	GAMES AT POSITION	DL	BFW
1908	NY N	64	160	38	48	6	2	0	11	36	7	—	.300	.448	.363	152	13	16	.921	-0	107	189	2b42,S12,3b4/lf	—	1.6
1909	NY N	42	130	16	24	2	0	0	8	13	1	—	.185	.264	.200	43	-8	10	.914	-3	90	106	O29(26/0/4),2b6,3b4/S	—	-1.5
1910	Bos N	106	380	51	95	20	3	3	32	30	15	34	.250	.329	.342	92	-3	13	.915	8	**116**	111	3b105	—	0.7
1911	Bos N	79	294	53	91	19	5	5	41	33	10	21	.310	.398	.459	129	12	26	.934	3	106	85	S74,3b4	—	2.1
	†NY N	69	247	37	66	14	4	1	26	14	7	19	.267	.325	.368	91	-3	22	.926	7	110	83	3b65,2b3/S	—	0.6
	Year	148	541	90	157	33	9	6	67	47	17	40	.290	.365	.418	112	9	48	.935	10	106	85	S75,3b69,2b3	—	2.7
1912	†NY N	140	482	72	127	20	9	2	47	57	7	34	.263	.350	.355	90	-6	37	.942	20	**117**	126	3b140	—	1.8
1913	†NY N	96	290	46	83	15	3	3	31	22	6	12	.286	.349	.390	110	4	23-15	.947	2	97	205	3b84,2b2	—	0.8
1914	Cin N	138	498	54	140	14	8	1	40	42	9	27	.281	.348	.347	104	3	46	.939	33	113	118	S137,1b2,M	—	4.8
1915	Cin N	155	579	61	153	14	10	1	42	34	8	21	.264	.314	.328	93	-6	35-16	.945	30	108	**141**	S153,1b2,M	—	4.0
1916	Cin N	79	281	30	75	14	2	1	24	21	5	12	.267	.329	.342	109	4	15-12	.931	-4	94	99	S65,3b12/lfM	—	0.5
	NY N	77	280	40	73	10	4	0	25	22	5	24	.261	.326	.325	106	2	19-16	.978	12	105	117	2b44,3b27,S9	—	1.8
	Year	156	561	70	148	24	6	1	49	43	10	36	.264	.327	.333	107	6	34-28	.926	8	97	105	S74,2b44,3b39/lf	—	2.3
1917	†NY N	114	417	69	98	10	8	2	31	31	13	36	.235	.308	.312	93	-3	12	.948	-9	95	**128**	2b113	—	-1.1
1918	Bos N	118	473	57	108	12	6	0	26	29	5	28	.228	.280	.279	74	-15	10	.961	2	**104**	99	2b99,1b12,S7	—	-1.2
1919	Bos N	73	275	27	77	8	5	1	25	13	6	11	.280	.327	.356	110	3	16	.953	-15	91	80	2b70/1	—	-1.2
	Chi N	52	193	15	53	4	4	0	17	10	8	7	.275	.336	.337	102	1	12	.987	-4	99	75	2b52	—	-0.3
	Year	125	468	42	130	12	9	1	42	23	**14**	18	.278	.331	.348	106	3	28	.967	-18	94	78	2b122/1	—	-1.5
1920	Chi N	91	305	39	59	9	2	0	19	20	8	21	.193	.261	.236	43	-22	8-9	.938	-4	93	87	2b59,3b28/1	—	-2.8
Total	13	1493	5284	705	1370	191	75	20	445	427	120	307	.259	.329	.335	96	-24	320-68	.954	80	98	108	2b490,3b473,S459,O31L,1b18	—	10.6

HERZOG, WHITEY Dorrel Norman Elvert; B11.9.1931 New Athens IL; BL/TL/5´11˝/(180–185); d4.17; M18/C4

YEAR	TM LG	G	AB	R	H	2B	3B	HR	RBI	BB-IB	HP	SO	AVG	OBP	SLG	AOPS	ABR	SB-CS	FA	FR	RNG	THR	GAMES AT POSITION	DL	BFW
1956	Was A	117	421	49	103	13	7	4	35	35-0	0	74	.245	.302	.337	69	-21	8-5	.980	-4	93	125	O103(15/84/7),1b5	0	-3.0
1957	Was A	36	78	7	13	3	0	0	4	13-0	2	12	.167	.301	.205	41	-6	1-2	.981	-1	108	0	O28(2/26/0)	0	-0.8
1958	Was A	8	5	0	0	0	0	0	0	1-0	0	5	.000	.167	.000	-51	-1	0-0	1.000	0	128	0	O7(0/5/2)	0	-0.1
	KC A	88	96	11	23	1	2	0	9	16-1	0	21	.240	.345	.292	77	-3	0-3	.968	-1	120	0	O37(29/7/1),1b22	0	-0.6
	Year	96	101	11	23	1	2	0	9	17-1	0	26	.228	.336	.277	71	-4	0-3	.972	-1	121	0	O44(29/12/3),1b22	0	-0.7
1959	KC A	38	123	25	36	7	1	1	9	34-0	0	23	.293	.446	.390	129	8	1-0	.963	2	120	107	O34(1/13/20)/1	81	0.9
1960	KC A	83	252	43	67	10	2	8	38	40-2	0	32	.266	.364	.417	111	5	0-1	.985	0	99	90	O69(29/0/42),1b2	39	0.1
1961	Bal A	113	323	39	94	11	6	5	35	50-1	1	41	.291	.387	.409	117	9	1-4	1.000	-7	86	31	O98(27/0/73)	0	-0.4
1962	Bal A	99	263	34	70	13	1	7	35	41-1	3	36	.266	.369	.403	116	7	2-3	.978	2	110	109	O70(13/1/59)	0	0.5
1963	Det A	52	53	5	8	2	1	0	7	11-3	1	17	.151	.303	.226	51	-3	0-0	.976	-1	31	55	1b7,O4(1/1/2)	0	-0.5
Total	8	634	1614	213	414	60	20	25	172	241-8	7	261	.257	.354	.365	96	-5	13-18	.982	-9	99	83	O450(117/137/206),1b37	120	-3.9

HESS, OTTO Otto C.; B10.10.1878 Bern, Switzerland; D2.25.1926 Tucson AZ; BL/TL/6´1˝/170; d8.3; ▲

YEAR	TM LG	G	AB	R	H	2B	3B	HR	RBI	BB-IB	HP	SO	AVG	OBP	SLG	AOPS	ABR	SB-CS	FA	FR	RNG	THR	GAMES AT POSITION	DL	BFW
1902	Cle A	7	14	2	1	0	0	0	1	2	0	—	.071	.188	.071	-27	-1	0	.870	1	124	0	P7	—	0.0
1904	Cle A	34	100	4	12	2	1	0	5	3	0	—	.120	.146	.160	-3	-12	0	.951	1	92	0	P21,O12(7/5/0)	—	-0.3
1905	Cle A	54	173	15	44	8	1	2	13	7	2	—	.254	.291	.347	101	0	2	.950	3	165	297	O28(27/0/1),P26	—	0.1
1906	Cle A	53	154	13	31	5	2	0	11	2	0	—	.201	.212	.260	48	-10	1	.949	-2	85	165	P43,O5C	—	-0.1
1907	Cle A	19	30	4	4	0	0	0	0	4	2	—	.133	.278	.133	31	-2	1	.941	-1	90	0	P17,O2L	—	0.0
1908	Cle A	9	14	0	0	0	0	0	0	1	0	—	.000	.067	.000	-78	-3	0	1.000	-0	140	0	P4,O4R	—	-0.3
1912	Bos N	33	94	10	23	4	4	0	10	0	0	26	.245	.245	.372	66	3	0	.951	-4	74	145	P33	—	0.0
1913	Bos N	35	83	9	26	0	1	2	11	7	0	15	.313	.367	.410	119	8	0	.945	1	103	141	P29	—	0.0
1914	Bos N	31	47	5	11	1	0	1	6	1	0	11	.234	.250	.319	69	-2	0	.947	1	140	293	P14,1b5	—	0.0
1915	Bos N	5	5	1	2	1	0	0	1	0	0	2	.400	.400	.600	210	1	0	.800	-0	106	0	P4/1	—	0.0
Total	10	280	714	63	154	21	9	5	58	27	4	54	.216	.248	.291	63	-18	4	.941	1	94	105	P198,O51(36/10/5),1b6	—	-0.6

HESS, TOM Thomas (b Thomas Heslin); B8.15.1875 Brooklyn NY; D12.15.1945 Albany NY; TR; d6.6

YEAR	TM LG	G	AB	R	H	2B	3B	HR	RBI	BB-IB	HP	SO	AVG	OBP	SLG	AOPS	ABR	SB-CS	FA	FR	RNG	THR	GAMES AT POSITION	DL	BFW
1892	Bal N	1	2	0	0	0	0	0	0	0	0	0	.000	.000	.000	-97	0	0	ø	0	*0*	*0*	/C	—	0.0

HESSMAN, MIKE Michael Steven; B3.5.1978 Fountain Valley CA; BR/TR/6´5˝/(210–215); [AtlN96 15/452]; d8.22

YEAR	TM LG	G	AB	R	H	2B	3B	HR	RBI	BB-IB	HP	SO	AVG	OBP	SLG	AOPS	ABR	SB-CS	FA	FR	RNG	THR	GAMES AT POSITION	DL	BFW
2003	Atl N	19	21	2	6	2	0	2	3	5-1	0	6	.286	.423	.667	179	3	0-0	.800	-1	123	0	O8(7/0/1),1b4,3b3	0	0.2
2004	Atl N	29	69	8	9	3	0	2	5	1-0	1	24	.130	.155	.261	5	-10	0-0	.962	1	57	72	1b16,3b7,O3L	0	-1.0
Total	2	48	90	10	15	5	0	4	8	6-1	1	30	.167	.227	.356	47	-7	0-0	.970	0	56	82	1b20,O11(10/0/1),3b10	0	-0.8

HETLING, GUS August Julius; B11.21.1885 St.Louis MO; D10.13.1962 Wichita KS; BR/TR/5´10˝/165; d10.6

YEAR	TM LG	G	AB	R	H	2B	3B	HR	RBI	BB-IB	HP	SO	AVG	OBP	SLG	AOPS	ABR	SB-CS	FA	FR	RNG	THR	GAMES AT POSITION	DL	BFW
1906	Det A	2	7	0	1	0	0	0	0	0	0	—	.143	.143	.143	-10	-1	0	1.000	-0	59	0	3b2	—	-0.1

HEUBEL, GEORGE George A.; B1849 , Germany; D1.22.1896 Philadelphia PA; 5´11.5˝/178; d5.20; U2

YEAR	TM LG	G	AB	R	H	2B	3B	HR	RBI	BB-IB	HP	SO	AVG	OBP	SLG	AOPS	ABR	SB-CS	FA	FR	RNG	THR	GAMES AT POSITION	DL	BFW
1871	Ath NA	17	75	18	23	4	2	0	13	2	—	0	.307	.325	.413	112	1	1-0	.758	0	160	0	O16R/1	—	0.2
1872	Oly NA	5	23	2	3	0	0	0	1	0	—	0	.130	.130	.130	-21	-3	0-0	.800	-1	0	0	O5C	—	-0.3
1876	NY N	1	4	0	0	0	0	0	0	0	—	0	.000	.000	.000	-99	-1	—	.750	-0	0	0	/1	—	-0.1
Total	2NA	22	98	20	26	4	2	0	14	2	—	0	.265	.280	.347	83	-2	1-0	.767	-0	124	0	O21(0/5/16)/1	—	-0.1

HEVING, JOHNNIE John Aloysius; B4.29.1896 Covington KY; D12.24.1968 Salisbury NC; BR/TR/6´0˝/175; d9.24; b-Joe

YEAR	TM LG	G	AB	R	H	2B	3B	HR	RBI	BB-IB	HP	SO	AVG	OBP	SLG	AOPS	ABR	SB-CS	FA	FR	RNG	THR	GAMES AT POSITION	DL	BFW
1920	StL A	1	1	0	0	0	0	0	0	0	0	0	.000	.000	.000	-97	0	0-0	ø	0	—	—	/H	—	0.0
1924	Bos A	45	109	15	31	5	1	0	11	10	0	7	.284	.345	.349	79	-3	0-0	.969	2	*101*	*148*	C29	—	0.0
1925	Bos A	45	119	14	20	7	0	0	6	12	0	7	.168	.244	.227	20	-15	0-1	.958	-0	*74*	*102*	C34	—	-1.2
1928	Bos A	82	158	11	41	7	2	0	11	11	0	10	.259	.308	.329	69	-7	1-1	.967	-5	*78*	*107*	C62	—	-1.0
1929	Bos A	76	188	26	60	4	3	0	23	8	2	7	.319	.354	.372	89	-4	1-2	.988	4	*110*	*123*	C55	—	0.4
1930	Bos A	75	220	15	61	5	3	0	17	11	0	14	.277	.312	.327	65	-12	2-0	.987	1	*155*	*88*	C71	—	-0.7
1931	†Phi A	42	113	8	27	3	2	1	12	6	0	8	.239	.277	.327	55	-8	0-0	.993	3	*126*	*65*	C40	—	-0.3
1932	Phi A	33	77	14	21	6	1	0	10	7	0	6	.273	.333	.377	81	-2	0-0	1.000	-0	*110*	*34*	C28	—	-0.1
Total	8	399	985	103	261	37	12	1	90	65	2	59	.265	.312	.330	66	-51	4-4	.981	3	*112*	*100*	C319	—	-2.9

HEYDON, MIKE Michael Edward "Ed"; B7.15.1874 MO; D10.13.1913 Indianapolis IN; BL/TR/6´0˝/?; d10.12

YEAR	TM LG	G	AB	R	H	2B	3B	HR	RBI	BB-IB	HP	SO	AVG	OBP	SLG	AOPS	ABR	SB-CS	FA	FR	RNG	THR	GAMES AT POSITION	DL	BFW
1898	Bal N	3	9	2	1	0	0	0	1	2	1	—	.111	.333	.111	28	-1	0	.917	-0	*95*	*131*	C3	—	-0.1
1899	Was N	3	3	0	0	0	0	0	0	2	0	—	.000	.400	.000	14	0	0	.833	-0	*85*	*147*	C2	—	0.0
1901	StL N	16	43	2	9	1	1	1	6	5	0	—	.209	.292	.349	90	-1	2	.941	-2	*97*	*69*	C13/cf	—	-0.2
1904	Chi A	4	10	0	1	1	0	0	1	1	1	—	.100	.250	.200	45	0	0	1.000	1	*153*	*123*	C4	—	0.1
1905	Was A	77	245	20	47	7	4	1	26	21	2	—	.192	.261	.265	70	-9	5	.955	9	*101*	***113***	C77	—	0.9
1906	Was A	49	145	14	23	7	1	0	10	14	1	—	.159	.237	.221	46	-9	2	.937	-6	*80*	*124*	C49	—	-1.1
1907	Was A	62	164	14	30	3	0	0	9	25	3	—	.183	.302	.201	66	-4	3	.961	-9	*85*	*92*	C57	—	-0.9
Total	7	214	619	52	111	19	6	2	53	70	8	—	.179	.271	.239	64	-24	12	.952	-7	*92*	*108*	C205/cf	—	-1.3

HIATT, JACK Jack E; B7.27.1942 Bakersfield CA; BR/TR/6´2˝/190; d9.7; C1

YEAR	TM LG	G	AB	R	H	2B	3B	HR	RBI	BB-IB	HP	SO	AVG	OBP	SLG	AOPS	ABR	SB-CS	FA	FR	RNG	THR	GAMES AT POSITION	DL	BFW
1964	LA A	9	16	2	6	0	0	0	2	2-0	0	3	.375	.444	.375	145	1	0-0	.889	-0	45	0	C3,1b2	0	0.1
1965	SF N	40	67	5	19	4	0	1	7	12-2	0	14	.284	.392	.388	118	2	0-0	.987	-2	79	95	C21,1b7	0	0.0
1966	SF N	18	23	2	7	2	0	0	1	4-0	0	5	.304	.407	.391	120	1	0-0	.982	1	180	109	1b7	0	0.2
1967	SF N	73	153	24	42	6	0	6	26	27-1	1	37	.275	.387	.431	136	8	0-0	.990	-2	90	109	1b36,C3,O2L	0	0.5
1968	SF N	90	224	14	52	10	2	4	34	41-4	1	61	.232	.351	.348	111	5	0-0	.994	2	109	97	C58,1b10	0	1.1
1969	SF N	69	194	18	38	4	0	7	34	48-5	0	58	.196	.352	.325	93	0	0-0	.992	2	146	118	C60,1b3	39	0.4
1970	Mon N	17	43	4	14	2	0	0	7	14-0	0	14	.326	.491	.372	135	4	0-0	.961	-3	45	0	C12,1b2	0	0.1
	Chi N	66	178	19	43	12	1	2	22	31-2	0	48	.242	.352	.354	80	-4	0-0	.990	6	87	100	C63,1b2	0	0.5
	Year	83	221	23	57	14	1	2	29	45-2	0	62	.258	.382	.357	91	-1	0-0	.986	3	80	84	C75,1b4	0	0.6
1971	Hou N	69	174	16	48	8	1	1	16	35-2	2	39	.276	.401	.351	119	7	0-1	.991	-2	87	90	C65/1	0	0.7
1972	Hou N	10	25	2	5	3	0	0	0	5-2	0	5	.200	.333	.320	89	0	0-0	1.000	-4	76	87	C10	53	-0.4
	Cal A	22	45	4	13	0	1	1	5	5-0	0	11	.289	.360	.400	133	2	0-0	1.000	-6	129	92	C17	0	-0.4
Total	9	483	1142	110	287	51	5	22	154	224-18	4	295	.251	.374	.363	109	26	0-1	.990	-9	102	95	C312,1b70,O2L	92	2.8

HIATT, PHIL Philip Farrell; B5.1.1969 Pensacola FL; BR/TR/6´3˝/200; [KCA90 8/234]; d4.7; Col Louisiana Tech

YEAR	TM LG	G	AB	R	H	2B	3B	HR	RBI	BB-IB	HP	SO	AVG	OBP	SLG	AOPS	ABR	SB-CS	FA	FR	RNG	THR	GAMES AT POSITION	DL	BFW
1993	KC A	81	238	30	52	12	1	7	36	16-0	7	82	.218	.285	.366	69	-11	6-3	.909	-3	98	55	3b70,D9	0	-1.3
1995	KC A	52	113	11	23	6	0	4	12	9-0	0	37	.204	.262	.363	59	-7	1-0	.957	2	105	195	O47(1/2/45),D2	15	-0.6
1996	Det A	7	21	3	4	0	1	0	1	2-0	0	11	.190	.261	.286	38	-2	0-0	1.000	1	135	161	3b3,O2(1/0/1)/D	0	-0.1

YEAR	TM LG	G	AB	R	H	2B	3B	HR	RBI	BB-IB	HP	SO	AVG	OBP	SLG	AOPS	ABR	SB-CS	FA	FR	RNG	THR	GAMES AT POSITION	DL	BFW
2001	LA N	30	50	6	12	3	0	2	6	3-1	0	19	.240	.283	.420	83	-1	0-0	1.000	-3	49	64	3b17,1b6	0	-0.5
Total	4	170	422	50	91	21	2	13	55	30-1	7	149	.216	.278	.367	67	-21	7-3	.920	-3	93	60	3b90,O49(2/2/46),D12,1b6	15	-2.5
HIBBS, JIM	James Kerr; B9.10.1944 Klamath Falls OR; BR/TR/6´0˝/190; [LAN66*S3/50]; d4.12; Col Stanford																								
1967	Cal A	3	3	0	0	0	0	0	0	0-0	0	2	.000	.000	.000	-99	-1	0-0	ø	0	—	—	/H	0	-0.1
HICKEY, EDDIE	Edward A.; B8.18.1872 Cleveland OH; D3.25.1941 Tacoma WA; d9.3																								
1901	Chi N	10	37	4	6	0	0	0	3	2	1	—	.162	.225	.162	14	-4	1	.743	-2	93	183	3b10	—	-0.6
HICKEY, MIKE	Michael Francis; B12.25.1871 Chicopee MA; D6.11.1918 Springfield MA; BR/TR/5´10.5˝/150; d9.14; Col Holy Cross																								
1899	Bos N	1	3	0	1	0	0	0	0	0	0	—	.333	.333	.333	76	0	0	.889	0	139	0	/2	—	0.0
HICKMAN, CHARLIE	Charles Taylor "Cheerful Charlie","Piano Legs"; B3.4.1876 Taylortown (Dunkard Twp.) PA; D4.19.1934 Morgantown WV; BR/TR/5´9˝/180; d9.8; Col West Virginia; OF(46/3/242); ▲																								
1897	†Bos N	2	3	1	2	0	0	1	2	0	0	—	.667	.667	1.667	476	2	0	1.000	0	55	1809	P2	—	0.0
1898	Bos N	19	58	4	15	2	0	0	7	1	1	—	.259	.283	.293	62	-3	0	1.000	-1	101	0	O7(6/1/0),1b6,P6	—	-0.3
1899	Bos N	19	63	15	25	2	7	0	15	2	2	—	.397	.433	.651	178	6	1	.941	-3	72	235	P11,O7(6/1/0)/1	—	0.0
1900	NY N	127	473	65	148	19	17	9	91	17	17	—	.313	.359	.482	137	21	10	.842	-4	99	105	3b120,O7R	—	1.7
1901	NY N	112	406	44	113	20	6	4	62	15	7	—	.278	.315	.387	107	3	5	.904	-3	132	59	O50(6/1/44),S23,3b15,P9,2b7,1b2	—	-0.1
1902	Bos A	28	108	13	32	5	2	3	16	3	4	—	.296	.339	.463	118	2	1	.939	-1	51	0	O27L	—	-0.1
	Cle A	102	426	61	161	31	11	8	94	12	3	—	.378	.399	.559	170	38	8	.966	-7	87	110	1b98,2b3/P	—	2.7
	Year	130	534	74	**193**	36	13	11	110	15	7	—	.361	.387	.539	159	39	9	.966	-8	87	110	1b98,O27L,2b3/P	—	2.6
1903	Cle A	131	522	64	154	31	11	12	97	17	6	—	.295	.325	.466	137	22	14	.972	-7	84	112	1b125,2b7	—	1.3
1904	Cle A	86	337	34	97	22	10	4	45	13	2	—	.288	.318	.448	142	15	9	.943	1	112	56	2b45,1b40/lf	—	1.6
	Det A	42	144	18	35	6	6	2	22	11	0	—	.243	.297	.410	126	4	3	.970	-2	91	99	1b39	—	0.1
	Year	128	481	52	132	28	16	6	67	24	2	—	.274	.312	.437	137	18	12	.969	-2	89	100	1b79,2b45/lf	—	1.7
1905	Det A	59	213	21	47	12	3	2	20	12	5	—	.221	.278	.333	93	-2	3	.940	3	136	238	O47R,1b12	—	-0.2
	Was A	88	360	48	112	25	9	2	46	9	2	—	.311	.332	.447	152	19	3	.922	6	119	83	2b85,1b3	—	2.8
	Year	147	573	69	159	37	12	4	66	21	7	—	.277	.311	.405	129	16	6	.922	9	119	83	2b85,O47R,1b15	—	2.6
1906	Was A	120	451	53	128	25	5	9	57	14	4	—	.284	.311	.421	135	16	9	.955	-1	100	70	O95R,1b18,3b5/2	—	1.2
1907	Was A	60	198	20	55	9	3	1	23	14	4	—	.278	.338	.369	136	8	4	.965	-2	87	84	1b30,O18R,2b3/P	—	0.5
	Chi A	21	23	1	6	2	0	0	1	4	0	—	.261	.370	.348	134	1	0	.667	-1	0	0	O3R	—	0.1
	Year	81	221	21	61	11	3	1	24	18	4	—	.276	.342	.367	135	9	4	.965	-2	87	84	1b30,O21R,2b3/P	—	0.6
1908	Cle A	65	197	16	46	6	1	2	16	9	1	—	.234	.271	.305	86	-3	2	.907	-1	150	121	O28R,1b20/2	—	-0.6
Total	12	1081	3982	478	1176	217	91	59	614	153	58	—	.295	.331	.440	133	149	72	.968	-22	90	106	1b394,O290R,2b152,3b140,P30,S23	—	10.7
HICKMAN, JIM	David James; B5.19.1892 Johnson City TN; D12.30.1958 Brooklyn NY; BR/TR/5´7.5˝/170; d9.17; Mil 1918																								
1915	Bal F	20	81	7	17	4	1	1	7	4	1	14	.210	.256	.321	60	-6	5	.963	4	101	242	O20C	—	-0.4
1916	Bro N	9	5	3	1	0	0	0	0	2	0	0	.200	.429	.200	94	0	1	1.000	0	141	0	O3(2/1/0)	—	0.0
1917	Bro N	114	370	46	81	15	4	6	36	17	0	66	.219	.253	.330	76	-12	14	.942	6	99	169	O101(26/71/3)	—	-1.3
1918	Bro N	53	167	14	39	4	7	1	16	8	3	31	.234	.281	.359	95	-2	5	.914	-1	92	132	O46(0/10/42)	—	-0.6
1919	Bro N	57	104	14	20	3	1	0	11	6	0	17	.192	.236	.240	43	-7	2	.962	1	107	95	O29(4/6/22)	—	-0.9
Total	5	253	727	84	158	26	13	8	70	37	4	128	.217	.259	.322	74	-27	27	.941	9	99	158	O199(32/108/67)	—	-3.2
HICKMAN, JIM	James Lucius; B5.10.1937 Henning TN; BR/TR/6´4˝/(195–205); d4.14																								
1962	NY N	140	392	54	96	18	2	13	46	47-2	3	96	.245	.328	.401	94	-3	4-4	.971	3	110	89	O124(7/84/33)	0	-0.6
1963	NY N	146	494	53	113	21	6	17	51	44-1	1	120	.229	.291	.399	96	-4	0-5	.963	-3	100	119	O82(19/42/22),3b59	0	-1.2
1964	NY N	139	409	48	105	14	1	11	57	36-4	2	90	.257	.319	.377	98	-1	0-1	.976	5	113	118	O113(39/89/19)/3	0	-0.1
1965	NY N	141	369	32	87	18	0	15	40	27-3	2	76	.236	.291	.407	98	-2	3-1	.965	-1	104	76	O91(35/44/16),1b30,3b14	0	-0.8
1966	NY N	58	160	15	38	7	0	4	16	13-0	1	34	.237	.299	.356	83	-4	2-1	.986	5	105	221	O45(16/8/23),1b17	86	-0.1
1967	LA N	65	98	7	16	6	1	0	10	14-1	0	28	.163	.268	.245	52	-6	1-1	1.000	3	125	145	O37(13/13/12),1b2,3b2/P	0	-0.5
1968	Chi N	75	188	22	42	6	3	5	23	18-2	1	38	.223	.290	.367	92	-2	1-1	.975	2	110	97	O66(3/20/49)	0	-0.4
1969	Chi N	134	338	38	80	11	2	21	54	47-3	0	74	.237	.326	.467	107	3	2-1	.981	-5	89	85	O125(5/9/116)	0	-0.7
1970	Chi N★	149	514	102	162	33	4	32	115	93-8	1	99	.315	.419	.582	148	38	0-1	.974	6	97	165	O79(2/53/28),1b74	0	3.5
1971	Chi N	117	383	50	98	13	2	19	60	50-7	3	61	.256	.342	.449	108	5	0-1	.982	-2	90	70	O69(1/3/66),1b44	15	-0.4
1972	Chi N	115	368	65	100	15	2	17	64	52-3	2	64	.272	.364	.462	120	11	3-1	.992	7	153	110	1b77,O27(1/0/26)	0	1.2
1973	Chi N	92	201	27	49	1	2	3	20	42-2	0	42	.244	.368	.313	86	-2	1-1	.988	-1	108	106	1b51,O13(3/0/11)	0	-0.7
1974	StL N	50	60	5	16	0	0	2	4	8-0	0	10	.267	.353	.367	101	0	0-0	.986	1	153	220	1b14/3	0	0.1
Total	13	1421	3974	518	1002	163	25	159	560	491-36	16	832	.252	.335	.426	106	33	17-19	.976	21	102	104	O871(144/365/421),1b309,3b77/P	101	-0.7
HICKS, BUDDY	Clarence Walter; B2.15.1927 Belvedere CA; BB/TR/5´10˝/170; d4.17																								
1956	Det A	26	47	5	10	2	0	0	5	3-0	0	2	.213	.260	.255	36	-4	0-1	1.000	-1	117	86	S16,2b6/3	0	-0.4
HICKS, JIM	James Edward; B5.18.1940 East Chicago IN; BR/TR/6´3˝/(185–205); d10.2; Col Illinois																								
1964	Chi A	2	0	0	0	0	0	0	0	0-0	0	0	ø	ø	ø	ø	0	0-0	ø	0	—	—	/R	0	0.0
1965	Chi A	13	19	2	5	1	0	1	2	0-0	0	9	.263	.263	.474	112	0	0-0	.750	-1	51	0	O5(3/0/2)	0	-0.1
1966	Chi A	18	26	3	5	0	1	0	1	1-0	0	5	.192	.222	.269	43	-2	0-0	1.000	-0	133	0	O10(2/0/8),1b2	0	-0.3
1969	StL N	19	44	5	8	0	2	1	3	4-0	0	14	.182	.250	.341	64	-3	0-0	1.000	1	111	216	O15R	0	-0.2
	Cal A	37	48	6	4	0	0	3	8	13-1	0	18	.083	.274	.271	57	-3	0-1	1.000	-2	92	0	O10(4/3/3),1b8	0	-0.6
1970	Cal A	4	4	0	1	0	0	0	0	0-0	0	2	.250	.250	.250	39	0	0-0	ø	0	—	—	/H	0	0.0
Total	5	93	141	16	23	1	3	5	14	18-1	0	48	.163	.256	.319	64	-8	0-1	.981	-1	105	100	O40(9/3/28),1b10	0	-1.2
HICKS, NAT	Nathan Woodhull; B4.19.1845 Hempstead NY; D4.21.1907 Hoboken NJ; BR/TR/6´1˝/186; d4.22; M2																								
1872	Mut NA	**56**	267	54	82	12	2	0	32	6	—	3	.307	.322	.367	119	8	3-0	.875	5	—	—	C54,O3R	—	0.9
1873	Mut NA	28	120	12	29	1	2	1	14	8	—	0	.242	.289	.308	77	-3	2-1	.778	2	—	—	C28	—	-0.1
1874	Phi NA	**58**	266	51	73	8	1	0	30	5	—	4	.274	.288	.312	89	-4	3-2	.823	7	—	—	C57,O4C/2M	—	0.3
1875	Mut NA	62	269	32	67	10	0	0	22	2	—	10	.249	.255	.286	83	-5	1-0	.819	5	—	—	C60,O5(0/1/4),M	—	0.1
1876	NY N	45	188	20	44	4	1	0	15	3	—	4	.234	.246	.266	81	-2	—	.741	-6	—	—	C45	—	-0.6
1877	Cin N	8	32	3	6	0	0	0	3	1	—	2	.188	.212	.188	30	-2	—	.868	0	—	—	C8	—	-0.2
Total	4NA	204	922	149	251	31	5	1	98	21	—	17	.272	.288	.320	94	-4	9-3	.828	19	—	—	C199,O12(0/5/7)/2	—	1.2
Total	2	53	220	23	50	4	1	0	18	4	—	6	.227	.241	.255	73	-4	—	.757	-6	—	—	C53	—	-0.8
HICKS, JOE	William Joseph; B4.7.1933 Ivy VA; BL/TR/6´0˝/180; d9.18; Col Virginia																								
1959	Chi A	6	7	0	3	0	0	0	0	1-0	0	1	.429	.500	.429	160	1	0-1	1.000	0	68	783	O4(1/2/1)	0	0.1
1960	Chi A	36	47	3	9	1	0	0	2	6-0	1	3	.191	.291	.213	40	-4	0-1	1.000	-2	65	0	O14(3/11/0)	0	-0.7
1961	Was A	12	29	2	5	0	0	1	1	0-0	0	4	.172	.172	.276	18	-4	0-1	1.000	1	105	194	O7(3/0/4)	0	-0.4
1962	Was A	102	174	20	39	4	2	6	14	15-0	0	34	.224	.286	.374	76	-7	3-1	.962	-0	106	58	O42(5/22/16)	0	-0.8
1963	NY N	56	159	16	36	6	1	5	22	7-0	3	31	.226	.272	.371	82	-4	0-2	.966	-1	103	40	O41(5/33/5)	0	-0.8
Total	5	212	416	41	92	11	3	12	39	29-0	4	73	.221	.278	.349	72	-18	3-6	.970	-3	100	71	O108(17/68/26)	0	-2.6
HIDALGO, RICHARD	Richard Jose; B6.28.1975 Caracas, Distrito Capital, Venez.; BR/TR/6´3˝/(190–220); d9.1																								
1997	†Hou N	19	62	8	19	5	0	2	6	4-0	1	18	.306	.358	.484	122	2	1-0	1.000	-3	77	0	O19(1/17/1)	0	0.0
1998	†Hou N	74	211	31	64	15	0	7	35	17-0	2	37	.303	.355	.474	120	6	3-3	.978	0	103	85	O72(9/57/14)	52	0.6
1999	Hou N	108	383	49	87	25	2	15	56	56-2	4	73	.227	.328	.420	90	-6	8-5	.991	9	101	238	O108(97/30/3)	56	0.0
2000	Hou N	153	558	118	175	42	3	44	122	56-3	21	110	.314	.391	.636	144	38	13-6	.984	14	**122**	77	O150(36/125/37)	0	4.8
2001	†Hou N	146	512	70	141	29	3	19	80	54-3	16	107	.275	.356	.455	102	3	3-5	.991	6	104	139	O144(23/128/37)	0	0.6
2002	Hou N	114	388	54	91	17	4	15	48	43-1	6	85	.235	.319	.415	85	-9	6-2	.995	3	108	90	O110(0/1/110)	17	-1.0
2003	Hou N	141	514	91	159	43	4	28	88	58-8	8	104	.309	.385	.572	139	30	9-7	.987	14	105	**249**	O137R/D	15	3.6
2004	Hou N	58	199	21	51	15	2	4	30	17-4	0	53	.256	.309	.412	83	-5	1-2	.982	3	115	131	O56R	0	-0.5
	NY N	86	324	46	74	11	1	21	52	27-3	5	76	.228	.296	.463	95	-5	3-2	.977	2	92	180	O86(5/0/83)	0	-0.7
	Year	144	523	67	125	26	3	25	82	44-7	5	129	.239	.301	.444	90	-10	4-4	.979	5	101	162	O142(5/0/139)	0	-1.2
2005	Tex A	88	308	43	68	12	0	16	43	26-1	4	74	.221	.289	.416	82	-9	1-2	.989	1	106	61	O85(0/3/83)/D	59	-1.2
Total	9	987	3459	531	929	214	19	171	560	358-25	67	737	.269	.345	.490	109	45	48-34	.987	49	106	142	O967(171/361/561),D2	199	6.2
HIETPAS, JOE	Joseph Carl; B5.1.1979 Appleton WI; BR/TR/6´3˝/220; [NYN01 16/492]; d10.3; Col Northwestern																								
2004	NY N	1	0	0	0	0	0	0	0	0-0	0	0	ø	ø	ø	ø	0	0-0	1.000	0	0	0	/C	0	0.0

YEAR	TM LG	G	AB	R	H	2B	3B	HR	RBI	BB-IB	HP	SO	AVG	OBP	SLG	AOPS	ABR	SB-CS	FA	FR	RNG	THR	GAMES AT POSITION	DL	BFW
Higbee, Mahlon	Mahlon Jesse; B8.16.1901 Louisville KY; D4.7.1968 Depauw IN; BR/TR/5´11˝/165; d9.27																								
1922	NY N	3	10	2	4	0	0	1	5	0	0	2	.400	.400	.700	177	1	0-0	1.000	-0	57	0	O3(2/0/1)	—	0.0
Higby	; d9.18																								
1872	Atl NA	1	4	0	0	0	0	0	0	0	—	0	.000	.000	.000	-85	-1	0-0	.667	-0	0	0	/rf	—	-0.1
Higdon, Bill	William Travis; B4.27.1924 Camp Hill AL; D8.30.1986 Pascagoula MS; BL/TR/6´1˝/193; d9.10; Col Auburn																								
1949	Chi A	11	23	3	7	3	0	0	1	6	0	3	.304	.448	.435	139	2	1-0	1.000	-0	71	314	O6C	0	0.2
Higgins, Kevin	Kevin Wayne; B1.22.1967 San Gabriel CA; BL/TR/5´11˝/185; [SDN89 12/312]; d5.29; Col Arizona St.																								
1993	SD N	71	181	17	40	4	1	0	13	16-0	3	17	.221	.294	.254	48	-13	0-1	.983	2	82	98	C59,3b4,1b3,O3(1/0/2)/2	0	-0.9
Higgins, Mark	Mark Douglas; B7.9.1963 Miami FL; BR/TR/6´2˝/210; [CleA84 S1/8]; d9.7; Col New Orleans																								
1989	Cle A	6	10	1	1	0	0	0	0	1-0	0	6	.100	.182	.100	-18	-2	0-0	1.000	0	146	39	1b5	0	-0.1
Higgins, Pinky	Michael Franklin "Mike"; B5.27.1909 Red Oak TX; D3.21.1969 Dallas TX; BR/TR/6´1˝/185; d6.25; Mil 1945; M8; Col Texas																								
1930	Phi A	14	24	1	6	2	0	0	0	4	0	5	.250	.357	.333	73	-1	0-0	1.000	-1	86	0	3b5,2b2/S	—	-0.2
1933	Phi A	**152**	567	85	178	34	12	13	99	61	2	53	.314	.383	.485	127	22	2-7	.947	-6	96	80	3b152	—	1.8
1934	Phi A☆	144	543	89	179	37	6	16	90	56	0	70	.330	.392	.508	136	28	9-2	.914	-15	89	116	3b144	—	1.8
1935	Phi A	133	524	69	155	32	4	23	94	42	2	62	.296	.350	.504	120	12	6-2	.947	-12	87	75	3b131	—	0.6
1936	Phi A★	146	550	89	159	32	2	12	80	67	0	61	.289	.366	.420	96	-3	7-4	.941	-11	94	93	3b145	—	-0.9
1937	Bos A	153	570	88	172	33	5	9	106	76	1	51	.302	.385	.425	100	2	2-6	.935	-21	81	94	3b152	—	-1.4
1938	Bos A	139	524	77	159	29	5	5	106	71	1	55	.303	.388	.406	95	-2	10-9	.914	-10	95	**112**	3b138	—	-0.8
1939	Det A	132	489	57	135	23	2	8	76	56	2	41	.276	.353	.380	81	-13	7-4	.914	-8	92	90	3b130	—	-1.5
1940	†Det A	131	480	70	130	24	3	13	76	61	3	31	.271	.357	.415	91	-6	4-2	.928	-7	91	66	3b129	—	-0.8
1941	Det A	147	540	79	161	28	3	11	73	67	2	45	.298	.378	.422	101	2	5-4	.946	2	101	51	3b145	0	0.9
1942	Det A	143	499	65	133	34	2	11	79	72	3	21	.267	.362	.409	108	7	3-7	.926	-15	87	92	3b137	0	-0.5
1943	Det A	138	523	62	145	20	1	10	84	57	1	31	.277	.349	.377	104	4	2-5	.940	-10	88	88	3b138	0	-0.7
1944	Det A★	148	543	79	161	32	4	7	76	81	4	34	.297	.392	.409	122	20	4-4	.954	-9	93	79	3b146	0	1.2
1946	Det A	18	60	2	13	3	1	0	8	5	0	6	.217	.277	.300	58	-3	0-1	.949	-2	85	71	3b17	0	-0.6
	†Bos A	64	200	18	55	11	1	2	28	24	1	24	.275	.356	.370	97	0	0-2	.947	-1	99	125	3b59	0	-0.1
	Year	82	260	20	68	14	2	2	36	29	1	30	.262	.338	.354	88	-3	0-3	.947	-2	96	114	3b76	0	-0.7
Total	14	1802	6636	930	1941	374	51	140	1075	800	22	590	.292	.370	.428	106	69	61-59	.935	-127	91	87	3b1768,2b2/S	0	-1.2
Higgins, Bob	Robert Stone; B9.23.1886 Fayetteville TN; D5.25.1941 Chattanooga TN; BR/TR/5´8˝/176; d9.13																								
1909	Cle A	8	23	0	2	0	0	0	0	0	0	—	.087	.087	.087	-43	-4	0	1.000	2	*119*	*101*	C8	—	-0.1
1911	Bro N	4	10	1	3	0	0	0	2	1	0	0	.300	.364	.300	90	0	1	.933	-0	*98*	*85*	C2/3	—	0.0
1912	Bro N	1	2	0	0	0	0	0	0	0	0	1	.000	.000	.000	-99	-1	0	.750	-0	*73*	*0*	/C	—	-0.1
Total	3	13	35	1	5	0	0	0	2	1	0	<u>1</u>	.143	.167	.143	-6	-5	1	.970	2	*111*	*91*	C11/3	—	-0.2
Higgins, Bill	William Edward; B9.8.1861 Wilmington DE; D4.25.1919 Wilmington DE; TR/5´9˝/155; d8.9																								
1888	Bos N	14	54	5	10	1	0	0	4	1	0	3	.185	.200	.204	28	-4	1	.906	2	104	210	2b14	—	-0.2
1890	StL AA	67	258	39	65	6	2	0	35	24	0	—	.252	.316	.291	69	-11	7	.951	13	105	122	2b67	—	0.3
	Syr AA	1	4	1	1	1	0	0	1	0	0	—	.250	.250	.500	135	0	0	1.000	1	122	188	/2	—	0.1
	Year	68	262	40	66	7	2	0	36	24	0	—	.252	.315	.294	70	-11	7	.952	14	105	123	2b68	—	0.4
Total	2	82	316	45	76	8	2	0	40	25	0	<u>3</u>	.241	.296	.278	64	-15	8	.943	16	105	139	2b82	—	0.2
Higginson, Bobby	Robert Leigh; B8.18.1970 Philadelphia PA; BL/TR/5´11˝/(180–195); [DetA92 12/336]; d4.26; Col Temple																								
1995	Det A	131	410	61	92	17	5	14	43	62-3	5	107	.224	.329	.393	88	-7	6-4	.985	6	102	159	O123(65/0/67),D2	0	-0.6
1996	Det A	130	440	75	141	35	0	26	81	65-7	1	66	.320	.404	.577	145	33	6-3	.963	-3	93	112	O123(63/19/57),D4	27	2.3
1997	Det A	146	546	94	163	30	5	27	101	70-2	3	85	.299	.379	.520	133	27	12-7	.972	9	99	**217**	O143(104/2/57),D2	15	2.8
1998	Det A	157	612	92	174	37	4	25	85	63-2	6	101	.284	.355	.480	114	12	3-3	.982	3	97	159	O153(17/0/136),D2	0	0.7
1999	Det A	107	377	51	90	18	0	12	46	64-2	2	66	.239	.351	.382	86	-7	4-6	.983	-2	102	33	O88R,D17	31	-1.4
2000	Det A	154	597	104	179	44	4	30	102	74-6	2	99	.300	.377	.538	130	28	15-3	.979	10	99	**215**	O145L,D10	0	3.0
2001	Det A	147	541	84	150	28	6	17	71	80-3	2	65	.277	.367	.445	117	15	20-12	.976	7	107	110	O142L,D5	16	1.6
2002	Det A	119	444	50	125	24	3	10	63	41-3	6	45	.282	.345	.417	107	5	12-5	.973	6	98	210	O117L/D	32	0.7
2003	Det A	130	469	61	110	13	4	14	52	59-3	3	73	.235	.320	.369	86	-10	8-8	.981	-2	102	57	O118(0/1/117),D8	26	-1.7
2004	Det A	131	448	63	110	24	2	12	64	70-5	7	84	.246	.353	.388	98	1	5-2	.975	2	95	170	O115R,D10	0	-0.3
2005	Det A	10	26	1	2	0	0	0	1	1-0	0	5	.077	.111	.077	-49	-6	0-0	1.000	-1	60	259	O7(1/0/6)/D	150	-0.7
Total	11	1362	4910	736	1336	270	33	187	709	649-36	37	796	.272	.358	.455	111	91	91-53	.977	33	99	150	O1274(654/22/643),D62	297	6.4
High, Andy	Andrew Aird "Handy Andy"; B11.21.1897 Ava IL; D2.22.1981 Sylvania OH; BL/TR/5´6˝/155; d4.12; C2; b–Charlie b–Hugh																								
1922	Bro N	153	579	82	164	27	10	6	65	59	4	26	.283	.354	.396	94	-5	3-12	.958	-3	102	106	3b130,S22/2	—	-0.1
1923	Bro N	123	426	51	115	23	9	3	37	47	1	13	.270	.344	.387	95	-2	4-1	.969	-4	97	90	3b80,S45,2b5	—	0.4
1924	Bro N	144	582	98	191	26	13	6	61	57	2	16	.328	.390	.448	128	24	3-6	.964	-9	91	62	2b133,S17/3	—	1.8
1925	Bro N	44	115	11	23	4	1	0	6	14	0	5	.200	.287	.252	40	-10	0-1	.938	-4	87	86	2b11,3b11,S3	—	-1.3
	Bos N	60	219	31	63	11	1	4	28	24	1	2	.288	.361	.402	104	2	3-5	.979	-5	94	72	3b60/2	—	-0.1
	Year	104	334	42	86	15	2	4	34	38	1	7	.257	.335	.350	80	-9	3-6	.963	-9	91	78	3b71,2b12,S3	—	-1.4
1926	Bos N	130	476	55	141	17	10	2	66	39	1	9	.296	.351	.387	108	5	4	.962	-11	97	99	3b81,2b49	—	0.0
1927	Bos N	113	384	59	116	15	9	4	46	26	2	11	.302	.350	.419	114	6	4	.915	-19	76	61	3b89,2b8,S2	—	-0.8
1928	†StL N	111	368	58	105	14	3	6	37	37	3	10	.285	.355	.389	93	-4	2	.935	-16	85	87	3b73,2b19	—	-1.4
1929	StL N	146	603	95	178	32	4	10	63	38	3	18	.295	.340	.411	84	-16	7	**.967**	-14	90	98	3b123,2b22	—	-2.0
1930	†StL N	72	215	34	60	12	2	2	29	23	0	6	.279	.349	.381	74	-9	1	.990	-6	81	63	3b48,2b3	—	-1.1
1931	†StL N	63	131	20	35	6	1	0	19	24	2	4	.267	.389	.328	91	0	0	1.000	-2	85	176	3b23,2b19	—	-0.1
1932	Cin N	84	191	16	36	4	2	0	12	23	0	6	.188	.276	.230	39	-16	1	.950	-6	89	32	3b46,2b12	—	-2.1
1933	Cin N	24	43	4	9	2	0	1	6	5	0	1	.209	.292	.326	77	-1	0	.966	1	115	82	3b11,2b2	—	0.0
1934	Phi N	47	68	4	14	2	0	0	7	9	0	3	.206	.299	.235	40	-6	1	.906	-2	74	184	3b14,2b2	—	-0.7
Total	13	1314	4400	618	1250	195	65	44	482	425	19	130	.284	.350	.388	94	-32	33-<u>25</u>	.956	-100	91	90	3b790,2b287,S89	—	-7.5
High, Charlie	Charles Edwin; B12.1.1898 Ava IL; D9.11.1960 Oak Grove OR; BL/TR/5´9˝/170; d9.5; b–Andy b–Hugh; Col St. Louis																								
1919	Phi A	11	29	2	2	0	0	0	1	3	1	4	.069	.182	.069	-28	-5	2	.944	-0	97	81	O9(0/1/8)	—	-0.6
1920	Phi A	17	65	7	20	2	1	1	6	3	4	6	.308	.375	.415	108	1	0-2	.882	-1	84	128	O17(0/2/15)	—	-0.2
Total	2	28	94	9	22	2	1	1	7	6	5	10	.234	.314	.309	68	-4	2-<u>2</u>	.904	-2	88	112	O26(0/3/23)	—	-0.8
High, Hugh	Hugh Jenken "Bunny"; B10.24.1887 Pottstown PA; D11.16.1962 St.Louis MO; BL/TL/5´7.5˝/155; d4.11; b–Andy b–Charlie																								
1913	Det A	87	183	18	42	6	1	0	16	28	1	24	.230	.335	.273	80	-3	6	.982	2	105	108	O52(3/43/7)	—	-0.5
1914	Det A	84	184	25	49	5	3	0	17	26	2	21	.266	.363	.326	104	2	7-6	.959	-6	88	31	O53(13/39/1)	—	-0.8
1915	NY A	119	427	51	110	19	7	1	43	62	3	47	.258	.356	.342	109	7	22-13	**.981**	-5	97	60	O117(44/71/1)	—	-0.6
1916	NY A	116	377	44	99	13	4	1	28	47	3	44	.263	.349	.326	101	2	13	.950	-2	97	98	O110(107/2/1)	—	-0.5
1917	NY A	103	365	37	86	11	6	1	19	48	3	31	.236	.329	.307	93	-2	8	.986	-3	88	108	O100(99/1/0)	—	-1.1
1918	NY A	7	10	1	0	0	0	0	0	1	0	1	.000	.091	.000	-71	-2	0	1.000	1	103	257	O4(2/1/1)	—	-0.2
Total	6	516	1546	176	386	54	21	3	123	212	12	168	.250	.345	.318	98	4	56-<u>19</u>	.972	-14	95	85	O436(268/157/11)	—	-3.7
Higham, Dick	Richard; B7.24.1851 Ipswich, England; D3.18.1905 Chicago IL; BL/TR/5´8.5˝/171; d6.1; M1/U2																								
1871	Mut NA	21	94	21	34	3	1	0	9	2	—	0	.362	.375	.415	139	6	3-2	.747	-5	93	86	2b12,O8R/C	—	0.1
1872	Bal NA	50	245	72	84	10	1	2	37	2	—	3	.343	.348	.416	128	7	4-5	.847	-2	—	—	C25,O24(0/2/22),2b5,3b2/1	—	0.4
1873	Mut NA	49	244	57	77	5	4	0	34	2	—	1	.316	.321	.369	104	1	2-2	.750	-9	34	202	O19(0/1/18),2b18,C17	—	-0.6
1874	Mut NA	**65**	333	58	87	14	3	1	38	4	—	0	.261	.270	.330	89	-5	5-3	**.852**	6	—	—	C48,O33(0/3/31)/2M	—	0.3
1875	Chi NA	42	208	44	49	5	3	0	12	0	—	0	.236	.236	.288	80	-4	6-2	.821	-5	—	—	C24,O14(0/3/11),2b13	—	-0.8
	Mut NA	15	64	12	25	5	0	0	10	0	—	1	.391	.391	.469	187	5	0-0	.739	-4	—	—	C8,2b6,O3R,1b2	—	0.1
	Year	57	272	56	74	10	3	0	22	0	—	1	.272	.272	.331	106	1	6-2	.802	-9	—	—	C32,2b19,O17(0/3/14),1b2	—	-0.7
1876	Har N	67	312	59	102	**21**	2	0	35	2	—	7	.327	.331	.407	134	10	—	.869	1	**168**	62	O59R,C13/S2	—	1.0
1878	Pro N	**62**	281	**60**	90	**22**	1	1	29	5	—	16	.320	.332	.416	145	14	—	.811	2	168	158	O62R/C	—	1.5
1880	Tro N	1	5	1	1	0	0	0	0	0	—	0	.200	.200	.200	34	0	—	ø	-1	0	0	/rfC	—	-0.2
Total	5NA	242	1188	264	356	42	12	3	140	10	—	5	.300	.306	.363	108	10	20-14	.836	-18	—	—	C123,O101(0/9/93),2b55,1b3,3b2	—	-0.5
Total	3	130	598	120	193	43	3	1	64	7	—	23	.323	.331	.410	138	24	—	.834	2	—	—	O122R,C15/2S	—	2.3

YEAR	TM LG	G	AB	R	H	2B	3B	HR	RBI	BB-IB	HP	SO	AVG	OBP	SLG	AOPS	ABR	SB-CS	FA	FR	RNG	THR	GAMES AT POSITION	DL	BFW
HILAND, JOHN	John William; B9.1860 Baltic CT; D4.10.1901 Philadelphia PA; BL/TL/5´8.5˝/165; d8.20																								
1885	Phi N	3	9	0	0	0	0	0	0	0	—	4	.000	.000	.000	-99	-2	—	.833	-1	59	0	2b3	—	-0.3
HILDEBRAND, GEORGE	George Albert; B9.6.1878 San Francisco CA; D5.30.1960 Reseda CA; BR/TR/5´8˝/170; d4.17; U22																								
1902	Bro N	11	41	3	9	1	0	0	5	3	1	—	.220	.289	.244	64	-2	0	1.000	2	135	0	O11L	—	0.0
HILDEBRAND, PALMER	Palmer Marion "Pete"; B12.23.1884 Shauck OH; D1.25.1960 N.Canton OH; BR/TR/5´10˝/170; d5.14																								
1913	StL N	26	55	3	9	2	0	0	1	1	2	10	.164	.207	.200	17	-6	1-2	.968	-1	81	103	C22/lf	—	-0.6
HILL, AARON	Aaron Walter; B3.21.1982 Visalia CA; BR/TR/5´11˝/195; [TorA03 1/13]; d5.20; Col LSU																								
2005	Tor A	105	361	49	99	25	3	3	40	34-0	5	41	.274	.342	.385	90	-4	2-1	.949	11	112	142	3b35,D34,2b22,S16	0	0.7
2006	Tor A	155	546	70	159	28	3	6	50	42-5	9	66	.291	.349	.386	87	-9	5-2	.987	15	**118**	**132**	2b112,S63/D	0	1.4
Total	2	260	907	119	258	53	6	9	90	76-5	14	107	.284	.346	.386	88	-13	7-3	.987	26	120	129	2b134,S79,D35,3b35	0	2.1
HILL, BELDEN	Belden L.; B8.24.1864 Kewanee IL; D10.22.1934 Cedar Rapids IA; BR/TR/5´10˝/170; d8.27																								
1890	Bal AA	9	30	3	5	2	0	0	2	3	3	—	.167	.306	.233	56	-1	6	.857	0	79	126	3b9	—	-0.1
HILL, DONNIE	Donald Earl; B11.12.1960 Pomona CA; BB/TR/5´10˝/(160–161); [OakA81 S1/1]; d7.25; Col Arizona St.																								
1983	Oak A	53	158	20	42	7	0	2	15	4-0	0	21	.266	.280	.348	77	-5	1-1	.961	-3	95	80	S53	0	-0.4
1984	Oak A	73	174	21	40	6	0	2	16	5-0	0	12	.230	.249	.299	55	-11	1-1	.949	-13	81	80	S66,2b4,3b2,D2	15	-2.0
1985	Oak A	123	393	45	112	13	2	3	48	23-2	0	33	.285	.321	.351	91	-5	9-4	.973	-29	90	68	2b122	0	-2.7
1986	Oak A	108	339	37	96	16	2	4	29	23-1	0	38	.283	.329	.378	99	-1	5-2	.984	-9	92	74	2b68,3b33,S2,D3	0	-0.7
1987	Chi A	111	410	57	98	14	6	9	46	30-1	1	35	.239	.290	.368	72	-18	1-0	.987	-11	98	95	2b84,3b32/D	30	-2.4
1988	Chi A	83	221	17	48	6	1	2	20	26-1	0	32	.217	.296	.281	64	-11	3-1	.975	-3	96	108	2b59,3b12,D5	0	-1.2
1990	Cal A	103	352	36	93	18	2	3	32	29-1	1	27	.264	.319	.352	90	-5	1-2	.990	10	115	125	2b60,S24,3b21,1b3/PD	17	0.7
1991	Cal A	77	209	36	50	8	1	1	20	30-1	0	21	.239	.335	.301	77	-6	1-0	.971	10	103	111	2b39,S29,1b3	0	0.7
1992	Min A	25	51	7	15	3	0	0	2	5-0	1	6	.294	.368	.353	99	0	0-0	.944	-0	118	97	S10,2b7,3b5/rf	39	0.1
Total	9	756	2307	276	594	91	14	26	228	175-7	3	225	.257	.308	.343	81	-62	22-11	.980	-50	97	90	2b443,S184,3b105,D12,1b6/rfP	101	-7.9
HILL, GLENALLEN	Glenallen; B3.22.1965 Santa Cruz CA; BR/TR/6´2˝/(210–230); [TorA83 9/219]; d7.31																								
1989	Tor A	19	52	4	15	0	0	1	7	3-0	0	12	.288	.327	.346	91	-1	2-1	.964	-1	92	0	O16(3/0/13),D3	0	-0.3
1990	Tor A	84	260	47	60	11	3	12	32	18-0	0	62	.231	.281	.435	95	-3	8-3	.983	-1	95	99	O60(27/1/34),D20	15	-0.6
1991	Tor A	35	99	14	25	5	2	3	11	7-0	0	24	.253	.296	.434	97	-1	2-2	.967	0	119	0	D16,O13(9/0/4)	0	-0.2
	Cle A	37	122	15	32	3	0	5	14	16-0	0	30	.262	.345	.410	108	1	4-2	.978	1	115	0	O33(12/26/1)/D	28	0.2
	Year	72	221	29	57	8	2	8	25	23-0	0	54	.258	.324	.421	103	0	6-4	.975	1	116	0	O46(21/26/5),D17	0	0.0
1992	Cle A	102	369	38	89	16	1	18	49	20-0	4	73	.241	.287	.436	101	-2	9-6	.956	-2	93	114	O59(50/1/8),D34	29	-0.7
1993	Cle A	66	174	19	39	7	2	5	25	11-1	1	50	.224	.268	.374	72	-8	7-3	.940	-3	93	44	O39(9/0/30),D18	0	-1.2
	Chi N	31	87	14	30	7	0	10	22	6-0	0	21	.345	.387	.770	202	12	1-0	.957	2	117	145	O21(18/0/4)	0	1.3
1994	Chi N	89	269	48	80	12	1	10	38	29-0	0	57	.297	.365	.461	114	6	19-6	.987	-3	97	0	O78(31/44/7)	0	0.3
1995	SF N	132	497	71	131	29	4	24	86	39-4	1	98	.264	.317	.483	110	5	25-5	.959	-6	88	105	O125(0/1/124)	0	-0.3
1996	SF N	98	379	56	106	26	0	19	67	33-3	6	95	.280	.344	.499	122	12	6-3	.960	-6	86	92	O98R	70	0.2
1997	†SF N	128	398	47	104	28	4	11	64	19-0	4	87	.261	.297	.435	92	-6	7-4	.947	-6	95	31	O97R,D7	0	-1.6
1998	Sea A	74	259	37	75	20	2	12	33	14-1	3	45	.290	.332	.521	117	6	1-1	.965	-3	98	58	O71L	0	0.1
	†Chi N	48	131	26	46	5	0	8	23	14-1	0	34	.351	.414	.573	151	10	0-0	.984	3	116	170	O34(28/0/6)	0	1.1
1999	Chi N	99	253	43	76	9	1	20	55	22-1	0	61	.300	.353	.581	132	11	5-1	.955	-4	81	92	O62(37/0/26),D4	15	0.5
2000	Chi N	64	168	23	44	4	1	11	29	10-2	0	43	.262	.303	.494	98	-2	0-1	.955	1	89	210	O29L,D9	8	-0.2
	†NY A	40	132	22	44	5	0	16	29	9-0	1	33	.333	.378	.735	176	14	0-0	1.000	-0	107	0	D24,O12L	0	1.1
2001	Ana A	16	66	4	9	0	0	1	2	0-0	0	20	.136	.136	.182	-17	-11	0-0	ø	0	0	0	D16	38	-1.2
Total	13	1162	3715	528	1005	187	21	186	586	270-13	20	845	.271	.321	.482	111	43	96-38	.964	-28	94	77	O847(336/73/452),D152	203	-1.5
HILL, HERMAN	Herman Alexander; B10.12.1945 Tuskegee AL; D12.14.1970 Valencia, Carabobo, Venez.; BL/TR/6´2˝/190; d9.2																								
1969	Min A	16	2	4	0	0	0	0	0	0-0	0	1	.000	.000	.000	-97	-1	1-2	ø	-0	0	0	O2C	0	-0.1
1970	Min A	27	22	8	2	0	0	0	0	0-0	0	6	.091	.091	.091	-49	-5	0-0	1.000	1	117	277	O14(2/10/2)	0	-0.4
Total	2	43	24	12	2	0	0	0	0	0-0	0	7	.083	.083	.083	-53	-6	1-2	1.000	1	106	251	O16(2/12/2)	0	-0.5
HILL, HUGH	Hugh Ellis; B7.21.1879 Ringgold GA; D9.6.1958 Cincinnati OH; BL/TR/5´11.5˝/168; d5.1; b–Bill																								
1903	Cle A	1	1	0	0	0	0	0	0	0	0	—	.000	.000	.000	-99	0	0	ø	0	—	—	/H	—	0.0
1904	StL N	23	93	13	21	2	1	3	4	2	0	—	.226	.242	.366	91	-2	3	1.000	0	67	122	O23L	—	-0.3
Total	2	24	94	13	21	2	1	3	4	2	0	—	.223	.240	.362	89	-2	3	1.000	0	67	122	O23L	—	-0.3
HILL, HUNTER	Hunter Benjamin; B6.21.1879 Austin TX; D2.22.1959 Austin TX; BR/TR; d7.1																								
1903	StL A	86	317	30	77	11	3	0	25	8	1	—	.243	.264	.297	70	-12	2	.923	1	99	113	3b86	—	-1.0
1904	StL A	58	219	19	47	3	0	0	14	6	3	—	.215	.246	.228	54	-12	4	.826	-18	70	56	3b56/lf	—	-3.3
	Was A	77	290	18	57	6	1	0	17	11	1	—	.197	.228	.224	44	-19	10	.895	-3	98	57	3b71,O5R	—	-2.3
	Year	135	509	37	104	9	1	0	31	17	4	—	.204	.236	.226	48	-31	14	.864	-21	85	57	3b127,O6(1/0/5)	—	-5.6
1905	Was A	104	374	37	78	12	1	1	24	32	4	—	.209	.278	.254	72	-11	10	.908	-1	100	109	3b103	—	-1.0
Total	3	325	1200	104	259	32	5	1	80	57	9	—	.216	.257	.253	62	-54	26	.895	-21	94	89	3b316,O6(1/0/5)	—	-7.6
HILL, JESSE	Jesse Terrill; B1.20.1907 Yates MO; D8.31.1993 Pasadena CA; BR/TR/5´9˝/165; d4.17; Col USC																								
1935	NY A	107	392	69	115	20	3	4	33	42	0	32	.293	.362	.390	100	0	14-4	.951	2	102	117	O94L	—	-0.2
1936	Was A	85	233	50	71	19	5	0	34	29	1	23	.305	.384	.429	106	3	11-0	.967	-2	86	124	O60(54/4/2)	—	0.1
1937	Was A	33	92	24	20	2	1	1	4	13	0	16	.217	.314	.293	57	-6	2-1	.986	1	122	0	O21(3/18/0)	—	-0.5
	Phi A	70	242	32	71	12	3	1	37	31	0	20	.293	.374	.380	92	-2	16-3	.954	-3	98	69	O68(3/65/0)	—	-0.4
	Year	103	334	56	91	14	4	2	41	44	0	36	.272	.357	.356	82	-8	18-4	.964	-2	104	51	O89(6/83/0)	—	-0.9
Total	3	295	959	175	277	53	12	6	108	115	1	91	.289	.366	.388	95	-5	43-8	.959	-2	100	94	O243(154/87/2)	—	-1.0
HILL, KOYIE	Koyie Dolan; B3.9.1979 Tulsa OK; BB/TR/6´0˝/190; [LAN00 4/117]; d9.5; Col Wichita St.																								
2003	LA N	3	3	0	1	1	0	0	0	0-0	0	2	.333	.333	.667	156	0	0-0	ø	0	—	—	/H	0	0.0
2004	Ari N	13	36	3	9	1	0	1	6	2-1	0	6	.250	.289	.361	63	-2	1-0	.984	-3	65	203	C11	47	-0.4
2005	Ari N	34	78	6	17	5	0	0	6	11-0	0	27	.218	.308	.282	55	-5	0-1	1.000	-3	105	78	C32	0	-0.7
Total	3	50	117	9	27	7	0	1	12	13-1	0	35	.231	.303	.316	60	-7	1-1	.995	-6	94	113	C43	47	-1.1
HILL, MARC	Marc Kevin; B2.18.1952 Elsberry MO; BR/TR/6´3˝/(200–240); [StLN70 10/234]; d9.28; C2																								
1973	StL N	1	3	0	0	0	0	0	0	0-0	0	1	.000	.000	.000	-99	-1	0-0	1.000	-0	49	0	/C	0	-0.1
1974	StL N	10	21	2	5	1	0	0	2	4-1	0	5	.238	.360	.286	82	0	0-0	1.000	2	432	45	C9	0	0.2
1975	SF N	72	182	14	39	4	0	5	23	25-5	0	27	.214	.305	.319	72	-7	0-0	.994	3	89	137	C60/3	0	-0.1
1976	SF N	54	131	11	24	5	0	3	15	10-2	1	19	.183	.243	.290	50	-9	0-1	.995	-0	108	73	C49/1	61	-0.8
1977	SF N	108	320	28	80	10	0	9	50	34-6	0	34	.250	.316	.366	84	-7	0-1	.989	-1	94	102	C102	0	-0.4
1978	SF N	117	358	20	87	15	1	3	36	45-8	1	39	.243	.329	.316	84	-7	1-2	.986	1	99	109	C116,1b2	0	-0.2
1979	SF N	63	169	20	35	3	0	3	15	26-5	0	25	.207	.308	.278	67	-7	0-1	.991	-4	96	145	C58/1	40	-0.9
1980	SF N	17	41	1	7	2	0	0	0	1-0	0	7	.171	.190	.220	15	-5	0-0	.972	-0	85	101	C14	0	-0.5
	Sea A	29	70	8	16	2	1	2	9	3-0	0	10	.229	.260	.371	70	-3	0-0	.991	1	151	111	C29	0	-0.2
1981	Chi A	16	6	0	0	0	0	0	0	0-0	0	1	.000	.000	.000	-99	-2	0-0	1.000	-1	0	91	C14/13	0	-0.3
1982	Chi A	53	88	9	23	2	0	3	13	6-0	1	13	.261	.313	.386	91	-1	0-0	.993	1	102	114	C49/13	0	0.1
1983	Chi A	58	133	11	30	6	0	1	11	9-2	0	24	.226	.275	.293	54	-8	0-1	.991	0	123	96	C55/1D	0	-0.7
1984	Chi A	77	193	15	45	10	1	5	20	9-0	2	26	.233	.275	.373	73	-7	0-1	.991	-2	108	77	C72,1b2	0	-0.7
1985	Chi A	40	75	5	10	2	0	0	4	12-0	0	9	.133	.253	.160	15	-9	0-0	.985	-0	101	56	C37/3	0	-0.8
1986	Chi A	22	19	2	3	0	0	0	1	1-0	0	3	.158	.238	.158	10	-2	0-0	1.000	4	110	139	C22	0	0.1
Total	14	737	1809	146	404	62	3	34	198	185-29	6	243	.223	.295	.317	69	-75	1-7	.990	3	106	104	C687,1b9,3b4,D2	101	-5.3
HILL, OLIVER	Oliver Clinton; B10.16.1909 Powder Springs GA; D9.20.1970 Decatur GA; BL/TR/5´11˝/178; d4.19																								
1939	Bos N	2	2	1	1	1	0	0	0	0	0	0	.500	.500	1.000	317	1	0	ø	0	—	—	/H	—	0.1

HILL, BOBBY William Robert; B4.3.1978 San Jose CA; BB/TR/5´10˝/(175–180); [ChiN00 2/43]; d5.10; Col Miami

YEAR	TM LG	G	AB	R	H	2B	3B	HR	RBI	BB-IB	HP	SO	AVG	OBP	SLG	AOPS	ABR	SB-CS	FA	FR	RNG	THR	GAMES AT POSITION	DL	BFW
2002	Chi N	59	190	26	48	7	2	4	20	17-4	4	42	.253	.327	.374	84	-5	6-1	.991	-2	84	98	2b55/S	0	-0.4
2003	Chi N	5	4	0	1	0	0	0	0	1-0	0	2	.250	.400	.250	73	0	0-0	1.000	-1	0	0	2b2	0	-0.1
	Pit N	1	3	1	1	0	0	0	0	1-0	0	0	.333	.500	.333	122	0	0-0	1.000	-0	96	0	/2	0	0.0
	Year	6	7	1	2	0	0	0	0	2-0	0	2	.286	.444	.286	94	0	0-0	1.000	-1	52	0	2b3	0	-0.1
2004	Pit N	126	233	28	62	7	2	2	27	20-2	12	39	.266	.353	.339	81	-6	0-3	.994	1	111	115	2b40,3b25	0	-0.4
2005	Pit N	58	93	12	25	6	0	0	11	9-0	2	17	.269	.343	.333	79	-2	0-0	.977	-2	90	119	3b24/2	0	-0.5
Total	4	249	523	67	137	20	4	6	58	48-6	18	100	.262	.343	.350	82	-13	6-4	.989	-5	93	103	2b99,3b49/S	0	-1.4

HILLEBRAND, HOMER Homer Hiller Henry; B10.10.1879 Freeport IL; D1.20.1974 Elsinore (now Lake Elsinore) CA; BR/TL/5´8˝/165; d4.24; Col Princeton; ▲

YEAR	TM LG	G	AB	R	H	2B	3B	HR	RBI	BB-IB	HP	SO	AVG	OBP	SLG	AOPS	ABR	SB-CS	FA	FR	RNG	THR	GAMES AT POSITION	DL	BFW
1905	Pit N	39	110	9	26	3	2	0	7	6	1	—	.236	.282	.300	72	-4	1	.978	-3	62	95	1b16,P10,O7(1/0/6),C3	—	-0.6
1906	Pit N	7	21	1	5	1	0	0	3	1	0	—	.238	.273	.286	71	1	0	1.000	1	125	442	P7	—	0.0
1908	Pit N	1	0	0	0	0	0	0	0	0	0	—	ø	ø	ø	ø	0	0	ø	-0	0	0	/P	—	0.0
Total	3	47	131	10	31	4	2	0	10	7	1	—	.237	.281	.298	72	-3	1	1.000	-2	92	204	P18,1b16,O7(1/0/6),C3	—	-0.6

HILLEBRAND, R. R. E.; d8.29

YEAR	TM LG	G	AB	R	H	2B	3B	HR	RBI	BB-IB	HP	SO	AVG	OBP	SLG	AOPS	ABR	SB-CS	FA	FR	RNG	THR	GAMES AT POSITION	DL	BFW
1902	Chi N	1	4	1	0	0	0	0	0	1	0	—	.000	.200	.000	-39	-1	0	1.000	-0	0	0	/rf	—	-0.1

HILLENBRAND, SHEA Shea Matthew; B7.27.1975 Mesa AZ; BR/TR/6´1˝/(200–210); [BosA96 10/301]; d4.2; Col Mesa (AZ) CC; [DL 1999 Bos A 34]

YEAR	TM LG	G	AB	R	H	2B	3B	HR	RBI	BB-IB	HP	SO	AVG	OBP	SLG	AOPS	ABR	SB-CS	FA	FR	RNG	THR	GAMES AT POSITION	DL	BFW
2001	Bos A	139	468	52	123	20	2	12	49	13-3	7	61	.263	.291	.391	78	-16	3-4	.941	-2	92	78	3b129,1b6/D	0	-1.9
2002	Bos A★	156	634	94	186	43	4	18	83	25-4	12	95	.293	.330	.459	106	4	4-2	.943	4	102	113	3b156	0	0.9
2003	Bos A	49	185	20	56	17	0	3	38	7-1	4	26	.303	.335	.443	101	1	1-0	.958	-1	87	64	3b29,1b28,D2	0	-0.2
	Ari N	85	330	40	88	18	1	17	59	17-3	2	44	.267	.302	.482	94	-4	0-0	.989	-5	76	75	1b56,3b34	20	-1.4
2004	Ari N	148	562	68	174	36	3	15	80	24-2	12	49	.310	.348	.464	102	1	2-0	.989	-5	90	93	1b131,3b17	0	-1.4
2005	Tor A★	152	594	91	173	36	2	18	82	26-2	**22**	79	.291	.343	.449	104	4	5-1	.991	-4	115	124	1b67,3b54,D33	0	-0.7
2006	Tor A	81	296	40	89	15	1	12	39	14-2	6	40	.301	.342	.480	106	2	1-2	.987	-5	128	99	D44,1b19,3b17	0	-0.7
	SF N	60	234	33	58	12	0	9	29	7-0	3	40	.248	.275	.415	74	-10	0-0	.998	-1	108	66	1b58,3b8	0	-1.5
Total	6	870	3303	438	947	197	13	104	459	133-17	68	434	.287	.325	.449	97	-18	16-9	.938	-18	94	92	3b444,1b365,D80	54	-6.9

HILLER, CHUCK Charles Joseph; B10.1.1934 Johnsburg IL; D10.20.2004 St.Pete Beach FL; BL/TR/5´11˝/(170–175); d4.11; C10; Col St. Thomas (MN)

YEAR	TM LG	G	AB	R	H	2B	3B	HR	RBI	BB-IB	HP	SO	AVG	OBP	SLG	AOPS	ABR	SB-CS	FA	FR	RNG	THR	GAMES AT POSITION	DL	BFW
1961	SF N	70	240	38	57	12	1	2	12	32-0	1	30	.237	.328	.321	76	-7	4-4	.973	-19	82	75	2b67	0	-2.1
1962	†SF N	161	602	94	166	22	2	3	48	55-3	8	49	.276	.341	.334	84	-11	5-4	.964	-6	97	110	2b161	0	-0.4
1963	SF N	111	417	44	93	10	2	6	33	20-0	2	23	.223	.261	.300	62	-21	3-2	.963	-14	95	78	2b109	0	-3.0
1964	SF N	80	205	21	37	8	1	1	17	17-0	1	23	.180	.243	.244	38	-17	1-1	.977	1	100	101	2b60/3	0	-1.2
1965	SF N	7	7	1	1	0	0	1	1	0-0	0	1	.143	.143	.571	88	0	0-0	1.000	-0	72	0	2b2	0	-0.1
	NY N	100	286	24	68	11	1	5	21	14-2	1	24	.238	.275	.336	74	-11	1-1	.959	-4	102	94	2b80,O4(3/0/1),3b2	0	-1.1
	Year	107	293	25	69	11	1	6	22	14-2	1	25	.235	.272	.341	74	-11	1-1	.959	-5	102	93	2b82,O4(3/0/1),3b2	0	-1.2
1966	NY N	108	254	25	71	8	2	2	14	15-0	5	22	.280	.332	.350	92	-3	0-0	.981	12	119	125	2b45,3b14,O9L	0	1.2
1967	NY N	25	54	0	5	3	0	0	3	2-0	0	11	.093	.125	.148	-22	-9	0-0	.968	2	115	123	2b14	38	-0.6
	Phi N	31	43	4	13	1	0	0	2	2-0	0	4	.302	.333	.326	88	-1	0-2	.947	-2	74	37	2b6	0	-0.3
	Year	56	97	4	18	4	0	0	5	4-0	0	15	.186	.218	.227	27	-9	0-2	.963	0	103	99	2b20	0	-0.9
1968	Pit N	11	13	2	5	1	0	0	1	0-0	0	0	.385	.385	.462	155	1	0-0	.857	-0	68	0	2b2	0	0.1
Total	8	704	2121	253	516	76	9	20	152	157-5	18	187	.243	.299	.316	72	-79	14-14	.967	-31	97	96	2b546,3b17,O13(12/0/1)	38	-7.5

HILLER, HOB Harvey Max; B5.12.1893 E.Mauch Chunk PA; D12.27.1956 Lehighton PA; BR/TR/5´8˝/162; d4.22

YEAR	TM LG	G	AB	R	H	2B	3B	HR	RBI	BB-IB	HP	SO	AVG	OBP	SLG	AOPS	ABR	SB-CS	FA	FR	RNG	THR	GAMES AT POSITION	DL	BFW
1920	Bos A	17	29	4	5	1	1	0	2	2	0	5	.172	.226	.276	34	-3	0-3	.905	1	116	113	3b6,S5,2b2/rf	—	-0.3
1921	Bos A	1	1	0	0	0	0	0	0	0	0	0	.000	.000	.000	-99	0	0-0	ø	0	—	—	/H	—	0.0
Total	2	18	30	4	5	1	1	0	2	2	0	5	.167	.219	.267	29	-3	0-3	.905	1	116	113	3b6,S5,2b2/rf	—	-0.3

HILLEY, ED Edward Garfield "Whitey"; B6.17.1879 Cleveland OH; D11.14.1956 Cleveland OH; BR/TR/5´10.5˝/170; d9.29

YEAR	TM LG	G	AB	R	H	2B	3B	HR	RBI	BB-IB	HP	SO	AVG	OBP	SLG	AOPS	ABR	SB-CS	FA	FR	RNG	THR	GAMES AT POSITION	DL	BFW
1903	Phi A	1	3	1	1	0	0	0	0	1	0	—	.333	.500	.333	147	0	0	.800	-0	35	655	/3	—	0.0

HILLIS, MACK Malcolm David; B7.23.1901 Cambridge MA; D6.16.1961 Cambridge MA; BR/TR/5´10˝/165; d9.13

YEAR	TM LG	G	AB	R	H	2B	3B	HR	RBI	BB-IB	HP	SO	AVG	OBP	SLG	AOPS	ABR	SB-CS	FA	FR	RNG	THR	GAMES AT POSITION	DL	BFW
1924	NY A	1	1	1	0	0	0	0	0	0	0	0	.000	.000	.000	-99	0	0-0	ø	-0	0	0	/2	—	0.0
1928	Pit N	11	36	6	9	2	3	1	7	0	0	6	.250	.250	.556	101	-1	1	.973	-1	111	96	2b8/3	—	-0.1
Total	2	12	37	7	9	2	3	1	7	0	0	6	.243	.243	.541	96	-1	1-0	.973	-1	109	94	2b9/3	—	-0.1

HILLY, PAT William Edward (b William Edward Hilgerink); B2.24.1887 Fostoria OH; D7.25.1953 Eureka MO; BR/TR/5´11˝/180; d5.7; Col Dayton

YEAR	TM LG	G	AB	R	H	2B	3B	HR	RBI	BB-IB	HP	SO	AVG	OBP	SLG	AOPS	ABR	SB-CS	FA	FR	RNG	THR	GAMES AT POSITION	DL	BFW
1914	Phi N	8	10	2	3	0	0	0	1	1	0	5	.300	.364	.300	92	0	0	1.000	0	138	0	O4R	—	0.0

HILTON, DAVE John David; B9.15.1950 Uvalde TX; BR/TR/5´11˝/185; [SDN71*1/1]; d9.10; C2; Col Rice

YEAR	TM LG	G	AB	R	H	2B	3B	HR	RBI	BB-IB	HP	SO	AVG	OBP	SLG	AOPS	ABR	SB-CS	FA	FR	RNG	THR	GAMES AT POSITION	DL	BFW
1972	SD N	13	47	2	10	2	1	0	5	3-0	0	6	.213	.260	.298	63	-3	1-0	.939	-3	73	43	3b13	0	-0.6
1973	SD N	70	234	21	46	9	0	5	16	19-6	1	35	.197	.260	.299	59	-14	2-1	.970	-10	94	120	3b47,2b23	0	-2.3
1974	SD N	74	217	17	52	8	2	1	12	13-1	0	28	.240	.281	.309	69	-10	3-5	.948	-5	91	117	3b55,2b15	0	-1.6
1975	SD N	4	8	0	0	0	0	0	0	0-0	0	0	.000	.000	.000	-99	-2	0-0	.900	1	142	0	3b4	58	-0.2
Total	4	161	506	40	108	19	3	6	33	35-7	1	69	.213	.265	.298	61	-29	6-6	.954	-16	91	107	3b119,2b38	58	-4.7

HIMES, JACK John Herby; B9.22.1878 Bryan OH; D12.16.1949 Joliet IL; BL/TR/6´2˝/180; d9.18

YEAR	TM LG	G	AB	R	H	2B	3B	HR	RBI	BB-IB	HP	SO	AVG	OBP	SLG	AOPS	ABR	SB-CS	FA	FR	RNG	THR	GAMES AT POSITION	DL	BFW
1905	StL N	12	41	3	6	0	0	0	0	1	0	—	.146	.167	.146	-7	-5	0	1.000	-0	74	0	O11(1/0/11)	—	-0.7
1906	StL N	40	155	10	42	5	2	0	14	7	1	—	.271	.307	.329	102	0	4	.977	4	197	158	O40(0/32/8)	—	0.2
Total	2	52	196	13	48	5	2	0	14	8	1	—	.245	.278	.291	79	-5	4	.981	4	172	126	O51(1/32/19)	—	-0.5

HINCH, A.J. Andrew Jay; B5.15.1974 Waverly IA; BR/TR/6´1˝/(200–207); [OakA96 3/75]; d4.1; Col Stanford

YEAR	TM LG	G	AB	R	H	2B	3B	HR	RBI	BB-IB	HP	SO	AVG	OBP	SLG	AOPS	ABR	SB-CS	FA	FR	RNG	THR	GAMES AT POSITION	DL	BFW
1998	Oak A	120	337	34	78	10	0	9	35	30-0	4	89	.231	.296	.341	68	-17	3-0	.986	-7	112	99	C118	0	-1.5
1999	Oak A	76	205	26	44	4	1	7	24	11-0	2	41	.215	.260	.346	55	-15	6-2	.987	-10	101	73	C73	0	-1.9
2000	Oak A	6	8	1	2	0	0	0	0	1-0	0	1	.250	.333	.250	52	-1	0-0	.900	-1	131	174	C5/D	0	-0.2
2001	KC A	45	121	10	19	3	0	6	15	8-1	3	26	.157	.226	.331	40	-11	1-1	.987	-1	125	62	C43,D2	0	-0.9
2002	KC A	72	197	25	49	7	1	7	27	18-0	3	35	.249	.321	.401	80	-6	3-3	.989	-5	80	62	C68	0	-0.7
2003	Det A	27	74	7	15	3	1	3	11	3-0	2	18	.203	.247	.392	70	-4	0-0	.983	-7	54	59	C27	42	-0.9
2004	Phi N	4	11	1	2	1	0	0	0	0-0	0	4	.182	.182	.273	15	-1	0-0	1.000	1	156	321	C4	0	-0.1
Total	7	350	953	104	209	28	3	32	112	71-1	14	214	.219	.280	.356	64	-55	13-6	.987	-30	101	81	C338,D3	42	-6.2

HINCHMAN, HARRY Harry Sibley; B8.4.1878 Philadelphia PA; D1.19.1933 Toledo OH; BB/TR/5´11˝/165; d7.29; b–Bill

YEAR	TM LG	G	AB	R	H	2B	3B	HR	RBI	BB-IB	HP	SO	AVG	OBP	SLG	AOPS	ABR	SB-CS	FA	FR	RNG	THR	GAMES AT POSITION	DL	BFW
1907	Cle A	15	51	3	11	3	1	0	9	5	0	—	.216	.286	.314	90	0	2	.904	3	135	106	2b15	—	0.3

HINCHMAN, BILL William White; B4.4.1883 Philadelphia PA; D2.20.1963 Columbus OH; BR/TR/5´11˝/190; d9.24; C1; b–Harry; OF(330/61/357)

YEAR	TM LG	G	AB	R	H	2B	3B	HR	RBI	BB-IB	HP	SO	AVG	OBP	SLG	AOPS	ABR	SB-CS	FA	FR	RNG	THR	GAMES AT POSITION	DL	BFW
1905	Cin N	17	51	10	13	4	1	0	10	13	1	—	.255	.415	.373	122	2	4	.905	-2	65	251	O12L,3b4/1	—	0.0
1906	Cin N	18	54	7	11	1	1	0	1	8	0	—	.204	.306	.259	73	-1	2	.963	1	153	415	O16(8/0/8)	—	-0.2
1907	Cle A	152	514	62	117	19	9	1	50	47	**15**	—	.228	.311	.305	96	-1	15	.958	-1	99	73	O148(128/14/8),1b4/2	—	-1.1
1908	Cle A	137	464	55	107	23	8	6	59	38	9	—	.231	.301	.353	112	6	9	.975	-9	146	45	O75(23/1/51),S51,1b4	—	-0.5
1909	Cle A	139	457	57	118	20	13	2	53	41	9	—	.258	.331	.372	117	9	22	.918	0	107	27	O131(87/38/6),S6	—	0.2
1915	Pit N	**156**	577	72	177	33	14	5	77	48	8	75	.307	.368	.438	146	32	17-17	.969	2	103	96	O156(6/0/151)	—	2.5
1916	Pit N	152	555	64	175	18	**16**	4	76	54	2	61	.315	.378	.427	146	30	10	.962	-5	107	54	O124(23/0/101),1b31	—	2.1
1917	Pit N	69	244	27	46	5	5	2	29	33	1	27	.189	.288	.275	71	-8	5	.945	-1	102	84	O48(41/8/0),1b20	—	-1.3
1918	Pit N	50	111	10	26	5	2	0	13	15	2	8	.234	.336	.315	96	0	1	1.000	2	77	245	O40(2/0/32),1b3	—	0.1
1920	Pit N	18	16	0	3	0	0	0	1	1	1	3	.188	.278	.188	34	-1	0-0	ø	0	—	—	/H	—	-0.1
Total	10	908	3043	364	793	128	69	20	369	298	48	<u>174</u>	.261	.336	.368	118	68	85-<u>17</u>	.954	-13	108	79	O750R,1b63,S57,3b4/2	—	1.7

HINES, HUNKEY Henry Fred; B9.29.1867 Elgin IL; D1.2.1928 Rockford IL; BR/TR/5´7˝/165; d5.16

YEAR	TM LG	G	AB	R	H	2B	3B	HR	RBI	BB-IB	HP	SO	AVG	OBP	SLG	AOPS	ABR	SB-CS	FA	FR	RNG	THR	GAMES AT POSITION	DL	BFW
1895	Bro N	2	8	3	2	0	0	0	1	2	0	0	.250	.400	.250	76	0	0	1.000	-0	0	0	O2R	—	0.0

HINES, MIKE Michael P.; B9.1862 , Ireland; D3.14.1910 Taunton MA; BR/TL/5´10˝/176; d5.1

YEAR	TM LG	G	AB	R	H	2B	3B	HR	RBI	BB-IB	HP	SO	AVG	OBP	SLG	AOPS	ABR	SB-CS	FA	FR	RNG	THR	GAMES AT POSITION	DL	BFW
1883	Bos N	63	231	38	52	13	1	0	16	7	—	36	.225	.248	.290	61	-11	—	.887	6	—	—	C59,O7(0/2/5)	—	0.1
1884	Bos N	35	132	16	23	3	0	0	3	3	—	24	.174	.193	.197	23	-12	—	.919	4	—	—	C35	—	-0.4
1885	Bos N	14	56	11	13	4	0	0	4	4	—	5	.232	.283	.304	93	0	—	.857	-2	49	0	O14R	—	-0.2
	Bro AA	3	13	1	1	0	1	0	1	0	0	—	.077	.077	.231	-6	-2	—	1.000	-1	—	—	C3	—	-0.2

YEAR	TM LG	G	AB	R	H	2B	3B	HR	RBI	BB-IB	HP	SO	AVG	OBP	SLG	AOPS	ABR	SB-CS	FA	FR	RNG	THR	GAMES AT POSITION	DL	BFW
	Pro N	1	3	0	0	0	0	0	0	0	—	2	.000	.000	.000	-99	-1	—	.636	-1	—	—	/C	—	-0.1
1888	Bos N	4	16	3	2	0	1	0	2	2	0	0	.125	.222	.250	49	-1	0	1.000	-1	0	0	O3(2/0/1)/C	—	-0.2
Total	4	120	451	69	91	20	3	0	26	16	0	<u>67</u>	.202	.229	.259	51	-27	0	.896	5	—	—	C99,O24(2/2/20)	—	-1.0
HINES, PAUL	Paul Aloysius; B3.1.1855 VA; D7.10.1935 Hyattsville MD; BR/TR/5´9.5˝/173; d4.20; OF NA(41/85/0); OF(27/1218/7)																								
1872	Nat NA	**11**	49	9	11	1	0	0	5	0	—	0	.224	.224	.245	38	-4	0-0	.862	-3	95	0	1b9,3b2/C	—	-0.5
1873	Was NA	**39**	181	33	60	6	3	1	29	1	—	2	.331	.335	.414	124	6	0-1	.798	-0	79	0	O36L,2b2/C	—	0.4
1874	Chi NA	**59**	271	47	80	10	2	0	34	4	—	4	.295	.305	.347	108	2	4-1	.877	3	73	157	O50(1/50/0),2b11,S2	—	0.4
1875	Chi NA	**69**	308	45	101	14	4	0	36	1	—	0	.328	.330	.399	151	15	6-9	.889	7	108	258	O39(4/35/0),2b30/CS	—	1.5
1876	Chi N	64	305	62	101	**21**	3	2	59	1	—	3	.331	.333	.439	139	11	—	**.923**	4	75	209	O64C/2	—	1.1
1877	Chi N	**60**	261	44	73	11	7	0	23	1	—	8	.280	.282	.375	94	-3	—	.806	-10	45	66	O49(24/18/7),2b11	—	-1.3
1878	Pro N	**62**	257	42	92	13	4	**4**	**50**	2	—	10	.358	.363	**.486**	178	20	—	.849	1	95	161	O61C/S	—	1.7
1879	Pro N	**85**	409	81	**146**	25	10	2	52	8	—	16	.357	.369	.482	181	**35**	—	.867	5	124	149	O85C	—	3.2
1880	Pro N	85	374	64	115	20	2	3	35	13	—	17	.307	.331	.396	150	20	—	**.927**	3	91	**251**	O75C,2b6,1b4	—	1.9
1881	Pro N	80	361	65	103	**27**	5	2	31	13	—	12	.285	.310	.404	125	11	—	.897	-2	69	65	O78C,2b4/1	—	0.5
1882	Pro N	**84**	379	73	117	28	10	4	34	10	—	14	.309	.326	.467	151	21	—	.861	-2	86	117	O82C,1b2	—	1.4
1883	Pro N	97	442	94	132	32	4	4	45	18	—	23	.299	.326	.416	120	11	—	.905	5	106	72	O89C,1b9	—	1.1
1884	†Pro N	**114**	490	94	148	**36**	10	3	41	44	—	28	.302	.360	.435	151	31	—	.895	-3	87	174	O108C,1b7/P	—	2.1
1885	Pro N	98	411	63	111	20	4	1	35	19	—	18	.270	.302	.345	112	6	—	.865	2	104	127	O92C,1b4/S32	—	0.4
1886	Was N	121	487	80	152	30	8	9	56	35	—	21	.312	.358	.462	160	36	21	.899	0	108	33	O92(1/91/0),3b15,1b10,S5,2b3	—	2.9
1887	Was N	123	478	83	147	32	5	10	72	48	8	24	.308	.380	.458	141	30	46	.886	-16	72	143	O109C,1b7,2b5,S4	—	0.9
1888	Ind N	133	513	84	144	26	3	4	58	41	8	45	.281	.343	.366	124	16	31	.912	-8	63	67	O125C,1b6,S2	—	0.3
1889	Ind N	121	486	77	148	27	1	6	72	49	5	22	.305	.374	.401	113	10	34	.964	3	121	108	1b109,O12C	—	0.3
1890	Pit N	31	121	11	22	1	0	0	9	11	1	7	.182	.256	.190	34	-10	6	.973	2	219	69	1b17,O14C	—	-0.8
	Bos N	69	273	41	72	12	3	2	48	32	4	20	.264	.350	.352	97	-1	9	.881	-11	36	96	O69(2/68/0)/1	—	-1.3
	Year	100	394	52	94	13	3	2	57	43	5	27	.239	.321	.302	80	-9	15	.871	-9	45	108	O83(2/82/0),1b18	—	-2.1
1891	Was AA	54	206	25	58	7	5	0	31	21	10	16	.282	.376	.364	117	6	6	.856	-3	99	197	O47C,1b8	—	0.0
Total	4NA	178	809	134	252	31	9	1	104	6	—	6	.311	.317	.376	122	19	10-11	.857	6	86	143	O125C,2b43,1b9,S3,C3,3b2	—	1.8
Total	16	1481	6253	1083	1881	368	84	56	751	366	36	304	.301	.343	.413	133	250	153	.887	-29	86	125	O1251C,1b185,2b31,3b16,S13/P	—	14.4
HINKLE, GORDIE	Daniel Gordon; B4.3.1905 Toronto OH; D3.19.1972 Houston TX; BR/TR/6´0˝/185; d4.19																								
1934	Bos A	27	75	7	13	6	1	0	9	7	0	23	.173	.244	.280	33	-8	0-0	.992	3	*110*	*73*	C26	—	-0.3
HINSHAW, GEORGE	George Addison; B10.23.1959 Los Angeles CA; BR/TR/6´0˝/185; [SDN80 11/265]; d9.19; Col La Verne																								
1982	SD N	6	15	1	4	0	0	0	1	3-1	0	5	.267	.389	.267	92	0	0-0	1.000	0	90	261	O6(1/0/5)	0	0.0
1983	SD N	7	16	1	7	1	0	0	4	0-0	0	4	.438	.438	.500	164	1	1-0	1.000	-1	60	0	3b5	0	0.1
Total	2	13	31	2	11	1	0	0	5	3-1	0	9	.355	.412	.387	129	1	1-0	1.000	-1	90	261	O6(1/0/5),3b5	0	0.1
HINSKE, ERIC	Eric Scott; B8.5.1977 Menasha WI; BL/TR/6´2˝/(225–235); [ChiN98 17/496]; d4.1; Col Arkansas																								
2002	Tor A	151	566	99	158	38	2	24	84	77-5	2	138	.279	.365	.481	119	17	13-1	.946	-8	97	55	3b148	0	1.2
2003	Tor A	124	449	74	109	45	3	12	63	59-1	1	104	.243	.329	.437	97	-1	12-2	.930	-7	97	61	3b124	31	-0.5
2004	Tor A	155	570	66	140	23	3	15	69	54-2	4	109	.246	.312	.375	75	-22	12-8	**.978**	-8	93	89	3b153/D	0	-2.8
2005	Tor A	147	477	79	125	31	2	15	68	46-4	8	121	.262	.333	.430	97	-1	8-4	.993	3	113	94	1b100,D43	0	-0.9
2006	Tor A	78	197	35	52	9	2	12	29	27-2	0	49	.264	.353	.513	115	4	1-1	1.000	-2	84	133	O30(1/0/30),D19,3b10,1b4	0	0.0
	Bos A	31	80	8	23	8	0	1	5	8-0	0	30	.287	.352	.425	98	0	1-1	1.000	-1	79	161	O15(5/0/10),1b12,D2	0	-0.2
	Year	109	277	43	75	17	2	13	34	35-2	0	79	.271	.353	.487	110	4	2-2	1.000	-3	83	141	O45(6/0/40),D21,1b16,3b10	0	-0.2
Total	5	686	2339	361	607	154	12	79	318	271-14	15	551	.260	.337	.437	98	-3	47-17	.953	-23	95	69	3b435,1b116,D65,O45(6/0/40)	31	-3.2
HINSON, PAUL	James Paul; B5.9.1904 Vanleer TN; D9.23.1960 Muskogee OK; BR/TR/5´10˝/150; d4.19																								
1928	Bos A	3	0	1	0	0	0	0	0	0	0	0	ø	ø	ø	ø	0	0-0	ø	0	—	—	/R	—	0.0
HINTON, CHUCK	Charles Edward; B5.3.1934 Rocky Mount NC; BR/TR/6´1˝/(180–197); d5.14; Col Shaw; OF(525/201/299)																								
1961	Was A	106	339	51	88	13	5	6	34	40-1	1	81	.260	.337	.381	93	-3	22-5	.963	1	100	91	O92(72/2/20)	0	-0.4
1962	Was A	151	542	73	168	25	6	17	75	47-0	0	66	.310	.361	.472	124	18	28-10	.988	-4	88	95	O136(54/28/67),2b12/S	0	1.0
1963	Was A	150	566	80	152	20	12	15	55	64-2	1	79	.269	.340	.426	115	11	25-9	.989	1	111	91	O125(86/7/45),3b19,1b6,S2	0	0.6
1964	Was A★	138	514	71	141	25	7	11	53	57-7	1	77	.274	.346	.414	112	9	17-6	.985	7	110	103	O131(131/1/1),3b2	0	1.0
1965	Cle A	133	431	59	110	17	6	18	54	53-2	1	65	.255	.336	.448	120	11	17-3	.966	-3	94	137	O72(33/43/4),1b40,2b23/3	0	0.8
1966	Cle A	123	348	46	89	9	3	12	50	35-2	1	66	.256	.323	.402	108	3	10-6	.973	-1	99	113	O104(53/57/11),1b6,2b2	0	-0.2
1967	Cle A	147	498	55	122	19	3	10	37	43-5	1	100	.245	.304	.355	94	-4	6-8	.976	-1	103	64	O136(26/53/92),2b5	0	-1.5
1968	Cal A	116	267	28	52	10	3	7	23	24-3	0	61	.195	.259	.333	82	-7	3-1	.987	4	148	112	1b48,O37(10/6/23),3b13,2b9	0	-0.7
1969	Cle A	94	121	18	31	3	2	3	19	8-2	1	22	.256	.303	.388	91	-2	2-0	.941	-2	106	0	O40(28/4/9),3b14	0	-0.5
1970	Cle A	107	195	24	62	4	0	9	29	25-1	0	34	.318	.392	.477	133	9	0-2	.994	-4	61	81	1b40,O35(17/0/22),C4,2b3,3b2	0	0.2
1971	Cle A	88	147	13	33	7	0	5	14	20-2	0	34	.224	.317	.374	87	-2	0-0	1.000	-4	75	166	1b20,O20(15/0/5),C5	0	-0.8
Total	11	1353	3968	518	1048	152	47	113	443	416-27	7	685	.264	.332	.412	108	43	130-50	.979	-7	101	95	O928L,1b160,2b54,3b51,C9,S3	0	-0.5
HINTON, JOHN	John Robert "Red"; B6.20.1876 Pittsburgh PA; D7.19.1920 Pittsburgh PA; BR/TR/6´0˝/200; d6.3																								
1901	Bos N	4	13	0	1	0	0	0	0	2	0	—	.077	.200	.077	-17	-2	0	.750	-2	69	0	3b4	—	-0.3
HINZO, TOMMY	Thomas Lee; B6.18.1964 San Diego CA; BB/TR/5´10˝/(170–175); [CleA86 7/161]; d7.16; Col Arizona																								
1987	Cle A	67	257	31	68	9	3	3	21	10-0	2	47	.265	.296	.358	72	-11	9-4	.973	1	110	96	2b67	0	-0.5
1989	Cle A	18	17	4	0	0	0	0	0	2-0	0	6	.000	.105	.000	-67	-4	1-2	.867	-4	64	42	2b6/SD	18	-0.8
Total	2	85	274	35	68	9	3	3	21	12-0	2	53	.248	.284	.336	64	-15	10-6	.968	-2	107	93	2b73/DS	18	-1.3
HISER, GENE	Gene Taylor; B12.11.1948 Baltimore MD; BL/TL/5´11˝/(175–180); [ChiN70 1/19]; d8.20; Col Maryland																								
1971	Chi N	17	29	4	6	0	0	0	1	4-0	0	8	.207	.303	.207	41	-2	1-0	1.000	0	111	0	O9(0/4/5)	0	-0.2
1972	Chi N	32	46	2	9	0	0	0	4	6-0	0	8	.196	.288	.196	36	-4	1-0	1.000	1	95	250	O15(4/2/9)	0	-0.3
1973	Chi N	100	109	15	19	3	0	1	6	11-1	1	17	.174	.254	.229	33	-10	4-5	.980	-4	81	0	O64(25/22/18)	0	-1.7
1974	Chi N	12	17	2	4	1	0	0	1	0-0	0	3	.235	.235	.294	45	-1	0-0	1.000	0	107	0	O8(6/1/1)	0	-0.2
1975	Chi N	45	62	11	15	3	0	0	6	11-1	0	7	.242	.351	.290	77	-1	0-1	1.000	0	117	0	O18(7/6/5)/1	0	-0.2
Total	5	206	263	34	53	7	0	1	18	32-2	1	43	.202	.289	.240	46	-18	6-6	.992	-3	95	46	O114(42/35/38)/1	0	-2.6
HISLE, LARRY	Larry Eugene; B5.5.1947 Portsmouth OH; BR/TR/6´2˝/(193–195); [PhiN65 2/38]; d4.10; C4																								
1968	Phi N	7	11	1	4	1	0	0	1	1-0	0	4	.364	.417	.455	162	1	0-0	1.000	0	112	0	O6C	0	0.1
1969	Phi N	145	482	75	128	23	5	20	56	48-8	5	152	.266	.338	.459	124	15	18-8	.977	7	111	137	O140(1/139/0)	0	2.0
1970	Phi N	126	405	52	83	22	4	10	44	53-2	3	139	.205	.299	.353	76	-14	5-5	.978	1	107	72	O121(0/86/36)	0	-1.8
1971	Phi N	36	76	7	15	3	0	0	3	6-1	0	22	.197	.256	.237	40	-6	1-0	.962	2	123	157	O27(19/8/0)	0	-0.5
1973	Min A	143	545	88	148	25	6	15	64	64-2	4	128	.272	.351	.422	112	10	11-4	.975	1	102	110	O143(49/93/3)	0	0.7
1974	Min A	143	510	68	146	20	7	19	79	48-5	8	112	.286	.353	.465	131	20	12-6	.979	-5	97	44	O137(74/52/26)	0	0.9
1975	Min A	80	255	37	80	9	2	11	51	27-3	1	39	.314	.376	.494	144	15	17-3	.976	-3	93	49	O58(37/26/9),D14	54	1.2
1976	Min A	155	581	81	158	19	5	14	96	56-4	4	93	.272	.335	.394	112	9	31-18	.984	11	109	142	O154(135/5/18)	0	1.2
1977	Min A★	141	546	95	165	36	3	28	**119**	56-5	6	106	.302	.369	.533	145	35	21-10	.974	-6	90	110	O134(68/65/6),D6	0	2.6
1978	Mil A★	142	520	96	151	24	0	34	115	67-3	5	90	.290	.374	.533	152	36	10-6	.978	-5	87	100	O87(67/22/1),D51	0	2.7
1979	Mil A	26	96	18	27	7	0	3	14	11-2	0	19	.281	.352	.448	115	2	1-0	1.000	0	77	254	D15,O10L	111	0.2
1980	Mil A	17	60	16	17	0	0	6	16	14-2	1	7	.283	.421	.583	178	7	1-1	ø	0	0	0	D17	120	0.6
1981	Mil A	27	87	11	20	4	0	4	11	6-0	2	17	.230	.289	.414	107	0	0-0	ø	0	0	0	D24	97	0.0
1982	Mil A	9	31	7	4	0	0	2	5	5-0	0	13	.129	.250	.323	59	-2	0-0	ø	0	—	—	D8	150	-0.2
Total	14	1197	4205	652	1146	193	32	166	674	462-37	39	941	.273	.347	.452	123	128	128-61	.978	2	101	103	O1017(460/502/99),D135	532	9.7
HITCHCOCK, JIM	James Franklin; B6.28.1911 Inverness AL; D6.23.1959 Montgomery AL; BR/TR/5´11˝/175; d8.24; b–Billy; Col Auburn																								
1938	Bos N	28	76	2	13	0	0	0	7	2	0	11	.171	.192	.171	1	-11	1	.881	-4	93	109	S24,3b2	—	-1.3
HITCHCOCK, BILLY	William Clyde; B7.31.1916 Inverness AL; D4.9.2006 Opelika AL; BR/TR/6´1.5˝/(180–185); d4.14; Mil 1943–45; M5/C7; b–Jim; Col Auburn																								
1942	Det A	85	280	27	59	8	1	0	29	26	1	21	.211	.280	.246	45	-20	2-2	.944	-3	93	86	S80/3	0	-1.9
1946	Det A	3	3	0	0	0	0	0	0	1	0	0	.000	.250	.000	-25	0	0-0	1.000	0	122	0	/2	0	0.0
	Was A	98	354	27	75	8	3	0	25	26	1	52	.212	.268	.251	48	-26	2-4	.966	-10	94	78	S53,3b46	0	-3.6
	Year	101	357	27	75	8	3	0	25	27	1	52	.210	.268	.249	48	-26	2-4	.966	-10	94	78	S53,3b46/2	0	-3.6

YEAR	TM LG	G	AB	R	H	2B	3B	HR	RBI	BB-IB	HP	SO	AVG	OBP	SLG	AOPS	ABR	SB-CS	FA	FR	RNG	THR	GAMES AT POSITION	DL	BFW
1947	StL A	80	275	25	61	2	2	1	28	21	0	34	.222	.277	.255	47	-20	3-0	.977	6	101	97	2b46,3b17,S7,1b5	0	-1.1
1948	Bos A	49	124	15	37	3	2	1	20	7	1	9	.298	.341	.379	87	-3	0-0	.951	3	109	114	2b15,3b15	0	0.1
1949	Bos A	55	147	22	30	6	1	0	9	17	1	11	.204	.291	.259	43	-12	2-3	.993	-5	75	95	1b29,2b8	0	-1.8
1950	Phi A	115	399	35	109	22	5	1	54	45	0	32	.273	.347	.361	83	-10	3-1	.967	-0	104	105	2b107/S	0	-0.4
1951	Phi A	77	222	27	68	10	4	1	36	21	2	23	.306	.371	.401	107	2	2-0	.929	5	116	161	3b45,2b23/1	0	0.8
1952	Phi A	119	407	45	100	8	4	1	56	39	4	45	.246	.318	.292	66	-18	1-1	.942	-1	101	109	3b104,1b13	0	-2.1
1953	Det A	22	38	8	8	0	0	0	0	3	0	3	.211	.268	.211	31	-4	0-0	.929	-0	103	50	3b12/2S	0	-0.4
Total	9	703	2249	231	547	67	22	5	257	206	10	230	.243	.310	.299	65	-111	15-11	.938	-4	105	111	3b240,2b201,S142,1b48	0	-10.4

Hoag, Myril Myril Oliver; B3.9.1908 Davis CA; D7.28.1971 High Springs FL; BR/TR/5´11˝/180; d4.15; Mil 1943

YEAR	TM LG	G	AB	R	H	2B	3B	HR	RBI	BB-IB	HP	SO	AVG	OBP	SLG	AOPS	ABR	SB-CS	FA	FR	RNG	THR	GAMES AT POSITION	DL	BFW
1931	NY A	44	28	6	4	2	0	0	3	1	0	8	.143	.172	.214	1	-4	0-0	1.000	2	162	337	O23(11/2/10)/3	—	-0.3
1932	†NY A	46	54	18	20	5	0	1	7	7	0	13	.370	.443	.519	156	5	1-1	.962	2	97	371	O35(27/2/9)/1	—	0.5
1934	NY A	97	251	45	67	8	2	3	34	21	0	21	.267	.324	.351	79	-9	1-3	.974	5	112	144	O86(29/17/50)	—	-0.7
1935	NY A	48	110	13	28	4	1	1	13	12	0	19	.255	.328	.336	76	-4	4-2	.986	2	120	88	O37(2/3/32)/3	—	-0.3
1936	NY A	45	156	23	47	9	4	3	34	7	3	16	.301	.343	.468	102	-1	3-1	.955	-2	95	64	O39(2/26/12)	—	-0.3
1937	†NY A	106	362	48	109	19	8	3	46	33	3	33	.301	.364	.423	97	-2	4-7	.955	-2	96	96	O99(24/9/70)	—	-1.0
1938	†NY A	85	267	28	74	14	3	0	48	25	2	31	.277	.344	.352	75	-10	4-3	.965	-2	94	91	O70(31/13/28)	—	-1.4
1939	StL A★	129	482	58	142	23	4	10	75	24	1	35	.295	.329	.421	89	-10	9-5	.971	-2	89	**153**	O117(11/49/60)/P	—	-1.5
1940	StL A	76	191	20	50	11	0	3	26	13	0	30	.262	.309	.366	73	-8	2-0	.971	-1	85	132	O46(1/1/44)	—	-1.0
1941	StL A	1	1	0	0	0	0	0	0	0	0	0	.000	.000	.000	-97	0	0-0	ø	0	—	—	/H	0	0.0
	Chi A	106	380	30	97	13	3	1	44	27	1	29	.255	.306	.313	65	-20	6-10	.957	-5	94	71	O99(75/25/0)	0	-3.2
	Year	107	381	30	97	13	3	1	44	27	1	29	.255	.306	.312	65	-20	6-10	.957	-5	94	71	O99(75/25/0)	0	-3.2
1942	Chi A	113	412	47	99	18	2	2	37	36	0	21	.240	.301	.308	73	-15	17-8	.972	2	98	146	O112(41/81/0)	0	-1.6
1944	Chi A	17	48	5	11	1	0	0	4	10	0	1	.229	.362	.250	77	-1	1-3	.969	-0	87	173	O14(0/13/1)	0	-0.2
	Cle A	67	277	33	79	9	3	1	27	25	1	23	.285	.347	.350	103	1	6-4	.947	-5	87	131	O66C	0	-0.6
	Year	84	325	38	90	10	3	1	31	35	1	24	.277	.349	.335	99	0	7-7	.950	-5	87	137	O80(0/79/1)	0	-0.8
1945	Cle A	40	128	10	27	5	3	0	3	11	1	18	.211	.279	.297	70	-5	1-2	.987	1	96	152	O33(0/27/6),P2	0	-0.7
Total	13	1020	3147	384	854	141	33	28	401	252	12	298	.271	.328	.364	83	-83	59-49	.965	-7	96	123	O876(254/334/322),P3,3b2/1	0	-12.3

Hoak, Don Donald Albert "Tiger"; B2.5.1928 Roulette PA; D10.9.1969 Pittsburgh PA; BR/TR/6´0˝/(165–185); d4.18; C1

YEAR	TM LG	G	AB	R	H	2B	3B	HR	RBI	BB-IB	HP	SO	AVG	OBP	SLG	AOPS	ABR	SB-CS	FA	FR	RNG	THR	GAMES AT POSITION	DL	BFW
1954	Bro N	88	261	41	64	9	5	7	26	25	4	39	.245	.318	.398	83	-7	8-3	.950	3	103	100	3b75	0	-0.3
1955	†Bro N	94	279	50	67	13	3	5	19	46-0	1	50	.240	.350	.362	87	-4	9-5	.960	15	120	112	3b78	0	1.1
1956	Chi N	121	424	51	91	18	4	5	37	41-0	1	46	.215	.283	.311	61	-23	8-3	.949	-13	80	87	3b110	0	-3.7
1957	Cin N★	149	529	78	155	**39**	2	19	89	74-5	4	54	.293	.381	.482	122	20	8-15	**.971**	0	93	**105**	3b149/2	0	1.7
1958	Cin N	114	417	51	109	30	0	6	50	43-4	2	36	.261	.333	.376	83	-8	6-8	.964	5	101	**136**	3b112/S	0	-0.6
1959	Pit N	**155**	564	60	166	29	3	8	65	71-4	4	75	.294	.374	.399	108	9	9-2	.961	7	106	127	3b155	0	1.7
1960	†Pit N	**155**	553	97	156	24	9	16	79	74-9	1	74	.282	.366	.445	120	17	3-2	.948	4	107	136	3b155	0	2.1
1961	Pit N	145	503	72	150	27	7	12	61	73-8	3	53	.298	.388	.451	122	19	4-2	.953	-4	95	107	3b143	0	1.5
1962	Pit N	121	411	63	99	14	8	5	48	49-5	1	49	.241	.320	.350	81	-11	4-2	**.969**	-1	101	92	3b116	0	-1.2
1963	Phi N	115	377	35	87	11	3	6	24	27-1	1	52	.231	.282	.324	75	-13	5-5	.958	10	110	90	3b106	0	-0.3
1964	Phi N	6	4	0	0	0	0	0	0	0-0	0	2	.000	.000	.000	-99	-1	0-0	ø	0	—	—	/H	0	-0.1
Total	11	1263	4322	598	1144	214	44	89	498	523-36	22	530	.265	.345	.396	98	-2	64-47	.959	28	101	111	3b1199/S2	0	1.9

Hobbs, Bill William Lee "Smokey"; B5.7.1893 Grants Lick KY; D1.5.1945 Hamilton OH; BR/TR/5´9.5˝/155; d8.9

YEAR	TM LG	G	AB	R	H	2B	3B	HR	RBI	BB-IB	HP	SO	AVG	OBP	SLG	AOPS	ABR	SB-CS	FA	FR	RNG	THR	GAMES AT POSITION	DL	BFW
1913	Cin N	4	4	0	0	0	0	0	0	0	0	3	.000	.000	.000	-99	-1	0	1.000	0	199	0	/23	—	-0.1
1916	Cin N	6	11	1	2	1	0	0	1	2	0	0	.182	.308	.273	81	0	1	.947	4	160	127	S6	—	0.4
Total	2	10	15	1	2	1	0	0	1	2	0	3	.133	.235	.200	32	-1	1	.947	4	160	127	S6/32	—	0.3

Hoblitzel, Dick Richard Carleton "Doc" (b Hoblitzell); B10.26.1888 Waverly WV; D11.14.1962 Parkersburg WV; BL/TL/6´0˝/172; d9.5; Mil 1918–20; Col Pittsburgh

YEAR	TM LG	G	AB	R	H	2B	3B	HR	RBI	BB-IB	HP	SO	AVG	OBP	SLG	AOPS	ABR	SB-CS	FA	FR	RNG	THR	GAMES AT POSITION	DL	BFW
1908	Cin N	32	114	8	29	3	2	0	8	7	2	—	.254	.309	.316	102	0	2	.985	2	123	79	1b32	—	0.1
1909	Cin N	142	517	59	159	23	11	4	67	44	2	—	.308	.364	.418	144	25	17	.982	-3	95	111	1b142	—	2.1
1910	Cin N	155	611	85	170	24	13	4	70	47	2	32	.278	.332	.380	112	7	28	.984	-7	80	71	1b148,2b7	—	-0.3
1911	Cin N	158	622	81	180	19	13	11	91	42	8	44	.289	.342	.415	116	9	32	.990	2	102	92	1b158	—	0.7
1912	Cin N	148	558	73	164	32	12	2	85	48	2	28	.294	.352	.405	110	7	23	.985	2	107	90	1b147	—	0.5
1913	Cin N	137	502	59	143	23	7	3	62	35	2	26	.285	.334	.376	103	1	18-12	.988	-5	82	105	1b134	—	-0.7
1914	Cin N	78	248	31	52	8	7	0	26	26	1	26	.210	.287	.298	72	-9	7	.988	-4	74	107	1b75	—	-1.7
	Bos A	69	229	31	73	10	3	0	33	19	6	21	.319	.386	.389	133	10	12-12	.979	-5	74	80	1b68	—	0.1
1915	†Bos A	124	399	54	113	15	12	2	61	38	4	26	.283	.351	.396	128	12	9-14	.987	-1	95	100	1b117	—	0.6
1916	†Bos A	130	417	57	108	17	1	0	39	47	3	28	.259	.338	.305	93	-2	10	.989	-1	95	102	1b126	—	-0.7
1917	Bos A	120	420	49	108	19	7	1	47	46	4	22	.257	.336	.343	108	5	12	.990	-8	73	97	1b118	—	-0.7
1918	Bos A	25	69	4	11	1	0	0	4	8	2	3	.159	.266	.174	33	-5	3	.996	1	118	171	1b19	—	-0.5
Total	11	1318	4706	591	1310	194	88	27	593	407	38	256	.278	.341	.374	111	60	173-38	.987	-28	91	96	1b1284,2b7	—	-0.5

Hobson, Butch Clell Lavern; B8.17.1951 Tuscaloosa AL; BR/TR/6´1˝/(190–193); [BosA73 8/185]; d9.7; M3; Col Alabama

YEAR	TM LG	G	AB	R	H	2B	3B	HR	RBI	BB-IB	HP	SO	AVG	OBP	SLG	AOPS	ABR	SB-CS	FA	FR	RNG	THR	GAMES AT POSITION	DL	BFW
1975	Bos A	2	4	0	1	0	0	0	0	0-0	0	2	.250	.250	.250	38	0	0-0	1.000	0	131	0	/3	0	0.0
1976	Bos A	76	269	34	63	7	5	8	34	15-1	0	62	.234	.272	.387	83	-7	0-1	.936	-6	97	87	3b76	0	-1.5
1977	Bos A	159	593	77	157	33	5	30	112	27-4	4	162	.265	.300	.489	100	-2	5-4	.946	-18	88	92	3b159	0	-2.3
1978	Bos A	147	512	65	128	26	2	17	80	50-3	0	122	.250	.312	.408	93	-5	1-0	.899	-8	98	98	3b133,D14	0	-1.5
1979	Bos A	146	528	74	138	26	7	28	93	30-2	0	78	.261	.298	.496	105	1	3-2	.935	-16	90	64	3b142/2	0	-1.8
1980	Bos A	93	324	35	74	6	0	11	39	25-2	0	69	.228	.281	.349	69	-15	1-1	.910	1	107	46	3b57,D36	30	-1.6
1981	Cal A	85	268	27	63	7	4	4	36	35-0	1	60	.235	.321	.336	90	-3	1-1	.929	-6	87	92	3b83,D2	0	-1.1
1982	NY A	30	58	2	10	2	0	0	3	1-0	0	14	.172	.183	.207	8	-7	0-0	.951	-1	76	78	D15,1b11	19	-0.9
Total	8	738	2556	314	634	107	23	98	397	183-12	5	569	.248	.297	.423	91	-38	11-9	.926	-53	93	83	3b651,D67,1b11/2	49	-10.7

Hock, Ed Edward Francis; B3.27.1899 Franklin Furnace OH; D11.21.1963 Portsmouth OH; BL/TL/5´10.5˝/165; d7.8

YEAR	TM LG	G	AB	R	H	2B	3B	HR	RBI	BB-IB	HP	SO	AVG	OBP	SLG	AOPS	ABR	SB-CS	FA	FR	RNG	THR	GAMES AT POSITION	DL	BFW
1920	StL N	1	0	0	0	0	0	0	0	0	0	0	ø	ø	ø	ø	0	0-0	ø	-0	0	0	/lf	—	0.0
1923	Cin N	2	0	0	0	0	0	0	0	0	0	0	ø	ø	ø	ø	0	0-0	ø	0	—	—	/R	—	0.0
1924	Cin N	16	10	7	1	0	0	0	0	0	1	2	.100	.182	.100	-23	-2	0-0	1.000	0	178	0	O2(1/2/0)	—	-0.1
Total	3	19	10	7	1	0	0	0	0	0	1	2	.100	.182	.100	-23	-2	0-0	1.000	0	164	0	O3(2/2/0)	—	-0.1

Hockett, Oris Oris Leon "Brown"; B9.29.1909 Amboy IN; D3.23.1969 Torrance CA; BL/TR/5´9˝/182; d9.4

YEAR	TM LG	G	AB	R	H	2B	3B	HR	RBI	BB-IB	HP	SO	AVG	OBP	SLG	AOPS	ABR	SB-CS	FA	FR	RNG	THR	GAMES AT POSITION	DL	BFW
1938	Bro N	21	70	8	23	5	1	1	8	4	0	9	.329	.365	.471	126	2	0	.893	-2	75	91	O17(4/13/0)	—	0.0
1939	Bro N	9	13	3	3	0	0	0	1	1	0	1	.231	.286	.231	39	-1	0	1.000	1	41	1401	/lf	—	-0.1
1941	Cle A	2	6	0	2	0	0	0	1	2	0	0	.333	.500	.333	130	1	0-0	1.000	-0	56	0	O2C	0	0.0
1942	Cle A	148	601	85	150	22	7	7	48	45	3	45	.250	.305	.344	88	-13	12-12	.980	-3	94	109	O145(0/2/144)	0	-2.6
1943	Cle A	141	601	70	166	33	4	2	51	45	4	45	.276	.331	.354	107	4	13-18	.960	-4	95	113	O139(35/81/26)	0	-1.0
1944	Cle A☆	124	457	47	132	29	5	1	50	35	0	27	.289	.339	.381	110	5	8-9	.986	-6	96	58	O110(45/65/1)	0	-0.7
1945	Chi A	106	417	46	122	23	4	2	55	27	3	30	.293	.340	.381	112	6	10-9	.982	-2	98	79	O106C	0	-0.1
Total	7	551	2165	259	598	112	21	13	214	159	10	157	.276	.329	.365	103	4	43-48	.974	-16	95	96	O520(85/269/171)	0	-4.5

Hocking, Denny Dennis Lee; B4.2.1970 Torrance CA; BB/TR (BR 1997–98p)/5´10˝/(174–188); [MinA89 52/1314]; d9.10; Col El Camino (CA) JC; OF(85/51/101)

YEAR	TM LG	G	AB	R	H	2B	3B	HR	RBI	BB-IB	HP	SO	AVG	OBP	SLG	AOPS	ABR	SB-CS	FA	FR	RNG	THR	GAMES AT POSITION	DL	BFW
1993	Min A	15	36	7	5	1	0	0	0	6-0	0	8	.139	.262	.167	18	-4	1-0	.971	-1	79	169	S12/2	0	-0.4
1994	Min A	11	31	3	10	3	0	0	2	0-0	0	4	.323	.323	.419	89	-1	2-0	1.000	-1	100	116	S10	0	0.0
1995	Min A	9	25	4	5	0	2	0	3	2-1	0	2	.200	.259	.360	59	-2	1-0	.971	1	110	116	S6	0	0.0
1996	Min A	49	127	16	25	6	0	1	10	8-0	0	24	.197	.243	.268	29	-14	3-3	.985	1	99	183	O33R,S6,2b2/1D	98	-1.4
1997	Min A	115	253	28	65	12	4	2	25	18-0	1	51	.257	.308	.360	72	-11	3-5	.975	5	99	130	S44,3b39,O20(7/2/12),2b15/1D	0	-0.4
1998	Min A	110	198	32	40	6	1	3	15	16-1	0	44	.202	.259	.288	42	-18	2-1	1.000	-6	99	88	2b47,S28,O24(17/1/7),3b11,1b2,D2	0	-2.1
1999	Min A	136	386	47	103	18	2	7	41	22-1	3	54	.267	.307	.378	71	-18	11-7	.987	-9	84	87	S61,2b56,O38(17/11/13),3b6,1b2	0	-2.1
2000	Min A	134	373	52	111	24	4	4	47	48-1	0	77	.298	.373	.416	94	-2	7-5	1.000	-4	97	261	O51(16/21/19),2b47,3b16,S15,1b12/D	0	-0.4
2001	Min A	112	327	34	82	16	2	3	25	29-1	2	67	.251	.315	.339	69	-14	6-1	.983	-3	93	105	S47,2b17,O16(6/5/5),1b11,3b6,D9	0	-1.4
2002	†Min A	102	260	28	65	13	0	2	25	24-0	1	44	.250	.310	.323	68	-12	0-2	.963	-15	91	82	2b56,S25,3b16,1b6,O5(0/1/4)	0	-2.3
2003	†Min A	83	188	22	45	10	2	3	22	15-0	0	37	.239	.291	.362	70	-8	0-1	1.000	-1	80	93	2b25,3b24,S17,1b10,O8(2/2/4),D2	17	-0.8
2004	Col N	55	94	7	19	2	0	0	4	7-0	0	20	.202	.257	.223	23	-11	0-1	.975	5	162	0	O30(20/8/4),S13,2b8,3b2	0	-0.5
2005	KC A	23	60	14	16	1	0	0	7	10-0	0	10	.267	.371	.283	81	-1	0-1	.976	6	120	123	2b13/3S	0	0.5
Total	13	954	2358	294	591	112	17	25	226	205-5	7	442	.251	.310	.344	67	-116	36-27	.983	-21	91	94	2b287,S285,O225R,3b121,1b45,D16	115	-11.3

YEAR	TM LG	G	AB	R	H	2B	3B	HR	RBI	BB-IB	HP	SO	AVG	OBP	SLG	AOPS	ABR	SB-CS	FA	FR	RNG	THR	GAMES AT POSITION	DL	BFW
HODAPP, JOHNNY	Urban John; B9.26.1905 Cincinnati OH; D6.14.1980 Cincinnati OH; BR/TR/6´0˝/185; d8.19																								
1925	Cle A	37	130	12	31	5	1	0	14	11	0	7	.238	.298	.292	50	-10	2-3	.960	2	109	98	3b37	—	-0.6
1926	Cle A	3	5	0	1	0	0	0	0	0	0	1	.200	.200	.200	5	-1	0-0	.750	-1	73	0	3b3	—	-0.1
1927	Cle A	79	240	25	73	15	3	5	40	14	0	23	.304	.343	.454	105	1	2-2	.935	1	108	120	3b67,1b4	—	0.4
1928	Cle A	116	449	51	145	31	6	2	73	20	0	20	.323	.352	.432	104	2	2-1	.944	2	109	102	3b101,1b13	—	0.9
1929	Cle A	90	294	30	96	12	7	4	51	15	1	14	.327	.361	.456	105	1	3-3	.977	8	115	68	2b72	—	1.0
1930	Cle A	**154**	635	111	**225**	**51**	8	9	121	32	1	29	.354	.386	.502	119	18	6-5	.970	10	106	97	2b154	—	2.9
1931	Cle A	122	468	71	138	19	4	2	56	27	2	23	.295	.336	.365	80	-14	1-5	.969	15	110	95	2b121	—	0.6
1932	Cle A	7	16	2	2	1	0	0	0	0	0	2	.125	.125	.188	-19	-3	0-0	1.000	-1	97	0	2b7	—	-0.3
	Chi A	68	176	21	40	8	0	3	20	11	0	3	.227	.273	.324	58	-12	1-0	.967	-5	94	0	O31(29/0/2),2b5,3b4	—	-1.6
	Year	75	192	23	42	9	0	3	20	11	0	5	.219	.261	.313	51	-15	1-0	.967	-6	94	0	O31(29/0/2),2b12,3b4	—	-1.9
1933	Bos A	115	413	55	129	27	5	3	54	33	1	14	.312	.365	.424	109	6	1-1	.960	-0	99	100	2b101,1b10	—	1.1
Total	9	791	2826	378	880	169	34	28	429	163	5	136	.311	.350	.425	98	-12	18-20	.967	32	106	92	2b460,3b212,O31(29/0/2),1b27	—	4.3
HODERLEIN, MEL	Melvin Anthony; B6.26.1923 Mt.Carmel OH; D5.21.2001 Mt.Carmel OH; BB/TR/5´10˝/185; d8.16																								
1951	Bos A	9	14	1	5	1	1	0	1	6	0	2	.357	.550	.571	185	2	0-1	1.000	0	87	217	2b3,3b3	0	0.2
1952	Was A	72	208	16	56	8	2	0	17	18	2	22	.269	.333	.327	87	-4	2-0	.978	-6	97	100	2b58	0	-0.7
1953	Was A	23	47	5	9	0	0	0	5	6	0	9	.191	.283	.191	31	-5	0-0	.953	-2	96	97	2b11,S2	0	-0.5
1954	Was A	14	25	0	4	1	0	0	1	1	0	4	.160	.192	.200	8	-3	0-0	.939	0	106	123	S6,2b5	0	-0.3
Total	4	118	294	22	74	10	3	0	24	31	2	37	.252	.327	.306	78	-10	2-1	.973	-8	97	103	2b77,S8,3b3	0	-1.3
HODES, CHARLIE	Charles; B1848 New York NY; D2.14.1875 Brooklyn NY; TR/5´11.5˝/175; d5.8																								
1871	Chi NA	**28**	130	32	36	4	1	2	25	7	—	0	.277	.314	.369	86	-4	3-0	.796	3	—	—	C20,3b10,O4(0/3/1)/S	—	0.0
1872	Tro NA	13	62	17	15	3	0	0	10	1	—	0	.242	.254	.290	66	-2	0-0	.759	-0	108	0	S5,O4C,C3/3	—	-0.2
1874	Atl NA	21	81	8	12	3	0	0	7	0	—	2	.148	.148	.185	7	-7	0-0	.825	-4	40	0	O18(0/13/5),C3,2b3/1	—	-0.9
Total	3NA	62	273	57	63	10	1	2	42	8	—	2	.231	.253	.297	63	-13	3-0	.820	-2	—	—	O26(0/20/6),C26,3b11,S6,2b3/1	—	-1.1
HODGE, GOMER	Harold Morris; B4.3.1944 Rutherfordton NC; BB/TR/6´2˝/185; d4.6																								
1971	Cle A	80	83	3	17	3	0	1	9	4-1	2	19	.205	.256	.277	47	-6	0-0	1.000	-1	63	132	1b3,3b3,2b2	0	-0.7
HODGES, BERT	Edward Burton; B5.25.1917 Knoxville TN; D1.8.2001 Knoxville TN; BL/TR/5´11˝/170; d4.14																								
1942	Phi N	8	11	0	2	0	0	0	0	1	0	0	.182	.250	.182	29	-1	0	1.000	-0	91	0	3b2	0	-0.1
HODGES, GIL	Gilbert Raymond (b Gilbert Ray Hodge); B4.4.1924 Princeton IN; D4.2.1972 West Palm Beach FL; BR/TR/6´1.5˝/(200–208); d10.3; Mil 1944–45; M9; Col St. Josephs (IN)																								
1943	Bro N	1	2	0	0	0	0	0	0	1	0	2	.000	.333	.000	0	0	1	.600	-0	82	438	/3	0	-0.1
1947	†Bro N	28	77	9	12	3	1	1	7	14	0	19	.156	.286	.260	44	-6	0	.958	-1	*97*	*153*	C24	0	-0.6
1948	Bro N	134	481	48	120	18	5	11	70	43	0	61	.249	.311	.376	82	-13	7	.986	-2	92	114	1b96,C38	0	-1.6
1949	†Bro N★	**156**	596	94	170	23	4	23	115	66	4	64	.285	.360	.453	112	10	10	**.995**	-4	82	**114**	1b156	0	0.0
1950	Bro N☆	153	561	98	159	26	2	32	113	73	1	73	.283	.367	.508	125	20	6	**.994**	-1	92	**114**	1b153	0	1.4
1951	Bro N★	**158**	582	118	156	25	3	40	103	93	5	99	.268	.374	.527	137	31	9-7	.992	7	**111**	**120**	1b158	0	3.2
1952	†Bro N☆	153	508	87	129	27	1	32	102	107	2	90	.254	.386	.500	142	33	2-4	.992	4	106	114	1b153	0	3.1
1953	†Bro N★	141	520	101	157	22	7	31	122	75	3	84	.302	.393	.550	139	31	1-4	.993	7	115	108	1b127,O24(18/0/6)	0	2.7
1954	Bro N★	**154**	579	106	176	23	5	42	130	74	1	84	.304	.373	.579	142	35	3-3	.995	7	109	94	1b154	0	3.1
1955	†Bro N★	150	546	75	158	24	5	27	102	80-3	3	91	.289	.377	.500	128	24	2-1	.991	2	106	112	1b139,O16(9/1/6)	0	1.8
1956	†Bro N	153	550	86	146	29	4	32	87	76-10	0	91	.265	.354	.507	119	16	3-3	.992	1	104	112	1b138,O30(22/0/8)/C	0	0.7
1957	Bro N★	150	579	94	173	28	7	27	98	63-6	2	91	.299	.366	.511	122	19	5-3	.990	3	103	100	1b150,3b2/2	0	1.3
1958	LA N	141	475	68	123	15	1	22	64	52-3	0	87	.259	.330	.434	98	-2	8-2	.992	3	98	**128**	1b122,3b15,O9(4/0/5)/C	0	-0.4
1959	†LA N	124	413	57	114	19	2	25	80	58-6	3	92	.276	.367	.513	123	14	3-2	**.992**	1	89	87	1b113,3b4	0	0.9
1960	LA N	101	197	22	39	8	1	8	30	26-1	1	37	.198	.291	.371	76	-7	0-1	.995	1	92	106	1b92,3b10	0	-1.0
1961	LA N	109	215	25	52	4	0	8	31	24-1	0	43	.242	.313	.372	76	-8	3-1	.998	-0	85	83	1b100	0	-1.1
1962	NY N	54	127	15	32	1	0	9	17	15-1	0	27	.252	.331	.472	111	2	0-0	.986	3	140	74	1b47	59	0.3
1963	NY N	11	22	2	5	0	0	0	3	3-0	0	2	.227	.320	.227	60	-1	0-0	1.000	2	185	129	1b10	14	0.0
Total	18	2071	7030	1105	1921	295	48	370	1274	943-31	25	1137	.273	.359	.487	119	198	63-31	.992	32	101	108	1b1908,O79(53/1/25),C64,3b32/2	73	13.7
HODGES, RON	Ronald Wray; B6.22.1949 Rocky Mount VA; BL/TR/6´1˝/(180–187); [NYN72*S2/47]; d6.13; Col Appalachian St.																								
1973	†NY N	45	127	5	33	2	0	1	18	11-2	0	19	.260	.314	.299	73	-5	0-1	.992	2	156	86	C40	0	-0.1
1974	NY N	59	136	16	30	4	0	4	14	19-3	0	11	.221	.310	.338	84	-3	0-0	.953	-7	81	63	C44	0	-0.8
1975	NY N	9	34	3	7	1	0	2	4	1-0	0	6	.206	.229	.412	77	-1	0-0	1.000	-1	79	137	C9	0	-0.2
1976	NY N	56	155	21	35	6	0	4	24	27-2	0	16	.226	.339	.342	99	1	2-0	.976	-8	119	72	C52	15	-0.5
1977	NY N	66	117	6	31	4	0	1	5	9-1	0	17	.265	.317	.325	75	-4	0-2	.992	-2	82	122	C27	0	-0.6
1978	NY N	47	102	4	26	4	1	0	7	10-0	1	11	.255	.322	.314	82	-2	1-2	.982	3	82	152	C30	0	0.1
1979	NY N	59	86	4	14	4	0	0	5	19-3	0	16	.163	.311	.209	47	-5	0-0	.980	-0	99	137	C22	0	-0.5
1980	NY N	36	42	4	10	2	0	0	5	10-1	0	13	.238	.377	.286	91	0	1-1	.982	2	88	196	C9	93	0.3
1981	NY N	35	43	5	13	2	0	1	6	5-2	0	8	.302	.375	.419	125	2	1-0	1.000	-2	56	102	C7	0	0.0
1982	NY N	80	228	26	56	12	1	5	27	41-6	0	40	.246	.358	.373	105	3	4-3	.980	0	96	100	C74	0	0.7
1983	NY N	110	250	20	65	12	0	0	21	49-6	2	42	.260	.383	.308	95	2	0-3	.971	-8	86	93	C96	0	-0.4
1984	NY N	64	106	5	22	3	0	1	11	23-0	1	18	.208	.351	.264	77	-2	1-1	.979	-1	81	97	C35	0	-0.2
Total	12	666	1426	119	342	56	2	19	147	224-26	4	217	.240	.342	.322	88	-14	10-13	.978	-20	97	99	C445	108	-2.2
HODGIN, RALPH	Elmer Ralph; B2.10.1915 Greensboro NC; BL/TR/5´10˝/170; d4.19; Mil 1945																								
1939	Bos N	32	48	4	10	1	0	0	4	3	0	4	.208	.255	.229	33	-5	0	1.000	-0	108	0	O9(2/0/7)	—	-0.5
1943	Chi A	117	407	52	128	22	8	1	50	20	6	24	.314	.356	.415	125	11	3-5	.945	-2	111	70	3b56,O42(17/0/25)	0	0.7
1944	Chi A	121	465	56	137	25	7	1	51	21	6	14	.295	.333	.385	106	2	3-1	.942	7	112	143	3b82,O33L	0	0.9
1946	Chi A	87	258	32	65	10	1	0	25	19	2	6	.252	.308	.298	73	-10	0-1	.983	-2	93	73	O57(49/0/8)	0	-1.7
1947	Chi A	59	180	26	53	10	3	1	24	13	3	4	.294	.352	.400	113	3	1-0	.990	0	103	66	O41(40/0/1)	64	0.0
1948	Chi A	114	331	28	88	11	5	1	34	21	0	11	.266	.310	.338	75	-14	0-3	.970	3	102	146	O79(39/2/40)	0	-1.6
Total	6	530	1689	198	481	79	24	4	188	97	17	63	.285	.330	.367	98	-13	7-10	.985	6	102	86	O261(180/2/81),3b138	64	-2.2
HODGSON, PAUL	Paul Joseph Denis; B4.14.1960 Montreal QC, Can.; BR/TR/6´2˝/190; d8.31																								
1980	Tor A	20	41	5	9	0	1	1	5	3-0	0	12	.220	.273	.341	65	-2	0-1	1.000	-1	80	126	O11(10/1/0),D3	0	-0.4
HOELSKOETTER, ART	Arthur William "Holley","Hoss" (aka Arthur William Hostetter); B9.30.1882 St.Louis MO; D8.3.1954 St.Louis MO; BR/TR/6´2˝/?; d9.10; OF(1/7/13); ▲																								
1905	StL N	24	83	7	20	2	1	0	5	3	0	—	.241	.267	.289	68	-4	1	.972	1	108	128	3b20,2b3/P	—	-0.2
1906	StL N	94	317	21	71	6	3	0	14	4	2	—	.224	.238	.262	58	-17	2	.943	-0	110	113	3b53,S16,P12,O12(1/1/11)/2	—	-1.6
1907	StL N	119	397	21	98	6	3	2	28	27	2	—	.247	.298	.292	88	-6	5	.927	2	109	96	2b73,1b27,C8,O8(0/6/2),P2,3b2	—	-0.4
1908	StL N	62	155	10	36	7	1	0	6	6	1	—	.232	.265	.290	81	-4	1	.948	-6	*67*	*112*	C41,3b2/12	—	-0.6
Total	4	299	952	59	225	21	8	2	53	40	5	—	.236	.271	.282	75	-31	9	.924	-2	106	94	2b78,3b77,C49,1b28,O20R,S16,P15	—	-2.8
HOEY, JACK	John Bernard; B11.10.1881 Watertown MA; D11.14.1947 Waterbury CT; BL/TL/5´9˝/185; d6.27; Col Holy Cross																								
1906	Bos A	94	361	27	88	8	4	0	24	14	1	—	.244	.274	.288	76	-11	10	.915	-7	59	0	O94L	—	-2.6
1907	Bos A	39	96	7	21	2	1	0	8	1	0	—	.219	.227	.260	56	-5	2	.857	-4	0	0	O21(17/4/0)	—	-1.1
1908	Bos A	13	43	5	7	0	0	0	3	0	0	—	.163	.163	.163	6	-5	1	1.000	1	189	0	O11R	—	-0.5
Total	3	146	500	39	116	10	5	0	35	15	1	—	.232	.256	.272	66	-21	13	.913	-10	60	0	O126(111/4/11)	—	-4.2
HOFFERTH, STEW	Stewart Edward; B1.27.1913 Logansport IN; D3.7.1994 Valparaiso IN; BR/TR/6´2˝/195; d4.19																								
1944	Bos N	66	180	14	36	8	0	1	26	11	0	5	.200	.246	.261	41	-14	0	.984	-1	*63*	*112*	C47	0	-1.3
1945	Bos N	50	170	13	40	2	0	3	15	14	1	11	.235	.297	.300	66	-8	1	.980	4	*102*	*140*	C45	0	-0.1
1946	Bos N	20	58	3	12	1	1	0	10	3	0	6	.207	.246	.259	43	-5	0	1.000	-1	*78*	*48*	C15	0	-0.6
Total	3	136	408	30	88	11	1	4	51	28	1	22	.216	.268	.277	52	-27	1	.985	2	*82*	*115*	C107	0	-2.0
HOFFMAN, DUTCH	Clarence Casper "Red"; B1.28.1904 Freeburg IL; D12.6.1962 Belleville IL; BR/TR/6´0˝/175; d4.23																								
1929	Chi A	107	337	27	87	16	5	3	37	24	0	28	.258	.307	.362	73	-15	6-3	.984	-0	106	45	O88(2/74/12)	—	-1.8

YEAR	TM LG	G	AB	R	H	2B	3B	HR	RBI	BB-IB	HP	SO	AVG	OBP	SLG	AOPS	ABR	SB-CS	FA	FR	RNG	THR	GAMES AT POSITION	DL	BFW
HOFFMAN, DANNY	Daniel John; B3.2.1880 Canton CT; D3.14.1922 Manchester CT; BL/TL/5´9˝/175; d4.20																								
1903	Phi A	74	248	29	61	5	7	2	22	6	1	—	.246	.267	.347	79	-7	7	.950	-0	57	0	O62(43/0/19)/P	—	-1.2
1904	Phi A	53	204	31	61	7	5	3	24	5	4	—	.299	.329	.426	131	6	9	.936	-0	87	70	O51(14/14/23)	—	0.4
1905	†Phi A	120	459	66	120	10	10	1	35	33	1	—	.261	.312	.333	103	0	**46**	.942	-3	93	141	O118(14/102/2)	—	-1.0
1906	Phi A	7	22	4	5	0	0	0	0	3	0	—	.227	.320	.227	70	-1	1	1.000	1	240	0	O7C	—	0.0
	NY A	100	320	34	82	10	6	0	23	27	2	—	.256	.318	.325	92	-3	32	.938	-3	67	46	O98C	—	-1.1
	Year	107	342	38	87	10	6	0	23	30	2	—	.254	.318	.319	91	-3	33	.943	-3	80	43	O105C	—	-1.1
1907	NY A	136	517	81	131	10	3	5	46	42	13	—	.253	.325	.313	96	-1	30	.953	4	116	90	O135C	—	-0.4
1908	StL A	99	363	41	91	9	7	1	25	23	5	—	.251	.304	.322	103	1	17	.962	9	168	270	O99(6/46/47)	—	0.6
1909	StL A	110	387	44	104	6	7	2	26	41	7	—	.269	.349	.336	125	12	24	.968	1	75	194	O110(0/109/1)	—	1.0
1910	StL A	106	380	20	90	11	5	0	27	34	4	—	.237	.306	.292	93	-3	16	.960	-2	97	92	O106(0/102/4)	—	-1.1
1911	StL A	24	81	11	17	3	2	0	7	12	2	—	.210	.326	.296	77	-2	3	.908	2	113	145	O23C	—	-0.2
Total	9	829	2981	361	762	71	52	14	235	226	39	—	.256	.316	.328	101	2	185	.951	8	100	122	O809(77/636/96)/P	—	-3.0
HOFFMAN, TEX	Edward Adolph; B11.30.1893 San Antonio TX; D5.19.1947 New Orleans LA; BL/TR/5´9˝/195; d7.11																								
1915	Cle A	9	13	1	2	0	0	0	2	1	0	5	.154	.214	.154	10	-1	0	.750	-1	59	0	3b3	—	-0.3
HOFFMAN, GLENN	Glenn Edward; B7.7.1958 Orange CA; BR/TR/6´2˝/(180–190); [BosA76 2/46]; d4.12; M1/C8; b–Trevor																								
1980	Bos A	114	312	37	89	15	4	4	42	19-2	2	41	.285	.326	.397	93	-3	2-4	.946	-3	103	85	3b110,S5,2b2	0	-0.8
1981	Bos A	78	242	28	56	10	0	1	20	12-0	1	25	.231	.271	.285	57	-14	0-1	.960	3	102	108	S78/3	0	-0.4
1982	Bos A	150	469	53	98	23	2	7	49	30-5	5	69	.209	.262	.311	54	-30	0-4	.972	16	104	112	S150	0	-0.1
1983	Bos A	143	473	56	123	24	1	4	41	30-1	2	76	.260	.306	.340	72	-18	1-1	.962	-6	96	93	S143	0	-0.9
1984	Bos A	64	74	8	14	4	0	0	4	5-0	0	10	.189	.241	.243	33	-7	0-1	.957	-3	88	99	S56,3b4,2b2	0	-0.8
1985	Bos A	96	279	40	77	17	2	6	34	25-0	5	40	.276	.343	.416	103	2	2-2	.975	5	99	115	S93,2b3,3b3	27	1.4
1986	Bos A	12	23	1	5	2	0	0	1	2-0	0	3	.217	.269	.304	59	-1	0-0	.923	-3	53	72	S11/3	76	-0.3
1987	Bos A	21	55	5	11	3	0	0	6	3-0	2	9	.200	.267	.255	38	-5	0-0	.984	2	122	103	S16,3b3,2b2	0	-0.1
	LA N	40	132	10	29	5	0	0	10	7-1	2	23	.220	.270	.258	42	-11	0-1	.966	-1	90	87	S40	0	-0.9
1989	Cal A	48	104	9	22	3	0	1	3	3-0	1	13	.212	.241	.269	44	-8	0-2	.982	-1	92	101	S23,3b18,2b4/1D	0	-0.8
Total	9	766	2163	247	524	106	9	23	210	136-9	20	309	.242	.291	.331	68	-95	5-16	.966	9	99	103	S615,3b140,2b13/D1	103	-3.7
HOFFMAN, IZZY	Harry C.; B1.5.1875 Bridgeport NJ; D11.13.1942 Philadelphia PA; BL/TL/5´9˝/160; d4.14																								
1904	Was A	10	30	1	3	1	0	0	1	2	0	—	.100	.156	.133	-8	-4	0	1.000	1	110	365	O9C	—	-0.4
1907	Bos N	19	86	17	24	3	1	0	3	6	0	—	.279	.326	.337	108	1	2	.897	-2	143	133	O19(3/1/16)	—	-0.2
Total	2	29	116	18	27	4	1	0	4	8	0	—	.233	.282	.284	79	-3	2	.939	-1	133	201	O28(3/10/16)	—	-0.6
HOFFMAN, JOHN	John Edward "Pork Chop"; B10.31.1943 Aberdeen SD; D12.27.2001 Seattle WA; BL/TR/6´0˝/195; d7.30																								
1964	Hou N	6	15	1	1	0	0	0	0	1-0	0	7	.067	.125	.067	-47	-3	0-0	1.000	-2	38	0	C5	0	-0.5
1965	Hou N	2	6	1	2	0	0	0	1	0-0	0	3	.333	.333	.333	95	0	0-0	1.000	-0	55	0	C2	0	0.0
Total	2	8	21	2	3	0	0	0	1	1-0	0	10	.143	.182	.143	-8	-3	0-0	1.000	-2	42	0	C7	0	-0.5
HOFFMAN, LARRY	Lawrence Charles; B7.18.1878 Chicago IL; D12.29.1948 Chicago IL; BR/TR/5´8˝/175; d7.4																								
1901	Chi N	6	22	2	7	1	0	0	6	0	1	—	.318	.348	.364	110	0	1	.800	-1	75	0	3b5/2	—	-0.1
HOFFMAN, RAY	Raymond Lamont; B6.14.1917 Detroit MI; BL/TR/6´0.5˝/175; d8.30																								
1942	Was A	7	19	2	1	0	0	0	2	1	0	1	.053	.100	.053	-57	-4	0-0	.815	1	135	0	3b6	0	-0.4
HOFFMAN, HICKEY	William A.; B1853 Cleveland OH; d5.10																								
1879	Cle N	2	6	0	0	0	0	0	0	0	—	3	.000	.000	.000	-99	-1	—	.857	0	—	—	C2/rf	—	-0.1
HOFFMEISTER, JESSE	Jesse H.; B6.1872 Toledo OH; D1.14.1933 Des Moines IA; TR; d7.24																								
1897	Pit N	48	188	33	58	6	9	3	36	8	0	—	.309	.337	.484	120	3	6	.792	-10	82	129	3b48	—	-0.5
HOFMAN, SOLLY	Arthur Frederick "Circus Solly"; B10.29.1882 St.Louis MO; D3.10.1956 St.Louis MO; BR/TR/6´0˝/160; d7.28; OF(77/557/79)																								
1903	Pit N	3	2	1	0	0	0	0	0	0	0	—	.000	.000	.000	-97	-1	0	ø	-0	0	0	O2(1/1/0)	—	-0.1
1904	Chi N	7	26	7	7	0	0	1	4	1	0	—	.269	.296	.385	110	0	2	1.000	0	296	560	O6(1/3/2)/S	—	0.0
1905	Chi N	86	287	43	68	14	4	1	38	20	1	—	.237	.289	.324	79	-8	15	.955	2	99	81	2b59,1b9,S9,3b3,O3(0/2/1)	—	-0.6
1906	†Chi N	64	195	30	50	2	3	2	20	20	0	—	.256	.326	.328	98	-1	13	.976	-1	84	205	O23(1/17/6),1b21,S9,2b4,3b4	—	-0.2
1907	Chi N	134	470	67	126	11	3	1	36	41	1	—	.268	.328	.311	94	-3	29	.938	-3	126	170	O69(12/23/35),S42,1b18,3b4,2b3	—	-0.9
1908	†Chi N	120	411	55	100	15	5	2	42	33	6	—	.243	.309	.319	96	-1	15	.955	-3	128	65	O50(0/50/2),1b37,2b22,3b9	—	-0.9
1909	Chi N	153	527	60	150	21	4	2	58	53	1	—	.285	.351	.351	115	10	20	.965	-2	71	115	O153(0/143/11)	—	0.1
1910	†Chi N	136	477	83	155	24	16	3	86	65	0	34	.325	.406	.461	154	33	29	.975	-0	97	124	O110(0/110/1),1b24/3	—	2.8
1911	Chi N	143	512	66	129	17	2	2	70	66	3	40	.252	.341	.305	81	-11	30	.968	-11	89	67	O107(2/107/0),1b36	—	-3.0
1912	Chi N	36	125	28	34	11	0	0	18	22	1	13	.272	.385	.360	105	2	5	.987	2	99	158	O27C,1b9	—	0.2
	Pit N	17	53	7	15	4	1	0	2	5	0	6	.283	.345	.396	104	0	0	1.000	2	113	133	O15C	—	0.1
	Year	53	178	35	49	15	1	0	20	27	1	19	.275	.374	.371	105	3	5	.991	3	104	150	O42C,1b9	—	0.3
1913	Pit N	28	83	11	19	5	2	0	7	8	0	6	.229	.297	.337	84	-2	3-3	.964	0	101	101	O24(0/23/2)	—	-0.3
1914	Bro F	147	515	65	148	25	12	5	83	54	2	41	.287	.357	.412	110	-1	34	.951	-1	96	92	2b108,1b22,O21(10/10/1)/S	—	-0.2
1915	Buf F	109	346	29	81	10	6	0	27	30	0	28	.234	.295	.298	66	-21	12	.961	3	91	157	O82(46/20/18),1b11,3b4,2b2/S	—	-2.5
1916	NY A	6	27	0	8	1	1	0	2	1	0	1	.296	.321	.407	116	0	1	1.000	1	107	206	O6C	—	0.1
	Chi N	5	16	2	5	2	1	0	2	2	0	2	.313	.389	.563	172	1	0	1.000	0	89	234	O4L	—	0.2
Total	14	1194	4072	554	1095	162	60	19	495	421	15	171	.269	.340	.352	102	-3	208-3	.967	-10	98	128	O702C,2b198,1b187,S63,3b25	—	-5.2
HOFMAN, BOBBY	Robert George; B10.5.1925 St.Louis MO; D4.5.1994 Chesterfield MO; BR/TR/5´11˝/(170–185); d4.19; C10																								
1949	NY N	19	48	4	10	0	0	0	3	5	1	6	.208	.296	.208	38	-4	0	.939	0	119	103	2b16	0	-0.3
1952	NY N	32	63	11	18	2	2	2	4	8	1	10	.286	.375	.476	134	3	0-0	.964	-0	104	93	2b21,3b2/1	0	0.4
1953	NY N	74	169	21	45	7	2	12	34	12	0	23	.266	.315	.544	117	3	1-1	.918	0	98	117	3b23,2b17	0	0.4
1954	NY N	71	125	12	28	5	0	8	30	17	1	15	.224	.317	.456	99	0	0-0	.994	-5	51	140	1b21,2b10,3b8	0	-0.5
1955	NY N	96	207	32	55	7	2	10	28	22-2	1	31	.266	.336	.464	110	3	0-2	1.000	-3	69	101	1b24,C19,2b19,3b5	0	-0.1
1956	NY N	47	56	1	10	1	0	0	2	6-0	1	8	.179	.270	.196	28	-6	0-0	1.000	0	*135*	*0*	C7,3b7,1b3,2b2	0	-0.5
1957	NY N	2	2	0	0	0	0	0	0	0-0	0	1	.000	.000	.000	-99	-1	0-0	ø	0	—	—	/H	0	-0.1
Total	7	341	670	81	166	22	6	32	101	70-2	5	94	.248	.322	.442	100	-2	1-3	.969	-7	104	93	2b85,1b49,3b45,C26	0	-0.7
HOFMANN, FRED	Fred "Bootnose"; B6.10.1894 St.Louis MO; D11.19.1964 St.Helena CA; BR/TR/5´11.5˝/175; d9.26; C13																								
1919	NY A	1	1	0	0	0	0	0	0	0	0	0	.000	.000	.000	-99	0	0	1.000	0	*0*	*446*	/C	—	0.0
1920	NY A	15	24	3	7	0	0	0	1	1	1	2	.292	.346	.292	68	-1	0-0	.905	-2	*84*	*33*	C14	—	-0.3
1921	NY A	23	62	7	11	1	1	1	5	5	1	13	.177	.250	.274	33	-7	0-0	.952	-1	*110*	*81*	C18/1	—	-0.6
1922	NY A	37	91	13	27	5	3	2	10	9	0	12	.297	.360	.484	116	2	0-0	.962	-2	*133*	*60*	C29	—	0.1
1923	†NY A	72	238	24	69	10	4	3	26	18	4	27	.290	.350	.403	96	-2	2-1	.979	-3	*124*	*55*	C70	—	0.0
1924	NY A	62	166	17	29	6	1	1	11	12	2	15	.175	.239	.241	24	-20	2-1	.991	2	*111*	*112*	C54	—	-1.4
1925	NY A	3	2	0	0	0	0	0	0	0	0	0	.000	.000	.000	-99	-1	0-0	1.000	0	*0*	*930*	/C	—	-0.1
1927	Bos A	87	217	20	59	19	1	0	24	21	2	26	.272	.342	.369	86	-4	2-0	.943	-10	*66*	*77*	C81	—	-0.8
1928	Bos A	78	199	14	45	8	1	0	16	11	1	25	.226	.270	.276	45	-16	0-1	.982	-1	*82*	*135*	C71	—	-1.3
Total	9	378	1000	98	247	49	11	7	93	77	11	120	.247	.308	.339	68	-49	6-3	.969	-16	*98*	*89*	C339/1	—	-4.4
HOGAN, HARRY	Harry Sweet; B11.1.1876 Syracuse NY; D1.24.1934 Syracuse NY; d8.13																								
1901	Cle A	1	4	0	0	0	0	0	0	0	0	—	.000	.000	.000	-99	-1	0	ø	-0	0	0	/rf	—	-0.1
HOGAN, SHANTY	James Francis; B3.21.1906 Somerville MA; D4.7.1967 Boston MA; BR/TR/6´1˝/240; d6.23																								
1925	Bos N	9	21	2	6	1	1	0	3	1	0	3	.286	.318	.429	97	0	0-0	1.000	-0	98	0	O5(2/0/3)	—	-0.1
1926	Bos N	4	14	1	4	1	1	0	5	0	0	0	.286	.286	.500	119	0	0	.852	-1	*76*	*113*	C4	—	0.0
1927	Bos N	71	229	24	66	17	1	3	32	9	3	23	.288	.324	.410	104	1	2	.985	1	*99*	*128*	C61	—	0.6
1928	NY N	131	411	48	137	25	2	10	71	42	8	25	.333	.406	.477	129	19	0	.978	-3	*140*	*56*	C124	—	2.3
1929	NY N	102	317	19	95	13	0	5	45	25	6	22	.300	.362	.388	86	-6	1	.979	1	***139***	*52*	C93	—	0.0
1930	NY N	122	389	60	132	26	2	13	75	21	3	24	.339	.378	.517	116	10	2	.982	-2	*103*	*89*	C96	—	1.3
1931	NY N	123	396	42	119	17	1	12	65	29	4	29	.301	.354	.439	115	8	1	**.996**	5	***144***	*88*	C113	—	1.9
1932	NY N	140	502	36	144	18	2	8	77	26	1	22	.287	.323	.378	90	-8	0	.983	-5	*98*	*93*	C136	—	-0.5

YEAR	TM LG	G	AB	R	H	2B	3B	HR	RBI	BB-IB	HP	SO	AVG	OBP	SLG	AOPS	ABR	SB-CS	FA	FR	RNG	THR	GAMES AT POSITION	DL	BFW
1933	Bos N	96	328	15	83	7	0	3	30	13	3	9	.253	.288	.302	75	-12	0	**.997**	2	***188***	*89*	C95	—	-0.4
1934	Bos N	92	279	20	73	5	2	4	34	16	6	13	.262	.316	.337	81	-8	0	.986	-1	*111*	*113*	C90	—	-0.4
1935	Bos N	59	163	9	49	8	0	2	25	21	4	8	.301	.394	.387	120	6	0	.990	-5	*88*	*79*	C56	—	0.5
1936	Was A	19	65	8	21	4	0	1	7	11	0	2	.323	.421	.431	117	2	0-1	.989	1	*91*	*81*	C19	—	0.4
1937	Was A	21	66	4	10	4	0	0	5	6	0	8	.152	.222	.212	10	-9	0-1	.979	1	*97*	*170*	C21	—	-0.7
Total	13	989	3180	288	939	146	12	61	474	220	38	188	.295	.348	.406	101	3	6-2	.985	-5	*124*	*88*	C908,O5(2/0/3)	—	4.9
Hogan, Kenny	Kenneth Sylvester; B10.9.1902 Cleveland OH; D1.2.1980 Cleveland OH; BL/TR/5´9˝/145; d10.2																								
1921	Cin N	1	2	0	0	0	0	0	0	0	0	1	.000	.000	.000	-99	-1	0-0	ø	-0	0	0	/cf	—	-0.1
1923	Cle A	1	0	0	0	0	0	0	0	0	0	0	ø	ø	ø	ø	0	0-0	ø	0	—	—	/R	—	0.0
1924	Cle A	2	1	0	0	0	0	0	0	0	0	0	.000	.000	.000	-99	0	0-0	ø	0	—	—	/H	—	0.0
Total	3	4	3	0	0	0	0	0	0	0	0	1	.000	.000	.000	-99	-1	0-0	.000	-0	0	0	/cf	—	-0.1
Hogan, Marty	Martin F.; B10.25.1869 Wednesbury, England; D8.15.1923 Youngstown OH; BR/TR/5´8˝/145; d8.6																								
1894	Cin N	6	23	4	3	0	0	0	3	1	0	4	.130	.167	.130	-27	-5	2	.846	-0	109	0	O6R	—	-0.4
	StL N	29	100	11	28	3	4	0	13	3	1	13	.280	.308	.390	67	-6	7	.887	1	121	517	O29(1/1/28)	—	-0.5
	Year	35	123	15	31	3	4	0	16	4	1	17	.252	.281	.341	49	-11	9	.879	1	119	423	O35(1/1/34)	—	-0.9
1895	StL N	5	18	2	3	1	0	0	2	3	0	0	.167	.286	.222	33	-2	2	.833	0	235	0	O5C	—	-0.1
Total	2	40	141	17	34	4	4	0	18	7	1	17	.241	.282	.326	47	-13	11	.869	1	137	355	O40(1/6/34)	—	-1.0
Hogan, Eddie	Mortimer Edward; B1862 IL; D3.17.1923 Chicago IL; BR; d9.27																								
1884	Mil U	11	37	6	3	1	0	0	—	7	—	—	.081	.227	.108	9	-4	—	.806	6	306	377	O11R	—	0.2
1887	NY AA	32	120	22	24	6	1	0	5	30	3	—	.200	.373	.267	84	0	12	.750	-6	108	88	O29(1/2/26),S4/3	—	-0.5
1888	Cle AA	78	269	60	61	16	6	0	24	50	10	—	.227	.368	.331	128	13	30	.896	-4	65	34	O78(26/0/52)	—	0.8
Total	3	121	426	88	88	23	7	0	<u>29</u>	87	13	—	.207	.357	.293	108	9	42	.844	-4	100	83	O118(27/2/89),S4/3	—	0.5
Hogan, Willie	William Henry; B9.14.1884 N.San Juan CA; D9.28.1974 San Jose CA; BR/TR/5´10˝/175; d4.12; b–George; Col Santa Clara																								
1911	Phi A	7	19	1	2	1	0	0	2	0	0	—	.105	.105	.158	-27	-3	0	.900	1	89	297	O6L	—	-0.3
	StL A	123	443	53	115	17	8	2	62	43	2	—	.260	.328	.348	92	-5	18	.929	11	116	133	O117(115/0/2),1b5	—	0.1
	Year	130	462	54	117	18	8	2	64	43	2	—	.253	.320	.340	87	-8	18	.928	12	**115**	139	O123(121/0/2),1b5	—	-0.2
1912	StL A	108	360	32	77	10	2	1	36	34	1	—	.214	.284	.261	58	-20	17	.972	10	117	107	O100(91/5/4)	—	-1.4
Total	2	238	822	86	194	28	10	3	100	77	3	—	.236	.304	.305	75	-28	35	.947	22	116	125	O223(212/5/6),1b5	—	-1.6
Hogg, Willy	Wilbert George "Sonny"; B4.21.1913 Detroit MI; D11.5.1973 Detroit MI; BR/TR/5´11.5˝/162; d6.1																								
1934	Bro N	2	1	0	0	0	0	0	0	0	0	0	.000	.000	.000	-99	0	0	ø	-0	0	0	/3	—	0.0
Hogriever, George	George C.; B3.17.1869 Cincinnati OH; D1.26.1961 Appleton WI; BR/TR/5´8˝/160; d4.24																								
1895	Cin N	69	239	61	65	8	7	2	34	36	3	17	.272	.374	.389	93	-2	41	.934	0	100	134	O66(10/48/8),2b3	—	-0.5
1901	Mil A	54	221	25	52	10	2	0	16	30	1	—	.235	.329	.299	79	-5	7	.901	-2	36	51	O54(49/5/0)	—	-1.0
Total	2	123	460	86	117	18	9	2	50	66	4	<u>17</u>	.254	.353	.346	87	-7	48	.920	-2	68	93	O120(59/53/8),2b3	—	-1.5
Hohman, Bill	William Henry; B11.27.1903 Brooklyn MD; D10.29.1968 Baltimore MD; BR/TR/6´0˝/178; d8.24																								
1927	Phi N	7	18	1	5	0	0	0	0	2	0	3	.278	.350	.278	69	-1	0	.917	0	102	226	O6L	—	-0.1
Hohnhorst, Eddie	Edward Hicks; B1.31.1885 Covington KY; D3.28.1916 Covington KY; BL/TL/6´1˝/175; d9.10																								
1910	Cle A	18	63	8	20	3	1	0	6	4	0	—	.317	.358	.397	135	2	3	.972	-1	77	117	1b18	—	0.1
1912	Cle A	15	54	5	11	1	0	0	2	2	0	—	.204	.232	.222	29	-5	5	.963	-1	90	120	1b15	—	-0.7
Total	2	33	117	13	31	4	1	0	8	6	0	—	.265	.301	.316	83	-3	8	.968	-2	83	118	1b33	—	-0.6
Hoiles, Chris	Christopher Allen; B3.20.1965 Bowling Green OH; BR/TR/6´0˝/(195–215); [DetA86 19/489]; d4.25; Col Eastern Michigan																								
1989	Bal A	6	9	0	1	1	0	0	1	1-0	0	3	.111	.200	.222	19	-1	0-0	1.000	1	0	0	C3,D3	0	0.0
1990	Bal A	23	63	7	12	3	0	1	6	5-1	0	12	.190	.250	.286	51	-4	0-0	1.000	-1	90	214	C7,1b6,D7	0	-0.6
1991	Bal A	107	341	36	83	15	0	11	31	29-1	1	61	.243	.304	.384	93	-4	0-2	**.998**	-7	112	93	C89,D13,1b2	0	-0.8
1992	Bal A	96	310	49	85	10	1	20	40	55-2	2	60	.274	.384	.506	144	19	0-2	.994	-9	80	63	C95/D	57	1.6
1993	Bal A	126	419	80	130	28	0	29	82	69-4	9	94	.310	.416	.585	159	37	1-1	.993	11	122	102	C124,D2	21	5.3
1994	Bal A	99	332	45	82	10	0	19	53	63-2	5	73	.247	.371	.449	105	4	2-0	.989	13	133	77	C98	0	2.1
1995	Bal A	114	352	53	88	15	1	19	58	67-3	4	80	.250	.373	.460	114	9	1-0	**.996**	3	101	110	C107,D6	15	1.7
1996	†Bal A	127	407	64	105	13	0	25	73	57-1	9	97	.258	.356	.474	110	6	0-1	.992	-10	79	86	C126/1	0	0.3
1997	†Bal A	99	320	45	83	15	0	12	49	51-3	10	86	.259	.375	.419	111	7	1-0	**1.000**	-2	78	72	C87,1b4/3D	31	1.1
1998	Bal A	97	267	36	70	12	0	15	56	38-0	4	50	.262	.358	.476	118	7	0-1	**.995**	-4	55	112	C83,1b6,D6	0	0.7
Total	10	894	2820	415	739	122	2	151	449	435-17	44	616	.262	.366	.467	118	80	5-7	.994	-6	96	90	C819,D46,1b19/3	124	11.4
Holbert, Aaron	Aaron Keith; B1.9.1973 Torrance CA; BR/TR/6´0˝/(160–180); [StLN90 1/18]; d4.14; b–Ray																								
1996	StL N	1	3	0	0	0	0	0	0	0-0	0	0	.000	.000	.000	-99	-1	0-0	1.000	-1	62	0	/2	0	-0.1
2005	Cin N	22	27	3	6	3	0	0	2	3-1	0	8	.222	.290	.333	66	-1	1-0	.950	1	90	133	2b4,1b2,3b2	0	0.0
Total	2	23	30	3	6	3	0	0	2	3-1	0	8	.200	.265	.300	50	-2	1-0	.952	1	86	113	2b5,3b2,1b2	0	-0.1
Holbert, Ray	Ray Arthur; B9.25.1970 Torrance CA; BR/TR/6´0˝/(175–185); [SDN88 3/58]; d5.2; b–Aaron																								
1994	SD N	5	5	1	1	0	0	0	0	0-0	0	4	.200	.200	.200	5	-1	0-0	ø	-0	0	0	/S	0	-0.1
1995	SD N	63	73	11	13	2	1	2	5	8-1	2	20	.178	.277	.315	57	-5	4-0	.940	0	103	113	S30,2b7/rf	33	-0.2
1998	Atl N	8	15	2	2	0	0	0	1	2-0	0	4	.133	.222	.133	0	-2	0-0	.952	1	112	132	S7	0	-0.1
	Mon N	2	5	0	0	0	0	0	0	0-0	0	1	.000	.000	.000	-99	-1	0-0	1.000	-0	102	0	/2	0	-0.2
	Year	10	20	2	2	0	0	0	1	2-0	0	5	.100	.174	.100	-24	-4	0-0	.952	1	112	132	S7/2	0	-0.3
1999	KC A	34	100	14	28	3	0	0	5	8-0	0	20	.280	.330	.310	63	-6	7-4	.987	-7	81	111	S22,2b11/3	0	-1.0
2000	KC A	3	4	0	1	0	0	0	0	0-0	0	2	.250	.250	.250	26	0	0-0	1.000	1	94	402	/23S	0	0.0
Total	5	115	202	28	45	5	1	2	11	18-1	2	51	.223	.290	.287	51	-15	11-4	.962	-6	94	116	S61,2b20,3b2/rf	33	-1.6
Holbert, Bill	William Henry; B3.14.1855 Baltimore MD; D3.20.1935 Laurel MD; BR/TR/?/197; d9.5; M1/U1; OF(12/19/38)																								
1876	Lou N	12	43	3	11	0	0	0	5	0	—	3	.256	.256	.256	60	-2	—	.843	6	—	—	C12	—	0.3
1878	Mil N	45	173	10	32	2	0	0	12	3	—	14	.185	.199	.197	28	-13	—	.818	5	229	76	O30R,C21	—	-0.7
1879	Syr N	59	229	11	46	0	0	0	21	1	—	20	.201	.204	.201	39	-14	—	.897	-0	—	—	C56,O4(0/3/1),M	—	-1.2
	Tro N	4	15	1	4	0	0	0	2	0	—	1	.267	.267	.267	82	0	—	.893	1	—	—	C4	—	0.0
	Year	63	244	12	50	0	0	0	23	1	—	21	.205	.208	.205	41	-15	—	.897	1	—	—	C60,O4(0/3/1)	—	-1.2
1880	Tro N	60	212	18	40	5	1	0	8	9	—	18	.189	.222	.222	48	-11	—	.911	11	—	—	C58,O3R	—	0.2
1881	Tro N	46	180	16	49	3	0	0	14	3	—	13	.272	.284	.289	77	-5	—	.918	7	—	—	C43,O3R	—	0.3
1882	Tro N	71	251	24	46	5	0	0	23	11	—	22	.183	.218	.203	38	-17	—	.892	15	—	—	C58,3b12,O3C	—	0.3
1883	NY AA	73	299	26	71	9	1	0	—	1	—	—	.237	.240	.274	62	-13	—	.920	**33**	—	—	C68,O5C/2	—	2.2
1884	†NY AA	65	255	28	53	5	0	0	—	7	2	—	.208	.235	.227	53	-13	—	.920	21	—	—	C59,O5(4/0/1)/S	—	1.2
1885	NY AA	56	202	13	35	3	0	0	13	8	0	—	.173	.205	.188	26	-17	—	.900	11	—	—	C39,O13(8/5/0),3b5	—	-0.3
1886	NY AA	48	171	8	35	4	2	0	13	6	0	—	.205	.232	.251	56	-9	4	.922	16	—	—	C45,O3C/S	—	0.9
1887	NY AA	69	255	20	58	4	3	0	32	7	0	—	.227	.248	.267	46	-19	12	.894	2	—	—	C60,1b8,S2/2	—	-1.0
1888	Bro AA	15	50	4	6	1	0	0	1	2	1	—	.120	.170	.140	-0	-6	0	.926	1	—	—	C15	—	-0.3
Total	12	623	2335	182	486	41	7	0	<u>144</u>	58	3	<u>91</u>	.208	.228	.232	47	-139	16	.907	128	—	—	C538,O69R,3b17,1b8,S4,2b2	—	1.9
Holbrook, Sammy	James Marbury; B7.17.1910 Meridian MS; D4.10.1991 Jackson MS; BR/TR/5´11˝/189; d4.25																								
1935	Was A	52	135	20	35	2	2	2	25	30	4	16	.259	.408	.348	101	2	0-0	.952	-12	*77*	*47*	C47	—	-0.7
Holden, Joe	Joseph Francis "Socks"; B6.4.1913 St.Clair PA; D5.10.1996 St.Clair PA; BL/TR/5´8˝/175; d6.14																								
1934	Phi N	10	14	1	1	0	0	0	0	0	0	2	.071	.071	.071	-54	-3	0	1.000	1	*98*	*255*	C6	—	-0.1
1935	Phi N	6	9	0	1	0	0	0	0	0	0	3	.111	.111	.111	-36	-2	1	1.000	-0	*0*	*0*	C4	—	-0.2
1936	Phi N	1	1	0	0	0	0	0	0	0	0	0	.000	.000	.000	-91	0	0	ø	0	—	—	/H	—	0.0
Total	3	17	24	1	2	0	0	0	0	0	0	5	.083	.083	.083	-49	-5	1	1.000	1	*68*	*178*	C10	—	-0.3

YEAR	TM LG	G	AB	R	H	2B	3B	HR	RBI	BB-IB	HP	SO	AVG	OBP	SLG	AOPS	ABR	SB-CS	FA	FR	RNG	THR	GAMES AT POSITION	DL	BFW
HOLDEN, BILL	William Paul; B9.7.1889 Birmingham AL; D9.14.1971 Pensacola FL; BR/TR/6´0˝/170; d9.11																								
1913	NY A	18	53	6	16	3	1	0	8	8	0	5	.302	.393	.396	131	2	0	.977	2	102	192	O16C	—	0.4
1914	NY A	50	165	12	30	3	2	0	12	16	0	26	.182	.254	.224	44	-12	2-4	.981	-1	106	52	O45(3/37/6)	—	-1.8
	Cin N	11	28	2	6	0	0	0	1	3	0	5	.214	.290	.214	49	-2	0	1.000	-0	86	112	O10(7/3/1)	—	-0.2
Total	2	79	246	20	52	6	3	0	21	27	0	36	.211	.289	.260	64	-12	2-4	.981	1	103	93	O71(10/56/7)	—	-1.6
HOLDSWORTH, JIM	James "Long Jim"; B7.14.1850 New York NY; D3.22.1918 New York NY; BR/TR; d5.14																								
1872	Cle NA	**22**	110	19	33	5	0	0	11	1	—	2	.300	.306	.345	106	1	3-2	.765	-2	78	200	S22	—	-0.1
	Eck NA	3	11	1	3	1	0	0	0	0	—	0	.273	.273	.364	111	0	0-0	.833	1	123	0	S3	—	0.1
	Year	25	121	20	36	6	0	0	11	1	—	2	.298	.303	.347	107	2	3-2	.774	-0	84	175	S25	—	0.0
1873	Mut NA	**53**	232	46	75	4	8	0	28	0	—	4	.323	.323	.409	116	4	1-0	.770	-14	75	92	S53	—	-0.9
1874	Phi NA	57	285	60	97	8	9	0	37	1	—	0	.340	.343	.432	142	11	1-2	.694	-22	60	119	3b31,S21,O6(0/3/3),2b2/1	—	-1.0
1875	Mut NA	**71**	324	45	92	12	1	0	23	1	—	3	.284	.286	.327	107	1	3-3	.780	-4	148	128	O45(0/43/2),S26	—	-0.3
1876	NY N	52	241	23	64	3	2	0	19	1	—	2	.266	.269	.295	101	1	—	.902	-1	118	46	O49C,2b3	—	-0.2
1877	Har N	55	260	26	66	5	2	0	20	2	—	8	.254	.260	.288	81	-5	—	.833	-4	108	62	O55C	—	-1.0
1882	Tro N	1	3	0	0	0	0	0	0	0	—	1	.000	.000	.000	-99	-1	—	1.000	1	443	0	/cf	—	0.0
1884	Ind AA	5	18	1	2	0	0	0	—	2	0	—	.111	.200	.111	4	-2	—	.929	1	103	613	O5C	—	-0.1
Total	4NA	206	962	171	300	30	18	0	99	3	—	9	.312	.314	.380	119	17	8-7	.747	-40	81	117	S125,O51(0/46/5),3b31,2b2/1	—	-2.2
Total	4	113	522	50	132	8	4	0	39	5	0	11	.253	.260	.284	85	-7	—	.875	-3	115	78	O110C,2b3	—	-1.3
HOLKE, WALTER	Walter Henry "Union Man"; B12.25.1892 St.Louis MO; D10.12.1954 St.Louis MO; BB/TL/6´1.5˝/185; d10.6; Def 1918; C1																								
1914	NY N	2	6	0	2	0	0	0	0	0	0	0	.333	.333	.333	102	0	0	.950	0	210	120	1b2	—	0.0
1916	NY N	34	111	16	39	4	2	0	13	6	1	16	.351	.390	.423	158	7	10	.997	-0	85	92	1b34	—	0.7
1917	†NY N	153	527	55	146	12	7	2	55	34	5	54	.277	.327	.338	107	4	13	.989	-6	83	**121**	1b153	—	-0.6
1918	NY N	88	326	38	82	17	4	1	27	10	1	26	.252	.276	.337	88	-6	10	.990	5	**120**	107	1b88	—	-0.3
1919	Bos N	137	518	48	151	14	6	0	48	21	5	25	.292	.325	.342	105	2	19	.993	6	115	108	1b136	—	0.5
1920	Bos N	144	551	53	162	15	11	3	64	28	1	31	.294	.329	.377	107	3	4-11	.991	-3	92	91	1b143	—	-0.7
1921	Bos N	150	579	60	151	15	10	3	63	17	2	41	.261	.284	.337	67	-30	8-11	**.997**	2	100	94	1b150	—	-4.0
1922	Bos N	105	395	35	115	9	4	0	46	14	1	23	.291	.317	.334	71	-18	6-8	.993	-4	81	81	1b105	—	-2.8
1923	Phi N	147	562	64	175	31	4	7	70	16	0	37	.311	.330	.418	86	-12	7-9	.991	-2	93	103	1b146/P	—	-2.3
1924	Phi N	148	563	60	169	23	6	6	64	25	0	33	.300	.330	.394	83	-14	3-8	.993	4	109	96	1b148	—	-2.2
1925	Phi N	39	86	11	21	5	0	1	17	3	0	6	.244	.270	.337	50	-7	0-0	.994	1	126	103	1b23	—	-0.6
	Cin N	65	232	24	65	8	4	1	20	17	0	12	.280	.329	.362	78	-8	1-3	.997	1	103	128	1b65	—	-1.1
	Year	104	318	35	86	13	4	2	37	20	0	18	.270	.314	.355	69	-15	1-3	.996	3	108	123	1b88	—	-1.7
Total	11	1212	4456	464	1278	153	58	24	487	191	16	304	.287	.318	.363	89	-79	81-50	.993	5	99	102	1b1193/P	—	-13.4
HOLLAHAN, BILL	William James "Happy"; B11.22.1896 New York NY; D11.27.1965 New York NY; BR/TR/5´8˝/165; d9.27																								
1920	Was A	3	4	0	1	0	0	0	1	1	0	2	.250	.400	.250	77	0	1-0	1.000	-0	54	0	3b3	—	0.0
HOLLAND, DUTCH	Robert Clyde; B10.12.1903 Middlesex NC; D6.16.1967 Lumberton NC; BR/TR/6´1˝/190; d8.16; Col North Carolina St.																								
1932	Bos N	39	156	15	46	11	1	1	18	12	0	20	.295	.345	.397	103	1	0	.990	-0	97	108	O39L	—	-0.2
1933	Bos N	13	31	3	8	3	0	0	3	3	0	8	.258	.324	.355	102	0	1	.867	-1	88	0	O7L	—	-0.1
1934	Cle A	50	128	19	32	12	1	2	13	13	0	11	.250	.319	.406	85	-3	0-0	.957	-2	85	48	O31(15/0/16)	—	-0.7
Total	3	102	315	37	86	26	2	3	34	28	0	39	.273	.332	.397	95	-2	1-0	.969	-4	92	78	O77(61/0/16)	—	-1.0
HOLLAND, WILL	Willard A.; B1862 Georgetown DE; D7.19.1930 Philadelphia PA; 5´10˝/180; d7.10																								
1889	Bal AA	40	143	13	27	1	2	0	16	9	2	28	.189	.247	.224	34	-13	4	.853	-11	85	73	S39/lf	—	-1.9
HOLLANDSWORTH, TODD	Todd Mathew; B4.20.1973 Dayton OH; BL/TL/6´2˝/(193–225); [LAN91 3/80]; d4.25																								
1995	†LA N	41	103	16	24	2	0	5	13	10-2	1	29	.233	.304	.398	91	-2	2-1	.938	-1	96	65	O37(9/25/3)	99	-0.3
1996	†LA N	149	478	64	139	26	4	12	59	41-1	2	93	.291	.348	.437	113	8	21-6	.978	-2	94	100	O142(122/18/9)	0	0.5
1997	LA N	106	296	39	73	20	2	4	31	17-2	0	60	.247	.286	.368	75	-12	5-5	.984	6	125	45	O99(80/30/4)	35	-0.8
1998	LA N	55	175	23	47	6	4	3	20	9-0	1	42	.269	.308	.400	89	-4	4-3	.957	-1	105	36	O51(48/10/1)	115	-0.6
1999	LA N	92	261	39	74	12	2	9	32	24-1	1	61	.284	.345	.448	104	1	5-2	.984	1	104	68	O67(27/34/9),1b13	40	0.1
2000	LA N	81	261	42	61	12	0	8	24	30-2	1	61	.234	.314	.372	76	-10	11-4	.987	1	98	163	O77(9/68/1)	0	-0.7
	Col N	56	167	39	54	8	0	11	23	11-1	0	38	.323	.365	.569	106	1	7-3	.988	1	87	223	O48(31/4/18)	0	0.1
	Year	137	428	81	115	20	0	19	47	41-3	1	99	.269	.333	.449	89	-8	18-7	.987	2	93	188	O125(40/72/19)	0	-0.6
2001	Col N	33	117	21	43	15	1	6	19	8-2	0	20	.368	.408	.667	142	8	5-0	.981	-1	90	111	O31(25/12/5)	149	0.7
2002	Col N	95	298	39	88	21	1	11	48	26-4	1	71	.295	.352	.483	104	2	7-8	.973	-0	94	140	O90(74/1/20)	0	-0.3
	Tex A	39	132	16	34	6	0	5	19	14-0	0	27	.258	.327	.417	94	-1	1-0	1.000	-3	89	0	O38(25/16/4)	16	-0.4
2003	†Fla N	93	228	32	58	23	3	3	20	22-4	0	55	.254	.317	.421	95	-2	2-3	.983	3	111	143	O64(61/0/3)/D	18	-0.1
2004	Chi N	57	148	28	47	6	2	8	22	17-3	1	26	.318	.392	.547	135	8	1-1	1.000	2	110	115	O36(4/0/32),1b3,D3	98	0.8
2005	Chi N	107	268	23	68	17	2	5	35	18-1	1	53	.254	.301	.388	77	-9	4-4	.980	-6	80	55	O95(92/0/6)/1	0	-1.8
	Atl N	24	35	3	6	0	0	1	1	5-0	0	13	.171	.275	.257	40	-3	0-1	1.000	-1	86	0	O9(6/0/3)/1	0	-0.4
	Year	131	303	26	74	17	2	6	36	23-1	1	66	.244	.298	.373	73	-12	4-5	.982	-6	80	51	O104(98/0/9),1b2	0	-2.2
2006	Cle A	56	156	21	37	12	1	6	27	4-1	0	33	.237	.253	.442	79	-6	0-1	.976	2	107	161	O44(30/2/15)/D	0	-0.5
	Cin N	34	68	6	18	6	0	1	8	6-0	0	19	.265	.324	.397	79	-2	0-1	1.000	-1	80	140	O20(1/0/19)	0	-0.4
Total	12	1118	3191	451	871	192	22	98	401	262-24	9	701	.273	.328	.439	97	-23	75-43	.980	2	99	102	O948(644/220/152),1b18,D5	570	-4.1
HOLLE, GARY	Gary Charles; B8.11.1954 Albany NY; BR/TL/6´6˝/208; [MilA76 13/292]; d6.2; Col Siena																								
1979	Tex A	5	6	0	1	1	0	0	0	1-0	0	0	.167	.286	.333	67	0	0-0	1.000	-0	0	128	/1	0	-0.1
HOLLIDAY, BUG	James Wear; B2.8.1867 St.Louis MO; D2.15.1910 Cincinnati OH; BR/TR/5´11˝/151; d4.17; U1; OF(211/598/92)																								
1889	Cin AA	135	563	107	181	28	7	**19**	104	43	2	59	.321	.372	.497	142	28	46	.923	-9	112	107	O135C	—	1.2
1890	Cin N	131	518	93	140	18	14	4	75	49	7	36	.270	.341	.382	111	6	50	.948	-5	89	118	O131C	—	-0.3
1891	Cin N	111	442	74	141	21	10	9	84	37	3	28	.319	.376	.473	145	24	30	.939	-8	78	107	O111(49/62/0)	—	1.1
1892	Cin N	152	602	114	177	23	16	**13**	91	57	1	39	.294	.356	.450	145	31	43	.933	-4	83	120	O152(1/78/77)/P	—	1.7
1893	Cin N	126	500	108	155	24	10	5	89	73	3	22	.310	.401	.428	117	14	32	.944	-12	67	90	O125(1/125/0)/1	—	-0.5
1894	Cin N	123	521	126	196	24	8	13	123	41	2	20	.376	.424	.528	124	19	33	.912	1	107	116	O121(111/5/8)/1	—	0.7
1895	Cin N	32	127	25	38	9	2	0	20	10	0	3	.299	.350	.402	90	-2	6	.940	-2	74	109	O32(5/27/0)	—	-0.5
1896	Cin N	29	84	17	27	4	0	0	8	9	1	4	.321	.394	.369	95	0	1	.925	-2	45	0	O16(10/3/3),1b5/SP	—	-0.2
1897	Cin N	61	195	50	61	9	4	2	20	27	1	—	.313	.399	.431	112	4	6	.940	-4	37	0	O42(32/6/4),S4,2b3,1b3	—	-0.2
1898	Cin N	30	106	21	25	2	1	0	7	14	0	—	.236	.325	.274	67	-4	5	.969	-1	28	118	O28(2/26/0)	—	-0.7
Total	10	930	3658	735	1141	162	72	65	621	360	20	211	.312	.377	.449	125	120	252	.934	-45	84	104	O893C,1b10,S5,2b3,P2	—	2.3
HOLLIDAY, MATT	Matthew Thomas; B1.15.1980 Stillwater OK; BR/TR/6´4˝/235; [ColN98 7/210]; d4.16																								
2004	Col N	121	400	65	116	31	3	14	57	31-0	6	86	.290	.349	.488	101	1	3-3	.963	-5	94	67	O115L	0	-0.8
2005	Col N	125	479	68	147	24	7	19	87	36-1	7	79	.307	.361	.505	112	8	14-3	.972	1	104	72	O123L	40	0.6
2006	Col N★	155	602	119	196	45	5	34	114	47-3	15	110	.326	.387	.586	133	30	10-5	.979	-4	91	95	O153L/D	0	2.0
Total	3	401	1481	252	459	100	15	67	258	114-4	28	275	.310	.368	.533	117	39	27-11	.972	-8	96	80	O391L/D	40	1.8
HOLLINGSHEAD, HOLLY	John Samuel (aka Samuel John Holly); B1.17.1853 Washington DC; D10.6.1926 Washington DC; d4.20; M2/U1																								
1872	Nat NA	9	44	12	14	1	1	0	6	1	—	0	.318	.333	.386	103	-1	0-0	.778	-4	70	45	2b9	—	-0.3
1873	Was NA	30	136	25	35	2	2	0	22	0	—	5	.257	.257	.301	67	-5	0-0	.824	2	119	0	O30C,2b2	—	-0.2
1875	Was NA	19	81	8	20	1	1	0	5	1	—	2	.247	.256	.284	91	-1	2-1	.826	2	202	126	O19(4/13/3),M	—	0.2
Total	3NA	58	261	45	69	4	4	0	33	2	—	7	.264	.270	.310	81	-7	2-1	.824	1	150	47	O49(4/43/3),2b11	—	-0.3
HOLLINS, DAMON	Damon Jamall; B6.12.1974 Fairfield CA; BR/TL/5´11˝/180; [AtlN92 4/117]; d4.24; [DL 2003 Atl N 29]																								
1998	Atl N	3	6	0	1	0	0	0	0	0-0	0	1	.167	.167	.167	-12	-1	0-0	1.000	-0	67	0	O3(2/0/1)	0	-0.1
	LA N	5	9	1	2	0	0	0	2	0-0	0	2	.222	.222	.222	18	-1	0-1	1.000	-0	103	0	O4(1/0/3)	0	-0.2
	Year	8	15	1	3	0	0	0	2	0-0	0	3	.200	.200	.200	6	-2	0-1	1.000	-0	89	0	O7(3/0/4)	0	-0.3
2004	Atl N	7	22	3	8	2	0	0	5	0-0	0	4	.364	.364	.455	109	0	0-0	1.000	0	84	337	O6(6/0/1)	0	0.0
2005	TB A	120	342	44	85	17	1	13	46	23-0	1	63	.249	.296	.418	89	-6	8-1	.977	8	110	165	O116(8/80/48)	0	0.2
2006	TB A	121	333	37	76	20	0	15	33	19-1	0	64	.228	.269	.423	76	-13	3-3	.982	4	112	93	O115(18/33/78),D3	0	-1.2
Total	4	256	712	85	172	39	1	28	86	42-1	1	134	.242	.284	.417	82	-21	11-5	.980	12	110	133	O244(35/113/131),D3	29	-1.3

YEAR	TM LG	G	AB	R	H	2B	3B	HR	RBI	BB-IB	HP	SO	AVG	OBP	SLG	AOPS	ABR	SB-CS	FA	FR	RNG	THR	GAMES AT POSITION	DL	BFW
Hollins, Dave	David Michael; B5.25.1966 Buffalo NY; BB/TR/6´1˝/(195–232); [SDN87 6/146]; d4.12; Col South Carolina																								
1990	Phi N	72	114	14	21	0	0	5	15	10-3	1	28	.184	.252	.316	56	-7	0-0	.932	-3	86	0	3b30/1	0	-1.1
1991	Phi N	56	151	18	45	10	2	6	21	17-1	3	26	.298	.378	.510	149	10	1-1	.922	-2	94	37	3b36,1b6	21	0.8
1992	Phi N	156	586	104	158	28	4	27	93	76-4	**19**	110	.270	.369	.469	137	30	9-6	.954	-18	84	83	3b156/1	0	1.4
1993	†Phi N★	143	543	104	148	30	4	18	93	85-5	5	109	.273	.372	.442	120	18	2-3	.914	-29	79	40	3b143	17	-1.0
1994	Phi N	44	162	28	36	7	1	4	26	23-0	4	32	.222	.328	.352	77	-5	1-0	.887	-13	61	31	3b43/rf	79	-1.7
1995	Phi N	65	205	46	47	12	2	7	25	53-4	5	38	.229	.393	.410	114	7	1-1	.988	-6	67	109	1b61	15	-0.5
	Bos A	5	13	2	2	0	0	0	1	4-0	0	7	.154	.353	.154	37	-1	0-0	1.000	0	111	0	O2R,D3	54	-0.1
1996	Min A	121	422	71	102	26	0	13	53	71-5	10	102	.242	.364	.396	90	-4	6-4	.953	0	102	82	3b116/SD	0	-0.3
	Sea A	28	94	17	33	3	0	3	25	13-2	3	15	.351	.438	.479	133	6	0-2	.961	2	105	122	3b28/1	0	0.6
	Year	149	516	88	135	29	0	16	78	84-7	13	117	.262	.377	.411	98	2	6-6	.955	2	103	90	3b144,D3/S1	0	0.3
1997	Ana A	149	572	101	165	29	2	16	85	62-2	8	124	.288	.363	.430	106	7	16-6	.922	-8	94	76	3b135,1b14	0	-0.1
1998	Ana A	101	363	60	88	16	2	11	39	44-2	7	69	.242	.334	.388	86	-7	11-3	.929	-2	94	99	3b91,1b7,D2	49	-0.8
1999	Tor A	27	99	12	22	5	0	2	6	5-0	0	22	.222	.260	.333	49	-8	0-0	ø	0	0	0	D23	33	-0.9
2001	Cle A	2	5	0	1	0	0	0	0	1-0	0	2	.200	.333	.200	44	0	0-0	ø	0	—	—	D2	0	0.0
2002	Phi N	14	17	1	2	0	0	0	0	0-0	1	3	.118	.167	.118	-25	-3	0-1	1.000	-0	45	106	1b5	142	-0.4
Total	12	983	3346	578	870	166	17	112	482	464-28	66	687	.260	.358	.420	106	43	47-27	.933	-80	89	70	3b778,1b96,D33,O3R/S	410	-4.1
Hollmig, Stan	Stanley Ernest "Hondo"; B1.2.1926 Fredericksburg TX; D12.4.1981 San Antonio TX; BR/TR/6´2.5˝/190; d4.19; Col Texas A&M																								
1949	Phi N	81	251	28	64	11	6	2	26	20	2	43	.255	.315	.371	85	-6	1	.958	-4	88	87	O66R	0	-1.2
1950	Phi N	11	12	1	3	2	0	0	1	0	0	3	.250	.250	.417	73	0	0	1.000	0	127	0	O3(2/0/1)	0	0.0
1951	Phi N	2	2	0	0	0	0	0	0	0	0	0	.000	.000	.000	-99	-1	0-0	ø	0	—	—	/H	0	-0.1
Total	3	94	265	29	67	13	6	2	27	20	2	46	.253	.310	.370	84	-7	1-0	.959	-4	89	85	O69(2/0/67)	0	-1.3
Hollocher, Charlie	Charles Jacob; B6.11.1896 St.Louis MO; D8.14.1940 Frontenac MO; BL/TR/5´7˝/154; d4.16																								
1918	†Chi N	**131**	509	72	**161**	23	6	2	38	47	4	30	.316	.379	.397	133	22	26	.929	-22	90	75	S131	—	1.0
1919	Chi N	115	430	51	116	14	5	3	26	44	7	19	.270	.347	.347	108	6	16	.941	6	105	107	S115	—	2.2
1920	Chi N	80	301	53	96	17	2	0	22	41	3	15	.319	.406	.389	126	13	20-14	.954	9	102	89	S80	—	2.9
1921	Chi N	140	558	71	161	28	8	3	37	43	2	13	.289	.342	.384	91	-6	5-16	**.963**	6	105	95	S137	—	1.0
1922	Chi N	152	592	90	201	37	8	3	69	58	5	5	.340	.403	.444	116	17	19-29	**.965**	-6	98	101	S152	—	2.0
1923	Chi N	66	260	46	89	14	2	1	28	26	4	5	.342	.410	.423	120	9	9-10	.963	-4	96	96	S65	—	1.0
1924	Chi N	76	286	28	70	12	4	2	21	18	1	7	.245	.292	.336	67	-14	4-11	.969	2	102	93	S71	—	-0.7
Total	7	760	2936	411	894	145	35	14	241	277	26	94	.304	.370	.392	110	47	99-80	.954	-9	100	94	S751	—	9.4
Holly, Ed	Edward William (b Edward William Ruthlavy); B7.6.1879 Chicago IL; D11.27.1973 Williamsport PA; BR/TR/5´10˝/165; d7.18																								
1906	StL N	10	34	1	2	0	0	0	7	5	0	—	.059	.179	.059	-27	-5	0	.939	-2	73	213	S10	—	-0.7
1907	StL N	150	545	55	125	18	3	1	40	36	5	—	.229	.283	.279	79	-14	16	.927	9	105	86	S147,2b3	—	0.0
1914	Pit F	100	350	28	86	9	4	0	26	17	0	52	.246	.281	.294	57	-28	14	.942	-3	95	87	S94,O2(1/0/1)/2	—	-2.5
1915	Pit F	16	42	8	11	2	0	0	5	5	1	6	.262	.354	.310	88	-1	3	.865	-4	77	106	S11,3b3	—	-0.5
Total	4	276	971	92	224	29	7	1	78	63	6	58	.231	.282	.278	67	-48	33	.931	1	99	92	S262,2b4,3b3,O2(1/0/1)	—	-3.7
Holm, Wattie	Roscoe Albert; B12.28.1901 Peterson IA; D5.19.1950 Everly IA; BR/TR/5´9.5˝/160; d4.15; Col Iowa																								
1924	StL N	81	293	40	86	10	4	0	23	8	2	16	.294	.317	.355	81	-9	1-4	.988	1	101	140	O64(1/63/0),C9,3b4	—	-1.1
1925	StL N	13	58	10	12	1	1	0	2	3	0	1	.207	.246	.259	28	-6	1-0	.976	1	127	50	O13(3/0/11)	—	-0.6
1926	†StL N	55	144	18	41	5	1	0	21	18	0	14	.285	.364	.333	85	-2	3	.962	-2	102	25	O39(26/0/13)	—	-0.7
1927	StL N	110	419	55	120	27	8	3	66	24	1	29	.286	.327	.411	93	-5	4	.967	-8	93	31	O97(55/25/18),3b9	—	-1.9
1928	†StL N	102	386	61	107	24	6	3	47	32	1	17	.277	.334	.394	88	-7	1	.918	-17	81	61	3b83,O7R	—	-1.8
1929	StL N	64	176	21	41	5	6	0	14	12	0	8	.233	.282	.330	50	-15	1	.944	2	116	90	O44(6/4/34)/3	—	-1.5
1932	StL N	11	17	2	3	1	0	0	1	3	1	1	.176	.333	.235	55	-1	0	1.000	-0	110	0	O4(2/0/2)	—	-0.1
Total	7	436	1493	207	410	73	26	6	174	100	5	86	.275	.322	.370	81	-45	11-4	.970	-22	103	65	O268(93/92/85),3b97,C9	—	-7.7
Holm, Billy	William Frederick Henry; B7.21.1912 Chicago IL; D7.27.1977 East Chicago IN; BR/TR/5´10.5˝/168; d9.24																								
1943	Chi N	7	15	0	1	0	0	0	0	2	0	4	.067	.176	.067	-29	-2	0	1.000	1	*152*	*83*	C7	0	-0.2
1944	Chi N	54	132	10	18	2	0	0	6	16	1	19	.136	.235	.152	10	-16	1	.979	-2	*97*	*92*	C50	0	-1.6
1945	Bos A	58	135	12	25	2	1	0	9	23	3	17	.185	.317	.215	54	-7	1-1	.980	-3	*105*	*113*	C57	0	-0.8
Total	3	119	282	22	44	4	1	0	15	41	4	40	.156	.272	.177	30	-25	2-1	.981	-4	*104*	*102*	C114	0	-2.6
Holman, Gary	Gary Richard; B1.25.1944 Long Beach CA; BL/TL/6´1˝/200; d6.26; Col USC																								
1968	Was A	75	85	10	25	5	1	0	7	13-1	0	15	.294	.388	.376	137	5	0-0	1.000	2	112	44	1b33,O10(3/0/8)	0	0.6
1969	Was A	41	31	1	5	1	0	0	2	4-0	0	7	.161	.257	.194	29	-3	0-0	1.000	-1	0	58	1b11,O3(1/0/2)	0	-0.4
Total	2	116	116	11	30	6	1	0	9	17-1	0	22	.259	.353	.328	107	2	0-0	1.000	1	90	47	1b44,O13(4/0/10)	0	0.2
Holmes, Fred	Frederick Clarence; B7.1.1878 Chicago IL; D2.13.1956 Norwood Park IL; BR/TR/5´7˝/145; d8.23																								
1903	NY A	1	0	0	0	0	0	0	0	1	0	—	ø	1.000	ø	207	0	0	.833	-0	0	0	/1	—	0.0
1904	Chi N	1	3	1	1	1	0	0	0	0	0	—	.333	.333	.667	206	0	0	1.000	0	*99*	*118*	/C	—	0.0
Total	2	2	3	1	1	1	0	0	0	1	0	—	.333	.500	.667	255	0	0	1.000	-0	*99*	*118*	/C1	—	0.0
Holmes, Ducky	Howard Elbert; B7.8.1883 Dayton OH; D9.18.1945 Dayton OH; BR/TR/5´10˝/160; d4.18; U1																								
1906	StL N	9	27	2	5	0	0	0	2	2	1	—	.185	.267	.185	43	-2	0	.979	-1	*78*	*91*	C9	—	-0.2
Holmes, Ducky	James William; B1.28.1869 Des Moines IA; D8.6.1932 Truro IA; BL/TR/5´6˝/170; d8.8; OF(564/37/285); ▲																								
1895	Lou N	40	161	33	60	10	2	3	20	12	3	9	.373	.426	.516	152	13	9	.780	-6	180	99	O29(0/3/26),S8,3b4,P2	—	0.5
1896	Lou N	47	141	22	38	3	2	0	18	13	7	5	.270	.360	.319	83	-3	8	.790	-7	142	81	O33(0/26/7),P2/S2	—	-0.9
1897	Lou N	2	4	0	0	0	0	0	0	1	0	—	.000	.200	.000	-46	-1	0	1.000	1	101	420	/S	—	0.0
	NY N	80	310	52	82	8	6	1	45	18	4	—	.265	.313	.339	74	-13	30	.905	-9	78	92	O78L/S	—	-2.5
	Year	82	314	52	82	8	6	1	45	19	4	—	.261	.312	.334	73	-13	30	.905	-8	78	92	O78L,S2	—	-2.5
1898	StL N	23	101	9	24	1	1	0	0	2	1	—	.238	.260	.267	50	-7	4	.900	1	183	367	O22(11/2/9)	—	-0.7
	Bal N	113	442	54	126	10	9	1	64	23	9	—	.285	.333	.355	96	-4	25	.935	2	79	116	O113L	—	-1.1
	Year	136	543	63	150	11	10	1	64	25	10	—	.276	.320	.339	87	-11	29	.930	3	96	**158**	O135(124/2/9)	—	-1.8
1899	Bal N	138	553	80	177	31	7	4	66	39	15	—	.320	.381	.423	114	11	50	.927	7	113	92	O138(137/0/1)	—	0.6
1901	Det A	131	537	90	158	28	10	4	62	37	6	—	.294	.347	.406	103	2	35	.907	-2	107	129	O131(2/0/131)	—	-0.5
1902	Det A	92	362	50	93	15	4	2	33	28	5	—	.257	.319	.337	80	-9	16	.950	4	131	195	O92(1/0/91)	—	-0.9
1903	Was A	21	71	13	16	3	1	1	8	5	1	—	.225	.286	.338	85	-1	10	.912	1	302	0	O14(0/3/11),3b4,2b2	—	-0.1
	Chi A	86	344	53	96	7	5	0	18	25	4	—	.279	.335	.328	104	2	25	.965	3	156	0	O82L,3b3	—	0.1
	Year	107	415	66	112	10	6	1	26	30	5	—	.270	.327	.330	101	1	35	.956	4	**179**	0	O96(82/3/11),3b7,2b2	—	0.0
1904	Chi A	68	251	42	78	11	9	1	19	14	3	—	.311	.354	.438	156	15	13	.975	1	110	174	O63(53/2/8)	—	1.4
1905	Chi A	92	328	42	66	15	2	0	22	19	6	—	.201	.258	.259	67	-12	11	.936	-4	105	48	O89(87/1/1)	—	-2.4
Total	10	933	3605	540	1014	142	58	17	375	236	64	14	.281	.336	.367	99	-7	236	.924	-6	117	110	O884L,3b11,S11,P4,2b3	—	-6.5
Holmes, Tommy	Thomas Francis "Kelly"; B3.29.1917 Brooklyn NY; BL/TL/5´10˝/180; d4.14; M2																								
1942	Bos N	141	558	56	155	24	4	4	41	64	1	10	.278	.353	.357	110	8	2	.990	5	105	117	O140(0/137/3)	0	1.1
1943	Bos N	152	629	75	170	33	10	5	41	58	2	20	.270	.334	.378	107	5	7	.993	-2	94	114	O152(2/149/1)	0	-0.2
1944	Bos N	**155**	631	93	195	42	6	13	73	61	2	11	.309	.372	.456	127	23	4	.991	-2	97	95	O155(2/154/0)	0	1.7
1945	Bos N✱	**154**	636	125	**224**	**47**	6	**28**	117	70	4	9	.352	.420	**.577**	**175**	**64**	15	.983	-2	98	89	O154(32/2/121)	0	5.1
1946	Bos N	149	568	80	176	35	6	6	79	58	3	14	.310	.377	.424	126	20	7	.987	5	104	115	O146R	0	2.2
1947	Bos N	150	618	90	**191**	33	3	9	53	44	5	16	.309	.360	.416	108	7	3	.989	6	109	90	O147R	0	0.7
1948	†Bos N★	139	585	85	190	35	7	6	61	46	1	20	.325	.375	.439	122	18	1	.983	-2	99	74	O137R	0	1.1
1949	Bos N	117	380	47	101	20	4	8	59	39	2	6	.266	.337	.403	103	1	1	.987	6	**112**	114	O103R	0	0.4
1950	Bos N	105	322	44	96	20	1	9	51	33	4	8	.298	.370	.450	122	11	0	1.000	1	104	100	O88R	0	0.9
1951	Bos N	27	29	1	5	2	0	0	5	3	0	4	.172	.250	.241	35	-3	0-0	1.000	-0	65	0	O3(2/0/1),M	0	-0.3
1952	†Bro N	31	36	2	4	1	0	0	1	4	0	4	.111	.200	.139	-4	-5	0-0	1.000	0	89	300	O6R	0	-0.5
Total	11	1320	4992	698	1507	292	47	88	581	480	24	122	.302	.366	.432	122	149	40-0	.989	16	102	101	O1231(38/442/753)	0	12.2
Holt, Red	James Emmett Madison; B7.25.1894 Dayton TN; D2.2.1961 Birmingham AL; BL/TL/5´11˝/175; d9.5																								
1925	Phi A	27	88	13	24	7	0	1	8	12	0	9	.273	.360	.386	84	-2	0-0	.986	-0	98	103	1b25	—	-0.3

YEAR	TM LG	G	AB	R	H	2B	3B	HR	RBI	BB-IB	HP	SO	AVG	OBP	SLG	AOPS	ABR	SB-CS	FA	FR	RNG	THR	GAMES AT POSITION	DL	BFW
HOLT, JIM	James William; B5.27.1944 Graham NC; BL/TR/6´0˝/(170–195); d4.17																								
1968	Min A	70	106	9	22	2	1	0	8	4-2	0	20	.208	.236	.245	44	-7	0-1	.973	-1	85	145	O38(23/2/14)/1	0	-1.1
1969	Min A	12	14	3	5	0	0	1	2	0-0	0	4	.357	.357	.571	152	1	0-0	1.000	-1	44	0	O5(1/0/4)/1	0	0.0
1970	†Min A	142	319	37	85	9	3	3	40	17-3	0	32	.266	.300	.342	76	-11	3-1	.995	2	111	36	O130(76/52/4),1b2	0	-1.4
1971	Min A	126	340	35	88	11	3	1	29	16-4	1	28	.259	.292	.318	71	-14	5-1	.986	0	104	75	O106(12/86/12),1b3	0	-1.7
1972	Min A	10	27	6	12	1	0	1	6	0-0	0	1	.444	.429	.593	197	3	0-0	.917	0	92	235	O7(2/0/5)/1	0	0.3
1973	Min A	132	441	52	131	25	3	11	58	29-4	2	43	.297	.341	.442	115	8	0-3	.990	5	105	94	O102(80/3/21),1b33	0	0.5
1974	Min A	79	197	24	50	11	0	0	16	14-2	1	16	.254	.302	.310	75	-6	0-0	.996	5	137	128	1b67,O5(2/0/3)	0	-0.5
	†Oak A	30	42	1	6	0	0	0	0	1-0	1	9	.143	.182	.143	-6	-6	0-0	1.000	1	143	81	1b17,D3	0	-0.6
	Year	109	239	25	56	11	0	0	16	15-2	2	25	.234	.282	.280	63	-11	0-0	.996	6	138	122	1b84,O5(2/0/3),D3	0	-1.1
1975	†Oak A	102	123	7	27	3	0	2	16	11-2	2	11	.220	.292	.293	68	-5	0-0	.991	0	117	102	1b52,O2L/CD	0	-0.7
1976	Oak A	4	7	0	2	2	0	0	2	1-0	0	2	.286	.375	.571	182	1	0-0	ø	0	—	—	D2	0	0.1
Total	9	707	1616	174	428	64	10	19	177	93-17	7	166	.265	.305	.352	84	-36	8-6	.988	12	104	76	O395(198/143/63),1b177,D9/C	0	-5.1
HOLT, ROGER	Roger Boyd; B4.8.1956 Daytona Beach FL; BB/TR/5´11˝/165; [NYA77 4/101]; d10.4; Col Florida																								
1980	NY A	2	6	0	1	0	0	0	1	1-0	0	2	.167	.286	.167	28	-1	0-0	1.000	1	150	0	2b2	0	0.0
HONAN, MARTY	Martin Weldon; B5.29.1869 Chicago IL; D8.20.1908 Chicago IL; d10.3																								
1890	Chi N	1	3	0	0	0	0	0	1	0	0	2	.000	.000	.000	-96	-1	0	.857	-1	*105*	*0*	/C	—	-0.1
1891	Chi N	5	12	1	2	0	1	0	3	1	0	3	.167	.231	.333	64	-1	0	.963	1	*141*	*170*	C5	—	0.1
Total	2	6	15	1	2	0	1	0	4	1	0	5	.133	.188	.267	32	-2	0	.941	0	*133*	*134*	C6	—	0.0
HOOD, ABIE	Albie Larrison; B1.31.1903 Sanford NC; D10.14.1988 Chesapeake VA; BL/TR/5´7˝/152; d7.15																								
1925	Bos N	5	21	2	6	2	0	1	2	1	0	0	.286	.318	.524	122	1	0-0	.920	-3	64	68	2b5	—	-0.2
HOOD, WALLY	Wallace James Sr.; B2.9.1895 Whittier CA; D5.2.1965 Hollywood CA; BR/TR/5´11.5˝/160; d4.15; s–Wally																								
1920	Bro N	7	14	4	2	1	0	0	1	4	0	4	.143	.333	.214	58	0	2-0	.944	1	125	126	O5(0/2/3)	—	0.0
	Pit N	2	1	1	0	0	0	0	0	1	0	0	.000	.500	.000	50	0	1-0	ø	0	—	—	/H	—	0.0
	Year	9	15	5	2	1	0	0	1	5	0	4	.133	.350	.200	59	0	3-0	.944	1	125	126	O5(0/2/3)	—	0.0
1921	Bro N	56	65	16	17	1	2	1	4	9	1	14	.262	.360	.385	94	0	2-2	.957	-1	99	0	O20(3/9/7)	—	-0.3
1922	Bro N	2	0	2	0	0	0	0	0	0	0	0	ø	ø	ø	ø	0	0-0	ø	0	—	—	/R	—	0.0
Total	3	67	80	23	19	2	2	1	5	14	1	18	.237	.358	.350	88	0	5-2	.951	-1	109	48	O25(3/11/10)	—	-0.3
HOOKS, ALEX	Alexander Marcus; B8.29.1906 Edgewood TX; D6.19.1993 Edgewood TX; BL/TL/6´1˝/183; d4.17; Col SMU																								
1935	Phi A	15	44	4	10	3	0	0	4	3	0	10	.227	.277	.295	48	-3	0-0	1.000	0	93	127	1b10	—	-0.4
HOOPER, HARRY	Harry Bartholomew; B8.24.1887 Bell Station CA; D12.18.1974 Santa Cruz CA; BL/TR/5´10˝/168; d4.16; HF1971; Col St. Marys (CA)																								
1909	Bos A	81	255	29	72	3	4	0	12	16	5	—	.282	.337	.325	107	2	15	.952	4	149	143	O74(62/4/8)	—	0.3
1910	Bos A	155	584	81	156	9	10	2	27	62	8	—	.267	.346	.327	108	7	40	.938	9	107	139	O155(9/4/142)	—	0.9
1911	Bos A	130	524	93	163	20	6	4	45	73	4	—	.311	.399	.395	123	20	38	.954	6	105	131	O130R	—	1.8
1912	†Bos A	147	590	98	143	20	12	2	53	66	7	—	.242	.326	.327	83	-13	29	.964	1	100	105	O147R	—	-2.0
1913	Bos A	148	586	100	169	29	12	4	40	60	5	51	.288	.359	.399	119	14	26	.968	8	110	114	O147(1/9/137)/P	—	1.4
1914	Bos A	142	530	85	137	23	15	1	41	58	4	47	.258	.336	.364	110	6	19-14	.973	10	113	128	O140(0/1/139)	—	0.9
1915	†Bos A	149	566	90	133	20	13	2	51	89	3	36	.235	.342	.327	103	4	22-20	.972	9	**111**	125	O149R	—	0.3
1916	†Bos A	151	575	75	156	20	11	1	37	80	1	35	.271	.361	.350	113	11	27-11	.966	5	111	104	O151R	—	1.1
1917	Bos A	151	559	89	143	21	11	3	45	80	6	40	.256	.355	.349	116	13	21	.971	-4	94	94	O151R	—	0.1
1918	†Bos A	**126**	474	81	137	26	13	1	44	75	4	25	.289	.391	.405	142	27	24	.963	-0	100	94	O126R	—	2.2
1919	Bos A	128	491	76	131	25	6	3	49	79	5	28	.267	.374	.360	113	13	23	.979	6	110	102	O128R	—	1.2
1920	Bos A	139	536	91	167	30	17	7	53	88	2	27	.312	.411	.470	139	33	16-18	.963	5	106	116	O139(2/0/137)	—	2.7
1921	Chi A	108	419	74	137	26	5	8	58	55	1	21	.327	.406	.470	125	17	13-7	.975	-3	95	83	O108R	—	0.6
1922	Chi A	152	602	111	183	35	8	11	80	68	5	33	.304	.379	.444	114	14	16-12	.962	5	106	112	O149R	—	0.5
1923	Chi A	145	576	87	166	32	4	10	65	68	7	22	.288	.370	.410	106	7	18-18	.960	-6	95	77	O143R	—	-1.3
1924	Chi A	130	476	107	156	27	8	10	62	65	4	26	.328	.413	.481	134	26	16-13	.986	10	112	128	O123R	—	2.4
1925	Chi A	127	442	62	117	23	5	6	55	54	5	21	.265	.351	.380	90	-6	12-8	.976	4	102	127	O124R	—	-1.1
Total	17	2309	8785	1429	2466	389	160	75	817	1136	76	412	.281	.368	.387	114	195	375-121	.966	68	106	112	O2284(74/18/2192)/P	—	12.0
HOOPER, KEVIN	Kevin James; B12.7.1976 Lawrence KS; BR/TR/5´10˝/160; [FlaN99 8/236]; d7.9; Col Wichita St.																								
2005	Det A	6	5	0	1	0	0	0	0	0-0	0	1	.200	.200	.200	7	-1	0-0	1.000	-0	110	0	O3L,S2/2	0	-0.1
2006	Det A	8	3	1	0	0	0	0	0	1-0	0	1	.000	.250	.000	-28	-1	0-0	1.000	1	158	221	2b3,3b2/D	0	0.0
Total	2	14	8	1	1	0	0	0	0	1-0	0	2	.125	.222	.125	-5	-2	0-0	1.000	0	84	88	2b4,O3L,3b2,S2/D	0	-0.1
HOOPER, MIKE	Michael H.; B2.7.1850 Baltimore MD; D12.2.1917 Baltimore MD; 5´6˝/165; d6.27																								
1873	Mar NA	3	14	3	3	1	0	0	2	0	—	0	.214	.214	.286	61	0	0-0	.833	-2	0	0	O2L/C	—	-0.1
HOOVER, CHARLIE	Charles E.; B9.21.1865 Mound City IL; BL/TR/5´8˝/170; d10.9																								
1888	KC AA	3	10	0	3	0	0	0	1	0	0	—	.300	.300	.300	87	0	0	.857	-0	—	—	C3	—	0.0
1889	KC AA	71	258	44	64	2	5	1	25	29	2	38	.248	.329	.306	76	-9	9	.916	-4	—	—	C66,3b4,O3L	—	-0.6
Total	2	74	268	44	67	2	5	1	26	29	2	38	.250	.328	.306	77	-9	9	.913	-4	—	—	C69,3b4,O3L	—	-0.6
HOOVER, PAUL	Paul Chester; B4.14.1976 Columbus OH; BR/TR/6´1˝/(200–210); [TBA97 23/714]; d9.8; Col Kent St.																								
2001	TB A	3	4	1	1	0	0	0	0	0-0	0	1	.250	.250	.250	33	0	0-0	1.000	-1	82	0	C2	0	-0.1
2002	TB A	5	17	1	3	0	0	0	2	0-0	0	5	.176	.176	.176	-6	-3	0-0	1.000	-2	52	308	C4	0	-0.4
2006	Fla N	4	5	0	2	0	0	0	1	0-0	0	0	.400	.400	.400	111	0	0-0	.875	-0	53	0	C3	0	0.0
Total	3	12	26	2	6	0	0	0	3	0-0	0	6	.231	.231	.231	23	-3	0-0	.966	-3	58	201	C9	0	-0.5
HOOVER, JOE	Robert Joseph; B4.15.1915 Brawley CA; D9.2.1965 Los Angeles CA; BR/TR/5´11˝/175; d4.21; Col Pomona (CA) JC																								
1943	Det A	144	575	78	140	15	8	4	38	36	1	101	.243	.289	.318	72	-22	6-5	.944	-8	90	94	S144	0	-2.1
1944	Det A	120	441	67	104	20	2	0	29	35	6	66	.236	.301	.290	66	-19	7-10	.932	15	102	**131**	S119/2	0	0.4
1945	†Det A	74	222	33	57	10	5	1	17	21	1	35	.257	.324	.360	92	-2	6-2	.944	-4	89	102	S68	0	-0.2
Total	3	338	1238	178	301	45	15	5	84	92	8	202	.243	.300	.316	73	-43	19-17	.939	3	94	109	S331/2	0	-1.9
HOOVER, BUSTER	William James; B4.12.1863 Philadelphia PA; D4.16.1924 Jersey City NJ; BR/TR/6´1˝/178; d4.17																								
1884	Phi U	63	275	76	100	20	8	0	—	12	—	—	.364	.390	.495	180	19	—	.780	0	141	113	O37L,S15,1b6,2b6/3	—	1.7
	Phi N	10	42	6	8	1	0	1	4	4	—	9	.190	.261	.286	75	-1	—	.929	-1	59	0	O10(6/4/0)	—	-0.2
1886	Bal AA	40	157	25	34	2	6	0	10	16	2	—	.217	.297	.306	91	-2	15	.839	-3	43	0	O40C	—	-0.5
1892	Cin N	14	51	7	9	0	0	0	2	5	0	4	.176	.250	.176	30	-4	1	.966	1	131	422	O14(12/1/2)	—	-0.4
Total	3	127	525	114	151	23	14	1	16	37	2	13	.288	.337	.390	129	12	16	.840	-2	93	101	O101(55/45/2),S15,2b6,1b6/3	—	0.6
HOPKINS, DON	Donald; B1.9.1952 West Point MS; BL/TR/6´0˝/175; d4.8																								
1975	†Oak A	82	6	25	1	0	0	0	0	2-0	0	0	.167	.375	.167	59	0	21-9	1.000	0	113	0	D20,O5(1/2/2)/R	0	0.1
1976	Oak A	3	0	0	0	0	0	0	0	0-0	0	0	ø	ø	ø	ø	0	0-1	ø	0	—	—	H2	0	0.0
Total	2	85	6	25	1	0	0	0	0	2-0	0	0	.167	.375	.167	59	0	21-10	1.000	0	113	0	D20,O5(1/2/2)	0	0.1
HOPKINS, GAIL	Gail Eason; B2.19.1943 Tulsa OK; BL/TR/5´10˝/(200–206); d6.29; Col Pepperdine																								
1968	Chi A	29	37	4	8	2	0	0	2	6-1	0	3	.216	.326	.270	81	-1	0-0	1.000	-1	32	79	1b7	0	-0.2
1969	Chi A	124	373	52	99	13	3	8	46	50-1	1	28	.265	.351	.381	101	1	2-1	.994	-2	91	103	1b101	0	-0.8
1970	Chi A	116	287	32	82	8	1	6	29	28-5	1	19	.286	.346	.383	99	0	0-0	.987	-1	101	115	1b77,C8	0	-0.6
1971	KC A	103	295	35	82	16	1	9	47	37-9	4	13	.278	.364	.431	126	11	3-1	.990	2	114	118	1b83	0	0.8
1972	KC A	53	71	1	15	2	0	0	5	7-1	0	4	.211	.282	.239	56	-4	0-0	.990	-2	34	86	1b13/3	0	-0.7
1973	KC A	74	138	17	34	6	1	2	16	29-2	2	15	.246	.380	.348	100	2	1-2	1.000	0	101	68	D36,1b10	0	0.0
1974	LA N	15	18	1	4	0	0	0	0	3-2	0	1	.222	.333	.222	60	-1	0-0	1.000	1	0	0	C2,1b2	0	0.0
Total	7	514	1219	142	324	47	6	25	145	160-21	8	83	.266	.352	.376	103	8	6-4	.991	-2	98	108	1b293,D36,C10/3	0	-1.5
HOPKINS, BUCK	John Winton "Sis"; B1.3.1883 Grafton VA; D10.2.1929 Phoebus VA; BL/TL/5´10˝/165; d7.22																								
1907	StL N	15	44	7	6	3	0	0	3	10	3	—	.136	.333	.205	71	0	2	.875	-3	0	0	O15C	—	-0.5

YEAR	TM LG	G	AB	R	H	2B	3B	HR	RBI	BB-IB	HP	SO	AVG	OBP	SLG	AOPS	ABR	SB-CS	FA	FR	RNG	THR	GAMES AT POSITION	DL	BFW
HOPKINS, MARTY	Meredith Hilliard; B2.22.1907 Wolfe City TX; D11.20.1963 Dallas TX; BR/TR/5´11˝/175; d4.17; Col Texas																								
1934	Phi N	10	25	6	3	2	0	0	3	7	0	5	.120	.313	.200	36	-2	0	1.000	-0	93	189	3b9	—	-0.2
	Chi A	67	210	22	45	7	0	2	28	42	1	26	.214	.348	.276	61	-11	0-3	.957	5	116	32	3b63	—	-0.5
1935	Chi A	59	144	20	32	3	0	2	17	36	0	23	.222	.378	.285	72	-4	1-0	.960	-4	102	83	3b49,2b5	—	-0.7
Total	2	136	379	48	80	12	0	4	48	85	1	54	.211	.357	.274	63	-17	1-3	.960	0	110	61	3b121,2b5	—	-1.4
HOPKINS, MIKE	Michael Joseph "Skinner"; B11.1.1872 Glasgow, Scotland; D2.5.1952 Pittsburgh PA; BR/TR/5´8˝/160; d8.24																								
1902	Pit N	1	2	0	2	1	0	0	0	0	0	—	1.000	1.000	1.500	648	1	0	1.000	0	*0*	*189*	/C	—	0.1
HOPP, JOHNNY	John Leonard "Hippity"; B7.18.1916 Hastings NE; D6.1.2003 Scottsbluff NE; BL/TL/5´10˝/175; d9.18; C2																								
1939	StL N	6	4	1	2	1	0	0	2	1	0	1	.500	.600	.750	246	1	0	1.000	0	342	258	1b2	—	0.1
1940	StL N	80	152	24	41	7	4	1	14	9	1	21	.270	.315	.388	88	-3	3	.967	2	125	44	O39(12/27/0),1b10	—	-0.2
1941	StL N	134	445	83	135	25	11	4	50	50	3	63	.303	.378	.436	121	13	15	.982	-1	107	60	O91(58/23/10),1b39	0	0.5
1942	†StL N	95	314	41	81	16	7	3	37	36	0	40	.258	.334	.382	102	1	14	.983	-4	85	116	1b88	0	-1.2
1943	†StL N	91	241	33	54	10	2	2	25	24	1	22	.224	.297	.307	71	-9	8	.950	1	113	23	O52(40/12/0),1b27	0	-1.3
1944	†StL N	139	527	106	177	35	9	11	72	58	2	47	.336	.404	.499	150	36	15	**.997**	-8	98	19	O131(1/130/0),1b6	0	2.5
1945	StL N	124	446	67	129	22	8	3	44	49	3	24	.289	.363	.395	108	5	14	.980	2	**113**	56	O104(2/26/89),1b15	0	0.1
1946	Bos N★	129	445	71	148	23	8	3	48	34	5	34	.333	.386	.440	133	19	21	.981	-2	94	96	1b68,O58(1/57/0)	0	1.4
1947	Bos N	134	430	74	124	20	2	2	32	58	2	30	.288	.376	.358	98	1	13	.980	-6	100	25	O125(0/123/2)	0	-0.7
1948	Pit N	120	392	64	109	15	12	1	31	40	0	25	.278	.345	.385	95	-3	5	1.000	-3	95	52	O80(1/71/8),1b25	0	-0.9
1949	Pit N	20	55	5	12	3	1	0	3	7	0	3	.218	.306	.309	64	-3	0	.929	-1	88	166	O7(2/0/5),1b6	0	-0.4
	Bro N	8	14	0	0	0	0	0	0	0	0	3	.000	.000	.000	-96	-4	0	1.000	1	105	393	O4(1/0/3),1b2	0	-0.3
	Pit N	85	316	50	106	11	4	5	36	30	0	26	.335	.393	.443	121	9	9	.994	-0	113	79	1b71,O9(2/0/7)	0	0.7
	Year	113	385	55	118	14	5	5	39	37	0	32	.306	.367	.408	105	3	9	.990	0	102	110	1b79,O20(5/0/15)	0	-0.0
1950	Pit N	106	318	51	108	24	5	8	47	43	1	17	.340	.420	.522	141	21	7	.990	-4	75	98	1b70,O7(2/2/3)	0	1.4
	†NY A	19	27	9	9	2	1	1	8	8	0	1	.333	.486	.593	180	4	0-1	1.000	0	71	23	1b12,O6L	0	0.3
1951	†NY A	46	63	10	13	1	0	2	4	9	0	11	.206	.306	.317	71	-3	2-0	.992	-2	55	83	1b25	0	-0.4
1952	NY A	15	25	4	4	0	0	0	2	2	1	3	.160	.250	.160	17	-3	2-0	1.000	1	119	156	1b12	0	-0.2
	Det A	42	46	5	10	1	0	0	3	6	0	7	.217	.308	.239	53	-3	0-0	1.000	-0	91	0	O4L/1	0	-0.3
	Year	57	71	9	14	1	0	0	5	8	1	10	.197	.287	.211	41	-6	2-0	1.000	0	115	150	1b13,O4L	0	-0.5
Total	14	1393	4260	698	1262	216	74	46	458	464	19	378	.296	.368	.414	113	79	128-1	.985	-23	104	44	O717(132/471/127),1b479	0	1.1
HOPPER, NORRIS	Norris Stephen; B3.24.1979 Shelby NC; BR/TR/5´10˝/200; [KCA98 8/227]; d8.20																								
2006	Cin N	21	39	6	14	1	0	1	5	6-0	0	4	.359	.435	.462	126	2	2-2	1.000	3	131	406	O15(1/2/13)	0	0.4
HORAN, SHAGS	Joseph Patrick; B9.6.1895 St.Louis MO; D2.13.1969 Torrance CA; BR/TR/5´10˝/170; d7.14																								
1924	NY A	22	31	4	9	1	0	0	7	1	0	5	.290	.313	.323	64	-2	0-0	1.000	0	89	156	O14(4/1/9)	—	-0.2
HORN, SAM	Samuel Lee; B11.2.1963 Dallas TX; BL/TL/6´5˝/(215–250); [BosA82 1/16]; d7.25																								
1987	Bos A	46	158	31	44	7	0	14	34	17-0	2	55	.278	.356	.589	140	9	0-1	ø	0	0	0	D40	0	0.7
1988	Bos A	24	61	4	9	0	0	2	8	11-3	0	20	.148	.274	.246	46	-4	0-0	ø	0	0	0	D16	0	-0.5
1989	Bos A	33	54	1	8	2	0	0	4	8-1	0	16	.148	.258	.185	25	-5	0-0	1.000	-0	0	0	D14,1b2	50	-0.6
1990	Bal A	79	246	30	61	13	0	14	45	32-1	0	62	.248	.332	.472	126	8	0-0	.970	-1	93	95	D63,1b10	21	0.5
1991	Bal A	121	317	45	74	16	0	23	61	41-4	3	99	.233	.326	.502	130	12	0-0	ø	0	0	0	D102	0	0.9
1992	Bal A	63	162	13	38	10	1	5	19	21-2	1	60	.235	.324	.401	99	0	0-0	ø	0	0	0	D46	0	-0.1
1993	Cle A	12	33	8	15	1	0	4	8	1-0	1	5	.455	.472	.848	250	7	0-0	ø	0	0	0	D11	0	0.6
1995	Tex A	11	9	0	1	0	0	0	0	1-0	0	6	.111	.200	.111	-16	-2	0-0	ø	0	—	—	/D	0	-0.2
Total	8	389	1040	132	250	49	1	62	179	132-11	7	323	.240	.328	.468	118	25	0-1	.972	-1	88	90	D293,1b12	71	1.3
HORNER, BOB	James Robert; B8.6.1957 Junction City KS; BR/TR/6´1˝/(195–220); [AtlN78 1/1]; d6.16; Col Arizona St.																								
1978	Atl N	89	323	50	86	17	1	23	63	24-2	2	42	.266	.313	.539	123	9	0-0	.956	10	110	108	3b89	0	1.8
1979	Atl N	121	487	66	153	15	1	33	98	22-6	3	74	.314	.346	.552	134	20	0-2	.930	-7	96	74	3b82,1b45	15	0.9
1980	Atl N	124	463	81	124	14	1	35	89	27-3	1	50	.268	.307	.529	129	14	3-1	.935	11	**115**	124	3b121/1	0	2.5
1981	Atl N	79	300	42	83	10	0	15	42	32-3	1	39	.277	.345	.460	127	10	2-3	.938	-11	89	50	3b79	0	-0.3
1982	†Atl N★	140	499	85	130	24	0	32	97	66-3	4	75	.261	.350	.501	133	22	3-5	.970	-14	86	92	3b137	0	0.5
1983	Atl N	104	386	75	117	25	1	20	68	50-2	1	63	.303	.383	.528	140	22	4-2	.958	-10	83	113	3b104/1	48	1.1
1984	Atl N	32	113	15	31	8	0	3	19	14-2	0	17	.274	.349	.425	110	2	0-0	.965	2	108	121	3b32	138	0.3
1985	Atl N	130	483	61	129	25	3	27	89	50-4	1	57	.267	.333	.499	124	14	1-1	1.000	-8	93	134	1b87,3b40	0	0.0
1986	Atl N	141	517	70	141	22	0	27	87	52-8	2	72	.273	.336	.472	117	11	1-4	.995	0	98	**123**	1b139	0	0.1
1988	StL N	60	206	15	53	9	1	3	33	32-6	1	23	.257	.348	.354	104	2	0-0	.990	1	106	98	1b57	105	-0.1
Total	10	1020	3777	560	1047	169	8	218	685	369-39	16	512	.277	.340	.499	127	126	14-18	.946	-27	96	97	3b684,1b330	306	6.8
HORNSBY, ROGERS	Rogers "Rajah"; B4.27.1896 Winters TX; D1.5.1963 Chicago IL; BR/TR/5´11˝/175; d9.10; M14/C3; HF1942; OF(6/1/13)																								
1915	StL N	18	57	5	14	2	0	0	4	2	0	6	.246	.271	.281	67	-2	0-2	.922	-2	82	163	S18	—	-0.4
1916	StL N	139	495	63	155	17	15	6	65	40	4	63	.313	.369	.444	150	28	17	.928	-0	112	56	3b83,S45,1b15/2	—	3.7
1917	StL N	145	523	86	171	24	**17**	8	66	45	4	34	.327	.385	**.484**	**170**	**42**	17	.939	19	112	**129**	S144	—	**7.8**
1918	StL N	115	416	51	117	19	11	5	60	40	3	43	.281	.349	.416	138	18	8	.933	9	**113**	113	S109,O3(0/1/2)	—	3.8
1919	StL N	**138**	512	68	163	15	9	8	71	48	7	41	.318	.384	.430	**154**	**34**	17	.933	9	106	106	3b72,S37,2b25,1b5	—	**5.1**
1920	StL N	149	589	96	**218**	**44**	20	9	**94**	60	3	50	**.370**	**.431**	**.559**	**190**	**69**	12-15	.962	7	**104**	94	2b149	—	**7.9**
1921	StL N	**154**	592	**131**	**235**	**44**	**18**	21	**126**	60	7	48	**.397**	**.458**	**.639**	**191**	**79**	13-13	.969	-2	100	87	2b142,O6L,S3,3b3/1	—	**7.7**
1922	StL N	**154**	623	**141**	**250**	**46**	14	**42**	**152**	65	1	50	**.401**	**.459**	**.722**	**210**	**100**	17-12	**.967**	-7	90	95	2b154	—	**8.9**
1923	StL N	107	424	89	163	32	10	17	83	55	3	29	**.384**	**.459**	**.627**	**188**	**56**	3-7	.962	-16	92	86	2b96,1b10	—	3.8
1924	StL N	143	536	**121**	**227**	**43**	14	25	94	**89**	2	32	**.424**	**.507**	**.696**	**223**	**99**	5-12	.965	-3	100	105	2b143	—	**9.3**
1925	StL N	138	504	133	203	41	10	**39**	**143**	83	2	39	**.403**	**.489**	**.756**	**208**	**85**	5-3	.954	-14	91	122	2b136,M	—	**6.8**
1926	†StL N	134	527	96	167	34	5	11	93	61	0	39	.317	.388	.463	123	19	3	.962	-31	94	100	2b134,M	—	-0.8
1927	NY N	**155**	568	**133**	205	32	9	26	125	**86**	4	38	.361	**.448**	.586	**176**	**64**	9	.972	2	107	106	2b155,M	—	6.8
1928	Bos N	140	486	99	188	42	7	21	94	**107**	1	41	**.387**	**.498**	**.632**	**204**	**83**	5	.973	-23	97	85	2b140,M	—	**6.1**
1929	†Chi N	**156**	602	**156**	229	47	8	39	149	87	1	65	.380	.459	**.679**	**178**	**76**	2	.973	-3	103	112	2b156	—	**6.8**
1930	Chi N	42	104	15	32	5	1	2	18	12	1	12	.308	.385	.433	96	0	0	.916	-3	99	104	2b25,M	—	-0.2
1931	Chi N	100	357	64	118	37	1	16	90	56	0	23	.331	.421	.574	162	34	1	.951	-8	103	58	2b69,3b26,M	—	3.0
1932	Chi N	19	58	10	13	2	0	1	7	10	2	4	.224	.357	.310	82	-1	0	1.000	-4	86	0	O10R,3b6,M	—	-0.5
1933	StL N	46	83	9	27	6	0	2	21	12	2	6	.325	.423	.470	147	6	1	.967	-3	86	90	2b17	—	0.4
	StL A	11	9	2	3	1	0	1	2	2	0	1	.333	.455	.778	208	1	0-0	ø	0	—	—	/HM	—	0.1
1934	StL A	24	23	2	7	2	0	1	11	7	1	4	.304	.484	.522	147	2	0-0	1.000	0	123	397	/3rfM	—	0.2
1935	StL A	10	24	1	5	3	0	0	3	3	0	6	.208	.296	.333	60	-1	0-0	1.000	-0	50	31	1b3,2b2/3M	—	-0.2
1936	StL A	2	5	1	2	0	0	0	2	1	0	0	.400	.500	.400	121	0	0-0	1.000	-0	0	0	/1M	—	0.0
1937	StL A	20	56	7	18	3	0	1	11	7	0	5	.321	.397	.429	107	1	0-0	.947	-3	93	90	2b17,M	—	-0.1
Total	23	2259	8173	1579	2930	541	169	301	1584	1038	48	679	.358	.434	.577	176	892	135-64	.965	-77	99	98	2b1561,S356,3b192,1b35,O20R	—	86.0
HORNUNG, JOE	Michael Joseph "Ubbo Ubbo"; B6.12.1857 Carthage NY; D10.30.1931 Howard Beach NY; BR/TR/5´8.5˝/164; d5.1; U2; OF(1051/1/5)																								
1879	Buf N	78	319	46	85	18	7	0	38	2	—	27	.266	.271	.367	105	1	—	.844	-1	69	57	O77(76/0/1)/1	—	-0.4
1880	Buf N	**85**	342	47	91	8	11	1	42	8	—	29	.266	.283	.363	115	4	—	.874	1	77	62	O67L,1b18,2b5/P	—	0.0
1881	Bos N	**83**	324	39	78	12	8	2	25	5	—	25	.241	.252	.346	90	-4	—	**.948**	12	86	149	O83(83/1/0)	—	0.2
1882	Bos N	**85**	388	67	117	14	11	1	50	2	—	25	.302	.305	.402	124	9	—	**.932**	12	75	114	O84L/1	—	1.6
1883	Bos N	**98**	446	**107**	124	25	13	8	66	8	—	54	.278	.291	.446	117	7	—	**.936**	7	67	96	O98L/3	—	1.0
1884	Bos N	115	518	119	139	27	10	7	51	17	—	80	.268	.292	.400	116	8	—	.916	2	60	33	O110L,1b6	—	0.6
1885	Bos N	25	109	14	22	4	1	1	7	1	—	20	.202	.209	.284	61	-5	—	.919	-2	23	0	O25L	—	-0.7
1886	Bos N	94	424	67	109	12	2	2	40	10	—	62	.257	.274	.309	79	-11	16	**.948**	5	62	33	O94L	—	-0.8
1887	Bos N	98	437	85	118	10	6	5	49	17	3	28	.270	.302	.355	81	-13	41	**.935**	12	128	87	O98L	—	-0.3
1888	Bos N	107	431	61	103	11	7	3	53	16	2	39	.239	.269	.318	84	-9	29	.947	-7	57	0	O107(106/0/1)	—	-1.8
1889	Bal AA	135	533	73	122	13	9	1	78	22	7	72	.229	.269	.293	59	-32	34	.913	12	126	179	O134(134/0/1)/3	—	-2.0
1890	NY N	120	513	62	122	18	5	0	65	12	2	37	.238	.258	.292	60	-29	39	.931	-1	94	109	O77(76/0/2),1b36,3b5,S2	—	-3.1
Total	12	1123	4784	787	1230	172	90	31	564	120	14	498	.257	.277	.350	90	-74	159	.922	51	82	83	O1054L,1b62,3b7,2b5,S2/P	—	-5.7

YEAR	TM LG	G	AB	R	H	2B	3B	HR	RBI	BB-IB	HP	SO	AVG	OBP	SLG	AOPS	ABR	SB-CS	FA	FR	RNG	THR	GAMES AT POSITION	DL	BFW
HORTON, TONY	Anthony Darrin; B12.6.1944 Santa Monica CA; BR/TR/6´3˝/(195–210); d7.31																								
1964	Bos A	36	126	9	28	5	0	1	8	3-0	0	20	.222	.238	.286	44	-10	0-0	1.000	1	112	205	O24L,1b8	0	-1.1
1965	Bos A	60	163	23	48	8	1	7	23	18-1	0	36	.294	.361	.485	131	7	0-2	.980	-2	90	91	1b44	0	0.2
1966	Bos A	6	22	0	3	0	0	0	2	0-0	0	5	.136	.136	.136	-19	-3	0-0	1.000	1	136	163	1b6	0	-0.3
1967	Bos A	21	39	2	12	3	0	0	9	0-0	0	5	.308	.300	.385	96	0	0-0	.929	-1	95	97	1b6	0	-0.2
	Cle A	106	363	35	102	13	4	10	44	18-3	4	52	.281	.321	.421	117	6	3-0	.991	-5	74	95	1b94	0	-0.4
	Year	127	402	37	114	16	4	10	53	18-3	4	57	.284	.319	.418	114	6	3-0	.987	-6	75	95	1b100	0	-0.6
1968	Cle A	133	477	57	119	29	3	14	59	34-5	3	56	.249	.302	.411	117	9	3-1	.992	-4	79	93	1b128	0	-0.4
1969	Cle A	159	625	77	174	25	4	27	93	37-3	2	91	.278	.319	.461	113	8	3-3	.989	2	101	95	1b157	0	-0.4
1970	Cle A	115	413	48	111	19	3	17	59	30-5	4	54	.269	.321	.453	107	3	3-2	.994	4	106	116	1b112	0	-0.3
Total	7	636	2228	251	597	102	15	76	297	140-17	13	319	.268	.313	.430	109	20	12-8	.990	-5	91	99	1b555,O24L	0	-2.9
HORTON, WILLIE	Willie Wattison; B10.18.1942 Arno VA; BR/TR/5´11˝/(190–210); d9.10; C2																								
1963	Det A	15	43	6	14	2	1	1	4	0-0	0	8	.326	.326	.488	120	1	2-0	1.000	-1	78	0	O9(8/0/1)	0	0.0
1964	Det A	25	80	6	13	1	3	1	10	11-2	1	20	.162	.272	.287	55	-5	0-0	.943	-2	88	0	O23(20/0/3)	0	-0.9
1965	Det A★	143	512	69	140	20	2	29	104	48-9	6	101	.273	.340	.490	132	21	5-9	.988	3	104	85	O141(111/0/34)/3	0	1.4
1966	Det A	146	526	72	138	22	6	27	100	44-4	3	103	.262	.321	.481	125	15	1-1	.979	-4	97	48	O137(129/0/20)	0	0.4
1967	Det A	122	401	47	110	20	3	19	67	36-0	4	80	.274	.338	.481	137	18	0-0	.971	1	99	79	O110(109/0/1)	0	1.4
1968	†Det A★	143	512	68	146	20	2	36	85	49-8	8	110	.285	.352	.543	165	39	0-3	.973	-6	88	70	O139L	0	2.8
1969	Det A	141	508	66	133	17	1	28	91	52-10	3	93	.262	.332	.465	117	10	3-3	.972	5	112	78	O136(135/0/3)	0	0.7
1970	Det A★	96	371	53	113	18	2	17	69	28-6	2	43	.305	.354	.501	133	15	0-1	.982	3	96	172	O96(96/0/2)	69	1.3
1971	Det A	119	450	64	130	25	1	22	72	37-8	7	75	.289	.349	.496	132	18	1-5	.963	-7	85	113	O118(106/0/29)	0	0.4
1972	†Det A	108	333	44	77	9	5	11	36	27-5	3	47	.231	.293	.387	98	-2	0-0	1.000	-4	86	96	O98(81/0/30)	15	-1.2
1973	Det A★	111	411	42	130	19	3	17	53	23-5	7	57	.316	.362	.501	133	17	1-4	.942	-9	89	31	O107L/D	18	0.1
1974	Det A	72	238	32	71	8	1	15	47	21-3	3	36	.298	.361	.529	149	14	0-1	.947	-4	91	48	O64L/D	83	0.6
1975	Det A	159	615	62	169	13	1	25	92	44-11	0	109	.275	.319	.421	104	1	1-2	ø	0	0	0	D159	0	-0.4
1976	Det A	114	401	40	105	17	0	14	56	49-7	2	63	.262	.342	.409	115	9	0-0	ø	0	0	0	D105	39	0.6
1977	Det A	1	4	0	1	0	0	0	0	0-0	0	0	.250	.250	.250	35	0	0-0	1.000	-0	49	0	/lf	0	-0.1
	Tex A	139	519	55	150	23	3	15	75	42-5	0	117	.289	.337	.432	108	5	2-3	.938	-1	89	0	D128,O10L	0	0.0
	Year	140	523	55	151	23	3	15	75	42-5	0	117	.289	.337	.430	107	5	2-3	.941	-1	85	0	D128,O11L	0	-0.1
1978	Cle A	50	169	15	42	7	0	5	22	15-4	1	25	.249	.314	.379	95	-1	3-0	ø	0	0	0	D48	0	-0.2
	Oak A	32	102	11	32	8	0	3	19	9-2	0	15	.314	.369	.480	144	6	0-1	.333	-0	104	0	D27/lf	0	0.5
	Tor A	33	122	12	25	6	0	3	19	4-0	0	29	.205	.228	.328	54	-8	0-0	ø	0	0	0	D30	0	-0.9
	Year	115	393	38	99	21	0	11	60	28-6	1	69	.252	.303	.389	94	-4	3-1	.841	-0	104	0	D105/lf	0	-0.6
1979	Sea A	162	646	77	180	19	5	29	106	42-4	4	112	.279	.326	.458	107	3	1-1	ø	0	0	0	D162	0	-0.2
1980	Sea A	97	335	32	74	10	1	8	36	39-2	4	70	.221	.306	.328	74	-12	0-4	ø	0	0	0	D92	48	-1.6
Total	18	2028	7298	873	1993	284	40	325	1163	620-95	58	1313	.273	.332	.457	119	164	20-38	.972	-26	95	79	O1190(1117/0/123),D753/3	272	4.7
HOSEY, DWAYNE	Dwayne Samuel; B3.11.1967 Sharon PA; BB/TR/5´10˝/175; [ChiA87 13/323]; d9.1; Col Pasadena (CA) City																								
1995	†Bos A	24	68	20	23	8	1	3	7	8-0	0	16	.338	.408	.618	157	6	6-0	1.000	0	103	111	O21(2/19/1)/D	0	0.7
1996	Bos A	28	78	13	17	2	2	1	3	7-0	0	17	.218	.282	.333	54	-6	6-3	.984	3	121	156	O26(7/20/0),D2	0	-0.3
Total	2	52	146	33	40	10	3	4	10	15-0	0	33	.274	.342	.466	102	0	12-3	.991	3	113	136	O47(9/39/1),D3	0	0.4
HOSEY, STEVE	Steven Bernard; B4.2.1969 Oakland CA; BR/TR/6´3˝/(215–225); [SFN89 1/14]; d8.29; Col Cal St.–Fresno																								
1992	SF N	21	56	6	14	1	0	1	6	0-0	0	15	.250	.241	.321	64	-3	1-1	.960	-2	81	0	O18R	0	-0.6
1993	SF N	3	2	0	1	1	0	0	1	1-0	0	1	.500	.667	1.000	350	1	0-0	ø	-0	0	0	/rf	0	0.1
Total	2	24	58	6	15	2	0	1	7	1-0	0	16	.259	.262	.345	77	-2	1-1	.960	-2	80	0	O19R	0	-0.5
HOSLEY, TIM	Timothy Kenneth; B5.10.1947 Spartanburg SC; BR/TR/5´10˝/(175–195); d9.8																								
1970	Det A	7	12	1	2	0	0	1	2	0-0	0	6	.167	.154	.417	55	-1	0-0	1.000	1	135	348	C4	0	0.0
1971	Det A	7	16	2	3	0	0	2	6	0-0	0	1	.188	.188	.563	101	0	0-0	1.000	0	126	0	C4/1	0	0.0
1973	Oak A	13	14	3	3	0	0	0	2	2-0	0	3	.214	.313	.214	53	-1	0-0	.952	-1	0	68	C13	0	-0.1
1974	Oak A	11	7	3	2	0	0	0	1	1-0	0	2	.286	.333	.286	98	0	0-0	1.000	1	87	0	C8/1	0	0.1
1975	Chi N	62	141	22	36	7	0	6	20	27-3	2	25	.255	.382	.433	120	5	1-1	.968	0	107	90	C53	0	0.7
1976	Oak A	37	55	4	9	2	0	1	4	8-0	0	12	.164	.270	.255	56	-3	0-0	.968	0	78	58	C37	0	-0.2
	Chi N	1	1	0	0	0	0	0	0	0-0	0	0	.000	.000	.000	-92	0	0-0	ø	0	—	—	/H	0	0.0
1977	Oak A	39	78	5	15	0	0	1	10	16-0	1	13	.192	.333	.231	59	-4	0-0	.955	2	69	100	C19,D12,1b3	0	-0.2
1978	Oak A	13	23	1	7	2	0	0	3	1-0	1	6	.304	.360	.391	117	1	0-0	.962	0	66	131	C6/D	0	0.1
1981	Oak A	18	21	2	2	0	0	1	5	2-0	0	5	.095	.174	.238	18	-2	0-0	.750	-0	0	0	/1D	0	-0.3
Total	9	208	368	43	79	11	0	12	53	57-3	4	73	.215	.324	.342	87	-5	1-1	.968	3	89	91	C144,D17,1b6	0	0.1
HOSTETLER, CHUCK	Charles Cloyd; B9.22.1903 McClellandtown PA; D2.18.1971 Fort Collins CO; BL/TR/6´0˝/175; d4.18																								
1944	Det A	90	265	42	79	9	2	0	20	21	0	31	.298	.350	.347	94	-2	4-4	.985	-1	96	109	O65(1/4/61)	0	-0.7
1945	†Det A	42	44	3	7	3	0	0	2	7	0	8	.159	.275	.227	43	-3	0-0	.889	-1	82	0	O8(6/1/1)	0	-0.4
Total	2	132	309	45	86	12	2	0	22	28	0	39	.278	.338	.330	87	-5	4-4	.979	-1	95	102	O73(7/5/62)	0	-1.1
HOSTETLER, DAVE	David Alan; B3.27.1956 Pasadena CA; BR/TR/6´4˝/(215–225); [MonN78 4/87]; d9.15; Col USC																								
1981	Mon N	5	6	1	3	0	0	1	1	0-0	0	2	.500	.500	1.000	307	1	0-0	1.000	-0	0	303	1b2	0	0.1
1982	Tex A	113	418	53	97	12	3	22	67	42-3	1	113	.232	.300	.433	104	1	2-2	.990	-9	70	105	1b109,D3	0	-1.6
1983	Tex A	94	304	31	67	9	2	11	46	42-1	5	103	.220	.323	.372	92	-3	0-2	1.000	-0	0	0	D88,1b2	0	-0.7
1984	Tex A	37	82	7	18	2	1	3	10	13-0	0	27	.220	.326	.378	91	-1	0-0	1.000	0	104	102	1b14,D13	0	-0.2
1988	Pit N	6	8	0	2	0	0	0	0	0-0	0	3	.250	.250	.250	44	-1	0-0	.944	0	241	0	1b4/C	0	-0.1
Total	5	255	818	92	187	23	6	37	124	97-4	6	248	.229	.313	.407	99	-3	2-4	.990	-10	73	104	1b131,D104/C	0	-2.5
HOTALING, PETE	Peter James "Monkey"; B12.16.1856 Mohawk NY; D7.3.1928 Cleveland OH; BR/TR/5´8˝/166; d5.1																								
1879	Cin N	**81**	369	64	103	20	9	1	27	12	—	17	.279	.302	.390	133	14	—	.843	0	107	116	O69(0/67/2),C8,2b6,3b3	—	1.1
1880	Cle N	78	325	40	78	17	8	0	41	10	—	30	.240	.263	.342	105	2	—	.896	-5	76	131	O78(2/76/0),C2	—	-0.7
1881	Wor N	77	317	51	98	15	3	1	35	18	—	12	.309	.346	.385	123	8	—	.862	-4	107	61	O74(2/72/1),C3	—	0.1
1882	Bos N	84	378	64	98	16	5	0	28	16	—	21	.259	.289	.328	97	-1	—	.865	0	84	139	O84(0/84/1)	—	-0.3
1883	Cle N	**100**	417	54	108	20	8	0	30	12	—	31	.259	.280	.345	90	-5	—	.829	-2	101	149	O100C	—	-0.9
1884	Cle N	102	408	69	99	16	6	3	27	28	—	50	.243	.291	.333	93	-4	—	.849	-1	113	144	O102(3/99/0)/2	—	-0.7
1885	Bro AA	94	370	73	95	9	5	1	34	49	4	—	.257	.350	.316	111	7	—	.893	-1	107	105	O94C	—	0.3
1887	Cle AA	126	505	108	151	28	13	3	94	53	7	—	.299	.373	.424	126	19	43	.903	-1	112	94	O126C	—	1.2
1888	Cle AA	98	403	67	101	7	6	0	55	26	7	—	.251	.307	.298	97	-1	35	.878	-10	64	187	O98C	—	-1.3
Total	9	840	3492	590	931	148	63	9	371	224	18	161	.267	.314	.353	108	39	78	.869	-23	97	126	O825(7/816/4),C13,2b7,3b3	—	-1.2
HOTTMAN, KEN	Kenneth Roger; B5.7.1948 Stockton CA; BR/TR/5´11˝/190; [ChiA68 S2/22]; d9.11; Col Sacramento (CA) City																								
1971	Chi A	6	16	1	2	0	0	0	0	1-0	0	2	.125	.176	.125	-13	-2	0-0	1.000	-1	65	0	O5L	0	-0.4
HOUCK, SADIE	Sargent Perry; B3.1856 Washington DC; D5.26.1919 Washington DC; BR/TR/5´7˝/151; d5.1																								
1879	Bos N	80	356	69	95	24	9	2	49	4	—	11	.267	.275	.402	117	6	—	.814	-10	144	168	O47(1/5/42),S33	—	-0.2
1880	Bos N	12	47	2	7	0	0	0	2	0	—	6	.149	.149	.149	1	-5	—	.786	-2	35	0	O12(0/2/10)	—	-0.6
	Pro N	49	184	27	37	7	7	1	22	3	—	6	.201	.214	.332	85	-3	—	.873	-1	82	0	O49(38/12/2)	—	-0.7
	Year	61	231	29	44	7	7	1	24	3	—	12	.190	.201	.294	68	-8	—	.855	-3	73	0	O61(38/14/12)	—	-1.3
1881	Det N	75	308	43	86	16	6	1	36	6	—	6	.279	.293	.380	106	1	—	.868	1	97	**166**	S75	—	0.5
1883	Det N	**101**	416	52	105	18	12	0	40	9	—	18	.252	.268	.353	91	-5	—	.852	4	103	122	S101	—	0.2
1884	Phi AA	**108**	472	93	140	19	14	0	—	7	8	—	.297	.318	.396	124	10	—	**.893**	22	**112**	117	S108/2	—	3.2
1885	Phi AA	93	388	74	99	10	9	0	54	10	7	—	.255	.286	.327	88	-7	—	.863	19	114	117	S93	—	1.3
1886	Bal AA	61	260	29	50	8	1	0	17	4	4	—	.192	.216	.231	41	-18	25	.849	-6	86	25	S55,2b5/cf	—	-2.0
	Was N	52	195	14	42	3	0	0	14	2	—	28	.215	.223	.231	41	-14	4	.858	2	107	59	S51/2	—	-1.0
1887	NY AA	10	33	3	5	1	0	0	0	3	1	—	.152	.243	.182	20	-3	2	.831	2	137	106	S10/2	—	-0.1
Total	8	641	2659	406	666	106	58	4	234	48	20	75	.250	.269	.338	91	-38	31	.863	31	104	111	S526,O109(39/20/54),2b8	—	0.6

YEAR	TM LG	G	AB	R	H	2B	3B	HR	RBI	BB-IB	HP	SO	AVG	OBP	SLG	AOPS	ABR	SB-CS	FA	FR	RNG	THR	GAMES AT POSITION	DL	BFW
Houk, Ralph	Ralph George "Major"; B8.9.1919 Lawrence KS; BR/TR/5´11˝/(191–193); d4.26; M20/C4																								
1947	†NY A	41	92	7	25	3	1	0	12	11	1	5	.272	.356	.326	91	-1	0-0	.987	0	*88*	*81*	C41	0	0.1
1948	NY A	14	29	3	8	2	0	0	3	0	0	0	.276	.276	.345	65	-2	0-0	1.000	3	*132*	*146*	C14	0	0.1
1949	NY A	5	7	0	4	0	0	0	1	0	0	1	.571	.571	.571	203	1	0-0	.889	-1	*49*	*0*	C5	0	0.0
1950	NY A	10	9	0	1	1	0	0	1	0	0	2	.111	.111	.222	-17	-2	0-0	.929	0	*0*	*0*	C9	0	-0.1
1951	NY A	3	5	0	1	0	0	0	2	0	0	1	.200	.200	.200	9	-1	0-0	1.000	-0	*0*	*447*	C3	0	-0.1
1952	†NY A	9	6	0	2	0	0	0	0	1	0	0	.333	.429	.333	121	0	0-0	.917	0	*0*	*0*	C9	0	0.1
1953	NY A	8	9	2	2	0	0	0	1	0	0	1	.222	.222	.222	21	-1	0-0	1.000	0	*0*	*0*	C8	0	-0.1
1954	NY A	1	1	0	0	0	0	0	0	0	0	0	.000	.000	.000	-99	0	0-0	ø	0	—	—	/H	0	0.0
Total	8	91	158	12	43	6	1	0	20	12	1	10	.272	.327	.323	79	-6	0-0	.981	2	*81*	*87*	C89	0	0.0
House, Frank	Henry Franklin "Pig"; B2.18.1930 Bessemer AL; D3.13.2005 Birmingham AL; BL/TR/6´2˝/190; d7.21; Mil 1952–53																								
1950	Det A	5	5	1	2	1	0	0	0	0	0	1	.400	.400	.600	148	0	0-0	1.000	0	*0*	*0*	C5	0	0.0
1951	Det A	18	41	3	9	2	0	1	4	6	0	2	.220	.319	.341	78	-1	1-1	.957	-0	*74*	*152*	C18	0	-0.1
1954	Det A	114	352	35	88	12	1	9	38	31	1	34	.250	.307	.366	87	-7	2-1	.992	2	*131*	*121*	C107	0	-0.1
1955	Det A	102	328	37	85	11	1	15	53	22-4	3	25	.259	.308	.436	102	-2	0-0	.987	-1	*100*	*115*	C93	0	0.2
1956	Det A	94	321	44	77	6	2	10	44	21-0	3	19	.240	.290	.364	72	-15	1-1	.986	-3	*133*	*101*	C88	0	-1.3
1957	Det A	106	348	31	90	9	0	7	36	35-13	1	26	.259	.327	.345	82	-8	1-1	.997	9	132	86	C97	0	0.5
1958	KC A	76	202	16	51	6	3	4	24	12-2	1	13	.252	.295	.371	81	-6	1-0	.992	-7	89	121	C55	0	-1.0
1959	KC A	98	347	32	82	14	3	1	30	20-6	2	23	.236	.282	.303	59	-20	0-3	.982	-8	96	75	C95	0	-2.5
1960	Cin N	23	28	0	5	2	0	0	3	0-0	0	2	.179	.179	.250	16	-3	0-0	1.000	1	132	108	C8	0	-0.2
1961	Det A	17	22	3	5	1	1	0	3	4-0	0	2	.227	.333	.364	87	0	0-0	.974	-1	73	76	C14	0	-0.1
Total	10	653	1994	202	494	64	11	47	235	151-25	11	147	.248	.302	.362	80	-62	6-7	.988	-9	*114*	*102*	C580	0	-4.6
House, J.R.	James Rodger; B11.11.1979 Charleston WV; BR/TR/5´10˝/(200–215); [PitN99 5/152]; d9.27																								
2003	Pit N	1	1	0	1	0	0	0	0	0-0	0	0	1.000	1.000	1.000	420	0	0-0	ø	0	—	—	/H	0	0.0
2004	Pit N	5	9	1	1	1	0	0	0	0-0	0	2	.111	.111	.222	-17	-2	0-0	1.000	0	0	0	C3	0	-0.1
2006	Hou N	4	9	0	0	0	0	0	0	0-0	0	2	.000	.000	.000	-97	-3	0-0	1.000	-0	81	0	C3,1b2	0	-0.3
Total	3	10	19	1	2	1	0	0	0	0-0	0	4	.105	.105	.158	-33	-5	0-0	1.000	0	31	0	C6,1b2	0	-0.4
Householder, Charlie	Charles F.; B1856 Harrisburg PA; D12.26.1908 Harrisburg PA; BR/TR/5´7˝/150; d4.20																								
1884	CP U	83	310	32	74	12	5	1	—	12	—	—	.239	.267	.319	78	-18	—	.796	-4	78	107	3b41,O40L,S3,P2	—	-2.0
Householder, Charlie	Charles W.; B2.8.1854 Philadelphia PA; D9.3.1913 Philadelphia PA; BL/TL/5´11˝/158; d5.2																								
1882	Bal AA	**74**	307	42	78	10	7	1	—	4	—	—	.254	.264	.342	111	4	—	.971	3	111	83	1b74,C3	—	0.0
1884	Bro AA	76	273	28	66	15	3	3	—	12	2	—	.242	.279	.352	104	1	—	.959	-4	132	87	1b40,C31,O6(2/2/1)/2	—	-0.4
Total	2	150	580	70	144	25	10	4	—	16	2	—	.248	.271	.347	108	5	—	.967	-1	118	84	1b114,C34,O6(2/2/1)/2	—	-0.4
Householder, Ed	Edward H.; B10.12.1869 Pittsburgh PA; D7.3.1924 Los Angeles CA; BL/TL/5´9.5˝/180; d4.17																								
1903	Bro N	12	43	5	9	0	0	0	9	2	0	—	.209	.244	.209	31	-4	3	.967	1	60	250	O12C	—	-0.4
Householder, Paul	Paul Wesley; B9.4.1958 Columbus OH; BB/TR/6´0˝/(180–200); [CinN76 2/47]; d8.26																								
1980	Cin N	20	45	3	11	1	1	0	7	1-0	0	13	.244	.261	.311	60	-3	1-0	1.000	0	81	234	O14(0/1/13)	0	-0.3
1981	Cin N	23	69	12	19	4	0	2	9	10-0	0	16	.275	.367	.420	123	2	3-1	1.000	-1	95	77	O19(1/6/13)	0	0.2
1982	Cin N	138	417	40	88	11	5	9	34	30-5	2	77	.211	.265	.326	65	-21	17-11	.992	8	106	**182**	O131(0/9/123)	0	-2.0
1983	Cin N	123	380	40	97	24	4	6	43	44-5	2	60	.255	.335	.387	96	-1	12-12	**.991**	2	109	80	O112(6/36/80)	22	-0.5
1984	Cin N	14	12	3	1	1	0	0	0	3-1	0	3	.083	.267	.167	23	-1	1-1	1.000	1	121	670	O10(3/1/6)	0	0.0
	StL N	13	14	1	2	0	0	0	0	0-0	0	3	.143	.143	.143	-20	-2	0-0	1.000	-1	64	0	O8(4/1/4)	0	-0.3
	Year	27	26	4	3	1	0	0	0	3-1	0	6	.115	.207	.154	3	-3	1-1	1.000	1	92	327	O18(7/2/10)	0	-0.3
1985	Mil A	95	299	41	77	15	0	11	34	27-0	1	60	.258	.320	.418	101	0	1-2	.986	2	105	90	O91(7/32/59),D3	0	-0.2
1986	Mil A	26	78	4	17	3	1	1	16	7-0	1	16	.218	.284	.321	64	-4	1-2	1.000	-1	89	87	O22(12/5/8),D3	0	-0.6
1987	Hou N	14	12	2	1	1	0	0	1	4-0	0	2	.083	.313	.167	33	-1	0-0	1.000	-1	64	0	O7(0/6/1)	0	-0.1
Total	8	466	1326	146	313	60	11	29	144	126-11	6	250	.236	.304	.363	84	-31	36-29	.991	10	104	123	O414(33/97/307),D6	22	-3.8
Houseman, John	John Franklin; B1.10.1870 , Netherlands; D11.4.1922 Chicago IL; ?/160; d9.11																								
1894	Chi N	4	15	5	6	3	1	0	4	5	1	3	.400	.571	.733	201	3	2	.950	1	107	129	S3/2	—	0.3
1897	StL N	80	278	34	68	6	6	0	21	28	7	—	.245	.329	.309	70	-12	16	.918	-1	102	61	2b41,O33(7/7/19),S5,3b3	—	-1.0
Total	2	84	293	39	74	9	7	0	25	33	8	3	.253	.344	.331	79	-9	18	.916	-0	102	69	2b42,O33(7/7/19),S8,3b3	—	-0.7
Houser, Ben	Benjamin Franklin; B11.30.1883 Shenandoah PA; D1.15.1952 Augusta ME; BL/TL/6´1˝/185; d5.2																								
1910	Phi A	34	69	9	13	3	2	0	7	7	0	—	.188	.263	.290	74	-2	0	1.000	-0	72	142	1b26	—	-0.3
1911	Bos N	20	71	11	18	1	0	1	9	8	0	6	.254	.329	.310	73	-2	2	.988	1	112	111	1b20	—	-0.2
1912	Bos N	108	332	38	95	17	3	8	52	22	1	29	.286	.332	.428	105	1	1	.986	-3	84	103	1b83	—	-0.4
Total	3	162	472	58	126	21	5	9	68	37	1	35	.267	.322	.390	96	-3	3	.989	-3	86	110	1b129	—	-0.9
Housie, Wayne	Wayne Tyrone; B5.20.1965 Hampton VA; BB/TR/5´9˝/165; [DetA86*8/199]; d9.17; Col Riverside (CA) CC																								
1991	Bos A	11	8	2	2	1	0	0	0	1-0	0	3	.250	.333	.375	91	0	1-0	1.000	-1	58	0	O4C,D2	0	0.0
1993	NY N	18	16	2	3	1	0	0	1	1-0	0	1	.188	.235	.250	30	-2	0-0	ø	-0	0	0	O2R	0	-0.2
Total	2	29	24	4	5	2	0	0	1	2-0	0	4	.208	.269	.292	51	-2	1-0	1.000	-1	45	0	O6(0/4/2),D2	0	-0.2
Houston, Tyler	Tyler Sam; B1.17.1971 Las Vegas NV; BL/TR/6´1˝/(205–218); [AtlN89 1/2]; d4.3																								
1996	Atl N	33	27	3	6	2	1	1	8	1-0	0	9	.222	.250	.481	82	-1	0-0	1.000	-0	59	55	1b11	0	-0.1
	Chi N	46	115	18	39	7	0	2	19	8-1	0	18	.339	.382	.452	115	3	3-2	.986	-5	66	101	C27,3b9,2b2/1lf	0	0.0
	Year	79	142	21	45	9	1	3	27	9-1	0	27	.317	.358	.458	108	2	3-2	.986	-5	66	101	C27,1b12,3b9,2b2/lf	0	-0.1
1997	Chi N	72	196	15	51	10	0	2	28	9-1	0	35	.260	.290	.342	63	-11	1-0	.986	-1	71	69	C41,3b12,1b2/2S	46	-0.9
1998	†Chi N	95	255	26	65	7	1	9	33	13-1	0	53	.255	.290	.396	76	-10	2-2	.993	-3	78	91	C63,3b12,1b7	29	-1.0
1999	Chi N	100	249	26	58	9	1	9	27	28-4	0	67	.233	.309	.386	75	-10	1-1	.901	-10	88	83	3b63,C18,1b2/rf	0	-1.9
	Cle A	13	27	2	4	1	0	1	3	3-0	0	11	.148	.233	.296	32	-3	0-0	1.000	-0	102	101	3b10/C	0	-0.3
2000	Mil N	101	284	30	71	15	0	18	43	17-3	0	72	.250	.292	.493	94	-5	2-1	.982	2	99	116	1b35,3b28,C23	17	-0.4
2001	Mil N	75	235	36	68	7	0	12	38	18-1	1	62	.289	.343	.472	110	3	0-0	.928	-2	102	107	3b62,1b3	78	0.1
2002	Mil N	76	255	25	77	15	2	7	33	14-3	4	41	.302	.347	.459	111	3	1-0	.947	-13	79	58	3b72/1	0	-0.9
	LA N	35	65	9	13	5	1	0	7	2-0	0	21	.200	.224	.308	40	-6	0-0	.981	-2	50	115	1b12,3b2	0	-0.8
	Year	111	320	34	90	20	3	7	40	16-3	4	62	.281	.323	.428	98	-2	1-0	.943	-15	80	57	3b74,1b13	0	-1.7
2003	Phi N	54	97	7	27	6	0	2	14	6-1	0	19	.278	.320	.402	94	-1	0-0	.936	-1	92	0	3b21/1	59	-0.2
Total	8	700	1805	197	479	84	6	63	253	119-15	5	408	.265	.312	.423	88	-38	10-6	.930	-35	94	81	3b291,C173,1b75,2b3,O2(1/0/1)/S	229	-6.4
Houtz, Lefty	Fred Fritz; B9.4.1875 Connersville IN; D2.15.1959 St.Marys OH; BL/TL/5´10˝/170; d7.23																								
1899	Cin N	5	17	1	4	0	1	0	0	4	0	—	.235	.381	.353	100	0	1	1.000	3	402	773	O5(1/4/0)	—	0.3
Hovley, Steve	Stephen Eugene; B12.18.1944 Ventura CA; BL/TL/5´10˝/(175–188); [AnaA66 35/665]; d6.26; Col Stanford																								
1969	Sea A	91	329	41	91	14	3	3	20	30-3	1	34	.277	.338	.365	98	-1	10-4	.989	4	106	136	O84(3/35/49)	0	0.0
1970	Mil A	40	135	17	38	9	0	0	16	17-1	1	11	.281	.366	.348	98	1	5-1	.958	-0	110	45	O38(0/4/38)	0	-0.1
	Oak A	72	100	8	19	1	0	0	1	5-1	0	11	.190	.229	.200	20	-11	3-0	1.000	1	113	66	O42(10/26/7)	0	-1.1
	Year	112	235	25	57	10	0	0	17	22-2	1	22	.243	.310	.285	66	-10	8-1	.977	1	111	54	O80(10/30/45)	0	-1.2
1971	Oak A	24	27	3	3	2	0	0	3	7-0	1	9	.111	.306	.185	45	-1	2-0	1.000	1	129	285	O11(4/3/4)	0	0.0
1972	KC A	105	196	24	53	5	1	3	24	24-2	1	29	.270	.351	.352	111	3	3-3	.982	3	102	184	O68(5/25/39)	0	0.4
1973	KC A	104	232	29	59	8	1	5	24	33-2	0	34	.254	.346	.323	83	-4	6-4	.975	1	103	113	O79(4/25/53),D15	0	-0.6
Total	5	436	1019	122	263	39	5	8	88	116-9	4	128	.258	.335	.330	88	-13	29-12	.982	10	106	125	O322(26/118/190),D15	0	-1.4
Howard, Chris	Christopher Hugh; B2.27.1966 San Diego CA; BR/TR/6´2˝/(200–220); [SeaA88 41/1056]; d9.15; Col Louisiana–Lafayette																								
1991	Sea A	9	6	1	1	1	0	0	0	1-0	0	2	.167	.286	.333	70	0	0-0	1.000	-1	218	265	C9	0	-0.1
1993	Sea A	4	1	0	0	0	0	0	0	0-0	0	0	.000	.000	.000	-98	0	0-0	1.000	-0	19	0	C4	0	-0.1
1994	Sea A	9	25	2	5	1	0	0	2	1-0	1	6	.200	.250	.240	29	-3	0-0	1.000	-0	0	86	C9	0	-0.2
Total	3	22	32	3	6	2	0	0	2	2-0	1	8	.188	.250	.250	33	-3	0-0	1.000	-2	67	136	C22	0	-0.4

HOWARD, DAVE David Austin "Del"; B5.1.1889 Washington DC; D1.26.1956 Dallas TX; BR/TR/5´11˝/165; d5.8; Col Cornell

YEAR	TM LG	G	AB	R	H	2B	3B	HR	RBI	BB-IB	HP	SO	AVG	OBP	SLG	AOPS	ABR	SB-CS	FA	FR	RNG	THR	GAMES AT POSITION	DL	BFW
1912	Was A	1	0	1	0	0	0	0	0	0	0	—	ø	ø	ø	ø	0	0	ø	0	—	—	/R	—	0.0
1915	Bro F	24	36	5	8	1	0	0	1	1	0	8	.222	.243	.250	39	-4	0	.925	1	134	0	2b12,O2(0/1/1)/S3	—	-0.2
Total	2	25	36	6	8	1	0	0	1	1	0	8	.222	.243	.250	39	-4	0	.925	1	134	0	2b12,O2(0/1/1)/3S	—	-0.2

HOWARD, DAVID David Wayne; B2.26.1967 Sarasota FL; BB/TR/6´0˝/(165–175); [KCA86 32/774]; d4.14; f–Bruce; Col Manatee (FL) CC; OF(20/25/28)

YEAR	TM LG	G	AB	R	H	2B	3B	HR	RBI	BB-IB	HP	SO	AVG	OBP	SLG	AOPS	ABR	SB-CS	FA	FR	RNG	THR	GAMES AT POSITION	DL	BFW
1991	KC A	94	236	20	51	7	0	1	17	16-0	1	45	.216	.267	.258	46	-17	3-2	.962	6	111	80	S63,2b26/3rfD	0	-0.7
1992	KC A	74	219	19	49	6	2	1	18	15-0	0	43	.224	.271	.283	54	-14	3-4	.976	1	97	116	S74,O2C	75	-0.9
1993	KC A	15	24	5	8	0	1	0	2	2-0	0	5	.333	.370	.417	108	0	1-0	.927	1	114	46	2b7,S3,3b2/cf	92	0.1
1994	KC A	46	83	9	19	4	0	1	13	11-0	0	23	.229	.309	.313	61	-5	3-2	1.000	5	118	43	3b25,S15,2b3/lfPD	0	0.1
1995	KC A	95	255	23	62	13	4	0	19	24-1	1	41	.243	.310	.325	64	-14	6-1	.994	12	105	102	2b41,S33,O30(11/16/8)/1D	21	0.2
1996	KC A	143	420	51	92	14	5	4	48	40-0	4	74	.219	.291	.305	51	-32	5-6	**.982**	13	**109**	**136**	S135,2b3,1b2/cf	0	-1.0
1997	KC A	80	162	24	39	8	1	1	13	10-1	1	31	.241	.287	.321	57	-10	2-2	.973	5	102	138	2b34,O23(5/2/17),S9,3b7,D5	18	-0.4
1998	StL N	46	102	15	25	1	1	2	12	12-2	0	22	.245	.322	.333	74	-4	0-0	1.000	-0	120	52	2b19,S16,3b14,O2(0/2/1)	102	-0.3
1999	StL N	52	82	3	17	4	0	1	6	7-3	2	27	.207	.286	.293	46	-7	0-2	.966	-2	91	44	S13,1b9,2b9,O5(3/1/1),3b4	74	-0.9
Total	9	645	1583	169	362	57	14	11	148	137-7	9	311	.229	.291	.303	56	-103	23-19	.976	41	108	116	S361,2b142,O66R,3b53,1b12,D9/P	382	-3.8

HOWARD, DOUG Douglas Lynn; B2.6.1948 Salt Lake City UT; BR/TR/6´3˝/(180–185); [AnaA70 8/183]; d9.6; Col Brigham Young

YEAR	TM LG	G	AB	R	H	2B	3B	HR	RBI	BB-IB	HP	SO	AVG	OBP	SLG	AOPS	ABR	SB-CS	FA	FR	RNG	THR	GAMES AT POSITION	DL	BFW
1972	Cal A	11	38	4	10	1	0	0	2	1-0	1	3	.263	.300	.289	80	-1	0-0	1.000	-1	63	375	O8L/13	0	-0.2
1973	Cal A	8	21	2	2	0	0	0	1	1-0	0	6	.095	.130	.095	-36	-4	0-0	1.000	-0	81	0	O6L/13	0	-0.5
1974	Cal A	22	39	5	9	0	1	0	5	2-0	0	1	.231	.268	.282	62	-2	1-0	1.000	-1	59	0	O8(2/6/0),1b5,D3	0	-0.3
1975	StL N	17	29	1	6	0	0	1	1	0-0	0	7	.207	.207	.310	40	-3	0-0	1.000	1	172	115	1b7	0	-0.2
1976	Cle A	39	90	7	19	4	0	0	13	3-2	1	13	.211	.237	.256	47	-6	1-1	.991	1	110	96	1b32,O2R,D4	0	-0.8
Total	5	97	217	19	46	5	1	1	22	7-2	2	30	.212	.239	.258	46	-16	2-1	.994	0	118	99	1b46,O24(16/6/2),D7,3b2	0	-2.0

HOWARD, ELSTON Elston Gene; B2.23.1929 St.Louis MO; D12.14.1980 New York NY; BR/TR/6´2˝/(196–208); d4.14; C11; Negro Lg 1948–50

YEAR	TM LG	G	AB	R	H	2B	3B	HR	RBI	BB-IB	HP	SO	AVG	OBP	SLG	AOPS	ABR	SB-CS	FA	FR	RNG	THR	GAMES AT POSITION	DL	BFW
1955	†NY A	97	279	33	81	8	7	10	43	20-5	1	36	.290	.336	.477	120	5	0-0	.978	5	98	191	O75(62/0/15),C9	0	0.7
1956	†NY A	98	290	35	76	8	3	5	34	21-6	1	30	.262	.312	.362	81	-9	0-1	.990	0	94	51	O65(62/0/5),C26	0	-1.1
1957	†NY A☆	110	356	33	90	13	4	8	44	16-6	0	43	.253	.283	.379	81	-11	2-5	.961	-4	53	144	O71(69/0/2),C32,1b2	0	-2.0
1958	†NY A☆	103	376	45	118	19	5	11	66	22-6	0	60	.314	.348	.479	131	14	1-1	.997	-2	103	101	C67,O24(17/0/8),1b5	0	1.5
1959	NY A☆	125	443	59	121	24	6	18	73	20-4	3	57	.273	.306	.476	116	7	0-1	.985	-3	87	98	1b50,C43,O28(18/0/10)	0	0.2
1960	†NY A★	107	323	29	79	11	3	6	39	28-7	0	43	.245	.298	.353	82	-9	3-0	.987	3	152	102	C91/lf	0	-0.2
1961	†NY A★	129	446	64	155	17	5	21	77	28-6	3	65	.348	.387	.549	156	33	0-3	.993	10	**196**	92	C111,1b9	0	4.5
1962	†NY A★	136	494	63	138	23	5	21	91	31-1	1	76	.279	.318	.474	115	8	1-1	.995	8	**229**	95	C129	0	2.2
1963	†NY A★	135	487	75	140	21	6	28	85	35-4	6	68	.287	.342	.528	141	25	0-0	.994	2	**203**	71	C132	0	3.4
1964	†NY A★	150	550	63	172	27	3	15	84	48-12	5	73	.313	.371	.455	127	21	1-1	**.998**	13	178	87	C146	0	4.2
1965	NY A☆	110	391	38	91	15	1	9	45	24-3	1	65	.233	.278	.345	77	-13	0-0	.991	2	106	105	C95,1b5/lf	32	-0.7
1966	NY A	126	410	38	105	19	2	6	35	37-9	1	65	.256	.317	.356	97	-1	0-0	.985	3	145	72	C100,1b13	0	0.6
1967	NY A	66	199	13	39	6	0	3	17	12-3	2	36	.196	.247	.271	56	-11	0-0	.984	0	104	79	C48/1	0	-1.0
	†Bos A	42	116	9	17	3	0	1	11	9-3	1	24	.147	.211	.198	21	-11	0-0	.996	3	109	73	C41	0	-0.7
	Year	108	315	22	56	9	0	4	28	21-6	3	60	.178	.233	.244	42	-23	0-0	.990	3	106	76	C89/1	0	-1.7
1968	Bos A	71	203	22	49	4	0	5	18	22-7	1	45	.241	.317	.335	93	-1	1-1	.995	-6	73	83	C68	0	-0.5
Total	14	1605	5363	619	1471	218	50	167	762	373-82	26	786	.274	.322	.427	108	47	9-14	.993	33	*162*	*90*	C1138,O265(230/0/40),1b85	32	11.1

HOWARD, FRANK Frank Oliver "Hondo","The Capital Punisher"; B8.8.1936 Columbus OH; BR/TR/6´7˝/(205–285); d9.10; M2/C20; Col Ohio St.

YEAR	TM LG	G	AB	R	H	2B	3B	HR	RBI	BB-IB	HP	SO	AVG	OBP	SLG	AOPS	ABR	SB-CS	FA	FR	RNG	THR	GAMES AT POSITION	DL	BFW
1958	LA N	8	29	3	7	1	0	1	2	1-0	0	11	.241	.267	.379	66	-1	0-0	1.000	1	105	207	O8(3/0/5)	0	-0.1
1959	LA N	9	21	2	3	0	1	1	6	2-0	0	9	.143	.217	.381	52	-2	0-0	1.000	0	115	0	O6(4/0/2)	0	-0.2
1960	LA N	117	448	54	120	15	2	23	77	32-1	3	108	.268	.320	.464	105	2	0-1	.984	-5	90	83	O115(22/0/94),1b4	0	-0.8
1961	LA N	92	267	36	79	10	2	15	45	21-3	1	50	.296	.347	.517	116	6	0-1	.934	-2	85	133	O65(20/0/46),1b7	0	-0.1
1962	LA N	141	493	80	146	25	6	31	119	39-10	1	108	.296	.346	.560	148	31	1-0	.972	2	88	189	O131(9/0/128)	0	2.4
1963	†LA N	123	417	58	114	16	1	28	64	33-4	4	116	.273	.330	.518	151	26	1-2	.960	-3	105	51	O111(6/0/107)	0	1.6
1964	LA N	134	433	60	98	13	2	24	69	51-10	0	113	.226	.303	.432	114	7	1-0	.979	-8	93	24	O122R	0	-0.9
1965	Was A	149	516	53	149	22	6	21	84	55-2	2	112	.289	.358	.477	138	25	0-0	.981	-5	90	65	O138(138/0/5)	0	1.4
1966	Was A	146	493	52	137	19	4	18	71	53-6	1	104	.278	.348	.442	127	17	1-1	.982	0	102	66	O135L	0	1.1
1967	Was A	149	519	71	133	20	2	36	89	60-7	5	155	.256	.338	.511	154	34	0-1	.986	-6	88	55	O141(141/0/3),1b4	0	2.3
1968	Was A★	158	598	79	164	28	3	**44**	106	54-12	6	141	.274	.338	**.552**	**173**	49	0-0	.955	-1	83	161	O107L,1b55	0	4.5
1969	Was A★	161	592	111	175	17	2	48	111	102-19	5	96	.296	.402	.574	180	65	1-0	.974	-16	73	36	O114(108/0/6),1b70	0	4.0
1970	Was A★	161	566	90	160	15	1	**44**	**126**	**132-29**	2	125	.283	.416	.546	172	61	1-2	.973	-9	83	83	O120(114/0/6),1b48	0	4.3
1971	Was A★	153	549	60	153	25	2	26	83	77-**20**	2	121	.279	.367	.474	144	32	1-0	.993	5	79	119	O100(95/0/5),1b68	0	3.0
1972	Tex A	95	287	28	70	9	0	9	31	42-8	1	55	.244	.341	.369	116	6	1-0	.981	-6	83	77	1b66,O21(20/0/1)	0	-0.6
	Det A	14	33	1	8	1	0	1	7	4-0	0	8	.242	.324	.364	101	0	0-0	.952	0	121	84	1b10/lf	0	0.0
	Year	109	320	29	78	10	0	10	38	46-8	1	63	.244	.340	.369	114	6	1-0	.978	-6	88	78	1b76,O22(21/0/1)	0	-0.6
1973	Det A	85	227	26	58	9	1	12	29	24-4	0	28	.256	.327	.463	113	3	0-1	.923	-0	0	0	D76,1b2	0	0.0
Total	16	1895	6488	864	1774	245	35	382	1119	782-135	33	1460	.273	.352	.499	143	361	8-9	.975	-52	89	86	O1435(923/0/530),1b334,D76	0	21.9

HOWARD, DEL George Elmer; B12.24.1877 Kenney IL; D12.24.1956 Seattle WA; BL/TR/6´0˝/180; d4.15; b–Ivan; OF(137/34/85)

YEAR	TM LG	G	AB	R	H	2B	3B	HR	RBI	BB-IB	HP	SO	AVG	OBP	SLG	AOPS	ABR	SB-CS	FA	FR	RNG	THR	GAMES AT POSITION	DL	BFW
1905	Pit N	123	435	56	127	18	5	2	63	27	8	—	.292	.345	.370	110	6	19	.978	-5	85	133	1b90,O28(1/0/27)/P	—	-0.2
1906	Bos N	147	545	46	142	19	8	1	54	26	10	—	.261	.306	.330	101	-1	17	.911	-12	128	106	O87L,2b45,S14,1b2	—	-1.9
1907	Bos N	50	187	20	51	4	2	1	13	11	5	—	.273	.330	.332	108	1	11	.969	-1	140	131	O45L,2b3	—	-0.2
	†Chi N	51	148	10	34	2	2	0	13	6	2	—	.230	.269	.270	65	-6	3	.972	-3	88	132	1b33,O8(0/3/6)	—	-1.1
	Year	101	335	30	85	6	4	1	26	17	7	—	.254	.304	.304	88	-5	14	.961	-4	121	113	O53(45/3/6),1b33,2b3	—	-1.3
1908	†Chi N	96	315	42	88	7	3	1	26	23	5	—	.279	.338	.330	109	3	11	.965	-3	101	46	O81(4/31/52),1b5	—	-0.3
1909	Chi N	69	203	25	40	4	2	1	24	18	6	—	.197	.282	.251	64	-8	6	.980	-0	101	120	1b57	—	-1.1
Total	5	536	1833	199	482	54	22	6	193	111	36	—	.263	.318	.326	98	-5	67	.946	-23	115	77	O249L,1b187,2b48,S14/P	—	-4.8

HOWARD, IVAN Ivan Chester; B10.12.1882 Kenney IL; D3.30.1967 Medford OR; BB/TR/5´10˝/170; d4.25; b–Del

YEAR	TM LG	G	AB	R	H	2B	3B	HR	RBI	BB-IB	HP	SO	AVG	OBP	SLG	AOPS	ABR	SB-CS	FA	FR	RNG	THR	GAMES AT POSITION	DL	BFW
1914	StL A	81	209	21	51	6	2	0	20	28	3	42	.244	.342	.292	94	0	14-10	.936	-4	93	75	3b34,1b28,O3(1/1/1)/S	—	-0.5
1915	StL A	113	324	43	90	10	7	2	43	43	3	48	.278	.368	.370	126	11	29-12	.992	8	132	93	1b48,3b23,O17(5/1/11),2b2,S2	—	2.0
1916	Cle A	81	246	20	46	11	5	0	23	30	9	34	.187	.298	.272	68	-9	9	.970	6	116	62	2b65,1b7	—	-0.2
1917	Cle A	27	39	7	4	0	0	0	0	3	0	5	.103	.167	.103	-17	-5	1	.833	-0	86	414	3b6,2b4,O4C	—	-0.7
Total	4	302	818	91	191	27	14	2	86	104	15	129	.233	.331	.308	92	-3	53-22	.990	9	125	68	1b83,2b71,3b63,O24(6/6/12),S3	—	0.6

HOWARD, LARRY Lawrence Rayford; B6.6.1945 Columbus OH; BR/TR/6´3˝/200; d8.9

YEAR	TM LG	G	AB	R	H	2B	3B	HR	RBI	BB-IB	HP	SO	AVG	OBP	SLG	AOPS	ABR	SB-CS	FA	FR	RNG	THR	GAMES AT POSITION	DL	BFW
1970	Hou N	31	88	11	27	6	0	2	16	10-3	0	23	.307	.378	.443	124	3	0-0	.993	-2	192	120	C26,1b2/rf	0	0.3
1971	Hou N	24	64	6	15	3	0	2	14	3-0	0	17	.234	.265	.375	83	-2	0-1	.992	3	149	122	C22	0	0.2
1972	Hou N	54	157	16	35	7	0	2	13	17-3	0	30	.223	.299	.306	74	-5	0-0	.980	-6	79	80	C53/lf	0	-0.9
1973	Hou N	20	48	3	8	3	0	0	4	5-2	0	12	.167	.245	.229	32	-4	0-0	.989	-1	99	152	C20	0	-0.5
	Atl N	4	8	0	1	0	0	0	0	2-0	0	3	.125	.300	.125	20	-1	0-0	1.000	-0	88	0	C2	0	-0.1
	Year	24	56	3	9	3	0	0	4	7-2	0	15	.161	.254	.214	31	-5	0-0	.990	-2	98	135	C22	0	-0.6
Total	4	133	365	36	86	19	0	6	47	37-8	0	85	.236	.305	.337	81	-9	0-1	.986	-6	118	104	C123,O2(1/0/1),1b2	0	-1.0

HOWARD, MATT Matthew Christopher; B9.22.1967 Fall River MA; BR/TR/5´10˝/170; [LAN89 34/890]; d5.17; Col Pepperdine

YEAR	TM LG	G	AB	R	H	2B	3B	HR	RBI	BB-IB	HP	SO	AVG	OBP	SLG	AOPS	ABR	SB-CS	FA	FR	RNG	THR	GAMES AT POSITION	DL	BFW
1996	NY A	35	54	9	11	1	0	1	9	2-0	0	8	.204	.228	.278	28	-6	1-0	.976	-8	72	54	2b30,3b6	0	-1.2

HOWARD, MIKE Michael Fredric; B4.2.1958 Seattle WA; BB/TR/6´2˝/(185–190); [LAN76 6/139]; d9.12

YEAR	TM LG	G	AB	R	H	2B	3B	HR	RBI	BB-IB	HP	SO	AVG	OBP	SLG	AOPS	ABR	SB-CS	FA	FR	RNG	THR	GAMES AT POSITION	DL	BFW
1981	NY N	14	24	4	4	1	0	0	3	4-0	0	6	.167	.276	.208	42	-2	2-0	.952	1	114	313	O14(6/1/7)	0	0.0
1982	NY N	33	39	5	7	0	0	1	3	6-0	1	7	.179	.298	.256	58	-2	2-0	1.000	2	111	272	O22(9/7/8),2b3	0	0.0
1983	NY N	1	3	0	1	0	0	0	1	0-0	0	1	.333	.333	.333	86	0	0-0	ø	-1	0	0	/rf	0	-0.1
Total	3	48	66	9	12	1	0	1	7	10-0	1	14	.182	.291	.242	54	-4	4-0	.980	3	106	274	O37(15/8/16),2b3	0	-0.1

HOWARD, PAUL Paul Joseph "Del"; B5.20.1884 Boston MA; D8.29.1968 Miami FL; BR/TR/5´8˝/170; d9.16

YEAR	TM LG	G	AB	R	H	2B	3B	HR	RBI	BB-IB	HP	SO	AVG	OBP	SLG	AOPS	ABR	SB-CS	FA	FR	RNG	THR	GAMES AT POSITION	DL	BFW
1909	Bos A	6	15	2	3	1	0	0	2	3	1	—	.200	.368	.267	99	0	0	1.000	-0	228	0	O6(4/0/2)	—	0.0

YEAR	TM LG	G	AB	R	H	2B	3B	HR	RBI	BB-IB	HP	SO	AVG	OBP	SLG	AOPS	ABR	SB-CS	FA	FR	RNG	THR	GAMES AT POSITION	DL	BFW
HOWARD, RYAN	Ryan James; B11.19.1979 St. Louis MO; BL/TL/6´4˝/(230–250); [PhiN01 5/140]; d9.1; Col Missouri St.																								
2004	Phi N	19	39	5	11	5	0	2	5	2-0	1	13	.282	.333	.564	122	1	0-0	1.000	1	133	164	1b8	0	0.1
2005	Phi N	88	312	52	90	17	2	22	63	33-8	1	100	.288	.356	.567	133	14	0-1	.993	-4	78	82	1b84	0	0.3
2006	Phi N★	159	581	104	182	25	1	**58**	**149**	108-37	9	181	.313	.425	.659	165	59	0-0	.991	-3	93	104	1b159	0	4.0
Total	3	266	932	161	283	47	3	82	217	143-45	11	294	.304	.399	.624	153	74	0-1	.992	-7	89	99	1b251	0	4.4
HOWARD, STEVE	Steven Bernard; B12.7.1963 Oakland CA; BR/TR/6´2˝/205; [OakA83*8/186]; d6.16																								
1990	Oak A	21	52	5	12	4	0	0	1	4-1	0	17	.231	.286	.308	68	-2	0-0	.933	-2	71	0	O14(4/3/8),D7	0	-0.4
HOWARD, THOMAS	Thomas Sylvester; B12.11.1964 Middletown OH; BB/TR (BL 1996–98)/6´2˝/(198–205); [SDN86 1/11]; d7.3; Col Ball St.																								
1990	SD N	20	44	4	12	2	0	0	0	0-0	0	11	.273	.273	.318	61	-2	0-1	.950	-1	92	0	O13(9/2/2)	0	-0.4
1991	SD N	106	281	30	70	12	3	4	22	24-4	1	57	.249	.309	.356	84	-6	10-7	.995	4	113	92	O86(34/41/14)	0	-0.4
1992	SD N	5	3	1	1	0	0	0	0	0-0	0	0	.333	.333	.333	88	0	0-0	ø	0	—	—	/H	0	0.0
	Cle A	117	358	36	99	15	2	2	32	17-1	0	60	.277	.308	.346	84	-8	15-8	.990	-2	96	90	O97(68/22/13),D2	0	-1.2
1993	Cle A	74	178	26	42	7	0	3	23	12-0	0	42	.236	.278	.326	63	-10	5-1	.977	2	106	129	O47(9/11/28),D7	0	-0.8
	Cin N	38	141	22	39	8	3	4	13	12-0	0	21	.277	.331	.461	109	1	5-6	.987	2	103	180	O37(27/12/0)	0	0.2
1994	Cin N	83	178	24	47	11	0	5	24	10-1	0	30	.264	.302	.410	84	-5	4-2	.965	1	106	83	O57(41/7/12)	0	-0.5
1995	†Cin N	113	281	42	85	15	2	3	26	20-0	1	37	.302	.350	.402	97	-1	17-8	.985	-0	102	58	O82(36/39/14)	0	-0.2
1996	Cin N	121	360	50	98	19	10	6	42	17-3	3	51	.272	.307	.431	91	-6	6-5	.982	1	97	146	O103(51/40/32)	19	-0.8
1997	†Hou N	107	255	24	63	16	1	3	22	26-1	3	48	.247	.323	.353	80	-7	1-2	1.000	0	93	163	O62(10/41/18)	0	-0.8
1998	LA N	47	76	9	14	4	0	2	4	3-0	0	15	.184	.215	.316	39	-7	1-0	1.000	1	102	207	O29(11/13/6)/D	0	-0.6
1999	StL N	98	195	16	57	10	0	6	28	17-0	2	26	.292	.353	.436	97	-1	1-1	.987	-2	100	0	O48(3/0/45)/D	0	-0.4
2000	StL N	86	133	13	28	4	1	6	28	7-0	1	34	.211	.255	.391	59	-9	1-0	.960	-2	75	101	O27(6/0/22)/1D	0	-1.1
Total	11	1015	2483	297	655	123	22	44	264	165-10	11	432	.264	.311	.384	84	-61	66-41	.986	4	100	106	O688(305/228/206),D14/1	19	-7.0
HOWARD, WILBUR	Wilbur Leon; B1.8.1949 Lowell NC; BB/TR/6´2˝/(170–175); [MilA68 19/441]; d9.4																								
1973	Mil A	16	39	3	8	0	0	0	1	2-1	0	10	.205	.244	.205	28	-4	0-1	.969	2	135	268	O12(5/0/7)/D	0	-0.2
1974	Hou N	64	111	19	24	4	0	2	5	5-0	0	18	.216	.250	.306	58	-7	4-5	1.000	2	103	137	O50(43/4/3)	0	-0.8
1975	Hou N	121	392	62	111	16	8	0	21	21-3	3	67	.283	.324	.365	98	-3	32-11	.995	2	101	112	O95(53/34/12)	0	-0.2
1976	Hou N	94	191	26	42	7	2	1	18	7-1	0	28	.220	.245	.293	58	-12	7-5	.961	1	107	65	O63(37/11/20),2b2	0	-1.5
1977	Hou N	87	187	22	48	6	0	2	13	5-1	0	30	.257	.276	.321	65	-10	11-1	.990	2	109	68	O62(46/15/4),2b4	0	-0.8
1978	Hou N	84	148	17	34	4	1	1	13	5-0	3	22	.230	.268	.291	60	-9	6-2	1.000	-3	78	103	O38(30/5/4),C3/2	20	-1.2
Total	6	466	1068	149	267	37	11	6	71	45-6	6	175	.250	.283	.322	73	-45	60-25	.987	7	103	105	O320(214/69/50),2b7,C3/D	20	-4.7
HOWARTH, JIM	James Eugene; B3.7.1947 Biloxi MS; BL/TL/5´11˝/175; d9.5; Col Mississippi St.																								
1971	SF N	7	13	3	3	1	0	0	2	3-0	0	3	.231	.375	.308	96	0	0-0	1.000	0	144	0	O6(2/1/3)	0	0.0
1972	SF N	74	119	16	28	4	0	1	7	16-1	0	18	.235	.326	.294	76	-3	3-2	1.000	-1	97	0	O25(8/17/0),1b4	0	-0.6
1973	SF N	65	90	8	18	1	1	0	7	7-0	0	8	.200	.258	.233	35	-8	0-0	1.000	0	102	79	O33(5/21/7)/1	0	-0.9
1974	SF N	6	4	0	0	0	0	0	0	0-0	0	0	.000	.000	.000	-96	-1	0-0	ø	-0	0	0	/lf	0	-0.1
Total	4	152	226	27	49	6	1	1	16	26-1	0	29	.217	.298	.265	58	-12	3-2	1.000	-1	103	36	O65(16/39/10),1b5	0	-1.6
HOWE, ART	Arthur Henry; B12.15.1946 Pittsburgh PA; BR/TR/6´2˝/(185–195); d7.10; M14/C5; Col Wyoming; [DL 1983 Hou N 182]																								
1974	†Pit N	29	74	10	18	4	1	1	5	9-0	0	13	.243	.321	.365	95	0	0-0	.937	1	110	216	3b20,S2	0	0.0
1975	Pit N	63	146	13	25	9	0	1	10	15-3	0	15	.171	.248	.253	39	-12	1-0	.938	-4	102	61	3b42,S3	0	-1.6
1976	Hou N	21	29	0	4	1	0	0	0	6-1	0	6	.138	.286	.172	35	-2	0-0	.938	0	90	99	3b8,2b2	0	-0.2
1977	Hou N	125	413	44	109	23	7	8	58	41-6	5	60	.264	.336	.412	108	4	0-1	.985	-1	101	89	2b96,3b19,S11	0	0.8
1978	Hou N	119	420	46	123	33	3	7	55	34-3	1	41	.293	.343	.436	126	14	2-3	.977	-9	92	81	2b107,3b11/1	0	1.1
1979	Hou N	118	355	32	88	15	2	6	33	36-5	1	37	.248	.316	.352	88	-6	3-1	.991	11	106	96	2b68,3b59,1b3	0	0.8
1980	†Hou N	110	321	34	91	12	5	10	46	34-6	1	29	.283	.350	.445	133	13	1-0	.986	-1	108	98	1b77,3b25,S5,2b3	0	0.8
1981	†Hou N	103	361	43	107	22	4	3	36	41-7	0	23	.296	.365	.404	126	13	1-3	.966	5	107	118	3b98,1b2	0	1.7
1982	Hou N	110	365	29	87	15	1	5	38	41-15	1	45	.238	.315	.326	87	-6	2-0	.972	8	111	118	3b72,1b35	38	-0.1
1984	StL N	89	139	17	30	5	0	2	12	18-1	0	18	.216	.300	.295	71	-5	0-2	.979	3	117	121	3b45,1b11,2b8,S5	0	-0.3
1985	StL N	4	3	0	0	0	0	0	0	0-0	0	0	.000	.000	.000	-99	-1	0-0	1.000	1	0	572	/13	0	0.0
Total	11	891	2626	268	682	139	23	43	293	275-47	9	287	.260	.329	.379	103	12	10-10	.965	14	106	108	3b400,2b284,1b130,S26	220	3.0
HOWE, SHORTY	John; B New York NY; d6.17																								
1890	NY N	19	64	4	11	0	0	0	4	3	1	2	.172	.221	.172	15	-7	3	.887	2	111	44	2b18/3	—	-0.4
1893	NY N	1	5	1	3	0	0	0	2	0	0	0	.600	.600	.600	218	1	1	.400	-1	69	0	/3	—	0.0
Total	2	20	69	5	14	0	0	0	6	3	1	2	.203	.247	.203	30	-6	4	.887	0	111	44	2b18,3b2	—	-0.4
HOWELL, DIXIE	Homer Elliott; B4.24.1920 Louisville KY; D10.5.1990 Binghamton NY; BR/TR/5´11˝/195; d5.6																								
1947	Pit N	76	214	23	59	11	0	4	25	27	0	34	.276	.357	.383	94	-1	1	.974	-4	*91*	*85*	C74	0	-0.1
1949	Cin N	64	172	17	42	6	1	2	18	8	2	21	.244	.286	.326	63	-10	0	.987	3	*117*	*138*	C56	0	-0.4
1950	Cin N	82	224	30	50	9	1	2	22	32	2	31	.223	.326	.299	65	-11	0	.986	-5	*74*	*83*	C81	0	-1.1
1951	Cin N	77	207	22	52	6	1	2	18	15	0	34	.251	.302	.319	66	-10	0-2	.987	0	*80*	*87*	C73	0	-0.7
1952	Cin N	17	37	4	7	1	1	2	4	3	0	9	.189	.250	.432	86	-1	0-0	.981	1	*83*	*165*	C16	0	0.0
1953	Bro N	1	1	0	0	0	0	0	0	0	0	1	.000	.000	.000	-98	0	0-0	ø	0	—	—	/H	0	0.0
1955	Bro N	16	42	2	11	4	0	0	5	1-0	0	7	.262	.273	.357	66	-2	0-0	.981	-1	*128*	*50*	C13	0	-0.2
1956	Bro N	7	13	0	3	2	0	0	1	1-1	0	3	.231	.267	.385	72	0	0-0	1.000	-0	*104*	*0*	C6	0	0.0
Total	8	340	910	98	224	39	4	12	93	87-1	4	140	.246	.314	.337	73	-35	1-2	.984	-5	*90*	*95*	C319	0	-2.5
HOWELL, JACK	Jack Robert; B8.18.1961 Tucson AZ; BL/TR/6´0˝/(185–201); d5.20; Col Arizona; OF(88/1/23)																								
1985	Cal A	43	137	19	27	4	0	5	18	16-2	0	33	.197	.279	.336	68	-6	1-1	.931	-2	98	132	3b42	0	-0.9
1986	†Cal A	63	151	26	41	14	2	4	21	19-0	0	28	.272	.349	.470	123	5	2-0	.977	-1	95	77	3b39,O8(7/0/1),D2	0	0.4
1987	Cal A	138	449	64	110	18	5	23	64	57-4	2	118	.245	.331	.461	111	6	4-3	.987	2	97	76	O89(78/0/15),3b48,2b13	0	0.4
1988	Cal A	154	500	59	127	32	2	16	63	46-8	6	130	.254	.323	.422	110	7	2-6	.953	-12	96	74	3b152,O2(1/1/0)	0	-0.7
1989	Cal A	144	474	56	108	19	4	20	52	52-9	3	125	.228	.308	.411	103	1	0-3	**.974**	23	**121**	**123**	3b142,O4(1/0/3)	0	2.3
1990	Cal A	105	316	35	72	19	1	8	33	46-5	1	61	.228	.326	.370	96	0	3-0	.939	-0	99	102	3b102/1S	17	0.0
1991	Cal A	32	81	11	17	2	0	2	7	11-0	0	11	.210	.304	.309	70	-3	1-1	.968	5	132	62	2b12,3b8,O5(1/0/4),1b3/D	24	0.1
	SD N	58	160	24	33	3	1	6	16	18-1	0	33	.206	.287	.350	76	-6	0-0	.985	6	114	106	3b54	0	0.0
1996	Cal A	66	126	20	34	4	1	8	21	10-0	0	30	.270	.324	.508	104	0	0-1	.884	-2	97	111	3b43,1b2/2D	33	-0.2
1997	Ana A	77	174	25	45	7	0	14	34	13-2	0	36	.259	.305	.540	116	3	1-0	.976	-2	80	134	3b24,D22,1b12	0	0.0
1998	Hou N	24	38	4	11	5	0	1	7	4-0	0	12	.289	.357	.500	126	2	0-0	1.000	1	145	66	1b10,3b2	131	0.2
1999	Hou N	37	33	2	7	2	0	1	1	8-0	0	9	.212	.366	.364	87	0	0-0	1.000	1	179	307	1b5,3b3,D2	107	0.0
Total	11	941	2639	345	632	129	16	108	337	300-31	12	626	.239	.318	.423	103	9	14-15	.958	19	105	107	3b659,O108L,1b33,D31,2b26/S	312	1.6
HOWELL, RED	Murray Donald "Porky"; B1.29.1909 Atlanta GA; D10.1.1950 Travelers Rest SC; BR/TR/6´0˝/215; d4.24																								
1941	Cle A	11	7	0	2	0	0	0	2	4	0	2	.286	.545	.286	132	1	0-0	ø	0	—	—	/H	0	0.1
HOWELL, PAT	Patrick O'Neal; B8.31.1968 Mobile AL; BB/TR/5´11˝/155; [NYN87 9/238]; d7.10																								
1992	NY N	31	75	9	14	1	0	0	1	2-0	1	15	.187	.218	.200	19	-8	4-2	1.000	2	129	0	O28C	0	-0.7
HOWELL, ROY	Roy Lee; B12.18.1953 Lompoc CA; BL/TR/6´1˝/(190–195); [TexA72 1/4]; d9.9																								
1974	Tex A	13	44	2	11	1	0	1	3	2-0	0	10	.250	.283	.341	81	-1	0-0	.906	-1	105	41	3b12	0	-0.2
1975	Tex A	125	383	43	96	15	2	10	51	39-6	3	79	.251	.322	.379	99	-1	2-2	.933	-2	100	**159**	3b115,D5	0	-0.3
1976	Tex A	140	491	55	124	28	2	8	53	30-8	1	106	.253	.295	.367	92	-6	1-0	.926	-6	98	95	3b130,D8	0	-1.3
1977	Tex A	7	17	0	0	0	0	0	0	2-0	0	4	.000	.105	.000	-68	-4	0-0	1.000	-0	135	0	O2L/13D	0	-0.5
	Tor A	96	364	41	115	17	1	10	44	42-2	1	76	.316	.386	.451	126	15	4-1	.953	-4	94	67	3b87,D8	0	1.0
	Year	103	381	41	115	17	1	10	44	44-2	1	80	.302	.374	.430	117	11	4-1	.954	-4	94	67	3b88,D10,O2L/1	0	0.5
1978	Tor A★	140	551	67	149	28	3	8	61	44-3	1	78	.270	.325	.376	95	-4	0-1	.950	8	106	97	3b131,O5R/D	0	0.2
1979	Tor A	138	511	60	126	28	4	15	72	42-4	6	91	.247	.310	.405	90	-8	1-4	.952	4	105	103	3b133,D4	16	-0.7
1980	Tor A	142	528	51	142	28	9	10	57	50-8	5	92	.269	.335	.413	100	0	0-0	.958	-14	92	79	3b138,D2	0	-1.6
1981	†Mil A	76	244	37	58	13	1	6	33	23-4	2	39	.238	.306	.373	100	0	0-0	.958	-4	93	97	3b53,D13,1b3/rf	0	-0.6
1982	†Mil A	98	300	31	78	11	2	4	38	21-2	0	39	.260	.305	.350	85	-7	0-2	.933	-0	117	43	D84,1b4,O2R	0	-1.0
1983	Mil A	69	194	23	54	9	6	4	25	15-0	0	29	.278	.330	.448	120	4	1-3	.960	1	284	217	D54,1b2	0	0.3

YEAR	TM LG	G	AB	R	H	2B	3B	HR	RBI	BB-IB	HP	SO	AVG	OBP	SLG	AOPS	ABR	SB-CS	FA	FR	RNG	THR	GAMES AT POSITION	DL	BFW
1984	Mil A	68	164	12	38	5	1	4	17	8-1	4	32	.232	.284	.348	76	-6	0-1	.907	0	107	110	3b46,1b4,D8	0	-0.7
Total	11	1112	3791	422	991	183	31	80	454	318-38	23	675	.261	.321	.389	97	-18	9-14	.944	-18	99	99	3b846,D189,1b14,O10(2/0/8)	16	-5.4
HOWERTON, BILL	William Ray "Hopalong"; B12.12.1921 Lompoc CA; D12.18.2001 Blakely PA; BL/TR/5´11˝/(180–185); d9.11; Col St. Marys (CA)																								
1949	StL N	9	13	1	4	1	0	0	1	0	0	2	.308	.308	.385	81	0	0	.900	0	123	0	O6(2/3/1)	0	-0.1
1950	StL N	110	313	50	88	20	8	10	59	47	0	60	.281	.375	.492	120	10	0	.969	-5	96	31	O94(32/54/11)	0	0.1
1951	StL N	24	65	10	17	4	1	1	4	10	0	12	.262	.360	.400	104	1	0-1	.949	1	106	132	O17(3/0/14)	0	0.0
	Pit N	80	219	29	60	12	2	11	37	26	0	44	.274	.351	.498	122	7	1-0	.950	-6	83	76	O53(4/38/11),3b4	0	0.0
	Year	104	284	39	77	16	3	12	41	36	0	56	.271	.353	.475	118	7	1-1	.950	-5	89	91	O70(7/38/25),3b4	0	0.0
1952	Pit N	13	25	3	8	1	1	0	4	6	0	5	.320	.452	.440	144	2	0-0	.900	-2	92	0	O5(0/2/3)/3	0	0.0
	NY N	11	15	2	1	1	0	0	1	3	0	2	.067	.222	.133	1	-2	0-0	1.000	-0	99	0	O3(0/1/2)	0	-0.2
	Year	24	40	5	9	2	1	0	5	9	0	7	.225	.367	.325	92	0	0-0	.938	-2	95	0	O8(0/3/5)/3	0	-0.2
Total	4	247	650	95	178	39	12	22	106	92	0	125	.274	.364	.472	117	18	1-1	.958	-12	94	53	O178(41/98/42),3b5	0	-0.2
HOWITT, DANN	Dann Paul John; B2.13.1964 Battle Creek MI; BL/TR/6´5˝/205; [OakA86 18/457]; d9.15; Col Cal St.–Fullerton																								
1989	Oak A	3	3	0	0	0	0	0	0	0-0	0	2	.000	.000	.000	-99	-1	0-0	1.000	-0	0	0	/1rf	0	-0.1
1990	Oak A	14	22	3	3	0	1	0	1	3-0	0	12	.136	.240	.227	33	-2	0-0	1.000	1	207	0	O11R,1b5/3	0	-0.1
1991	Oak A	21	42	5	7	1	0	1	3	1-0	0	12	.167	.182	.262	24	-5	0-0	1.000	1	126	0	O20(5/7/10)/1	0	-0.4
1992	Oak A	22	48	1	6	0	0	1	2	5-1	0	4	.125	.208	.188	12	-6	0-0	.951	3	109	311	O19(4/5/12),1b4/D	0	-0.4
	Sea A	13	37	6	10	4	1	1	8	3-0	0	5	.270	.302	.514	130	1	1-1	1.000	1	107	135	O11(10/0/1)	0	0.1
	Year	35	85	7	16	4	1	2	10	8-1	0	9	.188	.250	.329	65	-4	1-1	.970	3	108	235	O30(14/5/13),1b4/D	0	-0.3
1993	Sea A	32	76	6	16	3	1	2	8	4-0	0	18	.211	.250	.355	59	-5	0-0	1.000	1	110	85	O29(16/6/12),D2	0	-0.5
1994	Chi A	10	14	4	5	3	0	0	0	1-0	0	7	.357	.400	.571	148	1	0-0	1.000	-0	82	0	O7(1/1/5),1b4	0	0.1
Total	6	115	242	25	47	11	3	5	22	17-1	0	60	.194	.243	.326	57	-17	1-1	.987	5	116	126	O98(36/19/52),1b15,D3/3	0	-1.3
HOWLEY, DAN	Daniel Philip "Howling Dan","Dapper Dan"; B10.16.1885 Weymouth MA; D3.10.1944 Weymouth MA; BR/TR/6´0˝/187; d5.15; M6/C3																								
1913	Phi N	26	32	5	4	2	0	0	2	4	0	4	.125	.222	.188	17	-3	3	.954	1	111	52	C22	—	-0.1
HOWSER, DICK	Richard Dalton; B5.14.1936 Miami FL; D6.17.1987 Kansas City MO; BR/TR/5´8˝/(154–155); d4.11; M8/C10; Col Florida St.																								
1961	KC A★	158	611	108	171	29	6	3	45	92-0	5	38	.280	.377	.362	97	2	37-9	.950	-13	95	79	S157	0	0.7
1962	KC A	83	286	53	68	8	3	6	34	38-0	1	8	.238	.326	.350	79	-8	19-2	.962	-5	95	79	S72	46	-0.3
1963	KC A	15	41	4	8	0	0	0	1	7-1	0	3	.195	.313	.195	44	-3	0-0	.957	-2	81	100	S10	0	-0.4
	Cle A	49	162	25	40	5	0	1	10	22-0	0	18	.247	.333	.296	80	-4	9-3	.950	-11	76	66	S44	0	-1.0
	Year	64	203	29	48	5	0	1	11	29-1	0	21	.236	.329	.276	72	-7	9-3	.951	-13	77	73	S54	0	-1.4
1964	Cle A	162	637	101	163	23	4	3	52	76-1	2	39	.256	.335	.319	84	-11	20-7	.974	1	96	98	S162	0	0.6
1965	Cle A	107	307	47	72	8	2	1	6	57-0	1	25	.235	.354	.283	83	-4	17-4	.977	-3	87	90	S73,2b17	0	0.3
1966	Cle A	67	140	18	32	9	1	2	4	15-0	0	23	.229	.299	.350	87	-2	2-4	.986	-12	75	66	2b26,S26	0	-1.2
1967	NY A	63	149	18	40	6	0	0	10	25-0	2	15	.268	.381	.309	110	4	1-4	.990	-5	87	122	2b22,3b12,S3	46	-0.1
1968	NY A	85	150	24	23	2	1	0	3	35-0	2	17	.153	.321	.180	57	-6	0-1	.982	7	133	118	2b29,3b2/S	0	0.4
Total	8	789	2483	398	617	90	17	16	165	367-2	13	186	.248	.346	.318	86	-32	105-34	.963	-42	92	85	S548,2b94,3b14	92	-1.0
HOY, DUMMY	William Ellsworth; B5.23.1862 Houcktown OH; D12.15.1961 Cincinnati OH; BL/TR/5´6˝/160; d4.20																								
1888	Was N	**136**	503	77	138	10	8	2	29	69	11	48	.274	.374	.338	137	27	**82**	.897	7	117	148	O136(0/136/1)	—	2.9
1889	Was N	**127**	507	98	139	11	6	0	39	75	6	30	.274	.374	.320	100	5	35	.890	-4	121	80	O127(1/126/0)	—	-0.3
1890	Buf P	122	493	107	147	17	8	1	53	94	8	36	.298	.418	.371	122	25	39	.912	4	104	172	O122C/2	—	2.0
1891	StL AA	**139**	559	134	163	13	5	5	64	**117**	12	25	.292	.424	.360	108	10	59	.911	-2	107	62	O139C	—	0.3
1892	Was N	152	593	108	167	19	8	3	75	86	4	23	.282	.376	.356	125	23	60	.884	-15	66	55	O152(3/150/0)	—	-0.2
1893	Was N	**130**	564	106	138	12	6	0	45	66	13	9	.245	.337	.287	68	-23	48	.892	-4	119	148	O130C	—	-2.9
1894	Cin N	128	503	118	153	23	13	5	71	90	12	19	.304	.421	.431	102	5	28	.895	0	138	55	O128C	—	-0.2
1895	Cin N	107	429	93	119	21	12	3	55	52	6	8	.277	.363	.403	94	-4	50	.883	-5	86	163	O107(62/41/4)	—	-1.4
1896	Cin N	121	443	120	132	23	7	4	57	65	13	13	.298	.403	.409	107	7	50	.946	3	84	78	O120C	—	0.2
1897	Cin N	128	497	87	145	24	6	2	42	54	12	—	.292	.375	.376	92	-4	37	.934	5	55	147	O128C	—	-0.6
1898	Lou N	148	582	104	177	15	16	6	66	49	9	—	.304	.367	.416	126	18	37	.946	2	92	119	O148C	—	1.0
1899	Lou N	155	636	117	194	17	13	5	49	62	10	—	.305	.376	.396	112	11	33	.928	-11	87	128	O155C	—	-0.9
1901	Chi A	132	527	112	155	28	11	2	60	**86**	**14**	—	.294	.407	.400	128	27	27	.958	-3	92	164	O132C	—	1.6
1902	Cin N	72	279	48	81	15	2	2	20	41	4	—	.290	.389	.380	125	11	11	.933	-5	43	42	O72C	—	0.3
Total	14	1797	7115	1429	2048	248	121	40	725	1006	134	211	.288	.386	.374	109	138	596	.915	-25	95	113	O1796(66/1727/5)/2	—	1.8
HRBEK, KENT	Kent Alan; B5.21.1960 Minneapolis MN; BL/TR/6´4˝/(215–260); [MinA78 17/432]; d8.24																								
1981	Min A	24	67	5	16	5	0	1	7	5-1	1	9	.239	.301	.358	84	-1	0-0	1.000	-2	49	126	1b13,D8	0	-0.4
1982	Min A★	140	532	82	160	21	4	23	92	54-12	0	80	.301	.363	.485	127	19	3-1	.993	1	100	102	1b138,D2	0	1.2
1983	Min A	141	515	75	153	41	5	16	84	57-5	3	71	.297	.366	.489	129	22	4-6	.990	-1	100	97	1b137,D2	0	1.2
1984	Min A	149	559	80	174	31	3	27	107	65-15	4	87	.311	.383	.522	141	33	1-1	.990	-4	92	94	1b148/D	0	1.9
1985	Min A	158	593	78	165	31	2	21	93	67-12	2	87	.278	.351	.444	110	9	1-1	.995	1	102	91	1b156,D2	0	0.1
1986	Min A	149	550	85	147	27	1	29	91	71-9	6	81	.267	.353	.478	121	17	2-2	.992	-1	95	110	1b147/D	0	0.7
1987	†Min A	143	477	85	136	20	1	34	90	84-12	0	60	.285	.389	.545	140	29	5-2	.996	-10	69	103	1b137/D	0	1.0
1988	Min A	143	510	75	159	31	0	25	76	67-7	0	54	.312	.387	.520	148	35	0-3	.997	-5	78	109	1b105,D37	0	2.0
1989	Min A	109	375	59	102	17	0	25	84	53-4	1	35	.272	.360	.517	137	18	3-0	.995	3	109	89	1b89,D18	41	1.5
1990	Min A	143	492	61	141	26	0	22	79	69-8	7	45	.287	.377	.474	130	22	5-2	**.997**	3	103	98	1b120,D20/3	0	1.6
1991	†Min A	132	462	72	131	20	1	20	89	67-4	0	48	.284	.373	.461	124	16	4-4	.994	3	108	111	1b128	0	0.9
1992	Min A	112	394	52	96	20	0	15	58	71-9	0	56	.244	.357	.409	110	8	5-2	.997	1	99	91	1b104,D8	45	0.1
1993	Min A	123	392	60	95	11	1	25	83	71-6	1	57	.242	.357	.467	119	11	4-2	.995	2	107	103	1b115,D2	15	0.4
1994	Min A	81	274	34	74	11	0	10	53	37-6	1	28	.270	.353	.420	99	0	0-0	.997	-1	96	85	1b72,D4	26	-0.6
Total	14	1747	6192	903	1749	312	18	293	1086	838-110	26	798	.282	.367	.481	126	238	37-26	.994	-10	96	100	1b1609,D106/3	127	11.6
HRINIAK, WALT	Walter John; B5.22.1943 Natick MA; BL/TR/5´11˝/180; d9.10; C21																								
1968	Atl N	9	26	0	9	0	0	0	3	0-0	0	3	.346	.346	.346	108	0	0-0	.967	1	43	0	C9	0	0.1
1969	Atl N	7	7	0	1	0	0	0	0	2-0	0	1	.143	.333	.143	37	0	0-0	1.000	0	0	0	C6	25	0.0
	SD N	31	66	4	15	0	0	0	1	8-1	2	11	.227	.329	.227	60	-3	0-0	.981	-2	72	64	C19	15	-0.4
	Year	38	73	4	16	0	0	0	1	10-1	2	12	.219	.329	.219	58	-4	0-0	.982	-1	65	58	C25	0	-0.4
Total	2	47	99	4	25	0	0	0	4	10-1	2	15	.253	.333	.253	70	-3	0-0	.977	-1	59	42	C34	40	-0.3
HUBBARD, AL	Allen (aka Al West For 1 Game in 1883); B12.9.1860 Westfield MA; D12.14.1930 Newton MA; d9.13; Col Yale																								
1883	Phi AA	2	6	2	2	0	0	0	2	1	—	—	.333	.429	.333	136	0	—	.750	-1	45	0	/SC	—	0.0
HUBBARD, GLENN	Glenn Dee; B9.25.1957 Hahn Air Force Base, West Germany; BR/TR/5´7˝/(150–170); [AtlN75 20/473]; d7.14; C8																								
1978	Atl N	44	163	15	42	4	0	2	13	10-1	2	20	.258	.309	.319	68	-7	2-1	.979	2	101	107	2b44	32	-0.2
1979	Atl N	97	325	34	75	12	0	3	29	27-2	1	43	.231	.290	.295	57	-19	0-6	.968	-0	100	95	2b91	0	-1.7
1980	Atl N	117	431	55	107	21	3	9	43	49-2	0	69	.248	.322	.374	93	-3	7-5	.978	21	**113**	**130**	2b117	0	2.5
1981	Atl N	99	361	39	85	13	5	6	33	33-2	2	59	.235	.302	.349	84	-8	4-2	.991	-4	105	82	2b98	0	-0.7
1982	†Atl N	145	532	75	132	25	1	9	59	59-5	3	62	.248	.324	.350	87	-8	4-3	.983	19	109	125	2b144	0	1.9
1983	Atl N★	148	517	65	136	24	6	12	70	55-2	4	71	.263	.334	.402	97	-1	3-8	.985	25	110	112	2b148	0	3.0
1984	Atl N	120	397	53	93	27	2	9	43	55-6	4	61	.234	.331	.380	93	-2	4-1	.988	14	111	107	2b117	0	2.0
1985	Atl N	142	439	51	102	21	0	5	39	56-2	4	54	.232	.321	.314	75	-13	4-3	.989	**60**	**131**	**131**	2b140	0	5.6
1986	Atl N	143	408	42	94	16	1	4	36	66-14	4	74	.230	.340	.304	76	-11	3-2	.976	**40**	**118**	138	2b142	0	3.7
1987	Atl N	141	443	69	117	33	2	5	38	77-17	6	57	.264	.378	.381	99	4	1-1	.986	**28**	**118**	123	2b139	0	3.8
1988	†Oak A	105	294	35	75	12	2	3	33	33-0	3	50	.255	.334	.340	93	-2	1-3	.987	1	99	104	2b104/D	11	0.1
1989	Oak A	53	131	12	26	6	0	3	12	19-0	0	20	.198	.296	.313	75	-4	2-0	.968	7	109	142	2b48,D3	15	0.5
Total	12	1354	4441	545	1084	214	22	70	448	539-53	33	640	.244	.328	.349	85	-74	35-35	.983	212	112	117	2b1332,D4	58	20.5
HUBBARD, MIKE	Michael Wayne; B2.16.1971 Lynchburg VA; BR/TR/6´1˝/(180–205); [ChiN92 8/219]; d7.13; Col James Madison																								
1995	Chi N	15	23	2	4	0	0	0	1	2-0	0	2	.174	.240	.174	11	-3	0-0	.971	-3	80	98	C9	0	-0.6
1996	Chi N	21	38	1	4	0	0	1	4	0-0	0	15	.105	.103	.184	-25	-7	0-0	1.000	1	623	41	C14	0	-0.6
1997	Chi N	29	64	4	13	0	0	1	2	2-1	0	21	.203	.227	.250	24	-7	0-0	.992	1	89	70	C20/3	0	-0.5
1998	Mon N	32	55	3	8	1	0	1	3	0-0	1	17	.145	.161	.218	-2	-8	0-0	1.000	-6	32	129	C24/2	0	-1.3
2000	Atl N	2	1	0	0	0	0	0	0	0-0	0	1	.000	.000	.000	-99	0	0-0	1.000	0	0	0	/C	0	0.0

YEAR	TM LG	G	AB	R	H	2B	3B	HR	RBI	BB-IB	HP	SO	AVG	OBP	SLG	AOPS	ABR	SB-CS	FA	FR	RNG	THR	GAMES AT POSITION	DL	BFW
2001	Tex A	5	11	1	3	1	0	1	1	0-0	0	4	.273	.273	.636	126	0	0-0	1.000	-2	40	99	C5	116	-0.1
Total	6	104	192	11	32	2	0	4	11	4-1	1	60	.167	.187	.240	11	-25	0-0	.994	-9	158	88	C73/23	116	-3.1

HUBBARD, TRENIDAD Trenidad Aviel (b Trent Hubbard); B5.11.1964 Chicago IL; BR/TR/5´9˝/(180–203); [HouN86 12/302]; d7.7; Col Southern A&M

YEAR	TM LG	G	AB	R	H	2B	3B	HR	RBI	BB-IB	HP	SO	AVG	OBP	SLG	AOPS	ABR	SB-CS	FA	FR	RNG	THR	GAMES AT POSITION	DL	BFW
1994	Col N	18	25	3	7	1	1	1	3	3-0	0	4	.280	.357	.520	107	0	0-0	1.000	-1	53	0	O5(2/3/0)	0	-0.1
1995	†Col N	24	58	13	18	4	0	3	9	8-0	0	6	.310	.394	.534	111	1	2-1	1.000	-2	57	146	O16(4/14/0)	0	-0.1
1996	Col N	45	60	12	13	5	1	1	12	9-0	1	22	.217	.329	.383	70	-2	2-0	1.000	1	121	0	O19(3/16/0)	0	-0.1
	SF N	10	29	3	6	0	1	1	2	2-0	0	5	.207	.258	.379	67	-2	0-0	1.000	2	134	229	O9(8/1/0)	17	0.0
	Year	55	89	15	19	5	2	2	14	11-0	1	27	.213	.307	.382	68	-4	2-0	1.000	2	126	93	O28(11/17/0)	0	-0.1
1997	Cle A	7	12	3	3	1	0	0	0	1-0	0	3	.250	.308	.333	65	-1	2-0	1.000	-1	44	0	O6(5/1/0)	0	-0.1
1998	LA N	94	208	29	62	9	1	7	18	18-0	3	46	.298	.358	.452	118	5	9-5	.991	-1	97	90	O81(34/46/4)/3	38	0.4
1999	LA N	82	105	23	33	5	0	1	13	13-1	0	24	.314	.387	.390	103	1	4-3	.980	-1	97	76	O51(29/19/3)/C2	0	0.0
2000	Atl N	61	81	15	15	2	1	1	6	11-0	1	20	.185	.290	.272	43	-7	2-1	1.000	-1	89	68	O44(36/0/10)	0	-0.9
	Bal A	31	27	3	5	0	1	0	0	0-0	0	3	.185	.185	.259	11	-4	2-1	.929	-1	73	188	O24(11/0/14),D6	0	-0.4
2001	KC A	5	12	2	3	0	1	0	0	0-0	0	2	.250	.250	.417	65	-1	0-0	1.000	-1	38	0	O3(0/2/1)	0	-0.1
2002	SD N	89	129	16	27	5	0	1	7	14-0	0	28	.209	.285	.271	52	-9	9-6	.981	-1	91	129	O57(16/16/26),3b6,2b4/D	0	-1.1
2003	Chi N	10	16	2	4	1	0	0	2	4-0	1	3	.250	.429	.313	95	0	1-0	1.000	-1	69	0	O4(0/4/1)	0	0.0
Total	10	476	762	124	196	33	7	16	72	83-1	6	166	.257	.333	.382	85	-19	33-17	.989	-7	91	93	O319(148/122/59),D7,3b7,2b5/C	55	-2.5

HUBBS, KEN Kenneth Douglas; B12.23.1941 Riverside CA; D2.13.1964 Provo UT; BR/TR/6´2˝/180; d9.10

YEAR	TM LG	G	AB	R	H	2B	3B	HR	RBI	BB-IB	HP	SO	AVG	OBP	SLG	AOPS	ABR	SB-CS	FA	FR	RNG	THR	GAMES AT POSITION	DL	BFW
1961	Chi N	10	28	4	5	1	1	1	2	0-0	0	8	.179	.179	.393	46	-2	0-0	1.000	-2	84	43	2b8	0	-0.4
1962	Chi N	160	661	90	172	24	9	5	49	35-0	3	129	.260	.299	.346	71	-29	3-7	.983	4	107	93	2b159	0	-1.3
1963	Chi N	154	566	54	133	19	3	8	47	39-2	2	93	.235	.285	.322	71	-21	8-9	.974	19	116	111	2b152	0	1.1
Total	3	324	1255	148	310	44	13	14	98	74-2	5	230	.247	.290	.336	70	-52	11-16	.979	21	111	101	2b319	0	-0.6

HUBER, CLARENCE Clarence Bill "Gilly"; B10.27.1895 Tyler TX; D2.22.1965 Laredo TX; BR/TR/5´10˝/165; d9.17

YEAR	TM LG	G	AB	R	H	2B	3B	HR	RBI	BB-IB	HP	SO	AVG	OBP	SLG	AOPS	ABR	SB-CS	FA	FR	RNG	THR	GAMES AT POSITION	DL	BFW
1920	Det A	11	42	4	9	2	1	0	5	0	0	5	.214	.214	.310	39	-4	0-0	.907	1	103	0	3b11	—	-0.3
1921	Det A	1	0	0	0	0	0	0	0	0	0	0	ø	ø	ø	ø	0	0-0	1.000	-0	0	0	/3	—	0.0
1925	Phi N	124	436	46	124	28	5	5	54	17	0	33	.284	.311	.406	75	-17	3-5	.947	-9	94	72	3b120	—	-1.9
1926	Phi N	118	376	45	92	17	7	1	34	42	2	29	.245	.324	.335	74	-13	9	.956	9	111	110	3b115	—	0.2
Total	4	254	854	95	225	47	13	6	93	59	2	67	.263	.313	.370	73	-34	12-5	.948	1	102	85	3b247	—	-2.0

HUBER, JUSTIN Justin Patrick; B7.1.1982 Melbourne, Victoria, Australia; BR/TR/6´2˝/(195–200); d6.21

YEAR	TM LG	G	AB	R	H	2B	3B	HR	RBI	BB-IB	HP	SO	AVG	OBP	SLG	AOPS	ABR	SB-CS	FA	FR	RNG	THR	GAMES AT POSITION	DL	BFW
2005	KC A	25	78	6	17	3	0	0	6	5-0	1	20	.218	.271	.256	44	-6	0-0	.978	-1	75	99	1b19,D4	0	-0.9
2006	KC A	5	10	1	2	1	0	0	1	1-0	0	4	.200	.273	.300	49	-1	1-0	ø	0	—	—	D4	0	-0.1
Total	2	30	88	7	19	4	0	0	7	6-0	1	24	.216	.271	.261	44	-7	1-0	.978	-1	75	99	1b19,D8	0	-1.0

HUBER, OTTO Otto; B3.12.1914 Garfield NJ; D4.9.1989 Passaic NJ; BR/TR/5´10˝/165; d6.10

YEAR	TM LG	G	AB	R	H	2B	3B	HR	RBI	BB-IB	HP	SO	AVG	OBP	SLG	AOPS	ABR	SB-CS	FA	FR	RNG	THR	GAMES AT POSITION	DL	BFW
1939	Bos N	11	22	2	6	1	0	0	3	0	0	1	.273	.273	.318	63	-1	0	1.000	-0	99	0	2b4,3b4	—	-0.1

HUCKABY, KEN Kenneth Paul; B1.27.1971 San Leandro CA; BR/TR/6´1˝/(200–210); [LAN91 22/585]; d10.6; Col San Joaquin Delta (CA) JC

YEAR	TM LG	G	AB	R	H	2B	3B	HR	RBI	BB-IB	HP	SO	AVG	OBP	SLG	AOPS	ABR	SB-CS	FA	FR	RNG	THR	GAMES AT POSITION	DL	BFW
2001	Ari N	1	1	0	0	0	0	0	0	0-0	0	1	.000	.000	.000	-94	0	0-0	1.000	0	0	0	/C	0	0.0
2002	Tor A	88	273	29	67	6	1	3	22	9-1	0	44	.245	.270	.308	51	-20	0-0	.989	0	115	97	C88	0	-1.4
2003	Tor A	5	11	1	2	1	0	0	2	0-0	0	2	.182	.182	.273	17	-1	0-0	1.000	-0	35	0	C4	0	-0.1
2004	Tex A	8	25	2	4	1	0	0	0	3-0	0	10	.160	.250	.200	19	-3	0-0	1.000	2	99	109	C8	0	0.0
	Bal A	8	12	1	2	1	0	0	0	0-0	0	0	.167	.167	.250	7	-2	0-0	1.000	-1	71	99	C8	0	-0.2
	Tex A	8	13	1	1	1	0	0	0	2-0	0	2	.077	.200	.154	-6	-2	0-0	.939	-1	99	109	C8	0	-0.2
	Year	24	50	4	7	3	0	0	0	5-0	0	12	.140	.218	.200	10	-7	0-0	.983	1	81	100	C24	0	-0.4
2005	Tor A	35	87	8	18	4	0	0	6	5-0	0	19	.207	.250	.253	33	-8	0-0	.987	-2	123	160	C35	0	-0.8
2006	Bos A	8	5	0	1	0	0	0	1	0-0	0	0	.200	.200	.200	4	-1	0-0	1.000	-1	0	0	C8	0	-0.2
Total	6	161	427	42	95	14	1	3	31	19-1	0	78	.222	.256	.281	41	-37	0-0	.991	-2	109	108	C160	0	-2.9

HUDGENS, DAVE David Mark; B12.5.1956 Oroville CA; BL/TL/6´2˝/210; d9.4; C4; Col Arizona St.

YEAR	TM LG	G	AB	R	H	2B	3B	HR	RBI	BB-IB	HP	SO	AVG	OBP	SLG	AOPS	ABR	SB-CS	FA	FR	RNG	THR	GAMES AT POSITION	DL	BFW
1983	Oak A	6	7	0	1	0	0	0	0	0-0	0	3	.143	.143	.143	-22	-1	0-0	1.000	-0	0	0	1b3/D	0	-0.1

HUDGENS, JIMMY James Price; B8.24.1902 Newburg MO; D8.26.1955 St.Louis MO; BL/TR/6´0˝/180; d9.14

YEAR	TM LG	G	AB	R	H	2B	3B	HR	RBI	BB-IB	HP	SO	AVG	OBP	SLG	AOPS	ABR	SB-CS	FA	FR	RNG	THR	GAMES AT POSITION	DL	BFW
1923	StL N	6	12	2	3	1	0	0	0	3	0	3	.250	.400	.333	97	0	0-0	1.000	-0	210	0	1b3/2	—	0.0
1925	Cin N	3	7	0	3	1	1	0	0	1	0	1	.429	.500	.857	245	2	0-0	1.000	-0	71	103	1b3	—	0.1
1926	Cin N	17	20	2	5	1	0	0	1	1	0	0	.250	.286	.300	59	-1	0	1.000	0	129	50	1b6	—	-0.1
Total	3	26	39	4	11	3	1	0	1	5	0	4	.282	.364	.410	107	1	0-0	1.000	-0	138	50	1b12/2	—	0.0

HUDLER, REX Rex Allen; B9.2.1960 Tempe AZ; BR/TR/6´0˝/(180–202); [NYA78 1/18]; d9.9; OF(124/65/64); [DL 1987 Bal A 71]

YEAR	TM LG	G	AB	R	H	2B	3B	HR	RBI	BB-IB	HP	SO	AVG	OBP	SLG	AOPS	ABR	SB-CS	FA	FR	RNG	THR	GAMES AT POSITION	DL	BFW
1984	NY A	9	7	2	1	1	0	0	0	1-0	1	5	.143	.333	.286	76	0	0-0	1.000	-2	72	44	2b9	0	-0.2
1985	NY A	20	51	4	8	0	1	0	1	1-0	0	9	.157	.173	.196	1	-7	0-1	.977	4	115	124	2b16/1S	0	-0.3
1986	Bal A	14	1	1	0	0	0	0	0	0-0	0	0	.000	.000	.000	-99	0	1-0	.800	-2	36	0	2b13/3	0	-0.2
1988	Mon N	77	216	38	59	14	2	4	14	10-6	0	34	.273	.303	.412	99	-1	29-7	.978	-5	103	120	2b41,S27,O4(2/0/2)	0	0.1
1989	Mon N	92	155	21	38	7	0	6	13	6-2	1	23	.245	.278	.406	92	-2	15-4	.958	-5	99	113	2b38,O23(14/5/4),S18	0	-0.5
1990	Mon N	4	3	1	1	0	0	0	0	0-0	0	1	.333	.333	.333	87	0	0-0	ø	0	—	—	/H	0	0.0
	StL N	89	217	30	61	11	2	7	22	12-1	2	31	.281	.323	.447	109	2	18-10	.979	5	108	108	O45(17/3/27),2b10,1b6,3b6/S	0	0.6
	Year	93	220	31	62	11	2	7	22	12-1	2	32	.282	.323	.445	109	2	18-10	.979	5	108	108	O45(17/3/27),2b10,1b6,3b6/S	0	0.6
1991	StL N	101	207	21	47	10	2	1	15	10-1	0	29	.227	.260	.309	60	-12	12-8	.981	0	99	154	O58(28/21/10),1b12,2b5	0	-1.3
1992	StL N	61	98	17	24	4	0	3	5	2-0	1	23	.245	.265	.378	83	-3	2-6	.957	-1	108	89	2b16,O12(5/1/7),1b8	53	-0.6
1994	Cal A	56	124	17	37	8	0	8	20	6-0	0	28	.298	.326	.556	121	3	2-2	.971	3	109	149	2b22,O18L,3b4/1D	17	0.6
1995	Cal A	84	223	30	59	16	0	6	27	10-1	5	48	.265	.310	.417	88	-4	13-0	.986	4	104	126	2b52,O22(18/4/1),1b2,D3	0	0.4
1996	Cal A	92	302	60	94	20	3	16	40	9-0	3	54	.311	.337	.556	119	7	14-5	.982	-5	91	106	2b53,O21(8/14/0),1b7,D8	0	0.5
1997	Phi N	50	122	17	27	4	0	5	10	6-1	1	28	.221	.264	.377	66	-7	1-0	.962	1	104	76	O35(11/16/8),2b6	84	-0.6
1998	Phi N	25	41	2	5	1	0	0	2	4-0	0	12	.122	.200	.146	-7	-7	0-0	1.000	1	145	0	O9(3/1/5)/1	0	-0.6
Total	13	774	1767	261	461	96	10	56	169	77-12	14	325	.261	.296	.422	91	-31	107-43	.975	-1	102	115	2b281,O247L,S47,1b38,D15,3b11	225	-2.1

HUDSON, JOHNNY John Wilson "Mr. Chips"; B6.30.1912 Bryan TX; D11.7.1970 Bryan TX; BR/TR/5´10˝/160; d6.20

YEAR	TM LG	G	AB	R	H	2B	3B	HR	RBI	BB-IB	HP	SO	AVG	OBP	SLG	AOPS	ABR	SB-CS	FA	FR	RNG	THR	GAMES AT POSITION	DL	BFW
1936	Bro N	6	12	1	2	0	0	0	0	2	0	1	.167	.286	.167	24	-1	0	.889	-2	68	49	S4/2	—	-0.3
1937	Bro N	13	27	3	5	4	0	0	2	3	0	9	.185	.267	.333	61	-1	0	.867	-3	83	49	S11/2	—	-0.4
1938	Bro N	135	498	59	130	21	5	2	37	39	0	76	.261	.315	.335	77	-16	7	.963	-0	99	100	2b132,S3	—	-0.8
1939	Bro N	109	343	46	87	17	3	2	32	30	2	36	.254	.317	.338	74	-13	5	.959	-13	93	105	S50,2b45/3	—	-2.0
1940	Bro N	85	179	13	39	4	3	0	19	9	0	26	.218	.255	.274	43	-14	2	.921	-4	97	67	S38,2b27/3	—	-1.6
1941	Chi N	50	99	8	20	4	0	0	6	3	0	15	.202	.225	.242	33	-9	3	.907	-1	83	97	S17,2b13,3b10	0	-0.9
1945	NY N	28	11	8	0	0	0	0	0	1	0	1	.000	.083	.000	-75	-3	0	.875	1	112	406	3b5,2b2	0	-0.2
Total	7	426	1169	138	283	50	11	4	96	87	2	164	.242	.296	.314	65	-57	17	.962	-23	99	99	2b221,S123,3b17	0	-6.2

HUDSON, ORLANDO Orlando Thill; B12.12.1977 Darlington SC; BB/TR/6´0˝/(175–185); [TorA97 43/1280]; d7.24; Col Spartanburg Methodist (SC) JC

YEAR	TM LG	G	AB	R	H	2B	3B	HR	RBI	BB-IB	HP	SO	AVG	OBP	SLG	AOPS	ABR	SB-CS	FA	FR	RNG	THR	GAMES AT POSITION	DL	BFW
2002	Tor A	54	192	20	53	10	5	4	23	11-0	2	27	.276	.319	.443	97	-2	0-1	.986	9	104	139	2b52	0	1.0
2003	Tor A	142	474	54	127	21	6	9	57	39-1	5	87	.268	.328	.395	87	-9	5-4	.984	**45**	**123**	112	2b139	0	3.9
2004	Tor A	135	489	73	132	32	7	12	58	51-0	4	98	.270	.341	.438	96	-2	7-3	.984	**33**	**118**	104	2b133	23	3.5
2005	Tor A	131	461	62	125	25	5	10	63	30-1	3	65	.271	.315	.412	88	-8	7-1	**.991**	**28**	**112**	102	2b130	0	2.6
2006	Ari N	157	579	87	166	34	9	15	67	61-5	2	78	.287	.354	.454	100	0	9-6	.984	23	110	113	2b157	0	3.0
Total	5	619	2195	296	603	122	32	50	268	192-7	16	355	.275	.335	.428	94	-21	28-15	.986	139	115	111	2b611	23	14.0

HUELSMAN, FRANK Frank Elmer; B6.5.1874 St.Louis MO; D6.9.1959 Affton MO; BR/TR/6´2˝/210; d10.3

YEAR	TM LG	G	AB	R	H	2B	3B	HR	RBI	BB-IB	HP	SO	AVG	OBP	SLG	AOPS	ABR	SB-CS	FA	FR	RNG	THR	GAMES AT POSITION	DL	BFW
1897	StL N	2	7	0	2	1	0	0	0	0	0	—	.286	.286	.429	89	0	0	.000	-1	0	0	O2L	—	-0.1
1904	Chi A	3	6	0	1	1	0	0	0	0	0	—	.167	.167	.333	58	0	0	.000	-1	0	0	/cf	—	-0.1
	Det A	4	18	1	6	1	0	0	4	1	0	—	.333	.368	.389	144	1	1	1.000	-0	0	0	O4L	—	0.0
	Chi A	1	1	0	0	0	0	0	0	0	0	—	.000	.000	.000	-99	0	0	ø	0	—	—	/H	—	0.0
	StL A	20	68	6	15	2	1	0	1	6	2	—	.221	.303	.279	90	0	0	1.000	-2	0	0	O18R	—	-0.3
	Was A	84	303	21	75	19	4	2	30	24	5	—	.248	.313	.356	113	5	6	.960	-1	80	76	O84(82/2/0)	—	0.0
	Year	112	396	28	97	23	5	2	35	31	7	—	.245	.311	.343	110	5	7	.960	-3	65	62	O107(86/3/18)	—	-0.4

YEAR	TM LG	G	AB	R	H	2B	3B	HR	RBI	BB-IB	HP	SO	AVG	OBP	SLG	AOPS	ABR	SB-CS	FA	FR	RNG	THR	GAMES AT POSITION	DL	BFW
1905	Was A	121	421	48	114	28	8	3	62	31	8	—	.271	.333	.397	136	17	11	.929	-7	56	67	O116(115/0/1)	—	0.4
Total	3	235	824	76	213	52	13	5	97	62	15	—	.258	.322	.371	123	23	18	.941	-11	60	64	O225(203/3/19)	—	-0.1
HUFF, AUBREY	Aubrey Lewis; B12.20.1976 Marion OH; BL/TR/6´4˝/(221–230); [TBA98 5/162]; d8.2; Col Miami																								
2000	TB A	39	122	12	35	7	0	4	14	5-1	1	18	.287	.318	.443	92	-2	0-0	.939	-2	94	52	3b37	0	-0.4
2001	TB A	111	411	42	102	25	1	8	45	23-2	0	72	.248	.288	.372	73	-17	1-3	.918	-4	95	104	3b73,D20,1b19	0	-2.3
2002	TB A	113	454	67	142	25	0	23	59	37-7	1	55	.313	.364	.520	135	22	4-1	.987	-4	70	98	D53,1b45,3b14	0	1.1
2003	TB A	**162**	636	91	198	47	3	34	107	53-17	8	80	.311	.367	.555	143	39	2-3	.970	-7	96	87	O102R,D33,1b22,3b8	0	2.3
2004	TB A	157	600	92	178	27	2	29	104	56-6	6	74	.297	.360	.493	123	20	5-1	.943	-4	88	88	3b86,1b38,D34,O9(8/0/1)	0	1.1
2005	TB A	154	575	70	150	26	2	22	92	49-13	5	88	.261	.321	.428	100	-1	8-7	.986	3	112	114	O97R,D33,1b25,3b4	0	-0.7
2006	TB A	63	230	26	65	15	1	8	28	24-3	0	25	.283	.348	.461	109	3	0-0	.980	-1	96	118	3b60,D3	23	0.2
	Hou N	68	224	31	56	10	1	13	38	26-3	7	39	.250	.341	.478	105	2	0-0	.953	-3	66	66	O37R,3b30,1b3	0	-0.3
Total	7	867	3252	431	926	182	10	141	487	273-52	28	451	.285	.342	.477	115	66	20-15	.943	-23	92	92	3b312,0245(8/0/237),D176,1b152	23	1.0
HUFF, MIKE	Michael Kale; B8.11.1963 Honolulu HI; BR/TR/6´1˝/(180–190); [LAN85 16/402]; d8.7; Col Northwestern																								
1989	LA N	12	25	4	5	1	0	1	2	3-0	1	6	.200	.310	.360	92	0	0-1	1.000	0	122	0	O9(7/1/2)	0	0.0
1991	Cle A	51	146	28	35	6	1	2	10	25-0	4	30	.240	.364	.336	95	0	11-2	.990	-1	97	145	O48(8/39/5),2b2	0	0.0
	Chi A	51	97	14	26	4	1	1	15	12-2	2	18	.268	.357	.361	102	1	3-2	.986	-1	104	48	O48(9/14/35),2b2,D2	15	-0.1
	Year	102	243	42	61	10	2	3	25	37-2	6	48	.251	.361	.346	98	1	14-4	.988	-2	100	102	O96(17/53/40),2b4,D2	0	-0.1
1992	Chi A	60	115	13	24	5	0	0	8	10-1	1	24	.209	.273	.252	50	-8	1-2	1.000	-0	99	89	O56(10/3/45)/D	76	-1.0
1993	Chi A	43	44	4	8	2	0	1	6	9-0	1	15	.182	.321	.295	72	-1	1-0	1.000	-1	98	0	O43(31/8/7)	0	-0.2
1994	Tor A	80	207	31	63	15	3	3	25	27-2	3	27	.304	.392	.449	115	6	2-1	.992	2	106	111	O76(57/19/8)	15	0.6
1995	Tor A	61	138	14	32	9	1	1	9	22-0	1	21	.232	.337	.333	76	-4	1-1	.980	1	105	133	O55(9/33/15)	34	-0.3
1996	Tor A	11	29	5	5	0	1	0	0	1-0	0	5	.172	.200	.241	11	-4	0-0	1.000	-1	104	0	O9(1/4/4),3b3	0	-0.5
Total	7	369	801	113	198	42	7	9	75	109-5	13	146	.247	.344	.351	88	-10	19-9	.991	-0	103	94	0344(132/121/121),2b4,3b3,D3	140	-1.5
HUFFMAN, BEN	Benjamin Franklin; B7.18.1914 Rileyville VA; D2.22.2005 Luray VA; BL/TR/5´11.5˝/175; d4.23; Col Bridgewater (VA)																								
1937	StL A	76	176	18	48	9	0	1	24	10	3	7	.273	.323	.341	67	-9	1-0	.970	-6	*84*	77	C42	—	-1.2
HUG, ED	Edward Ambrose; B7.14.1880 Fayetteville OH; D5.11.1953 Cincinnati OH; BR/TR; d7.6																								
1903	Bro N	1	0	0	0	0	0	0	0	1	0	—	ø	1.000	ø	199	0	0	ø	0	*0*	*0*	/C	—	0.0
HUGGINS, MILLER	Miller James "Hug","Mighty Mite"; B3.27.1878 Cincinnati OH; D9.25.1929 New York NY; BB/TR/5´6.5˝/140; d4.15; M17; HF1964; Col Cincinnati																								
1904	Cin N	140	491	96	129	12	7	2	30	88	2	—	.263	.377	.328	108	9	13	.945	-2	101	78	2b140	—	0.9
1905	Cin N	149	564	117	154	11	8	1	38	**103**	7	—	.273	.392	.326	103	8	27	.945	**37**	**116**	108	2b149	—	4.7
1906	Cin N	146	545	81	159	11	7	0	26	71	3	—	.292	.376	.338	118	14	41	.948	22	**107**	128	2b146	—	4.1
1907	Cin N	**156**	561	64	139	12	4	1	31	**83**	1	—	.248	.346	.289	95	1	28	.961	4	99	**134**	2b156	—	0.6
1908	Cin N	135	498	65	119	14	5	0	23	58	2	—	.239	.321	.287	97	0	30	.959	6	102	116	2b135	—	0.8
1909	Cin N	57	159	18	34	3	1	0	6	28	1	—	.214	.335	.245	81	-2	11	.933	4	113	130	2b31,3b15	—	0.3
1910	StL N	151	547	101	145	15	6	1	36	**116**	6	46	.265	.399	.320	114	19	34	.963	6	107	81	2b151	—	2.7
1911	StL N	138	509	106	133	19	2	1	24	96	6	52	.261	.385	.312	99	6	37	.961	11	**111**	100	2b136	—	1.9
1912	StL N	120	431	82	131	15	4	0	29	87	1	31	.304	.422	.357	117	17	35	.943	-7	99	96	2b114	—	1.1
1913	StL N	121	382	74	109	12	0	0	27	92	7	49	.285	**.432**	.317	117	18	23-19	**.977**	4	102	91	2b113,M	—	2.3
1914	StL N	148	509	85	134	17	4	1	24	**105**	7	63	.263	.396	.318	115	18	32	.964	-8	98	109	2b147,M	—	1.3
1915	StL N	107	353	57	85	5	2	2	24	74	3	68	.241	.377	.283	101	6	13-12	.957	6	**111**	110	2b105,M	—	1.3
1916	StL N	18	9	2	3	0	0	0	0	2	1	3	.333	.500	.333	159	1	0	1.000	2	149	0	2b7,M	—	0.4
Total	13	1586	5558	948	1474	146	50	9	318	1003	47	312	.265	.382	.314	107	115	324-31	.956	84	105	105	2b1530,3b15	—	22.4
HUGHES, JOE	Joseph Thompson; B2.21.1880 Pardoe PA; D3.13.1951 Cleveland OH; BR/TR/5´10˝/165; d8.30; Col Geneva																								
1902	Chi N	1	3	0	0	0	0	0	0	0	0	—	.000	.000	.000	-99	-1	0	ø	-0	0	0	/rf	—	-0.1
HUGHES, KEITH	Keith Wills; B9.12.1963 Bryn Mawr PA; BL/TL/6´3˝/(205–210); d5.19																								
1987	NY A	4	4	0	0	0	0	0	0	0-0	0	2	.000	.000	.000	-99	-1	0-0	ø	0	—	—	/H	0	-0.1
	Phi N	37	76	8	20	2	0	0	10	7-0	1	11	.263	.333	.289	65	-4	0-0	.963	-2	88	0	O19(13/0/6)	0	-0.6
1988	Bal A	41	108	10	21	4	2	2	14	16-1	0	27	.194	.294	.324	76	-3	1-0	.969	1	95	220	O31R/D	0	-0.3
1990	NY N	8	9	0	0	0	0	0	0	0-0	0	4	.000	.000	.000	-99	-2	0-0	1.000	0	185	0	O5(4/1/0)	0	-0.2
1993	Cin N	3	4	0	0	0	0	0	0	0-0	0	0	.000	.000	.000	-99	-1	0-0	ø	-0	0	0	O2L	0	-0.1
Total	4	93	201	18	41	6	2	2	24	23-1	1	44	.204	.286	.284	57	-11	1-0	.969	-0	95	138	O57(19/1/37)/D	0	-1.3
HUGHES, BOBBY	Robert E.; B3.10.1971 Burbank CA; BR/TR/6´4˝/(229–237); [MilA92 2/50]; d4.2; Col USC																								
1998	Mil N	85	218	28	50	7	2	9	29	16-1	1	54	.229	.284	.404	77	-8	1-2	.995	-2	81	74	C72,O3R	0	-0.6
1999	Mil N	48	101	10	26	2	0	3	8	5-0	0	28	.257	.292	.366	65	-6	0-0	.988	-2	105	103	C44/D	68	-0.6
Total	2	133	319	38	76	9	2	12	37	21-1	1	82	.238	.287	.392	73	-14	1-2	.993	-3	88	83	C116,O3R/D	68	-1.2
HUGHES, ROY	Roy John "Jeep","Sage"; B1.11.1911 Cincinnati OH; D3.5.1995 Asheville NC; BR/TR/5´10.5˝/167; d4.16																								
1935	Cle A	82	266	40	78	15	3	0	14	18	1	17	.293	.340	.372	83	-7	13-3	.987	1	106	99	2b40,S29/3	—	0.0
1936	Cle A	152	638	112	188	35	9	0	63	57	4	40	.295	.356	.378	81	-19	20-9	.973	7	95	96	2b152	—	-0.2
1937	Cle A	104	346	57	96	12	6	1	40	40	0	22	.277	.352	.355	78	-11	11-6	.939	11	103	59	3b58,2b32	—	0.4
1938	StL A	58	96	16	27	3	0	2	13	12	0	11	.281	.361	.375	85	-2	3-0	.957	3	98	105	2b21,3b5,S2	—	0.2
1939	StL A	17	23	6	2	0	0	0	1	4	0	4	.087	.222	.087	-18	-4	0-0	1.000	1	108	129	2b6/S	—	-0.3
	Phi N	65	237	22	54	5	1	1	16	21	0	18	.228	.291	.270	53	-16	4	.984	-4	92	64	2b65	—	-1.6
1940	Phi N	1	0	0	0	0	0	0	0	0	0	0	ø	ø	ø	ø	0	0	1.000	-0	0	0	/2	—	0.0
1944	Chi N	126	478	86	137	16	6	1	28	35	1	30	.287	.337	.351	94	-4	16	.951	14	111	163	3b66,S52	0	1.4
1945	†Chi N	69	222	34	58	8	1	0	8	16	0	18	.261	.311	.306	73	-8	6	.931	-2	93	130	S36,2b21,3b9,1b2	0	-0.7
1946	Phi N	89	276	23	65	11	1	0	22	19	1	15	.236	.287	.283	64	-14	7	.942	-8	93	82	S34,3b31,2b7/1	0	-2.1
Total	9	763	2582	396	705	105	27	5	205	222	7	175	.273	.332	.340	78	-85	80-18	.980	22	97	91	2b345,3b170,S154,1b3	0	-2.9
HUGHES, TERRY	Terry Wayne; B5.13.1949 Spartanburg SC; BR/TR/6´1˝/185; [ChiN67 1/2]; d9.2																								
1970	Chi N	2	3	0	1	0	0	0	0	0-0	0	0	.333	.333	.333	71	0	0-0	ø	-0	0	0	/3rf	0	-0.1
1973	StL N	11	14	1	3	1	0	0	1	1-0	0	4	.214	.267	.286	53	-1	0-0	1.000	-0	110	277	3b5/1	0	-0.1
1974	Bos A	41	69	5	14	2	0	1	6	6-0	2	18	.203	.282	.275	58	-4	0-0	.958	-1	90	105	3b36/D	0	-0.5
Total	3	54	86	6	18	3	0	1	7	7-0	2	22	.209	.281	.279	58	-5	0-0	.961	-1	91	118	3b42/D1rf	0	-0.7
HUGHES, TOM	Thomas Franklin; B8.6.1907 Emmet AR; D8.10.1989 Beaumont TX; BL/TR/6´1˝/190; d9.9; Col Texas																								
1930	Det A	17	59	8	22	2	3	0	5	4	0	8	.373	.413	.508	130	2	0-1	.897	-2	83	0	O16(4/12/0)	—	-0.1
HUGHES, BILL	William R.; B11.25.1866 Blandinsville IL; D8.25.1943 Santa Ana CA; BL/TL; d9.28; ▲																								
1884	Was U	14	49	5	6	0	0	0	—	2	—	—	.122	.157	.122	-15	-8	—	.955	-0	82	33	1b9,O6(0/1/5)	—	-0.9
1885	Phi AA	4	16	3	3	1	1	0	1	1	1	—	.188	.278	.375	99	0	—	1.000	-0	0	0	O2R,P2	—	0.0
Total	2	18	65	8	9	1	1	0	1	3	1	—	.138	.188	.185	15	-8	—	.955	-1	82	33	1b9,O8(0/1/7),P2	—	-0.9
HUHN, EMIL	Emil Hugo "Hap"; B3.10.1892 North Vernon IN; D9.5.1925 Camden SC; BR/TR/6´0˝/180; d4.10																								
1915	New F	124	415	34	94	18	1	1	41	28	2	40	.227	.279	.282	61	-29	13	.985	-1	93	121	1b101,C16	—	-3.4
1916	Cin N	37	94	4	24	3	2	0	3	2	0	11	.255	.271	.330	86	-2	0	.989	-0	82	105	C18,1b14/rf	—	-0.2
1917	Cin N	23	51	2	10	1	2	0	3	2	0	5	.196	.226	.294	62	-3	1	.969	-1	*88*	*110*	C15/1	—	-0.3
Total	3	184	560	40	128	22	5	1	47	32	2	56	.229	.273	.291	65	-34	14	.986	-3	95	119	1b116,C49/rf	—	-3.9
HULEN, BILLY	William Franklin; B3.12.1870 Dixon CA; D10.2.1947 Santa Rosa CA; BL/TL/5´8˝/148; d5.2																								
1896	Phi N	88	339	87	90	18	7	0	38	55	0	20	.265	.368	.360	93	-1	23	.874	-19	85	101	S73,O12C,2b2	—	-1.5
1899	Was N	19	68	10	10	1	0	0	3	10	0	—	.147	.256	.162	16	-8	5	.902	-1	111	26	S19	—	-0.7
Total	2	107	407	97	100	19	7	0	41	65	0	20	.246	.350	.327	81	-9	28	.880	-20	90	86	S92,O12C,2b2	—	-2.2
HULETT, TIM	Timothy Craig; B1.12.1960 Springfield IL; BR/TR/6´0˝/(180–199); [ChiA80*S1/3]; d9.15; Col South Florida																								
1983	Chi A	6	5	0	1	0	0	0	0	0-0	0	0	.200	.200	.200	10	-1	1-0	.875	-1	76	56	2b6	0	-0.1
1984	Chi A	8	7	1	0	0	0	0	0	1-0	0	4	.000	.125	.000	-59	-2	1-0	1.000	3	116	0	3b4,2b3	0	0.2
1985	Chi A	141	395	52	106	19	4	5	37	30-1	4	81	.268	.324	.375	87	-7	6-4	.924	3	103	118	3b115,2b28/lf	0	-0.4
1986	Chi A	150	520	53	120	16	5	17	44	21-0	1	91	.231	.260	.379	69	-25	4-1	.951	2	96	72	3b89,2b66	0	-2.0

YEAR	TM LG	G	AB	R	H	2B	3B	HR	RBI	BB-IB	HP	SO	AVG	OBP	SLG	AOPS	ABR	SB-CS	FA	FR	RNG	THR	GAMES AT POSITION	DL	BFW
1987	Chi A	68	240	20	52	10	0	7	28	10-1	0	41	.217	.246	.346	54	-17	0-2	.953	-1	103	136	3b61,2b8	0	-1.8
1989	Bal A	33	97	12	27	5	0	3	18	10-0	0	17	.278	.343	.423	119	2	0-0	.976	-1	99	92	2b23,3b11	0	0.2
1990	Bal A	53	153	16	39	7	1	3	16	15-0	0	41	.255	.321	.373	96	-1	1-0	.961	9	135	101	3b24,2b16,D8	64	0.9
1991	Bal A	79	206	29	42	9	0	7	18	13-0	1	49	.204	.255	.350	68	-10	0-1	.976	-5	99	125	3b39,2b26,D15/S	0	-1.6
1992	Bal A	57	142	11	41	7	2	2	21	10-1	1	31	.289	.340	.408	105	1	0-1	.935	11	147	168	3b27,D13,2b10,S5	16	1.1
1993	Bal A	85	260	40	78	15	0	2	23	23-1	3	56	.300	.361	.381	96	-1	1-2	.963	15	126	202	3b75,S8,2b4,D2	0	1.4
1994	Bal A	36	92	11	21	2	1	2	15	12-0	0	24	.228	.314	.337	65	-5	0-0	.992	13	127	187	2b23,3b9,S6	0	0.8
1995	StL N	4	11	0	2	0	0	0	0	0-0	0	3	.182	.182	.182	-4	-2	0-0	.941	3	227	274	2b2/S	13	0.1
Total	12	720	2128	245	529	90	13	48	220	145-4	10	438	.249	.298	.371	79	-68	14-11	.947	51	109	125	3b454,2b215,D38,S21/lf	93	-1.2
Hulse, David	David Lindsey; B2.25.1968 San Angelo TX; BL/TL/5´11˝/170; [TexA90 13/360]; d8.11; Col Schreiner																								
1992	Tex A	32	92	14	28	4	0	0	2	3-0	0	18	.304	.326	.348	92	-1	3-1	.984	-2	96	0	O31(0/29/2)/D	0	-0.3
1993	Tex A	114	407	71	118	9	10	1	29	26-1	1	57	.290	.333	.369	92	-7	29-9	.988	-5	95	56	O112C,D2	18	-0.7
1994	Tex A	77	310	58	79	8	4	1	19	21-0	2	53	.255	.305	.316	60	-19	18-2	.978	-8	90	0	O76C/D	0	-2.1
1995	Mil A	119	339	46	85	11	6	3	47	18-2	0	60	.251	.285	.345	60	-21	15-3	.984	-10	84	34	O115(67/52/17)	0	-2.9
1996	Mil A	81	117	18	26	3	0	0	6	8-0	0	16	.222	.272	.248	31	-12	4-1	.990	0	105	42	O68(24/37/11),D4	33	-1.1
Total	5	423	1265	207	336	35	20	5	103	76-3	3	204	.266	.307	.337	69	-60	69-16	.985	-24	92	31	O402(91/306/30),D8	51	-7.1
Hulswitt, Rudy	Rudolph Edward; B2.23.1877 Newport KY; D1.16.1950 Louisville KY; BR/TR/5´8.5˝/165; d6.16; C3																								
1899	Lou N	1	0	0	0	0	0	0	0	0	0	—	ø	ø	ø	ø	0	0	.333	-2	42	0	/S	—	-0.1
1902	Phi N	128	497	59	135	11	7	0	38	30	2	—	.272	.316	.322	97	-3	12	.917	8	97	78	S125,3b3	—	1.0
1903	Phi N	138	519	56	128	22	9	1	58	28	2	—	.247	.288	.329	78	-17	10	.906	-1	98	83	S138	—	-1.2
1904	Phi N	113	406	36	99	11	4	1	36	16	2	—	.244	.276	.298	80	-11	8	.912	-11	89	95	S113	—	-1.9
1908	Cin N	119	386	27	88	5	7	1	28	30	2	—	.228	.287	.285	85	-7	7	.936	-8	95	100	S118/2	—	-1.3
1909	StL N	82	289	21	81	8	3	0	29	19	2	—	.280	.329	.329	111	3	7	.930	-7	96	61	S65,2b12	—	-0.2
1910	StL N	63	133	9	33	7	2	0	14	13	1	10	.248	.320	.331	93	-1	5	.854	-10	93	33	S30,2b2	—	-1.1
Total	7	644	2230	208	564	64	32	3	203	136	11	10	.253	.299	.314	89	-36	49	.915	-30	95	83	S590,2b15,3b3	—	-4.8
Hummel, John	John Edwin "Silent John"; B4.4.1883 Bloomsburg PA; D5.18.1959 Springfield MA; BR/TR/5´11˝/160; d9.12; Col Bloomsburg; OF(145/26/125)																								
1905	Bro N	30	109	19	29	3	4	0	7	9	0	—	.266	.322	.367	114	1	6	.962	2	100	120	2b30	—	0.4
1906	Bro N	97	286	20	57	6	4	1	21	36	0	—	.199	.289	.259	77	-7	10	.953	2	102	151	2b50,O21(15/1/4),1b15	—	-0.7
1907	Bro N	107	342	41	80	12	3	3	31	26	3	—	.234	.294	.313	98	-2	8	.951	9	115	102	2b44,O33(22/3/9),1b12,S8	—	0.6
1908	Bro N	**154**	594	51	143	11	12	4	41	34	2	—	.241	.284	.320	97	-5	20	.973	12	172	284	O95(92/4/2),2b43,S9,1b8	—	0.2
1909	Bro N	146	542	54	152	15	9	4	52	22	2	—	.280	.311	.363	113	4	16	.987	-11	50	77	1b54,2b38,S36,O17(0/6/11)	—	-0.8
1910	Bro N	153	578	67	141	21	13	5	74	57	2	81	.244	.314	.351	97	-4	21	**.965**	-18	94	96	2b153	—	-2.3
1911	Bro N	137	477	54	129	21	11	5	58	67	0	66	.270	.360	.392	115	10	16	**.972**	-4	96	105	2b127,1b4,S2	—	0.8
1912	Bro N	122	411	55	116	21	7	5	54	49	0	55	.282	.359	.404	113	8	7	.969	-5	98	73	2b58,O44R,1b11	—	0.2
1913	Bro N	67	198	20	48	7	7	2	24	13	1	23	.242	.292	.379	88	-4	4-1	.938	1	97	195	O28(3/0/25),S17,1b6,2b3	—	-0.3
1914	Bro N	73	208	25	55	8	9	0	20	16	0	25	.264	.317	.389	107	1	5	.982	-1	91	68	1b36,O19(5/4/11)/2S	—	-0.2
1915	Bro N	53	100	6	23	2	3	0	8	6	0	11	.230	.274	.310	75	-3	1-1	1.000	-2	105	0	O21(2/1/18),1b11/S	—	-0.7
1918	NY A	22	61	9	18	1	2	0	4	11	1	8	.295	.411	.377	135	3	5	.960	-3	91	0	O15(6/7/1),1b3/2	—	0.0
Total	12	1161	3906	421	991	128	84	29	394	346	11	269	.254	.316	.352	103	2	119-2	.963	-17	99	98	2b548,O293L,1b160,S74	—	-2.8
Hummel, Tim	Timothy Robert; B11.18.1978 Goshen NY; BR/TR/6´2˝/(190–205); [ChiA00 2/52]; d8.26; Col Old Dominion																								
2003	Cin N	26	84	9	19	5	0	2	10	8-0	0	13	.226	.290	.357	72	-4	0-0	.894	-3	90	0	3b20,S2/2	0	-0.7
2004	Cin N	56	110	10	24	4	0	1	7	8-2	2	17	.218	.281	.282	48	-9	1-0	.941	3	113	118	3b32,1b13/2S	0	-0.6
Total	2	82	194	19	43	9	0	3	17	16-2	2	30	.222	.285	.314	58	-13	1-0	.922	-1	103	64	3b52,1b13,S3,2b2	0	-1.3
Humphrey, Al	Albert; B2.28.1886 Ashtabula OH; D5.13.1961 Ashtabula OH; BL/TR/5´11˝/180; d9.1																								
1911	Bro N	8	27	4	5	0	0	0	0	3	0	7	.185	.267	.185	29	-3	0	.923	-1	82	0	O8(0/7/1)	—	-0.5
Humphrey, Terry	Terryal Gene; B8.4.1949 Chickasha OK; BR/TR/6´3˝/(180–190); [MonN69 39/873]; d9.5; Col Los Angeles (CA) City																								
1971	Mon N	9	26	1	5	1	0	0	1	0-0	0	4	.192	.192	.231	19	-3	0-0	.981	1	64	179	C9	0	-0.1
1972	Mon N	69	215	13	40	8	0	1	9	16-4	2	38	.186	.248	.237	38	-17	4-1	.986	-5	123	161	C65	0	-2.1
1973	Mon N	43	90	5	15	2	0	1	9	5-0	0	16	.167	.206	.222	19	-10	0-1	1.000	3	177	150	C35	0	-0.6
1974	Mon N	20	52	3	10	3	0	0	3	4-0	0	9	.192	.246	.250	38	-4	0-0	.990	5	84	299	C17	0	0.1
1975	Det A	18	41	0	10	0	0	0	1	2-0	0	6	.244	.279	.244	47	-3	0-0	1.000	-3	66	86	C18	79	-0.6
1976	Cal A	71	196	17	48	10	0	1	19	13-0	5	30	.245	.306	.311	87	-3	0-1	.980	-2	73	127	C71	0	-0.2
1977	Cal A	123	304	17	69	11	0	2	34	21-0	4	58	.227	.283	.283	58	-18	1-1	.989	2	78	**138**	C123	0	-1.2
1978	Cal A	53	114	11	25	4	1	1	9	6-0	2	12	.219	.264	.298	62	-6	0-1	.978	0	69	89	C52/23	0	-0.5
1979	Cal A	9	17	2	1	0	0	0	0	1-0	0	2	.059	.111	.059	-54	-4	0-0	.983	3	47	126	C9	70	-0.1
Total	9	415	1055	69	223	39	1	6	85	68-4	13	175	.211	.265	.267	51	-68	5-5	.986	4	91	141	C399/32	149	-5.3
Humphreys, Mike	Michael Butler; B4.10.1967 Dallas TX; BR/TR/6´0˝/(185–195); [SDN88 15/370]; d7.29; Col Texas Tech																								
1991	NY A	25	40	9	8	0	0	0	3	9-0	0	7	.200	.347	.200	55	-2	2-0	1.000	-1	90	0	O9(8/0/2),3b6,D7	0	-0.3
1992	NY A	4	10	0	1	0	0	0	0	0-0	0	1	.100	.100	.100	-44	-2	0-0	1.000	1	189	847	O2L/D	0	-0.1
1993	NY A	25	35	6	6	2	1	1	6	4-0	0	11	.171	.250	.371	68	-2	2-1	1.000	-2	69	0	O21(11/5/7),D3	0	-0.4
Total	3	54	85	15	15	2	1	1	9	13-0	0	19	.176	.283	.259	51	-6	4-1	1.000	-2	88	91	O32(21/5/9),D11,3b6	0	-0.8
Humphries, John	John Henry; B11.12.1861 N.Gower ON, Can.; D11.29.1933 Salinas CA; BL/TL/6´0˝/185; d7.7; Col Cornell																								
1883	NY N	29	107	5	12	1	0	0	4	1	—	22	.112	.120	.121	-26	-16	—	.815	-4	—	—	C20,O12(0/1/11)	—	-1.7
1884	Was AA	49	193	23	34	2	0	0	—	9	1	—	.176	.217	.187	37	-12	—	.890	-6	—	—	C35,O12(1/3/8),1b4	—	-1.5
	NY N	20	64	6	6	0	0	0	2	9	—	19	.094	.205	.094	-2	-7	—	.896	7	—	—	C20	—	0.1
Total	2	98	364	34	52	3	0	0	6	19	—	41	.143	.188	.151	9	-35	—	.876	-4	—	—	C75,O24(1/4/19),1b4	—	-3.1
Hundley, Randy	Cecil Randolph; B6.1.1942 Martinsville VA; BR/TR/6´0˝/(160–175); d9.27; C1; s–Todd																								
1964	SF N	2	1	1	0	0	0	0	0	0-0	0	1	.000	.000	.000	-98	0	0-0	ø	-1	0	0	C2	0	-0.1
1965	SF N	6	15	0	1	0	0	0	0	0-0	0	4	.067	.067	.067	-61	-3	0-0	1.000	2	62	140	C6	0	-0.1
1966	Chi N	149	526	50	124	22	3	19	63	35-3	3	113	.236	.285	.397	87	-10	1-3	.986	-11	99	**113**	C149	0	-1.5
1967	Chi N	152	539	68	144	25	3	14	60	44-6	2	75	.267	.322	.403	102	2	2-4	.996	-5	132	76	C152	0	0.4
1968	Chi N	160	553	41	125	18	4	7	65	39-6	4	69	.226	.280	.311	73	-18	1-0	.995	-7	148	105	C160	0	-1.9
1969	Chi N★	151	522	67	133	15	1	18	64	61-7	3	90	.255	.334	.391	91	-5	2-3	.992	17	125	123	C151	0	1.8
1970	Chi N	73	250	13	61	5	0	7	36	16-0	0	52	.244	.288	.348	62	-14	0-1	.990	6	177	99	C73	79	-0.5
1971	Chi N	9	21	1	7	1	0	0	2	0-0	0	2	.333	.333	.381	89	0	0-0	.979	3	109	172	C8	134	0.3
1972	Chi N	114	357	23	78	12	0	5	30	22-10	0	62	.218	.261	.294	53	-22	1-0	**.995**	6	87	87	C113	0	-1.2
1973	Chi N	124	368	35	83	11	1	10	43	30-8	0	51	.226	.283	.342	68	-17	5-6	.993	15	120	105	C122	0	0.3
1974	Min A	32	88	2	17	2	0	0	3	4-0	0	12	.193	.228	.216	27	-8	0-0	.965	1	80	204	C28	0	-0.7
1975	SD N	74	180	7	37	5	1	2	14	19-1	1	29	.206	.284	.278	61	-10	0-0	.970	1	100	100	C51	0	-0.7
1976	Chi N	13	18	3	3	2	0	0	1	1-0	0	4	.167	.200	.278	35	-2	0-0	.923	-0	48	88	C9	143	-0.2
1977	Chi N	2	4	0	0	0	0	0	0	0-0	0	1	.000	.000	.000	-90	-1	0-0	1.000	0	102	0	C2	0	-0.1
Total	14	1061	3442	311	813	118	13	82	381	271-41	13	565	.236	.292	.350	76	-108	12-17	.990	28	122	105	C1026	356	-4.2
Hundley, Todd	Todd Randolph; B5.27.1969 Martinsville VA; BB/TR (BL 1999p, 2000p)/5´11˝/(170–199); [NYN87 2/39]; d5.18; f–Randy; [DL 2004 LA N 183]																								
1990	NY N	36	67	8	14	6	0	0	2	6-0	0	18	.209	.274	.299	57	-4	0-0	.988	-1	109	49	C36	0	-0.4
1991	NY N	21	60	5	8	0	1	1	7	6-0	1	14	.133	.221	.217	24	-6	0-0	1.000	-5	88	101	C20	0	-1.1
1992	NY N	123	358	32	75	17	0	7	32	19-4	4	76	.209	.256	.316	62	-19	3-0	.996	1	89	86	C121	0	-1.2
1993	NY N	130	417	40	95	17	2	11	53	23-7	2	62	.228	.269	.357	68	-21	1-1	.988	-4	81	89	C123	0	-1.8
1994	NY N	91	291	45	69	10	1	16	42	25-4	3	73	.237	.303	.443	93	-5	2-1	.990	-1	128	88	C82	0	0.0
1995	NY N	90	275	39	77	11	0	15	51	42-5	5	64	.280	.382	.484	132	14	1-0	.987	-4	123	70	C89	40	1.5
1996	NY N★	153	540	85	140	32	1	41	112	79-15	3	146	.259	.356	.550	142	32	1-3	.992	-2	116	72	C150	0	3.8
1997	NY N✳	132	417	78	114	21	2	30	86	83-16	3	116	.273	.394	.549	152	34	2-3	.987	-10	113	62	C122/D	0	3.0
1998	NY N	53	124	8	20	4	0	3	12	16-0	1	55	.161	.261	.266	41	-11	1-1	.898	1	92	124	O34L,C2	117	-1.1
1999	LA N	114	376	49	78	14	0	24	55	44-3	4	113	.207	.295	.436	87	-10	3-0	.979	-9	68	107	C108	0	-1.1
2000	LA N	90	299	49	85	16	0	24	70	45-6	2	69	.284	.375	.579	145	21	0-1	.979	-11	64	106	C84/D	34	1.4
2001	Chi N	79	246	23	46	10	0	12	31	25-0	3	89	.187	.268	.374	66	-14	0-0	.993	-3	69	73	C70	37	-1.2
2002	Chi N	92	266	32	56	8	0	16	35	32-3	3	80	.211	.301	.421	88	-6	0-0	.984	6	71	105	C79/D	23	0.5

YEAR	TM LG	G	AB	R	H	2B	3B	HR	RBI	BB-IB	HP	SO	AVG	OBP	SLG	AOPS	ABR	SB-CS	FA	FR	RNG	THR	GAMES AT POSITION	DL	BFW
2003	LA N	21	33	2	6	1	0	2	11	8-0	0	13	.182	.341	.394	94	0	0-1	.981	-2	72	123	C10	121	-0.2
Total	14	1225	3769	495	883	167	7	202	599	453-63	34	988	.234	.320	.443	102	5	14-11	.988	-44	94	85	C1096,O34L,D3	555	2.1
HUNGLING, BERNIE	Bernard Herman "Bud"; B3.5.1896 Dayton OH; D3.30.1968 Dayton OH; BR/TR/6´2″/180; d4.14																								
1922	Bro N	39	102	9	23	1	2	1	13	6	0	20	.225	.269	.304	48	-8	2-0	.968	-1	*77*	*86*	C36	—	-0.7
1923	Bro N	2	4	0	0	0	0	0	0	0	0	2	.000	.000	.000	-99	-1	0-1	.667	-1	*47*	*0*	/C	—	-0.2
1930	StL A	10	31	4	10	2	0	0	2	5	0	3	.323	.417	.387	102	0	0-1	1.000	-2	*92*	*39*	C10	—	-0.1
Total	3	51	137	13	33	3	2	1	15	11	0	25	.241	.297	.314	57	-9	2-2	.968	-4	*80*	*75*	C47	—	-1.0
HUNNEFIELD, BILL	William Fenton "Wild Bill"; B1.5.1899 Dedham MA; D8.28.1976 Nantucket MA; BB/TR/5´10″/165; d4.17; Col Northeastern																								
1926	Chi A	131	470	81	129	26	4	3	48	37	1	28	.274	.329	.366	84	-12	24-9	.931	-5	97	94	S98,3b17,2b15	—	-0.3
1927	Chi A	112	365	45	104	25	1	2	36	25	1	24	.285	.332	.375	85	-8	15-13	.933	-17	93	97	S79,2b17/3	—	-1.7
1928	Chi A	94	333	42	98	8	3	2	24	26	3	24	.294	.351	.354	87	-6	16-6	.967	-10	94	99	2b82,S3/3	—	-1.2
1929	Chi A	47	127	13	23	5	0	0	9	7	0	3	.181	.224	.220	15	-16	5-2	.969	-2	101	107	2b29,3b4,S2	—	-1.6
1930	Chi A	31	81	11	22	2	0	1	5	4	1	10	.272	.314	.333	67	-4	1-1	.932	-6	74	88	S22/1	—	-0.8
1931	Cle A	21	71	13	17	4	1	0	4	9	0	4	.239	.325	.324	67	-3	3-1	.853	-6	84	73	S21/2	—	-0.7
	Bos N	11	21	2	6	0	0	0	1	0	0	2	.286	.286	.286	56	-1	0	.864	1	118	0	3b5,2b4	—	-0.1
	NY N	64	196	23	53	5	0	1	17	9	0	16	.270	.302	.311	67	-10	3	.951	-2	96	96	2b56,S5	—	-0.9
	Year	75	217	25	59	5	0	1	18	9	0	18	.272	.301	.309	66	-11	3	.951	-2	97	95	2b60,3b5,S5	—	-1.0
Total	6	511	1664	230	452	75	9	9	144	117	6	111	.272	.322	.344	76	-60	67-32	.925	-48	93	92	S230,2b204,3b28/1	—	-7.3
HUNT, RANDY	James Randall; B1.3.1960 Prattville AL; BR/TR/6´0″/185; [StLN81 S1/2]; d6.4; Col Alabama																								
1985	StL N	14	19	1	3	0	0	0	1	0-0	0	5	.158	.158	.158	-12	-3	0-1	1.000	-0	149	0	C13	0	-0.3
1986	Mon N	21	48	4	10	0	0	2	5	5-2	0	16	.208	.283	.333	70	-2	0-0	.960	2	77	84	C21	0	0.0
Total	2	35	67	5	13	0	0	2	6	5-2	0	21	.194	.250	.284	48	-5	0-1	.967	1	96	62	C34	0	-0.3
HUNT, KEN	Kenneth Lawrence; B7.13.1934 Grand Forks ND; D6.8.1997 Gardena CA; BR/TR/6´1″/(204–205); d9.10																								
1959	NY A	6	12	2	4	1	0	0	1	0-0	0	3	.333	.308	.417	108	0	0-0	1.000	1	154	0	O5R	0	0.0
1960	NY A	25	22	4	6	2	0	0	1	4-0	1	4	.273	.407	.364	117	1	0-0	.957	-0	103	0	O24(17/5/2)	0	0.0
1961	LA A	149	479	70	122	29	3	25	84	49-1	4	120	.255	.325	.484	103	1	8-2	.950	-6	96	88	O134(8/108/23)/2	0	-0.9
1962	LA A	13	11	4	2	0	0	1	1	1-0	0	5	.182	.250	.455	88	0	1-0	.867	-1	0	0	1b3	117	-0.1
1963	LA A	59	142	17	26	6	1	5	16	15-2	0	49	.183	.261	.345	72	-6	0-1	.972	-2	93	38	O50(22/2/27)	0	-1.1
	Was A	7	20	1	4	0	0	1	4	2-1	0	6	.200	.273	.350	73	-1	0-0	1.000	-0	112	0	O5(1/3/1)	0	-0.1
	Year	66	162	18	30	6	1	6	20	17-3	0	55	.185	.263	.346	73	-6	0-1	.976	-2	95	34	O55(23/5/28)	0	-1.2
1964	Was A	51	96	9	13	4	0	1	4	14-0	0	35	.135	.243	.208	28	-9	0-1	1.000	-1	101	49	O37(4/33/0)	0	-1.2
Total	6	310	782	107	177	42	4	33	111	85-4	5	222	.226	.303	.417	89	-14	9-4	.964	-10	98	66	O255(52/151/58),1b3/2	117	-3.4
HUNT, JOEL	Oliver Joel "Jodie"; B10.11.1905 Texico NM; D7.24.1978 Teague TX; BR/TR/5´10″/165; d4.27; Col Texas A&M																								
1931	StL N	4	1	2	0	0	0	0	0	0	0	1	.000	.000	.000	-96	0	0	ø	-0	0	0	/rf	—	0.0
1932	StL N	12	21	0	4	1	0	0	3	4	0	3	.190	.320	.238	51	-1	0	1.000	0	124	0	O5R	—	-0.1
Total	2	16	22	2	4	1	0	0	3	4	0	4	.182	.308	.227	45	-1	0	1.000	0	121	0	O6R	—	-0.1
HUNT, DICK	Richard M.; B1847 NY; D11.20.1895 New York NY; 5´9″/145; d5.7																								
1872	Eck NA	11	46	10	15	1	1	0	4	1	—	0	.326	.340	.391	147	3	0-1	.583	-1	257	0	O9(0/1/8),2b2	—	0.2
HUNT, RON	Ronald Kenneth; B2.23.1941 St.Louis MO; BR/TR/6´0″/(170–185); d4.16																								
1963	NY N	143	533	64	145	28	4	10	42	40-0	13	50	.272	.334	.396	109	7	5-4	.967	12	108	93	2b142/3	0	3.3
1964	NY N★	127	475	59	144	19	6	6	42	29-4	11	30	.303	.357	.406	117	11	6-2	.979	2	103	107	2b109,3b12	0	2.3
1965	NY N	57	196	21	47	12	1	1	10	14-2	6	19	.240	.309	.327	82	-4	2-7	.979	-2	101	58	2b46,3b6	85	-0.4
1966	NY N★	132	479	63	138	19	2	3	33	41-2	11	34	.288	.356	.355	101	3	8-10	.970	13	112	98	2b123/S3	0	2.5
1967	LA N	110	388	44	102	17	3	3	33	39-3	10	24	.263	.344	.345	107	5	2-1	.980	-12	92	91	2b90,3b8	0	0.1
1968	SF N	148	529	79	132	19	0	2	28	78-2	**25**	41	.250	.371	.297	103	9	6-6	.972	-11	101	82	2b147	0	1.1
1969	SF N	128	478	72	125	23	3	3	41	51-0	**25**	47	.262	.361	.341	99	3	9-2	.979	-7	106	91	2b125/3	0	0.6
1970	SF N	117	367	70	103	17	1	6	41	44-1	**26**	29	.281	.394	.381	110	9	1-2	.968	-22	82	75	2b85,3b16	0	-0.8
1971	Mon N	152	520	89	145	20	3	5	38	58-1	**50**	41	.279	.402	.358	115	18	5-7	.979	-8	97	78	2b133,3b19	0	1.7
1972	Mon N	129	443	56	112	20	0	0	18	51-4	**26**	29	.253	.363	.298	88	-2	9-2	.982	9	105	84	2b122,3b5	0	1.7
1973	Mon N	113	401	61	124	14	0	0	18	52-3	**24**	19	.309	.418	.344	110	11	10-7	.982	-7	94	79	2b102,3b14	24	1.0
1974	Mon N	115	403	66	108	15	0	0	26	55-0	14	17	.268	.375	.305	87	-3	2-5	.941	-3	103	104	3b75,2b31/S	0	-0.6
	StL N	12	23	1	4	0	0	0	0	3-0	2	2	.174	.321	.174	41	-2	0-0	1.000	-0	100	104	2b5	0	-0.2
	Year	127	426	67	112	15	0	0	26	58-0	**16**	19	.263	.372	.298	85	-5	2-5	.941	-3	103	104	3b75,2b36/S	0	-0.8
Total	12	1483	5235	745	1429	223	23	39	370	555-22	243	382	.273	.368	.347	104	65	65-55	.976	-34	101	87	2b1260,3b158,S2	109	12.3
HUNTER, BRIAN	Brian Lee; B3.5.1971 Portland OR; BR/TR/6´3″/180; [HouN89 2/35]; d6.27																								
1994	Hou N	6	24	2	6	1	0	0	0	1-0	0	6	.250	.280	.292	52	-2	2-1	.938	0	92	300	O6C	0	-0.1
1995	Hou N	78	321	52	97	14	5	2	28	21-0	2	52	.302	.346	.396	102	0	24-7	.955	4	106	204	O74C	18	0.8
1996	Hou N	132	526	74	145	27	2	5	35	17-0	2	92	.276	.297	.363	80	-17	35-9	.960	3	102	184	O127C	28	-0.8
1997	Det A	**162**	658	112	177	29	7	4	45	66-1	1	121	.269	.334	.353	81	-18	**74**-18	.990	-5	97	95	O162C	0	-1.0
1998	Det A	142	595	67	151	29	3	4	36	36-0	2	94	.254	.298	.333	63	-33	42-12	.988	5	105	124	O139C	0	-2.0
1999	Det A	18	55	8	13	2	1	0	0	5-0	1	11	.236	.311	.309	58	-4	0-3	1.000	2	120	100	O18C	0	-0.3
	Sea A	121	484	71	112	11	5	4	34	32-0	1	80	.231	.277	.300	49	-40	44-5	.985	8	111	189	O121(119/19/0)	15	-2.5
	Year	139	539	79	125	13	6	4	34	37-0	2	91	.232	.280	.301	50	-43	**44**-8	.988	10	112	**178**	O139(119/37/0)	0	-2.8
2000	Col N	72	200	36	55	4	1	1	13	21-0	1	31	.275	.347	.320	57	-13	15-3	.981	-0	96	103	O63(27/34/12)	0	-1.1
	Cin N	32	40	11	9	1	0	0	1	6-0	0	9	.225	.319	.250	47	-3	5-0	.971	3	115	558	O25(9/16/0)	0	0.1
	Year	104	240	47	64	5	1	1	14	27-0	1	40	.267	.342	.308	57	-15	20-3	.979	3	100	192	O88(36/50/12)	0	-1.0
2001	Phi N	83	145	22	40	6	0	2	16	16-0	0	25	.276	.344	.359	87	-2	14-3	1.000	3	110	161	O41(22/18/5)/D	18	0.2
2002	Hou N	98	201	32	54	16	3	3	20	16-0	2	39	.269	.329	.423	89	-3	5-0	1.000	2	105	150	O88C	37	0.1
2003	Hou N	56	98	13	23	6	1	0	13	6-0	1	21	.235	.278	.316	54	-7	0-0	.944	-2	80	85	O32(5/14/15)	0	-0.9
Total	10	1000	3347	500	882	146	28	25	241	243-1	13	581	.264	.313	.346	72	-142	260-61	.980	22	103	152	O896(182/715/32)/D	116	-7.5
HUNTER, BRIAN	Brian Ronald; B3.4.1968 Torrance CA; BR/TL/6´0″/(195–225); [AtlN87 8/194]; d5.31; Col Cerritos (CA) JC																								
1991	†Atl N	97	271	32	68	16	1	12	50	17-0	1	48	.251	.296	.450	101	0	0-2	.988	-1	102	97	1b85,O6(5/0/1)	0	-0.7
1992	†Atl N	102	238	34	57	13	2	14	41	21-3	0	50	.239	.292	.487	113	3	1-2	.997	5	118	81	1b92,O6(1/0/5)	0	0.3
1993	Atl N	37	80	4	11	3	1	0	8	2-1	0	15	.138	.153	.200	-5	-12	0-0	.994	0	99	143	1b29,O2R	30	-1.4
1994	Pit N	76	233	28	53	15	1	11	47	15-2	0	55	.227	.270	.442	81	-7	0-0	.991	1	113	115	1b59,O5L	0	-1.1
	Cin N	9	23	6	7	1	0	4	10	2-0	0	1	.304	.346	.870	208	3	0-0	1.000	0	114	0	O5(1/0/4)/1	0	0.3
	Year	85	256	34	60	16	1	15	57	17-2	0	56	.234	.277	.480	92	-4	0-0	.991	1	113	113	1b60,O10(6/0/4)	0	-0.8
1995	Cin N	40	79	9	17	6	0	1	9	11-1	1	21	.215	.312	.329	70	-3	2-1	.983	1	105	160	1b23,O4(3/0/1)	53	-0.4
1996	Sea A	75	198	21	53	10	0	7	28	15-2	4	43	.268	.327	.424	89	-4	0-1	.991	-0	43	85	1b41,O29(29/0/2),D2	0	-0.7
1998	StL N	62	112	11	23	9	1	4	13	7-0	1	23	.205	.258	.411	73	-5	1-1	.938	1	115	152	O25(16/0/11),1b10/D	0	-0.5
1999	†Atl N	114	181	28	45	12	1	6	30	31-1	4	40	.249	.367	.425	101	1	0-1	.991	2	115	100	1b101,O8L	0	-0.1
2000	Atl N	2	2	1	1	0	0	1	1	0-0	0	0	.500	.500	2.000	495	1	0-0	ø	0	—	—	/H	0	0.1
	Phi N	85	138	13	29	5	0	7	22	20-1	0	39	.210	.310	.399	78	-5	0-1	.994	1	106	64	1b40,O9(6/0/3)/D	0	-0.7
	Year	87	140	14	30	5	0	8	23	20-1	0	39	.214	.313	.421	84	-4	0-1	.994	1	106	64	1b40,O9(6/0/3)/D	0	-0.6
Total	9	699	1555	187	364	90	7	67	259	141-11	11	335	.234	.298	.430	89	-28	4-9	.991	10	104	99	1b481,O99(74/0/29),D4	83	-4.9
HUNTER, EDDIE	Edison Franklin; B2.6.1905 Bellevue KY; D3.14.1967 Colerain OH; BR/TR/5´7.5″/150; d8.5																								
1933	Cin N	1	0	0	0	0	0	0	0	0	0	0	ø	ø	ø	ø	0	0	ø	-0	0	0	/3	—	0.0
HUNTER, NEWT	Frederick Creighton; B1.5.1880 Chillicothe OH; D10.26.1963 Columbus OH; BR/TR/6´0″/180; d4.12; C5																								
1911	Pit N	65	209	35	53	10	6	2	24	25	4	43	.254	.345	.388	101	0	9	.989	-2	81	159	1b61	—	-0.3
HUNTER, GEORGE	George Henry; B7.8.1887 Buffalo NY; D1.11.1968 Harrisburg PA; BB/TL/5´8.5″/165; d5.4; twb–Bill; ▲																								
1909	Bro N	44	123	8	28	7	0	0	8	9	1	—	.228	.286	.285	80	-3	1	.871	-2	40	165	O23(4/1/18),P16	—	-0.5
1910	Bro N	1	0	0	0	0	0	0	0	0	0	0	ø	ø	ø	ø	0	0	ø	-0	0	0	/rf	—	0.0
Total	2	45	123	8	28	7	0	0	8	9	1	0	.228	.286	.285	80	-3	1	.871	-2	40	164	O24(4/1/19),P16	—	-0.5

HUNTER, BILLY Gordon William; B6.4.1928 Punxsutawney PA; BR/TR/6´0˝/(180–185); d4.14; M2/C14; Col Indiana (PA)

YEAR	TM LG	G	AB	R	H	2B	3B	HR	RBI	BB-IB	HP	SO	AVG	OBP	SLG	AOPS	ABR	SB-CS	FA	FR	RNG	THR	GAMES AT POSITION	DL	BFW
1953	StL A★	**154**	567	50	124	18	1	1	37	24	2	45	.219	.253	.259	38	-51	3-1	.970	14	108	91	S152	0	-2.4
1954	Bal A	125	411	28	100	9	5	2	27	21	2	38	.243	.281	.304	66	-22	5-4	.948	0	96	96	S124	0	-1.3
1955	NY A	98	255	14	58	7	1	3	20	15-2	0	18	.227	.269	.298	54	-18	9-2	.958	-1	100	123	S98	0	-1.0
1956	NY A	39	75	8	21	3	4	0	11	2-0	0	4	.280	.299	.427	93	-2	0-1	1.000	7	102	164	S32,3b4	32	0.6
1957	KC A	116	319	39	61	10	4	8	29	27-2	3	43	.191	.259	.323	58	-20	1-2	.974	-10	97	93	2b64,S35,3b17	0	-2.5
1958	KC A	22	58	6	9	1	1	2	11	5-0	0	7	.155	.222	.310	44	-5	1-1	.933	-4	105	60	S12,2b8/3	0	-0.8
	Cle A	76	190	21	37	10	2	0	9	17-1	1	37	.195	.263	.268	48	-13	4-1	.948	-3	91	114	S75,3b2	0	-1.2
	Year	98	248	27	46	11	3	2	20	22-1	1	44	.185	.254	.278	47	-18	5-2	.946	-7	93	106	S87,2b8,3b3	0	-2.0
Total	6	630	1875	166	410	58	18	16	144	111-5	8	192	.219	.264	.294	53	-131	23-12	.958	3	101	104	S528,2b72,3b24	32	-8.6

HUNTER, BUDDY Harold James; B8.9.1947 Omaha NE; BR/TR/5´10˝/170; [BosA69 3/61]; d7.1; Col Nebraska

YEAR	TM LG	G	AB	R	H	2B	3B	HR	RBI	BB-IB	HP	SO	AVG	OBP	SLG	AOPS	ABR	SB-CS	FA	FR	RNG	THR	GAMES AT POSITION	DL	BFW
1971	Bos A	8	9	2	2	1	0	0	0	2-0	0	1	.222	.364	.333	92	0	0-0	1.000	-1	97	42	2b6	0	-0.1
1973	Bos A	13	7	3	3	1	0	0	2	3-0	1	1	.429	.636	.571	228	2	0-0	1.000	1	50	604	3b3,2b2/D	0	0.3
1975	Bos A	1	1	0	0	0	0	0	0	0-0	0	0	.000	.000	.000	-92	0	0-0	.750	-0	61	264	/2	0	0.0
Total	3	22	17	5	5	2	0	0	2	5-0	1	2	.294	.478	.412	144	2	0-0	.968	-0	103	122	2b9,3b3/D	0	0.2

HUNTER, HERB Herbert Harrison; B12.25.1895 Boston MA; D7.25.1970 Orlando FL; BL/TR/6´0.5˝/165; d4.29

YEAR	TM LG	G	AB	R	H	2B	3B	HR	RBI	BB-IB	HP	SO	AVG	OBP	SLG	AOPS	ABR	SB-CS	FA	FR	RNG	THR	GAMES AT POSITION	DL	BFW
1916	NY N	21	28	3	7	0	0	1	4	0	0	5	.250	.250	.357	90	-1	0	1.000	-0	71	0	3b6,1b2	—	-0.1
	Chi N	2	4	0	0	0	0	0	0	0	0	0	.000	.000	.000	-90	-1	0	.750	-0	110	0	/3	—	-0.1
	Year	23	32	3	7	0	0	1	4	0	0	5	.219	.219	.313	65	-2	0	.941	-0	79	0	3b7,1b2	—	-0.2
1917	Chi N	3	3	0	0	0	0	0	0	0	0	0	.000	.000	.000	-93	-1	0	1.000	-0	0	0	/23	—	-0.1
1920	Bos A	4	12	2	1	0	0	0	0	1	0	1	.083	.154	.083	-38	-2	0-0	.857	-0	70	234	O4(3/1/0)	—	-0.3
1921	StL N	9	2	3	0	0	0	0	0	1	0	0	.000	.333	.000	-4	0	0-3	1.000	-0	0	632	/1	—	-0.1
Total	4	39	49	8	8	0	0	1	4	2	0	6	.163	.196	.224	24	-5	0-3	.905	-1	86	0	3b8,O4(3/1/0),1b3/2	—	-0.7

HUNTER, LEM Robert Lemuel; B1.16.1863 Warren OH; D11.9.1956 W.Lafayette OH; d9.1

YEAR	TM LG	G	AB	R	H	2B	3B	HR	RBI	BB-IB	HP	SO	AVG	OBP	SLG	AOPS	ABR	SB-CS	FA	FR	RNG	THR	GAMES AT POSITION	DL	BFW
1883	Cle N	1	4	1	1	0	0	0	0	0	—	2	.250	.250	.250	53	0	—	ø	-0	0	0	/rfP	—	0.0

HUNTER, TORII Torii Kedar; B7.18.1975 Pine Bluff AR; BR/TR/6´2˝/(201–220); [MinA93 1/20]; d8.22

YEAR	TM LG	G	AB	R	H	2B	3B	HR	RBI	BB-IB	HP	SO	AVG	OBP	SLG	AOPS	ABR	SB-CS	FA	FR	RNG	THR	GAMES AT POSITION	DL	BFW
1997	Min A	1	0	0	0	0	0	0	0	0-0	0	0	ø	ø	ø	ø	0	0-0	ø	0	—	—	/R	0	0.0
1998	Min A	6	17	0	4	1	0	0	2	2-0	0	6	.235	.316	.294	59	-1	0-1	1.000	-1	59	0	O6C	0	-0.3
1999	Min A	135	384	52	98	17	2	9	35	26-1	6	72	.255	.309	.380	72	-17	10-6	.997	2	104	98	O130(16/107/14)	0	-1.4
2000	Min A	99	336	44	94	14	7	5	44	18-2	2	68	.280	.318	.408	77	-13	4-3	.989	11	113	257	O99(1/98/0)	0	0.0
2001	Min A	148	564	82	147	32	5	27	92	29-0	8	125	.261	.306	.479	97	-4	9-6	.992	19	**121**	164	O147C	15	1.5
2002	†Min A★	148	561	89	162	37	4	29	94	35-3	5	118	.289	.334	.524	120	14	23-8	.992	-2	99	94	O146C/D	0	1.6
2003	†Min A	154	581	83	145	31	4	26	102	50-7	5	106	.250	.312	.451	95	-5	6-7	.991	3	107	73	O151C,D3	0	-0.1
2004	†Min A★	138	520	79	141	37	0	23	81	40-4	7	101	.271	.330	.475	104	3	21-7	.988	-3	98	80	O126C,D10	18	0.3
2005	Min A	98	372	63	100	24	1	14	56	34-3	6	65	.269	.337	.452	106	4	23-7	.987	-2	90	191	O93C,D5	65	0.6
2006	†Min A	147	557	86	155	21	2	31	98	45-2	5	108	.278	.336	.490	111	7	12-6	.989	0	100	118	O143C,D4	15	0.9
Total	10	1074	3892	578	1046	214	25	164	604	279-22	44	769	.269	.323	.463	99	-12	108-51	.991	27	104	127	O1041(17/1017/14),D23	113	3.1

HUNTER, BILL William Ellsworth; B7.8.1887 Buffalo NY; D4.10.1934 Buffalo NY; BL/TL/5´7.5˝/155; d8.6; twb–George

YEAR	TM LG	G	AB	R	H	2B	3B	HR	RBI	BB-IB	HP	SO	AVG	OBP	SLG	AOPS	ABR	SB-CS	FA	FR	RNG	THR	GAMES AT POSITION	DL	BFW
1912	Cle A	21	55	6	9	2	0	0	2	10	1	—	.164	.303	.200	43	-4	0	1.000	-1	100	43	O16C	—	-0.5

HUNTER, BILL William F.; B1855 St.Thomas ON, Can.; BR/5´7.5˝/160; d5.2

YEAR	TM LG	G	AB	R	H	2B	3B	HR	RBI	BB-IB	HP	SO	AVG	OBP	SLG	AOPS	ABR	SB-CS	FA	FR	RNG	THR	GAMES AT POSITION	DL	BFW
1884	Lou AA	2	7	1	1	0	0	0	—	0	0	—	.143	.143	.143	-7	-1	—	.667	-2	—	—	C2	—	-0.2

HUNTZ, STEVE Stephen Michael; B12.3.1945 Cleveland OH; BB/TR/6´1˝/(185–204); d9.19; Col Villanova; [DL 1965 StL N 142]

YEAR	TM LG	G	AB	R	H	2B	3B	HR	RBI	BB-IB	HP	SO	AVG	OBP	SLG	AOPS	ABR	SB-CS	FA	FR	RNG	THR	GAMES AT POSITION	DL	BFW
1967	StL N	3	6	1	1	0	0	0	0	1-0	0	2	.167	.286	.167	33	0	0-0	1.000	-2	40	0	2b2	0	-0.2
1969	StL N	71	139	13	27	4	0	3	13	27-7	0	34	.194	.325	.288	72	-4	0-0	.945	-4	93	113	S52,2b12,3b6	0	-0.4
1970	SD N	106	352	54	77	8	0	11	37	66-1	1	69	.219	.341	.335	86	-5	0-3	.958	6	115	109	S57,3b51	0	0.4
1971	Chi A	35	86	10	18	3	1	2	6	7-0	0	9	.209	.266	.337	69	-4	1-0	1.000	-2	95	83	2b14,S7,3b6	0	-0.4
1975	SD N	22	53	3	8	4	0	0	4	7-2	0	8	.151	.250	.226	35	-5	0-0	.939	2	116	257	3b16,2b2	0	-0.3
Total	5	237	636	81	131	19	1	16	60	108-10	1	122	.206	.320	.314	76	-18	1-3	.955	0	106	111	S116,3b79,2b30	142	-0.9

HUPPERT, DAVE David Blain; B4.17.1957 South Gate CA; BR/TR/6´1˝/190; d9.15; C1

YEAR	TM LG	G	AB	R	H	2B	3B	HR	RBI	BB-IB	HP	SO	AVG	OBP	SLG	AOPS	ABR	SB-CS	FA	FR	RNG	THR	GAMES AT POSITION	DL	BFW
1983	Bal A	2	0	0	0	0	0	0	0	0-0	0	0	ø	ø	ø	ø	0	0-0	1.000	0	0	0	C2	0	0.0
1985	Mil A	15	21	1	1	0	0	0	0	2-0	0	7	.048	.130	.048	-49	-4	0-0	.960	-1	78	74	C15	0	-0.5
Total	2	17	21	1	1	0	0	0	0	2-0	0	7	.048	.130	.048	-49	-4	0-0	.962	-0	74	70	C17	0	-0.5

HURDLE, CLINT Clinton Merrick; B7.30.1957 Big Rapids MI; BL/TR/6´3˝/195; [KCA75 1/9]; d9.18; M5/C6; OF(97/0/238)

YEAR	TM LG	G	AB	R	H	2B	3B	HR	RBI	BB-IB	HP	SO	AVG	OBP	SLG	AOPS	ABR	SB-CS	FA	FR	RNG	THR	GAMES AT POSITION	DL	BFW
1977	KC A	9	26	5	8	0	0	2	7	2-0	0	7	.308	.357	.538	139	1	0-0	1.000	0	121	0	O9R	0	0.1
1978	†KC A	133	417	48	110	25	5	7	56	56-1	1	84	.264	.348	.398	107	6	1-3	.958	-5	93	102	O78(41/0/42),1b52/3D	0	-0.6
1979	KC A	59	171	16	41	10	3	3	30	28-4	1	24	.240	.343	.386	96	0	0-1	.968	-2	96	60	O50(30/0/20)/3D	0	-0.4
1980	†KC A	130	395	50	116	31	2	10	60	34-5	2	61	.294	.349	.458	119	11	0-0	.960	-2	99	91	O126R	0	0.3
1981	†KC A	28	76	12	25	3	1	4	15	13-3	0	10	.329	.427	.553	181	8	0-0	1.000	2	119	57	O28(2/0/26)	75	0.9
1982	Cin N	19	34	2	7	1	0	0	1	2-2	1	6	.206	.270	.235	42	-3	0-1	.950	1	90	258	O17(17/0/1)	0	-0.3
1983	NY N	13	33	3	6	2	0	0	2	2-0	0	10	.182	.229	.242	31	-3	0-0	.800	-1	123	181	3b9/rf	0	-0.4
1985	NY N	43	82	7	16	4	0	3	7	13-3	1	20	.195	.313	.354	88	-1	0-1	1.000	-3	84	105	C17,O10(2/0/8)	0	-0.5
1986	StL N	78	154	18	30	5	1	3	15	26-0	1	38	.195	.311	.299	70	-6	0-0	.994	1	102	139	1b39,O10(5/0/5),C5,3b4	0	-0.7
1987	NY N	3	3	1	1	0	0	0	0	0-0	0	1	.333	.333	.333	81	0	0-0	1.000	-0	0	0	/1	0	0.0
Total	10	515	1391	162	360	81	12	32	193	176-18	7	261	.259	.341	.403	105	13	1-6	.965	-9	98	90	O329R,1b92,C22,3b15,D5	75	-1.6

HURLEY, JERRY Jeremiah; B4.1875 New York NY; D12.27.1919 New York NY; BR/TR; d9.23

YEAR	TM LG	G	AB	R	H	2B	3B	HR	RBI	BB-IB	HP	SO	AVG	OBP	SLG	AOPS	ABR	SB-CS	FA	FR	RNG	THR	GAMES AT POSITION	DL	BFW
1901	Cin N	9	21	1	1	0	0	0	0	1	1	—	.048	.130	.048	-51	-4	1	.938	-0	*120*	*74*	C7	—	-0.4
1907	Bro N	1	2	0	0	0	0	0	0	1	0	—	.000	.333	.000	5	0	0	1.000	-0	*107*	*113*	/C	—	0.0
Total	2	10	23	1	1	0	0	0	0	2	1	—	.043	.154	.043	-44	-4	1	.943	-0	*118*	*79*	C8	—	-0.4

HURLEY, JERRY Jeremiah Joseph; B6.15.1863 Boston MA; D9.17.1950 Boston MA; BR/TR/6´0˝/190; d5.1; Col Boston U.

YEAR	TM LG	G	AB	R	H	2B	3B	HR	RBI	BB-IB	HP	SO	AVG	OBP	SLG	AOPS	ABR	SB-CS	FA	FR	RNG	THR	GAMES AT POSITION	DL	BFW
1889	Bos N	1	4	0	0	0	0	0	0	0	0	0	.000	.000	.000	-94	-1	0	ø	-1	0	0	/rfC	—	-0.1
1890	Pit P	8	22	5	6	1	0	0	2	2	0	5	.273	.333	.318	81	0	0	.906	-0	*102*	*50*	C7/lf	—	0.0
1891	Cin AA	24	66	10	14	3	2	0	6	12	0	13	.212	.333	.318	80	-2	2	.862	-4	*89*	*51*	C24/rf1	—	-0.3
Total	3	33	92	15	20	4	2	0	8	14	0	18	.217	.321	.304	73	-3	2	.870	-4	*92*	*51*	C32,O3(1/0/2)/1	—	-0.4

HURLEY, DICK William H.; B1847 Honesdale PA; BL/5´7˝/160; d4.18

YEAR	TM LG	G	AB	R	H	2B	3B	HR	RBI	BB-IB	HP	SO	AVG	OBP	SLG	AOPS	ABR	SB-CS	FA	FR	RNG	THR	GAMES AT POSITION	DL	BFW
1872	Oly NA	2	7	0	0	0	0	0	0	0	—	1	.000	.000	.000	-99	-2	0-0	.667	-0	0	0	O2R	—	-0.1

HURST, DON Frank O'Donnell; B8.12.1905 Maysville KY; D12.6.1952 Los Angeles CA; BL/TL/6´0˝/215; d5.13; Col Ohio St.

YEAR	TM LG	G	AB	R	H	2B	3B	HR	RBI	BB-IB	HP	SO	AVG	OBP	SLG	AOPS	ABR	SB-CS	FA	FR	RNG	THR	GAMES AT POSITION	DL	BFW
1928	Phi N	107	396	73	113	23	4	19	64	68	1	40	.285	.391	.508	129	18	3	.989	5	119	87	1b104	—	1.5
1929	Phi N	**154**	589	100	179	29	4	31	125	80	3	36	.304	.390	.525	117	15	10	.985	5	117	88	1b154	—	0.9
1930	Phi N	119	391	78	128	19	3	17	78	46	2	22	.327	.401	.522	113	9	6	.984	-2	103	91	1b96,O7C	—	0.1
1931	Phi N	137	489	63	149	37	5	11	91	64	1	28	.305	.386	.468	119	16	8	.986	11	**139**	90	1b135	—	1.4
1932	Phi N	150	579	109	196	41	4	24	**143**	65	7	27	.339	.412	.547	139	34	10	**.993**	-2	92	81	1b150	—	1.8
1933	Phi N	147	550	58	147	27	8	8	76	48	1	32	.267	.327	.389	92	-5	3	.985	8	**128**	106	1b142	—	-1.1
1934	Phi N	40	130	16	34	9	0	2	21	12	0	7	.262	.324	.377	77	-4	1	.994	-1	84	113	1b34	—	-0.8
	Chi N	51	151	13	30	5	0	3	12	8	0	18	.199	.239	.291	42	-13	0	.986	-3	72	131	1b48	—	-2.0
	Year	91	281	29	64	14	0	5	33	20	0	25	.228	.279	.331	60	-16	1	.990	-4	77	123	1b82	—	-2.8
Total	7	905	3275	510	976	190	28	115	610	391	15	210	.298	.375	.478	113	70	41	.987	21	113	93	1b863,O7C	—	1.8

HURST, JIMMY Jimmy O'Neal; B3.1.1972 Tuscaloosa AL; BR/TR/6´6˝/225; [ChiA90 12/321]; d9.10; Col Three Rivers (MO) CC

YEAR	TM LG	G	AB	R	H	2B	3B	HR	RBI	BB-IB	HP	SO	AVG	OBP	SLG	AOPS	ABR	SB-CS	FA	FR	RNG	THR	GAMES AT POSITION	DL	BFW
1997	Det A	13	17	1	3	1	0	1	1	2-0	0	6	.176	.263	.412	73	-1	0-0	1.000	-0	97	0	O12(1/1/10)/D	0	-0.1

YEAR	TM LG	G	AB	R	H	2B	3B	HR	RBI	BB-IB	HP	SO	AVG	OBP	SLG	AOPS	ABR	SB-CS	FA	FR	RNG	THR	GAMES AT POSITION	DL	BFW
HUSKEY, BUTCH Robert Leon; B11.10.1971 Anadarko OK; BR/TR/6´3˝/244; [NYN89 7/190]; d9.8																									
1993	NY N	13	41	2	6	1	0	0	3	1-1	0	13	.146	.159	.171	-10	-6	0-0	.923	1	113	104	3b13	0	-0.6
1995	NY N	28	90	8	17	1	0	3	11	10-0	0	16	.189	.267	.300	52	-7	1-0	.925	3	124	52	3b27/lf	0	-0.3
1996	NY N	118	414	43	115	16	2	15	60	27-3	0	77	.278	.319	.435	102	-1	1-2	.984	-4	85	104	1b75,O40R,3b6	26	-1.2
1997	NY N	142	471	61	135	26	2	24	81	25-5	1	84	.287	.319	.503	118	9	8-5	.968	1	110	97	O92(30/0/72),1b22,3b15,D4	0	0.5
1998	NY N	113	369	43	93	18	0	13	59	26-3	1	66	.252	.300	.407	87	-8	7-6	.978	0	96	131	O103R/D	29	-1.3
1999	Sea A	74	262	44	76	9	0	15	49	27-0	0	45	.290	.353	.496	116	5	3-1	1.000	-1	109	32	O53(30/0/24),1b10/3D	0	0.2
	†Bos A	45	124	18	33	6	0	7	28	7-1	0	20	.266	.305	.484	94	-2	0-0	1.000	-0	61	449	D37,O4(2/0/2),3b2	0	-0.4
	Year	119	386	62	109	15	0	22	77	34-1	0	65	.282	.338	.492	108	3	3-1	1.000	-1	106	60	O57(32/0/26),D44,1b10,3b3	0	-0.2
2000	Min A	64	215	22	48	13	0	5	27	25-1	2	49	.223	.306	.353	63	-12	0-2	.975	2	123	196	D39,O15R,1b9	0	-1.3
	Col N	45	92	18	32	8	0	4	18	16-1	0	14	.348	.432	.565	124	4	1-1	1.000	0	103	88	O23(15/0/8),1b8	0	0.3
Total	7	642	2078	259	555	98	4	86	336	164-15	4	384	.267	.318	.442	97	-18	21-17	.976	3	104	104	O331(78/0/264),1b124,D88,3b64	55	-4.1
HUSON, JEFF Jeffrey Kent; B8.15.1964 Scottsdale AZ; BL/TR/6´3˝/(170–185); d9.2; Col Wyoming; OF(10/3/3); [DL 1994 Tex A 64]																									
1988	Mon N	20	42	7	13	2	0	0	3	4-2	0	3	.310	.370	.357	104	0	2-1	.932	-1	102	76	S15,2b2/3cf	0	0.0
1989	Mon N	32	74	1	12	5	0	0	2	6-3	0	6	.162	.225	.230	30	-7	3-0	.886	1	99	96	S20,2b9/3	0	-0.4
1990	Tex A	145	396	57	95	12	2	0	28	46-0	2	54	.240	.320	.280	70	-15	12-4	.960	6	97	**117**	S119,3b36,2b12	0	-0.1
1991	Tex A	119	268	36	57	8	3	2	26	39-0	0	32	.213	.312	.287	68	-11	8-3	.965	1	103	72	S116,2b2/3	23	-0.3
1992	Tex A	123	318	49	83	14	3	4	24	41-2	1	43	.261	.342	.362	102	2	18-6	.968	-3	99	113	S82,2b47,O2C/D	0	0.6
1993	Tex A	23	45	3	6	1	1	0	2	0-0	0	10	.133	.133	.200	-12	-7	0-0	.909	3	129	143	S12,2b5,3b2,D2	122	-0.4
1995	Bal A	66	161	24	40	4	2	1	19	15-1	1	20	.248	.315	.317	64	-9	5-4	1.000	-0	95	127	3b33,2b21/SD	0	-0.8
1996	Bal A	17	28	5	9	1	0	0	2	1-0	0	3	.321	.333	.357	78	-1	0-0	.973	0	86	133	2b12,3b3/rf	58	0.0
1997	Mil A	84	143	12	29	3	0	0	11	5-0	2	15	.203	.238	.224	22	-17	3-0	.989	-3	91	86	2b32,1b21,O9(8/0/1),3b2,D4	0	-1.8
1998	Sea A	31	49	8	8	1	0	1	4	5-0	0	6	.163	.241	.245	27	-5	1-1	1.000	-4	60	84	2b8,3b8,1b7/SrfD	0	-1.0
1999	Ana A	97	225	21	59	7	1	0	18	16-0	0	27	.262	.307	.302	58	-15	10-1	.993	-3	105	98	2b41,S22,3b9,1b8,O2L,D7	0	-1.3
2000	Chi N	70	130	19	28	7	1	0	11	13-1	0	9	.215	.287	.285	46	-11	2-1	1.000	-3	83	52	3b18,2b17,S17/1	0	-1.2
Total	12	827	1879	242	439	65	13	8	150	191-9	6	228	.234	.304	.295	64	-96	64-21	.956	-7	100	98	S405,2b208,3b114,1b37,D18,O16L	267	-6.7
HUSTA, CARL Carl Lawrence "Sox"; B4.8.1902 Egg Harbor City NJ; D11.6.1951 Kingston NY; BR/TR/5´11˝/176; d9.24																									
1925	Phi A	6	22	2	3	0	0	0	2	2	0	3	.136	.208	.136	-11	-4	0-0	.976	1	100	96	S6	—	-0.2
HUSTON, HARRY Harry Emanuel Kress; B10.14.1883 Bellefontaine OH; D10.13.1969 Blackwell OK; BR/TR/5´9˝/168; d9.3; Col Kansas																									
1906	Phi N	2	4	0	0	0	0	0	0	1	0	—	.000	.200	.000	-37	-1	0	1.000	0	*75*	*81*	C2	—	-0.1
HUSTON, WARREN Warren Llewellyn; B10.31.1913 Newtonville MA; D8.30.1999 Wareham MA; BR/TR/6´0˝/170; d6.24; Col Springfield																									
1937	Phi A	38	54	5	7	3	0	0	3	2	0	9	.130	.161	.185	-13	-10	0-1	.918	4	117	153	2b16,S15,3b2	—	-0.5
1944	Bos N	33	55	7	11	1	0	0	1	8	1	5	.200	.313	.218	49	-3	0	.979	2	121	45	3b20,2b5,S4	0	-0.1
Total	2	71	109	12	18	4	0	0	4	10	1	14	.165	.242	.202	19	-13	0-1	.964	6	124	106	3b22,2b21,S19	0	-0.6
HUTCHESON, JOE Joseph Johnson "Slug","Poodles"; B2.5.1905 Springtown TX; D2.23.1993 Tyler TX; BL/TR/6´2˝/200; d7.8; Col North Texas																									
1933	Bro N	55	184	19	43	4	1	6	21	15	1	13	.234	.295	.364	91	-3	1	.989	2	92	194	O45R	—	-0.3
HUTCHINSON, ED Edwin Forrest; B5.19.1867 Pittsburgh PA; D7.19.1934 Colfax CA; BL/TR/5´11˝/175; d6.17																									
1890	Chi N	4	17	0	1	1	0	0	0	0	0	0	.059	.059	.118	-47	-3	0	1.000	3	227	164	2b4	—	0.0
HUTSON, ROY Roy Lee; B2.27.1902 Luray MO; D5.20.1957 LaMesa CA; BL/TR/5´9˝/165; d9.20																									
1925	Bro N	7	8	1	4	0	0	0	1	1	0	1	.500	.556	.500	177	1	0-0	1.000	0	114	0	O4(3/0/1)	—	0.1
HUTTO, JIM James Neamon; B10.17.1947 Norfolk VA; BR/TR/5´11˝/195; [BosA65 7/135]; d4.17																									
1970	Phi N	57	92	7	17	2	0	3	12	5-0	0	20	.185	.222	.304	42	-8	0-0	1.000	0	102	197	O22(16/0/6),1b12,C5/3	0	-0.9
1975	Bal A	4	5	0	0	0	0	0	0	0-0	0	2	.000	.000	.000	-99	-1	0-0	1.000	-1	34	0	C3	0	-0.2
Total	2	61	97	7	17	2	0	3	12	5-0	0	22	.175	.212	.289	35	-9	0-0	1.000	-1	102	197	O22(16/0/6),1b12,C8/3	0	-1.1
HUTTON, TOM Thomas George; B4.20.1946 Los Angeles CA; BL/TL/5´11˝/(170–180); d9.16																									
1966	LA N	3	2	0	0	0	0	0	0	0-0	0	0	.000	.000	.000	-99	-1	0-0	1.000	-0	0	0	1b3	0	-0.1
1969	LA N	16	48	2	13	0	0	0	4	5-0	0	7	.271	.340	.271	78	-1	0-0	.993	4	217	88	1b16	0	0.2
1972	Phi N	134	381	40	99	16	2	4	38	56-4	0	24	.260	.354	.344	97	1	5-8	.992	4	106	90	1b87,O48(5/4/39)	0	-0.5
1973	Phi N	106	247	31	65	11	0	5	29	32-6	0	31	.263	.346	.368	96	0	3-1	.998	4	122	117	1b71	0	-0.1
1974	Phi N	96	208	32	50	6	3	4	33	30-8	0	13	.240	.331	.356	89	-3	2-2	.996	-2	87	108	1b39,O33L	0	-0.9
1975	Phi N	113	165	24	41	6	0	3	24	27-1	0	10	.248	.352	.339	89	-2	2-5	.994	5	148	132	1b71,O12R	0	-0.2
1976	†Phi N	95	124	15	25	5	1	1	13	27-0	0	11	.202	.342	.282	76	-3	1-2	1.000	3	125	92	1b72/rf	0	-0.3
1977	†Phi N	107	81	12	25	3	0	2	11	12-3	0	10	.309	.394	.420	114	2	1-1	.993	2	183	102	1b73,O9(7/0/2)	0	0.3
1978	Tor A	64	173	19	44	9	0	2	9	19-0	0	11	.254	.328	.341	87	-3	1-2	1.000	-2	91	63	O55(32/0/23),1b9	0	-0.8
	Mon N	39	59	4	12	3	0	0	5	10-2	0	5	.203	.319	.254	62	-3	0-0	1.000	-2	51	89	1b17,O5(3/1/1)	0	-0.5
1979	Mon N	86	83	14	21	2	1	1	13	10-0	0	7	.253	.333	.337	83	-2	0-0	1.000	3	221	64	1b25,O9R	0	0.0
1980	Mon N	62	55	2	12	2	0	0	5	4-0	0	10	.218	.267	.255	47	-4	0-0	1.000	-1	71	182	1b7,O4(1/0/3)/P	0	-0.5
1981	Mon N	31	29	1	3	0	0	0	2	2-0	0	1	.103	.161	.103	-23	-5	0-0	1.000	0	90	90	1b9,O2(1/0/1)	0	-0.5
Total	12	952	1655	196	410	63	7	22	186	234-24	0	140	.248	.339	.334	87	-24	15-21	.995	17	126	103	1b499,O178(82/5/91)/P	0	-3.9
HYATT, HAM Robert Hamilton; B11.1.1884 Buncombe Co. NC; D9.11.1963 Liberty Lake WA; BL/TR/6´1˝/185; d4.15																									
1909	†Pit N	49	67	9	20	3	4	0	7	3	0	—	.299	.329	.463	134	2	1	.933	3	583	592	O6(5/0/1),1b2	—	0.5
1910	Pit N	74	175	19	46	5	6	1	30	8	3	14	.263	.306	.377	94	-3	3	.986	-0	95	99	1b38,O4(0/3/1)	—	-0.4
1912	Pit N	46	97	13	28	3	1	0	22	6	0	8	.289	.330	.340	85	-2	2	.955	-2	83	48	O15(0/1/14),1b3	—	-0.5
1913	Pit N	63	81	8	27	6	2	4	16	3	2	8	.333	.372	.605	184	8	0	1.000	-0	42	46	1b5,O5(1/0/5)	—	0.8
1914	Pit N	74	79	2	17	3	1	1	15	7	2	14	.215	.295	.316	86	-1	1	.980	-2	0	39	1b7/C	—	-0.3
1915	StL N	106	295	23	79	8	9	2	46	28	3	24	.268	.337	.376	116	5	3-3	.991	-4	69	98	1b64,O25(0/1/26)	—	-0.2
1918	NY A	53	131	11	30	8	0	2	10	8	0	8	.229	.273	.336	82	-3	1	1.000	0	94	99	O25(21/2/2),1b5	—	-0.5
Total	7	465	925	85	247	36	23	10	146	63	10	76	.267	.321	.388	108	6	11-3	.989	-5	76	102	1b124,O80(27/7/49)/C	—	-0.6
HYERS, TIM Timothy James; B10.3.1971 Atlanta GA; BL/TL/6´1˝/195; [TorA90 2/71]; d4.4																									
1994	SD N	52	118	13	30	3	0	0	7	9-0	0	15	.254	.307	.280	56	-8	3-0	.986	0	103	82	1b41,O2R	49	-0.9
1995	SD N	6	5	0	0	0	0	0	0	0-0	0	1	.000	.000	.000	-99	-1	0-0	1.000	0	1166	0	/1	0	-0.1
1996	Det A	17	26	1	2	1	0	0	0	4-2	0	5	.077	.200	.115	-17	-5	0-0	1.000	-1	36	145	1b9/lfD	0	-0.5
1999	Fla N	58	81	8	18	4	1	2	12	14-0	0	11	.222	.333	.370	83	-2	0-0	1.000	-1	92	0	O15(12/0/4),1b14/D	0	-0.4
Total	4	133	230	22	50	8	1	2	19	27-2	0	32	.217	.298	.287	54	-16	3-0	.990	-1	91	90	1b65,O18(13/0/6),D3	49	-1.9
HYNES, PAT Patrick J.; B3.12.1884 St.Louis MO; D3.12.1907 St.Louis MO; TL; d9.27; ▲																									
1903	StL N	1	3	0	0	0	0	0	0	0	0	—	.000	.000	.000	-99	0	0	.500	-1	0	0	/P	—	0.0
1904	StL A	66	254	23	60	7	3	0	15	3	1	—	.236	.248	.287	74	-9	3	.901	-9	16	0	O63R,P5	—	-2.2
Total	2	67	257	23	60	7	3	0	15	3	1	—	.233	.245	.284	71	-9	3	.901	-9	16	0	O63R,P6	—	-2.2
HYZDU, ADAM Adam Davis; B12.6.1971 San Jose CA; BR/TR/6´2˝/220; [SFN90 1/15]; d9.8																									
2000	Pit N	12	18	2	7	2	0	1	4	0-0	0	4	.389	.389	.667	159	2	0-0	1.000	-0	92	0	O5(1/0/4)	0	0.1
2001	Pit N	51	72	7	15	1	0	5	9	4-0	1	18	.208	.260	.431	72	-4	0-1	1.000	-0	96	0	O27(8/1/18),1b4	0	-0.5
2002	Pit N	59	155	24	36	6	0	11	34	21-0	1	44	.232	.324	.484	108	1	0-0	1.000	-2	90	82	O50(10/36/13)/1	0	-0.1
2003	Pit N	51	63	16	13	5	0	1	8	10-0	1	21	.206	.320	.333	71	-2	0-0	1.000	0	98	103	O34(3/20/11)	0	-0.2
2004	Bos A	17	10	3	3	2	0	1	2	1-0	0	2	.300	.364	.800	180	1	0-0	1.000	-0	84	0	O14(11/0/4),D2	0	0.1
2005	SD N	17	20	1	3	1	0	0	4	3-0	0	4	.150	.250	.200	24	-2	1-0	1.000	2	126	338	O12(11/3/0)	0	-0.1
	†Bos A	12	16	1	4	1	0	0	0	2-0	0	3	.250	.333	.313	70	-1	0-0	.909	-1	89	0	O12(3/5/5)	0	-0.1
2006	Tex A	2	4	0	1	0	0	0	0	0-0	0	2	.250	.250	.250	30	0	0-0	1.000	0	143	0	/rf	0	0.0
Total	7	221	358	54	82	18	0	19	61	41-0	3	98	.229	.310	.439	92	-5	1-1	.995	-2	95	77	O155(47/65/56),1b5,D2	0	-0.8
IANNETTA, CHRIS Christopher Domenic; B4.8.1983 Providence RI; BR/TR/5´11˝/195; [ColN04 4/110]; d8.27; Col North Carolina																									
2006	Col N	21	77	12	20	4	0	2	10	13-2	1	17	.260	.370	.390	88	-1	0-1	1.000	0	72	63	C21	0	0.0

YEAR	TM LG	G	AB	R	H	2B	3B	HR	RBI	BB-IB	HP	SO	AVG	OBP	SLG	AOPS	ABR	SB-CS	FA	FR	RNG	THR	GAMES AT POSITION	DL	BFW
IBANEZ, RAUL	Raul Javier; B6.2.1972 New York NY; BL/TR/6´2˝/(200–220); [SeaA92 36/1006]; d8.1; Col Miami–Dade Kendall (FL) CC																								
1996	Sea A	4	5	0	0	0	0	0	0	0-0	1	1	.000	.167	.000	-53	-1	0-0	ø	0	—	—	D2	0	-0.1
1997	Sea A	11	26	3	4	0	1	1	4	0-0	0	6	.154	.154	.346	26	-3	0-0	1.000	-1	76	0	O8(2/0/6)/D	0	-0.4
1998	Sea A	37	98	12	25	7	1	2	12	5-0	0	22	.255	.291	.408	79	-3	0-0	1.000	-2	63	155	O17(6/0/12),1b16/D	90	-0.7
1999	Sea A	87	209	23	54	7	0	9	27	17-1	0	32	.258	.313	.421	86	-5	5-1	.988	1	120	42	O57(22/0/39),1b21/CD	16	-0.6
2000	†Sea A	92	140	21	32	8	0	2	15	14-1	1	25	.229	.301	.329	61	-8	2-0	.978	0	111	40	O76(35/0/44),1b3,D4	14	-0.9
2001	KC A	104	279	44	78	11	5	13	54	32-2	0	51	.280	.353	.495	109	3	0-2	.967	-1	87	147	O42(17/2/24),D33,1b10/3	0	-0.2
2002	KC A	137	497	70	146	37	6	24	103	40-5	2	76	.294	.346	.537	116	11	5-3	.989	-3	87	101	O55(42/0/16),1b49,D36	0	0.0
2003	KC A	157	608	95	179	33	5	18	90	49-5	3	81	.294	.345	.454	103	2	8-4	.988	1	95	115	O131(128/0/5),1b22,D12	0	-0.3
2004	Sea A	123	481	67	146	31	1	16	62	36-5	3	72	.304	.353	.472	119	13	1-2	.984	4	107	161	O112(110/0/3),1b10,D2	37	1.1
2005	Sea A	**162**	614	92	172	32	2	20	89	71-6	2	99	.280	.355	.436	118	17	9-4	.982	2	94	195	D101,O58(55/0/3),1b4	0	1.1
2006	Sea A	159	626	103	181	33	5	33	123	65-15	1	115	.289	.353	.516	130	27	2-4	.994	-1	98	96	O157L/D	0	1.8
Total	11	1073	3583	530	1017	199	26	138	579	329-40	13	580	.284	.344	.469	110	53	32-20	.987	1	98	117	O713(574/2/152),D194,1b135/3C	157	0.8
IGUCHI, TADAHITO	Tadahito; B12.4.1974 Tokyo, Japan; BR/TR/5´10˝/(185–200); d4.4; Col Aoyama Gakuin																								
2005	†Chi A	135	511	74	142	25	6	15	71	47-0	6	114	.278	.342	.438	103	2	15-5	.978	-14	96	104	2b133	0	-0.4
2006	Chi A	138	555	97	156	24	0	18	67	59-0	3	110	.281	.352	.422	97	-2	11-5	.988	-17	92	83	2b136/D	0	-1.1
Total	2	273	1066	171	298	49	6	33	138	106-0	9	224	.280	.347	.430	100	0	26-10	.983	-31	94	93	2b269/D	0	-1.5
INCAVIGLIA, PETE	Peter Joseph; B4.2.1964 Pebble Beach CA; BR/TR/6´1˝/(220–235); [MonN85 1/8]; d4.8; Col Oklahoma St.																								
1986	Tex A	153	540	82	135	21	2	30	88	55-2	4	185	.250	.320	.463	108	5	3-2	.921	-11	80	88	O114(1/0/112),D36	0	-1.2
1987	Tex A	139	509	85	138	26	4	27	80	48-1	1	168	.271	.332	.497	116	11	9-3	.945	-6	89	99	O132L,D6	0	0.0
1988	Tex A	116	418	59	104	19	3	22	54	39-3	7	153	.249	.321	.467	115	8	6-4	.989	3	92	229	O93L,D21	0	0.7
1989	Tex A	133	453	48	107	27	4	21	81	32-0	6	136	.236	.293	.453	106	2	5-7	.973	-3	93	108	O125(120/10/0),D5	15	-0.6
1990	Tex A	153	529	59	123	27	0	24	85	45-5	9	146	.233	.302	.420	100	-1	3-4	.974	2	98	138	O145(135/27/1),D2	0	-0.5
1991	Det A	97	337	38	72	12	1	11	38	36-0	1	92	.214	.290	.353	76	-12	1-3	.973	1	101	134	O54(50/0/4),D41	45	-1.4
1992	Hou N	113	349	31	93	22	1	11	44	25-2	3	99	.266	.319	.430	115	6	2-2	.970	6	108	163	O98(57/0/48)	0	0.9
1993	†Phi N	116	368	60	101	16	3	24	89	21-1	6	82	.274	.318	.530	126	11	1-1	.971	-2	100	63	O97(89/0/8)	0	0.5
1994	Phi N	80	244	28	56	10	1	13	32	16-3	1	71	.230	.278	.439	82	-8	1-0	.979	-3	89	60	O63L	0	-1.3
1996	Phi N	99	269	33	63	7	2	16	42	30-2	3	82	.234	.318	.454	100	-1	2-0	.969	-3	86	116	O71(70/0/2)	0	-0.6
	†Bal A	12	33	4	10	2	0	2	8	0-0	1	7	.303	.314	.545	115	1	0-0	1.000	0	85	275	O7L,D4	0	0.1
1997	Bal A	48	138	18	34	4	0	5	12	11-2	3	43	.246	.314	.384	84	-4	0-0	.952	-1	95	0	D26,O18(4/0/14)	6	-0.6
	NY A	5	16	1	4	0	0	0	0	0-0	0	3	.250	.250	.250	31	-2	0-0	ø	0	—	—	D5	0	-0.2
	Year	53	154	19	38	4	0	5	12	11-2	3	46	.247	.308	.370	79	-5	0-0	.952	-1	95	0	D31,O18(4/0/14)	0	-0.8
1998	Det A	7	14	0	1	0	0	0	0	1-0	0	6	.071	.133	.071	-44	-3	0-0	ø	-0	0	0	/lfD	0	-0.3
	†Hou N	13	16	0	2	1	0	0	2	1-0	0	4	.125	.176	.188	-4	-2	0-0	1.000	-0	92	0	O3L	15	-0.3
Total	12	1284	4233	546	1043	194	21	206	655	360-21	45	1277	.246	.310	.448	104	11	33-26	.966	-17	93	120	O1021(825/37/189),D150	81	-4.8
INFANTE, ALEXIS	Fermin Alexis (Carpio); B12.4.1961 Barquisimeto, Lara, Venez.; BR/TR/5´10˝/(175–188); d9.27																								
1987	Tor A	1	0	0	0	0	0	0	0	0-0	0	0	ø	ø	ø	ø	0	0-0	ø	0	—	—	/R	0	0.0
1988	Tor A	19	15	7	3	0	0	0	0	2-0	0	4	.200	.294	.200	41	-1	0-0	.909	-2	66	0	3b9,S2,D7	0	-0.3
1989	Tor A	20	12	1	2	0	0	0	0	0-0	0	1	.167	.167	.167	-6	-2	1-0	1.000	-1	90	100	S9,3b4/2D	0	-0.2
1990	Atl N	20	28	3	1	1	0	0	0	0-0	1	7	.036	.069	.071	-58	-6	0-0	.964	1	98	105	2b10,3b4,S3	0	-0.5
Total	4	60	55	11	6	1	0	0	0	2-0	1	12	.109	.155	.127	-20	-9	1-0	.933	-2	80	0	3b17,S14,2b11,D11	0	-1.0
INFANTE, OMAR	Omar Rafael; B12.26.1981 Puerto La Cruz, Anzoategui, Venezuela; BR/TR/6´0˝/(150–180); d9.7																								
2002	Det A	18	72	4	24	3	0	1	6	3-0	0	10	.333	.360	.417	110	1	0-1	.935	2	118	91	S16,2b2	0	0.3
2003	Det A	69	221	24	49	6	1	0	8	18-0	0	37	.222	.278	.258	45	-18	6-3	.962	16	125	124	S63,3b4,2b2	0	0.3
2004	Det A	142	503	69	133	27	9	16	55	40-3	1	112	.264	.317	.449	101	-1	13-7	.976	3	101	111	2b105,S23,3b10,O5C	0	0.8
2005	Det A	121	406	36	90	28	2	9	43	16-0	2	73	.222	.254	.367	64	-22	8-0	.988	12	98	116	2b69,S50	0	-0.1
2006	†Det A	78	224	35	62	11	4	4	25	14-0	3	45	.277	.325	.415	92	-3	3-2	.977	2	111	130	2b37,D17,S10,3b7,O4C	0	0.0
Total	5	428	1426	168	358	75	16	30	137	91-3	6	277	.251	.297	.389	81	-43	30-13	.981	34	102	118	2b215,S162,3b21,D17,O9C	0	1.3
INGE, BRANDON	Charles Brandon; B5.19.1977 Lynchburg VA; BR/TR/5´11˝/(185–195); [DetA98 2/57]; d4.3; Col Virginia Commonwealth																								
2001	Det A	79	189	13	34	11	0	0	15	9-0	0	41	.180	.215	.238	20	-22	1-4	.989	3	145	140	C79	42	-1.6
2002	Det A	95	321	27	65	15	3	7	24	24-0	4	101	.202	.266	.333	60	-19	1-3	.998	-1	117	72	C94/D	15	-1.5
2003	Det A	104	330	32	67	15	3	8	30	24-0	5	79	.203	.265	.339	61	-20	4-4	.996	4	77	**180**	C104	0	-0.9
2004	Det A	131	408	43	117	15	7	13	64	32-0	4	72	.287	.340	.453	110	5	5-4	.935	7	116	119	3b73,C39,O26(7/19/2)	19	1.3
2005	Det A	160	616	75	161	31	9	16	72	63-1	3	140	.261	.330	.419	100	0	7-6	.957	24	**116**	**149**	3b160,O2(1/1/0)	0	2.3
2006	†Det A	159	542	83	137	29	2	27	83	43-2	7	128	.253	.313	.463	100	-2	7-4	.960	**25**	**117**	108	3b159	0	2.2
Total	6	728	2406	273	581	116	24	71	288	195-3	23	561	.241	.302	.398	85	-58	25-25	.955	61	116	127	3b392,C316,O28(8/20/2)/D	76	1.8
INGERTON, SCOTTY	William John; B4.19.1886 Peninsula OH; D6.15.1956 Cleveland OH; BR/TR/6´1˝/172; d4.12																								
1911	Bos N	136	521	63	130	24	4	5	61	39	2	68	.250	.304	.340	74	-19	6	.942	13	104	58	3b58,O43(43/0/2),1b17,2b11,S4	—	-0.7
INGLETT, JOE	Joseph Steven; B6.29.1978 Sacramento CA; BL/TR/5´10˝/180; [CleA00 8/246]; d6.21; Col Nevada–Reno																								
2006	Cle A	64	201	26	57	8	3	2	21	14-0	1	39	.284	.332	.383	88	-4	5-1	.984	7	106	127	2b53,O9(6/3/0)/S	0	0.6
INGRAHAM, CHARLIE	Charles W.; B4.8.1860 IL; D2.18.1906 Chicago IL; 5´11˝/170; d7.4																								
1883	Bal AA	1	4	0	1	0	0	0	—	0	—	—	.250	.250	.250	60	0	—	.833	-1	—	—	/C	—	-0.1
INGRAM, GAREY	Garey Lamar; B7.25.1970 Columbus GA; BR/TR/5´11˝/(180–185); [LAN89 44/1146]; d5.15; Col Middle Georgia JC; [DL 1996 LA N 1]																								
1994	LA N	26	78	10	22	1	0	3	8	7-3	0	22	.282	.341	.410	100	0	0-0	.982	1	100	104	2b23	0	0.2
1995	LA N	44	55	5	11	2	0	0	3	9-0	0	8	.200	.313	.236	51	-4	3-0	.750	-0	100	0	3b12,2b7,O4L	0	-0.3
1997	LA N	12	9	2	4	0	0	0	1	1-0	0	3	.444	.500	.444	160	1	1-0	1.000	-0	87	0	O7(6/1/0)	0	0.1
Total	3	82	142	17	37	3	0	3	12	17-3	0	33	.261	.340	.345	85	-3	4-0	.985	1	100	109	2b30,3b12,O11(10/1/0)	1	-0.0
INGRAM, MEL	Melvin David; B7.4.1904 Asheville NC; D10.28.1979 Medford OR; BR/TR/5´11.5˝/175; d7.24; Col Gonzaga																								
1929	Pit N	3	0	1	0	0	0	0	0	0	0	0	ø	ø	ø	ø	0	0	ø	0	—	—	/R	—	0.0
INGRAM, RICCARDO	Riccardo Benay; B9.10.1966 Douglas GA; BR/TR/6´0˝/205; [DetA87 4/105]; d6.26; Col Georgia Tech																								
1994	Det A	12	23	3	5	0	0	0	2	1-0	0	2	.217	.240	.217	22	-3	0-1	1.000	0	94	224	O8(7/1/0)/D	0	-0.3
1995	Min A	4	8	0	1	0	0	0	1	2-0	0	1	.125	.300	.125	16	-1	0-0	ø	0	—	—	D3	0	-0.1
Total	2	16	31	3	6	0	0	0	3	3-0	0	3	.194	.257	.194	21	-4	0-1	1.000	0	94	224	O8(7/1/0),D4	0	-0.4
IORG, DANE	Dane Charles; B5.11.1950 Eureka CA; BL/TR/6´0˝/180; [PhiN71 D1/22]; d4.9; b–Garth; Col Brigham Young; OF(223/0/124)																								
1977	Phi N	12	30	3	5	1	0	0	2	1-0	0	3	.167	.194	.200	5	-4	0-0	.986	-0	95	108	1b9	0	-0.5
	StL N	30	32	2	10	1	0	0	4	5-0	0	4	.313	.395	.344	104	1	0-1	.875	-0	107	0	O7(4/0/3)	0	0.0
	Year	42	62	5	15	2	0	0	6	6-0	0	7	.242	.304	.274	57	-4	0-1	.986	-0	95	108	1b9,O7(4/0/3)	0	-0.5
1978	StL N	35	85	6	23	4	1	0	4	4-1	0	10	.271	.300	.341	80	-2	0-0	1.000	2	93	326	O25(8/0/18)	0	-0.1
1979	StL N	79	179	12	52	11	1	1	21	12-1	1	28	.291	.337	.380	94	-1	1-2	.964	-3	81	78	O39(22/0/20),1b10	0	-0.7
1980	StL N	105	251	33	76	23	1	3	36	20-2	0	34	.303	.349	.438	114	6	1-1	.991	-3	96	45	O63(49/0/14),1b5/3	0	0.0
1981	StL N	75	217	23	71	11	2	2	39	7-0	0	9	.327	.344	.424	113	3	2-0	.963	-6	82	0	O57(46/0/14),1b8,3b2	0	-0.5
1982	†StL N	102	238	17	70	14	1	0	34	23-3	0	23	.294	.352	.361	98	0	0-1	.971	-1	99	50	O63(47/0/17),1b10,3b2	0	-0.4
1983	StL N	58	116	6	31	9	1	0	11	10-2	1	11	.267	.321	.362	91	-1	1-0	.974	-1	115	0	O22(10/0/13),1b11	29	-0.3
1984	StL N	15	28	3	4	2	0	0	3	2-1	0	6	.143	.200	.214	17	-3	0-0	1.000	1	47	159	1b6,O5(3/0/2)	0	-0.3
	†KC A	78	235	27	60	16	2	5	30	13-3	0	15	.255	.287	.404	90	-4	0-1	.995	-2	86	109	1b43,O22(18/0/4)/3D	0	-0.9
1985	†KC A	64	130	7	29	9	1	1	21	8-2	0	16	.223	.268	.331	62	-7	0-1	1.000	-2	90	0	O32(13/0/19),1b2/3D	15	-1.0
1986	SD N	90	106	10	24	2	1	2	11	2-0	0	21	.226	.239	.321	55	-7	0-0	1.000	-3	31	84	1b10,3b6,O3L,P2	0	-1.1
Total	10	743	1647	149	455	103	11	14	216	107-15	2	180	.276	.317	.378	91	-19	5-7	.977	-18	95	57	O338L,1b114,3b13,D7,P2	44	-5.8
IORG, GARTH	Garth Ray; B10.12.1954 Arcata CA; BR/TR/5´11˝/(165–175); [NYA73 8/181]; d4.9; C2; b–Dane; OF(13/1/0)																								
1978	Tor A	19	49	3	8	0	0	0	3	3-0	1	4	.163	.218	.163	11	-6	0-0	.966	2	108	124	2b18	0	-0.3
1980	Tor A	80	222	24	55	10	1	2	14	12-0	0	39	.248	.286	.329	65	-11	2-1	.988	11	118	137	2b32,3b20,O14(13/1/0),1b11/SD	0	0.1
1981	Tor A	70	215	17	52	11	0	0	10	7-1	1	31	.242	.269	.293	58	-12	2-3	.963	0	107	92	2b46,3b17,S2/1D	0	-1.0
1982	Tor A	129	417	45	119	20	5	1	36	12-2	4	38	.285	.307	.365	78	-13	3-2	.946	1	103	84	3b100,2b30/D	0	-1.2

YEAR	TM LG	G	AB	R	H	2B	3B	HR	RBI	BB-IB	HP	SO	AVG	OBP	SLG	AOPS	ABR	SB-CS	FA	FR	RNG	THR	GAMES AT POSITION	DL	BFW
1983	Tor A	122	375	40	103	22	5	2	39	13-3	1	45	.275	.298	.376	80	-11	7-0	.976	-6	108	69	3b85,2b39/S	0	-1.4
1984	Tor A	121	247	24	56	10	3	1	25	5-0	1	16	.227	.244	.304	49	-18	1-3	.945	0	97	**127**	3b112,2b7,S2/D	0	-2.0
1985	†Tor A	131	288	33	90	22	1	7	37	21-3	0	26	.313	.358	.469	121	9	3-6	.951	-2	108	114	3b104,2b23	0	0.5
1986	Tor A	137	327	30	85	19	1	3	44	20-0	1	47	.260	.303	.352	76	-11	3-0	.955	-19	99	68	3b90,2b52,S2	0	-2.8
1987	Tor A	122	310	35	65	11	0	4	30	21-0	2	52	.210	.262	.284	44	-25	2-2	.982	-13	90	71	2b91,3b28,D5	0	-3.3
Total	9	931	2450	251	633	125	16	20	238	114-9	11	298	.258	.292	.347	72	-98	23-17	.955	-25	105	101	3b556,2b338,O14L,1b12,D10,S8	0	-11.4

IOTT, HAPPY Frederick Bidds "Happy Jack","Biddo" (b Frederick Hoyot); B7.7.1876 Houlton ME; D2.17.1941 Island Falls ME; BR/TR/5´10˝/175; d9.16

YEAR	TM LG	G	AB	R	H	2B	3B	HR	RBI	BB-IB	HP	SO	AVG	OBP	SLG	AOPS	ABR	SB-CS	FA	FR	RNG	THR	GAMES AT POSITION	DL	BFW
1903	Cle A	3	10	1	2	0	0	0	0	2	0	—	.200	.333	.200	64	0	1	.875	-0	0	0	O3C	—	-0.1

IRELAN, HAL Harold "Grump"; B8.5.1890 Burnetts Creek (now Burnettsville) IN; D7.16.1944 Carmel IN; BB/TR/5´7˝/165; d4.23

YEAR	TM LG	G	AB	R	H	2B	3B	HR	RBI	BB-IB	HP	SO	AVG	OBP	SLG	AOPS	ABR	SB-CS	FA	FR	RNG	THR	GAMES AT POSITION	DL	BFW
1914	Phi N	67	165	16	39	8	0	1	16	21	1	22	.236	.326	.303	82	-3	3	.909	4	112	67	2b44,S3,1b2,3b2	—	0.2

IRELAND, TIM Timothy Neal; B3.14.1953 Oakland CA; BR/TR (BB 1981)/6´0˝/180; [MonN73 25/563]; d9.20; Col Chabot (CA) JC

YEAR	TM LG	G	AB	R	H	2B	3B	HR	RBI	BB-IB	HP	SO	AVG	OBP	SLG	AOPS	ABR	SB-CS	FA	FR	RNG	THR	GAMES AT POSITION	DL	BFW
1981	KC A	4	0	1	0	0	0	0	0	0-0	0	0	ø	ø	ø	-ø	0	0-1	1.000	-0	0	0	1b4	0	-0.1
1982	KC A	7	7	2	1	0	0	0	0	1-0	0	1	.143	.250	.143	11	-1	0-0	1.000	-0	145	119	2b4,O2R/3	24	-0.1
Total	2	11	7	3	1	0	0	0	0	1-0	0	1	.143	.250	.143	11	-1	0-1	1.000	-0	145	119	2b4,1b4,O2R/3	24	-0.2

IRVIN, MONTE Monford; B2.25.1919 Haleburg AL; BR/TR/6´1˝/195; d7.8; HF1973; Negro Lg 1937–48 Mil 1943–45

YEAR	TM LG	G	AB	R	H	2B	3B	HR	RBI	BB-IB	HP	SO	AVG	OBP	SLG	AOPS	ABR	SB-CS	FA	FR	RNG	THR	GAMES AT POSITION	DL	BFW
1949	NY N	36	76	7	17	3	2	0	7	17	0	11	.224	.366	.316	84	-1	0	1.000	1	89	379	O10R,1b5,3b5	0	0.0
1950	NY N	110	374	61	112	19	5	15	66	52	5	41	.299	.392	.497	131	18	3	.979	3	126	136	1b59,O49(20/0/30)/3	0	1.7
1951	†NY N	151	558	94	174	19	11	24	**121**	89	9	44	.312	.415	.514	147	40	12-2	.996	5	94	94	O112(89/0/27),1b39	0	3.7
1952	NY N*	46	126	10	39	2	1	4	21	10	1	11	.310	.365	.437	120	3	0-1	1.000	-1	83	147	O32(30/1/1)	98	0.0
1953	NY N	124	444	72	146	21	5	21	97	55	3	34	.329	.406	.541	142	28	2-0	.973	4	109	107	O113(102/0/13)	0	2.5
1954	†NY N	135	432	62	113	13	3	19	64	70	2	23	.262	.363	.438	108	6	7-4	.976	2	106	86	O128(126/0/2)/13	0	0.0
1955	NY N	51	150	16	38	7	1	1	17	17-0	3	15	.253	.337	.333	80	-4	3-0	.961	2	108	121	O45(44/0/4)	0	-0.4
1956	Chi N	111	339	44	92	13	3	15	50	41-5	0	41	.271	.346	.460	118	8	1-0	.991	10	125	108	O96L	0	1.3
Total	8	764	2499	366	731	97	31	99	443	351-5	23	220	.293	.383	.475	126	98	28-7	.983	27	106	102	O585(507/1/87),1b104,3b7	98	8.8

IRWIN, ARTHUR Arthur Albert "Doc","Sandy"; B2.14.1858 Toronto ON, Can.; D7.16.1921 , At Sea Atlantic Ocean N.Y. To Boston; BL/TR/5´8.5˝/158; d5.1; M8/U1; b–John

YEAR	TM LG	G	AB	R	H	2B	3B	HR	RBI	BB-IB	HP	SO	AVG	OBP	SLG	AOPS	ABR	SB-CS	FA	FR	RNG	THR	GAMES AT POSITION	DL	BFW
1880	Wor N	**85**	352	53	91	19	4	1	35	11	—	27	.259	.281	.344	102	0	—	.895	**29**	**126**	134	S82,3b3/C	—	3.2
1881	Wor N	50	206	27	55	8	2	0	24	7	—	4	.267	.291	.325	88	-3	—	.851	-7	97	65	S50	—	-0.8
1882	Wor N	**84**	333	30	73	12	4	0	30	14	—	34	.219	.251	.279	68	-12	—	.837	17	131	93	3b51,S33	—	0.6
1883	Pro N	**98**	406	67	116	22	7	0	44	12	—	38	.286	.306	.374	103	1	—	.856	-8	98	**127**	S94,2b4	—	-0.4
1884	†Pro N	102	404	73	97	14	3	2	44	28	—	52	.240	.289	.304	89	-4	—	.881	-10	96	109	S102/P	—	-1.0
1885	Pro N	59	218	16	39	2	1	0	14	14	—	29	.179	.228	.197	40	-14	—	.875	2	109	94	S58/32	—	-0.9
1886	Phi N	101	373	51	87	6	6	0	34	35	—	39	.233	.299	.282	77	-10	24	.891	1	102	82	S100/3	—	-0.6
1887	Phi N	100	374	65	95	14	8	2	56	48	3	26	.254	.344	.350	88	-6	19	.892	-14	87	96	S100	—	-1.4
1888	Phi N	125	448	51	98	12	4	0	28	33	3	56	.219	.277	.263	69	-15	19	.900	10	102	95	S122,2b3	—	-0.1
1889	Phi N	18	73	9	16	5	0	0	10	6	0	6	.219	.278	.288	53	-5	6	.845	-3	90	101	S18	—	-0.7
	Was N	85	313	49	73	10	5	0	32	42	1	37	.233	.326	.297	79	-8	9	.895	12	107	108	S85/P2M	—	0.6
	Year	103	386	58	89	15	5	0	42	48	1	43	.231	.317	.295	73	-13	15	.888	8	104	107	S103/P2	—	-0.1
1890	Bos P	96	354	60	92	17	1	0	45	57	1	29	.260	.364	.314	77	-10	16	.878	2	**106**	115	S96	—	-0.4
1891	Bos AA	6	17	1	2	0	0	0	0	2	2	1	.118	.286	.118	16	-2	0	.778	-1	90	330	S6,M	—	-0.2
1894	Phi N	1	0	0	0	0	0	0	0	0	0	0	ø	ø	ø	ø	0	0	ø	-0	0	0	/SM	—	0.0
Total	13	1010	3871	552	934	141	45	5	396	309	10	378	.241	.299	.305	81	-88	93	.881	30	103	106	S947,3b56,2b9,P2/C	—	-2.1

IRWIN, CHARLIE Charles Edwin; B2.15.1869 Clinton IL; D9.21.1925 Chicago IL; BL/TR/5´10˝/160; d9.3

YEAR	TM LG	G	AB	R	H	2B	3B	HR	RBI	BB-IB	HP	SO	AVG	OBP	SLG	AOPS	ABR	SB-CS	FA	FR	RNG	THR	GAMES AT POSITION	DL	BFW
1893	Chi N	21	82	14	25	6	2	0	13	10	2	1	.305	.394	.427	120	3	4	.910	2	94	112	S21	—	0.4
1894	Chi N	130	504	85	149	25	9	8	100	64	10	23	.296	.386	.429	91	-8	35	.819	-4	93	130	3b68,S62	—	-0.6
1895	Chi N	3	10	4	2	0	0	0	0	2	0	1	.200	.333	.200	37	-1	0	.900	-1	84	113	S3	—	-0.1
1896	Cin N	127	476	77	141	16	6	1	67	26	4	17	.296	.338	.361	79	-16	31	**.931**	7	98	**162**	3b127	—	-0.6
1897	Cin N	**134**	505	89	146	26	6	0	74	47	9	—	.289	.360	.364	86	-10	27	.940	-6	90	117	3b134	—	-1.1
1898	Cin N	136	501	77	120	14	5	3	55	31	10	—	.240	.297	.305	68	-22	18	.940	12	105	104	3b136	—	-0.8
1899	Cin N	90	314	42	73	4	8	1	52	26	2	—	.232	.295	.306	64	-17	26	.909	-10	84	47	3b78,S6,2b3/1	—	-2.3
1900	Cin N	87	333	59	91	15	6	1	44	14	6	—	.273	.314	.363	89	-6	9	.931	-8	91	137	3b61,S16,O6(1/0/5),2b3	—	-1.1
1901	Cin N	67	260	25	62	12	2	0	25	14	3	—	.238	.285	.300	75	-8	13	.893	4	105	126	3b67	—	-0.3
	Bro N	65	242	25	52	13	2	0	20	14	4	—	.215	.269	.285	59	-12	4	.956	-4	82	68	3b65	—	-1.4
	Year	132	502	50	114	25	4	0	45	28	7	—	.227	.277	.293	67	-21	17	.921	-0	94	97	3b132	—	-1.7
1902	Bro N	131	458	59	125	14	0	2	43	39	12	—	.273	.346	.317	104	4	13	.927	-9	89	136	3b130/S	—	-0.1
Total	10	991	3685	556	986	145	46	16	493	287	62	42	.268	.331	.345	82	-93	180	.921	-16	94	118	3b866,S109,O6(1/0/5),2b6/1	—	-8.0

IRWIN, JOHN John; B7.21.1861 Toronto ON, Can.; D2.28.1934 Boston MA; BL/TR/5´10˝/168; d5.31; b–Arthur

YEAR	TM LG	G	AB	R	H	2B	3B	HR	RBI	BB-IB	HP	SO	AVG	OBP	SLG	AOPS	ABR	SB-CS	FA	FR	RNG	THR	GAMES AT POSITION	DL	BFW
1882	Wor N	1	4	0	0	0	0	0	0	0	—	2	.000	.000	.000	-98	-1	—	.636	-1	0	171	/1	—	-0.2
1884	Bos U	105	432	81	101	22	6	1	—	15	—	—	.234	.260	.319	76	-26	—	.780	4	103	73	3b105	—	-1.8
1886	Phi AA	3	13	4	3	1	0	0	1	0	0	—	.231	.231	.308	67	-1	0	.714	-1	58	0	S2/3	—	-0.1
1887	Was N	8	31	6	11	2	0	2	3	3	1	6	.355	.429	.613	198	4	6	.875	-2	77	67	S5,3b4	—	0.3
1888	Was N	37	126	14	28	5	2	0	8	5	2	18	.222	.263	.294	83	-2	15	.860	-2	102	58	S27,3b10	—	-0.3
1889	Was N	58	228	42	66	11	4	0	25	25	4	14	.289	.370	.373	114	6	10	.868	1	104	116	3b58	—	0.7
1890	Buf P	77	308	62	72	11	4	0	34	43	4	19	.234	.335	.295	75	-8	18	.883	8	106	105	3b64,1b12/2	—	0.0
1891	Bos AA	19	72	6	16	2	2	0	15	6	0	9	.222	.282	.306	69	-3	6	.882	-0	166	0	O17(9/0/9),3b2/S	—	-0.3
	Lou AA	14	55	7	15	1	1	0	7	5	1	6	.273	.344	.327	93	0	1	.795	-5	77	47	3b14	—	-0.4
	Year	33	127	13	31	3	3	0	22	11	1	15	.244	.309	.315	80	-4	7	.882	-5	166	0	O17(9/0/9),3b16/S	—	-0.7
Total	8	322	1269	222	312	55	19	3	93	102	12	74	.246	.308	.326	87	-31	56	.829	4	101	88	3b258,S35,O17(9/0/9),1b13/2	—	-2.1

IRWIN, TOMMY Thomas Andrew; B12.20.1912 Altoona PA; D4.25.1996 Altoona PA; BR/TR/5´11˝/165; d10.1; Col North Carolina

YEAR	TM LG	G	AB	R	H	2B	3B	HR	RBI	BB-IB	HP	SO	AVG	OBP	SLG	AOPS	ABR	SB-CS	FA	FR	RNG	THR	GAMES AT POSITION	DL	BFW
1938	Cle A	3	9	1	1	0	0	0	0	3	0	1	.111	.333	.111	16	-1	0-0	1.000	0	110	121	S3	—	-0.1

IRWIN, WALT Walter Kingsley; B9.23.1897 Henrietta PA; D8.18.1976 Spring Lake MI; BR/TR/5´10.5˝/170; d4.24

YEAR	TM LG	G	AB	R	H	2B	3B	HR	RBI	BB-IB	HP	SO	AVG	OBP	SLG	AOPS	ABR	SB-CS	FA	FR	RNG	THR	GAMES AT POSITION	DL	BFW
1921	StL N	4	1	1	0	0	0	0	0	0	0	1	.000	.000	.000	-99	0	0-0	ø	0	—	—	/H	—	0.0

IRWIN, ED William Edward; B1882 Philadelphia PA; D2.5.1916 Philadelphia PA; BR/TR; d5.18

YEAR	TM LG	G	AB	R	H	2B	3B	HR	RBI	BB-IB	HP	SO	AVG	OBP	SLG	AOPS	ABR	SB-CS	FA	FR	RNG	THR	GAMES AT POSITION	DL	BFW
1912	Det A	1	3	0	2	0	2	0	0	0	0	—	.667	.667	2.000	675	2	0	.500	-1	72	0	/3	—	0.1

ISALES, ORLANDO Orlando (Pizarro); B12.22.1959 Santurce, PR; BR/TR/5´9˝/175; d9.11

YEAR	TM LG	G	AB	R	H	2B	3B	HR	RBI	BB-IB	HP	SO	AVG	OBP	SLG	AOPS	ABR	SB-CS	FA	FR	RNG	THR	GAMES AT POSITION	DL	BFW
1980	Phi N	3	5	1	2	0	1	0	3	1-0	0	0	.400	.500	.800	241	1	0-0	1.000	-0	105	0	O2R	0	0.1

ISBELL, FRANK William Frank "Bald Eagle"; B8.21.1875 Delevan NY; D7.15.1941 Wichita KS; BL/TR/5´11˝/190; d5.1; OF(15/33/54); ▲

YEAR	TM LG	G	AB	R	H	2B	3B	HR	RBI	BB-IB	HP	SO	AVG	OBP	SLG	AOPS	ABR	SB-CS	FA	FR	RNG	THR	GAMES AT POSITION	DL	BFW
1898	Chi N	45	159	17	37	4	0	0	8	3	1	—	.233	.252	.258	46	-12	3	.956	-4	103	0	O28(4/12/11),P13,3b3,2b3,S2	—	-1.3
1901	Chi A	**137**	556	93	143	15	8	3	70	36	7	—	.257	.311	.329	79	-16	**52**	.980	13	**139**	109	1b137,2b2/PS3	—	-0.5
1902	Chi A	137	515	62	130	14	4	4	59	14	3	—	.252	.276	.318	67	-24	38	.986	10	**125**	**128**	1b133,S4/PC	—	-1.6
1903	Chi A	**138**	546	52	132	25	9	2	59	12	6	—	.242	.266	.332	82	-13	26	.984	4	122	99	1b117,3b19,2b2/Srf	—	-1.1
1904	Chi A	96	314	27	66	10	3	1	34	16	3	—	.210	.255	.271	69	-11	19	.986	-1	137	102	1b57,2b27,O5R,S4	—	-1.4
1905	Chi A	94	341	55	101	21	11	2	45	15	5	—	.296	.335	.440	151	18	15	.964	1	100	198	2b43,O41(2/5/34),1b9,S2	—	1.8
1906	†Chi A	143	549	71	153	18	11	0	57	30	7	—	.279	.324	.352	115	8	37	.949	-18	97	93	2b132,O14(4/7/3)/PC	—	-1.0
1907	Chi A	125	486	60	118	19	7	0	41	22	4	—	.243	.281	.311	92	-6	22	.957	9	106	114	2b119,O5L/PS	—	0.4
1908	Chi A	84	320	31	79	15	3	1	49	19	4	—	.247	.297	.322	103	1	18	.990	0	111	114	1b65,2b18	—	0.0
1909	Chi A	120	433	33	97	17	6	0	33	23	1	—	.224	.265	.291	79	-12	23	.994	2	105	106	1b101,O9C,2b5	—	-1.4
Total	10	1119	4219	501	1056	158	62	13	455	190	41	—	.250	.289	.326	89	-67	253	.986	16	126	111	1b619,2b351,O103R,3b23,P17,S15,C2	—	-6.1

ISHIKAWA, TRAVIS Travis Takashi; B9.24.1983 Seattle WA; BL/TL/6´3˝/200; [SFN02 21/637]; d4.18

YEAR	TM LG	G	AB	R	H	2B	3B	HR	RBI	BB-IB	HP	SO	AVG	OBP	SLG	AOPS	ABR	SB-CS	FA	FR	RNG	THR	GAMES AT POSITION	DL	BFW
2006	SF N	12	24	1	7	3	1	0	4	1-0	0	6	.292	.320	.500	105	0	0-0	1.000	2	203	113	1b10	0	0.1

YEAR	TM LG	G	AB	R	H	2B	3B	HR	RBI	BB-IB	HP	SO	AVG	OBP	SLG	AOPS	ABR	SB-CS	FA	FR	RNG	THR	GAMES AT POSITION	DL	BFW
IVIE, MIKE	Michael Wilson; B8.8.1952 Atlanta GA; BR/TR/6´3˝/(200–215); [SDN70 1/1]; d9.4																								
1971	SD N	6	17	0	8	0	0	0	3	1-1	1	1	.471	.526	.471	197	2	0-0	1.000	-2	33	95	C6	0	0.1
1974	SD N	12	34	1	3	0	0	1	3	2-0	0	8	.088	.139	.176	-13	-5	0-0	.986	-0	85	105	1b11	0	-0.7
1975	SD N	111	377	36	94	16	2	8	46	20-2	4	63	.249	.291	.366	88	-8	4-4	.989	-4	122	117	1b78,3b61/C	15	-1.8
1976	SD N	140	405	51	118	19	5	7	70	30-8	5	41	.291	.345	.415	126	12	6-6	.995	1	105	100	1b135,C2,3b2	0	0.4
1977	SD N	134	489	66	133	29	2	9	66	39-4	2	57	.272	.326	.395	103	1	3-2	.992	-4	99	91	1b105,3b25	0	-0.9
1978	SF N	117	318	34	98	14	3	11	55	27-6	2	45	.308	.363	.475	138	15	3-0	.995	-8	54	77	1b76,O22L	0	0.4
1979	SF N	133	402	58	115	18	3	27	89	47-7	1	80	.286	.359	.547	155	29	5-1	.995	-2	89	77	1b98,O24L,3b4/2	0	2.3
1980	SF N	79	286	21	69	16	1	4	25	19-2	0	40	.241	.288	.346	79	-9	1-2	.993	-5	72	79	1b72	17	-2.0
1981	SF N	7	17	1	5	2	0	0	3	0-0	0	1	.294	.278	.412	102	0	0-0	1.000	1	150	63	1b5	0	0.0
	Hou N	19	42	2	10	3	0	0	6	2-0	0	11	.238	.267	.310	69	-2	0-1	.989	2	172	78	1b10	111	-0.1
	Year	26	59	3	15	5	0	0	9	2-0	0	12	.254	.270	.339	78	-2	0-1	.992	3	165	74	1b15	0	-0.1
1982	Hou N	7	6	0	2	0	0	0	0	1-0	0	0	.333	.429	.333	125	0	0-0	ø	0	—	—	/H	0	0.0
	Det A	80	259	35	60	12	1	14	38	24-3	2	51	.232	.299	.448	102	0	0-0	ø	0	0	0	D79	0	-0.2
1983	Det A	12	42	4	9	4	0	0	7	2-1	0	4	.214	.244	.310	54	-3	0-0	1.000	-0	82	76	1b12	0	-0.4
Total	11	857	2694	309	724	133	17	81	411	214-34	17	402	.269	.324	.421	112	32	22-16	.993	-22	93	89	1b602,3b92,D79,O46L,C9/2	143	-2.9
IZQUIERDO, HANK	Enrique Roberto (Valdes); B3.20.1931 Matanzas, Cuba; BR/TR/5´11˝/175; d8.9																								
1967	Min A	16	26	4	7	2	0	0	2	1-0	0	2	.269	.296	.346	83	-1	0-0	.986	2	125	115	C16	0	0.2
IZTURIS, CESAR	Cesar D.; B2.10.1980 Barquisimeto, Lara, Venez.; BB/TR/5´9˝/(175–190); d6.23; b–Maicer																								
2001	Tor A	46	134	19	36	6	2	2	9	2-0	0	15	.269	.279	.388	72	-6	8-1	.988	1	108	103	2b41,S6	0	-0.2
2002	LA N	135	439	43	102	24	2	1	31	14-1	0	39	.232	.253	.303	49	-34	7-7	.979	-12	91	103	S128/2D	0	-3.9
2003	LA N	158	558	47	140	21	6	1	40	25-8	0	70	.251	.282	.315	57	-37	10-5	.977	18	104	106	S158	0	-0.7
2004	†LA N	159	670	90	193	32	9	4	62	43-2	0	70	.288	.330	.381	84	-17	25-9	.985	-12	92	105	S159	0	-1.4
2005	LA N✻	106	444	48	114	19	2	2	31	25-1	4	51	.257	.302	.322	63	-24	8-8	.977	8	110	94	S106	56	-1.0
2006	LA N	32	119	10	30	7	1	1	12	7-3	2	6	.252	.302	.353	68	-6	1-3	.955	8	133	56	3b28,S2/2	78	0.1
	Chi N	22	73	4	17	2	0	0	6	5-0	0	8	.233	.282	.260	40	-7	0-1	.975	-1	83	69	S21	15	-0.7
	Year	54	192	14	47	9	1	1	18	12-3	2	14	.245	.295	.318	57	-13	1-4	.955	7	133	56	3b28,S23/2	0	-0.6
Total	6	658	2437	261	632	111	22	11	191	121-15	6	259	.259	.295	.336	65	-131	59-34	.979	9	98	102	S580,2b43,3b28/D	149	-7.8
IZTURIS, MAICER	Maicer; B9.12.1980 Barquisimeto, Lara, Venezuela; BB/TR/5´8˝/(150–160); d8.27; b–Cesar																								
2004	Mon N	32	107	10	22	5	2	1	4	10-1	2	20	.206	.286	.318	54	-8	4-0	.937	1	117	110	S23,2b10	0	-0.4
2005	†LA A	77	191	18	47	8	4	1	15	17-2	0	21	.246	.306	.346	76	-7	9-3	.911	-3	105	96	3b45,S29/2cf	53	-0.6
2006	LA A	104	352	64	103	21	3	5	44	38-1	3	35	.293	.365	.412	105	4	14-6	.936	-7	94	76	3b87,S10,2b4,D2	46	-0.2
Total	3	213	650	92	172	34	9	7	63	65-4	5	76	.265	.335	.377	87	-11	27-9	.928	-9	97	82	3b132,S62,2b15,D2/cf	99	-1.2
JABLONSKI, RAY	Raymond Leo "Jabbo"; B12.17.1926 Chicago IL; D11.25.1985 Chicago IL; BR/TR/5´10˝/(175–185); d4.14																								
1953	StL N	**157**	604	64	162	23	5	21	112	34	1	61	.268	.308	.427	89	-12	2-2	.932	-18	93	86	3b157	0	-3.0
1954	StL N★	152	611	80	181	33	3	12	104	49	2	42	.296	.345	.419	99	-1	9-4	.925	-10	**99**	90	3b149/1	0	-1.1
1955	Cin N	74	221	28	53	9	0	9	28	13-1	3	35	.240	.289	.403	77	-8	0-1	.872	-6	84	64	3b28,O28L	0	-1.5
1956	Cin N	130	407	42	104	25	1	15	66	37-6	7	57	.256	.324	.432	96	-1	2-4	.970	-20	80	59	3b127/2	0	-2.3
1957	NY N	107	305	37	88	15	1	9	57	31-2	0	47	.289	.346	.433	110	5	0-2	.941	-0	108	130	3b70,1b6/lf	0	0.4
1958	SF N	82	230	28	53	15	1	12	46	17-2	2	50	.230	.287	.461	97	-2	2-0	.946	-6	90	21	3b57	0	-0.8
1959	StL N	60	87	11	22	4	0	3	14	8-0	0	19	.253	.313	.402	84	-2	1-0	.900	-2	86	98	3b19/S	0	-0.4
	KC A	25	65	4	17	1	0	2	8	3-0	0	11	.262	.294	.369	79	-2	0-0	.947	-2	82	116	3b17	0	-0.4
1960	KC A	21	32	3	7	1	0	0	3	4-0	0	8	.219	.297	.250	52	-2	0-0	.944	1	129	0	3b6	0	-0.2
Total	8	808	2562	297	687	126	11	83	438	196-11	15	330	.268	.320	.423	94	-25	16-13	.936	-64	93	80	3b630,O29L,1b7/S2	0	-9.3
JACKLITSCH, FRED	Frederick Lawrence; B5.24.1876 Brooklyn NY; D7.18.1937 Brooklyn NY; BR/TR/5´9˝/180; d6.6																								
1900	Phi N	5	11	0	2	1	0	0	3	0	0	—	.182	.182	.273	25	-1	0	1.000	-1	*68*	*61*	C3	—	-0.2
1901	Phi N	33	120	14	30	4	3	0	24	12	2	—	.250	.328	.333	90	-1	2	.971	-0	*98*	*107*	C30/3	—	0.2
1902	Phi N	38	114	8	23	4	0	0	8	9	3	—	.202	.278	.237	59	-5	2	.927	-9	*75*	*96*	C29/cf	—	-1.2
1903	Bro N	60	176	31	47	8	3	1	21	33	2	—	.267	.389	.364	118	6	4	.975	-13	*65*	*112*	C53/2cf	—	-0.1
1904	Bro N	26	77	8	18	3	1	0	8	7	3	—	.234	.322	.299	94	0	7	.957	-6	85	129	1b11,2b8,C5	—	-0.6
1905	NY A	1	3	1	0	0	0	0	1	1	0	—	.000	.250	.000	-17	0	0	1.000	-0	*119*	*105*	/C	—	0.0
1907	Phi N	73	202	19	43	7	0	0	17	27	2	—	.213	.312	.248	76	-4	7	.984	13	*123*	*113*	C58,1b6/rf	—	1.6
1908	Phi N	37	86	6	19	3	0	0	7	14	1	—	.221	.337	.256	87	0	3	.976	5	*134*	*104*	C30	—	0.8
1909	Phi N	20	32	6	10	1	1	0	1	10	0	—	.313	.476	.406	173	4	1	.964	-1	*101*	*84*	C11/2	—	0.4
1910	Phi N	25	51	7	10	3	0	0	2	5	0	9	.196	.268	.255	51	-3	0	.989	2	*105*	*119*	C13,1b2/23	—	0.0
1914	Bal F	122	337	40	93	21	4	2	48	52	2	66	.276	.376	.380	103	-1	7	**.988**	4	*110*	*102*	C118	—	1.3
1915	Bal F	49	135	20	32	9	0	2	13	31	2	25	.237	.387	.348	104	1	2	.992	-4	*101*	*83*	C45/S	—	0.0
1917	Bos N	1	0	0	0	0	0	0	0	0	0	0	ø	ø	ø	ø	0	0	1.000	-0	*0*	*0*	/C	—	0.0
Total	13	490	1344	160	327	64	12	5	153	201	17	100	.243	.349	.320	95	-4	35	.978	-11	*103*	*103*	C397,1b19,2b11,O3(0/2/1),3b2/S	—	2.2
JACKSON, CHARLIE	Charles Herbert "Lefty"; B2.7.1894 Granite City IL; D5.27.1968 Radford VA; BL/TL/5´9˝/150; d8.20; Mil 1918																								
1915	Chi A	1	1	0	0	0	0	0	0	0	0	1	.000	.000	.000	-97	0	0	ø	0	—	—	/H	—	0.0
1917	Pit N	41	121	7	29	3	2	0	1	10	1	22	.240	.303	.298	82	-2	4	.986	2	106	122	O36(20/1/15)	—	-0.3
Total	2	42	122	7	29	3	2	0	1	10	1	23	.238	.301	.295	80	-2	4	.986	2	106	122	O36(20/1/15)	—	-0.3
JACKSON, CHUCK	Charles Leo; B3.19.1963 Seattle WA; BR/TR/6´0˝/(185–190); [HouN84 7/175]; d5.26; Col Hawaii–Manoa; [DL 1990 SF N 80]																								
1987	Hou N	35	71	3	15	3	0	1	6	7-0	0	19	.211	.282	.296	55	-5	1-1	.957	3	137	177	3b16,O13(1/12/0)/S	0	-0.2
1988	Hou N	46	83	7	19	5	1	1	8	7-4	0	16	.229	.286	.349	86	-2	1-1	.908	1	107	170	3b32,S3,O3(0/1/2)	0	-0.1
1994	Tex A	1	2	0	0	0	0	0	0	0-0	0	0	.000	.000	.000	-99	-1	0-0	ø	-0	0	0	/3	0	-0.1
Total	3	82	156	10	34	8	1	2	14	14-4	0	35	.218	.281	.321	69	-8	2-2	.928	3	117	171	3b49,O16(1/13/2),S4	80	-0.4
JACKSON, CONOR	Conor Sims; B5.7.1982 Austin TX; BR/TR/6´3˝/225; [AriN03 1/19]; d7.28; Col California																								
2005	Ari N	40	85	8	17	3	0	2	8	12-0	1	11	.200	.303	.306	58	-5	0-0	.973	-1	103	116	1b20/lf	0	-0.8
2006	Ari N	140	485	75	141	26	1	15	79	54-2	9	73	.291	.368	.441	101	3	1-0	.990	-2	97	108	1b129/D	0	-1.0
Total	2	180	570	83	158	29	1	17	87	66-2	10	84	.277	.358	.421	95	-2	1-0	.988	-3	98	109	1b149/Dlf	0	-1.8
JACKSON, DAMIAN	Damian Jacques; B8.16.1973 Los Angeles CA; BR/TR/5´11˝/(160–185); [CleA91 44/1148]; d9.12; Col Laney (CA) JC; OF(75/59/20)																								
1996	Cle A	5	10	2	3	2	0	0	1	1-0	0	4	.300	.364	.500	116	0	0-0	1.000	3	191	266	S5	0	0.3
1997	Cle A	8	9	2	1	0	0	0	0	0-0	1	1	.111	.200	.111	-15	-2	1-0	1.000	-0	91	111	S5/2	0	-0.1
	Cin N	12	27	6	6	2	1	1	2	4-1	0	7	.222	.323	.481	105	0	1-1	1.000	0	93	68	S6,2b3	0	0.1
1998	Cin N	13	38	4	12	5	0	0	7	6-0	0	4	.316	.400	.447	124	2	2-0	.972	-1	87	60	S10,O3(0/3/1)	0	0.2
1999	SD N	133	388	56	87	20	2	9	39	53-3	3	105	.224	.320	.356	77	-14	34-10	.940	7	105	110	S100,2b21,O3(2/0/1)	0	0.4
2000	SD N	138	470	68	120	27	6	6	37	62-2	3	108	.255	.345	.377	88	-8	28-6	.955	13	115	100	S88,2b36,O17L	0	1.6
2001	SD N	122	440	67	106	21	6	4	38	44-2	6	128	.241	.316	.343	77	-16	23-6	.986	0	99	98	2b118,S3,O2C	40	-0.7
2002	Det A	81	245	31	63	20	1	1	25	21-0	3	36	.257	.320	.359	84	-5	12-3	.981	-7	96	99	2b56,S6,O6(3/3/0),3b2,D5	15	-0.7
2003	†Bos A	109	161	34	42	7	0	1	13	8-0	0	28	.261	.294	.323	61	-9	16-8	.960	-1	106	54	2b38,O38(13/13/12),S18,3b3,1b2,D9	0	-0.8
2004	Chi N	7	15	1	1	0	0	1	1	3-2	0	6	.067	.222	.267	25	-2	0-0	.957	2	129	222	2b5	0	0.1
	KC A	14	15	1	2	2	0	0	2	1-0	0	6	.133	.188	.267	16	-2	0-0	1.000	-1	88	0	O5(1/1/3)/2SD	0	-0.2
2005	†SD N	118	275	44	70	9	0	5	23	30-1	4	45	.255	.335	.342	82	-7	15-2	1.000	-2	112	181	O52(37/15/1),2b35,S26,3b8	0	-0.4
2006	Was N	67	116	16	23	6	1	4	10	12-0	4	39	.198	.295	.371	73	-5	1-3	.957	-7	103	0	O26(2/22/2),S16,2b11,3b6	16	-1.2
Total	11	827	2209	332	536	121	17	32	198	245-11	24	517	.243	.323	.356	79	-68	133-39	.982	7	100	100	2b325,S284,O152L,3b19,D16,1b2	71	-1.4
JACKSON, DARRIN	Darrin Jay; B8.22.1962 Los Angeles CA; BR/TR/6´0˝/(170–198); [ChiN81 2/28]; d6.17																								
1985	Chi N	5	11	0	1	0	0	0	0	0-0	0	3	.091	.091	.091	-45	-2	0-0	1.000	-1	82	0	O4C	0	-0.3
1987	Chi N	7	5	2	4	1	0	0	0	0-0	0	0	.800	.800	1.000	359	2	0-0	1.000	-0	46	0	O5(2/3/0)	0	0.2
1988	Chi N	100	188	29	50	11	3	6	20	5-1	1	28	.266	.287	.452	105	0	4-1	.983	0	104	45	O74(11/46/20)	0	0.0
1989	Chi N	45	83	7	19	4	0	1	8	6-1	0	17	.229	.281	.313	65	-4	1-2	.970	4	124	231	O39(10/9/20)	0	-0.1
	SD N	25	87	10	18	3	0	3	12	7-4	0	17	.207	.260	.345	73	-3	0-2	.954	-0	95	154	O24C	0	-0.5
	Year	70	170	17	37	7	0	4	20	13-5	0	34	.218	.270	.329	68	-7	1-4	.962	3	109	191	O63(10/33/20)	0	-0.6
1990	SD N	58	113	10	29	3	0	3	9	5-1	0	24	.257	.286	.363	77	-4	3-0	.985	-1	99	68	O39(4/30/5)	0	-0.4

YEAR	TM LG	G	AB	R	H	2B	3B	HR	RBI	BB-IB	HP	SO	AVG	OBP	SLG	AOPS	ABR	SB-CS	FA	FR	RNG	THR	GAMES AT POSITION	DL	BFW
1991	SD N	122	359	51	94	12	1	21	49	27-2	2	66	.262	.315	.476	116	6	5-3	.992	2	113	39	O98(21/79/0)/P	0	0.7
1992	SD N	155	587	72	146	23	5	17	70	26-4	4	106	.249	.283	.392	88	-12	14-3	.996	14	108	205	O153(5/152/2)	0	0.4
1993	Tor A	46	176	15	38	8	0	5	19	8-0	0	53	.216	.250	.347	57	-11	0-2	.989	-4	88	63	O46(0/10/37)	0	-1.7
	NY N	31	87	4	17	1	0	1	7	2-0	0	22	.195	.211	.241	22	-10	0-0	1.000	2	98	301	O26(10/16/0)	44	-0.8
1994	Chi A	104	369	43	115	17	3	10	51	27-3	3	56	.312	.362	.455	111	5	7-1	.996	3	117	31	O102(0/16/92)	0	0.5
1997	Min A	49	130	19	33	2	1	3	21	4-0	0	21	.254	.272	.354	62	-8	2-0	.990	2	101	216	O44C	0	-0.5
	Mil A	26	81	7	22	7	0	2	15	2-0	0	10	.272	.289	.432	84	-2	2-1	1.000	3	117	155	O26(21/9/3)	0	0.0
	Year	75	211	26	55	9	1	5	36	6-0	0	31	.261	.279	.384	70	-10	4-1	.994	4	107	193	O70(21/53/3)	0	-0.5
1998	Mil N	114	204	20	49	13	1	4	20	9-0	1	37	.240	.276	.373	67	-10	1-1	.982	-1	95	89	O94(55/43/5),D2	7	-1.2
1999	Chi A	73	149	22	41	9	1	4	16	3-0	0	20	.275	.288	.430	79	-5	4-1	.972	3	118	82	O64(46/25/3),D3	17	-0.3
Total	12	960	2629	311	676	114	15	80	317	131-16	11	480	.257	.293	.403	87	-58	43-17	.989	27	107	117	O838(185/510/187),D5/P	68	-4.0
JACKSON, GEORGE	George Christopher "Hickory"; B1.2.1882 Springfield MO; D11.25.1972 Cleburne TX; BR/TR/6´0.5˝/180; d8.2																								
1911	Bos N	39	147	28	51	11	2	0	25	12	2	21	.347	.404	.449	128	6	12	.929	-2	98	75	O39(38/1/0)	—	0.3
1912	Bos N	110	397	55	104	13	5	4	48	38	10	72	.262	.342	.350	88	-6	22	.943	1	96	119	O107(96/11/0)	—	-1.0
1913	Bos N	3	10	2	3	0	0	0	0	0	0	2	.300	.300	.300	70	0	0	.875	0	90	254	O3C	—	0.0
Total	3	152	554	85	158	24	7	4	73	50	12	95	.285	.357	.375	98	0	34	.938	-1	96	111	O149(134/15/0)	—	-0.7
JACKSON, HENRY	Henry Everett; B6.23.1861 Union City IN; D9.14.1932 Chicago IL; BR/TR/6´2˝/185; d9.13																								
1887	Ind N	10	38	1	10	1	0	0	3	0	0	12	.263	.263	.289	55	-2	2	.933	-1	82	112	1b10	—	-0.4
JACKSON, JIM	James Benner; B11.28.1877 Philadelphia PA; D10.9.1955 Philadelphia PA; BR/TR/5´6.5˝/165; d4.26; Col Penn																								
1901	Bal A	99	364	42	91	17	3	2	50	20	1	—	.250	.291	.330	69	-16	11	**.971**	2	32	34	O96(35/59/2)	—	-1.7
1902	NY N	37	116	14	21	5	1	0	15	16	0	—	.181	.280	.241	62	-5	6	.899	-2	88	0	O36(32/2/2)	—	-0.9
1905	Cle A	109	426	60	109	12	4	2	31	34	4	—	.256	.317	.317	100	0	15	.951	4	135	115	O106(104/0/2),3b3	—	-0.2
1906	Cle A	105	374	44	80	13	2	0	38	38	2	—	.214	.290	.259	73	-10	25	.975	-7	37	75	O104(103/1/0)	—	-2.6
Total	4	350	1280	160	301	47	10	4	134	108	7	—	.235	.298	.297	79	-31	57	.959	-2	71	69	O342(274/62/6),3b3	—	-5.4
JACKSON, JOE	Joseph Jefferson "Shoeless Joe"; B7.16.1889 Pickens Co. SC; D12.5.1951 Greenville SC; BL/TR/6´1˝/200; d8.25; Def 1918																								
1908	Phi A	5	23	0	3	0	0	0	3	0	0	—	.130	.130	.130	-14	-3	0	.875	-0	221	0	O5C	—	-0.4
1909	Phi A	5	17	3	3	0	0	0	3	1	0	—	.176	.222	.176	26	-1	0	.833	-1	0	0	O4(3/1/0)	—	-0.3
1910	Cle A	20	75	15	29	2	5	1	11	8	0	—	.387	.446	.587	220	10	4	.977	-0	103	67	O20(0/15/5)	—	0.9
1911	Cle A	147	571	126	233	45	19	7	83	56	8	—	.408	**.468**	.590	192	71	41	.958	5	98	129	O147(0/47/100)	—	6.5
1912	Cle A	154	572	121	**226**	44	**26**	3	90	54	12	—	.395	.458	.579	190	67	35	.950	14	**118**	143	O150(0/19/131)	—	7.1
1913	Cle A	148	528	109	**197**	**39**	17	7	71	80	5	26	.373	.460	**.551**	190	**63**	26	.930	1	95	126	O148R	—	5.9
1914	Cle A	122	453	61	153	22	13	3	53	41	5	34	.338	.399	.464	153	29	22-15	.967	2	107	91	O119(0/31/88)	—	2.6
1915	Cle A	83	303	42	99	16	9	3	45	28	3	11	.327	.389	.469	154	19	10-10	.961	-2	100	113	O50(5/0/44),1b30	—	1.4
	Chi A	45	158	21	43	4	5	2	36	24	3	12	.272	.378	.399	129	6	6-10	.947	-2	89	101	O45(19/26/0)	—	-0.1
	Year	128	461	63	142	20	14	5	81	52	6	23	.308	.385	.445	145	25	16-20	.953	-4	94	107	O95(24/26/44),1b30	—	1.3
1916	Chi A	**155**	592	91	202	40	**21**	3	78	46	5	25	.341	.393	.495	165	44	24-14	.975	-4	94	84	O155(131/1/23)	—	3.6
1917	†Chi A	146	538	91	162	20	17	5	75	57	7	25	.301	.375	.429	142	27	13	.984	6	111	84	O145(134/0/11)	—	2.8
1918	Chi A	17	65	9	23	2	2	1	20	8	0	1	.354	.425	.492	175	6	3	1.000	-0	109	45	O17(14/0/3)	—	0.5
1919	†Chi A	139	516	79	181	31	14	7	96	60	4	10	.351	.422	.506	159	42	9	.967	-3	92	105	O139(133/0/6)	—	3.3
1920	Chi A	146	570	105	218	42	**20**	12	121	56	7	14	.382	.444	.589	172	59	9-12	.965	-3	101	71	O145L	—	4.5
Total	13	1332	4981	873	1772	307	168	54	785	519	59	158	.356	.423	.517	169	439	202-61	.962	13	101	102	O1289(584/145/559),1b30	—	38.3
JACKSON, KEN	Kenneth Bernard; B8.21.1963 Shreveport LA; BR/TR/5´9˝/170; [PhiN82 S1/17]; d9.12; Col Angelina (TX) JC																								
1987	Phi N	8	16	1	4	2	0	0	2	1-1	1	4	.250	.333	.375	84	0	0-0	.955	-1	94	33	S8	0	-0.1
JACKSON, LOU	Louis Clarence; B7.26.1935 Riverton LA; D5.27.1969 Tokyo, Japan; BL/TR/5´10˝/(168–170); d7.23; Col Grambling St.																								
1958	Chi N	24	35	5	6	2	1	1	6	1-0	0	9	.171	.194	.371	46	-3	0-1	1.000	-1	67	0	O12(4/4/6)	0	-0.5
1959	Chi N	6	4	2	1	0	0	0	1	0-0	0	2	.250	.250	.250	34	0	0-0	ø	0	—	—	/H	0	0.0
1964	Bal A	4	8	0	3	0	0	0	0	0-0	0	2	.375	.375	.375	110	0	0-0	1.000	0	223	0	/lf	0	0.0
Total	3	34	47	7	10	2	1	1	7	1-0	0	13	.213	.229	.362	55	-3	0-1	1.000	-1	88	0	O13(5/4/6)	0	-0.5
JACKSON, RANDY	Ransom Joseph "Handsome Ransom"; B2.10.1926 Little Rock AR; BR/TR/6´1.5˝/(180–185); d5.2; Col Texas																								
1950	Chi N	34	111	13	25	4	3	3	6	7	0	25	.225	.271	.396	74	-5	4	.911	-4	95	48	3b27	0	-0.9
1951	Chi N	145	557	78	153	24	6	16	76	47	1	44	.275	.332	.425	101	-1	14-3	.956	7	103	86	3b143	0	0.8
1952	Chi N	116	379	44	88	8	5	9	34	27	1	42	.232	.285	.351	75	-15	6-5	.958	-2	104	79	3b104/lf	0	-1.8
1953	Chi N	139	498	61	142	22	8	19	66	42	0	61	.285	.341	.476	108	4	8-4	.949	4	104	79	3b133	0	0.7
1954	Chi N★	126	484	77	132	17	6	19	67	44	2	55	.273	.333	.450	102	0	2-1	.955	-4	**99**	85	3b124	0	-0.5
1955	Chi N★	138	499	73	132	13	7	21	70	58-6	1	58	.265	.340	.445	107	4	0-2	.949	-12	92	102	3b134	0	-0.8
1956	†Bro N	101	307	37	84	15	7	8	53	28-3	2	38	.274	.333	.446	101	0	2-1	.993	22	129	164	3b80	0	2.2
1957	Bro N	48	131	7	26	1	0	2	16	9-0	0	20	.198	.246	.252	32	-13	0-0	.976	-2	88	135	3b34	68	-1.5
1958	LA N	35	65	8	12	3	0	1	4	5-1	0	10	.185	.243	.277	36	-6	0-0	.964	5	135	205	3b17	0	-0.1
	Cle A	29	91	7	22	3	1	4	13	3-0	0	18	.242	.266	.429	90	-2	0-0	.901	3	118	81	3b24	0	0.1
1959	Cle A	3	7	0	1	0	0	0	0	0-0	0	1	.143	.143	.143	-22	-1	0-0	1.000	-1	69	0	3b2	0	-0.2
	Chi N	41	74	7	18	5	1	1	10	11-1	0	10	.243	.341	.378	92	0	0-0	.941	-4	77	68	3b22/lf	0	-0.4
Total	10	955	3203	412	835	115	44	103	415	281-11	7	382	.261	.320	.421	94	-35	36-16	.955	13	103	95	3b844,O2L	68	-2.4
JACKSON, REGGIE	Reginald Martinez; B5.18.1946 Wyncote PA; BL/TL/6´0˝/(195–208); [OakA66 1/2]; d6.9; HF1993; Col Arizona St.																								
1967	KC A	35	118	13	21	4	4	1	6	10-0	5	46	.178	.269	.305	72	-4	1-1	.933	-3	89	44	O34(19/3/14)	0	-1.0
1968	Oak A	154	553	82	138	13	6	29	74	50-5	5	171	.250	.316	.452	137	22	14-4	.959	6	108	169	O151(1/9/147)	0	2.2
1969	Oak A★	152	549	**123**	151	36	3	47	118	114-**20**	12	142	.275	.410	**.608**	**189**	**70**	13-5	.964	-2	99	116	O150(0/10/144)	0	6.3
1970	Oak A	149	426	57	101	21	2	23	66	75-11	8	135	.237	.359	.458	128	18	26-17	.956	-3	100	97	O142(0/49/113)	0	1.0
1971	†Oak A★	150	567	87	157	29	3	32	80	63-5	6	161	.277	.352	.508	145	32	16-10	.977	6	103	156	O145(0/3/145)	0	3.3
1972	†Oak A★	135	499	72	132	25	2	25	75	59-7	8	125	.265	.350	.473	151	31	9-8	.971	-8	95	53	O135(0/92/43)	15	2.0
1973	†Oak A★	151	539	**99**	158	28	2	**32**	**117**	76-11	7	111	.293	.383	**.531**	**164**	**47**	22-8	.971	-1	106	42	O145(0/1/144),D3	0	4.1
1974	†Oak A★	148	506	90	146	25	1	29	93	86-**20**	4	105	.289	.391	.514	**170**	49	25-5	.968	6	115	83	O127(0/3/126),D19	0	5.3
1975	†Oak A★	157	593	91	150	39	3	**36**	104	67-5	3	133	.253	.329	.511	138	28	17-8	.965	5	109	107	O147R,D9	0	2.7
1976	Bal A	134	498	84	138	27	2	27	91	54-7	4	108	.277	.351	**.502**	**157**	35	28-7	.964	1	104	87	O121(0/16/111),D11	0	3.5
1977	†NY A★	146	525	93	150	39	2	32	110	74-4	3	129	.286	.375	.550	150	38	17-3	.949	-4	97	80	O127R,D18	0	3.0
1978	†NY A✳	139	511	82	140	13	5	27	97	58-2	9	133	.274	.356	.477	135	23	14-11	.986	-3	97	77	O104R,D35	0	1.4
1979	NY A★	131	465	78	138	24	2	29	89	65-3	2	107	.297	.382	.544	150	33	9-8	.986	1	104	74	O125R,D3	24	2.6
1980	†NY A★	143	514	94	154	22	4	**41**	111	83-15	2	122	.300	.398	.597	172	52	1-2	.962	-4	96	45	O94R,D46	0	4.0
1981	†NY A★	94	334	33	79	17	1	15	54	46-2	1	82	.237	.330	.428	119	8	0-3	.974	-2	93	73	O61R,D33	9	0.1
1982	†Cal A★	153	530	92	146	17	1	**39**	101	85-12	2	156	.275	.375	.532	145	34	4-5	.972	-17	75	64	O139R,D5	0	0.9
1983	Cal A✳	116	397	43	77	14	1	14	49	52-5	4	140	.194	.290	.340	74	-14	0-2	.986	-4	74	121	D62,O47R	0	-2.3
1984	Cal A★	143	525	67	117	17	2	25	81	55-7	3	141	.223	.300	.406	93	-6	8-4	1.000	-0	107	0	D134,O3R	0	-1.0
1985	Cal A	143	460	64	116	27	0	27	85	78-12	1	138	.252	.360	.487	130	21	1-2	.944	-8	75	120	O81R,D52	0	0.7
1986	†Cal A	132	419	65	101	12	2	18	58	92-11	3	115	.241	.379	.408	116	13	1-1	.833	1	99	698	D121,O4R	0	1.0
1987	Oak A	115	336	42	74	14	1	15	43	33-0	4	97	.220	.297	.402	89	-6	2-1	1.000	-2	83	0	D79,O20R	0	-1.1
Total	21	2820	9864	1551	2584	463	49	563	1702	1375-164	96	2597	.262	.356	.490	139	524	228-115	.967	-34	99	92	O2102(20/186/1939),D630	48	38.7
JACKSON, SONNY	Roland Thomas; B7.9.1944 Washington DC; BL/TR/5´9˝/155; d9.27; C8																								
1963	Hou N	1	3	0	0	0	0	0	0	0-0	0	1	.000	.000	.000	-99	-1	0-0	.833	1	306	0	/S	0	0.0
1964	Hou N	9	23	3	8	1	0	0	1	2-0	0	3	.348	.400	.391	131	1	1-0	.870	-3	72	32	S7	0	-0.2
1965	Hou N	10	23	1	3	0	0	0	0	1-0	0	1	.130	.167	.130	-16	-4	1-1	.969	-2	74	74	S8/3	0	-0.5
1966	Hou N	150	596	80	174	6	5	3	25	42-0	3	53	.292	.341	.334	95	-4	49-14	.951	-3	98	81	S150	0	1.2
1967	Hou N	129	520	67	123	18	3	0	25	36-1	0	45	.237	.285	.283	66	-24	22-9	.943	-8	93	80	S128	21	-2.1
1968	Atl N	105	358	37	81	8	2	1	19	25-6	3	35	.226	.282	.268	66	-15	16-6	.952	-15	100	68	S99	32	-2.3
1969	†Atl N	98	318	41	76	3	5	1	27	35-2	2	33	.239	.317	.289	71	-12	12-7	.961	-9	93	100	S97	0	-1.1
1970	Atl N	103	328	60	85	14	3	0	20	45-1	1	27	.259	.347	.320	76	-9	11-4	.933	-13	92	83	S87	0	-1.2
1971	Atl N	149	547	58	141	20	5	2	25	35-1	1	45	.258	.302	.324	73	-19	7-6	.980	-7	85	87	O145C	0	-3.4
1972	Atl N	60	126	20	30	6	3	0	8	7-0	0	9	.238	.278	.333	67	-6	1-0	.976	4	117	101	S17,O10(0/9/1),3b6	25	0.0
1973	Atl N	117	206	29	43	5	2	0	12	22-0	1	13	.209	.283	.252	47	-14	6-3	.981	-1	94	56	O56(48/4/4),S36	0	-1.4

YEAR	TM LG	G	AB	R	H	2B	3B	HR	RBI	BB-IB	HP	SO	AVG	OBP	SLG	AOPS	ABR	SB-CS	FA	FR	RNG	THR	GAMES AT POSITION	DL	BFW
1974	Atl N	5	7	0	3	0	0	0	0	0-0	0	0	.429	.429	.429	135	0	0-1	1.000	0	131	0	/rf	0	0.0
Total	12	936	3055	396	767	81	28	7	162	250-11	11	265	.251	.308	.303	73	-107	126-51	.949	-57	96	81	S630,O212(48/158/6),3b7	78	-11.0
Jackson, Ron	Ronald Harris; B10.22.1933 Kalamazoo MI; BR/TR/6´7˝/(225–230); d6.15; Col Western Michigan																								
1954	Chi A	40	93	10	26	4	0	4	10	6	2	20	.280	.333	.452	111	1	2-1	.988	-3	55	74	1b35	0	-0.3
1955	Chi A	40	74	10	15	1	1	2	7	8-2	0	22	.203	.277	.324	61	-5	1-0	.988	-1	77	93	1b29	0	-0.7
1956	Chi A	22	56	7	12	3	0	1	4	10-1	0	13	.214	.333	.321	73	-2	1-0	1.000	1	114	116	1b19	0	-0.2
1957	Chi A	13	60	4	19	3	0	2	8	1-1	0	12	.317	.328	.467	114	1	0-0	.992	-1	64	90	1b13	0	-0.1
1958	Chi A	61	146	19	34	4	0	7	21	18-0	2	46	.233	.323	.404	101	0	2-0	.997	-2	77	99	1b38	0	-0.3
1959	Chi A	10	14	3	3	1	0	1	2	1-0	1	0	.214	.313	.500	121	0	0-0	1.000	-0	53	126	1b5	0	0.0
1960	Bos A	10	31	1	7	2	0	0	0	1-0	0	6	.226	.250	.290	44	-2	0-0	.973	-0	97	134	1b9	0	-0.3
Total	7	196	474	54	116	18	1	17	52	45-4	5	119	.245	.315	.395	92	-7	6-1	.992	-7	76	97	1b148	0	-1.9
Jackson, Ron	Ronnie Damien; B5.9.1953 Birmingham AL; BR/TR/6´0˝/(205–217); [AnaA71 2/37]; d9.12; C9; OF(51/1/4)																								
1975	Cal A	13	39	2	9	2	0	0	2	2-0	0	10	.231	.268	.282	60	-2	1-1	.947	0	97	160	O9L,3b3/D	0	-0.3
1976	Cal A	127	410	44	93	18	3	8	40	30-1	7	58	.227	.289	.344	91	-6	5-4	.950	4	100	109	3b114,2b7,O4(3/0/1),D6	0	-0.3
1977	Cal A	106	292	38	71	15	2	8	28	24-2	1	42	.243	.301	.390	90	-4	3-2	.990	2	121	99	1b43,3b30,D20,O3L/S	0	-0.5
1978	Cal A	105	387	49	115	18	6	6	57	16-1	9	31	.297	.337	.421	116	7	2-3	.994	-5	116	86	1b75,3b31/rfD	32	-0.3
1979	Min A	159	583	85	158	40	5	14	68	51-5	9	59	.271	.337	.429	101	2	3-1	.994	13	**128**	**125**	1b157/S3lf	0	0.5
1980	Min A	131	396	48	105	29	3	5	42	28-5	3	41	.265	.316	.391	87	-7	1-8	.991	4	**124**	121	1b119,O15(14/1/0),3b2/D	0	-1.2
1981	Min A	54	175	17	46	9	0	4	28	10-0	1	15	.263	.305	.383	92	-2	2-2	.988	0	109	80	1b36,O7(6/0/1),3b3,D6	0	-0.5
	Det A	31	95	12	27	8	1	1	12	8-0	0	11	.284	.337	.421	114	2	4-1	1.000	-0	90	103	1b29	0	0.1
	Year	85	270	29	73	17	1	5	40	18-0	1	26	.270	.316	.396	99	0	6-3	.993	-0	101	89	1b65,O7(6/0/1),D6,3b3	0	-0.4
1982	†Cal A	53	142	15	47	6	0	2	19	10-0	2	12	.331	.381	.415	118	4	0-1	.994	-2	89	140	1b37,3b9	0	-0.1
1983	Cal A	102	348	41	80	16	1	8	39	27-2	3	33	.230	.291	.351	76	-12	2-2	.957	2	110	103	3b38,1b35,D16,O15(14/0/1)	0	-1.4
1984	Cal A	33	91	5	15	2	1	0	5	7-1	0	13	.165	.222	.209	21	-10	0-0	.990	-1	90	103	1b21,3b9/lf	0	-1.3
	Bal A	12	28	0	8	2	0	0	2	0-0	0	4	.286	.286	.357	78	-1	0-2	.960	2	94	344	3b10	0	0.0
	Year	45	119	5	23	4	1	0	7	7-1	0	17	.193	.236	.244	34	-11	0-2	.990	0	90	103	1b21,3b19/lf	0	-1.3
Total	10	926	2986	356	774	165	22	56	342	213-17	35	329	.259	.314	.385	93	-29	23-27	.993	18	116	112	1b552,3b250,O56L,D51,2b7,S2	32	-5.3
Jackson, Ryan	Ryan Dewitte; B11.15.1971 Orlando FL; BL/TL/6´2˝/(185–205); [FlaN94 7/180]; d3.31; Col Duke																								
1998	Fla N	111	260	26	65	15	1	5	31	20-0	1	73	.250	.305	.373	82	-7	1-1	.973	-5	82	90	1b44,O32(10/0/23),D5	0	-1.6
1999	Sea A	32	68	4	16	3	0	0	10	6-0	1	19	.235	.299	.279	51	-5	3-3	.989	-0	97	94	1b29/lf	0	-0.7
2001	Det A	79	118	19	25	4	2	2	11	5-0	1	26	.212	.250	.331	52	-9	3-1	1.000	-2	128	114	1b35,O34(19/0/15),D5	0	-1.2
2002	Det A	4	6	0	2	1	1	0	0	1-0	0	2	.333	.429	.833	233	1	0-0	1.000	-0	73	0	O3(2/1/0)	0	0.1
Total	4	226	452	49	108	23	4	7	52	32-0	3	120	.239	.292	.354	72	-20	7-5	.983	-7	95	96	1b108,O70(32/1/38),D10	0	-3.4
Jackson, Sam	Samuel; B3.24.1849 Ripon, England; D8.4.1930 Clifton Springs NY; BR/TR/5´5.5˝/160; d5.9																								
1871	Bos NA	16	76	17	17	5	3	0	11	1	—	4	.224	.234	.368	68	-3	0-1	.818	-1	110	22	2b14/Scf	—	-0.4
1872	Atl NA	4	12	0	2	0	0	0	0	0	—	0	.167	.167	.167	2	-2	0-0	.667	-1	317	0	O3L/23	—	-0.2
Total	2NA	20	88	17	19	5	3	0	11	1	—	4	.216	.225	.341	58	-5	0-1	.810	-2	108	22	2b15,O4(3/1/0)/3S	—	-0.6
Jackson, Travis	Travis Calvin "Stonewall"; B11.2.1903 Waldo AR; D7.27.1987 Waldo AR; BR/TR/5´10.5˝/160; d9.27; C4; HF1982																								
1922	NY N	3	8	1	0	0	0	0	0	0	0	2	.000	.000	.000	-99	-2	0-0	.909	0	120	113	S3	—	-0.2
1923	†NY N	96	327	45	90	12	7	4	37	22	0	40	.275	.321	.391	88	-7	3-3	.943	3	112	86	S60,3b31/2	—	0.3
1924	†NY N	151	596	81	180	26	8	11	76	21	0	56	.302	.326	.428	103	0	6-7	.937	0	102	107	S151	—	1.5
1925	NY N	112	411	51	117	15	2	9	59	24	2	43	.285	.327	.397	87	-9	8-3	.942	2	99	95	S110	—	0.5
1926	NY N	111	385	64	126	24	8	8	51	20	1	26	.327	.362	.494	130	15	2	.962	-1	97	111	S108/rf	—	2.5
1927	NY N	127	469	67	149	29	4	14	98	32	1	30	.318	.363	.486	126	16	8	.952	26	**113**	116	S124,3b2	—	5.4
1928	NY N	150	537	73	145	35	6	14	77	56	0	46	.270	.339	.436	101	0	8	.952	28	**111**	125	S149	—	4.2
1929	NY N	149	551	92	162	21	12	21	94	64	0	56	.294	.367	.490	111	7	10	**.969**	15	107	123	S149	—	3.5
1930	NY N	116	431	70	146	27	8	13	82	32	1	25	.339	.386	.529	121	14	6	.956	9	**109**	91	S115	—	3.1
1931	NY N	145	555	65	172	26	10	5	71	36	1	23	.310	.353	.420	110	6	13	**.970**	10	102	88	S145	—	2.6
1932	NY N	52	195	23	50	17	1	4	38	13	2	16	.256	.310	.415	95	-1	1	.925	-4	95	98	S52	—	-0.1
1933	†NY N	53	122	11	30	5	0	0	12	8	0	11	.246	.292	.287	67	-5	2	.890	2	96	175	S21,3b21	—	-0.1
1934	NY N★	137	523	75	140	26	7	16	101	37	0	71	.268	.316	.436	102	-1	1	.945	10	**109**	87	S130,3b9	—	1.8
1935	NY N	128	511	74	154	20	12	9	80	29	1	64	.301	.340	.440	110	5	3	.947	-9	92	70	3b128	—	0.1
1936	†NY N	126	465	41	107	8	1	7	53	18	1	56	.230	.260	.297	50	-34	0	.952	-2	101	61	3b116,S9	—	-3.1
Total	15	1656	6086	833	1768	291	86	135	929	412	10	565	.291	.337	.433	102	4	71-13	.952	90	105	105	S1326,3b307/rf2	—	22.0
Jackson, Bo	Vincent Edward; B11.30.1962 Bessemer AL; BR/TR/6´1˝/(222–235); [KCA86 4/105]; d9.2; Col Auburn; [DL 1992 Chi A 182]																								
1986	KC A	25	82	9	17	2	1	2	9	7-0	2	34	.207	.286	.329	65	-4	3-1	.886	-3	67	133	O23R/D	0	-0.8
1987	KC A	116	396	46	93	17	2	22	53	30-0	5	158	.235	.296	.455	93	-6	10-4	.955	-7	82	132	O113(95/21/3)/D	0	-1.6
1988	KC A	124	439	63	108	16	4	25	68	25-6	1	146	.246	.287	.472	107	1	27-6	.973	3	100	162	O121(103/5/15),D2	31	0.5
1989	KC A★	135	515	86	132	15	6	32	105	39-8	3	172	.256	.310	.495	124	13	26-9	.967	4	100	172	O110(110/1/0),D24	15	1.5
1990	KC A	111	405	74	110	16	1	28	78	44-2	2	128	.272	.342	.523	142	21	15-9	.952	2	102	154	O97(36/61/0),D10	39	2.1
1991	Chi A	23	71	8	16	4	0	3	14	12-1	0	25	.225	.333	.408	107	1	0-1	ø	0	0	0	D21	147	0.0
1993	†Chi A	85	284	32	66	9	0	16	45	23-1	0	106	.232	.289	.433	93	-5	0-2	.989	4	108	190	O47(28/0/19),D36	0	-0.5
1994	Cal A	75	201	23	56	7	0	13	43	20-2	1	72	.279	.344	.507	115	4	1-0	.964	-0	104	110	O46(43/0/3),D9	0	0.2
Total	8	694	2393	341	598	86	14	141	415	200-20	14	841	.250	.309	.474	111	25	82-32	.962	2	96	154	O557(415/88/63),D104	414	1.4
Jackson, Bill	William Riley; B4.4.1881 Pittsburgh PA; D9.24.1958 Peoria IL; BL/TL/5´11.5˝/160; d4.30																								
1914	Chi F	26	25	2	1	0	0	0	1	3	0	5	.040	.143	.040	-52	-6	0	.917	1	152	178	O6(2/2/2),1b4	—	-0.6
1915	Chi F	50	98	15	16	1	0	1	12	14	0	15	.163	.268	.204	36	-10	3	.983	0	109	71	1b36/cf	—	-1.2
Total	2	76	123	17	17	1	0	1	13	17	0	20	.138	.243	.171	18	-16	3	.984	1	105	76	1b40,O7(2/3/2)	—	-1.8
Jacobs, Jake	Lamar Gary; B6.9.1937 Youngstown OH; BR/TR/6´0˝/(175–180); d9.13; Col Ohio U.																								
1960	Was A	6	2	0	0	0	0	0	0	0-0	0	0	.000	.000	.000	-99	-1	0-0	ø	0	—	—	/H	0	-0.1
1961	Min A	4	8	0	2	0	0	0	0	0-0	0	2	.250	.250	.250	32	-1	0-0	1.000	-1	49	0	O3C	0	-0.1
Total	2	10	10	0	2	0	0	0	0	0-0	0	2	.200	.200	.200	7	-2	0-0	1.000	-1	49	0	O3C	0	-0.2
Jacobs, Mike	Michael James; B10.30.1980 Chula Vista CA; BL/TR/6´2˝/200; [NYN99 38/1156]; d8.21; Col Grossmont (CA) JC																								
2005	NY N	30	100	19	31	7	0	11	23	10-0	1	22	.310	.375	.710	181	11	0-0	.984	-3	59	108	1b28	0	0.6
2006	Fla N	136	469	54	123	37	1	20	77	45-2	1	105	.262	.325	.473	107	4	3-0	.993	-3	87	103	1b124/D	0	-0.8
Total	2	166	569	73	154	44	1	31	100	55-2	2	127	.271	.334	.515	120	15	3-0	.991	-6	82	104	1b152/D	0	-0.2
Jacobs, Mike	Morris Elmore; B12.1877 Louisville KY; D3.21.1949 Louisville KY; d7.16																								
1902	Chi N	5	19	1	4	0	0	0	2	0	0	—	.211	.211	.211	31	-2	0	.880	-1	87	66	S5	—	-0.3
Jacobs, Otto	Otto Albert; B4.19.1889 Chicago IL; D11.19.1955 Chicago IL; BR/TR/5´9˝/180; d6.13																								
1918	Chi A	29	73	4	15	3	1	0	3	5	0	8	.205	.256	.274	59	-4	0	.955	-2	*119*	*83*	C21	—	-0.5
Jacobs, Ray	Raymond Frederick; B1.2.1902 Salt Lake City UT; D4.5.1952 Los Angeles CA; BR/TR/6´0˝/160; d4.20																								
1928	Chi N	2	2	0	0	0	0	0	0	0	0	1	.000	.000	.000	-99	-1	0	ø	0	—	—	/H	—	-0.1
Jacobs, Spook	Robert Forrest Vandergrift; B11.4.1925 Cheswold DE; BR/TR/5´8.5˝/155; d4.13																								
1954	Phi A	132	508	63	131	11	1	0	26	60	0	22	.258	.336	.283	71	-19	17-3	.974	-16	88	91	2b131	0	-2.4
1955	KC A	13	23	7	6	0	0	0	1	3-0	1	0	.261	.370	.261	71	-1	1-2	1.000	-2	78	109	2b7	0	-0.2
1956	KC A	32	97	13	21	3	0	0	5	15-1	0	5	.216	.321	.247	52	-6	4-1	.968	-2	92	116	2b31	0	-0.5
	Pit N	11	37	4	6	2	0	0	1	2-0	1	5	.162	.225	.216	20	-4	0-2	.926	-3	79	71	2b11	0	-0.8
Total	3	188	665	87	164	16	1	0	33	80-1	2	32	.247	.329	.274	65	-30	22-8	.971	-22	88	94	2b180	0	-3.9
Jacobsen, Bucky	Larry William; B8.31.1975 Riverton WY; BR/TR/6´4˝/220; [MilA97 7/217]; d7.16; Col Lewis-Clark St.; [DL 2005 Sea A 140]																								
2004	Sea A	42	160	17	44	9	0	9	28	14-0	1	47	.275	.335	.500	120	4	0-0	.984	-1	97	73	1b21,D20	0	0.1

YEAR	TM LG	G	AB	R	H	2B	3B	HR	RBI	BB-IB	HP	SO	AVG	OBP	SLG	AOPS	ABR	SB-CS	FA	FR	RNG	THR	GAMES AT POSITION	DL	BFW
JACOBSON, MERWIN	Merwin John William "Jake"; B3.7.1894 New Britain CT; D1.13.1978 Baltimore MD; BL/TL/5´11.5˝/165; d9.8																								
1915	NY N	8	24	0	2	0	0	0	0	1	0	5	.083	.120	.083	-40	-4	0	.909	0	90	164	O5(0/2/3)	—	-0.5
1916	Chi N	4	13	2	3	0	0	0	0	1	0	4	.231	.286	.231	54	-1	2	1.000	-0	120	0	O4R	—	-0.1
1926	Bro N	110	288	41	71	9	2	0	23	36	0	24	.247	.330	.292	70	-11	5	.975	-0	106	61	O86(2/53/32)	—	-1.6
1927	Bro N	11	6	4	0	0	0	0	1	0	0	1	.000	.000	.000	-99	-2	0	1.000	0	142	0	O3R	—	-0.2
Total	4	133	331	47	76	9	2	0	24	38	0	34	.230	.309	.269	59	-18	7	.973	-0	106	64	O98(2/55/42)	—	-2.4
JACOBSON, BABY DOLL	William Chester; B8.16.1890 Cable IL; D1.16.1977 Orion IL; BR/TR/6´3˝/215; d4.14; Mil 1918																								
1915	Det A	37	65	5	14	6	2	0	4	5	1	14	.215	.282	.369	90	-1	0-2	.983	-1	69	103	1b10,O7(3/5/0)	—	-0.3
	StL A	34	115	13	24	6	1	1	9	10	4	26	.209	.295	.304	82	-2	3-3	.981	-1	105	55	O32(3/3/26)	—	-0.6
	Year	71	180	18	38	12	3	1	13	15	5	40	.211	.290	.328	84	-4	3-5	.984	-1	104	70	O39(6/8/26),1b10	—	-0.9
1917	StL A	148	529	53	131	23	7	4	55	31	4	67	.248	.294	.340	97	-4	10	.975	3	108	95	O131(0/54/77),1b11	—	-1.1
1919	StL A	120	455	70	147	31	8	4	51	24	4	47	.323	.362	.453	125	14	9	.949	-3	107	61	O106(17/73/16),1b8	—	0.4
1920	StL A	**154**	609	97	216	34	14	9	122	46	2	37	.355	.402	.501	134	29	11-7	.979	10	116	94	O154(0/120/34)/1	—	2.7
1921	StL A	151	599	90	211	38	14	5	90	42	3	30	.352	.398	.487	118	16	8-8	.982	-1	107	39	O142(0/141/1),1b10	—	0.7
1922	StL A	145	555	88	176	22	16	9	102	46	9	36	.317	.379	.463	114	11	19-6	.969	-1	108	62	O137(11/125/1),1b7	—	0.5
1923	StL A	147	592	76	183	29	6	8	81	29	2	27	.309	.343	.419	95	-7	6-6	.974	4	111	61	O146C	—	-1.0
1924	StL A	152	579	103	184	41	12	19	97	35	4	45	.318	.361	.528	120	13	6-8	.986	10	**119**	48	O152C	—	1.4
1925	StL A	142	540	103	184	30	9	15	76	45	1	26	.341	.392	.513	122	16	8-11	.965	-4	90	120	O139C	—	0.4
1926	StL A	50	182	18	52	15	1	2	21	9	0	14	.286	.319	.412	86	-4	1-2	.964	-3	94	47	O50C	—	-1.0
	Bos A	98	394	44	120	36	1	6	69	22	2	22	.305	.344	.447	109	4	4-1	.980	-9	85	68	O98(6/57/36)	—	-1.0
	Year	148	576	62	172	51	2	8	90	31	2	36	.299	.337	.436	101	-1	5-3	.975	-13	88	62	O148(6/107/36)	—	-2.0
1927	Bos A	45	155	11	38	9	3	0	24	5	2	12	.245	.278	.342	61	-10	1-0	.979	-0	99	94	O39L	—	-1.2
	Cle A	32	103	13	26	5	0	0	13	6	1	4	.252	.300	.301	56	-7	0-0	.932	-2	104	33	O31C	—	-1.0
	Phi A	17	35	3	8	3	0	1	5	0	0	3	.229	.229	.400	57	-2	0-0	1.000	-1	69	0	O14(9/2/3)	—	-0.4
	Year	94	293	27	72	17	3	1	42	11	3	19	.246	.280	.334	59	-19	1-0	.959	-3	99	63	O84(48/33/3)	—	-2.6
Total	11	1472	5507	787	1714	328	94	83	819	355	39	410	.311	.357	.450	111	66	86-54	.973	1	106	71	O1378(88/1098/194),1b47	—	-1.5
JACOBY, BROOK	Brook Wallace; B11.23.1959 Philadelphia PA; BR/TR/5´11˝/(175–195); [AtlN79*7/153]; d9.13; C1; Col Ventura (CA) JC																								
1981	Atl N	11	10	0	2	0	0	0	1	0-0	0	3	.200	.200	.200	14	-1	0-0	1.000	2	229	695	3b3	0	0.0
1983	Atl N	4	8	0	0	0	0	0	0	0-0	0	1	.000	.000	.000	-93	-2	0-0	1.000	-1	63	0	3b2	0	-0.3
1984	Cle A	126	439	64	116	19	3	7	40	32-0	3	73	.264	.314	.369	88	-7	3-2	.951	-23	81	71	3b126/S	42	-3.3
1985	Cle A	161	606	72	166	26	3	20	87	48-3	0	120	.274	.324	.426	105	3	2-3	.958	-8	98	78	3b161/2	0	-0.8
1986	Cle A★	158	583	83	168	30	4	17	80	56-5	0	137	.288	.350	.441	115	12	2-1	.941	-12	100	79	3b158	0	-0.2
1987	Cle A	155	540	73	162	26	4	32	69	75-2	3	73	.300	.387	.541	141	33	2-3	.946	-5	94	65	3b144,1b7,D4	0	2.4
1988	Cle A	152	552	59	133	25	0	9	49	48-2	1	101	.241	.300	.335	76	-17	2-3	.975	2	103	91	3b151	0	-1.6
1989	Cle A	147	519	49	141	26	5	13	64	62-3	3	90	.272	.348	.416	114	10	2-5	.955	-14	92	64	3b144,D3	0	-0.5
1990	Cle A★	155	553	77	162	24	4	14	75	63-6	2	58	.293	.365	.427	121	17	1-4	.981	-15	90	86	3b99,1b78	0	-0.4
1991	Cle A	66	231	14	54	9	1	4	24	16-2	2	32	.234	.289	.333	71	-10	0-1	.988	1	95	63	1b55,3b15	17	-1.3
	Oak A	56	188	14	40	12	0	0	20	11-1	1	22	.213	.255	.277	51	-13	2-0	.982	-6	78	92	3b52,1b3	0	-1.9
	Year	122	419	28	94	21	1	4	44	27-3	3	54	.224	.274	.308	63	-22	2-1	.987	-6	85	97	3b67,1b58	0	-3.2
1992	Cle A	120	291	30	76	7	0	4	36	28-2	1	54	.261	.324	.326	85	-6	0-3	.957	-1	105	115	3b111,1b10	0	-0.8
Total	11	1311	4520	535	1220	204	24	120	545	439-26	16	764	.270	.334	.405	103	19	16-25	.958	-82	95	80	3b1166,1b153,D7/2S	59	-8.7
JACOBY, HARRY	Harry M.; B Philadelphia PA; D7.22.1900 Philadelphia PA; d5.2																								
1882	Bal AA	31	121	17	21	1	1	1	—	7	—	—	.174	.219	.223	53	-5	—	.776	7	112	83	3b19,O13R	—	0.2
1885	Bal AA	11	43	4	6	2	0	0	1	2	0	—	.140	.178	.186	15	-4	—	.896	-5	75	46	2b11	—	-0.8
Total	2	42	164	21	27	3	1	1	1	9	0	—	.165	.208	.213	43	-9	—	.776	3	112	83	3b19,O13R,2b11	—	-0.6
JAHA, JOHN	John Emil; B5.27.1966 Portland OR; BR/TR/6´1˝/(195–240); [MilA84 14/358]; d7.9																								
1992	Mil A	47	133	17	30	3	1	2	10	12-1	2	30	.226	.291	.308	71	-5	10-0	1.000	-1	89	87	1b38/lfD	0	-0.7
1993	Mil A	153	515	78	136	21	0	19	70	51-4	8	109	.264	.337	.416	103	2	13-9	.992	7	121	92	1b150/23	0	-0.4
1994	Mil A	84	291	45	70	14	0	12	39	32-3	10	75	.241	.332	.412	87	-5	3-3	.989	-2	96	103	1b73,D11	0	-1.4
1995	Mil A	88	316	59	99	20	2	20	65	36-0	4	66	.313	.389	.579	140	18	2-1	.997	2	113	122	1b81,D6	49	1.3
1996	Mil A	148	543	108	163	28	1	34	118	85-1	5	118	.300	.398	.543	130	26	3-1	.992	1	108	113	1b85,D63	0	1.5
1997	Mil A	46	162	25	40	7	0	11	26	25-1	3	40	.247	.354	.494	118	4	1-0	.992	-1	82	125	1b27,D20	120	0.0
1998	Mil N	73	216	29	45	6	1	7	38	49-3	6	66	.208	.366	.343	87	-2	1-3	.994	-5	64	134	1b57,D8	63	-1.3
1999	Oak A★	142	457	93	126	23	0	35	111	101-2	9	129	.276	.414	.556	149	39	2-0	1.000	1	153	79	D121,1b8	0	3.0
2000	Oak A	33	97	14	17	1	0	1	5	33-0	3	38	.175	.398	.216	63	-3	1-0	ø	0	0	0	D30	123	-0.4
2001	Oak A	12	45	2	4	3	0	0	8	6-0	0	15	.089	.192	.156	-5	-7	0-0	ø	0	0	0	D12	71	-0.8
Total	10	826	2775	470	730	126	5	141	490	430-15	50	686	.263	.369	.465	114	67	36-17	.993	1	104	107	1b519,D279/32lf	426	0.8
JAHN, ART	Arthur Charles; B12.2.1895 Struble IA; D1.9.1948 Little Rock AR; BR/TR/6´0˝/180; d7.2																								
1925	Chi N	58	226	30	68	10	8	0	37	11	1	20	.301	.336	.416	90	-4	2-2	.985	0	98	91	O58L	—	-0.9
1928	NY N	10	29	7	8	1	0	1	7	2	0	5	.276	.323	.414	91	0	0	1.000	1	108	148	O8(7/1/0)	—	-0.1
	Phi N	36	94	8	21	4	0	0	11	4	2	11	.223	.270	.266	39	-8	0	.978	-1	97	48	O29(2/0/27)	—	-1.1
	Year	46	123	15	29	5	0	1	18	6	2	16	.236	.282	.301	51	-9	0	.985	-0	100	77	O37(9/1/27)	—	-1.2
Total	2	104	349	45	97	15	8	1	55	17	3	36	.278	.317	.375	76	-12	2-2	.985	-0	99	86	O95(67/1/27)	—	-2.1
JAMES, ART	Arthur; B8.2.1952 Detroit MI; BL/TL/6´0˝/160; [DetA72*6/112]; d4.10; Col Macomb (MI) CC																								
1975	Det A	11	40	2	9	2	0	0	1	1-0	0	3	.225	.244	.275	44	-3	1-2	1.000	2	149	0	O11(0/4/7)	0	-0.2
JAMES, BERT	Berton Hulon "Jesse"; B7.7.1886 Coopertown TN; D1.2.1959 Adairville KY; BL/TR/5´11˝/175; d9.18																								
1909	StL N	6	21	1	6	0	0	0	0	4	0	—	.286	.400	.286	120	1	1	.909	0	119	477	O6R	—	0.1
JAMES, CHARLIE	Charles Wesley; B12.22.1937 St.Louis MO; BR/TR/6´1˝/195; d8.2; Col Missouri																								
1960	StL N	43	50	5	9	1	0	2	5	1-0	0	12	.180	.196	.320	35	-5	0-0	.917	-1	84	94	O37(23/7/9)	0	-0.6
1961	StL N	108	349	43	89	19	2	4	44	15-1	3	59	.255	.288	.355	64	-18	2-2	.962	-5	96	41	O90(39/4/56)	0	-2.8
1962	StL N	129	388	50	107	13	4	8	59	10-1	4	58	.276	.301	.392	77	-13	3-4	.988	-5	89	85	O116(17/1/104)	0	-2.6
1963	StL N	116	347	34	93	14	2	10	45	10-0	2	64	.268	.291	.406	91	-5	2-1	.994	4	115	70	O101(82/1/25)	0	-0.6
1964	†StL N	88	233	24	52	9	1	5	17	11-1	1	58	.223	.261	.335	61	-12	0-0	.963	-2	89	90	O60(46/0/14)	0	-1.8
1965	Cin N	26	39	2	8	0	0	0	2	1-0	0	9	.205	.225	.205	21	-4	0-0	.909	-0	103	0	O7(3/0/4)	0	-0.5
Total	6	510	1406	158	358	56	9	29	172	48-3	10	260	.255	.283	.369	71	-57	7-7	.976	-8	97	70	O411(210/13/212)	0	-8.9
JAMES, CLEO	Cleo Joel; B8.31.1940 Clarksdale MS; BR/TR/5´10˝/(175–176); d4.15; Col Riverside (CA) CC																								
1968	LA N	10	10	2	2	1	0	0	0	0-0	0	6	.200	.200	.300	52	-1	0-0	1.000	-0	94	0	O2L	0	-0.1
1970	Chi N	100	176	33	37	7	2	3	14	17-5	5	24	.210	.298	.324	59	-10	5-0	1.000	0	95	159	O90(5/83/2)	0	-1.0
1971	Chi N	54	150	25	43	7	0	2	13	10-0	6	16	.287	.353	.373	93	-1	6-2	.979	1	97	170	O48(1/35/14),3b2	0	-0.1
1973	Chi N	44	45	9	5	0	0	0	0	1-0	0	6	.111	.130	.111	-30	-8	5-0	.960	1	103	154	O22(14/8/1)	0	-0.7
Total	4	208	381	69	87	15	2	5	27	28-5	11	52	.228	.299	.318	63	-20	16-2	.988	1	96	161	O162(22/126/17),3b2	0	-1.9
JAMES, DION	Dion; B11.9.1962 Philadelphia PA; BL/TL/6´1˝/(170–185); [MilA80 1/25]; d9.16																								
1983	Mil A	11	20	1	2	0	0	0	1	2-0	0	2	.100	.182	.100	-21	-3	1-0	1.000	-0	78	220	O9(4/8/1),D2	0	-0.4
1984	Mil A	128	387	52	114	19	5	1	30	32-1	3	41	.295	.351	.377	106	4	10-10	.989	3	106	104	O118(2/30/93)	0	0.1
1985	Mil A	18	49	5	11	1	0	0	3	6-0	0	6	.224	.309	.245	54	-3	0-0	1.000	-3	67	0	O11C,D3	124	-0.6
1987	Atl N	134	494	80	154	37	6	10	61	70-2	2	63	.312	.397	.472	125	21	10-8	**.996**	-8	92	55	O126(29/99/0)	0	1.1
1988	Atl N	132	386	46	99	17	5	3	30	58-5	1	59	.256	.353	.350	99	2	9-9	.987	-4	93	82	O120(86/49/3)	0	-0.7
1989	Atl N	63	170	15	44	7	0	1	11	25-2	1	23	.259	.355	.318	92	0	1-3	1.000	1	106	0	O46(26/1/23),1b8	0	-0.2
	Cle A	71	245	26	75	11	0	4	29	24-4	0	26	.306	.368	.400	114	5	1-4	.976	1	115	52	O37(26/10/0),D27,1b2	0	0.3
1990	Cle A	87	248	28	68	15	2	1	22	27-3	1	23	.274	.347	.363	99	1	5-3	.996	-4	87	84	1b35,O33(24/8/0),D10	0	-0.6
1992	NY A	67	145	24	38	8	0	3	17	22-0	1	15	.262	.359	.379	108	3	1-0	1.000	-4	77	44	O46(8/12/27),D5	0	-0.2
1993	NY A	115	343	62	114	21	2	7	36	31-1	2	31	.332	.390	.466	133	17	0-0	.966	-8	82	82	O103(91/14/1)/1D	0	0.6
1995	†NY A	85	209	22	60	6	1	2	26	20-2	0	16	.287	.346	.354	84	-5	4-1	.968	-2	77	0	O29(23/0/6),D27,1b6	0	-0.8
1996	NY A	6	12	1	2	0	0	0	0	1-0	0	2	.167	.231	.167	3	-2	1-0	1.000	-1	56	0	O4(3/0/1)/D	0	-0.2
Total	11	917	2708	362	781	142	21	32	266	318-20	11	307	.288	.364	.392	107	40	43-38	.986	-29	93	64	O682(322/242/155),D76,1b52	124	-1.6

JAMES, CHRIS Donald Chris; B10.4.1962 Rusk TX; BR/TR/6´1˝/(190–202); d4.23; Col Blinn (TX) JC; OF(322/51/229)

YEAR	TM LG	G	AB	R	H	2B	3B	HR	RBI	BB-IB	HP	SO	AVG	OBP	SLG	AOPS	ABR	SB-CS	FA	FR	RNG	THR	GAMES AT POSITION	DL	BFW
1986	Phi N	16	46	5	13	3	0	1	5	1-0	0	13	.283	.298	.413	91	-1	0-0	1.000	-1	90	0	O11(4/7/0)	76	-0.2
1987	Phi N	115	358	48	105	20	6	17	54	27-0	2	67	.293	.344	.525	123	10	3-1	.990	2	109	78	O108(96/16/5)	0	0.9
1988	Phi N	150	566	57	137	24	1	19	66	31-2	3	73	.242	.283	.389	90	-9	7-4	.989	-2	110	124	O116(8/27/101),3b31	0	-1.5
1989	Phi N	45	179	14	37	4	0	2	19	4-0	0	23	.207	.223	.263	39	-15	3-1	.985	-2	89	155	O37L,3b11	0	-2.0
	SD N	87	303	41	80	13	2	11	46	22-2	1	45	.264	.314	.429	111	3	2-1	.987	1	101	75	O79(50/0/29),3b6	0	0.2
	Year	132	482	55	117	17	2	13	65	26-2	1	68	.243	.281	.367	84	-12	5-2	.986	-1	97	101	O116(87/0/29),3b17	0	-1.8
1990	Cle A	140	528	62	158	32	4	12	70	31-4	4	71	.299	.341	.443	118	12	4-3	1.000	0	95	124	D124,O14(12/1/1)	0	0.7
1991	Cle A	115	437	31	104	16	2	5	41	18-2	4	61	.238	.273	.318	63	-23	3-4	1.000	1	103	86	D60,O39(25/0/18),1b15	27	-2.8
1992	SF N	111	248	25	60	10	4	5	32	14-2	2	45	.242	.285	.375	91	-4	2-3	.974	2	109	82	O62(60/0/2)	17	-0.5
1993	Hou N	65	129	19	33	10	1	6	19	15-2	1	34	.256	.333	.488	122	4	2-0	.958	4	121	195	O34(16/0/18)	0	0.7
	Tex A	8	31	5	11	1	0	3	7	3-0	0	6	.355	.412	.677	193	4	0-0	1.000	-0	105	0	O7(4/0/4)	0	0.3
1994	Tex A	52	133	28	34	8	4	7	19	20-0	3	38	.256	.361	.534	127	5	0-0	1.000	-2	87	75	O48(1/0/47)	42	0.1
1995	KC A	26	58	6	18	3	0	2	7	6-0	1	10	.310	.373	.466	117	2	1-0	1.000	0	130	0	D14,O5L	66	0.1
	Bos A	16	24	2	4	1	0	0	1	1-0	0	4	.167	.200	.208	6	-3	0-0	1.000	1	141	0	O8(4/0/4),D6	15	-0.3
	Year	42	82	8	22	4	0	2	8	7-0	1	14	.268	.326	.390	85	-2	1-0	1.000	1	137	0	D20,O13(9/0/4)	0	-0.2
Total	10	946	3040	343	794	145	24	90	386	193-14	21	490	.261	.307	.413	98	-15	27-17	.987	3	105	98	O568L,D204,3b48,1b15	243	-4.3

JAMES, SKIP Philip Robert; B10.21.1949 Elmhurst IL; BL/TL/6´0˝/190; [SFN71 5/114]; d9.12; Col Kansas

YEAR	TM LG	G	AB	R	H	2B	3B	HR	RBI	BB-IB	HP	SO	AVG	OBP	SLG	AOPS	ABR	SB-CS	FA	FR	RNG	THR	GAMES AT POSITION	DL	BFW
1977	SF N	10	15	3	4	1	0	0	3	2-0	0	3	.267	.353	.333	85	0	0-0	1.000	1	134	53	1b9	0	0.0
1978	SF N	41	21	5	2	1	0	0	3	4-0	0	5	.095	.240	.143	10	-2	1-0	1.000	1	143	92	1b27	0	-0.2
Total	2	51	36	8	6	2	0	0	6	6-0	0	8	.167	.286	.222	42	-2	1-0	1.000	1	139	77	1b36	0	-0.2

JAMES, BERNIE Robert Byrne; B9.2.1905 Angleton TX; D8.1.1994 San Antonio TX; BB/TR/5´9.5˝/150; d5.6

YEAR	TM LG	G	AB	R	H	2B	3B	HR	RBI	BB-IB	HP	SO	AVG	OBP	SLG	AOPS	ABR	SB-CS	FA	FR	RNG	THR	GAMES AT POSITION	DL	BFW
1929	Bos N	46	101	12	31	3	2	0	9	9	1	13	.307	.369	.376	89	-2	3	.940	-7	74	75	2b32/cf	—	-0.7
1930	Bos N	8	11	1	2	1	0	0	1	0	0	1	.182	.182	.273	8	-2	0	.941	0	118	53	2b7	—	-0.1
1933	NY N	60	125	22	28	2	1	1	10	8	0	12	.224	.271	.280	58	-7	5	.948	1	105	78	2b26,S6,3b5	—	-0.4
Total	3	114	237	35	61	6	3	1	20	17	1	26	.257	.310	.321	70	-11	8	.944	-5	91	75	2b65,S6,3b5/cf	—	-1.2

JAMIESON, CHARLIE Charles Devine "Cuckoo"; B2.7.1893 Paterson NJ; D10.27.1969 Paterson NJ; BL/TL/5´8.5˝/165; d9.20; ▲

YEAR	TM LG	G	AB	R	H	2B	3B	HR	RBI	BB-IB	HP	SO	AVG	OBP	SLG	AOPS	ABR	SB-CS	FA	FR	RNG	THR	GAMES AT POSITION	DL	BFW
1915	Was A	17	68	9	19	3	2	0	7	6	0	9	.279	.338	.382	113	1	0	1.000	3	111	232	O17L	—	0.3
1916	Was A	64	145	16	36	4	0	0	13	18	0	18	.248	.331	.276	83	-2	5	.913	0	105	105	O41(24/2/15),1b4/P	—	-0.4
1917	Was A	20	35	4	6	2	0	0	2	6	0	5	.171	.293	.229	60	-1	0	.875	-1	104	0	O9L/P	—	-0.3
	Phi A	85	345	41	92	6	2	0	27	37	2	36	.267	.341	.296	96	-1	8	.937	-4	86	104	O83R	—	-1.1
	Year	105	380	45	98	8	2	0	29	43	2	41	.258	.336	.289	92	-2	8	.930	-5	87	96	O92(9/0/83)/P	—	-1.4
1918	Phi A	110	416	50	84	11	2	0	11	54	2	30	.202	.297	.238	61	-18	11	.970	-2	94	101	O102(0/1/101),P5	—	-2.9
1919	Cle A	26	17	3	6	2	1	0	2	0	0	2	.353	.353	.588	153	1	2	.750	-0	58	0	P4,O3(0/2/1)	—	0.0
1920	†Cle A	108	370	69	118	17	7	1	40	41	1	26	.319	.388	.411	108	5	2-9	.966	2	100	122	O98(93/5/0),1b4	—	0.1
1921	Cle A	140	536	94	166	33	10	1	46	67	1	27	.310	.387	.414	103	5	8-4	.974	3	100	108	O137(125/19/0)	—	-0.2
1922	Cle A	145	567	87	183	29	11	3	57	54	6	22	.323	.388	.429	112	11	15-9	.978	3	100	107	O144(141/2/1),P2	—	0.3
1923	Cle A	152	644	130	**222**	36	12	2	51	80	6	37	.345	.422	.447	129	31	18-14	.974	5	109	95	O152L	—	2.2
1924	Cle A	143	594	98	213	34	8	3	54	47	2	15	.359	.407	.458	121	19	21-12	.974	2	106	72	O139L	—	1.0
1925	Cle A	138	557	109	165	24	5	4	42	72	3	26	.296	.380	.379	92	-5	14-18	.955	5	108	101	O135L	—	-1.3
1926	Cle A	143	555	89	166	33	7	2	45	53	1	22	.299	.361	.395	96	-3	9-7	.960	2	100	108	O143L	—	-1.2
1927	Cle A	127	489	73	151	23	6	0	36	64	5	14	.309	.394	.380	101	4	7-9	.969	4	106	96	O127L	—	-0.4
1928	Cle A	112	433	63	133	18	4	1	37	56	1	20	.307	.388	.374	100	2	3-12	.984	16	111	**195**	O111L	—	0.6
1929	Cle A	102	364	56	106	22	1	0	26	50	1	12	.291	.378	.357	87	-4	2-13	.980	-3	93	84	O93L	—	-1.8
1930	Cle A	103	366	64	110	22	1	1	52	36	3	20	.301	.368	.374	85	-7	5-2	.955	-4	90	106	O95(93/2/0)	—	-1.5
1931	Cle A	28	43	7	13	2	1	0	4	5	0	1	.302	.375	.395	97	0	1-1	.833	-1	82	0	O7(6/1/0)	—	-0.2
1932	Cle A	16	16	0	1	1	0	0	0	2	1	3	.063	.211	.125	-10	-3	0-0	1.000	1	87	739	O2R	—	-0.2
Total	18	1779	6560	1062	1990	322	80	18	552	748	35	345	.303	.378	.385	101	35	131-110	.967	29	101	108	O1638(1408/34/203),P13,1b8	—	-7.0

JANOWICZ, VIC Victor Felix; B2.26.1930 Elyria OH; D2.27.1996 Columbus OH; BR/TR/5´9˝/(185–190); d5.31; Col Ohio St.

YEAR	TM LG	G	AB	R	H	2B	3B	HR	RBI	BB-IB	HP	SO	AVG	OBP	SLG	AOPS	ABR	SB-CS	FA	FR	RNG	THR	GAMES AT POSITION	DL	BFW
1953	Pit N	42	123	10	31	3	1	2	8	5	1	31	.252	.287	.341	63	-7	0-1	.937	-9	*59*	*111*	C35	0	-1.5
1954	Pit N	41	73	10	11	3	0	0	2	7	1	23	.151	.235	.192	13	-9	0-0	.904	0	106	98	3b18/lf	0	-1.0
Total	2	83	196	20	42	6	1	2	10	12	2	54	.214	.267	.286	44	-16	0-1	.937	-9	*59*	*111*	C35,3b18/lf	0	-2.5

JANSEN, RAY Raymond William; B1.16.1889 St.Louis MO; D3.19.1934 St.Louis MO; BR/TR/5´11˝/155; d9.30

YEAR	TM LG	G	AB	R	H	2B	3B	HR	RBI	BB-IB	HP	SO	AVG	OBP	SLG	AOPS	ABR	SB-CS	FA	FR	RNG	THR	GAMES AT POSITION	DL	BFW
1910	StL A	1	5	0	4	0	0	0	0	0	0	—	.800	.800	.800	428	2	0	.700	-0	122	0	/3	—	0.2

JANTZEN, HEINIE Walter Charles; B4.9.1890 Chicago IL; D4.1.1948 Hines IL; BR/TR/5´11.5˝/170; d6.29

YEAR	TM LG	G	AB	R	H	2B	3B	HR	RBI	BB-IB	HP	SO	AVG	OBP	SLG	AOPS	ABR	SB-CS	FA	FR	RNG	THR	GAMES AT POSITION	DL	BFW
1912	StL A	31	119	10	22	0	1	1	8	4	1	—	.185	.218	.227	28	-12	3	1.000	3	111	132	O31R	—	-1.1

JANVRIN, HAL Harold Chandler "Childe Harold"; B8.27.1892 Haverhill MA; D3.1.1962 Boston MA; BR/TR/5´11.5˝/168; d7.9; Mil 1918; OF(17/4/1)

YEAR	TM LG	G	AB	R	H	2B	3B	HR	RBI	BB-IB	HP	SO	AVG	OBP	SLG	AOPS	ABR	SB-CS	FA	FR	RNG	THR	GAMES AT POSITION	DL	BFW
1911	Bos A	9	27	2	4	1	0	0	1	3	1	—	.148	.258	.185	25	-3	0	.733	-2	75	0	3b5,1b4	—	-0.5
1913	Bos A	87	276	18	57	5	1	3	25	23	2	27	.207	.272	.264	56	-16	17	.923	-10	97	49	S48,3b19,2b8,1b6	—	-2.4
1914	Bos A	145	492	65	117	18	6	1	51	38	3	50	.238	.296	.305	81	-12	29-20	.919	-18	89	78	2b59,1b57,S20,3b6	—	-3.4
1915	†Bos A	99	316	41	85	9	1	0	37	14	8	27	.269	.317	.304	88	-5	8-14	.917	-17	90	73	S64,3b20,2b8	—	-2.2
1916	†Bos A	117	310	32	69	11	4	0	26	32	2	32	.223	.299	.284	75	-9	6	.921	-12	81	130	S59,2b39,1b4,3b4	—	-2.0
1917	Bos A	55	127	21	25	3	0	0	8	11	1	13	.197	.266	.220	49	-8	2	.940	-0	107	137	2b38,S10/1	—	-0.8
1919	Was A	61	208	17	37	4	1	1	13	19	2	17	.178	.253	.221	34	-18	8	.927	-22	75	65	2b56,S2	—	-4.3
	StL N	7	14	1	3	1	0	0	1	2	0	2	.214	.313	.286	86	0	0	1.000	-1	38	0	2b2/S3	—	-0.1
1920	StL N	87	270	33	74	8	4	1	28	17	0	19	.274	.317	.344	93	-3	5-6	.926	-1	82	120	S27,1b25,O20(16/4/0),2b6	—	-0.5
1921	StL N	18	32	5	9	1	0	0	5	1	0	0	.281	.303	.313	65	-2	1-0	.968	0	94	126	1b9/2	—	-0.2
	Bro N	44	92	8	18	4	0	0	14	7	0	6	.196	.253	.239	30	-9	3-1	.922	-4	91	46	S17,2b10,1b8,3b5/rf	—	-1.2
	Year	62	124	13	27	5	0	0	19	8	0	6	.218	.265	.258	38	-11	4-1	.922	-4	81	65	1b17,S17,2b11,3b5/rf	—	-1.4
1922	Bro N	30	57	7	17	3	1	0	1	4	0	4	.298	.344	.386	89	-1	0-0	.889	-3	111	60	2b15,S4,3b2/1lf	—	-0.3
Total	10	759	2221	250	515	68	18	6	210	171	19	197	.232	.292	.287	70	-86	79-41	.907	-90	87	92	S252,2b242,1b115,3b62,O22L	—	-17.9

JARVIS, ROY Leroy Gilbert; B6.27.1926 Shawnee OK; D1.13.1990 Oklahoma City OK; BR/TR/5´9˝/160; d4.30; Mil 1944–46

YEAR	TM LG	G	AB	R	H	2B	3B	HR	RBI	BB-IB	HP	SO	AVG	OBP	SLG	AOPS	ABR	SB-CS	FA	FR	RNG	THR	GAMES AT POSITION	DL	BFW
1944	Bro N	1	1	0	0	0	0	0	0	0	0	1	.000	.000	.000	-99	0	0	1.000	-0	*0*	*0*	/C	0	0.0
1946	Pit N	2	4	0	1	0	0	0	0	1	0	1	.250	.400	.250	84	0	0	.800	-1	*44*	*0*	/C	0	-0.1
1947	Pit N	18	45	4	7	1	0	1	4	6	0	5	.156	.255	.244	32	-4	0	.967	-1	*94*	*100*	C15	0	-0.4
Total	3	21	50	4	8	1	0	1	4	7	0	7	.160	.263	.240	34	-4	0	.955	-1	*88*	*90*	C17	0	-0.5

JATA, PAUL Paul; B9.4.1949 Astoria NY; BR/TR/6´1˝/190; [DetA67 5/95]; d4.19

YEAR	TM LG	G	AB	R	H	2B	3B	HR	RBI	BB-IB	HP	SO	AVG	OBP	SLG	AOPS	ABR	SB-CS	FA	FR	RNG	THR	GAMES AT POSITION	DL	BFW
1972	Det A	32	74	8	17	2	0	0	3	7-0	0	14	.230	.296	.257	63	-3	0-1	.991	0	104	72	1b12,O10(5/0/5)/C	0	-0.5

JAVIER, AL Ignacio Alfredo (b Ignacio Alfredo Wilkes (Javier)); B2.4.1954 San Pedro de Macoris, D.R.; BR/TR/5´11˝/160; d9.9

YEAR	TM LG	G	AB	R	H	2B	3B	HR	RBI	BB-IB	HP	SO	AVG	OBP	SLG	AOPS	ABR	SB-CS	FA	FR	RNG	THR	GAMES AT POSITION	DL	BFW
1976	Hou N	8	24	1	5	0	0	0	0	2-1	0	5	.208	.269	.208	40	-2	0-0	1.000	-1	57	0	O7(4/0/4)	0	-0.4

JAVIER, JULIAN Manuel Julian (Liranzo); B8.9.1936 San Francisco de Macoris, D.R.; BR/TR/6´1˝/(174–175); d5.28; s–Stan

YEAR	TM LG	G	AB	R	H	2B	3B	HR	RBI	BB-IB	HP	SO	AVG	OBP	SLG	AOPS	ABR	SB-CS	FA	FR	RNG	THR	GAMES AT POSITION	DL	BFW
1960	StL N	119	451	55	107	19	8	4	21	21-1	1	72	.237	.273	.341	62	-25	19-4	.962	17	**109**	102	2b119	0	0.4
1961	StL N	113	445	58	124	14	3	2	41	30-1	2	51	.279	.326	.337	70	-19	11-4	.966	4	106	102	2b113	30	-0.4
1962	StL N	155	598	97	157	25	5	7	39	47-0	1	73	.263	.316	.356	73	-22	26-9	.977	-3	99	105	2b151,S4	0	-1.0
1963	StL N★	161	609	82	160	27	9	9	46	24-1	6	86	.263	.296	.381	86	-12	18-10	.969	-9	95	100	2b161	0	-0.7
1964	†StL N	155	535	66	129	19	5	12	65	30-7	1	82	.241	.282	.363	74	-19	9-7	.966	3	100	114	2b154	0	-0.4
1965	StL N	77	229	34	52	6	4	2	23	8-2	3	44	.227	.260	.314	56	-14	5-5	.975	-5	98	103	2b69	46	-1.5
1966	StL N	147	460	52	105	13	5	7	31	26-2	1	63	.228	.269	.324	64	-23	11-5	.981	4	104	114	2b145	0	-0.8
1967	†StL N	140	520	68	146	16	3	14	64	25-3	1	92	.281	.314	.404	106	2	6-7	.965	-18	93	87	2b138	0	-0.6
1968	†StL N★	139	519	54	135	25	4	4	52	24-2	1	61	.260	.291	.347	93	-6	10-3	.976	-25	88	89	2b139	0	-2.0
1969	StL N	143	493	59	139	28	2	10	42	40-11	1	74	.282	.336	.408	107	4	8-4	.967	-19	98	86	2b141	0	-0.5
1970	StL N	139	513	62	129	16	3	2	42	24-6	1	70	.251	.284	.306	57	-32	6-4	.980	16	**113**	92	2b137	0	-0.7
1971	StL N	90	259	32	67	6	4	3	28	9-3	2	33	.259	.286	.347	76	-9	5-1	.978	-4	95	90	2b80/3	0	-0.8

YEAR	TM LG	G	AB	R	H	2B	3B	HR	RBI	BB-IB	HP	SO	AVG	OBP	SLG	AOPS	ABR	SB-CS	FA	FR	RNG	THR	GAMES AT POSITION	DL	BFW
1972	†Cin N	44	91	3	19	2	0	2	12	6-0	0	11	.209	.255	.297	60	-5	1-0	.896	-3	94	154	3b19,2b5/1	0	-0.9
Total	13	1622	5722	722	1469	216	55	78	506	314-39	21	812	.257	.296	.355	78	-180	135-63	.972	-40	100	99	2b1552,3b20,S4/1	76	-9.9
JAVIER, STAN	Stanley Julian Antonio (Negrin); B1.9.1964 San Francisco de Macoris, D.R.; BB/TR/6´0˝/(180–202); d4.15; f–Julian; OF(465/691/492)																								
1984	NY A	7	7	1	1	0	0	0	0	0-0	0	1	.143	.143	.143	-21	-1	0-0	1.000	-1	53	0	O5(0/3/3)	0	-0.2
1986	Oak A	59	114	13	23	8	0	0	8	16-0	1	27	.202	.305	.272	63	-5	8-0	1.000	3	120	50	O51(3/49/0),D2	0	0.0
1987	Oak A	81	151	22	28	3	1	2	9	19-3	0	33	.185	.276	.258	46	-12	3-2	.983	2	105	138	O71(8/52/15),1b6/D	29	-1.1
1988	†Oak A	125	397	49	102	13	3	2	35	32-1	2	63	.257	.313	.320	81	-10	20-1	.980	2	102	108	O115(69/45/29),1b4,D2	15	-0.7
1989	†Oak A	112	310	42	77	12	3	1	28	31-1	1	45	.248	.317	.316	82	-7	12-2	.991	5	113	65	O107(23/28/72)/12	15	-0.3
1990	Oak A	19	33	4	8	0	2	0	3	3-0	0	6	.242	.306	.364	90	-1	0-0	1.000	1	130	0	O13(4/4/5),D2	0	0.0
	LA N	104	276	56	84	9	4	3	24	37-2	0	44	.304	.384	.399	119	8	15-7	1.000	6	123	51	O87(9/70/12)	0	1.4
1991	LA N	121	176	21	36	5	3	1	11	16-0	0	36	.205	.268	.284	57	-10	7-1	.986	-1	95	43	O69(49/7/18),1b2	0	-1.3
1992	LA N	56	58	6	11	3	0	1	5	6-2	1	11	.190	.277	.293	62	-3	1-2	1.000	-1	83	0	O27(15/2/11)	0	-0.5
	Phi N	74	276	36	72	14	1	0	24	31-0	2	43	.261	.338	.319	87	-3	17-1	.986	11	127	189	O74(27/49/1)	0	1.1
	Year	130	334	42	83	17	1	1	29	37-2	3	54	.249	.327	.314	83	-6	18-3	.987	10	121	165	O101(42/51/12)	0	0.6
1993	Cal A	92	237	33	69	10	4	3	28	27-1	1	33	.291	.362	.405	104	1	12-2	.981	-4	96	66	O64(36/16/16),1b12,2b2/D	0	-0.2
1994	Oak A	109	419	75	114	23	0	10	44	49-1	2	76	.272	.349	.399	100	1	24-7	.986	1	104	55	O108(12/102/1)/13	0	0.5
1995	Oak A	130	442	81	123	20	2	8	56	49-3	4	63	.278	.353	.387	98	-1	36-5	**1.000**	9	**118**	49	O124(32/101/1)/3	0	1.3
1996	SF N	71	274	44	74	25	0	2	22	25-0	2	51	.270	.336	.383	91	-3	14-2	.984	4	119	53	O71(0/53/18)	91	0.3
1997	†SF N	142	440	69	126	16	4	8	50	56-1	5	70	.286	.368	.395	104	4	25-3	.977	0	112	28	O130(5/46/94),1b3	0	0.5
1998	SF N	135	417	63	121	13	5	4	49	65-4	1	63	.290	.385	.374	107	6	21-5	.986	-7	98	0	O121(6/29/95)	0	-0.1
1999	SF N	112	333	49	92	15	1	3	30	29-4	1	55	.276	.335	.354	80	-10	13-6	.976	-1	98	76	O94(51/3/42)	0	-1.3
	†Hou N	20	64	12	21	4	1	0	4	9-0	0	8	.328	.405	.422	113	2	3-1	1.000	-0	94	106	O18(7/6/10)/D	0	0.1
	Year	132	397	61	113	19	2	3	34	38-4	1	63	.285	.347	.365	86	-8	16-7	.980	-1	97	81	O112(58/9/52)/D	0	-1.2
2000	†Sea A	105	342	61	94	18	5	5	40	42-2	0	64	.275	.351	.401	92	-4	4-3	.993	-4	85	124	O88(47/13/38),1b3,D4	0	-1.0
2001	†Sea A	89	281	44	82	14	1	4	33	36-1	2	47	.292	.375	.391	109	5	11-1	.993	-1	105	25	O76(62/13/11),1b6,D2	17	0.4
Total	17	1763	5047	781	1358	225	40	57	503	578-26	25	839	.269	.345	.363	93	-43	246-51	.988	23	107	66	O1513C,1b38,D15,2b3,3b2	167	-1.1
JEANES, TEX	Ernest Lee; B12.19.1900 Maypearl TX; D4.5.1973 Longview TX; BR/TR/6´0˝/176; d4.20; Col Trinity (TX)																								
1921	Cle A	5	3	2	2	1	0	0	4	1	0	0	.667	.750	1.000	338	1	0-0	1.000	1	49	854	O5(1/2/1)	—	0.2
1922	Cle A	1	1	0	0	0	0	0	0	1	0	0	.000	.500	.000	39	0	0-0	ø	-0	0	0	/Plf	—	0.0
1925	Was A	15	19	2	5	1	0	1	4	3	0	2	.263	.364	.474	113	0	1-0	1.000	-1	90	0	O13(1/10/2)	—	0.0
1926	Was A	21	30	6	7	2	0	0	3	0	0	3	.233	.233	.300	39	-3	0-0	1.000	1	133	0	O14(3/10/1)	—	-0.2
1927	NY N	11	20	5	6	0	0	0	0	2	0	2	.300	.364	.300	79	-1	0	1.000	1	123	166	O6(4/0/2)/P	—	0.0
Total	5	53	73	15	20	4	0	1	11	7	0	7	.274	.338	.370	85	-3	1-0	1.000	1	114	102	O39(10/22/6),P2	—	0.0
JEFFCOAT, HAL	Harold Bentley; B9.6.1924 W.Columbia SC; BR/TR/5´10.5˝/(185–198); d4.20; b–George; ▲																								
1948	Chi N	134	473	53	132	16	4	4	42	24	1	68	.279	.315	.355	85	-12	8	.976	3	102	146	O119C	0	-1.2
1949	Chi N	108	363	43	89	18	6	2	26	20	1	48	.245	.286	.344	70	-17	12	.963	0	97	148	O101(1/68/32)	0	-1.9
1950	Chi N	66	179	21	42	13	1	2	18	6	0	23	.235	.259	.352	60	-11	7	.967	0	91	177	O53(12/11/31)	0	-1.2
1951	Chi N	113	278	44	76	20	2	4	27	16	1	23	.273	.315	.403	90	-4	8-4	.989	5	102	175	O87(14/39/34)	0	-0.1
1952	Chi N	102	297	29	65	17	2	4	30	15	1	40	.219	.259	.330	61	-16	7-2	.996	10	108	209	O95C	0	-0.8
1953	Chi N	106	183	22	43	3	1	4	22	21	0	26	.235	.314	.328	66	-9	5-0	.973	5	113	116	O100(2/99/0)	0	-0.6
1954	Chi N	56	31	13	8	2	1	1	6	1	0	7	.258	.265	.484	94	-1	2-0	.889	0	112	69	P43,O3C	0	0.0
1955	Chi N	52	23	3	4	0	0	1	1	2-0	0	9	.174	.240	.304	43	1	0-0	.903	1	144	85	P50	0	0.0
1956	Cin N	49	54	5	8	2	0	0	5	3-0	0	20	.148	.193	.185	2	-1	0-1	.969	3	**148**	178	P38	0	0.0
1957	Cin N	53	69	13	14	3	1	4	11	5-0	1	20	.203	.267	.449	82	6	0-0	.958	-1	90	202	P37	0	0.0
1958	Cin N	50	9	2	5	0	0	0	0	1-0	0	2	.556	.600	.556	198	1	0-0	1.000	2	158	219	P49/cf	0	0.1
1959	Cin N	17	1	1	1	1	0	0	0	0-0	0	0	1.000	1.000	2.000	655	1	0-0	1.000	0	57	378	P17	0	0.0
	StL N	12	3	0	0	0	0	0	0	0-0	0	3	.000	.000	.000	-94	0	0-0	1.000	-0	104	0	P11	0	0.0
	Year	29	4	1	1	1	0	0	0	0-0	0	3	.250	.250	.500	90	0	0-0	1.000	-0	78	208	P28	0	0.0
Total	12	918	1963	249	487	95	18	26	188	114-0	5	289	.248	.291	.355	73	-62	49-7	.978	29	102	160	O559(29/435/97),P245	0	-5.7
JEFFERIES, GREGG	Gregory Scott; B8.1.1967 Burlingame CA; BB/TR/5´10˝/(170–185); [NYN85 1/20]; d9.6																								
1987	NY N	6	6	0	3	1	0	0	2	0-0	0	0	.500	.500	.667	214	1	0-0	ø	0	—	—	/H	0	0.1
1988	†NY N	29	109	19	35	8	2	6	17	8-0	0	10	.321	.364	.596	180	11	5-1	.979	-2	81	181	3b20,2b10	0	1.0
1989	NY N	141	508	72	131	28	2	12	56	39-8	5	46	.258	.314	.392	106	3	21-6	.975	-26	78	66	2b123,3b20	0	-1.8
1990	NY N	153	604	96	171	**40**	3	15	68	46-2	5	40	.283	.337	.434	111	9	11-2	.976	-1	88	86	2b118,3b34	0	1.3
1991	NY N	136	486	59	132	19	2	9	62	47-2	2	38	.272	.336	.374	101	1	26-5	.982	-15	87	42	2b77,3b51	16	-0.9
1992	KC A	152	604	66	172	36	3	10	75	43-4	1	29	.285	.329	.404	102	1	19-9	.939	2	106	87	3b146/2D	0	0.4
1993	StL N★	142	544	89	186	24	3	16	83	62-7	2	32	.342	.408	.485	140	33	46-9	.993	-7	84	110	1b140/2	0	2.1
1994	StL N★	103	397	52	129	27	1	12	55	45-12	1	26	.325	.391	.489	129	18	12-5	.993	-7	77	111	1b102	0	0.3
1995	Phi N	114	480	69	147	31	2	11	56	35-5	0	26	.306	.349	.448	109	6	9-5	.994	-5	76	112	1b59,O55L	15	-0.6
1996	Phi N	104	404	59	118	17	3	7	51	36-6	1	21	.292	.348	.401	97	-1	20-6	.998	5	108	94	1b53,O51L	60	0.0
1997	Phi N	130	476	68	122	25	3	11	48	53-7	2	27	.256	.333	.391	90	-7	12-6	.986	1	101	69	O124L	15	-1.0
1998	Phi N	125	483	65	142	22	3	8	48	29-4	1	27	.294	.331	.402	93	-6	11-3	.994	-4	82	100	O121L	0	-1.3
	Ana A	19	72	7	25	6	0	1	10	0-0	0	5	.347	.347	.472	108	1	1-0	1.000	0	113	0	O15L,1b3	0	0.0
1999	Det A	70	205	22	41	8	0	6	18	13-1	4	11	.200	.258	.327	48	-17	3-4	1.000	0	239	41	D45,1b3,2b2,O2L	47	-1.9
2000	Det A	41	142	18	39	8	0	2	14	16-1	0	10	.275	.344	.373	84	-3	0-2	.994	-3	122	116	1b20,2b14,3b6/lfD	124	-0.7
Total	14	1465	5520	761	1593	300	27	126	663	472-59	24	348	.289	.344	.421	106	50	196-63	.994	-62	87	108	1b380,O369L,2b346,3b277,D48	277	-3.0
JEFFERSON, REGGIE	Reginald Jirod; B9.25.1968 Tallahassee FL; BL/TL (BB 1991–93)/6´4˝/(210–215); [CinN86 3/72]; d5.18																								
1991	Cin N	5	7	1	1	0	0	1	1	1-0	0	2	.143	.250	.571	119	0	0-0	1.000	0	113	346	1b2	0	0.0
	Cle A	26	101	10	20	3	0	2	12	3-0	0	22	.198	.219	.287	39	-9	0-0	.993	2	133	122	1b26	16	-0.8
1992	Cle A	24	89	8	30	6	2	1	6	1-0	1	17	.337	.352	.483	133	3	0-0	.993	0	110	66	1b15,D7	89	0.3
1993	Cle A	113	366	35	91	11	2	10	34	28-7	5	78	.249	.310	.372	82	-10	1-3	.976	-0	111	87	D88,1b15	0	-1.7
1994	Sea A	63	162	24	53	11	0	8	32	17-5	1	32	.327	.392	.543	135	9	0-0	.981	1	156	143	D32,1b13,O2L	20	0.7
1995	†Bos A	46	121	21	35	8	0	5	26	9-1	0	24	.289	.333	.479	107	1	0-0	1.000	1	152	127	D32,1b7,O2L	71	0.0
1996	Bos A	122	386	67	134	30	4	19	74	25-5	3	89	.347	.388	.593	142	24	0-0	.969	0	89	44	D49,O45L,1b16	0	1.7
1997	Bos A	136	489	74	156	33	1	13	67	24-5	7	93	.319	.358	.470	112	8	1-2	.975	-1	81	108	D119,1b12	0	0.0
1998	Bos A	62	196	24	60	16	1	8	31	21-2	1	40	.306	.374	.520	127	8	0-0	.953	0	124	57	D48,1b7	75	0.5
1999	Bos A	83	206	21	57	13	1	5	17	17-0	2	54	.277	.338	.422	89	-3	0-0	1.000	0	278	0	D58,1b2	11	-0.6
Total	9	680	2123	285	637	131	11	72	300	146-25	20	451	.300	.349	.474	111	31	2-5	.986	5	129	100	D433,1b115,O49L	282	0.1
JEFFERSON, STAN	Stanley; B12.4.1962 New York NY; BB/TR/5´11˝/(175–180); [NYN83 1/20]; d9.7; Col Bethune–Cookman																								
1986	NY N	14	24	6	5	1	0	1	3	2-0	1	8	.208	.296	.375	86	-1	0-0	1.000	-0	98	0	O7(1/7/0)	0	-0.1
1987	SD N	116	422	59	97	8	7	8	29	39-2	2	92	.230	.296	.339	71	-19	34-11	.987	-0	103	50	O107(61/83/0)	39	-1.9
1988	SD N	49	111	16	16	1	2	1	4	9-0	1	22	.144	.211	.216	25	-11	5-1	1.000	-3	84	0	O38(10/27/0)	0	-1.6
1989	NY A	10	12	1	1	0	0	0	1	0-0	0	4	.083	.083	.083	-53	-2	1-1	1.000	-1	53	0	O7(0/2/6)/D	0	-0.3
	Bal A	35	127	19	33	7	0	4	20	4-0	1	22	.260	.284	.409	97	-1	9-3	.988	2	106	125	O32(1/8/26),D2	0	0.1
	Year	45	139	20	34	7	0	4	21	4-0	1	26	.245	.267	.381	84	-4	10-4	.988	1	102	116	O39(1/10/32),D3	0	-0.2
1990	Bal A	10	19	1	0	0	0	0	0	2-0	0	8	.000	.095	.000	-73	-5	1-0	1.000	-1	93	0	O5(0/3/5)/D	0	-0.5
	Cle A	49	98	21	27	8	0	2	10	8-0	2	18	.276	.333	.418	112	2	8-4	.985	2	103	247	O34(23/11/1),D5	0	0.4
	Year	59	117	22	27	8	0	2	10	10-0	2	26	.231	.295	.350	82	-3	9-4	.987	2	102	212	O39(23/14/6),D6	0	-0.1
1991	Cin N	13	19	2	1	0	0	0	0	1-0	0	3	.053	.100	.053	-54	-4	2-0	1.000	-1	56	0	O5(4/1/1)	0	-0.5
Total	6	296	832	125	180	25	9	16	67	65-2	7	177	.216	.276	.326	66	-40	60-20	.990	-2	99	76	O235(100/142/39),D9	39	-4.4
JEFFRIES, IRV	Irvine Franklin; B9.10.1905 Louisville KY; D6.8.1982 Louisville KY; BR/TR/5´10˝/175; d4.30; Col Kentucky																								
1930	Chi A	40	97	14	23	3	0	2	11	3	2	2	.237	.275	.330	54	-7	1-2	.976	-1	97	135	3b20,S13	—	-0.6
1931	Chi A	79	223	29	50	10	0	2	16	14	0	9	.224	.270	.296	52	-16	3-0	.949	1	102	42	3b61,2b6,S5/cf	—	-1.2
1934	Phi N	56	175	28	43	6	0	4	19	15	0	10	.246	.305	.349	66	-8	2	.962	3	101	147	2b52/3	—	-0.2
Total	3	175	495	71	116	19	0	8	46	32	2	21	.234	.284	.321	58	-31	6-2	.955	3	100	60	3b82,2b58,S18/cf	—	-2.0
JELIC, CHRIS	Christopher John; B12.16.1963 Bethlehem PA; BR/TR/5´11˝/180; [KCA85 2/45]; d9.30; Col Pittsburgh																								
1990	NY N	4	11	2	1	0	0	1	1	0-0	0	3	.091	.091	.364	19	-1	0-0	1.000	-1	22	0	O4L	0	-0.2

YEAR	TM LG	G	AB	R	H	2B	3B	HR	RBI	BB-IB	HP	SO	AVG	OBP	SLG	AOPS	ABR	SB-CS	FA	FR	RNG	THR	GAMES AT POSITION	DL	BFW
Jelincich, Frank	Frank Anthony "Jelly"; B9.3.1917 San Jose CA; D6.27.1992 Rochester MN; BR/TR/6´2˝/198; d9.6; Mil 1942–45																								
1941	Chi N	4	8	0	1	0	0	0	2	1	0	2	.125	.222	.125	-1	-1	0	1.000	-0	45	0	O2L	0	-0.1
Jelks, Greg	Gregory Dion; B8.16.1961 Cherokee AL; BR/TR/6´2˝/188; d8.20; Col Gadsden St. (AL) CC																								
1987	Phi N	10	11	2	1	1	0	0	0	3-0	0	4	.091	.286	.182	26	-1	0-0	.750	-0	67	0	3b4,1b2/lf	0	-0.2
Jeltz, Steve	Larry Steven; B5.28.1959 Paris, France; BB/TR (BR 1983–85)/5´11˝/(170–190); [PhiN80 9/221]; d7.17; Col Kansas																								
1983	Phi N	13	8	0	1	0	1	0	1	1-0	0	2	.125	.222	.375	63	-1	0-0	1.000	-1	43	201	2b4,S2,3b2	0	-0.1
1984	Phi N	28	68	7	14	0	1	1	7	7-1	0	11	.206	.276	.279	57	-4	2-1	.992	7	123	61	S27/3	0	0.5
1985	Phi N	89	196	17	37	4	1	0	12	26-4	0	55	.189	.283	.219	42	-15	1-1	.958	-3	98	87	S86	0	-1.1
1986	Phi N	145	439	44	96	11	4	0	36	65-9	1	97	.219	.320	.262	60	-22	6-3	.967	-5	100	100	S141	0	-1.3
1987	Phi N	114	293	37	68	9	6	0	12	39-4	1	54	.232	.324	.304	65	-14	1-2	.971	-6	91	97	S114/lf	0	-1.1
1988	Phi N	148	379	39	71	11	4	0	27	59-8	0	58	.187	.295	.237	54	-21	3-0	.976	-4	97	93	S148	0	-1.6
1989	Phi N	116	263	28	64	7	3	4	25	45-6	1	44	.243	.356	.338	99	1	4-2	.985	3	90	59	S63,3b30,2b23/cf	0	0.9
1990	KC A	74	103	11	16	4	0	0	10	6-0	0	21	.155	.200	.194	11	-12	1-1	.977	-0	99	92	2b34,S23,O13(1/1/11),3b3,D3	0	-1.2
Total	8	727	1749	183	367	46	20	5	130	248-32	3	342	.210	.308	.268	61	-88	18-10	.971	-9	97	90	S604,2b61,3b36,O15(2/2/11),D3	0	-5.0
Jenkins, Geoff	Geoffrey Scott; B7.21.1974 Olympia WA; BL/TR/6´1˝/(200–210); [MilA95 1/9]; d4.24; Col USC																								
1998	Mil N	84	262	33	60	12	1	9	28	20-4	2	61	.229	.288	.385	74	-11	1-3	.968	0	92	134	O81(81/0/1)	0	-1.4
1999	Mil N	135	447	70	140	43	3	21	82	35-7	7	87	.313	.371	.564	132	22	5-1	.974	11	109	187	O128L	0	2.7
2000	Mil N	135	512	100	155	36	4	34	94	33-6	15	135	.303	.360	.588	136	26	11-1	.975	7	101	145	O131L	22	2.8
2001	Mil N	105	397	60	105	21	1	20	63	36-7	8	120	.264	.334	.474	109	5	4-2	.986	6	107	115	O104L	47	0.7
2002	Mil N	67	243	35	59	17	1	10	29	22-1	6	60	.243	.320	.444	100	0	1-2	.992	4	103	172	O66L	104	0.0
2003	Mil N☆	124	487	81	144	30	2	28	95	58-10	6	120	.296	.375	.538	136	26	0-0	**1.000**	3	97	142	O123L/D	41	2.3
2004	Mil N	157	617	88	163	36	6	27	93	46-10	12	152	.264	.325	.473	103	1	3-1	.996	-1	94	117	O156L	0	-0.5
2005	Mil N	148	538	87	157	42	1	25	86	56-9	**19**	138	.292	.375	.513	130	25	0-0	.984	11	115	128	O144R,D2	0	2.9
2006	Mil N	147	484	62	131	26	1	17	70	56-8	11	129	.271	.357	.434	101	2	4-1	.977	2	102	101	O133R	0	-0.2
Total	9	1102	3987	616	1114	263	20	191	640	362-62	86	1002	.279	.350	.499	116	96	29-11	.984	43	103	135	O1066(789/0/278),D3	214	9.3
Jenkins, John	John Robert; B7.7.1896 Bosworth MO; D8.3.1968 Columbia MO; BR/TR/5´8˝/160; d8.5																								
1922	Chi A	5	3	0	0	0	0	0	1	0	0	2	.000	.000	.000	-99	-1	0-0	.000	-1	0	0	/2S	—	-0.1
Jenkins, Joe	Joseph Daniel; B10.12.1890 Shelbyville TN; D6.21.1974 Fresno CA; BR/TR/5´11˝/170; d4.30; Mil 1918																								
1914	StL A	19	32	0	4	1	1	0	0	1	0	11	.125	.152	.219	12	-4	2	.931	-3	*79*	*34*	C9	—	-0.6
1917	Chi A	10	9	0	1	0	0	0	2	0	0	5	.111	.111	.111	-32	-1	0	ø	0	*0*	*0*	/C	—	-0.2
1919	Chi A	11	19	0	3	1	0	0	1	1	0	1	.158	.200	.211	15	-2	1	.824	-1	*121*	*102*	C4	—	-0.3
Total	3	40	60	0	8	2	1	0	3	2	0	17	.133	.161	.200	6	-7	3	.891	-4	*93*	*58*	C14	—	-1.1
Jenkins, Tom	Thomas Griffith "Tut"; B4.10.1898 Camden AL; D5.3.1979 Weymouth MA; BL/TR/6´1.5˝/174; d9.15																								
1925	Bos A	15	64	9	19	2	1	0	5	3	1	4	.297	.338	.359	77	-2	0-0	.938	-2	94	0	O15L	—	-0.5
1926	Bos A	21	50	3	9	1	1	0	6	3	0	7	.180	.226	.240	22	-6	0-0	1.000	-1	96	0	O13(12/1/0)	—	-0.8
	Phi A	6	23	3	4	2	0	0	0	0	0	2	.174	.174	.261	12	-3	0-0	1.000	0	115	0	O6(5/0/1)	—	-0.4
	Year	27	73	6	13	3	1	0	6	3	0	9	.178	.211	.247	19	-9	0-0	1.000	-1	102	0	O19(17/1/1)	—	-1.2
1929	StL A	21	22	1	4	0	1	0	0	4	0	8	.182	.308	.273	49	-2	0-0	1.000	-0	66	0	O3(0/1/2)	—	-0.2
1930	StL A	2	8	1	2	1	1	0	3	0	0	1	.250	.250	.625	110	0	0-0	1.000	-0	98	0	O2R	—	0.0
1931	StL A	81	230	20	61	7	2	3	25	17	0	25	.265	.316	.352	73	-10	1-3	.952	-2	89	119	O58R	—	-1.4
1932	StL A	25	62	5	20	1	0	0	5	1	0	6	.323	.333	.339	70	-3	0-0	.939	1	111	197	O12R	—	-0.2
Total	6	171	459	42	119	14	6	3	44	28	1	53	.259	.303	.336	64	-26	1-3	.958	-4	95	86	O109(32/2/75)	—	-3.5
Jennings, Alamazoo	Alfred Gorden; B11.30.1850 Newport KY; D11.2.1894 Cincinnati OH; d8.15; U2																								
1878	Mil N	1	2	0	0	0	0	0	0	1	—	0	.000	.333	.000	16	0	—	.429	-2	—	—	/C	—	-0.2
Jennings, Hughie	Hugh Ambrose "Ee-Yah"; B4.2.1869 Pittston PA; D2.1.1928 Scranton PA; BR/TR/5´8.5˝/165; d6.1; M16/C5; HF1945; Col Mansfield																								
1891	Lou AA	88	351	51	103	10	8	1	58	17	9	35	.293	.342	.376	107	1	12	.891	6	100	118	S68,1b17,3b3	—	0.7
1892	Lou N	152	594	65	133	16	4	2	61	30	9	30	.224	.272	.274	71	-21	28	.907	15	105	111	S152	—	0.1
1893	Lou N	23	88	6	12	3	0	0	9	3	1	3	.136	.174	.170	-9	-14	0	.899	4	109	102	S23	—	-0.8
	Bal N	16	55	6	14	0	0	1	6	4	3	3	.255	.339	.309	71	-2	0	.886	-3	79	70	S15/rf	—	-0.4
	Year	39	143	12	26	3	0	1	15	7	4	6	.182	.240	.224	25	-16	0	.895	1	98	91	S38/rf	—	-1.2
1894	†Bal N	128	501	134	168	28	16	4	109	37	**27**	17	.335	.411	.479	109	7	37	**.928**	**33**	112	129	S128	—	3.5
1895	†Bal N	**131**	529	159	204	41	7	4	125	24	**32**	17	.386	.444	.512	142	35	53	**.940**	**37**	102	**147**	S131	—	**6.3**
1896	†Bal N	130	521	125	209	27	9	0	121	19	**51**	11	.401	.472	.488	151	43	70	**.928**	31	107	**138**	S130	—	**6.7**
1897	†Bal N	117	439	133	156	26	9	2	79	42	**46**	—	.355	.463	.469	146	36	60	**.933**	23	105	128	S116	—	**5.5**
1898	Bal N	143	534	135	175	25	11	1	87	78	**46**	—	.328	.454	.421	149	44	28	.929	3	96	97	S115,2b27/rf	—	**4.9**
1899	Bro N	16	41	7	7	0	2	0	6	9	2	—	.171	.346	.268	68	-2	4	.825	-5	64	80	S11,1b4	—	-0.5
	Bal N	2	8	2	3	0	2	0	2	0	0	—	.375	.375	.875	227	1	0	1.000	-0	93	0	2b2	—	0.1
	Bro N	51	175	35	57	3	8	0	34	13	17	—	.326	.424	.434	133	9	14	.987	-0	239	68	1b46/2S	—	0.8
	Year	69	224	44	67	3	12	0	42	22	19	—	.299	.408	.420	124	8	18	.985	-5	110	90	1b50,S12,2b3	—	0.4
1900	†Bro N	115	441	61	120	18	6	1	69	31	20	—	.272	.348	.347	87	-7	31	.982	5	119	111	1b112,2b2	—	-0.2
1901	Phi N	82	302	38	79	21	2	1	39	25	12	—	.262	.342	.354	100	2	13	.979	-3	85	57	1b80/2S	—	-0.3
1902	Phi N	78	290	32	79	13	4	1	32	14	11	—	.272	.330	.355	111	4	8	.983	2	118	81	1b69,S5,2b4	—	0.5
1903	Bro N	6	17	2	4	0	0	0	1	1	1	—	.235	.316	.235	60	-1	1	1.000	-0	0	0	O4(1/0/3)	—	-0.1
1907	Det A	1	4	0	1	1	0	0	0	0	0	—	.250	.250	.500	133	0	0	.750	-1	99	0	/2SM	—	-0.1
1909	Det A	2	4	1	2	0	0	0	2	0	0	—	.500	.500	.500	207	0	0	1.000	0	182	477	1b2,M	—	0.1
1910	Det A	1	0	0	0	0	0	0	0	0	0	—	ø	ø	ø	ø	0	0	ø	0	—	—	/RM	—	0.0
1912	Det A	1	1	0	0	0	0	0	0	0	0	—	.000	.000	.000	-99	0	0	ø	0	—	—	/HM	—	0.0
1918	Det A	1	0	0	0	0	0	0	0	0	0	0	ø	ø	ø	ø	0	0	1.000	-0	0	0	/1M	—	0.0
Total	18	1284	4895	992	1526	232	88	18	840	347	287	116	.312	.391	.406	118	135	359	.922	146	103	122	S897,1b331,2b38,O6(1/0/5),3b3	—	26.8
Jennings, Doug	James Douglas; B9.30.1964 Atlanta GA; BL/TL/5´10˝/(165–195); [CalA84*2/31]; d4.8; Col Brevard (FL) CC																								
1988	Oak A	71	101	9	21	6	0	1	15	21-1	2	28	.208	.346	.297	87	0	0-1	1.000	-0	107	119	O23(16/0/7),1b14,D2	34	-0.2
1989	Oak A	4	4	0	0	0	0	0	0	0-0	0	2	.000	.000	.000	-99	-1	0-0	1.000	-0	76	0	O3L	0	-0.1
1990	†Oak A	64	156	19	30	7	2	2	14	17-0	2	48	.192	.275	.301	65	-7	0-3	.984	-3	90	46	O45(33/0/15),1b4,D8	0	-1.3
1991	Oak A	8	9	0	1	0	0	0	0	2-0	0	2	.111	.273	.111	11	-1	0-1	1.000	1	151	0	O6L	0	-0.1
1993	Chi N	42	52	8	13	3	1	2	8	3-0	2	10	.250	.316	.462	106	0	0-0	1.000	-1	41	153	1b10	0	-0.1
Total	5	189	322	36	65	16	3	5	37	43-1	6	90	.202	.302	.317	76	-9	0-5	.991	-4	98	63	O77(58/0/22),1b28,D10	34	-1.8
Jennings, Robin	Robin Christopher; B4.11.1972 Singapore, Singapore; BL/TL/6´2˝/(205–210); [ChiN91 33/865]; d4.18; Col Manatee (FL) CC; [DL 1998 Chi N 69]																								
1996	Chi N	31	58	7	13	5	0	0	4	3-0	1	9	.224	.274	.310	52	-4	1-0	1.000	1	109	319	O11R	0	-0.3
1997	Chi N	9	18	1	3	1	0	0	2	0-0	0	2	.167	.158	.222	1	-3	0-0	1.000	-1	72	0	O5(4/2/0)	0	-0.3
1999	Chi N	5	5	0	1	0	0	0	0	0-0	0	2	.200	.200	.200	2	-1	0-0	ø	0	—	—	/H	77	-0.1
2001	Oak A	20	52	4	13	3	0	0	4	2-0	0	6	.250	.273	.308	54	-3	0-0	1.000	-1	67	154	O13(3/0/12),1b6,D2	0	-0.5
	Col N	1	3	0	0	0	0	0	0	0-0	0	1	.000	.000	.000	-83	-1	0-0	.000	-1	0	0	/lf	0	-0.1
	Cin N	27	77	10	22	5	2	3	14	5-1	0	11	.286	.329	.519	108	1	0-0	.893	1	89	233	O15R,1b8	0	0.0
	Year	28	80	10	22	5	2	3	14	5-1	0	12	.275	.318	.500	100	0	0-0	.862	0	83	217	O16(1/0/15),1b8	0	-0.1
Total	4	93	213	22	52	14	2	3	24	10-1	1	31	.244	.279	.371	66	-11	1-0	.942	0	84	204	O45(8/2/38),1b14,D2	146	-1.3
Jennings, Bill	William Lee; B9.28.1925 St.Louis MO; BR/TR/6´2˝/175; d7.19; Col Washington–St. Louis																								
1951	StL A	64	195	20	35	10	2	0	13	26	0	42	.179	.276	.251	42	-16	1-0	.953	-8	91	74	S64	0	-2.0
Jensen, Woody	Forrest Docenus; B8.11.1907 Bremerton WA; D10.5.2001 Wichita KS; BL/TL/5´10.5˝/160; d4.20; Col Western Washington																								
1931	Pit N	73	267	43	65	5	4	3	17	10	2	18	.243	.276	.326	62	-16	4	.974	3	116	51	O67(64/3/0)	—	-1.7
1932	Pit N	7	5	2	0	0	0	0	0	0	0	2	.000	.000	.000	-99	-1	0	ø	-0	0	0	/lf	—	-0.1
1933	Pit N	70	196	29	58	7	3	0	15	8	2	2	.296	.330	.362	98	-1	1	.980	-1	106	30	O40L	—	-0.4
1934	Pit N	88	283	34	82	13	4	0	27	4	2	13	.290	.304	.364	76	-10	2	.993	-0	107	23	O66(46/17/4)	—	-1.3
1935	Pit N	143	627	97	203	28	7	8	62	15	4	14	.324	.344	.429	103	1	9	.977	-6	93	59	O140(138/0/2)	—	-1.3

YEAR	TM LG	G	AB	R	H	2B	3B	HR	RBI	BB-IB	HP	SO	AVG	OBP	SLG	AOPS	ABR	SB-CS	FA	FR	RNG	THR	GAMES AT POSITION	DL	BFW
1936	Pit N	153	696	98	197	34	10	10	58	16	6	19	.283	.305	.404	87	-15	2	.975	-2	104	52	O153(152/1/0)	—	-2.5
1937	Pit N	124	509	77	142	23	9	5	45	15	1	29	.279	.301	.389	86	-12	2	.963	-2	103	58	O120(88/32/0)	—	-2.0
1938	Pit N	68	125	12	25	4	0	0	10	1	1	3	.200	.213	.232	22	-14	0	.900	-4	85	0	O38(15/21/2)	—	-1.9
1939	Pit N	12	12	0	2	0	0	0	1	0	0	0	.167	.167	.167	-10	-2	0	1.000	1	0	1636	O3(0/1/2)	—	-0.1
Total	9	738	2720	392	774	114	37	26	235	69	18	100	.285	.307	.382	84	-70	20	.972	-12	102	50	O628(544/75/10)	—	-11.3
Jensen, Jackie	Jack Eugene; B3.9.1927 San Francisco CA; D7.14.1982 Charlottesville VA; BR/TR/5´11˝/190; d4.18; Col California																								
1950	†NY A	45	70	13	12	2	2	1	5	7	0	8	.171	.247	.300	41	-7	4-0	.947	0	120	0	O23(17/0/7)	0	-0.7
1951	NY A	56	168	30	50	8	1	8	25	18	1	18	.298	.369	.500	138	8	8-2	.974	2	101	158	O48(21/27/1)	0	0.9
1952	NY A	7	19	3	2	1	1	0	2	4	0	4	.105	.261	.263	49	-1	1-0	1.000	-1	77	0	O5C	0	-0.2
	Was A★	144	570	80	163	29	5	10	80	63	3	40	.286	.360	.407	117	13	17-6	.977	3	102	135	O143(0/7/142)	0	1.4
	Year	151	589	83	165	30	6	10	82	67	3	44	.280	.357	.402	115	12	18-6	.978	2	101	132	O148(0/12/142)	0	1.2
1953	Was A	147	552	87	147	32	8	10	84	73	5	51	.266	.357	.408	109	8	18-8	.983	-8	95	65	O146(0/1/145)	0	-0.5
1954	Bos A	152	580	92	160	25	7	25	117	79	2	52	.276	.359	.472	115	12	**22**-7	.986	-11	88	90	O151(8/106/44)	0	-0.3
1955	Bos A★	152	574	95	158	27	6	26	**116**	89-8	3	63	.275	.369	.479	118	15	16-7	.977	-4	96	90	O150R	0	0.6
1956	Bos A	151	578	80	182	23	**11**	20	97	89-5	1	43	.315	.405	.497	123	20	11-3	.962	-5	93	108	O151R	0	1.1
1957	Bos A	145	544	82	153	29	2	23	103	75-3	2	66	.281	.367	.469	121	17	8-5	.960	1	97	148	O144(4/0/143)	0	1.3
1958	Bos A★	154	548	83	157	31	0	35	**122**	99-7	3	65	.286	.396	.535	144	37	9-4	.981	-2	96	102	O153(2/0/153)	0	3.1
1959	Bos A	148	535	101	148	31	0	28	**112**	88-3	0	67	.277	.372	.492	131	25	20-5	.982	11	**117**	146	O146(0/7/142)	0	3.3
1961	Bos A	137	498	64	131	21	2	13	66	66-2	3	69	.263	.350	.392	96	-1	9-8	.986	7	105	137	O131(2/0/129)	0	-0.4
Total	11	1438	5236	810	1463	259	45	199	929	750-28	23	546	.279	.369	.460	119	146	143-55	.977	-7	99	113	O1391(54/153/1207)	0	9.6
Jensen, Marcus	Marcus Christian; B12.14.1972 Oakland CA; BB/TR/6´4˝/(195–204); [SFN90 1/33]; d4.14																								
1996	SF N	9	19	4	4	1	0	0	4	8-0	0	7	.211	.444	.263	95	1	0-0	.955	1	154	166	C7	0	0.2
1997	SF N	30	74	5	11	2	0	1	3	7-1	0	23	.149	.222	.216	16	-9	0-0	.983	-7	113	134	C28	0	-1.5
	Det A	8	11	1	2	0	0	0	1	1-0	0	5	.182	.250	.182	15	-1	0-0	.964	0	0	0	C8	0	-0.1
1998	Mil N	2	2	0	0	0	0	0	0	0-0	0	2	.000	.000	.000	-98	-1	0-0	1.000	0	0	0	/C	0	-0.1
1999	StL N	16	34	5	8	5	0	1	1	6-1	0	12	.235	.350	.471	103	0	0-0	.988	3	185	130	C14	0	0.4
2000	Min A	52	139	16	29	7	1	3	14	24-0	0	36	.209	.325	.338	64	-7	0-1	.993	2	153	81	C49/D	0	-0.3
2001	Bos A	1	4	0	1	0	0	0	0	0-0	0	1	.250	.250	.250	32	0	0-0	1.000	1	0	321	/C	0	0.1
	Tex A	11	25	0	4	1	0	0	2	0-0	0	9	.160	.160	.200	-6	-4	0-0	1.000	-2	70	97	C11	0	-0.6
	Year	12	29	0	5	1	0	0	2	0-0	0	10	.172	.172	.207	-1	-4	0-0	1.000	-1	61	127	C12	0	-0.5
2002	Mil N	16	35	2	4	0	0	1	4	4-2	0	11	.114	.200	.200	7	-5	0-0	.976	2	155	175	C15	0	-0.3
Total	7	145	343	33	63	16	1	6	29	50-4	0	106	.184	.287	.289	48	-26	0-1	.985	-1	135	113	C134/D	0	-2.2
Jessee, Dan	Daniel Edward; B2.22.1901 Olive Hill KY; D4.30.1970 Venice FL; BL/TR/5´10˝/165; d8.14; Col Pacific (OR)																								
1929	Cle A	1	0	0	0	0	0	0	0	0	0	0	ø	ø	ø	ø	0	0-0	ø	0	—	—	/R	—	0.0
Jestadt, Garry	Garry Arthur; B3.19.1947 Chicago IL; BR/TR/6´2˝/(180–190); [ChiN65 7/121]; d9.17																								
1969	Mon N	6	6	1	0	0	0	0	1	0-0	0	0	.000	.000	.000	-99	-2	0-0	.667	-1	0	0	/S	0	-0.2
1971	Chi N	3	3	0	0	0	0	0	0	0-0	0	0	.000	.000	.000	-87	-1	0-0	ø	-0	0	0	/3	0	-0.1
	SD N	75	189	17	55	13	0	0	13	11-0	0	24	.291	.328	.360	102	0	1-3	.935	2	129	65	3b49,2b23/S	0	0.2
	Year	78	192	17	55	13	0	0	13	11-0	0	24	.286	.324	.354	98	-1	1-3	.935	1	128	64	3b50,2b23/S	0	0.1
1972	SD N	92	256	15	63	5	1	6	22	13-2	0	21	.246	.281	.344	83	-7	0-0	.944	-17	80	80	2b48,3b25,S3	0	-2.3
Total	3	176	454	33	118	18	1	6	36	24-2	0	45	.260	.296	.344	87	-10	1-3	.942	-16	111	81	3b75,2b71,S5	0	-2.4
Jeter, Derek	Derek Sanderson; B6.26.1974 Pequannock NJ; BR/TR/6´3˝/(185–195); [NYA92 1/6]; d5.29																								
1995	NY A	15	48	5	12	4	1	0	7	3-0	0	11	.250	.294	.375	73	-2	0-0	.962	-4	83	81	S15	0	-0.4
1996	†NY A	157	582	104	183	25	6	10	78	48-1	9	102	.314	.370	.430	103	3	14-7	.969	-2	96	80	S157	0	1.3
1997	†NY A	159	654	116	190	31	7	10	70	74-0	10	125	.291	.370	.405	104	5	23-12	.975	-6	96	88	S159	0	1.2
1998	†NY A★	149	626	**127**	203	25	8	19	84	57-1	5	119	.324	.384	.481	129	26	30-6	.986	-22	88	97	S148	15	1.9
1999	†NY A★	158	627	134	**219**	37	9	24	102	91-5	12	116	.349	.438	.552	154	56	19-8	.978	-32	83	83	S158	0	3.4
2000	†NY A★	148	593	119	201	31	4	15	73	68-4	12	99	.339	.416	.481	128	29	22-4	.961	-36	79	80	S148	14	0.7
2001	†NY A★	150	614	110	191	35	3	21	74	56-3	10	99	.311	.377	.480	123	22	27-3	.974	-27	81	78	S150	6	1.0
2002	†NY A★	157	644	124	191	26	0	18	75	73-2	7	114	.297	.373	.421	112	13	32-3	.977	-40	80	73	S156/D	0	-0.9
2003	†NY A	119	482	87	156	25	3	10	52	43-2	13	88	.324	.393	.450	124	18	11-5	.968	-31	80	70	S118	42	-0.2
2004	†NY A★	154	643	111	188	44	1	23	78	46-1	14	99	.292	.352	.471	112	12	23-4	.981	-5	92	101	S154	0	2.1
2005	†NY A	159	654	122	202	25	5	19	70	77-3	11	117	.309	.389	.450	124	25	14-5	.979	9	102	95	S157/D	0	4.5
2006	†NY A★	154	623	118	214	39	3	14	97	69-4	12	102	.343	.417	.483	133	34	34-5	.975	-21	90	87	S150,D5	0	2.9
Total	12	1679	6790	1277	2150	347	50	183	860	705-26	115	1191	.317	.388	.463	122	241	249-62	.975	-215	88	85	S1670,D7	77	17.5
Jeter, Johnny	John; B10.24.1944 Shreveport LA; BR/TR/6´1˝/180; d6.14; s–Shawn; Col Grambling St.																								
1969	Pit N	28	29	7	9	1	1	1	6	3-1	0	15	.310	.375	.517	151	2	1-1	1.000	-0	79	186	O20(16/1/4)	0	0.1
1970	†Pit N	85	126	27	30	3	2	2	12	13-1	1	34	.238	.314	.341	76	-5	9-5	1.000	-1	90	96	O56(35/10/11)	0	-0.7
1971	SD N	18	75	8	24	4	0	1	3	2-0	0	16	.320	.338	.413	119	2	2-0	.967	2	87	66	O17C	0	0.4
1972	SD N	110	326	25	72	4	3	7	21	18-4	2	92	.221	.266	.316	70	-15	11-5	.987	-1	109	20	O91C	0	-1.9
1973	Chi A	89	300	38	72	14	4	7	26	9-0	0	74	.240	.260	.383	77	-11	4-3	.955	-3	97	63	O72(19/27/29),D3	0	-1.8
1974	Cle A	6	17	3	6	1	0	0	1	1-0	0	6	.353	.389	.412	131	1	1-2	.833	-1	57	0	O6(5/1/0)	0	-0.1
Total	6	336	873	108	213	27	10	18	69	46-6	3	237	.244	.283	.360	81	-26	28-16	.975	-4	98	55	O262(75/147/44),D3	0	-4.0
Jeter, Shawn	Shawn Darrell; B6.28.1966 Shreveport LA; BL/TR/6´2˝/185; [TorA85 7/183]; d6.13; f–Johnny																								
1992	Chi A	13	18	1	2	0	0	0	0	0-0	0	7	.111	.111	.111	-38	-3	0-0	.909	-0	114	0	O8(1/1/6),D3	0	-0.4
Jethroe, Sam	Samuel "Jet"; B1.20.1918 E.St.Louis IL; D6.16.2001 Erie PA; BB/TR/6´1˝/178; d4.18; Negro Lg 1938–48																								
1950	Bos N	141	582	100	159	28	8	18	58	52	5	93	.273	.338	.442	110	7	**35**	.969	3	98	148	O141C	0	0.6
1951	Bos N	148	572	101	160	29	10	18	65	57	11	88	.280	.356	.460	127	21	**35**-5	.974	-2	94	142	O140(13/127/2)	0	2.0
1952	Bos N	151	608	79	141	23	7	13	58	68	9	112	.232	.318	.357	90	-8	28-9	.970	-4	102	66	O151(1/150/0)	0	-1.4
1954	Pit N	2	1	0	0	0	0	0	0	0	0	0	.000	.000	.000	-99	0	0-0	1.000	0	153	0	/rf	0	0.0
Total	4	442	1763	280	460	80	25	49	181	177	25	293	.261	.337	.418	108	20	98-14	.971	-3	98	117	O433(14/418/3)	0	1.2
Jewett, Nat	Nathan W.; B12.25.1844 New York NY; D2.23.1914 Bronx NY; 5´9˝/137; d7.4																								
1872	Eck NA	2	8	1	1	0	0	0	0	0	—	0	.125	.125	.125	-27	-1	0-0	.700	-2	—	—	C2	—	-0.2
Jimenez, Houston	Alfonso (Gonzales); B10.30.1957 Mexico City, Distrito Federal, Mexico; BR/TR/5´8˝/(140–150); d6.13																								
1983	Min A	36	86	5	15	5	1	0	9	4-0	0	11	.174	.207	.256	27	-9	0-1	.969	-1	97	110	S36	0	-0.7
1984	Min A	108	298	28	60	11	1	0	19	15-0	0	34	.201	.238	.245	33	-27	0-1	.959	-12	94	104	S107	0	-3.1
1987	Pit N	5	6	0	0	0	0	0	0	1-0	0	2	.000	.143	.000	-57	-1	0-0	1.000	1	0	0	2b2,S2	0	0.0
1988	Cle A	9	21	1	1	0	0	0	1	0-0	0	2	.048	.048	.048	-71	-5	0-0	.973	5	173	84	2b7,S2	0	0.0
Total	4	158	411	34	76	16	2	0	29	20-0	0	49	.185	.221	.234	25	-42	0-2	.962	-7	96	107	S147,2b9	0	-3.8
Jimenez, D'Angelo	D'Angelo; B12.21.1977 Santo Domingo, D.R.; BB/TR/6´0˝/(160–215); d9.15; [DL 2000 NY A 142]																								
1999	NY A	7	20	3	8	2	0	0	4	3-0	0	4	.400	.478	.500	152	2	0-0	1.000	-0	101	295	3b6/2	0	0.1
2001	SD N	86	308	45	85	19	0	3	33	39-4	0	68	.276	.355	.367	95	-1	2-3	.948	4	107	91	S85	0	0.8
2002	SD N	87	321	39	77	11	4	3	33	34-1	0	63	.240	.311	.327	75	-12	4-2	.975	17	110	123	2b54,3b32/P	0	0.8
	Chi A	27	108	22	31	4	3	1	11	16-0	1	10	.287	.384	.407	107	1	2-1	.988	5	109	147	2b17,S10/3	0	0.8
2003	Chi A	73	271	35	69	11	5	7	26	32-1	0	46	.255	.332	.410	91	-4	4-3	.977	-6	90	99	2b68,3b2	0	-0.7
	Cin N	73	290	34	84	13	2	7	31	34-0	2	43	.290	.365	.421	110	5	7-4	.990	-2	99	105	2b73,3b2	0	0.7
2004	Cin N	152	563	76	152	28	3	12	67	82-1	2	99	.270	.364	.394	98	1	13-7	.990	-18	93	77	2b146,S5	0	-0.9
2005	Cin N	35	105	14	24	7	0	0	5	14-0	0	23	.229	.319	.295	62	-5	2-1	.983	-1	93	99	2b27	0	-0.5
2006	Tex A	20	57	7	12	3	0	1	8	10-0	0	6	.211	.328	.316	68	-2	0-0	.944	-5	73	111	2b16,3b2	0	-0.6
	†Oak A	8	14	1	1	0	0	0	0	6-2	0	7	.071	.350	.071	19	-1	0-0	.667	-3	47	0	3b3,S3,2b2	0	-0.4
	Year	28	71	8	13	3	0	1	8	16-2	0	13	.183	.333	.268	59	-4	0-0	.946	-8	70	102	2b18,3b5,S3	0	-1.0
Total	7	568	2057	276	543	98	17	34	218	270-9	5	369	.264	.349	.378	93	-16	34-21	.983	-9	95	97	2b404,S103,3b48/P	142	0.1
Jimenez, Elvio	Felix Elvio (Rivera); B1.6.1940 San Pedro de Macoris, D.R.; BR/TR/5´9˝/170; d10.4; b–Manny																								
1964	NY A	1	6	0	2	0	0	0	0	0-0	0	0	.333	.333	.333	85	0	0-0	1.000	0	153	0	/lf	0	0.0

YEAR	TM LG	G	AB	R	H	2B	3B	HR	RBI	BB-IB	HP	SO	AVG	OBP	SLG	AOPS	ABR	SB-CS	FA	FR	RNG	THR	GAMES AT POSITION	DL	BFW
JIMENEZ, MANNY	Manuel Emilio (Rivera); B11.19.1938 San Pedro de Macoris, D.R.; BL/TR/6´1˝/(185–195); d4.11; b–Elvio																								
1962	KC A	139	479	48	144	24	2	11	69	31-3	11	34	.301	.354	.428	105	4	0-1	.985	-5	82	109	O122(116/0/6)	0	-0.8
1963	KC A	60	157	12	44	9	0	0	15	16-2	5	14	.280	.361	.338	93	0	0-1	.960	2	91	233	O40(33/0/8)	0	-0.1
1964	KC A	95	204	19	46	7	0	12	38	15-1	5	24	.225	.293	.436	97	-1	0-0	.939	-2	83	146	O49(46/0/4)	0	-0.5
1966	KC A	13	35	1	4	0	1	0	1	6-0	0	4	.114	.244	.171	22	-4	0-0	.909	-1	55	182	O12(8/0/4)	0	-0.6
1967	Pit N	50	56	3	14	2	0	2	10	1-0	1	4	.250	.276	.393	89	-1	0-0	1.000	-1	69	0	O6L	0	-0.2
1968	Pit N	66	66	7	20	1	1	1	11	6-0	5	15	.303	.403	.394	142	4	0-0	.857	-1	87	0	O5L	0	0.4
1969	Chi N	6	6	0	1	0	0	0	0	0-0	0	2	.167	.167	.167	-6	-1	0-0	ø	0	—	—	/H	0	-0.1
Total	7	429	1003	90	273	43	4	26	144	75-6	27	97	.272	.337	.401	100	1	0-2	.966	-7	83	138	O234(214/0/22)	0	-1.9
JIMERSON, CHARLTON	Charlton Maxwell; B9.22.1979 San Leandro CA; BR/TR/6´3˝/210; [HouN01 5/146]; d9.14; Col Miami																								
2005	Hou N	1	0	0	0	0	0	0	0	0-0	0	0	ø	ø	ø	ø	0	0-0	ø	-0	0	0	/cf	0	0.0
2006	Hou N	17	6	2	2	0	0	1	1	0-0	0	3	.333	.333	.833	180	1	2-0	1.000	0	175	0	O9(0/1/9)	0	0.1
Total	2	18	6	2	2	0	0	1	1	0-0	0	3	.333	.333	.833	180	1	2-0	1.000	0	164	0	O10(0/2/9)	0	0.1
JOHJIMA, KENJI	Kenji; B6.8.1976 Nagasaki, Japan; BR/TR/6´0˝/200; d4.3																								
2006	Sea A	144	506	61	147	25	1	18	76	20-1	13	46	.291	.332	.451	107	4	3-1	.993	-4	124	95	C144	0	0.9
JOHNS, KEITH	Robert Keith; B7.19.1971 Callahan FL; BR/TR/6´1˝/175; [StLN92 6/167]; d5.23; Col U. of Mississippi																								
1998	Bos A	2	0	0	0	0	0	0	0	1-0	0	0	ø	1.000	ø	187	0	0-0	1.000	0	150	755	/2D	0	0.1
JOHNS, TOMMY	Thomas Pearce; B9.7.1851 Baltimore MD; D4.13.1927 Baltimore MD; d5.14																								
1873	Mar NA	1	4	0	0	0	0	0	0	0	—	0	.000	.000	.000	-99	-1	0-0	.000	-1	0	0	/lf	—	-0.1
JOHNS, PETE	William R.; B1.17.1888 Cleveland OH; D8.9.1964 Cleveland OH; BR/TR/5´10˝/165; d8.25																								
1915	Chi A	28	100	7	21	2	1	0	11	8	1	11	.210	.275	.250	56	-6	2-7	.943	0	102	112	3b28	—	-0.7
1918	StL A	46	89	5	16	1	1	0	11	4	0	6	.180	.215	.213	30	-8	0	.990	-1	177	60	1b10,S4,3b4,O4(1/3/0),2b2	—	-1.0
Total	2	74	189	12	37	3	2	0	22	12	1	17	.196	.248	.233	44	-14	2-7	.929	-0	100	105	3b32,1b10,O4(1/3/0),S4,2b2	—	-1.7
JOHNSON, ABBIE	Albert J.; B1.19.1874 Ontario, Can; D11.28.1960 Detroit MI; 5´9.5˝/165; d9.1																								
1896	Lou N	25	87	10	20	2	1	0	14	4	0	6	.230	.264	.276	44	-7	0	.937	-3	87	84	2b25	—	-0.8
1897	Lou N	49	165	16	40	6	1	0	23	13	1	—	.242	.302	.291	59	-10	2	.882	-9	92	67	2b34,S12	—	-1.4
Total	2	74	252	26	60	8	2	0	37	17	1	6	.238	.289	.286	54	-17	2	.904	-12	90	74	2b59,S12	—	-2.2
JOHNSON, ALEX	Alexander; B12.7.1942 Helena AR; BR/TR/6´0˝/(200–205); d7.25																								
1964	Phi N	43	109	18	33	7	1	4	18	6-1	1	26	.303	.345	.495	135	5	1-2	.980	1	105	60	O35(34/0/1)	0	0.4
1965	Phi N	97	262	27	77	9	3	8	28	15-3	2	60	.294	.337	.443	120	6	4-4	.966	0	102	89	O82(76/9/1)	0	0.3
1966	StL N	25	86	7	16	0	1	2	6	5-1	0	18	.186	.231	.279	41	-7	1-1	.962	-2	65	139	O22L	0	-1.1
1967	StL N	81	175	20	39	9	2	1	12	9-0	3	26	.223	.271	.314	68	-7	6-3	.970	5	113	231	O57(5/6/48)	0	-0.5
1968	Cin N	149	603	79	188	32	6	2	58	26-4	3	71	.312	.342	.395	114	10	16-6	.947	-0	103	86	O140(140/0/1)	0	0.4
1969	Cin N	139	523	86	165	18	4	17	88	25-1	9	69	.315	.350	.463	122	14	11-8	.927	-2	101	71	O132L	0	0.5
1970	Cal A★	156	614	85	202	26	6	14	86	35-9	7	68	**.329**	.370	.459	132	25	17-2	.959	-0	98	112	O156(155/0/1)	0	1.9
1971	Cal A	65	242	19	63	8	0	2	21	15-3	2	34	.260	.308	.318	84	-6	5-2	.926	-7	76	81	O61L	97	-1.7
1972	Cle A	108	356	31	85	10	1	8	37	22-10	1	40	.239	.283	.340	82	-9	6-8	.955	-5	88	60	O95L	0	-2.4
1973	Tex A	158	624	62	179	26	3	8	68	32-5	2	82	.287	.322	.377	100	-2	10-5	.987	1	94	148	D116,O41(40/1/0)	0	-0.6
1974	Tex A	114	453	57	132	14	3	4	41	28-4	4	59	.291	.338	.362	104	2	20-9	.956	4	108	114	O81L,D32	0	0.2
	NY A	10	28	3	6	1	0	1	2	0-0	0	3	.214	.214	.357	63	-2	0-0	ø	-0	0	0	/lfD	0	-0.2
	Year	124	481	60	138	15	3	5	43	28-4	4	62	.287	.331	.362	102	0	20-9	.956	4	107	113	O82L,D36	0	0.0
1975	NY A	52	119	15	31	5	1	1	15	7-1	0	21	.261	.297	.345	83	-3	2-3	1.000	-1	83	0	D28,O7(5/0/2)	0	-0.5
1976	Det A	125	429	41	115	15	2	6	45	19-1	2	49	.268	.298	.354	88	-8	14-10	.954	-5	90	111	O90L,D19	0	-2.0
Total	13	1322	4623	550	1331	180	33	78	525	244-43	36	626	.288	.326	.392	105	18	113-63	.953	-10	97	100	O1000(937/16/54),D199	97	-5.3
JOHNSON, TONY	Anthony Clair; B6.23.1956 Memphis TN; BR/TR/6´3˝/195; [MonN77 26/631]; d9.27; Col LeMoyne–Owen (TN)																								
1981	Mon N	2	1	0	0	0	0	0	0	0-0	0	0	.000	.000	.000	-97	0	0-0	ø	-0	0	0	/lf	0	0.0
1982	Tor A	70	98	17	23	2	1	3	14	11-1	0	26	.235	.309	.367	79	-3	3-13	.979	2	108	176	O28(25/2/2),D28	0	-0.7
Total	2	72	99	17	23	2	1	3	14	11-1	0	26	.232	.306	.364	77	-3	3-13	.979	2	107	175	O29(26/2/2),D28	0	-0.7
JOHNSON, BEN	Benjamin Joseph; B6.18.1981 Memphis TN; BR/TR/6´1˝/200; [StLN99 4/127]; d6.26																								
2005	†SD N	31	75	10	16	8	1	3	13	11-1	0	23	.213	.310	.467	106	1	0-2	.962	0	115	0	O29(13/9/11)	0	0.0
2006	SD N	58	120	19	30	5	2	4	12	14-2	1	36	.250	.333	.425	98	-1	3-0	1.000	3	122	58	O43(22/17/4)	27	0.2
Total	2	89	195	29	46	13	3	7	25	25-3	1	59	.236	.324	.441	101	0	3-2	.986	3	119	35	O72(35/26/15)	27	0.2
JOHNSON, BOB	Bobby Earl; B7.31.1959 Dallas TX; BR/TR/6´3˝/195; [TexA77 9/217]; d9.1																								
1981	Tex A	6	18	2	5	0	0	2	4	1-0	0	3	.278	.316	.611	170	1	0-0	1.000	-0	118	0	C5/1	0	0.1
1982	Tex A	20	56	4	7	2	0	2	7	3-0	1	22	.125	.183	.268	23	-6	0-1	1.000	0	146	122	C14,1b3	0	-0.6
1983	Tex A	72	175	18	37	6	1	5	16	16-0	1	55	.211	.280	.343	72	-7	3-0	1.000	4	137	75	C62,1b10	0	-0.1
Total	3	98	249	24	49	8	1	9	27	20-0	2	80	.197	.261	.345	67	-12	3-1	1.000	4	138	81	C81,1b14	0	-0.6
JOHNSON, BRIAN	Brian David; B1.8.1968 Oakland CA; BR/TR/6´2˝/(200–210); [NYA89 16/415]; d4.5; Col Stanford																								
1994	SD N	36	93	7	23	4	1	3	16	5-0	0	21	.247	.283	.409	81	-3	0-0	1.000	3	66	178	C24,1b5	0	0.1
1995	SD N	68	207	20	52	9	0	3	29	11-2	1	39	.251	.287	.338	68	-10	0-0	.993	2	111	87	C55,1b2	0	-0.4
1996	†SD N	82	243	18	66	13	1	8	35	4-2	4	36	.272	.290	.432	93	-4	0-0	.989	-2	95	88	C66/13	0	-0.2
1997	Det A	45	139	13	33	6	1	2	18	5-1	0	19	.237	.262	.338	56	-10	1-0	.987	-10	80	66	C43,D2	0	-1.6
	†SF N	56	179	19	50	7	2	11	27	14-7	2	26	.279	.333	.525	124	5	0-1	.995	3	127	101	C55,1b2	0	1.1
1998	SF N	99	308	34	73	8	1	13	34	28-4	5	67	.237	.310	.396	89	-6	0-2	.994	-3	132	81	C95/lf	33	-0.4
1999	Cin N	45	117	12	27	7	0	5	18	9-0	0	31	.231	.286	.419	73	-5	0-0	.995	4	147	82	C39	48	0.1
2000	KC A	37	125	9	26	6	0	4	18	4-0	0	28	.208	.229	.352	43	-11	0-0	.991	-1	68	90	C37	0	-1.0
2001	LA N	3	4	0	1	0	0	0	1	0-0	0	1	.250	.250	.250	32	0	0-0	1.000	-0	0	0	C2	0	0.0
Total	8	471	1415	132	351	60	6	49	196	80-16	12	268	.248	.291	.403	81	-44	1-3	.993	-3	108	91	C416,1b10,D2/lf3	81	-2.3
JOHNSON, CALEB	Caleb Clark; B5.23.1844 Fulton IL; D3.7.1925 Sterling IL; d5.20																								
1871	Cle NA	16	67	10	15	1	0	0	7	0	—	1	.224	.224	.239	35	-5	1-0	.736	-4	81	88	2b10,O6R	—	-0.6
JOHNSON, CHARLIE	Charles Cleveland "Home Run"; B3.12.1885 Slatington PA; D8.28.1940 Marcus Hook PA; BL/TL/5´9˝/150; d9.21																								
1908	Phi N	6	16	2	4	0	1	0	2	1	1	—	.250	.333	.375	122	0	0	1.000	-0	0	0	O4(1/3/0)	—	0.0
JOHNSON, CHARLES	Charles Edward; B7.20.1971 Fort Pierce FL; BR/TR/6´2˝/(215–225); [FlaN92 1/28]; d5.6; Col Miami																								
1994	Fla N	4	11	5	5	1	0	1	4	1-0	0	4	.455	.462	.818	227	2	0-0	1.000	1	0	106	C4	0	0.3
1995	Fla N	97	315	40	79	15	1	11	39	46-2	4	71	.251	.351	.410	99	0	0-2	.992	4	145	122	C97	23	1.0
1996	Fla N	120	386	34	84	13	1	13	37	40-6	2	91	.218	.292	.358	73	-16	1-0	**.995**	19	**203**	114	C120	35	1.1
1997	†Fla N★	124	416	43	104	26	1	19	63	60-6	3	109	.250	.347	.454	113	9	0-2	**1.000**	14	153	**128**	C123	0	2.9
1998	Fla N	31	113	13	25	5	0	7	23	16-0	0	30	.221	.315	.451	106	1	0-1	.990	-6	112	80	C31	0	-0.4
	LA N	102	346	31	75	13	0	12	35	29-1	1	99	.217	.279	.358	70	-17	0-1	.992	6	154	107	C100	0	-0.5
	Year	133	459	44	100	18	0	19	58	45-1	1	129	.218	.289	.381	78	-16	0-2	.992	-0	144	101	C131	0	-0.9
1999	Bal A	135	426	58	107	19	1	16	54	55-2	4	107	.251	.340	.413	95	-3	0-0	.994	5	128	97	C135	0	0.9
2000	Bal A	84	286	52	84	16	0	21	55	32-0	0	69	.294	.364	.570	138	16	2-0	.994	-9	119	72	C83/D	0	1.2
	†Chi A	44	135	24	44	8	0	10	36	20-0	1	37	.326	.411	.607	149	11	0-0	.987	-7	144	97	C43	0	0.6
	Year	128	421	76	128	24	0	31	91	52-0	1	106	.304	.379	.582	142	27	2-0	.992	-16	127	80	C126/D	0	1.8
2001	Fla N★	128	451	51	117	32	0	18	75	38-2	4	133	.259	.321	.450	100	-1	0-0	.996	3	128	110	C125	0	1.0
2002	Fla N	83	244	18	53	19	0	6	36	31-7	0	61	.217	.301	.369	79	-7	0-0	.994	0	106	**135**	C82	27	-0.2
2003	Col N	108	356	49	82	20	0	20	61	49-2	1	84	.230	.320	.455	88	-6	1-3	.993	-5	143	114	C107	0	-0.5
2004	Col N	109	305	42	72	20	0	13	47	49-1	5	91	.236	.350	.430	89	-4	2-1	.988	-7	74	91	C91	0	-0.4
2005	TB A	19	46	5	9	4	0	0	5	9-0	0	11	.196	.327	.283	66	-2	0-0	.959	-5	59	148	C19	0	-0.6
Total	12	1188	3836	465	940	211	4	167	570	475-29	25	997	.245	.330	.433	97	-17	6-10	.993	13	136	109	C1160/D	85	6.4

YEAR	TM LG	G	AB	R	H	2B	3B	HR	RBI	BB-IB	HP	SO	AVG	OBP	SLG	AOPS	ABR	SB-CS	FA	FR	RNG	THR	GAMES AT POSITION	DL	BFW
JOHNSON, CLIFF	Clifford; B7.22.1947 San Antonio TX; BR/TR/6´4˝/(212–225); [HouN66 5/83]; d9.13																								
1972	Hou N	5	4	0	1	0	0	0	0	2-0	0	0	.250	.500	.250	122	0	0-0	1.000	1	0	0	/C	0	0.1
1973	Hou N	7	20	6	6	2	0	2	6	1-0	1	7	.300	.364	.700	190	2	0-0	1.000	-0	68	169	1b5	0	0.2
1974	Hou N	83	171	26	39	4	1	10	29	33-1	3	45	.228	.357	.439	129	7	0-1	.978	-2	66	82	C28,1b21	0	0.4
1975	Hou N	122	340	52	94	16	1	20	65	46-5	5	64	.276	.370	.506	152	24	1-0	.991	-14	70	84	1b47,C41/lf	0	0.9
1976	Hou N	108	318	36	72	21	2	10	49	62-6	4	59	.226	.359	.399	125	13	0-0	.977	-14	54	104	C66,O20L,1b16	0	0.1
1977	Hou N	51	144	22	43	8	0	10	23	23-2	4	30	.299	.409	.563	171	15	0-1	.946	1	85	205	O34(33/0/4),1b10	0	1.4
	†NY A	56	142	24	42	8	0	12	31	20-0	6	23	.296	.405	.606	172	15	0-1	1.000	2	721	108	D25,C15,1b11	0	1.6
1978	†NY A	76	174	20	32	9	1	6	19	30-5	1	32	.184	.307	.351	86	-3	0-0	.975	-5	101	72	D39,C22/1	0	-0.8
1979	NY A	28	64	11	17	6	0	2	6	10-4	0	7	.266	.360	.453	121	2	0-0	1.000	-1	92	99	D22,C4	0	0.1
	Cle A	72	240	37	65	10	0	18	61	24-1	5	39	.271	.343	.538	135	11	2-0	ø	-0	0	0	D62/C	0	0.9
	Year	100	304	48	82	16	0	20	67	34-5	5	46	.270	.347	.520	132	14	2-0	1.000	-1	85	91	D84,C5	0	1.0
1980	Cle A	54	174	25	40	3	1	6	28	25-5	0	30	.230	.320	.362	87	-3	0-1	ø	0	0	0	D45	0	-0.5
	Chi N	68	196	28	46	8	0	10	34	29-5	1	35	.235	.335	.429	103	1	0-0	.992	-6	53	90	1b46,O3L/C	0	-0.8
1981	†Oak A	84	273	40	71	8	0	17	59	28-2	3	60	.260	.329	.476	136	12	5-3	1.000	-1	24	41	D68,1b9	0	0.9
1982	Oak A	73	214	19	51	10	0	7	31	26-2	2	41	.238	.324	.383	97	0	1-2	.987	1	134	88	D48,1b11	27	-0.2
1983	Tor A	142	407	59	108	23	1	22	76	67-8	5	69	.265	.373	.489	127	17	0-1	1.000	0	98	106	D130,1b6	0	1.3
1984	Tor A	127	359	51	109	23	1	16	61	50-4	3	62	.304	.390	.507	141	22	0-1	1.000	-1	0	0	D109,1b2	0	1.8
1985	Tex A	82	296	31	76	17	1	12	56	31-2	3	44	.257	.330	.443	108	4	0-0	ø	0	0	0	D82	38	0.1
	†Tor A	24	73	4	20	0	0	1	10	9-0	0	15	.274	.349	.315	83	-2	0-0	.947	-1	57	225	D21,1b3	0	-0.3
	Year	106	369	35	96	17	1	13	66	40-2	3	59	.260	.334	.417	103	2	0-0	.947	-1	57	225	D103,1b3	0	-0.2
1986	Tor A	107	336	48	84	12	1	15	55	52-1	4	57	.250	.355	.426	109	5	0-1	1.000	0	124	244	D95/1	15	0.2
Total	15	1369	3945	539	1016	188	10	196	699	568-53	50	719	.258	.355	.459	125	142	9-12	.993	-40	72	97	D746,1b189,C179,O58(57/0/4)	80	7.4
JOHNSON, DAN	Daniel Ryan; B8.10.1979 Coon Rapids MN; BL/TR/6´2˝/(220–225); [OakA01 7/221]; d5.27; Col Nebraska																								
2005	Oak A	109	375	54	103	21	0	15	58	50-1	1	52	.275	.355	.451	115	10	0-1	.994	-3	87	118	1b101,D5	0	-0.3
2006	Oak A	91	286	30	67	13	1	9	37	40-2	0	45	.234	.323	.381	85	-6	0-0	.995	6	133	132	1b85,D2	0	-0.7
Total	2	200	661	84	170	34	1	24	95	90-3	1	97	.257	.341	.421	102	4	0-1	.994	3	108	124	1b186,D7	0	-1.0
JOHNSON, DARRELL	Darrell Dean; B8.25.1928 Horace NE; D5.3.2004 Fairfield CA; BR/TR/6´1˝/(170–180); d4.20; M8/C8																								
1952	StL A	29	78	9	22	2	1	0	9	11	0	4	.282	.371	.333	94	0	0-0	.990	1	*103*	*137*	C22	0	0.2
	Chi A	22	37	3	4	0	0	0	1	5	0	9	.108	.214	.108	-8	-5	1-0	.955	2	*89*	*125*	C21	0	-0.3
	Year	51	115	12	26	2	1	0	10	16	0	13	.226	.321	.261	62	-6	1-0	.974	2	*98*	*132*	C43	0	-0.1
1957	NY A	21	46	4	10	1	0	1	8	3-0	1	10	.217	.275	.304	61	-3	0-0	1.000	-1	69	107	C20	0	-0.3
1958	NY A	5	16	1	4	0	0	0	0	0-0	0	2	.250	.250	.250	39	-1	0-0	1.000	1	104	318	C4	0	-0.1
1960	StL N	8	2	0	0	0	0	0	0	1-0	0	0	.000	.333	.000	1	0	0-0	1.000	0	60	0	C8	0	0.0
1961	Phi N	21	61	4	14	1	0	0	3	3-0	1	8	.230	.277	.246	41	-5	0-0	.982	1	71	223	C21	0	-0.3
	†Cin N	20	54	3	17	2	0	1	6	1-0	0	2	.315	.321	.407	92	-1	0-0	1.000	2	59	184	C20	0	0.2
	Year	41	115	7	31	3	0	1	9	4-0	1	10	.270	.298	.322	65	-6	0-0	.991	3	65	204	C41	0	-0.1
1962	Cin N	2	4	0	0	0	0	0	0	2-1	0	0	.000	.333	.000	-2	0	0-0	1.000	1	44	220	C2	0	0.1
	Bal A	6	22	0	4	0	0	0	1	0-0	0	4	.182	.182	.182	-2	-3	0-0	1.000	-2	70	171	C6	0	-0.5
Total	6	134	320	24	75	6	1	2	28	26-1	2	39	.234	.294	.278	57	-18	1-0	.988	5	*78*	*164*	C124	0	-1.0
JOHNSON, DAVEY	David Allen; B1.30.1943 Orlando FL; BR/TR/6´1˝/(170–182); d4.13; M14; Col Texas A&M																								
1965	Bal A	20	47	5	8	3	0	0	1	5-0	0	6	.170	.245	.234	38	-4	3-0	.929	1	113	61	3b9,2b3,S2	0	-0.2
1966	†Bal A	131	501	47	129	20	3	7	56	31-3	1	64	.257	.298	.351	88	-8	3-4	.971	-4	98	95	2b126,S3	0	-0.1
1967	Bal A	148	510	62	126	30	3	10	64	59-10	4	82	.247	.325	.376	109	7	4-5	.981	-2	96	97	2b144,3b3	0	1.8
1968	Bal A★	145	504	50	122	24	4	9	56	44-5	5	80	.242	.308	.359	102	1	7-3	.978	-5	99	103	2b127,S34	0	1.1
1969	†Bal A✳	142	511	52	143	34	1	7	57	57-2	3	52	.280	.351	.391	108	7	3-4	.984	-2	98	118	2b142,S2	0	1.5
1970	†Bal A★	149	530	68	149	27	1	10	53	66-8	0	68	.281	.360	.392	106	6	2-1	.990	1	98	118	2b149,S2	0	1.8
1971	†Bal A	142	510	67	144	26	1	18	72	51-5	5	55	.282	.351	.443	123	16	3-1	.984	4	100	**125**	2b140	0	3.1
1972	Bal A	118	376	31	83	22	3	5	32	52-8	4	68	.221	.320	.335	92	-2	1-1	**.990**	10	103	**127**	2b116	0	1.7
1973	Atl N★	157	559	84	151	25	0	43	99	81-9	9	93	.270	.370	.546	140	31	5-3	.966	-17	94	97	2b156	0	2.6
1974	Atl N	136	454	56	114	18	0	15	62	75-6	3	59	.251	.358	.390	106	6	1-2	.993	-4	116	113	1b73,2b71	0	0.0
1975	Atl N	1	1	0	1	1	0	0	1	0-0	0	0	1.000	1.000	2.000	695	1	0-0	ø	0	—	—	/H	0	0.1
1977	†Phi N	78	156	23	50	9	1	8	36	23-1	2	20	.321	.408	.545	147	11	1-1	1.000	0	79	112	1b43,2b9,3b6	16	1.0
1978	Phi N	44	89	14	17	2	0	2	14	10-0	2	19	.191	.284	.281	58	-5	0-0	.930	-3	92	105	2b15,3b9,1b7	0	-0.8
	Chi N	24	49	5	15	1	1	2	6	5-0	2	9	.306	.393	.490	130	2	0-0	.839	-1	108	57	3b12	0	0.1
	Year	68	138	19	32	3	1	4	20	15-0	4	28	.232	.323	.355	85	-3	0-0	.844	-4	94	35	3b21,2b15,1b7	0	-0.7
Total	13	1435	4797	564	1252	242	18	136	609	559-57	40	675	.261	.340	.404	110	69	33-25	.980	-20	98	111	2b1198,1b123,S43,3b39	16	13.7
JOHNSON, DERON	Deron Roger; B7.17.1938 San Diego CA; D4.23.1992 Poway CA; BR/TR/6´2˝/(200–209); d9.20; C13; OF(216/1/32)																								
1960	NY A	6	4	0	2	1	0	0	0	0-0	0	0	.500	.500	.750	247	1	0-0	.750	-1	99	0	3b5	0	0.0
1961	NY A	13	19	1	2	0	0	0	2	2-0	0	5	.105	.182	.105	-20	-3	0-0	1.000	2	158	0	3b8	0	-0.2
	KC A	83	283	31	61	11	3	8	42	14-1	1	44	.216	.252	.360	61	-17	0-1	.948	5	97	146	O59(28/1/30),3b19,1b3	0	-1.6
	Year	96	302	32	63	11	3	8	44	16-1	1	49	.209	.247	.344	57	-20	0-1	.948	6	97	146	O59(28/1/30),3b27,1b3	0	-1.8
1962	KC A	17	19	1	2	1	0	0	0	3-0	0	8	.105	.227	.158	6	-3	0-0	1.000	-1	0	0	1b2,3b2,O2R	0	-0.3
1964	Cin N	140	477	63	130	24	4	21	79	37-0	2	98	.273	.326	.472	118	11	4-3	.990	4	107	99	1b131,O10L/3	0	0.7
1965	Cin N	159	616	92	177	30	7	32	**130**	52-9	2	97	.287	.340	.515	129	23	0-4	.948	-12	85	96	3b159	0	0.9
1966	Cin N	142	505	75	130	25	3	24	81	39-5	2	87	.257	.309	.461	103	2	1-2	.980	-8	95	68	O106L,1b71,3b18	0	-1.4
1967	Cin N	108	361	39	81	18	1	13	53	22-2	2	104	.224	.270	.388	78	-10	0-1	.997	-4	86	84	1b81,3b24	0	-2.1
1968	Atl N	127	342	29	71	11	1	8	33	35-2	3	79	.208	.285	.316	80	-8	0-1	.996	-3	87	120	1b97,3b21	0	-1.9
1969	Phi N	138	475	51	121	19	4	17	80	60-4	0	111	.255	.333	.419	114	9	4-2	1.000	-10	79	28	O72L,3b50,1b18	0	-0.7
1970	Phi N	159	574	66	147	28	3	27	93	72-7	0	132	.256	.338	.456	114	10	0-0	.995	-10	71	83	1b154,3b3	0	-1.2
1971	Phi N	158	582	74	154	29	0	34	95	72-8	2	146	.265	.347	.490	134	26	0-1	.995	-4	100	**111**	1b136,3b22	0	1.2
1972	Phi N	96	230	19	49	4	1	9	31	26-4	3	69	.213	.298	.357	84	-5	0-1	.982	-3	82	98	1b62	16	-1.4
1973	Phi N	12	36	3	6	2	0	1	5	5-0	1	10	.167	.279	.306	62	-2	0-0	.976	-0	101	137	1b10	0	-0.3
	†Oak A	131	464	61	114	14	2	19	81	59-7	1	116	.246	.330	.407	112	7	0-1	.994	-2	51	124	D107,1b23	0	0.0
1974	Oak A	50	174	16	34	1	2	7	23	11-2	0	37	.195	.239	.345	72	-8	1-0	.991	-2	66	70	1b28,D23	15	-1.3
	Mil A	49	152	14	23	3	0	6	18	21-2	0	41	.151	.253	.289	56	-9	1-0	.833	-0	144	300	D46,1b2	0	-1.1
	Bos A	11	25	0	3	0	0	0	2	0-0	0	6	.120	.115	.120	-29	-4	0-0	ø	0	—	—	D8	0	-0.5
	Year	110	351	30	60	4	2	13	43	32-4	0	84	.171	.237	.305	57	-21	2-0	.983	-2	69	80	D77,1b30	0	-2.9
1975	Chi A	148	555	66	129	25	1	18	72	48-0	1	117	.232	.292	.378	88	-10	0-1	.994	-2	80	82	D93,1b55	0	-1.9
	Bos A	3	10	2	6	0	0	1	3	2-0	0	0	.600	.667	.900	313	3	0-0	1.000	-1	0	134	1b2/D	0	0.2
	Year	151	565	68	135	25	1	19	75	50-0	1	117	.239	.300	.388	92	-7	0-1	.994	-3	77	84	D94,1b57	0	-1.7
1976	Bos A	15	38	3	5	1	1	0	0	5-1	0	11	.132	.233	.211	27	-4	0-0	1.000	-1	40	110	1b5,D9	0	-0.5
Total	16	1765	5941	706	1447	247	33	245	923	585-54	20	1318	.244	.311	.420	102	9	11-18	.993	-53	85	97	1b880,3b332,D287,O249L	31	-13.4
JOHNSON, DON	Donald Spore "Pep"; B12.7.1911 Chicago IL; D4.6.2000 Laguna Beach CA; BR/TR/6´0˝/170; d9.26; f–Ernie; Col Oregon St.																								
1943	Chi N	10	42	5	8	2	0	0	1	2	0	4	.190	.227	.238	35	-4	0	.957	2	105	126	2b10	0	-0.1
1944	Chi N☆	154	608	50	169	37	1	2	71	28	1	48	.278	.311	.352	87	-11	8	.947	-1	100	94	2b154	0	-0.4
1945	†Chi N✳	138	557	94	168	23	2	2	58	32	3	34	.302	.343	.361	98	-2	9	.975	15	108	111	2b138	0	2.0
1946	Chi N	83	314	37	76	10	1	1	19	26	3	39	.242	.306	.290	71	-12	6	.981	-9	96	72	2b83	0	-1.8
1947	Chi N	120	402	33	104	17	2	3	26	24	1	45	.259	.302	.333	71	-18	2	.970	-2	100	91	2b108,3b6	0	-1.4
1948	Chi N	6	12	0	3	0	0	0	0	0	0	1	.250	.250	.250	37	-1	1	1.000	-1	53	235	2b2,3b2	0	-0.2
Total	6	511	1935	219	528	89	6	8	175	112	8	171	.273	.315	.337	83	-48	26	.966	4	102	95	2b495,3b8	0	-1.9
JOHNSON, ED	Edwin Cyril; B3.31.1899 Morganfield KY; D7.3.1975 Morganfield KY; BL/TR/5´9˝/160; d9.26																								
1920	Was A	4	13	1	3	0	0	0	2	3	0	2	.231	.375	.231	65	0	0-0	.625	-2	66	0	O4R	—	-0.2
JOHNSON, ELMER	Elmer Ellsworth "Hickory"; B6.12.1884 Beard IN; D10.31.1966 Hollywood FL; BR/TR/5´9˝/185; d4.24																								
1914	NY N	11	12	0	2	1	0	0	0	1	0	3	.167	.231	.250	44	-1	0	.947	-1	*119*	*70*	C11	—	-0.1

JOHNSON, ERIK Erik Anthony; B10.11.1965 Oakland CA; BR/TR/5´11˝/175; [SFN87 18/464]; d7.8; Col California–Santa Barbara

YEAR	TM LG	G	AB	R	H	2B	3B	HR	RBI	BB-IB	HP	SO	AVG	OBP	SLG	AOPS	ABR	SB-CS	FA	FR	RNG	THR	GAMES AT POSITION	DL	BFW
1993	SF N	4	5	1	2	2	0	0	0	0-0	0	1	.400	.400	.800	219	1	0-0	1.000	-1	0	0	2b2/3S	0	0.0
1994	SF N	5	13	0	2	0	0	0	0	0-0	0	4	.154	.154	.154	-20	-2	0-0	1.000	0	95	317	2b2/S	0	-0.2
Total	2	9	18	1	4	2	0	0	0	0-0	0	5	.222	.222	.333	45	-1	0-0	1.000	-0	78	259	2b4,S2/3	0	-0.2

JOHNSON, ERNIE Ernest Rudolph; B4.29.1888 Chicago IL; D5.1.1952 Monrovia CA; BL/TR/5´9˝/151; d8.5; s–Don

YEAR	TM LG	G	AB	R	H	2B	3B	HR	RBI	BB-IB	HP	SO	AVG	OBP	SLG	AOPS	ABR	SB-CS	FA	FR	RNG	THR	GAMES AT POSITION	DL	BFW
1912	Chi A	21	42	7	11	0	1	0	5	1	0	—	.262	.279	.310	70	-2	0	.984	2	112	91	S16	—	0.1
1915	StL F	152	512	58	123	18	10	7	67	46	2	35	.240	.305	.355	81	-21	32	.942	16	102	117	S152	—	0.6
1916	StL A	74	236	29	54	9	3	0	19	30	3	23	.229	.323	.292	89	-2	13	.936	-3	106	90	S60,3b12	—	-0.1
1917	StL A	80	199	28	49	6	2	2	20	12	2	16	.246	.296	.327	93	-3	13	.924	9	105	51	S39,2b18,3b14	—	1.0
1918	StL A	29	34	7	9	1	0	0	0	0	1	2	.265	.286	.294	77	-1	4	.821	-2	100	47	S11/3	—	-0.3
1921	Chi A	142	613	93	181	28	7	1	51	29	1	24	.295	.328	.369	78	-21	22-13	.947	21	**112**	115	S141	—	1.4
1922	Chi A	144	603	85	153	17	3	0	56	40	4	30	.254	.304	.292	56	-39	21-18	.952	-1	101	103	S141	—	-2.5
1923	Chi A	12	53	5	10	2	0	0	1	3	1	5	.189	.246	.226	25	-6	2-1	.922	-2	89	137	S12	—	-0.6
	†NY A	19	38	6	17	1	1	1	8	1	0	1	.447	.462	.605	176	4	0-0	.977	-1	80	97	S15/3	—	0.3
	Year	31	91	11	27	3	1	1	9	4	1	6	.297	.333	.385	88	-2	2-1	.944	-3	85	121	S27/3	—	-0.3
1924	NY A	64	119	24	42	4	8	3	12	11	1	7	.353	.412	.597	158	9	1-6	.955	-1	102	94	2b27,S9,3b2	—	0.7
1925	NY A	76	170	30	48	5	1	5	17	8	0	10	.282	.315	.412	85	-5	6-3	.955	-8	95	100	2b34,S28,3b2	—	-1.0
Total	10	813	2619	372	697	91	36	19	256	181	15	153	.266	.317	.350	80	-87	114-41	.944	31	103	105	S624,2b79,3b32	—	-0.4

JOHNSON, FRANK Frank Herbert; B7.22.1942 El Paso TX; BR/TR/6´1˝/155; d9.7

YEAR	TM LG	G	AB	R	H	2B	3B	HR	RBI	BB-IB	HP	SO	AVG	OBP	SLG	AOPS	ABR	SB-CS	FA	FR	RNG	THR	GAMES AT POSITION	DL	BFW
1966	SF N	15	32	2	7	0	0	0	0	2-0	0	7	.219	.265	.219	35	-3	0-1	1.000	-1	91	0	O13(8/2/7)	0	-0.5
1967	SF N	8	10	3	3	0	0	0	0	1-0	0	2	.300	.364	.300	93	0	0-0	.889	0	152	0	O3(2/1/1)	0	0.0
1968	SF N	67	174	11	33	2	0	1	7	12-2	1	23	.190	.246	.218	40	-13	1-0	.944	1	105	73	3b36,O8(4/5/0),S5,2b3	0	-1.3
1969	SF N	7	10	2	1	0	0	0	0	0-0	0	1	.100	.100	.100	-44	-2	0-0	1.000	0	115	0	O7(5/1/1)	0	-0.2
1970	SF N	67	161	25	44	1	2	3	31	19-3	2	18	.273	.357	.360	94	-1	1-1	.979	-0	100	110	O33(29/1/4),1b27	0	-0.4
1971	SF N	32	49	4	4	1	0	0	5	3-0	0	9	.082	.132	.102	-33	-9	0-0	.975	-2	28	73	1b9,O4(3/0/1)	0	-1.3
Total	6	196	436	47	92	4	2	4	43	37-5	3	60	.211	.277	.257	52	-28	2-2	.979	-2	103	56	O68(51/10/14),1b36,3b36,S5,2b3	0	-3.7

JOHNSON, GARY Gerald Clyde; B10.29.1975 Palo Alto CA; BL/TL/6´3˝/210; [AnaA99 19/581]; d4.26; Col Brigham Young/California

YEAR	TM LG	G	AB	R	H	2B	3B	HR	RBI	BB-IB	HP	SO	AVG	OBP	SLG	AOPS	ABR	SB-CS	FA	FR	RNG	THR	GAMES AT POSITION	DL	BFW
2003	Ana A	5	8	1	3	1	0	0	0	1-0	0	1	.375	.444	.500	155	1	0-1	1.000	0	139	0	O4(2/0/2)	0	0.1

JOHNSON, HOWARD Howard Michael; B11.29.1960 Clearwater FL; BB/TR/5´11˝/(175–195); [DetA79*S1/12]; d4.14; OF(99/86/36)

YEAR	TM LG	G	AB	R	H	2B	3B	HR	RBI	BB-IB	HP	SO	AVG	OBP	SLG	AOPS	ABR	SB-CS	FA	FR	RNG	THR	GAMES AT POSITION	DL	BFW
1982	Det A	54	155	23	49	5	0	4	14	16-1	1	30	.316	.384	.426	121	5	7-4	.901	-7	70	111	3b33,D10,O9(3/1/5)	0	-0.3
1983	Det A	27	66	11	14	0	0	3	5	7-0	1	10	.212	.297	.348	79	-2	0-0	.851	-1	101	67	3b21,D2	0	-0.4
1984	†Det A	116	355	43	88	14	1	12	50	40-1	1	67	.248	.324	.394	98	-1	10-6	.944	-11	87	101	3b108,S9/1O(1/1/0)D	0	-1.3
1985	NY N	126	389	38	94	18	4	11	46	34-10	0	78	.242	.300	.393	95	-4	6-4	.941	-10	85	131	3b113,S7/lf	0	-1.6
1986	†NY N	88	220	30	54	14	0	10	39	31-8	1	64	.245	.341	.445	118	6	8-1	.903	-2	106	191	3b45,S34/lf	21	0.7
1987	NY N	157	554	93	147	22	1	36	99	83-18	5	113	.265	.364	.504	133	27	32-10	.938	-16	91	70	3b140,S38,O2L	0	1.5
1988	†NY N	148	495	85	114	21	1	24	68	86-25	3	104	.230	.343	.422	125	18	23-7	.951	-13	83	95	3b131,S52	0	1.1
1989	NY N★	153	571	**104**	164	41	3	36	101	77-8	1	126	.287	.369	.559	170	52	41-8	.910	-40	69	75	3b143,S31	0	2.2
1990	NY N	154	590	89	144	37	3	23	90	69-12	0	100	.244	.319	.434	106	5	34-8	.913	2	92	92	3b92,S73	0	1.7
1991	NY N★	156	564	108	146	34	4	**38**	**117**	78-12	1	120	.259	.342	.535	146	34	30-16	.927	-3	89	70	3b104,O30R,S28	0	3.4
1992	NY N	100	350	48	78	19	0	7	43	55-5	2	79	.223	.329	.337	91	-2	22-5	.981	-9	88	58	O98(16/84/1)	64	-1.0
1993	NY N	72	235	32	56	8	2	7	26	43-3	0	43	.238	.354	.379	98	1	6-4	.944	2	104	105	3b67	94	0.3
1994	Col N	93	227	30	48	10	2	10	40	39-2	0	73	.211	.323	.405	77	-8	11-3	.979	-1	95	66	O62L/1	0	-0.9
1995	Chi N	87	169	26	33	4	1	7	22	34-0	1	46	.195	.330	.355	82	-4	1-1	.926	-4	98	86	3b34,O13L,2b8,1b3/S	0	-0.8
Total	14	1531	4940	760	1229	247	22	228	760	692-105	17	1053	.249	.340	.446	118	127	231-77	.929	-114	87	94	3b1031,S273,O217L,D16,2b8,1b5	179	4.6

JOHNSON, SPUD John Ralph; B1860 , Can; BL/TL/5´9˝/175; d4.18

YEAR	TM LG	G	AB	R	H	2B	3B	HR	RBI	BB-IB	HP	SO	AVG	OBP	SLG	AOPS	ABR	SB-CS	FA	FR	RNG	THR	GAMES AT POSITION	DL	BFW
1889	Col AA	116	459	91	130	14	10	2	79	39	12	47	.283	.355	.370	112	8	34	.879	-4	108	76	O69R,3b44,1b2/S	—	0.4
1890	Col AA	135	538	106	186	23	18	1	**113**	48	10	—	.346	.409	.461	168	46	43	.926	-13	55	24	O135(96/0/39)	—	2.7
1891	Cle N	80	327	49	84	8	3	1	46	22	8	23	.257	.319	.309	80	-9	16	.872	-4	84	46	O79R/1	—	-1.3
Total	3	331	1324	246	400	45	31	4	238	109	30	70	.302	.368	.392	125	45	93	.899	-21	75	42	O283(96/0/187),3b44,1b3/S	—	1.8

JOHNSON, KEITH Keith; B4.17.1971 Hanford CA; BR/TR/5´11˝/200; [LAN92 4/115]; d4.17; Col Pacific (CA)

YEAR	TM LG	G	AB	R	H	2B	3B	HR	RBI	BB-IB	HP	SO	AVG	OBP	SLG	AOPS	ABR	SB-CS	FA	FR	RNG	THR	GAMES AT POSITION	DL	BFW
2000	Ana A	6	4	2	2	0	0	0	0	2-0	0	0	.500	.667	.500	196	1	0-0	1.000	1	0	0	1b3,2b2/S	0	0.2

JOHNSON, KELLY Kelly Andrew; B2.22.1981 Austin TX; BL/TR/6´1˝/205; [AtlN00 1/38]; d5.29; [DL 2006 Atl N 182]

YEAR	TM LG	G	AB	R	H	2B	3B	HR	RBI	BB-IB	HP	SO	AVG	OBP	SLG	AOPS	ABR	SB-CS	FA	FR	RNG	THR	GAMES AT POSITION	DL	BFW
2005	†Atl N	87	290	46	70	12	3	9	40	40-1	1	75	.241	.334	.397	90	-4	2-1	1.000	7	114	135	O79L/D	0	0.0

JOHNSON, LANCE Kenneth Lance; B7.6.1963 Cincinnati OH; BL/TL/5´11˝/(155–165); [StLN84 6/139]; d7.10; Col South Alabama

YEAR	TM LG	G	AB	R	H	2B	3B	HR	RBI	BB-IB	HP	SO	AVG	OBP	SLG	AOPS	ABR	SB-CS	FA	FR	RNG	THR	GAMES AT POSITION	DL	BFW
1987	†StL N	33	59	4	13	2	1	0	7	4-1	0	6	.220	.270	.288	47	-5	6-1	.931	-2	89	0	O25(3/6/17)	0	-0.6
1988	Chi A	33	124	11	23	4	1	0	6	6-0	0	11	.185	.223	.234	28	-12	6-2	.970	-5	76	71	O31C/D	0	-1.7
1989	Chi A	50	180	28	54	8	2	0	16	17-0	0	24	.300	.360	.367	107	2	16-3	.983	1	119	0	O45(42/8/0)/D	0	0.5
1990	Chi A	151	541	76	154	18	9	1	51	33-2	1	45	.285	.325	.357	93	-7	36-22	.973	-3	100	72	O148(6/148/0)/D	0	-1.1
1991	Chi A	159	588	72	161	14	**13**	0	49	26-2	1	58	.274	.304	.342	80	-19	26-11	.995	6	105	136	O157(0/157/2)	0	-1.2
1992	Chi A	157	567	67	158	15	**12**	3	47	34-4	1	33	.279	.318	.363	92	-9	41-14	.987	-1	98	121	O157C	0	-0.7
1993	†Chi A	147	540	75	168	18	**14**	0	47	36-1	0	33	.311	.354	.396	103	1	35-7	.980	9	114	90	O146C	0	1.6
1994	Chi A	106	412	56	114	11	**14**	3	54	26-5	2	23	.277	.321	.393	84	-12	26-6	**1.000**	7	119	19	O103C/D	0	0.0
1995	Chi A	142	607	98	**186**	18	12	10	57	32-2	1	31	.306	.341	.425	102	-1	40-6	.991	-1	98	119	O140C/D	0	0.6
1996	NY N★	160	682	117	**227**	31	**21**	9	69	33-8	1	40	.333	.362	.479	127	22	50-12	.971	3	105	111	O157C	0	3.2
1997	NY N	72	265	43	82	10	6	1	24	33-2	0	21	.309	.385	.404	112	5	15-10	.975	-1	100	125	O66C	45	0.5
	Chi N	39	145	17	44	6	2	4	15	9-1	0	10	.303	.342	.455	104	0	5-2	.963	-1	109	0	O39C/D	0	0.0
	Year	111	410	60	126	16	8	5	39	42-3	0	31	.307	.370	.422	109	5	20-12	.971	-2	103	83	O105C/D	0	0.5
1998	†Chi N	85	304	51	85	8	4	2	21	26-1	0	22	.280	.335	.352	79	-10	10-6	.975	-4	91	112	O78C	77	-1.2
1999	Chi N	95	335	46	87	11	6	1	21	37-0	0	20	.260	.332	.337	71	-15	13-3	.988	6	115	132	O91C	72	-0.6
2000	NY A	18	30	6	9	1	0	0	2	0-0	0	7	.300	.300	.333	61	-2	2-0	1.000	-1	51	0	O4(2/0/2),D2	0	-0.2
Total	14	1447	5379	767	1565	175	117	34	486	352-29	7	384	.291	.334	.386	94	-62	327-105	.983	13	104	96	O1387(53/1327/21),D8	194	-0.9

JOHNSON, LAMAR Lamar; B9.2.1950 Bessemer AL; BR/TR/6´2˝/(207–232); [ChiA68 3/54]; d5.18; C9

YEAR	TM LG	G	AB	R	H	2B	3B	HR	RBI	BB-IB	HP	SO	AVG	OBP	SLG	AOPS	ABR	SB-CS	FA	FR	RNG	THR	GAMES AT POSITION	DL	BFW
1974	Chi A	10	29	1	10	0	0	0	2	0-0	0	3	.345	.333	.345	96	0	0-0	1.000	-0	67	159	1b7,D3	0	-0.1
1975	Chi A	8	30	2	6	3	0	1	1	1-0	0	5	.200	.226	.400	73	-1	0-0	.960	-1	63	82	1b6,D2	0	-0.2
1976	Chi A	82	222	29	71	11	1	4	33	19-1	2	37	.320	.372	.432	136	10	2-1	.983	-1	100	87	D35,1b34/lf	0	0.7
1977	Chi A	118	374	52	113	12	5	18	65	24-3	0	53	.302	.342	.505	128	13	1-1	.990	2	113	86	D68,1b45	0	0.9
1978	Chi A	148	498	52	136	23	2	8	72	43-2	2	46	.273	.329	.376	98	-1	6-5	.992	4	114	91	1b108,D36	0	-0.5
1979	Chi A	133	479	60	148	29	1	12	74	41-1	2	56	.309	.363	.449	118	13	8-2	.987	4	124	81	1b94,D37	0	1.1
1980	Chi A	147	541	51	150	26	3	13	81	47-5	0	53	.277	.331	.409	103	2	2-3	.990	5	129	102	1b80,D66	0	0.0
1981	Chi A	41	134	10	37	7	0	1	15	5-1	0	14	.276	.298	.351	89	-2	0-2	.989	-1	81	121	1b36,D2	0	-0.7
1982	Tex A	105	324	37	84	11	0	7	38	31-0	1	40	.259	.326	.358	92	-4	3-5	.982	-2	56	59	D77,1b12	0	-0.9
Total	9	792	2631	294	755	122	12	64	381	211-13	7	307	.287	.338	.415	109	30	22-19	.989	9	112	92	1b422,D326/lf	0	0.3

JOHNSON, LARRY Larry Doby; B8.17.1950 Cleveland OH; BR/TR/6´0˝/(180–185); [CleA68 9/186]; d10.3

YEAR	TM LG	G	AB	R	H	2B	3B	HR	RBI	BB-IB	HP	SO	AVG	OBP	SLG	AOPS	ABR	SB-CS	FA	FR	RNG	THR	GAMES AT POSITION	DL	BFW
1972	Cle A	1	2	0	1	0	0	0	0	0-0	0	1	.500	.500	.500	191	0	0-0	1.000	0	0	0	/C	0	0.1
1974	Cle A	1	0	1	0	0	0	0	0	0-0	0	0	ø	ø	ø	ø	0	0-0	ø	0	—	—	/R	0	0.0
1975	Mon N	1	3	0	1	1	0	0	1	1-0	0	1	.333	.500	.667	211	1	0-0	1.000	-0	54	0	/C	0	0.0
1976	Mon N	6	13	0	2	1	0	0	0	0-0	0	2	.154	.154	.231	8	-2	0-0	1.000	-0	57	70	C5	0	-0.2
1978	Chi A	3	8	0	1	0	0	0	0	1-0	0	4	.125	.222	.125	0	-1	0-0	.857	-1	27	414	C2/D	0	-0.2
Total	5	12	26	1	5	2	0	0	1	2-0	0	8	.192	.250	.269	45	-2	0-0	.975	-1	47	120	C9/D	0	-0.3

JOHNSON, LOU Louis Brown "Slick"; B9.22.1934 Lexington KY; BR/TR/5´11˝/(170–175); d4.17; Col Kentucky St.

YEAR	TM LG	G	AB	R	H	2B	3B	HR	RBI	BB-IB	HP	SO	AVG	OBP	SLG	AOPS	ABR	SB-CS	FA	FR	RNG	THR	GAMES AT POSITION	DL	BFW
1960	Chi N	34	68	6	14	2	1	0	1	5-1	1	19	.206	.270	.265	48	-5	3-1	1.000	4	122	257	O25(8/4/13)	0	-0.2
1961	LA A	1	0	0	0	0	0	0	0	0-0	0	0	ø	ø	ø	ø	0	0-0	ø	-0	0	0	/lf	0	0.0
1962	Mil N	61	117	22	33	4	5	2	13	11-0	1	27	.282	.349	.453	116	2	6-1	1.000	-0	101	47	O55(38/20/1)	0	0.2
1965	†LA N	131	468	57	121	24	1	12	58	24-8	16	81	.259	.315	.391	105	3	15-6	.985	-2	99	45	O128(124/11/3)	0	-0.5

YEAR	TM LG	G	AB	R	H	2B	3B	HR	RBI	BB-IB	HP	SO	AVG	OBP	SLG	AOPS	ABR	SB-CS	FA	FR	RNG	THR	GAMES AT POSITION	DL	BFW
1966	†LA N	152	526	71	143	20	2	17	73	21-4	**14**	75	.272	.316	.414	110	6	8-10	.985	4	107	86	O148(104/2/65)	0	-0.1
1967	LA N	104	330	39	89	14	1	11	41	24-5	7	52	.270	.330	.418	124	10	4-3	.976	3	105	128	O91(81/1/11)	0	0.8
1968	Chi N	62	205	14	50	14	3	1	14	6-2	7	23	.244	.289	.356	87	-3	3-1	.970	-5	97	0	O57(1/0/56)	0	-1.3
	Cle A	65	202	25	52	11	1	5	23	9-2	4	24	.257	.298	.396	112	2	6-1	.989	2	101	166	O57(41/0/20)	0	0.3
1969	Cal A	67	133	10	27	8	0	0	9	10-1	3	19	.203	.272	.263	53	-8	5-1	.935	-0	102	86	O44(23/0/23)	42	-1.0
Total	8	677	2049	244	529	97	14	48	232	110-23	53	320	.258	.311	.389	103	7	50-24	.981	5	103	85	O606(421/38/192)	42	-1.8
JOHNSON, MARK	Mark Landon; B9.12.1975 Wheat Ridge CO; BL/TR/6´0˝/(185–200); [ChiA94 1/26]; d9.14																								
1998	Chi A	7	23	2	2	0	2	0	1	1-0	0	8	.087	.125	.261	-3	-4	0-0	1.000	0	219	99	C7	0	-0.3
1999	Chi A	73	207	27	47	11	0	4	16	36-0	2	58	.227	.344	.338	75	-7	3-1	.993	2	117	92	C72,D2	0	0.0
2000	Chi A	75	213	29	48	11	0	3	23	27-0	1	40	.225	.315	.319	59	-13	3-2	.992	6	103	161	C74/D	0	-0.2
2001	Chi A	61	173	21	43	6	1	5	18	23-1	2	31	.249	.338	.382	86	-3	2-1	.992	3	126	103	C61	0	0.4
2002	Chi A	86	263	31	55	8	1	4	18	30-1	3	52	.209	.297	.293	56	-17	0-0	.994	-3	105	116	C85	0	-1.4
2003	Oak A	13	27	3	3	1	0	0	3	3-0	1	4	.111	.219	.148	2	-4	0-0	1.000	2	108	85	C13	0	-0.2
2004	Mil N	7	11	1	1	0	0	0	2	3-1	0	2	.091	.267	.091	4	-2	0-0	.952	-2	45	138	C5	0	-0.3
Total	7	322	917	114	199	37	4	16	81	123-3	9	195	.217	.313	.318	63	-50	8-4	.993	8	113	118	C317,D3	0	-2.0
JOHNSON, MARK	Mark Patrick; B10.17.1967 Worcester MA; BL/TL/6´4˝/230; [PitN90 20/537]; d4.26; Col Dartmouth																								
1995	Pit N	79	221	32	46	6	1	13	28	37-2	2	66	.208	.326	.421	93	-2	5-2	.986	-4	82	101	1b70	0	-1.1
1996	Pit N	127	343	55	94	24	0	13	47	44-3	5	64	.274	.361	.458	111	7	6-4	.994	6	126	92	1b100/lf	0	0.5
1997	Pit N	78	219	30	47	10	0	4	29	43-1	2	78	.215	.345	.315	74	-7	1-1	.992	1	106	102	1b63/D	0	-1.1
1998	Ana A	10	14	1	1	0	0	0	0	0-0	0	6	.071	.071	.071	-62	-3	0-0	1.000	-0	78	121	1b5,D2	0	-0.3
2000	NY N	21	22	2	4	0	0	1	6	5-0	0	9	.182	.333	.318	70	-1	0-0	1.000	1	0	113	1b4/lfD	0	-0.1
2001	NY N	71	118	17	30	6	1	6	23	16-1	0	31	.254	.338	.475	116	3	0-2	.991	-3	93	110	1b21,O19(12/0/7),D3	0	-0.2
2002	NY N	42	51	5	7	4	0	1	4	9-0	0	18	.137	.267	.275	45	-4	0-0	.989	-0	97	84	1b15/lf	0	-0.5
Total	7	428	988	142	229	50	2	38	137	154-7	9	272	.232	.338	.402	93	-7	12-9	.991	-0	105	98	1b278,O22(15/0/7),D7	0	-2.8
JOHNSON, NICK	Nicholas Robert; B9.19.1978 Sacramento CA; BL/TL/6´3˝/(224–225); [NYA96 3/89]; d8.21; [DL 2000 NY A 181]																								
2001	NY A	23	67	6	13	2	0	2	8	7-0	4	15	.194	.308	.313	64	-3	0-0	1.000	-1	67	44	1b15,D6	0	-0.5
2002	†NY A	129	378	56	92	15	0	15	58	48-5	12	98	.243	.347	.402	99	1	1-3	.988	2	114	95	1b78,D50,O2L	25	-0.6
2003	†NY A	96	324	60	92	19	0	14	47	70-4	8	57	.284	.422	.472	138	23	5-2	.991	-2	87	92	1b60,D34	70	1.3
2004	Mon N	73	251	35	63	16	0	7	33	40-2	3	58	.251	.359	.398	92	-1	6-3	.994	-3	88	118	1b73	98	-1.0
2005	Was N	131	453	66	131	35	3	15	74	80-8	12	87	.289	.408	.479	138	30	3-8	.996	4	113	101	1b129	29	2.1
2006	Was N	147	500	100	145	46	0	23	77	110-15	13	99	.290	.428	.520	149	45	10-3	.988	-1	102	71	1b147	0	3.1
Total	6	599	1973	323	536	133	3	76	297	355-34	52	414	.272	.395	.458	125	95	25-19	.992	-0	102	91	1b502,D90,O2L	403	4.4
JOHNSON, OTIS	Otis L.; B11.5.1883 Fowler IN; D11.9.1915 Johnson City NY; BB/TR/5´9˝/185; d4.12																								
1911	NY A	71	209	21	49	9	6	3	36	39	3	—	.234	.363	.378	100	1	12	.907	-8	94	116	S47,2b15,3b3	—	-0.4
JOHNSON, PAUL	Paul Oscar; B9.2.1896 N.Grosvenor Dale CT; D2.14.1973 McAllen TX; BR/TR/5´8˝/160; d9.13																								
1920	Phi A	18	72	6	15	0	0	0	5	4	0	8	.208	.250	.208	22	-8	1-1	.933	-2	76	97	O18(13/4/1)	—	-1.1
1921	Phi A	48	127	17	40	6	2	1	10	9	0	17	.315	.360	.417	97	-1	0-2	.969	-3	91	28	O32(6/24/2)	—	-0.6
Total	2	66	199	23	55	6	2	1	15	13	0	25	.276	.321	.342	71	-9	1-3	.958	-5	86	53	O50(19/28/3)	—	-1.7
JOHNSON, RANDY	Randall Glenn; B6.10.1956 Escondido CA; BR/TR/6´1˝/(185–190); [NYN78 11/263]; d4.27; Col San Jose St.																								
1982	Atl N	27	46	5	11	5	0	0	6	6-1	2	4	.239	.345	.348	94	0	0-1	.955	2	123	102	2b13,3b4	0	0.2
1983	Atl N	86	144	22	36	3	0	1	17	20-3	1	27	.250	.345	.292	73	-4	1-3	.991	8	110	204	3b53,2b4	0	0.2
1984	Atl N	91	294	28	82	13	0	5	30	21-6	1	21	.279	.329	.374	91	-3	4-7	.939	6	117	110	3b81	19	0.0
Total	3	204	484	55	129	21	0	6	53	47-10	4	52	.267	.336	.347	86	-7	5-11	.956	16	115	136	3b138,2b17	19	0.4
JOHNSON, RANDY	Randall Stuart; B8.15.1958 Miami FL; BL/TL/6´2˝/(189–195); [ChiA79*3/62]; d7.5; Col Miami–Dade Kendall (FL) CC																								
1980	Chi A	12	20	0	4	0	0	0	3	2-0	1	4	.200	.280	.200	41	-2	0-0	ø	-0	0	0	/1lfD	0	-0.2
1982	Min A	89	234	26	58	10	0	10	33	30-2	0	46	.248	.325	.419	102	1	0-0	1.000	-0	71	0	D67,O2R	0	-0.2
Total	2	101	254	26	62	10	0	10	36	32-2	1	50	.244	.321	.402	97	-1	0-0	1.000	-0	85	0	D71,O3(1/0/2)/1	0	-0.4
JOHNSON, REED	Reed Cameron; B12.8.1976 Riverside CA; BR/TR/5´10˝/180; [TorA99 17/523]; d4.17; Col Cal St.–Fullerton																								
2003	Tor A	114	412	79	121	21	2	10	52	20-1	20	67	.294	.353	.427	102	1	5-3	.977	-7	82	104	O111(53/5/71)	0	-1.0
2004	Tor A	141	537	68	145	25	2	10	61	28-2	12	98	.270	.320	.380	77	-18	6-3	.989	0	98	121	O137(57/33/53),D4	0	-2.0
2005	Tor A	142	398	55	107	21	6	8	58	22-1	16	82	.269	.332	.412	92	-5	5-6	.990	-3	94	88	O139(118/9/35)	0	-1.2
2006	Tor A	134	461	86	147	34	2	12	49	33-4	**21**	81	.319	.390	.479	119	15	8-2	.996	3	96	**162**	O133(100/16/30)/D	0	1.4
Total	4	531	1808	288	520	101	12	40	220	103-8	69	328	.288	.348	.423	97	-7	24-14	.989	-7	93	120	O520(328/63/189),D5	0	-2.8
JOHNSON, FOOTER	Richard Allan "Treads"; B2.15.1932 Dayton OH; BL/TL/5´11˝/175; d6.15; Col Duke																								
1958	Chi N	8	5	1	0	0	0	0	0	0-0	0	1	.000	.000	.000	-99	-1	0-0	ø	0	—	—	/H	0	-0.1
JOHNSON, BOB	Robert Lee "Indian Bob"; B11.26.1905 Pryor OK; D7.6.1982 Tacoma WA; BR/TR/6´0˝/180; d4.12; b–Roy; OF(1592/162/24)																								
1933	Phi A	142	535	103	155	44	4	21	93	85	0	74	.290	.387	.505	133	28	8-3	.952	-0	97	111	O142(127/1/15)	—	1.9
1934	Phi A	141	547	111	168	26	6	34	92	58	1	60	.307	.375	.563	144	32	12-8	.967	9	107	147	O139L	—	3.0
1935	Phi A★	147	582	103	174	29	5	28	109	78	2	76	.299	.384	.510	130	26	2-4	.946	4	106	107	O147L	—	1.9
1936	Phi A	153	566	91	165	29	14	25	121	88	2	71	.292	.389	.525	126	22	6-6	.962	5	108	114	O131(131/1/0),2b22/1	—	1.7
1937	Phi A	138	477	91	146	32	6	25	108	98	1	65	.306	.425	.556	148	38	9-7	.976	10	111	135	O133(129/6/0),2b2	—	3.6
1938	Phi A★	152	563	114	176	27	9	30	113	87	2	73	.313	.406	.552	142	36	9-8	.963	8	106	**158**	O150(29/122/0),2b3/3	—	3.5
1939	Phi A☆	150	544	115	184	30	9	23	114	99	0	59	.338	.440	.553	156	49	15-5	.967	9	108	145	O150(138/14/0)/2	—	4.8
1940	Phi A☆	138	512	93	137	25	4	31	103	83	4	64	.268	.374	.514	130	23	8-2	.962	6	102	**149**	O136(116/13/8)	—	2.1
1941	Phi A	149	552	98	152	30	8	22	107	95	3	75	.275	.385	.478	130	26	6-4	.990	7	105	161	O122(118/4/0),1b28	0	2.2
1942	Phi A★	149	550	78	160	35	7	13	80	82	1	61	.291	.384	.451	135	28	3-2	.963	5	102	157	O149(148/0/1)	0	2.5
1943	Was A★	117	438	65	116	22	8	7	63	64	3	50	.265	.362	.400	127	16	11-5	.996	8	106	153	O88L,3b19,1b10	0	2.0
1944	Bos A★	144	525	106	170	40	8	17	106	95	4	67	.324	**.431**	.528	**175**	**57**	2-7	.977	5	91	**203**	O142L	0	5.3
1945	Bos A✱	143	529	71	148	27	7	12	74	63	4	56	.280	.358	.425	124	16	5-3	.975	4	101	122	O140(140/1/0)	0	1.2
Total	13	1863	6920	1239	2051	396	95	288	1283	1075	24	851	.296	.393	.506	139	397	96-64	.968	79	104	143	O1769L,1b39,2b28,3b20	0	35.7
JOHNSON, BOB	Robert Wallace; B3.4.1936 Omaha NE; BR/TR/5´10˝/(170–180); d4.19																								
1960	KC A	76	146	12	30	4	0	1	9	19-1	1	23	.205	.301	.253	51	-10	2-0	.947	0	96	91	S30,2b27,3b11	0	-0.6
1961	Was A	61	224	27	66	13	1	6	28	19-2	1	26	.295	.350	.442	113	4	4-2	.956	-0	109	89	S57,2b2,3b2	0	0.9
1962	Was A	135	466	58	134	20	2	12	43	32-1	1	50	.288	.334	.416	102	0	9-6	.944	-3	97	93	3b72,S50,2b3/lf	0	0.0
1963	Bal A	82	254	34	75	10	0	8	32	18-0	2	35	.295	.347	.429	120	7	5-1	.987	2	107	122	2b50,1b8,S7,3b5	0	1.4
1964	Bal A	93	210	18	52	8	2	3	29	9-1	1	37	.248	.281	.348	74	-8	0-0	.964	-9	80	65	S18,1b15,2b15/3lf	0	-1.7
1965	Bal A	87	273	36	66	13	2	5	27	15-2	1	34	.242	.282	.359	80	-8	1-0	.996	-9	75	84	1b34,S23,3b13,2b5	0	-1.8
1966	Bal A	71	157	13	34	5	0	1	10	12-1	1	24	.217	.276	.268	58	-8	0-1	.966	-2	102	105	2b20,1b17,3b3	0	-1.0
1967	Bal A	4	3	1	1	0	0	0	0	1-0	0	1	.333	.500	.333	152	0	0-0	ø	0	—	—	/H	0	0.0
	NY N	90	230	26	80	8	3	5	27	12-0	0	29	.348	.377	.474	145	13	1-1	.987	-1	95	107	2b39,1b23,S14/3	0	1.5
1968	Cin N	16	15	2	4	0	0	0	1	1-0	0	2	.267	.313	.267	71	-1	0-0	.500	-1	92	0	S2/1	0	-0.2
	Atl N	59	187	15	49	5	1	0	11	10-3	0	20	.262	.298	.299	80	-5	0-0	.948	5	116	114	3b48,2b4	0	0.0
	Year	75	202	17	53	5	1	0	12	11-3	0	22	.262	.299	.297	79	-5	0-0	.948	4	116	114	3b48,2b4,S2/1	0	-0.2
1969	StL N	19	29	1	6	0	0	1	2	2-0	0	4	.207	.258	.310	58	-2	0-0	.833	-1	91	157	3b4/1	0	-0.2
	Oak A	51	67	5	23	1	0	1	9	3-1	1	4	.343	.375	.403	124	2	0-0	1.000	0	125	176	1b7,2b2	0	0.2
1970	Oak A	30	46	6	8	1	0	1	2	3-0	1	2	.174	.235	.261	39	-4	2-1	.952	1	137	86	3b6/1	0	-0.3
Total	11	874	2307	254	628	88	11	44	230	156-12	10	291	.272	.320	.377	95	-20	24-12	.956	-17	100	82	S201,2b167,3b166,1b107,O2L	0	-1.8
JOHNSON, RON	Ronald David; B3.23.1956 Long Beach CA; BR/TR/6´3˝/(215–220); [KCA78 24/595]; d9.12; Col Cal St.–Fresno																								
1982	KC A	8	14	2	4	2	0	0	0	4-0	0	3	.286	.444	.429	140	1	0-0	.976	-0	74	80	1b7	0	0.0
1983	KC A	9	27	2	7	0	0	0	1	3-0	0	1	.259	.333	.259	65	-1	0-0	.971	-1	64	134	1b7,C2	0	-0.3
1984	Mon N	5	5	0	1	0	0	0	1	0-0	0	2	.200	.200	.200	13	-1	0-0	1.000	-0	0	0	1b2/rf	0	-0.1
Total	3	22	46	4	12	2	0	0	2	7-0	0	6	.261	.358	.304	84	-1	0-0	.974	-2	64	107	1b16,C2/rf	0	-0.4

YEAR	TM LG	G	AB	R	H	2B	3B	HR	RBI	BB-IB	HP	SO	AVG	OBP	SLG	AOPS	ABR	SB-CS	FA	FR	RNG	THR	GAMES AT POSITION	DL	BFW
JOHNSON, RONDIN	Rondin Allen; B12.16.1958 Bremerton WA; BB/TR/5´10˝/160; [KCA80 6/146]; d9.3; Col Washington																								
1986	KC A	11	31	1	8	0	1	0	2	0-0	0	3	.258	.258	.323	56	-2	0-0	1.000	3	135	94	2b11	0	0.1
JOHNSON, RONTREZ	Rontrez Demon; B12.8.1976 Marshall TX; BR/TR/5´10˝/180; [BosA95 16/438]; d3.31																								
2003	KC A	8	3	3	1	0	0	0	0	0-0	0	2	.333	.333	.333	72	0	0-0	.000	-1	0	0	O6C,D2	0	-0.1
JOHNSON, ROY	Roy Cleveland; B2.23.1903 Pryor OK; D9.10.1973 Tacoma WA; BL/TR/5´9˝/175; d4.18; b–Bob																								
1929	Det A	148	640	128	201	**45**	14	10	69	67	0	60	.314	.379	.475	118	17	20-16	.928	6	103	153	O146(91/37/23)	—	1.1
1930	Det A	125	462	84	127	30	13	2	35	40	0	46	.275	.333	.409	85	-11	17-10	.936	5	106	**153**	O118(7/2/110)	—	-1.4
1931	Det A	151	621	107	173	37	**19**	8	55	72	2	51	.279	.355	.438	104	3	33-21	.960	11	105	**165**	O150(0/5/148)	—	0.4
1932	Det A	49	195	33	49	14	2	3	22	20	1	26	.251	.324	.390	81	-6	7-2	.929	-1	103	78	O48R	—	-0.8
	Bos A	94	349	70	104	24	4	11	47	44	1	41	.298	.378	.484	125	14	13-4	.930	-8	86	85	O85(14/16/56)	—	0.2
	Year	143	544	103	153	38	6	14	69	64	2	67	.281	.359	.450	109	7	20-6	.930	-9	92	82	O133(14/16/104)	—	-0.6
1933	Bos A	133	483	88	151	30	7	10	95	55	4	36	.313	.387	.466	126	19	13-10	.922	1	104	116	O125(26/10/95)	—	1.1
1934	Bos A	143	569	85	182	43	10	7	119	54	0	36	.320	.379	.467	109	8	11-5	.948	-5	92	102	O137L	—	-0.4
1935	Bos A	145	553	70	174	33	9	3	66	74	3	34	.315	.398	.423	105	7	11-12	.944	2	91	184	O142L	—	0.0
1936	†NY A	63	147	21	39	8	2	1	19	21	1	14	.265	.361	.367	83	-4	3-1	.944	-0	105	74	O33(28/0/3)	—	-0.5
1937	NY A	12	51	5	15	3	0	0	6	3	0	2	.294	.333	.353	73	-2	1-0	.840	-2	85	0	O12L	—	-0.4
	Bos N	85	260	24	72	8	3	3	22	38	0	29	.277	.369	.365	110	5	5	.965	-1	98	105	O63L/3	—	0.0
1938	Bos N	7	29	2	5	0	0	0	1	1	0	5	.172	.200	.172	4	-4	1	.769	-2	67	0	O7L	—	-0.7
Total	10	1155	4359	717	1292	275	83	58	556	489	12	380	.296	.369	.437	107	46	135-81	.938	6	99	131	O1066(527/70/483)/3	—	-1.4
JOHNSON, ROY	Roy Edward; B6.27.1959 Parkin AR; BL/TL/6´4˝/(205–220); [MonN80 5/125]; d7.3; Col Tennessee St.																								
1982	Mon N	17	32	2	7	2	0	0	2	1-0	0	6	.219	.235	.281	44	-2	0-0	1.000	-0	108	0	O11(0/9/3)	0	-0.3
1984	Mon N	16	33	2	5	2	0	1	2	7-0	0	10	.152	.300	.303	73	-1	1-0	.938	-1	87	0	O10(9/0/1)	0	-0.2
1985	Mon N	3	5	0	0	0	0	0	0	0-0	0	3	.000	.000	.000	-99	-1	0-0	ø	-1	0	0	O3(0/1/2)	0	-0.2
Total	3	36	70	4	12	4	0	1	4	8-0	0	19	.171	.253	.271	48	-4	1-0	.971	-2	90	0	O24(9/10/6)	0	-0.7
JOHNSON, STAN	Stanley Lucius; B2.12.1937 Dallas TX; BL/TL/5´10˝/(180–185); d9.18; Col San Francisco																								
1960	Chi A	5	6	1	1	0	0	1	1	0-0	0	1	.167	.167	.667	116	0	0-1	1.000	-0	70	0	O2L	0	-0.1
1961	KC A	3	3	1	0	0	0	0	0	2-0	0	1	.000	.400	.000	17	0	0-0	ø	-0	0	0	O2R	0	-0.1
Total	2	8	9	2	1	0	0	1	1	2-0	0	2	.111	.273	.444	89	0	0-1	1.000	-1	30	0	O4(2/0/2)	0	-0.2
JOHNSON, TIM	Timothy Evald; B7.22.1949 Grand Forks ND; BL/TR/6´1˝/(170–185); d4.24; M1/C4																								
1973	Mil A	136	465	39	99	10	2	0	32	29-2	1	93	.213	.259	.243	43	-36	6-3	.962	-13	94	100	S135	0	-3.4
1974	Mil A	93	245	25	60	7	7	0	25	11-1	1	48	.245	.278	.331	75	-9	4-3	.970	-1	106	94	S64,2b26/3lfD	0	-0.2
1975	Mil A	38	85	6	12	1	0	0	2	6-0	0	17	.141	.198	.153	0	-11	3-0	1.000	-4	105	91	2b11,3b11,S10,1b2,D3	77	-1.4
1976	Mil A	105	273	25	75	4	3	0	14	19-0	2	32	.275	.327	.311	89	-4	4-1	.980	-14	93	76	2b100,3b17/1S	0	-1.3
1977	Mil A	30	33	5	2	1	0	0	2	5-1	0	10	.061	.179	.091	-22	-6	1-0	.929	-2	18	0	2b10,S6,3b4/lfD	49	-0.6
1978	Mil A	3	3	1	0	0	0	0	0	2-0	0	0	.000	.400	.000	21	0	0-0	1.000	-2	0	0	S2	0	-0.2
	Tor A	68	79	9	19	2	0	0	3	8-0	1	16	.241	.315	.266	65	-3	0-1	.975	1	95	57	S49,2b13	0	-0.1
	Year	71	82	10	19	2	0	0	3	10-0	1	16	.232	.319	.256	63	-4	0-1	.975	-2	89	53	S51,2b13	0	-0.3
1979	Tor A	43	86	6	16	2	1	0	6	8-0	0	15	.186	.255	.233	32	-8	0-1	.958	3	87	138	2b25,3b9,1b7	0	-0.5
Total	7	516	1269	116	283	27	13	0	84	88-4	5	231	.223	.274	.265	55	-77	18-9	.965	-31	97	95	S267,2b185,3b42,1b10,D8,O2L	126	-7.7
JOHNSON, WALLACE	Wallace Darnell; B12.25.1956 Gary IN; BB/TR/5´11˝/(170–185); [MonN79 6/140]; d9.8; C5; Col Indiana St.																								
1981	†Mon N	11	9	1	2	0	1	0	3	1-1	0	1	.222	.300	.444	106	0	1-1	1.000	0	135	388	/2	0	0.0
1982	Mon N	36	57	5	11	0	2	0	2	5-0	0	5	.193	.258	.263	44	-5	4-1	.952	-2	71	90	2b13	0	-0.6
1983	Mon N	3	2	1	1	0	0	0	0	1-0	0	0	.500	.667	.500	228	1	1-0	ø	0	—	—	/H	0	0.1
	SF N	7	8	0	1	0	0	0	1	0-0	0	0	.125	.125	.125	-31	-1	0-0	1.000	0	73	168	/2	0	-0.1
	Year	10	10	1	2	0	0	0	1	1-0	0	0	.200	.273	.200	34	-1	1-0	1.000	0	73	168	/2	0	0.0
1984	Mon N	17	24	3	5	0	0	0	4	5-0	0	4	.208	.345	.208	61	-1	0-0	.968	0	134	126	1b4	0	-0.1
1986	Mon N	61	127	13	36	3	1	1	10	7-0	0	9	.283	.321	.346	84	-3	6-3	.991	-0	98	89	1b27	0	-0.5
1987	Mon N	75	85	7	21	5	0	1	14	7-0	0	6	.247	.298	.341	68	-4	5-0	.972	-1	44	91	1b9	0	-0.4
1988	Mon N	86	94	7	29	5	1	0	3	12-1	0	15	.309	.387	.383	116	3	0-2	.989	1	116	49	1b13/2	0	0.2
1989	Mon N	85	114	9	31	3	1	2	17	7-0	0	12	.272	.309	.368	93	-1	1-0	.972	-1	77	92	1b18	0	-0.4
1990	Mon N	47	49	6	8	1	0	1	5	7-2	1	6	.163	.281	.245	48	-3	1-0	1.000	-1	0	285	1b7	15	-0.5
Total	9	428	569	52	145	17	6	5	59	52-4	1	58	.255	.316	.332	80	-14	19-7	.983	-5	86	98	1b78,2b16	15	-2.3
JOHNSON, BILL	William F. "Sleepy Bill"; B9.1862 NJ; D7.17.1942 Chester PA; BL/TL/?/167; d6.27																								
1884	Phi U	1	4	0	0	0	0	0	—	0	—	—	.000	.000	.000	-99	-1	—	ø	-0	0	0	/lf	—	-0.1
1887	Ind N	11	42	3	8	0	0	0	3	0	1	6	.190	.209	.190	12	-5	5	.765	-1	120	0	O11R	—	-0.5
1890	Bal AA	24	95	15	28	2	3	0	6	7	1	—	.295	.350	.379	110	1	8	.865	3	151	347	O24R	—	0.2
1891	Bal AA	129	480	101	130	13	14	2	79	89	4	55	.271	.389	.369	116	13	32	.877	3	120	103	O129(60/24/46)	—	1.1
1892	Bal N	4	15	2	2	0	0	0	2	2	0	0	.133	.235	.133	12	-2	0	.667	-1	0	0	O4(1/0/3)	—	-0.3
Total	5	169	636	121	168	15	17	2	90	98	6	61	.264	.368	.351	105	6	45	.867	3	121	128	O169(62/24/84)	—	0.4
JOHNSON, BILL	William Lawrence; B10.18.1892 Chicago IL; D11.5.1950 Los Angeles CA; BL/TR/5´11˝/170; d9.22																								
1916	Phi A	4	15	1	4	1	0	0	1	0	0	4	.267	.267	.333	84	0	0	1.000	-1	70	0	O4C	—	-0.1
1917	Phi A	48	109	7	19	2	2	1	8	8	1	14	.174	.237	.257	51	-7	4	.900	-2	70	142	O30(2/1/27)	—	-1.1
Total	2	52	124	8	23	3	2	1	9	8	1	18	.185	.241	.266	55	-7	4	.909	-2	70	129	O34(2/5/27)	—	-1.2
JOHNSON, BILLY	William Russell "Bull"; B8.30.1918 Montclair NJ; D6.20.2006 Augusta GA; BR/TR/5´10˝/180; d4.22; Mil 1944–46																								
1943	†NY A	**155**	592	70	166	24	6	5	94	53	4	30	.280	.344	.367	107	5	3-5	.966	13	106	120	3b155	0	2.0
1946	NY A	85	296	51	77	14	5	4	35	31	2	42	.260	.334	.382	98	-1	1-0	.955	5	108	97	3b74	0	0.5
1947	†NY A★	132	494	67	141	19	8	10	95	44	6	43	.285	.351	.417	114	8	1-2	.952	-17	81	54	3b132	0	-1.1
1948	NY A	127	446	59	131	20	6	12	64	41	4	30	.294	.358	.446	114	7	0-0	.947	3	94	122	3b118	0	0.9
1949	†NY A	113	329	48	82	11	3	8	56	48	2	44	.249	.348	.374	91	-5	1-0	.951	-3	93	95	3b81,1b21/2	0	-0.8
1950	†NY A	108	327	44	85	16	2	6	40	42	1	30	.260	.346	.376	87	-6	1-0	.958	-3	94	113	3b100,1b5	0	-0.9
1951	NY A	15	40	5	12	3	0	0	4	7	0	0	.300	.404	.375	116	1	0-1	.960	-2	83	0	3b13	0	-0.1
	StL N	124	442	52	116	23	1	14	64	46	6	49	.262	.340	.414	101	1	5-3	**.976**	10	**115**	**106**	3b124	0	1.0
1952	StL N	94	282	23	71	10	2	2	34	34	3	21	.252	.339	.323	84	-5	1-0	.951	4	112	79	3b89	0	-0.2
1953	StL N	11	5	0	1	1	0	0	1	1	0	1	.200	.333	.400	90	0	0-0	1.000	1	172	206	3b11	0	0.1
Total	9	964	3253	419	882	141	33	61	487	347	28	290	.271	.346	.391	102	5	13-11	.959	10	100	98	3b897,1b26/2	0	1.4
JOHNSON, RUSS	William Russell; B2.22.1973 Baton Rouge LA; BR/TR/5´10˝/180; [HouN94 S1/30]; d4.8; Col Louisiana St.																								
1997	†Hou N	21	60	7	18	1	0	2	9	6-0	0	14	.300	.364	.417	107	1	1-1	.963	-2	93	99	3b14,2b3	0	-0.2
1998	Hou N	8	13	2	3	1	0	0	0	1-0	1	5	.231	.333	.308	72	0	1-0	1.000	1	174	0	3b5/2	0	0.1
1999	†Hou N	83	156	24	44	10	0	5	23	20-0	0	31	.282	.358	.442	104	1	2-3	.944	7	109	201	3b36,2b15,S2	0	0.8
2000	Hou N	26	45	4	8	0	0	0	3	2-0	0	10	.178	.213	.178	-0	-7	1-1	1.000	-4	67	71	S5,3b4,2b3	0	-1.0
	TB A	74	185	28	47	8	0	2	17	25-0	1	30	.254	.344	.330	73	-7	4-1	.967	9	135	108	3b49,2b18,S11	0	0.3
2001	TB A	85	248	32	73	19	2	4	33	34-0	1	57	.294	.380	.435	117	8	2-2	.922	-4	91	116	3b36,2b33,S6,D2	15	0.5
2002	TB A	45	111	15	24	5	0	1	12	16-1	1	22	.216	.320	.288	65	-5	5-2	.984	-5	75	99	3b27,S2/2D	73	-1.0
2005	NY A	22	18	5	4	2	0	0	0	1-0	1	4	.222	.300	.333	69	-1	0-0	1.000	-2	50	0	3b8,1b7,O3R/2D	0	-0.3
Total	7	364	836	117	221	46	2	14	97	105-1	5	173	.264	.348	.374	89	-10	16-10	.957	0	103	120	3b179,2b75,S26,D10,1b7,O3R	88	-0.8
JOHNSTON, GREG	Gregory Bernard; B2.12.1955 Los Angeles CA; BL/TL/6´0˝/175; [SFN75 12/272]; d7.27; Col Citrus (CA) JC																								
1979	SF N	42	74	5	15	2	0	1	7	2-0	0	17	.203	.224	.270	37	-7	0-0	.966	1	118	110	O17(13/1/5)	0	-0.7
1980	Min A	14	27	3	5	3	0	0	1	2-0	0	4	.185	.233	.296	43	-2	0-0	1.000	-0	106	0	O14C	0	-0.2
1981	Min A	7	16	2	2	0	0	0	0	2-0	0	5	.125	.222	.125	2	-2	0-0	1.000	0	76	307	O6C	0	-0.2
Total	3	63	117	10	22	5	0	1	8	6-0	0	26	.188	.226	.256	33	-11	0-0	.985	1	105	115	O37(13/21/5)	0	-1.1

JOHNSTON, JIMMY James Harle; B12.10.1889 Cleveland TN; D2.14.1967 Chattanooga TN; BR/TR/5´10˝/160; d5.3; C1; b–Doc; OF(72/112/177)

YEAR	TM LG	G	AB	R	H	2B	3B	HR	RBI	BB-IB	HP	SO	AVG	OBP	SLG	AOPS	ABR	SB-CS	FA	FR	RNG	THR	GAMES AT POSITION	DL	BFW
1911	Chi A	1	2	0	0	0	0	0	2	0	0	—	.000	.000	.000	-99	-1	0	1.000	-0	100	0	/cf	—	-0.1
1914	Chi N	50	101	9	23	3	2	1	8	4	1	9	.228	.264	.327	76	-4	3	.929	4	119	246	O28(2/22/4),2b4	—	-0.1
1916	†Bro N	118	425	58	107	13	8	1	26	35	3	38	.252	.313	.327	94	-3	22-19	.964	4	104	119	O106(8/45/55)	—	-0.9
1917	Bro N	103	330	33	89	10	4	0	25	23	2	28	.270	.321	.324	96	-2	16	.958	0	103	90	O66(37/24/5),1b14,S4,2b3,3b3	—	-0.6
1918	Bro N	123	484	54	136	16	8	0	27	33	1	31	.281	.328	.347	106	3	22	.956	4	98	121	O96(20/5/75),1b21,3b4/2	—	0.2
1919	Bro N	117	405	56	114	11	4	1	23	29	3	26	.281	.334	.336	100	0	11	.960	-2	105	84	2b87,O14(1/8/6),1b2/S	—	-0.1
1920	†Bro N	**155**	635	87	185	17	12	1	52	43	2	23	.291	.338	.361	98	-2	19-15	.934	-7	96	88	3b146,O7R,S3	—	-0.7
1921	Bro N	**152**	624	104	203	41	14	5	56	45	1	26	.325	.372	.460	115	14	28-16	.935	7	103	**120**	3b150,S3	—	3.0
1922	Bro N	138	567	110	181	20	7	4	49	38	2	17	.319	.364	.400	98	-2	18-9	.947	0	97	105	2b62,S50,3b26	—	0.8
1923	Bro N	151	625	111	203	29	11	4	60	53	0	15	.325	.378	.426	115	14	16-13	.948	14	99	92	2b84,S52,3b14	—	3.5
1924	Bro N	86	315	51	94	11	2	2	29	27	1	10	.298	.356	.365	97	-1	5-6	.939	-4	93	80	S63,3b10,1b4/rf	—	0.1
1925	Bro N	123	431	63	128	13	3	2	43	45	4	15	.297	.369	.355	88	-6	7-5	.886	-20	75	66	3b81,O20(2/0/18),1b8,S2	—	-2.2
1926	Bos N	23	57	7	14	1	0	1	5	10	0	3	.246	.358	.316	91	0	2	.865	-3	89	128	3b14,2b2/lf	—	-0.2
	NY N	37	69	11	16	0	0	0	5	6	0	5	.232	.293	.232	43	-5	0	1.000	-2	60	0	O14(1/7/6)	—	-0.8
	Year	60	126	18	30	1	0	1	10	16	0	8	.238	.324	.270	64	-6	2	1.000	-5	62	0	O15(2/7/6),3b14,2b2	—	-1.0
Total	13	1377	5070	754	1493	185	75	22	410	391	20	246	.294	.347	.374	100	5	169-83	.926	-4	93	88	3b448,O354R,2b243,S178,1b49	—	1.9

JOHNSTON, JOHNNY John Thomas; B3.28.1890 Longview TX; D3.7.1940 San Diego CA; BL/TR/5´11˝/172; d4.10

YEAR	TM LG	G	AB	R	H	2B	3B	HR	RBI	BB-IB	HP	SO	AVG	OBP	SLG	AOPS	ABR	SB-CS	FA	FR	RNG	THR	GAMES AT POSITION	DL	BFW
1913	StL A	111	380	37	85	14	4	2	27	42	4	51	.224	.308	.297	79	-9	11	.965	10	107	152	O107L	—	-0.5

JOHNSTON, REX Rex David; B11.8.1937 Colton CA; BB/TR/6´1.5˝/202; d4.15; Col USC

YEAR	TM LG	G	AB	R	H	2B	3B	HR	RBI	BB-IB	HP	SO	AVG	OBP	SLG	AOPS	ABR	SB-CS	FA	FR	RNG	THR	GAMES AT POSITION	DL	BFW
1964	Pit N	14	7	1	0	0	0	0	0	3-1	0	0	.000	.300	.000	-7	-1	0-0	1.000	-0	52	0	O8(6/2/0)	0	-0.1

JOHNSTON, DICK Richard Frederick; B4.6.1863 Kingston NY; D4.4.1934 Detroit MI; BR/TR/5´8˝/155; d8.12

YEAR	TM LG	G	AB	R	H	2B	3B	HR	RBI	BB-IB	HP	SO	AVG	OBP	SLG	AOPS	ABR	SB-CS	FA	FR	RNG	THR	GAMES AT POSITION	DL	BFW
1884	Ric AA	39	146	23	41	5	5	2	—	2	0	—	.281	.291	.425	132	4	—	.865	8	143	254	O37C,S2	—	1.0
1885	Bos N	26	111	17	26	6	3	1	23	0	—	15	.234	.234	.369	96	-1	—	.842	1	174	306	O26C	—	0.0
1886	Bos N	109	413	48	99	18	9	1	57	3	—	70	.240	.245	.334	77	-13	11	.892	14	133	117	O109C	—	-0.3
1887	Bos N	**127**	507	87	131	13	20	5	77	16	0	35	.258	.281	.393	84	-14	52	.933	23	151	209	O127C	—	0.3
1888	Bos N	135	585	102	173	31	**18**	12	68	15	1	33	.296	.314	.472	144	26	35	.898	4	131	67	O135C	—	2.5
1889	Bos N	132	539	80	123	16	4	5	67	41	2	60	.228	.285	.301	59	-32	34	.917	-8	87	139	O132C	—	-3.9
1890	Bos P	2	9	0	1	0	0	0	0	0	0	1	.111	.111	.111	-38	-2	0	.800	0	313	0	O2C	—	-0.1
	NY P	77	306	37	74	9	7	1	43	18	2	25	.242	.288	.327	59	-20	7	.897	-0	123	106	O76(12/62/2),S2	—	-1.9
	Year	79	315	37	75	9	7	1	43	18	2	26	.238	.284	.321	56	-22	7	.894	0	127	104	O78(12/64/2),S2	—	-2.0
1891	Cin AA	99	376	59	83	11	2	6	51	38	5	44	.221	.301	.309	69	-17	12	.895	-2	115	102	O99(0/99/1)	—	-2.0
Total	8	746	2992	453	751	109	68	33	386	133	10	283	.251	.285	.366	86	-69	151	.903	40	126	137	O743(12/729/3),S4	—	-4.4

JOHNSTON, DOC Wheeler Roger; B9.9.1887 Cleveland TN; D2.17.1961 Chattanooga TN; BL/TL/6´0˝/170; d10.3; b–Jimmy

YEAR	TM LG	G	AB	R	H	2B	3B	HR	RBI	BB-IB	HP	SO	AVG	OBP	SLG	AOPS	ABR	SB-CS	FA	FR	RNG	THR	GAMES AT POSITION	DL	BFW
1909	Cin N	3	10	1	0	0	0	0	1	0	0	—	.000	.000	.000	-99	-2	0	1.000	0	142	0	1b3	—	-0.2
1912	Cle A	43	164	22	46	7	4	1	11	11	0	—	.280	.326	.390	101	-1	8	.991	-1	76	142	1b41	—	-0.3
1913	Cle A	133	530	74	135	19	12	2	39	35	7	65	.255	.309	.347	89	-9	19	.989	-1	92	105	1b133	—	-1.4
1914	Cle A	104	340	43	83	15	1	0	23	28	5	46	.244	.311	.294	79	-8	14-9	.987	-7	65	86	1b90,O2C	—	-1.9
1915	Pit N	147	543	71	144	19	12	5	64	38	13	40	.265	.328	.372	113	8	26-17	.991	-12	61	84	1b147	—	-0.9
1916	Pit N	114	404	33	86	10	10	0	39	20	7	42	.213	.262	.287	68	-16	17	.987	-3	87	71	1b110	—	-2.5
1918	Cle A	74	273	30	62	12	2	0	25	26	3	19	.227	.301	.286	70	-9	12	.989	-3	83	58	1b73	—	-1.6
1919	Cle A	102	331	42	101	17	3	1	33	25	3	18	.305	.359	.384	102	1	21	.984	-4	89	117	1b98	—	-0.5
1920	†Cle A	147	535	68	156	24	10	2	71	28	5	32	.292	.333	.385	87	-11	13-7	.992	-1	95	105	1b147	—	-1.5
1921	Cle A	118	384	53	114	20	7	2	46	29	4	15	.297	.353	.401	90	-6	2-9	.988	-2	95	110	1b116	—	-1.6
1922	Phi A	71	260	41	65	11	7	1	29	24	1	15	.250	.316	.358	73	-11	7-6	.990	-5	74	73	1b65	—	-2.0
Total	11	1056	3774	478	992	154	68	14	381	264	48	292	.263	.319	.351	88	-64	139-48	.989	-37	83	94	1b1023,O2C	—	-14.4

JOHNSTON, FRED Wilfred Ivy; B7.9.1899 Charlotte NC; D7.14.1959 Tyler TX; BR/TR/5´11.5˝/170; d6.29; Col North Carolina St.

YEAR	TM LG	G	AB	R	H	2B	3B	HR	RBI	BB-IB	HP	SO	AVG	OBP	SLG	AOPS	ABR	SB-CS	FA	FR	RNG	THR	GAMES AT POSITION	DL	BFW
1924	Bro N	4	4	1	1	0	0	0	0	0	0	1	.250	.250	.250	35	0	0-0	.667	-0	123	0	/23	—	-0.1

JOHNSTONE, JAY John William; B11.20.1945 Manchester CT; BL/TR/6´1˝/(175–190); d7.30; OF(258/521/572)

YEAR	TM LG	G	AB	R	H	2B	3B	HR	RBI	BB-IB	HP	SO	AVG	OBP	SLG	AOPS	ABR	SB-CS	FA	FR	RNG	THR	GAMES AT POSITION	DL	BFW
1966	Cal A	61	254	35	67	12	4	3	17	11-1	1	36	.264	.297	.378	95	-3	3-3	.975	-2	96	52	O61(41/12/13)	0	-0.9
1967	Cal A	79	230	18	48	7	1	2	10	5-0	0	37	.209	.226	.274	49	-16	3-2	.973	3	118	95	O63(0/62/1)	0	-1.7
1968	Cal A	41	115	11	30	4	1	0	3	7-0	0	15	.261	.303	.313	90	-2	2-1	.984	2	100	233	O29(1/21/7)	21	-0.1
1969	Cal A	148	540	64	146	20	5	10	59	38-5	5	75	.270	.321	.381	101	-1	3-9	.983	3	104	139	O144C	0	-0.4
1970	Cal A	119	320	34	76	10	5	11	39	24-6	1	53	.237	.290	.403	93	-5	1-0	.981	-1	99	124	O100(2/88/10)	0	-0.8
1971	Chi A	124	388	53	101	14	1	16	40	38-4	3	50	.260	.329	.425	110	5	10-5	.968	-2	95	136	O119(11/92/23)	0	0.0
1972	Chi A	113	261	27	49	9	0	4	17	25-2	0	42	.188	.259	.268	56	-14	2-1	.988	-2	94	109	O97(13/85/6)	0	-2.1
1973	Oak A	23	28	1	3	1	0	0	3	2-0	0	4	.107	.167	.143	-13	-4	0-1	1.000	1	204	0	O7(3/1/3),2b2,D4	0	-0.4
1974	Phi N	64	200	30	59	10	4	6	30	24-4	0	28	.295	.371	.475	129	8	5-5	.968	-2	88	109	O59(31/1/40)	0	0.2
1975	Phi N	122	350	50	115	19	2	7	54	42-7	0	39	.329	.397	.454	130	16	7-3	.976	3	95	181	O101(0/3/100)	0	1.5
1976	†Phi N	129	440	62	140	38	4	5	53	41-5	2	39	.318	.373	.457	131	19	5-5	.982	8	121	88	O122(2/0/120),1b6	0	2.2
1977	†Phi N	112	363	64	103	18	4	15	59	38-3	2	38	.284	.349	.479	115	8	3-7	1.000	4	103	146	O91(4/0/87),1b19	0	0.5
1978	Phi N	35	56	3	10	2	0	0	4	6-0	0	9	.179	.258	.214	33	-5	0-2	.988	0	161	173	1b8,O7(3/0/4)	0	-0.7
	†NY A	36	65	6	17	0	0	1	6	4-0	3	10	.262	.329	.308	83	-1	0-1	1.000	-0	110	0	O22(8/0/14),D5	0	-0.3
1979	NY A	23	48	7	10	1	0	1	7	2-0	0	7	.208	.240	.292	43	-4	1-0	1.000	1	127	0	O19(14/4/1),D3	0	-0.4
	SD N	75	201	10	59	8	2	0	32	18-3	0	21	.294	.348	.353	99	0	1-3	.985	-0	80	142	O45(35/7/4),1b22	0	-0.4
1980	LA N	109	251	31	77	15	2	2	20	24-1	2	29	.307	.372	.406	120	8	3-2	.965	3	101	202	O61(5/0/57)	0	0.8
1981	†LA N	61	83	8	17	3	0	3	6	7-0	0	13	.205	.267	.349	77	-3	0-1	.957	1	93	334	O16(8/0/8),1b2	0	-0.3
1982	LA N	21	13	1	1	1	0	0	2	5-1	0	2	.077	.316	.154	42	-1	0-0	ø	0	—	—	/H	0	-0.1
	Chi N	98	269	39	67	13	1	10	43	40-8	0	41	.249	.343	.416	108	4	0-2	.982	4	106	140	O86(34/0/58)	0	0.3
	Year	119	282	40	68	14	1	10	45	45-9	0	43	.241	.341	.404	106	4	0-2	.982	4	106	140	O86(34/0/58)	0	0.2
1983	Chi N	86	140	16	36	7	0	6	22	20-6	3	24	.257	.362	.436	115	3	1-1	.935	-1	90	127	O44(36/0/8)	0	0.1
1984	Chi N	52	73	8	21	2	2	0	3	7-4	0	18	.288	.350	.370	94	-1	0-0	1.000	-2	64	0	O15(7/1/8)	33	-0.3
1985	†LA N	17	15	0	2	1	0	0	2	1-1	0	2	.133	.188	.200	9	-2	0-0	ø	0	—	—	/H	112	-0.2
Total	20	1748	4703	578	1254	215	38	102	531	429-61	22	632	.267	.329	.394	102	9	50-54	.979	21	101	128	O1308R,1b57,D12,2b2	166	-3.5

JOK, STAN Stanley Edward "Tucker"; B5.3.1926 Buffalo NY; D3.6.1972 Buffalo NY; BR/TR/6´0˝/(190–195); d4.13

YEAR	TM LG	G	AB	R	H	2B	3B	HR	RBI	BB-IB	HP	SO	AVG	OBP	SLG	AOPS	ABR	SB-CS	FA	FR	RNG	THR	GAMES AT POSITION	DL	BFW
1954	Phi N	3	3	0	0	0	0	0	0	0	0	2	.000	.000	.000	-99	-1	0-0	ø	0	—	—	/H	0	-0.1
	Chi A	3	12	1	2	0	0	0	2	1	0	2	.167	.231	.167	10	-2	0-0	1.000	0	101	180	3b3	0	-0.1
1955	Chi A	6	4	3	1	0	0	1	2	1-0	0	1	.250	.333	1.000	260	1	0-0	.857	-0	112	0	3b3/lf	0	0.1
Total	2	12	19	4	3	0	0	1	4	2-0	0	5	.158	.227	.316	47	-2	0-0	.941	0	105	116	3b6/lf	0	-0.1

JOLLEY, SMEAD Smead Powell "Guinea","Smudge"; B1.14.1902 Wesson AR; D11.17.1991 Alameda CA; BL/TR/6´3.5˝/210; d4.17

YEAR	TM LG	G	AB	R	H	2B	3B	HR	RBI	BB-IB	HP	SO	AVG	OBP	SLG	AOPS	ABR	SB-CS	FA	FR	RNG	THR	GAMES AT POSITION	DL	BFW
1930	Chi A	152	616	76	193	38	12	16	114	28	3	52	.313	.346	.492	114	10	3-1	.950	-0	93	146	O151(68/0/83)	—	-0.1
1931	Chi A	54	110	5	33	11	0	3	28	7	2	4	.300	.353	.482	125	4	0-0	.857	-3	76	60	O23(8/0/15)	—	0.0
1932	Chi A	12	42	3	15	3	0	0	7	3	1	0	.357	.413	.429	127	2	1-0	.923	-1	63	158	O11(7/0/4)	—	0.1
	Bos A	137	531	57	164	27	5	18	99	27	2	29	.309	.345	.480	115	8	0-5	.943	-3	90	131	O126(120/0/6),C5	—	-0.3
	Year	149	573	60	179	30	5	18	106	30	3	29	.312	.350	.476	116	10	1-5	.942	-4	88	133	O137(127/0/10),C5	—	-0.2
1933	Bos A	118	411	47	116	32	4	9	65	24	2	20	.282	.325	.445	103	1	1-1	.955	-0	92	132	O102(87/0/15)	—	-0.5
Total	4	473	1710	188	521	111	21	46	313	89	10	105	.305	.343	.475	112	25	5-7	.944	-8	90	134	O413(290/0/123),C5	—	-0.8

JONES B Johnstown PA; d7.14

YEAR	TM LG	G	AB	R	H	2B	3B	HR	RBI	BB-IB	HP	SO	AVG	OBP	SLG	AOPS	ABR	SB-CS	FA	FR	RNG	THR	GAMES AT POSITION	DL	BFW
1884	Was AA	4	17	2	5	0	0	0	—	1	0	—	.294	.333	.294	120	0	—	1.000	0	0	0	O4L	—	0.0

JONES ; d4.30

YEAR	TM LG	G	AB	R	H	2B	3B	HR	RBI	BB-IB	HP	SO	AVG	OBP	SLG	AOPS	ABR	SB-CS	FA	FR	RNG	THR	GAMES AT POSITION	DL	BFW
1885	NY AA	1	4	0	1	0	0	0	0	0	0	—	.250	.250	.250	61	0	—	1.000	1	156	0	/3	—	0.1

JONES, ADAM Adam La Marque; B8.1.1985 San Diego CA; BR/TR/6´2˝/200; [SeaA03 1/37]; d7.14

YEAR	TM LG	G	AB	R	H	2B	3B	HR	RBI	BB-IB	HP	SO	AVG	OBP	SLG	AOPS	ABR	SB-CS	FA	FR	RNG	THR	GAMES AT POSITION	DL	BFW
2006	Sea A	32	74	6	16	4	0	1	8	2-0	0	22	.216	.237	.311	43	-7	3-1	.960	5	120	455	O26C	0	-0.1

YEAR	TM LG	G	AB	R	H	2B	3B	HR	RBI	BB-IB	HP	SO	AVG	OBP	SLG	AOPS	ABR	SB-CS	FA	FR	RNG	THR	GAMES AT POSITION	DL	BFW
Jones, Andruw	Andruw Rudolf; B4.23.1977 Willemstad, Curacao; BR/TR/6´1˝/(185–210); d8.15																								
1996	†Atl N	31	106	11	23	7	1	5	13	7-0	0	29	.217	.265	.443	78	-4	3-0	.975	6	141	256	O29(0/12/20)	0	0.2
1997	†Atl N	153	399	60	92	18	1	18	70	56-2	4	107	.231	.329	.416	93	-4	20-11	.977	17	**126**	**202**	O147(2/57/95)	0	1.1
1998	†Atl N	159	582	89	158	33	8	31	90	40-8	4	129	.271	.321	.515	117	11	27-4	.995	20	118	**215**	O159C	0	3.6
1999	†Atl N	**162**	592	97	163	35	5	26	84	76-11	9	103	.275	.365	.483	113	13	24-12	.981	17	**122**	145	O162C	0	3.1
2000	†Atl N★	161	656	122	199	36	6	36	104	59-0	9	100	.303	.366	.541	127	25	21-6	.996	5	110	91	O161C	0	3.2
2001	†Atl N	161	625	104	157	25	2	34	104	56-3	3	142	.251	.312	.461	96	-6	11-4	.987	11	**117**	111	O161C	0	0.8
2002	†Atl N★	154	560	91	148	34	0	35	94	83-4	10	135	.264	.366	.512	129	25	8-3	.993	-1	106	56	O154C/D	0	2.6
2003	†Atl N★	156	595	101	165	28	2	36	116	53-2	5	125	.277	.338	.513	119	15	4-3	.993	2	105	93	O155C	0	1.8
2004	†Atl N	154	570	85	149	34	4	29	91	71-9	3	147	.261	.345	.488	112	10	6-6	.993	4	104	128	O154C	0	1.4
2005	†Atl N★	160	586	95	154	24	3	**51**	**128**	64-13	15	112	.263	.347	.575	136	28	5-3	.995	-4	94	131	O159C	0	2.7
2006	Atl N☆	156	565	107	148	29	0	41	129	82-9	13	127	.262	.363	.531	125	22	4-1	.995	-2	103	55	O153C,D2	0	2.1
Total	11	1607	5836	962	1556	303	32	342	1023	647-61	75	1256	.267	.345	.505	117	135	133-53	.990	75	111	123	O1594(2/1487/115),D3	0	22.6
Jones, Charlie	Charles Claude "Casey"; B6.2.1876 Butler PA; D4.2.1947 Two Harbors MN; BR/TR/6´1˝/165; d5.2; Col Grove City																								
1901	Bos A	10	41	6	6	2	0	0	6	1	0	—	.146	.167	.195	0	-6	2	.929	-2	0	0	O10(0/8/2)	—	-0.7
1904	Chi A	5	17	2	4	0	1	0	1	1	0	—	.235	.278	.353	103	0	0	1.000	1	411	0	O5C	—	0.1
1905	Was A	142	544	68	113	18	4	2	41	31	3	—	.208	.254	.267	68	-21	24	.971	14	153	161	O142C	—	-1.5
1906	Was A	131	497	56	120	11	11	3	42	24	5	—	.241	.283	.326	95	-5	34	.961	5	124	181	O128C/2	—	-0.7
1907	Was A	121	437	48	116	14	10	0	37	22	2	—	.265	.304	.343	115	5	26	.967	-2	43	58	O111(12/90/8),2b5,1b4,S2	—	-0.2
1908	StL A	74	263	37	61	11	2	0	17	14	3	—	.232	.279	.289	84	-5	14	.963	2	182	107	O72(0/70/2)	—	-0.7
Total	6	483	1799	217	420	56	28	5	144	93	13	—	.233	.276	.304	87	-32	100	.966	17	122	130	O468(12/443/12),2b6,1b4,S2	—	-3.7
Jones, Charlie	Charles F.; B10.24.1861 New York NY; D9.15.1922 New York NY; d6.28																								
1884	Bro AA	25	90	10	16	1	0	0	—	5	0	—	.178	.221	.189	35	-6	—	.871	-5	94	75	2b13,3b11,O2(1/0/1)	—	-1.0
Jones, Charley	Charles Wesley "Baby" (b Benjamin Wesley Rippay); B4.30.1850 Alamance Co. NC; BR/TR/5´11.5˝/202; d5.4; U2																								
1875	Wes NA	12	47	4	13	2	4	0	10	0	—	5	.277	.277	.489	152	2	1-1	.800	-2	103	0	O12L	—	0.1
	Har NA	1	4	1	0	0	0	0	0	0	—	1	.000	.000	.000	-95	-1	0-0	.667	-0	0	0	/cf	—	-0.1
	Year	13	51	5	13	2	4	0	10	0	—	6	.255	.255	.451	133	1	1-1	.778	-2	93	0	O13(12/1/0)	—	0.0
1876	Cin N	64	276	40	79	17	4	4	38	7	—	17	.286	.304	.420	162	21	—	.857	1	99	69	O64(10/53/1)	—	1.6
1877	Cin N	17	69	16	21	3	3	1	10	4	—	8	.304	.342	.478	176	6	—	.920	1	95	70	1b10,O8(5/3/0)	—	0.5
	Chi N	2	8	1	3	1	0	0	2	1	—	0	.375	.444	.500	176	1	—	1.000	1	251	0	O2C	—	0.1
	Cin N	38	163	36	51	8	7	1	26	10	—	17	.313	.353	.466	175	15	—	.838	10	136	0	O38L	—	2.0
	Year	57	240	53	75	12	10	2	38	15	—	25	.313	.353	.471	176	22	—	.845	12	163	102	O48(43/5/0),1b10	—	**2.6**
1878	Cin N	**61**	261	50	81	11	7	3	39	4	—	17	.310	.321	.441	163	18	—	.896	4	53	42	O61(51/10/0)	—	1.7
1879	Bos N	83	355	**85**	112	22	10	**9**	**62**	**29**	—	38	.315	.367	.510	182	32	—	**.933**	13	109	54	O83L	—	3.6
1880	Bos N	66	280	44	84	15	3	5	37	11	—	27	.300	.326	.429	159	17	—	.826	-4	71	98	O66(66/1/0)	—	0.9
1883	Cin AA	90	391	84	115	15	12	10	80	20	—	—	.294	.328	.471	146	18	—	.876	-0	69	58	O90(16/75/0)	—	1.3
1884	Cin AA	**112**	472	117	148	19	17	7	71	37	10	—	.314	**.376**	.470	166	34	—	.887	-1	52	0	O112(63/51/0)	—	2.7
1885	Cin AA	**112**	487	108	157	19	17	5	35	21	9	—	.322	.362	.462	156	29	—	.891	11	114	161	O112L	—	3.3
1886	Cin AA	127	500	87	135	22	10	6	68	61	6	—	.270	.356	.390	130	18	3	.879	2	107	24	O127L	—	1.5
1887	Cin AA	41	153	28	48	7	4	2	40	19	3	—	.314	.400	.451	134	7	7	.900	1	106	151	O41(41/1/0)	—	0.6
	NY AA	62	247	30	63	11	3	3	29	12	6	—	.255	.306	.360	89	-4	8	.917	4	182	246	O62(6/50/7),P2/1	—	-0.1
	Year	103	400	58	111	18	7	5	69	31	9	—	.278	.343	.395	107	4	15	.910	5	**152**	**208**	O103(47/51/7),P2/1	—	0.5
1888	KC AA	6	25	2	4	0	1	0	5	1	0	—	.160	.192	.240	36	-2	1	.750	-1	98	0	O6L	—	-0.3
Total	11	881	3687	728	1101	170	98	56	542	237	34	124	.299	.347	.443	150	210	19	.882	43	98	79	O872(624/246/8),1b11,P2	—	19.4
Jones, Chris	Christopher Carlos; B12.16.1965 Utica NY; BR/TR/6´2˝/(205–219); [CinN84 3/59]; d4.21																								
1991	Cin N	52	89	14	26	1	2	2	6	2-0	0	31	.292	.304	.416	98	-1	2-1	1.000	-1	82	99	O26(18/3/9)	0	-0.3
1992	Hou N	54	63	7	12	2	1	1	4	7-0	0	21	.190	.271	.302	65	-3	3-0	.931	-3	77	0	O43(17/5/25)	0	-0.6
1993	Col N	86	209	29	57	11	4	6	31	10-1	0	48	.273	.305	.450	85	-5	9-4	.983	-2	92	71	O70(16/52/4)	0	-0.7
1994	Col N	21	40	6	12	2	1	0	2	2-1	0	14	.300	.333	.400	77	-1	0-1	.941	-2	70	0	O14(4/13/0)	0	-0.3
1995	NY N	79	182	33	51	6	2	8	31	13-1	1	45	.280	.327	.467	111	2	2-1	.976	2	111	117	O52(25/0/28),1b5	0	0.2
1996	NY N	89	149	22	36	7	0	4	18	12-1	2	42	.242	.307	.369	81	-4	1-0	.957	-2	104	0	O66(17/8/44),1b5	0	-0.7
1997	SD N	92	152	24	37	9	0	7	25	16-0	2	45	.243	.322	.441	104	1	7-2	.951	1	97	176	O61(24/19/25)	19	0.1
1998	Ari N	20	31	3	6	1	0	0	3	3-0	0	9	.194	.265	.226	31	-3	0-0	1.000	-0	107	0	O8(1/0/7)	0	-0.3
	SF N	43	90	14	17	2	1	2	10	8-0	0	28	.189	.250	.300	48	-7	2-1	.941	-2	84	77	O29(5/0/24),D2	0	-1.0
	Year	63	121	17	23	3	1	2	13	11-0	0	37	.190	.254	.281	43	-11	2-1	.956	-2	89	61	O37(6/0/31),D2	0	-1.3
2000	Mil N	12	16	3	3	2	0	0	1	1-0	0	4	.188	.235	.313	37	-2	0-0	1.000	0	157	0	O2R	0	-0.1
Total	9	548	1021	155	257	43	11	30	131	74-4	5	287	.252	.303	.404	86	-23	26-10	.967	-8	95	77	O371(127/100/168),1b10,D2	19	-3.7
Jones, Chris	Christopher Dale; B7.13.1957 Los Angeles CA; BL/TL/6´0˝/183; [HouN79 25/625]; d6.8; Col San Diego St.																								
1985	Hou N	31	25	0	5	0	0	0	1	3-0	0	7	.200	.286	.200	39	-2	0-0	1.000	1	161	0	O15(2/9/4)	0	-0.1
1986	SF N	3	1	0	0	0	0	0	0	0-0	0	0	.000	.000	.000	-99	0	1-0	ø	0	—	—	/H	0	0.0
Total	2	34	26	0	5	0	0	0	1	3-0	0	7	.192	.276	.192	34	-2	1-0	1.000	1	161	0	O15(2/9/4)	0	-0.1
Jones, Clarence	Clarence Woodrow; B11.7.1941 Zanesville OH; BL/TL/6´2˝/205; d4.20; C15																								
1967	Chi N	53	135	13	34	7	0	2	16	14-3	0	33	.252	.314	.348	88	-2	0-0	.978	-3	95	0	O31(2/0/29),1b13	0	-0.8
1968	Chi N	5	2	0	0	0	0	0	0	2-0	0	1	.000	.500	.000	56	0	0-0	1.000	-0	0	0	/1	0	0.0
Total	2	58	137	13	34	7	0	2	16	16-3	0	34	.248	.318	.343	88	-2	0-0	.978	-3	95	0	O31(2/0/29),1b14	0	-0.8
Jones, Cleon	Cleon Joseph; B8.4.1942 Plateau AL; BR/TL/6´0˝/(185–200); d9.14; Col Alabama A&M																								
1963	NY N	6	15	1	2	0	0	0	1	0-0	0	4	.133	.133	.133	-23	-2	0-0	1.000	-0	82	0	O5(1/5/0)	0	-0.3
1965	NY N	30	74	2	11	1	0	1	9	2-0	0	23	.149	.171	.203	5	-10	1-0	1.000	0	92	184	O23(2/18/3)	0	-1.1
1966	NY N	139	495	74	136	16	4	8	57	30-2	3	62	.275	.318	.372	94	-5	16-8	.979	1	102	115	O129(3/107/35)	0	-0.8
1967	NY N	129	411	46	101	10	5	5	30	19-6	4	57	.246	.282	.331	77	-14	12-2	.977	-1	99	83	O115(20/86/21)	0	-1.8
1968	NY N	147	509	63	151	29	4	14	55	31-3	5	98	.297	.341	.452	136	22	23-12	.963	-2	99	82	O139(117/28/18)	0	1.5
1969	†NY N★	137	483	92	164	25	4	12	75	64-10	7	60	.340	.422	.482	150	35	16-8	.991	5	112	62	O122(121/1/0),1b15	0	3.4
1970	NY N	134	506	71	140	25	8	10	63	57-2	5	87	.277	.352	.417	105	4	12-3	.981	6	110	109	O130(125/6/1)	0	0.4
1971	NY N	136	505	63	161	24	6	14	69	53-6	2	87	.319	.382	.473	142	29	6-5	.981	3	**112**	51	O132(132/1/0)	0	2.5
1972	NY N	106	375	39	92	15	1	5	52	30-4	4	83	.245	.305	.331	83	-8	1-6	.986	1	94	152	O84(71/5/14),1b20	0	-1.6
1973	†NY N	92	339	48	88	13	0	11	48	28-6	3	51	.260	.315	.395	98	-1	1-1	.967	-2	95	98	O92(73/13/8)	36	-0.9
1974	NY N	124	461	62	130	23	1	13	60	38-3	6	79	.282	.343	.421	114	8	3-3	.970	0	101	99	O120(117/3/3)	0	0.1
1975	NY N	21	50	2	12	1	0	0	2	3-0	0	6	.240	.283	.260	53	-3	0-0	1.000	-2	50	0	O12L	50	-0.6
1976	Chi A	12	40	2	8	1	0	0	3	5-0	1	5	.200	.304	.225	56	-2	0-0	1.000	-2	49	0	O8L,D3	0	-0.5
Total	13	1213	4263	565	1196	183	33	93	524	360-42	40	702	.281	.339	.404	110	53	91-48	.978	7	102	92	O1111(802/273/103),1b35,D3	86	0.3
Jones, Cobe	Coburn Dyas; B8.21.1907 Denver CO; D6.3.1969 Denver CO; BB/TR/5´7˝/155; d9.27; Col Colorado																								
1928	Pit N	1	2	0	1	0	0	0	0	0	0	0	.500	.500	.500	156	0	0	1.000	-0	89	0	/S	—	0.0
1929	Pit N	25	63	6	16	5	1	0	4	1	0	5	.254	.266	.365	53	-5	1	.919	-6	69	80	S15	—	-0.9
Total	2	26	65	6	17	5	1	0	4	1	0	5	.262	.273	.369	56	-5	1	.921	-6	70	78	S16	—	-0.9
Jones, Darryl	Darryl Lee; B6.5.1951 Meadville PA; BR/TR/5´10˝/175; [NYA72 5/110]; d6.6; b–Lynn; Col Westminster (PA)																								
1979	NY A	18	47	6	12	5	1	0	6	2-0	0	7	.255	.286	.404	85	-1	0-0	1.000	0	103	0	D15,O2(1/0/1)	0	-0.2
Jones, Davy	David Jefferson "Kangaroo"; B6.30.1880 Cambria WI; D3.30.1972 Mankato MN; BL/TR/5´10˝/165; d9.15; Col Northern Illinois																								
1901	Mil A	14	52	12	9	0	0	3	5	11	1	—	.173	.328	.346	91	0	4	.911	0	0	0	O14L	—	-0.1
1902	StL A	15	49	4	11	1	1	0	3	6	0	—	.224	.309	.286	67	-2	5	.973	3	212	662	O15R	—	0.0
	Chi N	64	243	41	74	12	3	0	14	38	0	—	.305	.399	.379	144	15	12	.955	-4	32	45	O64(0/47/17)	—	0.9
1903	Chi N	130	497	64	140	18	3	1	62	53	1	—	.282	.352	.336	99	1	15	.970	1	82	79	O130(0/97/33)	—	-0.3
1904	Chi N	98	336	44	82	11	5	3	39	41	2	—	.244	.330	.333	105	3	14	.932	-9	68	0	O97(0/1/97)	—	-1.1
1906	Det A	84	323	41	84	12	2	0	24	41	2	—	.260	.347	.310	103	3	21	.981	3	96	122	O83(0/82/1)	—	0.2
1907	†Det A	126	491	101	134	10	6	0	27	60	4	—	.273	.357	.318	111	9	30	.971	13	92	52	O125(121/4/0)	—	1.6
1908	†Det A	56	121	17	25	2	1	0	10	13	0	—	.207	.284	.240	68	-4	11	.960	2	139	196	O32(4/26/2)	—	-0.4

YEAR	TM LG	G	AB	R	H	2B	3B	HR	RBI	BB-IB	HP	SO	AVG	OBP	SLG	AOPS	ABR	SB-CS	FA	FR	RNG	THR	GAMES AT POSITION	DL	BFW
1909	†Det A	69	204	44	57	2	2	0	10	28	1	—	.279	.369	.309	110	4	12	.982	-2	56	65	O57(42/13/2)	—	-0.1
1910	Det A	113	377	77	100	6	6	0	24	51	6	—	.265	.362	.313	105	4	25	.956	2	104	97	O101(95/6/0)	—	0.0
1911	Det A	98	341	78	93	10	0	0	19	41	2	—	.273	.354	.302	80	-7	25	.950	1	96	108	O92L	—	-1.0
1912	Det A	99	316	54	93	5	2	0	24	38	0	—	.294	.370	.323	102	2	16	.962	-0	88	121	O81(72/5/4)	—	-0.2
1913	Chi A	12	21	2	6	0	0	0	0	9	0	0	.286	.500	.286	132	2	1	.867	-0	79	197	O9L	—	0.2
1914	Pit F	97	352	58	96	9	8	2	24	42	3	16	.273	.355	.361	96	-7	15	.970	6	123	73	O93L	—	-0.6
1915	Pit F	14	49	6	16	0	1	0	4	6	0	0	.327	.400	.367	118	1	1	.926	-1	102	60	O13L	—	-0.1
1918	Det A	1	2	0	0	0	0	0	0	0	0	1	.000	.000	.000	-99	-1	0	1.000	0	0	0	/O(1/1/0)	—	-0.1
Total	15	1090	3774	643	1020	98	40	9	289	478	22	<u>17</u>	.270	.356	.325	102	23	207	.962	15	89	89	O1007(556/282/171)	—	-1.1
JONES, DAX	Dax Xenos; B8.4.1970 Pittsburgh PA; BR/TR/6'0"/180; [SFN91 8/219]; d7.11; Col Creighton																								
1996	SF N	34	58	7	10	0	2	1	7	8-0	0	12	.172	.269	.293	50	-5	2-2	1.000	2	124	117	O33(0/29/4)	0	-0.3
JONES, FIELDER	Fielder Allison; B8.13.1871 Shinglehouse PA; D3.13.1934 Portland OR; BL/TR/5'11"/180; d4.18; M10																								
1896	Bro N	104	395	82	140	10	8	3	46	48	2	15	.354	.427	.443	137	24	18	.928	-4	71	170	O103R	—	1.3
1897	Bro N	135	548	134	172	15	10	1	49	61	9	—	.314	.392	.383	111	12	48	.941	3	113	**210**	O135(2/0/133)	—	0.7
1898	Bro N	146	596	89	181	15	9	1	69	46	8	—	.304	.362	.364	108	7	36	.946	-8	84	142	O144(0/4/144),S2	—	-0.7
1899	Bro N	102	365	75	104	8	2	2	38	54	9	—	.285	.390	.334	97	2	18	.946	-5	75	52	O96(2/89/6)	—	-0.8
1900	†Bro N	136	552	106	171	26	4	4	54	57	9	—	.310	.383	.393	108	8	33	.957	-1	82	61	O136C	—	-0.1
1901	Chi A	133	521	120	162	16	3	2	65	84	6	—	.311	.412	.365	120	21	38	.937	-2	112	134	O133(0/5/128)	—	1.2
1902	Chi A	135	532	98	171	16	5	0	54	57	3	—	.321	.390	.370	117	15	33	.972	10	142	**322**	O135C	—	1.8
1903	Chi A	136	530	71	152	18	5	0	45	47	3	—	.287	.348	.340	112	10	21	**.985**	-1	73	78	O136C	—	0.2
1904	Chi A	149	547	72	133	14	5	3	42	53	5	—	.243	.316	.303	100	2	25	.977	2	92	104	O149C,M	—	-0.4
1905	Chi A	153	568	91	139	17	12	2	38	73	4	—	.245	.335	.327	115	12	20	.970	7	129	153	O153C,M	—	1.3
1906	†Chi A	144	496	77	114	22	4	2	34	83	5	—	.230	.346	.302	106	9	26	**.988**	3	125	143	O144C,M	—	0.6
1907	Chi A	154	559	72	146	18	1	0	47	67	5	—	.261	.345	.297	109	10	17	.973	-1	91	143	O154C,M	—	0.1
1908	Chi A	149	529	92	134	11	7	1	50	86	8	—	.253	.366	.306	121	18	26	.968	-4	101	125	O149C,M	—	0.8
1914	StL F	5	3	0	1	0	0	0	0	1	0	0	.333	.500	.333	123	0	0	ø	0	—	—	/HM	—	0.0
1915	StL F	7	6	1	0	0	0	0	0	0	0	0	.000	.000	.000	-95	-2	0	1.000	-0	82	0	O3(0/1/2),M	—	-0.2
Total	15	1788	6747	1180	1920	206	75	21	631	817	76	<u>15</u>	.285	.368	.347	112	148	359	.964	-0	101	143	O1770(4/1255/516),S2	—	5.8
JONES, FRANK	Frank M.; B8.25.1858 Princeton IL; D2.4.1936 Marietta OH; BL; d7.2																								
1884	Det N	2	8	0	1	0	0	0	0	0	—	1	.125	.125	.125	-22	-1	—	.667	-1	83	0	/Srf	—	-0.2
JONES, DEACON	Grover William; B4.18.1934 White Plains NY; BL/TR/5'10"/(185–190); d9.8; C11; Col Ithaca																								
1962	Chi A	18	28	3	9	2	0	0	8	4-2	0	6	.321	.394	.393	117	1	0-0	.962	-0	92	63	1b6	0	0.0
1963	Chi A	17	16	4	3	0	1	1	2	2-1	1	2	.188	.316	.500	127	0	0-0	1.000	0	145	531	/1	0	0.1
1966	Chi A	5	5	0	2	0	0	0	0	0-0	0	0	.400	.400	.400	140	0	0-0	ø	0	—	—	/H	0	0.0
Total	3	40	49	7	14	2	1	1	10	6-3	1	8	.286	.368	.429	122	1	0-0	.966	-0	100	131	1b7	0	0.1
JONES, HAL	Harold Marion; B4.9.1936 Louisiana MO; BR/TR/6'2"/194; d4.25																								
1961	Cle A	12	35	2	6	0	0	2	4	2-0	0	12	.171	.216	.343	48	-3	0-0	.974	-2	42	147	1b10	0	-0.6
1962	Cle A	5	16	2	5	1	0	0	1	0-0	1	4	.313	.353	.375	99	0	0-0	.969	-0	99	30	1b4	0	0.0
Total	2	17	51	4	11	1	0	2	5	2-0	1	16	.216	.259	.353	64	-3	0-0	.973	-2	59	112	1b14	0	-0.6
JONES, HENRY	Henry Monroe; B5.10.1857 NY; D5.31.1955 Manistee MI; BB/5'6"/149; d8.20																								
1884	Det N	34	127	24	28	3	1	0	3	16	—	18	.220	.308	.260	86	-1	—	.897	-1	95	45	2b16,O11R,S7	—	-0.1
JONES, HOWIE	Howard "Cotton" (b Howard Painter); B3.1.1897 Irwin PA; D7.15.1972 Jeannette PA; BL/TL/5'11"/165; d9.5																								
1921	StL N	3	2	0	0	0	0	0	0	0	0	1	.000	.000	.000	-99	-1	0-0	ø	-0	0	0	/lf	—	-0.1
JONES, JACQUE	Jacque Dewayne; B4.25.1975 San Diego CA; BL/TL/5'10"/(176–205); [MinA96 2/37]; d6.9; Col USC																								
1999	Min A	95	322	54	93	24	2	9	44	17-1	4	63	.289	.329	.460	94	-3	3-4	.980	9	117	175	O93(1/82/19)	0	0.5
2000	Min A	154	523	66	149	26	5	19	76	26-4	0	111	.285	.319	.463	89	-11	7-5	.994	7	112	119	O147(90/63/1)	0	-0.6
2001	Min A	149	475	57	131	25	0	14	49	39-2	3	92	.276	.335	.417	91	-6	12-9	.983	4	108	100	O140(137/2/2),D5	0	-0.6
2002	†Min A	149	577	96	173	37	2	27	85	37-2	2	129	.300	.341	.511	119	15	6-7	.986	13	119	136	O143L,D3	0	2.1
2003	†Min A	136	517	76	157	33	1	16	69	21-2	4	105	.304	.333	.464	104	3	13-1	.977	-0	108	34	O101(90/0/11),D29	16	0.0
2004	†Min A	151	555	69	141	22	1	24	80	40-2	10	117	.254	.315	.427	89	-11	13-10	.994	2	108	52	O142(0/2/141),D3	0	-1.6
2005	Min A	142	523	74	130	22	4	23	73	51-12	5	120	.249	.319	.438	98	-3	13-4	.986	1	99	125	O132(0/10/123),D9	0	-0.6
2006	Chi N	149	533	73	152	31	1	27	81	35-6	5	116	.285	.334	.499	108	5	9-1	.976	2	107	63	O143R	0	0.1
Total	8	1125	4025	565	1126	220	16	159	557	266-31	33	853	.280	.328	.461	99	-11	76-41	.985	38	109	98	O1041(461/159/440),D49	16	-0.7
JONES, DALTON	James Dalton; B12.10.1943 McComb MS; BL/TR/6'1"/(177–185); d4.17; OF(12/0/8)																								
1964	Bos A	118	374	37	86	16	4	6	39	22-2	1	38	.230	.274	.342	67	-17	6-3	.959	-7	87	74	2b85/S3	0	-1.8
1965	Bos A	112	367	41	99	13	5	5	37	28-0	2	45	.270	.325	.373	92	-4	8-1	.930	0	108	86	3b81,2b8	0	-0.2
1966	Bos A	115	252	26	59	11	5	4	23	22-4	3	27	.234	.303	.365	83	-6	1-2	.962	-11	82	74	2b70,3b3	0	-1.3
1967	†Bos A	89	159	18	46	6	2	3	25	11-3	0	23	.289	.333	.409	110	2	0-1	.912	-3	107	113	3b30,2b19/1	0	-0.1
1968	Bos A	111	354	38	83	13	0	5	29	17-0	1	53	.234	.271	.314	72	-12	1-1	.996	-10	85	120	1b56,2b26,3b8	0	-2.8
1969	Bos A	111	336	50	74	18	3	3	33	39-3	2	36	.220	.303	.318	71	-12	1-1	.992	-2	105	91	1b81,3b9/2	0	-2.2
1970	Det A	89	191	29	42	7	0	6	21	33-4	1	33	.220	.333	.351	89	-2	1-1	.985	-4	90	90	2b35,3b18,1b10	0	-0.5
1971	Det A	83	138	15	35	5	0	5	11	9-1	1	21	.254	.304	.399	94	-2	1-3	1.000	-5	72	0	O16(10/0/8),3b13,1b3/2	0	-0.9
1972	Det A	7	7	0	0	0	0	0	0	0-0	0	2	.000	.000	.000	-97	-2	0-0	ø	0	—	—	/H	0	-0.2
	Tex A	72	151	14	24	2	0	4	19	10-1	0	31	.159	.207	.252	39	-12	1-0	.979	-4	76	68	3b23,2b17,1b7,O2L	0	-1.8
	Year	79	158	14	24	2	0	4	19	10-1	0	33	.152	.199	.241	32	-14	1-0	.979	-4	76	68	3b23,2b17,1b7,O2L	0	-2.0
Total	9	907	2329	268	548	91	19	41	237	191-18	11	309	.235	.295	.343	79	-67	20-13	.967	-45	85	76	2b262,3b186,1b158,O18L/S	0	-11.8
JONES, JAKE	James Murrell; B11.23.1920 Epps LA; D12.13.2000 Delhi LA; BR/TR/6'3"/197; d9.20; Mil 1942–45																								
1941	Chi A	3	11	0	0	0	0	0	0	0	0	4	.000	.000	.000	-99	-3	0-0	1.000	-1	0	0	1b3	0	-0.4
1942	Chi A	7	20	2	3	1	0	0	0	2	0	2	.150	.227	.200	21	-2	1-0	.961	-1	60	51	1b5	0	-0.3
1946	Chi A	24	79	10	21	5	1	3	13	2	0	13	.266	.284	.468	112	0	0-0	.986	-3	40	108	1b20	0	-0.4
1947	Chi A	45	171	15	41	7	1	3	20	13	1	25	.240	.297	.345	81	-5	1-0	.988	-1	100	115	1b43	0	-0.7
	Bos A	109	404	50	95	14	3	16	76	41	3	60	.235	.310	.403	91	-6	5-4	.991	-3	91	108	1b109	0	-1.4
	Year	154	575	65	136	21	4	19	96	54	4	85	.237	.306	.386	88	-11	6-4	.990	-3	94	**110**	1b152	0	-2.1
1948	Bos A	36	105	3	21	4	0	1	8	11	0	26	.200	.276	.267	43	-9	1-0	.993	2	122	114	1b31	0	-0.8
Total	5	224	790	80	181	31	5	23	117	69	4	130	.229	.294	.368	80	-25	8-4	.989	-6	91	108	1b211	0	-4.0
JONES, JIM	James Tilford "Sheriff"; B12.25.1876 London KY; D5.6.1953 London KY; BR/TR/5'10"/162; d6.29; Col Centre; ▲																								
1897	Lou N	2	4	2	1	1	0	0	0	1	0	—	.250	.400	.500	141	1	0	ø	-0	0	0	/P	—	0.0
1901	NY N	21	91	10	19	4	3	0	5	4	1	—	.209	.250	.319	67	-4	2	.900	-0	137	124	O20R/P	—	-0.5
1902	NY N	67	249	16	59	11	1	0	19	13	0	—	.237	.275	.289	75	-8	7	.897	-2	94	82	O67(49/3/15)	—	-1.5
Total	3	90	344	28	79	16	4	0	24	18	1	—	.230	.270	.299	74	-11	9	.898	-3	105	92	O87(49/3/35),P2	—	-2.0
JONES, JASON	Jason Dewey; B10.17.1976 Marietta GA; BB/TR/6'3"/210; [TexA99 13/405]; d7.23; Col Kennesaw St.																								
2003	Tex A	40	107	11	23	6	0	3	11	10-0	3	21	.215	.298	.355	67	-5	0-1	.978	1	97	241	O27(14/0/13),1b3,D6	0	-0.5
JONES, JEFF	Jeffrey Raymond; B10.22.1957 Philadelphia PA; BR/TR/6'2"/200; [CinN79 20/516]; d4.4; Col Iowa																								
1983	Cin N	16	44	6	10	3	0	0	5	11-0	1	13	.227	.379	.295	90	0	2-0	1.000	0	109	109	O13(8/0/5)/1	0	0.1
JONES, BINKY	John Joseph; B7.11.1899 St.Louis MO; D5.13.1961 St.Louis MO; BR/TR/5'9"/154; d4.15																								
1924	Bro N	10	37	0	4	1	0	0	2	0	0	3	.108	.108	.135	-36	-7	0-0	.898	-1	90	109	S10	—	-0.8
JONES, JOHN	John William "Skins"; B5.13.1901 Coatesville PA; D11.3.1956 Baltimore MD; BL/TL/5'11"/185; d9.26; Col Penn St.																								
1923	Phi A	1	4	0	1	0	0	0	1	0	0	1	.250	.250	.250	31	0	0-0	1.000	-0	105	0	/cf	—	-0.1
1932	Phi A	4	6	0	1	0	0	0	0	0	0	3	.167	.167	.167	-13	-1	0-0	1.000	-0	89	0	/rf	—	-0.1
Total	2	5	10	0	2	0	0	0	1	0	0	4	.200	.200	.200	4	-1	0-0	1.000	-0	101	0	O2(0/1/1)	—	-0.2

YEAR	TM LG	G	AB	R	H	2B	3B	HR	RBI	BB-IB	HP	SO	AVG	OBP	SLG	AOPS	ABR	SB-CS	FA	FR	RNG	THR	GAMES AT POSITION	DL	BFW
JONES, CHIPPER	Larry Wayne; B4.24.1972 DeLand FL; BB/TR/6´4˝/(185–230); [AtlN90 1/1]; d9.11; [DL 1994 Atl N 131]																								
1993	Atl N	8	3	2	2	1	0	0	0	1-0	0	1	.667	.750	1.000	355	1	0-0	1.000	-1	48	0	S3	0	0.1
1995	†Atl N	140	524	87	139	22	3	23	86	73-1	0	99	.265	.353	.450	106	5	8-4	.931	1	97	104	3b123,O20(15/0/5)	0	0.6
1996	†Atl N★	157	598	114	185	32	5	30	110	87-0	0	88	.309	.393	.530	134	31	14-1	.947	-30	75	52	3b118,S38/rf	5	0.7
1997	†Atl N★	157	597	100	176	41	3	21	111	76-8	0	88	.295	.371	.479	120	19	20-5	.955	-25	81	76	3b152,O5(3/0/3)	0	-0.3
1998	†Atl N★	160	601	123	188	29	5	34	107	96-1	1	93	.313	.404	.547	150	46	16-6	.971	-5	89	111	3b158	0	4.2
1999	†Atl N	157	567	116	181	41	1	45	110	126-18	2	94	.319	.441	.633	170	**67**	25-3	.950	-34	76	42	3b156/S	0	3.5
2000	†Atl N★	156	579	118	180	38	1	36	111	95-10	2	64	.311	.404	.566	145	42	14-7	.944	-4	100	91	3b152,S6	0	3.8
2001	†Atl N★	159	572	113	189	33	5	38	102	98-20	2	82	.330	.427	.605	162	56	9-10	.945	-25	83	51	3b149,O8L/D	0	2.9
2002	†Atl N	158	548	90	179	35	1	26	100	107-23	2	89	.327	.435	.536	155	50	8-2	.975	-6	94	81	O152L	0	3.9
2003	†Atl N	153	555	103	169	33	2	27	106	94-13	1	83	.305	.402	.517	139	36	2-2	.968	-14	74	97	O149L/D	0	1.5
2004	†Atl N	137	472	69	117	20	1	30	96	84-8	4	96	.248	.362	.485	117	13	2-0	.975	-5	100	78	3b96,O29L,D7	19	0.8
2005	†Atl N	109	358	66	106	30	0	21	72	72-5	0	56	.296	.412	.556	150	30	5-1	.980	-6	92	101	3b101	42	2.4
2006	Atl N	110	411	87	133	28	3	26	86	61-4	1	73	.324	.409	.596	152	34	6-1	.936	-4	92	111	3b105,D2	44	3.0
Total	13	1761	6385	1188	1944	383	30	357	1197	1070-111	15	1006	.304	.402	.542	142	430	129-42	.953	-158	88	80	3b1310,O364(356/0/9),S48,D11	241	27.1
JONES, LEVIN	Levin; B Baltimore MD; d5.14																								
1873	Mar NA	1	4	0	3	0	0	0	1	0	—	0	.750	.750	.750	450	2	0-0	.800	-0	0	0	/cf	—	0.1
1874	Bal NA	2	7	0	1	0	0	0	1	0	—	0	.143	.143	.143	-8	-1	0-0	.875	-0	—	—	/Crf	—	-0.1
Total	2NA	3	11	0	4	0	0	0	2	0	—	0	.364	.364	.364	139	1	0-0	.800	-1	—	—	O2(0/1/1)/C	—	0.0
JONES, LYNN	Lynn Morris; B1.1.1953 Meadville PA; BR/TR/5´9˝/(165–175); [CinN74 10/239]; d4.13; C5; b–Darryl; Col Thiel																								
1979	Det A	95	213	33	63	8	0	4	26	17-0	1	22	.296	.349	.390	96	-1	9-6	.980	-0	102	73	O84(20/42/25),D6	0	-0.3
1980	Det A	30	55	9	14	2	2	0	6	10-0	0	5	.255	.364	.364	99	0	1-0	1.000	1	125	0	O17(4/4/9),D6	86	0.1
1981	Det A	71	174	19	45	5	0	2	19	18-1	1	10	.259	.328	.322	86	-3	1-2	.989	-1	88	146	O60(9/0/52),D4	0	-0.7
1982	Det A	58	139	15	31	3	1	0	14	7-0	0	14	.223	.259	.259	43	-11	0-2	1.000	1	102	103	O56(5/2/49)/D	0	-1.3
1983	Det A	49	64	9	17	1	2	0	6	3-0	0	6	.266	.299	.344	78	-2	1-0	.968	1	102	198	O31(9/1/22),D6	0	-0.2
1984	†KC A	47	103	11	31	6	0	1	10	4-0	1	9	.301	.330	.388	98	0	1-3	.962	-4	81	0	O45(13/7/29)	86	-0.7
1985	†KC A	110	152	12	32	7	0	0	9	8-0	3	15	.211	.261	.257	43	-12	0-1	.983	-1	100	60	O100(57/21/32),D2	0	-1.5
1986	KC A	67	47	1	6	2	0	0	1	6-0	0	5	.128	.226	.170	10	-6	0-0	.971	-3	82	0	O62(37/8/19)/2D	0	-0.9
Total	8	527	947	109	239	34	5	7	91	73-1	6	86	.252	.308	.321	73	-35	13-14	.983	-6	96	78	O455(154/85/237),D28/2	172	-5.5
JONES, MACK	Mack F. "Mack the Knife"; B11.6.1938 Atlanta GA; D6.8.2004 Atlanta GA; BL/TR/6´1˝/(180–204); d7.13																								
1961	Mil N	28	104	13	24	3	2	0	12	12-2	2	28	.231	.322	.298	70	-4	4-4	1.000	-4	70	103	O26C	0	-1.0
1962	Mil N	91	333	51	85	17	4	10	36	44-3	7	100	.255	.354	.420	110	6	5-1	.973	-10	84	39	O91(0/9/85)	0	-1.0
1963	Mil N	93	228	36	50	11	4	3	22	26-5	7	59	.219	.317	.342	91	-2	8-4	.978	-4	97	24	O80(12/69/0)	0	-0.8
1965	Mil N	143	504	78	132	18	7	31	75	29-1	9	122	.262	.313	.510	127	15	8-2	.980	-8	93	29	O133(31/119/0)	0	0.4
1966	Atl N	118	417	60	110	14	1	23	66	39-4	8	85	.264	.335	.468	120	11	16-10	.981	-5	103	13	O112(1/112/3)/1	0	0.3
1967	Atl N	140	454	72	115	23	4	17	50	64-4	9	108	.253	.355	.434	127	18	10-6	.985	-3	95	98	O126(26/100/0)	0	1.2
1968	Cin N	103	234	40	59	9	1	10	34	28-3	5	46	.252	.341	.427	123	7	2-3	.988	-7	77	29	O60(24/34/3)	0	-0.3
1969	Mon N	135	455	73	123	23	5	22	79	67-8	15	110	.270	.379	.488	141	27	6-7	.959	2	105	88	O129(125/5/0)	0	2.2
1970	Mon N	108	271	51	65	11	3	14	32	59-0	13	74	.240	.398	.458	129	14	5-3	.968	-2	96	59	O87(85/2/0)	0	0.8
1971	Mon N	43	91	11	15	3	0	3	9	15-1	2	24	.165	.296	.297	67	-4	1-0	.952	0	101	76	O27L	0	-0.5
Total	10	1002	3091	485	778	132	31	133	415	383-31	77	756	.252	.347	.444	120	88	65-40	.976	-40	95	53	O871(331/476/91)/1	0	1.3
JONES, RED	Morris E.; B11.2.1911 Timpson TX; D6.30.1974 Lincoln CA; BL/TR/6´3˝/190; d4.16																								
1940	StL N	12	11	0	1	0	0	0	1	1	0	2	.091	.167	.091	-26	-2	0	1.000	0	139	0	/lf	—	-0.2
JONES, RICKY	Ricky Miron; B6.4.1958 Tupelo MS; BR/TR/6´3˝/186; [BalA80 15/390]; d9.3; Col West Georgia																								
1986	Bal A	16	33	2	6	2	0	0	4	6-0	0	8	.182	.308	.242	53	-2	0-0	1.000	4	124	105	2b11,3b6	0	0.3
JONES, BOB	Robert Oliver; B10.11.1949 Elkton MD; BL/TL/6´2˝/(170–215); [TexA67 36/665]; d10.1; C3																								
1974	Tex A	2	5	0	0	0	0	0	0	0-0	0	1	.000	.000	.000	-99	-1	0-0	1.000	0	143	0	O2L	0	-0.1
1975	Tex A	9	11	2	1	0	0	0	0	3-0	0	3	.091	.286	.091	11	-1	0-0	1.000	0	123	0	O5(3/1/1)/D	0	-0.1
1976	Cal A	78	166	22	35	6	0	6	17	14-3	1	30	.211	.273	.355	89	-3	3-0	.990	1	91	182	O62(17/25/21),D2	0	-0.4
1977	Cal A	14	17	3	3	0	0	1	3	4-0	0	5	.176	.318	.353	90	-0	0-0	ø	0	—	—	D6	0	0.0
1981	Tex A	10	34	4	9	1	0	3	7	1-0	0	7	.265	.286	.559	145	2	0-1	1.000	3	106	601	O10(1/0/9)	0	0.4
1983	Tex A	41	72	5	16	4	0	1	11	5-1	2	17	.222	.284	.319	69	-3	0-2	1.000	0	124	0	O11(6/0/5),D11/1	0	-0.4
1984	Tex A	64	143	14	37	4	0	4	22	10-1	1	19	.259	.308	.371	85	-3	1-1	1.000	-0	103	155	O22(11/0/11),1b15,D4	18	-0.5
1985	Tex A	83	134	14	30	2	0	5	23	11-1	1	30	.224	.284	.351	72	-5	1-0	1.000	-3	81	0	O30(8/1/22),D10,1b4	0	-0.9
1986	Tex A	13	21	1	2	0	0	0	3	2-0	0	5	.095	.174	.095	-24	-4	0-0	.909	-1	100	0	O9(5/0/4),1b2	0	-0.5
Total	9	314	603	65	133	17	0	20	86	50-6	5	117	.221	.282	.348	78	-18	5-4	.992	1	97	152	O151(53/27/73),D34,1b22	18	-2.5
JONES, BOB	Robert Walter "Ducky"; B12.2.1889 Clayton CA; D8.30.1964 San Diego CA; BL/TR/6´0˝/170; d4.11																								
1917	Det A	46	77	16	12	1	2	0	2	4	0	8	.156	.198	.221	28	-7	3	.938	-1	114	19	2b18,3b8	—	-0.9
1918	Det A	74	287	43	79	14	4	0	21	17	2	16	.275	.320	.352	107	1	7	.947	-5	93	48	3b63,1b6/O	—	-0.2
1919	Det A	127	439	37	114	18	6	1	57	34	1	39	.260	.314	.335	84	-10	11	.944	-22	85	71	3b127	—	-3.0
1920	Det A	81	265	35	66	6	3	1	18	22	1	13	.249	.309	.306	65	-14	3-4	.942	0	100	65	3b67,2b5/S	—	-1.2
1921	Det A	141	554	82	168	23	9	1	72	37	1	24	.303	.348	.383	87	-12	8-9	.950	9	**106**	45	3b141	—	0.4
1922	Det A	124	455	65	117	10	6	3	44	36	2	18	.257	.314	.325	69	-22	8-5	**.962**	10	**105**	95	3b119	—	-0.4
1923	Det A	100	372	51	93	15	4	1	40	29	1	13	.250	.306	.320	66	-19	7-6	.954	7	107	100	3b97	—	-0.7
1924	Det A	110	393	52	107	27	4	0	47	20	0	20	.272	.308	.361	73	-17	1-5	.956	-2	100	76	3b106	—	-1.4
1925	Det A	50	148	18	35	6	0	0	15	9	0	5	.236	.280	.277	42	-13	1-1	.985	6	119	66	3b46	—	-0.5
Total	9	853	2990	399	791	120	38	7	316	208	8	156	.265	.314	.337	75	-113	49-30	.953	3	101	72	3b774,2b23,1b6/SO	—	-7.9
JONES, RON	Ronald Glen; B6.11.1964 Seguin TX; D6.4.2006 Houston TX; BL/TR/5´10˝/(200–214); d8.26; Col Wharton Co. (TX) JC																								
1988	Phi N	33	124	15	36	6	1	8	26	2-0	0	14	.290	.295	.548	136	5	0-0	1.000	2	115	65	O32R	0	0.6
1989	Phi N	12	31	7	9	0	0	2	4	9-1	0	1	.290	.450	.484	167	3	1-0	1.000	2	142	191	O12(3/0/10)	166	0.6
1990	Phi N	24	58	5	16	2	0	3	7	9-0	0	9	.276	.373	.466	129	2	0-1	1.000	-1	82	94	O16(8/0/8)	95	0.1
1991	Phi N	28	26	0	4	2	0	0	3	2-0	0	9	.154	.214	.231	25	-3	0-0	ø	0	—	—	/H	56	-0.4
Total	4	97	239	27	65	10	1	13	40	22-1	0	33	.272	.330	.485	128	7	1-1	1.000	3	111	95	O60(11/0/50)	317	0.9
JONES, ROSS	Ross A.; B1.14.1960 Miami FL; BR/TR/6´2˝/(180–185); [LAN80 1/9]; d4.2; Col Miami																								
1984	NY N	17	10	2	1	1	0	0	1	3-0	0	4	.100	.308	.200	46	-1	0-0	.833	-1	90	92	S6/23	0	-0.1
1986	Sea A	11	21	0	2	0	0	0	0	0-0	0	4	.095	.095	.095	-47	-4	0-1	1.000	-0	79	53	S4,2b3,3b2/D	0	-0.5
1987	KC A	39	114	10	29	4	2	0	10	5-0	1	15	.254	.285	.325	61	-7	1-0	.974	1	112	65	S36,2b3	0	-0.2
Total	3	67	145	12	32	5	2	0	11	8-0	1	23	.221	.261	.283	46	-12	1-1	.971	-0	109	65	S46,2b7,3b3/D	0	-0.8
JONES, RUPPERT	Ruppert Sanderson; B3.12.1955 Dallas TX; BL/TL/5´10˝/(170–189); [KCA73 3/57]; d8.1																								
1976	KC A	28	51	9	11	1	1	1	7	3-0	0	16	.216	.259	.333	72	-2	0-2	1.000	-1	87	0	O17(2/7/9),D3	0	-0.5
1977	Sea A★	160	597	85	157	26	8	24	76	55-3	2	120	.263	.324	.454	111	7	13-9	.981	9	114	99	O155C,D4	0	1.5
1978	Sea A	129	472	48	111	24	3	6	46	55-2	0	85	.235	.312	.337	83	-10	22-6	.985	6	107	116	O128C	34	-0.2
1979	Sea A	**162**	622	109	166	29	9	21	78	85-4	3	78	.267	.356	.444	112	12	33-12	.989	4	102	121	O161C	0	1.7
1980	NY A	83	328	38	73	11	3	9	42	34-3	3	50	.223	.299	.357	81	-9	18-8	.988	2	108	70	O82C	85	-0.7
1981	SD N	105	397	53	99	34	1	4	39	43-2	0	66	.249	.318	.370	105	3	7-9	.993	3	103	119	O104C	0	0.4
1982	SD N★	116	424	69	120	20	2	12	61	62-11	1	90	.283	.373	.425	131	20	18-15	.984	-2	105	42	O114C	15	1.6
1983	SD N	133	335	42	78	12	3	12	49	35-4	0	58	.233	.305	.394	95	-3	11-11	.981	1	106	67	O111C,1b5	0	-0.5
1984	†Det A	79	215	26	61	12	1	12	37	21-0	0	47	.284	.346	.516	136	10	2-4	1.000	5	112	104	O73(61/24/0),D2	0	1.2
1985	Cal A	125	389	66	90	17	2	21	67	57-2	0	82	.231	.328	.447	110	6	7-4	.995	11	112	255	O73(31/18/31),D43	0	1.3
1986	†Cal A	126	393	73	90	21	3	17	49	64-5	3	87	.229	.339	.427	109	6	10-3	.981	-6	93	68	O121(28/10/96)	0	-0.4
1987	Cal A	85	192	25	47	8	2	8	28	20-2	0	38	.245	.316	.432	99	-1	2-1	.965	-3	91	34	O66(52/3/21),D3	0	-0.6
Total	12	1331	4415	643	1103	215	38	147	579	534-38	12	817	.250	.330	.416	106	39	143-84	.986	28	105	99	O1205(174/917/157),D55,1b5	134	4.8

YEAR	TM LG	G	AB	R	H	2B	3B	HR	RBI	BB-IB	HP	SO	AVG	OBP	SLG	AOPS	ABR	SB-CS	FA	FR	RNG	THR	GAMES AT POSITION	DL	BFW
JONES, JACK	Ryerson L. "Ri","Angel Sleeves"; B Cincinnati OH; BR/TR; d8.13																								
1883	Lou AA	2	7	1	0	0	0	0	—	0	—	—	.000	.000	.000	-99	-2	—	.500	-1	0	0	O2C/S	—	-0.2
1884	Cin U	69	272	36	71	5	1	2	—	12	—	—	.261	.292	.309	76	-16	—	.858	-1	109	146	S41,2b19,3b10	—	-1.4
Total	2	71	279	37	71	5	1	2	—	12	—	—	.254	.285	.301	73	-18	—	.857	-2	109	143	S42,2b19,3b10,O2C	—	-1.6
JONES, TERRY	Terry Lee; B2.15.1971 Birmingham AL; BB/TR/5´10˝/(160–170); [ColN93 40/1136]; d9.8; Col North Alabama																								
1996	Col N	12	10	6	3	0	0	0	1	0-0	0	3	.300	.273	.300	48	-1	0-0	1.000	-0	91	0	O4C	0	-0.1
1998	Mon N	60	212	30	46	7	2	1	15	21-1	0	46	.217	.288	.283	52	-15	16-4	.988	5	121	113	O60C	0	-0.7
1999	Mon N	17	63	4	17	1	1	0	3	3-0	0	14	.270	.303	.317	60	-4	1-2	1.000	3	134	235	O17(5/12/0)	0	-0.1
2000	Mon N	108	168	30	42	8	2	0	13	10-1	0	32	.250	.292	.321	54	-12	7-2	.970	3	111	163	O78(55/26/7)	16	-0.8
2001	Mon N	30	77	8	20	5	0	0	2	2-0	0	11	.260	.278	.325	56	-5	3-0	.977	2	109	195	O22(10/13/2)	142	-0.3
Total	5	227	530	78	128	21	5	1	34	36-2	0	106	.242	.289	.306	54	-37	27-8	.984	13	117	151	O181(70/115/9)	158	-2.0
JONES, TOM	Thomas; B1.22.1877 Honesdale PA; D6.19.1923 Danville PA; BR/TR/6´1˝/195; d8.25																								
1902	Bal A	37	159	22	45	8	4	0	14	2	0	—	.283	.292	.384	83	-5	1	.955	-2	110	94	1b37/2	—	-0.6
1904	StL A	**156**	625	53	152	15	10	2	68	15	8	—	.243	.270	.309	88	-11	16	.988	1	107	87	1b134,2b23,O4R	—	-1.5
1905	StL A	135	504	44	122	16	2	0	48	30	4	—	.242	.290	.282	86	-8	19	.985	7	**119**	92	1b135	—	-0.4
1906	StL A	144	539	51	136	22	6	0	30	24	5	—	.252	.290	.315	94	-5	27	.985	11	**129**	101	1b143	—	0.4
1907	StL A	**155**	549	52	137	17	3	0	34	34	4	—	.250	.298	.291	88	-7	24	.983	2	106	101	1b155	—	-0.9
1908	StL A	**155**	549	43	135	14	2	1	50	30	4	—	.246	.290	.284	86	-9	18	.986	-2	93	118	1b155	—	-1.5
1909	StL A	97	337	30	84	9	3	0	29	18	6	—	.249	.299	.294	94	-3	13	.989	7	121	120	1b95,3b2	—	0.3
	†Det A	44	153	13	43	9	0	0	18	5	3	—	.281	.317	.340	103	0	9	.984	3	131	104	1b44	—	0.3
	Year	141	490	43	127	18	3	0	47	23	9	—	.259	.305	.308	97	-2	22	.988	9	124	115	1b139,3b2	—	0.6
1910	Det A	135	432	32	110	12	4	1	45	35	10	—	.255	.325	.308	92	-3	22	.985	-4	89	81	1b135	—	-1.1
Total	8	1058	3847	340	964	122	34	4	336	193	44	—	.251	.294	.303	90	-51	149	.984	22	109	100	1b1033,2b24,O4R,3b2	—	-5.0
JONES, TRACY	Tracy Donald; B3.31.1961 Hawthorne CA; BR/TR/6´3˝/(180–220); [CinN83*S1/1]; d4.7; Col Loyola Marymount																								
1986	Cin N	46	86	16	30	3	0	2	10	9-1	0	5	.349	.406	.453	133	4	7-1	1.000	2	125	82	O24(23/3/0),1b2	76	0.6
1987	Cin N	117	359	53	104	17	3	10	44	23-0	3	40	.290	.333	.437	100	-1	31-8	.990	0	109	36	O95(56/34/17)	0	0.0
1988	Cin N	37	83	9	19	1	0	1	9	8-2	1	6	.229	.304	.277	66	-4	9-0	.955	-0	105	0	O25(3/0/23)	42	-0.3
	Mon N	53	141	20	47	5	1	2	15	12-1	1	12	.333	.390	.426	127	5	9-6	1.000	-4	73	99	O43(26/9/15)	0	0.1
	Year	90	224	29	66	6	1	3	24	20-3	2	18	.295	.358	.371	105	2	18-6	.980	-4	85	63	O68(29/9/38)	0	-0.2
1989	SF N	40	97	5	18	4	0	0	12	5-3	1	14	.186	.233	.227	33	-9	2-1	1.000	-4	69	0	O30(9/5/22)	0	-1.5
	Det A	46	158	17	41	10	0	3	26	16-1	1	16	.259	.326	.380	102	1	1-1	.986	-1	102	0	O36(34/0/3),D8	46	-0.2
1990	Det A	50	118	15	27	4	1	4	9	6-0	3	13	.229	.283	.381	83	-3	1-1	.952	1	91	237	O27L,D20	0	-0.4
	Sea A	25	86	8	26	4	0	2	15	3-0	2	12	.302	.341	.419	110	1	0-1	1.000	-1	92	0	O18(18/1/0),D5	56	-0.1
	Year	75	204	23	53	8	1	6	24	9-0	5	25	.260	.307	.397	94	-2	1-2	.973	-1	91	126	O45(45/1/0),D25	0	-0.5
1991	Sea A	79	175	30	44	8	1	3	24	18-2	1	22	.251	.321	.360	89	-3	2-0	1.000	-0	108	0	D37,O36(35/0/3)	30	-0.4
Total	6	493	1303	173	356	56	6	27	164	100-10	13	140	.273	.329	.388	96	-9	62-19	.988	-9	98	46	O334(231/52/83),D70,1b2	250	-2.2
JONES, NIPPY	Vernal Leroy; B6.29.1925 Los Angeles CA; D10.3.1995 Sacramento CA; BR/TR/6´1˝/(185–195); d6.8																								
1946	†StL N	16	12	3	4	0	0	0	1	2	0	2	.333	.429	.333	113	0	0	.800	0	127	319	2b3	0	0.1
1947	StL N	23	73	6	18	4	0	1	5	2	0	10	.247	.267	.342	58	-5	0	.935	-2	103	57	2b13,O2R	0	-0.6
1948	StL N	132	481	58	122	21	9	10	81	36	1	45	.254	.307	.397	84	-12	2	.986	-8	78	107	1b128	0	-2.5
1949	StL N	110	380	51	114	20	2	8	62	16	1	20	.300	.330	.426	97	-3	1	.984	-7	74	113	1b98	0	-1.3
1950	StL N	13	26	0	6	1	0	0	6	3	0	1	.231	.310	.269	52	-2	0	.983	-0	79	147	1b8	90	-0.2
1951	StL N	80	300	20	79	12	0	3	41	9	1	13	.263	.287	.333	66	-15	1-2	.991	-0	100	115	1b71	0	-1.8
1952	Phi N	8	30	3	5	0	0	1	5	0	0	4	.167	.167	.267	19	-4	0-0	.976	0	123	125	1b8	0	-0.4
1957	†Mil N	30	79	5	21	2	1	2	8	3-1	0	7	.266	.293	.392	88	-2	0-0	.994	0	110	96	1b20/rf	0	-0.3
Total	8	412	1381	146	369	60	12	25	209	71-1	3	102	.267	.304	.382	81	-43	4-2	.987	-17	84	111	1b333,2b16,O3R	90	-7.0
JONES, BILL	William; B Syracuse NY; d5.17																								
1882	Bal AA	4	15	1	1	0	0	0	—	0	—	—	.067	.067	.067	-59	-2	—	1.000	1	248	0	O2(0/1/1),C2	—	-0.2
1884	Phi U	4	14	2	2	0	0	0	—	1	—	—	.143	.200	.143	6	-2	—	.862	-1	—	—	C4/rf	—	-0.3
Total	2	8	29	3	3	0	0	0	—	1	—	—	.103	.133	.103	-25	-4	—	.857	-1	—	—	C6,O3(0/1/2)	—	-0.5
JONES, BILL	William Dennis "Midget"; B4.8.1887 Hartland NB, Can.; D10.10.1946 Boston MA; BL/TR/5´6.5˝/157; d6.20																								
1911	Bos N	24	51	6	11	2	1	0	3	15	0	7	.216	.394	.294	87	0	1	.867	-1	97	127	O18C	—	-0.2
1912	Bos N	3	2	0	1	0	0	0	2	0	0	1	.500	.500	.500	171	0	0	ø	0	—	—	/H	—	0.0
Total	2	27	53	6	12	2	1	0	5	15	0	8	.226	.397	.302	89	0	1	.867	-1	97	127	O18C	—	-0.2
JONES, TEX	William Roderick; B8.4.1885 Marion KS; D2.26.1938 Wichita KS; BR/TR/6´0˝/192; d4.13																								
1911	Chi A	9	31	4	6	1	0	0	4	3	0	—	.194	.265	.226	39	-3	1	1.000	3	198	153	1b9	—	0.0
JONES, TIM	William Timothy; B12.1.1962 Sumter SC; BL/TR/5´10˝/175; [StLN85 2/46]; d7.26; Col The Citadel																								
1988	StL N	31	52	2	14	0	0	0	3	4-0	0	10	.269	.321	.269	70	-2	4-1	.955	3	110	121	S9,2b8/3	0	0.2
1989	StL N	42	75	11	22	6	0	0	7	7-1	1	8	.293	.353	.373	107	1	1-0	1.000	-3	102	58	2b12,S12,3b5/Clf	0	-0.1
1990	StL N	67	128	9	28	7	1	1	12	12-1	1	20	.219	.291	.313	65	-6	3-4	.944	-0	110	96	S29,2b19,3b6/P	0	-0.5
1991	StL N	16	24	1	4	2	0	0	2	2-1	0	6	.167	.222	.250	35	-2	0-1	1.000	-5	70	95	S14,2b4	0	-0.7
1992	StL N	67	145	9	29	4	0	0	3	11-1	0	29	.200	.256	.228	39	-12	5-2	.972	-9	85	126	S34,2b28,3b2/cf	33	-1.9
1993	StL N	29	61	13	16	6	0	0	1	9-0	1	8	.262	.366	.361	96	0	2-2	.976	2	120	94	S21,2b7	0	0.3
Total	6	252	485	45	113	25	1	1	28	45-4	3	81	.233	.300	.295	67	-21	15-10	.964	-13	98	98	S119,2b78,3b14,O2(1/1/0)/PC	33	-2.7
JONES, WILLIE	Willie Edward "Puddin' Head"; B8.16.1925 Dillon SC; D10.18.1983 Cincinnati OH; BR/TR/6´1˝/(192–200); d9.10																								
1947	Phi N	18	62	5	14	0	1	0	10	7	0	0	.226	.304	.258	53	-4	2	.909	1	110	90	3b17	0	-0.4
1948	Phi N	17	60	9	20	2	0	2	9	3	0	5	.333	.365	.467	126	2	0	.926	1	95	34	3b17	0	0.3
1949	Phi N	149	532	71	130	35	1	19	77	65	1	66	.244	.328	.421	102	2	3	.948	-6	98	63	3b145	0	-0.5
1950	†Phi N★	**157**	610	100	163	28	6	25	88	61	3	40	.267	.337	.456	108	5	5	.954	-5	95	95	3b157	0	0.0
1951	Phi N★	148	564	79	161	28	5	22	81	60	4	47	.285	.358	.470	123	18	6-2	.966	-8	91	95	3b147	0	1.0
1952	Phi N	147	541	60	135	12	3	18	72	53	6	36	.250	.323	.383	96	-4	5-3	**.969**	5	97	**135**	3b147	0	0.1
1953	Phi N	149	481	61	108	16	2	19	70	85	1	45	.225	.342	.385	90	-6	1-1	**.975**	1	93	**124**	3b147	0	-0.5
1954	Phi N	142	535	64	145	28	3	12	56	61	0	54	.271	.342	.402	94	-4	4-1	**.968**	2	96	95	3b141	0	-0.2
1955	Phi N	146	516	65	133	20	3	16	81	77-5	3	51	.258	.352	.401	103	4	6-2	**.960**	-7	84	86	3b146	0	-0.3
1956	Phi N	149	520	88	144	20	4	17	78	92-6	1	49	.277	.383	.429	121	19	5-4	**.973**	-1	89	91	3b149	0	1.8
1957	Phi N	133	440	58	96	19	2	9	47	61-3	0	41	.218	.310	.332	76	-14	1-0	.966	-10	81	85	3b126	0	-2.5
1958	Phi N	118	398	52	108	15	1	14	60	49-4	2	45	.271	.351	.420	105	4	1-2	**.967**	-11	84	61	3b110/1	0	-0.8
1959	Phi N	47	160	23	43	9	1	7	24	19-2	0	14	.269	.343	.469	113	3	0-0	.975	-2	92	71	3b46	0	0.0
	Cle A	11	18	1	4	1	0	0	1	1-0	0	3	.222	.263	.278	51	-1	0-0	.929	2	179	422	3b4	0	0.1
	Cin N	72	233	33	58	12	1	7	31	28-1	1	26	.249	.330	.399	91	-3	0-2	.966	-3	84	86	3b68	0	-0.6
1960	Cin N	79	149	16	40	7	0	3	27	31-3	0	16	.268	.388	.376	110	4	1-0	.962	-5	83	79	3b46/2	0	0.0
1961	Cin N	9	7	1	0	0	0	0	0	2-0	0	3	.000	.222	.000	-34	-1	0-0	.000	-0	0	0	/3	0	-0.2
Total	15	1691	5826	786	1502	252	33	190	812	755-24	22	541	.258	.343	.410	102	24	40-17	.963	-45	91	93	3b1614/21	0	-2.7
JONNARD, BUBBER	Clarence James; B11.23.1897 Nashville TN; D8.23.1977 New York NY; BR/TR/6´1˝/185; d10.1; C6; twb–Claude																								
1920	Chi A	2	5	0	0	0	0	0	0	0	0	1	.000	.000	.000	-99	-1	0-0	.857	-0	*0*	*142*	/C	—	-0.1
1922	Pit N	10	21	4	5	0	1	0	2	2	0	4	.238	.304	.333	64	-1	0-0	.974	1	*124*	*85*	C10	—	0.0
1926	Phi N	19	34	3	4	1	0	0	2	3	0	4	.118	.189	.147	-8	-5	0	.949	-1	*89*	*116*	C15	—	-0.5
1927	Phi N	53	143	18	42	6	0	0	14	7	0	7	.294	.327	.336	77	-5	0	.967	-7	*82*	*82*	C41	—	-1.0
1929	StL N	18	31	1	3	0	0	0	2	0	0	6	.097	.097	.097	-51	-8	0	.957	1	*128*	*81*	C18	—	-0.6
1935	Phi N	1	1	0	0	0	0	0	0	0	0	1	.000	.000	.000	-91	0	0	1.000	-0	*0*	*0*	/C	—	0.0
Total	6	103	235	26	54	7	1	0	20	12	0	23	.230	.267	.268	41	-20	0-0	.960	-6	*93*	*88*	C86	—	-2.2

YEAR	TM LG	G	AB	R	H	2B	3B	HR	RBI	BB-IB	HP	SO	AVG	OBP	SLG	AOPS	ABR	SB-CS	FA	FR	RNG	THR	GAMES AT POSITION	DL	BFW
Joost, Eddie	Edwin David; B6.5.1916 San Francisco CA; BR/TR/6´0˝/175; d9.11; Def 1944; M1																								
1936	Cin N	13	26	1	4	1	0	0	1	2	0	5	.154	.214	.192	11	-3	0	.947	-0	114	127	S7,2b5	—	-0.3
1937	Cin N	6	12	0	1	0	0	0	0	0	0	0	.083	.083	.083	-57	-3	0	.875	-0	110	83	2b6	—	-0.3
1939	Cin N	42	143	23	36	6	3	0	14	12	0	15	.252	.310	.336	73	-6	1	.957	-2	92	104	2b32,S6	—	-0.6
1940	†Cin N	88	278	24	60	7	2	1	24	32	2	40	.216	.301	.266	57	-16	4	.960	-2	98	117	S78,2b7,3b4	—	-1.2
1941	Cin N	152	537	67	136	25	4	4	40	69	2	59	.253	.340	.337	91	-5	9	.942	-8	93	105	S147,2b4,1b2/3	0	-0.2
1942	Cin N	142	562	65	126	30	3	6	41	62	5	57	.224	.307	.320	84	-11	9	.933	-15	94	109	S130,2b15	0	-1.5
1943	Bos N	124	421	34	78	16	3	2	20	68	0	80	.185	.299	.252	61	-19	5	.945	3	122	125	3b67,2b60,S4	0	-1.3
1945	Bos N	35	141	16	35	7	1	0	9	13	0	7	.248	.312	.312	73	-5	0	.945	-7	80	92	2b19,3b16	0	-1.1
1947	Phi A	151	540	76	111	22	3	13	64	114	4	110	.206	.348	.330	87	-5	6-6	.956	-0	98	97	S151	0	0.3
1948	Phi A	135	509	99	127	22	2	16	55	119	1	87	.250	.393	.395	110	12	2-4	.973	7	98	113	S135	0	2.6
1949	Phi A★	144	525	128	138	25	3	23	81	149	4	80	.263	.429	.453	138	38	2-1	.969	7	99	**110**	S144	0	5.1
1950	Phi A	131	476	79	111	12	3	18	58	103	3	68	.233	.373	.384	96	-1	5-1	.956	-5	98	109	S131	0	0.3
1951	Phi A	140	553	107	160	28	5	19	78	106	6	70	.289	.409	.461	132	29	10-8	.974	7	100	112	S140	0	4.3
1952	Phi A☆	146	540	94	132	26	3	20	75	122	5	94	.244	.388	.415	116	17	5-8	.962	-5	100	87	S146	0	2.0
1953	Phi A	51	177	39	44	6	0	6	15	45	0	24	.249	.401	.384	109	5	3-2	.958	-8	90	92	S51	0	0.1
1954	Phi A	19	47	7	17	3	0	1	9	10	0	10	.362	.474	.489	163	5	0-1	.963	-1	92	65	S9,3b5/2M	0	0.4
1955	Bos A	55	119	15	23	2	0	5	17	17-2	1	21	.193	.299	.336	65	-6	0-0	.932	1	112	144	S20,2b17,3b2	0	-0.3
Total	17	1574	5606	874	1339	238	35	134	601	1043-2	33	827	.239	.361	.366	99	26	61-31	.958	-28	97	106	S1299,2b166,3b95,1b2	0	8.3
Jordan, Dutch	Adolf Otto; B1.5.1880 Pittsburgh PA; D12.23.1972 W.Allegheny PA; BR/TR/5´10˝/185; d4.25																								
1903	Bro N	78	267	27	63	11	1	0	21	19	1	—	.236	.289	.285	66	-12	9	.928	-12	91	73	2b54,3b18,O4(1/0/3)/1	—	-2.3
1904	Bro N	87	252	21	45	10	2	0	19	13	2	—	.179	.225	.234	43	-17	7	.958	-19	82	77	2b70,3b11,1b4	—	-3.8
Total	2	165	519	48	108	21	3	0	40	32	3	—	.208	.258	.260	55	-29	16	.945	-31	86	75	2b124,3b29,1b5,O4(1/0/3)	—	-6.1
Jordan, Buck	Baxter Byerly; B1.16.1907 Cooleemee NC; D3.18.1993 Salisbury NC; BL/TR/6´0˝/170; d9.15																								
1927	NY N	5	5	0	1	0	0	0	0	0	0	3	.200	.200	.200	7	-1	0	ø	0	—	—	/H	—	-0.1
1929	NY N	2	2	1	1	1	0	0	0	0	0	0	.500	.500	1.000	262	1	0	1.000	-0	0	592	/1	—	0.0
1931	Was A	9	18	3	4	2	0	0	1	1	0	3	.222	.263	.333	56	-1	0-0	.978	-1	0	95	1b7	—	-0.2
1932	Bos N	49	212	27	68	12	3	2	29	4	0	5	.321	.333	.434	109	2	1	.991	-2	89	115	1b49	—	-0.5
1933	Bos N	152	588	77	168	29	9	4	46	34	2	22	.286	.327	.386	112	8	4	.991	-3	93	104	1b150	—	-1.0
1934	Bos N	124	489	68	152	26	9	2	58	35	1	19	.311	.358	.413	114	10	3	.989	-3	92	93	1b117	—	-0.5
1935	Bos N	130	470	62	131	24	5	5	35	19	0	17	.279	.307	.383	91	-7	3	.983	2	112	79	1b95,3b8,O2R	—	-1.4
1936	Bos N	138	555	81	179	27	5	3	66	45	2	22	.323	.375	.405	118	15	2	.993	1	104	**129**	1b136	—	0.3
1937	Bos N	8	8	1	2	0	0	0	0	0	0	0	.250	.250	.250	40	-1	0	ø	0	—	—	/H	—	-0.1
	Cin N	98	316	45	89	14	3	1	28	25	0	14	.282	.334	.354	92	-4	6	.989	-1	96	91	1b76	—	-1.1
	Year	106	324	46	91	14	3	1	28	25	0	14	.281	.332	.352	91	-4	6	.989	-1	96	91	1b76	—	-1.2
1938	Cin N	9	7	0	2	0	0	0	0	2	0	0	.286	.444	.286	107	0	0	ø	0	—	—	/H	—	0.0
	Phi N	87	310	31	93	18	1	0	18	17	0	4	.300	.336	.365	95	-2	1	.973	0	98	126	3b58,1b17	—	-0.2
	Year	96	317	31	95	18	1	0	18	19	0	4	.300	.339	.363	96	-2	1	.973	0	98	126	3b58,1b17	—	-0.2
Total	10	811	2980	396	890	153	35	17	281	182	5	109	.299	.340	.391	106	20	20-0	.990	-8	98	102	1b648,3b66,O2R	—	-4.8
Jordan, Brian	Brian O'Neal; B3.29.1967 Baltimore MD; BR/TR/6´1˝/(205–225); [StLN88 1/30]; d4.8; Col Richmond																								
1992	StL N	55	193	17	40	9	4	5	22	10-1	1	48	.207	.250	.373	76	-7	7-2	.991	-1	92	133	O53(27/9/21)	30	-1.0
1993	StL N	67	223	33	69	10	6	10	44	12-0	4	35	.309	.351	.543	137	10	6-6	.973	-1	96	101	O65(23/37/12)	0	0.7
1994	StL N	53	178	14	46	8	2	5	15	16-0	1	40	.258	.320	.410	89	-3	4-3	.991	5	114	165	O46(18/9/22)/1	33	0.0
1995	StL N	131	490	83	145	20	4	22	81	22-4	11	79	.296	.339	.488	113	7	24-9	.996	2	107	45	O126(0/13/116)	0	0.6
1996	†StL N	140	513	82	159	36	1	17	104	29-4	7	84	.310	.349	.483	118	13	22-5	.994	11	**120**	103	O136(0/13/128)/1	14	2.1
1997	StL N	47	145	17	34	5	0	0	10	10-1	6	21	.234	.311	.269	53	-10	6-1	1.000	1	112	84	O44(0/14/30)	117	-0.8
1998	StL N	150	564	100	178	34	7	25	91	40-1	9	66	.316	.368	.534	135	27	17-5	.970	2	102	118	O141(0/33/123)/3D	0	2.6
1999	†Atl N★	153	576	100	163	28	4	23	115	51-2	9	81	.283	.346	.465	105	3	13-8	.990	2	101	94	O150R	0	-0.2
2000	†Atl N	133	489	71	129	26	0	17	77	38-1	5	80	.264	.320	.421	87	-11	10-2	.990	6	111	87	O130R	15	-0.9
2001	†Atl N	148	560	82	165	32	3	25	97	31-3	6	88	.295	.334	.496	111	7	3-2	.991	10	112	117	O144(0/1/144),D2	0	1.0
2002	LA N	128	471	65	134	27	3	18	80	34-3	6	86	.285	.338	.469	117	10	2-2	.982	2	99	134	O125(121/0/4),D3	15	0.7
2003	LA N	66	224	28	67	9	0	6	28	23-3	4	30	.299	.372	.420	110	4	1-1	.990	-3	91	59	O62(54/14/3),D2	96	-0.1
2004	Tex A	61	212	27	47	13	1	5	23	16-2	1	35	.222	.275	.363	63	-12	2-2	.990	0	109	35	O44(1/0/44),D17	83	-1.4
2005	†Atl N	76	231	25	57	8	2	3	24	14-0	3	46	.247	.295	.338	66	-12	2-0	1.000	3	99	175	O62(45/0/17)	59	-1.1
2006	Atl N	48	91	11	21	2	0	3	10	7-0	1	23	.231	.287	.352	63	-5	0-0	.986	-1	87	93	1b25,O6(3/2/1)	76	-0.7
Total	15	1456	5160	755	1454	267	37	184	821	353-25	74	842	.282	.333	.455	104	21	119-48	.988	37	106	102	O1334(292/145/945),D27,1b27/3	538	1.5
Jordan, Slats	Clarence Veasey; B9.27.1878 Baltimore MD; D12.7.1953 Catonsville MD; BL/TL/6´1˝/190; d9.28																								
1901	Bal A	1	3	0	0	0	0	0	0	0	0	—	.000	.000	.000	-96	-1	0	.867	-1	0	0	/1	—	-0.1
1902	Bal A	1	4	0	0	0	0	0	0	0	0	—	.000	.000	.000	-96	-1	0	ø	-0	0	0	/rf	—	-0.1
Total	2	2	7	0	0	0	0	0	0	0	0	—	.000	.000	.000	-96	-2	0	.000	-1	0	0	/rf1	—	-0.2
Jordan, Jimmy	James William "Lord"; B1.13.1908 Tucapau (now Startex) SC; D12.4.1957 Gastonia NC; BR/TR/5´9˝/157; d4.20																								
1933	Bro N	70	211	16	54	12	1	0	17	4	0	6	.256	.270	.322	71	-8	3	.969	6	113	77	S51,2b11	—	0.2
1934	Bro N	97	369	34	98	17	2	0	43	9	1	32	.266	.285	.322	66	-19	1	.956	-6	102	52	S51,2b41,3b9	—	-1.9
1935	Bro N	94	295	26	82	7	0	0	30	9	1	17	.278	.302	.302	64	-15	3	.983	19	121	103	2b46,S28,3b5	—	0.8
1936	Bro N	115	398	26	93	15	1	2	28	15	0	21	.234	.262	.291	48	-30	1	.970	-17	86	78	2b98,S9,3b6	—	-4.0
Total	4	376	1273	102	327	51	4	2	118	37	2	76	.257	.279	.308	60	-72	8	.969	2	98	93	2b196,S139,3b20	—	-4.9
Jordan, Kevin	Kevin Wayne; B10.9.1969 San Francisco CA; BR/TR/6´1˝/(193–207); [NYA90 20/542]; d8.8; Col Nebraska																								
1995	Phi N	24	54	6	10	1	0	2	6	2-1	1	9	.185	.228	.315	41	-5	0-0	.984	5	127	139	2b9/3	0	0.1
1996	Phi N	43	131	15	37	10	0	3	12	5-0	1	20	.282	.309	.427	93	-2	2-1	1.000	1	68	93	1b30,2b7/3	105	-0.3
1997	Phi N	84	177	19	47	8	0	6	30	3-0	0	26	.266	.273	.412	79	-6	0-1	.987	-4	59	73	1b25,3b12,2b6/D	0	-1.3
1998	Phi N	112	250	23	69	13	0	2	27	8-1	2	30	.276	.303	.352	72	-11	0-0	1.000	2	100	103	1b24,2b22,3b6,D8	0	-1.0
1999	Phi N	120	347	36	99	17	3	4	51	24-1	6	34	.285	.339	.386	83	-9	0-0	.943	7	96	115	3b62,2b33,1b13	0	-0.2
2000	Phi N	109	337	30	74	16	2	5	36	17-0	1	41	.220	.257	.323	46	-29	0-1	.988	-4	101	70	2b47,3b39,1b9	0	-3.1
2001	Phi N	68	113	9	27	5	0	1	13	14-2	0	21	.239	.323	.310	68	-5	0-0	.948	-2	43	67	1b10,2b10,3b10	0	-0.7
Total	7	560	1409	138	363	70	5	23	175	73-5	11	181	.258	.297	.363	70	-67	2-3	.977	4	110	104	2b134,3b131,1b111,D9	105	-6.5
Jordan, Mike	Michael Henry "Mitty"; B2.7.1863 Lawrence MA; D9.25.1940 Lawrence MA; 5´7.5˝/155; d8.21																								
1890	Pit N	37	125	8	12	1	0	0	6	15	3	19	.096	.210	.104	-9	-16	5	.947	4	161	0	O37(29/8/0)	—	-1.2
Jordan, Ricky	Paul Scott; B5.26.1965 Richmond CA; BR/TR/6´3˝/(185–210); [PhiN83 1/22]; d7.17																								
1988	Phi N	69	273	41	84	15	1	11	43	7-2	0	39	.308	.324	.491	128	8	1-1	.992	-4	75	74	1b69	0	-0.1
1989	Phi N	144	523	63	149	22	3	12	75	23-5	5	62	.285	.317	.407	107	3	4-3	.993	-9	71	100	1b140	0	-1.7
1990	Phi N	92	324	32	78	21	0	5	44	13-6	5	39	.241	.277	.352	73	-12	2-0	.995	-7	68	114	1b84	21	-2.6
1991	Phi N	101	301	38	82	21	3	9	49	14-2	2	49	.272	.304	.452	112	4	0-2	.987	-6	75	75	1b72	0	-0.8
1992	Phi N	94	276	33	84	19	0	4	34	5-0	0	44	.304	.313	.417	106	1	3-0	.995	-5	74	91	1b54,O11L	35	-0.7
1993	†Phi N	90	159	21	46	4	1	5	18	8-1	1	32	.289	.324	.421	100	-1	0-0	.990	-5	23	100	1b33	0	-0.8
1994	Phi N	72	220	29	62	14	2	8	37	6-1	1	32	.282	.303	.473	97	-2	0-0	.993	-7	45	108	1b49	0	-1.3
1996	Sea A	15	28	4	7	0	0	1	4	1-0	1	6	.250	.290	.357	65	-2	0-0	1.000	-1	32	114	1b9,D2	121	-0.3
Total	8	677	2104	261	592	116	10	55	304	77-17	15	303	.281	.308	.424	103	-1	10-6	.993	-44	66	95	1b510,O11L,D2	177	-8.3
Jordan, Scott	Scott Allan; B5.27.1963 Waco TX; BR/TR/6´0˝/178; [CleA85 4/89]; d9.2; Col Georgia Tech																								
1988	Cle A	7	9	0	1	0	0	0	1	0-0	0	3	.111	.111	.111	-36	-2	0-0	1.000	0	109	0	O6(0/5/1)	0	-0.2
Jordan, Tom	Thomas Jefferson; B9.5.1919 Lawton OK; BR/TR/6´1.5˝/195; d9.4																								
1944	Chi A	14	45	2	12	1	1	0	3	1	0	0	.267	.283	.333	77	-2	0-0	.947	-1	*130*	*94*	C14	0	-0.2
1946	Chi A	10	15	1	4	2	1	0	0	0	0	1	.267	.267	.533	124	0	0-0	1.000	0	*65*	*0*	C2	0	0.1
	Cle A	14	35	2	7	1	0	1	3	3	0	1	.200	.263	.314	65	-2	1-1	.974	-3	*86*	*141*	C13	0	-0.5
	Year	24	50	3	11	3	1	1	3	3	0	2	.220	.264	.380	83	-2	1-1	.980	-3	*82*	*111*	C15	0	-0.4

THE BATTER REGISTER

YEAR	TM LG	G	AB	R	H	2B	3B	HR	RBI	BB-IB	HP	SO	AVG	OBP	SLG	AOPS	ABR	SB-CS	FA	FR	RNG	THR	GAMES AT POSITION	DL	BFW
1948	StL A	1	1	0	0	0	0	0	0	0	0	0	.000	.000	.000	-97	0	0-0	ø	0	—	—	/H	0	0.0
Total	3	39	96	5	23	4	2	1	6	4	0	2	.240	.270	.354	78	-4	1-1	.963	-4	*108*	*102*	C29	0	-0.6
Jordan, Tim	Timothy Joseph; B2.14.1879 New York NY; D9.13.1949 Bronx NY; BL/TL/6´1˝/170; d8.10																								
1901	Was A	6	20	2	4	1	0	0	2	3	0	—	.200	.304	.250	56	-1	0	.941	-1	66	61	1b6	—	-0.2
1903	NY A	2	8	2	1	0	0	0	0	0	0	—	.125	.125	.125	-23	-1	0	.889	-1	0	327	1b2	—	-0.2
1906	Bro N	129	450	67	118	20	8	**12**	78	59	3	—	.262	.352	.422	153	28	16	.978	-9	79	71	1b126	—	1.8
1907	Bro N	147	485	43	133	15	8	4	53	74	1	—	.274	.371	.363	141	26	10	.980	-6	89	97	1b143	—	2.0
1908	Bro N	148	515	58	127	18	5	**12**	60	59	3	—	.247	.328	.371	128	17	9	.982	-15	61	81	1b146	—	-0.1
1909	Bro N	103	330	47	90	20	3	3	36	59	2	—	.273	.386	.379	142	20	13	.983	-9	57	75	1b95	—	1.1
1910	Bro N	5	5	1	1	0	0	1	3	0	0	2	.200	.200	.800	195	0	0	ø	0	—	—	/H	—	0.0
Total	7	540	1813	220	474	74	24	32	232	254	9	2	.261	.355	.382	139	89	48	.980	-40	72	83	1b518	—	4.4
Jorgens, Art	Arndt Ludwig; B5.18.1905 Modum, Norway; D3.1.1980 Evanston IL; BR/TR/5´9˝/160; d4.26; b–Orville																								
1929	NY A	18	34	6	11	3	0	0	4	6	0	7	.324	.425	.412	125	2	0-4	.979	-0	*103*	*74*	C15	—	0.1
1930	NY A	16	30	7	11	3	0	0	1	2	0	4	.367	.406	.467	126	1	0-0	.960	-1	*104*	*101*	C16	—	0.1
1931	NY A	46	100	12	27	1	2	0	14	9	0	3	.270	.330	.320	76	-4	0-1	.962	-3	*104*	*66*	C40	—	-0.5
1932	NY A	56	151	13	33	7	1	2	19	14	0	11	.219	.285	.318	59	-10	0-0	.967	-1	*107*	*80*	C56	—	-0.8
1933	NY A	21	50	9	11	3	0	2	13	12	0	3	.220	.371	.400	111	1	1-0	.982	1	*185*	*22*	C19	—	0.4
1934	NY A	58	183	14	38	6	1	0	20	23	0	24	.208	.296	.251	45	-15	2-0	.984	3	*109*	*69*	C56	—	-0.8
1935	NY A	36	84	6	20	2	0	0	8	12	0	10	.238	.333	.262	59	-5	0-0	1.000	4	*134*	*77*	C33	—	0.1
1936	NY A	31	66	5	18	3	1	0	5	2	0	3	.273	.294	.348	60	-5	0-0	.990	2	*150*	*92*	C30	—	-0.1
1937	NY A	13	23	3	3	1	0	0	3	2	0	5	.130	.200	.174	-5	-4	0-0	1.000	0	*121*	*69*	C11	—	-0.3
1938	NY A	9	17	3	4	2	0	0	2	3	0	3	.235	.350	.353	77	0	0-0	.923	0	*105*	*142*	C8	—	0.0
1939	NY A	3	0	1	0	0	0	0	0	0	0	0	ø	ø	ø	ø	0	0-0	1.000	0	*0*	*0*	C2	—	0.0
Total	11	307	738	79	176	31	5	4	89	85	0	73	.238	.317	.310	66	-39	3-5	.978	7	*120*	*73*	C286	—	-1.8
Jorgensen, Pinky	Carl; B11.21.1914 Laton CA; D5.2.1996 Santa Cruz CA; BR/TR/6´1˝/195; d9.14; Col St. Marys (CA)																								
1937	Cin N	6	14	1	4	0	0	0	1	1	0	2	.286	.333	.286	73	-1	0	.875	0	80	362	O4L	—	-0.1
Jorgensen, Spider	John Donald; B11.3.1919 Folsom CA; D11.6.2003 Rancho Cugamonga CA; BL/TR/5´9˝/155; d4.15; Col Sacramento (CA) City																								
1947	†Bro N	129	441	57	121	29	8	5	67	58	1	45	.274	.360	.410	100	1	4	.949	-3	98	**123**	3b128	0	-0.2
1948	Bro N	31	90	15	27	6	2	1	13	16	1	13	.300	.411	.444	127	4	1	.887	-6	74	82	3b24	0	-0.1
1949	†Bro N	53	134	15	36	5	1	1	14	23	0	13	.269	.376	.343	90	-1	0	.946	-2	90	84	3b36	0	-0.3
1950	Bro N	2	2	0	0	0	0	0	1	1	0	0	.000	.333	.000	-4	0	0	1.000	-0	104	0	/3	0	0.0
	NY N	24	37	5	5	0	0	0	4	5	0	2	.135	.238	.135	1	-5	0	.913	0	110	85	3b5	0	-0.5
	Year	26	39	5	5	0	0	0	5	6	0	2	.128	.244	.128	1	-6	0	.917	0	110	79	3b6	0	-0.5
1951	NY N	28	51	5	12	0	0	2	8	3	1	2	.235	.291	.353	72	-2	0-0	1.000	-1	95	0	O11R/3	0	-0.3
Total	5	267	755	97	201	40	11	9	107	106	3	75	.266	.359	.384	95	-3	5-0	.940	-11	94	109	3b195,O11R	0	-1.4
Jorgensen, Mike	Michael; B8.16.1948 Passaic NJ; BL/TL/6´0˝/(185–195); [NYN66 4/61]; d9.10; M1																								
1968	NY N	8	14	0	2	1	0	0	0	0-0	0	4	.143	.143	.214	6	-2	0-0	1.000	-0	49	134	1b4	0	-0.3
1970	NY N	76	87	15	17	3	1	3	4	10-1	0	23	.195	.278	.356	68	-4	2-2	.992	2	112	77	1b50,O10(0/9/1)	0	-0.5
1971	NY N	45	118	16	26	1	1	5	11	11-1	3	24	.220	.303	.373	91	-2	1-2	.951	-2	95	0	O31(4/25/4)/1	0	-0.5
1972	Mon N	113	372	48	86	12	3	13	47	53-7	4	75	.231	.332	.384	102	2	12-13	.995	-1	115	104	1b76,O28(2/26/0)	0	-0.9
1973	Mon N	138	413	49	95	16	2	9	47	64-4	3	49	.230	.336	.344	86	-6	16-7	**.995**	4	**112**	93	1b123,O11(9/2/0)	0	-1.0
1974	Mon N	131	287	45	89	16	1	11	59	70-5	2	39	.310	.444	.488	153	25	3-5	.998	6	121	98	1b91,O29(28/1/0)	0	2.5
1975	Mon N	144	445	58	116	18	0	18	67	79-8	7	75	.261	.378	.422	117	13	3-3	.994	5	**114**	114	1b133,O6(5/1/0)	0	0.8
1976	Mon N	125	343	36	87	13	0	6	23	52-9	0	48	.254	.349	.344	93	-1	7-1	.989	3	136	104	1b81,O41(25/0/16)	0	-0.4
1977	Mon N	19	20	3	4	1	0	0	0	3-0	0	4	.200	.304	.250	52	-1	0-0	1.000	1	283	61	1b5	0	0.0
	Oak A	66	203	18	50	4	1	8	32	25-2	2	44	.246	.329	.394	99	0	3-2	.989	2	121	77	1b48,O20(6/1/13),D2	51	-0.1
1978	Tex A	96	97	20	19	3	0	1	9	18-1	0	10	.196	.319	.258	64	-4	3-1	.994	5	144	94	1b78,O9(2/4/4)/D	0	-0.1
1979	Tex A	90	157	21	35	7	0	6	16	14-1	2	29	.223	.293	.382	82	-4	0-2	.988	3	129	103	1b60,O20(4/7/9),D2	30	-0.4
1980	NY N	119	321	43	82	11	0	7	43	46-6	0	55	.255	.349	.355	98	1	0-3	.995	-1	88	70	1b72,O31(9/0/22)	0	-0.7
1981	NY N	86	122	8	25	5	2	3	15	12-1	0	24	.205	.270	.352	77	-4	4-0	.991	1	88	76	1b40,O19(4/0/15)	0	-0.5
1982	NY N	120	114	16	29	6	0	2	14	21-3	0	24	.254	.370	.360	105	2	2-0	.991	-2	57	140	1b56,O16(1/0/15)	0	-0.2
1983	NY N	38	24	5	6	3	0	1	3	2-0	1	4	.250	.333	.500	129	1	0-1	1.000	-0	92	143	1b19	0	0.0
	Atl N	57	48	5	12	1	0	1	8	8-0	0	8	.250	.351	.333	86	-1	0-0	1.000	0	89	169	1b19,O6L	0	-0.1
	Year	95	72	10	18	4	0	2	11	10-0	1	12	.250	.345	.389	100	0	0-1	1.000	0	90	156	1b38,O6L	0	-0.1
1984	Atl N	31	26	4	7	1	0	0	5	3-1	0	6	.269	.333	.308	79	-1	0-1	1.000	-1	0	0	1b8,O4(1/0/3)	0	-0.2
	StL N	59	98	5	24	4	2	1	12	10-1	0	17	.245	.315	.357	90	-1	0-0	.991	1	123	164	1b39	0	-0.2
	Year	90	124	9	31	5	2	1	17	13-2	0	23	.250	.319	.347	87	-2	0-1	.992	1	115	153	1b47,O4(1/0/3)	0	-0.4
1985	†StL N	72	112	14	22	6	0	0	11	31-0	1	27	.196	.375	.250	79	-1	2-1	.994	-2	78	133	1b49,O2L	0	-0.5
Total	17	1633	3421	429	833	132	13	95	426	532-51	25	589	.243	.347	.373	99	12	58-44	.994	23	114	102	1b1052,O283(108/76/102),D5	81	-3.3
Jorgensen, Ryan	Ryan Wayne; B5.4.1979 Jacksonville FL; BR/TR/6´2˝/220; [ChiN00 7/193]; d8.8; Col Louisiana St.																								
2005	Fla N	4	4	0	0	0	0	0	0	0-0	0	3	.000	.000	.000	-99	-1	0-0	1.000	-1	32	0	C3	0	-0.2
Jorgensen, Terry	Terry Allen; B9.2.1966 Kewaunee WI; BR/TR/6´4˝/(208–213); [MinA87 2/35]; d9.10; Col Wisconsin–Oshkosh																								
1989	Min A	10	23	1	4	1	0	0	2	4-0	0	5	.174	.296	.217	44	-2	0-0	.958	1	120	223	3b9	0	0.0
1992	Min A	22	58	5	18	1	0	0	5	3-0	1	11	.310	.349	.328	89	-1	1-2	1.000	3	111	127	1b13,3b9,S2	0	0.1
1993	Min A	59	152	15	34	7	0	1	12	10-0	0	21	.224	.270	.289	50	-11	1-0	.982	6	115	113	3b45,1b9,S6	0	-0.5
Total	3	91	233	21	56	9	0	1	19	17-0	1	37	.240	.292	.292	59	-14	2-2	.975	10	117	152	3b63,1b22,S8	0	-0.4
Jose, Felix	Domingo Felix Andujar (b Domingo Felix Andujar (Jose)); B5.2.1965 Santo Domingo, D.R.; BB/TR/6´1˝/(184–221); d9.2																								
1988	Oak A	8	6	2	2	1	0	0	1	0-0	0	1	.333	.333	.500	134	0	1-0	1.000	1	235	0	O6(1/0/5)	0	0.1
1989	Oak A	20	57	3	11	2	0	0	5	4-0	0	13	.193	.246	.228	35	-5	0-1	.974	1	109	174	O19(4/0/16)	0	-0.5
1990	Oak A	101	341	42	90	12	0	8	39	16-0	5	65	.264	.306	.370	92	-5	8-2	.977	3	111	87	O92(26/24/53),D7	0	-0.3
	StL N	25	85	12	23	4	1	3	13	8-0	0	16	.271	.333	.447	112	1	4-4	1.000	-2	90	0	O23(1/2/21)	0	-0.2
1991	StL N★	154	568	69	173	40	6	8	77	50-8	2	113	.305	.360	.438	123	18	20-12	.990	-2	90	130	O153R	0	1.2
1992	StL N	131	509	62	150	22	3	14	75	40-8	1	100	.295	.347	.432	122	14	28-12	.979	3	102	119	O127R	23	1.6
1993	KC A	149	499	64	126	24	3	6	43	36-5	1	95	.253	.303	.349	70	-21	31-13	.972	-8	91	66	O144(0/10/136)/D	0	-3.2
1994	KC A	99	366	56	111	28	1	11	55	35-6	0	75	.303	.362	.475	109	5	10-12	.980	-3	96	94	O98R	12	-0.4
1995	KC A	9	30	2	4	1	0	0	1	2-0	0	9	.133	.188	.167	-7	-5	0-0	1.000	2	108	417	O7R	0	-0.4
2000	NY A	20	29	4	7	0	0	1	5	2-0	0	9	.241	.281	.345	61	-2	0-1	.929	-0	103	0	O14(6/0/8),D2	29	-0.3
2002	Ari N	13	19	5	5	0	0	2	4	4-0	0	8	.263	.360	.579	137	1	0-0	1.000	-1	70	0	O5(1/0/4)	0	0.0
2003	Ari N	18	18	1	6	1	0	1	6	6-1	0	3	.333	.500	.556	162	2	0-0	ø	-0	0	0	/rfD	0	0.2
Total	11	747	2527	322	708	135	14	54	324	203-28	9	507	.280	.334	.409	102	3	102-57	.980	-6	97	101	O689(39/36/629),D11	64	-2.2
Joseph, Rick	Ricardo Emelindo (Harrigan); B8.24.1939 San Pedro de Macoris, D.R.; D9.8.1979 Santiago, D.R.; BR/TR/6´1˝/(190–210); d6.18																								
1964	KC A	17	54	3	12	2	0	0	1	3-0	0	11	.222	.263	.259	45	-4	0-1	.981	-1	76	123	1b12,3b3	0	-0.6
1967	Phi N	17	41	4	9	2	0	1	5	4-0	0	10	.220	.289	.341	79	-1	0-0	1.000	1	139	87	1b13	0	-0.1
1968	Phi N	66	155	20	34	5	0	3	12	16-2	1	35	.219	.295	.310	82	-3	0-1	.992	1	96	91	1b30,3b14/lf	0	-0.4
1969	Phi N	99	264	35	72	15	0	6	37	22-2	1	57	.273	.329	.398	106	2	2-1	.956	-2	95	111	3b58,1b17/2	0	-0.1
1970	Phi N	71	119	7	27	2	1	3	10	6-1	0	28	.227	.264	.336	61	-7	0-0	.917	-6	71	0	O12L,1b10,3b9	0	-1.5
Total	5	270	633	69	154	26	1	13	65	51-5	2	141	.243	.300	.349	84	-13	2-3	.933	-6	93	137	3b84,1b82,O13L/2	0	-2.7
Josephson, Duane	Duane Charles; B6.3.1942 New Hampton IA; D1.30.1997 New Hampton IA; BR/TR/6´0˝/(185–195); d9.15; Col Northern Iowa; [DL 1973 Bos A 9]																								
1965	Chi A	4	9	2	1	0	0	0	0	2-0	0	4	.111	.273	.111	14	-1	0-0	1.000	1	60	0	C4	0	0.0
1966	Chi A	11	38	3	9	1	0	0	3	3-0	0	3	.237	.293	.263	65	-2	0-0	.974	2	105	226	C11	0	0.1
1967	Chi A	62	189	11	45	5	1	1	9	6-0	0	24	.238	.262	.291	65	-9	0-3	1.000	-4	103	102	C59	24	-1.3
1968	Chi A★	128	434	35	107	16	6	6	45	18-2	6	52	.247	.284	.353	92	-6	2-4	.990	16	95	118	C122	0	1.7
1969	Chi A	52	162	19	39	6	2	1	20	13-0	1	17	.241	.296	.321	71	-6	0-0	.984	-2	80	111	C47	62	-0.6
1970	Chi A	96	285	28	90	12	1	4	41	24-2	3	28	.316	.370	.407	112	5	0-1	.985	-9	76	77	C84	21	-0.1
1971	Bos A	91	306	38	75	14	1	10	39	22-4	0	35	.245	.294	.395	88	-6	2-0	.989	-2	99	55	C87	0	-0.3

YEAR	TM LG	G	AB	R	H	2B	3B	HR	RBI	BB-IB	HP	SO	AVG	OBP	SLG	AOPS	ABR	SB-CS	FA	FR	RNG	THR	GAMES AT POSITION	DL	BFW
1972	Bos A	26	82	11	22	4	1	1	7	4-0	1	11	.268	.310	.378	98	0	0-2	.980	-4	95	58	1b16,C6	64	-0.7
Total	8	470	1505	147	388	58	12	23	164	92-8	11	174	.258	.303	.358	89	-25	4-10	.989	-2	94	95	C420,1b16	180	-1.2
Joshua, Von	Von Everett; B5.1.1948 Oakland CA; BL/TL/5´10˝/170; d9.2; C4; Col Chabot (CA) JC/Laney (CA) JC																								
1969	LA N	14	8	2	2	0	0	0	0	0-0	0	2	.250	.250	.250	43	-1	1-0	.800	-1	74	0	O8(7/0/2)	0	-0.1
1970	LA N	72	109	23	29	1	3	1	8	6-2	0	24	.266	.302	.358	80	-4	2-2	.941	-0	104	61	O41(21/10/16)	0	-0.6
1971	LA N	11	7	2	0	0	0	0	0	0-0	0	1	.000	.000	.000	-99	-2	0-0	1.000	1	317	0	O5(4/1/0)	0	-0.1
1973	LA N	75	159	19	40	4	1	2	17	8-2	1	29	.252	.288	.327	74	-6	7-2	.984	-3	82	77	O46(42/1/4)	27	-1.1
1974	†LA N	81	124	11	29	5	1	1	16	7-5	1	17	.234	.276	.315	69	-6	3-2	.943	-5	67	0	O35(12/17/6)	0	-1.2
1975	SF N	129	507	75	161	25	10	7	43	32-0	1	75	.318	.359	.448	119	11	20-10	**.993**	1	98	141	O117C	0	1.0
1976	SF N	42	156	13	41	5	2	0	2	4-2	0	20	.263	.280	.321	68	-7	1-3	.948	-5	76	133	O35(3/33/0)	0	-1.5
	Mil A	107	423	44	113	13	5	5	28	18-3	0	58	.267	.295	.357	93	-6	8-10	.982	2	99	131	O105(26/82/0)/D	0	-1.0
1977	Mil A	144	536	58	140	25	7	9	49	21-4	0	74	.261	.286	.384	81	-16	12-9	.970	-11	90	86	O140C	0	-2.8
1979	LA N	94	142	22	40	7	1	3	14	7-1	0	23	.282	.315	.408	98	-1	1-1	.967	-0	103	95	O46(11/10/28)	0	-0.2
1980	SD N	53	63	8	15	2	1	2	7	5-1	0	15	.238	.294	.397	98	-1	0-1	1.000	0	120	0	O12(3/8/1),1b2	18	-0.1
Total	10	822	2234	277	610	87	31	30	184	108-20	3	338	.273	.306	.380	91	-39	55-40	.975	-20	93	104	O590(129/419/57),1b2/D	45	-7.7
Jourdan, Ted	Theodore Charles; B9.5.1895 New Orleans LA; D9.23.1961 New Orleans LA; BL/TL/6´0˝/175; d9.18; Mil 1918																								
1916	Chi A	3	2	0	0	0	0	0	0	1	0	1	.000	.333	.000	1	0	2	ø	0	—	—	/H	—	0.0
1917	Chi A	17	34	2	5	0	1	0	2	1	0	3	.147	.171	.206	15	-4	0	.973	-0	101	47	1b14	—	-0.5
1918	Chi A	7	10	1	1	0	0	0	1	0	0	0	.100	.100	.100	-39	-2	0	1.000	-0	0	0	1b2	—	-0.2
1920	Chi A	48	150	16	36	5	2	0	8	17	5	17	.240	.337	.300	70	-6	3-2	.982	-4	71	163	1b40	—	-1.0
Total	4	75	196	19	42	5	3	0	11	19	5	21	.214	.300	.270	56	-12	5-2	.981	-4	74	140	1b56	—	-1.7
Joy, Pop	Aloysius C.; B6.11.1860 Washington DC; D6.28.1937 Washington DC; d6.3																								
1884	Was U	36	130	12	28	0	0	0	—	2	—	—	.215	.227	.215	36	-14	—	.966	0	69	112	1b36	—	-1.5
Joyce, George	George W.; B1847 Washington DC; D11.9.1895 Washington DC; d8.14																								
1886	Was N	1	0	0	0	0	0	0	0	0	—	0	ø	ø	ø	ø	0	0	ø	-0	0	0	/cf	—	0.0
Joyce, Bill	William Michael "Scrappy Bill"; B9.21.1865 St.Louis MO; D5.8.1941 St.Louis MO; BL/TR/5´11˝/185; d4.19; M3																								
1890	Bro P	**133**	489	121	123	18	18	1	78	**123**	12	77	.252	.413	.368	103	7	43	.811	-13	97	90	3b133	—	-0.3
1891	Bos AA	65	243	76	75	9	15	3	51	63	5	27	.309	.460	.506	179	29	36	.849	-0	104	124	3b64/1	—	2.5
1892	Bro N	97	372	89	91	15	12	6	45	82	8	55	.245	.392	.398	144	25	23	.862	-20	76	56	3b94,O3L	—	0.6
1894	Was N	99	355	103	126	25	14	17	89	87	12	33	.355	.496	.648	179	52	21	.866	4	100	126	3b99	—	4.3
1895	Was N	127	479	110	149	26	13	17	97	**96**	14	56	.311	.440	.526	150	41	29	.846	-4	93	78	3b127	—	3.1
1896	Was N	81	310	85	97	16	10	8	51	67	12	20	.313	.452	.506	152	28	32	.888	-5	108	76	3b48,2b33	—	2.1
	NY N	49	165	36	61	9	2	5	43	34	10	14	.370	.502	.539	180	24	13	.883	2	102	55	3b49,M	—	2.2
	Year	130	475	121	158	25	12	**13**	94	101	22	34	.333	.470	.518	162	52	45	.885	-3	105	65	3b97,2b33	—	4.3
1897	NY N	110	389	111	118	15	13	3	64	81	17	—	.303	.444	.432	135	27	35	.851	-6	90	124	3b107,1b2,M	—	1.9
1898	NY N	145	508	91	131	20	9	10	91	88	18	—	.258	.386	.392	127	23	34	.966	8	**142**	91	1b130,3b14,2b2,M	—	2.9
Total	8	906	3310	822	971	153	106	70	609	721	108	282	.293	.435	.467	144	256	266	.851	-35	95	91	3b735,1b133,2b35,O3L	—	19.3
Joyner, Wally	Wallace Keith; B6.16.1962 Atlanta GA; BL/TL/6´2˝/(185–207); [CalA83 3/67]; d4.8; Col Brigham Young																								
1986	†Cal A★	154	593	82	172	27	3	22	100	57-8	2	58	.290	.348	.457	120	16	5-2	.989	6	113	**113**	1b152	0	1.3
1987	Cal A	149	564	100	161	33	1	34	117	72-12	5	64	.285	.366	.528	139	33	8-2	.993	-8	83	**114**	1b149	0	1.6
1988	Cal A	158	597	81	176	31	2	13	85	55-14	5	51	.295	.356	.419	120	17	8-2	.995	10	122	107	1b156	0	1.7
1989	Cal A	159	593	78	167	30	2	16	79	46-7	6	58	.282	.335	.420	115	11	3-2	**.997**	-3	90	**114**	1b159	0	-0.4
1990	Cal A	83	310	35	83	15	0	8	41	41-4	1	34	.268	.350	.394	111	6	2-1	.995	4	116	104	1b83	84	0.4
1991	Cal A	143	551	79	166	34	3	21	96	52-4	1	66	.301	.360	.488	133	24	2-0	.994	6	112	108	1b141	0	2.0
1992	KC A	149	572	66	154	36	2	9	66	55-4	4	50	.269	.336	.386	99	0	11-5	.993	13	**131**	**113**	1b145,D4	0	0.3
1993	KC A	141	497	83	145	36	3	15	65	66-13	3	67	.292	.375	.467	118	14	5-9	.994	19	**145**	102	1b140	0	1.9
1994	KC A	97	363	52	113	20	3	8	57	47-3	0	43	.311	.386	.449	110	7	3-2	.991	2	108	100	1b86,D11	18	0.0
1995	KC A	131	465	69	144	28	0	12	83	69-10	2	65	.310	.394	.447	118	15	3-2	**.998**	11	**132**	116	1b126,D2	0	1.4
1996	†SD N	121	433	59	120	29	1	8	65	69-8	3	71	.277	.377	.404	112	11	5-3	**.997**	1	100	96	1b119	39	0.1
1997	SD N	135	455	59	149	29	2	13	83	51-5	2	51	.327	.390	.486	138	27	3-5	**.996**	0	100	80	1b131	15	1.5
1998	†SD N	131	439	58	131	30	1	12	80	51-8	1	44	.298	.370	.453	125	17	1-2	.993	-1	93	114	1b127	0	0.5
1999	SD N	110	323	34	80	14	2	5	43	58-6	2	54	.248	.363	.350	89	-4	0-1	.995	4	112	122	1b105/D	39	-0.8
2000	†Atl N	119	224	24	63	12	0	5	32	31-3	1	31	.281	.365	.402	96	0	0-0	.992	2	119	110	1b55,D7	0	-0.2
2001	Ana A	53	148	14	36	5	1	3	14	13-0	0	18	.243	.304	.351	71	-6	1-1	.997	-1	90	108	1b39,D9	0	-1.0
Total	16	2033	7127	973	2060	409	26	204	1106	833-109	38	825	.289	.362	.440	117	188	60-39	.994	63	111	108	1b1913,D34	195	10.3
Jude, Frank	Frank; B11.11.1884 Libby MN; D5.4.1961 Brownsville TX; BR/TR/5´7˝/150; d7.9																								
1906	Cin N	80	308	31	64	6	4	1	31	16	6	—	.208	.261	.263	61	-15	7	.965	-0	152	44	O80R	—	-2.1
Judge, Joe	Joseph Ignatius; B5.25.1894 Brooklyn NY; D3.11.1963 Washington DC; BL/TL/5´8.5˝/155; d9.20; C2																								
1915	Was A	12	41	7	17	2	0	0	9	4	3	6	.415	.500	.463	185	5	2-3	.990	-0	82	149	1b10,O2R	—	0.4
1916	Was A	103	336	42	74	10	8	0	28	54	3	44	.220	.333	.298	91	-2	18	.986	4	112	94	1b103	—	-0.1
1917	Was A	102	393	62	112	15	15	2	30	50	2	40	.285	.369	.415	141	19	17	.988	-1	95	103	1b100	—	1.7
1918	Was A	**130**	502	56	131	23	7	1	46	49	4	32	.261	.332	.341	105	3	20	.985	0	102	94	1b130	—	0.0
1919	Was A	135	521	83	150	33	12	2	31	81	2	35	.288	.386	.409	124	20	23	.988	-4	87	92	1b133	—	1.4
1920	Was A	126	493	103	164	19	15	5	51	65	5	34	.333	.416	.462	136	27	12-12	.992	-7	76	88	1b124	—	1.5
1921	Was A	153	622	87	187	26	11	7	72	68	3	35	.301	.372	.412	105	5	21-6	.996	-3	90	105	1b152	—	-0.5
1922	Was A	148	591	84	174	32	15	10	81	50	6	20	.294	.355	.450	114	10	5-15	.996	5	107	**122**	1b147	—	0.1
1923	Was A	113	405	56	127	24	6	2	63	58	5	20	.314	.406	.417	123	17	11-7	**.993**	8	**126**	**131**	1b112	—	1.7
1924	†Was A	140	516	71	167	38	9	3	79	53	6	21	.324	.393	.450	121	17	13-8	.994	-2	89	**118**	1b140	—	0.5
1925	†Was A	112	376	65	118	31	5	8	66	55	3	21	.314	.406	.487	128	18	7-12	**.993**	3	106	**117**	1b109	—	1.1
1926	Was A	134	453	70	132	25	11	7	92	53	1	25	.291	.367	.442	113	8	7-5	.994	9	125	96	1b128	—	0.8
1927	Was A	137	522	68	161	29	11	2	71	45	2	22	.308	.366	.418	104	3	10-5	**.996**	-6	77	80	1b136	—	-1.1
1928	Was A	153	542	78	166	31	10	3	93	80	1	19	.306	.396	.417	115	15	16-4	.996	1	99	**106**	1b149	—	0.8
1929	Was A	143	543	83	171	35	8	6	71	73	1	33	.315	.397	.442	115	15	12-5	**.996**	3	105	103	1b142	—	0.9
1930	Was A	126	442	83	144	29	11	10	80	60	3	29	.326	.410	.509	131	22	13-6	**.998**	2	101	**111**	1b117	—	1.6
1931	Was A	35	74	11	21	3	0	0	9	8	0	8	.284	.354	.324	79	-2	0-0	.994	1	115	78	1b15	—	-0.3
1932	Was A	82	291	45	75	16	3	3	29	37	1	19	.258	.343	.364	84	-6	3-3	.997	1	102	123	1b78	—	-1.1
1933	Bro N	42	112	7	24	2	1	0	9	7	0	10	.214	.261	.250	48	-8	1	.989	0	100	110	1b28	—	-1.1
	Bos A	35	108	20	32	8	1	0	22	13	0	4	.296	.372	.389	103	1	2-1	1.000	0	89	95	1b29	—	-0.2
1934	Bos A	10	15	3	5	2	0	0	2	2	0	1	.333	.412	.467	118	1	0-0	1.000	-0	82	49	1b2	—	0.0
Total	20	2171	7898	1184	2352	433	159	71	1034	965	51	478	.298	.378	.420	115	188	213-92	.993	15	99	104	1b2084,O2R	—	8.1
Judnich, Wally	Walter Franklin; B1.24.1916 San Francisco CA; D7.10.1971 Glendale CA; BL/TL/6´1˝/205; d4.16; Mil 1943–45																								
1940	StL A	137	519	97	157	27	7	24	89	54	0	71	.303	.368	.520	125	18	8-5	**.989**	-5	96	68	O133C	—	0.9
1941	StL A	146	546	90	155	40	6	14	83	80	2	45	.284	.377	.456	116	14	5-5	.980	2	102	95	O140C	0	1.1
1942	StL A	132	457	78	143	22	6	17	82	74	4	41	.313	.413	.499	153	35	3-2	**.991**	-6	97	43	O122C	0	2.6
1946	StL A	142	511	60	134	23	4	15	72	60	0	54	.262	.340	.411	104	3	0-4	**.995**	5	**111**	63	O137(6/131/1)	0	0.2
1947	StL A	144	500	58	129	24	3	18	64	60	0	62	.258	.338	.426	109	5	2-5	.989	-6	84	100	1b129,O15(0/14/1)	0	-0.7
1948	†Cle A	79	218	36	56	13	3	2	29	56	1	23	.257	.411	.372	112	7	2-3	.970	-5	85	121	O49(0/35/14),1b20	0	0.0
1949	Pit N	10	35	5	8	1	0	0	1	1	0	2	.229	.250	.257	35	-3	0	1.000	0	112	0	O8C	0	-0.3
Total	7	790	2786	424	782	150	29	90	420	385	7	298	.281	.369	.452	119	79	20-24	.988	-14	101	71	O604(6/583/16),1b149	0	3.8
Judy, Lyle	Lyle Leroy "Punch"; B11.15.1913 Lawrenceville IL; D1.15.1991 Ormond Beach FL; BR/TR/5´10˝/150; d9.17																								
1935	StL N	8	11	2	0	0	0	0	0	2	0	2	.000	.154	.000	-53	-2	2	1.000	0	80	142	2b5	—	-0.2
Juelich, Red	John Samuel; B9.20.1916 St.Louis MO; D12.25.1970 St.Louis MO; BR/TR/5´11.5˝/170; d5.30																								
1939	Pit N	17	46	5	11	0	2	0	4	2	0	4	.239	.271	.326	61	-3	0	.935	-3	84	81	2b10,3b2	—	-0.6

YEAR	TM LG	G	AB	R	H	2B	3B	HR	RBI	BB-IB	HP	SO	AVG	OBP	SLG	AOPS	ABR	SB-CS	FA	FR	RNG	THR	GAMES AT POSITION	DL	BFW
JUMONVILLE, GEORGE	George Benedict; B5.16.1917 Mobile AL; D12.12.1996 Mobile AL; BR/TR/6´0˝/175; d9.13																								
1940	Phi N	11	34	0	3	0	0	0	0	1	1	6	.088	.139	.088	-38	-7	0	.952	-2	79	58	S10/3	—	-0.9
1941	Phi N	6	7	1	3	0	0	1	2	0	0	0	.429	.429	.857	266	1	0	1.000	0	178	0	/2S	0	0.2
Total	2	17	41	1	6	0	0	1	2	1	1	6	.146	.186	.220	12	-6	0	.953	-2	81	56	S11/23	0	-0.7
JURAK, ED	Edward James; B10.24.1957 Los Angeles CA; BR/TR/6´2˝/(165–187); [BosA75 3/63]; d6.30																								
1982	Bos A	12	21	3	7	0	0	0	7	2-0	0	4	.333	.375	.333	96	0	0-0	.923	1	127	76	3b11/cf	0	0.1
1983	Bos A	75	159	19	44	8	4	0	18	18-1	1	25	.277	.350	.377	94	-1	1-2	.943	5	104	100	S38,1b19,3b12/2D	0	0.4
1984	Bos A	47	66	6	16	3	1	1	7	12-0	0	12	.242	.359	.364	96	0	0-2	1.000	2	158	104	1b19,2b14,3b9,S2	0	0.1
1985	Bos A	26	13	4	3	0	0	0	0	1-0	0	3	.231	.286	.231	42	-1	0-0	.833	1	119	0	3b7,S3/1lfD	0	0.0
1988	Oak A	3	1	1	0	0	0	0	0	0-0	0	0	.000	.000	.000	-99	0	0-0	ø	-0	0	0	/3D	0	0.0
1989	SF N	30	42	2	10	0	0	0	1	5-0	0	5	.238	.319	.238	63	-2	0-0	.875	-1	97	143	S6,3b5,2b4,O2(1/0/1)/1	0	-0.3
Total	6	193	302	35	80	11	5	1	33	38-1	1	49	.265	.346	.344	88	-4	1-4	.941	7	103	98	S49,3b45,1b40,2b19,D8,O4(2/1/1)	0	0.3
JURGES, BILLY	William Frederick; B5.9.1908 Bronx NY; D3.3.1997 Clearwater FL; BR/TR/5´11˝/175; d5.4; M2/C6																								
1931	Chi N	88	293	34	59	15	5	0	23	25	0	41	.201	.264	.287	47	-22	2	.963	9	122	121	3b54,2b33,S3	—	-1.0
1932	†Chi N	115	396	40	100	24	4	2	52	19	1	26	.253	.288	.348	71	-17	1	**.964**	**30**	**119**	116	S108,3b5	—	2.1
1933	Chi N	143	487	49	131	17	6	5	50	26	5	39	.269	.313	.359	92	-6	3	.958	23	**108**	114	S143	—	2.8
1934	Chi N	100	358	43	88	15	2	8	33	19	3	34	.246	.289	.366	76	-13	1	.966	-1	98	107	S98	—	-0.6
1935	†Chi N	146	519	69	125	33	1	1	59	42	5	39	.241	.304	.314	66	-24	3	**.964**	**25**	**107**	**132**	S146	—	1.2
1936	Chi N	118	429	51	120	25	1	1	42	23	3	25	.280	.321	.350	79	-12	4	.960	14	104	120	S116	—	1.0
1937	Chi N☆	129	450	53	134	18	10	1	65	42	6	41	.298	.365	.389	101	1	2	**.975**	-13	91	97	S128	—	-0.3
1938	†Chi N	137	465	53	114	18	3	1	47	58	5	53	.245	.335	.303	75	-14	3	.953	-5	97	100	S136	—	-0.9
1939	NY N☆	138	543	84	155	21	11	6	63	47	6	34	.285	.349	.398	99	-1	3	**.965**	**20**	**107**	102	S137	—	2.8
1940	NY N✱	63	214	23	54	3	3	2	36	25	6	14	.252	.347	.322	85	-4	2	.967	3	100	100	S63	—	0.4
1941	NY N	134	471	50	138	25	2	5	61	47	3	36	.293	.361	.386	108	6	0	.957	6	**107**	105	S134	0	2.3
1942	NY N	127	464	45	119	7	1	2	30	43	3	42	.256	.324	.289	79	-12	1	.978	6	103	95	S124	0	0.4
1943	NY N	136	481	46	110	8	2	4	29	53	4	38	.229	.310	.279	70	-18	2	.955	4	96	69	S99,3b28	0	-0.6
1944	NY N	85	246	28	52	2	1	1	23	23	0	20	.211	.279	.240	47	-17	4	.961	5	115	75	3b61,S10/2	0	-1.1
1945	NY N	61	176	22	57	3	1	3	24	24	0	11	.324	.405	.403	123	6	2	.937	2	110	38	3b44,S8	0	0.9
1946	Chi N	82	221	26	49	9	2	0	17	43	1	28	.222	.351	.281	82	-3	3	.976	-1	103	68	S73,3b7,2b2	0	0.0
1947	Chi N	14	40	5	8	2	0	1	2	9	0	9	.200	.347	.325	83	-1	0	.925	-1	103	137	S14	0	-0.1
Total	17	1816	6253	721	1613	245	55	43	656	568	51	530	.258	.325	.335	82	-151	36	.964	126	103	104	S1540,3b199,2b36	0	9.3
JUST, JOE	Joseph Erwin (b Joseph Erwin Juszczak); B1.8.1916 Milwaukee WI; D11.22.2003 Franklin WI; BR/TR/5´11˝/185; d5.13																								
1944	Cin N	11	11	0	2	0	0	0	0	0	1	2	.182	.250	.182	24	-1	0	.923	-0	*95*	*0*	C10	0	-0.1
1945	Cin N	14	34	2	5	0	0	0	2	4	0	7	.147	.237	.147	8	-4	0	.947	-1	*84*	*73*	C14	0	-0.5
Total	2	25	45	2	7	0	0	0	2	4	1	9	.156	.240	.156	12	-5	0	.941	-1	*87*	*56*	C24	0	-0.6
JUSTICE, DAVID	David Christopher; B4.14.1966 Cincinnati OH; BL/TL/6´3˝/(195–200); [AtlN85 4/94]; d5.24; Col Thomas More																								
1989	Atl N	16	51	7	12	3	0	1	3	3-1	1	9	.235	.291	.353	81	-1	2-1	1.000	-2	80	0	O16(3/0/13)	0	-0.4
1990	Atl N	127	439	76	124	23	2	28	78	64-4	0	92	.282	.373	.535	139	24	11-6	.981	-3	89	92	1b69,O61R	0	1.6
1991	†Atl N	109	396	67	109	25	1	21	87	65-9	3	81	.275	.377	.503	138	22	8-8	.968	-1	93	109	O106R	54	1.7
1992	†Atl N	144	484	78	124	19	5	21	72	79-8	2	85	.256	.359	.446	120	15	2-4	.976	7	112	85	O140R	15	1.8
1993	†Atl N★	157	585	90	158	15	4	40	120	78-12	3	90	.270	.357	.515	128	22	3-5	.985	-0	102	74	O157R	0	1.2
1994	Atl N★	104	352	61	110	16	2	19	59	69-5	2	45	.313	.427	.531	143	25	2-4	.947	-2	100	83	O102R	0	1.7
1995	†Atl N	120	411	73	104	17	2	24	78	73-5	2	68	.253	.365	.479	116	11	4-2	.984	3	104	97	O120R	15	0.8
1996	Atl N	40	140	23	45	9	0	6	25	21-1	1	22	.321	.409	.514	135	8	1-1	1.000	4	118	115	O40R	137	0.9
1997	†Cle A✱	139	495	84	163	31	1	33	101	80-11	0	79	.329	.418	.596	156	43	3-5	.984	-6	81	64	O78(74/0/5),D61	17	2.8
1998	†Cle A	146	540	94	151	39	2	21	88	76-7	0	98	.280	.363	.476	113	12	9-3	1.000	-1	95	0	D123,O21(19/0/2)	0	0.5
1999	†Cle A	133	429	75	123	18	0	21	88	94-11	2	90	.287	.413	.476	121	18	1-3	.977	-2	89	119	O93(79/0/15),D34	0	0.8
2000	Cle A	68	249	46	66	14	1	21	58	38-2	0	49	.265	.361	.582	129	11	1-1	.977	-2	95	72	O47(25/2/23),D20	0	0.5
	†NY A	78	275	43	84	17	0	20	60	39-1	1	42	.305	.391	.585	145	19	1-0	.985	6	116	177	O60(43/1/25),D18	0	2.0
	Year	146	524	89	150	31	1	41	118	77-3	1	91	.286	.377	.584	138	30	2-1	.982	4	106	129	O107(68/3/48),D38	0	2.5
2001	†NY A	111	381	58	92	16	1	18	51	54-5	0	83	.241	.333	.430	99	0	1-2	.981	4	121	308	D85,O25(16/0/11)	46	-0.2
2002	†Oak A	118	398	54	106	18	3	11	49	70-3	1	66	.266	.376	.410	110	8	4-1	.985	-3	92	74	O75(53/0/23),D37	27	0.1
Total	14	1610	5625	929	1571	280	24	305	1017	903-85	18	999	.279	.378	.500	127	237	53-46	.978	1	100	95	O1141(312/3/842),D378,1b69	311	15.8
JUTZE, SKIP	Alfred Henry; B5.28.1946 Bayside NY; BR/TR/5´11˝/190; [StLN68*S4/74]; d9.1; Col Central Connecticut																								
1972	StL N	21	71	1	17	2	0	0	5	1-0	0	16	.239	.247	.268	47	-5	0-1	.964	0	135	242	C17	0	-0.5
1973	Hou N	90	278	18	62	6	0	0	18	19-5	1	37	.223	.273	.245	45	-21	0-1	.984	-8	93	92	C86	0	-2.7
1974	Hou N	8	13	0	3	0	0	0	1	1-0	0	1	.231	.267	.231	48	-1	0-0	1.000	-2	105	196	C7	0	-0.2
1975	Hou N	51	93	9	21	2	0	0	6	2-0	0	4	.226	.242	.247	39	-8	1-0	.988	-6	82	49	C47	0	-1.3
1976	Hou N	42	92	7	14	2	3	0	6	4-0	0	16	.152	.186	.239	22	-10	0-0	.986	-3	76	108	C42	0	-1.2
1977	Sea A	42	109	10	24	2	0	3	15	7-1	0	12	.220	.267	.321	60	-6	0-4	.984	-5	61	107	C40	0	-1.1
Total	6	254	656	45	141	14	3	3	51	34-6	1	86	.215	.253	.259	44	-51	1-6	.983	-23	87	106	C239	0	-7.0
KADING, JACK	John Frederick; B11.17.1884 Waukesha WI; D6.2.1964 Chicago IL; BR/TR/6´3˝/190; d9.12																								
1910	Pit N	8	23	5	7	2	1	0	4	4	0	5	.304	.407	.478	149	2	0	1.000	1	166	124	1b8	—	0.3
1914	Chi F	3	3	0	0	0	0	0	0	0	0	0	.000	.000	.000	-99	-1	0	ø	0	—	—	/H	—	-0.1
Total	2	11	26	5	7	2	1	0	4	4	0	5	.269	.367	.423	123	1	0	1.000	1	166	124	1b8	—	0.2
KAFORA, JAKE	Frank Jacob "Tomatoes"; B10.16.1888 Chicago IL; D3.23.1928 Chicago IL; BR/TR/6´0˝/180; d10.5																								
1913	Pit N	1	1	0	0	0	0	0	0	0	1	1	.000	.500	.000	52	0	0	1.000	-0	43	0	/C	—	0.0
1914	Pit N	21	23	2	3	0	0	0	0	0	2	6	.130	.200	.130	-1	-3	0	1.000	-1	*98*	*55*	C17	—	-0.3
Total	2	22	24	3	3	0	0	0	0	0	3	7	.125	.222	.125	4	-3	0	1.000	-1	*95*	*52*	C18	—	-0.3
KAHDOT, IKE	Isaac Leonard "Chief"; B10.22.1899 Georgetown OK; D3.31.1999 Oklahoma City OK; BR/TR/5´5.5˝/145; d9.5; Col Haskell																								
1922	Cle A	4	2	0	0	0	0	0	0	0	0	1	.000	.000	.000	-99	-1	0-0	1.000	0	160	0	3b2	—	0.0
KAHL, NICK	Nicholas Alexander; B4.10.1879 Coulterville IL; D7.13.1959 Sparta IL; BR/TR/5´9˝/185; d5.2																								
1905	Cle A	40	135	16	29	4	1	0	21	4	2	—	.215	.248	.259	60	-6	1	.940	-3	106	37	2b32/Scf	—	-1.1
KAHLE, BOB	Robert Wayne; B11.23.1915 New Castle IN; D12.16.1988 Inglewood CA; BR/TR/6´0˝/170; d4.21																								
1938	Bos N	8	3	2	1	0	0	0	0	0	0	0	.333	.333	.333	93	0	0	ø	0	—	—	/H	—	0.0
KAHN, OWEN	Owen Earle "Jack"; B6.5.1905 Richmond VA; D1.17.1981 Richmond VA; BR/TR/5´11˝/160; d5.24; Col William and Mary																								
1930	Bos N	1	0	1	0	0	0	0	0	0	0	0	ø	ø	ø	ø	0	0	ø	0	—	—	/R	—	0.0
KAHOE, MIKE	Michael Joseph; B9.3.1873 Yellow Springs OH; D5.14.1949 Akron OH; BR/TR/6´0˝/185; d9.22																								
1895	Cin N	3	4	0	0	0	0	0	0	0	0	0	.000	.000	.000	-96	-1	0	1.000	-0	*122*	*0*	C3	—	-0.1
1899	Cin N	14	42	2	7	1	1	0	4	0	0	—	.167	.167	.238	10	-5	1	.957	2	*131*	*117*	C13	—	-0.2
1900	Cin N	52	175	18	33	3	3	1	9	4	2	—	.189	.215	.257	31	-17	3	.963	5	*117*	*98*	C51/S	—	-0.8
1901	Cin N	4	13	0	4	0	0	0	0	1	0	—	.308	.357	.308	100	0	0	1.000	-1	*98*	*64*	C4	—	-0.1
	Chi N	67	237	21	53	12	2	1	21	8	0	—	.224	.249	.304	62	-12	5	.974	4	*95*	*99*	C63,1b6	—	-0.2
	Year	71	250	21	57	12	2	1	21	9	0	—	.228	.255	.304	64	-12	5	.974	3	*95*	*97*	C67,1b6	—	-0.3
1902	Chi N	7	18	0	4	1	0	0	2	0	0	—	.222	.222	.278	56	-1	0	.875	-1	*114*	*81*	C4,3b2/S	—	-0.1
	StL A	55	197	21	48	9	2	2	28	6	1	—	.244	.270	.340	69	-9	4	.967	0	*115*	*80*	C53	—	-0.3
1903	StL A	77	244	26	46	7	5	0	23	11	1	—	.189	.227	.258	46	-16	1	.971	2	*119*	*79*	C71,O2(0/1/1)	—	-0.8
1904	StL A	72	236	9	51	6	1	0	12	8	0	—	.216	.242	.250	59	-11	4	.968	-3	*95*	*113*	C69	—	-0.9
1905	Phi N	16	51	2	13	2	0	0	4	1	0	—	.255	.269	.294	70	-2	1	.975	1	*116*	*98*	C15	—	0.1
1907	Chi N	5	10	0	4	0	0	0	1	0	0	—	.400	.400	.400	142	0	0	1.000	-1	*79*	*76*	C3/1	—	0.0
	Was A	17	47	3	9	1	0	0	1	0	0	—	.191	.191	.213	31	-4	0	.976	-1	*90*	*130*	C15	—	-0.4
1908	Was A	17	27	1	5	1	0	0	0	0	0	—	.185	.185	.222	35	-2	0	.983	2	*129*	*62*	C11	—	0.1
1909	Was A	4	8	0	1	0	0	0	0	0	0	—	.125	.125	.125	-22	-1	2	.867	-1	*92*	*131*	C3	—	-0.2
Total	11	410	1309	103	278	43	14	4	105	39	4	0	.212	.237	.276	52	-81	21	.968	9	*108*	*95*	C378,1b7,O2(0/1/1),3b2,S2	—	-3.9

YEAR	TM LG	G	AB	R	H	2B	3B	HR	RBI	BB-IB	HP	SO	AVG	OBP	SLG	AOPS	ABR	SB-CS	FA	FR	RNG	THR	GAMES AT POSITION	DL	BFW
KAISER, AL	Alfred Edward "Deerfoot"; B8.3.1886 Cincinnati OH; D4.11.1969 Cincinnati OH; BR/TR/5´9˝/165; d4.18																								
1911	Chi N	26	84	16	21	0	5	0	7	7	0	12	.250	.308	.369	89	-2	6	.905	-3	74	99	O22(1/21/0)	—	-0.7
	Bos N	66	197	20	40	5	2	2	15	10	2	26	.203	.249	.279	44	-16	4	.922	-1	99	86	O58(35/21/2)	—	-2.0
	Year	92	281	36	61	5	7	2	22	17	2	38	.217	.267	.306	57	-18	10	.918	-4	92	90	O80(36/42/2)	—	-2.7
1912	Bos N	4	13	0	0	0	0	0	0	0	0	3	.000	.000	.000	-98	-4	0	.900	0	94	167	O4L	—	-0.4
1914	Ind F	59	187	22	43	10	0	1	16	17	2	41	.230	.301	.299	58	-13	6	.918	-3	112	42	O50(40/10/0)/1	—	-2.0
Total	3	155	481	58	104	15	7	3	38	34	4	82	.216	.274	.295	53	-35	16	.917	-7	100	73	O134(80/52/2)/1	—	-5.1
KALAHAN, JOHN	John Joseph; B9.30.1878 Philadelphia PA; D6.20.1952 Philadelphia PA; BR/TR/6´0˝/165; d9.29																								
1903	Phi A	1	5	0	0	0	0	0	0	0	0	—	.000	.000	.000	-96	-1	0	1.000	-0	*106*	*118*	/C	—	-0.2
KALBFUS, CHARLIE	Charles Henry "Skinny"; B12.28.1864 Washington DC; D11.18.1941 Washington DC; BR/TR/5´11˝/145; d4.18																								
1884	Was U	1	5	1	1	0	0	0	—	0	—	—	.200	.200	.200	22	-1	—	ø	0	0	0	/rf	—	-0.1
KALIN, FRANK	Frank Bruno "Fats" (b Frank Bruno Kalinkiewicz); B10.3.1917 Steubenville OH; D1.12.1975 Weirton WV; BR/TR/6´0˝/200; d9.25; Mil 1943–45																								
1940	Pit N	3	3	0	0	0	0	0	1	2	0	0	.000	.400	.000	19	0	0	.667	-1	67	0	O2(1/0/1)	—	-0.1
1943	Chi A	4	4	0	0	0	0	0	0	0	0	0	.000	.000	.000	-99	-1	0-0	ø	0	—	—	/H	0	-0.1
Total	2	7	7	0	0	0	0	0	1	2	0	0	.000	.222	.000	-34	-1	0-0	.667	-1	67	0	O2(1/0/1)	0	-0.2
KALINE, AL	Albert William; B12.19.1934 Baltimore MD; BR/TR/6´2˝/(175–185); d6.25; HF1980; OF(16/484/2040)																								
1953	Det A	30	28	9	7	0	0	1	2	1	1	5	.250	.300	.357	78	-1	1-0	1.000	0	92	239	O20(5/11/4)	0	-0.1
1954	Det A	138	504	42	139	18	3	4	43	22	0	45	.276	.305	.347	80	-16	9-5	.971	7	108	157	O135R	0	-1.4
1955	Det A★	152	588	121	**200**	24	8	27	102	82-12	5	57	**.340**	.421	.546	163	54	6-8	.979	3	103	115	O152R	0	4.9
1956	Det A★	153	617	96	194	32	10	27	128	70-4	1	55	.314	.383	.530	139	33	7-1	.984	**12**	110	**156**	O153(1/12/142)	0	3.9
1957	Det A★	149	577	83	170	29	4	23	90	43-7	3	38	.295	.343	.478	120	14	11-9	.985	7	111	116	O145(5/21/137)	0	1.5
1958	Det A★	146	543	84	170	34	7	16	85	54-6	2	47	.313	.374	.490	127	21	7-4	.994	20	119	**192**	O145R	0	3.7
1959	Det A★	136	511	86	167	19	2	27	94	72-**12**	4	42	.327	.410	**.530**	149	37	10-4	.989	5	115	46	O136(0/122/15)	0	3.6
1960	Det A★	147	551	77	153	29	4	15	68	65-3	3	47	.278	.354	.426	108	7	19-4	.987	-4	103	56	O142C	0	-0.1
1961	Det A★	153	586	116	190	**41**	7	19	82	66-2	4	42	.324	.393	.515	138	33	14-1	.990	13	**123**	81	O147(1/22/141)/3	0	3.8
1962	Det A★	100	398	78	121	16	6	29	94	47-3	1	39	.304	.376	.593	152	28	4-0	.983	9	121	140	O100R	57	3.0
1963	Det A★	145	551	89	172	24	3	27	101	54-**12**	4	48	.312	.375	.514	142	31	6-4	.992	-5	98	54	O140(0/2/140)	0	1.8
1964	Det A✳	146	525	77	154	31	5	17	68	75-6	3	51	.293	.383	.469	134	27	4-1	.990	7	119	74	O136R	0	2.6
1965	Det A★	125	399	72	112	18	2	18	72	72-11	0	49	.281	.388	.471	142	25	6-0	.985	-8	90	36	O112(0/62/51)/3	0	1.4
1966	Det A★	142	479	85	138	29	1	29	88	81-7	5	66	.288	.392	.534	161	42	5-5	**.993**	1	103	93	O136(0/86/53)	0	3.8
1967	Det A✳	131	458	94	141	28	2	25	78	83-10	1	47	.308	.411	.541	176	47	8-2	.983	7	107	182	O130(0/1/130)	30	5.1
1968	†Det A	102	327	49	94	14	1	10	53	55-7	3	39	.287	.392	.428	145	21	6-4	.978	0	115	26	O74(4/0/75),1b22	36	1.7
1969	Det A	131	456	74	124	17	0	21	69	54-4	1	61	.272	.346	.447	117	10	1-2	.966	-0	101	109	O118R,1b9	0	0.3
1970	Det A	131	467	64	130	24	4	16	71	77-5	1	49	.278	.377	.450	127	20	2-2	.988	4	111	60	O91R,1b52	0	1.6
1971	Det A★	133	405	69	119	19	2	15	54	82-9	7	57	.294	.416	.462	144	28	4-6	**1.000**	-2	96	82	O129(0/3/128),1b5	0	2.1
1972	†Det A	106	278	46	87	11	2	10	32	28-5	2	33	.313	.374	.475	148	17	1-0	.991	-1	91	109	O84R,1b11	15	1.3
1973	Det A	91	310	40	79	13	0	10	45	29-4	3	28	.255	.320	.394	95	-2	4-1	1.000	-1	108	31	O63R,1b36	0	-0.8
1974	Det A★	147	558	71	146	28	2	13	64	65-2	1	75	.262	.337	.389	105	5	2-2	ø	0	0	0	D146	0	0.1
Total	22	2834	10116	1622	3007	498	75	399	1583	1277-131	55	1020	.297	.376	.480	134	481	137-65	.986	74	108	101	O2488R,D146,1b135,3b2	138	43.8
KAMM, WILLIE	William Edward; B2.2.1900 San Francisco CA; D12.21.1988 Belmont CA; BR/TR/5´10.5˝/170; d4.18																								
1923	Chi A	149	544	57	159	39	9	6	87	62	1	82	.292	.366	.430	110	8	18-13	.960	8	106	104	3b149	—	2.4
1924	Chi A	147	528	58	134	28	6	6	93	64	2	59	.254	.337	.364	83	-13	10-9	**.971**	9	105	119	3b146	—	0.4
1925	Chi A	152	509	82	142	32	4	6	83	**90**	4	36	.279	.391	.393	105	8	11-13	**.957**	-0	102	108	3b152	—	1.5
1926	Chi A	143	480	63	141	24	10	0	62	77	4	24	.294	.396	.385	108	9	12-4	**.978**	16	**110**	72	3b142	—	3.4
1927	Chi A	148	540	85	146	32	13	0	59	70	0	18	.270	.354	.378	92	-5	8-9	**.972**	3	96	75	3b146	—	0.5
1928	Chi A	**155**	552	70	170	30	12	1	84	73	2	22	.308	.391	.411	112	13	17-9	**.977**	-0	89	113	3b155	—	2.2
1929	Chi A	147	523	72	140	33	6	3	63	75	3	23	.268	.363	.371	90	-5	12-5	**.978**	4	98	97	3b145	—	0.9
1930	Chi A	112	331	49	89	21	6	3	47	51	1	20	.269	.368	.396	97	0	5-4	.939	13	**111**	97	3b106	—	1.7
1931	Chi A	18	59	9	15	4	1	0	9	7	0	6	.254	.333	.356	86	-1	1-1	.938	1	94	119	3b18	—	0.0
	Cle A	114	410	68	121	31	4	0	66	64	1	13	.295	.392	.390	100	3	13-9	.947	4	100	139	3b114	—	1.1
	Year	132	469	77	136	35	5	0	75	71	1	19	.290	.384	.386	99	3	14-10	.945	5	**99**	**136**	3b132	—	1.1
1932	Cle A	148	524	76	150	34	9	3	83	75	3	36	.286	.379	.403	96	-1	6-3	.967	9	**110**	84	3b148	—	1.3
1933	Cle A	133	447	59	126	17	2	1	47	54	0	27	.282	.359	.336	81	-10	6-3	**.984**	3	99	79	3b131	—	-0.2
1934	Cle A	121	386	52	104	23	3	0	42	62	1	38	.269	.372	.345	84	-6	7-1	**.978**	9	109	107	3b118	—	0.7
1935	Cle A	6	18	2	6	0	0	0	1	0	0	1	.333	.333	.333	72	-1	0-1	.875	-1	69	0	3b4	—	-0.2
Total	13	1693	5851	802	1643	348	85	29	826	824	22	405	.281	.372	.384	97	-1	126-84	.967	77	102	99	3b1674	—	15.7
KAMPOURIS, ALEX	Alexis William; B11.13.1912 Sacramento CA; D5.29.1993 Sacramento CA; BR/TR/5´8˝/155; d7.31; Mil 1944–45																								
1934	Cin N	19	66	6	13	1	0	0	3	3	2	18	.197	.254	.212	27	-7	2	.946	-1	105	73	2b16	—	-0.7
1935	Cin N	148	499	46	123	26	5	7	62	32	2	84	.246	.295	.361	77	-17	8	.957	-3	95	115	2b141,S6	—	-1.0
1936	Cin N	122	355	43	85	10	4	5	46	24	1	46	.239	.289	.332	72	-16	3	.969	22	**115**	115	2b119/lf	—	1.3
1937	Cin N	146	458	62	114	21	4	17	71	60	5	65	.249	.342	.424	112	8	2	.961	9	100	97	2b146	—	2.6
1938	Cin N	21	74	13	19	1	0	2	7	10	1	13	.257	.353	.351	97	0	0	.973	0	104	94	2b21	—	0.1
	NY N	82	268	35	66	9	1	5	37	27	1	50	.246	.318	.343	81	-7	0	.972	13	108	120	2b79	—	1.1
	Year	103	342	48	85	10	1	7	44	37	2	63	.249	.325	.345	84	-7	0	.972	13	107	115	2b100	—	1.2
1939	NY N	74	201	23	50	12	2	5	29	30	1	41	.249	.349	.403	101	1	0	.973	11	111	97	2b62,3b11	—	1.5
1941	Bro N	16	51	8	16	4	2	2	9	11	1	8	.314	.444	.588	181	6	0	.987	-1	102	91	2b15	0	0.6
1942	Bro N	10	21	3	5	2	1	0	3	0	0	4	.238	.238	.429	92	0	0	.970	1	99	167	2b9	0	0.1
1943	Bro N	19	44	9	10	4	1	0	4	17	1	6	.227	.452	.364	136	4	0	.946	-3	86	73	2b18	0	0.2
	Was A	51	145	24	30	4	0	2	13	30	5	25	.207	.361	.276	91	0	7-1	.936	-2	92	204	3b33,2b10/rf	0	0.0
Total	9	708	2182	272	531	94	20	45	284	244	20	360	.243	.325	.367	91	-28	22-1	.964	47	103	105	2b636,3b44,S6,O2(1/0/1)	0	5.8
KANE, FRANK	Francis Thomas "Sugar" (aka Frank Thomas Kiley in 1915); B3.9.1895 Whitman MA; D12.2.1962 Brockton MA; BL/TR/5´11.5˝/175; d9.13																								
1915	Bro F	3	10	2	2	0	1	0	2	0	0	0	.200	.200	.400	67	-1	0	1.000	1	107	304	O2L	—	0.0
1919	NY A	1	1	0	0	0	0	0	0	0	0	0	.000	.000	.000	-99	0	0	ø	0	—	—	/H	—	0.0
Total	2	4	11	2	2	0	1	0	2	0	0	0	.182	.182	.364	52	-1	0	1.000	1	107	304	O2L	—	0.0
KANE, JIM	James Joseph "Shamus"; B11.27.1881 Scranton PA; D10.2.1947 Omaha NE; BL/TL/6´2˝/225; d4.21																								
1908	Pit N	55	145	16	35	3	3	0	22	12	0	—	.241	.299	.303	93	-1	5	.966	-2	98	118	1b40	—	-0.5
KANE, JOHN	John Francis; B9.24.1882 Chicago IL; D1.28.1934 St.Anthony ID; BR/TR/5´6˝/138; d4.11																								
1907	Cin N	79	262	40	65	9	4	3	19	22	8	—	.248	.325	.347	106	2	20	.959	-2	98	0	O42(38/0/4),3b25,S6,2b2	—	-0.2
1908	Cin N	130	455	61	97	11	7	3	23	43	13	—	.213	.299	.288	90	-4	30	**.981**	2	96	53	O127(0/120/7)/2	—	-0.9
1909	Chi N	20	45	6	4	1	0	0	5	2	1	—	.089	.146	.111	-20	-6	1	.917	2	238	0	O8(6/1/1),S3,3b3,2b2	—	-0.5
1910	†Chi N	32	62	11	15	0	0	1	12	9	0	10	.242	.338	.290	84	-1	2	1.000	-2	100	0	O18(9/9/1),2b6,3b4,S2	—	-0.4
Total	4	261	824	118	181	21	11	7	59	76	22	10	.220	.303	.297	89	-9	53	.975	-0	101	36	O195(53/130/13),3b32,2b11,S11	—	-2.0
KANE, JOHN	John Francis; B2.19.1900 Chicago IL; D7.25.1956 Chicago IL; BB/TR/5´10.5˝/162; d9.3																								
1925	Chi A	14	56	6	10	1	0	0	3	0	1	3	.179	.193	.196	-1	-9	0-0	.935	1	116	125	S8,2b6	—	-0.7
KANE, TOM	Thomas Joseph "Sugar"; B12.15.1906 Chicago IL; D11.26.1973 Chicago IL; BR/TR/5´10.5˝/160; d8.3																								
1938	Bos N	2	2	0	0	0	0	0	0	2	0	0	.000	.500	.000	53	0	0	1.000	-1	67	0	2b2	—	0.0
KANE, JERRY	William Jeremiah; B4.4.1866 Collinsville IL; D6.16.1949 E.St.Louis IL; BR/TR/6´0˝/175; d5.2																								
1890	StL AA	8	25	3	5	0	0	0	2	2	0	—	.200	.259	.200	31	-2	0	.907	-1	57	46	1b5,C4	—	-0.3
KANEHL, ROD	Roderick Edwin "Hot Rod"; B4.1.1934 Wichita KS; D12.14.2004 Palm Springs CA; BR/TR/6´1˝/180; d4.15; OF(42/56/7)																								
1962	NY N	133	351	52	87	10	2	4	27	23-2	1	36	.248	.296	.322	65	-18	8-6	.944	12	111	123	2b62,3b30,O20(10/7/3),1b3,S2	0	-0.1
1963	NY N	109	191	26	46	6	0	1	9	5-0	2	26	.241	.268	.288	59	-10	6-3	.974	-2	115	252	O58(30/26/4),3b13,2b12,1b3	0	-1.4
1964	NY N	98	254	25	59	7	1	1	11	7-0	1	18	.232	.256	.280	52	-17	3-1	.988	10	103	83	2b34,O25(2/23/0),3b19,1b2	0	-0.5
Total	3	340	796	103	192	23	3	6	47	35-2	4	80	.241	.277	.300	60	-45	17-10	.950	21	104	105	2b108,O103C,3b62,1b8,S2	0	-2.0

YEAR	TM LG	G	AB	R	H	2B	3B	HR	RBI	BB-IB	HP	SO	AVG	OBP	SLG	AOPS	ABR	SB-CS	FA	FR	RNG	THR	GAMES AT POSITION	DL	BFW
Kapler, Gabe	Gabriel Stefan; B8.31.1975 Hollywood CA; BR/TR/6´2˝/(190–210); [DetA95 57/1488]; d9.20; Col Moorpark (CA) JC																								
1998	Det A	7	25	3	5	0	1	0	0	1-0	0	4	.200	.231	.280	32	-3	2-0	1.000	-1	73	0	O6R/D	0	-0.3
1999	Det A	130	416	60	102	22	4	18	49	42-0	2	74	.245	.315	.447	91	-7	11-5	.981	-2	101	52	O128(0/114/32),D2	0	-0.8
2000	Tex A	116	444	59	134	32	1	14	66	42-2	0	57	.302	.360	.473	108	6	8-4	.969	3	109	77	O116(0/84/40)	36	0.7
2001	Tex A	134	483	77	129	29	1	17	72	61-2	3	70	.267	.348	.437	103	4	23-6	.997	0	101	105	O133C/D	21	0.8
2002	Tex A	72	196	25	51	12	1	0	17	8-0	0	30	.260	.285	.332	63	-11	5-2	.977	4	106	241	O64(31/23/18)/1D	22	-0.7
	Col N	40	119	12	37	4	3	2	17	8-0	1	23	.311	.359	.445	97	-1	6-2	1.000	2	106	152	O38(15/1/23)	0	0.1
2003	Col N	39	67	10	15	2	0	0	4	8-1	0	18	.224	.307	.254	43	-5	2-0	.970	2	94	304	O29(15/2/13)	0	-0.4
	†Bos A	68	158	29	46	11	1	4	23	14-0	0	23	.291	.349	.449	104	1	4-2	.932	-2	82	199	O61(25/8/30)/1	0	-0.2
2004	†Bos A	136	290	51	79	14	1	6	33	15-0	2	49	.272	.311	.390	77	-10	5-4	.978	-1	98	112	O127(18/17/101),D2	0	-1.4
2005	Bos A	36	97	15	24	7	0	1	9	3-0	2	15	.247	.282	.351	65	-5	1-0	1.000	0	109	0	O36(8/12/22)	15	-0.5
2006	Bos A	72	130	21	33	7	0	2	12	14-0	3	15	.254	.340	.354	78	-4	1-1	1.000	2	101	173	O68(21/14/37)	0	-0.3
Total	9	850	2425	362	655	140	13	64	302	216-5	13	378	.270	.331	.418	90	-35	68-26	.981	7	101	113	O806(133/408/322),D7,1b2	94	-3.0
Kappel, Heinie	Henry; B9.1863 Philadelphia PA; D8.27.1905 Philadelphia PA; BR/TR/5´8˝/160; d5.22; b–Joe																								
1887	Cin AA	23	78	11	22	3	2	0	15	2	1	—	.282	.309	.372	87	-2	3	.667	-2	93	74	3b9,O7(2/0/5),2b6/S	—	-0.3
1888	Cin AA	36	143	18	37	4	4	1	15	2	1	—	.259	.274	.364	98	-1	20	.790	-11	93	95	S25,2b10/3	—	-1.0
1889	Col AA	46	173	25	47	7	5	3	21	21	1	28	.272	.354	.422	127	6	10	.791	-1	94	45	S23,3b23	—	0.5
Total	3	105	394	54	106	14	11	4	51	25	3	28	.269	.318	.391	109	3	33	.796	-14	94	68	S49,3b33,2b16,O7(2/0/5)	—	-0.8
Kappel, Joe	Joseph; B4.27.1857 Philadelphia PA; D7.8.1929 Philadelphia PA; BR/5´11˝/175; d5.26; b–Heinie																								
1884	Phi N	4	15	1	1	0	0	0	0	0	—	2	.067	.067	.067	-61	-3	—	.727	-4	—	—	C4	—	-0.6
1890	Phi AA	56	208	29	50	8	1	1	22	20	1	—	.240	.310	.303	81	-5	12	.851	-4	146	0	O23(11/8/5),S18,3b11,C3,2b2	—	-0.7
Total	2	60	223	30	51	8	1	1	22	20	1	2	.229	.295	.287	73	-8	12	.851	-7	—	—	O23(11/8/5),S18,3b11,C7,2b2	—	-1.3
Karkovice, Ron	Ronald Joseph; B8.8.1963 Union NJ; BR/TR/6´1˝/(215–219); [ChiA82 1/14]; d8.17																								
1986	Chi A	37	97	13	24	7	0	4	13	9-0	1	37	.247	.315	.443	101	0	1-0	.996	8	87	132	C37	0	1.0
1987	Chi A	39	85	7	6	0	0	2	7	7-0	2	40	.071	.160	.141	-19	-15	3-0	.982	6	444	100	C37/D	0	-0.7
1988	Chi A	46	115	10	20	4	0	3	9	7-0	1	30	.174	.228	.287	43	-9	4-2	.995	6	169	121	C46	0	-0.1
1989	Chi A	71	182	21	48	9	2	3	24	10-0	2	56	.264	.306	.385	96	-1	0-0	.986	12	152	135	C68,D2	0	1.4
1990	Chi A	68	183	30	45	10	0	6	20	16-1	1	52	.246	.308	.399	99	-1	2-0	.994	3	193	102	C64,D2	0	0.7
1991	Chi A	75	167	25	41	13	0	5	22	15-1	1	42	.246	.310	.413	101	0	0-0	.988	6	129	115	C69/lf	45	0.9
1992	Chi A	123	342	39	81	12	1	13	50	30-1	3	89	.237	.302	.392	94	-4	10-4	.990	1	109	85	C119/rf	0	0.4
1993	†Chi A	128	403	60	92	17	1	20	54	29-1	6	126	.228	.287	.424	91	-7	2-2	.994	20	**166**	124	C127	16	1.9
1994	Chi A	77	207	33	44	9	1	11	29	36-2	0	68	.213	.325	.425	94	-2	0-3	.993	-0	141	70	C76	25	0.1
1995	Chi A	113	323	44	70	14	1	13	51	39-0	5	84	.217	.306	.387	83	-8	2-3	.991	-4	95	123	C113	0	-0.6
1996	Chi A	111	355	44	78	22	0	10	38	24-2	1	93	.220	.270	.366	62	-22	0-0	.993	11	133	118	C111	0	-0.4
1997	Chi A	51	138	10	25	3	0	6	18	11-0	3	32	.181	.248	.333	54	-10	0-0	.996	-4	120	72	C51	0	-1.1
Total	12	939	2597	336	574	120	6	96	335	233-8	26	749	.221	.289	.383	80	-79	24-14	.992	64	147	109	C918,D5,O2(1/0/1)	86	3.5
Karlon, Bill	William John "Hank"; B1.21.1909 Palmer MA; D12.7.1964 Ware MA; BR/TR/6´1˝/190; d4.28																								
1930	NY A	2	5	0	0	0	0	0	0	0	0	1	.000	.000	.000	-99	-2	0-0	1.000	-0	74	0	/lf	—	-0.2
Karow, Marty	Martin Gregory (b Martin Gregory Karowsky); B7.18.1904 Braddock PA; D4.27.1986 Bryan TX; BR/TR/5´10.5˝/170; d6.21; Col Ohio St.																								
1927	Bos A	6	10	0	2	1	0	0	0	0	0	2	.200	.200	.300	29	-1	0-0	1.000	0	95	318	S3,3b2	—	0.0
Karros, Eric	Eric Peter; B11.4.1967 Hackensack NJ; BR/TR/6´4˝/(205–226); [LAN88 6/140]; d9.1; Col UCLA																								
1991	LA N	14	14	0	1	1	0	0	1	1-0	0	6	.071	.133	.143	-23	-2	0-0	1.000	-0	74	225	1b10	0	-0.3
1992	LA N	149	545	63	140	30	1	20	88	37-3	2	103	.257	.304	.426	106	3	2-4	.993	8	**116**	93	1b143	0	0.0
1993	LA N	158	619	74	153	27	2	23	80	34-1	2	82	.247	.287	.409	89	-13	0-1	.992	9	118	97	1b157	0	-1.8
1994	LA N	111	406	51	108	21	1	14	46	29-1	2	53	.266	.310	.426	97	-3	2-0	.991	13	139	96	1b109	0	0.1
1995	†LA N	143	551	83	164	29	3	32	105	61-4	4	115	.298	.369	.535	146	36	4-4	.995	0	96	94	1b143	0	2.2
1996	†LA N	154	608	84	158	29	1	34	111	53-2	1	121	.260	.316	.479	114	9	8-0	.990	1	102	109	1b154	0	-0.2
1997	LA N	**162**	628	86	167	28	0	31	104	61-2	2	116	.266	.329	.459	112	8	15-7	.992	-2	95	74	1b162	0	-0.7
1998	LA N	139	507	59	150	20	1	23	87	47-1	3	93	.296	.355	.475	123	16	7-2	.991	5	111	115	1b136,D2	24	0.9
1999	LA N	153	578	74	176	40	0	34	112	53-0	2	119	.304	.362	.550	134	28	8-5	.991	9	126	93	1b151	0	2.3
2000	LA N	155	584	84	146	29	0	31	106	63-2	4	122	.250	.321	.459	100	-2	4-3	.995	14	129	103	1b153/D	0	-0.1
2001	LA N	121	438	42	103	22	0	15	63	41-2	3	101	.235	.303	.388	82	-12	3-1	.996	-2	90	93	1b119	24	-2.4
2002	LA N	142	524	52	142	26	1	13	73	37-1	6	74	.271	.323	.399	95	-5	4-2	**.997**	11	**131**	97	1b142	0	-0.6
2003	†Chi N	114	336	37	96	16	1	12	40	28-1	0	46	.286	.340	.446	101	0	1-1	.992	-2	83	117	1b97	0	-0.9
2004	Oak A	40	103	8	20	6	0	2	11	7-1	0	16	.194	.243	.311	44	-9	1-0	.989	3	174	110	1b22,D10	0	-0.8
Total	14	1755	6441	797	1724	324	11	284	1027	552-21	31	1167	.268	.325	.454	108	54	59-30	.993	68	112	98	1b1698,D13	48	-2.3
Karst, John	John Gottlieb "King"; B10.15.1893 Philadelphia PA; D5.21.1976 Cape May Court House NJ; BL/TR/5´11.5˝/175; d10.6; Col Penn																								
1915	Bro N	1	0	0	0	0	0	0	0	0	0	0	ø	ø	ø	ø	0	0	1.000	0	149	2105	/3	—	0.0
Kasko, Eddie	Edward Michael; B6.27.1932 Linden NJ; BR/TR/6´0˝/(180–183); d4.18; M4																								
1957	StL N	134	479	59	131	16	5	1	35	33-7	0	53	.273	.319	.334	75	-17	6-1	.961	-7	**101**	97	3b120,S13/2	0	-2.3
1958	StL N	104	259	20	57	8	1	2	22	21-6	0	25	.220	.277	.282	47	-20	1-2	.961	-5	93	99	S77,2b12/3	0	-1.9
1959	Cin N	118	329	39	93	14	1	2	31	14-5	0	38	.283	.309	.350	74	-12	2-2	.976	11	106	119	S84,3b31,2b2	0	0.5
1960	Cin N	126	479	56	140	21	1	6	51	46-0	6	37	.292	.359	.378	101	2	9-9	.966	10	120	146	3b86,2b33,S15	0	1.5
1961	†Cin N★	126	469	64	127	22	1	2	27	32-1	4	36	.271	.320	.335	74	-17	4-3	.964	-10	91	90	S112,3b12,2b6	0	-1.7
1962	Cin N	134	533	74	148	26	2	4	41	35-1	5	44	.278	.326	.356	81	-13	3-3	.941	-4	95	89	3b114,S21	0	-1.8
1963	Cin N	76	199	25	48	9	0	3	10	21-4	0	29	.241	.311	.332	83	-4	0-2	.959	2	93	87	3b48,S15/2	0	-0.2
1964	Hou N	133	448	45	109	16	1	0	22	37-8	1	52	.243	.302	.283	70	-17	4-6	**.978**	13	108	105	S128,3b2	0	0.5
1965	Hou N	68	215	18	53	7	1	1	10	11-1	4	20	.247	.296	.302	74	-8	1-3	.976	-5	94	83	S59,3b2	58	-1.0
1966	Bos A	58	136	11	29	7	0	1	12	15-0	0	19	.213	.291	.287	61	-6	1-0	.976	7	117	71	S20,3b10,2b8	27	0.3
Total	10	1077	3546	411	935	146	13	22	261	265-33	20	353	.264	.317	.331	76	-112	31-31	.971	12	100	101	S544,3b426,2b63	85	-6.1
Kata, Matt	Matthew John; B3.14.1978 Avon Lake OH; BB/TR/6´1˝/(180–195); [AriN99 9/268]; d6.15; Col Vanderbilt																								
2003	Ari N	78	288	42	74	16	5	7	29	25-0	1	53	.257	.315	.420	84	-7	3-2	.988	2	95	88	2b52,3b23,S6	0	-0.2
2004	Ari N	42	162	17	40	9	2	2	13	13-2	0	29	.247	.301	.364	67	-8	4-1	.989	8	112	99	2b38,3b3/S	127	0.3
2005	Ari N	30	31	6	6	2	1	0	0	5-0	0	4	.194	.306	.323	62	-2	0-1	1.000	2	131	274	2b7	0	0.0
	Phi N	10	6	1	1	0	0	0	0	0-0	0	2	.167	.167	.167	-12	-1	0-0	ø	-1	0	0	2b3/SrfD	0	-0.2
	Year	40	37	7	7	2	1	0	0	5-0	0	6	.189	.286	.297	51	-3	0-1	1.000	1	111	232	2b10/SrfD	0	-0.2
Total	3	160	487	66	121	27	8	9	42	43-2	1	88	.248	.308	.392	76	-18	7-4	.989	12	103	99	2b100,3b26,S8/Drf	127	-0.1
Katt, Ray	Raymond Frederick; B5.9.1927 New Braunfels TX; D10.19.1999 New Braunfels TX; BR/TR/6´2˝/(190–200); d9.16; C3; Col Texas A&M																								
1952	NY N	9	27	4	6	0	0	0	1	1	0	5	.222	.250	.222	32	-3	0-0	1.000	1	*249*	*53*	C8	0	-0.1
1953	NY N	8	29	2	5	1	0	0	1	1	0	3	.172	.200	.207	6	-4	0-0	.975	-0	*112*	*141*	C8	0	-0.4
1954	NY N	86	200	26	51	7	1	9	33	19	0	29	.255	.314	.435	94	-3	1-0	.973	-3	*146*	*89*	C82	0	-0.2
1955	NY N	124	326	27	70	7	2	7	28	22-4	2	38	.215	.268	.313	54	-23	0-0	.987	-5	*115*	*89*	C122	0	-2.3
1956	NY N	37	101	10	23	4	0	7	14	6-1	1	16	.228	.278	.475	98	-1	0-1	.978	1	*117*	*125*	C37	0	0.1
	StL N	47	158	11	41	4	0	6	20	6-1	1	24	.259	.289	.399	83	-4	0-1	.984	-2	*94*	*61*	C47	0	-0.5
	Year	84	259	21	64	8	0	13	34	12-2	2	40	.247	.285	.429	89	-5	0-2	.982	-1	*103*	*87*	C84	0	-0.4
1957	NY N	72	165	11	38	3	1	2	17	15-1	2	35	.230	.294	.297	62	-9	1-0	.981	0	163	133	C68	0	-0.6
1958	StL N	19	41	1	7	1	0	1	4	4-0	0	6	.171	.239	.268	34	-4	0-0	.971	-0	55	156	C14	0	-0.4
1959	StL N	15	24	0	7	2	0	0	2	0-0	0	8	.292	.292	.375	71	-1	0-0	.976	0	0	82	C14	0	-0.1
Total	8	417	1071	92	248	29	4	32	120	74-7	6	164	.232	.282	.356	69	-52	2-2	.981	-8	*124*	*98*	C400	0	-4.5

YEAR	TM LG	G	AB	R	H	2B	3B	HR	RBI	BB-IB	HP	SO	AVG	OBP	SLG	AOPS	ABR	SB-CS	FA	FR	RNG	THR	GAMES AT POSITION	DL	BFW
KAUFF, BENNY	Benjamin Michael; B1.5.1890 Pomeroy OH; D11.17.1961 Columbus OH; BL/TL/5´8˝/157; d4.20; Mil 1918																								
1912	NY A	5	11	4	3	0	0	0	2	3	0	—	.273	.429	.273	96	0	1	1.000	-1	76	0	O4C	—	0.0
1914	Ind F	154	571	**120**	**211**	**44**	13	8	95	72	8	55	**.370**	**.447**	.534	150	37	**75**	.953	9	107	123	O154(33/54/68)	—	3.7
1915	Bro F	136	483	92	165	23	11	12	83	85	6	50	**.342**	**.446**	**.509**	**170**	**43**	**55**	.959	11	103	**161**	O136C	—	**4.7**
1916	NY N	154	552	71	146	22	15	9	74	68	3	65	.264	.348	.408	139	26	40-26	.962	-4	91	117	O154C	—	1.2
1917	†NY N	153	559	89	172	22	4	5	68	59	5	54	.308	.379	.388	140	29	30	.976	-11	96	57	O153(3/150/0)	—	0.9
1918	NY N	67	270	41	85	19	4	2	39	16	1	30	.315	.355	.437	144	14	9	.952	-5	83	118	O67C	—	0.5
1919	NY N	135	491	73	136	27	7	10	67	39	3	45	.277	.334	.422	128	16	21	.950	-6	92	103	O134C	—	0.1
1920	NY N	55	157	31	43	12	3	3	26	25	2	14	.274	.380	.446	138	9	3-7	.960	-6	76	120	O51C	—	-0.2
Total	8	859	3094	521	961	169	57	49	454	367	28	313	.311	.389	.450	146	174	234-33	.960	-12	95	112	O853(36/750/68)	—	10.9
KAUFFMAN, DICK	Howard Richard; B6.22.1888 E.Lewisburg PA; D4.16.1948 Mifflinburg PA; BB/TR/6´3˝/190; d9.17; Col Susquehanna																								
1914	StL A	7	15	1	4	1	0	0	2	0	0	3	.267	.267	.333	83	0	0	.967	-1	0	0	1b7	—	-0.2
1915	StL A	37	124	9	32	8	2	0	14	5	2	27	.258	.298	.355	99	-1	0-3	.984	-1	90	135	1b32/rf	—	-0.4
Total	2	44	139	10	36	9	2	0	16	5	2	30	.259	.295	.353	97	-1	0-3	.982	-2	81	121	1b39/rf	—	-0.6
KAUFMANN, TONY	Anthony Charles; B12.16.1900 Chicago IL; D6.4.1982 Elgin IL; BR/TR/5´11˝/165; d9.23; C4; ▲																								
1921	Chi N	2	5	0	2	1	0	0	0	0	0	1	.400	.400	.600	161	1	0-0	1.000	-1	29	0	P2	—	0.0
1922	Chi N	38	45	4	9	2	1	1	4	2	0	14	.200	.234	.356	49	1	0-0	.933	-1	79	0	P37	—	0.0
1923	Chi N	33	74	10	16	2	0	2	10	7	0	17	.216	.284	.324	60	3	0-0	.962	-1	85	124	P33	—	0.0
1924	Chi N	35	76	6	24	5	0	1	14	3	0	10	.316	.342	.421	102	6	0-0	.981	-2	75	123	P34	—	0.0
1925	Chi N	31	78	8	15	7	0	2	13	2	0	17	.192	.213	.359	42	2	0-0	.981	-0	93	210	P31	—	0.0
1926	Chi N	30	60	9	15	2	0	1	7	2	0	10	.250	.274	.333	62	2	1	**1.000**	-2	81	87	P26	—	0.0
1927	Chi N	9	16	2	5	0	0	1	6	4	0	4	.313	.450	.500	154	3	0	1.000	2	155	176	P9	—	0.0
	Phi N	8	7	1	1	0	0	1	2	0	0	1	.143	.143	.571	83	0	0	1.000	-0	72	0	P5/lf	—	0.0
	StL N	1	0	0	0	0	0	0	0	0	0	0	ø	ø	ø	ø	0	0	ø	0	0	0	/P	—	0.0
	Year	18	23	3	6	0	0	2	8	4	0	5	.261	.370	.522	136	1	0	1.000	1	133	130	P15/lf	—	0.0
1928	StL N	5	0	0	0	0	0	0	0	0	0	0	ø	ø	ø	ø	0	0	1.000	-0	86	0	P4	—	0.0
1929	NY N	39	32	18	1	0	0	0	1	6	0	4	.031	.184	.031	-43	-7	3	.964	1	131	0	O16(4/8/4)	—	-0.7
1930	StL N	2	3	1	1	0	0	0	0	1	0	1	.333	.500	.333	103	0	0	1.000	-0	50	0	P2	—	0.0
1931	StL N	20	18	1	2	0	0	0	0	1	0	3	.111	.158	.111	-26	-3	0	.929	-0	107	0	P15/lf	—	0.0
1935	StL N	7	0	2	0	0	0	0	0	0	0	0	ø	ø	ø	ø	0	0	1.000	0	119	0	P3	—	0.0
Total	12	260	414	62	91	19	1	9	57	28	0	82	.220	.269	.336	57	8	4-0	.972	-5	86	107	P202,O18(6/8/4)	—	-0.7
KAVANAGH, CHARLIE	Charles Hugh "Silk"; B6.6.1891 Chicago IL; D9.6.1973 Reedsburg WI; BR/TR/5´9˝/165; d6.11																								
1914	Chi A	6	5	0	1	0	0	0	0	0	1	2	.200	.333	.200	62	0	0	ø	0	—	—	/H	—	0.0
KAVANAGH, LEO	Leo Daniel; B8.9.1894 Chicago IL; D8.10.1950 Chicago IL; BR/TR/5´9˝/180; d4.22																								
1914	Chi F	5	11	0	3	0	0	0	1	1	0	0	.273	.333	.273	70	-1	0	1.000	-0	76	123	S5	—	-0.1
KAVANAGH, MARTY	Martin Joseph; B6.13.1891 Harrison NJ; D7.28.1960 Taylor MI; BR/TR/6´0˝/187; d4.18																								
1914	Det A	128	439	60	109	21	6	4	35	41	4	42	.248	.318	.351	98	-1	16-14	.929	-11	102	79	2b115,1b4	—	-1.3
1915	Det A	113	332	55	98	14	13	4	49	42	2	44	.295	.378	.452	141	16	8-8	.987	-11	88	70	1b44,2b42,S2,O2L/3	—	0.3
1916	Det A	58	78	6	11	4	0	0	5	9	1	15	.141	.239	.192	29	-7	0	1.000	-1	98	69	O11(1/0/10),2b2/3	—	-0.9
	Cle A	19	44	4	11	2	1	1	10	2	0	5	.250	.283	.409	102	0	0	.894	-1	123	55	2b9/13	—	-0.1
	Year	77	122	10	22	6	1	1	15	11	1	20	.180	.254	.270	55	-7	0	1.000	-2	98	69	O11(1/0/10),2b11,3b2/1	—	-1.0
1917	Cle A	14	14	1	0	0	0	0	0	3	0	2	.000	.176	.000	-43	-2	0	1.000	0	48	408	O2C	—	-0.2
1918	Cle A	13	38	4	8	2	0	0	6	7	1	7	.211	.348	.263	77	-1	1	.967	-1	68	107	1b12	—	-0.3
	StL N	12	44	6	8	1	0	1	8	3	0	1	.182	.234	.273	56	-2	1	1.000	-2	95	0	O8R,2b4	—	-0.5
	Det A	13	44	2	12	3	0	0	9	11	0	6	.273	.418	.341	135	3	0	.964	-2	73	76	1b12	—	0.1
Total	5	370	1033	138	257	47	20	10	122	118	8	122	.249	.330	.362	104	6	26-22	.926	-28	101	71	2b172,1b73,O23(3/2/18),3b3,S2	—	-2.9
KAVANAUGH	; d9.11																								
1872	Eck NA	5	23	3	6	1	0	0	4	0	—	0	.261	.261	.304	86	0	0-0	.921	-0	0	0	1b4,O2R	—	0.0
KAY, BILL	Walter Brocton "King Bill"; B2.14.1878 New Castle VA; D12.3.1945 Roanoke VA; BL/TR/6´2˝/180; d8.12; Col Roanoke																								
1907	Was A	25	60	8	20	1	1	0	7	0	0	—	.333	.333	.383	139	2	0	1.000	1	74	0	O12(0/1/11)	—	0.2
KAZAK, EDDIE	Edward Terrance (b Edward Terrance Tkaczuk); B7.18.1920 Steubenville OH; D12.15.1999 Austin TX; BR/TR/6´0˝/175; d9.29																								
1948	StL N	6	22	1	6	3	0	0	2	0	0	2	.273	.273	.409	78	-1	0	.900	-0	92	221	3b6	0	-0.1
1949	StL N★	92	326	43	99	15	3	6	42	29	1	17	.304	.362	.423	105	2	0	.926	-2	103	132	3b80,2b5	0	0.0
1950	StL N	93	207	21	53	2	2	5	23	18	1	19	.256	.319	.357	74	-8	0	.936	1	107	83	3b48	0	-0.8
1951	StL N	11	33	2	6	2	0	0	4	5	0	5	.182	.289	.242	44	-2	0-0	.933	-1	85	46	3b10	0	-0.4
1952	StL N	3	2	1	0	0	0	0	0	0	0	0	.000	.000	.000	-99	-1	0-0	1.000	0	143	0	/3	0	-0.1
	Cin N	13	15	1	1	0	1	0	0	0	0	2	.067	.067	.200	-29	-3	0-0	.667	-1	54	0	3b3/1	0	-0.4
	Year	16	17	2	1	0	1	0	0	0	0	2	.059	.059	.176	-37	-3	0-0	.750	-1	78	0	3b4/1	0	-0.5
Total	5	218	605	69	165	22	6	11	71	52	2	45	.273	.332	.383	87	-13	0-0	.927	-4	102	114	3b148,2b5/1	0	-1.8
KAZANSKI, TED	Theodore Stanley; B1.25.1934 Hamtramck MI; BR/TR/6´1˝/175; d6.25																								
1953	Phi N	95	360	39	78	17	5	2	27	26	3	53	.217	.275	.308	52	-26	1-1	.949	-18	85	93	S95	0	-3.5
1954	Phi N	39	104	7	14	2	0	1	8	4	0	14	.135	.164	.183	-9	-17	0-1	.945	-4	95	111	S38	0	-2.0
1955	Phi N	9	12	1	1	0	0	1	1	1-0	0	1	.083	.154	.333	25	-1	0-0	1.000	0	94	77	S4,3b4	0	-0.1
1956	Phi N	117	379	35	80	11	1	4	34	20-6	1	41	.211	.251	.277	43	-31	0-2	.979	-16	88	97	2b116/S	0	-4.2
1957	Phi N	62	185	15	49	7	1	3	11	17-1	0	20	.265	.327	.362	88	-3	1-1	.968	-7	98	217	3b36,2b22,S3	0	-0.9
1958	Phi N	95	289	21	66	12	2	3	35	22-2	4	34	.228	.291	.315	62	-16	2-3	.988	-23	84	94	2b59,S22,3b16	0	-3.6
Total	6	417	1329	118	288	49	9	14	116	90-9	8	163	.217	.269	.299	51	-94	4-8	.981	-68	85	95	2b197,S163,3b56	0	-14.3
KEARNEY, BOB	Robert Henry; B10.3.1956 San Antonio TX; BR/TR/6´0˝/(180–190); [SFN77 14/348]; d9.25; Col Texas																								
1979	SF N	2	0	0	0	0	0	0	0	1-0	0	0	ø	1.000	ø	212	0	0-0	ø	-0	0	0	/C	0	0.0
1981	Oak A	1	0	0	0	0	0	0	0	0-0	0	0	ø	ø	ø	ø	0	0-0	ø	-0	0	0	/C	0	0.0
1982	Oak A	22	71	7	12	3	0	0	5	3-0	2	10	.169	.218	.211	21	-8	0-0	.970	4	102	132	C22	0	-0.3
1983	Oak A	108	298	33	76	11	0	8	32	21-1	4	50	.255	.312	.372	93	-3	1-4	.982	2	116	105	C101,D3	0	0.1
1984	Sea A	133	431	39	97	24	1	7	43	18-0	2	72	.225	.257	.334	63	-22	7-5	.988	7	106	118	C133	0	-1.0
1985	Sea A	108	305	24	74	14	1	6	27	11-1	4	59	.243	.277	.354	71	-13	1-1	**.995**	5	114	119	C108	0	-0.4
1986	Sea A	81	204	23	49	10	0	6	25	12-1	0	35	.240	.281	.377	77	-7	0-2	.989	13	89	175	C79	0	0.8
1987	Sea A	24	47	5	8	4	1	0	1	1-0	0	9	.170	.188	.298	25	-5	0-0	.981	5	270	103	C24	0	0.0
Total	8	479	1356	131	316	66	3	27	133	67-3	12	235	.233	.274	.346	70	-58	9-12	.987	35	113	124	C469,D3	0	-0.8
KEARNS, AUSTIN	Austin Ryan; B5.20.1980 Lexington KY; BR/TR/6´3˝/(220–245); [CinN98 1/7]; d4.17																								
2002	Cin N	107	372	66	117	24	3	13	56	54-3	6	81	.315	.407	.500	133	20	6-3	.983	5	111	117	O103(13/6/95)	34	2.1
2003	Cin N	82	292	39	77	11	0	15	58	41-1	5	68	.264	.364	.455	118	8	5-2	.990	4	113	100	O80(0/40/51)	82	1.1
2004	Cin N	64	217	28	50	10	2	9	32	28-0	1	71	.230	.321	.419	91	-3	2-1	.975	-2	103	27	O60(0/1/60)	105	-0.8
2005	Cin N	112	387	62	93	26	1	18	67	48-2	8	107	.240	.333	.452	104	2	0-0	.988	9	117	135	O107(0/2/107)	0	0.7
2006	Cin N	87	325	53	89	21	1	16	50	35-2	5	85	.274	.351	.492	107	4	7-1	.991	8	122	118	O85R	0	0.9
	Was N	63	212	33	53	12	1	8	36	41-2	5	50	.250	.381	.429	113	6	2-3	.968	5	124	102	O60(0/5/59)	0	0.7
	Year	150	537	86	142	33	2	24	86	76-4	10	135	.264	.363	.467	110	10	9-4	.981	13	**123**	111	O145(0/5/144)	0	1.6
Total	5	515	1805	281	479	104	8	79	299	247-10	30	462	.265	.361	.463	113	37	22-10	.984	30	115	106	O495(13/54/457)	221	4.7
KEARNS, TEDDY	Edward Joseph; B1.1.1900 Trenton NJ; D12.21.1949 Trenton NJ; BR/TR/5´11˝/180; d10.1																								
1920	Phi A	1	1	0	0	0	0	0	0	0	0	0	.000	.000	.000	-99	0	0-0	ø	0	—	—	/H	—	0.0
1924	Chi N	4	16	0	4	0	1	0	1	1	0	1	.250	.294	.375	77	-1	0-0	1.000	0	96	98	1b4	—	-0.1
1925	Chi N	3	2	0	1	0	0	0	0	0	0	0	.500	.500	.500	154	0	0-0	1.000	-0	0	265	1b3	—	0.0
Total	3	8	19	0	5	0	1	0	1	1	0	1	.263	.300	.368	76	-1	0-0	1.000	0	86	116	1b7	—	-0.1

YEAR	TM LG	G	AB	R	H	2B	3B	HR	RBI	BB-IB	HP	SO	AVG	OBP	SLG	AOPS	ABR	SB-CS	FA	FR	RNG	THR	GAMES AT POSITION	DL	BFW
Kearns, Tom	Thomas J. "Dasher"; B11.9.1859 Rochester NY; D12.7.1938 Buffalo NY; BR/TR/5´7˝/160; d8.26																								
1880	Buf N	2	7	0	0	0	0	0	0	0	—	0	.000	.000	.000	-98	-1	—	.667	-2	—	—	C2	—	-0.4
1882	Det N	4	13	2	4	2	0	0	1	0	—	4	.308	.308	.462	143	1	—	.733	-2	86	0	2b4	—	-0.1
1884	Det N	21	79	9	16	0	1	0	7	2	—	10	.203	.222	.228	45	-5	—	.810	-8	80	58	2b21	—	-1.1
Total	3	27	99	11	20	2	1	0	8	2	—	14	.202	.218	.242	48	-5	—	.801	-12	—	—	2b25,C2	—	-1.6
Kearse, Eddie	Paul Edward "Truck"; B2.23.1916 San Francisco CA; D7.15.1968 Eureka CA; BR/TR/6´1˝/195; d6.13																								
1942	NY A	11	26	2	5	0	0	0	2	3	0	1	.192	.276	.192	34	-2	1-0	1.000	2	*184*	*143*	C11	0	0.1
Keating, Chick	Walter Francis; B8.8.1891 Philadelphia PA; D7.13.1959 Philadelphia PA; BR/TR/5´9.5˝/155; d9.26																								
1913	Chi N	2	5	1	1	1	0	0	0	0	0	1	.200	.200	.400	69	0	0	1.000	-1	26	0	S2	—	-0.1
1914	Chi N	20	30	3	3	0	1	0	0	6	0	9	.100	.250	.167	25	-3	0	.951	-0	97	72	S14	—	-0.3
1915	Chi N	4	8	1	0	0	0	0	0	0	0	3	.000	.000	.000	-99	-2	1	.750	-1	82	0	S2	—	-0.3
1926	Phi N	4	2	0	0	0	0	0	0	0	0	0	.000	.000	.000	-95	-1	0	1.000	-1	86	0	2b2,S2/3	—	-0.1
Total	4	30	45	5	4	1	1	0	0	6	0	13	.089	.196	.156	4	-6	1	.903	-3	86	50	S20,2b2/3	—	-0.8
Keatley, Greg	Gregory Steven; B9.12.1953 Princeton WV; BR/TR/6´2˝/200; [ChiN76 5/103]; d9.27; Col South Carolina																								
1981	KC A	2	0	0	0	0	0	0	0	0-0	0	0	ø	ø	ø	ø	0	0-0	1.000	0	0	0	C2	0	0.0
Keedy, Pat	Charles Patrick; B1.10.1958 Birmingham AL; BR/TR/6´4˝/(204–223); [CalA79 5/119]; d9.10; Col Auburn																								
1985	Cal A	3	4	1	2	1	0	1	1	0-0	0	0	.500	.500	1.500	422	2	0-1	ø	-1	0	0	3b2/lf	0	0.1
1987	Chi A	17	41	6	7	1	0	2	2	2-0	0	14	.171	.209	.341	41	-4	1-0	.943	4	131	113	3b11,1b2/2SlfD	0	0.0
1989	Cle A	9	14	3	3	2	0	0	1	2-0	0	5	.214	.313	.357	87	0	0-0	1.000	1	85	0	O3L,3b2/1SD	0	0.1
Total	3	29	59	10	12	4	0	3	4	4-0	0	19	.203	.254	.424	77	-2	1-1	.929	5	140	154	3b15,O5L,1b3,D2,S2/2	0	0.2
Keeler, Willie	William Henry "Wee Willie","Hit 'Em Where They Ain't" (b William Henry O'Kelleher); B3.3.1872 Brooklyn NY; D1.1.1923 Brooklyn NY; BL/TL/5´4.5˝/140; d9.30; HF1939																								
1892	NY N	14	53	7	17	3	0	0	6	3	1	3	.321	.368	.377	128	2	5	.878	-2	77	52	3b14	—	0.0
1893	NY N	7	24	5	8	2	1	1	7	5	0	1	.333	.448	.625	183	3	3	.667	-3	0	0	O3C,2b2,S2	—	0.0
	Bro N	20	80	14	25	1	1	1	9	4	1	4	.313	.353	.387	101	0	2	.833	-2	96	83	3b12,O8L	—	-0.2
	Year	27	104	19	33	3	2	2	16	9	1	5	.317	.377	.442	121	3	5	.833	-5	96	83	3b12,O11(8/3/0),2b2,S2	—	-0.2
1894	†Bal N	**129**	590	165	219	27	22	5	94	40	18	6	.371	.427	.517	121	19	32	.938	2	116	81	O128R/2	—	1.1
1895	†Bal N	**131**	565	162	213	24	15	4	78	37	14	12	.377	.429	.494	134	28	47	.964	10	107	126	O131R	—	2.5
1896	†Bal N	126	544	153	210	22	13	4	82	37	7	9	.386	.432	.496	142	33	67	.969	3	110	144	O126(2/0/124)	—	2.5
1897	†Bal N	129	564	145	**239**	27	19	0	74	35	7	—	**.424**	.464	.539	164	52	64	.970	-2	65	61	O129R	—	3.7
1898	Bal N	129	561	126	**216**	7	2	1	44	31	3	—	**.385**	.420	.410	136	26	28	.961	-1	78	53	O128R/3	—	1.7
1899	Bro N	141	570	**140**	216	12	13	1	61	37	9	—	.379	.425	.451	137	29	45	.979	-0	103	74	O141R	—	2.0
1900	†Bro N	136	563	106	**204**	13	12	4	68	30	7	—	.362	.402	.449	127	19	41	.940	6	121	82	O136R/2	—	1.6
1901	Bro N	136	595	123	202	18	12	2	43	21	7	—	.339	.369	.420	125	17	23	**.985**	-2	111	99	O125R,3b10,2b3	—	0.9
1902	Bro N	133	559	86	186	20	5	0	38	21	7	—	.333	.365	.386	131	19	19	**.978**	0	78	119	O133R	—	1.4
1903	NY A	132	512	95	160	14	7	0	32	32	13	—	.313	.368	.367	114	10	24	.935	-8	74	120	O128(0/5/123),3b4	—	-0.4
1904	NY A	143	543	78	186	14	8	2	40	35	7	—	.343	.390	.409	146	28	21	.935	-3	103	**188**	O142R	—	2.1
1905	NY A	149	560	81	169	14	4	4	38	43	5	—	.302	.357	.363	115	10	19	.968	1	116	29	O137(3/0/134),2b12,3b3	—	0.6
1906	NY A	152	592	96	180	8	3	2	33	40	5	—	.304	.353	.338	106	4	23	.987	-2	83	75	O152(1/0/151)	—	-0.5
1907	NY A	107	423	50	99	5	2	0	17	15	3	—	.234	.265	.255	61	-19	7	.969	-2	96	145	O107R	—	-2.9
1908	NY A	91	323	38	85	3	1	1	14	31	5	—	.263	.337	.288	102	2	14	.936	-1	90	65	O88(2/0/86)	—	-0.3
1909	NY A	99	360	44	95	7	5	1	32	24	10	—	.264	.327	.319	104	2	10	.968	-6	74	69	O95R	—	-0.9
1910	NY N	19	10	5	3	0	0	0	0	3	0	1	.300	.462	.300	123	1	1	1.000	-0	84	0	O2(1/1/0)	—	0.1
Total	19	2123	8591	1719	2932	241	145	33	810	524	129	36	.341	.388	.415	125	285	495	.960	-12	96	96	O2039(17/9/2013),3b44,2b19,S2	—	15.0
Keely, Bob	Robert William; B8.22.1909 St.Louis MO; D5.20.2001 Sarasota FL; BR/TR/6´0˝/175; d7.25; C12																								
1944	StL N	1	0	0	0	0	0	0	0	0	0	0	ø	ø	ø	ø	0	0	1.000	0	*0*	*0*	/C	0	0.0
1945	StL N	1	1	0	0	0	0	0	0	0	0	0	.000	.000	.000	-98	0	0	1.000	-0	*0*	*0*	/C	0	0.0
Total	2	2	1	0	0	0	0	0	0	0	0	0	.000	.000	.000	-98	0	0	1.000	-0	*0*	*0*	C2	0	0.0
Keen, Bill	William Brown "Buster"; B8.16.1892 Oglethorpe GA; D7.16.1947 South Point OH; BR/TR/6´0˝/181; d8.8																								
1911	Pit N	6	7	0	0	0	0	0	0	1	0	4	.000	.125	.000	-61	-2	0	1.000	-0	0	0	/1	—	-0.2
Keenan, Jim	James William; B2.10.1858 New Haven CT; D9.21.1926 Cincinnati OH; BR/TR/5´10˝/186; d5.17; OF(0/1/12); ▲																								
1875	NH NA	5	13	1	1	0	0	0	0	0	—	0	.077	.077	.077	-53	-2	0-0	.800	-4	—	—	C3,3b2/lf	—	-0.5
1880	Buf N	2	7	1	1	0	0	0	0	1	—	1	.143	.250	.143	36	0	—	.947	2	—	—	C2	—	0.1
1882	Pit AA	25	96	10	21	7	0	1	—	1	—	—	.219	.227	.323	87	-1	—	.906	-0	—	—	C22,O3(0/1/2)/S	—	0.1
1884	Ind AA	68	249	36	73	14	4	3	—	16	3	—	.293	.343	.418	151	15	—	.923	-2	—	—	C59,1b6,O2R/SP	—	1.6
1885	Cin AA	36	132	16	35	2	2	1	15	8	0	—	.265	.307	.333	100	0	—	.926	0	—	—	C33,1b4/P	—	0.2
1886	Cin AA	44	148	31	40	4	3	3	24	18	2	—	.270	.357	.399	132	6	0	.915	0	—	—	C30,O7R,3b5,1b4,P2	—	0.7
1887	Cin AA	47	174	19	44	4	1	0	17	11	1	—	.253	.301	.287	63	-9	7	.934	8	—	—	C38,1b11	—	0.1
1888	Cin AA	85	313	38	73	9	8	1	40	22	5	—	.233	.294	.323	93	-4	9	.946	3	—	—	C69,1b16	—	0.3
1889	Cin AA	87	300	52	86	10	11	6	60	48	6	35	.287	.395	.453	137	15	18	.962	4	—	—	C66,1b21/3	—	1.9
1890	Cin N	54	202	21	28	4	2	3	19	19	1	36	.139	.216	.223	28	-19	5	.950	9	*124*	*105*	C50,1b2/rf3	—	-0.5
1891	Cin N	75	252	30	51	7	5	4	33	33	3	39	.202	.302	.317	80	-7	2	.974	-4	133	89	1b41,C34/3	—	-1.1
Total	10	523	1873	254	452	61	36	22	208	177	21	111	.241	.314	.348	99	-4	41	.935	18	*111*	*93*	C403,1b105,O13R,3b8,P4,S2	—	3.4
Keerl, George	George Henry; B4.10.1847 Baltimore MD; D9.9.1923 Menominee MI; BR/TR/5´7˝/145; d5.4																								
1875	Chi NA	6	23	2	3	0	0	0	3	0	—	2	.130	.130	.130	-9	-2	0-0	.815	-2	98	0	2b6	—	-0.4
Keesey, Jim	James Ward; B10.27.1902 Perryville MD; D9.5.1951 Boise ID; BR/TR/6´0.5˝/170; d9.6																								
1925	Phi A	5	5	1	2	0	0	0	1	0	0	2	.400	.400	.400	97	0	0-0	1.000	-0	0	0	1b2	—	0.0
1930	Phi A	11	12	2	3	1	0	0	2	1	0	2	.250	.308	.333	60	-1	0-0	.909	-0	0	233	1b3	—	-0.1
Total	2	16	17	3	5	1	0	0	3	1	0	4	.294	.333	.353	71	-1	0-0	.923	-1	0	179	1b5	—	-0.1
Keister, Bill	William Hoffman "Wagon Tongue"; B8.17.1871 Baltimore MD; D8.19.1924 Baltimore MD; BL/TR/5´5.5˝/168; d5.20																								
1896	Bal N	15	58	8	14	3	0	0	5	3	2	5	.241	.302	.293	56	-4	4	.923	-4	80	47	2b8,3b6	—	-0.6
1898	Bos N	10	30	5	5	2	0	0	4	0	0	—	.167	.167	.233	14	-3	0	1.000	2	111	170	S4,2b4/rf	—	-0.2
1899	Bal N	136	523	96	172	22	16	3	73	16	16	—	.329	.368	.449	117	10	33	.895	-21	95	79	S90,2b46/lf	—	-0.4
1900	StL N	126	497	78	149	26	10	1	72	25	11	—	.300	.347	.398	106	4	32	.927	-23	97	59	2b116,S7,3b3	—	-1.2
1901	Bal A	115	442	78	145	20	**21**	2	93	18	8	—	.328	.365	.482	128	14	24	.851	-21	93	71	S112	—	-0.3
1902	Was A	119	483	82	145	33	9	9	90	14	7	—	.300	.329	.462	117	9	27	.912	-3	108	172	O65(0/12/53),2b40,3b14,S2	—	0.4
1903	Phi N	100	400	53	128	27	7	3	63	14	6	—	.320	.352	.445	131	14	11	.940	5	167	30	O100R	—	1.4
Total	7	621	2433	400	758	133	63	18	400	90	50	5	.312	.349	.440	116	44	131	.870	-64	94	74	S215,2b214,O167(1/12/154),3b23	—	-0.9
Keliher, Mickey	Maurice Michael; B1.11.1890 Washington DC; D9.7.1930 Washington DC; BL/TL/6´0˝/175; d9.10																								
1911	Pit N	3	7	0	0	0	0	0	0	0	0	5	.000	.000	.000	-96	-2	0	.875	0	142	164	1b3	—	-0.2
1912	Pit N	2	0	1	0	0	0	0	0	0	0	0	ø	ø	ø	ø	0	0	ø	0	—	—	/R	—	0.0
Total	2	5	7	1	0	0	0	0	0	0	0	5	.000	.000	.000	-96	-2	0	.875	0	142	164	1b3	—	-0.2
Kell, Skeeter	Everett Lee; B10.11.1929 Swifton AR; BR/TR/5´9˝/160; d4.19; b–George; Col Arkansas																								
1952	Phi A	75	213	24	47	8	3	0	17	14	2	18	.221	.275	.286	53	-14	5-1	.963	-6	101	79	2b68	0	-1.6
Kell, George	George Clyde; B8.23.1922 Swifton AR; BR/TR/5´9˝/175; d9.28; HF1983; b–Skeeter; Col Arkansas St.																								
1943	Phi A	1	5	1	1	0	1	0	1	0	0	0	.200	.200	.600	131	0	0-0	1.000	0	116	0	/3	0	0.0
1944	Phi A	139	514	51	138	15	3	0	44	22	1	23	.268	.300	.309	75	-18	5-2	.958	-2	95	103	3b139	0	-1.9
1945	Phi A	147	567	50	154	30	3	4	56	27	1	15	.272	.306	.356	92	-8	2-0	**.964**	22	**114**	106	3b147	0	1.7
1946	Phi A	26	87	3	26	6	1	0	11	10	1	6	.299	.378	.391	116	2	0-0	.979	4	107	80	3b26	0	0.6
	Det A	105	434	67	142	19	9	4	41	30	0	14	.327	.371	.440	119	10	3-2	.984	1	93	102	3b105/1	0	1.1
	Year	131	521	70	168	25	10	4	52	40	1	20	.322	.372	.432	118	12	3-2	**.983**	5	**96**	**98**	3b131/1	0	1.7
1947	Det A★	152	588	75	188	29	5	5	93	61	3	16	.320	.387	.412	118	16	9-11	.962	16	**110**	93	3b152	0	3.1
1948	Det A☆	92	368	47	112	24	3	2	44	33	5	15	.304	.369	.402	102	2	2-2	.969	-7	82	92	3b92	0	-0.6

YEAR	TM LG	G	AB	R	H	2B	3B	HR	RBI	BB-IB	HP	SO	AVG	OBP	SLG	AOPS	ABR	SB-CS	FA	FR	RNG	THR	GAMES AT POSITION	DL	BFW
1949	Det A★	134	522	97	179	38	9	3	59	71	3	13	**.343**	.424	.467	136	29	7-5	.975	-3	97	76	3b134	0	2.5
1950	Det A★	**157**	641	114	**218**	**56**	6	8	101	66	1	18	.340	.403	.484	122	23	3-3	**.982**	-2	99	96	3b157	0	1.9
1951	Det A★	147	598	92	**191**	**36**	3	2	59	61	4	18	.319	.386	.400	112	12	10-3	**.960**	7	**103**	109	3b147	0	2.0
1952	Det A	39	152	11	45	8	0	1	17	15	0	13	.296	.359	.368	102	1	0-1	.959	-1	96	79	3b39	0	0.0
	Bos A✳	75	276	41	88	15	2	6	40	31	1	10	.319	.390	.453	124	10	0-1	.959	-5	93	83	3b73	0	0.5
	Year	114	428	52	133	23	2	7	57	46	1	23	.311	.379	.423	117	11	0-2	.959	-5	94	82	3b112	0	0.5
1953	Bos A★	134	460	68	141	41	2	12	73	52	5	22	.307	.383	.483	126	18	5-2	**.972**	-12	90	83	3b124,O7L	0	0.6
1954	Bos A	26	93	15	24	3	0	0	10	15	0	3	.258	.361	.290	72	-3	0-0	.920	-3	89	96	3b25	0	-0.6
	Chi A✳	71	233	25	66	10	0	5	48	18	0	12	.283	.323	.391	95	-2	1-1	.996	-7	41	111	1b32,3b31,O2(2/0/1)	0	-1.1
	Year	97	326	40	90	13	0	5	58	33	0	15	.276	.334	.362	88	-5	1-1	.936	-10	90	96	3b56,1b32,O2(2/0/1)	0	-1.7
1955	Chi A	128	429	44	134	24	1	8	81	51-2	6	36	.312	.389	.429	118	13	2-2	**.976**	-15	85	46	3b105,1b24/lf	0	-0.3
1956	Chi A	21	80	7	25	5	0	1	11	8-0	0	6	.313	.371	.412	106	1	0-0	1.000	-2	81	0	3b18,1b4	0	-0.2
	Bal A★	102	345	45	90	17	2	8	37	25-3	3	31	.261	.313	.391	93	-5	0-1	.974	-3	91	105	3b97,1b2/2	0	-0.9
	Year	123	425	52	115	22	2	9	48	33-3	3	37	.271	.324	.395	96	-4	0-1	**.978**	-6	89	89	3b115,1b6/2	0	-1.1
1957	Bal A★	99	310	28	92	9	0	9	44	25-2	2	16	.297	.352	.413	116	6	2-0	.979	-5	91	132	3b80,1b22	0	0.1
Total	15	1795	6702	881	2054	385	50	78	870	621-7	36	287	.306	.367	.414	111	107	51-36	.969	-16	97	93	3b1692,1b85,O10(10/0/1)/2	0	8.5
KELLEHER, DUKE	Albert Aloysius; B9.30.1893 New York NY; D9.28.1947 Staten Island NY; TR/5´7˝/180; d8.18; Col Princeton																								
1916	NY N	1	0	0	0	0	0	0	0	0	0	0	ø	ø	ø	ø	0	0	ø	-0	0	0	/C	—	0.0
KELLEHER, FRANKIE	Francis Eugene; B8.22.1916 San Francisco CA; D4.13.1979 Stockton CA; BR/TR/6´1˝/195; d7.18; Mil 1944–45; Col St. Marys (CA)																								
1942	Cin N	38	110	13	20	3	1	3	12	16	0	20	.182	.286	.309	74	-4	0	.986	-1	100	47	O30L	0	-0.6
1943	Cin N	9	10	1	0	0	0	0	0	2	0	0	.000	.167	.000	-51	-2	0	1.000	-0	94	0	/rf	0	-0.2
Total	2	47	120	14	20	3	1	3	12	18	0	20	.167	.275	.283	64	-6	0	.986	-1	100	45	O31(30/0/1)	0	-0.8
KELLEHER, JOHN	John Patrick; B9.13.1893 Brookline MA; D8.21.1960 Brighton MA; BR/TR/5´11˝/150; d7.31																								
1912	StL N	8	12	0	4	1	0	0	1	0	0	2	.333	.333	.417	107	0	0	1.000	0	109	360	3b3	—	0.1
1916	Bro N	2	3	0	0	0	0	0	0	0	0	0	.000	.000	.000	-97	-1	0	1.000	-1	54	0	/S3	—	-0.2
1921	Chi N	95	301	31	93	11	7	4	47	16	1	16	.309	.346	.432	104	1	2-5	.947	3	108	103	3b37,2b27,1b11,S11/lf	—	0.6
1922	Chi N	63	193	23	50	7	1	0	20	15	1	14	.259	.316	.306	60	-11	5-7	.932	2	110	123	3b46,S7,1b4	—	-0.7
1923	Chi N	66	193	27	59	10	0	6	21	14	0	9	.306	.353	.451	110	3	2-4	.975	-7	86	74	1b22,S14,3b11,2b6	—	-0.4
1924	Bos N	1	1	0	0	0	0	0	0	0	0	1	.000	.000	.000	-99	0	0-0	ø	0	—	—	/H	—	0.0
Total	6	235	703	81	206	29	8	10	89	45	2	42	.293	.337	.400	92	-8	9-16	.924	-2	106	117	3b98,1b37,2b33,S33/lf	—	-0.6
KELLEHER, MICK	Michael Dennis; B7.25.1947 Seattle WA; BR/TR/5´9˝/(165–176); [StLN69 3/68]; d9.1; C4; Col Puget Sound																								
1972	StL N	23	63	5	10	2	1	0	1	6-0	0	15	.159	.232	.222	30	-6	0-0	.984	3	92	107	S23	0	0.0
1973	StL N	43	38	4	7	2	0	0	2	4-1	1	11	.184	.279	.237	44	-3	0-0	.955	-1	97	91	S42	0	-0.2
1974	Hou N	19	57	4	9	0	0	0	2	5-0	0	10	.158	.226	.158	9	-7	1-1	.944	3	122	105	S18	0	-0.2
1975	StL N	7	4	0	0	0	0	0	0	0-0	0	1	.000	.000	.000	-96	-1	0-0	.909	1	129	94	S7	0	0.0
1976	Chi N	124	337	28	77	12	1	0	22	15-3	2	32	.228	.264	.270	48	-23	0-4	.980	5	106	97	S101,3b22,2b5	0	-0.9
1977	Chi N	63	122	14	28	5	2	0	11	9-2	1	12	.230	.288	.303	53	-8	0-0	.976	6	116	94	2b40,S14/3	16	0.0
1978	Chi N	68	95	8	24	1	0	0	6	7-0	0	11	.253	.304	.263	53	-6	4-1	1.000	8	129	110	3b37,2b17,S10	0	0.4
1979	Chi N	73	142	14	36	4	1	0	10	7-0	2	9	.254	.296	.296	57	-8	2-0	.966	13	106	108	3b32,2b29,S14	0	0.7
1980	Chi N	105	96	12	14	1	1	0	4	9-1	0	17	.146	.217	.177	11	-12	1-3	.974	5	109	98	2b57,3b31,S17	0	-0.6
1981	Det A	61	77	10	17	4	0	0	6	7-0	0	10	.221	.282	.273	59	-4	0-0	.930	-1	82	68	3b39,2b11,S9	0	-0.5
1982	Det A	2	1	0	0	0	0	0	0	0-0	0	0	.000	.000	.000	-99	0	0-0	1.000	0	285	0	/23	0	0.0
	Cal A	34	49	9	8	1	0	0	1	5-0	1	5	.163	.255	.184	22	-5	1-1	.965	1	100	81	S28,3b6	0	-0.2
	Year	36	50	9	8	1	0	0	1	5-0	1	5	.160	.250	.180	20	-5	1-1	.965	1	100	81	S28,3b7/2	0	-0.2
Total	11	622	1081	108	230	32	6	0	65	74-7	7	133	.213	.266	.253	43	-83	9-10	.976	43	105	95	S283,3b169,2b160	16	-1.5
KELLER, CHARLIE	Charles Ernest "King Kong"; B9.12.1916 Middletown MD; D5.23.1990 Frederick MD; BL/TR/5´10˝/190; d4.22; Mer 1944–45; C2; b–Hal; Col Maryland																								
1939	†NY A	111	398	87	133	21	6	11	83	81	0	49	.334	.447	.500	144	31	6-3	.969	-4	96	64	O105(47/0/58)	—	1.9
1940	NY A★	138	500	102	143	18	15	21	93	**106**	0	65	.286	.411	.508	142	34	8-2	.967	-3	104	44	O136(65/0/71)	—	2.3
1941	†NY A★	140	507	102	151	24	10	33	122	102	1	65	.298	.416	.580	163	48	6-4	.980	2	108	59	O137L	0	4.0
1942	†NY A	152	544	106	159	24	9	26	108	114	2	61	.292	.417	.513	164	50	14-2	.985	-2	98	83	O152L	0	4.2
1943	†NY A✳	141	512	97	139	15	11	31	86	**106**	0	60	.271	.396	.525	**167**	**45**	7-5	.994	2	105	70	O141L	0	4.0
1945	NY A	44	163	26	49	7	4	10	34	31	0	21	.301	.412	.577	178	16	0-2	1.000	3	112	97	O44L	0	1.6
1946	NY A★	150	538	98	148	29	10	30	101	113	4	101	.275	.405	.533	158	46	1-4	.979	-3	102	40	O149(146/0/3)	0	3.2
1947	NY A✳	45	151	36	36	6	1	13	36	41	1	18	.238	.404	.550	165	15	0-0	.967	-1	97	75	O43L	0	1.1
1948	NY A	83	247	41	66	15	2	6	44	41	0	25	.267	.372	.417	111	5	1-1	.977	-4	97	23	O66L	0	-0.4
1949	NY A	60	116	17	29	4	1	3	16	25	2	15	.250	.392	.379	104	2	2-0	.976	-3	83	0	O31(29/0/2)	0	-0.2
1950	Det A	50	51	7	16	1	3	2	16	13	0	6	.314	.453	.569	155	5	0-0	1.000	-0	101	0	O6(1/0/5)	0	0.4
1951	Det A	54	62	6	16	2	0	3	21	11	0	12	.258	.370	.435	117	2	0-0	1.000	1	127	0	O8(4/0/4)	0	0.2
1952	NY A	2	1	0	0	0	0	0	0	0	0	1	.000	.000	.000	-99	0	0-0	ø	-0	0	0	/lf	0	0.0
Total	13	1170	3790	725	1085	166	72	189	760	784	10	499	.286	.410	.518	152	299	45-23	.980	-12	102	58	O1019(876/0/143)	0	22.3
KELLER, HAL	Harold Kefauver; B7.7.1927 Middletown MD; BL/TR/6´1˝/200; d9.13; b–Charlie; Col Maryland																								
1949	Was A	3	3	1	1	0	0	0	0	0	0	0	.333	.333	.333	78	0	0-0	ø	0	—	—	/H	0	0.0
1950	Was A	11	28	1	6	3	0	1	5	2	0	2	.214	.267	.429	79	-1	0-0	1.000	-1	*71*	*0*	C8	0	-0.2
1952	Was A	11	23	2	4	2	0	0	0	1	0	1	.174	.208	.261	31	-2	0-0	.967	-0	*93*	*62*	C11	0	-0.2
Total	3	25	54	4	11	5	0	1	5	3	0	3	.204	.246	.352	60	-3	0-0	.982	-1	*82*	*30*	C19	0	-0.4
KELLERT, FRANK	Frank William; B7.6.1924 Oklahoma City OK; D11.19.1976 Oklahoma City OK; BR/TR/6´2.5˝/185; d4.18; Col Oklahoma St.																								
1953	StL A	2	4	0	0	0	0	0	0	0	0	0	.000	.000	.000	-98	-1	0-0	1.000	-0	0	0	/1	0	-0.1
1954	Bal A	10	34	3	7	2	0	0	1	5	0	4	.206	.308	.265	62	-2	0-0	1.000	-1	33	75	1b9	0	-0.4
1955	†Bro N	39	80	12	26	4	2	4	19	9-0	0	10	.325	.385	.575	149	6	0-1	.983	-0	97	64	1b22	0	0.4
1956	Chi N	71	129	10	24	3	1	4	17	12-1	0	22	.186	.254	.318	54	-9	0-0	.991	2	122	100	1b27	0	-0.9
Total	4	122	247	25	57	9	3	8	37	26-1	0	36	.231	.301	.389	85	-6	0-1	.990	-0	97	82	1b59	0	-1.0
KELLETT, RED	Donald Stafford; B7.15.1909 Brooklyn NY; D11.3.1970 Ft.Lauderdale FL; BR/TR/6´0˝/185; d7.2; Col Penn																								
1934	Bos A	9	9	0	0	0	0	0	0	1	0	5	.000	.100	.000	-68	-2	0-0	.778	-0	103	0	S4,2b2/3	—	-0.2
KELLEY, JOE	Joseph James; B12.9.1871 Cambridge MA; D8.14.1943 Baltimore MD; BR/TR/5´11˝/190; d7.27; M5/C1; HF1971; OF(1131/328/8)																								
1891	Bos N	12	45	7	11	1	1	0	3	2	0	7	.244	.277	.311	63	-2	0	.852	-0	104	0	O12(12/1/0)	—	-0.3
1892	Pit N	56	205	26	49	7	7	0	28	17	0	21	.239	.297	.341	93	-3	8	.919	2	151	215	O56C	—	-0.4
	Bal N	10	33	3	7	0	0	0	4	4	1	7	.212	.316	.212	59	-1	2	.824	-2	0	0	O10C	—	-0.3
	Year	66	238	29	56	7	7	0	32	21	1	28	.235	.300	.324	88	-4	10	.908	-0	132	188	O66C	—	-0.7
1893	Bal N	125	502	120	153	27	16	9	76	77	4	44	.305	.401	.476	131	22	33	.940	6	104	85	O125(18/107/1)	—	1.6
1894	†Bal N	**129**	507	165	199	48	20	6	111	107	5	36	.393	.502	.602	158	55	46	.951	2	74	60	O129L	—	3.4
1895	†Bal N	**131**	518	148	189	26	19	10	134	77	10	29	.365	.456	.546	154	44	54	.946	1	101	125	O131(130/1/0)	—	2.6
1896	†Bal N	131	519	148	189	31	19	8	100	91	12	19	.364	.469	.543	164	54	**87**	.958	3	107	70	O131(129/0/2)	—	3.8
1897	†Bal N	131	505	113	183	31	9	5	118	70	7	—	.362	.447	.489	147	39	44	.959	-0	84	93	O130L,S3,3b2	—	2.3
1898	Bal N	124	464	71	149	18	15	2	110	56	3	—	.321	.398	.438	137	23	24	.969	2	111	118	O122(39/83/0),3b2	—	1.5
1899	Bro N	143	538	108	175	21	14	6	93	70	7	—	.325	.410	.450	133	26	31	.977	10	121	124	O143L	—	2.2
1900	†Bro N	121	454	90	145	23	17	6	91	53	6	—	.319	.398	.485	135	21	26	.959	1	115	71	O77L,1b32,3b13	—	1.4
1901	Bro N	120	492	77	151	22	12	4	65	40	3	—	.307	.363	.425	124	15	18	.975	7	126	107	1b115,3b5	—	1.9
1902	Bal A	60	222	50	69	17	7	1	34	34	1	—	.311	.405	.464	134	12	12	.973	0	119	146	O48(1/47/0),3b8,1b5	—	0.9
	Cin N	40	156	24	50	9	2	1	12	15	0	—	.321	.380	.423	135	7	3	.971	4	183	178	O20(18/2/0),2b10,3b9,S2,M	—	1.1
1903	Cin N	105	383	85	121	22	4	3	45	51	4	—	.316	.402	.418	120	12	18	.947	-4	90	0	O67(61/6/0),S12,2b11,3b8,1b6,M	—	0.5
1904	Cin N	123	449	75	126	21	13	0	63	49	6	—	.281	.359	.385	119	11	15	.988	0	99	105	1b117,O6(0/3/3)/2M	—	1.0
1905	Cin N	90	321	43	89	7	6	1	37	27	7	—	.277	.346	.346	96	-1	8	.974	-2	99	0	O85(84/0/1),1b2,M	—	-0.9
1906	Cin N	129	465	43	106	19	11	1	53	44	4	—	.228	.300	.323	90	-6	9	.966	-4	87	136	O122L,1b3/S3	—	-1.9
1908	Bos N	73	228	25	59	8	2	2	17	27	2	—	.259	.342	.338	119	6	5	.938	-0	93	75	O51(38/12/1),1b11,M	—	0.3
Total	17	1853	7006	1421	2220	358	194	65	1194	911	82	163	.317	.402	.451	132	334	443	.955	24	102	93	O1465L,1b291,3b48,2b22,S18	—	20.7

YEAR	TM LG	G	AB	R	H	2B	3B	HR	RBI	BB-IB	HP	SO	AVG	OBP	SLG	AOPS	ABR	SB-CS	FA	FR	RNG	THR	GAMES AT POSITION	DL	BFW
Kelley, Mike	Michael Joseph; B12.2.1875 Templeton MA; D6.6.1955 Minneapolis MN; BR/TR/6´0˝/210; d7.15																								
1899	Lou N	76	282	48	68	11	2	3	33	21	6	—	.241	.307	.326	74	-10	10	.974	-0	104	88	1b76	—	-1.0
Kelliher, Frank	Francis Mortimer "Yucka"; B5.23.1899 Somerville MA; D3.4.1956 Somerville MA; BL/TL/5´9.5˝/175; d9.19																								
1919	Was A	1	1	0	0	0	0	0	0	0	0	0	.000	.000	.000	-99	0	0	ø	0	—	—	/H	—	0.0
Kellogg, Nate	Nathaniel Monroe; B9.28.1858 Rochester IA; D7.19.1923 Brooklyn NY; 5´9˝/175; d8.27																								
1885	Det N	5	17	4	2	1	0	0	0	1	—	5	.118	.167	.176	11	-2	—	.783	-2	75	65	S5	—	-0.3
Kellogg, Bill	William Dearstyne; B5.25.1884 Albany NY; D12.12.1971 Baltimore MD; BR/TR/5´10˝/153; d4.14																								
1914	Cin N	71	126	14	22	0	1	0	7	14	1	28	.175	.262	.190	34	-10	7	.988	-1	87	104	1b38,2b11,O2C/3	—	-1.3
Kelly, Red	Albert Michael; B11.15.1884 Union IL; D2.4.1961 Zephyrhills FL; BR/TR/5´11.5˝/165; d6.18; Col Notre Dame																								
1910	Chi A	14	45	6	7	0	1	0	1	7	2	—	.156	.296	.200	58	-2	0	1.000	-0	103	58	O14R	—	-0.3
Kelly, Charlie	Charles H.; d6.14																								
1883	Phi N	2	7	1	1	0	1	0	0	0	—	3	.143	.143	.429	71	0	—	.700	-0	93	270	3b2	—	-0.1
1886	Phi AA	1	3	0	0	0	0	0	0	0	0	—	.000	.000	.000	-99	-1	0	.333	-1	68	0	/S	—	-0.2
Total	2	3	10	1	1	0	1	0	0	0	0	3	.100	.100	.300	19	-1	0	.700	-2	93	270	3b2/S	—	-0.3
Kelly, Pat	Dale Patrick; B8.27.1955 Santa Maria CA; BR/TR/6´3˝/210; [AnaA73 3/55]; d5.28																								
1980	Tor A	3	7	0	2	0	0	0	0	0-0	0	4	.286	.286	.286	55	0	0-0	1.000	1	0	0	C3	0	0.1
Kelly, George	George Lange "Highpockets"; B9.10.1895 San Francisco CA; D10.13.1984 Burlingame CA; BR/TR/6´4˝/190; d8.18; Mil 1918; C11; HF1973; b–Ren; OF(27/16/19)																								
1915	NY N	17	38	2	6	0	0	1	4	1	0	9	.158	.179	.237	27	-4	0-1	.983	0	96	31	1b9,O4C	—	-0.5
1916	NY N	49	76	4	12	2	1	0	3	6	0	24	.158	.220	.211	34	-6	1	.981	-2	38	73	1b13,O7(0/2/5)/3	—	-0.9
1917	NY N	11	7	0	0	0	0	0	0	0	0	3	.000	.000	.000	-99	-2	0	1.000	1	66	1005	O4(3/0/1)/P12	—	-0.1
	Pit N	8	23	2	2	0	1	0	0	1	0	9	.087	.125	.174	-9	-3	0	.971	-1	58	73	1b8	—	-0.5
	Year	19	30	2	2	0	1	0	0	1	0	12	.067	.097	.133	-30	-5	0	.972	-0	56	98	1b9,O4(3/0/1)/P2	—	-0.6
1919	NY N	32	107	12	31	6	2	1	14	3	1	15	.290	.315	.411	119	2	1	.994	-3	61	108	1b32	—	-0.1
1920	NY N	**155**	590	69	157	22	11	11	**94**	41	6	92	.266	.320	.397	106	3	6-16	.994	4	109	**120**	1b155	—	-0.1
1921	†NY N	149	587	95	181	42	9	**23**	122	40	3	73	.308	.356	.528	131	24	4-12	.990	12	**138**	**136**	1b149	—	2.2
1922	†NY N	151	592	96	194	33	8	17	107	30	3	65	.328	.363	.497	119	14	12-3	.993	9	**129**	122	1b151	—	1.4
1923	†NY N	145	560	82	172	23	5	16	103	47	1	64	.307	.362	.452	115	11	14-7	.993	-6	78	102	1b145	—	-0.3
1924	†NY N	144	571	91	185	37	9	21	**136**	38	5	52	.324	.371	.531	143	33	7-2	.993	-3	89	108	1b125,O14(5/9/0),2b5/3	—	2.2
1925	NY N	147	586	87	181	29	3	20	99	35	2	54	.309	.350	.471	112	9	5-2	.981	16	107	113	2b108,1b25,O17(8/0/9)	—	2.4
1926	NY N	136	499	70	151	24	4	13	80	36	2	52	.303	.352	.445	115	9	4	**.993**	7	118	101	1b114,2b18	—	0.9
1927	Cin N	61	222	27	60	16	4	5	21	11	1	23	.270	.308	.446	103	0	1	.992	-1	117	138	1b49,2b13,O2L	—	-0.4
1928	Cin N	116	402	46	119	33	7	3	58	28	2	35	.296	.345	.435	104	2	2	.991	8	141	133	1b99,O13(9/0/4)	—	0.3
1929	Cin N	147	577	73	169	45	9	5	103	33	1	61	.293	.332	.428	91	-9	7	.993	5	112	111	1b147	—	-1.3
1930	Cin N	51	188	18	54	10	1	5	35	7	0	20	.287	.313	.431	81	-6	1	.993	2	111	95	1b50	—	-0.7
	Chi N	39	166	22	55	6	1	3	19	7	1	16	.331	.362	.434	91	-3	0	.998	3	120	79	1b39	—	-0.2
	Year	90	354	40	109	16	2	8	54	14	1	36	.308	.336	.432	86	-9	1	.995	4	115	88	1b89	—	-0.9
1932	Bro N	64	202	23	49	9	1	4	22	22	0	27	.243	.317	.356	82	-5	0	.984	-2	95	100	1b62/cf	—	-1.2
Total	16	1622	5993	819	1778	337	76	148	1020	386	28	694	.297	.342	.452	110	69	65-43	.992	49	111	113	1b1373,2b145,O62L,3b2/P	—	3.1
Kelly, Pat	Harold Patrick; B7.30.1944 Philadelphia PA; D10.2.2005 Chambersburg PA; BL/TL/6´1˝/(185–195); d9.6; Mil 1967																								
1967	Min A	8	1	1	0	0	0	0	0	0-0	0	1	.000	.000	.000	-93	0	0-0	ø	0	—	—	/H	0	0.0
1968	Min A	12	35	2	4	2	0	1	2	3-0	1	10	.114	.205	.257	37	-3	0-2	.955	1	114	183	O10(2/5/4)	0	-0.4
1969	KC A	112	417	61	110	20	4	8	32	49-3	5	70	.264	.348	.388	104	3	40-13	.980	-7	110	157	O107(2/44/63)	0	1.1
1970	KC A	136	452	56	106	16	1	6	38	76-3	2	105	.235	.347	.314	83	-7	34-16	.963	7	118	103	O118(1/3/115)	0	-0.5
1971	Chi A	67	213	32	62	6	3	3	22	36-4	1	29	.291	.394	.390	120	7	14-9	.991	3	97	198	O61(0/1/61)	0	0.7
1972	Chi A	119	402	57	105	14	7	5	24	55-1	4	69	.261	.355	.368	113	8	32-9	.968	-3	89	110	O109R	0	0.4
1973	Chi A★	144	550	77	154	24	5	1	44	65-1	2	91	.280	.355	.347	96	-1	22-15	.978	-2	96	100	O141(0/3/138)/D	0	-1.1
1974	Chi A	122	424	60	119	16	3	4	21	46-0	2	58	.281	.354	.361	103	3	18-11	.976	-4	83	56	D67,O53(1/0/52)	0	-0.5
1975	Chi A	133	471	73	129	21	7	9	45	58-2	2	69	.274	.353	.406	113	9	18-10	**.991**	-1	103	45	O115R,D14	0	0.2
1976	Chi A	107	311	42	79	20	3	5	34	45-1	3	45	.254	.349	.386	116	8	15-7	.950	-2	87	67	D63,O26(14/0/12)	0	0.5
1977	Bal A	120	360	50	92	13	0	10	49	53-6	4	75	.256	.353	.375	106	5	25-7	.984	-7	95	27	O109(91/1/33)/D	0	-0.3
1978	Bal A	100	274	38	75	12	1	11	40	34-1	2	58	.274	.357	.445	132	12	10-8	.969	-6	86	64	O80(73/1/7),D2	0	0.3
1979	†Bal A	68	153	25	44	11	0	9	25	20-1	1	25	.288	.367	.536	147	11	4-5	1.000	-2	90	0	O24(23/0/1),D18	0	0.6
1980	Bal A	89	200	38	52	10	1	3	26	34-0	0	54	.260	.363	.365	103	2	16-2	1.000	0	88	205	O36(34/2/0),D30	0	0.4
1981	Cle A	48	75	8	16	4	0	1	16	14-2	0	9	.213	.333	.307	87	-1	2-4	1.000	0	113	0	D18,O8(3/0/5)	0	-0.2
Total	15	1385	4338	620	1147	189	35	76	418	588-25	29	768	.264	.354	.377	107	56	250-118	.978	-9	99	96	O997(244/60/715),D214	0	1.2
Kelly, Jim	James Robert (Also Played Under Real Name of Robert John Taggert in 1918); B2.1.1884 Bloomfield NJ; D4.10.1961 Kingsport TN; BL/TR/5´10.5˝/180; d4.24																								
1914	Pit N	32	44	4	10	2	1	0	3	2	0	3	.227	.261	.318	75	-2	0	1.000	0	114	105	O7(1/0/6)	—	-0.2
1915	Pit F	148	524	68	154	12	17	4	50	35	2	46	.294	.340	.405	110	-4	38	.952	13	**117**	138	O148(14/4/133)	—	0.2
1918	Bos N	35	146	19	48	1	4	0	4	9	2	9	.329	.376	.390	140	6	4	.955	-1	109	49	O35L	—	0.5
Total	3	215	714	91	212	15	22	4	57	46	4	58	.297	.343	.396	114	0	42	.954	13	115	119	O190(50/4/139)	—	0.5
Kelly, Tom	Jay Thomas; B8.15.1950 Graceville MN; BL/TL/5´11˝/188; [MilA68 8/178]; d5.11; M16/C4																								
1975	Min A	49	127	11	23	5	0	1	11	15-0	0	22	.181	.262	.244	45	-9	0-0	.985	1	105	85	1b43,O2(1/0/1)	0	-1.2
Kelly, John	John Benedict; B3.13.1879 Clifton Heights PA; D3.19.1944 Baltimore MD; 5´9˝/165; d4.11																								
1907	StL N	53	197	12	37	5	0	0	6	13	2	—	.188	.245	.213	45	-12	7	.968	-3	92	0	O52(0/16/36)	—	-2.0
Kelly, John	John Francis "Honest John","Father"; B3.3.1859 Paterson NJ; D4.13.1908 Paterson NJ; BR/TR/6´0˝/185; d6.7																								
1879	Cle N	1	4	0	1	0	0	0	0	0	—	0	.250	.250	.250	66	0	—	.571	-1	—	—	/C1	—	-0.1
1882	Cle N	30	104	6	14	2	0	0	5	1	—	24	.135	.143	.154	-5	-12	—	.800	-13	—	—	C30	—	-2.1
1883	Bal AA	48	202	18	46	9	2	0	—	3	—	—	.228	.239	.292	68	-7	—	.803	-16	—	—	C38,O13(0/1/12)	—	-1.9
	Phi N	1	3	0	0	0	0	0	0	0	—	2	.000	.000	.000	-99	-1	—	1.000	1	484	0	/cf	—	0.0
1884	Cin U	38	142	23	40	5	1	1	—	6	—	—	.282	.311	.352	93	-5	—	.865	-3	—	—	C37,O2(0/1/1)	—	-0.5
	Was U	4	14	1	5	1	0	0	—	0	—	—	.357	.357	.429	142	0	—	.967	1	—	—	C3/rf	—	0.1
	Year	42	156	24	45	6	1	1	—	6	—	—	.288	.315	.359	97	-5	—	.874	-2	—	—	C40,O3(0/1/2)	—	-0.4
Total	4	122	469	48	106	17	3	1	5	10	—	26	.226	.242	.281	63	-25	—	.831	-31	—	—	C109,O17(0/3/14)/1	—	-4.5
Kelly, Kick	John O. "Diamond John"; B10.31.1856 New York NY; D3.27.1926 Malba NY; 6´0.5˝/185; d5.1; M2/U4																								
1879	Syr N	10	36	4	4	1	0	0	2	0	—	6	.111	.111	.139	-20	-4	—	.827	-2	—	—	C8,1b2	—	-0.6
	Tro N	6	22	1	5	0	0	0	0	0	—	1	.227	.227	.227	54	-1	—	.789	-2	—	—	C3,O2R/3	—	-0.3
	Year	16	58	5	9	1	0	0	2	0	—	7	.155	.155	.172	9	-5	—	.817	-4	—	—	C11,1b2,O2R/3	—	-0.9
Kelly, Joe	Joseph Henry; B9.23.1886 Weir City KS; D8.16.1977 St.Joseph MO; BR/TR/5´10˝/175; d4.14; Mil 1918																								
1914	Pit N	141	508	47	113	19	9	1	48	39	4	59	.222	.283	.301	77	-16	21	.946	-3	100	90	O139C	—	-3.0
1916	Chi N	54	169	18	43	7	1	2	15	9	1	16	.254	.296	.343	87	-3	10	.953	-1	102	76	O46(16/25/6)	—	-0.7
1917	Bos N	116	445	41	99	9	8	3	36	26	2	45	.222	.268	.299	78	-13	21	.946	6	112	104	O116(87/29/0)	—	-1.5
1918	Bos N	47	155	20	36	2	4	0	15	6	1	12	.232	.265	.297	74	-6	12	.933	-1	102	82	O45(22/18/0)	—	-1.0
1919	Bos N	18	64	3	9	1	0	0	3	0	1	11	.141	.154	.156	-7	-8	2	.943	0	94	146	O16L	—	-1.0
Total	5	376	1341	129	300	38	22	6	117	80	9	143	.224	.272	.298	75	-46	66	.945	1	104	95	O362(141/211/6)	—	-7.2
Kelly, Joe	Joseph James; B4.23.1900 New York NY; D11.24.1967 Lynbrook NY; BL/TL/6´0˝/180; d4.13																								
1926	Chi N	65	176	16	59	15	3	0	32	7	0	11	.335	.361	.455	117	4	0	.953	-3	85	81	O39(25/0/14)	—	-0.2
1928	Chi N	32	52	3	11	1	0	1	7	1	2	3	.212	.255	.288	42	-5	0	.974	-0	112	101	1b10	—	-0.5
Total	2	97	228	19	70	16	3	1	39	8	2	14	.307	.336	.417	100	-1	0	.953	-3	85	81	O39(25/0/14),1b10	—	-0.7

YEAR	TM LG	G	AB	R	H	2B	3B	HR	RBI	BB-IB	HP	SO	AVG	OBP	SLG	AOPS	ABR	SB-CS	FA	FR	RNG	THR	GAMES AT POSITION	DL	BFW
Kelly, Kenny	Kenneth Alphonso; B1.26.1979 Plant City FL; BR/TR/6´3˝/(180–190); [TBA97 2/82]; d9.7; [DL 2002 Sea A 26]																								
2000	TB A	2	1	0	0	0	0	0	0	0-0	0	0	.000	.000	.000	-99	0	0-0	ø	0	—	—	/D	0	0.0
2005	Cin N	7	9	2	3	0	0	0	2	0-0	0	3	.333	.333	.333	75	0	0-1	1.000	0	135	0	O4(1/2/1)	23	-0.1
	Was N	17	4	3	1	1	0	0	0	1-0	0	3	.250	.400	.500	140	0	1-1	ø	-0	0	0	O2R/D	0	0.0
	Year	24	13	5	4	1	0	0	2	1-0	0	6	.308	.357	.385	97	0	1-2	1.000	-0	103	0	O6(1/2/3)/D	0	-0.1
Total	2	26	14	5	4	1	0	0	2	1-0	0	6	.286	.333	.357	82	0	1-2	1.000	-0	103	0	O6(1/2/3),D2	49	-0.1
Kelly, King	Michael Joseph; B12.31.1857 Troy NY; D11.8.1894 Boston MA; BR/TR/5´10˝/170; d5.1; M3; HF1945; OF(2/8/742); ▲																								
1878	Cin N	60	237	29	67	7	1	0	27	7	—	7	.283	.303	.321	116	5	—	.765	8	**199**	118	O47R,C17,3b2	—	1.3
1879	Cin N	77	345	78	120	20	12	2	47	8	—	14	.348	.363	.493	**188**	32	—	.832	10	128	73	3b33,O29(0/2/27),C21/2	—	**3.9**
1880	Chi N	84	344	72	100	17	9	1	60	12	—	22	.291	.315	.401	133	11	—	.779	-1	**203**	41	O64R,C17,3b14/S2P	—	1.0
1881	Chi N	82	353	84	114	**27**	3	2	55	16	—	14	.323	.352	.433	139	16	—	.841	2	170	79	O72R,C11,3b8	—	1.7
1882	Chi N	**84**	377	81	115	**37**	4	1	55	10	—	27	.305	.323	.432	133	14	—	.810	2	90	87	S42,O38R,C12,3b3/1	—	1.5
1883	Chi N	**98**	428	92	109	28	10	3	61	16	—	35	.255	.282	.388	93	-5	—	.813	5	**218**	**174**	O82R,C38,2b3,3b2/P	—	0.1
1884	Chi N	108	452	**120**	160	28	5	13	95	46	—	24	.354	**.414**	.524	178	**41**	—	.794	-5	232	45	O63R,C28,S12,3b10,1b2,P2/2	—	3.3
1885	†Chi N	107	438	**124**	126	24	7	9	75	46	—	24	.288	.355	.436	136	17	—	.867	3	208	117	O69(0/1/69),C37,2b6,3b2,1b2	—	2.1
1886	†Chi N	118	451	**155**	175	32	11	4	79	83	—	33	**.388**	**.483**	.534	182	48	53	.811	7	210	64	O56(0/1/55),C53,1b9,3b8,2b6,S5	—	**5.2**
1887	Bos N	116	484	120	156	34	11	8	63	55	1	40	.322	.393	.488	141	29	84	.856	-14	105	100	O61(1/0/61),2b30,C24,P3,S2,3b2,M	—	1.5
1888	Bos N	107	440	85	140	22	11	9	71	31	4	39	.318	.368	.480	164	31	56	.905	0	—	—	C76,O34R	—	3.7
1889	Bos N	125	507	120	149	**41**	5	9	78	65	2	40	.294	.376	.448	121	15	68	.848	-6	112	109	O113R,C23	—	0.9
1890	Bos P	89	340	83	111	18	6	4	66	52	2	22	.326	.419	.450	124	12	51	.915	6	*154*	*104*	C56,S27,O6(0/2/4),1b4,3b2/PM	—	1.8
1891	Cin AA	82	283	56	84	15	7	1	53	51	2	28	.297	.408	.410	124	10	22	.904	8	*88*	*156*	C66,3b8,O7(0/2/5),2b6,1b5,P3/SM	—	1.9
	Bos AA	4	15	2	4	0	0	1	4	0	0	2	.267	.267	.467	111	0	1	.950	0	*136*	*91*	C4	—	0.0
	Year	86	298	58	88	15	7	2	57	51	2	30	.295	.402	.413	123	10	23	.906	8	*125*	*82*	C70,3b8,O7(0/2/5),2b6,1b5,P3/S	—	1.9
	Bos N	16	52	7	12	1	0	0	5	6	1	10	.231	.322	.250	60	-3	6	.844	-2	*125*	*82*	C11,O6R	—	-0.4
1892	†Bos N	78	281	40	53	7	0	2	41	39	0	32	.189	.287	.235	53	-15	24	.912	6	*133*	*107*	C72,O2(1/0/1),3b2,1b2/P	—	-0.2
1893	NY N	20	67	9	18	1	0	0	15	6	0	5	.269	.329	.284	63	-4	3	.895	-3	*98*	*136*	C17/rf	—	-0.4
Total	16	1455	5894	1357	1813	359	102	69	950	549	12	418	.308	.368	.438	136	254	368	.820	27	179	104	O750R,C583,3b96,S90,2b54,1b25,P12	—	28.9
Kelly, Mike	Michael Raymond; B6.2.1970 Los Angeles CA; BR/TR/6´4˝/(195–200); [AtlN91 1/2]; d4.5; Col Arizona St.																								
1994	Atl N	30	77	14	21	10	1	2	9	2-0	1	17	.273	.300	.506	101	0	0-1	.962	-3	71	0	O25(19/6/1)	0	-0.4
1995	Atl N	97	137	26	26	6	1	3	17	11-0	2	49	.190	.258	.314	48	-11	7-3	.940	-4	90	0	O83(58/8/17)	0	-1.5
1996	Cin N	19	49	5	9	4	0	1	7	9-0	2	11	.184	.333	.327	74	-1	4-0	.972	1	110	128	O17(6/10/1)	0	0.0
1997	Cin N	73	140	27	41	13	2	6	19	10-0	0	30	.293	.338	.543	124	5	6-1	.978	4	138	89	O59(17/11/31)/D	0	0.8
1998	TB A	106	279	39	67	11	2	10	33	22-1	0	80	.240	.295	.401	77	-11	13-6	1.000	-1	96	84	O93(43/0/51),D6	20	-1.3
1999	Col N	2	2	0	1	1	0	0	1	0-0	0	0	.500	.500	1.000	212	0	0-0	ø	-0	0	0	/rf	0	0.0
Total	6	327	684	111	165	45	6	22	86	54-1	5	187	.241	.300	.421	84	-18	30-11	.978	-3	101	61	O278(143/35/102),D7	20	-2.4
Kelly, Pat	Patrick Franklin; B10.14.1967 Philadelphia PA; BR/TR/6´0˝/(180–182); [NYA88 9/235]; d5.20; Col West Chester																								
1991	NY A	96	298	35	72	12	4	3	23	15-0	5	52	.242	.287	.339	73	-12	12-1	.926	3	102	93	3b80,2b19	0	-0.6
1992	NY A	106	318	38	72	22	2	7	27	25-1	10	72	.226	.301	.374	89	-5	8-5	.978	-4	100	92	2b101/D	16	-0.6
1993	NY A	127	406	49	111	24	1	7	51	24-0	5	68	.273	.317	.389	93	-5	14-11	.978	11	110	108	2b125	0	1.1
1994	NY A	93	286	35	80	21	2	3	41	19-1	5	51	.280	.330	.399	91	-3	6-5	.978	5	107	**127**	2b93	15	0.5
1995	†NY A	89	270	32	64	12	1	4	29	23-0	5	65	.237	.307	.333	68	-13	8-3	.983	6	105	100	2b87/D	41	-0.2
1996	NY A	13	21	4	3	0	0	0	2	2-0	0	9	.143	.217	.143	-6	-4	0-1	.970	2	137	69	2b10,D3	147	-0.2
1997	NY A	67	120	25	29	6	1	2	10	14-1	1	37	.242	.324	.358	79	-4	8-1	.981	0	100	123	2b48,D16	39	-0.1
1998	StL N	53	153	18	33	5	0	4	14	13-0	2	48	.216	.284	.327	61	-9	5-1	.964	-1	108	77	2b41,O3L,S2	0	-0.7
1999	Tor A	37	116	17	31	7	0	6	20	10-0	0	23	.267	.318	.483	101	0	0-1	.962	-4	97	76	2b35,D2	0	-0.2
Total	9	681	1988	253	495	109	11	36	217	145-3	33	425	.249	.307	.369	81	-55	61-29	.977	18	105	105	2b559,3b80,D23,O3L,S2	258	-1.0
Kelly, Speed	Robert Brown; B8.19.1884 Bryan OH; D5.6.1949 Goshen IN; BR/TR/6´2˝/185; d7.13; Col Chicago																								
1909	Was A	17	42	3	6	2	1	0	1	3	0	—	.143	.200	.238	40	-3	1	.852	-1	99	207	3b10,2b3/cf	—	-0.4
Kelly, Roberto	Roberto Conrado (Gray) "Bobby"; B10.1.1964 Panama City, Pan; BR/TR/6´2˝/(182–202); d7.29																								
1987	NY A	23	52	12	14	3	0	1	7	5-0	0	15	.269	.328	.385	90	-1	9-3	.955	0	112	0	O17(0/16/1),D2	0	0.0
1988	NY A	38	77	9	19	4	1	1	7	3-0	0	15	.247	.272	.364	78	-3	5-2	.986	2	114	95	O30(1/28/2),D3	64	-0.1
1989	NY A	137	441	65	133	18	3	9	48	41-3	6	89	.302	.369	.417	122	13	35-12	.984	-0	99	124	O137C	17	1.6
1990	NY A	**162**	641	85	183	32	4	15	61	33-0	4	148	.285	.323	.418	105	3	42-17	.988	-2	103	60	O160(11/151/0)/D	0	0.3
1991	NY A	126	486	68	130	22	2	20	69	45-2	5	77	.267	.333	.444	113	8	32-9	.986	-4	91	121	O125(52/73/0)	38	0.5
1992	NY A★	152	580	81	158	31	2	10	66	41-4	4	96	.272	.322	.384	98	-2	28-5	.983	2	103	91	O146(47/99/0)	0	0.2
1993	Cin N★	78	320	44	102	17	3	9	35	17-0	2	43	.319	.354	.475	120	8	21-5	.995	0	102	77	O77C	82	1.2
1994	Cin N	47	179	29	54	8	0	3	21	11-1	3	35	.302	.351	.397	95	-1	9-8	.992	1	108	83	O47C	0	0.0
	Atl N	63	255	44	73	15	3	6	24	24-0	0	36	.286	.345	.439	100	0	10-3	.985	-4	88	94	O63C	0	-0.2
	Year	110	434	73	127	23	3	9	45	35-1	3	71	.293	.347	.422	98	-1	19-11	.988	-3	96	89	O110C	0	-0.2
1995	Mon N	24	95	11	26	4	0	1	9	7-1	2	14	.274	.337	.347	78	-3	4-3	1.000	-3	75	78	O24C	0	-0.6
	†LA N	112	409	47	114	19	2	6	48	15-5	4	65	.279	.306	.379	87	-9	15-7	.969	-8	88	34	O110(61/48/2)	0	-1.8
	Year	136	504	58	140	23	2	7	57	22-6	6	79	.278	.312	.373	85	-12	19-10	.974	-11	86	42	O134(61/72/2)	0	-2.4
1996	Min A	98	322	41	104	17	4	6	47	23-0	7	53	.323	.375	.457	109	4	10-2	.990	-2	101	67	O93(6/40/54),D2	15	0.2
1997	Min A	75	247	39	71	19	2	5	37	17-0	2	50	.287	.336	.441	100	0	7-4	1.000	-3	94	30	O59(1/1/57),D12	15	-0.5
	†Sea A	30	121	19	36	7	0	7	22	5-0	1	17	.298	.328	.529	120	3	2-1	1.000	-0	107	60	O29(28/1/0)/D	0	0.2
	Year	105	368	58	107	26	2	12	59	22-0	3	67	.291	.333	.470	106	3	9-5	1.000	-3	99	41	O88(29/2/57),D13	0	-0.3
1998	†Tex A	75	257	48	83	7	3	16	46	8-0	3	46	.323	.349	.560	125	8	0-2	.976	6	118	133	O71(14/41/31),D2	40	1.1
1999	†Tex A	87	290	41	87	17	1	8	37	21-0	5	57	.300	.355	.448	98	-1	6-1	.981	-3	94	80	O85(18/37/37)	0	-0.4
2000	NY A	10	25	4	3	1	0	1	1	1-0	1	6	.120	.185	.280	16	-3	0-0	1.000	-0	112	0	O10(7/3/0)	165	-0.3
Total	14	1337	4797	687	1390	241	30	124	585	317-16	49	862	.290	.337	.430	105	24	235-84	.985	-18	99	82	O1283(246/886/184),D23	436	1.4
Kelly, Van	Van Howard; B3.18.1946 Charlotte NC; BL/TR/5´11˝/(175–180); d6.13																								
1969	SD N	73	209	16	51	7	1	3	15	12-2	0	24	.244	.285	.330	74	-8	0-1	.971	-2	103	117	3b49,2b10	0	-1.1
1970	SD N	38	89	9	15	3	0	1	9	15-0	0	21	.169	.288	.236	44	-7	0-1	.971	2	104	46	3b27/2	0	-0.6
Total	2	111	298	25	66	10	1	4	24	27-2	0	45	.221	.286	.302	65	-15	0-2	.971	-0	103	94	3b76,2b11	0	-1.7
Kelly, Bill	William Henry "Big Bill"; B12.28.1898 Syracuse NY; D4.8.1990 Syracuse NY; BR/TR/6´0˝/190; d9.6; Col Dean (MA) JC																								
1920	Phi A	9	13	0	3	1	0	0	0	0	0	2	.231	.231	.308	41	-1	0-0	1.000	0	111	0	1b2	—	-0.1
1928	Phi N	23	71	6	12	1	1	0	5	7	0	20	.169	.244	.211	19	-9	0	.991	1	119	88	1b23	—	-0.9
Total	2	32	84	6	15	2	1	0	5	7	0	22	.179	.242	.226	22	-10	0-0	.992	1	119	83	1b25	—	-1.0
Kelly, Bill	William J.; B New York NY; d5.4																								
1871	Kek NA	18	67	16	15	1	1	0	7	6	—	1	.224	.288	.269	60	-3	0-0	.833	0	47	241	O18(1/4/14)	—	-0.1
Kelly, Billy	William Joseph; B5.1.1886 Baltimore MD; D6.3.1940 Detroit MI; BR/TR/6´0.5˝/183; d5.2																								
1910	StL N	2	2	1	0	0	0	0	0	1	0	0	.000	.333	.000	-1	0	0	ø	-0	*0*	*0*	/C	—	0.0
1911	Pit N	6	8	0	1	0	0	0	0	0	0	2	.125	.125	.125	-29	-1	0	1.000	1	*173*	*0*	/C	—	-0.1
1912	Pit N	48	132	20	42	3	2	1	11	2	0	16	.318	.328	.394	99	-1	8	.990	-4	*124*	*66*	C39	—	-0.2
1913	Pit N	48	82	11	22	2	2	0	9	2	2	12	.268	.302	.341	87	-2	1-1	.960	1	98	81	C40	—	0.1
Total	4	104	224	32	65	5	4	1	20	5	2	30	.290	.312	.362	89	-4	9-1	.977	-3	*114*	*71*	C81	—	-0.2
Kelsey, Billy	George William; B8.24.1881 Covington OH; D4.25.1968 Springfield OH; BR/TR/5´10˝/150; d10.4																								
1907	Pit N	2	5	1	2	0	0	0	0	0	0	—	.400	.400	.400	149	0	0	1.000	-0	*142*	*85*	C2	—	0.0
Keltner, Ken	Kenneth Frederick "Butch"; B10.31.1916 Milwaukee WI; D12.12.1991 New Berlin WI; BR/TR/6´0˝/190; d10.2; Mil 1945																								
1937	Cle A	1	1	0	0	0	0	0	1	0	0	0	.000	.000	.000	-99	0	0-0	1.000	0	144	0	/3	—	0.0
1938	Cle A	149	576	86	159	31	9	26	113	33	3	75	.276	.319	.497	103	-3	4-3	.956	-10	90	69	3b149	—	-0.7
1939	Cle A	**154**	587	84	191	35	11	13	97	51	0	41	.325	.379	.489	125	20	6-6	**.974**	5	94	**138**	3b154	—	2.8
1940	Cle A★	149	543	67	138	24	10	15	77	51	3	56	.254	.322	.418	93	-8	10-5	.953	-6	89	105	3b148	—	-0.8
1941	Cle A★	149	581	83	156	31	13	23	84	51	2	56	.269	.330	.485	119	11	2-2	**.971**	20	**108**	**129**	3b149	0	3.5

YEAR	TM LG	G	AB	R	H	2B	3B	HR	RBI	BB-IB	HP	SO	AVG	OBP	SLG	AOPS	ABR	SB-CS	FA	FR	RNG	THR	GAMES AT POSITION	DL	BFW
1942	Cle A★	152	624	72	179	34	4	6	78	20	3	36	.287	.312	.383	101	-3	4-3	**.945**	11	**111**	**135**	3b151	0	1.4
1943	Cle A★	110	427	47	111	31	3	4	39	36	0	20	.260	.317	.375	109	4	2-2	.969	3	104	120	3b107	0	0.9
1944	Cle A★	149	573	74	169	41	9	13	91	53	0	29	.295	.355	.466	139	27	4-3	.968	12	109	120	3b149	0	4.2
1946	Cle A★	116	398	47	96	17	1	13	45	30	0	38	.241	.294	.387	95	-5	0-3	.965	-2	92	77	3b112	0	-0.8
1947	Cle A	151	541	49	139	29	3	11	76	59	1	45	.257	.331	.383	101	0	5-4	.972	-5	95	116	3b150	0	-0.5
1948	†Cle A★	153	558	91	166	24	4	31	119	89	1	52	.297	.395	.522	146	37	2-1	.969	-2	106	105	3b153	0	3.3
1949	Cle A	80	246	35	57	9	2	8	30	38	0	26	.232	.335	.382	91	-4	0-1	.980	-1	108	75	3b69	0	-0.5
1950	Bos A	13	28	2	9	2	0	0	2	3	0	6	.321	.387	.393	91	0	0-0	.947	-1	80	0	3b8/1	0	-0.1
Total	13	1526	5683	737	1570	308	69	163	852	514	13	480	.276	.338	.441	113	76	39-33	.965	26	100	110	3b1500/1	0	12.7
Kelton, David	David Wayne; B12.17.1979 Dothan AL; BR/TR/6´3˝/(195–200); [ChiN98 2/46]; d6.8																								
2003	Chi N	10	12	1	2	1	0	0	1	0-0	0	5	.167	.167	.250	6	-2	0-0	1.000	0	160	0	O2L	0	-0.1
2004	Chi N	8	10	1	1	1	0	0	0	0-0	0	3	.100	.100	.200	-24	-2	0-0	1.000	-0	85	0	O3(2/0/1)	0	-0.2
Total	2	18	22	2	3	2	0	0	1	0-0	0	8	.136	.136	.227	-8	-4	0-0	1.000	0	124	0	O5(4/0/1)	0	-0.3
Kelty, John	John James "Chief"; B3.10.1871 Jersey City NJ; D4.13.1929 Jersey City NJ; 5´10˝/175; d4.19																								
1890	Pit N	59	207	24	49	10	2	1	27	22	4	42	.237	.322	.319	98	1	10	.898	-1	65	40	O59L	—	-0.1
Kemmer, Bill	William Edward (b William Edward Kemmerer); B11.15.1873 PA; D6.8.1945 Washington DC; BR/TR/6´2˝/195; d6.3																								
1895	Lou N	11	38	5	7	0	0	1	3	2	0	4	.184	.225	.263	27	-4	0	.809	1	113	189	3b9,1b2	—	-0.3
Kemmler, Rudy	Rudolph (b Rudolph Kemler); B1860 Chicago IL; D6.20.1909 Chicago IL; BR/TR/5´11˝/206; d7.26																								
1879	Pro N	2	7	0	1	0	0	0	0	0	—	1	.143	.143	.143	-6	-1	—	.833	1	—	—	C2	—	0.0
1881	Cle N	1	3	0	0	0	0	0	0	0	—	1	.000	.000	.000	-99	-1	—	1.000	1	—	—	/C	—	0.0
1882	Cin AA	3	11	0	1	1	0	0	—	0	—	—	.091	.091	.182	-10	-1	—	.909	-0	—	—	C3/rf	—	-0.1
	Pit AA	24	99	7	25	4	0	0	—	1	—	—	.253	.260	.293	90	-1	—	.920	3	—	—	C23/rf	—	0.4
	Year	27	110	7	26	5	0	0	—	1	—	—	.236	.243	.282	79	-2	—	.919	2	—	—	C26,O2R	—	0.3
1883	Col AA	84	318	27	66	6	2	0	—	13	—	—	.208	.239	.239	59	-13	—	.872	-8	—	—	C82,O2C	—	-1.2
1884	Col AA	61	211	28	42	3	3	0	—	15	0	—	.199	.252	.242	67	-6	—	.906	-12	—	—	C58,1b2/lf	—	-1.3
1885	Pit AA	18	64	2	13	2	1	0	5	2	1	—	.203	.239	.266	60	-3	—	.870	-3	—	—	C18	—	-0.4
1886	StL AA	35	123	13	17	2	0	0	6	8	1	—	.138	.197	.154	10	-13	0	.914	4	—	—	C32,1b3	—	-0.6
1889	Col AA	8	26	2	3	0	0	0	0	3	0	3	.115	.207	.115	-8	-4	0	.930	1	—	—	C8	—	-0.2
Total	8	236	862	79	168	18	6	0	<u>11</u>	42	2	<u>5</u>	.195	.234	.230	52	-43	0	.894	-15	—	—	C227,1b5,O5(1/2/2)	—	-3.4
Kemp, Matt	Matthew Ryan; B9.23.1984 Midwest City OK; BR/TR/6´2˝/230; [LAN03 6/181]; d5.28																								
2006	LA N	52	154	30	39	7	1	7	23	9-1	0	53	.253	.289	.448	86	-4	6-0	.929	-6	73	104	O46(11/29/10)	0	-0.8
Kemp, Steve	Steven F; B8.7.1954 San Angelo TX; BL/TL/6´0˝/(190–195); [DetA76*1/1]; d4.7; Col USC																								
1977	Det A	151	552	75	142	29	4	18	88	71-0	5	93	.257	.343	.422	103	4	3-3	.981	-10	84	89	O148L	0	-1.3
1978	Det A	159	582	75	161	18	4	15	79	97-3	1	87	.277	.379	.399	116	16	2-3	.977	-2	93	100	O157L	0	0.7
1979	Det A★	134	490	88	156	26	3	26	105	68-2	2	70	.318	.398	.543	148	35	5-6	.976	-0	92	135	O120(117/0/3),D11	0	2.7
1980	Det A	135	508	88	149	23	3	21	101	69-3	4	64	.293	.376	.474	130	23	5-1	.995	2	106	61	O85L,D46	0	2.0
1981	Det A	105	372	52	103	18	4	9	49	70-5	1	48	.277	.389	.419	129	17	9-3	.986	-2	99	60	O92L,D12	0	1.3
1982	Chi A	160	580	91	166	23	1	19	98	89-8	3	83	.286	.381	.428	122	21	7-7	.976	-12	86	64	O154L,D2	0	0.2
1983	NY A	109	373	53	90	17	3	12	49	41-3	2	37	.241	.318	.399	100	0	1-0	.987	3	109	69	O101(25/0/86),D2	18	-0.3
1984	NY A	94	313	37	91	12	1	7	41	40-0	1	54	.291	.369	.403	118	9	4-1	.972	-5	93	40	O75L,D12	16	0.1
1985	Pit N	92	236	19	59	13	2	2	21	25-1	0	54	.250	.317	.347	88	-4	1-0	1.000	0	105	26	O63L	13	-0.6
1986	Pit N	13	16	1	3	0	0	1	1	4-0	0	6	.188	.350	.375	97	0	1-0	1.000	1	183	0	O4L	0	0.1
1988	Tex A	16	36	2	8	0	0	0	2	2-0	0	9	.222	.256	.222	36	-3	1-0	1.000	-0	91	0	O5(5/0/1)/1D	0	-0.3
Total	11	1168	4058	581	1128	179	25	130	634	576-25	19	605	.278	.367	.431	118	118	39-24	.982	-25	95	78	O1004(925/0/90),D92/1	47	4.6
Kendall, Fred	Fred Lyn; B1.31.1949 Torrance CA; BR/TR/6´1˝/(185–190); [CinN67 4/68]; d9.8; C7; s-Jason																								
1969	SD N	10	26	2	4	0	0	0	0	2-0	0	5	.154	.214	.154	5	-3	0-0	1.000	0	150	103	C9	0	-0.3
1970	SD N	4	9	0	0	0	0	0	1	0-0	0	0	.000	.000	.000	-99	-3	0-0	1.000	-1	93	0	C2/1lf	0	-0.4
1971	SD N	49	111	2	19	1	0	1	7	7-3	0	16	.171	.220	.207	23	-12	1-0	1.000	0	62	91	C39/13	0	-1.1
1972	SD N	91	273	18	59	3	4	6	18	11-3	1	42	.216	.247	.322	66	-15	0-0	.995	1	85	99	C82/1	0	-1.1
1973	SD N	145	507	39	143	22	3	10	59	30-4	1	35	.282	.320	.396	107	3	3-1	.984	-9	100	100	C138	0	0.0
1974	SD N	141	424	32	98	15	2	8	45	49-7	0	33	.231	.308	.333	84	-9	0-1	.983	-18	77	104	C133	0	-2.4
1975	SD N	103	286	16	57	12	1	0	24	26-5	0	28	.199	.265	.248	46	-21	0-1	.977	-10	74	126	C85	0	-2.9
1976	SD N	146	456	30	112	17	0	2	39	36-4	3	42	.246	.302	.296	77	-14	1-1	.994	-11	114	90	C146	0	-2.0
1977	Cle A	103	317	18	79	13	1	3	39	16-1	1	27	.249	.283	.325	68	-14	0-1	.991	-22	68	74	C102/D	0	-3.2
1978	Bos A	20	41	3	8	1	0	0	4	1-0	0	2	.195	.205	.220	20	-4	0-0	1.000	0	134	102	1b13,C5/D	0	-0.5
1979	SD N	46	102	8	17	2	0	1	6	11-2	0	7	.167	.248	.216	29	-10	0-0	.977	1	92	133	C40,1b2	0	-0.9
1980	SD N	19	24	2	7	0	0	0	2	0-0	0	3	.292	.292	.292	68	-1	0-0	.938	-1	85	83	C14/1	0	-0.2
Total	12	877	2576	170	603	86	11	31	244	189-29	6	240	.234	.285	.312	72	-103	5-5	.987	-70	88	99	C795,1b19,D2/3lf	0	-15.0
Kendall, Jason	Jason Daniel; B6.26.1974 San Diego CA; BR/TR/6´0˝/(181–205); [PitN92 1/23]; d4.1; f-Fred																								
1996	Pit N★	130	414	54	124	23	5	3	42	35-11	15	30	.300	.372	.401	101	2	5-2	.980	-6	69	110	C129	0	0.5
1997	Pit N	144	486	71	143	36	4	8	49	49-2	31	53	.294	.391	.434	115	14	18-6	.990	18	110	112	C142	0	4.2
1998	Pit N★	149	535	95	175	36	3	12	75	51-3	**31**	51	.327	.411	.473	132	29	26-5	.992	8	103	79	C144	0	5.0
1999	Pit N	78	280	61	93	20	3	8	41	38-3	12	32	.332	.428	.511	137	19	22-3	.988	13	142	132	C75	91	3.7
2000	Pit N★	152	579	112	185	33	6	14	58	79-3	15	79	.320	.412	.470	123	24	22-12	.991	3	102	92	C147	0	3.5
2001	Pit N	157	606	84	161	22	2	10	53	44-4	20	48	.266	.335	.358	78	-20	13-14	.985	-11	94	85	C133,O27(18/0/10)	0	-2.5
2002	Pit N	145	545	59	154	25	3	3	44	49-1	9	29	.283	.350	.356	85	-10	15-8	.990	-2	100	109	C143	0	-0.3
2003	Pit N	150	587	84	191	29	3	6	58	49-3	25	40	.325	.399	.416	112	14	8-7	.989	-15	114	71	C146	0	0.8
2004	Pit N	147	574	86	183	32	0	3	51	60-2	19	41	.319	.399	.390	106	10	11-8	.991	14	120	126	C146	0	3.2
2005	Oak A	150	601	70	163	28	1	0	53	50-0	20	39	.271	.345	.321	80	-14	8-3	.993	-1	80	65	C147,D3	0	-0.4
2006	†Oak A	143	552	76	163	23	0	1	50	53-2	12	54	.295	.367	.342	88	-7	11-5	.995	6	110	92	C141/D	0	0.8
Total	11	1545	5759	852	1735	307	30	68	574	557-34	209	496	.301	.381	.400	103	61	159-73	.990	27	103	96	C1493,O27(18/0/10),D4	91	18.5
Kenders, Al	Albert Daniel George; B4.4.1937 Barrington NJ; BR/TR/6´0˝/185; d8.14																								
1961	Phi N	10	23	0	4	1	0	0	1	1-0	0	0	.174	.208	.217	13	-3	0-0	1.000	-3	49	65	C10	0	-0.5
Kendrick, Howie	Howard Joseph; B7.12.1983 Jacksonville FL; BR/TR/5´10˝/195; [AnaA02 10/294]; d4.26; Col St.Johns River (FL) CC																								
2006	LA A	72	267	25	76	21	1	4	30	9-2	4	44	.285	.314	.416	91	-4	6-0	.994	1	114	130	1b44,2b28/3D	0	-0.4
Kenna, Eddie	Edward Aloysius "Scrap Iron"; B9.30.1897 San Francisco CA; D8.21.1972 San Francisco CA; BR/TR/5´7.5˝/150; d6.2																								
1928	Was A	41	118	14	35	4	2	1	20	14	1	8	.297	.376	.390	102	1	1-5	.942	-1	*116*	*108*	C33	—	0.0
Kennedy, Adam	Adam Thomas; B1.10.1976 Riverside CA; BL/TR/6´1˝/(180–192); [StLN97 1/20]; d8.21; Col Cal St.–Northridge																								
1999	StL N	33	102	12	26	10	1	1	16	3-0	2	8	.255	.284	.402	71	-5	0-1	.971	-2	91	78	2b29	0	-0.6
2000	Ana A	156	598	82	159	33	11	9	72	28-5	3	73	.266	.300	.403	74	-26	22-8	.976	-13	96	100	2b155	0	-2.7
2001	Ana A	137	478	48	129	25	3	6	40	27-3	11	71	.270	.318	.372	81	-13	12-7	.984	2	107	81	2b131,D5	12	-0.5
2002	†Ana A	144	474	65	148	32	6	7	52	19-1	7	80	.312	.345	.449	112	7	17-4	.983	9	101	**120**	2b139/cfD	0	2.4
2003	Ana A	143	449	71	121	17	1	13	49	45-4	9	73	.269	.344	.399	100	1	22-9	**.990**	-3	97	96	2b140/D	15	0.6
2004	Ana A	144	468	70	130	20	5	10	48	41-7	13	92	.278	.351	.406	101	1	15-5	.982	-10	92	83	2b144	0	0.0
2005	†LA A	129	416	49	125	23	0	2	37	29-1	7	64	.300	.354	.370	97	-1	19-4	.991	-12	93	91	2b127	29	-0.3
2006	LA A	139	451	50	123	26	6	4	55	39-5	5	72	.273	.334	.384	89	-7	16-10	.984	-16	92	89	2b133,D2	0	-1.6
Total	8	1025	3436	447	961	186	33	52	369	231-26	57	533	.280	.332	.398	92	-43	123-48	.983	-45	97	94	2b998,D9/cf	56	-2.7
Kennedy, Ed	Edward; B4.1.1856 Carbondale PA; D5.20.1905 New York NY; 5´6˝/150; d5.1																								
1883	NY AA	94	356	57	78	6	7	2	—	17	—	—	.219	.255	.292	72	-12	—	.884	-8	54	0	O94L	—	-1.9
1884	†NY AA	103	378	49	72	6	2	1	—	16	1	—	.190	.225	.225	49	-21	—	.915	7	68	165	O100(99/1/0)/S2C	—	-1.5
1885	NY AA	96	349	35	71	8	4	2	21	12	4	—	.203	.238	.266	62	-15	—	.841	2	94	32	O96(95/1/0)	—	-1.4
1886	Bro AA	6	22	1	4	0	0	0	2	2	0	—	.182	.250	.182	36	-2	1	.909	-0	0	0	O6(3/4/0)	—	-0.2
Total	4	299	1105	142	225	20	13	5	<u>23</u>	47	5	—	.204	.239	.259	60	-50	1	.878	1	71	66	O296(291/6/0)/C2S	—	-5.0

YEAR	TM LG	G	AB	R	H	2B	3B	HR	RBI	BB-IB	HP	SO	AVG	OBP	SLG	AOPS	ABR	SB-CS	FA	FR	RNG	THR	GAMES AT POSITION	DL	BFW
Kennedy, Jim	James Earl; B11.1.1946 Tulsa OK; BL/TR/5´9˝/160; d6.14; b–Junior																								
1970	StL N	12	24	1	3	0	0	0	0	0-0	0	0	.125	.125	.125	-32	-5	0-0	.909	-1	88	80	S7,2b5	0	-0.5
Kennedy, John	John Edward; B5.29.1941 Chicago IL; BR/TR/6´0˝/185; d9.5; Mil 1968																								
1962	Was A	14	42	6	11	0	1	1	2	2-0	0	7	.262	.295	.381	81	-1	0-1	.974	-1	96	72	S9,3b2	0	-0.2
1963	Was A	36	62	3	11	1	1	0	4	6-0	1	22	.177	.261	.226	38	-5	2-0	.954	3	125	110	3b26,S2	0	-0.2
1964	Was A	148	482	55	111	16	4	7	35	29-2	5	119	.230	.280	.324	68	-22	3-3	.941	5	111	90	3b106,S49,2b2	0	-1.5
1965	†LA N	104	105	12	18	3	0	1	5	8-1	2	33	.171	.243	.229	36	-9	1-0	.971	-6	78	91	3b95,S5	0	-1.5
1966	†LA N	125	274	15	55	9	2	3	24	10-1	5	64	.201	.241	.281	49	-20	1-2	.965	-3	104	102	3b87,S28,2b15	0	-2.2
1967	NY A	78	179	22	35	4	0	1	17	17-0	1	35	.196	.265	.235	52	-11	2-1	.915	-4	103	99	S36,3b34,2b2	0	-1.3
1969	Sea A	61	128	18	30	3	1	4	14	14-1	1	25	.234	.315	.367	91	-2	4-0	.916	-1	86	99	S33,3b23	65	0.0
1970	Mil A	25	55	8	14	2	0	2	6	5-0	0	9	.255	.317	.400	96	0	0-1	.921	-7	73	70	2b16,3b5,S4/1	0	-0.7
	Bos A	43	129	15	33	7	1	4	17	6-1	1	14	.256	.292	.419	88	-2	0-0	.960	3	110	66	3b33,2b2	0	0.1
	Year	68	184	23	47	9	1	6	23	11-1	1	23	.255	.299	.413	91	-3	0-1	.962	-4	111	95	3b38,2b18,S4/1	0	-0.6
1971	Bos A	74	272	41	75	12	5	5	22	14-0	4	42	.276	.320	.412	99	-1	1-1	.974	-15	89	73	2b37,S33,3b5	0	-1.1
1972	Bos A	71	212	22	52	11	1	2	22	18-4	3	40	.245	.311	.335	88	-3	0-1	.962	-7	100	128	2b32,S27,3b11	0	-0.6
1973	Bos A	67	155	17	28	9	1	1	16	12-0	2	45	.181	.246	.271	44	-12	0-0	.980	-1	93	129	2b31,3b24,D9	0	-1.1
1974	Bos A	10	15	3	2	0	0	1	1	1-0	0	6	.133	.188	.333	44	-1	0-0	.778	-2	85	139	2b6,3b4	0	-0.3
Total	12	856	2110	237	475	77	17	32	185	142-10	25	461	.225	.281	.323	70	-89	14-10	.953	-36	102	93	3b455,S226,2b143,D9/1	65	-10.6
Kennedy, John	John Irvin; B10.12.1926 Jacksonville FL; D4.27.1998 Jacksonville FL; BR/TR/5´10˝/175; d4.22																								
1957	Phi N	5	2	1	0	0	0	0	0	0-0	0	1	.000	.000	.000	-99	-1	0-0	.500	0	113	1293	3b2	0	-0.1
Kennedy, Junior	Junior Raymond; B8.9.1950 Fort Gibson OK; BR/TR/6´0˝/(175–185); [BalA68 1/10]; d8.9; b–Jim																								
1974	Cin N	22	19	2	3	0	0	0	0	6-1	0	4	.158	.360	.158	49	-1	0-0	.909	-4	64	30	2b17,3b5	0	-0.5
1978	Cin N	89	157	22	40	2	2	0	11	31-2	1	28	.255	.381	.293	90	0	4-1	.979	-2	99	93	2b71,3b4	0	0.1
1979	Cin N	83	220	29	60	7	0	1	17	28-0	0	31	.273	.355	.318	85	-3	4-3	.980	-4	100	94	2b59,S5,3b4	0	-0.4
1980	Cin N	104	337	31	88	16	3	1	34	36-6	0	34	.261	.325	.335	88	-4	3-1	.988	1	102	91	2b103	0	0.2
1981	Cin N	27	44	5	11	1	0	0	5	1-0	0	5	.250	.255	.273	53	-3	0-0	.980	-1	87	142	2b16,3b5	0	-0.3
1982	Chi N	105	242	22	53	3	1	2	25	21-1	0	34	.219	.278	.264	51	-16	1-4	.978	-2	106	87	2b71,S28,3b7	0	-1.5
1983	Chi N	17	22	3	3	0	0	0	3	1-0	0	6	.136	.167	.136	-12	-3	0-0	1.000	-0	110	90	2b7,3b4/S	0	-0.4
Total	7	447	1041	114	258	29	6	4	95	124-10	1	142	.248	.325	.299	75	-30	12-9	.982	-11	101	92	2b344,S34,3b29	0	-2.8
Kennedy, Doc	Michael Joseph; B8.11.1853 Brooklyn NY; D5.23.1920 Grove NY; BR/TR/5´9.5˝/185; d5.1																								
1879	Cle N	49	193	19	56	8	2	1	18	2	—	10	.290	.297	.368	119	4	—	.891	3	—	—	C46,1b4	—	0.7
1880	Cle N	66	250	26	50	10	1	0	18	5	—	12	.200	.216	.248	58	-10	—	.899	-2	—	—	C65,O2(1/1/0)	—	-1.0
1881	Cle N	39	150	19	47	7	1	0	15	5	—	13	.313	.335	.373	129	5	—	.920	2	—	—	C35,O3(2/1/0)/3	—	0.7
1882	Cle N	1	3	0	1	0	0	0	0	1	—	0	.333	.500	.333	180	0	—	.857	2	—	—	/C	—	0.2
1883	Buf N	5	19	3	6	0	0	0	2	2	—	2	.316	.381	.316	113	0	—	.583	-2	0	0	O4(1/3/0)/1	—	-0.2
Total	5	160	615	67	160	25	4	1	53	15	—	37	.260	.278	.319	98	-1	—	.901	4	—	—	C147,O9(4/5/0),1b5/3	—	0.4
Kennedy, Ray	Raymond Lincoln; B5.19.1895 Pittsburgh PA; D1.18.1969 Casselberry FL; BR/TR/5´9˝/165; d9.8																								
1916	StL A	1	1	0	0	0	0	0	0	0	0	0	.000	.000	.000	-99	0	0	ø	0	—	—	/H	—	0.0
Kennedy, Bob	Robert Daniel; B8.18.1920 Chicago IL; D4.7.2005 Mesa AZ; BR/TR/6´2˝/(190–193); d9.14; Mil 1942–45, 1952; M4/C5; s–Terry; OF(204/30/601)																								
1939	Chi A	3	8	0	2	0	0	0	1	0	0	0	.250	.250	.250	27	-1	0-0	.750	-1	90	0	3b2	—	-0.1
1940	Chi A	154	606	74	153	23	3	3	52	42	0	58	.252	.301	.315	59	-37	3-7	.938	-5	97	94	3b154	—	-3.7
1941	Chi A	76	257	16	53	9	3	1	29	17	0	23	.206	.255	.276	41	-23	5-3	.934	0	102	100	3b71	0	-2.0
1942	Chi A	113	412	37	95	18	5	0	38	22	0	41	.231	.270	.299	61	-23	11-7	.956	7	110	101	3b96,O16(13/0/3)	0	-1.5
1946	Chi A	113	411	43	106	13	5	5	34	24	1	42	.258	.300	.350	85	-11	6-8	.965	4	95	194	O75(59/12/4),3b29	0	-1.4
1947	Chi A	115	428	47	112	19	3	6	48	18	0	38	.262	.291	.362	84	-12	3-4	.968	-4	93	103	O106(14/1/91)/3	0	-2.1
1948	Chi A	30	113	4	28	8	1	0	14	4	0	17	.248	.274	.336	64	-6	0-2	.970	0	97	141	O30(25/0/5)	0	-0.9
	†Cle A	66	73	10	22	3	2	0	5	4	0	6	.301	.338	.397	98	-1	0-0	1.000	2	107	173	O50(2/0/48),2b2/1	0	0.0
	Year	96	186	14	50	11	3	0	19	8	0	23	.269	.299	.360	77	-7	0-2	.981	2	101	152	O80(27/0/53),2b2/1	0	-0.9
1949	Cle A	121	424	49	117	23	5	9	57	37	0	40	.276	.334	.417	100	-2	5-5	.990	4	100	131	O98(1/0/98),3b21	0	-0.2
1950	Cle A	146	540	79	157	27	5	9	54	53	1	31	.291	.355	.409	99	-2	3-4	.987	2	102	108	O144(0/10/138)	0	-0.5
1951	Cle A	108	321	30	79	15	4	7	29	34	1	33	.246	.320	.383	95	-3	4-2	.968	2	101	143	O106(1/0/105)	0	-0.4
1952	Cle A	22	40	6	12	3	1	0	12	9	0	5	.300	.429	.425	148	3	1-0	1.000	2	120	0	O13(1/5/8),3b3	0	0.5
1953	Cle A	100	161	22	38	5	0	3	22	19	1	11	.236	.320	.323	76	-5	0-2	1.000	0	107	57	O89(42/2/52)	0	-0.8
1954	Cle A	1	0	0	0	0	0	0	0	0	0	0	ø	ø	ø	ø	0	0-0	ø	-0	0	0	/If	0	0.0
	Bal A	106	323	37	81	13	2	6	45	28	0	43	.251	.306	.359	90	-6	2-1	.938	-4	95	73	3b71,O21(12/0/9)	0	-1.1
	Year	107	323	37	81	13	2	6	45	28	0	43	.251	.306	.359	90	-6	2-1	.938	-4	95	73	3b71,O22(13/0/9)	0	-1.1
1955	Bal A	26	70	10	10	1	0	0	5	10-0	0	10	.143	.250	.157	12	-9	0-1	1.000	-0	111	0	O14R,1b6/3	0	-1.0
	Chi A	83	214	28	65	10	2	9	43	16-0	0	16	.304	.352	.495	122	6	0-2	.938	-6	85	132	3b55,O20(4/0/16),1b3	0	-0.2
	Year	109	284	38	75	11	2	9	48	26-0	0	26	.264	.326	.412	97	-2	0-3	.938	-7	85	131	3b56,O34(4/0/30),1b9	0	-1.2
1956	Chi A	8	13	0	1	0	0	0	0	2-0	0	4	.077	.200	.077	-24	-2	0-0	1.000	-0	53	393	3b6	0	-0.3
	Det A	70	177	17	41	5	0	4	22	24-2	2	19	.232	.328	.328	74	-6	2-2	.931	-3	111	113	O30(21/0/9),3b27	0	-1.0
	Year	78	190	17	42	5	0	4	22	26-2	2	23	.221	.320	.311	67	-9	2-2	.909	-3	76	92	3b33,O30(21/0/9)	0	-1.3
1957	Chi A	4	2	0	0	0	0	0	0	0-0	0	1	.000	.000	.000	-99	-1	0-0	ø	0	—	—	/H	0	-0.1
	Bro N	19	31	5	4	1	0	1	4	1-0	0	5	.129	.156	.258	8	-4	0-0	1.000	-2	44	0	O9(8/0/1),3b3	0	-0.6
Total	16	1484	4624	514	1176	196	41	63	514	364-2	6	443	.254	.309	.355	80	-145	45-50	.978	-3	100	117	O822R,3b540,1b10,2b2	0	-17.4
Kennedy, Sherman	Sherman Montgomery; B11.1.1878 Conneaut OH; D8.15.1945 Pasadena TX; BB/TR/5´10˝/165; d5.1																								
1902	Chi N	1	5	0	0	0	0	0	0	0	0	—	.000	.000	.000	-99	-1	0	1.000	-0	0	0	/cf	—	-0.2
Kennedy, Terry	Terrence Edward; B6.4.1956 Euclid OH; BL/TR/6´3˝/(220–230); [StLN77 1/6]; d9.4; f–Bob; Col Florida St.																								
1978	StL N	10	29	0	5	0	0	0	2	4-2	0	3	.172	.273	.172	27	-3	0-0	.980	-0	130	65	C10	0	-0.3
1979	StL N	33	109	11	31	7	0	2	17	6-2	0	20	.284	.319	.404	95	-1	0-0	.993	-5	85	67	C32	0	-0.5
1980	StL N	84	248	28	63	12	3	4	34	28-3	0	34	.254	.325	.375	92	-2	0-0	.967	-4	76	78	C41,O28L	0	-0.6
1981	SD N★	101	382	32	115	24	1	2	41	22-6	2	53	.301	.341	.385	116	7	0-2	.964	-8	96	121	C100	0	0.4
1982	SD N	153	562	75	166	42	1	21	97	26-9	5	91	.295	.328	.486	134	23	1-0	.990	-11	121	65	C139,1b12	0	1.9
1983	SD N☆	149	549	47	156	27	2	17	98	51-15	2	89	.284	.342	.434	119	13	1-3	.986	-7	92	101	C143,1b4	0	1.2
1984	†SD N	148	530	54	127	16	1	14	57	33-8	2	99	.240	.284	.353	78	-17	1-2	.982	-8	119	71	C147	0	-2.1
1985	SD N★	143	532	54	139	27	1	10	74	31-10	0	102	.261	.301	.372	88	-10	0-0	.986	6	113	110	C140,1b5	0	0.2
1986	SD N	141	432	46	114	22	1	12	57	37-7	2	74	.264	.324	.403	102	0	0-3	.990	1	104	95	C123	0	0.6
1987	Bal A★	143	512	51	128	13	1	18	62	35-6	1	112	.250	.299	.385	81	-15	1-0	.993	-10	95	106	C142	0	-1.8
1988	Bal A	85	265	20	60	10	0	3	16	15-0	1	53	.226	.269	.298	60	-14	0-0	.994	-13	78	112	C79	0	-2.4
1989	†SF N	125	355	19	85	15	0	5	34	35-7	0	56	.239	.306	.324	83	-8	1-3	.986	3	128	101	C121,1b2	0	0.0
1990	SF N	107	303	25	84	22	0	2	26	31-7	0	38	.277	.342	.370	100	1	1-2	.991	-11	122	78	C103	0	-0.6
1991	SF N	69	171	12	40	7	1	3	13	11-4	1	31	.234	.283	.339	77	-6	0-0	.978	-3	87	190	C58,1b2	0	-0.6
Total	14	1491	4979	474	1313	244	12	113	628	365-86	16	855	.264	.314	.386	96	-32	6-15	.985	-69	105	97	C1378,O28L,1b25	0	-4.6
Kennedy, Ed	William Edward; B4.5.1861 Bellevue KY; D12.22.1912 Cheyenne WY; BR/TR/5´7˝/160; d5.17																								
1884	Cin U	13	48	6	10	1	1	0	—	1	—	—	.208	.224	.271	46	-5	—	.857	0	97	143	3b8,S4/rf	—	-0.4
Kenney, Jerry	Gerald T; B6.30.1945 St.Louis MO; BL/TR/6´1˝/(160–170); d9.5; Mil 1968																								
1967	NY A	20	58	4	18	2	0	1	5	10-0	0	8	.310	.412	.397	145	4	2-1	.952	-2	98	51	S18	0	0.3
1969	NY A	130	447	49	115	14	2	2	34	48-2	1	36	.257	.328	.311	83	-9	25-14	.975	14	122	133	3b83,O31C,S10	0	0.5
1970	NY A	140	404	46	78	10	7	4	35	52-2	0	44	.193	.284	.282	60	-23	20-6	.960	16	**122**	80	3b135,2b2	0	-0.5
1971	NY A	120	325	50	85	10	3	0	20	56-3	1	38	.262	.368	.311	100	3	9-8	.953	10	119	111	3b109,S5/1	0	1.2
1972	NY A	50	119	16	25	2	0	0	7	16-2	0	13	.210	.304	.227	61	-5	3-0	.969	3	112	136	S45/3	0	0.3
1973	Cle A	5	16	0	4	0	1	0	2	2-0	0	0	.250	.316	.375	97	0	0-0	1.000	-1	94	31	2b5	0	-0.1
Total	6	465	1369	165	325	38	13	7	103	184-9	2	139	.237	.326	.299	81	-30	59-29	.962	40	121	104	3b328,S78,O31C,2b7/1	0	1.7

YEAR	TM LG	G	AB	R	H	2B	3B	HR	RBI	BB-IB	HP	SO	AVG	OBP	SLG	AOPS	ABR	SB-CS	FA	FR	RNG	THR	GAMES AT POSITION	DL	BFW
Kenney, John	John; d5.2																								
1872	Atl NA	5	19	0	0	0	0	0	1	0	—	1	.000	.000	.000	-85	-4	0-0	.692	-2	76	125	2b3,O3(2/0/1)	—	-0.5
Kent, Jeff	Jeffrey Franklin; B3.7.1968 Bellflower CA; BR/TR/6´1˝/(185–220); [TorA89 20/523]; d4.12; Col California																								
1992	Tor A	65	192	36	46	13	1	8	35	20-0	6	47	.240	.324	.443	109	3	2-1	.915	-3	87	43	3b49,2b17,1b3	0	0.0
	NY N	37	113	16	27	8	1	3	15	7-0	1	29	.239	.289	.407	96	-1	0-2	.980	1	95	99	2b34/3S	0	0.0
1993	NY N	140	496	65	134	24	0	21	80	30-2	8	88	.270	.320	.446	104	2	4-4	.969	-20	90	92	2b127,3b12,S2	0	-1.2
1994	NY N	107	415	53	121	24	5	14	68	23-3	10	84	.292	.341	.475	112	6	1-4	.976	-6	101	114	2b107	0	0.5
1995	NY N	125	472	65	131	22	3	20	65	29-3	8	89	.278	.327	.464	110	5	3-3	.984	-8	100	94	2b122	15	0.3
1996	NY N	89	335	45	97	20	1	9	39	21-1	1	56	.290	.331	.436	106	2	4-3	.925	11	116	132	3b89	0	1.3
	†Cle A	39	102	16	27	7	0	3	16	10-0	1	22	.265	.328	.422	90	-1	2-1	.992	1	93	116	1b20,2b9,3b6,D5	0	-0.1
1997	†SF N	155	580	90	145	38	2	29	121	48-6	13	133	.250	.316	.472	107	4	11-3	.979	19	110	116	2b148,1b13	0	2.9
1998	SF N	137	526	94	156	37	3	31	128	48-4	9	110	.297	.359	.555	145	33	9-4	.972	5	**108**	103	2b134/1	30	4.4
1999	SF N★	138	511	86	148	40	2	23	101	61-3	5	112	.290	.366	.511	128	23	13-6	.984	-9	93	107	2b133/1	18	1.9
2000	†SF N★	159	587	114	196	41	7	33	125	90-6	9	107	.334	.424	.596	166	63	12-9	.986	1	103	104	2b150,1b16	0	6.4
2001	SF N★	159	607	84	181	49	6	22	106	65-4	11	96	.298	.369	.507	133	32	7-6	.987	8	**110**	110	2b140,1b30	0	4.2
2002	†SF N	152	623	102	195	42	2	37	108	52-3	4	101	.313	.368	.565	147	40	5-1	.978	2	102	**125**	2b149,1b9	6	4.8
2003	Hou N	130	505	77	150	39	1	22	93	39-2	5	85	.297	.351	.509	115	11	6-2	.983	1	96	100	2b128	21	1.9
2004	†Hou N★	145	540	96	156	34	8	27	107	49-3	6	96	.289	.348	.531	121	16	7-3	.989	7	95	88	2b139,D2	0	2.9
2005	LA N★	149	553	100	160	36	0	29	105	72-8	8	85	.289	.377	.512	130	26	6-2	.978	8	104	99	2b140,1b14	0	3.9
2006	†LA N	115	407	61	119	27	3	14	68	55-8	8	69	.292	.385	.477	119	14	1-2	.985	9	109	109	2b108,1b9	36	2.6
Total	15	2041	7564	1200	2189	501	45	345	1380	719-56	113	1409	.289	.356	.504	125	278	93-56	.981	28	102	104	2b1785,3b157,1b116,D7,S3	126	36.7
Kenworthy, Dick	Richard Lee; B4.1.1941 Red Oak IA; BR/TR/5´9˝/(165–170); d9.8; Col Missouri																								
1962	Chi A	3	4	0	0	0	0	0	0	0-0	0	3	.000	.000	.000	-99	-1	0-0	1.000	1	159	346	2b2	0	0.0
1964	Chi A	2	2	0	0	0	0	0	0	0-0	0	1	.000	.000	.000	-99	-1	0-0	ø	0	—	—	/H	0	-0.1
1965	Chi A	3	1	0	0	0	0	0	0	1-0	1	0	.000	.667	.000	113	0	0-0	ø	0	—	—	/H	0	0.0
1966	Chi A	9	25	1	5	0	0	0	0	0-0	0	0	.200	.200	.200	16	-3	0-0	.875	-3	66	0	3b6	0	-0.6
1967	Chi A	50	97	9	22	4	1	4	11	4-0	1	17	.227	.262	.412	101	-1	0-2	.971	-2	100	28	3b35	0	-0.4
1968	Chi A	58	122	2	27	2	0	0	2	5-0	0	21	.221	.252	.238	48	-8	0-1	.938	-1	111	56	3b38	0	-1.1
Total	6	125	251	12	54	6	1	4	13	10-0	2	42	.215	.250	.295	63	-14	0-3	.948	-5	103	40	3b79,2b2	0	-2.2
Kenworthy, Bill	William Jennings "Duke"; B7.4.1886 Cambridge OH; D9.21.1950 Eureka CA; BB/TR/5´7˝/165; d8.28																								
1912	Was A	12	38	6	9	1	0	0	2	2	1	—	.237	.293	.263	59	-2	3	1.000	1	80	261	O12(7/5/0)	—	-0.2
1914	KC F	146	545	93	173	40	14	15	91	36	**11**	44	.317	.372	.525	148	26	37	.952	22	100	**143**	2b145	—	5.1
1915	KC F	122	396	59	118	30	7	3	52	28	7	32	.298	.355	.432	126	7	20	.936	-4	97	93	2b108,O7R	—	0.5
1917	StL A	5	10	1	1	0	0	0	1	1	0	1	.100	.182	.100	-14	-1	1	.889	1	118	226	2b4	—	-0.1
Total	4	285	989	159	301	71	21	18	146	67	19	77	.304	.360	.473	135	30	61	.945	20	99	123	2b257,O19(7/5/7)	—	5.3
Keough, Joe	Joseph William; B1.7.1946 Pomona CA; BL/TL/6´0˝/185; [OakA65 2/21]; d8.7; b–Marty; Col Mt. San Antonio (CA) JC																								
1968	Oak A	34	98	7	21	2	1	2	18	8-0	0	11	.214	.274	.316	82	-3	1-0	.962	1	106	127	O29(28/0/1)/1	0	-0.3
1969	KC A	70	166	17	31	2	0	0	7	13-0	2	13	.187	.254	.199	28	-16	5-2	1.000	-0	104	73	O49(3/26/21)/1	0	-1.9
1970	KC A	57	183	28	59	6	2	4	21	23-3	0	18	.322	.396	.443	131	8	1-1	.985	0	102	91	O34(18/1/15),1b18	95	0.5
1971	KC A	110	351	34	87	14	2	3	30	35-5	1	26	.248	.316	.325	83	-8	0-6	.982	-6	88	63	O100(1/7/93)	0	-2.2
1972	KC A	56	64	8	14	2	0	0	5	8-1	2	7	.219	.324	.250	73	-2	2-0	1.000	-1	58	125	O16(9/2/5)	0	-0.4
1973	Chi A	5	1	1	0	0	0	0	0	0-0	0	0	.000	.000	.000	-97	0	0-0	ø	0	—	—	/H	0	0.0
Total	6	332	863	95	212	26	5	9	81	87-9	5	75	.246	.317	.319	82	-21	9-9	.984	-7	94	81	O228(59/36/135),1b20	95	-4.3
Keough, Marty	Richard Martin; B4.14.1934 Oakland CA; BL/TL/6´0˝/(180–181); d4.21; b–Joe s–Matt																								
1956	Bos A	3	2	1	0	0	0	0	0	1-0	0	0	.000	.333	.000	-5	0	0-0	ø	0	—	—	/H	0	0.0
1957	Bos A	9	17	1	1	0	0	0	0	4-0	0	3	.059	.238	.059	-14	-3	0-0	1.000	1	153	0	O7(0/2/5)	0	-0.2
1958	Bos A	68	118	21	26	3	3	1	9	7-0	0	29	.220	.262	.322	57	-7	1-1	.974	-4	84	0	O25(1/21/3),1b2	0	-1.3
1959	Bos A	96	251	40	61	13	5	7	27	26-0	3	40	.243	.320	.418	97	-1	3-1	.993	1	104	131	O69C,1b3	0	-0.2
1960	Bos A	38	105	15	26	6	1	1	9	8-1	0	8	.248	.296	.352	73	-4	2-2	1.000	1	99	204	O29(1/28/0)	0	-0.5
	Cle A	65	149	19	37	5	0	3	11	9-0	1	23	.248	.294	.342	74	-6	2-3	.986	-2	91	96	O42(2/25/16)	0	-1.0
	Year	103	254	34	63	11	1	4	20	17-1	1	31	.248	.295	.346	74	-10	4-5	.992	-1	94	142	O71(3/53/16)	0	-1.5
1961	Was A	135	390	57	97	18	9	9	34	32-1	2	60	.249	.307	.410	92	-6	12-5	.978	4	109	106	O100(63/25/18),1b10	0	-0.7
1962	Cin N	111	230	34	64	8	2	7	27	21-4	4	31	.278	.346	.422	102	1	3-1	.968	4	107	65	O71(48/17/10),1b29	0	0.2
1963	Cin N	95	172	21	39	8	2	6	21	25-4	4	37	.227	.337	.401	109	3	1-4	.992	0	122	114	1b46,O28(4/3/22)	0	-0.1
1964	Cin N	109	276	29	71	9	1	9	28	22-1	1	58	.257	.314	.395	95	-2	1-2	.991	-2	95	91	O81(1/11/71),1b4	0	-0.9
1965	Cin N	62	43	14	5	0	0	0	3	3-0	1	14	.116	.191	.116	-10	-6	0-0	.988	-0	80	51	1b32,O4(3/0/1)	0	-0.8
1966	Atl N	17	17	1	1	0	0	0	1	1-0	0	6	.059	.111	.059	-50	-3	0-0	1.000	-1	0	0	1b4,O3(2/0/1)	0	-0.5
	Chi N	33	26	3	6	1	0	0	5	5-0	1	9	.231	.375	.269	82	0	1-0	1.000	-0	65	0	O5(2/2/1)	0	0.0
	Year	50	43	4	7	1	0	0	6	6-0	1	15	.163	.280	.186	32	-4	1-0	.667	-1	51	0	O8(4/2/2),1b4	0	-0.5
Total	11	841	1796	256	434	71	23	43	176	164-11	17	318	.242	.309	.379	86	-34	26-19	.984	3	101	95	O464(127/203/148),1b130	0	-6.0
Keppinger, Jeff	Jeffrey Scott; B4.21.1980 Miami FL; BR/TR/6´0˝/180; [PitN01 4/114]; d8.20; Col Georgia; [DL 2005 NY N 24]																								
2004	NY N	33	116	9	33	2	0	3	9	6-0	0	7	.284	.317	.379	82	-4	2-1	.987	1	107	104	2b32	0	-0.1
2006	KC A	22	60	11	16	2	0	2	8	5-1	0	6	.267	.323	.400	87	-1	0-0	.947	1	114	105	3b12,1b4/2lfD	0	0.0
Total	2	55	176	20	49	4	0	5	17	11-1	0	13	.278	.319	.386	84	-5	2-1	.987	2	107	109	2b33,3b12,1b4,D3/lf	24	-0.1
Kerins, John	John Nelson; B7.15.1858 Indianapolis IN; D9.8.1919 Louisville KY; BR/TR/5´10˝/177; d5.1; M2/U3; OF(13/9/49)																								
1884	Ind AA	94	364	58	78	10	3	6	—	6	1	—	.214	.229	.308	76	-10	—	**.972**	6	**142**	47	1b87,C5,O5(0/2/3)/3	—	-1.0
1885	Lou AA	**112**	456	65	111	9	16	3	51	20	4	—	.243	.281	.353	100	-2	—	.947	3	111	100	1b96,C19,O3R/3	—	-0.5
1886	Lou AA	120	487	113	131	19	9	4	50	66	3	—	.269	.360	.370	122	13	26	.933	**28**	—	—	C65,1b47,O7(2/2/3)/S	—	3.7
1887	Lou AA	112	476	101	140	18	**19**	5	57	38	2	—	.294	.349	.443	118	8	49	.970	14	78	79	1b74,C35,O5(1/1/3)	—	1.6
1888	Lou AA	83	319	38	75	11	4	2	41	25	3	—	.235	.297	.313	98	0	16	.844	-4	29	64	O47(10/2/35),C33,1b4,3b2/2M	—	-0.2
1889	Lou AA	2	9	2	3	1	0	0	3	0	0	1	.333	.333	.444	123	0	0	.500	-1	0	0	O2R/C	—	0.0
	Bal AA	16	53	7	15	2	0	0	12	2	1	4	.283	.321	.321	82	-1	2	.981	-1	131	28	1b9,C4,O2C/S	—	-0.2
	Year	18	62	9	18	3	0	0	15	2	1	5	.290	.323	.339	87	-1	2	.981	-2	131	28	1b9,C5,O4(0/2/2)/S	—	-0.2
1890	StL AA	18	63	8	8	2	0	0	3	8	0	—	.127	.225	.159	12	-7	2	.968	1	148	143	1b17/CM	—	-0.7
Total	7	557	2227	392	561	72	51	20	217	165	14	5	.252	.308	.357	102	1	95	.963	47	—	—	1b334,C163,O71R,3b4,S2/2	—	2.7
Kerlin, Orie	Orie Milton "Cy"; B1.23.1891 Summerfield LA; D10.29.1974 Shreveport LA; BL/TR/5´7˝/149; d6.6; Col Louisiana St.																								
1915	Pit F	3	1	0	0	0	0	0	0	0	0	0	.000	.000	.000	-99	0	0	ø	-0	*0*	*0*	C3	—	0.0
Kern, Bill	William George; B2.28.1933 Coplay PA; BR/TR/6´2˝/185; d9.19; Col Muhlenberg																								
1962	KC A	8	16	1	4	0	0	1	1	0-0	0	3	.250	.250	.438	77	-1	0-0	1.000	1	53	1257	O3L	0	0.0
Kernan, Joe	Joseph; B Baltimore MD; d4.14																								
1873	Mar NA	2	8	1	3	0	0	0	1	0	—	0	.375	.375	.375	160	1	0-0	.700	0	126	0	/2cf	—	0.0
Kernek, George	George Boyd; B1.12.1940 Holdenville OK; BL/TL/6´3˝/(170–180); d9.5; Col Oklahoma																								
1965	StL N	10	31	6	9	3	1	0	3	2-0	0	4	.290	.333	.452	109	0	0-0	.972	-0	107	165	1b7	0	0.0
1966	StL N	20	50	5	12	0	1	0	3	4-0	1	9	.240	.309	.280	65	-2	1-0	.984	-0	95	129	1b16	0	-0.4
Total	2	30	81	11	21	3	2	0	6	6-0	1	13	.259	.318	.346	82	-2	1-0	.980	-1	99	141	1b23	0	-0.4
Kerns, Russ	Russell Eldon; B11.10.1920 Fremont OH; D8.21.2000 Placerville CA; BL/TR/6´0˝/188; d8.18																								
1945	Det A	1	1	0	0	0	0	0	0	0	0	0	.000	.000	.000	-94	0	0-0	ø	0	—	—	/H	0	0.0
Kerr, John	John Francis; B11.26.1898 San Francisco CA; D10.19.1993 Long Beach CA; BR/TR (BB 1923–24)/5´8˝/158; d5.1; C1																								
1923	Det A	19	42	4	9	1	0	0	1	4	0	5	.214	.283	.238	39	-4	0-0	.877	1	120	81	S15	—	-0.2
1924	Det A	17	11	3	3	0	0	0	1	0	0	0	.273	.273	.273	42	-1	0-0	ø	0	0	0	3b3,O2R	—	-0.1
1929	Chi A	127	419	50	108	20	4	1	39	31	1	24	.258	.310	.332	66	-22	9-8	.971	17	**113**	110	2b122/S	—	-0.2
1930	Chi A	70	266	37	77	11	6	3	27	21	4	23	.289	.351	.410	95	-2	4-2	.980	-1	100	100	2b52,S20	—	0.0
1931	Chi A	128	444	51	119	17	2	2	50	35	2	22	.268	.324	.329	77	-15	9-3	.968	1	102	103	2b117,3b7/S	—	-0.6

YEAR	TM LG	G	AB	R	H	2B	3B	HR	RBI	BB-IB	HP	SO	AVG	OBP	SLG	AOPS	ABR	SB-CS	FA	FR	RNG	THR	GAMES AT POSITION	DL	BFW
1932	Was A	51	132	14	36	6	1	0	15	13	0	3	.273	.338	.333	75	-5	3-2	.954	-2	96	81	2b17,S14,3b8	—	-0.5
1933	†Was A	28	40	5	8	0	0	0	0	3	0	2	.200	.256	.200	22	-5	0-0	.966	1	112	84	2b16/3	—	-0.3
1934	Was A	31	103	8	28	4	0	0	12	8	0	13	.272	.324	.311	67	-5	1-1	.971	4	131	116	3b17,2b13	—	0.0
Total	8	471	1457	172	388	59	13	6	145	115	7	92	.266	.323	.337	73	-59	26-16	.970	21	105	103	2b337,S51,3b36,O2	—	-1.9
Kerr, Doc	John Jonas; B1.17.1882 Dellroy OH; D6.9.1937 Baltimore MD; BB/TR/5´10.5˝/190; d4.22																								
1914	Pit F	42	71	3	17	4	2	1	7	10	0	13	.239	.333	.394	99	-1	0	.970	0	*105*	*111*	C18	—	0.0
	Bal F	14	34	4	9	1	1	0	1	1	0	6	.265	.286	.353	71	-2	1	.979	2	*137*	*81*	C13/1	—	0.1
	Year	56	105	7	26	5	3	1	8	11	0	19	.248	.319	.381	90	-3	1	.974	3	*118*	*98*	C31/1	—	0.1
1915	Bal F	3	6	1	2	0	0	0	0	1	0	0	.333	.429	.333	112	0	0	1.000	-1	*83*	*75*	C2/1	—	-0.1
Total	2	59	111	8	28	5	3	1	8	12	0	19	.252	.325	.378	91	-3	1	.975	2	*117*	*97*	C33,1b2	—	0.0
Kerr, Buddy	John Joseph; B11.6.1922 Astoria NY; D11.7.2006 New York NY; BR/TR/6´2˝/180; d9.8																								
1943	NY N	27	98	14	28	3	0	2	12	8	2	5	.286	.352	.378	110	1	1	.955	3	103	57	S27	0	0.6
1944	NY N	150	548	68	146	31	4	9	63	37	3	32	.266	.316	.387	97	-3	14	.954	**19**	**106**	90	S149	0	2.8
1945	NY N	149	546	53	136	20	3	4	40	41	2	34	.249	.304	.319	72	-21	5	.964	**30**	**111**	101	S148	0	2.1
1946	NY N	145	497	50	124	20	3	6	40	53	2	31	.249	.324	.338	87	-8	7	**.982**	8	101	83	S126,3b18	0	0.8
1947	NY N	138	547	73	157	23	5	7	49	36	0	49	.287	.331	.386	89	-10	2	.977	12	**106**	88	S138	0	1.1
1948	NY N★	144	496	41	119	16	4	0	46	56	0	36	.240	.317	.288	64	-24	9	.967	4	106	88	S143	0	-1.1
1949	NY N	90	220	16	46	4	0	0	19	21	2	23	.209	.284	.227	39	-19	0	.959	3	106	85	S89	0	-1.1
1950	Bos N	155	507	45	115	24	6	2	46	50	0	50	.227	.296	.310	64	-27	0	.965	2	100	96	S155	0	-1.6
1951	Bos N	69	172	18	32	4	0	1	18	22	1	20	.186	.282	.227	41	-14	0-0	.969	7	107	86	S63,2b5	0	-0.3
Total	9	1067	3631	378	903	145	25	31	333	324	12	280	.249	.312	.328	76	-125	38-0	.967	89	105	90	S1038,3b18,2b5	0	3.3
Kerr, Mel	John Melville; B5.22.1903 Souris MB, Can.; D8.9.1980 Vero Beach FL; BL/TL/5´11.5˝/155; d9.16																								
1925	Chi N	1	0	1	0	0	0	0	0	0	0	0	ø	ø	ø	ø	0	0-0	ø	0	—	—	/R	—	0.0
Kerwin, Dan	Daniel Patrick (b Daniel Patrick Kervin); B7.9.1874 Philadelphia PA; D7.13.1960 Philadelphia PA; BL/TL/5´9˝/164; d9.27																								
1903	Cin N	2	6	1	4	1	0	0	1	2	1	—	.667	.778	.833	323	2	0	.500	-1	0	0	O2L	—	0.1
Kessinger, Don	Donald Eulon; B7.17.1942 Forrest City AR; BB/TR (BR 1964–65)/6´1˝/(170–175); d9.7; M1; s–Keith; Col U. of Mississippi																								
1964	Chi N	4	12	1	2	0	0	0	0	0-0	0	1	.167	.167	.167	-6	-2	0-0	1.000	-0	107	77	S4	0	-0.2
1965	Chi N	106	309	19	62	4	3	0	14	20-1	2	44	.201	.252	.233	37	-26	1-2	.948	11	113	113	S105	0	-0.8
1966	Chi N	150	533	50	146	8	2	1	43	26-5	0	46	.274	.306	.302	70	-22	13-7	.951	-17	100	74	S148	0	-2.8
1967	Chi N	145	580	61	134	10	7	0	42	33-1	4	80	.231	.275	.272	55	-34	6-13	.973	-4	102	97	S143	0	-3.2
1968	Chi N★	160	655	63	157	14	7	1	32	38-1	2	86	.240	.283	.287	67	-26	9-9	.962	**27**	112	112	S159	0	1.5
1969	Chi N★	158	664	109	181	38	6	4	53	61-4	1	70	.273	.332	.366	85	-11	11-8	**.976**	**25**	109	112	S157	0	3.3
1970	Chi N★	154	631	100	168	21	14	1	39	66-6	2	59	.266	.337	.349	75	-22	12-6	.972	12	103	98	S154	0	0.9
1971	Chi N★	155	617	77	159	18	6	2	38	52-6	3	54	.258	.318	.316	70	-23	15-8	.966	11	103	103	S154	0	0.7
1972	Chi N★	149	577	77	158	20	6	1	39	67-8	2	44	.274	.351	.334	86	-8	8-7	.965	17	**110**	106	S146	0	2.7
1973	Chi N	160	577	52	151	22	3	0	43	57-18	0	44	.262	.327	.310	72	-20	6-6	.964	**27**	**110**	114	S158	0	2.5
1974	Chi N★	153	599	83	155	20	7	1	42	62-7	4	54	.259	.332	.321	80	-15	7-7	.958	7	103	91	S150	0	0.9
1975	Chi N	154	601	77	146	26	10	0	46	68-2	1	47	.243	.317	.319	75	-20	4-7	.967	7	102	112	S140,3b13	0	0.2
1976	StL N	145	502	55	120	22	6	1	40	61-5	1	51	.239	.320	.313	79	-12	3-0	.969	-2	98	**120**	S113,2b31,3b2	0	0.1
1977	StL N	59	134	14	32	4	0	0	7	14-1	0	26	.239	.309	.269	57	-8	0-0	.978	4	98	155	S26,2b24,3b4	0	-0.1
	Chi A	39	119	12	28	3	2	0	11	13-2	0	7	.235	.308	.294	66	-6	2-1	.959	-6	69	104	S21,2b13,3b9	0	-0.9
1978	Chi A	131	431	35	110	18	1	1	31	36-1	0	34	.255	.312	.309	74	-14	2-4	.974	-18	91	85	S123,2b9	0	-2.2
1979	Chi A	56	110	14	22	6	0	1	7	10-1	0	12	.200	.264	.282	48	-8	1-0	.988	-9	84	65	S54/12M	0	-1.2
Total	16	2078	7651	899	1931	254	80	14	527	684-69	22	759	.252	.314	.312	72	-277	100-85	.966	92	104	102	S1955,2b78,3b28/1	0	1.4
Kessinger, Keith	Robert Keith; B2.19.1967 Forrest City AR; BB/TR/6´2˝/185; [BalA89 36/921]; d9.15; f–Don; Col U. of Mississippi																								
1993	Cin N	11	27	4	7	1	0	1	3	4-0	0	4	.259	.344	.407	103	0	0-0	.935	-2	91	100	S11	0	-0.1
Kessler, Henry	Henry "Lucky"; B1847 Brooklyn NY; D1.9.1900 Franklin PA; BR/TR/5´10˝/144; d8.4																								
1873	Atl NA	1	5	0	1	0	0	0	1	0	—	0	.200	.200	.200	21	0	0-0	.882	0	355	0	/1	—	0.0
1874	Atl NA	14	56	8	17	1	0	0	4	0	—	2	.304	.304	.321	114	1	0-0	.737	-4	—	—	C9,2b4,O4(2/2/0)/3	—	-0.2
1875	Atl NA	25	105	17	26	2	0	0	7	1	—	2	.248	.255	.267	93	0	0-2	.794	-3	107	29	S18,O7(0/4/3),C3/12	—	-0.3
1876	Cin N	59	248	26	64	5	0	0	11	7	—	10	.258	.278	.278	100	2	—	.788	-8	85	106	S46,O16(0/2/14)	—	-0.3
1877	Cin N	6	20	0	2	0	0	0	0	2	—	1	.100	.182	.100	-10	-2	—	.500	-5	—	—	C5/1	—	-0.7
Total	3NA	40	166	25	44	3	0	0	12	1	—	4	.265	.269	.283	98	1	0-2	.794	-7	—	—	S18,C12,O11(2/6/3),2b5,1b2/3	—	-0.5
Total	2	65	268	26	66	5	0	0	11	9	—	11	.246	.271	.265	91	0	—	.794	-13	—	—	S46,O16(0/2/14),C5/1	—	-1.0
Ketchum, Fred	Frederick L.; B7.27.1875 Elmira NY; D3.12.1908 Cortland NY; BL/TR/5´8˝/157; d9.12																								
1899	Lou N	15	61	13	18	1	0	0	5	0	1	—	.295	.306	.311	70	-3	2	1.000	-2	0	0	O15(4/1/10)	—	-0.5
1901	Phi A	5	22	5	5	0	0	0	2	0	0	—	.227	.227	.227	25	-2	0	.875	-1	0	0	O5L	—	-0.3
Total	2	20	83	18	23	1	0	0	7	0	1	—	.277	.286	.289	58	-5	2	.960	-3	0	0	O20(9/1/10)	—	-0.8
Ketter, Phil	Philip (b Philip Ketterer); B4.13.1884 St.Louis MO; D4.9.1965 St.Louis MO; TR; d5.23																								
1912	StL A	2	6	1	2	0	0	0	0	0	0	—	.333	.333	.333	94	0	0	1.000	-1	*68*	*121*	C2	—	-0.1
Khalifa, Sammy	Sam; B12.5.1963 Fontana CA; BR/TR/5´11˝/(170–180); [PitN82 1/7]; d6.25																								
1985	Pit N	95	320	30	76	14	3	2	31	34-8	0	56	.237	.307	.319	77	-10	5-2	.967	9	106	75	S95	0	1.0
1986	Pit N	64	151	8	28	6	0	0	4	19-6	0	28	.185	.276	.225	39	-12	0-2	.961	6	112	87	S60,2b6	0	-0.2
1987	Pit N	5	17	1	3	0	0	0	2	0-0	0	2	.176	.176	.176	-6	-3	0-0	.917	-4	43	37	S5	0	-0.7
Total	3	164	488	39	107	20	3	2	37	53-14	0	86	.219	.294	.285	62	-25	5-4	.964	11	106	78	S160,2b6	0	0.1
Kibbie, Hod	Horace Kent; B7.18.1903 Ft.Worth TX; D10.19.1975 Ft.Worth TX; BR/TR/5´10˝/150; d6.13; Col Texas																								
1925	Bos N	11	41	5	11	2	0	0	2	5	0	6	.268	.348	.317	78	-1	0-0	.904	-2	95	38	2b8,S3	—	-0.2
Kibble, Jack	John Westly "Happy"; B1.2.1892 Seatonville IL; D12.13.1969 Roundup MT; BB/TR/5´9.5˝/154; d9.10																								
1912	Cle A	5	8	1	0	0	0	0	0	0	1	—	.000	.111	.000	-65	-2	0	1.000	2	171	721	3b4/2	—	0.1
Kiefer, Steve	Steven George; B10.18.1960 Chicago IL; BR/TR/6´1˝/(175–185); [OakA81*1/16]; d9.3; b–Mark; Col Fullerton (CA) JC																								
1984	Oak A	23	40	7	7	1	2	0	2	2-0	0	10	.175	.209	.300	43	-3	2-1	.904	-4	92	61	S17,3b2,D3	0	-0.6
1985	Oak A	40	66	8	13	1	1	1	10	1-0	0	18	.197	.203	.288	37	-6	0-0	.881	-4	88	119	3b34,D2	0	-1.0
1986	Mil A	2	6	0	0	0	0	0	0	0-0	0	4	.000	.000	.000	-97	-2	0-0	1.000	2	155	175	S2	0	0.1
1987	Mil A	28	99	17	20	4	0	5	17	7-0	1	28	.202	.257	.394	68	-5	0-0	.966	-4	84	62	3b26,2b4	0	-0.8
1988	Mil A	7	10	2	3	1	0	1	1	2-0	1	3	.300	.462	.700	218	2	0-0	1.000	0	151	206	2b4,3b4	0	0.2
1989	NY A	5	8	0	1	0	0	0	0	0-0	0	5	.125	.125	.125	-30	-1	0-0	1.000	-1	24	0	3b5	16	-0.3
Total	6	105	229	34	44	7	3	7	30	12-0	2	68	.192	.234	.341	55	-15	2-1	.920	-10	82	80	3b71,S19,2b8,D5	16	-2.4
Kielty, Bobby	Robert Michael; B8.5.1976 Fontana CA; BB/TR/6´1˝/(215–225); d4.10; Col U. of Mississippi																								
2001	Min A	37	104	8	26	8	0	2	14	8-2	1	25	.250	.297	.385	77	-3	3-0	.956	-1	95	107	O34(11/11/17)/D	0	-0.4
2002	†Min A	112	289	49	84	14	3	12	46	52-4	5	66	.291	.405	.484	131	15	4-1	1.000	0	102	95	O82(9/34/50),D11,1b5	0	1.2
2003	Min A	75	238	40	60	13	0	9	32	42-2	3	56	.252	.370	.420	105	3	6-2	.972	-2	94	50	O36(1/2/33),D32	0	-0.1
	Tor A	62	189	31	44	13	1	4	25	29-4	4	36	.233	.342	.376	87	-2	2-1	.989	-3	87	69	O60(3/1/56),1b3	0	-0.8
	Year	137	427	71	104	26	1	13	57	71-6	7	92	.244	.358	.400	97	1	8-3	.981	-5	90	61	O96(4/3/89),D32,1b3	0	-0.9
2004	Oak A	83	238	29	51	14	1	7	31	35-0	3	47	.214	.321	.370	80	-6	1-0	.990	-4	90	31	O67(51/0/21),D11	0	-1.3
2005	Oak A	116	377	55	99	20	0	10	57	50-3	2	67	.263	.350	.395	99	1	3-2	.983	-2	95	102	O96(58/0/42),D17	0	-0.5
2006	†Oak A	81	270	35	73	20	1	8	36	22-0	2	49	.270	.329	.441	99	0	2-0	.993	-1	99	64	O73(44/0/31),D3	0	-0.4
Total	6	566	1705	247	437	102	6	52	241	238-15	20	346	.256	.351	.415	100	8	21-6	.986	-12	95	76	O448(177/48/250),D75,1b8	0	-2.3
Kienzle, Bill	William H.; B Philadelphia PA; BL/TL/5´8˝/166; d9.15																								
1882	Phi AA	9	33	8	11	3	2	0	9	5	—	—	.333	.421	.545	210	4	—	.842	-1	47	0	O9C	—	0.2
1884	Phi U	**67**	299	76	76	13	8	0	—	21	—	—	.254	.303	.351	106	-6	—	.772	-5	107	62	O67C	—	-1.2
Total	2	76	332	84	87	16	10	0	9	26	—	—	.262	.316	.370	117	-2	—	.781	-7	100	55	O76C	—	-1.0

Kieschnick, Brooks Michael Brooks; B6.6.1972 Robstown TX; BL/TR/6´4˝/(220–250); [ChiN93 1/10]; d4.3; Col Texas; ▲

YEAR	TM LG	G	AB	R	H	2B	3B	HR	RBI	BB-IB	HP	SO	AVG	OBP	SLG	AOPS	ABR	SB-CS	FA	FR	RNG	THR	GAMES AT POSITION	DL	BFW
1996	Chi N	25	29	6	10	2	0	1	6	3-0	0	8	.345	.406	.517	137	2	0-0	.833	-1	68	0	O8(4/0/5)	0	0.1
1997	Chi N	39	90	9	18	2	0	4	12	12-0	0	21	.200	.294	.356	67	-5	1-0	.952	0	104	76	O27(26/0/1)	0	-0.5
2000	Cin N	14	12	0	0	0	0	0	0	1-0	0	5	.000	.077	.000	-76	-3	0-0	1.000	0	0	0	/1	0	-0.3
2001	Col N	35	42	5	10	2	1	3	9	3-0	0	13	.238	.289	.548	91	-1	0-0	.818	-1	106	0	O12(8/0/4)/1	15	-0.1
2003	Mil N	70	70	12	21	1	0	7	12	6-0	0	13	.300	.355	.614	147	4	0-0	1.000	0	145	346	P42,O3L,D4	0	0.1
2004	Mil N	77	63	2	17	3	0	1	7	5-1	0	16	.270	.324	.365	77	6	0-0	1.000	-1	33	0	P32	25	0.0
Total	6	260	306	34	76	10	1	16	46	30-1	0	76	.248	.315	.444	91	3	1-0	1.000	-2	95	191	P74,O50(41/0/10),D4,1b2	40	-0.7

Kiger, Mark Mark Winston; B5.30.1980 San Diego CA; BR/TR/5´10˝/180; [OakA02 5/158]; d10.13; Col Florida

YEAR	TM LG	G	AB	R	H	2B	3B	HR	RBI	BB-IB	HP	SO	AVG	OBP	SLG	AOPS	ABR	SB-CS	FA	FR	RNG	THR	GAMES AT POSITION	DL	BFW
2006	†Oak A	0	0	0	0	0	0	0	0	0-0	0	0	ø	ø	ø	ø	0	0-0	.000	0	—	—	/H	0	0.0

Kilduff, Pete Peter John; B4.4.1893 Weir City KS; D2.14.1930 Pittsburg KS; BR/TR/5´7˝/155; d4.18; Mil 1918

YEAR	TM LG	G	AB	R	H	2B	3B	HR	RBI	BB-IB	HP	SO	AVG	OBP	SLG	AOPS	ABR	SB-CS	FA	FR	RNG	THR	GAMES AT POSITION	DL	BFW
1917	NY N	31	78	12	16	3	0	1	12	4	1	11	.205	.253	.282	66	-3	2	.954	-1	97	160	2b21,S5/3	—	-0.5
	Chi N	56	202	23	56	9	5	0	15	12	2	19	.277	.324	.371	105	1	11	.920	-14	76	83	S51,2b5	—	-1.1
	Year	87	280	35	72	12	5	1	27	16	3	30	.257	.304	.346	95	-2	13	.917	-15	77	79	S56,2b26/3	—	-1.6
1918	Chi N	30	93	7	19	2	2	0	13	7	1	7	.204	.267	.269	62	-4	1	.935	-4	82	162	2b30	—	-0.8
1919	Chi N	31	88	5	24	4	2	0	8	10	2	5	.273	.360	.364	117	2	1	.974	-3	105	129	3b14,2b8,S7	—	0.1
	Bro N	32	73	9	22	3	1	0	8	12	1	11	.301	.407	.370	132	4	5	.862	-4	91	134	3b26/2	—	0.1
	Year	63	161	14	46	7	3	0	16	22	3	16	.286	.382	.366	124	6	6	.903	-7	96	132	3b40,2b9,S7	—	0.2
1920	†Bro N	141	478	62	130	26	8	0	58	58	0	43	.272	.351	.360	101	3	2-9	.967	7	101	**111**	2b134,3b5	—	1.1
1921	Bro N	107	372	45	107	15	10	3	45	31	1	36	.288	.344	.406	94	-3	6-6	.963	12	**106**	107	2b105/3	—	1.0
Total	5	428	1384	163	374	62	28	4	159	134	8	132	.270	.338	.364	98	0	28-15	.963	-7	101	117	2b304,S63,3b47	—	-0.1

Kiley, John John Frederick; B7.1.1859 Dedham MA; D12.18.1940 Norwood MA; BL/TL/5´7˝/147; d5.1

YEAR	TM LG	G	AB	R	H	2B	3B	HR	RBI	BB-IB	HP	SO	AVG	OBP	SLG	AOPS	ABR	SB-CS	FA	FR	RNG	THR	GAMES AT POSITION	DL	BFW
1884	Was AA	14	56	9	12	2	2	0	—	3	1	—	.214	.267	.321	103	0	—	.571	-3	36	0	O14(13/1/1)	—	-0.3
1891	Bos N	1	2	0	0	0	0	0	0	1	1	1	.000	.500	.000	45	0	0	1.000	0	121	0	/P	—	0.0
Total	2	15	58	9	12	2	2	0	0	4	2	1	.207	.281	.310	102	0	0	.571	-3	36	0	O14(13/1/1)/P	—	-0.3

Kilhullen, Pat Joseph Isadore; B8.10.1890 Carbondale PA; D10.25.1922 San Leandro CA; BR/TR/5´9˝/175; d6.10; Col Villanova

YEAR	TM LG	G	AB	R	H	2B	3B	HR	RBI	BB-IB	HP	SO	AVG	OBP	SLG	AOPS	ABR	SB-CS	FA	FR	RNG	THR	GAMES AT POSITION	DL	BFW
1914	Pit N	1	1	0	0	0	0	0	0	0	0	0	.000	.000	.000	-99	0	0	ø	-0	*0*	*0*	/C	—	0.0

Killebrew, Harmon Harmon Clayton "Killer"; B6.29.1936 Payette ID; BR/TR/5´11˝/(193–214); d6.23; HF1984; OF(470/0/1)

YEAR	TM LG	G	AB	R	H	2B	3B	HR	RBI	BB-IB	HP	SO	AVG	OBP	SLG	AOPS	ABR	SB-CS	FA	FR	RNG	THR	GAMES AT POSITION	DL	BFW
1954	Was A	9	13	1	4	1	0	0	3	2	0	3	.308	.400	.385	122	1	0-0	1.000	-1	47	0	2b3	0	0.0
1955	Was A	38	80	12	16	1	0	4	7	9-0	0	31	.200	.281	.363	76	-3	0-0	.935	2	112	67	3b23,2b3	0	-0.1
1956	Was A	44	99	10	22	2	0	5	13	10-0	0	39	.222	.291	.394	80	-3	0-0	.951	-0	106	72	3b20,2b4	0	-0.4
1957	Was A	9	31	4	9	2	0	2	5	2-0	0	8	.290	.333	.548	139	1	0-0	.947	-1	106	130	3b7/2	0	0.1
1958	Was A	13	31	2	6	0	0	0	2	0-0	1	12	.194	.212	.194	15	-4	0-0	1.000	-0	89	61	3b9	0	-0.4
1959	Was A★	153	546	98	132	20	2	**42**	105	90-1	7	116	.242	.354	.516	137	28	3-2	.938	-3	105	65	3b150,O4L	0	2.4
1960	Was A	124	442	84	122	19	1	31	80	71-3	1	106	.276	.375	.534	145	28	1-0	.987	-9	71	106	1b71,3b65	0	1.6
1961	Min A★	150	541	94	156	20	7	46	122	107-6	3	109	.288	.405	.606	159	47	1-2	.987	-5	86	92	1b119,3b45,O2L	0	3.3
1962	Min A	155	552	85	134	21	1	**48**	**126**	106-6	4	142	.243	.366	.545	137	30	1-2	.967	-8	86	63	O151L,1b4	0	1.3
1963	Min A★	142	515	88	133	18	0	**45**	96	72-4	3	105	.258	.349	**.555**	147	32	0-0	.987	-1	93	80	O137L	0	2.5
1964	Min A★	158	577	95	156	11	1	**49**	111	93-5	**8**	135	.270	.377	.548	153	43	0-0	.971	-10	88	13	O157(157/0/1)	0	2.4
1965	†Min A★	113	401	78	108	16	1	25	75	72-12	4	69	.269	.384	.501	144	25	0-0	.988	-9	81	124	1b72,3b44/lf	0	1.3
1966	Min A★	**162**	569	89	160	27	1	39	110	**103-18**	2	98	.281	.391	.538	155	44	0-2	.951	-16	89	66	3b107,1b42,O18L	0	2.6
1967	Min A★	163	547	105	147	24	1	**44**	113	**131-15**	3	111	.269	.408	.558	170	54	1-0	.992	-6	84	93	1b160,3b3	0	4.2
1968	Min A★	100	295	40	62	7	2	17	40	70-9	2	70	.210	.361	.420	130	14	0-0	.994	5	128	95	1b77,3b11	53	1.6
1969	†Min A★	**162**	555	106	153	20	2	**49**	**140**	**145-20**	5	84	.276	**.427**	.584	176	64	8-2	.929	-14	97	67	3b105,1b80	0	4.6
1970	†Min A★	157	527	96	143	20	1	41	113	128-23	2	84	.271	.411	.546	161	49	0-3	.948	-25	79	59	3b138,1b28	0	2.2
1971	Min A★	147	500	61	127	19	1	28	**119**	**114**-14	0	96	.254	.386	.464	138	30	3-2	.997	-12	109	74	1b90,3b64	0	1.2
1972	Min A	139	433	53	100	13	2	26	74	94-12	1	91	.231	.367	.450	136	23	0-1	.992	11	**140**	92	1b130	0	2.7
1973	Min A	69	248	29	60	9	1	5	32	41-2	1	59	.242	.352	.347	93	-1	0-0	.998	5	130	93	1b57,D9	54	0.0
1974	Min A	122	333	28	74	7	0	13	54	45-6	0	61	.222	.312	.360	91	-4	0-0	.992	-2	131	93	D57,1b33	0	-0.5
1975	KC A	106	312	25	62	13	0	14	44	54-4	1	70	.199	.317	.375	93	-2	1-2	1.000	-1	0	126	D92,1b6	0	-0.6
Total	22	2435	8147	1283	2086	290	24	573	1584	1559-160	48	1699	.256	.376	.509	142	496	19-18	.992	-96	97	96	1b969,3b791,O470L,D158,2b11	107	32.0

Killefer, Red Wade; B4.13.1885 Bloomingdale MI; D9.4.1958 Los Angeles CA; BR/TR/5´9˝/175; d9.16; b–Bill; Col Michigan; OF(135/135/27)

YEAR	TM LG	G	AB	R	H	2B	3B	HR	RBI	BB-IB	HP	SO	AVG	OBP	SLG	AOPS	ABR	SB-CS	FA	FR	RNG	THR	GAMES AT POSITION	DL	BFW
1907	Det A	1	4	0	0	0	0	0	0	0	0	—	.000	.000	.000	-97	-1	0	1.000	0	0	0	/rf	—	-0.1
1908	Det A	28	75	9	16	1	0	0	11	3	1	—	.213	.253	.227	54	-4	4	.956	-5	90	171	2b16,S7,3b4	—	-1.0
1909	Det A	23	61	6	17	2	2	1	4	3	3	—	.279	.343	.426	137	2	2	.912	-1	115	53	2b17/rf	—	0.1
	Was A	40	121	11	21	1	0	0	5	13	2	—	.174	.265	.182	43	-7	4	.957	-4	36	0	O24(6/17/1),3b6,C3,2b3/S	—	-1.4
	Year	63	182	17	38	3	2	1	9	16	5	—	.209	.291	.264	76	-5	6	.957	-5	36	0	O25(6/17/2),2b20,3b6,C3/S	—	-1.3
1910	Was A	106	345	35	79	17	1	0	24	29	**16**	—	.229	.318	.284	93	0	17	.940	-4	97	94	2b88,O12(6/0/6)	—	-0.5
1914	Cin N	42	141	16	39	6	1	0	12	20	5	18	.277	.386	.333	111	3	11	.968	-4	80	103	O37(1/18/18),2b5/3	—	-0.3
1915	Cin N	155	555	75	151	25	11	1	41	38	**19**	33	.272	.340	.362	110	8	12-18	.970	1	102	93	O150(79/73/0),1b2	—	-0.4
1916	Cin N	70	234	29	57	9	1	1	18	21	8	8	.244	.327	.303	96	0	7	.966	-0	102	83	O68(43/27/0)	—	-0.4
	NY N	2	1	0	1	0	0	0	1	1	0	0	1.000	1.000	1.000	544	1	0	ø	0	—	—	/H	—	0.1
	Year	72	235	29	58	9	1	1	19	22	8	8	.247	.332	.306	99	1	7	.966	-0	102	83	O68(43/27/0)	—	-0.3
Total	7	467	1537	181	381	61	16	3	116	128	54	59	.248	.328	.314	98	2	57-18	.965	-18	93	88	O293L,2b129,3b11,S8,C3,1b2	—	-3.9

Killefer, Bill William "Reindeer Bill"; B10.10.1887 Bloomingdale MI; D7.3.1960 Elsmere DE; BR/TR/5´10.5˝/170; d9.13; M9/C6; b–Red; Col St. Edwards

YEAR	TM LG	G	AB	R	H	2B	3B	HR	RBI	BB-IB	HP	SO	AVG	OBP	SLG	AOPS	ABR	SB-CS	FA	FR	RNG	THR	GAMES AT POSITION	DL	BFW
1909	StL A	11	29	0	4	0	0	0	1	0	0	—	.138	.138	.138	-14	-4	2	.905	0	*99*	*166*	C11	—	-0.3
1910	StL A	74	193	14	24	2	2	0	7	12	2	—	.124	.184	.155	7	-21	0	.938	3	*89*	*124*	C73	—	-1.3
1911	Phi N	6	16	3	3	0	0	0	2	0	0	2	.188	.188	.188	5	-2	0	.975	1	*91*	*137*	C6	—	-0.1
1912	Phi N	85	268	18	60	6	3	1	21	4	2	14	.224	.241	.280	40	-24	6	.973	11	*92*	*118*	C85	—	-0.6
1913	Phi N	120	360	25	88	14	3	0	24	4	1	17	.244	.255	.300	56	-22	2-4	.988	8	111	**117**	C118/1	—	-0.5
1914	Phi N	98	299	27	70	10	1	0	27	8	3	17	.234	.261	.274	56	-17	3	.978	4	*77*	*117*	C90	—	-0.5
1915	†Phi N	105	320	26	76	9	2	0	24	18	4	14	.237	.287	.278	70	-12	5-3	.972	10	*117*	*97*	C104	—	0.8
1916	Phi N	97	286	22	62	5	4	3	27	8	3	14	.217	.246	.294	63	-14	2	**.985**	-1	111	92	C91	—	-0.8
1917	Phi N	125	409	28	112	12	0	0	31	15	4	21	.274	.306	.303	84	-8	4	**.984**	11	*119*	*89*	C120/lf	—	1.5
1918	†Chi N	104	331	30	77	10	3	0	22	17	3	10	.233	.276	.281	68	-13	5	.982	7	*110*	*95*	C104	—	0.4
1919	Chi N	103	315	17	90	10	2	0	22	15	2	8	.286	.322	.330	96	-2	5	**.987**	14	*107*	*95*	C100	—	2.3
1920	Chi N	62	191	16	42	7	1	0	16	8	8	5	.220	.280	.267	56	-10	2-2	.977	12	*114*	*117*	C61	—	0.8
1921	Chi N	45	133	11	43	1	0	0	16	4	3	4	.323	.357	.331	83	-3	3-3	.964	-1	*98*	*103*	C42,M	—	-0.2
Total	13	1035	3150	237	751	86	21	4	240	113	35	126	.238	.273	.283	63	-152	39-12	.976	79	*105*	*105*	C1005/lf1	—	1.5

Kimball, Gene Eugene Boynton; B8.31.1850 Rochester NY; D8.2.1882 Rochester NY; 5´10˝/160; d5.4

YEAR	TM LG	G	AB	R	H	2B	3B	HR	RBI	BB-IB	HP	SO	AVG	OBP	SLG	AOPS	ABR	SB-CS	FA	FR	RNG	THR	GAMES AT POSITION	DL	BFW
1871	Cle NA	**29**	131	18	25	1	0	0	9	3	—	2	.191	.209	.198	19	-13	5-1	.743	-7	83	59	2b17,O9(2/1/7),S6,3b2	—	-1.3

Kimble, Dick Richard Lewis; B7.27.1915 Buchtel OH; D5.7.2001 Toledo OH; BL/TR/5´9˝/160; d8.20; Col Ohio U.

YEAR	TM LG	G	AB	R	H	2B	3B	HR	RBI	BB-IB	HP	SO	AVG	OBP	SLG	AOPS	ABR	SB-CS	FA	FR	RNG	THR	GAMES AT POSITION	DL	BFW
1945	Was A	20	49	5	12	1	1	0	1	5	0	2	.245	.315	.306	88	-1	0-0	.950	-3	96	69	S15	0	-0.3

Kimm, Bruce Bruce Edward; B6.29.1951 Cedar Rapids IA; BR/TR/5´11˝/(170–175); [ChiA69 7/145]; d5.4; M1/C12

YEAR	TM LG	G	AB	R	H	2B	3B	HR	RBI	BB-IB	HP	SO	AVG	OBP	SLG	AOPS	ABR	SB-CS	FA	FR	RNG	THR	GAMES AT POSITION	DL	BFW
1976	Det A	63	152	13	40	8	0	1	6	15-0	0	20	.263	.329	.336	91	-1	4-3	.970	2	113	139	C61,D2	0	0.3
1977	Det A	14	25	2	2	1	0	0	1	0-0	1	4	.080	.115	.120	-34	-5	0-1	.958	-1	110	85	C12,D2	0	-0.6
1979	Chi N	9	11	0	1	0	0	0	0	0-0	0	0	.091	.091	.091	-46	-2	0-1	.969	1	69	72	C9	0	-0.2
1980	Chi A	100	251	20	61	10	1	0	19	17-0	0	26	.243	.290	.291	60	-14	1-3	.985	-3	107	84	C98	0	-1.4
Total	4	186	439	35	104	19	1	1	26	32-0	1	50	.237	.290	.292	62	-22	5-8	.977	-1	108	104	C180,D4	0	-1.9

Kimmick, Wally Walter Lyons; B5.30.1897 Turtle Creek PA; D7.24.1989 Boswell PA; BR/TR/5´11˝/174; d9.13

YEAR	TM LG	G	AB	R	H	2B	3B	HR	RBI	BB-IB	HP	SO	AVG	OBP	SLG	AOPS	ABR	SB-CS	FA	FR	RNG	THR	GAMES AT POSITION	DL	BFW
1919	StL N	2	1	1	0	0	0	0	0	1	0	0	.000	.500	.000	61	0	1	1.000	0	130	0	/S	—	0.0
1921	Cin N	3	6	0	1	0	0	0	1	0	0	1	.167	.167	.167	-12	-1	0-0	.667	-0	94	359	3b2	—	-0.1
1922	Cin N	39	89	11	22	2	1	0	12	3	0	12	.247	.272	.292	46	-7	0-0	.965	2	109	109	S30,2b3/3	—	-0.3
1923	Cin N	29	80	11	18	2	1	0	6	5	0	15	.225	.271	.275	45	-7	3-0	.972	6	127	78	2b17,3b4/S	—	0.1

YEAR	TM LG	G	AB	R	H	2B	3B	HR	RBI	BB-IB	HP	SO	AVG	OBP	SLG	AOPS	ABR	SB-CS	FA	FR	RNG	THR	GAMES AT POSITION	DL	BFW
1925	Phi N	70	141	16	43	3	2	1	10	22	0	26	.305	.399	.376	91	-1	0-3	.904	-3	106	51	S28,3b21,2b13	—	-0.2
1926	Phi N	20	28	0	6	2	1	0	2	3	0	7	.214	.290	.357	70	-1	0	1.000	-2	0	0	1b5,S4,3b4/2	—	-0.3
Total	6	163	345	39	90	9	5	1	31	34	0	61	.261	.327	.325	67	-17	4-3	.933	3	107	84	S64,2b34,3b32,1b5	—	-0.8
Kindall, Jerry	Gerald Donald "Slim"; B5.27.1935 St.Paul MN; BR/TR (BB 1960p)/6´2.5˝/175; d7.1; Col Minnesota																								
1956	Chi N	32	55	7	9	1	1	0	0	6-1	0	17	.164	.246	.218	27	-6	1-0	.956	0	102	101	S18	0	-0.4
1957	Chi N	72	181	18	29	3	0	6	12	8-0	0	48	.160	.196	.276	25	-20	1-0	.920	-5	99	47	2b28,3b19,S9	0	-2.4
1958	Chi N	3	6	0	1	1	0	0	0	0-0	0	3	.167	.167	.333	29	-1	0-0	1.000	-0	78	116	2b3	0	-0.1
1960	Chi N	89	246	17	59	16	2	2	23	5-3	0	52	.240	.253	.346	63	-13	4-3	.966	8	116	101	2b82,S2	0	0.0
1961	Chi N	96	310	37	75	22	3	9	44	18-0	2	89	.242	.288	.419	84	-8	2-2	.950	2	102	110	2b50,S47	0	0.1
1962	Cle A	154	530	51	123	21	1	13	55	45-9	0	107	.232	.290	.349	74	-21	4-3	.978	23	**113**	112	2b154	0	1.5
1963	Cle A	86	234	27	48	4	1	5	20	18-0	2	71	.205	.266	.295	58	-14	3-1	.958	-6	86	69	S46,2b37,1b4	0	-1.4
1964	Cle A	23	25	5	9	1	0	2	2	2-0	0	7	.360	.407	.640	188	3	0-0	.989	2	169	85	1b23	0	0.4
	Min A	62	128	8	19	2	0	1	6	7-1	1	44	.148	.199	.188	8	-16	0-0	.969	-1	100	76	2b51,S7/1	0	-1.5
	Year	85	153	13	28	3	0	3	8	9-1	1	51	.183	.233	.261	37	-13	0-0	.969	1	100	76	2b51,1b24,S7	0	-1.1
1965	Min A	125	342	41	67	12	1	6	36	36-3	3	97	.196	.274	.289	59	-18	2-2	.963	-4	98	105	2b106,3b10,S7	0	-1.4
Total	9	742	2057	211	439	83	9	44	198	145-17	8	535	.213	.266	.327	62	-114	17-11	.967	19	107	101	2b511,S136,3b29,1b28	0	-5.2
Kiner, Ralph	Ralph McPherran; B10.27.1922 Santa Rita NM; BR/TR/6´2˝/(190–195); d4.16; HF1975																								
1946	Pit N	144	502	63	124	17	3	**23**	81	74	1	109	.247	.345	.430	116	10	3	.969	-5	102	47	O140(64/76/0)	0	-0.1
1947	Pit N	152	565	118	177	23	4	**51**	127	98	2	81	.313	.417	**.639**	**172**	**58**	1	.983	8	**115**	69	O152L	0	**5.3**
1948	Pit N★	**156**	555	104	147	19	5	**40**	123	112	3	61	.265	.391	.533	145	37	1	.975	3	**111**	47	O154L	0	2.7
1949	Pit N★	152	549	116	170	19	5	**54**	**127**	**117**	1	61	.310	.432	**.658**	**183**	**67**	6	.979	-3	94	95	O152L	0	**5.1**
1950	Pit N★	150	547	112	149	21	6	**47**	118	122	3	79	.272	.408	.590	154	45	2	.965	-5	89	115	O150L	0	2.8
1951	Pit N★	151	531	**124**	164	31	6	**42**	109	**137**	2	57	.309	**.452**	**.627**	182	69	2-1	.967	-9	94	82	O94L,1b58	0	5.0
1952	Pit N☆	149	516	90	126	17	2	**37**	87	**110**	7	77	.244	.384	.500	140	31	3-0	.970	-10	85	81	O149L	0	1.1
1953	Pit N	41	148	27	40	6	1	7	29	25	2	21	.270	.383	.466	121	5	1-0	1.000	1	93	154	O41L	0	0.4
	Chi N★	117	414	73	117	14	2	28	87	75	1	67	.283	.394	.529	135	23	1-1	.964	-5	98	65	O116L	0	1.1
	Year	158	562	100	157	20	3	35	116	100	3	88	.279	.391	.512	131	28	2-1	.973	-4	97	88	O157L	0	1.5
1954	Chi N	147	557	88	159	36	5	22	73	76	2	90	.285	.371	.487	121	18	2-0	.971	1	105	67	O147L	0	1.0
1955	Cle A	113	321	56	78	13	0	18	54	65-1	0	46	.243	.367	.452	116	8	0-0	.986	-6	90	32	O87L	0	-0.2
Total	10	1472	5205	971	1451	216	39	369	1015	1011-1	24	749	.279	.398	.548	148	371	22-2	.974	-30	99	74	O1382(1306/76/0),1b58	0	24.2
King, Chick	Charles Gilbert; B11.10.1930 Paris TN; BR/TR/6´2˝/(185–190); d8.27; Col Memphis																								
1954	Det A	11	28	4	6	0	1	0	3	3	0	8	.214	.290	.286	59	-2	0-0	.958	1	105	138	O7C	0	-0.2
1955	Det A	7	21	3	5	0	0	0	0	1-0	0	2	.238	.273	.238	39	-2	0-0	.923	-1	100	0	O6L	0	-0.3
1956	Det A	6	9	0	2	0	0	0	0	1-0	0	4	.222	.300	.222	40	-1	0-0	.800	-0	109	0	O3L	0	-0.1
1958	Chi N	8	8	1	2	0	0	0	1	3-1	0	1	.250	.455	.250	95	0	0-0	1.000	-1	75	0	O7C	0	-0.1
1959	Chi N	7	3	3	0	0	0	0	0	0-0	0	1	.000	.000	.000	-99	-1	0-0	1.000	-0	79	0	/cf	0	-0.1
	StL N	5	7	0	3	0	0	0	1	0-0	0	2	.429	.375	.429	121	0	0-0	1.000	0	136	0	O4(1/3/0)	0	0.0
	Year	12	10	3	3	0	0	0	1	0-0	0	3	.300	.273	.300	59	-1	0-0	1.000	0	118	0	O5(1/4/0)	0	-0.1
Total	5	44	76	11	18	0	1	0	5	8-1	0	18	.237	.306	.263	56	-6	0-0	.947	-1	102	49	O28(10/18/0)	0	-0.8
King, Lee	Edward Lee; B3.28.1894 Waltham MA; D9.7.1938 Chelsea MA; BR/TR/5´10˝/160; d6.24; Mil 1918; Col Massachusetts																								
1916	Phi A	42	144	13	27	1	2	0	8	7	1	15	.188	.230	.222	38	-12	4	1.000	-5	81	53	O22(21/2/1),S11,3b5,2b2	—	-1.9
1919	Bos N	2	1	0	0	0	0	0	0	0	0	0	.000	.000	.000	-99	0	0	ø	0	—	—	/H	—	0.0
Total	2	44	145	13	27	1	2	0	8	7	1	15	.186	.229	.221	37	-12	4	1.000	-5	81	53	O22(21/2/1),S11,3b5,2b2	—	-1.9
King, Hal	Harold; B2.1.1944 Oviedo FL; BL/TR/6´1˝/(195–200); d9.6																								
1967	Hou N	15	44	2	11	1	2	0	6	2-0	0	9	.250	.283	.364	87	-1	0-0	1.000	-1	57	139	C11	0	-0.2
1968	Hou N	27	55	4	8	2	1	0	2	7-0	0	16	.145	.242	.218	40	-4	0-0	.968	-3	38	58	C19	0	-0.7
1970	Atl N	89	204	29	53	8	0	11	30	32-6	2	41	.260	.364	.461	113	4	1-0	.985	-8	80	73	C62	0	-0.1
1971	Atl N	86	198	14	41	9	0	5	19	29-5	4	43	.207	.320	.328	79	-4	0-0	.983	-2	146	90	C60	0	-0.4
1972	Tex A	50	122	12	22	5	0	4	12	25-1	3	35	.180	.333	.320	98	1	0-0	.970	-5	106	90	C38	0	-0.3
1973	†Cin N	35	43	5	8	0	0	4	10	6-0	0	10	.186	.286	.465	109	0	0-0	1.000	-1	131	0	C9	0	-0.1
1974	Cin N	20	17	1	3	1	0	0	3	3-0	0	4	.176	.300	.235	52	-1	0-0	1.000	-0	0	199	C5	0	-0.1
Total	7	322	683	67	146	26	3	24	82	104-12	9	158	.214	.325	.366	92	-5	1-0	.982	-21	102	83	C204	0	-1.9
King, Jim	James Hubert; B8.27.1932 Elkins AR; BL/TR/6´0˝/185; d4.17																								
1955	Chi N	113	301	43	77	12	3	11	45	24-1	2	39	.256	.312	.425	95	-3	2-1	.990	7	111	141	O93(17/0/76)	0	0.0
1956	Chi N	118	317	32	79	13	2	15	54	30-5	1	40	.249	.313	.445	103	1	1-2	.990	12	123	189	O82(69/0/14)	0	0.8
1957	StL N	22	35	1	11	0	0	0	2	4-2	0	2	.314	.385	.314	89	0	0-0	1.000	-1	57	0	O8(1/3/4)	0	-0.2
1958	SF N	34	56	8	12	2	1	2	8	10-1	1	8	.214	.343	.393	96	0	0-1	1.000	-1	85	0	O15(9/0/6)	0	-0.2
1961	Was A	110	263	43	71	12	1	11	46	38-3	2	45	.270	.363	.449	118	8	4-0	.980	1	97	127	O91(25/0/67)/C	0	0.5
1962	Was A	132	333	39	81	15	0	11	35	55-9	3	37	.243	.353	.387	101	2	4-2	.979	5	104	173	O101(20/0/81)	0	0.2
1963	Was A	136	459	61	106	16	5	24	62	45-3	1	43	.231	.300	.444	106	2	3-0	.987	2	95	164	O123(2/0/122)	0	-0.4
1964	Was A	134	415	46	100	15	1	18	56	55-7	5	65	.241	.335	.412	108	5	3-1	.973	10	**122**	147	O121R	0	0.8
1965	Was A	120	258	46	55	10	2	14	49	44-2	5	50	.213	.337	.430	119	7	1-0	.993	4	106	163	O88(1/0/87)	0	0.7
1966	Was A	117	310	41	77	14	2	10	30	38-2	0	41	.248	.330	.403	111	5	4-0	.987	1	105	92	O85R	0	0.1
1967	Was A	47	100	10	21	2	2	1	12	15-0	3	13	.210	.328	.300	91	-1	1-1	.962	-1	111	0	O31R/C	0	-0.4
	Chi A	23	50	2	6	1	0	0	2	4-0	0	16	.120	.185	.140	-3	-6	0-0	1.000	-1	83	0	O12(1/0/12)	0	-0.9
	Cle A	19	21	2	3	0	0	0	0	1-0	0	2	.143	.182	.143	-3	-3	0-0	1.000	-0	54	0	/rf	0	-0.3
	Year	89	171	14	30	3	2	1	14	20-0	3	31	.175	.272	.234	53	-10	1-1	.971	-3	101	0	O44(1/0/44)/C	0	-1.6
Total	11	1125	2918	374	699	112	19	117	401	363-35	23	401	.240	.326	.411	104	17	23-8	.984	36	107	140	O851(145/3/707),C2	0	0.7
King, Jeff	Jeffrey Wayne; B12.26.1964 Marion IN; BR/TR/6´1˝/(180–190); [PitN86 1/1]; d6.2; Col Arkansas																								
1989	Pit N	75	215	31	42	13	3	5	19	20-1	2	34	.195	.266	.353	79	-6	4-2	.995	-1	79	112	1b46,3b13,2b7/S	0	-1.1
1990	†Pit N	127	371	46	91	17	1	14	53	21-1	1	50	.245	.283	.410	92	-6	3-3	.938	6	**114**	117	3b115/1	0	0.0
1991	Pit N	33	109	16	26	1	1	4	18	14-3	1	15	.239	.328	.376	99	0	3-1	.975	-4	93	0	3b33	131	-0.4
1992	†Pit N	130	480	56	111	21	2	14	65	27-3	2	56	.231	.272	.371	82	-14	4-6	.953	-2	109	137	3b73,1b32,2b32,S6/rf	0	-1.9
1993	Pit N	158	611	82	180	35	3	9	98	59-4	4	54	.295	.356	.406	105	6	8-6	.964	14	**113**	108	3b156,2b2,S2	0	2.0
1994	Pit N	94	339	36	89	23	0	5	42	30-1	0	38	.263	.316	.375	80	-10	3-2	.955	7	106	**182**	3b91/2	15	-0.2
1995	Pit N	122	445	61	118	27	2	18	87	55-5	1	63	.265	.342	.456	107	5	7-4	.942	-2	102	100	3b84,1b35,2b8,S2	15	0.1
1996	Pit N	155	591	91	160	36	4	30	111	70-3	2	95	.271	.346	.497	116	13	15-1	.997	3	89	93	1b92,2b71,3b17	0	1.5
1997	KC A	155	543	84	129	30	1	28	112	89-4	2	96	.238	.341	.451	103	3	16-5	**.996**	21	**155**	**110**	1b150,D2	0	1.2
1998	KC A	131	486	83	128	17	1	24	93	42-1	2	73	.263	.319	.451	95	-5	10-2	.995	6	120	110	1b112,D16,3b4	16	-0.8
1999	KC A	21	72	14	17	2	0	3	11	15-1	3	10	.236	.385	.389	96	0	2-0	.990	1	127	110	1b20/D	20	0.0
Total	11	1201	4262	600	1091	222	18	154	709	442-27	20	584	.256	.324	.425	99	-14	75-32	.953	48	109	119	3b586,1b488,2b121,D19,S11/rf	197	0.4
King, Lee	Lee; B12.26.1892 Hundred WV; D9.16.1967 Shinnston WV; BR/TR/5´8˝/160; d9.20																								
1916	Pit N	8	18	0	2	0	0	0	1	0	0	7	.111	.111	.111	-31	-3	0	.714	-1	57	211	O8(2/0/4)	—	-0.4
1917	Pit N	111	381	32	95	14	5	1	35	15	2	58	.249	.281	.320	82	-9	8	.968	8	112	121	O102(7/0/95)	—	-0.8
1918	Pit N	36	112	9	26	3	2	1	11	11	0	15	.232	.301	.321	87	-2	3	.909	-5	88	0	O36(32/0/4)	—	-0.9
1919	NY N	21	20	5	2	1	0	0	1	1	0	6	.100	.143	.150	-12	-3	0	.667	-1	52	0	O7(2/1/3)	—	-0.4
1920	NY N	93	261	32	72	11	4	7	42	21	2	38	.276	.335	.429	120	6	3-7	.951	-16	73	61	O84(0/83/1)	—	-1.9
1921	NY N	39	94	17	21	4	2	0	7	13	1	6	.223	.324	.309	68	-4	0-2	.921	-0	86	164	O35(0/24/12)/1	—	-0.6
	Phi N	64	216	25	58	19	4	4	32	8	1	37	.269	.298	.449	88	-4	1-4	.911	-2	94	114	O57(55/1/2)	—	-1.2
	Year	103	310	42	79	23	6	4	39	21	2	43	.255	.306	.406	83	-8	1-6	.914	-2	92	129	O92(55/25/14)/1	—	-1.8
1922	Phi N	19	53	8	12	5	1	2	13	8	0	6	.226	.328	.472	95	0	0-0	.946	-1	102	54	O15(11/4/0)	—	-0.2
	†NY N	20	34	6	6	3	0	0	2	5	0	2	.176	.282	.265	41	-3	1-0	1.000	-0	77	61	1b5,O5(0/1/4)	—	-0.3
	Year	39	87	14	18	8	1	2	15	13	0	8	.207	.310	.391	76	-3	1-0	.961	-1	107	40	O20(11/5/4),1b5	—	-0.5
Total	7	411	1189	134	294	60	18	15	144	82	6	175	.247	.299	.366	87	-22	16-13	.940	-17	93	92	O349(109/114/125),1b6	—	-6.7

YEAR	TM LG	G	AB	R	H	2B	3B	HR	RBI	BB-IB	HP	SO	AVG	OBP	SLG	AOPS	ABR	SB-CS	FA	FR	RNG	THR	GAMES AT POSITION	DL	BFW
King, Lynn	Lynn Paul "Dig"; B11.28.1907 Villisca IA; D5.11.1972 Atlantic IA; BL/TR/5´9˝/165; d9.21; Col Drake																								
1935	StL N	8	22	6	4	0	0	0	0	4	0	1	.182	.308	.182	34	-2	2	1.000	1	130	0	O6C	—	-0.1
1936	StL N	78	100	12	19	2	1	0	10	9	0	14	.190	.257	.230	32	-10	2	.984	2	128	55	O34(7/12/15)	—	-0.8
1939	StL N	89	85	10	20	2	0	0	11	15	0	3	.235	.350	.259	62	-4	2	.982	2	132	78	O44(14/29/1)	—	-0.2
Total	3	175	207	28	43	4	1	0	21	28	0	18	.208	.302	.237	45	-16	6	.986	5	130	54	O84(21/47/16)	—	-1.1
King, Mart	Marshal Ney; B12.1849 Troy NY; D10.19.1911 Troy NY; TR/5´9.5˝/176; d5.8																								
1871	Chi NA	20	101	23	21	1	0	2	16	8	—	1	.208	.266	.277	51	-7	5-0	.786	-2	0	0	O11(1/10/0),C9,S3/3	—	-0.6
1872	Tro NA	3	11	0	0	0	0	0	1	0	—	1	.000	.000	.000	-99	-3	0-0	.857	-0	0	0	O3C	—	-0.2
Total	2NA	23	112	23	21	1	0	2	17	8	—	2	.188	.242	.250	39	-10	5-0	.810	-2	0	0	O14(1/13/0),C9,S3/3	—	-0.8
King, Sam	Samuel Warren; B5.17.1852 Peabody MA; D8.11.1922 Peabody MA; BL/TL/6´0˝/?; d5.1																								
1884	Was AA	12	45	3	8	2	0	0	—	1	1	—	.178	.213	.222	48	-2	—	.912	-1	96	85	1b12	—	-0.4
King, Steve	Stephen F.; B1842 Troy NY; D7.8.1895 Troy NY; 5´9˝/175; d5.9																								
1871	Tro NA	**29**	144	45	57	10	6	0	34	1	—	1	.396	.400	.549	167	12	3-3	.833	3	182	0	O29L	—	1.0
1872	Tro NA	**25**	128	33	39	8	0	0	20	1	—	2	.305	.310	.367	106	1	1-1	.776	1	183	203	O25L	—	0.2
Total	2NA	54	272	78	96	18	6	0	54	2	—	3	.353	.358	.463	139	13	4-4	.807	4	182	96	O54L	—	1.2
Kingdon, Wes	Westcott William; B7.4.1900 Los Angeles CA; D4.19.1975 San Juan Capistrano CA; BR/TR/5´8˝/148; d6.12																								
1932	Was A	18	34	10	11	3	1	0	3	5	0	2	.324	.410	.471	129	2	0-0	.929	-1	92	122	3b8,S4	—	0.1
Kingery, Mike	Michael Scott; B3.29.1961 St.James MN; BL/TL/6´0˝/(180–185); d7.7																								
1986	KC A	62	209	25	54	8	5	3	14	12-2	0	30	.258	.296	.388	83	-6	7-3	.973	-1	88	166	O59(1/13/51)	0	-0.8
1987	Sea A	120	354	38	99	25	4	9	52	27-0	2	43	.280	.329	.449	100	0	7-9	.992	14	118	219	O114(0/6/111),D4	0	0.7
1988	Sea A	57	123	21	25	6	0	1	9	19-1	1	23	.203	.313	.276	64	-5	3-1	.989	3	106	174	O44(9/24/13),1b10	0	-0.3
1989	Sea A	31	76	14	17	3	0	2	6	7-0	0	14	.224	.286	.342	75	-3	1-1	1.000	3	137	0	O23(2/20/1)	0	0.0
1990	SF N	105	207	24	61	7	1	0	24	12-0	1	19	.295	.335	.338	89	-3	6-1	.978	4	107	175	O95(15/9/74)	0	0.0
1991	SF N	91	110	13	20	2	2	0	8	15-1	0	21	.182	.280	.236	48	-8	1-0	.975	-0	113	0	O38(14/2/22),1b6	0	-0.9
1992	Oak A	12	28	3	3	0	0	0	1	1-0	0	3	.107	.138	.107	-32	-5	0-0	1.000	-1	78	0	O10(2/6/2)	0	-0.6
1994	Col N	105	301	56	105	27	8	4	41	30-2	2	26	.349	.402	.532	123	11	5-7	.979	-1	96	111	O98(20/77/2)/1	0	0.9
1995	†Col N	119	350	66	94	18	4	8	37	45-1	0	40	.269	.351	.411	78	-10	13-5	.979	-8	86	84	O108C,1b5	0	-1.6
1996	Pit N	117	276	32	68	12	2	3	27	23-2	1	29	.246	.304	.337	67	-13	2-1	.985	-3	93	59	O83(5/64/16)	0	-1.6
Total	10	819	2034	292	546	108	26	30	219	191-9	7	248	.268	.330	.391	86	-42	45-28	.984	9	101	128	O672(68/329/292),1b22,D4	0	-4.2
Kingman, Dave	David Arthur "Kong"; B12.21.1948 Pendleton OR; BR/TR/6´6˝/(210–218); [SFN70 S1/1]; d7.30; Col USC; OF(508/0/144)																								
1971	†SF N	41	115	17	32	10	2	6	24	9-0	1	35	.278	.328	.557	151	7	5-0	.981	-3	78	67	1b20,O14(7/0/7)	0	0.3
1972	SF N	135	472	65	106	17	4	29	83	51-2	4	140	.225	.303	.462	113	6	16-6	.932	4	120	104	3b59,1b56,O22L	0	0.7
1973	SF N	112	305	54	62	10	1	24	55	41-3	2	122	.203	.300	.479	108	2	8-5	.910	3	114	64	3b60,1b46,P2	0	0.2
1974	SF N	121	350	41	78	18	2	18	55	37-2	3	125	.223	.302	.440	102	-1	8-8	.983	1	128	110	1b91,3b21,O2R	0	-0.7
1975	NY N	134	502	65	116	22	1	36	88	34-5	4	153	.231	.284	.494	117	6	7-5	.958	4	108	61	O71(68/0/3),1b58,3b12	0	0.2
1976	NY N★	123	474	70	113	14	1	37	86	28-4	5	135	.238	.286	.506	128	12	7-4	.959	1	99	119	O111(5/0/106),1b16	38	0.7
1977	NY N	58	211	22	44	7	0	9	28	13-3	3	66	.209	.263	.370	70	-10	3-2	.974	-1	104	0	O45(26/0/20),1b17	0	-1.4
	SD N	56	168	16	40	9	0	11	39	12-1	2	48	.238	.292	.488	118	3	2-3	.964	3	100	171	O28L,1b13,3b2	0	0.3
	Year	114	379	38	84	16	0	20	67	25-4	5	114	.222	.276	.422	91	-7	5-5	.970	2	79	0	O73(54/0/20),1b30,3b2	0	-1.1
	Cal A	10	36	4	7	2	0	2	4	1-0	1	16	.194	.237	.417	77	-1	0-0	.974	-1	94	77	1b8,O2L	0	-0.2
	NY A	8	24	5	6	2	0	4	7	2-0	1	13	.250	.333	.833	207	3	0-1	ø	0	—	—	D6	0	0.3
	Year	18	60	9	13	4	0	6	11	3-0	2	29	.217	.277	.583	130	2	0-1	.974	-1	94	77	1b8,D6,O2L	0	0.1
1978	Chi N	119	395	65	105	17	4	28	79	39-8	6	111	.266	.336	.542	128	13	3-4	.978	-3	89	98	O100L,1b6	25	0.6
1979	Chi N✳	145	532	97	153	19	5	**48**	115	45-7	4	131	.288	.343	**.613**	143	28	4-2	.954	-0	93	111	O139L	0	2.3
1980	Chi N★	81	255	31	71	8	0	18	57	21-3	0	44	.278	.329	.522	125	7	2-2	.941	2	93	194	O61(63/0/1),1b2	48	0.6
1981	NY N	100	353	40	78	11	3	22	59	55-7	1	105	.221	.326	.456	121	9	6-0	.974	-5	92	100	1b56,O48L	0	0.0
1982	NY N	149	535	80	109	9	1	**37**	99	59-9	4	156	.204	.285	.432	98	-4	4-0	.986	-14	71	79	1b143	0	-2.7
1983	NY N	100	248	25	49	7	0	13	29	22-1	1	57	.198	.265	.383	78	-9	2-1	.994	-5	76	109	1b50,O5R	0	-1.8
1984	Oak A	147	549	68	147	23	1	35	118	44-8	6	119	.268	.321	.505	135	24	2-1	1.000	-2	34	41	D139,1b9	0	1.8
1985	Oak A	158	592	66	141	16	0	30	91	62-6	2	114	.238	.309	.417	105	2	3-2	1.000	-1	22	55	D149,1b9	0	-0.4
1986	Oak A	144	561	70	118	19	0	35	94	33-3	3	126	.210	.255	.431	90	-12	3-3	.895	-1	0	129	D140,1b3	0	-1.8
Total	16	1941	6677	901	1575	240	25	442	1210	608-72	53	1816	.236	.302	.478	114	85	85-49	.957	-18	96	100	O648L,1b603,D434,3b154,P2	111	-1.0
Kingman, Harry	Henry Lees; B4.3.1892 Tientsin, China; D12.27.1982 Oakland CA; BL/TL/6´1.5˝/165; d7.1; Col Springfield																								
1914	NY A	4	3	0	0	0	0	0	0	1	0	2	.000	.250	.000	-24	0	0	1.000	-0	0	0	/1	—	-0.1
Kingsale, Eugene	Eugene Humphrey; B8.20.1976 Solito, Aruba; BB/TR/6´3˝/(170–194); d9.3																								
1996	Bal A	3	0	0	0	0	0	0	0	0-0	0	0	ø	ø	ø	ø	0	0-0	1.000	0	226	0	O2C	0	0.0
1998	Bal A	11	2	1	0	0	0	0	0	0-0	0	1	.000	.000	.000	-99	-1	0-0	1.000	0	99	0	O4C	0	-0.1
1999	Bal A	28	85	9	21	2	0	0	7	5-0	2	13	.247	.301	.271	50	-6	1-3	.980	-3	80	68	O24C,D2	0	-0.9
2000	Bal A	26	88	13	21	2	1	0	9	2-0	0	14	.239	.253	.284	38	-9	1-2	.954	1	105	179	O24C/D	145	-0.8
2001	Bal A	3	4	0	0	0	0	0	0	0-0	0	2	.000	.000	.000	-99	-1	1-1	1.000	-0	38	0	/cf	0	-0.2
	Sea A	10	15	4	5	0	0	0	1	2-0	1	2	.333	.444	.333	116	1	2-0	1.000	0	117	0	O9(5/1/3)	0	0.1
	Year	13	19	4	5	0	0	0	1	2-0	1	4	.263	.364	.263	73	-1	3-1	1.000	-0	103	0	O10(5/2/3)	0	-0.1
2002	Sea A	2	3	0	2	0	0	0	0	0-0	0	0	.667	.667	.667	265	1	0-0	1.000	0	129	0	O2(0/1/1)	0	0.1
	SD N	89	216	27	60	10	3	2	28	20-0	3	47	.278	.346	.380	100	0	9-2	.985	4	116	116	O82(26/17/50)	0	0.3
2003	Det A	39	120	11	25	3	1	1	8	10-0	0	17	.208	.265	.275	46	-10	1-3	.985	-4	84	0	O30(8/23/0),D4	20	-1.4
Total	7	211	533	65	134	17	5	3	53	39-0	6	96	.251	.307	.319	68	-25	15-11	.979	-3	101	86	O178(39/97/54),D7	165	-2.9
Kinkade, Mike	Michael A.; B5.6.1973 Livonia MI; BR/TR/6´1˝/210; [MilA95 9/236]; d9.8; Col Washington St.																								
1998	NY N	3	2	2	0	0	0	0	0	0-0	0	0	.000	.000	.000	-99	-1	0-0	ø	-0	0	0	/3	0	-0.1
1999	NY N	28	46	3	9	2	1	2	6	3-0	2	9	.196	.275	.413	74	-2	1-0	1.000	-0	77	168	O17(12/0/8),3b3/C1	0	-0.3
2000	NY N	2	2	0	0	0	0	0	0	0-0	0	1	.000	.000	.000	-99	-1	0-0	ø	-0	0	0	/rf	0	-0.1
	Bal A	3	7	0	3	1	0	0	1	0-0	1	0	.429	.500	.571	179	1	0-0	1.000	0	0	0	/1D	0	0.1
2001	Bal A	61	160	19	44	5	0	4	16	14-0	3	31	.275	.345	.381	96	-1	2-1	.962	-1	95	63	O32(29/0/3),3b10,D10,1b3,C2	30	-0.3
2002	LA N	37	50	7	19	5	0	2	11	4-0	6	10	.380	.483	.600	194	8	1-0	1.000	-1	128	74	1b11,O8L	0	0.6
2003	LA N	88	162	25	35	7	0	5	14	13-2	16	38	.216	.335	.352	82	-4	1-3	.914	-3	70	0	O36(34/0/2),1b13,3b2/D	0	-1.0
Total	6	222	429	56	110	20	1	13	48	34-2	28	89	.256	.350	.399	99	0	5-4	.953	-6	78	48	O94(83/0/14),1b29,3b16,D13,C3	30	-1.1
Kinloch, Billy	William Francis; B3.21.1874 Providence RI; D2.15.1931 New York NY; d8.1																								
1895	StL N	1	3	0	1	0	0	0	0	0	0	2	.333	.333	.333	73	0	0	1.000	0	46	608	/3	—	0.0
Kinsella, Bob	Robert Francis "Red"; B1.5.1899 Springfield IL; D12.30.1951 Los Angeles CA; BL/TR/5´9.5˝/165; d9.20																								
1919	NY N	3	9	1	2	0	0	0	0	0	0	3	.222	.222	.222	34	-1	1	.500	-1	32	0	O3(2/0/1)	—	-0.2
1920	NY N	1	3	0	1	0	0	0	1	0	0	2	.333	.333	.333	93	0	0-0	.500	-0	66	0	/rf	—	-0.1
Total	2	4	12	1	3	0	0	0	1	0	0	5	.250	.250	.250	49	-1	1-0	.500	-1	43	0	O4(2/0/2)	—	-0.3
Kinsler, Ian	Ian Michael; B6.22.1982 Tucson AR; BR/TR/6´0˝/200; [TexA03 17/496]; d4.3; Col Nissouri																								
2006	Tex A	120	423	65	121	27	1	14	55	40-1	3	64	.286	.347	.454	106	4	11-4	.973	22	114	110	2b119	43	3.1
Kinsler, William	William H.; B11.9.1867 New York NY; D8.10.1963 Miami Beach FL; d6.8																								
1893	NY N	1	3	1	0	0	0	0	0	1	0	1	.000	.250	.000	-31	-1	0	1.000	-0	0	0	/rf	—	-0.1
Kinslow, Tom	Thomas F.; B1.12.1866 Washington DC; D2.22.1901 Washington DC; BR/TR/5´10˝/160; d6.4																								
1886	Was N	3	8	1	2	0	0	0	1	0	—	1	.250	.250	.250	57	0	0	1.000	-0	—	—	C3	—	0.0
1887	NY AA	2	6	0	0	0	0	0	0	0	0	—	.000	.000	.000	-99	-2	0	1.000	0	—	—	C2	—	-0.1
1890	Bro P	64	242	30	64	11	6	4	46	10	2	22	.264	.299	.409	83	-8	2	.909	14	*128*	*93*	C64	—	0.9
1891	Bro N	61	228	22	54	6	0	0	33	9	0	22	.237	.266	.263	55	-14	3	.922	-6	*97*	*82*	C61	—	-1.3
1892	Bro N	66	246	37	75	6	11	2	40	13	1	17	.305	.342	.443	142	10	4	.933	2	*104*	*112*	C66	—	1.7
1893	Bro N	78	312	38	76	8	4	4	45	11	1	13	.244	.272	.333	63	-19	4	.932	-1	*99*	*94*	C76,O2R	—	-1.1

YEAR	TM LG	G	AB	R	H	2B	3B	HR	RBI	BB-IB	HP	SO	AVG	OBP	SLG	AOPS	ABR	SB-CS	FA	FR	RNG	THR	GAMES AT POSITION	DL	BFW
1894	Bro N	62	223	39	68	5	6	2	41	20	0	11	.305	.362	.408	92	-3	4	.907	-10	*90*	*79*	C61/1	—	-0.7
1895	Pit N	19	62	10	14	2	0	0	5	2	0	2	.226	.250	.258	33	-6	1	.962	-3	*87*	*66*	C18	—	-0.6
1896	Lou N	8	25	4	7	0	1	0	7	1	0	5	.280	.308	.360	78	-1	0	.810	-2	*76*	*60*	C5/1	—	-0.2
1898	Was N	3	9	0	1	0	0	0	0	0	0	—	.111	.111	.111	-36	-2	0	.800	-1	*72*	*172*	C3/1	—	-0.2
	StL N	14	53	5	15	2	1	0	4	1	1	—	.283	.309	.358	89	-1	0	.925	-1	*74*	*120*	C14	—	-0.1
	Year	17	62	5	16	2	1	0	4	1	1	—	.258	.281	.323	72	-3	0	.909	-2	*74*	*127*	C17/1	—	-0.3
Total	10	380	1414	186	376	40	29	12	222	67	5	93	.266	.301	.361	81	-46	18	.923	-9	*102*	*93*	C373,1b3,O2R	—	-1.7
KINZIE, WALT	Walter Harris; B3.1858 KS; D11.5.1909 Chicago IL; BR/TR/5´10.5˝/161; d7.17																								
1882	Det N	13	53	5	5	0	1	0	2	0	—	8	.094	.094	.132	-28	-8	—	.852	-2	96	28	S13	—	-0.9
1884	Chi N	19	82	4	13	3	0	2	8	0	—	13	.159	.159	.268	29	-7	—	.831	-2	97	112	S17,3b2	—	-0.7
	StL AA	2	9	0	1	0	0	0	—	0	0	—	.111	.111	.111	-26	-1	—	.727	-2	62	0	2b2	—	-0.3
Total	2	34	144	9	19	3	1	2	10	0	0	21	.132	.132	.208	6	-16	—	.840	-6	97	75	S30,2b2,3b2	—	-1.9
KIPPERT, ED	Edward August "Kickapoo"; B1.3.1879 Detroit MI; D6.3.1960 Detroit MI; BR/TR/5´10.5˝/180; d4.14																								
1914	Cin N	2	2	0	0	0	0	0	0	0	0	0	.000	.000	.000	-97	0	0	1.000	-0	71	0	O2(1/1/0)	—	-0.1
KIRBY, JIM	James Herschel; B5.5.1923 Nashville TN; BR/TR/5´11˝/175; d5.1																								
1949	Chi N	3	2	0	1	0	0	0	0	0	0	0	.500	.500	.500	174	0	0	ø	0	—	—	/H	0	0.0
KIRBY, LA RUE	La Rue; B12.30.1889 Eureka MI; D6.10.1961 Lansing MI; BB/TR/6´0˝/185; d8.7; ▲																								
1912	NY N	3	5	1	1	1	0	0	0	0	0	0	.200	.200	.400	60	0	0	1.000	0	109	0	P3	—	0.0
1914	StL F	52	195	21	48	6	3	2	18	14	2	30	.246	.303	.338	71	-11	5	.973	2	103	107	O50(0/49/1)	—	-1.4
1915	StL F	61	178	15	38	7	2	0	16	17	0	31	.213	.282	.275	54	-13	3	.969	-0	93	128	O52(9/40/4)/P	—	-1.7
Total	3	116	378	37	87	14	5	2	34	31	2	61	.230	.292	.310	63	-24	8	.971	2	98	117	O102(9/89/5),P4	—	-3.1
KIRBY, WAYNE	Wayne Leonard; B1.22.1964 Williamsburg VA; BL/TR/5´10˝/(185–190); [LAN83*13/291]; d9.12																								
1991	Cle A	21	43	4	9	2	0	0	5	2-0	0	6	.209	.239	.256	38	-4	1-2	1.000	2	133	95	O21(5/1/17)	0	-0.3
1992	Cle A	21	18	9	3	1	0	1	1	3-0	0	2	.167	.286	.389	88	0	0-3	1.000	0	205	0	O2(1/0/1),D4	0	-0.1
1993	Cle A	131	458	71	123	19	5	6	60	37-2	3	58	.269	.323	.371	87	-9	17-5	.983	14	110	**227**	O123(2/15/113),D5	0	0.2
1994	Cle A	78	191	33	56	6	0	5	23	13-0	1	30	.293	.341	.403	90	-3	11-4	.959	-4	92	56	O68(8/6/55),D2	0	-0.7
1995	†Cle A	101	188	29	39	10	2	1	14	13-0	1	32	.207	.260	.298	44	-16	10-3	.990	-1	93	81	O68(1/34/35),D7	0	-1.6
1996	Cle A	27	16	3	4	1	0	0	1	2-0	0	2	.250	.333	.313	65	-1	0-1	1.000	-1	80	0	O18(2/5/11)	0	-0.2
	†LA N	65	188	23	51	10	1	1	11	17-1	1	17	.271	.333	.351	86	-3	4-2	.969	-2	91	87	O53(8/47/0)	0	-0.5
1997	LA N	46	65	6	11	2	0	0	4	10-0	0	12	.169	.280	.200	30	-7	0-0	1.000	2	121	136	O26(9/16/2)	0	-0.5
1998	NY N	26	31	5	6	0	1	0	0	1-0	0	9	.194	.219	.258	26	-4	1-1	1.000	1	115	239	O19(3/4/12)	0	-0.3
Total	8	516	1198	183	302	51	9	14	119	98-3	6	168	.252	.309	.345	74	-47	44-21	.981	11	103	140	O398(39/128/246),D18	0	-4.0
KIRK, TOM	Thomas Daniel; B9.27.1927 Philadelphia PA; D8.1.1974 Philadelphia PA; BL/TL/5´10.5˝/182; d6.24																								
1947	Phi A	1	1	0	0	0	0	0	0	0	0	0	.000	.000	.000	-98	0	0-0	ø	0	—	—	/H	0	0.0
KIRKE, JAY	Judson Fabian; B6.16.1888 Fleischmanns NY; D8.31.1968 New Orleans LA; BL/TR/6´0˝/195; d9.28; OF(102/2/38)																								
1910	Det A	8	25	3	5	1	0	0	3	1	0	—	.200	.231	.240	44	-2	1	.917	-2	86	39	2b7/lf	—	-0.4
1911	Bos N	20	89	9	32	5	5	0	12	2	1	6	.360	.380	.528	142	4	3	.929	-1	94	110	O14L,1b3/2S3	—	0.3
1912	Bos N	103	359	53	115	11	4	4	62	9	1	46	.320	.339	.407	102	-1	7	.903	-0	82	211	O72(62/0/10),3b14,S2/1	—	-0.4
1913	Bos N	18	38	3	9	2	0	0	3	1	2	6	.237	.293	.289	65	-2	0-1	.923	2	93	344	O13(3/2/8)	—	0.0
1914	Cle A	67	242	18	66	10	2	1	25	7	1	30	.273	.296	.343	89	-5	5-10	.974	1	113	57	O42(22/0/20),1b18	—	-0.9
1915	Cle A	87	339	35	105	19	2	2	40	14	5	21	.310	.346	.395	120	7	5-6	.986	-1	97	79	1b87	—	0.3
1918	NY N	17	56	1	14	1	0	0	3	1	0	3	.250	.263	.268	63	-3	0	.978	1	121	86	1b16	—	-0.3
Total	7	320	1148	122	346	49	13	7	148	35	10	112	.301	.328	.385	103	-2	21-17	.927	0	93	165	O142L,1b125,3b15,2b8,S3	—	-1.4
KIRKLAND, WILLIE	Willie Charles; B2.17.1934 Siluria AL; BL/TR/6´1˝/(195–206); d4.15																								
1958	SF N	122	418	48	108	25	6	14	56	43-7	5	69	.258	.332	.447	107	4	3-2	.961	-2	93	134	O115(5/0/112)	0	-0.2
1959	SF N	126	463	64	126	22	3	22	68	42-3	3	84	.272	.335	.475	116	9	5-3	.969	-1	99	90	O117(13/0/109)	0	0.4
1960	SF N	146	515	59	130	21	10	21	65	44-8	4	86	.252	.315	.454	115	8	12-7	.978	2	99	127	O143(3/0/143)	0	0.5
1961	Cle A	146	525	84	136	22	5	27	95	48-4	1	77	.259	.318	.474	113	7	7-0	.974	6	107	114	O138R	0	0.5
1962	Cle A	137	419	56	84	9	1	21	72	43-3	0	62	.200	.272	.377	76	-17	9-1	.972	6	109	170	O125(0/12/121)	0	-1.7
1963	Cle A	127	427	51	98	13	2	15	47	45-5	1	99	.230	.303	.375	90	-6	8-2	.984	3	102	159	O112(5/64/45)	0	-0.8
1964	Bal A	66	150	14	30	5	0	3	22	17-4	1	26	.200	.281	.293	62	-8	3-2	.989	5	109	266	O58(2/10/48)	0	-0.5
	Was A	32	102	8	22	6	0	5	13	6-0	0	30	.216	.259	.422	86	-2	0-0	.907	-3	84	0	O27(12/1/15)	0	-0.8
	Year	98	252	22	52	11	0	8	35	23-4	1	56	.206	.272	.345	72	-10	3-2	.964	2	100	166	O85(14/11/63)	0	-1.3
1965	Was A	123	312	38	72	9	1	14	54	19-1	0	65	.231	.270	.401	91	-5	3-2	.987	2	111	64	O92(32/5/67)	0	-0.9
1966	Was A	124	163	21	31	2	1	6	17	16-3	0	50	.190	.261	.325	68	-7	2-0	.983	-0	91	141	O68(50/0/19)	0	-1.0
Total	9	1149	3494	443	837	134	29	148	509	323-38	15	648	.240	.304	.422	99	-17	52-19	.974	18	102	129	O995(122/92/817)	0	-4.5
KIRKPATRICK, ED	Edgar Leon; B10.8.1944 Spokane WA; BL/TR/5´11.5˝/(185–200); d9.13; OF(236/62/291)																								
1962	LA A	3	6	0	0	0	0	0	0	0-0	0	2	.000	.000	.000	-99	-2	0-0	1.000	1	0	0	/C	0	-0.1
1963	LA A	34	77	4	15	5	0	2	7	6-0	1	19	.195	.259	.338	71	-3	1-0	.986	1	30	143	C14,O10L	0	-0.2
1964	LA A	75	219	20	53	13	3	2	22	23-6	2	30	.242	.315	.356	97	-1	2-2	.969	-2	86	102	O63(63/0/1)	0	-0.7
1965	Cal A	19	73	8	19	5	0	3	8	3-0	0	9	.260	.289	.452	110	1	1-2	.969	0	82	246	O19R	0	-0.1
1966	Cal A	117	312	31	60	7	4	9	44	51-8	5	67	.192	.313	.327	87	-4	7-4	.994	-3	93	77	O102(17/0/86),1b3	0	-1.4
1967	Cal A	3	8	0	0	0	0	0	0	0-0	0	2	.000	.000	.000	-99	-2	0-0	1.000	-1	0	0	C2/lf	0	-0.3
1968	Cal A	89	161	23	37	4	0	1	15	25-2	1	32	.230	.332	.273	89	-1	1-3	.982	-1	92	104	O45(12/1/34),C4,1b2	0	-0.6
1969	KC A	120	315	40	81	11	4	14	49	43-4	3	42	.257	.348	.451	121	9	3-5	.995	7	119	139	O82(29/24/32),C8,1b2,3b2/2	0	1.2
1970	KC A	134	424	59	97	17	2	18	62	55-8	1	65	.229	.319	.406	98	-1	4-4	.978	-2	79	**163**	C89,O19(8/3/8),1b16	0	-0.2
1971	KC A	120	365	46	80	12	1	9	46	48-8	2	60	.219	.308	.332	83	-8	3-4	.992	6	112	62	O61(30/16/18),C59	0	-0.2
1972	KC A	113	364	43	100	15	1	9	43	51-9	3	50	.275	.365	.396	128	14	3-5	.991	-3	85	98	C108/1	0	1.7
1973	KC A	126	429	61	113	24	3	6	45	46-6	1	48	.263	.333	.375	93	-3	3-7	.990	-0	96	43	O108(27/11/72),C14,D8	0	-1.0
1974	†Pit N	116	271	32	67	9	0	6	38	51-13	2	30	.247	.367	.347	104	4	1-2	.993	-1	99	122	1b59,O14(0/2/12),C6	0	-0.2
1975	†Pit N	89	144	15	34	5	0	5	16	18-2	0	22	.236	.319	.375	92	-2	1-0	1.000	-0	99	82	1b28,O14(8/0/6)	0	-0.4
1976	Pit N	83	146	14	34	9	0	0	16	14-2	0	15	.233	.294	.295	68	-6	1-0	.990	0	114	90	1b25,O9(3/4/2)/3	0	-0.8
1977	Pit N	21	28	5	4	2	0	1	4	8-0	0	6	.143	.324	.321	74	-1	1-0	.972	0	107	145	1b10,O2(1/1/0)/3	0	-0.1
	Tex A	20	48	2	9	1	0	0	3	4-1	0	11	.188	.250	.208	26	-5	2-0	1.000	1	148	0	O6(5/0/1),1b3/CD	0	-0.4
	Mil A	29	77	8	21	4	0	0	6	10-1	1	8	.273	.364	.325	89	-1	0-1	.973	-1	103	0	O22L/3D	0	-0.3
	Year	49	125	10	30	5	0	0	9	14-2	1	19	.240	.321	.280	65	-5	2-1	.980	-1	112	0	O28(27/0/1),D8,1b3/C3	0	-0.7
Total	16	1311	3467	411	824	143	18	85	424	456-70	22	518	.238	.327	.363	96	-12	34-39	.989	1	100	80	O577R,C306,1b149,D16,3b5/2	0	-4.1
KIRKPATRICK, ENOS	Enos Claire; B12.9.1884 Pittsburgh PA; D4.14.1964 Pittsburgh PA; BR/TR/5´10˝/175; d8.24; Col Duquesne																								
1912	Bro N	32	94	13	18	1	1	0	6	9	1	15	.191	.269	.223	37	-8	5	.968	5	129	85	3b29,S3	—	-0.3
1913	Bro N	48	89	13	22	4	1	1	5	3	2	18	.247	.287	.348	79	-3	5-1	.897	-2	71	51	S10,1b8,2b6,3b4	—	-0.4
1914	Bal F	55	174	22	44	7	2	2	16	18	2	30	.253	.330	.351	83	-7	10	.932	-1	80	25	3b36,S11,O3(2/0/1)/1	—	-0.6
1915	Bal F	68	171	22	41	8	2	0	19	24	1	15	.240	.337	.310	80	-6	12	.911	-3	94	72	3b28,2b21,1b5,S5	—	-0.9
Total	4	203	528	70	125	20	6	3	46	54	6	78	.237	.315	.314	74	-24	32-1	.936	-1	101	59	3b97,S29,2b27,1b14,O3(2/0/1)	—	-2.2
KIRRENE, JOE	Joseph John; B10.4.1931 San Francisco CA; BR/TR/6´2˝/195; d10.1; Mil 1952–53																								
1950	Chi A	1	4	0	1	0	0	0	0	0	0	1	.250	.250	.250	29	0	0-0	1.000	-0	59	0	/3	0	-0.1
1954	Chi A	9	23	4	7	1	0	0	4	5	1	2	.304	.448	.348	116	1	1-0	.947	-1	77	173	3b9	0	0.0
Total	2	10	27	4	8	1	0	0	4	5	1	3	.296	.424	.333	105	1	1-0	.952	-1	75	154	3b10	0	-0.1
KISH, ERNIE	Ernest Alexander; B2.6.1918 Washington DC; D12.21.1993 Kirtland OH; BL/TR/5´9.5˝/170; d7.29; Col Ohio U.																								
1945	Phi A	43	110	10	27	5	1	0	10	9	3	9	.245	.320	.309	83	-2	0-3	.932	-2	85	118	O30(13/8/11)	0	-0.7
KISSINGER, BILL	William Francis "Shang"; B8.15.1871 Dayton KY; D4.20.1929 Cincinnati OH; BR/TR/5´11˝/185; d5.30; ▲																								
1895	Bal N	2	5	1	1	0	0	0	0	0	0	1	.200	.200	.200	3	0	0	1.000	-0	80	0	P2	—	0.0
	StL N	33	97	8	24	6	1	0	8	0	0	11	.247	.247	.330	49	-8	1	.975	-3	97	87	P24,S4,O4(1/0/3)/3	—	-0.4
	Year	35	102	9	25	6	1	0	8	0	0	12	.245	.245	.324	46	-9	1	**.976**	-3	96	81	P26,S4,O4(1/0/3)/3	—	-0.4

YEAR	TM LG	G	AB	R	H	2B	3B	HR	RBI	BB-IB	HP	SO	AVG	OBP	SLG	AOPS	ABR	SB-CS	FA	FR	RNG	THR	GAMES AT POSITION	DL	BFW
1896	StL N	23	73	8	22	4	0	0	12	0	0	4	.301	.301	.356	76	-3	0	.906	0	127	155	P20,O3L/3	—	-0.1
1897	StL N	14	39	7	13	3	2	0	6	3	0	—	.333	.381	.513	138	2	0	.786	-1	0	0	O7(6/1/0),P7	—	0.0
Total	3	72	214	24	60	13	3	0	26	3	0	16	.280	.290	.369	73	-9	1	.935	-4	111	105	P53,O14(10/1/3),S4,3b2	—	-0.5
Kitsos, Chris	Christopher Anestos; B2.11.1928 New York NY; D6.7.2004 Mobile AL; BB/TR/5´9˝/165; d4.21																								
1954	Chi N	1	0	0	0	0	0	0	0	0	0	0	ø	ø	ø	ø	0	0-0	1.000	0	191	0	/S	0	0.0
Kittle, Ron	Ronald Dale; B1.5.1958 Gary IN; BR/TR/6´4˝/(200–220); d9.2																								
1982	Chi A	20	29	3	7	2	0	1	7	3-0	0	12	.241	.313	.414	97	0	0-0	1.000	-1	43	0	O5R,D3	0	-0.1
1983	†Chi A★	145	520	75	132	19	3	35	100	39-8	8	150	.254	.314	.504	116	9	8-3	.964	-13	83	67	O139L,D2	0	-0.9
1984	Chi A	139	466	67	100	15	0	32	74	49-5	6	137	.215	.295	.453	99	-2	3-6	.972	-1	87	166	O124L,D7	0	-1.0
1985	Chi A	116	379	51	87	12	0	26	58	31-1	5	92	.230	.295	.467	101	-1	1-4	.989	-2	92	67	O57L,D57	21	-0.8
1986	Chi A	86	296	34	63	11	0	17	48	28-0	3	87	.213	.282	.422	87	-6	2-1	1.000	1	93	244	D62,O20L	0	-0.8
	NY A	30	80	8	19	2	0	4	12	7-1	0	23	.237	.292	.412	92	-1	2-0	1.000	0	106	0	D24/lf	0	-0.2
	Year	116	376	42	82	13	0	21	60	35-1	3	110	.218	.284	.420	88	-8	4-1	.673	1	94	232	D86,O21L	0	-1.0
1987	NY A	59	159	21	44	5	0	12	28	10-1	1	36	.277	.318	.535	123	4	0-1	1.000	1	198	1409	D49,O2L	40	0.3
1988	Cle A	75	225	31	58	8	0	18	43	16-1	8	65	.258	.323	.533	133	9	0-0	ø	0	0	0	D63	0	0.7
1989	Chi A	51	169	26	51	10	0	11	37	22-1	1	42	.302	.378	.556	165	15	0-1	.982	-2	67	132	1b27,D17,O5L	113	1.1
1990	Chi A	83	277	29	68	14	0	16	43	24-2	3	77	.245	.311	.469	118	6	0-0	.987	-4	38	115	D54,1b25	0	-0.1
	Bal A	22	61	4	10	2	0	2	3	2-0	1	14	.164	.203	.295	39	-5	0-0	1.000	-1	42	37	D13,1b5	0	-0.7
	Year	105	338	33	78	16	0	18	46	26-2	4	91	.231	.293	.438	104	0	0-0	.989	-4	39	104	D67,1b30	0	-0.8
1991	Chi A	17	47	7	9	0	0	2	7	5-0	2	9	.191	.291	.319	72	-2	0-0	.982	-1	75	89	1b15	0	-0.4
Total	10	843	2708	356	648	100	3	176	460	236-20	38	744	.239	.306	.473	109	26	16-16	.974	-21	87	121	O353(348/0/5),D351,1b72	174	-2.9
Kittridge, Malachi	Malachi Jeddidah "Jeddidah"; B10.12.1869 Clinton MA; D6.23.1928 Gary IN; BR/TR/5´7˝/170; d4.19; M1																								
1890	Chi N	96	333	46	67	8	3	3	35	39	1	53	.201	.287	.270	60	-17	7	.944	5	*112*	*95*	C96	—	-0.4
1891	Chi N	79	296	26	62	8	5	2	27	17	0	28	.209	.252	.291	58	-17	4	.940	5	***132***	*91*	C79	—	-0.5
1892	Chi N	69	229	19	41	5	0	0	10	11	0	27	.179	.217	.201	26	-21	2	.945	8	*105*	*100*	C69	—	-0.6
1893	Chi N	70	255	32	59	9	5	2	30	17	0	15	.231	.279	.329	62	-15	3	.939	4	*90*	*116*	C70	—	-0.4
1894	Chi N	51	168	36	53	8	2	0	23	26	0	20	.315	.407	.387	87	-3	2	.925	-5	*80*	*71*	C51	—	-0.3
1895	Chi N	60	212	30	48	6	3	3	29	16	1	9	.226	.284	.325	53	-16	6	.976	0	*95*	*84*	C59	—	-0.9
1896	Chi N	65	215	17	48	4	1	1	19	14	1	14	.223	.274	.265	41	-19	6	.962	-0	*93*	*90*	C64/P	—	-1.2
1897	Chi N	79	262	25	53	5	5	1	30	22	0	—	.202	.264	.271	40	-24	9	.952	-1	*87*	*99*	C79	—	-1.6
1898	Lou N	86	287	27	70	8	5	1	31	15	0	—	.244	.281	.317	72	-12	9	.944	-13	*81*	*103*	C86	—	-1.6
1899	Lou N	46	131	11	26	2	1	0	13	26	1	—	.198	.335	.229	56	-7	3	.975	6	*116*	*110*	C44	—	0.3
	Was N	44	133	14	20	3	0	0	11	10	1	—	.150	.215	.173	7	-17	2	.949	-4	*78*	*118*	C43	—	-1.6
	Year	90	264	25	46	5	1	0	24	36	2	—	.174	.278	.201	32	-24	5	.962	3	*98*	*114*	C87	—	-1.3
1901	Bos N	114	381	24	96	14	0	2	40	32	1	—	.252	.312	.304	72	-13	2	**.984**	17	***130***	*97*	C113	—	1.5
1902	Bos N	80	255	18	60	7	0	2	30	24	1	—	.235	.304	.286	81	-5	4	.981	6	*110*	*97*	C72	—	0.9
1903	Bos N	32	99	10	21	2	0	0	6	11	0	—	.212	.291	.232	52	-6	1	.981	4	*98*	*85*	C30	—	0.1
	Was A	60	192	8	41	4	1	0	16	10	0	—	.214	.252	.245	49	-12	1	.978	-8	*74*	*118*	C60	—	-1.5
1904	Was A	81	265	11	64	7	0	0	24	8	1	—	.242	.266	.268	70	-9	2	.982	-5	*73*	***118***	C79,M	—	-0.7
1905	Was A	77	238	16	39	8	0	0	14	15	0	—	.164	.213	.197	32	-18	1	.978	7	*96*	*112*	C76	—	-0.5
1906	Was A	22	68	5	13	0	0	0	3	1	0	—	.191	.203	.191	25	-6	0	.946	-3	*81*	*72*	C22	—	-0.8
	Cle A	5	10	0	1	0	0	0	0	0	0	—	.100	.100	.100	-38	-2	0	.938	-1	*118*	*35*	C5	—	-0.2
	Year	27	78	5	14	0	0	0	3	1	0	—	.179	.190	.179	16	-8	0	.945	-4	*86*	*67*	C27	—	-1.0
Total	16	1216	4029	375	882	108	31	17	391	314	8	166	.219	.277	.274	56	-239	64	.961	22	*99*	*100*	C1197/P	—	-10.0
Klassen, Danny	Daniel Victor; B9.22.1975 Leamington ON, Can.; BR/TR/6´0˝/(175–190); [MilA93 2/65]; d7.4; [DL 2001 Ari N 189]																								
1998	Ari N	29	108	12	21	2	1	3	8	9-0	1	33	.194	.263	.315	51	-8	1-1	.964	-3	97	95	2b29	0	-1.0
1999	Ari N	1	1	0	1	0	0	0	0	0-0	0	0	1.000	1.000	1.000	406	0	0-0	ø	0	—	—	/H	0	0.0
2000	Ari N	29	76	13	18	3	0	2	8	8-0	1	24	.237	.318	.355	67	-4	1-1	.962	-2	93	115	3b25,S3	54	-0.5
2002	Ari N	4	3	0	1	0	0	0	0	0-0	0	1	.333	.333	.333	69	0	0-0	1.000	-0	146	0	3b2/S	24	0.0
2003	Det A	22	73	9	18	3	1	1	7	4-0	0	26	.247	.286	.356	71	-3	0-1	1.000	4	105	131	3b13,2b4,S3	0	0.1
Total	5	85	261	34	59	8	2	6	23	21-0	2	84	.226	.289	.341	63	-15	2-3	.978	-1	98	120	3b40,2b33,S7	267	-1.4
Klaus, Bobby	Robert Francis; B12.27.1937 Spring Grove IL; BR/TR/5´10˝/170; d4.21; b–Billy; Col Illinois																								
1964	Cin N	40	93	10	17	5	1	2	6	4-0	0	13	.183	.212	.323	48	-7	1-0	.972	-1	83	82	2b18,3b11,S3	0	-0.6
	NY N	56	209	25	51	8	3	2	11	25-0	0	30	.244	.325	.340	90	-2	3-4	.986	-3	115	71	2b25,3b28,S5	0	-0.4
	Year	96	302	35	68	13	4	4	17	29-0	0	43	.225	.291	.334	76	-10	4-4	.981	-4	102	75	2b43,3b39,S8	0	-1.0
1965	NY N	119	288	30	55	12	0	2	12	45-0	1	49	.191	.302	.253	61	-13	1-6	.968	7	110	116	2b72,S28,3b25	0	-0.3
Total	2	215	590	65	123	25	4	6	29	74-0	1	92	.208	.297	.295	69	-22	5-10	.973	3	107	100	2b115,3b64,S36	0	-1.3
Klaus, Billy	William Joseph; B12.9.1928 Spring Grove IL; BL/TR/5´10˝/(160–165); d4.16; b–Bobby																								
1952	Bos N	7	4	3	0	0	0	0	0	1	0	1	.000	.200	.000	-42	-1	0-0	.500	-1	0	0	S4	0	-0.2
1953	Mil N	2	2	1	0	0	0	0	1	0	0	0	.000	.000	.000	-99	-1	0-0	ø	0	—	—	/H	0	-0.1
1955	Bos A	135	541	83	153	26	2	7	60	60-0	0	44	.283	.351	.377	89	-7	6-0	.955	-3	104	72	S126,3b8	0	0.1
1956	Bos A	135	520	91	141	29	5	7	59	90-0	1	43	.271	.378	.387	92	-3	1-0	.945	2	**113**	79	3b106,S26	0	0.1
1957	Bos A	127	477	76	120	18	4	10	42	55-0	0	53	.252	.326	.369	85	-9	2-0	.961	21	114	112	S118	0	2.3
1958	Bos A	61	88	5	14	4	0	1	7	5-0	0	16	.159	.204	.239	20	-10	0-0	.883	-6	88	22	S27	0	-1.5
1959	Bal A	104	321	33	80	11	0	3	25	51-1	0	38	.249	.350	.312	86	-4	2-4	.970	-3	104	77	S59,3b49/2	0	-0.4
1960	Bal A	46	43	8	9	2	0	1	6	9-0	0	9	.209	.346	.326	84	-1	0-0	.960	2	104	129	2b30,S12,3b2	0	0.2
1961	Was A	91	251	26	57	8	2	7	30	30-3	2	34	.227	.311	.359	81	-7	2-2	.961	-1	114	31	3b51,S18/2lf	0	-0.7
1962	Phi N	102	248	30	51	8	2	4	20	29-3	1	43	.206	.290	.302	61	-14	1-1	.983	2	96	53	3b53,S30,2b11	0	-1.0
1963	Phi N	11	18	1	1	0	0	0	0	1-0	0	4	.056	.105	.056	-53	-4	0-0	1.000	-1	50	0	S5,3b3	0	-0.5
Total	11	821	2513	357	626	106	15	40	250	331-7	4	285	.249	.335	.351	82	-61	14-7	.955	12	106	85	S425,3b272,2b43/lf	0	-1.7
Klee, Ollie	Ollie Chester "Babe"; B5.20.1900 Piqua OH; D2.9.1977 Toledo OH; BL/TL/5´9.5˝/160; d8.10; Col Ohio St.																								
1925	Cin N	3	1	0	0	0	0	0	0	0	0	1	.000	.000	.000	-99	0	0-0	ø	-0	0	0	/cf	—	0.0
Klein, Chuck	Charles Herbert; B10.7.1904 Indianapolis IN; D3.28.1958 Indianapolis IN; BL/TR/6´0˝/185; d7.30; C4; HF1980																								
1928	Phi N	64	253	41	91	14	4	11	34	14	1	22	.360	.396	.577	146	16	0	.978	-0	95	109	O63R	—	1.0
1929	Phi N	149	616	126	219	45	6	**43**	145	54	0	61	.356	.407	.657	149	45	5	.966	-1	96	117	O149(0/25/123)	—	3.0
1930	Phi N	**156**	648	**158**	250	**59**	8	40	170	54	4	50	.386	.436	.687	155	58	4	.960	21	102	**217**	O156R	—	**5.7**
1931	Phi N	148	594	**121**	200	34	10	**31**	**121**	59	1	49	.337	.398	**.584**	149	40	7	.971	-2	94	121	O148(90/17/43)	—	3.0
1932	Phi N	**154**	650	**152**	**226**	50	15	**38**	137	60	1	49	.348	.404	**.646**	158	53	**20**	.960	7	96	**179**	O154R	—	4.9
1933	Phi N★	**152**	606	101	**223**	**44**	7	**28**	**120**	56	1	36	**.368**	**.422**	**.602**	168	**55**	15	.986	8	103	142	O152(0/1/152)	—	**5.6**
1934	Chi N★	115	435	78	131	27	2	20	80	47	2	38	.301	.372	.510	136	23	3	.962	-3	97	76	O110(97/1/15)	—	1.3
1935	†Chi N	119	434	71	127	14	4	21	73	41	1	42	.293	.355	.488	123	13	4	.958	-3	94	94	O111R	—	0.3
1936	Chi N	29	109	19	32	5	0	5	18	16	0	14	.294	.384	.477	128	5	0	.917	-1	104	89	O29R	—	0.2
	Phi N	117	492	83	152	30	7	20	86	33	0	45	.309	.352	.520	120	12	6	.930	-3	96	105	O117(2/0/115)	—	0.2
	Year	146	601	102	184	35	7	25	104	49	0	59	.306	.358	.512	122	17	6	.927	-4	98	102	O146(2/0/144)	—	0.4
1937	Phi N	115	406	74	132	20	2	15	57	39	1	21	.325	.386	.495	127	16	3	.949	-2	94	120	O102(29/0/75)	—	0.8
1938	Phi N	129	458	53	113	22	2	8	61	38	0	30	.247	.304	.356	83	-11	7	.960	0	106	81	O119(3/0/118)	—	-1.8
1939	Phi N	25	47	8	9	2	1	1	9	10	0	4	.191	.333	.340	84	-1	1	1.000	0	100	108	O11R/1	—	-0.1
	Pit N	85	270	37	81	16	4	11	47	26	0	17	.300	.361	.511	134	12	1	.951	-3	96	75	O66(30/0/37)	—	0.5
	Year	110	317	45	90	18	5	12	56	36	0	21	.284	.357	.486	127	11	2	.958	-3	97	79	O77(30/0/48)/1	—	0.4
1940	Phi N	116	354	39	77	16	2	7	37	44	0	30	.218	.304	.333	79	-10	2	.984	-0	106	58	O96(6/0/90)	—	-1.6
1941	Phi N	50	73	6	9	0	0	1	3	10	0	6	.123	.229	.164	12	-9	0	.958	-0	101	106	O14(2/0/12)	0	-1.0
1942	Phi N	14	14	0	1	0	0	0	0	0	0	2	.071	.071	.071	-61	-3	0	ø	0	—	—	/H	0	-0.3
1943	Phi N	12	20	0	2	0	0	0	3	0	0	3	.100	.100	.100	-44	-4	1	.000	-1	0	0	O2L	0	-0.5
1944	Phi N	4	7	1	1	0	0	0	0	0	0	2	.143	.143	.143	-20	-1	0	1.000	0	141	0	/rf	0	-0.1
Total	17	1753	6486	1168	2076	398	74	300	1201	601	12	521	.320	.379	.543	135	309	79	.962	17	98	122	O1600(261/44/1305)/1	0	21.1

YEAR	TM LG	G	AB	R	H	2B	3B	HR	RBI	BB-IB	HP	SO	AVG	OBP	SLG	AOPS	ABR	SB-CS	FA	FR	RNG	THR	GAMES AT POSITION	DL	BFW
KLEIN, LOU	Louis Frank; B10.22.1918 New Orleans LA; D6.20.1976 Metairie LA; BR/TR/5´11˝/170; d4.21; Mil 1944–45; M3/C6																								
1943	†StL N	154	627	91	180	28	14	7	62	50	2	70	.287	.342	.410	112	8	9	.973	-4	98	**141**	2b126,S51	0	1.4
1945	StL N	19	57	12	13	4	1	1	6	14	1	9	.228	.389	.386	113	2	0	.929	-1	81	110	S7,O7(4/0/3),3b4,2b2	0	0.1
1946	StL N	23	93	12	18	3	0	1	4	9	0	7	.194	.265	.258	47	-7	1	.975	-1	93	140	2b23	0	-0.7
1949	StL N	58	114	25	25	6	0	2	12	22	2	20	.219	.355	.325	80	-2	0	.890	-2	111	68	S21,2b9,3b7	0	-0.3
1951	Cle A	2	2	0	0	0	0	0	0	0	0	1	.000	.000	.000	-99	-1	0-0	ø	0	—	—	/H	0	-0.1
	Phi A	49	144	22	33	7	0	5	17	10	0	12	.229	.279	.382	76	-6	0-0	.975	0	106	117	2b42	0	-0.3
	Year	51	146	22	33	7	0	5	17	10	0	13	.226	.276	.377	74	-6	0-0	.975	0	106	117	2b42	0	-0.4
Total	5	305	1037	162	269	48	15	16	101	105	5	119	.259	.330	.381	97	-6	10-0	.975	-8	99	135	2b202,S79,3b11,O7(4/0/3)	0	0.1
KLEINOW, RED	John Peter; B7.20.1877 Milwaukee WI; D10.9.1929 New York NY; BR/TR/5´10˝/165; d5.3; Col St. Edwards																								
1904	NY A	68	209	12	43	8	4	0	16	15	0	—	.206	.259	.282	68	-8	4	.966	-4	88	104	C62,3b2/rf	—	-0.7
1905	NY A	88	253	23	56	6	3	1	24	20	2	—	.221	.284	.281	71	-8	7	.978	-3	111	99	C83,1b3	—	-0.5
1906	NY A	96	268	30	59	9	3	0	31	24	1	—	.220	.287	.276	69	-9	8	.974	1	103	103	C95/1	—	0.0
1907	NY A	90	269	30	71	6	4	0	26	24	1	—	.264	.327	.316	97	-1	5	.970	-2	90	100	C86/1	—	0.6
1908	NY A	96	279	16	47	3	2	1	13	22	3	—	.168	.237	.204	43	-17	5	.973	-9	78	117	C89,2b2	—	-2.1
1909	NY A	78	206	24	47	11	4	0	15	25	1	—	.228	.315	.320	100	1	7	.966	-3	90	95	C77	—	0.5
1910	NY A	6	12	2	5	0	0	0	2	1	0	—	.417	.462	.417	166	1	2	1.000	0	108	86	C5	—	0.2
	Bos A	50	147	9	22	1	0	1	8	20	0	—	.150	.251	.177	34	-11	3	.968	1	110	84	C49	—	-0.5
	Year	56	159	11	27	1	0	1	10	21	0	—	.170	.267	.195	44	-10	5	.970	1	110	84	C54	—	-0.3
1911	Bos A	8	14	0	3	0	0	0	0	2	0	—	.214	.313	.214	48	-1	1	1.000	0	98	125	C8	—	0.0
	Phi N	4	8	0	1	1	0	0	0	0	0	1	.125	.125	.250	4	-1	0	1.000	0	95	88	C4	—	-0.1
Total	8	584	1665	146	354	45	20	3	135	153	8	1	.213	.282	.269	71	-54	42	.972	-19	95	101	C558,1b5,2b2,3b2/rf	—	-2.6
KLESKO, RYAN	Ryan Anthony; B6.12.1971 Westminster CA; BL/TL/6´3˝/(220–235); [AtlN89 5/116]; d9.12																								
1992	Atl N	13	14	0	0	0	0	0	1	0-0	1	5	.000	.067	.000	-75	-3	0-0	1.000	-1	0	134	1b5	0	-0.4
1993	Atl N	22	17	3	6	1	0	2	5	3-1	0	4	.353	.450	.765	213	3	0-0	1.000	-0	0	0	1b3,O2L	0	0.2
1994	Atl N	92	245	42	68	13	3	17	47	26-3	1	48	.278	.344	.563	128	9	1-0	.921	-7	72	96	O74L,1b6	0	0.0
1995	†Atl N	107	329	48	102	25	2	23	70	47-10	2	72	.310	.396	.608	154	26	5-4	.942	-10	79	40	O102L,1b4	15	1.2
1996	†Atl N	153	528	90	149	21	4	34	93	68-10	2	129	.282	.364	.530	125	19	6-3	.975	-9	82	78	O144L,1b2	0	0.4
1997	†Atl N	143	467	67	122	23	6	24	84	48-5	4	130	.261	.334	.490	111	6	4-4	.969	-9	89	40	O130L,1b22	0	-0.9
1998	†Atl N	129	427	69	117	29	1	18	70	56-5	3	66	.274	.359	.473	118	12	5-3	.994	-3	81	139	O120L,1b7	0	0.5
1999	†Atl N	133	404	55	120	28	2	21	80	53-8	2	69	.297	.376	.532	129	18	5-2	.989	-8	81	85	1b75,O53L/D	0	0.4
2000	SD N	145	494	88	140	33	2	26	92	91-9	1	81	.283	.393	.516	136	31	23-7	.992	-1	101	99	1b136,O4(2/0/2)	0	1.9
2001	SD N★	146	538	105	154	34	6	30	113	88-7	3	89	.286	.384	.539	148	40	23-4	.991	-5	88	83	1b145	0	2.5
2002	SD N	146	540	90	162	39	1	29	95	76-11	4	86	.300	.388	.537	154	44	6-2	.993	-3	100	93	1b112,O31R/D	0	3.0
2003	SD N	121	397	47	100	18	0	21	67	65-5	3	83	.252	.354	.456	122	14	2-5	.994	6	119	75	1b111/D	28	0.9
2004	SD N	127	402	58	117	32	2	9	66	73-6	1	67	.291	.399	.448	125	19	3-2	.986	-2	90	44	O104L,1b18,D3	20	1.2
2005	†SD N	137	443	61	110	19	1	18	58	75-2	1	80	.248	.358	.418	108	6	3-4	.981	3	101	116	O121L/1D	0	0.4
2006	†SD N	6	4	0	3	1	0	0	2	2-0	0	0	.750	.833	1.000	387	2	0-0	ø	0	—	—	/H	170	0.2
Total	15	1620	5249	823	1470	316	30	272	943	771-82	28	1009	.280	.372	.507	130	246	86-40	.974	-50	84	76	O885(852/0/33),1b647,D9	233	11.5
KLEVEN, JAY	Jay Allen; B12.2.1949 Oakland CA; BR/TR/6´2˝/190; d6.20; Col Cal St.–Hayward																								
1976	NY N	2	5	0	1	0	0	0	2	0-0	0	1	.200	.200	.200	14	-1	0-0	1.000	0	0	0	C2	0	0.0
KLIMCHOCK, LOU	Louis Stephen; B10.15.1939 Hostetter PA; BL/TR/5´11˝/(176–180); d9.27																								
1958	KC A	2	10	2	2	0	0	1	1	0-0	0	1	.200	.200	.500	84	0	0-0	1.000	-0	114	67	2b2	0	-0.1
1959	KC A	17	66	10	18	1	0	4	13	1-0	0	6	.273	.284	.470	101	0	0-0	.949	-3	94	94	2b16	0	-0.2
1960	KC A	10	10	0	3	0	0	0	0	0-0	0	0	.300	.300	.300	62	-1	0-0	ø	-0	0	0	/2	0	-0.1
1961	KC A	57	121	8	26	4	1	1	16	5-0	0	13	.215	.244	.289	42	-10	0-0	.976	-5	60	44	1b11,O7(4/0/3),3b6/2	0	-1.6
1962	Mil N	8	8	0	0	0	0	0	0	0-0	0	2	.000	.000	.000	-99	-2	0-0	ø	0	—	—	/H	0	-0.2
1963	Was A	9	14	1	2	0	0	0	2	0-0	0	1	.143	.143	.143	-20	-2	0-0	1.000	0	140	63	2b3	0	-0.2
	Mil N	24	46	6	9	1	0	0	1	0-0	0	12	.196	.196	.217	19	-5	0-1	.988	0	121	190	1b12	0	-0.6
1964	Mil N	10	21	3	7	2	0	0	2	1-0	0	2	.333	.364	.429	121	1	0-0	1.000	-2	50	0	3b4,2b2	0	-0.1
1965	Mil N	34	39	3	3	0	0	0	3	2-0	0	8	.077	.119	.077	-42	-7	0-0	.923	1	256	0	1b4	0	-0.7
1966	NY N	5	5	0	0	0	0	0	0	0-0	0	3	.000	.000	.000	-99	-1	0-0	ø	0	—	—	/H	0	-0.1
1968	Cle A	11	15	0	2	0	0	0	3	1-1	0	0	.133	.176	.133	-2	-2	0-0	.500	-2	41	0	3b4/12	0	-0.5
1969	Cle A	90	258	26	74	13	2	6	26	18-3	0	14	.287	.331	.422	107	2	0-0	.934	-13	78	67	3b56,2b21/C	0	-1.1
1970	Cle A	41	56	5	9	0	0	1	2	3-1	1	9	.161	.213	.214	18	-6	0-0	1.000	-2	41	124	1b5,2b5	0	-0.9
Total	12	318	669	64	155	21	3	13	69	31-5	1	71	.232	.264	.330	63	-33	0-1	.906	-26	73	55	3b70,2b52,1b33,O7(4/0/3)/C	0	-6.4
KLINE, BOBBY	John Robert; B1.27.1929 St.Petersburg FL; BR/TR/6´0˝/179; d4.11																								
1955	Was A	77	140	12	31	5	0	0	9	11-0	2	27	.221	.288	.257	50	-10	0-0	.943	7	107	108	S69,2b4,3b3/P	0	0.1
KLING, JOHNNY	John "Noisy"; B11.13.1875 Kansas City MO; D1.31.1947 Kansas City MO; BR/TR/5´9.5˝/160; d9.11; M1; b–Bill																								
1900	Chi N	15	51	8	15	3	1	0	7	2	0	—	.294	.321	.392	100	0	0	.901	-2	94	85	C15	—	-0.1
1901	Chi N	74	256	26	70	6	3	0	21	9	1	—	.273	.301	.320	83	-6	8	.952	-9	87	101	C69/1rf	—	-0.9
1902	Chi N	115	436	50	126	19	3	0	59	29	0	—	.289	.333	.346	113	7	25	.974	8	107	107	C113/S	—	2.7
1903	Chi N	132	491	67	146	29	13	3	68	22	2	—	.297	.330	.428	118	9	23	.969	8	116	106	C132	—	2.8
1904	Chi N	123	452	41	110	18	0	2	46	16	1	—	.243	.271	.296	75	-14	7	.974	-4	120	99	C104,O10(9/0/1),1b6	—	-0.9
1905	Chi N	111	380	26	83	8	6	1	52	28	0	—	.218	.272	.279	62	-19	13	.966	6	115	95	C106,O4R/1	—	-0.2
1906	†Chi N	107	343	45	107	15	8	2	46	23	1	—	.312	.357	.420	134	12	14	**.982**	14	**163**	101	C96,O3R	—	3.9
1907	†Chi N	104	334	44	95	15	8	1	43	27	2	—	.284	.342	.386	120	7	9	**.987**	9	114	91	C98,1b2	—	2.9
1908	†Chi N	126	424	51	117	23	5	4	59	21	3	—	.276	.315	.382	117	7	16	.979	2	108	108	C117,O6(1/1/4),1b2	—	2.4
1910	†Chi N	91	297	31	80	17	2	2	32	37	2	27	.269	.354	.360	109	5	3	.979	5	**135**	88	C86	—	1.9
1911	Chi N	27	80	8	14	3	2	1	5	8	0	14	.175	.250	.300	54	-5	1	.969	5	170	93	C25	—	0.2
	Bos N	75	241	32	54	8	1	2	24	30	0	29	.224	.310	.290	63	-12	0	.951	-12	75	115	C71/3	—	-1.8
	Year	102	321	40	68	11	3	3	29	38	0	43	.212	.295	.293	61	-17	1	.956	-6	100	109	C96/3	—	-1.6
1912	Bos N	81	252	26	80	10	3	2	30	15	0	30	.317	.356	.405	106	1	3	.958	-0	94	107	C74,M	—	0.7
1913	Cin N	80	209	20	57	7	6	0	23	14	0	14	.273	.318	.364	95	-2	2-1	.975	4	108	107	C63	—	0.8
Total	13	1261	4246	475	1154	181	61	20	515	281	12	114	.272	.319	.357	100	-10	124-1	.971	36	115	101	C1169,O24(10/1/13),1b12/3S	—	14.4
KLING, RUDY	Rudolph A.; B3.23.1870 St.Louis MO; D3.14.1937 St.Louis MO; BR/TR/5´10˝/178; d9.21																								
1902	StL N	4	10	1	2	0	0	0	0	4	0	—	.200	.429	.200	99	0	1	.842	-2	63	151	S4	—	-0.1
KLINGER, JOE	Joseph John; B8.2.1902 Canonsburg PA; D7.31.1960 Little Rock AR; BR/TR/6´0˝/190; d9.13																								
1927	NY N	3	5	0	2	0	0	0	0	0	0	2	.400	.400	.400	115	0	0	1.000	0	141	0	/lf	—	0.0
1930	Chi A	4	8	0	3	0	0	0	1	0	0	0	.375	.375	.375	94	0	0-0	1.000	-1	0	0	C2,1b2	—	-0.1
Total	2	7	13	0	5	0	0	0	1	0	0	2	.385	.385	.385	102	0	0-0	1.000	-0	0	178	1b2,C2/lf	—	-0.1
KLOZA, NAP	John Clarence; B9.7.1903 , Poland; D6.11.1962 Milwaukee WI; BR/TR/5´11˝/180; d8.16																								
1931	StL A	3	7	1	1	0	0	0	0	1	0	4	.143	.250	.143	5	-1	0-0	1.000	0	33	682	O3R	—	-0.1
1932	StL A	19	13	4	2	0	1	0	2	4	0	4	.154	.353	.308	69	-1	0-0	1.000	0	115	0	O3(1/2/0)	—	-0.1
Total	2	22	20	5	3	0	1	0	2	5	0	8	.150	.320	.250	48	-2	0-0	1.000	0	59	467	O6(1/2/3)	—	-0.2
KLUGMANN, JOE	Josie; B3.26.1895 St.Louis MO; D7.18.1951 Moberly MO; BR/TR/5´11˝/175; d9.23																								
1921	Chi N	6	21	3	6	0	0	0	2	1	1	2	.286	.348	.286	69	-1	0-1	.969	-0	90	37	2b5	—	-0.1
1922	Chi N	2	2	0	0	0	0	0	0	0	0	0	.000	.000	.000	-98	-1	0-0	1.000	1	129	274	2b2	—	0.0
1924	Bro N	31	79	7	13	2	1	0	3	2	0	9	.165	.185	.215	7	-11	0-0	.929	-3	85	107	2b28/S	—	-1.3
1925	Cle A	38	85	12	28	9	2	0	12	8	0	4	.329	.387	.482	119	2	3-1	.959	-3	100	79	2b29,1b4,3b2	—	0.0
Total	4	77	187	22	47	11	3	0	17	11	1	15	.251	.296	.342	67	-11	3-2	.947	-5	93	90	2b64,1b4,3b2/S	—	-1.4

YEAR	TM LG	G	AB	R	H	2B	3B	HR	RBI	BB-IB	HP	SO	AVG	OBP	SLG	AOPS	ABR	SB-CS	FA	FR	RNG	THR	GAMES AT POSITION	DL	BFW
KLUMPP, ELMER	Elmer Edward; B8.26.1906 St.Louis MO; D10.18.1996 Menomonee Falls WI; BR/TR/6´0˝/184; d4.17																								
1934	Was A	12	15	2	2	0	0	0	0	0	1	1	.133	.188	.133	-17	-3	0-0	.889	-1	*194*	*94*	C11	—	-0.3
1937	Bro N	5	11	0	1	0	0	0	2	1	0	4	.091	.167	.091	-28	-2	0	1.000	1	*98*	*0*	C3	—	-0.1
Total	2	17	26	2	3	0	0	0	2	1	1	5	.115	.179	.115	-21	-5	0-0	.943	-1	*156*	*57*	C14	—	-0.4
KLUSMAN, BILLY	William F.; B3.24.1865 Cincinnati OH; D6.24.1907 Cincinnati OH; BR/TR/5´10.5˝/185; d6.21																								
1888	Bos N	28	107	9	18	4	0	2	11	5	0	13	.168	.205	.262	47	-6	3	.914	-6	89	62	2b28	—	-1.1
1890	StL AA	15	65	9	18	4	1	1	11	1	0	—	.277	.288	.415	94	-1	1	.896	-1	116	55	2b15	—	-0.1
Total	2	43	172	18	36	8	1	3	22	6	0	13	.209	.236	.320	66	-7	4	.908	-6	98	60	2b43	—	-1.2
KLUSZEWSKI, TED	Theodore Bernard "Big Klu"; B9.10.1924 Argo IL; D3.29.1988 Cincinnati OH; BL/TL/6´2˝/(225–245); d4.18; C9; Col Indiana																								
1947	Cin N	9	10	1	1	0	0	0	2	1	0	2	.100	.182	.100	-23	-2	0	1.000	-0	0	115	1b2	0	-0.2
1948	Cin N	113	379	49	104	23	4	12	57	18	0	32	.274	.307	.451	107	1	1	.990	2	106	80	1b98	0	0.0
1949	Cin N	136	531	63	164	26	2	8	68	19	0	24	.309	.333	.411	97	-4	3	.989	-6	84	97	1b134	0	-1.4
1950	Cin N	134	538	76	165	37	0	25	111	33	1	28	.307	.348	.515	123	16	3	.987	-12	66	83	1b131	0	0.0
1951	Cin N	154	607	74	157	35	2	13	77	35	2	33	.259	.301	.387	83	-16	6-2	**.997**	-7	80	81	1b154	0	-2.8
1952	Cin N	135	497	62	159	24	11	16	86	47	4	28	.320	.383	.509	146	30	3-3	**.993**	-8	76	97	1b133	0	1.8
1953	Cin N★	149	570	97	180	25	0	40	108	55	4	34	.316	.380	.570	142	35	2-0	**.995**	-15	62	**115**	1b147	0	1.2
1954	Cin N★	149	573	104	187	28	3	**49**	**141**	78	3	35	.326	.407	.642	165	54	0-2	**.996**	-2	94	**117**	1b149	0	4.2
1955	Cin N★	153	612	116	**192**	25	0	47	113	66-**25**	4	40	.314	.382	.585	144	39	1-1	**.995**	-8	81	**118**	1b153	0	2.1
1956	Cin N★	138	517	91	156	14	1	35	102	49-22	3	31	.302	.362	.536	130	21	1-0	.990	-5	90	101	1b131	0	0.9
1957	Cin N	69	127	12	34	7	0	6	21	5-3	1	5	.268	.301	.465	95	-1	0-0	.989	0	106	70	1b23	32	-0.2
1958	Pit N	100	301	29	88	13	4	4	37	26-6	1	16	.292	.348	.402	101	1	0-0	.994	-5	74	103	1b72	0	-0.8
1959	Pit N	60	122	11	32	10	1	2	17	5-1	0	14	.262	.291	.410	85	-3	0-0	1.000	-0	91	94	1b20	0	-0.4
	†Chi A	31	101	11	30	2	1	2	10	9-3	0	10	.297	.351	.396	107	1	0-1	1.000	-2	67	69	1b29	0	-0.3
1960	Chi A	81	181	20	53	9	0	5	39	22-5	0	10	.293	.364	.425	116	4	0-1	.997	-2	80	113	1b39	0	0.0
1961	LA A	107	263	32	64	12	0	15	39	24-5	0	23	.243	.303	.460	91	-4	0-0	.989	-5	67	99	1b66	0	-1.2
Total	15	1718	5929	848	1766	290	29	279	1028	492-70	23	365	.298	.353	.498	122	172	20-10	.993	-73	81	99	1b1481	32	2.9
KLUTTS, MICKEY	Gene Ellis; B9.20.1954 Montebello CA; BR/TR/5´11˝/(170–189); [NYA72 4/86]; d7.7; [DL 1978 Oak A 21]																								
1976	NY A	2	3	0	0	0	0	0	0	0-0	0	1	.000	.000	.000	-99	-1	0-0	.875	-0	83	0	S2	0	-0.1
1977	NY A	5	15	3	4	1	0	1	4	2-0	1	1	.267	.389	.533	149	1	0-1	1.000	2	168	155	3b4/S	24	0.2
1978	NY A	1	2	1	2	1	0	0	0	0-0	1	0	1.000	1.000	1.500	605	2	0-0	.750	0	92	555	/3	27	0.2
1979	Oak A	24	73	3	14	2	1	1	4	7-0	0	20	.192	.262	.288	51	-5	0-1	.882	-3	105	60	S10,2b8,3b6,D2	130	-0.8
1980	Oak A	75	197	20	53	14	0	4	21	13-1	0	41	.269	.313	.401	100	0	1-4	.947	-7	92	35	3b62,S8,2b7/D	64	-0.8
1981	†Oak A	15	46	9	17	0	0	5	11	2-1	0	9	.370	.396	.696	217	6	0-0	.957	-3	69	51	3b14	141	0.3
1982	Oak A	55	157	10	28	8	0	0	14	9-0	0	18	.178	.222	.229	25	-16	0-0	.946	-3	94	63	3b49	21	-2.0
1983	Tor A	22	43	3	11	0	0	3	5	1-1	1	11	.256	.289	.465	97	0	0-1	1.000	-4	57	94	3b17,D2	0	-0.5
Total	8	199	536	49	129	26	1	14	59	34-3	3	101	.241	.289	.371	83	-13	1-7	.948	-18	91	57	3b153,S21,2b15,D5	428	-3.5
KLUTTZ, CLYDE	Clyde Franklin; B12.12.1917 Rockwell NC; D5.12.1979 Salisbury NC; BR/TR/6´0˝/(195–198); d4.20; Col Catawba																								
1942	Bos N	72	210	21	56	10	1	1	31	7	1	13	.267	.294	.338	86	-5	0	.979	-3	*75*	*92*	C57	0	-0.4
1943	Bos N	66	207	13	51	7	0	0	20	15	0	9	.246	.297	.280	68	-9	0	.973	-3	*58*	*158*	C55	0	-0.9
1944	Bos N	81	229	20	64	12	2	2	19	13	0	14	.279	.318	.376	91	-3	0	.980	1	*64*	*155*	C58	0	0.1
1945	Bos N	25	81	9	24	4	1	0	10	2	0	6	.296	.313	.370	89	-2	0	.987	0	*106*	*123*	C19	0	0.0
	NY N	73	222	25	62	14	0	4	21	15	2	10	.279	.331	.396	100	0	1	.978	-1	*161*	*115*	C57	0	0.2
	Year	98	303	34	86	18	1	4	31	17	2	16	.284	.326	.389	97	-2	1	.981	-1	*146*	*117*	C76	0	0.2
1946	NY N	5	8	0	3	0	0	0	1	0	0	1	.375	.375	.375	112	0	0	.857	-1	*49*	*0*	C2	0	0.0
	StL N	52	136	8	36	7	0	0	14	10	0	10	.265	.315	.316	76	-4	0	.980	3	*149*	*105*	C49	0	0.1
	Year	57	144	8	39	7	0	0	15	10	0	11	.271	.318	.319	78	-4	0	.976	2	*146*	*102*	C51	0	0.1
1947	Pit N	73	232	26	70	9	2	6	42	17	2	18	.302	.355	.435	106	1	1	.987	2	*91*	*150*	C69	0	0.7
1948	Pit N	94	271	26	60	12	2	4	20	20	0	19	.221	.275	.325	61	-16	3	.978	2	*104*	***156***	C91	0	-0.9
1951	StL A	4	4	2	2	1	0	0	1	1	0	0	.500	.600	.750	256	1	0-0	1.000	0	*0*	*509*	/C	0	0.1
	Was A	53	159	15	49	9	0	1	22	20	1	8	.308	.389	.384	111	4	0-0	.968	-6	*96*	*65*	C46	0	0.0
	Year	57	163	17	51	10	0	1	23	21	1	8	.313	.395	.393	115	5	0-0	.968	-6	*94*	*73*	C47	0	0.1
1952	Was A	58	144	7	33	5	0	1	11	12	1	11	.229	.293	.285	63	-7	0-0	.979	1	*107*	*88*	C52	30	-0.5
Total	9	656	1903	172	510	90	8	19	212	132	7	119	.268	.318	.354	86	-40	5-0	.978	-5	*98*	*126*	C556	30	-1.5
KMAK, JOE	Joseph Robert; B5.3.1963 Napa CA; BR/TR/6´0˝/185; [SFN85 10/238]; d4.6; Col California–Santa Barbara																								
1993	Mil A	51	110	9	24	5	0	0	7	14-0	2	13	.218	.317	.264	59	-6	6-2	1.000	-2	88	114	C50	0	-0.5
1995	Chi N	19	53	7	13	3	0	1	6	6-0	1	12	.245	.328	.358	83	-1	0-0	1.000	-3	118	91	C18/3	35	-0.3
Total	2	70	163	16	37	8	0	1	13	20-0	3	25	.227	.321	.294	67	-7	6-2	1.000	-5	97	107	C68/3	35	-0.8
KNABE, OTTO	Franz Otto "Dutch"; B6.12.1884 Carrick PA; D5.17.1961 Philadelphia PA; BR/TR/5´8˝/175; d10.3; M2																								
1905	Pit N	3	10	0	3	1	0	0	2	3	0	—	.300	.462	.400	154	1	0	.786	0	130	247	3b3	—	0.1
1907	Phi N	129	444	67	113	16	9	1	34	52	5	—	.255	.339	.338	114	8	18	.960	2	95	129	2b121,O5(1/0/3)	—	1.2
1908	Phi N	151	555	63	121	26	8	0	27	49	7	—	.218	.290	.294	84	-9	27	.969	10	**104**	102	2b151	—	0.2
1909	Phi N	113	402	40	94	13	3	0	34	35	8	—	.234	.308	.281	82	-8	9	.938	5	101	105	2b110/lf	—	-0.2
1910	Phi N	137	510	73	133	18	6	1	44	47	3	42	.261	.327	.325	87	-8	15	.954	14	97	119	2b136	—	0.7
1911	Phi N	142	528	99	125	15	6	1	42	94	0	35	.237	.352	.294	80	-10	23	.950	2	100	88	2b142	—	-0.6
1912	Phi N	126	426	56	120	11	4	0	46	55	2	20	.282	.366	.326	85	-7	16	.952	2	101	93	2b123	—	-0.4
1913	Phi N	148	571	70	150	25	7	2	53	45	3	26	.263	.320	.342	85	-11	14-18	.959	6	106	97	2b148	—	-0.6
1914	Bal F	147	469	45	106	26	2	2	42	53	2	28	.226	.307	.303	65	-29	10	.956	2	99	98	2b144,M	—	-2.6
1915	Bal F	103	320	38	81	16	2	1	25	37	2	16	.253	.334	.325	83	-10	7	.975	5	98	129	2b94/rfM	—	-0.4
1916	Pit N	28	89	4	17	3	1	0	9	6	2	6	.191	.258	.247	55	-5	1	.962	-3	103	27	2b28	—	-0.9
	Chi N	51	145	17	40	8	0	0	7	9	2	18	.276	.327	.331	92	-1	3	.939	3	113	113	2b42/S3rf	—	0.4
	Year	79	234	21	57	11	1	0	16	15	4	24	.244	.300	.299	79	-5	4	.948	0	109	77	2b70/S3rf	—	-0.5
Total	11	1278	4469	572	1103	178	48	8	365	485	36	191	.247	.325	.313	84	-89	143-18	.957	47	101	104	2b1239,O8(2/0/5),3b4/S	—	-3.1
KNAUPP, COTTON	Henry Antone; B8.13.1889 San Antonio TX; D7.6.1967 New Orleans LA; BR/TR/5´9˝/165; d8.30																								
1910	Cle A	18	59	3	14	3	1	0	11	8	1	—	.237	.338	.322	105	1	1	.884	-7	91	81	S18	—	-0.6
1911	Cle A	13	39	2	4	1	0	0	0	0	0	—	.103	.103	.128	-35	-7	3	.964	2	118	57	S13	—	-0.5
Total	2	31	98	5	18	4	1	0	11	8	1	—	.184	.252	.245	48	-6	4	.913	-6	100	73	S31	—	-1.1
KNICELY, ALAN	Alan Lee; B5.19.1955 Harrisonburg VA; BR/TR/6´0.5˝/(194–195); [HouN74 3/63]; d8.12																								
1979	Hou N	7	6	0	0	0	0	0	0	2-0	0	3	.000	.250	.000	-27	-1	0-0	1.000	-1	0	0	C3/3	0	-0.2
1980	Hou N	1	1	0	0	0	0	0	0	0-0	0	1	.000	.000	.000	-99	0	0-0	ø	0	—	—	/H	0	0.0
1981	Hou N	3	7	2	4	0	0	2	2	0-0	0	1	.571	.571	1.429	480	3	0-0	1.000	1	0	0	C2/lf	0	0.4
1982	Hou N	59	133	10	25	2	0	2	12	14-3	1	30	.188	.270	.248	50	-9	0-1	.977	0	119	91	C23,O16(1/0/15)/3	0	-1.0
1983	Cin N	59	98	11	22	3	0	2	10	16-3	0	28	.224	.333	.316	78	-2	0-2	1.000	0	82	113	C31,O8(3/0/5),1b2	0	-0.3
1984	Cin N	10	29	0	4	0	0	0	5	3-0	0	6	.138	.200	.138	2	-4	0-0	.984	-2	92	76	1b8/C	0	-0.6
1985	Cin N	48	158	17	40	9	0	5	26	16-2	1	34	.253	.322	.405	98	0	0-0	.968	-9	73	75	C46	0	-0.8
	Phi N	7	7	0	0	0	0	0	0	0-0	0	4	.000	.000	.000	-98	-2	0-0	1.000	-0	0	335	/1	0	-0.2
	Year	55	165	17	40	9	0	5	26	16-2	1	38	.242	.310	.388	91	-2	0-0	.968	-10	73	75	C46/1	0	-1.0
1986	StL N	34	82	8	16	3	0	1	6	17-0	0	21	.195	.330	.268	68	-3	1-1	.995	-0	104	125	1b29,C2	0	-0.5
Total	8	228	521	48	111	17	0	12	61	68-8	2	128	.213	.303	.315	73	-18	1-4	.979	-10	83	84	C108,1b40,O25(5/0/20),3b2	0	-3.2
KNICKERBOCKER, AUSTIN	Austin Jay; B10.15.1918 Bangall NY; D2.18.1997 Clinton Corners NY; BR/TR/5´11˝/185; d4.19																								
1947	Phi A	21	48	8	12	3	2	0	2	3	0	4	.250	.294	.396	89	-1	0-1	.943	1	117	110	O14(2/2/10)	0	-0.1
KNICKERBOCKER, BILL	William Hart; B12.29.1911 Los Angeles CA; D9.8.1963 Sebastopol CA; BR/TR/5´11˝/170; d4.12																								
1933	Cle A	80	279	20	63	16	3	2	32	11	0	30	.226	.255	.326	51	-21	1-4	.939	2	104	97	S80	—	-1.4
1934	Cle A	146	593	82	188	32	5	4	67	25	2	40	.317	.347	.408	93	-8	6-6	.962	-7	96	**114**	S146	—	-0.5
1935	Cle A	132	540	77	161	34	5	0	55	27	0	31	.298	.332	.380	82	-15	2-12	.956	9	108	105	S128	—	-0.1
1936	Cle A	155	618	81	182	35	3	8	73	56	1	30	.294	.354	.400	85	-15	5-14	.952	-1	98	92	S155	—	-0.7

YEAR	TM LG	G	AB	R	H	2B	3B	HR	RBI	BB-IB	HP	SO	AVG	OBP	SLG	AOPS	ABR	SB-CS	FA	FR	RNG	THR	GAMES AT POSITION	DL	BFW
1937	StL A	121	491	53	128	29	5	4	61	30	0	32	.261	.303	.365	67	-26	3-2	.958	-9	103	73	S115,2b6	—	-2.5
1938	NY A	46	128	15	32	8	3	1	21	11	0	10	.250	.309	.383	73	-6	0-0	.982	1	96	117	2b34,S3	—	-0.3
1939	NY A	6	13	2	2	1	0	0	1	0	0	0	.154	.154	.231	-3	-2	0-0	1.000	1	111	97	2b2,S2	—	-0.1
1940	NY A	45	124	17	30	8	1	1	10	14	3	8	.242	.333	.347	80	-3	1-1	.985	-0	103	147	S19,3b17	—	-0.2
1941	Chi A	89	343	51	84	23	2	7	29	41	2	27	.245	.329	.385	89	-5	6-5	.970	-13	90	113	2b88	0	-1.3
1942	Phi A	87	289	25	73	12	0	1	19	29	1	30	.253	.323	.304	77	-8	1-2	.964	-10	93	85	2b81/S	0	-1.4
Total	10	907	3418	423	943	198	27	28	368	244	9	238	.276	.326	.374	79	-109	25-46	.955	-28	101	98	S649,2b211,3b17	0	-8.5
Knight, Lon	Alonzo P.; B6.16.1853 Philadelphia PA; D4.23.1932 Philadelphia PA; BR/TR/5´11.5˝/165; d9.4; M2/U3; ▲																								
1875	Ath NA	13	47	5	6	2	0	0	2	0	—	2	.128	.128	.170	2	-5	2-0	.875	-0	112	113	P13/S	—	-0.1
1876	Phi N	55	240	32	60	9	3	0	24	2	—	2	.250	.256	.313	89	-3	—	.804	-6	92	56	P34,1b13,O9(0/3/6),2b6	—	-0.6
1880	Wor N	49	201	31	48	11	3	0	21	5	—	8	.239	.257	.323	88	-3	—	.863	2	181	49	O49R	—	0.0
1881	Det N	83	340	67	92	16	3	1	52	23	—	21	.271	.317	.344	104	2	—	.890	0	98	**184**	O82R/21	—	0.2
1882	Det N	**86**	347	39	72	12	6	0	24	16	—	21	.207	.242	.277	66	-13	—	.867	-1	130	50	O84R,1b2	—	-1.4
1883	Phi AA	97	429	98	108	23	9	1	53	21	—	—	.252	.287	.354	96	-3	—	.858	-1	120	235	O93R,3b3,2b2,M	—	-0.4
1884	Phi AA	**108**	484	94	131	18	12	1	—	10	1	—	.271	.287	.364	104	0	—	.911	11	176	**198**	O108R,P2/1M	—	0.9
1885	Phi AA	29	119	17	25	1	1	0	14	9	1	—	.210	.271	.235	58	-6	—	.921	4	174	295	O29R/P	—	-0.2
	Pro N	25	81	8	13	1	0	0	8	11	—	17	.160	.261	.173	44	-4	—	.957	3	144	353	O25(0/4/22)/P	—	-0.2
Total	7	532	2241	386	549	91	37	3	196	97	—	69	.245	.277	.323	89	-30	—	.887	11	140	170	O479(0/7/473),P38,1b17,2b9,3b3	—	-1.7
Knight, Ray	Charles Ray; B12.28.1952 Albany GA; BR/TR/6´2˝/(182–195); [CinN70 10/238]; d9.10; M3/C5; OF(9/0/1)																								
1974	Cin N	14	11	1	2	1	0	0	2	1-0	0	2	.182	.250	.273	47	-1	0-0	1.000	-1	78	0	3b14	0	-0.2
1977	Cin N	80	92	8	24	5	1	1	13	9-1	0	16	.261	.324	.370	84	-2	1-1	.941	-1	96	120	3b37,2b17,O5L,S3	0	-0.3
1978	Cin N	83	65	7	13	3	0	1	4	3-0	0	13	.200	.235	.292	46	-5	0-0	.868	-0	115	35	3b60,2b4,O3(2/0/1)/1S	21	-0.6
1979	†Cin N	150	551	64	175	37	4	10	79	38-4	3	57	.318	.360	.454	122	17	4-4	.962	-10	92	101	3b149	0	0.5
1980	Cin N★	162	618	71	163	39	7	14	78	36-9	4	62	.264	.307	.417	103	0	1-2	.969	-11	89	80	3b162	0	-1.5
1981	Cin N	106	386	43	100	23	1	6	34	33-3	4	51	.259	.322	.370	97	-1	2-4	.957	-7	88	110	3b105	0	-1.2
1982	Hou N★	158	609	72	179	36	6	6	70	48-9	5	58	.294	.344	.402	119	16	2-5	.990	2	78	111	1b96,3b67	0	1.0
1983	Hou N	145	507	43	154	36	4	9	70	42-9	4	62	.304	.355	.444	129	20	0-3	.993	-11	73	**128**	1b143	0	-0.1
1984	Hou N	88	278	15	62	10	0	2	29	14-1	1	30	.223	.259	.281	56	-17	0-3	.946	-6	89	77	3b54,1b24	0	-2.8
	NY N	27	93	13	26	4	0	1	6	7-1	1	13	.280	.337	.355	96	0	0-0	.962	-5	73	92	3b27,1b3	0	-0.6
	Year	115	371	28	88	14	0	3	35	21-2	2	43	.237	.279	.299	67	-17	0-3	.951	-11	83	82	3b81,1b27	0	-3.4
1985	NY N	90	271	22	59	12	0	6	36	13-1	1	32	.218	.252	.328	64	-14	1-1	.958	-9	81	46	3b73,2b2/1	12	-2.6
1986	†NY N	137	486	51	145	24	2	11	76	40-2	4	63	.298	.351	.424	117	11	2-1	.948	-19	81	86	3b132/1	0	-1.1
1987	Bal A	150	563	46	144	24	0	14	65	39-3	6	90	.256	.310	.373	82	-15	0-0	.956	12	**113**	113	3b130,D14,1b6	0	-0.5
1988	Det A	105	299	34	65	12	2	3	33	20-0	3	30	.217	.271	.301	63	-15	1-1	.991	-4	84	95	1b64,D25,3b11,O2L	0	-2.4
Total	13	1495	4829	490	1311	266	27	84	595	343-43	36	579	.271	.321	.390	100	-6	14-25	.957	-70	92	96	3b1021,1b339,D39,2b23,O10L,S4	33	-12.4
Knight, John	John Wesley "Schoolboy"; B10.6.1885 Philadelphia PA; D12.19.1965 Walnut Creek CA; BR/TR/6´2.5˝/180; d4.14; Col Penn																								
1905	Phi A	88	325	28	66	12	1	3	29	9	1	—	.203	.227	.274	58	-17	4	.895	-26	79	39	S79,3b4	—	-4.5
1906	Phi A	74	253	29	49	7	2	3	20	19	0	—	.194	.250	.273	62	-11	6	.922	2	102	98	3b67,2b7	—	-0.8
1907	Phi A	40	139	6	29	7	1	0	12	10	2	—	.209	.272	.273	72	-4	1	.862	-3	90	115	3b40	—	-0.6
	Bos A	98	360	31	78	9	3	2	29	19	0	—	.217	.256	.275	70	-13	8	.924	3	104	136	3b92,2b4	—	-0.8
	Year	138	499	37	107	16	4	2	41	29	2	—	.214	.260	.275	71	-17	9	.906	-0	100	**130**	3b132,2b4	—	-1.4
1909	NY A	116	360	46	85	8	5	0	40	37	2	—	.236	.311	.286	88	-4	15	.901	-4	97	81	S76,1b19,2b17,3b3	—	-0.7
1910	NY A	117	414	58	129	25	4	3	45	34	6	—	.312	.372	.413	138	19	23	.929	-2	97	143	S79,1b23,2b7,3b4/rf	—	2.1
1911	NY A	132	470	69	126	16	7	3	62	42	11	—	.268	.342	.351	88	-8	18	.907	-6	89	99	S82,1b27,2b21/3	—	-0.8
1912	Was A	32	93	10	15	2	1	0	9	16	0	—	.161	.284	.204	40	-7	4	.926	-5	71	107	2b27,1b5	—	-1.2
1913	NY A	70	250	24	59	10	0	0	24	25	2	27	.236	.310	.276	72	-8	7	.980	8	148	95	1b50,2b21	—	-0.1
Total	8	767	2664	301	636	96	24	14	270	211	24	27	.239	.300	.309	84	-53	86	.909	-33	90	91	S316,3b211,1b124,2b104/rf	—	-7.4
Knight, Joe	Jonah William "Quiet Joe"; B9.28.1859 Port Stanley ON, Can.; D10.16.1938 Lynhurst ON, Can.; BL/TL/5´11˝/185; d5.16; ▲																								
1884	Phi N	6	24	2	6	3	0	0	2	0	—	2	.250	.250	.375	98	1	—	.789	-0	115	0	P6	—	0.0
1890	Cin N	127	481	67	150	26	8	4	67	38	4	31	.312	.367	.424	131	18	17	.925	-6	51	0	O127L	—	0.8
Total	2	133	505	69	156	29	8	4	69	38	4	33	.309	.362	.422	130	19	17	.925	-7	51	0	O127L,P6	—	0.8
Knisely, Pete	Peter Cole; B8.11.1887 Waynesburg PA; D7.1.1948 Brownsville PA; BR/TR/5´9˝/185; d9.4																								
1912	Cin N	21	67	10	22	7	3	0	7	4	1	5	.328	.375	.522	148	4	3	.939	-1	92	207	O13C,2b3/S	—	0.2
1913	Chi N	2	2	0	0	0	0	0	0	0	0	1	.000	.000	.000	-99	-1	0	ø	0	—	—	/H	—	-0.1
1914	Chi N	37	69	5	9	0	1	0	5	5	1	6	.130	.200	.159	7	-8	0	.975	2	116	130	O17(10/1/6)	—	-0.8
1915	Chi N	64	134	12	33	9	0	0	17	15	2	18	.246	.331	.313	95	0	1-2	.940	-3	98	109	O33(8/9/16),2b9	—	-0.5
Total	4	124	272	27	64	16	4	0	29	24	4	30	.235	.307	.324	86	-5	4-2	.951	-2	102	138	O63(18/23/22),2b12/S	—	-1.2
Knoblauch, Chuck	Edward Charles; B7.7.1968 Houston TX; BR/TR/5´9˝/(169–181); [MinA89 1/25]; d4.9; Col Texas A&M																								
1991	†Min A	151	565	78	159	24	6	1	50	59-0	4	40	.281	.351	.350	91	-5	25-5	.975	2	107	104	2b148,S2	0	0.4
1992	Min A★	155	600	104	178	19	6	2	56	88-1	5	60	.297	.384	.358	107	10	34-13	.992	-8	96	107	2b154/SD	0	0.9
1993	Min A	153	602	82	167	27	4	2	41	65-1	9	44	.277	.354	.346	89	-7	29-11	.988	-2	100	98	2b148,S6/cf	0	0.1
1994	Min A★	109	445	85	139	**45**	3	5	51	41-2	10	56	.312	.381	.461	115	13	35-6	.994	-21	91	84	2b109/S	0	0.2
1995	Min A	136	538	107	179	34	8	11	63	78-3	10	95	.333	.424	.487	136	33	46-18	.985	-9	98	94	2b136,S2	0	3.2
1996	Min A★	153	578	140	197	35	**14**	13	72	98-6	19	74	.341	.448	.517	142	44	45-14	**.988**	-17	93	94	2b151,D2	0	3.5
1997	Min A★	156	611	117	178	26	10	9	58	84-6	17	84	.291	.390	.411	108	11	62-10	.985	-7	101	105	2b154/SD	0	2.0
1998	†NY A	150	603	117	160	25	4	17	64	76-1	**18**	70	.265	.361	.405	104	6	31-12	.981	1	100	106	2b149/D	0	1.5
1999	†NY A	150	603	120	176	36	4	18	68	83-0	21	57	.292	.393	.454	118	21	28-9	.963	-20	94	68	2b150	0	1.0
2000	†NY A	102	400	75	113	22	2	5	26	46-0	8	45	.283	.366	.385	92	-3	15-7	.958	-13	86	82	2b82,D20	28	-1.2
2001	†NY A	137	521	66	130	20	3	9	44	58-1	14	73	.250	.339	.351	82	-12	38-9	.989	-2	89	133	O108L,D24	0	-1.3
2002	KC A	80	300	41	63	9	0	6	22	28-1	4	32	.210	.284	.300	50	-22	19-3	.980	-0	96	115	O74L,D2	44	-2.1
Total	12	1632	6366	1132	1839	322	64	98	615	804-22	139	730	.289	.378	.406	105	89	407-117	.982	-96	97	95	2b1381,O183(182/1/0),D51,S13	72	8.2
Knode, Mike	Kenneth Thomson; B11.8.1895 Westminster MD; D12.20.1980 South Bend IN; BR/TR/5´10˝/160; d6.28; b–Ray; Col Michigan																								
1920	StL N	42	65	11	15	1	1	0	12	5	2	6	.231	.306	.277	71	-2	0-1	.824	-1	85	102	O9(2/0/7),2b4,S2,3b2	—	-0.4
Knode, Ray	Robert Troxell "Bob"; B1.28.1901 Westminster MD; D4.13.1982 Battle Creek MI; BL/TL/5´10˝/160; d6.30; b–Mike; Col Michigan																								
1923	Cle A	22	38	7	11	0	0	2	4	2	0	4	.289	.325	.447	102	0	1-0	.992	0	105	100	1b21	—	-0.1
1924	Cle A	11	37	6	9	1	0	0	4	3	0	0	.243	.300	.270	47	-3	2-1	.992	1	130	141	1b10	—	-0.3
1925	Cle A	45	108	13	27	5	0	0	11	10	0	4	.250	.314	.296	55	-7	3-3	.990	1	107	120	1b34	—	-0.8
1926	Cle A	31	24	6	8	1	1	0	2	2	0	3	.333	.385	.458	118	1	0-0	.984	0	148	97	1b11	—	0.1
Total	4	109	207	32	55	7	1	2	21	17	0	11	.266	.321	.338	69	-9	6-4	.990	2	114	118	1b76	—	-1.1
Knoedler, Justin	Justin Joseph; B7.17.1980 Springfield IL; BR/TR/6´2˝/(210–215); [SFN01 5/166]; d10.3; Col Miami																								
2004	SF N	1	1	0	0	0	0	0	0	0-0	0	0	.000	.000	.000	-97	0	0-0	1.000	0	0	0	/C	0	0.0
2005	SF N	8	10	0	1	0	0	0	0	0-0	1	1	.100	.182	.100	-23	-2	0-0	1.000	-0	0	0	C4	0	-0.2
2006	SF N	5	7	0	1	0	0	0	0	0-0	0	1	.143	.143	.143	-26	-1	0-0	1.000	-0	41	0	C5	0	-0.1
Total	3	14	18	0	2	0	0	0	0	0-0	1	2	.111	.158	.111	-28	-3	0-0	1.000	-0	17	0	C10	0	-0.3
Knoll, Punch	Charles Elmer; B10.7.1881 Evansville IN; D2.8.1960 Evansville IN; BR/TR/5´7.5˝/170; d4.27																								
1905	Was A	79	244	24	52	10	5	0	29	9	2	—	.213	.247	.295	75	-8	3	.927	-1	75	63	O63(10/0/53),C5,1b2	—	-1.3
Knoop, Bobby	Robert Frank; B10.18.1938 Sioux City IA; BR/TR/6´1˝/(170–183); d4.13; M1/C21																								
1964	LA A	**162**	486	42	105	8	1	7	38	46-6	5	109	.216	.289	.280	66	-23	3-2	.978	**38**	**119**	123	2b161	0	2.9
1965	Cal A	142	465	47	125	24	4	7	43	31-5	0	101	.269	.313	.383	99	-1	3-2	.971	**23**	**117**	107	2b142	0	3.5
1966	Cal A★	161	590	54	137	18	**11**	17	72	43-8	1	144	.232	.282	.386	94	-8	1-5	**.981**	22	**113**	**129**	2b161	0	2.8
1967	Cal A	159	511	51	125	18	5	9	38	44-13	1	136	.245	.305	.352	98	-2	2-2	.986	9	102	107	2b159	0	2.1
1968	Cal A	152	494	48	123	20	4	3	39	35-6	3	128	.249	.301	.324	93	-5	3-2	.981	19	110	**114**	2b151	0	3.0
1969	Cal A	27	71	5	14	1	0	1	6	13-1	0	16	.197	.318	.254	65	-3	1-3	.977	2	99	95	2b27	0	0.0
	Chi A	104	345	34	79	14	1	6	41	35-3	2	68	.229	.301	.328	73	-12	2-0	.985	31	123	113	2b104	21	2.6
	Year	131	416	39	93	15	1	7	47	48-4	2	84	.224	.304	.315	72	-15	3-3	.984	**33**	**118**	110	2b131	0	2.6

YEAR	TM LG	G	AB	R	H	2B	3B	HR	RBI	BB-IB	HP	SO	AVG	OBP	SLG	AOPS	ABR	SB-CS	FA	FR	RNG	THR	GAMES AT POSITION	DL	BFW
1970	Chi A	130	402	34	92	13	2	5	36	34-4	2	79	.229	.290	.308	63	-20	0-1	.984	27	**123**	120	2b126	0	1.5
1971	KC A	72	161	14	33	8	1	1	11	15-1	0	36	.205	.270	.286	59	-9	1-0	.968	-8	95	103	2b52/3	0	-1.4
1972	KC A	44	97	8	23	5	0	0	7	9-1	0	16	.237	.299	.289	77	-3	0-0	.972	4	113	145	2b33,3b4	0	0.3
Total	9	1153	3622	337	856	129	29	56	331	305-48	14	833	.236	.296	.334	83	-86	16-17	.980	167	113	116	2b1116,3b5	21	17.3
Knorr, Randy	Randy Duane; B11.12.1968 San Gabriel CA; BR/TR/6´2˝/(205–230); [TorA86 10/263]; d9.5; C1																								
1991	Tor A	3	1	0	0	0	0	0	0	1-0	0	1	.000	.500	.000	49	0	0-0	1.000	1	0	0	C3	0	0.1
1992	Tor A	8	19	1	5	0	0	1	2	1-1	0	5	.263	.300	.421	95	0	0-0	1.000	1	392	147	C8	41	0.1
1993	†Tor A	39	101	11	25	3	2	4	20	9-0	0	29	.248	.309	.436	96	-1	0-0	1.000	-3	67	98	C39	0	-0.2
1994	Tor A	40	124	20	30	2	0	7	19	10-0	1	35	.242	.301	.427	85	-4	0-0	.993	-2	72	89	C40	0	-0.3
1995	Tor A	45	132	18	28	8	0	3	16	11-0	0	28	.212	.273	.341	58	-8	0-0	.971	-6	66	83	C45	41	-1.1
1996	Hou N	37	87	7	17	5	0	1	7	5-2	1	18	.195	.245	.287	44	-7	0-1	1.000	5	160	116	C33	0	-0.1
1997	Hou N	4	8	1	3	0	0	1	1	0-0	0	2	.375	.375	.750	192	1	0-0	1.000	1	85	251	C3,1b2	15	0.2
1998	Fla N	15	49	4	10	4	1	2	11	1-0	0	10	.204	.216	.449	75	-2	0-0	.989	-4	59	79	C15	0	-0.5
1999	Hou N	13	30	2	5	1	0	0	0	1-0	0	8	.167	.194	.200	-0	-5	0-0	1.000	-1	66	0	C11	0	-0.5
2000	Tex A	15	34	5	10	2	0	2	2	0-0	0	3	.294	.294	.529	101	0	0-0	.985	-1	90	150	C15	0	-0.1
2001	Mon N	34	91	13	20	2	0	3	10	8-0	1	22	.220	.287	.341	63	-5	0-0	.989	-8	48	89	C27	0	-1.1
Total	11	253	676	82	153	27	3	24	88	47-3	3	161	.226	.278	.382	71	-31	0-1	.990	-15	87	94	C239,1b2	97	-3.5
Knothe, George	George Bertram; B1.12.1898 Bayonne NJ; D7.3.1981 Toms River NJ; BR/TR/5´10˝/165; d4.25; b–Fritz; Col Penn																								
1932	Phi N	6	12	2	1	1	0	0	0	0	0	0	.083	.083	.167	-31	-2	0	.923	-1	98	120	2b5	—	-0.3
Knothe, Fritz	Wilfred Edgar; B5.1.1903 Passaic NJ; D3.27.1963 Passaic NJ; BR/TR/5´10.5˝/180; d4.12; b–George																								
1932	Bos N	89	344	45	82	19	1	1	36	39	1	37	.238	.318	.308	72	-12	5	.947	-6	98	45	3b87	—	-1.5
1933	Bos N	44	158	15	36	5	2	1	6	13	1	25	.228	.291	.304	76	-5	1	.978	-3	91	148	3b33,S9	—	-0.7
	Phi N	41	113	10	17	2	0	0	11	6	0	19	.150	.193	.168	3	-14	2	.949	9	127	151	3b32,2b4	—	-0.4
	Year	85	271	25	53	7	2	1	17	19	1	44	.196	.251	.247	42	-21	3	.961	5	110	150	3b65,S9,2b4	—	-1.1
Total	2	174	615	70	135	26	3	2	53	58	2	81	.220	.289	.281	59	-31	8	.953	-1	103	88	3b152,S9,2b4	—	-2.6
Knott, Jon	Jonathan David; B8.4.1978 Manassas VA; BR/TR/6´3˝/220; d5.30; Col Mississippi St.																								
2004	SD N	9	14	1	3	2	0	0	1	1-0	0	5	.214	.267	.357	62	-1	0-0	1.000	-0	81	0	O5L	0	-0.1
2006	SD N	3	3	0	0	0	0	0	0	0-0	0	1	.000	.000	.000	-99	-1	0-0	ø	0	—	—	/H	0	-0.1
Total	2	12	17	1	3	2	0	0	1	1-0	0	6	.176	.222	.294	33	-2	0-0	1.000	-0	81	0	O5L	0	-0.2
Knotts, Joe	Joseph Steven; B3.3.1884 Greensboro PA; D9.15.1950 Philadelphia PA; BR/TR/5´9˝/170; d9.18																								
1907	Bos N	3	8	0	0	0	0	0	0	1	0	—	.000	.111	.000	-65	-2	0	1.000	-0	*77*	*118*	C3	—	-0.2
Knouff, Ed	Edward "Fred"; B6.1868 Philadelphia PA; D9.14.1900 Philadelphia PA; BR/TR/?/160; d7.1; ▲																								
1885	Phi AA	14	48	5	9	0	0	0	2	2	0	—	.188	.220	.188	28	-4	—	.867	1	126	442	P14/rf	—	0.0
1886	Bal AA	1	3	0	0	0	0	0	0	0	1	—	.000	.250	.000	-20	0	0	1.000	1	324	0	/P	—	0.0
1887	Bal AA	9	31	4	9	0	0	0	3	1	0	—	.290	.313	.290	73	-1	1	.889	0	109	356	P9,O3(2/0/1)	—	0.0
	StL AA	15	56	4	10	1	2	0	6	1	1	—	.179	.207	.268	29	-6	1	.800	-2	0	0	O9(0/4/5),P6	—	-0.5
	Year	24	87	8	19	1	2	0	9	2	1	—	.218	.244	.276	43	-7	2	.897	-2	96	412	P15,O12(2/4/6)	—	-0.5
1888	StL AA	9	31	1	3	0	0	0	1	3	1	—	.097	.200	.097	-3	-2	1	.842	-2	62	0	P9	—	0.0
	Cle AA	2	6	0	1	1	0	0	0	1	0	—	.167	.286	.333	101	0	0	1.000	1	252	0	P2/2	—	0.0
	Year	11	37	1	4	1	0	0	1	4	1	—	.108	.214	.135	12	-4	1	.880	-1	81	0	P11/2	—	0.0
1889	Phi AA	3	12	2	3	1	0	0	2	1	0	1	.250	.308	.333	84	0	1	1.000	-1	40	0	P3	—	0.0
Total	5	53	187	16	35	3	2	0	14	9	3	1	.187	.236	.225	35	-13	4	.891	-2	103	272	P44,O13(2/4/7)/2	—	-0.5
Knowdell, Jake	Jacob Augustus; B7.27.1840 Brooklyn NY; 5´7.5˝/148; d5.15																								
1874	Atl NA	24	86	8	12	1	1	0	3	1	—	3	.140	.149	.174	4	-8	1-0	.824	-2	—	—	C21,O4L	—	-0.8
1875	Atl NA	43	163	17	32	2	0	0	9	1	—	3	.196	.201	.209	49	-7	0-1	.781	-10	—	—	C33,S11,O4(0/3/1)/2	—	-1.5
1878	Mil N	4	14	2	3	1	0	0	2	0	—	3	.214	.214	.286	59	-1	—	.875	-2	—	—	C2/rfS	—	-0.3
Total	2NA	67	249	25	44	3	1	0	12	2	—	6	.177	.183	.197	32	-15	1-1	.796	-12	—	—	C54,S11,O8(4/3/1)/2	—	-2.3
Knowles, Jimmy	James "Darby"; B9.5.1856 Toronto ON, Can.; D2.11.1912 Jersey City NJ; BR/5´9˝/160; d5.2																								
1884	Pit AA	46	182	19	42	5	7	0	—	5	2	—	.231	.259	.335	94	-2	—	.961	-0	95	80	1b46	—	-0.6
	Bro AA	41	153	19	36	5	1	1	—	3	1	—	.235	.255	.301	80	-3	—	.953	1	176	122	1b30,3b11	—	-0.5
	Year	87	335	38	78	10	8	1	—	8	3	—	.233	.257	.319	87	-5	—	.958	0	127	97	1b76,3b11	—	-1.1
1886	Was N	115	443	43	94	16	11	3	35	15	—	73	.212	.238	.318	73	-15	20	.899	21	113	103	2b62,3b53	—	0.9
1887	NY AA	16	60	12	15	1	1	0	6	1	0	—	.250	.262	.300	59	-4	6	.934	-2	85	60	2b16/3	—	-0.4
1890	Roc AA	123	491	83	138	12	8	5	84	59	1	—	.281	.359	.369	124	16	55	.881	7	111	99	3b123	—	2.2
1892	NY N	16	59	9	9	1	0	0	7	6	0	8	.153	.231	.169	22	-5	2	.792	-4	81	92	3b15/S	—	-0.8
Total	5	357	1388	185	334	40	28	9	132	89	4	81	.241	.288	.329	92	-13	83	.861	23	109	101	3b203,2b78,1b76/S	—	0.8
Knox, Andy	Andrew Jackson "Dasher"; B1.6.1864 Philadelphia PA; D9.14.1940 Philadelphia PA; BR/TR; d9.19																								
1890	Phi AA	21	75	6	19	3	0	0	8	9	0	—	.253	.333	.293	85	-1	5	.963	-2	63	65	1b21	—	-0.4
Knox, Cliff	Clifford Hiram "Bud"; B1.7.1902 Coalville IA; D9.24.1965 Oskaloosa IA; BB/TR/5´11.5˝/178; d7.1																								
1924	Pit N	6	18	1	4	0	0	0	2	2	0	0	.222	.300	.222	41	-1	0-0	.917	1	*191*	*133*	C6	—	0.0
Knox, John	John Clinton; B7.26.1948 Newark NJ; BL/TR/6´0˝/170; [DetA70 8/193]; d8.1; Col Bowling Green																								
1972	†Det A	14	13	1	1	1	0	0	0	1-0	0	2	.077	.143	.154	-11	-2	0-0	1.000	3	226	281	2b4	0	0.1
1973	Det A	12	32	1	9	1	0	0	3	3-0	0	3	.281	.343	.313	80	-1	1-1	1.000	-3	74	52	2b9	0	-0.4
1974	Det A	55	88	11	27	1	1	0	6	6-0	0	13	.307	.351	.341	96	-1	5-4	.956	-2	92	117	2b33/3D	0	-0.1
1975	Det A	43	86	8	23	1	0	0	2	10-0	0	9	.267	.344	.279	74	-3	1-2	.980	-3	101	67	2b23,3b3,D3	0	-0.5
Total	4	124	219	21	60	4	1	0	11	20-0	0	27	.274	.335	.301	79	-7	7-7	.973	-5	97	93	2b69,D5,3b4	0	-0.9
Koback, Nick	Nicholas Nicholie; B7.19.1935 Hartford CT; BR/TR/6´0˝/187; d7.29																								
1953	Pit N	7	16	1	2	0	1	0	0	1	0	4	.125	.176	.250	10	-2	0-0	1.000	-2	*44*	*192*	C6	0	-0.4
1954	Pit N	4	10	0	0	0	0	0	0	0	0	8	.000	.000	.000	-99	-3	0-0	1.000	-0	*79*	0	C4	0	-0.3
1955	Pit N	5	7	0	2	0	0	0	0	0-0	0	1	.286	.286	.286	53	0	0-0	1.000	0	0	*401*	C2	0	0.0
Total	3	16	33	1	4	0	1	0	0	1-0	0	13	.121	.147	.182	-15	-5	0-0	1.000	-2	*51*	*147*	C12	0	-0.7
Koch, Barney	Barnett; B3.23.1923 Campbell NE; D6.6.1987 Tacoma WA; BR/TR/5´8˝/140; d7.23; Col Oregon																								
1944	Bro N	33	96	11	21	2	0	0	1	3	0	9	.219	.242	.240	37	-8	0	.956	-5	87	59	2b29/S	0	-1.2
Kocher, Brad	Bradley Wilson; B1.16.1888 White Haven PA; D1.13.1965 White Haven PA; BR/TR/5´11˝/188; d4.24																								
1912	Det A	29	63	5	13	3	1	0	9	2	0	—	.206	.231	.286	49	-5	0	.904	-6	*81*	*107*	C24	—	-0.9
1915	NY N	4	11	3	5	0	1	0	2	0	0	1	.455	.455	.636	243	2	0	1.000	-1	*85*	*140*	C3	—	0.1
1916	NY N	34	65	1	7	2	0	0	1	2	0	10	.108	.134	.138	-17	-9	0	.978	-4	101	48	C30	—	-1.3
Total	3	67	139	9	25	5	2	0	12	4	0	11	.180	.203	.245	34	-12	0	.943	-10	*90*	*83*	C57	—	-2.1
Koegel, Pete	Peter John; B7.31.1947 Mineola NY; BR/TR/6´6.5˝/(225–230); [OakA65 4/79]; d9.1																								
1970	Mil A	7	8	2	2	0	0	1	1	1-0	0	3	.250	.333	.625	158	1	0-0	1.000	-0	60	0	/lf	0	0.0
1971	Mil A	2	3	0	0	0	0	0	0	2-0	0	2	.000	.400	.000	22	0	0-0	1.000	-0	0	0	/1	0	0.0
	Phi N	12	26	1	6	1	0	0	3	2-0	0	7	.231	.286	.269	58	-1	0-0	1.000	-1	53	87	C7/lf	0	-0.3
1972	Phi N	41	49	3	7	2	0	0	1	6-0	0	16	.143	.236	.184	20	-5	0-0	1.000	-1	81	81	1b8,C5,3b4,O2R	0	-0.7
Total	3	62	86	6	15	3	0	1	5	11-0	0	28	.174	.268	.244	45	-5	0-0	.971	-3	49	68	C12,1b9,3b4,O4(2/0/2)	0	-1.0
Koehler, Ben	Benard James; B1.26.1877 Schoerndorn, Germany; D5.21.1961 South Bend IN; BR/TR/5´10.5˝/175; d4.23																								
1905	StL A	142	536	55	127	14	6	2	47	32	4	—	.237	.285	.297	89	-8	22	.969	1	**170**	**336**	O124C,1b12,2b6	—	-1.5
1906	StL A	66	186	27	41	1	1	0	15	24	4	—	.220	.322	.237	79	-3	9	.957	-2	142	363	O52(1/34/17),2b7/S3	—	-0.7
Total	2	208	722	82	168	15	7	2	62	56	8	—	.233	.295	.281	87	-11	31	.966	-1	163	343	O176(1/158/17),2b13,1b12/3S	—	-2.2
Koehler, Pip	Horace Levering; B1.16.1902 Gilbert PA; D12.8.1986 Tacoma WA; BR/TR/5´10˝/165; d4.22; Col Penn St.																								
1925	NY N	12	2	1	0	0	0	0	0	0	0	1	.000	.000	.000	-99	-1	0-0	1.000	0	178	0	O3(1/0/2)	—	0.0

KOELLING, BRIAN Brian Wayne; B6.11.1969 Cincinnati OH; BR/TR/6´1˝/185; [CinN91 14/379]; d8.21; Col Bowling Green

YEAR	TM LG	G	AB	R	H	2B	3B	HR	RBI	BB-IB	HP	SO	AVG	OBP	SLG	AOPS	ABR	SB-CS	FA	FR	RNG	THR	GAMES AT POSITION	DL	BFW
1993	Cin N	7	15	2	1	0	0	0	0	0-0	1	2	.067	.125	.067	-47	-3	0-0	.941	-0	146	58	2b3,S2	0	-0.3

KOENECKE, LEN Leonard George; B1.18.1904 Baraboo WI; D9.17.1935 Toronto ON, Can.; BL/TR/5´11˝/180; d4.12

YEAR	TM LG	G	AB	R	H	2B	3B	HR	RBI	BB-IB	HP	SO	AVG	OBP	SLG	AOPS	ABR	SB-CS	FA	FR	RNG	THR	GAMES AT POSITION	DL	BFW
1932	NY N	42	137	33	35	5	0	4	14	11	2	13	.255	.320	.380	89	-2	3	.924	-4	87	0	O35L	—	-0.8
1934	Bro N	123	460	79	147	31	7	14	73	70	1	38	.320	.411	.509	152	37	8	**.994**	0	102	72	O121C	—	3.3
1935	Bro N	100	325	43	92	13	2	4	27	43	1	45	.283	.369	.372	102	3	0	.966	-4	101	42	O91(16/68/7)	—	-0.4
Total	3	265	922	155	274	49	9	22	114	124	4	96	.297	.383	.441	125	38	11	.976	-8	100	51	O247(51/189/7)	—	2.1

KOENIG, MARK Mark Anthony; B7.19.1904 San Francisco CA; D4.22.1993 Willows CA; BB/TR/6´0˝/180; d9.8; ▲

YEAR	TM LG	G	AB	R	H	2B	3B	HR	RBI	BB-IB	HP	SO	AVG	OBP	SLG	AOPS	ABR	SB-CS	FA	FR	RNG	THR	GAMES AT POSITION	DL	BFW
1925	NY A	28	110	14	23	6	1	0	4	5	0	4	.209	.243	.282	34	-12	0-1	.944	-2	95	99	S28	—	-1.0
1926	†NY A	147	617	93	167	26	8	5	62	43	1	37	.271	.319	.363	79	-22	4-3	.931	2	101	90	S141	—	-0.4
1927	†NY A	123	526	99	150	20	11	3	62	25	2	21	.285	.320	.382	84	-15	3-2	.936	12	**109**	**121**	S122	—	1.0
1928	†NY A	132	533	89	170	19	10	4	63	32	2	19	.319	.360	.415	106	3	3-5	.923	-19	89	98	S125	—	-0.3
1929	NY A	116	373	44	109	27	5	3	41	23	1	17	.292	.335	.416	99	-2	1-1	.911	-9	96	97	S61,3b37/2	—	-0.2
1930	NY A	21	74	9	17	5	0	0	9	6	1	5	.230	.296	.297	53	-5	0-0	.905	1	105	120	S19	—	-0.2
	Det A	76	267	37	64	9	2	1	16	20	1	15	.240	.295	.300	50	-21	2-0	.922	-8	92	98	S70,P2,3b2/rf	—	-1.9
	Year	97	341	46	81	14	2	1	25	26	2	20	.238	.295	.299	51	-26	2-0	.918	-8	95	103	S89,P2,3b2/rf	—	-2.1
1931	Det A	106	364	33	92	24	4	1	39	14	1	12	.253	.282	.349	63	-21	8-2	.955	-19	88	83	2b55,S35,P3	—	-3.1
1932	†Chi N	33	102	15	36	5	1	3	11	3	1	5	.353	.377	.510	137	5	0	.932	8	120	133	S31	—	1.4
1933	Chi N	80	218	32	62	12	1	3	25	15	0	9	.284	.330	.390	105	2	5	.922	3	100	173	3b37,S26,2b2	—	0.7
1934	Cin N	151	633	60	172	26	6	1	67	15	0	24	.272	.289	.336	68	-30	5	.930	-3	104	92	3b64,S58,2b26,1b4	—	-2.4
1935	NY N	107	396	40	112	12	0	3	37	13	0	18	.283	.306	.336	74	-15	0	.968	-4	105	64	2b64,S21,3b15	—	-1.3
1936	†NY N	42	58	7	16	4	0	1	7	8	1	4	.276	.373	.397	109	1	0	.905	-1	121	97	S10,2b8,3b3	—	0.1
Total	12	1162	4271	572	1190	195	49	28	443	222	11	190	.279	.316	.367	81	-132	31-14	.927	-39	100	103	S747,3b158,2b156,P5,1b4/rf	—	-7.6

KOHLER, HENRY Henry C.; B5.5.1852 Baltimore MD; D8.27.1934 Baltimore MD; d7.12

YEAR	TM LG	G	AB	R	H	2B	3B	HR	RBI	BB-IB	HP	SO	AVG	OBP	SLG	AOPS	ABR	SB-CS	FA	FR	RNG	THR	GAMES AT POSITION	DL	BFW
1871	Kek NA	3	12	0	2	1	0	0	1	0	—	0	.167	.167	.250	17	-1	0-0	ø	-1	—	—	C2,1b2/3	—	-0.1
1873	Mar NA	**6**	25	2	3	0	0	0	1	0	—	1	.120	.120	.120	-38	-4	0-0	.686	-3	48	0	3b6/C1cf	—	-0.5
1874	Bal NA	2	4	0	0	0	0	0	0	0	—	0	.000	.000	.000	-99	-1	0-0	.714	-1	426	0	/1	—	-0.1
Total	3NA	11	41	2	5	1	0	0	2	0	—	1	.122	.122	.146	-24	-6	0-0	.700	-5	—	—	3b7,1b4,C3/cf	—	-0.7

KOKOS, DICK Richard Jerome (b Richard Jerome Kokoszka); B2.28.1928 Chicago IL; D4.9.1986 Chicago IL; BL/TL/5´8.5˝/(170–175); d7.8; Mil 1951–52

YEAR	TM LG	G	AB	R	H	2B	3B	HR	RBI	BB-IB	HP	SO	AVG	OBP	SLG	AOPS	ABR	SB-CS	FA	FR	RNG	THR	GAMES AT POSITION	DL	BFW
1948	StL A	71	258	40	77	15	3	4	40	28	3	32	.298	.374	.426	110	4	4-3	.964	0	92	166	O71R	0	0.2
1949	StL A	143	501	80	131	28	1	23	77	66	3	91	.261	.351	.459	109	5	3-5	.981	7	109	124	O138R	0	0.6
1950	StL A	143	490	77	128	27	5	18	67	88	1	73	.261	.375	.447	106	5	8-8	.970	3	**110**	70	O127(81/0/50)	0	-0.1
1953	StL A	107	299	41	72	12	0	13	38	56	0	53	.241	.361	.411	106	4	0-5	.963	-2	97	82	O83(61/0/22)	0	-0.4
1954	Bal A	11	10	1	2	0	0	1	1	4	0	3	.200	.429	.500	166	1	0-0	1.000	0	112	0	/lf	0	0.1
Total	5	475	1558	239	410	82	9	59	223	242	7	252	.263	.365	.441	108	19	15-21	.971	9	104	105	O420(143/0/281)	0	0.4

KOLB, GARY Gary Alan; B3.13.1940 Rock Falls IL; BL/TR/6´0˝/195; d9.7; Col Illinois

YEAR	TM LG	G	AB	R	H	2B	3B	HR	RBI	BB-IB	HP	SO	AVG	OBP	SLG	AOPS	ABR	SB-CS	FA	FR	RNG	THR	GAMES AT POSITION	DL	BFW
1960	StL N	9	3	1	0	0	0	0	0	0-0	0	0	.000	.000	.000	-92	-1	0-0	1.000	0	196	0	O2(1/1/1)	0	-0.1
1962	StL N	6	14	1	5	0	0	0	0	1-0	0	3	.357	.400	.357	96	0	0-0	1.000	0	126	0	O6(1/0/5)	0	0.0
1963	StL N	75	96	23	26	1	5	3	10	22-0	0	26	.271	.403	.479	141	6	2-1	.981	-2	91	44	O58(25/0/35)/C3	0	0.2
1964	Mil N	36	64	7	12	1	0	0	2	6-1	0	10	.188	.257	.203	31	-6	3-2	1.000	-4	96	0	O14(5/3/7),3b7,2b6,C2	0	-1.1
1965	Mil N	24	27	3	7	0	0	0	1	1-0	0	6	.259	.286	.259	54	-2	0-0	1.000	0	121	0	O13(9/3/2)	0	-0.2
	NY N	40	90	8	15	2	0	1	7	3-0	0	28	.167	.191	.222	17	-10	3-0	.976	1	87	298	O29(10/10/9)/13	0	-1.1
	Year	64	117	11	22	2	0	1	8	4-0	0	34	.188	.213	.231	26	-12	3-0	.981	1	93	241	O42(19/13/11)/13	0	-1.3
1968	Pit N	74	119	16	26	4	1	2	6	11-2	0	17	.218	.285	.319	82	-3	2-1	.900	-1	102	137	O25(6/1/18),C10,3b4/2	0	-0.5
1969	Pit N	29	37	4	3	1	0	0	3	2-0	0	14	.081	.128	.108	-34	-7	0-0	1.000	-1	100	0	C7	0	-0.8
Total	7	293	450	63	94	9	6	6	29	46-3	0	104	.209	.281	.296	65	-23	10-4	.965	-7	97	116	O147(57/18/77),C20,3b13,2b7/1	0	-3.6

KOLLOWAY, DON Donald Martin "Butch","Cab"; B8.4.1918 Posen IL; D6.30.1994 Blue Island IL; BR/TR/6´3˝/(190–200); d9.16; Mil 1943–45

YEAR	TM LG	G	AB	R	H	2B	3B	HR	RBI	BB-IB	HP	SO	AVG	OBP	SLG	AOPS	ABR	SB-CS	FA	FR	RNG	THR	GAMES AT POSITION	DL	BFW
1940	Chi A	10	40	5	9	1	0	0	3	0	0	3	.225	.225	.250	23	-5	1-0	.922	-2	94	115	2b10	—	-0.6
1941	Chi A	71	280	33	76	8	3	3	24	6	2	12	.271	.292	.354	71	-13	11-4	.955	-8	106	64	2b62,1b4	0	-1.6
1942	Chi A	147	601	72	164	**40**	4	3	60	30	3	39	.273	.311	.368	92	-8	16-14	.966	-4	99	108	2b116,1b33	0	-0.9
1943	Chi A	85	348	29	75	14	4	1	33	9	0	30	.216	.235	.287	53	-23	11-7	.968	1	97	118	2b85	0	-1.9
1946	Chi A	123	482	45	135	23	4	3	53	9	0	29	.280	.293	.363	86	-12	14-6	.972	5	110	119	2b90,3b31	0	-0.1
1947	Chi A	124	485	49	135	25	4	2	35	17	0	34	.278	.303	.359	87	-11	11-4	.962	6	109	104	2b99,1b11,3b8	0	0.1
1948	Chi A	119	417	60	114	14	4	6	38	18	0	18	.273	.303	.369	81	-14	2-4	.966	11	109	94	2b83,3b18	0	0.0
1949	Chi A	4	4	0	0	0	0	0	0	0	0	0	.000	.000	.000	-99	-1	0-0	ø	-0	0	0	3b2	0	-0.1
	Det A	126	483	71	142	19	3	2	47	49	2	25	.294	.361	.358	91	-6	7-7	.956	-16	86	98	2b62,1b57,3b7	0	-2.1
	Year	130	487	71	142	19	3	2	47	49	2	26	.292	.359	.355	89	-8	7-7	.956	-16	86	98	2b62,1b57,3b9	0	-2.2
1950	Det A	125	467	55	135	20	4	6	62	29	0	28	.289	.331	.388	81	-15	1-3	.989	2	107	**120**	1b118/2	0	-1.7
1951	Det A	78	212	28	54	7	0	1	17	15	1	12	.255	.307	.302	65	-11	2-3	.992	6	139	106	1b59	0	-0.7
1952	Det A	65	173	19	42	9	0	2	21	7	2	19	.243	.280	.329	69	-8	0-2	.979	1	132	51	1b32,2b8	0	-0.8
1953	Phi A	2	1	0	0	0	0	0	0	0	0	1	.000	.000	.000	-96	0	0-0	ø	-0	0	0	/3	0	0.0
Total	12	1079	3993	466	1081	180	30	29	393	189	10	251	.271	.305	.353	80	-127	76-54	.964	2	103	103	2b616,1b314,3b67	0	-10.4

KOLSETH, KARL Karl Dickey "Koley"; B12.25.1892 Cambridge MA; D5.3.1956 Cumberland MD; BL/TR/6´0˝/182; d9.30

YEAR	TM LG	G	AB	R	H	2B	3B	HR	RBI	BB-IB	HP	SO	AVG	OBP	SLG	AOPS	ABR	SB-CS	FA	FR	RNG	THR	GAMES AT POSITION	DL	BFW
1915	Bal F	6	23	1	6	1	1	0	1	1	0	0	.261	.292	.391	89	-1	0	.915	-2	57	132	1b6	—	-0.3

KOMMERS, FRED Frederick Raymond "Bugs"; B3.31.1886 Chicago IL; D6.14.1943 Chicago IL; BL/TR/6´0˝/175; d6.25

YEAR	TM LG	G	AB	R	H	2B	3B	HR	RBI	BB-IB	HP	SO	AVG	OBP	SLG	AOPS	ABR	SB-CS	FA	FR	RNG	THR	GAMES AT POSITION	DL	BFW
1913	Pit N	40	155	14	36	5	4	0	22	10	0	29	.232	.279	.316	73	-6	1-6	.979	-3	103	18	O40C	—	-1.4
1914	StL F	76	244	33	75	9	8	3	41	24	3	33	.307	.376	.447	117	2	7	.908	-1	97	121	O67(3/36/28)	—	-0.2
	Bal F	16	42	5	9	1	0	1	1	7	1	10	.214	.340	.310	75	-2	0	.938	-2	86	0	O12(11/1/0)	—	-0.4
	Year	92	286	38	84	10	8	4	42	31	4	43	.294	.371	.427	111	0	7	.911	-2	95	103	O79(14/37/28)	—	-0.6
Total	2	132	441	52	120	15	12	4	64	41	4	72	.272	.340	.388	99	-6	8-6	.938	-5	98	73	O119(14/77/28)	—	-2.0

KOMMINSK, BRAD Brad Lynn; B4.4.1961 Lima OH; BR/TR/6´2˝/205; [AtlN79 1/4]; d8.14

YEAR	TM LG	G	AB	R	H	2B	3B	HR	RBI	BB-IB	HP	SO	AVG	OBP	SLG	AOPS	ABR	SB-CS	FA	FR	RNG	THR	GAMES AT POSITION	DL	BFW
1983	Atl N	19	36	2	8	2	0	0	4	5-0	0	7	.222	.317	.278	62	-2	0-0	.944	-0	90	148	O13(1/0/12)	0	-0.3
1984	Atl N	90	301	37	61	10	0	8	36	29-0	2	77	.203	.276	.316	62	-15	18-8	.993	-6	87	35	O80(28/2/50)	0	-2.6
1985	Atl N	106	300	52	68	12	3	4	21	38-1	1	71	.227	.314	.327	75	-9	10-8	.959	-1	107	36	O92(28/1/63)	0	-1.6
1986	Atl N	5	5	1	2	0	0	0	1	0-0	0	1	.400	.400	.400	116	0	0-1	1.000	-0	95	0	3b2,O2R	0	-0.1
1987	Mil A	7	15	0	1	0	0	0	0	1-0	0	7	.067	.125	.067	-46	-3	1-0	1.000	0	142	0	O5R/D	0	-0.3
1989	Cle A	71	198	27	47	8	2	8	33	24-0	1	55	.237	.319	.419	105	1	8-2	.995	4	113	90	O68(2/66/2)	25	0.6
1990	SF N	8	5	2	1	0	0	0	0	1-0	0	2	.200	.333	.200	52	0	0-0	1.000	-1	58	0	O7(2/2/3)	0	-0.1
	Bal A	46	101	18	24	4	0	3	8	14-1	2	29	.238	.342	.366	101	1	1-1	1.000	0	100	101	O40(6/12/26),D2	0	0.0
1991	Oak A	24	25	1	3	1	0	0	2	2-0	0	9	.120	.185	.160	-4	-4	1-0	1.000	-0	88	178	O22(7/8/8)	0	-0.4
Total	8	376	986	140	215	37	5	23	105	114-2	6	258	.218	.301	.336	75	-31	39-20	.984	-4	101	63	O329(74/91/171),D3,3b2	25	-4.8

KONERKO, PAUL Paul Henry; B3.5.1976 Providence RI; BR/TR/6´3˝/(205–220); [LAN94 1/13]; d9.8

YEAR	TM LG	G	AB	R	H	2B	3B	HR	RBI	BB-IB	HP	SO	AVG	OBP	SLG	AOPS	ABR	SB-CS	FA	FR	RNG	THR	GAMES AT POSITION	DL	BFW
1997	LA N	6	7	0	1	0	0	0	0	1-0	0	2	.143	.250	.143	7	-1	0-0	1.000	-1	0	605	/13	0	-0.2
1998	LA N	49	144	14	31	1	0	4	16	10-0	2	30	.215	.272	.306	55	-10	0-1	.995	1	107	54	1b23,3b11,O11L	0	-1.2
	Cin N	26	73	7	16	3	0	3	13	6-0	1	10	.219	.284	.384	74	-3	0-0	1.000	1	110	0	3b9,1b7,O7L,D3	0	-0.3
	Year	75	217	21	47	4	0	7	29	16-0	3	40	.217	.276	.332	62	-13	0-1	.996	1	118	48	1b30,3b20,O18L,D3	0	-1.5
1999	Chi A	142	513	71	151	31	4	24	81	45-0	2	68	.294	.352	.511	115	10	1-0	.995	3	113	87	1b92,D46/3	0	0.3
2000	†Chi A	143	524	84	156	31	1	21	97	47-0	10	72	.298	.363	.481	108	7	1-0	.991	-7	89	109	1b122,3b7,D7	0	-1.0
2001	Chi A	156	582	92	164	35	0	32	99	54-6	9	89	.282	.349	.507	115	13	1-0	.994	-3	95	101	1b144,D11	0	-0.3
2002	Chi A★	151	570	81	173	30	0	27	104	44-2	9	72	.304	.359	.498	121	17	0-0	.993	-5	85	102	1b140,D7	0	0.0
2003	Chi A	137	444	49	104	19	0	18	65	43-7	4	50	.234	.305	.399	81	-13	0-0	**.998**	5	112	**120**	1b119,D14	0	-1.7
2004	Chi A	155	563	84	156	22	0	41	117	69-5	6	107	.277	.359	.535	125	21	1-0	.995	-2	93	**125**	1b139,D16	0	0.6
2005	†Chi A★	158	575	98	163	24	0	40	100	81-10	5	109	.283	.375	.534	133	29	0-0	.996	-5	87	118	1b146,D11	0	1.0
2006	Chi A★	152	566	97	177	30	0	35	113	60-3	8	104	.313	.381	.551	135	30	1-0	.995	-6	82	99	1b140,D12	0	1.1
Total	10	1275	4561	677	1292	226	5	245	805	460-33	56	713	.283	.353	.496	115	100	5-1	.995	-18	94	107	1b1073,D127,3b29,O18L	0	-1.7

YEAR	TM LG	G	AB	R	H	2B	3B	HR	RBI	BB-IB	HP	SO	AVG	OBP	SLG	AOPS	ABR	SB-CS	FA	FR	RNG	THR	GAMES AT POSITION	DL	BFW
KONETCHY, ED	Edward Joseph "Big Ed"; B9.3.1885 LaCrosse WI; D5.27.1947 Ft.Worth TX; BR/TR/6´2.5˝/195; d6.29; ▲																								
1907	StL N	91	331	34	83	11	9	2	30	26	6	—	.251	.317	.356	115	5	13	.975	4	125	94	1b91	—	0.8
1908	StL N	**154**	545	46	135	19	12	5	50	38	10	—	.248	.309	.354	117	9	16	.986	11	**128**	85	1b154	—	2.0
1909	StL N	152	576	88	165	23	14	4	80	65	7	—	.286	.366	.396	145	31	25	.985	5	**117**	87	1b152	—	3.6
1910	StL N	144	520	87	157	23	16	3	78	78	4	59	.302	.397	.425	145	32	18	**.991**	9	123	90	1b144/P	—	**3.9**
1911	StL N	**158**	571	90	165	**38**	13	6	88	81	7	63	.289	.384	.433	132	27	27	**.991**	-6	79	91	1b158	—	1.7
1912	StL N	143	538	81	169	26	13	8	82	62	4	66	.314	.389	.455	134	25	25	.991	6	114	92	1b142/lf	—	2.6
1913	StL N	140	504	75	139	18	17	8	68	53	7	41	.276	.353	.427	124	15	27-25	**.995**	8	**119**	92	1b140/P	—	1.7
1914	Pit N	154	563	56	140	23	9	4	51	32	2	48	.249	.291	.343	92	-8	20	**.995**	5	109	94	1b154	—	-0.8
1915	Pit F	152	576	79	181	31	18	10	93	41	3	52	.314	.363	.483	138	18	27	**.994**	0	95	103	1b152	—	1.5
1916	Bos N	**158**	566	76	147	29	13	3	70	43	7	46	.260	.320	.373	117	11	13	.990	9	**124**	**121**	1b158	—	1.8
1917	Bos N	130	474	56	129	19	13	2	54	36	5	40	.272	.330	.380	125	13	16	**.994**	2	99	82	1b129	—	1.3
1918	Bos N	119	437	33	103	15	5	2	56	32	2	35	.236	.291	.307	86	-8	5	**.992**	-2	85	102	1b112,O6(1/4/1)/P	—	-1.4
1919	Bro N	132	486	46	145	24	9	1	47	29	3	39	.298	.342	.391	117	10	14	**.994**	6	114	86	1b132	—	1.4
1920	†Bro N	131	497	62	153	22	12	5	63	33	1	18	.308	.352	.431	120	12	3-2	.990	0	99	85	1b130	—	0.9
1921	Bro N	55	197	25	53	6	5	3	23	19	1	21	.269	.336	.396	90	-3	3-3	.987	-1	93	104	1b54	—	-0.8
	Phi N	72	268	38	86	17	4	8	59	21	4	17	.321	.379	.504	122	9	3-0	.986	5	139	70	1b71	—	1.0
	Year	127	465	63	139	23	9	11	82	40	5	38	.299	.361	.458	109	6	6-3	.986	4	119	85	1b125	—	0.2
Total	15	2085	7649	972	2150	344	182	74	992	689	73	545	.281	.346	.403	122	198	255-30	.990	60	110	93	1b2073,O7(2/4/1),P3	—	21.2
KONNICK, MIKE	Michael Aloysius; B1.13.1889 Glen Lyon PA; D7.9.1971 Wilkes–Barre PA; BR/TR/5´9˝/180; d10.3																								
1909	Cin N	2	5	0	2	1	0	0	1	0	0	—	.400	.400	.600	211	1	0	1.000	-0	*82*	*73*	C2	—	0.0
1910	Cin N	1	3	0	0	0	0	0	0	1	0	0	.000	.250	.000	-27	0	0	1.000	-0	72	0	/S	—	-0.1
Total	2	3	8	0	2	1	0	0	1	1	0	0	.250	.333	.375	117	1	0	1.000	-1	*82*	*73*	C2/S	—	-0.1
KONOPKA, BRUCE	Bruno Bruce; B9.16.1919 Hammond IN; D9.27.1996 Denver CO; BL/TL/6´2˝/190; d6.7; Mil 1943–45; Col USC																								
1942	Phi A	5	10	2	3	0	0	0	1	1	0	0	.300	.364	.300	88	0	0-0	1.000	-0	68	110	1b3	0	0.0
1943	Phi A	2	2	0	0	0	0	0	0	0	0	1	.000	.000	.000	-99	-1	0-0	ø	0	—	—	/H	0	-0.1
1946	Phi A	38	93	7	22	4	1	0	9	4	0	8	.237	.268	.301	59	-5	0-0	.994	2	129	75	1b20/lf	0	-0.5
Total	3	45	105	9	25	4	1	0	10	5	0	9	.238	.273	.295	59	-6	0-0	.995	2	123	78	1b23/lf	0	-0.6
KOONCE, GRAY	Graham Clinton; B5.15.1975 El Cajon CA; BL/TL/6´4˝/220; [DetA93 60/1561]; d9.20																								
2003	Oak A	6	8	0	1	1	0	0	0	0-0	0	6	.125	.125	.250	-4	-1	0-0	1.000	1	216	169	1b5	0	-0.1
KOONS, HARRY	Henry M.; B8.18.1862 Camden NJ; D4.5.1932 Camden NJ; BR/TR/5´8˝/174; d4.17																								
1884	Alt U	21	78	8	18	2	1	0	—	2	—	—	.231	.250	.282	60	-6	—	.866	5	126	39	3b21/C	—	-0.1
	CP U	1	3	0	0	0	0	0	—	0	—	—	.000	.000	.000	-99	-1	—	ø	-0	0	0	/3	—	-0.1
	Year	22	81	8	18	2	1	0	—	2	—	—	.222	.241	.272	55	-7	—	.866	5	125	39	3b22/C	—	-0.2
KOPACZ, GEORGE	George Felix "Sonny"; B2.26.1941 Chicago IL; BL/TL/6´1˝/(192–195); d9.18																								
1966	Atl N	6	9	1	0	0	0	0	0	1-0	0	5	.000	.100	.000	-68	-2	0-0	.909	-1	0	0	1b2	0	-0.3
1970	Pit N	10	16	1	3	0	0	0	0	0-0	0	5	.188	.188	.188	1	-2	0-0	1.000	-1	0	99	1b3	0	-0.3
Total	2	16	25	2	3	0	0	0	0	1-0	0	10	.120	.154	.120	-24	-4	0-0	.964	-1	0	59	1b5	0	-0.6
KOPF, WALLY	Walter Henry; B7.10.1899 Stonington CT; D4.30.1979 Hamilton Co. OH; BB/TR/5´11˝/168; d10.1; b–Larry; Col Dartmouth																								
1921	NY N	2	3	0	1	0	0	0	0	1	0	1	.333	.500	.333	125	0	0-0	1.000	1	222	435	3b2	—	0.1
KOPF, LARRY	William Lorenz (aka Fred Brady in 1913); B11.3.1890 Bristol CT; D10.15.1986 Anderson Twp. OH; BB/TR/5´9˝/160; d9.2; Def 1918; b–Wally; Col Fordham																								
1913	Cle A	6	10	2	3	1	0	0	1	0	0	0	.300	.300	.400	102	0	0	.923	1	146	150	2b4/3	—	0.2
1914	Phi A	37	69	8	13	2	2	0	12	8	3	14	.188	.300	.275	76	-2	6	.899	-3	85	62	S13,3b8,2b5	—	-0.2
1915	Phi A	118	386	39	87	10	2	1	33	41	9	45	.225	.314	.269	77	-10	5-9	.920	-7	92	71	S74,3b42,2b2	—	-1.4
1916	Cin N	11	40	2	11	2	0	0	5	1	0	8	.275	.293	.325	92	0	1	.942	-1	103	89	S11	—	-0.1
1917	Cin N	148	573	81	146	19	8	2	26	28	6	48	.255	.297	.326	95	-5	17	.916	-9	100	88	S145	—	-0.4
1919	†Cin N	135	503	51	136	18	5	0	58	28	3	27	.270	.313	.326	95	-4	18	.943	-35	86	75	S135	—	-3.3
1920	Cin N	126	458	56	112	15	6	0	59	35	5	24	.245	.305	.303	76	-14	14-13	.929	-33	85	90	S123,2b2,3b2/cf	—	-4.3
1921	Cin N	107	367	36	80	8	3	1	25	43	6	20	.218	.310	.264	56	-22	3-14	.947	-17	93	81	S93,2b4,3b3/lf	—	-3.3
1922	Bos N	126	466	59	124	6	3	1	37	45	1	22	.266	.332	.298	67	-22	8-9	.944	-12	93	82	2b78,S33,3b13	—	-2.8
1923	Bos N	39	138	15	38	3	1	0	10	13	0	6	.275	.338	.312	75	-5	0-3	.905	-5	99	110	S37,2b4	—	-0.7
Total	10	853	3010	349	750	84	30	5	266	242	33	214	.249	.312	.302	78	-84	72-48	.928	-120	92	84	S664,2b99,3b69,O2(1/1/0)	—	-16.3
KOPP, MERLIN	Merlin Henry "Manny"; B1.2.1892 Toledo OH; D5.6.1960 Sacramento CA; BB/TR (BR 1915)/5´8˝/158; d8.2; Mil 1918																								
1915	Was A	16	32	2	8	0	0	0	0	5	0	7	.250	.351	.250	79	-1	1	.933	-1	109	0	O9(8/0/1)	—	-0.1
1918	Phi A	96	363	60	85	7	7	0	18	42	4	55	.234	.320	.292	84	-7	22	.972	10	108	149	O96L	—	-0.2
1919	Phi A	75	235	34	53	2	4	1	12	42	2	43	.226	.348	.281	77	-6	16	.924	-3	95	101	O65(58/7/0)	—	-1.2
Total	3	187	630	96	146	9	11	1	30	89	6	105	.232	.332	.286	81	-14	39	.953	7	103	125	O170(162/7/1)	—	-1.5
KOPPE, JOE	Joseph (b Joseph Kopchia); B10.19.1930 Detroit MI; D9.27.2006 Ann Arbor MI; BR/TR/5´10˝/(165–170); d8.9																								
1958	Mil N	16	9	3	4	0	0	0	0	1-0	0	1	.444	.500	.444	167	1	0-0	.833	1	131	194	S3	0	0.2
1959	Phi N	126	422	68	110	18	7	7	28	41-0	2	80	.261	.327	.386	88	-7	7-7	.954	13	106	103	S113,2b11	0	1.4
1960	Phi N	58	170	13	29	6	1	1	13	23-3	1	47	.171	.272	.235	41	-14	3-2	.956	-6	91	76	S55,3b2	39	-1.6
1961	Phi N	6	3	1	0	0	0	0	0	0-0	0	0	.000	.000	.000	-99	-1	0-0	.800	-1	53	118	S5	0	-0.2
	LA A	91	338	46	85	12	2	5	40	45-0	1	77	.251	.339	.343	75	-11	3-3	.947	-3	99	89	S88,2b3/3	0	-0.6
1962	LA A	128	375	47	85	16	0	4	40	73-3	2	84	.227	.352	.301	81	-6	2-1	.957	-1	108	85	S118,2b5,3b4	0	0.4
1963	LA A	76	143	11	30	4	1	1	12	9-1	1	30	.210	.258	.273	53	-9	0-0	.962	4	116	66	S19,3b18,2b14,O3R	0	-0.4
1964	LA A	54	113	10	29	4	1	0	6	14-1	0	16	.257	.339	.310	91	-1	0-0	.945	9	129	115	S31,2b13,3b3	0	1.1
1965	Cal A	23	33	3	7	1	0	1	2	3-1	0	10	.212	.278	.333	75	-1	1-0	.979	4	158	90	2b10,S4,3b4	0	0.4
Total	8	578	1606	202	379	61	12	19	141	209-9	7	345	.236	.324	.324	76	-49	16-13	.952	20	105	92	S436,2b56,3b32,O3R	39	0.7
KOPSHAW, GEORGE	George Karl; B7.5.1895 Passaic NJ; D12.26.1934 Lynchburg VA; BR/TR/5´11.5˝/176; d8.4																								
1923	StL N	2	5	1	1	1	0	0	0	0	0	1	.200	.200	.400	56	0	0-0	1.000	-1	*54*	*0*	/C	—	-0.1
KORCHECK, STEVE	Stephen Joseph "Hoss"; B8.11.1932 McClellandtown PA; BR/TR/6´1˝/205; d9.6; Mil 1956–57; Col George Washington																								
1954	Was A	2	7	0	1	0	0	0	0	0	0	2	.143	.143	.143	-23	-1	0-0	.857	-1	*50*	*0*	C2	0	-0.2
1955	Was A	13	36	3	10	2	0	0	2	0-0	1	5	.278	.297	.333	73	-1	0-0	1.000	0	*86*	*207*	C12	0	-0.1
1958	Was A	21	51	6	4	2	1	0	1	1-1	0	16	.078	.096	.157	-32	-9	0-0	.975	-2	52	179	C20	0	-1.2
1959	Was A	22	51	3	8	2	0	0	4	5-0	0	13	.157	.228	.196	19	-6	0-0	.974	4	67	55	C22	0	-0.1
Total	4	58	145	12	23	6	1	0	7	6-1	1	36	.159	.196	.214	13	-17	0-0	.976	1	*66*	*129*	C56	0	-1.6
KORES, ART	Arthur Emil "Dutch"; B7.22.1886 Milwaukee WI; D3.26.1974 Milwaukee WI; BR/TR/5´9˝/167; d7.24																								
1915	StL F	60	201	18	47	9	2	1	22	21	0	13	.234	.306	.313	71	-11	6	.960	16	127	141	3b60	—	0.8
KOSCO, ANDY	Andrew John; B10.5.1941 Youngstown OH; BR/TR/6´3˝/(200–210); d8.13																								
1965	Min A	23	55	3	13	4	0	1	6	1-0	0	15	.236	.241	.364	69	-2	0-0	1.000	1	90	442	O14R,1b2	0	-0.2
1966	Min A	57	158	11	35	5	0	2	13	7-1	0	31	.222	.251	.291	53	-10	0-1	.986	0	109	95	O40(31/7/5),1b5	0	-1.3
1967	Min A	9	28	4	4	1	0	0	4	2-0	0	4	.143	.200	.179	12	-3	0-0	.923	-0	112	0	O7R	0	-0.4
1968	NY A	131	466	47	112	19	1	15	59	16-2	3	71	.240	.268	.382	99	-3	2-2	.960	-1	97	166	O95(1/0/94),1b28	0	-1.4
1969	LA N	120	424	51	105	13	2	19	74	21-2	1	66	.248	.282	.422	102	-2	0-1	.981	-4	88	88	O109(38/0/76),1b3	0	-1.3
1970	LA N	74	224	21	51	12	0	8	27	1-0	0	40	.228	.230	.388	65	-13	1-1	.981	-1	102	55	O58(3/0/55)/1	0	-1.6
1971	Mil A	98	264	27	60	6	2	10	39	24-5	0	57	.227	.291	.379	90	-5	1-3	.988	-1	118	87	O45(26/0/19),1b29,3b12	0	-1.1
1972	Cal A	49	142	15	34	4	2	6	13	5-1	1	23	.239	.267	.423	110	0	1-0	.985	1	108	86	O36(24/0/13)	0	-0.1
	Bos A	17	47	5	10	2	1	3	6	2-0	1	9	.213	.260	.489	113	0	0-0	1.000	-0	90	116	O12L	0	0.0
	Year	66	189	20	44	6	3	9	19	7-1	2	32	.233	.265	.439	110	1	1-0	.988	1	103	94	O48(36/0/13)	0	-0.1
1973	†Cin N	47	118	17	33	7	0	9	21	13-6	0	26	.280	.346	.568	157	9	0-0	1.000	-4	82	39	O36(1/7/28)/1	0	0.4
1974	Cin N	33	37	3	7	2	0	0	5	7-1	0	8	.189	.311	.243	59	-2	0-0	.846	-2	65	0	3b8/rf	40	-0.4
Total	10	658	1963	204	464	75	8	73	267	99-18	6	350	.236	.273	.394	92	-31	5-8	.979	-10	98	107	O453(136/14/312),1b69,3b20	40	-7.4

YEAR	TM LG	G	AB	R	H	2B	3B	HR	RBI	BB-IB	HP	SO	AVG	OBP	SLG	AOPS	ABR	SB-CS	FA	FR	RNG	THR	GAMES AT POSITION	DL	BFW
Koshorek, Clem	Clement John "Scooter"; B6.20.1925 Royal Oak MI; D9.8.1991 Royal Oak MI; BR/TR/5´4.5˝/165; d4.15																								
1952	Pit N	98	322	27	84	17	0	0	15	26	2	39	.261	.320	.314	74	-10	4-7	.949	4	117	124	S33,2b27,3b26	0	-0.5
1953	Pit N	1	1	0	0	0	0	0	0	0	0	1	.000	.000	.000	-99	0	0-0	ø	0	—	—	/H	55	0.0
Total	2	99	323	27	84	17	0	0	15	26	2	40	.260	.319	.313	74	-10	4-7	.949	4	117	124	S33,2b27,3b26	55	-0.5
Koskie, Corey	Cordel Leonard; B6.28.1973 Anola MB, Can.; BL/TR/6´3˝/(217–220); [MinA94 26/715]; d9.9; Col Des Moines Area (IA) CC																								
1998	Min A	11	29	2	4	0	0	1	2	2-0	0	10	.138	.194	.241	12	-4	0-0	.941	-2	68	82	3b10	0	-0.6
1999	Min A	117	342	42	106	21	0	11	58	40-4	5	72	.310	.387	.468	112	7	4-4	.962	0	109	72	3b79,O25R,D12	0	0.6
2000	Min A	146	474	79	142	32	4	9	65	77-7	4	104	.300	.400	.441	106	8	5-4	.966	-5	90	113	3b139/D	0	0.3
2001	Min A	153	562	100	155	37	2	26	103	68-9	12	118	.276	.362	.488	116	14	27-6	.964	-1	103	79	3b150,D2	0	1.8
2002	†Min A	140	490	71	131	37	3	15	69	72-4	9	127	.267	.368	.447	112	12	10-11	.969	4	101	76	3b138/D	16	1.4
2003	†Min A	131	469	76	137	29	2	14	69	77-5	7	113	.292	.393	.452	120	17	11-5	.973	-6	96	73	3b131	23	1.2
2004	†Min A	118	422	68	106	24	2	25	71	49-10	12	103	.251	.342	.495	113	8	9-3	.963	-3	98	79	3b115/D	15	0.6
2005	Tor A	97	354	49	88	20	0	11	36	44-3	4	90	.249	.337	.398	91	-4	4-1	.968	2	103	144	3b76,D19	67	-0.2
2006	Mil N	76	257	29	67	23	0	12	33	29-3	3	58	.261	.343	.490	109	4	1-2	.967	9	109	85	3b70	88	1.2
Total	9	989	3399	516	936	223	13	124	506	458-45	56	795	.275	.367	.458	110	62	71-36	.966	-1	100	88	3b908,D36,O25R	209	6.3
Koslofski, Kevin	Kevin Craig; B9.24.1966 Decatur IL; BL/TR/5´8˝/(165–175); [KCA84 20/512]; d6.28																								
1992	KC A	55	133	20	33	0	2	3	13	12-0	1	23	.248	.313	.346	82	-4	2-1	.991	4	110	190	O52(15/18/23)	0	0.0
1993	KC A	15	26	4	7	0	0	1	2	4-0	1	5	.269	.387	.385	101	0	0-1	1.000	3	123	459	O13(3/4/7)/D	0	0.2
1994	KC A	2	4	2	1	0	0	0	0	2-1	0	1	.250	.500	.250	97	0	0-0	.750	0	75	1130	O2(0/1/1)	0	0.0
1996	Mil A	25	42	5	9	3	2	0	6	4-1	1	12	.214	.298	.381	67	-2	0-0	.972	-0	106	0	O22(6/14/2)/D	0	-0.2
Total	4	97	205	31	50	3	4	4	21	22-2	3	41	.244	.325	.356	82	-6	2-2	.983	7	110	202	O89(24/37/33),D2	0	0.0
Kosman, Mike	Michael Thomas; B11.26.1917 Hamtramck MI; D12.10.2002 Lafayette IN; BR/TR/5´9˝/160; d4.20; Col Indiana																								
1944	Cin N	1	0	0	0	0	0	0	0	0	0	0	ø	ø	ø	ø	0	0	ø	0	—	—	/R	0	0.0
Koster, Fred	Frederick Charles "Fritz"; B12.21.1905 Louisville KY; D4.24.1979 St.Matthews KY; BL/TL/5´10.5˝/165; d4.27; Col Louisville																								
1931	Phi N	76	151	21	34	2	2	0	8	14	0	21	.225	.291	.265	47	-11	4	.923	0	102	120	O41(6/14/22)	—	-1.3
Kostro, Frank	Frank Jerry; B8.4.1937 Windber PA; BR/TR/6´2˝/(190–195); d9.2																								
1962	Det A	16	41	5	11	3	0	0	3	1-0	0	6	.268	.279	.341	66	-2	0-0	.967	0	102	115	3b11	0	-0.2
1963	Det A	31	52	4	12	1	0	0	0	9-0	0	13	.231	.344	.250	67	-2	0-0	.929	0	122	0	3b6,1b3,O3(1/0/2)	0	-0.2
	LA A	43	99	6	22	2	1	2	10	6-0	0	17	.222	.264	.323	68	-5	0-0	.960	-2	85	154	3b19,1b5,O3(1/0/2)	0	-0.7
	Year	74	151	10	34	3	1	2	10	15-0	0	30	.225	.293	.298	68	-7	0-0	.953	-2	93	120	3b25,1b8,O6(2/0/4)	0	-0.9
1964	Min A	59	103	10	28	5	0	3	12	4-0	1	21	.272	.303	.408	96	-1	0-0	.912	-4	92	51	3b12,2b7,O2L/1	0	-0.5
1965	Min A	20	31	2	5	2	0	0	1	4-0	0	5	.161	.250	.226	37	-2	0-0	.923	1	89	128	2b7,3b6,O2(1/0/1)	0	-0.2
1967	Min A	32	31	4	10	0	0	0	2	3-0	0	2	.323	.382	.323	102	0	0-0	1.000	-1	30	0	O3(2/0/1)/3	0	-0.1
1968	Min A	63	108	9	26	4	1	0	9	6-1	0	20	.241	.274	.296	71	-4	0-0	1.000	0	101	192	O24(14/0/10),1b5	0	-0.5
1969	Min A	2	2	0	0	0	0	0	0	0-0	0	1	.000	.000	.000	-97	-1	0-0	ø	0	—	—	/H	0	-0.1
Total	7	266	467	40	114	17	2	5	37	33-1	1	85	.244	.291	.321	74	-17	0-0	.926	-5	98	136	3b55,O37(21/0/16),2b14,1b14	0	-2.5
Kotchman, Casey	Casey John; B2.22.1983 St. Petersburg FL; BL/TL/6´3˝/(210–215); [AnaA01 1/13]; d5.9																								
2004	†Ana A	38	116	7	26	6	0	0	15	7-3	4	11	.224	.289	.276	51	-8	3-0	.988	-3	71	70	1b34,D2	0	-1.2
2005	†LA A	47	126	16	35	5	0	7	22	15-0	0	18	.278	.352	.484	124	4	1-1	1.000	-1	70	84	1b20,D20	0	0.1
2006	LA A	29	79	6	12	2	0	1	6	7-0	0	13	.152	.221	.215	14	-10	0-1	1.000	1	105	65	1b26	146	-1.2
Total	3	114	321	29	73	13	0	8	43	29-3	4	42	.227	.298	.343	70	-14	4-2	.995	-3	82	71	1b80,D22	146	-2.3
Kotsay, Mark	Mark Steven; B12.2.1975 Whittier CA; BL/TL/6´0˝/(180–205); [FlaN96 1/9]; d7.11; Col Cal St.–Fullerton																								
1997	Fla N	14	52	5	10	1	1	0	4	4-0	0	7	.192	.250	.250	33	-5	3-0	1.000	2	108	331	O14C	0	-0.3
1998	Fla N	154	578	72	161	25	7	11	68	34-2	1	61	.279	.318	.403	94	-7	10-5	.984	19	118	211	O145(0/46/107),1b3	0	0.7
1999	Fla N	148	495	57	134	23	9	8	50	29-5	0	50	.271	.306	.402	83	-15	7-6	.981	13	107	**246**	O129R,1b19	0	-0.9
2000	Fla N	152	530	87	158	31	5	12	57	42-2	0	46	.298	.347	.443	104	2	19-9	.990	11	111	173	O142(0/9/139),1b2	0	0.8
2001	SD N	119	406	67	118	29	1	10	58	48-1	2	58	.291	.366	.441	117	12	13-5	.986	4	115	72	O111(1/106/5)	15	1.7
2002	SD N	153	578	82	169	27	7	17	61	59-0	3	89	.292	.359	.452	123	18	11-9	.989	5	106	144	O147C	0	2.3
2003	SD N	128	482	64	128	28	4	7	38	56-3	1	82	.266	.343	.384	98	-1	6-3	.991	14	**116**	200	O126C	17	1.4
2004	Oak A	148	606	78	190	37	3	15	63	55-5	2	70	.314	.370	.459	116	15	8-5	.984	-2	94	151	O145C/D	0	1.4
2005	Oak A	139	582	75	163	35	1	15	82	40-3	1	51	.280	.325	.421	98	-2	5-5	.987	-8	88	107	O137C,D2	0	-0.9
2006	†Oak A	129	502	57	138	29	3	7	59	44-1	2	55	.275	.332	.386	88	-8	6-3	.993	-8	91	98	O127C,1b4/D	0	-1.4
Total	10	1284	4811	644	1369	265	41	102	540	411-22	12	569	.285	.340	.420	102	9	88-50	.987	48	105	159	O1223(1/857/380),1b28,D4	32	4.8
Kouzmanoff, Kevin	Kevin; B7.25.1981 Newport Beach CA; BR/TR/6´1˝/210; [CleA03 6/168]; d9.2; Col Nevada–Reno																								
2006	Cle A	16	56	4	12	2	0	3	11	5-0	0	12	.214	.279	.411	78	-2	0-0	.857	-0	104	0	D14,3b2	0	-0.3
Kowitz, Brian	Brian Mark; B8.7.1969 Baltimore MD; BL/TL/5´10˝/182; [AtlN90 9/237]; d6.4; Col Clemson																								
1995	Atl N	10	24	3	4	1	0	0	3	2-0	1	5	.167	.259	.208	24	-3	0-1	1.000	-1	53	0	O8(2/1/5)	0	-0.5
Koy, Ernie	Ernest Anyz "Chief"; B9.17.1909 Sealy TX; BR/TR/6´0˝/200; d4.19; Mil 1943–45; Col Texas																								
1938	Bro N	142	521	78	156	29	13	11	76	38	4	76	.299	.352	.468	121	13	15	.984	-0	104	66	O135(54/64/18)/3	—	0.8
1939	Bro N	125	425	57	118	37	5	8	67	39	0	64	.278	.338	.445	105	3	11	.962	0	106	56	O114(110/3/3)	—	-0.3
1940	Bro N	24	48	9	11	2	1	1	8	3	0	3	.229	.275	.375	73	-2	1	1.000	-0	105	0	O19(11/5/2)	—	-0.3
	StL N	93	348	44	108	19	5	8	52	28	4	59	.310	.368	.463	121	10	12	.970	-3	99	30	O91L	—	0.2
	Year	117	396	53	119	21	6	9	60	31	4	62	.301	.357	.452	115	8	13	.973	-4	100	27	O110(102/5/2)	—	-0.1
1941	StL N	13	40	5	8	1	0	2	4	1	0	8	.200	.220	.375	61	-2	0	1.000	-0	98	0	O12L	0	-0.3
	Cin N	67	204	24	51	11	2	2	27	14	1	22	.250	.301	.353	84	-5	1	.990	-2	90	89	O49(42/1/6)	0	-0.9
	Year	80	244	29	59	12	2	4	31	15	1	30	.242	.288	.357	80	-7	1	.991	-2	91	76	O61(54/1/6)	0	-1.2
1942	Cin N	3	2	0	0	0	0	0	0	0	0	2	.000	.000	.000	-99	-1	0	ø	0	—	—	/H	0	-0.1
	Phi N	91	258	21	63	9	3	4	26	14	0	50	.244	.283	.349	89	-5	0	.981	-1	100	73	O78(28/52/4)	0	-1.0
	Year	94	260	21	63	9	3	4	26	14	0	52	.242	.281	.346	87	-6	0	.981	-1	100	73	O78(28/52/4)	0	-1.1
Total	5	558	1846	238	515	108	29	36	260	137	9	284	.279	.332	.427	107	11	40	.977	-7	101	57	O498(348/125/33)/3	0	-1.9
Kozar, Al	Albert Kenneth; B7.5.1921 McKees Rocks PA; BR/TR/5´9.5˝/173; d4.19																								
1948	Was A	150	577	61	144	25	8	1	58	66	0	52	.250	.327	.326	76	-20	4-2	.967	-21	98	74	2b149	0	-3.2
1949	Was A	105	350	46	94	15	2	4	31	25	2	23	.269	.321	.357	81	-11	2-1	.977	-8	94	75	2b102	0	-1.4
1950	Was A	20	55	7	11	1	0	0	3	5	0	8	.200	.267	.218	27	-6	0-0	.962	-0	113	69	2b15	0	-0.5
	Chi A	10	10	4	3	0	0	1	2	0	0	3	.300	.300	.600	129	0	0-0	1.000	1	154	190	2b4/3	0	0.2
	Year	30	65	11	14	1	0	1	5	5	0	11	.215	.271	.277	42	-6	0-0	.968	1	118	84	2b19/3	0	-0.3
Total	3	285	992	118	252	41	10	6	94	96	2	86	.254	.321	.334	76	-37	6-3	.971	-27	98	75	2b270/3	0	-4.9
Kracher, Joe	Joseph Peter "Jug"; B11.4.1913 Philadelphia PA; D12.24.1981 San Angelo TX; BR/TR/5´11˝/185; d9.17																								
1939	Phi N	5	5	1	1	0	0	0	0	2	0	1	.200	.429	.200	76	0	0	1.000	-1	*0*	*0*	C2	—	0.0
Kraft, Clarence	Clarence Otto "Big Boy"; B6.9.1887 Evansville IN; D3.26.1958 Fort Worth TX; BR/TR/6´0˝/190; d5.1																								
1914	Bos N	3	3	0	1	0	0	0	0	0	0	1	.333	.333	.333	99	0	0	1.000	-0	0	0	/1	—	0.0
Kranepool, Ed	Edward Emil; B11.8.1944 New York NY; BL/TL/6´3˝/(205–215); d9.22																								
1962	NY N	3	6	0	1	1	0	0	0	0-0	0	1	.167	.167	.333	30	-1	0-0	1.000	1	292	0	1b3	0	0.0
1963	NY N	86	273	22	57	12	2	2	14	18-0	0	50	.209	.256	.289	56	-15	4-2	.954	-1	89	131	O55(6/0/50),1b20	0	-2.2
1964	NY N	119	420	47	108	19	4	10	45	32-2	2	50	.257	.310	.393	100	-1	0-1	.991	2	113	91	1b104,O6(0/1/5)	0	-0.6
1965	NY N☆	153	525	44	133	24	4	10	53	39-7	2	71	.253	.303	.371	94	-5	1-4	.992	1	104	101	1b147	0	-1.5
1966	NY N	146	464	51	118	15	2	16	57	41-9	3	66	.254	.316	.399	100	0	1-1	.992	4	**113**	98	1b132,O11L	0	-0.4
1967	NY N	141	469	37	126	17	1	10	54	37-15	1	51	.269	.321	.373	100	0	0-4	.992	3	107	101	1b139	0	-0.7
1968	NY N	127	373	29	86	13	1	3	20	19-5	2	39	.231	.271	.295	70	-14	0-3	.994	4	113	105	1b113,O2L	0	-2.0
1969	†NY N	112	353	36	84	9	2	11	49	37-7	0	32	.238	.307	.368	87	-7	3-2	.993	2	106	110	1b106,O2L	0	-1.3
1970	NY N	43	47	2	8	0	0	0	3	5-0	0	2	.170	.250	.170	15	-6	0-0	1.000	-0	74	113	1b8	0	-0.7
1971	NY N	122	421	61	118	20	4	14	58	38-6	1	33	.280	.340	.447	122	11	0-4	**.998**	-1	88	83	1b108,O11(6/0/5)	0	0.1

YEAR	TM LG	G	AB	R	H	2B	3B	HR	RBI	BB-IB	HP	SO	AVG	OBP	SLG	AOPS	ABR	SB-CS	FA	FR	RNG	THR	GAMES AT POSITION	DL	BFW
1972	NY N	122	327	28	88	15	1	8	34	34-13	1	35	.269	.336	.394	110	4	1-0	.996	0	96	95	1b108/rf	0	-0.2
1973	†NY N	100	284	28	68	12	2	1	35	30-4	0	28	.239	.310	.306	72	-10	1-0	.998	1	104	108	1b51,O32(31/0/1)	0	-1.5
1974	NY N	94	217	20	65	11	1	4	24	18-0	0	14	.300	.350	.415	115	4	1-0	.977	-4	80	50	O33(32/0/1),1b24	0	-0.3
1975	NY N	106	325	42	105	16	0	4	43	27-6	0	21	.323	.370	.409	121	10	1-1	.997	0	94	82	1b82,O4L	0	0.3
1976	NY N	123	415	47	121	17	1	10	49	35-4	0	38	.292	.344	.410	119	10	1-0	.996	-4	70	88	1b86,O31(23/0/8)	0	-0.2
1977	NY N	108	281	28	79	17	0	10	40	23-7	0	20	.281	.330	.448	112	4	1-4	.984	2	99	0	O42(10/0/32),1b41	0	0.1
1978	NY N	66	81	7	17	2	0	3	19	8-2	1	12	.210	.280	.346	79	-3	0-0	1.000	-0	68	0	O12(3/0/9),1b3	0	-0.4
1979	NY N	82	155	7	36	5	0	2	17	13-2	1	18	.232	.287	.303	65	-7	0-1	1.000	1	119	84	1b29,O8(2/0/6)	0	-0.9
Total	18	1853	5436	536	1418	225	25	118	614	454-89	14	581	.261	.316	.377	97	-26	15-27	.994	10	104	97	1b1304,O250(132/1/118)	0	-12.4
KRAUSE, CHARLIE	Charles Frederick; B10.2.1873 Detroit MI; D3.30.1948 Eloise (now part of Westland) MI; TR/5´6˝/?; d7.27																								
1901	Cin N	1	4	0	1	0	0	0	0	0	0	—	.250	.250	.250	48	0	0	ø	-0	0	0	/2	—	0.0
KRAVITZ, DANNY	Daniel "Dusty","Beak"; B12.21.1930 Lopez PA; BL/TR/5´11˝/(195–200); d4.17																								
1956	Pit N	32	68	6	18	2	2	2	10	5-1	0	9	.265	.311	.441	103	0	1-1	.944	-0	*116*	*115*	C26,3b2	0	0.0
1957	Pit N	19	41	2	6	1	0	0	4	2-0	-0	10	.146	.186	.171	-3	-6	0-0	1.000	3	53	58	C15	0	-0.3
1958	Pit N	45	100	9	24	3	2	1	5	11-5	0	10	.240	.313	.340	76	-4	0-0	.967	-5	100	122	C37	0	-0.7
1959	Pit N	52	162	18	41	9	1	3	21	5-1	0	14	.253	.274	.377	72	-7	0-1	.986	-5	65	89	C45	0	-1.0
1960	Pit N	8	6	0	0	0	0	0	0	1-0	0	2	.000	.143	.000	-57	-1	0-0	1.000	0	0	0	/C	0	-0.1
	KC A	59	175	17	41	7	2	4	14	11-1	0	19	.234	.280	.366	73	-7	0-0	.971	-4	70	37	C47	0	-1.0
Total	5	215	552	52	130	22	7	10	54	35-8	0	64	.236	.280	.355	70	-25	1-2	.973	-11	*80*	*81*	C171,3b2	0	-3.1
KREEVICH, MIKE	Michael Andreas; B6.10.1908 Mt.Olive IL; D4.25.1994 Pana IL; BR/TR/5´7.5˝/168; d9.7																								
1931	Chi N	5	12	0	2	0	0	0	0	0	0	6	.167	.167	.167	-10	-2	1	1.000	0	77	371	O4(1/1/2)	—	-0.2
1935	Chi A	6	23	3	10	2	0	0	2	1	0	0	.435	.458	.522	149	2	1-1	1.000	-2	44	0	3b6	—	0.0
1936	Chi A	137	550	99	169	32	11	5	69	61	2	46	.307	.378	.433	96	-3	10-5	.964	-2	92	136	O133(17/65/57)	—	-0.9
1937	Chi A	144	583	94	176	29	**16**	12	73	43	0	45	.302	.350	.468	104	1	10-1	**.988**	4	103	96	O138(6/138/1)	—	0.2
1938	Chi A★	129	489	73	145	26	12	6	73	55	3	23	.297	.371	.436	99	-1	13-5	.975	-1	105	55	O127(0/127/1)	—	-0.4
1939	Chi A	145	541	85	175	30	8	5	77	59	0	40	.323	.390	.436	108	8	23-10	.975	9	105	146	O139C,3b4	—	1.4
1940	Chi A	144	582	86	154	27	10	8	55	34	0	49	.265	.305	.387	77	-22	15-7	.982	7	107	109	O144C	—	-1.7
1941	Chi A	121	436	44	101	16	8	0	37	35	0	26	.232	.289	.305	58	-28	17-5	**.994**	-2	98	74	O113C	0	-3.0
1942	Phi A	116	444	57	113	19	1	1	30	47	0	31	.255	.326	.309	79	-11	7-9	.981	-0	106	49	O107C	0	-1.6
1943	StL A	60	161	24	41	6	0	0	10	26	0	13	.255	.358	.292	89	-1	4-1	.993	5	112	132	O51(3/47/1)	0	-0.3
1944	†StL A	105	402	55	121	15	6	5	44	27	2	24	.301	.348	.405	108	4	3-3	.986	-3	102	42	O100(0/93/7)	0	-0.3
1945	StL A	84	295	34	70	11	1	2	21	37	0	27	.237	.322	.302	78	-8	4-1	.991	2	112	46	O81C	0	-0.8
	Was A	45	158	22	44	8	2	1	23	21	0	9	.278	.363	.373	124	5	7-5	.971	-2	96	62	O40C	0	0.2
	Year	129	453	56	114	19	3	3	44	58	0	36	.252	.337	.327	92	-3	11-6	.985	0	107	51	O121C	0	-0.6
Total	12	1241	4676	676	1321	221	75	45	514	446	7	339	.283	.346	.391	92	-56	115-53	.982	15	103	90	O1177(27/1095/69),3b10	0	-6.8
KREHMEYER, CHARLIE	Charles L.; B7.5.1863 St.Louis MO; D2.10.1926 St.Louis MO; BL/TL/5´11˝/179; d7.8																								
1884	StL AA	21	70	3	16	0	1	0	5	2	0	—	.229	.250	.257	64	-3	—	.619	-3	87	0	O15(5/9/1),C7/1	—	-0.6
1885	Lou AA	7	31	4	7	1	1	0	5	1	0	—	.226	.250	.323	80	-1	—	.909	-2	—	—	C4,O2(1/0/1)/1	—	-0.2
	StL N	1	3	0	0	0	0	0	0	0	—	2	.000	.000	.000	-99	-1	—	.429	-2	—	—	/C	—	-0.3
Total	2	29	104	7	23	1	2	0	10	3	—	2	.221	.243	.269	64	-5	—	.571	-7	—	—	O17(6/9/2),C12,1b2	—	-1.1
KREITNER, MICKEY	Albert Joseph; B10.9.1922 Nashville TN; D3.6.2003 Nashville TN; BR/TR/6´3˝/190; d9.28																								
1943	Chi N	3	8	0	3	0	0	0	2	1	0	2	.375	.444	.375	140	0	0	1.000	-0	*67*	*0*	C3	0	0.0
1944	Chi N	39	85	3	13	2	0	0	1	8	1	16	.153	.234	.176	17	-9	0	.992	-0	*93*	*109*	C39	0	-0.8
Total	2	42	93	3	16	2	0	0	3	9	1	18	.172	.252	.194	27	-9	0	.992	-0	*91*	*100*	C42	0	-0.8
KREITZ, RALPH	Ralph Wesley "Red"; B11.13.1885 Plum Creek (now Lexington) NE; D7.20.1941 Portland OR; BR/TR/5´9.5˝/175; d8.1																								
1911	Chi A	7	17	0	4	1	0	0	0	2	0	—	.235	.316	.294	73	-1	0	1.000	-1	*127*	*58*	C7	—	-0.1
KREMERS, JIMMY	James Edward; B10.8.1965 Little Rock AR; BL/TR/6´3˝/205; [AtlN88 2/33]; d6.5; Col Arkansas																								
1990	Atl N	29	73	7	8	1	1	1	2	6-1	0	27	.110	.177	.192	1	-10	0-0	.992	-5	77	69	C27	0	-1.5
KRENCHICKI, WAYNE	Wayne Richard; B9.17.1954 Trenton NJ; BL/TR/6´1˝/(175–180); [BalA76*S1/7]; d6.15; Col Miami																								
1979	Bal A	16	21	1	4	1	0	0	0	0-0	0	0	.190	.190	.238	15	-3	0-0	.875	-2	71	0	3b7,2b6	0	-0.5
1980	Bal A	9	14	1	2	0	0	0	0	1-0	0	3	.143	.200	.143	-4	-2	0-0	1.000	-0	73	91	S6/2D	0	-0.2
1981	Bal A	33	56	7	12	4	0	0	6	4-0	0	9	.214	.267	.286	59	-3	0-0	.964	1	119	109	S16,2b7,3b6/D	0	-0.1
1982	Cin N	94	187	19	53	6	1	2	21	13-1	0	23	.283	.324	.358	92	-2	5-3	.955	4	106	96	3b70,2b9	0	0.1
1983	Cin N	51	77	6	21	2	0	0	11	8-2	1	4	.273	.345	.299	78	-2	0-0	.980	-1	103	85	3b39/2	0	-0.3
	Det A	59	133	18	37	7	0	1	16	11-0	1	27	.278	.333	.353	93	-1	0-0	.934	0	87	124	3b48,2b6,S6,1b3	0	-0.1
1984	Cin N	97	181	18	54	9	2	6	22	19-3	0	23	.298	.358	.470	127	7	0-1	.967	2	111	71	3b62,1b3,2b3	0	0.8
1985	Cin N	90	173	16	47	9	0	4	25	28-4	0	20	.272	.369	.393	109	3	0-0	.967	1	97	128	3b52,2b3	0	0.4
1986	Mon N	101	221	21	53	6	2	2	23	22-3	0	32	.240	.306	.312	72	-9	2-4	.991	3	91	86	1b41,3b24/2lf	0	-1.0
Total	8	550	1063	107	283	44	5	15	124	106-13	2	141	.266	.330	.359	92	-12	7-8	.955	8	102	102	3b308,1b47,2b37,S28,D2/lf	0	-0.9
KRESS, CHUCK	Charles Steven; B12.9.1921 Philadelphia PA; BL/TL/6´0˝/190; d4.16																								
1947	Cin N	11	27	4	4	0	0	0	0	6	0	4	.148	.303	.148	23	-3	0	.983	1	157	85	1b8	0	-0.2
1949	Cin N	27	29	3	6	3	0	0	3	3	0	5	.207	.281	.310	58	-2	0	.974	-0	100	103	1b16	0	-0.2
	Chi A	97	353	45	98	17	6	1	44	39	0	44	.278	.349	.368	93	-4	6-7	.994	1	102	105	1b95	0	-0.7
1950	Chi A	3	8	0	0	0	0	0	0	0	0	2	.000	.000	.000	-99	-2	0-0	1.000	-0	78	94	1b2	0	-0.3
1954	Det A	24	37	4	7	0	1	0	3	1	0	4	.189	.211	.243	24	-4	0-1	.971	-0	121	74	1b7/rf	0	-0.5
	Bro N	13	12	1	1	0	0	0	2	0	0	0	.083	.083	.083	-55	-3	0-0	.500	-0	0	505	/1	0	-0.3
Total	4	175	466	57	116	20	7	1	52	49	0	59	.249	.320	.328	74	-18	6-8	.990	1	106	103	1b129/rf	0	-2.2
KRESS, RED	Ralph; B1.2.1905 Columbia CA; D11.29.1962 Los Angeles CA; BR/TR/5´11.5˝/165; d9.24; C15; OF(22/0/103); ▲																								
1927	StL A	7	23	3	7	2	1	1	3	3	0	3	.304	.385	.609	150	2	0-0	.974	1	114	91	S7	—	0.3
1928	StL A	150	560	78	153	26	10	3	81	48	1	70	.273	.332	.371	82	-15	4-4	.929	-17	91	118	S150	—	-1.6
1929	StL A	147	557	82	170	38	4	9	107	52	1	54	.305	.366	.436	102	2	5-8	**.946**	2	100	**113**	S146	—	1.7
1930	StL A	**154**	614	94	192	43	8	16	112	50	2	56	.313	.366	.487	110	9	3-12	.938	-11	95	111	S123,3b31	—	1.0
1931	StL A	150	605	87	188	46	8	16	114	46	1	48	.311	.360	.493	118	14	3-16	.936	-5	94	86	3b84,O40R,S38,1b10	—	0.4
1932	StL A	14	52	2	9	0	1	2	9	4	0	6	.173	.232	.327	41	-5	1-1	.909	1	95	193	3b14	—	-0.4
	Chi A	135	515	83	147	42	4	9	57	47	1	36	.285	.346	.435	108	6	6-3	.956	11	94	214	O64(16/0/49),S53,3b19/1	—	1.6
	Year	149	567	85	156	42	5	11	66	51	1	42	.275	.336	.425	101	0	7-4	.956	12	94	214	O64(16/0/49),S53,3b33/1	—	1.2
1933	Chi A	129	467	47	116	20	5	10	78	37	0	40	.248	.304	.377	83	-14	4-4	.978	-5	99	96	1b111,O8R	—	-2.9
1934	Chi A	8	14	3	4	0	0	0	1	3	0	3	.286	.412	.286	80	0	0-0	1.000	-2	28	0	2b3	—	-0.2
	Was A	56	171	18	39	4	3	4	24	17	0	19	.228	.298	.357	71	-9	3-0	.993	-0	74	64	1b30,O10(6/0/4),2b6/S3	—	-1.0
	Year	64	185	21	43	4	3	4	25	20	0	22	.232	.307	.351	72	-9	3-0	.993	-3	74	64	1b30,O10(6/0/4),2b9/S3	—	-1.2
1935	Was A	84	252	32	75	13	4	2	42	25	0	16	.298	.361	.405	101	0	3-3	.964	11	112	137	S53,1b5,P3,O2R/2	—	1.3
1936	Was A	109	391	51	111	20	6	8	51	39	0	25	.284	.349	.427	96	-4	6-0	.927	4	101	121	S64,2b33,1b5	—	0.6
1938	StL A	150	566	74	171	33	3	7	79	69	0	47	.302	.378	.408	97	-1	5-4	**.965**	-12	86	90	S150	—	-0.2
1939	StL A	13	43	5	12	1	0	0	8	6	0	2	.279	.367	.302	72	-2	1-0	.933	-1	84	123	S13	—	-0.2
	Det A	51	157	19	38	7	0	1	22	17	0	16	.242	.316	.306	55	-10	2-1	.959	1	93	104	S25,2b16,3b4	—	-0.6
	Year	64	200	24	50	8	0	1	30	23	0	18	.250	.327	.305	59	-12	3-1	.951	-1	90	110	S38,2b16,3b4	—	-0.8
1940	Det A	33	99	13	22	3	1	1	11	10	0	12	.222	.294	.303	50	-7	0-0	.924	5	109	29	3b17,S12	—	-0.1
1946	NY N	1	1	0	0	0	0	0	0	1	0	0	.000	.500	.000	48	0	0	1.000	1	377	1785	/P	0	0.0
Total	14	1391	5087	691	1454	298	58	89	799	474	6	453	.286	.347	.420	96	-34	46-56	.944	-19	96	110	S835,3b170,1b162,O124R,2b59,P4	0	-0.3
KREUTER, CHAD	Chadden Michael; B8.26.1964 Greenbrae CA; BB/TR (BR 1989p, 90)/6´2˝/(190–200); [TexA85 5/109]; d9.14; Col Pepperdine																								
1988	Tex A	16	51	3	14	2	1	1	5	7-0	0	13	.275	.362	.412	113	1	0-0	.990	1	77	118	C16	0	0.3
1989	Tex A	87	158	16	24	3	0	5	9	27-0	0	40	.152	.274	.266	52	-10	0-1	.992	-1	65	73	C85	0	-0.8
1990	Tex A	22	22	2	1	1	0	0	2	8-0	0	9	.045	.290	.091	14	-2	0-0	.977	-4	100	94	C20/D	0	-0.6
1991	Tex A	3	4	0	0	0	0	0	0	0-0	0	1	.000	.000	.000	-99	-1	0-0	1.000	0	0	0	/C	0	-0.1
1992	Det A	67	190	22	48	9	0	2	16	20-1	0	38	.253	.321	.332	83	-4	0-1	.983	3	158	112	C62/D	0	0.2

YEAR	TM LG	G	AB	R	H	2B	3B	HR	RBI	BB-IB	HP	SO	AVG	OBP	SLG	AOPS	ABR	SB-CS	FA	FR	RNG	THR	GAMES AT POSITION	DL	BFW
1993	Det A	119	374	59	107	23	3	15	51	49-4	3	92	.286	.371	.484	128	16	2-1	.988	1	121	116	C112/1D	0	2.3
1994	Det A	65	170	17	38	8	0	1	19	28-0	0	36	.224	.327	.288	61	-9	0-1	.987	2	143	123	C64/1lf	0	-0.4
1995	Sea A	26	75	12	17	5	0	1	8	5-0	2	22	.227	.293	.333	62	-4	0-0	.976	2	99	122	C23	17	-0.1
1996	Chi A	46	114	14	25	8	0	3	18	13-0	2	29	.219	.308	.368	74	-5	0-0	.990	1	78	146	C38,1b2	72	-0.1
1997	Chi A	19	37	6	8	2	1	1	3	8-0	0	9	.216	.356	.405	101	0	0-1	.984	-0	120	69	C13,1b2	0	0.0
	Ana A	70	218	19	51	7	1	4	18	21-0	0	57	.234	.301	.330	64	-12	0-2	.994	6	134	122	C67,D2	0	-0.2
	Year	89	255	25	59	9	2	5	21	29-0	0	66	.231	.310	.341	70	-12	0-3	.992	6	132	115	C80,1b2,D2	0	-0.2
1998	Chi A	93	245	26	62	9	1	2	33	32-1	3	45	.253	.345	.322	77	-7	1-0	.985	-5	107	99	C91	0	-0.7
	Ana A	3	7	1	1	1	0	0	0	1-0	0	4	.143	.250	.286	38	-1	0-0	.882	-2	48	116	C3	0	-0.2
	Year	96	252	27	63	10	1	2	33	33-1	3	49	.250	.343	.321	76	-8	1-0	.981	-6	105	100	C94	0	-0.9
1999	KC A	107	324	31	73	15	0	5	35	34-1	6	65	.225	.309	.318	59	-20	0-0	.994	-7	81	130	C101/D	0	-1.9
2000	LA N	80	212	32	56	13	0	6	28	54-0	2	48	.264	.416	.410	116	9	1-0	.994	6	194	100	C78	0	1.8
2001	LA N	73	191	21	41	11	1	6	17	41-2	1	52	.215	.355	.377	96	0	0-0	1.000	7	123	97	C70/D	0	1.1
2002	LA N	41	95	8	25	5	0	2	12	10-4	1	31	.263	.333	.379	94	-1	1-0	.986	0	95	131	C41	17	0.1
2003	Tex A	7	18	0	2	1	0	0	0	3-0	0	2	.111	.238	.167	9	-2	0-0	1.000	-2	64	0	C7	0	-0.4
Total	16	944	2505	289	593	123	8	54	274	361-13	20	593	.237	.335	.357	83	-52	5-7	.990	9	117	110	C892,D8,1b6/lf	106	0.3
Krichell, Paul	Paul Bernard; B12.19.1882 New York NY; D6.4.1957 Bronx NY; BR/TR/5´7˝/150; d5.12																								
1911	StL A	28	82	6	19	3	0	0	8	4	1	—	.232	.276	.268	54	-5	2	.943	-3	*75*	*105*	C25	—	-0.7
1912	StL A	59	161	19	35	6	0	0	8	19	1	—	.217	.304	.255	62	-7	2	.959	-3	*88*	*88*	C59	—	-0.5
Total	2	87	243	25	54	9	0	0	16	23	2	—	.222	.295	.259	60	-12	4	.955	-6	*84*	*93*	C84	—	-1.2
Krieg, Bill	William Frederick; B1.29.1859 Petersburg IL; D3.25.1930 Chillicothe IL; BR/TR/5´8˝/180; d4.20																								
1884	CP U	71	279	35	69	15	4	0	—	11	—	—	.247	.276	.330	84	-14	—	.932	9	—	—	C52,O20(13/6/2)/S1	—	-0.1
1885	Chi N	1	3	0	0	0	0	0	0	0	—	2	.000	.000	.000	-88	-1	—	.800	1	344	0	/rf	—	0.0
	Bro AA	17	60	7	9	4	0	1	5	2	0	—	.150	.177	.267	39	-4	—	.910	-3	—	—	C12,1b5	—	-0.6
1886	Was N	27	98	11	25	6	3	1	15	3	—	12	.255	.277	.408	115	2	2	.975	-1	57	55	1b27	—	-0.1
1887	Was N	25	95	9	24	4	1	2	17	7	1	5	.253	.311	.379	97	0	2	.973	-1	96	62	1b16,O9(7/2/0)	—	-0.2
Total	4	141	535	62	127	29	8	4	37	23	1	19	.237	.270	.344	85	-17	4	.929	5	—	—	C64,1b49,O30(20/8/3)/S	—	-1.0
Kroeger, Josh	Joshua J.; B8.31.1982 Davenport IA; BL/TL/6´2˝/200; [AriN00 4/129]; d9.2																								
2004	Ari N	22	54	5	9	3	0	0	2	1-0	0	21	.167	.182	.222	3	-8	0-1	1.000	1	133	0	O19(11/2/8)	0	-0.7
Kroner, John	John Harold; B11.13.1908 St.Louis MO; D8.26.1968 St.Louis MO; BR/TR/6´0˝/185; d9.29																								
1935	Bos A	2	4	1	1	0	0	0	0	1	0	1	.250	.400	.250	67	0	0-0	1.000	-0	65	0	3b2	—	0.0
1936	Bos A	84	298	40	87	17	8	4	62	26	0	24	.292	.349	.443	89	-6	2-3	.964	-4	101	79	2b38,3b28,S18/rf	—	-0.6
1937	Cle A	86	283	29	67	14	1	2	26	22	0	25	.237	.292	.314	52	-21	1-1	.969	3	99	105	2b64,3b11	—	-1.3
1938	Cle A	51	117	13	29	16	0	1	17	19	0	6	.248	.353	.410	92	-1	0-1	.974	6	102	130	2b31,1b7,3b3/S	—	0.6
Total	4	223	702	83	184	47	9	7	105	68	0	56	.262	.327	.385	75	-28	3-5	.968	5	100	103	2b133,3b44,S19,1b7/rf	—	-1.3
Krsnich, Mike	Michael; B9.24.1931 W.Allis WI; BR/TR/6´1˝/190; d4.23; b–Rocky																								
1960	Mil N	4	9	0	3	1	0	0	2	0-0	0	0	.333	.333	.444	120	0	0-0	1.000	0	143	0	O3L	0	0.0
1962	Mil N	11	12	0	1	1	0	0	2	0-0	0	4	.083	.083	.167	-36	-2	0-0	1.000	0	91	0	O3L/13	0	-0.2
Total	2	15	21	0	4	2	0	0	4	0-0	0	4	.190	.190	.286	28	-2	0-0	1.000	1	122	0	O6L/31	0	-0.2
Krsnich, Rocky	Rocco Peter; B8.5.1927 W.Allis WI; BR/TR/6´1˝/170; d9.13; b–Mike																								
1949	Chi A	16	55	7	12	3	1	1	9	6	0	4	.218	.295	.364	76	-2	0-1	.935	2	116	104	3b16	0	-0.1
1952	Chi A	40	91	11	21	7	2	1	15	12	1	9	.231	.327	.385	97	0	0-0	.959	6	114	92	3b37	0	0.6
1953	Chi A	64	129	9	26	8	0	1	14	12	0	11	.202	.270	.287	49	-9	0-2	.929	4	122	80	3b57	0	-0.6
Total	3	120	275	27	59	18	3	3	38	30	1	24	.215	.294	.335	70	-11	0-3	.942	12	118	89	3b110	0	-0.1
Krueger, Otto	Arthur William "Oom Paul"; B9.17.1876 Chicago IL; D2.20.1961 St.Louis MO; BR/TR/5´7˝/165; d9.16																								
1899	Cle N	13	44	4	10	1	0	0	2	8	1	—	.227	.358	.250	73	-1	1	.763	-2	83	113	3b9,S2,2b2	—	-0.2
1900	StL N	12	35	8	14	3	2	1	3	10	1	—	.400	.543	.686	240	8	0	.852	-6	79	45	2b12	—	0.3
1901	StL N	**142**	520	77	143	16	12	2	79	50	13	—	.275	.353	.363	114	11	19	.881	-10	98	73	3b142	—	0.5
1902	StL N	128	467	55	124	7	8	0	46	29	3	—	.266	.313	.315	98	-2	14	.897	3	**112**	114	S107,3b18	—	0.4
1903	Pit N	80	256	42	63	6	8	1	28	21	8	—	.246	.323	.344	87	-5	5	.884	-1	97	171	S29,O28L,3b13,2b3	—	-0.7
1904	Pit N	86	268	34	52	6	2	1	26	29	4	—	.194	.282	.243	61	-11	8	.905	-3	113	78	O33(23/0/10),S32,3b10	—	-1.6
1905	Phi N	46	114	10	21	1	1	0	12	13	1	—	.184	.273	.211	47	-7	1	.930	-5	92	119	S23,O6(0/3/3)/3	—	-1.3
Total	7	507	1704	230	427	40	33	5	196	160	31	—	.251	.326	.322	94	-7	48	.902	-24	107	117	S193,3b193,O67(51/3/13),2b17	—	-2.6
Krueger, Ernie	Ernest George; B12.27.1890 Chicago IL; D4.22.1976 Waukegan IL; BR/TR/5´10.5˝/185; d8.4; Mil 1918; Col Lake Forest																								
1913	Cle A	5	6	0	0	0	0	0	0	0	0	2	.000	.000	.000	-97	-2	0	1.000	0	*78*	*159*	C4	—	-0.2
1915	NY A	10	29	3	5	1	0	0	0	0	1	5	.172	.200	.207	22	-3	0-1	.905	-3	*83*	*80*	C8	—	-0.6
1917	NY N	8	10	0	0	0	0	0	0	0	0	4	.000	.000	.000	-99	-2	0	.857	-1	*70*	*0*	C5	—	-0.4
	Bro N	31	81	10	22	2	2	1	6	5	2	7	.272	.330	.383	115	1	1	.979	1	*103*	*87*	C23	—	0.4
	Year	39	91	10	22	2	2	1	6	5	2	11	.242	.296	.341	94	-1	1	.973	-1	*101*	*81*	C28	—	0.0
1918	Bro N	30	87	4	25	4	2	0	7	4	0	9	.287	.319	.379	113	1	2	.986	3	*92*	*128*	C23	—	0.7
1919	Bro N	80	226	24	56	7	4	5	36	19	2	25	.248	.312	.381	105	1	4	.963	0	*91*	*104*	C66	—	0.8
1920	†Bro N	52	146	21	42	4	2	1	17	16	0	13	.288	.358	.363	104	1	2-0	.959	-3	*95*	*103*	C46	—	0.2
1921	Bro N	65	163	18	43	11	4	3	20	14	0	12	.264	.322	.436	95	-1	2-2	.969	-2	*85*	*73*	C52	—	0.0
1925	Cin N	37	88	7	27	4	0	1	7	6	0	8	.307	.351	.386	90	-1	1-2	.946	-3	*74*	*69*	C30	—	-0.3
Total	8	318	836	87	220	33	14	11	93	64	5	85	.263	.319	.376	97	-5	12-5	.964	-8	*90*	*94*	C257	—	0.6
Krug, Chris	Everett Ben; B12.25.1939 Los Angeles CA; BR/TR/6´4˝/200; d5.30; C1; Col Riverside (CA) CC																								
1965	Chi N	60	169	16	34	5	0	5	24	13-2	1	52	.201	.258	.320	61	-9	0-1	.980	2	107	117	C58	0	-0.5
1966	Chi N	11	28	1	6	1	0	0	1	1-0	0	8	.214	.241	.250	36	-2	0-0	1.000	1	61	163	C10	0	-0.1
1969	SD N	8	17	0	1	0	0	0	0	1-0	0	6	.059	.111	.059	-53	-4	0-0	.938	-1	106	145	C7	0	-0.4
Total	3	79	214	17	41	6	0	5	25	15-2	1	66	.192	.245	.290	50	-15	0-1	.980	2	101	126	C75	0	-1.0
Krug, Gene	Gary Eugene; B2.12.1955 Garden City KS; BL/TL/6´4˝/225; [ChiN77 29/689]; d4.29; Col Oklahoma																								
1981	Chi N	7	5	0	2	0	0	0	0	1-0	0	1	.400	.500	.400	149	0	0-0	ø	0	—	—	/H	0	0.0
Krug, Henry	Henry Charles; B12.4.1876 San Francisco CA; D1.14.1908 San Francisco CA; BR/TR; d7.26																								
1902	Phi N	53	198	20	45	3	3	0	14	7	2	—	.227	.261	.273	65	-9	2	.947	-4	108	98	O28L,2b13,S9,3b6	—	-1.5
Krug, Marty	Martin John; B9.10.1888 Koblenz, Germany; D6.27.1966 Glendale CA; BR/TR/5´9˝/165; d5.29																								
1912	Bos A	20	39	6	12	2	1	0	7	5	0	—	.308	.386	.410	122	1	2	.895	-1	83	141	S11,2b4	—	0.0
1922	Chi N	127	450	67	124	23	4	4	60	43	3	43	.276	.343	.371	82	-11	7-9	.937	-7	93	111	3b104,2b23/S	—	-1.1
Total	2	147	489	73	136	25	5	4	67	48	3	43	.278	.346	.374	85	-10	9-9	.937	-8	93	111	3b104,2b27,S12	—	-1.1
Kruger, Art	Arthur Theodore; B3.16.1881 San Antonio TX; D11.28.1949 Hondo (now part of Downey) CA; BR/TR/6´0˝/185; d4.11																								
1907	Cin N	100	317	25	74	10	9	0	28	18	5	—	.233	.285	.322	87	-6	10	.972	2	88	96	O96(26/70/1)	—	-1.0
1910	Cle A	47	168	14	26	4	2	0	10	15	3	—	.155	.237	.202	37	-12	10	.947	2	99	126	O47L	—	-1.5
	Bos N	1	1	0	0	0	0	0	0	0	0	0	.000	.000	.000	-96	0	0	ø	0	—	—	/H	—	0.0
	Cle A	15	55	5	12	2	1	0	4	5	1	—	.218	.295	.291	82	-1	2	.974	1	99	126	O15L	—	-0.1
1914	KC F	122	441	45	114	24	7	4	47	23	1	59	.259	.297	.372	85	-19	11	.963	-2	99	83	O120(7/113/0)	—	-3.1
1915	KC F	80	240	24	57	9	2	2	26	12	1	29	.237	.277	.317	70	-15	5	.984	1	101	94	O66(33/3/30)	—	-1.9
Total	4	365	1222	113	283	49	21	6	115	73	11	88	.232	.281	.321	76	-53	38	.968	3	98	95	O344(128/186/31)	—	-7.6
Kruk, John	John Martin; B2.9.1961 Charleston WV; BL/TL/5´10˝/(190–220); [SDN81 S3/62]; d4.7; Col Allegany (MD) CC																								
1986	SD N	122	278	33	86	16	2	4	38	45-0	0	58	.309	.403	.424	132	15	2-4	.981	-2	90	98	O74(70/0/6),1b9	0	0.9
1987	SD N	138	447	72	140	14	2	20	91	73-15	0	93	.313	.406	.488	142	29	18-10	.996	2	107	99	1b101,O29L	0	2.4
1988	SD N	120	378	54	91	17	1	9	44	80-12	0	68	.241	.369	.362	114	11	5-3	.995	-2	77	114	1b63,O55(29/0/26)	0	0.3
1989	SD N	31	76	7	14	0	0	3	6	17-0	0	14	.184	.333	.303	83	-1	0-0	.962	2	103	231	O27(2/0/25)	16	-0.1
	Phi N	81	281	46	93	13	6	5	38	27-2	0	39	.331	.386	.473	146	16	3-0	.983	-3	85	136	O72(63/0/12),1b7	25	1.3

YEAR	TM LG	G	AB	R	H	2B	3B	HR	RBI	BB-IB	HP	SO	AVG	OBP	SLG	AOPS	ABR	SB-CS	FA	FR	RNG	THR	GAMES AT POSITION	DL	BFW
	Year	112	357	53	107	13	6	8	44	44-2	0	53	.300	.374	.437	132	15	3-0	.977	-1	90	161	O99(65/0/37),1b7	0	1.2
1990	Phi N	142	443	52	129	25	8	7	67	69-16	0	70	.291	.386	.431	125	18	10-5	.986	-2	89	35	O87(68/0/21),1b61	0	1.1
1991	Phi N☆	152	538	84	158	27	6	21	92	67-16	1	100	.294	.367	.483	140	29	7-0	.997	-3	74	81	1b102,O52(36/11/6)	0	2.0
1992	Phi N★	144	507	86	164	30	4	10	70	92-8	1	88	.323	.423	.458	151	40	3-5	.993	-11	73	93	1b121,O35(6/0/29)	0	2.1
1993	†Phi N★	150	535	100	169	33	5	14	85	111-10	0	87	.316	.430	.475	145	42	6-2	.993	-10	70	72	1b144	0	1.9
1994	Phi N	75	255	35	77	17	0	5	38	42-4	0	51	.302	.395	.427	114	8	4-1	.995	-0	97	81	1b69	28	0.2
1995	Chi A	45	159	13	49	7	0	2	23	26-0	0	33	.308	.399	.390	113	4	0-1	.909	-0	0	118	D42/1	16	0.1
Total	10	1200	3897	582	1170	199	34	100	592	649-83	2	701	.300	.397	.446	134	211	58-31	.995	-31	85	88	1b678,O431(303/11/125),D42	85	12.2

KRYHOSKI, DICK Richard David; B3.24.1925 Leonia NJ; BL/TL/6´2˝/200; d4.19

YEAR	TM LG	G	AB	R	H	2B	3B	HR	RBI	BB-IB	HP	SO	AVG	OBP	SLG	AOPS	ABR	SB-CS	FA	FR	RNG	THR	GAMES AT POSITION	DL	BFW
1949	NY A	54	177	18	52	10	3	1	27	9	2	17	.294	.335	.401	94	-2	2-4	.983	-1	96	82	1b51	0	-0.5
1950	Det A	53	169	20	37	10	0	4	19	8	1	11	.219	.258	.349	53	-13	0-1	.991	-1	94	110	1b47	0	-1.5
1951	Det A	119	421	58	121	19	4	12	57	28	2	29	.287	.335	.437	107	2	1-2	.991	3	110	91	1b112	0	0.1
1952	StL A	111	342	38	83	13	1	11	42	23	3	42	.243	.296	.383	86	-8	2-0	.989	-4	85	102	1b86	0	-1.5
1953	StL A	104	338	35	94	18	4	16	50	26	2	33	.278	.333	.497	119	7	0-5	.992	5	120	90	1b88	0	0.6
1954	Bal A	100	300	32	78	13	2	1	34	19	2	24	.260	.305	.327	80	-9	0-0	.992	2	105	80	1b69	0	-1.2
1955	KC A	28	47	2	10	2	0	0	2	6-0	0	7	.213	.302	.255	50	-3	0-1	.988	0	107	81	1b14	0	-0.4
Total	7	569	1794	203	475	85	14	45	231	119-0	12	163	.265	.314	.403	93	-26	5-13	.990	5	103	92	1b467	0	-4.4

KRYNZEL, DAVE David Benjamin; B11.7.1981 Dayton OH; BL/TL/6´1˝/180; [MilN00 1/11]; d9.1

YEAR	TM LG	G	AB	R	H	2B	3B	HR	RBI	BB-IB	HP	SO	AVG	OBP	SLG	AOPS	ABR	SB-CS	FA	FR	RNG	THR	GAMES AT POSITION	DL	BFW
2004	Mil N	16	41	6	9	1	0	0	3	3-0	3	15	.220	.319	.244	48	-3	0-0	.968	3	160	187	O10(0/2/8)	0	-0.1
2005	Mil N	5	7	0	0	0	0	0	0	0-0	0	3	.000	.000	.000	-99	-2	0-0	1.000	-0	95	0	/cf	0	-0.2
Total	2	21	48	6	9	1	0	0	3	3-0	3	18	.188	.278	.208	28	-5	0-0	.970	3	154	170	O11(0/3/8)	0	-0.3

KUBEK, TONY Anthony Christopher; B10.12.1936 Milwaukee WI; BL/TR/6´3˝/(190–193); d4.20; OF(80/46/31)

YEAR	TM LG	G	AB	R	H	2B	3B	HR	RBI	BB-IB	HP	SO	AVG	OBP	SLG	AOPS	ABR	SB-CS	FA	FR	RNG	THR	GAMES AT POSITION	DL	BFW
1957	†NY A	127	431	56	128	21	3	3	39	24-3	3	48	.297	.335	.381	98	-2	6-6	.938	1	98	82	O50(29/23/0),S41,3b38/2	0	-0.1
1958	†NY A☆	138	559	66	148	21	1	2	48	25-3	1	57	.265	.295	.317	72	-23	5-4	.961	**21**	**111**	**112**	S134,O3(0/1/2)/12	0	0.9
1959	NY A★	132	512	67	143	25	7	6	51	24-3	2	46	.279	.313	.391	95	-5	3-3	.968	10	107	102	S67,O53(22/15/26),3b17/2	0	0.8
1960	†NY A	147	568	77	155	25	3	14	62	31-5	3	42	.273	.312	.401	98	-5	3-0	.968	8	108	101	S136,O29(22/6/1)	0	1.4
1961	†NY A★	153	617	84	170	38	6	8	46	27-1	1	60	.276	.306	.395	91	-10	1-3	.959	18	106	**132**	S145	0	1.9
1962	†NY A	45	169	28	53	6	1	4	17	12-0	0	17	.314	.357	.432	115	3	2-1	.954	8	115	134	S35,O6L	0	1.4
1963	†NY A	135	557	72	143	21	3	7	44	28-6	2	68	.257	.294	.343	79	-17	4-2	.980	8	103	113	S132/cf	0	0.3
1964	NY A	106	415	46	95	16	3	8	31	26-3	1	55	.229	.275	.340	69	-18	4-1	.978	7	107	98	S99	0	-0.3
1965	NY A	109	339	26	74	5	3	5	35	20-0	0	48	.218	.258	.295	58	-20	1-3	.964	-4	97	112	S93,O3(1/0/2)/1	0	-1.8
Total	9	1092	4167	522	1109	178	30	57	373	217-24	13	441	.266	.303	.364	85	-97	29-23	.967	77	106	113	S882,O145L,3b55,2b3,1b2	0	4.5

KUBEL, JASON Jason James; B5.25.1982 Belle Fourche SD; BL/TR/5´11˝/200; [MinA00 12/342]; d8.31; [DL 2005 Min A 183]

YEAR	TM LG	G	AB	R	H	2B	3B	HR	RBI	BB-IB	HP	SO	AVG	OBP	SLG	AOPS	ABR	SB-CS	FA	FR	RNG	THR	GAMES AT POSITION	DL	BFW
2004	†Min A	23	60	10	18	2	0	2	7	6-0	0	9	.300	.358	.433	104	0	1-1	1.000	1	97	220	O10(2/0/8),D9	0	0.0
2006	Min A	73	220	23	53	8	0	8	26	12-0	0	45	.241	.279	.386	70	-11	2-0	.953	-3	76	53	O37(30/0/7),D30	0	-1.6
Total	2	96	280	33	71	10	0	10	33	18-0	0	54	.254	.297	.396	78	-11	3-1	.966	-3	80	87	O47(32/0/15),D39	183	-1.6

KUBIAK, TED Theodore Rodger; B5.12.1942 New Brunswick NJ; BB/TR/6´0˝/175; d4.14; Mil 1968

YEAR	TM LG	G	AB	R	H	2B	3B	HR	RBI	BB-IB	HP	SO	AVG	OBP	SLG	AOPS	ABR	SB-CS	FA	FR	RNG	THR	GAMES AT POSITION	DL	BFW
1967	KC A	53	102	6	16	2	1	0	5	12-0	0	20	.157	.243	.196	33	-9	0-0	.984	-3	95	60	S20,2b10,3b5	0	-1.1
1968	Oak A	48	120	10	30	5	2	0	8	8-1	2	18	.250	.305	.325	96	-1	1-1	.929	-5	86	81	2b24,S12	0	-0.4
1969	Oak A	92	305	38	76	9	1	2	27	25-2	1	35	.249	.304	.305	75	-11	2-0	.976	2	100	103	S42,2b33	0	-0.1
1970	Mil A	158	540	63	136	9	6	4	41	72-16	0	51	.252	.340	.313	81	-13	4-9	.989	-12	90	105	2b91,S73	0	-1.3
1971	Mil A	89	260	26	59	6	5	3	17	41-3	0	31	.227	.330	.323	87	-4	0-5	.971	-4	88	75	2b48,S39	0	-0.3
	StL N	32	72	8	18	3	2	1	10	11-3	0	12	.250	.345	.389	104	1	1-0	.959	-5	82	68	S17,2b14	0	-0.2
1972	Tex A	46	116	5	26	3	0	0	7	12-3	1	12	.224	.300	.250	68	-4	0-1	.990	-4	91	84	2b25,S15/3	0	-0.7
	†Oak A	51	94	14	17	4	1	0	8	9-0	0	11	.181	.250	.245	51	-6	0-0	.988	1	104	112	2b49/3	0	-0.3
	Year	97	210	19	43	7	1	0	15	21-3	1	23	.205	.278	.248	60	-10	0-1	.989	-3	99	101	2b74,S15,3b2	0	-1.0
1973	†Oak A	106	182	15	40	6	1	3	17	12-1	0	19	.220	.267	.313	66	-9	1-1	.973	3	111	102	2b83,S26,3b2	0	-0.1
1974	Oak A	99	220	22	46	3	0	0	18	18-0	0	15	.209	.268	.223	45	-16	1-1	.995	-10	96	101	2b71,S19,3b14,D2	0	-2.2
1975	Oak A	20	28	2	7	1	0	0	4	2-0	0	2	.250	.300	.286	68	-1	0-0	1.000	-0	83	106	S7,3b7,2b6	0	-0.1
	SD N	87	196	13	44	5	0	0	14	24-5	0	18	.224	.308	.250	60	-10	3-1	.954	-3	105	104	3b64,2b11/1	0	-1.3
1976	SD N	96	212	16	50	5	2	0	26	25-2	0	28	.236	.314	.278	76	-6	0-3	.971	-7	99	124	3b27,2b25,S6/1	0	-1.3
Total	10	977	2447	238	565	61	21	13	202	271-36	4	272	.231	.307	.289	72	-89	13-22	.981	-45	95	94	2b490,S276,3b121,1b2,D2	0	-9.4

KUBISZYN, JACK John Henry; B12.19.1936 Buffalo NY; BR/TR/5´11˝/170; d4.23; Col Alabama

YEAR	TM LG	G	AB	R	H	2B	3B	HR	RBI	BB-IB	HP	SO	AVG	OBP	SLG	AOPS	ABR	SB-CS	FA	FR	RNG	THR	GAMES AT POSITION	DL	BFW
1961	Cle A	25	42	4	9	0	0	0	0	2-0	0	5	.214	.250	.214	26	-5	0-0	1.000	2	111	0	3b8,S7,2b2	0	-0.2
1962	Cle A	25	59	3	10	2	0	1	2	5-0	0	7	.169	.231	.254	32	-6	0-0	.964	0	100	133	S18/3	0	-0.4
Total	2	50	101	7	19	2	0	1	2	7-0	0	12	.188	.239	.238	30	-11	0-0	.969	3	103	145	S25,3b9,2b2	0	-0.6

KUBSKI, GIL Gilbert Thomas; B10.12.1954 Longview TX; BL/TR/6´3˝/185; [AnaA75*S1/12]; d9.2; Col Cal St.–Northridge

YEAR	TM LG	G	AB	R	H	2B	3B	HR	RBI	BB-IB	HP	SO	AVG	OBP	SLG	AOPS	ABR	SB-CS	FA	FR	RNG	THR	GAMES AT POSITION	DL	BFW
1980	Cal A	22	63	11	16	3	0	0	6	6-0	0	10	.254	.319	.302	72	-2	1-1	1.000	2	111	164	O20(1/0/19)	0	-0.2

KUCZEK, STEVE Stanislaw Leo; B12.28.1924 Amsterdam NY; BR/TR/6´0˝/160; d9.29; Col Colgate

YEAR	TM LG	G	AB	R	H	2B	3B	HR	RBI	BB-IB	HP	SO	AVG	OBP	SLG	AOPS	ABR	SB-CS	FA	FR	RNG	THR	GAMES AT POSITION	DL	BFW
1949	Bos N	1	1	0	1	1	0	0	0	0	0	0	1.000	1.000	2.000	723	1	0	ø	0	—	—	/H	0	0.1

KUEHNE, BILL William J. (b William J. Knelme); B10.24.1858 Leipzig, Saxony (now Germany); D10.27.1921 Sulphur Springs OH; BR/TR/5´8˝/185; d5.1; OF(33/9/30)

YEAR	TM LG	G	AB	R	H	2B	3B	HR	RBI	BB-IB	HP	SO	AVG	OBP	SLG	AOPS	ABR	SB-CS	FA	FR	RNG	THR	GAMES AT POSITION	DL	BFW
1883	Col AA	95	374	38	85	8	14	1	—	2	—	—	.227	.231	.332	86	-6	—	.833	-3	99	138	3b69,2b18,S7,O3(1/2/0)	—	-0.6
1884	Col AA	**110**	415	48	98	13	16	5	—	9	1	—	.236	.254	.381	113	5	—	.881	11	110	123	3b110	—	1.7
1885	Pit AA	104	411	54	93	9	19	0	43	15	2	—	.226	.257	.341	89	-7	—	.865	-5	98	107	3b97,S7	—	-0.9
1886	Pit AA	117	481	73	98	16	17	1	48	19	2	—	.204	.237	.314	72	-18	26	.899	1	126	0	O54(24/5/24),3b47,1b18	—	-1.7
1887	Pit N	102	402	68	120	18	15	1	41	14	1	39	.299	.324	.425	115	7	17	.883	-13	101	101	S91,3b4,1b4,O3(0/1/2)	—	-0.3
1888	Pit N	**138**	524	60	123	22	11	3	62	9	2	68	.235	.250	.336	94	-5	34	.910	1	111	98	3b75,S63	—	-0.1
1889	Pit N	97	390	43	96	20	5	5	57	9	0	36	.246	.263	.362	81	-12	15	.885	-2	100	109	3b75,O13(8/1/4),2b5,S2,1b2	—	-1.1
1890	Pit P	126	528	66	126	21	12	5	73	28	0	37	.239	.277	.352	74	-22	21	.850	7	**111**	88	3b126	—	-1.1
1891	Col AA	68	261	32	56	9	0	2	22	10	0	22	.215	.244	.272	50	-18	21	.885	0	101	144	3b68	—	-1.4
	Lou AA	39	152	25	41	3	1	1	17	7	1	13	.270	.306	.322	81	-5	9	.896	-1	99	107	3b39	—	-0.4
	Year	107	413	57	97	12	1	3	39	17	1	35	.235	.267	.291	62	-22	30	.889	-0	100	130	3b107	—	-1.8
1892	Lou N	76	287	22	48	4	5	0	36	13	0	36	.167	.203	.216	29	-26	6	.874	-4	95	141	3b76	—	-2.7
	StL N	6	24	1	4	1	0	0	0	0	1	3	.167	.200	.208	25	-2	1	.895	-0	98	0	3b5/S	—	-0.2
	Cin N	6	24	3	5	1	0	1	4	1	0	5	.208	.240	.375	87	-1	0	.941	0	107	356	3b4,2b2	—	0.0
	StL N	1	4	0	0	0	0	0	0	0	0	1	.000	.000	.000	-99	-1	0	1.000	1	98	0	/3	—	0.0
	Year	89	339	26	57	6	5	1	40	14	1	45	.168	.203	.224	32	-29	7	.880	-3	97	154	3b86,2b2/S	—	-2.9
Total	10	1085	4277	533	993	145	115	25	403	136	10	260	.232	.258	.337	82	-111	150	.875	-5	104	115	3b796,S171,O73L,2b25,1b24	—	-8.8

KUENN, HARVEY Harvey Edward; B12.4.1930 W.Allis WI; D2.28.1988 Peoria AZ; BR/TR/6´2˝/(182–197); d9.6; M3/C12; Col Wisconsin–Madison; OF(354/163/343)

YEAR	TM LG	G	AB	R	H	2B	3B	HR	RBI	BB-IB	HP	SO	AVG	OBP	SLG	AOPS	ABR	SB-CS	FA	FR	RNG	THR	GAMES AT POSITION	DL	BFW
1952	Det A	19	80	2	26	2	2	0	8	2	1	1	.325	.349	.400	107	0	2-1	.962	1	96	91	S19	0	0.3
1953	Det A★	155	679	94	**209**	33	7	2	48	50	1	31	.308	.356	.386	101	1	6-5	.973	-24	89	68	S155	0	-1.0
1954	Det A☆	**155**	656	81	**201**	28	6	5	48	29	1	13	.306	.335	.390	100	-2	9-9	.966	5	104	86	S155	0	1.5
1955	Det A★	145	620	101	190	**38**	5	8	62	40-3	1	27	.306	.347	.423	109	7	8-3	.956	-26	88	95	S141	0	-0.6
1956	Det A★	146	591	96	**196**	32	7	12	88	55-3	3	34	.332	.387	.470	126	23	9-5	**.968**	-14	92	90	S141/lf	0	1.9
1957	Det A★	151	624	74	173	30	6	9	44	47-4	0	28	.277	.327	.388	92	-7	5-8	.955	-37	82	97	S136,3b17/1	0	-3.7
1958	Det A☆	139	561	73	179	**39**	3	8	54	51-8	0	34	.319	.373	.442	116	14	5-10	.984	4	109	119	O138C	0	0.9
1959	Det A★	139	561	99	**198**	**42**	7	9	71	48-1	1	37	**.353**	.402	.501	140	32	7-2	.988	-4	98	79	O137(0/23/116)	0	2.4
1960	Cle A★	126	474	65	146	24	0	9	54	55-6	1	25	.308	.379	.416	119	14	3-0	.966	-2	104	95	O119(2/2/117),3b5	0	0.9
1961	SF N	131	471	60	125	22	4	5	46	47-2	1	34	.265	.329	.361	87	-8	5-4	.988	-6	100	124	O93(67/0/31),3b32/S	0	-1.9
1962	†SF N	130	487	73	148	23	5	10	68	49-3	1	37	.304	.365	.433	116	12	3-6	.970	-3	98	45	O105(99/0/10),3b30	0	0.2
1963	SF N	120	417	61	121	13	2	6	31	44-3	2	38	.290	.358	.374	113	8	2-1	.975	-16	87	118	O64(45/0/27),3b53	0	-1.2
1964	SF N	111	351	42	92	16	2	4	22	35-4	1	32	.262	.329	.353	91	-3	0-1	.952	-8	73	39	O88(65/0/36),1b11,3b2	0	-1.8
1965	SF N	23	59	4	14	0	0	0	6	10-0	1	3	.237	.352	.237	69	-2	3-1	1.000	-0	72	0	O14(12/0/2),1b7	0	-0.3
	Chi N	54	120	11	26	5	0	0	6	22-1	0	13	.217	.336	.258	69	-4	1-0	.975	-1	80	202	O35(31/0/4)/1	0	-0.6
	Year	77	179	15	40	5	0	0	12	32-1	1	16	.223	.341	.251	69	-6	4-1	.981	-1	78	139	O49(43/0/6),1b8	0	-0.9
1966	Chi N	3	3	0	1	0	0	0	0	0-0	0	1	.333	.333	.333	85	0	0-0	ø	-0	0	0	/lf	0	0.0

YEAR	TM LG	G	AB	R	H	2B	3B	HR	RBI	BB-IB	HP	SO	AVG	OBP	SLG	AOPS	ABR	SB-CS	FA	FR	RNG	THR	GAMES AT POSITION	DL	BFW
	Phi N	86	159	15	47	9	0	0	15	10-1	0	16	.296	.333	.352	92	-1	0-0	1.000	-3	85	0	O31L,1b13/3	0	-0.7
	Year	89	162	15	48	9	0	0	15	10-1	0	17	.296	.333	.352	92	-1	0-0	1.000	-3	84	0	O32L,1b13/3	0	-0.7
Total	15	1833	6913	951	2092	356	56	87	671	594-39	15	404	.303	.357	.408	108	84	68-56	.978	-136	96	89	O826L,S748,3b140,1b33	0	-3.7
KUHEL, JOE	Joseph Anthony; B6.25.1906 Cleveland OH; D2.26.1984 Kansas City KS; BL/TL/6´0˝/180; d7.31; M2																								
1930	Was A	18	63	9	18	3	3	0	17	5	1	6	.286	.348	.429	95	-1	1-0	.981	-1	87	84	1b16	—	-0.2
1931	Was A	139	524	70	141	34	8	8	85	47	5	45	.269	.335	.410	94	-5	7-5	.991	-6	77	**121**	1b139	—	-2.3
1932	Was A	101	347	52	101	21	5	4	52	32	1	19	.291	.353	.415	99	0	5-2	.994	-2	89	98	1b85	—	-0.9
1933	†Was A	**153**	602	89	194	34	10	11	107	59	2	48	.322	.385	.467	126	22	17-8	**.996**	-6	76	115	1b153	—	0.2
1934	Was A	63	263	49	76	12	3	3	25	30	1	14	.289	.364	.392	99	0	2-7	.994	-4	72	116	1b63	—	-1.1
1935	Was A	151	633	99	165	25	9	2	74	78	4	44	.261	.345	.338	80	-18	5-4	.991	1	104	109	1b151	—	-3.0
1936	Was A	149	588	107	189	42	8	16	118	64	4	30	.321	.392	.502	126	24	15-7	.993	-2	92	110	1b149	—	0.8
1937	Was A	136	547	73	155	24	11	6	61	63	0	39	.283	.357	.400	95	-5	6-3	.993	3	109	116	1b136	—	-1.4
1938	Chi A	117	412	67	110	27	4	8	51	72	0	35	.267	.376	.410	95	-2	9-7	.988	-8	79	95	1b111	—	-1.9
1939	Chi A	139	546	107	164	24	9	15	56	64	2	51	.300	.376	.460	110	8	18-5	.992	-4	89	107	1b136	—	-0.6
1940	Chi A	**155**	603	111	169	28	8	27	94	87	3	59	.280	.374	.488	120	18	12-5	.988	-5	91	93	1b155	—	0.0
1941	Chi A	153	600	99	150	39	5	12	63	70	3	55	.250	.331	.392	92	-7	20-5	.994	0	100	94	1b151	0	-1.8
1942	Chi A	115	413	60	103	14	4	4	52	60	2	22	.249	.347	.332	94	-2	22-9	.991	-3	91	103	1b112	0	-1.4
1943	Chi A	153	531	55	113	21	1	5	46	76	7	45	.213	.319	.284	77	-13	14-8	.995	2	103	107	1b153	0	-2.0
1944	Was A	139	518	90	144	26	7	4	51	68	2	40	.278	.364	.378	117	14	11-6	.987	-1	98	94	1b138	0	0.6
1945	Was A	142	533	73	152	29	13	2	75	79	1	31	.285	.378	.400	137	28	10-5	.989	-6	87	91	1b141	0	1.5
1946	Was A	14	20	2	3	0	0	0	2	5	0	2	.150	.320	.150	36	-1	0-0	1.000	0	125	61	1b5	0	-0.1
	Chi A	64	238	24	65	9	3	4	20	21	1	24	.273	.335	.387	105	1	4-4	.994	-1	95	122	1b63	0	-0.3
	Year	78	258	26	68	9	3	4	22	26	1	26	.264	.333	.368	100	0	4-4	.994	-1	97	119	1b68	0	-0.4
1947	Chi A	3	3	0	0	0	0	0	0	0	0	3	.000	.000	.000	-99	-1	0-0	ø	0	—	—	/H	0	-0.1
Total	18	2104	7984	1236	2212	412	111	131	1049	980	39	612	.277	.359	.406	104	60	178-90	.992	-42	92	105	1b2057	0	-14.0
KUHN, WALT	Charles Walter "Red"; B2.2.1887 Fresno CA; D6.14.1935 Fresno CA; BR/TR/5´7˝/162; d4.18																								
1912	Chi A	76	178	16	36	7	0	0	10	20	1	—	.202	.286	.242	53	-10	4	.966	5	*102*	*103*	C75/2	—	0.0
1913	Chi A	26	50	5	8	1	0	0	5	13	0	8	.160	.333	.180	52	-2	1	.980	0	*124*	*89*	C24	—	0.0
1914	Chi A	17	40	4	11	1	0	0	0	8	0	11	.275	.396	.300	111	1	2-3	.987	1	*121*	*85*	C16	—	0.3
Total	3	119	268	25	55	9	0	0	15	41	1	19	.205	.313	.239	62	-11	7-3	.971	7	*109*	*98*	C115/2	—	0.3
KUHN, KENNY	Kenneth Harold; B3.20.1937 Louisville KY; BL/TR/5´10.5˝/175; d7.7																								
1955	Cle A	4	6	0	2	0	0	0	0	1-0	0	0	.333	.429	.333	103	0	1-0	1.000	-1	72	0	S4	41	0.0
1956	Cle A	27	22	7	6	1	0	0	2	0-0	0	4	.273	.273	.318	54	-2	0-1	1.000	1	92	127	S17,2b5	0	-0.1
1957	Cle A	40	53	5	9	0	0	0	5	4-0	0	9	.170	.228	.170	10	-7	0-0	.974	-5	54	30	2b14,3b2/S	0	-1.1
Total	3	71	81	12	17	1	0	0	7	5-0	0	13	.210	.256	.222	30	-9	1-1	.963	-5	89	90	S22,2b19,3b2	41	-1.2
KUHNS, CHARLIE	Charles Benton; B10.27.1876 Freeport PA; D7.15.1922 Pittsburgh PA; 5´9˝/160; d6.4																								
1897	Pit N	1	3	0	0	0	0	0	0	1	0	—	.000	.250	.000	-32	-1	0	.667	-0	120	0	/3	—	-0.1
1899	Bos N	7	18	2	5	0	0	0	3	2	0	—	.278	.350	.278	67	-1	0	.813	-1	95	214	S3,3b3	—	-0.2
Total	2	8	21	2	5	0	0	0	3	3	0	—	.238	.333	.238	53	-2	0	.733	-1	112	0	3b4,S3	—	-0.3
KUIPER, DUANE	Duane Eugene; B6.19.1950 Racine WI; BL/TR/6´0˝/175; [CleA72*S1/21]; d9.9; Col Southern Illinois																								
1974	Cle A	10	22	7	11	2	0	0	4	2-0	0	2	.500	.542	.591	227	4	1-1	1.000	1	115	73	2b8	0	0.5
1975	Cle A	90	346	42	101	11	1	0	25	30-0	8	26	.292	.362	.329	96	0	19-18	.972	-14	90	107	2b87/D	20	-1.1
1976	Cle A	135	506	47	133	13	6	0	37	30-2	1	42	.263	.303	.312	82	-13	10-17	**.987**	17	99	115	2b128,1b5,D2	0	0.9
1977	Cle A	148	610	62	169	15	8	1	50	37-1	7	55	.277	.324	.333	82	-16	11-11	.985	-3	95	105	2b148	0	-1.2
1978	Cle A	149	547	52	155	18	6	0	43	19-1	4	35	.283	.311	.338	84	-13	4-9	.979	-12	93	89	2b149	0	-2.1
1979	Cle A	140	479	46	122	9	5	0	39	37-7	4	27	.255	.313	.294	65	-24	4-9	**.988**	-5	92	88	2b140	0	-2.3
1980	Cle A	42	149	10	42	5	0	0	9	13-3	0	8	.282	.337	.315	80	-4	0-1	.995	-5	88	90	2b42	126	-0.6
1981	Cle A	72	206	15	53	6	0	0	14	8-2	0	13	.257	.284	.286	65	-10	1-1	.983	-11	90	53	2b72	22	-1.8
1982	SF N	107	218	26	61	9	1	0	17	32-0	2	24	.280	.375	.330	100	2	2-2	.978	-8	90	85	2b51	0	-0.4
1983	SF N	72	176	14	44	2	2	0	14	27-6	2	13	.250	.353	.284	82	-3	0-1	.988	-13	87	49	2b64	41	-1.5
1984	SF N	83	115	8	23	1	0	0	11	12-5	0	10	.200	.273	.209	39	-9	0-1	.969	4	109	99	2b31/1	0	-0.5
1985	SF N	9	5	0	3	0	0	0	0	1-0	0	0	.600	.667	.600	269	1	0-0	ø	0	—	—	/H	29	0.1
Total	12	1057	3379	329	917	91	29	1	263	248-27	28	255	.271	.325	.316	81	-85	52-71	.983	-49	93	92	2b920,1b6,D3	238	-10.0
KUNKEL, JEFF	Jeffrey William; B3.25.1962 W.Palm Beach FL; BR/TR/6´2˝/(180–190); [TexA83 1/3]; d7.23; f-Bill; Col Rider; OF(14/30/5); [DL 1991 Tex A 182]																								
1984	Tex A	50	142	13	29	2	3	3	7	2-0	1	35	.204	.218	.324	47	-11	4-3	.922	-1	96	85	S48/D	0	-0.8
1985	Tex A	2	4	1	1	0	0	0	0	0-0	0	3	.250	.250	.250	37	0	0-0	1.000	1	192	171	S2	0	0.1
1986	Tex A	8	13	3	3	0	0	1	2	0-0	0	2	.231	.231	.462	80	0	0-0	.769	-4	53	0	S5/D	0	-0.4
1987	Tex A	15	32	1	7	0	0	1	2	0-0	1	10	.219	.242	.313	45	-3	0-1	.955	1	103	140	2b10,3b3,O3(1/2/0)/1SD	30	-0.2
1988	Tex A	55	154	14	35	8	3	2	15	4-1	1	35	.227	.250	.357	67	-8	0-1	.949	4	111	101	2b28,S19,3b10,O6(4/2/0)/PD	0	-0.3
1989	Tex A	108	293	39	79	21	2	8	29	20-0	3	75	.270	.323	.437	110	4	3-2	.936	-5	92	60	S59,O30(5/24/3),2b8,3b4/PD	0	0.2
1990	Tex A	99	200	17	34	11	1	3	17	11-0	2	66	.170	.221	.280	39	-17	2-1	.958	5	103	101	S67,3b15,2b13,O5(1/2/2)/D	32	-0.8
1992	Chi N	20	29	0	4	2	0	0	1	0-0	0	8	.138	.138	.207	-3	-4	0-0	1.000	2	172	90	S6,2b3,O3L	0	-0.2
Total	8	357	867	88	192	44	9	18	73	37-1	8	234	.221	.259	.355	69	-39	9-8	.940	3	97	80	S207,2b62,O47C,3b32,D12,P2/1	244	-2.4
KUNTZ, RUSTY	Russell Jay; B2.4.1955 Orange CA; BR/TR/6´3˝/190; [ChiA77 11/261]; d9.1; C11; Col Cal St.–Stanislaus																								
1979	Chi A	5	11	0	1	0	0	0	0	2-0	0	6	.091	.231	.091	-9	-2	0-0	1.000	2	183	444	O5(1/1/3)	0	0.0
1980	Chi A	36	62	5	14	4	0	0	3	5-0	0	13	.226	.284	.290	58	-3	1-0	.979	1	106	145	O34(19/9/6)	0	-0.3
1981	Chi A	67	55	15	14	2	0	0	4	6-0	1	8	.255	.339	.291	84	-1	1-0	1.000	0	111	0	O51(28/13/13),D5	0	-0.1
1982	Chi A	21	26	4	5	1	0	0	3	2-0	0	8	.192	.250	.231	33	-2	0-0	1.000	-1	83	0	O21(1/20/1)	0	-0.4
1983	Chi A	28	42	6	11	1	0	0	1	6-0	0	13	.262	.354	.286	75	-1	1-0	.976	-1	103	0	O27(2/25/0)/D	0	-0.2
	Min A	31	100	13	19	3	0	3	5	12-0	0	28	.190	.274	.310	59	-6	0-0	.986	-0	90	172	O30(0/27/3)	0	-0.7
	Year	59	142	19	30	4	0	3	6	18-0	0	41	.211	.298	.303	64	-7	1-0	.982	-1	95	112	O57(2/52/3)/D	0	-0.9
1984	†Det A	84	140	32	40	12	0	2	22	25-1	1	28	.286	.393	.414	125	7	2-2	.987	-4	84	80	O67(12/22/37),D10	0	0.1
1985	Det A	5	5	0	0	0	0	0	0	2-0	0	2	.000	.286	.000	-13	-1	0-1	.000	-0	0	0	/1D	0	-0.1
Total	7	277	441	75	104	23	0	5	38	60-1	2	106	.236	.328	.322	80	-9	5-3	.988	-3	97	89	O235(63/117/63),D19/1	0	-1.7
KUROWSKI, WHITEY	George John; B4.19.1918 Reading PA; D12.9.1999 Sinking Spring PA; BR/TR/5´11˝/193; d9.23																								
1941	StL N	5	9	1	3	2	0	0	2	0	1	2	.333	.400	.556	157	1	0	1.000	-0	75	0	3b4	0	0.0
1942	†StL N	115	366	51	93	17	3	9	42	33	6	60	.254	.326	.391	102	0	7	.944	6	101	119	3b104/Slf	0	1.1
1943	†StL N☆	139	522	69	150	24	8	13	70	31	2	54	.287	.330	.439	116	8	3	.952	-4	89	135	3b137,S2	0	0.6
1944	†StL N★	149	555	95	150	25	7	20	87	58	2	40	.270	.341	.449	119	13	2	**.965**	-1	92	95	3b146,2b9/S	0	1.4
1945	StL N✱	133	511	84	165	27	3	21	102	45	5	45	.323	.383	.511	144	29	1	.964	-4	90	**130**	3b131,S6	0	2.6
1946	†StL N★	142	519	76	156	32	5	14	89	72	5	47	.301	.391	.462	136	26	2	**.966**	-3	91	88	3b138	0	2.4
1947	StL N★	146	513	108	159	27	6	27	104	87	**10**	56	.310	.420	.544	148	38	4	.954	-15	88	71	3b141	0	2.2
1948	StL N	77	220	34	47	8	0	2	33	42	5	28	.214	.352	.277	68	-8	0	.939	-7	85	79	3b65	0	-1.5
1949	StL N	10	14	0	2	0	0	0	0	1	0	0	.143	.200	.143	-6	-2	0	1.000	-0	57	0	3b2	71	-0.2
Total	9	916	3229	518	925	162	32	106	529	369	36	332	.286	.366	.455	124	105	19	.957	-29	91	103	3b868,S10,2b9/lf	71	8.6
KUSICK, CRAIG	Craig Robert; B9.30.1948 Milwaukee, Wis. D.Sept.27, 2006 St.Paul, Minn; BR/TR/6´3˝/(210–230); d9.8; Col Wisconsin–La Crosse																								
1973	Min A	15	48	4	12	2	0	0	4	7-0	1	9	.250	.357	.292	81	-1	0-0	.989	-1	75	81	1b11,O2L,D2	0	-0.3
1974	Min A	76	201	36	48	7	1	8	26	35-1	1	36	.239	.353	.403	114	5	0-0	.996	3	112	85	1b75	0	0.3
1975	Min A	57	156	14	37	8	0	6	27	21-1	5	23	.237	.346	.404	110	3	0-0	.990	1	102	121	1b51	0	0.0
1976	Min A	109	266	33	69	13	0	11	36	35-0	1	44	.259	.344	.432	125	9	5-1	.977	2	160	127	D79,1b23	0	0.9
1977	Min A	115	268	34	68	12	0	12	45	49-5	3	60	.254	.370	.433	121	10	3-1	.972	-2	71	74	D85,1b23	0	0.5
1978	Min A	77	191	23	33	3	2	4	20	37-2	1	38	.173	.305	.272	63	-9	3-2	.987	2	145	76	D35,1b27,O9L	0	-1.0
1979	Min A	24	54	8	13	4	0	3	6	3-0	0	11	.241	.281	.481	97	0	0-0	1.000	0	100	151	D12,1b8	0	-0.1
	Tor A	24	54	3	11	1	0	2	7	7-0	1	7	.204	.302	.333	72	-2	0-0	.978	1	129	88	1b20/PD	0	-0.2
	Year	48	108	11	24	5	0	5	13	10-0	1	18	.222	.292	.407	85	-3	0-0	.983	1	123	101	1b28,D13/P	0	-0.3
Total	7	497	1238	155	291	50	3	46	171	194-9	13	228	.235	.342	.392	105	15	11-4	.988	6	113	96	1b238,D214,O11L/P	0	0.1

THE BATTER REGISTER

KUSNYER, ART Arthur William; B12.19.1945 Akron OH; BR/TR/6´2˝/(197–198); [ChiA66 37/698]; d9.21; C25; Col Kent St.

YEAR	TM LG	G	AB	R	H	2B	3B	HR	RBI	BB-IB	HP	SO	AVG	OBP	SLG	AOPS	ABR	SB-CS	FA	FR	RNG	THR	GAMES AT POSITION	DL	BFW
1970	Chi A	4	10	0	1	0	0	0	0	0-0	0	4	.100	.100	.100	-43	-2	0-0	.941	0	20	152	C3	0	-0.2
1971	Cal A	6	13	0	2	0	0	0	0	0-0	0	3	.154	.154	.154	-14	-2	0-0	.958	-1	93	332	C6	0	-0.3
1972	Cal A	64	179	13	37	2	1	2	13	16-3	1	33	.207	.276	.263	64	-8	0-0	.975	-4	69	95	C63	0	-1.1
1973	Cal A	41	64	5	8	2	0	0	3	2-0	0	12	.125	.149	.156	-14	-10	0-1	.979	-4	98	77	C41	0	-1.3
1976	Mil A	15	34	2	4	1	0	0	3	1-1	1	5	.118	.167	.147	-8	-5	1-0	.938	-2	117	87	C14	0	-0.7
1978	KC A	9	13	1	3	1	0	1	2	2-0	0	4	.231	.333	.538	137	1	0-0	.946	2	56	110	C9	0	0.3
Total	6	139	313	21	55	6	1	3	21	21-4	2	61	.176	.231	.230	37	-26	1-1	.970	-9	80	102	C136	0	-3.3

KUSTUS, JOE Joseph J. "Jul"; B9.5.1882 Detroit MI; D4.27.1916 Eloise (now part of Westland) MI; BR/TR/5´10˝/?; d4.17

YEAR	TM LG	G	AB	R	H	2B	3B	HR	RBI	BB-IB	HP	SO	AVG	OBP	SLG	AOPS	ABR	SB-CS	FA	FR	RNG	THR	GAMES AT POSITION	DL	BFW
1909	Bro N	53	173	12	25	5	0	1	11	11	2	—	.145	.204	.191	23	-16	9	.951	0	87	61	O50(1/18/31)	—	-2.0

KUTCHER, RANDY Randy Scott; B4.20.1960 Anchorage AK; BR/TR/5´11˝/175; [SFN79 4/96]; d6.19; OF(26/78/52)

YEAR	TM LG	G	AB	R	H	2B	3B	HR	RBI	BB-IB	HP	SO	AVG	OBP	SLG	AOPS	ABR	SB-CS	FA	FR	RNG	THR	GAMES AT POSITION	DL	BFW
1986	SF N	71	186	28	44	9	1	7	16	11-0	0	41	.237	.279	.409	92	-3	6-5	.990	-2	115	138	O51(7/44/1),S13,3b4,2b3	0	-0.6
1987	SF N	14	16	7	3	1	1	0	1	1-0	0	5	.188	.235	.375	61	-1	1-0	1.000	1	147	0	O6(1/4/1),2b2,3b2/S	0	0.0
1988	Bos A	19	12	2	2	1	0	0	0	0-0	0	2	.167	.167	.250	14	-1	0-1	1.000	1	92	548	O7(5/0/2),3b2,D7	0	-0.1
1989	Bos A	77	160	28	36	10	3	2	18	11-0	0	46	.225	.273	.363	73	-6	3-0	.982	1	116	0	O57(11/21/25),3b6/CD	15	-0.6
1990	†Bos A	63	74	18	17	4	1	1	5	13-0	0	18	.230	.345	.351	90	-1	3-3	1.000	3	114	0	O34(2/9/23),3b11,2b5,D5	0	0.2
Total	5	244	448	83	102	25	6	10	40	36-0	0	112	.228	.285	.377	82	-12	13-9	.989	4	115	69	O155C,3b25,D18,S14,2b10/C	15	-1.1

KUTINA, JOE Joseph Peter; B1.16.1885 Chicago IL; D4.13.1945 Chicago IL; BR/TR/6´2˝/205; d9.6

YEAR	TM LG	G	AB	R	H	2B	3B	HR	RBI	BB-IB	HP	SO	AVG	OBP	SLG	AOPS	ABR	SB-CS	FA	FR	RNG	THR	GAMES AT POSITION	DL	BFW
1911	StL A	26	101	12	26	6	2	3	15	2	1	—	.257	.279	.446	105	0	2	.981	-1	92	127	1b26	—	-0.2
1912	StL A	69	205	18	42	9	3	1	18	13	3	—	.205	.262	.293	61	-11	0	.985	-2	79	109	1b51/lf	—	-1.5
Total	2	95	306	30	68	15	5	4	33	15	4	—	.222	.268	.343	76	-11	2	.984	-3	83	115	1b77/lf	—	-1.7

KVASNAK, AL Alexander; B1.11.1921 Sagamore PA; D9.26.2002 Arcadia CA; BR/TR/6´1˝/170; d4.15; Mil 1942–45

YEAR	TM LG	G	AB	R	H	2B	3B	HR	RBI	BB-IB	HP	SO	AVG	OBP	SLG	AOPS	ABR	SB-CS	FA	FR	RNG	THR	GAMES AT POSITION	DL	BFW
1942	Was A	5	11	3	2	0	0	0	0	2	0	1	.182	.308	.182	40	-1	0-0	1.000	0	109	0	O3(1/0/2)	0	-0.1

KYLE, ANDY Andrew Ewing; B10.29.1889 Toronto ON, Can.; D9.6.1971 Toronto ON, Can.; BL/TL/5´8˝/160; d9.7

YEAR	TM LG	G	AB	R	H	2B	3B	HR	RBI	BB-IB	HP	SO	AVG	OBP	SLG	AOPS	ABR	SB-CS	FA	FR	RNG	THR	GAMES AT POSITION	DL	BFW
1912	Cin N	9	21	3	7	1	0	0	4	4	0	2	.333	.440	.381	129	1	0	1.000	1	112	112	O7(2/5/0)	—	0.1

LAABS, CHET Chester Peter; B4.30.1912 Milwaukee WI; D1.26.1983 Warren MI; BR/TR/5´8˝/175; d5.5; Def 1944; Mil 1945

YEAR	TM LG	G	AB	R	H	2B	3B	HR	RBI	BB-IB	HP	SO	AVG	OBP	SLG	AOPS	ABR	SB-CS	FA	FR	RNG	THR	GAMES AT POSITION	DL	BFW
1937	Det A	72	242	31	58	13	5	8	37	24	0	66	.240	.308	.434	83	-8	6-2	.971	-5	92	39	O62(22/40/0)	—	-1.3
1938	Det A	64	211	26	50	7	3	7	37	15	0	52	.237	.288	.398	66	-13	3-2	.971	0	102	91	O53(22/32/0)	—	-1.3
1939	Det A	5	16	1	5	1	1	0	2	2	0	0	.313	.389	.500	117	0	0-0	.933	1	112	283	O5L	—	0.1
	StL A	95	317	52	95	20	5	10	62	33	1	62	.300	.368	.489	115	6	4-1	.972	-2	96	107	O79(3/70/6)	—	0.3
	Year	100	333	53	100	21	6	10	64	35	1	62	.300	.369	.489	115	7	4-1	.969	-1	97	119	O84(8/70/6)	—	0.4
1940	StL A	105	218	32	59	11	5	10	40	34	1	59	.271	.372	.505	122	7	3-3	.969	-1	99	77	O63(25/29/10)	—	0.3
1941	StL A	118	392	64	109	23	6	15	59	51	0	59	.278	.361	.482	117	9	5-2	.982	-1	102	66	O100(21/15/64)	0	0.3
1942	StL A	144	520	90	143	21	7	27	99	88	0	88	.275	.380	.498	144	30	0-3	.970	-3	92	124	O139(36/25/80)	0	1.9
1943	StL A★	151	580	83	145	27	7	17	85	73	4	105	.250	.338	.409	115	11	5-7	.976	5	101	136	O150(125/24/6)	0	0.6
1944	†StL A	66	201	28	47	10	2	5	23	29	0	33	.234	.330	.378	96	-1	3-1	1.000	1	101	76	O55(38/0/18)	0	-0.3
1945	StL A	35	109	15	26	4	3	1	8	16	3	17	.239	.352	.358	101	1	0-0	.986	-0	107	37	O35(34/2/2)	0	-0.2
1946	StL A	80	264	40	69	13	0	16	52	20	1	50	.261	.316	.492	117	5	3-1	.987	2	110	83	O72(6/0/66)	0	0.5
1947	Phi A	15	32	5	7	1	0	1	5	4	0	4	.219	.306	.344	79	-1	0-0	1.000	1	105	199	O7(6/0/1)	0	-0.1
Total	11	950	3102	467	813	151	44	117	509	389	10	595	.262	.346	.452	113	46	32-22	.977	-3	99	98	O820(343/237/253)	0	0.8

LABANDEIRA, JOSH John Joshua; B2.25.1979 Tulare CA; BR/TR/5´7˝/180; [MonN01 6/172]; d9.17; Col Cal St.–Fresno

YEAR	TM LG	G	AB	R	H	2B	3B	HR	RBI	BB-IB	HP	SO	AVG	OBP	SLG	AOPS	ABR	SB-CS	FA	FR	RNG	THR	GAMES AT POSITION	DL	BFW
2004	Mon N	7	14	0	0	0	0	0	0	0-0	0	4	.000	.000	.000	-96	-4	0-0	.833	-3	49	0	S3,2b2	0	-0.7

LABOY, COCO Jose Alberto; B7.3.1939 Ponce, PR; BR/TR/5´10˝/(170–172); d4.8

YEAR	TM LG	G	AB	R	H	2B	3B	HR	RBI	BB-IB	HP	SO	AVG	OBP	SLG	AOPS	ABR	SB-CS	FA	FR	RNG	THR	GAMES AT POSITION	DL	BFW
1969	Mon N	157	562	53	145	29	1	18	83	40-2	4	96	.258	.308	.409	100	-1	0-2	.944	5	104	94	3b156	0	0.3
1970	Mon N	137	432	37	86	26	1	5	53	31-5	2	81	.199	.254	.299	48	-32	0-2	.946	-7	90	81	3b132,2b3	0	-4.1
1971	Mon N	76	151	10	38	4	0	1	14	11-0	0	19	.252	.302	.298	70	-6	0-1	.937	-2	93	54	3b65,2b2	0	-0.9
1972	Mon N	28	69	6	18	2	0	3	14	10-3	0	16	.261	.350	.420	117	2	0-0	.980	-3	90	61	3b24,2b3,S2	83	-0.2
1973	Mon N	22	33	2	4	1	0	1	2	5-1	0	8	.121	.237	.242	32	-3	0-0	.889	-1	88	87	3b20/2	0	-0.4
Total	5	420	1247	108	291	62	2	28	166	97-11	6	220	.233	.289	.354	77	-40	0-5	.944	-8	97	83	3b397,2b9,S2	83	-5.3

LACHANCE, CANDY George Joseph; B2.14.1870 Putnam CT; D8.18.1932 Waterville CT; BB/TR/6´1˝/183; d8.15

YEAR	TM LG	G	AB	R	H	2B	3B	HR	RBI	BB-IB	HP	SO	AVG	OBP	SLG	AOPS	ABR	SB-CS	FA	FR	RNG	THR	GAMES AT POSITION	DL	BFW
1893	Bro N	11	35	1	6	1	0	0	6	2	1	12	.171	.237	.200	17	-4	0	.654	-4	*104*	73	C6,O5(4/0/1)	—	-0.7
1894	Bro N	69	261	48	83	13	8	5	52	16	1	32	.318	.360	.487	110	3	20	.979	-8	52	72	1b56,C11,O3R	—	-0.3
1895	Bro N	128	541	102	170	23	9	8	111	29	8	48	.314	.358	.434	113	9	37	.983	-6	78	98	1b126,O3R	—	0.2
1896	Bro N	89	348	60	99	10	13	7	58	23	1	32	.284	.331	.448	110	2	17	.986	-4	77	115	1b89	—	-0.1
1897	Bro N	126	520	86	160	28	16	4	90	15	5	—	.308	.333	.446	111	4	26	.978	-4	90	110	1b126	—	0.0
1898	Bro N	136	526	62	130	23	7	5	65	31	8	—	.247	.299	.346	85	-12	23	.988	-16	56	116	1b74,S48,O13(11/2/0)	—	-2.5
1899	Bal N	125	472	65	145	23	10	1	75	21	10	—	.307	.350	.405	101	-1	31	.984	-7	65	102	1b125	—	-0.7
1901	Cle A	133	548	81	166	22	9	1	75	7	2	—	.303	.314	.381	96	-5	11	.979	-3	85	89	1b133	—	-0.9
1902	Bos A	**138**	541	60	151	13	4	6	56	18	5	—	.279	.309	.351	80	-16	8	.983	-12	59	106	1b138	—	-2.9
1903	†Bos A	**141**	522	60	134	22	6	1	53	28	7	—	.257	.303	.328	85	-9	12	.984	-11	64	107	1b141	—	-2.5
1904	Bos A	**157**	573	55	130	19	5	1	47	23	7	—	.227	.265	.283	69	-20	7	**.992**	-14	59	**111**	1b157	—	-4.2
1905	Bos A	12	41	1	6	1	0	0	5	6	0	—	.146	.255	.171	36	-3	0	.988	-1	80	117	1b12	—	-0.4
Total	12	1265	4928	681	1380	198	87	39	693	219	55	124	.280	.318	.379	93	-52	192	.984	-90	69	104	1b1177,S48,O24(15/2/7),C17	—	-15.0

LACHEMANN, RENE Rene George; B5.4.1945 Los Angeles CA; BR/TR/6´0˝/(198–200); d5.4; M8/C18; b–Marcel; Col USC

YEAR	TM LG	G	AB	R	H	2B	3B	HR	RBI	BB-IB	HP	SO	AVG	OBP	SLG	AOPS	ABR	SB-CS	FA	FR	RNG	THR	GAMES AT POSITION	DL	BFW
1965	KC A	92	216	20	49	7	1	9	29	12-3	0	57	.227	.264	.394	87	-5	0-0	.980	-7	54	66	C75	0	-1.0
1966	KC A	7	5	0	1	0	0	0	0	0-0	0	1	.200	.200	.400	70	0	0-0	1.000	0	0	0	C6	0	0.0
1968	Oak A	19	60	3	9	1	0	0	4	1-0	1	11	.150	.177	.167	5	-7	0-0	.967	-7	59	46	C16	0	-1.6
Total	3	118	281	23	59	9	1	9	33	13-3	1	69	.210	.245	.345	70	-12	0-0	.978	-14	54	60	C97	0	-2.6

LACOCK, PETE Ralph Pierre; B1.17.1952 Burbank CA; BL/TL/6´3˝/(200–210); [ChiN70*1/20]; d9.6

YEAR	TM LG	G	AB	R	H	2B	3B	HR	RBI	BB-IB	HP	SO	AVG	OBP	SLG	AOPS	ABR	SB-CS	FA	FR	RNG	THR	GAMES AT POSITION	DL	BFW
1972	Chi N	5	6	3	3	0	0	0	4	0-0	0	1	.500	.429	.500	167	0	1-0	1.000	-0	68	0	O3R	0	0.0
1973	Chi N	11	16	1	4	1	0	0	3	1-0	0	2	.250	.294	.313	63	-1	0-0	1.000	1	97	401	O5R	0	0.0
1974	Chi N	35	110	9	20	4	1	1	8	12-2	1	16	.182	.268	.264	47	-8	0-0	.974	2	114	170	O22R,1b11	0	-0.8
1975	Chi N	106	249	30	57	8	1	6	30	37-7	0	27	.229	.324	.341	82	-5	0-2	.988	3	136	95	1b53,O26(11/0/15)	0	-0.8
1976	Chi N	106	244	34	54	9	2	8	28	42-6	1	37	.221	.337	.373	93	-1	1-4	.975	-4	85	117	1b54,O19(7/0/12)	0	-1.2
1977	†KC A	88	218	25	66	12	1	3	29	15-1	1	25	.303	.345	.408	105	2	2-1	.990	2	122	98	1b29,D26,O12(8/1/3)	0	0.1
1978	†KC A	118	322	44	95	21	2	5	48	21-2	0	27	.295	.335	.419	109	4	1-0	.993	-6	74	104	1b106	0	-0.7
1979	KC A	132	408	54	113	25	4	3	56	37-7	1	26	.277	.334	.380	91	-4	2-1	**.997**	2	107	95	1b108,D16	0	-0.8
1980	†KC A	114	156	14	32	6	0	1	18	17-1	1	10	.205	.284	.263	51	-10	1-0	.997	-1	117	109	1b86,O29(26/0/5)	0	-1.4
Total	9	715	1729	214	444	86	11	27	224	182-26	5	171	.257	.326	.366	89	-23	8-8	.991	-0	102	100	1b447,O116(52/1/65),D42	0	-5.6

LACY, LEE Leondaus; B4.10.1948 Longview TX; BR/TR/6´1˝/(175–195); [LAN69*2/29]; d6.30; Col Laney (CA) JC; OF(417/77/594)

YEAR	TM LG	G	AB	R	H	2B	3B	HR	RBI	BB-IB	HP	SO	AVG	OBP	SLG	AOPS	ABR	SB-CS	FA	FR	RNG	THR	GAMES AT POSITION	DL	BFW
1972	LA N	60	243	34	63	7	3	0	12	19-0	0	37	.259	.312	.313	79	-7	5-3	.973	-2	104	113	2b58	0	-0.5
1973	LA N	57	135	14	28	2	0	0	8	15-1	0	34	.207	.287	.222	44	-10	2-3	.965	-5	90	112	2b41	0	-1.5
1974	†LA N	48	78	13	22	6	0	0	8	2-0	0	14	.282	.293	.359	87	-2	2-0	.968	-2	99	75	2b34/3	0	-0.2
1975	LA N	101	306	44	96	11	5	7	40	22-1	0	29	.314	.356	.451	129	10	5-9	.935	-7	77	63	2b43,O43(37/3/8)/S	0	0.1
1976	Atl N	50	180	25	49	4	2	3	20	6-1	1	12	.272	.299	.367	83	-5	2-2	.969	-11	80	88	2b44,O5(1/4/1)/3	0	-1.4
	LA N	53	158	17	42	7	1	0	14	16-2	0	13	.266	.330	.323	88	-2	1-2	.979	-1	102	38	O37(5/23/10),3b3,2b2	0	-0.6
	Year	103	338	42	91	11	3	3	34	22-3	1	25	.269	.314	.346	86	-7	3-4	.970	-12	79	85	2b46,O42(6/27/11),3b4	0	-2.0
1977	†LA N	75	169	28	45	7	0	6	21	10-0	0	21	.266	.306	.414	91	-3	4-0	1.000	-2	60	0	O32(18/0/18),2b22,3b12	25	-0.3
1978	†LA N	103	245	29	64	16	4	13	40	27-4	1	30	.261	.335	.518	136	11	7-4	.971	-4	99	70	O44(17/0/27),2b24,3b9/S	0	0.7
1979	†Pit N	84	182	17	45	9	3	5	15	22-2	1	36	.247	.327	.412	96	-1	6-1	.973	-3	94	102	O41L,2b5	0	-0.4
1980	Pit N	109	278	45	93	20	4	7	33	28-3	2	33	.335	.394	.511	147	18	18-9	.984	9	120	130	O88(86/3/0),3b3	0	2.5
1981	Pit N	78	213	31	57	11	4	2	10	11-2	1	29	.268	.307	.385	91	-3	24-3	.977	5	115	153	O63(34/1/29)/3	0	0.4
1982	Pit N	121	359	66	112	16	3	5	31	32-4	1	57	.312	.369	.415	114	7	40-15	.965	1	105	106	O113(40/17/71),3b2	0	0.9
1983	Pit N	108	288	40	87	12	3	4	13	22-2	0	36	.302	.352	.406	106	2	31-13	1.000	4	120	44	O98(59/24/28)	0	0.6

YEAR	TM LG	G	AB	R	H	2B	3B	HR	RBI	BB-IB	HP	SO	AVG	OBP	SLG	AOPS	ABR	SB-CS	FA	FR	RNG	THR	GAMES AT POSITION	DL	BFW
1984	Pit N	138	474	66	152	26	3	12	70	32-2	0	61	.321	.362	.464	131	19	21-11	**.996**	13	115	171	O127(78/0/88),2b2	0	2.8
1985	Bal A	121	492	69	144	22	4	9	48	39-0	2	95	.293	.343	.409	108	6	10-3	.984	1	100	117	O115(0/1/115),D5	35	0.2
1986	Bal A	130	491	77	141	18	0	11	47	37-2	0	71	.287	.334	.391	98	-1	4-6	.992	3	104	101	O120R,D3	0	-0.5
1987	Bal A	87	258	35	63	13	3	7	28	32-0	0	49	.244	.326	.399	94	-2	3-2	.973	5	100	228	O80(1/1/79),D4	20	-0.1
Total	16	1523	4549	650	1303	207	42	91	458	372-26	9	657	.286	.339	.410	107	37	185-86	.983	5	107	124	O1006R,2b275,3b32,D12,S2	80	2.7
LACY, GUY	Osceola Guy; B6.12.1897 Cleveland TN; D11.19.1953 Cleveland TN; BR/TR/5´11.5˝/170; d5.7																								
1926	Cle A	13	24	2	4	0	0	1	2	2	1	2	.167	.259	.292	43	-2	0-0	.976	-0	104	83	2b11,3b2	—	-0.2
LADD, HI	Arthur Clifford; B2.9.1870 Willimantic CT; D5.7.1948 Cranston RI; BL/TR/6´4˝/180; d7.12																								
1898	Pit N	1	1	0	0	0	0	0	0	0	0	—	.000	.000	.000	-99	0	0	ø	0	—	—	/H	—	0.0
	Bos N	1	4	1	1	0	0	0	0	0	0	—	.250	.250	.250	41	0	0	1.000	0	0	0	/lf	—	0.0
	Year	2	5	1	1	0	0	0	0	0	0	—	.200	.200	.200	14	-1	0	1.000	0	0	0	/lf	—	0.0
LADEW, STEVE	Stephen F.; B St.Louis MO; d9.27																								
1889	KC AA	2	4	0	0	0	0	0	0	0	0	3	.000	.000	.000	-94	-1	0	1.000	0	0	0	/lfP	—	-0.1
LAFATA, JOE	Joseph Joseph; B8,3.1921 Detroit MI; D5.6.2004 Roseville MI; BL/TL/6´0˝/163; d4.17																								
1947	NY N	62	95	13	21	1	0	2	18	15	1	18	.221	.333	.295	68	-4	1	.974	1	93	241	O19(20/1/0),1b2	0	-0.5
1948	NY N	1	1	0	0	0	0	0	0	0	0	1	.000	.000	.000	-99	0	0	ø	0	—	—	/H	0	0.0
1949	NY N	64	140	18	33	2	2	3	16	9	0	23	.236	.282	.343	67	-7	1	.984	-4	51	97	1b47	60	-1.3
Total	3	127	236	31	54	3	2	5	34	24	1	42	.229	.303	.322	67	-11	2	.985	-4	49	101	1b49,O19(20/1/0)	60	-1.8
LAFFERTY, FLIP	Frank Bernard; B5.4.1854 Scranton PA; D2.8.1910 Wilmington DE; TR; d9.15; ▲																								
1876	Phi N	1	3	0	0	0	0	0	0	0	—	0	.000	.000	.000	-99	-1	—	.750	0	141	1747	/P	—	0.0
1877	Lou N	4	17	2	1	1	0	0	0	0	—	4	.059	.059	.118	-39	-3	—	.750	-1	0	0	O4C	—	-0.3
Total	2	5	20	2	1	1	0	0	0	0	—	4	.050	.050	.100	-46	-4	—	.750	-1	0	0	O4C/P	—	-0.3
LAFOREST, TY	Byron Joseph (b Biron Joseph La Forest); B4.18.1917 Edmundston NB, Can.; D5.5.1947 Arlington MA; BR/TR/5´9˝/165; d8.4																								
1945	Bos A	52	204	25	51	7	4	2	16	10	0	35	.250	.285	.353	83	-6	4-4	.966	4	111	121	3b45,O5(3/0/2)	0	-0.2
LAFOREST, PETE	Pierre Luc; B1.27.1978 Hull QC, Can.; BL/TR/6´2˝/(200–210); d9.2; Col Fort Scott (KS) CC																								
2003	TB A	19	48	0	8	2	0	0	6	1-0	1	14	.167	.196	.208	8	-6	0-0	1.000	-1	29	0	D12,C4	0	-0.8
2005	TB A	25	64	5	11	3	0	1	4	6-1	0	23	.172	.243	.266	36	-6	0-1	1.000	-6	125	121	C21/1D	0	-1.1
Total	2	44	112	5	19	5	0	1	10	7-1	1	37	.170	.223	.241	24	-12	0-1	1.000	-7	110	103	C25,D14/1	0	-1.9
LAFRANCOIS, ROGER	Roger Victor; B8.2.1956 Norwich CT; BL/TR/6´2˝/202; [BosA77 8/195]; d5.27; Col Oklahoma																								
1982	Bos A	8	10	1	4	1	0	0	1	0-0	0	0	.400	.400	.500	137	1	0-0	1.000	0	0	0	C8	0	0.1
LAGA, MIKE	Michael Russell; B6.14.1960 Ridgewood NJ; BL/TL/6´2˝/210; [DetA80*1/17]; d9.1; Col Bergen (NJ) CC																								
1982	Det A	27	88	6	23	9	0	3	11	4-0	0	23	.261	.293	.466	104	0	1-0	.994	-3	33	127	1b19,D8	0	-0.4
1983	Det A	12	21	2	4	0	0	0	2	1-0	0	9	.190	.227	.190	17	-2	0-0	1.000	0	97	180	1b5,D6	0	-0.3
1984	Det A	9	11	1	6	0	0	0	1	1-0	0	2	.545	.583	.545	215	2	0-0	1.000	0	100	101	1b4,D4	0	0.2
1985	Det A	9	36	3	6	1	0	2	6	0-0	0	9	.167	.167	.361	40	-3	0-0	.974	1	163	123	1b4,D5	0	-0.3
1986	Det A	15	45	6	9	1	0	3	8	5-1	0	13	.200	.280	.422	88	-1	0-0	1.000	-1	80	111	1b12,D2	109	-0.2
	StL N	18	46	7	10	4	0	3	8	5-1	1	18	.217	.308	.500	119	1	0-0	1.000	2	169	105	1b16	0	0.3
1987	StL N	17	29	4	4	1	0	1	4	2-1	0	7	.138	.182	.276	22	-3	0-0	.973	1	143	170	1b12	0	-0.3
1988	StL N	41	100	5	13	0	0	1	4	2-0	0	21	.130	.147	.160	-12	-15	0-0	1.000	-0	91	133	1b37	101	-1.9
1989	SF N	17	20	1	4	1	0	1	7	1-0	0	6	.200	.238	.400	82	-1	0-0	1.000	-0	62	0	1b4	0	-0.1
1990	SF N	23	27	4	5	1	0	2	4	1-0	1	7	.185	.241	.444	87	-1	0-0	1.000	1	132	114	1b10	0	-0.1
Total	9	188	423	39	84	18	0	16	55	22-3	2	115	.199	.241	.355	63	-23	1-0	.996	-0	98	124	1b123,D25	210	-3.1
LAHOUD, JOE	Joseph Michael; B4.14.1947 Danbury CT; BL/TL/6´0˝/(188–198); d4.10; Col New Haven																								
1968	Bos A	29	78	5	15	1	0	1	6	16-0	0	16	.192	.330	.244	71	-2	0-2	.926	-3	61	162	O25(3/1/22)	0	-0.8
1969	Bos A	101	218	32	41	5	0	9	21	40-0	1	43	.188	.317	.335	79	-6	2-1	.979	-3	89	73	O66(24/12/33)/1	0	-1.2
1970	Bos A	17	49	6	12	1	0	2	5	7-1	0	6	.245	.339	.388	94	0	0-0	.963	2	109	401	O13(9/0/5)	0	0.1
1971	Bos A	107	256	39	55	9	3	14	32	40-3	4	45	.215	.330	.438	108	3	2-2	.993	3	109	91	O69(7/0/63)	0	0.2
1972	Mil A	111	316	35	75	9	3	12	34	45-7	0	54	.237	.331	.399	119	7	3-4	.974	-1	109	30	O97(38/0/63)	0	0.1
1973	Mil A	96	225	29	46	9	0	5	26	27-1	5	36	.204	.302	.311	74	-7	5-5	1.000	4	130	87	D41,O40(2/0/39)	0	-0.7
1974	Cal A	127	325	46	88	16	3	13	44	47-3	3	57	.271	.367	.458	144	20	4-5	.976	1	99	105	O106(70/0/39),D10	0	1.5
1975	Cal A	76	192	21	41	6	2	6	33	48-2	1	33	.214	.372	.359	116	7	2-1	1.000	-1	91	54	D35,O29(7/0/22)	39	0.3
1976	Cal A	42	96	8	17	4	0	0	4	18-2	2	16	.177	.319	.219	63	-3	0-0	.962	-0	114	0	O26(21/1/6),D3	0	-0.5
	Tex A	38	89	10	20	3	1	1	5	10-1	0	16	.225	.303	.315	79	-2	1-0	1.000	-0	65	0	D22,O5(4/0/1)	0	-0.3
	Year	80	185	18	37	7	1	1	9	28-3	2	32	.200	.312	.265	71	-6	1-0	.964	-1	110	0	O31(25/1/7),D25	0	-0.8
1977	†KC A	34	65	8	17	5	0	2	8	11-1	0	16	.262	.364	.431	116	2	1-0	.952	0	83	247	O15(13/0/2),D4	0	0.2
1978	KC A	13	16	0	2	0	0	0	0	0-0	0	1	.125	.125	.125	-29	-3	0-0	ø	-0	0	0	/rfD	0	-0.3
Total	11	791	1925	239	429	68	12	65	218	309-21	16	339	.223	.334	.372	103	16	20-20	.979	1	102	88	O492(198/14/296),D116/1	39	-1.4
LAIRD, GERALD	Gerald Lee; B11.13.1979 Westminster CA; BR/TR/6´2˝/(190–225); [OakA98 2/45]; d4.30; Col Cal St.–Fullerton																								
2003	Tex A	19	44	9	12	2	1	1	4	5-0	1	11	.273	.360	.432	101	0	0-0	.986	-2	178	98	C16	0	-0.1
2004	Tex A	49	147	20	33	6	0	1	16	12-0	2	35	.224	.287	.286	50	-11	0-1	.983	2	138	128	C49	63	-0.6
2005	Tex A	13	40	7	9	2	0	1	4	2-0	0	7	.225	.262	.350	59	-2	0-0	.957	-2	75	113	C13/rf	0	-0.4
2006	Tex A	78	243	46	72	20	1	7	22	12-0	2	54	.296	.332	.473	106	2	3-1	.986	1	145	137	C71/rf	0	0.7
Total	4	159	474	82	126	30	2	10	46	31-0	5	107	.266	.315	.401	84	-11	3-2	.983	-2	140	128	C149,O2R	63	-0.4
LAJESKIE, DICK	Richard Edward; B1.8.1926 Passaic NJ; D8.15.1976 Ramsey NJ; BR/TR/5´11˝/175; d9.10																								
1946	NY N	6	10	3	2	0	0	0	0	3	1	2	.200	.429	.200	81	0	0	.964	3	179	42	2b4	0	0.3
LAJOIE, NAP	Napoleon "Larry"; B9.5.1874 Woonsocket RI; D2.7.1959 Daytona Beach FL; BR/TR/6´1˝/195; d8.12; M5; HF1937; OF(4/5/18)																								
1896	Phi N	39	175	36	57	12	7	4	42	1	0	11	.326	.330	.543	129	5	7	.995	-3	53	107	1b39	—	0.2
1897	Phi N	127	545	107	197	40	23	9	127	15	12	—	.361	.392	**.569**	156	39	20	.984	-6	61	77	1b108,O19(2/0/18),3b2	—	2.7
1898	Phi N	147	608	113	197	**43**	11	6	**127**	21	7	—	.324	.354	.461	139	27	25	.949	0	90	101	2b146/1	—	3.2
1899	Phi N	77	312	70	118	19	9	6	70	12	10	—	.378	.419	.554	172	29	13	.954	16	105	145	2b67,O5C	—	4.2
1900	Phi N	102	451	95	152	33	12	7	92	10	8	—	.337	.362	.510	140	22	22	**.954**	22	**114**	**152**	2b102/3	—	4.4
1901	Phi A	131	544	**145**	**232**	**48**	14	**14**	**125**	24	13	—	**.426**	**.463**	**.643**	**196**	**69**	27	**.960**	22	99	111	2b119,S12	—	**8.1**
1902	Phi A	1	4	0	1	0	0	0	1	0	0	—	.250	.250	.250	37	0	1	1.000	-0	98	0	/2	—	0.0
	Cle A	86	348	81	132	35	5	7	64	19	6	—	.379	.421	.569	180	38	19	.974	23	105	133	2b86	—	5.6
	Year	87	352	81	133	35	5	7	65	19	6	—	**.378**	.419	.565	178	37	20	.974	23	105	132	2b87	—	**5.6**
1903	Cle A	125	485	90	167	41	11	7	93	24	3	—	**.344**	.379	**.518**	**170**	**41**	21	.955	**39**	111	**146**	2b122/13	—	**8.1**
1904	Cle A	140	553	92	**208**	**49**	15	5	**102**	27	8	—	**.376**	**.413**	**.546**	**204**	**64**	29	.962	2	90	155	2b95,S44,1b2	—	**7.4**
1905	Cle A	65	249	29	82	12	2	2	41	17	2	—	.329	.377	.418	150	14	11	.991	8	105	165	2b59,1b5,M	—	2.4
1906	Cle A	152	602	88	**214**	**48**	9	0	91	30	6	—	.355	.392	.465	170	48	20	**.973**	21	**108**	**188**	2b130,3b15,S7,M	—	**7.6**
1907	Cle A	137	509	53	152	30	6	2	63	30	6	—	.299	.345	.393	134	19	24	**.969**	**45**	**120**	**211**	2b128,1b9,M	—	**7.0**
1908	Cle A	**157**	581	77	168	32	6	2	74	47	9	—	.289	.352	.375	136	24	15	**.964**	**47**	**114**	**178**	2b156/1M	—	**8.0**
1909	Cle A	128	469	56	152	33	7	1	47	35	6	—	.324	.378	.431	149	27	13	.959	**23**	110	**135**	2b120,1b8,M	—	5.7
1910	Cle A	159	591	94	**227**	**51**	7	4	76	60	5	—	**.384**	.445	.514	198	**69**	26	.966	13	102	110	2b149,1b10	—	**8.9**
1911	Cle A	90	315	36	115	20	1	2	60	26	4	—	.365	.420	.454	142	19	13	.990	-5	61	88	1b41,2b37	—	1.3
1912	Cle A	117	448	66	165	34	4	0	90	28	7	—	.368	.414	.462	146	27	18	.959	9	97	147	2b97,1b20	—	3.6
1913	Cle A	137	465	66	156	25	2	1	68	33	15	17	.335	.398	.404	131	20	17	**.970**	15	102	136	2b126	—	3.8
1914	Cle A	121	419	37	108	14	3	0	50	32	2	15	.258	.313	.305	83	-9	14-15	.959	8	96	152	2b80,1b31	—	-0.3
1915	Phi A	129	490	40	137	24	5	1	61	11	4	16	.280	.301	.355	100	-4	10-6	.962	17	104	118	2b110,S10,1b5,3b2	—	1.7
1916	Phi A	113	426	33	105	14	4	2	35	14	1	26	.246	.272	.312	79	-14	15	.973	**27**	**107**	119	2b105,1b5,O2L	—	1.6
Total	21	2480	9589	1504	3242	657	163	82	1599	516	134	85	.338	.380	.466	150	574	380-21	.963	341	104	144	2b2035,1b286,S73,O26R,3b21	—	95.2

YEAR	TM LG	G	AB	R	H	2B	3B	HR	RBI	BB-IB	HP	SO	AVG	OBP	SLG	AOPS	ABR	SB-CS	FA	FR	RNG	THR	GAMES AT POSITION	DL	BFW
LAKE, EDDIE	Edward Erving "Sparky"; B3.18.1916 Antioch CA; D6.7.1995 Castro Valley CA; BR/TR/5´7˝/160; d9.26; ▲																								
1939	StL N	2	4	0	1	0	0	0	0	1	0	0	.250	.400	.250	74	0	0	.857	-1	66	112	S2	—	-0.1
1940	StL N	32	66	12	14	3	0	2	7	12	1	17	.212	.342	.348	86	-1	1	.957	-4	87	47	2b17,S6	—	-0.4
1941	StL N	45	76	9	8	2	0	0	0	15	0	22	.105	.253	.132	10	-9	3	.903	1	79	141	S15,3b15,2b5	0	-0.7
1943	Bos A	75	216	26	43	10	0	3	16	47	1	35	.199	.345	.287	84	-2	3-6	.961	3	107	103	S63	0	0.5
1944	Bos A	57	126	21	26	5	0	0	8	23	0	22	.206	.329	.246	66	-4	5-2	.927	-1	97	125	S41,P6,2b3/3	0	-0.3
1945	Bos A	133	473	81	132	27	1	11	51	106	1	37	.279	**.412**	.410	136	29	9-7	.948	24	**112**	**128**	S130/2	0	6.5
1946	Det A	**155**	587	105	149	24	1	8	31	103	4	69	.254	.369	.339	93	-1	15-9	.947	-21	88	99	S155	0	-1.3
1947	Det A	**158**	602	96	127	19	6	12	46	120	1	54	.211	.343	.322	83	-10	11-10	.943	-29	90	86	S158	0	-3.2
1948	Det A	64	198	51	52	6	0	2	18	57	0	20	.263	.427	.323	99	4	3-3	.972	-3	96	95	2b45,3b17	0	0.3
1949	Det A	94	240	38	47	9	1	1	15	61	0	33	.196	.359	.254	63	-10	2-8	.959	-7	98	103	S38,2b19,3b18	0	-1.6
1950	Det A	20	7	3	0	0	0	0	1	1	0	3	.000	.125	.000	-64	-2	0-0	ø	-0	0	0	/S3	0	-0.2
Total	11	835	2595	442	599	105	9	39	193	546	8	312	.231	.366	.323	91	-6	52-45	.947	-38	97	104	S609,2b90,3b52,P6	0	-0.5
LAKE, FRED	Frederick Lovett; B10.16.1866 Cornwallis NS (now Canada); D11.24.1931 Boston MA; BR/TR/5´10˝/170; d5.7; M3																								
1891	Bos N	5	7	1	1	0	0	0	0	2	0	4	.143	.333	.143	36	0	0	1.000	1	*162*	*106*	C4/rf	—	0.0
1894	Lou N	16	42	8	12	2	0	1	10	11	4	6	.286	.474	.405	122	3	2	.864	-3	80	226	2b6,S5,C5	—	0.1
1897	†Bos N	19	62	2	15	4	0	0	5	1	0	—	.242	.254	.306	45	-5	2	.970	2	*150*	*93*	C18	—	-0.2
1898	Pit N	5	13	1	1	0	0	0	1	2	0	—	.077	.200	.077	-20	-2	0	1.000	-0	64	165	1b3	—	-0.2
1910	Bos N	3	1	0	0	0	0	0	0	1	0	0	.000	.500	.000	46	0	0	ø	0	—	—	/HM	—	0.0
Total	5	48	125	12	29	6	0	1	16	17	4	10	.232	.342	.304	68	-4	4	.930	-1	*137*	*90*	C27,2b6,S5,1b3/rf	—	-0.3
LAKE, STEVE	Steven Michael; B3.14.1957 Inglewood CA; BR/TR/6´1˝/(180–202); [BalA75 3/71]; d4.9																								
1983	Chi N	38	85	9	22	4	1	1	7	2-2	1	6	.259	.284	.365	75	-3	0-0	1.000	2	101	164	C32	0	0.0
1984	†Chi N	25	54	4	12	4	0	2	7	0-0	1	7	.222	.232	.407	72	-2	0-0	.955	-1	151	164	C24	81	-0.2
1985	Chi N	58	119	5	18	2	0	1	11	3-1	1	21	.151	.177	.193	4	-16	1-0	.995	3	179	152	C55	0	-1.2
1986	Chi N	10	19	4	8	1	0	0	4	1-1	0	2	.421	.450	.474	144	1	0-0	1.000	-1	64	126	C10	0	0.0
	StL N	26	49	4	12	1	0	2	10	2-0	0	5	.245	.275	.388	81	-2	0-0	.976	2	253	144	C26	0	0.1
	Year	36	68	8	20	2	0	2	14	3-1	0	7	.294	.324	.412	100	0	0-0	.983	1	201	139	C36	0	0.1
1987	†StL N	74	179	19	45	7	2	2	19	10-4	0	18	.251	.289	.346	66	-9	0-0	.996	-1	169	101	C59	0	-0.8
1988	StL N	36	54	5	15	3	0	1	4	3-0	2	15	.278	.339	.389	107	1	0-0	.983	-1	117	126	C19	0	0.1
1989	Phi N	58	155	9	39	5	1	2	14	12-4	0	20	.252	.304	.335	83	-4	0-0	.990	7	127	162	C55	35	0.7
1990	Phi N	29	80	4	20	2	0	0	6	3-1	1	12	.250	.286	.275	55	-5	0-0	.993	5	294	130	C28	42	0.1
1991	Phi N	58	158	12	36	4	1	1	11	2-1	0	26	.228	.237	.285	47	-12	0-0	.993	-2	116	81	C58	0	-1.2
1992	Phi N	20	53	3	13	2	0	1	2	1-0	0	8	.245	.255	.340	68	-2	0-0	.975	-3	80	72	C17	45	-0.5
1993	Chi N	44	120	11	27	6	0	5	13	4-3	0	19	.225	.250	.400	71	-6	0-0	.985	-0	260	100	C41	0	-0.3
Total	11	476	1125	89	267	41	5	18	108	43-17	6	159	.237	.268	.331	64	-59	1-0	.989	10	166	124	C424	203	-3.2
LAKEMAN, AL	Albert Wesley "Moose"; B12.31.1918 Cincinnati OH; D5.25.1976 Spartanburg SC; BR/TR/6´2˝/195; d4.19; C5																								
1942	Cin N	20	38	0	6	1	0	0	2	3	1	10	.158	.238	.184	24	-4	0	.970	1	*99*	*120*	C17	0	-0.2
1943	Cin N	22	55	5	14	2	1	0	6	3	0	11	.255	.293	.327	80	-2	0	1.000	0	*108*	*88*	C21	0	-0.1
1944	Cin N	1	1	0	0	0	0	0	0	0	0	1	.000	.000	.000	-99	0	0	ø	0	—	—	/H	0	0.0
1945	Cin N	76	258	22	66	9	4	8	31	17	1	45	.256	.304	.415	101	-2	0	.963	-8	*84*	*73*	C74	0	-0.5
1946	Cin N	23	30	0	4	0	0	0	4	2	0	7	.133	.188	.133	-9	-4	0	1.000	-0	*119*	*110*	C6	0	-0.5
1947	Cin N	2	2	0	0	0	0	0	0	0	0	1	.000	.000	.000	-99	-1	0	ø	0	—	—	/H	0	-0.1
	Phi N	55	182	11	29	3	0	6	19	5	1	39	.159	.186	.275	22	-22	0	.995	-3	82	77	1b29,C23	0	-2.5
	Year	57	184	11	29	3	0	6	19	5	1	40	.158	.184	.272	20	-23	0	.995	-3	82	77	1b29,C23	0	-2.6
1948	Phi N	32	68	2	11	2	0	1	4	5	0	22	.162	.219	.235	23	-8	0	1.000	-2	*61*	*55*	C22/P	0	-0.8
1949	Bos N	3	6	0	1	0	0	0	0	1	0	0	.167	.286	.167	26	-1	0	1.000	0	180	130	1b2	0	0.0
1954	Det A	5	6	0	0	0	0	0	0	0	0	1	.000	.000	.000	-99	-2	0-0	1.000	0	*0*	*0*	C4	0	-0.1
Total	9	239	646	40	131	17	5	15	66	36	3	137	.203	.248	.314	55	-46	0-0	.974	-11	*84*	*76*	C167,1b31/P	0	-4.8
LAKER, TIM	Timothy John; B11.27.1969 Encino CA; BR/TR/6´3˝/(195–225); [MonN88 6/154]; d8.18; Col Oxnard (CA) JC; [DL 1996 Mon N 182]																								
1992	Mon N	28	46	8	10	3	0	0	4	2-0	0	14	.217	.250	.283	51	-3	1-1	.991	2	83	37	C28	0	-0.1
1993	Mon N	43	86	3	17	2	1	0	7	2-0	1	16	.198	.222	.244	24	-9	2-0	.987	-3	65	67	C43	0	-1.1
1995	Mon N	64	141	17	33	8	1	3	20	14-4	1	38	.234	.306	.369	75	-5	0-1	.977	-5	81	100	C61	0	-0.7
1997	Bal A	7	14	0	0	0	0	0	1	2-0	0	9	.000	.118	.000	-66	-4	0-0	.966	-2	51	67	C7	0	-0.5
1998	TB A	3	5	1	1	0	0	0	0	1-0	0	1	.200	.333	.200	42	0	0-1	1.000	-0	0	0	C2/D	0	-0.1
	Pit N	14	24	2	9	1	0	1	2	1-0	0	3	.375	.385	.542	144	1	0-0	1.000	-1	42	157	1b4/C	0	0.1
1999	Pit N	6	9	0	3	0	0	0	0	0-0	0	2	.333	.333	.333	69	0	0-0	1.000	0	77	0	C2	0	0.0
2001	Cle A	16	33	5	6	0	0	1	5	6-0	0	8	.182	.308	.273	53	-2	0-0	.988	-1	47	69	C14/P	0	-0.2
2003	Cle A	52	162	17	39	11	0	3	21	9-1	0	38	.241	.281	.364	69	-8	2-2	.983	-1	110	106	C50,D2	0	-0.5
2004	Cle A	44	117	12	25	2	0	3	17	7-1	1	28	.214	.262	.308	50	-9	0-0	.984	-2	79	88	C41/P	0	-0.8
2005	TB A	1	1	0	0	0	0	0	0	0-0	0	1	.000	.000	.000	-99	0	0-0	1.000	-0	0	0	/C	0	0.0
2006	Cle A	4	13	1	4	1	0	0	2	0-0	0	4	.308	.308	.385	81	0	0-0	1.000	-1	23	114	C4	0	-0.1
Total	11	282	651	66	147	28	2	11	79	44-6	3	162	.226	.276	.326	59	-39	5-5	.983	-14	81	86	C254,1b4,D3,P2	182	-4.0
LALLY, DAN	Daniel J.; B8.12.1867 Jersey City NJ; D4.14.1936 Milwaukee WI; BL/TR/5´11.5˝/210; d8.19																								
1891	Pit N	41	143	24	32	6	2	1	17	16	4	20	.224	.319	.315	87	-2	0	.839	-4	39	0	O41(0/4/37)	—	-0.5
1897	StL N	88	359	57	102	16	5	2	42	9	7	—	.284	.315	.373	83	-10	12	.896	-0	70	68	O85(83/1/1),1b3	—	-1.6
Total	2	129	502	81	134	22	7	3	59	25	11	20	.267	.316	.357	84	-12	12	.885	-4	62	49	O126(83/5/38),1b3	—	-2.1
LAMANNO, RAY	Raymond Simond; B11.17.1919 Oakland CA; D2.9.1994 Berkeley CA; BR/TR/6´0˝/185; d9.11; Mil 1943–45																								
1941	Cin N	1	0	0	0	0	0	0	0	0	1	0	ø	1.000	ø	197	0	0	1.000	-0	*0*	*0*	/C	0	0.0
1942	Cin N	111	371	40	98	12	2	12	43	31	2	54	.264	.324	.404	113	5	0	.978	-6	*97*	*105*	C104	0	0.5
1946	Cin N★	85	239	18	58	12	0	1	30	11	3	26	.243	.285	.305	70	-10	0	.974	3	*121*	*114*	C61	0	-0.5
1947	Cin N	118	413	33	106	21	3	5	50	28	2	39	.257	.307	.358	77	-15	0	.986	6	*100*	*113*	C109	0	-0.3
1948	Cin N	127	385	31	93	12	0	0	27	48	2	32	.242	.329	.273	67	-16	2	.978	-13	*71*	*71*	C125	0	-2.3
Total	5	442	1408	122	355	57	5	18	150	118	10	151	.252	.314	.338	82	-36	2	.980	-11	*94*	*98*	C400	0	-2.6
LAMAR, BILL	William Harmong "Good Time Bill"; B3.21.1897 Rockville MD; D5.24.1970 Rockport MA; BL/TR/6´1˝/185; d9.19; Mil 1918																								
1917	NY A	11	41	2	10	0	0	0	3	0	0	2	.244	.244	.244	48	-3	1	1.000	-1	98	55	O11(10/1/0)	—	-0.5
1918	NY A	28	110	12	25	3	0	0	2	6	0	2	.227	.267	.255	56	-6	2	.884	-3	88	73	O27(8/17/2)	—	-1.3
1919	NY A	11	16	1	3	1	0	0	0	2	0	1	.188	.278	.250	48	-1	1	1.000	-1	79	0	O3(0/1/2)/1	—	-0.2
	Bos A	48	148	18	43	5	1	0	14	5	0	9	.291	.314	.338	88	-3	3	.922	-2	80	154	O36(6/29/1)	—	-0.7
	Year	59	164	19	46	6	1	0	14	7	0	10	.280	.310	.329	83	-4	4	.926	-2	80	143	O39(6/30/3)/1	—	-0.9
1920	†Bro N	24	44	5	12	4	0	0	4	0	0	1	.273	.273	.364	79	-1	0-0	1.000	-0	81	109	O12(0/6/6)	—	-0.2
1921	Bro N	3	3	2	1	0	0	0	0	0	0	0	.333	.333	.333	74	0	0-0	ø	-0	0	0	/cf	—	0.0
1924	Phi A	87	367	68	121	22	5	7	48	18	0	21	.330	.361	.474	113	5	8-8	.971	2	96	136	O87L	—	-0.1
1925	Phi A	138	568	85	202	39	8	3	77	21	0	17	.356	.379	.468	107	5	2-6	.953	1	98	118	O131L	—	-0.6
1926	Phi A	116	419	62	119	17	6	5	50	18	1	15	.284	.315	.389	78	-15	4-5	.954	-2	96	102	O107L	—	-2.6
1927	Phi A	84	324	48	97	23	3	4	47	16	1	10	.299	.334	.426	91	-5	4-8	.952	-5	84	109	O79(76/3/0)	—	-1.8
Total	9	550	2040	303	633	114	23	19	245	86	2	78	.310	.339	.417	94	-24	25-27	.952	-10	93	114	O494(425/58/11)/1	—	-8.0
LAMB, DAVID	David Christian; B6.6.1975 West Hills CA; BB/TR/6´2˝/165; [BalA93 2/61]; d4.12																								
1999	TB A	55	124	18	28	5	1	1	13	10-0	0	18	.226	.284	.306	50	-10	0-1	.945	3	100	142	S35,2b15,D3	18	-0.4
2000	NY N	7	5	1	1	0	0	0	0	1-0	0	1	.200	.333	.200	41	0	0-0	1.000	-1	140	0	3b3,2b2,S2	0	-0.1
2002	†Min A	7	10	0	1	0	0	0	0	0-0	0	2	.100	.100	.100	-45	-2	0-0	1.000	-1	31	147	S4,2b2/3	0	-0.2
Total	3	69	139	19	30	5	1	1	13	11-0	0	21	.216	.273	.288	43	-12	0-1	.949	2	95	136	S41,2b19,3b4,D3	18	-0.7
LAMB, LYMAN	Laymon Raymond; B3.17.1895 Lincoln NE; D10.5.1955 Fayetteville AR; BR/TR/5´7˝/150; d9.14																								
1920	StL A	9	24	4	9	2	0	0	4	0	0	7	.375	.375	.458	116	1	2-0	1.000	-1	97	0	O7(5/2/0)	—	0.0
1921	StL A	45	134	18	34	9	2	1	17	4	1	12	.254	.281	.373	62	-8	0-0	.942	-4	94	0	3b25,2b7,O6(2/0/4)	—	-1.0
Total	2	54	158	22	43	11	2	1	21	4	1	19	.272	.294	.386	70	-7	2-0	.942	-4	94	0	3b25,O13(7/2/4),2b7	—	-1.0

YEAR	TM LG	G	AB	R	H	2B	3B	HR	RBI	BB-IB	HP	SO	AVG	OBP	SLG	AOPS	ABR	SB-CS	FA	FR	RNG	THR	GAMES AT POSITION	DL	BFW
LAMB, MIKE	Michael Robert; B8.9.1975 West Covina CA; BL/TR/6´1˝/(190–195); [TexA97 7/227]; d4.23; Col Cal St.–Fullerton; OF(26/0/6)																								
2000	Tex A	138	493	65	137	25	2	6	47	34-6	4	60	.278	.328	.373	77	-18	0-2	.913	-11	89	91	3b135,D2	0	-2.7
2001	Tex A	76	284	42	87	18	0	4	35	14-1	5	27	.306	.348	.412	97	-1	2-1	.914	-5	95	102	3b74	0	-0.6
2002	Tex A	115	314	54	89	13	0	9	33	33-5	3	48	.283	.354	.411	101	1	0-0	.987	-0	115	104	1b52,D21,O16(12/0/5),3b14,C3/2	0	-0.4
2003	Tex A	28	38	3	5	0	0	0	2	2-0	1	7	.132	.190	.132	-11	-6	1-0	1.000	-0	209	0	1b5,O2L/3D	0	-0.6
2004	†Hou N	112	278	38	80	14	3	14	58	31-3	0	63	.288	.356	.511	117	7	1-1	.919	5	109	98	3b57,1b10,2b7/D	0	1.1
2005	†Hou N	125	322	41	76	13	5	12	53	22-1	1	65	.236	.284	.419	81	-11	1-1	.989	3	92	102	1b68,3b15,O13(12/0/1)/D	0	-1.3
2006	Hou N	126	381	70	117	22	3	12	45	35-6	0	55	.307	.361	.475	110	6	2-4	.990	7	117	110	1b68,3b36,2b2	0	0.7
Total	7	720	2110	313	591	105	13	57	273	171-22	14	325	.280	.335	.423	93	-22	7-9	.921	-2	99	94	3b332,1b203,O31L,D31,2b10,C3	0	-3.8
LAMER, PETE	Pierre; B12.27.1873 New York NY; D10.24.1931 Brooklyn NY; TR/5´10˝/170; d9.10																								
1902	Chi N	2	9	2	2	0	0	0	0	0	0	—	.222	.222	.222	38	-1	0	.857	-0	*131*	*95*	C2	—	-0.1
1907	Cin N	1	2	0	0	0	0	0	0	0	0	—	.000	.000	.000	-96	0	0	1.000	-0	*39*	*309*	/C	—	-0.1
Total	2	3	11	2	2	0	0	0	0	0	0	—	.182	.182	.182	13	-1	0	.867	-0	*119*	*123*	C3	—	-0.2
LAMONT, GENE	Gene William; B12.25.1946 Rockford IL; BL/TR/6´1˝/(190–195); [DetA65 1/13]; d9.2; M8/C12																								
1970	Det A	15	44	3	13	3	1	1	4	2-0	1	9	.295	.340	.477	122	1	0-0	1.000	-0	83	135	C15	0	0.2
1971	Det A	7	15	2	1	0	0	0	1	0-0	0	5	.067	.067	.067	-60	-3	0-0	.952	1	215	76	C7	0	-0.2
1972	Det A	1	0	0	0	0	0	0	0	0-0	0	0	ø	ø	ø	ø	0	0-0	1.000	0	0	0	/C	0	0.0
1974	Det A	60	92	9	20	4	0	3	8	7-0	0	19	.217	.273	.359	78	-3	0-0	.974	1	95	112	C60	0	-0.1
1975	Det A	4	8	1	3	1	0	0	1	0-0	0	2	.375	.375	.500	139	0	1-0	.944	1	38	110	C4	0	0.1
Total	5	87	159	15	37	8	1	4	14	9-0	1	35	.233	.278	.371	80	-5	1-0	.977	2	100	114	C87	0	0.0
LAMOTTE, BOBBY	Robert Eugene; B2.15.1898 Savannah GA; D11.2.1970 Chatham GA; BR/TR/5´11˝/160; d9.1																								
1920	Was A	4	3	0	0	0	0	0	0	1	0	1	.000	.250	.000	-31	-1	0-0	.750	0	139	0	/S3	—	0.0
1921	Was A	16	41	5	8	0	0	0	2	5	0	0	.195	.283	.195	25	-5	0-0	.940	1	118	19	S12	—	-0.3
1922	Was A	68	214	22	54	10	2	1	23	15	2	21	.252	.307	.332	70	-10	6-1	.954	5	106	87	3b62,S6	—	0.0
1925	StL A	97	356	61	97	20	4	2	51	34	1	22	.272	.338	.368	75	-14	5-5	.926	-0	96	114	S93,3b3	—	-0.4
1926	StL A	36	79	11	16	4	3	0	9	11	0	6	.203	.300	.329	61	-5	0-0	.919	-2	97	110	S30/3	—	-0.4
Total	5	221	693	99	175	34	9	3	85	66	3	50	.253	.320	.341	69	-35	11-6	.927	3	97	100	S142,3b67	—	-1.1
LAMPARD, KEITH	Christopher Keith; B12.20.1945 Warrington, England; BL/TR/6´2˝/(185–200); [HouN65 2/24]; d9.15; Col Oregon																								
1969	Hou N	9	12	2	3	0	0	1	2	0-0	0	3	.250	.250	.500	107	0	0-0	1.000	1	180	1408	/lf	0	0.1
1970	Hou N	53	72	8	17	8	1	0	5	5-0	1	24	.236	.295	.375	81	-2	0-0	1.000	2	119	294	O16(13/0/4),1b2	0	-0.1
Total	2	62	84	10	20	8	1	1	7	5-0	1	27	.238	.289	.393	85	-2	0-0	1.000	3	125	403	O17(14/0/4),1b2	0	0.0
LAMPKIN, TOM	Thomas Michael; B3.4.1964 Cincinnati OH; BL/TR/5´11˝/(183–198); [CleA86 11/265]; d9.10; Col Portland																								
1988	Cle A	4	4	0	0	0	0	0	0	1-0	0	0	.000	.200	.000	-38	-1	0-0	1.000	-1	0	0	C3	0	-0.1
1990	SD N	26	63	4	14	0	1	1	4	4-1	0	9	.222	.269	.302	56	-4	0-1	.971	-0	115	149	C20	0	-0.4
1991	SD N	38	58	4	11	3	1	0	3	3-0	0	9	.190	.230	.276	40	-5	0-0	1.000	-1	76	82	C11	0	-0.5
1992	SD N	9	17	3	4	0	0	0	0	6-0	1	1	.235	.458	.235	100	1	2-0	1.000	-1	116	93	C7/lf	0	0.0
1993	Mil A	73	162	22	32	8	0	4	25	20-3	0	26	.198	.280	.321	63	-8	7-3	.978	0	107	78	C60,O3(2/0/1)/D	0	-0.5
1995	SF N	65	76	8	21	2	0	1	9	9-1	1	8	.276	.360	.342	89	-1	2-0	1.000	3	332	141	C17,O6L	0	0.3
1996	SF N	66	177	26	41	8	0	6	29	20-2	5	22	.232	.324	.379	87	-3	1-5	.992	15	222	122	C53	58	1.3
1997	StL N	108	229	28	56	8	1	7	22	28-5	4	30	.245	.335	.380	87	-4	2-1	.989	-6	85	99	C86	0	-0.5
1998	StL N	93	216	25	50	12	1	6	28	24-5	7	32	.231	.328	.380	86	-4	3-2	.986	-4	111	82	C62,O5(4/0/1),1b2	0	-0.5
1999	Sea A	76	206	29	60	11	2	9	34	13-1	5	32	.291	.345	.495	113	3	1-3	.985	-3	107	160	C56,O2L,D2	0	0.2
2000	Sea A	36	103	15	26	6	1	7	23	9-1	3	17	.252	.325	.534	116	2	0-0	.987	-2	81	134	C28,D3	106	0.2
2001	†Sea A	79	204	28	46	10	0	5	22	18-1	7	41	.225	.309	.348	77	-7	1-0	.995	3	153	58	C71/rfD	0	0.1
2002	SD N	104	281	32	61	10	1	10	37	38-7	3	59	.217	.313	.367	87	-6	4-2	.992	-6	121	84	C94	0	-0.6
Total	13	777	1796	224	422	78	8	56	236	193-27	36	286	.235	.319	.381	86	-37	23-17	.989	-2	126	100	C568,O18(15/0/3),D7,1b2	164	-1.0
LANCELLOTTI, RICK	Richard Anthony; B7.5.1956 Providence RI; BL/TL/6´3˝/(195–210); [PitN77 11/278]; d8.27; Col Rowan																								
1982	SD N	17	39	2	7	2	0	0	4	2-0	0	8	.179	.220	.231	28	-4	0-0	1.000	-1	48	156	1b7,O3(2/0/1)	0	-0.6
1986	SF N	15	18	2	4	0	0	2	6	0-0	0	7	.222	.222	.556	113	0	0-0	1.000	1	0	0	/1rf	0	0.0
1990	Bos A	4	8	0	0	0	0	0	1	0-0	0	3	.000	.000	.000	-95	-2	0-0	1.000	0	146	186	1b2	0	-0.2
Total	3	36	65	4	11	2	0	2	11	2-0	0	18	.169	.191	.292	35	-6	0-0	1.000	-0	68	158	1b10,O4(2/0/2)	0	-0.8
LAND, GROVER	Grover Cleveland; B9.22.1884 Frankfort KY; D7.22.1958 Phoenix AZ; BR/TR/6´0˝/190; d9.2; C7																								
1908	Cle A	8	16	1	3	0	0	0	2	0	0	—	.188	.188	.188	22	-1	0	.955	-0	*149*	*54*	C8	—	-0.2
1909	Cle A	1	4	0	2	0	0	0	1	0	0	—	.500	.500	.500	207	0	0	1.000	0	*142*	*85*	/C	—	0.1
1910	Cle A	34	111	4	23	0	0	0	7	2	1	—	.207	.228	.207	36	-9	1	.982	0	*91*	*95*	C33	—	-0.6
1911	Cle A	35	107	5	15	1	2	0	10	3	0	—	.140	.164	.187	-2	-15	2	.961	-1	*87*	*119*	C34/1	—	-1.4
1913	Cle A	17	47	3	11	1	0	0	9	4	2	1	.234	.321	.255	67	-2	1	.924	1	*122*	*96*	C17	—	0.1
1914	Bro F	102	335	24	92	6	2	0	29	12	3	23	.275	.306	.304	67	-21	7	.970	-7	*86*	*107*	C97	—	-2.1
1915	Bro F	96	290	25	75	13	2	0	22	6	2	20	.259	.279	.317	68	-18	3	.960	-10	*81*	*112*	C81	—	-2.2
Total	7	293	910	62	221	21	6	0	80	27	8	44	.243	.271	.279	55	-66	14	.964	-17	*89*	*107*	C271/1	—	-6.3
LAND, DOC	William Gilbert (b Doc Burrell Land); B5.14.1903 Binnsville MS; D4.14.1986 Livingston AL; BL/TL/5´11˝/165; d10.6; Col Alabama																								
1929	Was A	1	3	0	0	0	0	0	0	1	0	0	.000	.250	.000	-30	-1	0-0	1.000	-0	54	0	/cf	—	-0.1
LANDENBERGER, KEN	Kenneth Henry "Red"; B7.29.1928 Lyndhurst OH; D7.28.1960 Cleveland OH; BL/TL/6´3˝/200; d9.20; Col Ohio U.																								
1952	Chi A	2	5	0	1	0	0	0	0	0	0	2	.200	.200	.200	11	-1	0-0	1.000	0	135	0	/1	0	-0.1
LANDESTOY, RAFAEL	Rafael Silvialdo (Santana); B5.28.1953 Bani, D.R.; BB/TR (BR 1977)/5´10˝/(163–180); d8.27; C3; OF(12/4/7)																								
1977	†LA N	15	18	6	5	0	0	0	0	3-0	0	2	.278	.381	.278	80	0	2-0	1.000	-1	129	110	2b8,S3	0	-0.1
1978	Hou N	59	218	18	58	5	1	0	9	8-0	0	23	.266	.292	.298	70	-10	7-4	.980	-5	92	68	S50,O3(1/2/0),2b2	0	-1.1
1979	Hou N	129	282	33	76	9	6	0	30	29-5	1	24	.270	.338	.344	92	-3	13-4	.971	-6	95	112	2b114,S3	0	-0.3
1980	†Hou N	149	393	42	97	13	8	1	27	31-2	3	37	.247	.306	.328	84	-10	23-12	.991	-3	84	111	2b94,S65,3b3	0	-0.4
1981	Hou N	35	74	6	11	1	1	0	4	16-4	0	9	.149	.300	.189	44	-5	4-1	.966	-6	82	82	2b31	0	-0.9
	Cin N	12	11	2	2	0	0	0	1	1-0	0	0	.182	.250	.182	24	-1	1-0	1.000	-1	29	0	2b3	0	-0.2
	Year	47	85	8	13	1	1	0	5	17-4	0	9	.153	.294	.188	41	-6	5-1	.967	-6	80	79	2b34	0	-1.1
1982	Cin N	73	111	11	21	3	0	1	9	8-1	1	14	.189	.250	.243	38	-9	2-0	1.000	5	120	326	3b21,2b16,O3L,S2	0	-0.4
1983	Cin N	7	5	0	0	0	0	0	0	0-0	0	0	.000	.000	.000	-97	-1	0-0	1.000	-1	0	272	1b2/3lf	0	-0.2
	†LA N	64	64	6	11	1	1	1	1	3-0	0	8	.172	.209	.266	31	-6	0-2	1.000	3	104	142	2b14,3b10,O10(6/1/3)/S	0	-0.4
	Year	71	69	6	11	1	1	1	1	3-0	0	8	.159	.194	.246	21	-8	0-2	1.000	2	104	142	2b14,3b11,O11(7/1/3),1b2/S	0	-0.6
1984	LA N	53	54	10	10	0	0	1	2	1-0	0	6	.185	.200	.241	23	-6	2-1	.886	-2	85	99	2b14,3b11,O5(1/1/4)	0	-0.8
Total	8	596	1230	134	291	32	17	4	83	100-12	5	123	.237	.296	.300	70	-51	54-24	.976	-16	90	107	2b296,S124,3b46,O22L,1b2	0	-4.8
LANDIS, JIM	James Henry; B3.9.1934 Fresno CA; BR/TR/6´1˝/(170–180); d4.16; Col Contra Costa (CA) JC																								
1957	Chi A	96	274	38	58	11	3	2	16	45-2	3	61	.212	.329	.296	72	-9	14-4	.985	5	110	138	O90(11/38/44)	0	-0.6
1958	Chi A	142	523	72	145	23	7	15	64	52-1	8	80	.277	.351	.434	117	12	19-7	.986	-5	96	114	O142C	0	0.3
1959	†Chi A	149	515	78	140	26	7	5	60	78-5	8	68	.272	.370	.379	109	10	20-9	.993	6	109	96	O148C	0	1.0
1960	Chi A	148	494	89	125	25	6	10	49	80-4	9	84	.253	.365	.389	106	7	23-6	.985	3	104	146	O147C	0	0.6
1961	Chi A	140	534	87	151	18	8	22	85	65-0	4	71	.283	.362	.470	123	17	19-5	.988	8	113	120	O139C	0	2.3
1962	Chi A★	149	534	82	122	21	6	15	61	80-3	9	105	.228	.337	.375	92	-4	19-7	.995	-1	108	29	O144C	0	-0.8
1963	Chi A	133	396	56	89	6	6	13	45	47-4	6	75	.225	.316	.369	93	-4	8-6	**.993**	1	109	91	O124C	0	-0.7
1964	Chi A	106	298	30	62	8	4	1	18	36-1	6	64	.208	.305	.272	64	-14	5-0	.995	-1	94	119	O101C	0	-1.8
1965	KC A	118	364	46	87	15	1	3	36	57-1	3	84	.239	.346	.310	90	-2	8-3	.985	2	115	0	O108(0/108/1)	0	-0.3
1966	Cle A	85	158	23	35	5	1	3	14	20-1	2	25	.222	.317	.323	84	-3	2-1	1.000	-1	107	0	O61(18/37/17)	0	-0.6
1967	Det A	25	48	4	10	0	0	2	4	7-0	0	12	.208	.304	.333	87	-1	0-2	.952	1	105	316	O12(6/1/6)	0	-0.1
	Bos A	5	7	1	1	0	0	1	1	1-0	0	3	.143	.250	.571	126	0	0-0	1.000	0	117	0	O5R	0	0.0
	Year	30	55	5	11	0	0	3	5	8-0	0	15	.200	.297	.364	92	-1	0-2	.960	1	78	253	O17(6/1/11)	0	-0.1
	Hou N	50	143	19	36	11	1	1	14	20-0	1	35	.252	.341	.364	107	2	2-1	1.000	1	78	253	O44(28/3/14)	0	0.1
Total	11	1346	4288	625	1061	169	50	93	467	588-22	59	767	.247	.344	.375	100	11	139-51	.989	18	106	99	O1265(63/1132/87)	0	-0.6

LANDREAUX, KEN Kenneth Francis; B12.22.1954 Los Angeles CA; BL/TR/5´10˝/(164–190); [AnaA76 1/6]; d9.11; Col Arizona St.

YEAR	TM LG	G	AB	R	H	2B	3B	HR	RBI	BB-IB	HP	SO	AVG	OBP	SLG	AOPS	ABR	SB-CS	FA	FR	RNG	THR	GAMES AT POSITION	DL	BFW
1977	Cal A	23	76	6	19	5	1	0	5	5-1	0	15	.250	.296	.342	76	-3	1-1	.970	4	114	358	O22C	0	0.1
1978	Cal A	93	260	37	58	7	5	5	23	20-4	2	20	.223	.284	.346	79	-9	7-3	.986	1	97	137	O83(32/23/35)/D	0	-1.0
1979	Min A	151	564	81	172	27	5	15	83	37-4	4	57	.305	.347	.450	110	7	10-3	.981	-15	81	99	O147(49/98/0)	0	-0.9
1980	Min A★	129	484	56	136	23	11	7	62	39-4	2	42	.281	.334	.417	98	-2	8-6	.976	-14	79	93	O120(54/68/0),D6	0	-1.9
1981	†LA N	99	390	48	98	16	4	7	41	25-3	1	42	.251	.297	.367	92	-6	18-4	**1.000**	-9	86	62	O95C	0	-1.5
1982	LA N	129	461	71	131	23	7	7	50	39-2	4	54	.284	.341	.410	114	8	31-10	.986	-5	100	44	O117(1/116/0)	0	0.6
1983	†LA N	141	481	63	135	25	3	17	66	34-5	2	52	.281	.328	.451	115	8	30-11	.990	-3	98	68	O137(7/131/2)	0	0.7
1984	LA N	134	438	39	110	11	5	11	47	29-3	1	35	.251	.295	.374	88	-9	10-9	.986	-15	79	46	O129(9/105/18)	15	-2.8
1985	†LA N	147	482	70	129	26	2	12	50	33-2	1	37	.268	.311	.405	102	0	15-5	.975	-8	94	55	O140(11/126/4)	0	-0.8
1986	LA N	103	283	34	74	13	2	4	29	22-3	1	39	.261	.313	.364	94	-3	10-5	.955	-2	98	128	O85(20/69/1)	37	-0.6
1987	LA N	115	182	17	37	4	0	6	23	16-2	1	28	.203	.269	.324	58	-12	5-3	.951	1	96	190	O63(15/6/45)	0	-1.2
Total	11	1264	4101	522	1099	180	45	91	479	299-33	19	421	.268	.317	.400	99	-21	145-60	.981	-63	90	87	O1138(198/859/105),D7	52	-9.3

LANDRITH, HOBIE Hobert Neal; B3.16.1930 Decatur IL; BL/TR/5´10˝/(170–175); d7.30; C1; Col Michigan St.

YEAR	TM LG	G	AB	R	H	2B	3B	HR	RBI	BB-IB	HP	SO	AVG	OBP	SLG	AOPS	ABR	SB-CS	FA	FR	RNG	THR	GAMES AT POSITION	DL	BFW
1950	Cin N	4	14	1	3	0	0	0	1	2	0	1	.214	.313	.214	41	-1	0	1.000	-1	*107*	*118*	C4	100	-0.2
1951	Cin N	4	13	3	5	1	0	0	0	1	0	1	.385	.429	.462	137	1	0-0	1.000	1	*82*	*99*	C4	0	0.2
1952	Cin N	15	50	1	13	4	0	0	4	0	0	4	.260	.260	.340	65	-2	0-1	1.000	0	*101*	*101*	C14	0	-0.2
1953	Cin N	52	154	15	37	3	1	3	16	12	1	8	.240	.299	.331	64	-9	2-0	.985	0	*134*	*53*	C47	0	-0.6
1954	Cin N	48	81	12	16	0	0	5	14	18	0	9	.198	.340	.383	86	-1	1-0	.986	2	*181*	*116*	C42	0	0.2
1955	Cin N	43	87	9	22	3	0	4	7	10-1	0	14	.253	.330	.425	93	-1	0-1	1.000	3	*117*	*131*	C27	44	0.2
1956	Chi N	111	312	22	69	10	3	4	32	39-15	1	38	.221	.307	.311	69	-13	0-2	.975	-2	*75*	***136***	C99	0	-1.2
1957	StL N	75	214	18	52	6	0	3	26	25-1	0	27	.243	.318	.313	70	-8	1-2	.987	6	113	121	C67	0	0.0
1958	StL N	70	144	9	31	4	0	3	13	26-4	0	21	.215	.335	.306	68	-6	0-1	.992	1	58	74	C45	0	-0.3
1959	SF N	109	283	30	71	14	0	3	29	43-7	0	23	.251	.345	.332	85	-4	0-4	.992	12	126	126	C109	0	1.1
1960	SF N	71	190	18	46	10	0	1	20	23-2	0	11	.242	.321	.311	79	-5	1-1	.966	-7	72	85	C70	0	-0.9
1961	SF N	43	71	11	17	4	0	2	10	12-3	0	7	.239	.337	.380	97	0	0-0	.985	0	101	117	C30	0	0.1
1962	NY N	23	45	6	13	3	0	1	7	8-0	0	3	.289	.389	.422	118	2	0-0	.968	-2	55	91	C21	0	0.1
	Bal A	60	167	18	37	4	1	4	17	19-1	1	9	.222	.302	.329	75	-6	0-0	.982	-1	79	177	C60	0	-0.4
1963	Bal A	2	1	0	0	0	0	0	0	0-0	0	0	.000	.000	.000	-99	0	0-0	1.000	0	0	0	/C	0	0.0
	Was A	42	103	6	18	3	0	1	7	15-1	0	12	.175	.280	.233	46	-7	0-0	.978	0	70	185	C37	29	-0.6
	Year	44	104	6	18	3	0	1	7	15-1	0	12	.173	.277	.231	44	-7	0-0	.978	0	70	184	C38	0	-0.6
Total	14	772	1929	179	450	69	5	34	203	253-35	3	188	.233	.320	.327	76	-60	5-12	.983	14	*98*	*120*	C677	173	-2.5

LANDRUM, CED Cedric Bernard; B9.3.1963 Butler AL; BL/TR/5´7˝/167; d5.28; Col North Alabama

YEAR	TM LG	G	AB	R	H	2B	3B	HR	RBI	BB-IB	HP	SO	AVG	OBP	SLG	AOPS	ABR	SB-CS	FA	FR	RNG	THR	GAMES AT POSITION	DL	BFW
1991	Chi N	56	86	28	20	2	1	0	6	10-0	0	18	.233	.313	.279	65	-4	27-5	.968	-1	104	0	O44(25/18/8)	0	-0.1
1993	NY N	22	19	2	5	1	0	0	1	0-0	0	5	.263	.263	.316	55	-1	0-0	ø	-0	0	0	O3L	0	-0.1
Total	2	78	105	30	25	3	1	0	7	10-0	0	23	.238	.304	.286	63	-5	27-5	.968	-1	102	0	O47(28/18/8)	0	-0.2

LANDRUM, DON Donald Leroy; B2.16.1936 Santa Rosa CA; D1.9.2003 Pittsburg CA; BL/TR/6´0˝/180; d9.28

YEAR	TM LG	G	AB	R	H	2B	3B	HR	RBI	BB-IB	HP	SO	AVG	OBP	SLG	AOPS	ABR	SB-CS	FA	FR	RNG	THR	GAMES AT POSITION	DL	BFW
1957	Phi N	2	7	1	1	1	0	0	0	2-0	0	1	.143	.333	.286	71	0	0-0	1.000	1	171	0	O2C	0	0.0
1960	StL N	13	49	7	12	0	1	2	3	4-0	1	6	.245	.315	.408	88	-1	3-0	1.000	1	124	107	O13(2/13/3)	0	0.1
1961	StL N	28	66	5	11	2	0	1	3	5-0	0	14	.167	.225	.242	22	-7	1-0	1.000	2	114	233	O25(6/20/4)/2	0	-0.6
1962	StL N	32	35	11	11	0	0	0	3	4-1	0	2	.314	.375	.314	82	-1	2-0	1.000	-1	97	0	O26(16/4/7)	0	-0.1
	Chi N	83	238	29	67	5	2	1	15	30-0	3	31	.282	.369	.332	87	-3	9-2	.969	-2	98	73	O59(1/41/18)	0	-0.6
	Year	115	273	40	78	5	2	1	18	34-1	3	33	.286	.370	.330	85	-4	11-2	.973	-2	98	61	O85(17/45/25)	0	-0.7
1963	Chi N	84	227	27	55	4	1	1	10	13-1	4	42	.242	.294	.282	64	-10	6-3	.972	-5	82	85	O57(0/55/3)	0	-1.9
1964	Chi N	11	11	2	0	0	0	0	0	1-0	0	2	.000	.083	.000	-71	-3	0-0	1.000	1	42	1462	/cf	0	-0.2
1965	Chi N	131	425	60	96	20	4	6	34	36-3	10	84	.226	.300	.334	77	-12	14-8	.988	-2	102	49	O115(3/111/1)	0	-1.9
1966	SF N	72	102	9	19	4	0	1	7	9-0	1	18	.186	.259	.255	42	-8	1-1	.968	4	104	313	O54(38/14/3)	0	-0.6
Total	8	456	1160	151	272	36	8	12	75	104-5	19	200	.234	.307	.310	69	-45	36-14	.982	-1	99	102	O352(66/261/39)/2	0	-5.8

LANDRUM, JESSE Jesse Glenn; B7.31.1912 Crockett TX; D6.27.1983 Beaumont TX; BR/TR/5´11.5˝/175; d4.26; Col Texas A&M

YEAR	TM LG	G	AB	R	H	2B	3B	HR	RBI	BB-IB	HP	SO	AVG	OBP	SLG	AOPS	ABR	SB-CS	FA	FR	RNG	THR	GAMES AT POSITION	DL	BFW
1938	Chi A	4	6	0	0	0	0	0	1	0	0	2	.000	.000	.000	-98	-2	0-0	1.000	-0	109	156	2b3	—	-0.2

LANDRUM, TITO Terry Lee; B10.25.1954 Joplin MO; BR/TR/5´11˝/175; d7.23

YEAR	TM LG	G	AB	R	H	2B	3B	HR	RBI	BB-IB	HP	SO	AVG	OBP	SLG	AOPS	ABR	SB-CS	FA	FR	RNG	THR	GAMES AT POSITION	DL	BFW
1980	StL N	35	77	6	19	2	2	0	7	6-0	1	17	.247	.306	.325	74	-3	3-2	.976	-1	93	65	O29(17/8/6)	0	-0.5
1981	StL N	81	119	13	31	5	4	0	10	6-0	1	14	.261	.297	.370	86	-3	4-2	1.000	2	94	190	O67(43/6/24)	0	-0.2
1982	StL N	79	72	12	20	3	0	2	14	8-0	1	18	.278	.358	.403	109	1	0-1	1.000	2	111	124	O56(24/6/29)	0	0.2
1983	StL N	6	5	0	1	0	1	0	0	1-0	0	2	.200	.333	.600	153	0	1-0	1.000	-0	72	0	O5(4/0/1)	0	0.0
	†Bal A	26	42	8	13	2	0	1	4	1-0	0	11	.310	.318	.429	107	0	0-2	1.000	2	140	0	O26(11/4/15)	0	0.1
1984	StL N	105	173	21	47	9	1	3	26	10-1	0	27	.272	.306	.387	97	-1	3-4	.979	-3	90	30	O88(55/20/25)	0	-0.8
1985	†StL N	85	161	21	45	8	2	4	21	19-1	0	30	.280	.356	.429	119	4	1-4	1.000	1	108	65	O73(10/0/67)	21	0.2
1986	StL N	96	205	24	43	7	1	2	17	20-2	1	41	.210	.279	.283	57	-12	3-1	.993	7	123	135	O78(9/4/70)	0	-0.8
1987	StL N	30	50	5	10	1	0	0	6	7-2	0	14	.200	.298	.220	39	-4	1-1	1.000	3	148	114	O23(2/7/17)/1	34	-0.2
	LA N	51	67	8	16	3	0	1	4	3-0	1	16	.239	.282	.328	63	-4	1-1	.971	1	124	107	O31(19/0/14)	0	-0.3
	Year	81	117	13	26	4	0	1	10	10-2	1	30	.222	.289	.282	52	-8	2-2	.987	4	136	110	O54(21/7/31)/1	0	-0.5
1988	Bal A	13	24	2	3	0	1	0	2	4-0	0	6	.125	.250	.208	30	-2	0-0	1.000	-1	90	0	O12(5/0/8)/D	0	-0.3
Total	9	607	995	120	248	40	12	13	111	85-6	5	196	.249	.309	.353	84	-24	17-18	.992	13	109	93	O488(199/55/276)/D1	55	-2.6

LANE, CHAPPY George M.; B Pittsburgh PA; BR/?/165; d5.16

YEAR	TM LG	G	AB	R	H	2B	3B	HR	RBI	BB-IB	HP	SO	AVG	OBP	SLG	AOPS	ABR	SB-CS	FA	FR	RNG	THR	GAMES AT POSITION	DL	BFW
1882	Pit AA	57	214	26	38	8	2	3	—	5	—	—	.178	.196	.276	60	-8	—	.974	5	111	108	1b43,O13(0/12/1),C2	—	-0.7
1884	Tol AA	57	215	26	49	9	5	1	—	2	2	—	.228	.242	.330	82	-5	—	.948	2	125	79	1b46,O9(5/0/4),3b2/C	—	-0.7
Total	2	114	429	52	87	17	7	4	—	7	2	—	.203	.219	.303	72	-13	—	.961	7	118	93	1b89,O22(5/12/5),C3,3b2	—	-1.4

LANE, HUNTER James Hunter "Dodo"; B7.20.1900 Pulaski TN; D9.12.1994 Memphis TN; BR/TR/5´11˝/165; d5.13; Col Tennessee

YEAR	TM LG	G	AB	R	H	2B	3B	HR	RBI	BB-IB	HP	SO	AVG	OBP	SLG	AOPS	ABR	SB-CS	FA	FR	RNG	THR	GAMES AT POSITION	DL	BFW
1924	Bos N	7	15	0	1	0	0	0	0	1	0	1	.067	.125	.067	-49	-3	0-0	.909	-1	62	0	3b4/2	—	-0.4

LANE, JASON Jason Dean; B12.22.1976 Santa Rosa CA; BR/TL/6´2˝/220; [HouN99 6/203]; d5.10; Col USC

YEAR	TM LG	G	AB	R	H	2B	3B	HR	RBI	BB-IB	HP	SO	AVG	OBP	SLG	AOPS	ABR	SB-CS	FA	FR	RNG	THR	GAMES AT POSITION	DL	BFW
2002	Hou N	44	69	12	20	3	1	4	10	10-1	0	12	.290	.375	.536	128	3	1-1	.980	3	118	226	O38(11/1/27)	0	0.5
2003	Hou N	18	27	5	8	2	0	4	10	0-0	0	2	.296	.296	.815	167	2	0-0	1.000	-1	68	0	O10(3/6/2)	0	0.1
2004	†Hou N	107	136	21	37	10	2	4	19	16-0	1	33	.272	.348	.463	105	1	1-0	.984	-0	98	110	O76(35/17/24),1b3	0	0.0
2005	†Hou N	145	517	65	138	34	4	26	78	32-1	7	105	.267	.316	.499	108	4	6-2	.976	-6	94	54	O141(4/6/137)	0	-0.8
2006	Hou N	112	288	44	58	10	0	15	45	49-0	2	75	.201	.318	.392	80	-9	1-2	1.000	-1	102	25	O98(6/5/89)/1	0	-1.4
Total	5	426	1037	147	261	59	7	53	162	107-2	10	227	.252	.324	.475	103	1	9-5	.985	-6	98	64	O363(59/35/279),1b4	0	-1.6

LANE, MARVIN Marvin; B1.18.1950 Sandersville GA; BR/TR/5´11˝/180; [DetA68 10/222]; d9.4

YEAR	TM LG	G	AB	R	H	2B	3B	HR	RBI	BB-IB	HP	SO	AVG	OBP	SLG	AOPS	ABR	SB-CS	FA	FR	RNG	THR	GAMES AT POSITION	DL	BFW
1971	Det A	8	14	0	2	0	0	0	1	1-0	0	3	.143	.200	.143	-1	-2	0-0	1.000	-0	90	0	O6(3/0/3)	0	-0.3
1972	Det A	8	6	2	0	0	0	0	0	0-0	0	2	.000	.000	.000	-97	-1	0-0	1.000	-0	96	0	O3(1/1/1)	0	-0.2
1973	Det A	6	8	2	2	0	0	1	2	2-0	0	2	.250	.400	.625	174	1	0-0	1.000	0	147	0	O4(3/0/3)	0	0.1
1974	Det A	50	103	16	24	4	1	2	9	19-1	0	24	.233	.352	.350	99	1	2-0	.986	1	105	127	O46(40/2/6)/D	0	0.0
1976	Det A	18	48	3	9	1	0	0	5	6-0	0	11	.188	.273	.208	42	-3	0-0	.960	-1	84	116	O15(10/5/0)	0	-0.5
Total	5	90	179	23	37	5	1	3	17	28-1	0	42	.207	.313	.296	74	-4	2-0	.983	0	101	106	O74(57/8/13)/D	0	-0.9

LANE, DICK Richard Harrison; B6.28.1927 Highland Park MI; BR/TR/5´11˝/178; d6.20; Col Detroit Mercy

YEAR	TM LG	G	AB	R	H	2B	3B	HR	RBI	BB-IB	HP	SO	AVG	OBP	SLG	AOPS	ABR	SB-CS	FA	FR	RNG	THR	GAMES AT POSITION	DL	BFW
1949	Chi A	12	42	4	5	0	0	0	4	5	0	3	.119	.213	.119	-11	-7	0-1	1.000	1	103	245	O11L	0	-0.7

LANG, DON Donald Charles; B3.15.1915 Selma CA; BR/TR/6´0˝/175; d7.4

YEAR	TM LG	G	AB	R	H	2B	3B	HR	RBI	BB-IB	HP	SO	AVG	OBP	SLG	AOPS	ABR	SB-CS	FA	FR	RNG	THR	GAMES AT POSITION	DL	BFW
1938	Cin N	21	50	5	13	3	1	1	11	2	0	7	.260	.288	.420	95	-1	0	.976	1	106	155	3b15/2S	—	0.1
1948	StL N	117	323	30	87	14	1	4	31	47	1	38	.269	.364	.356	90	-3	2	.964	4	106	97	3b95,2b2	0	0.1
Total	2	138	373	35	100	17	2	5	42	49	1	45	.268	.355	.365	91	-4	2	.966	5	106	104	3b110,2b3/S	0	0.2

LANGE, BILL William Alexander "Little Eva"; B6.6.1871 San Francisco CA; D7.23.1950 San Francisco CA; BR/TR/6´1.5˝/190; d4.27; OF(15/702/2)

YEAR	TM LG	G	AB	R	H	2B	3B	HR	RBI	BB-IB	HP	SO	AVG	OBP	SLG	AOPS	ABR	SB-CS	FA	FR	RNG	THR	GAMES AT POSITION	DL	BFW
1893	Chi N	117	469	92	132	8	7	8	88	52	4	20	.281	.358	.380	98	-2	47	.888	-5	93	70	2b57,O40(14/27/0),3b8,S7,C7	—	-0.5
1894	Chi N	113	449	86	146	17	9	6	91	56	2	18	.325	.402	.443	98	-2	66	.912	4	136	207	O111(1/108/2),S2/3	—	-0.3
1895	Chi N	123	478	120	186	27	16	10	98	55	4	24	.389	.456	.575	155	39	67	.924	7	152	140	O123C	—	3.1

YEAR	TM LG	G	AB	R	H	2B	3B	HR	RBI	BB-IB	HP	SO	AVG	OBP	SLG	AOPS	ABR	SB-CS	FA	FR	RNG	THR	GAMES AT POSITION	DL	BFW
1896	Chi N	122	469	114	153	21	16	4	92	65	5	24	.326	.414	.465	126	19	84	.932	6	105	67	O121C/C	—	1.5
1897	Chi N	118	479	119	163	24	14	5	83	48	5	—	.340	.406	.480	129	19	**73**	.946	1	102	116	O118C	—	1.1
1898	Chi N	113	442	79	141	16	11	5	69	36	5	—	.319	.377	.439	134	18	22	.970	6	120	113	O111C,1b2	—	1.6
1899	Chi N	107	416	81	135	21	7	1	58	38	1	—	.325	.382	.416	122	13	41	.976	7	147	281	O94C,1b14	—	1.3
Total	7	813	3202	691	1056	134	80	39	579	350	26	86	.330	.400	.458	123	104	400	.942	26	125	144	O718C,2b57,1b16,S9,3b9,C8	—	7.8

LANGERHANS, RYAN Ryan David; B2.20.1980 San Antonio TX; BL/TL/6´3˝/(195–205); [AtlN98 3/101]; d4.28

YEAR	TM LG	G	AB	R	H	2B	3B	HR	RBI	BB-IB	HP	SO	AVG	OBP	SLG	AOPS	ABR	SB-CS	FA	FR	RNG	THR	GAMES AT POSITION	DL	BFW
2002	Atl N	1	1	0	0	0	0	0	0	0-0	0	0	.000	.000	.000	-99	0	0-0	ø	-0	0	0	/lf	0	0.0
2003	Atl N	16	15	2	4	0	0	0	0	0-0	0	6	.267	.267	.267	40	-1	0-0	1.000	1	109	305	O14(3/4/9)	0	-0.1
2005	†Atl N	128	326	48	87	22	3	8	42	37-3	5	75	.267	.348	.426	102	1	0-2	.995	-1	102	55	O114(54/19/48)	0	-0.4
2006	Atl N	131	315	46	76	16	3	7	28	50-8	3	91	.241	.350	.378	86	-6	1-2	.995	-1	103	40	O119(104/24/2)	0	-0.9
Total	4	276	657	96	167	38	6	15	70	87-11	8	172	.254	.347	.399	92	-6	1-4	.995	-1	103	54	O248(162/47/59)	0	-1.4

LANGFORD, SAM Elton; B5.21.1900 Briggs TX; D7.31.1993 Plainview TX; BL/TR/6´0˝/180; d4.13

YEAR	TM LG	G	AB	R	H	2B	3B	HR	RBI	BB-IB	HP	SO	AVG	OBP	SLG	AOPS	ABR	SB-CS	FA	FR	RNG	THR	GAMES AT POSITION	DL	BFW
1926	Bos A	1	1	1	0	0	0	0	0	0	0	0	.000	.000	.000	-99	0	0-0	ø	0	—	—	/H	—	0.0
1927	Cle A	20	67	10	18	5	0	1	7	5	3	7	.269	.347	.388	90	-1	0-1	1.000	-1	91	58	O20(1/18/1)	—	-0.3
1928	Cle A	110	427	50	118	17	8	4	50	21	1	35	.276	.312	.382	81	-14	3-8	.972	-8	93	46	O107(32/76/0)	—	-2.9
Total	3	131	495	61	136	22	8	5	57	26	4	42	.275	.316	.382	81	-15	3-9	.976	-10	93	48	O127(33/94/1)	—	-3.2

LANGSFORD, BOB Robert William (b Robert Hugo Lankswert); B8.5.1865 Louisville KY; D1.10.1907 Louisville KY; BL/TL/5´7˝/168; d6.18

YEAR	TM LG	G	AB	R	H	2B	3B	HR	RBI	BB-IB	HP	SO	AVG	OBP	SLG	AOPS	ABR	SB-CS	FA	FR	RNG	THR	GAMES AT POSITION	DL	BFW
1899	Lou N	1	4	0	0	0	0	0	0	0	0	—	.000	.000	.000	-99	-1	0	1.000	-0	63	0	/S	—	-0.1

LANIER, HAL Harold Clifton; B7.4.1942 Denton NC; BR/TR (BB 1967p, 68–70)/6´2˝/(180–186); d6.18; M3/C7; f–Max

YEAR	TM LG	G	AB	R	H	2B	3B	HR	RBI	BB-IB	HP	SO	AVG	OBP	SLG	AOPS	ABR	SB-CS	FA	FR	RNG	THR	GAMES AT POSITION	DL	BFW
1964	SF N	98	383	40	105	16	3	2	28	5-0	0	44	.274	.283	.347	75	-14	2-1	.979	12	108	88	2b98,S3	0	0.7
1965	SF N	159	522	41	118	15	9	0	39	21-4	0	67	.226	.256	.289	52	-35	2-1	.976	-6	97	86	2b158/S	0	-2.9
1966	SF N	149	459	37	106	14	2	3	37	16-7	0	49	.231	.256	.290	50	-31	1-0	.991	5	104	111	2b112,S41	0	-1.5
1967	SF N	151	525	37	112	16	3	0	42	16-2	2	61	.213	.239	.255	42	-41	2-2	.974	20	**109**	107	S137,2b34	0	-0.8
1968	SF N	151	486	37	100	14	1	0	27	12-0	0	57	.206	.222	.239	39	-37	2-2	**.979**	17	104	94	S150	0	-0.9
1969	SF N	150	495	37	113	9	1	0	35	25-5	0	68	.228	.263	.251	46	-37	0-1	.969	24	**116**	118	S150	0	0.4
1970	SF N	134	438	33	101	13	1	2	41	21-4	0	41	.231	.265	.279	46	-34	1-2	.967	8	101	103	S130,2b4,1b2	0	-1.2
1971	†SF N	109	206	21	48	8	0	1	13	15-3	0	26	.233	.283	.286	63	-10	0-0	.957	-5	83	76	3b83,2b13,S8,1b3	0	-1.6
1972	NY A	60	103	5	22	3	0	0	6	2-0	1	13	.214	.234	.243	43	-7	1-2	.973	1	107	148	3b47,S9,2b3	0	-0.7
1973	NY A	35	86	9	18	3	0	0	5	3-0	1	10	.209	.244	.244	39	-7	0-0	.960	-2	99	107	S26,2b8/3	0	-0.6
Total	10	1196	3703	297	843	111	20	8	273	136-25	4	436	.228	.255	.275	50	-253	11-11	.971	73	107	104	S655,2b430,3b131,1b5	0	-9.1

LANIER, RIMP Lorenzo; B10.19.1948 Tuskegee AL; BL/TR/5´8˝/150; d9.11

YEAR	TM LG	G	AB	R	H	2B	3B	HR	RBI	BB-IB	HP	SO	AVG	OBP	SLG	AOPS	ABR	SB-CS	FA	FR	RNG	THR	GAMES AT POSITION	DL	BFW
1971	Pit N	6	4	0	0	0	0	0	0	0-0	1	1	.000	.200	.000	-39	-1	0-0	ø	0	—	—	/H	0	-0.1

LANKFORD, RAY Raymond Lewis; B6.5.1967 Los Angeles CA; BL/TL/5´11˝/(180–200); [StLN87 3/72]; d8.21; Col Modesto (CA) JC

YEAR	TM LG	G	AB	R	H	2B	3B	HR	RBI	BB-IB	HP	SO	AVG	OBP	SLG	AOPS	ABR	SB-CS	FA	FR	RNG	THR	GAMES AT POSITION	DL	BFW
1990	StL N	39	126	12	36	10	1	3	12	13-0	0	27	.286	.353	.452	119	3	8-2	.989	1	113	57	O35C	0	0.5
1991	StL N	151	566	83	142	23	**15**	9	69	41-1	1	114	.251	.301	.392	93	-8	44-20	.984	0	107	89	O149C	0	-0.6
1992	StL N	153	598	87	175	40	6	20	86	72-6	5	147	.293	.371	.480	143	35	42-24	.996	-4	102	53	O153C	0	3.3
1993	StL N	127	407	64	97	17	3	7	45	81-7	3	111	.238	.366	.346	93	0	14-14	.978	-4	97	93	O121C	15	-0.4
1994	StL N	109	416	89	111	25	5	19	57	58-3	4	113	.267	.359	.488	119	12	11-10	.978	-2	99	87	O104C	0	1.0
1995	StL N	132	483	81	134	35	2	25	82	63-6	2	110	.277	.360	.513	126	19	24-8	.990	-2	98	100	O129C	0	2.0
1996	†StL N	149	545	100	150	36	8	21	86	79-10	3	133	.275	.366	.486	123	20	35-7	**.997**	4	105	122	O144C	0	3.0
1997	StL N★	133	465	94	137	36	3	31	98	95-10	0	125	.295	.411	.585	158	43	21-11	.971	-6	99	64	O131C	21	3.8
1998	StL N	154	533	94	156	37	1	31	105	86-5	3	151	.293	.391	.540	143	36	26-5	.986	-5	98	77	O145C/D	0	3.6
1999	StL N	122	422	77	129	32	1	15	63	49-3	3	110	.306	.380	.493	117	12	14-4	.987	3	106	92	O106(105/2/0)/D	19	1.2
2000	†StL N	128	392	73	99	16	3	26	65	70-1	4	148	.253	.367	.508	117	10	5-6	.973	-4	90	63	O117(116/2/0)/D	0	0.1
2001	StL N	91	264	38	62	18	3	15	39	44-8	2	105	.235	.345	.496	112	5	4-2	.966	-1	96	98	O85L	0	0.2
	SD N	40	125	20	36	10	1	4	19	18-1	2	40	.288	.386	.480	132	7	6-0	.985	-2	92	49	O38(21/16/2)	0	0.5
	Year	131	389	58	98	28	4	19	58	62-9	4	145	.252	.358	.491	118	12	10-2	.971	-3	95	83	O123(106/16/2)	0	0.7
2002	SD N	81	205	20	46	7	1	6	26	30-3	2	61	.224	.326	.356	88	-4	2-2	.953	2	105	131	O59(59/3/0)/D	68	-0.4
2004	StL N	92	200	36	51	14	1	6	22	29-4	2	55	.255	.349	.425	99	1	2-2	.956	-2	95	38	O70(66/4/0)	41	-0.4
Total	14	1701	5747	968	1561	356	54	238	874	828-68	36	1550	.272	.364	.477	122	191	258-117	.983	-22	100	83	O1586(452/1138/2),D4	164	17.4

LANNING, RED Lester Alfred; B5.13.1895 Harvard IL; D6.13.1962 Bristol CT; BL/TL/5´9˝/165; d6.20; Col Wesleyan; ▲

YEAR	TM LG	G	AB	R	H	2B	3B	HR	RBI	BB-IB	HP	SO	AVG	OBP	SLG	AOPS	ABR	SB-CS	FA	FR	RNG	THR	GAMES AT POSITION	DL	BFW
1916	Phi A	19	33	5	6	2	0	0	1	10	0	9	.182	.372	.242	89	0	0	.909	-1	82	0	O9(7/0/6),P6	—	-0.1

LANSFORD, CARNEY Carney Ray; B2.7.1957 San Jose CA; BR/TR/6´2˝/195; [CalA75 3/49]; d4.8; C3; b–Jody

YEAR	TM LG	G	AB	R	H	2B	3B	HR	RBI	BB-IB	HP	SO	AVG	OBP	SLG	AOPS	ABR	SB-CS	FA	FR	RNG	THR	GAMES AT POSITION	DL	BFW
1978	Cal A	121	453	63	133	23	2	8	52	31-2	4	67	.294	.339	.406	114	8	20-9	.942	-21	75	80	3b117,S2/D	26	-1.4
1979	†Cal A	157	654	114	188	30	5	19	79	39-2	3	115	.287	.329	.436	108	5	20-8	**.983**	-15	82	93	3b157	0	-1.0
1980	Cal A	151	602	87	157	27	3	15	80	50-2	0	93	.261	.312	.390	94	-6	14-5	.955	-20	79	88	3b150	0	-2.7
1981	Bos A	102	399	61	134	23	3	4	52	34-3	2	28	**.336**	.389	.439	130	17	15-10	.951	-2	97	104	3b86,D16	0	1.3
1982	Bos A	128	482	65	145	28	4	11	63	46-2	2	48	.301	.359	.444	114	10	9-4	.968	-15	86	77	3b114,D13	27	-0.6
1983	Oak A	80	299	43	92	16	2	10	45	22-4	3	33	.308	.357	.475	135	14	3-8	.957	-6	94	105	3b78/S	19	0.5
1984	Oak A	151	597	70	179	31	5	14	74	40-6	3	62	.300	.342	.439	123	18	9-3	.957	-2	97	90	3b151	0	1.4
1985	Oak A	98	401	51	111	18	2	13	46	18-1	4	27	.277	.311	.429	109	3	2-3	.976	-27	64	59	3b97	33	-2.6
1986	Oak A	151	591	80	168	16	4	19	72	39-2	5	51	.284	.332	.421	112	7	16-7	.982	-18	85	78	3b100,1b60/2D	0	-1.4
1987	Oak A	151	554	89	160	27	4	19	76	60-11	9	44	.289	.366	.455	124	21	27-8	**.980**	3	100	60	3b142,1b17,D4	0	2.3
1988	†Oak A★	150	556	80	155	20	2	7	57	35-4	7	35	.279	.327	.360	96	-4	29-8	**.979**	-12	87	72	3b143,1b9/2D	0	-1.2
1989	†Oak A	148	551	81	185	28	2	2	52	51-2	9	25	.336	.398	.405	132	26	37-15	.957	-20	77	55	3b136,1b15,D3	0	0.8
1990	†Oak A	134	507	58	136	15	1	3	50	45-4	6	50	.268	.333	.320	87	-8	16-14	**.970**	-9	89	116	3b126,1b5,D5	15	-1.9
1991	Oak A	5	16	0	1	0	0	0	1	0-0	0	2	.063	.063	.063	-69	-4	0-0	1.000	-2	53	0	3b4/D	176	-0.6
1992	†Oak A	135	496	65	130	30	1	7	75	43-0	7	39	.262	.325	.369	100	1	7-2	.965	-20	79	52	3b119,1b18/SD	0	-2.0
Total	15	1862	7158	1007	2074	332	40	151	874	553-45	64	719	.290	.343	.411	111	108	224-104	.966	-186	85	80	3b1720,1b124,D49,S4,2b2	296	-9.1

LANSFORD, JODY Joseph Dale; B1.15.1961 San Jose CA; BR/TR/6´5˝/225; [SDN79 1/14]; d7.31; b–Carney

YEAR	TM LG	G	AB	R	H	2B	3B	HR	RBI	BB-IB	HP	SO	AVG	OBP	SLG	AOPS	ABR	SB-CS	FA	FR	RNG	THR	GAMES AT POSITION	DL	BFW
1982	SD N	13	22	6	4	0	0	0	3	6-0	0	4	.182	.345	.182	58	-1	0-1	.986	-1	74	208	1b9	0	-0.2
1983	SD N	12	8	1	2	0	0	1	2	0-0	0	3	.250	.250	.625	139	0	0-0	1.000	0	98	88	1b8	0	0.0
Total	2	25	30	7	6	0	0	1	5	6-0	0	7	.200	.324	.300	82	-1	0-1	.988	-1	79	185	1b17	0	-0.2

LANSING, MIKE Michael Thomas; B4.3.1968 Rawlins WY; BR/TR/6´0˝/(180–195); [MiaI90 5/155]; d4.7; Col Wichita St.

YEAR	TM LG	G	AB	R	H	2B	3B	HR	RBI	BB-IB	HP	SO	AVG	OBP	SLG	AOPS	ABR	SB-CS	FA	FR	RNG	THR	GAMES AT POSITION	DL	BFW
1993	Mon N	141	491	64	141	29	1	3	45	46-2	5	56	.287	.352	.369	90	-5	23-5	.942	10	118	171	3b81,S51,2b25	0	1.2
1994	Mon N	106	394	44	105	21	2	5	35	30-3	7	37	.266	.328	.368	81	-11	12-8	.983	1	93	111	2b82,3b27,S12	0	-0.6
1995	Mon N	127	467	47	119	30	2	10	62	28-2	3	65	.255	.299	.392	78	-15	27-4	.991	15	107	97	2b127,S2	15	1.0
1996	Mon N	159	641	99	183	40	2	11	53	44-1	10	85	.285	.341	.406	94	-5	23-8	.985	-2	93	93	2b159,S2	0	0.3
1997	Mon N	144	572	86	161	45	2	20	70	45-2	5	92	.281	.338	.472	111	9	11-5	.987	-3	96	111	2b144	0	1.3
1998	Col N	153	584	73	161	39	2	12	66	39-4	5	88	.276	.325	.411	76	-19	10-3	.987	6	100	114	2b153/3	0	-0.5
1999	Col N	35	145	24	45	9	0	4	15	7-0	1	22	.310	.344	.455	80	-4	2-0	.990	8	103	154	2b35	136	0.5
2000	Col N	90	365	62	94	14	6	11	47	31-1	0	49	.258	.315	.419	68	-19	8-2	.983	-7	94	101	2b88	0	-2.0
	Bos A	49	139	10	27	4	0	0	13	7-1	0	26	.194	.230	.223	16	-18	0-0	1.000	-6	89	47	2b49/3	0	-2.1
2001	Bos A	106	352	45	88	23	0	8	34	22-1	1	50	.250	.294	.384	77	-12	3-3	.966	-4	89	84	S76,2b31	28	-1.0
Total	9	1110	4150	554	1124	254	17	84	440	299-17	37	570	.271	.324	.401	83	-99	119-38	.986	17	97	103	2b893,S143,3b110	179	-1.9

LAPAN, PETE Peter Nelson; B6.25.1891 Easthampton MA; D1.5.1953 Norwalk CA; BR/TR/5´7˝/165; d9.16

YEAR	TM LG	G	AB	R	H	2B	3B	HR	RBI	BB-IB	HP	SO	AVG	OBP	SLG	AOPS	ABR	SB-CS	FA	FR	RNG	THR	GAMES AT POSITION	DL	BFW
1922	Was A	11	34	7	11	1	0	1	6	3	0	4	.324	.378	.441	119	1	1-0	.958	0	*106*	*119*	C11	—	0.2
1923	Was A	2	2	0	0	0	0	0	0	0	0	0	.000	.000	.000	-99	-1	0-0	ø	0	—	—	/H	—	-0.1
Total	2	13	36	7	11	1	0	1	6	3	0	4	.306	.359	.417	107	0	1-0	.958	0	*106*	*119*	C11	—	0.1

LAPOINTE, RALPH Ralph Robert; B1.8.1922 Winooski VT; D9.13.1967 Burlington VT; BR/TR/5´11˝/185; d4.15; Col Vermont

YEAR	TM LG	G	AB	R	H	2B	3B	HR	RBI	BB-IB	HP	SO	AVG	OBP	SLG	AOPS	ABR	SB-CS	FA	FR	RNG	THR	GAMES AT POSITION	DL	BFW
1947	Phi N	56	211	33	65	7	0	1	15	17	1	15	.308	.362	.355	95	-1	8	.956	-5	100	81	S54	0	-0.3
1948	StL N	87	222	27	50	3	0	0	15	18	0	19	.225	.283	.239	40	-18	1	.965	5	101	107	2b44,S25/3	0	-1.0
Total	2	143	433	60	115	10	0	1	30	35	1	34	.266	.322	.296	66	-19	9	.955	-0	102	96	S79,2b44/3	0	-1.3

YEAR	TM LG	G	AB	R	H	2B	3B	HR	RBI	BB-IB	HP	SO	AVG	OBP	SLG	AOPS	ABR	SB-CS	FA	FR	RNG	THR	GAMES AT POSITION	DL	BFW
LaPorte, Frank	Frank Breyfogle "Pot"; B2.6.1880 Uhrichsville OH; D9.25.1939 Newcomerstown OH; BR/TR/5´8˝/175; d9.29																								
1905	NY A	11	40	4	16	1	0	1	12	1	0	—	.400	.415	.500	170	3	1	.918	-2	90	145	2b11	—	0.1
1906	NY A	123	454	60	120	23	9	2	54	22	1	—	.264	.300	.368	99	-2	10	.904	-4	94	106	3b114,2b5/lf	—	-0.3
1907	NY A	130	470	56	127	20	11	0	48	27	5	—	.270	.317	.360	107	3	10	.896	-6	95	58	3b64,O63(14/13/36)/1	—	-0.5
1908	Bos A	62	156	14	37	1	3	0	15	12	1	—	.237	.296	.282	86	-3	3	.950	6	126	80	2b27,3b12,O5(0/2/3)	—	0.4
	NY A	39	145	7	38	3	4	1	15	8	0	—	.262	.301	.359	113	1	3	.934	-2	99	111	2b26,O11(3/0/8)	—	-0.1
	Year	101	301	21	75	4	7	1	30	20	1	—	.249	.298	.319	98	-1	6	.942	4	112	96	2b53,O16(3/2/11),3b12	—	0.3
1909	NY A	89	309	35	92	19	3	0	31	18	2	—	.298	.340	.379	126	9	5	.938	-16	89	99	2b83	—	-0.7
1910	NY A	124	432	43	114	14	6	2	67	33	3	—	.264	.321	.338	100	0	16	.959	-4	106	83	2b79,O23(17/1/5),3b15	—	-0.5
1911	StL A	136	507	71	159	37	12	2	82	34	4	—	.314	.361	.446	130	19	4	.950	-3	**105**	**120**	2b133,3b3	—	1.8
1912	StL A	80	266	32	83	11	4	1	38	20	3	—	.312	.367	.395	122	7	7	.944	1	102	154	2b39,O32R	—	0.8
	Was A	40	136	13	42	9	1	0	17	12	0	—	.309	.365	.390	115	3	3	.939	-0	107	84	2b37	—	0.3
	Year	120	402	45	125	20	5	1	55	32	3	—	.311	.366	.393	120	10	10	.941	1	105	119	2b76,O32R	—	1.1
1913	Was A	79	242	25	61	5	4	0	18	17	3	16	.252	.309	.306	78	-7	10	.952	4	108	142	3b46,2b13,O12(4/0/8)	—	-0.3
1914	Ind F	133	505	86	157	27	12	4	**107**	36	4	36	.311	.361	.436	105	-3	15	.956	4	100	124	2b132	—	0.2
1915	New F	148	550	55	139	28	9	3	56	48	1	33	.253	.314	.353	93	-15	14	.960	-1	99	**117**	2b146	—	-1.5
Total	11	1194	4212	501	1185	198	78	16	560	288	27	85	.281	.331	.377	107	15	101	.952	-23	101	114	2b731,3b254,O147(39/16/92)/1	—	-0.3
Lapp, Jack	John Walker; B9.10.1884 Frazer PA; D2.6.1920 Philadelphia PA; BL/TR/5´8˝/160; d9.11																								
1908	Phi A	13	35	4	5	0	1	0	1	5	1	—	.143	.268	.200	49	-2	0	.947	-3	*67*	*109*	C13	—	-0.5
1909	Phi A	21	56	8	19	3	1	0	10	3	0	—	.339	.373	.429	150	3	1	.938	1	*130*	*99*	C19	—	0.7
1910	†Phi A	71	192	18	45	4	3	0	17	20	1	—	.234	.310	.286	88	-2	0	.980	7	*112*	*89*	C63	—	1.1
1911	†Phi A	68	167	35	59	10	3	1	26	24	0	—	.353	.435	.467	154	13	4	.972	-1	*112*	*68*	C57,1b4	—	1.6
1912	Phi A	91	281	26	82	15	6	1	35	19	0	—	.292	.337	.399	114	4	3	.958	-4	***127***	*88*	C83	—	0.7
1913	†Phi A	82	238	23	54	4	4	1	20	37	2	26	.227	.336	.290	85	-3	1	.968	-8	*105*	*100*	C78/1	—	-0.6
1914	†Phi A	69	199	22	46	7	2	0	19	31	1	14	.231	.338	.286	91	-1	1-4	.977	-6	*86*	*96*	C67	—	-0.3
1915	Phi A	112	312	26	85	16	5	2	31	30	2	29	.272	.340	.375	118	6	5-2	.967	-14	*60*	*116*	C89,1b12	—	-0.1
1916	Chi A	40	101	6	21	0	1	0	7	8	0	10	.208	.266	.228	48	-7	1	.989	3	147	115	C34	—	-0.2
Total	9	567	1581	168	416	59	26	5	166	177	7	79	.263	.340	.343	105	11	16-6	.969	-25	*103*	*96*	C503,1b17	—	2.4
Larker, Norm	Norman Howard John; B12.27.1930 Beaver Meadows PA; BL/TL/6´0˝/(169–200); d4.15																								
1958	LA N	99	253	32	70	16	5	4	29	29-0	3	21	.277	.352	.427	103	2	1-1	.985	-1	88	111	O43(41/0/2),1b35	0	-0.3
1959	†LA N	108	311	37	90	14	1	8	49	26-1	2	25	.289	.344	.418	96	-1	0-1	.990	5	119	125	1b55,O30(22/0/8)	0	-0.1
1960	LA N★	133	440	56	142	26	3	5	78	36-2	1	24	.323	.368	.430	112	9	1-0	.993	5	107	103	1b119,O2L	0	0.8
1961	LA N	97	282	29	76	16	1	5	38	24-7	1	22	.270	.326	.387	82	-7	0-0	.995	2	100	107	1b86/rf	0	-0.9
1962	Hou N	147	506	58	133	19	5	9	63	70-7	7	47	.263	.358	.374	105	6	1-1	.991	5	109	93	1b135,O6L	0	0.2
1963	Mil N	64	147	15	26	6	0	1	14	24-2	2	24	.177	.297	.238	58	-7	0-2	.992	4	148	88	1b42	0	-0.6
	SF N	19	14	0	1	0	0	0	0	2-0	0	2	.071	.188	.071	-22	-2	0-0	.929	-0	107	143	1b11	0	-0.3
	Year	83	161	15	27	6	0	1	14	26-2	2	26	.168	.288	.224	51	-9	0-2	.987	4	145	92	1b53	0	-0.9
Total	6	667	1953	227	538	97	15	32	271	211-19	16	165	.275	.347	.390	97	0	3-5	.991	20	111	101	1b483,O82(71/0/11)	0	-1.2
Larkin	; d5.29																								
1884	Was U	17	70	11	17	0	0	0	—	4	—	—	.243	.284	.243	63	-5	—	.726	-4	52	113	3b17	—	-0.8
Larkin, Barry	Barry Louis; B4.28.1964 Cincinnati OH; BR/TR/6´0˝/(180–196); [CinN85 1/4]; d8.13; b–Stephen; Col Michigan																								
1986	Cin N	41	159	27	45	4	3	3	19	9-1	0	21	.283	.320	.403	95	-2	8-0	.976	3	113	104	S36,2b3	0	0.6
1987	Cin N	125	439	64	107	16	2	12	43	36-3	5	52	.244	.306	.371	76	-16	21-6	.965	-2	102	110	S119	19	-0.4
1988	Cin N★	151	588	91	174	32	5	12	56	41-3	8	24	.296	.347	.429	118	14	40-7	.960	9	105	90	S148	0	4.3
1989	Cin N☆	97	325	47	111	14	4	4	36	20-5	2	23	.342	.375	.446	132	13	10-5	.976	20	118	76	S82	52	4.1
1990	†Cin N★	158	614	85	185	25	6	7	67	49-3	7	49	.301	.358	.396	103	4	30-5	.977	21	107	110	S156	0	4.2
1991	Cin N★	123	464	88	140	27	4	20	69	55-1	3	64	.302	.378	.506	141	26	24-6	.976	23	107	109	S119	17	**6.2**
1992	Cin N	140	533	76	162	32	6	12	78	63-8	4	58	.304	.377	.454	132	24	15-4	.983	15	102	94	S140	19	5.5
1993	Cin N★	100	384	57	121	20	3	8	51	51-6	1	33	.315	.394	.445	124	15	14-1	.965	3	98	95	S99	60	2.7
1994	Cin N✱	110	427	78	119	23	5	9	52	64-3	0	58	.279	.369	.419	106	6	26-2	.980	2	95	97	S110	0	2.0
1995	†Cin N★	131	496	98	158	29	6	15	66	61-2	3	49	.319	.394	.492	131	24	51-5	.980	-12	90	105	S130	0	3.0
1996	Cin N★	152	517	117	154	32	4	33	89	96-3	7	52	.298	.410	.567	153	44	36-10	.975	4	99	89	S151	0	6.0
1997	Cin N✱	73	224	34	71	17	3	4	20	47-6	3	24	.317	.440	.473	137	16	14-3	.980	-1	100	98	S63,D2	74	2.1
1998	Cin N	145	538	93	166	34	10	17	72	79-5	2	69	.309	.397	.504	134	29	26-3	.979	-18	88	94	S145	7	2.6
1999	Cin N★	161	583	108	171	30	4	12	75	93-5	2	57	.293	.390	.420	103	6	30-8	.978	-21	90	89	S161	0	0.0
2000	Cin N★	102	396	71	124	26	5	11	41	48-0	1	31	.313	.389	.487	116	11	14-6	.973	-16	91	72	S102/D	23	0.3
2001	Cin N	45	156	29	40	12	0	2	17	27-2	2	25	.256	.373	.372	89	-1	3-2	.951	-4	98	92	S44	130	-0.2
2002	Cin N	145	507	72	124	37	2	7	47	44-9	3	57	.245	.305	.367	74	-18	13-4	.979	2	105	108	S135	0	-0.6
2003	Cin N	70	241	39	68	16	1	2	18	22-0	1	32	.282	.345	.382	94	-2	2-0	.962	-4	103	99	S60	84	-0.2
2004	Cin N★	111	346	55	100	15	3	8	44	34-1	1	39	.289	.352	.419	101	0	2-0	.988	-10	97	65	S85	0	-0.3
Total	19	2180	7937	1329	2340	441	76	198	960	939-66	55	817	.295	.371	.444	115	193	379-77	.975	13	100	95	S2085,D3,2b3	485	41.9
Larkin, Ed	Edward Francis; B7.1.1885 Wyalusing PA; D3.28.1934 Wyalusing PA; BR/TR/5´8˝/?; d10.2; Col Lehigh																								
1909	Phi A	2	6	0	1	0	0	0	1	1	0	—	.167	.286	.167	42	0	0	.769	-1	*111*	*54*	C2	—	-0.2
Larkin, Gene	Eugene Thomas; B10.24.1962 Flushing NY; BB/TR/6´3˝/(195–212); [MinA84 20/504]; d5.21; Col Columbia																								
1987	†Min A	85	233	23	62	11	2	4	28	25-3	2	31	.266	.340	.382	88	-4	1-4	.989	-2	66	72	D40,1b26	0	-0.9
1988	Min A	149	505	56	135	30	2	8	70	68-8	**15**	55	.267	.368	.382	108	9	3-2	.994	-5	69	98	D86,1b60	0	-0.2
1989	Min A	136	446	61	119	25	1	6	46	54-6	9	57	.267	.353	.368	98	1	5-2	.992	-4	76	90	1b67,D41,O32(1/0/31)	0	-0.8
1990	Min A	119	401	46	108	26	4	5	42	42-2	5	55	.269	.343	.392	99	1	5-3	1.000	-2	87	161	O47R,D43,1b28	16	-0.6
1991	†Min A	98	255	34	73	14	1	2	19	30-3	1	21	.286	.361	.373	99	1	2-3	.968	-5	79	37	O47(2/0/48),1b39/23D	15	-0.8
1992	Min A	115	337	38	83	18	1	6	42	28-6	4	43	.246	.308	.359	84	-7	7-2	.992	-2	91	124	1b55,O43R,D4	0	-1.3
1993	Min A	56	144	17	38	7	1	1	19	21-3	2	16	.264	.357	.347	92	-1	0-1	1.000	-4	74	65	O28(4/0/25),1b18,3b2,D3	99	-0.7
Total	7	758	2321	275	618	131	12	32	266	268-31	38	278	.266	.348	.374	97	0	23-17	.992	-23	78	102	1b293,D221,O197(7/0/193),3b3/2	130	-5.3
Larkin, Terry	Frank S.; D9.16.1894 Brooklyn NY; BR/TR; d5.20; ▲																								
1876	NY N	1	4	0	0	0	0	0	0	0	—	0	.000	.000	.000	-99	-1	—	.500	-0	141	0	/P	—	0.0
1877	Har N	58	228	28	52	6	5	1	18	5	—	23	.228	.245	.311	83	-4	—	.885	-1	100	0	P56,3b2/2	—	-0.1
1878	Chi N	58	226	33	65	9	4	0	32	**17**	—	17	.288	.337	.363	122	6	—	.858	-4	86	0	P56/lf3	—	-0.2
1879	Chi N	60	228	26	50	12	2	0	18	8	—	24	.219	.246	.289	71	-7	—	.918	-7	74	47	P58,O3(2/1/0)	—	-0.3
1880	Tro N	6	20	1	3	1	0	0	1	3	—	4	.150	.261	.200	56	-1	—	1.000	0	105	684	P5,O2(0/1/1)/S	—	0.0
1884	Ric AA	40	139	17	28	1	4	0	—	9	3	—	.201	.265	.266	75	-4	—	.907	4	109	79	2b40	—	0.1
Total	6	223	845	105	198	29	15	1	69	42	3	68	.234	.273	.308	88	-11	—	.884	-8	87	32	P176,2b41,O6(3/2/1),3b3/S	—	-0.5
Larkin, Henry	Henry E. "Ted"; B1.12.1860 Reading PA; D1.31.1942 Reading PA; BR/TR/5´10˝/175; d5.1; M1																								
1884	Phi AA	85	326	59	90	21	9	3	37	15	8	—	.276	.324	.423	133	11	—	.856	-6	47	0	O85(30/55/0),2b2	—	0.3
1885	Phi AA	108	453	114	149	**37**	14	8	88	26	6	—	.329	.373	.525	171	36	—	.882	9	120	**239**	O108(48/61/0)	—	3.7
1886	Phi AA	**139**	565	133	180	**36**	16	2	74	59	7	—	.319	**.390**	.450	161	41	32	.866	5	91	44	O139L	—	3.7
1887	Phi AA	126	497	105	154	22	12	3	88	48	8	—	.310	.380	.421	123	16	37	.895	2	93	0	O93(86/7/0),1b23,2b10	—	1.1
1888	Phi AA	135	546	92	147	28	12	7	101	33	13	—	.269	.326	.403	134	20	20	.967	-8	80	87	1b122,2b14	—	0.2
1889	Phi AA	133	516	105	164	23	12	3	74	83	16	41	.318	.428	.426	145	37	11	.973	-5	79	118	1b131/32	—	1.7
1890	Cle P	125	506	93	167	32	15	5	112	65	12	18	.330	.419	.482	153	43	5	.978	-8	64	78	1b125/cfM	—	1.9
1891	Phi AA	133	526	94	147	27	14	10	93	66	15	56	.279	.376	.441	133	23	2	.974	-7	73	92	1b111,O23(5/0/18)	—	0.5
1892	Was N	119	464	76	130	13	7	8	96	39	8	21	.280	.346	.390	126	14	21	.969	2	116	115	1b117,O2R	—	1.4
1893	Was N	81	319	54	101	20	3	4	73	50	8	5	.317	.422	.436	132	18	1	.963	-9	64	80	1b81	—	0.7
Total	10	1184	4718	925	1429	259	114	53	836	484	101	141	.303	.380	.440	142	259	129	.971	-23	80	96	1b710,O451(308/124/20),2b27/3	—	15.2
Larkin, Stephen	Stephen Karari; B7.24.1973 Cincinnati OH; BL/TL/6´0˝/190; [TexA94 10/281]; d9.27; b–Barry; Col Texas																								
1998	Cin N	1	3	0	1	0	0	0	0	0-0	0	1	.333	.333	.333	75	0	0-0	1.000	-0	0	0	/1	0	0.0

YEAR	TM LG	G	AB	R	H	2B	3B	HR	RBI	BB-IB	HP	SO	AVG	OBP	SLG	AOPS	ABR	SB-CS	FA	FR	RNG	THR	GAMES AT POSITION	DL	BFW
LARMORE, BOB	Robert McKahan "Red"; B12.6.1896 Anderson IN; D1.15.1964 St.Louis MO; BR/TR/5´10.5˝/185; d5.14; Col Missouri																								
1918	StL N	4	7	0	2	0	0	0	1	0	0	2	.286	.286	.286	77	0	0	.778	-1	85	0	S2	—	-0.1
LAROCCA, GREG	Gregory Mark; B11.10.1972 Oswego NY; BR/TR/5´11˝/185; [SDN94 10/262]; d9.7; Col Massachusetts																								
2000	SD N	13	27	1	6	2	0	0	2	1-0	0	4	.222	.250	.296	40	-3	0-0	1.000	-4	54	0	3b8,S4,2b2	0	-0.6
2002	Cle A	21	52	12	14	3	1	0	4	6-0	2	6	.269	.367	.365	94	0	1-0	.800	-4	62	43	3b15,2b3/D	0	-0.4
2003	Cle A	5	9	3	3	1	0	0	0	1-0	0	1	.333	.400	.444	123	0	0-0	1.000	1	156	0	3b2	0	0.1
Total	3	39	88	16	23	6	1	0	6	8-0	2	11	.261	.337	.352	81	-3	1-0	.857	-8	71	31	3b25,2b5,S4/D	0	-0.9
LAROCHE, ADAM	David Adam; B11.6.1979 Orange Co. CA; BL/TL/6´3˝/(180–185); [AtlN00 29/880]; d4.7; f–Dave; Col Seminole St. (OK) JC																								
2004	†Atl N	110	324	45	90	27	1	13	45	27-1	1	78	.278	.333	.488	108	4	0-0	.994	-6	74	130	1b98	34	-1.0
2005	†Atl N	141	451	53	117	28	0	20	78	39-7	4	87	.259	.320	.455	100	-1	0-2	.994	0	104	105	1b125	0	-1.1
2006	Atl N	149	492	89	140	38	1	32	90	55-5	2	128	.285	.354	.561	129	21	0-2	.996	6	117	96	1b142	0	1.4
Total	3	400	1267	187	347	93	2	65	213	121-13	7	293	.274	.337	.504	114	24	0-4	.995	-0	102	108	1b365	34	-0.7
LAROQUE, SAM	Simeon Henry Jean; B2.26.1863 St.Mathias QC, Can.; D6.5.1933 Highland Park MI; BR/TR/5´11˝/190; d7.30																								
1888	Det N	2	9	1	4	0	0	0	2	1	0	1	.444	.500	.444	201	1	0	.789	-1	86	300	2b2	—	0.1
1890	Pit N	111	434	59	105	20	4	1	40	35	12	29	.242	.316	.313	95	-1	27	.925	-9	102	81	2b78,S31,1b2/lf	—	-0.5
1891	Pit N	1	4	0	0	0	0	0	0	0	0	1	.000	.000	.000	-99	-1	0	.714	-0	97	0	/3	—	-0.1
	Lou AA	10	35	6	11	2	1	1	8	5	2	8	.314	.429	.514	172	4	1	.875	-4	71	92	2b10/1	—	0.0
Total	3	124	482	66	120	22	5	2	50	41	14	39	.249	.326	.328	101	3	28	.916	-14	98	89	2b90,S31,1b3/3lf	—	-0.5
LAROSE, VIC	Victor Raymond; B12.23.1944 Los Angeles CA; BR/TR/5´11˝/185; d9.13																								
1968	Chi N	4	2	0	0	0	0	0	0	0-0	1	1	.000	.333	.000	6	0	0-0	1.000	-0	103	0	2b2,S2	0	0.0
LAROSS, HARRY	Harry Raymond "Spike"; B1.2.1888 Easton PA; D3.22.1954 Chicago IL; BR/TR/5´11.5˝/170; d6.24																								
1914	Cin N	22	48	7	11	1	0	0	5	2	0	10	.229	.260	.250	50	-3	4	.739	-2	63	143	O20(10/10/0)	—	-0.7
LARSEN, SWEDE	Erling Adeli; B11.15.1913 Jersey City NJ; D10.8.2005 Tucson AZ; BR/TR/5´11˝/170; d6.17; Col Colgate																								
1936	Bos N	3	1	0	0	0	0	0	0	0	0	0	.000	.000	.000	-99	0	0	1.000	-0	0	0	2b2	—	-0.1
LARSON, BRANDON	Brandon John; B5.24.1976 San Angelo TX; BR/TR/6´0˝/210; [CinN97 1/14]; d5.4; Col Louisiana St.																								
2001	Cin N	14	33	2	4	2	0	0	1	2-0	0	10	.121	.171	.182	-8	-5	0-0	.939	2	131	125	3b9	0	-0.3
2002	Cin N	23	51	8	14	2	0	4	13	6-1	1	10	.275	.362	.549	131	2	1-0	1.000	0	100	0	O9L,3b5,1b2	41	0.2
2003	Cin N	32	89	6	9	1	0	1	9	13-0	0	31	.101	.212	.146	-3	-14	2-2	.943	5	117	168	3b24,O3L	43	-1.0
2004	Cin N	40	118	13	25	6	0	3	14	14-0	2	35	.212	.304	.339	68	-6	1-0	.937	-5	85	67	3b35	94	-1.0
Total	4	109	291	29	52	11	0	8	37	35-1	3	86	.179	.271	.299	49	-23	4-2	.943	2	104	125	3b73,O12L,1b2	178	-2.1
LARUE, JASON	Michael Jason; B3.19.1974 Houston TX; BR/TR/5´11˝/(200–205); [CinN95 5/139]; d6.15; Col Dallas Baptist																								
1999	Cin N	36	90	12	19	7	0	3	10	11-1	2	32	.211	.311	.389	73	-4	4-1	.990	3	154	120	C35	0	0.2
2000	Cin N	31	98	12	23	3	0	5	12	5-2	4	19	.235	.299	.418	76	-4	0-0	.991	7	148	60	C31	0	0.4
2001	Cin N	121	364	39	86	21	2	12	43	27-4	9	106	.236	.303	.404	77	-13	3-3	.991	14	194	**161**	C107,3b3,O2L/1	0	0.6
2002	Cin N	113	353	42	88	17	1	12	52	27-6	13	117	.249	.324	.405	88	-6	1-2	.994	2	**171**	103	C110	7	0.2
2003	Cin N	118	379	52	87	23	1	16	50	33-4	20	111	.230	.321	.422	97	-2	3-3	.984	-10	115	70	C114/1lf	0	-0.4
2004	Cin N	114	390	46	98	24	2	14	55	26-5	24	108	.251	.334	.431	98	-1	0-2	.989	-7	150	72	C111/rfD	15	-0.1
2005	Cin N	110	361	38	94	27	0	14	60	41-7	13	101	.260	.355	.452	110	6	0-0	.993	-4	106	111	C109/rf	0	1.0
2006	Cin N	72	191	22	37	5	0	8	21	27-9	8	51	.194	.317	.346	66	-10	1-0	.995	7	145	99	C63	15	0.1
Total	8	715	2226	263	532	127	6	84	303	197-38	93	645	.239	.325	.415	90	-34	12-11	.991	12	146	101	C680,O5(3/0/2),3b3,1b2/D	37	2.0
LARUSSA, TONY	Anthony; B10.4.1944 Tampa FL; BR/TR/6´1˝/(175–190); d5.10; M28/C1; [DL 1967 KC A 24]																								
1963	KC A	34	44	4	11	1	1	0	1	7-0	0	12	.250	.346	.318	85	-1	0-0	.957	-5	65	98	S14,2b3	0	-0.5
1968	Oak A	5	3	0	1	0	0	0	0	0-0	0	0	.333	.333	.333	107	0	0-0	ø	0	—	—	/H	0	0.0
1969	Oak A	8	8	0	0	0	0	0	0	0-0	0	1	.000	.000	.000	-99	-2	0-0	ø	0	—	—	/H	0	-0.2
1970	Oak A	52	106	6	21	4	1	0	6	15-1	1	19	.198	.301	.255	57	-6	0-0	.969	-0	100	115	2b44	0	-0.4
1971	Oak A	23	8	3	0	0	0	0	0	0-0	0	4	.000	.000	.000	-99	-2	0-0	.833	-0	27	122	2b7,S4,3b2	0	-0.2
	Atl N	9	7	1	2	0	0	0	0	1-0	0	1	.286	.375	.286	84	0	0-0	.933	-1	64	138	2b9	0	-0.1
1973	Chi N	1	0	1	0	0	0	0	0	0-0	0	0	ø	ø	ø	ø	0	0-0	ø	0	—	—	/R	0	0.0
Total	6	132	176	15	35	5	2	0	7	23-1	1	37	.199	.292	.250	53	-11	0-0	.963	-7	92	116	2b63,S18,3b2	24	-1.4
LARY, LYN	Lynford Hobart "Broadway"; B1.28.1906 Armona CA; D1.9.1973 Downey CA; BR/TR/6´0˝/165; d5.11																								
1929	NY A	80	236	48	73	9	2	5	26	24	3	15	.309	.380	.428	115	6	4-1	.943	2	104	115	3b55,S14,2b2	—	1.2
1930	NY A	117	464	93	134	20	8	3	52	45	4	40	.289	.357	.386	92	-5	14-2	.940	-4	97	84	S113	—	0.5
1931	NY A	**155**	610	100	171	35	9	10	107	88	6	54	.280	.376	.416	115	16	13-10	.946	4	98	97	S155	—	2.9
1932	NY A	91	280	56	65	14	4	3	39	52	3	28	.232	.358	.343	87	-3	9-3	.941	-1	94	86	S80,1b5,2b2,3b2/lf	—	0.2
1933	NY A	52	127	25	28	3	3	0	13	28	0	17	.220	.361	.291	79	-3	2-1	.938	0	89	106	3b28,S16,1b3/lf	—	-0.1
1934	NY A	1	0	0	0	0	0	0	0	1	0	0	ø	1.000	ø	189	0	0-0	.800	-0	0	288	/1	—	0.0
	Bos A	129	419	58	101	20	4	2	54	66	0	51	.241	.344	.322	68	-19	12-5	**.965**	-7	95	80	S129	—	-1.4
	Year	130	419	58	101	20	4	2	54	67	0	51	.241	.346	.322	68	-18	12-5	.965	-7	95	80	S129/1	—	-1.4
1935	Was A	39	103	8	20	4	0	0	7	12	0	10	.194	.278	.233	35	-10	3-0	.953	-3	91	71	S30	—	-1.0
	StL A	93	371	78	107	25	7	2	35	64	2	43	.288	.396	.410	104	5	25-4	.962	10	100	100	S93	—	2.4
	Year	132	474	86	127	29	7	2	42	76	2	53	.268	.371	.371	90	-4	28-4	.960	6	98	94	S123	—	1.4
1936	StL A	**155**	619	112	179	30	6	2	52	117	2	54	.289	.404	.367	89	-5	**37**-9	.956	-2	101	77	S155	—	0.8
1937	Cle A	**156**	644	110	187	46	7	8	77	88	3	64	.290	.378	.421	100	3	18-8	.963	8	99	95	S156	—	2.1
1938	Cle A	141	568	94	152	36	4	3	51	88	0	65	.268	.366	.361	84	-11	23-6	.964	-2	93	91	S141	—	0.0
1939	Cle A	3	2	0	0	0	0	0	0	0	0	1	.000	.000	.000	-99	-1	0-0	.000	-1	0	0	S2	—	-0.1
	Bro N	29	31	7	5	1	1	0	1	12	1	6	.161	.409	.258	80	0	1	.947	-1	84	130	S12,3b7	—	0.0
	StL N	34	75	11	14	3	0	0	9	16	0	15	.187	.330	.227	49	-5	1	.961	-4	90	58	S30,3b3	—	-0.7
	Year	63	106	18	19	4	1	0	10	28	1	21	.179	.356	.236	59	-5	2	.958	-5	89	73	S42,3b10	—	-0.7
1940	StL A	27	54	5	3	1	1	0	3	4	1	7	.056	.136	.111	-35	-11	0-0	.952	0	101	95	S12/2	—	-1.0
Total	12	1302	4603	805	1239	247	56	38	526	705	25	470	.269	.369	.372	90	-43	162-49	.956	-0	97	88	S1138,3b95,1b9,2b5,O2L	—	5.8
LASSETTER, DON	Donald O'Neal; B3.27.1933 Newnan GA; BR/TR/6´3˝/200; d9.21; Col Georgia																								
1957	StL N	4	13	2	2	0	1	0	0	1-0	0	3	.154	.214	.308	37	-1	0-0	1.000	0	146	0	O3L	0	-0.1
LATHAM, CHRIS	Christopher Joseph; B5.26.1973 Coeur D'Alene ID; BB/TR/6´0˝/(185–198); [LAN91 11/299]; d4.12																								
1997	Min A	15	22	4	4	1	0	0	1	0-0	0	8	.182	.182	.227	6	-3	0-0	.917	-1	89	0	O10(0/8/3)	0	-0.4
1998	Min A	34	94	14	15	1	0	1	5	13-0	0	36	.160	.262	.202	22	-11	4-2	.972	0	110	56	O32(13/15/5)	0	-1.1
1999	Min A	14	22	1	2	0	0	0	3	0-0	0	13	.091	.083	.091	-51	-5	0-0	1.000	-1	80	0	O14(6/5/4)	0	-0.6
2001	Tor A	43	73	12	20	3	1	2	10	10-1	1	28	.274	.369	.425	106	1	4-1	1.000	3	122	162	O31(15/2/14)	0	0.3
2003	NY A	4	2	3	2	0	0	0	0	0-0	0	0	1.000	1.000	1.000	436	1	1-0	1.000	0	193	0	O2(0/1/1)	0	0.1
Total	5	110	213	34	43	5	1	3	19	23-1	1	85	.202	.280	.277	46	-17	9-3	.980	1	109	78	O89(34/31/27)	0	-1.7
LATHAM, JUICE	George Warren "Jumbo"; B9.6.1852 Utica NY; D5.26.1914 Utica NY; BR/TR/5´8˝/164; d4.19; M2																								
1875	Bos NA	16	78	23	21	4	0	0	13	0	—	2	.269	.269	.321	100	0	0-0	.927	0	154	206	1b16	—	0.1
	NH NA	20	76	6	15	1	0	0	5	0	—	4	.197	.197	.211	48	-3	6-0	.954	2	219	113	1b14,S4,3b3,M	—	0.0
	Year	36	154	29	36	5	0	0	18	0	—	6	.234	.234	.266	78	-3	6-0	.941	2	184	163	1b30,S4,3b3	—	0.1
1877	Lou N	59	278	42	81	10	6	0	22	5	—	6	.291	.304	.371	94	-4	—	.950	2	127	113	1b59	—	-0.4
1882	Phi AA	74	323	47	92	10	2	0	38	10	—	—	.285	.306	.328	107	1	—	**.972**	-0	64	89	1b74,M	—	-0.5
1883	Lou AA	88	368	60	92	7	6	0	—	12	—	—	.250	.274	.302	92	-2	—	.955	-1	110	132	1b67,2b14,S9	—	-0.8
1884	Lou AA	77	308	31	52	3	3	0	23	8	3	—	.169	.197	.198	31	-23	—	.961	3	121	**160**	1b76/3	—	-2.5
Total	4	298	1277	180	317	30	17	0	83	35	3	6	.248	.270	.298	83	-28	—	.960	3	104	124	1b276,2b14,S9/3	—	-4.2
LATHAM, ARLIE	Walter Arlington "The Freshest Man On Earth"; B3.15.1860 W.Lebanon NH; D11.29.1952 Garden City NY; BR/TR/5´8˝/150; d7.5; M1/C2/U2; OF(2/0/11)																								
1880	Buf N	22	79	9	10	3	1	0	3	1	—	8	.127	.138	.190	10	-7	—	.887	-0	104	32	S12,O10R/C	—	-0.7
1883	StL AA	**98**	406	86	96	12	7	0	—	18	—	—	.236	.269	.300	79	-10	—	.866	21	125	**162**	3b98/C	—	1.1
1884	StL AA	**110**	474	115	130	17	12	1	—	18	6	—	.274	.309	.367	116	7	—	.864	**37**	**148**	**138**	3b110/C	—	4.1

YEAR	TM LG	G	AB	R	H	2B	3B	HR	RBI	BB-IB	HP	SO	AVG	OBP	SLG	AOPS	ABR	SB-CS	FA	FR	RNG	THR	GAMES AT POSITION	DL	BFW
1885	†StL AA	110	485	84	100	15	3	1	35	18	5	—	.206	.242	.256	55	-25	—	.875	0	104	118	3b109,C2	—	-2.1
1886	†StL AA	134	578	**152**	174	23	8	1	47	55	6	—	.301	.368	.374	127	18	60	.827	-0	106	132	3b133/2	—	1.8
1887	†StL AA	136	627	163	198	35	10	2	83	45	5	—	.316	.366	.413	106	2	129	.877	0	106	92	3b132,2b5,C2	—	0.4
1888	†StL AA	133	570	119	151	19	5	2	31	43	8	—	.265	.325	.326	98	-2	**109**	.882	3	101	123	3b133/S	—	0.2
1889	StL AA	118	512	110	126	13	3	4	49	42	11	30	.246	.317	.307	69	-23	69	.883	9	100	117	3b116,2b3	—	-1.0
1890	Chi P	52	214	47	49	7	2	1	20	22	3	22	.229	.310	.294	59	-13	32	.880	1	102	105	3b52	—	-0.8
	Cin N	41	164	35	41	6	2	0	15	23	1	18	.250	.346	.311	92	-1	20	.853	3	115	158	3b41/rf	—	0.2
1891	Cin N	135	533	119	145	20	10	7	53	74	11	35	.272	.372	.386	120	16	87	.879	21	**122**	125	3b135/C	—	3.4
1892	Cin N	152	622	111	148	20	4	0	44	60	5	55	.238	.310	.283	81	-13	66	.883	-6	103	122	3b142,2b9/lf	—	-1.5
1893	Cin N	127	531	101	150	18	6	2	49	62	10	20	.282	.368	.350	89	-7	57	.892	-13	94	99	3b127	—	-1.5
1894	Cin N	131	534	132	167	23	6	4	60	61	9	24	.313	.392	.401	88	-9	62	.861	-12	97	93	3b129,2b2	—	-1.4
1895	Cin N	112	460	93	143	14	6	2	69	42	5	25	.311	.375	.380	91	-6	48	.861	-13	92	85	3b108,1b3/2	—	-1.4
1896	StL N	8	35	3	7	0	0	0	5	4	0	3	.200	.282	.200	29	-3	2	.744	-2	80	137	3b8,M	—	-0.5
1899	Was N	6	6	1	1	0	0	0	0	1	0	—	.167	.286	.167	26	-1	0	1.000	0	0	0	/lf2	—	-0.1
1909	NY N	4	2	1	0	0	0	0	0	0	0	—	.000	.000	.000	-99	0	1	1.000	0	217	0	2b2	—	0.0
Total	17	1629	6832	1481	1836	245	85	27	563	589	85	240	.269	.334	.341	91	-77	742	.870	48	108	118	3b1573,2b24,O13R,S13,C8,1b3	—	0.2

LATHERS, CHICK Charles Ten Eyck; B10.22.1888 Dearborn MI; D7.26.1971 Petoskey MI; BL/TR/6´0˝/180; d5.1; Col Michigan

YEAR	TM LG	G	AB	R	H	2B	3B	HR	RBI	BB-IB	HP	SO	AVG	OBP	SLG	AOPS	ABR	SB-CS	FA	FR	RNG	THR	GAMES AT POSITION	DL	BFW
1910	Det A	41	82	4	19	2	0	0	3	8	0	—	.232	.300	.256	70	-3	0	.926	2	128	162	3b14,2b7,S4	—	0.0
1911	Det A	29	45	5	10	1	0	0	4	5	1	—	.222	.314	.244	54	-3	0	.867	-2	115	101	2b9,3b8,S4,1b3	—	-0.4
Total	2	70	127	9	29	3	0	0	7	13	1	—	.228	.305	.252	64	-6	0	.933	0	131	111	3b22,2b16,S8,1b3	—	-0.4

LATIMER, TACKS Clifford Wesley; B11.30.1877 Loveland OH; D4.24.1936 Loveland OH; BR/TR/6´0˝/160; d10.1

YEAR	TM LG	G	AB	R	H	2B	3B	HR	RBI	BB-IB	HP	SO	AVG	OBP	SLG	AOPS	ABR	SB-CS	FA	FR	RNG	THR	GAMES AT POSITION	DL	BFW
1898	NY N	5	17	1	5	1	0	0	1	0	0	—	.294	.294	.353	88	0	0	.889	-1	*89*	*168*	C4,O2R	—	-0.1
1899	Lou N	9	29	3	8	1	0	0	4	2	0	—	.276	.323	.310	74	-1	1	.980	2	*113*	*84*	C8/1	—	0.1
1900	Pit N	4	12	1	4	1	0	0	2	0	0	—	.333	.333	.417	106	0	0	.947	-0	*126*	*99*	C4	—	0.0
1901	Bal A	1	4	0	1	0	0	0	0	0	0	—	.250	.250	.250	37	0	0	1.000	-0	*133*	*0*	/C	—	0.0
1902	Bro N	8	24	0	1	0	0	0	0	0	0	—	.042	.042	.042	-74	-5	0	.947	-1	*81*	*136*	C8	—	-0.6
Total	5	27	86	5	19	3	0	0	7	2	0	—	.221	.239	.256	41	-6	1	.949	-0	*104*	*110*	C25,O2R/1	—	-0.6

LAU, CHARLIE Charles Richard; B4.12.1933 Romulus MI; D3.18.1984 Key Colony Beach FL; BL/TR/6´0˝/(175–190); d9.12; C15

YEAR	TM LG	G	AB	R	H	2B	3B	HR	RBI	BB-IB	HP	SO	AVG	OBP	SLG	AOPS	ABR	SB-CS	FA	FR	RNG	THR	GAMES AT POSITION	DL	BFW
1956	Det A	3	9	1	2	0	0	0	0	0-0	0	1	.222	.222	.222	18	-1	0-0	1.000	0	*0*	*0*	C3	0	-0.1
1958	Det A	30	68	8	10	1	2	0	6	12-2	2	15	.147	.293	.221	41	-5	0-0	.985	1	147	206	C27	0	-0.4
1959	Det A	2	6	0	1	0	0	0	0	0-0	0	2	.167	.167	.167	-8	-1	0-0	1.000	1	0	0	C2	0	0.0
1960	Mil N	21	53	4	10	2	0	0	2	6-1	0	10	.189	.271	.226	41	-4	0-0	1.000	4	110	157	C16	0	0.1
1961	Mil N	28	82	3	17	5	0	0	5	14-3	1	11	.207	.323	.268	65	-3	1-1	.968	-3	100	89	C25	0	-0.5
	Bal A	17	47	3	8	0	0	1	4	1-1	0	3	.170	.188	.234	12	-6	0-0	.990	2	83	37	C17	0	-0.3
1962	Bal A	81	197	21	58	11	2	6	37	7-1	1	11	.294	.319	.462	115	3	1-0	.996	-4	51	58	C56	0	0.1
1963	Bal A	29	48	4	9	2	0	0	6	1-0	0	5	.188	.204	.229	22	-5	0-0	.964	1	115	85	C8	0	-0.4
	KC A	62	187	15	55	11	0	3	26	14-3	0	17	.294	.340	.401	102	1	1-0	.982	-11	59	101	C50	0	-0.8
	Year	91	235	19	64	13	0	3	32	15-3	0	22	.272	.313	.366	88	-4	1-0	.979	-10	66	99	C58	0	-1.2
1964	KC A	43	118	11	32	7	1	2	9	10-1	0	18	.271	.326	.398	98	0	0-0	.990	-7	48	67	C35	0	-0.6
	Bal A	62	158	16	41	15	1	1	14	17-5	1	27	.259	.333	.386	100	1	0-0	.992	-1	77	54	C47	0	0.2
	Year	105	276	27	73	22	2	3	23	27-6	1	45	.264	.330	.391	99	1	0-0	.991	-8	65	60	C82	0	-0.4
1965	Bal A	68	132	15	39	5	2	2	18	17-5	0	18	.295	.371	.409	120	4	0-0	.989	-4	159	61	C35	0	0.2
1966	Bal A	18	12	1	6	2	1	0	5	4-0	0	1	.500	.588	.833	320	4	0-0	ø	0	—	—	/H	113	0.4
1967	Bal A	11	8	0	1	1	0	0	3	2-1	0	2	.125	.273	.250	65	0	0-0	ø	0	—	—	/H	0	0.0
	Atl N	52	45	3	9	1	0	1	5	4-1	0	9	.200	.265	.289	59	-2	0-0	ø	0	—	—	/H	0	-0.3
Total	11	527	1170	105	298	63	9	16	140	109-24	5	150	.255	.318	.365	89	-14	3-1	.988	-20	*85*	*84*	C321	113	-2.4

LAUDER, BILLY William; B2.23.1874 New York NY; D5.20.1933 Norwalk CT; BR/TR/5´10˝/160; d6.25; C1; Col Brown

YEAR	TM LG	G	AB	R	H	2B	3B	HR	RBI	BB-IB	HP	SO	AVG	OBP	SLG	AOPS	ABR	SB-CS	FA	FR	RNG	THR	GAMES AT POSITION	DL	BFW
1898	Phi N	97	361	42	95	14	7	2	67	19	0	—	.263	.300	.357	92	-5	6	.866	-19	82	42	3b97	—	-2.1
1899	Phi N	151	583	74	156	17	6	3	90	34	2	—	.268	.310	.333	79	-18	15	.893	-14	91	104	3b151	—	-2.7
1901	Phi A	2	8	1	1	0	0	0	0	0	0	—	.125	.125	.125	-29	-1	0	.833	0	111	0	3b2	—	-0.1
1902	NY N	127	490	42	115	20	1	0	43	10	0	—	.235	.250	.280	64	-22	19	.908	2	97	106	3b123,O4(2/0/2)	—	-1.8
1903	NY N	108	395	52	111	13	0	0	53	14	1	—	.281	.307	.314	74	-14	19	.908	-8	90	99	3b108	—	-1.8
Total	5	485	1837	211	478	64	14	5	253	77	3	—	.260	.291	.318	76	-60	59	.894	-38	91	90	3b481,O4(2/0/2)	—	-8.5

LAUDNER, TIM Timothy Jon; B6.7.1958 Mason City IA; BR/TR/6´3˝/(195–218); [MinA79 3/63]; d8.28; Col Missouri; [DL 1990 Min A 17]

YEAR	TM LG	G	AB	R	H	2B	3B	HR	RBI	BB-IB	HP	SO	AVG	OBP	SLG	AOPS	ABR	SB-CS	FA	FR	RNG	THR	GAMES AT POSITION	DL	BFW
1981	Min A	14	43	4	7	2	0	2	5	3-1	1	17	.163	.234	.349	62	-2	0-0	1.000	-0	108	51	C12,D2	0	-0.2
1982	Min A	93	306	37	78	19	1	7	33	34-2	0	74	.255	.328	.392	94	-2	0-2	.976	-12	74	107	C93	0	-1.1
1983	Min A	62	168	20	31	9	0	6	18	15-0	0	49	.185	.250	.345	60	-10	0-0	.986	-2	67	96	C57,D4	0	-0.9
1984	Min A	87	262	31	54	16	1	10	35	18-0	1	78	.206	.258	.389	73	-10	0-0	.978	10	137	126	C81,D2	0	0.3
1985	Min A	72	164	16	39	5	0	7	19	12-0	1	45	.238	.292	.396	82	-5	0-1	.969	-6	110	94	C68/1	0	-0.8
1986	Min A	76	193	21	47	10	0	10	29	24-0	3	56	.244	.333	.451	109	3	1-0	.984	-13	115	67	C68	0	-0.7
1987	†Min A	113	288	30	55	7	1	16	43	23-0	1	80	.191	.252	.389	64	-16	1-0	.987	-3	92	79	C101,1b7,D2	0	-1.5
1988	Min A★	117	375	38	94	18	1	13	54	36-0	1	89	.251	.316	.408	99	-1	0-0	.992	5	88	84	C109,1b3,D4	0	1.0
1989	Min A	100	239	24	53	11	1	6	27	25-0	0	65	.222	.293	.351	77	-8	1-0	.991	-2	86	111	C68,D19,1b11	0	-0.7
Total	9	734	2038	221	458	97	5	77	263	190-3	8	553	.225	.292	.391	83	-51	3-3	.984	-24	96	95	C657,D33,1b22	17	-4.6

LAUER, CHUCK John Charles; B4.5.1865 Pittsburgh PA; D5.14.1915 Buffalo NY; TR; d7.17; ▲

YEAR	TM LG	G	AB	R	H	2B	3B	HR	RBI	BB-IB	HP	SO	AVG	OBP	SLG	AOPS	ABR	SB-CS	FA	FR	RNG	THR	GAMES AT POSITION	DL	BFW
1884	Pit AA	13	44	5	5	0	0	0	—	0	0	—	.114	.114	.114	-26	-6	—	.938	-1	60	0	O10(0/2/8),P3/1	—	-0.5
1889	Pit N	4	16	2	3	0	0	0	1	0	0	5	.188	.188	.188	5	-2	0	.815	0	—	—	C3/lf	—	-0.1
1890	Chi N	2	8	1	2	1	0	0	2	0	0	0	.250	.250	.375	78	0	0	.833	-1	*103*	*100*	C2	—	-0.1
Total	3	19	68	8	10	1	0	0	3	0	0	5	.147	.147	.162	-5	-8	0	.944	-1	55	0	O11(1/2/8),C5,P3/1	—	-0.7

LAUGHLIN, BEN Benjamin; d4.28

YEAR	TM LG	G	AB	R	H	2B	3B	HR	RBI	BB-IB	HP	SO	AVG	OBP	SLG	AOPS	ABR	SB-CS	FA	FR	RNG	THR	GAMES AT POSITION	DL	BFW
1873	Res NA	12	51	3	12	0	0	0	5	0	—	1	.235	.235	.235	43	-3	0-0	.698	-3	105	108	2b12	—	-0.5

LAUTERBORN, BILL William Bernard; B6.9.1879 Hornell NY; D4.19.1965 Andover NY; BR/TR/5´6˝/140; d9.20; Col Fordham

YEAR	TM LG	G	AB	R	H	2B	3B	HR	RBI	BB-IB	HP	SO	AVG	OBP	SLG	AOPS	ABR	SB-CS	FA	FR	RNG	THR	GAMES AT POSITION	DL	BFW
1904	Bos N	20	69	7	19	2	0	0	2	1	0	—	.275	.286	.304	85	-1	1	.943	-2	99	29	2b20	—	-0.3
1905	Bos N	67	200	11	37	1	1	0	9	12	2	—	.185	.238	.200	32	-17	1	.843	-10	91	0	3b29,2b23,S3,O2C	—	-2.7
Total	2	87	269	18	56	3	1	0	11	13	2	—	.208	.250	.227	45	-18	2	.929	-11	101	33	2b43,3b29,S3,O2C	—	-3.0

LAVAGETTO, COOKIE Harry Arthur (b Attilio H. Lavagetto); B12.1.1912 Oakland CA; D8.10.1990 Orinda CA; BR/TR/6´0˝/170; d4.17; Mil 1942–45; M5/C12

YEAR	TM LG	G	AB	R	H	2B	3B	HR	RBI	BB-IB	HP	SO	AVG	OBP	SLG	AOPS	ABR	SB-CS	FA	FR	RNG	THR	GAMES AT POSITION	DL	BFW
1934	Pit N	87	304	41	67	16	3	3	46	32	0	39	.220	.295	.322	64	-16	6	.961	-12	89	83	2b83	—	-2.2
1935	Pit N	78	231	27	67	9	4	0	19	18	0	15	.290	.341	.364	87	-4	1	.951	-9	92	49	2b42,3b15	—	-1.0
1936	Pit N	60	197	21	48	15	2	2	26	15	1	13	.244	.300	.371	78	-6	0	.951	-4	94	123	2b37,3b13/S	—	-0.8
1937	Bro N	149	503	64	142	26	6	8	70	74	1	41	.282	.375	.406	110	10	13	.949	-7	93	92	2b100,3b45	—	1.1
1938	Bro N☆	137	487	68	133	34	6	6	79	68	2	31	.273	.364	.405	109	8	15	.929	-8	91	114	3b132,2b4	—	0.5
1939	Bro N☆	153	587	93	176	28	5	10	87	78	5	30	.300	.387	.416	112	13	14	.948	-5	96	113	3b149	—	1.3
1940	Bro N★	118	448	56	115	21	3	4	43	70	3	32	.257	.361	.344	90	-3	4	.932	-14	84	74	3b116	—	-1.3
1941	†Bro N★	132	441	75	122	24	7	1	78	80	0	21	.277	.388	.370	109	9	7	.938	-18	87	87	3b120	0	-0.5
1946	Bro N	88	242	36	57	9	1	3	27	38	0	17	.236	.339	.318	86	-3	3	.927	-4	91	118	3b67	0	-0.8
1947	†Bro N	41	69	6	18	1	0	3	11	12	0	5	.261	.370	.406	102	0	0	.961	1	100	116	3b18,1b3	0	0.2
Total	10	1043	3509	487	945	183	37	40	486	485	12	244	.269	.360	.377	98	8	63	.936	-79	91	99	3b675,2b266,1b3/S	0	-3.5

LAVALLIERE, MIKE Michael Eugene; B8.18.1960 Charlotte NC; BL/TR/5´9˝/(180–210); d9.9; Col Massachusetts–Lowell

YEAR	TM LG	G	AB	R	H	2B	3B	HR	RBI	BB-IB	HP	SO	AVG	OBP	SLG	AOPS	ABR	SB-CS	FA	FR	RNG	THR	GAMES AT POSITION	DL	BFW
1984	Phi N	6	7	0	0	0	0	0	0	2-0	0	2	.000	.222	.000	-32	-1	0-0	1.000	1	0	90	C6	0	0.0
1985	StL N	12	34	2	5	1	0	0	6	7-0	0	3	.147	.273	.176	34	-3	0-0	1.000	-0	159	54	C12	0	-0.3
1986	StL N	110	303	18	71	10	2	3	30	36-5	1	37	.234	.318	.310	74	-10	0-1	.988	8	**167**	84	C108	0	0.2
1987	Pit N	121	340	33	102	19	0	1	36	43-9	1	32	.300	.377	.365	97	1	0-0	.992	19	**136**	**148**	C112	0	2.4
1988	Pit N	120	352	24	92	18	0	2	47	50-10	2	34	.261	.353	.330	99	2	3-2	.987	8	111	123	C114	0	1.7
1989	Pit N	68	190	15	60	10	0	2	23	29-7	0	24	.316	.406	.400	136	11	0-2	.991	-10	69	66	C65	78	0.4
1990	†Pit N	96	279	27	72	15	0	3	31	44-8	2	20	.258	.362	.344	99	2	0-3	.990	5	114	113	C95	0	1.1
1991	†Pit N	108	336	25	97	11	2	3	41	33-4	2	27	.289	.351	.360	103	2	2-1	**.998**	-3	91	95	C105	0	0.5

YEAR	TM LG	G	AB	R	H	2B	3B	HR	RBI	BB-IB	HP	SO	AVG	OBP	SLG	AOPS	ABR	SB-CS	FA	FR	RNG	THR	GAMES AT POSITION	DL	BFW
1992	†Pit N	95	293	22	75	13	1	2	29	44-14	1	21	.256	.350	.328	95	0	0-3	.994	-1	98	133	C92/3	0	0.3
1993	Pit N	1	5	0	1	0	0	0	0	0-0	0	0	.200	.200	.200	7	-1	0-0	1.000	1	77	0	/C	0	0.0
	†Chi A	37	97	6	25	2	0	0	8	4-0	0	14	.258	.282	.278	54	-7	0-1	1.000	5	250	213	C37	0	0.0
1994	Chi A	59	139	6	39	4	0	1	24	20-0	1	15	.281	.368	.331	85	-2	0-2	.991	3	77	116	C57	0	0.3
1995	Chi A	46	98	7	24	6	0	1	19	9-0	0	15	.245	.303	.337	71	-4	0-0	.996	5	140	182	C46	34	0.3
Total	12	879	2473	185	663	109	5	18	294	321-57	10	244	.268	.351	.338	93	-10	5-15	.992	41	119	117	C850/3	112	6.9
LAVAN, DOC	John Leonard (b John Leonard Laven); B10.28.1890 Grand Rapids MI; D5.29.1952 Detroit MI; BR/TR/5´8.5˝/151; d6.22; Col Michigan																								
1913	StL A	46	149	8	21	2	1	0	4	10	3	46	.141	.210	.168	11	-17	3	.899	-5	101	132	S46	—	-2.1
	Phi A	5	14	1	1	0	1	0	1	0	0	0	.071	.071	.214	-17	-2	0	1.000	0	107	0	S5	—	-0.2
	Year	51	163	9	22	2	2	0	5	10	3	46	.135	.199	.172	9	-19	3	.906	-5	101	122	S51	—	-2.3
1914	StL A	75	239	21	63	7	4	1	21	17	2	39	.264	.318	.339	101	-1	6-12	.916	-14	89	60	S74	—	-1.4
1915	StL A	157	514	44	112	17	7	1	48	42	3	83	.218	.281	.284	72	-19	13-19	.913	9	104	**139**	S157	—	-0.4
1916	StL A	110	343	32	81	13	1	0	19	32	2	38	.236	.305	.280	80	-8	7	.950	26	**121**	**140**	S106	—	2.7
1917	StL A	118	355	19	85	8	5	0	30	19	3	34	.239	.284	.290	78	-11	5	.923	13	107	**135**	S110,2b7	—	1.0
1918	Was A	117	464	44	129	17	2	0	45	14	2	21	.278	.302	.323	90	-8	12	.917	-18	91	96	S117/cf	—	-2.0
1919	StL N	100	356	25	86	12	2	1	25	11	0	30	.242	.264	.295	72	-13	4	.929	9	105	110	S99	—	0.3
1920	StL N	142	516	52	149	21	10	1	63	19	3	38	.289	.318	.374	102	-1	11-14	.942	10	103	108	S138	—	1.8
1921	StL N	150	560	58	145	23	11	2	82	23	2	30	.259	.291	.350	70	-26	7-7	.950	**21**	104	110	S150	—	1.0
1922	StL N	89	264	24	60	8	1	0	27	13	3	10	.227	.271	.265	41	-24	3-1	.937	5	102	92	S82,3b5	—	-1.0
1923	StL N	50	111	10	22	6	0	1	12	9	1	7	.198	.264	.279	44	-9	0-3	.924	-2	99	119	S40,3b4,1b3/2	—	-0.8
1924	StL N	4	6	0	0	0	0	0	0	0	0	0	.000	.000	.000	-99	-2	0-0	1.000	1	124	0	2b2,S2	—	-0.1
Total	12	1163	3891	338	954	134	45	7	377	209	24	376	.245	.288	.308	75	-141	71-56	.930	54	103	114	S1126,2b10,3b9,1b3/cf	—	-1.2
LAVIGNE, ART	Arthur David; B1.26.1885 Worcester MA; D7.18.1950 Worcester MA; BR/TR/5´10˝/162; d4.24																								
1914	Buf F	51	90	10	14	2	0	0	4	7	0	25	.156	.216	.178	8	-13	0	.967	4	*125*	*112*	C34,1b3	—	-0.7
LAVIN, JOHNNY	John; B Troy NY; 5´11˝/175; d9.10																								
1884	StL AA	16	52	9	11	2	0	0	—	3	1	—	.212	.268	.250	68	-2	—	.750	-2	41	0	O16(0/15/1)	—	-0.4
LAW, RUDY	Rudy Karl; B10.7.1956 Waco TX; BL/TL/6´1˝/(165–176); d9.12																								
1978	LA N	11	12	2	3	0	0	0	1	1-0	0	2	.250	.308	.250	57	-1	3-1	1.000	-1	49	0	O6(3/3/0)	0	-0.1
1980	LA N	128	388	55	101	5	4	1	23	23-1	3	27	.260	.306	.302	72	-15	40-13	.988	-1	98	97	O106(5/102/0)	0	-1.4
1982	Chi A	121	336	55	107	15	8	3	32	23-0	0	41	.318	.361	.438	118	8	36-10	.973	-2	102	38	O94(4/90/0),D3	0	0.9
1983	†Chi A	141	501	95	142	20	7	3	34	42-2	2	36	.283	.340	.369	92	-5	77-12	**.994**	-5	94	69	O132C,D3	0	0.1
1984	Chi A	136	487	68	122	14	7	6	37	39-6	3	42	.251	.309	.345	77	-16	29-17	.985	-5	97	62	O130(10/122/0)	0	-2.2
1985	Chi A	125	390	62	101	21	6	4	36	27-0	3	40	.259	.311	.374	83	-9	29-6	.987	5	108	116	O120(104/32/0),D3	15	-0.4
1986	KC A	87	307	42	80	26	5	1	36	29-0	2	22	.261	.327	.388	92	-3	14-6	.987	-4	94	40	O77(54/3/36),D2	56	-0.9
Total	7	749	2421	379	656	101	37	18	199	184-9	13	210	.271	.325	.366	88	-41	228-65	.986	-14	98	72	O665(180/484/36),D11	71	-4.0
LAW, VANCE	Vance Aaron; B10.1.1956 Boise ID; BR/TR/6´2˝/(185–190); [PitN78 39/758]; d6.1; f–Vern; Col Brigham Young; OF(6/7/2)																								
1980	Pit N	25	74	11	17	2	2	0	3	3-0	0	7	.230	.260	.311	57	-5	2-0	.964	-2	93	79	2b11,S8/3	0	-0.5
1981	Pit N	30	67	1	9	0	1	0	3	2-0	0	15	.134	.157	.164	-8	-10	1-1	1.000	-1	99	99	2b19,S7,3b2	0	-1.0
1982	Chi A	114	359	40	101	20	1	5	54	26-1	1	46	.281	.327	.384	95	-2	4-2	.953	3	102	96	S85,3b39,2b10/lf	0	0.9
1983	†Chi A	145	408	55	99	21	5	4	42	51-1	1	56	.243	.325	.348	83	-9	3-1	.966	9	104	106	3b139,2b3,S2/cfD	0	-0.1
1984	Chi A	151	481	60	121	18	2	17	59	41-2	1	75	.252	.309	.403	91	-6	4-1	.955	-16	87	112	3b137,2b22,O5C,S4	0	-2.3
1985	Mon N	147	519	75	138	30	6	10	52	86-0	2	96	.266	.369	.405	124	20	6-5	.985	4	100	111	2b126,1b20,3b11/rf	0	3.1
1986	Mon N	112	360	37	81	17	2	5	44	37-1	1	66	.225	.298	.325	72	-14	3-5	.993	10	105	97	2b94,1b20,3b13,P3/rf	0	-0.1
1987	Mon N	133	436	52	119	27	1	12	56	51-5	0	62	.273	.347	.422	99	1	8-5	.980	-12	96	83	2b106,3b22,1b17,P3	0	-0.7
1988	Chi N★	151	556	73	163	29	2	11	78	55-4	3	79	.293	.358	.412	116	13	1-4	.953	-10	92	83	3b150/lf	0	0.2
1989	†Chi N	130	408	38	96	22	3	7	42	38-0	0	73	.235	.296	.355	81	-10	2-2	.949	-16	82	74	3b119/lf	0	-2.8
1991	Oak A	74	134	11	28	7	1	0	9	18-0	0	27	.209	.303	.276	65	-6	0-0	.951	-7	78	82	3b67,S3,O3L/1P	15	-1.3
Total	11	1212	3802	453	972	193	26	71	442	408-14	9	602	.256	.326	.376	93	-28	34-26	.956	-38	92	93	3b700,2b391,S109,1b58,O14C,P7/D	15	-4.6
LAWING, GARLAND	Garland Frederick "Knobby"; B8.29.1918 Gastonia NC; D9.27.1996 Murrells Inlet SC; BR/TR/6´1˝/180; d5.29																								
1946	Cin N	2	3	0	0	0	0	0	0	0	0	2	.000	.000	.000	-99	-1	0	ø	-0	0	0	/cf	0	-0.1
	NY N	8	12	2	2	0	0	0	0	0	0	3	.167	.167	.167	-5	-2	0	1.000	-0	109	0	O4(3/0/1)	0	-0.2
	Year	10	15	2	2	0	0	0	0	0	0	5	.133	.133	.133	-24	-3	0	1.000	-0	105	0	O5(3/1/1)	0	-0.3
LAWLESS, TOM	Thomas James; B12.19.1956 Erie PA; BR/TR/5´11˝/(165–170); [CinN78 17/433]; d7.15; Col Behrend																								
1982	Cin N	49	165	19	35	6	0	0	4	9-0	0	30	.212	.253	.248	41	-13	16-5	.978	6	104	134	2b47	0	-0.3
1984	Cin N	43	80	10	20	2	0	1	2	8-1	0	12	.250	.318	.313	74	-3	6-3	1.000	-5	75	49	2b23,3b6	0	-0.7
	Mon N	11	17	1	3	1	0	0	0	0-0	0	4	.176	.176	.235	15	-2	1-0	1.000	-2	80	69	2b9	0	-0.3
	Year	54	97	11	23	3	0	1	2	8-1	0	16	.237	.295	.299	65	-4	7-3	1.000	-7	76	54	2b32,3b6	0	-1.0
1985	†StL N	47	58	8	12	3	1	0	8	5-0	0	4	.207	.270	.293	58	-3	2-1	.971	1	137	145	3b13,2b11	0	-0.2
1986	StL N	46	39	5	11	1	0	0	3	2-0	0	8	.282	.310	.308	73	-1	8-1	.875	-1	86	125	3b12,2b7/lf	0	-0.1
1987	†StL N	19	25	5	2	1	0	0	0	3-0	0	5	.080	.179	.120	-19	-4	2-0	1.000	0	142	132	2b7,3b3/rf	15	-0.4
1988	StL N	54	65	9	10	2	1	1	3	7-0	0	9	.154	.236	.262	42	-5	6-0	1.000	-1	81	47	3b24,O6(4/0/2),2b5/1	0	-0.5
1989	Tor A	59	70	20	16	1	0	0	3	7-0	0	12	.229	.295	.243	55	-4	12-1	1.000	-1	95	0	O16(7/0/9),3b12,D12,2b7/C	0	-0.4
1990	Tor A	15	12	1	1	0	0	0	1	0-0	0	1	.083	.083	.083	-52	-2	0-2	.800	1	88	0	3b4,O2L/2D	0	-0.2
Total	8	343	531	78	110	17	2	2	24	41-1	0	85	.207	.263	.258	46	-37	53-13	.988	-2	98	108	2b117,3b74,O26(14/0/12),D17/C1	15	-3.1
LAWLOR, MIKE	Michael H.; B3.11.1854 Troy NY; D8.3.1918 Troy NY; TR/6´0˝/180; d5.27																								
1880	Tro N	4	9	1	1	0	0	0	0	1	—	1	.111	.200	.111	8	-1	—	.867	-0	—	—	C4	—	-0.1
1884	Was U	2	7	0	0	0	0	0	—	0	—	—	.000	.000	.000	-99	-2	—	1.000	1	—	—	C2	—	-0.1
Total	2	6	16	1	1	0	0	0	0	1	—	1	.063	.118	.063	-39	-3	—	.920	1	—	—	C6	—	-0.2
LAWRENCE, JIM	James Ross; B2.12.1939 Hamilton ON, Can.; BL/TR/6´1˝/185; d5.30																								
1963	Cle A	2	0	0	0	0	0	0	0	0-0	0	0	ø	ø	ø	ø	0	0-0	.750	-1	4	0	C2	0	-0.1
LAWRENCE, JOE	Joseph Dudley; B2.13.1977 Lake Charles LA; BR/TR/6´2˝/190; [TorA96 1/16]; d4.8																								
2002	Tor A	55	150	16	27	4	0	2	15	16-0	2	38	.180	.262	.247	37	-14	2-1	.967	-7	97	64	2b49/D	0	-1.8
LAWRENCE, BILL	William Henry; B3.11.1906 San Mateo CA; D6.15.1997 Redwood City CA; BR/TR/6´4˝/194; d4.13; Col Santa Clara																								
1932	Det A	25	46	10	10	1	0	0	3	5	0	5	.217	.294	.239	38	-4	0-2	1.000	3	124	189	O15(0/8/7)	—	-0.3
LAWRY, OTIS	Otis Carroll "Rabbit"; B11.1.1893 Fairfield ME; D10.23.1965 China ME; BL/TR/5´8˝/133; d6.28; Mil 1918; Col Maine																								
1916	Phi A	41	123	10	25	0	0	0	4	9	1	21	.203	.263	.203	42	-9	4	.905	-4	101	67	2b29,O5(3/2/0)	—	-1.4
1917	Phi A	30	55	7	9	1	0	0	1	2	0	9	.164	.193	.182	15	-6	1	.921	-2	97	36	2b17/lf	—	-0.9
Total	2	71	178	17	34	1	0	0	5	11	1	30	.191	.242	.197	34	-15	5	.911	-6	100	57	2b46,O6(4/2/0)	—	-2.3
LAWTON, MARCUS	Marcus Dwayne; B8.18.1965 Gulfport MS; BB/TR/6´1˝/160; [NYN83 6/136]; d8.11; b–Matt																								
1989	NY A	10	14	1	3	0	0	0	0	0-0	0	3	.214	.214	.214	21	-2	1-0	.818	-0	116	0	O8(7/0/1)/D	0	-0.2
LAWTON, MATT	Matthew; B11.30.1971 Gulfport MS; BL/TR/5´10˝/(186–200); [MinA91 13/336]; d9.5; b–Marcus; Col Mississippi Gulf Coast CC																								
1995	Min A	21	60	11	19	4	1	1	12	7-0	3	11	.317	.414	.467	128	3	1-1	.972	-1	90	112	O19(1/12/8)/D	0	0.2
1996	Min A	79	252	34	65	7	1	6	42	28-1	4	28	.258	.339	.365	77	-9	4-4	.985	9	133	85	O75(1/18/60)/D	0	-0.2
1997	Min A	142	460	74	114	29	3	14	60	76-3	10	81	.248	.366	.415	102	4	7-4	.976	1	101	109	O138(58/24/66)	0	0.0
1998	Min A	152	557	91	155	36	6	21	77	86-6	15	64	.278	.387	.478	121	20	16-8	.990	14	**119**	112	O151(12/47/100)	0	2.9
1999	Min A	118	406	58	105	18	0	7	54	57-7	6	42	.259	.353	.355	79	-12	26-4	.982	-3	102	41	O109(10/6/103),D6	39	-1.4
2000	Min A★	156	561	84	171	44	2	13	88	91-8	7	63	.305	.405	.460	112	15	23-7	.983	-4	100	45	O143(67/3/83),D9	0	0.7
2001	Min A	103	376	71	110	25	0	10	51	63-6	3	46	.293	.396	.439	114	11	19-6	.980	-1	106	33	O94R,D7	0	0.7
	NY N	48	183	24	45	11	1	3	13	22-0	8	34	.246	.352	.366	93	-1	10-2	1.000	-0	103	33	O48R	0	-0.2
2002	Cle A	114	416	71	98	19	2	15	57	59-0	8	34	.236	.342	.399	94	-2	8-9	.975	5	114	97	O108(23/0/85),D3	41	-0.3
2003	Cle A	99	374	57	93	19	0	15	53	47-0	7	47	.249	.343	.420	100	1	10-3	.993	-4	89	87	O74(62/0/13),D21	60	-0.6
2004	Cle A★	150	591	109	164	25	0	20	70	74-3	11	84	.277	.366	.421	109	10	23-9	.986	-1	96	112	O142(124/0/19),D3	0	0.6

YEAR	TM LG	G	AB	R	H	2B	3B	HR	RBI	BB-IB	HP	SO	AVG	OBP	SLG	AOPS	ABR	SB-CS	FA	FR	RNG	THR	GAMES AT POSITION	DL	BFW
2005	Chi N	19	78	8	19	2	0	1	5	4-0	1	8	.244	.289	.308	55	-5	1-0	.971	-1	102	0	O19(18/0/3)	0	-0.7
	Pit N	101	374	53	102	28	1	10	44	58-0	9	61	.273	.380	.433	113	10	16-9	.995	2	106	71	O98R	0	0.8
	Year	120	452	61	121	30	1	11	49	62-0	10	69	.268	.366	.412	103	5	17-9	.992	2	100	0	O117(18/0/101)	0	0.1
	NY A	21	48	6	6	0	0	2	4	7-0	2	8	.125	.263	.250	38	-4	1-0	.969	-1	100	0	O19(8/0/12)	0	-0.6
2006	Sea A	11	27	5	7	0	0	0	1	2-0	0	2	.259	.310	.259	53	-2	0-0	1.000	-1	83	0	O7(1/5/2),D2	0	-0.3
Total	12	1334	4763	756	1273	267	17	138	631	681-34	94	613	.267	.368	.417	102	39	165-66	.984	17	105	77	O1244(385/115/794),D53	140	1.6

LAYDEN, GENE Eugene Francis; B3.14.1894 Pittsburgh PA; D12.12.1984 Pittsburgh PA; BL/TL/5´10˝/160; d7.29

YEAR	TM LG	G	AB	R	H	2B	3B	HR	RBI	BB-IB	HP	SO	AVG	OBP	SLG	AOPS	ABR	SB-CS	FA	FR	RNG	THR	GAMES AT POSITION	DL	BFW
1915	NY A	3	7	2	2	0	0	0	0	0	0	1	.286	.286	.286	71	0	0-1	.750	-0	94	0	O2C	—	-0.1

LAYDEN, PETE Peter John; B12.30.1919 Dallas TX; D7.18.1982 Edna TX; BR/TR/5´11˝/185; d4.20; Col Texas

YEAR	TM LG	G	AB	R	H	2B	3B	HR	RBI	BB-IB	HP	SO	AVG	OBP	SLG	AOPS	ABR	SB-CS	FA	FR	RNG	THR	GAMES AT POSITION	DL	BFW
1948	StL A	41	104	11	26	2	1	0	4	6	1	10	.250	.297	.288	55	-7	4-2	.973	1	99	146	O30(1/24/5)	0	-0.7

LAYNE, HERMAN Herman; B2.13.1901 New Haven WV; D8.27.1973 Gallipolis OH; BR/TR/5´11˝/165; d4.16; Col West Virginia

YEAR	TM LG	G	AB	R	H	2B	3B	HR	RBI	BB-IB	HP	SO	AVG	OBP	SLG	AOPS	ABR	SB-CS	FA	FR	RNG	THR	GAMES AT POSITION	DL	BFW
1927	Pit N	11	6	3	0	0	0	0	0	1	0	0	.000	.143	.000	-55	-1	0	.000	-1	0	0	O2(1/1/0)	—	-0.2

LAYNE, HILLIS Ivoria Hillis "Tony"; B2.23.1918 Whitwell TN; BL/TR/6´0˝/170; d9.16; Mil 1942–43

YEAR	TM LG	G	AB	R	H	2B	3B	HR	RBI	BB-IB	HP	SO	AVG	OBP	SLG	AOPS	ABR	SB-CS	FA	FR	RNG	THR	GAMES AT POSITION	DL	BFW
1941	Was A	13	50	8	14	2	0	0	6	4	0	5	.280	.333	.320	77	-2	1-1	.953	-0	108	39	3b13	0	-0.1
1944	Was A	33	87	6	17	2	0	0	8	6	2	10	.195	.263	.218	40	-7	2-0	.949	1	106	32	3b18,2b3	0	-0.5
1945	Was A	61	147	23	44	5	4	1	14	10	2	7	.299	.352	.408	132	5	0-1	.956	-3	88	57	3b33	0	0.2
Total	3	107	284	37	75	9	4	1	28	20	4	22	.264	.321	.335	92	-4	3-2	.953	-2	97	46	3b64,2b3	0	-0.4

LAYTON, LES Lester Lee; B11.18.1921 Nardin OK; BR/TR/6´0˝/165; d4.24; Col Oklahoma

YEAR	TM LG	G	AB	R	H	2B	3B	HR	RBI	BB-IB	HP	SO	AVG	OBP	SLG	AOPS	ABR	SB-CS	FA	FR	RNG	THR	GAMES AT POSITION	DL	BFW
1948	NY N	63	91	14	21	4	4	2	12	6	1	21	.231	.286	.429	90	-2	1	.951	0	112	84	O20(12/3/3)	0	-0.2

LAZOR, JOHNNY John Paul; B9.9.1912 Taylor WA; D12.9.2002 Renton WA; BL/TR/5´9.5˝/180; d4.22

YEAR	TM LG	G	AB	R	H	2B	3B	HR	RBI	BB-IB	HP	SO	AVG	OBP	SLG	AOPS	ABR	SB-CS	FA	FR	RNG	THR	GAMES AT POSITION	DL	BFW
1943	Bos A	83	208	21	47	10	2	0	13	21	0	25	.226	.297	.293	72	-7	5-6	.979	3	102	153	O63(51/7/8)	0	-1.0
1944	Bos A	16	24	0	2	1	0	0	0	1	0	0	.083	.120	.125	-30	-4	0-0	1.000	1	85	694	O6(1/0/5)/C	0	-0.4
1945	Bos A	101	335	35	104	19	2	5	45	18	0	17	.310	.346	.424	120	7	3-2	.961	-6	88	76	O81(12/0/73)	0	-0.5
1946	Bos A	23	29	1	4	0	0	1	4	2	0	11	.138	.194	.241	20	-3	0-0	1.000	-0	95	0	O7(3/0/4)	0	-0.4
Total	4	223	596	57	157	30	4	6	62	42	0	53	.263	.312	.357	92	-7	8-8	.971	-3	94	123	O157(67/7/90)/C	0	-2.3

LAZZERI, TONY Anthony Michael "Poosh 'Em Up Tony"; B12.6.1903 San Francisco CA; D8.6.1946 San Francisco CA; BR/TR/5´11.5˝/170; d4.13; C1; HF1991

YEAR	TM LG	G	AB	R	H	2B	3B	HR	RBI	BB-IB	HP	SO	AVG	OBP	SLG	AOPS	ABR	SB-CS	FA	FR	RNG	THR	GAMES AT POSITION	DL	BFW
1926	†NY A	**155**	589	79	162	28	14	18	114	54	2	96	.275	.338	.462	109	3	16-7	.961	-18	95	90	2b149,S5/3	—	-0.8
1927	†NY A	153	570	92	176	29	8	18	102	69	0	82	.309	.383	.482	127	22	22-14	.971	8	**111**	104	2b113,S38,3b9	—	3.5
1928	†NY A	116	404	62	134	30	11	10	82	43	1	50	.332	.397	.535	148	28	15-5	.956	-7	97	92	2b110	—	2.4
1929	NY A	147	545	101	193	37	11	18	106	68	4	45	.354	.429	.561	164	54	9-10	.969	1	97	112	2b147	—	5.2
1930	NY A	143	571	109	173	34	15	9	121	60	3	62	.303	.372	.462	115	13	4-4	.971	2	99	79	2b77,3b60,S8/1lf	—	2.0
1931	NY A	135	484	67	129	27	7	8	83	79	1	80	.267	.371	.401	109	9	18-9	.958	-4	100	96	2b90,3b39	—	1.2
1932	†NY A	142	510	79	153	28	16	15	113	82	2	64	.300	.399	.506	140	32	11-11	.978	4	91	84	2b134,3b5	—	3.9
1933	NY A☆	139	523	94	154	22	12	18	104	73	2	62	.294	.383	.486	137	28	15-7	.968	-12	88	80	2b138	—	2.4
1934	NY A	123	438	59	117	24	6	14	67	71	0	64	.267	.369	.445	117	12	11-1	.976	-15	91	91	2b92,3b30	—	0.5
1935	NY A	130	477	72	130	18	6	13	83	63	3	75	.273	.361	.417	107	5	11-5	.970	-21	85	103	2b118,S9	—	-0.7
1936	†NY A	150	537	82	154	29	6	14	109	97	1	65	.287	.397	.441	110	12	8-5	.968	-37	84	92	2b148,S2	—	-1.4
1937	†NY A	126	446	56	109	21	3	14	70	71	0	76	.244	.348	.399	87	-9	7-1	.966	-9	101	84	2b125	—	-0.8
1938	†Chi N	54	120	21	32	5	0	5	23	22	0	30	.267	.380	.433	120	4	0	.946	-5	88	94	S25,3b7,2b4/lf	—	0.1
1939	Bro N	14	39	6	11	2	0	3	6	10	2	7	.282	.451	.564	165	4	1	.914	-2	97	124	2b11,3b2	—	0.4
	NY N	13	44	7	13	0	0	1	8	7	0	6	.295	.392	.364	103	0	0	.889	-2	86	45	3b13	—	-0.1
	Year	27	83	13	24	2	0	4	14	17	2	13	.289	.422	.458	133	5	1	.897	-4	87	42	3b15,2b11	—	0.3
Total	14	1740	6297	986	1840	334	115	178	1191	869	21	864	.292	.380	.467	122	217	148-79	.967	-115	94	93	2b1456,3b166,S87,O2L/1	—	17.8

LEACH, FREDDY Frederick; B11.23.1897 Springfield MO; D12.10.1981 Hagerman ID; BL/TR/5´11˝/183; d5.24

YEAR	TM LG	G	AB	R	H	2B	3B	HR	RBI	BB-IB	HP	SO	AVG	OBP	SLG	AOPS	ABR	SB-CS	FA	FR	RNG	THR	GAMES AT POSITION	DL	BFW
1923	Phi N	52	104	5	27	4	0	1	16	3	0	14	.260	.280	.327	54	-7	1-2	.950	-2	97	0	O26(17/9/1)	—	-1.0
1924	Phi N	8	28	6	13	2	1	2	7	2	0	1	.464	.500	.821	221	5	0-0	1.000	-0	67	172	O7L	—	0.4
1925	Phi N	65	292	47	91	15	4	5	28	5	0	21	.312	.323	.442	86	-7	1-2	.952	-5	97	32	O65C	—	-1.5
1926	Phi N	129	492	73	162	29	7	11	71	16	1	33	.329	.352	.484	117	10	6	.979	6	105	126	O123(48/84/8)	—	0.9
1927	Phi N	140	536	69	164	30	4	12	83	21	8	32	.306	.342	.444	108	4	2	.981	16	107	**182**	O140(18/123/5)	—	1.4
1928	Phi N	145	588	83	179	36	11	13	96	30	4	30	.304	.342	.469	107	3	4	.978	7	108	109	O120(93/22/7),1b25	—	0.0
1929	NY N	113	411	74	119	22	6	8	47	17	4	14	.290	.324	.431	85	-11	10	.974	-12	78	32	O95(94/0/1)	—	-2.8
1930	NY N	126	544	90	178	19	13	13	71	22	7	25	.327	.361	.482	104	1	3	.978	-5	85	125	O124L	—	-1.2
1931	NY N	129	515	75	159	30	5	6	61	29	2	9	.309	.348	.421	109	5	4	.976	-1	100	98	O125L	—	-0.2
1932	Bos N	84	223	21	55	9	2	1	29	18	1	10	.247	.306	.318	71	-9	1	.977	-2	100	43	O50(8/22/21)	—	-1.4
Total	10	991	3733	543	1147	196	53	72	509	163	27	189	.307	.341	.446	101	-6	32-4	.975	3	98	104	O875(534/325/43),1b25	—	-5.4

LEACH, JALAL Jalal Donnell; B3.14.1969 San Francisco CA; BL/TL/6´2˝/200; [NYA90 7/192]; d9.5; Col Pepperdine

YEAR	TM LG	G	AB	R	H	2B	3B	HR	RBI	BB-IB	HP	SO	AVG	OBP	SLG	AOPS	ABR	SB-CS	FA	FR	RNG	THR	GAMES AT POSITION	DL	BFW
2001	SF N	8	10	0	1	0	0	0	1	2-0	0	3	.100	.250	.100	-5	-2	0-0	1.000	-1	35	0	O3(1/0/2)	0	-0.2

LEACH, RICK Richard Max; B5.4.1957 Ann Arbor MI; BL/TL/6´0˝/(190–195); [DetA79 1/13]; d4.30; Col Michigan

YEAR	TM LG	G	AB	R	H	2B	3B	HR	RBI	BB-IB	HP	SO	AVG	OBP	SLG	AOPS	ABR	SB-CS	FA	FR	RNG	THR	GAMES AT POSITION	DL	BFW
1981	Det A	54	83	9	16	3	1	1	11	16-1	0	15	.193	.320	.289	75	-2	0-1	1.000	-1	132	122	1b32,O15R,D2	0	-0.5
1982	Det A	82	218	23	52	7	2	3	12	21-2	0	29	.239	.303	.330	74	-8	4-0	.995	-3	88	98	1b56,O14(4/0/10),D4	35	-1.3
1983	Det A	99	242	22	60	17	0	3	26	19-1	1	21	.248	.305	.355	83	-5	2-2	.994	2	113	87	1b73,O13(2/0/11),D3	0	-0.8
1984	Tor A	65	88	11	23	6	2	0	7	8-0	0	14	.261	.320	.375	89	-1	0-0	1.000	3	93	132	O23(5/1/17),1b15/PD	0	0.0
1985	Tor A	16	35	2	7	0	1	0	1	3-1	0	9	.200	.263	.257	42	-3	0-0	.987	0	106	141	1b10,O4(1/0/3)	0	-0.3
1986	Tor A	110	246	35	76	14	1	5	39	13-3	0	24	.309	.335	.435	107	2	0-0	.978	-4	79	0	D42,O39(19/0/20),1b7	0	-0.5
1987	Tor A	98	195	26	55	13	1	3	25	25-2	3	25	.282	.371	.405	104	2	0-1	.981	-2	95	53	O43(21/0/22),D30,1b5	0	-0.2
1988	Tor A	87	199	21	55	13	1	0	23	18-3	0	27	.276	.336	.352	92	-2	0-1	1.000	2	107	51	O49(14/0/36),D25,1b4	0	-0.2
1989	Tex A	110	239	32	65	14	1	1	23	32-7	1	33	.272	.358	.351	99	1	2-1	.951	-1	96	59	D44,O41(37/0/3),1b4	0	-0.2
1990	SF N	78	174	24	51	13	0	2	16	21-0	1	20	.293	.372	.402	117	5	0-2	.989	2	109	109	O52(13/0/40),1b7	0	0.5
Total	10	799	1719	205	460	100	10	18	183	176-20	6	217	.268	.335	.369	94	-11	8-8	.983	-3	95	59	O293(116/1/177),1b213,D156/P	35	-3.5

LEACH, TOMMY Thomas William; B11.4.1877 French Creek NY; D9.29.1969 Haines City FL; BR/TR/5´6.5˝/150; d9.28; OF(74/996/13)

YEAR	TM LG	G	AB	R	H	2B	3B	HR	RBI	BB-IB	HP	SO	AVG	OBP	SLG	AOPS	ABR	SB-CS	FA	FR	RNG	THR	GAMES AT POSITION	DL	BFW
1898	Lou N	3	10	0	1	0	0	0	0	0	0	—	.100	.100	.100	-43	-2	0	.727	-1	116	0	3b3/2	—	-0.2
1899	Lou N	106	406	75	117	10	6	5	57	37	1	—	.288	.349	.379	100	-1	19	.908	-5	105	108	3b80,S25,2b2	—	-0.3
1900	†Pit N	51	160	20	34	1	2	1	16	21	0	—	.213	.304	.262	57	-9	8	.864	0	97	110	3b31,S8,2b7,O4(2/0/2)	—	-0.7
1901	Pit N	98	374	64	114	12	13	2	44	20	4	—	.305	.347	.422	119	7	16	.903	10	112	105	3b92,S4	—	1.9
1902	Pit N	135	514	97	143	14	**22**	**6**	85	45	4	—	.278	.341	.426	132	17	25	.926	12	112	66	3b134	—	3.4
1903	†Pit N	127	507	97	151	16	17	7	87	40	2	—	.298	.352	.438	121	11	22	.879	4	**111**	129	3b127	—	1.8
1904	Pit N	146	579	92	149	15	12	2	56	45	5	—	.257	.316	.335	98	-2	23	.907	**36**	**128**	115	3b146	—	4.0
1905	Pit N	131	499	71	128	10	14	2	53	37	1	—	.257	.309	.345	92	-6	17	.988	9	117	92	O71(16/51/6),3b58,2b2,S2	—	0.1
1906	Pit N	133	476	66	136	10	7	1	39	33	1	—	.286	.333	.342	106	2	21	.929	-2	103	58	3b65,O60(15/44/1)/S	—	-0.1
1907	Pit N	149	547	102	166	19	12	4	43	40	1	—	.303	.352	.404	135	20	43	.980	5	96	136	O111(2/109/0),3b33,S6/2	—	2.4
1908	Pit N	152	583	93	151	24	16	5	41	54	2	—	.259	.324	.381	125	15	24	.937	-7	96	109	3b150,O2C	—	1.5
1909	†Pit N	151	587	**126**	153	29	8	6	43	66	2	—	.261	.337	.368	110	7	27	.969	-5	59	75	O138C,3b13	—	-0.4
1910	Pit N	135	529	83	143	24	5	4	52	38	0	62	.270	.319	.357	92	-7	18	.966	4	**113**	76	O131C,S2/2	—	-1.0
1911	Pit N	108	386	60	92	12	6	3	43	46	2	50	.238	.323	.324	78	-11	19	.987	4	111	126	O89(1/89/0),S13/3	—	-1.2
1912	Pit N	28	97	24	29	4	2	0	19	12	0	9	.299	.376	.381	109	1	6	.986	2	109	103	O24C	—	0.2
	Chi N	82	265	50	64	10	3	2	32	55	3	20	.242	.378	.325	93	1	14	.975	-0	100	93	O73C,3b4	—	-0.5
	Year	110	362	74	93	14	5	2	51	67	3	29	.257	.377	.340	98	2	20	.978	2	102	95	O97C,3b4	—	-0.3
1913	Chi N	131	456	**99**	131	23	10	6	32	77	1	44	.287	.391	.421	132	22	21-10	**.990**	-0	99	93	O121(3/118/0),3b2	—	1.6
1914	Chi N	153	577	80	152	24	9	7	46	79	1	50	.263	.353	.373	116	13	16	.968	3	108	103	O136C,3b16	—	0.8
1915	Cin N	107	335	42	75	7	5	0	17	56	2	38	.224	.338	.275	85	-3	20-14	.959	-2	98	85	O96(17/81/0)	—	-1.3
1918	Pit N	30	72	14	14	2	3	0	5	19	0	5	.194	.363	.306	101	1	2	.952	-1	95	128	O23(18/0/4),S3	—	0.0
Total	19	2156	7959	1355	2143	266	172	63	810	820	32	278	.269	.340	.370	108	76	361-24	.975	68	98	91	O1079C,3b955,S64,2b14	—	12.0

LEAHY, DAN Daniel C.; B8.8.1870 Knoxville TN; D12.30.1903 Knoxville TN; 5´9˝/155; d9.2

YEAR	TM LG	G	AB	R	H	2B	3B	HR	RBI	BB-IB	HP	SO	AVG	OBP	SLG	AOPS	ABR	SB-CS	FA	FR	RNG	THR	GAMES AT POSITION	DL	BFW
1896	Phi N	2	6	0	2	1	0	0	1	1	0	2	.333	.429	.500	146	0	0	.857	0	121	0	S2	—	0.1

YEAR	TM LG	G	AB	R	H	2B	3B	HR	RBI	BB-IB	HP	SO	AVG	OBP	SLG	AOPS	ABR	SB-CS	FA	FR	RNG	THR	GAMES AT POSITION	DL	BFW
LEAHY, TOM Thomas Joseph; B6.2.1869 New Haven CT; D6.11.1951 New Haven CT; BR/TR/5´7.5˝/168; d5.18; Col Holy Cross																									
1897	Pit N	24	92	10	24	3	3	0	12	7	1	—	.261	.320	.359	82	-3	3	.935	-4	52	0	O13(7/4/2),C6,3b6	—	-0.6
	Was N	19	52	12	20	2	1	0	7	9	7	—	.385	.529	.462	164	7	6	.727	-1	237	0	O10(2/8/0),3b5,2b3/C	—	0.5
	Year	43	144	22	44	5	4	0	19	16	8	—	.306	.405	.396	115	4	9	.881	-5	108	0	O23(9/12/2),3b11,C7,2b3	—	-0.1
1898	Was N	15	55	10	10	2	0	0	5	8	1	—	.182	.297	.218	48	-3	6	.913	0	99	51	3b12,2b3	—	-0.2
1901	Mil A	33	99	18	24	6	2	0	10	11	5	—	.242	.348	.343	97	0	3	.941	-6	*70*	*106*	C28,O2R/2	—	-0.2
	Phi A	5	15	1	5	1	0	0	1	1	0	—	.333	.375	.400	110	0	0	1.000	-0	0	0	O2L/CS	—	0.0
	Year	38	114	19	29	7	2	0	11	12	5	—	.254	.351	.351	99	1	3	.944	-6	*74*	*109*	C29,O4(2/0/2)/2S	—	-0.2
1905	StL N	35	97	3	22	1	3	0	7	8	0	—	.227	.286	.299	77	-3	0	.946	-7	*79*	*92*	C29	—	-0.8
Total	4	131	410	54	105	15	9	0	42	44	14	—	.256	.348	.337	93	-2	18	.942	-17	*77*	*98*	C65,O27(11/12/4),3b23,2b7/S	—	-1.3
LEAR, FRED Frederick Francis "King"; B4.7.1894 New York NY; D10.13.1955 E.Orange NJ; BR/TR/6´0.5˝/180; d6.7; Col Villanova																									
1915	Phi A	2	2	0	0	0	0	0	0	0	0	2	.000	.000	.000	-99	-1	0	.600	-1	0	0	3b2	—	-0.1
1918	Chi N	2	1	0	0	0	0	0	0	1	0	0	.000	.500	.000	56	0	0	ø	0	—	—	/H	—	0.0
1919	Chi N	40	76	8	17	3	1	1	11	8	1	11	.224	.306	.329	90	-1	2	.990	-3	40	94	1b9,2b9,S3	—	-0.4
1920	NY N	31	87	12	22	0	1	1	7	8	1	15	.253	.323	.310	83	-2	0-2	.951	-1	101	163	3b24/2	—	-0.3
Total	4	75	166	20	39	3	2	2	18	17	2	28	.235	.314	.313	84	-4	2-2	.924	-4	96	155	3b26,2b10,1b9,S3	—	-0.8
LEARD, BILL William Wallace "Wild Bill"; B10.14.1885 Oneida NY; D1.15.1970 San Francisco CA; BR/TR/5´10˝/155; d7.21																									
1917	Bro N	3	3	0	0	0	0	0	0	0	0	1	.000	.000	.000	-97	-1	0	ø	-0	0	0	/2	—	-0.1
LEARY, JACK John J.; B7.1857 New Haven CT; TL/5´11˝/186; d8.21; ▲																									
1880	Bos N	1	3	1	0	0	0	0	0	1	—	0	.000	.250	.000	-7	0	—	1.000	1	940	0	/rfP	—	0.0
1881	Det N	3	11	2	3	1	1	0	4	1	—	1	.273	.333	.545	165	1	—	.833	-0	145	0	O2(0/1/1),P2	—	0.0
1882	Pit AA	60	257	32	75	7	3	1	—	5	—	—	.292	.305	.354	128	7	—	.759	-9	93	33	3b33,O27(0/8/19),P3/12	—	-0.2
	Bal AA	4	18	3	4	1	0	0	—	0	—	—	.222	.222	.278	73	0	—	.900	-0	105	0	P3/cf	—	0.0
	Year	64	275	35	79	8	3	1	—	5	—	—	.287	.300	.349	124	7	—	.759	-9	93	33	3b33,O28(0/9/19),P6/12	—	-0.2
1883	Lou AA	40	165	16	31	1	3	3	—	2	—	—	.188	.198	.285	58	-8	—	.816	-4	91	121	S40	—	-0.9
	Bal AA	3	11	1	2	0	2	0	—	0	—	—	.182	.182	.545	122	0	—	.727	-1	69	228	2b3	—	-0.1
	Year	43	176	17	33	1	5	3	—	2	—	—	.188	.197	.301	62	-8	—	.816	-5	91	121	S40,2b3	—	-1.0
1884	Alt U	8	33	1	3	0	0	0	—	1	—	—	.091	.118	.091	-36	-7	—	.692	-2	0	0	O6(4/2/0),P3/3	—	-0.6
	CP U	10	40	0	7	1	0	0	—	0	—	—	.175	.175	.200	14	-5	—	.840	-2	83	0	2b4,3b3,O3C,P2	—	-0.6
	Year	18	73	1	10	1	0	0	—	1	—	—	.137	.149	.151	-9	-12	—	.625	-4	79	0	O9(4/5/0),P5,3b4,2b4	—	-1.2
Total	5	129	538	56	125	11	9	4	4	10	—	1	.232	.246	.309	84	-12	—	.816	-17	91	121	S40,O40(4/15/21),3b37,P14,2b8/1	—	-2.4
LEARY, JOHN John Louis "Jack"; B5.2.1891 Waltham MA; D8.18.1961 Waltham MA; BR/TR/5´11.5˝/180; d4.14																									
1914	StL A	144	533	35	141	28	7	0	45	10	3	71	.265	.282	.343	91	-9	9-15	.987	-3	94	99	1b130,C15	—	-2.0
1915	StL A	75	227	19	55	10	0	0	15	5	3	36	.242	.268	.286	69	-10	2-4	.985	-2	118	164	1b53,C11	—	-1.4
Total	2	219	760	54	196	38	7	0	60	15	6	107	.258	.278	.326	85	-19	11-19	.987	-5	100	116	1b183,C26	—	-3.4
LEATHERS, HAL Harold Langford "Chuck"; B12.2.1898 Selma CA; D4.12.1977 Modesto CA; BL/TR/5´8˝/152; d9.13																									
1920	Chi N	9	23	3	7	1	0	1	0	1	0	1	.304	.333	.478	129	1	1-0	.825	-2	89	0	S6,2b3	—	0.0
LEBER, EMIL Emil Bohmiel; B5.15.1881 Cleveland OH; D11.6.1924 Cleveland OH; BR/TR/5´11˝/170; d9.2																									
1905	Cle A	2	6	1	0	0	0	0	0	1	0	—	.000	.143	.000	-53	-1	0	1.000	0	137	0	3b2	—	-0.1
LEBOURVEAU, BEVO De Witt Wiley; B8.24.1896 Dana CA; D12.10.1947 Nevada City CA; BL/TR/5´11˝/175; d9.9; Col Santa Clara																									
1919	Phi N	17	63	4	17	0	0	0	0	10	0	8	.270	.370	.270	88	0	2	1.000	2	82	275	O15(15/0/2)	—	0.1
1920	Phi N	84	261	29	67	7	2	3	12	11	3	36	.257	.295	.333	76	-8	9-6	.949	3	91	195	O72(51/17/4)	—	-1.0
1921	Phi N	93	281	42	83	12	5	6	35	29	0	51	.295	.361	.438	102	1	4-5	.911	-6	89	76	O76(27/1/48)	—	-1.1
1922	Phi N	74	167	24	45	8	3	2	20	24	2	29	.269	.368	.389	87	-3	0-3	.920	-3	92	81	O42(33/4/5)	—	-0.9
1929	Phi A	12	16	1	5	0	1	0	2	5	0	1	.313	.476	.438	132	1	0-1	1.000	0	116	0	O3(0/2/1)	—	0.1
Total	5	280	788	100	217	27	11	11	69	79	5	125	.275	.345	.379	91	-9	15-15	.935	-4	90	134	O208(126/24/60)	—	-2.8
LECROY, MATTHEW Matthew Hanks; B12.13.1975 Belton SC; BR/TR/6´2˝/(225–230); [MinA97 1/50]; d4.3; Col Clemson																									
2000	Min A	56	167	18	29	10	0	5	17	17-2	2	38	.174	.254	.323	43	-15	0-0	.988	3	124	76	C49,1b3,D3	0	-0.9
2001	Min A	15	40	6	17	5	0	3	12	0-0	1	8	.425	.429	.775	200	6	0-1	1.000	0	72	338	C3,1b2,D9	0	0.5
2002	†Min A	63	181	19	47	11	1	7	27	13-1	0	38	.260	.306	.448	95	-2	0-2	.976	-1	31	205	D41,1b8,C6	0	-0.6
2003	†Min A	107	345	39	99	19	0	17	64	25-1	4	82	.287	.342	.490	112	6	0-1	.980	-8	71	95	D64,C22,1b17	0	-0.6
2004	†Min A	88	264	25	71	14	0	9	39	16-0	5	60	.269	.321	.424	90	-4	0-0	.967	-7	55	26	D30,C26,1b23	33	-1.3
2005	Min A	101	304	33	79	5	0	17	50	41-2	4	85	.260	.354	.444	109	4	0-0	.986	-3	61	115	D63,1b23/C	0	-0.4
2006	Was N	39	67	5	16	3	0	2	9	11-0	1	17	.239	.350	.373	91	-1	0-0	.968	-6	29	47	C13,1b6,D2	0	-0.6
Total	7	469	1368	145	358	67	1	60	218	123-6	17	328	.262	.328	.444	98	-6	0-4	.982	-23	87	68	D212,C120,1b82	33	-3.9
LEDEE, RICKY Ricardo Alberto; B11.22.1973 Ponce, PR; BL/TL/6´1˝/(160–225); [NYA90 16/435]; d6.14																									
1998	†NY A	42	79	13	19	5	2	1	12	7-0	0	29	.241	.299	.392	82	-2	3-1	.981	1	95	263	O42(36/3/4)	0	-0.2
1999	†NY A	88	250	45	69	13	5	9	40	28-5	0	73	.276	.346	.476	109	3	4-3	.942	-1	107	71	O77(69/6/3),D5	0	0.0
2000	NY A	62	191	23	46	11	1	7	31	26-2	1	39	.241	.332	.419	91	-3	7-3	.979	-1	101	37	O49(46/4/1),D10	0	-0.5
	Cle A	17	63	13	14	2	1	2	8	8-0	0	9	.222	.310	.381	71	-3	0-0	1.000	1	119	99	O17(12/0/6)	0	-0.2
	Tex A	58	213	23	50	6	3	4	38	25-2	1	50	.235	.317	.347	68	-11	6-3	.977	-1	110	0	O57(20/3/42)	0	-1.3
	Year	137	467	59	110	19	5	13	77	59-4	2	98	.236	.322	.381	77	-17	13-6	.981	-1	108	28	O123(78/7/49),D10	0	-2.0
2001	Tex A	78	242	33	56	21	1	2	36	23-0	3	58	.231	.303	.351	71	-10	3-3	.979	-2	102	24	O72(6/10/60)	73	-1.4
2002	Phi N	96	203	33	46	13	1	8	23	35-0	1	50	.227	.342	.419	106	2	1-2	1.000	-2	98	0	O51(10/40/5)	0	0.0
2003	Phi N	121	255	37	63	15	2	13	46	34-5	0	59	.247	.334	.475	117	6	0-0	1.000	-3	80	156	O71(29/42/1),D2	0	0.2
2004	Phi N	73	123	19	35	7	0	7	26	22-2	0	27	.285	.393	.512	127	6	2-0	1.000	3	109	282	O22(9/13/1)	15	0.8
	SF N	31	53	6	6	2	0	0	4	5-0	1	20	.113	.200	.151	-6	-9	1-0	.960	-1	103	0	O15(1/3/11),D2	0	-0.9
	Year	104	176	25	41	9	0	7	30	27-2	1	47	.233	.337	.403	88	-3	3-0	.987	2	107	181	O37(10/16/12),D2	0	-0.1
2005	LA N	102	237	31	66	16	1	7	39	20-1	3	55	.278	.335	.443	103	1	0-0	.975	-6	72	63	O69(57/0/17)	33	-0.7
2006	LA N	43	53	4	13	5	0	1	8	2-0	0	10	.245	.273	.396	68	-3	1-0	1.000	-2	37	0	O9(7/0/2)	73	-0.4
	NY N	27	32	4	3	1	0	1	1	4-0	0	6	.094	.194	.219	6	-5	0-0	1.000	-0	84	0	O4(2/0/3)	0	-0.5
	Year	70	85	8	16	6	0	2	9	6-0	0	16	.188	.242	.329	45	-7	1-0	1.000	-2	54	0	O13(9/0/5)	0	-0.9
Total	9	838	1994	284	486	117	17	62	312	239-17	10	485	.244	.325	.413	91	-28	28-15	.979	-14	97	73	O555(304/124/156),D19	194	-5.1
LEDESMA, AARON Aaron David; B6.3.1971 Union City CA; BR/TR/6´2˝/200; [NYN90 2/57]; d7.2; Col Chabot (CA) JC																									
1995	NY N	21	33	4	8	0	0	0	3	6-1	0	7	.242	.359	.242	65	-1	0-0	.875	-1	113	0	3b10,1b2,S2	0	-0.2
1997	Bal A	43	88	24	31	5	1	2	11	13-0	1	9	.352	.437	.500	149	7	1-0	.973	-3	87	79	2b22,3b11,1b5,S4	0	0.5
1998	TB A	95	299	30	97	16	3	0	29	9-1	1	51	.324	.344	.398	91	-4	9-7	.971	16	110	154	S58,2b19,3b7,1b2,D6	0	1.5
1999	TB A	93	294	32	78	15	0	0	30	14-1	3	35	.265	.305	.316	58	-19	1-1	.978	12	95	99	S50,3b26,2b17,1b4/D	37	-0.3
2000	Col N	32	40	4	9	2	0	0	3	2-0	1	9	.225	.279	.275	33	-4	0-0	1.000	0	58	0	3b5,1b3	0	-0.4
Total	5	284	754	94	223	38	4	2	76	44-3	6	111	.296	.338	.365	80	-21	11-8	.974	24	102	126	S114,3b59,2b58,1b16,D7	37	1.1
LEDWITH, MIKE Michael; B Brooklyn NY; D1.2.1929 Bronx NY; d8.19																									
1874	Atl NA	1	4	1	1	0	0	0	1	0	—	0	.250	.250	.250	69	0	0-0	.600	-1	—	—	/C	—	-0.1
LEE, CARLOS Carlos (Noriel); B6.20.1976 Aguadulce, Pan; BR/TR/6´2˝/(220–240); d5.7																									
1999	Chi A	127	492	66	144	32	2	16	84	13-0	4	72	.293	.312	.463	94	-6	4-2	.981	-2	103	47	O105L,D16,1b5	0	-1.2
2000	†Chi A	152	572	107	172	29	2	24	92	38-1	3	94	.301	.345	.484	104	2	13-4	.990	-4	92	113	O149L,D2	0	-0.6
2001	Chi A	150	558	75	150	33	3	24	84	38-2	6	85	.269	.321	.468	99	-2	17-7	.969	-1	97	117	O130L,D17	0	-0.7
2002	Chi A	140	492	82	130	26	2	26	80	75-4	2	73	.264	.359	.484	118	14	1-4	.996	-2	93	103	O137L,D2	0	0.6
2003	Chi A	158	623	100	181	35	1	31	113	37-2	4	91	.291	.331	.499	111	9	18-4	.978	1	103	89	O156L/D	0	0.6
2004	Chi A	153	591	103	180	37	0	31	99	54-3	7	86	.305	.366	.525	125	22	11-5	**1.000**	4	101	137	O148L,D5	0	2.0
2005	Mil N★	**162**	618	85	164	41	0	32	114	57-7	2	87	.265	.324	.487	110	8	13-4	.981	4	108	90	O162L	0	0.7
2006	Mil N★	102	388	60	111	18	0	28	81	38-4	2	39	.286	.347	.549	125	13	12-2	.974	-6	84	82	O98L,D4	0	0.5
	Tex A	59	236	42	76	19	1	9	35	20-2	0	26	.322	.369	.525	129	11	7-0	.976	-5	84	28	O51L,D8	0	0.5
Total	8	1203	4570	720	1308	270	11	221	782	370-25	30	653	.286	.340	.495	111	71	96-32	.984	-11	98	96	O1136L,D55,1b5	0	2.4

LEE, CLIFF Clifford Walker; B8.4.1896 Lexington NE; D8.25.1980 Denver CO; BR/TR/6´1˝/175; d5.15

YEAR	TM LG	G	AB	R	H	2B	3B	HR	RBI	BB-IB	HP	SO	AVG	OBP	SLG	AOPS	ABR	SB-CS	FA	FR	RNG	THR	GAMES AT POSITION	DL	BFW
1919	Pit N	42	112	5	22	2	4	0	2	6	0	8	.196	.237	.286	55	-7	2	.962	-6	*116*	*54*	C28,O6(2/2/2)	—	-1.2
1920	Pit N	37	76	9	18	2	2	0	8	4	0	14	.237	.275	.316	67	-3	0-1	.974	0	*93*	*124*	C19,O2(1/1/0)	—	-0.3
1921	Phi N	88	286	31	88	14	4	4	29	13	0	34	.308	.338	.427	94	-3	5-2	.987	-5	79	101	1b48,O27(2/1/24),C2	—	-1.2
1922	Phi N	122	422	65	136	29	6	17	77	32	1	43	.322	.371	.540	121	12	2-3	.967	-4	92	92	O89(83/0/6),1b18/3	—	-0.1
1923	Phi N	107	355	54	114	20	4	11	47	20	0	39	.321	.357	.493	110	4	3-3	.959	-2	98	58	O83(54/0/32),1b16	—	-0.5
1924	Phi N	21	56	4	14	3	2	1	7	2	0	5	.250	.276	.429	77	-2	0-1	1.000	1	116	82	O13R,1b4	—	-0.3
	Cin N	6	6	1	2	1	0	0	2	0	0	2	.333	.333	.500	122	0	0-0	ø	-0	0	0	/rf	—	0.0
	Year	27	62	5	16	4	2	1	9	2	0	7	.258	.281	.435	82	-2	0-1	1.000	0	115	81	O14R,1b4	—	-0.3
1925	Cle A	77	230	43	74	15	6	4	42	21	0	33	.322	.378	.491	118	6	2-1	.951	1	105	113	O70(0/15/56)	—	0.3
1926	Cle A	21	40	4	7	1	0	1	2	6	0	8	.175	.283	.275	45	-3	0-0	1.000	0	121	0	O9(6/1/2),C3	—	-0.4
Total	8	521	1583	216	475	87	28	38	216	104	1	186	.300	.344	.462	103	4	14-11	.960	-15	99	80	O300(148/20/136),1b86,C52/3	—	-3.7

LEE, DEREK Derek Gerald; B7.28.1966 Chicago IL; BL/TR/6´1˝/200; [ChiA88 42/1078]; d6.27; Col South Florida

YEAR	TM LG	G	AB	R	H	2B	3B	HR	RBI	BB-IB	HP	SO	AVG	OBP	SLG	AOPS	ABR	SB-CS	FA	FR	RNG	THR	GAMES AT POSITION	DL	BFW
1993	Min A	15	33	3	5	1	0	0	4	1-0	0	4	.152	.176	.182	-3	-5	0-0	1.000	-1	83	0	O13(9/0/4)	0	-0.6

LEE, DERREK Derrek Leon; B9.6.1975 Sacramento CA; BR/TR/6´5˝/(205–245); [SDN93 1/14]; d4.28

YEAR	TM LG	G	AB	R	H	2B	3B	HR	RBI	BB-IB	HP	SO	AVG	OBP	SLG	AOPS	ABR	SB-CS	FA	FR	RNG	THR	GAMES AT POSITION	DL	BFW
1997	SD N	22	54	9	14	3	0	1	4	9-0	0	24	.259	.365	.370	99	0	0-0	1.000	1	119	95	1b21	0	0.0
1998	Fla N	141	454	62	106	29	1	17	74	47-1	10	120	.233	.318	.414	97	-2	5-2	.993	10	132	103	1b132	0	-0.3
1999	Fla N	70	218	21	45	9	1	5	20	17-1	0	70	.206	.263	.326	51	-18	2-1	.994	3	119	89	1b66	0	-1.9
2000	Fla N	158	477	70	134	18	3	28	70	63-6	4	123	.281	.368	.507	125	17	0-3	.993	6	117	96	1b147	0	1.0
2001	Fla N	158	561	83	158	37	4	21	75	50-1	8	126	.282	.346	.474	114	11	4-2	.994	6	115	**116**	1b156	0	0.4
2002	Fla N	**162**	581	95	157	35	7	27	86	98-8	5	164	.270	.378	.494	133	30	19-9	.992	5	113	96	1b162	0	2.2
2003	†Fla N	155	539	91	146	31	2	31	92	88-7	10	131	.271	.379	.508	135	30	21-8	.996	2	101	**104**	1b155	0	2.0
2004	Chi N	161	605	90	168	39	1	32	98	68-4	8	128	.278	.356	.504	116	15	12-5	.996	11	115	89	1b161	0	1.2
2005	Chi N★	158	594	120	**199**	**50**	3	46	107	85-23	5	109	**.335**	.418	**.662**	**173**	**65**	15-3	.996	11	120	91	1b158	0	**6.3**
2006	Chi N	50	175	30	50	9	0	8	30	25-1	0	41	.286	.368	.474	113	4	8-4	.988	-0	96	89	1b47/D	101	0.0
Total	10	1235	4258	671	1177	260	22	216	656	550-52	50	1036	.276	.363	.500	124	152	86-37	.994	55	115	98	1b1205/D	101	10.9

LEE, DUD Ernest Holford (aka Ernest Dudley in 1920-21); B8.22.1899 Denver CO; D1.7.1971 Denver CO; BL/TR/5´9˝/150; d10.3

YEAR	TM LG	G	AB	R	H	2B	3B	HR	RBI	BB-IB	HP	SO	AVG	OBP	SLG	AOPS	ABR	SB-CS	FA	FR	RNG	THR	GAMES AT POSITION	DL	BFW
1920	StL A	1	2	2	2	0	0	0	1	0	0	0	1.000	1.000	1.000	418	1	1-0	.333	-1	47	0	/S	—	0.0
1921	StL A	72	180	18	30	4	2	0	11	14	2	34	.167	.235	.211	14	-24	1-1	.922	-1	94	63	S31,2b30,3b3	—	-2.0
1924	Bos A	94	288	36	73	9	4	0	29	40	3	17	.253	.350	.313	72	-11	8-4	.937	-6	92	96	S90	—	-0.7
1925	Bos A	84	255	22	57	7	3	0	19	34	0	19	.224	.315	.275	51	-19	2-3	.924	13	109	127	S84	—	0.1
1926	Bos A	2	7	2	1	0	0	0	0	0	1	0	.143	.250	.143	4	-1	0-0	1.000	-0	64	112	S2	—	-0.1
Total	5	253	732	80	163	20	9	0	60	88	6	70	.223	.311	.275	50	-54	12-8	.928	4	99	103	S208,2b30,3b3	—	-2.7

LEE, HAL Harold Burnham "Sheriff"; B2.15.1905 Ludlow MS; D9.4.1989 Pascagoula MS; BR/TR/5´11˝/180; d4.19; Col Mississippi College

YEAR	TM LG	G	AB	R	H	2B	3B	HR	RBI	BB-IB	HP	SO	AVG	OBP	SLG	AOPS	ABR	SB-CS	FA	FR	RNG	THR	GAMES AT POSITION	DL	BFW
1930	Bro N	22	37	5	6	0	0	1	4	4	0	5	.162	.244	.243	19	-5	0	1.000	0	112	0	O12(10/0/1)	—	-0.5
1931	Phi N	44	131	13	29	10	0	2	12	10	1	18	.221	.282	.344	62	-7	0	.967	1	110	45	O38(26/11/2)	—	-0.8
1932	Phi N	149	595	76	180	42	10	18	85	36	1	45	.303	.343	.497	110	8	6	.965	9	114	114	O148(136/12/0)	—	0.9
1933	Phi N	46	167	25	48	12	2	0	12	18	1	13	.287	.360	.383	100	1	1	.981	1	100	141	O45L	—	0.0
	Bos N	88	312	32	69	15	9	1	28	18	1	26	.221	.266	.337	77	-11	1	.977	2	106	84	O87(85/2/0)	—	-1.5
	Year	134	479	57	117	27	11	1	40	36	2	39	.244	.300	.353	87	-9	2	.978	3	104	103	O132(130/2/0)	—	-1.5
1934	Bos N	139	521	70	152	23	6	8	79	47	2	43	.292	.353	.405	111	8	3	.985	3	114	54	O128L,2b4	—	0.3
1935	Bos N	112	422	49	128	18	6	0	39	18	1	25	.303	.333	.374	98	-3	0	.962	6	116	86	O110(98/0/12)	—	-0.2
1936	Bos N	152	565	46	143	24	7	3	64	52	2	50	.253	.318	.336	82	-15	4	.973	-8	96	43	O150L	—	-3.0
Total	7	752	2750	316	755	144	40	33	323	203	9	225	.275	.326	.392	95	-24	15	.973	14	108	77	O718(678/25/15),2b4	—	-4.8

LEE, LEONIDAS Leonidas Pyrrhus (b Leonidas Pyrrhus Funkhouser); B12.13.1860 St.Louis MO; D6.11.1912 Hendersonville NC; d7.17; Col Princeton

YEAR	TM LG	G	AB	R	H	2B	3B	HR	RBI	BB-IB	HP	SO	AVG	OBP	SLG	AOPS	ABR	SB-CS	FA	FR	RNG	THR	GAMES AT POSITION	DL	BFW
1877	StL N	4	18	0	5	1	0	0	0	0	—	1	.278	.278	.333	97	0	—	.667	-2	0	0	O4(1/2/1)/S	—	-0.2

LEE, LERON Leron; B3.4.1948 Bakersfield CA; BL/TR/6´0˝/(192–196); [StLN66 1/7]; d9.5

YEAR	TM LG	G	AB	R	H	2B	3B	HR	RBI	BB-IB	HP	SO	AVG	OBP	SLG	AOPS	ABR	SB-CS	FA	FR	RNG	THR	GAMES AT POSITION	DL	BFW
1969	StL N	7	23	3	5	1	0	0	0	3-0	0	8	.217	.308	.261	60	-1	0-0	1.000	-0	60	230	O7(4/0/3)	0	-0.2
1970	StL N	121	264	28	60	13	1	6	23	24-4	1	66	.227	.290	.352	70	-11	5-1	.969	-2	98	68	O77(1/0/76)	0	-1.6
1971	StL N	25	28	3	5	1	0	1	2	4-0	0	12	.179	.281	.321	67	-1	0-1	.800	-1	55	0	O8(5/0/4)	0	-0.3
	SD N	79	256	29	70	20	2	4	21	18-4	0	45	.273	.321	.414	114	4	4-5	.920	-5	66	128	O68L	0	-0.6
	Year	104	284	32	75	21	2	5	23	22-4	0	57	.264	.317	.405	107	2	4-6	.914	-6	65	121	O76(73/0/4)	0	-0.9
1972	SD N	101	370	50	111	23	7	12	47	29-4	3	58	.300	.353	.497	151	23	2-5	.975	3	105	93	O96(96/0/1)	40	2.0
1973	SD N	118	333	36	79	7	2	3	30	33-3	1	61	.237	.306	.297	74	-12	4-0	.970	2	100	126	O84(72/0/14)	0	-1.4
1974	Cle A	79	232	18	54	13	0	5	25	15-2	0	42	.233	.279	.353	82	-6	3-2	.958	4	108	121	O62(60/0/2),D2	0	-0.6
1975	Cle A	13	23	3	3	1	0	0	0	2-0	1	5	.130	.231	.174	16	-3	1-0	1.000	0	113	0	O5L,D3	0	-0.3
	LA N	48	43	2	11	4	0	0	2	3-1	0	9	.256	.298	.349	84	-1	0-0	1.000	-0	40	0	O4L	0	-0.1
1976	LA N	23	45	1	6	0	1	0	2	2-1	0	9	.133	.170	.178	-1	-6	0-0	1.000	-2	71	0	O10R	0	-0.9
Total	8	614	1617	173	404	83	13	31	152	133-19	6	315	.250	.307	.375	94	-14	19-14	.962	-1	94	104	O421(315/0/110),D5	40	-4.0

LEE, MANUEL Manuel Lora "Manny" (b Manuel Lora (Lee)); B6.17.1965 San Pedro de Macoris, D.R.; BB/TR/5´9˝/(150–166); d4.10

YEAR	TM LG	G	AB	R	H	2B	3B	HR	RBI	BB-IB	HP	SO	AVG	OBP	SLG	AOPS	ABR	SB-CS	FA	FR	RNG	THR	GAMES AT POSITION	DL	BFW
1985	†Tor A	64	40	9	8	0	0	0	0	2-0	0	9	.200	.238	.200	21	-4	1-4	.971	1	98	97	2b38,S8,3b5,D8	0	-0.4
1986	Tor A	35	78	8	16	0	1	1	7	4-0	0	10	.205	.241	.269	38	-7	0-1	.990	-2	110	71	2b29,S5,3b2	0	-0.8
1987	Tor A	56	121	14	31	2	3	1	11	6-0	0	13	.256	.289	.347	67	-6	2-0	.966	6	107	130	2b27,S26/D	0	0.3
1988	Tor A	116	381	38	111	16	3	2	38	26-1	0	64	.291	.333	.365	95	-2	3-3	.988	8	102	106	2b98,S23,3b8,D2	28	0.9
1989	†Tor A	99	300	27	78	9	2	3	34	20-1	0	60	.260	.305	.333	81	-8	4-2	.985	-5	85	114	2b40,S28,3b17,D13/rf	37	-1.0
1990	Tor A	117	391	45	95	12	4	6	41	26-0	0	90	.243	.288	.340	74	-15	3-1	**.993**	-12	89	93	2b112,S9	0	-2.4
1991	†Tor A	138	445	41	104	18	3	0	29	24-0	2	107	.234	.274	.288	54	-28	7-2	.967	-20	91	68	S138	0	-3.8
1992	†Tor A	128	396	49	104	10	1	3	39	50-0	0	73	.263	.343	.316	82	-8	6-2	.987	-11	89	88	S128	0	-0.9
1993	Tex A	73	205	31	45	3	1	1	12	22-3	2	39	.220	.300	.259	54	-13	2-4	.968	1	104	83	S72/D	80	-0.8
1994	Tex A	95	335	41	93	18	2	2	38	21-0	0	66	.278	.319	.361	74	-13	3-1	.967	-1	105	95	S85,2b13	15	-0.7
1995	StL N	1	1	1	1	0	0	0	0	0-0	0	0	1.000	1.000	1.000	422	0	0-0	.800	-0	206	0	/2	36	0.1
Total	11	922	2693	304	686	88	20	19	249	201-5	4	531	.255	.305	.323	72	-104	31-20	.972	-35	96	85	S522,2b358,3b32,D25/rf	196	-9.5

LEE, TERRY Terry James; B3.13.1962 San Francisco CA; BR/TR/6´5˝/(215–220); d9.3; Col Chemeketa (OR) CC

YEAR	TM LG	G	AB	R	H	2B	3B	HR	RBI	BB-IB	HP	SO	AVG	OBP	SLG	AOPS	ABR	SB-CS	FA	FR	RNG	THR	GAMES AT POSITION	DL	BFW
1990	Cin N	12	19	1	4	1	0	0	3	2-0	0	2	.211	.273	.263	50	-1	0-0	1.000	0	113	40	1b6	0	-0.1
1991	Cin N	3	6	0	0	0	0	0	0	0-0	0	2	.000	.000	.000	-96	-2	0-0	1.000	1	413	0	1b2	0	0.0
Total	2	15	25	1	4	1	0	0	3	2-0	0	4	.160	.214	.200	17	-3	0-0	1.000	1	193	29	1b8	0	-0.1

LEE, TRAVIS Travis Reynolds; B5.26.1975 San Diego CA; BL/TL/6´3˝/(210–225); d3.31; Col San Diego St.

YEAR	TM LG	G	AB	R	H	2B	3B	HR	RBI	BB-IB	HP	SO	AVG	OBP	SLG	AOPS	ABR	SB-CS	FA	FR	RNG	THR	GAMES AT POSITION	DL	BFW
1998	Ari N	146	562	71	151	20	2	22	72	67-5	0	123	.269	.346	.429	102	2	8-1	.998	-2	96	92	1b146	15	-1.2
1999	Ari N	120	375	57	89	16	2	9	50	58-4	0	50	.237	.337	.363	77	-13	17-3	**.997**	2	105	90	1b114,O2R	26	-1.6
2000	Ari N	72	224	34	52	13	0	8	40	25-1	0	46	.232	.308	.397	74	-9	5-1	.983	5	125	105	O55(0/2/54),1b23	14	-0.7
	Phi N	56	180	19	43	11	1	1	14	40-0	2	33	.239	.381	.328	82	-3	3-0	1.000	2	126	121	1b47,O10L	0	-0.4
	Year	128	404	53	95	24	1	9	54	65-1	2	79	.235	.342	.366	78	-12	8-1	.996	7	117	128	1b70,O65(10/2/54)	0	-1.1
2001	Phi N	157	555	75	143	34	2	20	90	71-5	4	109	.258	.341	.434	105	5	3-4	.996	-7	81	101	1b156	0	-1.6
2002	Phi N	153	536	55	142	26	2	13	70	54-10	0	104	.265	.331	.394	96	-4	5-3	.996	-6	83	103	1b148	0	-2.2
2003	TB A	145	542	75	149	37	3	19	70	64-4	0	97	.275	.348	.459	114	12	6-2	.998	0	99	93	1b142,D2	15	0.0
2004	NY A	7	19	1	2	1	0	0	2	1-1	0	3	.105	.150	.158	-20	-3	0-0	1.000	0	120	52	1b6	174	-0.3
2005	TB A	129	404	54	110	22	2	12	49	35-4	1	66	.272	.331	.426	101	1	7-4	.996	2	106	86	1b124	18	-0.6
2006	TB A	114	343	35	77	11	2	11	31	42-1	2	73	.224	.312	.364	75	-13	5-2	**.998**	1	101	100	1b112	0	-2.0
Total	9	1099	3740	476	958	191	16	115	488	457-35	9	704	.256	.337	.408	95	-25	59-20	.997	-2	96	97	1b1018,O67(10/2/56),D2	262	-10.6

LEE, BILLY William Joseph; B1.9.1894 Bayonne NJ; D1.6.1984 West Hazleton PA; BR/TR/5´9˝/165; d4.15

YEAR	TM LG	G	AB	R	H	2B	3B	HR	RBI	BB-IB	HP	SO	AVG	OBP	SLG	AOPS	ABR	SB-CS	FA	FR	RNG	THR	GAMES AT POSITION	DL	BFW
1915	StL A	18	59	2	11	1	0	0	4	6	0	5	.186	.262	.203	41	-4	1-1	1.000	2	121	100	O15(7/6/2)/3	—	-0.4
1916	StL A	7	11	1	2	0	0	0	0	1	0	1	.182	.250	.182	31	-1	0	1.000	-0	105	0	O4(0/2/2)	—	-0.1
Total	2	25	70	3	13	1	0	0	4	7	0	6	.186	.260	.200	39	-5	1-1	1.000	2	119	87	O19(7/8/4)/3	—	-0.5

YEAR	TM LG	G	AB	R	H	2B	3B	HR	RBI	BB-IB	HP	SO	AVG	OBP	SLG	AOPS	ABR	SB-CS	FA	FR	RNG	THR	GAMES AT POSITION	DL	BFW
LEE, WATTY Wyatt Arnold; B8.12.1879 Lynch Station VA; D3.6.1936 Washington DC; BL/TL/5´10.5˝/171; d4.30; ▲																									
1901	Was A	43	129	15	33	6	3	0	12	7	2	—	.256	.304	.349	82	-3	0	.948	1	108	120	P36,O7(2/1/4)	—	0.0
1902	Was A	109	391	61	100	21	5	4	45	33	3	—	.256	.319	.366	89	-6	8	.916	2	118	40	O96(22/20/54),P13	—	-0.8
1903	Was A	75	231	17	48	8	4	0	13	18	0	—	.208	.265	.277	62	-11	5	.930	5	110	136	O47(0/10/37),P22	—	-0.6
1904	Pit N	8	12	1	4	0	1	0	0	0	0	—	.333	.333	.500	152	1	0	.889	-0	111	0	P5	—	0.0
Total	4	235	763	94	185	35	13	4	70	58	5	—	.242	.300	.338	80	-19	13	.917	8	117	72	O150(24/31/95),P76	—	-1.4
LEEK, GENE Eugene Harold; B7.15.1936 San Diego CA; BR/TR/6´0˝/185; d4.22; Col Arizona																									
1959	Cle A	13	36	7	8	3	0	1	5	2-0	0	7	.222	.263	.389	80	-1	0-0	.955	-2	73	0	3b13/S	0	-0.3
1961	LA A	57	199	16	45	9	1	5	20	7-0	2	54	.226	.260	.357	57	-13	0-1	.958	18	126	105	3b49,S7/lf	0	0.5
1962	LA A	7	14	0	2	0	0	0	0	0-0	0	6	.143	.143	.143	-24	-2	0-0	1.000	-1	58	152	3b4	0	-0.3
Total	3	77	249	23	55	12	1	6	25	9-0	2	67	.221	.254	.349	55	-16	0-1	.959	15	114	92	3b66,S8/lf	0	-0.1
LEEPER, DAVE David Dale; B10.30.1959 Santa Ana CA; BL/TL/5´11˝/170; [KCA81 1/23]; d9.10; Col USC																									
1984	KC A	4	6	1	0	0	0	0	0	0-0	0	1	.000	.000	.000	-99	-2	0-0	1.000	0	134	0	O2L/D	0	-0.2
1985	KC A	15	34	1	3	0	0	0	4	1-0	0	3	.088	.114	.088	-43	-7	0-0	.929	-1	86	0	O8(2/0/6)	0	-0.8
Total	2	19	40	2	3	0	0	0	4	1-0	0	4	.075	.098	.075	-51	-9	0-0	.944	-1	94	0	O10(4/0/6)/D	0	-1.0
LEES, GEORGE George Edward; B2.2.1895 Bethlehem PA; D1.2.1980 Harrisburg PA; BR/TR/5´9˝/150; d5.7; Col Lehigh																									
1921	Chi A	20	42	3	9	2	0	0	4	0	0	3	.214	.214	.262	21	-5	0-1	.951	-2	*84*	*75*	C16	—	-0.6
LEFEBVRE, JIM James Kenneth; B1.7.1942 Inglewood CA; BB/TR/6´0˝/185; d4.12; M6/C11																									
1965	†LA N	157	544	57	136	21	4	12	69	71-7	2	92	.250	.337	.369	106	6	3-5	.970	0	100	104	2b156	0	2.0
1966	†LA N★	152	544	69	149	23	3	24	74	48-6	3	72	.274	.333	.460	129	20	1-1	.980	3	106	90	2b119,3b40	0	3.4
1967	LA N	136	494	51	129	18	5	8	50	44-11	3	64	.261	.322	.366	106	3	1-5	.955	5	106	78	3b92,2b34,1b5	0	0.9
1968	LA N	84	286	23	69	12	1	5	31	26-4	1	55	.241	.304	.343	102	1	0-0	.978	-4	92	92	2b62,3b16,O5L,1b3	0	0.1
1969	LA N	95	275	29	65	15	2	4	44	48-10	1	37	.236	.349	.349	103	3	2-1	.985	1	116	107	3b44,2b37,1b6	0	0.6
1970	LA N	109	314	33	79	15	1	4	44	29-2	1	42	.252	.314	.344	80	-9	1-1	.988	-9	94	84	2b70,3b21/1	0	-1.4
1971	LA N	119	388	40	95	14	2	12	68	39-6	2	55	.245	.314	.384	103	1	0-2	.988	-6	92	109	2b102,3b7	0	0.1
1972	LA N	70	169	11	34	8	0	5	24	17-6	0	30	.201	.271	.337	74	-6	0-0	.987	-0	105	124	2b33,3b11	0	-0.5
Total	8	922	3014	313	756	126	18	74	404	322-52	13	447	.251	.323	.378	105	19	8-15	.979	-11	100	99	2b613,3b231,1b15,O5L	0	5.2
LEFEBVRE, JOE Joseph Henry; B2.22.1956 Concord NH; BL/TR/5´10˝/(170–180); [NYA77 3/75]; d5.22; C5; Col Eckerd; [DL 1985 Phi N 182]																									
1980	†NY A	74	150	26	34	1	1	8	21	27-3	0	30	.227	.345	.407	107	2	0-0	.975	-4	81	88	O71(20/3/52)	0	-0.4
1981	SD N	86	246	31	63	13	4	8	31	35-7	2	33	.256	.352	.439	135	12	6-4	.994	4	111	95	O84(0/2/83)	0	1.2
1982	SD N	102	239	25	57	9	0	4	21	18-2	1	50	.238	.292	.326	78	-7	0-0	.972	-2	98	115	3b39,O36(18/2/18),C3	0	-1.2
1983	SD N	18	20	1	5	0	0	0	1	2-0	0	3	.250	.318	.250	61	-1	0-0	1.000	1	23	611	O6R,3b4,C2	0	-0.1
	†Phi N	101	258	34	80	20	8	8	38	31-6	3	46	.310	.388	.543	157	20	5-3	.990	-4	90	103	O74(22/0/58),3b9,C3	0	1.4
	Year	119	278	35	85	20	8	8	39	33-6	3	49	.306	.383	.522	151	19	5-3	.990	-3	87	123	O80(22/0/64),3b13,C5	0	1.3
1984	Phi N	52	160	22	40	9	0	3	18	23-4	2	37	.250	.348	.363	99	1	0-2	.966	0	101	133	O47(16/0/34)/3	105	-0.2
1986	Phi N	14	18	0	2	0	0	0	0	3-0	0	5	.111	.238	.111	-1	-2	0-0	1.000	-0	95	0	O3R	0	-0.3
Total	6	447	1091	139	281	52	13	31	130	139-22	8	204	.258	.344	.414	115	25	11-9	.986	-5	95	102	O321(76/7/254),3b53,C8	287	0.4
LEFEBVRE, BILL Wilfred Henry "Lefty"; B11.11.1915 Natick RI; BL/TL/5´11.5˝/180; d6.10; Mil 1945; Col Holy Cross; ▲																									
1938	Bos A	1	1	1	1	0	0	1	1	0	0	0	1.000	1.000	4.000	1048	1	0-0	ø	-0	0	0	/P	—	0.0
1939	Bos A	7	10	3	3	0	0	0	1	2	0	2	.300	.417	.300	83	1	0-0	1.000	-1	45	0	P5	—	0.0
1943	Was A	7	14	0	4	3	0	0	1	1	0	0	.286	.333	.500	148	2	0-0	1.000	-0	92	249	P6	0	0.0
1944	Was A	60	62	4	16	2	2	0	8	12	0	9	.258	.378	.355	115	2	0-0	.933	-0	99	209	P24,1b2	0	0.0
Total	4	75	87	8	24	5	2	1	11	15	0	11	.276	.382	.414	129	6	0-0	.960	-1	84	171	P36,1b2	0	0.0
LEFEVRE, AL Alfred Modesto; B9.16.1898 New York NY; D1.21.1982 Glen Cove NY; BR/TR/5´10.5˝/160; d6.28; Col Fordham																									
1920	NY N	17	27	5	4	0	1	0	0	0	0	13	.148	.148	.222	5	-3	0-0	1.000	3	142	115	S9,2b6/3	—	-0.1
LEFLER, WADE Wade Hampton; B6.5.1896 Cooleemee NC; D3.6.1981 Hickory NC; BL/TR/5´11˝/162; d4.16; Col Duke																									
1924	Bos N	1	1	0	0	0	0	0	0	0	0	1	.000	.000	.000	-99	0	0-0	ø	0	—	—	/H	—	0.0
	Was A	5	8	0	5	3	0	0	4	0	0	0	.625	.625	1.000	325	3	0-0	1.000	0	121	0	/rf	—	0.2
Total	1	6	9	0	5	3	0	0	4	0	0	1	.556	.556	.889	279	3	0-0	1.000	0	121	0	/rf	—	0.2
LEFLORE, RON Ronald; B6.16.1948 Detroit MI; BR/TR/6´0˝/(197–200); d8.1																									
1974	Det A	59	254	37	66	8	1	2	13	13-0	3	58	.260	.301	.323	77	-8	23-9	.935	-2	92	181	O59C	0	-1.0
1975	Det A	136	550	66	142	13	6	8	37	33-1	2	139	.258	.302	.347	80	-16	28-20	.973	-3	94	144	O134C	0	-2.5
1976	Det A★	135	544	93	172	23	8	4	39	51-2	2	111	.316	.376	.410	125	18	58-20	.973	5	104	142	O132C/D	19	2.6
1977	Det A	154	652	100	212	30	10	16	57	37-1	4	121	.325	.363	.475	121	18	39-19	.972	-12	88	107	O152C	0	0.7
1978	Det A	155	666	**126**	198	30	3	12	62	65-7	4	104	.297	.361	.405	112	12	**68**-16	.976	-5	98	85	O155C	0	1.6
1979	Det A	148	600	110	180	22	10	9	57	52-2	0	95	.300	.355	.415	104	3	78-14	.990	0	101	85	O113C,D34	0	1.3
1980	Mon N	139	521	95	134	21	11	4	39	62-1	1	99	.257	.337	.363	93	-4	**97**-19	.957	2	96	153	O130L	0	0.8
1981	Chi A	82	337	46	83	10	4	0	24	28-0	1	70	.246	.304	.300	76	-10	36-11	.960	-2	96	110	O82(76/7/0)	0	-1.2
1982	Chi A	91	334	58	96	15	4	4	25	22-1	0	91	.287	.331	.392	97	-2	28-14	.939	-5	88	140	O83(2/81/0),D2	0	-0.6
Total	9	1099	4458	731	1283	172	57	59	353	363-15	17	888	.288	.342	.392	102	11	455-142	.968	-22	96	123	O1040(208/833/0),D37	19	1.7
LEGETT, LOU Louis Alfred "Doc"; B6.1.1901 New Orleans LA; D3.6.1988 New Orleans LA; BR/TR/5´10˝/166; d5.8																									
1929	Bos N	39	81	7	13	2	0	0	6	3	0	18	.160	.190	.185	-7	-14	2	.914	-1	*108*	*128*	C28	—	-1.3
1933	Bos A	8	5	1	1	1	0	0	1	0	0	0	.200	.200	.400	56	0	0-0	1.000	0	*0*	*0*	C2	—	0.0
1934	Bos A	19	38	4	11	0	0	0	1	2	0	4	.289	.325	.289	56	-3	0-0	.977	0	*91*	*88*	C17	—	-0.2
1935	Bos A	2	0	1	0	0	0	0	0	0	0	0	ø	ø	ø	ø	0	0-0	ø	0	—	—	/R	—	0.0
Total	4	68	124	13	25	3	0	0	8	5	0	22	.202	.233	.226	16	-17	2-0	.938	-1	*101*	*113*	C47	—	-1.5
LEGG, GREG Gregory Lynn; B4.21.1960 San Jose CA; BR/TR/6´1˝/185; [PhiN82 22/559]; d4.18; Col Southeastern Oklahoma																									
1986	Phi N	11	20	2	9	1	0	0	1	0-0	0	3	.450	.450	.500	156	1	0-0	.941	1	143	167	2b4/S	0	0.3
1987	Phi N	3	2	1	0	0	0	0	0	0-0	0	0	.000	.000	.000	-97	-1	0-0	1.000	0	158	674	/2S3	0	0.0
Total	2	14	22	3	9	1	0	0	1	0-0	0	3	.409	.409	.455	132	0	0-0	.952	1	144	205	2b5,S2/3	0	0.3
LEHAN, JAMES James Francis; B5.14.1856 Hartford CT; D7.18.1946 Hartford CT; d4.26																									
1884	Was U	3	12	1	4	2	0	0	—	0	—	—	.333	.333	.500	155	1	—	.688	-1	104	0	S3/lf3	—	0.0
LEHANE, MIKE Michael Patrick; B4.15.1865 New York NY; BR/6´1.5˝/180; d4.17																									
1890	Col AA	**140**	512	54	108	19	5	0	56	43	3	—	.211	.276	.268	65	-22	13	**.982**	10	**131**	**127**	1b140	—	-2.2
1891	Col AA	137	511	59	110	12	7	1	52	34	3	77	.215	.268	.272	58	-29	16	**.981**	7	**125**	**128**	1b137	—	-3.0
Total	2	277	1023	113	218	31	12	1	108	77	6	77	.213	.272	.270	61	-51	29	.982	17	128	127	1b277	—	-5.2
LEHNER, PAUL Paul Eugene "Peanuts","Gulliver"; B7.1.1920 Dolomite AL; D12.27.1967 Birmingham AL; BL/TL/5´9˝/165; d9.10																									
1946	StL A	16	45	6	10	1	2	0	5	1	0	5	.222	.239	.333	56	-3	0-0	.941	-1	72	178	O12(0/11/1)	0	-0.5
1947	StL A	135	483	59	120	25	9	7	48	28	3	29	.248	.294	.381	85	-12	5-5	.980	-8	97	12	O127(2/125/0)	0	-2.6
1948	StL A	103	333	23	92	15	4	2	46	30	0	19	.276	.336	.363	84	-8	0-2	.974	-5	94	59	O89C,1b2	0	-1.6
1949	StL A	104	297	25	68	13	0	3	37	16	1	20	.229	.271	.303	50	-23	0-2	.987	1	114	25	O56(12/35/10),1b18	0	-2.5
1950	Phi A	114	427	48	132	17	5	9	52	32	0	33	.309	.357	.436	104	1	1-1	.981	4	105	119	O101(80/7/15)	0	-0.2
1951	Phi A	9	28	1	4	1	0	0	1	1	0	1	.143	.172	.179	-5	-4	0-0	1.000	1	103	183	O6L	0	-0.4
	Chi A	23	72	9	15	3	1	0	3	10	0	4	.208	.305	.278	60	-4	0-0	.980	1	97	171	O20(8/13/9)	0	-0.4
	StL A	21	67	2	9	5	0	1	2	6	0	5	.134	.205	.254	23	-7	0-1	1.000	-1	105	0	O18(1/17/0)	0	-0.9
	Cle A	12	13	2	3	0	0	0	1	1	0	2	.231	.286	.231	43	-1	0-0	1.000	-0	78	0	/lf	0	-0.1
	Year	65	180	14	31	9	1	1	7	18	0	12	.172	.247	.250	35	-17	0-1	.991	0	101	109	O45(16/30/9)	0	-1.8
1952	Bos A	3	3	0	2	0	0	0	2	2	0	0	.667	.800	.667	288	1	0-0	1.000	0	131	0	O2R	0	0.1
Total	7	540	1768	175	455	80	21	22	197	127	4	118	.257	.309	.364	78	-60	6-11	.981	-8	101	63	O432(110/297/37),1b20	0	-9.1
LEHR, CLARENCE Clarence Emanuel "King"; B5.16.1886 Escanaba MI; D1.31.1948 Highland Park MI; BR/TR/5´11˝/165; d5.18																									
1911	Phi N	23	27	2	4	0	0	0	2	0	0	7	.148	.148	.148	-17	-4	0	1.000	1	85	0	O5(1/1/3),2b4,S4	—	-0.4

YEAR	TM LG	G	AB	R	H	2B	3B	HR	RBI	BB-IB	HP	SO	AVG	OBP	SLG	AOPS	ABR	SB-CS	FA	FR	RNG	THR	GAMES AT POSITION	DL	BFW
LEIBER, HANK	Henry Edward; B1.17.1911 Phoenix AZ; D11.8.1993 Tucson AZ; BR/TR/6´1.5˝/205; d4.16; Col Arizona; ▲																								
1933	NY N	6	10	1	2	0	0	0	0	0	0	2	.200	.200	.200	15	-1	0	1.000	1	88	804	/lf	—	-0.1
1934	NY N	63	187	17	45	5	3	2	25	4	0	13	.241	.257	.332	58	-12	1	.971	-3	86	94	O51(2/49/0)	—	-1.7
1935	NY N	154	613	110	203	37	4	22	107	48	**10**	29	.331	.389	.512	143	37	0	.965	-22	83	38	O154C	—	1.1
1936	†NY N	101	337	44	94	19	7	9	67	37	1	41	.279	.352	.457	118	8	1	.961	-8	77	150	O86(7/78/1)/1	—	-0.2
1937	†NY N	51	184	24	54	7	3	4	32	15	0	27	.293	.347	.429	108	2	1	.988	-6	80	30	O46(1/42/3)	—	-0.5
1938	NY N★	98	360	50	97	18	4	12	65	31	0	45	.269	.327	.442	109	3	0	.974	-9	84	81	O89(2/86/4)	—	-0.8
1939	Chi N	112	365	65	113	16	1	24	88	59	4	42	.310	.411	.556	155	30	1	.977	-2	101	63	O98C	—	2.5
1940	Chi N✱	117	440	68	133	24	2	17	86	45	3	68	.302	.371	.482	136	22	1	.985	-6	85	101	O103(0/53/52),1b12	—	1.1
1941	Chi N✱	53	162	20	35	5	0	7	25	16	1	25	.216	.291	.377	90	-3	0	.964	-2	94	53	O29(23/2/5),1b15	0	-0.8
1942	NY N	58	147	11	32	6	0	4	23	19	2	27	.218	.315	.340	91	-1	0	.990	-0	103	58	O41(1/40/0)/P	0	-0.3
Total	10	813	2805	410	808	137	24	101	518	274	21	319	.288	.356	.462	122	85	5	.973	-58	87	77	O698(37/602/65),1b28/P	0	0.3
LEIBOLD, NEMO	Harry Loran; B2.17.1892 Butler IN; D2.4.1977 Detroit MI; BL/TR/5´6.5˝/157; d4.12																								
1913	Cle A	93	286	37	74	11	6	0	12	21	0	43	.259	.309	.339	87	-6	16	.945	-2	93	109	O74(4/66/2)	—	-1.3
1914	Cle A	115	402	46	106	13	3	0	32	54	2	56	.264	.354	.311	96	0	12-14	.931	4	99	**159**	O107(0/90/17)	—	-0.5
1915	Cle A	57	207	28	53	5	4	0	4	24	2	16	.256	.339	.319	95	-1	5-3	.969	5	113	124	O52C	—	0.0
	Chi A	36	74	10	17	1	0	0	11	15	0	11	.230	.360	.243	78	-1	1-3	1.000	3	114	157	O22(10/12/0)	—	0.0
	Year	93	281	38	70	6	4	0	15	39	2	27	.249	.345	.299	91	-2	6-6	.978	8	113	134	O74(10/64/0)	—	0.0
1916	Chi A	45	82	5	20	1	2	0	13	7	0	7	.244	.303	.305	82	-2	7	1.000	-1	95	48	O24(2/16/6)	—	-0.4
1917	†Chi A	125	428	59	101	12	6	0	29	74	1	34	.236	.350	.292	94	0	27	.961	3	104	117	O122(16/4/102)	—	-0.2
1918	Chi A	116	440	57	110	14	7	0	31	63	0	32	.250	.344	.314	97	0	15	.979	7	111	104	O114(95/7/12)	—	0.2
1919	†Chi A	122	434	81	131	18	2	0	26	72	2	30	.302	.404	.353	113	12	17	.928	8	103	162	O122(7/1/114)	—	1.5
1920	Chi A	108	413	61	91	16	3	1	28	55	3	30	.220	.316	.281	59	-23	7-15	.977	6	102	130	O105(3/4/98)	—	-2.6
1921	Bos A	123	467	88	143	26	6	0	31	41	1	27	.306	.363	.388	94	-3	13-7	.949	-1	98	100	O117(0/107/10)	—	-0.9
1922	Bos A	81	271	42	70	8	1	1	18	41	2	14	.258	.360	.306	76	-8	1-6	.966	2	100	126	O71(1/66/4)	—	-1.1
1923	Bos A	12	18	1	2	0	0	0	0	1	0	2	.111	.158	.111	-28	-3	0-1	.909	0	88	218	O10C	—	-0.4
	Was A	95	315	68	96	13	4	1	22	53	2	16	.305	.408	.381	114	10	7-6	.980	-2	88	137	O84C	—	0.4
	Year	107	333	69	98	13	4	1	22	54	2	18	.294	.396	.366	106	6	7-7	.977	-2	88	141	O94C	—	0.0
1924	†Was A	84	246	41	72	6	4	0	20	42	1	10	.293	.398	.350	97	1	7-5	.994	1	102	114	O70(4/52/14)	—	-0.1
1925	†Was A	56	84	14	23	1	1	0	7	8	0	7	.274	.337	.310	66	-4	1-0	.972	0	97	144	O26(2/22/2)/3	—	-0.4
Total	13	1268	4167	638	1109	145	49	3	284	571	16	335	.266	.357	.327	91	-28	136-60	.961	35	101	126	O1120(144/593/381)/3	—	-5.8
LEIFER, ELMER	Elmer Edwin; B5.23.1893 Clarington OH; D9.26.1948 Everett WA; BL/TR/5´9.5˝/170; d9.7																								
1921	Chi A	9	10	0	3	0	0	0	1	0	0	4	.300	.300	.300	54	-1	0-0	1.000	-0	67	0	/3lf	—	-0.1
LEIGHTON, JOHN	John Atkinson; B10.4.1861 Peabody MA; D10.31.1956 Lynn MA; BL/TL/5´11˝/170; d7.12																								
1890	Syr AA	7	27	6	8	2	0	0	0	3	0	—	.296	.367	.370	131	1	2	.938	-0	0	0	O7C	—	0.1
LEINHAUSER, BILL	William Charles; B11.4.1893 Philadelphia PA; D4.14.1978 Elkins Park PA; BR/TR/5´10˝/150; d5.18																								
1912	Det A	1	4	0	0	0	0	0	0	0	0	—	.000	.000	.000	-99	-1	0	1.000	1	0	5707	/cf	—	0.0
LEIP, ED	Edgar Ellsworth; B11.29.1910 Trenton NJ; D11.24.1983 Zephyrhills FL; BR/TR/5´9˝/160; d9.16; Mil 1942–45																								
1939	Was A	9	32	4	11	1	0	0	2	2	0	4	.344	.382	.375	102	0	0-1	.951	-0	110	102	2b8	—	0.0
1940	Pit N	3	5	2	1	0	0	0	0	0	0	0	.200	.200	.200	11	-1	0	1.000	-0	81	183	2b2	—	-0.1
1941	Pit N	15	25	1	5	0	2	0	3	1	0	2	.200	.231	.360	65	-2	1	.889	0	120	84	2b7/3	0	-0.1
1942	Pit N	3	0	0	0	0	0	0	0	0	0	0	ø	ø	ø	ø	0	0	ø	0	—	—	/R	0	0.0
Total	4	30	62	7	17	1	2	0	5	3	0	6	.274	.308	.355	80	-3	1-1	.931	0	111	101	2b17/3	0	-0.2
LEIUS, SCOTT	Scott Thomas; B9.24.1965 Yonkers NY; BR/TR/6´3˝/(180–208); [MinA86 13/325]; d9.3; Col Concordia (NY)																								
1990	Min A	14	25	4	6	1	0	1	4	2-0	0	2	.240	.296	.400	87	0	0-0	1.000	2	96	174	S12/3	0	0.2
1991	†Min A	109	199	35	57	7	2	5	20	30-1	0	35	.286	.378	.417	115	5	5-5	.953	2	101	88	3b79,S19,O2C	0	0.7
1992	Min A	129	409	50	102	18	2	2	35	34-0	1	61	.249	.309	.318	73	-15	6-5	.955	-0	105	63	3b125,S10	0	-1.5
1993	Min A	10	18	4	3	0	0	0	2	2-0	0	4	.167	.227	.167	14	-2	0-0	.947	2	126	153	S9	165	0.0
1994	Min A	97	350	57	86	16	1	14	49	37-0	1	58	.246	.318	.417	87	-7	2-4	.969	-1	103	87	3b95,S2	0	-0.8
1995	Min A	117	372	51	92	16	5	4	45	49-3	2	54	.247	.335	.349	79	-11	2-1	.945	-4	99	144	3b112,S7,D3	0	-1.3
1996	Cle A	27	43	3	6	4	0	1	3	2-0	0	8	.140	.178	.302	18	-6	0-0	1.000	-1	76	0	3b8,1b7,2b6/D	20	-0.6
1998	KC A	17	46	2	8	0	0	0	4	1-0	0	6	.174	.191	.174	-4	-7	0-0	.867	-1	91	118	3b15,S2/D	21	-0.8
1999	KC A	37	74	8	15	1	0	1	10	4-0	1	8	.203	.244	.257	29	-8	1-0	.971	1	140	188	1b13,3b10,S2/2D	92	-0.7
Total	9	557	1536	214	375	63	10	28	172	161-4	5	236	.244	.316	.353	77	-51	16-15	.954	1	102	98	3b445,S63,1b20,D11,2b7,O2C	298	-4.8
LEJA, FRANK	Frank John; B2.7.1936 Holyoke MA; D5.3.1991 Boston MA; BL/TL/6´4˝/205; d5.1																								
1954	NY A	12	5	2	1	0	0	0	0	0	0	1	.200	.200	.200	10	-1	0-0	1.000	-0	0	0	1b6	0	-0.1
1955	NY A	7	2	1	0	0	0	0	0	0-0	0	1	.000	.000	.000	-99	-1	0-0	1.000	-0	0	507	1b2	0	-0.1
1962	LA A	7	16	0	0	0	0	0	0	1-0	0	6	.000	.059	.000	-85	-4	0-0	.953	-0	108	120	1b4	0	-0.5
Total	3	26	23	3	1	0	0	0	0	1-0	0	8	.043	.083	.043	-67	-6	0-0	.958	-1	97	134	1b12	0	-0.7
LEJEUNE, LARRY	Sheldon Aldenbert; B7.22.1885 Chicago IL; D4.21.1952 Eloise (now part of Westland) MI; BR/TR/6´0˝/185; d5.10																								
1911	Bro N	6	19	2	3	0	0	0	2	2	0	8	.158	.238	.158	12	-2	2	.818	-1	82	0	O6C	—	-0.4
1915	Pit N	18	65	4	11	0	1	0	2	2	1	7	.169	.206	.200	23	-6	4-3	.940	2	105	192	O18C	—	-0.7
Total	2	24	84	6	14	0	1	0	4	4	1	15	.167	.213	.190	21	-8	6-3	.918	1	100	151	O24C	—	-1.1
LEJOHN, DON	Donald Everett; B5.13.1934 Daisytown PA; D2.25.2005 California PA; BR/TR/5´10˝/175; d6.30																								
1965	†LA N	34	78	2	20	2	0	0	7	5-0	0	13	.256	.301	.282	70	-3	0-1	.959	-0	101	80	3b26	0	-0.4
LELIVELT, JACK	John Frank; B11.14.1885 Chicago IL; D1.20.1941 Seattle WA; BL/TL/5´11.5˝/175; d6.24; b–Bill																								
1909	Was A	91	318	25	93	8	6	0	24	19	1	—	.292	.334	.355	124	7	8	.970	6	116	104	O91(41/35/15)	—	0.9
1910	Was A	110	347	40	92	10	3	0	33	40	1	—	.265	.343	.311	110	5	20	.964	6	112	126	O86(80/5/1),1b7	—	0.8
1911	Was A	72	225	29	72	12	4	0	22	22	2	—	.320	.386	.409	124	8	7	.939	2	93	134	O49(36/0/13),1b7	—	0.7
1912	NY A	36	149	12	54	6	7	2	23	4	1	—	.362	.383	.537	153	9	7	.963	-2	95	76	O36C	—	0.4
1913	NY A	18	28	2	6	0	1	0	4	2	0	2	.214	.267	.286	61	-2	1	1.000	1	110	128	O5C	—	-0.2
	Cle A	23	23	0	9	2	0	0	7	0	0	3	.391	.391	.478	150	1	1	ø	-0	0	0	/cf	—	0.1
	Year	41	51	2	15	2	1	0	11	2	0	5	.294	.321	.373	101	0	2	1.000	0	108	125	O6C	—	-0.1
1914	Cle A	34	64	6	21	5	1	0	13	2	0	10	.328	.348	.438	131	2	2-3	.933	-1	87	0	O13(0/7/6)/1	—	-0.1
Total	6	384	1154	114	347	43	22	2	126	89	5	15	.301	.353	.381	124	30	46-3	.962	11	107	110	O281(157/88/35),1b15	—	2.6
LEMASTER, JOHNNIE	Johnnie Lee; B6.19.1954 Portsmouth OH; BR/TR/6´2˝/(160–180); [SFN73 1/6]; d9.2																								
1975	SF N	22	74	4	14	4	0	2	9	4-0	1	15	.189	.241	.324	54	-5	2-1	.967	-3	93	92	S22	0	-0.5
1976	SF N	33	100	9	21	3	2	0	9	2-0	0	21	.210	.223	.280	42	-8	2-0	.937	7	122	95	S31	0	0.3
1977	SF N	68	134	13	20	5	1	0	8	13-3	0	27	.149	.223	.201	15	-16	2-1	.934	-3	103	66	S54,3b2	0	-1.5
1978	SF N	101	272	23	64	18	3	1	14	21-1	1	45	.235	.293	.335	77	-9	6-6	.966	-7	96	87	S96,2b2	0	-0.7
1979	SF N	108	343	42	87	11	2	3	29	23-1	2	55	.254	.304	.324	77	-12	9-5	.959	-1	96	88	S106	0	-0.3
1980	SF N	135	405	33	87	16	6	3	31	25-5	0	57	.215	.257	.306	60	-23	0-1	.957	-15	93	74	S134	0	-2.8
1981	SF N	104	324	27	82	9	1	0	28	24-7	1	46	.253	.306	.287	71	-12	3-7	.964	-10	94	92	S103	0	-1.5
1982	SF N	130	436	34	94	14	1	2	30	31-10	0	78	.216	.267	.266	50	-29	13-4	.963	-12	95	86	S130	17	-2.8
1983	SF N	141	534	81	128	16	1	6	30	60-3	2	96	.240	.317	.307	76	-16	39-19	.964	-12	97	71	S139	0	-1.3
1984	SF N	132	451	46	98	13	2	4	32	31-5	0	97	.217	.265	.282	56	-28	17-5	.964	5	104	89	S129	0	-0.9
1985	SF N	12	16	1	0	0	0	0	0	1-0	0	5	.000	.059	.000	-86	-4	0-0	.955	-3	49	29	S10	45	-0.7
	Cle A	11	20	0	3	0	0	0	2	0-0	0	6	.150	.150	.150	-18	-3	0-1	.949	-0	83	137	S10	0	-0.3
	Pit N	22	58	4	9	0	0	1	6	5-2	0	12	.155	.222	.207	21	-6	1-0	.983	10	129	108	S21	32	0.6
1987	Oak A	20	24	3	2	0	0	0	1	1-0	0	4	.083	.120	.083	-48	-5	0-1	1.000	0	133	445	3b8,S7,2b5/D	0	-0.5
Total	12	1039	3191	320	709	109	19	22	229	241-37	7	564	.222	.277	.289	60	-176	94-51	.961	-44	98	84	S992,3b10,2b7/D	94	-12.9

LEMBO, STEVE Stephen Neal; B11.13.1926 Brooklyn NY; D12.4.1989 Flushing NY; BR/TR/6´1˝/185; d9.16

YEAR	TM LG	G	AB	R	H	2B	3B	HR	RBI	BB-IB	HP	SO	AVG	OBP	SLG	AOPS	ABR	SB-CS	FA	FR	RNG	THR	GAMES AT POSITION	DL	BFW
1950	Bro N	5	6	0	1	0	0	0	0	1	0	0	.167	.286	.167	22	-1	0	1.000	2	*0*	*196*	C5	0	0.1
1952	Bro N	2	5	0	1	0	0	0	1	0	0	1	.200	.200	.200	11	-1	0-0	1.000	0	*0*	*0*	C2	0	0.0
Total	2	7	11	0	2	0	0	0	1	1	0	1	.182	.250	.182	18	-2	0-0	1.000	2	*0*	*125*	C7	0	0.1

LEMKE, MARK Mark Alan; B8.13.1965 Utica NY; BB/TR/5´9˝/167; [AtlN83 27/677]; d9.17

YEAR	TM LG	G	AB	R	H	2B	3B	HR	RBI	BB-IB	HP	SO	AVG	OBP	SLG	AOPS	ABR	SB-CS	FA	FR	RNG	THR	GAMES AT POSITION	DL	BFW
1988	Atl N	16	58	8	13	4	0	0	2	4-0	0	5	.224	.274	.293	60	-3	0-2	.970	1	100	98	2b16	0	-0.3
1989	Atl N	14	55	4	10	2	1	2	10	5-0	0	7	.182	.250	.364	72	-2	0-1	1.000	-1	97	88	2b14	0	-0.4
1990	Atl N	102	239	22	54	13	0	0	21	21-3	0	22	.226	.286	.280	54	-14	0-1	.989	19	120	145	3b45,2b44/S	49	0.5
1991	†Atl N	136	269	36	63	11	2	2	23	29-2	0	27	.234	.305	.312	71	-10	1-2	.978	9	110	115	2b110,3b15	0	0.0
1992	†Atl N	155	427	38	97	7	4	6	26	50-11	0	39	.227	.307	.304	70	-17	0-3	.984	-13	96	81	2b145,3b13	0	-3.0
1993	†Atl N	151	493	52	124	19	2	7	49	65-13	0	50	.252	.335	.341	81	-12	1-2	.982	18	105	123	2b150	0	1.3
1994	Atl N	104	350	40	103	15	0	3	31	38-12	0	37	.294	.363	.363	87	-5	0-3	**.994**	9	101	95	2b103	0	0.7
1995	†Atl N	116	399	42	101	16	5	5	38	44-4	0	40	.253	.325	.356	76	-13	2-2	.990	-1	100	94	2b115	23	-0.9
1996	†Atl N	135	498	64	127	17	0	5	37	53-1	0	48	.255	.323	.319	67	-23	5-2	.977	11	**113**	93	2b133	17	-0.5
1997	Atl N	109	351	33	86	17	1	2	26	33-2	0	51	.245	.306	.316	64	-18	2-0	.980	17	114	122	2b104	39	0.3
1998	Bos A	31	91	10	17	4	0	0	7	6-0	0	15	.187	.232	.231	22	-11	0-1	1.000	-7	86	91	2b31	125	-1.6
Total	11	1069	3230	349	795	125	15	32	270	348-48	0	341	.246	.317	.324	71	-128	11-19	.984	61	105	102	2b965,3b73/S	253	-3.9

LEMON, CHET Chester Earl; B2.12.1955 Jackson MS; BR/TR/6´0˝/(185–196); [OakA72 1/22]; d9.9

YEAR	TM LG	G	AB	R	H	2B	3B	HR	RBI	BB-IB	HP	SO	AVG	OBP	SLG	AOPS	ABR	SB-CS	FA	FR	RNG	THR	GAMES AT POSITION	DL	BFW
1975	Chi A	9	35	2	9	2	0	0	1	2-0	0	6	.257	.297	.314	72	-1	1-0	.923	-3	57	0	3b6/cfD	0	-0.4
1976	Chi A	132	451	46	111	15	5	4	38	28-0	7	65	.246	.298	.328	83	-10	13-7	.992	8	108	136	O131(1/130/0)	0	-0.6
1977	Chi A	150	553	99	151	38	4	19	67	52-1	11	88	.273	.343	.459	118	14	8-7	.978	23	**132**	114	O149C	0	3.5
1978	Chi A★	105	357	51	107	24	6	13	55	39-2	8	46	.300	.377	.510	147	23	5-9	.983	11	120	137	O95(0/84/12),D10	15	3.0
1979	Chi A★	148	556	79	177	**44**	2	17	86	56-6	**13**	68	.318	.391	.496	138	32	7-11	.977	-0	101	101	O147C/D	0	2.7
1980	Chi A	147	514	76	150	32	6	11	51	71-6	12	56	.292	.388	.442	128	23	6-6	.981	-5	93	117	O139C/2D	0	1.6
1981	Chi A	94	328	50	99	23	6	9	50	33-0	**13**	48	.302	.384	.491	154	24	5-8	.984	-2	103	38	O93C	0	2.0
1982	Det A	125	436	75	116	20	1	19	52	56-2	**15**	69	.266	.368	.447	122	15	1-4	.984	-3	93	128	O121(0/29/93)/D	0	0.6
1983	Det A	145	491	78	125	21	5	24	69	54-1	**20**	70	.255	.350	.464	125	18	0-7	.988	1	104	68	O145C	0	1.4
1984	†Det A★	141	509	77	146	34	6	20	76	51-9	7	83	.287	.357	.495	134	24	5-5	.995	4	110	65	O140C/D	0	2.6
1985	Det A	145	517	69	137	28	4	18	68	45-3	10	93	.265	.334	.439	110	7	0-2	.990	-0	105	65	O144C	0	0.5
1986	Det A	126	403	45	101	21	3	12	53	39-3	8	53	.251	.326	.407	99	-1	2-1	.985	-0	101	95	O124C	0	-0.2
1987	†Det A	146	470	75	130	30	3	20	75	70-1	8	82	.277	.376	.481	131	24	0-0	.992	-1	100	66	O145C	0	2.0
1988	Det A	144	512	67	135	29	4	17	64	59-6	7	65	.264	.346	.436	122	16	1-2	.974	-1	99	92	O144R	0	1.0
1989	Det A	127	414	45	98	19	2	7	47	46-3	8	71	.237	.323	.343	90	-4	1-5	.985	-7	86	75	O111R,D13	0	-1.7
1990	Det A	104	322	39	83	16	4	5	32	48-3	4	61	.258	.359	.379	106	4	3-2	.973	4	111	107	O96(0/3/94),D6	15	0.5
Total	16	1988	6868	973	1875	396	61	215	884	749-46	151	1024	.273	.355	.442	120	208	58-76	.984	26	104	93	O1925(1/1473/454),D40,3b6/2	30	18.5

LEMON, JIM James Robert; B3.23.1928 Covington VA; D5.14.2006 Brandon MS; BR/TR/6´4˝/200; d8.20; M1/C7

YEAR	TM LG	G	AB	R	H	2B	3B	HR	RBI	BB-IB	HP	SO	AVG	OBP	SLG	AOPS	ABR	SB-CS	FA	FR	RNG	THR	GAMES AT POSITION	DL	BFW
1950	Cle A	12	34	4	6	1	0	1	1	3	0	12	.176	.243	.294	38	-3	0-0	.824	-1	74	168	O10L	0	-0.5
1953	Cle A	16	46	5	8	1	0	1	5	3	0	15	.174	.224	.261	32	-5	0-0	.913	-1	90	130	O11L,1b2	0	-0.7
1954	Was A	37	128	12	30	2	3	2	13	9	0	34	.234	.283	.344	76	-5	0-0	.951	-4	88	0	O33(1/0/32)	0	-1.1
1955	Was A	10	25	3	5	2	0	1	3	3-0	0	4	.200	.286	.400	88	-1	0-0	.923	-1	102	0	O6(1/0/5)	0	-0.1
1956	Was A	146	538	77	146	21	**11**	27	96	65-2	2	138	.271	.349	.502	123	15	2-4	.963	4	107	104	O141(12/0/130)	0	1.3
1957	Was A	137	518	58	147	23	6	17	64	49-3	3	94	.284	.345	.450	118	12	1-7	.971	-7	96	41	O131R,1b3	0	-0.3
1958	Was A	142	501	65	123	15	9	26	75	50-3	1	120	.246	.314	.467	114	7	2-4	.978	-2	101	70	O137(2/0/135)	0	-0.1
1959	Was A	147	531	73	148	18	3	33	100	46-0	1	99	.279	.334	.510	130	19	5-2	.969	-1	102	46	O142(117/0/25)	0	1.0
1960	Was A★	148	528	81	142	10	1	38	100	67-**8**	7	114	.269	.354	.508	133	23	2-0	.960	-4	88	112	O145L	0	1.2
1961	Min A	129	423	57	109	26	1	14	52	44-2	4	98	.258	.329	.423	95	-2	1-1	.940	-2	95	92	O120(120/0/1)	0	-1.1
1962	Min A	12	17	1	3	0	0	1	5	3-0	0	4	.176	.286	.353	72	-1	0-0	1.000	-1	23	0	O3(2/0/1)	119	-0.2
1963	Min A	7	17	0	2	0	0	0	1	1-0	0	5	.118	.167	.118	-18	-3	0-0	.800	-1	60	0	O4L	0	-0.4
	Phi N	31	59	6	16	2	0	2	6	8-1	0	18	.271	.353	.407	121	2	0-0	.963	0	117	0	O18(16/0/4)	0	0.1
	Chi A	36	80	4	16	0	1	1	8	12-0	0	32	.200	.304	.262	62	-4	0-0	.979	-2	61	144	1b25	0	-0.8
Total	12	1010	3445	446	901	121	35	164	529	363-19	18	787	.262	.332	.460	114	54	13-18	.961	-23	98	73	O901(441/0/464),1b30	119	-1.7

LEMON, BOB Robert Granville; B9.22.1920 San Bernardino CA; D1.11.2000 Long Beach CA; BL/TR/6´0˝/185; d9.9; Mil 1943–45; M8/C6; HF1976; ▲

YEAR	TM LG	G	AB	R	H	2B	3B	HR	RBI	BB-IB	HP	SO	AVG	OBP	SLG	AOPS	ABR	SB-CS	FA	FR	RNG	THR	GAMES AT POSITION	DL	BFW
1941	Cle A	5	4	0	1	0	0	0	0	0	0	1	.250	.250	.250	34	0	0-0	1.000	0	103	0	/3	0	0.0
1942	Cle A	5	5	0	0	0	0	0	0	0	0	3	.000	.000	.000	-99	-1	0-0	.500	-0	107	0	/3	0	-0.2
1946	Cle A	55	89	9	16	3	0	1	4	7	0	18	.180	.240	.247	39	-8	0-1	.976	5	173	484	P32,O12C	0	-0.2
1947	Cle A	47	56	11	18	4	3	2	5	6	0	9	.321	.387	.607	179	5	0-0	.983	4	**170**	242	P37,O2(0/1/1)	0	0.2
1948	†Cle A☆	52	119	20	34	9	0	5	21	8	0	23	.286	.331	.487	119	13	0-0	.965	8	**166**	238	P43	0	0.0
1949	Cle A☆	46	108	17	29	6	2	7	19	10	0	20	.269	.331	.556	135	15	0-0	.963	6	137	137	P37	0	0.0
1950	Cle A★	72	136	21	37	9	1	6	26	13	1	25	.272	.340	.485	113	17	0-0	.957	5	131	158	P44	0	0.0
1951	Cle A★	56	102	11	21	4	1	3	13	9	0	22	.206	.270	.353	72	4	0-0	.976	4	132	138	P42	0	0.0
1952	Cle A★	54	124	14	28	5	0	2	9	4	0	21	.226	.250	.315	60	6	0-0	.982	6	149	186	P42	0	0.0
1953	Cle A☆	51	112	12	26	9	1	2	17	7	0	20	.232	.277	.384	79	8	2-0	.972	8	**159**	**466**	P41	0	0.0
1954	†Cle A★	40	98	11	21	4	1	2	10	6	0	24	.214	.257	.337	61	5	0-0	.963	4	131	263	P36	0	0.0
1955	Cle A	49	78	11	19	0	0	1	9	13-0	0	16	.244	.344	.282	69	5	0-0	.983	2	121	144	P35	0	0.0
1956	Cle A	43	93	8	18	0	0	5	12	9-0	1	21	.194	.272	.355	63	4	0-0	.934	4	148	186	P39	0	0.0
1957	Cle A	25	46	2	3	1	0	1	1	0-0	0	14	.065	.065	.152	-43	-3	0-0	1.000	3	159	265	P21	0	0.0
1958	Cle A	15	13	1	3	0	0	0	1	1-0	0	4	.231	.286	.231	45	0	0-0	1.000	1	172	256	P11	31	0.0
Total	15	615	1183	148	274	54	9	37	147	93-0	2	241	.232	.288	.386	82	70	2-1	.969	59	146	228	P460,O14(0/13/1),3b2	31	-0.2

LENHARDT, DON Donald Eugene "Footsie"; B10.4.1922 Alton IL; BR/TR/6´3˝/190; d4.18; C4; Col Illinois

YEAR	TM LG	G	AB	R	H	2B	3B	HR	RBI	BB-IB	HP	SO	AVG	OBP	SLG	AOPS	ABR	SB-CS	FA	FR	RNG	THR	GAMES AT POSITION	DL	BFW
1950	StL A	139	480	75	131	22	6	22	81	90	2	94	.273	.390	.481	118	14	3-2	.988	-9	73	87	1b86,O39L,3b10	0	-0.1
1951	StL A	31	103	9	27	3	0	5	18	6	0	13	.262	.303	.437	95	-1	1-0	.982	-2	97	0	O27L/1	0	-0.5
	Chi A	64	199	23	53	9	1	10	45	24	2	25	.266	.351	.472	124	6	1-1	.983	-2	98	50	O53L,1b2	0	0.0
	Year	95	302	32	80	12	1	15	63	30	2	38	.265	.335	.460	114	4	2-1	.983	-3	98	34	O80L,1b3	0	-0.5
1952	Bos A	30	105	18	31	4	0	7	24	15	0	18	.295	.383	.533	142	6	0-1	.981	-2	94	0	O27L	0	0.2
	Det A	45	144	18	27	2	1	3	13	28	0	18	.188	.320	.278	67	-6	0-1	.989	3	102	191	O43L	0	-0.7
	StL A	18	48	5	13	4	1	1	5	4	0	8	.271	.327	.458	114	1	0-0	1.000	1	110	0	O11(10/1/0),1b2	0	0.0
	Year	93	297	41	71	10	2	11	42	47	0	44	.239	.343	.397	102	1	0-2	.988	2	100	103	O81(80/1/0),1b2	0	-0.5
1953	StL A	97	303	37	96	15	0	10	35	41	1	41	.317	.400	.465	131	14	1-2	.969	1	96	143	O77(72/0/5),3b6	0	1.0
1954	Bal A	13	33	2	5	1	0	0	1	3	0	9	.152	.222	.182	12	-4	0-0	1.000	0	84	0	O7L,1b2	0	-0.5
	Bos A	44	66	5	18	4	0	3	17	3	1	9	.273	.310	.470	101	0	0-0	1.000	-1	87	0	O13L/3	0	-0.1
	Year	57	99	7	23	5	0	3	18	6	1	18	.232	.280	.374	74	-4	0-0	1.000	-0	86	0	O20L,1b2/3	0	-0.6
Total	5	481	1481	192	401	64	9	61	239	214	6	235	.271	.365	.450	114	30	6-7	.980	-11	97	82	O297(291/1/5),1b93,3b17	0	-0.7

LENNON, PATRICK Patrick Orlando; B4.27.1968 Whiteville NC; BR/TR/6´2˝/(200–240); [SeaA86 1/8]; d9.15

YEAR	TM LG	G	AB	R	H	2B	3B	HR	RBI	BB-IB	HP	SO	AVG	OBP	SLG	AOPS	ABR	SB-CS	FA	FR	RNG	THR	GAMES AT POSITION	DL	BFW
1991	Sea A	9	8	2	1	1	0	0	1	3-0	0	1	.125	.364	.250	73	0	0-0	1.000	0	438	0	/lfD	0	0.0
1992	Sea A	1	2	0	0	0	0	0	0	0-0	0	0	.000	.000	.000	-99	-1	0-0	1.000	-0	0	314	/1	0	-0.1
1996	KC A	14	30	5	7	3	0	0	1	7-0	0	10	.233	.378	.333	82	0	0-0	.947	-0	105	0	O11L/D	0	-0.1
1997	Oak A	56	116	14	34	6	1	1	14	15-0	0	35	.293	.374	.388	99	0	0-1	.948	-1	110	0	O36(23/1/12),D17	23	-0.2
1998	Tor A	2	4	1	2	2	0	0	0	0-0	0	1	.500	.500	1.000	276	1	0-0	1.000	0	172	0	O2R	0	0.1
1999	Tor A	9	29	3	6	2	0	1	6	2-0	1	12	.207	.281	.379	65	-2	0-0	1.000	2	159	204	O8(5/0/4)	0	0.0
Total	6	91	189	25	50	14	1	2	22	27-0	1	59	.265	.359	.381	92	-2	0-1	.962	2	121	37	O58(40/1/18),D23/1	23	-0.3

LENNON, BOB Robert Albert "Arch"; B9.15.1928 Brooklyn NY; D6.14.2005 Dix Hills NY; BL/TL/6´0˝/(195–200); d9.9

YEAR	TM LG	G	AB	R	H	2B	3B	HR	RBI	BB-IB	HP	SO	AVG	OBP	SLG	AOPS	ABR	SB-CS	FA	FR	RNG	THR	GAMES AT POSITION	DL	BFW
1954	NY N	3	3	0	0	0	0	0	0	0	0	0	.000	.000	.000	-99	-1	0-0	ø	0	—	—	/H	0	-0.1
1956	NY N	26	55	3	10	1	0	0	1	4-1	0	17	.182	.233	.200	19	-6	0-0	.885	-1	79	174	O21(5/1/18)	0	-0.8
1957	Chi N	9	21	2	3	1	0	1	3	1-0	0	9	.143	.182	.333	35	-2	0-0	1.000	-1	43	0	O4C	0	-0.4
Total	3	38	79	5	13	2	0	1	4	5-1	0	26	.165	.212	.228	19	-9	0-0	.900	-2	72	138	O25(5/5/18)	0	-1.3

YEAR	TM LG	G	AB	R	H	2B	3B	HR	RBI	BB-IB	HP	SO	AVG	OBP	SLG	AOPS	ABR	SB-CS	FA	FR	RNG	THR	GAMES AT POSITION	DL	BFW
LENNON, BILL	William H.; B1848 Brooklyn NY; D8.19.1910 Philadelphia PA; 5´7˝/145; d5.4; M1/U2																								
1871	Kek NA	12	48	5	11	3	0	0	5	1	—	0	.229	.245	.292	52	-3	1-0	.887	-2	—	—	C12,S2/rfM	—	-0.3
1872	Nat NA	**11**	54	11	11	1	0	0	6	0	—	0	.204	.204	.222	26	-5	0-0	.765	-5	—	—	C11/1	—	-0.7
1873	Mar NA	5	19	2	4	0	0	0	2	0	—	0	.211	.211	.211	32	-1	0-0	.942	-1	0	0	1b4/C3	—	-0.2
Total	3NA	28	121	18	26	4	0	0	13	1	—	0	.215	.221	.248	38	-9	1-0	.817	-9	—	—	C24,1b5,S2/3rf	—	-1.2
LENNOX, ED	James Edgar "Eggie"; B11.3.1883 Camden NJ; D10.26.1939 Camden NJ; BR/TR/5´10˝/174; d8.8																								
1906	Phi A	6	17	1	1	1	0	0	0	1	0	—	.059	.111	.118	-28	-2	0	.909	3	145	0	3b6	—	0.1
1909	Bro N	126	435	33	114	18	9	2	44	47	2	—	.262	.337	.359	120	10	11	**.959**	-3	88	115	3b121	—	1.1
1910	Bro N	110	367	19	95	19	4	3	32	36	5	39	.259	.333	.357	104	2	7	.950	-16	78	97	3b100	—	-1.2
1912	Chi N	27	81	13	19	4	1	1	16	12	2	10	.235	.347	.346	90	-1	1	.934	-3	84	38	3b24	—	-0.3
1914	Pit F	124	430	71	134	25	10	11	84	71	4	38	.312	.414	.493	148	25	19	.954	-17	87	65	3b123	—	1.2
1915	Pit F	55	53	1	16	3	1	1	9	7	0	12	.302	.383	.453	136	2	0	1.000	1	135	0	3b3	—	0.3
Total	6	448	1383	138	379	70	25	18	185	174	13	99	.274	.361	.400	122	36	38	.953	-35	86	87	3b377	—	1.2
LENTINE, JIM	James Matthew; B7.16.1954 Los Angeles CA; BR/TR/6´0˝/175; [StLN75 12/280]; d9.3; Col La Verne																								
1978	StL N	8	11	1	2	0	0	0	1	0-0	1	0	.182	.250	.182	22	-1	1-0	1.000	-0	72	0	O3(2/0/1)	0	-0.2
1979	StL N	11	23	2	9	1	0	0	1	3-0	0	6	.391	.462	.435	143	2	0-1	1.000	1	99	221	O8(3/2/3)	0	0.2
1980	StL N	9	10	1	1	0	0	0	1	0-0	0	2	.100	.100	.100	-42	-2	0-0	1.000	-0	79	0	O6(5/1/0)	0	-0.2
	Det A	67	161	19	42	8	1	1	17	28-1	2	30	.261	.377	.342	96	1	2-1	.963	2	102	156	O55(40/10/6),D9	0	0.1
Total	3	95	205	23	54	9	1	1	20	31-1	3	38	.263	.368	.332	91	0	3-2	.969	2	99	148	O72(50/13/10),D9	0	-0.1
LENZ, DAVID	David; B1.1.1851 , Germany; D5.21.1886 Brooklyn NY; d5.7																								
1872	Eck NA	4	12	2	1	0	0	0	0	0	—	0	.083	.083	.083	-57	-2	0-0	.733	-3	—	—	C4	—	-0.4
LEON, EDDIE	Eduardo Antonio; B8.11.1946 Tucson AZ; BR/TR/6´0˝/(170–175); [CleA67 S2/35]; d9.9; Col Arizona																								
1968	Cle A	6	1	0	0	0	0	0	0	0-0	0	1	.000	.000	.000	-99	0	0-0	1.000	1	114	406	S6	0	0.1
1969	Cle A	64	213	20	51	6	0	3	19	19-3	0	37	.239	.300	.310	69	-9	2-2	.952	-1	94	110	S64	0	-0.2
1970	Cle A	152	549	58	136	20	4	10	56	47-2	2	89	.248	.308	.353	79	-17	1-2	.982	17	100	111	2b141,S23/3	0	1.1
1971	Cle A	131	429	35	112	12	2	4	35	34-5	1	69	.261	.317	.326	75	-14	3-5	.983	0	95	93	2b107,S24	0	-0.6
1972	Cle A	89	225	14	45	2	1	4	16	20-1	1	47	.200	.265	.271	59	-12	0-2	.993	2	108	95	2b36,S35	0	-0.6
1973	Chi A	127	399	37	91	10	3	3	30	34-0	3	103	.228	.291	.291	63	-20	1-5	.972	-6	95	95	S122,2b3	0	-1.4
1974	Chi A	31	46	1	5	1	0	0	3	2-0	0	12	.109	.143	.130	-20	-7	0-0	.962	4	101	126	S21,2b7,3b2/D	0	-0.2
1975	NY A	1	0	0	0	0	0	0	0	0-0	0	0	ø	ø	ø	ø	0	0-0	ø	-0	0	0	/S	0	0.0
Total	8	601	1862	165	440	51	10	24	159	156-11	7	358	.236	.296	.313	69	-79	7-16	.963	17	97	108	S296,2b294,3b3/D	0	-1.8
LEON, JOSE	Jose Geraldo (Vega); B12.8.1976 Cayey, PR; BR/TR/6´0˝/(175–220); [StLN94 22/614]; d6.16																								
2002	Bal A	36	89	8	22	2	0	3	10	3-0	1	20	.247	.280	.371	75	-4	1-0	1.000	0	92	132	1b17,3b12,O2L,D2	0	-0.4
2003	Bal A	21	54	6	13	1	0	0	0	3-0	2	18	.241	.305	.259	51	-4	0-0	.963	0	103	196	3b10,1b7,D3	0	-0.4
2004	Bal A	31	66	4	12	2	0	2	8	2-0	0	19	.182	.203	.303	31	-7	0-0	1.000	2	145	93	1b16,3b6,D5	0	-0.6
Total	3	88	209	18	47	5	0	5	18	8-0	3	57	.225	.262	.321	54	-15	1-0	.996	2	104	121	1b40,3b28,D10,O2L	0	-1.4
LEONARD	; d9.12																								
1892	StL N	1	0	0	0	0	0	0	0	1	0	0	ø	1.000	ø	219	0	1	ø	-0	0	0	/rf	—	0.0
LEONARD, ANDY	Andrew Jackson; B6.1.1846 Co. Cavan, Ireland; D8.21.1903 Boston MA; BR/TR/5´7˝/168; d5.5																								
1871	Oly NA	31	148	33	43	8	3	0	30	3	—	1	.291	.305	.385	102	1	14-3	.863	-2	98	105	2b19,O11L/S	—	0.1
1872	Bos NA	46	241	57	84	7	1	2	42	0	—	2	.349	.349	.411	126	6	8-5	.828	-4	176	0	O38L,3b6,2b4/S	—	0.2
1873	Bos NA	58	300	81	96	13	6	0	60	2	—	0	.320	.325	.403	105	0	27-9	.750	1	**259**	84	O45(45/0/1),2b12,1b2/S	—	0.3
1874	Bos NA	**71**	339	68	106	18	4	0	50	2	—	2	.313	.317	.389	119	6	11-3	.807	0	81	80	O51L,2b11,S11	—	0.6
1875	Bos NA	80	396	87	127	14	6	1	74	2	—	6	.321	.324	.394	143	15	14-8	.806	-2	101	0	O73L,S3,3b3,2b2	—	1.4
1876	Bos N	64	303	53	85	10	2	0	27	4	—	6	.281	.290	.327	103	1	—	.925	2	109	157	O35L,2b30	—	0.2
1877	Bos N	58	272	46	78	5	0	0	27	5	—	5	.287	.300	.305	88	-4	—	.875	-3	68	186	O37L,S21	—	-0.8
1878	Bos N	**60**	262	41	68	8	5	0	16	3	—	19	.260	.268	.328	88	-4	—	.777	-7	51	45	O60L	—	-1.4
1880	Cin N	33	133	15	28	3	0	1	17	8	—	11	.211	.255	.256	75	-3	—	.833	-7	90	69	S23,3b10	—	-0.8
Total	5NA	286	1424	326	456	60	20	3	256	9	—	11	.320	.324	.397	121	28	74-28	.787	-6	149	37	O218(218/0/1),2b48,S17,3b9,1b2	—	2.6
Total	4	215	970	155	259	26	7	1	87	20	—	41	.267	.282	.311	91	-10	—	.856	-14	70	114	O132L,S44,2b30,3b10	—	-2.8
LEONARD, JEFFREY	Jeffrey; B9.22.1955 Philadelphia PA; BR/TR/6´2˝/(187–205); d9.2																								
1977	LA N	11	10	1	3	0	1	0	2	1-0	0	4	.300	.364	.500	128	0	0-0	1.000	0	123	0	O10(6/0/4)	0	0.0
1978	Hou N	8	26	2	10	2	0	0	4	1-0	0	2	.385	.407	.462	152	2	0-1	1.000	1	112	199	O8(4/2/2)	0	0.2
1979	Hou N	134	411	47	119	15	5	0	47	46-7	2	68	.290	.360	.350	102	2	23-10	.959	-6	98	65	O123(4/22/100)	0	-0.8
1980	†Hou N	88	216	29	46	7	5	3	20	19-2	0	46	.213	.274	.333	76	-8	4-1	.979	0	100	161	O56(3/9/44),1b11	0	-1.1
1981	Hou N	7	18	1	3	1	1	0	3	0-0	0	4	.167	.158	.333	41	-2	1-0	1.000	-1	63	0	1b2,O2R	0	-0.2
	SF N	37	127	20	39	11	3	4	26	12-3	1	21	.307	.371	.535	160	10	4-2	1.000	1	114	91	O28(8/19/4),1b5	0	1.1
	Year	44	145	21	42	12	4	4	29	12-3	1	25	.290	.346	.510	146	8	5-2	1.000	1	112	85	O30(8/19/6),1b7	0	0.9
1982	SF N	80	278	32	72	16	1	9	49	19-2	2	65	.259	.306	.421	104	1	18-5	.958	-7	90	36	O74(56/17/2)/1	57	-0.7
1983	SF N	139	516	74	144	17	7	21	87	35-2	1	116	.279	.323	.461	119	10	26-7	.975	4	96	171	O136(127/12/2)	0	1.3
1984	SF N	136	514	76	155	27	2	21	86	47-3	0	123	.302	.357	.484	139	26	17-7	.970	-0	92	135	O131(116/18/4)	0	2.2
1985	SF N	133	507	49	122	20	3	17	62	21-5	1	107	.241	.272	.393	88	-12	11-6	.977	-3	92	115	O126(125/3/0)	0	-2.1
1986	SF N	89	341	48	95	11	3	6	42	20-1	3	62	.279	.322	.381	99	-2	16-3	.970	-1	95	69	O87L	67	-0.5
1987	†SF N★	131	503	70	141	29	4	19	63	21-6	2	68	.280	.309	.467	108	3	16-7	.966	-7	84	85	O127(127/1/0)	0	-0.8
1988	SF N	44	160	12	41	8	1	2	20	9-1	0	24	.256	.292	.356	90	-3	7-5	.987	-4	90	0	O43L	9	-0.8
	Mil A	94	374	45	88	19	0	8	44	16-1	3	68	.235	.270	.350	72	-15	10-4	.985	-2	98	73	O91L,D2	0	-1.9
1989	Sea A★	150	566	69	144	20	1	24	93	38-2	5	125	.254	.301	.420	100	-2	6-1	.982	1	105	137	D123,O26(25/0/1)	0	-0.5
1990	Sea A	134	478	39	120	20	0	10	75	37-6	3	97	.251	.305	.356	84	-11	4-2	.983	-9	80	0	O79(74/0/6),D48	0	-2.4
Total	14	1415	5045	614	1342	223	37	144	723	342-41	23	1000	.266	.312	.411	102	-1	163-61	.974	-31	93	93	O1147(896/103/171),D173,1b19	133	-7.0
LEONARD, JOE	Joseph Howard; B11.15.1894 W.Chicago IL; D5.1.1920 Washington DC; BL/TR/5´7.5˝/156; d4.24; Mil 1918																								
1914	Pit N	53	126	17	25	2	2	0	4	12	0	21	.198	.268	.246	56	-7	4	.909	-6	88	53	3b38/S	—	-1.3
1916	Cle A	3	2	1	0	0	0	0	0	0	0	1	.000	.000	.000	-94	0	0	1.000	0	102	0	/2	—	0.0
	Was A	42	168	20	46	7	0	0	14	22	0	23	.274	.358	.315	103	2	4	.952	-7	75	78	3b42	—	-0.4
	Year	45	170	21	46	7	0	0	14	22	0	24	.271	.354	.312	101	1	4	.952	-7	75	78	3b42/2	—	-0.4
1917	Was A	99	297	30	57	6	7	0	23	45	2	40	.192	.302	.259	72	-9	6	.925	-2	89	158	3b68,1b19/Srf	—	-1.1
1919	Was A	71	198	26	51	8	3	2	20	20	1	28	.258	.329	.359	94	-2	3	.944	-7	80	96	2b28,3b25,1b4/lf	—	-0.8
1920	Was A	1	0	0	0	0	0	0	0	0	0	0	ø	ø	ø	ø	0	0-0	ø	0	—	—	/R	—	0.0
Total	5	269	791	94	179	23	12	2	61	99	3	113	.226	.315	.293	82	-16	17-0	.937	-21	85	114	3b173,2b29,1b23,O2(1/0/1),S2	—	-3.6
LEONARD, MARK	Mark David; B8.14.1964 Mountain View CA; BL/TR/6´0˝/(195–212); [SFN86 29/709]; d7.21; Col California–Santa Barbara																								
1990	SF N	11	17	3	3	1	0	1	2	3-0	0	8	.176	.300	.412	97	0	0-0	1.000	0	112	0	O7(2/0/5)	28	0.0
1991	SF N	64	129	14	31	7	1	2	14	12-1	1	25	.240	.306	.357	89	-2	0-1	1.000	-4	74	0	O34(24/0/12)	0	-0.7
1992	SF N	55	128	13	30	7	0	4	16	16-0	3	31	.234	.331	.383	108	2	0-1	.984	1	98	132	O37(33/0/4)	57	0.1
1993	Bal A	10	15	1	1	1	0	0	3	3-0	0	7	.067	.190	.133	-2	-2	0-0	.833	0	133	0	O4L,D3	0	-0.2
1994	SF N	14	11	2	4	1	1	0	2	3-0	0	2	.364	.500	.636	201	2	0-0	1.000	0	111	0	O2L	0	0.2
1995	SF N	14	21	4	4	1	0	1	4	5-1	0	2	.190	.346	.381	94	0	0-0	1.000	-0	99	0	O6(1/0/5)	0	0.0
Total	6	168	321	37	73	18	2	8	41	42-2	4	75	.227	.319	.371	97	0	0-2	.985	-3	90	59	O90(66/0/26),D3	85	-0.6
LEONE, JUSTIN	Justin Paul; B3.9.1977 Las Vegas NV; BR/TR/6´1˝/(190–210); [SeaA99 13/395]; d7.2; Col St. Martins																								
2004	Sea A	31	102	15	22	5	0	6	13	9-0	3	32	.216	.298	.441	94	-1	1-0	.901	-3	93	44	3b28,S2/D	47	-0.4
2006	SD N	1	1	0	0	0	0	0	0	0-0	0	0	.000	.000	.000	-99	0	0-0	ø	0	—	—	/H	0	0.0
Total	2	32	103	15	22	5	0	6	13	9-0	3	32	.214	.296	.437	92	-1	1-0	.901	-3	93	44	3b28,S2/D	47	-0.4
LEOVICH, JOHN	John Joseph; B5.5.1918 Portland OR; D2.3.2000 Lincoln City OR; BR/TR/6´0.5˝/200; d5.1; Col Oregon St.																								
1941	Phi A	1	2	0	1	1	0	0	0	0	0	0	.500	.500	1.000	296	1	0-0	ø	-0	*0*	*0*	/C	0	0.0

YEAR	TM LG	G	AB	R	H	2B	3B	HR	RBI	BB-IB	HP	SO	AVG	OBP	SLG	AOPS	ABR	SB-CS	FA	FR	RNG	THR	GAMES AT POSITION	DL	BFW
LEPCIO, TED	Thaddeus Stanley; B7.28.1930 Utica NY; BR/TR/5´10˝/(175–180); d4.15; Col Seton Hall																								
1952	Bos A	84	274	34	72	17	2	5	26	24	3	41	.263	.329	.394	93	-2	3-3	.972	8	113	98	2b57,3b25/S	0	0.8
1953	Bos A	66	161	17	38	4	2	4	11	17	1	24	.236	.313	.360	77	-6	0-0	.981	11	121	126	2b34,S20,3b11	0	0.8
1954	Bos A	116	398	42	102	19	4	8	45	42	3	62	.256	.328	.384	86	-7	3-4	.971	8	107	94	2b80,3b24,S14	0	0.7
1955	Bos A	51	134	19	31	9	0	6	15	12-0	4	36	.231	.313	.433	91	-2	1-1	.943	3	107	78	3b45	0	0.1
1956	Bos A	83	284	34	74	10	0	15	51	30-1	3	77	.261	.335	.454	96	-2	1-3	.966	3	103	105	2b57,3b22	0	0.3
1957	Bos A	79	232	24	56	10	2	9	37	29-1	1	61	.241	.328	.418	97	-1	0-0	.976	5	110	122	2b68	0	0.9
1958	Bos A	50	136	10	27	3	0	6	14	12-1	1	47	.199	.268	.353	65	-7	0-1	.980	-1	100	90	2b40	0	-0.6
1959	Bos A	3	3	1	1	1	0	0	1	0-0	0	2	.333	.333	.667	160	0	0-0	1.000	0	158	0	/2	0	0.0
	Det A	76	215	25	60	8	0	7	24	17-2	0	49	.279	.332	.414	98	-1	2-0	.951	-3	90	87	S35,2b24,3b11	0	0.1
	Year	79	218	26	61	9	0	7	25	17-2	0	51	.280	.332	.417	99	0	2-0	.951	-3	90	87	S35,2b25,3b11	0	0.1
1960	Phi N	69	141	16	32	7	0	2	8	17-1	2	41	.227	.315	.319	75	-4	0-3	.942	-8	89	32	3b50,S14,2b5	0	-1.4
1961	Chi A	5	2	0	0	0	0	0	0	1-1	0	0	.000	.333	.000	-2	0	0-0	.000	-0	0	0	/3	0	-0.1
	Min A	47	112	11	19	3	1	7	19	8-0	1	31	.170	.230	.402	62	-7	1-0	.919	-1	73	74	3b35,2b22,S6	0	-0.6
	Year	52	114	11	19	3	1	7	19	9-1	1	31	.167	.232	.395	62	-7	1-0	.895	-1	72	73	3b36,2b22,S6	0	-0.7
Total	10	729	2092	233	512	91	11	69	251	209-7	19	471	.245	.318	.398	87	-39	11-15	.972	24	107	107	2b388,3b224,S90	0	1.0
LEPINE, PETE	Louis Joseph; B9.5.1876 Montreal QC, Can.; D12.3.1949 Woonsocket RI; BL/TL/5´10˝/142; d7.21																								
1902	Det A	30	96	8	20	3	2	1	19	8	1	—	.208	.276	.313	62	-5	1	1.000	1	115	274	O19R,1b8	—	-0.5
LEPPERT, DON	Don Eugene "Tiger"; B11.20.1930 Memphis TN; BL/TR/5´8˝/175; d4.11																								
1955	Bal A	40	70	6	8	0	1	0	2	9-0	0	10	.114	.213	.143	-2	-10	1-1	.937	-7	72	72	2b35	0	-1.7
LEPPERT, DON	Donald George; B10.19.1931 Indianapolis IN; BR/TR/6´2˝/220; d6.18; C18; Col Wabash																								
1961	Pit N	22	60	6	16	2	1	3	5	1-0	0	11	.267	.279	.483	97	-1	0-0	.968	1	157	81	C21	0	0.1
1962	Pit N	45	139	14	37	6	1	3	18	12-2	1	21	.266	.327	.388	92	-2	0-1	.989	1	83	60	C44	0	0.1
1963	Was A☆	73	211	20	50	11	0	6	24	20-2	1	29	.237	.305	.374	90	-3	0-0	.984	-5	93	34	C60	0	-0.5
1964	Was A	50	122	6	19	3	0	3	12	11-1	0	32	.156	.224	.254	33	-11	0-0	.990	-2	72	103	C43	0	-1.2
Total	4	190	532	46	122	22	2	15	59	44-5	2	93	.229	.289	.363	78	-17	0-1	.985	-4	92	63	C168	0	-1.5
LERCHEN, DUTCH	Bertram Roe; B4.4.1889 Detroit MI; D1.7.1962 Detroit MI; BR/TR/5´8˝/160; d8.14																								
1910	Bos A	6	15	1	0	0	0	0	0	1	0	—	.000	.063	.000	-78	-3	0	.929	-2	37	87	S6	—	-0.6
LERCHEN, GEORGE	George Edward; B12.1.1922 Detroit MI; BB/TR (BL 1953)/5´11˝/175; d4.15																								
1952	Det A	14	32	1	5	1	0	1	3	7	0	10	.156	.308	.281	64	-1	1-0	1.000	-1	97	0	O7(0/3/4)	0	-0.2
1953	Cin N	22	17	2	5	1	0	0	2	5	0	6	.294	.455	.353	113	1	0-0	1.000	0	102	0	/cf	0	0.1
Total	2	36	49	3	10	2	0	1	5	12	0	16	.204	.361	.306	82	0	1-0	1.000	-1	97	0	O8(0/4/4)	0	-0.1
LERIAN, WALT	Walter Irvin "Peck"; B2.10.1903 Baltimore MD; D10.22.1929 Baltimore MD; BR/TR/5´11˝/170; d4.16																								
1928	Phi N	96	239	28	65	16	2	2	25	41	3	29	.272	.385	.381	97	1	1	.977	-5	*75*	*126*	C74	—	0.1
1929	Phi N	105	273	28	61	13	2	6	25	53	2	37	.223	.354	.352	71	-12	0	**.986**	-2	*92*	*119*	C103	—	-0.7
Total	2	201	512	56	126	29	4	8	50	94	5	66	.246	.368	.365	83	-11	1	.982	-8	*84*	*122*	C177	—	-0.6
LESHER, BRIAN	Brian Herbert; B3.5.1971 Wilrijk, Belgium; BR/TL/6´5˝/(205–222); [OakA92 25/704]; d8.25; Col Delaware																								
1996	Oak A	26	82	11	19	3	0	5	16	5-0	1	17	.232	.281	.451	83	-3	0-0	.977	-1	89	129	O25(14/0/14)/1	0	-0.4
1997	Oak A	46	131	17	30	4	1	4	16	9-0	0	30	.229	.275	.366	67	-7	4-1	.958	2	106	152	O32(31/0/3),1b3,D3	0	-0.6
1998	Oak A	7	7	0	1	1	0	0	1	0-0	0	3	.143	.143	.286	8	-1	0-0	1.000	2	108	1788	O4L/1	41	0.1
2000	Sea A	5	5	1	4	1	1	0	3	1-0	0	0	.800	.833	1.400	459	3	1-0	1.000	0	154	0	1b4	0	0.3
2002	Tor A	24	38	2	5	1	0	0	2	4-0	0	15	.132	.209	.158	1	-5	0-0	1.000	1	122	24	1b12,O5(3/0/2),D3	0	-0.5
Total	5	108	263	31	59	10	2	9	38	19-0	1	65	.224	.275	.380	68	-13	5-1	.970	4	102	186	O66(52/0/19),1b21,D6	41	-1.1
LESLIE, ROY	Roy Reid; B8.23.1894 Bailey TX; D4.9.1972 Sherman TX; BR/TR/6´1˝/175; d9.6																								
1917	Chi N	7	19	1	4	0	0	0	1	1	0	5	.211	.250	.211	39	-1	1	.969	-0	102	90	1b6	—	-0.2
1919	StL N	12	24	2	5	1	0	0	4	4	0	3	.208	.321	.250	78	0	0	.957	-0	111	142	1b9	—	-0.1
1922	Phi N	141	513	44	139	23	2	6	50	37	0	49	.271	.320	.359	68	-24	3-7	.990	-5	86	102	1b139	—	-3.8
Total	3	160	556	47	148	24	2	6	55	42	0	57	.266	.318	.349	68	-25	4-7	.988	-5	88	103	1b154	—	-4.1
LESLIE, SAM	Samuel Andrew "Sambo"; B7.26.1905 Moss Point MS; D1.21.1979 Pascagoula MS; BL/TL/6´0˝/192; d10.6																								
1929	NY N	1	1	0	0	0	0	0	1	0	0	0	.000	.000	.000	-99	0	0	1.000	-0	85	0	/lf	—	0.0
1930	NY N	2	2	0	1	0	0	0	0	0	0	1	.500	.500	.500	146	0	0	ø	0	—	—	/H	—	0.0
1931	NY N	53	53	11	16	4	0	3	5	1	0	2	.302	.315	.547	131	2	3	1.000	0	110	0	1b6	—	0.2
1932	NY N	77	75	5	22	4	0	1	15	2	2	5	.293	.329	.387	94	-1	0	1.000	-0	0	0	1b2	—	-0.1
1933	NY N	40	137	21	44	12	3	3	27	12	1	9	.321	.380	.518	157	10	0	.990	-0	95	111	1b35	—	0.7
	Bro N	96	364	41	104	11	4	5	46	23	7	14	.286	.340	.379	110	4	1	.982	-6	81	57	1b95	—	-1.1
	Year	136	501	62	148	23	7	8	73	35	8	23	.295	.351	.417	123	15	1	.984	-6	85	72	1b130	—	-0.4
1934	Bro N	146	546	75	181	29	6	9	102	69	3	34	.332	.409	.456	138	33	5	.993	5	112	93	1b138	—	2.4
1935	Bro N	142	520	72	160	30	7	5	93	55	5	19	.308	.379	.421	117	15	4	.989	0	101	108	1b138	—	0.3
1936	†NY N	117	417	49	123	19	5	6	54	23	2	16	.295	.335	.408	100	-1	0	.991	1	104	110	1b99	—	-1.0
1937	†NY N	72	191	25	59	7	2	3	30	20	2	12	.309	.380	.414	114	4	1	.990	4	128	142	1b44	—	0.4
1938	NY N	76	154	12	39	7	1	1	16	11	1	6	.253	.307	.331	75	-5	0	.988	-2	76	91	1b32	—	-1.0
Total	10	822	2460	311	749	123	28	36	389	216	23	118	.304	.366	.421	117	61	14	.989	0	101	98	1b589/lf	—	0.8
LETCHAS, CHARLIE	Charlie; B10.3.1915 Thomasville GA; D3.14.1995 Tampa FL; BR/TR/5´10˝/150; d9.16; Mil 1945–46																								
1939	Phi N	12	44	2	10	2	0	1	3	1	0	2	.227	.244	.341	57	-3	0	.933	-1	97	117	2b12	—	-0.3
1941	Was A	2	8	0	1	0	0	0	1	1	0	1	.125	.222	.125	-6	-1	0-0	.800	-1	121	74	2b2	0	-0.2
1944	Phi N	116	396	29	94	8	0	0	33	32	2	27	.237	.298	.258	59	-21	0	.968	4	101	146	2b47,3b32,S29	0	-1.3
1946	Phi N	6	13	1	3	0	0	0	0	1	0	1	.231	.286	.231	49	-1	0	1.000	0	89	204	2b4	0	0.0
Total	4	136	461	32	108	10	0	1	37	35	2	31	.234	.291	.262	58	-26	0-0	.959	3	100	142	2b65,3b32,S29	0	-1.8
LETCHER, TOM	Frederick Thomas; B1.1868 Bryan OH; BL/6´0˝/?; d9.27																								
1891	Mil AA	6	21	3	4	1	0	0	2	0	0	1	.190	.190	.238	19	-2	1	.857	1	241	1241	O6(1/0/5)	—	-0.1
LEVAN, JESSE	Jesse Roy; B7.15.1926 Reading PA; D11.30.1998 Reading PA; BL/TR/6´0˝/172; d9.27																								
1947	Phi N	2	9	3	4	0	0	0	1	0	0	0	.444	.444	.444	142	0	0	1.000	-0	60	0	O2L	0	0.0
1954	Was A	7	10	1	3	0	0	0	0	0	0	0	.300	.300	.300	68	-1	0-0	ø	-0	0	0	3b4/1	0	-0.1
1955	Was A	16	16	1	3	0	0	1	4	0-0	0	2	.188	.188	.375	51	-1	0-0	ø	0	—	—	/H	0	-0.1
Total	3	25	35	5	10	0	0	1	5	0-0	0	2	.286	.286	.371	80	-2	0-0	.000	-0	0	0	3b4,O2L/1	0	-0.2
LEVEY, JIM	James Julius; B9.13.1906 Pittsburgh PA; D3.14.1970 Dallas TX; BB/TR (BR 1930–31)/5´10.5˝/154; d9.17																								
1930	StL A	8	37	7	9	2	0	0	3	3	0	2	.243	.300	.297	50	-3	0-0	.958	1	102	117	S8	—	-0.1
1931	StL A	139	498	53	104	19	2	5	38	35	2	83	.209	.264	.285	43	-43	13-8	.920	-12	96	**114**	S139	—	-4.2
1932	StL A	152	568	59	159	30	8	4	63	21	4	48	.280	.310	.382	74	-24	6-4	.939	-19	94	83	S152	—	-3.0
1933	StL A	141	529	43	103	10	4	2	36	26	3	68	.195	.237	.240	25	-59	4-6	.945	-6	97	89	S138	—	-5.4
Total	4	440	1632	162	375	61	14	11	140	85	9	201	.230	.272	.305	48	-129	23-18	.936	-36	96	95	S437	—	-12.7
LEVIS, CHARLIE	Charles H.; B6.21.1860 St.Louis MO; D10.16.1926 St.Louis MO; BR; d4.17																								
1884	Bal U	87	373	59	85	11	4	5	—	3	—	—	.228	.234	.319	60	-30	—	.955	-0	89	100	1b87	—	-3.5
	Was U	1	3	0	0	0	0	0	—	0	—	—	.000	.000	.000	-99	-1	—	1.000	0	0	0	/1	—	-0.1
	Year	88	376	59	85	11	4	5	—	3	—	—	.226	.232	.316	59	-31	—	.955	-0	128	86	1b88	—	-3.6
	Ind AA	3	10	0	2	0	0	0	—	0	0	—	.200	.200	.200	32	-1	—	1.000	0	128	86	1b3	—	-0.1
1885	Bal AA	1	4	2	1	0	0	0	0	0	1	—	.250	.400	.250	110	0	—	.889	-0	0	0	/1	—	0.0
Total	2	92	390	61	88	11	4	5	0	3	1	—	.226	.234	.313	59	-32	—	.956	-0	88	97	1b92	—	-3.7

YEAR	TM LG	G	AB	R	H	2B	3B	HR	RBI	BB-IB	HP	SO	AVG	OBP	SLG	AOPS	ABR	SB-CS	FA	FR	RNG	THR	GAMES AT POSITION	DL	BFW
LEVIS, JESSE	Jesse; B4.14.1968 Philadelphia PA; BL/TR/5´9˝/(180–200); [CleA89 4/98]; d4.24; Col North Carolina																								
1992	Cle A	28	43	2	12	4	0	1	3	0-0	0	5	.279	.279	.442	100	0	0-0	.985	0	104	54	C21/D	0	0.0
1993	Cle A	31	63	7	11	2	0	0	4	2-0	0	10	.175	.197	.206	9	-8	0-0	.991	1	89	103	C29	0	-0.6
1994	Cle A	1	1	0	1	0	0	0	0	0-0	0	0	1.000	1.000	1.000	414	0	0-0	ø	0	—	—	/H	0	0.0
1995	Cle A	12	18	1	6	2	0	0	3	1-0	0	0	.333	.333	.444	108	0	0-0	1.000	-1	50	168	C12	0	0.0
1996	Mil A	104	233	27	55	6	1	1	21	38-0	2	15	.236	.348	.283	60	-13	0-0	**.998**	9	106	83	C90,D6	0	0.0
1997	Mil A	99	200	19	57	7	0	1	19	24-0	1	17	.285	.361	.335	83	-4	1-0	.994	0	90	82	C78,D8	0	0.0
1998	Mil N	22	37	4	13	0	0	0	4	7-2	2	6	.351	.468	.351	121	2	1-0	1.000	2	89	36	C14	0	-0.1
1999	Cle A	10	26	0	4	0	0	0	3	1-0	1	6	.154	.214	.154	-4	-4	0-0	1.000	-0	93	42	C9	143	0.4
2001	Mil N	12	33	6	8	2	0	0	3	3-0	0	7	.242	.306	.303	59	-2	0-0	.984	-2	87	38	C11	0	-0.4
Total	9	319	654	66	167	23	1	3	60	76-2	6	66	.255	.336	.307	68	-29	2-0	.995	8	95	79	C264,D15	0	-0.3
LEVY, ED	Edward Clarence (b Edward Clarence Whitner); B10.28.1916 Birmingham AL; BR/TR/6´5.5˝/190; d4.16; Col Rollins																								
1940	Phi N	1	1	0	0	0	0	0	0	0	0	0	.000	.000	.000	-99	0	0	ø	0	—	—	/H	—	0.0
1942	NY A	13	41	5	5	0	0	0	3	4	0	5	.122	.200	.122	-9	-6	1-0	.992	1	132	142	1b13	0	-0.6
1944	NY A	40	153	12	37	11	2	4	29	6	0	19	.242	.270	.418	92	-3	1-1	.962	-2	96	67	O36L	0	-0.7
Total	3	54	195	17	42	11	2	4	32	10	0	24	.215	.254	.354	70	-9	2-1	.962	-0	96	67	O36L,1b13	0	-1.3
LEWIS, ALLAN	Allan Sydney "The Panamanian Express"; B12.12.1941 Colon, Pan; BB/TR/6´0˝/170; d4.11																								
1967	KC A	34	6	7	1	0	0	0	0	0-0	0	3	.167	.167	.167	-1	-1	14-5	ø	0	—	—	/H	0	0.1
1968	Oak A	26	4	9	1	0	0	0	0	1-0	0	0	.250	.400	.250	105	0	8-4	ø	-0	0	0	/lf	0	0.0
1969	Oak A	12	1	2	0	0	0	0	0	0-0	0	0	.000	.000	.000	-99	0	0-0	ø	0	—	—	/H	0	0.0
1970	Oak A	25	8	8	2	0	0	1	1	0-0	0	0	.250	.250	.625	138	0	7-1	1.000	-0	63	0	O2L	0	0.1
1972	†Oak A	24	10	5	2	1	0	0	2	0-0	0	1	.200	.200	.300	50	-1	8-3	.900	0	143	0	O6(5/0/1)	0	0.0
1973	†Oak A	35	0	16	0	0	0	0	0	0-0	0	0	ø	ø	ø	ø	0	7-4	1.000	0	456	0	/lfD	0	0.0
Total	6	156	29	47	6	1	0	1	3	1-0	0	4	.207	.233	.345	69	-2	44-17	.923	0	116	0	O10(9/0/1),D6	0	0.2
LEWIS, DARREN	Darren Joel; B8.28.1967 Berkeley CA; BR/TR/6´0˝/(175–195); [OakA88 18/463]; d8.21; Col California																								
1990	Oak A	25	35	4	8	0	0	0	1	7-0	1	4	.229	.372	.229	74	-1	2-0	1.000	0	107	0	O23(3/16/5),D2	0	0.0
1991	SF N	72	222	41	55	5	3	1	15	36-0	2	30	.248	.358	.311	92	-1	13-7	1.000	2	113	62	O68C	0	0.1
1992	SF N	100	320	38	74	8	1	1	18	29-0	1	46	.231	.295	.272	65	-15	28-8	1.000	-0	104	63	O94C	0	-1.3
1993	SF N	136	522	84	132	17	7	2	48	30-0	7	40	.253	.302	.324	70	-24	46-15	**1.000**	3	106	62	O131C	15	-1.5
1994	SF N	114	451	70	116	15	**9**	4	29	53-0	4	50	.257	.340	.357	85	-10	30-13	.993	-3	97	79	O113C	0	-0.9
1995	SF N	74	309	47	78	10	3	1	16	17-0	6	37	.252	.303	.314	65	-16	21-7	.995	2	110	48	O73C	0	-1.1
	†Cin N	58	163	19	40	3	0	0	8	17-0	2	20	.245	.324	.264	57	-10	11-11	.992	3	116	126	O57C	0	-0.7
	Year	132	472	66	118	13	3	1	24	34-0	8	57	.250	.311	.297	62	-26	32-18	.994	5	112	77	O130C	0	-1.8
1996	Chi A	141	337	55	77	12	2	4	53	45-1	3	40	.228	.321	.312	65	-18	21-5	.990	-6	104	0	O138(1/137/0)	0	-1.8
1997	Chi A	81	77	15	18	1	0	0	5	11-0	0	14	.234	.330	.247	55	-5	11-4	1.000	4	127	70	O64C,D6	0	0.0
	LA N	26	77	7	23	3	1	1	10	6-0	0	17	.299	.349	.403	103	0	3-2	.980	2	124	75	O25(23/2/1)	0	0.1
1998	†Bos A	155	585	95	157	25	3	8	63	70-0	8	94	.268	.352	.362	85	-11	29-12	.992	2	108	61	O152(4/109/55)/D	0	-0.7
1999	†Bos A	135	470	63	113	14	6	2	40	45-0	5	52	.240	.311	.309	58	-31	16-10	.994	1	107	50	O130(0/88/51),D2	0	-2.9
2000	Bos A	97	270	44	65	12	0	2	17	22-0	3	34	.241	.305	.307	54	-19	10-5	.981	-3	90	112	O89(18/41/37),D5	14	-2.2
2001	Bos A	82	164	18	46	9	1	1	12	8-0	3	25	.280	.326	.366	82	-4	5-5	1.000	3	106	143	O69(27/21/29),D6	0	-0.3
2002	Chi N	58	79	7	19	3	1	0	7	7-0	3	11	.241	.326	.304	67	-4	1-3	1.000	3	119	192	O47(22/18/9)	0	-0.2
Total	13	1354	4081	607	1021	137	37	27	342	403-1	48	514	.250	.323	.322	72	-169	247-107	.994	11	106	67	O1273(98/1032/187),D22	29	-13.4
LEWIS, FRED	Frederick Deshaun; B12.9.1980 Hattiesburg MS; BL/TR/6´2˝/190; [SDN02 2/66]; d9.1; Col Southern																								
2006	SF N	13	11	5	5	1	0	0	2	0-0	0	3	.455	.455	.545	154	1	0-0	.889	0	184	0	O6(6/1/0)	0	0.1
LEWIS, FRED	Frederick Miller; B10.13.1858 Buffalo NY; D6.5.1945 Utica NY; BB/TR/5´10.5˝/194; d7.2																								
1881	Bos N	27	114	17	25	6	0	0	9	7	—	5	.219	.264	.272	72	-3	—	.837	-3	82	90	O27(0/3/24)	—	-0.6
1883	Phi N	38	160	21	40	7	0	0	18	4	—	13	.250	.268	.294	78	-4	—	.814	-1	91	55	O38C	—	-0.5
	StL AA	49	209	37	63	8	4	1	33	1	—	—	.301	.305	.392	116	3	—	.848	-3	61	0	O49C	—	-0.2
1884	StL AA	73	300	59	97	25	3	0	—	16	4	—	.323	.366	.427	152	18	—	.853	-1	100	46	O73C	—	1.3
	StL U	8	30	6	9	1	0	0	—	3	—	—	.300	.364	.333	108	0	—	.909	-1	0	0	O8C	—	-0.2
1885	StL N	45	181	12	53	9	0	1	27	9	—	10	.293	.326	.359	130	6	—	.957	7	216	173	O45(9/37/0)	—	1.1
1886	Cin AA	77	324	72	103	14	6	2	32	20	4	—	.318	.365	.417	140	14	8	.884	-4	88	41	O76C/3	—	0.6
Total	5	317	1318	224	390	70	13	4	119	60	8	28	.296	.330	.378	124	34	8	.866	-6	102	59	O316(9/284/24)/3	—	1.5
LEWIS, DUFFY	George Edward; B4.18.1888 San Francisco CA; D6.17.1979 Salem NH; BR/TR/5´10.5˝/165; d4.16; Mil 1918; C5; Col St. Marys (CA)																								
1910	Bos A	151	541	64	153	29	7	8	68	32	4	—	.283	.328	.407	127	15	10	.944	12	106	147	O149L	—	1.9
1911	Bos A	130	469	64	144	32	4	7	86	25	10	—	.307	.355	.437	122	13	11	.939	5	93	145	O125L	—	1.2
1912	†Bos A	**154**	581	85	165	36	9	6	109	52	3	—	.284	.346	.408	110	7	9	.947	6	103	120	O154L	—	0.6
1913	Bos A	149	551	54	164	31	12	0	90	30	2	55	.298	.336	.397	112	6	12	.960	11	105	**159**	O142L/P3	—	1.1
1914	Bos A	146	510	53	142	37	9	2	79	57	5	41	.278	.357	.398	127	18	22-31	.952	-3	92	105	O142L	—	0.3
1915	†Bos A	152	557	69	162	31	7	2	76	45	4	63	.291	.348	.382	122	14	14-7	.952	-6	93	80	O152L	—	0.2
1916	†Bos A	152	563	56	151	29	5	1	56	33	4	56	.268	.313	.343	97	-4	16	.970	-3	98	80	O151(136/15/0)	—	-1.6
1917	Bos A	150	553	55	167	29	9	1	65	29	5	54	.302	.342	.392	125	14	8	.972	5	108	96	O150L	—	1.4
1919	NY A	**141**	559	67	152	23	4	7	89	17	0	42	.272	.293	.365	84	-15	8	.985	-8	86	86	O141L	—	-3.1
1920	NY A	107	365	34	99	8	1	4	61	24	2	32	.271	.320	.332	70	-16	2-8	.961	-1	93	114	O99(98/0/1)	—	-2.3
1921	Was A	27	102	11	19	4	1	0	14	8	1	10	.186	.252	.245	29	-11	1-1	.980	-1	88	96	O27(26/0/1)	—	-1.4
Total	11	1459	5351	612	1518	289	68	38	793	352	40	353	.284	.333	.384	108	41	113-47	.959	16	98	112	O1432(1415/15/2)/3P	—	-1.7
LEWIS, JACK	John David; B2.14.1884 Pittsburgh PA; D2.25.1956 Steubenville OH; BR/TR/5´8˝/158; d9.16																								
1911	Bos A	18	59	7	16	0	0	0	6	7	2	—	.271	.368	.271	80	-1	2	.931	0	106	88	2b18	—	-0.1
1914	Pit F	117	394	32	92	14	5	1	48	17	6	46	.234	.276	.302	58	-31	9	.949	3	103	77	2b115/S	—	-2.8
1915	Pit F	82	231	24	61	6	5	0	26	8	1	31	.264	.292	.333	76	-12	7	.962	-0	102	107	2b45,S11,O6R,1b5/3	—	-1.2
Total	3	217	684	63	169	20	10	1	80	32	9	77	.247	.290	.310	66	-44	18	.951	2	103	86	2b178,S12,O6R,1b5/3	—	-4.1
LEWIS, BUDDY	John Kelly; B8.10.1916 Gastonia NC; BL/TR/6´1˝/175; d9.16; Mil 1942–45																								
1935	Was A	8	28	0	3	0	0	0	2	0	0	5	.107	.107	.107	-46	-6	0-0	.941	0	111	129	3b6	—	-0.6
1936	Was A	143	601	100	175	21	13	6	67	47	4	46	.291	.347	.399	89	-14	6-6	.933	6	**108**	105	3b139	—	-0.3
1937	Was A	156	668	107	210	32	6	10	79	52	3	44	.314	.367	.425	104	3	11-5	.938	-20	91	99	3b156	—	-1.0
1938	Was A★	151	656	122	194	35	9	12	91	58	1	35	.296	.354	.431	103	1	17-9	.912	-5	103	109	3b151	—	0.2
1939	Was A	140	536	87	171	23	**16**	10	75	72	2	27	.319	.402	.478	134	28	10-9	.933	11	**114**	117	3b134	—	3.9
1940	Was A	148	600	101	190	38	10	6	63	74	1	36	.317	.393	.443	124	24	15-10	.960	1	96	127	O112R,3b36	—	1.8
1941	Was A	149	569	97	169	29	11	9	72	82	0	30	.297	.386	.434	122	20	10-7	.972	3	116	169	O96R,3b49	0	1.7
1945	Was A	69	258	42	86	14	7	2	37	37	3	15	.333	.423	.465	172	25	1-2	.981	3	107	113	O69R	0	2.4
1946	Was A	150	582	82	170	28	13	7	45	59	2	26	.292	.359	.421	125	18	5-3	.970	2	101	119	O145(8/1/137)	0	1.6
1947	Was A★	140	506	67	132	15	4	6	48	51	1	27	.261	.330	.342	89	-8	6-6	.968	0	101	118	O130R	0	-1.3
1949	Was A	95	257	25	63	14	4	3	28	41	3	12	.245	.355	.366	93	-2	2-2	.979	2	114	69	O67R	0	-0.3
Total	11	1349	5261	830	1563	249	93	71	607	573	20	303	.297	.368	.420	112	89	83-59	.927	4	102	109	3b671,O619(8/1/611)	0	8.1
LEWIS, JOHNNY	Johnny Joe; B8.10.1939 Greenville AL; BL/TR/6´1˝/(185–192); d4.14; C9																								
1964	StL N	40	94	10	22	2	2	2	7	13-1	0	23	.234	.324	.362	86	-2	2-2	.966	1	105	143	O36(2/0/34)	0	-0.3
1965	NY N	148	477	64	117	15	3	15	45	59-4	3	117	.245	.331	.384	105	4	4-7	.975	4	100	163	O142(0/48/101)	0	-0.2
1966	NY N	65	166	21	32	6	1	5	20	21-0	0	43	.193	.282	.331	72	-6	2-0	.988	-2	94	64	O49(11/8/31)	0	-1.1
1967	NY N	13	34	2	4	1	0	0	2	2-0	0	11	.118	.167	.147	-10	-5	0-0	1.000	1	107	180	O10(2/0/9)	0	-0.5
Total	4	266	771	97	175	24	6	22	74	95-5	3	194	.227	.313	.359	90	-9	8-9	.977	4	100	140	O237(15/56/175)	0	-2.1
LEWIS, MARK	Mark David; B11.30.1969 Hamilton OH; BR/TR/6´1˝/(185–195); [CleA88 1/2]; d4.26																								
1991	Cle A	84	314	29	83	15	1	0	30	15-0	0	45	.264	.293	.318	70	-13	2-2	.966	-12	95	84	2b50,S36	0	-2.2
1992	Cle A	122	413	44	109	21	0	5	30	25-1	3	69	.264	.308	.351	86	-8	4-5	.954	-11	95	93	S121/3	0	-1.2
1993	Cle A	14	52	6	13	2	0	1	5	0-0	0	7	.250	.250	.346	58	-3	3-0	.964	-3	82	116	S13	0	-0.4
1994	Cle A	20	73	6	15	5	0	1	8	2-0	0	13	.205	.227	.315	37	-7	1-0	.902	-5	92	50	S13,3b6/2	0	-1.1

YEAR	TM LG	G	AB	R	H	2B	3B	HR	RBI	BB-IB	HP	SO	AVG	OBP	SLG	AOPS	ABR	SB-CS	FA	FR	RNG	THR	GAMES AT POSITION	DL	BFW
1995	†Cin N	81	171	25	58	13	1	3	30	21-2	0	33	.339	.407	.480	133	9	0-3	.968	-1	105	56	3b72,2b2,S2	0	0.7
1996	Det A	145	545	69	147	30	3	11	55	42-0	5	109	.270	.326	.396	82	-16	6-1	.987	-9	98	81	2b144/D	0	-1.5
1997	†SF N	118	341	50	91	14	6	10	42	23-2	4	62	.267	.318	.431	97	-3	3-2	.945	-15	84	93	3b69,2b29/D	12	-1.7
1998	Phi N	142	518	52	129	21	2	9	54	48-2	3	111	.249	.312	.349	75	-19	3-3	.978	7	106	83	2b140	0	-0.6
1999	Cin N	88	173	18	44	16	0	6	28	7-1	0	24	.254	.280	.451	79	-6	0-0	.938	-8	78	129	3b52,2b2	0	-1.3
2000	Cin N	11	19	1	2	1	0	0	3	1-0	0	3	.105	.150	.158	-22	-4	0-0	.909	1	134	0	3b5	0	-0.3
	Bal A	71	163	19	44	17	0	2	21	12-0	1	31	.270	.322	.411	89	-3	7-2	.857	-6	91	52	3b29,2b21,S14,D4	15	-0.5
2001	Cle A	6	13	1	1	0	0	0	0	0-0	0	4	.077	.077	.077	-57	-3	0-0	.889	0	123	225	3b4,2b3	0	-0.3
Total	11	902	2795	320	736	155	13	48	306	196-8	16	511	.263	.312	.380	82	-76	29-18	.977	-62	100	83	2b392,3b238,S199,D6	27	-10.4
Lewis, Phil	Philip; B10.7.1883 Pittsburgh PA; D8.8.1959 Port Wentworth GA; BR/TR/6´0˝/195; d4.14; Col Cornell																								
1905	Bro N	118	433	32	110	9	2	3	33	16	1	—	.254	.282	.305	81	-12	16	.904	-3	97	120	S118	—	-1.2
1906	Bro N	136	452	40	110	8	4	0	37	43	0	—	.243	.309	.279	90	-5	14	.922	-20	98	80	S135	—	-2.3
1907	Bro N	136	475	52	118	11	1	0	30	23	2	—	.248	.286	.276	83	-11	16	.938	-23	90	80	S136	—	-3.4
1908	Bro N	118	415	22	91	5	6	1	30	13	0	—	.219	.243	.267	66	-19	9	.943	-2	96	94	S116	—	-2.0
Total	4	508	1775	146	429	33	13	4	130	95	3	—	.242	.281	.282	80	-47	55	.926	-48	95	93	S505	—	-8.9
Lewis, Bill	William Henry "Buddy"; B10.15.1904 Ripley TN; D10.24.1977 Memphis TN; BR/TR/5´9˝/165; d6.3																								
1933	StL N	15	35	8	14	1	0	1	8	2	0	3	.400	.432	.514	161	3	0	1.000	0	*79*	*99*	C8	—	0.4
1935	Bos N	6	4	1	0	0	0	0	0	1	0	1	.000	.200	.000	-45	-1	0	ø	-0	*0*	*0*	/C	—	-0.1
1936	Bos N	29	62	11	19	2	0	0	3	12	0	7	.306	.419	.339	113	2	0	.967	-2	*134*	65	C21	—	0.1
Total	3	50	101	20	33	3	0	1	11	15	0	11	.327	.414	.386	124	4	0	.981	-2	*114*	77	C30	—	0.4
Leyritz, Jim	James Joseph; B12.27.1963 Lakewood OH; BR/TR/6´0˝/(190–220); d6.8; Col Kentucky; OF(25/0/30)																								
1990	NY A	92	303	28	78	13	1	5	25	27-1	7	51	.257	.331	.356	92	-3	2-3	.929	-14	76	40	3b69,O14(10/0/4),C11	0	-1.7
1991	NY A	32	77	8	14	3	0	0	4	13-0	0	15	.182	.300	.221	46	-5	0-1	.909	-5	65	64	3b18,C5,1b3/D	0	-1.0
1992	NY A	63	144	17	37	6	0	7	26	14-1	6	22	.257	.341	.444	121	4	0-1	.990	3	70	188	D31,C18,1b2,3b2,O2R/2	0	0.6
1993	NY A	95	259	43	80	14	0	14	53	37-3	8	59	.309	.410	.525	154	21	0-0	.993	-2	79	106	1b29,O28(6/0/23),D21,C12	0	1.5
1994	NY A	75	249	47	66	12	0	17	58	35-1	6	61	.265	.365	.518	130	11	0-0	1.000	-1	153	47	C37,D25,1b10	0	1.0
1995	†NY A	77	264	37	71	12	0	7	37	37-2	8	73	.269	.374	.394	101	2	1-1	.993	-5	70	77	C46,1b18,D15	0	-0.2
1996	†NY A	88	265	23	70	10	0	7	40	30-3	9	68	.264	.355	.381	87	-4	2-0	.995	-2	106	87	C55,3b13,D12,1b5,O3L,2b2	0	-0.3
1997	Ana A	84	294	47	81	7	0	11	50	37-2	3	56	.276	.357	.412	101	1	1-1	1.000	4	100	172	C58,1b15,D13	0	0.7
	Tex A	37	85	11	24	4	0	0	14	23-0	3	22	.282	.446	.329	101	2	1-0	.984	-2	62	184	C11,1b9,D9	0	0.0
	Year	121	379	58	105	11	0	11	64	60-2	6	78	.277	.379	.393	101	3	2-1	.998	2	94	174	C69,1b24,D22	0	0.7
1998	Bos A	52	129	17	37	6	0	8	24	21-1	2	34	.287	.385	.519	132	7	0-0	1.000	0	34	0	D39/C1	0	0.5
	†SD N	62	143	17	38	10	0	4	18	21-0	7	40	.266	.384	.420	120	6	0-0	.987	-1	117	37	C24,1b20/3lf	0	0.5
1999	SD N	50	134	17	32	5	0	8	21	15-1	4	37	.239	.331	.455	105	0	0-0	.994	1	54	86	C24,1b19/3	37	0.1
	†NY A	31	66	8	15	4	1	0	5	13-1	0	17	.227	.354	.318	75	-2	0-0	.986	1	191	102	D14,1b9/C3	0	-0.2
2000	NY A	24	55	2	12	0	0	1	4	7-0	1	14	.218	.317	.273	52	-4	0-0	1.000	-1	53	0	D15,C2/1	0	-0.5
	LA N	41	60	3	12	1	0	1	8	7-0	1	12	.200	.294	.267	45	-5	0-0	1.000	-2	80	108	1b8,O6(5/0/1),C3	0	-0.7
Total	11	903	2527	325	667	107	2	90	387	337-16	65	581	.264	.362	.415	106	31	7-7	.995	-23	104	101	C308,D195,1b149,3b105,O54R,2b3	37	0.3
Lezcano, Carlos	Carlos Manuel (Rubio); B9.30.1955 Arecibo, PR; BR/TR/6´2˝/185; d4.10; Col Florida St.																								
1980	Chi N	42	88	15	18	4	1	3	12	11-0	1	29	.205	.294	.375	81	-2	1-2	.948	-1	98	158	O39C	0	-0.4
1981	Chi N	7	14	1	1	0	0	0	2	0-0	0	4	.071	.071	.071	-56	-3	0-0	1.000	0	118	0	O5(1/0/4)	0	-0.3
Total	2	49	102	16	19	4	1	3	14	11-0	1	33	.186	.267	.333	63	-5	1-2	.952	-1	100	142	O44(1/39/4)	0	-0.7
Lezcano, Sixto	Sixto Joaquin (Curras); B11.28.1953 Arecibo, PR; BR/TR/5´11˝/(165–190); d9.10																								
1974	Mil A	15	54	5	13	2	0	2	9	4-0	0	9	.241	.283	.389	95	-1	1-1	.972	2	101	245	O15R	0	0.0
1975	Mil A	134	429	55	106	19	3	11	43	46-1	4	93	.247	.324	.382	99	-1	5-5	.977	-3	98	95	O129(0/2/128),D2	0	-1.1
1976	Mil A	145	513	53	146	19	5	7	56	51-2	2	112	.285	.348	.382	117	11	14-10	.973	6	**111**	94	O142(64/17/66),D3	0	1.0
1977	Mil A	109	400	50	109	21	4	21	49	52-1	2	78	.273	.358	.503	132	18	6-5	.988	9	111	142	O108R	24	2.0
1978	Mil A	132	442	62	129	21	4	15	61	64-6	1	83	.292	.377	.459	135	22	3-3	.979	5	95	184	O127R,D3	0	2.1
1979	Mil A	138	473	84	152	29	3	28	101	77-5	3	74	.321	.414	.573	164	46	4-3	.986	-4	94	93	O135R/D	0	3.3
1980	Mil A	112	411	51	94	19	3	18	55	39-3	3	75	.229	.298	.421	98	-3	1-1	.983	1	101	94	O108R,D4	0	-0.8
1981	StL N	72	214	26	57	8	2	5	28	40-2	0	40	.266	.376	.393	115	6	0-1	.973	-6	79	87	O65(32/0/34)	0	-0.4
1982	SD N	138	470	73	136	26	6	16	84	78-10	2	69	.289	.388	.472	150	34	2-1	.990	9	104	161	O134R	0	3.8
1983	SD N	97	317	41	74	11	2	8	49	47-3	1	66	.233	.331	.356	94	-2	0-0	.968	2	101	128	O91R	0	-0.5
	†Phi N	18	39	8	11	1	0	0	7	5-0	0	9	.282	.364	.308	88	0	1-0	1.000	1	97	300	O15(2/1/13)	0	0.0
	Year	115	356	49	85	12	2	8	56	52-3	1	75	.239	.334	.351	93	-2	1-0	.971	3	101	146	O106(2/1/104)	0	-0.5
1984	Phi N	109	256	36	71	6	2	14	40	38-1	0	43	.277	.371	.480	135	12	0-1	.981	3	118	67	O87(4/0/83)	0	1.2
1985	Pit N	72	116	16	24	2	0	3	9	35-3	1	17	.207	.392	.302	98	2	0-0	.967	-0	99	92	O40(25/0/16)	0	0.0
Total	12	1291	4134	560	1122	184	34	148	591	576-37	19	768	.271	.360	.440	124	144	37-31	.980	24	101	120	O1196(127/20/1058),D13	24	10.6
Libby, Steve	Stephen Augustus; B12.8.1853 Scarborough ME; D3.31.1935 Milford CT; 6´1.5˝/168; d5.10																								
1879	Buf N	1	2	0	0	0	0	0	0	0	—	1	.000	.000	.000	-98	0	—	1.000	0	0	0	/1	—	0.0
Libke, Al	Albert Walter; B9.12.1918 Tacoma WA; D3.7.2003 Wenatchee WA; BL/TR/6´4˝/215; d4.19; ▲																								
1945	Cin N	130	449	41	127	23	5	4	53	34	2	62	.283	.336	.383	102	0	6	.963	1	96	131	O108(27/0/82),P4,1b2	0	-0.6
1946	Cin N	124	431	32	109	22	1	5	42	43	1	50	.253	.322	.343	92	-5	0	.972	-4	86	121	O115R/P	0	-1.3
Total	2	254	880	73	236	45	6	9	95	77	3	112	.268	.329	.364	97	-5	6	.967	-4	91	126	O223(27/0/197),P5,1b2	0	-1.9
Libran, Frankie	Francisco (Rosas); B5.6.1948 Mayaguez, PR; BR/TR/6´0˝/175; d9.3																								
1969	SD N	10	10	1	1	1	0	0	1	1-0	0	2	.100	.182	.200	7	-1	0-0	1.000	-2	85	41	S9	0	-0.2
Lickert, John	John Wilbur; B4.4.1960 Pittsburgh PA; BR/TR/5´11˝/175; [BosA78 13/336]; d9.19																								
1981	Bos A	1	0	0	0	0	0	0	0	0-0	0	0	ø	ø	ø	ø	0	0-0	1.000	0	0	0	/C	0	0.0
Liddell, Dave	David Alexander (b Desmond Lane Liddell); B6.15.1966 Los Angeles CA; BR/TR/6´0˝/190; [ChiN84 4/83]; d6.3																								
1990	NY N	1	1	1	1	0	0	0	0	0-0	0	0	1.000	1.000	1.000	451	0	0-0	1.000	0	0	0	/C	0	0.0
Lieberthal, Mike	Michael Scott; B1.18.1972 Glendale CA; BR/TR/6´0˝/(170–190); [PhiN90 1/3]; d6.30																								
1994	Phi N	24	79	6	21	3	1	1	5	3-0	1	5	.266	.301	.367	72	-4	0-0	.969	-5	106	29	C22	0	-0.7
1995	Phi N	16	47	1	12	2	0	0	4	5-0	0	5	.255	.327	.298	66	-2	0-0	.991	0	71	89	C14	0	-0.1
1996	Phi N	50	166	21	42	8	0	7	23	10-0	2	30	.253	.297	.428	90	-3	0-0	.990	5	154	93	C43	39	0.4
1997	Phi N	134	455	59	112	27	1	20	77	44-1	4	76	.246	.314	.442	98	-3	3-4	.988	4	126	93	C129/D	0	0.9
1998	Phi N	86	313	39	80	15	3	8	45	17-1	7	44	.256	.304	.399	84	-8	2-1	.988	6	**151**	78	C83	40	0.3
1999	Phi N★	145	510	84	153	33	1	31	96	44-7	11	86	.300	.363	.551	127	20	0-0	**.997**	4	153	73	C143	0	3.1
2000	Phi N★	108	389	55	108	30	0	15	71	40-3	6	53	.278	.352	.470	106	4	2-0	.993	1	140	98	C106	36	1.1
2001	Phi N	34	121	21	28	8	0	2	11	12-2	3	21	.231	.316	.347	75	-4	0-0	.992	4	189	56	C33	148	0.1
2002	Phi N	130	476	46	133	29	2	15	52	38-2	14	58	.279	.349	.443	115	10	0-1	.993	-9	143	82	C129	0	0.9
2003	Phi N	131	508	68	159	30	1	13	81	38-2	12	59	.313	.373	.453	124	18	0-0	.990	-13	77	64	C131	0	1.4
2004	Phi N	131	476	58	129	31	1	17	61	37-2	11	69	.271	.335	.447	98	-2	1-1	.993	-7	90	76	C129	0	-0.1
2005	Phi N	118	392	48	103	25	0	12	47	35-14	11	35	.263	.335	.418	94	-3	0-0	.993	-8	91	70	C117	0	-0.3
2006	Phi N	67	209	22	57	14	0	9	36	8-0	6	19	.273	.316	.469	93	-2	0-0	.991	12	111	143	C60	61	1.2
Total	13	1174	4141	528	1137	255	10	150	609	331-34	88	560	.275	.338	.450	104	21	8-7	.992	-9	122	81	C1139/D	324	8.2
Liefer, Jeff	Jeffrey David; B8.17.1974 Fontana CA; BL/TR/6´3˝/(195–210); [ChiA95 1/25]; d4.7; Col Cal St.–Long Beach																								
1999	Chi A	45	113	8	28	7	1	0	14	8-0	0	28	.248	.295	.327	58	-7	2-0	1.000	2	106	114	O17(14/0/3),1b15,D7	0	-0.6
2000	Chi A	5	11	0	2	0	0	0	0	0-0	0	4	.182	.182	.182	-7	-2	0-0	1.000	-0	51	0	O5R/1	13	-0.2
2001	Chi A	83	254	36	65	13	0	18	39	20-1	2	69	.256	.313	.520	108	2	0-1	1.000	-7	73	90	O38(35/0/4),1b15,3b15,D10	0	-0.7
2002	Chi A	76	204	28	47	8	0	7	26	19-2	0	60	.230	.295	.373	73	-8	0-0	1.000	-3	94	58	O36(24/0/12),1b31,D6	0	-1.4
2003	Mon N	35	88	6	17	3	0	3	18	3-0	0	26	.193	.217	.330	40	-8	0-1	.980	-3	56	125	1b21	0	-1.3
	TB A	9	25	4	3	1	0	1	3	3-1	0	13	.120	.214	.280	30	-3	0-0	.929	-0	89	0	3b6/lfD	0	-0.3
2004	Mil N	16	28	2	6	2	0	1	5	2-0	0	8	.214	.258	.393	67	-1	0-0	1.000	-0	72	0	O3R,D3	0	-0.2

YEAR	TM LG	G	AB	R	H	2B	3B	HR	RBI	BB-IB	HP	SO	AVG	OBP	SLG	AOPS	ABR	SB-CS	FA	FR	RNG	THR	GAMES AT POSITION	DL	BFW
2005	Cle A	19	56	5	11	2	0	1	8	1-0	0	15	.196	.211	.286	31	-6	0-0	.950	-0	108	88	1b5,O3R,D9	0	-0.6
Total	7	288	779	89	179	36	1	31	113	56-4	2	223	.230	.281	.398	74	-33	2-2	1.000	-11	87	75	O103(74/0/30),1b88,D37,3b21	13	-5.3

LIESE, FRED Frederick Richard; B10.7.1885 WI; D6.30.1967 Los Angeles CA; BL/TL/5´8˝/150; d4.14; Col Wisconsin–Madison

YEAR	TM LG	G	AB	R	H	2B	3B	HR	RBI	BB-IB	HP	SO	AVG	OBP	SLG	AOPS	ABR	SB-CS	FA	FR	RNG	THR	GAMES AT POSITION	DL	BFW
1910	Bos N	5	4	0	0	0	0	0	0	1	0	2	.000	.200	.000	-39	-1	0	ø	0	—	—	/H	—	-0.1

LILLARD, GENE Robert Eugene; B11.12.1913 Santa Barbara CA; D4.12.1991 Goleta CA; BR/TR/5´10.5˝/178; d5.8; b–Bill; ▲

YEAR	TM LG	G	AB	R	H	2B	3B	HR	RBI	BB-IB	HP	SO	AVG	OBP	SLG	AOPS	ABR	SB-CS	FA	FR	RNG	THR	GAMES AT POSITION	DL	BFW
1936	Chi N	19	34	6	7	1	0	0	2	3	0	8	.206	.270	.235	36	-3	0	.947	-1	81	98	S4,3b3	—	-0.4
1939	Chi N	23	10	3	1	0	0	0	0	6	0	3	.100	.438	.100	51	1	0	1.000	0	98	0	P20	—	0.0
1940	StL N	2	0	0	0	0	0	0	0	0	0	0	ø	ø	ø	ø	0	0	1.000	0	99	0	P2	—	0.0
Total	3	44	44	9	8	1	0	0	2	9	0	11	.182	.321	.205	43	-2	0	1.000	-1	98	0	P22,S4,3b3	—	-0.4

LILLARD, BILL William Beverly; B1.10.1918 Goleta CA; BR/TR/5´10˝/170; d9.11; b–Gene

YEAR	TM LG	G	AB	R	H	2B	3B	HR	RBI	BB-IB	HP	SO	AVG	OBP	SLG	AOPS	ABR	SB-CS	FA	FR	RNG	THR	GAMES AT POSITION	DL	BFW
1939	Phi A	7	19	4	6	1	0	0	1	3	0	1	.316	.409	.368	102	0	0-0	.974	2	128	70	S7	—	0.2
1940	Phi A	73	206	26	49	8	2	1	21	28	1	28	.238	.332	.311	69	-9	0-1	.921	-13	90	72	S69/2	—	-1.7
Total	2	80	225	30	55	9	2	1	22	31	1	29	.244	.339	.316	72	-9	0-1	.927	-12	94	72	S76/2	—	-1.5

LILLIE, JIM James J. "Grasshopper" (b James J. Lilly); B7.27.1861 New Haven CT; D11.9.1890 Kansas City MO; BR; d5.17; ▲

YEAR	TM LG	G	AB	R	H	2B	3B	HR	RBI	BB-IB	HP	SO	AVG	OBP	SLG	AOPS	ABR	SB-CS	FA	FR	RNG	THR	GAMES AT POSITION	DL	BFW
1883	Buf N	50	201	25	47	7	3	1	29	1	—	31	.234	.238	.313	64	-9	—	.835	-6	82	132	O47(12/34/1),P3,C2/S32	—	-1.4
1884	Buf N	**114**	471	68	105	12	5	3	53	5	—	71	.223	.231	.289	60	-23	—	.852	16	**180**	**197**	O114R,P2	—	-0.7
1885	Buf N	**112**	430	49	107	13	3	2	30	6	—	39	.249	.259	.307	80	-11	—	.862	2	112	121	O112(21/4/89),S3/1	—	-1.0
1886	KC N	114	416	37	73	9	0	0	22	11	—	80	.175	.197	.197	19	-41	13	.884	11	132	75	O114L/P	—	-3.0
Total	4	390	1518	179	332	41	11	6	134	23	—	221	.219	.230	.272	54	-84	13	.863	23	135	131	O387(147/38/204),P6,S4,C2/123	—	-6.1

LILLIS, BOB Robert Perry; B6.2.1930 Altadena CA; BR/TR/5´11˝/160; d8.17; M4/C22; Col USC

YEAR	TM LG	G	AB	R	H	2B	3B	HR	RBI	BB-IB	HP	SO	AVG	OBP	SLG	AOPS	ABR	SB-CS	FA	FR	RNG	THR	GAMES AT POSITION	DL	BFW
1958	LA N	20	69	10	27	3	1	1	5	4-0	1	2	.391	.421	.507	143	4	1-2	.964	-3	92	75	S19	0	0.3
1959	LA N	30	48	7	11	2	0	0	2	3-1	0	4	.229	.275	.271	43	-4	0-0	.919	2	110	109	S20	0	0.0
1960	LA N	48	60	6	16	4	0	0	6	2-1	0	6	.267	.290	.333	66	-3	2-0	.982	6	103	148	S23,3b14/2	0	0.5
1961	LA N	19	9	0	1	0	0	0	1	1-0	0	1	.111	.200	.111	-13	-1	0-0	1.000	-1	39	0	3b12/2S	0	-0.2
	StL N	86	230	24	50	4	0	0	21	7-2	2	13	.217	.245	.235	26	-24	3-3	.928	-1	102	65	S56,2b24	0	-2.1
	Year	105	239	24	51	4	0	0	22	8-2	2	14	.213	.243	.230	25	-26	3-3	.924	-2	101	64	S57,2b25,3b12	0	-2.3
1962	Hou N	129	457	38	114	12	4	1	30	28-1	0	23	.249	.292	.300	64	-24	7-3	.972	16	105	96	S99,2b33,3b9	0	0.2
1963	Hou N	147	469	31	93	13	1	1	19	15-1	4	35	.198	.229	.237	37	-39	3-4	.957	-5	99	79	S124,2b19,3b6	0	-3.8
1964	Hou N	109	332	31	89	11	2	0	17	11-1	0	10	.268	.291	.313	75	-12	4-9	.995	7	100	87	2b52,S43,3b12	0	-0.2
1965	Hou N	124	408	34	90	12	1	0	20	20-6	6	10	.221	.267	.255	51	-27	2-2	.968	-15	89	80	S104,3b9,2b6	0	-3.5
1966	Hou N	68	164	14	38	6	0	0	11	7-0	0	4	.232	.260	.268	52	-11	1-1	.951	-7	78	82	2b35,S18,3b6	0	-1.5
1967	Hou N	37	82	3	20	1	0	0	5	1-0	0	8	.244	.253	.256	48	-6	0-1	.947	-0	109	70	S23,2b3,3b2	0	-0.5
Total	10	817	2328	198	549	68	9	3	137	99-13	13	116	.236	.270	.277	54	-147	23-25	.959	-0	99	85	S530,2b174,3b70	0	-10.8

LIMMER, LOU Louis; B3.10.1925 New York NY; BL/TL/6´2˝/(185–190); d4.22

YEAR	TM LG	G	AB	R	H	2B	3B	HR	RBI	BB-IB	HP	SO	AVG	OBP	SLG	AOPS	ABR	SB-CS	FA	FR	RNG	THR	GAMES AT POSITION	DL	BFW
1951	Phi A	94	214	25	34	9	1	5	30	28	0	40	.159	.256	.280	44	-18	1-0	.988	3	124	113	1b58	0	-1.6
1954	Phi A	115	316	41	73	10	3	14	32	35	0	37	.231	.305	.415	96	-3	2-3	.988	3	115	84	1b79	0	-0.6
Total	2	209	530	66	107	19	4	19	62	63	0	77	.202	.285	.360	75	-21	3-3	.988	5	119	95	1b137	0	-2.2

LINARES, RUFINO Rufino (b Rufino De La Cruz (Linares)); B2.28.1951 San Pedro de Macoris, D.R.; D5.16.1998 San Pedro de Macoris, D.R.; BR/TR/6´0˝/(165–190); d4.10; [DL 1983 Atl N 182]

YEAR	TM LG	G	AB	R	H	2B	3B	HR	RBI	BB-IB	HP	SO	AVG	OBP	SLG	AOPS	ABR	SB-CS	FA	FR	RNG	THR	GAMES AT POSITION	DL	BFW
1981	Atl N	78	253	27	67	9	2	5	25	9-2	0	28	.265	.289	.375	87	-5	8-4	.963	3	107	119	O60L	0	-0.5
1982	Atl N	77	191	28	57	7	1	2	17	7-0	1	29	.298	.325	.377	94	-2	5-2	1.000	3	104	113	O53(51/0/4)	0	-0.1
1984	Atl N	34	58	4	12	3	0	1	10	6-0	0	12	.207	.273	.310	62	-3	0-0	.958	1	101	241	O13(12/0/1)	0	-0.2
1985	Cal A	18	43	7	11	2	0	3	11	2-0	0	5	.256	.283	.512	114	1	2-0	1.000	0	140	0	D14,O2R	0	0.1
Total	4	207	545	66	147	21	3	11	63	24-2	1	74	.270	.299	.380	89	-9	15-6	.977	7	105	128	O128(123/0/7),D14	182	-0.7

LIND, ADAM Adam Alan; B7.17.1983 Anderson IN; BL/TL/6´2˝/195; [TorA04 3/83]; d9.2; Col South Alabama

YEAR	TM LG	G	AB	R	H	2B	3B	HR	RBI	BB-IB	HP	SO	AVG	OBP	SLG	AOPS	ABR	SB-CS	FA	FR	RNG	THR	GAMES AT POSITION	DL	BFW
2006	Tor A	18	60	8	22	8	0	2	8	5-0	0	12	.367	.415	.600	152	5	0-0	1.000	0	109	0	D15,O2L	0	0.4

LIND, CARL Henry Carl "Hooks"; B9.19.1903 New Orleans LA; D8.4.1946 New York NY; BR/TR/6´0˝/160; d9.14; Col Tulane

YEAR	TM LG	G	AB	R	H	2B	3B	HR	RBI	BB-IB	HP	SO	AVG	OBP	SLG	AOPS	ABR	SB-CS	FA	FR	RNG	THR	GAMES AT POSITION	DL	BFW
1927	Cle A	12	37	2	5	0	0	0	1	5	1	7	.135	.256	.135	4	-5	1-0	.969	1	120	92	2b11/S	—	-0.3
1928	Cle A	154	650	102	191	42	4	1	54	36	0	48	.294	.331	.375	84	-15	8-3	.960	5	101	**114**	2b154	—	-0.5
1929	Cle A	66	225	19	54	8	1	0	13	13	0	17	.240	.282	.284	44	-19	0-2	.957	10	101	158	2b64/3	—	-0.7
1930	Cle A	24	69	8	17	3	0	0	6	3	0	7	.246	.278	.290	43	-6	0-1	.940	8	127	142	S22,2b2	—	0.3
Total	4	256	981	131	267	53	5	1	74	57	1	79	.272	.313	.339	69	-45	9-6	.960	24	102	125	2b231,S23/3	—	-1.2

LIND, JACK Jackson Hugh; B6.8.1946 Denver CO; BB/TR/6´0˝/170; d9.10; C4; Col Arizona St.

YEAR	TM LG	G	AB	R	H	2B	3B	HR	RBI	BB-IB	HP	SO	AVG	OBP	SLG	AOPS	ABR	SB-CS	FA	FR	RNG	THR	GAMES AT POSITION	DL	BFW
1974	Mil A	9	17	4	4	2	0	0	1	3-0	0	2	.235	.350	.353	103	0	0-0	1.000	-2	73	85	S5,2b4	0	-0.1
1975	Mil A	17	20	1	1	0	0	0	0	2-0	0	12	.050	.136	.050	-45	-4	1-0	.919	1	136	52	S9,3b6/1	0	-0.2
Total	2	26	37	5	5	2	0	0	1	5-0	0	14	.135	.238	.189	23	-4	1-0	.943	-1	111	65	S14,3b6,2b4/1	0	-0.3

LIND, JOSE Jose (Salgado) "Chico"; B5.1.1964 Toa Baja, PR; BR/TR/5´11˝/(170–180); d8.28

YEAR	TM LG	G	AB	R	H	2B	3B	HR	RBI	BB-IB	HP	SO	AVG	OBP	SLG	AOPS	ABR	SB-CS	FA	FR	RNG	THR	GAMES AT POSITION	DL	BFW
1987	Pit N	35	143	21	46	8	4	0	11	8-1	0	12	.322	.358	.434	107	1	2-1	.995	6	127	55	2b35		
1988	Pit N	154	611	82	160	24	4	2	49	42-0	0	75	.262	.308	.324	83	-14	15-4	.987	1	104	84	2b153	0	0.9
1989	Pit N	153	578	52	134	21	3	2	48	39-7	2	64	.232	.280	.289	66	-27	15-1	.976	-10	101	95	2b151	0	-0.8
1990	†Pit N	152	514	46	134	28	5	1	48	35-19	1	52	.261	.305	.340	81	-14	8-0	.991	20	111	103	2b152	0	-3.2
1991	†Pit N	150	502	53	133	16	6	3	54	30-10	2	56	.265	.306	.339	83	-13	7-4	.989	**26**	**112**	111	2b149	0	1.2
1992	†Pit N	135	468	38	110	14	1	0	39	26-12	1	29	.235	.275	.269	55	-28	3-1	**.992**	9	109	100	2b134	0	1.8
1993	KC A	136	431	33	107	13	2	0	37	13-0	2	36	.248	.271	.288	48	-33	3-2	**.994**	-10	92	88	2b136	0	-1.6
1994	KC A	85	290	34	78	16	2	1	31	16-1	0	34	.269	.306	.348	65	-15	9-5	.988	-9	95	86	2b84/D	0	-3.5
1995	KC A	29	97	4	26	3	0	0	6	3-0	0	8	.268	.290	.299	52	-7	0-1	.992	-4	91	95	2b29	0	-1.9
	Cal A	15	43	5	7	2	0	0	1	3-0	0	4	.163	.217	.209	12	-6	0-0	1.000	1	105	114	2b15	0	-1.0
	Year	44	140	9	33	5	0	0	7	6-0	0	12	.236	.267	.271	40	-13	0-1	.995	-3	96	101	2b44	0	-0.4
Total	9	1044	3677	368	935	145	27	9	324	215-50	8	370	.254	.295	.316	70	-156	62-19	.988	29	105	95	2b1038/D	0	-1.4
																								0	-8.5

LINDBECK, EM Emerit Desmond; B8.27.1935 Kewanee IL; BL/TR/6´0˝/185; d4.22; Col Illinois

YEAR	TM LG	G	AB	R	H	2B	3B	HR	RBI	BB-IB	HP	SO	AVG	OBP	SLG	AOPS	ABR	SB-CS	FA	FR	RNG	THR	GAMES AT POSITION	DL	BFW
1960	Det A	2	1	0	0	0	0	0	0	1-0	0	0	.000	.500	.000	46	0	0-0	ø	0	—	—	/H	0	0.0

LINDELL, JOHNNY John Harlan; B8.30.1916 Greeley CO; D8.27.1985 Newport Beach CA; BR/TR/6´4.5˝/(217–220); d4.18; Mil 1945; ▲

YEAR	TM LG	G	AB	R	H	2B	3B	HR	RBI	BB-IB	HP	SO	AVG	OBP	SLG	AOPS	ABR	SB-CS	FA	FR	RNG	THR	GAMES AT POSITION	DL	BFW
1941	NY A	1	1	0	0	0	0	0	0	0	0	0	.000	.000	.000	-99	0	0-0	ø	0	—	—	/H		
1942	NY A	27	24	1	6	1	0	0	4	0	0	5	.250	.250	.292	53	1	0-0	.923	-0	66	279	P23	0	0.0
1943	†NY A☆	122	441	53	108	17	**12**	4	51	51	4	55	.245	.329	.365	102	0	2-5	.966	-2	96	123	O122(3/55/66)	0	0.0
1944	NY A	149	594	91	178	33	**16**	18	103	44	3	56	.300	.351	.500	137	25	5-4	.986	4	110	61	O149(2/148/0)	0	-0.9
1945	NY A	41	159	26	45	6	3	1	20	17	3	10	.283	.363	.377	110	2	2-1	.982	-1	102	59	O41C	0	2.5
1946	NY A	102	332	41	86	10	5	10	40	32	2	47	.259	.328	.410	104	0	4-1	.982	-1	98	141	O74(5/31/39),1b14	0	0.0
1947	†NY A	127	476	66	131	18	7	11	67	32	1	70	.275	.322	.412	104	0	1-2	.978	6	**112**	72	O118(102/10/11)	0	-0.3
1948	NY A	88	309	58	98	17	2	13	55	35	0	50	.317	.387	.511	139	16	0-0	.994	2	99	125	O79(72/1/7)	0	-0.4
1949	†NY A	78	211	33	51	10	0	6	27	35	0	27	.242	.350	.374	92	-2	3-0	.983	-1	96	102	O65(63/3/1)	0	1.2
1950	NY A	7	21	2	4	0	0	0	2	4	0	2	.190	.320	.190	34	-2	0-0	.857	-1	70	0	O6L	0	-0.6
	StL N	36	113	16	21	5	2	5	16	15	1	24	.186	.287	.398	74	-5	0	.984	-1	96	45	O33(29/4/0)	0	-0.3
1953	Pit N	58	91	11	26	6	1	4	15	16	2	15	.286	.404	.505	136	6	0-0	.962	2	139	74	P27,1b2	0	-0.8
	Phi N	11	18	3	7	1	0	0	2	6	0	2	.389	.542	.444	162	2	0-0	1.000	-1	76	0	P5,O2R	0	0.1
	Year	69	109	14	33	7	1	4	17	22	2	17	.303	.429	.495	141	8	0-0	.964	1	132	65	P32,1b2,O2R	0	0.0
1954	Phi N	7	5	0	1	0	0	0	2	2	0	3	.200	.429	.200	70	0	0-0	ø	0	—	—	/H	0	0.1
Total	12	854	2795	401	762	124	48	72	404	289	16	366	.273	.344	.429	113	43	17-13	.980	6	103	92	O689(282/293/126),P55,1b16	0	0.0
																								0	0.5

LINDEMAN, JIM James William; B1.10.1962 Evanston IL; BR/TR/6´1˝/200; [StLN83 1/24]; d9.3; Col Bradley

YEAR	TM LG	G	AB	R	H	2B	3B	HR	RBI	BB-IB	HP	SO	AVG	OBP	SLG	AOPS	ABR	SB-CS	FA	FR	RNG	THR	GAMES AT POSITION	DL	BFW
1986	StL N	19	55	7	14	1	0	1	6	2-0	0	10	.255	.276	.327	67	-3	1-1	.992	0	116	90	1b17/3lf	0	-0.4
1987	†StL N	75	207	20	43	13	0	8	28	11-0	3	56	.208	.253	.386	66	-11	3-1	.976	2	99	141	O49(1/0/48),1b20	47	-1.2
1988	StL N	17	43	3	9	1	0	2	7	2-0	0	9	.209	.244	.372	73	-2	0-0	.941	-0	95	0	O12(4/0/8),1b3	74	-0.3

YEAR TM LG	G	AB	R	H	2B	3B	HR	RBI	BB-IB	HP	SO	AVG	OBP	SLG	AOPS	ABR	SB-CS	FA	FR	RNG	THR	GAMES AT POSITION	DL	BFW
1989 StL N	73	45	8	5	1	0	0	2	3-0	0	18	.111	.163	.133	-13	-7	0-0	.989	1	118	141	1b42,O5(3/0/2)	31	-0.7
1990 Det A	12	32	5	7	1	0	2	8	2-0	0	13	.219	.265	.438	92	-1	0-0	1.000	-0	0	0	D10/1rf	0	-0.1
1991 Phi N	65	95	13	32	5	0	0	12	13-1	0	14	.337	.413	.389	129	5	0-1	1.000	-2	81	85	O30(14/6/10)/1	0	0.2
1992 Phi N	29	39	6	10	1	0	1	6	3-0	0	11	.256	.310	.359	89	-1	0-0	1.000	-1	72	0	O9(4/0/7)	95	-0.2
1993 Hou N	9	23	2	8	3	0	0	0	0-0	0	7	.348	.348	.478	122	1	0-0	1.000	1	131	162	1b9	0	0.1
1994 NY N	52	137	18	37	8	1	7	20	6-2	1	35	.270	.303	.496	106	0	0-0	.948	-2	95	51	O33(21/0/14),1b4	0	-0.3
Total 9	351	676	82	165	34	1	21	89	42-3	4	173	.244	.289	.391	83	-19	4-3	.970	-2	93	85	O140(48/6/90),1b97,D10/3	247	-2.9
LINDEMANN, BOB	John Frederick Mann; B6.5.1881 Philadelphia PA; D12.19.1951 Williamsport PA; BB/TR/6´0˝/175; d8.28																							
1901 Phi A	3	9	0	1	0	0	0	0	0	0	—	.111	.111	.111	-37	-2	0	.600	-0	294	0	O3R	—	-0.2
LINDEN, TODD	Todd Anthony; B6.30.1980 Edmonds WA; BB/TR/6´3˝/(210–220); [SFN01 1/41]; d8.18; Col Louisiana St./Washington																							
2003 SF N	18	38	2	8	1	0	1	6	1-0	0	8	.211	.231	.316	40	-4	0-0	.929	-1	82	0	O13(9/0/6)	0	-0.5
2004 SF N	16	32	6	5	1	0	0	1	5-0	1	7	.156	.289	.188	26	-3	0-0	1.000	-2	62	0	O11(7/0/4)	0	-0.5
2005 SF N	60	171	20	37	8	0	4	13	10-0	5	54	.216	.280	.333	58	-11	3-0	.983	3	126	0	O52(18/0/40)	0	-1.0
2006 SF N	61	77	15	21	4	2	2	5	9-0	1	20	.273	.356	.455	105	1	1-0	1.000	0	102	95	O47(40/0/12)	0	0.0
Total 4	155	318	43	71	14	2	7	25	25-0	7	89	.223	.294	.346	65	-17	4-0	.983	1	109	23	O123(74/0/62)	0	-2.0
LINDEN, WALT	Walter Charles; B3.27.1924 Chicago IL; BR/TR/6´1˝/190; d4.30; Col Illinois																							
1950 Bos N	3	5	0	2	1	0	0	0	1	0	0	.400	.500	.600	201	1	0	1.000	-0	*0*	*0*	C3	0	0.1
LINDSAY, CHRIS	Christian Haller "Pinky","The Crab"; B7.24.1878 Beaver Co. PA; D1.25.1941 Cleveland OH; BR/TR/6´0˝/190; d7.6																							
1905 Det A	88	329	38	88	14	1	0	31	18	5	—	.267	.315	.316	100	0	10	.978	0	102	106	1b88	—	-0.1
1906 Det A	141	499	59	112	16	2	0	33	45	3	—	.224	.293	.265	73	-14	18	.977	-7	86	98	1b122,2b17/3	—	-2.6
Total 2	229	828	97	200	30	3	0	64	63	8	—	.242	.301	.285	83	-14	28	.978	-7	93	101	1b210,2b17/3	—	-2.7
LINDSAY, BILL	William Gibbons; B2.24.1881 Madison NC; D7.14.1963 Greensboro NC; BL/TR/5´10.5˝/165; d6.21; Col Guilford																							
1911 Cle A	19	66	6	16	2	0	0	5	1	1	—	.242	.265	.273	49	-5	2	.883	1	123	43	3b15/2	—	-0.3
LINDSEY, DOUG	Michael Douglas; B9.22.1967 Austin TX; BR/TR/6´2˝/200; [PhiN87 6/156]; d10.6; Col Seminole St. (OK) JC																							
1991 Phi N	1	3	0	0	0	0	0	0	0-0	0	3	.000	.000	.000	-99	-1	0-0	1.000	0	0	0	/C	0	-0.1
1993 Phi N	2	2	0	1	0	0	0	0	0-0	0	1	.500	.500	.500	171	0	0-0	1.000	0	0	0	C2	0	0.0
Chi A	2	1	0	0	0	0	0	0	0-0	0	0	.000	.000	.000	-99	0	0-0	1.000	0	0	0	C2	0	0.0
Total 2	5	6	0	1	0	0	0	0	0-0	0	4	.167	.167	.167	-8	-1	0-0	1.000	0	0	0	C5	0	-0.1
LINDSEY, ROD	Rodney Lee; B1.28.1976 Opelika AL; BR/TR/5´8˝/175; [SDN94 39/1074]; d9.2																							
2000 Det A	11	3	6	1	1	0	0	0	0-0	1	1	.333	.500	.667	194	1	2-1	1.000	-1	48	0	O7(2/4/2)	0	0.0
LINDSEY, BILL	William Donald; B4.12.1960 Staten Island NY; BR/TR/6´3˝/195; d7.18; Col Broward (FL) CC																							
1987 Chi A	9	16	2	3	0	0	0	1	0-0	0	3	.188	.176	.188	-0	-2	0-0	1.000	1	226	196	C9	0	-0.1
LINDSTROM, CHUCK	Charles William; B9.7.1936 Chicago IL; BR/TR/5´11˝/170; d9.28; f–Freddie; Col Northwestern																							
1958 Chi A	1	1	1	1	0	1	0	1	1-0	0	0	1.000	1.000	3.000	975	1	0-0	1.000	-0	0	0	/C	0	0.1
LINDSTROM, FREDDIE	Frederick Charles (b Frederick Anthony Lindstrom); B11.21.1905 Chicago IL; D10.4.1981 Chicago IL; BR/TR/5´11˝/170; d4.15; HF1976; s–Chuck																							
1924 †NY N	52	79	19	20	3	1	0	4	6	1	10	.253	.314	.316	71	-3	3-1	.911	3	122	134	2b23,3b11	—	0.1
1925 NY N	104	356	43	102	15	12	4	33	22	2	20	.287	.332	.430	97	-4	5-9	.957	-3	88	58	3b96/2S	—	-0.3
1926 NY N	140	543	90	164	19	9	9	76	39	2	21	.302	.351	.420	108	5	11	.962	-1	97	103	3b138/rf	—	1.2
1927 NY N	138	562	107	172	36	8	7	58	40	2	40	.306	.354	.436	111	8	10	.968	2	107	85	3b87,O51L	—	1.2
1928 NY N	153	646	99	**231**	39	9	14	107	25	2	21	.358	.383	.511	131	27	15	**.958**	15	**112**	**132**	3b153	—	4.9
1929 NY N	130	549	99	175	23	6	15	91	30	0	28	.319	.354	.464	101	-1	10	.966	6	104	**140**	3b128	—	1.1
1930 NY N	148	609	127	231	39	7	22	106	48	0	33	.379	.425	.575	142	42	15	.953	4	103	96	3b148	—	4.7
1931 NY N	78	303	38	91	12	6	5	36	26	0	12	.300	.356	.429	113	5	5	.975	-7	96	45	O73R,2b4	—	-0.6
1932 NY N	144	595	83	161	26	5	15	92	27	1	28	.271	.303	.407	91	-10	6	.982	-5	88	156	O128C,3b15	—	-1.8
1933 Pit N	138	538	70	167	39	10	5	55	33	0	22	.310	.350	.448	127	18	1	.988	6	**112**	73	O130(20/111/0)	—	2.1
1934 Pit N	97	383	59	111	24	4	4	49	23	2	21	.290	.333	.405	94	-3	1	.990	1	97	127	O92L	—	-0.7
1935 †Chi N	90	342	49	94	22	4	3	62	10	1	13	.275	.297	.389	82	-9	1	.979	-5	95	113	O50C,3b33	—	-1.4
1936 Bro N	26	106	12	28	4	0	0	10	5	0	7	.264	.297	.302	61	-6	1	.982	1	95	214	O26(24/2/0)	—	-0.6
Total 13	1438	5611	895	1747	301	81	103	779	334	13	276	.311	.351	.449	110	69	84-10	.959	17	101	108	3b809,O551(187/291/74),2b28/S	—	9.9
LINHART, CARL	Carl James; B12.14.1929 Zborov, Czechoslovakia; BL/TR/5´11˝/184; d8.2																							
1952 Det A	3	2	0	0	0	0	0	0	0	0	0	.000	.000	.000	-99	-1	0-0	ø	0	—	—	/H	0	-0.1
LINIAK, COLE	Cole Edward; B8.23.1976 Encinitas CA; BR/TR/6´1˝/(190–195); [BosA95 7/186]; d9.3																							
1999 Chi N	12	29	3	7	2	0	0	2	1-0	0	4	.241	.267	.310	46	-2	0-1	1.000	-3	52	73	3b10	0	-0.5
2000 Chi N	3	3	0	0	0	0	0	0	0-0	0	2	.000	.000	.000	-99	-1	0-0	ø	0	—	—	/H	0	-0.1
Total 2	15	32	3	7	2	0	0	2	1-0	0	6	.219	.242	.281	32	-3	0-1	1.000	-3	52	73	3b10	0	-0.6
LINTON, BOB	Claud Clarence; B4.18.1902 Emerson AR; D4.3.1980 Destin FL; BL/TR/6´0˝/185; d4.26; Col Wyoming																							
1929 Pit N	17	18	0	2	0	0	0	1	1	0	2	.111	.158	.111	-31	-4	0	1.000	0	*125*	*220*	C8	—	-0.3
LINTZ, LARRY	Larry; B10.10.1949 Martinez CA; BB/TR/5´9˝/150; [MonN71 6/125]; d7.16; Col San Jose St.																							
1973 Mon N	52	116	20	29	1	0	0	3	17-0	1	18	.250	.351	.259	69	-4	12-4	.945	-2	109	86	2b34,S15	0	-0.2
1974 Mon N	113	319	60	76	10	1	0	20	44-0	2	50	.238	.334	.276	68	-12	50-7	.961	-7	98	77	2b67,S31/3	0	-0.3
1975 Mon N	46	132	18	26	0	0	0	3	23-0	0	18	.197	.316	.197	43	-10	17-9	.970	-4	95	69	2b39,S2	0	-1.1
StL N	27	18	6	5	1	0	0	1	3-0	0	2	.278	.381	.333	95	0	4-0	.889	2	98	0	2b6,S6	0	0.3
Year	73	150	24	31	1	0	0	4	26-0	0	20	.207	.324	.213	49	-9	21-9	.963	-3	95	63	2b45,S8	0	-0.8
1976 Oak A	68	1	21	0	0	0	0	0	2-0	0	0	.000	.667	.000	111	0	31-11	1.000	-1	66	0	D19,2b5,O3(1/0/2)	0	0.2
1977 Oak A	41	30	11	4	1	0	0	0	8-1	1	13	.133	.333	.167	42	-2	13-5	1.000	-1	94	106	2b28,S2/3D	0	-0.1
1978 Cle A	3	0	1	0	0	0	0	0	0-0	0	0	ø	ø	ø	ø	0	1-2	ø	0	—	—	/R	0	-0.1
Total 6	350	616	137	140	13	1	0	27	97-1	4	101	.227	.336	.252	63	-28	128-38	.962	-13	99	77	2b179,S56,D24,O3(1/0/2),3b2	0	-1.3
LINZ, PHIL	Philip Francis; B6.4.1939 Baltimore MD; BR/TR/6´1˝/(170–180); d4.13																							
1962 NY A	71	129	28	37	8	0	1	14	6-2	0	17	.287	.316	.372	88	-2	6-2	.937	-7	80	69	S21,3b8,2b5,O2R	0	-0.7
1963 †NY A	72	186	22	50	9	0	2	12	15-0	2	18	.269	.328	.349	91	-2	1-6	.963	0	113	118	S22,3b13,O12(2/5/5),2b6	0	-0.2
1964 †NY A	112	368	63	92	21	3	5	25	43-2	2	61	.250	.332	.364	92	-3	3-4	.952	7	115	123	S55,3b41,2b5,O3(1/2/0)	0	0.9
1965 NY A	99	285	37	59	12	1	2	16	30-1	0	33	.207	.281	.277	60	-15	2-1	.954	3	101	74	S71,3b4,O4R/2	0	-0.6
1966 Phi N	40	70	4	14	3	0	0	6	2-0	0	14	.200	.222	.243	29	-7	0-0	.971	-4	90	91	3b14,S6,2b3	0	-1.1
1967 Phi N	23	18	4	4	2	0	1	5	2-0	0	1	.222	.300	.500	124	1	0-0	.833	-3	29	0	S7/3	0	-0.2
NY N	24	58	8	12	2	0	0	1	4-0	1	10	.207	.270	.241	48	-4	0-0	.964	-2	88	104	2b11,S8/3lf	0	-0.5
Year	47	76	12	16	4	0	1	6	6-0	1	11	.211	.277	.303	66	-3	0-0	.963	-4	64	25	S15,2b11,3b2/lf	0	-0.7
1968 NY N	78	258	19	54	7	0	0	17	10-0	2	41	.209	.243	.236	45	-18	1-0	.968	-11	88	98	2b71	0	-2.7
Total 7	519	1372	185	322	64	4	11	96	112-5	7	195	.235	.295	.311	72	-50	13-13	.952	-15	102	92	S190,2b102,3b82,O22(4/7/11)	0	-5.1
LIPON, JOHNNY	John Joseph "Skids"; B11.10.1922 Martins Ferry OH; D8.17.1998 Houston TX; BR/TR/6´0˝/(170–175); d8.16; Mil 1943–45; M1/C4																							
1942 Det A	34	131	5	25	2	0	0	9	7	0	7	.191	.232	.206	22	-14	1-3	.945	3	98	107	S34	0	-0.9
1946 Det A	14	20	4	6	0	0	0	1	5	0	3	.300	.440	.300	103	0	0-0	.933	1	87	160	S8/3	0	0.1
1948 Det A	121	458	65	133	18	8	5	52	68	2	22	.290	.384	.397	105	5	4-4	.970	-10	94	76	S117/23	0	0.1
1949 Det A	127	439	57	110	14	6	3	59	75	2	24	.251	.362	.330	84	-9	2-4	.965	0	99	107	S120	0	-0.2
1950 Det A	147	601	104	176	27	6	2	63	81	1	26	.293	.378	.368	89	-8	9-6	.958	9	106	**120**	S147	0	0.9
1951 Det A	129	487	56	129	15	1	0	38	49	2	27	.265	.335	.300	72	-18	7-6	.949	-11	98	87	S125	0	-2.1
1952 Det A	39	136	17	30	4	2	0	12	16	0	6	.221	.303	.279	62	-7	3-1	.978	-2	92	49	S39	0	-0.7
Bos A	79	234	25	48	8	1	0	18	32	0	20	.205	.301	.248	50	-15	1-1	.982	12	113	121	S69,3b7	0	0.1
Year	118	370	42	78	12	3	0	30	48	0	26	.211	.301	.259	54	-22	4-2	**.981**	10	**105**	95	S108,3b7	0	-0.6
1953 Bos A	60	145	18	31	7	0	0	13	14	0	16	.214	.283	.262	46	-11	1-0	.951	2	105	86	S58	0	-0.5
StL A	7	9	0	2	0	0	0	1	0	0	1	.222	.222	.222	20	-1	0-0	1.000	-1	148	0	3b6/2	0	-0.2
Year	67	154	18	33	7	0	0	14	14	0	17	.214	.280	.260	44	-12	1-0	.951	1	105	86	S58,3b6/2	0	-0.7

YEAR	TM LG	G	AB	R	H	2B	3B	HR	RBI	BB-IB	HP	SO	AVG	OBP	SLG	AOPS	ABR	SB-CS	FA	FR	RNG	THR	GAMES AT POSITION	DL	BFW
1954	Cin N	1	1	0	0	0	0	0	0	0	0	0	.000	.000	.000	-97	0	0-0	ø	0	—	—	/H	0	0.0
Total	9	758	2661	351	690	95	24	10	266	347	7	152	.259	.346	.324	77	-78	28-25	.961	2	101	98	S717,3b15,2b2	0	-3.4

LIPSCOMB, NIG Gerard; B2.24.1911 Rutherfordton NC; D2.27.1978 Huntersville NC; BR/TR/6´0˝/175; d4.23; ▲

YEAR	TM LG	G	AB	R	H	2B	3B	HR	RBI	BB-IB	HP	SO	AVG	OBP	SLG	AOPS	ABR	SB-CS	FA	FR	RNG	THR	GAMES AT POSITION	DL	BFW
1937	StL A	36	96	11	31	9	1	0	8	11	1	10	.323	.398	.438	110	2	0-0	.963	-0	97	130	2b27,P3/3	—	0.3

LIPSKI, BOB Robert Peter; B7.7.1938 Scranton PA; BL/TR/6´1˝/180; d4.28

YEAR	TM LG	G	AB	R	H	2B	3B	HR	RBI	BB-IB	HP	SO	AVG	OBP	SLG	AOPS	ABR	SB-CS	FA	FR	RNG	THR	GAMES AT POSITION	DL	BFW
1963	Cle A	2	1	0	0	0	0	0	0	0-0	0	1	.000	.000	.000	-99	0	0-0	1.000	0	0	0	C2	0	0.0

LIRIANO, NELSON Nelson Arturo (Bonilla); B6.3.1964 Puerto Plata, D.R.; BB/TR/5´10˝/(165–185); d8.25

YEAR	TM LG	G	AB	R	H	2B	3B	HR	RBI	BB-IB	HP	SO	AVG	OBP	SLG	AOPS	ABR	SB-CS	FA	FR	RNG	THR	GAMES AT POSITION	DL	BFW
1987	Tor A	37	158	29	38	6	2	2	10	16-2	0	22	.241	.310	.342	71	-7	13-2	.995	3	99	120	2b37	0	0.0
1988	Tor A	99	276	36	73	6	2	3	23	11-0	2	40	.264	.297	.333	76	-10	12-5	.961	-14	90	104	2b80,D11/3	0	-2.1
1989	†Tor A	132	418	51	110	26	3	5	53	43-0	2	51	.263	.331	.376	101	2	16-7	.980	-14	95	97	2b122,D5	0	-0.8
1990	Tor A	50	170	16	36	7	2	1	15	16-0	1	20	.212	.282	.294	60	-9	3-5	.983	-8	93	84	2b49	0	-1.7
	Min A	53	185	30	47	5	7	0	13	22-0	0	24	.254	.332	.357	87	-3	5-2	.968	-9	95	83	2b50/SD	0	-1.0
	Year	103	355	46	83	12	9	1	28	38-0	1	44	.234	.308	.327	75	-12	8-7	.975	-16	94	84	2b99,D2/S	0	-2.7
1991	KC A	10	22	5	9	0	0	0	1	0-0	0	2	.409	.409	.409	126	1	0-1	1.000	1	116	69	2b10	0	0.1
1993	Col N	48	151	28	46	6	3	2	15	18-2	0	22	.305	.376	.424	98	0	6-4	.975	-8	87	69	S35,2b16/3	0	-0.5
1994	Col N	87	255	39	65	17	5	3	31	42-5	0	44	.255	.357	.396	83	-5	0-2	.973	-8	96	81	2b79,S3,3b2	0	-1.0
1995	Pit N	107	259	29	74	12	1	5	38	24-3	2	34	.286	.347	.398	95	-2	2-2	.981	-11	86	84	2b67,3b5/S	0	-1.0
1996	Pit N	112	217	23	58	14	2	3	30	14-2	0	22	.267	.308	.392	81	-6	2-0	.984	-2	105	79	2b36,3b9,S5	0	-0.6
1997	LA N	76	88	10	20	6	0	1	11	6-1	0	12	.227	.274	.330	62	-5	0-0	.949	-4	76	103	2b17,1b2/3S	11	-0.8
1998	Col N	12	17	0	0	0	0	0	0	0-0	0	7	.000	.000	.000	-83	-4	0-0	1.000	-2	43	90	2b3/S	0	-0.6
Total	11	823	2216	296	576	105	27	25	240	212-15	7	300	.260	.324	.366	84	-48	59-30	.976	-73	94	92	2b566,S47,3b19,D18,1b2	11	-10.0

LIS, JOE Joseph Anthony; B8.15.1946 Somerville NJ; BR/TR/6´0˝/(185–195); d9.5

YEAR	TM LG	G	AB	R	H	2B	3B	HR	RBI	BB-IB	HP	SO	AVG	OBP	SLG	AOPS	ABR	SB-CS	FA	FR	RNG	THR	GAMES AT POSITION	DL	BFW
1970	Phi N	13	37	1	7	2	0	1	4	5-0	0	11	.189	.286	.324	65	-2	0-0	.947	0	121	0	O9L	0	-0.2
1971	Phi N	59	123	16	26	6	0	6	10	16-0	2	43	.211	.308	.407	102	0	0-1	.978	-2	77	102	O35L	0	-0.4
1972	Phi N	62	140	13	34	6	0	6	18	30-1	1	34	.243	.380	.414	122	6	0-1	.996	2	97	90	1b30,O14(8/0/6)	0	0.5
1973	Min A	103	253	37	62	11	1	9	25	28-1	3	66	.245	.325	.403	100	0	0-1	.987	-1	99	93	1b96/D	0	-0.7
1974	Min A	24	41	5	8	0	0	0	3	5-0	1	12	.195	.298	.195	43	-3	0-0	.992	-1	78	83	1b18	0	-0.5
	Cle A	57	109	15	22	3	0	6	16	14-1	0	30	.202	.293	.394	97	-1	1-0	1.000	-2	81	85	1b31,3b9/lfD	0	-0.4
	Year	81	150	20	30	3	0	6	19	19-1	1	42	.200	.294	.340	82	-4	1-0	.997	-3	80	84	1b49,3b9,D9/lf	0	-0.9
1975	Cle A	9	13	4	4	2	0	2	8	3-0	1	3	.308	.444	.923	285	3	0-0	1.000	-0	62	51	1b8/D	0	0.3
1976	Cle A	20	51	4	16	1	0	2	7	8-0	0	8	.314	.400	.451	152	4	0-0	1.000	-1	72	79	1b17/D	0	0.2
1977	Sea A	9	13	1	3	0	0	0	1	1-0	0	2	.231	.286	.231	43	-1	0-0	1.000	-1	55	136	1b4/C	0	-0.2
Total	8	356	780	96	182	31	1	32	92	110-3	8	209	.233	.332	.399	105	6	1-3	.992	-5	90	89	1b204,O59(53/0/6),D12,3b9/C	0	-1.4

LISI, RICK Riccardo Patrick Emilio; B3.17.1956 Halifax NS, Can.; BR/TR/6´0˝/175; [TexA74 13/290]; d5.9

YEAR	TM LG	G	AB	R	H	2B	3B	HR	RBI	BB-IB	HP	SO	AVG	OBP	SLG	AOPS	ABR	SB-CS	FA	FR	RNG	THR	GAMES AT POSITION	DL	BFW
1981	Tex A	9	16	6	5	0	0	0	1	4-0	0	0	.313	.450	.313	129	1	0-1	1.000	-1	79	0	O8(0/2/6)	0	0.0

LISTACH, PAT Patrick Alan; B9.12.1967 Natchitoches LA; BB/TR/5´9˝/(170–180); [MilA88 5/133]; d4.8; Col Arizona St.; [DL 1996 NY A 38]

YEAR	TM LG	G	AB	R	H	2B	3B	HR	RBI	BB-IB	HP	SO	AVG	OBP	SLG	AOPS	ABR	SB-CS	FA	FR	RNG	THR	GAMES AT POSITION	DL	BFW
1992	Mil A	149	579	93	168	19	6	1	47	55-0	1	124	.290	.352	.349	99	-1	54-18	.966	2	104	107	S148/2cf	0	1.8
1993	Mil A	98	356	50	87	15	1	3	30	37-0	3	70	.244	.319	.317	73	-13	18-9	.975	-10	100	92	S95,O6C	46	-1.5
1994	Mil A	16	54	8	16	3	0	0	2	3-0	0	8	.296	.333	.352	73	-2	2-1	.958	2	122	113	S16	110	0.1
1995	Mil A	101	334	35	73	8	2	0	25	25-0	2	61	.219	.276	.254	37	-31	13-3	1.000	11	112	118	2b59,S36,O11(1/10/1),3b2	0	-1.4
1996	Mil A	87	317	51	76	16	2	1	33	36-0	1	51	.240	.317	.312	58	-20	25-5	.982	-7	97	154	O68(2/66/0),2b12,S7	15	-2.0
1997	Hou N	52	132	13	24	2	2	0	6	11-2	1	24	.182	.247	.227	27	-15	4-2	.951	-10	85	75	S31,O6(1/4/1)	0	-2.3
Total	6	503	1772	250	444	63	13	5	143	167-2	8	338	.251	.316	.309	67	-82	116-38	.967	-13	103	103	S333,O92(4/87/2),2b72,3b2	209	-5.3

LISTER, PETE Morris Elmer; B7.21.1881 Savanna IL; D3.27.1947 St.Petersburg FL; BR/TR/6´0˝/190; d9.14

YEAR	TM LG	G	AB	R	H	2B	3B	HR	RBI	BB-IB	HP	SO	AVG	OBP	SLG	AOPS	ABR	SB-CS	FA	FR	RNG	THR	GAMES AT POSITION	DL	BFW
1907	Cle A	22	65	5	18	2	0	0	4	3	1	—	.277	.319	.308	99	0	2	.974	-1	83	141	1b22	—	-0.2

LITTLE, SCOTT Dennis Scott; B1.19.1963 E.St.Louis IL; BR/TR/6´0˝/198; [NYN84*7/158]; d7.27; Col Missouri

YEAR	TM LG	G	AB	R	H	2B	3B	HR	RBI	BB-IB	HP	SO	AVG	OBP	SLG	AOPS	ABR	SB-CS	FA	FR	RNG	THR	GAMES AT POSITION	DL	BFW
1989	Pit N	3	4	0	1	0	0	0	0	0-0	0	1	.250	.250	.250	45	0	0-0	1.000	1	84	3020	/rf	0	0.1

LITTLE, HARRY Henry Alexander; B11.9.1850 Pocahontas MO; D2.17.1927 Bremen Twp. (Cook Co.) IL; TR; d7.16

YEAR	TM LG	G	AB	R	H	2B	3B	HR	RBI	BB-IB	HP	SO	AVG	OBP	SLG	AOPS	ABR	SB-CS	FA	FR	RNG	THR	GAMES AT POSITION	DL	BFW
1877	StL N	3	12	2	2	0	0	0	0	1	—	6	.167	.231	.167	29	-1	—	1.000	-0	0	0	O3C	—	-0.1
	Lou N	1	3	0	0	0	0	0	0	1	—	1	.000	.250	.000	-13	0	—	.857	0	145	0	/2	—	0.0
	Year	4	15	2	2	0	0	0	0	2	—	7	.133	.235	.133	19	-1	—	1.000	-0	0	0	O3C/2	—	-0.1

LITTLE, MARK Mark Travis; B7.11.1972 Edwardsville IL; BR/TR/6´0˝/(190–195); [TexA94 8/225]; d9.12; Col Memphis

YEAR	TM LG	G	AB	R	H	2B	3B	HR	RBI	BB-IB	HP	SO	AVG	OBP	SLG	AOPS	ABR	SB-CS	FA	FR	RNG	THR	GAMES AT POSITION	DL	BFW
1998	StL N	7	12	0	1	0	0	0	0	2-0	0	5	.083	.214	.083	-18	-2	1-0	1.000	0	128	0	O7(3/0/4)	0	-0.2
2001	Col N	51	85	18	29	6	0	3	13	1-1	4	20	.341	.378	.518	107	1	5-2	1.000	3	102	303	O29(13/14/6)	113	0.4
2002	Col N	61	105	20	21	5	2	0	5	13-0	4	28	.200	.311	.286	52	-7	2-1	.970	3	118	130	O36(16/11/16)	0	-0.5
	NY N	3	3	0	0	0	0	0	0	0-0	0	1	.000	.000	.000	-99	-1	0-1	ø	-0	0	0	/rf	0	-0.1
	†Ari N	15	22	8	6	0	1	0	2	2-0	4	5	.273	.429	.364	101	0	0-0	1.000	0	113	0	O12(4/2/7)	0	0.0
	Year	79	130	28	27	5	3	0	7	15-0	8	34	.208	.327	.292	58	-8	2-2	.975	2	116	101	O49(20/13/24)	0	-0.6
2004	Cle A	11	20	0	4	0	0	0	2	0-0	2	7	.200	.261	.200	27	-2	0-0	1.000	0	89	284	O11(4/5/4)	0	-0.2
Total	4	148	247	46	61	11	3	3	22	18-1	14	66	.247	.332	.352	70	-11	8-4	.986	6	110	169	O96(40/32/38)	113	-0.6

LITTLE, BRYAN Richard Bryan "Twig"; B10.8.1959 Houston TX; BB/TR/5´10˝/(155–160); [MonN80 9/229]; d7.29; C3; Col Texas A&M

YEAR	TM LG	G	AB	R	H	2B	3B	HR	RBI	BB-IB	HP	SO	AVG	OBP	SLG	AOPS	ABR	SB-CS	FA	FR	RNG	THR	GAMES AT POSITION	DL	BFW
1982	Mon N	29	42	6	9	0	0	0	3	4-0	0	6	.214	.277	.214	39	-3	2-1	1.000	-5	72	23	2b16,S10	0	-0.8
1983	Mon N	106	350	48	91	15	3	1	36	50-1	2	22	.260	.352	.329	91	-2	4-5	.968	-18	79	83	S66,2b51	0	-1.4
1984	Mon N	85	266	31	65	11	1	0	9	34-0	1	19	.244	.332	.293	80	-6	2-3	.982	-7	93	109	2b77,S2	0	-1.0
1985	Chi A	73	188	35	47	9	1	2	27	26-0	3	21	.250	.345	.340	86	-3	0-1	.989	6	107	92	2b68,3b2/S	0	0.6
1986	Chi A	20	35	3	6	1	0	0	2	4-0	0	4	.171	.256	.200	25	-4	0-0	1.000	2	102	67	2b12,S7/3	0	-0.1
	NY A	14	41	3	8	1	0	0	0	2-0	0	7	.195	.233	.220	24	-4	0-0	.975	4	120	114	2b14	0	0.1
	Year	34	76	6	14	2	0	0	2	6-0	0	11	.184	.244	.211	25	-8	0-0	.983	6	114	97	2b26,S7/3	0	0.0
Total	5	327	922	126	226	37	5	3	77	120-1	6	79	.245	.333	.306	79	-22	8-10	.987	-18	99	92	2b238,S86,3b3	0	-2.6

LITTLE, JACK William Arthur; B3.12.1891 Mart TX; D7.27.1961 Dallas TX; BR/TR/5´11˝/175; d7.2; Col Baylor

YEAR	TM LG	G	AB	R	H	2B	3B	HR	RBI	BB-IB	HP	SO	AVG	OBP	SLG	AOPS	ABR	SB-CS	FA	FR	RNG	THR	GAMES AT POSITION	DL	BFW
1912	NY A	3	12	2	3	0	0	0	0	1	1	—	.250	.357	.250	70	0	2	1.000	0	85	216	O3C	—	0.0

LITTLEJOHN, DENNIS Dennis Gerald; B10.4.1954 Santa Monica CA; BR/TR/6´2˝/200; [SFN76*S1/2]; d7.9; Col USC

YEAR	TM LG	G	AB	R	H	2B	3B	HR	RBI	BB-IB	HP	SO	AVG	OBP	SLG	AOPS	ABR	SB-CS	FA	FR	RNG	THR	GAMES AT POSITION	DL	BFW
1978	SF N	2	0	0	0	0	0	0	0	0-0	0	0	ø	ø	ø	ø	0	0-0	ø	-0	0	0	C2	0	0.0
1979	SF N	63	193	15	38	6	1	1	13	21-4	0	46	.197	.272	.254	49	-14	0-0	.986	-2	69	129	C63	0	-1.3
1980	SF N	13	29	2	7	1	0	0	2	7-1	0	7	.241	.368	.276	92	0	0-0	.983	2	108	103	C10	0	0.2
Total	3	78	222	17	45	7	1	1	15	28-5	0	53	.203	.286	.257	55	-14	0-0	.985	-0	74	125	C75	0	-1.1

LITTLETON, LARRY Larry Marvin; B4.3.1954 Charlotte NC; BR/TR/6´1˝/185; [PitN76*S1/6]; d4.12; Col Georgia

YEAR	TM LG	G	AB	R	H	2B	3B	HR	RBI	BB-IB	HP	SO	AVG	OBP	SLG	AOPS	ABR	SB-CS	FA	FR	RNG	THR	GAMES AT POSITION	DL	BFW
1981	Cle A	26	23	2	0	0	0	0	1	3-0	0	6	.000	.111	.000	-65	-5	0-0	1.000	-2	57	0	O24(19/6/1)	0	-0.8

LITTON, GREG Jon Gregory; B7.13.1964 New Orleans LA; BR/TR/6´0˝/(175–190); [SFN84*1/10]; d5.2; Col Pensacola (FL) JC; OF(42/0/50)

YEAR	TM LG	G	AB	R	H	2B	3B	HR	RBI	BB-IB	HP	SO	AVG	OBP	SLG	AOPS	ABR	SB-CS	FA	FR	RNG	THR	GAMES AT POSITION	DL	BFW
1989	†SF N	71	143	12	36	5	3	4	17	7-0	1	29	.252	.291	.413	102	-1	0-2	.953	-2	103	30	3b34,2b15,S9,O6(4/0/2),C2	0	-0.4
1990	SF N	93	204	17	50	9	1	1	24	11-0	1	45	.245	.284	.314	67	-10	1-0	.985	3	89	257	O56(14/0/42),2b18,S7,3b5	12	-0.7
1991	SF N	59	127	13	23	7	1	1	15	11-0	1	25	.181	.250	.276	50	-9	0-2	.989	3	158	150	1b15,2b15,3b11,S9,O6(2/0/4)/CP	17	-0.7
1992	SF N	68	140	9	32	5	0	4	15	11-0	0	33	.229	.285	.350	83	-4	0-1	.992	-1	98	124	2b31,3b10,1b8,S3/lf	0	-0.5
1993	Sea A	72	174	25	52	17	0	3	25	18-2	1	30	.299	.366	.448	116	5	0-1	1.000	1	83	327	O22(21/0/2),2b17,1b13,D12,3b7,S5	0	0.4
1994	Bos A	11	21	2	2	0	0	0	1	0-0	0	5	.095	.091	.095	-48	-5	0-0	1.000	0	76	0	2b4,1b3,3b2/D	0	-0.4
Total	6	374	809	78	195	43	5	13	97	53-2	4	167	.241	.293	.355	81	-24	1-6	.997	4	90	118	2b100,O91R,3b69,1b39,S33,D13,C3/P	29	-2.3

LITTRELL, JACK Jack Napier; B1.22.1929 Louisville KY; BR/TR/6´0˝/179; d4.19

YEAR	TM LG	G	AB	R	H	2B	3B	HR	RBI	BB-IB	HP	SO	AVG	OBP	SLG	AOPS	ABR	SB-CS	FA	FR	RNG	THR	GAMES AT POSITION	DL	BFW
1952	Phi A	4	2	0	0	0	0	0	0	1	0	2	.000	.333	.000	-2	0	0-0	1.000	0	150	345	S2/3	0	0.0
1954	Phi A	9	30	7	9	2	0	1	3	6	0	3	.300	.417	.467	141	2	1-0	.976	-1	84	123	S9	0	0.2
1955	KC A	37	70	7	14	0	1	0	1	4-0	0	12	.200	.243	.229	27	-8	0-0	.947	-1	93	77	S22,1b6,2b4	0	-0.8

YEAR	TM LG	G	AB	R	H	2B	3B	HR	RBI	BB-IB	HP	SO	AVG	OBP	SLG	AOPS	ABR	SB-CS	FA	FR	RNG	THR	GAMES AT POSITION	DL	BFW
1957	Chi N	61	153	8	29	4	2	1	13	9-1	0	43	.190	.233	.261	34	-15	0-0	.944	-2	97	77	S47,2b6,3b5	0	-1.3
Total	4	111	255	22	52	6	3	2	17	20-1	0	60	.204	.261	.275	45	-21	1-0	.949	-4	95	85	S80,2b10,1b6,3b6	0	-1.9
LITWHILER, DANNY	Daniel Webster; B8.31.1916 Ringtown PA; BR/TR/5´10.5˝/198; d4.25; Mil 1945–46; C1; Col Bloomsburg																								
1940	Phi N	36	142	10	49	2	2	5	17	3	1	13	.345	.363	.493	139	6	1	.986	2	103	152	O34(2/3/31)	—	0.6
1941	Phi N	151	590	72	180	29	6	18	66	39	2	43	.305	.350	.466	134	23	1	.964	13	**118**	113	O150(148/0/2)	0	2.8
1942	Phi N★	**151**	591	59	160	25	9	9	56	27	7	42	.271	.310	.389	109	3	2	**1.000**	-3	95	83	O151(130/0/24)	0	-0.9
1943	Phi N	36	139	23	36	6	0	5	17	11	0	14	.259	.313	.410	113	2	1	.989	4	113	142	O34L	0	0.3
	†StL N	80	258	40	72	14	3	7	31	19	2	31	.279	.333	.438	117	5	1	1.000	3	107	115	O70L	0	0.4
	Year	116	397	63	108	20	3	12	48	30	2	45	.272	.326	.428	115	6	2	**.996**	7	109	125	O104L	0	0.7
1944	†StL N	140	492	53	130	25	5	15	82	37	**10**	56	.264	.328	.427	109	5	2	.974	-2	104	60	O136L	0	-0.5
1946	StL N	6	5	0	0	0	0	0	0	1	0	1	.000	.167	.000	-49	-1	0	ø	0	—	—	/H	0	-0.1
	Bos N	79	247	29	72	12	2	8	38	19	2	23	.291	.347	.453	125	7	1	.985	-1	105	39	O65L,3b2	0	0.2
	Year	85	252	29	72	12	2	8	38	20	2	24	.286	.343	.444	121	6	1	.985	-1	105	39	O65L,3b2	0	0.1
1947	Bos N	91	226	38	59	5	2	7	31	25	1	43	.261	.337	.394	96	-2	1	.976	-1	101	49	O66(64/0/1)	0	-0.7
1948	Bos N	13	33	0	9	2	0	0	6	4	2	2	.273	.385	.333	97	0	0	1.000	1	114	128	O8L	0	0.0
	Cin N	106	338	51	93	19	2	14	44	48	0	41	.275	.365	.467	128	14	1	.988	3	105	51	O83(5/1/77),3b15	0	1.4
	Year	119	371	51	102	21	2	14	50	52	2	43	.275	.367	.456	125	14	1	.990	4	106	59	O91(13/1/77),3b15	0	1.4
1949	Cin N	102	292	35	85	18	1	11	48	44	0	42	.291	.384	.473	127	12	0	.987	0	101	94	O82(11/1/71),3b3	0	1.0
1950	Cin N	54	112	15	29	4	0	6	12	20	0	21	.259	.371	.455	116	3	0	.958	-1	105	0	O29(8/0/21)	0	0.1
1951	Cin N	12	29	3	8	1	0	2	3	2	0	5	.276	.323	.517	120	1	0-0	.933	-1	103	0	O7R	0	0.0
Total	11	1057	3494	428	982	162	32	107	451	299	27	377	.281	.342	.438	119	78	11-0	.982	17	105	83	O915(681/5/234),3b20	0	4.6
LIVINGSTON, PADDY	Patrick Joseph; B1.14.1880 Cleveland OH; D9.19.1977 Cleveland OH; BR/TR/5´8˝/197; d9.2; C1																								
1901	Cle A	1	2	0	0	0	0	0	0	0	1	—	.000	.333	.000	-2	0	0	1.000	-0	*79*	*159*	/C	—	0.0
1906	Cin N	50	139	8	22	1	4	0	8	12	7	—	.158	.259	.223	48	-8	0	.960	2	*101*	*108*	C47	—	-0.2
1909	Phi A	64	175	15	41	6	4	0	15	15	8	—	.234	.323	.314	99	0	4	.969	10	*125*	*121*	C64	—	1.8
1910	Phi A	37	120	11	25	4	3	0	9	6	3	—	.208	.264	.292	75	-4	2	.968	4	*111*	*112*	C37	—	0.4
1911	Phi A	27	71	9	17	4	0	0	8	7	1	—	.239	.316	.296	72	-2	1	.977	3	*121*	*106*	C26	—	0.3
1912	Cle A	20	47	5	11	2	1	0	3	1	2	—	.234	.280	.319	69	-2	0	.976	1	*93*	*91*	C14	—	-0.1
1917	StL N	7	20	0	4	0	0	0	2	0	0	1	.200	.200	.200	23	-2	2	1.000	0	*120*	*81*	C6	—	-0.1
Total	7	206	574	48	120	17	12	0	45	41	22	1	.209	.287	.280	73	-18	9	.969	19	*113*	*111*	C195	—	2.1
LIVINGSTON, MICKEY	Thompson Orville; B11.15.1914 Newberry SC; D4.3.1983 Houston TX; BR/TR/6´1.5˝/185; d9.17; Mil 1944																								
1938	Was A	2	4	0	3	2	0	0	1	0	0	1	.750	.750	1.250	421	2	0-0	.667	-1	*0*	*0*	C2	—	0.1
1941	Phi N	95	207	16	42	6	1	0	18	20	1	38	.203	.276	.242	49	-14	2	.974	-3	*75*	*94*	C71/1	0	-1.4
1942	Phi N	89	239	20	49	6	1	2	22	25	1	20	.205	.283	.264	64	-11	0	.987	-7	*67*	*97*	C78,1b6	0	-1.6
1943	Phi N	84	265	25	66	9	2	3	18	19	2	18	.249	.304	.332	87	-5	1	.988	1	*94*	*109*	C84,1b2	0	0.0
	Chi N	36	111	11	29	5	1	4	16	12	0	8	.261	.333	.432	122	3	1	1.000	-1	*122*	*59*	C31,1b4	0	0.4
	Year	120	376	36	95	14	3	7	34	31	2	26	.253	.313	.362	98	-2	2	**.991**	0	*102*	*95*	C115,1b6	0	0.4
1945	†Chi N	71	224	19	57	4	2	2	23	19	4	6	.254	.324	.317	80	-6	2	.990	3	*153*	*70*	C68/1	0	0.1
1946	Chi N	66	176	14	45	14	0	2	20	20	2	19	.256	.338	.369	103	1	0	.981	-1	*111*	*78*	C56	0	0.3
1947	Chi N	19	33	2	7	2	0	0	3	1	0	5	.212	.235	.273	36	-3	0	1.000	-0	*86*	*0*	C7	0	-0.3
	NY N	5	6	0	1	0	0	0	0	1	0	2	.167	.286	.167	23	-1	0	.800	-0	*0*	*0*	/C	0	-0.1
	Year	24	39	2	8	2	0	0	3	2	0	7	.205	.244	.256	34	-4	0	.970	-0	*74*	*0*	C8	0	-0.4
1948	NY N	45	99	9	21	4	1	2	12	21	0	11	.212	.350	.333	85	-1	1	.980	-0	*111*	*54*	C42	0	0.0
1949	NY N	19	57	6	17	2	0	4	12	2	1	8	.298	.333	.544	132	2	0	.985	-1	*85*	*61*	C19	0	0.2
	Bos N	28	64	6	15	2	1	0	6	3	2	5	.234	.290	.297	61	-4	0	.977	0	*100*	*104*	C22	0	-0.3
	Year	47	121	12	32	4	1	4	18	5	3	13	.264	.310	.413	95	-1	0	.980	-1	*93*	*84*	C41	0	-0.1
1951	Bro N	2	5	0	2	0	0	0	2	1	0	0	.400	.500	.400	142	0	0-0	1.000	0	*0*	*364*	C2	0	0.0
Total	10	561	1490	128	354	56	9	19	153	144	13	141	.238	.310	.326	82	-37	7-0	.984	-10	*100*	*85*	C483,1b14	0	-2.6
LIVINGSTONE, SCOTT	Scott Louis; B7.15.1965 Dallas TX; BL/TR/6´0˝/(185–198); [DetA88 2/56]; d7.19; Col Texas A&M																								
1991	Det A	44	127	19	37	5	0	2	11	10-0	0	25	.291	.341	.378	97	0	2-1	.980	-3	89	80	3b43	0	-0.4
1992	Det A	117	354	43	100	21	0	4	46	21-1	0	36	.282	.319	.376	94	-3	1-3	.962	-4	100	86	3b112	0	-0.8
1993	Det A	98	304	39	89	10	2	2	39	19-1	0	32	.293	.328	.359	86	-6	1-3	.955	-10	85	58	3b62,D32	0	-1.8
1994	Det A	15	23	0	5	1	0	0	1	1-0	0	4	.217	.250	.261	32	-2	0-0	1.000	0	0	142	1b5/3D	0	-0.2
	SD N	57	180	11	49	12	1	2	10	6-0	0	22	.272	.294	.383	78	-6	2-2	.942	-0	100	89	3b50	0	-0.7
1995	SD N	99	196	26	66	15	0	5	32	15-1	0	22	.337	.380	.490	132	9	2-1	.991	-1	67	94	1b43,3b13,2b4	0	0.5
1996	†SD N	102	172	20	51	4	1	2	20	9-0	0	22	.297	.331	.366	88	-4	0-1	.993	-1	87	130	1b22,3b16	20	-0.6
1997	SD N	23	26	1	4	1	0	0	3	2-0	0	1	.154	.214	.192	8	-4	0-0	.750	1	154	0	3b3,1b2/2	27	-0.3
	StL N	42	41	3	7	1	0	0	3	1-0	0	10	.171	.182	.195	1	-6	1-0	1.000	-1	47	0	3b2/rfD	21	-0.6
	Year	65	67	4	11	2	0	0	6	3-0	0	11	.164	.194	.194	4	-10	1-0	.778	0	111	0	3b5,1b2/2rfD	0	-0.9
1998	Mon N	76	110	1	23	6	0	0	12	5-2	0	15	.209	.237	.264	34	-11	1-1	.938	0	113	0	3b17,1b3,D5	0	-1.1
Total	8	673	1533	163	431	76	4	17	177	89-5	0	189	.281	.317	.369	86	-33	10-12	.958	-19	97	74	3b319,1b75,D43,2b5/rf	68	-6.0
LIZOTTE, ABEL	Abel; B4.13.1870 Lewiston ME; D12.4.1926 Wilkes–Barre PA; 5´8˝/174; d9.17																								
1896	Pit N	7	29	3	3	0	0	0	3	2	0	2	.103	.161	.103	-31	-6	1	.952	1	163	72	1b7	—	-0.4
LLENAS, WINSTON	Winston Enriquillo (Davila); B9.23.1943 Santiago, D.R.; BR/TR/5´10˝/(165–168); d8.15; C1																								
1968	Cal A	16	39	5	5	1	0	0	1	2-0	1	5	.128	.190	.154	5	-4	0-0	.800	-2	85	0	3b9	0	-0.8
1969	Cal A	34	47	4	8	2	0	0	0	2-0	0	10	.170	.204	.213	17	-5	0-0	.929	-1	93	88	3b9	0	-0.7
1972	Cal A	44	64	3	17	3	0	0	7	3-0	0	8	.266	.290	.313	86	-1	0-0	.950	-1	95	137	3b10,2b2,O2L	0	-0.2
1973	Cal A	78	130	16	35	1	0	1	25	10-0	1	16	.269	.317	.300	83	-3	0-0	1.000	2	77	38	2b20,3b11,O4L,D4	0	-0.1
1974	Cal A	72	138	16	36	6	0	2	17	11-1	0	19	.261	.301	.348	96	-1	0-0	1.000	-1	91	82	O32(25/0/7),2b15,D10,3b2	15	-0.3
1975	Cal A	56	113	6	21	4	0	0	11	10-0	0	11	.186	.250	.221	37	-9	0-1	1.000	4	111	94	2b12,O10(9/0/1),1b6,3b3,D6	0	-0.6
Total	6	300	531	50	122	17	0	3	61	38-1	2	69	.230	.277	.279	65	-23	0-1	1.000	1	89	62	2b49,O48(40/0/8),3b44,D20,1b6	15	-2.7
LOAN, MIKE	William Joseph; B9.27.1894 Philadelphia PA; D11.21.1966 Springfield PA; BR/TR/5´11˝/185; d9.18; Col Villanova																								
1912	Phi N	1	2	1	1	0	0	0	0	0	0	0	.500	.500	.500	163	0	0	1.000	-0	*44*	*0*	/C	—	0.0
LOANE, BOB	Robert Kenneth; B8.5.1914 Berkeley CA; D12.11.2002 Monterey CA; BR/TR/6´0˝/190; d7.29																								
1939	Was A	3	9	2	0	0	0	0	1	4	0	4	.000	.308	.000	-16	-1	0-0	.909	1	89	715	O3C	—	0.0
1940	Bos N	13	22	4	5	3	0	0	1	2	0	5	.227	.292	.364	84	0	2	1.000	2	114	364	O10(2/8/0)	—	0.1
Total	2	16	31	6	5	3	0	0	2	6	0	9	.161	.297	.258	54	-1	2-0	.969	3	106	478	O13(2/11/0)	—	0.1
LOBERT, FRANK	Frank John; B11.26.1883 Williamsport PA; D5.29.1932 Pittsburgh PA; BR/TR/6´0˝/180; d6.6; b–Hans																								
1914	Bal F	11	30	3	6	0	1	0	2	0	0	0	.200	.200	.267	26	-4	0	.870	-2	31	96	3b7/2	—	-0.6
LOBERT, HANS	John Bernard "Honus"; B10.18.1881 Wilmington DE; D9.14.1968 Philadelphia PA; BR/TR/5´9˝/170; d9.21; M2/C11; b–Frank; Col Carnegie Mellon																								
1903	Pit N	5	13	1	1	1	0	0	0	1	0	—	.077	.143	.154	-15	-2	1	.778	-1	86	0	3b3/2S	—	-0.3
1905	Chi N	14	46	7	9	2	0	0	1	3	1	—	.196	.260	.239	47	-3	4	.918	-1	90	137	3b13/cf	—	-0.4
1906	Cin N	79	268	39	83	5	5	0	19	19	5	—	.310	.366	.366	123	7	20	.959	-7	99	98	3b35,S31,2b10/cf	—	0.2
1907	Cin N	148	537	61	132	9	12	1	41	37	4	—	.246	.299	.313	88	-9	30	.941	-16	89	111	S142,3b5	—	-2.3
1908	Cin N	**155**	570	71	167	17	18	4	63	46	2	—	.293	.348	.407	145	27	47	.921	-21	91	89	3b99,S35,O21L	—	1.0
1909	Cin N	122	425	50	90	13	5	4	52	48	8	—	.212	.304	.294	86	-6	30	.921	-13	84	104	3b122	—	-1.8
1910	Cin N	93	314	43	97	6	6	3	40	30	0	9	.309	.369	.395	128	10	41	.932	1	99	85	3b90	—	1.4
1911	Phi N	147	541	94	154	20	9	9	72	66	5	31	.285	.368	.405	115	11	40	.954	-18	78	62	3b147	—	-0.2
1912	Phi N	65	257	37	84	12	5	2	33	19	0	13	.327	.373	.436	113	4	13	.976	-8	76	38	3b64	—	-0.2
1913	Phi N	150	573	98	172	28	11	7	55	42	5	34	.300	.353	.424	117	12	41-21	**.974**	-16	83	67	3b145,S3/2	—	0.2
1914	Phi N	135	505	83	139	24	5	1	52	49	3	32	.275	.343	.349	99	1	31	**.943**	-23	68	52	3b133,S2	—	-2.1
1915	NY N	106	386	46	97	18	4	0	38	25	4	24	.251	.304	.319	94	-3	14-15	.950	-4	95	65	3b103	—	-0.7
1916	NY N	48	76	6	17	3	2	0	11	5	0	8	.224	.272	.316	84	-2	2	.961	2	115	97	3b20	—	0.0
1917	NY N	50	52	4	10	1	0	1	5	5	1	5	.192	.276	.269	70	-2	2	.906	1	114	167	3b21	—	-0.1
Total	14	1317	4563	640	1252	159	82	32	482	395	38	156	.274	.337	.366	109	45	316-36	.944	-123	85	74	3b1000,S214,O23(21/2/0),2b12	—	-5.3

YEAR	TM LG	G	AB	R	H	2B	3B	HR	RBI	BB-IB	HP	SO	AVG	OBP	SLG	AOPS	ABR	SB-CS	FA	FR	RNG	THR	GAMES AT POSITION	DL	BFW
LOCHHEAD, HARRY Robert Henry; B3.29.1876 Stockton CA; D8.22.1909 Stockton CA; BR/TR/5′11″/172; d4.16																									
1899	Cle N	148	541	52	129	7	1	1	43	21	10	—	.238	.280	.261	52	-36	23	.909	12	104	78	S146/2P	—	-1.5
1901	Det A	1	4	2	2	0	0	0	0	0	1	—	.500	.600	.500	198	1	0	.857	-0	108	0	/S	—	0.0
	Phi A	9	34	3	3	0	0	0	2	3	0	—	.088	.162	.088	-28	-6	0	.757	-6	71	33	S9	—	-1.1
	Year	10	38	5	5	0	0	0	2	3	1	—	.132	.214	.132	-3	-5	0	.773	-6	76	29	S10	—	-1.1
Total	2	158	579	57	134	7	1	1	45	24	11	—	.231	.275	.252	48	-41	23	.903	6	102	75	S156/P2	—	-2.6
LOCK, DON Don Wilson; B7.27.1936 Wichita KS; BR/TR/6′2″/(195–205); d7.17; Col Wichita St.																									
1962	Was A	71	225	30	57	6	2	12	37	30-0	0	63	.253	.336	.458	114	4	4-5	.973	3	111	52	O67(67/1/0)	0	0.2
1963	Was A	149	531	71	134	20	1	27	82	70-3	2	151	.252	.338	.446	119	14	7-3	.980	6	109	144	O146(10/135/9)	0	1.7
1964	Was A	152	512	73	127	17	4	28	80	79-3	1	137	.248	.346	.461	124	17	4-2	.987	9	105	182	O149(0/135/25)	0	2.2
1965	Was A	143	418	52	90	15	1	16	39	57-4	5	115	.215	.315	.371	96	-1	1-3	.969	-1	101	115	O136C	0	-0.7
1966	Was A	138	386	52	90	13	1	16	48	57-5	2	126	.233	.333	.396	110	6	2-6	.977	5	112	115	O129(0/126/4)	0	0.6
1967	Phi N	112	313	46	79	13	1	14	51	43-4	5	98	.252	.349	.435	123	10	9-5	.973	-0	93	172	O97(1/96/1)	0	0.9
1968	Phi N	99	248	27	52	7	2	8	34	26-0	0	64	.210	.283	.351	90	-3	3-4	.955	-0	110	45	O78(8/46/27)	0	-0.8
1969	Phi N	4	4	0	0	0	0	0	0	0-0	0	1	.000	.000	.000	-99	-1	0-0	ø	-0	0	0	/lf	0	-0.1
	Bos A	53	58	8	13	1	0	1	2	11-0	0	21	.224	.348	.293	77	-1	0-1	1.000	-1	89	0	O28(15/9/4),1b4	0	-0.3
Total	8	921	2695	359	642	92	12	122	373	373-19	15	776	.238	.331	.417	111	45	30-29	.976	21	105	127	O831(102/684/70),1b4	0	3.7
LOCKE, MARSHALL Marshall Pinkney Wilder; B3.12.1857 Ashland OH; D3.6.1940 Ashland OH; d7.5																									
1884	Ind AA	7	29	5	7	0	1	0	5	0	0	—	.241	.241	.310	81	-1	—	.800	-1	87	0	O7(0/3/4)	—	-0.1
LOCKHART, KEITH Keith Virgil; B11.10.1964 Whittier CA; BL/TR/5′10″/170; [CinN86 11/280]; d4.5; Col Oral Roberts																									
1994	SD N	27	43	4	9	0	0	2	6	4-0	1	10	.209	.286	.349	68	-2	1-0	1.000	1	56	0	3b13,2b5/Srf	0	-0.1
1995	KC A	94	274	41	88	19	3	6	33	14-2	4	21	.321	.355	.478	114	5	8-1	.974	4	109	134	2b61,3b17,D14	0	1.2
1996	KC A	138	433	49	118	33	3	7	55	30-4	2	40	.273	.319	.411	83	-11	11-6	.975	-5	106	121	2b84,3b55/D	0	-1.1
1997	†Atl N	96	147	25	41	5	3	6	32	14-0	1	17	.279	.337	.476	111	2	0-0	.983	-2	100	124	2b20,3b11,D4	16	0.0
1998	†Atl N	109	366	50	94	21	0	9	37	29-0	1	37	.257	.311	.388	84	-9	2-2	.984	6	109	117	2b97/3D	0	0.1
1999	†Atl N	108	161	20	42	3	1	1	21	19-0	1	21	.261	.337	.311	67	-8	3-1	1.000	-1	111	97	2b25,3b10,D4	0	-0.8
2000	†Atl N	113	275	32	73	12	3	2	32	29-7	0	31	.265	.331	.353	75	-11	4-1	.979	3	111	90	2b74,3b18	0	-0.4
2001	†Atl N	104	178	17	39	6	0	3	12	16-1	2	22	.219	.289	.303	53	-13	1-2	1.000	-6	89	98	2b47,3b4	0	-1.7
2002	†Atl N	128	296	34	64	13	3	5	32	27-9	1	50	.216	.282	.331	61	-17	0-1	.979	5	116	101	2b89/3	0	-0.9
2003	SD N	62	95	18	23	5	1	3	8	13-0	1	19	.242	.339	.411	104	1	0-1	.986	-3	75	78	2b27,3b3	59	-0.2
Total	10	979	2268	290	591	117	17	44	268	195-23	14	268	.261	.319	.385	82	-63	30-15	.981	3	107	109	2b529,3b133,D25/rfS	75	-3.9
LOCKLEAR, GENE Gene; B7.19.1949 Lumberton NC; BL/TR/5′10″/165; d4.5																									
1973	Cin N	29	26	6	5	0	0	0	0	2-0	1	5	.192	.276	.192	33	-2	0-0	1.000	-1	71	0	O5(1/0/4)	0	-0.3
	SD N	67	154	20	37	6	1	3	25	21-1	0	22	.240	.330	.351	97	0	9-4	.952	2	103	78	O37L	0	0.0
	Year	96	180	26	42	6	1	3	25	23-1	1	27	.233	.322	.328	87	-3	9-4	.954	1	101	72	O42(38/0/4)	0	-0.3
1974	SD N	39	74	7	20	3	2	1	3	4-0	0	12	.270	.308	.405	103	0	0-1	1.000	0	97	121	O12(8/0/4)	0	-0.1
1975	SD N	100	237	31	76	11	1	5	27	22-4	1	26	.321	.378	.439	136	11	4-2	.970	-0	97	106	O51(50/0/2)	0	0.9
1976	SD N	43	67	9	15	3	0	0	8	4-1	0	15	.224	.264	.269	57	-4	0-0	.952	-1	103	0	O11L	0	-0.5
	NY A	13	32	2	7	1	0	0	1	2-0	0	7	.219	.265	.250	51	-2	0-0	1.000	-1	70	0	O3L,D6	0	-0.3
1977	NY A	1	5	1	3	0	0	0	2	0-0	0	0	.600	.600	.600	230	1	0-0	.667	-0	111	0	/lf	0	0.1
Total	5	292	595	76	163	24	4	9	66	55-6	2	87	.274	.335	.373	105	4	13-7	.962	0	98	83	O120(111/0/10),D6	0	-0.2
LOCKLIN, STU Stuart Carlton; B7.22.1928 Appleton WI; BL/TL/6′1.5″/190; d6.23; Col Wisconsin–Madison																									
1955	Cle A	16	18	4	3	1	0	0	0	3-0	0	4	.167	.286	.222	37	-2	0-0	1.000	-0	65	0	O7(0/4/3)	0	-0.2
1956	Cle A	9	6	0	1	0	0	0	0	0-0	0	1	.167	.167	.167	-12	-1	0-0	1.000	0	151	0	/rf	0	-0.1
Total	2	25	24	4	4	1	0	0	0	3-0	0	5	.167	.259	.208	26	-3	0-0	1.000	-0	77	0	O8(0/4/4)	0	-0.3
LOCKMAN, WHITEY Carroll Walter; B7.25.1926 Lowell NC; BL/TR/6′1″/(175–180); d7.5; Mil 1945–46; M3/C7																									
1945	NY N	32	129	16	44	9	0	3	18	13	2	10	.341	.410	.481	145	8	1	.961	-4	87	40	O32C	0	0.4
1947	NY N	2	2	0	1	0	0	0	1	0	0	0	.500	.500	.500	165	0	0	ø	0	—	—	/H	0	0.0
1948	NY N	146	584	117	167	24	10	18	59	68	1	63	.286	.361	.454	119	14	8	.987	-3	102	52	O144(53/91/0)	0	0.5
1949	NY N	151	617	97	186	32	7	11	65	62	3	31	.301	.368	.429	113	12	12	.973	1	104	78	O151L	0	0.2
1950	NY N	129	532	72	157	28	5	6	52	42	2	29	.295	.349	.400	96	-3	1	.978	4	103	109	O128(123/6/0)	0	-0.9
1951	†NY N	153	614	85	173	27	7	12	73	50	3	32	.282	.339	.407	99	-2	4-5	.986	0	104	111	1b119,O34L	0	-0.9
1952	NY N★	**154**	606	99	176	17	4	13	58	67	2	52	.290	.363	.396	110	9	2-4	.992	2	105	115	1b154	0	0.5
1953	NY N	150	607	85	179	22	4	9	61	52	0	36	.295	.351	.389	91	-8	3-4	.989	5	114	88	1b120,O30(0/3/28)	0	-1.1
1954	†NY N	148	570	73	143	17	3	16	60	59	0	31	.251	.318	.375	80	-17	2-2	.987	-7	85	97	1b145,O2(1/1/0)	0	-3.3
1955	NY N	147	576	76	157	19	0	15	49	39-2	3	34	.273	.320	.384	86	-12	3-3	.983	-4	105	68	O81(79/2/1),1b68	0	-2.5
1956	NY N	48	169	13	46	7	1	1	10	16-2	0	17	.272	.333	.343	83	-4	0-2	.960	-1	95	122	O39(38/1/1),1b7	0	-0.8
	StL N	70	193	14	48	0	2	0	10	18-4	0	8	.249	.311	.269	59	-11	2-2	.955	-4	94	56	O57(32/23/8),1b2	0	-1.9
	Year	118	362	27	94	7	3	1	20	34-6	0	25	.260	.322	.304	70	-15	2-4	.957	-5	94	85	O96(70/24/9),1b9	0	-2.7
1957	NY N	133	456	51	113	9	4	7	30	39-3	2	19	.248	.308	.331	73	-18	5-5	.991	-1	98	114	1b102,O27(22/3/4)	0	-2.7
1958	SF N	92	122	15	29	5	0	2	7	13-4	0	8	.238	.311	.328	71	-5	0-0	1.000	-2	101	0	O25(23/0/4),2b15,1b7	0	-0.8
1959	Bal A	38	69	7	15	1	1	0	2	8-0	0	4	.217	.299	.261	56	-4	0-0	.992	-1	37	126	1b22,2b5/rf	0	-0.6
	Cin N	52	84	10	22	5	1	0	7	4-0	0	6	.262	.292	.345	68	-4	0-0	.971	-2	124	95	1b20,2b6/3cf	0	-0.6
1960	Cin N	21	10	6	2	0	0	1	1	2-0	1	3	.200	.385	.500	138	1	0-0	1.000	-0	0	171	1b5	0	0.0
Total	15	1666	5940	836	1658	222	49	114	563	552-15	19	383	.279	.342	.391	95	-44	43-27	.989	-16	96	104	1b771,O752(556/163/47),2b26/3	0	-14.5
LOCKWOOD, SKIP Claude Edward; B8.17.1946 Boston MA; BR/TR/6′0″/(180–200); d4.23; ▲																									
1965	KC A	42	33	4	4	0	0	0	0	7-0	1	11	.121	.293	.121	23	-3	0-0	1.000	0	62	147	3b7	0	-0.3
1969	Sea A	6	7	0	0	0	0	0	0	0-0	0	2	.000	.000	.000	-99	-1	0-0	1.000	0	145	330	P6	0	0.0
1970	Mil A	27	53	2	12	1	0	1	2	1-0	0	11	.226	.236	.302	49	2	0-0	.970	-2	71	56	P27	0	0.0
1971	Mil A	36	62	2	5	1	0	1	4	5-0	0	20	.081	.149	.145	-17	-1	0-0	**1.000**	-3	54	98	P33	0	0.0
1972	Mil A	31	53	3	7	0	0	0	0	3-0	1	12	.132	.193	.132	-2	-1	0-1	.958	-3	49	50	P29	0	0.0
1973	Mil A	37	0	0	0	0	0	0	0	0-0	0	0	ø	ø	ø	ø	0	0-0	.944	-0	98	56	P37	0	0.0
1974	Cal A	37	0	0	0	0	0	0	0	0-0	0	0	ø	ø	ø	ø	0	0-0	1.000	-0	93	116	P37	0	0.0
1975	NY N	24	6	0	1	0	0	0	1	0-0	0	0	.167	.167	.167	-8	0	0-0	.800	-1	42	0	P24	0	0.0
1976	NY N	56	18	2	6	1	0	0	2	2-0	0	3	.333	.400	.389	130	3	0-1	.867	-0	78	139	P56	0	0.0
1977	NY N	63	15	1	3	0	0	0	1	0-0	0	1	.200	.200	.200	8	0	0-0	.875	-2	38	0	P63	0	0.0
1978	NY N	57	11	1	2	1	0	1	1	0-0	0	5	.182	.182	.545	99	1	0-0	.900	-2	35	106	P57	0	0.0
1979	NY N	28	2	0	0	0	0	0	0	0-0	0	1	.000	.000	.000	-99	0	0-0	.800	-1	50	220	P27	103	0.0
1980	Bos A	24	0	0	0	0	0	0	0	0-0	0	0	ø	ø	ø	ø	0	0-0	1.000	-1	44	0	P24	0	0.0
Total	13	468	260	15	40	4	0	3	11	18-0	2	66	.154	.214	.204	19	0	0-2	.947	-13	64	78	P420,3b7	103	-0.3
LOCKWOOD, MILO Milo Hathaway; B4.7.1858 Solon OH; D10.9.1897 Economy PA; 5′10″/160; d4.17; ▲																									
1884	Was U	20	67	9	14	1	0	0	—	8	—	—	.209	.293	.224	61	-5	—	.773	1	46	284	O11(1/7/3),P11,3b3	—	-0.2
LODIGIANI, DARIO Dario Antonio; B6.6.1916 San Francisco CA; BR/TR/5′8″/150; d4.18; Mil 1943–45; C2																									
1938	Phi A	93	325	36	91	15	1	6	44	34	7	25	.280	.361	.388	90	-5	3-0	.953	-6	98	77	2b80,3b13	—	-0.4
1939	Phi A	121	393	46	102	22	4	6	44	42	4	18	.260	.337	.382	85	-9	2-0	.944	-3	104	43	3b89,2b28	—	-0.6
1940	Phi A	1	1	0	0	0	0	0	0	0	0	0	.000	.000	.000	-99	0	0-0	ø	0	—	—	/H	—	0.0
1941	Chi A	87	322	39	77	19	2	4	40	31	5	19	.239	.316	.348	76	-11	0-4	.962	4	99	146	3b86	0	-0.5
1942	Chi A	59	168	9	47	7	0	0	15	18	1	10	.280	.353	.321	92	-1	3-4	.944	4	117	55	3b43,2b7	0	0.4
1946	Chi A	44	155	12	38	8	0	0	13	16	2	14	.245	.324	.297	77	-4	4-0	.935	-3	99	45	3b44	0	-0.7
Total	6	405	1364	142	355	71	7	16	156	141	19	86	.260	.338	.358	84	-30	12-8	.947	-4	103	82	3b275,2b115	0	-1.8
LODUCA, PAUL Paul Anthony; B4.12.1972 Brooklyn NY; BR/TR/5′10″/(185–210); [LAN93 25/690]; d6.21; Col Arizona St.																									
1998	LA N	6	14	2	4	1	0	0	1	0-0	0	1	.286	.286	.357	71	-1	0-0	1.000	0	83	259	C4	0	0.0
1999	LA N	36	95	11	22	1	0	3	11	10-4	2	9	.232	.312	.337	69	-5	1-2	.990	0	103	119	C34	0	-0.3
2000	LA N	34	65	6	16	2	0	2	8	6-0	0	8	.246	.301	.369	74	-3	0-2	.992	4	117	206	C20,O8(7/0/2)/3	0	0.2
2001	LA N	125	460	71	147	28	0	25	90	39-2	6	30	.320	.374	.543	144	30	2-4	.991	-7	105	123	C99,1b33,O5(4/0/1)/D	22	2.5

YEAR	TM LG	G	AB	R	H	2B	3B	HR	RBI	BB-IB	HP	SO	AVG	OBP	SLG	AOPS	ABR	SB-CS	FA	FR	RNG	THR	GAMES AT POSITION	DL	BFW
2002	LA N	149	580	74	163	38	1	10	64	34-2	10	31	.281	.330	.402	97	-3	3-1	.992	2	83	116	C137,1b18,O9L	0	0.8
2003	LA N★	147	568	64	155	34	2	7	52	44-6	10	54	.273	.335	.377	88	-10	0-2	.987	**34**	74	**207**	C123,1b22,O6L	0	2.9
2004	LA N★	91	349	41	105	18	1	10	49	22-0	6	27	.301	.351	.444	106	3	2-4	.995	-3	77	130	C81,O9L,1b3	0	0.3
	Fla N	52	186	27	48	11	1	3	31	14-0	3	22	.258	.314	.376	83	-5	2-1	.997	-1	64	156	C49	0	-0.2
	Year	143	535	68	153	29	2	13	80	36-0	9	49	.286	.338	.421	98	-2	4-5	.996	-4	72	**140**	C130,O9L,1b3	0	0.1
2005	Fla N★	132	445	45	126	23	1	6	57	34-5	4	31	.283	.334	.380	93	-5	4-3	.991	-8	68	118	C128	0	-0.5
2006	†NY N★	124	512	80	163	39	1	5	49	24-0	6	38	.318	.355	.428	102	2	3-0	.987	-10	79	103	C118,D3	0	0.1
Total	9	896	3274	421	949	195	7	71	412	227-19	47	251	.290	.341	.419	101	3	17-19	.991	12	81	136	C793,1b76,O37(35/0/3),D4/3	22	5.8
Loepp, George	George Herbert; B9.11.1901 Detroit MI; D9.4.1967 Los Angeles CA; BR/TR/5´11˝/170; d8.29																								
1928	Bos A	15	51	6	9	3	1	0	3	5	0	12	.176	.250	.275	38	-5	0-0	.949	0	103	128	O14(1/10/6)	—	-0.5
1930	Was A	50	134	23	37	7	1	0	14	20	3	9	.276	.382	.343	85	-2	0-4	.958	-1	97	109	O48(12/34/3)	—	-0.5
Total	2	65	185	29	46	10	2	0	17	25	3	21	.249	.347	.324	73	-7	0-4	.956	-0	99	114	O62(13/44/9)	—	-1.0
Lofton, James	James O'Neal; B3.6.1974 Los Angeles CA; BB/TR/5´10˝/170; [CinN93 13/372]; d9.19; Col Los Angeles (CA) City																								
2001	Bos A	8	26	1	5	1	0	0	1	1-0	0	4	.192	.214	.231	20	-3	2-1	.920	-1	84	78	S7	0	-0.4
Lofton, Kenny	Kenneth; B5.31.1967 E.Chicago IN; BL/TL/6´0˝/(180–190); [HouN88 17/428]; d9.14; Col Arizona																								
1991	Hou N	20	74	9	15	1	0	0	0	5-0	0	19	.203	.253	.216	35	-7	2-1	.977	-0	101	107	O20C	0	-0.7
1992	Cle A	148	576	96	164	15	8	5	42	68-3	2	54	.285	.362	.365	105	5	**66**-12	.982	7	104	170	O143C	0	2.1
1993	Cle A	148	569	116	185	28	8	1	42	81-6	1	83	.325	.408	.408	120	20	**70**-14	.979	5	105	138	O146C	0	3.6
1994	Cle A★	112	459	105	**160**	32	9	12	57	52-5	2	56	.349	.412	.536	142	30	**60**-12	.993	1	91	214	O112C	0	3.8
1995	†Cle A★	118	481	93	149	22	**13**	7	53	40-6	1	49	.310	.362	.453	109	5	**54**-15	.970	-5	86	197	O114C,D2	15	0.8
1996	†Cle A★	154	662	132	210	35	4	14	67	61-3	0	82	.317	.372	.446	106	7	**75**-17	.975	-5	95	138	O152C	0	1.3
1997	†Atl N✳	122	493	90	164	20	6	5	48	64-5	2	83	.333	.409	.428	119	16	27-20	.983	1	108	88	O122C	39	1.7
1998	†Cle A★	154	600	101	169	31	6	12	64	87-1	2	80	.282	.371	.413	101	3	54-10	.978	-4	86	**199**	O154C	0	0.9
1999	†Cle A★	120	465	110	140	28	6	7	39	79-2	6	84	.301	.405	.432	109	10	25-6	.989	-3	91	159	O119C/D	32	1.2
2000	Cle A	137	543	107	151	23	5	15	73	79-3	4	72	.278	.369	.422	98	-1	30-7	.989	3	109	64	O135C/D	14	0.7
2001	†Cle A	133	517	91	135	21	4	14	66	47-1	2	69	.261	.322	.398	86	-11	16-8	.981	-2	105	45	O130C	16	-1.0
2002	Chi A	93	352	68	91	20	6	8	42	49-0	0	51	.259	.348	.418	99	0	22-8	1.000	0	103	67	O92C	0	0.3
	†SF N	46	180	30	48	10	3	3	9	23-0	1	22	.267	.353	.406	102	1	7-3	1.000	3	113	126	O44C	0	0.4
2003	Pit N	84	339	58	94	19	4	9	26	28-1	2	29	.277	.333	.437	98	-1	18-5	1.000	1	101	107	O81C	0	0.2
	†Chi N	56	208	39	68	13	4	3	20	18-2	2	22	.327	.381	.471	119	6	12-4	.974	-1	99	116	O55C	0	0.7
	Year	140	547	97	162	32	8	12	46	46-3	4	51	.296	.352	.450	106	5	30-9	.991	-0	100	111	O136C	0	0.9
2004	†NY A	83	276	51	76	10	7	3	18	31-1	1	27	.275	.346	.395	94	-3	7-3	.989	4	109	117	O74(0/65/10),D4	30	0.2
2005	Phi N	110	367	67	123	15	5	2	36	32-2	2	41	.335	.392	.420	109	6	22-3	.981	3	103	166	O97C/D	17	1.3
2006	†LA N	129	469	79	141	15	12	3	41	45-1	0	42	.301	.360	.403	95	-4	32-5	.988	-9	89	74	O120C,D2	11	-0.6
Total	16	1967	7630	1442	2283	358	110	123	743	889-42	30	965	.299	.372	.423	106	82	599-153	.984	-3	99	131	O1910(0/1901/10),D11	174	16.9
Loftus, Dick	Richard Joseph; B3.7.1901 Concord MA; D1.21.1972 Concord MA; BL/TR/6´0˝/155; d4.20																								
1924	Bro N	46	81	18	22	6	0	0	8	7	0	2	.272	.330	.346	84	-2	1-0	1.000	1	111	49	O29(6/14/9)/1	—	-0.2
1925	Bro N	51	131	16	31	6	0	0	13	5	2	5	.237	.275	.282	44	-11	2-0	.977	2	114	83	O38(3/0/35)	—	-1.1
Total	2	97	212	34	53	12	0	0	21	12	2	7	.250	.296	.307	59	-13	3-0	.985	2	113	71	O67(9/14/44)/1	—	-1.3
Loftus, Tom	Thomas Joseph; B11.15.1856 St.Louis MO; D4.16.1910 Dubuque IA; BR/?/168; d8.17; M9																								
1877	StL N	3	11	2	2	0	0	0	0	0	—	1	.182	.182	.182	16	-1	—	.778	1	434	0	O3(1/0/2)	—	0.0
1883	StL AA	6	22	1	4	0	0	0	—	2	—	—	.182	.250	.182	39	-1	—	.882	-1	0	0	O6C	—	-0.2
Total	2	9	33	3	6	0	0	0	0	2	—	1	.182	.229	.182	32	-2	—	.846	1	148	0	O9(1/6/2)	—	-0.2
Logan, Nook	Exavier Prente; B11.28.1979 Natchez MS; BB/TR/6´2˝/180; [DetA00 3/78]; d7.21; Col Copiah–Lincoln (MS) CC																								
2004	Det A	47	133	12	37	5	2	0	10	13-0	0	24	.278	.340	.346	83	-3	8-2	.984	3	112	146	O46C	0	0.1
2005	Det A	129	322	47	83	12	5	1	17	21-3	1	52	.258	.305	.335	72	-14	23-6	.979	2	109	60	O123C,D3	0	-0.7
2006	Was N	27	90	13	27	3	1	1	8	6-1	0	20	.300	.337	.389	91	-1	2-1	.983	-2	94	0	O26C	0	-0.3
Total	3	203	545	72	147	20	8	2	35	40-4	1	96	.270	.319	.347	78	-18	33-9	.981	3	107	72	O195C,D3	0	-0.9
Logan, Johnny	John "Yatcha"; B3.23.1927 Endicott NY; BR/TR/5´11˝/(175–186); d4.17																								
1951	Bos N	62	169	14	37	7	1	0	16	18	1	13	.219	.298	.272	59	-10	0-0	.958	2	102	91	S58	0	-0.5
1952	Bos N	117	456	56	129	21	3	4	42	31	4	33	.283	.334	.368	98	-2	1-2	**.972**	13	**107**	99	S117	0	1.8
1953	Mil N	150	611	100	167	27	8	11	73	41	7	33	.273	.326	.398	93	-7	2-2	**.975**	21	105	**115**	S150	0	2.5
1954	Mil N	**154**	560	66	154	17	7	8	66	51	6	51	.275	.339	.373	92	-7	2-0	**.969**	13	103	107	S154	0	1.9
1955	Mil N★	**154**	595	95	177	**37**	5	13	83	58-1	4	58	.297	.360	.442	118	17	3-3	.963	5	108	97	S154	0	3.4
1956	Mil N	148	545	69	153	27	5	15	46	46-2	5	49	.281	.340	.431	113	10	3-0	.968	4	107	106	S148	0	2.7
1957	†Mil N☆	129	494	59	135	19	7	10	49	31-2	4	49	.273	.319	.401	100	-2	5-0	.960	**25**	**115**	114	S129	0	3.5
1958	†Mil N★	145	530	54	120	20	0	11	53	40-1	5	57	.226	.286	.326	68	-26	1-2	.959	18	**110**	112	S144	0	0.3
1959	Mil N☆	138	470	59	137	17	0	13	50	57-9	3	45	.291	.369	.411	118	14	1-3	.975	-1	101	97	S138	0	2.3
1960	Mil N	136	482	52	118	14	4	7	42	43-6	2	40	.245	.309	.334	82	-13	1-1	.956	-1	103	96	S136	0	-0.3
1961	Mil N	18	19	0	2	1	0	0	1	1-0	0	3	.105	.150	.158	-19	-3	0-0	1.000	-1	88	142	S2	0	-0.4
	Pit N	27	52	5	12	4	0	0	5	4-0	0	8	.231	.286	.308	57	-3	0-0	1.000	0	113	212	3b7,S6	0	-0.3
	Year	45	71	5	14	5	0	0	6	5-0	0	11	.197	.250	.268	38	-6	0-0	.964	-1	95	99	S8,3b7	0	-0.7
1962	Pit N	44	80	7	24	3	0	1	12	7-0	0	6	.300	.348	.375	96	0	0-0	.980	1	109	164	3b19	0	0.1
1963	Pit N	81	181	15	42	2	1	0	9	23-5	2	27	.232	.325	.254	69	-6	0-0	.920	-4	98	110	S44,3b4	0	-0.8
Total	13	1503	5244	651	1407	216	41	93	547	451-26	43	472	.268	.330	.378	95	-38	19-13	.965	93	106	104	S1380,3b30	0	16.2
Lohman, Pete	George F.; B10.21.1864 Washington Co. MN; D11.21.1928 Los Angeles CA; BR/TR; d5.11																								
1891	Was AA	32	109	18	21	1	4	1	11	16	1	17	.193	.302	.303	77	-4	1	.914	-3	*87*	*86*	C21,O8(1/1/6),3b4/S2	—	-0.4
Lohr, Howard	Howard Sylvester; B6.3.1892 Philadelphia PA; D6.9.1977 Philadelphia PA; BR/TR/6´0˝/165; d6.17																								
1914	Cin N	18	47	6	10	1	1	0	7	0	0	8	.213	.213	.277	44	-4	2	.926	-1	89	68	O17(0/17/1)	—	-0.6
1916	Cle A	3	7	0	1	0	0	0	1	0	0	1	.143	.143	.143	-13	-1	1	1.000	-0	104	0	O3R	—	-0.1
Total	2	21	54	6	11	1	1	0	8	0	0	9	.204	.204	.259	36	-5	3	.933	-1	91	59	O20(0/17/4)	—	-0.7
Lohrke, Jack	Jack Wayne "Lucky"; B2.25.1924 Los Angeles CA; BR/TR/6´0˝/(175–180); d4.18																								
1947	NY N	112	329	44	79	12	4	11	35	46	2	29	.240	.337	.401	95	-3	3	.939	-2	94	108	3b111	0	-0.5
1948	NY N	97	280	35	70	15	1	5	31	30	0	30	.250	.323	.364	85	-6	3	.898	-4	94	64	3b50,2b36	0	-0.8
1949	NY N	55	180	32	48	11	4	5	22	16	2	12	.267	.333	.456	110	2	3	.969	1	135	36	2b23,3b19,S15	0	0.5
1950	NY N	30	43	4	8	0	0	0	4	4	0	8	.186	.255	.186	18	-5	0	.958	0	101	145	3b16/2	0	-0.5
1951	†NY N	23	40	3	8	0	0	1	3	10	0	2	.200	.360	.275	73	-1	0-0	.943	-1	103	84	3b17/S	0	-0.2
1952	Phi N	25	29	4	6	0	0	0	1	4	0	3	.207	.303	.207	44	-2	0-0	1.000	1	113	123	S5,3b3/2	0	-0.1
1953	Phi N	12	13	3	2	0	0	0	0	1	0	2	.154	.214	.154	-2	-2	0-0	.750	0	178	0	2b2,S2/3	0	-0.2
Total	7	354	914	125	221	38	9	22	96	111	4	86	.242	.327	.375	87	-17	9-0	.928	-5	94	96	3b217,2b63,S23	0	-1.8
Lois, Alberto	Alberto (b Alberto Louis (Pie)); B5.6.1956 Hato Mayor, D.R.; BR/TR/5´9˝/(160–175); d9.8; [DL 1980 Pit N 133]																								
1978	Pit N	3	4	0	1	0	1	0	0	0-0	0	1	.250	.250	.750	162	0	0-0	1.000	0	160	0	O2(2/1/0)	0	0.0
1979	Pit N	11	0	6	0	0	0	0	0	0-0	0	0	ø	ø	ø	ø	0	1-1	ø	0	—	—	/R	0	0.0
Total	2	14	4	6	1	0	1	0	0	0-0	0	1	.250	.250	.750	162	0	1-1	1.000	0	160	0	O2(2/1/0)	133	0.0
Lolich, Ron	Ronald John; B9.19.1946 Portland OR; BR/TR/6´1˝/185; [ChiA65 8/197]; d7.18																								
1971	Chi A	2	8	0	1	1	0	0	0	0-0	0	2	.125	.125	.250	4	-1	0-0	1.000	-1	29	0	O2R	0	-0.2
1972	Cle A	24	80	4	15	1	0	2	8	4-1	0	20	.188	.224	.275	47	-6	0-0	1.000	-1	97	64	O22(4/0/19)	0	-0.9
1973	Cle A	61	140	16	32	7	0	2	15	7-0	0	27	.229	.265	.321	63	-7	0-2	.909	-2	80	121	O32(5/0/27),D12	0	-1.2
Total	3	87	228	20	48	9	0	4	23	11-1	0	49	.211	.246	.303	56	-14	0-2	.953	-4	86	91	O56(9/0/48),D12	0	-2.3
Lollar, Sherm	John Sherman; B8.23.1924 Durham AR; D9.24.1977 Springfield MO; BR/TR/6´1˝/(180–195); d4.20; C5; Col Pittsburg St. (KS)																								
1946	Cle A	28	62	7	15	6	0	1	9	5	0	9	.242	.299	.387	97	0	0-1	.990	-2	*106*	*114*	C24	0	-0.1
1947	†NY A	11	32	4	7	0	1	1	6	1	0	5	.219	.242	.375	71	-2	0-1	1.000	0	*89*	*44*	C9	0	-0.1
1948	NY A	22	38	0	8	0	0	0	4	1	0	6	.211	.231	.211	18	-5	0-0	.976	1	*109*	*118*	C10	0	-0.4

THE BATTER REGISTER

YEAR	TM LG	G	AB	R	H	2B	3B	HR	RBI	BB-IB	HP	SO	AVG	OBP	SLG	AOPS	ABR	SB-CS	FA	FR	RNG	THR	GAMES AT POSITION	DL	BFW
1949	StL A	109	284	28	74	9	1	8	49	32	2	22	.261	.340	.384	88	-6	0-1	.988	-2	98	107	C93	0	-0.4
1950	StL A☆	126	396	55	111	22	3	13	65	64	8	25	.280	.391	.449	110	8	2-0	.981	-4	93	**152**	C109	0	0.9
1951	StL A	98	310	44	78	21	0	8	44	43	4	26	.252	.350	.397	99	0	1-0	**.995**	-3	91	**138**	C85/3	0	0.2
1952	Chi A	132	375	35	90	15	0	13	50	54	12	34	.240	.354	.384	104	4	1-0	.989	-3	71	80	C120	0	0.7
1953	Chi A	113	334	46	96	19	0	8	54	47	8	29	.287	.388	.416	114	9	1-0	**.994**	1	85	106	C107/1	0	1.5
1954	Chi A☆	107	316	31	77	13	0	7	34	37	7	28	.244	.334	.351	85	-5	0-1	.993	2	113	107	C93	0	0.0
1955	Chi A☆	138	426	67	111	13	1	16	61	68-12	10	34	.261	.374	.408	108	7	2-2	.995	12	119	84	C136	0	2.5
1956	Chi A★	136	450	55	132	28	2	11	75	53-4	16	34	.293	.383	.438	116	13	2-0	**.993**	3	**145**	67	C132	0	2.1
1957	Chi A	101	351	33	90	11	2	11	70	35-2	13	24	.256	.342	.393	101	1	2-0	.998	3	95	91	C96	0	1.0
1958	Chi A☆	127	421	53	115	16	0	20	84	57-3	8	37	.273	.367	.454	128	18	2-1	.987	3	89	92	C116	0	2.7
1959	†Chi A★	140	505	63	134	22	3	22	84	55-6	9	49	.265	.345	.451	119	13	4-3	.993	10	84	**116**	C122,1b24	0	2.7
1960	Chi A★	129	421	43	106	23	0	7	46	42-3	8	39	.252	.326	.356	87	-7	2-0	**.995**	4	120	127	C123	0	0.4
1961	Chi A	116	337	38	95	10	1	7	41	37-10	6	22	.282	.360	.380	100	1	0-0	**.998**	-7	113	121	C107	0	-0.1
1962	Chi A	84	220	17	59	12	0	2	26	32-9	3	23	.268	.369	.350	95	0	1-0	.991	-7	74	99	C66	34	-0.3
1963	Chi A	35	73	4	17	4	0	0	6	8-0	1	7	.233	.317	.288	72	-2	0-0	.981	-2	118	172	C23,1b2	0	-0.3
Total	18	1752	5351	623	1415	244	14	155	808	671-49	115	453	.264	.357	.402	104	47	20-10	.992	10	101	106	C1571,1b27/3	34	13.0
LOMAN, DOUG	Douglas Edward; B5.9.1958 Bakersfield CA; BL/TL/5´11˝/185; [MilA78*2/33]; d9.3; Col Bakersfield (CA) JC																								
1984	Mil A	23	76	13	21	4	0	2	12	15-2	1	7	.276	.402	.408	129	4	0-2	.967	3	108	249	O23(21/0/4)	0	0.5
1985	Mil A	24	66	10	14	3	2	0	7	1-0	0	12	.212	.221	.318	46	-5	0-0	1.000	3	100	344	O20(0/8/15)	0	-0.3
Total	2	47	142	23	35	7	2	2	19	16-2	1	19	.246	.325	.366	92	-1	0-2	.981	6	105	290	O43(21/8/19)	0	0.2
LOMASNEY, STEVE	Steven James; B8.29.1977 Melrose MA; BR/TR/6´0˝/195; [BosA95 5/130]; d10.3																								
1999	Bos A	1	2	0	0	0	0	0	0	0-0	0	2	.000	.000	.000	-97	-1	0-0	1.000	2	0	1103	/C	0	0.1
LOMBARD, GEORGE	George Paul; B9.14.1975 Atlanta GA; BL/TR/6´0˝/(208–212); [AtlN94 2/61]; d9.4; [DL 2001 Atl N 190, 2002 Atl N 80]																								
1998	Atl N	6	6	2	2	0	0	1	1	0-0	0	1	.333	.333	.833	195	1	1-0	1.000	-0	87	0	O2R	0	0.1
1999	Atl N	6	6	1	2	0	0	0	0	1-0	0	2	.333	.429	.333	97	0	2-0	1.000	0	129	0	O4(2/0/2)	0	0.0
2000	Atl N	27	39	8	4	0	0	0	2	1-0	1	14	.103	.146	.103	-36	-8	4-0	1.000	0	93	170	O15(5/0/11)	0	-0.7
2002	Det A	72	241	34	58	11	3	5	13	20-1	1	78	.241	.300	.373	81	-7	13-2	.982	-2	100	54	O69(29/40/1),D2	0	-0.7
2003	TB A	13	37	8	8	1	0	1	4	0-0	1	6	.216	.237	.324	47	-3	1-0	.964	1	121	160	O13(3/0/11)	0	-0.2
2006	Was N	20	21	2	3	0	0	1	1	5-0	0	10	.143	.308	.286	56	-1	2-0	.933	1	142	412	O8(3/0/5)	0	0.0
Total	6	144	350	55	77	12	3	8	21	27-1	3	111	.220	.281	.340	65	-18	23-2	.978	1	104	94	O111(42/40/32),D2	270	-1.5
LOMBARDI, ERNIE	Ernesto Natali "Schnozz","Bocci"; B4.6.1908 Oakland CA; D9.26.1977 Santa Cruz CA; BR/TR/6´3˝/230; d4.15; HF1986																								
1931	Bro N	73	182	20	54	7	1	4	23	12	0	12	.297	.340	.412	102	0	1	.984	1	105	80	C50	—	0.4
1932	Cin N	118	413	43	125	22	9	11	68	41	4	19	.303	.371	.479	131	18	0	.963	-9	91	115	C110	—	1.6
1933	Cin N	107	350	30	99	21	1	4	47	16	4	17	.283	.322	.383	102	1	2	.972	-9	94	94	C95	—	-0.3
1934	Cin N	132	417	42	127	19	4	9	62	16	3	22	.305	.335	.434	107	2	0	.989	-2	99	95	C111	—	0.7
1935	Cin N	120	332	36	114	23	3	12	64	16	3	6	.343	.379	.539	148	22	0	.983	-4	88	121	C82	—	2.2
1936	Cin N☆	121	387	42	129	23	2	12	68	19	7	16	.333	.375	.496	142	22	1	.962	-9	96	94	C105	—	1.8
1937	Cin N☆	120	368	41	123	22	1	9	59	14	2	17	.334	.362	.473	132	15	1	.973	-12	74	109	C90	—	0.8
1938	Cin N★	129	489	60	167	30	1	19	95	40	0	14	**.342**	.391	.524	154	35	0	.985	-2	**127**	102	C123	—	4.1
1939	†Cin N★	130	450	43	129	26	2	20	85	35	3	19	.287	.342	.487	120	11	0	.984	1	113	111	C120	—	1.9
1940	†Cin N★	109	376	50	120	22	0	14	74	31	7	14	.319	.382	.489	137	20	0	.989	-1	113	60	C101	—	2.5
1941	Cin N	117	398	33	105	12	1	10	60	36	0	14	.264	.325	.374	96	-3	1	.983	-4	77	117	C116	0	0.0
1942	Bos N★	105	309	32	102	14	0	11	46	37	1	12	**.330**	.403	.482	162	25	1	.980	-12	76	92	C85	0	1.8
1943	NY N★	104	295	19	90	7	0	10	51	16	3	11	.305	.347	.431	123	7	1	.971	-10	80	88	C73	0	0.2
1944	NY N	117	373	37	95	13	0	10	58	33	1	25	.255	.317	.370	93	-4	0	.968	-9	105	90	C100	0	-0.8
1945	NY N✳	115	368	46	113	7	1	19	70	43	5	11	.307	.387	.486	140	19	0	.983	3	**160**	88	C96	0	2.8
1946	NY N	88	238	19	69	4	1	12	39	18	3	24	.290	.347	.466	129	8	0	.978	-0	87	110	C63	0	1.1
1947	NY N	48	110	8	31	5	0	4	21	7	0	9	.282	.325	.436	100	0	0	.980	-1	163	96	C24	0	-0.1
Total	17	1853	5855	601	1792	277	27	190	990	430	46	262	.306	.358	.460	126	198	8	.979	-78	102	99	C1544	0	20.7
LOMBARDI, PHIL	Phillip Arden; B2.20.1963 Abilene TX; BR/TR/6´2˝/(200–205); [NYA81 3/77]; d4.26																								
1986	NY A	20	36	6	10	3	0	2	6	4-0	1	7	.278	.366	.528	140	2	0-0	.867	0	100	255	O8L,C3	0	0.2
1987	NY A	5	8	0	1	0	0	0	0	0-0	0	2	.125	.125	.125	-34	-2	0-0	1.000	1	61	367	C3	0	-0.1
1989	NY N	18	48	4	11	1	0	1	3	5-0	0	8	.229	.302	.313	79	-1	0-0	.980	-2	56	22	C16/1	0	-0.3
Total	3	43	92	10	22	4	0	3	9	9-0	1	17	.239	.314	.380	95	-1	0-0	.975	-1	56	38	C22,O8L/1	0	-0.2
LOMBARDOZZI, STEVE	Stephen Paul; B4.26.1960 Malden MA; BR/TR/6´0˝/(175–183); [MinA81 9/218]; d7.12; Col Florida																								
1985	Min A	28	54	10	20	4	1	0	6	6-0	0	6	.370	.426	.481	141	3	3-2	.982	5	130	117	2b26	0	0.9
1986	Min A	156	453	53	103	20	5	8	33	52-2	1	76	.227	.308	.347	76	-15	3-1	**.991**	7	102	106	2b155	0	0.0
1987	†Min A	136	432	51	103	19	3	8	38	33-1	4	66	.238	.298	.352	69	-20	5-1	.977	-2	97	94	2b133	0	-1.4
1988	Min A	103	287	34	60	15	2	3	27	35-2	2	48	.209	.295	.307	68	-12	2-5	.986	-9	95	94	2b90,S12,3b5	0	-1.9
1989	Hou N	21	37	5	8	3	1	1	3	4-1	0	9	.216	.293	.432	108	0	0-0	.922	-4	82	77	2b18/3	0	-0.4
1990	Hou N	2	1	0	0	0	0	0	0	1-0	0	1	.000	.500	.000	51	0	0-0	ø	0	—	—	/H	43	0.0
Total	6	446	1264	153	294	61	12	20	107	131-6	7	206	.233	.307	.347	75	-44	13-9	.983	-2	100	99	2b422,S12,3b6	43	-2.8
LONERGAN, WALTER	Walter E.; B9.22.1885 Boston MA; D1.23.1958 Lexington MA; BR/TR/5´7˝/156; d8.17																								
1911	Bos A	10	26	2	7	0	0	0	1	1	0	—	.269	.296	.269	59	-2	1	.935	-1	80	104	2b7/S3	—	-0.2
LONEY, JAMES	James Anthony; B5.7.1984 Houston TX; BL/TL/6´0˝/200; [LAN02 1/19]; d4.4																								
2006	†LA N	48	102	20	29	6	5	4	18	8-1	1	10	.284	.342	.559	125	3	1-0	.996	-1	92	79	1b39,O2R	0	0.0
LONG	; d8.29																								
1888	Lou AA	1	2	0	0	0	0	0	0	1	0	—	.000	.333	.000	11	0	0	ø	0	0	0	/rf	—	0.0
LONG, DAN	Daniel W.; B8.27.1867 Boston MA; D4.30.1929 Sausalito CA; d8.27																								
1890	Bal AA	21	77	19	12	0	0	0	2	14	2	—	.156	.301	.156	33	-6	16	.939	0	159	0	O21C	—	-0.6
LONG, HERMAN	Herman C. "Germany","Flying Dutchman"; B4.13.1866 Chicago IL; D9.17.1909 Denver CO; BL/TR/5´8.5˝/160; d4.17																								
1889	KC AA	136	574	137	158	32	6	3	60	64	10	63	.275	.358	.368	101	1	89	.874	31	108	110	S128,2b8/lf	—	3.0
1890	Bos N	101	431	95	108	15	3	8	52	40	4	34	.251	.320	.355	90	-7	49	.898	7	100	121	S101	—	0.2
1891	Bos N	139	577	129	163	21	12	9	75	80	8	51	.282	.377	.407	115	10	60	.902	15	95	**143**	S139	—	2.6
1892	†Bos N	151	646	115	181	33	6	6	78	44	8	36	.280	.334	.378	105	2	57	.889	15	105	**145**	S141,O12(11/1/0)/3	—	2.2
1893	Bos N	128	552	**149**	159	22	6	6	58	73	5	32	.288	.376	.382	94	-5	38	.883	16	110	**144**	S123,2b5	—	1.4
1894	Bos N	104	475	136	154	28	11	12	79	35	4	17	.324	.375	.505	103	-1	24	.885	1	105	125	S98,O5L,2b3	—	0.3
1895	Bos N	125	540	109	170	23	10	9	75	31	3	13	.315	.355	.444	98	-5	36	.892	-13	94	100	S123,2b2	—	-1.0
1896	Bos N	120	502	106	173	26	8	6	101	26	5	16	.345	.383	.464	116	10	38	.897	9	103	110	S120	—	2.1
1897	†Bos N	107	450	89	145	32	7	3	69	23	2	—	.322	.358	.444	105	1	22	.905	-3	97	109	S107/lf	—	0.3
1898	Bos N	144	589	99	156	21	10	6	99	39	0	—	.265	.311	.365	89	-12	20	.923	-1	97	124	S142,2b2	—	-0.5
1899	Bos N	145	578	91	153	30	8	6	100	45	3	—	.265	.321	.375	83	-16	20	.929	-15	87	**138**	S143,1b2	—	-2.1
1900	Bos N	125	486	80	127	19	4	**12**	66	44	2	—	.261	.325	.391	86	-11	26	.937	-8	99	71	S125	—	-1.1
1901	Bos N	138	518	54	112	14	6	3	68	25	1	—	.216	.254	.284	51	-34	20	**.946**	-7	97	112	S138	—	-3.6
1902	Bos N	120	437	40	101	11	0	2	44	31	1	—	.231	.284	.270	70	-15	24	**.946**	20	103	123	S107,2b13	—	0.9
1903	NY A	22	80	6	15	3	0	0	8	2	0	—	.188	.207	.225	28	-7	3	.889	-4	87	83	S22	—	-1.1
	Det A	69	239	21	53	12	0	0	23	10	1	—	.222	.256	.272	60	-11	11	.879	-1	88	89	S38,2b31	—	-1.2
	Year	91	319	27	68	15	0	0	31	12	1	—	.213	.244	.260	52	-18	14	.883	-5	88	87	S60,2b31	—	-2.3
1904	Phi N	1	4	0	1	0	0	0	0	0	0	—	.250	.250	.250	56	0	0	.889	0	102	0	/2	—	0.0
Total	16	1875	7678	1456	2129	342	97	91	1055	612	57	262	.277	.335	.383	93	-100	537	.906	63	99	119	S1795,2b65,O19(18/1/0),1b2/3	—	2.4
LONG, JIMMIE	James Albert; B6.29.1898 Ft.Dodge IA; D9.14.1970 Ft.Dodge IA; BR/TR/5´11˝/160; d9.12																								
1922	Chi A	3	3	0	0	0	0	0	0	1	0	0	.000	.250	.000	-30	-1	0-0	1.000	-0	0	0	C2	—	-0.1

YEAR	TM LG	G	AB	R	H	2B	3B	HR	RBI	BB-IB	HP	SO	AVG	OBP	SLG	AOPS	ABR	SB-CS	FA	FR	RNG	THR	GAMES AT POSITION	DL	BFW

LONG, JIM James M.; B11.15.1862 Louisville KY; D12.12.1932 Louisville KY; 5´10˝/160; d8.9

YEAR	TM LG	G	AB	R	H	2B	3B	HR	RBI	BB-IB	HP	SO	AVG	OBP	SLG	AOPS	ABR	SB-CS	FA	FR	RNG	THR	GAMES AT POSITION	DL	BFW
1891	Lou AA	6	25	5	6	0	0	0	4	3	2	6	.240	.367	.240	75	0	1	.857	1	186	435	O6(4/2/0)	—	0.0
1893	Bal N	55	226	31	48	8	1	2	25	16	4	27	.212	.276	.283	48	-18	23	.893	-1	86	48	O55L	—	-1.9
Total	2	61	251	36	54	8	1	2	29	19	6	33	.215	.286	.279	51	-18	24	.890	0	96	86	O61(59/2/0)	—	-1.9

LONG, JEOFF Jeffrey Keith; B10.9.1941 Covington KY; BR/TR/6´1˝/200; d7.31

YEAR	TM LG	G	AB	R	H	2B	3B	HR	RBI	BB-IB	HP	SO	AVG	OBP	SLG	AOPS	ABR	SB-CS	FA	FR	RNG	THR	GAMES AT POSITION	DL	BFW
1963	StL N	5	5	0	1	0	0	0	0	0-0	0	1	.200	.200	.200	14	-1	0-0	ø	0	—	—	/H	0	-0.1
1964	StL N	28	43	5	10	1	0	1	4	6-0	1	18	.233	.340	.326	81	-1	0-0	.833	-1	88	0	O4R,1b3	0	-0.3
	Chi A	23	35	0	5	0	0	0	5	4-0	0	15	.143	.225	.143	7	-4	0-0	1.000	0	207	142	1b5,O5L	0	-0.5
Total	2	56	83	5	16	1	0	1	9	10-0	1	34	.193	.284	.241	48	-6	0-0	.750	-1	82	0	O9(5/0/4),1b8	0	-0.9

LONG, DALE Richard Dale; B2.6.1926 Springfield MO; D1.27.1991 Palm Coast FL; BL/TL/6´4˝/(210–215); d4.21; C1

YEAR	TM LG	G	AB	R	H	2B	3B	HR	RBI	BB-IB	HP	SO	AVG	OBP	SLG	AOPS	ABR	SB-CS	FA	FR	RNG	THR	GAMES AT POSITION	DL	BFW
1951	Pit N	10	12	1	2	0	0	1	1	0	0	3	.167	.167	.417	50	-1	0-0	1.000	-0	0	0	/1	0	-0.1
	StL A	34	105	11	25	5	1	2	11	10	1	22	.238	.310	.362	79	-3	0-0	.988	-1	96	74	1b28/lf	0	-0.5
1955	Pit N	131	419	59	122	19	**13**	16	79	48-6	1	72	.291	.362	.513	132	18	0-1	.988	6	120	105	1b119	0	1.7
1956	Pit N★	148	517	64	136	20	7	27	91	54-11	0	85	.263	.326	.485	119	12	1-0	.982	-4	94	80	1b138	0	0.0
1957	Pit N	7	22	0	4	1	0	0	5	4-0	0	10	.182	.296	.227	48	-1	0-0	1.000	0	113	125	1b7	0	-0.2
	Chi N	123	397	55	121	19	0	21	62	52-4	1	63	.305	.383	.511	141	24	1-1	.995	-2	88	89	1b104	0	1.6
	Year	130	419	55	125	20	0	21	67	56-4	1	73	.298	.378	.496	136	23	1-1	.995	-2	89	91	1b111	0	1.4
1958	Chi N	142	480	68	130	26	4	20	75	66-9	2	64	.271	.357	.467	119	14	2-0	.992	-2	90	100	1b137,C2	0	0.4
1959	Chi N	110	296	34	70	10	3	14	37	31-2	0	53	.236	.306	.432	96	-3	0-0	.985	-4	88	102	1b85	0	-1.1
1960	SF N	37	54	4	9	0	0	3	6	7-1	0	7	.167	.262	.333	66	-3	0-0	1.000	0	100	73	1b10	0	-0.3
	†NY A	26	41	6	15	3	1	3	10	5-1	0	6	.366	.435	.707	216	7	0-0	.988	-1	73	41	1b11	0	0.5
1961	Was A	123	377	52	94	20	4	17	49	39-5	1	41	.249	.317	.459	107	3	0-0	.983	-6	88	106	1b95	0	-0.9
1962	Was A	67	191	17	46	8	0	4	24	18-0	1	22	.241	.307	.346	77	-6	5-1	.996	0	100	119	1b51	0	-0.8
	†NY A	41	94	12	28	4	0	4	17	18-0	0	9	.298	.404	.468	140	6	1-0	.992	1	115	106	1b31	0	0.6
	Year	108	285	29	74	12	0	8	41	36-0	1	31	.260	.340	.386	98	0	6-1	.995	1	105	114	1b82	0	-0.2
1963	NY A	14	15	1	3	0	0	0	0	1-0	0	3	.200	.250	.200	28	-1	0-0	.917	-0	0	136	1b2	0	-0.2
Total	10	1013	3020	384	805	135	33	132	467	353-39	7	460	.267	.341	.464	116	66	10-3	.988	-13	96	96	1b819,C2/lf	0	0.7

LONG, RYAN Ryan Marcus; B2.3.1973 Houston TX; BR/TR/6´2˝/215; [KCA91 1/45]; d7.16

YEAR	TM LG	G	AB	R	H	2B	3B	HR	RBI	BB-IB	HP	SO	AVG	OBP	SLG	AOPS	ABR	SB-CS	FA	FR	RNG	THR	GAMES AT POSITION	DL	BFW
1997	KC A	6	9	2	2	0	0	0	2	0-0	1	3	.222	.300	.222	38	-1	0-0	1.000	1	157	0	O5(1/0/4)/D	0	0.0

LONG, TERRENCE Terrence Deon; B2.29.1976 Montgomery AL; BL/TL/6´1˝/(190–200); [NYN94 1/20]; d4.14

YEAR	TM LG	G	AB	R	H	2B	3B	HR	RBI	BB-IB	HP	SO	AVG	OBP	SLG	AOPS	ABR	SB-CS	FA	FR	RNG	THR	GAMES AT POSITION	DL	BFW
1999	NY N	3	3	0	0	0	0	0	0	0-0	0	2	.000	.000	.000	-99	-1	0-0	ø	0	—	—	/H	0	-0.1
2000	†Oak A	138	584	104	168	34	4	18	80	43-1	1	77	.288	.336	.452	99	-2	5-0	.971	-11	94	29	O137C	0	-1.0
2001	†Oak A	**162**	629	90	178	37	4	12	85	52-8	0	103	.283	.335	.412	96	-4	9-3	.980	-10	92	51	O162(62/74/28)	0	-1.5
2002	†Oak A	**162**	587	71	141	32	4	16	67	48-6	2	96	.240	.298	.390	82	-16	3-6	.980	-13	90	58	O162C	0	-2.7
2003	†Oak A	140	486	64	119	22	2	14	61	31-4	3	67	.245	.293	.385	77	-17	4-1	.984	-7	94	40	O137(75/0/74)/D	0	-2.9
2004	SD N	136	288	31	85	19	4	3	28	19-4	1	51	.295	.335	.420	100	0	3-2	.986	2	109	59	O87(61/28/9)/D	0	0.0
2005	KC A	137	455	62	127	21	3	6	53	30-0	0	56	.279	.321	.378	89	-8	3-3	.986	2	92	202	O121(103/6/17),D4	0	-1.0
2006	NY A	12	36	6	6	1	0	0	2	4-0	0	8	.167	.250	.194	17	-4	0-0	.958	1	127	182	O10(2/2/7)/D	0	-0.4
Total	8	890	3068	428	824	166	21	69	376	227-23	7	460	.269	.318	.404	89	-52	27-15	.980	-36	94	70	O816(303/409/135),D7	0	-9.6

LONG, TOM Thomas Augustus; B6.1.1890 Coffeeville AL; D6.15.1972 Mobile AL; BR/TR/5´10.5˝/165; d9.11

YEAR	TM LG	G	AB	R	H	2B	3B	HR	RBI	BB-IB	HP	SO	AVG	OBP	SLG	AOPS	ABR	SB-CS	FA	FR	RNG	THR	GAMES AT POSITION	DL	BFW
1911	Was A	14	48	1	11	3	0	0	5	1	0	—	.229	.245	.292	50	-3	4	.875	-2	78	56	O13(4/0/9)	—	-0.6
1912	Was A	1	1	0	0	0	0	0	0	0	0	—	.000	.000	.000	-99	0	0	ø	0	—	—	/H	—	0.0
1915	StL N	140	507	61	149	21	**25**	2	61	31	4	50	.294	.339	.446	137	19	19-15	.927	-3	95	118	O136(2/51/87)	—	0.8
1916	StL N	119	403	37	118	11	10	1	33	10	1	43	.293	.312	.377	112	3	21-14	.945	-5	85	108	O106(3/12/94)	—	-0.8
1917	StL N	144	530	49	123	12	14	3	41	37	2	44	.232	.285	.325	89	-9	21	.919	-19	75	54	O137(30/0/109)	—	-3.9
Total	5	418	1489	148	401	47	49	6	140	79	7	137	.269	.309	.379	110	10	65-29	.928	-28	85	91	O392(39/63/299)	—	-4.5

LONGMIRE, TONY Anthony Eugene; B8.12.1968 Vallejo CA; BL/TR/6´1˝/(197–202); [PitN86 8/186]; d9.3; [DL 1992 Phi N 182, 1996 Phi N 182]

YEAR	TM LG	G	AB	R	H	2B	3B	HR	RBI	BB-IB	HP	SO	AVG	OBP	SLG	AOPS	ABR	SB-CS	FA	FR	RNG	THR	GAMES AT POSITION	DL	BFW
1993	†Phi N	11	13	1	3	0	0	0	1	0-0	0	1	.231	.231	.231	24	-1	0-0	1.000	0	166	0	O2L	0	-0.1
1994	Phi N	69	139	10	33	11	0	0	17	10-1	1	27	.237	.289	.317	58	-8	2-1	.941	-1	85	159	O32(13/0/21)	0	-1.0
1995	Phi N	59	104	21	37	7	0	3	19	11-1	1	19	.356	.419	.510	144	7	1-1	1.000	1	103	186	O23(19/2/2)	56	0.7
Total	3	139	256	32	73	18	0	3	37	21-2	2	47	.285	.340	.391	91	-2	3-2	.967	1	94	165	O57(34/2/23)	420	-0.4

LONNETT, JOE Joseph Paul; B2.7.1927 Beaver Falls PA; BR/TR/5´10˝/180; d4.22; C14

YEAR	TM LG	G	AB	R	H	2B	3B	HR	RBI	BB-IB	HP	SO	AVG	OBP	SLG	AOPS	ABR	SB-CS	FA	FR	RNG	THR	GAMES AT POSITION	DL	BFW
1956	Phi N	16	22	2	4	0	0	0	0	2-0	0	7	.182	.250	.182	19	-3	0-0	1.000	-0	*64*	*117*	C7	0	-0.3
1957	Phi N	67	160	12	27	5	0	5	15	22-1	1	39	.169	.272	.294	54	-10	0-0	.997	-3	116	63	C65	0	-1.1
1958	Phi N	17	50	0	7	2	0	0	2	2-0	0	11	.140	.167	.180	-6	-8	0-0	.988	0	72	149	C15	0	-0.7
1959	Phi N	43	93	8	16	1	0	1	10	14-2	1	17	.172	.284	.215	36	-8	0-1	.983	-8	86	60	C43	0	-1.5
Total	4	143	325	22	54	8	0	6	27	40-3	2	74	.166	.259	.246	37	-29	0-1	.992	-11	*98*	*76*	C130	0	-3.6

LOOK, BRUCE Bruce Michael; B6.9.1943 Lansing MI; BL/TR/5´11˝/185; d4.17; b–Dean; Col Michigan St.

YEAR	TM LG	G	AB	R	H	2B	3B	HR	RBI	BB-IB	HP	SO	AVG	OBP	SLG	AOPS	ABR	SB-CS	FA	FR	RNG	THR	GAMES AT POSITION	DL	BFW
1968	Min A	59	118	7	29	4	0	0	9	20-3	0	24	.246	.353	.280	89	0	0-1	.996	1	81	89	C41	0	0.2

LOOK, DEAN Dean Zachary; B7.23.1937 Lansing MI; BR/TR/5´11˝/185; d9.22; b–Bruce; Col Michigan St.

YEAR	TM LG	G	AB	R	H	2B	3B	HR	RBI	BB-IB	HP	SO	AVG	OBP	SLG	AOPS	ABR	SB-CS	FA	FR	RNG	THR	GAMES AT POSITION	DL	BFW
1961	Chi A	3	6	0	0	0	0	0	0	0-0	0	1	.000	.000	.000	-99	-2	0-0	1.000	-0	57	0	/lf	0	-0.2

LOPATA, STAN Stanley Edward "Stash"; B9.12.1925 Delray MI; BR/TR/6´2˝/(210–220); d9.19

YEAR	TM LG	G	AB	R	H	2B	3B	HR	RBI	BB-IB	HP	SO	AVG	OBP	SLG	AOPS	ABR	SB-CS	FA	FR	RNG	THR	GAMES AT POSITION	DL	BFW
1948	Phi N	6	15	2	2	1	0	0	2	0	0	4	.133	.133	.200	-11	-2	0	1.000	0	*59*	*126*	C4	0	-0.2
1949	Phi N	83	240	31	65	9	2	8	27	21	0	44	.271	.330	.425	104	0	1	.973	-2	*86*	*75*	C58	0	0.1
1950	†Phi N	58	129	10	27	2	2	1	11	22	0	25	.209	.325	.279	61	-7	1	.974	1	*104*	*66*	C51	0	-0.4
1951	Phi N	3	5	0	0	0	0	0	0	0	0	0	.000	.000	.000	-99	-1	0-0	1.000	0	*0*	*0*	/C	0	-0.1
1952	Phi N	57	179	25	49	9	1	4	27	36	0	33	.274	.395	.402	123	8	1-1	.987	4	*101*	*80*	C55	0	1.4
1953	Phi N	81	234	34	56	12	3	8	31	28	0	39	.239	.321	.419	91	-3	3-1	.987	2	*114*	*71*	C80	0	0.3
1954	Phi N	86	259	42	75	14	5	14	42	33	1	37	.290	.369	.544	136	13	1-3	.989	6	*123*	*74*	C75/1	0	2.2
1955	Phi N★	99	303	49	82	9	3	22	58	58-6	2	62	.271	.388	.538	146	21	4-1	.995	7	*109*	*86*	C66,1b24	0	3.0
1956	Phi N☆	146	535	96	143	33	7	32	95	75-10	1	93	.267	.353	.535	138	30	5-2	.982	-19	*74*	*54*	C102,1b39	0	1.4
1957	Phi N	116	388	50	92	18	2	18	67	56-7	1	81	.237	.331	.433	108	5	2-2	.988	-2	60	82	C108	0	0.7
1958	Phi N	86	258	36	64	9	0	9	33	60-9	2	63	.248	.391	.388	109	7	0-1	.987	-4	92	70	C80	0	0.6
1959	Mil N	25	48	0	5	0	0	0	4	3-0	0	13	.104	.157	.104	-31	-9	0-0	1.000	-2	45	0	C11,1b2	0	-1.1
1960	Mil N	7	8	0	1	0	0	0	0	1-0	0	3	.125	.222	.125	-2	-1	0-0	.944	1	0	0	C4	0	0.0
Total	13	853	2601	375	661	116	25	116	397	393-32	7	497	.254	.351	.452	115	61	18-11	.986	-9	*91*	72	C695,1b66	0	7.9

LOPES, DAVEY David Earl; B5.3.1945 E.Providence RI; BR/TR/5´9˝/170; [LAN68*S2/26]; d9.22; M3/C16; Col Washburn Topeka; OF(86/98/66)

YEAR	TM LG	G	AB	R	H	2B	3B	HR	RBI	BB-IB	HP	SO	AVG	OBP	SLG	AOPS	ABR	SB-CS	FA	FR	RNG	THR	GAMES AT POSITION	DL	BFW
1972	LA N	11	42	6	9	4	0	0	1	7-0	0	6	.214	.327	.310	83	-1	4-0	.964	-2	91	77	2b11	0	-0.1
1973	LA N	142	535	77	147	13	5	6	37	62-6	5	77	.275	.352	.351	100	1	36-16	.984	-2	101	**115**	2b135,O5(0/2/3),S2/3	0	1.1
1974	†LA N	145	530	95	141	26	3	10	35	66-3	4	71	.266	.350	.383	109	8	59-18	.965	-12	93	93	2b143	0	1.2
1975	LA N	155	618	108	162	24	6	8	41	91-3	2	93	.262	.358	.359	104	6	**77**-12	.979	-17	92	78	2b137,O24(0/23/1),S14	0	1.0
1976	LA N	117	427	72	103	17	7	4	20	56-1	4	49	.241	.333	.342	93	-3	**63**-10	.964	-17	94	96	2b100,O19C	25	-0.4
1977	†LA N	134	502	85	142	19	5	11	53	73-3	2	69	.283	.372	.406	109	9	47-12	.979	13	108	108	2b130	0	3.5
1978	†LA N★	151	587	93	163	25	4	17	58	71-3	0	70	.278	.355	.421	116	13	45-4	.974	12	106	111	2b147,O2C	0	4.3
1979	LA N★	153	582	109	154	20	6	28	73	97-4	4	88	.265	.372	.464	129	26	44-4	.981	-31	84	83	2b152	0	1.2
1980	LA N★	141	553	79	139	15	3	10	49	58-2	1	71	.251	.321	.344	89	-8	23-7	.980	-5	98	106	2b140	0	-0.3
1981	†LA N★	58	214	35	44	2	0	5	17	22-1	3	35	.206	.289	.285	66	-10	20-2	.993	3	99	97	2b55	15	-0.1
1982	Oak A	128	450	58	109	19	3	11	42	40-1	1	51	.242	.304	.371	88	-8	28-12	.977	-16	92	91	2b125,O6C	0	-1.6
1983	Oak A	147	494	64	137	13	4	17	67	51-7	2	61	.277	.341	.423	117	11	22-4	.983	-25	85	96	2b123,D12,O7(0/2/5),3b5	0	-0.5
1984	Oak A	72	230	32	59	11	1	9	36	31-1	1	36	.257	.343	.430	121	7	12-0	.965	-4	100	179	O42(3/8/31),2b17,3b5,D9	30	0.5
	†Chi N	16	17	5	4	1	0	0	0	6-0	0	5	.235	.435	.294	100	1	3-0	1.000	-1	123	0	O9(2/1/6),2b2	0	0.0
1985	Chi N	99	275	52	78	11	0	11	44	46-1	0	37	.284	.383	.444	120	9	47-4	.991	-6	83	44	O79(46/25/17),3b4/2	0	0.9
1986	Chi N	59	157	38	47	8	2	6	22	31-0	2	16	.299	.419	.490	140	10	17-6	.902	2	110	66	3b32,O22(21/0/2)	0	1.3
	†Hou N	37	98	11	23	2	1	1	13	12-0	0	9	.235	.315	.306	75	-3	8-2	1.000	3	121	270	O19(9/10/1),3b5	0	0.0

YEAR	TM LG	G	AB	R	H	2B	3B	HR	RBI	BB-IB	HP	SO	AVG	OBP	SLG	AOPS	ABR	SB-CS	FA	FR	RNG	THR	GAMES AT POSITION	DL	BFW
	Year	96	255	49	70	10	3	7	35	43-0	2	25	.275	.381	.420	117	7	25-8	1.000	5	121	156	O41(30/10/3),3b37	0	1.3
1987	Hou N	47	43	4	10	2	0	1	6	13-2	0	8	.233	.411	.349	108	1	2-1	.857	-1	73	0	O5L	68	0.1
Total	16	1812	6354	1023	1671	232	50	155	614	833-38	31	852	.263	.349	.388	106	69	557-114	.977	-107	95	97	2b1418,O239C,3b52,D21,S16	138	12.1
LOPEZ, AL	Alfonso Ramon; B8.20.1908 Tampa FL; D10.30.2005 Tampa FL; BR/TR/5´11˝/165; d9.27; M17; HF1977																								
1928	Bro N	3	12	0	0	0	0	0	0	0	0	0	.000	.000	.000	-99	-4	0	1.000	-1	*111*	*0*	C3	—	-0.4
1930	Bro N	128	421	60	130	20	4	6	57	33	2	35	.309	.362	.418	89	-7	3	.983	9	*104*	*101*	C126	—	0.8
1931	Bro N	111	360	38	97	13	4	0	40	28	1	33	.269	.324	.328	76	-12	1	.977	-5	*102*	*113*	C105	—	-1.1
1932	Bro N	126	404	44	111	18	6	1	43	34	0	35	.275	.331	.356	87	-7	3	.976	-4	*95*	*124*	C125	—	-0.3
1933	Bro N	126	372	39	112	11	4	3	41	21	0	39	.301	.338	.376	108	3	10	.991	14	*96*	***129***	C124/2	—	2.5
1934	Bro N★	140	439	58	120	23	2	7	54	49	2	44	.273	.349	.383	101	2	2	.982	-7	*93*	*99*	C137,2b2,3b2	—	0.3
1935	Bro N	128	379	50	95	12	4	3	39	35	1	36	.251	.316	.327	75	-13	2	.980	6	*115*	*99*	C126	—	0.0
1936	Bos N	128	426	46	103	12	5	7	50	41	2	41	.242	.311	.343	81	-12	1	.975	8	***145***	*108*	C127/1	—	0.4
1937	Bos N	105	334	31	68	11	1	3	38	35	1	57	.204	.281	.269	55	-21	3	.984	11	***191***	*93*	C102	—	-0.3
1938	Bos N	71	236	19	63	6	1	1	14	11	2	24	.267	.305	.314	78	-8	5	.989	4	*169*	*98*	C71	—	0.1
1939	Bos N	131	412	32	104	22	1	8	49	40	0	45	.252	.319	.369	91	-6	1	.986	4	***147***	*107*	C129	—	0.6
1940	Bos N	36	119	20	35	3	1	2	17	6	0	8	.294	.328	.387	102	0	1	.987	2	*100*	*152*	C36	—	0.3
	Pit N	59	174	15	45	6	2	1	24	13	0	13	.259	.310	.333	78	-5	5	.992	1	*72*	*99*	C59	—	-0.2
	Year	95	293	35	80	9	3	3	41	19	0	21	.273	.317	.355	87	-6	6	**.990**	2	*83*	*120*	C95	—	0.1
1941	Pit N★	114	317	33	84	9	1	5	43	31	0	23	.265	.330	.347	91	-4	0	.980	1	*106*	*91*	C114	0	0.3
1942	Pit N	103	289	17	74	8	2	1	26	34	2	17	.256	.338	.308	88	-4	0	**.995**	5	*88*	*102*	C99	0	0.7
1943	Pit N	118	372	40	98	9	4	1	39	44	0	25	.263	.341	.317	88	-5	2	**.991**	11	*137*	*104*	C116/3	0	1.4
1944	Pit N	115	331	27	76	12	1	1	34	34	1	24	.230	.303	.281	62	-16	4	**.984**	6	*100*	*118*	C115	0	-0.4
1945	Pit N	91	243	22	53	8	0	0	18	35	0	12	.218	.317	.251	57	-13	1	.992	3	*82*	*94*	C91	0	-0.5
1946	Pit N	56	150	13	46	2	0	1	12	23	0	14	.307	.399	.340	108	3	1	.985	-1	*68*	*125*	C56	0	0.5
1947	Cle A	61	126	9	33	1	0	0	14	9	0	13	.262	.311	.270	64	-6	1-1	1.000	2	*167*	*152*	C57	0	-0.3
Total	19	1950	5916	613	1547	206	43	51	652	556	14	538	.261	.326	.337	83	-135	46-1	.985	70	*116*	*108*	C1918,3b3,2b3/1	0	4.4
LOPEZ, ART	Arturo (Rodriguez); B5.8.1937 Mayaguez, PR; BL/TL/5´9˝/170; d4.12; Col New Jersey City																								
1965	NY A	38	49	5	7	0	0	0	0	1-0	0	6	.143	.160	.143	-13	-7	0-0	.958	0	125	0	O16(3/0/14)	0	-0.9
LOPEZ, CARLOS	Carlos Antonio (Morales); B9.27.1948 Mazatlan, Sinaloa, Mexico; BR/TR/6´0˝/(162–190); d9.17																								
1976	Cal A	9	10	1	0	0	0	0	0	2-0	0	3	.000	.167	.000	-52	-2	2-0	1.000	-1	59	0	O4(1/0/4)/D	0	-0.3
1977	Sea A	99	297	39	84	18	1	8	34	14-1	3	61	.283	.319	.431	103	1	16-4	.972	5	103	198	O90(0/7/87),D2	21	0.5
1978	Bal A	129	193	21	46	6	0	4	20	9-1	1	34	.238	.273	.332	74	-7	5-7	.988	5	102	166	O114(0/41/91)/D	0	-0.7
Total	3	237	500	61	130	24	1	12	54	25-2	4	98	.260	.298	.384	90	-8	23-11	.979	9	102	180	O208(1/48/182),D4	21	-0.5
LOPEZ, FELIPE	Felipe; B5.12.1980 Bayamon, PR; BB/TR/6´0˝/(175–185); [TorA98 1/8]; d8.3																								
2001	Tor A	49	177	21	46	5	4	5	23	12-1	0	39	.260	.304	.418	87	-4	4-3	.940	1	114	74	3b47,S3	0	-0.3
2002	Tor A	85	282	35	64	15	3	8	34	23-1	1	90	.227	.287	.387	74	-11	5-4	.975	-8	94	98	S79,3b2/D	0	-1.4
2003	Cin N	59	197	28	42	7	2	2	13	28-1	1	59	.213	.313	.299	64	-10	8-5	.928	-12	101	65	S50,3b8,2b3	0	-1.9
2004	Cin N	79	264	35	64	18	2	7	31	25-0	3	81	.242	.314	.405	86	-6	1-1	.957	1	108	86	S51,3b24,2b2	0	-0.1
2005	Cin N★	148	580	97	169	34	5	23	85	57-2	1	111	.291	.352	.486	117	14	15-7	.970	-26	91	77	S140,2b7/3	0	0.0
2006	Cin N	85	343	55	92	14	1	9	30	47-1	0	66	.268	.355	.394	87	-6	23-6	.959	-14	93	87	S84	0	-1.0
	Was N	71	274	43	77	13	2	2	22	34-0	2	60	.281	.362	.365	92	-2	21-6	.947	-21	83	75	S71	0	-1.5
	Year	156	617	98	169	27	3	11	52	81-1	2	126	.274	.358	.381	89	-8	44-12	.954	-35	0	0	S155	0	-2.5
Total	6	576	2117	314	554	106	19	56	238	226-6	8	506	.262	.333	.409	92	-25	77-32	.959	-79	93	82	S478,3b82,2b12/D	0	-6.2
LOPEZ, HECTOR	Hector Headley (Swainson); B7.9.1929 Colon, Pan; BR/TR/5´11˝/(168–182); d5.12; OF(477/21/172)																								
1955	KC A	128	483	50	140	15	2	15	68	33-1	3	58	.290	.337	.422	103	0	1-4	.936	10	116	122	3b93,2b36	0	1.1
1956	KC A	151	561	91	153	27	3	18	69	63-3	3	73	.273	.347	.428	104	3	4-5	.940	3	105	89	3b121,O20C,2b8,S4	0	0.4
1957	KC A	121	391	51	115	19	4	11	35	41-5	0	66	.294	.357	.448	118	10	1-6	.937	6	109	**103**	3b111,2b4,O3(2/0/1)	0	1.3
1958	KC A	151	564	84	147	28	4	17	73	49-2	2	61	.261	.317	.415	99	-1	2-2	.974	8	113	111	2b96,3b55/Slf	0	1.4
1959	KC A	35	135	22	38	10	3	6	24	8-0	1	23	.281	.324	.533	129	5	1-0	.933	-10	80	63	2b33	0	-0.2
	NY A	112	406	60	115	16	2	16	69	28-1	6	54	.283	.336	.451	119	9	3-1	.926	-3	99	116	3b76,O35L	0	0.4
	Year	147	541	82	153	26	5	22	93	36-1	7	77	.283	.333	.471	122	14	4-1	.926	-13	99	116	3b76,O35L,2b33	0	0.2
1960	†NY A	131	408	66	116	14	6	9	42	46-0	4	64	.284	.361	.414	116	9	1-1	.976	2	101	119	O106(93/0/17),2b5/3	0	0.5
1961	†NY A	93	243	27	54	7	2	3	22	24-1	1	38	.222	.292	.305	64	-13	1-0	.977	3	102	148	O72(65/0/9)	0	-1.3
1962	†NY A	106	335	45	92	19	1	6	48	33-2	0	53	.275	.338	.391	99	0	0-1	.984	2	108	62	O84(64/0/21)/23	0	-0.3
1963	†NY A	130	433	54	108	13	4	14	52	35-5	0	71	.249	.304	.395	95	-4	1-2	.957	-2	86	138	O124(104/0/21)/2	0	-1.4
1964	†NY A	127	285	34	74	9	3	10	34	24-2	1	54	.260	.317	.418	101	0	1-1	.971	-2	100	50	O103(80/1/31)/3	0	-0.7
1965	NY A	111	283	25	74	12	2	7	39	26-2	1	61	.261	.322	.392	104	1	0-0	.942	-6	82	74	O75(20/0/55),1b2	0	-1.0
1966	NY A	54	117	14	25	4	1	4	16	8-0	1	20	.214	.268	.368	84	-3	0-0	.936	-2	91	64	O29(13/0/17)	0	-0.7
Total	12	1450	4644	623	1251	193	37	136	591	418-24	23	696	.269	.330	.415	104	16	16-23	.967	10	95	100	O652L,3b459,2b184,S5,1b2	0	-0.5
LOPEZ, JAVY	Javier (Torres); B11.5.1970 Ponce, PR; BR/TR/6´3˝/(185–230); d9.18																								
1992	†Atl N	9	16	3	6	2	0	0	2	0-0	0	1	.375	.375	.500	137	1	0-0	1.000	-1	46	57	C9	0	0.0
1993	Atl N	8	16	1	6	1	1	1	2	0-0	1	2	.375	.412	.750	199	2	0-0	.975	2	104	138	C7	0	0.4
1994	Atl N	80	277	27	68	9	0	13	35	17-0	5	61	.245	.299	.419	82	-8	0-2	.995	0	80	83	C75	0	-0.4
1995	†Atl N	100	333	37	105	11	4	14	51	14-0	2	57	.315	.344	.498	114	5	0-1	.988	2	113	60	C93	0	1.3
1996	†Atl N	138	489	56	138	19	1	23	69	28-5	3	84	.282	.322	.466	100	-2	1-6	.994	21	104	91	C135	0	2.4
1997	†Atl N★	123	414	52	122	28	1	23	68	40-10	5	82	.295	.361	.534	130	18	1-1	.993	7	117	85	C117	16	3.1
1998	†Atl N★	133	489	73	139	21	1	34	106	30-1	6	85	.284	.328	.540	126	15	5-3	**.995**	24	146	76	C128/D	0	4.6
1999	Atl N	65	246	34	78	18	1	11	45	20-2	3	41	.317	.375	.533	127	10	0-3	.991	2	90	89	C60,D4	95	1.3
2000	†Atl N	134	481	60	138	21	1	24	89	35-3	4	80	.287	.337	.484	106	3	0-0	.993	0	105	67	C132	0	1.0
2001	†Atl N	128	438	45	117	16	1	17	66	28-3	10	82	.267	.322	.425	91	-7	1-0	.989	3	101	97	C127	0	0.4
2002	†Atl N	109	347	31	81	15	0	11	52	26-8	8	63	.233	.299	.372	76	-13	0-1	.986	13	100	132	C103	15	0.6
2003	†Atl N★	129	457	89	150	29	3	43	109	33-5	4	90	.328	.378	.687	171	45	0-1	.994	4	109	89	C120,D3	0	5.4
2004	Bal A	150	579	83	183	33	3	23	86	47-4	6	97	.316	.370	.503	127	23	0-0	.994	-3	93	87	C132,D21	0	2.5
2005	Bal A	103	395	47	110	24	1	15	49	19-2	7	68	.278	.322	.458	105	2	0-1	.994	-0	73	100	C75,D28/1	61	0.5
2006	Bal A	76	279	30	74	15	1	8	31	18-0	2	60	.265	.314	.412	89	-5	0-0	1.000	-4	57	89	D53,C21	15	-1.0
	Bos A	18	63	6	12	5	0	0	4	2-0	0	16	.190	.215	.270	24	-7	0-0	.990	-4	58	55	C17	0	-1.0
	Year	94	342	36	86	20	1	8	35	20-0	2	76	.251	.297	.386	76	-13	0-0	.996	-8	57	74	D53,C38	0	-2.0
Total	15	1503	5319	674	1527	267	19	260	864	357-43	66	969	.287	.337	.491	112	82	8-19	.992	66	103	87	C1351,D110/1	202	21.1
LOPEZ, JOSE	Jose Celestino; B11.24.1983 Anzoategui, Venezuela; BR/TR/6´2˝/(170–200); d7.31																								
2004	Sea A	57	207	28	48	13	0	5	22	8-0	1	31	.232	.263	.367	65	-11	0-1	.956	-18	77	67	S57/3	0	-2.5
2005	Sea A	54	190	18	47	19	0	2	25	6-0	4	25	.247	.282	.379	80	-5	4-2	.979	9	109	95	2b51/3	0	0.6
2006	Sea A★	151	603	78	170	28	8	10	79	26-1	9	80	.282	.319	.405	92	-9	5-2	.978	-7	99	90	2b150	0	-0.8
Total	3	262	1000	124	265	60	8	17	126	40-1	14	136	.265	.300	.392	84	-25	9-5	.978	-17	101	91	2b201,S57,3b2	0	-2.7
LOPEZ, LUIS	Luis; B10.5.1973 Brooklyn NY; BR/TR/6´0˝/205; d4.29; Col Coastal Carolina																								
2001	Tor A	41	119	10	29	4	0	3	10	8-1	0	16	.244	.291	.353	67	-6	0-0	.936	1	113	87	3b28,1b5,D4	0	-0.4
2004	Mon N	11	26	0	4	0	0	0	0	0-0	1	9	.154	.185	.154	-10	-4	0-0	1.000	-1	45	94	1b8	0	-0.6
Total	2	52	145	10	33	4	0	3	10	8-1	1	25	.228	.273	.317	53	-10	0-0	.936	0	113	87	3b28,1b13,D4	0	-1.0
LOPEZ, LUIS	Luis Antonio; B9.1.1964 Brooklyn NY; BR/TR/6´1˝/190; [LAN83 2/48]; d9.14																								
1990	LA N	6	6	0	0	0	0	0	0	0-0	0	2	.000	.000	.000	-99	-2	0-0	1.000	-0	0	333	/1	0	-0.2
1991	Cle A	35	82	7	18	4	1	0	7	4-1	1	7	.220	.261	.293	53	-5	0-0	1.000	-1	86	138	C12,1b10/3lfD	0	-0.7
Total	2	41	88	7	18	4	1	0	7	4-1	1	9	.205	.245	.273	43	-7	0-0	1.000	-2	86	138	C12,1b11,D6/lf3	0	-0.9
LOPEZ, LUIS	Luis Manuel (Santos); B9.4.1970 Cidra, PR; BB/TR/5´11˝/(166–185); d9.7; OF(8/0/1); [DL 1995 SD N 160]																								
1993	SD N	17	43	1	5	1	0	0	1	0-0	0	8	.116	.114	.140	-32	-8	0-0	.983	-2	90	65	2b15	0	-1.0
1994	SD N	77	235	29	65	16	1	2	20	15-2	3	39	.277	.325	.379	86	-5	3-2	.941	1	104	89	S43,2b29,3b5	0	0.0
1996	†SD N	63	139	10	25	3	0	2	11	9-1	1	35	.180	.233	.245	28	-15	0-0	.981	-7	92	76	S35,2b22,3b2	49	-1.9
1997	NY N	78	178	19	48	12	1	1	19	12-2	4	42	.270	.330	.365	86	-4	2-4	.966	9	113	117	S45,2b20,3b4	0	0.7

YEAR	TM LG	G	AB	R	H	2B	3B	HR	RBI	BB-IB	HP	SO	AVG	OBP	SLG	AOPS	ABR	SB-CS	FA	FR	RNG	THR	GAMES AT POSITION	DL	BFW
1998	NY N	117	266	37	67	13	2	2	22	20-3	4	60	.252	.312	.338	74	-10	2-2	.975	-3	93	81	2b50,S39,3b11,O9(8/0/1)	0	-1.1
1999	NY N	68	104	11	22	4	0	2	13	12-0	3	33	.212	.308	.308	60	-6	1-1	.971	-1	106	93	S33,2b16,3b9	0	-0.5
2000	Mil N	78	201	24	53	14	0	6	27	9-1	5	35	.264	.309	.423	84	-5	1-2	.959	-1	100	120	S45,2b22,3b6	0	-0.3
2001	Mil N	92	222	22	60	8	3	4	18	14-2	5	44	.270	.326	.387	86	-5	0-1	.922	0	93	150	3b46,S17,2b15	0	-0.4
2002	Mil N	6	8	1	0	0	0	0	1	2-0	0	1	.000	.200	.000	-42	-2	0-0	1.000	-2	22	0	S4	49	-0.3
	Bal A	52	109	10	23	6	0	2	9	3-0	0	20	.211	.232	.321	47	-9	1-0	.967	-6	114	60	S22,2b12/1D	0	-1.2
2004	Bal A	56	88	7	16	5	0	1	8	3-0	1	20	.182	.211	.273	27	-10	0-0	.944	-2	92	116	S14,3b11,1b6,2b6,D8	0	-1.1
2005	Cin N	17	27	0	6	3	0	0	2	1-0	0	6	.222	.250	.333	51	-2	0-0	.900	-1	60	0	3b6,2b4	105	-0.3
Total	11	721	1620	171	390	85	7	22	151	100-11	26	343	.241	.293	.343	67	-81	10-12	.959	-14	101	102	S297,2b211,3b100,D9,O9L,1b7	363	-7.4

Lopez, Mendy Mendy (Aude); B10.15.1973 Pimentel, D.R.; BR/TR/6´2˝/(190–200); d6.3

YEAR	TM LG	G	AB	R	H	2B	3B	HR	RBI	BB-IB	HP	SO	AVG	OBP	SLG	AOPS	ABR	SB-CS	FA	FR	RNG	THR	GAMES AT POSITION	DL	BFW
1998	KC A	74	206	18	50	10	2	1	15	12-0	1	40	.243	.286	.325	57	-13	5-2	.955	12	115	123	S72,3b2	0	0.3
1999	KC A	7	20	2	8	0	1	0	3	0-0	1	5	.400	.429	.500	131	1	0-0	1.000	-1	96	120	2b6/S	0	0.0
2000	Fla N	4	3	0	0	0	0	0	0	1-0	0	1	.000	.250	.000	-31	-1	0-0	ø	0	—	—	/H	0	-0.1
2001	Hou N	10	15	3	4	0	0	1	3	2-0	1	4	.267	.389	.467	112	0	0-0	1.000	-1	44	0	2b3,3b2	0	-0.1
	Pit N	22	43	5	10	3	1	0	4	4-1	0	16	.233	.292	.349	65	-2	0-0	.970	2	101	89	2b9,S6,3b4	0	0.0
	Year	32	58	8	14	3	1	1	7	6-1	1	20	.241	.318	.379	78	-2	0-0	.975	1	90	72	2b12,3b6,S6	0	-0.1
2002	Pit N	3	3	0	0	0	0	0	0	0-0	0	3	.000	.000	.000	-98	-1	0-0	ø	0	—	—	/H	0	-0.1
2003	KC A	52	94	13	26	5	1	3	11	4-0	0	28	.277	.306	.447	89	-2	2-0	1.000	-1	206	50	1b17,3b13,2b11,S4,O3(1/0/2)	58	-0.2
2004	KC A	18	38	4	4	0	0	1	4	4-0	1	9	.105	.209	.184	4	-6	0-0	.941	-3	61	80	2b6,3b4,S4,O4(2/0/2),1b2	0	-0.8
Total	7	190	422	45	102	18	5	6	40	27-1	4	106	.242	.292	.351	64	-24	7-2	.957	8	115	126	S87,2b35,3b25,1b19,O7(3/0/4)	58	-1.0

Lopez, Pedro Pedro Michel; B4.28.1984 Moca, D.R.; BR/TR/6´1˝/160; d5.1

YEAR	TM LG	G	AB	R	H	2B	3B	HR	RBI	BB-IB	HP	SO	AVG	OBP	SLG	AOPS	ABR	SB-CS	FA	FR	RNG	THR	GAMES AT POSITION	DL	BFW
2005	Chi A	2	7	1	2	0	0	0	2	0-0	0	1	.286	.286	.286	51	-1	0-0	1.000	0	166	319	/2S	0	0.0

Lopez, Mickey Raymond Michael; B11.17.1973 Miami FL; BB/TR/5´9˝/170; [MilA95 13/348]; d9.6; Col Florida St.

YEAR	TM LG	G	AB	R	H	2B	3B	HR	RBI	BB-IB	HP	SO	AVG	OBP	SLG	AOPS	ABR	SB-CS	FA	FR	RNG	THR	GAMES AT POSITION	DL	BFW
2004	Sea A	6	4	1	1	0	0	0	0	1-0	1	0	.250	.500	.250	110	0	0-0	1.000	0	139	0	2b3,D3	0	0.0

Lord, Bris Bristol Robotham "The Human Eyeball"; B9.21.1883 Upland PA; D11.13.1964 Prince Frederick MD; BR/TR/5´9˝/185; d4.21

YEAR	TM LG	G	AB	R	H	2B	3B	HR	RBI	BB-IB	HP	SO	AVG	OBP	SLG	AOPS	ABR	SB-CS	FA	FR	RNG	THR	GAMES AT POSITION	DL	BFW
1905	†Phi A	66	238	38	57	14	0	0	13	14	1	—	.239	.285	.298	83	-4	3	.963	1	142	216	O61(4/38/19)	—	-0.6
1906	Phi A	118	434	50	101	13	7	1	44	27	2	—	.233	.281	.302	80	-11	12	.941	-3	91	130	O115(5/103/7)	—	-2.2
1907	Phi A	57	170	12	31	3	0	1	11	14	1	—	.182	.249	.218	48	-10	2	.951	-2	88	0	O53(10/40/4)/P	—	-1.6
1909	Cle A	69	249	26	67	7	3	1	25	8	1	—	.269	.295	.333	94	-3	10	.992	7	154	215	O67(48/3/16)	—	0.0
1910	Cle A	58	210	23	46	8	7	0	17	12	2	—	.219	.268	.324	84	-5	4	.958	4	90	184	O56(24/0/32)	—	-0.4
	†Phi A	70	279	54	78	13	11	1	20	23	1	—	.280	.337	.416	137	11	6	.980	1	112	61	O70(64/4/2)	—	0.8
	Year	128	489	77	124	21	18	1	37	35	3	—	.254	.307	.376	114	5	10	.972	5	103	112	O126(88/4/34)	—	0.4
1911	†Phi A	134	574	92	178	37	11	3	55	35	5	—	.310	.355	.429	120	14	15	.963	3	109	78	O132(122/1/9)	—	1.0
1912	Phi A	97	378	63	90	12	9	0	25	34	5	—	.238	.309	.317	82	-9	15	.942	-2	92	105	O97(19/0/78)	—	-1.6
1913	Bos N	73	235	22	59	12	1	6	26	8	0	22	.251	.276	.387	86	-5	7-6	.914	-6	85	59	O62(25/3/35)	—	-1.6
Total	8	742	2767	380	707	119	49	13	236	175	18	22	.256	.304	.348	95	-22	74-6	.957	2	106	113	O713(321/192/202)/P	—	-6.2

Lord, Harry Harry Donald; B3.8.1882 Porter ME; D8.9.1948 Westbrook ME; BL/TR/5´10.5˝/165; d9.25; M1; Col Bates

YEAR	TM LG	G	AB	R	H	2B	3B	HR	RBI	BB-IB	HP	SO	AVG	OBP	SLG	AOPS	ABR	SB-CS	FA	FR	RNG	THR	GAMES AT POSITION	DL	BFW
1907	Bos A	10	38	4	6	1	0	0	3	1	0	—	.158	.179	.184	16	-4	1	.919	0	106	0	3b10	—	-0.4
1908	Bos A	145	560	61	145	15	6	2	37	22	8	—	.259	.297	.318	97	-3	23	.902	-8	94	83	3b144	—	-0.9
1909	Bos A	136	534	89	168	12	7	0	31	20	8	—	.315	.349	.363	122	12	36	.929	-10	95	59	3b134	—	0.7
1910	Bos A	77	288	25	72	5	5	1	32	14	4	—	.250	.294	.313	88	-5	17	.927	-5	92	105	3b70/S	—	-0.9
	Chi A	44	165	26	49	6	3	0	10	14	0	—	.297	.352	.370	132	6	17	.952	-5	85	76	3b44	—	0.2
	Year	121	453	51	121	11	8	1	42	28	4	—	.267	.315	.333	103	0	34	.935	-10	89	94	3b114/S	—	-0.7
1911	Chi A	141	561	103	180	18	18	3	61	32	6	—	.321	.364	.433	126	16	43	.941	-19	80	117	3b138	—	0.1
1912	Chi A	151	570	81	152	19	12	5	54	52	5	—	.267	.333	.368	104	2	30	.895	-25	79	77	3b106,O45(32/4/9)	—	-2.2
1913	Chi A	150	547	62	144	18	12	1	42	45	7	39	.263	.327	.346	98	-3	24	.924	-29	81	70	3b150	—	-3.0
1914	Chi A	21	69	8	13	1	1	1	3	5	0	3	.188	.243	.275	57	-4	2-2	.933	-2	101	0	3b19/lf	—	-0.7
1915	Buf F	97	359	50	97	12	6	1	21	21	0	15	.270	.311	.345	83	-15	15	.946	-8	94	100	3b92/rfM	—	-2.2
Total	9	972	3691	509	1026	107	70	14	294	226	38	57	.278	.326	.356	104	2	208-2	.924	-111	88	82	3b907,O47(33/4/10)/S	—	-9.3

Lord, Carlton William Carlton; B1.7.1900 Philadelphia PA; D8.15.1947 Chester PA; BR/TR/5´11˝/170; d7.12

YEAR	TM LG	G	AB	R	H	2B	3B	HR	RBI	BB-IB	HP	SO	AVG	OBP	SLG	AOPS	ABR	SB-CS	FA	FR	RNG	THR	GAMES AT POSITION	DL	BFW
1923	Phi N	17	47	3	11	2	0	0	2	2	0	3	.234	.265	.277	39	-4	0-1	.833	-2	100	40	3b14	—	-0.5

Loretta, Mark Mark David; B8.14.1971 Santa Monica CA; BR/TR/6´0˝/(175–190); [MilA93 7/207]; d9.4; Col Northwestern

YEAR	TM LG	G	AB	R	H	2B	3B	HR	RBI	BB-IB	HP	SO	AVG	OBP	SLG	AOPS	ABR	SB-CS	FA	FR	RNG	THR	GAMES AT POSITION	DL	BFW
1995	Mil A	19	50	13	13	3	0	1	3	4-0	1	7	.260	.327	.380	79	-2	1-1	.979	-3	100	64	S13,2b4/D	0	-0.3
1996	Mil A	73	154	20	43	3	0	1	13	14-0	0	15	.279	.339	.318	65	-8	2-1	.989	-2	107	91	2b28,3b23,S21	0	-0.7
1997	Mil A	132	418	56	120	17	5	5	47	47-2	2	60	.287	.354	.388	95	-3	5-5	.980	5	105	148	2b63,S44,1b19,3b15/D	0	0.6
1998	Mil N	140	434	55	137	29	0	6	54	42-1	7	47	.316	.382	.424	111	9	9-6	.992	6	79	119	1b70,S56,3b22,2b13/lf	0	1.5
1999	Mil N	153	587	93	170	34	5	5	67	52-1	10	59	.290	.354	.390	89	-9	4-1	.986	-4	92	92	S74,1b66,2b17,3b14	0	-1.1
2000	Mil N	91	352	49	99	21	1	7	40	37-2	1	38	.281	.350	.406	91	-4	0-3	.995	-1	107	95	S90/2	75	0.0
2001	Mil N	102	384	40	111	14	2	2	29	28-0	7	46	.289	.346	.352	84	-9	1-2	.992	2	104	98	2b52,3b39,S9/PD	48	-0.4
2002	Mil N	86	217	23	58	14	0	2	19	23-1	5	32	.267	.350	.359	88	-3	0-0	.991	-7	88	67	3b47,S12,1b5,2b3	0	-0.9
	Hou N	21	66	10	28	4	0	2	8	9-0	0	5	.424	.481	.576	167	7	1-1	.944	-1	66	58	3b10,S6,2b3/D	0	0.7
	Year	107	283	33	86	18	0	4	27	32-1	5	37	.304	.381	.410	108	5	1-1	.984	-7	84	65	3b57,S18,2b6,1b5/D	0	-0.2
2003	SD N	154	589	74	185	28	4	13	72	54-2	3	62	.314	.372	.441	123	19	5-4	**.990**	-6	97	84	2b150,S3	0	2.0
2004	SD N★	154	620	108	208	47	2	16	76	58-3	9	45	.335	.391	.495	136	36	5-3	.987	4	102	112	2b154	0	4.6
2005	†SD N	105	404	54	113	16	1	3	38	45-4	8	34	.280	.360	.347	92	-3	8-4	.987	-17	85	91	2b105/3	60	-1.5
2006	Bos A★	155	635	75	181	33	0	5	59	49-1	12	63	.285	.345	.361	82	-15	4-1	.994	1	98	104	2b138,1b11,D6	0	-0.7
Total	12	1385	4910	670	1466	263	20	68	525	462-17	65	513	.299	.363	.402	100	15	45-32	.988	-20	98	103	2b731,S328,1b171,3b171,D13/Plf	183	3.8

Loucks, Scott Scott Gregory; B11.11.1956 Anchorage AK; BR/TR/6´0˝/178; [HouN77 5/118]; d9.1; Col Southeastern Oklahoma; [DL 1984 Hou N 61]

YEAR	TM LG	G	AB	R	H	2B	3B	HR	RBI	BB-IB	HP	SO	AVG	OBP	SLG	AOPS	ABR	SB-CS	FA	FR	RNG	THR	GAMES AT POSITION	DL	BFW
1980	Hou N	8	3	4	1	0	0	0	0	0-0	0	2	.333	.333	.333	94	0	0-0	1.000	-0	52	0	O4(0/2/2)	0	0.0
1981	Hou N	10	7	2	4	0	0	0	0	1-0	0	3	.571	.625	.571	256	2	1-0	1.000	-0	91	0	O5C	0	0.2
1982	Hou N	44	49	6	11	2	0	0	3	3-0	0	17	.224	.269	.265	54	-3	4-1	.978	3	114	343	O37C	0	0.0
1983	Hou N	7	14	2	3	0	0	0	0	1-0	0	4	.214	.267	.214	37	-1	2-2	1.000	1	127	533	O6(1/5/0)	0	0.0
1985	Pit N	4	7	1	2	2	0	0	1	2-0	0	2	.286	.444	.571	184	1	0-0	1.000	-0	63	0	O4(3/0/1)	0	0.1
Total	5	73	80	15	21	4	0	0	4	7-0	0	28	.262	.322	.313	83	-1	7-3	.985	3	108	304	O56(4/49/3)	61	0.3

Louden, Baldy William P.; B8.27.1883 Pittsburgh PA; D12.8.1935 Piedmont WV; BR/TR/5´11˝/175; d9.13

YEAR	TM LG	G	AB	R	H	2B	3B	HR	RBI	BB-IB	HP	SO	AVG	OBP	SLG	AOPS	ABR	SB-CS	FA	FR	RNG	THR	GAMES AT POSITION	DL	BFW
1907	NY A	4	9	4	1	0	0	0	0	2	0	—	.111	.273	.111	21	-1	1	.750	-0	111	0	3b3	—	-0.1
1912	Det A	122	403	57	97	12	4	1	36	58	11	—	.241	.352	.298	89	-2	27	.951	18	126	81	2b87,3b26,S5	—	1.8
1913	Det A	76	191	28	46	4	5	0	23	24	6	22	.241	.344	.314	94	-1	6	.906	1	106	67	2b30,3b26,S6,O5(0/1/4)	—	0.1
1914	Buf F	126	431	73	135	11	4	6	63	52	3	41	.313	.391	.399	113	3	35	.931	-19	81	83	S115	—	-0.8
1915	Buf F	141	469	67	132	18	5	4	48	64	4	45	.281	.372	.367	106	0	30	.978	12	104	100	2b88,S27,3b19	—	1.7
1916	Cin N	134	439	38	96	16	4	1	32	54	6	54	.219	.313	.280	85	-6	12	**.968**	17	111	107	2b108,S23	—	1.6
Total	6	603	1942	267	507	61	22	12	202	254	30	162	.261	.355	.334	98	-7	111	.961	28	113	94	2b313,S176,3b74,O5(0/1/4)	—	4.3

Loudenslager, Charlie Charles Edward; B5.21.1881 Baltimore MD; D10.31.1933 Baltimore MD; TR/5´9˝/186; d4.15

YEAR	TM LG	G	AB	R	H	2B	3B	HR	RBI	BB-IB	HP	SO	AVG	OBP	SLG	AOPS	ABR	SB-CS	FA	FR	RNG	THR	GAMES AT POSITION	DL	BFW
1904	Bro N	1	2	0	0	0	0	0	0	0	0	—	.000	.000	.000	-99	0	0	1.000	-0	70	0	/2	—	-0.1

Loughlin B Baltimore MD; d5.9

YEAR	TM LG	G	AB	R	H	2B	3B	HR	RBI	BB-IB	HP	SO	AVG	OBP	SLG	AOPS	ABR	SB-CS	FA	FR	RNG	THR	GAMES AT POSITION	DL	BFW
1883	Bal AA	1	5	0	2	0	0	0	—	0	—	—	.400	.400	.400	154	0	—	ø	-0	0	0	/rf	—	0.0

Loughran, Bill William H.; B6.1862 New York NY; D8.7.1917 New York NY; d6.6; Col Manhattan

YEAR	TM LG	G	AB	R	H	2B	3B	HR	RBI	BB-IB	HP	SO	AVG	OBP	SLG	AOPS	ABR	SB-CS	FA	FR	RNG	THR	GAMES AT POSITION	DL	BFW
1884	NY N	9	29	4	3	1	1	0	3	7	—	11	.103	.278	.207	54	-1	—	.857	-2	—	—	C9/rf	—	-0.3

Lovelace, Tom Thomas Rivers; B10.19.1897 Wolfe City TX; D7.12.1979 Dallas TX; BR/TR/5´11˝/170; d9.23

YEAR	TM LG	G	AB	R	H	2B	3B	HR	RBI	BB-IB	HP	SO	AVG	OBP	SLG	AOPS	ABR	SB-CS	FA	FR	RNG	THR	GAMES AT POSITION	DL	BFW
1922	Pit N	1	1	0	0	0	0	0	0	0	0	0	.000	.000	.000	-99	0	0-0	ø	0	—	—	/H	—	0.0

THE BATTER REGISTER

YEAR	TM LG	G	AB	R	H	2B	3B	HR	RBI	BB-IB	HP	SO	AVG	OBP	SLG	AOPS	ABR	SB-CS	FA	FR	RNG	THR	GAMES AT POSITION	DL	BFW
LOVETT, LEN	Leonard Walker; B7.17.1852 Lancaster Co. PA; D11.18.1922 Newark DE; BR/TR; d8.4; ▲																								
1873	Res NA	1	5	1	2	0	0	0	1	0	—	0	.400	.400	.400	149	1	0-0	.500	-0	68	0	/P	—	0.0
1875	Cen NA	6	21	2	5	1	0	0	2	1	—	5	.238	.273	.286	103	0	0-0	.700	-0	136	0	O6(1/0/5)	—	0.0
Total	2NA	7	26	3	7	1	0	0	3	1	—	5	.269	.296	.308	113	1	0-0	.700	-1	136	0	O6(1/0/5)/P	—	0.0
LOVETT, MEM	Merritt Marwood; B6.15.1912 Chicago IL; D9.19.1995 Downers Grove IL; BR/TR/5´9.5˝/165; d9.4																								
1933	Chi A	1	1	0	0	0	0	0	0	0	0	0	.000	.000	.000	-99	0	0-0	ø	0	—	—	/H	—	0.0
LOVIGLIO, JAY	John Paul; B5.30.1956 Freeport NY; BR/TR/5´9˝/160; d9.2; Col Suffolk (NY) CC																								
1980	Phi N	16	5	7	0	0	0	0	0	1-0	0	0	.000	.167	.000	-47	-1	1-2	1.000	-1	60	0	/2	0	-0.2
1981	Chi A	14	15	5	4	0	0	0	2	1-0	0	1	.267	.313	.267	69	-1	2-2	.786	0	100	347	3b4,2b3,D2	0	-0.1
1982	Chi A	15	31	5	6	0	0	0	2	1-0	0	4	.194	.219	.194	14	-4	2-1	.964	1	107	72	2b13,D2	0	-0.3
1983	Chi N	1	1	0	0	0	0	0	0	0-0	0	1	.000	.000	.000	-95	0	0-0	ø	0	—	—	/H	0	0.0
Total	4	46	52	17	10	0	0	0	4	3-0	0	6	.192	.236	.192	21	-6	5-5	.971	0	99	57	2b17,D4,3b4	0	-0.6
LOVITTO, JOE	Joseph; B1.6.1951 San Pedro CA; D5.19.2001 Arlington TX; BB/TR/6´0˝/185; [TexA69*1/2]; d4.15																								
1972	Tex A	117	330	23	74	9	1	1	19	37-2	2	54	.224	.306	.267	74	-10	13-11	.976	4	109	114	O103(8/77/23)	0	-1.2
1973	Tex A	26	44	3	6	1	0	0	0	5-0	0	7	.136	.224	.159	10	-5	1-0	.898	0	80	109	3b20,O3(0/2/1)	0	-0.5
1974	Tex A	113	283	27	63	9	3	2	26	25-4	0	36	.223	.285	.297	69	-11	6-8	.972	-5	92	119	O107(0/105/2),1b5	0	-2.2
1975	Tex A	50	106	17	22	3	0	1	8	13-1	0	16	.208	.289	.264	59	-6	2-2	.985	-1	89	150	O38(18/25/0),1b2/CD	40	-0.8
Total	4	306	763	70	165	22	4	4	53	80-7	2	113	.216	.291	.271	66	-32	22-21	.975	-2	99	120	O251(26/209/26),3b20,1b7,D2/C	40	-4.7
LOVULLO, TOREY	Salvatore Anthony; B7.25.1965 Santa Monica CA; BB/TR/6´0˝/(180–185); [DetA87 5/131]; d9.10; Col UCLA; OF(1/0/2)																								
1988	Det A	12	21	2	8	1	1	1	2	1-0	0	2	.381	.409	.667	203	3	0-0	1.000	-0	101	53	2b9,3b3	0	0.3
1989	Det A	29	87	8	10	2	0	1	4	14-0	0	20	.115	.233	.172	18	-9	0-0	1.000	-1	37	81	1b18,3b11	0	-1.2
1991	NY A	22	51	0	9	2	0	0	2	5-1	0	7	.176	.250	.216	30	-5	0-0	.940	1	106	33	3b22	0	-0.4
1993	Cal A	116	367	42	92	20	0	6	30	36-1	1	49	.251	.318	.354	78	-11	7-6	.981	-0	98	121	2b91,3b14,S9,O2R/1	0	-0.8
1994	Sea A	36	72	9	16	5	0	2	7	9-1	0	13	.222	.309	.375	73	-3	1-0	1.000	2	113	87	2b20,3b5,D2	0	0.0
1996	Oak A	65	82	15	18	4	0	3	9	11-0	2	17	.220	.323	.378	78	-3	1-2	1.000	-1	94	160	1b42,3b11,2b2/SlfD	0	-0.5
1998	Cle A	6	19	1	4	1	0	0	1	1-0	0	2	.211	.250	.263	33	-2	0-0	.947	0	112	111	2b5/3	0	-0.2
1999	Phi N	17	38	3	8	0	0	2	5	3-0	0	11	.211	.268	.368	58	-3	0-0	1.000	-0	219	109	1b6,2b6	0	-0.3
Total	8	303	737	80	165	35	1	15	60	80-3	3	121	.224	.301	.335	69	-33	9-8	.984	0	99	109	2b133,1b67,3b67,S10,D6,O3R	0	-3.1
LOW, FLETCHER	Fletcher; B4.7.1893 Essex MA; D6.6.1973 Hanover NH; BR/TR/5´10.5˝/175; d10.7; Col Dartmouth																								
1915	Bos N	1	4	1	1	0	1	0	1	0	0	0	.250	.250	.750	207	0	0	1.000	-0	50	0	/3	—	0.0
LOWE, CHARLIE	Charles; B Baltimore MD; d9.24																								
1872	Atl NA	7	31	2	5	0	0	0	3	0	—	2	.161	.161	.161	-0	-4	0-0	.827	-1	88	30	2b7	—	-0.4
LOWE, DICK	Richard Alvern; B1.28.1854 Evansville WI; D6.28.1922 Janesville WI; d6.26																								
1884	Det N	1	3	0	1	0	0	0	0	0	—	1	.333	.333	.333	117	0	—	.125	-3	—	—	/C	—	-0.3
LOWE, BOBBY	Robert Lincoln "Link"; B7.10.1865 Pittsburgh PA; D12.8.1951 Detroit MI; BR/TR/5´10˝/150; d4.19; M1; OF(173/56/11)																								
1890	Bos N	52	207	35	58	13	2	2	21	26	2	32	.280	.366	.391	112	3	15	.951	-7	88	14	S24,O15(3/11/1),3b12	—	-0.3
1891	Bos N	125	497	92	129	19	5	6	74	53	9	54	.260	.342	.354	92	-6	43	.927	-5	99	82	O107(64/38/5),2b17,S2/3P	—	-1.2
1892	†Bos N	124	475	79	115	16	7	3	57	37	8	47	.242	.308	.324	83	-11	36	.928	11	120	74	O90(87/3/0),3b14,S13,2b10	—	-0.6
1893	Bos N	126	526	130	157	19	5	14	89	55	4	29	.298	.369	.433	105	1	22	.936	1	104	111	2b121,S5	—	0.6
1894	Bos N	**133**	613	158	212	34	11	17	115	50	6	25	.346	.401	.520	112	9	23	.927	-7	98	106	2b130,S2/3	—	0.6
1895	Bos N	100	417	102	124	12	7	7	62	40	8	16	.297	.370	.410	94	-5	24	.954	10	106	**126**	2b100	—	0.8
1896	Bos N	73	306	59	98	11	4	2	48	20	4	12	.320	.370	.402	98	-2	15	.965	18	117	104	2b73	—	1.6
1897	†Bos N	123	499	87	154	24	8	5	106	32	4	—	.309	.355	.419	98	-3	16	.952	-9	101	84	2b123	—	-0.6
1898	Bos N	147	559	65	152	11	7	4	94	29	3	—	.272	.311	.338	82	-16	12	.958	12	100	124	2b145,S2	—	0.3
1899	Bos N	152	559	81	152	5	9	4	88	35	1	—	.272	.316	.335	72	-24	17	.954	-1	99	129	2b148,S4	—	-1.7
1900	Bos N	127	474	65	132	11	5	3	71	26	5	—	.278	.323	.342	74	-18	15	.951	-9	93	78	2b127	—	-2.0
1901	Bos N	129	491	47	125	11	1	3	47	17	3	—	.255	.284	.299	63	-24	22	.912	-6	88	**110**	3b111,2b18	—	-2.6
1902	Chi N	121	480	44	119	13	3	0	35	12	5	—	.248	.274	.287	75	-15	17	.956	18	111	136	2b119,3b2	—	0.3
1903	Chi N	32	105	14	28	5	3	0	15	4	4	—	.267	.319	.371	99	-1	5	.948	2	118	125	2b22,1b6/3	—	0.2
1904	Pit N	1	1	0	0	0	0	0	0	0	0	—	.000	.000	.000	-97	0	0	ø	0	—	—	/H	—	0.0
	Det A	140	506	47	105	14	6	0	40	17	2	—	.208	.236	.259	58	-25	15	.964	0	98	103	2b140,M	—	-2.7
1905	Det A	58	181	17	35	7	2	0	9	13	2	—	.193	.255	.254	61	-8	3	.980	2	196	0	O24(17/3/4),3b22,2b6,S4/1	—	-0.8
1906	Det A	41	145	11	30	3	0	1	12	4	1	—	.207	.233	.248	49	-9	3	.915	4	114	14	S19,2b17,3b5	—	-0.4
1907	Det A	17	37	2	9	2	0	0	5	4	0	—	.243	.317	.297	93	0	0	.870	-2	101	0	3b10,O4(2/1/1),S2	—	-0.2
Total	18	1821	7078	1135	1934	230	85	71	988	474	71	215	.273	.325	.360	86	-154	303	.951	33	102	109	2b1316,O240L,3b179,S77,1b7/P	—	-8.7
LOWELL, MIKE	Michael Averett; B2.24.1974 San Juan, PR; BR/TR/6´4˝/(193–212); [NYA95 20/562]; d9.13; Col Florida International																								
1998	NY A	8	15	1	4	0	0	0	0	0-0	0	1	.267	.267	.267	41	-1	0-0	1.000	-1	66	182	3b7	0	-0.2
1999	Fla N	97	308	32	78	15	0	12	47	26-1	5	69	.253	.317	.419	90	-5	0-0	.981	-3	97	82	3b83	54	-0.8
2000	Fla N	140	508	73	137	38	0	22	91	54-4	9	75	.270	.344	.474	111	9	4-0	.968	4	102	74	3b136	15	1.3
2001	Fla N	146	551	65	156	37	0	18	100	43-3	10	79	.283	.340	.448	107	6	1-2	.976	10	103	**138**	3b144	0	1.5
2002	Fla N★	160	597	88	165	44	0	24	92	65-5	4	92	.276	.346	.471	118	16	4-3	.969	1	94	109	3b159	0	1.8
2003	†Fla N★	130	492	76	136	27	1	32	105	56-6	3	78	.276	.350	.530	132	22	3-1	**.973**	-3	93	119	3b128,D2	28	1.9
2004	Fla N★	158	598	87	175	44	1	27	85	64-8	6	77	.293	.365	.505	129	26	5-1	.982	-3	92	114	3b154,D3	0	2.4
2005	Fla N	150	500	56	118	36	1	8	58	46-1	2	58	.236	.298	.360	77	-17	4-0	**.983**	-1	94	**134**	3b135,2b8	0	-1.6
2006	Bos A	153	573	79	163	47	1	20	80	47-5	4	61	.284	.339	.475	106	6	2-2	.987	21	108	123	3b153	0	2.5
Total	9	1142	4142	557	1132	288	4	163	658	401-33	43	590	.273	.339	.463	110	62	23-9	.977	24	98	113	3b1099,2b8,D5	97	8.8
LOWENSTEIN, JOHN	John Lee; B1.27.1947 Wolf Point MT; BL/TR/6´0˝/(175–181); [CleA68 18/402]; d9.2; Col California–Riverside; OF(687/49/201)																								
1970	Cle A	17	43	5	11	3	1	1	6	1-0	0	9	.256	.273	.442	90	-1	1-0	1.000	4	146	96	2b10,3b2,O2L/S	0	0.4
1971	Cle A	58	140	15	26	5	0	4	9	16-1	0	28	.186	.269	.307	57	-8	1-5	.986	0	87	93	2b29,O18(7/5/8),S3	31	-0.8
1972	Cle A	68	151	16	32	8	1	6	21	20-0	0	43	.212	.304	.397	104	1	2-4	1.000	3	91	219	O58(27/3/29),1b2	0	0.0
1973	Cle A	98	305	42	89	16	1	6	40	23-0	0	41	.292	.338	.410	108	3	5-3	.931	1	70	166	O51(12/4/36),2b25,3b8/1D	0	0.3
1974	Cle A	140	508	65	123	14	2	8	48	53-2	2	85	.242	.313	.325	85	-9	36-17	.986	5	99	89	O100(88/8/7),3b28,1b12,2b4	0	-0.8
1975	Cle A	91	265	37	64	5	1	12	33	28-2	0	28	.242	.313	.404	101	0	15-10	.983	-4	82	77	O36(19/3/17),D31,3b8,2b2	0	-0.7
1976	Cle A	93	229	33	47	8	2	2	14	25-3	0	35	.205	.283	.284	67	-9	11-8	.972	-1	90	203	O61(13/19/29),D11,1b9	0	-1.5
1977	Cle A	81	149	24	36	6	1	4	12	21-1	0	29	.242	.335	.376	96	0	1-8	1.000	-1	100	46	O39(18/5/17),D19/1	0	-0.6
1978	Tex A	77	176	28	39	8	3	5	21	37-2	2	29	.222	.363	.386	110	4	16-3	.926	-2	92	51	3b25,D21,O16(14/0/2)	0	0.3
1979	†Bal A	97	197	33	50	8	2	11	34	30-3	1	37	.254	.351	.482	128	8	16-4	.992	4	116	106	O72(44/1/41)/13D	15	1.1
1980	Bal A	104	196	38	61	8	0	4	27	32-1	0	29	.311	.403	.413	128	9	7-3	.992	1	106	69	O91(88/0/3),D3	23	0.8
1981	Bal A	83	189	19	47	7	0	6	20	22-1	1	32	.249	.329	.381	105	1	7-6	.990	-4	86	77	O73(67/0/10),D4	0	-0.6
1982	Bal A	122	322	69	103	15	2	24	66	54-10	1	59	.320	.415	.602	178	36	7-6	**1.000**	-2	102	35	O111(110/0/2)	0	2.9
1983	†Bal A	122	310	52	87	13	2	15	60	49-1	1	55	.281	.374	.481	137	17	2-1	.982	-4	86	120	O107(106/1/0)/2D	0	1.0
1984	Bal A	105	270	34	64	13	0	8	28	33-3	1	54	.237	.319	.374	94	-2	1-0	.971	-3	85	137	O67L,D22,1b2	18	-0.7
1985	Bal A	12	26	0	2	0	0	0	2	2-0	0	3	.077	.138	.077	-39	-5	0-0	1.000	0	129	0	O4L,D6	0	-0.5
Total	16	1368	3476	510	881	137	18	116	441	446-30	9	596	.253	.337	.403	108	45	128-78	.984	-2	94	108	O906L,D125,3b72,2b71,1b28,S4	87	0.6
LOWERY, TERRELL	Quenton Terrell; B10.25.1970 Oakland CA; BR/TR/6´3˝/(180–195); [TexA91 2/63]; d9.13; Col Loyola Marymount																								
1997	Chi N	9	14	2	4	0	0	0	0	3-0	0	3	.286	.412	.286	84	0	1-0	1.000	2	106	921	O6(5/2/0)	0	0.2
1998	Chi N	24	15	2	3	1	0	0	1	3-0	0	7	.200	.333	.267	58	-1	0-0	.929	-1	101	0	O22(2/20/0)	0	-0.1
1999	TB A	66	185	25	48	15	1	2	17	19-0	1	53	.259	.330	.384	81	-5	0-2	.971	-2	87	133	O60(29/36/1)	0	-0.8
2000	SF N	24	34	13	15	4	0	1	5	7-0	1	8	.441	.548	.647	214	7	1-0	.917	-1	72	0	O20(13/0/8)/D	0	0.5
Total	4	123	248	42	70	20	1	3	23	32-0	2	71	.282	.367	.407	98	1	2-2	.964	-2	87	147	O108(49/58/9)/D	0	-0.2
LOWREY, PEANUTS	Harry Lee; B8.27.1917 Culver City CA; D7.2.1986 Inglewood CA; BR/TR/5´8.5˝/(170–172); d4.14; Mil 1944; C17; OF(548/387/62)																								
1942	Chi N	27	58	4	11	0	0	1	4	4	0	4	.190	.242	.241	43	-4	0	.978	2	112	143	O19(7/15/0)	0	-0.4
1943	Chi N	130	480	59	140	25	12	1	63	35	0	24	.292	.340	.400	115	7	13	.982	6	106	121	O113C,S16,2b3	0	1.2
1945	†Chi N	143	523	72	148	22	7	7	89	48	0	27	.283	.343	.392	106	3	11	.987	4	95	176	O138(125/14/0),S2	0	0.0

YEAR	TM LG	G	AB	R	H	2B	3B	HR	RBI	BB-IB	HP	SO	AVG	OBP	SLG	AOPS	ABR	SB-CS	FA	FR	RNG	THR	GAMES AT POSITION	DL	BFW
1946	Chi N★	144	540	75	139	24	5	4	54	56	1	22	.257	.328	.343	92	-6	10	.979	2	100	127	O126(73/60/0),3b20	0	-1.2
1947	Chi N	115	448	56	126	17	5	5	37	38	1	26	.281	.339	.375	93	-5	2	.945	10	117	132	3b91,O25(18/6/1),2b6	0	0.3
1948	Chi N	129	435	47	128	12	3	2	54	34	1	31	.294	.347	.349	93	-5	2	.983	-0	98	119	O103(63/43/0),3b9,2b2/S	0	-1.0
1949	Chi N	38	111	18	30	5	0	2	10	9	0	8	.270	.325	.369	88	-2	3	.966	-2	95	46	O31(28/3/1)/3	0	-0.6
	Cin N	89	309	48	85	16	2	2	25	37	1	11	.275	.354	.359	91	-3	1	.995	6	112	102	O78(77/1/0)	0	-0.3
	Year	127	420	66	115	21	2	4	35	46	1	19	.274	.347	.362	90	-5	4	.989	4	108	88	O109(105/4/1)/3	0	-0.9
1950	Cin N	91	264	34	60	14	0	1	11	36	0	7	.227	.320	.292	62	-14	0	.987	2	107	81	O72(66/2/6)/2	0	-1.6
	StL N	17	56	10	15	0	0	1	4	6	1	1	.268	.349	.321	74	-2	0	1.000	1	96	85	2b6,3b5,O4(3/1/0)	0	-0.1
	Year	108	320	44	75	14	0	2	15	42	1	8	.234	.325	.297	64	-16	0	.982	3	106	78	O76(69/3/6),2b7,3b5	0	-1.7
1951	StL N	114	370	52	112	19	5	5	40	35	2	12	.303	.366	.422	111	6	0-1	.983	-8	92	75	O85(13/74/0),3b11,2b3	0	-0.5
1952	StL N	132	374	48	107	18	2	1	48	34	4	13	.286	.352	.353	96	-1	3-2	.978	-5	96	42	O106(63/35/6),3b6	0	-1.1
1953	StL N	104	182	26	49	9	2	5	27	15	0	21	.269	.325	.423	93	-2	1-0	1.000	-3	87	56	O38(3/10/25),2b10/3	0	-0.5
1954	StL N	74	61	6	7	1	2	0	5	9	0	9	.115	.222	.197	12	-8	0-0	1.000	-0	104	0	O12(3/1/9)	0	-0.8
1955	Phi N	54	106	9	20	4	0	0	8	7-0	0	10	.189	.237	.226	25	-12	2-0	.973	-1	95	73	O28(6/9/14),2b2/1	0	-1.3
Total	13	1401	4317	564	1177	186	45	37	479	403-0	11	226	.273	.336	.362	92	-48	48-3	.983	13	100	108	O978L,3b144,2b33,S19/1	0	-7.9
LOWRY, DWIGHT	Dwight (b Dwight Lowery); B10.23.1957 Lumberton NC; D7.10.1997 Jamestown NY; BL/TR/6´3˝/210; [DetA80 11/278]; d4.3; Col North Carolina																								
1984	Det A	32	45	8	11	2	0	2	7	3-0	0	11	.244	.292	.422	95	0	0-0	1.000	1	107	83	C31	0	0.1
1986	Det A	56	150	21	46	4	0	3	18	17-0	4	19	.307	.392	.393	114	4	0-0	.992	-5	97	72	C55/1rf	0	0.1
1987	Det A	13	25	0	5	2	0	0	1	0-0	0	6	.200	.200	.280	26	-3	0-0	1.000	-2	63	45	C12/1	0	-0.4
1988	Min A	7	7	0	0	0	0	0	0	0-0	0	2	.000	.000	.000	-97	-2	0-0	1.000	0	26	214	C5	0	-0.2
Total	4	108	227	29	62	8	0	5	26	20-0	4	38	.273	.343	.374	95	-1	0-0	.995	-5	94	75	C103,1b2/rf	0	-0.4
LOWRY, JOHN	John D.; B Baltimore MD; d6.26																								
1875	Was NA	6	22	2	3	0	0	0	0	1	—	0	.136	.174	.136	10	-2	0-1	.727	-1	0	0	O6C	—	-0.3
LOZADO, WILLIE	William; B5.12.1959 New York NY; BR/TR/6´0˝/166; d7.16; Col Miami–Dade Wolfson (FL) CC																								
1984	Mil A	43	107	15	29	8	2	1	20	12-0	0	23	.271	.339	.411	112	2	0-3	.925	-4	90	121	3b36,S6/2D	0	-0.3
LUBRATICH, STEVE	Steven George; B5.1.1955 Oakland CA; BR/TR/6´0˝/170; d9.27; Col California–Riverside																								
1981	Cal A	7	21	2	3	1	0	0	1	0-0	0	2	.143	.143	.190	-5	-3	1-0	1.000	2	139	185	3b6	0	-0.1
1983	Cal A	57	156	12	34	9	0	0	7	4-0	0	17	.218	.236	.276	41	-13	0-1	.949	9	105	130	S23,3b22,2b14	0	-0.2
Total	2	64	177	14	37	10	0	0	8	4-0	0	19	.209	.225	.266	36	-16	1-1	.988	10	134	143	3b28,S23,2b14	0	-0.3
LUBY, HUGH	Hugh Max "Hal"; B6.13.1913 Blackfoot ID; D5.4.1986 Eugene OR; BR/TR/5´10˝/185; d9.10; Mil 1945; Col Creighton																								
1936	Phi A	9	38	3	7	1	0	0	3	0	1	7	.184	.205	.211	3	-6	2-0	.880	-3	98	48	2b9	—	-0.8
1944	NY N	111	323	30	82	10	2	2	35	52	4	15	.254	.364	.316	93	0	2	.943	13	107	129	3b65,2b45/1	0	1.5
Total	2	120	361	33	89	11	2	2	38	52	5	22	.247	.349	.305	83	-6	4-0	.943	9	107	129	3b65,2b54/1	0	0.7
LUCADELLO, JOHNNY	John; B2.22.1919 Thurber TX; D10.30.2001 San Antonio TX; BB/TR/5´11˝/160; d9.24; Mil 1942–45																								
1938	StL A	7	20	1	3	1	0	0	0	0	0	0	.150	.150	.200	-13	-4	0-0	.909	-1	64	0	3b6	—	-0.4
1939	StL A	9	30	0	7	2	0	0	4	2	0	4	.233	.281	.300	48	-2	0-0	.912	-3	75	58	2b7	—	-0.5
1940	StL A	17	63	15	20	4	2	2	10	6	2	4	.317	.394	.540	137	3	1-0	.968	1	107	116	2b16	—	0.5
1941	StL A	107	351	58	98	22	4	2	31	48	0	23	.279	.366	.382	95	-1	5-2	.962	-13	98	87	2b70,S12,3b6/lf	0	-0.9
1946	StL A	87	210	21	52	7	1	1	15	36	0	20	.248	.358	.305	82	-3	0-1	.942	-5	98	52	3b37,2b19	0	-0.8
1947	NY A	12	12	0	1	0	0	0	0	1	0	5	.083	.154	.083	-33	-2	0-0	1.000	-1	0	0	2b5	0	-0.3
Total	6	239	686	95	181	36	7	5	60	93	2	56	.264	.353	.359	88	-9	6-3	.965	-22	94	88	2b117,3b49,S12/lf	0	-2.4
LUCAS, RED	Charles Fred "The Nashville Narcissus"; B4.28.1902 Columbia TN; D7.9.1986 Nashville TN; BL/TR/5´9.5˝/170; d4.19; ▲																								
1923	NY N	3	2	0	0	0	0	0	0	0	0	1	.000	.000	.000	-99	0	0-0	1.000	1	257	0	P3	—	0.0
1924	Bos N	33	33	5	11	1	0	0	5	1	0	4	.333	.353	.364	96	0	0-0	1.000	1	107	95	P27,3b2	—	0.0
1925	Bos N	6	20	1	3	0	0	0	2	2	0	4	.150	.227	.150	-2	-3	0-0	.968	-0	109	122	2b6	—	-0.3
1926	Cin N	66	76	15	23	4	4	0	14	10	0	13	.303	.384	.461	130	3	0	1.000	1	94	52	P39/2	—	-0.1
1927	Cin N	80	150	14	47	5	2	0	28	12	1	10	.313	.368	.373	102	1	0	.983	-4	97	84	P37,2b5,S3/lf	—	-0.3
1928	Cin N	39	73	8	23	2	1	0	7	4	0	6	.315	.351	.370	90	6	0	**1.000**	-0	95	137	P27	—	0.0
1929	Cin N	76	140	15	41	6	0	0	13	13	0	15	.293	.353	.336	75	12	1	.949	0	105	89	P32	—	0.0
1930	Cin N	80	113	18	38	4	1	2	19	17	0	4	.336	.423	.442	115	16	0	**1.000**	-3	70	69	P33	—	0.0
1931	Cin N	97	153	15	43	4	0	0	17	12	0	9	.281	.333	.307	78	12	0	.984	1	108	88	P29	—	0.0
1932	Cin N	76	150	13	43	11	2	0	19	10	1	9	.287	.335	.387	97	15	0	.973	-0	98	126	P31	—	0.0
1933	Cin N	75	122	14	35	6	1	1	15	12	1	6	.287	.356	.377	111	13	0	**1.000**	0	107	198	P29	—	0.0
1934	Pit N	68	105	11	23	5	1	0	8	6	0	16	.219	.261	.286	45	3	1	.939	-3	67	98	P29	—	0.0
1935	Pit N	47	66	6	21	6	0	0	10	7	1	11	.318	.392	.409	112	8	0	.968	-1	87	77	P20	—	0.0
1936	Pit N	69	108	11	26	4	1	0	14	8	0	17	.241	.293	.296	58	4	0	.976	-1	88	175	P27	—	0.0
1937	Pit N	59	82	8	22	3	0	0	17	7	0	6	.268	.326	.305	72	5	0	1.000	-2	70	76	P20	—	0.0
1938	Pit N	33	46	1	5	0	0	0	2	3	0	2	.109	.163	.109	-24	-2	0	1.000	-1	82	98	P13	—	0.0
Total	16	907	1439	155	404	61	13	3	190	124	4	133	.281	.340	.347	84	93	2-0	.981	-14	93	107	P396,2b12,S3,3b2/lf	—	-0.7
LUCAS, FRED	Frederick Warrington "Fritz"; B1.19.1903 Vineland NJ; D3.11.1987 Cambridge MD; BR/TR/5´10˝/165; d7.15																								
1935	Phi N	20	34	1	9	0	0	0	2	3	0	6	.265	.324	.265	55	-2	0	.944	-0	105	0	O10(4/3/3)	—	-0.3
LUCAS, JOHNNY	John Charles "Buster"; B2.10.1903 Glen Carbon IL; D10.31.1970 Maryville IL; BR/TL/5´10˝/186; d4.15																								
1931	Bos A	3	2	0	0	0	0	0	0	0	0	1	.000	.000	.000	-99	-1	0-0	ø	-0	0	0	O2(1/1/0)	—	-0.1
1932	Bos A	1	1	0	0	0	0	0	0	0	0	0	.000	.000	.000	-99	0	0-0	ø	0	—	—	/H	—	0.0
Total	2	4	3	0	0	0	0	0	0	0	0	1	.000	.000	.000	-99	-1	0-0	.000	-0	0	0	O2(1/1/0)	—	-0.1
LUCE, FRANK	Frank Edward; B12.6.1896 Spencer OH; D2.3.1942 Milwaukee WI; BL/TR/5´11˝/180; d9.17																								
1923	Pit N	9	12	2	6	0	0	0	3	2	0	2	.500	.571	.500	181	2	2-1	1.000	-0	89	0	O5(3/1/1)	—	0.1
LUDERUS, FRED	Frederick William; B9.12.1885 Milwaukee WI; D1.5.1961 Three Lakes WI; BL/TR/5´11.5˝/185; d9.23																								
1909	Chi N	11	37	8	11	1	1	1	9	3	1	—	.297	.366	.459	152	2	0	.950	-2	67	88	1b11	—	0.0
1910	Chi N	24	54	5	11	1	1	0	3	4	0	3	.204	.259	.259	52	-4	0	.975	-1	88	93	1b17	—	-0.5
	Phi N	21	68	10	20	5	2	0	14	9	1	5	.294	.385	.426	132	3	2	.985	1	111	135	1b19	—	0.3
	Year	45	122	15	31	6	3	0	17	13	1	8	.254	.331	.352	98	0	2	.981	-0	101	117	1b36	—	-0.2
1911	Phi N	146	551	69	166	24	11	16	99	40	4	76	.301	.353	.472	128	17	6	.985	-2	92	102	1b146	—	1.2
1912	Phi N	148	572	77	147	31	5	10	69	44	7	65	.257	.318	.381	85	-13	8	.990	10	**128**	96	1b146	—	-0.6
1913	Phi N	155	588	67	154	32	7	18	86	34	2	51	.262	.304	.432	105	1	5-8	.984	1	104	90	1b155	—	-0.4
1914	Phi N	121	443	55	110	16	5	12	55	33	5	31	.248	.308	.388	100	-1	2	.975	1	**114**	72	1b121	—	-0.3
1915	†Phi N	141	499	55	157	36	7	7	62	42	7	36	.315	.376	.457	150	31	9-7	.993	10	**129**	107	1b141	—	4.0
1916	Phi N	146	508	52	143	26	3	5	53	41	5	32	.281	.341	.374	115	10	8	.982	-2	99	109	1b146	—	0.6
1917	Phi N	**154**	522	57	136	24	4	5	72	65	6	35	.261	.349	.351	110	10	5	.991	4	109	102	1b154	—	1.1
1918	Phi N	**125**	468	54	135	23	2	5	67	42	3	33	.288	.351	.378	115	10	4	.988	6	119	95	1b125	—	1.4
1919	Phi N	**138**	509	60	149	30	6	5	49	54	4	48	.293	.365	.405	123	16	6	.985	9	**131**	92	1b138	—	2.4
1920	Phi N	16	32	1	5	2	0	0	4	3	0	6	.156	.229	.219	28	-3	0-1	.983	0	114	143	1b7	—	-0.4
Total	12	1346	4851	570	1344	251	54	84	642	414	45	421	.277	.340	.403	113	79	55-16	.986	37	113	97	1b1326	—	8.8
LUDWICK, RYAN	Ryan Andrew; B7.13.1978 Satellite Beach FL; BR/TL/6´3˝/(203–210); [OakA99 2/60]; d6.5; b–Eric; Col Nevada–Las Vegas																								
2002	Tex A	23	81	10	19	6	0	1	9	7-0	0	24	.235	.295	.346	68	-4	2-1	1.000	-3	75	0	O22(2/21/1)	0	-0.7
2003	Tex A	8	26	3	4	1	0	0	0	4-0	0	9	.154	.267	.192	23	-3	0-0	1.000	-0	98	0	O8(4/0/6)	0	-0.4
	Cle A	39	136	14	36	7	1	7	26	8-1	0	39	.265	.306	.485	104	0	2-0	1.000	1	108	105	O32(13/0/19),D4	20	0.1
	Year	47	162	17	40	8	1	7	26	12-1	0	48	.247	.299	.438	90	-3	2-0	1.000	1	106	83	O40(17/0/25),D4	0	-0.3
2004	Cle A	15	50	3	11	2	0	2	4	2-0	2	14	.220	.278	.380	72	-2	0-0	.970	-0	114	0	O15R	92	-0.3
2005	Cle A	19	41	8	9	0	0	4	5	7-0	0	13	.220	.333	.512	125	1	0-1	.957	-0	105	0	O15(9/0/6),D3	0	0.0
Total	4	104	334	38	79	16	1	14	44	28-1	2	99	.237	.299	.416	86	-8	4-2	.989	-3	99	39	O92(28/21/47),D7	112	-1.3
LUDWIG, BILL	William Lawrence; B5.27.1882 Louisville KY; D9.5.1947 Louisville KY; BR/TR; d4.16																								
1908	StL N	66	187	15	34	2	2	0	8	16	0	—	.182	.246	.214	50	-11	3	.952	-10	*65*	*127*	C62	—	-1.8

LUEBBE, ROY Roy John; B9.17.1900 Parkersburg IA; D8.21.1985 Papillion NE; BB/TR/6´0˝/175; d8.22

YEAR	TM LG	G	AB	R	H	2B	3B	HR	RBI	BB-IB	HP	SO	AVG	OBP	SLG	AOPS	ABR	SB-CS	FA	FR	RNG	THR	GAMES AT POSITION	DL	BFW
1925	NY A	8	15	1	0	0	0	0	3	2	0	6	.000	.118	.000	-69	-4	0-0	1.000	1	*103*	*81*	C8	—	-0.3

LUFF, HENRY Henry T.; B9.14.1856 Philadelphia PA; D10.11.1916 Philadelphia PA; 5´11˝/175; d4.19; ▲

YEAR	TM LG	G	AB	R	H	2B	3B	HR	RBI	BB-IB	HP	SO	AVG	OBP	SLG	AOPS	ABR	SB-CS	FA	FR	RNG	THR	GAMES AT POSITION	DL	BFW
1875	NH NA	38	166	15	45	10	3	2	18	0	—	5	.271	.271	.404	150	10	3-3	.689	-5	99	161	3b30,P10,O4(0/1/3)/S	—	0.2
1882	Det N	3	11	1	3	2	0	0	1	0	—	0	.273	.273	.455	129	0	—	.667	-2	90	231	2b3/cf	—	-0.1
	Cin AA	28	120	16	28	2	2	0	6	2	—	—	.233	.246	.283	74	-4	—	.922	-2	95	112	1b27/rf	—	-0.8
1883	Lou AA	6	23	1	4	0	0	0	2	0	—	—	.174	.174	.174	13	-2	—	.868	-1	0	65	1b4,O2(0/1/1)	—	-0.3
1884	Phi U	26	111	9	30	4	2	0	—	4	—	—	.270	.296	.342	101	-3	—	.733	-4	57	0	O12(11/0/1),1b6,3b5,2b3	—	-0.7
	KC U	5	19	0	1	0	0	0	—	1	—	—	.053	.100	.053	-60	-4	—	.444	-3	82	0	3b4,O4(3/1/1)	—	-0.7
	Year	31	130	9	31	4	2	0	—	5	—	—	.238	.267	.300	78	-7	—	.706	-7	51	0	O16(14/1/2),3b9,1b6,2b3	—	-1.4
Total	3	68	284	27	66	8	4	0	9	7	—	0	.232	.251	.289	73	-13	—	.911	-12	107	108	1b37,O20(14/3/4),3b9,2b6	—	-2.6

LUGO, JULIO Julio Cesar; B11.16.1975 Santa Cruz de Barahona, D.R.; BR/TR/6´0˝/(165–170); [HouN94 43/1193]; d4.15; b–Ruddy; Col Connors St. (OK) JC

YEAR	TM LG	G	AB	R	H	2B	3B	HR	RBI	BB-IB	HP	SO	AVG	OBP	SLG	AOPS	ABR	SB-CS	FA	FR	RNG	THR	GAMES AT POSITION	DL	BFW
2000	Hou N	116	420	78	119	22	5	10	40	37-0	4	93	.283	.346	.431	88	-8	22-9	.951	-9	93	84	S60,2b45,O6(3/1/2)	0	-0.9
2001	†Hou N	140	513	93	135	20	3	10	37	46-0	5	116	.263	.326	.372	76	-19	12-11	.964	15	106	101	S133,O8(6/0/2),2b2	0	0.5
2002	Hou N	88	322	45	84	15	1	8	35	28-3	2	74	.261	.322	.388	80	-9	9-3	.976	-10	88	62	S84	48	-1.3
2003	Hou N	22	65	6	16	3	0	0	2	9-1	0	12	.246	.338	.292	63	-3	2-1	.966	-1	95	83	S22	0	-0.3
	TB A	117	433	58	119	13	4	15	53	35-0	4	88	.275	.333	.427	101	0	10-3	.970	3	104	93	S117	0	1.2
2004	TB A	157	581	83	160	41	4	7	75	54-0	5	106	.275	.338	.396	94	-4	21-5	.963	2	104	97	S143,2b8,D5	0	1.1
2005	TB A	158	616	89	182	36	6	6	57	61-0	6	72	.295	.362	.403	106	7	39-11	.968	2	95	85	S156	0	2.4
2006	TB A	73	289	53	89	17	1	12	27	27-0	3	47	.308	.373	.498	124	11	18-4	.957	-2	98	82	S73	31	1.5
	†LA N	49	146	16	32	5	1	0	10	12-0	1	29	.219	.278	.267	42	-13	6-5	.980	5	122	92	2b29,3b16,S8,O3(1/0/2)	0	-0.7
Total	7	920	3385	521	936	172	25	68	336	309-4	30	637	.277	.340	.402	91	-38	139-52	.965	3	99	88	S796,2b84,O17(10/1/6),3b16,D5	79	3.5

LUKACHYK, ROB Robert James; B7.24.1968 Jersey City NJ; BL/TR/6´0˝/185; [ChiA87 10/245]; d7.5; Col Brookdale (NJ) CC

YEAR	TM LG	G	AB	R	H	2B	3B	HR	RBI	BB-IB	HP	SO	AVG	OBP	SLG	AOPS	ABR	SB-CS	FA	FR	RNG	THR	GAMES AT POSITION	DL	BFW
1996	Mon N	2	2	0	0	0	0	0	0	0-0	0	1	.000	.000	.000	-98	-1	0-0	ø	0	—	—	/H	0	-0.1

LUKE, MATT Matthew Clifford; B2.26.1971 Long Beach CA; BL/TL/6´5˝/220; [NYA92 8/214]; d4.3; Col California

YEAR	TM LG	G	AB	R	H	2B	3B	HR	RBI	BB-IB	HP	SO	AVG	OBP	SLG	AOPS	ABR	SB-CS	FA	FR	RNG	THR	GAMES AT POSITION	DL	BFW
1996	NY A	1	0	1	0	0	0	0	0	0-0	0	0	ø	ø	ø	ø	0	0-0	ø	0	—	—	/R	0	0.0
1998	LA N	33	77	10	22	7	0	3	11	3-0	0	18	.286	.313	.494	113	1	0-0	.958	-13	23	62	O15(13/0/2),1b12	0	-1.4
	Cle A	2	2	0	0	0	0	0	0	0-0	0	2	.000	.000	.000	-96	-1	0-0	ø	0	—	—	/H	0	-0.1
	LA N	69	160	24	34	5	1	9	23	14-2	1	42	.213	.278	.425	86	-4	2-1	1.000	-3	23	62	O48(36/0/12),1b6	0	-1.0
1999	Ana A	18	30	4	9	0	0	3	6	2-0	0	10	.300	.344	.600	135	1	0-0	1.000	1	101	0	O6(2/0/4),1b4	69	0.2
Total	3	123	269	39	65	12	1	15	40	19-2	1	70	.242	.293	.461	98	-3	2-1	.991	-15	55	90	O69(51/0/18),1b22	69	-2.3

LUKON, EDDIE Edward Paul "Mongoose"; B8.5.1920 Burgettstown PA; D11.7.1996 Canonsburg PA; BL/TL/5´10˝/168; d8.6; Mil 1943–45

YEAR	TM LG	G	AB	R	H	2B	3B	HR	RBI	BB-IB	HP	SO	AVG	OBP	SLG	AOPS	ABR	SB-CS	FA	FR	RNG	THR	GAMES AT POSITION	DL	BFW
1941	Cin N	23	86	6	23	3	0	0	3	6	0	6	.267	.315	.302	74	-3	1	.980	1	110	103	O22R	0	-0.4
1945	Cin N	2	8	1	1	0	0	0	0	0	0	1	.125	.125	.125	-31	-1	0	1.000	0	126	0	O2C	0	-0.1
1946	Cin N	102	312	31	78	8	8	12	34	26	1	29	.250	.310	.442	116	3	3	.985	-3	97	59	O83(72/0/11)	0	-0.6
1947	Cin N	86	200	26	41	6	1	11	33	28	1	36	.205	.306	.410	89	-4	0	1.000	1	99	101	O55(33/0/25)	0	-0.6
Total	4	213	606	64	143	17	9	23	70	60	2	72	.236	.307	.408	99	-5	4	.989	-2	100	77	O162(105/2/58)	0	-1.7

LUM, MIKE Michael Ken-Wai; B10.27.1945 Honolulu HI; BL/TL/6´0˝/(180–185); d9.12; C3

YEAR	TM LG	G	AB	R	H	2B	3B	HR	RBI	BB-IB	HP	SO	AVG	OBP	SLG	AOPS	ABR	SB-CS	FA	FR	RNG	THR	GAMES AT POSITION	DL	BFW
1967	Atl N	9	26	1	6	0	0	0	1	1-0	0	4	.231	.259	.231	42	-2	0-1	.944	1	114	287	O6C	0	-0.2
1968	Atl N	122	232	22	52	7	3	3	21	14-2	4	35	.224	.277	.319	79	-6	3-5	.976	3	103	160	O95(74/7/21)	0	-0.9
1969	†Atl N	121	168	20	45	8	0	1	22	16-4	0	18	.268	.326	.333	86	-3	0-0	.992	7	134	70	O89(56/16/21)	0	0.2
1970	Atl N	123	291	25	74	17	2	7	28	17-0	5	43	.254	.306	.399	83	-8	3-2	.988	5	120	67	O98(36/33/35)	0	-0.6
1971	Atl N	145	454	56	122	14	1	13	55	47-5	5	43	.269	.340	.390	101	1	0-3	.990	9	106	106	O125(10/17/104)/1	0	0.4
1972	Atl N	123	369	40	84	14	2	9	38	50-4	3	52	.228	.323	.350	84	-6	1-4	.976	6	**117**	55	O109(30/20/62),1b2	0	-0.7
1973	Atl N	138	513	74	151	26	6	16	82	41-7	6	89	.294	.351	.462	116	11	2-5	.991	-1	79	95	1b84,O64(48/2/14)	0	-0.1
1974	Atl N	106	361	50	84	11	2	11	50	45-12	2	49	.233	.319	.366	89	-6	0-2	.994	-6	75	117	1b60,O50(24/9/25)	38	-2.0
1975	Atl N	124	364	32	83	8	2	8	36	39-7	0	38	.228	.302	.327	72	-14	2-4	.992	-3	90	83	1b60,O38(1/32/5)	0	-2.5
1976	†Cin N	84	136	15	31	5	1	3	20	22-1	1	24	.228	.331	.346	92	-1	0-1	1.000	-4	80	0	O38(33/2/5)	0	-0.7
1977	Cin N	81	125	14	20	1	0	5	16	9-1	1	33	.160	.221	.288	35	-12	2-0	1.000	-1	108	0	O24(12/1/11),1b8	0	-1.4
1978	Cin N	86	146	15	39	7	1	6	23	22-4	0	18	.267	.361	.452	126	5	0-0	.987	3	97	305	O43(10/26/9),1b7	0	0.8
1979	Atl N	111	217	27	54	6	0	6	27	18-1	0	34	.249	.304	.359	76	-7	0-2	.998	1	106	100	1b51,O3L	0	-1.0
1980	Atl N	93	83	7	17	3	0	0	5	18-3	0	19	.205	.343	.241	66	-3	0-0	1.000	0	105	0	O19L,1b10	0	-0.3
1981	Atl N	10	11	1	1	0	0	0	0	2-1	0	2	.091	.231	.091	-6	-2	0-0	1.000	0	157	0	/lf	0	-0.1
	Chi N	41	58	5	14	1	0	2	7	5-2	1	5	.241	.308	.362	86	-1	0-0	.923	-2	64	0	O14(12/0/3)/1	0	-0.4
	Year	51	69	6	15	1	0	2	7	7-3	1	7	.217	.295	.319	72	-3	0-0	.938	-2	72	0	O15(13/0/3)/1	0	-0.5
Total	15	1517	3554	404	877	128	20	90	431	366-54	28	506	.247	.319	.370	89	-54	13-29	.986	19	108	80	O816(369/171/315),1b284	38	-9.5

LUMLEY, HARRY Harry Garfield "Judge"; B9.29.1880 Forest City PA; D5.22.1938 Binghamton NY; BL/TL/5´10˝/183; d4.14; M1

YEAR	TM LG	G	AB	R	H	2B	3B	HR	RBI	BB-IB	HP	SO	AVG	OBP	SLG	AOPS	ABR	SB-CS	FA	FR	RNG	THR	GAMES AT POSITION	DL	BFW
1904	Bro N	150	577	79	161	23	**18**	**9**	78	41	4	—	.279	.331	.428	137	22	30	.955	4	141	144	O150R	—	2.1
1905	Bro N	130	505	50	148	19	10	7	47	36	0	—	.293	.340	.412	134	19	22	.912	-0	128	88	O129R	—	1.4
1906	Bro N	133	484	72	157	23	12	9	61	48	1	—	.324	.386	**.477**	**184**	**45**	35	.949	2	81	126	O131R	—	4.5
1907	Bro N	127	454	47	121	23	11	9	66	31	2	—	.267	.316	.425	144	19	18	.959	-2	95	178	O118R	—	1.4
1908	Bro N	127	440	36	95	13	12	4	39	29	1	—	.216	.266	.327	93	-6	4	.955	-3	93	177	O116R	—	-1.7
1909	Bro N	55	172	13	43	8	3	0	14	16	0	—	.250	.314	.331	104	1	1	.948	2	123	57	O52R,M	—	0.0
1910	Bro N	8	21	3	3	0	0	0	0	3	1	6	.143	.280	.143	25	-2	0	.833	-1	80	0	O4R	—	-0.3
Total	7	730	2653	300	728	109	66	38	305	204	9	6	.274	.328	.408	135	98	110	.946	1	110	134	O700R	—	7.4

LUMPE, JERRY Jerry Dean; B6.2.1933 Lincoln MO; BL/TR/6´2˝/(179–190); d4.17; C1

YEAR	TM LG	G	AB	R	H	2B	3B	HR	RBI	BB-IB	HP	SO	AVG	OBP	SLG	AOPS	ABR	SB-CS	FA	FR	RNG	THR	GAMES AT POSITION	DL	BFW
1956	NY A	20	62	12	16	3	0	0	4	5-2	0	11	.258	.313	.306	66	-3	1-1	.916	1	105	135	S17/3	0	0.0
1957	†NY A	40	103	15	35	6	2	0	11	9-0	0	13	.340	.389	.437	128	4	2-2	.956	-2	90	139	3b30,S6	0	0.2
1958	†NY A	81	232	34	59	8	4	3	32	23-2	1	21	.254	.319	.362	92	-3	1-2	.943	5	109	117	3b65,S5	0	0.2
1959	NY A	18	45	2	10	0	0	0	2	6-5	0	7	.222	.314	.222	52	-3	0-0	1.000	1	100	144	3b12,S4/2	0	-0.2
	KC A	108	403	47	98	11	5	3	28	41-1	0	32	.243	.313	.318	72	-15	2-1	.986	7	107	105	2b61,S56,3b4	0	0.0
	Year	126	448	49	108	11	5	3	30	47-6	0	39	.241	.313	.308	70	-18	2-1	.987	8	107	107	2b62,S60,3b16	0	-0.2
1960	KC A	146	574	69	156	19	3	8	53	48-1	0	49	.272	.326	.357	85	-13	1-1	.982	9	100	99	2b134,S15	0	0.7
1961	KC A	148	569	81	167	29	9	3	54	48-0	2	39	.293	.348	.392	96	-3	1-0	.979	21	**111**	93	2b147	0	3.0
1962	KC A	156	641	89	193	34	10	10	83	44-0	0	38	.301	.341	.432	103	2	0-2	.986	-5	98	90	2b156,S2	0	0.9
1963	KC A	157	595	75	161	26	7	5	59	58-3	0	44	.271	.333	.363	91	-6	3-2	.988	-1	101	92	2b155	0	0.6
1964	Det A☆	158	624	75	160	21	6	6	46	50-3	2	61	.256	.312	.338	80	-17	2-1	.983	-17	92	94	2b158	0	-2.1
1965	Det A	145	502	72	129	15	3	4	39	56-1	3	34	.257	.333	.323	87	-7	7-0	.985	-9	92	89	2b139	0	-0.4
1966	Det A	113	385	30	89	14	3	1	26	24-1	0	44	.231	.275	.291	62	-19	0-3	.991	1	95	94	2b95	0	-1.3
1967	Det A	81	177	19	41	4	0	4	17	16-2	0	18	.232	.295	.322	80	-4	0-0	.963	1	108	75	2b54,3b6	0	0.0
Total	12	1371	4912	620	1314	190	52	47	454	428-21	8	411	.268	.325	.356	87	-87	20-15	.984	13	99	93	2b1100,3b118,S105	0	1.6

LUNA, HECTOR Hector R.; B2.1.1980 Monte Cristi, D.R.; BR/TR/6´1˝/170; d4.8; OF(28/3/23)

YEAR	TM LG	G	AB	R	H	2B	3B	HR	RBI	BB-IB	HP	SO	AVG	OBP	SLG	AOPS	ABR	SB-CS	FA	FR	RNG	THR	GAMES AT POSITION	DL	BFW
2004	†StL N	83	173	25	43	7	2	3	22	13-0	2	37	.249	.304	.364	72	-8	6-3	.947	6	123	130	S24,2b19,3b16,O10(8/2/0)	0	0.0
2005	†StL N	64	137	26	39	10	2	1	18	9-0	4	25	.285	.344	.409	95	-1	10-2	.947	6	113	348	O25(3/1/21),2b22,3b7,S6	0	0.7
2006	StL N	76	223	27	65	14	1	4	21	21-1	1	34	.291	.355	.417	96	-1	5-3	.976	-7	94	98	2b41,O18(17/0/1),S14,1b6,3b2/D	0	-0.6
	Cle A	37	127	14	35	7	1	2	17	6-0	0	26	.276	.306	.394	83	-3	0-1	.947	-2	92	102	2b20,S10,3b2/rfD	0	-0.4
Total	3	260	660	92	182	38	6	10	78	49-1	7	122	.276	.330	.397	87	-13	21-9	.973	3	98	110	2b102,O54L,S54,3b27,1b6,D3	0	-0.3

LUNAR, FERNANDO Fernando Jose; B5.25.1977 Cantaura, Anzoategui, Venez.; BR/TR/6´1˝/190; d5.8

YEAR	TM LG	G	AB	R	H	2B	3B	HR	RBI	BB-IB	HP	SO	AVG	OBP	SLG	AOPS	ABR	SB-CS	FA	FR	RNG	THR	GAMES AT POSITION	DL	BFW
2000	Atl N	22	54	5	10	1	0	0	5	3-1	3	15	.185	.267	.204	21	-7	0-2	.993	4	60	109	C22	0	-0.3
	Bal A	9	16	0	2	0	0	0	1	0-0	1	4	.125	.176	.125	-23	-3	0-0	1.000	3	0	177	C9	0	0.0
2001	Bal A	64	167	8	41	7	0	0	16	7-0	3	32	.246	.287	.287	55	-11	0-0	.987	-3	97	124	C64	0	-1.0
2002	Bal A	2	0	0	0	0	0	0	0	0-0	0	0	ø	ø	ø	ø	0	0-0	1.000	0	0	0	C2	0	0.0
Total	3	97	237	13	53	8	0	0	22	10-1	7	51	.224	.275	.257	42	-21	0-2	.990	4	82	124	C97	0	-1.3

YEAR	TM LG	G	AB	R	H	2B	3B	HR	RBI	BB-IB	HP	SO	AVG	OBP	SLG	AOPS	ABR	SB-CS	FA	FR	RNG	THR	GAMES AT POSITION	DL	BFW
LUND, DON	Donald Andrew; B5.18.1923 Detroit MI; BR/TR/6´0˝/200; d7.3; C2; Col Michigan																								
1945	Bro N	4	3	0	0	0	0	0	0	1	0	1	.000	.250	.000	-27	0	0	ø	0	—	—	/H	0	0.0
1947	Bro N	11	20	5	6	2	0	2	5	3	0	7	.300	.391	.700	178	2	0	1.000	0	118	0	O5L	0	0.2
1948	Bro N	27	69	9	13	4	0	1	5	5	0	16	.188	.243	.290	42	-6	1	.977	1	105	136	O25(17/0/8)	0	-0.6
	StL A	63	161	21	40	7	4	3	25	10	3	17	.248	.305	.398	84	-5	0-0	1.000	-0	95	115	O45(21/0/25)	0	-0.7
1949	Det A	2	2	0	0	0	0	0	0	0	0	1	.000	.000	.000	-99	-1	0-0	ø	0	—	—	/H	0	-0.1
1952	Det A	8	23	1	7	0	0	0	1	3	0	3	.304	.385	.304	93	0	0-1	1.000	0	99	220	O7R	0	0.0
1953	Det A	131	421	51	108	21	4	9	47	39	2	65	.257	.323	.390	93	-5	3-3	.980	5	109	118	O123(37/29/69)	0	-0.6
1954	Det A	35	54	4	7	2	0	0	3	4	0	3	.130	.186	.167	-2	-8	1-0	.971	0	107	99	O31(19/3/11)	0	-0.8
Total	7	281	753	91	181	36	8	15	86	65	5	113	.240	.305	.369	81	-23	5-4	.983	7	106	118	O236(99/32/120)	0	-2.6
LUND, GORDY	Gordon Thomas; B2.23.1941 Iron Mountain MI; BR/TR/5´11˝/170; d8.1																								
1967	Cle A	3	8	1	2	1	0	0	0	0-0	0	2	.250	.250	.375	82	0	0-0	.667	-2	51	182	S2	0	-0.2
1969	Sea A	20	38	4	10	0	0	0	1	5-1	0	7	.263	.349	.263	74	-1	1-1	.927	-2	99	88	S17/23	0	-0.2
Total	2	23	46	5	12	1	0	0	1	5-1	0	9	.261	.333	.283	76	-1	1-1	.902	-4	92	101	S19/32	0	-0.4
LUNDSTEDT, TOM	Thomas Robert; B4.10.1949 Davenport IA; BB/TR/6´4˝/(195–205); [ChiN70 S1/17]; d8.31; Col Michigan																								
1973	Chi N	4	5	0	0	0	0	0	0	0-0	0	1	.000	.000	.000	-93	-1	0-0	1.000	-0	45	0	C4	0	-0.2
1974	Chi N	22	32	1	3	0	0	0	0	5-0	0	7	.094	.216	.094	-11	-5	0-0	.987	-1	81	59	C22	0	-0.6
1975	Min A	18	28	2	3	0	0	0	1	4-1	0	5	.107	.219	.107	-5	-4	0-0	1.000	-2	51	59	C14,D2	0	-0.5
Total	3	44	65	3	6	0	0	0	1	9-1	0	13	.092	.203	.092	-15	-10	0-0	.993	-3	67	54	C40,D2	0	-1.3
LUNSFORD, TREY	James Lewis; B5.25.1979 Odessa TX; BR/TR/6´1˝/195; [SFN00 33/991]; d9.12; Col Texas Tech																								
2002	SF N	3	3	0	2	1	0	0	1	0-0	0	1	.667	.667	1.000	343	1	0-0	.800	-1	46	0	C3	0	0.0
2003	SF N	1	1	0	0	0	0	0	0	0-0	0	0	.000	.000	.000	-99	0	0-0	ø	-0	0	0	/C	0	-0.1
Total	2	4	4	0	2	1	0	0	1	0-0	0	1	.500	.500	.750	228	1	0-0	.800	-1	40	0	C4	0	-0.1
LUNTE, HARRY	Harry August; B9.15.1892 St.Louis MO; D7.27.1965 St.Louis MO; BR/TR/5´11.5˝/165; d5.19																								
1919	Cle A	26	77	2	15	2	0	0	2	1	1	7	.195	.215	.221	21	-8	0	.935	-1	105	69	S24	—	-0.8
1920	†Cle A	23	71	6	14	0	0	0	7	5	0	6	.197	.250	.197	19	-8	0-1	.979	4	121	115	S21,2b2	—	-0.4
Total	2	49	148	8	29	2	0	0	9	6	1	13	.196	.232	.209	20	-16	0-1	.955	3	112	90	S45,2b2	—	-1.2
LUPIEN, TONY	Ulysses John; B4.23.1917 Chelmsford MA; D7.9.2004 Norwich VT; BL/TL/5´10.5˝/185; d9.12; Mil 1945; Col Harvard																								
1940	Bos A	10	19	5	9	3	2	0	4	1	0	1	.474	.500	.842	232	4	0-0	1.000	-0	79	109	1b8	—	0.3
1942	Bos A	128	463	63	130	25	7	3	70	50	0	20	.281	.351	.384	103	2	10-12	.992	-7	79	102	1b121	0	-1.8
1943	Bos A	154	608	65	155	21	9	4	47	54	1	23	.255	.317	.339	90	-9	16-9	.993	3	108	105	1b153	0	-1.5
1944	Phi N	153	597	82	169	23	9	5	52	56	2	29	.283	.347	.377	107	5	18	.992	2	104	95	1b151	0	-0.1
1945	Phi N	15	54	1	17	1	0	0	3	6	0	0	.315	.383	.333	103	0	2	1.000	3	163	89	1b15	0	0.2
1948	Chi A	**154**	617	69	152	19	3	6	54	74	0	38	.246	.327	.316	74	-23	11-7	.993	-4	91	99	1b154	0	-3.2
Total	6	614	2358	285	632	92	30	18	230	241	3	111	.268	.337	.355	94	-21	57-28	.993	-3	98	100	1b602	0	-6.1
LUPLOW, AL	Alvin David; B3.13.1939 Saginaw MI; BL/TR/5´11˝/(178–180); d9.16; Col Michigan St.																								
1961	Cle A	5	18	0	1	0	0	0	0	2-0	0	6	.056	.150	.056	-44	-4	0-0	1.000	1	89	510	O5(1/0/4)	0	-0.3
1962	Cle A	97	318	54	88	15	3	14	45	36-0	6	44	.277	.359	.475	127	12	1-0	.960	1	102	86	O86(70/0/24)	0	0.8
1963	Cle A	100	295	34	69	6	2	7	27	33-2	3	62	.234	.316	.339	85	-6	4-4	.994	5	110	138	O85(14/0/73)	0	-0.7
1964	Cle A	19	18	1	2	0	0	0	1	1-0	0	8	.111	.158	.111	-24	-3	0-0	1.000	1	223	0	O5(0/1/4)	0	-0.3
1965	Cle A	53	45	3	6	2	0	1	4	3-0	0	14	.133	.188	.244	22	-5	0-1	1.000	0	214	0	O6(2/1/3)	0	-0.5
1966	NY N	111	334	31	84	9	1	7	31	38-3	2	46	.251	.331	.347	91	-3	2-6	.987	-5	89	65	O101(16/24/71)	0	-1.6
1967	NY N	41	112	11	23	1	0	3	9	8-1	1	19	.205	.260	.295	61	-6	0-0	.966	-0	105	59	O33(6/16/16)	0	-0.8
	Pit N	55	103	13	19	1	0	1	8	6-0	1	14	.184	.232	.223	32	-9	1-0	.961	3	116	280	O25(15/2/8)	0	-0.8
	Year	96	215	24	42	2	0	4	17	14-1	2	33	.195	.247	.260	47	-15	1-0	.963	3	110	157	O58(21/18/24)	0	-1.6
Total	7	481	1243	147	292	34	6	33	125	127-6	13	213	.235	.311	.352	85	-24	8-11	.977	5	102	111	O346(124/44/203)	0	-4.2
LUSADER, SCOTT	Scott Edward; B9.30.1964 Chicago IL; BL/TL/5´10˝/165; [DetA85 6/158]; d9.1; Col Florida																								
1987	Det A	23	47	8	15	3	1	1	8	5-1	0	7	.319	.377	.489	135	2	1-0	.967	-1	98	0	O22(6/3/16)/D	0	0.1
1988	Det A	16	16	3	1	0	0	1	3	1-0	0	4	.063	.111	.250	-0	-2	0-0	1.000	-0	98	0	O4(2/2/2),D6	0	-0.3
1989	Det A	40	103	15	26	4	0	1	8	9-0	0	21	.252	.310	.320	80	-3	3-0	.933	-2	99	0	O33(4/8/24)/D	32	-0.5
1990	Det A	45	87	13	21	2	0	2	16	12-0	0	8	.241	.324	.333	86	-1	0-0	.982	-2	90	51	O42(12/5/27),D2	0	-0.4
1991	NY A	11	7	2	1	0	0	0	1	1-0	0	3	.143	.250	.143	12	-1	0-1	1.000	-0	86	0	O4(1/3/0)/D	47	-0.1
Total	5	135	260	41	64	9	1	5	36	28-1	0	43	.246	.313	.346	86	-5	4-1	.961	-6	95	20	O105(25/21/69),D11	79	-1.2
LUSH, ERNIE	Ernest Benjamin; B11.1.1885 Bridgeport CT; D2.26.1937 Detroit MI; BR/TL; d7.20; b–Billy; Col Niagara																								
1910	StL N	1	4	0	0	0	0	0	0	1	0	1	.000	.200	.000	-42	-1	0	1.000	-0	55	0	/cf	—	-0.1
LUSH, JOHNNY	John Charles; B10.8.1885 Williamsport PA; D11.18.1946 Beverly Hills CA; BL/TL/5´9.5˝/165; d4.22; ▲																								
1904	Phi N	106	369	39	102	22	3	2	42	27	6	—	.276	.336	.369	122	10	12	.950	-8	71	94	1b62,O33R,P7	—	-0.1
1905	Phi N	6	16	3	5	0	0	0	1	1	1	—	.313	.389	.313	114	0	0	.667	-1	0	0	O3(0/2/1),P2	—	-0.1
1906	Phi N	76	212	28	56	7	1	0	15	14	0	—	.264	.310	.307	92	-2	6	.907	4	111	76	P37,O22(0/6/16),1b2	—	0.1
1907	Phi N	17	40	5	8	1	1	0	5	1	0	—	.200	.220	.275	56	-2	1	1.000	-0	114	386	P8,O4(0/3/1)	—	-0.2
	StL N	27	82	6	23	2	3	0	5	5	0	—	.280	.322	.378	123	2	4	.917	-1	88	141	P20,O7(0/3/4)	—	-0.1
	Year	44	122	11	31	3	4	0	10	6	0	—	.254	.289	.344	101	-1	5	.941	-1	95	210	P28,O11(0/6/5)	—	-0.3
1908	StL N	45	89	7	15	2	0	0	2	7	0	—	.169	.229	.191	36	1	1	.926	0	102	0	P38	—	0.0
1909	StL N	45	92	11	22	5	0	0	14	6	1	—	.239	.293	.293	87	-1	2	.945	-1	98	0	P34,O3R	—	-0.1
1910	StL N	47	93	8	21	1	3	0	10	8	0	11	.226	.287	.301	74	4	2	.928	-2	89	86	P36	—	0.0
Total	7	369	993	107	252	40	11	2	94	69	8	11	.254	.307	.322	98	12	28	.926	-9	101	75	P182,O72(0/14/58),1b64	—	-0.5
LUSH, BILLY	William Lucas; B11.10.1873 Bridgeport CT; D8.28.1951 Hawthorne NY; BB/TR/5´7˝/165; d9.3; b–Ernie																								
1895	Was N	5	18	2	6	0	0	0	2	2	0	1	.333	.400	.333	91	0	0	.692	-2	0	0	O5(4/0/1)	—	-0.2
1896	Was N	97	352	74	87	9	11	4	45	66	2	49	.247	.369	.369	95	-1	28	.885	-0	155	117	O91(10/14/68),2b3	—	-0.5
1897	Was N	3	12	1	0	0	0	0	0	2	0	—	.000	.143	.000	-61	-3	0	1.000	0	208	0	O3R	—	-0.2
1901	Bos N	7	27	2	5	1	1	0	3	3	0	—	.185	.267	.296	58	-2	0	.960	2	188	406	O7C	—	0.0
1902	Bos N	120	413	68	92	8	1	2	19	76	2	—	.223	.346	.262	87	-1	30	.952	9	152	127	O116(10/104/2)/3	—	0.2
1903	Det A	119	423	71	116	18	14	1	33	70	1	—	.274	.379	.390	135	22	14	.968	8	138	125	O101(89/0/12),3b12,2b3,S3	—	2.5
1904	Cle A	138	477	76	123	13	8	1	50	72	3	—	.258	.359	.325	118	14	12	.959	2	71	101	O138(125/13/0)	—	0.9
Total	7	489	1722	294	429	49	35	8	152	291	8	50	.249	.360	.332	107	29	84	.943	20	124	120	O461(238/138/86),3b13,2b6,S3	—	2.7
LUSKEY, CHARLIE	Charles Melton; B4.6.1876 Washington DC; D12.20.1962 Bethesda MD; BR/TR/5´7˝/165; d9.12																								
1901	Was A	11	41	8	8	3	1	0	3	2	0	—	.195	.233	.317	52	-3	0	.818	-2	88	0	O8L,C3	—	-0.4
LUTENBERG, LUKE	Charles William; B10.4.1864 Quincy IL; D12.24.1938 Quincy IL; BR/TR/6´2˝/225; d7.7																								
1894	Lou N	70	255	43	49	10	4	0	23	23	9	21	.192	.282	.263	34	-28	4	.977	2	104	124	1b68,2b2	—	-2.0
LUTTRELL, LYLE	Lyle Kenneth; B2.22.1930 Bloomington IL; D7.11.1984 Chattanooga TN; BR/TR/6´0˝/180; d5.15; Col Illinois Wesleyan																								
1956	Was A	38	122	17	23	5	3	2	9	8-0	3	19	.189	.254	.328	53	-9	5-1	.939	-5	91	71	S37	0	-1.0
1957	Was A	19	45	4	9	4	0	0	5	3-0	0	8	.200	.250	.289	47	-3	0-0	.927	-7	66	49	S17	0	-1.0
Total	2	57	167	21	32	9	3	2	14	11-0	3	27	.192	.253	.317	52	-12	5-1	.936	-13	84	65	S54	0	-2.0
LUTZ, RED	Louis William; B12.17.1898 Cincinnati OH; D2.22.1984 Cincinnati OH; BR/TR/5´10˝/170; d5.31																								
1922	Cin N	1	1	0	1	1	0	0	0	0	0	0	1.000	1.000	2.000	669	1	0-0	ø	0	0	0	/C	—	0.1
LUTZ, JOE	Rollin Joseph; B2.18.1925 Keokuk IA; BL/TL/6´0˝/195; d4.17; C3																								
1951	StL A	14	36	7	6	0	1	0	2	6	0	9	.167	.286	.222	38	-3	0-0	1.000	-1	60	85	1b11	0	-0.4

YEAR	TM LG	G	AB	R	H	2B	3B	HR	RBI	BB-IB	HP	SO	AVG	OBP	SLG	AOPS	ABR	SB-CS	FA	FR	RNG	THR	GAMES AT POSITION	DL	BFW
LUTZKE, RUBE	Walter John; B11.17.1897 Milwaukee WI; D3.6.1938 Granville WI; BR/TR/5´11˝/175; d4.18																								
1923	Cle A	143	511	71	131	20	6	3	65	59	4	57	.256	.338	.337	78	-16	9-6	.939	16	**113**	89	3b141,S2	—	0.9
1924	Cle A	106	341	37	83	18	3	0	42	38	5	46	.243	.328	.314	65	-17	4-0	.947	17	**113**	**140**	3b103,2b3	—	0.6
1925	Cle A	81	238	31	52	9	0	1	16	26	0	29	.218	.295	.269	44	-21	2-4	.936	0	108	77	3b69,2b10	—	-1.7
1926	Cle A	142	475	42	124	28	6	0	59	34	2	35	.261	.313	.345	71	-21	6-3	.960	-3	99	**124**	3b142	—	-1.4
1927	Cle A	100	311	35	78	12	3	0	41	22	3	29	.251	.307	.309	60	-19	2-1	.938	4	105	124	3b98	—	-0.9
Total	5	572	1876	216	468	87	18	4	223	179	14	196	.249	.319	.321	66	-94	23-14	.945	34	107	113	3b553,2b13,S2	—	-2.5
LUULOA, KEITH	Keith H. M.; B12.24.1974 Honolulu HI; BR/TR/6´0˝/185; [CalA93 33/915]; d5.17; Col Modesto (CA) JC																								
2000	Ana A	6	18	3	6	0	0	0	0	1-0	0	1	.333	.368	.333	77	-1	0-0	.833	-2	42	60	S4,2b3	0	-0.2
LUZINSKI, GREG	Gregory Michael; B11.22.1950 Chicago IL; BR/TR/6´1˝/(210–256); [PhiN68 1/11]; d9.9; C4																								
1970	Phi N	8	12	0	2	0	0	0	0	3-0	0	5	.167	.333	.167	39	-1	0-1	1.000	1	170	46	1b3	0	-0.1
1971	Phi N	28	100	13	30	8	0	3	15	12-0	2	32	.300	.386	.470	141	6	2-0	.996	6	189	70	1b28	0	1.1
1972	Phi N	150	563	66	158	33	5	18	68	42-4	3	114	.281	.332	.453	119	13	0-4	.960	-1	99	93	O145(145/0/1),1b2	0	0.1
1973	Phi N	161	610	76	174	26	4	29	97	51-9	7	135	.285	.346	.484	124	19	3-3	**.993**	-7	87	67	O159L	0	0.2
1974	Phi N	85	302	29	82	14	1	7	48	29-3	0	76	.272	.330	.394	99	-1	3-0	.981	5	100	189	O82L	81	0.1
1975	Phi N★	161	596	85	179	35	3	34	**120**	89-**17**	8	151	.300	.394	.540	151	43	3-6	.966	-12	83	84	O159L	0	2.1
1976	†Phi N★	149	533	74	162	28	1	21	95	50-2	**11**	107	.304	.369	.478	136	26	1-2	.964	-9	84	91	O144L	0	1.0
1977	†Phi N★	149	554	99	171	35	3	39	130	80-14	3	140	.309	.394	.594	154	44	3-2	.964	-10	78	118	O148L	0	2.8
1978	†Phi N★	155	540	85	143	32	2	35	101	100-15	11	135	.265	.388	.526	151	41	8-7	.984	-11	85	58	O154L	0	2.4
1979	Phi N	137	452	47	114	23	1	18	81	56-5	**10**	103	.252	.343	.427	105	5	3-3	.946	-16	73	35	O125L	0	-1.7
1980	†Phi N	106	368	44	84	19	1	19	56	60-5	**6**	100	.228	.342	.440	111	7	3-0	.993	-14	74	28	O105L	47	-1.1
1981	Chi A	104	378	55	100	15	1	21	62	58-1	3	80	.265	.365	.476	143	22	0-0	ø	0	0	0	D103	0	2.0
1982	Chi A	159	583	87	170	37	1	18	102	89-11	6	120	.292	.386	.451	130	29	1-1	ø	0	0	0	D156	0	2.4
1983	†Chi A	144	502	73	128	26	1	32	95	70-6	11	117	.255	.352	.502	128	21	2-1	1.000	0	122	98	D139,1b2	0	1.6
1984	Chi A	125	412	47	98	13	0	13	58	56-3	3	80	.238	.329	.364	88	-5	5-1	ø	0	0	0	D114	0	-0.8
Total	15	1821	6505	880	1795	344	24	307	1128	845-95	84	1495	.276	.363	.478	128	269	37-31	.972	-66	85	82	O1221(1221/0/1),D512,1b35	128	12.1
LYDEN, MITCH	Mitchell Scott; B12.14.1964 Portland OR; BR/TR/6´3˝/225; [NYA83 4/93]; d6.16																								
1993	Fla N	6	10	2	3	0	0	1	1	0-0	0	3	.300	.300	.600	126	0	0-0	1.000	-1	93	0	C2	0	-0.1
LYDY, SCOTT	Donald Scott; B10.26.1968 Mesa AZ; BR/TR/6´5˝/195; [OakA89 2/56]; d5.18; Col South Mountain (AZ) CC																								
1993	Oak A	41	102	11	23	5	0	2	7	8-0	1	39	.225	.288	.333	70	-4	2-0	.958	-0	100	101	O38(17/5/16),D2	0	-0.5
LYNCH, JERRY	Gerald Thomas; B7.17.1930 Bay City MI; BL/TR/6´1˝/(180–202); d4.15																								
1954	Pit N	98	284	27	68	4	5	8	36	20	1	43	.239	.290	.373	73	-13	2-2	.965	3	95	201	O83(46/4/36)	0	-1.4
1955	Pit N	88	282	43	80	18	6	5	28	22-4	0	33	.284	.331	.443	106	2	2-2	.950	1	85	224	O71(40/0/32),C2	0	0.0
1956	Pit N	19	19	1	3	0	1	0	0	1-0	0	4	.158	.200	.263	24	-2	0-0	1.000	0	166	0	/lf	103	-0.2
1957	Cin N	67	124	11	32	4	1	4	13	6-1	0	18	.258	.290	.403	79	-4	0-0	1.000	-1	109	0	O24(1/0/22),C2	0	-0.5
1958	Cin N	122	420	58	131	20	5	16	68	18-1	0	54	.312	.338	.498	112	6	1-4	.970	-7	89	65	O101(1/0/101)	0	-0.5
1959	Cin N	117	379	49	102	16	3	17	58	29-1	1	50	.269	.320	.462	103	1	2-0	.979	1	103	70	O98(97/0/1)	0	-0.3
1960	Cin N	102	159	23	46	8	2	6	27	16-3	1	25	.289	.356	.478	124	5	0-0	.913	-2	87	48	O32(31/0/1)	0	0.2
1961	†Cin N	96	181	33	57	13	2	13	50	27-6	1	25	.315	.407	.624	166	18	2-2	.948	-3	83	71	O44(42/0/2)	0	1.3
1962	Cin N	114	288	41	81	15	4	12	57	24-4	1	38	.281	.335	.486	115	5	3-3	.970	-0	84	165	O73(70/0/3)	0	0.1
1963	Cin N	22	32	5	8	3	0	2	9	1-0	1	5	.250	.294	.531	129	1	0-0	1.000	-1	72	0	O7(4/0/3)	0	0.0
	Pit N	88	237	26	63	6	3	10	36	22-2	1	28	.266	.328	.443	120	6	0-1	.960	-6	75	58	O64L	0	-0.4
	Year	110	269	31	71	9	3	12	45	23-2	2	33	.264	.324	.454	121	7	0-1	.962	-6	75	54	O71(68/0/3)	0	-0.4
1964	Pit N	114	297	35	81	14	2	16	66	26-3	1	57	.273	.328	.495	130	11	0-1	.983	-11	55	0	O78(77/0/1)	0	-0.4
1965	Pit N	73	121	7	34	1	0	5	16	8-3	1	26	.281	.328	.413	108	1	0-2	.903	-2	76	85	O26(23/0/3)	0	-0.3
1966	Pit N	64	56	5	12	1	0	1	6	4-1	0	10	.214	.267	.286	54	-4	0-0	1.000	0	157	0	O4L	0	-0.4
Total	13	1184	2879	364	798	123	34	115	470	224-29	9	416	.277	.329	.463	110	33	12-17	.964	-27	86	98	O706(501/4/205),C4	103	-2.8
LYNCH, HENRY	Henry W.; B4.8.1866 Worcester MA; D11.23.1925 Worcester MA; BB/5´7˝/143; d9.21																								
1893	Chi N	4	14	0	3	2	0	0	2	1	0	1	.214	.267	.357	66	-1	0	.833	-1	0	0	O4R	—	-0.1
LYNCH, DANNY	Matt Dan "Dummy"; B2.7.1926 Dallas TX; D6.30.1978 Plano TX; BR/TR/5´11˝/174; d9.14; Col SMU																								
1948	Chi N	7	7	3	2	0	0	1	1	1	0	1	.286	.375	.714	197	1	0	1.000	0	160	0	/2	0	0.1
LYNCH, MIKE	Michael Joseph; B9.10.1875 St.Paul MN; D4.1.1947 Jennings Lodge OR; TR/5´10˝/155; d4.24																								
1902	Chi N	7	28	4	4	0	0	0	0	2	0	—	.143	.200	.143	6	-3	0	.929	-0	117	0	O7C	—	-0.4
LYNCH, TOM	Thomas James; B4.3.1860 Bennington VT; D3.28.1955 Cohoes NY; BL/TR/5´10.5˝/170; d8.18; U12; Col Gallaudet																								
1884	Wil U	16	58	6	16	3	1	0	—	5	—	—	.276	.333	.362	108	-1	—	.846	-0	—	—	C8,O8L/1	—	-0.1
	Phi N	13	48	7	15	4	2	0	3	4	—	5	.313	.365	.479	171	4	—	.860	-0	—	—	C7,O7(1/6/0)	—	0.4
1885	Phi N	13	53	7	10	3	0	0	1	10	—	3	.189	.317	.245	86	0	—	.838	2	171	268	O13(9/4/0)	—	0.1
Total	2	42	159	20	41	10	3	0	4	19	—	8	.258	.337	.358	119	3	—	.887	1	—	—	O28(18/10/0),C15/1	—	0.4
LYNCH, WALT	Walter Edward "Jabber"; B4.15.1897 Buffalo NY; D12.21.1976 Daytona Beach FL; TR/6´0˝/176; d7.8; Col Niagara																								
1922	Bos A	3	2	1	1	0	0	0	0	0	0	0	.500	.500	.500	163	0	0-0	1.000	0	*0*	*0*	C3	—	0.0
LYNN, BYRD	Byrd "Birdie"; B3.13.1889 Unionville IL; D2.5.1940 Napa CA; BR/TR/5´11˝/165; d4.16																								
1916	Chi A	31	40	4	9	1	0	0	3	4	1	7	.225	.311	.250	68	-1	2	.952	4	219	259	C13	—	0.4
1917	†Chi A	35	72	7	16	2	0	0	5	7	1	11	.222	.300	.250	67	-3	1	.959	1	*145*	*55*	C29	—	0.0
1918	Chi A	5	8	0	2	0	0	0	0	2	0	1	.250	.400	.250	95	0	0	1.000	-1	*95*	*132*	C4	—	0.0
1919	†Chi A	29	66	4	15	4	0	0	4	4	0	9	.227	.271	.288	57	-4	0	.982	1	*121*	*94*	C28	—	-0.1
1920	Chi A	16	25	0	8	2	1	0	3	1	0	3	.320	.346	.480	117	0	0-0	1.000	-0	*133*	*78*	C14	—	0.1
Total	5	116	211	15	50	9	1	0	15	18	2	31	.237	.303	.289	72	-8	3-0	.969	5	*147*	*107*	C88	—	0.4
LYNN, FRED	Fredric Michael; B2.3.1952 Chicago IL; BL/TL/6´1˝/(185–191); [BosA73 2/41]; d9.5; Col USC																								
1974	Bos A	15	43	5	18	2	2	2	10	6-2	1	6	.419	.490	.698	226	7	0-0	1.000	-1	70	238	O12(6/4/2)/D	0	0.6
1975	†Bos A★	145	528	**103**	175	**47**	7	21	105	62-10	3	90	.331	.401	**.566**	159	42	10-5	.983	2	105	107	O144C	0	4.1
1976	Bos A★	132	507	76	159	32	8	10	65	48-2	1	67	.314	.367	.467	130	20	14-9	.984	4	102	134	O128(0/127/1),D5	0	2.1
1977	Bos A★	129	497	81	129	29	5	18	76	51-2	3	63	.260	.327	.447	99	-1	2-3	.994	-2	100	78	O125C/D	30	-0.4
1978	Bos A★	150	541	75	161	33	3	22	82	75-11	1	50	.298	.380	.492	131	24	3-6	.984	-6	94	107	O149C	0	1.6
1979	Bos A★	147	531	116	177	42	1	39	122	82-4	4	79	**.333**	**.423**	**.637**	**173**	**57**	2-2	.987	-0	99	107	O143C/D	0	5.3
1980	Bos A★	110	415	67	125	32	3	12	61	58-3	0	39	.301	.383	.480	129	19	12-0	.994	2	99	143	O110C	0	2.3
1981	Cal A★	76	256	28	56	8	1	5	31	38-4	3	42	.219	.322	.316	85	-4	1-2	.978	-3	95	96	O69C	0	-0.8
1982	†Cal A★	138	472	89	141	38	1	21	86	58-4	3	72	.299	.374	.517	142	29	7-8	.991	-10	89	68	O133C	0	1.7
1983	Cal A★	117	437	56	119	20	3	22	74	55-10	2	83	.272	.352	.483	129	17	2-2	.993	-11	82	105	O113C,D2	0	0.5
1984	Cal A	142	517	84	140	28	4	23	79	77-8	2	97	.271	.366	.474	131	24	2-2	.982	0	96	132	O140(0/62/112)	0	1.8
1985	Bal A	124	448	59	118	12	1	23	68	53-6	1	100	.263	.339	.449	117	10	7-3	.994	-5	95	77	O123C	0	0.4
1986	Bal A	112	397	67	114	13	1	23	67	53-1	2	59	.287	.371	.499	136	21	2-2	.984	-10	88	36	O107C/D	16	0.9
1987	Bal A	111	396	49	100	24	0	23	60	39-6	1	72	.253	.320	.487	113	7	3-7	.991	-7	90	46	O101C,D8	15	-0.3
1988	Bal A	87	301	37	76	13	1	18	37	28-1	0	66	.252	.312	.482	123	8	2-2	.991	-0	105	25	O83(0/64/21),D2	28	0.6
	Det A	27	90	9	20	1	0	7	19	5-0	1	16	.222	.265	.467	106	0	0-0	1.000	1	96	178	O22(19/3/0),D3	0	0.0
	Year	114	391	46	96	14	1	25	56	33-1	1	82	.246	.302	.478	119	8	2-2	.992	0	103	56	O105(19/67/21),D5	0	0.6
1989	Det A	117	353	44	85	11	1	11	46	47-1	1	71	.241	.328	.371	100	0	1-1	.992	1	97	140	O68L,D46	15	-0.3
1990	SD N	90	196	18	47	3	1	6	23	22-2	1	44	.240	.315	.357	85	-4	2-0	1.000	-4	89	29	O55(42/6/8)	0	-0.9
Total	17	1969	6925	1063	1960	388	43	306	1111	857-77	30	1116	.283	.360	.484	128	276	72-54	.988	-49	95	95	O1825(135/1584/144),D70	104	19.2
LYNN, JERRY	Jerome Edward; B4.14.1916 Scranton PA; D9.25.1972 Scranton PA; BR/TR/5´10˝/164; d9.19																								
1937	Was A	1	3	0	2	1	0	0	0	0	0	0	.667	.667	1.000	329	1	0-0	1.000	0	93	275	/2	—	0.1
LYON, RUSS	Russell Mayo; B6.26.1913 Ball Ground GA; D12.24.1975 Charleston SC; BR/TR/6´1˝/230; d4.21; Col Georgia Tech																								
1944	Cle A	7	11	1	2	0	0	0	0	1	0	1	.182	.250	.182	25	-1	0-0	.909	0	*95*	*175*	C3	0	-0.1

Lyons, Barry Barry Stephen; B6.3.1960 Biloxi MS; BR/TR/6´1˝/(200–205); [NYN82 15/371]; d4.19; Col Delta St.

YEAR	TM LG	G	AB	R	H	2B	3B	HR	RBI	BB-IB	HP	SO	AVG	OBP	SLG	AOPS	ABR	SB-CS	FA	FR	RNG	THR	GAMES AT POSITION	DL	BFW
1986	NY N	6	9	1	0	0	0	0	2	1-1	0	2	.000	.100	.000	-71	-2	0-0	.941	-2	36	0	C3	0	-0.4
1987	NY N	53	130	15	33	4	1	4	24	8-1	2	24	.254	.301	.392	87	-3	0-0	.984	-6	85	79	C49	0	-0.8
1988	NY N	50	91	5	21	7	1	0	11	3-0	0	12	.231	.253	.330	70	-4	0-0	.979	-4	78	108	C32/1	0	-0.7
1989	NY N	79	235	15	58	13	0	3	27	11-1	2	28	.247	.283	.340	82	-6	0-1	.980	-1	86	87	C76	28	-0.3
1990	NY N	24	80	8	19	0	0	2	7	2-0	1	9	.237	.265	.313	58	-5	0-0	.980	-1	56	84	C23	54	-0.5
	LA N	3	5	1	1	0	0	1	2	0-0	0	1	.200	.200	.800	165	0	0-0	1.000	-0	0	0	C2	0	0.0
	Year	27	85	9	20	0	0	3	9	2-0	1	10	.235	.261	.341	64	-5	0-0	.980	-1	55	82	C25	0	-0.5
1991	LA N	9	9	0	0	0	0	0	0	0-0	0	2	.000	.000	.000	-99	-2	0-0	1.000	1	153	0	C6	0	-0.2
	Cal A	2	5	0	1	0	0	0	0	0-0	0	0	.200	.200	.200	11	-1	0-0	1.000	0	142	0	1b2	0	-0.1
1995	Chi A	27	64	8	17	2	0	5	16	4-0	0	14	.266	.304	.531	118	1	0-0	.987	1	41	215	C16,1b4,D6	0	0.2
Total	7	253	628	53	150	26	2	15	89	29-3	5	92	.239	.275	.358	77	-22	0-1	.981	-12	77	93	C207,1b7,D6	82	-2.8

Lyons, Denny Dennis Patrick Aloysius; B3.12.1866 Cincinnati OH; D1.2.1929 W.Covington KY; BR/TR/5´10˝/185; d9.18

YEAR	TM LG	G	AB	R	H	2B	3B	HR	RBI	BB-IB	HP	SO	AVG	OBP	SLG	AOPS	ABR	SB-CS	FA	FR	RNG	THR	GAMES AT POSITION	DL	BFW
1885	Pro N	4	16	3	2	1	0	0	1	0	—	3	.125	.125	.188	-0	-2	—	.824	-0	95	0	3b4	—	-0.2
1886	Phi AA	32	123	22	26	3	1	0	11	8	4	—	.211	.281	.252	67	-5	7	.807	-5	89	22	3b32	—	-0.8
1887	Phi AA	**137**	570	128	209	43	14	6	102	47	6	—	.367	.421	.523	162	48	73	.866	-5	78	**144**	3b137	—	3.6
1888	Phi AA	111	456	93	135	22	5	6	83	41	7	—	.296	.363	.406	147	25	39	.878	-12	82	76	3b111	—	1.4
1889	Phi AA	131	510	135	168	36	4	9	82	79	7	44	.329	.426	.469	157	43	10	.860	9	107	**125**	3b130/1	—	4.5
1890	Phi AA	88	339	79	120	29	5	7	73	57	10	—	.354	**.461**	**.531**	**193**	44	21	.909	10	105	93	3b88	—	4.7
1891	StL AA	120	451	124	142	24	3	11	84	88	18	58	.315	.445	.455	137	25	9	.871	-5	93	87	3b120	—	1.9
1892	NY N	108	389	71	100	16	7	8	51	59	3	37	.257	.359	.396	130	16	11	.871	-7	86	77	3b108	—	1.0
1893	Pit N	**131**	490	103	150	19	16	3	105	97	9	29	.306	.430	.429	131	28	19	.918	4	99	102	3b131	—	2.7
1894	Pit N	72	257	52	82	14	4	4	51	43	4	13	.319	.424	.451	112	8	14	.897	4	102	90	3b72	—	0.9
1895	StL N	34	132	24	39	6	0	2	25	15	3	7	.295	.380	.386	99	1	3	.889	-5	71	37	3b34	—	-0.3
1896	Pit N	118	436	77	134	25	6	4	71	67	5	25	.307	.406	.420	123	19	13	.893	-16	81	86	3b116	—	0.4
1897	Pit N	37	131	22	27	6	4	2	17	22	6	—	.206	.346	.359	90	-1	5	.989	-1	76	73	1b35,3b2	—	-0.2
Total	13	1123	4300	933	1334	244	69	62	756	623	82	216	.310	.407	.442	138	249	224	.882	-30	91	95	3b1085,1b36	—	19.6

Lyons, Ed Edward Hoyte "Mouse"; B5.12.1923 Winston–Salem NC; BR/TR/5´9˝/165; d9.15; C1

YEAR	TM LG	G	AB	R	H	2B	3B	HR	RBI	BB-IB	HP	SO	AVG	OBP	SLG	AOPS	ABR	SB-CS	FA	FR	RNG	THR	GAMES AT POSITION	DL	BFW
1947	Was A	7	26	2	4	0	0	0	0	2	0	2	.154	.214	.154	3	-3	0-0	1.000	3	127	123	2b7	0	0.0

Lyons, Harry Harry Pratt; B3.25.1866 Chester PA; D6.29.1912 Mauricetown NJ; BR/TR/5´10.5˝/157; d8.29

YEAR	TM LG	G	AB	R	H	2B	3B	HR	RBI	BB-IB	HP	SO	AVG	OBP	SLG	AOPS	ABR	SB-CS	FA	FR	RNG	THR	GAMES AT POSITION	DL	BFW
1887	Phi N	1	4	0	0	0	0	0	0	1	0	0	.000	.200	.000	-38	-1	0	.500	-1	0	0	/lf	—	-0.1
	†StL AA	2	8	2	1	0	0	0	1	0	0	—	.125	.125	.125	-27	-1	2	1.000	1	178	280	/2rf	—	-0.1
1888	†StL AA	123	499	66	97	10	5	4	63	20	3	—	.194	.230	.259	51	-30	36	.891	5	163	115	O122(0/112/10),3b2/S2	—	-2.8
1889	NY N	5	20	1	2	0	1	0	2	2	0	0	.100	.182	.200	6	-3	0	1.000	-1	0	0	O5(0/1/4)	—	-0.3
1890	Roc AA	**133**	584	83	152	11	11	3	58	27	1	—	.260	.294	.332	91	-10	47	.921	10	113	79	O132(130/0/2),3b2/CP	—	-0.2
1892	NY N	96	411	67	98	5	2	0	53	33	1	29	.238	.297	.260	70	-15	25	.910	-1	101	29	O96(10/86/0)	—	-2.1
1893	NY N	47	187	27	51	5	2	0	21	14	0	6	.273	.323	.321	71	-8	10	.917	-1	104	166	O47(1/46/0)	—	-1.0
Total	6	407	1713	246	401	31	21	7	198	97	5	35	.234	.277	.289	69	-68	120	.908	13	122	87	O404(142/245/17),3b4,2b2/PCS	—	-6.6

Lyons, Pat Patrick Jerry; B3.1860 Belleville ON, Can.; D1.20.1914 Springfield OH; BR/TR/5´7˝/155; d7.21

YEAR	TM LG	G	AB	R	H	2B	3B	HR	RBI	BB-IB	HP	SO	AVG	OBP	SLG	AOPS	ABR	SB-CS	FA	FR	RNG	THR	GAMES AT POSITION	DL	BFW
1890	Cle N	11	38	2	2	1	0	0	1	4	0	4	.053	.143	.079	-36	-7	0	.839	-5	84	44	2b11	—	-1.0

Lyons, Steve Stephen John; B6.3.1960 Tacoma WA; BL/TR/6´3˝/(190–195); [BosA81 1/19]; d4.15; Col Oregon St.; OF(59/237/43)

YEAR	TM LG	G	AB	R	H	2B	3B	HR	RBI	BB-IB	HP	SO	AVG	OBP	SLG	AOPS	ABR	SB-CS	FA	FR	RNG	THR	GAMES AT POSITION	DL	BFW
1985	Bos A	133	371	52	98	14	3	5	30	32-0	1	64	.264	.322	.358	83	-9	12-9	.973	-6	96	64	O114(2/111/2)/3SD	0	-1.6
1986	Bos A	59	124	20	31	7	2	1	14	12-2	0	23	.250	.312	.363	84	-3	2-3	.972	2	106	158	O55C	0	-0.2
	Chi A	42	123	10	25	2	1	0	6	7-0	1	24	.203	.248	.236	33	-12	2-3	.987	1	105	96	O35(22/6/7),3b3/1D	0	-1.3
	Year	101	247	30	56	9	3	1	20	19-2	1	47	.227	.280	.300	58	-15	4-6	.978	2	106	129	O90(22/61/7),3b3/1D	0	-1.5
1987	Chi A	76	193	26	54	11	1	1	19	12-0	0	37	.280	.320	.363	79	-6	3-1	.971	7	114	132	3b51,O15(6/8/2)/2D	0	0.0
1988	Chi A	146	472	59	127	28	3	5	45	32-1	1	59	.269	.313	.373	92	-5	1-2	.927	8	113	**190**	3b128,O14(0/8/6),2b4,C2/1	0	0.3
1989	Chi A	140	443	51	117	21	3	2	50	35-3	1	68	.264	.317	.339	87	-7	9-6	.982	2	101	109	2b70,1b40,3b28,O20(10/1/9),S3/CD	0	-0.6
1990	Chi A	94	146	22	28	6	1	1	11	10-1	1	41	.192	.245	.267	45	-11	1-0	.991	0	105	123	1b61,2b15,O7(2/3/3),3b5/SDP	0	-1.3
1991	Bos A	87	212	15	51	10	1	4	17	11-2	0	35	.241	.277	.354	70	-9	10-3	1.000	2	106	0	O45(8/36/3),2b16,3b12,1b2/SDP	0	-0.6
1992	Atl N	11	14	0	1	0	1	0	1	0-0	0	4	.071	.071	.214	-21	-2	0-0	1.000	-0	86	0	O6(2/0/4),2b2	0	-0.3
	Mon N	16	13	2	3	0	0	0	1	1-0	0	3	.231	.286	.231	48	-1	1-2	1.000	0	76	0	O8(7/1/0)/1	0	-0.1
	Year	27	27	2	4	0	1	0	2	1-0	0	7	.148	.179	.222	13	-3	1-2	1.000	-0	138	0	O14(9/1/4),2b2/1	0	-0.4
	Bos A	21	28	3	7	0	1	0	2	2-0	0	1	.250	.300	.321	69	-1	0-1	1.000	1	140	67	1b8,O5(0/2/3)/2D	0	-0.1
1993	Bos A	28	23	4	3	1	0	0	0	2-0	0	5	.130	.200	.174	1	-3	1-2	1.000	1	85	0	O10(0/6/4),2b9/C13D	0	-0.3
Total	9	853	2162	264	545	100	17	19	196	156-9	5	364	.252	.301	.340	77	-69	42-32	.979	17	102	81	O334C,3b229,2b118,1b115,D24,S6,C4,P2	0	-6.1

Lyons, Terry Terence Hilbert; B12.14.1908 New Holland OH; D9.9.1959 Dayton OH; BR/TR/6´0.5˝/165; d4.19

YEAR	TM LG	G	AB	R	H	2B	3B	HR	RBI	BB-IB	HP	SO	AVG	OBP	SLG	AOPS	ABR	SB-CS	FA	FR	RNG	THR	GAMES AT POSITION	DL	BFW
1929	Phi N	1	0	0	0	0	0	0	0	0	0	0	ø	ø	ø	ø	0	0	ø	0	0	0	/1	—	0.0

Lyons, Bill William Allen; B4.26.1958 Alton IL; BR/TR/6´1˝/175; d7.20; Col Southern Illinois

YEAR	TM LG	G	AB	R	H	2B	3B	HR	RBI	BB-IB	HP	SO	AVG	OBP	SLG	AOPS	ABR	SB-CS	FA	FR	RNG	THR	GAMES AT POSITION	DL	BFW
1983	StL N	42	60	3	10	1	1	0	3	1-0	0	11	.167	.180	.217	9	-8	3-2	.985	-2	107	90	2b23,3b8,S2	0	-1.0
1984	StL N	46	73	13	16	3	0	0	3	9-1	0	13	.219	.305	.260	61	-3	3-1	.991	6	110	163	2b25,S11,3b3	0	0.4
Total	2	88	133	16	26	4	1	0	6	10-1	0	24	.195	.252	.241	38	-11	6-3	.989	4	109	134	2b48,S13,3b11	0	-0.6

Lytle, Dad Edward Benson "Pop"; B3.10.1862 Racine WI; D12.21.1950 Long Beach CA; BR/TR/5´11˝/160; d8.11

YEAR	TM LG	G	AB	R	H	2B	3B	HR	RBI	BB-IB	HP	SO	AVG	OBP	SLG	AOPS	ABR	SB-CS	FA	FR	RNG	THR	GAMES AT POSITION	DL	BFW
1890	Chi N	1	4	1	0	0	0	0	0	0	0	1	.000	.000	.000	-96	-1	0	1.000	1	370	0	/rf	—	0.0
	Pit N	15	55	2	8	1	0	0	0	8	0	9	.145	.254	.164	25	-5	0	.837	-5	89	0	2b8,O7(0/4/3)	—	-0.8
	Year	16	59	3	8	1	0	0	0	8	0	10	.136	.239	.153	16	-6	0	.824	-4	80	0	O8(0/4/4),2b8	—	-0.8

Lyttle, Jim James Lawrence; B5.20.1946 Hamilton OH; BL/TR/6´0˝/(178–186); [NYA66 1/10]; d5.17; Col Florida St.

YEAR	TM LG	G	AB	R	H	2B	3B	HR	RBI	BB-IB	HP	SO	AVG	OBP	SLG	AOPS	ABR	SB-CS	FA	FR	RNG	THR	GAMES AT POSITION	DL	BFW
1969	NY A	28	83	7	15	4	0	0	4	4-0	0	19	.181	.218	.229	26	-8	1-2	.983	1	98	196	O28C	0	-0.9
1970	NY A	87	126	20	39	7	1	3	14	10-1	0	26	.310	.355	.452	128	5	3-6	.989	1	109	72	O70(2/4/64)	0	0.2
1971	NY A	49	86	7	17	5	0	1	7	8-2	1	18	.198	.271	.291	63	-4	0-2	1.000	-0	100	65	O29(3/6/20)	0	-0.7
1972	Chi A	44	82	8	19	5	2	0	5	1-0	0	28	.232	.241	.341	70	-3	0-1	1.000	-1	87	93	O21(0/16/5)	9	-0.6
1973	Mon N	49	116	12	30	5	1	4	19	9-2	0	14	.259	.305	.422	98	-1	0-2	.974	4	104	164	O36(29/7/0)	0	0.1
1974	Mon N	25	9	1	3	0	0	0	2	1-1	0	3	.333	.364	.333	101	0	0-0	1.000	1	88	433	O18(14/5/0)	0	0.0
1975	Mon N	44	55	7	15	4	0	0	6	13-3	0	6	.273	.406	.345	106	1	0-1	1.000	-1	66	144	O16(5/8/3)	0	0.0
1976	Mon N	42	85	6	23	4	1	1	8	7-1	0	13	.271	.326	.376	94	-1	0-0	.977	2	101	199	O29(12/0/20)	0	0.0
	LA N	23	68	3	15	3	0	0	5	8-4	0	12	.221	.303	.265	63	-3	0-1	1.000	4	104	441	O18(1/17/1)	0	0.0
	Year	65	153	9	38	7	1	1	13	15-5	0	25	.248	.315	.327	80	-4	0-1	.990	6	102	313	O47(13/17/21)	0	0.0
Total	8	391	710	71	176	37	5	9	70	61-14	1	139	.248	.305	.352	85	-14	4-15	.988	8	100	164	O265(66/91/113)	9	-1.9

Maas, Kevin Kevin Christian; B1.20.1965 Castro Valley CA; BL/TL/6´3˝/(203–209); [NYA86 22/572]; d6.29; Col California

YEAR	TM LG	G	AB	R	H	2B	3B	HR	RBI	BB-IB	HP	SO	AVG	OBP	SLG	AOPS	ABR	SB-CS	FA	FR	RNG	THR	GAMES AT POSITION	DL	BFW
1990	NY A	79	254	42	64	9	0	21	41	43-10	3	76	.252	.367	.535	148	17	1-2	.983	-2	95	92	1b57,D18	0	1.0
1991	NY A	148	500	69	110	14	1	23	63	83-3	4	128	.220	.333	.390	99	1	5-1	.983	-1	92	71	D109,1b36	0	-0.6
1992	NY A	98	286	35	71	12	0	11	35	25-4	0	63	.248	.305	.406	99	-1	3-1	.986	-3	37	83	D62,1b22	0	-0.7
1993	NY A	59	151	20	31	4	0	9	25	24-2	1	32	.205	.316	.411	97	-1	1-1	.984	-1	70	144	D31,1b17	0	-0.5
1995	Min A	22	57	5	11	4	0	1	5	7-2	0	11	.193	.281	.316	55	-4	0-0	.936	-2	25	82	D12,1b8	16	-0.6
Total	5	406	1248	171	287	43	1	65	169	182-21	8	310	.230	.329	.422	107	12	10-5	.982	-9	82	89	D232,1b140	16	-1.4

Mabry, John John Steven; B10.17.1970 Wilmington DE; BL/TR/6´4˝/(195–210); [StLN91 6/155]; d4.23; Col West Chester; OF(189/11/386)

YEAR	TM LG	G	AB	R	H	2B	3B	HR	RBI	BB-IB	HP	SO	AVG	OBP	SLG	AOPS	ABR	SB-CS	FA	FR	RNG	THR	GAMES AT POSITION	DL	BFW
1994	StL N	6	23	2	7	3	0	0	3	2-0	0	4	.304	.360	.435	106	0	0-0	1.000	1	145	0	O6R	0	0.1
1995	StL N	129	388	35	119	21	1	5	41	24-5	2	45	.307	.347	.405	97	-2	0-3	.994	5	118	124	1b73,O39(11/0/29)	0	-0.5
1996	†StL N	151	543	63	161	30	2	13	74	37-11	3	84	.297	.342	.431	103	2	3-2	.994	-10	78	103	1b146,O14(1/0/13)	0	-2.0
1997	StL N	116	388	40	110	19	0	5	36	39-9	3	77	.284	.352	.371	90	-5	0-1	1.000	-3	86	165	O78(4/6/71),1b49/3	35	-1.4
1998	StL N	142	377	41	94	22	0	9	46	30-6	1	76	.249	.305	.379	79	-12	0-2	.971	-5	98	205	O80(46/0/37),3b38,1b16	0	-2.0
1999	Sea A	87	262	34	64	14	0	9	33	20-1	0	60	.244	.297	.401	77	-10	2-1	.989	5	113	251	O43(7/2/35),3b24,1b20/D	51	-0.8
2000	Sea A	48	103	18	25	5	0	1	7	10-0	2	31	.243	.322	.320	65	-5	0-1	.862	-5	71	122	3b22,O19(7/0/12),1b3/PD	19	-1.0

YEAR	TM LG	G	AB	R	H	2B	3B	HR	RBI	BB-IB	HP	SO	AVG	OBP	SLG	AOPS	ABR	SB-CS	FA	FR	RNG	THR	GAMES AT POSITION	DL	BFW
	SD N	48	123	17	28	8	0	7	25	5-0	0	38	.228	.256	.463	82	-4	0-0	.980	-1	94	60	O32(2/0/30),1b2	0	-0.6
2001	StL N	5	7	0	0	0	0	0	0	0-0	0	2	.000	.000	.000	-98	-2	0-0	1.000	-0	0	192	1b2,O2R	0	-0.3
	Fla N	82	147	14	32	7	0	6	20	13-1	5	44	.218	.299	.388	79	-5	1-0	.958	-2	82	111	O39(3/2/34)/1PD	34	-0.8
	Year	87	154	14	32	7	0	6	20	13-1	5	46	.208	.287	.370	71	-7	1-0	.958	-2	80	109	O41(3/2/36),1b3/PD	0	-1.1
2002	Phi N	21	21	1	6	0	0	0	3	1-1	0	5	.286	.304	.286	65	-1	0-0	1.000	0	194	0	/1rf	0	-0.1
	†Oak A	89	193	27	53	13	1	11	40	14-1	1	37	.275	.322	.523	122	5	1-1	.978	2	106	40	O53(33/0/21),1b50	0	0.4
2003	Sea A	64	104	12	22	6	0	3	16	15-2	3	21	.212	.328	.356	85	-2	0-0	.957	1	86	140	O22(8/0/14),D12,1b9	23	-0.2
2004	†StL N	87	240	32	71	11	0	13	40	26-5	1	63	.296	.363	.504	121	7	0-1	.986	0	94	0	O57(39/1/25),3b20,1b14	0	0.5
2005	†StL N	112	246	26	59	15	1	8	32	20-1	0	63	.240	.295	.407	80	-8	0-0	.965	-7	65	40	O70(23/0/49),3b18,1b14	0	-1.7
2006	Chi N	107	210	16	43	8	1	5	25	23-0	1	57	.205	.283	.324	55	-15	0-0	.994	3	120	61	1b51,O11(5/0/7),3b2,D2	0	-1.5
Total	13	1294	3375	378	894	182	6	95	441	279-43	22	707	.265	.323	.407	90	-57	7-12	.983	-15	93	117	O566R,1b451,3b125,D21,P2	162	-11.9
MacDonald, Harvey	Harvey Forsyth; B5.18.1898 New York NY; D10.4.1965 Manoa PA; BL/TL/5´11˝/170; d6.12; Col Albright																								
1928	Phi N	13	16	0	4	0	0	0	2	2	0	3	.250	.333	.250	53	-1	0	1.000	-0	94	0	O2R	—	-0.1
Macey	B Columbus OH; d10.2																								
1890	Phi AA	1	1	0	0	0	0	0	0	0	0	—	.000	.000	.000	-99	0	0	1.000	-1	*56*	*0*	/C	—	-0.1
MacFarlane, Mike	Michael Andrew; B4.12.1964 Stockton CA; BR/TR/6´1˝/(200–210); [KCA85 4/97]; d7.23; Col Santa Clara																								
1987	KC A	8	19	0	4	1	0	0	3	2-0	0	2	.211	.286	.263	46	-1	0-0	1.000	-1	120	184	C8	0	-0.2
1988	KC A	70	211	25	56	15	0	4	26	21-2	1	37	.265	.332	.393	102	1	0-0	.994	-12	90	75	C68	0	-0.8
1989	KC A	69	157	13	35	6	0	2	19	7-0	2	27	.223	.263	.299	59	-9	0-0	.996	5	153	98	C59,D4	0	-0.2
1990	KC A	124	400	37	102	24	4	6	58	25-2	7	69	.255	.306	.380	93	-4	1-0	.991	-12	100	40	C112,D5	0	-1.0
1991	KC A	84	267	34	74	18	2	13	41	17-0	6	52	.277	.330	.506	128	9	1-0	.993	-0	197	80	C69,D4	60	1.3
1992	KC A	129	402	51	94	28	3	17	48	30-2	**15**	89	.234	.310	.445	106	3	1-5	.993	3	102	78	C104,D13	0	1.0
1993	KC A	117	388	55	106	27	0	20	67	40-2	16	83	.273	.360	.497	121	12	2-5	.985	12	101	**136**	C114	0	2.9
1994	KC A	92	314	53	80	17	3	14	47	35-1	**18**	71	.255	.359	.462	105	3	1-0	.993	6	80	82	C81,D8	0	1.3
1995	†Bos A	115	364	45	82	18	1	15	51	38-0	14	78	.225	.319	.404	85	-8	2-1	.993	2	125	99	C111,D3	0	0.1
1996	KC A	112	379	58	104	24	2	19	54	31-5	7	57	.274	.339	.499	108	4	3-3	.993	-1	144	100	C99,D9	0	0.8
1997	KC A	82	257	34	61	14	2	8	35	24-3	6	47	.237	.316	.401	83	-7	0-2	.991	-7	192	46	C81	33	-0.9
1998	KC A	3	11	1	1	0	0	0	0	0-0	0	2	.091	.091	.091	-50	-2	0-0	1.000	0	201	214	C3	0	-0.2
	Oak A	78	207	28	52	12	0	7	34	12-0	4	34	.251	.301	.411	85	-5	1-0	.989	4	119	72	C70	0	0.3
	Year	81	218	29	53	12	0	7	34	12-0	4	36	.243	.291	.394	78	-8	1-0	.990	4	123	79	C73	0	0.1
1999	Oak A	81	226	24	55	17	0	4	31	13-0	1	52	.243	.282	.372	68	-11	0-0	.997	3	110	129	C79/D	15	-0.4
Total	13	1164	3602	458	906	221	17	129	514	295-17	97	700	.252	.322	.430	98	-15	12-16	.992	2	123	87	C1058,D47	108	4.0
MacGamwell, Ed	Edward M.; B1.10.1878 Buffalo NY; D5.26.1924 Albany NY; BL/TL; d4.14																								
1905	Bro N	4	16	0	4	0	0	0	0	1	0	—	.250	.294	.250	68	-1	0	.951	-1	74	0	1b4	—	-0.1
Macha, Ken	Kenneth Edward; B9.29.1950 Monroeville PA; BR/TR/6´2˝/(205–217); [PitN72 6/143]; d9.14; M4/C12; b–Mike; Col Pittsburgh																								
1974	Pit N	5	5	1	3	1	0	0	1	0-0	0	0	.600	.600	.800	297	1	0-0	1.000	0	0	0	/C	0	0.2
1977	Pit N	35	95	2	26	4	0	0	11	6-0	0	17	.274	.317	.316	68	-4	1-1	.964	-6	73	0	3b17,1b11,O4(3/0/1)	0	-1.2
1978	Pit N	29	52	5	11	1	1	0	5	12-1	0	10	.212	.354	.269	74	-1	2-0	.970	-4	65	120	3b21	0	-0.6
1979	Mon N	25	36	8	10	3	1	0	4	2-1	1	9	.278	.333	.417	103	0	0-0	1.000	1	99	70	3b13,1b2,O2R/C	0	0.1
1980	Mon N	49	107	10	31	5	1	1	8	11-1	1	17	.290	.361	.383	106	1	0-2	.910	-6	78	73	3b33,1b2/Crf	0	-0.7
1981	Tor A	37	85	4	17	2	0	0	6	8-0	0	15	.200	.266	.224	41	-6	1-1	.892	-1	108	78	3b19,1b16/CD	0	-0.9
Total	6	180	380	30	98	16	3	1	35	39-3	2	68	.258	.329	.324	79	-9	4-4	.938	-17	82	70	3b103,1b31,O7(3/0/4),C4,D2	0	-3.1
Macha, Mike	Michael William; B2.17.1954 Victoria TX; BR/TR/5´11˝/180; [AtlN76*S1/10]; d4.20; b–Ken; Col Rice																								
1979	Atl N	6	13	2	2	0	0	0	1	1-0	0	5	.154	.214	.154	2	-2	0-0	.769	0	152	0	3b3	0	-0.1
1980	Tor A	5	8	0	0	0	0	0	0	0-0	0	1	.000	.000	.000	-96	-2	0-0	.778	1	146	265	3b2/C	0	-0.2
Total	2	11	21	2	2	0	0	0	1	1-0	0	6	.095	.136	.095	-34	-4	0-0	.773	1	150	102	3b5/C	0	-0.3
Machado, Alejandro	Alejandro Jose; B4.26.1982 Caracas, Distrito Capital, Venezuela; BB/TR/6´0˝/185; d9.2																								
2005	†Bos A	10	5	4	1	1	0	0	0	1-0	0	1	.200	.333	.400	90	0	0-0	1.000	-2	95	0	O6(2/3/1),2b3/SD	0	-0.1
Machado, Anderson	Anderson Javier; B1.25.1981 Caracas, Distrito Capital, Venezuela; BB/TR/5´11˝/(160–170); d9.27; [DL 2004 Phi N 25]																								
2003	Phi N	1	0	0	0	0	0	0	0	0-0	0	0	ø	ø	ø	ø	0	1-0	ø	0	—	—	/R	0	0.0
2004	Cin N	17	56	6	15	5	1	0	4	10-2	0	26	.268	.379	.393	102	1	3-1	.937	-7	74	63	S17	0	-0.5
2005	Cin N	2	2	0	0	0	0	0	0	0-0	0	1	.000	.000	.000	-99	-1	0-0	ø	0	—	—	/H	94	-0.1
	Col N	4	10	1	0	0	0	0	2	2-0	0	5	.000	.154	.000	-46	-2	0-0	.929	-2	53	35	S4	0	-0.5
	Year	6	12	1	0	0	0	0	2	2-0	0	6	.000	.133	.000	-54	-3	0-0	.929	-2	53	35	S4	0	-0.6
Total	3	24	68	7	15	5	1	0	6	12-2	0	32	.221	.333	.324	73	-2	4-1	.935	-10	70	58	S21	119	-1.1
Machado, Robert	Robert Alexis; B6.3.1973 Puerto Cabello, Carabobo, Venez.; BR/TR/6´1˝/(205–220); d7.24																								
1996	Chi A	4	6	1	4	1	0	0	2	0-0	0	0	.667	.667	.833	288	2	0-0	1.000	-2	65	176	C4	0	0.0
1997	Chi A	10	15	1	3	0	1	0	2	1-0	0	6	.200	.250	.333	52	-1	0-0	1.000	0	58	237	C10	0	-0.1
1998	Chi A	34	111	14	23	6	0	3	15	7-0	0	22	.207	.254	.342	54	-8	0-0	.981	-2	95	113	C34	0	-0.7
1999	Mon N	17	22	3	4	1	0	0	0	2-0	0	6	.182	.250	.227	23	-3	0-0	1.000	-0	0	55	C17	0	-0.2
2000	Sea A	8	14	2	3	0	0	1	1	1-0	0	4	.214	.267	.429	73	-1	0-0	1.000	2	246	0	C8	0	0.2
2001	Chi N	52	135	13	30	10	0	2	13	7-3	1	26	.222	.266	.341	57	-9	0-0	.997	1	77	125	C47	0	-0.5
2002	Chi N	22	58	5	16	4	0	1	5	5-0	0	11	.276	.333	.397	91	-1	0-0	.985	3	92	231	C21/1	0	0.3
	Mil N	51	153	14	39	10	1	2	17	12-4	1	30	.255	.310	.373	80	-4	0-0	.987	-1	78	122	C48,1b2	0	-0.3
	Year	73	211	19	55	14	1	3	22	17-4	1	41	.261	.316	.379	83	-5	0-0	.987	2	82	151	C69,1b3	0	0.0
2003	Bal A	18	49	8	13	1	0	1	3	6-0	0	12	.265	.345	.347	84	-1	0-0	.990	1	62	200	C18	0	0.1
2004	Bal A	37	73	5	11	3	0	1	3	4-0	0	18	.151	.195	.233	11	-10	0-0	.994	6	272	136	C35	0	-0.2
Total	9	253	636	66	146	36	2	11	61	45-7	2	135	.230	.282	.344	63	-36	0-0	.991	8	104	137	C242,1b3	0	-1.4
Machemer, Dave	David Ritchie; B5.24.1951 St.Joseph MO; BR/TR/5´11.5˝/180; [AnaA72 4/82]; d6.21; Col Central Michigan																								
1978	Cal A	10	22	6	6	1	0	1	2	2-0	0	1	.273	.333	.455	123	1	0-1	1.000	-4	76	0	2b5,3b3/S	0	-0.4
1979	Det A	19	26	8	5	1	0	0	2	3-0	0	2	.192	.276	.231	37	-2	0-3	.972	-1	84	111	2b11/lfD	0	-0.4
Total	2	29	48	14	11	2	0	1	4	5-0	0	3	.229	.302	.333	74	-1	0-4	.978	-5	82	80	2b16,3b3/DlfS	0	-0.8
Macias, Jose	Jose Prado (Salazar); B1.25.1972 Panama City, Pan; BB/TR/5´10˝/(173–190); d5.12; OF(57/110/36)																								
1999	Det A	5	4	2	1	0	0	1	2	0-0	0	1	.250	.250	1.000	196	0	0-0	1.000	1	216	0	/2	0	0.1
2000	Det A	73	173	25	44	3	5	2	24	18-0	1	24	.254	.328	.364	76	-7	2-0	.976	-2	106	106	2b39,3b26,O3(0/1/2)/SD	0	-0.6
2001	Det A	137	488	62	131	24	6	8	51	32-0	3	54	.268	.316	.391	87	-10	21-6	.955	12	120	146	3b89,O29(3/22/4),2b18,D2	0	0.5
2002	Det A	33	107	10	25	4	0	0	6	8-0	1	13	.234	.291	.271	53	-7	3-2	.964	-1	129	49	2b17,O10(0/9/1),3b8	0	-0.7
	Mon N	90	231	33	59	17	1	7	33	13-0	1	44	.255	.294	.429	84	-6	5-6	.978	6	110	230	O49C,3b22,2b6,S4	20	0.1
2003	Mon N	111	272	31	65	15	2	4	22	11-1	2	45	.239	.273	.353	60	-17	4-3	.977	-0	97	157	O62(41/15/8),3b25,2b4/D	0	-1.8
2004	Chi N	98	194	23	52	6	3	3	22	5-0	2	38	.268	.292	.376	69	-10	4-1	1.000	-2	101	231	O28(8/7/13),3b18,2b16	10	-1.1
2005	Chi N	112	177	15	45	8	0	1	13	6-0	0	24	.254	.274	.316	54	-12	4-3	.913	0	69	49	3b23,2b20,O20(5/7/8)	0	-1.2
Total	7	659	1646	201	422	77	17	26	173	93-1	10	243	.256	.298	.371	74	-69	43-21	.948	14	106	95	3b211,O201C,2b121,S5,D4	30	-4.7
Mack, Connie	Cornelius Alexander "The Tall Tactician" (b McGillicuddy); B12.22.1862 E.Brookfield MA; D2.8.1956 Philadelphia PA; BR/TR/6´1˝/150; d9.11; M53; HF1937; s–Earle																								
1886	Was N	10	36	4	13	2	1	0	5	0	—	2	.361	.361	.472	164	3	0	.957	5	—	—	C10	—	0.7
1887	Was N	82	314	35	63	6	1	0	20	8	3	17	.201	.228	.226	28	-30	26	.906	1	—	—	C76,O5(2/2/1),2b2	—	-1.9
1888	Was N	85	300	49	56	5	6	3	29	17	8	18	.187	.249	.273	71	-9	31	.916	10	—	—	C79,O4(2/0/2)/S1	—	0.6
1889	Was N	98	386	51	113	16	1	0	42	15	8	12	.293	.333	.339	93	-4	26	.891	7	—	—	C45,O34(1/0/33),1b22	—	0.4
1890	Buf P	123	503	95	134	15	12	0	53	47	**20**	13	.266	.353	.344	94	-1	16	.925	-22	*81*	*104*	C112,O9(0/1/8),1b5	—	-1.2
1891	Pit N	75	280	43	60	10	0	0	29	19	9	11	.214	.286	.250	58	-14	4	.926	8	*104*	*97*	C72,1b3	—	0.0
1892	Pit N	97	346	39	84	9	4	1	31	21	6	22	.243	.298	.301	81	-9	11	**.951**	23	*113*	*134*	C92,O3(1/0/2)/1	—	2.1
1893	Pit N	37	133	22	38	3	1	0	15	10	5	9	.286	.358	.323	83	-3	4	.941	4	*98*	*117*	C37	—	0.4
1894	Pit N	70	231	33	57	7	1	1	21	21	4	14	.247	.320	.299	50	-19	8	.948	2	*102*	*96*	C70,M	—	-0.8
1895	Pit N	14	49	12	15	2	0	0	4	7	1	1	.306	.404	.347	100	1	1	.962	-2	*88*	*93*	C12/1M	—	0.0
1896	Pit N	33	120	9	26	4	1	0	16	5	0	8	.217	.248	.267	37	-11	0	.974	0	112	87	1b28,C5,M	—	-0.9
Total	11	724	2698	392	659	79	28	5	265	170	64	127	.244	.305	.300	72	-96	127	.927	35	*98*	*109*	C610,1b61,O55(6/3/46),2b2/S	—	-0.6

MACK, DENNY Dennis Joseph (b Dennis Joseph McGee); B1851 Easton PA; D4.10.1888 Wilkes–Barre PA; BR/TR/5´7˝/164; d5.6; M1/U2; Col Villanova; ▲

YEAR	TM LG	G	AB	R	H	2B	3B	HR	RBI	BB-IB	HP	SO	AVG	OBP	SLG	AOPS	ABR	SB-CS	FA	FR	RNG	THR	GAMES AT POSITION	DL	BFW
1871	Rok NA	**25**	122	34	30	7	1	0	17	8	—	7	.246	.292	.320	79	-2	12-0	.936	1	**162**	104	1b24,P3/Slf	—	0.1
1872	Ath NA	**47**	205	68	59	9	1	0	34	**23**	—	9	.288	.360	.341	116	6	9-5	.948	-1	349	87	1b26,S21	—	0.3
1873	Phi NA	48	205	55	60	5	0	0	19	15	—	9	.293	.341	.317	92	-2	6-2	.938	3	86	109	1b42,O5(1/1/3),S3/2	—	0.2
1874	Phi NA	56	246	48	51	8	4	0	22	2	—	3	.207	.214	.272	53	-13	4-0	.900	-4	77	159	1b56	—	-1.2
1876	StL N	48	180	32	39	5	0	1	7	11	—	5	.217	.262	.261	79	-3	—	.886	-5	89	106	S41,2b5,O2(1/1/0)	—	-0.6
1880	Buf N	17	59	5	12	0	0	0	3	5	—	7	.203	.266	.203	60	-2	—	.940	1	99	72	S16/2	—	-0.1
1882	Lou AA	72	264	41	48	3	1	0	—	16	—	—	.182	.229	.201	49	-13	—	.898	2	100	85	S49,2b24,O5(1/3/1),M	—	-0.8
1883	Pit AA	60	224	26	44	5	3	0	—	13	—	—	.196	.241	.246	59	-9	—	.844	5	112	83	S38,1b25/2	—	-0.4
Total	4NA	176	778	205	200	29	6	0	92	48	—	28	.257	.300	.310	85	-11	31-7	.927	-2	143	123	1b148,S25,O6(2/1/3),P3/2	—	-0.6
Total	4	197	727	104	143	13	4	1	10	45	—	12	.197	.244	.230	60	-27	—	.886	2	100	89	S144,2b31,1b25,O7(2/4/1)	—	-1.9

MACK, EARLE Earle Thaddeus (b McGillicuddy); B2.1.1890 Spencer MA; D2.4.1967 Upper Darby Twp. PA; BL/TR/5´8˝/140; d10.5; M2/C27; f–Connie; Col Niagara

YEAR	TM LG	G	AB	R	H	2B	3B	HR	RBI	BB-IB	HP	SO	AVG	OBP	SLG	AOPS	ABR	SB-CS	FA	FR	RNG	THR	GAMES AT POSITION	DL	BFW
1910	Phi A	1	4	0	2	0	1	0	0	0	0	—	.500	.500	1.000	372	1	0	1.000	-0	*118*	*105*	/C	—	0.1
1911	Phi A	2	4	0	0	0	0	0	0	0	0	—	.000	.000	.000	-99	-1	0	ø	-0	0	0	3b2	—	-0.1
1914	Phi A	2	8	0	0	0	0	0	1	0	0	0	.000	.000	.000	-99	-2	1	1.000	-0	83	0	1b2	—	-0.2
Total	3	5	16	0	2	0	1	0	1	0	0	0	.125	.125	.250	11	-2	1	1.000	-0	83	0	1b2,3b2/C	—	-0.2

MACK, REDDY Joseph (b Joseph McNamara); B5.2.1866 , Ireland; D12.30.1916 Newport KY; 5´8˝/182; d9.16

YEAR	TM LG	G	AB	R	H	2B	3B	HR	RBI	BB-IB	HP	SO	AVG	OBP	SLG	AOPS	ABR	SB-CS	FA	FR	RNG	THR	GAMES AT POSITION	DL	BFW
1885	Lou AA	11	41	7	10	1	0	0	5	2	1	—	.244	.295	.268	79	-1	—	.885	1	103	193	2b11	—	0.1
1886	Lou AA	137	483	82	118	23	11	1	56	68	4	—	.244	.342	.344	109	6	13	.900	6	103	99	2b137	—	1.5
1887	Lou AA	128	478	117	147	23	8	1	69	83	5	—	.308	.415	.395	124	21	22	.912	1	99	91	2b128	—	2.1
1888	Lou AA	112	446	77	97	13	5	3	34	52	15	—	.217	.320	.289	98	2	18	.907	5	103	81	2b112	—	1.1
1889	Bal AA	136	519	84	125	24	7	1	87	60	8	69	.241	.329	.320	84	-10	23	.897	-7	93	112	2b135/cf	—	-1.0
1890	Bal AA	26	95	14	27	3	5	0	11	10	3	—	.284	.370	.421	127	3	7	.932	3	109	67	2b26	—	0.6
Total	6	550	2062	381	524	87	36	6	262	275	36	69	.254	.352	.340	104	21	83	.905	9	100	97	2b549/cf	—	4.4

MACK, JOE Joseph John (b Joseph John Maciarz); B1.4.1912 Chicago IL; D12.19.1998 Atlanta GA; BB/TL/5´11.5˝/185; d4.17

YEAR	TM LG	G	AB	R	H	2B	3B	HR	RBI	BB-IB	HP	SO	AVG	OBP	SLG	AOPS	ABR	SB-CS	FA	FR	RNG	THR	GAMES AT POSITION	DL	BFW
1945	Bos N	66	260	30	60	13	1	3	44	34	0	39	.231	.320	.323	79	-7	1	.991	-0	102	92	1b65	0	-1.1

MACK, QUINN Quinn David; B9.11.1965 Los Angeles CA; BL/TL/5´10˝/185; d6.16; b–Shane; Col California–Santa Barbara

YEAR	TM LG	G	AB	R	H	2B	3B	HR	RBI	BB-IB	HP	SO	AVG	OBP	SLG	AOPS	ABR	SB-CS	FA	FR	RNG	THR	GAMES AT POSITION	DL	BFW
1994	Sea A	5	21	1	5	3	0	0	2	1-0	0	3	.238	.273	.381	65	-1	2-0	1.000	-0	84	0	O4(3/1/0)/D	0	-0.1

MACK, RAY Raymond James (b Raymond James Mlckovsky); B8.31.1916 Cleveland OH; D5.7.1969 Bucyrus OH; BR/TR/6´0˝/200; d9.9; Mil 1945; Col Case Western Reserve

YEAR	TM LG	G	AB	R	H	2B	3B	HR	RBI	BB-IB	HP	SO	AVG	OBP	SLG	AOPS	ABR	SB-CS	FA	FR	RNG	THR	GAMES AT POSITION	DL	BFW
1938	Cle A	2	6	2	2	0	1	0	2	0	0	1	.333	.333	.667	147	0	0-0	1.000	1	102	0	2b2	—	0.1
1939	Cle A	36	112	12	17	4	1	1	6	12	1	19	.152	.240	.232	22	-14	0-2	.976	1	94	131	2b34/3	—	-1.1
1940	Cle A★	146	530	60	150	21	5	12	69	51	0	77	.283	.346	.409	98	-3	4-2	.965	-5	94	**117**	2b146	—	0.2
1941	Cle A	145	500	54	114	22	4	9	44	54	0	69	.228	.303	.342	74	-20	8-4	.970	-2	93	114	2b145	0	-1.2
1942	Cle A	143	481	43	108	14	6	2	45	41	2	51	.225	.288	.291	67	-23	9-3	.969	-1	**104**	117	2b143	0	-1.4
1943	Cle A	**153**	545	56	120	25	2	7	62	47	2	61	.220	.285	.312	79	-16	8-3	.967	-4	98	116	2b153	0	-1.2
1944	Cle A	83	284	24	66	15	3	0	29	28	0	45	.232	.301	.306	77	-9	4-1	.951	2	103	117	2b83	0	-0.1
1946	Cle A	61	171	13	35	6	2	1	9	23	0	27	.205	.299	.281	67	-8	2-2	.970	-3	93	103	2b61	0	-0.8
1947	NY A	1	0	0	0	0	0	0	0	0	0	0	ø	ø	ø	ø	0	0-0	ø	0	—	—	/R	0	0.0
	Chi N	21	78	9	17	6	0	2	12	5	1	15	.218	.274	.372	73	-3	0	.965	4	118	92	2b21	0	0.2
Total	9	791	2707	273	629	113	24	34	278	261	6	365	.232	.301	.330	76	-96	35-17	.966	-7	98	115	2b788/3	0	-5.3

MACK, SHANE Shane Lee; B12.7.1963 Los Angeles CA; BR/TR/6´0˝/(185–190); [SDN84 1/11]; d5.25; b–Quinn; Col UCLA; [DL 1989 SD N 31]

YEAR	TM LG	G	AB	R	H	2B	3B	HR	RBI	BB-IB	HP	SO	AVG	OBP	SLG	AOPS	ABR	SB-CS	FA	FR	RNG	THR	GAMES AT POSITION	DL	BFW
1987	SD N	105	238	28	57	11	3	4	25	18-0	3	47	.239	.299	.361	77	-8	4-6	.982	-1	108	28	O91(0/90/2)	0	-1.1
1988	SD N	56	119	13	29	3	0	0	12	14-0	3	21	.244	.336	.269	78	-3	5-1	.983	4	111	214	O55(9/46/6)	0	0.2
1990	Min A	125	313	50	102	10	4	8	44	29-1	5	69	.326	.392	.460	129	12	13-4	.988	8	114	145	O109(23/43/51),D4	0	2.0
1991	†Min A	143	442	79	137	27	8	18	74	34-1	6	79	.310	.363	.529	138	22	13-9	.977	3	110	76	O140(48/36/81)/D	0	2.1
1992	Min A	156	600	101	189	31	6	16	75	64-1	**15**	106	.315	.394	.467	135	30	26-14	.988	-1	101	88	O155(150/9/4)	0	2.6
1993	Min A	128	503	66	139	30	4	10	61	41-1	4	76	.276	.335	.412	99	-1	15-5	.986	9	114	107	O128(64/67/2)	15	0.7
1994	Min A	81	303	55	101	21	2	15	61	32-1	6	51	.333	.402	.564	146	22	4-1	.990	4	120	39	O75(66/24/0),D4	30	2.2
1997	Bos A	60	130	13	41	7	0	3	17	9-1	3	24	.315	.368	.438	109	2	2-1	1.000	-5	83	0	O45(3/43/0),D5	25	-0.2
1998	Oak A	3	2	1	0	0	0	0	0	0-0	0	0	.000	.000	.000	-99	-1	0-0	ø	0	—	—	/H	0	-0.1
	KC A	66	207	30	58	15	1	6	29	15-0	6	36	.280	.345	.449	101	0	8-2	.982	-2	91	54	O32(30/0/3),D21	59	-0.2
	Year	69	209	31	58	15	1	6	29	15-0	6	36	.278	.342	.445	99	0	8-2	.982	-2	91	54	O32(30/0/3),D21	0	-0.3
Total	9	923	2857	436	853	155	28	80	398	256-6	51	509	.299	.364	.456	119	75	90-43	.985	19	108	87	O830(393/358/149),D35	160	8.2

MACKANIN, PETE Peter; B8.1.1951 Chicago IL; BR/TR/6´2˝/(180–196); [TexA69 4/71]; d7.3; M1/C7; OF(4/0/1)

YEAR	TM LG	G	AB	R	H	2B	3B	HR	RBI	BB-IB	HP	SO	AVG	OBP	SLG	AOPS	ABR	SB-CS	FA	FR	RNG	THR	GAMES AT POSITION	DL	BFW
1973	Tex A	44	90	3	9	2	0	0	2	4-0	1	26	.100	.146	.122	-24	-15	0-0	.947	-5	95	75	S33,3b10	0	-1.7
1974	Tex A	2	6	0	1	0	1	0	0	0-0	0	2	.167	.167	.500	88	0	0-0	1.000	2	151	293	S2	0	0.2
1975	Mon N	130	448	59	101	19	6	12	44	31-4	2	99	.225	.276	.375	76	-17	11-5	.966	14	111	115	2b127/S3	0	0.6
1976	Mon N	114	380	36	85	15	2	8	33	15-1	2	66	.224	.256	.337	64	-19	6-2	.965	3	105	90	2b100,3b8,S3/lf	0	-1.0
1977	Mon N	55	85	9	19	2	2	1	6	4-1	0	17	.224	.258	.329	58	-6	3-1	1.000	2	89	96	2b9,S8,3b5,O4(3/0/1)	0	-0.2
1978	Phi N	5	8	0	2	0	0	0	1	0-0	0	4	.250	.250	.250	39	-1	0-0	1.000	0	190	0	/13	0	0.0
1979	Phi N	13	9	2	1	0	0	1	2	1-0	0	2	.111	.200	.444	68	-1	0-0	1.000	2	231	0	2b2,S2,3b2	30	0.1
1980	Min A	108	319	31	85	18	0	4	35	14-2	0	34	.266	.296	.361	74	-12	6-2	.968	5	108	111	2b71,S30,1b4,3b3,D5	0	0.0
1981	Min A	77	225	21	52	7	1	4	18	7-2	1	40	.231	.256	.324	63	-11	1-2	.980	-5	110	80	2b31,S28,1b10,3b4,D6	0	-1.5
Total	9	548	1570	161	355	63	12	30	141	76-10	6	290	.226	.263	.339	65	-82	27-12	.968	19	108	103	2b340,S107,3b34,1b15,D11,O5L	30	-3.5

MACKENZIE, ERIC Eric Hugh; B8.29.1932 Glendon AL, Can.; BL/TR/6´0˝/185; d4.23

YEAR	TM LG	G	AB	R	H	2B	3B	HR	RBI	BB-IB	HP	SO	AVG	OBP	SLG	AOPS	ABR	SB-CS	FA	FR	RNG	THR	GAMES AT POSITION	DL	BFW
1955	KC A	1	1	0	0	0	0	0	0	0-0	0	0	.000	.000	.000	-99	0	0-0	ø	0	*0*	*0*	/C	0	0.0

MACKENZIE, GORDON Henry Gordon; B7.9.1937 St.Petersburg FL; BR/TR/5´11˝/175; d8.13; C7

YEAR	TM LG	G	AB	R	H	2B	3B	HR	RBI	BB-IB	HP	SO	AVG	OBP	SLG	AOPS	ABR	SB-CS	FA	FR	RNG	THR	GAMES AT POSITION	DL	BFW
1961	KC A	11	24	1	3	0	0	0	1	1-0	0	6	.125	.160	.125	-22	-4	0-0	1.000	-0	94	0	C7	0	-0.4

MACKIEWICZ, FELIX Felix Thaddeus; B11.20.1917 Chicago IL; D12.20.1993 Olivette MO; BR/TR/6´2˝/195; d9.7; Col Purdue

YEAR	TM LG	G	AB	R	H	2B	3B	HR	RBI	BB-IB	HP	SO	AVG	OBP	SLG	AOPS	ABR	SB-CS	FA	FR	RNG	THR	GAMES AT POSITION	DL	BFW
1941	Phi A	5	14	3	4	0	1	0	0	1	0	0	.286	.333	.429	103	0	0-0	1.000	-0	86	0	O3(0/1/2)	0	-0.1
1942	Phi A	6	14	3	3	2	0	0	2	0	0	4	.214	.214	.357	59	-1	0-0	1.000	1	94	526	O3(0/2/1)	0	0.0
1943	Phi A	9	16	1	1	0	0	0	0	2	0	8	.063	.167	.063	-32	-3	0-0	1.000	0	123	0	O3(0/2/1)	0	-0.3
1945	Cle A	120	359	42	98	14	7	2	37	44	2	41	.273	.356	.368	115	7	5-5	.987	7	109	131	O112C	0	1.2
1946	Cle A	78	258	35	67	15	4	0	16	16	1	32	.260	.305	.349	88	-5	5-1	.983	-0	105	48	O72(0/71/1)	0	-0.7
1947	Cle A	2	5	0	0	0	0	0	0	0	0	2	.000	.000	.000	-99	-1	0-0	1.000	0	119	0	O2C	0	-0.1
	Was A	3	6	1	1	1	0	0	0	0	0	1	.167	.167	.333	38	-1	0-0	1.000	-0	85	0	O3C	0	-0.1
	Year	5	11	1	1	1	0	0	0	0	0	3	.091	.091	.182	-26	-2	0-0	1.000	-0	103	0	O5C	0	-0.2
Total	6	223	672	85	174	32	12	2	55	63	3	88	.259	.325	.351	97	-4	10-6	.986	7	107	100	O198(0/193/5)	0	-0.1

MACKO, STEVE Steven Joseph; B9.6.1954 Burlington IA; D11.15.1981 Arlington TX; BL/TR/5´10˝/160; [ChiN77 5/116]; d8.18; Col Baylor; [DL 1981 Chi N 177]

YEAR	TM LG	G	AB	R	H	2B	3B	HR	RBI	BB-IB	HP	SO	AVG	OBP	SLG	AOPS	ABR	SB-CS	FA	FR	RNG	THR	GAMES AT POSITION	DL	BFW
1979	Chi N	19	40	2	9	1	0	0	3	4-0	0	8	.225	.295	.250	46	-3	0-0	1.000	3	93	80	2b10,3b4	0	0.0
1980	Chi N	6	20	2	6	2	0	0	2	0-0	0	3	.300	.300	.400	86	0	0-0	1.000	1	149	227	S3,3b2/2	38	0.1
Total	2	25	60	4	15	3	0	0	5	4-0	0	11	.250	.297	.300	59	-3	0-0	1.000	4	85	70	2b11,3b6,S3	215	0.1

MACKOWIAK, ROB Robert William; B6.20.1976 Oak Lawn IL; BL/TR/5´10˝/(168–200); [PitN96 53/1499]; d5.19; Col South Suburban (IL) JC; OF(74/173/253)

YEAR	TM LG	G	AB	R	H	2B	3B	HR	RBI	BB-IB	HP	SO	AVG	OBP	SLG	AOPS	ABR	SB-CS	FA	FR	RNG	THR	GAMES AT POSITION	DL	BFW
2001	Pit N	83	214	30	57	15	2	4	21	15-5	3	52	.266	.319	.411	86	-5	4-3	.986	2	94	121	O46(10/0/40),2b21,3b2/1	29	-0.3
2002	Pit N	136	385	57	94	22	0	16	48	42-5	7	120	.244	.328	.426	95	-3	9-3	.988	1	86	139	O106(2/42/76),3b26,2b3	0	-0.3
2003	Pit N	77	174	20	47	4	4	6	19	15-2	4	53	.270	.342	.443	101	0	6-0	1.000	-4	93	0	O30(8/8/14),3b19,2b15	0	-0.3
2004	Pit N	155	491	65	121	22	6	17	75	50-2	6	114	.246	.319	.420	90	-8	13-4	.974	0	86	188	O118(25/19/79),3b55/1	0	-0.9
2005	Pit N	142	463	57	126	21	3	9	58	43-4	3	100	.272	.337	.389	90	-7	8-4	.952	4	114	148	3b65,O63(1/41/23),2b20,1b3	0	-0.2
2006	Chi A	112	255	31	74	12	1	5	23	28-3	3	59	.290	.365	.404	97	0	5-2	.974	-6	89	53	O96(28/63/21),3b6,D2	0	-0.6
Total	6	705	1982	260	519	96	16	57	244	193-21	26	498	.262	.333	.413	92	-23	45-16	.981	-3	89	127	O459R,3b173,2b59,1b5,D2	29	-2.6

MACLIN, LONNIE Lonnie Lee; B2.17.1967 Clayton MO; BL/TL/5´11˝/185; [StLN86 S3/63]; d9.7; Col St. Louis–Meramec (MO) CC

YEAR	TM LG	G	AB	R	H	2B	3B	HR	RBI	BB-IB	HP	SO	AVG	OBP	SLG	AOPS	ABR	SB-CS	FA	FR	RNG	THR	GAMES AT POSITION	DL	BFW
1993	StL N	12	13	2	1	0	0	0	1	0-0	0	5	.077	.071	.077	-59	-3	1-0	1.000	-1	64	0	O5L	0	-0.3

YEAR	TM LG	G	AB	R	H	2B	3B	HR	RBI	BB-IB	HP	SO	AVG	OBP	SLG	AOPS	ABR	SB-CS	FA	FR	RNG	THR	GAMES AT POSITION	DL	BFW
MACON, MAX	Max Cullen; B10.14.1915 Pensacola FL; D8.5.1989 Jupiter FL; BL/TL/6´3˝/175; d4.21; Mil 1945–46; ▲																								
1938	StL N	46	36	5	11	0	0	0	3	2	0	4	.306	.342	.306	75	-1	0	.946	1	123	120	P38/rf	—	0.0
1940	Bro N	2	1	0	1	0	0	0	0	0	0	0	1.000	1.000	1.000	427	0	0	ø	-0	0	0	P2	—	0.0
1942	Bro N	26	43	4	12	2	1	0	1	2	0	4	.279	.311	.372	98	3	1	.960	-0	83	0	P14	0	0.0
1943	Bro N	45	55	7	9	0	0	0	6	0	0	1	.164	.164	.164	-5	-8	1	1.000	0	121	174	P25,1b3	0	-0.1
1944	Bos N	106	366	38	100	15	3	3	36	12	0	23	.273	.296	.355	79	-11	7	.977	-2	106	115	1b72,O22(21/2/0)/P	0	-1.8
1947	Bos N	1	1	0	0	0	0	0	0	0	0	0	.000	.000	.000	-99	0	0	1.000	0	267	0	/P	0	0.0
Total	6	226	502	54	133	17	4	3	46	16	0	32	.265	.288	.333	72	-17	9	.965	-1	112	97	P81,1b75,O23(21/2/1)	0	-1.9
MACPHEE, WADDY	Walter Scott; B12.23.1899 Brooklyn NY; D1.20.1980 Charlotte NC; BR/TR/5´8˝/140; d9.27; Col Princeton																								
1922	NY N	2	7	2	2	0	1	0	0	1	0	0	.286	.375	.571	140	0	0-0	.889	0	116	0	3b2	—	0.1
MACULLAR, JIMMY	James F. "Little Mac"; B1.16.1855 Boston MA; D4.8.1924 Baltimore MD; BR/TL/5´6˝/155; d5.5; M1/U1																								
1879	Syr N	64	246	24	52	9	0	0	13	3	—	27	.211	.221	.248	61	-9	—	.865	-4	93	100	S37,O26C,2b4/3M	—	-1.2
1882	Cin AA	79	299	44	70	6	6	0	22	14	—	—	.234	.268	.294	85	-5	—	.922	-4	68	122	O79C	—	-1.1
1883	Cin AA	14	48	4	8	2	0	0	4	4	—	—	.167	.231	.208	40	-3	—	.900	-2	53	0	O14(2/6/7)/S	—	-0.4
1884	Bal AA	107	360	73	73	16	6	4	—	36	8	—	.203	.290	.314	93	-1	—	.866	-2	93	87	S107	—	0.0
1885	Bal AA	100	320	52	61	7	6	3	26	49	4	—	.191	.306	.278	87	-2	—	.877	-0	94	90	S98,O2R/P	—	0.0
1886	Bal AA	85	268	49	55	7	1	0	26	49	2	—	.205	.332	.239	82	-2	23	.852	-8	81	81	S82,O2C/2P	—	-0.6
Total	6	449	1541	246	319	47	19	7	91	155	14	27	.207	.285	.276	83	-22	23	.865	-19	90	88	S325,O123(2/113/9),2b5,P2/3	—	-3.3
MADDEN, GENE	Eugene; B6.5.1890 Elm Grove WV; D4.6.1949 Utica NY; BL/TR/5´10˝/155; d4.20																								
1916	Pit N	1	1	0	0	0	0	0	0	0	0	0	.000	.000	.000	-99	0	0	ø	0	—	—	/H	—	0.0
MADDEN, FRANK	Francis A. "Red"; B10.17.1892 Pittsburgh PA; D4.30.1952 Pittsburgh PA; d7.4																								
1914	Pit F	2	2	0	1	0	0	0	1	0	0	0	.500	.500	.500	174	0	0	ø	-0	0	0	/C	—	0.0
MADDEN, BUNNY	Thomas Francis; B9.14.1882 Boston MA; D1.20.1954 Cambridge MA; BR/TR/5´10˝/190; d6.3; Col Villanova																								
1909	Bos A	10	17	0	4	0	0	0	1	0	0	—	.235	.235	.235	48	-1	0	.941	1	141	86	C7	—	0.0
1910	Bos A	14	35	4	13	3	0	0	4	3	1	—	.371	.436	.457	175	3	0	.938	-3	102	65	C12	—	0.2
1911	Bos A	4	15	2	3	0	0	0	2	2	0	—	.200	.294	.200	39	-1	0	1.000	-1	82	50	C4	—	-0.2
	Phi N	28	76	4	21	1	1	0	4	0	0	13	.276	.276	.316	65	-4	0	.924	-1	94	110	C22	—	-0.3
Total	3	56	143	10	41	4	1	0	11	5	1	13	.287	.315	.329	87	-3	0	.935	-4	101	90	C45	—	-0.3
MADDEN, TOMMY	Thomas Joseph; B7.31.1883 Philadelphia PA; D7.26.1930 Philadelphia PA; BL/TL/5´11˝/160; d9.10																								
1906	Bos N	4	15	1	4	0	0	0	0	1	0	—	.267	.313	.267	83	0	0	1.000	0	243	0	O4L	—	-0.1
1910	NY A	1	1	0	0	0	0	0	0	0	0	—	.000	.000	.000	-95	0	0	ø	0	—	—	/H	—	0.0
Total	2	5	16	1	4	0	0	0	0	1	0	—	.250	.294	.250	71	0	0	1.000	0	243	0	O4L	—	-0.1
MADDERN, CLARENCE	Clarence James; B9.26.1921 Lowell AZ; D8.9.1986 Tucson AZ; BR/TR/6´1˝/185; d9.19																								
1946	Chi N	3	3	0	0	0	0	0	0	0	1	0	.000	.250	.000	-27	0	0	1.000	0	149	0	O2L	0	0.0
1948	Chi N	80	214	16	54	12	1	4	27	10	5	25	.252	.301	.374	85	-5	0	.981	1	95	154	O55(48/0/10)	0	-0.8
1949	Chi N	10	9	1	3	0	0	1	2	2	0	0	.333	.455	.667	202	1	0	1.000	0	352	0	/1	0	0.2
1951	Cle A	11	12	0	2	0	0	0	0	0	0	1	.167	.167	.167	-10	-2	0-0	.667	-0	86	0	/lf	0	-0.2
Total	4	104	238	17	59	12	1	5	29	12	6	26	.248	.301	.370	84	-6	0-0	.973	1	96	147	O58(51/0/10)/1	0	-0.8
MADDOX, ELLIOTT	Elliott; B12.21.1947 East Orange NJ; BR/TR/5´11˝/(180–185); [DetA68 S1/20]; d4.7; Col Michigan; OF(77/472/189)																								
1970	Det A	109	258	30	64	13	4	3	24	30-1	3	42	.248	.332	.364	91	-3	2-3	.919	3	103	101	3b40,O37(28/1/9),S19/2	0	-0.1
1971	Was A	128	258	38	56	8	2	1	18	51-3	0	42	.217	.344	.275	82	-4	10-4	.990	8	116	154	O103(12/84/10),3b12	0	0.2
1972	Tex A	98	294	40	74	7	2	0	10	49-4	2	53	.252	.361	.289	99	2	20-10	.990	3	102	126	O94(11/70/14)	0	0.3
1973	Tex A	100	172	24	41	1	0	1	17	29-2	3	28	.238	.356	.262	80	-3	5-4	.981	5	107	176	O89(22/58/11),3b7/D	15	0.0
1974	NY A	137	466	75	141	26	2	3	45	69-4	4	48	.303	.395	.386	127	21	6-5	.986	9	103	**202**	O135(1/112/25),2b2/3	0	2.7
1975	NY A	55	218	36	67	10	3	1	23	21-0	7	24	.307	.382	.394	122	7	9-3	1.000	4	110	131	O55C/2	107	1.1
1976	†NY A	18	46	4	10	2	0	0	3	4-1	0	3	.217	.275	.261	59	-2	0-1	1.000	0	80	248	O13(0/6/7),D2	138	-0.3
1977	Bal A	49	107	14	28	7	0	2	9	13-0	4	9	.262	.357	.383	110	2	2-2	.990	1	119	0	O45(1/44/0)/3	99	0.3
1978	NY N	119	389	43	100	18	2	2	39	71-1	2	38	.257	.370	.329	101	4	2-11	.988	4	115	152	O79(0/13/72),3b43/1	20	0.2
1979	NY N	86	224	21	60	13	0	1	12	20-0	3	27	.268	.335	.339	87	-3	3-2	.985	4	116	126	O65(2/26/40),3b11	22	-0.1
1980	NY N	130	411	35	101	16	1	4	34	52-5	**6**	44	.246	.336	.319	86	-6	1-9	.956	3	96	106	3b115,O4(0/3/1),1b2	0	-0.8
Total	11	1029	2843	360	742	121	16	18	234	409-21	34	358	.261	.358	.334	99	15	60-54	.989	44	109	149	O719C,3b230,S19,2b4,1b3,D3	401	3.5
MADDOX, GARRY	Garry Lee; B9.1.1949 Cincinnati OH; BR/TR/6´3˝/(170–195); [SFN68*2/38]; d4.25																								
1972	SF N	125	458	62	122	26	7	12	58	14-3	4	97	.266	.293	.432	102	-1	13-6	.979	-1	101	94	O121(20/96/6)	0	-0.5
1973	SF N	144	587	81	187	30	10	11	76	24-2	6	73	.319	.350	.460	118	13	24-10	.969	-4	107	44	O140C	0	0.7
1974	SF N	135	538	74	153	31	3	8	50	29-3	3	64	.284	.322	.398	97	-3	21-9	.986	-3	105	37	O131C	0	-0.8
1975	SF N	17	52	4	7	1	0	1	4	6-1	1	3	.135	.237	.212	24	-5	1-1	1.000	2	106	346	O13C	0	-0.4
	Phi N	99	374	50	109	25	8	4	46	36-5	5	54	.291	.359	.433	114	7	24-3	.983	13	121	169	O97C	36	2.2
	Year	116	426	54	116	26	8	5	50	42-6	6	57	.272	.344	.406	103	2	25-4	.985	15	**119**	**192**	O110C	0	1.8
1976	†Phi N	146	531	75	175	37	6	6	68	42-8	4	59	.330	.377	.456	132	23	29-12	.989	14	**123**	114	O144C	0	3.7
1977	†Phi N	139	571	85	167	27	10	14	74	24-8	4	58	.292	.323	.448	100	-2	22-6	.977	3	111	77	O138C	15	0.2
1978	†Phi N	155	598	62	172	34	3	11	68	39-11	2	89	.288	.332	.410	105	3	33-7	.983	6	112	81	O154C	0	1.4
1979	Phi N	148	548	70	154	28	6	13	61	17-5	4	71	.281	.304	.425	94	-7	26-13	.996	17	**123**	130	O140C	0	1.1
1980	†Phi N	143	549	59	142	31	3	11	73	18-5	0	52	.259	.278	.386	80	-16	25-5	.976	1	107	71	O143C	0	-1.4
1981	†Phi N	94	323	37	85	7	1	5	40	17-1	1	42	.263	.295	.337	77	-10	9-4	.977	8	115	139	O94C	0	-0.3
1982	Phi N	119	412	39	117	27	2	8	61	12-0	0	32	.284	.303	.417	97	-3	7-5	**.992**	3	104	135	O111C	33	-0.1
1983	†Phi N	97	324	27	89	14	2	4	32	17-5	1	31	.275	.312	.367	88	-6	7-6	.977	-2	105	26	O95C	15	-0.9
1984	Phi N	77	241	29	68	11	0	5	19	13-1	0	29	.282	.316	.390	97	-2	3-2	1.000	3	110	93	O69C	57	0.0
1985	Phi N	105	218	22	52	8	1	4	23	13-2	1	26	.239	.281	.339	72	-9	4-2	.980	-0	104	88	O94C	0	-1.0
1986	Phi N	6	7	1	3	0	0	0	1	2-0	0	1	.429	.556	.429	169	1	0-1	1.000	-1	25	0	O3C	14	0.0
Total	15	1749	6331	777	1802	337	62	117	754	323-60	36	781	.285	.320	.413	100	-17	248-92	.983	59	111	93	O1687(20/1660/6)	170	3.9
MADDOX, JERRY	Jerry Glenn; B7.28.1953 Whittier CA; BR/TR/6´2˝/200; [AtlN75 8/186]; d6.3; Col Arizona St.																								
1978	Atl N	7	14	1	3	0	0	0	1	1-0	0	2	.214	.267	.214	32	-1	0-0	.909	-1	90	0	3b5	0	-0.2
MADISON, ART	Arthur M.; B1.14.1871 Clarksburg MA; D1.27.1933 N.Adams MA; BR/TR/5´9˝/165; d9.9																								
1895	Phi N	11	34	6	12	3	0	0	8	1	0	1	.353	.371	.441	109	0	4	.955	-1	96	0	S6,2b3,3b2	—	0.0
1899	Pit N	42	118	20	32	2	4	0	19	11	1	—	.271	.338	.356	91	-2	1	.953	-5	89	71	2b19,S15,3b2	—	-0.5
Total	2	53	152	26	44	5	4	0	27	12	1	1	.289	.345	.375	95	-2	5	.926	-6	90	82	2b22,S21,3b4	—	-0.5
MADISON, SCOTTI	Charles Scott; B9.12.1959 Pensacola FL; BB/TR/5´11˝/(185–195); [MinA80 3/64]; d7.6; Col Vanderbilt																								
1985	Det A	6	11	0	0	0	0	0	1	2-0	0	0	.000	.143	.000	-53	-2	0-0	1.000	0	0	0	/CD	0	-0.2
1986	Det A	2	7	0	0	0	0	0	1	0-0	0	3	.000	.000	.000	-99	-2	0-0	.667	-0	51	580	/3D	22	-0.2
1987	KC A	7	15	4	4	3	0	0	0	1-0	0	5	.267	.313	.467	100	0	0-0	1.000	-2	141	234	1b4,C3	0	-0.2
1988	KC A	16	35	4	6	2	0	0	2	4-0	0	5	.171	.256	.229	36	-3	1-0	1.000	1	0	0	C4,O3(2/0/1),1b2,D4	0	-0.2
1989	Cin N	40	98	13	17	7	0	1	7	8-2	1	9	.173	.241	.276	46	-7	0-1	1.000	1	99	81	3b26	0	-0.6
Total	5	71	166	21	27	12	0	1	11	15-2	1	22	.163	.232	.253	37	-14	1-1	.985	-1	97	103	3b27,D8,C8,1b6,O3(2/0/1)	22	-1.4
MADJESKI, ED	Edward William (b Edward William Majewski); B7.20.1908 Far Rockaway NY; D11.11.1994 Montgomery OH; BR/TR/5´11˝/178; d5.2; Col Seton Hall																								
1932	Phi A	17	35	4	8	0	0	0	3	3	0	6	.229	.289	.229	35	-3	0-0	1.000	1	99	133	C8	—	-0.2
1933	Phi A	51	142	17	40	4	0	0	17	4	0	21	.282	.301	.310	62	-8	0-0	.958	-4	86	61	C41	—	-0.9
1934	Phi A	8	8	1	3	1	0	0	2	0	0	1	.375	.375	.500	129	0	0-0	.000	-1	0	0	/C	—	0.0
	Chi A	85	281	36	62	14	2	5	32	14	1	31	.221	.260	.338	52	-22	2-0	.973	-3	64	123	C79	—	-1.8
	Year	93	289	37	65	15	2	5	34	14	1	32	.225	.263	.343	54	-21	2-0	.971	-4	64	123	C80	—	-1.8
1937	NY N	5	15	0	3	0	0	0	2	0	0	2	.200	.200	.200	9	-2	0	1.000	-1	104	111	C5	—	-0.3
Total	4	166	481	58	116	19	2	5	56	21	1	61	.241	.274	.320	53	-35	2-0	.970	-7	73	107	C134	—	-3.2

YEAR	TM LG	G	AB	R	H	2B	3B	HR	RBI	BB-IB	HP	SO	AVG	OBP	SLG	AOPS	ABR	SB-CS	FA	FR	RNG	THR	GAMES AT POSITION	DL	BFW
MADLOCK, BILL	Bill; B1.2.1951 Memphis TN; BR/TR/5´11˝/(180–210); [TexA70*S5/99]; d9.7; C2; Col Southeastern (IA) CC																								
1973	Tex A	21	77	16	27	5	3	1	5	7-0	1	9	.351	.412	.532	170	7	3-2	.918	-4	79	47	3b21	0	0.3
1974	Chi N	128	453	65	142	21	5	9	54	42-8	5	39	.313	.374	.442	123	14	11-7	.946	-8	96	55	3b121	31	0.6
1975	Chi N★	130	514	77	182	29	7	7	64	42-5	3	34	**.354**	.402	.479	138	27	9-7	.943	-3	102	59	3b128	0	2.4
1976	Chi N	142	514	68	174	36	1	15	84	56-15	**11**	27	**.339**	.412	.500	146	34	15-11	.961	-9	93	85	3b136	0	2.5
1977	SF N	140	533	70	161	28	1	12	46	43-14	6	33	.302	.360	.426	110	8	13-10	.949	-20	86	77	3b126,2b6	0	-1.5
1978	SF N	122	447	76	138	26	3	15	44	48-11	3	39	.309	.378	.481	144	27	16-5	.974	-8	102	78	2b114,1b3	0	2.8
1979	SF N	69	249	37	65	9	2	7	41	18-3	0	19	.261	.309	.398	99	-2	11-3	.976	-9	88	78	2b63,1b5	0	-0.6
	†Pit N	85	311	48	102	17	3	7	44	34-8	1	22	.328	.390	.469	128	13	21-8	.969	-9	89	82	3b85	0	0.5
	Year	154	560	85	167	26	5	14	85	52-11	1	41	.298	.355	.438	116	12	32-11	.969	-18	89	82	3b85,2b63,1b5	0	-0.1
1980	Pit N	137	494	62	137	22	4	10	53	45-12	4	33	.277	.341	.399	103	2	16-10	.955	-16	85	99	3b127,1b12	0	-1.7
1981	Pit N★	82	279	35	95	23	1	6	45	34-7	3	17	**.341**	.412	.495	150	21	18-6	.956	-0	102	139	3b78	0	2.2
1982	Pit N	154	568	92	181	33	3	19	95	48-16	4	39	.319	.368	.488	134	26	18-6	.952	-7	93	101	3b146,1b3	0	1.9
1983	Pit N★	130	473	68	153	21	0	12	68	49-10	2	24	**.323**	.386	.444	127	18	3-4	.958	-16	82	106	3b126	0	0.0
1984	Pit N	103	403	38	102	16	0	4	44	26-5	1	29	.253	.297	.323	75	-14	3-1	.942	-11	85	112	3b98/1	49	-2.8
1985	Pit N	110	399	49	100	23	1	10	41	39-2	5	42	.251	.323	.388	99	0	3-3	.940	-11	92	58	3b98,1b12	0	-1.4
	†LA N	34	114	20	41	4	0	2	15	10-0	3	11	.360	.422	.447	147	8	7-1	.948	4	107	165	3b32	0	1.3
	Year	144	513	69	141	27	1	12	56	49-2	8	53	.275	.345	.402	110	8	10-4	.943	-7	95	82	3b130,1b12	0	-0.1
1986	LA N	111	379	38	106	17	0	10	60	30-4	5	43	.280	.336	.404	112	6	3-3	.910	-2	97	48	3b101,1b2	35	0.2
1987	LA N	21	61	5	11	1	0	3	7	6-0	1	5	.180	.265	.344	61	-4	0-0	.912	-2	84	86	3b16/1	23	-0.6
	†Det A	87	326	56	91	17	0	14	50	28-1	10	45	.279	.351	.460	118	9	4-3	.989	-2	78	94	D64,1b22/3	0	0.4
Total	15	1806	6594	920	2008	348	34	163	860	605-121	68	510	.305	.365	.442	122	200	174-90	.948	-132	92	86	3b1440,2b183,D64,1b61	138	6.5
MADRID, SAL	Salvador; B6.9.1920 El Paso TX; D2.24.1977 Ft.Wayne IN; BR/TR/5´9˝/165; d9.17																								
1947	Chi N	8	24	0	3	1	0	0	1	1	0	6	.125	.160	.167	-14	-4	0	.956	2	118	126	S8	0	-0.1
MAGADAN, DAVE	David Joseph; B9.30.1962 Tampa FL; BL/TR/6´3˝/(190–215); [NYN83 2/32]; d9.7; C4; Col Alabama																								
1986	NY N	10	18	3	8	0	0	0	3	3-0	0	1	.444	.524	.444	173	2	0-0	1.000	1	128	130	1b9	0	0.2
1987	NY N	85	192	21	61	13	1	3	24	22-2	0	22	.318	.386	.443	124	8	0-0	.981	5	122	86	3b50,1b13	11	1.2
1988	†NY N	112	314	39	87	15	0	1	35	60-4	2	39	.277	.393	.334	116	11	0-1	.988	2	93	95	1b71,3b48	15	1.0
1989	NY N	127	374	47	107	22	3	4	41	49-6	1	37	.286	.367	.393	123	13	1-0	.991	3	117	98	1b87,3b28	0	1.1
1990	NY N	144	451	74	148	28	6	6	72	74-4	2	55	.328	.417	.457	142	31	2-1	**.998**	4	98	79	1b113,3b19	0	2.8
1991	NY N	124	418	58	108	23	0	4	51	83-3	2	50	.258	.378	.342	106	9	1-1	.996	4	105	94	1b122	0	0.4
1992	NY N	99	321	33	91	9	1	3	28	56-3	0	44	.283	.390	.346	111	8	1-0	.941	-14	81	70	3b93,1b2	57	-0.7
1993	Fla N	66	227	22	65	12	0	4	29	44-4	1	30	.286	.400	.392	108	5	0-1	.961	5	105	115	3b63,1b2	0	1.0
	Sea A	71	228	27	59	11	0	1	21	36-3	0	33	.259	.356	.320	83	-4	2-0	.991	2	78	106	1b41,3b27,D2	0	-0.5
1994	Fla N	74	211	30	58	7	0	1	17	39-0	1	25	.275	.386	.322	85	-2	0-0	.958	-4	96	73	3b48,1b16	32	-0.7
1995	Hou N	127	348	44	109	24	0	2	51	71-9	0	56	.313	.428	.399	129	20	2-1	.922	-8	92	64	3b100,1b11	0	1.2
1996	Chi N	78	169	23	43	10	0	3	17	29-3	0	23	.254	.360	.367	90	-1	0-2	.963	-4	96	72	3b51,1b10	60	-0.6
1997	Oak A	128	271	38	82	10	1	4	30	50-1	2	40	.303	.414	.391	112	8	1-0	.940	4	113	134	3b49,1b30,D25	0	0.9
1998	Oak A	35	109	12	35	8	0	1	13	13-1	0	12	.321	.390	.422	114	3	0-1	.918	4	126	195	3b30,1b7	135	0.6
1999	SD N	116	248	20	68	12	1	2	30	45-2	0	36	.274	.377	.355	96	1	1-3	.969	-2	94	79	3b52,1b42	0	-0.3
2000	SD N	95	132	13	36	7	0	2	21	32-1	0	23	.273	.410	.371	107	4	0-0	.952	2	93	63	3b29,1b8,S2,D2	18	0.5
2001	SD N	91	128	12	32	7	0	1	12	12-0	1	20	.250	.317	.328	73	-5	0-0	.950	-2	83	74	3b22,1b9/2SD	0	-0.7
Total	16	1582	4159	516	1197	218	13	42	495	718-46	12	546	.288	.390	.377	112	111	11-11	.951	0	98	92	3b709,1b593,D31,S3/2	328	7.4
MAGALLANES, EVER	Everardo (Espinoza); B11.6.1965 El Sauz, Chihuahua, Mexico; BL/TR/5´10˝/165; [CleA87 10/255]; d5.17; Col Texas A&M																								
1991	Cle A	3	2	0	0	0	0	0	0	1-0	0	1	.000	.333	.000	1	0	0-0	1.000	-0	98	0	S2	0	0.0
MAGEE, LEE	Leo Christopher (b Leopold Christopher Hoernschemeyer); B6.4.1889 Cincinnati OH; D3.14.1966 Columbus OH; BB/TR/5´11˝/165; d7.4; M1; OF(230/285/8)																								
1911	StL N	26	69	9	18	1	1	0	8	8	1	8	.261	.338	.304	82	-2	4	.975	-2	83	91	2b18,S3	—	-0.3
1912	StL N	128	458	60	133	13	8	0	40	39	1	29	.290	.347	.354	94	-4	16	.956	6	104	134	O85L,2b23,1b6/S	—	-0.2
1913	StL N	137	531	54	142	13	7	2	31	34	2	30	.267	.314	.330	85	-11	23-26	.982	11	104	**134**	O108(108/3/1),2b22,1b6,S2	—	-1.0
1914	StL N	142	529	59	150	23	4	2	40	42	1	24	.284	.337	.353	107	4	36	.970	1	91	115	O102(2/100/0),1b39,2b6	—	-0.3
1915	Bro F	121	452	87	146	19	10	4	49	22	1	19	.323	.356	.436	123	5	34	.937	1	100	99	2b115,1b2,M	—	0.9
1916	NY A	131	510	57	131	18	4	3	45	50	1	31	.257	.324	.325	93	-4	29-25	.975	-1	99	91	O128(21/107/0),2b2	—	-1.8
1917	NY A	51	173	17	38	4	1	0	8	13	1	18	.220	.278	.254	62	-8	3	.938	-4	84	100	O50(2/48/0)	—	-1.7
	StL A	36	112	11	19	1	0	0	4	6	0	6	.170	.212	.179	20	-11	3	.971	6	124	137	3b20,2b6,1b5/rf	—	-0.5
	Year	87	285	28	57	5	1	0	12	19	1	24	.200	.252	.225	46	-19	6	.938	2	84	99	O51(2/48/1),3b20,2b6,1b5	—	-2.2
1918	Cin N	119	459	61	133	22	13	0	28	28	0	19	.290	.331	.394	123	11	19	.956	7	101	**139**	2b114,3b3	—	2.2
1919	Bro N	45	181	16	43	7	2	0	7	5	1	8	.238	.262	.298	67	-8	5	.938	-3	104	64	2b36,3b9	—	-1.1
	Chi N	79	267	36	78	12	4	1	17	18	1	16	.292	.339	.378	115	5	14	.978	-5	85	128	O45(12/27/6),S13,3b10,2b7	—	-0.2
	Year	124	448	52	121	19	6	1	24	23	2	24	.270	.309	.346	95	-3	19	.978	-8	85	128	O45(12/27/6),2b43,3b19,S13	—	-1.3
Total	9	1015	3741	467	1031	133	54	12	277	265	9	208	.276	.325	.350	98	-23	186-51	.969	17	97	116	O519C,2b349,1b58,3b42,S19	—	-4.0
MAGEE, SHERRY	Sherwood Robert; B8.6.1884 Clarendon PA; D3.13.1929 Philadelphia PA; BR/TR/5´11˝/179; d6.29; U1; OF(1601/140/125)																								
1904	Phi N	95	364	51	101	15	12	3	57	14	2	—	.277	.308	.409	125	8	11	.921	5	165	52	O94(19/1/74)/1	—	1.0
1905	Phi N	**155**	603	100	180	24	17	5	98	44	8	—	.299	.354	.420	135	25	48	.963	10	92	122	O155L	—	2.6
1906	Phi N	**154**	563	77	159	36	8	6	67	52	5	—	.282	.348	.407	135	23	55	.982	12	95	44	O154L	—	2.9
1907	Phi N	140	503	75	165	28	12	4	**85**	53	4	—	.328	.396	.455	169	41	46	.978	8	68	154	O139L	—	4.5
1908	Phi N	143	508	79	144	30	16	2	57	49	11	—	.283	.359	.417	143	25	40	.970	3	85	124	O142L	—	2.3
1909	Phi N	143	522	60	141	33	14	2	66	43	11	—	.270	.339	.398	128	16	38	.970	-7	54	0	O143L	—	0.1
1910	Phi N	154	519	**110**	172	39	17	6	**123**	94	12	36	**.331**	**.445**	**.507**	**172**	**53**	49	.974	-12	92	47	O154(126/23/5)	—	3.4
1911	Phi N	121	445	79	128	32	5	15	94	49	6	33	.288	.366	.483	135	20	22	**.981**	1	103	81	O120(120/0/1)	—	1.6
1912	Phi N	132	464	79	142	25	9	6	66	55	7	54	.306	.388	.438	118	12	30	.963	-11	96	43	O124L,1b6	—	-0.4
1913	Phi N	138	470	92	144	36	6	11	70	38	9	36	.306	.369	.479	136	22	23-8	.968	-11	92	41	O123(106/8/9),1b4	—	0.8
1914	Phi N	146	544	96	**171**	**39**	11	15	**103**	55	3	42	.314	.380	**.509**	154	35	25	.940	5	115	39	O67L,S39,1b32,2b8	—	4.2
1915	Bos N	156	571	72	160	34	12	2	87	54	7	39	.280	.350	.392	130	22	15-12	.981	7	109	95	O135(34/102/0),1b21	—	2.0
1916	Bos N	122	419	44	101	17	5	3	54	44	6	52	.241	.322	.327	104	3	10	.978	-7	95	45	O120(102/3/19),1b2/S	—	-1.1
1917	Bos N	72	246	24	63	8	4	1	29	13	3	23	.256	.302	.333	100	-1	7	.954	2	109	89	O65(63/0/2),1b2	—	-0.2
	Cin N	45	137	17	44	8	4	0	23	16	2	7	.321	.400	.438	164	11	4	.989	4	110	141	O41(29/0/12),1b2	—	1.5
	Year	117	383	41	107	16	8	1	52	29	5	30	.279	.338	.371	124	11	11	.967	6	109	109	O106(92/0/14),1b4	—	1.3
1918	Cin N	115	400	46	119	15	13	2	**76**	37	9	18	.298	.370	.415	142	20	14	.981	-2	93	100	1b66,O38(34/2/1),2b6	—	1.7
1919	†Cin N	56	163	11	35	6	1	0	21	26	4	19	.215	.337	.264	84	-1	4	.990	-3	106	17	O47(44/1/2)/23	—	-0.7
Total	16	2087	7441	1112	2169	425	166	83	1176	736	109	359	.291	.364	.427	137	334	441-20	.970	5	96	71	O1861L,1b136,S40,2b15/3	—	26.2
MAGEE, WENDELL	Wendell Errol; B8.3.1972 Hattiesburg MS; BR/TR/6´0˝/(219–220); [PhiN94 12/338]; d8.16; Col Samford																								
1996	Phi N	38	142	9	29	7	0	2	14	9-0	0	33	.204	.252	.296	44	-12	0-0	.978	3	120	94	O37(6/18/18)	0	-1.0
1997	Phi N	38	115	7	23	4	0	1	9	9-1	0	20	.200	.254	.261	37	-11	1-4	.960	4	129	129	O38C	0	-0.8
1998	Phi N	20	75	9	22	6	1	1	11	7-0	0	11	.293	.354	.440	107	1	0-0	.941	-1	86	80	O19L	0	-0.1
1999	Phi N	12	14	4	5	1	0	2	5	1-0	0	4	.357	.400	.857	204	2	0-0	1.000	0	133	0	O4(1/2/1)	0	0.2
2000	Det A	91	186	31	51	4	2	7	31	10-0	0	28	.274	.310	.430	86	-5	1-0	1.000	-2	88	95	O76(18/5/56),D6	21	-0.9
2001	Det A	90	207	26	44	11	4	5	17	23-1	1	44	.213	.293	.377	77	-7	3-0	.992	2	97	208	O74(21/36/19),D11	23	-0.6
2002	Det A	97	347	34	94	19	1	6	35	10-0	1	64	.271	.289	.383	81	-11	2-4	.982	8	115	125	O91(5/78/9),D4	0	-0.3
Total	7	386	1086	120	268	52	8	24	122	69-2	2	204	.247	.291	.376	75	-43	7-8	.981	13	107	129	O339(70/177/103),D21	44	-3.5
MAGGERT, HARL	Harl Vestin; B2.13.1883 Cromwell IN; D1.7.1963 Fresno CA; BL/TR/5´8˝/155; d9.4; s–Harl																								
1907	Pit N	3	6	1	0	0	0	0	0	2	0	—	.000	.250	.000	-21	-1	1	1.000	0	0	0	O2L	—	-0.1
1912	Phi A	74	242	39	62	8	6	1	13	36	2	—	.256	.357	.351	107	3	10	.939	-5	90	64	O61(39/17/5)	—	-0.5
Total	2	77	248	40	62	8	6	1	13	38	2	—	.250	.354	.343	104	2	11	.942	-5	87	62	O63(41/17/5)	—	-0.6
MAGGERT, HARL	Harl Warren; B5.4.1914 Los Angeles CA; D7.10.1986 Citrus Heights CA; BR/TR/6´0˝/190; d4.19; f–Harl																								
1938	Bos N	66	89	12	25	3	0	3	19	10	0	20	.281	.354	.416	123	3	0	.944	0	94	153	O10(8/0/2),3b8	—	0.3

YEAR	TM LG	G	AB	R	H	2B	3B	HR	RBI	BB-IB	HP	SO	AVG	OBP	SLG	AOPS	ABR	SB-CS	FA	FR	RNG	THR	GAMES AT POSITION	DL	BFW
MAGNER, STUBBY	Edmund Burke; B2.10.1888 Kalamazoo MI; D9.6.1956 Chillicothe OH; BR/TR/5´3˝/135; d7.12; Col Cornell																								
1911	NY A	13	33	3	7	0	0	0	4	4	0	—	.212	.297	.212	40	-3	1	.970	0	100	137	S6,2b5	—	-0.2
MAGNER, JOHN	John T.; B1855 St.Louis MO; 5´7.5˝/170; d7.14; U1																								
1879	Cin N	1	4	0	0	0	0	0	1	0	—	1	.000	.000	.000	-99	-1	—	.500	-1	0	0	/cf	—	-0.1
MAGOON, GEORGE	George Henry "Maggie","Topsy"; B3.27.1875 St.Albans ME; D12.6.1943 Rochester NH; BR/TR/5´10˝/160; d6.29																								
1898	Bro N	93	343	35	77	7	0	1	39	30	3	—	.224	.293	.254	57	-19	7	.925	10	113	94	S93	—	-0.4
1899	Bal N	62	207	26	53	8	3	0	31	26	5	—	.256	.353	.324	82	-4	7	.923	0	101	84	S62	—	-0.1
	Chi N	59	189	24	43	5	1	0	21	24	6	—	.228	.333	.265	67	-7	5	.896	5	107	154	S59	—	0.0
	Year	121	396	50	96	13	4	0	52	50	11	—	.242	.344	.295	75	-11	12	.909	5	104	118	S121	—	-0.1
1901	Cin N	127	460	47	116	16	7	1	53	52	2	—	.252	.331	.324	97	0	15	.919	-18	90	78	S112,2b15	—	-1.4
1902	Cin N	45	162	29	44	9	2	0	23	13	5	—	.272	.344	.352	105	1	7	.930	3	116	102	2b41,S3	—	0.5
1903	Cin N	42	139	6	30	6	0	0	9	19	1	—	.216	.314	.259	58	-7	2	.971	2	97	75	2b32,3b9	—	-0.5
	Chi A	94	334	32	76	11	3	0	25	30	6	—	.228	.303	.278	79	-7	4	.936	-25	89	81	2b94	—	-3.3
Total	5	522	1834	199	439	62	16	2	201	194	28	—	.239	.321	.294	78	-43	47	.916	-23	101	99	S329,2b182,3b9	—	-5.2
MAGRANN, TOM	Thomas Joseph; B12.9.1963 Hollywood FL; BR/TR/6´3˝/177; d9.7; Col Broward (FL) CC																								
1989	Cle A	9	10	0	0	0	0	0	0	0-0	0	4	.000	.000	.000	-98	-3	0-0	1.000	1	34	163	C9	0	-0.2
MAGRUDER, CHRIS	Christopher James; B4.26.1977 Tacoma WA; BB/TR/5´11˝/200; [SFN98 2/72]; d9.4; Col Washington																								
2001	Tex A	17	29	3	5	0	0	0	1	1-0	1	5	.172	.226	.172	7	-4	0-0	1.000	2	150	225	O12(8/1/3)	0	-0.2
2002	Cle A	87	258	34	56	15	1	6	29	15-2	1	55	.217	.261	.353	60	-15	2-0	.987	-1	102	51	O83(45/20/27)	0	-1.7
2003	Cle A	9	26	3	9	2	1	1	3	3-0	1	6	.346	.433	.615	173	3	0-1	1.000	-1	76	0	O8(5/0/3)	0	0.1
2004	Mil N	56	89	11	21	6	1	2	10	8-2	2	21	.236	.310	.393	80	-3	0-1	1.000	0	102	100	O24(10/0/16)	0	-0.3
2005	Mil N	101	138	16	28	9	0	2	13	7-1	5	33	.203	.265	.312	51	-10	3-0	.964	-1	103	0	O45(5/9/31)	0	-1.1
Total	5	270	540	67	119	32	3	11	56	34-5	10	120	.220	.277	.352	64	-29	5-2	.985	-1	103	53	O172(73/30/80)	0	-3.2
MAGUIRE, FREDDIE	Frederick Edward; B5.10.1899 Roxbury MA; D11.3.1961 Boston MA; BR/TR/5´11˝/155; d9.22; Col Holy Cross																								
1922	NY N	5	12	4	4	0	0	0	1	0	0	1	.333	.333	.333	72	-1	1-0	.944	1	140	77	2b3	—	0.1
1923	†NY N	41	30	11	6	1	0	0	2	2	0	4	.200	.250	.233	29	-3	1-0	.881	5	149	205	2b16/3	—	0.2
1928	Chi N	140	574	67	160	24	7	1	41	25	3	38	.279	.312	.350	74	-23	6	.976	**49**	**112**	**140**	2b138	—	2.9
1929	Bos N	138	496	54	125	26	8	0	41	19	3	40	.252	.284	.337	55	-37	8	.971	8	102	114	2b138/S	—	-2.3
1930	Bos N	146	516	54	138	21	5	0	52	20	2	22	.267	.297	.328	53	-41	4	.969	-2	97	104	2b146	—	-3.5
1931	Bos N	148	492	36	112	18	2	0	26	16	5	26	.228	.259	.272	45	-39	3	**.976**	10	**105**	103	2b148	—	-2.0
Total	6	618	2120	226	545	90	22	1	163	82	13	131	.257	.289	.322	57	-144	23-0	.971	71	105	116	2b589/S3	—	-4.6
MAGUIRE, JACK	Jack; B2.5.1925 St.Louis MO; D9.28.2001 Kerrville TX; BR/TR/5´11˝/165; d4.18																								
1950	NY N	29	40	3	7	2	0	0	3	3	0	13	.175	.233	.225	21	-5	0	1.000	2	114	429	O9(4/0/5),1b2	0	-0.3
1951	NY N	16	20	6	8	1	1	1	4	2	0	2	.400	.455	.700	204	3	0-0	1.000	1	133	233	O8R	0	0.4
	Pit N	8	5	1	0	0	0	0	0	1	0	0	.000	.167	.000	-50	-1	0-0	1.000	1	205	0	/23	0	-0.1
	Year	24	25	7	8	1	1	1	4	3	0	2	.320	.393	.560	151	2	0-0	1.000	2	98	95	O8R/23	0	0.3
	StL A	41	127	15	31	2	1	1	14	12	0	21	.244	.309	.299	63	-7	1-0	.969	-1	98	95	O26L,3b5,2b2	0	-1.0
Total	2	94	192	25	46	5	2	2	21	18	0	36	.240	.305	.318	66	-10	1-0	.979	3	105	166	O43(30/0/13),3b6,2b3,1b2	0	-1.0
MAHADY, JIM	James Bernard; B4.22.1901 Cortland NY; D8.9.1936 Cortland NY; BR/TR/5´11˝/170; d10.2																								
1921	NY N	1	0	0	0	0	0	0	0	0	0	0	ø	ø	ø	ø	0	0-0	1.000	0	133	0	/2	—	0.0
MAHAN, ART	Arthur Leo; B6.8.1913 Somerville MA; BL/TL/5´11˝/178; d4.30; Col Villanova																								
1940	Phi N	146	544	55	133	24	5	2	39	40	1	37	.244	.297	.318	73	-21	4	.992	4	109	100	1b145/P	—	-3.1
MAHAR, FRANK	Frank Edward; B12.4.1878 Natick MA; D12.5.1961 Somerville MA; TR/5´10.5˝/?; d8.29																								
1902	Phi N	1	1	0	0	0	0	0	0	0	0	—	.000	.000	.000	-99	0	0	ø	0	—	—	/H	—	0.0
MAHARG, BILLY	William Joseph; B3.19.1881 Philadelphia PA; D11.20.1953 Philadelphia PA; BR/TR/5´4.5˝/155; d5.18																								
1912	Det A	1	1	0	0	0	0	0	0	0	0	—	.000	.000	.000	-99	0	0	1.000	0	215	0	/3	—	0.0
1916	Phi N	1	1	0	0	0	0	0	0	0	0	0	.000	.000	.000	-97	0	0	ø	-0	0	0	/rf	—	0.0
Total	2	2	2	0	0	0	0	0	0	0	0	0	.000	.000	.000	-99	0	0	.000	0	0	0	/rf3	—	0.0
MAHER, TOM	Thomas Francis; B7.6.1870 Philadelphia PA; D8.25.1929 Philadelphia PA; d4.24																								
1902	Phi N	1	0	0	0	0	0	0	0	0	0	—	ø	ø	ø	ø	0	0	ø	0	—	—	/R	—	0.0
MAHLBERG, GREG	Gregory John; B8.8.1952 Milwaukee WI; BR/TR/5´10˝/(180–181); d9.24; Col Wisconsin–Madison																								
1978	Tex A	1	1	0	0	0	0	0	0	0-0	0	0	.000	.000	.000	-99	0	0-0	1.000	-0	0	584	/C	0	0.0
1979	Tex A	7	17	2	2	0	0	1	1	2-0	0	4	.118	.211	.294	35	-2	0-0	1.000	-2	62	0	C7	0	-0.4
Total	2	8	18	2	2	0	0	1	1	2-0	0	4	.111	.200	.278	28	-2	0-0	1.000	-2	57	44	C8	0	-0.4
MAHONEY, DAN	Daniel J.; B3.20.1864 Springfield MA; D1.31.1904 Springfield MA; BR/TR/5´9.5˝/165; d8.20																								
1892	Cin N	5	21	1	4	0	1	0	1	1	0	4	.190	.227	.286	56	-1	0	.943	1	*124*	*120*	C5	—	0.0
1895	Was N	6	12	2	2	0	0	0	1	0	0	0	.167	.167	.167	-14	-2	0	1.000	-1	*73*	*117*	C2/1	—	-0.2
Total	2	11	33	3	6	0	1	0	2	1	0	4	.182	.206	.242	28	-3	0	.949	1	*118*	*120*	C7/1	—	-0.2
MAHONEY, DANNY	Daniel Joseph; B9.6.1888 Haverhill MA; D9.28.1960 Utica NY; BR/TR/5´6.5˝/145; d5.15; Col Holy Cross																								
1911	Cin N	1	0	0	0	0	0	0	0	0	0	0	ø	ø	ø	ø	0	0	ø	0	—	—	/R	—	0.0
MAHONEY, MIKE	George W. "Big Mike"; B12.5.1873 Boston MA; D1.3.1940 Boston MA; BR/6´4˝/220; d5.18; Col Georgetown																								
1897	Bos N	2	2	1	1	0	0	0	1	0	0	—	.500	.500	.500	155	0	0	1.000	0	*0*	*0*	/CP	—	0.0
1898	StL N	2	7	0	0	0	0	0	0	0	0	—	.000	.000	.000	-98	-2	0	.920	-0	106	81	1b2	—	-0.2
Total	2	4	9	1	1	0	0	0	1	0	0	—	.111	.111	.111	-36	-2	0	.920	-0	106	81	1b2/PC	—	-0.2
MAHONEY, JIM	James Thomas "Moe"; B5.26.1934 Englewood NJ; BR/TR/6´0˝/(170–175); d7.28; C7																								
1959	Bos A	31	23	10	3	0	0	1	4	3-0	0	7	.130	.231	.261	33	-2	0-0	.940	3	119	70	S30	0	0.1
1961	Was A	43	108	10	26	0	1	0	6	5-0	0	23	.241	.274	.259	44	-9	1-2	.968	6	116	143	S31,2b2	0	-0.1
1962	Cle A	41	74	12	18	4	0	3	5	3-2	0	14	.243	.269	.419	86	-2	0-0	.964	1	104	103	S23,2b8/3	0	0.1
1965	Hou N	5	5	0	1	0	0	0	0	0-0	0	3	.200	.200	.200	14	-1	0-0	1.000	-1	34	257	S5	0	-0.1
Total	4	120	210	32	48	4	1	4	15	11-2	0	47	.229	.266	.314	57	-14	1-2	.962	9	110	122	S89,2b10/3	0	0.0
MAHONEY, MIKE	Michael John; B12.5.1972 Des Moines IA; BR/TR/6´1˝/200; [AtlN95 39/1093]; d9.8; Col Creighton																								
2000	Chi N	4	7	1	2	1	0	0	1	1-0	1	0	.286	.444	.429	124	0	0-0	1.000	-1	104	0	C4	0	-0.1
2002	Chi N	16	29	2	6	3	0	0	3	1-1	0	10	.207	.233	.310	42	-2	0-0	1.000	2	0	154	C16	0	0.0
2005	StL N	26	64	5	10	1	0	1	6	4-1	1	10	.156	.217	.219	15	-8	0-0	.984	-2	157	0	C25	0	-0.9
Total	3	46	100	8	18	5	0	1	10	6-2	2	20	.180	.241	.260	31	-10	0-0	.991	-2	108	45	C45	0	-1.0
MAIER, MITCH	Mitchell William; B6.30.1982 Petoskey MI; BL/TR/6´2˝/210; [KCA03 1/30]; d9.23; Col Toledo																								
2006	KC A	5	13	3	2	0	0	0	0	2-0	0	4	.154	.267	.154	13	-2	0-0	.800	-1	58	0	O4(2/0/2)/D	0	-0.3
MAIER, BOB	Robert Phillip; B9.5.1915 Dunellen NJ; D8.4.1993 S.Plainfield NJ; BR/TR/5´8˝/180; d4.17																								
1945	†Det A	132	486	58	128	25	7	1	34	38	0	32	.263	.317	.350	88	-8	7-11	.936	-15	85	80	3b124,O5L	0	-2.6
MAILHO, EMIL	Emil Pierre "Lefty"; B12.16.1909 Berkeley CA; BL/TL/5´10˝/165; d4.14; Col California																								
1936	Phi A	21	18	5	1	0	0	0	0	5	0	3	.056	.261	.056	-18	-3	0-0	1.000	0	123	0	/lf	—	-0.3
MAISEL, CHARLIE	Charles Louis; B4.21.1894 Catonsville MD; D8.25.1953 Baltimore MD; BR/TR/6´0˝/?; d10.2																								
1915	Bal F	1	4	0	0	0	0	0	0	0	0	0	.000	.000	.000	-97	-1	0	1.000	0	*138*	*90*	/C	—	-0.1

MAISEL, FRITZ Frederick Charles "Flash"; B12.23.1889 Catonsville MD; D4.22.1967 Baltimore MD; BR/TR/5´7.5˝/170; d8.11; b–George

YEAR	TM LG	G	AB	R	H	2B	3B	HR	RBI	BB-IB	HP	SO	AVG	OBP	SLG	AOPS	ABR	SB-CS	FA	FR	RNG	THR	GAMES AT POSITION	DL	BFW
1913	NY A	51	187	33	48	4	3	0	12	34	0	20	.257	.371	.310	99	1	25	.950	-2	91	44	3b51	—	0.1
1914	NY A	150	548	78	131	23	9	2	47	76	2	69	.239	.334	.325	98	1	**74**-17	.928	-17	85	91	3b148	—	-0.2
1915	NY A	135	530	77	149	16	6	4	46	48	1	35	.281	.342	.357	109	5	51-12	.940	-9	88	96	3b134	—	0.7
1916	NY A	53	158	18	36	5	0	0	7	20	1	18	.228	.318	.259	72	-5	4	.980	-4	95	33	O26C,3b11,2b4	—	-1.0
1917	NY A	113	404	46	80	4	4	0	20	36	2	18	.198	.267	.228	51	-24	29	.967	-3	97	92	2b100,3b7	—	-2.8
1918	StL A	90	284	43	66	4	2	0	16	46	1	17	.232	.341	.261	84	-3	11	.949	-3	94	67	3b79/rf	—	-0.5
Total	6	592	2111	295	510	56	24	6	148	260	7	177	.242	.327	.299	88	-25	194-29	.938	-38	89	83	3b430,2b104,O27(0/26/1)	—	-3.7

MAISEL, GEORGE George John; B3.12.1892 Catonsville MD; D11.20.1968 Baltimore MD; BR/TR/5´10.5˝/180; d5.1; b–Fritz

YEAR	TM LG	G	AB	R	H	2B	3B	HR	RBI	BB-IB	HP	SO	AVG	OBP	SLG	AOPS	ABR	SB-CS	FA	FR	RNG	THR	GAMES AT POSITION	DL	BFW
1913	StL A	11	18	2	3	2	0	0	1	1	0	7	.167	.211	.278	44	-1	0	.833	-1	80	0	O5(2/3/0)	—	-0.2
1916	Det A	8	5	2	0	0	0	0	0	0	0	2	.000	.000	.000	-97	-1	0	.857	1	210	457	3b3	—	0.0
1921	Chi N	111	393	54	122	7	2	0	43	11	3	13	.310	.334	.338	78	-12	17-7	.978	-1	102	84	O108(0/107/1)	—	-1.6
1922	Chi N	38	84	9	16	1	1	0	6	8	0	2	.190	.261	.226	26	-9	1-3	1.000	0	103	77	O26(2/13/11)	—	-1.1
Total	4	168	500	67	141	10	3	0	50	20	3	24	.282	.314	.314	66	-23	18-10	.979	-0	102	81	O139(4/123/12),3b3	—	-2.9

MAJESKI, HANK Henry "Heeney"; B12.13.1916 Staten Island NY; D8.9.1991 Staten Island NY; BR/TR/5´9˝/180; d5.17; Mil 1943–45

YEAR	TM LG	G	AB	R	H	2B	3B	HR	RBI	BB-IB	HP	SO	AVG	OBP	SLG	AOPS	ABR	SB-CS	FA	FR	RNG	THR	GAMES AT POSITION	DL	BFW
1939	Bos N	106	367	35	100	16	1	7	54	18	2	30	.272	.310	.379	91	-6	2	.945	10	113	118	3b99	—	0.7
1940	Bos N	3	3	0	0	0	0	0	0	0	0	0	.000	.000	.000	-99	-1	0	ø	0	—	—	/H	—	-0.1
1941	Bos N	19	55	5	8	5	0	0	3	1	0	13	.145	.161	.236	11	-7	0	.911	0	104	86	3b11	0	-0.6
1946	NY A	8	12	1	1	0	1	0	0	0	0	3	.083	.083	.250	-9	-2	0-0	.750	-1	73	0	3b2	0	-0.3
	Phi A	78	264	25	66	14	3	1	25	26	1	13	.250	.320	.337	84	-6	3-2	.967	11	114	134	3b72	0	0.5
	Year	86	276	26	67	14	4	1	25	26	1	16	.243	.310	.333	80	-8	3-2	.964	10	113	131	3b74	0	0.2
1947	Phi A	141	479	54	134	26	5	8	72	53	5	31	.280	.358	.405	110	7	1-0	**.988**	8	104	**119**	3b134,S4/2	0	1.5
1948	Phi A	148	590	88	183	41	4	12	120	48	6	43	.310	.368	.454	118	14	2-1	**.975**	3	103	72	3b142,S8	0	1.6
1949	Phi A	114	448	62	124	26	5	9	67	29	4	23	.277	.326	.417	99	-4	0-1	.957	-5	96	138	3b113	0	-0.9
1950	Chi A	122	414	47	128	18	2	6	46	42	3	34	.309	.377	.406	103	2	1-4	.970	8	106	**132**	3b112	0	0.8
1951	Chi A	12	35	4	9	4	0	0	6	1	0	0	.257	.278	.371	76	-1	0-0	.950	0	116	156	3b9	0	-0.1
	Phi A	89	323	41	92	19	4	5	42	35	2	24	.285	.358	.415	106	3	1-2	.974	13	123	95	3b88	0	1.5
	Year	101	358	45	101	23	4	5	48	36	2	24	.282	.351	.411	104	2	1-2	.972	13	122	99	3b97	0	1.4
1952	Phi A	34	117	14	30	2	2	2	20	19	1	10	.256	.365	.359	96	0	0-1	.976	3	114	109	3b34	0	0.3
	Cle A	36	54	7	16	2	0	0	9	7	0	7	.296	.377	.333	106	1	0-0	.913	-1	80	182	3b11,2b3	0	0.0
	Year	70	171	21	46	4	2	2	29	26	1	17	.269	.369	.351	101	1	0-1	.966	3	108	122	3b45,2b3	0	0.3
1953	Cle A	50	50	6	15	1	0	2	12	3	1	8	.300	.352	.440	116	1	0-0	1.000	-1	85	84	2b10,3b7/lf	0	0.0
1954	†Cle A	57	121	10	34	4	0	3	17	7	0	14	.281	.320	.388	92	-2	0-0	.990	1	99	98	2b25,3b10	0	0.0
1955	Cle A	36	48	3	9	2	0	2	6	8-0	2	3	.188	.322	.354	80	-1	0-0	1.000	-1	75	137	3b9,2b4	0	-0.2
	Bal A	16	41	2	7	1	0	0	2	2-1	0	4	.171	.209	.195	10	-5	0-0	1.000	-2	93	81	3b8,2b5	0	-0.7
	Year	52	89	5	16	3	0	2	8	10-1	2	7	.180	.275	.281	50	-6	0-0	1.000	-3	86	103	3b17,2b9	0	-0.9
Total	13	1069	3421	404	956	181	27	57	501	299-1	27	260	.279	.342	.398	100	-7	10-11	.968	48	107	113	3b861,2b48,S12/lf	0	4.0

MAJEWSKI, VAL Walter V.; B6.19.1981 New Brunswick NJ; BL/TL/6´2˝/200; [BalA02 3/76]; d8.20; Col Rutgers; [DL 2005 Bal A 183]

YEAR	TM LG	G	AB	R	H	2B	3B	HR	RBI	BB-IB	HP	SO	AVG	OBP	SLG	AOPS	ABR	SB-CS	FA	FR	RNG	THR	GAMES AT POSITION	DL	BFW
2004	Bal A	9	13	3	2	1	0	0	1	0-0	0	1	.154	.154	.231	-2	-2	0-0	1.000	1	158	0	O4(0/3/1),D3	0	-0.1

MAKSUDIAN, MIKE Michael Bryant; B5.28.1966 Belleville IL; BL/TR/5´11˝/(200–220); d9.2; Col South Alabama

YEAR	TM LG	G	AB	R	H	2B	3B	HR	RBI	BB-IB	HP	SO	AVG	OBP	SLG	AOPS	ABR	SB-CS	FA	FR	RNG	THR	GAMES AT POSITION	DL	BFW
1992	Tor A	3	3	0	0	0	0	0	0	0-0	0	0	.000	.000	.000	-95	-1	0-0	ø	0	0	0	/1	0	-0.1
1993	Min A	5	12	2	2	1	0	0	2	4-0	0	2	.167	.353	.250	71	0	0-0	1.000	1	233	93	1b4/3	13	0.1
1994	Chi N	26	26	6	7	2	0	0	4	10-0	0	4	.269	.472	.346	118	2	0-1	1.000	1	120	170	1b3,C2,3b2	0	0.2
Total	3	34	41	8	9	3	0	0	6	14-0	0	6	.220	.411	.293	91	1	0-1	1.000	2	187	119	1b8,3b3,C2	13	0.2

MALAVE, JOSE Jose Francisco; B5.31.1971 Cumana, Sucre, Venez.; BR/TR/6´2˝/212; d5.23

YEAR	TM LG	G	AB	R	H	2B	3B	HR	RBI	BB-IB	HP	SO	AVG	OBP	SLG	AOPS	ABR	SB-CS	FA	FR	RNG	THR	GAMES AT POSITION	DL	BFW
1996	Bos A	41	102	12	24	3	0	4	17	2-0	1	25	.235	.257	.382	58	-7	0-0	.978	-3	82	55	O38(8/0/30)	19	-1.0
1997	Bos A	4	4	0	0	0	0	0	0	0-0	0	2	.000	.000	.000	-98	-1	0-0	1.000	0	129	0	O4L	0	-0.1
Total	2	45	106	12	24	3	0	4	17	2-0	1	27	.226	.248	.368	52	-8	0-0	.979	-2	84	53	O42(12/0/30)	19	-1.1

MALAY, CHARLIE Charles Francis; B6.13.1879 Brooklyn NY; D9.18.1949 Brooklyn NY; BB/TR/5´11.5˝/175; d4.24; s–Joe

YEAR	TM LG	G	AB	R	H	2B	3B	HR	RBI	BB-IB	HP	SO	AVG	OBP	SLG	AOPS	ABR	SB-CS	FA	FR	RNG	THR	GAMES AT POSITION	DL	BFW
1905	Bro N	102	349	33	88	7	2	1	31	22	2	—	.252	.300	.292	83	-8	13	.932	-3	101	66	2b75,O25(1/23/1)/S	—	-1.2

MALAY, JOE Joseph Charles; B10.25.1905 Brooklyn NY; D3.19.1989 Bridgeport CT; BL/TL/6´0˝/175; d9.7; f–Charlie

YEAR	TM LG	G	AB	R	H	2B	3B	HR	RBI	BB-IB	HP	SO	AVG	OBP	SLG	AOPS	ABR	SB-CS	FA	FR	RNG	THR	GAMES AT POSITION	DL	BFW
1933	NY N	8	24	0	3	0	0	0	2	0	0	0	.125	.125	.125	-29	-4	0	1.000	2	195	49	1b8	—	-0.3
1935	NY N	1	1	0	1	0	0	0	0	0	0	0	1.000	1.000	1.000	447	0	0	ø	0	—	—	/H	—	0.0
Total	2	9	25	0	4	0	0	0	2	0	0	0	.160	.160	.160	-9	-4	0	1.000	2	195	49	1b8	—	-0.3

MALDONADO, CANDY Candido (Guadarrama); B9.5.1960 Humacao, PR; BR/TR/6´0˝/(185–220); d9.7

YEAR	TM LG	G	AB	R	H	2B	3B	HR	RBI	BB-IB	HP	SO	AVG	OBP	SLG	AOPS	ABR	SB-CS	FA	FR	RNG	THR	GAMES AT POSITION	DL	BFW
1981	LA N	11	12	0	1	0	0	0	0	0-0	0	5	.083	.083	.083	-55	-2	0-0	1.000	0	140	0	O9(4/0/5)	0	-0.3
1982	LA N	6	4	0	0	0	0	0	0	1-1	0	2	.000	.200	.000	-41	-1	0-0	1.000	1	253	0	O3(3/0/1)	0	0.0
1983	†LA N	42	62	5	12	1	1	1	6	5-0	0	14	.194	.254	.290	50	-4	0-0	1.000	-2	81	0	O33(12/3/19)	0	-0.8
1984	LA N	116	254	25	68	14	0	5	28	19-0	1	29	.268	.318	.382	97	-1	0-3	.955	-5	89	96	O102(7/31/67),3b4	0	-1.0
1985	†LA N	121	213	20	48	7	1	5	19	19-4	0	40	.225	.288	.338	76	-7	1-1	.984	1	92	161	O113(44/57/24)	0	-0.9
1986	SF N	133	405	49	102	31	3	18	85	20-4	3	77	.252	.289	.477	114	5	4-4	.983	1	93	147	O101(47/6/62)/3	0	0.1
1987	†SF N	118	442	69	129	28	4	20	85	34-4	6	78	.292	.346	.509	130	18	8-8	.973	-8	82	89	O116(4/0/115)	40	0.3
1988	SF N	142	499	53	127	23	1	12	68	37-1	7	89	.255	.311	.377	102	1	6-5	.962	-4	96	75	O139R	0	-0.9
1989	†SF N	129	345	39	75	23	0	9	41	37-4	3	69	.217	.296	.362	91	-4	4-1	.974	1	100	118	O116R	0	-0.6
1990	Cle A	155	590	76	161	32	2	22	95	49-4	5	134	.273	.330	.446	116	12	3-5	.993	5	106	101	O134(104/0/41),D20	0	1.1
1991	Mil A	34	111	11	23	6	0	5	20	13-0	0	23	.207	.288	.396	90	-2	1-0	.976	-2	88	0	O24(12/0/13)	75	-0.4
	†Tor A	52	177	26	49	9	0	7	28	23-4	6	53	.277	.375	.446	122	6	3-0	.990	-2	95	71	O52(52/0/1),D9	0	0.4
	Year	86	288	37	72	15	0	12	48	36-4	6	76	.250	.342	.427	111	5	4-0	.986	-4	93	50	O76(64/0/14),D9	0	0.0
1992	†Tor A	137	489	64	133	25	4	20	66	59-3	7	112	.272	.357	.462	122	15	2-2	.978	1	96	138	O132(129/0/4),D4	0	1.1
1993	Chi N	70	140	8	26	5	0	3	15	13-0	1	40	.186	.260	.286	46	-11	0-0	.914	-1	86	134	O41(29/0/14)	0	-1.4
	Cle A	28	81	11	20	2	0	5	20	11-2	0	18	.247	.333	.457	111	1	0-1	.976	-1	90	65	O26(2/0/25),D2	0	-0.2
1994	Cle A	42	92	14	18	5	1	5	12	19-1	0	31	.196	.333	.435	95	-1	1-1	1.000	-0	87	0	D25,O5L	0	-0.2
1995	Tor A	61	160	22	43	13	0	7	25	25-0	2	45	.269	.368	.481	120	6	1-1	.988	-3	87	66	O58(26/0/38)/D	0	0.0
	Tex A	13	30	6	7	3	0	2	5	7-0	0	5	.233	.378	.533	130	2	0-1	1.000	1	111	165	O11(9/0/4)	0	0.2
	Year	74	190	28	50	16	0	9	30	32-0	2	50	.263	.370	.489	122	7	1-2	.990	-2	91	82	O69(35/0/42)/D	0	0.2
Total	15	1410	4106	498	1042	227	17	146	618	391-32	41	864	.254	.322	.424	107	33	34-33	.977	-20	94	103	O1215(489/97/688),D61,3b5	115	-3.5

MALDONADO, CARLOS Carlos Luis; B1.3.1979 Maracaibo, Venezuela; BR/TR/6´1˝/245; d9.8

YEAR	TM LG	G	AB	R	H	2B	3B	HR	RBI	BB-IB	HP	SO	AVG	OBP	SLG	AOPS	ABR	SB-CS	FA	FR	RNG	THR	GAMES AT POSITION	DL	BFW
2006	Pit N	8	19	0	2	0	0	0	0	1-1	0	10	.105	.150	.105	-32	-4	1-0	.968	-3	61	71	C8	0	-0.7

MALER, JIM James Michael; B8.16.1958 New York NY; BR/TR/6´4˝/230; [SeaA78*1/5]; d9.3; Col Miami

YEAR	TM LG	G	AB	R	H	2B	3B	HR	RBI	BB-IB	HP	SO	AVG	OBP	SLG	AOPS	ABR	SB-CS	FA	FR	RNG	THR	GAMES AT POSITION	DL	BFW
1981	Sea A	12	23	1	8	1	0	0	2	2-0	1	1	.348	.423	.391	130	1	1-0	1.000	-0	71	126	1b5,D2	0	0.1
1982	Sea A	64	221	18	50	8	3	4	26	12-3	3	35	.226	.274	.344	66	-11	0-0	.991	2	108	95	1b57,D5	0	-1.3
1983	Sea A	26	66	5	12	1	0	1	3	5-0	2	11	.182	.260	.242	38	-6	0-3	1.000	0	88	58	1b19,D5	0	-0.8
Total	3	102	310	24	70	10	3	5	31	19-3	6	47	.226	.283	.326	65	-16	1-3	.994	2	102	90	1b81,D12	0	-2.0

MALINOSKY, TONY Anthony Francis; B10.5.1909 Collinsville IL; BR/TR/5´10.5˝/165; d4.26; Col Whittier

YEAR	TM LG	G	AB	R	H	2B	3B	HR	RBI	BB-IB	HP	SO	AVG	OBP	SLG	AOPS	ABR	SB-CS	FA	FR	RNG	THR	GAMES AT POSITION	DL	BFW
1937	Bro N	35	79	7	18	2	0	0	3	9	0	11	.228	.307	.253	53	-5	0	.833	-6	88	132	3b13,S11	—	-1.1

MALKMUS, BOBBY Robert Edward; B7.4.1931 Newark NJ; BR/TR/5´9˝/(165–180); d6.1

YEAR	TM LG	G	AB	R	H	2B	3B	HR	RBI	BB-IB	HP	SO	AVG	OBP	SLG	AOPS	ABR	SB-CS	FA	FR	RNG	THR	GAMES AT POSITION	DL	BFW
1957	Mil N	13	22	6	2	0	1	0	0	3-0	0	3	.091	.200	.182	4	-3	0-0	.972	2	127	115	2b7	0	-0.1
1958	Was A	41	70	5	13	2	1	0	3	4-0	0	15	.186	.230	.243	31	-7	0-0	.964	2	102	90	2b26,3b2/S	0	-0.4
1959	Was A	6	0	0	0	0	0	0	0	0-0	0	0	ø	ø	ø	ø	0	0-0	ø	0	—	—	/R	0	0.0
1960	Phi N	79	133	16	28	4	1	1	12	11-0	0	28	.211	.267	.278	51	-9	2-2	1.000	1	112	162	S29,2b23,3b12	0	-0.7
1961	Phi N	121	342	39	79	8	2	7	31	20-1	2	43	.231	.276	.327	61	-20	1-3	.988	24	109	124	2b58,S34,3b25	0	0.9
1962	Phi N	8	5	3	1	1	0	0	0	0-0	0	1	.200	.200	.400	58	0	0-0	1.000	1	227	265	/S	0	0.1
Total	6	268	572	69	123	15	5	8	46	38-1	2	90	.215	.265	.301	53	-39	3-5	.982	30	107	110	2b114,S65,3b39	0	-0.2

YEAR	TM LG	G	AB	R	H	2B	3B	HR	RBI	BB-IB	HP	SO	AVG	OBP	SLG	AOPS	ABR	SB-CS	FA	FR	RNG	THR	GAMES AT POSITION	DL	BFW
Mallett, Jerry	Gerald Gordon; B9.18.1935 Bonne Terre MO; BR/TR/6´5˝/205; d9.19; Col Baylor																								
1959	Bos A	4	15	1	4	0	0	0	1	1-0	0	3	.267	.313	.267	58	-1	0-0	1.000	2	131	696	O4C	0	0.1
Mallon, Les	Leslie Clyde; B11.21.1905 Sweetwater TX; D4.17.1991 Granbury TX; BR/TR/5´8˝/160; d4.14																								
1931	Phi N	122	375	41	116	19	2	1	45	29	0	40	.309	.359	.379	91	-4	0	.956	6	103	88	2b97,1b5,S3,3b3	—	0.8
1932	Phi N	103	347	44	90	16	0	5	31	28	2	28	.259	.318	.349	71	-14	1	.955	-24	85	77	2b88,3b5	—	-3.2
1934	Bos N	42	166	23	49	6	1	0	18	15	0	12	.295	.354	.343	95	-1	0	.967	-5	103	69	2b42	—	-0.3
1935	Bos N	116	412	48	113	24	2	2	25	28	1	37	.274	.322	.357	89	-6	3	.975	-9	97	74	2b73,3b36/rf	—	-0.9
Total	4	383	1300	156	368	65	5	8	119	100	3	117	.283	.336	.359	85	-25	4	.962	-32	96	79	2b300,3b44,1b5,S3/rf	—	-3.6
Mallonee, Ben	Howard Bennett "Lefty"; B3.31.1894 Baltimore MD; D2.19.1978 Baltimore MD; BL/TL/5´6˝/150; d9.14																								
1921	Phi A	7	25	2	6	1	0	0	4	1	0	2	.240	.269	.280	40	-2	1-0	1.000	0	96	126	O6C	—	-0.2
Mallonee, Jule	Julius Norris; B4.4.1900 Charlotte NC; D12.26.1934 Charlotte NC; BL/TR/6´2˝/180; d8.4																								
1925	Chi A	2	3	1	0	0	0	0	0	1	0	0	.000	.250	.000	-34	-1	0-0	1.000	-0	62	0	/cf	—	-0.1
Mallory, Jim	James Baugh "Sunny Jim"; B9.1.1918 Lawrenceville VA; D8.6.2001 Greenville NC; BR/TR/6´1˝/170; d9.8; Col North Carolina																								
1940	Was A	4	12	2	2	0	0	0	0	1	0	1	.167	.231	.167	5	-2	0-0	1.000	0	130	0	O3(1/1/1)	—	-0.2
1945	StL N	13	43	3	10	2	0	0	5	0	0	2	.233	.233	.279	41	-4	0	.923	-0	99	126	O11(8/3/2)	0	-0.4
	NY N	37	94	10	28	1	0	0	9	6	0	7	.298	.340	.309	80	-3	1	.979	-0	94	127	O21(8/9/4)	0	-0.4
	Year	50	137	13	38	3	0	0	14	6	0	9	.277	.308	.299	68	-6	1	.959	-0	96	127	O32(16/12/6)	0	-0.8
Total	2	54	149	15	40	3	0	0	14	7	0	10	.268	.301	.289	63	-9	1-0	.964	0	99	114	O35(17/13/7)	0	-1.0
Mallory, Sheldon	Sheldon; B7.16.1953 Argo IL; BL/TL/6´2˝/172; d4.10; Col Manatee (FL) CC																								
1977	Oak A	64	126	19	27	4	1	0	5	11-0	3	18	.214	.291	.262	53	-8	12-5	.977	1	112	127	O45(9/17/21),1b4,D7	29	-0.7
Malloy, Marty	Marty Thomas; B4.6.1972 Gainesville FL; BL/TR/5´10˝/160; d9.6; Col Santa Fe (FL) CC																								
1998	†Atl N	11	28	3	5	1	0	1	1	2-0	0	2	.179	.233	.321	44	-2	0-0	1.000	1	106	93	2b10	0	-0.1
2002	Fla N	24	25	1	3	0	0	0	1	2-0	0	8	.120	.185	.120	-18	-4	0-0	1.000	-0	72	98	2b3,3b2	0	-0.5
Total	2	35	53	4	8	1	0	1	2	4-0	0	10	.151	.211	.226	15	-6	0-0	1.000	1	100	94	2b13,3b2	0	-0.6
Malmberg, Harry	Harry William "Swede"; B7.31.1925 Fairfield AL; D10.29.1976 San Francisco CA; BR/TR/6´1˝/170; d4.12; C2																								
1955	Det A	67	208	25	45	5	2	0	19	29-2	0	19	.216	.310	.260	56	-12	0-1	.985	3	109	91	2b65	0	-0.5
Malone, Eddie	Edward Russell; B6.16.1920 Chicago IL; D6.1.2006 Laguna Hills CA; BR/TR/5´10˝/175; d7.17																								
1949	Chi A	55	170	17	46	7	2	1	16	29	0	19	.271	.377	.353	97	0	2-1	.990	-2	*83*	*85*	C51	0	0.1
1950	Chi A	31	71	2	16	2	0	0	10	10	0	8	.225	.321	.254	50	-5	0-0	1.000	1	*70*	*119*	C21	0	-0.3
Total	2	86	241	19	62	9	2	1	26	39	0	27	.257	.361	.324	83	-5	2-1	.993	-0	*79*	*94*	C72	0	-0.2
Malone, Fergy	Fergus G.; B1842 , Ireland; D1.1.1905 Seattle WA; BR/TL/5´8˝/156; d5.20; M3/U1																								
1871	Ath NA	27	134	33	46	7	1	1	33	9	—	4	.343	.385	.433	136	7	9-3	.856	9	—	—	C27	—	1.1
1872	Ath NA	41	213	46	60	5	3	0	39	4	—	5	.282	.295	.333	92	-2	3-0	**.884**	5	—	—	C24,1b17	—	0.2
1873	Phi NA	**53**	259	59	75	11	2	0	41	14	—	7	.290	.326	.347	96	-1	6-1	.898	5	—	—	C53/SM	—	0.3
1874	Chi NA	47	223	33	56	5	0	0	28	4	—	0	.251	.264	.274	72	-7	2-1	.820	3	—	—	C47,M	—	-0.3
1875	Phi NA	29	123	15	28	2	1	0	10	1	—	2	.228	.234	.260	69	-4	1-0	.919	-3	25	53	1b22,C6,O2C	—	-0.5
1876	Phi N	22	96	14	22	2	0	0	6	0	—	1	.229	.229	.250	60	-4	—	.777	-2	—	—	C20,O3R/S	—	-0.5
1884	Phi U	1	4	0	1	0	0	0	—	0	—	—	.250	.250	.250	56	0	—	.818	-1	—	—	/CM	—	-0.1
Total	5NA	197	952	186	265	30	7	1	151	32	—	18	.278	.302	.328	93	-7	21-5	.856	19	—	—	C157,1b39,O2C/S	—	0.8
Total	2	23	100	14	23	2	0	0	6	0	—	1	.230	.230	.250	60	-4	—	.780	-3	—	—	C21,O3R/S	—	-0.6
Malone, Lew	Lewis Aloysius; B3.13.1897 Baltimore MD; D2.17.1972 Brooklyn NY; BR/TR/5´11˝/175; d5.31; Mil 1918																								
1915	Phi A	76	201	17	41	4	4	1	17	21	1	40	.204	.283	.279	70	-8	7-1	.919	-6	87	44	2b43,3b12,O4R,S2	—	-1.2
1916	Phi A	5	4	1	0	0	0	0	0	1	0	2	.000	.200	.000	-42	-1	0	1.000	-0	0	0	/S	—	-0.1
1917	Bro N	1	0	1	0	0	0	0	0	0	0	0	ø	ø	ø	ø	0	0	ø	0	—	—	/R	—	0.0
1919	Bro N	51	162	9	33	7	3	0	11	6	0	18	.204	.232	.284	54	-10	1	.934	-7	83	66	3b47,2b2,S2	—	-1.7
Total	4	133	367	28	74	11	7	1	28	28	1	60	.202	.260	.278	62	-19	8-1	.910	-13	84	65	3b59,2b45,S5,O4R	—	-3.0
Malone, Martin	Martin; d6.20; ▲																								
1872	Eck NA	5	16	2	6	0	0	0	3	1	—	3	.375	.412	.375	169	2	0-1	.333	-3	0	0	O3(0/1/2),P2,2b2	—	-0.1
Maloney, John	John; d9.15																								
1876	NY N	2	7	1	2	0	1	0	2	0	—	1	.286	.286	.571	206	1	—	.800	-0	0	0	O2C	—	0.0
1877	Har N	1	4	0	1	0	0	0	0	0	—	0	.250	.250	.250	65	0	—	.250	-1	0	0	/cf	—	-0.1
Total	2	3	11	1	3	0	1	0	2	0	—	1	.273	.273	.455	152	1	—	.556	-2	0	0	O3C	—	-0.1
Maloney, Pat	Patrick William; B1.19.1888 Grosvenor Dale CT; D6.27.1979 Pawtucket RI; BR/TR/6´0˝/150; d6.19																								
1912	NY A	25	79	9	17	1	0	0	4	6	1	—	.215	.279	.228	43	-6	3	.926	-1	111	55	O20C	—	-0.8
Maloney, Billy	William Alphonse; B6.5.1878 Lewiston ME; D9.2.1960 Breckenridge TX; BL/TR/5´10˝/177; d5.2																								
1901	Mil A	86	290	42	85	3	4	0	22	7	8	—	.293	.328	.331	87	-5	11	.952	-4	*78*	***124***	C72,O8C	—	-0.2
1902	StL A	30	112	8	23	3	0	0	11	6	2	—	.205	.258	.232	37	-9	0	.906	-3	112	194	O23(1/0/22),C7	—	-1.2
	Cin N	27	89	13	22	4	0	1	7	2	1	—	.247	.272	.326	77	-3	8	.848	-0	199	0	O18(10/6/2),C7	—	-0.3
1905	Chi N	145	558	78	145	17	14	2	56	43	11	—	.260	.325	.351	98	-2	**59**	.954	-1	90	96	O145(0/12/134)	—	-1.0
1906	Bro N	151	566	71	125	15	7	0	32	49	3	—	.221	.286	.272	80	-13	38	.966	9	102	130	O151(0/149/2)	—	-1.3
1907	Bro N	144	502	51	115	7	10	0	32	31	10	—	.229	.287	.283	86	-10	25	.967	1	89	99	O144C	—	-1.8
1908	Bro N	113	359	31	70	5	7	3	17	24	5	—	.195	.255	.273	71	-13	14	.947	2	87	130	O103(5/95/3),C4	—	-1.8
Total	6	696	2476	294	585	54	42	6	177	162	40	—	.236	.294	.299	83	-55	155	.954	5	94	111	O592(16/414/163),C90	—	-7.6
Malzone, Frank	Frank James; B2.28.1930 Bronx NY; BR/TR/5´10˝/(180–185); d9.17																								
1955	Bos A	6	20	2	7	1	0	0	1	1-0	0	3	.350	.381	.400	101	0	0-0	1.000	2	152	103	3b4	0	0.2
1956	Bos A	27	103	15	17	3	1	2	11	9-0	0	8	.165	.230	.272	29	-11	1-0	.931	2	117	77	3b26	0	-0.9
1957	Bos A★	153	634	82	185	31	5	15	103	31-1	1	41	.292	.323	.427	98	-3	2-1	**.954**	21	**120**	101	3b153	0	1.8
1958	Bos A★	**155**	627	76	185	30	2	15	87	33-3	4	53	.295	.333	.421	100	-1	1-3	.950	17	**118**	106	3b155	0	1.5
1959	Bos A★	**154**	604	90	169	34	2	19	92	42-6	1	58	.280	.323	.437	103	2	6-0	.953	10	**109**	**131**	3b154	0	1.2
1960	Bos A★	152	595	60	161	30	2	14	79	36-4	4	42	.271	.313	.398	89	-10	2-3	.948	13	**108**	103	3b151	0	0.1
1961	Bos A	151	590	74	157	21	4	14	87	44-3	1	49	.266	.314	.386	85	-14	1-3	.950	1	101	137	3b149	0	-1.4
1962	Bos A	156	619	74	175	20	3	21	95	35-2	0	43	.283	.319	.426	96	-5	0-1	.967	8	104	106	3b156	0	0.1
1963	Bos A★	151	580	66	169	25	2	15	71	31-5	3	45	.291	.327	.419	105	3	0-2	.964	3	99	64	3b148	0	0.5
1964	Bos A☆	148	537	62	142	19	0	13	56	37-1	2	43	.264	.312	.372	86	-10	0-0	.959	6	97	89	3b143	0	-0.5
1965	Bos A	106	364	40	87	20	0	3	34	28-0	1	38	.239	.293	.319	70	-14	1-1	.969	-1	97	101	3b96	0	-1.6
1966	Cal A	82	155	6	32	5	0	2	12	10-1	0	11	.206	.253	.277	54	-9	0-0	.925	-0	100	56	3b35	0	-1.0
Total	12	1441	5428	647	1486	239	21	133	728	337-26	17	434	.274	.315	.399	91	-72	14-14	.955	80	107	103	3b1370	0	-0.0
Mancuso, Gus	August Rodney "Blackie"; B12.5.1905 Galveston TX; D10.26.1984 Houston TX; BR/TR/5´10˝/185; d4.30; C1; b–Frank																								
1928	StL N	11	38	2	7	0	1	0	3	0	0	5	.184	.184	.237	9	-5	0	.984	2	*138*	*90*	C11	—	-0.2
1930	†StL N	76	227	39	83	17	2	7	59	18	1	16	.366	.415	.551	127	10	1	.969	1	*114*	*100*	C61	—	1.4
1931	†StL N	67	187	13	49	16	1	1	23	18	0	13	.262	.327	.374	85	-3	2	.972	5	*100*	*140*	C56	—	0.5
1932	StL N	103	310	25	88	23	1	5	43	30	0	15	.284	.347	.413	100	1	0	.977	4	*74*	***125***	C82	—	1.0
1933	†NY N	144	481	39	127	17	2	6	56	48	0	21	.264	.331	.345	95	-2	0	.972	-1	*105*	*102*	C142	—	0.6
1934	NY N	122	383	32	94	14	0	7	46	27	0	19	.245	.295	.337	70	-17	0	.977	5	*110*	*108*	C122	—	-0.4
1935	NY N★	128	447	33	133	18	2	5	56	30	0	16	.298	.342	.380	95	-3	1	.972	-4	***117***	*99*	C126	—	0.1
1936	†NY N	139	519	55	156	21	3	9	63	39	1	28	.301	.351	.405	104	3	0	.977	7	*134*	*111*	C138	—	1.8
1937	†NY N★	86	287	30	80	17	1	4	39	17	0	20	.279	.319	.387	90	-4	1	.982	11	*159*	***110***	C81	—	1.2
1938	NY N	52	158	19	55	8	0	2	15	17	0	13	.348	.411	.437	132	8	0	.977	3	*127*	*77*	C44	—	1.3
1939	Chi N	80	251	17	58	10	0	2	17	24	0	19	.231	.298	.295	59	-14	0	.981	2	*127*	*93*	C76	—	-0.8
1940	Bro N	60	144	16	33	8	0	0	16	13	0	7	.229	.293	.285	56	-8	0	.982	5	*123*	*92*	C56	—	-0.1

YEAR	TM LG	G	AB	R	H	2B	3B	HR	RBI	BB-IB	HP	SO	AVG	OBP	SLG	AOPS	ABR	SB-CS	FA	FR	RNG	THR	GAMES AT POSITION	DL	BFW
1941	StL N	106	328	25	75	13	1	2	37	37	1	19	.229	.309	.293	66	-14	0	.989	8	125	101	C105	0	0.0
1942	StL N	5	13	0	1	0	0	0	1	0	0	0	.077	.077	.077	-51	-2	0	.917	-1	0	0	C3	0	-0.3
	NY N	39	109	4	21	1	1	0	8	14	0	7	.193	.285	.220	48	-7	1	.982	2	129	92	C38	0	-0.3
	Year	44	122	4	22	1	1	0	9	14	0	7	.180	.265	.205	38	-10	1	.977	1	120	86	C41	0	-0.6
1943	NY N	94	252	11	50	5	0	2	20	28	2	16	.198	.284	.242	52	-15	0	.974	-4	80	96	C77	0	-1.6
1944	NY N	78	195	15	49	4	1	1	25	30	0	20	.251	.351	.297	84	-3	0	.976	2	107	111	C72	0	0.2
1945	Phi N	70	176	11	35	5	0	0	16	28	0	10	.199	.309	.227	52	-10	2	.988	-2	69	123	C70	0	-0.9
Total	17	1460	4505	386	1194	197	16	53	543	418	5	264	.265	.328	.351	85	-85	8	.977	45	113	105	C1360	0	3.5

Mancuso, Frank Frank Octavius; B5.23.1918 Houston TX; BR/TR/6´0˝/195; d4.18; b–Gus

YEAR	TM LG	G	AB	R	H	2B	3B	HR	RBI	BB-IB	HP	SO	AVG	OBP	SLG	AOPS	ABR	SB-CS	FA	FR	RNG	THR	GAMES AT POSITION	DL	BFW
1944	†StL A	88	244	19	50	11	0	1	24	20	2	32	.205	.271	.262	50	-16	1-0	.953	-6	91	70	C87	0	-1.8
1945	StL A	119	365	39	98	13	3	1	38	46	2	44	.268	.354	.329	94	-1	0-2	.989	-4	101	74	C115	0	0.1
1946	StL A	87	262	22	63	8	3	3	23	30	2	31	.240	.323	.328	78	-7	1-0	.973	-14	62	74	C85	0	-1.9
1947	Was A	43	131	5	30	5	1	0	13	5	0	11	.229	.257	.282	51	-9	0-0	.958	-4	96	92	C35	0	-1.2
Total	4	337	1002	85	241	37	7	5	98	101	6	118	.241	.314	.306	74	-33	2-2	.972	-28	88	75	C322	0	-4.8

Manda, Carl Carl Alan; B11.16.1886 Little River KS; D3.9.1983 Artesia NM; BR/TR/5´10˝/170; d9.11

YEAR	TM LG	G	AB	R	H	2B	3B	HR	RBI	BB-IB	HP	SO	AVG	OBP	SLG	AOPS	ABR	SB-CS	FA	FR	RNG	THR	GAMES AT POSITION	DL	BFW
1914	Chi A	9	15	2	4	0	0	0	1	3	0	3	.267	.389	.267	99	0	1	.971	3	144	60	2b7	—	0.3

Maney, Vincent Stephen Vincent; B10.14.1886 Batavia NY; D3.13.1952 Batavia NY; BR/TR/6´0˝/175; d5.18

YEAR	TM LG	G	AB	R	H	2B	3B	HR	RBI	BB-IB	HP	SO	AVG	OBP	SLG	AOPS	ABR	SB-CS	FA	FR	RNG	THR	GAMES AT POSITION	DL	BFW
1912	Det A	1	2	0	0	0	0	0	0	1	1	—	.000	.500	.000	48	0	0	.833	-0	71	315	/S	—	0.0

Mangan, Jim James Daniel; B9.24.1929 San Francisco CA; BR/TR/5´10˝/190; d4.16; Mil 1953–54; Col Santa Clara

YEAR	TM LG	G	AB	R	H	2B	3B	HR	RBI	BB-IB	HP	SO	AVG	OBP	SLG	AOPS	ABR	SB-CS	FA	FR	RNG	THR	GAMES AT POSITION	DL	BFW
1952	Pit N	11	13	1	2	0	0	0	2	1	0	3	.154	.214	.154	4	-2	0-0	.833	-1	47	279	C4	0	-0.2
1954	Pit N	14	26	2	5	0	0	0	2	4	0	9	.192	.300	.192	32	-3	0-0	1.000	-0	53	88	C7	0	-0.2
1956	NY N	20	20	2	2	0	0	0	1	4-0	0	6	.100	.250	.100	-1	-3	0-0	1.000	0	153	0	C15	0	-0.2
Total	3	45	59	5	9	0	0	0	5	9-0	0	18	.153	.265	.153	15	-8	0-0	.985	-0	96	72	C26	0	-0.6

Mangual, Angel Angel Luis (Guilbe); B3.19.1947 Juana Diaz, PR; BR/TR/5´10˝/(178–180); d9.15; b–Pepe

YEAR	TM LG	G	AB	R	H	2B	3B	HR	RBI	BB-IB	HP	SO	AVG	OBP	SLG	AOPS	ABR	SB-CS	FA	FR	RNG	THR	GAMES AT POSITION	DL	BFW
1969	Pit N	6	4	1	1	1	0	0	0	0-0	0	0	.250	.250	.500	108	0	0-0	.000	-0	0	0	O3(2/0/1)	0	0.0
1971	†Oak A	94	287	32	82	8	1	4	30	17-1	0	27	.286	.324	.362	96	-2	1-4	.988	-2	99	66	O81(17/57/9)	21	-0.8
1972	†Oak A	91	272	19	67	13	2	5	32	14-1	1	48	.246	.285	.364	97	-2	0-1	.971	3	112	81	O74(2/22/52)	0	-0.4
1973	†Oak A	74	192	20	43	4	1	3	13	8-1	1	34	.224	.257	.302	60	-11	1-1	.947	-1	103	72	O50(14/17/21),D14,1b2/2	0	-1.5
1974	†Oak A	115	365	37	85	14	4	9	43	17-2	0	59	.233	.265	.367	86	-9	3-0	.961	0	104	111	O74(26/28/29),D37/3	0	-1.2
1975	Oak A	62	109	13	24	3	0	1	6	3-0	0	18	.220	.241	.275	46	-8	0-1	.978	-1	95	60	O39(21/6/14),D15	0	-1.1
1976	Oak A	8	12	0	2	1	0	0	1	0-0	0	1	.167	.167	.250	22	-1	0-1	1.000	0	61	429	O7R	0	-0.2
Total	7	450	1241	122	304	44	8	22	125	59-5	2	187	.245	.279	.346	83	-33	5-8	.969	-1	103	85	O328(82/130/133),D66,1b2/32	21	-5.2

Mangual, Pepe Jose Manuel (Guilbe); B5.23.1952 Ponce, PR; BR/TR/5´10˝/165; d9.6; b–Angel

YEAR	TM LG	G	AB	R	H	2B	3B	HR	RBI	BB-IB	HP	SO	AVG	OBP	SLG	AOPS	ABR	SB-CS	FA	FR	RNG	THR	GAMES AT POSITION	DL	BFW
1972	Mon N	8	11	2	3	0	0	0	0	1-0	0	5	.273	.333	.273	73	0	0-1	1.000	-1	37	0	O3(2/0/1)	0	-0.2
1973	Mon N	33	62	9	11	2	1	3	7	6-0	0	18	.177	.246	.387	71	-3	2-4	.966	-1	85	0	O22(20/1/1)	0	-0.6
1974	Mon N	23	61	10	19	3	0	0	4	5-0	0	15	.311	.353	.361	98	0	5-0	1.000	-2	69	0	O22(18/2/8)	0	-0.2
1975	Mon N	140	514	84	126	16	2	9	45	74-1	4	115	.245	.340	.337	85	-8	33-11	.972	-11	88	90	O138(1/135/2)	0	-2.1
1976	Mon N	66	215	34	56	9	1	3	16	50-2	2	49	.260	.403	.353	111	7	17-7	.968	1	106	77	O62(34/36/1)	0	0.6
	NY N	41	102	15	19	5	2	1	9	10-0	0	32	.186	.259	.304	62	-5	7-3	.985	1	104	116	O38(12/22/5)	0	-0.6
	Year	107	317	49	75	14	3	4	25	60-2	2	81	.237	.361	.338	98	2	24-10	.973	2	105	89	O100(46/58/6)	0	0.0
1977	NY N	8	7	1	1	0	0	0	2	1-0	0	4	.143	.250	.143	9	-1	0-0	.833	0	241	0	O4(2/2/0)	0	-0.1
Total	6	319	972	155	235	35	6	16	83	147-3	6	238	.242	.341	.340	88	-10	64-26	.972	-14	92	78	O289(89/198/18)	0	-3.2

Mangus, George George Graham; B5.22.1890 Red Creek NY; D8.10.1933 Rutland MA; BL/TR/5´11.5˝/165; d8.20

YEAR	TM LG	G	AB	R	H	2B	3B	HR	RBI	BB-IB	HP	SO	AVG	OBP	SLG	AOPS	ABR	SB-CS	FA	FR	RNG	THR	GAMES AT POSITION	DL	BFW
1912	Phi N	10	25	2	5	3	0	0	3	1	0	6	.200	.231	.320	47	-2	0	.750	-2	80	0	O5L	—	-0.4

Manion, Clyde Clyde Jennings "Pete"; B10.30.1896 Big River MO; D9.4.1967 Detroit MI; BR/TR/5´11˝/175; d5.5

YEAR	TM LG	G	AB	R	H	2B	3B	HR	RBI	BB-IB	HP	SO	AVG	OBP	SLG	AOPS	ABR	SB-CS	FA	FR	RNG	THR	GAMES AT POSITION	DL	BFW
1920	Det A	32	80	4	22	4	1	0	8	4	1	7	.275	.318	.350	79	-3	0-0	.940	-3	92	114	C30	—	-0.3
1921	Det A	12	10	0	2	0	0	0	2	2	1	2	.200	.385	.200	53	-1	0-0	1.000	0	80	312	C3	—	0.0
1922	Det A	42	69	9	19	4	1	0	12	4	0	6	.275	.315	.362	79	-2	0-1	.932	-3	83	47	C22/1	—	-0.5
1923	Det A	23	22	0	3	0	0	0	2	2	0	2	.136	.208	.136	-8	-4	0-0	.857	-1	82	147	C3/1	—	-0.4
1924	Det A	14	13	1	3	0	0	0	2	1	0	1	.231	.286	.231	35	-1	0-0	.750	-1	61	0	C3/1	—	-0.2
1926	Det A	75	176	15	35	4	0	0	14	24	0	16	.199	.295	.222	36	-16	1-1	.972	-3	87	102	C74	—	-1.6
1927	Det A	1	0	0	0	0	0	0	0	1	0	0	ø	1.000	ø	174	0	0-0	ø	0	—	—	/H	—	0.0
1928	StL A	76	243	25	55	5	1	2	31	15	1	18	.226	.274	.280	44	-20	3-0	.980	5	100	83	C71	—	-1.0
1929	StL A	35	111	16	27	2	0	0	11	15	0	3	.243	.333	.261	53	-7	1-0	.976	3	155	80	C34	—	-0.1
1930	StL A	57	148	12	32	1	0	1	11	24	0	17	.216	.326	.243	45	-12	0-1	.985	7	141	144	C56	—	-0.2
1932	Cin N	49	135	7	28	4	0	0	12	14	0	16	.207	.282	.237	43	-11	0	.970	1	88	92	C47	—	-0.8
1933	Cin N	36	84	3	14	1	0	0	3	8	0	7	.167	.239	.179	21	-9	0	.981	2	93	114	C34	—	-0.5
1934	Cin N	25	54	4	10	0	0	0	4	4	0	7	.185	.241	.185	16	-6	0	1.000	2	93	135	C24	—	-0.4
Total	13	477	1145	96	250	25	3	3	112	118	3	102	.218	.293	.253	45	-92	5-3	.973	9	106	102	C401,1b3	—	-6.0

Mankowski, Phil Philip Anthony; B1.9.1953 Buffalo NY; BL/TR/6´0˝/180; [DetA70 9/218]; d8.30

YEAR	TM LG	G	AB	R	H	2B	3B	HR	RBI	BB-IB	HP	SO	AVG	OBP	SLG	AOPS	ABR	SB-CS	FA	FR	RNG	THR	GAMES AT POSITION	DL	BFW
1976	Det A	24	85	9	23	2	1	1	4	4-0	0	8	.271	.300	.353	88	-2	0-0	.971	2	103	211	3b23	0	0.1
1977	Det A	94	286	21	79	7	3	3	27	16-4	2	41	.276	.318	.353	79	-9	1-2	.964	12	118	103	3b85/2	0	0.2
1978	Det A	88	222	28	61	8	0	4	20	22-3	2	28	.275	.344	.365	97	0	2-3	.972	2	106	148	3b80/D	0	0.0
1979	Det A	42	99	11	22	4	0	0	8	10-4	0	16	.222	.286	.263	50	-7	0-0	.963	2	104	121	3b36/D	55	-0.5
1980	NY N	8	12	1	2	1	0	0	1	2-0	0	4	.167	.286	.250	51	-1	0-0	.571	-1	93	0	3b3	147	-0.2
1982	NY N	13	35	2	8	1	0	0	4	1-0	0	6	.229	.237	.257	42	-3	0-1	.957	-0	107	123	3b13	0	-0.4
Total	6	269	739	72	195	23	4	8	64	55-11	4	103	.264	.315	.338	79	-22	3-6	.962	17	110	131	3b240,D2/2	202	-0.8

Manlove, Charlie Charles Henry Weeks "Chick"; B10.8.1862 Philadelphia PA; D2.12.1952 Altoona PA; BR/TR/5´9˝/165; d5.31

YEAR	TM LG	G	AB	R	H	2B	3B	HR	RBI	BB-IB	HP	SO	AVG	OBP	SLG	AOPS	ABR	SB-CS	FA	FR	RNG	THR	GAMES AT POSITION	DL	BFW
1884	Alt U	2	7	1	3	0	0	0	—	0	—	—	.429	.429	.429	159	0	—	1.000	-1	—	—	/Ccf	—	0.0
	NY N	3	10	0	0	0	0	0	0	0	—	4	.000	.000	.000	-98	-2	—	.833	-0	—	—	C3/rf	—	-0.2
Total	1	5	17	1	3	0	0	0	0	0	—	4	.176	.176	.176	9	-2	—	.880	-1	—	—	C4,O2(0/1/1)	—	-0.2

Mann, Garth Ben Garth "Red"; B11.16.1915 Brandon TX; D9.11.1980 Italy TX; BR/TR/6´0˝/155; d5.14

YEAR	TM LG	G	AB	R	H	2B	3B	HR	RBI	BB-IB	HP	SO	AVG	OBP	SLG	AOPS	ABR	SB-CS	FA	FR	RNG	THR	GAMES AT POSITION	DL	BFW
1944	Chi N	1	0	1	0	0	0	0	0	0	0	0	ø	ø	ø	ø	0	0	ø	0	—	—	/R	0	0.0

Mann, Fred Fred J.; B4.1.1858 Sutton VT; D4.6.1916 Springfield MA; BL/TR/5´10.5˝/178; d5.1; OF(39/444/28)

YEAR	TM LG	G	AB	R	H	2B	3B	HR	RBI	BB-IB	HP	SO	AVG	OBP	SLG	AOPS	ABR	SB-CS	FA	FR	RNG	THR	GAMES AT POSITION	DL	BFW
1882	Wor N	19	77	12	18	5	0	0	7	2	—	15	.234	.253	.299	74	-2	—	.703	-5	81	75	3b18/1	—	-0.6
	Phi AA	29	121	13	28	7	4	0	—	4	—	—	.231	.256	.355	98	-1	—	.798	-7	68	109	3b29	—	-0.7
1883	Col AA	96	394	61	98	18	13	1	—	18	—	—	.249	.282	.368	117	9	—	.854	-4	104	194	O82(2/80/0),1b9,3b6/S	—	0.1
1884	Col AA	99	366	70	101	12	18	7	—	25	11	—	.276	.341	.464	174	31	—	.857	-8	65	79	O97C,2b2	—	1.8
1885	Pit AA	99	391	60	99	17	6	0	41	31	6	—	.253	.318	.327	106	4	—	.908	-10	59	69	O97C,3b3	—	-0.8
1886	Pit AA	116	440	85	110	16	14	2	60	45	11	—	.250	.335	.364	119	11	26	.878	-4	71	100	O116(0/115/1)	—	0.2
1887	Cle AA	64	259	45	80	15	7	2	41	23	9	—	.309	.385	.444	135	13	25	.879	0	102	142	O64(37/0/27)	—	1.0
	Phi AA	55	229	42	63	14	6	0	32	15	6	—	.275	.336	.389	102	0	16	.917	-2	85	114	O55C	—	-0.3
	Year	119	488	87	143	29	13	2	73	38	15	—	.293	.362	.418	119	13	41	.896	-2	95	130	O119(37/55/27)	—	0.7
Total	6	577	2277	388	597	104	68	12	181	163	43	15	.262	.323	.383	122	65	67	.881	-40	78	112	O511C,3b56,1b10,2b2/S	—	0.7

Mann, Johnny John Leo; B2.4.1898 Fontanet IN; D3.31.1977 Terre Haute IN; BR/TR/5´11˝/160; d4.18

YEAR	TM LG	G	AB	R	H	2B	3B	HR	RBI	BB-IB	HP	SO	AVG	OBP	SLG	AOPS	ABR	SB-CS	FA	FR	RNG	THR	GAMES AT POSITION	DL	BFW
1928	Chi A	6	6	0	2	0	0	0	1	1	0	0	.333	.429	.333	104	0	0-0	1.000	0	125	0	3b2	—	0.0

Mann, Kelly Kelly John; B8.17.1967 Santa Monica CA; BR/TR/6´3˝/215; [ChiN85 20/520]; d9.4

YEAR	TM LG	G	AB	R	H	2B	3B	HR	RBI	BB-IB	HP	SO	AVG	OBP	SLG	AOPS	ABR	SB-CS	FA	FR	RNG	THR	GAMES AT POSITION	DL	BFW
1989	Atl N	7	24	1	5	2	0	0	1	0-0	1	6	.208	.240	.292	50	-2	0-0	1.000	2	88	165	C7	0	0.1
1990	Atl N	11	28	2	4	1	0	1	2	0-0	0	6	.143	.143	.286	14	-3	0-0	1.000	-2	78	108	C10	0	-0.6
Total	2	18	52	3	9	3	0	1	3	0-0	1	12	.173	.189	.288	30	-5	0-0	1.000	-1	83	135	C17	0	-0.5

YEAR	TM LG	G	AB	R	H	2B	3B	HR	RBI	BB-IB	HP	SO	AVG	OBP	SLG	AOPS	ABR	SB-CS	FA	FR	RNG	THR	GAMES AT POSITION	DL	BFW
MANN, LES	Leslie "Major"; B11.18.1892 Lincoln NE; D1.14.1962 Pasadena CA; BR/TR/5´9˝/172; d4.30																								
1913	Bos N	120	407	54	103	24	7	3	51	18	4	73	.253	.291	.369	86	-9	7-16	.960	1	103	95	O120(12/103/6)	—	-2.0
1914	†Bos N	126	389	44	96	16	11	4	40	24	1	50	.247	.292	.375	99	-3	9	.952	10	104	**161**	O123(5/104/14)	—	-0.1
1915	Chi F	135	470	74	144	12	**19**	4	58	36	1	40	.306	.357	.438	131	9	18	.969	5	110	97	O130(94/7/33)/S	—	0.8
1916	Chi N	127	415	46	113	13	9	2	29	19	2	31	.272	.307	.361	95	-3	11-7	.972	-3	99	77	O115(74/20/26)	—	-1.3
1917	Chi N	117	444	63	121	19	10	1	44	27	1	46	.273	.316	.367	101	0	14	.953	-1	88	141	O116(106/11/2)	—	-0.7
1918	†Chi N	129	489	69	141	27	7	2	55	38	2	45	.288	.342	.384	118	11	21	.961	-5	88	107	O129L	—	0.0
1919	Chi N	80	299	31	68	8	8	1	22	11	1	29	.227	.257	.318	72	-12	12	.982	1	101	101	O78L	—	-1.6
	Bos N	40	145	15	41	6	4	3	20	9	1	14	.283	.329	.441	136	6	7	.929	2	97	165	O40L	—	0.6
	Year	120	444	46	109	14	12	4	42	20	2	43	.245	.281	.358	92	-6	19	.962	2	100	123	O118L	—	-1.0
1920	Bos N	115	424	48	117	7	8	3	32	38	4	42	.276	.341	.351	104	2	7-7	.980	0	99	102	O110(102/0/8)	—	-0.4
1921	StL N	97	256	57	84	12	7	7	30	23	3	28	.328	.390	.512	140	14	5-5	.969	3	105	114	O79(1/66/12)	—	1.3
1922	StL N	84	147	42	51	14	1	2	20	16	1	12	.347	.415	.497	141	10	0-1	.978	1	109	78	O57(10/47/0)	—	0.8
1923	StL N	38	89	20	33	5	2	5	11	9	1	5	.371	.434	.640	184	11	0-0	.979	1	104	135	O26(5/6/16)	—	1.0
	Cin N	8	1	1	0	0	0	0	0	0	0	0	.000	.000	.000	-99	0	0-0	ø	0	—	—	/H	—	0.0
	Year	46	90	21	33	5	2	5	11	9	1	5	.367	.430	.633	181	10	0-0	.979	1	104	135	O26(5/6/16)	—	1.0
1924	Bos N	32	102	13	28	7	4	0	10	8	1	10	.275	.333	.422	105	1	1-0	1.000	1	104	121	O28(7/0/21)	—	0.0
1925	Bos N	60	184	27	63	11	4	2	20	5	4	11	.342	.373	.478	127	7	6-1	.992	3	107	110	O57(5/11/41)	—	0.6
1926	Bos N	50	129	23	39	8	2	1	20	9	0	9	.302	.348	.419	116	3	5	.966	2	108	142	O46(17/17/16)	—	0.3
1927	Bos N	29	66	8	17	3	1	0	6	8	0	3	.258	.338	.333	87	-1	2	.955	2	101	202	O24(5/3/17)	—	-0.1
	NY N	29	67	13	22	4	1	2	10	8	0	7	.328	.400	.507	142	4	2	1.000	-0	85	142	O22(15/5/2)	—	0.3
	Year	58	133	21	39	7	2	2	16	16	0	10	.293	.369	.421	116	3	4	.973	1	94	175	O46(20/8/19)	—	0.2
1928	NY N	82	193	29	51	7	1	2	25	18	1	9	.264	.330	.342	76	-7	2	.952	-3	91	64	O68(3/14/63)	—	-1.3
Total	16	1498	4716	677	1332	203	106	44	503	324	28	464	.282	.332	.398	109	43	129-37	.966	18	100	113	O1368(708/414/277)/S	—	-1.8
MANNING, JIMMY	James H.; B1.31.1862 Fall River MA; D10.22.1929 Edinburg TX; BB/TR/5´7˝/157; d5.16; M1																								
1884	Bos N	89	345	52	83	8	6	2	35	19	—	47	.241	.280	.316	88	-5	—	.878	-3	95	97	O73(1/72/0),S9,2b9,3b3	—	-0.9
1885	Bos N	84	306	34	63	8	9	2	27	19	—	36	.206	.252	.310	84	-6	—	.898	7	130	131	O83(12/63/8)/S	—	-0.1
	Det N	20	78	15	21	4	0	1	9	4	—	10	.269	.305	.359	114	1	—	.802	-6	83	113	S20	—	-0.4
	Year	104	384	49	84	12	9	3	36	23	—	46	.219	.263	.320	90	-4	—	.898	1	130	131	O83(12/63/8),S21	—	-0.5
1886	Det N	26	97	14	18	2	3	0	7	6	—	10	.186	.233	.268	50	-6	7	.947	0	85	158	O26L/S	—	-0.6
1887	Det N	13	52	5	10	1	0	0	3	5	1	4	.192	.276	.212	36	-4	3	.867	-5	0	0	O10L,S3	—	-0.8
1889	KC AA	132	506	68	103	16	7	3	68	54	13	61	.204	.297	.281	61	-27	58	.927	-8	154	63	O69L,2b63/S3	—	-2.9
Total	5	364	1384	188	298	39	25	8	149	107	14	168	.215	.278	.297	73	-47	68	.903	-15	118	102	O261(118/135/8),2b72,S35,3b4	—	-5.7
MANNING, JACK	John E.; B12.20.1853 Braintree MA; D8.15.1929 Boston MA; BR/TR/5´8.5˝/158; d4.23; M1; OF NA(2/2/69); OF(2/16/605); ▲																								
1873	Bos NA	31	154	28	41	4	1	0	21	1	—	14	.266	.271	.305	65	-8	5-2	.920	-1	168	132	1b28,O7(2/0/5)	—	-0.5
1874	Bal NA	42	174	32	61	8	2	0	18	2	—	2	.351	.358	.420	149	9	0-0	.839	-5	109	0	P22,2b22,S4/13	—	-0.1
	Har NA	1	5	1	1	0	0	0	0	0	—	0	.200	.200	.200	27	0	0-0	.167	-2	38	0	/3	—	-0.2
	Year	43	179	33	62	8	2	0	18	2	—	2	.346	.354	.413	146	9	0-0	.793	-7	109	0	P22,2b22,S4,3b2/1	—	-0.3
1875	Bos NA	77	348	71	94	11	3	1	46	2	—	9	.270	.274	.328	104	1	5-5	.802	-1	151	117	O65(0/2/64),P27,1b3/3	—	0.3
1876	Bos N	**70**	288	52	76	13	0	2	25	7	—	5	.264	.281	.330	101	1	—	.777	-4	85	0	O56(0/1/55),P34/S2	—	-0.3
1877	Cin N	57	252	47	80	16	7	0	36	5	—	6	.317	.331	.437	157	17	—	.742	-10	87	30	S26,1b17,O12(1/10/1),P10,2b2,M	—	0.5
1878	Bos N	**60**	248	41	63	10	1	0	23	10	—	16	.254	.283	.302	86	-4	—	.753	-15	57	45	O59(0/3/56),P3	—	-1.8
1880	Cin N	48	190	20	41	6	3	2	17	7	—	15	.216	.244	.311	87	-2	—	.798	-3	108	45	O47(0/2/47)/1	—	-0.6
1881	Buf N	1	1	0	0	0	0	0	0	0	—	0	.000	.000	.000	-99	0	—	1.000	1	1112	0	/lf	—	0.0
1883	Phi N	98	420	60	112	31	5	0	37	20	—	37	.267	.300	.364	110	8	—	.853	7	167	108	O98R	—	1.2
1884	Phi N	104	424	71	115	29	4	5	52	40	—	67	.271	.334	.394	134	20	—	.847	0	129	194	O104R	—	1.7
1885	Phi N	107	445	61	114	24	4	3	40	37	—	27	.256	.313	.348	116	10	—	.896	-6	106	119	O107R	—	0.3
1886	Bal AA	137	556	78	124	18	7	1	45	50	3	—	.223	.291	.286	83	-10	24	.887	-9	71	72	O137R	—	-1.8
Total	3NA	151	681	132	197	23	6	1	85	5	—	25	.289	.294	.345	105	2	10-7	.781	-8	139	108	O72R,P49,1b32,2b22,S4,3b3	—	-0.5
Total	9	682	2824	430	725	147	31	13	275	176	3	173	.257	.301	.345	108	40	24	.844	-39	106	94	O621R,P47,S27,1b18,2b3	—	-0.8
MANNING, RICK	Richard Eugene; B9.2.1954 Niagara Falls NY; BL/TR/6´1˝/180; [CleA72 1/2]; d5.23																								
1975	Cle A	120	480	69	137	16	5	3	35	44-2	2	62	.285	.347	.358	100	0	19-11	.974	10	115	133	O118(28/69/32)/D	0	0.6
1976	Cle A	138	552	73	161	24	7	6	43	41-1	0	75	.292	.337	.393	115	10	16-10	.987	-2	99	82	O136C	0	0.4
1977	Cle A	68	252	33	57	7	3	5	18	21-0	0	35	.226	.282	.337	71	-11	9-5	.990	1	111	43	O68C	72	-1.0
1978	Cle A	148	566	65	149	27	3	3	50	38-1	1	62	.263	.309	.337	83	-13	12-12	.995	-3	98	78	O144C	0	-2.0
1979	Cle A	144	560	67	145	12	2	3	51	55-3	1	48	.259	.323	.304	71	-22	30-8	.986	7	110	97	O141C/D	0	-1.2
1980	Cle A	140	471	55	110	17	4	3	52	63-11	2	66	.234	.321	.306	73	-16	12-6	.990	1	104	76	O139C	0	-1.6
1981	Cle A	**103**	360	47	88	15	3	4	33	40-2	0	57	.244	.318	.336	90	-4	25-3	.987	8	116	101	O103C	0	0.8
1982	Cle A	152	562	71	152	18	2	8	44	54-5	0	60	.270	.334	.352	88	-8	12-8	.978	-7	93	98	O152C	0	-1.7
1983	Cle A	50	194	20	54	6	0	1	10	12-1	0	22	.278	.319	.325	75	-7	7-3	.987	-1	104	31	O50C	0	-0.8
	Mil A	108	375	40	86	14	4	3	33	26-4	1	40	.229	.279	.312	68	-18	11-2	.991	-1	107	14	O108C	0	-1.8
	Year	158	569	60	140	20	4	4	43	38-5	1	62	.246	.292	.316	70	-24	18-5	.990	-2	106	20	O158C	0	-2.6
1984	Mil A	119	341	53	85	10	5	7	31	34-1	1	32	.249	.318	.370	93	-4	5-7	.987	-13	84	31	O114C/D	0	-1.9
1985	Mil A	79	216	19	47	9	1	2	18	14-0	0	19	.218	.265	.296	54	-14	1-0	.976	-2	101	50	O74(1/57/17),D2	19	-1.7
1986	Mil A	89	205	31	52	7	3	8	27	17-2	1	20	.254	.310	.434	98	-1	5-3	.988	4	115	81	O83(40/29/18),D5	0	0.0
1987	Mil A	97	114	21	26	7	1	0	13	12-0	0	18	.228	.299	.307	60	-6	4-0	.958	-1	102	45	O78(21/8/51),D2	0	-0.8
Total	13	1555	5248	664	1349	189	43	56	458	471-33	9	616	.257	.317	.341	84	-114	168-78	.985	-1	104	75	O1508(90/1317/118),D12	91	-12.7
MANNING, TIM	Timothy Edward; B12.3.1853 Henley–On–Thames, England; D6.11.1934 Oak Park IL; BR/TR/5´10˝/170; d5.1																								
1882	Pro N	21	76	7	8	0	0	0	8	5	—	13	.105	.160	.105	-13	-9	—	.787	-9	79	72	S17,C4	—	-1.7
1883	Bal AA	35	121	23	26	5	0	0	—	14	—	—	.215	.296	.256	77	-2	—	.913	3	106	53	2b35	—	0.2
1884	Bal AA	91	341	49	70	14	5	2	—	26	7	—	.205	.275	.293	82	-6	—	.907	-2	96	73	2b91	—	-0.5
1885	Bal AA	43	157	17	32	8	1	0	16	10	3	—	.204	.265	.268	70	-5	—	.919	2	103	99	2b41,3b3	—	-0.1
	Pro N	10	35	3	2	1	0	0	0	1	—	11	.057	.083	.086	-47	-6	—	.854	-3	74	69	S10	—	-0.8
Total	4	200	730	99	138	28	6	2	24	56	—	24	.189	.256	.252	63	-28	—	.911	-10	100	75	2b167,S27,C4,3b3	—	-2.9
MANNO, DON	Donald D.; B5.4.1915 Williamsport PA; D3.11.1995 Williamsport PA; BR/TR/6´1˝/190; d9.22; Col West Chester																								
1940	Bos N	3	7	1	2	0	0	1	4	0	0	2	.286	.286	.714	177	1	0	1.000	0	134	0	O2R	—	0.1
1941	Bos N	22	30	2	5	1	0	0	4	3	0	7	.167	.242	.200	27	-3	0	1.000	-1	94	0	O5L,3b3/1	0	-0.4
Total	2	25	37	3	7	1	0	1	8	3	0	9	.189	.250	.297	56	-2	0	1.000	-1	109	0	O7(5/0/2),3b3/1	0	-0.3
MANRIQUE, FRED	Fred Eloy (Reyes); B11.5.1961 Edo Bolivar, Venezuela; BR/TR/6´1˝/175; d8.23																								
1981	Tor A	14	28	1	4	0	0	0	1	0-0	1	12	.143	.172	.143	-8	-4	0-1	.949	1	124	144	S11,3b2/D	0	-0.3
1984	Tor A	10	9	0	3	0	0	0	1	0-0	0	1	.333	.333	.333	82	0	0-0	.938	1	136	204	2b9/D	0	0.1
1985	Mon N	9	13	5	4	1	1	1	1	1-0	0	3	.308	.357	.769	218	2	0-0	1.000	1	115	0	2b2,S2/3	0	0.3
1986	StL N	13	17	2	3	0	0	1	1	1-0	0	1	.176	.222	.353	56	-1	1-0	1.000	-2	60	0	3b4/2	0	-0.3
1987	Chi A	115	298	30	77	13	3	4	29	19-1	1	69	.258	.302	.362	74	-12	5-3	.984	-4	105	120	2b92,S23,D5	0	-0.9
1988	Chi A	140	345	43	81	10	6	5	37	21-1	3	54	.235	.283	.342	75	-13	6-5	.985	5	105	108	2b129,S12/D	0	-0.6
1989	Chi A	65	187	23	56	13	1	2	30	8-1	2	30	.299	.333	.412	111	3	0-4	.961	-9	90	91	2b57,S2/3D	0	-0.6
	Tex A	54	191	23	55	12	0	2	22	9-0	0	33	.288	.318	.382	95	-1	4-1	.963	-4	87	112	S37,2b17,3b6	0	-0.2
	Year	119	378	46	111	25	1	4	52	17-1	2	63	.294	.326	.397	103	1	4-5	.952	-12	89	86	2b74,S39,3b7/D	0	-0.8
1990	Min A	69	228	22	54	10	0	5	29	4-0	2	35	.237	.254	.346	63	-12	2-0	.974	-7	96	103	2b67/D	0	-1.7
1991	Oak A	9	21	2	3	0	0	0	0	2-0	0	1	.143	.217	.143	2	-3	0-0	.955	-0	83	52	S7,2b2	0	-0.3
Total	9	498	1337	151	340	59	11	20	151	65-3	9	239	.254	.292	.360	79	-41	18-14	.976	-17	101	106	2b376,S94,3b14,D10	0	-4.5
MANSELL, JOHN	John; B1859 Auburn NY; D2.20.1925 Romulus NY; BL/5´10˝/168; d5.9; b–Mike b–Tom																								
1882	Phi AA	31	126	17	30	3	1	0	17	4	—	—	.238	.262	.278	77	-3	—	.791	-5	54	0	O31C	—	-0.9
MANSELL, MIKE	Michael R.; B1.15.1858 Auburn NY; D12.4.1902 Auburn NY; BL/5´11˝/175; d5.1; b–John b–Tom																								
1879	Syr N	67	242	24	52	4	2	1	13	5	—	45	.215	.231	.260	69	-7	—	.881	15	71	103	O67L	—	0.3
1880	Cin N	53	187	22	36	6	2	2	12	4	—	37	.193	.209	.278	64	-7	—	.865	12	102	196	O53L	—	0.2
1882	Pit AA	**79**	347	59	96	**18**	**16**	2	—	7	—	—	.277	.291	.438	150	17	—	.829	3	86	55	O79L	—	1.6

YEAR	TM LG	G	AB	R	H	2B	3B	HR	RBI	BB-IB	HP	SO	AVG	OBP	SLG	AOPS	ABR	SB-CS	FA	FR	RNG	THR	GAMES AT POSITION	DL	BFW
1883	Pit AA	96	412	90	106	12	13	3	—	25	—	—	.257	.300	.371	120	10	—	.883	3	59	39	O96L	—	0.9
1884	Pit AA	27	100	15	14	0	3	1	—	7	1	—	.140	.204	.230	42	-6	—	.796	-1	60	110	O27(24/0/3)	—	-0.8
	Phi AA	20	70	6	14	1	1	0	—	5	0	—	.200	.253	.243	59	-3	—	.762	-2	48	0	O20(16/4/0)	—	-0.5
	Ric AA	29	113	21	34	2	5	0	—	8	3	—	.301	.363	.407	153	7	—	.763	-3	106	125	O29(0/2/27)	—	0.3
	Year	76	283	42	62	3	9	1	—	20	4	—	.219	.280	.304	90	-3	—	.775	-6	72	82	O76(40/6/30)	—	-1.0
Total	5	371	1471	237	352	43	42	9	25	61	4	82	.239	.271	.344	106	11	—	.854	26	76	86	O371(335/6/30)	—	2.0
Mansell, Tom	Thomas E. "Brick"; B1.1.1855 Auburn NY; D10.6.1934 Auburn NY; BL/TR/5´8˝/160; d5.1; b–John b–Mike																								
1879	Tro N	40	177	29	43	6	0	0	11	3	—	9	.243	.256	.277	81	-3	—	.742	-7	31	82	O40(38/2/0)	—	-1.2
	Syr N	1	4	0	1	0	0	0	0	0	—	0	.250	.250	.250	74	0	—	1.000	-0	0	0	/rf	—	0.0
	Year	41	181	29	44	6	0	0	11	3	—	9	.243	.255	.276	81	-3	—	.747	-7	30	80	O41(38/2/1)	—	-1.2
1883	Det N	34	131	22	29	4	1	0	10	8	—	13	.221	.266	.267	66	-5	—	.758	-4	149	73	O34R/P	—	-0.8
	StL AA	28	112	23	45	8	1	0	24	7	—	—	.402	.437	.491	188	11	—	.786	-6	18	0	O28(25/2/1)	—	0.4
1884	Cin AA	65	266	49	66	4	6	0	23	15	5	—	.248	.301	.308	94	-2	—	.752	-10	25	0	O65(41/25/1)	—	-1.2
	Col AA	23	77	9	15	1	3	0	6	6	1	—	.195	.262	.286	85	-1	—	.667	-3	85	0	O23L	—	-0.4
	Year	88	343	58	81	5	9	0	29	21	6	—	.236	.292	.303	93	-3	—	.739	-12	39	0	O88(64/25/1)	—	-1.6
Total	3	191	767	132	199	23	11	0	74	39	6	22	.259	.300	.318	100	0	—	.751	-29	54	33	O191(127/29/37)/P	—	-3.2
Mantilla, Felix	Felix (Lamela); B7.29.1934 Isabela, PR; BR/TR/6´0˝/160; d6.21; OF(74/76/10); [DL 1967 Chi N 81]																								
1956	Mil N	35	53	9	15	1	1	0	3	1-0	1	8	.283	.309	.340	79	-2	0-1	1.000	5	144	138	S15,3b3	0	0.4
1957	†Mil N	71	182	28	43	9	1	4	21	14-2	2	34	.236	.296	.363	82	-5	2-0	.931	1	102	110	S35,2b13,3b7/cf	0	0.0
1958	†Mil N	85	226	37	50	5	1	7	19	20-2	0	20	.221	.282	.345	72	-10	2-0	.987	-8	96	81	O43(12/33/0),2b21,S5,3b2	0	-1.8
1959	Mil N	103	251	26	54	5	0	3	19	16-1	2	31	.215	.266	.271	48	-19	6-1	.970	-3	104	97	2b60,S23,3b9,O7C	0	-1.7
1960	Mil N	63	148	21	38	7	0	3	11	7-1	1	16	.257	.291	.365	86	-3	3-1	.956	-9	68	67	2b26,S25,O8(3/5/0)	0	-1.0
1961	Mil N	45	93	13	20	3	0	1	5	10-0	1	16	.215	.298	.280	58	-6	1-1	.933	-3	91	98	S19,2b10,O10(2/6/2),3b6	0	-0.8
1962	NY N	141	466	54	128	17	4	11	59	37-0	5	51	.275	.330	.399	94	-4	3-1	.948	-7	107	126	3b95,S25,2b14	0	-0.8
1963	Bos A	66	178	27	56	8	0	6	15	20-1	0	14	.315	.384	.461	131	8	2-1	.965	-1	93	117	S27,O11C,2b5	0	0.9
1964	Bos A	133	425	69	123	20	1	30	64	41-1	4	46	.289	.357	.553	142	24	0-1	.984	-3	82	93	O48(36/5/8),2b45,3b7,S6	0	2.3
1965	Bos A★	150	534	60	147	17	2	18	92	79-5	8	84	.275	.374	.416	118	16	7-3	.976	-23	86	78	2b123,O27(20/8/0),1b2	0	0.2
1966	Hou N	77	151	16	33	5	0	6	22	11-0	2	32	.219	.279	.371	85	-3	1-0	.990	-4	41	89	1b14,3b14,2b9/lf	25	-0.8
Total	11	969	2707	360	707	97	10	89	330	256-13	26	352	.261	.329	.403	100	-4	27-10	.977	-55	89	80	2b326,S180,O156C,3b143,1b16	106	-3.1
Mantle, Mickey	Mickey Charles "The Commerce Comet"; B10.20.1931 Spavinaw OK; D8.13.1995 Dallas TX; BB/TR/5´11˝/(175–201); d4.17; C1; HF1974; OF(129/1745/146)																								
1951	†NY A	96	341	61	91	11	5	13	65	43	0	74	.267	.349	.443	117	7	8-7	.959	-5	90	74	O86(0/3/85)	0	-0.1
1952	†NY A☆	142	549	94	171	37	7	23	87	75	0	111	.311	.394	.530	166	**48**	4-1	.968	-6	90	132	O141(0/121/20)/3	0	3.9
1953	†NY A★	127	461	105	136	24	3	21	92	79	0	90	.295	.398	.497	145	31	8-4	.982	-3	97	95	O121(0/116/4)/S	0	2.3
1954	NY A★	146	543	**129**	163	17	12	27	102	102	0	107	.300	.408	.525	160	47	5-2	.975	-4	88	156	O144(0/143/1),S4/2	0	3.8
1955	†NY A★	147	517	121	158	25	**11**	**37**	99	**113**-6	3	97	.306	**.431**	**.611**	**181**	**62**	8-1	.995	-1	97	129	O145C,S2	0	**5.5**
1956	†NY A★	150	533	**132**	188	22	5	**52**	**130**	112-6	2	99	**.353**	.464	**.705**	**213**	**90**	10-1	.990	0	100	105	O144C	0	**8.1**
1957	†NY A★	144	474	**121**	173	28	6	34	94	**146**-23	0	75	.365	.512	.665	223	**94**	16-3	.979	-10	93	62	O139C	0	**8.0**
1958	†NY A★	150	519	**127**	158	21	1	**42**	97	**129-13**	2	120	.304	.443	.592	**189**	**71**	18-3	.977	-13	91	60	O150C	0	**5.5**
1959	NY A★	144	541	104	154	23	4	31	75	93-6	2	126	.285	.390	.514	**152**	**41**	21-3	**.995**	-1	102	72	O143C	0	3.6
1960	†NY A★	153	527	**119**	145	17	6	**40**	94	111-6	1	125	.275	.399	.558	**166**	**51**	14-3	.991	-11	89	100	O150C	0	3.6
1961	†NY A★	153	514	**132**	163	16	6	54	128	**126**-9	0	112	.317	.448	**.687**	**210**	**86**	12-1	.983	-6	99	77	O150C	0	7.5
1962	†NY A★	123	377	96	121	15	1	30	89	**122**-9	1	78	.321	**.486**	**.605**	**198**	**63**	9-0	.978	-10	87	73	O117(0/94/23)	0	**5.0**
1963	†NY A✳	65	172	40	54	8	0	15	35	40-4	0	32	.314	.441	.622	197	25	2-1	.990	-2	99	74	O52C	35	2.2
1964	†NY A★	143	465	92	141	25	2	35	111	99-**18**	0	102	.303	**.423**	.591	**177**	**53**	6-3	.978	-16	80	36	O132(17/102/13)	0	3.4
1965	NY A✳	122	361	44	92	12	1	19	46	73-7	0	76	.255	.379	.452	136	20	4-1	.966	-1	102	54	O108L	0	1.5
1966	NY A	108	333	40	96	12	1	23	56	57-5	0	76	.288	.389	.538	171	32	1-1	1.000	-7	91	40	O97(4/93/0)	0	2.4
1967	NY A★	144	440	63	108	17	0	22	55	107-7	1	113	.245	.391	.434	150	34	1-1	.993	4	115	92	1b131	0	3.3
1968	NY A★	144	435	57	103	14	1	18	54	106-7	1	97	.237	.385	.398	143	29	6-2	.988	-2	99	102	1b131	0	2.3
Total	18	2401	8102	1677	2415	344	72	536	1509	1733-126	13	1710	.298	.421	.557	173	884	153-38	.982	-92	93	87	O2019C,1b262,S7/23	35	71.8
Manto, Jeff	Jeffrey Paul; B8.23.1964 Bristol PA; BR/TR/6´3˝/210; [CalA85 14/355]; d6.7; C1; Col Temple																								
1990	Cle A	30	76	12	17	5	1	2	14	21-1	0	18	.224	.392	.395	121	3	0-1	.990	1	132	103	1b25,3b5	0	0.3
1991	Cle A	47	128	15	27	7	0	2	13	14-0	4	22	.211	.306	.313	72	-5	2-0	.929	-1	97	203	3b32,1b14,C5/lf	0	-0.6
1993	Phi N	8	18	0	1	0	0	0	0	0-0	1	3	.056	.105	.056	-56	-4	0-0	1.000	-0	84	0	3b6/S	0	-0.5
1995	Bal A	89	254	31	65	9	0	17	38	24-0	2	69	.256	.325	.492	107	1	0-3	.959	-2	91	117	3b69,D13,1b4	17	-0.2
1996	Bos A	10	30	5	8	3	1	2	4	3-0	1	6	.267	.353	.633	140	2	0-0	.963	4	134	99	2b4,S4	32	0.6
	Sea A	21	54	7	10	3	0	1	4	9-0	0	12	.185	.302	.296	52	-4	0-1	.971	0	104	82	3b16/lfD	0	-0.4
	Bos A	12	18	3	2	0	0	0	2	5-0	0	6	.111	.304	.111	11	-2	0-0	.960	3	146	77	3b10/1	0	0.0
	Year	43	102	15	20	6	1	3	10	17-0	1	24	.196	.317	.363	70	-5	0-1	.967	7	118	80	3b26,2b4,S4,D2/lf1	0	0.2
1997	Cle A	16	30	3	8	3	0	2	7	1-0	0	10	.267	.290	.567	112	0	0-0	1.000	-2	72	0	3b7,1b6/lf	0	-0.2
1998	Cle A	7	14	3	1	0	0	0	1	1-0	0	5	.071	.133	.071	-43	-3	0-0	1.000	-5	0	23	1b4,3b2/2	0	-0.9
	Det A	16	30	6	8	2	0	1	3	3-0	1	11	.267	.353	.433	102	0	1-0	.977	-2	0	68	1b10/lfD	0	-0.2
	Cle A	8	23	5	7	1	0	2	5	1-0	0	5	.304	.333	.609	133	1	0-1	1.000	-3	12	0	3b6,1b3	0	-0.3
	Year	31	67	14	16	3	0	3	9	5-0	1	21	.239	.301	.418	82	-2	1-1	.979	-10	18	54	1b17,3b8,D6/2lf	0	-1.4
1999	Cle A	12	25	5	5	0	0	1	2	11-0	0	11	.200	.444	.320	95	1	0-0	1.000	1	110	148	3b10/1	0	0.2
	NY A	6	8	0	1	0	0	0	0	2-0	0	4	.125	.300	.125	14	-1	0-0	1.000	0	112	80	1b3/3	0	-0.1
	Year	18	33	5	6	0	0	1	2	13-0	0	15	.182	.413	.273	78	0	0-0	1.000	1	108	146	3b11,1b4	0	0.1
2000	Col N	7	5	2	4	2	0	1	4	2-0	0	0	.800	.857	1.800	444	3	0-0	1.000	0	0	1047	/13	0	0.3
Total	9	289	713	97	164	35	2	31	97	97-1	9	182	.230	.329	.415	93	-8	3-6	.960	-6	92	123	3b165,1b72,D21,2b5,S5,C5,O4L	49	-2.0
Manuel, Charlie	Charles Fuqua; B1.4.1944 Northfork WV; BL/TR/6´4˝/(180–200); d4.8; M5/C8																								
1969	†Min A	83	164	14	34	6	0	2	24	28-4	0	33	.207	.320	.280	68	-6	1-0	.967	-3	82	69	O46(41/1/4)	0	-1.1
1970	†Min A	59	64	4	12	0	0	1	7	6-2	1	17	.188	.260	.234	39	-5	0-0	1.000	-1	66	0	O11(9/0/2)	0	-0.7
1971	Min A	18	16	1	2	1	0	0	1	1-0	0	8	.125	.176	.188	3	-2	0-0	ø	-0	0	0	/rf	0	-0.2
1972	Min A	63	122	6	25	5	0	1	8	4-0	1	16	.205	.233	.270	48	-8	0-0	.977	1	91	233	O28(20/0/9)	0	-0.9
1974	LA N	4	3	0	1	0	0	0	1	1-0	0	0	.333	.500	.333	141	0	0-0	ø	0	—	—	/H	0	0.0
1975	LA N	15	15	0	2	0	0	0	2	0-0	0	3	.133	.133	.133	-27	-3	0-0	ø	0	—	—	/H	0	-0.3
Total	6	242	384	25	76	12	0	4	43	40-6	2	77	.198	.273	.260	52	-24	1-0	.973	-3	83	120	O86(70/1/16)	0	-3.2
Manuel, Jerry	Jerry; B12.23.1953 Hahira GA; BB/TR (BR 1981–82)/6´0˝/(155–165); [DetA72 1/20]; d9.18; M6/C9																								
1975	Det A	6	18	0	1	0	0	0	0	0-0	0	4	.056	.056	.056	-66	-4	0-0	.944	2	140	99	2b6	0	-0.1
1976	Det A	54	43	4	6	1	0	0	2	3-0	1	9	.140	.213	.163	11	-5	1-0	.921	-1	108	64	2b47,S4/D	0	-0.4
1980	Mon N	7	6	0	0	0	0	0	0	0-0	0	2	.000	.000	.000	-98	-2	0-0	.941	1	142	0	S7	0	0.0
1981	†Mon N	27	55	10	11	5	0	3	10	6-1	0	11	.200	.270	.455	102	0	0-0	.987	-3	80	115	2b23,S2	107	-0.2
1982	SD N	2	5	0	1	0	1	0	1	1-0	0	0	.200	.333	.600	166	0	0-0	1.000	-2	0	172	/2S3	0	-0.1
Total	5	96	127	14	19	6	1	3	13	10-1	1	26	.150	.214	.283	41	-11	1-0	.949	-2	99	91	2b77,S14/3D	107	-0.8
Manush, Frank	Frank Henry; B9.18.1883 Tuscumbia AL; D1.5.1965 Laguna Beach CA; BR/TR/5´10.5˝/175; d8.31; b–Heinie																								
1908	Phi A	23	77	6	12	2	1	0	0	2	1	—	.156	.188	.208	27	-6	2	.933	-4	71	89	3b20,2b2	—	-1.2
Manush, Heinie	Henry Emmett; B7.20.1901 Tuscumbia AL; D5.12.1971 Sarasota FL; BL/TL/6´1˝/200; d4.20; C2; HF1964; b–Frank																								
1923	Det A	109	308	59	103	20	5	4	54	20	**17**	21	.334	.406	.471	133	15	3-5	.953	-6	93	61	O79(72/0/7)	—	0.2
1924	Det A	120	422	83	122	24	8	9	68	27	**16**	30	.289	.355	.448	108	3	14-5	.979	-7	97	35	O106(99/1/6)/1	—	-1.0
1925	Det A	99	278	46	84	14	3	5	47	24	2	21	.302	.362	.428	101	0	8-3	.982	0	98	107	O73(13/56/5)	—	-0.2
1926	Det A	136	498	95	188	35	8	14	86	31	6	28	**.378**	.421	.564	153	37	11-5	.967	-6	96	60	O120(11/104/5)	—	2.6
1927	Det A	151	593	102	177	31	18	6	90	47	4	29	.298	.354	.442	104	1	12-8	.971	-9	94	60	O149(3/147/0)	—	-1.4
1928	StL A	**154**	638	104	**241**	**47**	20	13	108	39	0	14	.378	.414	.575	153	46	16-5	.992	-2	104	40	O154L	—	3.3
1929	StL A	142	574	85	204	**45**	10	6	81	43	1	24	.355	.401	.500	126	23	9-9	.987	-5	93	77	O141L	—	0.5
1930	StL A	49	198	26	65	16	4	2	29	5	0	7	.328	.345	.480	103	0	3-1	.990	3	105	147	O48L	—	0.0
	Was A	88	356	74	129	33	8	7	65	26	0	17	.362	.406	.559	141	22	4-3	.988	-3	93	78	O86L	—	1.2
	Year	137	554	100	194	49	12	9	94	31	0	24	.350	.385	.531	128	22	7-4	.989	-0	97	102	O134L	—	1.2
1931	Was A	146	616	110	189	41	11	6	70	36	6	27	.307	.351	.438	106	4	3-3	.977	-12	86	50	O143L	—	-1.5

YEAR	TM LG	G	AB	R	H	2B	3B	HR	RBI	BB-IB	HP	SO	AVG	OBP	SLG	AOPS	ABR	SB-CS	FA	FR	RNG	THR	GAMES AT POSITION	DL	BFW
1932	Was A	149	625	121	214	41	14	14	116	36	5	29	.342	.383	.520	133	29	7-2	.988	-1	101	54	O146L	—	1.9
1933	†Was A	**153**	658	115	**221**	32	**17**	5	95	36	2	18	.336	.372	.459	120	17	6-4	.982	-3	99	64	O150L	—	0.5
1934	Was A★	137	556	88	194	42	11	11	89	36	3	23	.349	.392	.523	140	31	7-3	.980	-2	105	43	O131(130/1/0)	—	2.0
1935	Was A	119	479	68	131	26	9	4	56	35	4	17	.273	.328	.390	88	-10	2-0	.985	2	102	84	O111L	—	-1.3
1936	Bos A	82	313	43	91	15	5	0	45	17	1	11	.291	.329	.371	69	-16	1-3	.966	-4	90	57	O72L	—	-2.2
1937	Bro N	132	466	57	155	25	7	4	73	40	3	24	.333	.389	.442	123	16	6	.970	-6	94	64	O123R	—	0.3
1938	Bro N	17	51	9	12	3	1	0	6	5	0	4	.235	.304	.333	73	-2	1	1.000	1	118	88	O12R	—	-0.2
	Pit N	15	13	2	4	1	1	0	4	2	0	0	.308	.400	.538	155	1	0	ø	0	—	—	/H	—	0.1
	Year	32	64	11	16	4	2	0	10	7	0	4	.250	.324	.375	90	-1	1	1.000	1	118	88	O12R	—	-0.1
1939	Pit N	10	12	0	0	0	0	0	1	1	0	1	.000	.077	.000	-79	-3	0	1.000	-0	74	0	/rf	—	-0.3
Total	17	2008	7654	1287	2524	491	160	110	1183	506	70	345	.330	.377	.479	121	214	113-59	.979	-59	97	62	O1845(1379/309/159)/1	—	4.5
MANWARING, KIRT	Kirt Dean; B7.15.1965 Elmira NY; BR/TR/5´11˝/(185–203); [SFN86 2/31]; d9.15; Col Coastal Carolina																								
1987	SF N	6	7	0	1	0	0	0	0	0-0	1	1	.143	.250	.143	8	-1	0-0	.909	-1	206	0	C6	0	-0.2
1988	SF N	40	116	12	29	7	0	1	15	2-0	3	21	.250	.279	.336	80	-3	0-1	.979	-3	109	92	C40	0	-0.5
1989	†SF N	85	200	14	42	4	2	0	18	11-1	4	28	.210	.264	.250	49	-14	2-1	.982	1	148	86	C81	15	-1.0
1990	SF N	8	13	0	2	0	1	0	1	0-0	0	3	.154	.154	.308	24	-2	0-0	1.000	0	92	0	C8	0	-0.1
1991	SF N	67	178	16	40	9	0	0	19	9-0	3	22	.225	.271	.275	56	-10	1-1	.988	1	131	90	C67	41	-0.7
1992	SF N	109	349	24	85	10	5	4	26	29-0	5	42	.244	.311	.335	87	-7	2-1	.994	7	**172**	127	C108	15	0.7
1993	SF N	130	432	48	119	15	1	5	49	41-13	6	76	.275	.345	.350	90	-5	1-3	**.998**	7	**154**	122	C130	0	0.9
1994	SF N	97	316	30	79	17	1	1	29	25-3	3	50	.250	.308	.320	67	-15	1-1	.993	2	108	102	C97	0	-0.6
1995	SF N	118	379	21	95	15	2	4	36	27-6	10	72	.251	.314	.332	73	-15	1-0	.990	-12	121	77	C118	0	-1.9
1996	SF N	49	145	9	34	6	0	1	14	16-1	3	24	.234	.319	.297	66	-7	0-1	.993	-1	120	161	C49	43	-0.5
	Hou N	37	82	5	18	3	0	0	4	3-0	2	16	.220	.264	.256	41	-7	0-0	.995	2	113	194	C37	0	-0.4
	Year	86	227	14	52	9	0	1	18	19-1	5	40	.229	.300	.282	58	-14	0-1	.994	1	117	**173**	C86	0	-0.9
1997	Col N	104	337	22	76	6	4	1	27	30-0	2	78	.226	.291	.276	41	-29	1-5	.994	-16	87	84	C100	0	-4.0
1998	Col N	110	291	30	72	12	3	2	26	38-3	3	49	.247	.339	.330	64	-14	1-5	.988	-2	90	116	C108	0	-1.1
1999	Col N	48	137	17	41	7	1	2	14	12-1	5	23	.299	.374	.409	79	-4	0-0	.981	-6	72	83	C44/D	33	-0.7
Total	13	1008	2982	248	733	111	20	21	278	243-28	50	505	.246	.311	.318	68	-133	10-19	.991	-20	123	106	C993/D	147	-10.1
MAPES, CLIFF	Clifford Franklin; B3.13.1922 Sutherland NE; D12.5.1996 Pryor OK; BL/TR/6´3˝/205; d4.20																								
1948	NY A	53	88	19	22	11	1	1	12	6	0	13	.250	.298	.432	94	-1	1-1	.958	3	109	321	O21(9/6/6)	0	0.1
1949	†NY A	111	304	56	75	13	3	7	38	58	1	50	.247	.369	.378	98	0	6-0	.976	6	103	**186**	O108(4/58/49)	0	0.5
1950	†NY A	108	356	60	88	14	6	12	61	47	2	61	.247	.338	.421	96	-4	1-6	.950	-4	93	105	O102(4/21/80)	0	-1.1
1951	NY A	45	51	6	11	3	1	2	8	4	0	14	.216	.273	.431	92	-1	0-0	1.000	0	115	0	O34(2/3/29)	0	-0.1
	StL A	56	201	32	55	7	2	7	30	26	1	33	.274	.360	.433	110	3	0-1	.983	0	100	100	O53(15/12/31)	0	0.0
	Year	101	252	38	66	10	3	9	38	30	1	47	.262	.343	.433	109	2	0-1	.986	0	103	82	O87(17/15/60)	0	-0.1
1952	Det A	86	193	26	38	7	0	9	23	27	0	42	.197	.295	.373	84	-5	0-1	.967	-2	94	87	O63(5/18/43)	0	-0.9
Total	5	459	1193	199	289	55	13	38	172	168	4	213	.242	.338	.406	97	-8	8-9	.969	4	99	135	O381(39/118/238)	0	-1.5
MAPLE, HOWARD	Howard Albert "Mape"; B7.20.1903 Adrian MO; D11.9.1970 Portland OR; BL/TR/5´7˝/175; d5.19; Col Oregon St.																								
1932	Was A	44	41	6	10	0	1	0	7	7	1	7	.244	.367	.293	74	-1	0-0	1.000	-1	*153*	*86*	C41	—	-0.2
MAPPES, GEORGE	George Richard "Dick"; B12.25.1865 St.Louis MO; D2.20.1934 St.Louis MO; 5´8˝ /200; d9.23																								
1885	Bal AA	6	19	2	4	0	1	0	0	1	0	—	.211	.250	.316	79	-1	—	.875	-2	76	43	2b6	—	-0.2
1886	StL N	6	14	1	2	0	0	0	0	1	—	5	.143	.200	.143	6	-2	0	1.000	-1	—	—	C3,3b2/2	—	-0.2
Total	2	12	33	3	6	0	1	0	0	2	—	5	.182	.229	.242	48	-3	0	.848	-3	—	—	2b7,C3,3b2	—	-0.4
MARANVILLE, RABBIT	Walter James Vincent; B11.11.1891 Springfield MA; D1.5.1954 New York NY; BR/TR/5´5˝/155; d9.10; Mil 1918; M1; HF1954																								
1912	Bos N	26	86	8	18	2	0	0	8	9	1	14	.209	.292	.233	44	-7	1	.929	1	110	90	S26	—	-0.4
1913	Bos N	143	571	68	141	13	8	2	48	68	3	62	.247	.330	.308	81	-12	25-19	.949	17	**106**	93	S143	—	1.4
1914	†Bos N	156	586	74	144	23	6	4	78	45	6	56	.246	.306	.326	88	-9	28	.938	**50**	**116**	**168**	S156	—	**5.5**
1915	Bos N	149	509	51	124	23	6	2	43	45	2	65	.244	.308	.324	96	-3	18-12	.941	20	103	107	S149	—	3.0
1916	Bos N	155	604	79	142	16	13	4	38	50	2	69	.235	.296	.325	94	-5	32-15	**.947**	23	101	**133**	S155	—	3.4
1917	Bos N	142	561	69	146	19	13	3	43	40	2	47	.260	.312	.357	111	6	27	.947	14	100	106	S142	—	3.3
1918	Bos N	11	38	3	12	0	1	0	3	4	0	0	.316	.381	.368	134	2	0	.932	-1	89	43	S11	—	0.2
1919	Bos N	131	480	44	128	18	10	5	43	36	1	23	.267	.319	.377	113	7	12	.941	**26**	108	**126**	S131	—	4.6
1920	Bos N	134	493	48	131	19	15	1	43	28	0	24	.266	.305	.371	98	-4	14-11	.948	15	105	97	S133	—	2.1
1921	Pit N	153	612	90	180	25	12	1	70	47	3	38	.294	.347	.379	90	-8	25-12	.962	-17	97	94	S153	—	-0.7
1922	Pit N	**155**	672	115	198	26	15	0	63	61	2	43	.295	.355	.378	88	-11	24-13	.961	3	95	104	S138,2b18	—	0.7
1923	Pit N	141	581	78	161	19	9	1	41	42	1	34	.277	.327	.346	76	-21	14-11	**.965**	11	**101**	**111**	S141	—	0.5
1924	Pit N	152	594	62	158	33	20	2	71	35	0	53	.266	.307	.399	86	-14	18-14	**.973**	5	103	**123**	2b152	—	-0.5
1925	Chi N	75	266	37	62	10	3	0	23	29	0	20	.233	.308	.293	54	-18	6-5	.955	2	102	106	S74,M	—	-0.8
1926	Bro N	78	234	32	55	8	5	0	24	26	0	24	.235	.312	.312	69	-10	7	.948	7	102	79	S60,2b18	—	0.4
1927	StL N	9	29	0	7	1	0	0	0	2	0	2	.241	.290	.276	51	-2	0	.962	2	121	125	S9	—	0.1
1928	†StL N	112	366	40	88	14	10	1	34	36	1	27	.240	.310	.342	69	-18	3	.969	-9	98	87	S112,2b2	—	-1.4
1929	Bos N	146	560	87	159	26	10	0	55	47	4	33	.284	.344	.366	79	-18	13	.961	21	**110**	108	S145/2	—	1.7
1930	Bos N	142	558	85	157	26	8	2	43	48	5	23	.281	.344	.367	75	-23	9	**.965**	-14	91	96	S138,3b4	—	-1.9
1931	Bos N	145	562	69	146	22	5	0	33	56	2	34	.260	.329	.317	77	-17	9	.949	-24	93	103	S137,2b11	—	-3.1
1932	Bos N	149	571	67	134	20	4	0	37	46	3	28	.235	.295	.284	59	-33	4	**.975**	4	103	104	2b149	—	-1.9
1933	Bos N	143	478	46	104	15	4	0	38	36	1	34	.218	.274	.266	59	-26	2	.971	-28	87	106	2b142	—	-4.8
1935	Bos N	23	67	3	10	2	0	0	5	3	0	3	.149	.186	.179	-2	-10	0	.963	-3	94	110	2b20	—	-1.1
Total	23	2670	10078	1255	2605	380	177	28	884	839	39	756	.258	.318	.340	82	-254	291-112	.952	126	102	109	S2153,2b513,3b4	—	10.3
MARION, RED	John Wyeth; B3.14.1914 Richburg SC; D3.13.1975 San Jose CA; BR/TR/6´2˝/175; d9.16; b–Marty																								
1935	Was A	4	11	1	2	1	0	1	1	0	0	2	.182	.182	.545	85	0	0-0	.833	0	67	463	O3(1/1/1)	—	0.0
1943	Was A	14	17	2	3	0	0	0	1	3	0	1	.176	.300	.176	42	-1	0-0	1.000	0	119	0	O4L	0	-0.1
Total	2	18	28	3	5	1	0	1	2	3	0	3	.179	.258	.321	63	-1	0-0	.923	0	93	232	O7(5/1/1)	0	-0.1
MARION, MARTY	Martin Whiteford "Slats","The Octopus"; B12.1.1917 Richburg SC; BR/TR/6´2˝/(167–170); d4.16; M6/C2; b–Red; [DL 1951 StL N 76]																								
1940	StL N	125	435	44	121	18	1	3	46	21	0	34	.278	.311	.345	76	-14	9	.949	-8	95	101	S125	—	-1.4
1941	StL N	**155**	547	50	138	22	3	3	58	42	2	48	.252	.308	.320	72	-20	8	.954	2	101	103	S155	0	-0.7
1942	†StL N	147	485	66	134	**38**	5	0	54	48	1	50	.276	.343	.375	102	3	8	.960	6	99	113	S147	0	2.1
1943	†StL N★	129	418	38	117	15	3	1	52	32	2	37	.280	.334	.337	90	-5	1	.970	16	103	**138**	S128	0	2.2
1944	†StL N★	144	506	50	135	26	2	6	63	43	0	50	.267	.324	.362	91	-6	1	**.972**	3	98	**126**	S144	0	0.9
1945	StL N✱	123	430	63	119	27	5	1	59	39	2	39	.277	.340	.370	95	-3	2	.967	-6	97	**114**	S122	0	0.1
1946	†StL N★	146	498	51	116	29	4	3	46	59	3	53	.233	.318	.325	79	-12	1	.973	**18**	**104**	**125**	S145	0	1.5
1947	StL N★	149	540	57	147	19	6	4	74	49	1	58	.272	.334	.352	79	-16	3	**.981**	16	99	**123**	S141	0	0.8
1948	StL N✱	144	567	70	143	26	4	4	43	37	0	54	.252	.298	.333	67	-27	1	**.974**	10	103	106	S142	0	-0.8
1949	StL N☆	134	515	61	140	31	2	5	70	37	2	42	.272	.323	.369	81	-13	0	.976	12	106	99	S134	0	0.7
1950	StL N★	106	372	36	92	10	2	4	40	44	0	55	.247	.327	.317	67	-17	1	.978	2	100	112	S101	0	-0.9
1952	StL A	67	186	16	46	11	0	2	19	19	1	17	.247	.320	.339	81	-4	0-2	.980	-6	89	118	S63,M	0	-0.8
1953	StL A	3	7	0	0	0	0	0	0	0	0	0	.000	.000	.000	-98	-2	0-0	1.000	-1	0	0	3b2,M	0	-0.3
Total	13	1572	5506	602	1448	272	37	36	624	470	14	537	.263	.323	.345	81	-136	35-2	.969	65	100	115	S1547,3b2	76	3.4
MARIS, ROGER	Roger Eugene (b Roger Eugene Maras); B9.10.1934 Hibbing MN; D12.14.1985 Houston TX; BL/TR/6´0˝/(185–204); d4.16																								
1957	Cle A	116	358	61	84	9	5	14	51	60-5	1	79	.235	.344	.405	106	3	8-4	.975	7	111	148	O112(26/87/8)	0	0.5
1958	Cle A	51	182	26	41	5	1	9	27	17-2	0	33	.225	.287	.412	94	-2	4-2	.967	4	114	190	O47(0/27/23)	0	0.0
	KC A	99	401	61	99	14	3	19	53	28-1	2	52	.247	.298	.439	99	-3	0-0	.975	-3	91	108	O99(0/21/90)	0	-1.0
	Year	150	583	87	140	19	4	28	80	45-3	2	85	.240	.294	.431	97	-5	4-2	.972	1	98	133	O146(0/48/113)	0	-1.0
1959	KC A★	122	433	69	118	21	7	16	72	58-5	3	53	.273	.359	.464	123	14	2-1	.975	4	112	110	O117(0/6/113)	31	1.4
1960	†NY A★	136	499	98	141	18	7	39	**112**	70-4	3	65	.283	.371	**.581**	164	42	2-2	.985	-0	106	71	O131(0/7/128)	0	3.7
1961	†NY A★	161	590	**132**	159	16	4	**61**	**142**	94-0	7	67	.269	.372	.620	170	57	0-0	.968	-14	82	75	O160(0/11/156)	0	3.1
1962	†NY A★	157	590	92	151	34	1	33	100	87-11	6	78	.256	.356	.485	128	25	1-0	.991	-6	98	47	O154(0/64/103)	0	1.1
1963	†NY A	90	312	53	84	14	1	23	53	35-3	2	40	.269	.346	.542	146	19	1-0	.988	3	107	114	O86(0/1/86)	0	1.7

YEAR	TM LG	G	AB	R	H	2B	3B	HR	RBI	BB-IB	HP	SO	AVG	OBP	SLG	AOPS	ABR	SB-CS	FA	FR	RNG	THR	GAMES AT POSITION	DL	BFW
1964	†NY A	141	513	86	144	12	2	26	71	62-1	6	78	.281	.364	.464	127	19	3-0	.996	-6	94	68	O137(0/32/105)	0	0.6
1965	NY A	46	155	22	37	7	0	8	27	29-1	0	29	.239	.357	.439	126	6	0-0	.971	-3	90	38	O43R	0	0.0
1966	NY A	119	348	37	81	9	2	13	43	36-3	3	60	.233	.307	.382	101	0	0-0	.993	-7	82	60	O95(0/1/94)	0	-1.4
1967	†StL N	125	410	64	107	18	7	9	55	52-3	4	61	.261	.346	.405	117	10	0-0	.991	2	111	63	O118(0/2/118)	0	0.5
1968	†StL N	100	310	25	79	18	2	5	45	24-3	1	38	.255	.307	.374	106	2	0-0	.983	3	120	62	O84R	0	0.1
Total	12	1463	5101	826	1325	195	42	275	851	652-42	38	733	.260	.345	.476	128	192	21-9	.982	-17	100	84	O1383(26/259/1151)	31	10.3
Markakis, Nick	Nicholas William; B11.17.1983 Woodstock GA; BL/TL/6´2˝/195; [BalA03 1/7]; d4.3; Col Young Harris (GA) JC																								
2006	Bal A	147	491	72	143	25	2	16	62	43-3	3	72	.291	.351	.448	108	6	2-0	.994	8	**116**	95	O145(26/9/127)	0	0.8
Markland, Gene	Cleneth Eugene "Mousey"; B12.26.1919 Detroit MI; D6.15.1999 Barefoot Bay FL; BR/TR/5´10˝/160; d4.25																								
1950	Phi A	5	8	2	1	0	0	0	0	3	0	0	.125	.364	.125	30	-1	0-0	1.000	-0	92	31	2b5	0	-0.1
Marnie, Harry	Harry Sylvester; B7.6.1918 Philadelphia PA; D1.7.2002 Philadelphia PA; BR/TR/6´1˝/178; d9.15; Mil 1943–45																								
1940	Phi N	11	34	4	6	0	0	0	4	4	0	2	.176	.263	.176	24	-3	0	.984	4	132	123	2b11	—	0.1
1941	Phi N	61	158	12	38	3	3	0	11	13	0	25	.241	.298	.297	71	-7	0	.990	2	93	91	2b39,S16,3b3	0	-0.2
1942	Phi N	24	30	3	5	0	0	0	0	1	0	2	.167	.194	.167	6	-4	1	.971	5	155	175	2b11,S7/3	0	0.1
Total	3	96	222	19	49	3	3	0	15	18	0	29	.221	.279	.261	55	-14	1	.987	10	107	105	2b61,S23,3b4	0	0.0
Marolewski, Fred	Fred Daniel "Fritz"; B10.6.1928 Chicago IL; BR/TR/6´2.5˝/205; d9.19																								
1953	StL N	1	0	0	0	0	0	0	0	0	0	0	ø	ø	ø	ø	0	0-0	ø	0	0	0	/1	0	0.0
Marquardt, Ollie	Albert Ludwig; B9.22.1902 Toledo OH; D2.7.1968 Port Clinton OH; BR/TR/5´9˝/156; d4.14																								
1931	Bos A	17	39	4	7	1	0	0	2	3	0	4	.179	.238	.205	18	-5	0-1	.946	-2	105	66	2b13/S3	—	-0.6
Marquez, Gonzalo	Gonzalo Enrique (Moya); B3.31.1946 Carupano, Sucre, Venez.; D12.20.1984 Valencia, Carabobo, Venez.; BL/TL/5´11˝/180; d8.11																								
1972	†Oak A	23	21	2	8	0	0	0	4	3-0	1	4	.381	.462	.381	166	2	1-1	.929	-0	119	90	1b2	0	0.2
1973	Oak A	23	25	1	6	1	0	0	2	0-0	0	4	.240	.240	.280	48	-2	0-0	ø	-0	0	0	2b2/1rfD	0	-0.2
	Chi N	19	58	5	13	2	0	1	4	3-1	1	4	.224	.270	.310	57	-3	0-0	.994	2	135	103	1b18	0	-0.3
1974	Chi N	11	11	1	0	0	0	0	0	1-1	0	2	.000	.083	.000	-72	-3	0-0	1.000	0	0	0	/1	0	-0.3
Total	3	76	115	9	27	3	0	1	10	7-2	2	14	.235	.286	.287	62	-6	1-1	.989	2	132	101	1b22,2b2/Drf	0	-0.6
Marquez, Luis	Luis Angel (Sanchez) "Canena"; B10.28.1925 Aguadilla, PR; D3.1.1988 Aguadilla, PR; BR/TR/5´10.5˝/(174–190); d4.18; Negro Lg 1945–48																								
1951	Bos N	68	122	19	24	5	1	0	11	10	3	20	.197	.274	.254	46	-9	4-4	1.000	3	123	67	O43(21/23/3)	0	-0.8
1954	Chi N	17	12	2	1	0	0	0	0	2	0	4	.083	.214	.083	-19	-2	3-0	1.000	1	140	0	O14(4/10/0)	0	-0.1
	Pit N	14	9	3	1	0	0	0	0	4	0	0	.111	.385	.111	37	-1	0-0	1.000	0	136	0	O4(1/1/2)	0	0.0
	Year	31	21	5	2	0	0	0	0	6	0	4	.095	.296	.095	7	-3	3-0	1.000	1	139	0	O18(5/11/2)	0	-0.1
Total	2	99	143	24	26	5	1	0	11	16	3	24	.182	.278	.231	40	-12	7-4	1.000	4	125	57	O61(26/34/5)	0	-0.9
Marquis, Bob	Robert Rudolph; B12.23.1924 Oklahoma City OK; BL/TL/6´1˝/170; d4.17																								
1953	Cin N	40	44	9	12	1	1	2	3	4	0	11	.273	.333	.477	107	0	0-0	.905	-0	116	0	O10(2/8/0)	0	0.0
Marquis, Roger	Roger Julian "Noonie"; B4.5.1937 Holyoke MA; D7.19.2004 Holyoke MA; BL/TL/6´0˝/190; d9.25																								
1955	Bal A	1	1	0	0	0	0	0	0	0-0	0	0	.000	.000	.000	-99	0	0-0	ø	-0	0	0	/rf	0	0.0
Marr, Lefty	Charles W.; B9.19.1862 Cincinnati OH; D1.11.1912 New Britain CT; BL/TR/5´9˝/180; d10.3																								
1886	Cin AA	8	29	2	8	1	1	0	2	1	1	—	.276	.323	.379	116	0	1	.696	-2	61	0	O8C	—	-0.2
1889	Col AA	**139**	546	110	167	26	**15**	1	75	87	6	32	.306	.407	.414	141	35	29	.856	7	106	101	3b66,O47(0/1/47),S26,1b2/C	—	3.6
1890	Cin N	130	527	91	157	17	12	1	73	46	6	29	.298	.361	.381	117	11	44	.930	-7	115	152	O64R,3b63,S3	—	0.4
1891	Cin N	72	286	32	74	9	7	0	32	25	2	15	.259	.323	.339	92	-3	16	.835	-9	58	0	O72R	—	-1.1
	Cin AA	14	57	9	11	1	0	0	4	7	0	4	.193	.281	.211	38	-5	2	.923	-1	42	0	O14R	—	-0.5
Total	4	363	1445	244	417	54	35	2	186	166	15	80	.289	.368	.379	118	38	92	.853	-11	80	57	O205(0/9/197),3b129,S29,1b2/C	—	2.2
Marrero, Eli	Elieser; B11.17.1973 Havana, Cuba; BR/TR/6´1˝/180; [StLN93 3/88]; d9.3; OF(125/56/117)																								
1997	StL N	17	45	4	11	2	0	2	7	2-1	0	13	.244	.271	.422	80	-2	4-0	.969	1	122	173	C17	0	0.1
1998	StL N	83	254	28	62	18	1	4	20	28-5	0	42	.244	.318	.370	81	-7	6-2	.991	0	133	95	C73,1b2	13	-0.1
1999	StL N	114	317	32	61	13	1	6	34	18-4	1	56	.192	.236	.297	34	-34	11-2	.987	0	143	119	C96,1b20	0	-2.6
2000	†StL N	53	102	21	23	3	1	5	17	9-0	3	16	.225	.302	.422	80	-4	5-0	1.000	5	277	118	C38,1b7	60	0.4
2001	†StL N	86	203	37	54	11	3	6	23	15-2	0	36	.266	.312	.438	90	-4	6-3	.984	5	129	66	C65,O15(8/0/7),1b6	0	0.4
2002	†StL N	131	397	63	104	19	1	18	66	40-11	0	72	.262	.327	.451	102	0	14-2	.985	6	104	166	O106(39/36/46),C44,1b4	0	0.7
2003	StL N	41	107	10	24	4	2	2	20	7-0	0	18	.224	.267	.355	62	-6	0-1	.980	3	114	73	O31(10/6/21),C6,1b2	112	-0.5
2004	†Atl N	90	250	37	80	18	1	10	40	23-1	1	50	.320	.374	.520	128	11	4-1	.992	2	101	161	O73(47/4/25)	44	1.1
2005	KC A	32	88	11	14	4	0	4	9	7-0	1	18	.159	.222	.341	51	-7	1-0	.967	-1	90	263	O20(8/5/7),1b9,D2	0	-0.8
	Bal A	22	50	8	11	3	2	3	10	4-0	0	20	.220	.268	.540	111	0	0-0	.966	-1	100	0	O16(7/3/6)	68	-0.1
	Year	54	138	19	25	7	2	7	19	11-0	1	38	.181	.239	.413	73	-6	1-0	.966	-2	95	133	O36(15/8/13),1b9,D2	0	-0.9
2006	Col N	30	60	7	13	3	0	4	10	11-1	1	16	.217	.347	.467	97	0	3-0	1.000	3	189	132	1b7,O6(3/0/3),C5	0	0.3
	NY N	25	33	4	6	1	0	2	5	4-0	1	15	.182	.282	.394	74	-1	2-0	.909	-0	86	0	O7(3/2/2),C2/13	0	-0.2
	Year	55	93	11	19	4	0	6	15	15-1	2	31	.204	.324	.441	91	-1	5-0	.923	3	106	175	O13(6/2/5),1b8,C7/3	0	0.1
Total	10	724	1906	262	463	99	12	66	261	168-25	8	372	.243	.303	.411	83	-54	56-11	.987	23	141	101	C346,O274L,1b58,D2/3	297	-1.3
Marrero, Oreste	Oreste Vilato (Vazquez); B10.31.1969 Bayamon, PR; BL/TL/6´0˝/195; d8.12																								
1993	Mon N	32	81	10	17	5	1	1	4	14-0	0	16	.210	.326	.333	74	-3	1-3	.991	-1	93	121	1b32	0	-0.6
1996	LA N	10	8	2	3	1	0	0	1	1-0	0	3	.375	.444	.500	158	1	0-0	1.000	0	0	0	/1	0	0.1
Total	2	42	89	12	20	6	1	1	5	15-0	0	19	.225	.337	.348	81	-2	1-3	.991	-1	93	120	1b33	0	-0.5
Marriott, William	William Earl; B4.18.1893 Pratt KS; D8.11.1969 Berkeley CA; BL/TR/6´0˝/170; d9.6; Mil 1918																								
1917	Chi N	3	6	0	0	0	0	0	0	0	0	1	.000	.000	.000	-93	-1	0	.667	-0	77	0	/lf	—	-0.2
1920	Chi N	14	43	7	12	4	2	0	5	6	0	5	.279	.367	.465	135	2	1-1	.892	-3	94	31	2b14	—	-0.1
1921	Chi N	30	38	3	12	1	1	0	7	4	0	1	.316	.381	.395	105	0	0-1	.826	-1	81	53	2b6/S3lf	—	-0.1
1925	Bos N	103	370	37	99	9	1	1	40	28	2	26	.268	.322	.305	67	-18	3-8	.928	-3	103	74	3b89/lf	—	-1.7
1926	Bro N	109	360	39	96	13	9	3	42	17	2	20	.267	.303	.378	84	-10	12	.927	-6	97	37	3b104	—	-1.0
1927	Bro N	6	9	0	1	0	1	0	1	2	0	2	.111	.273	.333	61	-1	0	.889	0	105	0	3b2	—	0.0
Total	6	265	826	86	220	27	14	4	95	57	4	55	.266	.317	.347	78	-28	16-10	.925	-14	100	57	3b196,2b20,O3L/S	—	-3.1
Marsans, Armando	Armando; B10.3.1887 Matanzas, Cuba; D9.3.1960 Havana, Cuba; BR/TR/5´10˝/157; d7.4; OF(51/459/71)																								
1911	Cin N	58	138	17	36	2	2	0	11	15	3	11	.261	.346	.304	86	-2	11	.968	-3	99	48	O34(5/16/13)/13	—	-0.7
1912	Cin N	110	416	59	132	19	7	1	38	20	3	17	.317	.353	.404	110	4	35	.975	-1	106	77	O98(7/82/13),1b6	—	-0.3
1913	Cin N	118	435	49	129	7	6	0	38	17	3	25	.297	.327	.340	91	-6	37-11	.963	-2	98	106	O94(3/56/37),1b22,3b2/S	—	-1.0
1914	Cin N	36	124	16	37	3	0	0	22	14	1	6	.298	.374	.323	105	1	13	.916	-1	100	85	O36L	—	-0.1
	StL F	9	40	5	14	0	2	0	2	3	0	0	.350	.395	.450	123	1	4	.927	-1	88	244	2b7,S2	—	0.0
1915	StL F	36	124	16	22	3	0	0	6	14	0	5	.177	.261	.202	29	-13	5	.975	2	94	164	O35C	—	-1.5
1916	StL A	151	528	51	134	12	1	1	60	57	6	41	.254	.333	.286	91	-5	46-26	.977	-2	95	111	O150C	—	-1.8
1917	StL A	75	257	31	59	12	0	0	20	20	0	6	.230	.285	.276	74	-8	11	.963	-5	100	33	O67C,3b5/2	—	-1.9
	NY A	25	88	10	20	4	0	0	15	8	0	3	.227	.292	.273	72	-3	6	.974	2	113	107	O25C	—	-0.3
	Year	100	345	41	79	16	0	0	35	28	0	9	.229	.287	.275	73	-11	17	.967	-3	104	55	O92C,3b5/2	—	-2.2
1918	NY A	37	123	13	29	5	1	0	9	5	0	3	.236	.266	.293	67	-5	3	.943	-4	91	45	O36(0/28/8)	—	-1.3
Total	8	655	2273	267	612	67	19	2	221	173	16	117	.269	.325	.318	88	-36	171-37	.967	-13	99	90	O575C,1b29,2b8,3b8,S3	—	-8.9
Marsh, Fred	Fred Francis; B1.5.1924 Valley Falls KS; D10.26.2006 Corry PA; BR/TR/5´10˝/180; d4.19																								
1949	Cle A	1	0	0	0	0	0	0	0	0	0	0	ø	ø	ø	ø	0	0-0	ø	0	—	—	/R	0	0.0
1951	StL A	130	445	44	108	21	4	4	43	36	0	56	.243	.299	.335	69	-20	4-4	.928	3	**103**	**113**	3b117,S3,2b2	0	-1.8
1952	StL A	11	24	3	5	1	0	0	1	5	0	4	.208	.345	.250	65	-1	0-1	.963	0	109	86	2b9,S3	0	0.0
	Was A	9	24	1	1	0	0	0	1	1	0	4	.042	.080	.042	-68	-6	0-0	1.000	-2	59	103	2b5,O2L	0	-0.8
	StL A	76	223	25	64	8	1	2	26	22	0	29	.287	.351	.359	95	-1	3-2	.945	-10	97	216	S57,3b21	0	-0.9
	Year	96	271	29	70	9	1	2	28	28	0	37	.258	.328	.321	79	-7	3-3	.945	-12	89	109	S60,3b21,2b14,O2L	0	-1.7
1953	Chi A	67	95	22	19	1	0	2	2	13	1	26	.200	.303	.274	55	-6	0-3	.940	3	101	158	3b32,S17,1b5,2b2	0	-0.3

YEAR	TM LG	G	AB	R	H	2B	3B	HR	RBI	BB-IB	HP	SO	AVG	OBP	SLG	AOPS	ABR	SB-CS	FA	FR	RNG	THR	GAMES AT POSITION	DL	BFW
1954	Chi A	62	98	21	30	5	2	0	4	9	0	16	.306	.364	.398	105	1	4-2	.975	10	132	158	3b36,S3,1b2/rf	0	1.1
1955	Bal A	89	303	30	66	7	1	2	19	35-1	1	33	.218	.300	.267	58	-18	1-2	.983	-17	82	89	2b76,3b18,S16	30	-3.0
1956	Bal A	20	24	2	3	0	0	0	0	4-0	0	3	.125	.250	.125	2	-3	1-0	.929	-1	99	115	S8,3b8,2b5	0	-0.4
Total	7	465	1236	148	296	43	8	10	96	125-1	2	171	.239	.310	.311	69	-54	13-14	.928	-13	107	121	3b232,S107,2b99,1b7,O3(2/0/1)	30	-6.1
MARSH, TOM	Thomas Owen; B12.27.1965 Toledo OH; BR/TR/6´2˝/(180–190); [PhiN88 16/406]; d6.5; Col Toledo																								
1992	Phi N	42	125	7	25	3	2	2	16	2-0	1	23	.200	.215	.304	47	-10	0-1	.971	-1	105	0	O35(25/0/12)	31	-1.3
1994	Phi N	8	18	3	5	1	1	0	3	1-0	0	1	.278	.316	.444	94	0	0-0	.889	-0	95	0	O7(3/0/4)	0	-0.1
1995	Phi N	43	109	13	32	3	1	3	15	4-0	0	25	.294	.316	.422	93	-2	0-1	.939	0	102	141	O29(24/4/1)	16	-0.3
Total	3	93	252	23	62	7	4	5	34	7-0	1	49	.246	.266	.365	71	-12	0-2	.952	-1	103	56	O71(52/4/17)	47	-1.7
MARSHALL, CHARLIE	Charles Anthony (b Charles Anthony Marchlewicz); B8.28.1919 Wilmington DE; BR/TR/5´10.5˝/178; d6.14																								
1941	StL N	1	0	0	0	0	0	0	0	0	0	0	ø	ø	ø	ø	0	0	1.000	-0	*0*	*0*	/C	0	0.0
MARSHALL, DAVE	David Lewis; B1.14.1943 Artesia CA; BL/TR/6´1˝/(190–205); d9.7; Col Long Beach (CA) City																								
1967	SF N	1	0	0	0	0	0	0	0	0-0	0	0	ø	ø	ø	ø	0	0-0	ø	0	—	—	/R	0	0.0
1968	SF N	76	174	17	46	5	1	1	16	20-2	1	37	.264	.338	.322	101	1	2-1	.924	-4	78	93	O50(24/0/28)	0	-0.6
1969	SF N	110	267	32	62	7	1	2	33	40-3	5	68	.232	.340	.288	79	-6	1-8	.956	-5	85	70	O87(79/0/17)	0	-1.8
1970	NY N	92	189	21	46	10	1	6	29	17-0	0	43	.243	.304	.402	87	-4	4-1	.973	-0	102	76	O43(12/0/33)	0	-0.6
1971	NY N	100	214	28	51	9	1	3	21	26-3	2	54	.238	.322	.332	87	-3	3-1	.989	-1	100	59	O64(25/0/39)	0	-0.7
1972	NY N	72	156	21	39	5	0	4	11	22-1	1	28	.250	.346	.359	102	1	3-3	.972	-2	107	0	O42(1/4/38)	0	-0.3
1973	SD N	39	49	4	14	5	0	0	4	8-0	1	9	.286	.390	.388	128	3	0-1	1.000	-1	100	0	O8R	0	0.1
Total	7	490	1049	123	258	41	4	16	114	133-9	10	239	.246	.333	.338	91	-8	13-15	.966	-11	93	60	O294(141/4/163)	0	-3.9
MARSHALL, DOC	Edward Harbert "Eddie"; B6.4.1906 New Albany MS; D9.1.1999 Lake San Marcos CA; BR/TR/5´11˝/150; d9.28; Col U. of Mississippi																								
1929	NY N	5	15	6	6	2	0	0	2	1	0	0	.400	.438	.533	140	1	0	1.000	-1	94	0	2b5	—	0.0
1930	NY N	78	223	33	69	5	3	0	21	13	1	9	.309	.350	.359	73	-10	0	.947	-1	96	92	S45,2b17,3b5	—	-0.6
1931	NY N	68	194	15	39	6	2	0	10	8	0	8	.201	.233	.253	31	-20	1	.956	2	103	102	2b47,S11,3b3	—	-1.4
1932	NY N	68	226	18	56	8	1	0	28	6	1	11	.248	.270	.292	52	-16	1	.922	-3	98	100	S63	—	-1.4
Total	4	219	658	72	170	21	6	0	61	28	2	28	.258	.291	.309	56	-45	2	.931	-3	96	98	S119,2b69,3b8	—	-3.4
MARSHALL, JOE	Joseph Hanley "Home Run Joe"; B2.19.1876 Audubon MN; D9.11.1931 Santa Monica CA; BR/TR/5´8˝/170; d9.7																								
1903	Pit N	10	23	2	6	1	2	0	2	0	0	—	.261	.261	.478	106	0	0	1.000	-2	71	115	S3,O3(2/1/0)/2	—	-0.2
1906	StL N	33	95	2	15	1	2	0	7	6	1	—	.158	.216	.211	34	-8	0	.903	1	246	0	O23R,1b4	—	-0.9
Total	2	43	118	4	21	2	4	0	9	6	1	—	.178	.224	.263	50	-8	0	.903	-1	242	0	O26(2/1/23),1b4,S3/2	—	-1.1
MARSHALL, KEITH	Keith Alan; B7.2.1951 San Francisco CA; BR/TR/6´2˝/173; [KCA69 5/117]; d4.7																								
1973	KC A	8	9	0	2	1	0	0	3	1-0	0	4	.222	.300	.333	73	0	0-0	1.000	-0	94	0	O8(5/2/2)	0	-0.1
MARSHALL, MIKE	Michael Allen; B1.12.1960 Libertyville IL; BR/TR/6´5˝/(215–220); [LAN78 6/151]; d9.7																								
1981	†LA N	14	25	2	5	3	0	0	1	1-0	1	4	.200	.259	.320	66	-1	0-0	1.000	-1	0	200	1b3,3b3,O2(1/0/1)	0	-0.3
1982	LA N	49	95	10	23	3	0	5	9	13-1	1	23	.242	.336	.432	118	2	2-0	1.000	-2	79	0	O19(3/0/16),1b13	0	-0.1
1983	†LA N	140	465	47	132	17	1	17	65	43-4	5	127	.284	.347	.434	116	10	7-3	.976	-6	92	46	O109R,1b33	0	-0.2
1984	LA N☆	134	495	68	127	27	0	21	65	40-6	3	93	.257	.315	.438	110	6	4-3	.981	-1	95	102	O118(116/0/4),1b15	21	-0.1
1985	†LA N	135	518	72	152	27	2	28	95	37-6	3	137	.293	.342	.515	140	26	3-10	.991	-5	86	106	O125(1/0/124),1b7	28	1.1
1986	LA N	103	330	47	77	11	0	19	53	27-3	4	90	.233	.298	.439	108	2	4-4	.963	-3	89	112	O97(1/0/97)	15	-0.7
1987	LA N	104	402	45	118	19	0	16	72	18-2	4	79	.294	.327	.460	109	4	0-5	.987	-9	80	60	O102R	38	-1.2
1988	†LA N	144	542	63	150	27	2	20	82	24-7	7	93	.277	.314	.445	119	11	4-1	.966	-2	86	98	O90R,1b53	0	0.3
1989	LA N	105	377	41	98	21	1	11	42	33-4	5	78	.260	.325	.408	111	5	2-5	.978	-5	95	38	O102R	31	-0.5
1990	NY N	53	163	24	39	8	1	6	27	7-0	3	40	.239	.278	.411	88	-3	0-2	.993	-0	88	77	1b42/rf	15	-0.7
	†Bos A	30	112	10	32	6	1	4	12	4-0	1	26	.286	.316	.464	110	1	0-0	1.000	0	157	95	D14,1b8,O8R	0	0.0
1991	Bos A	22	62	4	18	4	0	1	7	0-0	0	19	.290	.290	.403	85	-1	0-0	.979	-2	0	114	1b5,O4(1/0/3),D7	16	-0.4
	Cal A	2	7	0	0	0	0	0	0	0-0	0	1	.000	.000	.000	-99	-2	0-0	1.000	0	157	239	/1D	0	-0.2
	Year	24	69	4	18	4	0	1	7	0-0	0	20	.261	.261	.362	67	-3	0-0	.984	-2	31	138	D8,1b6,O4(1/0/3)	0	-0.6
Total	11	1035	3593	433	971	173	8	148	530	247-33	37	810	.270	.321	.446	114	60	26-33	.978	-35	89	78	O777(123/0/657),1b180,D22,3b3	164	-3.0
MARSHALL, MAX	Milo May; B9.18.1913 Randolph IA; D9.16.1993 Salem OR; BL/TR/6´1˝/180; d5.10; Mil 1944–45																								
1942	Cin N	131	530	49	135	17	6	7	43	34	1	38	.255	.301	.349	90	-9	4	.976	-11	91	27	O129(43/11/79)	0	-3.0
1943	Cin N	132	508	55	120	11	8	4	39	34	2	52	.236	.287	.313	74	-19	8	.981	-5	92	89	O129R	0	-3.5
1944	Cin N	66	229	36	56	13	2	4	23	21	0	10	.245	.308	.371	94	-2	3	.965	1	104	89	O59(1/0/58)	0	-0.6
Total	3	329	1267	140	311	41	16	15	105	89	3	100	.245	.297	.339	84	-30	15	.975	-16	94	63	O317(44/11/266)	0	-7.1
MARSHALL, JIM	Rufus James; B5.25.1931 Danville IL; BL/TL/6´1˝/190; d4.15; M4/C1; Col Compton (CA) CC																								
1958	Bal A	85	191	17	41	4	3	5	19	18-1	0	30	.215	.280	.346	76	-7	3-2	1.000	-2	77	101	1b52,O8(3/0/5)	0	-1.2
	Chi N	26	81	12	22	2	0	5	11	12-0	1	13	.272	.372	.481	126	3	1-0	.992	-3	84	94	1b15,O11R	0	0.0
1959	Chi N	108	294	39	74	10	1	11	40	33-1	0	39	.252	.324	.405	95	-2	0-1	.997	2	114	105	1b72,O8(7/0/3)	0	-0.5
1960	SF N	75	118	19	28	2	2	2	13	17-1	0	24	.237	.331	.339	90	-2	0-1	.968	-3	68	86	1b28,O6L	0	-0.7
1961	SF N	44	36	5	8	0	0	1	7	3-0	0	8	.222	.275	.306	58	-2	0-0	1.000	0	133	117	1b4,O2(1/0/1)	0	-0.2
1962	NY N	17	32	6	11	1	0	3	4	3-0	0	6	.344	.400	.656	175	3	0-0	1.000	-0	123	136	1b5/rf	0	0.3
	Pit N	55	100	13	22	5	1	2	12	15-0	0	19	.220	.319	.350	80	-3	1-0	1.000	1	104	116	1b26	0	-0.3
	Year	72	132	19	33	6	1	5	16	18-0	0	25	.250	.338	.424	103	1	1-0	1.000	1	107	120	1b31/rf	0	0.0
Total	5	410	852	111	206	24	7	29	106	101-3	1	139	.242	.320	.388	93	-10	5-4	.994	-5	96	103	1b202,O36(17/0/21)	0	-2.6
MARSHALL, WILLARD	Willard Warren; B2.8.1921 Richmond VA; D11.5.2000 Norwood NJ; BL/TR/6´1˝/(190–205); d4.14; Mil 1943–45; Col Wake Forest																								
1942	NY N★	116	401	41	103	9	2	11	59	26	3	20	.257	.307	.372	98	-3	1	.975	1	94	**157**	O107(67/46/1)	0	-0.7
1946	NY N	131	510	63	144	18	3	13	48	33	1	29	.282	.327	.406	107	2	3	.978	-4	89	125	O125(51/59/15)	0	-0.9
1947	NY N★	**155**	587	102	171	19	6	36	107	67	2	30	.291	.366	.528	134	26	3	.972	9	108	142	O155R	0	3.0
1948	NY N	143	537	72	146	21	8	14	86	64	1	34	.272	.350	.419	107	5	2	.983	1	93	148	O142R	0	0.1
1949	NY N★	141	499	81	153	19	3	12	70	78	1	20	.307	.401	.429	123	19	4	.974	2	105	100	O138(2/0/136)	0	1.7
1950	Bos N	105	298	38	70	10	2	5	40	36	1	5	.235	.319	.332	77	-10	1	.958	4	101	191	O85(14/9/64)	0	-0.9
1951	Bos N	136	469	65	132	24	7	11	62	48	2	18	.281	.351	.433	118	11	0-3	**1.000**	-3	93	99	O136R	0	0.4
1952	Bos N	21	66	5	15	4	1	2	11	4	0	4	.227	.271	.409	89	-1	0-0	.938	0	82	186	O16R	0	-0.2
	Cin N	107	397	52	106	23	1	8	46	37	2	21	.267	.333	.390	100	0	0-1	.985	2	97	138	O105R	0	-0.2
	Year	128	463	57	121	27	2	10	57	41	2	25	.261	.324	.393	99	-1	0-1	.979	2	95	145	O121R	0	-0.4
1953	Cin N	122	357	51	95	14	6	17	62	41	0	28	.266	.342	.482	111	5	0-0	.995	5	102	157	O95R	0	0.6
1954	Chi A	47	71	7	18	2	0	1	7	11	0	9	.254	.349	.324	84	-1	0-0	.960	-1	84	99	O29(7/0/22)	0	-0.3
1955	Chi A	22	41	6	7	0	0	0	6	13-1	0	1	.171	.364	.171	48	-2	0-0	.957	-1	105	0	O12(4/0/8)	9	-0.3
Total	11	1246	4233	583	1160	163	39	130	604	458-1	13	219	.274	.347	.423	109	51	14-4	.979	15	98	135	O1145(145/114/895)	9	2.3
MARSHALL, BILL	William Henry; B2.14.1911 Dorchester MA; D5.5.1977 Sacramento CA; BR/TR/5´8.5˝/156; d6.20																								
1931	Bos A	1	0	1	0	0	0	0	0	0	0	0	ø	ø	ø	ø	0	0-0	ø	0	—	—	/R	—	0.0
1934	Cin N	6	8	0	1	0	0	0	0	0	0	2	.125	.125	.125	-34	-2	0	.875	0	133	0	2b2	—	-0.1
Total	2	7	8	1	1	0	0	0	0	0	0	2	.125	.125	.125	-34	-2	0-0	.875	0	133	0	2b2	—	-0.1
MARSHALL, DOC	William Riddle; B9.22.1875 Butler PA; D12.11.1959 Clinton IL; BR/TR/6´0˝/185; d4.15; Col Grove City																								
1904	Phi N	8	20	1	2	0	0	0	1	0	0	—	.100	.100	.100	-40	-3	0	.944	1	*87*	*185*	C7	—	-0.2
	NY N	1	0	0	0	0	0	0	0	0	0	—	ø	ø	ø	ø	0	0	ø	-0	*0*	*0*	/C	—	0.0
	Bos N	13	43	3	9	0	1	0	2	2	0	—	.209	.244	.256	56	-2	2	.955	0	*87*	*126*	C10/lf	—	-0.2
	NY N	10	17	3	6	1	0	0	2	1	0	—	.353	.389	.412	141	1	0	.955	1	*0*	*0*	C2,O2(1/0/1)/2	—	0.2
	Year	32	80	7	17	1	1	0	5	3	0	—	.213	.241	.250	52	-5	2	.952	1	*98*	*145*	C20,O3(2/0/1)/2	—	-0.2
1906	NY N	38	102	8	17	3	2	0	7	7	2	—	.167	.234	.235	45	-7	7	1.000	1	169	0	O16(1/3/13),C13,1b2	—	-0.6
	StL N	39	123	6	34	4	1	0	10	6	1	—	.276	.315	.325	104	0	1	.961	1	*87*	*108*	C38	—	0.5
	Year	77	225	14	51	7	3	0	17	13	3	—	.227	.278	.284	76	-7	8	.969	2	*90*	*108*	C51,O16(1/3/13),1b2	—	-0.1
1907	StL N	84	268	19	54	8	2	2	18	12	4	—	.201	.246	.269	64	-12	2	.952	-3	*81*	***123***	C83	—	-0.8
1908	StL N	6	14	0	1	0	0	0	1	0	0	—	.071	.071	.071	-57	-2	0	1.000	1	*74*	*92*	C6	—	-0.2
	Chi N	12	20	4	6	0	1	0	3	0	0	—	.300	.300	.400	118	0	0	1.000	2	*120*	*197*	C4,O3(0/1/2)	—	0.2

YEAR	TM LG	G	AB	R	H	2B	3B	HR	RBI	BB-IB	HP	SO	AVG	OBP	SLG	AOPS	ABR	SB-CS	FA	FR	RNG	THR	GAMES AT POSITION	DL	BFW
	Year	18	34	4	7	0	1	0	4	0	0	—	.206	.206	.265	49	-2	0	1.000	3	*83*	*113*	C10,O3(0/1/2)	—	0.0
1909	Bro N	50	149	7	30	7	1	0	10	6	0	—	.201	.232	.262	55	-8	3	.968	-4	*88*	*96*	C49/rf	—	-0.9
Total	5	261	756	51	159	23	8	2	54	34	7	—	.210	.251	.270	64	-33	15	.961	-1	*86*	*115*	C213,O23(3/4/17),1b2/2	—	-2.0

MARTE, ANDY Andy Manuel; B10.21.1983 Villa Tapia, D.R.; BR/TR/6´1˝/(185–190); d6.7

YEAR	TM LG	G	AB	R	H	2B	3B	HR	RBI	BB-IB	HP	SO	AVG	OBP	SLG	AOPS	ABR	SB-CS	FA	FR	RNG	THR	GAMES AT POSITION	DL	BFW
2005	Atl N	24	57	3	8	2	1	0	4	7-0	0	13	.140	.227	.211	18	-7	0-1	.857	-9	48	36	3b17	0	-1.7
2006	Cle A	50	164	20	37	15	1	5	23	13-0	1	38	.226	.287	.421	83	-4	0-0	.962	6	114	135	3b50	0	0.1
Total	2	74	221	23	45	17	2	5	27	20-0	1	51	.204	.270	.367	66	-11	0-1	.949	-3	99	112	3b67	0	-1.6

MARTEL, DOC Leon Alphonse "Marty"; B6.29.1883 Weymouth MA; D10.11.1947 Washington DC; BR/TR/6´0˝/185; d7.6; Col Georgetown

YEAR	TM LG	G	AB	R	H	2B	3B	HR	RBI	BB-IB	HP	SO	AVG	OBP	SLG	AOPS	ABR	SB-CS	FA	FR	RNG	THR	GAMES AT POSITION	DL	BFW
1909	Phi N	24	41	1	11	3	1	0	7	4	0	—	.268	.333	.390	123	1	0	.974	3	*109*	*130*	C12	—	0.5
1910	Bos N	10	31	0	4	0	0	0	1	2	0	3	.129	.182	.129	-9	-4	0	.980	-0	101	91	1b10	—	-0.5
Total	2	34	72	1	15	3	1	0	8	6	0	3	.208	.269	.278	64	-3	0	.974	2	*109*	*130*	C12,1b10	—	0.0

MARTIN, AL Albert De Groot (aka Albert May in 1872); B8.1847 NY; D3.17.1915 Brooklyn NY; d5.7

YEAR	TM LG	G	AB	R	H	2B	3B	HR	RBI	BB-IB	HP	SO	AVG	OBP	SLG	AOPS	ABR	SB-CS	FA	FR	RNG	THR	GAMES AT POSITION	DL	BFW
1872	Eck NA	4	18	2	5	0	0	0	1	0	—	0	.278	.278	.278	84	0	0-0	.700	-2	69	59	2b4	—	-0.2
1874	Atl NA	7	29	1	4	0	0	0	1	0	—	1	.138	.138	.138	-13	-3	0-0	.646	-3	102	57	2b6/lf	—	-0.5
1875	Atl NA	6	26	1	3	0	0	0	1	0	—	0	.115	.115	.115	-22	-3	0-0	.909	-0	0	0	O6C	—	-0.3
Total	3NA	17	73	4	12	0	0	0	3	0	—	1	.164	.164	.164	9	-6	0-0	.662	-6	89	58	2b10,O7(1/6/0)	—	-1.0

MARTIN, AL Albert Lee; B11.24.1967 West Covina CA; BL/TL/6´2˝/(207–220); [AtlN85 8/198]; d7.28

YEAR	TM LG	G	AB	R	H	2B	3B	HR	RBI	BB-IB	HP	SO	AVG	OBP	SLG	AOPS	ABR	SB-CS	FA	FR	RNG	THR	GAMES AT POSITION	DL	BFW
1992	Pit N	12	12	1	2	0	1	0	2	0-0	0	5	.167	.154	.333	39	-1	0-0	1.000	0	119	0	O7L	0	-0.1
1993	Pit N	143	480	85	135	26	8	18	64	42-5	1	122	.281	.338	.481	117	10	16-9	.975	-6	94	73	O136(81/63/6)	0	0.3
1994	Pit N	82	276	48	79	12	4	9	33	34-3	2	56	.286	.367	.457	112	5	15-6	.979	-1	89	177	O77(67/13/0)	32	0.3
1995	Pit N	124	439	70	124	25	3	13	41	44-6	2	92	.282	.351	.442	105	3	20-11	.977	-0	97	124	O121(95/42/0)	0	0.1
1996	Pit N	155	630	101	189	40	1	18	72	54-2	2	116	.300	.354	.452	108	8	38-12	.965	-16	78	58	O152(142/26/0)	0	-0.8
1997	Pit N	113	423	64	123	24	7	13	59	45-7	3	83	.291	.359	.473	115	9	23-7	.957	-13	63	114	O110L	33	-0.5
1998	Pit N	125	440	57	105	15	2	12	47	32-2	5	91	.239	.296	.364	72	-19	20-3	.985	2	99	89	O114L,D2	0	-1.8
1999	Pit N	143	541	97	150	36	8	24	63	49-5	1	119	.277	.337	.506	109	6	20-3	.952	-13	80	38	O133L	0	-0.8
2000	SD N	93	346	62	106	13	6	11	27	28-5	2	54	.306	.360	.474	116	7	6-8	.950	-7	79	77	O89L	0	-0.4
	†Sea A	42	134	19	31	2	4	4	9	8-0	2	31	.231	.283	.396	71	-7	4-1	.963	3	117	163	O35(20/7/9),D2	0	-0.4
2001	†Sea A	100	283	41	68	15	2	7	42	37-4	2	59	.240	.330	.382	93	-3	9-3	.971	2	109	81	O73(72/1/1),D16	0	-0.3
2003	TB A	100	238	19	60	12	2	3	26	17-4	2	51	.252	.306	.357	76	-8	2-2	1.000	0	112	0	D57,O13(8/0/5)/1	0	-1.2
Total	11	1232	4242	664	1172	220	48	132	485	390-43	24	879	.276	.339	.444	103	10	173-65	.969	-49	87	89	O1060(938/152/21),D77/1	65	-5.6

MARTIN, BILLY Alfred Manuel; B5.16.1928 Berkeley CA; D12.25.1989 Johnson City NY; BR/TR/5´11.5˝/(165–175); d4.18; Mil 1954–55; M16/C4

YEAR	TM LG	G	AB	R	H	2B	3B	HR	RBI	BB-IB	HP	SO	AVG	OBP	SLG	AOPS	ABR	SB-CS	FA	FR	RNG	THR	GAMES AT POSITION	DL	BFW
1950	NY A	34	36	10	9	1	0	1	8	3	0	3	.250	.308	.361	73	-2	0-0	.976	-2	75	82	2b22/3	0	-0.3
1951	†NY A	51	58	10	15	1	2	0	2	4	2	9	.259	.328	.345	85	-1	0-1	.988	9	137	171	2b23,S6,3b2/cf	0	0.8
1952	†NY A	109	363	32	97	13	3	3	33	22	8	31	.267	.323	.344	91	-5	3-6	.984	18	112	**130**	2b107	0	1.8
1953	†NY A	149	587	72	151	24	6	15	75	43	6	56	.257	.314	.395	94	-8	6-7	.985	2	100	**117**	2b146,S18	0	0.4
1955	†NY A	20	70	8	21	2	0	1	9	7-1	0	9	.300	.354	.371	100	0	1-2	.977	2	106	161	2b17,S3	0	0.3
1956	†NY A★	121	458	76	121	24	5	9	49	30-0	3	56	.264	.310	.397	90	-9	7-3	.980	-6	98	**114**	2b105,3b16	0	-0.7
1957	NY A	43	145	12	35	5	2	1	12	3-0	1	14	.241	.257	.324	60	-9	2-1	.947	1	103	105	2b26,3b13	0	-0.6
	KC A	73	265	33	68	9	3	9	27	12-0	3	20	.257	.295	.415	91	-5	7-1	.987	-13	87	80	2b52,3b20,S2	0	-1.4
	Year	116	410	45	103	14	5	10	39	15-0	4	34	.251	.282	.383	80	-13	9-2	.973	-12	92	89	2b78,3b33,S2	0	-2.0
1958	Det A	131	498	56	127	19	1	7	42	16-0	3	62	.255	.279	.339	65	-24	5-3	.958	-13	88	106	S88,3b41	0	-3.1
1959	Cle A	73	242	37	63	7	0	9	24	8-2	3	18	.260	.290	.401	92	-4	0-2	.997	-12	84	85	2b67,3b4	30	-1.3
1960	Cin N	103	317	34	78	17	1	3	16	27-5	0	34	.246	.304	.334	74	-11	0-1	.975	-14	87	96	2b97	0	-1.9
1961	Mil N	6	6	1	0	0	0	0	0	0-0	0	1	.000	.000	.000	-99	-2	0-0	ø	0	—	—	/H	0	-0.2
	Min A	108	374	44	92	15	5	6	36	13-0	3	42	.246	.275	.361	65	-20	3-2	.963	-7	94	95	2b105/S	0	-1.9
Total	11	1021	3419	425	877	137	28	64	333	188-8	32	355	.257	.300	.369	81	-100	34-29	.980	-34	97	108	2b767,S118,3b97/cf	30	-8.1

MARTIN, PHONNEY Alphonse Case; B8.4.1845 New York NY; D5.24.1933 Hollis NY; 5´7˝/148; d4.26; M1; ▲

YEAR	TM LG	G	AB	R	H	2B	3B	HR	RBI	BB-IB	HP	SO	AVG	OBP	SLG	AOPS	ABR	SB-CS	FA	FR	RNG	THR	GAMES AT POSITION	DL	BFW
1872	Tro NA	**25**	119	27	36	2	1	0	14	0	—	1	.303	.303	.336	95	-1	0-0	.780	-2	0	0	O25R,P8	—	-0.1
	Eck NA	18	78	13	15	1	1	0	9	2	—	3	.192	.213	.231	43	-4	3-2	.833	1	98	0	P10,O9R,M	—	0.0
	Year	**43**	197	40	51	3	2	0	23	2	—	4	.259	.266	.294	76	-4	3-2	.776	-1	59	0	O34R,P18	—	-0.1
1873	Mut NA	31	140	12	31	1	0	0	14	0	—	4	.221	.221	.229	34	-11	1-1	.680	-6	0	0	O30R,P6	—	-1.0
Total	2NA	74	337	52	82	4	2	0	37	2	—	8	.243	.248	.267	58	-16	4-3	.747	-7	33	0	O64R,P24	—	-1.1

MARTIN, BABE Boris Michael (b Boris Michael Martinovich); B3.28.1920 Seattle WA; BR/TR/5´11.5˝/194; d9.25

YEAR	TM LG	G	AB	R	H	2B	3B	HR	RBI	BB-IB	HP	SO	AVG	OBP	SLG	AOPS	ABR	SB-CS	FA	FR	RNG	THR	GAMES AT POSITION	DL	BFW
1944	StL A	2	4	0	3	1	0	0	1	0	0	0	.750	.750	1.000	376	1	0-0	1.000	-0	82	0	/lf	0	0.1
1945	StL A	54	185	13	37	5	2	2	16	11	0	24	.200	.245	.281	50	-13	0-1	.992	6	117	162	O48(43/0/6),1b6	0	-1.1
1946	StL A	3	9	0	2	0	0	0	1	1	0	2	.222	.300	.222	45	-1	0-0	1.000	0	*107*	*0*	C2	0	0.0
1948	Bos A	4	4	0	2	0	0	0	0	0	0	1	.500	.500	.500	158	0	0-0	ø	0	*0*	*0*	/C	0	0.0
1949	Bos A	2	2	0	0	0	0	0	0	0	0	0	.000	.000	.000	-93	-1	0-0	ø	0	*0*	*0*	/C	0	-0.1
1953	StL A	4	2	0	0	0	0	0	0	1	0	0	.000	.333	.000	-4	0	0-0	ø	0	*0*	*0*	/C	0	0.0
Total	6	69	206	13	44	6	2	2	18	13	0	27	.214	.260	.291	56	-14	0-1	.992	6	117	160	O49(44/0/6),1b6,C5	0	-1.1

MARTIN, FRANK Frank; B2.28.1879 Chicago IL; D9.30.1924 Chicago IL; d6.30

YEAR	TM LG	G	AB	R	H	2B	3B	HR	RBI	BB-IB	HP	SO	AVG	OBP	SLG	AOPS	ABR	SB-CS	FA	FR	RNG	THR	GAMES AT POSITION	DL	BFW
1897	Lou N	2	8	1	2	0	0	0	0	0	0	—	.250	.250	.250	33	-1	0	.813	-1	117	0	2b2	—	-0.1
1898	Chi N	1	4	0	0	0	0	0	0	0	0	—	.000	.000	.000	-99	-1	0	1.000	-0	56	0	/2	—	-0.1
1899	NY N	17	54	5	14	2	0	0	1	2	1	—	.259	.298	.296	66	-3	0	.824	-0	97	171	3b17	—	-0.2
Total	3	20	66	6	16	2	0	0	1	2	1	—	.242	.275	.273	52	-5	0	.824	-1	97	171	3b17,2b3	—	-0.4

MARTIN, HERSH Hershel Ray; B9.19.1909 Birmingham AL; D11.17.1980 Cuba MO; BB/TR/6´2˝/190; d4.23

YEAR	TM LG	G	AB	R	H	2B	3B	HR	RBI	BB-IB	HP	SO	AVG	OBP	SLG	AOPS	ABR	SB-CS	FA	FR	RNG	THR	GAMES AT POSITION	DL	BFW
1937	Phi N	141	579	102	164	35	7	8	49	69	2	66	.283	.362	.409	101	3	11	.978	-3	98	76	O139(3/136/0)	—	-0.4
1938	Phi N☆	120	466	58	139	36	6	3	39	34	1	48	.298	.347	.421	113	9	8	.965	-2	105	73	O116(0/115/2)	—	0.4
1939	Phi N	111	393	59	111	28	5	1	22	42	2	27	.282	.355	.387	102	2	4	.976	3	112	61	O95(9/73/13)	—	0.2
1940	Phi N	33	83	10	21	6	1	0	5	9	0	9	.253	.326	.349	90	-1	1	.979	1	92	257	O23(0/19/4)	—	0.0
1944	NY A	85	328	49	99	12	4	9	47	34	2	26	.302	.371	.445	128	12	5-2	.964	0	97	114	O80(78/2/0)	0	0.8
1945	NY A	117	408	53	109	18	6	7	53	65	0	31	.267	.368	.392	115	10	4-1	.984	1	104	86	O102(97/3/2)	0	0.6
Total	6	607	2257	331	643	135	29	28	215	253	7	207	.285	.359	.408	109	35	33-3	.974	0	103	86	O555(187/348/21)	0	1.6

MARTIN, JERRY Jerry Lindsey; B5.11.1949 Columbia SC; BR/TR/6´1˝/(190–195); d9.7; f–Barney; Col Furman

YEAR	TM LG	G	AB	R	H	2B	3B	HR	RBI	BB-IB	HP	SO	AVG	OBP	SLG	AOPS	ABR	SB-CS	FA	FR	RNG	THR	GAMES AT POSITION	DL	BFW
1974	Phi N	13	14	2	3	1	0	0	1	1-0	0	5	.214	.267	.286	52	-1	0-0	1.000	-1	59	0	O11(6/3/2)	0	-0.2
1975	Phi N	57	113	15	24	7	1	2	11	11-4	1	16	.212	.288	.345	71	-4	2-2	.979	2	111	143	O49(8/41/0)	0	-0.3
1976	†Phi N	130	121	30	30	7	0	2	15	7-0	0	28	.248	.287	.355	79	-3	3-2	.975	-2	100	0	O110(73/23/15)/1	0	-0.8
1977	†Phi N	116	215	34	56	16	3	6	28	18-2	4	42	.260	.328	.447	100	0	6-4	.984	-1	95	91	O106(45/18/51)/1	0	-0.3
1978	†Phi N	128	266	40	72	13	4	9	36	28-3	1	65	.271	.339	.451	118	6	9-5	.987	4	105	147	O112(48/22/55)	0	0.7
1979	Chi N	150	534	74	145	34	3	19	73	38-3	3	85	.272	.321	.453	100	0	2-4	.981	-9	88	113	O144(0/140/4)	0	-1.2
1980	Chi N	141	494	57	112	22	2	23	73	38-6	2	107	.227	.281	.419	87	-10	8-3	.978	-12	83	85	O129(5/103/42)	0	-2.6
1981	SF N	72	241	23	58	5	3	4	25	21-2	3	52	.241	.308	.336	86	-5	6-2	.993	-5	86	88	O64(10/58/0)	0	-1.1
1982	KC A	147	519	52	138	22	1	15	65	38-0	2	138	.266	.316	.399	95	-4	1-1	.980	1	110	39	O142(11/3/134),D3	0	-1.1
1983	KC A	13	44	4	14	2	0	2	13	1-0	0	7	.318	.313	.500	125	1	1-0	.957	-2	80	0	O13R	156	-0.1
1984	NY N	51	91	6	14	1	0	3	5	6-0	0	29	.154	.206	.264	32	-9	0-0	1.000	2	123	169	O30(9/0/21),1b3	0	-0.8
Total	11	1018	2652	337	666	130	17	85	345	207-20	16	574	.251	.307	.409	93	-29	38-23	.982	-22	96	87	O910(215/411/337),1b5,D3	156	-7.8

MARTIN, JACK John Christopher; B4.19.1887 Plainfield NJ; D7.4.1980 Plainfield NJ; BR/TR/5´9˝/159; d4.25

YEAR	TM LG	G	AB	R	H	2B	3B	HR	RBI	BB-IB	HP	SO	AVG	OBP	SLG	AOPS	ABR	SB-CS	FA	FR	RNG	THR	GAMES AT POSITION	DL	BFW
1912	NY A	71	231	30	52	6	1	0	17	37	6	—	.225	.347	.260	70	-7	14	.898	-2	104	77	S65,3b4/2	—	-0.4
1914	Bos N	33	85	10	18	2	0	0	5	6	0	7	.212	.264	.235	49	-5	0	.949	0	96	167	3b26/12	—	-0.5
	Phi N	83	292	26	74	5	3	0	21	27	1	29	.253	.319	.291	77	-8	6	.930	-3	96	73	S83	—	-0.6
	Year	116	377	36	92	7	3	0	26	33	1	36	.244	.307	.279	71	-13	6	.930	-3	96	73	S83,3b26/12	—	-1.1
Total	2	187	608	66	144	13	4	0	43	70	7	36	.237	.323	.271	71	-20	20	.915	-5	100	75	S148,3b30,2b2/1	—	-1.5

Martin, Pepper Johnny Leonard Roosevelt "The Wild Horse of the Osage"; B2.29.1904 Temple OK; D3.5.1965 McAlester OK; BR/TR/5´8˝/170; d4.16; C1

YEAR TM LG	G	AB	R	H	2B	3B	HR	RBI	BB-IB	HP	SO	AVG	OBP	SLG	AOPS	ABR	SB-CS	FA	FR	RNG	THR	GAMES AT POSITION	DL	BFW
1928 †StL N	39	13	11	4	0	0	0	0	1	1	2	.308	.400	.308	86	0	2	1.000	0	157	0	O4R	—	0.0
1930 StL N	6	1	5	0	0	0	0	0	0	0	0	.000	.000	.000	-97	0	0	ø	0	—	—	/H	—	0.0
1931 †StL N	123	413	68	124	32	8	7	75	30	2	40	.300	.351	.467	114	8	16	.967	0	99	116	O110C	—	0.5
1932 StL N	85	323	47	77	19	6	4	34	30	1	31	.238	.305	.372	79	-10	9	.976	-3	86	178	O69(5/64/0),3b15	—	-1.4
1933 StL N★	145	599	**122**	189	36	12	8	57	67	3	46	.316	.387	.456	133	28	**26**	.943	-5	93	68	3b145	—	2.9
1934 †StL N★	110	454	76	131	25	11	5	49	32	1	41	.289	.337	.425	96	-3	**23**	.936	-5	96	50	3b107/P	—	-0.4
1935 StL N★	135	539	121	161	41	6	9	54	33	2	58	.299	.341	.447	106	5	20	.904	-14	86	108	3b114,O16(1/5/10)	—	-0.6
1936 StL N	143	572	121	177	36	11	11	76	58	0	66	.309	.373	.469	126	21	**23**	.976	-7	93	97	O127(0/3/124),3b15/P	—	0.6
1937 StL N☆	98	339	60	103	27	8	5	38	33	0	50	.304	.366	.475	124	12	9	.973	7	110	154	O82(0/40/42),3b5	—	1.5
1938 StL N	91	269	34	79	18	2	2	38	18	1	34	.294	.340	.398	97	-1	4	.986	-2	107	21	O62(1/38/23),3b4	—	-0.5
1939 StL N	88	281	48	86	17	7	3	37	30	1	35	.306	.375	.448	113	6	6	.975	-4	99	105	O51(8/37/8),3b22	—	0.1
1940 StL N	86	228	28	72	15	4	3	39	22	1	24	.316	.378	.456	122	7	6	.974	4	102	211	O63(16/10/40),3b2	—	0.8
1944 StL N	40	86	15	24	4	0	2	4	15	0	11	.279	.386	.395	118	3	2	.980	-1	105	46	O29(0/7/22)	0	0.1
Total 13	1189	4117	756	1227	270	75	59	501	369	13	438	.298	.358	.443	112	76	146	.973	-28	99	117	O613(31/314/273),3b429,P2	0	3.6

Martin, J. C. Joseph Clifton; B12.13.1936 Axton VA; BL/TR/6´2˝/(185–200); d9.10; C1

YEAR TM LG	G	AB	R	H	2B	3B	HR	RBI	BB-IB	HP	SO	AVG	OBP	SLG	AOPS	ABR	SB-CS	FA	FR	RNG	THR	GAMES AT POSITION	DL	BFW
1959 Chi A	3	4	0	1	0	0	0	1	0-0	0	1	.250	.250	.250	38	0	0-0	.667	-0	104	0	3b2	0	-0.1
1960 Chi A	7	20	0	2	1	0	0	2	0-0	0	6	.100	.100	.150	-34	-4	0-0	1.000	-1	74	0	3b5/1	0	-0.5
1961 Chi A	110	274	26	63	8	3	5	32	21-2	2	31	.230	.290	.336	68	-14	1-2	.988	7	106	81	1b60,3b36	0	-1.0
1962 Chi A	18	26	0	2	0	0	0	2	0-0	0	3	.077	.077	.077	-59	-6	0-0	1.000	-2	69	0	C6/13	0	-0.7
1963 Chi A	105	259	25	53	11	1	5	28	26-6	1	35	.205	.278	.313	67	-11	0-0	.983	14	128	125	C98,1b3/3	0	0.6
1964 Chi A	122	294	23	58	10	1	4	22	16-7	2	30	.197	.241	.279	46	-22	0-0	.986	9	177	107	C120	0	-1.0
1965 Chi A	119	230	21	60	12	0	2	21	24-10	2	29	.261	.333	.339	98	0	2-1	.982	-5	96	89	C112,1b4,3b2	0	-0.2
1966 Chi A	67	157	13	40	5	3	2	20	14-6	1	24	.255	.316	.363	103	0	0-0	.982	-5	77	63	C63	33	-0.2
1967 Chi A	101	252	22	59	12	1	4	22	30-4	1	41	.234	.317	.337	97	0	4-4	.987	6	87	77	C96/1	0	1.0
1968 NY N	78	244	20	55	9	2	3	31	21-3	5	31	.225	.298	.316	84	-4	0-0	.994	-5	79	125	C53,1b14	21	-0.9
1969 †NY N	66	177	12	37	5	1	4	21	12-1	0	32	.209	.257	.316	59	-10	0-0	.996	-4	121	33	C48,1b2	0	-1.3
1970 Chi N	40	77	11	12	1	0	1	4	20-7	1	11	.156	.333	.208	44	-5	0-0	.983	-0	128	119	C36,1b3	0	-0.4
1971 Chi N	47	125	13	33	5	0	2	17	12-6	2	16	.264	.336	.352	83	-2	1-1	.996	2	72	125	C43/lf	0	0.2
1972 Chi N	25	50	3	12	3	0	0	7	5-1	0	9	.240	.304	.300	66	-2	1-0	.970	-3	41	29	C17	41	-0.4
Total 14	908	2189	189	487	82	12	32	230	201-53	17	299	.222	.291	.315	72	-80	9-8	.987	13	110	94	C692,1b89,3b47/lf	95	-4.9

Martin, Mike Joseph Michael; B12.3.1958 Portland OR; BL/TR/6´2˝/193; [SDN78*S1/6]; d8.15; Col Linn–Benton (OR) CC

YEAR TM LG	G	AB	R	H	2B	3B	HR	RBI	BB-IB	HP	SO	AVG	OBP	SLG	AOPS	ABR	SB-CS	FA	FR	RNG	THR	GAMES AT POSITION	DL	BFW
1986 Chi N	8	13	1	1	1	0	0	0	2-1	0	4	.077	.200	.154	-1	-2	0-0	1.000	-3	43	101	C8	0	-0.5

Martin, Joe Joseph Samuel "Silent Joe"; B1.1.1876 Hollidaysburg PA; D5.25.1964 Altoona PA; BL/TR/5´9.5˝/155; d4.28

YEAR TM LG	G	AB	R	H	2B	3B	HR	RBI	BB-IB	HP	SO	AVG	OBP	SLG	AOPS	ABR	SB-CS	FA	FR	RNG	THR	GAMES AT POSITION	DL	BFW
1903 Was A	35	119	11	27	4	5	0	7	5	0	—	.227	.258	.345	78	-4	2	.892	-4	106	66	2b15,3b13,O7(1/0/6)	—	-0.8
StL A	44	173	18	37	6	4	0	7	6	2	—	.214	.249	.295	64	-8	0	.983	-2	138	281	O38(4/0/34),2b6/3	—	-1.2
Year	79	292	29	64	10	9	0	14	11	2	—	.219	.252	.315	70	-12	2	.959	-6	119	242	O45(5/0/40),2b21,3b14	—	-2.0

Martin, Norberto Norberto Edonal (McDonald); B12.10.1966 San Pedro de Macoris, D.R.; BR/TR/5´10˝/(164–182); d9.20

YEAR TM LG	G	AB	R	H	2B	3B	HR	RBI	BB-IB	HP	SO	AVG	OBP	SLG	AOPS	ABR	SB-CS	FA	FR	RNG	THR	GAMES AT POSITION	DL	BFW
1993 Chi A	8	14	3	5	0	0	0	2	1-0	0	1	.357	.400	.357	107	0	0-0	.957	1	88	181	2b5/D	0	0.1
1994 Chi A	45	131	19	36	7	1	1	16	9-0	0	16	.275	.317	.366	78	-4	4-2	.982	-6	79	69	2b28,S6,3b5,O2L/D	0	-0.8
1995 Chi A	72	160	17	43	7	4	2	17	3-0	1	25	.269	.281	.400	79	-6	5-0	.950	2	95	112	2b17,O12(5/0/7),D10,3b9,S7	0	-0.2
1996 Chi A	70	140	30	49	7	0	1	14	6-0	0	17	.350	.374	.421	106	1	10-2	.943	7	94	158	S24,D22,2b10,3b3	60	0.9
1997 Chi A	71	213	24	64	7	1	2	27	6-0	0	31	.300	.320	.371	82	-6	1-4	.960	-12	71	77	S28,3b17,2b9,D6	36	-1.6
1998 Ana A	79	195	20	42	2	0	1	13	6-0	0	29	.215	.236	.241	25	-22	3-1	.982	4	110	108	2b54,D10,3b5,O5L,S2	15	-1.5
1999 Tor A	9	27	3	6	2	0	0	0	4-0	2	4	.222	.364	.296	70	-1	0-0	.974	1	126	148	2b8/S	0	0.1
Total 7	354	880	116	245	32	6	7	89	35-0	3	123	.278	.306	.352	72	-38	23-9	.976	-3	103	101	2b131,S68,D50,3b39,O19(12/0/7)	111	-3.0

Martin, Russell Russell Nathan; B2.15.1983 East York ON, Can.; BR/TR/5´11˝/200; [LAN02 17/511]; d5.5; Col Chipola (FL) JC

YEAR TM LG	G	AB	R	H	2B	3B	HR	RBI	BB-IB	HP	SO	AVG	OBP	SLG	AOPS	ABR	SB-CS	FA	FR	RNG	THR	GAMES AT POSITION	DL	BFW
2006 †LA N	121	415	65	117	26	4	10	65	45-8	4	57	.282	.355	.436	102	2	10-5	.993	9	93	127	C117/D	0	1.8

Martin, Stu Stuart McGuire; B11.19.1912 Rich Square NC; D1.11.1997 Severn NC; BL/TR/6´0˝/155; d4.14; Col Guilford

YEAR TM LG	G	AB	R	H	2B	3B	HR	RBI	BB-IB	HP	SO	AVG	OBP	SLG	AOPS	ABR	SB-CS	FA	FR	RNG	THR	GAMES AT POSITION	DL	BFW
1936 StL N☆	92	332	63	99	21	4	6	41	29	1	27	.298	.356	.440	114	6	17	.949	-14	92	105	2b83,S3	—	-0.2
1937 StL N	90	223	34	58	6	1	1	17	32	0	18	.260	.353	.309	80	-5	3	.946	-6	96	102	2b48,1b9/S	—	-0.9
1938 StL N	114	417	54	116	26	2	1	27	30	1	28	.278	.328	.357	84	-9	4	.967	-4	99	95	2b99	—	-0.6
1939 StL N	120	425	60	114	26	7	3	30	33	3	40	.268	.325	.384	85	-9	4	**.977**	-2	97	96	2b107/1	—	-0.5
1940 StL N	112	369	45	88	12	6	4	32	33	0	35	.238	.301	.336	71	-15	4	.972	-16	78	22	3b73,2b33	—	-2.8
1941 Pit N	88	233	37	71	13	2	0	19	10	3	17	.305	.341	.378	103	1	2	.972	-0	105	87	2b53,3b2/1	0	0.4
1942 Pit N	42	120	16	27	4	2	1	12	8	0	10	.225	.273	.317	71	-5	1	.979	-8	84	81	2b30/1S	0	-1.2
1943 Chi N	64	118	13	26	4	0	0	5	15	0	10	.220	.308	.254	64	-5	1	.980	3	119	99	2b22,3b8,1b2	0	-0.2
Total 8	722	2237	322	599	112	24	16	183	190	8	185	.268	.327	.361	86	-41	36	.966	-47	97	95	2b475,3b83,1b14,S5	0	-6.0

Martin, Gene Thomas Eugene; B1.12.1947 Americus GA; BL/TR/6´0.5˝/190; [TexA65 3/43]; d7.28

YEAR TM LG	G	AB	R	H	2B	3B	HR	RBI	BB-IB	HP	SO	AVG	OBP	SLG	AOPS	ABR	SB-CS	FA	FR	RNG	THR	GAMES AT POSITION	DL	BFW
1968 Was A	9	11	1	4	1	0	1	1	0-0	0	1	.364	.364	.727	232	2	0-0	ø	-1	0	0	O2L	0	0.1

Martin, Joe William Joseph "Smokey Joe"; B8.28.1911 Seymour MO; D9.28.1960 Buffalo NY; BR/TR/5´11.5˝/181; d4.27; Col California–Santa Barbara

YEAR TM LG	G	AB	R	H	2B	3B	HR	RBI	BB-IB	HP	SO	AVG	OBP	SLG	AOPS	ABR	SB-CS	FA	FR	RNG	THR	GAMES AT POSITION	DL	BFW
1936 NY N	7	15	0	4	1	0	0	2	0	1	4	.267	.313	.333	75	-1	0	1.000	0	104	193	3b7	—	0.0
1938 Chi A	1	0	0	0	0	0	0	0	0	0	0	ø	ø	ø	ø	0	0-0	ø	0	—	—	/R	—	0.0
Total 2	8	15	0	4	1	0	0	2	0	1	4	.267	.313	.333	75	-1	0-0	1.000	0	104	193	3b7	—	0.0

Martin, Billy William Gloyd; B2.13.1894 Washington DC; D9.14.1949 Arlington VA; BR/TR/5´8.5˝/170; d10.6; Col Georgetown

YEAR TM LG	G	AB	R	H	2B	3B	HR	RBI	BB-IB	HP	SO	AVG	OBP	SLG	AOPS	ABR	SB-CS	FA	FR	RNG	THR	GAMES AT POSITION	DL	BFW
1914 Bos N	1	3	0	0	0	0	0	0	0	0	0	.000	.000	.000	-99	-1	0	.500	-1	57	0	/S	—	-0.2

Martinez, Sandy Angel Sandy (Martinez); B10.3.1970 Villa Mella, D.R.; BL/TR/6´2˝/(200–215); d6.24

YEAR TM LG	G	AB	R	H	2B	3B	HR	RBI	BB-IB	HP	SO	AVG	OBP	SLG	AOPS	ABR	SB-CS	FA	FR	RNG	THR	GAMES AT POSITION	DL	BFW
1995 Tor A	62	191	12	46	12	0	2	25	7-0	1	45	.241	.270	.335	57	-13	0-0	.986	1	178	80	C61	0	-0.7
1996 Tor A	76	229	17	52	9	3	3	18	16-0	4	58	.227	.288	.332	57	-16	0-0	.993	4	131	91	C75	15	-0.7
1997 Tor A	3	2	1	0	0	0	0	0	1-0	0	1	.000	.333	.000	-3	0	0-0	.933	0	32	209	C3	0	0.0
1998 †Chi N	45	87	7	23	9	1	0	7	13-0	1	21	.264	.363	.391	96	0	1-0	.985	3	116	64	C33	0	0.4
1999 Chi N	17	30	1	5	0	0	1	1	0-0	0	11	.167	.167	.267	7	-4	0-0	.959	0	490	0	C12	28	-0.3
2000 Fla N	10	18	1	4	2	0	0	0	0-0	0	8	.222	.222	.333	40	-2	0-0	1.000	1	161	0	C9	0	0.0
2001 Mon N	1	1	0	0	0	0	0	0	0-0	0	0	.000	.000	.000	-99	0	0-0	1.000	0	6	0	/C	188	0.0
2004 Cle A	1	2	0	0	0	0	0	0	0-0	0	1	.000	.000	.000	-99	-1	0-0	1.000	0	20	539	/C	0	0.0
Bos A	3	4	0	0	0	0	0	0	0-0	0	2	.000	.000	.000	-94	-1	0-0	1.000	-1	0	0	C3	0	-0.2
Year	4	6	0	0	0	0	0	0	0-0	0	3	.000	.000	.000	-97	-2	0-0	1.000	-1	8	210	C4	0	-0.2
Total 8	218	564	39	130	32	4	6	51	37-0	6	147	.230	.284	.333	58	-37	1-0	.988	9	158	79	C198	231	-1.5

Martinez, Carlos Carlos Alberto Escobar (b Carlos Alberto Escobar (Martinez)); B8.11.1964 LaGuaira, Vargas, Venez.; D1.24.2006 LaGuaira, Vargas, Venez.; BR/TR/6´5˝/(175–215); d9.2

YEAR TM LG	G	AB	R	H	2B	3B	HR	RBI	BB-IB	HP	SO	AVG	OBP	SLG	AOPS	ABR	SB-CS	FA	FR	RNG	THR	GAMES AT POSITION	DL	BFW
1988 Chi A	17	55	5	9	1	0	0	0	0-0	0	12	.164	.164	.182	-3	-8	1-0	.909	0	118	40	3b15,D2	0	-0.8
1989 Chi A	109	350	44	105	22	0	5	32	21-2	1	57	.300	.340	.406	112	5	4-1	.912	-5	98	106	3b68,1b34,O10L/D	21	-0.1
1990 Chi A	92	272	18	61	6	5	4	24	10-2	0	40	.224	.252	.327	62	-16	0-4	.988	-6	75	84	1b82/lfD	0	-2.9
1991 Cle A	72	257	22	73	14	0	5	30	10-2	2	43	.284	.310	.397	95	-2	3-2	.968	-4	63	125	D41,1b31	0	-1.0
1992 Cle A	69	228	23	60	9	1	5	35	7-0	1	21	.263	.283	.377	86	-5	1-2	.996	-6	95	152	1b37,3b28,D4	53	-1.4
1993 Cle A	80	262	26	64	10	0	5	31	20-3	0	29	.244	.295	.340	71	-11	1-1	.934	-7	78	89	3b35,1b22,D19	0	-2.1
1995 Cal A	26	61	7	11	1	0	1	9	6-2	1	7	.180	.265	.246	34	-6	0-0	.968	1	112	374	3b16,1b4,D2	0	-0.5
Total 7	465	1485	145	383	63	6	25	161	74-11	5	209	.258	.293	.359	81	-43	10-10	.986	-26	74	98	1b210,3b162,D72,O11L	74	-8.8

Martinez, Carmelo Carmelo (Salgado); B7.28.1960 Dorado, PR; BR/TR/6´2˝/(185–225); d8.22

YEAR TM LG	G	AB	R	H	2B	3B	HR	RBI	BB-IB	HP	SO	AVG	OBP	SLG	AOPS	ABR	SB-CS	FA	FR	RNG	THR	GAMES AT POSITION	DL	BFW
1983 Chi N	29	89	8	23	3	0	6	16	4-0	0	19	.258	.287	.494	108	0	0-0	.992	0	94	104	1b26/3lf	0	-0.1
1984 †SD N	149	488	64	122	28	2	13	66	68-4	4	82	.250	.340	.395	107	7	1-3	.976	11	113	128	O142L,1b2	0	1.1
1985 SD N	150	514	64	130	28	1	21	72	87-4	3	82	.253	.362	.434	123	19	0-4	.978	5	102	115	O150L,1b3	7	1.7
1986 SD N	113	244	28	58	10	0	9	25	35-2	1	46	.238	.333	.389	102	1	1-1	.978	1	90	152	O60L,1b26/3	0	-0.1
1987 SD N	139	447	59	122	21	2	15	70	70-5	3	82	.273	.372	.430	117	13	5-5	.968	-1	94	137	O78L,1b65	0	0.5

YEAR	TM LG	G	AB	R	H	2B	3B	HR	RBI	BB-IB	HP	SO	AVG	OBP	SLG	AOPS	ABR	SB-CS	FA	FR	RNG	THR	GAMES AT POSITION	DL	BFW
1988	SD N	121	365	48	86	12	0	18	65	35-3	0	57	.236	.301	.416	106	2	1-1	.993	8	117	164	O64(55/0/11),1b41	0	0.6
1989	SD N	111	267	23	59	12	2	6	39	32-3	0	54	.221	.302	.348	86	-5	0-0	.982	3	96	166	O65L,1b32	0	-0.5
1990	Phi N	71	198	23	48	8	0	8	31	29-0	0	37	.242	.339	.404	104	1	2-1	.994	-1	98	120	1b43,O20(20/0/1)	15	-0.2
	†Pit N	12	19	3	4	1	0	2	4	1-0	0	5	.211	.250	.579	125	0	0-0	1.000	1	216	240	1b5,O2L	0	0.1
	Year	83	217	26	52	9	0	10	35	30-0	0	42	.240	.332	.419	106	2	2-1	.995	0	106	128	1b48,O22(22/0/1)	0	-0.1
1991	Pit N	11	16	1	4	0	0	0	0	1-0	0	2	.250	.294	.250	55	-1	0-0	.945	-1	31	65	1b8	0	-0.3
	KC A	44	121	17	25	6	0	4	17	27-3	0	25	.207	.351	.355	95	0	0-1	.991	3	127	95	1b43/D	0	0.0
	Cin N	53	138	12	32	5	0	6	19	15-1	0	37	.232	.301	.399	93	-1	0-0	.985	0	72	88	1b25,O16L	0	-0.3
Total	9	1003	2906	350	713	134	7	108	424	404-25	11	528	.245	.337	.408	108	36	10-16	.980	30	105	134	O598(588/0/12),1b319,3b2/D	22	2.5
Martinez, Tino	Constantino; B12.7.1967 Tampa FL; BL/TR/6´2˝/(205–230); [SeaA88 1/14]; d8.20; Col Tampa																								
1990	Sea A	24	68	4	15	4	0	0	5	9-0	0	9	.221	.308	.279	66	-3	0-0	1.000	0	95	157	1b23	0	-0.4
1991	Sea A	36	112	11	23	2	0	4	9	11-0	0	24	.205	.272	.330	67	-5	0-0	.993	2	119	103	1b29,D5	0	-0.6
1992	Sea A	136	460	53	118	19	2	16	66	42-9	2	77	.257	.316	.411	103	0	2-1	.995	4	116	88	1b78,D47	0	-0.3
1993	Sea A	109	408	48	108	25	1	17	60	45-9	5	56	.265	.343	.456	111	6	0-3	.997	-2	85	98	1b103,D6	55	-0.6
1994	Sea A	97	329	42	86	21	0	20	61	29-2	1	52	.261	.320	.508	107	2	1-2	.997	1	94	88	1b82,D8	0	-0.4
1995	†Sea A★	141	519	92	152	35	3	31	111	62-15	4	91	.293	.369	.551	135	26	0-0	.993	4	104	71	1b139/D	0	1.7
1996	†NY A	155	595	82	174	28	0	25	117	68-4	2	85	.292	.364	.466	109	8	2-1	**.996**	-2	88	91	1b151,D3	0	-0.6
1997	†NY A★	158	594	96	176	31	2	44	141	75-14	3	75	.296	.371	.577	146	40	3-1	.994	7	116	102	1b150,D9	0	3.2
1998	†NY A	142	531	92	149	33	1	28	123	61-3	6	83	.281	.355	.505	127	22	2-1	.992	1	103	109	1b142	0	1.0
1999	†NY A	159	589	95	155	27	2	28	105	69-7	3	86	.263	.341	.458	104	2	3-4	.995	7	115	85	1b158	0	-0.4
2000	†NY A	155	569	69	147	37	4	16	91	52-9	8	74	.258	.328	.422	90	-10	4-1	.994	-1	94	86	1b154	0	-2.1
2001	†NY A	154	589	89	165	24	2	34	113	42-2	2	89	.280	.329	.501	114	9	1-2	.996	5	105	91	1b149,D3	0	0.1
2002	†StL N	150	511	63	134	25	1	21	75	58-9	2	71	.262	.337	.438	102	1	3-2	.996	-2	94	106	1b149	0	-1.3
2003	StL N	138	476	66	130	25	2	15	69	53-7	9	71	.273	.352	.429	105	4	1-1	**.997**	0	102	91	1b126,D5	0	-0.7
2004	TB A	138	458	63	120	20	1	23	76	66-9	9	72	.262	.362	.461	116	12	3-1	.997	-1	95	90	1b114,D19	0	0.1
2005	†NY A	131	303	43	73	9	0	17	49	38-3	3	54	.241	.328	.439	103	1	2-0	.991	-3	87	95	1b122/D	0	-0.9
Total	16	2023	7111	1008	1925	365	21	339	1271	780-102	59	1069	.271	.344	.471	112	115	27-20	.995	20	101	93	1b1869,D107	55	-2.2
Martinez, Dave	David; B9.26.1964 New York NY; BL/TL/5´10˝/(150–190); [ChiN83*S3/53]; d6.15; Col Valencia (FL) CC; [DL 2002 Atl N 183]																								
1986	Chi N	53	108	13	15	1	1	1	7	6-0	1	22	.139	.190	.194	6	-14	4-2	.988	2	114	117	O46(9/39/1)	0	-1.3
1987	Chi N	142	459	70	134	18	8	8	36	57-4	2	96	.292	.372	.418	105	4	16-8	.980	2	101	149	O139(14/134/3)	0	0.5
1988	Chi N	75	256	27	65	10	1	4	34	21-5	2	46	.254	.311	.348	86	-4	7-3	.970	-3	96	66	O72(0/70/2)	0	-0.8
	Mon N	63	191	24	49	3	5	2	12	17-3	0	48	.257	.316	.356	88	-3	16-6	.992	0	97	86	O60(1/44/22)	0	-0.3
	Year	138	447	51	114	13	6	6	46	38-8	2	94	.255	.313	.351	87	-8	23-9	.979	-3	96	75	O132(1/114/24)	0	-1.1
1989	Mon N	126	361	41	99	16	7	3	27	27-2	0	57	.274	.324	.382	100	-1	23-4	.967	-4	86	144	O118(0/104/38)	0	-0.3
1990	Mon N	118	391	60	109	13	5	11	39	24-2	1	48	.279	.321	.422	107	2	13-11	.989	2	105	110	O108(0/103/22)/P	0	0.1
1991	Mon N	124	396	47	117	18	5	7	42	20-3	3	54	.295	.332	.419	112	5	16-7	.982	2	98	152	O112(36/34/54)	0	0.6
1992	Cin N	135	393	47	100	20	5	3	31	42-4	0	54	.254	.323	.354	90	-5	12-8	.991	2	104	145	O111(3/105/6),1b21	0	-0.6
1993	SF N	91	241	28	58	12	1	5	27	27-3	0	39	.241	.317	.361	84	-6	6-3	.993	1	96	163	O73(3/43/34)	35	-0.5
1994	SF N	97	235	23	58	9	3	4	27	21-1	2	22	.247	.314	.362	79	-8	3-4	1.000	2	110	103	O58(3/3/53),1b25	0	-1.0
1995	Chi A	119	303	49	93	16	4	5	37	32-2	1	41	.307	.371	.436	115	7	8-2	.976	-2	102	77	O59(30/5/32),1b47/PD	0	0.1
1996	Chi A	146	440	85	140	20	8	10	53	52-1	3	52	.318	.393	.468	122	16	15-7	.988	1	106	65	O121(3/73/73),1b23	0	1.3
1997	Chi A	145	504	78	144	16	6	12	55	55-7	3	69	.286	.356	.413	104	3	12-6	.996	4	105	103	O105(4/45/75),1b52/D	0	0.2
1998	TB A	90	309	31	79	11	0	3	20	35-4	2	52	.256	.334	.320	70	-13	8-7	.994	3	100	153	O86(0/2/85)/1D	68	-1.4
1999	TB A	143	514	79	146	25	5	6	66	60-3	5	76	.284	.361	.387	90	-6	13-6	.985	-7	90	91	O140(2/52/93)	0	-1.5
2000	TB A	29	104	12	27	4	2	1	12	10-1	0	17	.260	.319	.365	75	-4	1-4	1.000	2	88	274	O28R	0	-0.5
	Chi N	18	54	5	10	1	1	0	1	2-0	0	8	.185	.214	.241	15	-7	1-0	1.000	-0	104	0	O10(9/1/0),1b9	0	-0.8
	Tex A	38	119	14	32	4	1	2	12	14-2	1	20	.269	.351	.370	82	-3	2-1	1.000	4	130	93	O35R,1b4	0	-0.1
	Tor A	47	180	29	56	10	1	2	22	24-0	1	28	.311	.393	.411	101	1	4-2	.982	6	108	249	O47R	0	0.4
	Year	114	403	55	115	18	4	5	46	48-3	2	65	.285	.362	.387	87	-6	7-7	.992	11	109	209	O110R,1b4	0	-0.1
2001	†Atl N	120	237	33	68	11	3	2	20	21-0	1	44	.287	.347	.384	88	-4	3-3	1.000	-0	91	76	O52(27/0/28),1b10/D	0	-0.7
Total	16	1919	5795	795	1599	238	72	91	580	567-47	28	893	.276	.341	.389	95	-40	183-94	.986	15	100	123	O1580(144/857/731),1b192,D8,P2	286	-6.5
Martinez, Domingo	Domingo Emilio (La Fontaine); B8.4.1967 Santo Domingo, D.R.; BR/TR/6´2˝/215; d9.11																								
1992	Tor A	7	8	2	5	0	0	1	3	0-0	0	1	.625	.625	1.000	332	2	0-0	1.000	-1	0	113	1b7	0	0.2
1993	Tor A	8	14	2	4	0	0	1	3	1-0	0	7	.286	.333	.500	119	0	0-0	1.000	1	172	75	1b7/3	0	0.0
Total	2	15	22	4	9	0	0	2	6	1-0	0	8	.409	.435	.682	194	2	0-0	1.000	-0	101	91	1b14/3	0	0.2
Martinez, Edgar	Edgar; B1.2.1963 New York NY; BR/TR/5´11˝/(175–210); d9.12																								
1987	Sea A	13	43	6	16	5	2	0	5	2-0	1	5	.372	.413	.581	152	3	0-0	1.000	0	91	50	3b12/D	0	0.3
1988	Sea A	14	32	0	9	4	0	0	5	4-0	0	7	.281	.351	.406	109	1	0-0	.929	-4	46	65	3b13	0	-0.3
1989	Sea A	65	171	20	41	5	0	2	20	17-1	3	26	.240	.314	.304	74	-5	2-1	.949	-6	80	106	3b61	0	-1.1
1990	Sea A	144	487	71	147	27	2	11	49	74-3	5	62	.302	.397	.433	131	24	1-4	.928	-5	95	65	3b143,D2	0	1.9
1991	Sea A	150	544	98	167	35	1	14	52	84-9	8	72	.307	.405	.452	137	32	0-3	.962	3	103	91	3b144,D2	0	3.4
1992	Sea A★	135	528	100	181	**46**	3	18	73	54-2	4	61	**.343**	.404	.544	162	45	14-4	.943	2	100	129	3b103,D28,1b2	0	4.9
1993	Sea A	42	135	20	32	7	0	4	13	28-1	0	19	.237	.366	.378	99	1	0-0	.889	-7	41	42	D24,3b16	126	-0.7
1994	Sea A	89	326	47	93	23	1	13	51	53-3	3	42	.285	.387	.482	120	12	6-2	.950	5	100	119	3b64,D23	20	1.5
1995	†Sea A★	**145**	511	**121**	182	**52**	0	29	113	116-19	8	87	**.356**	**.479**	.628	**184**	**73**	4-3	.800	-2	47	0	D138,3b4,1b3	0	**5.8**
1996	Sea A★	139	499	121	163	52	2	26	103	123-12	8	84	.327	.464	.595	165	60	3-3	.967	-1	41	89	D134,1b4,3b2	22	4.6
1997	†Sea A★	155	542	104	179	35	1	28	108	119-11	11	86	.330	.456	.554	163	60	2-4	.986	0	100	86	D144,1b7/3	0	4.7
1998	Sea A	154	556	86	179	46	1	29	102	106-4	3	96	.322	**.429**	.565	156	52	1-1	1.000	2	277	101	D147,1b4	0	4.2
1999	Sea A	142	502	86	169	35	1	24	86	97-6	6	99	.337	**.447**	.554	156	49	7-2	1.000	-0	84	47	D134,1b5	0	3.8
2000	†Sea A★	153	556	100	180	31	0	37	**145**	96-8	5	95	.324	.423	.579	154	50	3-0	1.000	0	99	215	D146,1b2	0	3.9
2001	†Sea A★	132	470	80	144	40	1	23	116	93-9	9	90	.306	.423	.543	163	50	4-1	1.000	-0	0	0	D127/1	18	4.1
2002	Sea A	97	328	42	91	23	0	15	59	67-8	6	69	.277	.403	.485	141	24	1-1	ø	0	0	0	D91	62	1.8
2003	Sea A★	145	497	72	146	25	0	24	98	92-7	7	95	.294	.406	.489	144	37	0-1	ø	0	0	0	D140	0	2.7
2004	Sea A	141	486	45	128	23	0	12	63	58-10	2	107	.263	.342	.385	94	-3	1-0	ø	0	0	0	D122/3	0	-0.9
Total	18	2055	7213	1219	2247	514	15	309	1261	1283-113	89	1202	.312	.418	.515	147	565	49-30	.946	-13	95	93	D1403,3b564,1b28	248	44.6
Martinez, Felix	Felix (Mata); B5.18.1974 Nagua, D.R.; BB/TR/6´0˝/180; d9.3																								
1997	KC A	16	31	3	7	1	1	0	3	6-0	0	8	.226	.351	.323	75	-1	0-0	.975	-3	73	106	S12,D2	0	-0.3
1998	KC A	34	85	7	11	1	1	0	5	5-0	1	21	.129	.187	.165	-7	-14	3-1	.956	-1	96	123	S32,2b2	0	-1.2
1999	KC A	6	7	1	1	0	0	0	0	0-0	0	0	.143	.143	.143	-26	-1	0-0	ø	-2	0	0	S2/2	0	-0.3
2000	TB A	106	299	42	64	11	4	2	17	32-0	8	68	.214	.305	.298	55	-21	9-3	.976	34	124	116	S106	0	2.0
2001	TB A	77	219	24	54	13	1	1	14	10-0	5	46	.247	.294	.329	65	-11	6-5	.944	-6	92	100	S67,2b10	18	-1.2
Total	5	239	641	77	137	26	7	3	39	53-0	14	143	.214	.287	.290	50	-48	18-9	.964	22	107	111	S219,2b13,D2	18	-1.0
Martinez, Tony	Gabriel Antonio (Diaz); B3.18.1940 Perico, Cuba; D8.24.1991 Miami FL; BR/TR/5´10˝/(165–170); d4.9; Mil 1970																								
1963	Cle A	43	141	10	22	4	0	0	8	5-0	0	18	.156	.184	.184	4	-18	1-1	.961	-12	78	77	S41	0	-3.0
1964	Cle A	9	14	1	3	1	0	0	2	0-0	0	2	.214	.214	.286	38	-1	0-1	1.000	3	144	261	2b4/S	0	0.1
1965	Cle A	4	3	0	0	0	0	0	0	0-0	0	0	.000	.000	.000	-99	-1	0-0	ø	0	—	—	/H	0	-0.1
1966	Cle A	17	17	2	5	0	0	0	0	1-0	0	6	.294	.333	.294	82	0	1-1	.833	-1	112	0	S5,2b4	0	-0.1
Total	4	73	175	13	30	5	0	0	10	6-0	0	26	.171	.198	.200	13	-20	2-3	.958	-11	78	81	S47,2b8	0	-3.1
Martinez, Greg	Gregory Alfred; B1.27.1972 Las Vegas NV; BB/TR/5´10˝/168; [MilA93 24/683]; d3.31; Col Barstow (CA) CC																								
1998	Mil N	13	3	2	0	0	0	0	0	1-0	0	2	.000	.250	.000	-26	-1	2-0	ø	-1	0	0	O6L	0	-0.1
Martinez, Buck	John Albert; B11.7.1948 Redding CA; BR/TR/5´10˝/(185–200); [PhiN67*2/32]; d6.18; Mil 1970; M2																								
1969	KC A	72	205	14	47	6	1	4	23	8-2	0	25	.229	.258	.327	62	-11	0-0	.972	3	125	83	C55/rf	0	-0.6
1970	KC A	6	9	1	1	0	0	0	0	2-0	0	1	.111	.273	.111	10	-1	0-0	.958	-0	72	315	C5	0	-0.1
1971	KC A	22	46	3	7	2	0	0	1	5-0	0	9	.152	.231	.196	23	-5	0-1	.968	-0	106	46	C21	0	-0.5
1973	KC A	14	32	2	8	1	0	1	6	4-0	0	5	.250	.333	.375	92	0	0-0	.966	-1	187	57	C14	0	0.0
1974	KC A	43	107	10	23	3	1	1	8	14-0	2	19	.215	.317	.290	71	-4	0-1	.977	-0	101	58	C38	0	-0.3
1975	KC A	80	226	15	51	9	2	3	23	21-0	1	28	.226	.293	.323	72	-8	1-0	.980	-4	76	107	C79	0	-1.0

YEAR	TM LG	G	AB	R	H	2B	3B	HR	RBI	BB-IB	HP	SO	AVG	OBP	SLG	AOPS	ABR	SB-CS	FA	FR	RNG	THR	GAMES AT POSITION	DL	BFW
1976	†KC A	95	267	24	61	13	3	5	34	16-1	0	45	.228	.269	.356	82	-7	0-0	.991	3	89	108	C94	16	0.0
1977	KC A	29	80	3	18	4	0	1	9	3-0	0	12	.225	.253	.313	53	-5	0-1	.993	1	116	66	C28	0	-0.4
1978	Mil A	89	256	26	56	10	1	1	20	14-1	0	42	.219	.255	.277	51	-17	1-1	.978	-1	120	75	C89	0	-1.5
1979	Mil A	69	196	17	53	8	0	4	26	8-0	0	25	.270	.296	.372	80	-6	0-1	.967	-5	133	100	C68/P	0	-0.8
1980	Mil A	76	219	16	49	9	0	3	17	12-0	1	33	.224	.266	.306	58	-13	1-0	.985	6	115	101	C76	0	-0.4
1981	Tor A	45	128	13	29	8	1	4	21	11-0	1	16	.227	.287	.398	92	-1	1-0	.991	2	105	88	C45	0	0.3
1982	Tor A	96	260	26	63	17	0	10	37	24-1	0	34	.242	.301	.423	90	-4	1-1	.988	8	170	90	C93	0	0.8
1983	Tor A	88	221	27	56	14	0	10	33	29-0	0	39	.253	.337	.452	109	3	0-1	.989	-2	149	67	C85	0	0.4
1984	Tor A	102	232	24	51	13	1	5	37	29-0	2	49	.220	.301	.349	79	-6	0-3	.995	-1	126	68	C98/D	0	-0.5
1985	Tor A	42	99	11	16	3	0	4	14	10-0	1	12	.162	.239	.313	50	-7	0-0	.988	3	112	109	C42	89	-0.2
1986	Tor A	81	160	13	29	8	0	2	12	20-0	0	25	.181	.271	.269	47	-12	0-0	.994	-1	112	76	C78/D	0	-1.1
Total	17	1049	2743	245	618	128	10	58	321	230-5	8	419	.225	.284	.343	73	-104	5-10	.984	10	119	87	C1008,D2/Prf	105	-5.9
Martinez, Jose	Jose (Azcuiz); B7.26.1942 Cardenas, Cuba; BR/TR/5´10˝/180; d4.12; C15																								
1969	Pit N	77	168	20	45	6	0	1	16	9-0	1	32	.268	.309	.321	79	-5	1-3	.975	6	113	123	2b42,S20,3b5,O2L	0	0.3
1970	Pit N	19	20	1	1	0	0	0	0	1-0	0	5	.050	.095	.050	-60	-5	0-0	1.000	2	40	0	3b7,2b4/S	0	-0.3
Total	2	96	188	21	46	6	0	1	16	10-0	1	37	.245	.286	.293	63	-10	1-3	.966	7	116	126	2b46,S21,3b12,O2L	0	0.0
Martinez, Manny	Manuel (De Jesus); B10.3.1970 San Pedro de Macoris, D.R.; BR/TR/6´2˝/(169–185); d6.14																								
1996	Sea A	9	17	3	4	2	1	0	3	3-0	0	5	.235	.350	.471	105	0	2-0	1.000	1	103	563	O8(2/4/3)	0	0.2
	Phi N	13	36	2	8	0	2	0	0	1-0	1	11	.222	.263	.333	56	-3	2-1	.955	1	112	168	O11(1/1/10)	0	-0.2
1998	Pit N	73	180	21	45	11	2	6	24	9-0	2	44	.250	.290	.433	87	-4	0-3	.989	-3	95	0	O62(26/37/3)	0	-0.9
1999	Mon N	137	331	48	81	12	7	2	26	17-0	0	51	.245	.279	.341	59	-23	19-6	.968	5	108	208	O126(0/126/1)	15	-1.4
Total	3	232	564	74	138	25	12	8	53	30-0	3	111	.245	.284	.374	69	-30	23-10	.974	4	104	154	O207(29/168/17)	15	-2.3
Martinez, Marty	Orlando (Oliva); B8.23.1941 Havana, Cuba; BB/TR (BR 1962)/6´1˝/(170–175); d5.2; M1/C4																								
1962	Min A	37	18	13	3	0	1	0	3	3-0	0	4	.167	.286	.278	51	-1	0-0	.920	-3	84	50	S11/3	0	-0.3
1967	Atl N	44	73	14	21	2	1	0	5	11-1	1	11	.288	.384	.342	112	2	0-1	.920	-0	110	123	S25,2b9,C3,3b2/1	34	0.4
1968	Atl N	113	356	34	82	5	3	0	12	29-4	2	28	.230	.291	.261	67	-14	6-6	.955	-7	97	124	S54,3b37,2b16,C14	0	-1.9
1969	Hou N	78	198	14	61	5	4	0	15	10-1	0	21	.308	.340	.374	102	0	0-0	1.000	-2	79	116	O21L,S17,3b15,C7/P2	21	-0.2
1970	Hou N	75	150	12	33	3	0	0	12	9-0	0	22	.220	.264	.240	38	-14	0-0	.990	-3	97	68	S29,3b10,C6,2b4	0	-1.4
1971	Hou N	32	62	4	16	3	1	0	4	3-0	0	6	.258	.292	.339	81	-2	1-0	.968	-1	103	80	2b9,S7,1b4,3b3	16	-0.1
1972	StL N	9	7	0	3	0	0	0	2	0-0	0	1	.429	.429	.429	145	0	0-0	1.000	-0	57	0	S3,2b2/3	0	0.0
	Oak A	22	40	3	5	0	0	0	1	3-0	0	6	.125	.186	.125	-7	-5	0-0	.944	1	70	68	2b17,S6/3	0	-0.4
	Tex A	26	41	3	6	1	1	0	3	2-0	0	8	.146	.182	.220	21	-4	0-1	.944	-2	57	38	S5,3b4/2	22	-0.7
	Year	48	81	6	11	1	1	0	4	5-0	0	14	.136	.184	.173	8	-10	0-1	.946	-1	69	67	2b18,S11,3b5	0	-1.1
Total	7	436	945	97	230	19	11	0	57	70-6	3	107	.243	.296	.287	69	-38	7-8	.950	-16	99	101	S157,3b74,2b59,C30,O21L,1b5/P	93	-4.6
Martinez, Pablo	Pablo Made (Valera); B6.29.1969 Sabana Grande, D.R.; BB/TR/5´10˝/155; d7.20																								
1996	Atl N	4	2	1	1	0	0	0	0	0-0	0	0	.500	.500	.500	155	0	0-1	1.000	-1	63	172	/S	0	-0.1
Martinez, Ramon	Ramon E.; B10.10.1972 Philadelphia PA; BR/TR/6´1˝/(170–190); d6.20; Col Vernon (TX) JC; OF(3/0/1)																								
1998	SF N	19	19	4	6	1	0	0	0	4-0	0	2	.316	.435	.368	120	1	0-0	1.000	2	113	176	2b14	0	0.3
1999	SF N	61	144	21	38	6	0	5	19	14-0	0	17	.264	.327	.410	91	-2	1-2	.992	5	124	114	2b27,S12,3b11/D	15	0.3
2000	†SF N	88	189	30	57	13	2	6	25	15-1	1	22	.302	.354	.487	118	5	3-2	.991	-6	87	112	S44,2b32,1b2,3b2	0	0.1
2001	SF N	128	391	48	99	18	3	5	37	38-6	5	52	.253	.323	.353	81	-11	1-2	.974	2	89	66	3b70,2b42,S24	0	-0.7
2002	†SF N	72	181	26	49	10	2	4	25	14-2	4	26	.271	.335	.414	100	0	2-0	.950	-4	93	138	S40,2b17,1b4,O3L,3b2	15	-0.1
2003	†Chi N	108	293	30	83	16	1	3	34	24-1	2	50	.283	.333	.375	85	-6	0-1	.979	-1	80	111	2b42,3b37,S32,1b2	0	-0.4
2004	Chi N	102	260	22	64	15	1	3	30	26-3	1	40	.246	.313	.346	69	-12	1-0	.977	4	101	96	S73,3b24,2b6	15	-0.2
2005	Det A	19	56	4	15	1	0	0	5	3-0	0	4	.268	.300	.286	60	-3	0-0	.955	-2	95	60	S12,2b4,1b2/3	20	-0.4
	Phi N	33	56	7	16	2	0	1	9	3-0	1	7	.286	.317	.375	82	-1	0-0	1.000	-1	108	116	1b10,3b3,S3/2	0	-0.3
2006	†LA N	82	176	20	49	7	1	2	24	15-1	1	20	.278	.339	.364	80	-5	0-0	1.000	-4	94	67	2b39,3b20,S12/1rf	0	-0.7
Total	9	712	1765	212	476	89	10	29	208	156-14	15	240	.270	.330	.381	86	-34	8-7	.968	-5	99	113	S252,2b224,3b170,1b21,O4L/D	65	-2.1
Martinez, Chito	Reyenaldo Ignacio; B12.19.1965 Belize City, British Honduras (Belize); BL/TL/5´10˝/(180–185); [KCA84 6/148]; d7.5																								
1991	Bal A	67	216	32	58	12	1	13	33	11-0	0	51	.269	.303	.514	126	6	1-1	.982	1	102	106	O54(1/0/53)/1D	0	0.5
1992	Bal A	83	198	26	53	10	1	5	25	31-4	2	47	.268	.366	.404	114	5	0-1	.973	0	101	117	O52R,D4	0	0.3
1993	Bal A	8	15	0	0	0	0	0	0	4-2	0	4	.000	.211	.000	-36	-3	0-0	1.000	-1	37	0	O5R,D2	0	-0.4
Total	3	158	429	58	111	22	2	18	58	46-6	2	102	.259	.330	.445	114	8	1-2	.978	1	100	109	O111(1/0/110),D10/1	0	0.4
Martinez, Hector	Rodolfo Hector (Santos); B5.11.1939 Las Villas, Cuba; D12.1999 , Cuba; BR/TR/5´10˝/(160–170); d9.30																								
1962	KC A	1	1	0	0	0	0	0	0	0-0	0	1	.000	.000	.000	-96	0	0-0	ø	0	—	—	/H	0	0.0
1963	KC A	6	14	2	4	0	0	1	3	1-0	1	3	.286	.375	.500	135	1	0-1	1.000	-0	100	0	O3C	0	0.0
Total	2	7	15	2	4	0	0	1	3	1-0	1	4	.267	.353	.467	120	1	0-1	1.000	-0	100	0	O3C	0	0.0
Martinez, Ted	Teodoro Noel (Encarnacion); B12.10.1947 Santa Cruz de Barahona, D.R.; BR/TR (BB 1973p)/6´0˝/(158–160); d7.18; [DL 1976 Oak A 29]																								
1970	NY N	4	16	0	1	0	0	0	0	0-0	0	3	.063	.063	.063	-66	-4	0-0	1.000	0	76	153	2b4/S	0	-0.3
1971	NY N	38	125	16	36	5	2	1	10	4-2	3	22	.288	.323	.384	100	0	6-0	.976	-7	83	120	S23,2b13,3b3/lf	17	-0.3
1972	NY N	103	330	22	74	5	5	1	19	12-2	1	49	.224	.254	.279	52	-22	7-4	.994	-12	72	39	2b47,S42,O15(6/4/5),3b2	0	-3.1
1973	†NY N	92	263	34	67	11	0	1	14	13-2	2	38	.255	.294	.308	68	-12	3-5	.941	-8	91	58	S44,O21(4/18/0),3b14,2b5	0	-1.8
1974	NY N	116	334	32	73	15	7	2	43	14-4	0	40	.219	.247	.323	60	-20	3-2	.952	-1	96	83	S75,3b12,2b11,O10(1/9/0)	0	-1.3
1975	StL N	16	21	1	4	2	0	0	2	0-0	0	2	.190	.190	.286	29	-2	0-0	1.000	0	118	0	O7(3/0/4),2b2/S3	0	-0.2
	†Oak A	86	87	7	15	0	0	0	3	2-0	1	9	.172	.200	.172	6	-11	1-1	.955	-8	77	74	S45,2b31,3b14	0	-1.7
1977	LA N	67	137	21	41	6	1	1	10	2-0	0	20	.299	.309	.380	83	-4	3-4	.992	3	109	192	2b27,S13,3b12	38	0.1
1978	LA N	54	55	13	14	1	0	1	5	4-1	1	14	.255	.317	.327	80	-2	3-2	.912	0	88	68	S17,3b16,2b10	0	0.0
1979	LA N	81	112	19	30	5	1	0	2	4-1	0	16	.268	.293	.330	71	-5	3-2	.769	-14	42	74	3b23,S21,2b18	0	-1.8
Total	9	657	1480	165	355	50	16	7	108	55-12	8	213	.240	.270	.309	62	-82	29-20	.956	-46	88	82	S282,2b168,3b97,O54(15/31/9)	84	-10.4
Martinez, Victor	Victor Jesus; B12.23.1978 Ciudad Bolivar, Bolivar, Venezuela; BB/TR/6´2˝/(170–195); d9.10																								
2002	Cle A	12	32	2	9	1	0	1	5	3-0	0	2	.281	.333	.406	96	0	0-0	.983	-2	40	100	C9/D	0	-0.2
2003	Cle A	49	159	15	46	4	0	1	16	13-0	1	21	.289	.345	.333	81	-4	1-1	.996	3	108	102	C40,D5	24	0.2
2004	Cle A★	141	520	77	147	38	1	23	108	60-11	5	69	.283	.359	.492	124	20	0-1	.994	-11	72	102	C132,D8	0	1.6
2005	Cle A	147	547	73	167	33	0	20	80	63-9	5	78	.305	.378	.475	131	26	0-1	.995	-2	79	92	C142,D2	0	3.3
2006	Cle A	153	572	82	181	37	0	16	93	71-8	3	78	.316	.391	.465	127	26	0-0	.990	-17	70	74	C133,1b22,D3	0	1.5
Total	5	502	1830	249	550	113	1	61	302	210-28	14	248	.301	.373	.463	123	68	1-3	.993	-28	76	91	C456,1b22,D19	24	6.4
Marty, Joe	Joseph Anton; B9.1.1913 Sacramento CA; D10.4.1984 Sacramento CA; BR/TR/6´0˝/182; d4.22; Mil 1942–45; Col St. Marys (CA)																								
1937	Chi N	88	290	41	84	17	2	5	44	28	2	30	.290	.356	.414	104	2	3	.976	-3	97	60	O84(1/83/0)	—	-0.3
1938	†Chi N	76	235	32	57	8	3	7	35	18	3	26	.243	.305	.391	88	-5	0	.987	-2	93	113	O68(0/64/6)	—	-0.9
1939	Chi N	23	76	6	10	1	0	2	10	4	0	13	.132	.175	.224	6	-11	2	.933	-0	73	273	O21(1/1/19)	—	-1.2
	Phi N	91	299	32	76	12	6	9	44	24	0	27	.254	.310	.425	98	-3	1	.974	3	103	151	O79(6/56/18)/P	—	-0.2
	Year	114	375	38	86	13	6	11	54	28	0	40	.229	.283	.384	79	-13	3	.968	3	97	174	O100(7/57/37)/P	—	-1.4
1940	Phi N	123	455	52	123	21	8	13	50	17	1	50	.270	.298	.437	105	-1	2	.974	-1	104	74	O118(0/115/3)	—	-0.5
1941	Phi N	137	477	60	128	19	3	8	39	51	4	41	.268	.344	.371	105	4	6	.964	-8	93	71	O132(0/131/1)	0	-0.8
Total	5	538	1832	223	478	78	22	44	222	142	10	187	.261	.318	.400	97	-14	14	.972	-11	97	95	O502(8/450/47)/P	0	-3.9
Martyn, Bob	Robert Gordon; B8.15.1930 Weiser ID; BL/TR/6´0˝/(175–176); d6.18; Col Linfield																								
1957	KC A	58	131	10	35	2	4	1	12	11-3	0	20	.267	.322	.366	87	-3	1-3	.976	1	105	119	O49(13/9/28)	0	-0.5
1958	KC A	95	226	25	59	10	7	2	23	26-5	0	36	.261	.336	.394	99	0	1-4	.967	2	107	97	O63(27/1/45)	0	-0.3
1959	KC A	1	1	0	0	0	0	0	0	0-0	0	0	.000	.000	.000	-98	0	0-0	ø	0	—	—	/R	0	0.0
Total	3	154	358	35	94	12	11	3	35	37-8	0	56	.263	.330	.383	94	-3	2-7	.970	3	106	106	O112(40/10/73)	0	-0.8
Martz, Gary	Gary Arthur; B1.10.1951 Spokane WA; BR/TR/6´4˝/210; [MilA69 5/115]; d7.8																								
1975	KC A	1	1	0	0	0	0	0	0	0-0	0	0	.000	.000	.000	-98	0	0-0	1.000	0	411	0	/lf	0	0.0

YEAR	TM LG	G	AB	R	H	2B	3B	HR	RBI	BB-IB	HP	SO	AVG	OBP	SLG	AOPS	ABR	SB-CS	FA	FR	RNG	THR	GAMES AT POSITION	DL	BFW
MARZANO, JOHN	John Robert; B2.14.1963 Philadelphia PA; BR/TR/5´11˝/(185–197); [BosA84 1/14]; d7.31; Col Temple																								
1987	Bos A	52	168	20	41	11	0	5	24	7-0	3	41	.244	.283	.399	77	-6	0-1	.986	4	114	97	C52	0	0.0
1988	Bos A	10	29	3	4	1	0	0	1	1-0	0	3	.138	.167	.172	-5	-4	0-0	1.000	3	86	111	C10	0	0.0
1989	Bos A	7	18	5	8	3	0	1	3	0-0	0	2	.444	.421	.778	224	3	0-0	1.000	-1	98	113	C7	0	0.2
1990	Bos A	32	83	8	20	4	0	0	6	5-0	0	10	.241	.281	.289	58	-5	0-1	1.000	3	84	100	C32	0	-0.1
1991	Bos A	49	114	10	30	8	0	0	9	1-0	1	16	.263	.271	.333	64	-6	0-0	.985	-3	130	122	C48	0	-0.6
1992	Bos A	19	50	4	4	2	1	0	1	2-0	1	12	.080	.132	.160	-17	-8	0-0	.968	-2	79	87	C18/D	111	-0.9
1995	Tex A	2	6	1	2	0	0	0	0	0-0	0	0	.333	.333	.333	72	0	0-0	1.000	-0	27	281	C2	0	0.0
1996	Sea A	41	106	8	26	6	0	0	6	7-0	4	15	.245	.316	.302	57	-7	0-0	.986	-2	123	35	C39	0	-0.6
1997	Sea A	39	87	7	25	3	0	1	10	7-0	0	15	.287	.340	.356	82	-2	0-0	.976	-2	85	105	C37/D	0	-0.3
1998	Sea A	50	133	13	31	7	1	4	12	9-1	9	24	.233	.325	.391	84	-3	0-0	.997	4	92	95	C48/D	0	0.4
Total	10	301	794	79	191	45	2	11	72	39-1	18	138	.241	.289	.344	67	-38	0-2	.988	5	103	94	C293,D3	111	-1.9
MASHORE, CLYDE	Clyde Wayne; B5.29.1945 Concord CA; BR/TR/5´11˝/(182–184); d7.11; s–Damon																								
1969	Cin N	2	1	1	0	0	0	0	0	0-0	0	0	.000	.000	.000	-95	0	0-0	ø	0	—	—	/H	0	0.0
1970	Mon N	13	25	2	4	0	0	1	3	4-2	0	11	.160	.276	.280	49	-2	0-0	1.000	-1	77	0	O10(2/8/0)	0	-0.3
1971	Mon N	66	114	20	22	5	0	1	7	10-1	0	22	.193	.258	.263	47	-8	1-0	.967	-2	91	0	O47(19/29/5)/3	38	-1.2
1972	Mon N	93	176	23	40	7	1	3	23	14-1	0	41	.227	.278	.330	73	-7	6-1	.988	-2	87	85	O74(23/8/46)	0	-1.1
1973	Mon N	67	103	12	21	3	0	3	14	15-0	0	28	.204	.300	.320	71	-4	4-3	.958	3	102	189	O44(43/3/1)/2	20	-0.3
Total	5	241	419	58	87	15	1	8	47	43-4	0	102	.208	.278	.305	64	-21	11-4	.974	-3	91	84	O175(87/48/52)/23	58	-2.9
MASHORE, DAMON	Damon Wayne; B10.31.1969 Ponce, PR; BR/TR/5´11˝/(195–209); [OakA91 9/255]; d6.5; f–Clyde; Col Arizona																								
1996	Oak A	50	105	20	28	7	1	3	12	16-0	1	31	.267	.366	.438	104	1	4-0	.985	-1	94	45	O48(35/7/15)	48	0.0
1997	Oak A	92	279	55	69	10	2	3	18	50-1	5	82	.247	.370	.330	85	-4	5-4	.991	9	108	246	O89(28/71/6)	64	0.4
1998	Ana A	43	98	13	23	6	0	2	11	9-0	3	22	.235	.318	.357	74	-4	1-0	1.000	-1	95	54	O35(1/7/28),D7	0	-0.5
Total	3	185	482	88	120	23	3	8	41	75-1	9	135	.249	.359	.359	87	-7	10-4	.991	7	102	161	O172(64/85/49),D7	112	-0.1
MASI, PHIL	Philip Samuel; B1.6.1916 Chicago IL; D3.29.1990 Mt.Prospect IL; BR/TR/5´10˝/(175–180); d4.23																								
1939	Bos N	46	114	14	29	7	2	1	14	9	1	15	.254	.315	.377	92	-2	0	.960	-1	*148*	*93*	C42	—	-0.1
1940	Bos N	63	138	11	27	4	1	1	14	14	0	14	.196	.270	.261	50	-10	0	.966	-1	*105*	*126*	C52	—	-0.8
1941	Bos N	87	180	17	40	8	2	3	18	16	0	13	.222	.286	.339	79	-6	4	.978	-5	*95*	*95*	C83	0	-0.7
1942	Bos N	57	87	14	19	3	1	0	9	12	0	4	.218	.313	.276	74	-3	2	.961	0	*75*	*159*	C39,O4(1/0/4)	0	-0.1
1943	Bos N	80	238	27	65	9	1	2	28	27	0	20	.273	.347	.345	102	1	7	.991	-7	*57*	*128*	C73	0	-0.2
1944	Bos N	89	251	33	69	13	5	3	23	31	0	20	.275	.355	.402	108	3	4	.977	-1	*65*	*141*	C63,1b12,3b2	0	0.5
1945	Bos N✳	114	371	55	101	25	4	7	46	42	1	32	.272	.348	.418	112	6	9	.980	1	*101*	*114*	C95,1b7	0	1.2
1946	Bos N★	133	397	52	106	17	5	3	62	55	1	41	.267	.358	.358	102	2	5	.981	-8	*81*	*87*	C124	0	0.1
1947	Bos N★	126	411	54	125	22	4	9	50	47	1	27	.304	.377	.443	120	12	7	**.989**	-3	*82*	*111*	C123	0	1.5
1948	†Bos N★	113	376	43	95	19	0	5	44	35	1	26	.253	.318	.343	80	-10	2	.988	0	*93*	*76*	C109	0	-0.5
1949	Bos N	37	105	13	22	2	0	0	6	14	0	10	.210	.303	.229	47	-8	1	.993	-1	*100*	*87*	C37	0	-0.7
	Pit N	48	135	16	37	6	1	2	13	17	0	16	.274	.355	.378	94	-1	1	.994	1	*118*	*109*	C44,1b2	0	0.2
	Year	85	240	29	59	8	1	2	19	31	0	26	.246	.332	.313	74	-8	2	**.994**	0	*110*	*99*	C81,1b2	0	-0.5
1950	Chi A	122	377	38	105	17	2	7	55	49	3	36	.279	.366	.390	96	-1	2-1	**.996**	2	*73*	*108*	C114	0	0.6
1951	Chi A	84	225	24	61	11	2	4	28	32	2	27	.271	.367	.391	107	3	1-0	.979	0	*80*	*54*	C78	0	0.7
1952	Chi A	30	63	9	16	1	1	0	7	10	0	10	.254	.356	.302	84	-1	0-0	.956	-1	*72*	*66*	C25	0	-0.1
Total	14	1229	3468	420	917	164	31	47	417	410	10	311	.264	.344	.370	97	-15	45-1	.983	-24	*87*	*102*	C1101,1b21,O4(1/0/4),3b2	0	1.6
MASKREY, HARRY	Harry H.; B12.21.1861 Mercer PA; D8.17.1930 Mercer PA; d9.21; b–Leech																								
1882	Lou AA	1	4	0	0	0	0	0	—	0	—	—	.000	.000	.000	-99	-1	—	.000	-1	0	0	/cf	—	-0.1
MASKREY, LEECH	Samuel Leech; B2.11.1854 Mercer PA; D4.1.1922 Mercer PA; BR/TR/5´8˝/150; d5.2; b–Harry																								
1882	Lou AA	76	288	30	65	14	2	0	—	9	—	—	.226	.249	.288	85	-3	—	.902	-2	60	58	O76(75/0/1)/2	—	-0.6
1883	Lou AA	96	361	50	73	13	8	1	—	10	—	—	.202	.224	.291	70	-11	—	.914	10	103	46	O96(45/41/14)/S	—	-0.3
1884	Lou AA	105	412	48	103	13	4	0	36	17	1	—	.250	.281	.301	94	-2	—	.896	4	88	81	O103(97/0/7),3b3/S	—	0.0
1885	Lou AA	109	423	54	97	8	11	1	46	19	4	—	.229	.269	.307	82	-10	—	.899	-4	48	59	O108L,3b3	—	-1.5
1886	Lou AA	5	19	1	3	1	0	0	2	1	0	—	.158	.200	.211	27	-2	0	.800	-1	0	0	O5(3/0/2)	—	-0.2
	Cin AA	27	98	7	19	3	1	0	10	5	1	—	.194	.240	.245	51	-6	4	.926	-1	91	116	O26(0/7/19),3b2	—	-0.6
	Year	32	117	8	22	4	1	0	12	6	1	—	.188	.234	.239	47	-7	4	.915	-2	79	101	O31(3/7/21),3b2	—	-0.8
Total	5	418	1601	190	360	52	26	2	94	61	6	—	.225	.256	.294	80	-34	4	.904	6	75	64	O414(328/48/43),3b8,S2/2	—	-3.2
MASON, CHARLIE	Charles E.; B6.25.1853 New Orleans LA; D10.21.1936 Philadelphia PA; BR/TR/?/175; d4.26; M1																								
1875	Cen NA	12	47	5	11	0	0	0	3	0	—	1	.234	.234	.234	69	-1	0-0	.719	-0	174	0	O10(3/0/7),1b2/C	—	-0.1
	Was NA	8	33	2	3	0	0	0	1	0	—	3	.091	.091	.091	-38	-4	0-0	.909	2	251	0	O8L/P	—	-0.1
	Year	20	80	7	14	0	0	0	4	0	—	4	.175	.175	.175	23	-6	0-0	.796	2	205	0	O18(11/0/7),1b2/CP	—	-0.2
1883	Phi AA	1	2	0	1	0	0	0	1	0	—	—	.500	.500	.500	204	0	—	ø	-0	0	0	/rf	—	0.0
MASON, DON	Donald Stetson; B12.20.1944 Boston MA; BL/TR/5´11˝/160; d4.14																								
1966	SF N	42	25	8	3	0	0	1	1	0-0	0	2	.120	.120	.240	-3	-4	0-1	.905	0	99	56	2b9	0	-0.4
1967	SF N	4	3	0	0	0	0	0	0	0-0	0	0	.000	.000	.000	-99	-1	0-0	1.000	-1	106	0	2b2	0	-0.1
1968	SF N	10	19	3	3	0	0	0	1	1-0	0	4	.158	.200	.158	8	-2	1-1	1.000	-2	63	0	2b5,S4,3b2	0	-0.5
1969	SF N	104	250	43	57	4	2	0	13	36-0	0	29	.228	.324	.260	67	-10	1-5	.956	2	108	127	2b51,3b21,S7	0	-0.7
1970	SF N	46	36	4	5	0	0	0	1	5-0	0	7	.139	.244	.139	5	-5	0-0	.950	-3	61	32	2b14	0	-0.7
1971	SD N	113	344	43	73	12	1	2	11	27-0	0	35	.212	.270	.270	57	-20	6-4	.965	-6	97	80	2b90,3b3	0	-2.2
1972	SD N	9	11	1	2	0	0	0	0	1-0	0	1	.182	.250	.182	26	-1	0-0	.692	-2	96	0	2b3	0	-0.3
1973	SD N	8	8	0	0	0	0	0	0	0-0	0	2	.000	.000	.000	-99	-2	0-0	.750	0	199	420	/2	0	-0.2
Total	8	336	696	102	143	16	3	3	27	70-0	0	80	.205	.278	.250	52	-45	8-11	.955	-10	99	91	2b175,3b26,S11	0	-5.1
MASON, JIM	James Percy; B8.14.1950 Mobile AL; BL/TR/6´2˝/(170–190); [TexA68 2/28]; d9.26																								
1971	Was A	3	9	0	3	0	0	0	0	1-0	0	3	.333	.400	.333	115	0	0-0	.955	2	144	54	S3	0	0.2
1972	Tex A	46	147	10	29	3	0	0	10	9-0	1	39	.197	.247	.218	41	-11	0-0	.948	-7	94	66	S32,3b10	0	-1.7
1973	Tex A	92	238	23	49	7	2	3	19	23-0	0	48	.206	.273	.290	62	-13	0-1	.947	-2	98	91	S74,2b19/3	0	-0.6
1974	NY A	152	440	41	110	18	6	5	37	35-1	0	87	.250	.302	.352	90	-7	1-2	.964	0	98	103	S152	0	1.0
1975	NY A	94	223	17	34	3	2	2	16	22-0	0	49	.152	.228	.211	25	-23	0-2	.955	-1	93	110	S93/2	0	-1.7
1976	†NY A	93	217	17	39	7	1	1	14	9-0	0	37	.180	.210	.235	31	-19	0-0	.966	5	108	123	S93	0	-0.6
1977	Tor A	22	79	10	13	3	0	0	2	7-0	0	10	.165	.233	.203	20	-9	1-1	.971	-3	82	66	S22	0	-0.9
	Tex A	36	55	9	12	3	0	1	7	6-0	0	10	.218	.290	.327	68	-2	0-0	.976	2	111	115	S32/3D	0	0.1
	Year	58	134	19	25	6	0	1	9	13-0	0	20	.187	.257	.254	40	-11	1-1	.973	-1	95	88	S54/3D	0	-0.8
1978	Tex A	55	105	10	20	4	0	0	3	5-0	0	17	.190	.227	.229	28	-10	0-0	.938	-4	103	84	S42,3b11/2D	0	-1.2
1979	Mon N	40	71	3	13	5	1	0	6	7-1	0	16	.183	.256	.282	47	-5	0-2	.966	-4	84	84	S33,3b6	0	-0.9
Total	9	633	1584	140	322	53	12	12	114	124-2	1	316	.203	.259	.275	54	-99	2-8	.959	-11	98	100	S576,3b29,2b21,D2	0	-6.3
MASSA, GORDON	Gordon Richard "Moose","Duke"; B9.2.1935 Cincinnati OH; BL/TR/6´3˝/210; d9.24; Mil 1959; Col Holy Cross																								
1957	Chi N	6	15	2	7	1	0	0	3	4-0	0	3	.467	.579	.533	205	3	0-0	1.000	-1	125	0	C6	0	0.2
1958	Chi N	2	2	0	0	0	0	0	0	0-0	0	2	.000	.000	.000	-99	-1	0-0	ø	0	—	—	/H	0	-0.1
Total	2	8	17	2	7	1	0	0	3	4-0	0	5	.412	.524	.471	172	2	0-0	1.000	-1	125	0	C6	0	0.1
MASSEY, ROY	Roy Hardee "Red"; B10.9.1890 Sevierville TN; D6.23.1954 Atlanta GA; BL/TR/5´11˝/170; d4.16; Col Tennessee																								
1918	Bos N	66	203	20	59	6	2	0	18	23	0	20	.291	.363	.340	120	6	1	.954	-2	91	106	O45(21/29/0),3b2/1S	—	0.1
MASSEY, BILL	William Harry "Big Bill"; B1.1871 Philadelphia PA; D10.9.1940 Manila, Philippines; BR/TR/5´11˝/168; d9.18																								
1894	Cin N	13	53	7	15	3	0	0	5	3	0	2	.283	.321	.340	57	-4	0	.991	-2	86	227	1b10,2b2/3	—	-0.4
MASSEY, MIKE	William Herbert; B9.28.1893 Galveston TX; D10.17.1971 Shreveport LA; BB/TR/6´0˝/195; d4.12; Col Texas																								
1917	Bos N	31	91	12	18	0	0	0	2	15	1	15	.198	.318	.198	63	-3	2	.900	-7	91	89	2b25	—	-1.1
MASTELLER, DAN	Dan Patrick; B3.17.1968 Toledo OH; BL/TL/6´0˝/190; [MinA89 11/295]; d6.23; Col Michigan St.																								
1995	Min A	71	198	21	47	12	0	3	21	18-0	1	19	.237	.303	.343	68	-9	1-2	.994	-2	81	112	1b48,O22(6/0/16),D8	0	-1.5

THE BATTER REGISTER

YEAR	TM LG	G	AB	R	H	2B	3B	HR	RBI	BB-IB	HP	SO	AVG	OBP	SLG	AOPS	ABR	SB-CS	FA	FR	RNG	THR	GAMES AT POSITION	DL	BFW
Mata, Victor	Victor Jose (Abreu); B6.17.1961 Santiago, D.R.; BR/TR/6´1˝/165; d7.22																								
1984	NY A	30	70	8	23	5	0	1	6	0-0	1	12	.329	.333	.443	118	2	1-1	.942	-2	92	0	O28(2/21/8)	0	-0.1
1985	NY A	6	7	1	1	0	0	0	0	0-0	0	0	.143	.143	.143	-22	-1	0-0	1.000	-1	27	0	O3(1/1/2)	0	-0.2
Total	2	36	77	9	24	5	0	1	6	0-0	1	12	.312	.316	.416	105	1	1-1	.943	-3	87	0	O31(3/22/10)	0	-0.3
Matchick, Tom	John Thomas; B9.7.1943 Hazleton PA; BL/TR/6´0˝/175; d9.2																								
1967	Det A	8	6	1	1	0	0	0	0	0-0	0	2	.167	.167	.167	-1	-1	0-0	1.000	0	0	0	/S	0	-0.1
1968	†Det A	80	227	18	46	6	2	3	14	10-3	4	46	.203	.248	.286	60	-11	0-2	.950	-2	94	99	S59,2b13,1b6	0	-1.2
1969	Det A	94	298	25	72	11	2	0	32	15-3	0	51	.242	.276	.292	57	-17	3-0	.972	-7	101	117	2b47,3b27,S6,1b2	0	-2.2
1970	Bos A	10	14	2	1	0	0	0	0	2-0	0	2	.071	.188	.071	-24	-2	0-1	1.000	-0	105	0	3b2/2S	0	-0.3
	KC A	55	158	11	31	3	2	0	11	5-2	1	23	.196	.226	.241	28	-16	0-0	.985	11	115	138	S43,2b10/3	21	0.0
	Year	65	172	13	32	3	2	0	11	7-2	1	25	.186	.222	.227	24	-18	0-1	.985	11	115	138	S44,2b11,3b3	0	-0.3
1971	Mil A	42	114	6	25	1	0	1	7	7-0	0	23	.219	.264	.254	48	-8	3-2	.979	0	98	90	3b41/2	0	-0.9
1972	Bal A	3	9	0	2	0	0	0	0	0-0	0	1	.222	.222	.222	31	-1	0-1	.857	-1	78	0	3b3	0	-0.2
Total	6	292	826	63	178	21	6	4	64	39-8	5	148	.215	.254	.270	49	-56	6-6	.967	1	100	113	S110,3b74,2b72,1b8	21	-4.9
Mateo, Henry	Henry Antonio (Valera); B10.14.1976 Santo Domingo, D.R.; BB/TR/5´11˝/(175–180); [MonN95 2/58]; d7.28																								
2001	Mon N	5	9	1	3	1	0	0	0	0-0	0	1	.333	.333	.444	99	0	0-0	.818	-1	104	0	2b2	0	-0.1
2002	Mon N	22	23	1	4	0	1	0	0	2-1	0	6	.174	.240	.261	30	-3	2-0	1.000	2	204	111	2b3,S2	0	0.0
2003	Mon N	100	154	29	37	3	1	0	7	11-0	3	38	.240	.304	.273	51	-11	11-1	.970	3	106	137	2b43,O10(2/2/6),S2,D3	0	-0.5
2004	Mon N	40	44	3	12	2	0	0	0	1-0	0	9	.273	.289	.318	55	-3	2-3	.879	2	138	109	2b9/lf	0	-0.2
2005	Was N	1	1	0	0	0	0	0	0	1-0	0	0	.000	.500	.000	49	0	0-0	1.000	-0	97	0	/2	118	0.0
2006	Was N	22	26	5	4	2	0	1	3	2-0	0	3	.154	.214	.346	42	-2	0-0	.875	-1	62	88	S3,3b2/cf	0	-0.4
Total	6	190	257	39	60	8	2	1	10	17-1	3	57	.233	.289	.292	51	-19	15-4	.948	4	114	121	2b58,O12(3/3/6),S7,D3,3b2	118	-1.2
Mateo, Ruben	Ruben Amaury; B2.10.1978 San Cristobal, D.R.; BR/TR/6´0˝/(185–210); d6.12																								
1999	Tex A	32	122	16	29	9	1	5	18	4-0	1	28	.238	.268	.451	74	-5	3-0	1.000	-3	80	156	O31C	76	-0.6
2000	Tex A	52	206	32	60	11	0	7	19	10-1	5	34	.291	.339	.447	96	-2	6-0	.980	1	102	150	O52C	120	0.1
2001	Tex A	40	129	18	32	5	2	1	13	9-0	6	28	.248	.322	.341	74	-5	1-0	.986	-3	92	0	O39R	0	-0.9
2002	Cin N	46	86	11	22	6	0	2	7	6-0	2	20	.256	.319	.395	84	-2	0-0	1.000	-1	93	84	O24(0/2/23)	0	-0.3
2003	Cin N	74	207	16	50	9	0	3	18	12-1	3	53	.242	.290	.329	65	-11	0-0	.982	-1	101	62	O54(4/14/39)	0	-1.4
2004	Pit N	19	33	4	8	0	0	3	7	5-1	1	6	.242	.359	.515	122	1	0-0	.933	-0	76	228	O10(2/5/4)/D	0	0.0
	KC A	32	93	9	18	4	3	0	7	3-0	2	20	.194	.235	.301	38	-9	1-1	1.000	2	101	274	O30(11/5/15)	0	-0.7
Total	6	295	876	106	219	44	6	21	89	49-3	20	189	.250	.303	.386	77	-33	11-1	.986	-4	95	117	O240(17/109/120)/D	196	-3.8
Matheny, Mike	Michael Scott; B9.22.1970 Columbus OH; BR/TR/6´3˝/(205–220); [MilA91 8/208]; d4.7; Col Michigan																								
1994	Mil A	28	53	3	12	3	0	1	2	3-0	2	13	.226	.293	.340	59	-3	0-1	.989	-1	83	98	C27	0	-0.3
1995	Mil A	80	166	13	41	9	1	0	21	12-0	2	28	.247	.306	.313	58	-10	2-1	.986	-2	125	60	C80	0	-0.8
1996	Mil A	106	313	31	64	15	2	8	46	14-0	3	80	.204	.243	.342	44	-28	3-2	.985	-5	114	97	C104/D	0	-2.4
1997	Mil A	123	320	29	78	16	1	4	32	17-0	7	68	.244	.294	.338	64	-17	0-1	.993	11	103	109	C121,1b2	0	0.1
1998	Mil N	108	320	24	76	13	0	6	27	11-0	7	63	.237	.278	.334	59	-20	1-0	.987	-12	84	83	C107	28	-2.5
1999	Tor A	57	163	16	35	6	0	3	17	12-0	1	37	.215	.271	.307	47	-14	0-0	.995	8	80	126	C57	0	-0.2
2000	StL N	128	417	43	109	22	1	6	47	32-8	4	96	.261	.317	.362	70	-19	0-0	.994	17	163	149	C124,1b8	0	0.5
2001	†StL N	121	381	40	83	12	0	7	42	28-5	4	76	.218	.276	.304	50	-29	0-1	.995	15	**210**	88	C121,1b2	0	-0.6
2002	†StL N	110	315	31	77	12	1	3	35	32-6	2	49	.244	.313	.317	68	-15	1-3	.994	3	127	91	C106/1	0	-0.6
2003	StL N	141	441	43	111	18	2	8	47	44-16	2	81	.252	.320	.356	78	-15	1-1	**1.000**	-2	155	53	C138,1b4	0	-0.9
2004	†StL N	122	385	28	95	22	1	5	50	23-7	3	83	.247	.292	.348	65	-21	0-2	**.999**	16	154	71	C122/1	15	0.2
2005	SF N	134	443	42	107	34	0	13	59	29-10	6	91	.242	.295	.406	80	-13	0-2	.999	10	106	145	C132	0	0.5
2006	SF N	47	160	10	37	8	0	3	18	9-2	2	30	.231	.276	.338	57	-11	0-0	.996	-7	111	108	C46	123	-1.4
Total	13	1305	3877	353	925	190	9	67	443	266-54	45	795	.239	.293	.344	64	-215	8-14	.994	52	132	99	C1285,1b18/D	166	-8.4
Mathes, Joe	Joseph John; B7.28.1891 Milwaukee WI; D12.21.1978 St.Louis MO; BB/TR/6´0.5˝/180; d9.19																								
1912	Phi A	4	14	0	2	0	0	0	0	0	1	—	.143	.200	.143	-2	-2	0	.889	-0	115	0	3b4	—	-0.2
1914	StL F	26	85	10	25	3	0	0	6	9	0	11	.294	.362	.329	85	-3	1	.938	-4	91	60	2b23	—	-0.6
1916	Bos N	2	0	0	0	0	0	0	0	0	0	0	ø	ø	ø	ø	0	0	.000	-1	0	0	2b2	—	-0.1
Total	3	32	99	10	27	3	0	0	6	9	1	11	.273	.339	.303	74	-5	1	.921	-5	90	59	2b25,3b4	—	-0.9
Mathews, Eddie	Edwin Lee; B10.13.1931 Texarkana TX; D2.18.2001 LaJolla CA; BL/TR/6´1˝/(185–200); d4.15; M3/C2; HF1978																								
1952	Bos N	145	528	80	128	23	5	25	58	59	1	115	.242	.320	.447	114	8	6-4	.957	-9	92	85	3b142	0	-0.1
1953	Mil N★	**157**	579	110	175	31	8	**47**	135	99	2	83	.302	.406	.627	**175**	65	1-3	.939	1	99	105	3b157	0	6.1
1954	Mil N	138	476	96	138	21	4	40	103	113	2	61	.290	.423	.603	**177**	58	10-3	.966	-2	**99**	**128**	3b127,O10L	0	5.4
1955	Mil N★	141	499	108	144	23	5	41	101	**109**-20	1	98	.289	.413	.601	175	58	3-4	.952	-7	98	84	3b137	0	4.9
1956	Mil N☆	151	552	103	150	21	2	37	95	91-17	1	86	.272	.373	.518	146	37	6-0	.944	-14	97	92	3b150	0	2.5
1957	†Mil N★	148	572	109	167	28	9	32	94	90-5	0	79	.292	.387	.540	157	48	3-1	.964	-5	**101**	98	3b147	0	4.3
1958	†Mil N☆	149	546	97	137	18	1	31	77	85-5	2	85	.251	.349	.458	123	19	5-0	.955	8	111	90	3b149	0	2.7
1959	Mil N★	148	594	118	182	16	8	**46**	114	80-2	3	71	.306	.390	.593	172	60	2-1	.961	2	103	92	3b148	0	6.0
1960	Mil N★	153	548	108	152	19	7	39	124	111-3	2	113	.277	.397	.551	**170**	**57**	7-3	.950	-14	92	85	3b153	0	4.3
1961	Mil N★	152	572	103	175	23	6	32	91	**93**-3	2	95	.306	.402	.535	156	49	12-7	.961	-7	96	107	3b151	0	4.1
1962	Mil N★	152	536	106	142	25	6	29	90	**101**-7	2	90	.265	.381	.496	138	32	4-2	.964	1	101	92	3b140,1b7	0	3.1
1963	Mil N	158	547	82	144	27	4	23	84	**124**-14	1	119	.263	**.399**	.453	147	41	3-4	**.968**	13	112	135	3b121,O42L	0	5.3
1964	Mil N	141	502	83	117	19	1	23	74	85-5	1	100	.233	.344	.412	112	10	2-2	.962	6	99	99	3b128,1b7	0	1.6
1965	Mil N	156	546	77	137	23	0	32	95	73-7	3	110	.251	.341	.469	125	19	1-0	.956	5	105	79	3b153	0	2.5
1966	Atl N	134	452	72	113	21	4	16	53	63-6	0	82	.250	.341	.420	109	7	1-1	.946	-0	99	**134**	3b127	0	0.6
1967	Hou N	101	328	39	78	13	2	10	38	48-12	1	65	.238	.333	.381	109	5	2-4	.987	-2	97	88	1b79,3b24	0	-0.3
	Det A	36	108	14	25	3	0	6	19	15-0	2	23	.231	.331	.426	121	3	0-0	.933	-2	76	0	3b21,1b13	0	0.0
1968	†Det A	31	52	4	11	0	0	3	8	5-1	0	12	.212	.281	.385	97	0	0-0	.974	1	95	151	1b6,3b6	85	0.0
Total	17	2391	8537	1509	2315	354	72	512	1453	1444-107	26	1487	.271	.376	.509	145	576	68-39	.956	-27	100	98	3b2181,1b112,O52L	85	53.0
Mathews, Nelson	Nelson Elmer; B7.21.1941 Columbia IL; BR/TR/6´4˝/195; d9.9; s–Timothy																								
1960	Chi N	3	8	1	2	0	0	0	0	0-0	0	2	.250	.250	.250	38	-1	0-0	1.000	0	147	0	O2R	0	-0.1
1961	Chi N	3	9	0	1	0	0	0	0	0-0	0	2	.111	.111	.111	-40	-2	0-0	1.000	-0	98	0	O2C	0	-0.2
1962	Chi N	15	49	5	15	2	0	2	13	5-0	2	4	.306	.393	.469	126	2	3-3	.962	-3	76	0	O14C	0	-0.1
1963	Chi N	61	155	12	24	3	2	4	10	16-2	0	48	.155	.234	.277	44	-11	3-4	.979	-3	93	36	O46C	0	-1.8
1964	KC A	157	573	58	137	27	5	14	60	43-7	1	143	.239	.293	.377	82	-14	2-3	.968	-1	109	47	O154C	0	-2.1
1965	KC A	67	184	17	39	7	7	2	15	24-4	0	49	.212	.300	.359	89	-3	0-2	.981	-2	100	37	O57(25/26/8)	0	-0.8
Total	6	306	978	93	218	39	14	22	98	88-13	3	248	.223	.288	.359	78	-29	8-12	.972	-8	103	40	O275(25/242/10)	0	-5.1
Mathews, Bobby	Robert T.; B11.21.1851 Baltimore MD; D4.17.1898 Baltimore MD; BR/TR/5´5.5˝/140; d5.4; U3; ▲																								
1871	Kek NA	**19**	89	15	24	3	1	0	10	2	—	0	.270	.286	.326	74	-2	2-1	.840	-1	79	145	P19	—	0.0
1872	Bal NA	50	222	36	50	2	0	0	22	3	—	2	.225	.236	.234	43	-16	3-1	.780	-5	75	95	P49,O8R,3b3	—	-0.3
1873	Mut NA	52	223	40	43	3	3	0	14	10	—	3	.193	.227	.233	37	-17	1-1	.780	-3	80	47	P52,O5R	—	-0.2
1874	Mut NA	**65**	298	46	72	6	1	0	30	3	—	4	.242	.249	.268	64	-12	2-0	.774	-2	94	108	P65/3lf	—	-0.1
1875	Mut NA	70	264	23	48	6	2	0	15	2	—	5	.182	.188	.220	39	-16	1-2	.838	-6	81	72	P70/lf	—	-0.2
1876	NY N	56	218	19	40	4	1	0	9	3	—	2	.183	.195	.211	40	-12	—	.810	-3	96	0	P56/rf	—	-0.1
1877	Cin N	15	59	5	10	0	0	0	0	1	—	2	.169	.183	.169	13	-5	—	.862	-3	79	0	P15/lfS	—	-0.2
1879	Pro N	43	173	25	35	2	0	1	10	7	—	12	.202	.233	.231	55	-8	—	.956	-4	99	0	P27,O21R,3b5	—	-0.8
1881	Pro N	16	57	6	11	1	0	0	4	5	—	6	.193	.258	.211	50	-3	—	.810	-2	82	264	P14,O5R	—	-0.2
	Bos N	19	71	2	12	2	0	0	4	0	—	5	.169	.169	.197	15	-7	—	.818	-2	74	0	O18(1/9/9),P5	—	-0.8
	Year	35	128	8	23	3	0	0	8	5	—	11	.180	.211	.203	32	-10	—	.811	-4	64	0	O23(1/9/14),P19	—	-1.0
1882	Bos N	45	169	17	38	6	0	0	13	8	—	18	.225	.260	.260	67	-6	—	.867	-8	63	67	P34,O13R/S	—	-0.7
1883	Phi AA	45	167	15	31	2	0	0	11	5	—	—	.186	.209	.198	29	-14	—	.874	-1	88	101	P44,O3(1/1/1)	—	-0.1
1884	Phi AA	49	184	26	34	5	1	0	—	7	0	—	.185	.215	.223	40	-12	—	.775	-3	90	57	P49/rf	—	-0.1
1885	Phi AA	48	179	22	30	3	0	0	12	10	0	—	.168	.212	.184	24	-15	—	.881	-0	96	55	P48/rf	—	0.0
1886	Phi AA	24	88	16	21	3	0	0	10	3	0	—	.239	.264	.273	67	-3	1	.843	-0	112	**266**	P24/rf	—	0.0
1887	Phi AA	7	25	5	5	0	0	0	0	4	0	—	.200	.310	.200	44	0	0	.889	0	118	386	P7	—	0.0

YEAR	TM LG	G	AB	R	H	2B	3B	HR	RBI	BB-IB	HP	SO	AVG	OBP	SLG	AOPS	ABR	SB-CS	FA	FR	RNG	THR	GAMES AT POSITION	DL	BFW
Total	5NA	256	1096	160	237	20	7	0	91	20	—	14	.216	.230	.247	49	-63	9-5	.801	-15	83	86	P255,O15(2/0/13),3b4	—	-0.8
Total	10	367	1390	158	267	28	2	1	73	53	0	45	.192	.222	.217	42	-85	1	.845	-25	91	76	P323,O65(3/10/53),3b5,S2	—	-3.0
MATHIS, JEFF	Jeffery Stephen; B3.31.1983 Marianna FL; BR/TR/6´0˝/(180–185); [AnaA01 1/33]; d8.12																								
2005	LA A	5	3	1	1	0	0	0	0	0-0	0	1	.333	.333	.333	81	0	0-0	1.000	0	0	0	C3,D2	0	0.0
2006	LA A	23	55	9	8	2	0	2	6	7-1	0	14	.145	.238	.291	38	-5	0-0	.970	-5	64	91	C20,D2	0	-0.9
Total	2	28	58	10	9	2	0	2	6	7-1	0	15	.155	.242	.293	40	-5	0-0	.971	-5	62	88	C23,D4	0	-0.9
MATHISON, JIMMY	James Michael Ignatius; B11.11.1878 Baltimore MD; D7.4.1911 Baltimore MD; TR; d8.29																								
1902	Bal A	29	91	12	24	2	1	0	7	9	6	—	.264	.368	.308	85	-1	2	.889	-4	85	86	3b28/S	—	-0.4
MATIAS, JOHN	John Roy; B8.15.1944 Honolulu HI; BL/TL/5´11˝/170; d4.7																								
1970	Chi A	58	117	7	22	2	0	2	6	3-1	1	22	.188	.215	.256	28	-12	1-0	.941	-0	55	219	O22(5/0/17),1b18	0	-1.4
MATOS, FRANCISCO	Francisco Aguirre (Mancebo); B7.23.1969 Santo Domingo, D.R.; BR/TR/6´1˝/160; d7.17																								
1994	Oak A	14	28	1	7	1	0	0	2	1-0	0	2	.250	.267	.286	49	-2	1-0	.925	-2	90	71	2b12,D2	0	-0.3
MATOS, JULIUS	Julius; B12.12.1974 New York NY; BR/TR/5´11˝/175; [CleA94 16/437]; d5.31; Col South Suburban (IL) JC																								
2002	SD N	76	185	19	44	3	0	2	19	9-0	2	33	.238	.279	.286	54	-13	1-1	.963	3	107	101	2b49,3b17,S4,O3R,1b2/D	0	-0.9
2003	KC A	28	57	7	15	1	0	2	7	1-0	0	12	.263	.276	.386	67	-3	1-0	1.000	-4	55	0	3b13,2b11,S2/rfD	0	-0.6
Total	2	104	242	26	59	4	0	4	26	10-0	2	45	.244	.278	.310	58	-16	2-1	.964	-1	109	98	2b60,3b30,S6,O4R,D2,1b2	0	-1.5
MATOS, LUIS	Luis David; B10.30.1978 Bayamon, PR; BR/TR/6´0˝/(179–215); [BalA96 10/291]; d6.19																								
2000	Bal A	72	182	21	41	6	3	1	17	12-0	3	30	.225	.281	.308	52	-14	13-4	.988	6	121	96	O69(1/44/25),D3	0	-0.7
2001	Bal A	31	98	16	21	7	0	4	12	11-0	1	30	.214	.300	.408	89	-2	7-0	.985	0	99	119	O31(1/23/10)	145	0.0
2002	Bal A	17	31	0	4	1	0	0	1	1-0	0	6	.129	.156	.161	-16	-5	1-0	1.000	-1	84	0	O14(2/6/7)/D	67	-0.6
2003	Bal A	109	439	70	133	23	3	13	45	28-0	7	90	.303	.353	.458	113	8	15-7	.987	4	108	101	O107(0/106/4),D2	0	1.3
2004	Bal A	89	330	36	74	18	0	6	28	19-2	5	60	.224	.275	.333	59	-21	12-4	.996	-2	99	68	O89C	74	-1.9
2005	Bal A	121	389	53	109	20	2	4	32	27-0	10	58	.280	.340	.373	91	-4	17-9	.984	4	107	129	O120C	39	0.2
2006	Bal A	55	121	14	25	7	1	2	5	10-0	2	21	.207	.278	.331	58	-8	7-0	1.000	-2	96	0	O47(31/9/13)/D	18	-0.8
	Was N	14	15	2	3	2	0	0	0	0-0	0	2	.200	.200	.333	35	-1	0-0	1.000	1	123	1431	O4(1/3/0)	0	-0.1
Total	7	508	1605	212	410	84	9	30	140	108-2	28	297	.255	.312	.375	81	-47	72-24	.989	10	106	96	O481(36/400/59),D7	343	-2.6
MATOS, PASCUAL	Pascual (Cuevas); B12.23.1974 Santa Cruz de Barahona, D.R.; BR/TR/6´2˝/160; d5.11																								
1999	Atl N	6	8	0	1	0	0	0	2	0-0	0	1	.125	.125	.125	-37	-2	0-0	1.000	0	59	0	C5	0	-0.1
MATRANGA, DAVE	David Michael; B1.8.1977 Orange CA; BR/TR/6´0˝/170; [HouN98 6/182]; d6.27; Col Pepperdine																								
2003	Hou N	6	5	1	1	0	0	1	1	0-0	0	2	.200	.200	.800	137	0	0-0	1.000	-0	0	0	2b2	0	0.0
2005	LA A	1	1	0	0	0	0	0	0	0-0	0	0	.000	.000	.000	-99	0	0-0	1.000	1	146	707	/2	0	0.0
Total	2	7	6	1	1	0	0	1	1	0-0	0	2	.167	.167	.667	100	0	0-0	1.000	0	58	283	2b3	0	0.0
MATSUI, HIDEKI	Hideki "Godzilla"; B6.12.1974 Ishikawa, Japan; BL/TR/6´1˝/(210–230); d3.31																								
2003	†NY A★	**163**	623	82	179	42	1	16	106	63-5	3	86	.287	.353	.435	109	9	2-2	.977	-1	94	147	O159(118/46/0),D4	0	0.4
2004	†NY A★	**162**	584	109	174	34	2	31	108	88-2	3	103	.298	.390	.522	136	33	3-0	.978	-1	96	91	O160(160/3/0)	0	2.5
2005	†NY A	**162**	629	108	192	45	3	23	116	63-7	3	78	.305	.367	.496	129	27	2-2	.990	-3	96	94	O142(115/28/4),D19	0	1.9
2006	†NY A	51	172	32	52	9	0	8	29	27-2	0	23	.302	.393	.494	129	8	1-0	.988	3	124	42	O36L,D13	123	0.9
Total	4	538	2008	331	597	130	6	78	359	241-16	9	290	.297	.372	.485	125	77	8-4	.982	-2	97	107	O497(429/77/4),D36	123	5.7
MATSUI, KAZUO	Kazuo; B10.23.1975 Osaka, Japan; BB/TR/5´10˝/185; d4.6																								
2004	NY N	114	460	65	125	32	2	7	44	40-4	2	97	.272	.331	.396	89	-7	14-3	.956	-2	102	94	S110,2b3	46	0.2
2005	NY N	87	267	31	68	9	4	3	24	14-1	5	43	.255	.300	.352	73	-11	6-1	.970	-6	102	79	2b71	52	-1.3
2006	NY N	38	130	10	26	6	0	1	7	6-1	0	19	.200	.235	.269	30	-14	2-0	.994	2	98	117	2b31	17	-1.0
	Col N	32	113	22	39	6	3	2	19	10-0	0	27	.345	.392	.504	119	3	8-1	.984	3	122	175	2b21,S3	0	0.9
	Year	70	243	32	65	12	3	3	26	16-1	0	46	.267	.310	.379	74	-10	10-1	.989	5	108	140	2b52,S3	0	-0.1
Total	3	271	970	128	258	53	9	13	94	70-6	7	186	.266	.318	.379	81	-29	30-5	.978	-2	105	108	2b126,S113	115	-1.2
MATTHEWS, GARY	Gary Nathaniel Jr.; B8.25.1974 San Francisco CA; BB/TR/6´3˝/(200–225); [SDN93 13/366]; d6.4; f–Gary; Col Mission (CA) JC																								
1999	SD N	23	36	4	8	0	0	0	7	9-0	0	9	.222	.378	.222	61	-2	2-0	1.000	-0	109	0	O17(6/2/10)	0	-0.2
2000	Chi N	80	158	24	30	1	2	4	14	15-1	1	28	.190	.264	.297	42	-15	3-0	.978	3	110	136	O61(46/21/1)	0	-1.2
2001	Chi N	106	258	41	56	9	1	9	30	38-2	1	55	.217	.320	.364	79	-8	5-3	.976	-2	98	78	O100(20/88/1)	0	-1.0
	Pit N	46	147	22	36	6	1	5	14	22-0	0	45	.245	.341	.401	89	-2	3-2	.971	-3	99	43	O44C	0	-0.4
	Year	152	405	63	92	15	2	14	44	60-2	1	100	.227	.328	.378	83	-10	8-5	.974	-5	98	66	O144(20/132/1)	0	-1.4
2002	NY N	2	1	0	0	0	0	0	0	0-0	0	0	.000	.000	.000	-99	0	0-0	ø	0	—	—	/H	0	0.0
	Bal A	109	344	54	95	25	3	7	38	43-1	1	69	.276	.355	.427	114	8	15-5	.969	-4	92	106	O100(16/16/76),D2	17	0.2
2003	Bal A	41	162	21	33	12	1	2	20	9-0	1	29	.204	.250	.327	51	-12	0-3	1.000	-1	95	110	O40C/D	0	-1.3
	SD N	103	306	50	83	19	1	4	22	34-0	1	66	.271	.346	.379	98	-1	12-5	.993	-2	98	45	O92(33/35/35)	0	-0.4
2004	Tex A	87	280	37	77	17	1	11	36	33-5	1	64	.275	.350	.461	106	3	5-1	.990	6	108	158	O85(3/30/66)	0	0.6
2005	Tex A	131	475	72	121	25	5	17	55	47-1	0	90	.255	.320	.436	96	-3	9-2	.982	3	104	109	O123(5/97/22)/D	24	0.1
2006	Tex A★	147	620	102	194	44	6	19	79	58-5	4	99	.313	.371	.495	123	22	10-7	.980	-6	93	110	O145(0/142/3)/D	9	1.6
Total	8	875	2787	427	733	158	21	78	315	308-15	10	554	.263	.336	.419	97	-10	64-28	.982	-7	99	101	O807(129/515/214),D5	50	-2.0
MATTHEWS, GARY	Gary Nathaniel Sr.; B7.5.1950 San Fernando CA; BR/TR/6´3˝/(188–205); [SFN68 1/17]; d9.6; C7; s–Gary																								
1972	SF N	20	62	11	18	1	1	4	14	7-2	0	13	.290	.357	.532	149	4	0-1	.971	-1	101	0	O19(10/0/9)	0	0.2
1973	SF N	148	540	74	162	22	10	12	58	58-7	1	83	.300	.367	.444	119	14	17-5	.983	1	93	110	O145(144/0/1)	0	0.9
1974	SF N	154	561	87	161	27	6	16	82	70-5	3	69	.287	.368	.442	121	17	11-9	.970	-1	95	85	O151(150/0/1)	0	0.6
1975	SF N	116	425	67	119	22	3	12	58	65-5	2	53	.280	.377	.431	120	13	13-4	.967	3	102	127	O113L	43	1.2
1976	SF N	156	587	79	164	28	4	20	84	75-3	1	94	.279	.359	.443	124	19	12-5	.975	-11	81	71	O156L	0	0.0
1977	Atl N	148	555	89	157	25	5	17	64	67-3	2	90	.283	.362	.438	102	3	22-8	.965	1	93	117	O145L	0	-0.1
1978	Atl N	129	474	75	135	20	5	18	62	61-2	2	92	.285	.366	.462	118	13	8-7	.969	-1	101	99	O127(1/0/127)	17	0.5
1979	Atl N★	156	631	97	192	34	5	27	90	60-5	0	75	.304	.363	.502	127	23	18-6	.974	-5	96	93	O156R	0	1.2
1980	Atl N	155	571	79	159	17	3	19	75	42-2	0	93	.278	.325	.419	106	3	11-3	.960	-8	95	64	O143(6/0/137)	0	-1.3
1981	†Phi N	101	359	62	108	21	3	9	67	59-2	3	42	.301	.398	.451	135	19	15-2	.963	-1	93	132	O100L	0	1.8
1982	Phi N	**162**	616	89	173	31	1	19	83	66-1	2	87	.281	.349	.427	113	12	21-4	.966	-2	91	116	O162L	0	0.7
1983	†Phi N	132	446	66	115	18	2	10	50	69-3	0	81	.258	.352	.374	104	4	13-9	.974	-3	86	136	O122L	0	-0.4
1984	†Chi N	147	491	101	143	21	2	14	82	**103**-2	3	97	.291	**.410**	.428	127	24	17-8	.955	-7	88	68	O145L	0	1.3
1985	Chi N	97	298	45	70	12	0	13	40	59-2	2	64	.235	.362	.406	105	4	2-0	.977	-2	85	130	O85L	39	0.0
1986	Chi N	123	370	49	96	16	1	21	46	60-1	0	59	.259	.361	.478	121	11	3-2	.940	-7	80	82	O105L	0	0.0
1987	Chi N	44	42	3	11	3	0	0	8	4-1	0	11	.262	.326	.333	72	-2	0-0	1.000	-0	92	0	O2L	0	-0.2
	Sea A	45	119	10	28	1	0	3	15	15-0	0	22	.235	.319	.319	67	-6	0-1	ø	0	0	0	D39	0	-0.7
Total	16	2033	7147	1083	2011	319	51	234	978	940-46	21	1125	.281	.364	.439	116	175	183-74	.968	-44	92	99	O1876(1446/0/431),D39	99	5.7
MATTHEWS, BOB	Robert; B Camden NJ; d9.25																								
1891	Phi AA	1	3	1	1	0	0	0	0	0	2	1	.333	.600	.333	167	1	0	ø	-0	0	0	/rf	—	0.0
MATTHEWS, WID	Wid Curry "Matty"; B10.20.1896 Raleigh IL; D10.5.1965 Hollywood CA; BL/TL/5´8.5˝/155; d4.18																								
1923	Phi A	129	485	52	133	11	6	1	25	50	1	27	.274	.343	.328	76	-17	16-16	.947	-15	95	20	O127(2/125/0)	—	-3.8
1924	Was A	53	169	25	51	10	4	0	13	11	3	4	.302	.355	.408	100	-1	3-8	.985	5	109	177	O44(1/43/0)	—	0.0
1925	Was A	10	9	2	4	0	0	0	1	0	0	1	.444	.444	.444	129	0	0-0	1.000	0	106	0	/cf	—	0.0
Total	3	192	663	79	188	21	10	1	39	61	4	32	.284	.348	.350	83	-18	19-24	.957	-10	98	58	O172(3/169/0)	—	-3.8
MATTHIAS, STEVE	Stephen J.; B1860 Mitchellville MD; D7.29.1891 Baltimore MD; BR/TR/5´8˝/160; d4.20																								
1884	CP U	37	142	24	39	7	1	0	—	5	—	—	.275	.299	.338	94	-5	—	.840	1	95	92	S36,O2C	—	-0.3
MATTICK, BOBBY	Robert James; B12.5.1915 Sioux City IA; D12.16.2004 Scottsdale AZ; BR/TR/5´11˝/178; d5.5; M2; f–Wally																								
1938	Chi N	1	1	0	1	0	0	0	0	1	0	0	1.000	1.000	1.000	439	0	0	ø	-0	0	0	/S	—	0.0
1939	Chi N	51	178	16	51	12	1	0	23	6	1	19	.287	.314	.365	80	-5	1	.927	4	110	84	S48	—	0.2
1940	Chi N	128	441	30	96	15	0	0	33	19	0	33	.218	.250	.252	39	-37	5	.946	8	108	103	S126/3	—	-2.1

YEAR	TM LG	G	AB	R	H	2B	3B	HR	RBI	BB-IB	HP	SO	AVG	OBP	SLG	AOPS	ABR	SB-CS	FA	FR	RNG	THR	GAMES AT POSITION	DL	BFW
1941	Cin N	20	60	8	11	3	0	0	7	8	0	7	.183	.279	.233	45	-4	1	.982	-1	90	97	S12,3b5/2	0	-0.4
1942	Cin N	6	10	0	2	1	0	0	0	0	0	1	.200	.200	.300	45	-1	0	1.000	0	91	85	S3	0	0.0
Total	5	206	690	54	161	31	1	0	64	33	1	60	.233	.269	.281	52	-47	7	.943	11	107	97	S190,3b6/2	0	-2.3
MATTICK, WALLY	Walter Joseph "Chick"; B3.12.1887 St.Louis MO; D11.5.1968 Los Altos CA; BR/TR/5´10˝/180; d4.11; s–Bobby																								
1912	Chi A	90	285	45	74	7	9	1	35	27	5	—	.260	.334	.358	101	0	16	.982	-5	91	69	O79(2/66/10)	—	-1.1
1913	Chi A	71	207	15	39	8	1	0	11	18	0	16	.188	.253	.237	44	-15	3	.977	2	91	152	O64(7/56/0)	—	-1.8
1918	StL N	8	14	0	2	0	0	0	1	2	2	3	.143	.333	.143	49	-1	0	1.000	0	84	182	O3R	—	-0.1
Total	3	169	506	60	115	15	10	1	47	47	7	19	.227	.302	.302	77	-16	19	.980	-3	91	106	O146(9/122/13)	—	-3.0
MATTIMORE, MIKE	Michael Joseph; B8.1858 North Bend PA; D4.28.1931 Butte MT; BL/TL/5´8.5˝/160; d5.3; ▲																								
1887	NY N	8	32	5	8	1	0	0	4	0	0	6	.250	.250	.281	50	-2	1	.889	-1	47	0	P7,O2C	—	-0.1
1888	Phi AA	41	142	22	38	6	5	0	12	12	2	—	.268	.333	.380	129	5	16	.915	4	137	338	P26,O16(1/1/15)	—	0.4
1889	Phi AA	23	73	10	17	1	2	1	8	9	2	7	.233	.333	.342	94	-1	6	.944	-2	0	0	O12(3/5/4),1b7,P5	—	-0.2
	KC AA	19	75	6	12	1	1	0	5	3	0	16	.160	.192	.200	11	-9	0	.844	-1	82	0	O19(19/1/0)/P	—	-0.9
	Year	42	148	16	29	2	3	1	13	12	2	23	.196	.265	.270	52	-10	6	.873	-3	56	0	O31(22/6/4),1b7,P6	—	-1.1
1890	Bro AA	33	129	14	17	1	1	0	7	16	2	—	.132	.238	.155	17	-13	11	.887	-4	106	0	P19,O14(0/1/13)	—	-0.8
Total	4	124	451	57	92	10	9	1	36	40	6	29	.204	.278	.273	64	-20	34	.853	-5	69	105	O63(23/10/32),P58,1b7	—	-1.6
MATTINGLY, DON	Donald Arthur "Donnie Baseball"; B4.20.1961 Evansville IN; BL/TL/6´0˝/(175–200); [NYA79 19/493]; d9.8; C3																								
1982	NY A	7	12	0	2	0	0	0	1	0-0	0	1	.167	.154	.167	-8	-2	0-0	1.000	2	200	603	O6(5/0/1)/1	0	0.0
1983	NY A	91	279	34	79	15	4	4	32	21-5	1	31	.283	.333	.409	107	2	0-0	.974	-5	86	97	O48(13/1/39),1b42/2	0	-0.7
1984	NY A★	153	603	91	**207**	**44**	2	23	110	41-8	1	33	**.343**	.381	.537	**158**	47	1-1	**.996**	16	**135**	**115**	1b133,O19(13/1/6)	0	5.3
1985	NY A★	159	652	107	211	**48**	3	35	**145**	56-13	2	41	.324	.371	.567	158	51	2-2	**.995**	-10	75	117	1b159	0	3.0
1986	NY A★	**162**	677	117	**238**	**53**	2	31	113	53-11	1	35	.352	.394	**.573**	**162**	**58**	0-0	**.996**	-2	88	101	1b160,3b3/D	0	4.5
1987	NY A★	141	569	93	186	38	2	30	115	51-13	1	38	.327	.378	.559	146	38	1-4	**.996**	-1	97	108	1b140/D	15	2.6
1988	NY A★	144	599	94	186	37	0	18	88	41-14	3	29	.311	.353	.462	128	22	1-0	.993	-2	98	105	1b143/lfD	18	1.1
1989	NY A★	158	631	79	191	37	2	23	113	51-18	1	30	.303	.351	.477	134	27	3-0	.995	-4	90	105	1b145,D17/rf	0	1.3
1990	NY A	102	394	40	101	16	0	5	42	28-13	3	20	.256	.308	.335	80	-11	1-0	.997	8	130	102	1b89,D13/lf	47	-1.0
1991	NY A	152	587	64	169	35	0	9	68	46-11	4	42	.288	.339	.394	103	3	2-0	.996	-3	88	**124**	1b127,D22	0	-0.9
1992	NY A	157	640	89	184	40	0	14	86	39-7	1	43	.287	.327	.416	108	5	3-0	**.997**	6	113	103	1b143,D15	0	0.2
1993	NY A	134	530	78	154	27	2	17	86	61-9	2	42	.291	.364	.445	120	16	0-0	**.998**	1	100	**116**	1b130,D5	27	0.5
1994	NY A	97	372	62	113	20	1	6	51	60-7	0	24	.304	.397	.411	114	11	0-0	**.998**	5	122	**123**	1b97	15	0.7
1995	†NY A	128	458	59	132	32	2	7	49	40-7	1	35	.288	.341	.413	97	-1	0-2	.994	0	98	91	1b125/D	0	-1.2
Total	14	1785	7003	1007	2153	442	20	222	1099	588-136	21	444	.307	.358	.471	127	266	14-9	.996	13	100	109	1b1634,D76,O76(33/2/47),3b3/2	122	15.4
MATTIS, RALPH	Ralph "Matty"; B8.24.1890 Roxborough PA; D9.13.1960 Williamsport PA; BR/TR/5´11˝/172; d4.22																								
1914	Pit F	36	85	14	21	4	1	0	8	9	1	11	.247	.326	.318	77	-4	2	.938	2	106	167	O24(12/0/12)	—	-0.3
MATTOX, CLOY	Cloy Mitchell "Monk"; B11.24.1902 Leesville VA; D8.3.1985 Danville VA; BL/TR/5´8˝/168; d9.1; b–Jim; Col VPI																								
1929	Phi A	3	6	0	1	0	0	0	0	1	0	1	.167	.286	.167	19	-1	0-0	.875	-0	*85*	*145*	C3	—	-0.1
MATTOX, JIM	James Powell; B12.17.1896 Leesville VA; D10.12.1973 Myrtle Beach SC; BL/TR/5´9.5˝/168; d4.30; b–Cloy; Col Washington and Lee																								
1922	Pit N	29	51	11	15	1	1	0	3	1	0	3	.294	.308	.353	69	-3	0-0	.984	1	*98*	*78*	C21	—	-0.1
1923	Pit N	22	32	4	6	1	1	0	1	0	2	5	.188	.235	.281	35	-3	0-0	.960	0	*111*	*139*	C8	—	-0.2
Total	2	51	83	15	21	2	2	0	4	1	2	8	.253	.279	.325	56	-6	0-0	.978	1	*102*	*97*	C29	—	-0.3
MATUSZEK, LEN	Leonard James; B9.27.1954 Toledo OH; BL/TR/6´2˝/(190–205); [PhiN76 5/113]; d9.3; Col Toledo																								
1981	Phi N	13	11	1	3	1	0	0	1	3-1	0	1	.273	.429	.364	120	1	0-1	1.000	1	0	538	/13	0	0.1
1982	Phi N	25	39	1	3	1	0	0	3	1-0	1	10	.077	.119	.103	-35	-7	0-1	.750	-2	83	0	3b8,1b3	16	-1.0
1983	Phi N	28	80	12	22	6	1	4	16	4-1	0	14	.275	.306	.525	128	3	0-1	1.000	-1	72	58	1b21	0	0.0
1984	Phi N	101	262	40	65	17	1	12	43	39-4	4	54	.248	.350	.458	125	10	4-3	.990	5	136	79	1b81/lf	43	1.1
1985	Tor A	62	151	23	32	6	2	2	15	11-0	0	24	.212	.259	.318	57	-9	2-1	1.000	0	126	63	D54,1b5	0	-1.1
	†LA N	43	63	10	14	2	1	3	13	8-2	1	14	.222	.307	.429	110	1	0-1	1.000	0	120	0	O17L,1b10/3	0	0.0
1986	LA N	91	199	26	52	7	0	9	28	21-1	1	47	.261	.333	.432	118	4	2-2	1.000	-0	80	116	O37(35/0/2),1b31	47	0.1
1987	LA N	16	15	0	1	0	0	0	0	1-0	0	4	.067	.125	.067	-49	-3	0-0	1.000	0	173	0	1b3	157	-0.3
Total	7	379	820	113	192	40	5	30	119	88-9	7	168	.234	.309	.405	99	0	8-10	.990	4	119	80	1b155,O55(53/0/2),D54,3b10	263	-1.1
MAUCH, GENE	Gene William "Skip"; B11.18.1925 Salina KS; D8.8.2005 Rancho Mirage CA; BR/TR/5´10˝/(165–175); d4.18; Mil 1944–45; M26/C1																								
1944	Bro N	5	15	2	2	1	0	0	2	2	0	3	.133	.235	.200	24	-1	0	1.000	-1	75	120	S5	0	-0.2
1947	Pit N	16	30	8	9	0	0	0	1	7	0	6	.300	.432	.300	95	0	0	.963	-3	88	0	2b6,S4	0	-0.2
1948	Bro N	12	13	1	2	0	0	0	0	1	0	4	.154	.214	.154	1	-2	0	.950	0	82	109	2b7/S	0	-0.2
	Chi N	53	138	18	28	3	2	1	7	26	0	10	.203	.329	.275	68	-6	1	.925	-3	90	130	2b26,S19	0	-0.6
	Year	65	151	19	30	3	2	1	7	27	0	14	.199	.320	.265	62	-8	1	.929	-3	89	127	2b33,S20	0	-0.8
1949	Chi N	72	150	15	37	6	2	1	7	21	0	15	.247	.339	.333	83	-3	3	.971	8	124	108	2b25,S19,3b7	0	0.7
1950	Bos N	48	121	17	28	5	0	1	15	14	1	9	.231	.316	.298	67	-6	1	.968	-3	95	82	2b28,3b7,S5	0	-0.6
1951	Bos N	19	20	5	2	0	0	0	1	7	0	4	.100	.333	.100	24	-2	0-0	1.000	-1	89	50	S10,3b3,2b2	0	-0.2
1952	StL N	7	3	0	0	0	0	0	0	1	0	2	.000	.250	.000	-25	0	0-0	.500	-1	0	0	S2	0	-0.1
1956	Bos A	7	25	4	8	0	0	0	1	3-0	0	3	.320	.393	.320	80	-1	0-0	.935	-1	100	85	2b6	0	-0.1
1957	Bos A	65	222	23	60	10	3	2	28	22-0	1	26	.270	.335	.369	88	-3	1-0	.962	-4	99	98	2b58	0	-0.3
Total	9	304	737	93	176	25	7	5	62	104-0	2	82	.239	.333	.312	75	-24	6-0	.958	-8	100	97	2b158,S65,3b17	0	-1.8
MAUER, JOE	Joseph Patrick; B4.19.1983 St. Paul MN; BL/TR/6´4˝/(220–225); [MinA01 1/1]; d4.5																								
2004	Min A	35	107	18	33	8	1	6	17	11-0	1	14	.308	.369	.570	139	6	1-0	.991	3	133	101	C32/D	136	1.0
2005	Min A	131	489	61	144	26	2	9	55	61-12	1	64	.294	.372	.411	107	7	13-1	.993	14	**191**	91	C116,D13	0	2.9
2006	†Min A★	140	521	86	181	36	4	13	84	79-21	1	54	**.347**	.429	.507	143	38	8-3	.996	8	177	81	C120,D17	0	5.0
Total	3	306	1117	165	358	70	7	28	156	151-33	3	132	.321	.399	.471	127	51	22-4	.994	25	178	88	C268,D31	136	8.9
MAUL, AL	Albert Joseph "Smiling Al"; B10.9.1865 Philadelphia PA; D5.3.1958 Philadelphia PA; BR/TR/6´0˝/175; d6.20; ▲																								
1884	Phi U	1	4	0	0	0	0	0	—	0	—	—	.000	.000	.000	-99	-1	—	1.000	-0	55	0	/P	—	0.0
1887	Phi N	16	56	15	17	2	2	1	4	15	0	10	.304	.451	.464	146	4	5	.818	-2	0	0	O8(7/1/0),P7,1b2	—	0.0
1888	Pit N	74	259	21	54	9	4	0	31	21	3	45	.208	.276	.274	83	-4	9	.975	0	59	115	1b38,O34(0/3/31),P3	—	-0.7
1889	Pit N	68	257	37	71	6	6	4	44	29	3	41	.276	.356	.393	120	7	18	.946	10	134	179	O64(39/0/25),P6	—	1.3
1890	Pit P	45	162	31	42	6	2	0	21	22	0	12	.259	.348	.321	86	-2	5	.904	5	123	205	P30,O15(11/3/1)/S	—	0.2
1891	Pit N	47	149	15	28	2	4	0	14	20	0	28	.188	.284	.255	59	-8	4	.878	1	132	223	O40(20/12/8),P8	—	-0.6
1893	Was N	44	134	10	34	8	4	0	12	33	1	14	.254	.405	.373	110	4	1	.889	-0	105	40	P37,O7(5/0/2)	—	0.0
1894	Was N	41	124	23	30	3	3	2	20	14	7	11	.242	.352	.363	75	-5	1	.877	2	129	0	P28,O12(1/0/11)	—	-0.1
1895	Was N	22	72	9	18	5	2	0	16	6	0	7	.250	.308	.375	76	-3	0	.933	0	104	255	P16,O4(2/0/2)	—	-0.1
1896	Was N	8	28	6	8	1	1	0	5	3	0	2	.286	.355	.393	97	2	0	.923	-1	65	169	P8	—	0.0
1897	Was N	1	1	0	0	0	0	0	0	0	0	—	.000	.000	.000	-99	0	0	1.000	0	219	0	/P	—	0.0
	Bal N	2	3	0	1	0	0	0	0	0	0	—	.333	.333	.333	76	0	0	1.000	-0	55	0	P2	—	0.0
	Year	3	4	0	1	0	0	0	0	0	0	—	.250	.250	.250	32	0	0	1.000	-0	88	0	P3	—	0.0
1898	Bal N	29	93	21	19	3	2	0	10	16	2	—	.204	.333	.280	75	-2	1	.978	-6	64	0	P28/cf	—	-0.3
1899	Bro N	4	11	2	3	0	0	0	0	1	0	—	.273	.333	.273	66	0	0	.900	0	137	0	P4	—	0.0
1900	Phi N	5	15	2	3	0	0	0	1	2	0	—	.200	.294	.200	38	0	0	.917	0	115	0	P5	—	0.0
1901	NY N	3	8	1	3	0	0	0	1	0	0	—	.375	.375	.375	123	1	0	1.000	0	145	0	P3	—	0.0
Total	15	410	1376	193	331	45	30	7	179	182	16	170	.241	.336	.332	91	-7	44	.910	9	105	94	P187,O185(85/20/80),1b40/S	—	-0.3
MAULDIN, MARK	Marshall Reese; B11.5.1914 Atlanta GA; D9.2.1990 Union City GA; BR/TR/5´11˝/170; d9.10																								
1934	Chi A	10	38	3	10	2	0	1	3	0	0	3	.263	.263	.395	66	-2	0-0	.906	-0	95	155	3b10	—	-0.2
MAURER, ROB	Robert John; B1.7.1967 Evansville IN; BL/TL/6´3˝/(200–210); [TexA88 6/141]; d9.8; Col Evansville; [DL 1993 Tex A 182]																								
1991	Tex A	13	16	0	1	1	0	0	2	2-0	1	6	.063	.211	.125	-5	-2	0-0	1.000	1	366	193	1b4,D2	0	-0.1
1992	Tex A	8	9	1	2	0	0	0	1	1-0	0	2	.222	.300	.222	50	-1	0-0	1.000	0	98	0	1b3/D	0	-0.1
Total	2	21	25	1	3	1	0	0	3	3-0	1	8	.120	.241	.160	14	-3	0-0	1.000	1	220	88	1b7,D3	182	-0.2

YEAR	TM LG	G	AB	R	H	2B	3B	HR	RBI	BB-IB	HP	SO	AVG	OBP	SLG	AOPS	ABR	SB-CS	FA	FR	RNG	THR	GAMES AT POSITION	DL	BFW
MAURO, CARMEN	Carmen Louis; B11.10.1926 St.Paul MN; D12.19.2003 Carmichael CA; BL/TR/6´0˝/(167–170); d10.1																								
1948	Chi N	3	5	2	1	0	0	1	1	2	0	0	.200	.429	.800	235	1	0	1.000	0	117	0	O2(0/1/1)	0	0.1
1950	Chi N	62	185	19	42	4	3	1	10	13	2	31	.227	.285	.297	54	-13	3	.946	-4	92	56	O49(18/1/30)	0	-1.9
1951	Chi N	13	29	3	5	1	0	0	3	2	1	6	.172	.250	.207	24	-3	0-0	.900	-0	97	166	O6(0/5/1)	0	-0.4
1953	Bro N	8	9	1	0	0	0	0	0	0	0	4	.000	.000	.000	-98	-3	0-0	1.000	0	96	0	/rf	0	-0.3
	Was A	17	23	1	4	0	1	0	2	1	0	3	.174	.208	.261	27	-3	0-0	1.000	1	114	344	O6(3/3/0)	0	-0.2
	Phi A	64	165	14	44	4	4	0	17	19	0	21	.267	.342	.339	81	-4	3-4	.969	2	108	135	O49(4/38/7)/3	0	-0.5
	Year	81	188	15	48	4	5	0	19	20	0	24	.255	.327	.330	76	-7	3-4	.971	3	108	151	O55(7/41/7)/3	0	-0.7
Total	4	167	416	40	96	9	8	2	33	37	3	65	.231	.298	.305	61	-25	6-4	.958	-1	100	104	O113(25/48/40)/3	0	-3.2
MAVIS, BOB	Robert Henry; B4.8.1918 Milwaukee WI; D3.1.2005 Little Rock AR; BL/TR/5´7˝/160; d9.17																								
1949	Det A	1	0	0	0	0	0	0	0	0	0	0	ø	ø	ø	ø	0	0-0	ø	0	—	—	/R	0	0.0
MAXVILL, DAL	Charles Dallan; B2.18.1939 Granite City IL; BR/TR/5´11˝/(157–160); d6.10; C7; Col Washington–St. Louis																								
1962	StL N	79	189	20	42	3	1	1	18	17-2	1	39	.222	.287	.265	46	-14	1-2	.962	-6	92	115	S76/3	0	-1.5
1963	StL N	53	51	12	12	2	0	0	3	6-0	0	11	.235	.316	.275	66	-2	0-0	.974	-5	68	84	S24,2b9,3b3	0	-0.6
1964	†StL N	37	26	4	6	0	0	0	4	0-0	0	7	.231	.231	.231	28	-3	1-0	.972	-2	91	154	2b15,S13/3rf	0	-0.3
1965	StL N	68	89	10	12	2	2	0	10	7-3	1	15	.135	.206	.202	14	-10	0-0	.993	0	97	132	2b49,S12	0	-0.8
1966	StL N	134	394	25	96	14	3	0	24	37-9	2	61	.244	.312	.294	69	-15	3-0	.967	18	**109**	125	S128,2b5/lf	0	1.4
1967	†StL N	152	476	37	108	14	4	1	41	48-12	1	66	.227	.297	.279	67	-20	0-2	.974	2	102	93	S148,2b7	0	-0.6
1968	†StL N	151	459	51	116	8	5	1	24	52-9	1	71	.253	.329	.298	91	-4	0-2	.969	-10	96	107	S151	0	-0.2
1969	StL N	132	372	27	65	10	2	2	32	44-2	1	52	.175	.263	.228	39	-30	1-1	.969	14	107	113	S131	0	-0.2
1970	StL N	152	399	35	80	5	2	0	28	51-3	0	56	.201	.287	.223	39	-34	0-0	**.982**	28	**118**	110	S136,2b22	0	0.8
1971	StL N	142	356	31	80	10	1	0	24	43-3	1	45	.225	.307	.258	60	-18	1-2	.979	11	**108**	89	S140	0	0.7
1972	StL N	105	276	22	61	6	1	1	23	31-4	0	47	.221	.299	.261	61	-14	0-1	.980	5	99	116	S95,2b11	0	0.1
	†Oak A	27	36	2	9	1	0	0	1	1-0	0	11	.250	.270	.278	66	-2	0-1	.983	-1	108	123	2b24,S4	0	-0.2
1973	Oak A	29	19	0	4	0	0	0	1	1-0	0	3	.211	.250	.211	32	-2	0-0	.966	-3	76	118	S18,2b11/3	0	-0.4
	Pit N	74	217	19	41	4	3	0	17	22-2	0	40	.189	.261	.235	40	-18	0-0	.971	7	109	105	S74	0	-0.3
1974	Pit N	8	22	3	4	0	0	0	0	2-0	0	4	.182	.250	.182	23	-2	0-0	.946	1	106	205	S8	0	-0.1
	†Oak A	60	52	3	10	0	0	0	2	8-0	0	10	.192	.300	.192	47	-3	0-0	1.000	-2	95	40	2b30,S29/3	23	-0.2
1975	Oak A	20	10	1	2	0	0	0	0	0-0	0	0	.200	.200	.200	14	-1	0-0	.955	-2	80	35	S20,2b2	0	-0.3
Total	14	1423	3443	302	748	79	24	6	252	370-49	8	538	.217	.293	.259	57	-192	7-11	.973	57	104	107	S1207,2b185,3b7,O2(1/0/1)	23	-2.7
MAXWELL, CHARLIE	Charles Richard "Smokey"; B4.8.1927 Lawton MI; BL/TL/5´11˝/(185–190); d9.20; Col Western Michigan																								
1950	Bos A	3	8	1	0	0	0	0	0	1	0	3	.000	.111	.000	-63	-2	0-0	1.000	0	124	0	O2R	0	-0.2
1951	Bos A	49	80	8	15	1	0	3	12	9	0	18	.188	.270	.313	52	-6	0-1	.926	-1	96	0	O13(5/0/8)	0	-0.8
1952	Bos A	8	15	0	1	1	0	0	0	3	0	11	.067	.222	.133	0	-2	0-0	.966	1	233	44	1b3,O3(0/1/2)	0	-0.1
1954	Bos A	74	104	9	26	4	1	0	5	12	0	21	.250	.328	.308	67	-4	3-0	1.000	-1	85	104	O27(21/3/6)	0	-0.5
1955	Bal A	4	4	0	0	0	0	0	0	0-0	0	1	.000	.000	.000	-99	-1	0-0	ø	0	—	—	/H	0	-0.1
	Det A	55	109	19	29	7	1	7	18	8-0	2	20	.266	.325	.541	134	4	0-0	.967	1	107	145	O26(22/0/4),1b2	0	0.4
	Year	59	113	19	29	7	1	7	18	8-0	2	21	.257	.315	.522	126	3	0-0	.967	1	107	145	O26(22/0/4),1b2	0	0.3
1956	Det A☆	141	500	96	163	14	3	28	87	79-1	2	74	.326	.414	.534	150	37	1-1	.987	6	107	121	O136(134/0/2)	0	3.4
1957	Det A★	138	492	75	136	23	3	24	82	76-7	5	84	.276	.377	.482	130	22	3-2	**.997**	10	114	80	O137(137/0/3)	0	2.4
1958	Det A	131	397	56	108	14	4	13	65	64-4	0	54	.272	.369	.426	111	8	6-1	.986	-2	99	64	O114(113/0/3),1b14	0	0.1
1959	Det A	145	518	81	130	12	2	31	95	81-5	6	91	.251	.357	.461	117	13	0-2	.986	6	109	71	O136L	0	0.9
1960	Det A	134	482	70	114	16	5	24	81	58-6	6	75	.237	.325	.440	102	0	5-0	**.996**	-0	98	57	O120L	0	-0.6
1961	Det A	79	131	11	30	4	2	5	18	20-2	1	24	.229	.333	.405	94	-1	0-0	.965	2	122	119	O25(22/0/4)	0	0.0
1962	Det A	30	67	5	13	2	0	1	9	8-1	0	10	.194	.273	.269	47	-5	0-0	.966	-0	109	0	O15R/1	0	-0.7
	Chi A	69	206	30	61	8	3	9	43	34-3	0	32	.296	.394	.495	139	12	0-0	.990	1	106	72	O56(49/0/7),1b6	0	1.0
	Year	99	273	35	74	10	3	10	52	42-4	0	42	.271	.365	.440	115	7	0-0	.985	1	107	56	O71(49/0/22),1b7	0	0.3
1963	Chi A	71	130	17	30	4	2	3	17	31-2	0	27	.231	.370	.362	111	3	0-0	1.000	-1	80	150	O24L,1b17	0	0.0
1964	Chi A	2	2	0	0	0	0	0	0	0-0	0	0	.000	.000	.000	-99	-1	0-0	ø	0	—	—	/H	0	-0.1
Total	14	1133	3245	478	856	110	26	148	532	484-31	22	545	.264	.360	.451	116	77	18-7	.988	23	105	83	O834(783/4/55),1b43	0	5.1
MAXWELL, JASON	Jason Ramond; B3.26.1972 Lewisburg TN; BR/TR/6´0˝/(180–185); [ChiN93 74/1667]; d9.1; Col Middle Tennessee																								
1998	Chi N	7	3	2	1	0	0	1	2	0-0	0	2	.333	.333	1.333	301	1	0-0	1.000	0	296	0	/2	0	0.1
2000	Min A	64	111	14	27	6	0	1	11	9-0	1	32	.243	.298	.324	56	-7	2-1	.967	4	133	114	2b30,3b19,S5,O2(0/1/1),D7	16	-0.2
2001	Min A	39	68	4	13	4	0	1	10	9-2	0	23	.191	.286	.294	51	-5	2-0	.893	-4	91	77	S12,3b11,2b9,D6	30	-0.7
Total	3	110	182	20	41	10	0	3	23	18-2	1	57	.225	.294	.330	58	-11	4-1	.974	1	124	82	2b40,3b30,S17,D13,O2(0/1/1)	46	-0.8
MAY, CARLOS	Carlos; B5.17.1948 Birmingham AL; BL/TR/6´0˝/215; [ChiA66 1/18]; d9.6; b–Lee																								
1968	Chi A	17	67	4	12	1	0	0	1	3-1	0	15	.179	.214	.194	24	-6	0-0	.960	-2	80	0	O17(15/0/2)	0	-1.1
1969	Chi A★	100	367	62	103	18	2	18	62	58-7	6	66	.281	.385	.488	137	20	1-4	.982	-4	83	126	O100(80/0/22)	0	0.9
1970	Chi A	150	555	83	158	28	4	12	68	79-9	3	96	.285	.373	.414	114	13	12-5	.991	-2	81	135	O141L,1b7	0	0.3
1971	Chi A	141	500	64	147	21	7	7	70	62-5	6	61	.294	.375	.406	119	15	16-7	.986	-2	93	85	1b130,O9L	17	0.3
1972	Chi A☆	148	523	83	161	26	3	12	68	79-14	9	70	.308	.405	.438	148	36	23-14	.983	-5	84	120	O145L,1b5	0	2.5
1973	Chi A	149	553	62	148	20	0	20	96	53-5	5	73	.268	.334	.412	106	4	8-6	.992	0	91	150	D75,O70L,1b2	0	-0.2
1974	Chi A	149	551	66	137	19	2	8	58	46-3	1	76	.249	.306	.334	82	-13	8-9	.988	1	98	122	O129L,D13	0	-2.2
1975	Chi A	128	454	55	123	19	2	8	53	67-13	9	46	.271	.373	.374	111	10	12-7	.989	3	129	98	1b63,O46L,D19	0	0.5
1976	Chi A	20	63	7	11	2	0	0	3	9-0	0	5	.175	.278	.206	43	-4	4-0	1.000	-1	92	0	D10,O9L	0	-0.5
	†NY A	87	288	38	80	11	2	3	40	34-2	5	32	.278	.358	.361	113	6	1-1	.950	-1	112	0	D71,O7L/1	0	0.4
	Year	107	351	45	91	13	2	3	43	43-2	5	37	.259	.344	.333	101	2	5-1	.807	-1	103	0	D81,O16L/1	0	-0.1
1977	NY A	65	181	21	41	7	1	2	16	17-4	1	24	.227	.292	.309	66	-8	0-0	1.000	-1	60	0	D53,O4(2/0/2)	0	-1.1
	Cal A	11	18	0	6	0	0	0	1	5-0	0	1	.333	.478	.333	130	1	0-0	1.000	0	107	43	1b3/D	0	0.1
	Year	76	199	21	47	7	1	2	17	22-4	1	25	.236	.311	.312	72	-7	0-0	1.000	-0	60	0	D54,O4(2/0/2),1b3	0	-1.0
Total	10	1165	4120	545	1127	172	23	90	536	512-63	45	565	.274	.357	.392	111	74	85-53	.984	-13	87	127	O677(653/0/26),D242,1b211	17	-0.1
MAY, DAVE	David La France; B12.23.1943 New Castle DE; BL/TR/5´10.5˝/(185–210); d7.28; s–Derrick																								
1967	Bal A	36	85	12	20	1	1	1	7	6-2	0	13	.235	.286	.306	75	-3	0-0	.969	-0	99	87	O19(1/0/18)	0	-0.5
1968	Bal A	84	152	15	29	6	3	0	7	19-3	1	27	.191	.285	.270	69	-5	3-3	.984	-4	83	43	O61(1/16/47)	0	-1.4
1969	†Bal A	78	120	8	29	6	0	3	10	9-0	2	23	.242	.305	.367	86	-2	2-1	.940	1	94	204	O40R	0	-0.3
1970	Bal A	25	31	6	6	0	1	1	6	4-0	0	4	.194	.286	.355	74	-1	0-0	1.000	-1	47	0	O9R	0	-0.3
	Mil A	100	342	36	82	8	1	7	31	44-6	2	56	.240	.329	.330	83	-8	8-6	.989	4	112	98	O99(0/99/1)	0	-0.7
	Year	125	373	42	88	8	2	8	37	48-6	2	60	.236	.325	.332	82	-9	8-6	.989	2	108	93	O108(0/99/10)	0	-1.0
1971	Mil A	144	501	74	139	20	3	16	65	50-4	3	59	.277	.343	.425	119	12	15-9	.975	5	109	113	O142(2/94/48)	0	1.3
1972	Mil A	143	500	49	119	20	2	9	45	47-8	3	56	.238	.306	.340	94	-4	11-13	.985	5	111	100	O138C	0	-0.5
1973	Mil A★	156	624	96	189	23	4	25	93	44-6	5	78	.303	.352	.473	133	25	6-7	.979	-7	97	76	O152C,D2	0	1.3
1974	Mil A	135	477	56	108	15	1	10	42	28-4	3	73	.226	.273	.325	72	-19	4-3	.989	1	100	109	O121(5/17/108),D8	0	-2.5
1975	Atl N	82	203	28	56	8	0	12	40	25-3	2	27	.276	.361	.493	131	8	1-1	.964	-0	101	90	O53(13/17/24)	0	0.6
1976	Atl N	105	214	27	46	5	3	3	23	26-3	1	31	.215	.300	.308	70	-8	5-1	.972	2	101	141	O60(41/0/19)	0	-0.9
1977	Tex A	120	340	46	82	14	1	7	42	32-1	4	43	.241	.311	.350	80	-9	4-3	.969	1	100	121	O111(21/2/92),D5	0	-1.3
1978	Mil A	39	77	9	15	4	0	2	11	9-1	2	10	.195	.295	.325	74	-3	0-0	.944	1	99	212	O16(4/7/5),D8	0	-0.2
	Pit N	5	4	0	0	0	0	0	0	1-0	0	1	.000	.200	.000	-38	-1	1-0	ø	0	—	—	/H	0	-0.1
Total	12	1252	3670	462	920	130	20	96	422	344-41	28	501	.251	.318	.375	97	-18	60-47	.978	6	102	104	O1021(88/542/411),D23	0	-5.5
MAY, DERRICK	Derrick Brant; B7.14.1968 Rochester NY; BL/TR/6´4˝/(205–235); [ChiN86 1/9]; d9.6; f–Dave																								
1990	Chi N	17	61	8	15	3	0	1	11	2-0	0	7	.246	.270	.344	63	-3	1-0	.972	0	104	89	O17L	0	-0.3
1991	Chi N	15	22	4	5	2	0	1	3	2-0	0	1	.227	.280	.455	102	0	0-0	1.000	1	111	365	O7L	0	0.1
1992	Chi N	124	351	33	96	11	0	8	45	14-4	3	40	.274	.306	.373	89	-6	5-3	.969	-8	81	65	O108(98/0/14)	0	-1.8
1993	Chi N	128	465	62	137	25	2	10	77	31-6	1	41	.295	.336	.422	103	2	10-3	.970	-3	95	90	O122(121/0/2)	0	-0.4
1994	Chi N	100	345	43	98	19	2	8	51	30-4	0	34	.284	.340	.420	97	-2	3-2	.994	-2	93	75	O92L	0	-0.6
1995	Mil A	32	113	15	28	3	1	1	9	5-0	1	18	.248	.286	.319	54	-8	0-1	.971	-0	106	48	O32L	0	-0.9
	Hou N	78	206	29	62	15	1	8	41	19-0	1	24	.301	.358	.500	133	10	5-0	.974	-4	91	0	O55(43/0/12)/1	0	0.5
1996	Hou N	109	259	24	65	12	3	5	33	30-8	2	33	.251	.330	.378	94	-2	2-2	.970	5	117	145	O71(70/0/3)	15	0.0
1997	Phi N	83	149	8	34	5	1	1	13	8-3	0	26	.228	.266	.295	48	-12	4-1	.961	3	113	167	O56(7/0/49)	0	-1.0

YEAR	TM LG	G	AB	R	H	2B	3B	HR	RBI	BB-IB	HP	SO	AVG	OBP	SLG	AOPS	ABR	SB-CS	FA	FR	RNG	THR	GAMES AT POSITION	DL	BFW
1998	Mon N	85	180	13	43	8	0	5	15	11-1	0	24	.239	.281	.367	71	-8	0-0	.984	-0	87	131	O48L,D2	0	-1.0
1999	Bal A	26	49	5	13	0	0	4	12	4-0	0	6	.265	.315	.510	111	0	0-0	1.000	1	119	491	O5(2/0/3),D9	0	0.1
Total	10	797	2200	244	596	103	10	52	310	156-26	8	254	.271	.319	.398	92	-29	30-12	.975	-6	96	92	O613(537/0/83),D11/1	15	-5.3
May, Jerry	Jerry Lee; B12.14.1943 Staunton VA; D6.30.1996 Swoope VA; BR/TR/6´2.5˝/(185–200); d9.19																								
1964	Pit N	11	31	1	8	0	0	0	3	3-0	0	9	.258	.314	.258	66	-1	0-0	.988	2	59	38	C11	0	0.1
1965	Pit N	4	2	0	1	0	0	0	1	0-0	0	0	.500	.500	.500	182	0	0-0	1.000	-1	0	0	C4	0	-0.1
1966	Pit N	42	52	6	13	4	0	1	2	2-1	1	15	.250	.291	.385	86	-1	0-1	.984	4	262	99	C41	0	0.4
1967	Pit N	110	325	23	88	13	2	3	22	36-19	3	55	.271	.348	.351	100	1	0-0	.993	-0	117	104	C110	21	0.7
1968	Pit N	137	416	26	91	15	2	1	33	41-12	3	80	.219	.293	.272	72	-13	0-0	.988	5	119	109	C135	0	-0.2
1969	Pit N	62	190	21	44	8	0	7	23	9-0	2	53	.232	.268	.384	84	-5	1-1	.994	-6	142	95	C52	30	-0.9
1970	Pit N	51	139	13	29	4	2	1	16	21-6	1	25	.209	.313	.288	63	-7	0-0	.994	11	110	185	C45	0	0.6
1971	KC A	71	218	16	55	13	2	1	24	27-8	0	37	.252	.329	.344	93	-1	0-0	.997	0	107	99	C71	34	0.2
1972	KC A	53	116	10	22	5	1	1	4	14-2	0	13	.190	.277	.276	65	-5	0-0	.979	-6	78	95	C41	0	-1.1
1973	KC A	11	30	4	4	1	1	0	2	3-0	1	5	.133	.235	.233	30	-3	0-0	.940	-3	42	32	C11	0	-0.6
	NY N	4	8	0	2	0	0	0	0	1-0	0	1	.250	.333	.250	64	0	0-0	1.000	0	0	0	C4	31	0.0
Total	10	556	1527	120	357	63	10	15	130	157-48	11	293	.234	.307	.318	81	-35	1-2	.990	7	117	106	C525	116	-0.9
May, Lee	Lee Andrew; B3.23.1943 Birmingham AL; BR/TR/6´3˝/(195–225); d9.1; C10; b–Carlos																								
1965	Cin N	5	4	1	0	0	0	0	0	0-0	0	1	.000	.000	.000	-94	-1	0-0	ø	0	—	—	/H	0	-0.1
1966	Cin N	25	75	14	25	5	1	2	10	0-0	0	14	.333	.333	.507	119	2	0-1	.972	-1	88	112	1b16	0	0.0
1967	Cin N	127	438	54	116	29	2	12	57	19-3	10	80	.265	.308	.422	97	-1	4-8	.994	1	91	88	1b81,O48(32/0/16)	0	-1.0
1968	Cin N	146	559	78	162	32	1	22	80	34-11	6	100	.290	.337	.469	132	21	4-7	.996	-1	91	91	1b122,O33(11/0/22)	0	1.1
1969	Cin N★	158	607	85	169	32	3	38	110	45-8	6	142	.278	.331	.529	132	23	5-4	.993	0	104	95	1b156,O7(5/0/2)	0	1.1
1970	†Cin N	153	605	78	153	34	2	34	94	38-5	2	125	.253	.297	.484	106	1	1-1	.993	-1	100	114	1b153	0	-1.2
1971	Cin N★	147	553	85	154	17	3	39	98	42-2	4	135	.278	.332	.532	143	28	3-0	.994	-5	88	109	1b143	18	1.3
1972	Hou N★	148	592	87	168	31	2	29	98	52-12	2	145	.284	.343	.490	138	28	3-1	.996	-3	86	109	1b146	0	1.4
1973	Hou N	148	545	65	147	24	3	28	105	34-10	2	122	.270	.310	.479	118	10	1-1	.993	-2	91	94	1b144	0	-0.4
1974	Hou N	152	556	59	149	26	0	24	85	17-2	7	97	.268	.294	.444	111	3	1-0	.994	2	106	103	1b145	0	-0.6
1975	Bal A	146	580	67	152	28	3	20	99	36-8	5	91	.262	.308	.424	112	7	1-2	.993	4	**113**	**134**	1b144,D2	0	-0.1
1976	Bal A	148	530	61	137	17	4	25	**109**	41-8	3	104	.258	.312	.447	129	16	4-1	.996	3	114	93	1b94,D52	0	1.2
1977	Bal A	150	585	75	148	16	2	27	99	38-5	0	119	.253	.296	.426	100	-3	2-2	.995	-3	88	123	1b110,D39	0	-1.3
1978	Bal A	148	556	56	137	16	1	25	80	31-5	1	110	.246	.286	.414	101	-3	5-2	.973	-0	83	105	D140,1b4	0	-0.8
1979	†Bal A	124	456	59	116	15	0	19	69	28-4	1	100	.254	.297	.412	93	-7	3-4	.913	-1	0	125	D117,1b2	0	-1.2
1980	Bal A	78	222	20	54	10	2	7	31	15-1	0	53	.243	.289	.401	89	-4	2-0	1.000	-0	71	70	D58,1b7	0	-0.6
1981	†KC A	26	55	3	16	3	0	0	8	3-0	0	14	.291	.328	.345	94	0	0-1	1.000	-1	47	142	1b8,D4	0	-0.2
1982	KC A	42	91	12	28	5	2	3	12	14-1	0	18	.308	.393	.505	146	6	0-0	.989	-1	79	102	1b32,D2	0	0.3
Total	18	2071	7609	959	2031	340	31	354	1244	487-85	49	1570	.267	.313	.459	116	126	39-35	.994	-8	97	106	1b1507,D414,O88(48/0/40)	18	-1.1
May, Pinky	Merrill Glend; B1.18.1911 Laconia IN; D9.4.2000 Corydon IN; BR/TR/5´11.5˝/165; d4.21; Mil 1944–45; s–Milt; Col Indiana																								
1939	Phi N	135	464	49	133	27	3	2	62	41	1	20	.287	.346	.371	95	-2	4	**.956**	10	**106**	109	3b132	—	1.2
1940	Phi N★	136	501	59	147	24	2	1	48	58	4	33	.293	.371	.355	105	7	2	.954	16	**118**	58	3b135/S	—	2.7
1941	Phi N	142	490	46	131	17	4	0	39	55	2	30	.267	.344	.318	91	-5	2	**.972**	**24**	**111**	107	3b140	0	2.4
1942	Phi N	115	345	25	82	15	0	0	18	51	1	17	.238	.338	.281	86	-3	3	.963	**19**	**123**	120	3b107	0	2.0
1943	Phi N	137	415	31	117	19	2	1	48	56	1	21	.282	.369	.345	111	8	2	**.963**	9	**108**	90	3b132	0	1.9
Total	5	665	2215	210	610	102	11	4	215	261	9	121	.275	.354	.337	98	5	13	.962	77	113	95	3b646/S	0	10.2
May, Milt	Milton Scott; B8.1.1950 Gary IN; BL/TR/6´0˝/(175–192); [PitN68 11/237]; d9.8; C14; f–Pinky																								
1970	Pit N	5	4	1	2	1	0	0	2	0-0	1	0	.500	.600	.750	260	1	0-0	ø	0	—	—	/H	0	0.1
1971	†Pit N	49	126	15	35	1	0	6	25	9-3	0	16	.278	.321	.429	111	1	0-0	1.000	4	330	97	C31	0	0.7
1972	†Pit N	57	139	12	39	10	0	0	14	10-2	0	13	.281	.325	.353	95	-1	0-0	.985	3	139	121	C33	0	0.4
1973	Pit N	101	283	29	76	8	1	7	31	34-12	2	26	.269	.349	.378	104	2	0-1	.973	-6	101	93	C79	0	0.0
1974	Hou N	127	405	47	117	17	4	7	54	39-8	1	33	.289	.349	.402	116	8	0-1	**.993**	3	97	**123**	C116	0	1.7
1975	Hou N	111	386	29	93	15	1	4	52	26-3	0	41	.241	.287	.316	73	-16	1-2	.986	8	87	**176**	C102	0	-0.4
1976	Det A	6	25	2	7	1	0	0	1	0-0	0	1	.280	.280	.320	72	-1	0-0	1.000	2	133	147	C6	135	0.1
1977	Det A	115	397	32	99	9	3	12	46	26-2	0	31	.249	.291	.378	78	-13	0-0	.986	6	117	106	C111	0	-0.2
1978	Det A	105	352	24	88	9	0	10	37	27-3	2	26	.250	.305	.361	85	-8	0-0	.979	2	108	95	C94	0	-0.2
1979	Det A	6	11	1	3	2	0	0	3	1-1	0	1	.273	.333	.455	107	0	0-0	1.000	0	35	0	C5	0	0.0
	Chi A	65	202	23	51	13	0	7	28	14-1	2	27	.252	.306	.421	94	-2	0-0	.981	2	106	105	C65	0	0.2
	Year	71	213	24	54	15	0	7	31	15-2	2	28	.254	.307	.423	94	-2	0-0	.982	2	103	100	C70	0	0.2
1980	SF N	111	358	27	93	16	2	6	50	25-4	1	40	.260	.305	.366	91	-5	0-1	.986	1	98	108	C103	16	0.0
1981	SF N	97	316	20	98	17	0	2	33	34-10	0	29	.310	.376	.383	120	9	1-4	.989	-4	82	93	C93	0	0.9
1982	SF N	114	395	29	104	19	0	9	39	28-8	0	38	.263	.311	.380	94	-4	0-1	.987	-4	79	144	C110	0	-0.4
1983	SF N	66	186	18	46	6	0	6	20	21-6	0	23	.247	.324	.376	96	-1	2-2	.981	-1	90	102	C56	7	0.0
	Pit N	7	12	0	3	0	0	0	0	1-1	0	1	.250	.308	.250	55	-1	0-0	1.000	1	52	242	C4	0	0.0
	Year	73	198	18	49	6	0	6	20	22-7	0	24	.247	.323	.369	93	-2	2-2	.983	-0	88	110	C60	0	0.0
1984	Pit N	50	96	4	17	3	0	1	8	10-1	0	15	.177	.255	.240	39	-8	0-1	.993	3	97	83	C26	0	-0.5
Total	15	1192	3693	313	971	147	11	77	443	305-65	9	361	.263	.318	.371	93	-39	4-13	.986	20	105	116	C1034	158	2.4
Mayberry, John	John Claiborn; B2.18.1949 Detroit MI; BL/TL/6´3˝/(215–239); [HouN67 1/6]; d9.10; C2																								
1968	Hou N	4	9	0	0	0	0	0	0	0-0	1	2	.000	.100	.000	-69	-2	0-0	1.000	-0	0	65	1b2	0	-0.3
1969	Hou N	5	4	0	0	0	0	0	0	1-0	0	1	.000	.200	.000	-40	-1	0-0	ø	0	—	—	/H	0	-0.1
1970	Hou N	50	148	23	32	3	2	5	14	21-6	2	33	.216	.318	.365	87	-3	1-1	.995	3	125	85	1b45	0	-0.3
1971	Hou N	46	137	16	25	0	1	7	14	13-2	2	32	.182	.260	.350	75	-5	0-0	.997	-4	57	68	1b37	0	-1.4
1972	KC A	149	503	65	150	24	3	25	100	78-13	3	74	.298	.394	.507	168	45	0-2	**.995**	-1	96	**120**	1b146	0	3.5
1973	KC A★	152	510	87	142	20	2	26	100	**122-17**	2	79	.278	**.417**	.478	142	35	3-0	.994	-6	84	110	1b149/D	0	1.8
1974	KC A★	126	427	63	100	13	1	22	69	77-11	6	72	.234	.358	.424	118	12	4-2	.990	-3	95	112	1b106,D16	0	0.1
1975	KC A	156	554	95	161	38	1	34	106	**119**-16	4	73	.291	.416	.547	**167**	**55**	5-3	.988	1	104	97	1b131,D27	0	4.5
1976	†KC A	161	594	76	138	22	2	13	95	82-7	2	73	.232	.322	.342	95	-2	3-2	.996	-3	93	105	1b160,D2	0	-1.8
1977	†KC A	153	543	73	125	22	1	23	82	83-9	7	86	.230	.336	.401	100	2	1-3	**.995**	-5	83	103	1b145,D8	0	-1.3
1978	Tor A	152	515	51	129	15	2	22	70	60-2	4	57	.250	.329	.416	107	5	1-2	.993	-13	60	101	1b139,D7	0	-1.8
1979	Tor A	137	464	61	127	22	1	21	74	69-7	5	60	.274	.372	.461	122	16	1-1	.995	-7	80	103	1b135	0	0.1
1980	Tor A	149	501	62	124	19	2	30	82	77-9	3	80	.248	.349	.473	119	13	0-0	.994	-5	86	106	1b136,D8	0	0.0
1981	Tor A	94	290	34	72	6	1	17	43	44-4	8	45	.248	.360	.452	126	11	1-1	.993	-8	67	97	1b80,D10	0	-0.2
1982	Tor A	17	33	7	9	0	0	2	3	7-1	1	5	.273	.405	.455	127	2	0-0	1.000	-1	36	94	D13,1b4	0	0.0
	NY A	69	215	20	45	7	0	8	27	28-2	5	38	.209	.313	.353	84	-4	0-0	.996	-2	78	104	1b63,D4	0	-1.0
	Year	86	248	27	54	7	0	10	30	35-3	6	43	.218	.326	.367	90	-3	0-0	.996	-3	75	103	1b67,D17	0	-1.0
Total	15	1620	5447	733	1379	211	19	255	879	881-106	55	810	.253	.360	.439	122	179	20-17	.994	-53	85	104	1b1478,D96	0	1.8
Maye, Lee	Arthur Lee; B12.11.1934 Tuscaloosa AL; D7.17.2002 Riverside CA; BL/TR/6´2˝/(185–190); d7.17																								
1959	Mil N	51	140	17	42	5	1	4	16	7-2	1	26	.300	.338	.436	114	2	2-2	.976	2	113	102	O44(24/0/21)	0	0.2
1960	Mil N	41	83	14	25	6	0	0	2	7-2	1	21	.301	.359	.373	110	2	5-0	.968	-1	89	67	O19(15/0/4)	0	0.1
1961	Mil N	110	373	68	101	11	5	14	41	36-2	3	50	.271	.337	.440	112	5	10-1	.972	-3	98	71	O96(26/0/72)	0	-0.2
1962	Mil N	99	349	40	85	10	0	10	41	25-2	1	58	.244	.294	.358	77	-12	9-3	.977	1	110	33	O94(38/60/2)	35	-1.5
1963	Mil N	124	442	67	120	22	7	11	34	36-2	3	52	.271	.329	.428	118	10	14-2	.983	1	108	57	O111(70/73/3)	0	1.0
1964	Mil N	153	588	96	179	**44**	5	10	74	34-3	4	54	.304	.346	.447	121	17	5-10	.961	-4	103	86	O135(54/92/0),3b5	0	0.6
1965	Mil N	15	53	8	16	2	0	2	7	2-0	1	6	.302	.339	.453	120	1	0-0	.962	1	93	295	O13(4/9/0)	0	0.1
	Hou N	108	415	38	104	17	7	3	36	20-3	1	37	.251	.285	.347	83	-11	1-5	.953	1	101	110	O103(92/11/3)	0	-1.8
	Year	123	468	46	120	19	7	5	43	22-3	2	43	.256	.291	.359	88	-10	1-5	.954	1	100	131	O116(96/20/3)	0	-1.7
1966	Hou N	115	358	38	103	12	4	9	36	20-5	0	26	.288	.323	.419	113	5	4-3	.949	-2	95	68	O97L	0	-0.3
1967	Cle A	115	297	43	77	20	4	9	27	26-4	1	47	.259	.321	.444	123	8	3-3	.981	-4	90	49	O77(23/10/54)/2	0	0.0
1968	Cle A	109	299	20	84	13	2	4	26	15-0	1	24	.281	.316	.378	112	3	0-0	.984	3	113	104	O80(71/0/10)/1	0	0.3
1969	Cle A	43	108	9	27	5	0	1	15	8-2	1	15	.250	.305	.324	75	-4	1-0	.982	1	125	0	O28(26/0/2)	0	-0.4
	Was A	71	238	41	69	9	3	9	26	20-0	0	25	.290	.345	.466	132	9	1-3	.944	-4	99	23	O65(6/4/56)	0	0.2
	Year	114	346	50	96	14	3	10	41	28-2	1	40	.277	.332	.422	112	5	2-3	.957	-3	107	16	O93(32/4/58)	0	-0.2

YEAR	TM LG	G	AB	R	H	2B	3B	HR	RBI	BB-IB	HP	SO	AVG	OBP	SLG	AOPS	ABR	SB-CS	FA	FR	RNG	THR	GAMES AT POSITION	DL	BFW
1970	Was A	96	255	28	67	12	1	7	30	21-1	1	32	.263	.321	.400	102	0	4-2	1.000	-5	71	104	O68(6/0/63)/3	0	-0.8
	Chi A	6	6	0	1	0	0	0	1	0-0	0	1	.167	.167	.167	-8	-1	0-0	ø	0	—	—	/H	0	-0.1
	Year	102	261	28	68	12	1	7	31	21-1	1	33	.261	.318	.395	99	-1	4-2	1.000	-5	71	104	O68(6/0/63)/3	0	-0.9
1971	Chi A	32	44	6	9	2	0	1	7	5-1	0	7	.205	.280	.318	69	-2	0-0	1.000	0	82	217	O10(2/0/8)	15	-0.2
Total	13	1288	4048	533	1109	190	39	94	419	282-29	19	481	.274	.323	.410	108	32	59-34	.970	-13	101	75	O1040(554/259/298),3b6/12	50	-2.8
Mayer, Ed	Edward H.; B8.16.1865 Marshall IL; D5.15.1946 Chicago IL; 5´8.5˝/155; d4.19																								
1890	Phi N	120	484	49	117	25	5	1	70	22	8	36	.242	.286	.320	75	-17	20	.878	-11	90	111	3b117,O4C	—	-2.3
1891	Phi N	68	268	24	50	2	4	0	31	14	4	29	.187	.238	.224	34	-24	7	.895	-3	103	65	3b31,O29(4/24/1),S7/2	—	-2.4
Total	2	188	752	73	167	27	9	1	101	36	12	65	.222	.269	.286	60	-41	27	.882	-13	93	102	3b148,O33(4/28/1),S7/2	—	-4.7
Mayer, Sam	Samuel Frankel (b Samuel Frankel Erskine); B2.28.1893 Atlanta GA; D7.1.1962 Atlanta GA; BR/TL/5´10˝/164; d9.14; b–Erskine																								
1915	Was A	11	29	5	7	0	0	1	4	4	0	2	.241	.333	.345	101	0	1-2	1.000	0	97	96	O9(1/0/8)/P1	—	-0.1
Mayer, Wally	Walter A.; B7.8.1890 Cincinnati OH; D11.18.1951 Minnetonka MN; BR/TR/5´11˝/168; d9.28; Mil 1918																								
1911	Chi A	1	3	0	0	0	0	0	0	2	0	—	.000	.400	.000	16	0	0	.900	-0	*190*	*64*	/C	—	0.0
1912	Chi A	9	9	1	0	0	0	0	0	1	0	—	.000	.100	.000	-73	-2	0	1.000	-0	*95*	*44*	C6	—	-0.2
1914	Chi A	40	85	7	14	3	1	0	5	14	1	23	.165	.290	.224	55	-4	1-1	.968	5	*133*	*109*	C33/3	—	0.3
1915	Chi A	22	54	3	12	3	1	0	5	5	0	8	.222	.288	.315	78	-2	0-2	.990	1	*181*	*61*	C20	—	0.0
1917	Bos A	4	12	2	2	0	0	0	0	5	0	2	.167	.412	.167	78	0	0	.964	1	*125*	*125*	C4	—	0.2
1918	Bos A	26	49	7	11	4	0	0	5	7	0	7	.224	.321	.306	91	0	0	.964	-0	*108*	*89*	C23	—	0.1
1919	StL A	30	62	2	14	4	1	0	5	8	0	11	.226	.314	.323	77	-2	0	.959	3	*107*	*123*	C25	—	0.3
Total	7	132	274	22	53	14	3	0	20	42	1	51	.193	.303	.266	68	-10	1-3	.969	8	*131*	*98*	C112/3	—	0.7
Mayes, Paddy	Adair Bushyhead; B3.17.1885 Locust Grove OK; D5.28.1963 Fayetteville AR; BL/TR/5´11˝/160; d6.11																								
1911	Phi N	5	5	1	0	0	0	0	0	1	1	2	.000	.286	.000	-17	-1	0	1.000	0	0	0	O2	—	0.0
Maynard, Buster	James Walter; B3.25.1913 Henderson NC; D9.7.1977 Durham NC; BR/TR/5´11˝/170; d9.17; Mil 1944–45																								
1940	NY N	7	29	6	8	2	2	1	2	2	0	6	.276	.323	.586	145	1	0	.929	-1	87	0	O7(0/3/4)	—	0.0
1942	NY N	89	190	17	47	4	1	4	32	19	1	19	.247	.319	.342	93	-2	3	.982	5	105	160	O58(7/48/4),3b10/2	0	0.2
1943	NY N	121	393	43	81	8	2	9	32	24	0	27	.206	.252	.305	60	-22	3	.965	-2	86	145	O74(25/39/13),3b22	0	-2.9
1946	NY N	7	4	2	0	0	0	0	0	1	0	1	.000	.200	.000	-41	-1	0	.750	-0	103	0	O3(0/1/2)	0	-0.1
Total	4	224	616	68	136	14	5	14	66	46	1	53	.221	.276	.328	74	-24	6	.967	2	93	140	O142(32/91/23),3b32/2	0	-2.8
Maynard, Chick	Le Roy Evans; B11.2.1896 Turners Falls MA; D1.31.1957 Bangor ME; BL/TR/5´9˝/150; d6.27; Col Dartmouth																								
1922	Bos A	12	24	1	3	0	0	0	0	3	0	2	.125	.222	.125	-8	-4	0-1	.872	-3	90	26	S12	—	-0.6
Mayne, Brent	Brent Danem; B4.19.1968 Loma Linda CA; BL/TR/6´1˝/(190–195); [KCA89 1/13]; d9.18; Col Cal St.–Fullerton																								
1990	KC A	5	13	2	3	0	0	0	1	3-0	0	3	.231	.375	.231	74	0	0-1	.970	0	52	74	C5	0	0.0
1991	KC A	85	231	22	58	8	0	3	31	23-4	0	42	.251	.315	.325	78	-7	2-4	.987	-0	82	104	C80/D	0	-0.4
1992	KC A	82	213	16	48	10	0	0	18	11-0	0	26	.225	.260	.272	49	-15	0-4	.990	3	146	94	C62,3b8/D	0	-1.0
1993	KC A	71	205	22	52	9	1	2	22	18-7	1	31	.254	.317	.337	71	-8	3-2	.995	-0	81	84	C68/D	0	-0.5
1994	KC A	46	144	19	37	5	1	2	20	14-1	0	27	.257	.323	.347	69	-7	1-0	.996	2	94	96	C42,D3	0	-0.2
1995	KC A	110	307	23	77	18	1	1	27	25-1	3	41	.251	.313	.326	65	-15	0-1	.995	11	108	57	C103	0	0.1
1996	NY N	70	99	9	26	6	0	1	6	12-1	0	22	.263	.342	.354	88	-1	0-1	1.000	-8	54	21	C21	0	-0.8
1997	Oak A	85	256	29	74	12	0	6	22	18-1	4	33	.289	.343	.406	95	-2	1-0	.996	-11	88	95	C83	0	-0.7
1998	SF N	94	275	26	75	15	0	3	32	37-3	1	47	.273	.359	.360	95	-1	2-1	.991	-6	88	70	C88	0	-0.2
1999	SF N	117	322	39	97	32	0	2	39	43-5	5	65	.301	.389	.419	113	9	2-2	.995	-1	96	116	C105	0	1.3
2000	Col N	117	335	36	101	21	0	6	64	47-13	1	48	.301	.381	.418	84	-6	1-3	.990	-0	101	79	C105/P	0	-0.1
2001	Col N	49	160	15	53	7	0	0	20	16-3	0	24	.331	.385	.375	83	-3	0-0	.997	8	118	114	C44/1	0	0.8
	KC A	51	166	13	40	4	1	2	20	10-2	1	17	.241	.283	.313	53	-12	1-2	.993	-2	101	91	C49	0	-1.1
2002	KC A	101	326	35	77	8	2	4	30	34-1	2	54	.236	.309	.310	59	-19	4-4	.993	-2	115	100	C99	28	-1.5
2003	KC A	113	372	39	91	17	1	6	36	32-5	3	59	.245	.307	.344	68	-17	0-2	.994	-4	104	102	C112	0	-1.4
2004	Ari N	36	94	9	24	6	1	0	10	13-4	0	17	.255	.343	.340	73	-3	1-0	.990	-1	105	213	C30/1	39	-0.2
	†LA N	47	96	5	18	0	0	0	5	14-4	0	24	.188	.286	.188	28	-10	0-0	1.000	-0	117	88	C47	0	-0.8
	Year	83	190	14	42	6	1	0	15	27-8	0	41	.221	.314	.263	52	-13	1-0	.995	-1	112	144	C77/1	0	-1.0
Total	15	1279	3614	359	951	178	8	38	403	370-55	21	580	.263	.332	.348	76	-117	18-27	.993	-13	101	93	C1143,3b8,D6,1b2/P	67	-6.7
Mayo, Eddie	Edward Joseph "Hotshot" (b Edward Joseph Mayoski); B4.15.1910 Holyoke MA; D11.27.2006 Banning CA; BL/TR/5´11˝/178; d5.22; C4																								
1936	†NY N	46	141	11	28	4	1	1	8	11	0	12	.199	.257	.262	40	-12	0	.981	3	111	191	3b40	—	-0.8
1937	Bos N	65	172	19	39	6	1	1	18	15	1	20	.227	.293	.291	65	-8	1	.956	-5	90	37	3b50	—	-1.2
1938	Bos N	8	14	2	3	0	0	1	4	1	0	0	.214	.267	.429	98	0	0	.923	1	114	332	3b6,S2	—	0.1
1943	Phi A	128	471	49	103	10	1	0	28	34	5	32	.219	.278	.244	54	-28	2-0	**.976**	0	93	74	3b123	0	-2.9
1944	Det A	154	607	76	151	18	3	5	63	57	4	23	.249	.317	.313	76	-18	9-13	.978	**34**	**114**	**121**	2b143,S11	0	2.2
1945	†Det A✳	134	501	71	143	24	3	10	54	47	0	29	.285	.347	.405	111	7	7-7	**.980**	20	**112**	115	2b124	0	3.5
1946	Det A	51	202	21	51	9	2	0	22	14	0	12	.252	.301	.317	68	-9	6-2	.965	-6	92	93	2b49	0	-1.2
1947	Det A	142	535	66	149	28	4	6	48	48	0	28	.279	.338	.379	96	-3	3-7	.983	-14	93	83	2b142	0	-1.1
1948	Det A	106	370	35	92	20	1	2	42	30	3	19	.249	.310	.324	67	-18	1-9	.975	-7	91	83	2b86,3b10	0	-2.3
Total	9	834	3013	350	759	119	16	26	287	257	13	175	.252	.313	.328	78	-89	29-38	.978	26	103	102	2b544,3b229,S13	0	-3.7
Mayo, Jackie	John Lewis; B7.26.1925 Litchfield IL; BL/TR/6´1˝/190; d9.19; Col Notre Dame																								
1948	Phi N	12	35	7	8	2	1	0	3	7	2	7	.229	.386	.343	101	1	1	1.000	1	114	114	O11L	0	0.1
1949	Phi N	45	39	3	5	0	0	0	2	4	0	5	.128	.209	.128	-8	-6	0	.889	0	123	117	O25(0/1/24)	0	-0.6
1950	†Phi N	18	36	1	8	3	0	0	3	2	0	5	.222	.263	.306	50	-3	0	.958	-0	113	0	O15L	0	-0.3
1951	Phi N	9	7	1	1	0	0	0	0	0	0	0	.143	.143	.143	-23	-1	0-0	1.000	0	147	0	O5L	0	-0.1
1952	Phi N	50	119	13	29	5	0	1	4	12	0	17	.244	.313	.311	74	-4	1-3	1.000	3	111	48	O27(24/1/2),1b6	0	-0.4
1953	Phi N	5	4	0	0	0	0	0	0	0	0	1	.000	.000	.000	-99	-1	0-0	ø	-0	0	0	/rf	0	-0.1
Total	6	139	240	25	51	10	1	1	12	25	2	35	.213	.292	.275	56	-14	2-3	.972	4	114	62	O84(55/2/27),1b6	0	-1.4
Mays, Willie	Willie Howard "The Say Hey Kid"; B5.6.1931 Westfield AL; BR/TR/5´11˝/(170–185); d5.25; Mil 1952–53; C6; HF1979; Negro Lg 1948–50																								
1951	†NY N	121	464	59	127	22	5	20	68	57	2	60	.274	.356	.472	120	13	7-4	.976	2	105	110	O121C	0	1.2
1952	NY N	34	127	17	30	2	4	4	23	16	1	17	.236	.326	.409	102	0	4-1	.991	4	110	161	O34C	0	0.4
1954	†NY N★	151	565	119	195	33	**13**	41	110	66	2	57	**.345**	.411	**.667**	176	61	8-5	.985	10	109	112	O151C	0	**6.2**
1955	NY N★	152	580	123	185	18	**13**	**51**	127	79-13	4	60	.319	.400	**.659**	**176**	**62**	24-4	.982	12	102	**195**	O152C	0	**6.8**
1956	NY N★	152	578	101	171	27	8	36	84	68-20	1	65	.296	.369	.557	146	37	**40**-10	.979	6	104	126	O152C	0	4.1
1957	NY N★	152	585	112	195	26	**20**	35	97	76-15	1	62	.333	.407	**.626**	**174**	**61**	**38**-19	.980	2	101	122	O150C	0	**5.7**
1958	SF N★	152	600	**121**	208	33	11	29	96	78-12	1	56	.347	.419	.583	**167**	**59**	**31**-6	.980	7	107	137	O151C	0	**6.2**
1959	SF N★	151	575	125	180	43	5	34	104	65-9	2	58	.313	.381	.583	157	47	**27**-4	.984	-4	102	73	O147(2/146/0)	0	4.0
1960	SF N★	153	595	107	**190**	29	12	29	103	61-11	4	70	.319	.381	.555	164	51	25-10	.981	4	105	108	O152C	0	5.0
1961	SF N★	154	572	**129**	176	32	3	40	123	81-15	2	77	.308	.393	.584	162	52	18-9	.980	-2	106	64	O153C	0	4.5
1962	†SF N★	162	621	130	189	36	5	**49**	141	78-11	4	85	.304	.384	.615	167	58	18-2	.991	7	115	57	O161C	0	**6.1**
1963	SF N★	157	596	115	187	32	7	38	103	66-5	2	83	.314	.380	.582	176	58	8-3	.981	3	110	68	O157C/S	0	**6.0**
1964	SF N★	157	578	121	171	21	9	**47**	111	82-13	1	72	.296	.383	**.607**	**171**	**54**	19-5	.984	4	110	103	O155C/1S3	0	5.8
1965	SF N★	157	558	118	177	21	3	**52**	112	76-16	0	71	.317	**.398**	**.645**	**184**	**62**	9-4	.983	10	110	163	O151(1/147/5)	0	**6.9**
1966	SF N★	152	552	99	159	29	4	37	103	70-11	2	81	.288	.368	.556	149	37	5-1	.982	5	113	79	O150(1/145/5)	0	3.9
1967	SF N★	141	486	83	128	22	2	22	70	51-7	2	92	.263	.334	.453	125	16	6-0	.976	-3	101	44	O134C	0	1.1
1968	SF N★	148	498	84	144	20	5	23	79	67-7	2	81	.289	.372	.488	158	36	12-6	.978	0	102	87	O142C/1	0	3.7
1969	SF N★	117	403	64	114	17	3	13	58	49-7	3	71	.283	.362	.437	125	14	6-2	.976	-10	87	63	O108(0/106/2)/1	0	0.3
1970	SF N★	139	478	94	139	15	2	28	83	79-3	3	90	.291	.390	.506	141	29	5-0	.975	-2	101	89	O129C,1b5	0	2.5
1971	†SF N★	136	417	82	113	24	5	18	61	**112**-11	3	123	.271	**.425**	.482	159	41	23-3	.970	-4	104	47	O84C,1b48	0	3.7
1972	SF N	19	49	8	9	2	0	0	3	17-1	0	5	.184	.394	.224	78	0	3-0	1.000	-1	91	0	O14C	0	-0.1
	NY N★	69	195	27	52	9	1	8	19	43-5	1	43	.267	.402	.446	143	13	1-5	.974	0	108	120	O49(1/48/0),1b11	0	1.1
	Year	88	244	35	61	11	1	8	22	60-6	1	48	.250	.400	.402	129	13	4-5	.979	-1	104	93	O63(1/62/0),1b11	0	1.0
1973	†NY N★	66	209	24	44	10	0	6	25	27-0	1	47	.211	.303	.344	80	-6	1-0	.991	1	115	85	O45(5/43/9),1b17	21	-0.7
Total	22	2992	10881	2062	3283	523	140	660	1903	1464-192	44	1526	.302	.384	.557	156	855	338-103	.981	50	106	100	O2842(10/2827/21),1b84,S2/3	21	84.4

YEAR	TM LG	G	AB	R	H	2B	3B	HR	RBI	BB-IB	HP	SO	AVG	OBP	SLG	AOPS	ABR	SB-CS	FA	FR	RNG	THR	GAMES AT POSITION	DL	BFW
MAZEROSKI, BILL	William Stanley "Maz"; B9.5.1936 Wheeling WV; BR/TR/5´11.5˝/(180–188); d7.7; C3; HF2001																								
1956	Pit N	81	255	30	62	8	1	3	14	18-1	0	24	.243	.293	.318	66	-13	0-0	.981	9	111	110	2b81	0	0.2
1957	Pit N	148	526	59	149	27	7	8	54	27-2	1	49	.283	.318	.407	96	-4	3-3	.978	5	109	105	2b144	0	1.1
1958	Pit N★	152	567	69	156	24	6	19	68	25-3	3	71	.275	.308	.439	98	-4	1-1	.980	17	**112**	110	2b152	0	2.3
1959	Pit N★	135	493	50	119	15	6	7	59	29-1	1	54	.241	.283	.339	66	-26	1-3	.981	-6	100	**121**	2b133	0	-2.3
1960	†Pit N★	151	538	58	147	21	5	11	64	40-15	1	50	.273	.320	.392	95	-5	4-0	**.989**	**30**	**109**	**144**	2b151	0	3.8
1961	Pit N	152	558	71	148	21	2	13	59	26-10	3	55	.265	.298	.380	79	-18	2-1	.975	**37**	**115**	**129**	2b152	0	3.2
1962	Pit N★	159	572	55	155	24	9	14	81	37-**16**	2	47	.271	.315	.418	95	-6	0-3	.985	**41**	**112**	**135**	2b159	0	4.7
1963	Pit N✳	142	534	43	131	22	3	8	52	32-6	0	46	.245	.286	.343	80	-14	2-0	.984	**56**	**127**	**153**	2b138	0	5.7
1964	Pit N☆	**162**	601	66	161	22	8	10	64	29-11	0	52	.268	.300	.381	91	-9	1-1	.975	**35**	**118**	**119**	2b162	0	4.1
1965	Pit N	130	494	52	134	17	1	6	54	18-5	2	34	.271	.294	.346	81	-13	2-1	**.988**	**26**	**116**	**142**	2b127	0	2.5
1966	Pit N	**162**	621	56	163	22	7	16	82	31-9	1	62	.262	.296	.398	91	-9	4-3	**.992**	**41**	**116**	**149**	2b162	0	4.8
1967	Pit N★	**163**	639	62	167	25	3	9	77	30-7	0	55	.261	.292	.352	84	-15	1-2	.981	21	**110**	116	2b163	0	2.1
1968	Pit N	143	506	36	127	18	2	3	42	38-10	2	38	.251	.304	.312	87	-8	3-4	.981	20	**114**	**124**	2b142	0	2.7
1969	Pit N	67	227	13	52	7	1	3	25	22-3	2	16	.229	.298	.308	73	-8	1-1	.988	14	113	115	2b65	0	1.0
1970	†Pit N	112	367	29	84	14	0	7	39	27-9	2	40	.229	.283	.324	63	-20	2-0	.987	20	114	128	2b102	0	0.7
1971	†Pit N	70	193	17	49	3	1	1	16	15-1	0	8	.254	.303	.295	71	-7	0-0	.986	-4	100	82	2b46,3b7	0	-1.0
1972	†Pit N	34	64	3	12	4	0	0	3	3-1	0	5	.188	.217	.250	35	-5	0-0	.986	1	106	96	2b15,3b3	19	-0.4
Total	17	2163	7755	769	2016	294	62	138	853	447-110	20	706	.260	.299	.367	84	-184	27-23	.983	362	113	127	2b2094,3b10	19	35.2
MAZZERA, MEL	Melvin Leonard "Mike"; B1.31.1914 Stockton CA; D12.17.1997 Stockton CA; BL/TL/5´11˝/180; d9.9																								
1935	StL A	12	30	4	7	2	0	1	2	4	0	9	.233	.324	.400	82	-1	0-0	.950	0	105	161	O10(4/3/3)	—	-0.1
1937	StL A	7	7	1	2	2	0	0	0	0	0	2	.286	.286	.571	110	0	0-0	ø	0	—	—	/H	—	0.0
1938	StL A	86	204	33	57	8	2	6	29	12	3	25	.279	.329	.426	88	-5	1-1	.976	2	93	230	O47(25/8/14)	—	-0.4
1939	StL A	33	110	21	33	5	2	3	22	10	1	20	.300	.364	.464	108	1	0-0	.983	0	105	57	O25(18/0/7)	—	0.0
1940	Phi N	69	156	16	37	5	4	0	13	19	0	15	.237	.320	.321	80	-4	1	.985	1	90	202	O42(26/2/16),1b11	—	-0.5
Total	5	207	507	75	136	22	8	10	66	45	4	71	.268	.333	.402	90	-9	2-1	.978	3	96	175	O124(73/13/40),1b11	—	-1.0
MAZZILLI, LEE	Lee Louis; B3.25.1955 New York NY; BB/TR/6´1˝/(180–195); [NYN73 1/14]; d9.7; M2/C5																								
1976	NY N	24	77	9	15	2	0	2	7	14-0	1	10	.195	.323	.299	82	-1	5-4	.983	2	112	165	O23(2/21/0)	0	0.0
1977	NY N	159	537	66	134	24	3	6	46	72-6	3	72	.250	.340	.339	86	-8	22-15	.992	3	108	95	O156C	0	-0.7
1978	NY N	148	542	78	148	28	5	16	61	69-6	1	82	.273	.353	.432	122	17	20-13	.987	-1	101	96	O144C	0	1.6
1979	NY N★	158	597	78	181	34	4	15	79	93-5	0	74	.303	.395	.449	134	32	34-12	.989	-5	94	111	O143C,1b15	0	2.9
1980	NY N	152	578	82	162	31	4	16	76	82-11	3	92	.280	.370	.431	125	22	41-15	.983	-4	83	99	1b92,O66C	0	1.7
1981	NY N	95	324	36	74	14	5	6	34	46-3	2	53	.228	.324	.358	95	-2	17-7	.970	-1	102	75	O89(51/40/0)	0	-0.4
1982	Tex A	58	195	23	47	8	0	4	17	28-0	1	26	.241	.339	.344	92	-1	11-6	.945	-2	88	65	O26(11/15/2),D24	40	-0.4
	NY A	37	128	20	34	2	0	6	17	15-0	1	15	.266	.347	.422	112	2	2-3	.995	-2	54	136	1b23,O2L,D9	0	-0.2
	Year	95	323	43	81	10	0	10	34	43-0	2	41	.251	.342	.375	100	1	13-9	.949	-4	89	60	D33,O28(13/15/2),1b23	0	-0.6
1983	Pit N	109	246	37	59	9	0	5	24	49-1	2	43	.240	.365	.337	95	1	15-5	.985	-1	102	122	O57(5/53/0),1b7	0	0.0
1984	Pit N	111	266	37	63	11	1	4	21	40-2	1	42	.237	.338	.331	89	-3	8-1	.989	-6	82	42	O74L,1b5	15	-1.1
1985	Pit N	92	117	20	33	8	0	1	9	29-1	0	17	.282	.425	.376	127	7	4-1	.986	-1	63	129	1b19,O5(3/3/0)	0	0.5
1986	Pit N	61	93	18	21	2	1	1	8	26-1	0	25	.226	.392	.301	92	1	3-3	1.000	-1	104	0	O18(16/3/0),1b7	0	-0.2
	†NY N	39	58	10	16	3	0	2	7	12-1	2	11	.276	.417	.431	137	4	1-1	1.000	-1	120	0	O10(8/0/2),1b8	0	0.2
	Year	100	151	28	37	5	1	3	15	38-2	2	36	.245	.401	.351	109	4	4-4	1.000	-2	110	0	O28(24/3/2),1b15	0	0.0
1987	NY N	88	124	26	38	8	1	3	24	21-3	0	14	.306	.399	.460	135	7	5-3	1.000	-1	87	101	O25(12/2/13),1b13	0	0.5
1988	†NY N	68	116	9	17	2	0	0	12	12-0	1	16	.147	.227	.164	16	-13	4-1	1.000	-1	100	147	O18(13/0/6),1b16	0	-1.6
1989	NY N	48	60	10	11	2	0	2	7	17-0	0	19	.183	.364	.317	100	1	3-0	.889	-1	93	0	O10(4/1/5),1b8	0	0.0
	†Tor A	28	66	12	15	3	0	4	11	17-1	2	16	.227	.395	.455	142	5	2-0	.944	-1	96	74	D19,1b2,O2R	0	0.4
Total	14	1475	4124	571	1068	191	24	93	460	642-41	20	627	.259	.359	.385	108	71	197-90	.986	-24	100	92	O868(201/647/30),1b215,D52	55	3.2
MCALEER, JIMMY	James Robert "Loafer"; B7.10.1864 Youngstown OH; D4.29.1931 Youngstown OH; BR/TR/6´0˝/175; d4.24; M11																								
1889	Cle N	110	447	66	105	6	6	0	35	30	4	49	.235	.289	.275	58	-26	37	.955	8	136	237	O110C	—	-2.0
1890	Cle P	86	341	58	91	8	7	1	42	37	1	33	.267	.340	.340	89	-4	21	.940	6	90	109	O86C	—	-0.1
1891	Cle N	136	565	97	135	16	11	1	61	49	5	47	.239	.305	.312	77	-18	51	.924	5	88	26	O136(124/13/0)	—	-1.5
1892	†Cle N	149	571	92	136	26	7	4	70	63	4	54	.238	.318	.329	92	-5	40	.948	9	75	135	O149C	—	-0.6
1893	Cle N	91	350	63	83	5	1	2	41	35	4	21	.237	.314	.274	53	-24	32	.928	-1	98	91	O91(2/89/0)	—	-2.6
1894	Cle N	64	253	36	73	15	1	2	40	13	3	17	.289	.331	.379	68	-14	14	.953	3	85	126	O64C	—	-1.2
1895	†Cle N	**132**	532	85	144	17	3	0	68	38	6	37	.271	.326	.314	62	-31	32	.934	-2	70	25	O132C	—	-3.4
1896	†Cle N	116	455	70	131	16	4	1	54	47	5	32	.288	.361	.347	82	-11	24	.958	3	108	133	O116C	—	-1.3
1897	Cle N	24	91	6	20	2	0	0	10	7	1	—	.220	.283	.242	37	-8	4	.947	-0	94	0	O24(1/23/0)	—	-0.9
1898	Cle N	106	366	47	87	3	0	0	48	46	5	—	.238	.331	.246	67	-13	7	.965	1	70	131	O104(1/102/1),2b2	—	-1.7
1901	Cle A	3	7	0	1	0	0	0	0	0	0	—	.143	.143	.143	-22	-1	0	1.000	-0	0	0	O2C/P3M	—	-0.1
1902	StL A	2	3	0	2	0	0	0	0	0	0	—	.667	.667	.667	274	1	0	ø	-0	0	0	O2(0/1/1),M	—	0.1
1907	StL A	2	0	0	0	0	0	0	0	0	0	—	ø	ø	ø	ø	0	0	ø	0	—	—	/RM	—	0.0
Total	13	1021	3981	620	1008	114	40	11	469	365	38	290	.253	.322	.310	72	-154	262	.944	31	90	106	O1016(128/887/2),2b2/3P	—	-15.3
MCALEESE, JACK	John James; B1877 Sharon PA; D11.15.1950 New York NY; BR/TR/5´8˝/?; d8.10																								
1901	Chi A	1	1	0	0	0	0	0	0	0	0	—	.000	.000	.000	-99	0	0	1.000	0	117	0	/P	—	0.0
1909	StL A	85	267	33	57	7	0	0	12	32	9	—	.213	.318	.240	82	-3	18	.910	-1	119	93	O79(27/32/20),3b2	—	-0.8
Total	2	86	268	33	57	7	0	0	12	32	9	—	.213	.317	.239	82	-3	18	.910	-1	119	93	O79(27/32/20),3b2/P	—	-0.8
MCALLESTER, BILL	William Lusk; B12.29.1889 Chattanooga TN; D3.3.1970 Chattanooga TN; BR/TR/6´0˝/175; d5.2; Col Tennessee																								
1913	StL A	49	85	3	13	4	0	0	6	11	0	12	.153	.250	.200	33	-7	2	.908	-2	*110*	*84*	C39	—	-0.8
MCALLISTER, SPORT	Lewis William; B7.23.1874 Austin MS; D7.17.1962 Wyandotte MI; BB/TR/5´11˝/180; d8.7; OF(17/10/123); ▲																								
1896	Cle N	8	27	2	6	2	0	0	1	0	1	2	.222	.250	.296	41	-2	1	.500	-1	0	0	O4R,C2/P	—	-0.3
1897	Cle N	43	137	23	30	5	1	0	11	12	1	—	.219	.287	.270	45	-11	3	.894	-4	59	0	O28(1/3/24),S4,P4,1b3,C2/2	—	-1.3
1898	Cle N	17	57	8	13	3	1	0	9	5	0	—	.228	.290	.316	75	-2	0	.941	0	87	0	P9,O8(0/4/4)	—	-0.1
1899	Cle N	113	418	29	99	6	8	1	31	19	2	—	.237	.273	.297	61	-24	5	.943	-11	95	107	O79(9/3/70),C17,3b7,1b6,S3,P3/2	—	-3.4
1901	Det A	90	306	45	92	9	4	3	57	15	5	—	.301	.344	.386	97	-2	17	.898	-13	*107*	92	C35,1b28,O11(5/0/6),3b10,S3	—	-1.1
1902	Det A	21	67	8	14	1	0	1	8	2	1	—	.209	.243	.269	41	-6	0	1.000	0	307	93	1b5,S5,2b3,C2,3b2/lf	—	-0.5
	Bal A	3	11	0	1	0	0	0	1	1	0	—	.091	.167	.091	-26	-2	0	.923	-0	118	0	2b2/1	—	-0.2
	Det A	45	162	11	34	4	2	0	24	3	1	—	.210	.229	.259	34	-15	1	.991	-1	307	93	1b21,O11(1/0/10),C7,3b4/S	—	-1.5
	Year	69	240	19	49	5	2	1	33	6	2	—	.204	.230	.254	33	-22	1	.992	-1	105	96	1b27,O12(2/0/10),C9,S6,3b6,2b5/D	—	-2.2
1903	Det A	78	265	31	69	8	2	0	22	10	4	—	.260	.297	.306	84	-5	5	.888	-6	96	80	S46,C18,O5R,3b4/1	—	-0.8
Total	7	418	1450	157	358	38	18	5	164	67	15	2	.247	.287	.308	67	-69	32	.914	-35	87	89	O147R,C83,1b65,S62,3b27,P17,2b7	—	-9.2
MCANANY, JIM	James; B9.4.1936 Los Angeles CA; BR/TR/5´10˝/(190–196); d9.19; Col USC																								
1958	Chi A	5	13	0	0	0	0	0	0	0-0	0	5	.000	.000	.000	-99	-4	0-0	1.000	0	149	0	O3R	0	-0.4
1959	†Chi A	67	210	22	58	9	3	0	27	19-4	1	26	.276	.339	.348	90	-3	2-1	.966	-0	92	167	O67(4/2/63)	0	-0.5
1960	Chi A	3	2	0	0	0	0	0	0	0-0	0	2	.000	.000	.000	-99	-1	0-0	ø	0	—	—	/H	0	-0.1
1961	Chi N	11	10	1	3	1	0	0	0	1-0	0	3	.300	.364	.400	101	0	0-0	ø	-0	0	0	/rf	0	0.0
1962	Chi N	7	6	0	0	0	0	0	0	1-0	0	2	.000	.143	.000	-56	-1	0-0	ø	0	—	—	/H	0	-0.1
Total	5	93	241	23	61	10	3	0	27	21-4	1	38	.253	.316	.320	75	-9	2-1	.968	-0	95	159	O71(4/2/67)	0	-1.1
MCANULTY, PAUL	Paul Michael; B2.24.1981 Oxnard CA; BL/TR/5´10˝/220; [SDN02 12/355]; d6.22; Col Cal St.–Long Beach																								
2005	SD N	22	24	4	5	0	0	0	0	3-1	1	7	.208	.321	.208	45	-2	1-0	1.000	-1	79	0	O6L/1	0	-0.2
2006	SD N	16	13	3	3	1	0	1	3	2-0	0	4	.231	.333	.538	125	0	0-0	ø	-0	0	0	/rf	0	0.0
Total	2	38	37	7	8	1	0	1	3	5-1	1	11	.216	.326	.324	73	-2	1-0	1.000	-1	74	0	O7(6/0/1)/1	0	-0.2
MCATEE, BUB	Michael James "Butch"; B3.1845 Troy NY; D10.18.1876 Troy NY; TR/5´9˝/160; d5.8																								
1871	Chi NA	26	135	34	37	8	2	0	10	5	—	2	.274	.300	.363	81	-5	5-3	.943	1	117	130	1b26	—	-0.2
1872	Tro NA	**25**	126	30	28	3	1	0	15	3	—	2	.222	.240	.262	54	-7	0-2	.948	1	67	70	1b25	—	-0.4
Total	2NA	51	261	64	65	11	3	0	25	8	—	4	.249	.271	.314	69	-12	5-5	.945	2	93	101	1b51	—	-0.6

YEAR	TM LG	G	AB	R	H	2B	3B	HR	RBI	BB-IB	HP	SO	AVG	OBP	SLG	AOPS	ABR	SB-CS	FA	FR	RNG	THR	GAMES AT POSITION	DL	BFW
McAuley, Ike	James Earl; B8.19.1891 Wichita KS; D4.6.1928 Des Moines IA; BR/TR/5´9.5˝/150; d9.10																								
1914	Pit N	15	24	3	3	0	0	0	0	0	0	8	.125	.125	.125	-27	-4	0	.900	0	104	266	S5,3b3,2b2	—	-0.4
1915	Pit N	5	15	0	2	1	0	0	0	0	0	6	.133	.133	.200	0	-2	0	.917	-1	90	90	S5	—	-0.3
1916	Pit N	4	8	1	2	0	0	0	1	0	0	1	.250	.250	.250	53	0	0	.938	0	83	178	S4	—	0.0
1917	StL N	3	7	0	2	0	0	0	1	0	0	1	.286	.286	.286	78	0	0	.833	-1	58	0	S3	—	-0.2
1925	Chi N	37	125	10	35	7	2	0	11	11	1	12	.280	.343	.368	80	-3	1-0	.949	-7	79	95	S37	—	-0.6
Total	5	64	179	14	44	8	2	0	13	11	1	28	.246	.293	.313	62	-9	1-0	.940	-9	81	109	S54,3b3,2b2	—	-1.5
McAuliffe, Gene	Eugene Leo; B2.28.1872 Randolph MA; D4.29.1953 Randolph MA; BR/TR/6´1˝/180; d8.17																								
1904	Bos N	1	2	0	1	0	0	0	0	0	0	—	.500	.500	.500	217	0	0	.667	-1	*75*	*156*	/C	—	0.0
McAuliffe, Dick	Richard John; B11.29.1939 Hartford CT; BL/TR/5´11˝/(175–176); d9.17																								
1960	Det A	8	27	2	7	0	1	0	1	2-0	0	6	.259	.310	.333	72	-1	0-0	.884	2	122	164	S7	0	0.1
1961	Det A	80	285	36	73	12	4	6	33	24-0	4	39	.256	.322	.389	87	-6	2-3	.933	-18	82	105	S55,3b22	0	-2.0
1962	Det A	139	471	50	124	20	5	12	63	64-3	0	76	.263	.349	.403	99	0	4-2	.965	-24	78	71	2b70,3b49,S16	0	-1.7
1963	Det A	150	568	77	149	18	6	13	61	64-1	0	75	.262	.334	.384	98	-1	11-5	.963	-21	91	91	S133,2b15	0	-0.9
1964	Det A	162	557	85	134	18	7	24	66	77-8	3	96	.241	.334	.427	109	7	8-5	.958	-6	100	89	S160	0	1.6
1965	Det A★	113	404	61	105	13	6	15	54	49-4	2	62	.260	.342	.433	118	9	6-9	.956	-8	91	98	S112	43	1.0
1966	Det A★	124	430	83	118	16	8	23	56	66-2	3	80	.274	.373	.509	148	28	5-7	.964	1	100	84	S105,3b15	0	3.8
1967	Det A★	153	557	92	133	16	7	22	65	105-4	7	118	.239	.364	.411	126	22	6-5	.965	-4	97	**115**	2b145,S43	0	3.3
1968	†Det A	151	570	**95**	142	24	10	16	56	82-8	2	99	.249	.344	.411	125	19	8-7	.986	-21	88	105	2b148,S5	0	1.2
1969	Det A	74	271	49	71	10	5	11	33	47-1	0	41	.262	.369	.458	125	10	2-5	.976	5	102	92	2b72	81	1.9
1970	Det A	146	530	73	124	21	1	12	50	101-7	3	62	.234	.358	.345	94	0	5-6	.975	14	105	91	2b127,S15,3b12	0	2.2
1971	Det A	128	477	67	99	16	6	18	57	53-4	5	67	.208	.293	.379	86	-10	4-1	.987	11	101	106	2b123,S7	0	1.0
1972	†Det A	122	408	47	98	16	3	8	30	59-7	2	59	.240	.339	.353	102	3	0-0	.975	-5	90	94	2b116,S3/3	0	0.6
1973	Det A	106	343	39	94	18	1	12	47	49-5	1	52	.274	.366	.437	118	9	0-4	.986	3	103	96	2b102,S2/D	0	1.8
1974	Bos A	100	272	32	57	13	1	5	24	39-5	1	40	.210	.310	.320	76	-7	2-0	.971	-6	91	99	2b53,3b40,S3,D3	0	-1.0
1975	Bos A	7	15	0	2	0	0	0	1	1-0	0	2	.133	.188	.133	-7	-2	0-0	.769	-2	73	105	3b7	0	-0.5
Total	16	1763	6185	888	1530	231	71	197	697	882-59	33	974	.247	.343	.403	108	80	63-59	.977	-78	95	98	2b971,S666,3b146,D4	124	12.4
McAvoy, George	George Robert; B3.12.1884 E.Liverpool OH; D8.19.1952 Miami FL; BL/TR; d7.17																								
1914	Phi N	1	1	0	0	0	0	0	0	0	0	0	.000	.000	.000	-94	0	0	ø	0	—	—	/H	—	0.0
McAvoy, Wickey	James Eugene; B10.20.1894 Rochester NY; D7.6.1973 Rochester NY; BR/TR/5´11˝/172; d9.29																								
1913	Phi A	4	9	0	1	0	0	0	0	0	1	4	.111	.200	.111	-9	-1	0	1.000	1	*132*	*156*	C4	—	0.0
1914	Phi A	8	16	1	2	0	1	0	0	0	0	4	.125	.125	.250	13	-2	0	.971	0	*94*	*127*	C8	—	-0.1
1915	Phi A	68	184	12	35	7	2	0	6	11	0	32	.190	.236	.250	47	-13	0-2	.931	-7	*64*	*150*	C64	—	-1.7
1917	Phi A	10	24	1	6	1	0	1	4	0	0	3	.250	.250	.417	105	0	0	.955	1	*85*	*182*	C8	—	0.1
1918	Phi A	83	271	14	66	5	3	0	32	13	2	23	.244	.283	.284	70	-11	5	.960	4	*87*	***119***	C74/P1rf	—	-0.1
1919	Phi A	62	170	10	24	5	2	0	11	14	0	21	.141	.207	.194	13	-20	1	.973	-3	*76*	*130*	C57	—	-2.1
Total	6	235	674	38	134	18	8	1	53	38	3	87	.199	.245	.254	47	-47	6-2	.954	-4	*79*	*133*	C215/rf1P	—	-3.9
McBride, Algie	Algernon Griggs; B5.23.1869 Washington DC; D1.10.1956 Georgetown OH; BL/TL/5´9˝/152; d5.12																								
1896	Chi N	9	29	2	7	1	1	1	7	7	0	3	.241	.389	.448	116	1	0	.917	-0	74	0	O9L	—	0.0
1898	Cin N	120	486	94	147	14	12	2	43	51	12	—	.302	.383	.393	114	10	16	.959	3	105	75	O120(4/115/1)	—	0.4
1899	Cin N	64	251	57	87	12	5	1	23	30	7	—	.347	.431	.446	138	15	5	.950	-1	88	84	O64(5/45/14)	—	0.9
1900	Cin N	112	436	59	120	15	8	4	59	25	4	—	.275	.320	.374	94	-5	12	.915	-5	73	140	O110(14/10/86)	—	-1.5
1901	Cin N	30	123	19	29	7	0	2	18	7	1	—	.236	.282	.341	86	-2	0	.968	-2	28	0	O28(11/19/0)	—	-0.5
	NY N	68	264	27	74	11	0	2	29	12	2	—	.280	.317	.345	95	-2	3	.948	-3	100	135	O65R	—	-0.7
	Year	98	387	46	103	18	0	4	47	19	3	—	.266	.306	.344	92	-4	3	.956	-5	78	93	O93(11/19/65)	—	-1.2
Total	5	403	1589	258	464	60	26	12	179	132	26	3	.292	.356	.385	108	17	36	.946	-8	87	96	O396(43/189/166)	—	-1.4
McBride, Bake	Arnold Ray; B2.3.1949 Fulton MO; BL/TR/6´2˝/(175–187); [StLN70 37/811]; d7.26; Col Westminster (MO)																								
1973	StL N	40	63	8	19	3	0	0	5	4-0	2	10	.302	.352	.349	97	0	0-1	.976	2	136	132	O17(1/16/0)	0	0.1
1974	StL N	150	559	81	173	19	5	6	56	43-9	13	57	.309	.369	.394	114	11	30-11	.990	1	105	97	O144C	0	1.1
1975	StL N	116	413	70	124	10	9	5	36	34-1	1	52	.300	.354	.404	106	2	26-8	.990	4	113	63	O107C	22	0.6
1976	StL N☆	72	272	40	91	13	4	3	24	18-0	6	28	.335	.386	.445	134	12	10-5	.981	4	116	118	O66C	89	1.6
1977	StL N	43	122	21	32	5	1	4	20	7-2	0	19	.262	.298	.418	92	-2	9-3	1.000	-3	75	118	O33C	0	-0.5
	†Phi N	85	280	55	95	20	5	11	41	25-2	3	25	.339	.392	.564	147	19	27-4	.986	2	102	125	O73(0/21/54)	0	2.2
	Year	128	402	76	127	25	6	15	61	32-4	3	44	.316	.364	.520	132	17	36-7	.990	-2	94	123	O106(0/54/54)	0	1.7
1978	†Phi N	122	472	68	127	20	4	10	49	28-3	5	68	.269	.315	.392	95	-4	28-3	**.996**	4	108	88	O119(0/1/118)	0	-0.1
1979	Phi N	151	582	82	163	16	12	12	60	41-3	4	77	.280	.328	.411	97	-4	25-14	.989	13	122	103	O147R	0	0.2
1980	†Phi N	137	554	68	171	33	10	9	87	26-4	5	58	.309	.342	.453	114	9	13-10	.990	2	112	53	O133(0/1/133)	0	0.4
1981	†Phi N	58	221	26	60	17	1	2	21	11-1	0	25	.271	.303	.385	90	-3	5-0	.987	-4	83	51	O56R	75	-0.9
1982	Cle A	27	85	8	31	3	3	0	13	2-1	0	12	.365	.375	.471	131	3	2-2	1.000	-1	103	0	O22R	114	0.1
1983	Cle A	70	230	21	67	8	1	1	18	9-2	1	26	.291	.318	.348	81	-6	8-2	.977	1	105	137	O46R,D15	52	-0.6
Total	11	1071	3853	548	1153	167	55	63	430	248-28	40	457	.299	.345	.420	108	37	183-63	.989	24	109	88	O963(1/389/576),D15	352	4.2
McBride, George	George Florian; B11.20.1880 Milwaukee WI; D7.2.1973 Milwaukee WI; BR/TR/5´11˝/170; d9.12; M1/C3																								
1901	Mil A	3	12	0	2	0	0	0	0	1	0	—	.167	.231	.167	12	-1	0	1.000	0	86	201	S3	—	-0.1
1905	Pit N	27	87	9	19	4	0	0	7	6	1	—	.218	.277	.264	60	-4	2	.902	-2	93	171	3b17,S8	—	-0.6
	StL N	81	281	22	61	1	2	2	34	14	4	—	.217	.264	.256	57	-16	10	.938	-4	106	90	S80/1	—	-1.7
	Year	108	368	31	80	5	2	2	41	20	5	—	.217	.267	.258	58	-20	12	.935	-5	106	90	S88,3b17/1	—	-2.3
1906	StL N	90	313	24	53	8	2	0	13	17	1	—	.169	.215	.208	33	-25	5	.944	2	103	101	S90	—	-2.3
1908	Was A	**155**	518	47	120	10	6	0	34	41	3	—	.232	.292	.274	92	-5	12	.948	33	106	**121**	S155	—	3.7
1909	Was A	**156**	504	38	118	16	0	0	34	36	7	—	.234	.294	.266	81	-10	17	**.935**	13	100	101	S156	—	0.9
1910	Was A	154	514	54	118	19	4	1	55	61	8	—	.230	.321	.288	95	0	11	.939	**33**	107	110	S154	—	4.1
1911	Was A	**154**	557	58	131	11	4	0	59	52	10	—	.235	.312	.269	64	-26	15	.941	27	110	106	S154	—	1.2
1912	Was A	152	521	56	118	13	7	1	52	38	7	—	.226	.288	.284	63	-26	17	**.941**	**28**	105	116	S152	—	1.2
1913	Was A	150	499	52	107	18	7	1	52	43	7	46	.214	.286	.285	66	-22	12	**.960**	9	100	109	S150	—	-0.3
1914	Was A	156	503	49	102	12	4	0	24	43	6	70	.203	.274	.243	53	-29	12-14	**.958**	10	97	**129**	S156	—	-1.2
1915	Was A	146	476	54	97	8	6	1	30	29	1	60	.204	.251	.252	50	-32	10-5	**.968**	7	96	98	S146	—	-1.5
1916	Was A	139	466	36	106	15	4	1	36	23	5	58	.227	.271	.283	67	-21	8	.957	14	101	104	S139	—	0.3
1917	Was A	50	141	6	27	3	0	0	9	10	4	17	.191	.265	.213	46	-9	1	.943	0	96	91	S41,3b6,2b2	—	-0.7
1918	Was A	18	53	2	7	0	0	0	1	0	0	11	.132	.132	.132	-21	-8	1	.986	1	106	84	S14,2b2	—	-0.7
1919	Was A	15	40	3	8	1	1	0	4	3	0	6	.200	.256	.275	49	-3	0	.932	-0	100	41	S15	—	-0.2
1920	Was A	13	41	6	9	1	0	0	3	2	0	3	.220	.256	.244	34	-4	0-0	.966	-3	84	62	S13	—	-0.6
Total	16	1659	5526	516	1203	140	47	7	447	419	64	271	.218	.281	.264	65	-241	133-19	.948	168	102	108	S1626,3b23,2b4/1	—	1.5
McBride, John	John F.; d10.12																								
1890	Phi AA	1	2	0	0	0	0	0	0	0	0	—	.000	.000	.000	-99	-1	0	1.000	1	632	0	/cf	—	0.0
McBride, Tom	Thomas Raymond; B11.2.1914 Bonham TX; D12.26.2001 Wichita Falls TX; BR/TR/6´0˝/190; d4.23																								
1943	Bos A	26	96	11	23	3	1	0	7	7	0	3	.240	.291	.292	70	-4	2-0	.984	-0	96	109	O24(0/21/3)	0	-0.5
1944	Bos A	71	216	29	53	7	3	0	24	8	1	13	.245	.276	.306	67	-10	4-0	.992	4	103	203	O57(23/14/22),1b5	0	-0.9
1945	Bos A	100	344	38	105	11	7	1	47	26	0	17	.305	.354	.387	112	4	2-2	.984	1	95	142	O81(15/50/22),1b11	0	0.2
1946	†Bos A	61	153	21	46	5	2	0	19	9	0	6	.301	.340	.359	90	-2	0-1	1.000	-2	93	37	O43(10/2/32)	0	-0.6
1947	Bos A	2	5	0	1	0	0	0	0	0	0	0	.200	.200	.200	11	-1	0-0	1.000	1	80	1087	/rf	0	0.0
	Was A	56	166	19	45	4	2	0	15	15	0	9	.271	.331	.319	84	-4	3-1	.972	-0	104	66	O51(43/4/5)/3	0	-0.7
	Year	58	171	19	46	4	2	0	15	15	0	9	.269	.328	.316	81	-5	3-1	.973	1	103	95	O52(43/4/6)/3	0	-0.7
1948	Was A	92	206	22	53	9	1	1	29	28	0	15	.257	.346	.325	81	-5	2-2	.983	5	108	204	O55(25/0/30)	0	-0.2
Total	6	408	1186	140	326	39	16	2	141	93	1	63	.275	.328	.340	88	-22	13-6	.985	9	100	141	O312(116/91/115),1b16/3	0	-2.7

YEAR	TM LG	G	AB	R	H	2B	3B	HR	RBI	BB-IB	HP	SO	AVG	OBP	SLG	AOPS	ABR	SB-CS	FA	FR	RNG	THR	GAMES AT POSITION	DL	BFW
McCabe, Swat	James Arthur; B11.20.1881 Towanda PA; D12.9.1944 Bristol CT; BL/TR/5´10˝/187; d9.23																								
1909	Cin N	3	11	2	6	1	0	0	0	0	0	—	.545	.545	.636	269	2	1	.625	-1	0	0	O3C	—	0.1
1910	Cin N	13	35	3	9	1	0	0	5	1	1	2	.257	.297	.286	73	-1	0	1.000	1	102	172	O9R	—	-0.1
Total	2	16	46	5	15	2	0	0	5	1	1	2	.326	.354	.370	118	1	1	.875	-0	74	125	O12(0/3/9)	—	0.0
McCabe, Joe	Joseph Robert; B8.27.1938 Indianapolis IN; BR/TR/6´0˝/190; d4.18; Col Purdue																								
1964	Min A	14	19	1	3	0	0	0	2	0-0	0	8	.158	.150	.158	-12	-3	0-0	1.000	-1	59	94	C12	0	-0.4
1965	Was A	14	27	1	5	0	0	1	5	4-0	0	13	.185	.281	.296	68	-1	1-0	.972	-3	182	218	C11	0	-0.4
Total	2	28	46	2	8	0	0	1	7	4-0	0	21	.174	.231	.239	36	-4	1-0	.986	-4	133	169	C23	0	-0.8
McCabe, Bill	William Francis; B10.28.1892 Chicago IL; D9.2.1966 Chicago IL; BB/TR (BL 1918)/5´9.5˝/180; d4.16																								
1918	†Chi N	29	45	9	8	0	1	0	5	4	0	7	.178	.245	.222	42	-3	2	.939	3	126	24	2b13,O4(1/0/2)	—	0.0
1919	Chi N	33	84	8	13	3	1	0	5	9	2	15	.155	.253	.214	41	-6	3	.950	-1	101	72	O20(0/1/19),S4/3	—	-0.9
1920	Chi N	3	2	1	1	0	0	0	0	0	0	0	.500	.500	.500	184	0	0-0	ø	0	—	—	/H	—	0.0
	†Bro N	41	68	10	10	0	0	0	3	2	0	6	.147	.171	.147	-8	-9	1-2	.882	0	111	92	S13,O6L,2b4,3b3	—	-1.0
	Year	44	70	11	11	0	0	0	3	2	0	6	.157	.181	.157	-2	-9	1-2	.882	0	111	92	S13,O6L,2b4,3b3	—	-1.0
Total	3	106	199	28	32	3	2	0	13	15	2	28	.161	.227	.196	26	-18	6-2	.943	2	103	86	O30(7/1/21),S17,2b17,3b4	—	-1.9
McCaffery, Harry	Harry Charles; B11.25.1858 St.Louis MO; D4.19.1928 St.Louis MO; BR/TR/5´10.5˝/185; d6.15; U1																								
1882	Lou AA	1	4	1	1	0	0	0	—	0	—	—	.250	.250	.250	73	0	—	1.000	-0	44	0	/2	—	0.0
	StL AA	38	153	23	42	8	6	0	—	3	—	—	.275	.288	.405	127	4	—	.891	3	196	337	O23(5/0/18),2b8,3b7/1	—	0.6
	Year	39	157	24	43	8	6	0	—	3	—	—	.274	.287	.401	125	3	—	.891	3	196	337	O23(5/0/18),2b9,3b7/1	—	0.6
1883	StL AA	5	18	0	1	0	0	0	1	1	—	—	.056	.105	.056	-44	-3	—	.900	2	332	2340	O5C	—	-0.1
Total	2	44	175	24	44	8	6	0	1	4	—	—	.251	.268	.366	107	1	—	.893	5	218	665	O28(5/5/18),2b9,3b7/1	—	0.5
McCaffrey, Sparrow	Charles P.; B1868 Philadelphia PA; D4.29.1894 Philadelphia PA; ?/120; d8.13																								
1889	Col AA	2	1	1	1	0	0	0	0	1	0	0	1.000	1.000	1.000	495	1	0	ø	-0	—	—	C2	—	0.0
McCall, Brian	Brian Allen "Bam"; B1.25.1943 Kentfield CA; BL/TL/5´10˝/175; d9.18																								
1962	Chi A	4	8	2	3	0	0	2	3	0-0	0	2	.375	.375	1.125	287	2	0-0	1.000	0	163	0	/cf	0	0.2
1963	Chi A	3	7	1	0	0	0	0	0	1-0	0	2	.000	.125	.000	-62	-2	0-0	1.000	-0	99	0	O2R	0	-0.2
Total	2	7	15	3	3	0	0	2	3	1-0	0	4	.200	.250	.600	126	0	0-0	1.000	0	124	0	O3(0/1/2)	0	0.0
McCandless, Jack	Scott Cook; B5.5.1891 Pittsburgh PA; D8.17.1961 Pittsburgh PA; BL/TR/6´0˝/170; d9.10																								
1914	Bal F	11	31	5	8	0	1	0	1	3	1	0	.258	.343	.323	79	-1	0	1.000	-0	94	91	O8(0/1/7)	—	-0.2
1915	Bal F	117	406	47	87	6	7	5	34	41	6	99	.214	.296	.300	66	-25	9	.945	1	100	111	O105(23/58/25)	—	-3.3
Total	2	128	437	52	95	6	8	5	35	44	7	99	.217	.299	.302	67	-26	9	.948	1	100	110	O113(23/59/32)	—	-3.5
McCann, Brian	Brian Michael; B2.20.1984 Athens GA; BL/TR/6´3˝/210; [AtlN02 2/64]; d6.10																								
2005	†Atl N	59	180	20	50	7	0	5	23	18-5	1	26	.278	.345	.400	94	-1	1-1	.991	1	119	46	C57	0	0.3
2006	Atl N★	130	442	61	147	34	0	24	93	41-8	3	54	.333	.388	.572	141	28	2-0	.989	-5	100	81	C124	16	3.0
Total	2	189	622	81	197	41	0	29	116	59-13	4	80	.317	.376	.523	128	27	3-1	.990	-4	106	70	C181	16	3.3
McCann, Emmett	Robert Emmett; B3.4.1902 Philadelphia PA; D4.15.1937 Philadelphia PA; BR/TR/5´11˝/150; d4.19																								
1920	Phi A	13	34	4	9	1	1	0	3	3	1	1	.265	.342	.353	83	-1	0-1	.907	-0	99	79	S11	—	-0.1
1921	Phi A	52	157	15	35	5	0	0	15	4	0	6	.223	.242	.255	27	-18	2-1	.949	-3	101	81	S32,3b9,2b2/1	—	-1.6
1926	Bos A	6	3	0	0	0	0	0	0	1	0	1	.000	.250	.000	-32	-1	0-0	1.000	-0	0	0	/S3	—	-0.1
Total	3	71	194	19	44	6	1	0	18	8	1	8	.227	.261	.268	36	-20	2-2	.939	-4	100	80	S44,3b10,2b2/1	—	-1.8
McCardell, Roger	Roger Morton; B8.29.1932 Gorsuch Mills MD; D11.13.1996 Wilmington DE; BR/TR/6´0˝/210; d5.8; Col Boston U.																								
1959	SF N	4	4	0	0	0	0	0	0	0-0	0	0	.000	.000	.000	-99	-1	0-0	1.000	-0	37	412	C3	0	-0.1
McCarren, Bill	William Joseph; B11.4.1895 Fortenia PA; D9.11.1983 Denver CO; BR/TR/5´11.5˝/170; d5.4																								
1923	Bro N	69	216	28	53	10	1	3	27	22	4	39	.245	.326	.343	79	-6	0-1	.927	-2	92	102	3b66/rf	—	-0.5
McCarthy, Alex	Alexander George; B5.12.1888 Chicago IL; D3.12.1978 Salisbury MD; BR/TR/5´9˝/150; d10.7; Col Notre Dame																								
1910	Pit N	3	12	1	1	0	1	0	0	0	0	2	.083	.083	.250	-3	-2	0	.875	0	115	187	S3	—	-0.2
1911	Pit N	50	150	18	36	5	1	2	31	14	0	24	.240	.305	.327	74	-6	4	.981	3	91	112	S33,2b11/3lf	—	0.0
1912	Pit N	111	401	53	111	12	4	1	41	30	3	26	.277	.332	.334	84	-9	8	.962	-9	95	119	2b105,3b4	—	-1.6
1913	Pit N	31	74	7	15	5	0	0	10	7	3	7	.203	.298	.270	66	-3	1-2	.902	-1	93	89	S12,3b12,2b6	—	-0.4
1914	Pit N	57	173	14	26	0	1	1	14	6	3	17	.150	.192	.179	11	-20	2	.975	6	118	139	3b36,2b10,S6	—	-1.4
1915	Pit N	21	49	3	10	0	1	0	3	5	1	10	.204	.291	.245	64	-2	1-2	.950	1	90	67	2b9,S5,3b4/1	—	-0.2
	Chi N	23	72	4	19	3	0	1	6	5	2	7	.264	.329	.347	105	1	2-3	.972	7	105	165	2b12,3b12/S	—	0.8
	Year	44	121	7	29	3	1	1	9	10	3	17	.240	.313	.306	88	-2	3-5	.964	8	99	126	2b21,3b16,S6/1	—	0.6
1916	Chi N	37	107	10	26	2	3	0	6	11	5	7	.243	.341	.318	93	0	1	.931	-2	106	76	2b34,S3	—	-0.2
	Pit N	50	146	11	29	3	0	0	3	15	2	10	.199	.282	.219	54	-7	3	.955	-4	84	95	S39,2b7,3b5	—	-1.0
	Year	87	253	21	55	5	3	0	9	26	7	17	.217	.308	.261	72	-7	4	.951	-6	83	92	S42,2b41,3b5	—	-1.2
1917	Pit N	49	151	15	33	4	0	0	8	11	1	13	.219	.276	.245	58	-7	1	.964	3	82	229	3b26,2b13,S9	—	-0.3
Total	8	432	1335	136	306	34	11	5	122	104	20	123	.229	.295	.282	67	-55	23-7	.957	3	100	111	2b207,S111,3b100/1lf	—	-4.5
McCarthy, Jerry	Jerome Francis; B5.23.1923 Brooklyn NY; D10.3.1965 Oceanside NY; BL/TL/6´1˝/205; d6.19; Col Penn																								
1948	StL A	2	3	0	1	0	0	0	0	0	0	0	.333	.333	.333	76	0	0-0	.600	-1	0	0	1b2	0	-0.1
McCarthy, Jack	John Arthur; B3.26.1869 Gilbertville MA; D9.11.1931 San Francisco CA; BL/TL/5´9˝/155; d8.3; Col Holy Cross																								
1893	Cin N	49	195	28	55	8	3	0	22	22	0	7	.282	.365	.354	86	-4	6	.887	-1	88	0	O47(10/1/37),1b2	—	-0.6
1894	Cin N	40	167	29	45	9	1	0	21	17	3	6	.269	.348	.335	63	-10	3	.895	2	142	0	O25(5/0/20),1b15	—	-0.7
1898	Pit N	137	537	75	155	13	12	4	78	34	4	—	.289	.336	.380	107	3	7	.935	4	98	93	O137L	—	-0.5
1899	Pit N	139	565	109	173	22	17	4	69	39	4	—	.306	.355	.427	114	9	28	.962	-5	88	105	O139(133/6/0)	—	-0.7
1900	Chi N	124	503	68	148	16	7	0	48	24	2	—	.294	.329	.354	92	-7	22	.944	-1	117	90	O123(96/1/26)	—	-1.6
1901	Cle A	86	343	60	110	14	7	0	32	30	4	—	.321	.382	.402	123	12	9	.949	1	83	183	O86(85/1/0)	—	0.7
1902	Cle A	95	359	45	102	31	5	0	41	24	0	—	.284	.329	.398	105	3	12	.944	-4	50	0	O95L	—	-0.6
1903	Cle A	108	415	47	110	20	8	0	43	19	1	—	.265	.299	.352	96	-2	15	.964	-3	84	173	O108L	—	-1.2
	Chi N	24	101	11	28	5	0	0	14	4	0	—	.277	.305	.327	82	-3	8	.947	-1	103	154	O24L	—	-0.5
1904	Chi N	115	432	36	114	14	2	0	51	23	4	—	.264	.307	.306	89	-6	14	.961	-7	56	0	O115(25/90/0)	—	-1.9
1905	Chi N	59	170	16	47	4	3	0	14	10	1	—	.276	.320	.335	92	-2	8	.986	2	191	410	O37(18/19/0),1b6	—	-0.2
1906	Bro N	91	322	23	98	13	1	0	35	20	1	—	.304	.347	.351	128	10	9	.924	2	122	38	O86(83/3/0)	—	0.8
1907	Bro N	25	91	4	20	2	0	0	8	2	0	—	.220	.237	.242	54	-5	4	1.000	-3	0	0	O25L	—	-1.1
Total	12	1092	4200	551	1205	171	66	8	476	268	24	13	.287	.333	.365	101	-2	145	.946	-12	91	91	O1047(844/121/83),1b23	—	-8.1
McCarthy, Johnny	John Joseph; B1.7.1910 Chicago IL; D9.13.1973 Mundelein IL; BL/TL/6´1.5˝/185; d9.2; Mil 1943–45																								
1934	Bro N	17	39	7	7	2	0	1	5	2	0	2	.179	.220	.308	42	-3	0	.961	1	157	170	1b13	—	-0.4
1935	Bro N	22	48	9	12	1	1	0	4	2	0	9	.250	.280	.313	60	-3	1	.982	-3	0	135	1b19	—	-0.7
1936	NY N	4	16	1	7	0	0	1	2	0	0	1	.438	.438	.625	185	2	1	.981	1	213	157	1b4	—	0.2
1937	†NY N	114	420	53	117	19	3	10	65	24	3	37	.279	.322	.410	96	-3	2	.987	3	112	**113**	1b110	—	-1.0
1938	NY N	134	470	55	128	13	4	8	59	39	1	28	.272	.329	.368	91	-7	3	.993	-3	92	114	1b125	—	-2.1
1939	NY N	50	80	12	21	6	1	1	11	3	1	8	.262	.298	.400	85	-2	0	1.000	-2	28	130	1b12,O4(0/1/3)/P	—	-0.5
1940	NY N	51	67	6	16	4	0	0	5	2	0	8	.239	.261	.299	53	-4	0	1.000	1	139	131	1b6	—	-0.4
1941	NY N	14	40	1	13	3	0	0	12	3	0	0	.325	.372	.400	115	1	0	.987	1	143	60	1b8/lf	0	0.1
1943	Bos N	78	313	32	95	24	6	2	33	10	1	19	.304	.327	.438	122	7	1	.996	-1	99	79	1b78	0	0.2
1946	Bos N	2	7	0	1	0	0	0	1	2	0	0	.143	.333	.143	37	0	0	1.000	-1	0	209	1b2	0	-0.1
1948	NY N	56	57	6	15	0	1	2	12	3	0	2	.263	.300	.404	88	-1	0	.966	-1	56	99	1b6	0	-0.2
Total	11	542	1557	182	432	72	16	25	209	90	6	114	.277	.319	.392	95	-13	8	.990	-2	99	109	1b383,O5(1/1/3)/P	0	-4.9

YEAR	TM LG	G	AB	R	H	2B	3B	HR	RBI	BB-IB	HP	SO	AVG	OBP	SLG	AOPS	ABR	SB-CS	FA	FR	RNG	THR	GAMES AT POSITION	DL	BFW
McCarthy, Joe	Joseph Nicodemus; B12.25.1881 Syracuse NY; D1.12.1937 Syracuse NY; BR/TR; d9.27; Col Niagara																								
1905	NY A	1	2	0	0	0	0	0	0	0	0	—	.000	.000	.000	-90	0	0	1.000	-0	*59*	*210*	/C	—	-0.1
1906	StL N	15	37	3	9	2	0	0	2	2	0	—	.243	.282	.297	84	-1	0	.984	-1	*77*	*99*	C15	—	-0.1
Total	2	16	39	3	9	2	0	0	2	2	0	—	.231	.268	.282	74	-1	0	.985	-1	*76*	*105*	C16	—	-0.2
McCarthy, Tommy	Thomas Francis Michael; B7.24.1863 Boston MA; D8.5.1922 Boston MA; BR/TR/5´7˝/170; d7.10; M1; HF1957; OF(514/32/647); ▲																								
1884	Bos U	53	209	37	45	2	2	0	—	6	—	—	.215	.237	.244	47	-20	—	.794	0	104	65	O48(41/2/7),P7	—	-1.7
1885	Bos N	40	148	16	27	2	0	0	11	5	—	25	.182	.209	.196	33	-11	—	.865	1	96	0	O40(39/0/1)	—	-1.0
1886	Phi N	8	27	6	5	2	1	0	3	2	—	3	.185	.241	.333	73	-1	1	.818	-1	82	0	O8R/P	—	-0.1
1887	Phi N	18	70	7	13	4	0	0	6	2	1	5	.186	.219	.243	27	-7	15	.897	-7	95	0	O8(6/2/0),2b5,S3,3b2	—	-1.2
1888	†StL AA	131	511	107	140	20	3	1	68	38	3	—	.274	.328	.331	100	-1	93	.931	26	**189**	**306**	O131(0/12/119),P2	—	2.1
1889	StL AA	**140**	604	136	176	24	7	2	63	46	6	26	.291	.348	.364	91	-10	57	.893	12	138	**200**	O140(1/3/137),2b2/P	—	0.1
1890	StL AA	133	548	137	192	28	9	6	69	66	11	—	.350	.430	.467	144	30	**83**	.893	6	107	135	O102(2/0/100),3b32/2M	—	3.0
1891	StL AA	134	570	124	176	20	6	8	92	49	10	19	.309	.374	.407	107	2	37	.898	1	124	129	O112(7/0/106),2b14,S12,3b2/P	—	0.2
1892	†Bos N	**152**	603	119	146	19	5	4	63	93	4	29	.242	.347	.310	91	-5	53	.883	0	119	86	O152(0/1/151)	—	-1.1
1893	Bos N	116	462	107	160	28	6	5	111	64	3	10	.346	.429	.465	128	20	46	.902	2	149	109	O108(88/3/17),2b7,S3	—	1.1
1894	Bos N	127	539	118	188	21	8	13	126	59	6	17	.349	.419	.490	110	8	43	.904	10	128	199	O127(119/9/0),S2/2P	—	0.5
1895	Bos N	117	452	90	131	13	2	2	73	72	3	12	.290	.391	.341	83	-9	18	.885	-10	94	57	O109L,2b9	—	-2.4
1896	Bro N	104	377	62	94	8	4	3	47	34	3	17	.249	.316	.316	71	-16	22	.920	-1	142	170	O103(102/0/1)	—	-2.2
Total	13	1273	5120	1066	1493	191	53	44	732	536	50	163	.292	.364	.375	99	-20	468	.897	39	130	146	O1188R,2b39,3b36,S20,P13	—	-2.7
McCarthy, Bill	William John; B2.14.1886 Boston MA; D2.4.1928 Washington DC; TR; d6.5; Col Fordham																								
1905	Bos N	1	3	0	0	0	0	0	0	0	0	—	.000	.000	.000	-99	-1	0	.667	-1	*153*	*80*	/C	—	-0.2
1907	Cin N	3	8	1	1	0	0	0	0	0	0	—	.125	.125	.125	-21	-1	0	1.000	-0	*110*	*164*	C3	—	-0.1
Total	2	4	11	1	1	0	0	0	0	0	0	—	.091	.091	.091	-43	-2	0	.842	-1	*126*	*133*	C4	—	-0.3
McCarton, Frank	Francis J.; B10.6.1854 New York NY; D6.17.1907 New York NY; d4.26																								
1872	Man NA	19	82	19	25	5	0	0	12	3	—	4	.305	.329	.366	121	3	0-0	.743	-3	52	0	O19(0/18/1)	—	0.0
McCarty, David	David Andrew; B11.23.1969 Houston TX; BR/TL/6´5˝/(207–215); [MinA91 1/3]; d5.17; Col Stanford																								
1993	Min A	98	350	36	75	15	2	2	21	19-0	1	80	.214	.257	.286	45	-28	2-6	.959	6	101	187	O67(38/2/34),1b36,D2	0	-2.8
1994	Min A	44	131	21	34	8	2	1	12	7-1	5	32	.260	.322	.374	78	-4	2-1	.981	3	157	80	1b32,O14(9/0/5)	0	-0.3
1995	Min A	25	55	10	12	3	1	0	4	4-0	1	18	.218	.279	.309	54	-4	0-1	.993	-1	93	101	1b18,O5(2/0/4)	0	-0.6
	SF N	12	20	1	5	1	0	0	2	2-0	0	4	.250	.318	.300	66	-1	1-0	.833	-1	97	0	O4R,1b2	0	-0.2
1996	SF N	91	175	16	38	3	0	6	24	18-0	2	43	.217	.294	.337	68	-8	2-1	.990	-1	71	114	1b51,O20(5/0/15)	21	-1.2
1998	Sea A	8	18	1	5	0	0	1	2	5-0	0	4	.278	.435	.444	128	1	1-0	1.000	-1	102	0	O5R,1b2	0	0.0
2000	KC A	103	270	34	75	14	2	12	53	22-1	0	68	.278	.329	.478	96	-2	0-0	.992	10	160	127	1b63,O11(7/0/4)/SD	0	0.2
2001	KC A	98	200	26	50	10	0	7	26	24-1	1	45	.250	.328	.405	85	-4	0-0	.988	2	128	133	1b68,O9(8/0/1),D7	0	-0.7
2002	KC A	13	32	3	3	1	0	1	2	2-0	0	10	.094	.147	.219	-4	-5	0-0	1.000	0	97	73	1b9,D2	0	-0.6
	TB A	12	34	2	6	0	0	1	2	4-0	2	9	.176	.300	.265	53	-2	0-0	1.000	1	102	176	O11L	0	-0.2
	Year	25	66	5	9	1	0	2	4	6-0	2	19	.136	.230	.242	24	-7	0-0	1.000	1	102	176	O11L,1b9,D2	0	-0.8
2003	Oak A	8	26	2	7	2	0	0	2	1-0	0	7	.269	.286	.346	68	-1	0-0	1.000	-1	55	0	O5L,1b3	0	-0.3
	†Bos A	16	27	4	11	3	0	1	6	2-0	0	7	.407	.448	.630	173	3	0-0	1.000	-1	72	0	O8(7/0/1),1b5/D	0	0.2
	Year	24	53	6	18	5	0	1	8	3-0	0	14	.340	.368	.491	122	2	0-0	1.000	-2	64	0	O13(12/0/1),1b8/D	0	-0.1
2004	Bos A	91	151	24	39	8	1	4	17	14-0	2	40	.258	.327	.404	85	-3	1-0	.991	3	132	89	1b67,O17(10/0/7),P3,D3	19	-0.3
2005	Bos A	13	4	2	2	0	0	0	2	2-0	0	0	.500	.667	.500	209	1	0-0	1.000	1	176	128	1b12/lf	0	0.1
Total	11	632	1493	182	362	68	8	36	175	126-3	14	367	.242	.305	.371	74	-57	9-9	.990	20	128	107	1b368,O177(103/2/80),D22,P3/S	40	-6.7
McCarty, Lew	George Lewis; B11.17.1888 Milton PA; D6.9.1930 Reading PA; BR/TR/5´11.5˝/192; d8.30																								
1913	Bro N	9	26	1	6	0	0	0	2	2	0	2	.231	.286	.231	47	-2	0	1.000	0	96	80	C9	—	-0.1
1914	Bro N	90	284	20	72	14	2	1	30	14	2	22	.254	.293	.327	83	-7	1	.970	-2	*88*	*102*	C84	—	-0.2
1915	Bro N	84	276	19	66	9	4	0	19	7	1	23	.239	.261	.301	68	-12	7-4	.969	-7	*85*	*107*	C81	—	-1.4
1916	Bro N	55	150	17	47	6	1	0	13	14	3	16	.313	.383	.367	127	6	4	.985	-1	94	99	C27,1b17	—	0.7
	NY N	25	68	6	27	3	4	0	9	7	0	9	.397	.453	.559	222	10	0	.993	1	114	78	C24	—	1.4
	Year	80	218	23	74	9	5	0	22	21	3	25	.339	.405	.427	155	15	4	.989	0	104	89	C51,1b17	—	2.1
1917	†NY N	56	162	15	40	3	2	2	19	14	1	6	.247	.311	.327	99	0	1	.979	-2	*107*	*56*	C54	—	0.2
1918	NY N	86	257	16	69	7	3	0	24	17	3	13	.268	.321	.319	97	-1	3	.975	-6	*97*	*65*	C75	—	0.0
1919	NY N	85	210	17	59	5	4	2	21	18	1	15	.281	.341	.371	115	4	2	.970	-6	*99*	*74*	C59	—	0.3
1920	NY N	36	38	2	5	0	0	0	0	4	0	2	.132	.214	.132	1	-5	2-0	1.000	1	*145*	*116*	C5	—	-0.3
	StL N	5	7	0	2	0	0	0	0	5	0	0	.286	.583	.286	160	1	0-0	1.000	-1	*82*	*138*	C3	—	0.1
	Year	41	45	2	7	0	0	0	0	9	0	2	.156	.296	.156	33	-3	2-0	1.000	1	*122*	*124*	C8	—	-0.2
1921	StL N	1	1	0	0	0	0	0	0	0	0	1	.000	.000	.000	-99	0	0-0	ø	0	—	—	/H	—	0.0
Total	9	532	1479	113	393	47	20	5	137	102	11	109	.266	.318	.335	97	-6	20-4	.975	-22	*96*	*85*	C421,1b17	—	0.7
McCarver, Tim	James Timothy; B10.16.1941 Memphis TN; BL/TR/6´1˝/(185–201); d9.10																								
1959	StL N	8	24	3	4	1	0	0	0	2-0	0	1	.167	.231	.208	17	-3	0-0	.971	-1	99	0	C6	0	-0.4
1960	StL N	10	10	3	2	0	0	0	0	0-0	0	2	.200	.200	.200	9	-1	0-0	1.000	-1	25	0	C5	0	-0.2
1961	StL N	22	67	5	16	2	1	1	6	0-0	0	5	.239	.239	.343	47	-5	0-0	.969	-1	92	150	C20	0	-0.6
1963	StL N	127	405	39	117	12	7	4	51	27-5	2	43	.289	.333	.383	97	-1	5-2	.994	-4	103	82	C126	0	0.1
1964	†StL N	143	465	53	134	19	3	9	52	40-15	1	44	.288	.343	.400	101	1	2-0	.987	-3	112	57	C137	0	0.6
1965	StL N	113	409	48	113	17	2	11	48	31-11	1	26	.276	.327	.408	97	-1	5-1	**.995**	1	105	69	C111	0	0.7
1966	StL N★	150	543	50	149	19	**13**	12	68	36-10	2	38	.274	.319	.424	105	2	9-6	.992	3	112	84	C148	0	1.2
1967	†StL N★	138	471	68	139	26	3	14	69	54-19	5	32	.295	.369	.452	137	24	8-8	**.997**	9	**172**	102	C130	0	4.1
1968	†StL N	128	434	35	110	15	6	5	48	26-8	1	31	.253	.295	.350	95	-4	4-3	.986	4	116	72	C109	0	0.6
1969	StL N	138	515	46	134	27	3	7	51	49-9	2	26	.260	.323	.365	93	-4	4-9	.986	6	88	81	C136	0	0.6
1970	Phi N	44	164	16	47	11	1	4	14	14-4	1	10	.287	.346	.439	111	3	2-2	.991	-1	70	73	C44	122	0.3
1971	Phi N	134	474	51	132	20	5	8	46	43-7	1	26	.278	.337	.392	106	4	5-3	.985	-9	59	125	C125	0	0.1
1972	Phi N	45	152	14	36	8	0	2	14	17-2	2	15	.237	.318	.329	83	-3	1-2	.989	-0	96	61	C40	0	-0.2
	Mon N	77	239	19	60	5	1	5	20	19-3	1	14	.251	.309	.343	83	-6	4-4	.990	7	100	126	C45,O14(14/0/1),3b6	0	0.2
	Year	122	391	33	96	13	1	7	34	36-5	3	29	.246	.313	.338	83	-8	5-6	.990	7	98	95	C85,O14(14/0/1),3b6	0	0.0
1973	StL N	130	331	30	88	16	4	3	49	38-6	2	31	.266	.339	.366	96	-1	2-0	.986	-7	67	88	1b77,C11	0	-1.3
1974	StL N	74	106	13	23	0	1	0	11	22-0	3	6	.217	.353	.236	71	-3	0-1	.969	-3	51	139	C21,1b6	0	-0.6
	Bos A	11	28	3	7	1	0	0	1	4-2	0	1	.250	.344	.286	77	-1	1-0	1.000	1	71	76	C8,D2	0	0.1
1975	Bos A	12	21	1	8	2	1	0	3	1-1	0	3	.381	.409	.571	161	2	0-0	.957	1	61	70	C7/1	0	0.2
	Phi N	47	59	6	15	2	0	1	7	14-3	0	7	.254	.397	.339	101	1	0-0	.984	1	61	129	C10/1	0	0.3
1976	†Phi N	90	155	26	43	11	2	3	29	35-2	1	14	.277	.409	.432	135	9	2-1	1.000	6	77	69	C41,1b2	0	1.8
1977	†Phi N	93	169	28	54	13	2	6	30	28-1	2	11	.320	.410	.527	145	12	3-5	.988	1	83	107	C42,1b3	0	1.4
1978	†Phi N	90	146	18	36	9	1	1	14	28-6	2	24	.247	.367	.342	100	2	2-2	.995	6	158	150	C34,1b11	0	0.8
1979	Phi N	79	137	13	33	5	1	1	12	19-5	1	12	.241	.333	.314	75	-4	2-0	.989	6	148	123	C31/lf	0	0.4
1980	Phi N	6	5	2	1	1	0	0	2	1-0	0	0	.200	.333	.400	97	0	0-0	1.000	-0	0	0	1b2	0	0.0
Total	21	1909	5529	590	1501	242	57	97	645	548-119	30	422	.271	.337	.388	102	23	61-49	.990	20	105	88	C1387,1b103,O15(15/0/1),3b6,D2	122	10.2
McCauley, Al	Allen A.; B3.4.1863 Indianapolis IN; D8.24.1917 Wayne Twnshp. IN; BL/TL/6´0˝/180; d6.21; ▲																								
1884	Ind AA	17	53	7	10	0	1	0	5	12	2	—	.189	.358	.226	97	1	—	1.000	1	144	286	P10,1b5,O3R	—	0.0
1890	Phi N	116	418	63	102	25	7	1	42	57	8	38	.244	.346	.344	99	1	8	.973	-6	63	107	1b116	—	-1.4
1891	Was AA	59	206	36	58	5	8	1	31	30	2	13	.282	.378	.398	128	8	9	.969	-1	95	71	1b59	—	0.2
Total	3	192	677	106	170	30	16	2	78	99	12	51	.251	.357	.352	107	10	17	.971	-6	73	97	1b180,P10,O3R	—	-1.2
McCauley, Jim	James Adelbert; B3.24.1863 Stanley NY; D9.14.1930 Canandaigua NY; BL/TR/6´0˝/180; d9.17; Col Union (NY)																								
1884	StL AA	1	2	0	0	0	0	0	—	0	0	—	.000	.000	.000	-97	0	—	.818	0	—	—	/C	—	0.0
1885	Buf N	24	84	4	15	2	1	0	7	11	—	12	.179	.274	.226	61	-3	—	.936	2	—	—	C21,O4C	—	0.1
	Chi N	3	6	1	1	0	0	0	0	2	—	3	.167	.375	.167	70	0	—	.800	-2	—	—	C2,O2R	—	-0.1
	Year	27	90	5	16	2	1	0	7	13	—	15	.178	.282	.222	62	-3	—	.927	1	—	—	C23,O6(0/4/2)	—	0.0
1886	Bro AA	11	30	5	7	1	0	0	3	11	0	—	.233	.439	.267	122	2	2	.846	-2	—	—	C11	—	0.1
Total	3	39	122	10	23	3	1	0	10	24	0	15	.189	.322	.230	76	-1	2	.893	-1	—	—	C35,O6(0/4/2)	—	0.1

YEAR	TM LG	G	AB	R	H	2B	3B	HR	RBI	BB-IB	HP	SO	AVG	OBP	SLG	AOPS	ABR	SB-CS	FA	FR	RNG	THR	GAMES AT POSITION	DL	BFW
McCauley, Pat	Patrick F.; B6.10.1870 Ware MA; D1.17.1917 Hoboken NJ; TR/5´10.5˝/156; d9.5																								
1893	StL N	5	16	0	1	0	0	0	0	0	1	1	.063	.063	.063	-67	-4	0	.808	-1	*83*	*136*	C5	—	-0.3
1896	Was N	26	84	14	21	3	0	3	11	7	0	8	.250	.315	.393	86	-2	3	.917	-2	*87*	*124*	C24/rf	—	-0.1
1903	NY A	6	19	0	1	0	0	0	1	0	0	—	.053	.053	.053	-64	-4	0	.920	-2	*99*	*51*	C6	—	-0.5
Total	3	37	119	14	23	3	0	3	12	7	1	9	.193	.244	.294	44	-10	3	.900	-4	*88*	*114*	C35/rf	—	-0.9
McCauley, Bill	William H.; B12.20.1869 Washington DC; D1.27.1926 Washington DC; d8.31																								
1895	Was N	1	2	0	0	0	0	0	0	0	0	0	.000	.000	.000	-99	-1	0	.714	0	143	0	/S	—	0.0
McChesney, Harry	Harry Vincent "Pud"; B6.1.1880 Pittsburgh PA; D8.11.1960 Pittsburgh PA; BR/TR/5´9˝/165; d9.17																								
1904	Chi N	22	88	9	23	6	2	0	11	4	0	—	.261	.293	.375	106	0	2	.967	-2	75	142	O22(0/1/21)	—	-0.3
McClain, Scott	Scott Michael; B5.19.1972 Simi Valley CA; BR/TR/6´3˝/(210–220); [BalA90 22/604]; d5.14																								
1998	TB A	9	20	2	2	0	0	0	0	2-0	1	6	.100	.217	.100	-13	-3	0-0	.966	-1	192	38	1b5,3b3	0	-0.4
2005	Chi N	13	14	1	2	1	0	0	1	2-0	0	2	.143	.250	.214	23	-2	0-0	1.000	-1	0	67	1b4,3b3	0	-0.3
Total	2	22	34	3	4	1	0	0	1	4-0	1	8	.118	.231	.147	2	-5	0-0	.978	-1	121	49	1b9,3b6	0	-0.7
McClanahan, Pete	Robert Hugh; B10.24.1906 Coldspring TX; D10.28.1987 Mont Belvieu TX; BR/TR/5´9˝/170; d4.24																								
1931	Pit N	7	4	2	2	0	0	0	0	2	0	0	.500	.667	.500	220	1	0	ø	0	—	—	/H	—	0.1
McClellan, Harvey	Harvey McDowell "Little Mac"; B12.22.1894 Cynthiana KY; D11.6.1925 Cynthiana KY; BR/TR/5´9.5˝/143; d5.31																								
1919	Chi A	7	12	2	4	0	0	0	1	1	0	1	.333	.385	.333	102	0	0	1.000	-0	141	330	3b3,S2	—	0.0
1920	Chi A	10	18	4	6	1	1	0	5	4	0	1	.333	.455	.500	153	2	2-0	.917	-2	54	0	S4,3b2	—	0.0
1921	Chi A	63	196	20	35	4	1	1	14	14	1	18	.179	.237	.224	18	-25	2-3	.968	14	123	40	2b21,S15,O15R,3b5	—	-1.0
1922	Chi A	91	301	28	68	17	3	2	28	16	3	32	.226	.272	.322	55	-21	3-2	.971	-3	103	111	3b71,S8,2b2/cf	—	-1.8
1923	Chi A	141	550	67	129	29	3	1	41	27	0	44	.235	.270	.304	52	-41	14-11	.958	-17	95	92	S139,2b2	—	-4.3
1924	Chi A	32	85	9	15	3	0	0	9	6	1	7	.176	.239	.212	17	-11	2-0	.938	2	120	64	S21,2b7/3rf	—	-0.6
Total	6	344	1162	130	257	54	8	4	98	68	5	103	.221	.267	.292	46	-96	23-16	.952	-7	99	90	S189,3b82,2b32,O17(0/1/16)	—	-7.7
McClellan, Bill	William Henry; B3.22.1856 Chicago IL; D7.3.1929 Chicago IL; BB/TL/5´5.5˝/156; d5.20																								
1878	Chi N	48	205	26	46	6	1	0	29	2	—	13	.224	.232	.263	59	-9	—	.866	-8	97	94	2b42,S5/rf	—	-1.5
1881	Pro N	68	259	30	43	3	1	0	16	15	—	21	.166	.212	.185	26	-21	—	.855	-7	91	117	S50,O17(0/1/16)/2	—	-2.5
1883	Phi N	80	326	42	75	21	4	1	33	19	—	18	.230	.272	.328	89	-2	—	.849	5	105	91	S78,O2C/3	—	0.5
1884	Phi N	111	450	71	116	13	2	3	33	28	—	43	.258	.301	.316	99	1	—	.852	-9	95	81	S111/cf	—	-0.4
1885	Bro AA	**112**	464	85	124	22	7	0	46	28	6	—	.267	.317	.345	108	5	—	.837	-7	78	117	3b57,2b55	—	0.1
1886	Bro AA	**141**	595	131	152	33	9	1	68	56	2	—	.255	.322	.346	108	7	43	.907	-8	98	97	2b141	—	0.3
1887	Bro AA	136	548	109	144	24	6	1	53	80	6	—	.263	.363	.334	94	-1	70	.879	-21	97	87	2b136	—	-1.4
1888	Bro AA	74	278	33	57	7	3	0	21	40	1	—	.205	.307	.252	80	-4	13	.905	-7	89	128	2b56,O18(0/1/17)	—	-0.9
	Cle AA	22	72	6	16	0	0	0	5	6	0	—	.222	.282	.222	64	-3	6	.875	-1	179	0	O15R,2b5,S2	—	-0.4
	Year	96	350	39	73	7	3	0	26	46	1	—	.209	.302	.246	77	-7	19	.897	-8	90	132	2b61,O33(0/1/32),S2	—	-1.3
Total	8	792	3197	533	773	129	33	6	304	274	15	95	.242	.305	.308	90	-27	132	.893	-63	97	97	2b436,S246,3b58,O54(0/5/49)	—	-6.2
McClendon, Lloyd	Lloyd Glenn; B1.11.1959 Gary IN; BR/TR/5´11˝/(195–212); [NYN80 8/183]; d4.6; M5/C5; Col Valparaiso																								
1987	Cin N	45	72	8	15	5	0	2	13	4-0	0	15	.208	.247	.361	57	-5	1-0	.981	-1	121	65	C12,1b5/3lf	0	-0.5
1988	Cin N	72	137	9	30	4	0	3	14	15-1	2	22	.219	.301	.314	75	-4	4-0	1.000	3	181	65	C23,O17(11/0/6),1b12,3b2	0	-0.1
1989	†Chi N	92	259	47	74	12	1	12	40	37-3	1	31	.286	.368	.479	134	12	6-4	.962	-5	92	90	O45L,1b28,3b6,C5	0	0.5
1990	Chi N	49	107	5	17	3	0	1	10	14-2	0	21	.159	.254	.215	29	-10	1-0	.980	3	117	0	O23L,C8,1b8	0	-0.9
	Pit N	4	3	1	1	0	0	1	2	0-0	0	1	.333	.333	1.333	347	1	0-0	ø	-0	0	0	/lf	0	0.1
	Year	53	110	6	18	3	0	2	12	14-2	0	22	.164	.256	.245	37	-9	1-0	.980	3	116	0	O24L,C8,1b8	0	-0.8
1991	†Pit N	85	163	24	47	7	0	7	24	18-0	2	23	.288	.366	.460	132	7	2-1	.966	-2	69	152	O32(14/0/18),1b22,C2	0	0.4
1992	†Pit N	84	190	26	48	8	1	3	20	28-0	2	24	.253	.350	.353	101	1	1-3	.964	-4	84	0	O60(10/0/50),1b18	0	-0.5
1993	Pit N	88	181	21	40	11	1	2	19	23-1	0	17	.221	.306	.326	70	-7	0-3	.967	-1	96	90	O61(21/0/47),1b6	0	-1.1
1994	Pit N	51	92	9	22	4	0	4	12	4-0	1	11	.239	.278	.413	76	-4	0-1	.967	-1	88	89	O20(12/0/9),1b2	0	-0.6
Total	8	570	1204	150	294	54	3	35	154	143-7	8	165	.244	.325	.381	94	-9	15-12	.966	-8	91	69	O260(138/0/130),1b101,C50,3b9	0	-2.7
McCleskey, Jeff	Jefferson Lamar; B11.6.1891 Americus GA; D5.11.1971 Americus GA; BL/TR/5´11˝/160; d9.8; Col Georgia																								
1913	Bos N	2	3	0	0	0	0	0	0	1	0	0	.000	.250	.000	-25	0	0	.750	-1	47	0	3b2	—	-0.1
McCloskey	B Brooklyn NY; d5.25																								
1875	Was NA	11	40	1	7	0	0	0	4	1	—	2	.175	.195	.175	31	-3	0-1	.673	-6	—	—	C11	—	-0.8
McCloskey, Bill	William George; B5.1854 PA; 5´8˝/155; d8.18																								
1884	Wil U	9	30	0	3	0	0	0	—	0	—	—	.100	.100	.100	-38	-6	—	.588	-0	262	0	O5(3/3/0),C5	—	-0.6
McClure, Hal	Harold Murray "Mac"; B8.8.1859 Lewisburg PA; D3.1.1919 Lewisburg PA; BR/TR/6´0˝/165; d5.10; Col Bucknell																								
1882	Bos N	2	6	1	2	0	0	0	0	0	—	1	.333	.333	.333	114	0	—	.750	-1	0	0	O2R	—	0.0
McClure, Larry	Lawrence Ledwith; B10.8.1884 Wayne WV; D9.1.1949 Huntington WV; BR/TR/5´6.5˝/130; d7.26; Col West Virginia																								
1910	NY A	1	1	0	0	0	0	0	0	0	0	—	.000	.000	.000	-95	0	0	ø	-0	0	0	/lf	—	0.0
McConnell, Amby	Ambrose Moses; B4.29.1883 N.Pownal VT; D5.20.1942 Utica NY; BL/TR/5´7˝/150; d4.17; Col Beloit																								
1908	Bos A	140	502	77	140	10	6	2	43	38	11	—	.279	.343	.335	117	10	31	.939	-16	95	86	2b126,S3	—	-0.5
1909	Bos A	121	453	61	108	7	8	0	36	34	6	—	.238	.300	.289	84	-8	26	.954	11	**112**	101	2b121	—	0.4
1910	Bos A	11	35	6	6	0	0	0	1	5	2	—	.171	.310	.171	50	-2	4	.959	-1	108	0	2b10	—	-0.3
	Chi A	33	120	13	33	2	3	0	5	7	1	—	.275	.320	.342	112	1	4	.952	-0	97	109	2b32	—	0.1
	Year	44	155	19	39	2	3	0	6	12	3	—	.252	.318	.303	97	-1	8	.954	-1	100	81	2b42	—	-0.2
1911	Chi A	104	396	45	111	11	5	1	34	23	7	—	.280	.331	.341	90	-6	7	**.973**	0	100	102	2b103	—	-0.4
Total	4	409	1506	202	398	30	22	3	119	107	27	—	.264	.324	.319	98	-5	72	.954	-6	102	94	2b392,S3	—	-0.7
McConnell, George	George Neely "Slats"; B9.16.1877 Shelbyville TN; D5.10.1964 Chattanooga TN; BR/TR/6´3˝/190; d4.13; ▲																								
1909	NY A	13	43	4	9	0	1	0	5	1	0	—	.209	.227	.256	52	-3	1	.964	2	154	116	1b11,P2	—	-0.2
1912	NY A	42	91	11	27	4	2	0	8	4	1	—	.297	.333	.385	99	0	0	.913	5	**146**	193	P23,1b2	—	0.2
1913	NY A	39	67	4	12	2	0	0	2	0	0	11	.179	.179	.209	13	-8	0	.965	4	140	115	P35/1	—	0.2
1914	Chi N	1	2	0	0	0	0	0	0	0	0	1	.000	.000	.000	-99	0	0	1.000	0	162	0	/P	—	0.0
1915	Chi F	53	125	14	31	6	2	1	18	0	1	16	.248	.254	.352	74	4	2	.974	3	113	144	P44	—	0.0
1916	Chi N	28	57	2	9	0	0	0	0	2	1	4	.158	.200	.158	10	-2	0	.952	2	111	218	P28	—	0.0
Total	6	176	385	35	88	12	5	1	33	7	3	32	.229	.248	.294	57	-9	3	.953	15	126	161	P133,1b14	—	0.2
McConnell, Sam	Samuel Faulkner; B6.8.1895 Philadelphia PA; D6.27.1981 Phoenixville PA; BL/TR/5´6.5˝/150; d4.19																								
1915	Phi A	6	11	1	2	1	0	0	0	1	0	3	.182	.250	.273	58	-1	0	.842	1	134	0	3b5	—	0.0
McCormack, Don	Donald Ross; B9.18.1955 Omak WA; BR/TR/6´3˝/205; [PhiN74 4/75]; d9.30																								
1980	Phi N	2	1	0	1	0	0	0	0	0-0	0	0	1.000	1.000	1.000	431	0	0-0	1.000	1	0	0	C2	0	0.1
1981	Phi N	3	4	0	1	0	0	0	0	0-0	0	1	.250	.250	.250	40	0	0-0	1.000	-0	0	165	C3	0	0.0
Total	2	5	5	0	2	0	0	0	0	0-0	0	1	.400	.400	.400	120	0	0-0	1.000	1	0	126	C5	0	0.1
McCormick, Frank	Frank Andrew "Buck"; B6.9.1911 New York NY; D11.21.1982 Manhasset NY; BR/TR/6´4˝/205; d9.11; C2																								
1934	Cin N	12	16	1	5	2	1	0	5	0	0	1	.313	.313	.563	132	1	0	.941	-1	0	76	1b2	—	0.0
1937	Cin N	24	83	5	27	5	0	0	9	2	0	4	.325	.341	.386	102	0	1	1.000	1	123	123	1b20,2b4/rf	—	-0.1
1938	Cin N★	**151**	640	89	**209**	40	4	5	106	18	3	17	.327	.348	.425	115	11	1	.995	-4	89	103	1b151	—	-0.7
1939	†Cin N★	**156**	630	99	**209**	41	4	18	**128**	40	2	16	.332	.374	.495	131	26	1	**.996**	1	97	**117**	1b156	—	1.3
1940	†Cin N★	**155**	618	93	**191**	**44**	3	19	127	52	5	26	.309	.367	.482	131	27	2	**.995**	-1	95	**130**	1b155	—	1.1
1941	Cin N★	**154**	603	77	162	31	5	17	97	40	4	13	.269	.318	.421	107	3	2	**.995**	-0	94	108	1b154	0	-1.2
1942	Cin N★	145	564	58	156	24	0	13	89	45	2	18	.277	.332	.388	111	7	1	.993	5	111	**124**	1b144	0	-0.2
1943	Cin N✳	126	472	56	143	28	0	8	59	29	1	15	.303	.345	.413	120	11	2	.995	4	**111**	116	1b120	0	0.9
1944	Cin N☆	153	581	85	177	37	3	20	102	57	4	17	.305	.371	.482	144	34	7	.992	12	**133**	122	1b153	0	3.8

YEAR	TM LG	G	AB	R	H	2B	3B	HR	RBI	BB-IB	HP	SO	AVG	OBP	SLG	AOPS	ABR	SB-CS	FA	FR	RNG	THR	GAMES AT POSITION	DL	BFW
1945	Cin N✻	152	580	68	160	33	0	10	81	56	5	22	.276	.345	.384	105	4	6	.994	4	**109**	90	1b151	0	0.1
1946	Phi N★	135	504	46	143	20	2	11	66	36	1	21	.284	.333	.397	110	4	2	**.999**	5	**108**	83	1b134	0	0.5
1947	Phi N	15	40	7	9	2	0	1	8	3	0	2	.225	.279	.350	69	-2	0	.989	-1	63	115	1b12	0	-0.3
	Bos N	81	212	24	75	18	2	2	43	11	0	8	.354	.386	.486	133	10	2	.996	-1	90	92	1b46	0	0.7
	Year	96	252	31	84	20	2	3	51	14	0	10	.333	.368	.464	123	8	2	.995	-2	85	96	1b58	0	0.4
1948	†Bos N	75	180	14	45	9	2	4	34	10	0	9	.250	.289	.389	84	-5	0	.987	2	126	112	1b50	0	-0.4
Total	13	1534	5723	722	1711	334	26	128	954	399	27	189	.299	.348	.434	118	131	27	.995	28	105	110	1b1448,2b4/rf	0	5.5
McCormick, Moose	Harry Elwood; B2.28.1881 Philadelphia PA; D7.9.1962 Lewisburg PA; BL/TL/5´11˝/180; d4.14; Col Bucknell																								
1904	NY N	59	203	28	54	9	5	1	26	13	4	—	.266	.323	.374	110	2	13	.916	-4	47	124	O55(2/52/1)	—	-0.5
	Pit N	66	238	25	69	10	6	2	23	13	2	—	.290	.332	.408	124	6	6	.940	-3	94	0	O66(18/0/48)	—	0.0
	Year	125	441	53	123	19	11	3	49	26	6	—	.279	.328	.392	118	8	19	.928	-7	72	58	O121(20/52/49)	—	-0.5
1908	Phi N	11	22	0	2	0	0	0	2	2	0	—	.091	.167	.091	-17	-3	0	1.000	0	0	0	O5L	—	-0.4
	NY N	73	252	31	76	16	3	0	32	4	1	—	.302	.315	.389	119	4	6	.901	-8	36	113	O65(59/0/12)	—	-0.9
	Year	84	274	31	78	16	3	0	34	6	1	—	.285	.302	.365	108	1	6	.910	-8	33	105	O70(64/0/12)	—	-1.3
1909	NY N	110	413	68	120	21	8	3	27	49	5	—	.291	.373	.402	138	20	4	.924	-10	90	198	O110(87/0/23)	—	0.5
1912	†NY N	42	39	4	13	4	1	0	8	6	0	9	.333	.422	.487	144	3	1	.667	-1	54	0	O6(1/1/4)/1	—	0.2
1913	†NY N	57	80	9	22	2	3	0	15	5	0	13	.275	.318	.375	97	-1	0	.909	-0	103	72	O15(0/2/13)	—	-0.2
Total	5	418	1247	165	356	62	26	6	133	92	12	22	.285	.340	.391	122	31	30	.920	-26	70	118	O322(172/55/101)/1	—	-1.3
McCormick, Jim	James Ambrose; B11.2.1868 Spencer MA; D2.1.1948 Saco ME; BR/TR/6´1˝/160; d9.10																								
1892	StL N	3	11	0	0	0	0	0	0	1	0	5	.000	.083	.000	-78	-2	0	1.000	-0	102	0	2b2/3	—	-0.2
McCormick, Jerry	John; B Philadelphia PA; D9.19.1905 Philadelphia PA; d5.1																								
1883	Bal AA	93	389	40	102	16	6	0	—	2	—	—	.262	.266	.334	89	-6	—	.799	1	101	87	3b93	—	-0.3
1884	Phi U	**67**	295	41	84	12	2	0	—	4	—	—	.285	.294	.339	99	-9	—	.811	11	118	118	3b54,2b5,O5(5/0/1),S3/P	—	0.3
	Was U	42	157	23	34	8	2	0	—	1	—	—	.217	.222	.293	57	-13	—	.792	-3	72	149	3b38,S4	—	-1.4
	Year	109	452	64	118	20	4	0	—	5	—	—	.261	.269	.323	84	-23	—	**.806**	9	101	129	3b92,S7,2b5,O5(5/0/1)/P	—	-1.1
Total	2	202	841	104	220	36	10	0	—	7	—	—	.262	.268	.328	86	-28	—	.802	9	101	108	3b185,S7,O5(5/0/1),2b5/P	—	-1.4
McCormick, Mike	Michael J. "Kid","Dude"; B5.1883 , Scotland; D11.18.1953 Jersey City NJ; BR/TR/5´3˝/155; d4.14																								
1904	Bro N	105	347	28	64	5	4	0	27	43	2	—	.184	.278	.222	56	-17	22	**.914**	-2	93	**181**	3b104/2	—	-1.7
McCormick, Mike	Myron Winthrop; B5.6.1917 Angels Camp CA; D4.13.1976 Los Angeles CA; BR/TR/6´0˝/200; d4.16; Mil 1943–45																								
1940	†Cin N	110	417	48	125	20	0	1	30	13	3	36	.300	.326	.355	87	-8	8	.986	2	102	102	O107(51/50/6)	—	-1.1
1941	Cin N	110	369	52	106	17	3	4	31	30	0	24	.287	.341	.382	103	1	4	.976	2	101	119	O101(82/19/0)	0	-0.2
1942	Cin N	40	135	18	32	2	3	1	11	13	0	7	.237	.304	.319	82	-3	0	.990	-0	104	61	O38(13/26/0)	67	-0.5
1943	Cin N	4	15	0	2	0	0	0	0	2	0	0	.133	.235	.133	8	-2	0	.909	-1	83	0	O4C	0	-0.3
1946	Cin N	23	74	10	16	2	0	0	5	8	0	4	.216	.293	.243	55	-4	0	1.000	-1	96	50	O21C	0	-0.7
	Bos N	59	164	23	43	6	2	1	16	11	0	7	.262	.309	.341	83	-4	0	.973	-1	110	27	O48(10/33/5)	0	-0.7
	Year	82	238	33	59	8	2	1	21	19	0	11	.248	.304	.311	75	-8	0	.982	-2	105	35	O69(10/54/5)	0	-1.4
1947	Bos N	92	284	42	81	13	7	3	36	20	0	21	.285	.332	.412	99	-2	1	.981	-3	94	84	O79(26/62/1)	0	-0.7
1948	†Bos N	115	343	45	104	22	7	1	39	32	0	34	.303	.363	.417	112	6	1	.975	-1	96	106	O100(56/34/20)	0	0.1
1949	†Bro N	55	139	17	29	5	1	2	14	14	0	12	.209	.281	.302	54	-9	1	1.000	0	97	106	O49(38/7/5)	0	-1.1
1950	NY N	4	4	0	0	0	0	0	0	0	0	2	.000	.000	.000	-99	-1	0	ø	0	—	—	/H	0	-0.1
	Chi A	55	138	16	32	4	3	0	10	16	0	6	.232	.312	.304	60	-9	0-1	.982	2	107	130	O44(2/42/0)	0	-0.7
1951	Was A	81	243	31	70	9	3	1	23	29	0	20	.288	.364	.362	98	0	1-2	.966	3	106	156	O62(24/12/28)	0	0.0
Total	10	748	2325	302	640	100	29	14	215	188	3	173	.275	.330	.361	90	-35	16-3	.980	3	101	100	O653(302/310/65)	67	-6.0
McCormick, Barry	William J.; B12.25.1874 Maysville KY; D1.28.1956 Cincinnati OH; TR/5´9˝/?; d9.25; U13																								
1895	Lou N	3	12	2	3	0	1	0	0	0	0	0	.250	.250	.417	75	-1	1	1.000	-1	96	141	S2/2	—	-0.1
1896	Chi N	45	168	22	37	3	1	1	23	14	0	30	.220	.280	.268	43	-14	9	.835	-5	98	93	3b35,S6,2b3/rf	—	-1.6
1897	Chi N	101	419	87	112	8	10	2	55	33	2	—	.267	.324	.348	75	-17	44	.851	2	108	137	3b56,S46/2	—	-1.1
1898	Chi N	137	530	76	131	15	9	2	78	47	5	—	.247	.314	.321	82	-13	15	.888	3	**112**	**171**	3b136/S2	—	-0.7
1899	Chi N	102	376	48	97	15	2	2	52	25	4	—	.258	.311	.324	76	-12	14	.941	1	110	124	2b99,S3	—	-0.6
1900	Chi N	110	379	35	83	13	5	3	48	38	1	—	.219	.292	.303	67	-17	8	.907	-9	98	94	S84,3b21,2b5	—	-2.0
1901	Chi N	115	427	45	100	15	6	1	32	31	1	—	.234	.288	.304	74	-14	12	.911	-4	103	103	S112,3b3	—	-1.4
1902	StL A	**139**	504	55	124	14	4	3	51	37	5	—	.246	.304	.308	71	-20	10	.905	-15	92	**142**	3b132,S7/cf	—	-3.0
1903	StL A	61	207	13	45	6	1	1	16	18	1	—	.217	.283	.271	69	-7	5	.969	-1	95	85	2b28,3b28,S4	—	-0.7
	Was A	63	219	14	47	10	2	0	23	10	2	—	.215	.255	.279	59	-11	3	.960	9	112	115	2b63	—	-0.2
	Year	124	426	27	92	16	3	1	39	28	3	—	.216	.269	.275	64	-18	8	.962	8	107	106	2b91,3b28,S4	—	-0.9
1904	Was A	113	404	36	88	11	1	0	39	27	4	—	.218	.274	.250	67	-14	9	.938	4	**109**	106	2b113	—	-1.1
Total	10	989	3645	433	867	110	42	15	417	280	25	30	.238	.297	.303	71	-140	130	.885	-18	103	145	3b411,2b314,S265,O2(0/1/1)	—	-12.5
McCosky, Barney	William Barney; B4.11.1917 Coal Run PA; D9.6.1996 Venice FL; BL/TR/6´1˝/184; d4.18; Mil 1943–45; [DL 1949 Phi A 129]																								
1939	Det A	147	611	120	190	33	14	4	58	70	2	45	.311	.384	.430	100	1	20-4	.986	3	108	57	O145C	—	0.3
1940	†Det A	143	589	123	**200**	39	**19**	4	57	67	1	41	.340	.408	.491	120	19	13-9	.983	-5	96	70	O141C	—	1.0
1941	Det A	127	494	80	160	25	8	3	55	61	3	33	.324	.401	.425	108	8	8-3	.985	-0	104	59	O122(21/101/0)	0	0.4
1942	Det A	154	600	75	176	28	11	7	50	68	0	37	.293	.365	.412	109	8	11-5	.981	0	105	58	O154(145/7/2)	0	0.0
1946	Det A	25	91	11	18	5	0	1	11	17	0	9	.198	.324	.286	67	-3	0-0	.966	-2	90	63	O24C	0	-0.7
	Phi A	92	308	33	109	17	4	1	34	43	0	13	.354	.433	.445	146	22	2-2	.981	-2	104	39	O85C	0	1.8
	Year	117	399	44	127	22	4	2	45	60	0	22	.318	.407	.409	127	18	2-2	.978	-4	101	45	O109C	0	1.1
1947	Phi A	137	546	77	179	22	7	1	52	57	4	29	.328	.395	.399	119	16	1-4	.983	-0	100	80	O136(114/23/0)	0	0.5
1948	Phi A	135	515	95	168	21	5	0	46	68	0	22	.326	.405	.386	111	11	1-3	.990	-2	96	94	O134L	0	-0.2
1950	Phi A	66	179	19	43	10	1	0	11	22	0	12	.240	.323	.307	63	-10	0-0	.987	-2	91	35	O42L	0	-1.4
1951	Phi A	12	27	4	8	2	0	1	1	3	0	4	.296	.367	.481	125	1	0-0	1.000	-0	101	0	O7(5/0/2)	0	-0.0
	Cin N	25	50	2	16	2	1	1	11	4	0	2	.320	.370	.460	120	1	0-0	1.000	-1	84	0	O11(4/7/1)	0	0.0
	Cle A	31	61	8	13	3	0	0	2	8	0	5	.213	.304	.262	57	-3	1-0	1.000	-0	107	0	O16(1/2/13)	0	-0.4
1952	Cle A	54	80	14	17	4	1	1	6	8	0	5	.213	.284	.325	74	-3	1-1	.944	-2	80	0	O19(11/0/9)	0	-0.6
1953	Cle A	22	21	3	4	3	0	0	3	1	0	4	.190	.227	.333	51	-1	0-0	ø	0	—	—	/H	0	-0.1
Total	11	1170	4172	664	1301	214	71	24	397	497	10	261	.312	.386	.414	109	67	58-31	.984	-13	101	63	O1036(477/535/27)	129	0.6
McCovey, Willie	Willie Lee "Stretch"; B1.10.1938 Mobile AL; BL/TL/6´4˝/(190–230); d7.30; HF1986																								
1959	SF N	52	192	32	68	9	5	13	38	22-1	4	35	.354	.429	.656	189	24	2-0	.989	-1	92	80	1b51	0	2.1
1960	SF N	101	260	37	62	15	3	13	51	45-4	0	53	.238	.349	.469	130	12	1-1	.985	-2	88	84	1b71	0	0.5
1961	SF N	106	328	59	89	12	3	18	50	37-3	5	60	.271	.350	.491	126	12	1-2	.985	-2	93	81	1b84	0	0.4
1962	†SF N	91	229	41	67	6	1	20	54	29-1	0	35	.293	.368	.590	156	17	3-3	.976	1	111	66	O57(45/0/12),1b17	0	1.5
1963	SF N★	152	564	103	158	19	5	**44**	102	50-5	11	119	.280	.350	.566	161	42	1-1	.942	-0	100	86	O135(134/0/2),1b23	0	3.6
1964	SF N	130	364	55	80	14	1	18	54	61-5	5	73	.220	.336	.412	108	6	2-1	.935	-5	80	111	O83(78/0/5),1b26	0	-0.5
1965	SF N	160	540	93	149	17	4	39	92	88-5	6	118	.276	.381	.539	152	40	0-4	.991	-6	83	87	1b156	0	2.5
1966	SF N★	150	502	85	148	26	6	36	96	76-10	6	100	.295	.391	.586	163	45	2-1	.984	-7	87	89	1b145	0	3.1
1967	SF N	135	456	73	126	17	4	31	91	71-17	6	110	.276	.378	.535	162	38	3-3	.989	1	108	112	1b127	0	3.3
1968	SF N★	148	523	81	153	16	4	**36**	**105**	72-20	5	71	.293	.378	**.545**	**176**	**49**	4-2	.985	3	115	91	1b146	0	4.9
1969	SF N★	149	491	101	157	26	2	**45**	**126**	121-**45**	4	66	.320	**.453**	**.656**	**211**	**80**	0-0	.992	-5	90	107	1b148	0	**6.5**
1970	SF N★	152	495	98	143	39	2	39	126	**137-40**	3	75	.289	.444	**.612**	**182**	**67**	0-0	.989	12	**132**	95	1b146	0	**6.5**
1971	†SF N★	105	329	45	91	13	0	18	70	64-**21**	4	57	.277	.396	.480	150	25	0-2	.983	-2	100	110	1b95	15	1.6
1972	SF N	81	263	30	56	8	0	14	35	38-5	2	45	.213	.316	.403	102	1	0-0	.986	-4	79	95	1b74	44	-1.0
1973	SF N	130	383	52	102	14	3	29	75	105-**25**	1	78	.266	.420	.546	160	36	1-0	.988	2	110	102	1b117	0	3.1
1974	SD N	128	344	53	87	19	1	22	63	96-9	1	76	.253	.416	.506	165	36	1-0	.987	-6	76	65	1b104	0	2.3
1975	SD N	122	413	43	104	17	0	23	68	57-8	3	80	.252	.345	.460	131	17	1-0	.986	1	113	107	1b115	0	1.0
1976	SD N	71	202	20	41	9	0	7	36	21-7	1	39	.203	.281	.351	85	-5	0-0	.991	7	163	108	1b51	0	-0.2
	Oak A	11	24	0	5	0	0	0	0	3-1	0	4	.208	.296	.208	51	-1	0-0	ø	0	—	—	D9	0	-0.2
1977	SF N	141	478	54	134	21	0	28	86	67-16	0	106	.280	.367	.500	130	21	3-0	.989	-7	78	95	1b136	0	0.7
1978	SF N	108	351	32	80	19	2	12	64	36-8	0	57	.228	.298	.396	96	-3	1-0	.987	-2	92	80	1b97	0	-1.1
1979	SF N	117	353	34	88	9	0	15	57	36-2	1	70	.249	.318	.402	103	0	0-2	.987	1	104	87	1b89	0	-0.5

YEAR	TM LG	G	AB	R	H	2B	3B	HR	RBI	BB-IB	HP	SO	AVG	OBP	SLG	AOPS	ABR	SB-CS	FA	FR	RNG	THR	GAMES AT POSITION	DL	BFW
1980	SF N	48	113	8	23	8	0	1	16	13-2	1	23	.204	.285	.301	68	-5	0-0	.992	-2	75	85	1b27	0	-0.8
Total	22	2588	8197	1229	2211	353	46	521	1555	1345-260	69	1550	.270	.374	.515	148	554	26-22	.987	-23	99	94	1b2045,O275(257/0/19),D9	59	39.3
McCoy, Art	Arthur Gray; B7.15.1864 Danville PA; D3.22.1904 Danville PA; ?/168; d7.8																								
1889	Was N	2	6	0	0	0	0	0	0	2	0	1	.000	.250	.000	-29	-1	0	.889	-1	38	0	2b2	—	-0.2
McCoy, Benny	Benjamin Jenison; B11.9.1915 Jenison MI; BL/TR/5´9˝/170; d9.14; Mil 1942–45																								
1938	Det A	7	15	2	3	1	0	0	0	1	0	2	.200	.250	.267	28	-2	0-0	.963	1	136	144	2b6/3	—	-0.1
1939	Det A	55	192	38	58	13	6	1	33	29	0	26	.302	.394	.448	107	3	3-1	.958	-1	101	87	2b34,S16	—	0.4
1940	Phi A	134	490	56	126	26	5	7	62	65	1	44	.257	.345	.373	88	-8	2-2	.951	-10	102	90	2b130/3	—	-1.0
1941	Phi A	141	517	86	140	12	7	8	61	95	0	50	.271	.384	.368	102	5	3-3	.963	-11	104	96	2b135	0	0.2
Total	4	337	1214	182	327	52	18	16	156	190	1	122	.269	.369	.381	97	-2	8-6	.957	-22	103	93	2b305,S16,3b2	0	-0.5
McCracken, Quinton	Quinton Antoine; B3.16.1970 Wilmington NC; BB/TR/5´7˝/(170–190); [ColN92 25/711]; d9.17; Col Duke																								
1995	Col N	3	1	0	0	0	0	0	0	0-0	0	1	.000	.000	.000	-78	0	0-0	ø	-0	0	0	/cf	0	0.0
1996	Col N	124	283	50	82	13	6	3	40	32-4	1	62	.290	.363	.410	84	-6	17-6	.957	-7	82	84	O93(8/85/4)	0	-1.1
1997	Col N	147	325	69	95	11	1	3	36	42-0	1	62	.292	.374	.360	76	-10	28-11	.980	-4	94	114	O132C	0	-1.0
1998	TB A	155	614	77	179	38	7	7	59	41-1	3	107	.292	.335	.410	91	-8	19-10	.992	5	95	193	O153(58/103/0)	0	-0.3
1999	TB A	40	148	20	37	6	1	1	18	14-0	1	23	.250	.317	.324	64	-8	6-5	.988	-2	96	43	O40(26/20/0)	132	-1.0
2000	TB A	15	31	5	4	0	0	0	2	6-0	0	4	.129	.270	.129	6	-4	0-1	1.000	-0	104	0	O11(9/3/0)	0	-0.5
2001	Min A	24	64	7	14	2	2	0	3	5-0	0	13	.219	.275	.313	52	-5	0-1	1.000	-1	85	0	O10(6/2/3),D9	0	-0.6
2002	†Ari N	123	349	60	108	27	8	3	40	32-0	2	68	.309	.367	.458	106	4	5-4	.995	4	110	100	O97(7/31/68)	0	0.5
2003	Ari N	115	203	17	46	5	2	0	18	15-2	0	34	.227	.276	.271	41	-18	5-1	.983	-5	75	42	O55(10/16/34)/D	0	-2.3
2004	Sea A	19	20	6	3	0	0	0	0	2-0	0	4	.150	.227	.150	1	-3	1-1	1.000	-0	72	287	O8(4/4/0),D6	0	-0.3
	Ari N	55	156	20	45	11	1	2	13	13-0	0	23	.288	.341	.410	88	-3	2-4	.979	-3	76	107	O37(27/3/10)	0	-0.8
2005	Ari N	134	215	23	51	4	3	1	13	23-4	1	35	.237	.313	.298	59	-13	4-0	.975	-4	80	95	O59(11/46/2)	0	-1.6
2006	Cin N	45	53	5	11	1	1	1	2	4-0	0	9	.208	.263	.321	46	-5	2-0	.955	1	127	0	O15(7/6/2)	0	-0.4
Total	12	999	2462	359	675	118	32	21	244	229-11	9	445	.274	.336	.374	78	-79	89-44	.984	-17	92	115	O711(173/452/123),D16	132	-9.4
McCraw, Tom	Tommy Lee; B11.21.1940 Malvern AR; BL/TL/6´0˝/(178–185); d6.4; C24; Col Santa Monica (CA) City																								
1963	Chi A	102	280	38	71	11	3	6	33	21-1	3	46	.254	.309	.379	94	-3	15-4	.993	-2	88	112	1b97	0	-0.8
1964	Chi A	125	368	47	96	11	5	6	36	32-4	4	65	.261	.325	.367	95	-3	15-7	.992	-3	89	125	1b84,O36(32/2/3)	0	-1.1
1965	Chi A	133	273	38	65	12	1	5	21	25-4	3	48	.238	.309	.344	91	-3	12-7	.993	-2	132	97	1b72,O64(37/31/3)	0	-0.9
1966	Chi A	151	389	49	89	16	4	5	48	29-7	5	40	.229	.288	.329	83	-9	20-11	.990	3	120	93	1b121,O41(29/0/16)	0	-1.4
1967	Chi A	125	453	55	107	18	3	11	45	33-2	1	55	.236	.288	.362	95	-4	24-10	.991	11	**140**	**114**	1b123,O6(1/4/1)	0	0.1
1968	Chi A	136	477	51	112	16	12	9	44	36-9	5	58	.235	.293	.375	101	-1	20-5	.986	3	119	107	1b135	0	-0.4
1969	Chi A	93	240	21	62	12	2	2	25	21-6	3	24	.258	.326	.350	85	-5	1-3	.989	-6	91	98	1b44,O41(11/16/17)	42	-1.6
1970	Chi A	129	332	39	73	11	2	6	31	21-3	4	50	.220	.273	.319	61	-18	12-3	.987	0	135	99	1b59,O49(21/12/18)	0	-2.2
1971	Was A	122	207	33	44	6	4	7	25	19-2	5	38	.213	.291	.382	95	-3	3-3	.958	-3	102	33	O60(26/1/37),1b30	0	-0.9
1972	Cle A	129	391	43	101	13	5	7	33	41-5	4	47	.258	.333	.371	106	3	12-10	1.000	1	103	37	O84(42/22/24),1b38	0	-0.4
1973	Cal A	99	264	25	70	7	0	3	24	30-1	2	42	.265	.343	.326	96	0	3-2	1.000	4	91	156	O34(32/1/1),1b25,D8	0	-0.1
1974	Cal A	56	119	21	34	8	0	3	17	12-2	0	13	.286	.348	.429	130	5	2-1	1.000	2	94	56	1b29,O12(7/0/5),D3	0	0.5
	Cle A	45	112	17	34	8	0	3	17	5-0	1	11	.304	.336	.455	128	4	0-1	.990	2	130	115	1b38/cf	0	0.3
	Year	101	231	38	68	16	0	6	34	17-2	1	24	.294	.343	.442	129	9	2-2	.994	3	115	91	1b67,O13(7/1/5),D3	0	0.8
1975	Cle A	23	51	7	14	1	1	2	5	7-2	0	7	.275	.362	.451	128	2	4-1	1.000	-1	79	96	1b16,O3L	0	0.0
Total	13	1468	3956	484	972	150	42	75	404	332-48	40	544	.246	.309	.362	94	-35	143-68	.991	8	116	106	1b911,O431(241/90/125),D11	42	-8.9
McCray, Rodney	Rodney Duncan; B9.13.1963 Detroit MI; BR/TR/5´10˝/175; [SDN84*9/219]; d4.30; Col West Los Angeles (CA) CC																								
1990	Chi A	32	6	8	0	0	0	0	0	1-0	0	4	.000	.143	.000	-58	-1	6-0	1.000	0	135	0	O13(3/7/4),D7	0	0.0
1991	Chi A	17	7	2	2	0	0	0	0	0-0	0	2	.286	.286	.286	60	0	1-1	1.000	1	162	0	O8(4/2/2),D6	0	0.0
1992	NY N	18	1	3	1	0	0	0	1	0-0	0	0	1.000	1.000	1.000	472	0	2-0	1.000	0	153	0	O13(1/1/11)	0	0.1
Total	3	67	14	13	3	0	0	0	1	1-0	0	6	.214	.267	.214	36	-1	9-1	1.000	1	150	0	O34(8/10/17),D13	0	0.1
McCrea, Frank	Francis William; B9.6.1896 Jersey City NJ; D2.25.1981 Dover NJ; BR/TR/5´9˝/155; d9.26																								
1925	Cle A	1	5	1	1	0	0	0	0	0	0	0	.200	.200	.200	2	-1	0-0	1.000	-0	*65*	*0*	/C	—	-0.1
McCredie, Walt	Walter Henry; B11.9.1876 Manchester IA; D7.29.1934 Portland OR; BL/TR/6´2˝/195; d4.20																								
1903	Bro N	56	213	40	69	5	0	0	20	24	2	—	.324	.397	.347	116	6	10	.925	-4	79	165	O56R	—	0.0
McCreery, Tom	Thomas Livingston; B10.19.1874 Beaver PA; D7.3.1941 Beaver PA; BB/TR/5´11˝/180; d6.8; Col Georgetown; OF(39/203/390); ▲																								
1895	Lou N	31	108	18	35	3	1	0	10	8	1	15	.324	.376	.370	99	0	3	.875	-4	49	0	O18R,P8,S4/31	—	-0.4
1896	Lou N	115	441	87	155	23	**21**	7	65	42	1	58	.351	.409	.546	156	34	26	.916	0	128	88	O111(0/2/109)/2P	—	2.4
1897	Lou N	91	344	55	96	5	6	4	40	40	0	—	.279	.354	.363	93	-3	13	.859	-6	100	74	O91(1/1/89)	—	-1.2
	NY N	49	177	36	53	8	5	1	28	22	1	—	.299	.380	.418	114	4	15	.900	-1	160	85	O45R,2b3	—	0.1
	Year	140	521	91	149	13	11	5	68	62	1	—	.286	.363	.382	100	1	28	.871	-6	120	78	O136(1/1/134),2b3	—	-1.1
1898	NY N	35	121	15	24	4	3	1	17	19	0	—	.198	.307	.306	78	-3	3	.820	-5	85	0	O35(1/0/35)	—	-0.9
	Pit N	53	190	33	59	5	7	2	20	26	0	—	.311	.394	.442	142	10	3	.934	-1	88	66	O51(0/46/5)	—	0.6
	Year	88	311	48	83	9	10	3	37	45	0	—	.267	.360	.389	117	7	6	.901	-6	87	39	O86(1/46/40)	—	-0.3
1899	Pit N	119	460	77	149	21	9	3	65	47	3	—	.324	.390	.428	125	17	11	.911	-12	102	48	O98(15/50/33),S9,2b7	—	0.0
1900	Pit N	43	132	20	29	4	3	1	13	16	0	—	.220	.304	.318	71	-5	2	.887	1	179	169	O35(17/1/17)/P	—	-0.6
1901	Bro N	91	335	47	97	11	14	3	53	32	2	—	.290	.355	.433	124	9	13	.947	1	83	70	O82(4/78/0),1b4,S2	—	0.6
1902	Bro N	112	430	49	105	8	4	4	57	29	2	—	.244	.295	.309	86	-8	16	.979	-1	94	97	1b108,O4(1/0/3)	—	-1.2
1903	Bro N	40	141	13	37	5	2	0	10	20	0	—	.262	.354	.326	97	0	5	.892	-3	72	149	O38(0/2/36)	—	-0.5
	Bos N	23	83	15	18	2	1	1	10	9	0	—	.217	.293	.301	72	-3	6	.900	-1	59	115	O23C	—	-0.5
	Year	63	224	28	55	7	3	1	20	29	0	—	.246	.332	.317	88	-3	11	.896	-4	67	136	O61(0/25/36)	—	-1.0
Total	9	802	2962	465	857	99	76	27	388	310	10	73	.289	.359	.401	113	52	116	.906	-30	106	83	O631R,1b113,S15,2b11,P10/3	—	-1.6
McCue, Frank	Frank Aloysius; B10.4.1898 Chicago IL; D7.5.1953 Chicago IL; BB/TR/5´9˝/150; d9.15																								
1922	Phi A	2	5	0	0	0	0	0	0	0	0	0	.000	.000	.000	-97	-1	0-0	ø	-0	0	0	3b2	—	-0.2
McCullough, Clyde	Clyde Edward; B3.4.1917 Nashville TN; D9.18.1982 San Francisco CA; BR/TR/5´11.5˝/(180–190); d4.28; Mil 1944–45; C4																								
1940	Chi N	9	26	4	4	1	0	0	1	5	0	5	.154	.290	.192	36	-2	0	1.000	1	*108*	*76*	C7	—	0.0
1941	Chi N	125	418	41	95	9	2	9	53	34	2	67	.227	.289	.323	75	-16	5	.982	-6	*89*	*93*	C119	0	-1.5
1942	Chi N	109	337	39	95	22	1	5	31	25	0	47	.282	.331	.398	117	7	7	.980	0	*110*	*108*	C97	0	1.3
1943	Chi N	87	266	20	63	5	2	2	23	24	1	33	.237	.302	.293	73	-9	6	.977	-10	*126*	*41*	C81	0	-1.6
1945	†Chi N	0	0	0	0	0	0	0	0	0	0	0	ø	ø	ø	ø	0	0	.000	0	—	—	/H	0	0.0
1946	Chi N	95	307	38	88	18	5	4	34	22	2	39	.287	.338	.417	116	5	2	.991	-3	*111*	*74*	C89	0	0.7
1947	Chi N	86	234	25	59	12	4	3	30	20	1	20	.252	.314	.376	86	-6	1	.984	4	*110*	*107*	C64	0	0.2
1948	Chi N☆	69	172	10	36	4	2	1	7	15	0	25	.209	.273	.273	50	-13	0	.973	1	*93*	*125*	C51	0	-0.9
1949	Pit N	91	241	30	57	9	3	4	21	24	4	30	.237	.316	.349	76	-8	1	.985	6	*122*	*100*	C90	0	0.2
1950	Pit N	103	279	28	71	16	4	6	34	31	5	35	.254	.340	.405	92	-3	3	.985	-4	*126*	*95*	C100	30	-0.2
1951	Pit N	92	259	26	77	9	2	8	39	27	1	31	.297	.366	.440	113	5	2-0	.988	6	*108*	*109*	C87	0	1.6
1952	Pit N	66	172	10	40	5	1	1	15	10	2	18	.233	.283	.291	58	-10	0-1	.981	4	*82*	*143*	C61/1	0	-0.4
1953	Chi N☆	77	229	21	59	3	2	6	23	15	0	23	.258	.303	.367	72	-10	0-0	.987	-2	*84*	*112*	C73	0	-0.9
1954	Chi N	31	81	9	21	7	0	3	17	5	1	5	.259	.310	.457	96	-1	0-0	.981	-2	*61*	*26*	C26,3b3	46	-0.2
1955	Chi N	44	81	7	16	0	0	0	10	8-3	1	15	.198	.272	.198	29	-8	0-0	.989	3	*77*	*79*	C37	0	-0.4
1956	Chi N	14	19	0	4	1	0	0	1	0-0	0	5	.211	.200	.263	27	-2	0-0	1.000	0	*60*	*129*	C7	0	-0.1
Total	16	1098	3121	308	785	121	28	52	339	265-3	20	398	.252	.314	.358	85	-71	27-1	.984	-2	*105*	*95*	C989,3b3/1	76	-2.2
McCurdy, Harry	Harry Henry “Hank”; B9.15.1899 Stevens Point WI; D7.21.1972 Houston TX; BL/TR/5´11˝/187; d7.4; Col Illinois																								
1922	StL N	13	27	3	8	2	2	0	5	1	0	1	.296	.321	.519	119	0	0-0	.967	-1	*95*	*94*	C9,1b2	—	0.0
1923	StL N	67	185	17	49	11	2	0	15	11	0	11	.265	.306	.346	73	-7	3-1	.969	-6	*94*	*68*	C58	—	-0.9
1926	Chi A	44	86	16	28	7	2	1	11	6	0	10	.326	.370	.488	127	3	0-1	.974	-2	*126*	*73*	C25,1b8	—	0.2
1927	Chi A	86	262	34	75	19	3	1	27	32	1	24	.286	.366	.393	99	1	6-4	.972	-1	*115*	*84*	C82	—	0.5
1928	Chi A	49	103	12	27	10	0	2	13	8	0	15	.262	.315	.417	92	-1	1-3	.964	-1	*130*	*52*	C34	—	-0.2
1930	Phi N	80	148	23	49	6	2	1	25	15	0	12	.331	.393	.419	90	-2	0	.966	-6	*76*	*95*	C41	—	-0.5

YEAR	TM LG	G	AB	R	H	2B	3B	HR	RBI	BB-IB	HP	SO	AVG	OBP	SLG	AOPS	ABR	SB-CS	FA	FR	RNG	THR	GAMES AT POSITION	DL	BFW
1931	Phi N	66	150	21	43	9	0	1	25	23	0	16	.287	.382	.367	95	0	2	.968	-3	*75*	*111*	C45	—	0.0
1932	Phi N	62	136	13	32	6	1	1	14	17	1	13	.235	.325	.316	65	-6	0	.974	-1	*89*	*76*	C42	—	-0.5
1933	Phi N	73	54	9	15	1	0	2	12	16	1	6	.278	.451	.407	130	3	0	ø	0	*0*	*0*	C2	—	0.4
1934	Cin N	3	6	0	0	0	0	0	1	0	0	0	.000	.000	.000	-99	-2	0	1.000	1	293	212	/1	—	-0.1
Total	10	543	1157	148	326	71	12	9	148	129	3	108	.282	.355	.387	92	-11	12-9	.970	-19	*100*	82	C338,1b11	—	-1.1
McDaniel, Terry	Terrence Keith; B12.6.1966 Kansas City MO; BB/TR/5´9˝/205; [NYN86*6/152]; d8.30																								
1991	NY N	23	29	3	6	1	0	0	2	1-0	0	11	.207	.233	.241	34	-3	2-0	1.000	1	128	0	O14(7/5/4)	0	-0.2
McDavid, Ray	Ray Darnell; B7.20.1971 San Diego CA; BL/TR/6´3˝/200; [SDN89 9/234]; d7.15; Col Arizona Western CC																								
1994	SD N	9	28	2	7	1	0	0	2	1-0	0	8	.250	.276	.286	48	-2	1-0	1.000	-1	83	0	O7(4/2/1)	0	-0.3
1995	SD N	11	17	2	3	0	0	0	0	2-0	0	6	.176	.263	.176	19	-2	1-1	1.000	-1	72	0	O7C	0	-0.3
Total	2	20	45	4	10	1	0	0	2	3-0	0	14	.222	.271	.244	37	-4	2-1	1.000	-1	79	0	O14(4/9/1)	0	-0.6
McDermott, Red	Frank A.; B11.12.1888 Philadelphia PA; D9.11.1964 Philadelphia PA; BR/TR/5´6˝/150; d8.6																								
1912	Det A	5	15	2	4	1	0	0	0	0	1	—	.267	.313	.333	87	0	1	1.000	0	86	186	O5L	—	0.0
McDermott, Mickey	Maurice Joseph "Maury"; B8.29.1929 Poughkeepsie NY; D8.7.2003 Phoenix AZ; BL/TL/6´2˝/(170–190); d4.24; C1; ▲																								
1948	Bos A	7	8	2	3	1	0	0	0	0	0	0	.375	.375	.500	125	1	0-0	1.000	1	197	0	P7	0	0.0
1949	Bos A	12	33	3	7	3	0	0	6	3	0	6	.212	.278	.303	50	1	0-0	.941	-0	94	0	P12	0	0.0
1950	Bos A	39	44	11	16	5	0	0	12	9	0	3	.364	.472	.477	131	7	0-0	.938	1	110	52	P38	0	0.0
1951	Bos A	43	66	8	18	1	1	1	6	3	1	14	.273	.314	.364	76	2	0-1	.950	2	114	196	P34	0	0.0
1952	Bos A	36	62	10	14	1	1	1	7	4	0	11	.226	.273	.323	60	2	0-0	.944	0	86	47	P30	0	0.0
1953	Bos A	45	93	9	28	8	0	1	13	2	0	13	.301	.316	.419	92	7	0-1	.957	1	120	124	P32	0	0.0
1954	Was A	54	95	7	19	3	0	0	4	7	0	12	.200	.255	.232	36	3	0-0	.955	1	118	72	P30	0	0.0
1955	Was A	70	95	10	25	4	0	1	10	6-0	1	16	.263	.311	.337	79	8	1-0	.943	0	115	54	P31	0	0.0
1956	†NY A	46	52	4	11	0	0	1	4	8-0	0	13	.212	.317	.269	58	3	0-0	1.000	-0	92	167	P23	0	0.0
1957	KC A	58	49	6	12	1	0	4	7	9-2	0	16	.245	.362	.510	133	2	0-0	.960	1	147	0	P29,1b2	0	0.0
1958	Det A	4	3	0	1	0	0	0	1	0-0	0	2	.333	.333	.333	78	0	0-0	ø	-0	0	0	P2	0	0.0
1961	StL N	22	14	1	1	1	0	0	3	0-0	0	4	.071	.071	.143	-41	-1	0-0	1.000	-0	63	0	P19	0	0.0
	KC A	7	5	0	1	1	0	0	1	1-0	0	2	.200	.333	.400	93	1	0-0	.500	-0	0	0	P4	0	0.0
Total	12	443	619	71	156	29	2	9	74	52-2	2	112	.252	.312	.349	76	36	1-2	.951	5	111	84	P291,1b2	0	0.0
McDermott, Terry	Terrence Michael; B3.20.1951 Rockville Cen. NY; BR/TR/6´3˝/205; [LAN69 1/8]; d9.12																								
1972	LA N	9	23	2	3	0	0	0	0	2-0	0	8	.130	.200	.130	-4	-3	0-0	1.000	-0	68	97	1b7	0	-0.4
McDermott, Sandy	Thomas Nathaniel; B3.15.1856 Zanesville OH; D11.23.1922 Mansfield OH; d6.18																								
1885	Bal AA	1	0	0	0	0	0	0	0	0	0	—	ø	ø	ø	ø	0	—	ø	-0	0	0	/2	—	0.0
McDonald	; d5.18																								
1872	Eck NA	1	4	0	0	0	0	0	0	0	—	0	.000	.000	.000	-99	-1	0-0	.333	-1	59	0	/S	—	-0.2
McDonald, Tex	Charles E. (b Charles C. Crabtree); B1.31.1891 Farmersville TX; D3.31.1943 Houston TX; BL/TR/5´10˝/160; d4.11																								
1912	Cin N	61	140	16	36	3	4	1	15	13	2	24	.257	.329	.357	90	-2	5	.915	-8	81	49	S42	—	-0.8
1913	Cin N	11	10	1	3	0	0	0	2	0	0	1	.300	.300	.300	72	0	0	ø	-0	0	0	/S	—	-0.1
	Bos N	62	145	24	52	4	4	0	18	15	1	17	.359	.422	.441	144	9	4-6	.869	-2	104	169	3b31,2b6/rf	—	0.7
	Year	73	155	25	55	4	4	0	20	15	1	18	.355	.415	.432	140	8	4-6	.869	-2	104	169	3b31,2b6/Srf	—	0.6
1914	Pit F	67	223	27	71	16	7	3	29	13	2	23	.318	.361	.493	132	6	9	.925	3	82	270	O29R,2b27,S5	—	0.8
	Buf F	69	250	32	74	13	6	3	32	20	2	26	.296	.353	.432	111	0	11	.953	-2	103	71	O61(2/1/58),2b10	—	-0.6
	Year	136	473	59	145	29	13	6	61	33	4	49	.307	.357	.461	121	5	20	.943	1	96	135	O90(2/1/87),2b37,S5	—	0.2
1915	Buf F	87	251	31	68	9	6	6	39	27	2	34	.271	.346	.426	114	1	5	.924	-5	96	53	O65(12/0/53)	—	-0.8
Total	4	357	1019	131	304	45	27	13	135	88	9	125	.298	.359	.434	118	14	34-6	.936	-14	96	101	O156(14/1/141),S48,2b43,3b31	—	-0.8
McDonald, Jack	Daniel; B1844 Brooklyn NY; D11.23.1880 Brooklyn NY; 5´11˝/154; d5.2																								
1872	Atl NA	15	62	9	16	3	1	0	4	0	—	1	.258	.258	.339	70	-3	0-0	.720	-2	0	0	O15(1/0/14)	—	-0.3
McDonald, Darnell	Darnell T.; B11.17.1978 Fort Collins CO; BR/TR/5´11˝/210; [BalA97 1/26]; d4.30; b–Donzell																								
2004	Bal A	17	32	3	5	1	0	0	1	2-0	0	6	.156	.206	.188	4	-5	1-0	1.000	-1	99	0	O13(1/4/8)/D	0	-0.5
McDonald, Dave	David Bruce; B5.20.1943 New Albany IN; BL/TR/6´3˝/(215–227); d9.15; Col Nebraska																								
1969	NY A	9	23	0	5	1	0	0	2	2-0	0	5	.217	.280	.261	54	-1	0-1	.960	-1	84	47	1b7	0	-0.3
1971	Mon N	24	39	3	4	2	0	1	4	4-0	0	14	.103	.178	.231	17	-4	0-0	.983	-1	81	146	1b8/lf	0	-0.6
Total	2	33	62	3	9	3	0	1	6	6-0	0	19	.145	.214	.242	30	-5	0-1	.972	-1	82	101	1b15/lf	0	-0.9
McDonald, Donzell	Donzell; B2.20.1975 Long Beach CA; BB/TR/5´11˝/180; [NYA95 22/618]; d4.19; b–Darnell; Col Yavapai (AZ) JC																								
2001	NY A	5	3	0	1	0	0	0	0	0-0	0	2	.333	.333	.333	76	0	0-0	1.000	-0	94	0	O3(1/2/0)	0	0.0
2002	KC A	10	22	3	4	2	0	0	1	4-0	0	5	.182	.296	.273	50	-1	1-0	1.000	-2	25	0	O7L	0	-0.3
Total	2	15	25	3	5	2	0	0	1	4-0	0	7	.200	.300	.280	53	-1	1-0	1.000	-2	35	0	O10(8/2/0)	0	-0.3
McDonald, Ed	Edward Cyril; B10.28.1886 Albany NY; D3.11.1946 Albany NY; BR/TR/6´0˝/180; d8.5																								
1911	Bos N	54	175	28	36	7	3	1	21	40	2	39	.206	.359	.297	78	-3	11	.955	-2	95	121	3b53/S	—	-0.4
1912	Bos N	121	459	70	119	23	6	2	34	70	5	91	.259	.363	.349	94	-1	22	.940	1	99	109	3b118	—	0.2
1913	Chi N	1	0	0	0	0	0	0	0	0	0	0	ø	ø	ø	ø	0	0	ø	0	—	—	/R	—	0.0
Total	3	176	634	98	155	30	9	3	55	110	7	130	.244	.362	.334	89	-4	33	.945	-1	98	113	3b171/S	—	-0.2
McDonald, Jim	James; B Philadelphia PA; BR/TR/6´0˝/180; d6.2																								
1902	NY N	2	9	0	3	0	0	0	1	0	0	—	.333	.333	.333	107	0	0	1.000	-0	0	0	O2R	—	0.0
McDonald, Jim	James Augustus; B8.6.1860 San Francisco CA; D9.14.1914 San Francisco CA; BR/5´9.5˝/180; d6.20																								
1884	Was U	2	6	0	1	0	0	0	—	0	—	—	.167	.167	.167	1	-1	—	.700	-1	—	—	/Crf	—	-0.2
	Pit AA	38	145	11	23	3	0	0	—	2	0	—	.159	.170	.179	14	-13	—	.795	-5	97	74	3b22,O15(1/12/2)/2	—	-1.7
1885	Buf N	5	14	0	0	0	0	0	0	0	—	4	.000	.000	.000	-97	-3	—	.875	1	135	102	S4/cf	—	-0.2
Total	2	45	165	11	24	3	0	0	0	2	—	4	.145	.156	.164	4	-17	—	.795	-5	—	—	3b22,O17(1/13/3),S4/2C	—	-2.1
McDonald, Jason	Jason Adam; B3.20.1972 Modesto CA; BB/TR/5´8˝/(182–190); [OakA93 4/125]; d6.5; Col Houston																								
1997	Oak A	78	236	47	62	11	4	4	14	36-0	1	49	.263	.361	.394	98	0	13-8	.961	-2	100	64	O74(17/66/0)	0	-0.2
1998	Oak A	70	175	25	44	9	0	1	16	27-0	3	33	.251	.359	.320	80	-4	10-4	.956	4	106	221	O60(11/33/25)	87	0.0
1999	Oak A	100	187	26	39	2	1	3	8	25-0	3	48	.209	.310	.278	54	-13	6-3	.993	4	113	85	O89(31/53/13)/2D	0	-0.9
2000	Tex A	38	94	15	22	5	0	3	13	17-0	1	25	.234	.357	.383	86	-2	4-4	.988	7	124	314	O32(11/3/26)	0	0.3
Total	4	286	692	113	167	27	5	11	51	105-0	8	155	.241	.347	.342	80	-19	33-19	.973	14	109	148	O255(70/155/64),D5/2	87	-0.8
McDonald, John	John Joseph; B9.24.1974 New London CT; BR/TR/5´11˝/(175–185); [CleA96 12/363]; d7.4; Col Providence																								
1999	Cle A	18	21	2	7	0	0	0	0	0-0	0	3	.333	.333	.333	67	-1	0-1	1.000	3	149	244	2b7,S6	0	0.2
2000	Cle A	9	9	0	4	0	0	0	0	0-0	0	1	.444	.444	.444	122	0	0-0	1.000	0	93	66	S7,2b2	0	0.1
2001	Cle A	17	22	1	2	1	0	0	0	1-0	1	7	.091	.167	.136	-18	-4	0-0	.955	-1	83	55	S9,2b3,3b3	0	-0.4
2002	Cle A	93	264	35	66	11	3	1	12	10-0	5	50	.250	.288	.326	62	-15	3-0	.986	12	118	107	2b64,S21,3b10/D	0	0.2
2003	Cle A	82	214	21	46	9	1	1	14	11-0	2	31	.215	.258	.280	43	-18	3-3	.980	-7	110	134	2b37,S27,3b23	50	-2.1
2004	Cle A	66	93	17	19	5	1	2	7	4-0	0	11	.204	.237	.344	51	-7	0-0	.947	9	119	128	S30,2b12,3b9,D8	0	0.4
2005	Tor A	37	93	8	27	3	0	0	12	6-0	2	12	.290	.340	.323	76	-3	5-0	.977	6	119	120	S32,2b5	0	0.6
	Det A	31	73	10	19	3	1	0	4	5-0	0	12	.260	.308	.329	71	-3	1-1	.951	6	137	146	S22,2b8/3	0	0.4
	Year	68	166	18	46	6	1	0	16	11-0	2	24	.277	.326	.325	74	-6	6-1	.966	12	126	130	S54,2b13/3	0	1.0
2006	Tor A	104	260	35	58	7	3	3	23	16-0	2	41	.223	.271	.308	48	-21	7-2	.960	7	105	120	S90,2b10,3b2	15	-0.6
Total	8	457	1049	129	248	39	9	7	72	53-0	12	168	.236	.279	.311	55	-72	19-7	.961	37	108	118	S244,2b148,3b48,D9	65	-1.2
McDonald, Joe	Malcolm Joseph; B4.9.1888 TX; D5.30.1963 Baytown TX; BR/TR/5´11˝/175; d9.6																								
1910	StL A	10	32	4	5	0	0	0	1	1	0	—	.156	.182	.156	6	-4	0	.821	-2	77	156	3b10	—	-0.6

YEAR	TM LG	G	AB	R	H	2B	3B	HR	RBI	BB-IB	HP	SO	AVG	OBP	SLG	AOPS	ABR	SB-CS	FA	FR	RNG	THR	GAMES AT POSITION	DL	BFW
McDonald, Keith	William Keith; B2.8.1973 Yokosuka, Japan; BR/TR/6´2˝/215; [StLN94 24/670]; d7.4; Col Pepperdine																								
2000	StL N	6	7	3	3	0	0	3	5	2-0	0	1	.429	.556	1.714	433	4	0-0	1.000	1	83	0	C4	0	0.4
2001	StL N	2	2	0	0	0	0	0	0	0-0	0	1	.000	.000	.000	-98	-1	0-0	1.000	0	0	0	C2	0	0.0
Total	2	8	9	3	3	0	0	3	5	2-0	0	2	.333	.455	1.333	323	3	0-0	1.000	1	66	0	C6	0	0.4
McDonnell, Jim	James William "Mack"; B8.15.1922 Gagetown MI; D4.24.1993 Detroit MI; BL/TR/5´11˝/165; d9.23																								
1943	Cle A	2	1	1	0	0	0	0	0	2	0	1	.000	.667	.000	108	0	0-0	1.000	-0	0	0	/C	0	0.0
1944	Cle A	20	43	5	10	0	0	0	4	4	0	3	.233	.298	.233	55	-3	0-0	.900	-2	91	73	C13	0	-0.4
1945	Cle A	28	51	3	10	2	0	0	8	2	0	4	.196	.226	.235	36	-4	0-0	.980	5	104	123	C23	0	0.1
Total	3	50	95	9	20	2	0	0	12	8	0	8	.211	.272	.232	48	-7	0-0	.953	2	97	101	C37	0	-0.3
McDonough, Ed	Edward Sebastian; B9.11.1886 Elgin IL; D9.2.1926 Elgin IL; BR/TR/6´0˝/160; d8.3; Col Notre Dame																								
1909	Phi N	1	1	0	0	0	0	0	0	0	0	—	.000	.000	.000	-99	0	0	1.000	0	0	294	/C	—	0.0
1910	Phi N	5	9	1	1	0	0	0	0	0	0	1	.111	.111	.111	-34	-2	0	1.000	-1	82	51	C4	—	-0.2
Total	2	6	10	1	1	0	0	0	0	0	0	1	.100	.100	.100	-40	-2	0	1.000	-0	70	87	C5	—	-0.2
McDougald, Gil	Gilbert James; B5.19.1928 San Francisco CA; BR/TR/6´1˝/(175–180); d4.20; Col San Francisco																								
1951	†NY A	131	402	72	123	23	4	14	63	56	4	54	.306	.396	.488	143	25	14-5	.949	-8	91	167	3b82,2b55	0	2.1
1952	†NY A★	152	555	65	146	16	5	11	78	57	4	73	.263	.336	.369	102	1	6-5	.968	16	**113**	**149**	3b117,2b38	0	1.9
1953	†NY A	141	541	82	154	27	7	10	83	60	5	65	.285	.361	.416	113	10	3-4	.953	7	105	**124**	3b136,2b26	0	1.7
1954	NY A	126	394	66	102	22	2	12	48	62	5	64	.259	.364	.416	118	12	3-4	.989	10	103	138	2b92,3b35	0	2.8
1955	†NY A	141	533	79	152	10	8	13	53	65-2	2	77	.285	.361	.407	109	6	6-4	**.985**	22	106	**127**	2b126,3b17	0	3.7
1956	†NY A☆	120	438	79	136	13	3	13	56	68-1	3	59	.311	.405	.443	128	20	3-8	.970	9	97	129	S92,2b31,3b5	0	3.5
1957	†NY A★	141	539	87	156	25	**9**	13	62	59-1	4	71	.289	.362	.442	121	16	2-5	.976	26	102	**132**	S121,2b21,3b7	0	5.3
1958	†NY A★	138	503	69	126	19	1	14	65	59-1	3	75	.250	.329	.376	98	-1	6-2	.977	3	99	**114**	2b115,S19	0	1.3
1959	NY A★	127	434	44	109	16	8	4	34	35-3	3	40	.251	.309	.353	85	-10	0-3	.989	7	106	117	2b53,S52,3b25	0	0.4
1960	†NY A	119	337	54	87	16	4	8	34	38-0	3	45	.258	.337	.401	105	2	2-4	.945	12	108	119	3b84,2b42	0	1.5
Total	10	1336	4676	697	1291	187	51	112	576	559-8	36	623	.276	.356	.410	112	81	45-44	.984	106	104	119	2b599,3b508,S284	0	24.2
McDougall, Marshall	Marshall James; B12.19.1978 Jacksonville FL; BR/TR/6´1˝/200; [OakA00 9/270]; d6.7; Col Florida St.; [DL 2006 Tex A 9]																								
2005	Tex A	18	18	3	3	1	0	0	0	0-0	0	10	.167	.167	.222	2	-3	0-0	1.000	-1	69	0	3b5,O3R,2b2/SD	0	-0.3
McDowell, Oddibe	Oddibe; B8.25.1962 Hollywood FL; BL/TL/5´9˝/(160–165); [TexA84 1/12]; d5.19; Col Arizona St.																								
1985	Tex A	111	406	63	97	14	5	18	42	36-2	3	85	.239	.304	.431	97	-3	25-7	.993	6	109	147	O103C,D4	0	0.5
1986	Tex A	154	572	105	152	24	7	18	49	65-5	1	112	.266	.341	.427	105	4	33-15	.991	-3	89	177	O148C/D	0	0.1
1987	Tex A	128	407	65	98	26	4	14	52	51-0	0	99	.241	.324	.428	97	-2	24-2	.989	-2	97	107	O125C	0	0.0
1988	Tex A	120	437	55	108	19	5	6	37	41-2	2	89	.247	.311	.355	85	-9	33-10	.989	-6	93	41	O113C,D3	0	-1.3
1989	Cle A	69	239	33	53	5	2	3	22	25-0	1	36	.222	.296	.297	67	-11	12-5	.992	1	99	136	O64(63/1/0),D2	0	-1.1
	Atl N	76	280	56	85	18	4	7	24	27-3	0	37	.304	.365	.471	135	13	15-10	.978	0	107	58	O68C	0	1.3
1990	Atl N	113	305	47	74	14	0	7	25	21-0	2	53	.243	.295	.357	75	-11	13-2	.971	-8	83	53	O72(12/60/1)	0	-1.8
1994	Tex A	59	183	34	48	5	1	1	15	28-0	0	39	.262	.355	.317	76	-6	14-2	.983	-1	103	66	O53(0/31/27),D2	30	-0.4
Total	7	830	2829	458	715	125	28	74	266	294-12	9	550	.253	.323	.395	94	-25	169-53	.987	-13	97	107	O746(75/649/28),D12	30	-2.7
McElveen, Pryor	Pryor Mynatt "Humpty"; B11.5.1881 Atlanta GA; D10.27.1951 Pleasant Hill TN; BR/TR/5´10˝/168; d4.26; Col Carson–Newman																								
1909	Bro N	81	258	22	51	8	1	3	25	14	1	—	.198	.242	.271	61	-13	6	.938	-3	93	111	3b37,O13(1/3/7),S10,1b5,2b5	—	-1.7
1910	Bro N	74	213	19	48	8	3	1	26	22	3	47	.225	.307	.305	81	-5	6	.943	-7	79	161	3b54,S6,2b3/C	—	-1.1
1911	Bro N	16	31	1	6	0	0	0	5	0	0	3	.194	.194	.194	9	-4	0	.929	-2	66	177	2b5/S	—	-0.6
Total	3	171	502	42	105	16	4	4	56	36	4	50	.209	.268	.281	67	-22	12	.941	-12	85	141	3b91,S17,2b13,O13(1/3/7),1b5/C	—	-3.4
McElwee, Lee	Leland Stanford; B5.23.1894 LaMesa CA; D2.8.1957 Union ME; BR/TR/5´10.5˝/160; d7.3; Col Bowdoin																								
1916	Phi A	54	155	9	41	3	0	0	10	8	0	17	.265	.301	.284	79	-4	0	.883	1	96	114	3b30,O9R,2b3/1S	—	-0.4
McElyea, Frank	Frank; B8.4.1918 Hawthorne Twp. IL; D4.19.1987 Evansville IN; BR/TR/6´6˝/221; d9.10; Mil 1943–45																								
1942	Bos N	7	4	2	0	0	0	0	0	0	0	0	.000	.000	.000	-99	-1	0	1.000	0	200	0	/lf	0	-0.1
McEwing, Joe	Joseph Earl; B10.19.1972 Bristol PA; BR/TR/5´10˝/(170–210); [StLN92 28/783]; d9.2; Col CC of Morris (NJ); OF(161/46/79)																								
1998	StL N	10	20	5	4	1	0	0	1	1-0	1	3	.200	.273	.250	39	-2	0-1	1.000	-1	83	106	2b6,O3(1/1/1)	0	-0.3
1999	StL N	152	513	65	141	28	4	9	44	41-8	6	87	.275	.333	.398	83	-13	7-4	.980	8	104	88	2b96,O66(32/23/19),3b6,1b2/S	0	-0.3
2000	†NY N	87	153	20	34	14	1	2	19	5-0	1	29	.222	.248	.366	56	-11	3-1	1.000	-3	94	74	O52(43/11/6),3b19,2b16,S4	0	-1.2
2001	NY N	116	283	41	80	17	3	8	30	17-0	10	57	.283	.342	.449	111	4	8-5	1.000	-0	89	71	O62(48/2/25),3b25,S12,2b5,1b3/D	0	0.3
2002	NY N	105	196	22	39	8	1	3	26	9-0	3	50	.199	.242	.296	44	-17	4-4	1.000	1	129	0	O35(10/1/24),S21,1b20,2b13,3b10	17	-1.7
2003	NY N	119	278	31	67	11	0	1	16	25-4	3	57	.241	.309	.291	61	-16	3-0	.995	4	89	88	2b55,S42,O18(16/1/2),1b5,3b2	0	-0.8
2004	NY N	75	138	17	35	3	1	1	16	9-4	0	32	.254	.297	.312	60	-9	4-1	.981	5	109	83	2b34,O15(8/6/1),S13,1b11/3	45	-0.2
2005	KC A	83	180	16	43	7	0	1	6	6-0	0	35	.239	.263	.294	50	-13	4-4	.962	7	124	40	3b29,1b20,2b11,S6,O5(3/1/1),D6	0	-0.7
2006	Hou N	7	6	0	0	0	0	0	0	0-0	0	2	.000	.000	.000	-97	-2	0-0	1.000	0	209	0	2b2	0	-0.1
Total	9	754	1767	217	443	89	10	25	158	113-16	24	352	.251	.302	.355	71	-79	33-20	.997	20	108	66	O256L,2b238,S99,3b92,1b61,D7	62	-5.0
McFadden, Guy	Guy G.; B9.3.1872 Topeka KS; D3.10.1911 Topeka KS; d8.24																								
1895	StL N	4	14	1	3	0	0	0	2	0	0	2	.214	.214	.214	11	-2	0	.968	-1	0	135	1b4	—	-0.2
McFadden, Leon	Leon; B4.26.1944 Little Rock AR; BR/TR/6´2˝/195; d9.6																								
1968	Hou N	16	47	2	13	1	0	0	1	6-2	0	10	.277	.358	.298	101	0	1-0	.968	-3	93	35	S16	0	-0.1
1969	Hou N	44	74	3	13	2	0	0	3	4-0	0	9	.176	.218	.203	19	-8	1-2	.944	-2	91	0	O17(4/0/13),S8	0	-1.1
1970	Hou N	2	0	0	0	0	0	0	0	0-0	0	0	ø	ø	ø	ø	0	0-0	ø	0	—	—	/R	0	0.0
Total	3	62	121	5	26	3	0	0	4	10-2	0	19	.215	.275	.240	50	-8	2-2	.966	-5	92	25	S24,O17(4/0/13)	0	-1.2
McFarlan, Alex	Alexander Shepherd; B11.11.1866 KY; D3.2.1939 Pewee Valley KY; 5´9˝/165; d6.19; b-Dan																								
1892	Lou N	14	42	2	7	0	0	0	1	8	0	11	.167	.300	.167	46	-2	1	.773	-2	57	0	O12R,2b2	—	-0.4
McFarland, Chris	Christopher; B8.17.1861 Fall River MA; D5.24.1918 New Bedford MA; 5´9˝/170; d4.19																								
1884	Bal U	3	14	2	3	1	0	0	—	0	—	—	.214	.214	.286	46	-1	—	.571	-1	0	0	O3C/P	—	-0.2
McFarland, Ed	Edward William; B8.3.1874 Cleveland OH; D11.28.1959 Cleveland OH; BR/TR/5´10˝/180; d7.7																								
1893	Cle N	8	22	5	9	2	1	0	6	1	1	2	.409	.458	.591	168	2	0	1.000	-1	0	0	O5C,3b2/C	—	0.0
1896	StL N	83	290	48	70	13	4	3	36	15	1	17	.241	.281	.345	67	-15	7	.961	1	85	**144**	C80,O2R	—	-0.6
1897	StL N	31	107	14	35	5	2	1	17	8	0	—	.327	.374	.439	117	2	2	.965	-5	68	124	C23,1b3,O3L/2	—	0.0
	Phi N	38	130	18	29	3	5	1	16	14	2	—	.223	.308	.346	75	-5	2	.951	-2	104	98	C37	—	-0.3
	Year	69	237	32	64	8	7	2	33	22	2	—	.270	.337	.388	93	-3	4	.957	-7	89	109	C60,1b3,O3L/2	—	-0.3
1898	Phi N	121	429	65	121	21	5	3	71	44	2	—	.282	.352	.375	113	8	4	.960	2	110	102	C121	—	2.0
1899	Phi N	96	324	59	108	22	9	2	57	36	2	—	.333	.403	.475	146	21	9	.968	11	109	103	C94	—	3.6
1900	Phi N	94	344	50	105	14	8	0	38	29	3	—	.305	.364	.392	110	5	9	**.963**	-12	78	112	C93/3	—	0.1
1901	Phi N	74	295	33	84	14	2	1	32	18	0	—	.285	.326	.356	96	-2	11	.970	2	99	**113**	C74	—	0.8
1902	Chi A	75	246	29	56	9	2	1	25	19	3	—	.228	.291	.293	65	-11	8	.967	7	128	90	C69/1	—	0.2
1903	Chi A	61	201	15	42	7	2	1	19	14	1	—	.209	.264	.279	66	-8	3	.968	0	110	101	C56/1	—	-0.2
1904	Chi A	50	160	22	44	11	3	0	20	17	1	—	.275	.348	.381	136	7	2	.975	-4	117	77	C49	—	0.9
1905	Chi A	80	250	24	70	13	4	0	31	23	2	—	.280	.345	.364	130	9	5	.973	8	132	94	C70	—	2.6
1906	†Chi A	12	23	0	4	1	0	0	3	3	0	—	.174	.269	.217	54	-1	0	.973	0	161	46	C7	—	0.0
1907	Chi A	52	138	11	39	9	1	0	8	12	0	—	.283	.340	.362	128	5	3	.972	-1	118	92	C43	—	0.9
1908	Bos A	19	48	5	10	2	1	0	4	1	0	—	.208	.224	.292	66	-2	0	.978	3	100	128	C13	—	0.3
Total	14	894	3007	398	826	146	49	13	383	254	18	19	.275	.335	.369	104	15	65	.967	10	106	105	C830,O10(3/5/2),1b5,3b3/2	—	10.3
McFarland, Herm	Hermas Walter; B3.11.1870 Des Moines IA; D9.21.1935 Richmond VA; BL/TR/5´6˝/150; d4.21																								
1896	Lou N	30	110	11	21	4	1	1	12	9	0	14	.191	.252	.273	40	-10	4	.833	-3	104	268	O28(3/18/9)/C	—	-1.3
1898	Cin N	19	64	10	18	1	3	0	11	7	1	—	.281	.361	.391	108	0	3	.968	-1	47	0	O17(13/3/1)	—	-0.2
1901	Chi A	132	473	83	130	21	9	4	59	75	9	—	.275	.384	.383	116	15	33	.946	5	82	83	O132L	—	1.2
1902	Chi A	7	27	5	5	0	0	0	4	2	0	—	.185	.241	.185	20	-3	1	1.000	-0	0	0	O7(2/0/5)	—	-0.3

YEAR	TM LG	G	AB	R	H	2B	3B	HR	RBI	BB-IB	HP	SO	AVG	OBP	SLG	AOPS	ABR	SB-CS	FA	FR	RNG	THR	GAMES AT POSITION	DL	BFW
	Bal A	61	242	54	78	19	6	3	36	36	4	—	.322	.418	.488	144	16	10	.965	4	146	52	O61C	—	1.6
	Year	68	269	59	83	19	6	3	40	38	4	—	.309	.402	.457	133	14	11	.967	4	132	47	O68(2/61/5)	—	1.3
1903	NY A	103	362	41	88	16	9	5	45	46	3	—	.243	.333	.378	106	4	13	.939	-3	79	72	O103(39/58/7)	—	-0.5
Total	5	352	1278	204	340	61	28	13	167	175	17	14	.266	.362	.388	110	22	64	.941	2	91	83	O348(189/140/22)/C	—	0.5
McFarland, Howie	Howard Alexander; B3.7.1910 El Reno OK; D4.7.1993 Wichita KS; BR/TR/6'0"/175; d7.16																								
1945	Was A	6	11	0	1	0	0	0	2	0	0	3	.091	.091	.091	-52	-2	0-0	1.000	0	61	639	O3(1/0/2)	0	-0.2
McFarlane, Orlando	Orlando Dejesus (Quesada); B6.28.1938 Oriente, Cuba; BR/TR/6'0"/180; d4.23																								
1962	Pit N	8	23	0	2	0	0	0	1	1-0	0	4	.087	.125	.087	-42	-5	0-0	1.000	-0	46	109	C8	0	-0.5
1964	Pit N	37	78	5	19	5	0	0	1	4-2	0	27	.244	.280	.308	66	-3	0-0	.983	-4	215	72	C35/rf	0	-0.7
1966	Det A	49	138	16	35	7	0	5	13	9-1	1	46	.254	.304	.413	102	0	0-0	.991	-2	116	78	C33	17	0.0
1967	Cal A	12	22	0	5	0	0	0	3	1-0	0	7	.227	.250	.227	47	-2	0-0	.935	-2	68	144	C6	39	-0.3
1968	Cal A	18	31	1	9	0	0	0	2	5-1	0	9	.290	.389	.290	112	1	0-0	.977	-0	46	56	C9	38	0.1
Total	5	124	292	22	70	12	0	5	20	20-4	1	93	.240	.290	.332	78	-9	0-0	.985	-9	129	82	C91/rf	94	-1.4
McGaffigan, Patsy	Mark Andrew; B9.12.1888 Carlyle IL; D12.22.1940 Carlyle IL; BR/TR/5'8"/140; d4.16; Mil 1918																								
1917	Phi N	19	60	5	10	1	0	0	6	0	0	7	.167	.167	.183	7	-7	1	.920	1	103	82	S17/rf	—	-0.5
1918	Phi N	54	192	17	39	3	2	1	8	16	1	23	.203	.268	.255	56	-10	3	.948	-8	98	84	2b53/S	—	-1.9
Total	2	73	252	22	49	4	2	1	14	16	1	30	.194	.245	.238	45	-17	4	.948	-7	98	84	2b53,S18/rf	—	-2.4
McGah, Eddie	Edward Joseph; B9.30.1921 Oakland CA; D9.30.2002 Oakland CA; BR/TR/6'0"/183; d4.26																								
1946	Bos A	15	37	2	8	1	1	0	1	7	0	7	.216	.341	.297	75	-1	0-0	.981	-1	*116*	*68*	C14	0	-0.2
1947	Bos A	9	14	1	0	0	0	0	2	3	0	0	.000	.176	.000	-45	-3	0-0	.964	1	*151*	*79*	C7	0	-0.1
Total	2	24	51	3	8	1	1	0	3	10	0	7	.157	.295	.216	41	-4	0-0	.975	-0	*127*	*71*	C21	0	-0.3
McGann, Ambrose	Ambrose J.; B1868 Baltimore MD; D2.2.1941 Baltimore MD; ?/170; d5.2																								
1895	Lou N	20	73	9	21	5	2	0	9	8	0	6	.288	.358	.411	105	1	6	.852	-2	86	25	S8,3b6,O5R	—	-0.1
McGann, Dan	Dennis Lawrence "Cap"; B7.15.1871 Shelbyville KY; D12.13.1910 Louisville KY; BB/TR/6'0"/190; d8.8																								
1896	Bos N	43	171	25	55	6	7	2	30	12	5	10	.322	.383	.474	118	4	2	.905	-11	89	64	2b43	—	-0.5
1898	Bal N	145	535	99	161	18	8	5	106	53	39	—	.301	.404	.393	126	22	33	.983	2	98	102	1b145	—	2.2
1899	Bro N	63	214	49	52	11	4	2	32	21	19	—	.243	.362	.360	96	0	16	.985	1	102	137	1b61	—	0.1
	Was N	76	280	65	96	9	8	5	58	14	18	—	.343	.410	.486	147	18	11	.990	3	101	77	1b76	—	1.8
	Year	139	494	114	148	20	12	7	90	35	**37**	—	.300	.389	.431	124	18	27	**.988**	4	101	105	1b137	—	1.9
1900	StL N	121	444	79	132	10	9	4	58	32	**24**	—	.297	.376	.387	112	8	26	**.990**	-1	85	63	1b121/2	—	0.6
1901	StL N	103	423	73	115	15	9	6	56	16	**23**	—	.272	.333	.392	116	8	17	.984	-3	85	**127**	1b103	—	0.3
1902	Bal A	68	250	40	79	10	8	0	42	19	6	—	.316	.378	.420	116	5	17	.987	3	113	117	1b68	—	0.7
	NY N	61	227	25	68	5	7	0	21	12	8	—	.300	.356	.383	130	7	12	.981	1	109	112	1b61	—	0.8
1903	NY N	129	482	75	130	21	6	3	50	32	12	—	.270	.331	.357	93	-5	36	**.988**	-1	85	97	1b129	—	-0.8
1904	NY N	141	517	81	148	22	6	6	71	36	**18**	—	.286	.354	.387	123	15	42	**.991**	3	98	119	1b141	—	1.6
1905	†NY N	136	491	88	147	23	14	5	75	55	**19**	—	.299	.391	.434	143	28	22	**.991**	5	102	101	1b136	—	3.1
1906	NY N	134	451	62	107	14	8	0	37	60	13	—	.237	.344	.304	100	3	30	**.995**	4	99	102	1b133	—	0.4
1907	NY N	81	262	29	78	9	1	2	36	29	7	—	.298	.383	.363	129	11	9	.994	5	113	95	1b81	—	1.6
1908	Bos N	135	475	52	114	8	5	2	55	38	**19**	—	.240	.321	.291	97	0	9	.988	6	125	**124**	1b121,2b9	—	0.5
Total	12	1436	5222	842	1482	181	100	42	727	429	230	10	.284	.364	.381	117	124	282	.989	16	100	105	1b1376,2b53	—	12.4
McGarr, Chippy	James B.; B5.10.1863 Worcester MA; D6.6.1904 Worcester MA; BR/TR/5'7"/168; d7.11; U1																								
1884	CP U	19	70	10	11	2	0	0	—	0	—	—	.157	.157	.186	4	-10	—	.905	-3	74	56	2b13,O6(5/0/1)	—	-1.2
1886	Phi AA	71	267	41	71	9	3	2	31	9	2	—	.266	.295	.345	99	-1	17	.850	-1	100	110	S71	—	0.0
1887	Phi AA	**137**	536	93	158	23	6	1	63	23	2	—	.295	.326	.366	93	-7	84	.875	-1	95	123	S137	—	-0.3
1888	StL AA	34	132	17	31	1	0	0	13	6	0	—	.235	.268	.242	58	-7	25	.895	-6	99	109	2b33/S	—	-1.1
1889	KC AA	25	108	22	31	3	0	0	16	6	1	11	.287	.330	.315	79	-3	12	.857	-2	78	282	3b11,O6(2/0/4),2b5,S3	—	-0.4
	Bal AA	3	7	1	1	0	0	0	0	1	0	1	.143	.250	.143	13	-1	0	.583	-2	53	0	S3	—	-0.3
	Year	28	115	23	32	3	0	0	16	7	1	12	.278	.325	.304	75	-4	12	.857	-5	78	282	3b11,O6(2/0/4),S6,2b5	—	-0.7
1890	Bos N	121	487	68	115	12	7	1	51	34	4	38	.236	.291	.296	66	-23	39	**.933**	-3	95	78	3b115,S5/rf	—	-2.1
1893	Cle N	63	249	38	77	12	0	0	28	20	1	15	.309	.363	.357	86	-5	24	.886	0	103	66	3b63	—	-0.3
1894	Cle N	128	523	94	144	24	6	2	74	28	3	29	.275	.316	.356	59	-37	31	.902	-6	95	90	3b128	—	-3.1
1895	†Cle N	113	422	86	114	14	2	2	59	35	1	33	.270	.328	.327	65	-23	19	.872	-5	98	93	3b109,2b4	—	-2.1
1896	†Cle N	113	455	68	122	16	4	1	53	22	0	30	.268	.302	.327	62	-26	16	.924	-7	96	132	3b113/C	—	-2.7
Total	10	827	3256	538	875	116	28	9	388	184	14	157	.269	.311	.330	71	-143	267	.903	-35	96	98	3b539,S220,2b55,O13(7/0/6)/C	—	-13.6
McGarr, Jim	James Vincent "Reds"; B11.9.1888 Philadelphia PA; D7.21.1981 Miami FL; BR/TR/5'9.5"/170; d5.18																								
1912	Det A	1	4	0	0	0	0	0	0	0	0	—	.000	.000	.000	-99	-1	0	.800	-0	124	0	/2	—	-0.1
McGarvey, Dan	Daniel Francis; B12.2.1887 Philadelphia PA; D3.7.1947 Philadelphia PA; BR; d5.18																								
1912	Det A	1	3	0	0	0	0	0	0	1	1	—	.000	.400	.000	18	0	0	.667	1	441	6688	/lf	—	0.1
McGeachy, Jack	John Charles; B5.23.1864 Clinton MA; D4.5.1930 Cambridge MA; BR/TR/5'8"/165; d6.17; ▲																								
1886	Det N	6	27	3	9	0	1	0	4	0	—	3	.333	.333	.407	120	0	2	.875	-1	89	0	O6L	—	0.0
	StL N	59	226	31	46	12	3	2	24	1	—	37	.204	.207	.310	59	-11	8	.880	0	138	173	O55C,2b2,3b2	—	-1.1
	Year	65	253	34	55	12	4	2	28	1	—	40	.217	.220	.320	66	-11	10	.880	-0	133	157	O61(6/55/0),2b2,3b2	—	-1.1
1887	Ind N	99	405	49	109	17	3	1	56	5	1	16	.269	.280	.333	72	-16	27	.894	4	125	85	O98(0/97/2)/3P	—	-1.2
1888	Ind N	118	452	45	99	15	2	0	30	5	2	21	.219	.231	.261	56	-23	49	.932	5	137	117	O117(2/6/109)/SP	—	-1.9
1889	Ind N	131	532	83	142	32	1	2	63	9	2	39	.267	.282	.342	72	-22	37	.918	8	144	170	O131R,P3	—	-1.4
1890	Bro P	104	443	84	108	24	4	1	65	19	2	12	.244	.278	.323	57	-30	21	.906	-3	81	24	O104(22/31/52)	—	-2.8
1891	Phi AA	50	201	24	46	4	3	2	13	6	1	12	.229	.255	.308	61	-12	9	.920	2	115	0	O50(4/12/34)	—	-1.0
	Bos AA	41	178	26	45	2	1	1	21	12	1	8	.253	.304	.292	72	-7	11	.910	-4	57	0	O41(38/0/3)	—	-1.0
	Year	91	379	50	91	6	4	3	34	18	2	20	.240	.278	.301	66	-19	20	.916	-2	89	0	O91(42/12/37)	—	-2.0
Total	6	608	2464	345	604	106	18	9	276	57	9	148	.245	.265	.314	65	-121	164	.909	11	119	94	O602(72/201/331),P5,3b3,2b2/S	—	-10.4
McGeary, Mike	Michael Henry; B1851 Philadelphia PA; BR/TR/5'7"/138; d5.9; M3																								
1871	Tro NA	**29**	148	42	39	4	0	0	12	6	—	0	.264	.292	.291	67	-6	**20-4**	**.897**	-1	—	—	C26,S3	—	-0.3
1872	Ath NA	**47**	225	68	81	9	2	0	35	2	—	1	.360	.366	.418	140	10	13-8	.867	5	—	—	C23,S23/rf	—	1.0
1873	Ath NA	**52**	275	63	83	8	1	0	31	1	—	1	.302	.304	.338	83	-7	4-6	.804	-5	95	105	S43,C14/3	—	-1.0
1874	Ath NA	54	271	61	87	10	2	0	22	1	—	2	.321	.324	.373	113	2	10-2	.837	8	—	—	C28,S26,O4R	—	0.9
1875	Phi NA	68	310	71	90	6	2	0	37	1	—	1	.290	.293	.323	109	2	19-4	.743	1	84	71	3b27,2b23,S18,O3(0/1/2),M	—	0.2
1876	StL N	61	276	48	72	3	0	0	30	2	—	1	.261	.266	.272	84	-4	—	.889	8	112	117	2b56,C5/cf3	—	0.5
1877	StL N	57	258	35	65	3	2	0	20	2	—	6	.252	.258	.279	73	-8	—	.883	6	102	82	2b39,3b19	—	0.1
1879	Pro N	**85**	374	62	103	7	2	0	35	5	—	13	.275	.285	.305	96	-2	—	.884	1	97	80	2b73,3b12	—	0.3
1880	Pro N	18	59	5	8	0	0	0	1	0	—	6	.136	.136	.136	-8	-6	—	.887	4	147	101	3b17,2b2/SM	—	-0.2
	Cle N	31	111	14	28	2	1	0	6	4	—	3	.252	.278	.288	94	-1	—	.887	-5	81	140	3b29,O2R	—	-0.5
	Year	49	170	19	36	2	1	0	7	4	—	9	.212	.230	.235	60	-7	—	.887	-1	99	129	3b46,2b2,O2R/S	—	-0.7
1881	Cle N	11	41	1	9	0	0	0	5	0	—	6	.220	.220	.220	41	-3	—	.724	-5	64	69	3b11,M	—	-0.7
1882	Det N	34	133	14	19	4	1	0	2	2	—	20	.143	.156	.188	10	-13	—	.928	4	102	51	S33,2b3	—	-0.7
Total	5NA	250	1229	305	380	37	7	0	137	11	—	5	.309	.315	.351	104	1	66-24	.807	9	—	—	S113,C91,3b28,2b23,O8(0/1/7)	—	0.8
Total	6	297	1252	179	304	19	6	0	99	15	—	55	.243	.252	.268	72	-37	—	.885	13	—	—	2b173,3b89,S34,C5,O3(0/1/2)	—	-1.2
McGee, Dan	Daniel Aloysius; B9.29.1911 New York NY; D12.4.1991 Lakehurst NJ; BR/TR/5'8.5"/152; d7.14																								
1934	Bos N	7	22	2	3	0	0	0	1	3	0	6	.136	.240	.136	4	-3	0	.951	1	118	79	S7	—	-0.1
McGee, Frank	Francis De Sales; B4.28.1899 Columbus OH; D1.30.1934 Columbus OH; BR/TR/5'11.5"/175; d9.19; Col Ohio St.																								
1925	Was A	2	3	0	0	0	0	0	0	0	0	1	.000	.000	.000	-99	-1	0-0	1.000	0	147	125	1b2	—	-0.1

McGee, Pat Patrick; B Philadelphia PA; D6.20.1889 New York NY; d9.24

YEAR	TM LG	G	AB	R	H	2B	3B	HR	RBI	BB-IB	HP	SO	AVG	OBP	SLG	AOPS	ABR	SB-CS	FA	FR	RNG	THR	GAMES AT POSITION	DL	BFW
1874	Atl NA	16	65	4	11	1	0	0	6	0	—	3	.169	.169	.185	15	-5	0-0	.795	-2	46	0	O15(6/9/0),S2/2	—	-0.6
1875	Mut NA	25	95	4	17	2	0	0	9	0	—	10	.179	.179	.200	30	-7	0-0	.848	-2	53	0	O25C	—	-0.8
	Atl NA	18	65	3	10	3	1	0	5	1	—	4	.154	.167	.231	42	-3	0-0	.912	5	381	229	O13C,2b6/3	—	0.1
	Year	43	160	7	27	5	1	0	14	1	—	14	.169	.174	.213	34	-10	0-0	.875	3	161	75	O38C,2b6/3	—	-0.7
Total	2NA	59	225	11	38	6	1	0	20	1	—	17	.169	.173	.204	29	-15	0-0	.849	1	125	52	O53(6/47/0),2b7,S2/3	—	-1.3

McGee, Willie Willie Dean; B11.2.1958 San Francisco CA; BB/TR/6´1˝/(160–195); [NYA77*S1/15]; d5.10; Col Diablo Valley (CA) JC

YEAR	TM LG	G	AB	R	H	2B	3B	HR	RBI	BB-IB	HP	SO	AVG	OBP	SLG	AOPS	ABR	SB-CS	FA	FR	RNG	THR	GAMES AT POSITION	DL	BFW
1982	†StL N	123	422	43	125	12	8	4	56	12-2	2	58	.296	.318	.391	95	-5	24-12	.958	-11	91	46	O117(1/116/0)	0	-1.7
1983	StL N★	147	601	75	172	22	8	5	75	26-2	0	98	.286	.314	.374	90	-10	39-8	.987	-4	97	93	O145C	25	-1.0
1984	StL N	145	571	82	166	19	11	6	50	29-2	1	80	.291	.325	.394	104	0	43-10	.985	3	103	126	O141C	15	0.8
1985	†StL N★	152	612	114	**216**	26	**18**	10	82	34-2	0	86	**.353**	.384	.503	148	36	56-16	.978	0	102	118	O149(3/146/0)	0	4.3
1986	StL N	124	497	65	127	22	7	7	48	37-7	1	82	.256	.306	.370	86	-11	19-16	**.991**	-1	102	114	O121C	24	-1.5
1987	†StL N★	153	620	76	177	37	11	11	105	24-5	2	90	.285	.312	.434	93	-8	16-4	.981	-8	93	100	O152C/S	0	-1.5
1988	StL N★	137	562	73	164	24	6	3	50	32-5	1	84	.292	.329	.372	100	-1	41-6	.975	-3	96	140	O135C	0	0.2
1989	StL N	58	199	23	47	10	2	3	17	10-0	1	34	.236	.275	.352	76	-7	8-6	.976	-2	97	80	O47C	60	-1.0
1990	StL N	125	501	76	168	32	5	3	62	38-6	1	86	**.335**	.382	.437	124	17	28-9	.957	4	105	**182**	O124(0/118/6)	0	2.3
	†Oak A	29	113	23	31	3	2	0	15	10-0	0	18	.274	.333	.336	91	-2	3-0	.986	0	103	73	O28C/D	0	-0.1
1991	SF N	131	497	67	155	30	3	4	43	34-3	2	74	.312	.357	.408	119	12	17-9	.978	-5	95	80	O128(0/89/48)	19	0.6
1992	SF N	138	474	56	141	20	2	1	36	29-3	1	88	.297	.339	.354	102	0	13-4	.976	1	95	150	O119(0/31/90)	0	0.0
1993	SF N	130	475	53	143	28	1	4	46	38-7	1	67	.301	.353	.389	102	2	10-9	.979	-3	93	98	O126R	19	-0.8
1994	SF N	45	156	19	44	3	0	5	23	15-2	0	24	.282	.337	.397	97	-1	3-0	.988	-1	98	64	O42R	65	-0.3
1995	†Bos A	67	200	32	57	11	3	2	15	9-0	0	41	.285	.311	.400	82	-6	5-2	.973	3	94	250	O64(3/27/47)	0	-0.4
1996	†StL N	123	309	52	95	15	2	5	41	18-2	2	60	.307	.348	.417	101	0	5-2	.962	1	95	149	O83(35/11/42),1b6	0	-0.1
1997	StL N	122	300	29	90	19	4	3	38	22-2	0	59	.300	.347	.420	100	0	8-2	.981	-1	87	154	O81(18/18/53),D3	17	-0.2
1998	StL N	120	269	27	68	10	1	3	34	14-5	0	49	.253	.287	.331	63	-15	7-2	.938	1	92	159	O88(56/6/38)/1D	0	-1.6
1999	StL N	132	271	25	68	7	0	0	20	17-3	0	60	.251	.293	.277	45	-23	7-4	.972	-4	89	58	O89(30/19/43),1b3	0	-2.7
Total	18	2201	7649	1010	2254	350	94	79	856	448-58	15	1238	.295	.333	.396	100	-22	352-121	.976	-31	97	117	O1979(146/1351/535),1b10,D7/S	244	-4.7

McGeehan, Dan Daniel De Sales; B6.7.1885 Jeddo PA; D7.12.1955 Hazleton PA; BR/TR/5´6˝/135; d4.22; b–Conny

YEAR	TM LG	G	AB	R	H	2B	3B	HR	RBI	BB-IB	HP	SO	AVG	OBP	SLG	AOPS	ABR	SB-CS	FA	FR	RNG	THR	GAMES AT POSITION	DL	BFW
1911	StL N	3	9	0	2	0	0	0	1	0	0	1	.222	.222	.222	25	-1	0	.818	-1	80	0	2b3	—	-0.2

McGhee, Ed Warren Edward; B9.29.1924 Perry AR; D2.13.1986 Memphis TN; BR/TR/5´11˝/(170–176); d9.20; Col Arkansas St.

YEAR	TM LG	G	AB	R	H	2B	3B	HR	RBI	BB-IB	HP	SO	AVG	OBP	SLG	AOPS	ABR	SB-CS	FA	FR	RNG	THR	GAMES AT POSITION	DL	BFW
1950	Chi A	3	6	0	1	0	1	0	0	0	0	1	.167	.167	.500	67	-1	0-0	1.000	-0	71	0	/rf	0	-0.1
1953	Phi A	104	358	36	94	11	4	1	29	32	3	43	.263	.328	.324	74	-13	4-3	.982	5	117	47	O99(1/97/1)	0	-1.3
1954	Phi A	21	53	5	11	2	0	2	9	4	0	8	.208	.259	.358	69	-3	0-1	.933	-0	115	0	O13(2/11/0)	0	-0.4
	Chi A	42	75	12	17	1	0	0	5	12	0	8	.227	.333	.240	57	-4	5-0	.982	2	102	227	O34(5/18/11)	0	-0.2
	Year	63	128	17	28	3	0	2	14	16	0	16	.219	.303	.289	62	-7	5-1	.960	2	107	138	O47(7/29/11)	0	-0.6
1955	Chi A	26	13	6	1	0	0	0	0	6-0	0	1	.077	.368	.077	24	-1	2-1	.923	0	131	0	O17(5/12/0)	0	-0.1
Total	4	196	505	59	124	14	5	3	43	54-0	3	61	.246	.321	.311	70	-22	11-5	.975	7	115	69	O164(13/138/13)	0	-2.1

McGhee, Bill William Mac "Fibber"; B9.5.1905 Shawmut AL; D3.10.1984 Decatur GA; BL/TL/5´10.5˝/185; d7.5

YEAR	TM LG	G	AB	R	H	2B	3B	HR	RBI	BB-IB	HP	SO	AVG	OBP	SLG	AOPS	ABR	SB-CS	FA	FR	RNG	THR	GAMES AT POSITION	DL	BFW
1944	Phi A	77	287	27	83	12	0	1	19	21	0	20	.289	.338	.341	96	-2	2-1	.989	-1	95	82	1b75	0	-0.7
1945	Phi A	93	250	24	63	6	1	0	19	24	1	16	.252	.320	.284	76	-7	3-2	.989	-3	86	47	O48(40/0/9),1b8	0	-1.5
Total	2	170	537	51	146	18	1	1	38	45	1	36	.272	.329	.315	87	-9	5-3	.990	-4	98	85	1b83,O48(40/0/9)	0	-2.2

McGilvray, Bill William Alexander "Big Bill"; B4.29.1883 Portland OR; D5.23.1952 Denver CO; BL/TL/6´0˝/160; d4.17; Col Stanford

YEAR	TM LG	G	AB	R	H	2B	3B	HR	RBI	BB-IB	HP	SO	AVG	OBP	SLG	AOPS	ABR	SB-CS	FA	FR	RNG	THR	GAMES AT POSITION	DL	BFW
1908	Cin N	2	2	0	0	0	0	0	0	0	0	—	.000	.000	.000	-99	0	0	ø	0	—	—	/H	—	-0.1

McGinley, Tim Timothy S.; B1854 Philadelphia PA; D11.2.1899 Oakland CA; 5´9.5˝/155; d4.21

YEAR	TM LG	G	AB	R	H	2B	3B	HR	RBI	BB-IB	HP	SO	AVG	OBP	SLG	AOPS	ABR	SB-CS	FA	FR	RNG	THR	GAMES AT POSITION	DL	BFW
1875	Cen NA	13	52	5	12	0	1	0	5	0	—	4	.231	.231	.269	80	-1	0-0	.646	-6	—	—	C12,O2R	—	-0.6
	NH NA	32	131	13	36	3	1	0	10	0	—	7	.275	.275	.313	119	3	1-1	.807	-7	—	—	C32,3b2	—	-0.3
	Year	45	183	18	48	3	2	0	15	0	—	11	.262	.262	.301	107	2	1-1	.762	-13	—	—	C44,O2R,3b2	—	-0.9
1876	Bos N	9	40	5	6	0	0	0	2	0	—	1	.150	.150	.150	0	-4	—	.600	-4	0	0	O6C,C3	—	-0.7

McGinn, Frank Frank J.; B1869 Cincinnati OH; D11.19.1897 Cincinnati OH; d6.9

YEAR	TM LG	G	AB	R	H	2B	3B	HR	RBI	BB-IB	HP	SO	AVG	OBP	SLG	AOPS	ABR	SB-CS	FA	FR	RNG	THR	GAMES AT POSITION	DL	BFW
1890	Pit N	1	4	0	0	0	0	0	0	0	0	2	.000	.000	.000	-99	-1	0	1.000	-0	0	0	/cf	—	-0.1

McGinnis, Russ Russell Brent; B6.18.1963 Coffeyville KS; BR/TR/6´3˝/225; [MilA85 14/341]; d6.3; Col Oklahoma

YEAR	TM LG	G	AB	R	H	2B	3B	HR	RBI	BB-IB	HP	SO	AVG	OBP	SLG	AOPS	ABR	SB-CS	FA	FR	RNG	THR	GAMES AT POSITION	DL	BFW
1992	Tex A	14	33	2	8	4	0	0	4	3-0	0	7	.242	.306	.364	89	0	0-0	1.000	-3	76	75	C10,1b2,3b2	0	-0.3
1995	KC A	3	5	1	0	0	0	0	0	1-0	0	1	.000	.167	.000	-51	-1	0-0	1.000	-1	0	0	/13lf	0	-0.2
Total	2	17	38	3	8	4	0	0	4	4-0	0	8	.211	.286	.316	68	-1	0-0	1.000	-4	76	75	C10,3b3,1b3/lf	0	-0.5

McGlone, John John T.; B1864 Brooklyn NY; D11.22.1927 Brooklyn NY; TR/5´10˝/165; d10.7

YEAR	TM LG	G	AB	R	H	2B	3B	HR	RBI	BB-IB	HP	SO	AVG	OBP	SLG	AOPS	ABR	SB-CS	FA	FR	RNG	THR	GAMES AT POSITION	DL	BFW
1886	Was N	4	15	2	1	0	0	0	1	0	—	3	.067	.067	.067	-64	-3	0	.846	-1	55	0	3b4	—	-0.4
1887	Cle AA	21	79	14	20	2	1	0	10	7	3	—	.253	.337	.304	82	-2	15	.854	1	90	75	3b21	—	-0.1
1888	Cle AA	55	203	22	37	1	3	1	22	16	2	—	.182	.249	.232	56	-10	26	.787	-6	89	65	3b48,O7C	—	-1.4
Total	3	80	297	38	58	3	4	1	33	23	5	3	.195	.265	.242	58	-15	41	.810	-7	88	65	3b73,O7C	—	-1.9

McGovern, Art Arthur John; B2.27.1882 St.John NB, Can.; D11.14.1915 Danvers MA; BR/TR/5´10˝/160; d4.21

YEAR	TM LG	G	AB	R	H	2B	3B	HR	RBI	BB-IB	HP	SO	AVG	OBP	SLG	AOPS	ABR	SB-CS	FA	FR	RNG	THR	GAMES AT POSITION	DL	BFW
1905	Bos A	15	44	1	5	1	0	0	1	4	1	—	.114	.204	.136	9	-4	0	.951	-2	*120*	*61*	C15	—	-0.6

McGowan, Beauty Frank Bernard; B11.8.1901 Branford CT; D5.6.1982 Hamden CT; BL/TR/5´11˝/190; d4.12

YEAR	TM LG	G	AB	R	H	2B	3B	HR	RBI	BB-IB	HP	SO	AVG	OBP	SLG	AOPS	ABR	SB-CS	FA	FR	RNG	THR	GAMES AT POSITION	DL	BFW
1922	Phi A	99	300	36	69	10	5	1	20	40	1	46	.230	.323	.307	63	-16	6-5	.965	6	108	145	O82(0/56/28)	—	-1.5
1923	Phi A	95	287	41	73	9	1	1	19	36	1	25	.254	.340	.303	69	-12	4-3	.971	2	99	132	O79(26/17/36)	—	-1.5
1928	StL A	47	168	35	61	13	4	2	18	16	2	15	.363	.425	.524	143	11	2-1	.962	-1	105	61	O47(0/11/37)	—	0.6
1929	StL A	125	441	62	112	26	6	2	51	61	1	34	.254	.346	.354	78	-13	5-2	.975	2	97	124	O117(0/34/84)	—	-1.9
1937	Bos N	9	12	0	1	0	0	0	0	1	0	2	.083	.154	.083	-37	-2	0	1.000	-0	89	0	O2R	—	-0.3
Total	5	375	1208	174	316	58	16	6	108	154	5	122	.262	.347	.351	80	-32	17-11	.970	9	101	122	O327(26/118/187)	—	-4.6

McGraw, John John Joseph "Mugsy","Little Napoleon"; B4.7.1873 Truxton NY; D2.25.1934 New Rochelle NY; BL/TR/5´7˝/155; d8.26; M33; HF1937

YEAR	TM LG	G	AB	R	H	2B	3B	HR	RBI	BB-IB	HP	SO	AVG	OBP	SLG	AOPS	ABR	SB-CS	FA	FR	RNG	THR	GAMES AT POSITION	DL	BFW
1891	Bal AA	33	115	17	31	3	5	0	14	12	4	17	.270	.359	.383	111	1	4	.811	-12	70	98	S21,O9R,2b3	—	-0.8
1892	Bal N	79	286	41	77	13	2	1	26	32	6	21	.269	.355	.339	107	4	15	.897	3	151	86	O34(8/6/20),2b34,S8,3b3	—	0.6
1893	Bal N	127	480	123	154	9	10	5	64	101	16	11	.321	.454	.412	129	28	38	.894	-17	90	82	S117,O11(10/0/1)	—	1.3
1894	†Bal N	124	512	156	174	18	14	1	92	91	13	12	.340	.451	.436	110	13	78	.892	1	107	98	3b118,2b6	—	1.2
1895	†Bal N	96	388	110	143	13	6	2	48	60	5	9	.369	.459	.448	131	22	61	.878	8	119	**148**	3b95/2	—	2.5
1896	†Bal N	23	77	20	25	2	2	0	14	11	2	4	.325	.422	.403	116	2	13	.833	-2	97	157	3b18/1	—	0.0
1897	†Bal N	106	391	90	127	15	3	0	48	99	9	—	.325	**.471**	.379	126	25	44	.886	-12	91	**134**	3b105	—	1.3
1898	Bal N	143	515	**143**	176	8	10	0	53	**112**	19	—	.342	.475	.396	148	44	43	.900	-8	97	96	3b137,O3C	—	3.5
1899	Bal N	117	399	**140**	156	13	3	1	33	**124**	14	—	.391	**.547**	.446	165	53	73	.945	1	102	85	3b117,M	—	4.9
1900	StL N	99	334	84	115	10	4	2	33	85	23	—	.344	**.505**	.416	157	38	29	.909	-6	97	58	3b99	—	3.1
1901	Bal A	73	232	71	81	14	9	0	28	61	**14**	—	.349	.508	.487	169	29	24	.890	-14	78	56	3b69,M	—	1.5
1902	Bal A	20	63	14	18	3	2	1	3	17	2	—	.286	.451	.444	143	5	5	.864	-5	63	202	3b19,M	—	0.0
	NY N	35	107	13	25	0	0	0	5	26	4	—	.234	.401	.234	98	3	7	.926	-2	99	96	S34,M	—	0.2
1903	NY N	12	11	2	3	0	0	0	1	1	3	—	.273	.467	.273	109	1	1	ø	-1	0	0	2b2,O2L/S3M	—	-0.1
1904	NY N	5	12	0	4	0	0	0	0	3	0	—	.333	.467	.333	142	1	0	.947	2	129	381	2b2,S2,M	—	0.3
1905	NY N	3	0	0	0	0	0	0	0	0	0	—	ø	ø	ø	ø	0	1	ø	-0	0	0	/lfM	—	0.0
1906	NY N	4	2	0	0	0	0	0	0	1	0	—	.000	.333	.000	4	0	0	ø	-0	0	0	/3M	—	0.0
Total	16	1099	3924	1024	1309	121	70	13	462	836	134	74	.334	.466	.410	135	269	436	.898	-65	99	102	3b782,S183,O60(21/9/30),2b48/1	—	19.5

McGriff, Fred Frederick Stanley "Crime Dog"; B10.31.1963 Tampa FL; BL/TL/6´3˝/(200–225); [NYA81 9/233]; d5.17

YEAR	TM LG	G	AB	R	H	2B	3B	HR	RBI	BB-IB	HP	SO	AVG	OBP	SLG	AOPS	ABR	SB-CS	FA	FR	RNG	THR	GAMES AT POSITION	DL	BFW
1986	Tor A	3	5	1	1	0	0	0	0	0-0	0	2	.200	.200	.200	9	-1	0-0	1.000	-0	0	0	/1D	0	-0.1
1987	Tor A	107	295	58	73	16	0	20	43	60-4	1	104	.247	.376	.505	128	14	3-2	.983	-1	84	56	D90,1b14	0	0.9
1988	Tor A	154	536	100	151	35	4	34	82	79-3	4	149	.282	.376	.552	156	41	6-1	**.997**	-3	90	113	1b153	0	2.9
1989	†Tor A	161	551	98	148	27	3	**36**	92	119-12	4	132	.269	.399	.525	**161**	**50**	7-4	.989	2	109	109	1b159,D2	0	4.0
1990	Tor A	153	557	91	167	21	1	35	88	94-12	2	108	.300	.400	.530	155	44	5-3	.996	10	124	99	1b147,D6	0	4.3

YEAR	TM LG	G	AB	R	H	2B	3B	HR	RBI	BB-IB	HP	SO	AVG	OBP	SLG	AOPS	ABR	SB-CS	FA	FR	RNG	THR	GAMES AT POSITION	DL	BFW
1991	SD N	153	528	84	147	19	1	31	106	105-**26**	2	135	.278	.396	.494	145	36	4-1	.990	-10	79	113	1b153	0	1.6
1992	SD N★	152	531	79	152	30	4	**35**	104	96-23	1	108	.286	.394	.556	164	47	8-6	.991	-0	100	89	1b151	0	3.8
1993	SD N	83	302	52	83	11	1	18	46	42-4	1	55	.275	.361	.497	127	12	4-3	.983	-7	75	77	1b83	0	-0.3
	†Atl N	68	255	59	79	18	1	19	55	34-2	1	51	.310	.392	.612	160	22	1-0	.992	0	100	114	1b66	0	1.7
	Year	151	557	111	162	29	2	37	101	76-6	2	106	.291	.375	.549	142	34	5-3	.987	-7	86	94	1b149	0	1.4
1994	Atl N★	113	424	81	135	25	1	34	94	50-8	1	76	.318	.389	.623	153	33	7-3	.994	-3	86	86	1b112	0	2.0
1995	†Atl N★	**144**	528	85	148	27	1	27	93	65-6	5	99	.280	.361	.489	117	14	3-6	.996	3	101	100	1b144	0	0.2
1996	†Atl N★	159	617	81	182	37	1	28	107	68-12	2	116	.295	.365	.494	117	16	7-3	.992	8	115	102	1b158	0	1.0
1997	†Atl N	152	564	77	156	25	1	22	97	68-4	4	112	.277	.356	.441	107	6	5-0	.990	-2	95	111	1b149	0	-0.8
1998	TB A	151	564	73	160	33	0	19	81	79-9	2	118	.284	.371	.443	109	10	7-2	.995	-4	88	**123**	1b135,D14	0	-0.6
1999	TB A	144	529	75	164	30	1	32	104	86-11	1	107	.310	.405	.552	139	34	1-0	.989	6	121	**109**	1b125,D18	0	2.6
2000	TB A★	158	566	82	157	18	0	27	106	91-10	0	120	.277	.373	.452	110	10	2-0	.993	-7	83	108	1b144,D10	0	-0.9
2001	TB A	97	343	40	109	18	0	19	61	40-9	0	69	.318	.387	.536	143	22	1-1	.986	4	120	85	1b74,D17	0	1.7
	Chi N	49	170	27	48	7	2	12	41	26-4	3	37	.282	.383	.559	145	12	0-1	.990	-2	77	85	1b49	0	0.5
2002	Chi N	146	523	67	143	27	2	30	103	63-6	4	99	.273	.353	.505	123	17	1-2	.993	-9	67	76	1b137,D2	0	-0.4
2003	LA N	86	297	32	74	14	0	13	40	31-4	1	66	.249	.322	.428	96	-2	0-0	.989	-3	85	114	1b79	65	-1.2
2004	TB A	27	72	7	13	3	0	2	7	9-2	0	19	.181	.272	.306	51	-5	0-0	1.000	-0	79	98	D14,1b6	0	-0.7
Total	19	2460	8757	1349	2490	441	24	493	1550	1305-171	39	1882	.284	.377	.509	133	432	72-38	.992	-19	96	102	1b2239,D175	65	22.2
McGriff, Terry	Terence Roy; B9.23.1963 Fort Pierce FL; BR/TR/6´2˝/(190–200); [CinN81 8/197]; d7.11																								
1987	Cin N	34	89	6	20	3	0	2	11	8-0	0	17	.225	.289	.326	60	-5	0-0	.983	2	98	111	C33	0	-0.2
1988	Cin N	35	96	9	19	3	0	1	4	12-0	0	31	.198	.284	.260	56	-5	1-0	.990	0	74	141	C32	0	-0.3
1989	Cin N	6	11	1	3	0	0	0	2	2-1	0	3	.273	.385	.273	88	0	0-0	.929	0	63	86	C6	0	0.1
1990	Cin N	2	4	0	0	0	0	0	0	0-0	0	1	.000	.000	.000	-96	-1	0-0	1.000	0	23	535	/C	0	-0.1
	Hou N	4	5	0	0	0	0	0	0	0-0	0	0	.000	.000	.000	-99	-1	0-0	.900	-1	54	0	C4	0	-0.3
	Year	6	9	0	0	0	0	0	0	0-0	0	1	.000	.000	.000	-99	-2	0-0	.938	-1	43	193	C5	0	-0.4
1993	Fla N	3	7	0	0	0	0	0	0	1-0	0	2	.000	.125	.000	-60	-2	0-0	1.000	-0	0	0	C3	0	-0.2
1994	StL N	42	114	10	25	6	0	0	13	13-1	2	11	.219	.308	.272	53	-7	0-0	.991	2	79	131	C39	0	-0.3
Total	6	126	326	26	67	12	0	3	30	36-2	2	65	.206	.287	.270	51	-21	1-0	.985	3	79	126	C118	0	-1.3
McGrillis, Mark	Mark Anthony; B10.22.1872 Philadelphia PA; D5.16.1935 Philadelphia PA; 6´0˝/148; d9.17; Col Penn																								
1892	StL N	1	3	0	0	0	0	0	0	0	0	1	.000	.000	.000	-99	-1	0	1.000	0	131	0	/3	—	-0.1
McGuckin, Joe	Joseph W.; B3.13.1862 Paterson NJ; D12.31.1903 Yonkers NY; 5´8.5˝/160; d8.27																								
1890	Bal AA	11	37	2	4	0	0	0	2	6	1	—	.108	.250	.108	6	-4	3	.962	3	200	230	O11R	—	-0.1
McGuinness, John	John James; B1857 , Ireland; D12.19.1916 Binghamton NY; 5´10.5˝/150; d5.6																								
1876	NY N	1	4	0	0	0	0	0	0	0	—	0	.000	.000	.000	-99	-1	—	.500	-2	79	0	/2C	—	-0.2
1879	Syr N	12	51	7	15	1	1	0	4	0	—	6	.294	.294	.353	126	1	—	.928	-1	94	129	1b12	—	0.0
1884	Phi U	53	220	25	52	8	1	0	—	5	—	—	.236	.253	.282	67	-15	—	.959	-0	81	88	1b48,2b5/S	—	-1.8
Total	3	66	275	32	67	9	2	0	4	5	—	6	.244	.257	.291	75	-15	—	.954	-2	84	96	1b60,2b6/SC	—	-2.0
McGuire, Jim	James A.; B2.4.1875 Dunkirk NY; D1.26.1917 Buffalo NY; TR; d9.10																								
1901	Cle A	18	69	4	16	2	0	0	3	0	0	—	.232	.232	.261	38	-6	0	.913	0	93	134	S18	—	-0.5
McGuire, Deacon	James Thomas; B11.18.1863 Youngstown OH; D10.31.1936 Duck Lake MI; BR/TR/6´1˝/185; d6.21; M6/C6																								
1884	Tol AA	45	151	12	28	7	0	1	—	5	1	—	.185	.217	.252	50	-8	—	.906	-6	—	—	C41,O4(1/3/0),S3	—	-1.0
1885	Det N	34	121	11	23	4	2	0	9	5	—	23	.190	.222	.256	54	-6	—	.920	9	—	—	C31,O3L	—	0.5
1886	Phi N	50	167	25	33	7	1	2	18	19	—	25	.198	.280	.287	72	-5	2	.899	-5	—	—	C49/rf	—	-0.6
1887	Phi N	41	150	22	46	6	6	2	23	11	2	8	.307	.362	.467	121	4	3	.884	-1	—	—	C41	—	0.5
1888	Phi N	12	51	7	17	4	2	0	11	4	0	9	.333	.382	.490	167	4	0	.800	-5	—	—	C10,3b2	—	0.0
	Det N	3	13	0	0	0	0	0	0	0	0	4	.000	.000	.000	-99	-3	0	.810	-2	—	—	C3	—	-0.5
	Year	15	64	7	17	4	2	0	11	4	0	13	.266	.309	.391	116	1	0	.802	-7	—	—	C13,3b2	—	-0.5
	Cle AA	26	94	15	24	1	3	1	13	7	4	—	.255	.333	.362	126	3	2	.891	-1	—	—	C17,1b6,O3R	—	0.2
1890	Roc AA	87	331	46	99	16	4	4	53	21	8	—	.299	.356	.408	135	14	8	.938	11	*115*	*86*	C71,1b15,O3(0/1/2)/P	—	2.6
1891	Was AA	114	413	55	125	22	10	3	66	43	10	34	.303	.382	.426	138	21	10	.911	-13	*87*	*111*	C98,O18R,3b3/1	—	1.3
1892	Was N	97	315	46	73	14	4	4	43	61	2	49	.232	.360	.340	115	9	7	.936	-15	*67*	*103*	C89,1b8/rf	—	0.2
1893	Was N	63	237	29	61	14	3	1	26	26	3	12	.257	.338	.354	86	-4	3	.889	-9	*78*	*98*	C50,1b12	—	-0.7
1894	Was N	104	425	67	130	18	6	6	78	33	7	19	.306	.366	.419	91	-6	11	.918	-17	*71*	*110*	C104	—	-1.1
1895	Was N	**133**	538	89	181	30	8	10	97	40	5	18	.336	.388	.478	124	18	17	.937	-1	*78*	***142***	C133/S	—	2.3
1896	Was N	108	389	60	125	25	3	2	70	30	6	14	.321	.379	.416	109	6	12	.936	-6	*87*	*92*	C98/1	—	0.8
1897	Was N	93	327	51	112	17	7	4	53	21	2	—	.343	.386	.474	127	12	9	.947	-1	*80*	*123*	C73,1b6	—	1.5
1898	Was N	131	489	59	131	18	3	1	57	24	6	—	.268	.310	.323	82	-12	10	.967	-8	*65*	*103*	C93,1b37,M	—	-1.2
1899	Was N	59	199	25	54	3	1	1	12	16	3	—	.271	.335	.312	79	-6	3	.973	-8	*77*	*110*	C56/1	—	-0.8
	Bro N	46	157	22	50	12	4	0	23	12	5	—	.318	.385	.446	125	6	4	.971	2	*92*	*107*	C46	—	1.0
	Year	105	356	47	104	15	5	1	35	28	8	—	.292	.357	.371	99	0	7	.972	-6	*84*	*109*	C102/1	—	0.2
1900	†Bro N	71	241	20	69	15	2	0	34	19	4	—	.286	.348	.365	91	-2	2	.952	-5	*93*	*97*	C69	—	-0.1
1901	Bro N	85	301	28	89	16	4	0	40	18	3	—	.296	.342	.375	105	2	4	.960	-9	*79*	*96*	C81,1b3	—	0.1
1902	Det A	73	229	27	52	14	1	2	23	24	0	—	.227	.300	.323	71	-8	0	.952	-6	*82*	*88*	C70	—	-0.8
1903	Det A	72	248	15	62	12	1	0	21	19	1	—	.250	.306	.306	87	-3	3	.960	-8	*77*	*96*	C69/1	—	-0.5
1904	NY A	101	322	17	67	12	2	0	20	27	3	—	.208	.276	.258	66	-11	2	.970	6	*95*	*108*	C97/1	—	0.5
1905	NY A	72	228	9	50	7	2	0	33	18	5	—	.219	.291	.268	69	-7	3	.975	-3	*114*	*85*	C71	—	-0.3
1906	NY A	51	144	11	43	5	0	0	14	12	3	—	.299	.365	.333	108	2	3	.966	0	*108*	*75*	C49/1	—	0.7
1907	NY A	1	1	0	0	0	0	0	0	0	0	—	.000	.000	.000	-93	0	0	1.000	0	*0*	*255*	/C	—	0.0
	Bos A	6	4	1	3	0	0	1	1	0	0	—	.750	.750	1.500	620	2	0	ø	0	—	—	/HM	—	0.2
	Year	7	5	1	3	0	0	1	1	0	0	—	.600	.600	1.200	470	2	0	1.000	0	*0*	*255*	/C	—	0.2
1908	Bos A	1	1	0	0	0	0	0	0	0	0	—	.000	.000	.000	-97	0	0	ø	0	—	—	/HM	—	0.0
	Cle A	1	4	0	1	1	0	0	2	0	0	—	.250	.250	.500	142	0	0	1.000	-0	0	0	/1	—	0.0
	Year	2	5	0	1	1	0	0	2	0	0	—	.200	.200	.400	93	0	0	1.000	-0	0	0	/1	—	0.0
1910	Cle A	1	3	0	1	0	0	0	0	0	1	—	.333	.500	.333	159	0	0	1.000	-1	*53*	*118*	/CM	—	0.0
1912	Det A	1	2	1	1	0	0	0	0	0	0	—	.500	.500	.500	192	0	0	.714	-0	*129*	*194*	/C	—	0.0
Total	26	1782	6295	770	1750	300	79	45	840	515	84	215	.278	.341	.372	101	22	118	.938	-101	*85*	*104*	C1612,1b94,O33(4/4/25),3b5,S4/P	—	4.8
McGuire, Mickey	M C Adolphus; B1.18.1941 Dayton OH; BR/TR/5´10˝/170; d9.7																								
1962	Bal A	6	4	0	0	0	0	0	0	0-0	0	0	.000	.000	.000	-99	-1	0-0	1.000	-1	51	0	S5	0	-0.2
1967	Bal A	10	17	2	4	0	0	0	2	0-0	0	2	.235	.235	.235	40	-1	0-0	1.000	-3	36	0	2b4	0	-0.5
Total	2	16	21	2	4	0	0	0	2	0-0	0	2	.190	.190	.190	11	-2	0-0	1.000	-4	51	0	S5,2b4	0	-0.7
McGuire, Ryan	Ryan Byron; B11.23.1971 Bellflower CA; BL/TL/6´2˝/(200–215); [BosA93 3/79]; d6.5; Col UCLA																								
1997	Mon N	84	199	22	51	15	2	3	17	19-1	0	34	.256	.320	.397	88	-4	1-4	.960	2	109	126	O44(21/2/22),1b30,D3	0	-0.6
1998	Mon N	130	210	17	39	9	0	1	10	32-0	0	55	.186	.292	.243	44	-17	0-0	.980	-2	101	66	1b78,O46(33/7/8)	0	-2.2
1999	Mon N	88	140	17	31	7	2	2	18	27-0	0	33	.221	.347	.343	79	-4	1-1	.997	8	165	71	1b58,O23(16/1/7)	0	0.1
2000	NY N	1	2	0	0	0	0	0	0	1-0	0	0	.000	.333	.000	-6	0	0-0	1.000	0	215	0	/rf	0	0.0
2001	Fla N	48	54	8	10	2	0	1	8	7-0	0	15	.185	.270	.278	46	-4	1-0	1.000	1	139	0	O9R,1b4	0	-0.4
2002	Bal A	17	26	0	2	1	0	0	2	2-0	0	7	.077	.143	.115	-32	-5	0-0	1.000	0	99	113	1b7/D	0	-0.5
Total	6	368	631	64	133	34	4	7	55	88-1	0	144	.211	.306	.311	63	-34	3-5	.992	10	124	84	1b177,O123(70/10/47),D4	0	-3.6
McGuire, Bill	William Patrick; B2.14.1964 Omaha NE; BR/TR/6´3˝/(195–215); [SeaA85 1/27]; d8.2; Col Nebraska																								
1988	Sea A	9	16	1	3	0	0	0	2	3-0	0	2	.188	.316	.188	43	-1	0-0	1.000	-3	69	54	C9	0	-0.3
1989	Sea A	14	28	2	5	0	0	1	4	2-0	0	6	.179	.233	.286	44	-2	0-0	1.000	2	119	63	C14	0	0.0
Total	2	23	44	3	8	0	0	1	6	5-0	0	8	.182	.265	.250	44	-3	0-0	1.000	-1	100	60	C23	0	-0.3
McGunnigle, Bill	William Henry "Gunner"; B1.1.1855 Boston MA; D3.9.1899 Brockton MA; BR/TR/5´9˝/155; d5.2; M5; ▲																								
1879	Buf N	47	171	22	30	0	1	0	5	5	—	24	.175	.199	.187	27	-13	—	.918	3	87	0	O34R,P14	—	-0.7
1880	Buf N	7	22	0	4	0	0	0	1	0	—	4	.182	.182	.182	23	-2	—	1.000	-2	54	0	P5,O3(1/1/1)	—	-0.2
	Wor N	1	4	0	0	0	0	0	0	0	—	2	.000	.000	.000	-92	-1	—	1.000	-0	0	0	/O(1/0/1)	—	-0.1

YEAR	TM LG	G	AB	R	H	2B	3B	HR	RBI	BB-IB	HP	SO	AVG	OBP	SLG	AOPS	ABR	SB-CS	FA	FR	RNG	THR	GAMES AT POSITION	DL	BFW
	Year	8	26	0	4	0	0	0	1	0	—	6	.154	.154	.154	5	-3	—	1.000	-2	54	0	P5,O4(2/1/2)	—	-0.3
1882	Cle N	1	5	2	1	0	0	0	0	0	—	1	.200	.200	.200	30	0	—	ø	-0	0	0	/cf	—	0.0
Total	3	56	202	24	35	0	1	0	6	5	—	31	.173	.193	.183	25	-16	—	.900	1	77	0	O39(2/2/36),P19	—	-1.0
McGwire, Mark	Mark David "Big Mac"; B10.1.1963 Pomona CA; BR/TR/6´5˝/(215–250); [OakA84 1/10]; d8.22; Col USC																								
1986	Oak A	18	53	10	10	1	0	3	9	4-0	1	18	.189	.259	.377	76	-2	0-1	.833	-4	78	40	3b16	0	-0.6
1987	Oak A★	151	557	97	161	28	4	**49**	118	71-8	5	131	.289	.370	**.618**	167	53	1-1	.992	-7	85	80	1b145,3b8,O3R	0	3.5
1988	†Oak A★	155	550	87	143	22	1	32	99	76-4	4	117	.260	.352	.478	135	26	0-0	.993	-10	78	97	1b154/rf	0	0.5
1989	†Oak A★	143	490	74	113	17	0	33	95	83-5	3	94	.231	.339	.467	131	21	1-1	.995	5	110	108	1b141,D2	15	1.6
1990	†Oak A★	156	523	87	123	16	0	39	108	**110**-9	7	116	.235	.370	.489	145	35	2-1	.997	-8	83	**108**	1b154,D2	0	1.6
1991	Oak A✳	154	483	62	97	22	0	22	75	93-3	3	116	.201	.330	.383	103	4	2-1	.997	-1	94	93	1b152	0	-0.7
1992	†Oak A★	139	467	87	125	22	0	42	104	90-12	5	105	.268	.385	**.585**	**178**	51	0-1	.995	-13	69	101	1b139	20	2.9
1993	Oak A	27	84	16	28	6	0	9	24	21-5	1	19	.333	.467	.726	229	17	0-1	1.000	-2	77	90	1b25	112	1.2
1994	Oak A	47	135	26	34	3	0	9	25	37-3	0	40	.252	.413	.474	139	10	0-0	.988	-3	74	89	1b40,D5	65	0.4
1995	Oak A✳	104	317	75	87	13	0	39	90	88-5	11	77	.274	.441	.685	199	51	1-1	.986	-1	98	85	1b91,D10	36	3.8
1996	Oak A★	130	423	104	132	21	0	**52**	113	116-16	8	112	.312	**.467**	**.730**	**199**	71	0-0	.990	-5	87	**125**	1b109,D18	22	5.0
1997	Oak A★	105	366	48	104	24	0	34	81	58-8	4	98	.284	.383	.628	160	33	1-0	.994	-3	90	94	1b101	0	2.0
	StL N	51	174	38	44	3	0	24	42	43-8	5	61	.253	.411	.684	181	22	2-0	.998	-1	88	101	1b50	0	1.6
1998	StL N★	155	509	130	152	21	0	**70**	147	**162**-28	6	155	.299	**.470**	**.752**	**217**	**96**	1-0	.992	-9	87	101	1b151	0	**7.1**
1999	StL N★	153	521	118	145	21	1	**65**	**147**	133-**21**	2	141	.278	.424	.697	**175**	63	0-0	.990	-6	89	97	1b151	0	4.1
2000	†StL N✳	89	236	60	72	8	0	32	73	76-12	7	78	.305	.483	.746	201	41	1-0	.998	-9	49	93	1b70	62	2.5
2001	†StL N	97	299	48	56	4	0	29	64	56-3	3	118	.187	.316	.492	104	0	0-0	.994	-8	62	95	1b90	42	-1.5
Total	16	1874	6187	1167	1626	252	6	583	1414	1317-150	75	1596	.263	.394	.588	163	592	12-8	.993	-83	85	98	1b1763,D37,3b24,O4R	374	35.0
McHale, Jim	James Bernard "J.B."; B12.17.1875 Miners Mills PA; D6.17.1959 Los Angeles CA; BR/TR/5´11˝/165; d4.14; Col St. Marys (CA)																								
1908	Bos A	21	67	9	15	2	2	0	7	4	1	—	.224	.278	.313	90	-1	4	.970	-1	104	0	O19(1/18/0)	—	-0.3
McHale, John	John Joseph; B9.21.1921 Detroit MI; BL/TR/6´0˝/200; d5.28; Mil 1943; Col Notre Dame																								
1943	Det A	4	3	0	0	0	0	0	0	1	0	1	.000	.250	.000	-23	0	0-0	ø	0	—	—	/H	0	0.0
1944	Det A	1	1	0	0	0	0	0	0	0	0	0	.000	.000	.000	-95	0	0-0	ø	0	—	—	/H	0	0.0
1945	†Det A	19	14	0	2	0	0	0	1	1	1	4	.143	.250	.143	14	-1	0-0	1.000	0	302	0	1b3	0	-0.1
1947	Det A	39	95	10	20	1	0	3	11	7	0	24	.211	.265	.316	59	-6	1-1	.995	-1	82	64	1b25	0	-0.8
1948	Det A	1	1	0	0	0	0	0	0	0	0	0	.000	.000	.000	-97	0	0-0	ø	0	—	—	/H	0	0.0
Total	5	64	114	10	22	1	0	3	12	9	1	29	.193	.258	.281	49	-7	1-1	.995	-0	87	63	1b28	0	-0.9
McHale, Bob	Robert Emmet "Rabbit"; B2.25.1872 Michigan Bluff CA; D6.9.1952 Sacramento CA; TR/5´11˝/152; d5.9																								
1898	Was N	11	33	5	6	2	0	0	7	1	3	—	.182	.270	.242	47	-2	1	.900	-1	0	0	O9C/S1	—	-0.3
McHenry, Austin	Austin Bush "Mac"; B9.22.1895 Wrightsville OH; D11.27.1922 Jefferson Twp. OH; BR/TR/5´11˝/152; d6.22																								
1918	StL N	80	272	32	71	12	6	1	29	21	2	24	.261	.319	.360	111	3	8	.952	1	89	159	O80L	—	0.0
1919	StL N	110	371	41	106	19	11	1	47	19	1	57	.286	.322	.404	125	10	7	.985	4	93	**164**	O103(73/26/7)	—	1.0
1920	StL N	137	504	66	142	19	11	10	65	25	0	73	.282	.316	.423	115	7	8-11	.952	4	102	129	O133(89/52/0)	—	0.2
1921	StL N	152	574	92	201	37	8	17	102	38	2	48	.350	.393	.531	145	37	10-20	.965	5	114	70	O152(146/0/6)	—	2.5
1922	StL N	64	238	31	72	18	3	5	43	14	1	27	.303	.344	.466	112	4	2-2	.935	5	104	171	O61L	—	0.3
Total	5	543	1959	262	592	105	39	34	286	117	6	229	.302	.343	.448	126	61	35-33	.960	19	102	128	O529(449/78/13)	—	4.0
McHenry, Vance	Vance Loren; B7.10.1956 Chico CA; BR/TR/5´9˝/165; [SeaA78 11/266]; d8.13; Col Nevada–Las Vegas																								
1981	Sea A	15	18	3	4	0	0	0	2	1-0	0	1	.222	.263	.222	39	-1	0-0	.893	-2	90	137	S13/D	0	-0.3
1982	Sea A	3	1	0	0	0	0	0	0	0-0	0	0	.000	.000	.000	-97	0	0-0	.500	-0	0	0	/SD	0	0.0
Total	2	18	19	3	4	0	0	0	2	1-0	0	1	.211	.250	.211	32	-1	0-0	.867	-2	88	135	S14,D2	0	-0.3
McIlveen, Irish	Henry Cooke; B7.27.1880 Belfast, Ireland; D10.18.1960 Lorain OH; BL/TL/5´11.5˝/180; d7.4; Col Penn St.																								
1906	Pit N	5	5	1	2	0	0	0	0	0	0	—	.400	.400	.400	143	0	0	1.000	0	100	0	P2	—	0.0
1908	NY A	44	169	17	36	3	3	0	8	14	1	—	.213	.277	.266	76	-5	6	.949	-1	77	0	O44(13/1/30)	—	-0.8
1909	NY A	4	3	0	0	0	0	0	0	1	0	—	.000	.250	.000	-20	0	0	ø	0	—	—	/H	—	0.0
Total	3	53	177	18	38	3	3	0	8	15	1	—	.215	.280	.266	76	-5	6	.949	-0	77	0	O44(13/1/30),P2	—	-0.8
McInnis, Stuffy	John Phalen "Jack"; B9.19.1890 Gloucester MA; D2.16.1960 Ipswich MA; BR/TR/5´9.5˝/162; d4.12; Mil 1918; M1																								
1909	Phi A	19	46	4	11	0	0	1	4	2	1	—	.239	.286	.304	85	-1	0	.886	-1	92	111	S14	—	-0.2
1910	Phi A	38	73	10	22	2	4	0	12	7	0	—	.301	.363	.438	152	4	3	.927	-4	83	80	S17,2b5,3b4/lf	—	0.1
1911	†Phi A	126	468	76	150	20	10	3	77	25	5	—	.321	.361	.425	121	11	23	.982	-15	85	122	1b97,S24	—	-0.4
1912	Phi A	**153**	568	83	186	25	13	3	101	49	3	—	.327	.384	.433	138	28	27	.984	3	110	**121**	1b153	—	2.7
1913	†Phi A	148	543	79	176	30	4	4	90	45	6	31	.324	.382	.416	137	26	16	**.992**	-1	89	110	1b148	—	2.2
1914	†Phi A	149	576	74	181	12	8	1	95	19	4	27	.314	.341	.368	118	8	25-19	**.995**	0	90	109	1b149	—	0.4
1915	Phi A	119	456	44	143	14	4	0	49	14	2	17	.314	.337	.362	113	4	8-8	.989	6	**116**	81	1b119	—	0.6
1916	Phi A	140	512	42	151	25	3	1	60	25	3	19	.295	.331	.361	114	6	7	.992	7	115	93	1b140	—	1.1
1917	Phi A	150	567	50	172	19	4	0	44	33	0	19	.303	.342	.351	113	7	18	.993	2	99	86	1b150	—	0.5
1918	†Bos A	117	423	40	115	11	5	0	56	19	2	10	.272	.306	.322	91	-7	10	**.992**	5	114	88	1b94,3b23	—	-0.4
1919	Bos A	120	440	32	134	12	5	1	58	23	1	11	.305	.341	.361	103	0	8	.995	3	104	**133**	1b118	—	0.0
1920	Bos A	148	559	50	166	21	3	2	71	18	2	19	.297	.321	.356	83	-16	6-11	**.996**	-2	92	118	1b148	—	-2.3
1921	Bos A	152	584	72	179	31	10	0	76	21	4	9	.307	.335	.394	88	-13	2-4	**.999**	4	103	109	1b152	—	-1.8
1922	Cle A	142	537	58	164	28	7	1	78	15	1	5	.305	.325	.389	85	-14	1-5	**.997**	-5	81	94	1b140	—	-2.8
1923	Bos N	154	607	70	191	23	9	2	95	26	0	12	.315	.343	.392	97	-4	7-8	.991	4	112	107	1b154	—	-1.1
1924	Bos N	146	581	57	169	23	7	1	59	15	2	6	.291	.311	.360	83	-16	9-3	.994	7	**118**	101	1b146	—	-1.8
1925	†Pit N	59	155	19	57	10	4	0	24	17	2	1	.368	.437	.484	126	7	1-1	.993	1	111	127	1b46	—	0.5
1926	Pit N	47	127	12	38	6	1	0	13	7	0	3	.299	.336	.362	83	-3	1	.988	-1	94	126	1b40	—	-0.6
1927	Phi N	1	0	0	0	0	0	0	0	0	0	0	ø	ø	ø	ø	0	0	1.000	-0	0	0	/1M	—	0.0
Total	19	2128	7822	872	2405	312	101	20	1062	380	38	189	.307	.343	.381	106	27	172-59	.993	15	102	106	1b1995,S55,3b27,2b5/lf	—	-3.3
McIntosh, Tim	Timothy Allen; B3.21.1965 Minneapolis MN; BR/TR/5´11˝/195; [MilA86 3/61]; d9.3; Col Minnesota																								
1990	Mil A	5	5	1	1	0	0	1	1	0-0	0	2	.200	.200	.800	168	0	0-0	.875	-1	107	0	C4	0	-0.1
1991	Mil A	7	11	2	4	1	0	1	1	0-0	0	4	.364	.364	.727	198	1	0-0	ø	-0	0	0	O4L/1D	0	0.1
1992	Mil A	35	77	7	14	3	0	0	6	3-0	2	9	.182	.229	.221	28	-8	1-3	.983	1	60	65	C14,O10(9/0/1),1b7,D3	15	-0.7
1993	Mil A	1	0	0	0	0	0	0	0	0-0	0	0	ø	ø	ø	ø	0	0-0	ø	-0	0	0	/C	0	0.0
	Mon N	20	21	2	2	1	0	0	2	0-0	0	7	.095	.095	.143	-36	-4	0-0	1.000	-0	72	0	O7(2/0/6),C5	0	-0.4
1996	NY A	3	3	0	0	0	0	0	0	0-0	0	0	.000	.000	.000	-99	-1	0-0	ø	-0	0	0	/C13	0	-0.1
Total	5	71	117	12	21	5	0	2	10	3-0	2	22	.179	.211	.274	34	-12	1-3	.973	-1	60	48	C25,O21(15/0/7),1b9,D5/3	15	-1.2
McIntyre, Matty	Matthew Martin; B6.12.1880 Stonington CT; D4.2.1920 Detroit MI; BL/TL/5´11˝/175; d7.3																								
1901	Phi A	82	308	38	85	12	4	0	46	30	3	—	.276	.346	.341	87	-5	11	.921	-4	72	0	O82L	—	-1.2
1904	Det A	152	578	74	146	11	10	2	46	44	4	—	.253	.310	.317	101	1	11	.959	12	94	85	O152(151/0/1)	—	0.5
1905	Det A	131	495	59	130	21	5	0	30	48	2	—	.263	.330	.325	107	5	9	.968	18	126	172	O131L	—	1.7
1906	Det A	133	493	63	128	19	11	0	39	56	2	—	.260	.338	.343	110	7	29	.982	12	147	198	O133(132/1/0)	—	1.3
1907	Det A	20	81	6	23	1	1	0	9	7	0	—	.284	.341	.321	107	1	3	1.000	3	119	170	O20L	—	0.3
1908	†Det A	151	569	**105**	168	24	13	0	28	83	7	—	.295	.392	.383	146	33	20	**.977**	16	97	81	O151L	—	4.6
1909	†Det A	125	476	65	116	18	9	1	34	54	3	—	.244	.325	.326	101	2	13	.975	-1	87	29	O122(119/3/0)	—	-0.7
1910	Det A	83	305	40	72	15	5	0	25	39	0	—	.236	.323	.318	94	-1	4	.946	2	103	110	O77(58/17/2)	—	-0.4
1911	Chi A	146	569	102	184	19	11	1	52	64	5	—	.323	.397	.401	127	22	17	.948	-3	105	76	O146(0/31/115)	—	1.1
1912	Chi A	49	84	10	14	0	0	0	10	14	2	—	.167	.300	.167	36	-6	3	1.000	-0	100	71	O25(14/1/10)	—	-0.8
Total	10	1072	3958	562	1066	140	69	4	319	439	28	—	.269	.346	.343	110	59	120	.964	56	105	98	O1039(858/53/128)	—	6.4
McIvor, Otto	Edward Otto; B7.26.1884 Greenville TX; D5.4.1954 Dallas TX; BB/TL/5´11.5˝/175; d4.18																								
1911	StL N	30	62	11	14	2	1	1	9	9	1	14	.226	.333	.339	91	-1	0	.926	-1	93	54	O17(3/6/8)	—	-0.3

YEAR	TM LG	G	AB	R	H	2B	3B	HR	RBI	BB-IB	HP	SO	AVG	OBP	SLG	AOPS	ABR	SB-CS	FA	FR	RNG	THR	GAMES AT POSITION	DL	BFW
McKay, Cody	Cody Dean; B1.11.1974 Vancouver BC, Can.; BL/TR/6´0˝/(210–212); [OakA96 9/255]; d9.22; f–Dave; Col Arizona St.																								
2002	Oak A	2	3	0	2	0	0	0	2	0-0	0	1	.667	.500	.667	258	1	0-0	1.000	0	0	0	/C	0	0.1
2004	StL N	35	74	7	17	2	0	0	6	2-0	2	14	.230	.269	.257	37	-7	0-0	1.000	-2	131	164	C18,3b7/1P	0	-0.8
Total	2	37	77	7	19	2	0	0	8	2-0	2	15	.247	.280	.273	45	-6	0-0	1.000	-2	124	155	C19,3b7/P1	0	-0.7
McKay, Dave	David Lawrence; B3.14.1950 Vancouver BC, Can.; BB/TR (BR 1975–76, 77p)/6´1˝/(190–195); d8.22; C23; s–Cody; Col Creighton																								
1975	Min A	33	125	8	32	4	1	2	16	6-0	1	14	.256	.291	.352	81	-4	1-1	.923	1	95	172	3b33	0	-0.3
1976	Min A	45	138	8	28	2	0	0	8	9-0	4	27	.203	.272	.217	44	-10	1-2	.911	-1	101	186	3b41,S2/D	0	-1.2
1977	Tor A	95	274	18	54	4	3	3	22	7-0	2	51	.197	.222	.266	32	-27	2-1	.968	-4	97	81	2b40,3b32,S20,D2	0	-2.8
1978	Tor A	145	504	59	120	20	8	7	45	20-2	1	91	.238	.268	.351	71	-21	4-4	.984	-2	98	96	2b140,S3,3b2/D	0	-1.7
1979	Tor A	47	156	19	34	9	0	0	12	7-0	1	19	.218	.256	.276	43	-12	1-1	.974	7	109	107	2b46,3b2	0	-0.3
1980	Oak A	123	295	29	72	16	1	1	29	10-0	6	57	.244	.283	.315	68	-13	1-1	.977	-8	91	72	2b62,3b54,S10	0	-1.9
1981	†Oak A	79	224	25	59	11	1	4	21	16-0	2	43	.263	.313	.375	103	1	4-1	.926	-4	93	52	3b43,2b38,S7	0	-0.2
1982	Oak A	78	212	25	42	4	1	4	17	11-0	0	35	.198	.235	.283	44	-17	6-1	.968	-9	88	68	2b59,3b16,S3	0	-2.3
Total	8	645	1928	191	441	70	15	21	170	86-2	17	337	.229	.266	.313	62	-103	20-12	.976	-20	97	89	2b385,3b223,S45,D4	0	-10.7
McKean, Ed	Edwin John "Mack"; B6.6.1864 Grafton OH; D8.16.1919 Cleveland OH; BR/TR/5´9˝/160; d4.16																								
1887	Cle AA	132	539	97	154	16	13	2	54	60	1	—	.286	.358	.375	108	7	76	.847	-5	95	87	S123,2b8,O4L	—	0.4
1888	Cle AA	131	548	94	164	21	15	6	68	28	6	—	.299	.340	.425	149	28	52	.909	5	100	65	S78,O48(43/4/1),2b9/3	—	3.1
1889	Cle N	123	500	88	159	22	8	5	75	42	4	25	.318	.375	.424	124	16	35	.907	9	105	101	S122/2	—	2.5
1890	Cle N	**136**	530	95	157	15	14	7	61	87	6	25	.296	.401	.417	141	31	23	.903	-12	97	91	S134,2b3	—	2.0
1891	Cle N	**141**	603	115	170	13	12	6	69	64	1	19	.282	.352	.373	107	4	14	.887	-12	99	82	S141	—	-0.4
1892	†Cle N	129	531	76	139	14	10	0	93	49	1	29	.262	.325	.326	93	-5	19	.862	-44	85	72	S129	—	-4.0
1893	Cle N	125	545	103	169	29	24	4	133	50	4	14	.310	.372	.473	117	9	16	.902	-3	100	112	S125	—	1.0
1894	Cle N	**130**	554	116	198	30	15	8	128	49	2	12	.357	.412	.509	116	13	33	.905	-20	91	81	S130	—	0.0
1895	†Cle N	**132**	569	131	194	32	17	8	119	46	7	26	.341	.397	.499	123	17	13	.907	-20	93	86	S132	—	0.3
1896	†Cle N	133	571	100	193	29	12	7	112	45	2	9	.338	.388	.468	118	13	13	.915	-34	88	113	S133	—	-1.2
1897	Cle N	125	523	83	143	21	14	2	78	40	4	—	.273	.330	.379	82	-16	15	.920	-28	90	82	S125	—	-3.2
1898	Cle N	151	604	89	172	23	1	9	94	56	1	—	.285	.346	.371	107	6	11	.932	-31	86	84	S151	—	-1.6
1899	StL N	67	277	40	72	7	3	3	40	20	0	—	.260	.310	.339	76	-10	4	.886	-9	94	93	S42,1b15,2b10	—	-1.5
Total	13	1655	6894	1227	2084	272	158	67	1124	636	39	159	.302	.365	.417	114	113	324	.900	-205	94	89	S1565,O52(47/4/1),2b31,1b15/3	—	-2.6
McKechnie, Bill	William Boyd "Deacon"; B8.7.1886 Wilkinsburg PA; D10.29.1965 Bradenton FL; BB/TR/5´10˝/160; d9.8; M25/C7; HF1962																								
1907	Pit N	3	8	0	1	0	0	0	0	0	0	—	.125	.125	.125	-21	-1	0	1.000	-0	97	0	3b2/2	—	-0.1
1910	Pit N	71	212	23	46	1	2	0	12	11	0	23	.217	.256	.241	42	-16	4	.971	4	106	98	2b36,S14,3b8,1b4	—	-1.2
1911	Pit N	104	321	40	73	8	7	2	37	28	2	18	.227	.293	.315	68	-15	9	.975	-0	98	99	1b57,2b17,S12,3b6	—	-1.6
1912	Pit N	24	73	8	18	0	1	0	4	4	0	5	.247	.286	.274	54	-5	2	.978	-0	104	0	3b13,S4,2b3,1b2	—	-0.4
1913	Bos N	1	4	1	0	0	0	0	0	0	1	1	.000	.200	.000	-39	-1	0	1.000	-0	94	0	/cf	—	-0.1
	NY A	45	112	7	15	0	0	0	8	8	1	17	.134	.198	.134	-2	-15	2	.950	4	114	143	2b28,S7,3b2	—	-1.1
1914	Ind F	149	570	107	173	24	6	2	38	53	5	36	.304	.368	.377	93	-11	47	.939	23	**117**	122	3b149	—	1.6
1915	New F	127	451	49	113	22	5	1	43	41	2	31	.251	.316	.328	86	-16	28	.956	1	96	98	3b117/rfM	—	-1.3
1916	NY N	71	260	22	64	9	1	0	17	7	1	20	.246	.269	.288	75	-8	7	.940	-2	98	87	3b71	—	-1.0
	Cin N	37	130	4	36	3	0	0	10	3	0	12	.277	.293	.300	84	-3	4	.960	-2	90	119	3b35	—	-0.4
	Year	108	390	26	100	12	1	0	27	10	1	32	.256	.277	.292	78	-11	11	.947	-4	95	97	3b106	—	-1.4
1917	Cin N	48	134	11	34	3	1	0	15	7	1	7	.254	.296	.291	84	-3	5	.943	-4	88	119	2b26,S13,3b4	—	-0.7
1918	Pit N	**126**	435	34	111	13	9	2	43	24	2	22	.255	.297	.340	91	-6	12	.966	-1	95	131	3b126	—	-0.4
1920	Pit N	40	133	13	29	3	1	1	13	4	0	7	.218	.241	.278	47	-9	7-4	.943	-2	90	78	3b20,S10,2b6/1	—	-1.1
Total	11	846	2843	319	713	86	33	8	240	190	15	199	.251	.301	.313	76	-109	127-4	.952	19	101	107	3b553,2b117,1b64,S60,O2(0/1/1)	—	-7.8
McKee, Frank	Frank; B Philadelphia PA; d6.11																								
1884	Was U	4	17	2	3	0	0	0	—	1	—	—	.176	.222	.176	23	-2	—	.200	-2	142	0	O3R,3b2/C	—	-0.3
McKee, Red	Raymond Ellis; B7.20.1890 Shawnee OH; D8.5.1972 Saginaw MI; BL/TR/5´11˝/180; d4.19																								
1913	Det A	68	187	18	53	3	4	1	20	21	1	21	.283	.359	.358	112	3	7	.950	-10	*83*	*104*	C62	—	-0.2
1914	Det A	34	64	7	12	1	1	0	8	14	1	16	.188	.342	.234	71	-1	1-2	.964	-5	*85*	*71*	C27	—	-0.5
1915	Det A	55	106	10	29	5	0	1	17	13	0	16	.274	.353	.349	105	1	1	.954	-5	*93*	*83*	C35	—	-0.1
1916	Det A	32	76	3	16	1	2	0	4	6	0	11	.211	.268	.276	61	-4	0	.955	-4	84	107	C26	—	-0.7
Total	4	189	433	38	110	10	7	2	49	54	2	64	.254	.339	.323	95	-1	9-2	.954	-24	*86*	*95*	C150	—	-1.5
McKeel, Walt	Walt Thomas; B1.17.1972 Wilson NC; BR/TR/6´2˝/200; [BosA90 3/91]; d9.14																								
1996	Bos A	1	0	0	0	0	0	0	0	0-0	0	0	ø	ø	ø	ø	0	0-0	ø	-0	0	0	/C	0	0.0
1997	Bos A	5	3	0	0	0	0	0	0	0-0	0	1	.000	.000	.000	-98	-1	0-0	1.000	0	0	0	C4/1	0	-0.1
2002	Col N	5	13	1	4	0	0	0	0	0-0	0	3	.308	.308	.308	55	-1	0-0	1.000	-2	26	0	C5	0	-0.2
Total	3	11	16	1	4	0	0	0	0	0-0	0	4	.250	.250	.250	29	-2	0-0	1.000	-2	21	0	C10/1	0	-0.3
McKeever, Jim	James; B4.19.1861 St.John NB (now Canada); D8.19.1897 Boston MA; BR/5´10˝/170; d4.17																								
1884	Bos U	16	66	13	9	0	0	0	—	0	—	—	.136	.136	.136	-17	-12	—	.869	-4	—	—	C12,O4R	—	-1.4
McKelvey, John	John Wellington; B8.27.1847 Rochester NY; D5.31.1944 Rochester NY; BR/TR/5´7.5˝/175; d4.19																								
1875	NH NA	43	188	26	43	3	1	0	10	5	—	8	.229	.249	.255	86	-1	3-1	.656	-9	88	68	O39(0/4/35),3b5	—	-0.6
McKelvy, Russ	Russell Errett; B9.8.1854 Swissvale PA; D10.19.1915 Omaha NE; BR/TR; d5.1; Col Allegheny; ▲																								
1878	Ind N	**63**	253	33	57	4	3	2	36	5	—	38	.225	.240	.289	84	-3	—	.846	5	113	82	O62C,P4	—	-0.1
1882	Pit AA	1	4	0	0	0	0	0	—	0	—	—	.000	.000	.000	-99	-1	—	ø	-0	0	0	/rf	—	-0.1
Total	2	64	257	33	57	4	3	2	36	5	—	38	.222	.237	.284	81	-4	—	.846	4	113	82	O63(0/62/1),P4	—	-0.2
McKenna, Ed	Edward J.; B St.Louis MO; d7.29																								
1874	Phi NA	1	4	0	0	0	0	0	0	0	—	1	.000	.000	.000	-97	-1	0-0	1.000	0	0	0	/1	—	-0.1
1877	StL N	1	5	0	1	0	0	0	0	0	—	1	.200	.200	.200	28	0	—	1.000	-0	0	0	/cf	—	-0.1
1884	Was U	32	117	19	22	1	0	0	—	4	—	—	.188	.215	.197	26	-14	—	.876	-8	—	—	C23,O10(0/2/8),3b7	—	-1.9
Total	2	33	122	19	23	1	0	0	0	4	—	1	.189	.214	.197	26	-14	—	1.000	-8	—	—	C23,O11(0/3/8),3b7	—	-2.0
McKeough, Dave	David J.; B12.1.1863 Utica NY; D7.11.1901 Utica NY; 5´7˝/158; d4.22																								
1890	Roc AA	62	218	38	49	5	0	0	20	29	0	—	.225	.316	.248	72	-6	14	.929	2	*114*	*112*	C47,S13,2b2/3	—	0.0
1891	Phi AA	15	54	4	14	1	1	0	3	8	0	6	.259	.355	.315	92	0	0	.854	-4	*109*	*84*	C14/S	—	-0.3
Total	2	77	272	42	63	6	1	0	23	37	0	6	.232	.324	.261	76	-6	14	.912	-2	*113*	*105*	C61,S14,2b2/3	—	-0.3
McKinney, Rich	Charles Richard; B11.22.1946 Piqua OH; BR/TR/5´11˝/185; [ChiA68 1/14]; d6.26; Col Ohio U.; OF(6/0/27)																								
1970	Chi A	43	119	12	20	5	0	4	17	11-0	1	25	.168	.242	.311	50	-8	3-2	.931	1	95	44	3b23,S11	0	-0.7
1971	Chi A	114	369	35	100	11	2	8	46	35-1	2	37	.271	.334	.377	99	0	0-0	.968	-8	93	79	2b67,O25R,3b5	0	-0.5
1972	NY A	37	121	10	26	2	0	1	7	7-0	0	13	.215	.258	.256	54	-7	1-0	.917	-1	110	86	3b33	0	-1.0
1973	Oak A	48	65	9	16	3	0	1	7	7-0	0	4	.246	.319	.338	89	-1	0-0	.900	-1	96	84	3b17,2b7,O3L,D6	0	-0.2
1974	Oak A	5	7	0	1	0	0	0	0	0-0	0	0	.143	.143	.143	-19	-1	0-0	1.000	-1	0	0	2b3	0	-0.3
1975	Oak A	8	7	0	1	0	0	0	2	1-0	0	2	.143	.200	.143	14	-1	0-0	1.000	-0	0	0	/1D	0	-0.1
1977	Oak A	86	198	13	35	7	0	6	21	16-0	0	43	.177	.236	.303	47	-15	0-1	.978	-2	101	93	1b32,D18,3b7,O5(3/0/2),2b3	0	-2.0
Total	7	341	886	79	199	28	2	20	100	77-1	3	124	.225	.286	.328	73	-33	4-3	.911	-12	103	77	3b85,2b80,1b33,O33R,D26,S11	0	-4.8
McKinney, Bob	Robert Francis; B10.4.1875 McSherrystown PA; D8.19.1946 Hanover PA; BR/TR/5´7˝/165; d7.23																								
1901	Phi A	2	2	0	0	0	0	0	0	0	0	—	.000	.000	.000	-96	-1	0	ø	-1	0	0	/23	—	-0.1
McKinnon, Alex	Alexander J.; B8.14.1856 Boston MA; D7.24.1887 Charlestown MA; BR/5´11.5˝/170; d5.1; M1																								
1884	NY N	**116**	470	66	128	21	13	3	73	8	—	62	.272	.285	.391	108	2	—	.955	-2	93	102	1b116	—	-0.9
1885	StL N	100	411	42	121	21	6	1	44	8	—	31	.294	.308	.382	130	13	—	**.978**	-2	77	96	1b100,M	—	0.2
1886	StL N	122	491	75	148	24	7	8	72	21	—	23	.301	.330	.428	138	22	10	.963	-6	79	105	1b119,O3C	—	0.5
1887	Pit N	48	200	26	68	16	4	1	30	8	0	9	.340	.365	.475	142	12	6	.977	3	139	101	1b48	—	0.9
Total	4	386	1572	209	465	82	30	13	219	45	0	125	.296	.315	.411	127	49	16	.967	-6	90	101	1b383,O3C	—	0.7

YEAR	TM LG	G	AB	R	H	2B	3B	HR	RBI	BB-IB	HP	SO	AVG	OBP	SLG	AOPS	ABR	SB-CS	FA	FR	RNG	THR	GAMES AT POSITION	DL	BFW
McKNIGHT, JIM	James Arthur; B6.1.1936 Bee Branch AR; D2.24.1994 Van Buren Co. AR; BR/TR/6´1˝/(180–185); d9.22; s–Jeff																								
1960	Chi N	3	6	0	2	0	0	0	1	0-0	0	1	.333	.333	.333	84	0	0-0	.667	-0	159	342	/2rf	0	-0.1
1962	Chi N	60	85	6	19	0	1	0	5	2-0	0	13	.224	.241	.247	30	-9	0-0	.955	3	161	218	3b9,O5R,2b2	0	-0.6
Total	2	63	91	6	21	0	1	0	6	2-0	0	14	.231	.247	.253	34	-9	0-0	.955	3	161	218	3b9,O6R,2b3	0	-0.7
McKNIGHT, JEFF	Jefferson Alan; B2.18.1963 Conway AR; BB/TR/6´0˝/(175–188); [NYN83*S2/29]; d6.6; f–Jim; Col Arkansas–Fort Smith [JC]; OF(10/0/6)																								
1989	NY N	6	12	2	3	0	0	0	0	2-0	0	1	.250	.357	.250	80	0	0-0	1.000	-1	97	101	2b4/13S	0	-0.2
1990	Bal A	29	75	11	15	2	0	1	4	5-0	1	17	.200	.259	.267	49	-5	0-0	1.000	-1	115	83	1b15,O8(4/0/4),2b5/SD	0	-0.7
1991	Bal A	16	41	2	7	1	0	0	2	2-0	0	7	.171	.209	.195	13	-5	1-0	1.000	-0	64	282	O7(6/0/1),1b2,D4	125	-0.6
1992	NY N	31	85	10	23	3	1	2	13	2-0	0	8	.271	.287	.400	94	-1	0-1	.980	1	113	89	2b14,1b9,3b3,S3/rf	0	-0.1
1993	NY N	105	164	19	42	3	1	2	13	13-0	1	31	.256	.311	.323	72	-7	0-0	.943	0	99	109	S29,2b15,1b10,3b9/C	0	-0.5
1994	NY N	31	27	1	4	1	0	0	2	4-0	0	12	.148	.250	.185	18	-3	0-0	1.000	-0	0	0	1b2	62	-0.3
Total	6	218	404	45	94	10	2	5	34	28-0	2	76	.233	.284	.304	63	-21	1-1	.996	-1	102	81	1b39,2b38,S34,O16L,3b13,D5/C	187	-2.4
McLANE, ED	Edward Cameron; B8.20.1881 Weston MA; D8.21.1975 Baltimore MD; BR/TR/5´10˝/179; d10.6; Col Fordham																								
1907	Bro N	1	2	0	0	0	0	0	0	0	1	—	.000	.333	.000	5	0	0	.333	-1	0	0	/rf	—	-0.1
McLARNEY, ART	Arthur James; B12.20.1908 Ft.Worden WA; D12.20.1984 Seattle WA; BB/TR/6´0˝/168; d8.23; Col Washington St.																								
1932	NY N	9	23	2	3	1	0	0	3	1	0	3	.130	.167	.174	-8	-4	0	1.000	-1	87	84	S7	—	-0.4
McLARRY, POLLY	Howard Zell; B3.25.1891 Leonard TX; D11.4.1971 Bonham TX; BL/TR/6´0˝/185; d9.2																								
1912	Chi A	2	2	0	0	0	0	0	0	0	0	—	.000	.000	.000	-99	-1	0	ø	0	—	—	/H	—	-0.1
1915	Chi N	68	127	16	25	3	0	1	12	14	0	20	.197	.277	.244	58	-6	2-2	.957	1	105	45	2b21,1b18	—	-0.6
Total	2	70	129	16	25	3	0	1	12	14	0	<u>20</u>	.194	.273	.240	56	-7	2-<u>2</u>	.957	1	105	45	2b21,1b18	—	-0.7
McLAUGHLIN, BARNEY	Bernard; B1857 , Ireland; D2.13.1921 Lowell MA; BR/TR; d8.2; b–Frank; ▲																								
1884	KC U	42	162	15	37	7	3	0	—	9	—	—	.228	.269	.309	86	-7	—	.762	-1	185	360	O24(4/3/17),2b12,P7,S2	—	-0.7
1887	Phi N	50	205	26	45	8	3	1	26	11	1	27	.220	.263	.302	53	-14	2	.879	-14	90	71	2b50	—	-2.2
1890	Syr AA	86	329	43	87	8	1	2	40	47	2	—	.264	.360	.313	110	8	13	.902	-6	96	82	S86	—	0.3
Total	3	178	696	84	169	23	7	3	<u>66</u>	67	3	<u>27</u>	.243	.312	.309	86	-13	15	.900	-22	97	80	S88,2b62,O24(4/3/17),P7	—	-2.6
McLAUGHLIN, FRANK	Francis Edward; B6.19.1856 Lowell MA; D4.5.1917 Lowell MA; BR/TR/5´9˝/160; d8.9; b–Barney; ▲																								
1882	Wor N	15	55	7	12	0	2	1	4	0	—	11	.218	.218	.345	76	-2	—	.760	-4	99	44	S14/cf	—	-0.5
1883	Pit AA	29	114	15	25	2	0	1	—	6	—	—	.219	.258	.263	71	-3	—	.802	-0	112	64	S25,O4(0/3/1),2b2,P2	—	-0.2
1884	Cin U	16	67	10	16	4	1	2	—	2	—	—	.239	.261	.418	95	-3	—	.740	-6	73	139	S16	—	-0.7
	CP U	15	67	11	16	4	1	0	—	1	—	—	.239	.250	.328	75	-4	—	.888	3	114	179	2b14/Srf	—	0.0
	KC U	32	123	17	28	11	0	1	—	9	—	—	.228	.280	.341	101	-3	—	.847	-6	105	58	2b10,O10(2/6/2),3b9,S5,P2	—	-0.7
	Year	63	257	38	60	19	2	3	—	12	—	—	.233	.268	.358	93	-10	—	.873	-9	111	134	2b24,S22,O11(2/6/3),3b9,P2	—	-1.4
Total	3	107	426	60	97	21	4	5	<u>4</u>	18	—	<u>11</u>	.228	.259	.331	85	-15	—	.769	-13	98	83	S61,2b26,O16(2/10/4),3b9,P4	—	-2.1
McLAUGHLIN, KID	James Anson "Sunshine"; B4.12.1888 Randolph NY; D11.17.1934 Allegany NY; BL/TR/5´8.5˝/158; d6.30; Col Colgate																								
1914	Cin N	3	2	1	0	0	0	0	0	0	0	0	.000	.000	.000	-97	0	0	1.000	0	130	0	O2C	—	-0.1
McLAUGHLIN, JIM	James Robert; B1.3.1902 St.Louis MO; D12.18.1968 Mount Vernon IL; BR/TR/5´8.5˝/168; d4.18																								
1932	StL A	1	1	0	0	0	0	0	1	0	0	0	.000	.000	.000	-95	0	0-0	ø	-0	0	0	/3	—	0.0
McLAUGHLIN, TOM	Thomas; B3.28.1860 Louisville KY; D7.21.1921 Louisville KY; TR; d7.17																								
1883	Lou AA	42	146	16	28	1	2	0	—	5	—	—	.192	.219	.226	47	-8	—	.844	2	118	129	S19,O17(8/9/1),1b5,3b2,2b2	—	-0.5
1884	Lou AA	98	335	41	67	11	6	0	21	22	6	—	.200	.262	.269	77	-7	—	.892	13	109	**171**	S94,3b4/2	—	0.8
1885	Lou AA	**112**	411	49	87	13	9	2	41	15	3	—	.212	.245	.302	72	-14	—	.883	-1	92	112	2b93,S19	—	-0.9
1886	NY AA	74	250	27	34	3	1	0	16	26	1	—	.136	.220	.156	20	-21	13	.886	7	102	62	S63,2b10/lf	—	-1.1
1891	Was AA	14	41	9	11	0	1	0	3	7	2	6	.268	.400	.317	111	1	3	.871	1	98	128	S14	—	0.2
Total	5	340	1183	142	227	28	19	2	<u>81</u>	75	12	<u>6</u>	.192	.247	.253	62	-49	16	.886	22	106	128	S209,2b106,O18(9/9/1),3b6,1b5	—	-1.5
McLAUGHLIN, BILL	William; B San Francisco CA; d5.3																								
1884	Was U	10	37	3	7	3	0	0	—	0	—	—	.189	.189	.270	39	-4	—	.696	-4	75	0	S9/3	—	-0.7
McLAURIN, RALPH	Ralph Edgar; B5.23.1885 Kissimmee FL; D2.11.1943 McColl SC; d9.5																								
1908	StL N	8	22	2	5	0	0	0	0	0	0	—	.227	.227	.227	47	-1	0	.875	-1	0	0	O6L	—	-0.3
McLEAN, LARRY	John Bannerman; B7.18.1881 Fredericton NB, Can.; D3.24.1921 Boston MA; BR/TR/6´5˝/228; d4.26																								
1901	Bos A	9	19	4	4	1	0	0	2	0	0	—	.211	.211	.263	31	-2	1	1.000	0	107	114	1b5	—	-0.1
1903	Chi N	1	4	0	0	0	0	0	0	1	0	—	.000	.200	.000	-42	-1	0	.889	0	*182*	*67*	/C	—	-0.1
1904	StL N	27	84	5	14	2	1	0	4	4	0	—	.167	.205	.214	31	-7	1	.954	-4	*88*	*52*	C24	—	-0.9
1906	Cin N	12	35	3	7	2	0	0	2	4	0	—	.200	.282	.257	65	-1	0	.954	-1	*101*	*90*	C12	—	-0.1
1907	Cin N	113	374	35	108	9	9	0	54	13	0	—	.289	.313	.361	107	0	4	.975	-0	*100*	*91*	C89,1b13	—	1.0
1908	Cin N	99	309	24	67	9	4	1	28	15	2	—	.217	.258	.282	74	-10	2	.963	-3	*108*	*101*	C69,1b19	—	-0.8
1909	Cin N	95	324	26	83	12	2	2	36	21	3	—	.256	.307	.324	97	-2	1	.978	-3	*89*	*106*	C95	—	0.5
1910	Cin N	127	423	27	126	14	7	2	71	26	1	23	.298	.340	.378	114	6	4	.983	7	*118*	*104*	C119	—	2.4
1911	Cin N	107	328	24	94	7	2	0	34	20	1	18	.287	.330	.320	85	-7	1	.968	14	*132*	*110*	C98	—	1.5
1912	Cin N	102	333	17	81	15	1	1	27	18	1	15	.243	.284	.303	63	-18	1	.973	-1	*94*	*109*	C98	—	-1.1
1913	StL N	48	152	7	41	9	0	0	12	6	0	9	.270	.297	.329	80	-4	0	.981	-7	71	112	C42	—	-0.8
	†NY N	30	75	3	24	4	0	0	9	4	0	4	.320	.354	.373	107	1	1	.953	-1	114	65	C28	—	0.2
	Year	78	227	10	65	13	0	0	21	10	0	13	.286	.316	.344	89	-3	1	.970	-8	86	96	C70	—	-0.6
1914	NY N	79	154	8	40	6	0	0	14	4	1	9	.260	.283	.299	76	-5	4	.973	-0	*133*	*69*	C74	—	-0.2
1915	NY N	13	33	0	5	0	0	0	4	0	0	1	.152	.152	.152	-9	-4	0	.985	1	*89*	*161*	C12	—	-0.4
Total	13	862	2647	183	694	90	26	6	298	136	9	<u>79</u>	.262	.301	.323	86	-54	20	.973	2	*106*	*100*	C761,1b37	—	1.1
McLEMORE, MARK	Mark Tremell; B10.4.1964 San Diego CA; BB/TR/5´11˝/(175–207); [CalA82 9/218]; d9.13; OF(250/21/147)																								
1986	Cal A	5	4	0	0	0	0	0	0	1-0	0	2	.000	.200	.000	-40	-1	0-1	1.000	2	171	86	2b2	0	0.0
1987	Cal A	138	433	61	102	13	3	3	41	48-0	0	72	.236	.310	.300	65	-21	25-8	.974	-8	93	**117**	2b132,S6,D3	0	-1.8
1988	Cal A	77	233	38	56	11	2	2	16	25-0	0	28	.240	.312	.330	83	-5	13-7	.979	4	107	138	2b63,3b5/D	70	0.1
1989	Cal A	32	103	12	25	3	1	0	14	7-0	1	19	.243	.295	.291	68	-5	6-1	.966	4	111	147	2b27/D	0	0.2
1990	Cal A	20	48	4	7	2	0	0	2	4-0	0	9	.146	.212	.188	13	-6	1-0	1.000	-5	79	62	2b8,S8/D	92	-1.0
	Cle A	8	12	2	2	0	0	0	0	0-0	0	6	.167	.167	.167	-7	-2	0-0	1.000	1	73	395	3b4,2b3/D	0	-0.1
	Year	28	60	6	9	2	0	0	2	4-0	0	15	.150	.203	.183	9	-7	1-0	1.000	-4	85	94	2b11,S8,3b4,D2	0	-1.1
1991	Hou N	21	61	6	9	1	0	0	2	6-0	0	13	.148	.221	.164	11	-7	0-1	.975	-1	103	83	2b19	47	-0.9
1992	Bal A	101	228	40	56	7	2	0	27	21-1	0	26	.246	.308	.294	68	-10	11-5	.978	2	103	121	2b70,D17	0	-0.6
1993	Bal A	148	581	81	165	27	5	4	72	64-4	1	92	.284	.353	.368	91	-6	21-15	.987	12	109	141	O124R,2b25,3b4/D	0	0.0
1994	Bal A	104	343	44	88	11	1	3	29	51-3	1	50	.257	.354	.321	72	-13	20-5	.981	2	99	98	2b96,O7R/D	0	-0.4
1995	Tex A	129	467	73	122	20	5	5	41	59-6	3	71	.261	.346	.358	81	-12	21-11	.986	-2	103	0	O73(69/0/5),2b66,D2	0	-1.2
1996	†Tex A	147	517	84	150	23	4	5	46	87-5	0	69	.290	.389	.379	91	-4	27-10	.985	24	109	113	2b147/rf	0	2.6
1997	Tex A	89	349	47	91	17	2	1	25	40-1	2	54	.261	.338	.330	71	-14	7-5	.980	-1	104	106	2b89/lf	70	-1.1
1998	†Tex A	126	461	79	114	15	1	5	53	89-1	2	64	.247	.369	.317	77	-12	12-4	.975	-5	94	90	2b122,D2	15	-0.9
1999	†Tex A	144	566	105	155	20	7	6	45	83-2	0	79	.274	.363	.366	83	-13	16-8	.983	10	106	102	2b135,O11(4/0/7)	0	0.3
2000	†Sea A	138	481	72	118	23	1	3	46	81-2	1	78	.245	.353	.316	73	-17	30-14	.987	-1	96	103	2b129,O14(14/1/0)	0	-1.0
2001	†Sea A	125	409	78	117	16	9	5	57	69-0	0	84	.286	.384	.406	116	12	39-7	.988	-5	97	121	O68(63/8/2),3b36,S35,2b9,D2	0	1.4
2002	Sea A	104	337	54	91	17	2	7	41	61-1	1	63	.270	.380	.395	111	8	18-10	.972	-2	109	45	O88(82/12/1),3b14,2b2/SD	0	0.4
2003	Sea A	99	309	34	72	15	2	2	37	38-0	2	71	.233	.318	.314	72	-12	5-5	.972	1	98	130	S38,3b29,O16L,D11,2b6	0	-1.0
2004	Oak A	77	250	29	62	14	0	2	21	41-3	1	33	.248	.355	.328	81	-5	0-2	.975	8	107	138	2b47,3b27/lf	36	0.4
Total	19	1832	6192	943	1602	255	47	53	615	875-29	15	983	.259	.349	.341	81	-145	272-119	.981	39	101	110	2b1197,O404L,3b119,S88,D47	330	-4.6
McLEOD, RALPH	Ralph Alton; B10.19.1916 N.Quincy MA; BL/TL/6´0˝/170; d9.14																								
1938	Bos N	6	7	1	2	1	0	0	0	0	0	2	.286	.286	.429	105	0	0	1.000	0	98	0	/lf	—	0.0

YEAR	TM LG	G	AB	R	H	2B	3B	HR	RBI	BB-IB	HP	SO	AVG	OBP	SLG	AOPS	ABR	SB-CS	FA	FR	RNG	THR	GAMES AT POSITION	DL	BFW
McLeod, Jim	Soule James; B9.12.1908 Jones LA; D8.3.1981 Little Rock AR; BR/TR/6´0˝/187; d5.22; Col Arkansas–Little Rock																								
1930	Was A	18	34	3	9	1	0	0	1	1	1	5	.265	.306	.294	53	-2	1-1	1.000	-1	101	0	3b10,S7	—	-0.2
1932	Was A	7	0	1	0	0	0	0	0	1	0	0	ø	1.000	ø	183	0	0-0	1.000	0	145	0	/S	—	0.0
1933	Phi N	67	232	20	45	6	1	0	15	12	1	25	.194	.237	.228	30	-21	1	.914	-3	101	85	3b67/S	—	-2.3
Total	3	92	266	24	54	7	1	0	16	14	2	30	.203	.248	.237	33	-23	2-1	.922	-3	101	76	3b77,S9	—	-2.5
McLouth, Nate	Nathan Richard; B10.28.1981 Muskegon MI; BL/TR/5´11˝/185; [PitN00 25/749]; d6.29																								
2005	Pit N	41	109	20	28	6	0	5	12	3-0	5	20	.257	.305	.450	95	-1	2-0	.958	-4	78	0	O29(0/21/8)	0	-0.5
2006	Pit N	106	270	50	63	16	2	7	16	18-0	5	59	.233	.293	.385	71	-13	10-1	.982	-6	81	35	O75(3/42/39)	51	-1.7
Total	2	147	379	70	91	22	2	12	28	21-0	10	79	.240	.296	.404	77	-14	12-1	.975	-10	80	25	O104(3/63/47)	51	-2.2
McMahon, Jack	John Henry; B10.15.1869 Waterbury CT; D12.30.1894 Bridgeport CT; BR/TR/5´10˝/165; d8.8																								
1892	NY N	40	147	21	33	5	7	1	24	10	1	9	.224	.278	.374	98	-2	3	.973	-3	74	68	1b36,C5	—	-0.4
1893	NY N	11	30	5	10	2	1	0	4	2	0	0	.333	.375	.467	122	1	0	.891	-1	101	103	C11	—	0.0
Total	2	51	177	26	43	7	8	1	28	12	1	9	.243	.295	.390	103	-1	3	.973	-4	74	68	1b36,C16	—	-0.4
McManus, Frank	Francis E.; B9.21.1875 Lawrence MA; D9.1.1923 Syracuse NY; TR/5´7˝/150; d9.14																								
1899	Was N	7	21	3	8	1	0	0	2	2	0	—	.381	.435	.429	139	1	3	.931	-1	78	162	C7	—	0.1
1903	Bro N	2	7	0	0	0	0	0	0	0	0	—	.000	.000	.000	-99	-2	0	.929	0	90	135	C2	—	-0.1
1904	Det A	1	0	0	0	0	0	0	0	0	0	—	ø	ø	ø	ø	0	0	ø	0	0	0	/C	—	0.0
	NY A	4	7	0	0	0	0	0	0	0	0	—	.000	.000	.000	-96	-2	0	.900	-1	81	0	C4	—	-0.2
	Year	5	7	0	0	0	0	0	0	0	0	—	.000	.000	.000	-97	-2	0	.900	-1	76	0	C5	—	-0.2
Total	3	14	35	3	8	1	0	0	2	2	0	—	.229	.270	.257	50	-3	3	.925	-1	80	125	C14	—	-0.2
McManus, Jim	James Michael; B7.20.1936 Brookline MA; BL/TL/6´4˝/215; d9.21																								
1960	KC A	5	13	3	4	0	0	1	2	1-0	0	2	.308	.357	.538	138	1	0-0	1.000	-0	48	34	1b3	0	0.0
McManus, Marty	Martin Joseph; B3.14.1900 Chicago IL; D2.18.1966 St.Louis MO; BR/TR/5´10.5˝/160; d9.26; M2																								
1920	StL A	1	3	0	1	0	1	0	1	0	0	0	.333	.333	1.000	236	0	0-0	.667	-1	95	0	/3	—	0.0
1921	StL A	121	412	49	107	19	8	3	64	27	2	30	.260	.308	.367	68	-22	5-3	.952	-12	91	87	2b96,3b13,1b9,S2	—	-2.9
1922	StL A	**154**	606	88	189	34	11	11	109	38	6	41	.312	.358	.459	108	5	9-6	.964	1	96	130	2b153/1	—	1.0
1923	StL A	**154**	582	86	180	35	10	15	94	49	4	50	.309	.367	.481	116	11	14-10	.960	-4	91	112	2b133,1b20	—	0.9
1924	StL A	123	442	71	147	23	5	5	80	55	2	40	.333	.409	.441	112	10	13-9	.972	8	102	103	2b119	—	2.0
1925	StL A	**154**	587	108	169	**44**	8	13	90	73	5	69	.288	.371	.457	104	4	5-11	.967	2	97	94	2b154/rf	—	0.6
1926	StL A	149	549	102	156	30	10	9	68	55	1	62	.284	.350	.424	97	-4	5-7	.958	12	104	113	3b84,2b61,1b4	—	1.3
1927	Det A	108	369	60	99	19	7	9	69	34	1	38	.268	.332	.431	95	-4	8-7	.960	0	95	93	S39,2b35,3b22,1b6	—	0.1
1928	Det A	139	500	78	144	37	5	8	73	51	1	32	.288	.355	.430	104	3	11-13	.955	2	101	69	3b92,1b45,S2	—	0.6
1929	Det A	154	599	99	168	32	8	18	90	60	1	52	.280	.347	.451	103	2	16-11	.972	7	101	89	3b150,S8	—	1.7
1930	Det A	132	484	74	155	40	4	9	89	59	2	28	.320	.396	.475	118	15	**23**-8	**.966**	7	100	**100**	3b130,S3/1	—	3.0
1931	Det A	107	362	39	98	17	3	3	53	49	2	22	.271	.361	.359	87	-6	7-3	.950	7	109	120	3b79,2b21/1	—	0.6
	Bos A	17	62	8	18	4	0	1	9	8	0	1	.290	.371	.403	110	1	1-1	1.000	6	151	299	3b11,2b7	—	0.7
	Year	124	424	47	116	21	3	4	62	57	2	23	.274	.362	.366	90	-5	8-4	.956	13	114	142	3b90,2b28/1	—	1.3
1932	Bos A	93	302	39	71	19	4	5	24	36	0	30	.235	.317	.374	80	-9	1-2	.969	1	107	80	2b49,3b30,S2/1M	—	-0.4
1933	Bos A	106	366	51	104	30	4	3	36	49	0	21	.284	.369	.413	108	6	3-0	.957	-2	97	73	3b76,2b26,1b4,M	—	0.8
1934	Bos N	119	435	56	120	18	0	8	47	32	3	42	.276	.330	.372	95	-3	5	.964	-6	103	92	2b73,3b37	—	-0.3
Total	15	1831	6660	1008	1926	401	88	120	996	675	30	558	.289	.357	.430	101	9	126-91	.965	29	98	104	2b927,3b725,1b92,S56/rf	—	9.7
McMath, Jimmy	Jimmy Lee; B8.10.1949 Tuscaloosa AL; BL/TL/6´1.5˝/180; [ChiN67 2/22]; d9.7																								
1968	Chi N	6	14	0	2	0	0	0	2	0-0	0	6	.143	.143	.143	-13	-2	0-0	1.000	0	135	0	O3L	0	-0.2
McMillan, George	George A. "Reddy"; B9.1.1863 Ontario, Can; D4.18.1920 Cleveland OH; 5´8˝/175; d8.11																								
1890	NY N	10	35	4	5	0	0	0	1	7	0	4	.143	.286	.143	26	-3	1	.800	-2	58	0	O10(1/0/9)	—	-0.4
McMillan, Norm	Norman Alexis "Bub"; B10.5.1895 Latta SC; D9.28.1969 Marion SC; BR/TR/6´0˝/175; d4.12; Col Clemson; OF(0/15/12)																								
1922	†NY A	33	78	7	20	1	2	0	11	6	0	10	.256	.310	.321	63	-5	4-1	.921	-3	92	0	O26(0/15/12),3b5	—	-0.8
1923	Bos A	131	459	37	116	24	5	0	42	28	2	44	.253	.299	.327	64	-25	13-5	.942	3	88	93	3b67,2b34,S28	—	-1.2
1924	StL A	76	201	25	56	12	2	0	27	12	4	17	.279	.332	.358	73	-8	6-4	.966	-3	96	94	2b37,3b19,S7,1b2	—	-0.8
1928	Chi N	49	123	11	27	2	2	1	12	13	1	19	.220	.299	.293	56	-8	0	.977	2	116	136	2b19,3b18	—	-0.5
1929	†Chi N	124	495	77	134	35	5	5	55	36	3	43	.271	.324	.392	76	-19	13	.944	6	101	111	3b120	—	-0.5
Total	5	413	1356	157	353	74	16	6	147	95	10	133	.260	.313	.352	69	-65	36-10	.944	5	95	93	3b229,2b90,S35,O26C,1b2	—	-3.8
McMillan, Roy	Roy David; B7.17.1929 Bonham TX; D11.2.1997 Bonham TX; BR/TR/5´11˝/(160–170); d4.17; M2/C7																								
1951	Cin N	85	199	21	42	4	0	1	8	17	0	26	.211	.273	.246	40	-17	0-0	.963	2	101	85	S54,3b12/2	0	-1.2
1952	Cin N	**154**	540	60	132	32	2	7	57	45	3	81	.244	.306	.350	82	-13	4-5	.971	10	**107**	97	S154	0	0.6
1953	Cin N	**155**	557	51	130	15	4	5	43	43	1	52	.233	.290	.302	54	-38	2-4	.972	10	**109**	**115**	S155	0	-1.6
1954	Cin N	**154**	588	86	147	21	2	4	42	47	5	54	.250	.308	.313	61	-33	4-2	.959	7	99	**124**	S154	0	-1.3
1955	Cin N	151	470	50	126	21	2	1	37	66-7	7	33	.268	.364	.328	81	-9	4-4	.969	**18**	**110**	**120**	S150	0	2.0
1956	Cin N★	150	479	51	126	16	7	3	62	76-9	5	54	.263	.366	.344	88	-5	4-3	**.975**	**29**	**114**	**108**	S150	0	3.7
1957	Cin N★	151	448	50	122	25	5	1	55	66-8	6	44	.272	.371	.357	91	-2	5-1	**.977**	-3	100	95	S151	0	0.7
1958	Cin N	145	393	48	90	18	3	1	25	47-5	1	33	.229	.312	.298	60	-22	5-2	**.980**	3	101	97	S145	0	-0.8
1959	Cin N	79	246	38	65	14	2	9	24	27-3	4	27	.264	.345	.447	106	3	0-2	.974	-1	94	113	S73	44	0.7
1960	Cin N	124	399	42	94	12	2	10	42	35-5	4	40	.236	.301	.351	77	-13	2-0	.964	-9	101	110	S116,2b10	0	-1.2
1961	Mil N	154	505	42	111	16	0	7	48	61-2	4	86	.220	.305	.293	65	-25	2-4	**.975**	-1	107	115	S154	0	-1.3
1962	Mil N	137	468	66	115	13	0	12	41	60-0	5	53	.246	.336	.350	87	-7	2-2	.972	13	107	115	S135	0	1.7
1963	Mil N	100	320	35	80	10	1	4	29	17-2	2	25	.250	.291	.325	78	-9	1-5	.979	5	105	122	S94	0	0.1
1964	Mil N	8	13	1	4	0	0	0	2	0-0	0	2	.308	.308	.308	73	-1	1-0	.933	-2	56	87	S8	0	-0.2
	NY N	113	379	30	80	8	2	1	25	14-2	4	16	.211	.246	.251	42	-30	3-1	.976	7	109	95	S111	0	-1.4
	Year	121	392	31	84	8	2	1	27	14-2	4	18	.214	.248	.253	43	-31	4-1	.975	5	107	95	S119	0	-1.6
1965	NY N	157	528	44	128	19	2	1	42	24-1	4	60	.242	.280	.292	64	-26	1-0	.964	5	108	88	S153	0	-1.0
1966	NY N	76	220	24	47	9	1	1	12	20-3	2	25	.214	.284	.277	59	-12	1-1	.975	1	104	86	S71	20	-0.6
Total	16	2093	6752	739	1639	253	35	68	594	665-47	57	711	.243	.314	.321	72	-259	41-36	.972	93	105	107	S2028,3b12,2b11	64	-1.1
McMillan, Tom	Thomas Erwin; B9.13.1951 Richmond VA; BR/TR/5´9˝/165; [CleA73 2/29]; d9.17; Col Jacksonville																								
1977	Sea A	2	5	0	0	0	0	0	0	0-0	0	0	.000	.000	.000	-99	-1	0-0	1.000	0	89	141	S2	0	-0.1
McMillan, Tommy	Thomas Law "Rebel"; B4.18.1888 Pittston PA; D7.15.1966 Orlando FL; BR/TR/5´5˝/130; d8.19; Col Georgia Tech																								
1908	Bro N	43	147	9	35	3	0	0	3	9	3	—	.238	.296	.259	80	-3	5	.873	-7	91	111	S29,O14C	—	-1.1
1909	Bro N	108	373	18	79	15	1	0	24	20	1	—	.212	.254	.257	61	-18	11	.914	-11	96	81	S105,2b2/3	—	-2.9
1910	Bro N	23	74	2	13	1	0	0	2	6	0	10	.176	.237	.189	26	-7	4	.898	-2	99	79	S23	—	-0.9
	Cin N	82	248	20	46	0	3	0	13	31	2	23	.185	.281	.210	46	-17	7	.927	8	111	95	S82	—	-0.7
	Year	105	322	22	59	1	3	0	15	37	2	33	.183	.271	.205	41	-24	11	.921	6	**108**	92	S105	—	-1.6
1912	NY A	41	149	24	34	2	0	0	12	15	1	—	.228	.303	.242	53	-9	18	.948	-3	92	91	S41	—	-1.0
Total	4	297	991	73	207	21	4	0	54	81	7	33	.209	.273	.238	56	-54	45	.917	-15	100	90	S280,O14C,2b2/3	—	-6.6
McMillon, Billy	William Edward; B11.17.1971 Alamogordo NM; BL/TL/5´11˝/(172–195); [FlaN93 8/239]; d7.26; Col Clemson																								
1996	Fla N	28	51	4	11	0	0	0	4	5-1	0	14	.216	.286	.216	36	-5	0-0	1.000	-1	92	0	O15L	0	-0.6
1997	Fla N	13	18	0	2	1	0	0	1	0-0	0	7	.111	.111	.167	-30	-3	0-0	1.000	0	110	0	O2L	0	-0.3
	Phi N	24	72	10	21	4	1	2	13	6-0	0	17	.292	.333	.458	110	1	2-1	.957	2	126	170	O21(19/0/2)	0	0.3
	Year	37	90	10	23	5	1	2	14	6-0	0	24	.256	.293	.400	84	-2	2-1	.960	3	125	155	O23(21/0/2)	0	0.0
2000	Det A	46	123	20	37	7	1	4	24	19-0	1	19	.301	.388	.472	120	4	1-0	.964	1	137	0	D24,O15(3/0/13)	0	0.3
2001	Det A	20	34	1	3	1	0	1	4	2-0	1	12	.088	.162	.206	-4	-5	0-0	1.000	0	111	0	O7(1/0/6),D3	0	-0.5
	Oak A	20	58	6	17	7	1	0	10	5-0	1	13	.293	.354	.448	111	1	1-0	.950	-2	60	106	O16(15/0/2)/D	77	-0.2
	Year	40	92	7	20	8	1	1	14	7-0	2	25	.217	.284	.359	69	-4	1-0	.967	-2	72	82	O23(16/0/8),D4	0	-0.7
2003	†Oak A	66	153	15	41	11	0	6	26	19-1	2	36	.268	.354	.458	112	3	0-0	.979	-2	98	0	O36(35/0/1),1b3,D9	0	0.0

YEAR	TM LG	G	AB	R	H	2B	3B	HR	RBI	BB-IB	HP	SO	AVG	OBP	SLG	AOPS	ABR	SB-CS	FA	FR	RNG	THR	GAMES AT POSITION	DL	BFW
2004	Oak A	52	92	10	17	4	0	3	11	8-0	1	22	.185	.255	.326	51	-7	0-1	1.000	-2	82	0	O21(20/0/1),1b3,D6	55	-0.9
Total	6	269	601	66	149	35	3	16	93	64-2	6	140	.248	.322	.396	88	-11	4-2	.974	-3	99	48	O133(110/0/25),D43,1b6	132	-1.9
McMullen, Hugh	Hugh Raphael; B12.16.1901 LaCygne KS; D5.23.1986 Whittier CA; BB/TR/6´1˝/180; d9.19																								
1925	NY N	5	15	1	2	1	0	0	0	0	0	3	.133	.133	.200	-17	-3	0-0	1.000	-1	*91*	*0*	C5	—	-0.3
1926	NY N	57	91	5	17	2	0	0	6	2	0	18	.187	.204	.209	11	-12	1	.942	-2	*86*	*104*	C56	—	-1.1
1928	Was A	1	1	0	0	0	0	0	0	0	0	1	.000	.000	.000	-99	0	0-0	ø	0	—	—	/H	—	0.0
1929	Cin N	1	1	0	0	0	0	0	0	0	0	0	.000	.000	.000	-99	0	0	1.000	0	*0*	*0*	/C	—	0.0
Total	4	64	108	6	19	3	0	0	6	2	0	22	.176	.191	.204	5	-15	1-0	.947	-3	*85*	*92*	C62	—	-1.4
McMullen, Ken	Kenneth Lee; B6.1.1942 Oxnard CA; BR/TR/6´3˝/(190–200); d9.17; OF(12/0/8)																								
1962	LA N	6	11	0	3	0	0	0	0	0-0	0	3	.273	.273	.273	50	-1	0-0	1.000	-0	35	0	O2L	0	-0.1
1963	LA N	79	233	16	55	9	0	5	28	20-2	1	46	.236	.297	.339	89	-3	1-2	.933	-3	95	85	3b71/2lf	0	-0.7
1964	LA N	24	67	3	14	0	0	1	2	3-1	0	7	.209	.243	.254	43	-5	0-1	.991	-2	92	82	1b13,3b4,O3(1/0/2)	0	-0.9
1965	Was A	150	555	75	146	18	6	18	54	47-4	4	90	.263	.323	.414	110	6	2-0	.954	6	102	98	3b142,O8(3/0/5)/1	0	1.2
1966	Was A	147	524	48	122	19	4	13	54	44-1	0	89	.233	.289	.359	87	-10	3-1	.951	-1	99	115	3b141,1b8/rf	0	-1.3
1967	Was A	146	563	73	138	22	2	16	67	46-2	1	84	.245	.301	.377	104	1	5-3	.965	9	108	**153**	3b145	0	1.0
1968	Was A	151	557	66	138	11	2	20	62	63-5	3	66	.248	.326	.382	119	12	1-3	.962	8	105	93	3b145,S11	0	2.1
1969	Was A	158	562	83	153	25	2	19	87	70-6	1	103	.272	.349	.425	123	18	4-5	.976	21	**110**	109	3b154	0	3.9
1970	Was A	15	59	5	12	2	0	0	3	5-0	0	10	.203	.266	.237	42	-5	0-0	.971	5	119	207	3b15	0	0.0
	Cal A	124	422	50	98	9	3	14	61	59-10	3	81	.232	.329	.367	95	-3	1-0	.959	8	102	139	3b122	0	0.5
	Year	139	481	55	110	11	3	14	64	64-10	3	91	.229	.321	.351	89	-7	1-0	.960	13	104	**147**	3b137	0	0.5
1971	Cal A	160	593	63	148	19	2	21	68	53-10	3	74	.250	.312	.395	107	3	1-1	.966	-6	98	84	3b158	0	-0.4
1972	Cal A	137	472	36	127	18	1	9	34	48-2	0	59	.269	.335	.369	116	9	1-2	.970	1	96	100	3b137	0	1.0
1973	LA N	42	85	6	21	5	0	5	18	6-1	0	13	.247	.297	.482	116	1	0-0	.922	5	145	71	3b24	0	0.6
1974	†LA N	44	60	5	15	1	0	3	12	2-0	0	12	.250	.274	.417	95	-1	0-0	1.000	0	104	0	3b7,2b3	0	-0.1
1975	LA N	39	46	4	11	1	1	2	14	7-0	0	12	.239	.340	.435	118	1	0-0	1.000	1	86	0	3b11,1b3	0	0.2
1976	Oak A	98	186	20	41	6	2	5	23	22-3	1	33	.220	.305	.355	97	-1	1-1	.952	-3	104	44	3b35,1b26,D23,O5L/2	0	-0.6
1977	Mil A	63	136	15	31	7	1	5	19	15-0	0	33	.228	.305	.404	91	-2	0-0	.978	1	138	109	D29,1b11,3b7	0	-0.3
Total	16	1583	5131	568	1273	172	26	156	606	510-47	17	815	.248	.316	.383	105	20	20-19	.961	51	103	108	3b1318,1b62,D52,O20L,S11,2b5	0	6.1
McMullin, Fred	Fred Drury; B10.13.1891 Scammon KS; D11.20.1952 Los Angeles CA; BR/TR/5´11˝/170; d8.27																								
1914	Det A	1	1	0	0	0	0	0	0	0	0	1	.000	.000	.000	-97	0	0	.667	-0	97	0	/S	—	0.0
1916	Chi A	68	187	8	48	3	0	0	10	19	2	30	.257	.332	.273	81	-4	9	.950	-3	93	113	3b63,S2/2	—	-0.5
1917	†Chi A	59	194	35	46	2	1	0	12	27	3	17	.237	.339	.258	81	-3	9	.932	-10	86	58	3b52,S2	—	-1.3
1918	Chi A	70	235	32	65	7	0	1	16	25	4	26	.277	.356	.319	103	2	8	.941	-3	102	69	3b69/2	—	0.1
1919	†Chi A	60	170	31	50	8	4	0	19	11	5	18	.294	.355	.388	108	2	4	.931	-2	100	157	3b46,2b5	—	0.1
1920	Chi A	46	127	14	25	1	4	0	13	9	1	13	.197	.255	.268	39	-12	1-1	.962	-3	94	81	3b29,2b3/S	—	-1.5
Total	6	304	914	120	234	21	9	1	70	91	15	105	.256	.333	.302	85	-15	31-1	.942	-21	95	94	3b259,2b10,S6	—	-3.1
McMullin, John	John F. "Lefty"; B1848 Philadelphia PA; D4.11.1881 Philadelphia PA; BR/TL/5´9˝/160; d5.9; ▲																								
1871	Tro NA	**29**	136	38	38	0	5	0	32	8	—	6	.279	.319	.353	92	-2	11-1	.871	-0	100	44	P29/S	—	0.0
1872	Mut NA	54	236	47	60	6	1	0	24	11	—	6	.254	.287	.288	83	-2	8-2	.871	3	46	0	O53(41/1/11),P3	—	0.3
1873	Ath NA	**52**	227	54	62	7	1	0	28	8	—	4	.273	.298	.313	75	-8	9-1	.822	-4	41	81	O51L/P	—	-0.6
1874	Ath NA	**55**	260	61	90	10	2	2	32	8	—	13	.346	.366	.423	140	10	4-3	.771	-6	62	80	O55(5/51/1)	—	0.3
1875	Phi NA	54	222	33	57	9	4	2	19	5	—	12	.257	.273	.360	114	3	6-10	.835	-1	47	132	O54(22/32/0),P4	—	0.0
Total	5NA	244	1081	233	307	32	13	4	135	40	—	41	.284	.310	.349	102	1	38-17	.827	-8	49	71	O213(119/84/12),P37/S	—	0.0
McNabb, Carl	Carl Mac "Skinny"; B1.25.1917 Stevenson AL; BR/TR/5´9˝/155; d4.20																								
1945	Det A	1	1	0	0	0	0	0	0	0	0	1	.000	.000	.000	-94	0	0-0	ø	0	—	—	/H	0	0.0
McNair, Eric	Donald Eric "Boob"; B4.12.1909 Meridian MS; D3.11.1949 Meridian MS; BR/TR/5´8.5˝/160; d9.20																								
1929	Phi A	4	8	2	4	1	0	0	3	0	0	0	.500	.500	.625	181	1	1-0	1.000	-0	75	0	S4	—	0.1
1930	†Phi A	78	237	27	63	12	2	0	34	9	1	19	.266	.296	.333	57	-16	5-2	.915	-11	78	68	S31,3b29,2b5/rf	—	-2.0
1931	†Phi A	79	280	41	76	10	1	5	33	11	3	19	.271	.306	.368	72	-12	1-4	.915	-4	98	220	3b47,2b16,S13	—	-1.3
1932	Phi A	135	554	87	158	**47**	3	18	95	28	3	29	.285	.323	.478	101	-1	8-4	.953	-12	92	111	S133	—	-0.2
1933	Phi A	89	310	57	81	15	4	7	48	15	3	32	.261	.302	.403	84	-9	2-1	.966	-2	95	99	S46,2b27	—	-0.5
1934	Phi A	151	599	80	168	20	4	17	82	35	1	42	.280	.321	.412	91	-12	7-8	.951	8	102	108	S151	—	0.6
1935	Phi A	137	526	55	142	22	2	4	57	35	3	33	.270	.319	.342	72	-23	3-7	.955	-17	91	95	S121,3b11,1b2	—	-3.2
1936	Bos A	128	494	68	141	36	2	4	74	27	5	34	.285	.329	.391	73	-22	3-3	.966	-10	91	96	S84,2b35,3b11	—	-2.1
1937	Bos A	126	455	60	133	29	4	12	76	30	3	33	.292	.340	.453	94	-5	10-7	.969	-6	99	91	2b106,S9,3b4/1	—	-0.4
1938	Bos A	46	96	9	15	1	1	0	7	3	0	6	.156	.182	.188	-7	-17	0-1	.870	1	119	58	S15,2b14,3b3	—	-1.3
1939	Chi A	129	479	62	155	18	5	7	82	38	1	41	.324	.375	.426	102	1	17-9	.937	1	97	134	3b103,2b19,S9	—	0.7
1940	Chi A	66	251	26	57	13	1	7	31	12	1	26	.227	.265	.371	62	-15	1-7	.958	-16	91	71	2b65/3	—	-2.9
1941	Det A	23	59	5	11	1	0	0	3	4	1	4	.186	.250	.203	19	-7	0-0	.970	-1	91	0	3b11,S3	0	-0.7
1942	Det A	26	68	5	11	2	0	1	4	3	0	5	.162	.197	.235	20	-7	0-1	.881	-5	76	67	S21	0	-1.3
	Phi A	34	103	8	25	2	0	0	4	11	0	5	.243	.316	.262	64	-5	1-0	.952	-5	92	60	S29/2	0	-0.7
	Year	60	171	13	36	4	0	1	8	14	0	10	.211	.270	.251	46	-13	1-1	.927	-10	86	63	S50/2	0	-2.0
Total	14	1251	4519	592	1240	229	29	82	633	261	25	328	.274	.318	.392	80	-149	59-54	.949	-79	94	99	S669,2b288,3b220,1b3/rf	0	-15.2
McNally, Mike	Michael Joseph "Minooka Mike"; B9.13.1893 Minooka PA; D5.29.1965 Bethlehem PA; BR/TR/5´11˝/150; d4.21; Mil 1918																								
1915	Bos A	23	53	7	8	0	1	0	0	3	0	7	.151	.196	.189	16	-6	0-2	.891	-1	92	154	3b18,2b5	—	-0.8
1916	†Bos A	87	135	28	23	0	0	0	9	10	0	19	.170	.228	.170	20	-14	9	.964	2	116	103	2b35,3b14,S7/cf	—	-1.2
1917	Bos A	42	50	9	15	1	0	0	2	6	0	3	.300	.375	.320	113	1	3	.935	3	118	60	3b14,S9,2b6	—	0.5
1919	Bos A	33	42	10	11	4	0	0	6	1	0	2	.262	.279	.357	83	-1	4	.950	5	125	86	S11,3b11,2b3	—	0.5
1920	Bos A	93	312	42	80	5	1	0	23	31	1	24	.256	.326	.279	64	-16	13-10	.930	-8	100	115	2b76,S8,1b6	—	-2.2
1921	†NY A	71	215	36	56	4	2	1	24	14	0	15	.260	.306	.312	56	-15	5-6	.974	14	132	60	3b49,2b16	—	0.1
1922	†NY A	52	143	20	36	2	2	0	18	16	1	14	.252	.331	.294	63	-8	3-0	.983	-2	94	95	3b34,2b9,S4/1	—	-0.7
1923	NY A	30	38	5	8	0	0	0	1	3	0	4	.211	.268	.211	27	-4	2-0	1.000	-1	116	77	S13,3b7,2b5	—	-0.4
1924	NY A	49	69	11	17	0	0	0	2	7	0	5	.246	.316	.246	46	-6	1-1	.985	5	119	125	2b25,3b13,S6	—	0.0
1925	Was A	12	21	1	3	0	0	0	0	1	0	4	.143	.182	.143	-17	-4	0-0	1.000	-1	91	97	3b7,S2/2	—	-0.4
Total	10	492	1078	169	257	16	6	1	85	92	2	97	.238	.299	.267	54	-73	40-19	.946	18	108	109	2b181,3b167,S60,1b7/cf	—	-4.6
McNamara, George	George Francis; B1.11.1901 Chicago IL; D6.12.1990 Hinsdale IL; BL/TR/6´0˝/175; d9.28																								
1922	Was A	3	11	3	3	0	0	0	1	1	0	2	.273	.333	.273	63	-1	0-0	1.000	-0	74	0	O3R	—	-0.1
McNamara, Jim	James Patrick; B6.10.1965 Nashua NH; BL/TR/6´4˝/210; [SFN86 5/110]; d4.9; Col North Carolina St.																								
1992	SF N	30	74	6	16	1	0	1	9	6-2	0	25	.216	.275	.270	58	-4	0-0	.993	-1	179	60	C30	0	-0.5
1993	SF N	4	7	0	1	0	0	0	1	0-0	0	1	.143	.143	.143	-24	-1	0-0	1.000	-0	144	0	C4	0	-0.2
Total	2	34	81	6	17	1	0	1	10	6-2	0	26	.210	.264	.259	51	-5	0-0	.993	-2	176	55	C34	0	-0.7
McNamara, Dinny	John Raymond; B9.16.1905 Lexington MA; D12.20.1963 Arlington MA; BL/TR/5´9˝/165; d7.2; Col Boston College																								
1927	Bos N	11	9	3	0	0	0	0	0	0	0	3	.000	.000	.000	-99	-3	0	1.000	1	180	0	O3C	—	-0.2
1928	Bos N	9	4	2	1	0	0	0	0	0	0	1	.250	.250	.250	33	0	0	1.000	1	198	0	O3(0/1/2)	—	0.0
Total	2	20	13	5	1	0	0	0	0	0	0	4	.077	.077	.077	-63	-3	0	1.000	1	188	0	O6(0/4/2)	—	-0.2
McNamara, Bob	Robert Maxey; B9.19.1916 Denver CO; BR/TR/5´10˝/170; d5.27; Col California																								
1939	Phi A	9	9	0	2	1	0	0	3	1	0	2	.222	.300	.333	63	0	0-0	1.000	-0	109	0	3b5,S2/12	—	-0.1
McNamara, Tom	Thomas Henry; B11.5.1895 Roxbury MA; D5.5.1974 Danvers MA; BR/TR/6´2˝/200; d6.25; Col Princeton																								
1922	Pit N	1	1	0	0	0	0	0	0	0	0	0	.000	.000	.000	-99	0	0-0	ø	0	—	—	/H	—	0.0
McNealy, Rusty	Robert Lee; B8.12.1958 Sacramento CA; BL/TL/5´8˝/160; [SeaA80 17/422]; d9.4; Col Florida International																								
1983	Oak A	15	4	5	0	0	0	0	0	0-0	0	0	.000	.000	.000	-99	-1	0-1	1.000	1	216	0	O5(1/4/1),D7	0	-0.1

McNeely, Earl George Earl; B5.12.1898 Sacramento CA; D7.16.1971 Sacramento CA; BR/TR/5´9˝/155; d8.9; C3

YEAR	TM LG	G	AB	R	H	2B	3B	HR	RBI	BB-IB	HP	SO	AVG	OBP	SLG	AOPS	ABR	SB-CS	FA	FR	RNG	THR	GAMES AT POSITION	DL	BFW
1924	†Was A	43	179	31	59	5	6	0	15	5	2	21	.330	.355	.425	104	-1	3-1	.973	-1	101	79	O42(0/42/2)	—	-0.2
1925	†Was A	122	385	76	110	14	2	3	37	48	9	54	.286	.378	.356	89	-5	15-16	.975	2	99	123	O112(7/103/2)/1	—	-0.9
1926	Was A	124	442	84	134	20	12	0	48	44	5	28	.303	.373	.403	105	3	18-6	.969	3	108	83	O118(65/52/2)	—	0.1
1927	Was A	73	185	40	51	10	4	0	16	11	1	13	.276	.320	.373	80	-6	11-4	.977	-1	98	83	O47(3/32/14),1b4	—	-0.8
1928	StL A	127	496	66	117	27	7	0	44	37	**8**	39	.236	.299	.319	61	-29	8-6	.984	5	100	150	O120(2/1/118)	—	-3.3
1929	StL A	69	230	27	56	8	1	1	18	7	2	13	.243	.272	.300	45	-19	2-1	.980	-3	91	74	O62(18/2/42)	—	-2.5
1930	StL A	76	235	33	64	19	1	0	20	22	2	14	.272	.340	.362	75	-8	8-3	.939	-2	86	94	O38(8/26/4),1b27	—	-1.2
1931	StL A	49	102	12	23	4	0	0	15	9	0	5	.225	.288	.265	45	-8	4-4	.969	-0	93	137	O37(2/23/12)/1	—	-0.9
Total	8	683	2254	369	614	107	33	4	213	183	29	187	.272	.335	.354	78	-73	69-41	.974	2	99	109	O576(105/281/196),1b33	—	-9.7

McNeely, Jeff Jeffrey Lavern; B10.18.1969 Monroe NC; BR/TR/6´2˝/200; [BosA89 2/53]; d9.5; Col Spartanburg Methodist (SC) JC

YEAR	TM LG	G	AB	R	H	2B	3B	HR	RBI	BB-IB	HP	SO	AVG	OBP	SLG	AOPS	ABR	SB-CS	FA	FR	RNG	THR	GAMES AT POSITION	DL	BFW
1993	Bos A	21	37	10	11	1	1	0	1	7-0	0	9	.297	.409	.378	106	1	6-0	.917	-3	73	0	O13C,D3	0	0.0

McNeil, Norm Norman Francis; B10.22.1892 Chicago IL; D4.11.1942 Buffalo NY; BR/TR/5´11˝/180; d6.21

YEAR	TM LG	G	AB	R	H	2B	3B	HR	RBI	BB-IB	HP	SO	AVG	OBP	SLG	AOPS	ABR	SB-CS	FA	FR	RNG	THR	GAMES AT POSITION	DL	BFW
1919	Bos A	5	9	0	3	0	0	0	1	1	0	0	.333	.400	.333	113	0	0	.818	-1	*91*	*68*	C5	—	-0.1

McNertney, Jerry Gerald Edward; B8.7.1936 Boone IA; BR/TR/6´1˝/(185–195); d4.16; C2; Col Iowa St.

YEAR	TM LG	G	AB	R	H	2B	3B	HR	RBI	BB-IB	HP	SO	AVG	OBP	SLG	AOPS	ABR	SB-CS	FA	FR	RNG	THR	GAMES AT POSITION	DL	BFW
1964	Chi A	73	186	16	40	5	0	3	23	19-4	3	24	.215	.290	.290	66	-8	0-0	.987	9	124	77	C69	0	0.4
1966	Chi A	44	59	3	13	0	0	0	1	7-0	0	6	.220	.303	.220	57	-3	1-1	.969	0	76	209	C37	0	-0.2
1967	Chi A	56	123	8	28	6	0	3	13	6-3	2	14	.228	.275	.350	87	-2	0-0	.996	4	81	214	C52	21	0.4
1968	Chi A	74	169	18	37	4	1	3	18	18-3	2	29	.219	.300	.308	84	-3	0-0	.985	6	88	114	C64/1	0	0.7
1969	Sea A	128	410	39	99	18	1	8	55	29-3	0	63	.241	.291	.349	79	-13	1-0	.988	-6	82	112	C122	0	-1.3
1970	Mil A	111	296	27	72	11	1	6	22	22-4	4	33	.243	.302	.348	79	-9	1-4	.984	-4	64	121	C94,1b13	0	-1.2
1971	StL N	56	128	15	37	4	2	4	22	12-1	0	14	.289	.343	.445	118	3	0-0	.985	-3	147	40	C36	0	0.2
1972	StL N	39	48	3	10	3	1	0	9	6-1	0	16	.208	.291	.313	73	-2	0-0	.982	2	159	205	C10	0	0.1
1973	Pit N	9	4	0	1	0	0	0	0	0-0	0	0	.250	.250	.250	40	0	0-0	1.000	-0	0	172	C9	0	0.0
Total	9	590	1423	129	337	51	6	27	163	119-19	11	199	.237	.298	.338	81	-37	3-5	.987	9	92	121	C493,1b14	21	-0.9

McNulty, Pat Patrick Howard; B2.27.1899 Cleveland OH; D5.4.1963 Hollywood CA; BL/TR/5´11˝/160; d9.5; Col Ohio St.

YEAR	TM LG	G	AB	R	H	2B	3B	HR	RBI	BB-IB	HP	SO	AVG	OBP	SLG	AOPS	ABR	SB-CS	FA	FR	RNG	THR	GAMES AT POSITION	DL	BFW
1922	Cle A	22	59	10	16	2	1	0	5	9	0	5	.271	.368	.339	85	-1	4-1	.956	-1	103	0	O22(1/19/2)	—	-0.3
1924	Cle A	101	291	46	78	13	5	0	26	33	2	22	.268	.347	.347	78	-9	10-7	.961	-2	93	106	O75(11/20/44)	—	-1.5
1925	Cle A	118	373	70	117	18	2	6	43	47	1	23	.314	.392	.421	105	4	7-7	.965	4	100	**157**	O111(3/29/81)	—	0.1
1926	Cle A	48	56	3	14	2	1	0	6	5	0	9	.250	.311	.321	65	-3	0-1	.909	0	68	387	O9(2/5/2)	—	-0.3
1927	Cle A	19	41	3	13	1	0	0	4	4	0	3	.317	.378	.341	87	-1	1-2	.906	-0	103	92	O12(1/11/0)	—	-0.2
Total	5	308	820	132	238	36	9	6	84	98	3	62	.290	.368	.378	91	-10	22-18	.957	1	97	128	O229(18/84/129)	—	-2.2

McNulty, Bill William Francis; B8.29.1946 Sacramento CA; BR/TR/6´4˝/(190–205); d7.9

YEAR	TM LG	G	AB	R	H	2B	3B	HR	RBI	BB-IB	HP	SO	AVG	OBP	SLG	AOPS	ABR	SB-CS	FA	FR	RNG	THR	GAMES AT POSITION	DL	BFW
1969	Oak A	5	17	0	0	0	0	0	0	0-0	0	10	.000	.000	.000	-99	-5	0-0	1.000	2	122	667	O5L	0	-0.3
1972	Oak A	4	10	0	1	0	0	0	0	2-0	0	1	.100	.250	.100	7	-1	0-0	.800	-2	35	0	3b3	0	-0.3
Total	2	9	27	0	1	0	0	0	0	2-0	0	11	.037	.103	.037	-61	-6	0-0	1.000	0	122	667	O5L,3b3	0	-0.6

McPhee, Bid John Alexander; B11.1.1859 Massena NY; D1.3.1943 San Diego CA; BR/TR/5´8˝/152; d5.2; M2; HF2000

YEAR	TM LG	G	AB	R	H	2B	3B	HR	RBI	BB-IB	HP	SO	AVG	OBP	SLG	AOPS	ABR	SB-CS	FA	FR	RNG	THR	GAMES AT POSITION	DL	BFW
1882	Cin AA	78	311	43	71	8	7	1	31	11	—	—	.228	.255	.309	84	-6	—	**.920**	-4	90	**130**	2b78	—	-0.7
1883	Cin AA	96	367	61	90	10	10	2	42	18	—	—	.245	.281	.343	95	-3	—	**.928**	4	97	**149**	2b96	—	0.4
1884	Cin AA	**112**	450	107	125	8	7	5	64	27	6	—	.278	.327	.360	118	8	—	.924	15	103	154	2b112	—	2.5
1885	Cin AA	110	431	78	114	12	4	0	46	19	7	—	.265	.306	.311	94	-3	—	**.936**	4	103	116	2b110	—	0.5
1886	Cin AA	140	560	139	150	23	12	**8**	70	59	5	—	.268	.343	.395	127	17	40	**.939**	27	**104**	**133**	2b140	—	**4.2**
1887	Cin AA	129	540	137	156	20	**19**	2	87	55	5	—	.289	.360	.407	111	7	95	.924	23	**109**	**147**	2b129	—	2.8
1888	Cin AA	111	458	88	110	12	10	4	51	43	5	—	.240	.312	.336	102	0	54	**.940**	26	107	**164**	2b111	—	2.8
1889	Cin AA	135	540	109	145	25	7	5	57	60	4	29	.269	.346	.369	100	0	63	**.946**	**37**	112	**133**	2b135/3	—	3.6
1890	Cin N	132	528	125	135	16	22	3	39	82	6	26	.256	.362	.386	119	13	55	.942	26	104	**130**	2b132	—	3.9
1891	Cin N	**138**	562	107	144	14	16	6	38	74	2	35	.256	.345	.370	107	5	33	**.954**	24	109	123	2b138	—	3.0
1892	Cin N	144	573	111	157	19	12	4	60	84	7	48	.274	.373	.370	127	22	44	.948	23	105	146	2b144	—	4.7
1893	Cin N	127	491	101	138	17	11	3	68	94	4	20	.281	.401	.379	105	7	25	.954	**31**	**109**	**168**	2b127	—	3.6
1894	Cin N	128	483	113	151	21	10	5	93	91	6	23	.313	.428	.429	103	6	33	.945	30	**113**	115	2b128	—	3.2
1895	Cin N	115	432	107	129	24	12	1	75	73	8	30	.299	.409	.417	109	9	30	.955	12	101	114	2b115	—	2.1
1896	Cin N	117	433	81	132	18	7	1	87	51	10	18	.305	.391	.386	98	0	48	**.978**	8	101	130	2b117	—	1.2
1897	Cin N	81	282	45	85	13	7	1	39	35	4	—	.301	.386	.408	103	1	9	.966	13	106	129	2b81	—	1.5
1898	Cin N	133	486	72	121	26	9	1	60	66	2	—	.249	.341	.346	91	-5	21	.956	-13	97	**145**	2b130,O3R	—	-1.1
1899	Cin N	112	377	60	105	17	7	1	65	40	7	—	.279	.358	.369	98	0	18	.955	-4	98	109	2b106/cf	—	0.1
Total	18	2138	8304	1684	2258	303	189	53	1072	982	88	229	.272	.355	.373	106	78	568	.944	283	104	136	2b2129,O4(0/1/3)/3	—	38.3

McPherson, Dallas Dallas Lyle; B7.23.1980 Greensboro NC; BL/TR/6´4˝/230; [AnaA01 2/57]; d9.10

YEAR	TM LG	G	AB	R	H	2B	3B	HR	RBI	BB-IB	HP	SO	AVG	OBP	SLG	AOPS	ABR	SB-CS	FA	FR	RNG	THR	GAMES AT POSITION	DL	BFW
2004	†Ana A	16	40	5	9	1	0	3	6	3-0	0	17	.225	.279	.475	95	-1	1-0	1.000	2	122	60	3b14	0	0.2
2005	LA A	61	205	29	50	14	2	8	26	14-0	1	64	.244	.295	.449	97	-2	3-3	.944	-7	83	154	3b60	87	-0.8
2006	LA A	40	115	16	30	4	0	7	13	6-0	0	40	.261	.298	.478	100	-1	1-0	.954	-2	98	79	3b31,1b6,D2	71	-0.3
Total	3	117	360	50	89	19	2	18	45	23-0	1	121	.247	.294	.461	98	-4	5-3	.955	-7	92	122	3b105,1b6,D2	158	-0.9

McQuaid, Mart Mortimer Martin; B6.28.1861 Chicago IL; D3.5.1928 Chicago IL; 5´9˝/160; d8.15

YEAR	TM LG	G	AB	R	H	2B	3B	HR	RBI	BB-IB	HP	SO	AVG	OBP	SLG	AOPS	ABR	SB-CS	FA	FR	RNG	THR	GAMES AT POSITION	DL	BFW
1891	StL AA	4	11	1	4	2	0	0	1	0	0	1	.364	.364	.545	139	0	1	1.000	0	88	112	2b3/lf	—	0.1
1898	Was N	1	4	0	0	0	0	0	0	0	0	—	.000	.000	.000	-99	-1	0	.333	-1	0	0	/lf	—	-0.2
Total	2	5	15	1	4	2	0	0	1	0	0	1	.267	.267	.400	82	-1	1	1.000	-1	88	112	2b3,O2L	—	-0.1

McQuaig, Jerry Gerald Joseph; B1.31.1912 Douglas GA; D2.5.2001 Buford GA; BR/TR/5´11˝/183; d8.25; Col Mercer

YEAR	TM LG	G	AB	R	H	2B	3B	HR	RBI	BB-IB	HP	SO	AVG	OBP	SLG	AOPS	ABR	SB-CS	FA	FR	RNG	THR	GAMES AT POSITION	DL	BFW
1934	Phi A	7	16	2	1	0	0	0	1	2	0	4	.063	.167	.063	-40	-3	0-0	.889	-1	95	0	O6(5/0/1)	—	-0.4

McQuery, Mox William Thomas; B6.28.1861 Garrard Co. KY; D6.12.1900 Cincinnati OH; 6´4˝/?; d8.20

YEAR	TM LG	G	AB	R	H	2B	3B	HR	RBI	BB-IB	HP	SO	AVG	OBP	SLG	AOPS	ABR	SB-CS	FA	FR	RNG	THR	GAMES AT POSITION	DL	BFW
1884	Cin U	35	132	31	37	5	0	2	—	8	—	—	.280	.321	.364	99	-4	—	.978	1	80	88	1b35	—	-0.5
1885	Det N	70	278	34	76	15	4	3	30	8	—	29	.273	.294	.388	119	5	—	.976	3	117	88	1b70	—	0.2
1886	KC N	122	449	62	111	27	4	4	38	36	—	44	.247	.303	.352	93	-4	4	.969	1	108	90	1b122	—	-1.3
1890	Syr AA	122	461	64	142	17	6	2	55	53	3	—	.308	.383	.384	141	27	26	.972	-1	94	93	1b122	—	1.3
1891	Was AA	68	261	40	63	9	4	2	37	18	6	19	.241	.305	.330	86	-5	3	.977	1	107	85	1b68	—	-0.9
Total	5	417	1581	231	429	73	18	13	160	123	9	92	.271	.327	.365	110	19	33	.973	5	103	90	1b417	—	-1.2

McQuillen, Glenn Glenn Richard "Red"; B4.19.1915 Strasburg VA; D6.8.1989 Baltimore MD; BR/TR/6´0˝/198; d6.16; Mil 1943–45; Col McDaniel

YEAR	TM LG	G	AB	R	H	2B	3B	HR	RBI	BB-IB	HP	SO	AVG	OBP	SLG	AOPS	ABR	SB-CS	FA	FR	RNG	THR	GAMES AT POSITION	DL	BFW
1938	StL A	43	116	14	33	4	0	0	13	4	0	12	.284	.308	.319	57	-8	0-1	.971	1	122	0	O30L	—	-0.8
1941	StL A	7	21	4	7	2	1	0	3	1	0	2	.333	.364	.524	128	1	0-1	.933	-0	108	0	O6(3/0/3)	0	0.0
1942	StL A	100	339	40	96	15	12	3	47	10	1	17	.283	.306	.425	103	-2	1-1	.969	-6	93	32	O77(68/0/9)	0	-1.3
1946	StL A	59	166	24	40	3	3	1	12	19	0	18	.241	.319	.313	73	-6	0-2	.977	3	94	299	O48(44/0/5)	0	-0.6
1947	StL A	1	1	0	0	0	0	0	0	0	0	0	.000	.000	.000	-98	0	0-0	ø	0	—	—	/H	0	0.0
Total	5	210	643	82	176	24	16	4	75	34	1	49	.274	.311	.379	87	-15	1-5	.970	-2	99	93	O161(145/0/17)	0	-2.7

McQuinn, George George Hartley; B5.29.1910 Arlington VA; D12.24.1978 Alexandria VA; BL/TL/5´11˝/165; d4.14

YEAR	TM LG	G	AB	R	H	2B	3B	HR	RBI	BB-IB	HP	SO	AVG	OBP	SLG	AOPS	ABR	SB-CS	FA	FR	RNG	THR	GAMES AT POSITION	DL	BFW
1936	Cin N	38	134	5	27	3	4	0	13	10	1	22	.201	.262	.284	50	-10	0	.992	1	111	100	1b38	—	-1.2
1938	StL A	148	602	100	195	42	7	12	82	58	1	49	.324	.384	.477	115	14	4-5	.992	1	95	92	1b148	—	0.0
1939	StL A☆	154	617	101	195	37	13	20	94	65	2	42	.316	.383	.515	125	22	6-5	.993	10	123	80	1b154	—	1.5
1940	StL A☆	151	594	78	166	39	10	16	84	57	0	58	.279	.343	.460	104	2	3-3	**.992**	9	**126**	112	1b150	—	-0.3
1941	StL A	130	495	93	147	28	4	18	80	74	0	30	.297	.388	.479	124	19	5-4	**.995**	7	117	102	1b125	0	1.3
1942	StL A☆	145	554	86	145	32	5	12	78	60	1	77	.262	.335	.403	105	3	1-1	.991	1	103	96	1b144	0	-0.9
1943	StL A	125	449	53	109	19	2	12	74	56	0	65	.243	.327	.374	103	1	4-3	.992	2	104	84	1b122	0	-0.3
1944	†StL A★	146	516	83	129	26	3	11	72	85	1	74	.250	.357	.376	103	5	4-3	**.994**	-6	80	93	1b146	0	-0.9
1945	StL A✶	139	483	69	134	31	3	7	61	65	1	51	.277	.364	.398	115	11	1-1	.991	4	107	82	1b136	0	0.9
1946	Phi A	136	484	47	109	23	6	3	35	64	1	62	.225	.317	.316	78	-14	4-2	.988	2	106	88	1b134	0	-1.7
1947	†NY A★	144	517	84	157	24	3	13	80	78	0	66	.304	.395	.437	132	25	0-2	.994	-2	89	98	1b142	0	1.8

YEAR	TM LG	G	AB	R	H	2B	3B	HR	RBI	BB-IB	HP	SO	AVG	OBP	SLG	AOPS	ABR	SB-CS	FA	FR	RNG	THR	GAMES AT POSITION	DL	BFW
1948	NY A★	94	302	33	75	11	4	11	41	40	0	38	.248	.336	.421	102	-1	0-2	.993	-1	90	106	1b90	0	-0.5
Total	12	1550	5747	832	1588	315	64	135	794	712	8	634	.276	.357	.424	109	77	32-31	.992	28	104	94	1b1529	0	-0.3
McRae, Brian	Brian Wesley; B8.27.1967 Bradenton FL; BB/TR/6´0˝/(180–195); [KCA85 1/17]; d8.7; f–Hal																								
1990	KC A	46	168	21	48	8	3	2	23	9-0	0	29	.286	.318	.405	103	0	4-3	1.000	1	110	47	O45C	0	0.1
1991	KC A	152	629	86	164	28	9	8	64	24-1	2	99	.261	.288	.372	81	-19	20-11	.993	-2	106	26	O150C	0	-2.1
1992	KC A	149	533	63	119	23	5	4	52	42-1	6	88	.223	.285	.308	65	-26	18-5	.993	1	102	95	O148C	0	-2.4
1993	KC A	153	627	78	177	28	9	12	69	37-1	4	105	.282	.325	.413	91	-10	23-14	.983	-6	98	48	O153C	0	-1.3
1994	KC A	114	436	71	119	22	6	4	40	54-3	6	67	.273	.359	.378	87	-8	28-8	.988	-12	85	34	O110C,D4	0	-1.4
1995	Chi N	137	580	92	167	38	7	12	48	47-1	7	92	.288	.348	.440	106	5	27-8	.991	-2	104	53	O137C	0	0.9
1996	Chi N	157	624	111	172	32	5	17	66	73-6	12	84	.276	.360	.425	103	4	37-9	.986	-12	92	24	O155C	0	-0.1
1997	Chi N	108	417	63	100	27	5	6	28	52-2	4	62	.240	.329	.372	81	-11	14-6	.996	-2	103	60	O107C	0	-1.0
	NY N	45	145	23	36	5	2	5	15	13-0	2	22	.248	.317	.414	94	-2	3-4	.957	-6	77	56	O41C	0	-0.8
	Year	153	562	86	136	32	7	11	43	65-2	6	84	.242	.326	.383	84	-13	17-10	.987	-7	96	59	O148C	0	-1.8
1998	NY N	159	552	79	146	36	5	21	79	80-3	5	90	.264	.360	.462	119	16	20-11	.987	-13	86	86	O154C	0	0.6
1999	NY N	96	298	35	66	12	1	8	36	39-1	5	57	.221	.320	.349	73	-13	2-6	.994	-11	80	24	O87C	0	-2.3
	Col N	7	23	1	6	2	0	1	1	2-0	2	7	.261	.370	.478	90	0	0-0	1.000	-1	90	0	O7C	0	-0.1
	Year	103	321	36	72	14	1	9	37	41-1	7	64	.224	.323	.358	75	-13	2-6	.994	-12	90	130	O94C	0	-2.4
	Tor A	31	82	11	16	3	1	3	11	16-1	2	22	.195	.340	.366	79	-2	0-1	1.000	-0	90	130	D15,O13C	0	-0.4
Total	10	1354	5114	734	1336	264	58	103	532	488-20	57	824	.261	.331	.396	91	-66	196-86	.990	-63	96	52	O1307C,D19	0	-10.3
McRae, Hal	Harold Abraham; B7.10.1945 Avon Park FL; BR/TR/5´11˝/(180–185); [CinN65 6/117]; d7.11; M6/C12; s–Brian; Col Florida A&M; OF(360/33/94)																								
1968	Cin N	17	51	1	10	1	0	0	2	4-2	0	14	.196	.255	.216	40	-4	1-1	.926	-6	70	84	2b16	0	-1.1
1970	†Cin N	70	165	18	41	6	1	8	23	15-2	1	23	.248	.313	.442	100	-1	0-2	.981	-3	89	41	O46(46/0/1),3b6/2	0	-0.7
1971	Cin N	99	337	39	89	24	2	9	34	11-0	2	35	.264	.291	.427	102	0	3-2	.966	-0	94	109	O91(66/28/0)	0	-0.5
1972	†Cin N	61	97	9	27	4	0	5	26	2-0	2	10	.278	.295	.474	125	2	0-0	.867	-3	101	0	O12(0/3/9),3b11	0	-0.1
1973	KC A	106	338	36	79	18	3	9	50	34-2	6	38	.234	.312	.385	89	-5	2-2	.963	-1	96	110	O64(3/0/63),D37,3b2	0	-1.0
1974	KC A	148	539	71	167	36	4	15	88	54-6	5	68	.310	.375	.475	136	27	11-8	.950	2	115	49	D90,O56(40/0/19)/3	0	2.3
1975	KC A★	126	480	58	147	38	6	5	71	47-7	4	47	.306	.366	.442	126	18	11-8	.986	-4	88	86	O114(112/2/0),D12/3	0	0.7
1976	†KC A★	149	527	75	175	34	5	8	73	64-7	8	43	.332	**.407**	.461	154	**39**	22-12	.970	0	104	95	D117,O31L	0	3.7
1977	†KC A	**162**	641	104	191	**54**	11	21	92	59-5	**13**	43	.298	.366	.515	136	33	18-14	.958	5	109	275	D115,O47L	0	3.2
1978	†KC A	156	623	90	170	39	5	16	72	51-6	6	62	.273	.329	.429	110	8	17-8	1.000	0	55	557	D153,O3L	0	0.4
1979	KC A	101	393	55	113	32	4	10	74	38-0	4	46	.288	.351	.466	117	10	5-4	ø	0	0	0	D100	52	0.7
1980	†KC A	124	489	73	145	39	5	14	83	29-4	8	56	.297	.342	.483	123	15	10-2	1.000	-1	99	0	D110,O9L	20	1.2
1981	†KC A	101	389	38	106	23	2	7	36	34-3	2	33	.272	.330	.396	110	5	3-4	.909	0	128	0	D97,O4(2/0/2)	0	0.1
1982	KC A★	159	613	91	189	**46**	8	27	**133**	55-7	5	61	.308	.369	.542	145	38	4-4	.500	-1	45	0	D158/lf	0	3.2
1983	KC A	157	589	84	183	41	6	12	82	50-7	10	68	.311	.372	.462	128	24	2-3	ø	0	0	0	D156	0	1.8
1984	†KC A	106	317	30	96	13	4	3	42	34-3	1	47	.303	.363	.397	112	6	0-3	ø	0	0	0	D94	0	0.2
1985	†KC A	112	320	41	83	19	0	14	70	44-3	1	45	.259	.349	.450	116	8	0-1	ø	0	0	0	D106	0	0.5
1986	KC A	112	278	22	70	14	0	7	37	18-4	1	39	.252	.298	.378	81	-8	0-0	ø	0	0	0	D75	0	-1.0
1987	KC A	18	32	5	10	3	0	1	9	5-1	0	1	.313	.405	.500	134	2	0-0	ø	0	—	—	D7	0	0.2
Total	19	2084	7218	940	2091	484	66	191	1097	648-69	79	779	.290	.351	.454	122	217	109-78	.966	-11	97	103	D1427,O478L,3b21,2b17	72	13.8
McRemer	; d6.20																								
1884	Was U	1	3	0	0	0	0	0	—	0	—	—	.000	.000	.000	-99	-1	—	1.000	0	0	0	/rf	—	-0.1
McReynolds, Kevin	Walter Kevin; B10.16.1959 Little Rock AR; BR/TR/6´1˝/(205–225); [SDN81 1/6]; d6.2; Col Arkansas																								
1983	SD N	39	140	15	31	3	1	4	14	12-1	0	29	.221	.277	.343	75	-5	2-1	.989	0	92	190	O38(3/32/10)	0	-0.6
1984	†SD N	147	525	68	146	26	6	20	75	34-8	0	69	.278	.317	.465	118	10	3-6	.991	10	113	122	O143C	0	1.8
1985	SD N	152	564	61	132	24	4	15	75	43-6	3	81	.234	.290	.371	85	-13	4-0	.993	9	111	125	O150C	0	-0.5
1986	SD N	158	560	89	161	31	6	26	96	66-6	1	83	.287	.358	.504	140	30	8-6	.977	2	102	96	O154(108/109/3)	0	2.8
1987	NY N	151	590	86	163	32	5	29	95	39-5	1	70	.276	.318	.495	117	11	14-1	.987	1	101	79	O150L	0	0.8
1988	†NY N	147	552	82	159	30	2	27	99	38-3	4	56	.288	.336	.496	143	28	21-0	.985	6	93	**213**	O147(147/1/0)	0	3.6
1989	NY N	148	545	74	148	25	3	22	85	46-10	1	74	.272	.326	.450	126	16	15-7	.969	8	112	129	O145L	0	2.1
1990	NY N	147	521	75	140	23	1	24	82	71-11	1	61	.269	.353	.455	122	16	9-2	.988	-2	88	147	O144L	0	1.2
1991	NY N	143	522	65	135	32	1	16	74	49-7	2	46	.259	.322	.416	107	5	6-6	.993	1	99	116	O141(125/33/2)	0	0.2
1992	KC A	109	373	45	92	25	0	13	49	67-3	0	48	.247	.357	.418	114	9	7-1	.986	-7	90	55	O106(94/0/12)/D	27	0.0
1993	KC A	110	351	44	86	22	4	11	42	37-6	1	56	.245	.316	.425	92	-5	2-2	.990	0	99	89	O104L/D	23	-0.8
1994	NY N	51	180	23	46	11	2	4	21	20-1	0	34	.256	.328	.406	92	-2	2-0	1.000	-0	100	34	O47L	62	-0.4
Total	12	1502	5423	727	1439	284	35	211	807	522-67	14	707	.265	.328	.447	115	100	93-32	.987	27	101	119	O1469(1067/468/27),D2	112	10.2
McShannic, Pete	Peter Robert; B3.20.1864 Pittsburgh PA; D11.30.1946 Toledo OH; BB/TR/5´7˝/190; d9.15																								
1888	Pit N	26	98	5	19	1	0	0	5	1	2	9	.194	.218	.204	38	-7	3	.907	-1	95	29	3b26	—	-0.7
McSorley, Trick	John Bernard; B12.6.1852 St.Louis MO; D2.9.1936 St.Louis MO; BR/TR/5´4˝/142; d5.6																								
1875	RS NA	15	52	4	11	0	0	0	2	0	—	3	.212	.212	.212	53	-2	3-0	.745	0	121	0	3b9,O7(6/1/0)	—	-0.1
1884	Tol AA	21	68	12	17	1	0	0	—	3	0	—	.250	.282	.265	77	-2	—	.974	1	150	207	1b16,O5L/3P	—	-0.2
1885	StL N	2	6	2	3	1	0	0	1	2	—	1	.500	.625	.667	340	2	—	.400	-2	29	0	3b2	—	0.0
1886	StL AA	5	20	1	3	3	0	0	0	0	0	—	.150	.150	.300	38	-1	0	.765	-3	66	0	S5	—	-0.4
Total	3	28	94	15	23	5	0	0	1	5	0	1	.245	.283	.298	85	-1	0	.745	-3	150	207	1b16,S5,O5L,3b3/P	—	-0.6
McSweeney, Paul	Paul A.; B4.3.1867 St.Louis MO; D8.12.1951 St.Louis MO; d9.20																								
1891	StL AA	3	12	2	3	1	0	0	2	0	1	0	.250	.308	.333	73	0	1	.643	-3	69	0	2b3/3	—	-0.3
McTamany, Jim	James Edward; B7.1.1863 Philadelphia PA; D4.16.1916 Lenni PA; BR/TR/5´8˝/190; d8.15																								
1885	Bro AA	35	131	21	36	7	2	1	13	9	0	—	.275	.321	.382	121	3	—	.896	-4	0	0	O35L	—	-0.1
1886	Bro AA	111	418	86	106	23	10	2	56	54	10	—	.254	.353	.371	126	15	18	.893	11	150	145	O111(0/107/4)	—	2.0
1887	Bro AA	134	520	123	134	22	10	1	68	76	12	—	.258	.365	.344	97	1	66	.918	6	147	162	O134C	—	0.2
1888	KC AA	130	516	94	127	12	10	4	41	67	11	—	.246	.345	.331	110	7	55	.913	0	121	87	O130(0/80/50)	—	0.4
1889	Col AA	**139**	529	113	146	21	7	4	52	116	1	66	.276	.407	.365	127	28	40	.902	-7	107	128	O139C	—	1.5
1890	Col AA	125	466	**140**	120	27	7	1	48	**112**	4	—	.258	.405	.352	132	30	43	.940	0	80	**198**	O125C	—	2.3
1891	Col AA	81	304	59	76	17	9	3	35	58	2	48	.250	.374	.395	127	13	20	.929	-3	71	137	O81C	—	0.7
	Phi AA	58	218	57	49	6	3	3	21	43	5	44	.225	.365	.321	96	1	13	.901	-1	97	47	O58(0/57/1)	—	-0.1
	Year	139	522	116	125	23	12	6	56	101	7	92	.239	.370	.364	114	14	33	.917	-4	82	99	O139(0/138/1)	—	0.6
Total	7	813	3102	693	794	135	58	19	334	535	45	158	.256	.373	.355	117	98	255	.913	3	109	130	O813(35/723/55)	—	6.9
McVey, Cal	Calvin Alexander; B8.30.1849 Montrose IA; D8.20.1926 San Francisco CA; BR/TR/5´9˝/170; d5.5; M3; OF NA(4/32/66); ▲																								
1871	Bos NA	29	153	43	**66**	9	5	0	43	1	—	2	.431	.435	.556	177	14	6-0	.873	2	—	—	C29,O5R/3	—	1.1
1872	Bos NA	46	237	56	76	10	2	0	41	1	—	1	.321	.324	.380	110	1	6-1	.869	6	—	—	C39,O11(2/0/9)/3	—	0.6
1873	Bal NA	38	192	49	73	5	5	2	35	3	—	2	.380	.390	.490	159	13	2-1	**.907**	-1	—	—	C25,O6(1/4/1),S5,2b4,1b3,3b2,M	—	0.8
1874	Bos NA	70	343	**91**	**123**	21	6	3	**71**	1	—	3	.359	.360	.481	159	20	5-0	.710	-2	91	0	O57(0/8/49),C23	—	1.7
1875	Bos NA	**82**	389	89	138	**36**	9	3	**87**	1	—	5	.355	.356	**.517**	193	35	7-0	.949	7	**129**	155	1b55,O23(1/20/2),C16,P3	—	3.7
1876	Chi N	63	308	62	107	15	0	1	53	2	—	4	.347	.352	.406	136	10	—	.959	4	110	**145**	1b55,P11,C6/lf3	—	0.9
1877	Chi N	**60**	266	58	98	9	7	0	36	8	—	11	.368	.387	.455	147	13	—	.859	-10	—	—	C40,3b17,P17/21	—	0.2
1878	Cin N	**61**	271	43	83	10	4	2	28	5	—	10	.306	.319	.395	147	14	—	.814	-10	82	89	3b61,C3,M	—	0.6
1879	Cin N	**81**	354	64	105	18	6	0	55	8	—	13	.297	.312	.381	134	13	—	.946	-7	27	101	1b72,O7(0/1/6),P3/3CM	—	0.2
Total	5NA	265	1314	328	476	81	27	8	277	7	—	13	.362	.366	.483	161	83	26-2	.876	12	—	—	C132,O102R,1b58,S5,2b4,3b4,P3	—	7.9
Total	4	265	1199	227	393	52	17	3	172	23	—	38	.328	.340	.407	140	50	—	.951	-23	—	—	1b128,3b80,C50,P31,O8(1/1/6)/2	—	1.9
McVey, George	George W.; B9.16.1865 Port Jervis NY; D5.3.1896 Quincy IL; BR/TR/6´1˝/185; d9.19																								
1885	Bro AA	6	21	2	3	0	0	0	1	2	0	—	.143	.217	.143	15	-2	—	.967	0	0	139	1b3,C3	—	-0.2
McWilliams, Bill	William Henry; B11.28.1910 Dubuque IA; D1.21.1997 Garland TX; BR/TR/6´0˝/185; d7.8; Col Iowa																								
1931	Bos A	2	2	0	0	0	0	0	0	0	0	1	.000	.000	.000	-99	-1	0-0	ø	0	—	—	/H	—	-0.1

THE BATTER REGISTER

YEAR	TM LG	G	AB	R	H	2B	3B	HR	RBI	BB-IB	HP	SO	AVG	OBP	SLG	AOPS	ABR	SB-CS	FA	FR	RNG	THR	GAMES AT POSITION	DL	BFW
Meacham, Bob	Robert Andrew; B8.25.1960 Los Angeles CA; BB/TR (BR 1987–88)/6´1˝/(175–180); [StLN81 1/8]; d6.30; C1; Col San Diego St.																								
1983	NY A	22	51	5	12	2	0	0	4	4-0	1	10	.235	.304	.275	62	-3	8-0	.929	4	124	103	S18,3b4	0	0.5
1984	NY A	99	360	62	91	13	4	2	25	32-0	3	70	.253	.312	.328	82	-9	9-5	.955	-12	91	87	S96,2b2	0	-1.1
1985	NY A	156	481	70	105	16	2	1	47	54-1	5	102	.218	.302	.266	59	-26	25-7	.963	-20	87	112	S155	0	-2.7
1986	NY A	56	161	19	36	7	1	0	10	17-0	3	39	.224	.309	.280	62	-8	3-6	.948	-4	101	100	S56	0	-0.8
1987	NY A	77	203	28	55	11	1	5	21	19-0	6	33	.271	.349	.409	101	1	6-5	.961	-5	94	93	S56,2b25/D	15	0.1
1988	NY A	47	115	18	25	9	0	0	7	14-0	2	22	.217	.308	.296	72	-4	7-1	.959	-7	81	101	S24,2b21,3b5	81	-0.8
Total	6	457	1371	202	324	58	8	8	114	140-1	20	276	.236	.313	.308	73	-49	58-24	.957	-44	92	101	S405,2b48,3b9/D	96	-4.8
Mead, Charlie	Charles Richard; B4.9.1921 Vermilion AL, Can.; BL/TR/6´1.5˝/185; d8.28																								
1943	NY N	37	146	9	40	6	1	1	13	10	0	15	.274	.321	.349	93	-2	3	.976	-0	100	77	O37(0/3/34)	0	-0.5
1944	NY N	39	78	5	14	1	0	1	8	5	0	7	.179	.229	.231	30	-8	0	.981	4	115	245	O23(13/3/7)	0	-0.5
1945	NY N	11	37	4	10	1	0	1	6	5	0	2	.270	.357	.378	103	0	0	.962	1	93	285	O11(0/1/11)	0	0.1
Total	3	87	261	18	64	8	1	3	27	20	0	24	.245	.299	.318	75	-10	3	.975	4	103	158	O71(13/7/52)	0	-0.9
Meadows, Louie	Michael Ray; B4.29.1961 Maysville NC; BL/TL/5´11˝/(189–190); [HouN82 2/43]; d7.3; Col North Carolina St.																								
1986	Hou N	6	6	1	2	0	0	0	0	0-0	0	0	.333	.333	.333	87	0	1-0	ø	-0	0	0	/rf	0	0.0
1988	Hou N	35	42	5	8	0	1	2	3	6-0	0	8	.190	.292	.381	95	0	4-2	1.000	1	128	237	O10(7/1/3)	0	0.1
1989	Hou N	31	51	5	9	0	0	3	10	1-0	0	14	.176	.189	.353	55	-4	1-2	1.000	-2	65	0	O14(12/0/4)/1	0	-0.6
1990	Hou N	15	14	3	2	0	0	0	0	2-0	0	4	.143	.250	.143	11	-2	0-0	1.000	-0	107	0	O9(7/0/2)	0	-0.2
	Phi N	15	14	1	1	0	0	0	0	1-0	0	2	.071	.133	.071	-42	-3	0-0	1.000	-1	32	0	O4(3/2/0)	0	-0.3
	Year	30	28	4	3	0	0	0	0	3-0	0	6	.107	.194	.107	-15	-4	0-0	1.000	-1	84	0	O13(10/2/2)	0	-0.5
Total	4	102	127	15	22	0	1	5	13	10-0	0	28	.173	.232	.307	54	-9	6-4	1.000	-1	91	82	O38(29/3/10)/1	0	-1.0
Meara, Charlie	Charles Edward "Goggy"; B4.16.1891 New York NY; D2.8.1962 Bronx NY; BL/TR/5´10˝/160; d6.1; Col Manhattan																								
1914	NY A	4	7	2	2	0	0	0	1	2	0	2	.286	.444	.286	120	0	0-1	1.000	-0	105	0	O3(0/2/2)	—	0.0
Meares, Pat	Patrick James; B9.6.1968 Salina KS; BR/TR/6´0˝/(184–188); [MinA90 12/329]; d5.5; Col Wichita St.; [DL 2002 Pit N 183, 2003 Pit N 183]																								
1993	Min A	111	346	33	87	14	3	0	33	7-0	1	52	.251	.266	.309	54	-23	4-5	.961	-0	101	105	S111	0	-1.7
1994	Min A	80	229	29	61	12	1	2	24	14-0	2	50	.266	.310	.354	71	-10	5-1	.963	-2	98	98	S79	15	-0.5
1995	Min A	116	390	57	105	19	4	12	49	15-0	11	68	.269	.311	.431	91	-7	10-4	.965	-3	100	93	S114,O3(0/2/1)	0	-0.1
1996	Min A	152	517	66	138	26	7	8	67	17-1	9	90	.267	.298	.391	72	-24	9-4	.965	-27	83	92	S150/cf	0	-3.6
1997	Min A	134	439	63	121	23	3	10	60	18-0	16	86	.276	.323	.410	89	-7	7-7	.969	15	**112**	**112**	S134	15	1.5
1998	Min A	149	543	56	141	26	3	9	70	24-1	6	86	.260	.296	.368	70	-25	7-4	.966	-9	96	100	S149	0	-2.2
1999	Pit N	21	91	15	28	4	0	0	7	9-0	2	20	.308	.382	.352	87	-1	0-0	.939	1	110	96	S21	150	0.1
2000	Pit N	132	462	55	111	22	2	13	47	36-6	8	91	.240	.305	.381	72	-21	1-0	.967	22	**115**	118	S126	0	0.9
2001	Pit N	87	270	27	57	11	1	4	25	10-3	2	45	.211	.244	.304	40	-25	0-2	.973	3	111	110	2b85	27	-1.9
Total	9	982	3287	401	849	157	24	58	382	150-11	57	588	.258	.299	.374	72	-143	43-27	.965	-1	101	103	S884,2b85,O4(0/3/1)	573	-7.5
Medeiros, Ray	Ray Antone "Pep"; B5.9.1926 Oakland CA; D6.6.2003 San Mateo CA; BR/TR/5´10˝/163; d4.25																								
1945	Cin N	1	0	0	0	0	0	0	0	0	0	0	ø	ø	ø	ø	0	0	ø	0	—	—	/R	0	0.0
Medina, Luis	Luis Main; B3.26.1963 Santa Monica CA; BR/TL/6´4˝/195; [CleA85 9/219]; d9.2; Col Arizona St.																								
1988	Cle A	16	51	10	13	0	0	6	8	2-0	2	18	.255	.309	.608	146	3	0-0	1.000	-0	86	111	1b16	0	0.1
1989	Cle A	30	83	8	17	1	0	4	8	6-0	0	35	.205	.258	.361	71	-4	0-1	.500	-1	48	0	D25,O3(1/0/2)/1	0	-0.6
1991	Cle A	5	16	0	1	0	0	0	0	1-0	0	7	.063	.118	.063	-48	-3	0-0	ø	0	—	—	D5	0	-0.4
Total	3	51	150	18	31	1	0	10	16	9-0	2	60	.207	.261	.413	84	-4	0-1	1.000	-1	85	110	D30,1b17,O3(1/0/2)	0	-0.9
Medwick, Joe	Joseph Michael "Ducky","Muscles"; B11.24.1911 Carteret NJ; D3.21.1975 St.Petersburg FL; BR/TR/5´10˝/187; d9.2; HF1968																								
1932	StL N	26	106	13	37	12	1	2	12	2	1	10	.349	.367	.538	136	5	3	.970	-1	95	96	O26(7/19/0)	—	0.4
1933	StL N	148	595	92	182	40	10	18	98	26	2	56	.306	.337	.497	129	20	5	.980	7	103	150	O147L	—	2.0
1934	†StL N★	149	620	110	198	40	**18**	18	106	21	1	83	.319	.343	.529	122	16	3	.960	3	105	97	O149(144/0/5)	—	1.0
1935	StL N★	**154**	634	132	224	46	13	23	126	30	4	59	.353	.386	.576	149	42	4	.965	3	108	74	O154L	—	3.4
1936	StL N★	**155**	636	115	**223**	**64**	13	18	**138**	34	4	33	.351	.387	.577	157	49	3	.985	14	**114**	141	O155L	—	5.2
1937	StL N★	**156**	633	**111**	**237**	**56**	10	**31**	**154**	41	2	50	**.374**	.414	**.641**	**179**	**68**	4	**.988**	4	107	81	O156L	—	6.0
1938	StL N★	146	590	100	190	**47**	8	21	**122**	42	2	41	.322	.369	.536	138	30	0	.974	8	109	105	O144L	—	3.0
1939	StL N★	150	606	98	201	48	8	14	117	45	2	44	.332	.380	.507	128	24	6	.976	5	106	113	O149L	—	2.1
1940	StL N	37	158	21	48	12	0	3	20	6	0	8	.304	.329	.437	104	1	0	.988	-1	101	37	O37L	—	-0.2
	Bro N★	106	423	62	127	18	12	14	66	26	3	28	.300	.345	.499	123	11	2	.980	4	107	92	O103L	—	0.9
	Year	143	581	83	175	30	12	17	86	32	3	36	.301	.341	.482	118	12	2	.982	3	105	77	O140L	—	0.7
1941	†Bro N★	133	538	100	171	33	10	18	88	38	1	35	.318	.364	.517	140	26	2	.983	-3	90	116	O131(130/0/1)	0	1.6
1942	Bro N★	142	553	69	166	37	4	4	96	32	0	25	.300	.338	.403	115	9	2	.990	-3	99	55	O140L	0	-0.1
1943	Bro N	48	173	13	47	10	0	0	25	10	1	8	.272	.315	.329	86	-3	1	.971	-3	88	60	O42L	0	-0.9
	NY N	78	324	41	91	20	3	5	45	9	0	14	.281	.300	.407	103	-1	0	.988	3	100	138	O74L,1b3	0	-0.3
	Year	126	497	54	138	30	3	5	70	19	1	22	.278	.306	.380	97	-4	1	.983	-0	96	113	O116L,1b3	0	-1.2
1944	NY N★	128	490	64	165	24	3	7	85	38	1	24	.337	.386	.441	133	21	2	.993	7	**114**	89	O122L	0	2.1
1945	NY N	26	92	14	28	4	0	3	11	2	0	2	.304	.319	.446	110	1	2	.979	-1	95	63	O23L	0	-0.2
	Bos N	66	218	17	62	13	0	0	26	12	1	12	.284	.325	.344	85	-4	3	1.000	2	97	261	O38L,1b15	0	-0.6
	Year	92	310	31	90	17	0	3	37	14	1	14	.290	.323	.374	93	-4	5	.992	1	96	185	O61L,1b15	0	-0.8
1946	Bro N	41	77	7	24	4	0	2	18	6	1	5	.312	.369	.442	128	3	0	1.000	-1	106	0	O18L/1	0	0.1
1947	StL N	75	150	19	46	12	0	4	28	16	0	12	.307	.373	.467	117	4	0	1.000	0	95	122	O43(7/0/36)	0	0.3
1948	StL N	20	19	0	4	0	0	0	2	1	0	2	.211	.250	.211	24	-2	0	ø	-0	0	0	/rf	0	-0.2
Total	17	1984	7635	1198	2471	540	113	205	1383	437	26	551	.324	.362	.505	133	320	42	.980	47	104	103	O1852(1790/19/43),1b19	0	25.6
Mee, Tommy	Thomas William "Judge"; B3.18.1890 Chicago IL; D5.16.1981 Chicago IL; BR/TR/5´8˝/165; d6.14																								
1910	StL A	8	19	1	3	2	0	0	1	0	0	—	.158	.158	.263	34	-1	0	.828	-1	116	0	S6/23	—	-0.3
Meek, Dad	Frank J.; B3.14.1867 St.Louis MO; D12.22.1922 St.Louis MO; 6´0˝/?; d5.10																								
1889	StL AA	2	2	2	1	0	0	0	1	0	0	0	.500	.500	.500	164	0	1	.667	0	—	—	C2	—	0.0
1890	StL AA	4	16	3	5	0	0	0	1	0	0	—	.313	.313	.313	74	-1	1	.913	1	*96*	*129*	C4	—	0.1
Total	2	6	18	5	6	0	0	0	2	0	0	0	.333	.333	.333	84	-1	2	.898	1	*96*	*129*	C6	—	0.1
Meeks, Sammy	Samuel Mack; B4.23.1923 Anderson SC; BR/TR/5´9˝/160; d4.29																								
1948	Was A	24	33	4	4	1	0	0	2	1	0	12	.121	.147	.152	-21	-6	0-0	.939	-1	93	120	S10/2	0	-0.6
1949	Cin N	16	36	10	11	2	0	2	6	2	0	6	.306	.342	.528	128	1	1	1.000	4	117	177	2b8,S3	0	0.5
1950	Cin N	39	95	7	27	5	0	1	8	6	0	14	.284	.327	.368	82	-2	1	.951	-2	95	89	S29,3b2	0	-0.3
1951	Cin N	23	35	4	8	0	0	0	2	0	0	4	.229	.229	.229	23	-4	1-0	.929	-1	47	215	3b4/S	0	-0.5
Total	4	102	199	25	50	8	0	3	18	9	0	36	.251	.284	.337	64	-11	3-0	.953	-1	97	104	S43,2b9,3b6	0	-0.9
Meier, Dutch	Arthur Ernst; B3.30.1879 St.Louis MO; D3.23.1948 Chicago IL; BR/TR/5´10˝/175; d5.12; Col Princeton																								
1906	Pit N	82	273	32	70	11	4	0	16	13	3	—	.256	.298	.326	90	-4	4	.975	-6	90	164	O52(29/6/18),S17	—	-1.2
Meier, Dave	David Keith; B8.8.1959 Helena MT; BR/TR/6´0˝/185; [MinA81 5/114]; d4.3; Col Stanford																								
1984	Min A	59	147	18	35	8	1	0	13	6-0	1	9	.238	.271	.306	57	-9	0-1	.978	-1	99	71	O50(41/0/10)/3D	0	-1.2
1985	Min A	71	104	15	27	6	0	1	8	18-0	1	12	.260	.374	.346	93	0	0-6	.987	-0	102	44	O63(55/3/4),D3	0	-0.4
1987	Tex A	13	21	4	6	1	0	0	0	0-0	0	4	.286	.286	.333	63	-1	0-0	.917	-0	100	0	O8(6/0/2)	0	-0.2
1988	Chi N	2	5	0	2	0	0	0	1	0-0	0	1	.400	.400	.400	124	0	0-0	1.000	-1	0	0	/3	0	-0.1
Total	4	145	277	37	70	15	1	1	22	24-0	2	26	.253	.316	.325	73	-10	0-7	.978	-2	100	54	O121(102/3/16),D7,3b2	0	-1.9
Meinert, Walt	Walter Henry; B12.11.1890 New York NY; D11.9.1958 Decatur IL; BL/TL/5´7.5˝/150; d9.6																								
1913	StL A	4	8	1	3	0	0	0	0	1	0	3	.375	.444	.375	144	1	1	1.000	-0	120	0	O2R	—	0.0
Meinke, Frank	Frank Louis; B10.18.1863 Chicago IL; D11.8.1931 Chicago IL; BR/5´10.5˝/172; d5.1; s-Bob; ▲																								
1884	Det N	92	341	28	56	5	7	6	24	6	—	89	.164	.179	.273	42	-23	—	.839	-2	100	135	S51,P35,O4(1/0/4),3b3,2b3	—	-1.3
1885	Det N	1	3	0	0	0	0	0	0	0	—	1	.000	.000	.000	-99	-1	—	1.000	0	0	0	/lfP	—	0.0
Total	2	93	344	28	56	5	7	6	24	6	—	90	.163	.177	.270	41	-24	—	.839	-2	100	135	S51,P36,O5(2/0/4),2b3,3b3	—	-1.3

YEAR	TM LG	G	AB	R	H	2B	3B	HR	RBI	BB-IB	HP	SO	AVG	OBP	SLG	AOPS	ABR	SB-CS	FA	FR	RNG	THR	GAMES AT POSITION	DL	BFW
MEINKE, BOB	Robert Bernard; B6.25.1887 Chicago IL; D12.29.1952 Chicago IL; BR/TR/5´10˝/135; d8.22; f–Frank																								
1910	Cin N	2	1	0	0	0	0	0	0	1	0	0	.000	.500	.000	51	0	0	1.000	1	144	0	S2	—	0.1
MEISTER, GEORGE	George B.; B6.5.1864 Dorzbach, Germany; D8.24.1908 Pittsburgh PA; ?/160; d8.15																								
1884	Tol AA	34	119	9	23	6	0	0	—	3	5	—	.193	.244	.244	58	-5	—	.817	-7	72	91	3b34	—	-1.1
MEISTER, JOHN	John F.; B5.10.1863 Allentown PA; D1.17.1923 Philadelphia PA; 5´8˝/175; d8.24																								
1886	NY AA	45	186	35	44	7	3	2	21	4	0	—	.237	.253	.339	92	-2	1	.906	-5	88	94	2b45	—	-0.5
1887	NY AA	39	158	24	35	6	2	1	21	16	2	—	.222	.301	.304	72	-5	9	.930	-5	91	248	O22C,2b14,3b3/S	—	-0.9
Total	2	84	344	59	79	13	5	3	42	20	2	—	.230	.276	.323	82	-7	10	.905	-10	89	96	2b59,O22C,3b3/S	—	-1.4
MEISTER, KARL	Karl Daniel "Dutch"; B5.15.1891 Marietta OH; D8.15.1967 Marietta OH; BR/TR/6´0˝/178; d8.10																								
1913	Cin N	4	7	1	2	1	0	0	2	0	0	4	.286	.286	.429	103	0	0	.667	-1	59	0	O4(1/3/0)	—	-0.1
MEIXELL, MOXIE	Merton Merrill; B10.18.1887 Lake Crystal MN; D8.17.1982 Los Angeles CA; BL/TL/5´10˝/168; d7.7																								
1912	Cle A	3	2	0	1	0	0	0	0	0	0	—	.500	.500	.500	181	0	0	ø	-0	0	0	/rf	—	0.0
MEJIA, MIGUEL	Miguel; B3.25.1975 San Pedro de Macoris, D.R.; BR/TR/6´1˝/155; d4.4																								
1996	†StL N	45	23	10	2	0	0	0	0	0-0	0	10	.087	.087	.087	-54	-5	6-3	.933	-0	112	0	O21(5/11/6)	30	-0.5
MEJIA, ROBERTO	Roberto Antonio (Diaz); B4.14.1972 Hato Mayor, D.R.; BR/TR/5´11˝/(160–183); d7.15																								
1993	Col N	65	229	31	53	14	5	5	20	13-1	1	63	.231	.275	.402	67	-11	4-1	.963	-1	102	88	2b65	0	-0.8
1994	Col N	38	116	11	28	8	1	4	14	15-2	0	33	.241	.326	.431	82	-3	3-1	.959	-5	91	79	2b34	0	-0.6
1995	Col N	23	52	5	8	1	0	1	4	0-0	1	17	.154	.167	.231	3	-7	0-1	.971	-5	73	42	2b16	0	-1.2
1997	StL N	7	14	0	1	1	0	0	2	0-0	0	5	.071	.067	.143	-46	-3	0-0	.900	-1	94	224	2b3/O(1/0/1)	170	-0.4
Total	4	133	411	47	90	24	6	10	40	28-3	2	118	.219	.270	.380	60	-24	7-3	.961	-11	95	82	2b118/O(1/0/1)	170	-3.0
MEJIAS, ROMAN	Roman (Gomez); B8.9.1930 Abreus, Cuba; BR/TR/6´0˝/(175–180); d4.13																								
1955	Pit N	71	167	14	36	8	1	3	21	9-0	0	13	.216	.256	.329	55	-11	1-3	.926	2	90	278	O44(30/1/14)	0	-1.2
1957	Pit N	58	142	12	39	7	4	2	15	6-1	1	13	.275	.309	.423	97	-1	2-2	1.000	1	88	241	O42(7/7/29)	0	-0.2
1958	Pit N	76	157	17	42	3	2	5	19	2-1	1	27	.268	.280	.408	82	-5	2-0	.973	5	132	103	O57(41/10/8)	0	-0.2
1959	Pit N	96	276	28	65	6	1	7	28	21-7	5	48	.236	.298	.341	71	-12	1-2	.970	1	97	136	O85(15/21/52)	0	-1.5
1960	Pit N	3	1	1	0	0	0	0	0	0-0	0	1	.000	.000	.000	-99	0	0-0	ø	0	—	—	/H	0	0.0
1961	Pit N	4	1	1	0	0	0	0	0	0-0	0	1	.000	.000	.000	-99	0	0-0	1.000	0	244	0	O2L	0	0.0
1962	Hou N	146	566	82	162	12	3	24	76	30-1	6	83	.286	.326	.445	114	8	12-4	.946	-6	94	90	O142(1/1/141)	0	-0.7
1963	Bos A	111	357	43	81	18	0	11	39	14-2	3	36	.227	.260	.370	72	-14	4-1	.973	-2	99	116	O86(7/65/15)	0	-1.9
1964	Bos A	62	101	14	24	3	1	2	4	7-1	1	16	.238	.294	.347	74	-4	0-0	.962	1	110	146	O37(14/13/11)	0	-0.4
Total	9	627	1768	212	449	57	12	54	202	89-13	17	238	.254	.294	.391	86	-39	22-12	.963	2	99	135	O495(117/118/270)	0	-6.1
MEJIAS, SAM	Samuel Elias; B5.9.1952 Santiago, D.R.; BR/TR/6´0˝/(160–180); d9.6; C7																								
1976	StL N	18	21	1	3	1	0	0	0	2-1	0	2	.143	.217	.190	16	-2	2-0	1.000	1	120	156	O17(3/1/13)	0	-0.1
1977	Mon N	74	101	14	23	4	1	3	8	2-0	0	17	.228	.243	.376	65	-6	1-0	.966	-0	101	106	O56(4/21/31)	0	-0.7
1978	Mon N	67	56	9	13	1	0	0	6	2-1	0	5	.232	.259	.250	43	-4	0-0	.949	0	98	142	O52(24/4/25)/P	0	-0.5
1979	Chi N	31	11	4	2	0	0	0	0	2-0	0	5	.182	.308	.182	34	-1	0-0	.875	-1	71	0	O23(15/5/3)	0	-0.2
	Cin N	7	2	1	1	0	0	0	0	0-0	0	0	.500	.500	.500	174	0	0-0	1.000	-0	48	0	O5C	0	0.0
	Year	38	13	5	3	0	0	0	0	2-0	0	5	.231	.333	.231	53	-1	0-0	.889	-1	68	0	O28(15/10/3)	0	-0.2
1980	Cin N	71	108	16	30	5	1	1	10	6-0	1	13	.278	.322	.370	94	-1	4-2	.989	3	106	160	O67(8/50/17)	0	0.1
1981	Cin N	66	49	6	14	2	0	0	7	2-1	0	9	.286	.302	.327	82	-1	1-0	.972	-1	83	73	O58(0/16/42)	0	-0.3
Total	6	334	348	51	86	13	2	4	31	16-3	1	51	.247	.281	.330	69	-15	8-2	.973	1	99	121	O278(54/102/131)/P	0	-1.7
MELE, DUTCH	Albert Ernest; B1.11.1915 New York NY; D2.12.1975 Hollywood FL; BL/TL/6´0.5˝/195; d9.14																								
1937	Cin N	6	14	1	2	1	0	0	1	1	0	1	.143	.200	.214	13	-2	0	1.000	-1	28	0	O5(2/0/3)	—	-0.3
MELE, SAM	Sabath Anthony; B1.21.1922 Astoria NY; BR/TR/6´1˝/187; d4.15; M7/C3; Col NYU																								
1947	Bos A	123	453	71	137	14	8	12	73	37	1	35	.302	.356	.448	114	7	0-3	.992	-1	95	126	O116(3/29/87)/1	0	0.1
1948	Bos A	66	180	25	42	12	1	2	25	13	2	21	.233	.292	.344	66	-9	1-1	.971	-1	104	60	O55(3/0/52)	0	-1.1
1949	Bos A	18	46	1	9	1	1	0	7	7	0	14	.196	.302	.261	46	-4	2-0	.955	-1	91	95	O11R	0	-0.4
	Was A	78	264	21	64	12	2	3	25	17	0	34	.242	.288	.337	67	-14	2-1	.966	0	98	119	O63(1/24/44),1b11	0	-1.6
	Year	96	310	22	73	13	3	3	32	24	0	48	.235	.290	.326	63	-18	4-1	.964	-0	97	115	O74(1/24/55),1b11	0	-2.0
1950	Was A	126	435	57	119	21	6	12	86	51	1	40	.274	.351	.432	105	2	2-0	.990	-0	94	102	O99(6/26/72),1b16	0	-0.2
1951	Was A	143	558	58	153	**36**	7	5	94	32	1	31	.274	.315	.391	92	-9	2-3	.993	2	108	90	O124(2/17/107),1b15	0	-1.2
1952	Was A	9	28	2	12	3	0	2	10	1	0	2	.429	.448	.750	237	5	0-0	.917	-1	94	0	O7(0/1/6)	0	0.4
	Chi A	123	423	46	105	18	2	14	59	48	2	40	.248	.328	.400	101	0	1-2	1.000	-6	86	95	O112R,1b3	0	-1.1
	Year	132	451	48	117	21	2	16	69	49	2	42	.259	.335	.421	109	4	1-2	.994	-7	86	90	O119(0/1/118),1b3	0	-0.7
1953	Chi A	140	481	64	132	26	8	12	82	58	0	47	.274	.353	.437	109	6	3-1	.996	-8	83	115	O138(0/4/138),1b2	0	-0.7
1954	Bal A	72	230	17	55	9	4	5	32	18	0	26	.239	.290	.378	90	-5	1-0	.962	-2	88	136	O62(40/0/24)	0	-1.0
	Bos A	42	132	22	42	6	0	7	23	12	2	12	.318	.378	.523	132	6	0-1	.994	-2	63	96	1b22,O13(3/0/13)	0	0.2
	Year	114	362	39	97	15	4	12	55	30	2	38	.268	.322	.431	107	2	1-1	.961	-4	87	132	O75(43/0/37),1b22	0	-0.8
1955	Bos A	14	31	1	4	2	0	0	1	0-0	0	7	.129	.125	.194	-13	-5	1-0	1.000	2	100	534	O7(6/0/1)	0	-0.3
	Cin N	35	62	4	13	1	0	2	7	5-0	1	13	.210	.279	.323	56	-4	0-1	.960	-0	110	0	O13(12/0/1)/1	0	-0.5
1956	Cle A	57	114	17	29	7	0	4	20	12-0	0	20	.254	.320	.421	94	-1	0-1	.969	1	96	175	O20(14/0/6),1b8	0	-0.2
Total	10	1046	3437	406	916	168	39	80	544	311-0	10	342	.267	.328	.408	97	-25	15-14	.985	-16	94	109	O840(90/101/674),1b79	0	-7.6
MELENDEZ, FRANCISCO	Francisco Javier (Villegas); B1.25.1964 Rio Piedras, PR; BL/TL/6´0˝/(170–190); d8.26																								
1984	Phi N	21	23	0	3	0	0	0	2	1-0	0	5	.130	.167	.130	-15	-4	0-0	1.000	1	174	35	1b10	0	-0.3
1986	Phi N	9	8	0	2	0	0	0	0	0-0	0	2	.250	.250	.250	37	-1	0-0	1.000	-0	0	0	1b2	0	-0.1
1987	SF N	12	16	2	5	0	0	1	1	0-0	0	3	.313	.313	.500	116	0	0-0	1.000	-1	0	0	1b5	0	0.0
1988	SF N	23	26	1	5	0	0	0	3	3-0	0	2	.192	.276	.192	38	-2	0-0	1.000	-1	0	119	1b6/lf	39	-0.3
1989	Bal A	9	11	1	3	0	0	0	3	1-0	0	2	.273	.308	.273	75	0	0-0	1.000	0	101	167	1b5	0	-0.1
Total	5	74	84	4	18	0	0	1	9	5-0	0	14	.214	.256	.250	43	-7	0-0	1.000	-1	83	79	1b28/lf	39	-0.8
MELENDEZ, LUIS	Luis Antonio (Santana); B8.11.1949 Aibonito, PR; BR/TR/6´0˝/165; d9.7																								
1970	StL N	21	70	11	21	1	0	0	8	2-0	0	12	.300	.315	.314	68	-3	3-0	1.000	0	90	179	O18(0/5/13)	0	-0.3
1971	StL N	88	173	25	39	3	1	0	11	24-1	0	29	.225	.320	.254	61	-8	2-0	.959	-1	100	97	O66(4/20/45)	22	-1.2
1972	StL N	118	332	32	79	11	3	5	28	25-0	1	34	.238	.292	.334	78	-10	5-4	.959	1	107	91	O105(4/69/40)	0	-1.4
1973	StL N	121	341	35	91	18	1	2	35	27-2	0	50	.267	.319	.343	84	-7	2-7	.990	2	103	131	O95(2/65/30)	0	-1.1
1974	StL N	83	124	15	27	4	3	0	8	11-0	1	9	.218	.283	.298	64	-6	2-2	.977	1	119	0	O46(23/22/10)/S	0	-0.7
1975	StL N	110	291	33	77	8	5	2	27	16-3	0	25	.265	.301	.347	77	-10	3-2	.983	-0	102	62	O89(36/49/7)	0	-1.4
1976	StL N	20	24	0	3	0	0	0	0	0-0	0	3	.125	.125	.125	-28	-4	0-0	1.000	1	163	0	O8(4/4/0)	0	-0.3
	SD N	72	119	15	29	5	0	0	5	3-1	0	12	.244	.260	.286	60	-7	1-1	.988	1	112	0	O60(24/29/10)	0	-0.8
	Year	92	143	15	32	5	0	0	5	3-1	0	15	.224	.238	.259	44	-11	1-1	.990	2	117	0	O68(28/33/10)	0	-1.1
1977	SD N	8	3	1	0	0	0	0	0	1-0	0	1	.000	.250	.000	-29	-1	0-0	1.000	0	172	0	O2C	31	0.0
Total	8	641	1477	167	366	50	13	9	122	109-7	2	175	.248	.299	.318	72	-56	18-16	.977	5	105	84	O489(97/265/155)/S	53	-7.2
MELHUSE, ADAM	Adam Michael; B3.27.1972 Santa Clara CA; BB/TR/6´2˝/(185–210); [TorA93 13/378]; d6.16; Col UCLA																								
2000	LA N	1	1	0	0	0	0	0	0	0-0	0	1	.000	.000	.000	-99	0	0-0	ø	0	—	—	/H	0	0.0
	Col N	23	23	3	4	0	1	0	4	3-0	0	5	.174	.269	.261	28	-3	0-0	1.000	-0	94	75	1b3/Crf	0	-0.3
	Year	24	24	3	4	0	1	0	4	3-0	0	6	.167	.259	.250	24	-3	0-0	1.000	-0	94	75	1b3/Crf	0	-0.3
2001	Col N	40	71	5	13	2	0	1	8	6-0	0	18	.183	.241	.254	25	-8	1-0	.991	-4	54	23	C23/1	0	-1.1
2003	†Oak A	40	77	13	23	7	0	5	14	9-0	0	19	.299	.372	.584	146	5	0-0	.993	0	93	95	C33,3b2/1	0	0.7
2004	Oak A	69	214	23	55	11	0	11	31	16-1	0	47	.257	.309	.463	98	-1	0-1	.995	-3	113	91	C64,3b3/1	0	-0.1
2005	Oak A	39	97	11	24	7	0	2	12	5-0	0	28	.247	.284	.381	76	-3	0-0	1.000	-1	127	71	C24,D8	0	-0.3
2006	†Oak A	49	128	10	28	8	0	4	18	9-1	1	34	.219	.273	.375	68	-6	0-1	1.000	-1	72	189	C24,D15,3b3,1b2	0	-0.7
Total	6	261	611	65	147	35	1	23	87	48-2	1	152	.241	.296	.414	81	-16	1-2	.996	-9	98	97	C169,D23,3b8,1b8/rf	0	-1.8

YEAR	TM LG	G	AB	R	H	2B	3B	HR	RBI	BB-IB	HP	SO	AVG	OBP	SLG	AOPS	ABR	SB-CS	FA	FR	RNG	THR	GAMES AT POSITION	DL	BFW
Melillo, Ski	Oscar Donald "Spinach"; B8.4.1899 Chicago IL; D11.14.1963 Chicago IL; BR/TR/5´8˝/150; d4.18; M1/C13																								
1926	StL A	99	385	54	98	18	5	1	30	32	2	31	.255	.315	.335	66	-20	6-7	.965	10	106	120	2b88,3b11	—	-0.7
1927	StL A	107	356	45	80	18	2	0	26	25	0	28	.225	.276	.287	45	-30	3-6	.935	3	99	122	2b101	—	-2.5
1928	StL A	51	132	9	25	2	0	0	9	9	0	11	.189	.241	.205	18	-16	2-1	.961	0	97	101	2b28,3b19	—	-1.4
1929	StL A	141	494	57	146	17	10	5	67	29	2	30	.296	.337	.401	86	-12	11-6	.973	**20**	110	**118**	2b141	—	1.2
1930	StL A	149	574	62	147	30	10	5	59	23	2	44	.256	.287	.369	63	-35	15-9	.979	25	**112**	110	2b148	—	-0.5
1931	StL A	151	617	88	189	34	11	2	75	37	0	29	.306	.346	.407	94	-7	7-11	.968	**35**	**113**	**123**	2b151	—	3.3
1932	StL A	**154**	612	71	148	19	11	3	66	36	2	42	.242	.286	.324	54	-44	6-6	.981	11	104	104	2b153	—	-2.2
1933	StL A	132	496	50	145	23	6	3	79	29	1	18	.292	.333	.381	83	-13	12-10	**.991**	**22**	105	**133**	2b130	—	1.6
1934	StL A	144	552	54	133	19	3	2	55	28	1	27	.241	.279	.297	45	-47	4-6	**.981**	17	102	110	2b141	—	-2.1
1935	StL A	19	62	8	13	3	0	0	5	8	0	4	.210	.300	.258	43	-5	0-0	.970	-0	108	73	2b18	—	-0.4
	Bos A	106	400	45	104	13	2	1	39	38	2	22	.260	.327	.310	61	-23	3-2	.973	17	109	120	2b105	—	0.1
	Year	125	462	53	117	16	2	1	44	46	2	26	.253	.324	.303	59	-28	3-2	.973	17	**109**	114	2b123	—	-0.3
1936	Bos A	98	327	39	74	12	4	0	32	28	0	16	.226	.287	.287	40	-32	0-0	.980	-7	87	107	2b93	—	-3.0
1937	Bos A	26	56	8	14	2	0	0	6	5	0	4	.250	.311	.286	50	-4	0-1	.939	-3	77	80	2b19,S2,3b2	—	-0.6
Total	12	1377	5063	590	1316	210	64	22	548	327	12	306	.260	.306	.340	64	-288	69-65	.973	151	105	115	2b1316,3b32,S2	—	-7.2
Mellana, Joe	Joseph Peter; B3.11.1905 Oakland CA; D11.1.1969 Larkspur CA; BR/TR/5´10˝/180; d9.21																								
1927	Phi A	4	7	1	2	0	0	0	2	0	0	1	.286	.286	.286	46	-1	0-0	.889	1	201	273	3b2	—	0.1
Mellor, Bill	William Harpin; B6.6.1874 Camden NJ; D11.5.1940 Bridgeton RI; BR/TR/6´0˝/190; d7.28; Col Virginia																								
1902	Bal A	10	36	4	13	3	0	0	5	3	0	—	.361	.410	.444	131	2	1	.978	-1	41	17	1b10	—	0.0
Melo, Juan	Juan Esteban; B11.11.1976 Bani, D.R.; BB/TR/6´3˝/160; d9.2																								
2000	SF N	11	13	0	1	0	0	0	1	0-0	0	5	.077	.077	.077	-65	-3	0-0	1.000	-2	57	0	2b6	0	-0.5
Meloan, Paul	Paul B. "Molly"; B8.23.1888 Paynesville MO; D2.11.1950 Taft CA; BL/TR/5´10.5˝/175; d8.2; Col Washington–St. Louis																								
1910	Chi A	65	222	23	54	6	6	0	23	17	6	—	.243	.314	.324	104	1	4	.948	4	90	192	O65R	—	0.2
1911	Chi A	1	3	0	1	0	0	0	1	0	0	—	.333	.333	.333	89	0	0	.000	-1	0	0	/rf	—	-0.1
	StL A	64	206	30	54	11	2	3	14	15	2	—	.262	.318	.379	98	-1	7	.904	-4	96	70	O54(1/0/53)	—	-0.7
	Year	65	209	30	55	11	2	3	15	15	2	—	.263	.319	.378	98	-1	7	.893	-4	94	69	O55(1/0/54)	—	-0.8
Total	2	130	431	53	109	17	8	3	38	32	8	—	.253	.316	.350	101	0	11	.923	-0	92	138	O120(1/0/119)	—	-0.6
Melton, Dave	David Olin; B10.3.1928 Pampa TX; BR/TR/6´0˝/185; d4.17; Col Stanford																								
1956	KC A	3	3	0	1	0	0	0	0	0-0	0	0	.333	.333	.333	76	0	0-0	1.000	0	139	0	O3L	121	0.0
1958	KC A	9	6	0	0	0	0	0	0	0-0	0	5	.000	.000	.000	-98	-2	0-0	1.000	0	280	0	O2L	0	-0.1
Total	2	12	9	0	1	0	0	0	0	0-0	0	5	.111	.111	.111	-39	-2	0-0	1.000	0	174	0	O5L	121	-0.1
Melton, Bill	William Edwin; B7.7.1945 Gulfport MS; BR/TR/6´2˝/(190–195); d5.4; Col Citrus (CA) JC																								
1968	Chi A	34	109	5	29	8	0	2	16	10-0	0	32	.266	.322	.394	117	2	1-1	.968	-0	114	89	3b33	0	0.2
1969	Chi A	157	556	67	142	26	2	23	87	56-7	5	106	.255	.326	.433	107	4	1-2	.952	-0	102	117	3b148,O11(3/0/8)	0	0.2
1970	Chi A	141	514	74	135	15	1	33	96	56-2	9	107	.263	.340	.488	123	15	2-4	1.000	7	86	171	O71R,3b70	0	1.8
1971	Chi A☆	150	543	72	146	18	2	**33**	86	61-5	11	87	.269	.352	.492	134	24	3-3	.968	24	115	90	3b148	0	4.9
1972	Chi A	57	208	22	51	5	0	7	30	23-2	0	31	.245	.319	.370	103	1	1-1	.935	3	104	110	3b56	97	0.4
1973	Chi A	152	560	83	155	29	1	20	87	75-7	2	66	.277	.363	.439	121	17	4-4	.953	10	109	104	3b151/D	0	2.7
1974	Chi A	136	495	63	120	17	0	21	63	59-3	5	60	.242	.326	.404	107	5	3-2	.939	-8	93	103	3b123,D11	0	-0.4
1975	Chi A	149	512	62	123	16	0	15	70	78-1	8	106	.240	.346	.359	99	2	5-4	.945	-8	93	78	3b138,D11	0	-0.8
1976	Cal A	118	341	31	71	17	3	6	42	44-2	2	53	.208	.300	.328	90	-4	2-0	.992	-5	88	102	D51,1b30,3b21	0	-1.2
1977	Cle A	50	133	17	32	11	0	0	14	17-0	2	21	.241	.331	.323	83	-2	1-3	1.000	-1	89	97	1b15,D14,3b13	0	-0.5
Total	10	1144	3971	496	1004	162	9	160	591	479-29	44	669	.253	.337	.419	112	64	23-24	.949	22	104	100	3b901,D88,O82(3/0/79),1b45	97	7.3
Meluskey, Mitch	Mitchell Wade; B9.18.1973 Yakima WA; BB/TR/6´0˝/185; [CleA92 12/322]; d8.30; [DL 2001 Det A 190]																								
1998	Hou N	8	8	1	2	1	0	0	0	1-0	0	4	.250	.333	.375	88	0	0-0	1.000	0	0	0	C3	0	0.0
1999	Hou N	10	33	4	7	1	0	1	3	5-1	0	6	.212	.316	.333	65	-2	1-0	1.000	-1	55	151	C10	161	-0.1
2000	Hou N	117	337	47	101	21	0	14	69	55-10	4	74	.300	.401	.487	115	10	1-0	.982	-8	83	81	C103/3	17	0.8
2002	Det A	8	27	3	6	0	0	0	1	5-0	1	3	.222	.353	.222	63	-1	0-0	1.000	-2	223	148	C8	162	-0.2
2003	Hou N	12	9	1	1	1	0	0	2	2-0	0	2	.111	.250	.222	30	-1	0-0	ø	0	—	—	/H	0	-0.2
Total	5	155	414	56	117	24	0	15	75	68-11	5	89	.283	.386	.449	106	6	2-0	.985	-9	91	91	C124/3	530	0.3
Melvin, Bob	Robert Paul; B10.28.1961 Palo Alto CA; BR/TR/6´4˝/(205–210); [DetA81*S1/2]; d5.25; M4/C4; Col California																								
1985	Det A	41	82	10	18	4	1	0	4	3-0	0	21	.220	.247	.293	47	-6	0-0	.989	3	91	72	C41	0	-0.2
1986	SF N	89	268	24	60	14	2	5	25	15-1	0	69	.224	.262	.347	71	-12	3-2	.988	6	103	140	C84/3	0	-0.3
1987	†SF N	84	246	31	49	8	0	11	31	17-3	0	44	.199	.249	.366	64	-14	0-4	.998	7	127	155	C78/1	15	-0.6
1988	SF N	92	273	23	64	13	1	8	27	13-0	0	46	.234	.268	.377	87	-6	0-2	.984	-4	149	68	C89/1	0	-0.7
1989	Bal A	85	278	22	67	10	1	1	32	15-3	0	53	.241	.279	.295	64	-14	1-4	.991	-10	99	88	C75,D9	15	-2.2
1990	Bal A	93	301	30	73	14	1	5	37	11-1	0	53	.243	.267	.346	73	-12	0-1	.997	-4	108	77	C76,D10/1	0	-1.3
1991	Bal A	79	228	11	57	10	0	1	23	11-2	0	46	.250	.279	.307	66	-11	0-0	.998	-1	91	85	C72,D4	0	-0.8
1992	KC A	32	70	5	22	5	0	0	6	5-0	0	13	.314	.351	.386	105	1	0-0	1.000	-0	102	106	C21,1b3	0	0.1
1993	Bos A	77	176	13	39	7	0	3	23	7-0	1	44	.222	.251	.313	49	-13	0-0	.994	-3	116	39	C76/1	15	-1.3
1994	NY A	9	14	2	4	0	0	1	3	0-0	0	3	.286	.286	.500	101	0	0-0	1.000	-1	64	178	C4,1b4/D	29	-0.1
	Chi A	11	19	3	3	0	0	0	1	1-0	0	4	.158	.200	.158	-6	-3	0-0	1.000	-0	53	0	C11	0	-0.3
	Year	20	33	5	7	0	0	1	4	1-0	0	7	.212	.235	.303	38	-3	0-0	1.000	-1	56	41	C15,1b4/D	0	-0.4
Total	10	692	1955	174	456	85	6	35	212	98-10	1	396	.233	.268	.337	68	-90	4-13	.993	-8	111	93	C627,D24,1b11/3	74	-7.7
Mench, Kevin	Kevin Ford; B1.7.1978 Wilmington DE; BR/TR/6´0˝/(225–230); [TexA99 4/118]; d4.9; Col Delaware																								
2002	Tex A	110	366	52	95	20	2	15	60	31-0	8	83	.260	.327	.448	102	1	1-1	.990	0	98	117	O106(57/1/62),D2	0	-0.4
2003	Tex A	38	125	15	40	12	0	2	11	10-0	3	17	.320	.381	.464	115	3	1-1	.984	-2	87	51	O35(34/3/2)	100	0.0
2004	Tex A	125	438	69	122	30	3	26	71	33-2	6	63	.279	.335	.539	119	11	0-0	.995	1	100	93	O109(53/5/62),D14	19	0.6
2005	Tex A	150	557	71	147	33	3	25	73	50-4	5	68	.264	.328	.469	106	5	4-3	.987	-1	97	97	O148(119/1/41)/D	0	-0.3
2006	Tex A	87	320	36	91	18	1	12	50	23-5	4	42	.284	.338	.459	104	2	1-0	.992	-4	89	65	O72(17/0/57),D15	0	-0.6
	Mil N	40	126	9	29	6	1	1	18	4-0	0	17	.230	.248	.317	45	-11	0-0	.985	1	112	62	O38L	0	-1.1
Total	5	550	1932	252	524	119	10	81	283	151-11	26	290	.271	.330	.469	104	11	7-5	.990	-6	97	90	O508(318/10/224),D32	119	-1.8
Mendez, Carlos	Carlos Alberto (Castillo); B6.18.1974 Caracas, Distrito Capital, Venezuela; BR/TR/6´0˝/210; d5.22																								
2003	Bal A	26	45	3	10	2	0	0	5	0-0	0	12	.222	.217	.267	28	-5	0-0	.939	-0	111	29	1b9,D8	0	-0.5
Mendez, Donaldo	Donaldo Alfonso; B6.7.1978 Barquisimeto, Lara, Venez.; BR/TR/6´1˝/155; d4.5																								
2001	SD N	46	118	11	18	2	1	1	5	5-2	3	37	.153	.206	.212	9	-17	1-2	.920	-6	94	72	S46	91	-2.1
2003	SD N	26	84	10	19	6	0	2	9	7-1	2	32	.226	.298	.369	81	-2	1-0	.951	-4	96	60	S26	0	-0.5
Total	2	72	202	21	37	8	1	3	14	12-3	5	69	.183	.245	.277	39	-19	2-2	.933	-11	95	67	S72	91	-2.6
Mendoza, Carlos	Carlos Ramon; B11.4.1974 Bolivar, Venezuela; BL/TL/5´11˝/(165–175); d9.3																								
1997	NY N	15	12	6	3	0	0	0	1	4-0	2	2	.250	.500	.250	109	1	0-0	1.000	-0	80	0	O3(2/3/0)	0	0.0
2000	Col N	13	10	0	1	0	0	0	0	1-0	0	4	.100	.182	.100	-21	-2	0-1	.000	-1	0	0	O3L	0	-0.3
Total	2	28	22	6	4	0	0	0	1	5-0	2	6	.182	.379	.182	48	-1	0-1	.833	-1	64	0	O6(5/3/0)	0	-0.3
Mendoza, Minnie	Cristobal Rigoberto (Carreras); B11.16.1933 Ceiba Del Agua, Cuba; BR/TR/6´0˝/180; d4.9; C1																								
1970	Min A	16	16	2	3	0	0	0	2	0-0	0	1	.188	.188	.188	4	-2	0-0	1.000	1	168	0	3b5,2b4	0	-0.2
Mendoza, Mario	Mario (Aizpuru); B12.26.1950 Chihuahua, Chihuahua, Mexico; BR/TR/5´11˝/(158–187); d4.26																								
1974	†Pit N	91	163	10	36	1	2	0	15	8-2	1	35	.221	.259	.252	45	-13	1-1	.964	-4	106	66	S87	0	-1.0
1975	Pit N	56	50	8	9	1	0	0	2	3-0	0	17	.180	.226	.200	19	-6	0-0	.952	-4	95	78	S53/3	0	-0.7
1976	Pit N	50	92	6	17	5	0	0	12	4-1	0	15	.185	.216	.239	29	-9	0-1	.967	1	107	111	S45,3b2/2	0	-0.5
1977	Pit N	70	81	5	16	3	0	0	4	3-0	0	10	.198	.226	.235	23	-9	0-0	.928	-5	99	100	S45,3b19/P	0	-1.2
1978	Pit N	57	55	5	12	1	0	1	3	2-1	3	9	.218	.283	.291	58	-3	3-1	.980	-1	114	53	2b21,3b18,S14	0	-0.3
1979	Sea A	148	373	26	74	10	3	1	29	9-0	1	62	.198	.216	.249	26	-40	3-0	.968	7	107	102	S148	0	-1.9

THE BATTER REGISTER

YEAR	TM LG	G	AB	R	H	2B	3B	HR	RBI	BB-IB	HP	SO	AVG	OBP	SLG	AOPS	ABR	SB-CS	FA	FR	RNG	THR	GAMES AT POSITION	DL	BFW
1980	Sea A	114	277	27	68	6	3	2	14	16-0	0	42	.245	.286	.310	63	-15	3-4	.959	-1	101	108	S114	0	-0.7
1981	Tex A	88	229	18	53	6	1	0	22	7-0	1	25	.231	.254	.266	54	-14	2-1	.970	6	109	97	S88	0	-0.1
1982	Tex A	12	17	1	2	0	0	0	0	0-0	0	4	.118	.118	.118	-37	-3	0-0	.882	-1	84	157	S12	0	-0.3
Total	9	686	1337	106	287	33	9	4	101	52-4	6	219	.215	.245	.262	41	-112	12-8	.961	-2	104	96	S606,3b40,2b22/P	0	-6.7

MENECHINO, FRANK Frank; B1.7.1971 Staten Island NY; BR/TR/5´8˝/(175–200); [ChiA93 45/1261]; d9.6; Col Alabama

YEAR	TM LG	G	AB	R	H	2B	3B	HR	RBI	BB-IB	HP	SO	AVG	OBP	SLG	AOPS	ABR	SB-CS	FA	FR	RNG	THR	GAMES AT POSITION	DL	BFW
1999	Oak A	9	9	0	2	0	0	0	0	0-0	0	4	.222	.222	.222	14	-1	0-0	1.000	0	100	139	S5/3	0	-0.1
2000	†Oak A	66	145	31	37	9	1	6	26	20-0	1	45	.255	.345	.455	103	1	1-4	.973	10	121	114	2b51,S5,3b4/PD	0	1.1
2001	†Oak A	139	471	82	114	22	2	12	60	79-0	19	97	.242	.369	.374	97	2	2-3	.978	18	111	**119**	2b136,S3/3D	0	2.4
2002	Oak A	38	132	22	27	7	0	3	15	20-0	1	32	.205	.312	.326	71	-5	0-0	.992	-5	103	51	2b32,3b4,S2/D	0	-0.9
2003	†Oak A	43	83	10	16	0	0	2	9	19-1	4	16	.193	.364	.265	71	-3	0-0	.986	-0	103	120	2b22,3b19,S3/D	0	-0.2
2004	Oak A	13	33	0	3	0	0	0	1	1-0	1	8	.091	.143	.091	-38	-7	0-0	.978	-1	111	33	2b12	18	-0.7
	Tor A	72	236	40	71	13	4	9	25	36-1	3	44	.301	.400	.504	126	10	0-2	1.000	-5	90	71	2b30,D19,S14,3b7/P	0	0.6
	Year	85	269	40	74	13	4	9	26	37-1	4	52	.275	.371	.454	108	4	0-2	.994	-6	96	61	2b42,D19,S14,3b7/P	0	-0.1
2005	Tor A	70	148	22	32	7	0	4	13	25-0	6	33	.216	.352	.345	82	-3	0-1	.991	6	121	137	2b26,D25,3b9/S	0	0.2
Total	7	450	1257	207	302	58	7	36	149	200-2	35	279	.240	.358	.383	94	-6	3-10	.982	23	110	104	2b309,D51,3b45,S33,P2	18	2.4

MENEFEE, JOCK John; B1.15.1868 Rowlesburg WV; D3.11.1953 Belle Vernon PA; BR/TR/6´0˝/165; d8.17; ▲

YEAR	TM LG	G	AB	R	H	2B	3B	HR	RBI	BB-IB	HP	SO	AVG	OBP	SLG	AOPS	ABR	SB-CS	FA	FR	RNG	THR	GAMES AT POSITION	DL	BFW
1892	Pit N	2	3	0	0	0	0	0	0	0	0	0	.000	.000	.000	-99	-1	0	1.000	0	0	0	/rfP	—	0.0
1893	Lou N	22	73	10	20	2	1	0	12	13	1	5	.274	.391	.329	100	1	2	.913	2	126	97	P15,O7(1/2/4)	—	0.1
1894	Lou N	29	79	7	13	1	0	0	4	8	1	7	.165	.250	.177	5	-12	2	.940	2	113	0	P28/2	—	0.1
	Pit N	13	47	6	12	1	2	0	7	3	0	3	.255	.300	.362	59	0	2	.909	2	142	0	P13	—	0.0
	Year	42	126	13	25	2	2	0	11	11	1	10	.198	.268	.246	26	-16	4	.928	4	123	0	P41/2	—	0.1
1895	Pit N	2	0	0	0	0	0	0	0	0	0	0	ø	ø	ø	ø	0	0	.667	0	220	0	P2	—	0.0
1898	NY N	1	5	0	0	0	0	0	0	0	0	—	.000	.000	.000	-99	-1	0	.750	0	135	0	/P	—	0.0
1900	Chi N	17	46	5	5	0	0	0	4	2	2	—	.109	.180	.109	-20	-3	0	.889	-2	71	126	P16	—	0.0
1901	Chi N	48	152	19	39	5	3	0	13	8	8	—	.257	.327	.329	94	-1	4	.913	-2	103	132	O24(5/1/18),P21,1b2/2	—	-0.3
1902	Chi N	65	216	24	50	4	1	0	15	15	7	—	.231	.303	.259	76	-5	4	.952	-5	62	130	O23(1/0/21),P22,1b18,3b2/2	—	-1.0
1903	Chi N	22	64	3	13	3	0	0	2	3	0	—	.203	.239	.250	40	-5	0	.896	3	140	0	P20,1b2	—	0.1
Total	9	221	685	74	152	16	7	0	57	52	19	15	.222	.295	.266	60	-27	14	.918	0	110	50	P139,O55(7/3/44),1b22,2b3,3b2	—	-1.0

MENKE, DENIS Denis John; B7.21.1940 Bancroft IA; BR/TR/6´0˝/(178–185); d4.14; C20; OF(3/0/2)

YEAR	TM LG	G	AB	R	H	2B	3B	HR	RBI	BB-IB	HP	SO	AVG	OBP	SLG	AOPS	ABR	SB-CS	FA	FR	RNG	THR	GAMES AT POSITION	DL	BFW
1962	Mil N	50	146	12	28	3	1	2	16	16-0	2	38	.192	.277	.267	49	-11	0-1	.980	2	104	99	2b20,3b15,S9,1b2/lf	0	-0.7
1963	Mil N	146	518	58	121	16	4	11	50	37-4	6	106	.234	.289	.344	83	-12	6-7	.976	8	112	109	S82,3b51,2b22/1lf	0	0.4
1964	Mil N	151	505	79	143	29	5	20	65	68-13	4	77	.283	.368	.479	137	27	4-2	.964	12	105	103	S141,2b15,3b6	0	5.3
1965	Mil N	71	181	16	44	13	1	4	18	18-3	1	28	.243	.313	.392	97	0	1-3	.967	2	108	86	S54,1b8,3b4	35	0.5
1966	Atl N	138	454	55	114	20	4	15	60	71-8	6	87	.251	.355	.412	112	10	0-7	.955	-19	91	83	S106,3b39,1b7	0	-0.3
1967	Atl N	129	418	37	95	14	3	7	39	65-5	3	62	.227	.333	.325	91	-3	5-7	.965	-21	92	94	S124,3b3	0	-1.5
1968	Hou N	150	542	56	135	23	6	6	56	64-6	6	81	.249	.334	.347	107	7	5-8	.982	-9	90	65	2b119,S35,1b5,3b4	0	0.9
1969	Hou N★	154	553	72	149	25	5	10	90	87-12	4	87	.269	.369	.387	115	14	2-7	.956	-11	90	83	S131,2b23,1b9/3	0	1.8
1970	Hou N★	154	562	82	171	26	6	13	92	82-10	5	80	.304	.392	.441	129	27	6-5	.954	-17	95	80	S133,2b21,1b5,3b5,O3(1/0/2)	0	2.6
1971	Hou N	146	475	57	117	26	3	1	43	59-4	2	68	.246	.328	.320	88	-5	4-5	.997	-4	89	103	1b101,3b32,S17,2b5	0	-1.8
1972	†Cin N	140	447	41	104	19	2	9	50	58-2	5	76	.233	.322	.345	96	-1	0-1	.955	-4	103	105	3b130,1b11	0	-0.8
1973	†Cin N	139	241	38	46	10	0	3	26	69-6	2	53	.191	.368	.270	85	0	1-1	.966	-0	104	123	3b123,S7,2b5/1	0	-0.1
1974	Hou N	30	29	2	3	1	0	0	1	4-0	0	10	.103	.206	.138	-1	-4	0-0	1.000	1	89	264	1b12,3b7,2b3,S2	0	-0.3
Total	13	1598	5071	605	1270	225	40	101	606	698-73	46	853	.250	.343	.370	104	49	34-54	.961	-60	97	92	S841,3b420,2b233,1b162,O5L	35	6.0

MENOSKY, MIKE Michael William "Leaping Mike"; B10.16.1894 Glen Campbell PA; D4.11.1983 Detroit MI; BL/TR/5´10˝/163; d4.18; Mil 1918; Col Indiana (PA)

YEAR	TM LG	G	AB	R	H	2B	3B	HR	RBI	BB-IB	HP	SO	AVG	OBP	SLG	AOPS	ABR	SB-CS	FA	FR	RNG	THR	GAMES AT POSITION	DL	BFW
1914	Pit F	68	140	26	37	4	1	2	9	16	3	30	.264	.352	.350	92	-3	5	.942	0	111	91	O41(6/3/32)	—	-0.5
1915	Pit F	17	21	3	2	0	0	0	1	2	1	0	.095	.208	.095	-13	-4	2	.917	-0	122	0	O9(6/1/2)	—	-0.4
1916	Was A	11	37	5	6	1	1	0	3	1	0	10	.162	.184	.243	29	-4	1	.952	2	92	265	O9(1/8/0)	—	-0.3
1917	Was A	114	322	46	83	12	10	1	34	45	6	55	.258	.359	.366	123	10	22	.982	11	121	126	O94(93/0/1)	—	1.8
1919	Was A	116	342	62	98	15	3	6	39	44	7	46	.287	.379	.401	120	11	13	.979	1	108	65	O103(87/15/1)	—	0.7
1920	Bos A	141	532	80	158	24	9	3	64	65	9	52	.297	.383	.393	110	11	23-19	.961	-5	93	89	O141L	—	-0.2
1921	Bos A	133	477	77	143	18	5	3	45	60	9	45	.300	.388	.377	99	2	12-6	.970	-4	97	72	O133L	—	-1.1
1922	Bos A	126	406	61	115	16	5	3	32	40	5	33	.283	.355	.369	90	-6	9-5	.977	6	108	108	O103(74/4/26)	—	-0.8
1923	Bos A	84	188	22	43	8	4	0	25	22	0	19	.229	.310	.314	64	-10	3-6	.920	3	96	214	O49(28/18/3)	—	-1.1
Total	9	810	2465	382	685	98	38	18	252	295	40	290	.278	.364	.370	100	7	90-36	.967	13	103	100	O682(569/49/65)	—	-1.9

MENSOR, ED Edward "The Midget"; B11.7.1885 Woodville (now Rogue River) OR; D4.20.1970 Salem OR; BB/TR/5´6˝/145; d7.15

YEAR	TM LG	G	AB	R	H	2B	3B	HR	RBI	BB-IB	HP	SO	AVG	OBP	SLG	AOPS	ABR	SB-CS	FA	FR	RNG	THR	GAMES AT POSITION	DL	BFW
1912	Pit N	39	99	19	26	3	2	0	1	23	0	12	.263	.402	.333	104	2	10	.955	-1	104	72	O32(0/20/12)	—	-0.1
1913	Pit N	44	56	9	10	1	0	0	1	8	1	13	.179	.292	.196	43	-4	2-4	.971	2	107	236	O18(1/16/1)/2S	—	-0.4
1914	Pit N	44	89	15	18	2	1	1	6	22	2	13	.202	.372	.281	99	2	2	.969	0	117	54	O25(4/10/11)	—	0.0
Total	3	127	244	43	54	6	3	1	8	53	3	38	.221	.367	.283	89	0	14-4	.964	1	110	95	O75(5/46/24)/S2	—	-0.5

MENZE, TED Theodore Charles; B11.4.1897 St.Louis MO; D12.23.1969 St.Louis MO; BR/TR/5´9˝/172; d4.23

YEAR	TM LG	G	AB	R	H	2B	3B	HR	RBI	BB-IB	HP	SO	AVG	OBP	SLG	AOPS	ABR	SB-CS	FA	FR	RNG	THR	GAMES AT POSITION	DL	BFW
1918	StL N	1	3	0	0	0	0	0	0	0	0	2	.000	.000	.000	-99	-1	0	1.000	-0	73	0	/lf	—	-0.1

MEOLI, RUDY Rudolph Bartholomew; B5.1.1951 Troy NY; BL/TR/5´9˝/(160–165); [AnaA69 4/75]; d9.9

YEAR	TM LG	G	AB	R	H	2B	3B	HR	RBI	BB-IB	HP	SO	AVG	OBP	SLG	AOPS	ABR	SB-CS	FA	FR	RNG	THR	GAMES AT POSITION	DL	BFW
1971	Cal A	7	3	0	0	0	0	0	0	0-0	0	1	.000	.000	.000	-99	-1	0-0	ø	0	—	—	/H	0	-0.1
1973	Cal A	120	305	36	68	12	1	2	23	31-1	0	38	.223	.290	.289	70	-12	2-4	.933	-11	90	94	S95,3b13,2b8	0	-1.4
1974	Cal A	36	90	9	22	2	0	0	3	8-0	0	10	.244	.306	.267	69	-3	2-4	.946	2	124	0	3b20,S8/12	0	-0.2
1975	Cal A	70	126	12	27	2	1	0	6	15-0	0	20	.214	.298	.246	59	-7	3-0	.976	-5	110	73	S28,3b15,2b11,D3	0	-0.9
1978	Chi N	47	29	10	3	0	1	0	2	6-0	0	4	.103	.257	.172	20	-3	1-0	.900	1	94	0	2b6,3b5	0	-0.2
1979	Phi N	30	73	2	13	4	1	0	6	9-1	0	15	.178	.268	.260	43	-6	2-0	.984	2	96	74	S16,2b15/3	0	-0.2
Total	6	310	626	69	133	20	4	2	40	69-2	0	88	.212	.289	.267	60	-32	10-8	.944	-11	94	91	S147,3b54,2b41,D3/1	0	-3.0

MERCADO, ORLANDO Orlando (Rodriguez); B11.7.1961 Arecibo, PR; BR/TR/6´0˝/(180–195); d9.13; C4

YEAR	TM LG	G	AB	R	H	2B	3B	HR	RBI	BB-IB	HP	SO	AVG	OBP	SLG	AOPS	ABR	SB-CS	FA	FR	RNG	THR	GAMES AT POSITION	DL	BFW
1982	Sea A	9	17	1	2	0	0	1	6	0-0	0	5	.118	.118	.294	8	-2	0-0	1.000	-2	82	54	C8/D	0	-0.4
1983	Sea A	66	178	10	35	11	2	1	16	14-0	1	27	.197	.256	.298	51	-12	2-2	.995	1	81	61	C65	0	-0.9
1984	Sea A	30	78	5	17	3	1	0	5	4-0	1	12	.218	.265	.282	52	-5	1-0	.992	-5	82	101	C29	0	-0.9
1986	Tex A	46	102	7	24	1	1	1	7	6-0	1	13	.235	.279	.294	56	-6	0-1	.996	7	81	115	C45	0	0.2
1987	Det A	10	22	2	3	0	0	0	1	2-0	0	0	.136	.208	.136	-6	-3	0-0	.980	1	115	79	C10	0	-0.2
	LA N	7	5	1	3	1	0	0	1	1-0	0	1	.600	.667	.800	294	2	0-0	1.000	-1	206	0	C7	0	0.1
1988	Oak A	16	24	3	3	0	0	1	1	3-0	0	8	.125	.222	.250	33	-2	0-0	.959	-3	97	37	C16	0	-0.5
1989	Min A	19	38	1	4	0	0	0	1	4-0	0	4	.105	.190	.105	-14	-6	1-0	1.000	3	146	75	C19	0	-0.2
1990	NY N	42	90	10	19	1	0	3	7	8-3	2	11	.211	.290	.322	68	-4	0-0	.991	-4	75	47	C40	0	-0.7
	Mon N	8	8	0	2	0	0	0	0	0-0	0	1	.250	.250	.250	39	-1	0-0	1.000	0	49	84	C8	0	-0.1
	Year	50	98	10	21	1	0	3	7	8-3	2	12	.214	.287	.316	66	-5	0-0	.992	-4	72	51	C48	0	-0.8
Total	8	253	562	40	112	17	4	7	45	42-3	5	82	.199	.259	.281	48	-39	4-3	.993	-3	88	74	C247/D	0	-3.6

MERCED, ORLANDO Orlando Luis (Villanueva); B11.2.1966 Hato Rey, PR; BL/TR (BB 1990–92)/5´11˝/(170–195); d6.27

YEAR	TM LG	G	AB	R	H	2B	3B	HR	RBI	BB-IB	HP	SO	AVG	OBP	SLG	AOPS	ABR	SB-CS	FA	FR	RNG	THR	GAMES AT POSITION	DL	BFW
1990	Pit N	25	24	3	5	1	0	0	0	1-0	0	9	.208	.240	.250	36	-2	0-0	ø	-0	0	0	/Crf	0	-0.2
1991	†Pit N	120	411	83	113	17	2	10	50	64-4	1	81	.275	.373	.399	119	13	8-4	.988	-4	90	100	1b105,O7R	0	0.2
1992	†Pit N	134	405	50	100	28	5	6	60	52-8	2	63	.247	.332	.385	104	3	5-4	.995	2	107	111	1b114,O17R	0	-0.3
1993	Pit N	137	447	68	140	26	4	8	70	77-10	1	64	.313	.414	.443	130	24	3-3	.965	8	114	158	O109R,1b42	0	2.4
1994	Pit N	108	386	48	105	21	3	9	51	42-5	1	58	.272	.343	.412	95	-3	4-1	.981	-5	87	71	O68R,1b55	0	-1.4
1995	Pit N	132	487	75	146	29	4	15	83	52-9	1	74	.300	.365	.468	116	12	7-2	.976	2	101	109	O107(4/0/104),1b35	0	0.7
1996	Pit N	120	453	69	130	24	1	17	80	51-5	0	74	.287	.357	.457	109	7	8-4	.988	10	107	179	O115R/1	47	1.1
1997	Tor A	98	368	45	98	23	2	9	40	47-1	3	62	.266	.352	.413	99	1	7-3	.985	5	103	169	O96R/1D	61	0.1
1998	Min A	63	204	22	59	12	0	5	33	17-3	1	29	.289	.345	.422	96	-1	1-4	.982	-0	94	115	1b38,O13R,D8	0	-0.6
	Bos A	9	9	0	0	0	0	0	2	2-0	0	3	.000	.167	.000	-46	-2	0-0	1.000	0	297	0	/rfD	0	-0.2
	Year	72	213	22	59	12	0	5	35	19-3	1	32	.277	.336	.404	90	-3	1-4	.982	0	94	115	1b38,O14R,D9	0	-0.8
	Chi N	12	10	2	3	0	0	1	5	1-0	0	2	.300	.333	.600	143	1	0-0	1.000	0	201	0	O4L	0	0.1
1999	Mon N	93	194	25	52	12	1	8	26	26-0	0	27	.268	.353	.464	109	3	2-1	.962	2	108	141	O44L,1b7,D2	27	0.3
2001	†Hou N	94	137	19	36	6	1	6	29	14-1	1	32	.263	.333	.453	94	-1	5-1	.975	-1	98	76	O31(11/0/21),3b2/1	19	-0.2

YEAR	TM LG	G	AB	R	H	2B	3B	HR	RBI	BB-IB	HP	SO	AVG	OBP	SLG	AOPS	ABR	SB-CS	FA	FR	RNG	THR	GAMES AT POSITION	DL	BFW
2002	Hou N	123	251	35	72	13	3	6	30	26-5	0	50	.287	.350	.434	98	0	4-0	.980	5	108	251	O56(20/0/44),1b7/3D	0	0.3
2003	Hou N	123	212	20	49	17	2	3	26	15-2	1	33	.231	.283	.373	66	-11	3-2	.959	2	106	293	O31(10/0/21),1b12,3b2,D7	0	-1.0
Total	13	1391	3998	564	1108	229	28	103	585	487-53	12	661	.277	.355	.426	106	44	57-29	.978	26	104	157	O700(93/0/617),1b418,D20,3b5/C	154	1.3
Mercedes, Henry	Henry Felipe (Perez); B7.23.1969 Santo Domingo, D.R.; BR/TR/6´1˝/(185–210); d4.22																								
1992	Oak A	9	5	1	4	0	1	0	1	0-0	0	1	.800	.800	1.200	476	2	0-0	.875	-1	41	0	C9	0	0.1
1993	Oak A	20	47	5	10	2	0	0	3	2-0	1	15	.213	.260	.255	41	-4	1-1	.987	-1	180	155	C18/D	0	-0.4
1995	KC A	23	43	7	11	2	0	0	9	8-0	1	13	.256	.370	.302	80	-1	0-0	.986	-4	92	90	C22	0	-0.4
1996	KC A	4	4	1	1	0	0	0	0	0-0	0	1	.250	.250	.250	27	0	0-0	1.000	-1	67	0	C4	0	-0.1
1997	Tex A	23	47	4	10	4	0	0	4	6-0	0	25	.213	.302	.298	54	-3	0-0	.988	-3	92	21	C23	0	-0.5
Total	5	79	146	18	36	8	1	0	17	16-0	2	55	.247	.325	.315	70	-6	1-1	.983	-11	115	82	C76/D	0	-1.3
Mercedes, Luis	Luis Roberto (Santana); B2.15.1968 San Pedro de Macoris, D.R.; BR/TR/6´0˝/(180–193); d9.8																								
1991	Bal A	19	54	10	11	2	0	0	2	4-0	0	9	.204	.259	.241	40	-4	0-0	1.000	-2	74	0	O15(13/0/3)/D	0	-0.7
1992	Bal A	23	50	7	7	2	0	0	4	8-0	1	9	.140	.267	.180	28	-5	0-1	.956	3	146	219	O16(1/2/13),D7	0	-0.2
1993	Bal A	10	24	1	7	2	0	0	0	5-0	0	4	.292	.414	.375	108	1	1-1	1.000	-0	68	172	O8R,D2	0	0.0
	SF N	18	25	1	4	0	1	0	3	1-0	2	3	.160	.250	.240	33	-3	0-1	1.000	-1	52	0	O5(1/3/1)	0	-0.4
Total	3	70	153	19	29	6	1	0	9	18-0	3	25	.190	.286	.242	47	-11	1-3	.976	-0	96	112	O44(15/5/25),D10	0	-1.3
Mercer, Win	George Barclay; B6.20.1874 Chester WV; D1.12.1903 San Francisco CA; BR/TR/5´7˝/140; d4.21; OF(21/25/30); ▲																								
1894	Was N	53	165	29	48	5	2	2	29	9	0	20	.291	.328	.382	73	-8	9	.944	1	108	40	P50,O4R	—	0.0
1895	Was N	64	201	26	51	9	1	1	26	12	3	33	.254	.306	.323	63	-11	7	.874	-6	82	74	P44,S7,O6(1/0/5),3b3/2	—	-0.7
1896	Was N	49	156	23	38	1	1	1	14	9	4	18	.244	.302	.282	54	-11	9	.856	0	98	86	P46/cf	—	0.0
1897	Was N	50	139	23	44	2	5	0	19	6	2	—	.317	.354	.403	100	8	7	.858	-2	88	149	P47	—	0.0
1898	Was N	80	249	38	80	3	5	2	25	18	1	—	.321	.369	.398	120	6	14	.863	-6	85	96	P33,S23,O19(2/17/0),3b5/2	—	-0.1
1899	Was N	108	375	73	112	6	7	1	35	32	4	—	.299	.360	.360	99	-1	16	.846	-10	78	68	3b62,P23,O16(15/0/1)/S1	—	-1.1
1900	NY N	76	248	32	73	4	0	0	27	26	2	—	.294	.366	.310	92	-1	15	.931	0	110	159	P33,3b19,O14R,S7,2b3	—	-0.1
1901	Was A	51	140	26	42	7	2	0	16	23	1	—	.300	.402	.379	119	5	10	.944	-1	97	58	P24,O16(3/7/6),1b7/S3	—	0.1
1902	Det A	35	100	8	18	2	0	0	6	6	0	—	.180	.226	.200	18	-2	1	.935	3	125	66	P35	—	0.0
Total	9	566	1773	278	506	39	23	7	197	141	17	71	.285	.344	.345	87	-15	88	.903	-19	101	89	P335,3b90,O76R,S39,1b8,2b5	—	-1.9
Mercer, John	John Locke; B6.22.1892 Taylortown LA; D12.22.1982 Shreveport LA; BL/TL/5´10.5˝/155; d6.25; Col Louisiana St.																								
1912	StL N	1	1	0	0	0	0	0	0	0	0	0	.000	.000	.000	-99	0	0	.500	-0	0	0	/1	—	-0.1
Merchant, Andy	James Anderson; B8.30.1950 Mobile AL; BL/TR/5´11˝/190; [BosA72 10/232]; d9.28; Col Auburn																								
1975	Bos A	1	4	1	2	0	0	0	0	1-0	0	0	.500	.600	.500	197	1	0-0	1.000	-1	73	232	/C	0	0.0
1976	Bos A	2	2	0	0	0	0	0	0	0-0	0	2	.000	.000	.000	-90	0	0-0	1.000	0	0	0	/C	0	0.0
Total	2	3	6	1	2	0	0	0	0	1-0	0	2	.333	.429	.333	110	1	0-0	1.000	-0	66	209	C2	0	0.0
Merewether, Art	Arthur Francis "Merry"; B7.7.1902 E.Providence RI; D2.2.1997 Bayside NY; BR/TR/5´9.5˝/155; d7.10; Col Brown																								
1922	Pit N	1	1	0	0	0	0	0	0	0	0	0	.000	.000	.000	-99	0	0-0	ø	0	—	—	/H	—	0.0
Merkle, Fred	Frederick Charles (b Carl Frederick Rudolf Merkle); B12.20.1888 Watertown WI; D3.2.1956 Daytona Beach FL; BR/TR/6´1˝/190; d9.21; C2																								
1907	NY N	15	47	0	12	1	0	0	5	1	0	—	.255	.271	.277	69	-2	0	.949	-1	88	65	1b15	—	-0.4
1908	NY N	38	41	6	11	2	1	1	7	4	0	—	.268	.333	.439	140	2	0	1.000	-1	33	106	1b11,O5(2/0/3)/23	—	0.1
1909	NY N	79	236	15	45	9	1	0	20	16	1	—	.191	.245	.237	49	-14	8	.976	-3	82	105	1b70/2	—	-2.1
1910	NY N	144	506	75	148	35	14	4	70	44	3	59	.292	.353	.441	131	18	23	.981	1	103	111	1b144	—	1.7
1911	†NY N	149	541	80	153	24	10	12	84	43	6	60	.283	.342	.431	112	6	49	.985	16	**143**	101	1b148	—	1.8
1912	†NY N	129	479	82	148	22	6	11	84	42	8	70	.309	.374	.449	121	13	37	.980	-1	101	122	1b129	—	0.9
1913	†NY N	153	563	78	147	30	12	3	69	41	3	60	.261	.315	.373	95	-5	35-18	.986	-4	88	121	1b153	—	-1.2
1914	NY N	146	512	71	132	25	7	7	63	52	1	80	.258	.327	.375	112	8	23	.990	4	110	114	1b146	—	0.8
1915	NY N	140	505	52	151	25	3	4	62	36	2	39	.299	.348	.384	129	17	20-15	.989	-2	88	101	1b110,O30(0/27/5)	—	1.1
1916	NY N	112	401	45	95	19	3	7	44	33	8	46	.237	.308	.352	108	4	17	.984	0	103	103	1b112	—	0.2
	†Bro N	23	69	6	16	1	0	0	2	7	1	4	.232	.312	.246	70	-2	2	.992	-1	60	43	1b15,O4(3/1/0)	—	-0.4
	Year	135	470	51	111	20	3	7	46	40	9	50	.236	.308	.336	102	2	19	.985	-0	98	97	1b127,O4(3/1/0)	—	-0.2
1917	Bro N	2	8	1	1	1	0	0	0	0	0	1	.125	.125	.250	13	-1	0	1.000	0	86	76	1b2	—	-0.1
	Chi N	146	549	65	146	30	9	3	57	42	4	60	.266	.323	.370	104	3	13	.983	-4	86	96	1b140,O6(5/1/0)	—	-0.5
	Year	148	557	66	147	31	9	3	57	42	4	61	.264	.320	.368	103	2	13	.983	-4	86	96	1b142,O6(5/1/0)	—	-0.6
1918	†Chi N	129	482	55	143	25	5	3	65	35	4	36	.297	.349	.388	122	13	21	.990	1	100	98	1b129	—	1.2
1919	Chi N	133	498	52	133	20	6	3	62	33	2	35	.267	.315	.349	99	-1	20	.985	-10	71	98	1b132/2	—	-1.6
1920	Chi N	92	330	33	94	20	4	3	38	24	1	32	.285	.335	.397	108	3	3-5	.985	1	105	89	1b85/lf	—	0.1
1925	NY A	7	13	4	5	1	0	0	1	1	0	1	.385	.429	.462	128	1	1-0	1.000	-0	48	124	1b5	—	0.0
1926	NY A	1	2	0	0	0	0	0	0	0	0	0	.000	.000	.000	-99	-1	0-0	1.000	-0	0	0	/1	—	-0.1
Total	16	1638	5782	720	1580	290	81	61	733	454	44	583	.273	.331	.383	109	62	272-38	.985	-5	98	105	1b1547,O46(11/29/8),2b3/3	—	1.5
Merloni, Lou	Louis William; B4.6.1971 Framingham MA; BR/TR/5´10˝/(194–200); [BosA93 10/275]; d5.10; Col Providence; OF(9/0/1)																								
1998	Bos A	39	96	10	27	6	0	1	15	7-1	2	20	.281	.343	.375	85	-2	1-0	.974	-2	94	72	2b32,3b5/S	75	-0.2
1999	†Bos A	43	126	18	32	7	0	1	13	8-0	2	16	.254	.307	.333	62	-7	0-0	.956	2	94	105	S24,3b9,2b8/1lfD	0	-0.3
2000	Bos A	40	128	10	41	11	2	0	18	4-1	1	22	.320	.341	.438	94	-1	1-0	.928	0	100	53	3b40	0	-0.1
2001	Bos A	52	146	21	39	10	0	3	13	6-0	3	31	.267	.306	.397	84	-3	2-1	.987	1	97	81	S45,2b5/3	15	0.1
2002	Bos A	84	194	28	48	12	2	4	18	20-0	5	35	.247	.332	.392	90	-2	1-2	.988	4	94	92	2b66,3b8,S5,1b3,O2(1/0/1)	0	0.4
2003	SD N	65	151	20	41	7	2	1	17	22-2	1	33	.272	.362	.364	101	1	2-3	.925	1	104	86	3b25,S23,2b10,1b2,O2L	26	0.3
	Bos A	15	30	4	7	1	0	0	1	4-0	0	8	.233	.324	.267	56	-2	0-0	1.000	1	53	148	2b7,3b7/lf	0	0.0
2004	Cle A	71	190	25	55	12	1	4	28	14-1	3	41	.289	.343	.426	104	1	1-2	.997	-1	64	62	1b42,3b10,2b7,O4L,D3	23	-0.3
2005	LA A	5	5	1	0	0	0	0	1	1-0	0	2	.000	.143	.000	-51	-1	0-0	1.000	2	220	0	3b4/1	154	0.0
2006	Cle A	9	19	1	4	1	0	0	1	2-0	0	5	.211	.286	.263	45	-2	1-0	1.000	-3	41	0	2b3,3b3,S3	0	-0.4
Total	9	423	1085	138	294	67	7	14	125	88-5	17	213	.271	.332	.384	87	-18	9-8	.977	6	92	88	2b138,3b112,S101,1b49,O10L,D6	293	-0.5
Merrill, Ed	Edward Mason; B5.22.1860 Maysville KY; D1.29.1946 Elmwood Park IL; 5´11˝/176; d5.5																								
1882	Lou AA	1	0	0	0	0	0	0	—	0	—	—	ø	ø	ø	ø	0	—	ø	-0	0	0	/cf	—	0.0
	Wor N	2	8	0	1	0	0	0	0	0	—	1	.125	.125	.125	-19	-1	—	.714	-0	112	0	3b2	—	-0.1
1884	Ind AA	55	196	14	35	3	1	0	—	6	1	—	.179	.207	.204	35	-13	—	.900	-3	96	60	2b55	—	-1.4
Total	2	58	204	14	36	3	1	0	0	6	1	1	.176	.204	.201	33	-14	—	.900	-4	96	60	2b55,3b2/cf	—	-1.5
Merriman, Lloyd	Lloyd Archer "Citation"; B8.2.1924 Clovis CA; D1.20.2004 Fresno CA; BL/TL/6´0˝/195; d4.24; Mil 1952–53; Col Stanford																								
1949	Cin N	103	287	35	66	12	5	4	26	21	1	36	.230	.285	.348	68	-14	2	.969	1	102	128	O86C	0	-1.5
1950	Cin N	92	298	44	77	15	3	2	31	30	2	23	.258	.330	.349	79	-9	6	.989	-4	93	65	O84(2/81/1)	0	-1.5
1951	Cin N	114	359	34	87	23	2	5	36	31	0	34	.242	.303	.359	76	-12	8-4	.997	6	117	55	O102(31/76/0)	0	-1.0
1954	Cin N	73	112	12	30	8	1	0	16	23	3	10	.268	.397	.357	98	1	3-0	.981	-0	112	0	O25(9/0/16)	0	0.1
1955	Chi A	1	1	0	0	0	0	0	0	0-0	0	0	.000	.000	.000	-97	0	0-0	ø	0	—	—	/H	0	0.0
	Chi N	72	145	15	31	6	1	1	8	21-0	0	21	.214	.311	.290	62	-8	1-0	.977	-1	95	73	O47(8/36/3)	0	-1.0
Total	5	455	1202	140	291	64	12	12	117	126-0	6	124	.242	.316	.345	75	-42	20-4	.985	2	105	73	O344(50/279/20)	0	-4.9
Merritt, George	George Washington; B4.14.1880 Paterson NJ; D2.21.1938 Memphis TN; TR/6´0˝/160; d9.6; ▲																								
1901	Pit N	4	11	2	3	0	1	0	0	0	2	—	.273	.385	.455	139	1	0	1.000	-0	82	0	P3	—	0.0
1902	Pit N	2	9	2	3	1	0	0	2	0	0	—	.333	.333	.444	135	0	0	1.000	1	297	0	O2L	—	0.1
1903	Pit N	9	27	4	4	0	1	0	3	2	1	—	.148	.233	.222	29	-3	1	.889	-1	0	0	O7(1/0/6)/P	—	-0.4
Total	3	15	47	8	10	1	2	0	5	2	3	—	.213	.288	.319	74	-2	1	.929	-1	93	0	O9(3/0/6),P4	—	-0.3
Merritt, Herm	Herman G.; B11.12.1900 Independence KS; D5.26.1927 Kansas City MO; BR/TR; d8.24																								
1921	Det A	20	46	3	17	1	2	0	6	1	1	5	.370	.396	.478	123	1	1-0	.882	-5	64	0	S17	—	-0.3
Merritt, John	John Howard; B10.12.1894 Tupelo MS; D11.3.1955 Tupelo MS; BR/TL/5´11˝/170; d9.27																								
1913	NY N	1	0	0	0	0	0	0	0	0	0	0	ø	ø	ø	ø	0	0	ø	-0	0	0	/rf	—	0.0

YEAR	TM LG	G	AB	R	H	2B	3B	HR	RBI	BB-IB	HP	SO	AVG	OBP	SLG	AOPS	ABR	SB-CS	FA	FR	RNG	THR	GAMES AT POSITION	DL	BFW
Merritt, Bill	William Henry; B7.30.1870 Lowell MA; D11.17.1937 Lowell MA; BR/TR/5´7˝/160; d8.8; Col Holy Cross																								
1891	Chi N	11	42	4	9	1	0	0	4	2	0	2	.214	.250	.238	42	-3	0	.955	-1	131	109	C11/1	—	-0.3
1892	Lou N	46	168	22	33	4	2	1	13	11	0	15	.196	.246	.262	58	-9	3	.940	-5	89	105	C46	—	-0.9
1893	Bos N	39	141	30	49	6	3	3	26	13	0	13	.348	.403	.496	128	5	3	.945	0	131	56	C37,O2L	—	0.7
1894	Bos N	10	26	3	6	1	0	0	6	8	0	0	.231	.412	.269	62	-1	0	.881	1	118	89	C8/cf	—	0.0
	Pit N	36	109	18	30	1	2	1	18	15	0	7	.275	.363	.349	73	-5	2	.952	0	102	130	C28,1b4,O2L	—	-0.2
	Cin N	30	117	17	38	6	1	1	22	10	2	3	.325	.388	.419	91	-2	4	.956	-1	99	115	C25,3b3/1rf	—	0.0
	Year	76	252	38	74	8	3	2	46	33	2	10	.294	.380	.373	80	-7	6	.942	0	103	118	C61,1b5,O4(2/1/1),3b3	—	-0.2
1895	Cin N	22	79	9	14	2	0	0	12	6	0	5	.177	.235	.203	13	-11	2	.955	0	103	100	C20/2	—	-0.7
	Pit N	67	239	32	68	5	1	0	27	18	2	16	.285	.340	.314	73	-9	2	.935	-7	88	93	C63,1b2	—	-0.8
	Year	89	318	41	82	7	1	0	39	24	2	21	.258	.314	.286	57	-20	4	.939	-6	92	95	C83,1b2/2	—	-1.5
1896	Pit N	77	282	26	82	8	2	1	42	18	1	10	.291	.336	.344	83	-7	3	.941	-6	84	121	C62,3b5,2b3,1b3,S2	—	-0.6
1897	Pit N	62	209	21	55	6	1	1	26	9	1	—	.263	.297	.316	64	-11	2	.946	-8	83	79	C53,1b7	—	-1.3
1899	Bos N	1	2	0	0	0	0	0	0	0	1	—	.000	.333	.000	-5	0	0	1.000	0	120	211	/C	—	0.0
Total	8	401	1414	182	384	40	12	8	196	110	7	71	.272	.327	.334	75	-53	21	.942	-25	96	99	C354,1b18,3b8,O6(4/1/1),2b4,S2	—	-4.1
Merson, Jack	John Warren; B1.17.1922 Elkridge MD; D4.28.2000 Elkridge MD; BR/TR/5´11˝/175; d9.14																								
1951	Pit N	13	50	6	18	2	2	1	14	1	0	7	.360	.373	.540	138	2	0-0	.987	2	122	64	2b13	0	0.5
1952	Pit N	111	398	41	98	20	2	5	38	22	1	38	.246	.287	.344	72	-15	1-1	.978	-0	99	107	2b81,3b27	0	-1.2
1953	Bos A	1	4	0	0	0	0	0	0	0	0	0	.000	.000	.000	-95	-1	0-0	.875	0	127	0	/2	0	-0.1
Total	3	125	452	47	116	22	4	6	52	23	1	45	.257	.294	.363	78	-14	1-1	.978	2	103	99	2b95,3b27	0	-0.8
Mertes, Sam	Samuel Blair "Sandow"; B8.6.1872 San Francisco CA; D3.12.1945 Villa Grande CA; BR/TR/6´0˝/225; d6.30; OF(687/182/110)																								
1896	Phi N	37	143	20	34	4	4	0	14	8	2	10	.238	.288	.322	61	-9	19	.907	-1	64	0	O35(1/33/1)/S2	—	-1.0
1898	Chi N	83	269	45	80	4	8	1	47	34	6	—	.297	.388	.383	121	8	27	.880	0	149	308	O60(4/5/53),S14,2b4,1b2	—	0.6
1899	Chi N	117	426	83	127	13	16	9	81	33	0	—	.298	.349	.467	126	12	45	.923	-2	122	93	O108(16/47/46),1b3/S	—	0.4
1900	Chi N	127	481	72	142	25	4	7	60	42	3	—	.295	.356	.407	114	10	38	.923	-4	112	133	O88(10/78/0),1b33,S7	—	0.0
1901	Chi A	**137**	545	94	151	16	17	5	98	52	6	—	.277	.347	.396	108	6	46	.940	-10	94	101	2b132,O5L	—	-0.3
1902	Chi A	129	497	60	140	23	7	1	79	37	2	—	.282	.334	.362	97	-2	46	.922	3	**160**	158	O120(111/0/9),S5,C2/P123	—	-0.5
1903	NY N	138	517	100	145	**32**	14	7	**104**	61	3	—	.280	.360	.437	122	15	45	**.973**	8	126	117	O137L/C1	—	1.4
1904	NY N	148	532	83	147	28	11	4	78	54	3	—	.276	.346	.393	123	15	47	.956	-2	90	21	O147(130/17/0)/S	—	0.5
1905	†NY N	150	551	81	154	27	17	5	108	56	5	—	.279	.351	.417	126	17	52	.960	-9	51	73	O150(149/2/0)	—	-0.1
1906	NY N	71	253	37	60	9	6	1	33	29	3	—	.237	.323	.332	102	1	21	.970	0	107	0	O71(71/0/1)	—	-0.4
	StL N	53	191	20	47	7	4	0	19	16	0	—	.246	.304	.325	100	0	10	.890	-5	63	0	O53L	—	-0.9
	Year	124	444	57	107	16	10	1	52	45	3	—	.241	.315	.329	101	0	31	.938	-5	89	0	O124(124/0/1)	—	-1.3
Total	10	1190	4405	695	1227	188	108	40	721	422	33	10	.279	.346	.398	114	73	396	.938	-22	106	92	O974L,2b138,1b40,S29,C3/3P	—	-0.3
Merullo, Lennie	Leonard Richard; B5.5.1917 Boston MA; BR/TR/5´11˝/168; d9.12; gs–Matt; Col Villanova																								
1941	Chi N	7	17	3	6	1	0	0	1	2	0	0	.353	.421	.412	140	1	1	.968	1	107	156	S7	0	0.3
1942	Chi N	143	515	53	132	23	3	2	37	35	5	45	.256	.310	.324	89	-8	14	.946	-1	102	93	S143	0	0.2
1943	Chi N	129	453	37	115	18	3	1	25	26	2	42	.254	.297	.313	78	-14	7	.940	-6	100	97	S125	0	-1.1
1944	Chi N	66	193	20	41	8	1	1	16	16	1	18	.212	.276	.280	57	-11	3	.937	1	101	86	S56/1	0	-0.6
1945	†Chi N	121	394	40	94	18	0	2	37	31	2	30	.239	.297	.299	68	-17	7	.948	1	99	96	S118	0	-0.8
1946	Chi N	65	126	14	19	8	0	0	7	11	0	13	.151	.219	.214	24	-13	2	.946	8	117	106	S44	0	-0.2
1947	Chi N	108	373	24	90	16	1	0	29	15	2	26	.241	.274	.290	52	-27	4	.949	6	101	116	S108	0	-1.4
Total	7	639	2071	191	497	92	8	6	152	136	12	174	.240	.291	.301	69	-89	38	.945	12	102	99	S601/1	0	-3.6
Merullo, Matt	Matthew Bates; B8.4.1965 Winchester MA; BL/TR/6´2˝/200; [ChiA86 7/179]; d4.12; gf–Lennie; Col North Carolina																								
1989	Chi A	31	81	5	18	1	0	1	8	6-0	0	14	.222	.273	.272	56	-5	0-1	.973	-4	78	45	C27/D	0	-0.8
1991	Chi A	80	140	8	32	1	0	5	21	9-1	0	18	.229	.268	.343	71	-6	0-0	.989	-3	64	163	C27,1b16,D6	0	-0.9
1992	Chi A	24	50	3	9	1	1	0	3	1-0	1	8	.180	.208	.240	26	-5	0-0	.971	-2	88	66	C16/D	0	-0.7
1993	Chi A	8	20	1	1	0	0	0	0	0-0	0	1	.050	.050	.050	-74	-5	0-0	ø	0	—	—	D6	0	-0.5
1994	Cle A	4	10	1	1	0	0	0	0	2-0	0	1	.100	.250	.100	-5	-2	0-0	.957	-2	35	0	C4	0	-0.3
1995	Min A	76	195	19	55	14	1	1	27	14-0	3	27	.282	.335	.379	86	-4	0-1	.987	-10	67	47	C46,D13,1b2	0	-1.1
Total	6	223	496	37	116	17	2	7	59	32-1	4	69	.234	.281	.319	64	-27	0-2	.981	-21	71	67	C120,D27,1b18	0	-4.3
Mesner, Steve	Stephan Mathias; B1.13.1918 Los Angeles CA; D4.6.1981 San Diego CA; BR/TR/5´9˝/178; d9.23																								
1938	Chi N	2	4	2	1	0	0	0	0	1	0	1	.250	.400	.250	80	0	0	.667	-1	80	0	/S	—	-0.1
1939	Chi N	17	43	7	12	4	0	0	6	3	1	4	.279	.340	.372	90	0	0	.927	1	124	109	S12/23	—	0.2
1941	StL N	24	69	8	10	1	0	0	10	5	0	6	.145	.203	.159	3	-9	0	.958	3	108	246	3b22	0	-0.6
1943	Cin N	137	504	53	137	26	1	0	52	26	1	20	.272	.309	.327	85	-10	6	.944	-1	102	130	3b130	0	-1.0
1944	Cin N	121	414	31	100	17	4	1	47	34	1	20	.242	.301	.309	75	-14	1	.951	-8	**99**	**120**	3b120	0	-2.2
1945	Cin N	150	540	52	137	19	1	1	52	52	2	18	.254	.322	.298	74	-18	4	.971	15	**113**	127	3b148,2b3	0	-0.1
Total	6	451	1574	153	397	67	6	2	167	121	5	69	.252	.308	.306	75	-51	11	.956	10	105	131	3b421,S13,2b4	0	-3.8
Messenger, Bobby	Charles Walter; B3.19.1884 Bangor ME; D7.10.1951 Bath ME; BB/TR/5´10.5˝/165; d8.30																								
1909	Chi A	31	112	18	19	1	1	0	0	13	2	—	.170	.268	.196	49	-6	7	.950	-2	102	126	O31R	—	-1.0
1910	Chi A	9	26	7	6	0	1	0	4	4	2	—	.231	.375	.308	119	1	3	.846	-0	66	190	O8L	—	0.0
1911	Chi A	13	17	4	2	0	1	0	0	3	0	—	.118	.250	.235	37	-2	0	.875	-1	97	0	O4L	—	-0.2
1914	StL A	1	2	0	0	0	0	0	0	0	0	0	.000	.000	.000	-99	-1	0	ø	0	0	0	/rf	—	-0.1
Total	4	54	157	29	27	1	3	0	4	20	4	0	.172	.282	.217	57	-8	10	.918	-3	94	126	O44(12/0/32)	—	-1.3
Messitt, Jack	Thomas John; B7.27.1874 Philadelphia PA; D9.22.1934 Chicago IL; 5´9˝/177; d9.14																								
1899	Lou N	3	11	0	1	0	0	0	0	0	0	—	.091	.091	.091	-50	-2	0	1.000	1	134	219	C3	—	-0.1
Metcalfe, Al	Alfred Tristram; B12.31.1852 Brooklyn NY; D9.2.1914 Brooklyn NY; d5.27																								
1875	Mut NA	8	32	2	7	0	0	0	1	0	—	3	.219	.219	.219	50	-2	2-0	.667	-1	113	0	3b5,O2R/S	—	-0.2
Metcalfe, Mike	Michael Henry; B1.2.1973 Quantico VA; BR/TR/5´10˝/175; [LAN94 3/76]; d9.18; Col Miami																								
1998	LA N	4	1	0	0	0	0	0	0	0-0	0	1	.000	.000	.000	-99	0	2-0	ø	-0	0	0	/2	0	0.0
2000	LA N	4	12	0	1	0	0	0	0	1-0	0	2	.083	.154	.083	-40	-3	0-0	1.000	-1	115	0	O4(3/1/0)/2	0	-0.3
Total	2	8	13	0	1	0	0	0	0	1-0	0	3	.077	.143	.077	-44	-3	2-0	1.000	-1	115	0	O4(3/1/0),2b2	0	-0.3
Metha, Scat	Frank Joseph; B12.13.1913 Los Angeles CA; D3.2.1975 Fountain Valley CA; BR/TR/5´11˝/165; d4.22																								
1940	Det A	26	37	6	9	0	1	0	3	2	0	8	.243	.282	.297	46	-3	0-1	.960	2	113	101	2b10,3b6	—	-0.1
Metheny, Bud	Arthur Beauregard; B6.1.1915 St.Louis MO; D1.2.2003 Virginia Beach VA; BL/TL/5´11˝/190; d4.27; Col William and Mary																								
1943	†NY A	103	360	51	94	18	2	9	36	39	0	34	.261	.333	.397	113	5	2-3	.963	-9	88	16	O91R	0	-1.1
1944	NY A	137	518	72	124	16	1	14	67	56	2	57	.239	.316	.355	89	-8	5-5	.956	-7	90	90	O132(11/0/121)	0	-2.5
1945	NY A	133	509	64	126	18	2	8	53	54	4	31	.248	.325	.338	88	-7	5-2	.984	-6	90	94	O128R	0	-2.2
1946	NY A	3	3	0	0	0	0	0	0	0	0	0	.000	.000	.000	-99	-1	0-0	ø	0	—	—	/H	0	-0.1
Total	4	376	1390	187	344	52	5	31	156	149	6	122	.247	.323	.359	94	-11	12-10	.968	-22	89	72	O351(11/0/340)	0	-5.9
Metkovich, Catfish	George Michael; B10.8.1920 Angels Camp CA; D5.17.1995 Costa Mesa CA; BL/TL/6´1˝/185; d7.16																								
1943	Bos A	78	321	34	79	14	4	5	27	19	3	38	.246	.294	.361	90	-6	1-3	.955	-3	92	100	O76(0/54/25),1b2	0	-1.4
1944	Bos A	134	549	94	152	28	8	9	59	31	3	57	.277	.319	.406	108	3	13-4	.962	0	102	97	O82(0/81/3),1b50	0	-0.1
1945	Bos A	138	539	65	140	26	3	5	62	51	6	70	.260	.331	.347	94	-3	19-6	.985	-3	101	108	1b97,O42(0/29/14)	0	-1.2
1946	†Bos A	86	281	42	69	15	2	4	25	36	1	39	.246	.333	.356	88	-4	8-3	.948	-7	88	48	O81(6/2/73)	0	-1.3
1947	Cle A	126	473	68	120	22	7	5	40	32	1	51	.254	.302	.362	86	-11	5-3	.989	-3	101	24	O119(0/119/2)/1	0	-1.8
1949	Chi A	93	338	50	80	9	4	5	45	41	1	24	.237	.321	.331	75	-13	5-4	.968	-8	94	17	O87(9/79/1)	0	-2.4
1951	Pit N	120	423	51	124	21	3	3	40	28	1	23	.293	.338	.378	90	-6	3-2	.994	-2	95	68	O69(3/66/0),1b37	0	-1.1
1952	Pit N	125	373	41	101	18	3	7	41	32	4	29	.271	.335	.391	98	-1	5-2	.988	-6	79	102	1b72,O33(5/21/8)	0	-1.0
1953	Pit N	26	41	5	6	0	1	1	7	6	0	3	.146	.255	.268	37	-4	0-0	1.000	-1	0	44	1b5,O4(0/3/1)	0	-0.5
	Chi N	61	124	19	29	9	0	2	12	16	1	10	.234	.326	.355	76	-4	2-1	1.000	-1	111	44	O38(10/11/18),1b7	0	-0.6
	Year	87	165	24	35	9	1	3	19	22	1	13	.212	.309	.333	66	-8	2-1	1.000	-1	110	77	O42(10/14/19),1b12	0	-1.1

YEAR	TM LG	G	AB	R	H	2B	3B	HR	RBI	BB-IB	HP	SO	AVG	OBP	SLG	AOPS	ABR	SB-CS	FA	FR	RNG	THR	GAMES AT POSITION	DL	BFW
1954	Mil N	68	123	7	34	5	1	1	15	15	1	15	.276	.352	.358	94	-1	0-0	1.000	2	129	110	1b18,O13R	0	0.0
Total	10	1055	3585	476	934	167	36	47	373	307	22	359	.261	.322	.367	91	-50	61-28	.976	-31	97	59	O644(33/465/158),1b289	0	-11.4

METRO, CHARLIE Charles (b Charles Moreskonich); B4.28.1919 Nanty Glo PA; BR/TR/5´11.5˝/178; d5.4; M2/C3

YEAR	TM LG	G	AB	R	H	2B	3B	HR	RBI	BB-IB	HP	SO	AVG	OBP	SLG	AOPS	ABR	SB-CS	FA	FR	RNG	THR	GAMES AT POSITION	DL	BFW
1943	Det A	44	40	12	8	0	0	0	2	3	0	6	.200	.256	.200	32	-3	1-1	.966	1	139	0	O14(1/11/2)	0	-0.3
1944	Det A	38	78	8	15	0	1	0	5	3	0	10	.192	.222	.218	25	-8	1-0	1.000	0	106	66	O20(9/10/2)	0	-0.9
	Phi A	24	40	4	4	0	0	0	1	7	0	6	.100	.234	.100	-3	-5	0-0	1.000	1	117	195	O11(9/0/2),3b5,2b2	0	-0.5
	Year	62	118	12	19	0	1	0	6	10	0	16	.161	.227	.178	16	-13	1-0	1.000	1	109	101	O31(18/10/4),3b5,2b2	0	-1.4
1945	Phi A	65	200	18	42	10	1	3	15	23	0	33	.210	.291	.315	76	-6	1-1	.972	-2	90	106	O57(53/1/4)	0	-1.2
Total	3	171	358	42	69	10	2	3	23	36	0	55	.193	.266	.257	51	-22	3-2	.980	0	100	94	O102(72/22/10),3b5,2b2	0	-2.9

METZ, LENNY Leonard Ray; B7.6.1899 Superior CO; D2.24.1953 Denver CO; BR/TR/5´10.5˝/170; d9.11

YEAR	TM LG	G	AB	R	H	2B	3B	HR	RBI	BB-IB	HP	SO	AVG	OBP	SLG	AOPS	ABR	SB-CS	FA	FR	RNG	THR	GAMES AT POSITION	DL	BFW
1923	Phi N	12	37	4	8	0	0	0	3	4	1	3	.216	.310	.216	37	-3	0-0	.969	0	75	83	2b6,S6	—	-0.2
1924	Phi N	7	7	1	2	0	0	0	1	1	0	0	.286	.375	.286	71	0	0-0	.846	-0	121	71	S6	—	0.0
1925	Phi N	11	14	1	0	0	0	0	0	0	0	2	.000	.000	.000	-92	-4	0-0	1.000	1	113	0	S9,2b2	—	-0.3
Total	3	30	58	6	10	0	0	0	4	5	1	5	.172	.250	.172	11	-7	0-0	.951	1	114	74	S21,2b8	—	-0.5

METZGER, ROGER Roger Henry; B10.10.1947 Fredericksburg TX; BB/TR (BL 1970, 80)/6´0˝/165; [ChiN69 1/16]; d6.16; Col St. Edwards

YEAR	TM LG	G	AB	R	H	2B	3B	HR	RBI	BB-IB	HP	SO	AVG	OBP	SLG	AOPS	ABR	SB-CS	FA	FR	RNG	THR	GAMES AT POSITION	DL	BFW
1970	Chi N	1	2	0	0	0	0	0	0	0-0	0	0	.000	.000	.000	-89	-1	0-0	.833	1	157	217	/S	0	0.0
1971	Hou N	150	562	64	132	14	**11**	0	26	44-4	4	50	.235	.294	.299	71	-23	15-6	.977	-4	96	100	S148	0	-0.9
1972	Hou N	**153**	641	84	142	12	3	2	38	60-1	1	71	.222	.288	.259	58	-35	23-9	.971	5	100	105	S153	0	-1.1
1973	Hou N	154	580	67	145	11	**14**	1	35	39-0	3	70	.250	.299	.322	73	-23	10-4	**.982**	-18	90	90	S149	0	-2.4
1974	Hou N	143	572	66	145	18	10	0	30	37-1	0	73	.253	.297	.320	76	-20	9-7	.976	-7	98	99	S143	18	-1.2
1975	Hou N	127	450	54	102	7	9	2	26	41-10	0	39	.227	.289	.296	68	-22	4-5	.977	16	**110**	104	S126	0	0.8
1976	Hou N	152	481	37	101	13	8	0	29	52-10	0	63	.210	.286	.270	64	-24	1-1	**.986**	0	98	97	S150,2b2	0	-0.6
1977	Hou N	97	269	24	50	9	6	0	16	32-3	0	24	.186	.272	.264	48	-20	2-0	.973	-9	96	93	S96/2	50	-2.0
1978	Hou N	45	123	11	27	4	1	0	6	12-3	0	9	.220	.287	.268	60	-7	0-0	.964	-4	88	97	S42/2	0	-0.7
	SF N	75	235	17	61	6	1	0	17	12-0	0	17	.260	.294	.294	67	-11	8-1	.974	-13	85	82	S74	0	-1.7
	Year	120	358	28	88	10	2	0	23	24-3	0	26	.246	.292	.285	65	-18	8-1	.970	-17	86	87	S116/2	0	-2.4
1979	SF N	94	259	24	65	7	8	0	31	23-2	0	31	.251	.311	.340	84	-7	11-3	.956	-1	98	80	S78,2b10/3	0	0.1
1980	SF N	28	27	5	2	0	0	0	0	3-0	0	2	.074	.167	.074	-32	-5	0-0	.971	-3	73	84	S13/2	0	-0.7
Total	11	1219	4201	453	972	101	71	5	254	355-34	8	449	.231	.291	.293	67	-198	83-36	.976	-38	97	96	S1173,2b15/3	68	-10.4

METZIG, WILLIAM William Andrew; B12.4.1918 Ft.Dodge IA; D3.12.2006 Lubbock TX; BR/TR/6´1˝/180; d9.19; Mil 1945

YEAR	TM LG	G	AB	R	H	2B	3B	HR	RBI	BB-IB	HP	SO	AVG	OBP	SLG	AOPS	ABR	SB-CS	FA	FR	RNG	THR	GAMES AT POSITION	DL	BFW
1944	Chi A	5	16	1	2	0	0	0	1	1	0	4	.125	.176	.125	-13	-2	0-0	1.000	1	118	65	2b5	0	-0.1

METZLER, ALEX Alexander; B1.4.1903 Fresno CA; D11.30.1973 Fresno CA; BL/TR/5´9˝/167; d9.16

YEAR	TM LG	G	AB	R	H	2B	3B	HR	RBI	BB-IB	HP	SO	AVG	OBP	SLG	AOPS	ABR	SB-CS	FA	FR	RNG	THR	GAMES AT POSITION	DL	BFW
1925	Chi N	9	38	2	7	2	0	0	2	3	0	7	.184	.244	.237	23	-4	0-0	1.000	2	96	351	O9C	—	-0.3
1926	Phi A	20	67	8	16	3	0	0	12	7	0	5	.239	.311	.284	53	-5	1-0	1.000	1	97	180	O17(15/1/1)	—	-0.4
1927	Chi A	134	543	87	173	29	11	3	61	61	9	39	.319	.396	.429	117	15	15-11	.965	7	109	111	O134(0/133/4)	—	1.5
1928	Chi A	139	464	71	141	18	14	3	55	77	6	30	.304	.410	.422	121	17	15-8	.968	-1	102	84	O134(50/43/46)	—	0.8
1929	Chi A	146	568	80	156	23	13	2	49	80	3	45	.275	.367	.371	92	-5	9-5	.960	-5	92	103	O142(132/10/0)	—	-2.0
1930	Chi A	56	79	12	14	4	0	0	5	11	0	6	.177	.278	.228	31	-8	0-2	.969	-0	99	85	O27(21/1/5)	—	-0.9
	StL A	56	209	30	54	6	3	1	23	21	0	12	.258	.326	.330	65	-11	5-1	.951	-6	85	46	O56(1/36/19)	—	-1.8
	Year	112	288	42	68	10	3	1	28	32	0	18	.236	.313	.302	57	-19	5-3	.955	-7	88	54	O83(22/37/24)	—	-2.7
Total	6	560	1968	290	561	85	41	9	207	260	18	144	.285	.374	.384	97	-1	45-27	.965	-2	99	101	O519(219/233/75)	—	-3.1

MEULENS, HENSLEY Hensley Filemon Acasio "Bam-Bam"; B6.23.1967 Willemstad, Curacao; BR/TR/6´3˝/(190–217); d8.23

YEAR	TM LG	G	AB	R	H	2B	3B	HR	RBI	BB-IB	HP	SO	AVG	OBP	SLG	AOPS	ABR	SB-CS	FA	FR	RNG	THR	GAMES AT POSITION	DL	BFW
1989	NY A	8	28	2	5	0	0	0	1	2-0	0	8	.179	.233	.179	18	-3	0-1	.875	2	141	68	3b8	0	-0.2
1990	NY A	23	83	12	20	7	0	3	10	9-0	3	25	.241	.337	.434	113	2	1-0	.963	2	106	205	O23L	0	0.3
1991	NY A	96	288	37	64	8	1	6	29	18-1	4	97	.222	.276	.319	64	-15	3-0	.967	2	110	106	O73(61/0/13),D13,1b7	0	-1.5
1992	NY A	2	5	1	3	0	0	1	1	1-0	0	0	.600	.667	1.200	414	2	0-0	1.000	0	113	814	3b2	0	0.2
1993	NY A	30	53	8	9	1	1	2	5	8-0	0	19	.170	.279	.340	67	-3	0-1	1.000	-2	93	0	O24(22/0/1),1b3/3	0	-0.5
1997	Mon N	16	24	6	7	1	0	2	6	4-0	0	10	.292	.379	.583	153	2	0-1	1.000	-1	65	0	O8L,1b3	0	0.0
1998	Ari N	7	15	1	1	0	0	1	1	0-0	0	6	.067	.067	.267	-18	-3	0-0	1.000	1	105	499	O4R	0	-0.2
Total	7	182	496	67	109	17	2	15	53	42-1	7	165	.220	.288	.353	76	-18	4-3	.972	4	105	118	O132(114/0/18),1b13,D13,3b11	0	-1.9

MEUSEL, IRISH Emil Frederick; B6.9.1893 Oakland CA; D3.1.1963 Long Beach CA; BR/TR/5´11.5˝/178; d10.1; C1; b–Bob

YEAR	TM LG	G	AB	R	H	2B	3B	HR	RBI	BB-IB	HP	SO	AVG	OBP	SLG	AOPS	ABR	SB-CS	FA	FR	RNG	THR	GAMES AT POSITION	DL	BFW
1914	Was A	1	2	0	0	0	0	0	0	0	0	0	.000	.000	.000	-96	0	0	1.000	-0	97	0	/lf	—	-0.1
1918	Phi N	124	473	48	132	25	6	4	62	30	1	21	.279	.323	.383	108	4	18	.972	2	106	94	O120(71/45/0),2b4	—	-0.1
1919	Phi N	135	521	65	159	26	7	5	59	15	2	13	.305	.327	.411	113	7	24	.968	-3	99	79	O128(59/15/54)	—	-0.3
1920	Phi N	138	518	75	160	27	8	14	69	32	0	27	.309	.349	.473	129	18	17-11	.929	-5	94	99	O129(99/0/43),1b3	—	0.6
1921	Phi N	84	343	59	121	21	7	12	51	18	0	17	.353	.385	.560	136	17	8-4	.929	0	87	160	O84(38/1/46)	—	1.0
	†NY N	62	243	37	80	12	6	2	36	15	2	12	.329	.373	.453	117	6	5-9	.971	0	93	133	O62(62/0/1)	—	-0.1
	Year	146	586	96	201	33	13	14	87	33	2	29	.343	.380	.515	129	23	13-13	.947	0	89	149	O146(100/1/47)	—	0.9
1922	†NY N	154	617	100	204	28	17	16	132	35	2	33	.331	.369	.509	123	18	12-10	.980	-10	88	79	O154L	—	-0.5
1923	†NY N	146	595	102	177	22	14	19	**125**	38	1	16	.297	.341	.477	115	9	8-8	.949	-9	90	75	O145L	—	-1.2
1924	†NY N	139	549	75	170	26	9	6	102	33	2	18	.310	.351	.423	109	6	11-7	.967	-8	100	28	O138L	—	-1.2
1925	NY N	135	516	82	169	35	8	21	111	26	3	19	.328	.363	.548	135	24	5-4	.959	-6	86	125	O126(118/0/8)	—	0.8
1926	NY N	129	449	51	131	25	10	6	65	16	4	18	.292	.322	.432	103	-1	5	.958	-4	92	100	O112L	—	-1.3
1927	Bro N	42	74	7	18	3	1	1	7	11	0	5	.243	.341	.351	85	-1	0	1.000	0	93	134	O17(11/0/6)	—	-0.2
Total	11	1289	4900	701	1521	250	93	106	819	269	17	199	.310	.348	.464	118	107	113-53	.959	-43	94	92	O1216(1008/61/158),2b4,1b3	—	-2.6

MEUSEL, BOB Robert William "Long Bob"; B7.19.1896 San Jose CA; D11.28.1977 Downey CA; BR/TR/6´3˝/190; d4.14; b–Irish

YEAR	TM LG	G	AB	R	H	2B	3B	HR	RBI	BB-IB	HP	SO	AVG	OBP	SLG	AOPS	ABR	SB-CS	FA	FR	RNG	THR	GAMES AT POSITION	DL	BFW
1920	NY A	119	460	75	151	40	7	11	83	20	2	72	.328	.359	.517	126	15	4-4	.947	-8	94	112	O64(16/0/48),3b45,1b2	—	0.4
1921	†NY A	149	598	104	190	40	16	24	135	34	2	88	.318	.356	.559	128	20	17-6	.934	4	97	143	O147(10/0/137)	—	1.3
1922	†NY A	121	473	61	151	26	11	16	84	40	3	58	.319	.376	.522	129	18	13-8	.950	2	88	**174**	O121(47/1/74)	—	1.1
1923	†NY A	132	460	59	144	29	10	9	91	31	2	52	.313	.359	.478	117	9	13-15	.953	-1	92	126	O121(78/0/43)	—	-0.3
1924	NY A	143	579	93	188	40	11	12	120	32	5	43	.325	.365	.494	120	14	26-14	.951	-4	92	110	O143(93/2/49),3b2	—	0.1
1925	NY A	**156**	624	101	181	34	12	**33**	**138**	54	1	55	.290	.348	.542	125	18	13-14	.985	-6	95	65	O131(86/0/46),3b27	—	0.1
1926	†NY A	108	413	73	130	22	3	12	81	37	1	32	.315	.373	.470	121	11	16-17	.960	-6	100	37	O107(68/1/38)	—	-0.5
1927	†NY A	135	516	75	174	47	9	8	103	45	2	58	.337	.393	.510	137	28	24-10	.950	-4	92	110	O131(83/0/48)	—	1.5
1928	†NY A	131	518	77	154	45	5	11	113	39	2	56	.297	.349	.467	116	12	6-9	.975	2	96	124	O131(87/0/44)	—	0.1
1929	NY A	100	391	46	102	15	3	10	57	17	0	42	.261	.292	.391	79	-15	2-5	.968	3	109	96	O96(56/0/40)	—	-2.0
1930	Cin N	113	443	62	128	30	8	10	62	26	1	63	.289	.330	.460	93	-7	9	.962	-3	95	100	O112(70/39/4)	—	-1.4
Total	11	1407	5475	826	1693	368	95	156	1067	375	21	619	.309	.356	.497	119	123	143-102	.958	-20	95	110	O1304(694/43/571),3b74,1b2	—	0.4

MEYER, BENNY Bernhard "Earache"; B1.21.1885 Hematite MO; D2.6.1974 Festus MO; BR/TR/5´9˝/170; d4.9; C6

YEAR	TM LG	G	AB	R	H	2B	3B	HR	RBI	BB-IB	HP	SO	AVG	OBP	SLG	AOPS	ABR	SB-CS	FA	FR	RNG	THR	GAMES AT POSITION	DL	BFW
1913	Bro N	38	87	12	17	0	1	1	10	10	0	14	.195	.278	.253	51	-6	8-3	.943	-1	97	98	O26(2/17/7)/C	—	-0.8
1914	Bal F	143	500	76	152	18	10	5	40	71	4	53	.304	.395	.410	116	6	23	.916	-9	94	71	O132(12/2/118),S4	—	-0.9
1915	Bal F	35	120	20	29	2	0	0	5	37	1	13	.242	.424	.258	91	0	6	.931	-4	96	22	O34R	—	-0.6
	Buf F	93	333	37	77	8	6	1	29	40	1	37	.231	.316	.300	72	-17	9	.947	-5	88	83	O88(73/0/15)	—	-2.9
	Year	128	453	57	106	10	6	1	34	77	2	50	.234	.348	.289	78	-17	15	.943	-9	90	65	O122(73/0/49)	—	-3.5
1925	Phi N	1	1	1	1	0	0	0	0	0	0	0	1.000	1.000	2.000	594	1	0-0	ø	-0	0	0	/2	—	0.1
Total	4	310	1041	146	276	29	17	7	84	158	6	117	.265	.365	.346	95	-16	46-3	.931	-19	93	71	O280(87/19/174),S4/2C	—	-5.1

MEYER, DAN Daniel Thomas; B8.3.1952 Hamilton OH; BL/TR/5´11˝/180; [DetA72 4/92]; d9.14; Col Arizona

YEAR	TM LG	G	AB	R	H	2B	3B	HR	RBI	BB-IB	HP	SO	AVG	OBP	SLG	AOPS	ABR	SB-CS	FA	FR	RNG	THR	GAMES AT POSITION	DL	BFW
1974	Det A	13	50	5	10	1	1	3	7	1-1	1	1	.200	.231	.440	86	-1	1-0	.967	0	122	0	O12L	0	-0.2
1975	Det A	122	470	56	111	17	3	8	47	26-1	2	25	.236	.277	.336	70	-20	8-3	.950	-2	88	77	O74L,1b46	17	-3.0
1976	Det A	105	294	37	74	8	4	2	16	17-0	0	22	.252	.292	.327	78	-9	10-0	.988	-4	82	122	O47L,1b19/D	0	-1.6
1977	Sea A	159	582	75	159	24	4	22	90	43-4	1	51	.273	.320	.442	107	4	11-8	.992	-1	97	98	1b159	0	-0.7
1978	Sea A	123	444	38	101	18	1	8	56	24-6	0	39	.227	.264	.327	66	-21	7-3	.989	-2	98	115	1b121,O2L/D	15	-3.1
1979	Sea A	144	525	72	146	21	7	20	74	29-10	4	35	.278	.317	.459	105	1	11-7	.936	-9	96	111	3b101,O31L,1b15	0	-1.0
1980	Sea A	146	531	56	146	25	6	11	71	31-4	1	42	.275	.314	.407	95	-5	8-4	.961	-11	76	112	O123L,3b5,1b4,D7	0	-2.1
1981	Sea A	83	252	26	66	10	1	3	22	10-1	1	16	.262	.291	.345	79	-7	4-3	.961	-4	91	137	3b49,O14(13/1/0),1b3,D3	13	-1.4
1982	Oak A	120	383	28	92	17	3	8	59	18-3	0	33	.240	.271	.363	76	-14	1-1	.990	-1	91	84	1b58,D38,O11(4/0/8)	0	-2.0

YEAR	TM LG	G	AB	R	H	2B	3B	HR	RBI	BB-IB	HP	SO	AVG	OBP	SLG	AOPS	ABR	SB-CS	FA	FR	RNG	THR	GAMES AT POSITION	DL	BFW
1983	Oak A	69	169	15	32	9	0	1	13	19-2	0	11	.189	.268	.260	50	-11	0-0	.987	-3	70	86	1b41,D12,O11(9/0/2)/3	39	-1.7
1984	Oak A	20	22	1	7	3	1	0	4	0-0	0	2	.318	.318	.545	142	1	0-0	.944	0	233	93	1b3/D	0	0.1
1985	Oak A	14	12	2	0	0	0	0	0	1-0	0	0	.000	.077	.000	-82	-3	0-0	ø	0	0	0	/3rfD	0	-0.3
Total	12	1118	3734	411	944	153	31	86	459	219-32	10	277	.253	.293	.379	85	-85	61-29	.991	-35	94	100	1b469,O326(315/1/11),3b157,D64	84	-17.0
MEYER, DREW	Drew Edward; B8.29.1981 Charleston SC; BL/TR/5´10˝/200; [TexA02 1/10]; d4.21; Col South Carolina																								
2006	Tex A	5	14	1	3	0	0	0	0	0-0	0	8	.214	.214	.214	11	-2	0-0	1.000	-2	64	43	2b3/Srf	0	-0.3
MEYER, GEORGE	George Francis; B8.3.1909 Chicago IL; D1.3.1992 Hoffman Estates IL; BR/TR/5´9˝/160; d9.3																								
1938	Chi A	24	81	10	24	2	2	0	9	11	1	17	.296	.387	.370	89	-1	3-1	.967	2	116	69	2b24	—	0.2
MEYER, DUTCH	Lambert Daniel; B10.6.1915 Waco TX; D1.19.2003 Fort Worth TX; BR/TR/5´10.5˝/181; d6.23; Mil 1943–44; Col TCU																								
1937	Chi N	1	0	0	0	0	0	0	0	0	0	0	ø	ø	ø	ø	0	0	ø	0	—	—	/R	—	0.0
1940	Det A	23	58	12	15	3	0	0	6	4	1	10	.259	.317	.310	58	-3	2-0	.960	-1	98	60	2b21	—	-0.3
1941	Det A	46	153	12	29	9	1	1	14	8	0	13	.190	.230	.281	31	-15	1-1	.972	2	92	77	2b40	0	-1.1
1942	Det A	14	52	5	17	3	0	2	9	4	1	4	.327	.386	.500	137	3	0-1	.989	5	124	146	2b14	0	0.8
1945	Cle A	130	524	71	153	29	8	7	48	40	0	32	.292	.342	.418	125	15	2-4	.978	-28	84	79	2b130	0	-0.8
1946	Cle A	72	207	13	48	5	3	0	16	26	1	16	.232	.321	.285	75	-7	0-1	.977	-10	91	67	2b64	0	-1.5
Total	6	286	994	113	262	49	12	10	93	82	3	75	.264	.322	.367	94	-7	5-7	.977	-32	90	79	2b269	0	-2.9
MEYER, LEO	Leo; B3.29.1888 Iowa City IA; D9.2.1968 Smyrna DE; TR; d9.27																								
1909	Bro N	7	23	1	3	0	0	0	0	2	0	—	.130	.200	.130	3	-3	0	.882	-1	89	63	S7	—	-0.4
MEYER, SCOTT	Scott William; B8.19.1957 Evergreen Park IL; BR/TR/6´1˝/195; [OakA78 5/108]; d9.10; Col Western Michigan																								
1978	Oak A	8	9	1	1	1	0	0	0	0-0	0	4	.111	.111	.222	-9	-1	0-0	1.000	-0	120	0	C7	0	-0.1
MEYER, JOEY	Tanner Joe; B5.10.1962 Honolulu HI; BR/TR/6´3˝/260; [MilA83 5/132]; d4.4; Col Hawaii–Manoa																								
1988	Mil A	103	327	22	86	18	0	11	45	23-2	1	88	.263	.313	.419	102	0	0-1	.986	-0	101	99	D66,1b33	0	-0.4
1989	Mil A	53	147	13	33	6	0	7	29	12-1	0	36	.224	.274	.408	93	-2	1-0	.982	-1	87	143	D31,1b18	0	-0.4
Total	2	156	474	35	119	24	0	18	74	35-3	1	124	.251	.300	.416	99	-2	1-1	.984	-1	97	113	D97,1b51	0	-0.8
MEYER, BILLY	William Adam; B1.14.1893 Knoxville TN; D3.31.1957 Knoxville TN; BR/TR/5´9.5˝/170; d9.6; M5																								
1913	Chi A	1	1	0	1	0	0	0	0	0	0	0	1.000	1.000	1.000	490	0	0	.857	0	*0*	*130*	/C	—	0.1
1916	Phi A	50	138	6	32	2	2	1	12	8	0	11	.232	.274	.297	75	-5	3	.961	-2	63	145	C48	—	-0.4
1917	Phi A	62	162	9	38	5	1	0	9	7	1	14	.235	.271	.278	68	-7	0	.962	1	*84*	*110*	C55	—	-0.1
Total	3	113	301	15	71	7	3	1	21	15	1	25	.236	.274	.289	73	-12	3	.960	-0	*74*	*126*	C104	—	-0.4
MEYERLE, LEVI	Levi Samuel "Long Levi"; B7.1845 Philadelphia PA; D11.4.1921 Philadelphia PA; BR/TR/6´1˝/177; d5.20; OF NA(2/0/29); ▲																								
1871	Ath NA	26	130	45	64	9	3	**4**	40	2	—	1	**.492**	**.500**	**.700**	**243**	**23**	4-0	.646	-9	67	32	3b26/P	—	0.9
1872	Ath NA	27	146	31	48	10	5	1	31	0	—	1	.329	.329	.486	147	7	0-0	.773	3	165	0	O26R/3	—	0.9
1873	Phi NA	48	238	53	83	14	4	3	59	2	—	0	.349	.354	.479	139	10	5-0	.746	-7	89	106	3b48/S	—	0.2
1874	Chi NA	53	254	65	100	19	1	1	45	3	—	4	**.394**	**.401**	.488	**182**	**23**	3-1	.833	-12	79	113	2b31,3b14,S5,O5(2/0/3)	—	0.7
1875	Phi NA	68	301	55	95	14	8	1	54	0	—	2	.316	.316	.425	149	13	7-2	.859	-6	98	99	2b36,3b20,1b16	—	0.5
1876	Phi N	55	256	46	87	12	8	0	34	3	—	2	.340	.347	.449	165	17	—	.791	-4	101	75	3b49,O3R,2b3,P2	—	1.3
1877	Cin N	27	107	11	35	7	2	0	15	0	—	4	.327	.327	.430	154	7	—	.822	0	99	88	S18,2b12/cf	—	0.7
1884	Phi U	3	11	0	1	1	0	0	—	0	—	—	.091	.091	.182	-21	-2	—	.789	-1	0	127	1b2/rf	—	-0.3
Total	5NA	222	1069	249	390	66	21	10	229	7	—	8	.365	.369	.494	166	76	19-3	.705	-30	76	99	3b109,2b67,O31R,1b16,S6/P	—	3.2
Total	3	85	374	57	123	20	10	0	<u>49</u>	3	—	<u>6</u>	.329	.334	.436	156	22	—	.791	-4	101	75	3b49,S18,2b15,O5(0/1/4),1b2,P2	—	1.7
MEYERS, CHAD	Chad William; B8.8.1975 Omaha NE; BR/TR/6´0˝/(185–190); [ChiN96 5/142]; d8.6; Col Creighton																								
1999	Chi N	43	142	17	33	9	0	0	4	9-1	3	27	.232	.292	.296	49	-11	4-2	.983	-7	89	71	2b32,O14(4/10/0)	0	-1.6
2000	Chi N	36	52	8	9	2	0	0	5	3-0	1	11	.173	.228	.212	13	-7	1-0	1.000	-1	94	115	2b8,3b8	0	-0.8
2001	Chi N	18	17	1	2	0	0	0	0	2-0	4	5	.118	.348	.118	29	-2	0-1	1.000	2	172	82	2b4,O4(2/2/0)/3	0	0.0
2003	Sea A	9	1	1	0	0	0	0	0	0-0	0	0	.000	.000	.000	-99	0	1-0	ø	-0	0	0	O3L,D6	0	0.0
Total	4	106	212	27	44	11	0	0	9	14-1	8	43	.208	.281	.259	39	-20	6-3	.987	-6	95	78	2b44,O21(9/12/0),3b9,D6	0	-2.4
MEYERS, HENRY	Henry L.; B1860 Philadelphia PA; D6.28.1898 Harrisburg PA; d8.30																								
1890	Phi AA	5	19	2	3	0	0	0	1	1	1	—	.158	.238	.158	17	-2	2	.684	-2	67	0	3b5	—	-0.4
MEYERS, CHIEF	John Tortes; B7.29.1880 Riverside CA; D7.25.1971 San Bernardino CA; BR/TR/5´11˝/194; d4.16																								
1909	NY N	90	220	15	61	10	5	1	30	22	6	—	.277	.359	.382	128	8	3	.963	2	*117*	*87*	C64	—	1.7
1910	NY N	127	365	25	104	18	0	1	62	40	4	18	.285	.362	.342	106	4	5	.969	2	*99*	*101*	C117	—	1.9
1911	†NY N	133	391	48	130	18	9	1	61	25	13	33	.332	.392	.432	126	14	7	.979	10	*130*	*76*	C128	—	3.3
1912	†NY N	126	371	60	133	16	5	6	54	47	8	20	.358	.441	.477	147	26	8	.973	5	*124*	*84*	C122	—	4.0
1913	†NY N	120	378	37	118	18	5	3	47	37	9	22	.312	.387	.410	127	15	7-9	.967	6	**117**	97	C116	—	3.0
1914	NY N	134	381	33	109	13	5	1	55	34	8	25	.286	.357	.354	116	8	4	.970	-2	*130*	*96*	C126	—	1.7
1915	NY N	110	289	24	67	10	5	1	26	26	7	18	.232	.311	.311	94	-2	4-4	**.986**	-6	*89*	*87*	C96	—	-0.1
1916	†Bro N	80	239	21	59	10	3	0	21	26	6	15	.247	.336	.314	97	1	2	.984	5	104	104	C74	—	1.4
1917	Bro N	47	132	8	28	3	0	0	3	13	0	7	.212	.283	.235	58	-6	4	.974	-4	*97*	*77*	C44	—	-0.8
	Bos N	25	68	5	17	4	4	0	4	4	2	4	.250	.311	.426	133	2	0	1.000	5	*124*	*123*	C24	—	1.1
	Year	72	200	13	45	7	4	0	7	17	2	11	.225	.292	.300	82	-4	4	.984	1	*107*	*94*	C68	—	0.3
Total	9	992	2834	276	826	120	41	14	363	274	63	<u>162</u>	.291	.367	.378	117	70	44-<u>13</u>	.974	24	*114*	*91*	C911	—	17.2
MEYERS, LOU	Lewis Henry "Crazy Horse"; B12.9.1859 Cincinnati OH; D11.30.1920 Cincinnati OH; BR/TR/5´11˝/165; d5.10																								
1884	Cin U	2	3	1	0	0	0	0	—	1	—	—	.000	.250	.000	-17	-1	—	.667	-1	—	—	C2/rf	—	-0.1
MICELOTTA, MICKEY	Robert Peter; B10.20.1928 Corona NY; BR/TR/5´11˝/170; d4.20																								
1954	Phi N	13	3	2	0	0	0	0	0	1	0	1	.000	.250	.000	-28	-1	0-0	1.000	0	145	0	/S	0	-0.1
1955	Phi N	4	4	0	0	0	0	0	0	0-0	0	0	.000	.000	.000	-99	-1	0-0	1.000	-0	74	184	S2	0	-0.1
Total	2	17	7	2	0	0	0	0	0	1-<u>0</u>	0	1	.000	.125	.000	-64	-2	0-0	1.000	-0	88	147	S3	0	-0.2
MICHAEL, GENE	Eugene Richard "Stick"; B6.2.1938 Kent OH; BB/TR/6´2˝/(182–185); d7.15; M4/C8; Col Kent St.																								
1966	Pit N	30	33	9	5	2	1	0	2	0-0	0	7	.152	.152	.273	15	-4	0-0	.903	1	115	220	S8,2b2/3	0	-0.3
1967	LA N	98	223	20	45	3	1	0	7	11-0	2	30	.202	.246	.224	39	-18	1-3	.950	-10	93	75	S83	0	-2.5
1968	NY A	61	116	8	23	3	0	1	8	2-0	1	23	.198	.218	.250	43	-8	3-2	.939	-5	95	79	S43/P	0	-1.2
1969	NY A	119	412	41	112	24	4	2	31	43-1	1	56	.272	.341	.364	101	1	7-4	.968	0	102	103	S118	0	1.6
1970	NY A	134	435	42	93	10	1	2	38	50-5	0	93	.214	.292	.255	55	-26	3-1	.957	-1	102	113	S123,3b4,2b3	0	-1.3
1971	NY A	139	456	36	102	15	0	3	35	48-8	3	64	.224	.299	.276	68	-19	3-3	.973	25	**117**	119	S136	0	2.2
1972	NY A	126	391	29	91	7	4	1	32	32-4	1	45	.233	.290	.279	72	-14	4-2	.969	24	117	126	S121	0	2.7
1973	NY A	129	418	30	94	11	1	3	47	26-0	0	51	.225	.270	.278	56	-25	1-3	.965	11	107	110	S129	0	-0.1
1974	NY A	81	177	19	46	9	0	0	13	14-0	0	24	.260	.313	.311	81	-4	0-0	.970	2	102	106	2b45,S39,3b2	0	0.3
1975	Det A	56	145	15	31	2	0	3	13	8-0	0	28	.214	.253	.290	51	-10	0-0	.938	0	98	109	S44,2b7,3b4	0	-0.5
Total	10	973	2806	249	642	86	12	15	226	234-18	8	421	.229	.288	.284	66	-127	22-18	.962	48	106	109	S844,2b57,3b11/P	0	0.9
MICHAELS, CASS	Casimir Eugene (Played in 1943 Under Real Name of Casimir Eugene Kwietniewski); B3.4.1926 Detroit MI; D11.12.1982 Grosse Pointe MI; BR/TR/5´11˝/175; d8.19																								
1943	Chi A	2	7	0	0	0	0	0	0	0	0	0	.000	.000	.000	-99	-2	0-0	1.000	-1	37	0	3b2	0	-0.3
1944	Chi A	27	68	4	12	4	1	0	5	2	0	5	.176	.200	.265	33	-6	0-0	.930	2	111	97	S21,3b3	0	-0.3
1945	Chi A	129	445	47	109	8	5	2	54	37	3	28	.245	.307	.299	78	-13	8-7	.936	8	105	93	S126/2	0	0.4
1946	Chi A	91	291	37	75	8	0	1	22	29	4	36	.258	.333	.296	80	-7	9-3	.957	1	104	112	2b66,3b13,S6	0	-0.1
1947	Chi A	110	355	31	97	15	4	3	34	39	3	28	.273	.350	.363	102	1	10-5	.982	9	111	126	2b60,3b44,S2	0	1.4
1948	Chi A	145	484	47	120	12	6	5	56	69	2	42	.248	.344	.329	82	-12	8-2	.957	16	111	100	S85,2b55/cf	0	1.3
1949	Chi A★	**154**	561	73	173	27	9	6	83	101	3	50	.308	.417	.421	126	25	5-7	.976	15	**111**	109	2b154	0	4.5
1950	Chi A	36	138	21	43	6	3	4	19	13	1	8	.312	.375	.486	122	4	0-0	.964	-3	80	122	2b35	0	0.2
	Was A★	106	388	48	97	8	4	4	47	55	1	39	.250	.345	.322	75	-14	2-3	.975	7	107	100	2b104	0	-0.2
	Year	142	526	69	140	14	7	8	66	68	2	47	.266	.352	.365	88	-10	2-3	.972	3	100	105	2b139	0	0.0
1951	Was A	138	485	59	125	20	4	4	45	61	1	41	.258	.342	.340	86	-8	1-1	.964	-22	100	84	2b128	0	-2.3
1952	Was A	22	86	10	20	4	1	1	7	7	0	15	.233	.290	.337	77	-3	0-0	.977	-2	106	92	2b22	0	-0.3

YEAR	TM LG	G	AB	R	H	2B	3B	HR	RBI	BB-IB	HP	SO	AVG	OBP	SLG	AOPS	ABR	SB-CS	FA	FR	RNG	THR	GAMES AT POSITION	DL	BFW
	StL A	55	166	21	44	8	2	3	25	23	0	16	.265	.354	.392	104	1	1-0	.916	-0	105	129	3b42,2b8	0	0.1
	Phi A	55	200	22	50	4	5	1	18	23	1	11	.250	.330	.335	80	-5	3-0	.993	-9	86	74	2b55	0	-1.2
	Year	132	452	53	114	16	8	5	50	53	1	42	.252	.332	.356	89	-7	4-0	.989	-11	92	81	2b85,3b42	0	-1.4
1953	Phi A	117	411	53	103	10	0	12	42	51	1	56	.251	.335	.363	85	-9	7-0	.970	-12	96	87	2b110	0	-1.1
1954	Chi A	101	282	35	74	13	2	7	44	56	4	31	.262	.392	.397	113	8	10-4	.958	-2	96	66	3b91,2b2	0	0.6
Total	12	1288	4367	508	1142	147	46	53	501	566	24	406	.262	.349	.353	92	-40	64-32	.973	6	103	101	2b800,S240,3b195/cf	0	2.7
MICHAELS, JASON	Jason Drew; B5.4.1976 Tampa FL; BR/TR/6´0˝/(204–205); [PhiN98 4/104]; d4.6; gf–John; Col Miami																								
2001	Phi N	6	6	0	1	0	0	0	1	0-0	0	2	.167	.167	.167	-14	-1	0-0	ø	-0	0	0	/lf	0	-0.1
2002	Phi N	81	105	16	28	10	3	2	11	13-1	1	33	.267	.347	.476	124	4	1-1	1.000	-1	76	254	O26(6/14/7)/3D	0	0.3
2003	Phi N	76	109	20	36	11	0	5	17	15-1	1	22	.330	.416	.569	166	11	0-0	.976	1	92	237	O38(23/5/13)	15	1.1
2004	Phi N	115	299	44	82	12	0	10	40	42-1	2	80	.274	.364	.415	99	0	2-2	.983	4	109	131	O78(39/44/12)/D	0	0.3
2005	Phi N	105	289	54	88	16	2	4	31	44-1	4	45	.304	.399	.415	111	7	3-3	.990	9	114	218	O91(22/75/13)	0	1.6
2006	Cle A	123	494	77	132	32	1	9	55	43-0	3	101	.267	.326	.391	89	-8	9-5	.991	-4	95	71	O118(117/0/1),D2	18	-1.5
Total	6	506	1302	211	367	81	6	30	155	157-4	11	283	.282	.360	.422	105	13	15-11	.988	10	102	142	O352(208/138/46),D5/3	33	1.7
MICHAELS, RALPH	Ralph Joseph; B5.3.1902 Etna PA; D8.5.1988 Monroeville PA; BR/TR/5´10.5˝/178; d4.16																								
1924	Chi N	8	11	0	4	0	0	0	2	0	0	1	.364	.364	.364	95	0	0-0	.929	-0	95	73	S4	—	0.0
1925	Chi N	22	50	10	14	1	0	0	6	6	0	9	.280	.357	.300	69	-2	1-0	.975	2	121	190	3b15/12S	—	0.1
1926	Chi N	2	0	1	0	0	0	0	0	0	0	0	ø	ø	ø	ø	0	0	ø	0	—	—	/H	—	0.0
Total	3	32	61	11	18	1	0	0	8	6	0	10	.295	.358	.311	73	-2	1-0	.975	2	121	190	3b15,S5/21	—	0.1
MICKELSON, ED	Edward Allen; B9.9.1926 Ottawa IL; BR/TR/6´3˝/(200–205); d9.18; Col Oklahoma St.																								
1950	StL N	5	10	1	1	0	0	0	0	2	0	3	.100	.250	.100	-4	-2	0	1.000	1	182	32	1b4	0	-0.1
1953	StL A	7	15	1	2	1	0	0	2	2	0	6	.133	.235	.200	18	-2	0-0	1.000	0	111	71	1b3	0	-0.2
1957	Chi N	6	12	0	0	0	0	0	1	0-0	0	4	.000	.000	.000	-99	-3	0-0	1.000	1	198	178	1b2	0	-0.3
Total	3	18	37	2	3	1	0	0	3	4-0	0	13	.081	.171	.108	-23	-7	0-0	1.000	2	162	80	1b9	0	-0.6
MIDKIFF, EZRA	Ezra Millington "Salt Rock"; B11.13.1882 Salt Rock WV; D3.20.1957 Huntington WV; BL/TR/5´10˝/180; d10.5																								
1909	Cin N	1	2	0	0	0	0	0	0	0	0	—	.000	.000	.000	-99	0	0	.000	-1	0	0	/3	—	-0.1
1912	NY A	21	86	9	21	1	0	0	9	7	0	—	.244	.301	.256	56	-5	4	.901	2	120	32	3b21	—	-0.3
1913	NY A	83	284	22	56	9	1	0	14	12	1	33	.197	.232	.236	37	-23	9	.957	14	121	105	3b76,S4,2b2	—	-0.8
Total	3	105	372	31	77	10	1	0	23	19	1	33	.207	.247	.239	41	-28	13	.942	15	120	90	3b98,S4,2b2	—	-1.2
MIENTKIEWICZ, DOUG	Douglas Andrew; B6.19.1974 Toledo OH; BL/TR/6´2˝/(193–205); [MinA95 5/128]; d9.18; Col Florida St.																								
1998	Min A	8	25	1	5	1	0	0	2	4-0	0	3	.200	.310	.240	45	-2	1-1	1.000	-1	61	50	1b8	0	-0.3
1999	Min A	118	327	34	75	21	3	2	32	43-3	4	51	.229	.324	.330	65	-17	1-1	**.997**	-2	89	91	1b110	0	-2.6
2000	Min A	3	14	0	6	0	0	0	4	0-0	0	0	.429	.400	.429	111	0	0-0	1.000	-1	0	109	1b3	0	-0.1
2001	Min A	151	543	77	166	39	1	15	74	67-6	9	92	.306	.387	.464	118	17	2-6	**.997**	-9	74	83	1b148,D2	0	-0.6
2002	†Min A	143	467	60	122	29	1	10	64	74-8	6	69	.261	.365	.392	99	3	1-2	.996	-6	81	90	1b143	0	-1.5
2003	†Min A	142	487	67	146	38	1	11	65	74-4	5	55	.300	.393	.450	119	17	4-1	.997	-8	78	83	1b139,O3R/23D	0	-0.2
2004	Min A	78	284	34	70	18	0	5	25	38-2	3	38	.246	.340	.363	82	-7	2-2	.994	-4	77	102	1b77	16	-1.7
	†Bos A	49	107	13	23	6	1	1	10	10-0	1	18	.215	.286	.318	54	-7	0-1	.997	2	116	58	1b47/2	0	-0.8
	Year	127	391	47	93	24	1	6	35	48-2	4	56	.238	.326	.350	74	-14	2-3	.995	-3	88	89	1b124/2	0	-2.5
2005	NY N	87	275	36	66	13	0	11	29	32-7	2	39	.240	.322	.407	92	-3	0-1	.995	-3	86	93	1b83	49	-1.3
2006	KC A	91	314	37	89	24	2	4	43	35-1	5	50	.283	.359	.411	102	2	3-0	.996	-2	88	101	1b90	63	-0.6
Total	9	870	2843	359	768	189	9	59	348	377-31	35	415	.270	.359	.405	98	3	14-15	.996	-34	82	89	1b848,O3R,D3,2b2/3	128	-9.7
MIERKOWICZ, ED	Edward Frank "Butch","Mouse"; B3.6.1924 Wyandotte MI; BR/TR/6´4˝/205; d8.31																								
1945	†Det A	10	15	0	2	2	0	0	2	1	0	3	.133	.188	.267	29	-1	0-0	1.000	-0	109	0	O6L	0	-0.2
1947	Det A	21	42	6	8	1	0	1	1	1	0	12	.190	.209	.286	36	-4	1-0	.947	-0	104	0	O10L	0	-0.5
1948	Det A	3	5	0	1	0	0	0	1	2	0	2	.200	.429	.200	69	0	0-0	1.000	0	128	0	/lf	0	0.0
1950	StL N	1	1	0	0	0	0	0	0	0	0	1	.000	.000	.000	-95	0	0	ø	0	—	—	/H	0	0.0
Total	4	35	63	6	11	3	0	1	4	4	0	18	.175	.224	.270	36	-5	1-0	.968	-0	108	0	O17L	0	-0.7
MIESKE, MATT	Matthew Todd; B2.13.1968 Midland MI; BR/TR/6´0˝/(185–195); [SDN90 17/471]; d5.3; Col Western Michigan																								
1993	Mil A	23	58	9	14	0	0	3	7	4-0	0	14	.241	.290	.397	83	-2	0-2	.936	-1	96	78	O22(1/9/12)	0	-0.4
1994	Mil A	84	259	39	67	13	1	10	38	21-0	3	62	.259	.320	.432	88	-5	3-5	.976	0	99	122	O80(6/0/80)/D	0	-0.9
1995	Mil A	117	267	42	67	13	1	12	48	27-0	4	45	.251	.323	.442	93	-3	2-4	.979	5	112	130	O108R,D2	0	-0.3
1996	Mil A	127	374	46	104	24	3	14	64	26-2	2	76	.278	.324	.471	95	-4	1-5	.996	7	**114**	95	O122(9/10/108)	0	-0.3
1997	Mil A	84	253	39	63	15	3	5	21	19-2	0	50	.249	.300	.391	78	-9	1-0	.962	-1	93	146	O74(26/0/52),D5	25	-1.2
1998	Chi N	77	97	16	29	7	0	1	12	11-1	1	17	.299	.373	.402	101	1	0-0	.974	-2	83	67	O62(50/3/12)	0	-0.2
1999	Sea A	24	41	11	15	0	0	4	7	2-1	0	9	.366	.395	.659	164	4	0-0	1.000	2	133	162	O20(6/3/13)/D	0	0.4
	†Hou N	54	109	13	31	5	0	5	22	6-1	0	22	.284	.316	.468	98	-1	0-0	1.000	2	120	69	O37(30/0/7)	0	0.0
2000	Hou N	62	81	7	14	1	2	1	5	7-0	1	17	.173	.247	.272	29	-9	0-0	.933	-1	75	0	O18(14/0/4)	9	-1.1
	Ari N	11	8	3	2	0	0	1	2	1-0	0	1	.250	.300	.625	130	0	0-0	1.000	0	886	0	/rf	0	0.1
	Year	73	89	10	16	1	2	2	7	8-0	1	18	.180	.253	.303	38	-9	0-0	.941	-1	85	0	O19(14/0/5)	0	-1.0
Total	8	663	1547	225	406	78	10	56	226	124-7	11	313	.262	.318	.434	89	-28	7-16	.979	12	105	110	O544(142/25/397),D9	34	-3.9
MIGGINS, LARRY	Lawrence Edward "Irish"; B8.20.1925 Bronx NY; BR/TR/6´4˝/195; d10.3; Col St. Thomas (MN)																								
1948	StL N	1	1	1	0	0	0	0	0	0	0	0	.000	.000	.000	-95	0	0	ø	0	—	—	/H	0	0.0
1952	StL N	42	96	7	22	5	1	2	10	3	0	19	.229	.253	.365	69	-5	0-1	.967	-2	87	0	O25(23/0/2)/1	0	-0.8
Total	2	43	97	8	22	5	1	2	10	3	0	19	.227	.250	.361	67	-5	0-1	.967	-2	87	0	O25(23/0/2)/1	0	-0.8
MIHALIC, JOHN	John Michael; B11.13.1911 Cleveland OH; D4.24.1987 Ft.Oglethorpe GA; BR/TR/5´11˝/172; d9.18																								
1935	Was A	6	22	4	5	3	0	0	6	2	0	3	.227	.292	.364	71	-1	1-0	.966	-0	96	133	S6	—	0.0
1936	Was A	25	88	15	21	2	1	0	8	14	0	14	.239	.343	.284	60	-5	2-1	.972	1	101	147	2b25	—	-0.2
1937	Was A	38	107	13	27	5	2	0	8	17	0	9	.252	.355	.336	79	-3	2-1	.981	1	98	126	2b28,S3	—	0.0
Total	3	69	217	32	53	10	3	0	22	33	0	26	.244	.344	.318	70	-9	5-2	.977	2	99	136	2b53,S9	—	-0.2
MIKSIS, EDDIE	Edward Thomas; B9.11.1926 Burlington NJ; D4.8.2005 Huntingdon Valley PA; BR/TR/6´0.5˝/(182–185); d6.17; Mil 1945; OF(34/106/88)																								
1944	Bro N	26	91	12	20	2	0	0	11	6	0	11	.220	.268	.242	45	-7	4	.896	-4	78	275	3b15,S10	0	-1.1
1946	Bro N	23	48	3	7	0	0	0	5	3	1	3	.146	.212	.146	2	-6	0	.970	-0	96	0	3b13/2	0	-0.7
1947	†Bro N	45	86	18	23	1	0	4	10	9	0	8	.267	.337	.419	96	-1	0	1.000	2	113	82	2b13,O11L,3b5,S2	0	0.0
1948	Bro N	86	221	28	47	7	1	2	16	19	1	27	.213	.278	.281	50	-16	5	.967	-1	96	66	2b54,3b22,S5	0	-1.4
1949	†Bro N	50	113	17	25	5	0	1	6	7	0	8	.221	.267	.292	48	-8	3	.978	4	111	79	3b29,S4,2b3/1	0	-0.5
1950	Bro N	51	76	13	19	2	1	2	10	5	0	10	.250	.296	.382	75	-3	3	.964	1	80	61	2b15,S15,3b7	0	-0.1
1951	Bro N	19	10	6	2	1	0	0	0	1	1	2	.200	.333	.300	70	0	0-0	1.000	1	150	699	3b6/2	0	0.1
	Chi N	102	421	48	112	13	3	4	35	33	0	36	.266	.319	.340	76	-15	11-5	.969	1	106	85	2b102	0	-0.7
	Year	121	431	54	114	14	3	4	35	34	1	38	.265	.320	.339	76	-15	11-5	.969	2	106	85	2b103,3b6	0	-0.6
1952	Chi N	93	383	44	89	20	1	2	19	20	1	32	.232	.272	.305	59	-22	4-4	.950	-14	91	63	2b54,S40	0	-3.2
1953	Chi N	142	577	61	145	17	6	8	39	33	1	59	.251	.293	.343	64	-32	13-4	.954	-15	96	91	2b92,S53	0	-3.4
1954	Chi N	38	99	9	20	3	0	2	3	3	0	9	.202	.225	.293	33	-10	1-0	.961	2	104	101	2b21,3b2/lf	0	-0.6
1955	Chi N	131	481	52	113	14	2	9	41	32-3	0	55	.235	.282	.328	62	-27	3-6	**.989**	-1	100	66	O111(0/76/41),3b18	0	-3.5
1956	Chi N	114	356	54	85	10	3	9	27	32-2	1	40	.239	.303	.360	79	-11	4-2	.975	1	99	55	3b48,O33(6/25/2),2b19,S2	0	-1.0
1957	StL N	49	38	3	8	0	0	1	2	7-1	0	7	.211	.333	.289	68	-2	0-0	1.000	-2	68	0	O31(11/3/18)	0	-0.4
	Bal A	1	1	0	0	0	0	0	0	0-0	0	0	.000	.000	.000	-99	0	0-0	ø	0	—	—	/H	0	0.0
1958	Bal A	3	2	0	0	0	0	0	0	0-0	0	1	.000	.000	.000	-99	-1	0-0	ø	-0	0	0	/S	0	-0.1
	Cin N	69	50	15	7	0	0	0	4	5-0	0	5	.140	.218	.140	-2	-7	1-1	1.000	-1	113	0	O32(5/2/27),3b14,2b7,S5/1	0	-0.8
Total	14	1042	3053	383	722	95	17	44	228	215-6	6	313	.236	.288	.322	62	-168	52-22	.962	-27	99	80	2b382,O219C,3b179,S137,1b2	0	-17.4
MILAN, HORACE	Horace Robert; B4.7.1894 Linden TN; D6.29.1955 Texarkana AR; BR/TR/5´9˝/175; d8.29; Mil 1918; b–Clyde																								
1915	Was A	11	27	6	11	1	1	0	7	8	0	7	.407	.543	.519	214	5	2	1.000	-1	79	0	O10(2/4/4)	—	0.4
1917	Was A	31	73	8	21	3	1	0	9	4	2	9	.288	.342	.356	114	1	4	.932	-1	120	0	O23L	—	-0.1
Total	2	42	100	14	32	4	2	0	16	12	2	16	.320	.404	.400	144	6	6	.944	-2	108	0	O33(25/4/4)	—	0.3

YEAR	TM LG	G	AB	R	H	2B	3B	HR	RBI	BB-IB	HP	SO	AVG	OBP	SLG	AOPS	ABR	SB-CS	FA	FR	RNG	THR	GAMES AT POSITION	DL	BFW
Milan, Clyde	Jesse Clyde "Deerfoot"; B3.25.1887 Linden TN; D3.3.1953 Orlando FL; BL/TR/5´9˝/168; d8.19; M1/C17; b–Horace																								
1907	Was A	48	183	22	51	3	3	0	9	8	4	—	.279	.323	.328	117	3	8	.929	4	203	68	O47(0/30/17)	—	0.5
1908	Was A	130	485	55	116	10	12	1	32	38	7	—	.239	.304	.315	110	5	29	.959	5	126	156	O122C	—	0.4
1909	Was A	130	400	36	80	12	4	1	15	31	6	—	.200	.268	.257	69	-14	10	.972	5	130	86	O120(29/89/2)	—	-1.7
1910	Was A	142	531	89	148	17	6	0	16	71	15	—	.279	.379	.333	129	23	44	.946	8	99	154	O142C	—	2.6
1911	Was A	**154**	616	109	194	24	8	3	35	74	7	—	.315	.395	.394	123	22	58	.957	7	102	131	O154C	—	1.8
1912	Was A	**154**	601	105	184	19	11	1	79	63	5	—	.306	.377	.379	116	13	**88**	.935	7	102	147	O154C	—	1.0
1913	Was A	154	579	92	174	18	9	3	54	58	3	25	.301	.367	.378	116	12	**75**	.932	-12	88	83	O154C	—	-1.2
1914	Was A	115	437	63	129	19	11	1	39	32	2	26	.295	.346	.396	118	8	38-21	.949	-6	96	71	O113(1/112/0)	—	-0.5
1915	Was A	153	573	83	165	13	7	2	66	53	5	32	.288	.353	.346	107	5	40-19	.946	-6	102	61	O151C	—	-1.0
1916	Was A	150	565	58	154	14	3	1	45	56	5	31	.273	.343	.313	98	0	34-21	.961	14	**114**	136	O149C	—	0.4
1917	Was A	155	579	60	170	15	4	0	48	58	6	26	.294	.364	.333	114	11	20	.962	-6	96	86	O153C	—	-0.6
1918	Was A	128	503	56	146	18	5	0	56	36	5	14	.290	.344	.346	110	5	26	.972	-4	95	90	O124C	—	-0.9
1919	Was A	88	321	43	92	12	6	0	37	40	3	16	.287	.371	.361	107	4	11	.953	-1	103	83	O86C	—	-0.2
1920	Was A	126	506	70	163	22	5	3	41	28	5	12	.322	.364	.403	106	4	10-12	.971	4	109	88	O123(115/0/8)	—	0.0
1921	Was A	113	406	55	117	19	11	1	40	37	2	13	.288	.351	.397	95	-4	4-5	.931	3	98	147	O99(34/15/52)	—	-0.9
1922	Was A	42	74	8	17	5	0	0	5	2	0	2	.230	.250	.297	44	-6	0-0	1.000	1	91	249	O12(3/0/9),M	—	-0.6
Total	16	1982	7359	1004	2100	240	105	17	617	685	80	197	.285	.353	.353	109	91	495-78	.953	21	106	109	O1903(182/1635/88)	—	-0.9
Milbourne, Larry	Lawrence William; B2.14.1951 Port Norris NJ; BB/TR/6´0˝/(153–165); d4.6; [DL 1985 Sea A 106]																								
1974	Hou N	112	136	31	38	2	1	0	9	10-0	0	14	.279	.329	.309	83	-3	6-2	.974	2	112	86	2b87,S8,O4L	0	0.2
1975	Hou N	73	151	17	32	1	2	1	9	6-1	1	14	.212	.245	.265	45	-12	1-2	.968	-2	95	130	2b43,S22	0	-1.1
1976	Hou N	59	145	22	36	4	0	0	7	14-0	1	10	.248	.319	.276	76	-4	6-1	.965	-3	98	84	2b32	0	-0.4
1977	Sea A	86	242	24	53	10	0	2	21	6-0	2	20	.219	.239	.285	44	-19	3-1	.982	4	112	108	2b41,S40/3D	0	-1.0
1978	Sea A	93	234	31	53	6	2	2	20	9-1	0	6	.226	.254	.295	54	-15	5-7	.989	4	96	65	3b32,S23,2b15,D10	0	-1.1
1979	Sea A	123	356	40	99	13	4	2	26	19-2	0	20	.278	.313	.354	78	-11	5-3	.981	3	113	92	S65,2b49,3b11	0	-0.3
1980	Sea A	106	258	31	68	6	6	0	26	19-4	1	13	.264	.313	.333	77	-9	7-6	.976	3	113	114	2b38,S34,3b6,D8	0	-0.2
1981	†NY A	61	163	24	51	7	2	1	12	9-2	1	14	.313	.351	.399	117	3	2-0	.955	-2	89	84	S39,2b14,3b3,D3	0	0.6
1982	NY A	14	27	2	4	1	0	0	0	1-0	0	4	.148	.179	.185	0	-4	0-1	.917	-2	62	0	S9,2b3,3b3	0	-0.5
	Min A	29	98	9	23	1	1	0	1	7-0	0	8	.235	.283	.265	51	-7	1-1	.981	-7	76	82	2b26	0	-1.3
	Cle A	82	291	29	80	11	4	2	25	12-0	2	20	.275	.301	.361	83	-8	2-5	.981	-3	99	83	2b63,S21,3b9/D	0	-0.8
	Year	125	416	40	107	13	5	2	26	20-0	2	32	.257	.289	.327	70	-18	3-7	.979	-12	93	87	2b92,S30,3b12/D	0	-2.6
1983	Phi N	41	66	3	16	0	1	0	4	4-0	0	7	.242	.282	.273	56	-4	2-1	.963	-3	83	39	2b27,S8,3b3	0	-0.6
	NY A	31	70	5	14	4	0	0	2	5-0	1	10	.200	.263	.257	45	-5	1-1	1.000	2	104	85	2b19,S6,3b4	0	-0.2
1984	Sea A	79	211	22	56	5	1	1	22	12-0	0	16	.265	.304	.313	72	-8	0-2	.900	-7	74	87	3b40,2b14,S5,D6	15	-1.6
Total	11	989	2448	290	623	71	24	11	184	133-10	9	176	.254	.293	.317	70	-106	41-33	.974	-10	102	98	2b471,S280,3b112,D29,O4L	121	-8.3
Miles, Aaron	Aaron Wade; B12.15.1976 Pittsburg CA; BB/TR/5´8˝/(170–180); [HouN95 19/529]; d9,11																								
2003	Chi A	8	12	3	4	3	0	0	2	0-0	0	0	.333	.333	.583	130	1	0-0	1.000	0	130	0	2b3,D2	0	0.1
2004	Col N	134	522	75	153	15	3	6	47	29-0	2	53	.293	.329	.368	72	-22	12-7	.984	10	**112**	81	2b128	0	-0.5
2005	Col N	99	324	37	91	12	3	2	28	8-1	4	38	.281	.306	.355	65	-17	4-2	.984	7	106	93	2b79/S	33	-0.6
2006	†StL N	135	426	48	112	20	5	2	30	38-9	2	42	.263	.324	.347	72	-18	2-1	.975	12	107	119	2b88,S39/3	0	0.1
Total	4	376	1284	163	360	50	11	10	107	75-10	8	133	.280	.322	.360	71	-56	18-10	.982	29	109	94	2b298,S40,D2/3	33	-0.9
Miles, Don	Donald Ray; B3.13.1936 Indianapolis IN; BL/TR/6´1˝/210; d9.9; Col Indianapolis																								
1958	LA N	8	22	2	4	0	0	0	0	0-0	1	6	.182	.217	.182	7	-3	0-0	1.000	1	194	0	O5L	0	-0.2
Miles, Dee	Wilson Daniel; B2.15.1909 Kellerman AL; D11.2.1976 Birmingham AL; BL/TR/6´0˝/175; d7.7																								
1935	Was A	60	215	28	57	5	2	0	29	7	1	13	.265	.291	.307	57	-15	6-4	.970	1	102	129	O45R	—	-1.6
1936	Was A	25	59	8	14	1	2	0	7	1	0	5	.237	.250	.322	43	-6	0-1	.958	0	103	102	O10(1/0/9)	—	-0.6
1939	Phi A	106	320	49	96	17	6	1	37	15	0	17	.300	.331	.400	88	-7	3-4	.968	-3	96	72	O77(1/20/57)	—	-1.3
1940	Phi A	88	236	26	71	9	6	1	23	8	1	18	.301	.327	.403	90	-5	1-1	.945	0	106	82	O50(15/18/18)	—	-0.7
1941	Phi A	80	170	14	53	7	1	0	15	4	1	8	.312	.331	.365	86	-4	0-1	1.000	2	115	73	O35(25/2/8)	0	-0.4
1942	Phi A	99	346	41	94	12	5	0	22	12	2	10	.272	.300	.335	79	-11	5-3	.984	0	99	109	O81(9/46/28)	0	-1.5
1943	Bos A	45	121	9	26	2	2	0	10	3	0	3	.215	.234	.264	45	-9	0-2	.968	-1	89	159	O25(1/24/0)	0	-1.2
Total	7	503	1467	175	411	53	24	2	143	50	5	74	.280	.306	.353	76	-57	15-16	.971	1	101	100	O323(52/110/165)	0	-7.3
Miley, Mike	Michael Wilfred; B3.30.1953 Yazoo City MS; D1.6.1977 Baton Rouge LA; BB/TR (BR 1975p)/6´1˝/185; [AnaA74 1/10]; d7.6; Col Louisiana St.																								
1975	Cal A	70	224	17	39	3	2	4	26	16-0	1	54	.174	.230	.259	41	-19	0-1	.939	-9	86	123	S70	0	-2.0
1976	Cal A	14	38	4	7	2	0	0	4	4-1	0	8	.184	.256	.237	50	-2	1-0	.981	-3	74	122	S14	0	-0.3
Total	2	84	262	21	46	5	2	4	30	20-1	1	62	.176	.234	.256	43	-21	1-1	.945	-11	84	123	S84	0	-2.3
Millan, Felix	Felix Bernardo (Martinez); B8.21.1943 Yabucoa, PR; BR/TR/5´11˝/172; d6.2																								
1966	Atl N	37	91	20	25	6	0	0	5	2-2	0	6	.275	.290	.341	74	-3	3-1	.973	-6	86	82	2b25/S3	0	-0.7
1967	Atl N	41	136	13	32	3	3	2	6	4-1	2	10	.235	.266	.346	75	-5	0-3	.972	6	118	102	2b41	0	0.3
1968	Atl N	149	570	49	165	22	2	1	33	22-7	6	26	.289	.321	.340	99	-1	6-6	.980	1	102	111	2b145	0	1.3
1969	†Atl N★	**162**	652	98	174	23	5	6	57	34-5	8	35	.267	.310	.345	83	-16	14-3	**.980**	-18	94	76	2b162	0	-2.2
1970	Atl N✳	142	590	100	183	25	5	2	37	35-2	5	23	.310	.352	.380	91	-7	16-5	.979	-11	89	95	2b142	0	-0.6
1971	Atl N★	143	577	65	167	20	8	2	45	37-7	3	22	.289	.332	.362	92	-6	11-7	.982	6	101	119	2b141	0	0.9
1972	Atl N	125	498	46	128	19	3	1	38	23-1	3	28	.257	.292	.313	67	-22	6-4	.987	-11	96	84	2b120	0	-2.7
1973	†NY N	153	638	82	185	23	4	3	37	35-3	6	22	.290	.332	.353	91	-9	2-2	.989	4	95	102	2b153	0	0.6
1974	NY N	136	518	50	139	15	2	1	33	31-2	8	14	.268	.317	.311	77	-16	5-1	.979	-10	87	96	2b134	0	-1.7
1975	NY N	**162**	676	81	191	37	2	1	56	36-2	**12**	28	.283	.329	.348	91	-8	1-6	.972	-23	86	89	2b162	0	-2.4
1976	NY N	139	531	55	150	25	2	1	35	41-5	7	19	.282	.341	.343	99	0	2-4	.977	-15	84	90	2b136	0	-0.7
1977	NY N	91	314	40	78	11	2	2	21	18-3	3	9	.248	.294	.315	66	-16	1-1	.977	-9	83	92	2b89	24	-2.1
Total	12	1480	5791	699	1617	229	38	22	403	318-40	63	242	.279	.322	.343	86	-109	67-43	.980	-85	93	95	2b1450/3S	24	-10.0
Millar, Kevin	Kevin Charles; B9.24.1971 Los Angeles CA; BR/TR/6´1˝/(185–215); d4.11; Col Lamar																								
1998	Fla N	2	2	1	1	0	0	0	0	1-0	0	0	.500	.667	.500	227	1	0-0	.833	1	221	704	3b2	161	0.1
1999	Fla N	105	351	48	100	17	4	9	67	40-2	7	64	.285	.362	.433	108	5	1-0	.995	-4	87	105	1b94/3lf	0	-0.6
2000	Fla N	123	259	36	67	14	3	14	42	36-0	8	47	.259	.364	.498	122	9	0-0	.989	6	159	79	1b34,O18(17/0/1),3b13,D6	0	1.1
2001	Fla N	144	449	62	141	39	5	20	85	39-2	5	70	.314	.374	.557	141	27	0-0	.986	-7	92	38	O86(27/0/66),1b15,3b10,D6	0	1.5
2002	Fla N	126	438	58	134	41	0	16	57	40-0	5	74	.306	.366	.509	134	22	0-2	.985	0	97	92	O108(89/0/22),1b2,3b2,D6	29	1.8
2003	†Bos A	148	544	83	150	30	1	25	96	60-5	5	108	.276	.348	.472	110	9	3-2	.996	6	115	98	1b101,O31(19/0/12),D19	0	0.4
2004	†Bos A	150	508	74	151	36	0	18	74	57-0	**17**	91	.297	.383	.474	116	14	1-1	.976	4	99	25	O74(20/0/55),1b69,D8	0	1.0
2005	†Bos A	134	449	57	122	28	1	9	50	54-0	8	74	.272	.355	.399	98	1	0-1	.992	9	**144**	82	1b110,O34(20/0/14)	0	0.0
2006	Bal A	132	430	64	117	26	0	15	64	59-3	12	74	.272	.374	.437	113	11	1-1	.995	5	119	86	1b98,D30	0	0.5
Total	9	1064	3430	483	983	231	14	126	535	386-12	67	602	.287	.366	.472	117	99	6-7	.994	20	121	93	1b523,O352(193/0/170),D75,3b28	190	5.8
Millard, Frank	Frank E.; B7.4.1865 E.St.Louis IL; D7.4.1892 Dallas TX; d5.4																								
1890	StL AA	1	1	0	0	0	0	0	0	1	0	—	.000	.500	.000	42	0	0	.625	-0	153	0	/2	—	0.0
Milledge, Lastings	Lastings Darnell; B4.5.1984 Bradenton FL; BR/TR/6´1˝/185; [NYN03 1/12]; d5.30																								
2006	NY N	56	166	14	40	7	2	4	22	12-4	5	39	.241	.310	.380	78	-6	1-2	.977	0	92	174	O50(26/0/24)	0	-0.8
Miller, Corky	Abraham Philip; B3.18.1976 Yucaipa CA; BR/TR/6´1˝/(225–245); d9.4; Col Nevada–Reno																								
2001	Cin N	17	49	5	9	2	0	3	7	4-0	2	16	.184	.263	.408	69	-3	1-0	.991	4	108	186	C17	0	0.2
2002	Cin N	39	114	9	29	10	0	3	15	9-2	4	20	.254	.328	.421	93	-1	0-0	.992	5	138	78	C38	0	0.6
2003	Cin N	14	30	4	8	0	0	0	1	5-0	2	7	.267	.395	.267	84	0	0-0	1.000	-0	45	99	C11	0	0.0
2004	Cin N	13	39	2	1	0	0	0	3	6-0	3	12	.026	.204	.026	-34	-8	0-0	.989	1	318	40	C12	0	-0.6
2005	Min A	5	12	0	0	0	0	0	0	0-0	0	2	.000	.000	.000	-98	-3	0-0	1.000	2	160	294	C4/D	0	-0.1
2006	Bos A	1	4	0	0	0	0	0	0	0-0	0	1	.000	.000	.000	-98	-1	0-0	1.000	-0	0	0	/C	0	-0.1
Total	6	89	248	20	47	12	0	6	26	24-2	11	58	.190	.285	.310	56	-16	1-0	.993	11	148	105	C83/D	0	-0.0

YEAR	TM LG	G	AB	R	H	2B	3B	HR	RBI	BB-IB	HP	SO	AVG	OBP	SLG	AOPS	ABR	SB-CS	FA	FR	RNG	THR	GAMES AT POSITION	DL	BFW
Miller, Dusty	Charles Bradley; B9.10.1868 Oil City PA; D9.3.1945 Memphis TN; BL/TR/5´11.5˝/170; d9.23; Col Niagara																								
1889	Bal AA	11	40	4	6	1	1	0	6	2	1	11	.150	.209	.225	23	-4	3	.636	-8	69	0	S8,O3(2/1/0)	—	-1.0
1890	StL AA	26	96	17	21	5	3	1	10	8	0	—	.219	.279	.365	78	-4	4	.872	3	195	351	O24(9/15/0),S3	—	-0.2
1895	Cin N	**132**	529	103	177	31	16	10	112	33	4	34	.335	.378	.510	123	15	43	.937	10	129	183	O132(0/11/121)	—	1.5
1896	Cin N	125	504	91	162	38	12	4	93	33	4	30	.321	.368	.468	112	7	76	.902	-2	122	176	O125(1/0/124)	—	-0.1
1897	Cin N	119	440	83	139	27	1	4	70	48	8	—	.316	.393	.409	105	5	29	.929	2	108	64	O119R	—	0.1
1898	Cin N	152	586	99	175	24	12	3	90	38	9	—	.299	.351	.396	106	3	32	.929	5	106	79	O152R	—	0.0
1899	Cin N	81	327	45	83	12	6	0	37	9	3	—	.254	.280	.327	65	-17	18	.927	6	144	123	O81(1/2/79)	—	-1.4
	StL N	10	39	3	8	1	0	0	3	3	1	—	.205	.279	.231	40	-3	1	.875	-1	64	249	O10C	—	-0.5
	Year	91	366	48	91	13	6	0	40	12	4	—	.249	.280	.317	62	-20	19	.921	4	135	137	O91(1/12/79)	—	-1.9
Total	7	656	2561	445	771	139	51	22	421	174	30	75	.301	.353	.421	103	2	206	.923	15	121	134	O646(13/39/595),S11	—	-1.6
Miller, Bruce	Charles Bruce; B3.4.1947 Fort Wayne IN; BR/TR/6´1˝/(175–185); [ChiA70 20/469]; d8.4; Col Indiana																								
1973	SF N	12	21	1	3	0	0	0	2	2-1	0	3	.143	.217	.143	2	-3	0-0	.900	0	124	0	3b4,2b3/S	0	-0.3
1974	SF N	73	198	19	55	7	1	0	16	11-2	1	15	.278	.316	.323	77	-6	1-1	.938	8	138	46	3b41,S13,2b9	0	0.4
1975	SF N	99	309	22	74	6	3	1	31	15-0	1	26	.239	.275	.288	55	-20	0-1	.949	5	97	101	3b68,2b21,S6	0	-1.4
1976	SF N	12	25	1	4	1	0	0	2	2-1	0	5	.160	.222	.200	20	-3	0-0	.920	-3	93	83	2b8,3b2	0	-0.5
Total	4	196	553	43	136	14	4	1	51	30-4	2	49	.246	.285	.291	59	-32	1-2	.944	11	111	78	3b115,2b41,S20	0	-1.8
Miller, Charlie	Charles Elmer; B1.4.1892 Warrensburg MO; D4.23.1972 Warrensburg MO; TR; d9.18																								
1912	StL A	1	2	0	0	0	0	0	0	0	0	—	.000	.000	.000	-99	-1	0	1.000	0	142	0	/S	—	0.0
Miller, Charlie	Charles Hess; B12.30.1877 Conestoga PA; D1.13.1951 Millersville PA; BR/TR/6´0˝/190; d10.2																								
1915	Bal F	1	1	0	0	0	0	0	0	0	0	0	.000	.000	.000	-97	0	0	ø	0	—	—	/H	—	0.0
Miller, Chuck	Charles Marion; B9.18.1889 Woodville OH; D6.16.1961 Houston TX; BL/TL/5´8.5˝/155; d9.19																								
1913	StL N	4	12	0	2	0	0	0	1	0	0	2	.167	.167	.167	-5	-2	0	1.000	-0	85	0	O3(2/0/1)	—	-0.2
1914	StL N	36	36	4	7	1	0	0	2	3	0	9	.194	.256	.222	43	-3	2	1.000	1	107	153	O14(6/5/2)	—	-0.2
Total	2	40	48	4	9	1	0	0	3	3	0	11	.188	.235	.208	31	-5	2	1.000	0	100	103	O17(8/5/3)	—	-0.4
Miller, Dusty	Dakin Evans; B9.3.1876 Malvern IA; D4.19.1950 Stockton CA; BL/TR/5´10˝/175; d4.17																								
1902	Chi N	51	187	17	46	4	1	0	13	7	7	—	.246	.299	.278	80	-4	10	.955	2	132	0	O51(46/1/4)	—	-0.6
Miller, Damian	Damian Donald; B10.13.1969 LaCrosse WI; BR/TR/6´2˝/(190–220); [MinA90 20/544]; d8.10; Col Viterbo																								
1997	Min A	25	66	5	18	1	0	2	13	2-0	0	12	.273	.282	.379	73	-3	0-0	1.000	-2	249	61	C20,D3	0	-0.3
1998	Ari N	57	168	17	48	14	2	3	14	11-2	2	43	.286	.337	.446	104	1	1-0	.986	1	121	94	C46,O2R/1D	0	0.5
1999	Ari N	86	296	35	80	19	0	11	47	19-3	2	78	.270	.316	.446	90	-5	0-0	.991	17	90	143	C86	0	1.6
2000	Ari N	100	324	43	89	24	0	10	44	36-4	1	74	.275	.347	.441	94	-2	2-2	.992	1	111	127	C97,1b2/S	0	0.4
2001	†Ari N	123	380	45	103	19	0	13	47	35-9	4	80	.271	.337	.424	89	-6	0-1	.993	**30**	92	126	C121	0	3.0
2002	†Ari N★	101	297	40	74	22	0	11	42	38-5	3	88	.249	.340	.434	93	-2	0-0	**.997**	12	122	108	C100	21	1.5
2003	†Chi N	114	352	34	82	19	1	9	36	39-6	1	91	.233	.310	.369	75	-13	1-0	.997	22	126	113	C114	0	1.6
2004	Oak A	110	397	39	108	25	0	9	58	39-0	2	87	.272	.339	.403	93	-3	0-1	**.999**	6	127	**128**	C109	0	0.9
2005	Mil N	114	385	50	105	25	1	9	43	37-6	4	94	.273	.340	.413	96	-1	0-1	.996	-3	104	109	C111	0	0.2
2006	Mil N	101	331	34	83	28	0	6	38	33-7	4	86	.251	.322	.390	82	-8	0-0	.997	-6	158	80	C98	0	-0.8
Total	10	931	2996	342	790	196	4	83	382	289-42	23	733	.264	.331	.415	90	-42	4-5	.995	77	119	114	C902,D5,1b3,O2R/S	21	8.6
Miller, Darrell	Darrell Keith; B2.26.1958 Washington DC; BR/TR/6´2˝/(200–205); [CalA79 9/223]; d8.14; Col Cal Poly–Pomona																								
1984	Cal A	17	41	5	7	0	0	0	1	4-0	0	9	.171	.244	.171	17	-5	0-0	.990	-1	76	114	1b16/lf	0	-0.7
1985	Cal A	51	48	8	18	2	1	2	7	1-0	1	10	.375	.400	.583	165	4	0-1	.952	2	126	205	O45(1/3/41)/C3D	22	0.5
1986	Cal A	33	57	6	13	2	1	0	4	4-0	0	8	.228	.274	.298	58	-3	0-0	1.000	-5	41	0	O23(11/3/9),C10,D2	0	-0.9
1987	Cal A	53	108	14	26	5	0	4	16	9-0	2	13	.241	.303	.398	89	-2	1-0	.984	0	171	144	C33,O18(14/0/4)/3D	47	-0.1
1988	Cal A	70	140	21	31	4	1	2	7	9-0	5	29	.221	.292	.307	70	-6	2-1	.987	1	99	113	C53,O8(7/2/0)/D	15	-0.3
Total	5	224	394	54	95	13	3	8	35	27-0	8	69	.241	.300	.350	80	-12	3-2	.987	-2	118	120	C97,O95(34/8/54),1b16,D8,3b2	84	-1.5
Miller, Bing	Edmund John; B8.30.1894 Vinton IA; D5.7.1966 Philadelphia PA; BR/TR/6´0˝/185; d4.16; C17; b–Ralph																								
1921	Was A	114	420	57	121	28	8	9	71	25	4	50	.288	.334	.457	105	1	3-4	.945	-0	102	89	O109(92/3/14)	—	-0.8
1922	Phi A	143	535	90	179	29	12	21	90	24	7	42	.335	.371	.551	134	23	10-10	.977	5	102	132	O139(15/90/36)	—	1.9
1923	Phi A	123	458	68	137	25	4	12	64	27	4	34	.299	.344	.450	106	2	9-3	.978	-2	103	67	O119(104/0/15)	—	-0.8
1924	Phi A	113	398	62	136	22	4	6	62	12	10	24	.342	.376	.462	114	7	11-5	.973	-3	94	89	O94(10/9/75),1b7	—	-0.2
1925	Phi A	124	474	78	151	29	10	10	81	19	8	14	.319	.355	.485	105	1	11-6	.975	-8	89	60	O115(22/0/96),1b12	—	-1.6
1926	Phi A	38	110	13	32	6	2	2	13	11	0	6	.291	.355	.436	100	0	4-1	1.000	-2	99	34	O34(10/0/26)/1	—	-0.3
	StL A	94	353	60	117	27	5	4	50	22	7	12	.331	.382	.470	116	8	7-9	.939	3	108	116	O94(26/16/54)	—	0.2
	Year	132	463	73	149	33	7	6	63	33	7	18	.322	.376	.462	112	8	11-10	.950	2	106	97	O128(36/16/80)/1	—	-0.1
1927	StL A	143	492	83	160	32	7	5	75	30	9	26	.325	.375	.449	109	6	8-7	.970	3	111	72	O126(37/61/29)	—	0.1
1928	Phi A	139	510	76	168	34	7	8	85	27	**8**	24	.329	.372	.471	117	12	10-6	.968	-1	107	60	O133(28/43/66)	—	0.2
1929	†Phi A	147	556	84	184	32	16	8	93	40	4	25	.331	.380	.489	118	13	24-10	.970	-1	107	64	O145(9/4/133)	—	0.2
1930	†Phi A	**154**	585	89	177	38	7	9	100	47	3	22	.303	.357	.438	96	-3	13-13	.976	4	**111**	78	O154(0/13/142)	—	-1.2
1931	†Phi A	137	534	75	150	43	5	8	77	36	**10**	16	.281	.338	.425	94	-5	5-3	.987	5	**115**	55	O137R	—	-0.8
1932	Phi A	95	305	40	90	17	4	7	58	20	2	11	.295	.343	.446	99	-1	7-3	.979	4	118	52	O84(5/0/79)	—	-0.2
1933	Phi A	67	120	22	33	7	1	2	17	12	1	7	.275	.346	.400	96	-1	4-2	1.000	-1	99	57	O30(10/3/18),1b6	—	-0.2
1934	Phi A	81	177	22	43	10	2	1	22	16	1	14	.243	.309	.339	70	-8	1-0	1.000	0	101	70	O46(4/0/42)	—	-1.0
1935	Bos A	78	138	18	42	8	1	3	26	10	1	8	.304	.356	.442	99	-1	0-1	.962	-0	101	99	O29(1/0/28)	—	-0.2
1936	Bos A	30	47	9	14	2	1	1	6	5	1	5	.298	.377	.447	97	0	0-0	1.000	0	88	141	O13(7/0/7)	—	-0.1
Total	16	1820	6212	946	1934	389	96	116	990	383	80	340	.311	.359	.461	108	54	127-83	.971	6	105	77	O1601(380/242/997),1b26	—	-4.8
Miller, Eddie	Edward Lee; B6.29.1957 San Pablo CA; BB/TR/5´9˝/(160–175); [TexA75 2/41]; d9.5																								
1977	Tex A	17	6	7	2	0	0	0	1	1-0	0	1	.333	.429	.333	110	0	3-1	1.000	-0	88	0	O2C,D3	0	0.0
1978	Atl N	6	21	5	3	1	0	0	2	2-0	1	4	.143	.250	.190	22	-2	3-0	1.000	-2	53	0	O5(2/3/0)	0	-0.3
1979	Atl N	27	113	12	35	1	0	0	5	5-1	2	24	.310	.350	.319	79	-3	15-2	.988	1	114	50	O27(1/27/0)	0	0.0
1980	Atl N	11	19	3	3	0	0	0	0	0-0	0	5	.158	.158	.158	-12	-3	1-2	1.000	-2	46	0	O9(1/8/0)	0	-0.6
1981	Atl N	50	134	29	31	3	1	0	7	7-1	3	29	.231	.285	.269	57	-8	23-5	.985	-0	101	72	O36(28/2/7)	23	-0.6
1982	Det A	14	25	3	1	0	0	0	0	4-0	3	4	.040	.250	.040	-14	-4	0-3	1.000	-0	80	195	O8(0/3/5)/D	23	-0.6
1984	SD N	13	14	4	4	0	1	1	2	0-0	0	4	.286	.286	.643	153	1	4-0	1.000	1	62	828	O8(0/4/4)	0	0.2
Total	7	138	332	63	79	5	2	1	17	19-2	9	71	.238	.297	.274	58	-19	49-13	.989	-3	95	98	O95(32/49/16),D4	46	-1.9
Miller, Eddie	Edward Robert "Eppie"; B11.26.1916 Pittsburgh PA; D7.31.1997 Lake Worth FL; BR/TR/5´9˝/180; d9.9																								
1936	Cin N	5	10	0	1	0	0	0	0	1	0	1	.100	.182	.100	-24	-2	0	.938	-1	112	54	S4/2	—	-0.2
1937	Cin N	36	60	3	9	3	1	0	5	3	0	8	.150	.190	.233	15	-7	0	.926	3	107	126	S30,3b4	—	-0.3
1939	Bos N	77	296	32	79	12	2	4	31	16	5	21	.267	.315	.361	88	-6	4	.970	10	106	141	S77	—	1.0
1940	Bos N★	151	569	78	157	33	3	14	79	41	5	43	.276	.330	.418	111	8	8	**.970**	15	99	**118**	S151	—	3.4
1941	Bos N★	154	585	54	140	27	3	6	68	35	5	72	.239	.288	.326	76	-20	8	**.966**	13	104	**120**	S154	0	0.4
1942	Bos N★	142	534	47	130	28	2	6	47	22	4	42	.243	.279	.337	81	-15	11	**.983**	6	**105**	93	S142	0	0.2
1943	Cin N★	154	576	49	129	26	4	2	71	33	4	43	.224	.271	.293	64	-28	8	**.979**	**24**	105	130	S154	0	0.9
1944	Cin N✳	**155**	536	48	112	21	5	4	55	41	3	41	.209	.269	.289	59	-30	9	.971	12	**106**	125	S155	0	-0.6
1945	Cin N	115	421	46	100	27	2	13	49	18	4	38	.238	.275	.404	89	-9	4	**.975**	6	105	95	S115	0	0.7
1946	Cin N✳	91	299	30	58	10	0	6	36	25	1	34	.194	.258	.288	57	-18	5	.970	16	111	161	S88	0	0.3
1947	Cin N✳	151	545	69	146	**38**	4	19	87	49	4	40	.268	.333	.457	109	5	5	.972	-6	94	91	S151	0	0.8
1948	Phi N	130	468	45	115	20	1	14	61	19	4	40	.246	.281	.382	79	-16	1	.966	-12	93	89	S122	0	-2.1
1949	Phi N	85	266	21	55	10	1	6	29	29	4	21	.207	.294	.320	66	-13	1	.986	-11	86	104	2b82/S	0	-2.0
1950	StL N	64	172	17	39	8	0	3	22	19	1	21	.227	.307	.326	64	-9	0	.980	10	120	96	S51/2	0	0.3
Total	14	1510	5337	539	1270	263	28	97	640	351	44	465	.238	.290	.352	80	-160	64	.972	85	103	114	S1395,2b84,3b4	0	2.8

YEAR	TM LG	G	AB	R	H	2B	3B	HR	RBI	BB-IB	HP	SO	AVG	OBP	SLG	AOPS	ABR	SB-CS	FA	FR	RNG	THR	GAMES AT POSITION	DL	BFW
MILLER, ED	Edwin Collins "Big Ed"; B11.24.1888 Annville PA; D4.17.1980 S.Lebanon Twp. PA; BR/TR/6´0˝/180; d6.29																								
1912	StL A	13	46	4	9	1	0	0	5	2	1	—	.196	.245	.217	34	-4	1	.951	-4	43	75	1b8,S5	—	-0.8
1914	StL A	41	58	8	8	0	1	0	4	4	2	13	.138	.219	.172	18	-6	1-3	.981	-2	66	162	1b8,2b5,O5R,3b2	—	-1.0
1918	Cle A	32	96	9	22	4	3	0	3	12	1	10	.229	.321	.333	89	-1	2	.977	2	126	118	1b22,O4(1/0/3)	—	0.0
Total	3	86	200	21	39	5	4	0	12	18	4	*23*	.195	.275	.260	58	-11	4-*3*	.972	-4	99	114	1b38,O9(1/0/8),2b5,S5,3b2	—	-1.8
MILLER, ELMER	Elmer; B7.28.1890 Sandusky OH; D11.28.1944 Beloit WI; BR/TR/6´0˝/175; d4.26																								
1912	StL N	12	37	5	7	1	0	0	3	4	0	9	.189	.268	.216	34	-3	1	1.000	1	118	66	O11(4/3/4)	—	-0.3
1915	NY A	26	83	4	12	1	0	0	3	4	1	14	.145	.193	.157	5	-10	0	.955	-2	92	34	O26(0/20/6)	—	-1.5
1916	NY A	43	152	12	34	3	2	1	18	11	1	18	.224	.280	.289	70	-6	8	.969	4	101	161	O42(18/9/15)	—	-0.5
1917	NY A	114	379	43	95	11	3	3	35	40	**9**	44	.251	.336	.319	99	1	11	.961	-4	91	108	O112(33/53/26)	—	-1.0
1918	NY A	67	202	18	49	9	2	1	22	19	3	17	.243	.317	.322	91	-2	4	.947	2	99	141	O62(3/53/6)	—	-0.5
1921	†NY A	56	242	41	72	9	8	4	36	19	3	16	.298	.356	.450	102	0	2-2	.947	-1	91	133	O56C	—	-0.4
1922	NY A	51	172	31	46	7	2	3	18	11	0	12	.267	.311	.384	79	-6	2-3	.982	1	95	150	O51(7/41/3)	—	-0.8
	Bos A	44	147	16	28	2	3	4	16	5	1	10	.190	.222	.327	42	-14	3-1	.957	-1	97	82	O35(2/33/0)	—	-1.6
	Year	95	319	47	74	9	5	7	34	16	1	22	.232	.271	.357	62	-20	5-4	.970	-0	96	120	O86(9/74/3)	—	-2.4
Total	7	413	1414	170	343	43	20	16	151	113	18	140	.243	.307	.335	80	-40	31-*6*	.960	-1	95	121	O395(67/268/60)	—	-6.6
MILLER, ELMER	Elmer Joseph "Lefty"; B4.17.1903 Detroit MI; D1.8.1987 Corona CA; BL/TL/5´11˝/189; d6.21; ▲																								
1929	Phi N	31	38	3	9	1	0	1	4	1	0	5	.237	.256	.342	44	-4	0	.750	2	82	0	P8,O4R	—	-0.1
MILLER, KOHLY	Frank Aloysius; B1.1874 Cumru Twp. PA; D3.29.1951 Reading PA; d9.16																								
1892	Was N	1	3	0	0	0	0	0	0	0	0	1	.000	.000	.000	-99	-1	0	.400	-1	74	0	/S	—	-0.2
	StL N	1	4	0	0	0	0	0	0	0	0	0	.000	.000	.000	-99	-1	0	.500	-1	0	0	/3	—	-0.2
	Year	2	7	0	0	0	0	0	0	0	0	1	.000	.000	.000	-99	-2	0	.400	-2	74	0	/S3	—	-0.4
1897	Phi N	3	11	2	2	0	0	0	1	2	0	—	.182	.308	.182	32	-1	0	.857	-2	45	104	2b3	—	-0.3
Total	2	5	18	2	2	0	0	0	1	2	0	*1*	.111	.200	.111	-13	-3	0	.857	-4	45	104	2b3/3S	—	-0.7
MILLER, GEORGE	George C.; B2.19.1853 Newport KY; D7.24.1929 Norwood OH; BR/TR/5´5˝/160; d9.6																								
1877	Cin N	11	37	4	6	1	0	0	3	5	—	2	.162	.262	.189	50	-1	—	.918	-0	—	—	C11	—	-0.1
1884	Cin AA	6	20	6	5	1	1	0	3	1	1	—	.250	.318	.400	127	1	—	.975	2	—	—	C6	—	0.3
Total	2	17	57	10	11	2	1	0	6	6	1	*2*	.193	.281	.263	79	0	—	.938	2	—	—	C17	—	0.2
MILLER, DOGGIE	George Frederick "Foghorn","Calliope"; B8.15.1864 Brooklyn NY; D4.6.1909 Ridgewood NY; BR/TR/5´6˝/145; d5.1; M1; OF(146/68/96)																								
1884	Pit AA	89	347	46	78	10	2	0	—	13	2	—	.225	.257	.265	71	-10	—	.798	-2	131	56	O49(48/0/1),C36,3b3/2	—	-1.0
1885	Pit AA	42	166	19	27	3	1	0	13	4	0	—	.163	.182	.193	19	-15	—	.893	-6	—	—	C33,O6(3/3/0),S2,3b2	—	-1.6
1886	Pit AA	83	317	70	80	15	1	2	36	43	1	—	.252	.343	.325	110	6	35	.918	-14	—	—	C61,O22(12/10/1)/2	—	-0.3
1887	Pit N	87	342	58	83	17	4	1	34	35	2	13	.243	.317	.325	85	-5	33	.928	-20	—	—	C73,O14(2/11/1)/3	—	-1.7
1888	Pit N	103	404	50	112	17	5	0	36	18	7	16	.277	.319	.344	122	11	27	.908	-12	—	—	C68,O32(25/5/2),3b4	—	0.3
1889	Pit N	104	422	77	113	25	3	6	56	31	2	11	.268	.321	.384	106	3	16	.889	-7	—	—	C76,O27(6/5/16),3b3	—	0.2
1890	Pit N	**138**	549	85	150	24	3	4	66	68	4	11	.273	.357	.350	120	19	32	.850	4	121	100	3b88,O25(1/2/22),S13,C10,2b6	—	2.3
1891	Pit N	135	548	80	156	19	6	4	57	59	3	26	.285	.357	.363	113	10	35	.938	-9	*105*	*110*	C41,S37,3b34,O24(22/0/2)/1	—	0.5
1892	Pit N	149	623	103	158	15	12	2	59	69	7	14	.254	.335	.326	99	0	28	.906	1	99	92	O76(24/30/23),C63,S19,3b2	—	0.4
1893	Pit N	41	154	23	28	6	1	0	17	17	5	8	.182	.284	.234	39	-13	3	.916	-1	*98*	*100*	C40	—	-0.9
1894	StL N	127	481	93	163	9	11	8	86	58	4	9	.339	.414	.453	109	8	17	.832	-11	90	73	3b52,C41,2b18,1b12,O4(2/0/2)/SM	—	0.1
1895	StL N	122	494	81	144	15	4	5	74	25	6	12	.291	.333	.368	82	-14	18	.829	-21	81	74	3b46,C47,O21R,S9,1b6	—	-2.6
1896	Lou N	98	324	54	89	17	4	1	33	27	2	9	.275	.334	.361	86	-6	16	.922	-11	*78*	*118*	C48,2b25,O8(1/2/5),3b8,1b3,S2	—	-1.1
Total	13	1318	5171	839	1381	192	57	33	*567*	467	45	*129*	.267	.333	.345	97	-6	260	.918	-108	*96*	*107*	C637,O308L,3b243,S83,2b51,1b22	—	-5.4
MILLER, HUGHIE	Hugh Stanley "Cotton"; B12.22.1886 St.Louis MO; D12.24.1945 Jefferson Barracks MO; BR/TR/6´1.5˝/175; d6.18																								
1911	Phi N	1	0	0	0	0	0	0	0	0	0	0	ø	ø	ø	ø	0	0	ø	0	—	—	/R	—	0.0
1914	StL F	132	490	51	109	20	5	0	46	27	1	57	.222	.264	.284	47	-44	4	.990	0	95	68	1b130	—	-5.1
1915	StL F	7	6	0	3	1	0	0	3	0	0	0	.500	.500	.667	216	1	0	1.000	-0	0	0	1b6	—	0.1
Total	3	140	496	51	112	21	5	0	49	27	1	57	.226	.267	.288	49	-43	4	.990	-0	94	67	1b136	—	-5.0
MILLER, JAKE	Jacob George (b Jacob George Muenzing); B12.1.1895 Baltimore MD; D8.24.1974 Towson MD; BR/TR/5´10˝/170; d7.15																								
1922	Pit N	3	11	0	1	0	0	0	0	2	0	0	.091	.231	.091	-14	-2	1-0	.889	-0	114	0	O3R	—	-0.2
MILLER, HACK	James Eldridge; B2.13.1913 Celeste TX; D11.21.1966 Dallas TX; BR/TR/5´11.5˝/215; d4.18; Col Southeastern Oklahoma																								
1944	Det A	5	5	1	1	0	0	1	3	1	0	1	.200	.333	.800	207	1	0-0	1.000	0	*0*	*269*	C5	0	0.1
1945	Det A	2	4	0	3	0	0	0	1	0	0	0	.750	.750	.750	315	1	0-0	1.000	0	*0*	*0*	C2	0	0.1
Total	2	7	9	1	4	0	0	1	4	1	0	1	.444	.500	.778	250	2	0-0	1.000	1	*0*	*152*	C7	0	0.2
MILLER, JIM	James McCurdy "Rabbit"; B10.2.1880 Pittsburgh PA; D2.7.1937 Pittsburgh PA; BR/TR/5´8˝/165; d9.9																								
1901	NY N	18	58	3	8	0	0	0	3	6	0	—	.138	.219	.138	5	-7	1	.936	-2	99	98	2b18	—	-0.9
MILLER, JOHN	John Allen; B3.14.1944 Alhambra CA; BR/TR/5´11˝/(175–195); d9.11																								
1966	NY A	6	23	1	2	0	0	1	2	0-0	0	9	.087	.087	.217	-16	-4	0-0	1.000	-1	0	49	1b3,O3L	0	-0.6
1969	LA N	26	38	3	8	1	0	1	1	2-0	0	9	.211	.250	.316	61	-2	0-0	1.000	-2	18	0	O6L,1b5,3b2/2	0	-0.5
Total	2	32	61	4	10	1	0	2	3	2-0	0	18	.164	.190	.279	33	-6	0-0	1.000	-3	44	0	O9L,1b8,3b2/2	0	-1.1
MILLER, DOTS	John Barney; B9.9.1886 Kearny NJ; D9.5.1923 Saranac Lake NY; BR/TR/5´11.5˝/170; d4.16; Mil 1918																								
1909	†Pit N	151	560	71	156	31	13	3	87	39	3	—	.279	.329	.396	115	8	14	**.953**	-12	102	113	2b150	—	-0.3
1910	Pit N	120	444	45	101	13	10	1	48	33	2	41	.227	.284	.309	69	-19	11	.946	-15	95	93	2b119/1S	—	-3.5
1911	Pit N	137	470	82	126	17	8	6	78	51	7	48	.268	.348	.377	99	-1	17	.943	-3	98	**137**	2b129	—	-0.1
1912	Pit N	148	567	74	156	33	12	4	87	37	4	45	.275	.324	.397	98	-4	18	.985	-0	102	**124**	1b147	—	-0.8
1913	Pit N	154	580	75	158	24	20	7	90	37	1	52	.272	.317	.419	114	7	20-13	.985	-4	92	86	1b150,S3	—	-0.2
1914	StL N	155	573	67	166	27	10	4	88	34	9	52	.290	.339	.393	119	12	16	.993	-6	107	97	1b91,S60,2b5	—	0.9
1915	StL N	150	553	73	146	17	10	2	72	43	6	48	.264	.324	.342	101	0	27-19	.991	3	99	102	1b94,2b55,3b9,S3	—	0.2
1916	StL N	143	505	47	120	22	7	1	46	40	5	49	.238	.300	.315	89	-6	18	.993	7	98	110	1b93,2b38,S21/3	—	0.0
1917	StL N	148	544	61	135	15	9	2	45	33	3	52	.248	.295	.320	91	-7	14	.960	17	112	135	2b92,1b46,S11	—	1.3
1919	StL N	101	346	38	80	10	4	1	24	13	3	23	.231	.265	.292	72	-13	6	.981	3	107	93	1b68,2b28	—	-1.3
1920	Phi N	98	343	41	87	12	2	1	27	16	1	17	.254	.289	.309	68	-14	13-6	.948	-7	87	115	2b59,3b17,S12,1b9/cf	—	-2.0
1921	Phi N	84	320	37	95	11	3	0	23	15	1	27	.297	.330	.350	74	-11	3-5	.940	3	110	132	3b41,1b38,2b6	—	-0.9
Total	12	1589	5805	711	1526	232	108	32	715	391	45	*454*	.263	.314	.357	95	-48	177-*43*	.988	-14	101	104	1b737,2b681,S111,3b68/cf	—	-6.7
MILLER, JOE	Joseph A.; B2.17.1861 Baltimore MD; D4.23.1928 Wheeling WV; BR/5´9.5˝/165; d5.1																								
1884	Tol AA	105	423	46	101	12	8	1	—	26	1	—	.239	.284	.312	91	-4	—	.864	2	98	102	S105	—	0.0
1885	Lou AA	98	339	44	62	9	5	0	24	28	2	—	.183	.249	.239	55	-17	—	.891	2	102	104	S79,3b11,2b8	—	-1.1
Total	2	203	762	90	163	21	13	1	*24*	54	3	—	.214	.269	.280	75	-21	—	.876	4	100	103	S184,3b11,2b8	—	-1.1
MILLER, JOE	Joseph Wick; B7.24.1850 , Germany; D8.28.1891 White Bear Lake MN; 5´10.5˝/169; d6.26																								
1872	Nat NA	1	4	0	1	0	0	0	0	0	—	0	.250	.250	.250	46	0	0-0	.923	-0	0	0	/1	—	0.0
1875	Wes NA	**13**	50	4	6	1	0	0	0	0	—	3	.120	.120	.140	-9	-5	0-0	.870	5	107	109	2b13	—	-0.1
	Chi NA	15	54	1	8	0	0	0	1	0	—	7	.148	.148	.148	3	-5	0-0	.788	-3	100	54	2b14/O(1/0/1)	—	-0.8
	Year	28	104	5	14	1	0	0	1	0	—	10	.135	.135	.144	-3	-11	0-0	.832	2	104	82	2b27/O(1/0/1)	—	-0.9
Total	2NA	29	108	5	15	1	0	0	1	0	—	10	.139	.139	.148	-1	-10	0-0	.832	2	104	82	2b27/O(1/0/1)1	—	-0.9
MILLER, KEITH	Keith Alan; B6.12.1963 Midland MI; BR/TR/5´11˝/(175–185); d6.16; Col Oral Roberts; OF(49/65/28)																								
1987	NY N	25	51	14	19	2	2	0	1	2-0	1	6	.373	.407	.490	142	3	8-1	.967	-2	97	74	2b16	64	0.3
1988	NY N	40	70	9	15	1	1	1	5	6-0	0	10	.214	.276	.300	68	-3	0-5	.946	-9	59	43	2b16,S8,3b6/rf	0	-1.4
1989	NY N	57	143	15	33	7	0	1	7	5-0	1	27	.231	.262	.301	63	-7	6-0	.967	-1	81	78	2b23,O14(0/10/4),S8,3b2	0	-0.7
1990	NY N	88	233	42	60	8	0	1	12	23-1	2	46	.258	.327	.305	76	-7	16-3	.980	8	133	40	O61(7/53/5),2b11,S4	39	0.3
1991	NY N	98	275	41	77	22	1	4	23	23-0	5	44	.280	.345	.411	113	5	14-4	.972	12	106	113	2b60,O28(14/2/17),3b2,S2	20	2.1
1992	KC A	106	416	57	118	24	4	4	38	31-0	14	46	.284	.352	.389	104	3	16-6	.971	-9	93	99	2b93,O16L/D	49	-0.2
1993	KC A	37	108	9	18	3	0	0	3	8-0	1	19	.167	.229	.194	15	-13	3-1	.889	-3	87	64	3b21,O4L,2b3,D6	94	-1.6

YEAR	TM LG	G	AB	R	H	2B	3B	HR	RBI	BB-IB	HP	SO	AVG	OBP	SLG	AOPS	ABR	SB-CS	FA	FR	RNG	THR	GAMES AT POSITION	DL	BFW
1994	KC A	5	15	1	2	0	0	0	0	0-0	0	3	.133	.133	.133	-29	-3	0-0	1.000	0	105	440	O4L,3b2	102	-0.3
1995	KC A	9	15	2	5	0	0	1	3	2-0	0	4	.333	.412	.533	141	1	0-0	1.000	1	156	938	O4(4/0/1),D4	0	0.2
Total	9	465	1326	190	347	67	8	12	92	100-1	24	205	.262	.323	.351	87	-21	63-20	.969	-3	94	98	2b222,O132C,3b33,S22,D11	368	-1.3
Miller, Ed	L. Edward; B Tecumseh MI; d7.18																								
1884	Tol AA	8	24	2	6	0	0	0	1	1	0	—	.250	.280	.250	72	-1	—	.615	-0	210	0	O8(6/1/2)	—	-0.1
Miller, Hack	Laurence H.; B1.1.1894 New York NY; D9.16.1971 Oakland CA; BR/TR/5´9˝/195; d9.22																								
1916	Bro N	3	3	0	1	0	1	0	1	1	0	1	.333	.500	1.000	345	1	0	1.000	-0	58	0	O3(0/2/1)	—	0.1
1918	†Bos A	12	29	2	8	2	0	0	4	0	0	4	.276	.276	.345	89	-1	0	1.000	-1	86	0	O10(9/1/0)	—	-0.2
1922	Chi N	122	466	61	164	28	5	12	78	26	2	39	.352	.389	.511	128	19	3-3	.959	-3	92	105	O116(115/0/2)	—	0.6
1923	Chi N	135	485	74	146	24	2	20	88	27	4	39	.301	.343	.482	116	9	6-5	.978	3	96	143	O129L	—	0.1
1924	Chi N	53	131	17	44	8	1	4	25	8	1	11	.336	.379	.504	133	6	1-0	.948	-3	92	35	O32L	—	0.1
1925	Chi N	24	86	10	24	3	2	2	9	2	1	9	.279	.303	.430	84	-3	0-1	.878	-3	83	55	O21L	—	-0.7
Total	6	349	1200	164	387	65	11	38	205	64	8	103	.322	.361	.490	120	31	10-9	.962	-6	93	109	O311(306/3/3)	—	0.0
Miller, Lemmie	Lemmie Earl; B6.2.1960 Dallas TX; BR/TR/6´1˝/190; [LAN81 2/50]; d5.22; Col Arizona St.																								
1984	LA N	8	12	1	2	0	0	0	0	1-0	0	2	.167	.231	.167	13	-1	0-0	1.000	-0	75	0	O5(4/0/1)	0	-0.2
Miller, Otto	Lowell Otto "Moonie"; B6.1.1889 Minden NE; D3.29.1962 Brooklyn NY; BR/TR/6´0˝/196; d7.16; C11																								
1910	Bro N	31	66	5	11	3	0	0	2	2	1	19	.167	.203	.212	22	-7	1	.987	6	*106*	*104*	C28	—	0.1
1911	Bro N	25	62	7	13	2	2	0	8	0	0	4	.210	.210	.306	46	-5	2	.927	-4	*79*	*124*	C22	—	-0.8
1912	Bro N	98	316	35	88	18	1	1	31	18	4	50	.278	.325	.351	88	-5	11	.975	8	*94*	*112*	C94	—	1.1
1913	Bro N	104	320	26	87	11	7	0	26	10	0	31	.272	.294	.350	81	-9	7-12	.971	9	103	103	C103/1	—	0.6
1914	Bro N	54	169	17	39	6	1	0	9	7	0	20	.231	.261	.278	59	-9	0	.964	-2	*89*	*98*	C50/1	—	-0.7
1915	Bro N	84	254	20	57	4	6	0	25	6	1	28	.224	.245	.287	60	-14	3	.981	2	*91*	*95*	C83	—	-0.4
1916	†Bro N	73	216	16	55	9	2	1	17	7	1	29	.255	.281	.329	85	-4	6	.968	4	103	80	C69	—	0.6
1917	Bro N	92	274	19	63	5	4	1	17	14	2	29	.230	.272	.288	70	-10	5	.979	0	*102*	*94*	C91	—	-0.3
1918	Bro N	75	228	8	44	6	1	0	8	9	2	20	.193	.230	.228	40	-17	1	.972	2	*90*	*99*	C62/1	—	-1.1
1919	Bro N	51	164	18	37	5	0	0	5	7	0	14	.226	.257	.256	53	-9	2	.966	-0	*89*	*94*	C51	—	-0.6
1920	†Bro N	90	301	16	87	9	2	0	33	9	1	18	.289	.312	.332	82	-7	0-5	**.986**	-2	*99*	*66*	C89	—	-0.4
1921	Bro N	91	286	22	67	8	6	1	27	9	1	26	.234	.260	.315	50	-22	2-1	.972	4	*87*	*104*	C91	—	-1.2
1922	Bro N	59	180	20	47	11	1	1	23	6	0	13	.261	.285	.350	63	-10	0-0	.968	-1	*76*	*114*	C57	—	-0.7
Total	13	927	2836	229	695	97	33	5	231	104	13	301	.245	.275	.308	67	-128	40-18	.973	25	*94*	*97*	C890,1b3	—	-3.8
Miller, Keith	Neal Keith; B3.7.1963 Dallas TX; BB/TR/5´11˝/(170–175); [PhiN84 16/413]; d4.23; Col Lubbock Christian																								
1988	Phi N	47	48	4	8	3	0	0	6	5-0	0	13	.167	.245	.229	36	-4	0-0	1.000	-0	57	0	O4(2/1/1),3b3/S	0	-0.5
1989	Phi N	8	10	0	3	1	0	0	0	0-0	0	3	.300	.300	.400	98	0	0-0	1.000	-0	69	0	O2C	0	0.0
Total	2	55	58	4	11	4	0	0	6	5-0	0	16	.190	.254	.259	46	-4	0-0	1.000	-1	62	0	O6(2/3/1),3b3/S	0	-0.5
Miller, Norm	Norman Calvin; B2.5.1946 Los Angeles CA; BL/TR/5´11˝/(175–195); d9.11; Mil 1967; Col Los Angeles Valley (CA) JC																								
1965	Hou N	11	15	2	3	0	1	0	1	1-0	0	7	.200	.250	.333	67	-1	0-0	1.000	-0	59	0	O2L	0	-0.1
1966	Hou N	11	34	1	5	0	0	1	3	2-1	0	8	.147	.194	.235	20	-4	0-0	1.000	1	100	0	O8(5/0/3),3b2	0	-0.4
1967	Hou N	64	190	15	39	9	3	1	14	19-2	0	42	.205	.278	.300	68	-8	2-0	.967	2	109	105	O53L	0	-1.0
1968	Hou N	79	257	35	61	18	2	6	28	22-1	5	48	.237	.304	.393	112	4	6-5	.971	-2	107	19	O74(2/7/65)	0	-0.3
1969	Hou N	119	409	58	108	21	4	4	50	47-3	7	77	.264	.348	.364	102	3	4-4	.984	-1	97	99	O114(8/14/97)	0	-0.4
1970	Hou N	90	226	29	54	9	0	4	29	41-7	1	33	.239	.357	.332	90	-2	3-1	.947	-1	90	147	O72(4/3/68)/C	0	-0.5
1971	Hou N	45	74	5	19	5	0	2	10	5-0	1	13	.257	.313	.405	105	0	0-0	1.000	-1	93	0	O20(0/6/15)/C	33	-0.2
1972	Hou N	67	107	18	26	4	0	4	13	13-0	1	23	.243	.331	.393	108	1	1-0	1.000	-2	82	72	O29(6/10/13)	0	-0.1
1973	Hou N	3	3	0	0	0	0	0	0	0-0	0	2	.000	.000	.000	-99	-1	0-0	ø	-0	0	0	/rf	0	-0.1
	Atl N	9	8	2	3	1	0	1	6	3-0	0	3	.375	.500	.875	267	2	0-0	.667	-0	39	0	/lf	131	0.2
	Year	12	11	2	3	1	0	1	6	3-0	0	5	.273	.400	.636	182	1	0-0	.667	-0	34	0	O2(1/0/1)	0	0.1
1974	Atl N	42	41	1	7	1	0	1	5	7-1	0	9	.171	.292	.268	55	-2	0-0	1.000	0	55	484	O4(1/0/4)	16	-0.3
Total	10	540	1364	166	325	68	10	24	159	160-15	15	265	.238	.323	.356	94	-8	16-10	.972	-5	98	87	O378(82/40/266),C2,3b2	180	-3.2
Miller, Orlando	Orlando (Salmon); B1.13.1969 Changuinola, Pan; BR/TR/6´1˝/180; d7.8																								
1994	Hou N	16	40	3	13	0	1	2	9	2-2	2	12	.325	.386	.525	142	2	1-0	1.000	-1	99	68	S11,2b3	0	0.2
1995	Hou N	92	324	36	85	20	1	5	36	22-8	5	71	.262	.319	.377	88	-6	3-4	.964	4	102	99	S89	15	0.4
1996	Hou N	139	468	43	120	26	2	15	58	14-4	10	116	.256	.291	.417	91	-8	3-7	.958	-13	95	85	S117,3b29	0	-1.5
1997	Det A	50	111	13	26	7	1	2	10	5-0	4	24	.234	.289	.369	71	-5	1-0	.979	-0	102	132	S31,D11,3b4,1b3	70	-0.4
Total	4	297	943	95	244	53	5	24	113	43-14	21	223	.259	.305	.402	90	-17	8-11	.964	-11	99	94	S248,3b33,D11,1b3,2b3	85	-1.3
Miller, Otto	Otis Louis; B2.2.1901 Belleville IL; D7.26.1959 Belleville IL; BR/TR/5´10.5˝/168; d4.17																								
1927	StL A	51	76	8	17	5	0	0	8	8	1	5	.224	.306	.289	53	-5	0-1	.938	-1	100	88	S35,3b11	—	-0.5
1930	Bos A	112	370	49	106	22	5	0	40	26	0	21	.286	.333	.373	82	-10	2-4	.948	-1	110	95	3b83,2b15	—	-0.7
1931	Bos A	107	389	38	106	12	1	0	43	15	1	20	.272	.301	.308	64	-21	1-1	.953	2	112	97	3b75,2b25	—	-1.4
1932	Bos A	2	2	0	0	0	0	0	0	0	0	0	.000	.000	.000	-99	-1	0-0	ø	0	—	—	/H	—	-0.1
Total	4	272	837	95	229	39	6	0	91	49	2	46	.274	.315	.335	71	-37	3-6	.949	-0	111	98	3b169,2b40,S35	—	-2.7
Miller, Ralph	Ralph Joseph; B2.29.1896 Ft.Wayne IN; D3.18.1939 Ft.Wayne IN; BR/TR/6´0˝/190; d4.14																								
1920	Phi N	97	338	28	74	14	1	0	28	11	1	32	.219	.246	.266	45	-24	3-4	.940	5	110	97	3b91,1b3,S2/lf	—	-1.9
1921	Phi N	57	204	19	62	10	0	3	26	6	1	10	.304	.327	.397	84	-5	3-5	.910	-1	99	88	S46,3b10	—	-0.1
1924	†Was A	9	15	1	2	0	0	0	0	1	0	1	.133	.188	.133	-17	-3	0-0	.941	0	120	67	2b3	—	-0.2
Total	3	163	557	48	138	24	1	3	54	18	2	43	.248	.274	.311	59	-32	6-9	.927	4	112	105	3b101,S48,2b3,1b3/lf	—	-2.2
Miller, Ray	Raymond Peter; B2.12.1888 Pittsburgh PA; D4.7.1927 Pittsburgh PA; BL/TL/5´10˝/168; d4.14; Mil 1918																								
1917	Cle A	19	21	1	4	1	0	0	2	8	0	3	.190	.414	.238	92	1	0	1.000	1	226	0	1b4	—	0.2
	Pit N	6	27	1	4	1	0	0	0	2	0	3	.148	.207	.185	20	-3	0	1.000	0	117	124	1b6	—	-0.3
Total	1	25	48	2	8	2	0	0	2	10	0	6	.167	.310	.208	56	-2	0	1.000	2	156	80	1b10	—	-0.1
Miller, Rick	Richard Alan; B4.19.1948 Grand Rapids MI; BL/TL/6´0˝/(175–185); [BosA69 2/37]; d9.4; Col Michigan St.																								
1971	Bos A	15	33	9	11	5	0	1	7	8-0	0	8	.333	.452	.576	180	4	0-2	.969	2	140	145	O14(4/4/6)	0	0.5
1972	Bos A	89	98	13	21	4	1	3	15	11-0	0	27	.214	.291	.367	90	-1	0-2	.967	5	114	313	O75(24/47/4)	0	0.2
1973	Bos A	143	441	65	115	17	7	6	43	51-2	3	59	.261	.339	.372	95	-2	12-7	.978	-0	107	46	O137(15/71/61)	0	-0.8
1974	Bos A	114	280	41	73	8	1	5	22	37-2	0	47	.261	.347	.350	94	-1	13-2	.989	9	115	116	O105(21/77/7)	0	0.8
1975	†Bos A	77	108	21	21	2	1	0	15	21-6	0	20	.194	.326	.231	55	-6	3-2	.981	5	136	78	O65(25/15/26)	0	-0.2
1976	Bos A	105	269	40	76	15	3	0	27	34-2	0	47	.283	.359	.361	101	2	11-10	.991	9	126	75	O82(17/37/32),D4	0	0.7
1977	Bos A	86	189	34	48	9	3	0	24	22-1	3	30	.254	.341	.333	76	-6	11-5	.992	-2	87	114	O79(2/29/48)/D	27	-0.9
1978	Cal A	132	475	66	125	25	4	1	37	54-1	4	70	.263	.341	.339	95	-1	3-13	.989	8	112	108	O129(0/93/36)	0	0.1
1979	†Cal A	120	427	60	125	15	5	2	28	50-1	1	69	.293	.367	.365	102	2	5-4	.989	8	**120**	42	O117C,D2	37	0.9
1980	Cal A	129	412	52	113	14	3	2	38	48-4	1	71	.274	.349	.337	91	-4	7-3	.984	7	108	147	O118(0/98/24)	0	0.2
1981	Bos A	97	316	38	92	17	2	2	33	28-1	1	36	.291	.349	.377	103	2	3-5	.987	-8	87	88	O95C	0	-0.9
1982	Bos A	135	409	50	104	13	2	4	38	40-2	2	41	.254	.323	.325	74	-14	5-6	.983	-10	87	76	O127C	0	-2.6
1983	Bos A	104	262	41	75	10	2	2	21	28-1	1	30	.286	.356	.363	92	-2	3-3	.993	0	102	91	O66(6/22/40),1b2,D2	0	-0.5
1984	Bos A	95	123	17	32	5	1	0	12	17-0	0	22	.260	.348	.317	82	-2	1-1	.974	-1	82	93	O31(0/21/10),1b8	0	-0.4
1985	Bos A	41	45	5	15	2	0	0	9	5-0	0	6	.333	.392	.378	110	1	1-0	1.000	0	127	0	O8(4/1/3),D4	29	0.1
Total	15	1482	3887	552	1046	161	35	28	369	454-23	16	583	.269	.346	.350	92	-28	78-65	.986	31	107	95	O1248(118/854/297),D13,1b10	93	-2.8
Miller, Rod	Rodney Carter; B1.16.1940 Portland OR; BL/TR/5´10˝/160; d9.28																								
1957	Bro N	1	1	0	0	0	0	0	0	0-0	0	1	.000	.000	.000	-91	0	0-0	ø	0	—	—	/H	0	0.0
Miller, Doc	Roy Oscar; B2.4.1883 Chatham ON, Can.; D7.31.1938 Jersey City NJ; BL/TL/5´10.5˝/170; d5.4																								
1910	Chi N	1	1	0	0	0	0	0	0	0	0	0	.000	.000	.000	-99	0	0	ø	0	—	—	/H	—	0.0
	Bos N	130	482	48	138	27	4	3	55	33	1	52	.286	.333	.378	103	1	17	.951	-8	98	52	O130(6/0/127)	—	-1.4
	Year	131	483	48	138	27	4	3	55	33	1	52	.286	.333	.377	102	0	17	.951	-8	98	52	O130(6/0/127)	—	-1.4
1911	Bos N	146	577	69	**192**	36	3	7	91	43	0	43	.333	.379	.442	120	15	32	.961	3	99	129	O146(0/3/143)	—	1.0

YEAR	TM LG	G	AB	R	H	2B	3B	HR	RBI	BB-IB	HP	SO	AVG	OBP	SLG	AOPS	ABR	SB-CS	FA	FR	RNG	THR	GAMES AT POSITION	DL	BFW
1912	Bos N	51	201	26	47	8	1	2	24	14	1	17	.234	.287	.313	63	-11	6	.948	2	91	156	O50R	—	-1.1
	Phi N	67	177	24	51	12	5	0	21	9	0	13	.288	.323	.412	94	-2	3	.986	2	96	160	O40R	—	-0.2
	Year	118	378	50	98	20	6	2	45	23	1	30	.259	.303	.360	78	-13	9	.964	4	93	158	O90R	—	-1.3
1913	Phi N	69	87	9	30	6	0	0	11	6	2	6	.345	.400	.414	127	4	2-1	.800	-2	61	0	O12R	—	0.1
1914	Cin N	93	192	8	49	7	2	0	33	16	0	18	.255	.313	.313	83	-4	4	.976	-2	105	34	O47(23/3/23)	—	-0.9
Total	5	557	1717	184	507	96	15	12	235	121	4	149	.295	.343	.390	102	3	64-1	.958	-5	97	100	O425(29/6/395)	—	-2.5
Miller, Rudy	Rudel Charles; B7.12.1900 Kalamazoo MI; D1.22.1994 Kalamazoo MI; BR/TR/6´1˝/180; d9.19; Col Western Michigan																								
1929	Phi A	2	4	1	1	0	0	0	1	3	0	0	.250	.571	.250	115	1	0-0	.750	-1	72	0	3b2	—	0.0
Miller, Tom	Thomas P. "Reddy"; B1850 Philadelphia PA; D5.29.1876 Philadelphia PA; d10.24																								
1874	Ath NA	4	16	1	8	0	0	0	5	0	—	0	.500	.500	.500	204	2	0-0	.793	0	—	—	C4/O(0/1/1)	—	0.1
1875	StL NA	56	214	18	35	2	0	0	12	1	—	8	.164	.167	.173	20	-15	2-0	.827	-4	—	—	C53,3b2	—	-1.7
Total	2NA	60	230	19	43	2	0	0	17	1	—	8	.187	.190	.196	37	-13	2-0	.824	-4	—	—	C57,3b2/O(0/1/1)	—	-1.6
Miller, Tom	Thomas Royall; B7.5.1897 Powhatan Court House VA; D8.13.1980 Richmond VA; BL/TR/5´11˝/180; d7.29; Col Richmond																								
1918	Bos N	2	2	0	0	0	0	0	0	0	0	0	.000	.000	.000	-99	0	1	ø	0	—	—	/H	—	-0.1
1919	Bos N	7	6	2	2	0	0	0	0	0	0	1	.333	.333	.333	105	0	0	ø	0	—	—	/H	—	0.0
Total	2	9	8	2	2	0	0	0	0	0	0	1	.250	.250	.250	53	0	1	ø	0	—	—	—	—	-0.1
Miller, Ward	Ward Taylor "Windy","Grump"; B7.5.1884 Mt.Carroll IL; D9.4.1958 Dixon IL; BL/TR/5´11˝/177; d4.14; Col Northern Illinois																								
1909	Pit N	15	56	2	8	0	1	0	4	4	1	—	.143	.213	.179	20	-5	2	.967	-2	50	0	O14C	—	-0.9
	Cin N	43	113	17	35	3	1	0	4	6	0	—	.310	.345	.354	118	2	9	.981	-0	61	0	O26(17/16/3)	—	0.0
	Year	58	169	19	43	3	2	0	8	10	1	—	.254	.300	.296	84	-4	11	.976	-2	57	0	O40(17/30/3)	—	-0.9
1910	Cin N	81	126	21	30	6	0	0	10	22	1	13	.238	.356	.286	92	0	10	.944	2	94	207	O26(0/11/15)	—	0.1
1912	Chi N	86	241	45	74	11	4	0	22	26	1	18	.307	.377	.386	109	4	11	.943	-5	90	70	O64(13/38/14)	—	-0.4
1913	Chi N	80	203	23	48	5	7	1	16	34	1	33	.236	.349	.345	98	0	13-15	.980	4	107	110	O63(47/11/5)	—	-0.1
1914	StL F	121	402	49	118	17	7	4	50	59	10	36	.294	.397	.400	112	4	18	.953	5	**115**	86	O111(74/31/6)	—	0.3
1915	StL F	154	536	80	164	19	9	1	63	79	5	39	.306	.400	.381	114	7	33	.963	4	111	85	O154L	—	0.5
1916	StL A	146	485	72	129	17	5	1	50	72	9	76	.266	.371	.328	116	13	25-21	.943	-9	96	69	O136(3/0/133)	—	-0.5
1917	StL A	43	82	13	17	1	1	1	2	16	2	15	.207	.350	.280	96	1	7	.966	-1	71	166	O25(12/4/9)	—	-0.1
Total	8	769	2244	322	623	79	35	8	221	318	30	230	.278	.375	.355	108	26	128-36	.957	-1	101	84	O619(320/125/185)	—	-1.1
Miller, Warren	Warren Lemuel "Gitz"; B7.14.1885 Philadelphia PA; D8.12.1956 Philadelphia PA; BL/TL/5´10˝/160; d7.29																								
1909	Was A	26	51	5	11	0	0	0	1	4	0	—	.216	.273	.216	57	-2	0	1.000	1	152	0	O15(1/10/4)	—	-0.3
1911	Was A	21	34	3	5	0	0	0	0	0	0	—	.147	.147	.147	-18	-6	0	.778	-1	72	104	O9(1/0/8)	—	-0.6
Total	2	47	85	8	16	0	0	0	1	4	0	—	.188	.225	.188	25	-8	0	.931	-0	123	38	O24(2/10/12)	—	-0.9
Miller, Bill	William Alexander; B5.23.1879 Bad Schwalbach, Germany; D9.8.1957 Ashtabula OH; BL/TL/6´2˝/170; d8.23																								
1902	Pit N	1	5	0	1	0	0	0	2	0	0	—	.200	.200	.200	23	0	0	ø	0	0	0	/rf	—	-0.1
Millette, Joe	Joseph Anthony; B8.12.1966 Walnut Creek CA; BR/TR/6´1˝/180; d7.16; Col St. Marys (CA)																								
1992	Phi N	33	78	5	16	0	0	0	2	5-2	2	10	.205	.271	.205	37	-7	1-0	.974	4	120	106	S26,3b3/2	0	-0.1
1993	Phi N	10	10	3	2	0	0	0	2	1-0	0	2	.200	.273	.200	29	-1	0-0	1.000	1	130	47	S7,3b3	0	0.1
Total	2	43	88	8	18	0	0	0	4	6-2	2	12	.205	.271	.205	36	-8	1-0	.978	5	121	98	S33,3b6/2	0	0.0
Milliard, Ralph	Ralph Gregory; B12.30.1973 Willemstad, Curacao; BR/TR/5´11˝/(170–175); d5.12; [DL 1999 Cin N 42]																								
1996	Fla N	24	62	7	10	2	0	0	1	14-1	0	16	.161	.312	.194	39	-5	2-0	.955	5	123	116	2b24	0	0.1
1997	Fla N	8	30	2	6	0	0	0	2	3-0	2	3	.200	.314	.200	40	-3	1-1	1.000	4	138	176	2b8	0	0.2
1998	NY N	10	1	3	0	0	0	0	0	0-0	0	1	.000	.000	.000	-99	0	0-0	.833	-1	77	0	2b5/S	0	-0.1
Total	3	42	93	12	16	2	0	0	3	17-1	2	20	.172	.310	.194	38	-8	3-1	.963	9	126	130	2b37/S	42	0.2
Millies, Wally	Walter Louis; B10.18.1906 Chicago IL; D2.28.1995 Oak Lawn IL; BR/TR/5´10.5˝/170; d9.23																								
1934	Bro N	2	7	0	0	0	0	0	0	0	0	0	.000	.000	.000	-99	-2	0	1.000	0	*55*	*0*	C2	—	-0.2
1936	Was A	74	215	26	67	10	2	0	25	11	0	8	.312	.345	.377	83	-6	1-0	.968	-0	*87*	*141*	C72	—	-0.2
1937	Was A	59	179	21	40	7	1	0	28	9	0	15	.223	.261	.274	36	-18	1-0	.971	0	*101*	*126*	C56	—	-1.4
1939	Phi N	84	205	12	48	3	0	0	12	9	1	5	.234	.270	.249	41	-17	0	.964	-10	*54*	***127***	C84	—	-2.4
1940	Phi N	26	43	1	3	0	0	0	0	4	0	4	.070	.149	.070	-39	-8	0	.958	0	*89*	*93*	C24	—	-0.7
1941	Phi N	1	2	0	0	0	0	0	0	0	0	0	.000	.000	.000	-99	-1	0	.800	0	*0*	*469*	/C	0	-0.1
Total	6	246	651	60	158	20	3	0	65	33	1	32	.243	.280	.283	47	-52	2-0	.966	-10	*79*	*129*	C239	0	-5.0
Milligan, Jocko	John; B8.8.1861 Philadelphia PA; D8.29.1923 Philadelphia PA; BR/TR/6´0˝/192; d5.1																								
1884	Phi AA	66	268	39	77	20	3	3	—	8	0	—	.287	.308	.418	126	7	—	**.939**	10	—	—	C65/cf	—	2.1
1885	Phi AA	67	265	35	71	15	4	2	39	7	1	—	.268	.289	.377	103	0	—	.935	9	—	—	C61,1b6,O2R	—	1.2
1886	Phi AA	75	301	52	76	17	3	5	45	21	0	—	.252	.301	.379	111	3	18	.919	1	—	—	C40,1b29,O5(0/4/1),3b2	—	0.4
1887	Phi AA	95	377	54	114	27	4	2	50	21	3	—	.302	.344	.411	110	5	8	.966	1	83	90	1b50,C47/cf	—	0.4
1888	†StL AA	63	219	19	55	6	2	5	37	17	2	—	.251	.311	.365	105	0	3	.941	9	—	—	C58,1b5	—	1.2
1889	StL AA	72	273	53	100	30	2	12	76	16	3	19	.366	.408	.623	170	22	2	.933	9	—	—	C66,1b9	—	3.0
1890	Phi P	62	234	38	69	9	3	3	57	19	6	19	.295	.363	.397	101	0	2	.893	2	*98*	*92*	C59,1b3	—	0.6
1891	Phi AA	118	455	75	138	**35**	12	11	106	56	15	51	.303	.397	.505	158	34	2	.939	-1	*108*	*77*	C87,1b32	—	3.2
1892	Was N	88	323	40	89	20	9	4	43	26	3	24	.276	.335	.430	135	13	2	.947	-4	*67*	*134*	C59,1b28	—	1.2
1893	Bal N	24	102	19	25	5	2	1	19	5	2	7	.245	.294	.363	73	-5	2	.981	2	149	74	1b22/C	—	-0.2
	NY N	42	147	16	34	5	6	1	25	14	1	14	.231	.302	.367	77	-6	2	.934	8	*99*	*152*	C42	—	0.5
	Year	66	249	35	59	10	8	2	44	19	3	21	.237	.299	.365	75	-11	4	.932	9	*99*	*148*	C43,1b22	—	0.3
Total	10	772	2964	440	848	189	50	49	497	210	36	134	.286	.341	.433	123	73	41	.930	44	*95*	*106*	C585,1b184,O9(0/6/3),3b2	—	13.6
Milligan, Randy	Randy Andre; B11.27.1961 San Diego CA; BR/TR/6´1˝/(215–235); [NYN81*1/3]; d9.12; Col San Diego Mesa (CA) JC																								
1987	NY N	3	1	0	0	0	0	0	0	1-0	0	1	.000	.500	.000	49	0	0-0	ø	0	—	—	/H	0	0.0
1988	Pit N	40	82	10	18	5	0	3	8	20-0	1	24	.220	.379	.390	122	4	1-2	.987	-1	98	128	1b25,O2L	0	0.1
1989	Bal A	124	365	56	98	23	5	12	45	74-2	3	75	.268	.394	.458	144	25	9-5	.995	1	109	100	1b117/D	0	1.9
1990	Bal A	109	362	64	96	20	1	20	60	88-3	2	68	.265	.408	.492	156	32	6-3	.990	5	121	115	1b98,D9	50	3.0
1991	Bal A	141	483	57	127	17	2	16	70	84-4	2	108	.263	.373	.406	120	16	0-5	.990	2	111	105	1b106,D25,O9L	0	0.8
1992	Bal A	137	462	71	111	21	1	11	53	106-0	4	81	.240	.383	.361	107	10	0-1	.994	-6	84	110	1b129,D6	0	-0.5
1993	Cin N	83	234	30	64	11	1	6	29	46-0	1	49	.274	.394	.406	114	7	0-2	.994	6	132	104	1b61,O9L	0	0.7
	Cle A	19	47	7	20	7	0	0	7	14-0	0	4	.426	.557	.574	204	9	0-0	1.000	-1	81	145	1b18/D	0	0.7
1994	Mon N	47	82	10	19	2	0	2	12	14-1	0	21	.232	.337	.329	76	-3	0-0	.978	2	140	116	1b33	0	-0.3
Total	8	703	2118	305	553	106	10	70	284	447-10	13	431	.261	.391	.420	127	100	16-18	.992	8	108	109	1b587,D42,O20L	50	6.4
Mills, Jack	Abbott Paige; B10.23.1889 S.Williamstown MA; D6.3.1973 Washington DC; BL/TR/6´0˝/165; d7.1; Col Williams																								
1911	Cle A	13	17	5	5	0	0	0	1	1	1	—	.294	.368	.294	85	0	1	1.000	1	147	185	3b7	—	0.1
Mills, Charlie	Charles F.; B9.1844 Brooklyn NY; D4.9.1874 Brooklyn NY; 6´0˝/?; d5.18; U2																								
1871	Mut NA	32	146	27	36	4	3	0	22	1	—	0	.247	.252	.315	68	-5	2-0	.866	-1	—	—	C29,O4R/3	—	-0.3
1872	Mut NA	6	31	6	4	0	0	0	2	0	—	0	.129	.129	.129	-22	-4	0-0	.667	-1	0	0	O4R,C3	—	-0.4
Total	2NA	38	177	33	40	4	3	0	24	1	—	0	.226	.230	.282	53	-9	2-0	.854	-2	—	—	C32,O8R/3	—	-0.7
Mills, Buster	Colonel Buster "Bus"; B9.16.1908 Ranger TX; D12.1.1991 Arlington TX; BR/TR/5´11.5˝/195; d4.18; Mil 1943–45; M1/C7; Col Oklahoma																								
1934	StL N	29	72	7	17	4	1	1	8	4	2	11	.236	.295	.361	70	-3	0	1.000	-1	104	0	O18(0/17/1)	—	-0.4
1935	Bro N	17	56	12	12	2	1	1	7	5	4	11	.214	.323	.339	80	-1	0	.971	-1	96	0	O17(11/6/0)	—	-0.3
1937	Bos A	123	505	85	149	25	8	7	58	46	6	41	.295	.361	.418	92	-6	11-8	.946	-5	94	84	O120(107/10/5)	—	-1.7
1938	StL A	123	466	66	133	24	4	3	46	43	3	46	.285	.350	.373	81	-13	7-8	.964	2	104	113	O113(106/6/1)	—	-1.7
1940	NY A	34	63	10	25	3	3	1	15	7	0	5	.397	.457	.587	176	7	0-0	1.000	-1	93	0	O14(12/0/2)	—	0.5
1942	Cle A	80	195	19	54	4	2	1	26	23	0	18	.277	.353	.333	99	0	5-4	.973	4	113	107	O53(13/37/3)	0	0.2
1946	Cle A	9	22	1	6	0	0	0	3	3	0	5	.273	.360	.273	84	0	0-1	1.000	-0	97	0	O6L	0	-0.1
Total	7	415	1379	200	396	62	19	14	163	131	15	137	.287	.355	.390	91	-16	23-21	.964	-2	101	85	O341(255/76/12)	0	-3.5

YEAR	TM LG	G	AB	R	H	2B	3B	HR	RBI	BB-IB	HP	SO	AVG	OBP	SLG	AOPS	ABR	SB-CS	FA	FR	RNG	THR	GAMES AT POSITION	DL	BFW
MILLS, EVERETT	Everett; B1.20.1845 Newark NJ; D6.22.1908 Newark NJ; 6´1˝/174; d5.5; M1																								
1871	Oly NA	**32**	157	38	43	6	4	1	24	3	—	1	.274	.287	.382	95	0	2-3	.967	3	98	120	1b32	—	0.2
1872	Bal NA	55	266	55	79	14	2	0	34	3	—	2	.297	.305	.365	100	-1	0-2	.931	1	91	87	1b55,M	—	0.0
1873	Bal NA	54	262	64	87	20	9	0	56	2	—	1	.332	.337	.477	139	12	1-0	**.949**	2	65	101	1b53/cf	—	1.1
1874	Har NA	**53**	244	39	69	6	1	0	19	4	—	2	.283	.294	.316	91	-3	1-1	.920	-2	88	58	1b53	—	-0.3
1875	Har NA	80	342	59	89	8	4	1	48	0	—	3	.260	.260	.316	94	-3	6-4	.945	2	78	**166**	1b80	—	0.0
1876	Har N	63	254	28	66	8	1	0	23	1	—	3	.260	.263	.299	80	-6	—	.939	-2	63	78	1b63	—	-1.0
Total	5NA	274	1271	255	367	54	20	2	181	12	—	9	.289	.295	.367	104	5	10-10	.941	6	82	111	1b273/cf	—	1.0
MILLS, FRANK	Frank Le Moyne; B5.13.1895 Knoxville OH; D8.31.1983 Youngstown OH; BL/TR/6´0˝/180; d9.22																								
1914	Cle A	4	8	0	1	0	0	0	0	1	0	2	.125	.222	.125	4	-1	0	.900	-1	*75*	*162*	C2	—	-0.2
MILLS, BRAD	James Bradley; B1.19.1957 Exeter CA; BL/TR/6´0˝/(190–195); [MonN79 17/426]; d6.8; C8; Col Arizona																								
1980	Mon N	21	60	1	18	1	0	0	8	5-1	0	6	.300	.348	.317	87	-1	0-1	.977	-1	78	131	3b18	0	-0.2
1981	†Mon N	17	21	3	5	1	0	0	1	2-1	0	1	.238	.304	.286	66	-1	0-0	1.000	-1	70	0	3b7,2b2	0	-0.2
1982	Mon N	54	67	6	15	3	0	1	2	5-0	0	11	.224	.278	.313	63	-3	0-0	.867	-3	60	84	3b13	0	-0.7
1983	Mon N	14	20	1	5	0	0	0	1	2-0	0	3	.250	.318	.250	59	-1	0-0	1.000	-0	102	0	3b3/1	16	-0.2
Total	4	106	168	11	43	5	0	1	12	14-2	0	21	.256	.311	.304	71	-6	0-1	.959	-5	74	92	3b41,2b2/1	16	-1.3
MILLS, RUPERT	Rupert Frank; B10.12.1892 Newark NJ; D7.20.1929 Lake Hopatcong NJ; BR/TR/6´2˝/185; d6.23; Col Notre Dame																								
1915	New F	41	134	12	27	5	1	0	16	6	1	21	.201	.241	.254	42	-13	6	.976	-0	108	110	1b37	—	-1.6
MILLS, BILL	William Henry; B11.2.1920 Boston MA; BR/TR/5´10˝/175; d5.19; Col Holy Cross																								
1944	Phi A	5	4	0	1	0	0	0	0	1	0	1	.250	.400	.250	89	0	0-0	ø	0	*0*	*0*	/C	0	0.0
MILNE, PETE	William James; B4.10.1925 Mobile AL; D4.11.1999 Mobile AL; BL/TR/6´1˝/180; d9.15																								
1948	NY N	12	27	0	6	0	1	0	2	1	0	6	.222	.250	.296	47	-2	0	.867	-1	90	0	O9(2/5/2)	0	-0.4
1949	NY N	31	29	5	7	1	0	1	6	3	0	6	.241	.313	.379	85	-1	0	1.000	0	130	0	/lf	0	-0.1
1950	NY N	4	4	1	1	0	1	0	1	0	0	1	.250	.250	.750	151	0	0	ø	0	—	—	/H	0	0.0
Total	3	47	60	6	14	1	2	1	9	4	0	13	.233	.281	.367	73	-3	0	.882	-1	94	0	O10(3/5/2)	0	-0.5
MILNER, BRIAN	Brian Tate; B11.17.1959 Fort Worth TX; BR/TR/6´2˝/200; [TorA78 7/158]; d6.23																								
1978	Tor A	2	9	3	4	0	1	0	2	0-0	0	1	.444	.444	.667	204	1	0-0	.800	-2	58	0	C2	0	-0.1
MILNER, EDDIE	Eddie James; B5.21.1955 Columbus OH; BL/TL/5´11˝/(170–175); [CinN76 21/503]; d9.2; Col Central St.																								
1980	Cin N	6	3	1	0	0	0	0	0	0-0	0	0	.000	.000	.000	-99	-1	0-0	ø	0	—	—	/H	0	-0.1
1981	Cin N	8	5	0	1	1	0	0	1	1-0	0	1	.200	.333	.400	108	0	0-0	1.000	-0	105	0	O4(2/0/2)	0	0.0
1982	Cin N	113	407	61	109	23	5	4	31	41-1	2	40	.268	.338	.378	100	0	18-12	.987	4	107	113	O107(65/30/37)	27	0.1
1983	Cin N	146	502	77	131	23	6	9	33	68-2	1	60	.261	.350	.384	100	1	41-12	.990	13	**118**	142	O139(0/138/1)	0	1.9
1984	Cin N	117	336	44	78	8	4	7	29	51-3	2	50	.232	.333	.342	87	-5	21-13	.983	14	**127**	162	O108C	37	0.9
1985	Cin N	145	453	82	115	19	7	3	33	61-3	1	31	.254	.342	.347	89	-5	35-13	.983	14	**122**	**173**	O135C	0	1.2
1986	Cin N	145	424	70	110	22	6	15	47	36-2	0	56	.259	.317	.446	104	1	18-11	.990	3	112	93	O127C	0	0.4
1987	†SF N	101	214	38	54	14	0	4	19	24-3	0	33	.252	.328	.374	90	-3	10-9	.993	-2	107	0	O84C	52	-0.6
1988	Cin N	23	51	3	9	1	0	0	2	4-0	0	9	.176	.236	.196	25	-5	2-2	.968	0	101	178	O15(2/11/2)	21	-0.6
Total	9	804	2395	376	607	111	28	42	195	286-14	6	280	.253	.333	.376	94	-17	145-72	.987	47	116	125	O719(69/633/42)	137	3.2
MILNER, JOHN	John David "The Hammer"; B12.28.1949 Atlanta GA; D1.4.2000 East Point GA; BL/TL/6´0˝/(182–185); [NYN68 14/301]; d9.15																								
1971	NY N	9	18	1	3	1	0	0	1	0-0	0	3	.167	.167	.222	9	-2	0-0	1.000	1	179	624	O3L	0	-0.1
1972	NY N	117	362	52	86	12	2	17	38	51-1	5	74	.238	.340	.423	117	9	2-1	.965	3	106	125	O91(88/0/3),1b10	0	0.7
1973	†NY N	129	451	69	108	12	3	23	72	62-6	1	84	.239	.329	.432	111	6	1-1	.989	-4	89	89	1b95,O29L	15	-0.8
1974	NY N	137	507	70	128	19	0	20	63	66-9	0	77	.252	.337	.408	109	6	10-2	.994	1	100	96	1b133	0	-0.2
1975	NY N	91	220	24	42	11	0	7	29	33-4	2	22	.191	.302	.336	79	-6	1-1	.985	6	113	92	O31(29/2/0),1b29	0	-0.4
1976	NY N	127	443	56	120	25	4	15	78	65-1	0	53	.271	.362	.447	135	22	0-7	.985	2	103	102	O112L,1b12	0	1.5
1977	NY N	131	388	43	99	20	3	12	57	61-7	0	55	.255	.353	.415	110	7	6-2	.994	1	99	107	1b87,O22(21/0/1)	0	0.3
1978	Pit N	108	295	39	80	17	0	6	38	34-6	0	25	.271	.342	.390	100	1	5-0	1.000	1	113	22	O69(68/0/1),1b28	0	0.0
1979	†Pit N	128	326	52	90	9	4	16	60	53-6	1	37	.276	.373	.475	124	12	3-5	.958	0	111	50	O64L,1b48	0	0.7
1980	Pit N	114	238	31	58	6	0	8	34	52-2	0	29	.244	.378	.370	106	4	2-2	.991	-4	85	111	1b70,O11(10/0/1)	0	-0.4
1981	Pit N	34	59	6	14	1	0	2	9	5-0	0	3	.237	.292	.356	80	-2	0-0	.980	-2	25	44	1b8,O8L	0	-0.5
	†Mon N	31	76	6	18	5	0	3	9	12-2	0	6	.237	.341	.421	112	1	0-1	.978	0	117	102	1b21	0	0.0
	Year	65	135	12	32	6	0	5	18	17-2	0	9	.237	.320	.393	98	0	0-1	.979	-2	96	89	1b29,O8L	0	-0.5
1982	Mon N	26	28	1	3	0	0	0	2	4-0	0	2	.107	.212	.107	-6	-4	0-0	1.000	0	88	193	1b5	18	-0.4
	Pit N	33	25	5	6	2	0	2	8	6-1	1	3	.240	.406	.560	160	2	1-0	1.000	0	0	1163	/1	0	0.3
	Year	59	53	6	9	2	0	2	10	10-1	1	5	.170	.308	.321	74	-2	1-0	1.000	0	85	229	1b6	0	-0.1
Total	12	1215	3436	455	855	140	16	131	498	504-45	10	473	.249	.344	.413	111	56	31-22	.991	6	99	102	1b547,O440(432/2/6)	33	0.7
MILOSEVICH, MIKE	Michael "Mollie"; B1.13.1915 Zeigler IL; D2.3.1966 E.Chicago IN; BR/TR/5´10.5˝/172; d4.30																								
1944	NY A	94	312	27	77	11	4	0	32	30	0	37	.247	.313	.308	75	-10	1-2	.954	5	100	121	S91	0	0.1
1945	NY A	30	69	5	15	2	0	0	7	6	1	6	.217	.289	.246	54	-4	0-0	.957	0	98	110	S22/2	0	-0.3
Total	2	124	381	32	92	13	4	0	39	36	1	43	.241	.309	.297	71	-14	1-2	.954	5	100	119	S113/2	0	-0.2
MINCHER, DON	Donald Ray; B6.24.1938 Huntsville AL; BL/TR/6´3˝/(205–213); d4.18																								
1960	Was A	27	79	10	19	4	1	2	5	11-0	0	11	.241	.330	.392	96	0	0-1	.977	-4	37	72	1b20	0	-0.6
1961	Min A	35	101	18	19	5	1	5	11	22-0	0	11	.188	.333	.406	91	-1	0-1	.969	-1	97	119	1b29	0	-0.4
1962	Min A	86	121	20	29	1	1	9	29	34-3	0	24	.240	.406	.488	134	7	0-0	.978	-1	89	99	1b25	0	0.5
1963	Min A	82	225	41	58	8	0	17	42	30-0	3	51	.258	.351	.520	138	12	0-0	.983	-4	76	85	1b60	0	0.5
1964	Min A	120	287	45	68	12	4	23	56	27-2	0	51	.237	.300	.547	130	10	0-0	.992	1	102	93	1b76	0	0.6
1965	†Min A	128	346	43	87	17	3	22	65	49-**15**	2	73	.251	.344	.509	134	16	1-3	.992	-5	79	94	1b99/lf	0	0.4
1966	Min A	139	431	53	108	30	0	14	62	58-9	2	68	.251	.340	.418	110	8	3-2	.992	3	106	73	1b130	0	0.4
1967	Cal A★	147	487	81	133	23	3	25	76	69-9	4	69	.273	.367	.487	157	36	0-3	.994	-1	97	96	1b142/rf	0	2.8
1968	Cal A	120	399	35	94	12	1	13	48	43-6	4	65	.236	.312	.368	110	5	0-2	.991	-2	92	**116**	1b113	0	-0.5
1969	Sea A★	140	427	53	105	14	0	25	78	78-13	5	69	.246	.366	.454	130	19	10-11	.995	6	113	91	1b122	0	1.4
1970	Oak A	140	463	62	114	18	0	27	74	56-11	3	71	.246	.327	.460	120	11	5-4	.990	-2	97	106	1b137	0	-0.1
1971	Oak A	28	92	9	22	6	1	2	8	20-3	0	14	.239	.375	.391	119	3	1-1	.996	3	134	55	1b27	0	0.4
	Was A	100	323	35	94	15	1	10	45	53-4	2	52	.291	.389	.437	142	20	2-1	.990	1	108	109	1b88	0	1.5
	Year	128	415	44	116	21	2	12	53	73-7	2	66	.280	.386	.427	136	23	3-2	.991	4	**114**	96	1b115	0	1.9
1972	Tex A	61	191	23	45	10	0	6	39	46-1	2	23	.236	.384	.382	135	11	2-1	.994	5	136	91	1b59	0	1.4
	†Oak A	47	54	2	8	1	0	0	5	10-0	0	16	.148	.281	.167	37	-4	0-2	.988	-1	68	69	1b11	0	-0.7
	Year	108	245	25	53	11	0	6	44	56-1	2	39	.216	.363	.335	114	8	2-3	.993	4	127	88	1b70	0	0.7
Total	13	1400	4026	530	1003	176	16	200	643	606-76	27	668	.249	.348	.450	127	153	24-32	.990	-3	99	95	1b1138,O2(1/0/1)	0	7.6
MINCHER, ED	Edward M.; B6.17.1851 Baltimore MD; D12.8.1918 Brooklyn NY; d5.4																								
1871	Kek NA	9	36	4	8	0	0	0	5	0	—	0	.222	.222	.222	28	-3	1-0	.852	0	0	0	O9L	—	-0.2
1872	Nat NA	**11**	53	5	5	0	0	0	4	0	—	1	.094	.094	.094	-36	-9	0-0	.837	2	83	0	O11L	—	-0.5
Total	2NA	20	89	9	13	0	0	0	9	0	—	1	.146	.146	.146	-11	-12	1-0	.842	2	47	0	O20L	—	-0.7
MINNEHAN, DAN	Daniel Joseph; B11.28.1865 Troy NY; D8.8.1929 Troy NY; BR/TR/5´10˝/145; d9.20																								
1895	Lou N	8	34	6	13	0	0	0	6	1	0	1	.382	.400	.382	109	0	0	.920	0	92	284	3b7,O2C	—	0.1
MINOR, DAMON	Damon Reed; B1.5.1974 Canton OH; BL/TL/6´7˝/230; [SFN96 12/342]; d9.2; b–Ryan; Col Oklahoma																								
2000	SF N	10	9	3	4	0	0	3	6	2-0	0	1	.444	.545	1.444	405	4	0-0	1.000	-0	0	0	1b4	0	0.3
2001	SF N	19	45	3	7	1	0	0	3	3-1	0	8	.156	.208	.178	1	-7	0-0	.989	-1	64	49	1b11	9	-0.9
2002	SF N	83	173	21	41	6	0	10	24	24-6	2	34	.237	.333	.445	107	2	0-0	.997	-1	89	105	1b44,D3	17	-0.2
2004	SF N	24	58	8	14	2	0	0	6	12-0	4	18	.241	.405	.276	78	-1	0-0	1.000	-0	94	100	1b17/D	0	-0.2
Total	4	136	285	35	66	9	0	13	39	41-7	6	61	.232	.338	.400	95	-2	0-0	.996	-2	84	92	1b76,D4	26	-1.0

MINOR, RYAN Ryan Dale; B1.5.1974 Canton OH; BR/TR/6´7˝/(225–245); [BalA96 33/981]; d9.13; b–Damon; Col Oklahoma

YEAR	TM LG	G	AB	R	H	2B	3B	HR	RBI	BB-IB	HP	SO	AVG	OBP	SLG	AOPS	ABR	SB-CS	FA	FR	RNG	THR	GAMES AT POSITION	DL	BFW
1998	Bal A	9	14	3	6	1	0	0	1	0-0	0	3	.429	.429	.500	143	1	0-0	.833	-0	87	0	3b6,1b3/D	0	0.0
1999	Bal A	46	124	13	24	7	0	3	10	8-0	0	43	.194	.241	.323	44	-11	1-0	.963	6	120	132	3b45/1	0	-0.5
2000	Bal A	32	84	4	11	1	0	0	3	3-0	1	20	.131	.170	.143	-20	-16	0-0	.927	-1	84	126	3b26,1b5	22	-1.6
2001	Mon N	55	95	10	15	2	0	2	13	9-0	1	31	.158	.234	.242	25	-11	0-1	.970	-6	64	0	3b24,O2L/1D	0	-1.7
Total	4	142	317	30	56	11	0	5	27	20-0	2	97	.177	.228	.259	26	-37	1-1	.951	-1	97	97	3b101,1b10,D4,O2L	22	-3.8

MINOSO, MINNIE Saturnino Orestes Armas (Arrieta) (b Saturnino Orestes Arrieta (Armas)); B11.29.1925 Havana, Cuba; BR/TR/5´10˝/175; d4.19; C4; Negro Lg 1945–48; OF(1512/83/87)

YEAR	TM LG	G	AB	R	H	2B	3B	HR	RBI	BB-IB	HP	SO	AVG	OBP	SLG	AOPS	ABR	SB-CS	FA	FR	RNG	THR	GAMES AT POSITION	DL	BFW
1949	Cle A	9	16	2	3	0	0	1	1	2	2	2	.188	.350	.375	94	0	0-1	1.000	-0	115	0	O7R	0	-0.1
1951	Cle A	8	14	3	6	2	0	0	2	1	2	1	.429	.529	.571	209	3	0-0	.952	-0	97	27	1b7	0	0.2
	Chi A★	138	516	109	167	32	14	10	74	71	14	41	.324	.419	.498	150	39	31-10	.961	-9	88	69	O82(44/2/41),3b68/S	0	2.8
	Year	146	530	112	173	34	**14**	10	76	72	**16**	42	.326	.422	.500	152	42	**31**-10	.961	-9	88	69	O82(44/2/41),3b68,1b7/S	0	3.0
1952	Chi A★	147	569	96	160	24	9	13	61	71	**14**	46	.281	.375	.424	121	17	**22**-16	.979	-4	92	107	O143(70/63/10),3b9/S	0	0.5
1953	Chi A★	151	556	104	174	24	8	15	104	74	**17**	43	.313	.410	.466	132	28	**25**-16	.967	2	96	146	O147(145/0/2),3b10	0	2.1
1954	Chi A★	153	568	119	182	29	**18**	19	116	77	**16**	46	.320	.411	**.535**	154	44	18-11	.978	6	103	133	O146(120/16/13),3b9	0	4.1
1955	Chi A	139	517	79	149	26	7	10	70	76-3	10	43	.288	.387	.424	115	14	19-8	.971	6	99	162	O138(135/2/7),3b2	0	1.3
1956	Chi A	151	545	106	172	29	**11**	21	88	86-4	**23**	40	.316	.425	.525	149	42	12-6	.974	-4	96	88	O148(147/0/1),3b8/1	0	2.9
1957	Chi A★	153	568	96	176	**36**	5	12	103	79-5	**21**	54	.310	.408	.454	136	34	18-15	.984	0	94	107	O152L/3	0	2.4
1958	Cle A	149	556	94	168	25	2	24	80	59-3	**15**	53	.302	.383	.484	141	32	14-14	.975	5	101	140	O147L/3	0	2.7
1959	Cle A★	148	570	92	172	32	0	21	92	54-2	**17**	46	.302	.377	.468	136	30	8-10	.985	10	105	145	O148L	0	2.9
1960	Chi A★	**154**	591	89	**184**	32	4	20	105	52-2	**13**	63	.311	.374	.481	132	27	17-13	.980	0	89	128	O154(152/0/5)	0	1.7
1961	Chi A	152	540	91	151	28	3	14	82	67-2	**16**	46	.280	.369	.420	114	14	9-4	.956	-1	97	90	O147L	0	0.5
1962	StL N	39	97	14	19	5	0	1	10	7-0	3	17	.196	.271	.278	44	-8	4-0	.972	-1	81	123	O27L	99	-0.9
1963	Was A	109	315	38	72	12	2	4	30	33-1	8	38	.229	.315	.317	79	-8	8-6	.955	-3	76	80	O74L,3b8	0	-1.6
1964	Chi A	30	31	4	7	0	0	1	5	5-1	1	3	.226	.351	.323	91	0	0-0	1.000	1	174	0	O5(4/0/1)	0	0.0
1976	Chi A	3	8	0	1	0	0	0	0	0-0	0	2	.125	.125	.125	-27	-1	0-0	ø	0	—	—	D3	0	-0.1
1980	Chi A	2	2	0	0	0	0	0	0	0-0	0	0	.000	.000	.000	-99	-1	0-0	ø	0	—	—	/H	0	-0.1
Total	17	1835	6579	1136	1963	336	83	186	1023	814-23	192	584	.298	.389	.459	130	306	205-130	.974	6	96	119	O1665L,3b116,1b8,D3,S2	99	21.3

MIRABELLI, DOUG Douglas Anthony; B10.18.1970 Kingman AZ; BR/TR/6´1˝/(210–228); [SFN92 5/131]; d8.27; Col Wichita St.

YEAR	TM LG	G	AB	R	H	2B	3B	HR	RBI	BB-IB	HP	SO	AVG	OBP	SLG	AOPS	ABR	SB-CS	FA	FR	RNG	THR	GAMES AT POSITION	DL	BFW
1996	SF N	9	18	2	4	1	0	0	1	3-0	0	4	.222	.333	.278	65	-1	0-0	1.000	-2	104	0	C8	0	-0.2
1997	SF N	6	7	0	1	0	0	0	0	1-0	0	3	.143	.250	.143	6	-1	0-0	1.000	0	158	0	C6	0	-0.1
1998	SF N	10	17	2	4	2	0	1	4	2-0	0	6	.235	.316	.529	123	1	0-0	.974	-0	115	253	C10	0	0.1
1999	SF N	33	87	10	22	6	0	1	10	9-1	1	25	.253	.327	.356	79	-3	0-0	1.000	-3	125	132	C30	0	-0.3
2000	†SF N	82	230	23	53	10	2	6	28	36-2	2	57	.230	.337	.370	84	-5	1-0	.985	-10	98	107	C80	0	-1.0
2001	Tex A	23	49	4	5	2	0	2	3	10-0	0	21	.102	.254	.265	36	-5	0-0	.990	-0	157	246	C23/D	0	-0.3
	Bos A	54	141	16	38	8	0	9	26	17-2	4	36	.270	.360	.518	129	6	0-0	.995	-1	65	141	C52/D	0	0.8
	Year	77	190	20	43	10	0	11	29	27-2	4	57	.226	.332	.453	104	1	0-0	.994	-1	91	171	C75,D2	0	0.5
2002	Bos A	57	151	17	34	7	0	7	25	17-0	3	33	.225	.312	.411	90	-2	0-0	1.000	-1	63	170	C50,D4	0	0.0
2003	†Bos A	62	163	23	42	13	0	6	18	11-0	1	36	.258	.307	.448	92	-2	0-0	.988	-3	62	114	C55,1b2,D4	0	-0.1
2004	†Bos A	59	160	27	45	12	0	9	32	19-0	3	46	.281	.368	.525	122	5	0-0	.993	-8	49	76	C53,D4	0	0.1
2005	†Bos A	50	136	16	31	7	0	6	18	14-0	2	48	.228	.309	.412	86	-3	2-0	.988	1	96	96	C43,D5	24	0.1
2006	SD N	14	22	1	4	1	0	0	0	4-0	0	5	.182	.308	.227	43	-2	0-0	1.000	-0	80	159	C9	0	-0.2
	Bos A	59	161	12	31	6	0	6	25	11-0	4	54	.193	.261	.342	53	-12	0-0	.994	-7	72	66	C57,D2	0	-1.5
Total	11	518	1342	153	314	75	2	53	190	154-5	20	374	.234	.320	.411	89	-24	3-0	.992	-33	82	118	C476,D21,1b2	24	-2.6

MIRANDA, WILLY Guillermo (Perez); B5.24.1926 Velasco, Cuba; D9.7.1996 Baltimore MD; BB/TR/5´9.5˝/(150–160); d5.6

YEAR	TM LG	G	AB	R	H	2B	3B	HR	RBI	BB-IB	HP	SO	AVG	OBP	SLG	AOPS	ABR	SB-CS	FA	FR	RNG	THR	GAMES AT POSITION	DL	BFW
1951	Was A	7	9	2	4	0	0	0	0	0	0	0	.444	.444	.444	143	0	0-0	.818	-1	40	0	S2/1	0	-0.1
1952	Chi A	12	8	1	2	1	0	0	0	3	0	0	.250	.455	.375	131	1	0-0	1.000	3	144	156	S4,3b4/2	0	0.4
	StL A	7	11	2	1	0	1	0	1	3	0	1	.091	.286	.273	54	-1	0-0	.900	-1	100	37	S7	0	-0.2
	Chi A	58	142	13	31	3	1	0	7	10	1	14	.218	.275	.254	47	-10	1-0	.975	6	144	156	S50/23	0	-0.2
	Year	77	161	16	34	4	2	0	8	16	1	15	.211	.287	.261	52	-10	1-0	.970	7	111	105	S61,3b5,2b2	0	0.0
1953	StL A	17	6	2	1	0	0	0	0	1	0	1	.167	.286	.167	24	-1	1-1	.933	1	106	77	S8,3b6	0	0.1
	NY A	48	58	12	13	0	0	1	5	5	0	10	.224	.286	.276	54	-4	1-1	.984	9	118	154	S45	0	0.6
	Year	65	64	14	14	0	0	1	5	6	0	11	.219	.286	.266	51	-5	2-2	.979	10	117	148	S53,3b6	0	0.7
1954	NY A	92	116	12	29	4	2	1	12	10	0	10	.250	.300	.345	82	-3	0-3	.948	9	107	146	S88,2b4/3	0	0.8
1955	Bal A	153	487	42	124	12	6	1	38	42-4	1	58	.255	.313	.310	74	-19	4-3	.958	20	**110**	105	S153/2	0	1.3
1956	Bal A	148	461	38	100	16	4	2	34	46-3	0	73	.217	.287	.282	55	-31	3-6	.962	4	103	99	S147	0	-1.6
1957	Bal A	115	314	29	61	3	0	0	20	24-2	0	42	.194	.249	.204	28	-32	2-1	.966	-3	101	91	S115	0	-2.8
1958	Bal A	102	214	15	43	6	0	1	8	14-2	0	25	.201	.250	.243	38	-19	1-1	.962	-8	91	111	S102	0	-2.1
1959	Bal A	65	88	8	14	5	0	0	7	7-0	0	16	.159	.221	.216	21	-10	0-0	.974	4	105	127	S47,3b11,2b5	0	-0.3
Total	9	824	1914	176	423	50	14	6	132	165-11	2	250	.221	.282	.271	54	-129	13-16	.962	43	104	107	S768,3b23,2b12/1	0	-4.1

MISSE, JOHN John Beverly; B5.30.1885 Highland KS; D3.18.1970 St.Joseph MO; BR/TR/5´8˝/150; d5.26

YEAR	TM LG	G	AB	R	H	2B	3B	HR	RBI	BB-IB	HP	SO	AVG	OBP	SLG	AOPS	ABR	SB-CS	FA	FR	RNG	THR	GAMES AT POSITION	DL	BFW
1914	StL F	99	306	28	60	8	1	0	22	36	0	52	.196	.281	.229	38	-31	3	.948	1	105	76	2b50,S48,3b2	—	-2.7

MITCHELL, CLARENCE Clarence Elmer; B2.22.1891 Franklin NE; D11.6.1963 Grand Island NE; BL/TL/5´11.5˝/190; d6.2; Mil 1918; C2; ▲

YEAR	TM LG	G	AB	R	H	2B	3B	HR	RBI	BB-IB	HP	SO	AVG	OBP	SLG	AOPS	ABR	SB-CS	FA	FR	RNG	THR	GAMES AT POSITION	DL	BFW
1911	Det A	5	4	2	2	0	0	0	0	1	0	—	.500	.600	.500	198	1	0	1.000	-1	52	0	P5	—	0.0
1916	Cin N	56	117	11	28	2	1	0	11	4	0	6	.239	.264	.274	67	-5	1	.985	-0	107	**290**	P29,1b9,O3L	—	-0.2
1917	Cin N	47	90	13	25	3	0	0	5	5	0	5	.278	.316	.311	97	0	0	.982	0	100	128	P32,1b6,O5L	—	0.0
1918	Bro N	10	24	2	6	1	1	0	2	0	0	3	.250	.250	.375	90	-1	0	.750	-1	51	0	O6R,1b2/P	—	-0.2
1919	Bro N	34	49	7	18	1	0	1	2	4	0	4	.367	.415	.449	156	6	0	.976	1	115	112	P23	—	0.0
1920	†Bro N	55	107	9	25	2	2	0	11	8	0	9	.234	.287	.290	64	-5	1-0	1.000	1	139	0	P19,1b11,O4(2/0/2)	—	-0.4
1921	Bro N	46	91	11	24	5	0	0	12	5	2	7	.264	.316	.319	66	-4	3-1	.945	3	127	**326**	P37,1b4	—	0.1
1922	Bro N	56	155	21	45	6	3	3	28	19	1	6	.290	.371	.426	106	2	0-0	.992	4	130	108	1b42,P5	—	0.2
1923	Phi N	53	78	10	21	3	2	1	9	4	0	11	.269	.305	.397	75	3	0-0	.880	-3	55	98	P29	—	0.0
1924	Phi N	69	102	7	26	3	0	0	13	2	1	7	.255	.276	.284	45	0	1-0	**1.000**	3	126	135	P30	—	0.0
1925	Phi N	52	92	7	18	2	0	0	13	5	0	9	.196	.237	.217	16	-12	2-0	**1.000**	4	132	289	P32,1b2	—	0.2
1926	Phi N	39	78	8	19	4	0	0	6	5	0	5	.244	.289	.295	55	-5	0	.986	4	140	107	P28,1b4	—	0.2
1927	Phi N	18	42	5	10	2	0	1	6	2	0	1	.238	.273	.357	67	2	0	.963	0	120	88	P13	—	0.0
1928	Phi N	5	4	0	1	0	0	0	0	0	0	0	.250	.250	.250	30	0	0	1.000	0	215	0	P3	—	0.0
	†StL N	19	56	0	7	1	0	0	1	0	0	3	.125	.125	.143	-30	-4	0	.982	2	137	164	P19	—	0.0
	Year	24	60	0	8	1	0	0	1	0	0	3	.133	.133	.150	-26	-4	0	.983	3	**140**	158	P22	—	0.0
1929	StL N	26	66	9	18	3	1	0	9	4	0	6	.273	.314	.348	63	4	1	.974	-1	96	132	P25	—	0.0
1930	StL N	1	2	0	1	0	0	0	0	0	0	0	.500	.500	.500	138	0	0	ø	-0	0	0	/P	—	0.0
	NY N	24	47	9	12	1	0	0	1	1	0	5	.255	.271	.277	33	0	0	1.000	2	134	60	P24	—	0.0
	Year	25	49	9	13	1	0	0	1	1	0	5	.265	.280	.286	38	1	0	1.000	2	131	59	P25	—	0.0
1931	NY N	27	73	5	16	2	0	1	4	2	0	4	.219	.240	.288	42	2	0	.885	-2	83	83	P27	—	0.0
1932	NY N	8	10	2	2	0	0	0	0	1	0	1	.200	.273	.200	30	0	0	.833	-1	48	0	P8	—	0.0
Total	18	650	1287	138	324	41	10	7	133	72	4	92	.252	.293	.315	64	-16	9-1	.972	15	114	155	P390,1b80,O18(12/0/8)	—	-0.1

MITCHELL, FRED Frederick Francis (b Frederick Francis Yapp); B6.5.1878 Cambridge MA; D10.13.1970 Newton MA; BR/TR/5´9.5˝/185; d4.27; M7/C3; OF(1/2/0); ▲

YEAR	TM LG	G	AB	R	H	2B	3B	HR	RBI	BB-IB	HP	SO	AVG	OBP	SLG	AOPS	ABR	SB-CS	FA	FR	RNG	THR	GAMES AT POSITION	DL	BFW
1901	Bos A	20	44	5	7	0	2	0	4	2	0	—	.159	.196	.250	23	-5	0	.875	-1	106	223	P17,2b2/S	—	-0.1
1902	Bos A	1	1	0	0	0	0	0	0	0	0	—	.000	.000	.000	-97	0	0	.667	0	171	2645	/P	—	0.0
	Phi A	20	48	7	9	1	1	0	3	1	0	—	.188	.204	.250	24	-5	1	.942	2	136	267	P18/cf	—	0.1
	Year	21	49	7	9	1	1	0	3	1	0	—	.184	.200	.245	22	-5	1	.927	2	137	352	P19/cf	—	0.1
1903	Phi N	29	95	11	19	4	0	0	10	0	0	—	.200	.200	.242	27	-1	0	.857	-3	81	150	P28	—	0.0
1904	Phi N	25	82	9	17	3	1	0	3	5	0	—	.207	.253	.268	63	-4	1	.981	3	154	0	P13,1b9,3b2/cf	—	0.0
	Bro N	8	24	3	7	1	1	0	6	1	1	—	.292	.346	.417	139	3	0	.906	1	128	341	P8	—	0.0
	Year	33	106	12	24	4	2	0	9	6	1	—	.226	.274	.302	80	-3	1	.952	4	144	129	P21,1b9,3b2/cf	—	0.0
1905	Bro N	27	79	4	15	0	0	0	8	4	1	—	.190	.238	.190	30	-7	0	.881	-1	123	113	P12,1b7,3b4/Slf	—	-0.6
1910	NY A	68	196	16	45	7	2	0	18	9	3	—	.230	.274	.286	71	-7	6	.968	-9	*96*	*90*	C62	—	-1.2
1913	Bos N	4	3	0	1	0	0	0	0	0	0	2	.333	.333	.333	89	0	0	ø	0	—	—	/H	—	0.0
Total	7	202	572	55	120	16	7	0	52	22	5	2	.210	.245	.262	52	-26	8	.904	-8	115	182	P97,C62,1b16,3b6,O3C,S2,2b2	—	-1.8

Mitchell, Johnny John Franklin; B8.9.1894 Detroit MI; D11.4.1965 Birmingham MI; BB/TR/5´8˝/155; d5.21

YEAR	TM LG	G	AB	R	H	2B	3B	HR	RBI	BB-IB	HP	SO	AVG	OBP	SLG	AOPS	ABR	SB-CS	FA	FR	RNG	THR	GAMES AT POSITION	DL	BFW
1921	NY A	13	42	4	11	1	0	0	2	4	0	4	.262	.326	.286	56	-3	1-0	.958	-4	110	44	S7,2b5	—	-0.6
1922	NY A	4	4	1	0	0	0	0	0	0	0	1	.000	.000	.000	-98	-1	0-0	1.000	-0	79	0	S4	—	-0.1
	Bos A	59	203	20	51	4	1	1	8	16	4	17	.251	.318	.296	61	-12	1-2	.962	-3	101	103	S58	—	-0.8
	Year	63	207	21	51	4	1	1	8	16	4	18	.246	.313	.290	58	-13	1-2	.963	-3	101	102	S62	—	-0.9
1923	Bos A	92	347	40	78	15	4	0	19	34	1	18	.225	.296	.291	55	-23	7-11	.961	4	102	87	S87,2b5	—	-1.2
1924	Bro N	64	243	42	64	10	0	1	16	37	0	22	.263	.361	.317	86	-3	3-1	.951	0	97	74	S64	—	0.5
1925	Bro N	97	336	45	84	8	3	0	18	28	0	19	.250	.308	.292	55	-23	2-0	.947	-2	95	89	S90	—	-1.4
Total	5	329	1175	152	288	38	8	2	63	119	5	81	.245	.317	.296	62	-65	14-14	.955	-5	99	87	S310,2b10	—	-3.6

Mitchell, Keith Keith Alexander; B8.6.1969 San Diego CA; BR/TR/5´10˝/(180–195); [AtlN87 4/90]; d7.23

YEAR	TM LG	G	AB	R	H	2B	3B	HR	RBI	BB-IB	HP	SO	AVG	OBP	SLG	AOPS	ABR	SB-CS	FA	FR	RNG	THR	GAMES AT POSITION	DL	BFW
1991	†Atl N	48	66	11	21	0	0	2	5	8-0	0	12	.318	.392	.409	119	2	3-1	.970	-1	91	89	O34(24/1/10)	0	0.1
1994	Sea A	46	128	21	29	2	0	5	15	18-0	1	22	.227	.324	.359	75	-5	0-0	.980	-4	84	0	O38(27/3/11),D6	41	-0.9
1996	Cin N	11	15	2	4	1	0	1	3	1-0	0	3	.267	.313	.533	116	0	0-0	.875	-0	109	0	O5(2/1/2)	0	0.0
1998	Bos A	23	33	4	9	2	0	0	6	7-1	0	5	.273	.400	.333	92	0	1-0	1.000	-1	60	0	D12,O10(4/0/6)	0	-0.2
Total	4	128	242	38	63	5	0	8	29	34-1	1	42	.260	.353	.380	91	-3	4-1	.969	-6	85	27	O87(57/5/29),D18	41	-1.0

Mitchell, Kevin Kevin Darnell; B1.13.1962 San Diego CA; BR/TR/5´11˝/(210–244); d9.4; OF(756/6/53); [DL 1993 SF N 24]

YEAR	TM LG	G	AB	R	H	2B	3B	HR	RBI	BB-IB	HP	SO	AVG	OBP	SLG	AOPS	ABR	SB-CS	FA	FR	RNG	THR	GAMES AT POSITION	DL	BFW
1984	NY N	7	14	0	3	0	0	0	1	0-0	0	3	.214	.214	.214	21	-2	0-1	.833	-0	81	457	3b5	0	-0.2
1986	†NY N	108	328	51	91	22	2	12	43	33-0	1	61	.277	.344	.466	124	11	3-3	.983	4	105	73	O68(40/6/29),S24,3b7,1b2	0	1.3
1987	SD N	62	196	19	48	7	1	7	26	20-3	0	38	.245	.313	.398	91	-3	0-0	.945	3	113	106	3b51,O3L	0	-0.1
	†SF N	69	268	49	82	13	1	15	44	28-1	2	50	.306	.376	.530	143	16	9-6	.962	-1	100	93	3b68,O3(2/0/1)/S	0	1.4
	Year	131	464	68	130	20	2	22	70	48-4	2	88	.280	.350	.474	121	13	9-6	.954	2	106	99	3b119,O6(5/0/1)/S	0	1.3
1988	SF N	148	505	60	127	25	7	19	80	48-7	5	85	.251	.319	.442	122	13	5-5	.943	-0	106	122	3b102,O40L	0	1.2
1989	†SF N★	154	543	100	158	34	6	**47**	**125**	87-**32**	3	115	.291	.387	**.635**	**194**	**67**	3-4	.978	-2	96	92	O147L,3b2	0	**6.2**
1990	SF N★	140	524	90	152	24	2	35	93	58-9	2	87	.290	.360	.544	151	35	4-7	.971	-0	97	87	O138L	0	2.9
1991	SF N	113	371	52	95	13	1	27	69	43-8	5	57	.256	.338	.515	142	19	2-3	.970	-1	97	108	O100L/1	22	1.5
1992	Sea A	99	360	48	103	24	0	9	67	35-4	3	46	.286	.351	.428	117	9	0-2	1.000	-1	98	91	O69L,D26	48	0.4
1993	Cin N	93	323	56	110	21	3	19	64	25-4	1	48	.341	.385	.601	160	26	1-0	.957	2	100	124	O87(85/0/2)	15	2.5
1994	Cin N	95	310	57	101	18	1	30	77	59-15	3	62	.326	.429	.681	186	41	2-0	.972	1	89	184	O89L/1	0	3.8
1996	Bos A	27	92	9	28	4	0	2	13	11-0	1	14	.304	.385	.413	100	0	0-0	.935	-3	78	0	O21(1/0/21),D4	63	-0.3
	Cin N	37	114	18	37	11	0	6	26	26-2	0	16	.325	.447	.579	166	13	0-0	.978	-1	102	0	O31L,1b3	0	1.0
1997	Cle A	20	59	7	9	1	0	4	11	9-2	1	11	.153	.275	.373	65	-3	1-0	.000	-0	0	0	D16/lf	0	-0.4
1998	Oak A	51	127	14	29	7	1	2	21	9-0	0	26	.228	.279	.346	62	-7	0-0	1.000	-1	88	0	D23,O10L,1b2	31	-0.9
Total	13	1223	4134	630	1173	224	25	234	760	491-87	27	719	.284	.360	.520	142	235	30-31	.971	-2	96	99	O807L,3b235,D69,S25,1b9	203	20.3

Mitchell, Dale Loren Dale; B8.23.1921 Colony OK; D1.5.1987 Tulsa OK; BL/TL/6´1˝/195; d9.15; Col Oklahoma

YEAR	TM LG	G	AB	R	H	2B	3B	HR	RBI	BB-IB	HP	SO	AVG	OBP	SLG	AOPS	ABR	SB-CS	FA	FR	RNG	THR	GAMES AT POSITION	DL	BFW
1946	Cle A	11	44	7	19	3	0	0	5	1	0	2	.432	.444	.500	175	4	1-0	1.000	-0	105	0	O11C	0	0.4
1947	Cle A	123	493	69	156	16	10	1	34	23	0	14	.316	.347	.396	109	3	2-5	.977	-6	88	101	O115(83/42/1)	0	-1.2
1948	†Cle A	141	608	82	204	30	8	4	56	45	2	17	.336	.383	.431	119	15	13-18	**.991**	0	96	113	O140(140/1/0)	0	0.1
1949	Cle A★	149	640	81	**203**	16	**23**	3	56	43	0	11	.317	.360	.428	110	4	10-3	**.994**	-3	95	87	O149L	0	-0.9
1950	Cle A	130	506	81	156	27	5	3	49	67	1	21	.308	.390	.399	106	7	3-7	.972	-11	87	33	O127L	0	-1.4
1951	Cle A	134	510	83	148	21	7	11	62	53	1	16	.290	.358	.424	117	11	7-7	.992	-9	89	32	O124L	0	-0.9
1952	Cle A★	134	511	61	165	26	3	5	58	52	1	9	.323	.387	.415	132	22	6-6	.992	-7	93	25	O128L	0	0.6
1953	Cle A	134	500	76	150	26	4	13	60	42	0	20	.300	.354	.446	118	11	3-1	.970	-10	90	23	O125L	0	-0.5
1954	†Cle A	53	60	6	17	1	0	1	6	9	0	1	.283	.377	.350	98	0	0-0	.889	-0	69	327	O6L/1	0	0.0
1955	Cle A	61	58	4	15	2	1	0	10	4-2	0	3	.259	.302	.328	68	-3	0-0	1.000	0	107	208	1b8,O3L	0	-0.3
1956	Cle A	38	30	2	4	0	0	0	6	7-1	0	2	.133	.297	.133	17	-3	0-0	ø	-0	0	0	/lf	0	-0.3
	†Bro N	19	24	3	7	1	0	0	1	0-0	0	3	.292	.292	.333	63	-1	0-0	1.000	-0	90	0	O2L	0	-0.2
Total	11	1127	3984	555	1244	169	61	41	403	346-3	5	119	.312	.368	.416	114	70	45-47	.985	-46	91	62	O931(888/54/1),1b9	0	-4.6

Mitchell, Mike Michael Francis; B12.12.1879 Springfield OH; D7.16.1961 Phoenix AZ; BR/TR/6´1˝/185; d4.11

YEAR	TM LG	G	AB	R	H	2B	3B	HR	RBI	BB-IB	HP	SO	AVG	OBP	SLG	AOPS	ABR	SB-CS	FA	FR	RNG	THR	GAMES AT POSITION	DL	BFW
1907	Cin N	148	558	64	163	17	12	3	47	37	3	—	.292	.339	.382	121	12	17	.962	24	**200**	186	O146(3/0/144),1b2	—	3.3
1908	Cin N	119	406	41	90	9	6	1	37	46	2	—	.222	.304	.281	89	-4	18	.959	2	110	56	O118(3/0/115)/1	—	-0.9
1909	Cin N	145	523	83	162	17	**17**	4	86	57	0	—	.310	.378	.430	152	30	37	.962	5	100	64	O145R/1	—	3.2
1910	Cin N	**156**	583	79	167	16	**18**	5	88	59	4	56	.286	.356	.401	126	17	35	.958	-2	99	92	O149(0/22/127),1b7	—	0.9
1911	Cin N	142	529	74	154	22	22	2	84	44	2	34	.291	.348	.427	121	11	35	.971	9	114	113	O140(1/0/139)	—	1.2
1912	Cin N	147	552	60	156	14	13	4	78	41	1	43	.283	.333	.377	97	-5	23	.947	-1	106	85	O144R	—	-1.3
1913	Chi N	82	279	37	73	11	6	4	35	32	1	33	.262	.340	.387	107	3	15-8	.941	1	100	119	O82(72/0/10)	—	0.0
	Pit N	54	199	25	54	8	2	1	16	14	0	15	.271	.319	.347	94	-2	8-10	.946	3	110	112	O54C	—	-0.5
	Year	136	478	62	127	19	8	5	51	46	1	48	.266	.331	.370	102	1	23-18	.943	4	104	116	O136(72/54/10)	—	-0.5
1914	Pit N	76	273	31	64	11	5	2	23	16	1	16	.234	.279	.333	86	-6	5	.984	6	124	81	O76R	—	-0.5
	Was A	55	193	20	55	5	3	1	20	22	1	19	.285	.361	.358	112	3	9-7	.957	2	98	142	O53(47/0/6)	—	0.2
Total	8	1124	4095	514	1138	130	104	27	514	368	15	216	.278	.340	.380	114	59	202-25	.959	49	118	103	O1107(126/76/905),1b11	—	5.6

Mitchell, Bobby Robert Van; B4.7.1955 Salt Lake City UT; BL/TL/5´10˝/170; [LAN77 7/176]; d9.1; Col USC

YEAR	TM LG	G	AB	R	H	2B	3B	HR	RBI	BB-IB	HP	SO	AVG	OBP	SLG	AOPS	ABR	SB-CS	FA	FR	RNG	THR	GAMES AT POSITION	DL	BFW
1980	LA N	9	3	1	1	0	0	0	0	1-0	0	0	.333	.500	.333	141	0	0-0	1.000	0	139	0	O8(0/7/1)	0	0.0
1981	LA N	10	8	0	1	0	0	0	0	1-0	0	4	.125	.222	.125	1	-1	0-0	1.000	0	122	0	O7(1/6/1)	0	-0.1
1982	Min A	124	454	48	113	11	6	2	28	54-4	2	53	.249	.331	.313	76	-14	8-9	.997	11	116	105	O121(5/115/6)	0	-0.7
1983	Min A	59	152	26	35	4	2	1	15	28-2	1	21	.230	.354	.303	79	-3	1-1	.990	-2	89	84	O44(1/43/0)	0	-0.6
Total	4	202	617	75	150	15	8	3	43	84-6	3	78	.243	.336	.308	76	-18	9-10	.996	8	110	98	O180(7/171/8)	0	-1.4

Mitchell, Bobby Robert Vance; B10.22.1943 Norristown PA; BR/TR/6´4˝/(185–190); d7.5

YEAR	TM LG	G	AB	R	H	2B	3B	HR	RBI	BB-IB	HP	SO	AVG	OBP	SLG	AOPS	ABR	SB-CS	FA	FR	RNG	THR	GAMES AT POSITION	DL	BFW
1970	NY A	10	22	1	5	2	0	0	4	2-0	1	3	.227	.320	.318	80	0	0-2	1.000	2	177	0	O7(0/2/5)	0	0.0
1971	Mil A	35	55	7	10	1	1	2	6	6-1	0	18	.182	.262	.345	72	-2	0-2	.974	2	121	228	O19(2/7/10)	0	-0.2
1973	Mil A	47	130	12	29	6	0	5	20	5-1	0	32	.223	.250	.385	78	-5	4-1	.960	-2	77	0	O20(10/0/10),D19	0	-0.8
1974	Mil A	88	173	27	42	6	2	5	20	18-1	1	46	.243	.314	.387	102	0	7-6	.969	-1	96	88	D53,O26(10/2/14)	0	-0.3
1975	Mil A	93	229	39	57	14	3	9	41	25-1	0	69	.249	.320	.454	117	5	3-4	.992	2	108	49	O72L,D11	0	0.2
Total	5	273	609	86	143	29	6	21	91	56-4	2	168	.235	.299	.406	99	-2	14-15	.984	3	107	68	O144(94/11/39),D83	0	-1.1

Mitterling, Ralph Ralph "Sarge"; B4.19.1890 Freeburg PA; D1.22.1956 Pittsburgh PA; BR/TR/5´10˝/165; d7.7; Col Springfield

YEAR	TM LG	G	AB	R	H	2B	3B	HR	RBI	BB-IB	HP	SO	AVG	OBP	SLG	AOPS	ABR	SB-CS	FA	FR	RNG	THR	GAMES AT POSITION	DL	BFW
1916	Phi A	13	39	1	6	0	0	0	2	3	0	6	.154	.214	.154	11	-4	0	.944	-1	85	86	O12(1/11/0)	—	-0.6

Mitterwald, George George Eugene; B6.7.1945 Berkeley CA; BR/TR/6´2˝/(195–206); d9.15; C5; Col Chabot (CA) JC

YEAR	TM LG	G	AB	R	H	2B	3B	HR	RBI	BB-IB	HP	SO	AVG	OBP	SLG	AOPS	ABR	SB-CS	FA	FR	RNG	THR	GAMES AT POSITION	DL	BFW
1966	Min A	3	5	1	1	0	0	0	0	0-0	0	0	.200	.200	.200	14	-1	0-0	1.000	1	0	0	C3	0	0.0
1968	Min A	11	34	1	7	1	0	0	1	3-0	0	8	.206	.270	.235	51	-2	0-0	.961	-1	67	36	C10	0	-0.2
1969	†Min A	69	187	18	48	8	0	5	13	17-1	3	47	.257	.327	.380	95	-1	0-1	.987	9	135	74	C63/lf	0	1.1
1970	†Min A	117	369	36	82	12	2	15	46	34-6	2	84	.222	.291	.388	84	-9	3-5	.996	26	141	128	C117	0	2.1
1971	Min A	125	388	38	97	13	1	13	44	39-9	0	104	.250	.316	.389	97	-2	3-3	.986	-3	102	97	C120	0	0.0
1972	Min A	64	163	12	30	4	1	1	8	9-2	0	37	.184	.225	.239	37	-13	0-1	.984	5	75	152	C61	0	-0.7
1973	Min A	125	432	50	112	15	0	16	64	39-0	5	111	.259	.326	.405	101	0	3-1	.992	4	97	99	C122,D3	0	1.0
1974	Chi N	78	215	17	54	7	0	7	28	18-4	2	42	.251	.310	.381	90	-3	1-3	.974	-6	65	142	C68	0	-0.7
1975	Chi N	84	200	19	44	4	3	5	26	19-7	0	42	.220	.285	.345	72	-9	0-0	.976	3	118	188	C59,1b10	0	-0.4
1976	Chi N	101	303	19	65	7	0	5	28	16-2	0	63	.215	.249	.287	49	-21	1-2	.981	-2	93	113	C64,1b25	0	-2.4
1977	Chi N	110	349	40	83	22	0	9	43	28-7	1	69	.238	.295	.378	72	-14	3-1	.989	10	108	130	C109/1	0	0.1
Total	11	887	2645	251	623	93	7	76	301	222-38	13	607	.236	.296	.362	80	-75	14-17	.987	47	105	118	C796,1b36,D3/lf	0	-0.1

Mize, Johnny John Robert "The Big Cat"; B1.7.1913 Demorest GA; D6.2.1993 Demorest GA; BL/TR/6´2˝/(205–223); d4.16; Mil 1943–45; C1; HF1981; Col Piedmont

YEAR	TM LG	G	AB	R	H	2B	3B	HR	RBI	BB-IB	HP	SO	AVG	OBP	SLG	AOPS	ABR	SB-CS	FA	FR	RNG	THR	GAMES AT POSITION	DL	BFW
1936	StL N	126	414	76	136	30	8	19	93	50	1	32	.329	.402	.577	162	36	1	.994	0	96	78	1b97,O8R	—	2.5
1937	StL N★	145	560	103	204	40	7	25	113	56	5	57	.364	.427	.595	171	56	2	.988	-14	67	91	1b144	—	2.9
1938	StL N	149	531	85	179	34	**16**	27	102	74	4	47	.337	.422	**.614**	172	53	0	.989	-0	100	96	1b140	—	3.9
1939	StL N★	153	564	104	197	44	14	**28**	108	92	4	49	**.349**	.444	**.626**	**174**	**62**	0	.987	-3	91	94	1b152	—	**4.3**
1940	StL N★	155	579	111	182	31	13	**43**	**137**	82	5	49	.314	.404	**.636**	**173**	**57**	7	.990	-6	82	83	1b153	—	3.6
1941	StL N★	126	473	67	150	**39**	8	16	100	70	1	45	.317	.406	.535	153	35	4	.994	4	107	110	1b122	—	2.7
1942	NY N★	142	541	97	165	25	7	26	**110**	60	5	39	.305	.380	**.521**	161	41	3	**.995**	-2	90	98	1b138	0	2.7

YEAR	TM LG	G	AB	R	H	2B	3B	HR	RBI	BB-IB	HP	SO	AVG	OBP	SLG	AOPS	ABR	SB-CS	FA	FR	RNG	THR	GAMES AT POSITION	DL	BFW
1946	NY N★	101	377	70	127	18	3	22	70	62	5	26	.337	.437	.576	185	44	3	.989	6	121	97	1b101	0	4.8
1947	NY N★	154	586	**137**	177	26	2	**51**	**138**	74	4	42	.302	.384	.614	160	48	2	**.996**	9	119	93	1b154	0	5.0
1948	NY N★	152	560	110	162	26	4	**40**	125	94	4	37	.289	.395	.564	156	45	4	.991	3	108	97	1b152	0	4.2
1949	NY N★	106	388	59	102	15	0	18	62	50	3	19	.263	.351	.441	111	6	1	.994	2	106	95	1b101	0	0.5
	†NY A	13	23	4	6	1	0	1	2	4	1	2	.261	.393	.435	119	1	0-0	.980	-0	77	87	1b6	0	0.0
1950	†NY A	90	274	43	76	12	0	25	72	29	2	24	.277	.351	.595	143	14	0-1	.996	-2	78	117	1b72	0	0.9
1951	†NY A	113	332	37	86	14	1	10	49	36	4	24	.259	.339	.398	102	1	1-0	.994	-3	81	119	1b93	0	-0.4
1952	†NY A	78	137	9	36	9	0	4	29	11	2	15	.263	.327	.416	112	2	0-0	.987	0	106	155	1b27	0	0.2
1953	†NY A★	81	104	6	26	3	0	4	27	12	2	17	.250	.339	.394	101	0	0-0	1.000	-0	89	171	1b15	0	-0.1
Total	15	1884	6443	1118	2011	367	83	359	1337	856	52	524	.312	.397	.562	157	501	28-1	.992	-7	96	97	1b1667,O8R	0	37.7

MIZEROCK, JOHN John Joseph; B12.8.1960 Punxsutawney PA; BL/TR/5´11˝/(180–190); [HouN79 1/8]; d4.12; M1/C3; [DL 1984 Hou N 79]

YEAR	TM LG	G	AB	R	H	2B	3B	HR	RBI	BB-IB	HP	SO	AVG	OBP	SLG	AOPS	ABR	SB-CS	FA	FR	RNG	THR	GAMES AT POSITION	DL	BFW
1983	Hou N	33	85	8	13	4	1	1	10	12-2	1	15	.153	.263	.259	48	-6	0-0	.967	-2	101	112	C33	23	-0.7
1985	Hou N	15	38	6	9	4	0	0	6	2-0	1	8	.237	.293	.342	79	-1	0-0	.966	2	74	121	C15	0	0.1
1986	Hou N	44	81	9	15	1	1	1	6	24-2	1	16	.185	.374	.259	81	-1	0-0	.987	-1	106	54	C42	0	0.0
1989	Atl N	11	27	1	6	0	0	0	2	0-0	0	3	.222	.222	.222	27	-3	0-0	1.000	1	301	73	C11	0	-0.1
Total	4	103	231	24	43	9	2	2	24	38-4	3	42	.186	.307	.268	64	-11	0-0	.979	0	118	87	C101	102	-0.7

MIZEUR, BILL William Francis "Bad Bill"; B6.22.1897 Nokomis IL; D8.27.1976 Decatur IL; BL/TR/6´0˝/180; d9.30

YEAR	TM LG	G	AB	R	H	2B	3B	HR	RBI	BB-IB	HP	SO	AVG	OBP	SLG	AOPS	ABR	SB-CS	FA	FR	RNG	THR	GAMES AT POSITION	DL	BFW
1923	StL A	1	1	0	0	0	0	0	0	0	0	0	.000	.000	.000	-95	0	0-0	ø	0	—	—	/H	—	0.0
1924	StL A	1	1	0	0	0	0	0	0	0	0	0	.000	.000	.000	-94	0	0-0	ø	0	—	—	/H	—	0.0
Total	2	2	2	0	0	0	0	0	0	0	0	0	.000	.000	.000	-94	0	0-0	ø	0	—	—	—	—	0.0

MOATES, DAVE David Allan; B1.30.1948 Great Lakes IL; BL/TL/5´9˝/165; [TexA69 S4/87]; d9.21; Col Florida St.

YEAR	TM LG	G	AB	R	H	2B	3B	HR	RBI	BB-IB	HP	SO	AVG	OBP	SLG	AOPS	ABR	SB-CS	FA	FR	RNG	THR	GAMES AT POSITION	DL	BFW
1974	Tex A	1	0	0	0	0	0	0	0	0-0	0	0	ø	ø	ø	ø	0	0-0	ø	0	—	—	/R	0	0.0
1975	Tex A	54	175	21	48	9	0	3	14	13-0	0	15	.274	.321	.377	99	0	9-2	.984	0	93	184	O51(1/49/1)/D	0	0.0
1976	Tex A	85	137	21	33	7	1	0	13	11-2	0	18	.241	.293	.307	75	-4	6-3	.991	3	102	137	O66(8/37/25),D7	0	-0.2
Total	3	140	312	42	81	16	1	3	27	24-2	0	33	.260	.309	.346	89	-4	15-5	.987	4	97	162	O117(9/86/26),D8	0	-0.2

MOELLER, CHAD Chad Edward; B2.18.1975 Upland CA; BR/TR/6´3˝/(210–215); [MinA96 7/187]; d6.20; Col USC

YEAR	TM LG	G	AB	R	H	2B	3B	HR	RBI	BB-IB	HP	SO	AVG	OBP	SLG	AOPS	ABR	SB-CS	FA	FR	RNG	THR	GAMES AT POSITION	DL	BFW
2000	Min A	48	128	13	27	3	1	1	9	9-0	0	33	.211	.261	.273	34	-13	1-0	.979	2	175	51	C48	16	-0.8
2001	Ari N	25	56	8	13	0	1	1	2	6-1	0	12	.232	.306	.321	59	-4	0-0	1.000	-4	82	112	C25	0	-0.6
2002	†Ari N	37	105	10	30	11	1	2	16	17-3	0	23	.286	.385	.467	112	3	0-1	.997	9	101	95	C35	0	1.3
2003	Ari N	78	239	29	64	17	1	7	29	23-11	2	59	.268	.335	.435	92	-3	1-2	.987	-5	84	93	C76	0	-0.4
2004	Mil N	101	317	25	66	13	1	5	27	21-1	4	74	.208	.265	.303	46	-26	0-1	.999	14	93	88	C100	0	-0.6
2005	Mil N	66	199	23	41	9	1	7	23	13-1	1	48	.206	.257	.367	61	-12	0-0	.994	7	90	80	C65	0	-0.2
2006	Mil N	29	98	9	18	3	0	2	5	4-0	2	26	.184	.231	.276	29	-11	0-0	.995	-0	71	102	C29	0	-0.9
Total	7	384	1142	117	259	56	6	25	111	93-17	9	275	.227	.289	.352	63	-66	2-4	.993	22	99	86	C378	16	-2.2

MOELLER, DANNY Daniel Edward; B3.23.1885 DeWitt IA; D4.14.1951 Florence AL; BB/TR/5´11˝/165; d9.24; Col Millikin

YEAR	TM LG	G	AB	R	H	2B	3B	HR	RBI	BB-IB	HP	SO	AVG	OBP	SLG	AOPS	ABR	SB-CS	FA	FR	RNG	THR	GAMES AT POSITION	DL	BFW
1907	Pit N	11	42	4	12	1	1	0	3	4	0	—	.286	.348	.357	119	1	2	.800	-1	76	327	O11R	—	-0.1
1908	Pit N	36	109	14	21	3	1	0	9	9	0	—	.193	.254	.239	57	-5	4	.950	-3	0	0	O27(3/1/23)	—	-1.2
1912	Was A	132	519	90	143	26	10	6	46	52	4	—	.276	.346	.399	112	8	30	.944	3	98	124	O132(31/0/101)	—	0.3
1913	Was A	153	589	88	139	15	10	5	42	72	3	103	.236	.322	.321	86	-10	62	.926	3	104	116	O153(16/0/137)	—	-1.6
1914	Was A	151	571	83	143	19	10	1	45	71	7	89	.250	.341	.324	96	-1	26-25	.930	-1	101	104	O150(1/1/149)	—	-1.4
1915	Was A	118	438	65	99	11	10	2	23	59	1	63	.226	.319	.311	87	-7	32-10	.952	-5	89	90	O116(21/0/95)	—	-1.6
1916	Was A	78	240	30	59	8	1	1	23	30	2	35	.246	.335	.300	92	-2	13	.963	4	101	165	O63(23/0/40)	—	-0.1
	Cle A	25	30	5	2	0	0	0	1	5	0	6	.067	.200	.067	-19	-4	2	1.000	-0	108	0	O8(3/2/3)/2	—	-0.5
	Year	103	270	35	61	8	1	1	24	35	2	41	.226	.319	.274	78	-6	15	.966	4	101	154	O71(26/2/43)/2	—	-0.6
Total	7	704	2538	379	618	83	43	15	192	302	17	296	.243	.328	.328	93	-20	171-35	.938	-2	95	113	O660(98/4/559)/2	—	-6.2

MOFFETT, JOE Joseph William; B6.1859 Wheeling VA (now West Virginia); D2.24.1935 San Bernardino CA; 6´0˝/179; d5.6; b–Sam

YEAR	TM LG	G	AB	R	H	2B	3B	HR	RBI	BB-IB	HP	SO	AVG	OBP	SLG	AOPS	ABR	SB-CS	FA	FR	RNG	THR	GAMES AT POSITION	DL	BFW
1884	Tol AA	56	204	17	41	5	3	0	—	2	0	—	.201	.209	.255	49	-12	—	.957	-5	46	115	1b38,3b11,2b4,O3(1/3/0)	—	-1.8

MOFFETT, SAM Samuel R.; B3.14.1857 Wheeling VA (now West Virginia); D5.5.1907 Butte MT; BR/TR/6´0˝/175; d5.15; b–Joe; ▲

YEAR	TM LG	G	AB	R	H	2B	3B	HR	RBI	BB-IB	HP	SO	AVG	OBP	SLG	AOPS	ABR	SB-CS	FA	FR	RNG	THR	GAMES AT POSITION	DL	BFW
1884	Cle N	67	256	26	47	12	2	0	15	8	—	56	.184	.208	.246	41	-17	—	.827	6	186	0	O42(13/1/28),P24,1b2/32	—	-0.7
1887	Ind N	11	41	6	5	1	0	0	1	1	0	6	.122	.143	.146	-20	-7	2	.857	-1	75	0	P6,O5(1/2/3)	—	-0.2
1888	Ind N	10	35	6	4	0	0	0	0	5	0	4	.114	.225	.114	11	-3	0	.750	-2	41	342	P7,O3C	—	-0.2
Total	3	88	332	38	56	13	2	0	16	14	0	66	.169	.202	.220	30	-27	2	.821	2	169	0	O50(14/6/31),P37,1b2/23	—	-1.1

MOHARDT, JOHN John Henry; B1.21.1898 Pittsburgh PA; D11.24.1961 LaJolla CA; BR/TR/5´10˝/165; d4.15; Col Notre Dame

YEAR	TM LG	G	AB	R	H	2B	3B	HR	RBI	BB-IB	HP	SO	AVG	OBP	SLG	AOPS	ABR	SB-CS	FA	FR	RNG	THR	GAMES AT POSITION	DL	BFW
1922	Det A	5	1	2	1	0	0	0	0	1	0	0	1.000	1.000	1.000	436	1	0-1	1.000	0	407	0	O3(1/1/1)	—	0.1

MOHLER, KID Ernest Follette; B12.13.1870 Oneida IL; D11.4.1961 San Francisco CA; BL/TL/5´4.5˝/145; d9.29

YEAR	TM LG	G	AB	R	H	2B	3B	HR	RBI	BB-IB	HP	SO	AVG	OBP	SLG	AOPS	ABR	SB-CS	FA	FR	RNG	THR	GAMES AT POSITION	DL	BFW
1894	Was N	3	9	0	1	0	0	0	0	2	0	4	.111	.273	.111	-5	-2	0	.952	1	106	65	2b3	—	-0.1

MOHR, DUSTAN Dustan Kyle; B6.19.1976 Hattiesburg MS; BR/TR/6´0˝/(210–215); [CleA97 9/291]; d8.29; Col Alabama

YEAR	TM LG	G	AB	R	H	2B	3B	HR	RBI	BB-IB	HP	SO	AVG	OBP	SLG	AOPS	ABR	SB-CS	FA	FR	RNG	THR	GAMES AT POSITION	DL	BFW
2001	Min A	20	51	6	12	2	0	0	4	5-0	0	17	.235	.298	.275	51	-4	1-1	1.000	2	139	0	O19(6/0/15)/D	0	-0.3
2002	†Min A	120	383	55	103	23	2	12	45	31-3	1	86	.269	.325	.433	96	-2	6-3	.992	5	115	62	O113(28/1/94),D3	0	-0.2
2003	Min A	121	348	50	87	22	0	10	36	33-0	1	106	.250	.314	.399	84	-8	5-2	.976	3	117	35	O110(30/11/77),D6	0	-0.8
2004	SF N	117	263	52	72	20	1	7	28	46-3	8	64	.274	.394	.437	112	7	0-3	.981	4	108	136	O95(43/6/55),D2	0	0.7
2005	Col N	98	266	34	57	10	3	17	38	23-2	2	94	.214	.280	.466	82	-8	1-2	.987	4	114	108	O76(17/10/55)	23	-0.7
2006	Bos A	21	40	5	7	1	0	2	3	3-0	0	20	.175	.233	.350	47	-3	0-0	1.000	0	109	0	O20(7/13/5)	0	-0.3
Total	6	497	1351	202	338	78	6	48	154	141-8	12	387	.250	.325	.423	90	-18	13-11	.985	18	115	73	O433(131/41/301),D12	23	-1.6

MOKAN, JOHNNIE John Leo; B9.23.1895 Buffalo NY; D2.10.1985 Buffalo NY; BR/TR/5´7˝/165; d4.15

YEAR	TM LG	G	AB	R	H	2B	3B	HR	RBI	BB-IB	HP	SO	AVG	OBP	SLG	AOPS	ABR	SB-CS	FA	FR	RNG	THR	GAMES AT POSITION	DL	BFW
1921	Pit N	19	52	7	14	3	2	0	9	5	0	3	.269	.333	.404	92	-1	0-0	.946	-0	122	0	O15(6/0/7)	—	-0.2
1922	Pit N	31	89	9	23	3	1	0	8	9	0	3	.258	.327	.315	65	-4	0-1	.903	-2	72	134	O23(3/0/20)	—	-0.7
	Phi N	47	151	20	38	7	1	3	27	16	1	25	.252	.327	.371	73	-6	1-0	.905	-3	83	113	O37(36/2/3),3b2	—	-1.1
	Year	78	240	29	61	10	2	3	35	25	1	28	.254	.327	.350	70	-10	1-1	.905	-5	79	120	O60(39/2/23),3b2	—	-1.8
1923	Phi N	113	400	76	125	23	3	10	48	53	6	31	.313	.401	.460	113	10	6-11	.969	5	101	**150**	O105(84/21/2)/3	—	0.5
1924	Phi N	96	366	50	95	15	1	7	44	30	3	27	.260	.321	.363	74	-13	7-5	.986	-2	95	90	O94(93/2/0)	—	-2.2
1925	Phi N	75	209	30	69	11	2	6	42	27	4	9	.330	.417	.488	120	7	3-5	.984	-4	97	21	O68(36/32/2)	—	0.0
1926	Phi N	127	456	68	138	23	5	6	62	41	4	31	.303	.365	.414	104	3	4	.967	-1	92	117	O123(67/0/67)	—	-0.7
1927	Phi N	74	213	22	61	13	2	0	33	25	0	21	.286	.361	.366	94	-1	5	.962	-2	91	95	O63(27/9/28)	—	-0.7
Total	7	582	1936	282	563	98	17	32	273	206	18	150	.291	.364	.409	97	-5	26-22	.966	-9	94	104	O528(352/66/129),3b3	—	-5.1

MOLE, FENTON Fenton Le Roy "Muscles"; B6.14.1925 San Leandro CA; BL/TL/6´1.5˝/200; d9.1

YEAR	TM LG	G	AB	R	H	2B	3B	HR	RBI	BB-IB	HP	SO	AVG	OBP	SLG	AOPS	ABR	SB-CS	FA	FR	RNG	THR	GAMES AT POSITION	DL	BFW
1949	NY A	10	27	2	5	2	1	0	2	3	0	5	.185	.267	.333	58	-2	0-0	1.000	1	117	160	1b8	0	-0.1

MOLINA, BENGIE Benjamin Jose; B7.20.1974 Rio Piedras, PR; BR/TR/5´11˝/(200–225); d9.21; b–Jose b–Yadier; Col Arizona Western CC

YEAR	TM LG	G	AB	R	H	2B	3B	HR	RBI	BB-IB	HP	SO	AVG	OBP	SLG	AOPS	ABR	SB-CS	FA	FR	RNG	THR	GAMES AT POSITION	DL	BFW
1998	Ana A	2	1	0	0	0	0	0	0	0-0	0	0	.000	.000	.000	-98	0	0-0	1.000	-0	0	0	C2	0	0.0
1999	Ana A	31	101	8	26	5	0	1	10	6-0	2	6	.257	.312	.337	66	-5	0-1	.991	8	127	109	C30	0	0.4
2000	Ana A	130	473	59	133	20	2	14	71	23-0	6	33	.281	.318	.421	84	-13	1-0	.991	10	105	**129**	C127,D2	0	0.5
2001	Ana A	96	325	31	85	11	0	6	40	16-3	8	51	.262	.309	.351	73	-13	0-1	.991	1	107	106	C94/D	53	-0.6
2002	†Ana A	122	428	34	105	18	0	5	47	15-3	4	34	.245	.274	.322	60	-26	0-0	**.999**	13	142	122	C121	15	-0.4
2003	Ana A	119	409	37	115	24	0	14	71	13-2	2	31	.281	.304	.443	98	-3	1-1	.993	13	128	147	C117	25	1.7
2004	†Ana A	97	337	36	93	13	0	10	54	18-1	2	35	.276	.313	.404	90	-6	0-1	.995	1	83	88	C89,D5	31	0.0
2005	†LA A	119	410	45	121	17	0	15	69	27-2	1	41	.295	.336	.446	110	5	0-2	.996	-3	111	93	C105,D11	25	0.7
2006	Tor A	117	433	44	123	20	1	19	57	19-1	4	47	.284	.319	.467	96	-4	1-1	.997	-5	77	68	C99,D16	0	-0.3
Total	9	833	2917	294	801	128	3	84	419	137-12	29	278	.275	.310	.407	87	-65	3-7	.994	38	110	110	C784,D35	149	2.0

MOLINA, IZZY Islay; B6.3.1971 New York NY; BR/TR/6´0˝/(200–224); [OakA90 22/610]; d8.15

YEAR	TM LG	G	AB	R	H	2B	3B	HR	RBI	BB-IB	HP	SO	AVG	OBP	SLG	AOPS	ABR	SB-CS	FA	FR	RNG	THR	GAMES AT POSITION	DL	BFW
1996	Oak A	14	25	0	5	2	0	0	1	1-0	0	3	.200	.231	.280	29	-3	0-0	1.000	-3	46	0	C12/D	0	-0.5
1997	Oak A	48	111	6	22	3	1	3	7	3-0	0	17	.198	.219	.324	40	-11	0-0	.992	-4	73	87	C48	0	-1.2
1998	Oak A	6	2	1	1	0	0	0	0	0-0	0	0	.500	.500	.500	163	0	0-0	1.000	0	32	0	C5	0	0.1

YEAR	TM LG	G	AB	R	H	2B	3B	HR	RBI	BB-IB	HP	SO	AVG	OBP	SLG	AOPS	ABR	SB-CS	FA	FR	RNG	THR	GAMES AT POSITION	DL	BFW
2002	Bal A	1	3	1	1	0	0	0	0	0-0	0	0	.333	.333	.333	82	0	0-0	1.000	0	54	390	/C	0	0.0
Total	4	69	141	8	29	5	1	3	8	4-0	0	20	.206	.228	.319	40	-14	0-0	.993	-6	68	80	C66/D	0	-1.6
MOLINA, JOSE	Jose Benjamin (Matta); B6.3.1975 Bayamon, PR; BR/TR/6´1˝/(195–220); [ChiN93 14/390]; d9.6; b–Bengie b–Yadier																								
1999	Chi N	10	19	3	5	1	0	0	1	2-1	0	4	.263	.333	.316	66	-1	0-0	1.000	1	100	150	C10	0	0.1
2001	Ana A	15	37	8	10	3	0	2	4	3-0	0	8	.270	.325	.514	114	1	0-0	1.000	2	77	230	C15	42	0.4
2002	†Ana A	29	70	5	19	3	0	0	5	5-0	0	15	.271	.312	.314	71	-3	0-2	.983	4	84	151	C29	0	0.2
2003	Ana A	53	114	12	21	4	0	0	6	1-0	3	26	.184	.210	.219	15	-14	0-0	.996	-2	112	82	C53	0	-1.3
2004	†Ana A	73	203	26	53	10	2	3	25	10-0	0	52	.261	.296	.374	76	-8	4-1	.994	9	126	156	C70,1b2	0	0.6
2005	†LA A	75	184	14	42	4	0	6	25	13-0	2	41	.228	.286	.348	70	-9	2-0	.993	18	142	170	C65,1b4,D5	0	1.3
2006	LA A	78	225	18	54	17	0	4	22	9-0	2	49	.240	.273	.369	67	-11	1-0	.986	12	129	133	C76,1b3	0	0.5
Total	7	333	852	86	204	42	2	15	88	43-1	7	195	.239	.280	.346	65	-45	7-3	.991	45	121	145	C318,1b9,D5	42	1.8
MOLINA, YADIER	Yadier B.; B7.13.1982 Bayamon, PR; BR/TR/5´11˝/225; [StLN00 4/113]; d6.3; b–Bengie b–Jose																								
2004	†StL N	51	135	12	36	6	0	2	15	13-3	0	20	.267	.329	.356	77	-5	0-1	.993	3	228	101	C51	0	0.1
2005	†StL N	114	385	36	97	15	1	8	49	23-3	2	30	.252	.295	.358	70	-18	2-3	.991	24	**403**	109	C114/1	40	1.3
2006	†StL N	129	417	29	90	26	0	6	49	26-2	8	41	.216	.274	.321	52	-31	1-2	.995	17	**191**	109	C127,1b4	0	-0.6
Total	3	294	937	77	223	47	1	16	113	62-8	10	91	.238	.291	.342	63	-54	3-6	.993	44	283	108	C292,1b5	40	0.8
MOLINARO, BOB	Robert Joseph; B5.21.1950 Newark NJ; BL/TR/6´0˝/(175–180); [DetA68 2/38]; d9.18																								
1975	Det A	6	19	2	5	0	1	0	1	1-0	0	0	.263	.300	.368	84	-1	0-0	1.000	0	83	243	O6R	0	-0.1
1977	Det A	4	4	0	1	1	0	0	0	0-0	0	2	.250	.250	.500	94	0	0-0	ø	0	—	—	/H	0	0.0
	Chi A	1	2	0	1	0	0	0	0	0-0	0	1	.500	.500	.500	174	0	1-0	1.000	-0	90	0	/rf	0	0.0
	Year	5	6	0	2	1	0	0	0	0-0	0	3	.333	.333	.500	119	0	1-0	1.000	-0	90	0	/rf	0	0.0
1978	Chi A	105	286	39	75	5	5	6	27	19-2	3	12	.262	.314	.378	93	-4	22-6	1.000	-3	88	58	O62(12/1/50),D32	0	-0.8
1979	Bal A	8	6	0	0	0	0	0	0	1-0	0	3	.000	.143	.000	-60	-1	1-0	1.000	0	164	0	O5L	0	-0.1
1980	Chi A	119	344	48	100	16	4	5	36	26-7	7	29	.291	.348	.404	107	4	18-7	.957	-2	97	93	O49L,D47	0	0.0
1981	Chi A	47	42	7	11	1	1	1	9	8-1	1	1	.262	.377	.405	132	2	1-0	1.000	0	114	0	O2(1/0/1),D4	0	0.2
1982	Chi N	65	66	6	13	1	0	1	12	6-1	0	5	.197	.264	.258	45	-5	1-1	1.000	-1	27	0	O4L	0	-0.7
	Phi N	19	14	0	4	0	0	0	2	3-1	0	1	.286	.412	.286	95	0	1-0	ø	0	—	—	/H	0	0.0
	Year	84	80	6	17	1	0	1	14	9-2	0	6	.213	.292	.262	54	-5	2-1	1.000	-1	27	0	O4L	0	-0.7
1983	Phi N	19	18	1	2	1	0	1	3	0-0	0	2	.111	.105	.333	19	-2	0-0	ø	0	—	—	/H	0	-0.3
	Det A	8	2	3	0	0	0	0	0	1-0	0	1	.000	.333	.000	1	0	1-1	ø	0	—	—	/D	0	0.0
Total	8	401	803	106	212	25	11	14	90	65-12	11	57	.264	.324	.375	94	-7	46-15	.980	-6	91	77	O129(71/1/58),D84	0	-1.8
MOLITOR, PAUL	Paul Leo "The Igniter"; B8.22.1956 St.Paul MN; BR/TR/6´0˝/(175–195); [MilA77 1/3]; d4.7; C4; HF2004; Col Minnesota; OF(4/43/4)																								
1978	Mil A	125	521	73	142	26	4	6	45	19-2	4	54	.273	.301	.372	88	-9	30-12	.976	5	108	100	2b91,S31/3D	0	0.7
1979	Mil A	140	584	88	188	27	16	9	62	48-5	2	48	.322	.372	.469	126	20	33-13	.979	6	**113**	97	2b122,S10,D8	0	3.5
1980	Mil A✳	111	450	81	137	29	2	9	37	48-4	3	48	.304	.372	.438	125	17	34-7	.971	6	104	123	2b91,S12/3D	24	3.3
1981	†Mil A	64	251	45	67	11	0	2	19	25-1	3	29	.267	.341	.335	99	1	10-6	.976	-2	90	129	O46(0/43/4),D16	101	-0.3
1982	†Mil A	160	666	**136**	201	26	8	19	71	69-1	1	93	.302	.366	.450	130	27	41-9	.942	-3	99	**150**	3b150,S4,D6	0	2.8
1983	Mil A	152	608	95	164	28	6	15	47	59-4	2	74	.270	.333	.410	112	9	41-8	.966	2	105	112	3b146,D2	0	1.5
1984	Mil A	13	46	3	10	1	0	0	6	2-0	0	8	.217	.245	.239	37	-4	1-0	.933	3	156	219	3b7,D4	152	-0.1
1985	Mil A★	140	576	93	171	28	3	10	48	54-6	1	80	.297	.356	.408	109	8	21-7	.953	3	101	115	3b135,D4	15	1.2
1986	Mil A	105	437	62	123	24	6	9	55	40-0	0	81	.281	.340	.426	104	2	20-5	.944	0	94	155	3b91,D10,O4L	54	0.3
1987	Mil A	118	465	**114**	164	**41**	5	16	75	69-2	2	67	.353	.438	.566	159	43	45-10	.947	-6	85	109	D58,3b41,2b19	45	3.9
1988	Mil A★	154	609	115	190	34	6	13	60	71-8	2	54	.312	.384	.452	132	28	41-10	.941	-5	96	96	3b105,D49/2	0	2.8
1989	Mil A	155	615	84	194	35	4	11	56	64-4	4	67	.315	.379	.439	132	28	27-11	.950	11	115	97	3b112,D28,2b16	11	4.1
1990	Mil A	103	418	64	119	27	6	12	45	37-4	1	51	.285	.343	.464	125	13	18-3	.988	7	112	87	2b60,1b37,3b2,D4	55	2.1
1991	Mil A★	158	665	**133**	**216**	32	**13**	17	75	77-16	6	62	.325	.399	.489	147	44	19-8	.986	-2	94	130	D112,1b46	0	3.6
1992	Mil A★	158	609	89	195	36	7	12	89	73-12	3	66	.320	.389	.461	141	36	31-6	.996	-5	70	117	D108,1b48	0	2.9
1993	†Tor A★	160	636	121	**211**	37	5	22	111	77-3	3	71	.332	.402	.509	142	39	22-4	.985	-2	79	78	D137,1b23	0	3.1
1994	Tor A★	**115**	454	86	155	30	4	14	75	55-4	1	48	.341	.410	.518	137	27	20-0	1.000	0	88	139	D110,1b5	0	2.3
1995	Tor A	130	525	63	142	31	2	15	60	61-1	5	57	.270	.350	.423	100	1	12-0	ø	0	0	0	D129	0	-0.3
1996	Min A	161	660	99	**225**	41	8	9	113	56-10	3	72	.341	.390	.468	115	17	18-6	.993	1	117	91	D143,1b17	0	0.9
1997	Min A	135	538	63	164	32	4	10	89	45-8	0	73	.305	.351	.435	104	3	11-4	.991	-0	97	64	D122,1b12	18	-0.3
1998	Min A	126	502	75	141	29	5	4	69	45-5	1	41	.281	.335	.382	86	-10	9-2	1.000	1	124	57	D115,1b9	24	-1.4
Total	21	2683	10835	1782	3319	605	114	234	1307	1094-100	47	1244	.306	.369	.448	122	340	504-131	.950	20	102	122	D1174,3b791,2b400,1b197,S57,O50C499		36.6
MOLLENKAMP, FRED	Frederick Henry; B3.15.1890 Cincinnati OH; D11.1.1948 Cincinnati OH; 6´2˝/195; d8.29																								
1914	Phi N	3	8	0	1	0	0	0	0	2	0	0	.125	.300	.125	26	-1	0	1.000	2	328	129	1b3	—	0.1
MOLLWITZ, FRITZ	Frederick August; B6.16.1890 Coburg, Germany; D10.3.1967 Bradenton FL; BR/TR/6´2˝/170; d9.26																								
1913	Chi N	2	7	1	3	0	0	0	0	0	0	0	.429	.429	.429	145	0	0	1.000	-0	0	0	1b2	—	0.0
1914	Chi N	13	20	0	3	0	0	0	1	0	0	3	.150	.150	.150	-11	-3	1	.962	-0	66	0	1b4/rf	—	-0.4
	Cin N	32	111	12	18	2	0	0	5	3	2	9	.162	.198	.180	12	-12	2	.991	1	112	105	1b32	—	-1.3
	Year	45	131	12	21	2	0	0	6	3	2	12	.160	.191	.176	9	-15	3	.989	1	108	97	1b36/rf	—	-1.7
1915	Cin N	153	525	36	136	21	3	1	51	15	1	49	.259	.281	.316	79	-15	19-11	**.996**	-0	95	**122**	1b153	—	-2.1
1916	Cin N	65	183	12	41	4	4	0	16	5	0	12	.224	.245	.290	65	-9	6	.981	-1	100	104	1b54	—	-1.2
	Chi N	33	71	1	19	2	0	0	11	7	0	6	.268	.333	.296	85	-1	4	.976	-1	123	95	1b19,O6(4/0/2)	—	-0.2
	Year	98	254	13	60	6	4	0	27	12	0	18	.236	.271	.291	71	-9	10	.980	-1	105	102	1b73,O6(4/0/2)	—	-1.4
1917	Pit N	36	140	15	36	4	1	0	12	8	0	8	.257	.297	.300	81	-3	4	.994	-1	87	69	1b36/2	—	-0.6
1918	Pit N	119	432	43	116	12	7	0	45	23	0	24	.269	.305	.329	90	-6	23	.990	-1	95	101	1b119	—	-1.1
1919	Pit N	56	168	11	29	2	4	0	12	15	2	18	.173	.249	.232	43	-12	9	.994	-3	69	91	1b53/rf	—	-1.8
	StL N	25	83	7	19	3	0	0	5	7	0	3	.229	.289	.265	71	-3	2	.994	1	102	139	1b25	—	-0.3
	Year	81	251	18	48	5	4	0	17	22	2	21	.191	.262	.243	52	-15	11	.994	-2	80	108	1b78/rf	—	-2.1
Total	7	534	1740	138	420	50	19	1	158	83	5	132	.241	.278	.294	72	-64	70-11	.991	-5	94	106	1b497,O8(4/0/4)/2	—	-9.0
MONACO, BLAS	Blas; B11.16.1915 San Antonio TX; D2.10.2000 San Antonio TX; BB/TR/5´11˝/170; d8.18																								
1937	Cle A	5	7	0	2	0	1	0	2	0	1	2	.286	.375	.571	134	0	0-0	1.000	0	107	0	2b3	—	0.0
1946	Cle A	12	6	2	0	0	0	0	0	1	0	1	.000	.143	.000	-62	-1	0-0	ø	0	—	—	/H	0	-0.1
Total	2	17	13	2	2	0	1	0	2	1	1	3	.154	.267	.308	53	-1	0-0	1.000	0	107	0	2b3	0	-0.1
MONAHAN, SHANE	Shane Hartland; B8.12.1974 Syosset NY; BL/TR/6´0˝/195; [SeaA95 2/33]; d7.9; Col Clemson																								
1998	Sea A	62	211	17	51	8	1	4	28	8-0	0	53	.242	.269	.346	58	-14	1-2	.992	2	111	91	O62(61/3/2)	0	-1.4
1999	Sea A	16	15	3	2	0	0	0	0	0-0	0	6	.133	.133	.133	-32	-3	0-0	1.000	-0	105	0	O9(7/0/3),D3	0	-0.3
Total	2	78	226	20	53	8	1	4	28	8-0	0	59	.235	.261	.332	52	-17	1-2	.992	1	111	86	O71(68/3/5),D3	0	-1.7
MONCEWICZ, FREDDIE	Frederick Alfred; B9.1.1903 Brockton MA; D4.23.1969 Brockton MA; BR/TR/5´8.5˝/175; d6.19; Col Boston College																								
1928	Bos A	3	1	0	0	0	0	0	0	0	0	1	.000	.000	.000	-99	0	0-0	1.000	0	101	0	S2	—	0.0
MONCHAK, ALEX	Alex; B12.22.1919 Bayonne NJ; BR/TR/6´0˝/180; d6.22; C17																								
1940	Phi N	19	14	1	2	0	0	0	0	0	0	6	.143	.143	.143	-22	-2	1	.833	-1	91	92	S9/2	—	-0.3
MONDAY, RICK	Robert James; B11.20.1945 Batesville AR; BL/TL/6´3˝/(195–200); [OakA65 1/1]; d9.3; Col Arizona St.																								
1966	KC A	17	41	4	4	1	1	0	2	6-0	0	16	.098	.213	.171	12	-5	1-1	.964	-1	88	130	O15C	0	-0.7
1967	KC A	124	406	52	102	14	6	14	58	42-2	2	107	.251	.322	.419	122	10	3-6	.972	8	109	**220**	O113(3/110/0)	0	1.5
1968	Oak A★	148	482	56	132	24	7	8	49	72-7	4	143	.274	.371	.402	141	27	14-6	.978	-3	94	121	O144C	0	2.3
1969	Oak A	122	399	57	108	17	4	12	54	72-11	5	100	.271	.388	.424	132	20	12-3	.964	-9	96	40	O119C	29	1.0
1970	Oak A	112	376	63	109	19	7	10	37	58-0	2	99	.290	.387	.457	136	20	17-11	.981	-3	103	45	O109C	0	1.5
1971	†Oak A	116	355	53	87	9	3	18	56	49-5	0	93	.245	.335	.439	121	9	6-9	.984	-5	94	93	O111C	0	-0.1
1972	Chi N	138	434	68	108	22	5	11	42	78-8	1	102	.249	.362	.399	105	6	12-9	**.996**	-10	87	78	O134(0/132/2)	0	-0.8
1973	Chi N	149	554	93	148	24	5	26	56	92-7	1	124	.267	.372	.469	122	19	5-12	.973	-9	93	101	O148C	0	0.4
1974	Chi N	142	538	84	158	19	7	20	58	70-6	2	94	.294	.375	.467	129	21	7-9	.984	-9	87	118	O139C	0	0.7
1975	Chi N	136	491	89	131	29	4	17	60	83-12	1	95	.267	.373	.446	121	16	8-3	.973	-7	96	74	O131C	0	0.7
1976	Chi N	137	534	107	145	20	5	32	77	60-8	2	125	.272	.346	.507	129	19	5-9	.993	-2	105	61	O103(5/99/0),1b32	0	1.0

YEAR	TM LG	G	AB	R	H	2B	3B	HR	RBI	BB-IB	HP	SO	AVG	OBP	SLG	AOPS	ABR	SB-CS	FA	FR	RNG	THR	GAMES AT POSITION	DL	BFW
1977	†LA N	118	392	47	90	13	1	15	48	60-6	0	109	.230	.330	.383	91	-5	1-4	.991	-16	78	43	O115(0/114/1),1b3	0	-2.3
1978	†LA N★	119	342	54	87	14	1	19	57	49-11	1	100	.254	.348	.468	126	12	2-4	.995	-6	92	50	O103(11/80/30)/1	0	0.3
1979	LA N	12	33	2	10	0	0	0	2	5-0	0	6	.303	.395	.303	95	0	0-0	.964	0	123	0	O10(0/8/3)	146	0.0
1980	LA N	96	194	35	52	7	1	10	25	28-3	1	49	.268	.363	.469	134	9	2-2	.969	-4	93	30	O50(1/31/25)	0	0.4
1981	†LA N	66	130	24	41	1	2	11	25	24-3	1	42	.315	.423	.608	199	17	1-2	.962	-3	85	40	O41(6/0/37)	0	1.3
1982	LA N	104	210	37	54	6	4	11	42	39-6	1	51	.257	.372	.481	142	13	2-1	.943	-5	70	116	O57(18/0/40),1b4	0	0.6
1983	†LA N	99	178	21	44	7	1	6	20	29-9	0	42	.247	.351	.399	108	3	0-0	.969	-2	97	41	O44(14/0/31),1b4	0	-0.1
1984	LA N	31	47	4	9	2	0	1	7	8-3	0	16	.191	.309	.298	71	-2	0-0	.987	-1	79	48	1b10,O2(2/0/1)	0	-0.3
Total	19	1986	6136	950	1619	248	64	241	775	924-107	24	1513	.264	.361	.443	124	209	98-91	.979	-85	93	86	O1688(60/1490/170),1b54	175	7.4
Mondesi, Raul	Raul Ramon (Avelino); B3.12.1971 San Cristobal, D.R.; BR/TR/5´11˝/(200–230); d7.19																								
1993	LA N	42	86	13	25	3	1	4	10	4-0	0	16	.291	.322	.488	120	2	4-1	.951	2	110	174	O40(20/6/17)	0	0.3
1994	LA N	112	434	63	133	27	8	16	56	16-5	2	78	.306	.333	.516	124	12	11-8	.965	1	94	**194**	O112(0/15/109)	0	0.8
1995	†LA N★	139	536	91	153	23	6	26	88	33-4	4	96	.285	.328	.496	123	14	27-4	.980	9	106	174	O138(0/24/114)	0	2.2
1996	†LA N	157	634	98	188	40	7	24	88	32-9	5	122	.297	.334	.495	123	18	14-7	.967	7	113	103	O157R	0	1.7
1997	LA N	159	616	95	191	42	5	30	87	44-7	6	105	.310	.360	.541	141	35	32-15	.989	9	118	87	O159R	0	3.6
1998	LA N	148	580	85	162	26	5	30	90	30-4	3	112	.279	.316	.497	116	9	16-10	.980	-9	92	67	O148(0/94/54)	0	-0.1
1999	LA N	159	601	98	152	29	5	33	99	71-6	3	134	.253	.332	.483	109	6	36-9	.982	-3	101	66	O158(0/1/158)	0	0.0
2000	Tor A	96	388	78	105	22	2	24	67	32-0	3	73	.271	.329	.523	108	3	22-6	.967	1	105	75	O96R	59	0.2
2001	Tor A	149	572	88	144	26	4	27	84	73-3	6	128	.252	.342	.453	105	4	30-11	.972	-1	89	179	O149R	0	-0.2
2002	Tor A	75	299	51	67	16	1	15	45	31-1	3	57	.224	.301	.435	90	-5	9-2	.984	-2	96	76	O62R,D13	0	-0.9
	†NY A	71	270	39	65	18	0	11	43	28-2	2	46	.241	.315	.430	97	-1	6-4	.969	-6	81	93	O70(0/11/59)/D	0	-1.0
	Year	146	569	90	132	34	1	26	88	59-3	5	103	.232	.308	.432	93	-6	15-6	.976	-8	88	85	O132(0/11/121),D14	0	-1.9
2003	NY A	98	361	56	93	23	3	16	49	38-6	2	66	.258	.330	.471	110	5	17-7	.986	3	103	129	O97R/D	0	0.4
	Ari N	45	162	27	49	8	1	8	22	18-0	1	31	.302	.372	.512	119	5	5-4	.964	-1	103	38	O43(0/2/42)	0	0.1
2004	Pit N	26	99	8	28	8	0	2	14	11-0	0	27	.283	.355	.424	100	0	0-2	.939	-1	94	135	O26(14/0/12)	0	-0.2
	Ana A	8	34	2	4	1	0	1	1	2-0	1	4	.118	.189	.235	10	-5	0-1	1.000	1	101	256	O7C/D	49	-0.4
2005	Atl N	41	142	17	30	7	1	4	17	12-3	0	35	.211	.271	.359	63	-8	0-1	.986	-3	86	87	O40R	0	-1.3
Total	13	1525	5814	909	1589	319	49	271	860	475-50	41	1130	.273	.331	.485	113	94	229-92	.976	7	101	114	O1502(34/160/1325),D16	108	5.2
Money, Don	Donald Wayne "Brooks"; B6.7.1947 Washington DC; BR/TR/6´1˝/(170–190); d4.10; OFL																								
1968	Phi N	4	13	1	3	2	0	0	2	2-1	0	4	.231	.333	.385	115	0	0-1	1.000	-1	65	137	S4	0	-0.1
1969	Phi N	127	450	41	103	22	2	6	42	43-5	1	83	.229	.296	.327	77	-14	1-3	.969	18	111	101	S126	0	1.8
1970	Phi N	120	447	66	132	25	4	14	66	43-6	7	68	.295	.361	.463	123	15	4-7	.961	5	96	119	3b119,S2	0	1.8
1971	Phi N	121	439	40	98	22	8	7	38	31-10	3	80	.223	.276	.358	79	-14	4-1	.953	7	110	132	3b68,O40L,2b20	0	-0.8
1972	Phi N	152	536	54	119	16	2	15	52	41-5	2	92	.222	.278	.343	74	-19	5-7	**.978**	15	102	**128**	3b151,S2	0	-0.8
1973	Mil A	145	556	75	158	28	2	11	61	53-3	3	53	.284	.347	.401	112	10	22-5	**.971**	-11	93	94	3b124,S21	0	0.3
1974	Mil A☆	159	629	85	178	32	3	15	65	62-5	2	80	.283	.346	.415	120	16	19-6	**.989**	-7	98	123	3b157/2D	0	1.2
1975	Mil A	109	405	58	112	16	1	15	43	31-1	3	51	.277	.331	.432	114	6	7-9	.951	-6	91	108	3b99,S7	27	-0.1
1976	Mil A★	117	439	51	117	18	4	12	62	47-2	0	50	.267	.333	.408	120	11	6-5	.958	-2	95	116	3b103,D10/S	0	0.8
1977	Mil A✳	152	570	86	159	28	3	25	83	57-2	7	70	.279	.348	.470	121	17	8-5	.981	18	**111**	112	2b116,O23L,3b15,D7	0	3.9
1978	Mil A★	137	518	88	152	30	2	14	54	48-2	7	70	.293	.361	.440	123	17	3-0	.994	6	100	105	1b61,2b36,3b25,D15,S2	0	2.2
1979	Mil A	92	350	52	83	20	1	6	38	40-0	2	47	.237	.316	.351	80	-9	1-0	1.000	-3	124	140	D33,3b26,1b19,2b16	45	-1.3
1980	Mil A	86	289	39	74	17	1	17	46	40-0	1	36	.256	.348	.498	132	13	0-0	.940	1	104	169	3b55,1b14,D14,2b2	0	1.1
1981	†Mil A	60	185	17	40	7	0	2	14	19-0	1	27	.216	.288	.286	70	-7	0-0	.977	-7	92	83	3b56/1D	0	-1.6
1982	†Mil A	96	275	40	78	14	3	16	55	32-2	1	38	.284	.360	.531	149	18	0-2	.923	3	117	66	D66,3b16,1b11/2	0	1.7
1983	Mil A	43	114	5	17	5	0	1	8	11-1	0	17	.149	.220	.219	24	-12	0-0	.980	4	142	0	D28,3b11,1b2	27	-0.9
Total	16	1720	6215	798	1623	302	36	176	729	600-45	40	866	.261	.328	.406	106	48	80-51	.968	39	99	118	3b1025,2b192,D176,S165,1b108,063L99		9.2
Monroe, Craig	Craig Keystone; B2.27.1977 Texarkana TX; BR/TR/6´1˝/(195–220); [TexA95 8/206]; d7.28																								
2001	Tex A	27	52	8	11	1	0	2	5	6-0	0	18	.212	.293	.346	66	-3	2-0	1.000	4	135	292	O24(6/0/21)/D	0	0.1
2002	Det A	13	25	3	3	1	0	1	1	0-0	1	5	.120	.154	.280	12	-3	0-2	.950	1	133	245	O9(4/0/5),D3	0	-0.3
2003	Det A	128	425	51	102	18	1	23	70	27-2	2	89	.240	.287	.449	95	-5	4-2	.970	1	99	122	O108(75/2/38),D13	0	-0.9
2004	Det A	128	447	65	131	27	3	18	72	29-1	2	79	.293	.337	.488	116	9	3-4	.960	0	106	72	O125(65/27/51),D2	17	0.5
2005	Det A	157	567	69	157	30	3	20	89	40-4	3	95	.277	.322	.446	105	3	8-3	.981	-7	89	113	O156(69/33/85)/D	0	-0.8
2006	†Det A	147	541	89	138	35	2	28	92	37-3	1	126	.255	.301	.482	101	-2	2-2	.980	-5	82	149	O116(113/8/0),D30	0	-1.2
Total	6	600	2057	285	542	112	9	92	329	139-10	9	412	.263	.310	.461	102	-1	19-13	.973	-6	95	120	O538(332/70/200),D50	17	-2.6
Monroe, Frank	Frank W.; B Hamilton OH; d7.18																								
1884	Ind AA	2	8	1	0	0	0	0	—	0	0	—	.000	.000	.000	-99	-2	—	1.000	-1	0	0	/rfC	—	-0.3
Monroe, John	John Allen; B8.24.1898 Farmersville TX; D6.19.1956 Conroe TX; BL/TR/5´10˝/160; d4.16																								
1921	NY N	19	21	4	3	0	0	1	3	3	1	6	.143	.280	.286	50	-2	0-0	.846	-1	98	44	2b8/S	—	-0.2
	Phi N	41	133	13	38	4	2	1	8	11	1	9	.286	.345	.368	82	-3	2-2	.938	4	122	85	2b28,3b9	—	0.2
	Year	60	154	17	41	4	2	2	11	14	2	15	.266	.335	.357	79	-4	2-2	.920	3	118	78	2b36,3b9/S	—	0.0
Montague, Ed	Edward Francis; B7.24.1905 San Francisco CA; D6.17.1988 Daly City CA; BR/TR/5´10˝/165; d5.14																								
1928	Cle A	32	51	12	12	0	1	0	3	6	2	7	.235	.339	.275	62	-3	0-0	.914	2	117	123	S15,3b9	—	0.0
1930	Cle A	58	179	37	47	5	2	1	16	37	1	38	.263	.392	.330	82	-3	1-5	.917	-7	91	76	S46,3b13	—	-0.6
1931	Cle A	64	193	27	55	8	3	1	26	21	1	22	.285	.358	.373	87	-3	3-4	.924	13	118	86	S64	—	1.2
1932	Cle A	66	192	29	47	5	1	0	24	21	2	24	.245	.326	.281	55	-13	3-3	.891	-14	88	75	S57,3b11	—	-2.2
Total	4	220	615	105	161	18	7	2	69	85	6	91	.262	.357	.324	74	-22	7-12	.912	-6	102	82	S182,3b33	—	-1.6
Montanez, Willie	Guillermo (Naranjo); B4.1.1948 Catano, PR; BL/TL/6´1˝/(185–193); d4.12																								
1966	Cal A	8	2	2	0	0	0	0	0	0-0	0	2	.000	.000	.000	-99	-1	1-0	1.000	0	0	1092	1b2	0	0.0
1970	Phi N	18	25	3	6	0	0	0	3	1-1	0	4	.240	.269	.240	38	-2	0-0	1.000	1	89	306	O10(1/0/9),1b5	0	-0.2
1971	Phi N	158	599	78	153	27	6	30	99	67-14	3	105	.255	.327	.471	125	19	4-7	.972	-6	93	114	O158(0/137/24),1b9	0	0.6
1972	Phi N	147	531	60	131	**39**	3	13	64	58-13	1	108	.247	.320	.405	103	3	1-3	.985	8	106	**201**	O130C,1b14	0	0.6
1973	Phi N	146	552	69	145	16	5	11	65	46-7	6	80	.263	.324	.370	90	-8	2-6	.994	-2	91	103	1b99,O51R	0	-2.3
1974	Phi N	143	527	55	160	33	1	7	79	32-6	3	57	.304	.343	.410	106	4	3-6	.992	-2	92	108	1b137/rf	0	-1.0
1975	Phi N	21	84	9	24	8	0	2	16	4-0	0	12	.286	.315	.452	107	1	1-0	.990	2	134	122	1b21	0	0.1
	SF N	135	518	52	158	26	2	8	85	45-8	4	50	.305	.359	.409	111	8	5-3	.994	-1	93	99	1b134	0	-0.3
	Year	156	602	61	182	34	2	10	101	49-8	4	62	.302	.353	.415	110	9	6-3	.993	1	99	102	1b155	0	-0.2
1976	SF N	60	230	22	71	15	2	2	20	15-5	1	15	.309	.351	.417	115	4	2-1	.989	3	125	108	1b58	0	0.3
	Atl N	103	420	52	135	14	0	9	64	21-6	0	32	.321	.353	.419	112	6	0-4	.986	-8	76	96	1b103	0	-1.2
	Year	163	650	74	206	29	2	11	84	36-11	1	47	.317	.352	.418	113	10	2-5	.987	-4	94	100	1b161	0	-0.9
1977	Atl N★	136	544	70	156	31	1	20	68	35-3	0	60	.287	.328	.458	98	-2	1-1	.992	-6	80	74	1b134	24	-1.7
1978	NY N	159	609	66	156	32	0	17	96	60-19	1	92	.256	.320	.392	102	1	9-4	.995	2	103	108	1b158	0	-0.7
1979	NY N	109	410	36	96	19	0	5	47	25-7	1	48	.234	.277	.317	64	-21	0-1	.989	3	115	107	1b108	0	-2.6
	Tex A	38	144	19	46	6	0	8	24	8-1	1	14	.319	.357	.528	137	7	0-1	.995	1	112	84	1b19,D17	0	0.5
1980	SD N	128	481	39	132	12	4	6	63	36-9	3	52	.274	.325	.353	97	-3	3-4	.994	4	114	107	1b124	0	-0.8
	Mon N	14	19	1	4	0	0	0	1	3-1	0	3	.211	.318	.211	49	-1	0-1	1.000	-0	86	0	1b4	0	-0.2
	Year	142	500	40	136	12	4	6	64	39-10	3	55	.272	.325	.348	94	-5	3-5	.994	4	113	104	1b128	0	-1.0
1981	Mon N	26	62	6	11	0	1	0	5	4-0	0	9	.177	.227	.210	24	-6	0-0	.992	1	128	86	1b16	0	-0.7
	Pit N	29	38	2	10	0	0	1	1	1-0	0	2	.263	.282	.342	73	-2	0-0	1.000	-1	23	81	1b11	0	-0.3
	Year	55	100	8	21	0	1	1	6	5-0	0	11	.210	.248	.260	42	-8	0-0	.995	-0	95	84	1b27	0	-1.0
1982	Pit N	36	32	4	9	1	0	0	1	3-3	0	3	.281	.343	.313	81	-1	0-0	1.000	0	178	166	1b2,O2L	0	-0.1
	Phi N	18	16	0	1	0	0	0	1	1-0	0	3	.063	.118	.063	-47	-3	0-0	1.000	0	190	0	1b6	0	-0.3
	Year	54	48	4	10	1	0	0	2	4-3	0	6	.208	.269	.229	39	-4	0-0	1.000	1	186	58	1b8,O2L	0	-0.4
Total	14	1632	5843	645	1604	279	25	139	802	465-103	24	751	.275	.327	.402	101	3	32-42	.992	0	99	101	1b1164,O352(2/267/85),D17	24	-10.3
Monteagudo, Rene	Rene (Miranda); B3.12.1916 Havana, Cuba; D9.14.1973 Hialeah FL; BL/TL/5´7˝/165; d9.6; s–Aurelio; ▲																								
1938	Was A	5	6	0	3	0	0	0	1	0	0	0	.500	.500	.500	162	1	0-0	1.000	-1	24	0	P5	—	0.0
1940	Was A	27	33	4	6	1	1	0	1	1	0	4	.182	.206	.273	24	0	0-0	.941	-1	60	83	P27	—	0.0
1944	Was A	10	38	2	11	2	0	0	4	0	0	1	.289	.289	.342	84	-1	0-0	.929	-0	82	201	O9R	0	-0.2

YEAR	TM LG	G	AB	R	H	2B	3B	HR	RBI	BB-IB	HP	SO	AVG	OBP	SLG	AOPS	ABR	SB-CS	FA	FR	RNG	THR	GAMES AT POSITION	DL	BFW
1945	Phi N	114	193	26	58	6	0	0	15	28	0	7	.301	.389	.332	104	3	2	.918	-2	82	196	O35(12/0/23),P14	0	-0.1
Total	4	156	270	32	78	9	1	0	21	29	0	12	.289	.358	.330	94	3	2-0	.889	-4	57	98	P46,O44(12/0/32)	0	-0.3
MONTEMAYOR, FELIPE	Felipe Angel "Monty"; B2.7.1928 Monterrey, Nuevo Leon, Mexico; BL/TL/6´2˝/(180–185); d4.14																								
1953	Pit N	28	55	5	6	4	0	0	2	4	3	13	.109	.210	.182	3	-8	0-0	1.000	1	100	205	O12(1/11/0)	0	-0.7
1955	Pit N	36	95	10	20	1	3	2	8	18-2	1	24	.211	.342	.347	85	-2	1-0	.957	-3	89	0	O28(6/14/9)	0	-0.5
Total	2	64	150	15	26	5	3	2	10	22-2	4	37	.173	.295	.287	55	-10	1-0	.974	-2	93	67	O40(7/25/9)	0	-1.2
MONTERO, MIGUEL	Miguel Angel; B7.9.1983 Caracas, Venezuela; BL/TR/5´11˝/195; d9.6																								
2006	Ari N	6	16	0	4	1	0	0	3	1-0	0	3	.250	.294	.313	53	-1	0-0	1.000	2	90	97	C5	0	0.1
MONTGOMERY, AL	Alvin Atlas; B7.3.1920 Loving NM; D4.26.1942 Waverly VA; BR/TR/5´10.5˝/185; d6.20																								
1941	Bos N	42	52	4	10	1	0	0	4	9	1	8	.192	.323	.212	55	-3	0	.976	-3	*95*	*92*	C30	0	-0.5
MONTGOMERY, RAY	Raymond James; B8.8.1969 Bronxville NY; BR/TR/6´3˝/195; [HouN90 13/359]; d7.3; Col Fordham																								
1996	Hou N	12	14	4	3	1	0	1	4	1-0	0	5	.214	.267	.500	104	0	0-0	1.000	0	121	0	O6(5/1/2)	0	0.0
1997	Hou N	29	68	8	16	4	1	0	4	5-0	0	18	.235	.276	.324	62	-4	0-0	1.000	1	94	195	O18(2/2/15)	103	-0.4
1998	Hou N	6	5	2	2	0	0	0	0	0-0	0	0	.400	.400	.400	114	0	0-0	1.000	0	155	0	O2(1/0/1)	6	0.0
Total	3	47	87	14	21	5	1	1	8	6-0	0	23	.241	.281	.356	71	-4	0-0	1.000	1	100	160	O26(8/3/18)	109	-0.4
MONTGOMERY, BOB	Robert Edward; B4.16.1944 Nashville TN; BR/TR/6´1˝/(195–210); d9.6																								
1970	Bos A	22	78	8	14	2	0	1	4	6-0	1	20	.179	.244	.244	34	-7	0-0	.981	0	99	143	C22	0	-0.6
1971	Bos A	67	205	19	49	11	2	2	24	16-4	3	43	.239	.300	.341	77	-6	1-0	.989	-6	93	68	C66	0	-0.9
1972	Bos A	24	77	7	22	1	0	2	7	3-0	0	17	.286	.309	.377	99	0	0-0	.985	-3	106	49	C22	0	-0.2
1973	Bos A	34	128	18	41	6	2	7	25	7-0	0	36	.320	.353	.563	146	7	0-0	.974	-0	80	118	C33	0	0.8
1974	Bos A	88	254	26	64	10	0	4	38	13-1	1	50	.252	.287	.339	75	-8	3-0	.977	-3	98	101	C79,D5	0	-0.8
1975	†Bos A	62	195	16	44	10	1	2	26	4-0	1	37	.226	.241	.318	54	-12	1-1	.987	-7	104	86	C53,1b6,D3	0	-1.8
1976	Bos A	31	93	10	23	3	1	3	13	5-1	0	20	.247	.283	.398	88	-2	0-1	.983	-3	102	77	C30/D	0	-0.4
1977	Bos A	17	40	6	12	2	0	2	7	4-0	1	9	.300	.370	.500	123	1	0-0	.982	-3	89	78	C15	0	-0.1
1978	Bos A	10	29	2	7	1	1	0	5	2-0	0	12	.241	.290	.345	71	-1	0-0	.976	-0	299	83	C10	0	-0.1
1979	Bos A	32	86	13	30	4	1	0	7	4-1	0	24	.349	.374	.419	109	1	1-0	.984	-4	71	32	C31	62	-0.2
Total	10	387	1185	125	306	50	8	23	156	64-7	7	268	.258	.296	.372	83	-27	6-2	.983	-30	100	85	C361,D9,1b6	62	-4.3
MONTOYO, CHARLIE	Jose Carlos (Diaz); B10.17.1965 Florida, PR; BR/TR/5´10˝/170; [MilA87 6/149]; d9.7; Col Louisiana Tech																								
1993	Mon N	4	5	1	2	1	0	0	3	0-0	0	0	.400	.400	.600	156	0	0-0	ø	-1	0	0	2b3	0	-0.1
MONTREUIL, AL	Allan Arthur; B8.23.1943 New Orleans LA; BR/TR/5´5˝/158; d9.1; Col Loyola–New Orleans																								
1972	Chi N	5	11	0	1	0	0	0	0	1-0	0	4	.091	.167	.091	-23	-2	0-0	1.000	-1	75	46	2b5	0	-0.3
MONZON, DAN	Daniel Francisco; B5.17.1946 Bronx NY; D1.21.1996 Santo Domingo, D.R.; BR/TR/5´10˝/182; [MinA67 S2/23]; d4.25; Col Buena Vista																								
1972	Min A	55	55	13	15	1	0	0	5	8-0	0	12	.273	.365	.291	92	0	1-0	.977	1	102	37	2b13,3b5,S3/lf	0	0.2
1973	Min A	39	76	10	17	1	1	0	4	11-0	1	9	.224	.326	.263	66	-3	1-0	.968	1	81	93	2b17,3b14/lf	0	-0.1
Total	2	94	131	23	32	2	1	0	9	19-0	1	21	.244	.342	.275	77	-3	2-0	.971	2	90	69	2b30,3b19,S3,O2L	0	0.1
MOOCK, JOE	Joseph Geoffrey; B3.12.1944 Plaquemine LA; BL/TR/6´1˝/180; [NYN65 3/42]; d9.1; Col Louisiana St.																								
1967	NY N	13	40	2	9	2	0	0	5	0-0	0	7	.225	.225	.275	43	-3	0-0	.917	1	114	166	3b12	0	-0.2
MOOLIC, GEORGE	George Henry "Prunes"; B3.12.1865 Lawrence MA; D2.19.1915 Methuen MA; BR/TR/5´7˝/145; d5.1																								
1886	Chi N	16	56	9	8	3	0	0	2	2	—	17	.143	.172	.196	10	-6	0	.945	3	—	—	C15,O2R	—	-0.2
MOON, WALLY	Wallace Wade; B4.3.1930 Bay AR; BL/TR/6´0˝/(169–175); d4.13; C1; Col Texas A&M																								
1954	StL N	151	635	106	193	29	9	12	76	71	1	73	.304	.371	.435	109	10	18-10	.978	-7	93	93	O148(10/139/0)	0	-0.4
1955	StL N	152	593	86	175	24	8	19	76	47-4	3	65	.295	.349	.459	113	10	11-11	.975	-5	93	70	O100(34/44/28),1b51	0	-0.5
1956	StL N	149	540	86	161	22	11	16	68	80-7	1	50	.298	.390	.469	129	25	12-9	.988	-0	92	97	O97(0/1/96),1b52	0	1.8
1957	StL N★	142	516	86	152	28	5	24	73	62-12	1	57	.295	.367	.508	131	23	5-6	.966	-9	88	82	O133(89/13/48)	0	0.7
1958	StL N	108	290	36	69	10	3	7	38	47-5	0	30	.238	.342	.366	85	-5	2-3	.984	-6	83	83	O82(31/8/54)	0	-1.6
1959	†LA N★	145	543	93	164	26	**11**	19	74	81-1	3	64	.302	.394	.495	126	23	15-6	.983	-4	84	119	O143(128/4/29)/1	0	1.1
1960	LA N	138	469	74	140	21	6	13	69	67-4	1	53	.299	.383	.452	121	16	6-10	.986	1	90	154	O127(115/0/18)	0	0.8
1961	LA N	134	463	79	152	25	3	17	88	89-9	1	79	.328	**.434**	.505	137	30	7-5	.970	-7	89	53	O133(126/0/19)	0	1.6
1962	LA N	95	244	36	59	9	1	4	31	30-3	1	33	.242	.326	.336	84	-5	5-2	.981	1	119	109	O36(24/0/12),1b32	0	-0.7
1963	LA N	122	343	41	90	13	2	8	48	45-5	1	43	.262	.345	.382	119	9	5-5	.962	-8	85	33	O96(48/3/60)	0	-0.5
1964	LA N	68	118	8	26	2	1	2	9	12-3	0	22	.220	.292	.305	74	-4	1-1	1.000	-2	89	0	O23(6/0/17)	0	-0.8
1965	†LA N	53	89	6	18	3	0	1	11	13-3	0	22	.202	.304	.270	67	-3	2-0	1.000	-1	82	91	O23(10/0/13)	0	-0.5
Total	12	1457	4843	737	1399	212	60	142	661	644-56	13	591	.289	.371	.445	117	129	89-68	.978	-47	89	89	O1141(621/212/394),1b136	0	1.0
MOORE, AL	Albert James; B8.4.1902 Brooklyn NY; D11.29.1974 , At Sea N.Y.To P.R; BR/TR/5´10˝/174; d9.27; Col St. Johns																								
1925	NY N	2	8	0	1	0	0	0	0	1	0	2	.125	.222	.125	-9	-1	0-1	1.000	-0	91	0	O2L	—	-0.2
1926	NY N	28	81	12	18	4	0	0	10	5	0	7	.222	.267	.272	46	-6	2	.966	2	97	199	O20(5/16/0)	—	-0.5
Total	2	30	89	12	19	4	0	0	10	6	0	9	.213	.263	.258	41	-7	2-1	.968	2	96	181	O22(7/16/0)	—	-0.7
MOORE, JUNIOR	Alvin Earl; B1.25.1953 Waskom TX; BR/TR/5´11˝/(177–185); [AtlN71 11/255]; d8.2																								
1976	Atl N	20	26	1	7	1	0	0	2	4-0	1	4	.269	.387	.308	93	0	0-0	.929	1	118	146	3b6/2lf	0	0.1
1977	Atl N	112	361	41	94	9	3	5	34	33-0	1	29	.260	.323	.343	71	-14	4-5	.942	4	103	58	3b104/2	0	-1.3
1978	Chi A	24	65	8	19	0	1	0	4	6-0	0	7	.292	.352	.323	90	-1	1-1	.857	0	87	0	D12,3b6,O5L	0	-0.1
1979	Chi A	88	201	24	53	6	2	1	23	12-0	0	20	.264	.300	.328	71	-9	0-2	.966	-2	95	91	O61(52/0/12),D10,2b2	0	-1.3
1980	Chi A	45	121	9	31	4	1	1	10	7-0	0	11	.256	.295	.331	72	-5	0-2	.929	-1	93	92	3b34,O3L/1D	0	-0.7
Total	5	289	774	83	204	20	7	7	73	62-0	2	71	.264	.318	.335	73	-29	5-10	.936	3	101	66	3b150,O70(61/0/12),D24,2b4/1	0	-3.3
MOORE, ANSE	Anselm Winn; B9.22.1917 Delhi LA; D10.29.1993 Pearl MS; BL/TR/6´1˝/190; d4.17																								
1946	Det A	51	134	16	28	4	0	1	8	12	1	9	.209	.279	.261	48	-9	1-1	.971	-0	99	81	O32(17/0/15)	0	-1.2
MOORE, ARCHIE	Archie Francis; B8.30.1941 Upper Darby PA; BL/TL/6´2˝/190; d4.20; Col Springfield																								
1964	NY A	31	23	4	4	2	0	0	1	2-0	0	9	.174	.240	.261	39	-2	0-0	1.000	0	75	0	O8(0/5/3),1b7	0	-0.2
1965	NY A	9	17	1	7	2	0	1	4	4-1	0	4	.412	.524	.706	248	4	0-0	.889	0	97	390	O5(1/0/5)	0	0.4
Total	2	40	40	5	11	4	0	1	5	6-1	0	13	.275	.370	.450	128	2	0-0	.929	0	88	223	O13(1/5/8),1b7	0	0.2
MOORE, CHARLEY	Charles Wesley; B12.1.1884 Jackson Co. IN; D7.29.1970 Portland OR; BR/TR/5´10˝/160; d4.16																								
1912	Chi N	5	9	2	2	0	1	0	2	0	0	1	.222	.222	.444	80	0	0	.800	0	81	0	S2/23	—	0.0
MOORE, CHARLIE	Charles William; B6.21.1953 Birmingham AL; BR/TR/5´11˝/(180–190); [MilA71 5/99]; d9.8																								
1973	Mil A	8	27	0	5	0	1	0	3	2-1	0	4	.185	.241	.259	42	-2	0-0	.981	2	67	197	C8	0	0.0
1974	Mil A	72	204	17	50	10	4	0	19	21-0	0	34	.245	.316	.333	87	-3	3-4	.985	0	78	62	C61,D6	0	-0.1
1975	Mil A	73	241	26	70	20	1	1	29	17-0	0	31	.290	.336	.394	105	2	1-5	.960	-2	105	87	C47,O22(16/0/6)/D	0	0.0
1976	Mil A	87	241	33	46	7	4	3	16	43-0	1	45	.191	.314	.290	80	-5	1-2	.969	1	89	149	C49,O28L/3D	0	-0.4
1977	Mil A	138	375	42	93	15	6	5	45	31-0	1	39	.248	.306	.360	81	-10	1-7	.980	-1	94	91	C137	0	-0.8
1978	Mil A	96	268	30	72	7	1	5	31	12-0	0	24	.269	.300	.358	84	-7	4-2	.983	4	**140**	68	C95	0	0.1
1979	Mil A	111	337	45	101	16	2	5	38	29-1	1	32	.300	.355	.404	104	2	8-5	.979	12	98	101	C106	0	1.8
1980	Mil A	111	320	42	93	13	2	2	30	24-2	0	28	.291	.336	.363	95	-2	10-5	.989	-1	139	68	C105	0	0.1
1981	†Mil A	48	156	16	47	8	3	1	9	12-0	0	13	.301	.351	.410	124	5	1-4	.970	1	106	79	C34,O8(3/0/5),D6	0	0.6
1982	†Mil A	133	456	53	116	22	4	6	45	29-2	1	49	.254	.299	.360	85	-11	2-10	.988	8	101	163	O115R,C20/2	0	-1.0
1983	Mil A	151	529	65	150	27	6	2	49	55-5	4	42	.284	.354	.369	107	7	11-4	.978	-7	95	76	O150R,C7/D	0	-0.7
1984	Mil A	70	188	13	44	7	1	2	17	10-0	1	26	.234	.275	.314	65	-9	0-4	.984	-1	108	61	O61(0/7/56),C7	17	-1.4
1985	Mil A	105	349	35	81	13	4	0	31	27-0	1	53	.232	.288	.292	60	-20	4-0	.977	5	114	123	C102,O3R	0	-0.9
1986	Mil A	80	235	24	61	12	3	3	39	21-1	0	38	.260	.317	.374	85	-5	5-5	.992	17	133	140	C72,O4(0/1/3)/2D	0	1.4
1987	Tor A	51	107	15	23	10	1	1	7	13-0	1	12	.215	.306	.355	73	-4	0-0	.984	2	82	64	C44,O5(2/0/3)	0	-0.1
Total	15	1334	4033	456	1052	187	43	36	408	346-12	11	470	.261	.319	.355	88	-62	51-57	.980	42	110	96	C894,O396(49/8/341),D18,2b2/3	17	-1.4

YEAR	TM LG	G	AB	R	H	2B	3B	HR	RBI	BB-IB	HP	SO	AVG	OBP	SLG	AOPS	ABR	SB-CS	FA	FR	RNG	THR	GAMES AT POSITION	DL	BFW
Moore, Dee	D C; B4.6.1914 Hedley TX; D7.2.1997 Williston ND; BR/TR/5´11˝/190; d9.12; Mil 1944–45																								
1936	Cin N	6	10	4	4	2	1	0	1	0	0	3	.400	.400	.800	230	2	0	1.000	-0	202	0	P2/C	—	0.1
1937	Cin N	7	13	2	1	0	0	0	0	1	1	2	.077	.200	.077	-23	-2	0	.931	1	*80*	*143*	C6	—	-0.1
1943	Bro N	37	79	8	20	3	0	0	12	11	0	8	.253	.344	.291	84	-1	1	.982	-4	*94*	*100*	C15,3b9	0	-0.5
	Phi N	37	113	13	27	4	1	1	8	15	0	8	.239	.328	.319	91	-1	0	.960	-1	*98*	*111*	C21,O6L,3b5/1	0	-0.1
	Year	74	192	21	47	7	1	1	20	26	0	16	.245	.335	.307	88	-2	1	.968	-5	*97*	*107*	C36,3b14,O6L/1	0	-0.6
1946	Phi N	11	13	2	1	0	0	0	1	7	0	3	.077	.400	.077	41	0	0	1.000	-0	*74*	*88*	C6,1b2	0	0.0
Total	4	98	228	29	53	9	2	1	22	34	1	24	.232	.335	.303	85	-2	1	.962	-4	*90*	*105*	C49,3b14,O6L,1b3,P2	0	-0.6
Moore, Gene	Eugene Jr. "Rowdy"; B8.26.1909 Lancaster TX; D3.12.1978 Jackson MS; BL/TL/5´11˝/175; d9.19; f–Gene																								
1931	Cin N	4	14	2	2	1	0	0	1	0	0	0	.143	.143	.214	-6	-2	0	1.000	0	111	0	O3L	—	-0.2
1933	StL N	11	38	6	15	3	2	0	8	4	0	10	.395	.452	.579	183	4	1	.967	-0	109	0	O10C	—	0.4
1934	StL N	9	18	2	5	1	0	0	1	2	0	2	.278	.350	.333	79	0	0	.923	-0	112	0	O3C	—	-0.1
1935	StL N	3	3	0	0	0	0	0	0	0	0	1	.000	.000	.000	-96	-1	0	ø	0	—	—	/H	—	-0.1
1936	Bos N	151	637	91	185	38	12	13	67	40	3	80	.290	.335	.449	117	12	6	.977	13	102	186	O151R	—	1.6
1937	Bos N☆	148	561	88	159	29	10	16	70	61	4	73	.283	.358	.456	132	24	11	.978	11	**113**	128	O148R	—	2.6
1938	Bos N	54	180	27	49	8	3	3	19	16	2	20	.272	.338	.400	114	3	1	.981	1	107	95	O47R	—	0.1
1939	Bro N	107	306	45	69	13	6	3	39	40	0	50	.225	.315	.337	73	-12	4	.961	-4	88	110	O86(2/1/83)/1	—	-2.0
1940	Bro N	10	26	3	7	2	0	0	2	1	0	3	.269	.296	.346	72	-1	0	1.000	-1	89	0	O6R	—	-0.2
	Bos N	103	363	46	106	24	1	5	39	25	0	32	.292	.338	.405	110	5	2	.986	6	108	147	O94(0/1/94)	—	0.5
	Year	113	389	49	113	26	1	5	41	26	0	35	.290	.335	.401	107	3	2	.986	5	107	140	O100(0/1/100)	—	0.3
1941	Bos N	129	397	42	108	17	8	5	43	45	2	37	.272	.349	.393	114	7	5	.968	5	106	147	O110(1/28/84)	0	0.7
1942	Was A	1	2	0	0	0	0	0	0	0	0	1	.000	.000	.000	-99	-1	0-0	ø	-0	0	0	/cf	0	-0.1
1943	Was A	92	254	41	68	14	3	2	39	19	1	29	.268	.321	.370	106	1	0-2	.985	2	105	119	O57(24/1/32)/1	0	-0.1
1944	†StL A	110	390	56	93	13	6	6	58	24	1	37	.238	.284	.349	76	-14	0-5	.968	2	110	77	O98R/1	0	-2.1
1945	StL A	110	354	48	92	16	2	5	50	40	1	26	.260	.337	.359	97	-1	1-3	.970	0	101	110	O100(1/0/99)	0	-0.8
Total	14	1042	3543	497	958	179	53	58	436	317	14	401	.270	.333	.400	105	24	31-10	.975	36	105	128	O914(31/45/842),1b3	0	0.2
Moore, Ferdie	Ferdinand De Paige; B2.22.1896 Camden NJ; D5.6.1947 Atlantic City NJ; 6´0˝/212; d10.2																								
1914	Phi A	2	4	1	2	0	0	0	1	0	0	2	.500	.500	.500	209	0	0	.895	-1	0	0	1b2	—	0.0
Moore, Gary	Gary Douglas; B2.24.1945 Tulsa OK; BR/TL/5´10˝/175; [LAN65 14/537]; d5.3; Col Texas																								
1970	LA N	7	16	2	3	0	2	0	0	0-0	0	1	.188	.188	.438	64	-1	1-0	1.000	-1	70	0	O5R/1	0	-0.2
Moore, Eddie	Graham Edward; B1.18.1899 Barlow KY; D2.10.1976 Ft.Myers FL; BR/TR/5´7˝/165; d9.25																								
1923	Pit N	6	26	6	7	1	0	0	1	2	0	3	.269	.321	.308	65	-1	1-0	.923	-3	63	63	S6	—	-0.3
1924	Pit N	72	209	47	75	8	4	2	13	27	2	12	.359	.437	.464	139	13	6-7	.988	3	105	134	O35(1/0/34),3b13,2b4	—	1.2
1925	†Pit N	142	547	106	163	29	8	6	77	73	2	26	.298	.383	.413	97	0	19-7	.952	-6	95	119	2b122,O15R,3b3	—	-0.2
1926	Pit N	43	132	19	30	8	1	0	19	12	0	6	.227	.292	.303	57	-8	3	.911	-6	84	119	2b24,3b9/S	—	-1.3
	Bos N	54	184	17	49	3	2	0	15	16	0	12	.266	.325	.304	77	-6	6	.973	-4	93	112	2b39,S14/3	—	-0.8
	Year	97	316	36	79	11	3	0	34	28	0	18	.250	.311	.304	68	-14	9	.950	-11	90	115	2b63,S15,3b10	—	-2.1
1927	Bos N	112	411	53	124	14	4	1	32	39	1	17	.302	.364	.363	103	3	5	.947	-8	93	65	3b52,2b39,O16(1/11/4)/S	—	-0.1
1928	Bos N	68	215	27	51	9	0	2	18	19	0	12	.237	.299	.307	62	-12	7	.958	5	112	161	O54L/2	—	-1.2
1929	Bro N	111	402	48	119	18	6	0	48	44	3	16	.296	.370	.371	86	-8	3	.955	-14	93	67	2b74,S36,O2R/3	—	-1.4
1930	Bro N	76	196	24	55	13	1	1	20	21	2	7	.281	.356	.372	77	-6	1	.991	2	111	111	2b23,O23(13/7/3),S17/3	—	-0.4
1932	NY N	37	87	9	23	3	0	1	6	9	1	6	.264	.340	.333	84	-2	1	.930	1	96	92	S21,3b6,2b5	—	0.1
1934	Cle A	27	65	4	10	2	0	0	8	10	0	4	.154	.267	.185	18	-8	0-0	.932	0	95	107	2b18,3b3,S2	—	-0.6
Total	10	748	2474	360	706	108	26	13	257	272	11	121	.285	.359	.366	89	-35	52-14	.956	-31	95	104	2b349,O145(69/18/58),S98,3b89	—	-5.0
Moore, Harry	Henry S.; d4.17																								
1884	Was U	111	461	77	155	23	5	1	—	19	—	—	.336	.363	.414	140	10	—	.820	-7	64	98	O105(102/2/1),S8	—	0.0
Moore, Jackie	Jackie Spencer; B2.19.1939 Jay FL; BR/TR/6´0˝/180; d4.18; M3/C26																								
1965	Det A	21	53	2	5	0	0	0	2	6-2	0	12	.094	.183	.094	-17	-8	0-0	.985	2	119	114	C20	0	-0.5
Moore, Jimmy	James William; B4.24.1903 Paris TN; D3.7.1986 Memphis TN; BR/TR/6´0.5˝/187; d4.17; Col Union (TN)																								
1930	Chi A	16	39	4	8	2	0	0	2	6	1	3	.205	.326	.256	52	-3	0-0	.900	1	94	311	O11L	—	-0.2
	†Phi A	15	50	10	19	3	0	2	12	2	0	4	.380	.404	.560	136	3	1-1	.958	-0	98	113	O13(8/1/4)	—	0.1
	Year	31	89	14	27	5	0	2	14	8	1	7	.303	.367	.427	100	0	1-1	.932	1	96	197	O24(19/1/4)	—	-0.1
1931	†Phi A	49	143	18	32	5	1	2	21	11	1	13	.224	.284	.315	54	-10	0-1	.973	2	105	118	O36(24/2/10)	—	-1.0
Total	2	80	232	32	59	10	1	4	35	19	2	20	.254	.316	.358	71	-10	1-2	.958	2	102	148	O60(43/3/14)	—	-1.1
Moore, Jerrie	Jeremiah S.; B1855 Windsor ON, Can.; D9.26.1890 Wayne MI; BL/5´11˝/170; d4.17																								
1884	Alt U	20	80	10	25	3	1	1	—	0	—	—	.313	.313	.412	117	-1	—	.800	-8	—	—	C12,O9(1/2/6)	—	-0.7
	Cle N	9	30	1	6	0	0	0	10	0	—	5	.200	.200	.200	25	-3	—	.887	-2	—	—	C9	—	-0.3
1885	Det N	6	23	2	4	1	0	0	0	1	—	3	.174	.208	.217	38	-2	—	.800	-2	—	—	C6	—	-0.3
Total	2	35	133	13	35	4	1	1	10	1	—	8	.263	.269	.331	83	-6	—	.830	-12	—	—	C27,O9(1/2/6)	—	-1.3
Moore, Johnny	John Francis; B3.23.1902 Waterville CT; D4.4.1991 Bradenton FL; BL/TR/5´10.5˝/175; d9.15																								
1928	Chi N	4	4	0	0	0	0	0	0	0	0	0	.000	.000	.000	-99	-1	0	ø	0	—	—	/H	—	-0.1
1929	Chi N	37	63	13	18	1	0	2	8	4	1	6	.286	.338	.397	81	-2	0	.971	1	110	100	O15(10/4/1)	—	-0.2
1931	Chi N	39	104	19	25	3	1	2	16	7	0	5	.240	.288	.346	69	-5	1	.964	0	95	193	O22(12/9/1)	—	-0.6
1932	†Chi N	119	443	59	135	24	5	13	64	22	3	38	.305	.342	.470	117	9	4	.983	-4	91	119	O109(4/91/14)	—	0.2
1933	Cin N	135	514	60	135	19	5	1	44	29	3	16	.263	.306	.325	81	-13	4	.974	3	102	118	O132(75/57/0)	—	-1.7
1934	Cin N	16	42	5	8	1	1	0	5	3	0	2	.190	.244	.262	36	-4	0	1.000	-0	109	0	O10R	—	-0.5
	Phi N	116	458	68	157	34	6	11	93	40	1	18	.343	.397	.515	125	18	7	.981	8	104	175	O115(10/0/108)	—	1.8
	Year	132	500	73	165	35	7	11	98	43	1	20	.330	.384	.494	120	15	7	.983	8	104	161	O125(10/0/118)	—	1.3
1935	Phi N	153	600	84	194	33	3	19	93	45	5	50	.323	.375	.483	117	15	4	.973	-10	78	117	O150(2/0/148)	—	-0.4
1936	Phi N	124	472	85	155	24	3	16	68	26	1	22	.328	.365	.494	117	11	1	.948	-6	96	54	O112(78/0/35)	—	-0.2
1937	Phi N	96	307	46	98	16	2	9	59	18	0	18	.319	.357	.472	114	6	2	.943	-0	93	147	O72(30/2/42)	—	0.1
1945	Chi N	7	6	0	1	0	0	0	2	1	0	1	.167	.286	.167	28	-1	0	ø	0	—	—	/H	0	-0.1
Total	10	846	3013	439	926	155	26	73	452	195	14	176	.307	.352	.449	109	33	23	.970	-9	94	120	O737(221/163/359)	0	-1.7
Moore, Jo-Jo	Joseph Gregg "The Gause Ghost"; B12.25.1908 Gause TX; D4.1.2001 Bryan TX; BL/TR/5´11˝/155; d9.17																								
1930	NY N	3	5	1	1	0	0	0	0	0	0	1	.200	.200	.200	-3	-1	0	1.000	-0	75	0	/cf	—	-0.1
1931	NY N	4	8	0	2	1	0	0	3	0	0	1	.250	.250	.375	68	0	1	1.000	-0	96	0	/lf	—	0.0
1932	NY N	86	361	53	110	15	2	2	27	20	0	18	.305	.341	.374	94	-3	4	.982	-3	88	115	O86(85/1/0)	—	-1.1
1933	†NY N	132	524	56	153	16	5	0	42	21	3	27	.292	.323	.342	91	-7	4	.966	2	90	**185**	O132(111/21/0)	—	-1.3
1934	NY N✳	139	580	106	192	37	4	15	61	31	5	23	.331	.370	.486	130	24	5	.954	-13	81	83	O131(112/20/0)	—	0.5
1935	NY N★	155	681	108	201	28	9	15	71	53	8	24	.295	.353	.429	111	10	5	.972	-1	98	96	O155L	—	0.1
1936	†NY N☆	152	649	110	205	29	9	7	63	37	6	27	.316	.358	.421	110	8	2	.981	8	94	**224**	O149L	—	0.8
1937	†NY N★	142	580	89	180	37	10	6	57	46	3	37	.310	.364	.440	116	13	7	.975	-8	83	120	O140L	—	-0.3
1938	NY N☆	125	506	76	153	23	6	11	56	22	3	27	.302	.335	.437	110	5	2	.978	-5	88	88	O114L	—	-0.7
1939	NY N	138	562	80	151	23	2	10	47	45	1	17	.269	.324	.370	85	-12	5	.986	3	95	159	O136L	—	-1.7
1940	NY N★	138	543	83	150	33	4	6	46	43	7	30	.276	.337	.385	98	-1	7	.982	-2	93	95	O133L	—	-1.1
1941	NY N	121	428	47	117	16	2	7	40	30	1	15	.273	.322	.369	93	-5	4	.972	-2	100	66	O116(112/4/0)	0	-1.3
Total	12	1335	5427	809	1615	258	53	79	513	348	37	247	.298	.344	.408	105	31	46	.975	-21	91	125	O1294(1248/47/0)	0	-6.2
Moore, Kelvin	Kelvin Orlando; B9.26.1957 Leroy AL; BR/TL/6´1˝/195; [OakA78 6/134]; d8.28; Col Jackson St.																								
1981	†Oak A	14	47	5	12	0	1	1	3	5-0	0	15	.255	.327	.362	102	0	1-0	1.000	-1	72	81	1b13	0	-0.2
1982	Oak A	21	67	6	15	1	1	2	6	3-0	0	23	.224	.250	.358	69	-3	0-1	.971	-2	75	57	1b20	0	-0.7
1983	Oak A	41	124	12	26	4	0	5	16	10-0	1	39	.210	.272	.363	78	-4	2-4	.994	-3	70	115	1b40	0	-1.0
Total	3	76	238	23	53	5	2	8	25	18-0	1	77	.223	.277	.361	80	-7	3-5	.989	-6	72	93	1b73	0	-1.9
Moore, Kerwin	Kerwin Lamar; B10.29.1970 Detroit MI; BB/TR/6´1˝/190; [KCA88 16/413]; d8.30																								
1996	Oak A	22	16	4	1	1	0	0	0	2-0	0	6	.063	.167	.125	-25	-3	1-0	1.000	-0	103	0	O18C,D2	0	-0.3

YEAR	TM LG	G	AB	R	H	2B	3B	HR	RBI	BB-IB	HP	SO	AVG	OBP	SLG	AOPS	ABR	SB-CS	FA	FR	RNG	THR	GAMES AT POSITION	DL	BFW
Moore, Molly	Maurice; TR; d6.30																								
1875	Atl NA	21	86	5	19	4	0	0	5	0	—	4	.221	.221	.267	79	-1	0-1	.747	-4	111	0	S14,1b8,O2R/C23	—	-0.5
Moore, Randy	Randolph Edward; B6.21.1906 Naples TX; D6.12.1992 Mt.Pleasant TX; BL/TR/6´0˝/185; d4.12; OF(66/13/339)																								
1927	Chi A	6	15	0	0	0	0	0	0	0	0	2	.000	.000	.000	-99	-5	0-0	1.000	1	119	257	O4R	—	-0.4
1928	Chi A	24	61	6	13	4	1	0	5	3	0	5	.213	.250	.311	47	-5	0-2	.946	0	117	63	O16(2/0/14)	—	-0.7
1930	Bos N	83	191	24	55	9	0	2	34	10	0	13	.288	.323	.366	69	-10	3	.986	1	113	121	O34(11/12/11),3b13	—	-0.9
1931	Bos N	83	192	19	50	8	1	3	34	13	1	3	.260	.311	.359	83	-5	1	.952	1	93	180	O29(17/1/11),3b22/2	—	-0.5
1932	Bos N	107	351	41	103	21	2	3	43	15	0	11	.293	.322	.390	94	-3	1	.987	-2	94	54	O41R,3b31,1b22/C	—	-0.9
1933	Bos N	135	497	64	150	23	7	8	70	40	2	16	.302	.356	.425	133	21	3	.979	-1	101	92	O122(12/0/110),1b10	—	1.2
1934	Bos N	123	422	55	120	21	2	7	64	40	0	16	.284	.346	.393	105	4	2	.965	-0	108	114	O72(16/0/56),1b37	—	-0.4
1935	Bos N	125	407	42	112	20	4	4	42	26	0	16	.275	.319	.373	93	-5	1	.950	1	104	130	O78(7/0/71),1b21	—	-1.0
1936	Bro N	42	88	4	21	3	0	0	14	8	0	1	.239	.302	.273	55	-5	0	.964	-2	91	0	O21R	—	-0.8
1937	Bro N	13	22	3	3	1	0	0	2	3	0	2	.136	.240	.182	16	-3	0	.889	-0	106	109	C10	—	-0.3
	StL N	8	7	0	0	0	0	0	0	0	0	0	.000	.000	.000	-98	-2	0	ø	-0	0	0	/lf	—	-0.2
	Year	21	29	3	3	1	0	0	2	3	0	2	.103	.188	.138	-10	-4	0	.889	-1	106	109	C10/lf	—	-0.5
Total	10	749	2253	258	627	110	17	27	308	158	3	85	.278	.326	.378	95	-18	11-2	.969	-2	103	104	O418R,1b90,3b66,C11/2	—	-4.9
Moore, Bobby	Robert Vincent; B10.27.1965 Cincinnati OH; BR/TR/5´9˝/165; [KCA87 16/405]; d9.5; Col Eastern Kentucky																								
1991	KC A	18	14	3	5	1	0	0	0	1-0	0	2	.357	.400	.429	128	1	3-2	1.000	0	102	0	O13(9/5/0)	0	0.0
Moore, Scott	Scott Alan; B11.17.1983 Long Beach CA; BL/TR/6´2˝/180; [DetA02 1/8]; d9.4																								
2006	Chi N	16	38	6	10	2	0	2	5	2-0	1	10	.263	.317	.474	97	0	0-0	.978	-2	63	22	1b6,3b5	0	-0.2
Moore, Terry	Terry Bluford; B5.27.1912 Vernon AL; D3.29.1995 Collinsville IL; BR/TR/5´11˝/195; d4.16; Mil 1943–45; M1/C7																								
1935	StL N	119	456	63	131	34	3	6	53	15	3	40	.287	.314	.414	90	-6	13	.984	7	109	109	O117C	—	-0.3
1936	StL N	143	590	85	156	39	4	5	47	37	1	52	.264	.309	.369	82	-15	9	.977	13	112	139	O133C	—	-0.5
1937	StL N	115	461	76	123	17	3	5	43	32	2	41	.267	.317	.349	79	-14	13	.988	8	112	100	O106C	—	-0.8
1938	StL N	94	312	49	85	21	3	4	21	46	0	19	.272	.366	.397	104	3	9	.987	4	114	77	O75C,3b6	—	0.6
1939	StL N★	130	417	65	123	25	2	17	77	43	1	38	.295	.362	.487	119	11	6	**.994**	8	102	**175**	O121C/P	—	1.6
1940	StL N★	136	537	92	163	33	4	17	64	42	2	44	.304	.356	.475	121	15	18	.987	13	**120**	104	O133C	—	2.5
1941	StL N★	122	493	86	145	26	4	6	68	52	2	31	.294	.364	.400	108	6	3	.984	0	95	140	O121(0/121/1)	0	0.3
1942	†StL N★	130	489	80	141	26	3	6	49	56	2	26	.288	.364	.391	112	9	10	.986	-8	92	80	O126C/3	0	-0.2
1946	†StL N	91	278	32	73	14	1	3	28	18	2	26	.263	.312	.353	85	-6	0	.982	-2	97	89	O66C	0	-1.0
1947	StL N	127	460	61	130	17	1	7	45	38	1	39	.283	.339	.370	84	-10	1	.983	-7	92	71	O120C	0	-2.1
1948	StL N	91	207	30	48	11	0	4	18	27	0	12	.232	.321	.343	75	-7	0	.993	-3	94	53	O71C	0	-1.1
Total	11	1298	4700	719	1318	263	28	80	513	406	16	368	.280	.340	.399	98	-14	82	.985	33	104	108	O1189(0/1189/1),3b7/P	0	-1.0
Moore, Scrappy	William Allen; B12.16.1892 St.Louis MO; D10.13.1964 Little Rock AR; BR/TR/5´8˝/153; d6.21; Col Vanderbilt																								
1917	StL A	4	8	1	1	0	0	0	0	1	0	0	.125	.222	.125	6	-1	0	.750	-0	100	651	3b2	—	-0.1
Moore, Bill	William Henry "Willie"; B12.12.1903 Kansas City MO; D5.24.1972 Kansas City MO; BL/TR/5´11˝/170; d9.7																								
1926	Bos A	5	18	2	3	0	0	0	0	0	0	2	.167	.167	.167	-13	-3	0-0	1.000	0	66	155	C5	—	-0.3
1927	Bos A	44	69	7	15	2	0	0	4	13	0	8	.217	.341	.246	56	-4	0-0	.938	-2	68	112	C42	—	-0.4
Total	2	49	87	9	18	2	0	0	4	13	0	10	.207	.310	.230	43	-7	0-0	.946	-2	68	119	C47	—	-0.7
Moore, Bill	William Ross; B10.10.1960 Los Angeles CA; BR/TL/6´1˝/185; [MonN83 6/146]; d7.19; Col Cal St.–Fullerton																								
1986	Mon N	6	12	0	2	0	0	0	0	0-0	0	4	.167	.167	.167	-8	-2	0-0	1.000	-0	59	61	1b3/rf	0	-0.2
Mora, Andres	Andres (Ibarra); B5.25.1955 Rio Bravo, Coahuila, Mexico; BR/TR/6´0˝/(162–205); d4.13																								
1976	Bal A	73	220	18	48	11	0	6	25	13-0	0	49	.218	.258	.350	83	-6	1-0	.951	0	99	152	D34,O31(30/0/2)	0	-0.8
1977	Bal A	77	233	32	57	8	2	13	44	5-1	1	53	.245	.261	.464	99	-2	0-0	1.000	-7	70	55	O57L/3D	0	-1.2
1978	Bal A	76	229	21	49	8	0	8	14	13-1	1	47	.214	.258	.354	75	-9	0-1	.978	1	105	100	O69L/D	0	-1.1
1980	Cle A	9	18	0	2	0	0	0	0	0-0	0	0	.111	.111	.111	-38	-3	0-0	1.000	-0	99	0	O3(2/0/1)	0	-0.4
Total	4	235	700	71	156	27	2	27	83	31-2	2	149	.223	.256	.383	83	-20	1-1	.978	-6	91	92	O160(158/0/3),D40/3	0	-3.5
Mora, Melvin	Melvin; B2.2.1972 Agua Negra, Yaracuy, Venez.; BR/TR/5´10˝/(180–200); d5.30; OF(170/158/29)																								
1999	†NY N	66	31	6	5	0	0	0	1	4-0	1	7	.161	.278	.161	16	-4	2-1	1.000	-1	98	0	O45(28/11/8),2b4,3b3/S	0	-0.4
2000	NY N	79	215	35	56	13	2	6	30	18-3	2	48	.260	.317	.423	91	-3	7-3	.958	-6	89	68	S44,O28(12/16/3),2b4,3b4	16	-0.5
	Bal A	53	199	25	58	9	3	2	17	17-0	4	32	.291	.359	.397	96	-1	5-8	.952	2	107	88	S52/2	0	0.3
2001	Bal A	128	436	49	109	28	0	7	48	41-2	14	91	.250	.329	.362	88	-6	11-4	.987	7	105	86	O88C,S43/2	0	0.6
2002	Bal A	149	557	86	130	30	4	19	64	70-2	20	108	.233	.338	.404	102	3	16-10	.989	16	109	152	O104(74/31/5),S41,2b12,D3	0	1.9
2003	Bal A★	96	344	68	109	17	1	15	48	49-0	12	71	.317	.418	.503	143	24	6-3	.994	5	102	205	O79(56/12/13),S11,2b6/1	32	2.7
2004	Bal A	140	550	111	187	41	0	27	104	66-0	11	95	.340	**.419**	.562	155	48	11-6	.948	6	102	86	3b137/SD	15	5.1
2005	Bal A★	149	593	86	168	30	1	27	88	50-0	10	112	.283	.348	.474	117	14	7-4	.957	5	103	84	3b148/D	0	1.9
2006	Bal A	155	624	96	171	25	0	16	83	54-1	14	99	.274	.342	.391	93	-6	11-1	.959	-10	93	53	3b154/2D	0	-1.3
Total	8	1015	3549	562	993	193	11	119	483	369-8	88	663	.280	.359	.441	112	69	76-40	.955	25	99	75	3b446,O344L,S193,2b29,D6/1	63	10.3
Morales, Jose	Jose Manuel (Hernandez); B12.30.1944 Frederiksted, V.I.; BR/TR/6´0˝/(187–210); d8.13; C9																								
1973	Oak A	6	14	0	4	1	0	0	1	1-0	0	5	.286	.313	.357	99	0	0-1	ø	0	—	—	D3	0	0.0
	Mon N	5	5	0	2	0	0	0	0	0-0	0	0	.400	.400	.400	118	0	0-0	ø	0	—	—	/H	0	0.0
1974	Mon N	25	26	3	7	4	0	1	5	1-0	0	7	.269	.296	.538	123	1	0-0	.800	-1	0	0	C2	0	0.0
1975	Mon N	93	163	18	49	6	1	2	24	14-9	0	21	.301	.354	.387	101	0	0-2	.983	5	191	103	1b27,O6L,C5	0	0.3
1976	Mon N	104	158	12	50	11	0	4	37	3-3	2	20	.316	.333	.462	119	4	0-0	.977	-0	208	73	1b21,C12	0	0.3
1977	Mon N	65	74	3	15	4	1	1	9	5-3	0	12	.203	.247	.324	55	-5	0-0	1.000	-2	51	104	C8,1b8	0	-0.8
1978	Min A	101	242	22	76	13	1	2	38	20-3	1	35	.314	.363	.401	113	5	0-1	ø	0	0	0	D77/C1lf	0	0.3
1979	Min A	92	191	21	51	5	1	2	27	14-5	2	27	.267	.319	.335	75	-7	0-0	1.000	-0	0	0	D77/1	0	-0.9
1980	Min A	97	241	36	73	17	2	8	36	22-4	1	19	.303	.361	.490	123	8	0-0	1.000	-0	0	0	D86,C2,1b2	6	0.5
1981	Bal A	38	86	6	21	3	0	2	14	3-0	0	13	.244	.270	.349	77	-3	0-0	1.000	-0	0	66	D22,1b3	0	-0.4
1982	Bal A	3	3	0	0	0	0	0	0	0-0	0	2	.000	.000	.000	-99	-1	0-0	ø	0	—	—	/H	0	-0.1
	LA N	35	30	1	9	1	0	1	8	4-0	0	8	.300	.382	.433	132	1	0-0	ø	0	—	—	/H	0	0.0
1983	†LA N	47	53	4	15	3	0	3	8	1-0	0	11	.283	.296	.509	119	1	0-0	.951	-1	84	77	1b4	0	0.0
1984	LA N	22	19	0	3	0	0	0	0	1-1	0	2	.158	.200	.158	2	-3	0-0	ø	0	—	—	/H	0	-0.3
Total	12	733	1305	126	375	68	6	26	207	89-28	6	182	.287	.332	.408	102	1	0-4	.981	1	166	96	D265,1b67,C30,O7L	6	-1.1
Morales, Jerry	Julio Ruben (Torres); B2.18.1949 Yabucoa, PR; BR/TR/5´10˝/(155–175); d9.5; C3																								
1969	SD N	19	41	5	8	2	0	1	6	5-0	0	7	.195	.283	.317	70	-2	0-2	1.000	2	105	259	O19(10/9/1)	0	-0.1
1970	SD N	28	58	6	9	0	1	1	4	3-0	0	11	.155	.197	.241	17	-7	0-0	.926	-2	86	0	O26(23/0/4)	0	-1.0
1971	SD N	12	17	1	2	0	0	0	1	2-0	0	2	.118	.211	.118	-5	-2	1-0	1.000	-0	89	0	O7(4/1/2)	0	-0.3
1972	SD N	115	347	38	83	15	7	4	18	35-3	0	54	.239	.307	.357	96	-3	4-6	.987	5	108	139	O96(34/56/12),3b4	0	-0.3
1973	SD N	122	388	47	109	23	2	9	34	27-3	0	55	.281	.325	.420	115	7	6-5	.991	2	107	77	O100(31/50/27)	0	0.4
1974	Chi N	151	534	70	146	21	7	15	82	46-3	2	63	.273	.330	.423	106	3	2-12	.975	-5	95	54	O143(83/32/41)	0	-1.4
1975	Chi N	153	578	62	156	21	0	12	91	50-9	5	65	.270	.328	.369	90	-7	3-7	.979	-3	95	111	O151(0/20/136)	0	-2.0
1976	Chi N	140	537	66	147	17	0	16	67	41-7	0	49	.274	.323	.395	95	-4	3-8	.983	-0	100	104	O136(3/8/131)	0	-1.4
1977	Chi N★	136	490	56	142	34	5	11	69	43-4	2	75	.290	.348	.447	101	1	0-3	.985	-13	81	98	O128(6/125/3)	0	-1.4
1978	StL N	130	457	44	109	19	8	4	46	33-1	1	44	.239	.288	.341	77	-16	4-4	.977	-4	102	56	O126(0/34/94)	0	-2.7
1979	Det A	129	440	50	93	23	1	14	56	30-0	2	56	.211	.260	.364	65	-23	10-4	.986	-7	88	75	O119(18/20/88),D7	0	-3.4
1980	NY N	94	193	19	49	7	1	3	30	13-2	1	31	.254	.293	.347	83	-5	2-3	.973	-2	94	97	O63(3/55/6)	0	-0.8
1981	Chi N	84	245	27	70	6	2	1	25	22-0	1	29	.286	.343	.339	90	-3	1-1	.986	-3	94	44	O72(17/49/8)	0	-0.8
1982	Chi N	65	116	14	33	2	2	4	30	9-1	0	7	.284	.333	.440	111	1	1-2	1.000	5	110	299	O41(12/36/4)	41	0.5
1983	Chi N	63	87	11	17	9	0	0	11	7-0	0	19	.195	.253	.299	51	-6	0-0	1.000	-0	89	109	O29(17/10/3)	15	-0.7
Total	15	1441	4528	516	1173	199	36	95	570	366-33	14	567	.259	.313	.382	91	-66	37-57	.983	-26	96	92	O1256(261/505/560),D7,3b4	56	-15.4
Morales, Kendry	Kendrys; B6.20.1983 Fomento, Cuba; BB/TR/6´1˝/220; d5.23																								
2006	LA A	57	197	21	46	10	1	5	22	17-1	0	28	.234	.293	.371	73	-8	1-1	.989	2	112	94	1b56	0	-1.1

YEAR	TM LG	G	AB	R	H	2B	3B	HR	RBI	BB-IB	HP	SO	AVG	OBP	SLG	AOPS	ABR	SB-CS	FA	FR	RNG	THR	GAMES AT POSITION	DL	BFW
Morales, Rich	Richard Angelo; B9.20.1943 San Francisco CA; BR/TR/5´11˝/170; d8.8; C2; Col San Mateo (CA) [JC]																								
1967	Chi A	8	10	0	0	0	0	0	0	0-0	0	2	.000	.000	.000	-99	-3	0-0	.944	-1	97	51	S7	0	-0.3
1968	Chi A	10	29	2	5	0	0	0	0	2-0	0	5	.172	.226	.172	22	-3	0-0	.966	0	186	260	S7,2b5	0	-0.2
1969	Chi A	55	121	12	26	0	1	0	6	7-0	2	18	.215	.269	.231	39	-10	1-0	.976	5	123	90	2b38,S13/3	0	-0.2
1970	Chi A	62	112	6	18	2	0	1	2	9-0	1	16	.161	.228	.205	20	-12	1-0	.967	-1	108	88	S24,3b20,2b12	21	-1.2
1971	Chi A	84	185	19	45	8	0	2	14	22-4	4	26	.243	.336	.319	84	-3	2-3	.976	-6	95	52	S57,3b18,2b3/rf	0	-0.5
1972	Chi A	110	287	24	59	7	1	2	20	19-2	3	49	.206	.261	.258	54	-17	2-3	.968	-5	94	76	S86,2b16,3b14	0	-1.5
1973	Chi A	7	4	1	0	0	0	0	1	1-0	0	1	.000	.200	.000	-38	-1	0-0	1.000	0	123	0	3b5,2b2	0	-0.1
	SD N	90	244	9	40	6	1	0	16	27-6	0	36	.164	.245	.197	27	-25	0-1	.988	15	113	90	2b79,S10	0	-0.5
1974	SD N	54	61	8	12	3	0	1	5	8-1	0	6	.197	.290	.295	67	-3	1-0	.933	0	99	71	S29,2b18,3b6/1	0	-0.1
Total	8	480	1053	81	205	26	3	6	64	95-13	10	159	.195	.267	.242	46	-77	7-7	.970	7	99	74	S233,2b173,3b64/1rf	21	-4.6
Morales, Willie	William Anthony; B9.7.1972 Tucson AZ; BR/TR/5´10˝/182; [OakA93 14/405]; d4.9																								
2000	Bal A	3	11	1	3	1	0	0	0	0-0	0	3	.273	.273	.364	62	-1	0-0	1.000	2	0	278	C3	25	0.1
Moran, Charlie	Charles Barthell "Uncle Charlie"; B2.22.1878 Nashville TN; D6.14.1949 Horse Cave KY; BR/TR/5´8˝/180; d9.9; U22; Col Vanderbilt; ▲																								
1903	StL N	4	14	2	6	0	0	0	1	0	0	—	.429	.429	.429	149	1	1	1.000	-1	46	0	P3/S	—	0.0
1908	StL N	21	63	2	11	1	2	0	2	0	0	—	.175	.175	.254	38	-5	0	.903	-5	65	133	C16	—	-1.0
Total	2	25	77	4	17	1	2	0	3	0	0	—	.221	.221	.286	61	-4	1	.903	-6	65	133	C16,P3/S	—	-1.0
Moran, Charles	Charles Vincent; B3.26.1879 Washington DC; D4.11.1934 Washington DC; TR; d4.29; Col Georgetown																								
1903	Was A	98	373	41	84	14	5	1	24	33	5	—	.225	.297	.298	77	-9	8	**.943**	6	100	106	S96,2b2	—	0.0
1904	Was A	62	243	27	54	10	0	0	7	23	0	—	.222	.289	.263	77	-5	7	.919	-6	94	85	S61/3	—	-1.1
	StL A	82	272	15	47	3	1	0	14	25	0	—	.173	.242	.191	40	-18	2	.937	-3	109	27	3b81/rf	—	-2.1
	Year	144	515	42	101	13	1	0	21	48	0	—	.196	.265	.225	58	-23	9	.938	-9	109	27	3b82,S61/rf	—	-3.2
1905	StL A	27	82	6	16	1	0	0	5	10	1	—	.195	.290	.207	62	-3	3	.954	-3	98	132	2b20,3b5	—	-0.7
Total	3	269	970	89	201	28	6	1	50	91	6	—	.207	.279	.252	66	-35	20	.935	-6	98	98	S157,3b87,2b22/rf	—	-3.9
Moran, Herbie	John Herbert; B2.16.1884 Costello PA; D9.21.1954 Clarkson NY; BL/TR/5´5˝/150; d4.16																								
1908	Phi A	19	59	4	9	0	0	0	4	6	1	—	.153	.242	.153	27	-5	1	.952	0	47	0	O19(0/10/9)	—	-0.6
	Bos N	8	29	3	8	0	0	0	2	2	2	—	.276	.364	.276	106	0	1	1.000	2	168	1021	O8L	—	0.2
1909	Bos N	8	31	8	7	1	0	0	0	5	0	—	.226	.333	.258	80	0	0	1.000	0	98	0	O8L	—	-0.1
1910	Bos N	20	67	11	8	0	0	0	3	13	2	14	.119	.280	.119	17	-6	6	.958	4	98	245	O20(11/0/9)	—	-0.4
1912	Bro N	130	508	77	140	18	10	1	40	69	5	38	.276	.368	.356	102	4	28	.961	2	98	118	O129(2/73/55)	—	-0.3
1913	Bro N	132	515	71	137	15	5	0	26	45	7	29	.266	.333	.315	83	-10	21-16	.950	-1	104	88	O129(3/6/121)	—	-1.9
1914	Cin N	107	395	43	93	10	5	1	35	41	3	29	.235	.312	.294	78	-10	26	.954	-7	93	70	O107(1/24/82)	—	-2.5
	†Bos N	41	154	24	41	3	1	0	4	17	2	11	.266	.347	.299	93	-1	4	.940	-5	80	70	O41(0/17/30)	—	-0.8
	Year	148	549	67	134	13	6	1	39	58	5	40	.244	.322	.295	82	-11	30	.950	-11	90	70	O148(1/41/112)	—	-3.3
1915	Bos N	130	419	59	84	13	5	0	21	66	8	41	.200	.320	.255	79	-7	16-10	.964	1	92	140	O123(15/12/101)	—	-1.3
Total	7	595	2177	300	527	60	26	2	135	264	30	162	.242	.332	.296	83	-35	103-26	.957	-4	96	118	O584(48/142/407)	—	-7.7
Moran, Pat	Patrick Joseph; B2.7.1876 Fitchburg MA; D3.7.1924 Orlando FL; BR/TR/5´10˝/180; d5.15; M9																								
1901	Bos N	52	180	12	38	5	1	2	18	3	1	—	.211	.228	.283	44	-14	3	.973	-2	130	55	C28,1b13,3b4,S3,O3R/2	—	-1.3
1902	Bos N	80	251	22	60	5	5	1	24	17	6	—	.239	.303	.311	89	-4	6	**.982**	3	107	99	C71,1b3/rf	—	0.7
1903	Bos N	109	389	40	102	25	5	7	54	29	11	—	.262	.331	.406	114	7	8	.967	13	97	**121**	C107/1	—	2.9
1904	Bos N	113	398	26	90	11	3	4	34	18	4	—	.226	.267	.299	77	-12	10	.957	1	86	107	C72,3b39,1b2	—	-0.3
1905	Bos N	85	267	22	64	11	5	2	22	8	3	—	.240	.270	.341	83	-7	3	**.986**	0	79	99	C78	—	0.1
1906	†Chi N	70	226	22	57	13	1	0	35	7	2	—	.252	.281	.319	82	-5	6	.979	8	161	97	C61	—	1.0
1907	†Chi N	65	198	8	45	5	1	1	19	10	2	—	.227	.271	.278	68	-8	5	.973	2	112	106	C59	—	0.0
1908	Chi N	50	150	12	39	5	1	0	12	13	1	—	.260	.323	.307	97	0	6	.968	-0	110	103	C45	—	0.5
1909	Chi N	77	246	18	54	11	1	1	23	16	4	—	.220	.278	.285	73	-8	2	.984	5	128	96	C74	—	0.5
1910	Phi N	68	199	13	47	7	1	0	11	17	3	16	.236	.306	.281	69	-8	6	.989	-0	94	104	C56	—	-0.3
1911	Phi N	34	103	2	19	3	0	0	8	3	0	13	.184	.208	.214	18	-12	0	.984	-2	86	104	C32	—	-1.1
1912	Phi N	13	26	1	3	1	0	0	1	1	0	7	.115	.148	.154	-16	-4	0	.955	-1	89	71	C13	—	-0.5
1913	Phi N	1	1	0	0	0	0	0	0	0	0	0	.000	.000	.000	-96	0	0	ø	0	—	—	/H	—	0.0
1914	Phi N	1	0	0	0	0	0	0	1	0	0	0	ø	ø	ø	ø	0	0	ø	-0	0	0	/C	—	0.0
Total	14	818	2634	198	618	102	24	18	262	142	37	36	.235	.283	.312	78	-75	55	.976	27	107	102	C697,3b43,1b19,O4R,S3/2	—	2.2
Moran, Al	Richard Alan; B12.5.1938 Detroit MI; BR/TR/6´1.5˝/(190–195); d4.9																								
1963	NY N	119	331	26	64	5	2	1	23	36-1	1	60	.193	.274	.230	46	-23	3-7	.951	-1	105	82	S116/3	0	-1.8
1964	NY N	16	22	2	5	0	0	0	4	2-0	0	2	.227	.280	.227	50	-1	0-0	.957	1	118	92	S15/3	0	0.0
Total	2	135	353	28	69	5	2	1	27	38-1	1	62	.195	.274	.229	46	-24	3-7	.951	-0	106	83	S131,3b2	0	-1.8
Moran, Roy	Roy Ellis "Deedle"; B9.17.1884 Vincennes IN; D7.18.1966 Atlanta GA; BR/TR/5´8˝/155; d9.3																								
1912	Was A	7	13	1	2	0	0	0	0	8	0	—	.154	.476	.154	82	1	3	.889	-0	73	157	O6(5/1/0)	—	0.0
Moran, Bill	William L.; B10.10.1869 Joliet IL; D4.8.1916 Joliet IL; 5´10.5˝/175; d5.7																								
1892	StL N	24	81	2	11	1	0	0	5	2	0	12	.136	.157	.148	-8	-11	0	.898	-5	96	91	C22,O2L	—	-1.3
1895	Chi N	15	55	8	9	2	1	1	9	3	1	2	.164	.220	.291	29	-6	2	.827	-3	94	109	C15	—	-0.7
Total	2	39	136	10	20	3	1	1	14	5	1	14	.147	.183	.206	10	-17	2	.871	-8	95	99	C37,O2L	—	-2.0
Moran, Billy	William Nelson; B11.27.1933 Montgomery AL; BR/TR/5´11˝/(180–185); d4.15																								
1958	Cle A	115	257	26	58	11	0	1	18	13-1	0	23	.226	.262	.280	51	-18	3-2	.960	-2	108	87	2b74,S38	0	-1.5
1959	Cle A	11	17	1	5	0	0	0	2	0-0	0	1	.294	.294	.294	64	-1	0-0	1.000	-2	85	43	2b6,S5	0	-0.2
1961	LA A	54	173	17	45	7	1	2	22	17-1	1	16	.260	.328	.347	73	-6	0-0	.966	-4	92	91	2b51,S2	0	-0.6
1962	LA A★	160	659	90	186	25	3	17	74	39-2	4	80	.282	.324	.407	99	-3	5-1	.986	18	108	92	2b160	0	2.9
1963	LA A	153	597	67	164	29	5	7	65	31-2	3	57	.275	.310	.375	98	-3	1-1	.973	9	**105**	100	2b151	0	1.9
1964	LA A	50	198	26	53	10	1	0	11	13-1	1	20	.268	.315	.328	88	-3	1-3	.929	-6	91	59	3b47,2b3/S	0	-1.1
	Cle A	69	151	14	31	6	0	1	10	18-3	1	16	.205	.291	.265	57	-8	0-1	.972	-1	94	60	3b42,2b15,1b2	0	-0.9
	Year	119	349	40	84	16	1	1	21	31-4	2	36	.241	.304	.301	73	-12	1-4	.947	-7	92	59	3b89,2b18,1b2/S	0	-2.0
1965	Cle A	22	24	1	3	0	0	0	0	0-0	2	5	.125	.222	.125	1	-3	0-0	1.000	-0	73	111	2b7/S	0	-0.3
Total	7	634	2076	242	545	88	10	28	202	133-10	11	218	.263	.308	.355	85	-45	10-8	.976	11	104	93	2b467,3b89,S47,1b2	0	0.2
Morandini, Mickey	Michael Robert; B4.22.1966 Kittanning PA; BL/TR/5´11˝/(167–182); [PhiN88 5/120]; d9.1; Col Indiana																								
1990	Phi N	25	79	9	19	4	0	1	3	6-0	0	19	.241	.294	.329	71	-3	3-0	.990	-4	98	78	2b25	0	-0.6
1991	Phi N	98	325	38	81	11	4	1	20	29-0	2	45	.249	.313	.317	79	-9	13-2	.986	-0	101	91	2b97	0	-0.5
1992	Phi N	127	422	47	112	8	8	3	30	25-2	0	64	.265	.305	.344	84	-11	8-3	.991	9	106	96	2b124,S3	0	0.2
1993	†Phi N	120	425	57	105	19	9	3	33	34-2	5	73	.247	.309	.355	79	-14	13-2	.990	-7	96	74	2b111	0	-1.3
1994	Phi N	87	274	40	80	16	5	2	26	34-5	4	33	.292	.378	.409	103	3	10-5	.985	1	100	85	2b79	0	0.7
1995	Phi N★	127	494	65	140	34	7	6	49	42-3	9	80	.283	.350	.417	101	1	9-6	.989	2	98	98	2b122	0	0.9
1996	Phi N	140	539	64	135	24	6	3	32	49-0	9	87	.250	.321	.334	73	-20	26-5	.982	-2	97	105	2b137	15	-1.2
1997	Phi N	150	553	83	163	40	2	1	39	62-0	8	91	.295	.371	.380	99	3	16-13	.990	-16	85	96	2b146/S	0	-0.7
1998	†Chi N	154	582	93	172	20	4	8	53	72-4	9	84	.296	.380	.385	99	2	13-1	**.993**	-22	92	72	2b152	0	-1.0
1999	Chi N	144	456	60	110	18	5	4	37	48-2	6	61	.241	.319	.329	65	-24	6-6	.991	-1	101	97	2b132	0	-2.0
2000	Phi N	91	302	31	76	13	3	0	22	29-1	4	54	.252	.324	.315	63	-17	5-2	.987	-8	88	85	2b85	0	-2.0
	Tor A	35	107	10	29	2	1	0	7	7-0	0	23	.271	.316	.308	57	-7	1-0	.993	-0	99	123	2b35	0	-0.5
Total	11	1298	4558	597	1222	209	54	32	351	437-19	56	714	.268	.338	.359	85	-96	123-45	.989	-47	96	91	2b1245,S4	15	-8.0
Morban, Jose	Jose; B10.2.1979 Santiago, D.R.; BR/TR/6´1˝/170; d4.6																								
2003	Bal A	61	71	14	10	0	0	2	5	3-0	1	21	.141	.187	.225	8	-10	8-0	1.000	-3	51	121	S14,D13,2b12/3	0	-1.0
Mordecai, Mike	Michael Howard; B12.13.1967 Birmingham AL; BR/TR/5´11˝/(175–185); [AtlN89 6/142]; d5.8; Col South Alabama; OF(1/1/2)																								
1994	Atl N	4	4	1	1	0	0	1	3	1-0	0	0	.250	.400	1.000	240	1	0-0	1.000	-0	105	0	S4	0	0.1
1995	†Atl N	69	75	10	21	6	0	3	11	9-0	0	16	.280	.353	.480	113	2	0-0	1.000	-2	84	165	2b21,1b9,3b6,S6/cf	0	0.0
1996	†Atl N	66	108	12	26	5	0	2	8	9-1	0	24	.241	.297	.343	65	-6	1-0	.985	0	113	113	2b20,3b10,S6/1	22	-0.4
1997	Atl N	61	81	8	14	2	1	0	3	6-0	0	16	.173	.227	.222	19	-10	0-1	1.000	-2	54	129	3b19,2b4,S4,1b3/rfD	0	-1.2

YEAR	TM LG	G	AB	R	H	2B	3B	HR	RBI	BB-IB	HP	SO	AVG	OBP	SLG	AOPS	ABR	SB-CS	FA	FR	RNG	THR	GAMES AT POSITION	DL	BFW
1998	Mon N	73	119	12	24	4	2	3	10	9-0	0	20	.202	.258	.345	58	-8	1-0	.953	-6	108	68	S30,2b21,3b11/1	30	-1.2
1999	Mon N	109	226	29	53	10	2	5	25	20-0	1	31	.235	.297	.363	69	-12	2-5	.962	-1	93	136	2b38,S38,3b32/1	0	-1.0
2000	Mon N	86	169	20	48	16	0	4	16	12-0	1	34	.284	.335	.450	95	-1	2-2	.937	-1	102	126	3b58,S10,2b9,1b3	0	-0.1
2001	Mon N	96	254	28	71	17	2	3	32	19-1	1	53	.280	.330	.398	88	-4	2-2	.974	-8	86	33	3b42,2b32,S4/C1rfD	0	-1.1
2002	Mon N	55	74	9	15	4	0	0	4	8-3	1	14	.203	.289	.257	43	-6	1-1	.931	-0	98	133	3b28,2b4,1b3,S3/lf	0	-0.6
	Fla N	38	77	10	22	4	0	0	7	5-1	1	13	.286	.337	.338	82	-2	1-1	.988	1	105	93	S24,3b7/1	0	0.0
	Year	93	151	19	37	8	0	0	11	13-4	2	27	.245	.313	.298	61	-8	2-2	.947	1	92	171	3b35,S27,2b4,1b4/lf	0	-0.6
2003	†Fla N	65	89	11	19	4	0	2	8	8-3	0	21	.213	.276	.326	59	-6	3-0	.976	-7	82	107	S14,2b12,3b12/1	0	-1.0
2004	Fla N	69	84	7	19	3	0	1	5	6-0	0	18	.226	.278	.298	51	-6	0-1	.929	2	107	226	3b19,2b4,S3/C	0	-0.4
2005	Fla N	2	2	0	0	0	0	0	0	0-0	0	1	.000	.000	.000	-99	-1	0-0	1.000	-0	104	0	/2S	0	-0.1
Total	12	793	1362	157	333	75	7	24	132	112-9	5	261	.244	.303	.363	72	-59	13-13	.956	-23	91	93	3b244,2b166,S147,1b24,O4R,C2,D2	52	-7.0
MOREHART, RAY	Raymond Anderson; B12.2.1899 Terrell TX; D1.13.1989 Dallas TX; BL/TR/5´9˝/157; d8.9; Col Austin																								
1924	Chi A	31	100	10	20	4	2	0	8	17	0	7	.200	.316	.280	56	-6	3-1	.873	-9	92	94	S27,2b2	—	-1.2
1926	Chi A	73	192	27	61	10	3	0	21	11	1	15	.318	.358	.401	101	0	3-11	.950	-5	103	61	2b48	—	-0.7
1927	NY A	73	195	45	50	7	2	1	20	29	0	18	.256	.353	.328	80	-5	4-4	.945	1	109	104	2b53	—	-0.3
Total	3	177	487	82	131	21	7	1	49	57	1	40	.269	.347	.347	83	-11	10-16	.946	-12	105	83	2b103,S27	—	-2.2
MOREJON, DANNY	Daniel (Torres); B7.21.1930 Havana, Cuba; BR/TR/6´1˝/175; d7.11																								
1958	Cin N	12	26	4	5	0	0	0	1	9-1	0	2	.192	.400	.192	60	-1	1-0	1.000	-2	74	0	O11(2/6/3)	0	-0.3
MORELAND, KEITH	Bobby Keith; B5.2.1954 Dallas TX; BR/TR/6´0˝/(186–200); [PhiN75 7/156]; d10.1; Col Texas; OF(119/0/560)																								
1978	Phi N	1	2	0	0	0	0	0	0	0-0	0	0	.000	.000	.000	-98	-1	0-0	1.000	-1	7	0	/C	0	-0.1
1979	Phi N	14	48	3	18	3	2	0	8	3-0	0	5	.375	.412	.521	146	3	0-0	1.000	-1	78	105	C13	0	0.3
1980	†Phi N	62	159	13	50	8	0	4	29	8-2	0	14	.314	.341	.440	111	2	3-1	.967	-1	80	128	C39,3b4,O2R	0	0.4
1981	†Phi N	61	196	16	50	7	0	6	37	15-1	1	13	.255	.307	.383	91	-3	1-2	.982	-3	72	112	C50,3b7,1b2,O2R	0	-0.5
1982	Chi N	138	476	50	124	17	2	15	68	46-8	3	71	.261	.326	.399	99	-1	0-6	.989	3	104	140	O86(54/0/35),C44,3b2	0	-0.3
1983	Chi N	154	533	76	161	30	3	16	70	68-8	3	73	.302	.378	.460	127	21	0-3	.976	-10	88	69	O151R,C3	0	0.3
1984	†Chi N	140	495	59	138	17	3	16	80	34-5	3	71	.279	.326	.422	101	0	1-4	.976	-8	89	97	O103(1/0/102),1b29,3b8,C3	0	-1.7
1985	Chi N	161	587	74	180	30	3	14	106	68-7	1	58	.307	.374	.440	117	15	12-3	.976	-8	87	103	O148R,1b12,3b11,C2	0	0.1
1986	Chi N	156	586	72	159	30	0	12	79	53-10	0	48	.271	.326	.384	90	-7	3-6	.980	-8	84	139	O121R,3b24,C13,1b12	0	-2.4
1987	Chi N	153	563	63	150	29	1	27	88	39-4	0	66	.266	.309	.465	99	-2	3-3	.934	7	106	102	3b150/1	0	0.2
1988	SD N	143	511	40	131	23	0	5	64	40-6	0	51	.256	.305	.331	86	-9	2-3	.994	-2	100	115	1b73,O64L,3b2	0	-2.1
1989	Det A	90	318	34	95	16	0	5	35	27-5	2	33	.299	.357	.396	114	7	3-2	1.000	-2	60	76	D51,1b31,3b12/C	0	0.1
	Bal A	33	107	11	23	4	0	1	10	4-0	0	12	.215	.243	.280	48	-8	0-0	ø	0	0	0	D29	0	-0.9
	Year	123	425	45	118	20	0	6	45	31-5	2	45	.278	.330	.367	98	-1	3-2	1.000	-2	60	76	D80,1b31,3b12/C	0	-0.8
Total	12	1306	4581	511	1279	214	14	121	674	405-56	13	515	.279	.335	.411	103	17	28-33	.979	-34	89	103	O677R,3b220,C169,1b160,D80	0	-6.6
MORELOCK, HARRY	A. Harry; B11.1869 Philadelphia PA; d8.21																								
1891	Phi N	4	14	1	1	0	0	0	0	3	0	3	.071	.235	.071	-9	-2	0	.824	-2	77	0	S4	—	-0.4
1892	Phi N	1	3	0	0	0	0	0	0	1	0	0	.000	.250	.000	-23	0	0	.600	-1	44	0	/3	—	-0.1
Total	2	5	17	1	1	0	0	0	0	4	0	3	.059	.238	.059	-11	-2	0	.824	-3	77	0	S4/3	—	-0.5
MORENO, JOSE	Jose De Los Santos (b Jose De Los Santos Mauricio (Moreno)); B11.1.1957 Santo Domingo, D.R.; BB/TR/6´0˝/175; d5.24																								
1980	NY N	37	46	6	9	2	1	2	9	3-2	0	12	.196	.240	.413	82	-2	1-0	.917	2	120	393	2b4,3b4	0	0.1
1981	SD N	34	48	5	11	2	0	0	6	1-1	0	8	.229	.245	.271	50	-3	4-1	1.000	1	101	176	O9(4/0/5)/2	0	-0.3
1982	Cal A	11	3	3	0	0	0	0	0	2-0	0	0	.000	.400	.000	21	0	0-2	1.000	-1	65	0	2b2/D	0	-0.1
Total	3	82	97	14	20	4	1	2	15	6-3	0	20	.206	.250	.330	66	-5	5-3	1.000	3	101	176	O9(4/0/5),2b7,3b4/D	0	-0.3
MORENO, OMAR	Omar Renan (Quintero); B10.24.1952 Puerto Armuelles, Pan; BL/TL/6´2˝/(170–188); d9.6																								
1975	Pit N	6	6	1	1	0	0	0	0	1-0	0	1	.167	.286	.167	28	-1	1-0	.000	-1	0	0	/lf	0	-0.1
1976	Pit N	48	122	24	33	4	1	2	12	16-0	1	24	.270	.357	.369	105	1	15-5	.960	1	111	146	O42C	0	0.4
1977	Pit N	150	492	69	118	19	9	7	34	38-5	1	102	.240	.295	.358	72	-21	53-16	.977	5	109	113	O147C	0	-1.2
1978	Pit N	155	515	95	121	15	7	2	33	81-4	3	104	.235	.339	.303	78	-13	**71**-22	.984	5	108	110	O152C	0	-0.1
1979	†Pit N	162	695	110	196	21	12	8	69	51-9	3	104	.282	.333	.381	89	-11	**77**-21	.975	5	111	88	O162C	0	0.2
1980	Pit N	**162**	676	87	168	20	**13**	2	36	57-11	2	101	.249	.306	.325	75	-24	96-33	.990	11	110	133	O162C	0	-0.4
1981	Pit N	**103**	434	62	120	18	8	1	35	26-4	3	76	.276	.319	.362	89	-7	39-14	.997	2	107	81	O103C	0	-0.2
1982	Pit N	158	645	82	158	18	9	3	44	44-2	1	121	.245	.292	.315	67	-29	60-26	.983	1	104	108	O157C	0	-2.7
1983	Hou N	97	405	48	98	12	11	0	25	22-3	1	72	.242	.282	.326	72	-18	30-13	.977	3	102	171	O97C	0	-1.5
	NY A	48	152	17	38	9	1	1	17	8-0	0	31	.250	.287	.342	75	-5	7-3	.992	-1	100	37	O48C	0	-0.7
1984	NY A	117	355	37	92	12	6	4	38	18-1	1	48	.259	.294	.361	84	-9	20-11	.985	-1	96	138	O108C/D	0	-1.1
1985	NY A	34	66	12	13	4	1	1	4	1-0	0	16	.197	.209	.333	46	-5	1-1	1.000	3	132	184	O26(3/19/4)/D	0	-0.2
	KC A	24	70	9	17	1	3	2	12	3-0	1	8	.243	.280	.429	91	-1	0-1	1.000	-3	67	83	O21(0/13/8)	0	-0.5
	Year	58	136	21	30	5	4	3	16	4-0	1	24	.221	.246	.382	70	-7	1-2	1.000	0	99	132	O47(3/32/12)/D	0	-0.7
1986	Atl N	118	359	46	84	18	6	4	27	21-2	0	77	.234	.276	.351	69	-16	17-16	.970	0	95	127	O97(18/12/71)	0	-2.3
Total	12	1382	4992	699	1257	171	87	37	386	387-41	17	885	.252	.306	.343	78	-159	487-182	.982	30	105	114	O1323(22/1221/83),D2	0	-10.4
MORGAN, CHET	Chester Collins "Chick"; B6.6.1910 Cleveland MS; D9.20.1991 Pasadena TX; BL/TR/5´9˝/160; d4.19																								
1935	Det A	14	23	2	4	1	0	0	1	5	0	0	.174	.321	.217	43	-2	0-0	.909	-0	110	0	O4L	—	-0.2
1938	Det A	74	306	50	87	6	1	0	27	20	1	12	.284	.330	.310	58	-20	5-6	.980	-2	96	85	O74(6/68/0)	—	-2.3
Total	2	88	329	52	91	7	1	0	28	25	1	12	.277	.330	.304	57	-22	5-6	.977	-2	97	80	O78(10/68/0)	—	-2.5
MORGAN, DAN	Daniel; B5.1853 MO; D1.30.1910 St.Louis MO; d5.4; ▲																								
1875	RS NA	**19**	69	11	18	4	0	0	1	5	—	4	.261	.311	.319	132	3	2-1	.824	-4	79	0	O10(3/7/0),P7,3b7	—	-0.1
1878	Mil N	14	56	2	11	0	0	0	5	3	—	9	.196	.237	.196	41	-4	—	.769	-4	47	0	O13(0/1/12),3b3/2	—	-0.7
MORGAN, ED	Edward Carre; B5.22.1904 Cairo IL; D4.9.1980 New Orleans LA; BR/TR/6´0.5˝/180; d4.11; Col Tulane																								
1928	Cle A	76	265	42	83	24	6	4	54	21	1	17	.313	.366	.494	123	8	5-5	.968	2	124	122	1b36,O21(0/18/3),3b14	—	0.8
1929	Cle A	93	318	60	101	19	10	3	37	37	2	24	.318	.392	.469	116	8	4-3	.908	-8	74	108	O80R	—	-0.6
1930	Cle A	150	584	122	204	47	11	26	136	62	1	66	.349	.413	.601	148	42	8-4	.987	-1	107	103	1b129,O19R	—	2.9
1931	Cle A	131	462	87	162	33	4	11	86	83	1	46	.351	.451	.511	144	35	4-5	.984	2	112	107	1b117,3b3	—	2.3
1932	Cle A	144	532	96	156	32	7	4	68	94	3	44	.293	.402	.402	102	6	7-6	.985	-10	81	88	1b142/3	—	-1.6
1933	Cle A	39	121	10	32	3	3	1	13	7	0	9	.264	.305	.364	73	-5	1-1	.997	2	128	65	1b32/lf	—	-0.6
1934	Bos A	138	528	95	141	28	4	3	79	81	2	46	.267	.367	.352	80	-13	7-1	.988	-6	80	94	1b137	—	-2.9
Total	7	771	2810	512	879	186	45	52	473	385	10	252	.313	.398	.467	117	81	36-25	.986	-18	97	97	1b593,O121(1/18/102),3b18	—	0.3
MORGAN, EDDIE	Edwin Willis "Pepper"; B11.19.1914 Brady Lake OH; D6.27.1982 Lakewood OH; BL/TL/5´10˝/160; d4.14; Col Miami–Ohio																								
1936	StL N	8	18	4	5	0	0	1	3	2	0	4	.278	.350	.444	113	0	0	.889	-1	102	0	O4R	—	0.0
1937	Bro N	31	48	4	9	3	0	0	5	9	0	7	.188	.316	.250	55	-3	0	.984	-2	24	83	1b7,O7(1/1/5)	—	-0.5
Total	2	39	66	8	14	3	0	1	8	11	0	11	.212	.325	.303	70	-3	0	.842	-2	90	123	O11(1/1/9),1b7	—	-0.5
MORGAN, BILL	Henry William; B10.1857 Washington DC; d8.17																								
1882	Pit AA	17	66	10	17	2	1	0	—	4	—	—	.258	.300	.318	114	1	—	.688	-6	0	418	O11R,C7	—	-0.4
1884	Ric AA	6	20	0	2	0	0	0	—	1	0	—	.100	.143	.100	-20	-3	—	.850	-2	—	—	C3,O2R/2	—	-0.4
	Bal U	2	9	1	2	0	0	0	—	1	—	—	.222	.300	.222	55	-1	—	.909	-1	—	—	/C2rf	—	-0.1
Total	2	25	95	11	21	2	1	0	—	6	—	—	.221	.267	.263	78	-3	—	.727	-9	—	—	O14R,C11,2b2	—	-0.9
MORGAN, RED	James Edward; B10.6.1883 Neola IA; D3.25.1981 New York NY; BR/TR/5´10.5˝/180; d6.20; Col Georgetown																								
1906	Bos A	88	307	20	66	6	3	1	21	16	7	—	.215	.270	.264	67	-12	7	.866	-11	82	98	3b88	—	-2.3
MORGAN, JOE	Joe Leonard; B9.19.1943 Bonham TX; BL/TR/5´7˝/(148–165); d9.21; HF1990																								
1963	Hou N	8	25	5	6	0	1	0	3	5-0	0	5	.240	.367	.320	106	0	1-0	.909	-2	83	57	2b7	0	-0.1
1964	Hou N	10	37	4	7	0	0	0	0	6-0	0	7	.189	.302	.189	44	-3	0-1	.949	-2	77	64	2b10	0	-0.5
1965	Hou N	157	601	100	163	22	12	14	40	**97**-1	3	77	.271	.373	.418	132	29	20-9	.969	-7	99	81	2b157	0	3.8
1966	Hou N✱	122	425	60	121	14	8	5	42	89-3	3	43	.285	.410	.391	134	25	11-8	.965	-17	91	79	2b117	40	1.9
1967	Hou N	133	494	73	136	27	11	6	42	81-5	2	51	.275	.378	.411	131	23	29-5	.979	1	97	77	2b130/lf	0	4.2

YEAR	TM LG	G	AB	R	H	2B	3B	HR	RBI	BB-IB	HP	SO	AVG	OBP	SLG	AOPS	ABR	SB-CS	FA	FR	RNG	THR	GAMES AT POSITION	DL	BFW
1968	Hou N	10	20	6	5	0	1	0	0	7-0	0	4	.250	.444	.350	144	2	3-0	.882	-4	44	64	2b5/lf	119	-0.1
1969	Hou N	147	535	94	126	18	5	15	43	110-1	1	74	.236	.365	.372	109	11	49-14	.972	3	90	95	2b132,O14(12/2/0)	0	2.9
1970	Hou N★	144	548	102	147	28	9	8	52	102-3	1	55	.268	.383	.396	114	15	42-13	.979	11	106	101	2b142	0	3.9
1971	Hou N	160	583	87	149	27	**11**	13	56	88-2	1	52	.256	.351	.407	118	16	40-8	.986	-7	100	89	2b157	0	2.7
1972	†Cin N★	149	552	**122**	161	23	4	16	73	**115**-1	6	44	.292	**.417**	.435	150	44	58-17	**.990**	-6	100	103	2b149	0	5.8
1973	†Cin N★	157	576	116	167	35	2	26	82	111-3	4	61	.290	.406	.493	155	49	67-15	.990	5	102	109	2b154	0	**7.4**
1974	Cin N★	149	512	107	150	31	3	22	67	120-8	3	69	.293	**.427**	.494	160	49	58-12	.982	2	97	110	2b142	0	7.0
1975	†Cin N★	146	498	107	163	27	6	17	94	**132**-3	3	52	.327	**.466**	.508	**169**	**57**	67-10	**.986**	2	103	112	2b142	0	**8.1**
1976	†Cin N★	141	472	113	151	30	5	27	111	114-8	1	41	.320	**.444**	**.576**	**186**	**60**	60-9	.981	-14	87	104	2b133	0	**6.7**
1977	Cin N★	153	521	113	150	21	6	22	78	117-2	2	58	.288	.417	.478	137	34	49-10	**.993**	-3	89	117	2b151	0	4.6
1978	Cin N★	132	441	68	104	27	0	13	75	79-3	2	40	.236	.347	.385	106	7	19-5	.980	-23	85	69	2b124	0	-0.7
1979	†Cin N★	127	436	70	109	26	1	9	32	93-11	1	45	.250	.379	.376	108	10	28-6	.980	-12	93	101	2b121	0	0.9
1980	†Hou N	141	461	66	112	17	5	11	49	**93**-6	0	47	.243	.367	.373	118	15	24-6	.988	-11	92	96	2b130	0	1.4
1981	SF N	90	308	47	74	16	1	8	31	66-7	0	37	.240	.371	.377	117	10	14-5	.991	-4	97	112	2b87	0	1.4
1982	SF N	134	463	68	134	19	4	14	61	85-4	2	60	.289	.400	.438	136	27	24-4	.989	-3	102	94	2b120,3b3	0	3.5
1983	†Phi N	123	404	72	93	20	1	16	59	89-1	4	54	.230	.370	.403	116	13	18-2	.971	17	107	96	2b117	15	4.1
1984	Oak A	116	365	50	89	21	0	6	43	66-4	1	39	.244	.356	.351	104	6	8-3	.977	-16	85	98	2b100,D5	0	-0.4
Total	22	2649	9277	1650	2517	449	96	268	1133	1865-76	40	1015	.271	.392	.427	133	499	689-162	.981	-89	96	97	2b2527,O16(14/2/0),D5,3b3	174	68.5
MORGAN, JOE	Joseph Michael; B11.19.1930 Walpole MA; BL/TR/5´10˝/(170–180); d4.14; M4/C5; Col Boston College																								
1959	Mil N	13	23	2	5	1	0	0	1	2-0	0	4	.217	.280	.261	49	-2	0-0	.913	-1	103	39	2b7	0	-0.2
	KC A	20	21	2	4	0	1	0	3	3-0	0	7	.190	.292	.286	58	-1	0-0	1.000	-1	63	0	3b2	0	-0.2
1960	Phi N	26	83	5	11	2	2	0	2	6-1	0	11	.133	.191	.205	8	-11	0-0	.971	1	106	79	3b24	0	-1.0
	Cle A	22	47	6	14	2	0	2	4	6-0	0	4	.298	.377	.468	131	2	0-0	.889	-0	109	47	3b12,O2R	0	0.2
1961	Cle A	4	10	0	2	0	0	0	0	1-0	0	3	.200	.273	.200	29	-1	0-0	1.000	-0	106	0	O2C	0	-0.1
1964	StL N	3	3	0	0	0	0	0	0	0-0	0	2	.000	.000	.000	-92	-1	0-0	ø	0	—	—	/H	0	-0.1
Total	4	88	187	15	36	5	3	2	10	18-1	0	31	.193	.263	.283	49	-14	0-0	.944	-1	105	66	3b38,2b7,O4(0/2/2)	0	-1.4
MORGAN, KEVIN	Kevin Lee; B3.3.1970 Lafayette LA; BR/TR/6´1˝/170; [DetA91 30/790]; d6.15; Col Southeastern Louisiana																								
1997	NY N	1	1	0	0	0	0	0	0	0-0	0	0	.000	.000	.000	-99	0	0-0	1.000	0	235	0	/3	0	0.0
MORGAN, RAY	Raymond Caryll; B6.14.1889 Baltimore MD; D2.15.1940 Baltimore MD; BR/TR/5´8.5˝/155; d8.7																								
1911	Was A	25	89	11	19	2	0	0	5	4	0	—	.213	.247	.236	36	-8	2	.900	-2	95	31	3b25	—	-0.9
1912	Was A	81	273	40	65	10	7	1	30	29	3	—	.238	.318	.337	87	-5	12	.939	-9	87	90	2b76,S4/3	—	-1.3
1913	Was A	138	481	58	131	19	8	0	57	68	6	63	.272	.369	.345	107	7	19	.950	-8	93	**141**	2b134,S4	—	0.2
1914	Was A	147	491	50	126	22	8	1	49	62	10	34	.257	.352	.340	104	5	24-17	.948	-13	90	**128**	2b146	—	-0.7
1915	Was A	62	193	21	45	5	4	0	21	30	2	15	.233	.342	.301	91	-1	6-5	.965	-3	100	114	2b57,S2,3b2	—	-0.4
1916	Was A	99	315	41	84	12	4	1	29	59	10	29	.267	.398	.340	123	14	14	.957	-11	94	104	2b82,S9,1b3/3	—	0.4
1917	Was A	101	338	32	90	9	1	1	33	40	1	29	.266	.346	.308	101	2	7	.961	-8	88	113	2b95,3b3	—	-0.5
1918	Was A	88	300	25	70	11	1	0	30	28	6	14	.233	.311	.277	79	-7	4	.959	-8	98	88	2b80,O2R	—	-1.6
Total	8	741	2480	278	630	90	33	4	254	320	38	184	.254	.348	.322	98	7	88-22	.953	-61	92	115	2b670,3b32,S19,1b3,O2R	—	-4.8
MORGAN, BOBBY	Robert Morris; B6.29.1926 Oklahoma City OK; BR/TR/5´9˝/(175–180); d4.18																								
1950	Bro N	67	199	38	45	10	3	7	21	32	3	43	.226	.342	.412	95	-1	0	.969	8	122	154	3b52,S10	0	0.7
1952	†Bro N	67	191	36	45	8	0	7	16	46	3	35	.236	.392	.387	115	7	2-2	.968	1	108	121	3b60,2b5,S4	0	0.7
1953	†Bro N	69	196	35	51	6	2	7	33	33	1	47	.260	.370	.418	103	2	2-2	.920	-2	98	99	3b36,S21	0	0.0
1954	Phi N	135	455	58	119	25	2	14	50	70	0	68	.262	.357	.418	102	3	3-1	.954	-19	93	91	S129,3b8,2b5	0	-0.5
1955	Phi N	136	483	61	112	20	2	10	49	73-0	0	72	.232	.331	.344	81	-11	6-4	.980	-17	87	87	2b88,S41,3b6/1	0	-1.9
1956	Phi N	8	25	1	5	0	0	0	1	6-0	0	4	.200	.355	.200	56	-1	0-0	.857	-1	94	101	3b5,2b3	0	-0.2
	StL N	61	113	14	22	7	0	3	20	15-0	0	24	.195	.287	.336	67	-5	0-2	.980	-1	101	52	2b13,3b11,S6	0	-0.6
	Year	69	138	15	27	7	0	3	21	21-0	0	28	.196	.300	.312	65	-6	0-2	.877	-1	102	70	3b16,2b16,S6	0	-0.8
1957	Phi N	2	0	0	0	0	0	0	0	0-0	0	0	ø	ø	ø	ø	0	0-0	1.000	-0	0	0	/2	0	0.0
	Chi N	125	425	43	88	20	2	5	27	52-1	1	87	.207	.294	.299	61	-23	5-0	.976	8	108	78	2b116,3b12	0	-0.6
	Year	127	425	43	88	20	2	5	27	52-1	1	87	.207	.294	.299	61	-23	5-0	.976	7	108	78	2b117,3b12	0	-0.6
1958	Chi N	1	1	0	0	0	0	0	0	0-0	0	1	.000	.000	.000	-99	0	0-0	ø	0	—	—	/H	0	0.0
Total	8	671	2088	286	487	96	11	53	217	327-1	8	381	.233	.338	.366	88	-29	18-11	.978	-25	99	79	2b231,S211,3b190/1	0	-2.4
MORGAN, VERN	Vernon Thomas; B8.8.1928 Emporia VA; D11.8.1975 Minneapolis MN; BL/TR/6´1˝/190; d8.10; C7; Col Richmond																								
1954	Chi N	24	64	3	15	2	0	0	2	1	0	10	.234	.242	.266	33	-6	0-0	.895	-3	91	38	3b15	0	-0.9
1955	Chi N	7	7	1	1	0	0	0	1	3-0	0	4	.143	.400	.143	52	0	0-0	.667	-1	62	0	3b2	0	-0.1
Total	2	31	71	4	16	2	0	0	3	4-0	0	14	.225	.263	.254	36	-6	0-0	.864	-4	88	34	3b17	0	-1.0
MORGAN, BILL	William; B1856 Brooklyn NY; D9.7.1908 New York NY; d8.6																								
1883	Pit AA	32	114	12	18	2	1	0	—	7	—	—	.158	.207	.193	31	-8	—	.825	-2	93	58	S21,O6(1/4/1),C5,2b2	—	-0.8
1884	Was AA	45	162	8	28	1	1	0	—	8	1	—	.173	.216	.191	39	-10	—	.781	-4	70	92	O31(17/2/13),C12,2b2,S2	—	-1.2
Total	2	77	276	20	46	3	2	0	—	15	1	—	.167	.212	.192	35	-18	—	.771	-6	64	84	O37(18/6/14),S23,C17,2b4	—	-2.0
MORHARDT, MOE	Meredith Goodwin; B1.16.1937 Manchester CT; BL/TL/6´1˝/185; d9.7; Col Connecticut																								
1961	Chi N	7	18	3	5	0	0	0	1	3-0	0	5	.278	.381	.278	78	0	0-0	.962	-1	65	157	1b7	0	-0.2
1962	Chi N	18	16	1	2	0	0	0	2	2-0	0	8	.125	.222	.125	-4	-2	0-0	ø	0	—	—	/H	0	-0.2
Total	2	25	34	4	7	0	0	0	3	5-0	0	13	.206	.308	.206	39	-2	0-0	.962	-1	65	157	1b7	0	-0.4
MORIARITY, GENE	Eugene John; B7.5.1855 Holyoke MA; BL/TL/5´8˝/130; d6.18; ▲																								
1884	Bos N	4	16	1	1	0	0	0	0	0	—	8	.063	.063	.063	-61	-3	—	.714	-0	131	0	O4(1/3/0)	—	-0.3
	Ind AA	10	37	4	8	0	2	0	4	0	0	—	.216	.216	.324	76	-1	—	.769	-1	76	0	O7R,P2/3	—	-0.2
1885	Det N	11	39	1	1	1	0	0	0	0	—	10	.026	.026	.051	-75	-7	—	.905	-0	59	0	O6(1/0/5),3b4/SP	—	-0.7
1892	StL N	47	177	20	31	4	1	3	19	4	3	37	.175	.207	.260	43	-13	7	.820	1	114	0	O47L	—	-1.6
Total	3	72	269	26	41	5	3	3	23	4	3	55	.152	.174	.227	24	-24	7	.822	-1	104	0	O64(49/3/12),3b5,P3/S	—	-2.8
MORIARTY, ED	Edward Jerome; B10.12.1912 Holyoke MA; D9.29.1991 Holyoke MA; BR/TR/5´10.5˝/180; d6.21; Col Holy Cross																								
1935	Bos N	8	34	4	11	2	1	1	1	0	0	6	.324	.324	.529	136	1	0	.923	-3	103	0	2b8	—	-0.1
1936	Bos N	6	6	1	1	0	0	0	0	0	0	1	.167	.167	.167	-11	-1	0	ø	0	—	—	/H	—	-0.1
Total	2	14	40	5	12	2	1	1	1	0	0	7	.300	.300	.475	114	0	0	.923	-3	103	0	2b8	—	-0.2
MORIARTY, GEORGE	George Joseph; B7.7.1885 Chicago IL; D4.8.1964 Miami FL; BR/TR/6´0˝/185; d9.27; M2/U22; b–Bill																								
1903	Chi N	1	5	1	0	0	0	0	0	0	0	—	.000	.000	.000	-99	-1	0	1.000	-0	39	0	/3	—	-0.2
1904	Chi N	4	13	0	0	0	0	0	0	1	0	—	.000	.071	.000	-77	-3	0	.778	-1	66	0	3b2,O2C	—	-0.4
1906	NY A	65	197	22	46	7	7	0	23	17	1	—	.234	.298	.340	90	-3	8	.912	0	98	82	3b39,O15(14/2/0),1b5/2	—	-0.3
1907	NY A	126	437	51	121	16	5	0	43	25	3	—	.277	.320	.336	101	0	28	.899	-9	93	81	3b91,1b22,O9(1/4/3),2b8/S	—	-0.7
1908	NY A	101	348	25	82	12	1	0	27	11	5	—	.236	.269	.276	76	-9	22	.976	7	85	108	1b52,3b28,O10(8/0/2),2b4	—	-0.4
1909	†Det A	133	473	43	129	20	4	1	39	24	1	—	.273	.309	.338	100	-1	34	**.939**	-1	**111**	84	3b106,1b24	—	0.1
1910	Det A	136	490	53	123	24	3	2	60	33	7	—	.251	.308	.324	92	-4	33	.927	1	**107**	88	3b134	—	0.0
1911	Det A	130	478	51	116	20	4	1	60	27	3	—	.243	.287	.308	63	-25	28	.929	-5	104	57	3b129/1	—	-2.6
1912	Det A	105	375	38	93	23	1	0	54	26	11	—	.248	.316	.315	83	-7	30	.987	-7	65	52	1b71,3b33	—	-1.5
1913	Det A	104	347	29	83	5	2	0	30	24	7	25	.239	.302	.265	67	-14	33	.938	-1	104	65	3b94,O7L	—	-1.4
1914	Det A	132	465	56	118	19	5	1	40	39	5	27	.254	.318	.323	90	-6	34-15	.956	16	**125**	91	3b126,1b3	—	1.7
1915	Det A	31	38	2	8	1	0	0	0	5	1	7	.211	.318	.237	63	-1	1-1	.875	-0	115	101	3b12/12cf	—	-0.2
1916	Chi A	7	5	1	1	0	0	0	0	2	0	0	.200	.429	.200	88	0	0	1.000	0	740	0	/13	—	0.1
Total	13	1075	3671	372	920	147	32	5	376	234	44	59	.251	.303	.312	84	-74	251-16	.931	0	108	79	3b796,1b180,O44(30/9/5),2b14/S	—	-5.8
MORIARTY, MIKE	Michael Thomas; B3.8.1974 Camden NJ; BR/TR/6´0˝/195; [MinA95 7/184]; d4.11; Col Seton Hall																								
2002	Bal A	8	16	0	3	1	0	0	3	0-0	0	2	.188	.188	.250	16	-2	0-1	1.000	3	146	0	S4,2b2/3	0	0.1
MORIARTY, BILL	William Joseph; B8.1883 Chicago IL; D12.25.1916 Elgin IL; BR/TR/6´2˝/180; d4.29; b–George																								
1909	Cin N	6	20	1	4	1	0	0	1	0	0	—	.200	.200	.250	40	-1	2	.944	-0	84	89	S6	—	-0.2

YEAR	TM LG	G	AB	R	H	2B	3B	HR	RBI	BB-IB	HP	SO	AVG	OBP	SLG	AOPS	ABR	SB-CS	FA	FR	RNG	THR	GAMES AT POSITION	DL	BFW
Morley, Bill	William M. (b William Morley Jennings); B1.23.1890 Holland MI; D5.14.1985 Lubbock TX; BR/TR/5´11˝/170; d9.8																								
1913	Was A	2	3	0	0	0	0	0	0	0	0	0	.000	.000	.000	-98	-1	0	ø	-0	0	0	/2	—	-0.1
Morman, Russ	Russell Lee; B4.28.1962 Independence MO; BR/TR/6´4˝/(215–225); [ChiA83 1/28]; d8.3; Col Wichita St.																								
1986	Chi A	49	159	18	40	5	0	4	17	16-0	2	36	.252	.324	.358	84	-3	1-0	.989	-4	72	85	1b47	0	-1.0
1988	Chi A	40	75	8	18	2	0	0	3	3-0	0	17	.240	.269	.267	51	-5	0-0	.981	-3	65	83	1b22,O10L,D3	0	-0.9
1989	Chi A	37	58	5	13	2	0	0	8	6-1	0	16	.224	.292	.259	59	-3	1-0	.988	-1	94	116	1b35/D	0	-0.5
1990	KC A	12	37	5	10	4	2	1	3	3-0	0	3	.270	.317	.568	147	2	0-0	1.000	0	57	238	O8L,1b3/D	0	0.2
1991	KC A	12	23	1	6	0	0	0	1	1-1	0	5	.261	.292	.261	54	-2	0-0	1.000	-0	81	47	1b8,O2L/D	0	-0.2
1994	Fla N	13	33	2	7	0	1	1	2	2-0	1	9	.212	.278	.364	63	-2	0-0	.987	1	157	153	1b8	0	-0.2
1995	Fla N	34	72	9	20	2	1	3	7	3-0	1	12	.278	.316	.458	99	-1	0-0	.955	-1	83	0	O18(6/0/12),1b3	21	-0.2
1996	Fla N	6	6	0	1	1	0	0	0	1-0	0	2	.167	.286	.333	64	0	0-0	1.000	-0	0	535	1b2	0	0.0
1997	Fla N	4	7	3	2	1	0	1	2	0-0	0	2	.286	.286	.857	193	1	1-0	1.000	0	0	1726	O2R/1	0	0.1
Total	9	207	470	51	117	17	4	10	43	35-2	4	102	.249	.304	.366	81	-13	3-0	.989	-8	87	95	1b129,O40(26/0/14),D6	21	-2.7
Morneau, Justin	Justin Ernest George; B5.15.1981 New Westminster BC, Can.; BL/TR/6´4˝/(200–230); [MinA99 3/89]; d6.10																								
2003	Min A	40	106	14	24	4	0	4	16	9-1	0	30	.226	.287	.377	71	-5	0-0	.971	0	152	32	D23,1b7	0	-0.6
2004	†Min A	74	280	39	76	17	0	19	58	28-8	2	54	.271	.340	.536	120	8	0-0	.995	1	106	113	1b61,D11	0	0.3
2005	Min A	141	490	62	117	23	4	22	79	44-8	4	94	.239	.304	.437	93	-6	0-2	.994	1	106	120	1b138/D	15	-1.7
2006	†Min A	157	592	97	190	37	1	34	130	53-9	5	93	.321	.375	.559	139	34	3-3	.994	10	123	93	1b153,D4	0	2.8
Total	4	412	1468	212	407	81	5	79	283	134-26	11	271	.277	.338	.501	115	31	3-5	.994	13	114	106	1b359,D39	15	0.8
Moronko, Jeff	Jeffrey Robert; B8.17.1959 Houston TX; BR/TR/6´2˝/190; [CleA80 6/140]; d9.1; Col Texas Wesleyan																								
1984	Cle A	7	19	1	3	1	0	0	3	3-0	0	5	.158	.273	.211	35	-2	0-0	.895	-0	69	190	3b6/D	0	-0.2
1987	NY A	7	11	0	1	0	0	0	0	0-0	1	2	.091	.167	.091	-29	-2	0-0	1.000	0	141	0	3b3,S2,O2(1/0/1)	0	-0.2
Total	2	14	30	1	4	1	0	0	3	3-0	1	7	.133	.235	.167	12	-4	0-0	.926	-0	91	132	3b9,O2(1/0/1),S2/D	0	-0.4
Morrill, John	John Francis "Honest John"; B2.19.1855 Boston MA; D4.2.1932 Brookline MA; BR/TR/5´10.5˝/155; d4.24; M8; OF(2/12/12); ▲																								
1876	Bos N	66	278	38	73	5	2	0	26	3	—	5	.263	.270	.295	87	-4	—	.857	5	110	133	2b37,C23,O5(1/3/1),1b3	—	0.3
1877	Bos N	**61**	242	47	73	5	1	0	28	6	—	15	.302	.319	.331	101	0	—	.864	-9	76	36	3b30,1b18,O11R,2b3	—	-0.8
1878	Bos N	**60**	233	26	56	5	1	0	23	5	—	16	.240	.256	.270	68	-9	—	.957	2	130	**139**	1b59/cf3	—	-0.8
1879	Bos N	**84**	348	56	98	18	5	0	49	14	—	32	.282	.309	.362	118	7	—	.878	1	87	34	3b51,1b33	—	0.7
1880	Bos N	**86**	342	51	81	16	8	2	44	11	—	37	.237	.261	.348	108	3	—	.966	2	220	114	1b46,3b40,P3	—	0.4
1881	Bos N	81	311	47	90	19	3	1	39	12	—	30	.289	.316	.379	123	9	—	.969	7	138	76	1b74,2b4,P3,3b2	—	1.3
1882	Bos N	83	349	73	101	19	11	2	54	18	—	29	.289	.324	.424	137	14	—	.964	-2	76	63	1b76,S3,2b2/cf3PM	—	0.5
1883	Bos N	97	404	83	129	33	16	6	68	15	—	68	.319	.344	.525	155	26	—	**.974**	-1	76	93	1b81,O7C,3b6,S2,2b2,P2,M	—	1.5
1884	Bos N	111	438	80	114	19	7	3	61	30	—	87	.260	.308	.356	109	5	—	.971	2	125	96	1b91,2b17,P7,3b2/lfM	—	-0.1
1885	Bos N	111	394	74	89	20	7	4	44	64	—	78	.226	.334	.343	124	15	—	.969	0	103	108	1b92,2b17,3b2,M	—	0.7
1886	Bos N	117	430	86	106	25	6	7	69	56	—	81	.247	.333	.381	120	13	9	.895	-8	87	78	S55,1b42,2b20/PM	—	0.3
1887	Bos N	**127**	504	79	141	32	6	12	81	37	1	86	.280	.330	.438	110	7	19	.984	4	109	102	1b127,M	—	0.0
1888	Bos N	135	486	60	96	18	7	4	39	55	2	68	.198	.282	.288	80	-9	21	.979	9	**147**	104	1b133,2b2,M	—	-1.3
1889	Was N	44	146	20	27	5	0	2	16	30	1	23	.185	.328	.260	69	-4	12	.980	-1	104	60	1b40,3b3/2PM	—	-0.8
1890	Bos P	2	7	1	1	0	0	0	2	2	0	1	.143	.333	.143	28	-1	0	.750	-1	88	0	/S1	—	-0.1
Total	15	1265	4912	821	1275	239	80	43	643	358	4	656	.260	.310	.367	111	72	61	.971	11	124	101	1b916,3b138,2b105,S61,O26C,C23,P18	—	1.8
Morris, Doyt	Doyt Theodore; B7.15.1916 Stanley NC; D7.4.1984 Gastonia NC; BR/TR/6´4˝/195; d6.6; Col Wake Forest																								
1937	Phi A	6	13	0	2	0	0	0	0	0	0	3	.154	.154	.154	-23	-3	0-0	1.000	0	111	0	O3(2/1/0)	—	-0.2
Morris, Jim	James A.; B Trenton NJ; d9.11																								
1884	Bal U	1	3	0	0	0	0	0	—	0	—	—	.000	.000	.000	-91	-1	—	ø	-0	0	0	/cfP	—	-0.1
Morris, John	John Daniel; B2.23.1961 N.Bellmore NY; BL/TL/6´1˝/185; [KCA82 1/10]; d8.5; Col Seton Hall																								
1986	StL N	39	100	8	24	0	1	1	14	7-2	0	15	.240	.287	.290	60	-6	6-2	.986	2	130	0	O31(5/4/26)	0	-0.5
1987	†StL N	101	157	22	41	6	4	3	23	11-4	1	22	.261	.314	.408	87	-4	5-2	.989	0	113	0	O74(2/8/68)	0	-0.5
1988	StL N	20	38	3	11	2	1	0	3	1-0	0	7	.289	.308	.395	99	0	0-0	.857	-2	65	0	O16(11/3/2)	151	-0.3
1989	StL N	96	117	8	28	4	1	2	14	4-0	0	22	.239	.264	.342	70	-5	1-0	1.000	-2	94	0	O51(10/11/32)	0	-0.8
1990	StL N	18	18	0	2	0	0	0	0	3-0	0	6	.111	.238	.111	-1	-2	0-0	1.000	-0	87	0	O6(0/1/5)	121	-0.3
1991	Phi N	85	127	15	28	2	1	1	6	12-4	1	25	.220	.293	.276	61	-7	2-0	.974	-0	104	51	O57(11/27/24)	0	-0.8
1992	Cal A	43	57	4	11	1	0	1	3	4-1	1	11	.193	.258	.263	46	-4	1-0	1.000	-1	94	0	O14(5/0/9),D6	18	-0.5
Total	7	402	614	60	145	15	8	8	63	42-11	3	108	.236	.288	.326	69	-28	15-4	.981	-3	106	12	O249(44/54/166),D6	290	-3.7
Morris, Walter	John Walter; B1.31.1880 Rockwall TX; D8.2.1961 Dallas TX; BR/TR/5´11˝/?; d8.31; Col Texas																								
1908	StL N	23	73	1	13	1	1	0	2	0	0	—	.178	.178	.219	28	-6	1	.938	2	103	109	S23	—	-0.4
Morris, P.	P.; B Rockford IL; d5.14																								
1884	Was U	1	3	0	0	0	0	0	—	0	—	—	.000	.000	.000	-99	-1	—	.750	-0	113	0	/S	—	-0.1
Morris, Warren	Warren Randall; B1.11.1974 Alexandria LA; BL/TR/5´11˝/(179–185); [TexA96 5/143]; d4.5; Col Louisiana St.																								
1999	Pit N	147	511	65	147	20	3	15	73	59-3	2	88	.288	.360	.427	99	-1	3-7	.979	3	104	111	2b144	0	0.7
2000	Pit N	144	528	68	137	31	2	3	43	65-3	2	78	.259	.341	.343	74	-20	7-10	.979	19	**114**	97	2b134	0	0.4
2001	Pit N	48	103	6	21	6	0	2	11	3-0	2	9	.204	.239	.320	42	-9	2-3	.965	2	122	105	2b29/3	19	-0.6
2002	Min A	4	7	0	0	0	0	0	0	0-0	0	1	.000	.000	.000	-97	-2	0-0	1.000	0	117	91	2b4	0	-0.2
2003	Det A	97	346	37	94	13	2	6	37	23-1	1	42	.272	.316	.373	86	-8	4-2	.987	12	111	138	2b89	0	0.8
Total	5	440	1495	176	399	70	7	26	164	150-7	7	218	.267	.334	.375	82	-40	16-22	.980	36	110	112	2b400/3	19	1.1
Morris, Hal	William Harold; B4.9.1965 Fort Rucker AL; BL/TL/6´4˝/(195–215); [NYA86 8/210]; d7.29; Col Michigan																								
1988	NY A	15	20	1	2	0	0	0	0	0-0	0	9	.100	.100	.100	-44	-4	0-0	1.000	0	125	0	O4(3/0/2)/D	0	-0.4
1989	NY A	15	18	2	5	0	0	0	4	1-0	0	4	.278	.316	.278	69	-1	0-0	1.000	-0	109	0	O5(2/0/3),1b2/D	0	-0.1
1990	†Cin N	107	309	50	105	22	3	7	36	21-4	1	32	.340	.381	.498	135	15	9-3	.995	1	104	104	1b80,O6L	0	1.2
1991	Cin N	136	478	72	152	33	1	14	59	46-7	1	61	.318	.374	.479	134	23	10-4	.992	6	116	103	1b128/lf	0	2.1
1992	Cin N	115	395	41	107	21	3	6	53	45-8	2	53	.271	.347	.385	105	4	6-6	**.999**	7	**116**	91	1b109	45	0.2
1993	Cin N	101	379	48	120	18	0	7	49	34-4	2	51	.317	.371	.420	112	7	2-2	.994	3	106	81	1b98	63	0.1
1994	Cin N	112	436	60	146	30	4	10	78	34-8	5	62	.335	.385	.491	128	19	6-2	.994	2	102	94	1b112	0	1.1
1995	†Cin N	101	359	53	100	25	2	11	51	29-7	1	58	.279	.333	.451	104	2	1-1	.994	5	119	**116**	1b99	25	-0.2
1996	Cin N	142	528	82	165	32	4	16	80	50-5	5	76	.313	.374	.479	122	18	7-5	.993	-2	95	94	1b140	15	0.4
1997	Cin N	96	333	42	92	20	1	1	33	23-2	3	43	.276	.328	.351	77	-11	3-1	.990	-3	86	101	1b89	44	-2.1
1998	KC A	127	472	50	146	27	2	1	40	32-6	1	52	.309	.350	.381	88	-8	1-0	.990	-2	127	98	1b46,O39L,D39	15	-1.5
1999	Cin N	80	102	10	29	9	0	0	16	10-0	0	21	.284	.348	.373	80	-3	0-0	.991	-1	78	112	1b25,O4L/D	28	-0.5
2000	Cin N	59	63	9	14	2	1	2	6	12-3	1	10	.222	.351	.381	84	-1	0-0	1.000	3	239	100	1b16/rfD	0	0.1
	Det A	40	106	15	33	7	0	1	8	19-1	0	16	.311	.416	.406	110	3	0-0	.990	1	109	101	1b38/lf	26	0.1
Total	13	1246	3998	535	1216	246	21	76	513	356-55	22	548	.304	.361	.433	110	63	45-24	.994	19	107	98	1b982,O61(56/0/6),D43	261	0.5
Morrison, Jim	James Forrest; B9.23.1952 Pensacola FL; BR/TR/5´11˝/(175–186); [PhiN74 5/99]; d9.18; Col Georgia Southern; OF(9/0/3)																								
1977	Phi N	5	7	3	3	0	0	0	1	1-0	0	1	.429	.500	.429	144	1	0-0	.875	-0	119	0	3b5	0	0.0
1978	†Phi N	53	108	12	17	1	1	3	10	10-1	1	21	.157	.235	.269	40	-9	1-1	.968	11	122	144	2b31,3b3/lf	0	0.3
1979	Chi A	67	240	38	66	14	0	14	35	15-0	4	48	.275	.324	.508	121	6	11-3	.982	5	100	102	2b48,3b29	0	1.4
1980	Chi A	**162**	604	66	171	40	0	15	57	36-2	8	74	.283	.329	.424	106	5	9-6	.969	9	101	96	2b161/SD	0	2.2
1981	Chi A	90	290	27	68	8	1	10	34	10-0	2	29	.234	.261	.372	83	-8	3-2	.956	9	108	92	3b87/2D	0	-0.1
1982	Chi A	51	166	17	37	7	3	7	19	13-0	0	15	.223	.279	.428	90	-3	0-1	.914	-10	85	101	3b50/D	0	-1.5
	Pit N	44	86	10	24	4	1	4	15	5-0	0	14	.279	.309	.488	117	2	2-0	.964	1	100	65	3b26,O2L/2S	0	0.3
1983	Pit N	66	158	16	48	7	2	6	25	9-1	2	25	.304	.347	.487	126	5	2-6	.973	1	104	119	2b28,3b26,S7	0	0.6
1984	Pit N	100	304	38	87	14	2	11	45	20-1	1	52	.286	.328	.454	119	6	0-1	.938	-4	98	89	3b61,2b26,S2/1	0	0.2
1985	Pit N	92	244	17	62	10	0	4	22	8-1	1	44	.254	.277	.344	74	-9	3-0	.961	1	90	106	3b59,2b15/lf	0	-0.8
1986	Pit N	154	537	58	147	35	4	23	88	47-5	4	88	.274	.334	.482	120	14	9-8	.946	-12	95	49	3b151/2S	0	-0.2
1987	Pit N	96	348	41	92	22	1	9	46	27-3	1	57	.264	.315	.411	91	-5	8-5	.975	4	105	89	3b82,S17,2b9	0	-0.1

YEAR	TM LG	G	AB	R	H	2B	3B	HR	RBI	BB-IB	HP	SO	AVG	OBP	SLG	AOPS	ABR	SB-CS	FA	FR	RNG	THR	GAMES AT POSITION	DL	BFW
	†Det A	34	117	15	24	1	1	4	19	2-0	1	26	.205	.221	.333	47	-10	2-1	.962	4	152	37	3b16,2b3,S3,O3(1/0/2)/1D	0	-0.5
1988	Det A	24	74	7	16	5	0	0	6	0-0	0	14	.216	.216	.284	40	-6	0-2	1.000	-0	0	130	D14,1b4,3b4,O2(1/0/1)/S	0	-0.8
	Atl N	51	92	6	14	2	0	2	13	10-1	0	13	.152	.229	.239	35	-8	0-1	.933	-2	84	34	3b20,O4L,P3	0	-1.0
Total	12	1089	3375	371	876	170	16	112	435	213-15	25	521	.260	.305	.419	98	-19	50-37	.949	16	100	79	3b619,2b324,S33,D25,O13L,1b6,P30		0.0
Morrison, Jon	Jonathan W.; B1859 London ON, Can.; BL/5´9.5˝/167; d8.1																								
1884	Ind AA	44	182	26	48	6	8	1	—	7	4	—	.264	.306	.401	132	6	—	.784	2	107	282	O44C	—	0.6
1887	NY AA	9	34	7	4	0	0	0	3	6	1	—	.118	.268	.118	10	-4	0	.600	-4	0	0	O9C	—	-0.7
Total	2	53	216	33	52	6	8	1	3	13	5	—	.241	.299	.356	110	2	0	.756	-2	89	235	O53C	—	-0.1
Morrison, Tom	Thomas J.; B8.1870 St.Louis MO; D3.27.1902 St.Louis MO; 5´3˝/145; d9.18																								
1895	Lou N	6	22	3	6	0	2	0	4	1	0	1	.273	.304	.455	100	0	0	1.000	-1	59	108	S3,3b3	—	-0.1
1896	Lou N	8	27	3	4	1	0	0	0	4	0	4	.148	.258	.185	19	-3	0	.864	1	131	0	3b5,O2R/S	—	-0.2
Total	2	14	49	6	10	1	2	0	4	5	0	5	.204	.278	.306	55	-3	0	.839	-1	117	0	3b8,S4,O2R	—	-0.3
Morrissey, Jack	John Albert "King"; B5.2.1876 Lansing MI; D10.30.1936 Lansing MI; BB/TR/5´10˝/160; d9.18																								
1902	Cin N	12	39	5	11	1	1	0	3	4	0	—	.282	.349	.359	108	0	0	.941	-1	96	87	2b11/lf	—	0.0
1903	Cin N	29	89	14	22	1	0	0	9	14	0	—	.247	.350	.258	67	-3	3	.922	-9	82	0	2b17,O8(6/2/0),S2	—	-1.3
Total	2	41	128	19	33	2	1	0	12	18	0	—	.258	.349	.289	78	-3	3	.930	-10	87	32	2b28,O9(7/2/0),S2	—	-1.3
Morrissey, John	John J.; B12.30.1856 Janesville WI; D4.29.1884 Janesville WI; d5.2; b–Tom																								
1881	Buf N	12	47	3	10	2	0	0	3	0	—	3	.213	.213	.255	47	-3	—	.865	-1	103	0	3b12	—	-0.4
Morrissey, Jo-Jo	Joseph Anselm; B1.16.1904 Warren RI; D5.2.1950 Worcester MA; BR/TR/6´1.5˝/178; d4.12; Col Holy Cross																								
1932	Cin N	89	269	15	65	10	1	0	13	14	1	15	.242	.282	.286	55	-17	2	.967	4	102	78	S45,2b42,3b12/lf	—	-0.9
1933	Cin N	148	534	43	123	20	0	0	26	20	2	22	.230	.261	.268	52	-34	5	.964	-6	113	98	2b88,S63,3b15	—	-3.3
1936	Chi A	17	38	3	7	1	0	0	6	2	0	3	.184	.225	.211	8	-6	0-0	.895	-1	97	103	3b9,S4/2	—	-0.5
Total	3	254	841	61	195	31	1	0	45	36	3	40	.232	.266	.271	51	-57	7-0	.971	-3	112	102	2b131,S112,3b36/lf	—	-4.7
Morrissey, Tom	Thomas J.; B5.1860 Janesville WI; D9.23.1941 Janesville WI; 5´11˝/180; d7.12; b–John																								
1882	Det N	2	7	1	2	0	0	0	0	0	—	2	.286	.286	.286	84	0	—	.714	-1	23	0	3b2	—	-0.1
1884	Mil U	**12**	47	3	8	2	0	0	—	0	—	—	.170	.170	.213	28	-6	—	.710	-1	71	147	3b12	—	-0.6
Total	2	14	54	4	10	2	0	0	0	0	—	2	.185	.185	.222	39	-6	—	.711	-2	64	125	3b14	—	-0.7
Morse, Mike	Michael John; B3.22.1981 Fort Lauderdale FL; BR/TR/6´4˝/(220–225); [ChiA00 3/82]; d5.31																								
2005	Sea A	72	230	27	64	10	1	3	23	18-0	8	50	.278	.349	.370	99	0	3-1	.946	-11	81	103	S55,O8L,D9	0	-0.7
2006	Sea A	21	43	5	16	5	0	0	11	3-0	0	7	.372	.396	.488	141	3	1-0	1.000	-1	85	295	O9(2/0/7),3b5,1b2/SD	0	0.2
Total	2	93	273	32	80	15	1	3	34	21-0	8	57	.293	.356	.388	106	3	4-1	.946	-12	81	103	S56,O17(10/0/7),D13,3b5,1b2	0	-0.5
Morse, Bud	Newell Obediah; B9.4.1904 Berkeley CA; D4.6.1987 Sparks NV; BL/TR/5´9˝/150; d9.14; Col Michigan																								
1929	Phi A	8	27	1	2	0	0	0	0	0	0	2	.074	.074	.074	-60	-7	0-0	.975	1	103	78	2b8	—	-0.6
Morse, Hap	Peter Raymond "Pete"; B12.6.1886 St.Paul MN; D6.19.1974 St.Paul MN; BR/TR/5´8˝/160; d4.18																								
1911	StL N	4	8	0	0	0	0	0	0	1	0	2	.000	.111	.000	-70	-2	0	.750	-1	89	0	S2/lf	—	-0.3
Morton, Charlie	Charles Hazen; B10.12.1854 Kingsville OH; D12.9.1921 Massillon OH; BR/TR/?/150; d5.2; M3/U1; ▲																								
1882	Pit AA	25	103	12	29	0	3	0	—	5	—	—	.282	.315	.340	127	3	—	.816	1	159	0	O25C,3b3/S	—	0.2
	StL AA	9	32	2	2	0	1	0	—	2	—	—	.063	.118	.125	-17	-4	—	.708	-4	79	48	2b7,O3(1/2/0)	—	-0.7
	Year	34	135	14	31	0	4	0	—	7	—	—	.230	.268	.289	90	-2	—	.821	-3	155	0	O28(1/27/0),2b7,3b3/S	—	-0.5
1884	Tol AA	32	111	11	18	6	2	0	—	7	0	—	.162	.212	.252	49	-6	—	.861	-0	79	78	3b16,O15(14/0/1),P3/2M	—	-0.5
1885	Det N	22	79	9	14	1	2	0	3	5	—	10	.177	.226	.241	51	-4	—	.750	-1	103	85	3b18,S4,M	—	-0.4
Total	3	88	325	34	63	7	8	0	3	19	—	10	.194	.238	.265	66	-11	—	.841	-4	144	0	O43(15/27/1),3b37,2b8,S5,P3	—	-1.4
Morton, Guy	Guy Jr. "Moose"; B11.4.1930 Tuscaloosa AL; BR/TR/6´2˝/200; d9.17; f–Guy; Col Alabama																								
1954	Bos A	1	1	0	0	0	0	0	0	0	0	1	.000	.000	.000	-90	0	0-0	ø	0	—	—	/H	0	0.0
Morton, Bubba	Wycliffe Nathaniel; B12.13.1931 Washington DC; D1.14.2006 Seattle WA; BR/TR/5´10.5˝/(175–180); d4.19; Col Howard																								
1961	Det A	77	108	26	31	5	1	2	19	9-1	1	25	.287	.342	.407	98	0	3-1	.952	0	107	73	O30(8/2/20)	0	-0.1
1962	Det A	90	195	30	51	6	3	4	17	32-0	0	32	.262	.366	.385	99	0	1-1	.991	3	111	159	O62(1/30/33),1b3	0	0.0
1963	Det A	6	11	2	1	0	0	0	2	2-0	0	1	.091	.231	.091	-5	-2	0-0	.875	-0	120	0	O3C	0	-0.2
	Mil N	15	28	1	5	0	0	0	4	2-1	1	3	.179	.258	.179	28	-3	0-0	1.000	0	129	0	O9(6/3/0)	0	-0.3
1966	Cal A	15	50	4	11	1	0	0	4	2-0	0	6	.220	.250	.240	43	-4	1-1	1.000	0	99	126	O14R	0	-0.5
1967	Cal A	80	201	23	63	9	3	0	32	22-1	2	29	.313	.387	.388	135	9	0-3	1.000	-2	96	31	O61(9/0/55)	0	0.3
1968	Cal A	81	163	13	44	6	0	1	18	14-0	4	18	.270	.341	.325	106	2	2-1	.985	-1	102	48	O50(3/0/47)/3	0	-0.2
1969	Cal A	87	172	18	42	10	1	7	32	28-1	3	29	.244	.356	.436	127	7	0-0	1.000	2	101	166	O49(6/0/43)/1	0	0.7
Total	7	451	928	117	248	37	8	14	128	111-4	11	143	.267	.351	.370	106	9	7-7	.988	2	104	96	O278(33/38/212),1b4/3	0	-0.3
Moryn, Walt	Walter Joseph "Moose"; B4.12.1926 St.Paul MN; D7.21.1996 Winfield IL; BL/TR/6´2˝/(205–215); d6.29																								
1954	Bro N	48	91	16	25	4	2	2	14	7	1	11	.275	.330	.429	94	-1	0-0	.881	0	95	199	O20(6/0/15)	0	-0.2
1955	Bro N	11	19	3	5	1	0	1	3	5-1	0	4	.263	.417	.474	132	1	0-0	.833	-1	67	0	O7(1/0/6)	0	0.0
1956	Chi N	147	529	69	151	27	3	23	67	50-2	3	67	.285	.348	.478	122	16	4-2	.983	6	104	144	O141(1/0/140)	0	1.8
1957	Chi N	149	568	76	164	33	0	19	88	50-6	3	90	.289	.348	.447	114	12	0-2	.960	4	105	123	O147R	0	1.0
1958	Chi N☆	143	512	77	135	26	7	26	77	62-7	**8**	83	.264	.350	.494	123	17	1-2	.978	-1	102	40	O141L	0	0.7
1959	Chi N	117	381	41	89	14	1	14	48	44-2	3	66	.234	.316	.386	87	-7	0-0	.989	-2	88	111	O104(97/1/9)	0	-1.5
1960	Chi N	38	109	12	32	4	0	2	11	13-0	0	19	.294	.366	.385	108	2	2-1	.964	0	103	89	O30(25/0/5)	0	0.0
	StL N	75	200	24	49	4	3	11	35	17-4	0	38	.245	.299	.460	97	-2	0-0	.990	1	107	90	O62(29/0/39)	0	-0.3
	Year	113	309	36	81	8	3	13	46	30-4	0	57	.262	.323	.434	101	0	2-1	.981	1	106	90	O92(54/0/44)	0	-0.3
1961	StL N	17	32	0	4	2	0	0	2	1-0	0	5	.125	.152	.188	-10	-5	0-0	.889	-1	83	0	O7(3/0/4)	0	-0.6
	Pit N	40	65	6	13	1	0	3	9	2-0	1	10	.200	.235	.354	53	-5	0-0	.950	1	105	261	O11(6/0/5)	0	-0.4
	Year	57	97	6	17	3	0	3	11	3-0	1	15	.175	.208	.299	31	-10	0-0	.931	0	97	163	O18(9/0/9)	0	-1.0
Total	8	785	2506	324	667	116	16	101	354	251-22	19	393	.266	.335	.446	108	28	7-7	.972	8	101	106	O670(309/1/370)	0	0.5
Moschitto, Ross	Rosaire Allen; B2.15.1945 Fresno CA; BR/TR/6´2˝/(175–177); d4.15; Mil 1966; Col Fresno (CA) City																								
1965	NY A	96	27	12	5	0	0	1	3	0-0	0	12	.185	.179	.296	35	-2	0-0	.941	-1	111	0	O89(10/55/24)	0	-0.4
1967	NY A	14	9	1	1	0	0	0	0	1-0	0	2	.111	.200	.111	-6	-1	0-0	1.000	0	46	736	O8(2/4/2)	0	-0.1
Total	2	110	36	13	6	0	0	1	3	1-0	0	14	.167	.184	.250	25	-3	0-0	.944	-0	105	65	O97(12/59/26)	0	-0.5
Moseby, Lloyd	Lloyd Anthony; B11.5.1959 Portland AR; BL/TR/6´3˝/(200–205); [TorA78 1/2]; d5.24; C1																								
1980	Tor A	114	389	44	89	24	1	9	46	25-4	4	85	.229	.281	.365	73	-15	4-6	.982	2	96	152	O104(12/6/86),D6	0	-1.9
1981	Tor A	100	378	36	88	16	2	9	43	24-3	1	86	.233	.278	.357	78	-12	11-8	.989	-3	99	62	O100(0/80/21)	0	-1.8
1982	Tor A	147	487	51	115	20	9	9	52	33-3	8	106	.236	.294	.370	75	-18	11-7	.992	-4	100	45	O145C	0	-2.3
1983	Tor A	151	539	104	170	31	7	18	81	51-4	5	85	.315	.376	.499	131	23	27-8	.983	4	104	116	O147C	0	2.8
1984	Tor A	158	592	97	166	28	**15**	18	92	78-9	8	122	.280	.368	.470	126	22	39-9	.990	4	108	77	O156C	0	3.0
1985	†Tor A	152	584	92	151	30	7	18	70	76-4	4	91	.259	.345	.426	108	7	37-15	.980	-10	93	70	O152C	0	-0.1
1986	Tor A★	152	589	89	149	24	5	21	86	64-3	6	122	.253	.329	.418	100	0	32-11	.984	-8	93	75	O147C,D3	0	-0.6
1987	Tor A	155	592	106	167	27	4	26	96	70-4	2	124	.282	.358	.473	116	14	39-7	.980	-17	78	107	O153C,D2	0	0.1
1988	Tor A	128	472	77	113	17	7	10	42	70-6	6	93	.239	.343	.369	99	1	31-8	.984	-9	91	34	O125(11/117/6)/D	16	-0.6
1989	†Tor A	135	502	72	111	25	3	11	43	56-1	6	101	.221	.306	.349	85	-9	24-7	.986	-12	88	45	O120C,D14	0	-2.0
1990	Det A	122	431	64	107	16	5	14	51	48-3	5	77	.248	.329	.406	104	2	17-5	.983	3	101	153	O116(14/104/0),D4	17	0.6
1991	Det A	74	260	37	68	15	1	6	35	21-2	3	43	.262	.321	.396	96	-1	8-1	.955	-4	98	28	O64L,D7	48	-0.5
Total	12	1588	5815	869	1494	273	66	169	737	616-46	58	1135	.257	.332	.414	102	14	280-92	.984	-55	96	82	O1529(101/1327/113),D37	81	-3.3
Moser, Arnie	Arnold Robert; B8.9.1915 Houston TX; D8.15.2002 Houston TX; BR/TR/5´11˝/165; d6.20																								
1937	Cin N	5	5	0	0	0	0	0	0	0	0	2	.000	.000	.000	-99	-1	0	ø	0	—	—	/H	—	-0.1

MOSES, JERRY Gerald Braheen; B8.9.1946 Yazoo City MS; BR/TR/6´3˝/(205–215); d5.9

YEAR	TM LG	G	AB	R	H	2B	3B	HR	RBI	BB-IB	HP	SO	AVG	OBP	SLG	AOPS	ABR	SB-CS	FA	FR	RNG	THR	GAMES AT POSITION	DL	BFW
1965	Bos A	4	4	1	1	0	0	1	1	0-0	0	2	.250	.250	1.000	224	1	0-0	ø	0	—	—	/H	0	0.1
1968	Bos A	6	18	2	6	0	0	2	4	1-0	0	4	.333	.368	.667	196	2	0-1	.963	-2	246	0	C6	0	0.0
1969	Bos A	53	135	13	41	9	1	4	17	5-1	1	23	.304	.326	.474	118	3	0-1	.981	-7	90	94	C36	0	-0.3
1970	Bos A☆	92	315	26	83	18	1	6	35	21-9	2	45	.263	.313	.384	86	-6	1-1	.990	6	103	71	C88/lf	0	0.4
1971	Cal A	69	181	12	41	8	2	4	15	10-4	0	34	.227	.266	.359	82	-6	0-0	.977	1	78	149	C63/rf	0	-0.2
1972	Cle A	52	141	9	31	3	0	4	14	11-3	3	29	.220	.290	.326	80	-4	0-0	.982	-1	130	118	C39,1b3	0	-0.3
1973	NY A	21	59	5	15	2	0	0	3	2-0	0	6	.254	.270	.288	61	-3	0-0	1.000	5	112	73	C17/D	0	0.2
1974	Det A	74	198	19	47	6	3	4	19	11-2	2	38	.237	.282	.359	81	-6	0-1	.985	-1	109	88	C74	23	-0.4
1975	SD N	13	19	1	3	2	0	0	1	2-0	0	3	.158	.238	.263	42	-1	0-0	.900	-1	51	0	C5	0	-0.3
	Chi A	2	2	1	1	0	1	0	0	0-0	0	0	.500	.500	1.500	442	1	0-0	1.000	-0	0	0	/1D	0	0.1
Total	9	386	1072	89	269	48	8	25	109	63-19	8	184	.251	.295	.381	89	-19	1-4	.984	1	104	95	C328,1b4,D2,O2(1/0/1)	23	-0.7

MOSES, JOHN John William; B8.9.1957 Los Angeles CA; BB/TL/5´10˝/(165–174); [SeaA80 16/396]; d8.23; C6; Col Arizona

YEAR	TM LG	G	AB	R	H	2B	3B	HR	RBI	BB-IB	HP	SO	AVG	OBP	SLG	AOPS	ABR	SB-CS	FA	FR	RNG	THR	GAMES AT POSITION	DL	BFW
1982	Sea A	22	44	7	14	5	1	1	3	4-0	0	5	.318	.375	.545	144	3	5-1	.947	-1	69	279	O19(8/3/9)	0	0.2
1983	Sea A	93	130	19	27	4	1	0	6	12-0	1	20	.208	.280	.254	46	-10	11-5	.979	3	87	297	O71(34/31/7),D10	0	-0.8
1984	Sea A	19	35	3	12	1	1	0	2	2-0	1	5	.343	.395	.429	128	1	1-0	1.000	-1	84	131	O19(7/14/0)/D	0	0.1
1985	Sea A	33	62	4	12	0	0	0	3	2-0	0	8	.194	.219	.194	14	-8	5-2	1.000	-3	71	85	O29(1/28/0)	0	-1.0
1986	Sea A	103	399	56	102	16	3	3	34	34-3	0	65	.256	.311	.333	75	-14	25-18	.987	-4	88	185	O93(2/91/0),1b7,D4	0	-1.9
1987	Sea A	116	390	58	96	16	4	3	38	29-2	3	49	.246	.301	.331	65	-20	23-15	.987	-3	94	120	O100(0/97/4),1b16,D5	0	-2.4
1988	Min A	105	206	33	65	10	3	2	12	15-2	2	21	.316	.366	.422	117	5	11-6	1.000	1	113	35	O82(29/20/43),D2	0	0.5
1989	Min A	129	242	33	68	12	3	1	31	19-1	1	23	.281	.333	.368	92	-2	14-7	.988	3	**117**	73	O108(39/26/63),1b2/PD	0	-0.1
1990	Min A	115	172	26	38	3	1	1	14	19-1	2	19	.221	.303	.267	58	-9	2-3	1.000	0	108	68	O85(16/23/52),D10,1b6,P2	0	-1.1
1991	Det A	13	21	5	1	1	0	0	1	2-0	0	7	.048	.130	.095	-36	-4	4-0	1.000	-1	91	0	O12(11/0/1)	0	-0.4
1992	Sea A	21	22	3	3	1	0	0	1	5-0	0	4	.136	.296	.182	36	-2	0-0	1.000	-1	95	0	O18(17/1/1)/D	0	-0.3
Total	11	769	1723	247	438	69	17	11	145	143-9	10	226	.254	.313	.333	75	-60	101-57	.990	-5	97	127	O636(164/334/180),D36,1b31,P3	0	-7.2

MOSES, WALLY Wallace; B10.8.1910 Uvalda GA; D10.10.1990 Vidalia GA; BL/TL/5´10˝/160; d4.17; C16

YEAR	TM LG	G	AB	R	H	2B	3B	HR	RBI	BB-IB	HP	SO	AVG	OBP	SLG	AOPS	ABR	SB-CS	FA	FR	RNG	THR	GAMES AT POSITION	DL	BFW
1935	Phi A	85	345	60	112	21	3	5	35	25	3	18	.325	.375	.446	113	6	3-4	.943	-1	101	103	O80R	—	0.0
1936	Phi A	146	585	98	202	35	11	7	66	62	2	32	.345	.410	.479	121	20	12-6	.974	0	101	93	O144(0/136/9)	—	1.5
1937	Phi A☆	**154**	649	113	208	48	13	25	86	54	2	38	.320	.374	.550	132	29	9-7	.958	5	108	111	O154R	—	2.2
1938	Phi A	142	589	86	181	29	8	8	49	58	0	31	.307	.369	.424	101	0	15-5	.966	4	**112**	87	O139R	—	-0.2
1939	Phi A	115	437	68	134	28	7	3	33	44	0	23	.307	.370	.423	105	3	7-4	.965	-1	96	119	O103(0/5/100)	—	-0.3
1940	Phi A	142	537	91	166	41	9	9	50	75	2	44	.309	.396	.469	126	23	6-4	.974	5	110	92	O133(0/2/131)	—	1.9
1941	Phi A	116	438	78	132	31	4	4	35	62	0	27	.301	.388	.418	116	13	3-3	.975	8	**114**	109	O109R	0	1.3
1942	Chi A	146	577	73	156	28	4	7	49	74	0	27	.270	.353	.369	106	6	16-10	.980	6	106	129	O145(3/14/130)	0	0.3
1943	Chi A	150	599	82	147	22	**12**	3	48	55	1	47	.245	.310	.337	89	-10	56-14	.979	7	**110**	106	O148(0/23/125)	0	-0.5
1944	Chi A	136	535	82	150	26	9	3	34	52	1	22	.280	.345	.379	108	6	21-7	.975	-2	100	77	O134R	0	-0.3
1945	Chi A✱	140	569	79	168	**35**	15	2	50	69	2	33	.295	.373	.420	134	25	11-5	.977	6	**115**	85	O139R	0	2.4
1946	Chi A	56	168	20	46	9	1	4	16	17	1	20	.274	.344	.411	115	3	2-2	1.000	-2	95	63	O36(2/14/22)	0	0.0
	†Bos A	48	175	23	36	11	3	2	17	14	1	15	.206	.268	.337	65	-9	2-4	.979	-1	98	72	O44(0/2/43)	0	-1.3
	Year	104	343	43	82	20	4	6	33	31	2	35	.239	.306	.373	88	-6	4-6	.989	-3	97	68	O80(2/16/65)	0	-1.3
1947	Bos A	90	255	32	70	18	2	2	27	27	0	16	.275	.344	.384	95	-1	3-0	.974	-4	93	47	O58R	0	-0.7
1948	Bos A	78	189	26	49	12	1	2	29	21	2	19	.259	.340	.365	83	-4	5-0	.981	1	108	61	O45R	0	-0.4
1949	Phi A	110	308	49	85	19	3	1	25	51	1	19	.276	.381	.367	102	3	1-3	.983	-0	100	88	O92(1/1/91)	0	-0.1
1950	Phi A	88	265	47	70	16	5	2	21	40	2	17	.264	.365	.385	94	-2	0-1	.987	3	107	128	O62(4/7/51)	0	-0.1
1951	Phi A	70	136	17	26	6	0	0	9	21	1	9	.191	.304	.235	46	-10	2-2	.984	1	112	51	O27R	0	-1.0
Total	17	2012	7356	1124	2138	435	110	89	679	821	21	457	.291	.364	.416	109	101	174-81	.973	35	106	96	O1792(10/204/1587)	0	4.7

MOSKIMAN, DOC William Bankhead; B12.20.1879 Oakland CA; D1.11.1953 San Leandro CA; BR/TR/6´0˝/170; d8.23

YEAR	TM LG	G	AB	R	H	2B	3B	HR	RBI	BB-IB	HP	SO	AVG	OBP	SLG	AOPS	ABR	SB-CS	FA	FR	RNG	THR	GAMES AT POSITION	DL	BFW
1910	Bos A	5	9	1	1	0	0	0	1	2	0	—	.111	.273	.111	20	-1	0	1.000	0	143	185	1b2/rf	—	-0.1

MOSOLF, JIM James Frederick; B8.21.1905 Puyallup WA; D12.28.1979 Dallas OR; BL/TR/5´10˝/186; d9.9

YEAR	TM LG	G	AB	R	H	2B	3B	HR	RBI	BB-IB	HP	SO	AVG	OBP	SLG	AOPS	ABR	SB-CS	FA	FR	RNG	THR	GAMES AT POSITION	DL	BFW
1929	Pit N	8	13	3	6	1	1	0	2	1	0	1	.462	.500	.692	188	2	0	1.000	0	128	0	O3L	—	0.2
1930	Pit N	40	51	16	17	2	1	0	9	8	0	7	.333	.424	.412	103	1	0	.765	-1	76	120	O12(1/1/9)/P	—	-0.1
1931	Pit N	39	44	7	11	1	0	1	8	8	0	5	.250	.365	.341	92	0	0	1.000	-1	73	0	O4(3/0/1)	—	-0.1
1933	Chi N	31	82	13	22	5	1	1	9	5	2	8	.268	.326	.390	104	0	0	.964	1	107	122	O22(19/3/0)	—	0.0
Total	4	118	190	39	56	9	3	2	28	22	2	21	.295	.374	.405	107	3	0	.929	-1	99	101	O41(26/4/10)/P	—	0.0

MOSQUERA, JULIO Julio Alberto (Cervantes); B1.29.1972 Panama City, Pan; BR/TR/6´0˝/(190–192); d8.17

YEAR	TM LG	G	AB	R	H	2B	3B	HR	RBI	BB-IB	HP	SO	AVG	OBP	SLG	AOPS	ABR	SB-CS	FA	FR	RNG	THR	GAMES AT POSITION	DL	BFW
1996	Tor A	8	22	2	5	2	0	0	2	0-0	1	3	.227	.261	.318	46	-2	0-1	1.000	1	203	0	C8	0	-0.1
1997	Tor A	3	8	0	2	1	0	0	0	0-0	0	2	.250	.250	.375	60	0	0-0	1.000	-0	135	151	C3	0	-0.1
2005	Mil N	1	1	0	0	0	0	0	0	0-0	0	0	.000	.000	.000	-99	0	0-0	ø	0	—	—	/H	0	0.0
Total	3	12	31	2	7	3	0	0	2	0-0	1	5	.226	.250	.323	45	-2	0-1	1.000	0	187	36	C11	0	-0.2

MOSS, CHARLIE Charles Crosby; B3.20.1911 Meridian MS; D10.9.1991 Meridian MS; BR/TR/5´10˝/160; d5.19; Col U. of Mississippi

YEAR	TM LG	G	AB	R	H	2B	3B	HR	RBI	BB-IB	HP	SO	AVG	OBP	SLG	AOPS	ABR	SB-CS	FA	FR	RNG	THR	GAMES AT POSITION	DL	BFW
1934	Phi A	10	10	3	2	0	0	0	1	0	0	0	.200	.200	.200	4	-1	0-0	1.000	-1	*56*	*0*	C6	—	-0.2
1935	Phi A	4	3	1	1	0	0	0	1	1	0	0	.333	.500	.333	120	0	0-0	ø	0	*0*	*0*	/C	—	0.0
1936	Phi A	33	44	2	11	1	1	0	10	6	0	5	.250	.340	.318	65	-2	1-0	.929	-2	*73*	*82*	C19	—	-0.4
Total	3	47	57	6	14	1	1	0	12	7	0	5	.246	.328	.298	58	-3	1-0	.935	-3	*70*	*72*	C26	—	-0.6

MOSS, HOWIE Howard Glenn; B10.17.1918 Gastonia NC; D5.7.1989 Baltimore MD; BR/TR/5´11.5˝/185; d4.14; Mil 1945

YEAR	TM LG	G	AB	R	H	2B	3B	HR	RBI	BB-IB	HP	SO	AVG	OBP	SLG	AOPS	ABR	SB-CS	FA	FR	RNG	THR	GAMES AT POSITION	DL	BFW
1942	NY N	7	14	0	0	0	0	0	0	0	0	4	.000	.000	.000	-99	-4	0	1.000	-0	105	0	O3(2/1/0)	0	-0.4
1946	Cin N	7	26	1	5	0	0	0	1	0	1	4	.192	.222	.192	19	-3	0	1.000	0	89	155	O6R	0	-0.3
	Cle A	8	32	2	2	0	0	0	0	3	0	9	.063	.143	.063	-44	-6	0-1	.857	-1	89	0	3b8	0	-0.9
Total	2	22	72	3	7	0	0	0	1	3	1	17	.097	.145	.097	-32	-13	0-1	1.000	-1	94	105	O9(2/1/6),3b8	0	-1.6

MOSS, LES John Lester; B5.14.1925 Tulsa OK; BR/TR/5´11˝/(188–205); d9.10; M2/C13

YEAR	TM LG	G	AB	R	H	2B	3B	HR	RBI	BB-IB	HP	SO	AVG	OBP	SLG	AOPS	ABR	SB-CS	FA	FR	RNG	THR	GAMES AT POSITION	DL	BFW
1946	StL A	12	35	4	13	3	0	0	5	3	1	5	.371	.436	.457	142	2	1-0	.968	-0	*66*	*64*	C12	0	0.3
1947	StL A	96	274	17	43	5	2	6	27	35	1	48	.157	.255	.255	41	-23	0-0	.983	-7	*73*	*106*	C96	0	-2.6
1948	StL A	107	335	35	86	12	1	14	46	39	0	50	.257	.334	.424	98	-2	0-0	.988	-8	*62*	*104*	C103	0	-0.6
1949	StL A	97	278	28	81	11	0	10	39	49	1	32	.291	.399	.439	117	8	0-1	.970	-3	*98*	*103*	C83	0	0.8
1950	StL A	84	222	24	59	6	0	8	34	26	0	32	.266	.343	.401	87	-5	0-1	.957	-3	*97*	*119*	C60	0	-0.5
1951	StL A	16	47	5	8	2	0	1	7	6	0	8	.170	.264	.277	45	-4	0-0	.967	-1	*101*	*171*	C12	0	-0.4
	Bos A	71	202	18	40	6	0	3	26	25	1	34	.198	.289	.272	48	-15	0-0	.984	-1	*119*	*63*	C69	0	-1.3
	Year	87	249	23	48	8	0	4	33	31	1	42	.193	.285	.273	47	-18	0-0	.981	-2	***116***	*81*	C81	0	-1.7
1952	StL A	52	118	11	29	3	0	3	12	15	0	13	.246	.331	.347	86	-2	0-1	.957	-3	*99*	*108*	C39	0	-0.4
1953	StL A	78	239	21	66	14	1	2	28	18	1	31	.276	.329	.368	86	-5	0-1	.978	-7	*87*	*86*	C71	0	-0.8
1954	Bal A	50	126	7	31	3	0	0	5	14	0	16	.246	.321	.270	68	-5	0-0	.972	-3	*81*	*120*	C38	0	-0.7
1955	Bal A	29	56	5	19	1	0	2	6	7-1	0	4	.339	.413	.464	146	4	0-1	1.000	1	*85*	*82*	C17	0	0.5
	Chi A	32	59	5	15	2	0	2	7	6-1	1	10	.254	.333	.390	91	-1	0-0	.990	1	*126*	*64*	C32	0	0.1
	Year	61	115	10	34	3	0	4	13	13-2	1	14	.296	.372	.426	116	3	0-1	.994	2	*108*	*72*	C49	0	0.6
1956	Chi A	56	127	20	31	4	0	10	22	18-0	0	15	.244	.338	.512	120	3	0-0	.994	-3	*130*	*65*	C49	0	0.1
1957	Chi A	42	115	10	31	3	0	2	12	20-1	0	18	.270	.375	.348	99	1	0-0	.980	-6	111	12	C39	0	-0.4
1958	Chi A	2	1	0	0	0	0	0	0	1-0	0	0	.000	.500	.000	51	0	0-0	ø	0	—	—	/H	0	0.0
Total	13	824	2234	210	552	75	4	63	276	282-3	6	316	.247	.333	.369	86	-44	1-5	.978	-43	*91*	*93*	C720	0	-5.9

MOSTIL, JOHNNY John Anthony "Bananas"; B6.1.1896 Chicago IL; D12.10.1970 Midlothian IL; BR/TR/5´8.5˝/168; d6.20

YEAR	TM LG	G	AB	R	H	2B	3B	HR	RBI	BB-IB	HP	SO	AVG	OBP	SLG	AOPS	ABR	SB-CS	FA	FR	RNG	THR	GAMES AT POSITION	DL	BFW
1918	Chi A	10	33	4	9	2	2	0	4	1	0	6	.273	.294	.455	125	1	1	.923	-2	88	123	2b9	—	-0.1
1921	Chi A	100	326	43	98	21	7	3	42	28	13	35	.301	.379	.436	109	5	10-12	.946	-3	94	103	O91(1/90/0)/2	—	-0.4
1922	Chi A	132	458	74	139	28	14	7	70	38	**14**	39	.303	.375	.472	120	13	14-10	.966	0	107	67	O123(18/105/0)	—	0.6
1923	Chi A	153	546	91	159	37	15	3	64	62	12	51	.291	.376	.430	113	11	41-16	.974	15	**116**	126	O143(0/135/8),3b5/S	—	2.3
1924	Chi A	118	385	75	125	22	5	4	49	45	4	41	.325	.401	.439	120	13	7-11	.974	7	109	130	O102(1/90/12)	—	1.2
1925	Chi A	153	605	**135**	181	36	16	2	50	**90**	**12**	52	.299	.400	.421	115	17	**43**-20	**.985**	-2	102	64	O153C	—	1.1
1926	Chi A	148	600	120	197	41	15	4	42	79	**10**	55	.328	.415	.467	135	33	**35**-14	.968	7	109	96	O147C	—	3.5

YEAR	TM LG	G	AB	R	H	2B	3B	HR	RBI	BB-IB	HP	SO	AVG	OBP	SLG	AOPS	ABR	SB-CS	FA	FR	RNG	THR	GAMES AT POSITION	DL	BFW
1927	Chi A	13	16	3	2	0	0	0	1	0	1	1	.125	.176	.125	-21	-3	1-0	.857	0	84	427	O6C	—	-0.2
1928	Chi A	133	503	69	136	19	8	0	51	66	4	54	.270	.360	.340	86	-8	23-20	.976	12	**115**	123	O131(0/120/11)	—	-0.4
1929	Chi A	12	35	4	8	3	0	0	3	6	0	2	.229	.341	.314	71	-1	1-1	.963	0	97	99	O11(0/10/1)	—	-0.2
Total	10	972	3507	618	1054	209	82	23	376	415	70	336	.301	.386	.427	113	81	176-104	.971	34	108	101	O907(20/856/32),2b10,3b5/S	—	7.4
MOTA, ANDY	Andres Alberto (Matos); B3.4.1966 Santo Domingo, D.R.; BR/TR/5´10˝/180; [HouN87 12/314]; d8.31; b–Jose f–Manny; Col Cal St.–Fullerton																								
1991	Hou N	27	90	4	17	2	0	1	6	1-0	0	17	.189	.198	.244	25	-9	2-0	.970	-8	86	78	2b27	0	-1.8
MOTA, JOSE	Jose Manuel (Matos); B3.16.1965 Santo Domingo, D.R.; BB/TR/5´9˝/155; [ChiA85 2/33]; d5.24; b–Andy f–Manny; Col Cal St.–Fullerton																								
1991	SD N	17	36	4	8	0	0	0	2	2-0	1	7	.222	.282	.222	42	-3	0-0	.962	-2	91	97	2b13,S3	0	-0.4
1995	KC A	2	2	0	0	0	0	0	0	0-0	0	0	.000	.000	.000	-98	-1	0-0	1.000	0	174	0	2b2	94	0.0
Total	2	19	38	4	8	0	0	0	2	2-0	1	7	.211	.268	.211	35	-4	0-0	.965	-1	95	92	2b15,S3	94	-0.4
MOTA, MANNY	Manuel Rafael (Geronimo); B2.18.1938 Santo Domingo, D.R.; BR/TR/5´11˝/(168–170); d4.16; C12; s–Andy s–Jose																								
1962	SF N	47	74	9	13	1	0	0	9	7-0	1	8	.176	.253	.189	22	-8	3-2	1.000	3	112	348	O27(22/2/4),3b7,2b3	0	-0.6
1963	Pit N	59	126	20	34	2	3	0	7	7-0	1	18	.270	.313	.333	86	-3	0-2	.953	-2	83	57	O37(35/2/2)/2	0	-0.8
1964	Pit N	115	271	43	75	8	3	5	32	10-0	3	31	.277	.309	.384	94	-3	4-1	.961	-0	99	99	O93(57/50/7)/C2	0	-0.6
1965	Pit N	121	294	47	82	7	6	4	29	22-0	2	32	.279	.330	.384	101	0	2-2	.985	-2	90	122	O95(35/60/15)	0	-0.6
1966	Pit N	116	322	54	107	16	7	5	46	25-1	4	28	.332	.383	.472	137	17	7-7	.994	-3	99	57	O96(45/52/12),3b4	0	1.0
1967	Pit N	120	349	53	112	14	8	4	56	14-2	2	46	.321	.343	.441	125	10	3-2	.988	4	96	181	O99(48/48/13),3b2	0	1.0
1968	Pit N	111	331	35	93	10	2	1	33	20-4	1	19	.281	.320	.332	99	-1	4-2	.981	-2	93	86	O92(50/31/22)/23	0	-0.8
1969	Mon N	31	89	6	28	1	1	0	0	6-0	0	11	.315	.358	.348	98	0	1-3	.907	-3	94	0	O22(1/17/5)	0	-0.5
	LA N	85	294	35	95	6	4	3	30	26-1	1	25	.323	.377	.401	127	10	5-4	.969	1	90	186	O80(75/4/10)	0	0.7
	Year	116	383	41	123	7	5	3	30	32-1	1	36	.321	.372	.389	120	10	6-7	.954	-1	91	146	O102(76/21/15)	0	0.2
1970	LA N	124	417	63	127	12	6	3	37	47-4	3	37	.305	.377	.384	109	6	11-6	.973	-0	95	106	O111(109/1/4)/3	0	0.0
1971	LA N	91	269	24	84	13	5	0	34	20-5	1	20	.312	.361	.398	121	7	4-3	.965	-4	88	67	O80(62/0/24)	0	-0.1
1972	LA N	118	371	57	120	16	5	5	48	27-6	5	15	.323	.375	.434	132	15	4-4	.993	-7	86	48	O99(96/3/0)	0	0.3
1973	LA N★	89	293	33	92	11	2	0	23	25-9	1	12	.314	.368	.365	108	4	1-3	1.000	-7	72	84	O74L	0	-0.9
1974	†LA N	66	57	5	16	2	0	0	16	5-4	1	4	.281	.328	.316	90	-1	0-0	1.000	-0	35	0	O3L	0	-0.1
1975	LA N	52	49	3	13	1	0	0	10	5-0	2	1	.265	.357	.286	83	-1	0-0	1.000	1	165	0	O5L	0	0.0
1976	LA N	50	52	1	15	3	0	0	13	7-3	0	5	.288	.367	.346	106	1	0-0	1.000	2	189	485	O6L	0	0.3
1977	†LA N	49	38	5	15	1	0	1	4	10-3	0	0	.395	.521	.500	174	5	1-1	1.000	0	116	0	/lf	0	0.5
1978	†LA N	37	33	2	10	1	0	0	6	3-1	0	4	.303	.361	.333	95	0	0-0	ø	0	—	—	/H	0	-0.1
1979	LA N	47	42	1	15	0	0	0	3	3-0	0	4	.357	.400	.357	110	1	0-0	ø	-0	0	0	/lf	0	0.1
1980	LA N	7	7	0	3	0	0	0	2	0-0	0	0	.429	.429	.429	144	0	0-0	ø	0	—	—	/H	0	0.0
1982	LA N	1	1	0	0	0	0	0	0	0-0	0	0	.000	.000	.000	-99	0	0-0	ø	0	—	—	/H	0	0.0
Total	20	1536	3779	496	1149	125	52	31	438	289-43	28	320	.304	.355	.389	112	59	50-42	.979	-21	92	104	O1021(725/270/118),3b15,2b6/C	0	-1.2
MOTLEY, DARRYL	Darryl De Wayne; B1.21.1960 Muskogee OK; BR/TR/5´9˝/196; [KCA78 2/51]; d8.10																								
1981	KC A	42	125	15	29	4	0	2	8	7-0	1	15	.232	.276	.312	70	-5	1-3	.968	3	114	112	O39(2/0/38)	0	-0.6
1983	KC A	19	68	9	16	1	2	3	11	2-0	1	8	.235	.264	.441	90	-2	2-1	.978	1	108	148	O18(3/2/15)/D	0	-0.1
1984	†KC A	146	522	64	148	25	6	15	70	28-2	1	73	.284	.319	.441	107	3	10-12	.984	2	106	76	O138(105/3/45)	0	-0.3
1985	†KC A	123	383	45	85	20	1	17	49	18-2	2	57	.222	.257	.413	80	-12	6-4	.967	-5	94	59	O114(44/0/76),D7	0	-2.2
1986	KC A	72	217	22	44	9	1	7	20	11-1	0	31	.203	.241	.350	57	-14	0-2	.979	-6	79	50	O66(3/1/62),D2	0	-2.4
	Atl N	5	10	1	2	1	0	0	0	1-1	0	1	.200	.273	.300	55	-1	0-0	1.000	-0	104	0	O3R	0	-0.1
1987	Atl N	6	8	0	0	0	0	0	1	0-0	0	1	.000	.000	.000	-96	-2	0-0	1.000	-0	97	0	O2L	0	-0.2
Total	6	413	1333	156	324	60	10	44	159	67-6	5	186	.243	.280	.402	85	-33	19-22	.976	-6	99	73	O380(159/6/239),D10	0	-5.9
MOTT, BITSY	Elisha Matthew; B6.12.1918 Arcadia FL; D2.25.2001 Brandon FL; BR/TR/5´8˝/155; d4.17																								
1945	Phi N	90	289	21	64	8	0	0	22	27	1	25	.221	.290	.249	52	-18	2	.944	12	110	119	S63,2b27,3b7	0	-0.1
MOTTOLA, CHAD	Charles Edward; B10.15.1971 Augusta GA; BR/TR/6´3˝/(220–235); [CinN92 1/5]; d4.23; Col Central Florida																								
1996	Cin N	35	79	10	17	3	0	3	6	6-1	0	16	.215	.271	.367	65	-4	2-2	1.000	0	98	134	O31(0/1/30)	0	-0.5
2000	Tor A	3	9	1	2	0	0	0	2	0-0	1	4	.222	.300	.222	34	-1	0-0	1.000	-0	103	0	O3R	0	-0.1
2001	Fla N	5	7	1	0	0	0	0	1	2-0	0	2	.000	.200	.000	-36	-1	0-0	1.000	1	142	575	O5(2/1/4)	0	0.0
2004	Bal A	6	14	2	2	1	0	1	3	2-0	0	3	.143	.250	.429	73	-1	0-0	1.000	-1	81	0	O5(3/0/2)	0	-0.1
2006	Tor A	10	16	3	4	2	0	0	0	0-0	0	3	.250	.250	.375	56	-1	0-0	1.000	-0	76	0	O5(3/0/2),D2	0	-0.1
Total	5	59	125	17	25	6	0	4	12	10-1	1	28	.200	.263	.344	57	-8	2-2	1.000	1	98	135	O49(8/2/41),D2	0	-0.8
MOTTON, CURT	Curtell Howard; B9.24.1940 Darnell LA; BR/TR/5´7.5˝/(164–175); d7.5; C1; Col California																								
1967	Bal A	27	65	5	13	2	0	2	9	5-0	2	14	.200	.267	.323	78	-2	0-1	.973	1	125	0	O18(18/0/1)	0	-0.3
1968	Bal A	83	217	27	43	7	0	8	25	31-0	1	43	.198	.298	.341	94	-1	1-3	.989	0	101	62	O54L	21	-0.5
1969	†Bal A	56	89	15	27	6	0	6	21	13-0	1	10	.303	.398	.573	167	8	3-1	1.000	-2	87	0	O20(16/0/4)	0	0.6
1970	Bal A	52	84	16	19	3	1	3	19	18-0	1	20	.226	.369	.393	108	2	1-2	1.000	0	104	90	O21(20/0/2)	0	0.1
1971	†Bal A	38	53	13	10	1	0	4	8	10-0	0	12	.189	.317	.434	110	1	0-0	1.000	0	94	138	O16(12/0/5)	0	0.0
1972	Mil A	6	6	1	1	0	0	1	2	1-0	0	2	.167	.286	.667	180	1	0-0	ø	-0	0	0	O3L	20	0.0
	Cal A	42	39	6	6	1	0	0	1	5-0	0	12	.154	.250	.179	31	-3	0-0	1.000	0	130	0	O9L	0	-0.4
	Year	48	45	7	7	1	0	1	3	6-0	0	14	.156	.255	.244	51	-3	0-0	1.000	0	122	0	O12L	0	-0.4
1973	Bal A	5	6	2	2	0	0	1	4	1-0	0	1	.333	.429	.833	247	1	0-0	ø	-0	0	0	/lfD	0	0.1
1974	†Bal A	7	8	0	0	0	0	0	0	2-0	0	2	.000	.200	.000	-39	-1	0-0	1.000	0	162	0	O2R/D	0	-0.1
Total	8	316	567	85	121	20	1	25	89	86-0	5	116	.213	.319	.384	105	6	5-7	.991	0	104	52	O144(133/0/14),D2	41	-0.5
MOTZ, FRANK	Frank H.; B10.1.1868 Freeburg PA; D3.18.1944 Akron OH; 6´0˝/160; d8.27																								
1890	Phi N	1	2	1	0	0	0	0	0	1	0	1	.000	.333	.000	-1	0	1	1.000	0	315	411	/1	—	0.0
1893	Cin N	43	156	16	40	7	1	2	25	19	4	10	.256	.352	.353	85	-3	3	.981	6	162	102	1b43	—	0.2
1894	Cin N	18	69	8	14	4	0	0	12	9	1	1	.203	.304	.261	36	-7	2	.995	4	174	80	1b18	—	-0.3
Total	3	62	227	25	54	11	1	2	37	29	5	12	.238	.337	.322	68	-10	6	.985	10	168	100	1b62	—	-0.1
MOULTON, ALLIE	Albert Theodore; B1.16.1886 Medway MA; D7.10.1968 Peabody MA; BR/TR/5´6˝/155; d9.25																								
1911	StL A	4	15	4	1	0	0	0	1	4	0	—	.067	.263	.067	-6	-2	0	.938	-0	133	0	2b4	—	-0.2
MOUNTAIN, FRANK	Frank Henry; B5.17.1860 Ft.Edward NY; D11.19.1939 Schenectady NY; BR/TR/5´11˝/185; d7.19; Col Union (NY); ▲																								
1880	Tro N	2	9	1	2	0	0	0	0	0	—	4	.222	.222	.222	49	0	—	1.000	0	118	0	P2	—	0.0
1881	Det N	7	25	0	4	1	1	0	4	2	—	8	.160	.222	.280	55	0	—	.923	-1	52	0	P7	—	0.0
1882	Wor N	5	16	1	1	0	0	0	1	0	—	5	.063	.063	.063	-58	-2	—	.889	-1	75	0	P5	—	0.0
	Phi AA	9	36	5	12	3	0	0	—	2	—	—	.333	.368	.417	154	2	—	.917	1	136	0	P8/rf	—	0.1
	Wor N	20	70	8	19	2	2	2	5	3	—	18	.271	.301	.443	132	2	—	.870	-2	75	0	P13,O6(1/5/0),1b2/S	—	-0.1
1883	Col AA	70	276	36	60	14	5	3	—	9	—	—	.217	.242	.337	92	-1	—	.848	1	101	99	P59,O12(8/4/0)	—	0.0
1884	Col AA	58	210	26	50	7	3	4	—	9	4	—	.238	.283	.357	117	5	—	.919	3	121	0	P42,O17(9/7/1)	—	0.2
1885	Pit AA	5	20	1	2	0	1	0	1	1	0	—	.100	.143	.200	8	-1	—	.846	0	131	0	P5	—	0.0
1886	Pit AA	18	55	6	8	1	1	0	2	13	1	—	.145	.319	.200	64	-1	3	.959	-0	100	87	1b16,P2	—	-0.3
Total	7	194	717	84	158	28	13	9	13	39	5	35	.220	.265	.333	96	4	3	.880	2	106	52	P143,O36(18/16/2),1b18/S	—	-0.1
MOUTON, JAMES	James Raleigh; B12.29.1968 Denver CO; BR/TR/5´9˝/175; [HouN91 7/183]; d4.4; Col St. Marys (CA)																								
1994	Hou N	99	310	43	76	11	0	2	16	27-0	5	69	.245	.315	.300	65	-16	24-5	.982	0	102	92	O96(1/19/80)	0	-1.5
1995	Hou N	104	298	42	78	18	2	4	27	25-1	4	59	.262	.326	.376	91	-4	25-8	1.000	-1	95	88	O94(38/22/38)	18	-0.5
1996	Hou N	122	300	40	79	15	1	3	34	38-2	0	55	.263	.343	.350	91	-3	21-9	.971	3	103	157	O108(79/29/5)	0	-0.1
1997	Hou N	86	180	24	38	9	1	3	23	18-0	2	30	.211	.287	.322	62	-10	9-7	1.000	-3	91	40	O61(9/39/14)	0	-1.4
1998	SD N	55	63	8	12	2	1	0	7	7-1	0	11	.190	.268	.254	42	-5	4-3	.969	-0	96	97	O33(16/4/14)/D	16	-0.6
1999	Mon N	95	122	18	32	5	1	2	13	18-1	2	31	.262	.364	.369	90	-1	6-2	.981	-0	92	127	O56(32/16/11)/D	0	-0.1
2000	Mil N	87	159	28	37	7	1	2	17	30-0	3	43	.233	.363	.327	77	-4	13-4	.989	1	99	127	O45(19/23/7)	0	-0.3
2001	Mil N	75	138	20	34	8	0	2	10	11-0	6	40	.246	.329	.348	77	-4	7-3	.965	2	111	102	O53(21/28/7)	15	-0.3
Total	8	723	1570	223	386	75	7	18	147	174-5	22	338	.246	.328	.337	78	-47	109-41	.983	1	99	106	O546(215/180/176),D2	49	-4.8

YEAR	TM LG	G	AB	R	H	2B	3B	HR	RBI	BB-IB	HP	SO	AVG	OBP	SLG	AOPS	ABR	SB-CS	FA	FR	RNG	THR	GAMES AT POSITION	DL	BFW
Mouton, Lyle	Lyle Joseph; B5.13.1969 Lafayette LA; BR/TR/6′4″/(230–240); [NYA91 5/126]; d6.7; Col Louisiana St.																								
1995	Chi A	58	179	23	54	16	0	5	27	19-0	2	46	.302	.373	.475	124	7	1-0	.990	3	105	166	O53(29/0/30),D2	0	0.8
1996	Chi A	87	214	25	63	8	1	7	39	22-4	2	50	.294	.361	.439	107	2	3-0	.970	-2	95	43	O47(21/0/29),D28	0	-0.2
1997	Chi A	88	242	26	65	9	0	5	23	14-1	1	66	.269	.308	.368	79	-8	4-4	.969	1	113	28	O67(16/0/55),D11	16	-1.0
1998	Bal A	18	39	5	12	2	0	2	7	4-0	0	8	.308	.372	.513	129	2	0-0	1.000	-0	89	135	O16(6/0/12),D2	0	0.1
1999	Mil N	14	17	2	3	1	0	1	3	2-0	0	3	.176	.263	.412	67	-1	0-0	1.000	-1	26	0	O3(2/0/1)	0	-0.2
2000	Mil N	42	97	14	27	7	1	2	16	10-0	1	29	.278	.349	.433	98	0	1-0	.978	3	98	301	O27(22/1/4)	19	0.2
2001	Fla N	21	17	1	1	0	0	0	1	0-0	0	7	.059	.059	.059	-72	-4	0-0	1.000	-1	54	0	O11(6/0/5)	0	-0.5
Total	7	328	805	96	225	43	2	22	116	71-5	6	209	.280	.339	.420	98	-2	9-4	.978	3	102	107	O224(102/1/136),D43	35	-0.8
Mowe, Ray	Raymond Benjamin; B7.12.1889 Rochester IN; D8.14.1968 Sarasota FL; BL/TR/5′7.5″/160; d9.25																								
1913	Bro N	5	9	0	1	0	0	0	0	0	1	1	.111	.200	.111	-10	-1	0	.941	0	102	98	S2	—	-0.1
Mowrey, Mike	Harry Harlan; B4.20.1884 Browns Mill PA; D3.20.1947 Chambersburg PA; BR/TR/5′10″/180; d9.24																								
1905	Cin N	7	30	4	8	1	0	0	6	1	0	—	.267	.290	.300	69	-1	0	.759	-1	116	110	3b7	—	-0.2
1906	Cin N	21	53	3	17	3	0	0	6	5	0	—	.321	.379	.377	130	2	2	.930	2	114	58	3b15/2S	—	0.4
1907	Cin N	138	448	43	113	16	6	1	44	35	1	—	.252	.308	.321	93	-4	10	.929	-16	84	87	3b127,S11	—	-1.8
1908	Cin N	77	227	17	50	9	1	0	23	12	2	—	.220	.266	.269	73	-7	5	.936	-5	102	90	3b56,S3,O3L/2	—	-1.3
1909	Cin N	38	115	10	22	5	0	0	5	20	0	—	.191	.311	.235	70	-3	2	.947	0	111	137	3b22,S13	—	-0.2
	StL N	12	29	3	7	1	0	0	4	4	0	—	.241	.333	.276	95	0	1	.921	-1	85	0	2b7,3b2	—	-0.1
	Year	50	144	13	29	6	0	0	9	24	0	—	.201	.315	.243	75	-3	3	.948	-1	112	135	3b24,S13,2b7	—	-0.3
1910	StL N	143	489	69	138	24	6	2	70	67	6	38	.282	.375	.368	121	16	21	.927	14	114	**139**	3b141	—	3.6
1911	StL N	137	471	59	126	29	7	0	61	59	5	46	.268	.355	.359	103	4	15	.944	7	107	96	3b134/S	—	1.5
1912	StL N	114	408	59	104	13	8	2	50	46	3	29	.255	.335	.341	87	-7	19	.931	2	105	**139**	3b108	—	-0.2
1913	StL N	132	450	61	117	18	4	0	33	53	3	40	.260	.342	.318	90	-4	21-15	.953	18	**121**	**129**	3b131	—	1.7
1914	Pit N	79	284	24	72	7	5	1	25	22	4	20	.254	.316	.324	94	-2	8	.960	-1	103	82	3b78	—	-0.1
1915	Pit F	151	521	56	146	26	6	1	49	66	5	39	.280	.367	.359	105	-1	40	**.959**	-17	90	72	3b151	—	-1.5
1916	†Bro N	144	495	57	121	22	6	0	60	50	5	60	.244	.320	.313	92	-3	16	**.965**	-2	99	87	3b144	—	0.0
1917	Bro N	83	271	20	58	9	5	0	25	29	1	25	.214	.292	.284	75	-7	7	.952	-1	103	102	3b80,2b2	—	-0.7
Total	13	1276	4291	485	1099	183	54	7	461	469	35	297	.256	.334	.329	96	-17	167-15	.944	-0	103	103	3b1196,S29,2b11,O3L	—	1.1
Mowry, Joe	Joseph Aloysius; B4.6.1908 St.Louis MO; D2.9.1994 St.Louis MO; BB/TR/6′0″/198; d5.13; Col Iowa																								
1933	Bos N	86	249	25	55	8	5	0	20	15	3	22	.221	.273	.293	67	-11	1	.994	1	108	37	O64(48/5/11)	—	-1.5
1934	Bos N	25	79	9	17	3	0	1	4	3	0	13	.215	.244	.291	46	-6	0	.976	1	112	66	O20(4/0/16)/2	—	-0.6
1935	Bos N	81	136	17	36	8	1	1	13	11	1	13	.265	.324	.360	91	-2	0	.970	1	107	137	O45(30/2/13)	—	-0.2
Total	3	192	464	51	108	19	6	2	37	29	4	48	.233	.284	.313	71	-19	1	.985	3	108	66	O129(82/7/40)/2	—	-2.3
Moynahan, Mike	Michael; B1856 Chicago IL; D4.9.1899 Chicago IL; BL/TR; d8.20																								
1880	Buf N	27	100	12	33	5	1	0	14	6	—	9	.330	.368	.400	157	6	—	.862	-3	91	99	S27	—	0.4
1881	Cle N	33	135	12	31	5	1	0	8	3	—	14	.230	.246	.281	69	-5	—	.883	-2	35	166	O32L/3	—	-0.9
	Det N	1	4	1	1	0	0	0	0	0	—	1	.250	.250	.250	55	0	—	.857	0	111	0	/3	—	0.0
	Year	34	139	13	32	5	1	0	8	3	—	15	.230	.246	.281	69	-5	—	.883	-2	35	166	O32L,3b2	—	-0.9
1883	Phi AA	95	400	90	124	18	10	1	67	31	—	—	.310	.360	.412	135	15	—	.833	-0	101	69	S95	—	1.5
1884	Phi AA	1	4	0	0	0	0	0	—	0	0	—	.000	.000	.000	-94	-1	—	.500	-1	0	0	/cf	—	-0.1
	Cle N	12	45	9	13	2	1	0	6	7	—	11	.289	.385	.378	136	2	—	.852	-1	107	0	2b6,S3,O3(1/0/2)	—	0.2
Total	4	169	688	124	202	30	13	1	95	47	—	35	.294	.339	.379	125	17	—	.837	-7	100	77	S125,O36(33/1/2),2b6,3b2	—	1.1
Mueller, Heinie	Clarence Francis; B9.16.1899 Creve Coeur MO; D1.23.1975 DeSoto MO; BL/TL/5′8″/158; d9.25																								
1920	StL N	4	22	0	7	1	0	0	1	2	0	4	.318	.375	.364	117	1	1-0	1.000	-0	110	0	O4(1/0/4)	—	0.0
1921	StL N	55	176	25	62	10	6	1	34	11	2	22	.352	.397	.494	137	9	2-4	.976	-1	102	76	O54(0/51/3)	—	0.5
1922	StL N	61	159	20	43	7	2	3	26	14	0	18	.270	.329	.396	91	-3	2-1	.947	1	96	143	O44(10/34/0)	—	-0.3
1923	StL N	78	265	39	91	16	9	5	41	18	3	16	.343	.392	.528	144	16	4-3	.963	3	108	100	O74(0/71/3)	—	1.5
1924	StL N	92	296	39	78	12	6	2	37	19	2	16	.264	.312	.365	82	-8	8-7	.962	-0	106	81	O53(2/42/9),1b27	—	-1.3
1925	StL N	78	243	33	76	16	4	1	26	17	3	11	.313	.365	.424	99	0	0-3	.955	0	103	95	O72(2/57/13)	—	-0.4
1926	StL N	52	191	36	51	7	5	3	28	11	7	6	.267	.330	.403	93	-2	8	.950	0	96	123	O51(0/21/30)	—	-0.5
	NY N	85	305	36	76	6	2	4	29	21	1	17	.249	.300	.321	68	-14	7	.950	1	97	135	O82(10/38/35)	—	-1.9
	Year	137	496	72	127	13	7	7	57	32	8	23	.256	.312	.353	78	-17	15	.950	1	97	**131**	O133(10/59/65)	—	-2.4
1927	NY N	84	190	33	55	6	1	3	19	25	4	12	.289	.384	.379	105	3	2	.944	-4	100	22	O56(49/5/2)/1	—	-0.4
1928	Bos N	42	151	25	34	3	1	0	19	17	3	9	.225	.316	.258	54	-10	1	.985	3	107	152	O41(4/37/0)	—	-0.8
1929	Bos N	46	93	10	19	2	1	0	11	12	1	12	.204	.302	.247	39	-9	2	1.000	-0	100	56	O24(4/11/10)	—	-1.0
1935	StL A	16	27	0	5	1	0	0	1	1	0	4	.185	.214	.222	12	-4	0-0	.955	0	204	127	1b3,O2(1/1/0)	—	-0.4
Total	11	693	2118	296	597	87	37	22	272	168	26	147	.282	.342	.389	94	-21	37-18	.960	3	102	101	O557(83/368/109),1b31	—	-5.0
Mueller, Don	Donald Frederick "Mandrake the Magician"; B4.14.1927 St.Louis MO; BL/TR/6′0″/(170–185); d8.2; f–Walter																								
1948	NY N	36	81	12	29	4	1	1	9	0	0	3	.358	.358	.469	121	2	0	.973	1	92	229	O22(18/1/1)	0	0.2
1949	NY N	51	56	5	13	4	0	0	1	5	0	6	.232	.295	.304	61	-3	0	1.000	-0	108	0	O6(2/0/4)	0	-0.3
1950	NY N	132	525	60	153	15	6	7	84	10	3	26	.291	.309	.383	80	-18	1	.986	-2	99	82	O125(3/0/122)	0	-2.3
1951	NY N	122	469	58	130	10	7	16	69	19	1	13	.277	.307	.431	95	-6	1-1	.983	-2	107	48	O115R	0	-1.2
1952	NY N	126	456	61	128	14	7	12	49	34	2	24	.281	.333	.421	107	3	2-1	.987	-3	99	73	O120R	0	-0.4
1953	NY N	131	480	56	160	12	2	6	60	19	1	13	.333	.360	.404	97	-3	2-0	.972	-4	94	82	O122(11/0/111)	0	-1.0
1954	†NY N★	153	619	90	**212**	35	8	4	71	22	2	17	.342	.363	.444	110	8	2-3	.979	-5	90	102	O153R	0	-0.3
1955	NY N★	147	605	67	185	21	4	8	83	19-4	3	12	.306	.326	.393	91	-9	1-2	.976	-14	86	41	O146R	0	-2.9
1956	NY N	138	453	38	122	12	1	5	41	15-2	0	7	.269	.290	.333	68	-21	0-1	.989	-9	89	41	O117R	0	-3.6
1957	NY N	135	450	45	116	7	1	6	37	13-3	1	16	.258	.280	.318	60	-26	2-0	.989	-1	86	**162**	O115R	0	-3.2
1958	Chi A	70	166	7	42	5	0	0	16	11-3	0	9	.253	.298	.283	62	-9	0-0	.968	-3	78	92	O43R	0	-1.4
1959	Chi A	4	4	0	2	0	0	0	0	0-0	0	0	.500	.500	.500	178	0	0-0	ø	0	—	—	/H	0	0.0
Total	12	1245	4364	499	1292	139	37	65	520	167-12	13	146	.296	.322	.390	89	-82	11-8	.982	-41	93	81	O1084(34/1/1047)	0	-16.4
Mueller, Heinie	Emmett Jerome; B7.20.1912 St.Louis MO; D10.3.1986 Orlando FL; BB/TR/5′6″/167; d4.19; Mil 1942–45																								
1938	Phi N	136	444	53	111	12	4	4	34	64	1	43	.250	.346	.322	87	-6	2	.967	-21	87	64	2b111,3b21	—	-2.0
1939	Phi N	115	341	46	95	19	4	9	43	33	0	34	.279	.342	.437	111	5	4	.964	-6	87	101	2b51,3b17,O17(4/0/13)/S	—	0.1
1940	Phi N	97	263	24	65	13	2	3	28	37	2	23	.247	.344	.346	95	-1	2	.966	-5	87	68	2b34,O31(29/0/2),3b13,1b2	—	-0.5
1941	Phi N	93	233	21	53	11	1	1	22	22	3	24	.227	.302	.296	72	-9	2	.980	2	94	106	2b29,O21(0/1/20),3b19	0	-0.5
Total	4	441	1281	144	324	55	11	17	127	156	6	124	.253	.337	.353	93	-11	10	.968	-30	88	79	2b225,3b70,O69(33/1/35),1b2/S	0	-2.9
Mueller, Ray	Ray Coleman "Iron Man"; B3.8.1912 Pittsburg KS; D6.29.1994 Lower Paxton Twp. PA; BR/TR/5′9″/175; d5.11; Mil 1945; C2																								
1935	Bos N	42	97	10	22	5	0	3	11	3	0	11	.227	.250	.371	70	-5	0	.978	-1	*87*	*174*	C40	—	-0.4
1936	Bos N	24	71	5	14	4	0	0	5	5	0	17	.197	.250	.254	38	-6	0	.986	-2	*158*	*55*	C23	—	-0.6
1937	Bos N	64	187	21	47	9	2	2	26	18	0	36	.251	.317	.353	90	-3	1	.995	6	*198*	*93*	C57	—	0.6
1938	Bos N	83	274	23	65	8	6	4	35	16	1	28	.237	.282	.354	82	-9	3	.993	2	*165*	*105*	C75	—	-0.2
1939	Pit N	86	180	14	42	8	1	2	18	14	0	22	.233	.289	.322	65	-9	0	.971	-1	*114*	*96*	C81	—	-0.7
1940	Pit N	4	3	1	1	0	0	0	1	2	0	0	.333	.600	.333	165	1	0	1.000	0	*59*	*211*	C4	—	0.1
1943	Cin N	141	427	50	111	19	4	8	52	56	1	42	.260	.347	.379	111	7	1	.988	20	*118*	***129***	C140	0	3.8
1944	Cin N★	**155**	555	54	159	24	4	10	73	53	4	47	.286	.353	.398	115	11	4	.983	1	***154***	*55*	C155	0	2.3
1946	Cin N	114	378	35	96	18	4	8	48	27	3	37	.254	.309	.386	100	-2	0	**.994**	10	*124*	***116***	C100	0	1.4
1947	Cin N	71	192	17	48	11	0	6	33	16	1	25	.250	.311	.401	88	-4	0	.984	0	*101*	*124*	C55	0	-0.1
1948	Cin N	14	34	2	7	1	0	0	2	4	0	3	.206	.289	.235	45	-3	0	.982	-0	*73*	*82*	C10	126	-0.2
1949	Cin N	32	106	7	29	4	0	1	13	5	2	13	.274	.319	.340	76	-4	1	1.000	-1	*121*	*107*	C31	0	-0.3
	NY N	56	170	17	38	2	2	5	23	13	0	14	.224	.279	.347	67	-9	1	.982	1	*92*	*85*	C56	0	-0.6
	Year	88	276	24	67	6	2	6	36	18	2	27	.243	.294	.344	70	-13	2	.988	-1	*103*	*93*	C87	0	-0.9
1950	NY N	4	11	0	1	1	0	0	0	0	0	2	.091	.091	.182	-30	-2	0	1.000	1	*113*	*0*	C4	0	-0.1
	Pit N	67	156	17	42	7	0	6	24	11	1	14	.269	.321	.429	92	-2	2	.996	2	*125*	*110*	C63	0	0.2
	Year	71	167	17	43	8	0	6	24	11	1	16	.257	.307	.413	85	-4	2	.996	3	*124*	*102*	C67	0	0.1
1951	Bos N	28	70	8	11	2	0	1	9	7	0	11	.157	.234	.229	27	-7	0-0	1.000	2	*78*	*163*	C23	0	-0.5
Total	14	985	2911	281	733	123	23	56	373	250	13	322	.252	.314	.368	91	-46	14-0	.988	40	*131*	*101*	C917	126	4.7

YEAR	TM LG	G	AB	R	H	2B	3B	HR	RBI	BB-IB	HP	SO	AVG	OBP	SLG	AOPS	ABR	SB-CS	FA	FR	RNG	THR	GAMES AT POSITION	DL	BFW
MUELLER, WALTER	Walter John; B12.6.1894 Central MO; D8.16.1971 St.Louis MO; BR/TR/5´8˝/160; d5.7; s–Don																								
1922	Pit N	32	122	21	33	5	1	2	18	5	1	7	.270	.305	.377	74	-5	1-0	.976	4	108	179	O31R	—	-0.3
1923	Pit N	40	111	11	34	4	4	0	20	4	1	6	.306	.336	.414	95	-1	2-2	.941	0	113	76	O26(19/0/7)	—	-0.3
1924	Pit N	30	50	6	13	1	1	0	8	4	1	4	.260	.327	.320	73	-2	1-0	1.000	2	96	409	O15(8/5/2)	—	0.0
1926	Pit N	19	62	8	15	0	1	0	3	0	0	2	.242	.242	.274	37	-6	0	.969	1	102	145	O15(14/0/1)	—	-0.6
Total	4	121	345	46	95	10	7	2	49	13	3	19	.275	.307	.362	74	-14	4-2	.966	8	107	165	O87(41/5/41)	—	-1.2
MUELLER, BILL	William Lawrence "Hawk"; B11.9.1920 Bay City MI; D10.24.2001 Glenview IL; BR/TR/6´1.5˝/180; d8.29; Mil 1943–45																								
1942	Chi A	26	85	5	14	1	0	0	5	12	1	9	.165	.276	.176	29	-8	2-1	.978	6	114	351	O26(0/23/3)	0	-0.2
1945	Chi A	13	9	3	0	0	0	0	0	2	0	1	.000	.182	.000	-47	-2	1-0	.778	-0	124	0	O7(0/5/2)	0	-0.2
Total	2	39	94	8	14	1	0	0	5	14	1	10	.149	.266	.160	22	-10	3-1	.960	6	115	323	O33(0/28/5)	0	-0.4
MUELLER, BILL	William Richard; B3.17.1971 Maryland Heights MO; BB/TR/5´10˝/(170–180); [SFN93 15/414]; d4.18; Col Missouri St.																								
1996	SF N	55	200	31	66	15	1	0	19	24-0	1	26	.330	.401	.415	119	7	0-0	.966	-2	95	141	3b45,2b8	0	0.6
1997	†SF N	128	390	51	114	26	3	7	44	48-1	3	71	.292	.369	.428	112	8	4-3	.956	4	103	97	3b122	17	1.3
1998	SF N	145	534	93	157	27	0	9	59	79-1	1	83	.294	.383	.395	112	13	3-3	.952	2	106	141	3b137,2b10	0	1.5
1999	SF N	116	414	61	120	24	0	2	36	65-1	3	52	.290	.388	.362	98	3	4-2	.958	-4	95	96	3b108,2b3	41	0.0
2000	†SF N	153	560	97	150	29	4	10	55	52-0	6	62	.268	.333	.387	88	-11	4-2	**.974**	-3	95	99	3b145,2b2	0	-1.2
2001	Chi N	70	210	38	62	12	1	6	23	37-3	3	19	.295	.403	.448	125	10	1-1	.942	0	96	64	3b64/2	91	1.0
2002	Chi N	103	353	51	94	19	4	7	37	51-2	0	41	.266	.355	.402	100	1	0-0	.973	1	92	103	3b101	36	0.2
	SF N	8	13	0	2	0	0	0	1	1-0	0	1	.154	.214	.154	-1	-2	0-0	1.000	-0	76	0	3b3	0	-0.2
	Year	111	366	51	96	19	4	7	38	52-2	0	42	.262	.350	.393	97	-1	0-0	.974	0	92	101	3b104	0	0.0
2003	†Bos A	146	524	85	171	45	5	19	85	59-2	7	77	**.326**	.398	.540	140	32	1-4	.951	1	105	101	3b135,2b10/SD	0	3.1
2004	†Bos A	110	399	75	113	27	1	12	57	51-1	4	56	.283	.365	.446	105	5	2-2	.943	-2	101	102	3b96,2b14	43	0.3
2005	†Bos A	150	519	69	153	34	3	10	62	59-3	6	74	.295	.369	.430	108	9	0-0	.972	-4	99	78	3b142,2b5	0	0.6
2006	LA N	32	107	12	27	7	0	3	15	17-3	1	9	.252	.357	.402	95	0	1-1	.905	0	110	128	3b30	143	0.0
Total	11	1216	4223	663	1229	265	22	85	493	543-17	35	571	.291	.373	.425	109	75	20-18	.958	-7	100	102	3b1128,2b53,D3/S	371	7.2
MULDOON, MIKE	Michael D.; B4.9.1858 Co. Westmeath, Ireland; 5´8˝/165; d5.1																								
1882	Cle N	**84**	341	50	84	17	5	6	45	10	—	28	.246	.268	.378	108	3	—	.880	3	103	158	3b61,O23(21/2/0)	—	0.6
1883	Cle N	98	378	54	86	22	3	0	29	10	—	39	.228	.247	.302	67	-14	—	.825	-9	88	77	3b98,O2R	—	-1.9
1884	Cle N	110	422	46	101	16	6	2	38	18	—	67	.239	.270	.320	82	-9	—	.833	-7	98	106	3b109/rf2	—	-1.3
1885	Bal AA	102	410	47	103	20	6	2	52	20	4	—	.251	.293	.344	102	1	—	.870	-2	98	106	3b101/2	—	0.1
1886	Bal AA	101	381	57	76	13	8	0	23	34	2	—	.199	.269	.276	72	-12	12	.912	3	101	68	2b57,3b44	—	-0.5
Total	5	495	1932	254	450	88	28	10	187	92	6	134	.233	.270	.323	86	-31	12	.846	-12	97	103	3b413,2b59,O26(21/2/3)	—	-3.0
MULLANE, TONY	Anthony John "Count","The Apollo of the Box"; B1.20.1859 Cork, Ireland; D4.25.1944 Chicago IL; BB/TR (BL 1882, TB 1882p, 1893p)/5´10.5˝/165; d8.27; OF(57/59/39); ▲																								
1881	Det N	5	19	0	5	0	0	0	1	0	—	0	.263	.263	.263	63	0	—	.882	0	83	0	P5	—	0.0
1882	Lou AA	77	303	46	78	13	1	0	—	13	—	—	.257	.288	.307	107	3	—	.959	10	117	**299**	P55,1b13,O12(1/12/1),2b2	—	0.5
1883	StL AA	83	307	38	69	11	6	0	33	13	—	—	.225	.256	.300	74	-9	—	.851	2	103	204	P53,O30(13/10/7),2b3,1b2	—	-0.2
1884	Tol AA	95	352	49	97	19	3	3	—	33	1	—	.276	.339	.372	127	12	—	.889	5	126	296	P67,O19(14/0/4),1b7,3b6/S2	—	0.4
1886	Cin AA	91	324	59	73	12	5	0	39	25	1	—	.225	.283	.293	78	-9	20	.899	-1	102	235	P63,O27(2/23/2),1b4,3b2/S2	—	-0.5
1887	Cin AA	56	199	35	44	6	3	3	23	16	4	—	.221	.292	.327	71	-8	20	.944	-1	85	**282**	P48,O9(7/2/0)	—	-0.1
1888	Cin AA	51	175	27	44	4	4	1	16	8	3	—	.251	.296	.337	97	-1	12	.888	-1	97	48	P44,1b4,O3R,2b2	—	-0.1
1889	Cin AA	63	196	53	58	16	4	0	29	27	2	21	.296	.387	.418	125	7	24	.920	-3	83	0	P33,3b18,O12(4/5/3),1b4	—	0.1
1890	Cin N	81	286	41	79	9	8	0	34	39	6	30	.276	.375	.364	116	7	19	.941	-7	78	0	O28(8/2/18),P25,3b21,S10/1	—	-0.2
1891	Cin N	64	209	16	31	1	2	0	10	18	4	33	.148	.229	.172	17	-22	4	.958	0	106	66	P51,O12(6/5/1),3b4	—	-0.3
1892	Cin N	39	118	14	20	3	1	0	9	9	3	8	.169	.246	.212	39	-9	4	.926	5	132	183	P37,1b2	—	0.2
1893	Cin N	16	52	11	15	0	0	1	6	5	3	3	.288	.383	.346	92	0	1	.939	0	107	113	P15/3	—	0.0
	Bal N	38	114	15	26	2	1	0	14	5	0	14	.228	.261	.263	39	-11	5	.943	2	110	107	P34,O2L/1	—	0.0
	Year	54	166	26	41	2	1	1	20	10	3	17	.247	.302	.289	56	-11	6	.942	2	109	109	P49,O2L/31	—	0.0
1894	Bal N	21	53	3	21	3	0	0	9	6	2	3	.396	.475	.453	119	5	2	.889	-1	73	128	P21	—	0.0
	Cle N	4	13	0	1	0	0	0	0	4	0	2	.077	.294	.077	-6	-1	1	.944	2	225	485	P4	—	0.0
	Year	25	66	3	22	3	0	0	9	10	2	5	.333	.436	.379	94	4	3	.911	1	105	204	P25	—	0.0
Total	13	784	2720	407	661	99	38	8	223	221	29	114	.243	.307	.316	87	-36	112	.918	13	106	180	P555,O154C,3b52,1b38,S12,2b9	—	-0.2
MULLEAVY, GREG	Gregory Thomas "Moe"; B9.25.1905 Detroit MI; D2.1.1980 Arcadia CA; BR/TR/5´9˝/167; d7.4; C7																								
1930	Chi A	77	289	27	76	14	5	0	28	20	0	23	.263	.311	.346	69	-14	5-2	.918	-8	99	91	S73	—	-1.2
1932	Chi A	1	3	0	0	0	0	0	0	0	0	0	.000	.000	.000	-99	-1	0-0	1.000	0	87	207	/2	—	-0.1
1933	Bos A	1	0	1	0	0	0	0	0	0	0	0	ø	ø	ø	ø	0	0-0	ø	0	—	—	/R	—	0.0
Total	3	79	292	28	76	14	5	0	28	20	0	23	.260	.308	.342	67	-15	5-2	.918	-8	99	91	S73/2	—	-1.3
MULLEN, CHARLIE	Charles George; B3.15.1889 Seattle WA; D6.6.1963 Seattle WA; BR/TR/5´10.5˝/155; d5.18																								
1910	Chi A	41	123	15	24	2	1	0	13	4	0	—	.195	.220	.228	42	-9	4	.982	1	115	145	1b37,O2R	—	-0.9
1911	Chi A	20	59	7	12	2	1	0	5	5	0	—	.203	.266	.271	51	-4	1	.969	0	107	27	1b20	—	-0.4
1914	NY A	93	323	33	84	8	0	0	44	33	2	55	.260	.332	.285	86	-4	11-17	.994	3	106	130	1b93	—	-0.9
1915	NY A	40	90	11	24	1	0	0	7	10	0	12	.267	.340	.278	85	-1	5-2	.982	1	120	0	1b27	—	-0.1
1916	NY A	59	146	11	39	9	1	0	18	9	0	13	.267	.310	.342	94	-1	7	.943	-5	73	72	2b20,1b17,O6(1/2/3)	—	-0.7
Total	5	253	741	77	183	22	3	0	87	61	2	80	.247	.306	.285	78	-19	28-19	.988	-0	109	100	1b194,2b20,O8(1/2/5)	—	-3.0
MULLEN, MOON	Ford Parker; B2.9.1917 Olympia WA; BL/TR/5´9˝/165; d4.18; Mil 1945; Col Oregon																								
1944	Phi N	118	464	51	124	9	4	0	31	28	4	32	.267	.315	.304	77	-15	4	.963	-6	98	81	2b114/3	0	-1.5
MULLEN, JOHN	John; B Philadelphia PA; BL/TL; d9.9																								
1876	Phi N	1	3	0	0	0	0	0	0	0	—	0	.000	.000	.000	-99	-1	—	.714	-0	—	—	/C	—	-0.1
MULLEN, MARTIN	Martin; B8.22.1852 Cleveland OH; D10.27.1915 Cleveland OH; d8.17																								
1872	Cle NA	1	4	1	0	0	0	0	0	0	—	0	.000	.000	.000	-99	-1	0-0	.400	-1	0	0	/rf	—	-0.1
MULLEN, BILLY	William John; B1.23.1896 St.Louis MO; D5.4.1971 St.Louis MO; BR/TR/5´8˝/160; d10.2																								
1920	StL A	2	4	0	0	0	0	0	0	0	0	0	.000	.000	.000	-97	-1	0-0	1.000	-0	71	0	/2	—	-0.2
1921	StL A	4	4	0	0	0	0	0	0	2	0	1	.000	.333	.000	-8	-1	0-0	1.000	0	90	0	3b2	—	0.0
1923	Bro N	4	11	1	3	0	0	0	0	0	0	0	.273	.273	.273	46	-1	0-0	.875	-0	115	0	3b4	—	-0.1
1926	Det A	11	13	2	1	0	0	0	0	5	0	1	.077	.333	.077	11	-1	1-0	.875	-1	87	0	3b9	—	-0.2
1928	StL A	15	18	2	7	1	0	0	2	3	0	4	.389	.476	.444	139	1	0-0	.867	0	111	141	3b6	—	0.1
Total	5	36	50	5	11	1	0	0	2	10	0	6	.220	.350	.240	56	-3	1-0	.884	-1	102	47	3b21/2	—	-0.4
MULLER, FREDDIE	Frederick William; B12.21.1907 Newark CA; D10.20.1976 Davis CA; BR/TR/5´10˝/170; d7.8																								
1933	Bos A	15	48	6	9	1	1	0	3	5	0	5	.188	.264	.250	37	-5	1-0	.923	-3	94	82	2b14	—	-0.6
1934	Bos A	2	1	1	0	0	0	0	0	1	0	0	.000	.500	.000	36	0	0-0	.800	-1	47	0	/23	—	-0.1
Total	2	17	49	7	9	1	1	0	3	6	0	5	.184	.273	.245	38	-5	1-0	.914	-3	91	77	2b15/3	—	-0.7
MULLIGAN, EDDIE	Edward Joseph; B8.27.1894 St.Louis MO; D3.15.1982 San Rafael CA; BR/TR/5´9˝/152; d9.23; Col St. Louis																								
1915	Chi N	11	22	5	8	1	0	0	2	5	0	1	.364	.481	.409	170	2	2-2	.907	0	91	233	S10/3	—	0.3
1916	Chi N	58	189	13	29	3	4	0	9	8	3	30	.153	.200	.212	24	-17	1	.888	-3	103	109	S58	—	-1.9
1921	Chi A	151	609	82	153	21	12	1	45	32	4	53	.251	.293	.330	59	-40	13-18	.955	-12	94	95	3b151/S	—	-4.4
1922	Chi A	103	372	39	87	14	8	0	31	22	1	32	.234	.278	.315	55	-26	7-7	.971	3	108	84	3b84,S7	—	-1.8
1928	Pit N	27	43	4	10	2	0	0	1	3	0	4	.233	.283	.279	45	-3	0	.929	0	92	253	3b6,2b4	—	-0.3
Total	5	350	1235	143	287	41	24	1	88	70	8	120	.232	.278	.307	54	-84	23-27	.961	-12	99	94	3b242,S76,2b4	—	-8.1
MULLIGAN, JOHN	John; d6.14																								
1884	Was U	1	4	2	1	0	0	0	—	0	—	—	.250	.250	.250	54	0	—	1.000	1	113	0	/3	—	0.0
MULLIGAN, SEAN	Sean Patrick; B4.25.1970 Lynwood CA; BR/TR/6´2˝/210; [SDN91 4/107]; d9.1; Col Illinois																								
1996	SD N	2	1	0	0	0	0	0	0	0-0	0	0	.000	.000	.000	-99	0	0-0	ø	0	—	—	/H	0	0.0

YEAR	TM LG	G	AB	R	H	2B	3B	HR	RBI	BB-IB	HP	SO	AVG	OBP	SLG	AOPS	ABR	SB-CS	FA	FR	RNG	THR	GAMES AT POSITION	DL	BFW
Mullin, Henry	Henry J.; B4.17.1862 St.John NB (now Canada); D11.8.1927 Beverly MA; BR/5´9˝/160; d6.4																								
1884	Was AA	34	120	13	17	3	1	0	—	8	0	—	.142	.195	.183	27	-9	—	.869	1	107	0	O34(4/29/1)/3	—	-0.8
	Bos U	2	8	1	0	0	0	0	—	0	—	—	.000	.000	.000	-99	-2	—	1.000	2	506	1163	O2C	—	0.0
Total	1	36	128	14	17	3	1	0	—	8	—	—	.133	.184	.172	18	-11	—	.882	3	137	88	O36(4/31/1)/3	—	-0.8
Mullin, Jim	James Henry; B10.16.1883 New York NY; D1.24.1925 Philadelphia PA; BR/TR/5´10˝/173; d6.1; Col Manhattan																								
1904	Phi A	22	52	5	14	1	0	1	5	3	1	—	.269	.321	.346	106	0	2	.985	-3	66	68	1b7,2b5,S2/lf	—	-0.3
	Was A	27	102	10	19	2	2	0	4	4	1	—	.186	.224	.245	49	-6	3	.981	5	111	98	2b27	—	-0.1
	Phi A	19	58	4	10	0	0	0	4	2	3	—	.172	.238	.172	29	-5	2	.984	-1	66	68	1b19	—	-0.6
	Year	68	212	19	43	3	2	1	13	9	5	—	.203	.252	.250	58	-10	7	.965	1	109	97	2b32,1b26,S2/lf	—	-1.0
1905	Was A	50	163	18	31	7	6	0	13	5	0	—	.190	.214	.307	67	-7	5	.928	-2	100	85	2b40,1b6	—	-1.0
Total	2	118	375	37	74	10	8	1	26	14	5	—	.197	.236	.275	62	-18	12	.946	-1	104	91	2b72,1b32,S2/lf	—	-2.0
Mullin, Pat	Patrick Joseph; B11.1.1917 Trotter PA; D8.14.1999 Brownsville PA; BL/TR/6´2˝/(180–190); d9.18; Mil 1942–45; C8																								
1940	Det A	4	4	0	0	0	0	0	0	0	0	0	.000	.000	.000	-91	-1	0-0	ø	-0	0	0	/cf	—	-0.1
1941	Det A	54	220	42	76	11	5	5	23	18	2	18	.345	.400	.509	126	8	5-1	.944	-4	93	52	O51C	53	0.3
1946	Det A	93	276	34	68	13	4	3	35	25	1	36	.246	.311	.355	81	-7	3-5	.949	-2	91	133	O75(0/1/75)	0	-1.3
1947	Det A☆	116	398	62	102	28	6	15	62	63	1	66	.256	.359	.470	126	14	3-8	.988	4	107	128	O106R	0	1.3
1948	Det A★	138	496	91	143	16	11	23	80	77	1	57	.288	.385	.504	132	21	1-2	.972	-2	101	75	O131(0/10/123)	0	1.4
1949	Det A	104	310	55	83	8	6	12	59	42	1	29	.268	.357	.448	112	4	1-2	.989	-2	98	73	O79(61/18/3)	0	-0.3
1950	Det A	69	142	16	31	5	0	6	23	20	0	23	.218	.315	.380	75	-6	1-4	1.000	1	94	164	O32(21/0/13)	0	-0.7
1951	Det A	110	295	41	83	11	6	12	51	40	0	38	.281	.367	.481	128	10	2-2	.939	-5	91	69	O83(76/4/6)	0	0.0
1952	Det A	97	255	29	64	13	5	7	35	31	0	30	.251	.332	.424	108	2	4-2	.979	3	102	151	O65(60/2/5)	0	0.1
1953	Det A	79	97	11	26	1	0	4	17	14	0	15	.268	.360	.402	107	1	0-1	.944	-1	83	133	O14(10/0/4)	0	0.0
Total	10	864	2493	381	676	106	43	87	385	330	6	312	.271	.358	.453	115	46	20-27	.970	-8	98	101	O637(228/87/335)	53	0.7
Mulliniks, Rance	Steven Rance; B1.15.1956 Tulare CA; BL/TR/6´0˝/(160–175); [CalA74 3/58]; d6.18																								
1977	Cal A	78	271	36	73	13	2	3	21	23-2	1	36	.269	.329	.365	92	-3	1-1	.963	3	101	83	S77	0	0.8
1978	Cal A	50	119	6	22	3	1	1	6	8-0	1	23	.185	.238	.252	40	-10	2-0	.953	-6	81	97	S47,D2	0	-1.2
1979	Cal A	22	68	7	10	0	0	1	8	4-0	1	14	.147	.192	.191	8	-9	0-0	.957	-5	68	92	S22	0	-1.2
1980	KC A	36	54	8	14	3	0	0	6	7-0	0	10	.259	.339	.315	81	-1	0-0	.981	-3	86	61	S18,2b14	0	-0.3
1981	KC A	24	44	6	10	3	0	0	5	2-0	0	7	.227	.261	.295	60	-2	0-1	.900	-1	94	129	2b10,S7,3b5	0	-0.3
1982	Tor A	112	311	32	76	25	0	4	35	37-1	1	49	.244	.326	.363	82	-6	3-2	.938	-5	91	84	3b102,S16	0	-1.2
1983	Tor A	129	364	54	100	34	3	10	49	57-5	1	43	.275	.373	.467	122	13	0-2	.971	-4	87	59	3b116,S15,2b2	0	0.7
1984	Tor A	125	343	41	111	21	5	3	42	33-3	1	44	.324	.383	.440	123	12	2-3	**.968**	-6	91	77	3b119,S3/2	0	0.4
1985	†Tor A	129	366	55	108	26	1	10	57	55-2	0	54	.295	.383	.454	126	15	2-0	**.971**	-9	88	97	3b119	0	0.5
1986	Tor A	117	348	50	90	22	0	11	45	43-1	1	60	.259	.340	.417	102	2	1-1	**.975**	5	108	90	3b110/2D	26	0.5
1987	Tor A	124	332	37	103	28	1	11	44	34-1	0	55	.310	.371	.500	126	13	1-1	.927	-5	98	113	3b96,D22/S	0	0.6
1988	Tor A	119	337	49	101	21	1	12	48	56-3	0	57	.300	.395	.475	142	22	1-0	1.000	-1	63	0	D108,3b7	20	1.7
1989	†Tor A	103	273	25	65	11	2	3	29	34-6	0	40	.238	.320	.326	84	-5	0-0	.985	2	106	236	D73,3b29	0	-0.6
1990	Tor A	57	97	11	28	4	0	2	16	22-2	0	19	.289	.417	.392	126	5	2-1	.949	-3	79	150	3b22,D10,1b3	0	0.2
1991	†Tor A	97	240	27	60	12	1	2	24	44-2	0	44	.250	.364	.333	91	-1	0-0	1.000	-2	44	0	D81,3b5	31	-0.5
1992	Tor A	3	2	1	1	0	0	0	0	1-0	0	0	.500	.667	.500	220	0	0-0	ø	0	—	—	D2	148	0.0
Total	16	1325	3569	445	972	226	17	73	435	460-28	7	555	.272	.354	.407	107	45	15-12	.961	-41	93	93	3b730,D303,S206,2b28,1b3	225	0.1
Mullins, Fran	Francis Joseph; B5.14.1957 Oakland CA; BR/TR/6´0˝/(180–182); [ChiA79 3/61]; d9.1; Col Santa Clara																								
1980	Chi A	21	62	9	12	4	0	0	3	9-0	0	8	.194	.292	.258	53	-4	0-1	.981	-1	85	173	3b21	0	-0.6
1984	SF N	57	110	8	24	8	0	2	10	9-0	0	29	.218	.277	.345	76	-4	3-1	.969	4	119	108	S28,3b28,2b4	55	0.2
1986	Cle A	28	40	3	7	4	0	0	5	2-0	0	11	.175	.209	.275	32	-4	0-0	.953	2	129	78	2b13,S11/1D	32	0.0
Total	3	106	212	20	43	16	0	2	18	20-0	0	48	.203	.269	.307	61	-12	3-2	.968	5	96	127	3b49,S39,2b17/D1	87	-0.4
Mulvey, Joe	Joseph H.; B10.27.1858 Providence RI; D8.21.1928 Philadelphia PA; BR/TR/5´11.5˝/178; d5.31																								
1883	Pro N	4	16	1	2	1	0	0	2	0	—	1	.125	.125	.188	-6	-2	—	.692	-2	77	0	S4	—	-0.4
	Phi N	3	12	2	6	1	0	0	3	0	—	1	.500	.500	.583	250	2	—	.750	-1	44	171	3b3	—	0.1
	Year	7	28	3	8	2	0	0	5	0	—	2	.286	.286	.357	96	0	—	.692	-3	77	0	S4,3b3	—	-0.3
1884	Phi N	100	401	47	92	11	2	2	32	4	—	49	.229	.237	.282	66	-16	—	.834	13	115	151	3b100	—	-0.1
1885	Phi N	107	443	74	119	25	6	6	64	3	—	18	.269	.274	.393	116	6	—	.848	-5	95	96	3b107	—	0.3
1886	Phi N	107	430	71	115	16	10	2	53	15	—	31	.267	.292	.365	98	-3	27	.879	-19	87	18	3b107/rf	—	-1.8
1887	Phi N	111	474	93	136	21	6	2	78	21	3	14	.287	.321	.369	86	-10	43	.865	-17	86	106	3b111	—	-2.2
1888	Phi N	100	398	37	86	12	3	0	39	9	1	33	.216	.235	.261	55	-21	18	.891	-13	89	72	3b100	—	-3.2
1889	Phi N	129	544	77	157	21	9	6	77	23	1	25	.289	.319	.393	90	-12	23	.893	1	104	83	3b129	—	-0.8
1890	Phi P	120	519	96	149	26	16	5	87	27	3	36	.287	.326	.428	98	-6	20	.857	-17	87	72	3b120	—	-1.6
1891	Phi AA	113	453	62	115	9	13	5	66	17	4	32	.254	.287	.364	86	-13	11	.894	1	96	98	3b113	—	-0.9
1892	Phi N	25	98	9	14	1	1	0	4	6	1	9	.143	.200	.173	13	-11	2	.883	2	105	139	3b25	—	-0.8
1893	Was N	55	226	21	53	9	4	0	19	7	2	8	.235	.264	.310	54	-16	2	.874	5	112	88	3b55	—	-0.9
1895	Bro N	13	49	8	15	4	1	0	8	2	0	0	.306	.333	.429	104	0	1	.917	1	99	50	3b13	—	0.1
Total	12	987	4063	598	1059	157	71	28	532	134	15	257	.261	.287	.355	84	-102	147	.871	-53	96	88	3b983,S4/rf	—	-12.2
Mumphrey, Jerry	Jerry Wayne; B9.9.1952 Tyler TX; BB/TR/6´2˝/(175–200); [StLN71 4/79]; d9.10																								
1974	StL N	5	2	2	0	0	0	0	0	0-0	0	0	.000	.000	.000	-99	-1	0-0	ø	-0	0	0	/lf	0	-0.1
1975	StL N	11	16	2	6	2	0	0	1	4-0	0	3	.375	.500	.500	170	2	0-0	1.000	1	174	0	O3R	0	0.3
1976	StL N	112	384	51	99	15	5	1	26	37-0	1	53	.258	.322	.331	85	-7	22-6	.993	5	113	98	O94(15/77/12)	0	-0.3
1977	StL N	145	463	73	133	20	10	2	38	47-6	1	70	.287	.354	.387	99	0	22-15	.971	6	111	100	O133(49/67/34)	0	0.2
1978	StL N	125	367	41	96	13	4	2	37	30-0	1	40	.262	.317	.335	83	-9	14-10	.995	-1	89	141	O116(48/30/48)	0	-1.4
1979	StL N	124	339	53	100	10	3	3	32	26-2	0	39	.295	.341	.369	93	-3	8-11	.984	-3	96	44	O114(83/19/20)	16	-1.3
1980	SD N	160	564	61	168	24	3	4	59	49-4	0	90	.298	.352	.372	110	8	52-5	.974	-3	100	97	O153C	0	1.4
1981	†NY A	80	319	44	98	11	5	6	32	24-1	0	27	.307	.354	.429	127	10	14-9	.966	3	112	113	O79C	0	1.3
1982	NY A	123	477	76	143	24	10	9	68	50-4	0	66	.300	.364	.449	124	16	11-3	.986	0	104	63	O123C	42	1.6
1983	NY A	83	267	41	70	11	4	7	36	28-2	0	33	.262	.327	.412	107	2	2-3	.983	7	113	154	O83C	0	0.7
	Hou N	44	143	17	48	10	2	1	17	22-3	1	23	.336	.425	.455	153	12	5-0	.990	-2	97	50	O43C	0	1.1
1984	Hou N★	151	524	66	152	20	3	9	83	56-7	0	79	.290	.355	.391	118	13	15-7	.988	-8	93	67	O137C	0	0.5
1985	Hou N	130	444	52	123	25	2	8	61	37-8	0	57	.277	.329	.396	105	3	6-7	.969	-2	100	81	O126(0/58/68)	0	-0.4
1986	Chi N	111	309	37	94	11	2	5	32	26-4	0	45	.304	.355	.401	101	1	2-3	.982	-0	102	64	O92(39/65/21)	0	-0.2
1987	Chi N	118	309	41	103	19	2	13	44	35-6	0	47	.333	.400	.534	139	18	1-1	.992	-1	94	105	O85(78/1/6)	0	1.4
1988	Chi N	63	66	3	9	2	0	0	9	7-2	0	16	.136	.219	.167	12	-7	0-0	1.000	-1	69	0	O4L	0	-0.9
Total	15	1585	4993	660	1442	217	55	70	575	478-49	4	688	.289	.349	.396	108	58	174-80	.981	2	102	90	O1386(317/935/212)	58	3.9
Munce, John	John Lewis "Big John"; B11.18.1857 Philadelphia PA; D3.15.1917 Philadelphia PA; 5´8.5˝/160; d8.19																								
1884	Wil U	7	21	1	4	0	0	0	—	1	—	—	.190	.227	.190	27	-3	—	.667	-0	136	0	O7(0/2/6)	—	-0.3
Munch, Jake	Jacob Ferdinand; B11.16.1890 Morton PA; D6.8.1966 Lansdowne PA; BL/TL/6´2.5˝/170; d5.27																								
1918	Phi A	22	30	3	8	0	1	0	0	0	0	5	.267	.267	.333	80	-1	0	.667	-1	67	0	O3(0/1/2),1b2	—	-0.2
Mundinger, George	George; B11.20.1854 New Orleans LA; D10.12.1910 Covington LA; BR/TR/6´2˝/200; d5.9																								
1884	Ind AA	3	8	1	2	0	0	0	3	0	0	—	.250	.250	.250	65	0	—	.750	-2	—	—	C3	—	-0.2
Mundy, Bill	William Edward; B6.28.1889 Salineville OH; D9.23.1958 Kalamazoo MI; BL/TL/5´10˝/154; d8.17																								
1913	Bos A	16	47	4	12	0	0	0	4	4	0	12	.255	.314	.255	65	-2	0	.952	-3	47	53	1b14	—	-0.5
Munn, Horatio	Horatio Brinsmade; B7.26.1851 Newark NJ; D2.17.1910 Brooklyn NY; d9.4																								
1875	Atl NA	1	4	0	0	0	0	0	0	0	—	0	.000	.000	.000	-99	-1	0-0	.833	-0	111	0	/2	—	-0.1
Munoz, Jose	Jose Luis; B11.11.1967 Chicago IL; BB/TR/5´11˝/165; [LAN87 20/508]; d4.7; Col Florida JC																								
1996	Chi A	17	27	7	7	0	0	0	1	4-0	0	1	.259	.355	.259	61	-1	0-0	.923	-3	72	51	2b7,S2/3lfD	0	-0.3

YEAR	TM LG	G	AB	R	H	2B	3B	HR	RBI	BB-IB	HP	SO	AVG	OBP	SLG	AOPS	ABR	SB-CS	FA	FR	RNG	THR	GAMES AT POSITION	DL	BFW
Munoz, Noe	Noe; B11.11.1967 San Cristobal, Estado de Mexico, Mexico; BR/TR/6´2˝/180; d4.30																								
1995	LA N	2	1	0	0	0	0	0	0	0-0	0	0	.000	.000	.000	-99	0	0-0	1.000	1	0	0	C2	0	0.0
Munoz, Pedro	Pedro Javier (Gonzalez); B9.19.1968 Ponce, PR; BR/TR/5´10˝/(170–208); d9.1																								
1990	Min A	22	85	13	23	4	1	0	5	2-0	0	16	.271	.281	.341	71	-4	3-0	.972	-2	81	69	O21(3/0/19)/D	0	-0.6
1991	Min A	51	138	15	39	7	1	7	26	9-0	1	31	.283	.327	.500	121	3	3-0	.989	3	116	114	O44(10/0/39),D2	15	0.6
1992	Min A	127	418	44	113	16	3	12	71	17-1	1	90	.270	.298	.409	93	-6	4-5	.987	-0	95	106	O122(7/0/117),D3	0	-1.1
1993	Min A	104	326	34	76	11	1	13	38	25-2	3	97	.233	.294	.393	82	-10	1-2	.983	-5	89	80	O102(64/0/41)	25	-1.9
1994	Min A	75	244	35	72	15	2	11	36	19-0	2	67	.295	.348	.508	117	6	0-0	.965	-2	102	26	O58(42/0/19),D12	0	0.0
1995	Min A	104	376	45	113	17	0	18	58	19-0	3	86	.301	.338	.489	112	5	0-3	.926	-3	57	225	D77,O25(1/0/24),1b3	0	-0.4
1996	Oak A	34	121	17	31	5	0	6	18	9-1	0	31	.256	.308	.446	89	-3	0-0	1.000	-3	56	0	D18,O14R	120	-0.7
Total	7	517	1708	203	467	75	8	67	252	100-4	10	418	.273	.315	.444	99	-9	11-10	.980	-12	92	89	O386(127/0/273),D113,1b3	160	-4.1
Munson, Red	Clarence Hanford; B7.31.1883 Cincinnati OH; D2.19.1957 Mishawaka IN; TR/5´11˝/?; d8.28																								
1905	Phi N	9	26	1	3	1	0	0	2	0	0	—	.115	.115	.154	-21	-4	0	.857	-1	*120*	*89*	C8	—	-0.4
Munson, Eric	Eric Walter; B10.3.1977 San Diego CA; BL/TR/6´3˝/(220–225); [DetA99 1/3]; d7.18; Col USC																								
2000	Det A	3	5	0	0	0	0	0	0	0-0	0	1	.000	.000	.000	-99	-2	0-0	.941	-1	0	167	1b3	0	-0.2
2001	Det A	17	66	4	10	3	1	1	6	3-0	0	21	.152	.188	.273	20	-8	0-1	.994	1	121	92	1b17	0	-0.9
2002	Det A	18	59	3	11	0	0	2	5	6-0	1	11	.186	.269	.288	51	-4	0-0	.970	0	121	88	D14,1b4	0	-0.5
2003	Det A	99	313	28	75	9	0	18	50	35-1	1	61	.240	.312	.441	102	0	3-0	.920	-13	90	79	3b91,D3	48	-1.1
2004	Det A	109	321	36	68	14	2	19	49	29-3	6	90	.212	.289	.445	91	-6	1-1	.934	4	111	119	3b94/CD	0	-0.1
2005	TB A	11	18	2	3	1	0	0	2	4-0	1	3	.167	.333	.222	58	-1	0-0	1.000	-1	33	0	3b2/1lfD	34	-0.2
2006	Hou N	53	141	10	28	6	0	5	19	11-1	3	32	.199	.269	.348	56	-10	0-0	.995	-6	124	114	C37,1b4/D	0	-1.3
Total	7	310	923	83	195	33	3	45	132	88-5	12	219	.211	.286	.400	80	-31	4-2	.928	-15	100	98	3b187,C38,1b29,D28/lf	82	-4.3
Munson, Joe	Joseph Martin Napoleon (b Joseph Martin Napoleon Carlson); B11.6.1899 Renovo PA; D2.24.1991 Drexel Hill PA; BL/TR/5´9˝/184; d9.18; Col Lehigh																								
1925	Chi N	9	35	5	13	3	1	0	3	3	1	1	.371	.436	.514	140	2	1-1	1.000	-0	95	80	O9R	—	0.1
1926	Chi N	33	101	17	26	2	2	3	15	8	1	4	.257	.318	.406	93	-2	0	.898	-2	95	67	O28(16/0/12)	—	-0.6
Total	2	42	136	22	39	5	3	3	18	11	2	5	.287	.349	.434	105	0	1-1	.922	-2	95	70	O37(16/0/21)	—	-0.5
Munson, Thurman	Thurman Lee; B6.7.1947 Akron OH; D8.2.1979 Canton OH; BR/TR/5´11˝/(190–195); [NYA68 1/4]; d8.8; Col Kent St.																								
1969	NY A	26	86	6	22	1	2	1	9	10-1	0	10	.256	.330	.349	94	-1	0-1	.986	1	207	103	C25	0	0.1
1970	NY A	132	453	59	137	25	4	6	53	57-6	7	56	.302	.386	.415	127	19	5-7	.989	14	**167**	96	C125	0	3.9
1971	NY A★	125	451	71	113	15	4	10	42	52-1	7	65	.251	.335	.368	105	3	6-5	**.998**	8	**221**	113	C117/rf	0	1.7
1972	NY A	140	511	54	143	16	3	7	46	47-5	3	58	.280	.343	.364	113	8	6-7	.977	5	**185**	77	C132	0	2.0
1973	NY A★	147	519	80	156	29	4	20	74	48-4	4	64	.301	.362	.487	141	28	4-6	.984	16	158	98	C142/D	0	4.9
1974	NY A★	144	517	64	135	19	2	13	60	44-12	1	66	.261	.316	.381	102	1	2-0	.974	6	123	70	C137,D4	0	1.4
1975	NY A★	157	597	83	190	24	3	12	102	45-8	6	52	.318	.366	.429	127	21	3-2	.972	18	151	111	C130,D22,1b2,O2(1/0/1)/3	0	4.5
1976	†NY A★	152	616	79	186	27	1	17	105	29-6	9	38	.302	.337	.432	126	18	14-11	.981	1	111	94	C121,D21,O11(2/0/9)	0	2.5
1977	†NY A★	149	595	85	183	28	5	18	100	39-8	2	55	.308	.351	.462	121	16	5-6	.984	3	111	92	C136,D10	0	2.3
1978	†NY A★	154	617	73	183	27	1	6	71	35-6	3	70	.297	.332	.373	101	1	2-3	.986	9	128	103	C125,D14,O13R	0	1.3
1979	NY A	97	382	42	110	18	3	3	39	32-2	0	37	.288	.340	.374	95	-2	1-2	.978	4	**181**	85	C88,1b3,D5	0	0.4
Total	11	1423	5344	696	1558	229	32	113	701	438-59	42	571	.292	.346	.410	116	112	48-50	.982	84	153	94	C1278,D77,O27(3/0/24),1b5/3	0	25.0
Munyan, John	John Baird; B11.14.1860 Chester PA; D2.18.1945 Endicott NY; d7.12																								
1887	Cle AA	16	58	9	14	1	1	0	6	3	0	—	.241	.279	.293	61	-3	4	.762	-1	64	0	O12(3/3/6),C3,3b2	—	-0.3
1890	Col AA	2	7	1	1	0	0	0	0	0	1	—	.143	.250	.143	17	-1	0	.667	0	281	0	O2C	—	-0.1
	StL AA	96	342	61	91	15	7	4	42	32	7	—	.266	.341	.386	100	-2	11	.939	-1	*100*	*99*	C83,O7L,2b5,3b3/S	—	0.3
	Year	98	349	62	92	15	7	4	42	32	8	—	.264	.339	.381	99	-3	11	.939	-1	*100*	*99*	C83,O9(7/2/0),2b5,3b3/S	—	0.2
1891	StL AA	60	176	41	41	4	3	0	19	41	4	39	.233	.389	.290	82	-3	13	.940	-4	*115*	*82*	C43,O12(4/0/8),S5,3b3	—	-0.3
Total	3	174	583	112	147	20	11	4	67	76	12	39	.252	.350	.345	90	-9	28	.937	-6	*105*	*94*	C129,O33(14/5/14),3b8,S6,2b5	—	-0.4
Murcer, Bobby	Bobby Ray; B5.20.1946 Oklahoma City OK; BL/TR/5´11˝/(165–185); d9.8; Mil 1967–68; OF(56/789/839)																								
1965	NY A	11	37	2	9	0	1	1	4	5-0	0	12	.243	.333	.378	102	0	0-0	.932	7	130	229	S11	0	0.8
1966	NY A	21	69	3	12	1	1	0	5	4-0	0	5	.174	.219	.217	27	-7	2-2	.931	-2	97	40	S18	0	-0.9
1969	NY A	152	564	82	146	24	4	26	82	50-2	3	103	.259	.319	.454	119	12	7-5	.964	-6	94	45	O118(0/27/99),3b31	0	0.0
1970	NY A	159	581	95	146	23	3	23	78	87-5	2	100	.251	.348	.420	117	14	15-10	.992	-4	93	139	O155C	0	0.6
1971	NY A★	146	529	94	175	25	6	25	94	91-13	0	60	.331	**.427**	.543	**182**	**61**	14-8	.985	-14	83	103	O143C	0	4.5
1972	NY A★	153	585	**102**	171	30	7	33	96	63-7	2	67	.292	.361	.537	169	48	11-9	.992	-4	97	105	O151C	0	4.3
1973	NY A★	160	616	83	187	29	2	22	95	50-6	3	67	.304	.357	.464	133	26	6-7	.985	-7	92	119	O160C	0	1.5
1974	NY A★	156	606	69	166	25	4	10	88	57-10	2	59	.274	.332	.378	107	6	14-5	.978	-5	85	178	O156(0/59/101)	0	-0.5
1975	SF N★	147	526	80	157	29	4	11	91	91-6	2	45	.298	.396	.432	127	24	9-5	.981	-11	77	108	O144(0/2/143)	0	0.7
1976	SF N	147	533	73	138	20	2	23	90	84-10	4	78	.259	.362	.433	122	17	12-7	.961	-6	96	88	O146R	0	0.5
1977	Chi N	154	554	90	147	18	3	27	89	80-13	3	77	.265	.355	.455	106	5	16-7	.980	-12	82	94	O150R/2S	0	-1.4
1978	Chi N	146	499	66	140	22	6	9	64	80-15	0	57	.281	.376	.403	106	7	14-5	.979	-16	79	74	O138(0/33/121)	0	-1.4
1979	Chi N	58	190	22	49	4	1	7	22	36-2	1	20	.258	.374	.400	102	2	2-3	1.000	2	111	95	O54R	0	0.0
	NY A	74	264	42	72	12	0	8	33	25-2	2	32	.273	.339	.409	103	1	1-1	.983	-2	98	87	O70(12/59/7)	0	-0.2
1980	†NY A	100	297	41	80	9	1	13	57	34-2	2	28	.269	.339	.438	116	6	2-0	.955	-4	90	59	O59(44/0/18),D33	0	0.0
1981	†NY A	50	117	14	31	6	0	6	24	12-1	0	15	.265	.331	.470	131	4	0-0	ø	0	0	0	D33	0	0.4
1982	NY A	65	141	12	32	6	0	7	30	12-2	1	15	.227	.288	.418	94	-2	2-1	ø	0	0	0	D47	0	-0.3
1983	NY A	9	22	2	4	2	0	1	1	1-0	0	1	.182	.217	.409	70	-1	0-0	ø	0	—	—	D5	0	-0.1
Total	17	1908	6730	972	1862	285	45	252	1043	862-96	27	841	.277	.357	.445	124	223	127-75	.981	-83	89	105	O1644R,D118,3b31,S30/2	0	8.5
Murch, Simmy	Simeon Augustus; B11.21.1880 Castine ME; D6.6.1939 Exeter NH; BR/TR/6´2˝/220; d9.20																								
1904	StL N	13	51	3	7	1	0	0	1	1	0	—	.137	.154	.157	-4	-6	0	.905	-1	101	166	2b6,3b6/S	—	-0.7
1905	StL N	4	9	0	1	0	0	0	0	0	0	—	.111	.111	.111	-35	-2	0	.750	-2	0	0	2b2/S	—	-0.4
1908	Bro N	6	11	1	2	1	0	0	0	1	0	—	.182	.250	.273	70	0	0	.964	-1	0	99	1b2	—	-0.1
Total	3	23	71	4	10	2	0	0	1	2	0	—	.141	.164	.169	3	-8	0	.880	-4	83	136	2b8,3b6,1b2,S2	—	-1.2
Murdoch, Wilbur	Wilbur Edwin; B3.14.1875 Avon NY; D10.29.1941 Los Angeles CA; TR; d8.29																								
1908	StL N	27	62	5	16	3	0	0	5	3	0	—	.258	.292	.306	96	0	4	.913	-2	0	0	O16(13/5/0)	—	-0.3
Murnane, Tim	Timothy Hayes; B6.4.1852 Naugatuck CT; D2.7.1917 Boston MA; BL/TR/5´9.5˝/172; d4.26; M1; Col Holy Cross																								
1872	Man NA	23	114	28	41	1	1	0	16	0	—	0	.360	.360	.386	137	5	1-2	.905	-4	0	62	1b23	—	0.1
1873	Ath NA	41	176	53	39	2	1	1	10	8	—	13	.222	.255	.261	49	-12	8-2	.785	-3	55	0	O30(0/24/6),1b10,2b6	—	-1.0
1874	Ath NA	21	82	11	17	2	0	0	11	1	—	3	.207	.217	.232	40	-6	0-1	.857	-3	132	0	O14(0/1/13),2b6,1b3	—	-0.7
1875	Phi NA	69	313	71	85	5	0	1	30	7	—	7	.272	.287	.297	100	-1	**30**-9	.918	1	86	74	1b31,O26(1/24/1),2b15	—	0.3
1876	Bos N	69	308	60	87	4	3	2	34	8	—	12	.282	.301	.334	109	3	—	.927	-4	44	130	1b65,O3(2/1/0)/2	—	-0.4
1877	Bos N	35	140	23	39	7	1	1	15	6	—	7	.279	.308	.364	107	1	—	.815	0	102	280	O30(0/25/5),1b5	—	0.0
1878	Pro N	49	188	35	45	6	1	0	14	8	—	12	.239	.270	.282	82	-3	—	.940	1	**168**	111	1b48/cf	—	-0.5
1884	Bos U	76	311	55	73	5	2	0	—	22	—	—	.235	.285	.264	68	-21	—	.950	-4	39	40	1b63,O16(1/0/15),M	—	-2.7
Total	4NA	154	685	163	182	10	2	2	67	16	—	23	.266	.282	.295	83	-14	39-14	.824	-9	47	0	O70(1/49/20),1b67,2b27	—	-1.3
Total	4	229	947	173	244	22	7	3	63	44	—	31	.258	.291	.305	90	-20	—	.938	-8	81	92	1b181,O50(3/27/20)/2	—	-3.6
Murphy	; d8.16																								
1884	Bos U	1	3	0	0	0	0	0	—	1	—	—	.000	.250	.000	-18	0	—	.333	-2	—	—	/Clf	—	-0.2
Murphy, Clarence	Clarence; d6.17																								
1886	Lou AA	1	3	0	0	0	0	0	0	0	0	—	.000	.000	.000	-95	-1	0	1.000	0	0	0	/lf	—	-0.1
Murphy, Connie	Cornelius David "Stone Face"; B11.1.1870 Northfield MA; D12.14.1945 New Bedford MA; BL/TR/5´8˝/155; d9.17																								
1893	Cin N	6	17	3	3	1	0	0	2	1	0	2	.176	.222	.235	21	-2	0	.917	-1	*115*	*30*	C4	—	-0.3
1894	Cin N	1	4	0	0	0	0	0	0	1	0	1	.000	.200	.000	-47	-1	0	.500	-1	*81*	*106*	/C	—	-0.1
Total	2	7	21	3	3	1	0	0	2	2	0	3	.143	.217	.190	6	-3	0	.857	-2	*108*	*45*	C5	—	-0.4

YEAR	TM LG	G	AB	R	H	2B	3B	HR	RBI	BB-IB	HP	SO	AVG	OBP	SLG	AOPS	ABR	SB-CS	FA	FR	RNG	THR	GAMES AT POSITION	DL	BFW
MURPHY, DALE	Dale Bryan; B3.12.1956 Portland OR; BR/TR/6´5˝/(185–227); [AtlN74 1/5]; d9.13																								
1976	Atl N	19	65	3	17	6	0	0	9	7-0	0	9	.262	.333	.354	90	0	0-0	.974	-1	59	151	C19	0	-0.1
1977	Atl N	18	76	5	24	8	1	2	14	0-0	0	8	.316	.316	.526	109	1	0-1	.954	-3	56	66	C18	0	-0.1
1978	Atl N	151	530	66	120	14	3	23	79	42-3	3	145	.226	.284	.394	80	-16	11-7	.984	2	116	81	1b129,C21	0	-2.2
1979	Atl N	104	384	53	106	7	2	21	57	38-5	2	67	.276	.340	.469	113	6	6-1	.980	-12	85	97	1b76,C27	55	-0.9
1980	Atl N★	156	569	98	160	27	2	33	89	59-9	1	133	.281	.349	.510	136	26	9-6	.985	-1	96	127	O154(4/129/21)/1	0	2.3
1981	Atl N	104	369	43	91	12	1	13	50	44-8	0	72	.247	.325	.390	102	1	14-5	.981	-2	92	151	O103(0/102/1),1b3	0	-0.1
1982	†Atl N★	**162**	598	113	168	23	2	36	**109**	93-9	3	134	.281	.378	.507	143	36	23-11	.979	-0	105	54	O162(65/118/8)	0	3.5
1983	Atl N★	**162**	589	131	178	24	4	36	**121**	90-12	2	110	.302	.393	**.540**	147	39	30-4	.985	-3	96	119	O160(28/136/2)	0	4.0
1984	Atl N★	**162**	607	94	176	32	8	**36**	100	79-20	2	134	.290	.372	**.547**	145	36	19-7	.987	-11	88	108	O160C	0	2.6
1985	Atl N★	**162**	616	**118**	185	32	2	**37**	111	**90**-15	1	141	.300	.388	.539	149	42	10-3	.980	-20	81	78	O161C	0	2.2
1986	Atl N★	160	614	89	163	29	7	29	83	75-5	2	141	.265	.347	.477	120	16	7-7	.981	-20	82	64	O159(0/155/6)	0	-0.7
1987	Atl N★	159	566	115	167	27	1	44	105	115-**29**	7	136	.295	.417	.580	155	50	16-6	.977	5	105	123	O159R	0	4.6
1988	Atl N	156	592	77	134	35	4	24	77	74-16	2	125	.226	.313	.421	105	4	3-5	.992	11	105	183	O156R	0	0.9
1989	Atl N	154	574	60	131	16	0	20	84	65-10	2	142	.228	.306	.361	89	-8	3-2	.985	-7	95	61	O151(0/82/70)	0	-2.0
1990	Atl N	97	349	38	81	14	0	17	55	41-11	1	84	.232	.312	.418	95	-3	9-2	.981	1	108	45	O97R	0	-0.4
	Phi N	57	214	22	57	9	1	7	28	20-3	0	46	.266	.328	.416	104	1	0-1	.992	-0	95	99	O55(1/1/53)	0	-0.2
	Year	154	563	60	138	23	1	24	83	61-14	1	130	.245	.318	.417	98	-2	9-3	.985	1	103	65	O152(1/1/150)	0	-0.6
1991	Phi N	153	544	66	137	33	1	18	81	48-3	0	93	.252	.309	.415	104	2	1-0	.983	-1	103	56	O147R	0	-0.3
1992	Phi N	18	62	5	10	1	0	2	7	1-0	0	13	.161	.175	.274	25	-6	0-0	.950	-3	68	0	O16(1/0/16)	156	-1.1
1993	Col N	26	42	1	6	1	0	0	7	5-1	0	15	.143	.224	.167	8	-5	0-0	1.000	0	91	148	O13(2/0/11)	0	-0.6
Total	18	2180	7960	1197	2111	350	39	398	1266	986-159	28	1748	.265	.346	.469	120	222	161-68	.983	-66	96	98	O1853(101/1044/747),1b209,C85	211	11.4
MURPHY, DANNY	Daniel Francis; B8.11.1876 Philadelphia PA; D11.22.1955 Jersey City NJ; BR/TR/5´9˝/175; d9.17; C6																								
1900	NY N	22	74	11	20	1	0	0	6	8	0	—	.270	.341	.284	77	-2	4	.888	-4	89	102	2b22	—	-0.4
1901	NY N	5	20	0	4	0	0	0	0	1	0	—	.200	.238	.200	29	-2	0	.895	-2	85	0	2b5	—	-0.4
1902	Phi A	76	291	48	91	11	8	1	48	13	4	—	.313	.351	.416	107	2	12	.963	-13	86	69	2b76	—	-1.0
1903	Phi A	133	513	66	140	31	11	1	60	13	3	—	.273	.295	.382	97	-3	17	.949	-13	88	73	2b133	—	-1.6
1904	Phi A	150	557	78	160	30	17	7	77	22	5	—	.287	.320	.440	132	18	22	.941	14	103	84	2b150	—	3.7
1905	†Phi A	151	537	71	149	34	4	6	71	42	8	—	.277	.339	.389	129	18	23	.955	-12	92	76	2b151	—	0.8
1906	Phi A	119	448	48	135	28	6	2	60	21	6	—	.301	.341	.404	129	14	17	.955	-11	90	95	2b119	—	0.4
1907	Phi A	124	469	51	127	23	3	2	57	30	2	—	.271	.317	.345	109	5	11	.965	7	101	73	2b122	—	1.4
1908	Phi A	142	525	51	139	28	7	4	66	32	2	—	.265	.309	.368	112	6	16	.963	7	110	146	O84(2/12/70),2b56,1b2	—	1.1
1909	Phi A	149	541	61	152	28	14	5	69	35	6	—	.281	.332	.412	132	18	19	**.977**	-4	87	126	O149R	—	0.8
1910	†Phi A	151	560	70	168	28	18	4	64	31	1	—	.300	.338	.436	143	24	18	.974	-3	102	74	O151R	—	-1.6
1911	†Phi A	141	508	104	167	27	11	6	66	50	8	—	.329	.398	.461	142	29	22	.961	7	87	**153**	O136R,2b4	—	2.8
1912	Phi A	36	130	27	42	6	2	2	20	16	1	—	.323	.401	.446	147	8	8	.891	-4	81	44	O36R	—	0.3
1913	Phi A	40	59	3	19	5	1	0	6	4	0	8	.322	.365	.441	139	3	0	1.000	-1	62	0	O9R	—	0.2
1914	Bro F	52	161	16	49	9	0	4	32	17	1	16	.304	.374	.435	121	3	4	.986	2	102	115	O46(1/0/45)	—	0.2
1915	Bro F	5	6	0	1	0	0	0	0	0	0	0	.167	.167	.167	-6	-1	0	1.000	-0	77	0	/2rf	—	-0.2
Total	16	1496	5399	705	1563	289	102	44	702	335	47	24	.289	.336	.405	124	140	193	.953	-32	94	79	2b839,O612(3/12/597),1b2	—	9.7
MURPHY, DANNY	Daniel Francis; B8.23.1942 Beverly MA; BL/TR/5´11˝/(180–185); d6.18; ▲																								
1960	Chi N	31	75	7	9	2	0	1	6	4-0	1	13	.120	.175	.187	-1	-11	0-0	.976	0	105	77	O21(0/16/5)	0	-1.2
1961	Chi N	4	13	3	5	0	0	2	3	1-0	0	5	.385	.429	.846	225	2	0-0	1.000	0	87	345	O4R	0	0.2
1962	Chi N	14	35	5	7	3	1	0	3	2-0	0	9	.200	.243	.343	53	-2	0-0	1.000	-2	39	0	O5(2/1/6)	0	-0.5
1969	Chi A	17	1	0	0	0	0	0	0	2-0	0	0	.000	.667	.000	95	1	0-0	1.000	-0	86	0	P17	0	0.0
1970	Chi A	51	6	3	2	0	0	1	1	2-0	0	2	.333	.500	.833	252	2	0-0	.933	-1	84	112	P51	0	0.0
Total	5	117	130	18	23	5	1	4	13	11-0	1	29	.177	.246	.323	53	-8	0-0	.947	-3	85	81	P68,O30(2/17/15)	0	-1.5
MURPHY, DANNY	Daniel Joseph "Handsome Dan"; B9.10.1864 Brooklyn NY; D12.14.1915 Brooklyn NY; ?/156; d4.26																								
1892	NY N	8	26	2	3	0	0	0	0	5	0	4	.115	.258	.115	14	-2	0	.900	-2	*69*	72	C8	—	-0.4
MURPHY, DAVE	David Francis "Dirty Dave"; B5.4.1876 Adams MA; D4.8.1940 Adams MA; TR; d8.28																								
1905	Bos N	3	11	0	2	0	0	0	1	0	0	—	.182	.182	.182	9	-1	0	1.000	-1	97	0	S2/3	—	-0.3
MURPHY, DAVID	David Matthew; B10.18.1981 Houston TX; BL/TL/6´4˝/190; [BosA03 1/17]; d9.2; Col Baylor																								
2006	Bos A	20	22	4	5	1	0	1	2	4-0	0	4	.227	.346	.409	92	0	0-0	1.000	-1	71	0	O16(6/8/2)/D	0	-0.1
MURPHY, DONNIE	Donald Rex; B3.10.1983 Lakewood CA; BR/TR/5´10˝/(180–200); [KCA02 5/138]; d9.18; Col Orange Coast (CA) JC																								
2004	KC A	7	27	1	5	3	0	0	3	0-0	0	7	.185	.185	.296	23	-3	1-0	1.000	-1	91	167	2b7	0	-0.3
2005	KC A	32	77	4	12	5	0	1	8	9-0	0	23	.156	.241	.260	36	-7	0-1	.972	-5	88	77	2b29,S2/D	15	-1.1
Total	2	39	104	5	17	8	0	1	11	9-0	0	30	.163	.228	.269	32	-10	1-1	.978	-6	89	98	2b36,S2/D	15	-1.4
MURPHY, DWAYNE	Dwayne Keith; B3.18.1955 Merced CA; BL/TR/6´1˝/(180–185); [OakA73 15/359]; d4.8; C6																								
1978	Oak A	60	52	15	10	2	0	0	5	7-0	0	14	.192	.279	.231	50	-3	0-1	1.000	2	121	88	O45(21/12/14),D5	0	-0.2
1979	Oak A	121	388	57	99	10	4	11	40	84-6	1	80	.255	.387	.387	116	13	15-11	.988	4	103	131	O118(2/115/3)	23	1.4
1980	Oak A	159	573	86	157	18	2	13	68	102-7	2	96	.274	.384	.380	118	19	26-15	.990	12	113	115	O158C	0	3.0
1981	†Oak A	107	390	58	98	10	3	15	60	73-6	2	91	.251	.369	.408	129	17	10-4	.985	3	109	89	O106C/D	0	2.1
1982	Oak A	151	543	84	129	15	1	27	94	94-2	3	122	.238	.349	.418	114	13	26-8	.983	10	109	137	O147C/SD	0	2.4
1983	Oak A	130	471	55	107	17	2	17	75	62-4	0	105	.227	.314	.380	96	-2	7-5	.979	3	108	91	O124C,D7	17	-0.1
1984	Oak A	153	559	93	143	18	2	33	88	74-1	3	111	.256	.342	.472	132	24	4-5	.988	11	111	138	O153C	0	3.3
1985	Oak A	152	523	77	122	21	3	20	59	84-3	3	123	.233	.340	.400	110	9	4-5	.989	-2	104	61	O150C	0	0.5
1986	Oak A	98	329	50	83	11	3	9	39	56-4	4	80	.252	.364	.386	113	8	3-1	.993	6	111	119	O97C/D	54	1.4
1987	Oak A	82	219	39	51	7	0	8	35	58-2	0	61	.233	.388	.374	112	7	4-4	.984	0	106	33	O79C/12	77	0.6
1988	Det A	49	144	14	36	5	0	4	19	24-2	1	26	.250	.361	.368	108	3	1-1	1.000	3	116	51	O43(4/35/10),D3	0	0.5
1989	Phi N	98	156	20	34	5	0	9	27	29-2	0	44	.218	.341	.423	117	4	0-1	.986	-1	99	52	O52(30/5/19)	0	0.2
Total	12	1360	4347	648	1069	139	20	166	609	747-39	19	953	.246	.356	.402	115	112	100-61	.987	53	109	102	O1272(57/1181/46),D18/21S	171	15.1
MURPHY, ED	Edward Joseph; B8.23.1918 Joliet IL; D12.10.1991 Joliet IL; BR/TR/5´11˝/190; d9.10; Mil 1943–45																								
1942	Phi N	13	28	2	7	2	0	0	4	2	0	4	.250	.300	.321	86	0	0	1.000	-0	72	126	1b8	0	-0.2
MURPHY, TONY	Francis J.; B7.1859 New York NY; D12.15.1915 New York NY; 5´6˝/145; d10.15																								
1884	NY AA	1	3	1	1	0	0	0	—	0	0	—	.333	.333	.333	121	0	—	1.000	-0	—	—	/C	—	0.0
MURPHY, FRANK	Francis Patrick; B4.6.1876 N.Tarrytown NY; D11.4.1912 Central Islip NY; BR/TR; d7.2; Col Fordham																								
1901	Bos N	45	176	13	46	5	3	1	18	4	1	—	.261	.282	.341	73	-7	6	.939	3	164	71	O45L	—	-0.6
	NY N	35	130	10	21	3	0	0	8	6	0	—	.162	.199	.185	12	-15	2	.847	-9	90	34	2b23,O12L	—	-2.4
	Year	80	306	23	67	8	3	1	26	10	1	—	.219	.246	.275	49	-21	8	.940	-6	149	59	O57L,2b23	—	-3.0
MURPHY, DUMMY	Herbert Courtland; B12.18.1886 Olney IL; D8.10.1962 Tallahassee FL; BR/TR/5´10˝/165; d4.14																								
1914	Phi N	9	26	1	4	1	0	0	3	0	1	4	.154	.185	.192	12	-3	0	.864	0	102	58	S9	—	-0.2
MURPHY, HOWARD	Howard; B1.1.1882 Birmingham AL; D10.5.1926 Fort Worth TX; BL/TR/5´8.5˝/150; d8.4																								
1909	StL N	25	60	3	12	0	0	0	3	4	0	—	.200	.250	.200	42	-4	1	.925	-1	86	0	O19C	—	-0.7
MURPHY, EDDIE	John Edward; B10.2.1891 Hancock NY; D2.21.1969 Dunmore PA; BL/TR/5´9˝/155; d8.26; Col Villanova																								
1912	Phi A	33	142	24	45	4	1	0	6	11	1	—	.317	.370	.359	113	3	7	.947	-0	90	118	O33R	—	0.0
1913	†Phi A	137	508	105	150	14	7	1	30	70	10	44	.295	.391	.356	122	18	21	.942	-11	85	72	O135R	—	0.0
1914	†Phi A	148	573	101	156	12	9	3	43	87	**12**	46	.272	.379	.340	121	19	36-32	.941	-7	92	80	O148R	—	0.1
1915	Phi A	68	260	37	60	3	4	0	17	29	3	15	.231	.315	.273	79	-7	13-3	.899	-2	78	125	O58R,3b6	—	-1.0
	Chi A	70	273	51	86	11	5	0	26	39	5	12	.315	.410	.392	136	14	20-12	.952	-2	104	81	O70(3/0/67)	—	1.0
	Year	138	533	88	146	14	9	0	43	68	8	27	.274	.365	.334	109	8	33-15	.933	-4	94	99	O128(3/0/125),3b6	—	0.0
1916	Chi A	51	105	14	22	5	1	0	4	9	2	5	.210	.284	.276	68	-4	3	1.000	-1	98	91	O24R/3	—	-0.7
1917	Chi A	53	51	9	16	2	1	0	16	5	1	1	.314	.386	.392	135	2	4	1.000	-1	48	0	O9(1/0/8)	—	0.2
1918	Chi A	91	286	36	85	9	3	0	23	22	1	18	.297	.350	.350	110	3	6	.958	-7	101	36	O63(1/0/62),2b8	—	-0.7

YEAR	TM LG	G	AB	R	H	2B	3B	HR	RBI	BB-IB	HP	SO	AVG	OBP	SLG	AOPS	ABR	SB-CS	FA	FR	RNG	THR	GAMES AT POSITION	DL	BFW
1919	†Chi A	30	35	8	17	4	0	0	5	7	0	0	.486	.571	.600	228	7	0	.917	0	111	163	O6(2/0/4)	—	0.7
1920	Chi A	58	118	22	40	2	1	0	19	12	1	4	.339	.405	.373	107	2	1-3	.886	2	75	340	O19R,3b3	—	0.2
1921	Chi A	6	5	1	1	0	0	0	0	0	0	0	.200	.200	.200	2	-1	0-0	ø	0	—	—	/H	—	-0.1
1926	Pit N	16	17	3	2	0	0	0	6	3	0	0	.118	.250	.118	2	-2	0	1.000	0	114	0	O3L	—	-0.3
Total	11	761	2373	411	680	66	32	4	195	294	36	145	.287	.374	.346	114	54	111-50	.942	-28	91	88	O568(10/0/558),3b10,2b8	—	-0.6
MURPHY, JOHN	John Patrick; B1879 New Haven CT; D4.20.1949 Andover MA; 5´7.5˝/160; d9.10																								
1902	StL N	1	3	1	2	1	0	0	1	1	0	—	.667	.750	1.000	458	1	0	1.000	-1	0	0	/3	—	0.1
1903	Det A	5	22	1	4	1	0	0	1	0	0	—	.182	.182	.227	23	-2	0	.852	-1	103	58	S5	—	-0.3
Total	2	6	25	2	6	2	0	0	2	1	0	—	.240	.269	.320	79	-1	0	.852	-1	103	58	S5/3	—	-0.2
MURPHY, LEO	Leo Joseph "Red"; B1.7.1889 Terre Haute IN; D8.12.1960 Racine WI; BR/TR/6´1˝/179; d5.2																								
1915	Pit N	31	41	4	4	0	0	0	4	4	0	12	.098	.178	.098	-16	-6	0	.932	-2	*77*	*118*	C20	—	-0.8
MURPHY, MIKE	Michael Jerome; B8.19.1888 Forestville PA; D10.26.1952 Johnson City NY; BR/TR/5´9˝/170; d5.17; Col Villanova																								
1912	StL N	1	1	0	0	0	0	0	1	0	0	0	.000	.000	.000	-99	0	0	ø	0	*0*	*0*	/C	—	0.0
1916	Phi A	14	27	0	3	0	0	0	1	1	0	3	.111	.143	.111	-25	-4	0	.973	-3	51	75	C12	—	-0.7
Total	2	15	28	0	3	0	0	0	2	1	0	3	.107	.138	.107	-28	-4	0	.973	-3	*50*	*74*	C13	—	-0.7
MURPHY, MORGAN	Morgan Edward; B2.14.1867 E.Providence RI; D10.3.1938 Providence RI; BR/TR/5´8˝/160; d4.22																								
1890	Bos P	68	246	38	56	10	2	2	32	24	2	31	.228	.301	.309	59	-15	16	.903	14	*154*	*83*	C67,S2/cf3	—	0.3
1891	Bos AA	106	402	60	87	11	4	4	54	36	5	58	.216	.289	.294	68	-18	17	**.954**	**27**	***140***	*99*	C104,O4(1/2/1)	—	1.5
1892	Cin N	74	234	29	46	8	2	2	24	25	1	57	.197	.277	.274	67	-9	4	.955	2	*118*	*69*	C74	—	0.0
1893	Cin N	57	200	25	47	5	1	1	19	14	3	35	.235	.295	.285	53	-14	1	.932	-3	*110*	*77*	C56/1	—	-1.0
1894	Cin N	76	261	42	70	9	0	1	37	26	1	36	.268	.337	.314	56	-19	6	.901	-6	*99*	*101*	C75/S3	—	-1.5
1895	Cin N	25	82	15	22	2	0	0	16	11	0	8	.268	.355	.293	66	-4	6	.907	-1	*104*	*85*	C25	—	-0.3
1896	StL N	49	175	12	45	5	2	0	11	8	0	14	.257	.290	.309	60	-11	1	.926	-6	*85*	*99*	C48	—	-1.1
1897	StL N	63	211	13	36	2	0	0	12	6	1	—	.171	.197	.180	-0	-31	1	.946	-12	*68*	*125*	C54,1b8	—	-3.4
1898	Pit N	5	16	0	2	0	0	0	2	1	0	—	.125	.176	.125	-14	-2	0	.957	1	*110*	*136*	C5	—	-0.1
	Phi N	25	86	6	17	3	0	0	11	6	1	—	.198	.258	.233	43	-6	0	.964	1	*111*	*118*	C25	—	-0.3
	Year	30	102	6	19	3	0	0	13	7	1	—	.186	.245	.216	34	-9	0	.963	2	*111*	*121*	C30	—	-0.4
1900	Phi N	11	36	2	10	0	1	0	3	0	0	—	.278	.278	.333	69	-2	0	.980	-0	*78*	*116*	C11	—	-0.1
1901	Phi A	9	28	5	6	1	0	0	6	0	0	—	.214	.214	.250	27	-3	1	.929	-0	*107*	*79*	C8/1	—	-0.2
Total	11	568	1977	247	444	56	12	10	227	157	14	239	.225	.286	.280	53	-134	53	.936	16	*114*	*94*	C552,1b10,O5(1/3/1),S3,3b2	—	-6.2
MURPHY, PAT	Patrick J.; B1.2.1857 Auburn MA; D5.16.1927 Worcester MA; TR/5´10˝/160; d9.2																								
1887	NY N	17	56	4	12	2	0	0	4	2	0	4	.214	.241	.250	38	-5	1	.847	-1	—	—	C17	—	-0.3
1888	†NY N	28	106	11	18	1	0	0	4	6	0	11	.170	.214	.179	27	-9	3	.913	2	—	—	C28	—	-0.4
1889	NY N	9	28	5	10	1	1	0	4	2	0	0	.357	.400	.571	168	2	0	.872	-1	—	—	C9	—	0.1
1890	NY N	32	119	14	28	5	1	0	9	14	1	13	.235	.321	.294	79	-3	3	.905	-4	*99*	*100*	C29,O3(1/1/1)/S	—	-0.4
Total	4	86	309	34	68	9	2	1	21	24	1	28	.220	.278	.272	64	-15	7	.895	-4	*99*	*100*	C83,O3(1/1/1)/S	—	-1.0
MURPHY, LARRY	Patrick Lawrence; B3.17.1857 Toronto ON, Can.; D10.6.1911 Indianapolis IN; BL/5´8˝/170; d5.30																								
1891	Was AA	101	400	73	106	15	3	1	35	63	5	27	.265	.372	.325	104	7	29	.874	-6	56	67	O101(69/3/30)	—	-0.1
MURPHY, DICK	Richard Lee; B10.25.1931 Cincinnati OH; BL/TL/5´11˝/170; d6.13; Mil 1955–57; Col Ohio U.																								
1954	Cin N	6	1	1	0	0	0	0	0	0	0	1	.000	.000	.000	-97	0	0-0	ø	0	—	—	/H	0	0.0
MURPHY, BUZZ	Robert Sylvester; B4.26.1895 Denver CO; D5.11.1938 Denver CO; BL/TL/5´8.5˝/155; d7.14																								
1918	Bos N	9	32	6	12	2	3	1	9	3	0	5	.375	.429	.719	259	6	0	1.000	-1	89	0	O9L	—	0.5
1919	Was A	79	252	19	66	7	4	0	28	19	5	32	.262	.326	.321	83	-6	5	.959	3	112	91	O73(19/54/0)	—	-0.8
Total	2	88	284	25	78	9	7	1	37	22	5	37	.275	.338	.366	101	0	5	.961	2	110	82	O82(28/54/0)	—	-0.3
MURPHY, TOMMY	Thomas Christian; B8.27.1979 Suffern NY; BB/TR/6´0˝/185; [AnaA00 3/80]; d5.4; Col Florida Atlantic																								
2006	LA A	48	70	12	16	4	1	1	6	5-0	0	21	.229	.276	.357	66	-4	4-1	1.000	4	127	182	O42(2/29/12),D2	0	0.1
MURPHY, BILLY	William Eugene; B5.7.1944 Pineville LA; BR/TR/6´1˝/191; d4.15																								
1966	NY N	84	135	15	31	4	1	3	13	7-0	1	34	.230	.271	.341	71	-6	1-2	.955	-1	76	255	O57(8/48/1)	0	-0.9
MURPHY, WILLIE	William H. "Gentle Willie"; B3.23.1864 Springfield MA; BL/5´11˝/198; d5.1																								
1884	Cle N	42	168	18	38	3	3	1	9	1	—	23	.226	.231	.298	63	-8	—	.720	-7	72	0	O42(34/3/5)	—	-1.5
	Was AA	5	21	3	10	0	0	0	—	1	2	—	.476	.542	.476	266	4	—	.700	0	0	0	O4L/3	—	0.4
Total	1	47	189	21	48	3	3	1	9	2	2	23	.254	.269	.317	83	-4	—	.718	-7	66	0	O46(38/3/5)/3	—	-1.1
MURPHY, YALE	William Henry "Tot","Midget"; B10.11.1869 Southborough MA; D2.14.1906 Westborough MA; BL/TR/5´3˝/125; d4.19; Col Yale																								
1894	†NY N	75	283	65	77	6	2	0	28	52	0	23	.272	.385	.307	69	-12	28	.898	-10	87	63	S49,O21(1/0/20),3b3/21	—	-1.5
1895	NY N	51	184	35	37	6	2	0	16	27	0	13	.201	.303	.255	46	-14	7	.944	-4	78	175	O33(29/2/2),S8,3b8/2	—	-1.7
1897	NY N	5	8	1	0	0	0	0	1	2	0	—	.000	.200	.000	-46	-2	0	.800	-2	46	0	S3,2b2	—	-0.3
Total	3	131	475	101	114	12	4	0	45	81	0	36	.240	.351	.282	59	-28	35	.890	-15	87	64	S60,O54(30/2/22),3b11,2b4/1	—	-3.5
MURRAY, TONY	Anthony Joseph; B4.30.1904 Chicago IL; D3.19.1974 Chicago IL; BR/TR/5´10.5˝/154; d10.6; Col DePaul																								
1923	Chi N	2	4	0	1	0	0	0	0	0	1	0	.250	.400	.250	75	0	0-0	1.000	-0	82	0	O2(1/2/1)	—	0.0
MURRAY, CALVIN	Calvin Duane; B7.30.1971 Dallas TX; BR/TR/5´11˝/(184–190); [SFN92 1/7]; d6.22; Col Texas																								
1999	SF N	15	19	1	5	2	0	0	5	2-0	0	4	.263	.333	.368	83	0	1-0	1.000	-1	66	0	O9(3/6/0)	0	-0.1
2000	†SF N	108	194	35	47	12	1	2	22	29-0	3	33	.242	.348	.345	82	-5	9-3	.980	0	108	61	O106(2/104/0)	0	-0.3
2001	SF N	106	326	54	80	14	2	6	25	32-0	3	57	.245	.319	.356	79	-11	8-8	.979	3	116	87	O104C	0	-0.7
2002	Tex A	37	77	16	13	5	1	0	1	6-0	1	15	.169	.238	.260	31	-8	4-0	1.000	2	105	150	O34(0/33/1),D2	0	-0.5
	SF N	11	12	0	0	0	0	0	0	1-0	0	2	.000	.077	.000	-80	-3	0-0	.917	1	122	458	O10(5/4/3)	0	-0.3
2004	Chi N	11	5	2	1	0	0	0	1	1-0	0	0	.200	.333	.200	41	0	0-0	1.000	1	246	0	O8(1/5/2)	0	0.0
Total	5	288	633	108	146	33	4	8	54	71-0	7	111	.231	.315	.333	71	-27	22-11	.981	6	112	94	O271(11/256/6),D2	0	-1.9
MURRAY, EDDIE	Eddie Clarence; B2.24.1956 Los Angeles CA; BB/TR/6´2˝/(180–225); [BalA73 3/63]; d4.7; C9; HF2003; b–Rich																								
1977	Bal A	160	611	81	173	29	2	27	88	48-6	1	104	.283	.333	.470	124	19	0-1	.992	-3	70	108	D111,1b42,O3L	0	0.9
1978	Bal A☆	**161**	610	85	174	32	3	27	95	70-7	1	97	.285	.356	.480	142	34	6-5	.997	3	101	115	1b157,3b3/D	0	2.7
1979	†Bal A	**159**	606	90	179	30	2	25	99	72-9	2	78	.295	.369	.475	131	28	10-2	.994	-1	96	109	1b157,D2	0	1.8
1980	Bal A	158	621	100	186	36	2	32	116	54-10	2	71	.300	.354	.519	139	32	7-2	.994	-9	76	115	1b154/D	0	1.4
1981	Bal A★	99	378	57	111	21	2	**22**	**78**	40-10	1	43	.294	.360	.534	156	27	2-3	**.999**	11	**136**	110	1b99	0	3.2
1982	Bal A★	151	550	87	174	30	1	32	110	70-**18**	1	82	.316	.391	.549	157	44	7-2	**.997**	3	106	90	1b149,D2	0	3.9
1983	†Bal A★	156	582	115	178	30	3	33	111	86-13	3	90	.306	.393	.538	**157**	**48**	5-1	.993	4	109	104	1b153,D2	0	4.2
1984	Bal A★	**162**	588	97	180	26	3	29	110	**107-25**	2	87	.306	**.410**	.509	157	**50**	10-2	.992	10	124	114	1b159,D3	0	5.1
1985	Bal A★	156	583	111	173	37	1	31	124	84-12	2	68	.297	.383	.523	150	43	5-2	.987	12	128	110	1b154,D2	0	4.4
1986	Bal A☆	137	495	61	151	25	1	17	84	78-7	0	49	.305	.396	.463	135	28	3-0	.989	-2	96	101	1b119,D16	28	1.8
1987	Bal A	160	618	89	171	28	3	30	91	73-6	0	80	.277	.352	.477	120	18	1-2	.993	12	127	112	1b156,D4	0	1.8
1988	Bal A	**161**	603	75	171	27	2	28	84	75-8	0	78	.284	.361	.474	136	29	5-2	.989	10	137	111	1b103,D58	0	3.0
1989	LA N	**160**	594	66	147	29	1	20	88	87-24	2	85	.247	.342	.401	114	13	7-2	**.996**	10	118	116	1b159,3b2	0	1.3
1990	LA N	155	558	96	184	22	3	26	95	82-**21**	1	64	.330	.414	.520	160	48	8-5	.992	1	99	91	1b150	0	3.9
1991	LA N★	153	576	69	150	23	1	19	96	55-17	0	74	.260	.321	.403	105	3	10-3	.995	6	110	100	1b149/3	0	0.0
1992	NY N	156	551	64	144	37	2	16	93	66-8	0	74	.261	.336	.423	116	13	4-2	.991	-5	87	101	1b154	0	-0.3
1993	NY N	154	610	77	174	28	1	27	100	40-4	0	61	.285	.325	.467	112	8	2-2	.988	2	108	101	1b154	0	-0.4
1994	Cle A	108	433	57	110	21	1	17	76	31-6	0	53	.254	.302	.425	84	-12	8-4	.988	-2	76	111	D82,1b26	0	-1.9
1995	†Cle A	113	436	68	141	21	0	21	82	39-5	0	65	.323	.375	.516	128	17	5-1	.984	3	162	85	D95,1b18	29	1.3
1996	Cle A	88	336	33	88	9	1	12	45	34-2	0	45	.262	.326	.402	84	-9	3-0	1.000	0	137	0	D87/1	0	-1.2
	†Bal A	64	230	36	59	12	0	10	34	27-4	0	42	.257	.327	.439	94	-2	1-0	ø	0	0	0	D62	0	-0.5
	Year	152	566	69	147	21	1	22	79	61-6	0	87	.260	.327	.417	88	-12	4-0	1.000	0	137	0	D149/1	0	-1.7
1997	Ana A	46	160	13	35	7	0	3	15	13-0	0	24	.219	.273	.319	55	-11	1-0	ø	0	0	0	D45	53	-1.3

YEAR	TM LG	G	AB	R	H	2B	3B	HR	RBI	BB-IB	HP	SO	AVG	OBP	SLG	AOPS	ABR	SB-CS	FA	FR	RNG	THR	GAMES AT POSITION	DL	BFW
	LA N	9	7	0	2	0	0	0	3	2-0	0	2	.286	.444	.286	103	0	0-0	ø	0	—	—	/H	0	0.0
Total	21	3026	11336	1627	3255	560	35	504	1917	1333-222	18	1516	.287	.359	.476	129	468	110-43	.993	66	108	106	1b2413,D573,3b6,O3L	110	35.1
MURRAY, ED	Edward Francis; B5.8.1895 Mystic CT; D11.8.1970 Cheyenne WY; BR/TR/5´6˝/145; d6.24; Col Trinity (CT)																								
1917	StL A	1	1	0	0	0	0	0	0	0	0	1	.000	.000	.000	-99	0	0	ø	-0	0	0	/S	—	0.0
MURRAY, GLENN	Glenn Everett; B11.23.1970 Manning SC; BR/TR/6´2˝/225; [MonN89 2/40]; d5.10																								
1996	Phi N	38	97	8	19	3	0	2	6	7-0	0	36	.196	.250	.289	41	-9	1-1	1.000	1	117	66	O27(1/2/24)	76	-0.8
MURRAY, JIM	James Oscar; B1.16.1878 Galveston TX; D4.25.1945 Galveston TX; BR/TL/5´10˝/180; d9.2																								
1902	Chi N	12	47	3	8	0	0	0	1	2	0	—	.170	.204	.170	16	-5	0	1.000	-1	64	0	O12R	—	-0.6
1911	StL A	31	102	8	19	5	0	3	11	5	0	—	.186	.224	.324	54	-7	0	.935	0	106	93	O25(0/1/24)	—	-0.8
1914	Bos N	39	112	10	26	4	2	0	12	6	1	24	.232	.277	.304	73	-4	2	.941	-4	75	32	O32(18/1/13)	—	-1.0
Total	3	82	261	21	53	9	2	3	24	13	1	24	.203	.244	.287	56	-16	2	.949	-5	86	51	O69(18/2/49)	—	-2.4
MURRAY, MIAH	Jeremiah J.; B1.1.1865 Boston MA; D1.11.1922 Boston MA; BR/TR/5´11.5˝/170; d5.17; U1																								
1884	Pro N	8	27	1	5	0	0	0	1	1	—	8	.185	.214	.185	27	-2	—	.836	-4	—	—	C7/cf1	—	-0.5
1885	Lou AA	12	43	4	8	0	0	0	3	2	1	—	.186	.239	.186	36	-3	—	.863	-1	—	—	C12,1b2	—	-0.2
1888	Was N	12	42	1	4	1	0	0	3	1	0	7	.095	.116	.119	-27	-6	0	.912	0	—	—	C10,1b2	—	-0.5
1891	Was AA	2	8	0	0	0	0	0	0	0	0	1	.000	.000	.000	-99	-2	0	1.000	1	*87*	*63*	C2	—	-0.1
Total	4	34	120	6	17	1	0	0	7	4	1	16	.142	.176	.150	3	-13	0	.884	-3	*87*	*63*	C31,1b5/cf	—	-1.3
MURRAY, RED	John Joseph; B3.4.1884 Arnot PA; D12.4.1958 Sayre PA; BR/TR/5´10.5˝/190; d6.16; Col Notre Dame																								
1906	StL N	46	144	18	37	9	7	1	16	9	1	—	.257	.305	.438	137	5	5	.962	-1	194	0	O34(4/11/20),C7	—	0.4
1907	StL N	132	485	46	127	10	10	7	46	24	3	—	.262	.301	.367	113	4	23	.935	3	132	82	O131(124/1/6)	—	-0.2
1908	StL N	**154**	593	64	167	19	15	7	62	37	8	—	.282	.332	.400	140	24	48	.914	-3	118	84	O154(0/89/67)	—	1.7
1909	NY N	149	570	74	150	15	12	**7**	91	45	2	—	.263	.319	.368	112	5	48	.947	2	142	22	O149(29/0/120)	—	0.1
1910	NY N	149	553	78	153	27	8	4	87	52	6	51	.277	.345	.376	110	7	57	.948	6	103	135	O148(24/0/124)	—	0.7
1911	†NY N	140	488	70	142	27	15	3	78	43	5	37	.291	.354	.426	114	8	48	.954	-6	95	75	O131(50/2/83)	—	-0.4
1912	†NY N	143	549	83	152	26	20	3	92	27	8	45	.277	.320	.413	97	-6	38	**.968**	5	109	101	O143(27/0/117)	—	-0.8
1913	†NY N	147	520	70	139	21	3	2	59	34	6	28	.267	.320	.331	85	-10	35-25	.965	9	110	127	O147(32/1/116)	—	-1.0
1914	NY N	86	139	19	31	6	3	0	23	9	0	7	.223	.270	.309	75	-5	11	1.000	0	114	48	O49(16/0/34)	—	-0.7
1915	NY N	45	127	12	28	1	2	3	11	7	0	15	.220	.261	.331	83	-4	2-3	.959	-0	96	111	O34(1/30/3)	—	-0.7
	Chi N	51	144	20	43	6	1	0	11	8	1	8	.299	.340	.354	110	2	6-5	.966	2	116	91	O40(7/11/25)/2	—	0.2
	Year	96	271	32	71	7	3	3	22	15	1	23	.262	.303	.343	98	-2	8-8	.963	2	107	100	O74(8/41/28)/2	—	-0.5
1917	NY N	22	22	1	1	1	0	0	3	4	0	3	.045	.192	.091	-12	-3	0	1.000	-0	117	0	O11(4/4/3)/C	—	-0.3
Total	11	1264	4334	555	1170	168	96	37	579	299	40	194	.270	.323	.379	108	27	321-33	.950	18	118	86	O1171(318/149/718),C8/2	—	-1.0
MURRAY, LARRY	Larry; B4.1.1953 Chicago IL; BB/TR/5´11˝/(179–180); [NYA71 5/115]; d9.7																								
1974	NY A	6	1	1	0	0	0	0	0	0-0	0	0	.000	.000	.000	-99	0	0-1	ø	-0	0	0	O3(1/1/2)	0	-0.1
1975	NY A	6	1	1	0	0	0	0	0	0-0	0	0	.000	.000	.000	-99	0	0-0	1.000	-0	66	0	O4(2/1/1)	0	0.0
1976	NY A	8	10	2	1	0	0	0	2	1-0	0	2	.100	.182	.100	-16	-1	2-0	1.000	0	84	340	O7(0/6/1)	0	-0.1
1977	Oak A	90	162	19	29	5	2	1	9	17-2	0	36	.179	.257	.253	40	-14	12-3	.992	0	101	83	O78(27/36/22)/SD	0	-1.3
1978	Oak A	11	12	1	1	0	0	0	0	3-0	0	2	.083	.267	.083	3	-1	0-0	1.000	-0	90	0	O6(5/0/1)	0	-0.2
1979	Oak A	105	226	25	42	11	2	2	20	28-1	0	34	.186	.275	.279	53	-15	6-6	.963	7	122	142	O90(24/12/57),2b3	0	-1.2
Total	6	226	412	49	73	16	4	3	31	49-3	0	74	.177	.264	.257	44	-31	20-10	.975	7	111	119	O188(59/56/84),2b3,D3/S	0	-2.9
MURRAY, RAY	Raymond Lee "Deacon"; B10.12.1917 Spring Hope NC; D4.9.2003 Fort Worth TX; BR/TR/6´3˝/204; d4.25																								
1948	Cle A	4	4	0	0	0	0	0	0	0	0	3	.000	.000	.000	-99	-1	0-0	ø	0	—	—	/H	0	-0.1
1950	Cle A	55	139	16	38	8	2	1	13	12	0	13	.273	.331	.381	85	-4	1-0	.972	-1	*122*	*116*	C45	0	-0.3
1951	Cle A	1	1	0	1	0	0	0	1	0	0	0	1.000	1.000	1.000	468	1	0-0	1.000	1	*0*	*0*	/C	0	0.1
	Phi A	40	122	10	26	6	0	0	13	14	0	8	.213	.294	.262	50	-8	0-0	.985	1	*136*	*147*	C39	0	-0.6
	Year	41	123	10	27	6	0	0	14	14	0	8	.220	.299	.268	53	-8	0-0	.986	1	*134*	*145*	C40	0	-0.5
1952	Phi A	44	136	14	28	5	0	1	10	9	0	13	.206	.255	.265	42	-11	0-0	.995	4	*129*	*191*	C42	0	-0.4
1953	Phi A	84	268	25	76	14	3	6	41	18	1	25	.284	.331	.425	99	-1	0-0	.989	4	*148*	*127*	C78	0	0.7
1954	Bal A	22	61	4	15	4	1	0	2	2	0	5	.246	.270	.344	73	-3	0-0	.989	0	*81*	*132*	C21	0	-0.2
Total	6	250	731	69	184	37	6	8	80	55	1	67	.252	.305	.352	75	-27	1-0	.987	8	*132*	*141*	C226	0	-0.8
MURRAY, RICH	Richard Dale; B7.6.1957 Los Angeles CA; BR/TR/6´4˝/195; [SFN75 6/128]; d6.7; b–Eddie																								
1980	SF N	53	194	19	42	8	2	4	24	11-1	0	48	.216	.259	.340	68	-9	2-1	.987	1	113	78	1b53	60	-1.2
1983	SF N	4	10	0	2	0	0	0	1	0-0	0	3	.200	.200	.200	11	-1	0-0	1.000	-0	63	57	1b3	0	-0.2
Total	2	57	204	19	44	8	2	4	25	11-1	0	51	.216	.256	.333	65	-10	2-1	.988	1	111	77	1b56	60	-1.4
MURRAY, BOBBY	Robert Hayes; B7.4.1894 St.Albans VT; D1.4.1979 Nashua NH; BL/TR/5´7˝/155; d9.24; Col Norwich																								
1923	Was A	10	37	2	7	1	0	0	2	1	0	4	.189	.211	.216	13	-5	1-0	1.000	2	121	0	3b10	—	-0.2
MURRAY, TOM	Thomas W.; B1866 Paterson NJ; BR/5´7˝/150; d6.20																								
1894	Phi N	1	2	0	0	0	0	0	0	0	0	2	.000	.000	.000	-99	-1	0	.833	-1	36	0	/S	—	-0.1
MURRAY, BILL	William Allenwood "Dasher"; B9.6.1893 Vinalhaven ME; D9.14.1943 Boston MA; BB/TR/5´11˝/165; d6.27; Col Brown																								
1917	Was A	8	21	2	3	0	1	0	4	2	0	2	.143	.217	.238	39	-2	1	.889	-2	79	85	2b6/S	—	-0.4
MURRELL, IVAN	Ivan Augustus (Peters); B4.24.1943 Bocas Del Toro, Pan; D10.8.2006 Stuart FL; BR/TR/6´2˝/(195–198); d9.28																								
1963	Hou N	2	5	1	1	0	0	0	0	0-0	0	2	.200	.200	.200	17	-1	0-0	1.000	0	106	0	O2C	0	-0.1
1964	Hou N	10	14	1	2	1	0	0	1	0-0	0	6	.143	.133	.214	-1	-2	0-0	1.000	-1	32	0	O5(4/0/1)	0	-0.3
1967	Hou N	10	29	2	9	0	0	0	1	1-1	0	9	.310	.333	.310	88	-1	1-0	.846	-1	102	0	O6(5/0/1)	0	-0.1
1968	Hou N	32	59	3	6	1	1	0	3	1-0	0	17	.102	.117	.153	-20	-9	0-0	.931	3	118	358	O15(4/2/9)	0	-0.8
1969	SD N	111	247	19	63	10	6	3	25	11-1	2	65	.255	.291	.381	90	-5	3-4	.959	3	114	82	O72(23/41/14),1b2	0	-0.5
1970	SD N	125	347	43	85	9	3	12	35	17-5	4	93	.245	.287	.392	83	-11	9-7	.970	5	109	133	O101(61/24/20)/1	0	-1.1
1971	SD N	103	255	23	60	6	3	7	24	7-1	3	60	.235	.263	.365	82	-8	5-2	.978	2	100	47	O72(55/16/2)	0	-1.0
1972	SD N	5	7	0	1	0	0	0	1	0-0	0	3	.143	.143	.143	-20	-1	0-0	1.000	0	106	0	/rf	34	-0.1
1973	SD N	93	210	23	48	13	1	9	21	2-0	0	52	.229	.236	.429	87	-6	2-0	.959	2	101	95	O37(10/18/12),1b24	0	-0.6
1974	Atl N	73	133	11	33	1	1	2	12	5-1	0	35	.248	.273	.316	63	-7	0-0	.983	3	130	149	O32(13/9/13),1b13	0	-0.6
Total	10	564	1306	126	308	41	15	33	123	44-9	9	342	.236	.265	.366	77	-51	20-13	.965	16	108	104	O343(175/112/73),1b40	34	-5.2
MURTAUGH, DANNY	Daniel Edward; B10.8.1917 Chester PA; D12.2.1976 Chester PA; BR/TR/5´9˝/165; d7.6; Mil 1943–45; M15/C2																								
1941	Phi N	85	347	34	76	8	1	0	11	26	1	31	.219	.275	.248	50	-24	**18**	.978	3	98	86	2b85/S	0	-1.6
1942	Phi N	144	506	48	122	16	4	0	27	49	2	39	.241	.311	.289	80	-13	13	.939	8	101	87	S60,3b53,2b32	0	0.3
1943	Phi N	113	451	65	123	17	4	1	35	57	2	23	.273	.357	.335	104	4	4	.974	3	99	104	2b113	0	1.5
1946	Phi N	6	19	1	4	1	0	1	3	2	0	2	.211	.286	.421	102	0	0	.958	-2	72	0	2b6	0	-0.2
1947	Bos N	3	8	0	1	0	0	0	0	1	0	2	.125	.222	.125	-6	-1	0	1.000	-0	91	71	2b2,3b2	0	-0.1
1948	Pit N	146	514	56	149	21	5	1	71	60	1	40	.290	.365	.356	94	-2	10	.979	3	101	111	2b146	0	0.9
1949	Pit N	75	236	16	48	7	2	2	24	29	0	17	.203	.291	.275	51	-16	2	.975	2	95	120	2b74	0	-1.0
1950	Pit N	118	367	34	108	20	5	2	37	47	1	42	.294	.376	.392	99	1	2	.976	3	104	103	2b108	0	0.9
1951	Pit N	77	151	9	30	7	0	1	11	16	2	19	.199	.284	.265	47	-11	0-0	.970	-0	98	105	2b65,3b3	0	-0.9
Total	9	767	2599	263	661	97	21	8	219	287	9	215	.254	.331	.317	81	-62	49-0	.975	19	100	102	2b631,S61,3b58	0	-0.2
MURTON, MATT	Matthew Henry; B10.3.1981 Fort Lauderdale FL; BR/TR/6´1˝/(215–220); [BosA03 1/32]; d7.8; Col Georgia Tech																								
2005	Chi N	51	140	19	45	3	2	7	14	16-4	0	22	.321	.386	.521	132	6	2-1	.969	-2	92	49	O43L	0	0.4
2006	Chi N	144	455	70	135	22	3	13	62	45-1	5	62	.297	.365	.444	104	3	5-2	.988	4	112	50	O133L	0	0.3
Total	2	195	595	89	180	25	5	20	76	61-5	5	84	.303	.370	.462	111	9	7-3	.984	2	107	50	O176L	0	0.7
MUSER, TONY	Anthony Joseph; B8.1.1947 Van Nuys CA; BL/TL/6´2˝/(175–200); d9.14; M6/C14; Col San Diego Mesa (CA) JC																								
1969	Bos A	2	9	0	1	0	0	0	1	1-0	0	1	.111	.200	.111	-11	-1	0-0	1.000	1	226	174	1b2	0	-0.1
1971	Chi A	11	16	2	5	0	1	0	1	1-0	0	1	.313	.353	.438	120	0	0-0	.963	0	182	44	1b4	0	0.0
1972	Chi A	44	61	6	17	2	2	1	9	2-0	0	6	.279	.302	.426	112	0	1-1	.986	-1	83	97	1b29/rf	0	-0.2

YEAR	TM LG	G	AB	R	H	2B	3B	HR	RBI	BB-IB	HP	SO	AVG	OBP	SLG	AOPS	ABR	SB-CS	FA	FR	RNG	THR	GAMES AT POSITION	DL	BFW
1973	Chi A	109	309	38	88	14	3	4	30	33-0	0	36	.285	.352	.388	105	3	8-4	.992	-3	86	106	1b89,D13,O2L	0	-0.6
1974	Chi A	103	206	16	60	5	1	1	18	6-0	1	22	.291	.313	.340	86	-4	1-4	.998	-4	51	108	1b80,D13	0	-1.5
1975	Chi A	43	111	11	27	3	0	0	6	7-1	0	8	.243	.286	.270	58	-6	2-1	.993	2	121	125	1b41	0	-0.7
	Bal A	80	82	11	26	3	0	0	11	8-0	0	9	.317	.374	.354	114	2	0-0	.996	-0	93	129	1b62	0	-0.1
	Year	123	193	22	53	6	0	0	17	15-1	0	17	.275	.324	.306	82	-4	2-1	.994	1	109	127	1b103	0	-0.8
1976	Bal A	136	326	25	74	7	1	1	30	21-4	0	34	.227	.270	.264	61	-17	1-1	.991	3	**121**	106	1b109,O12(8/4/0),D10	0	-2.2
1977	Bal A	120	118	14	27	6	0	0	7	13-5	0	16	.229	.301	.280	64	-5	1-2	.992	1	136	199	1b77,O11(5/6/0)/D	0	-0.6
1978	Mil A	15	30	0	4	1	1	0	5	3-0	0	5	.133	.212	.233	25	-3	0-0	.988	-0	95	61	1b12	0	-0.4
Total	9	663	1268	123	329	41	9	7	117	95-10	1	138	.259	.309	.323	82	-31	14-13	.992	-2	99	115	1b505,D37,O26(15/10/1)	0	-6.4
Musial, Stan	Stanley Frank "Stan the Man"; B11.21.1920 Donora PA; BL/TL/6´0˝/(175–180); d9.17; Mil 1945; HF1969																								
1941	StL N	12	47	8	20	4	0	1	7	2	0	1	.426	.449	.574	175	5	1	1.000	-0	93	113	O11(3/0/8)	0	0.4
1942	†StL N	140	467	87	147	32	10	10	72	62	2	25	.315	.397	.490	148	30	6	.984	7	**117**	74	O135(133/2/2)	0	3.2
1943	†StL N★	**157**	617	108	**220**	**48**	**20**	13	81	72	2	18	**.357**	**.425**	**.562**	**176**	**61**	9	.982	5	108	88	O155(34/10/117)	0	**5.7**
1944	†StL N★	146	568	112	**197**	**51**	14	12	94	90	5	28	.347	**.440**	**.549**	**174**	**61**	7	.987	3	105	99	O146(1/38/124)	0	**5.5**
1946	†StL N★	**156**	624	**124**	**228**	**50**	**20**	16	103	73	3	31	**.365**	.434	**.587**	**180**	**66**	7	.989	-3	83	135	1b114,O42L	0	**5.8**
1947	StL N★	149	587	113	183	30	13	19	95	80	4	24	.312	.398	.504	132	28	4	.994	-6	81	118	1b149	0	1.6
1948	StL N★	**155**	611	**135**	**230**	**46**	**18**	39	**131**	79	3	34	**.376**	**.450**	**.702**	**196**	**82**	7	.981	-2	98	85	O155(41/64/76),1b2	0	**7.2**
1949	StL N★	**157**	612	128	**207**	**41**	**13**	36	123	107	2	38	.338	**.438**	.624	174	67	3	**.991**	-10	89	74	O156(3/72/117)/1	0	5.1
1950	StL N★	146	555	105	192	41	7	28	109	87	3	36	**.346**	.437	**.596**	**161**	**53**	5	.964	-7	91	39	O77(56/14/10),1b69	0	3.8
1951	StL N★	152	578	**124**	205	30	**12**	32	108	98	1	40	**.355**	.449	.614	**182**	**70**	4-5	.974	2	102	150	O91(84/10/1),1b60	0	6.1
1952	StL N★	**154**	578	**105**	**194**	**42**	6	21	91	96	2	29	**.336**	.432	**.538**	**167**	**58**	7-7	.987	-10	94	49	O129(21/106/9),1b25/P	0	4.2
1953	StL N★	**157**	593	127	200	**53**	9	30	113	**105**	0	32	.337	**.437**	.609	169	**66**	3-4	.984	-9	92	66	O157(141/9/26)	0	4.4
1954	StL N★	**153**	591	**120**	195	**41**	9	35	126	103	4	39	.330	.428	.607	166	61	1-7	**.990**	-5	92	96	O152(8/0/147),1b10	0	4.7
1955	StL N★	**154**	562	97	179	30	5	33	108	80-19	**8**	39	.319	.408	.566	156	48	5-4	.992	7	**127**	99	1b110,O51(21/0/33)	0	4.5
1956	StL N★	**156**	594	87	184	33	6	27	**109**	75-15	3	39	.310	.386	.522	142	37	2-0	.993	6	**124**	**119**	1b103,O53(3/0/51)	0	3.6
1957	StL N★	134	502	82	176	38	3	29	102	66-**19**	2	34	**.351**	**.422**	.612	172	54	1-1	.992	1	102	**127**	1b130	0	4.7
1958	StL N★	135	472	64	159	35	2	17	62	72-**26**	1	26	.337	.423	.528	145	35	0-0	.989	7	**122**	112	1b124	0	3.5
1959	StL N★	115	341	37	87	13	2	14	44	60-11	0	25	.255	.364	.428	104	4	0-2	.990	3	114	105	1b90,O3L	0	0.1
1960	StL N★	116	331	49	91	17	1	17	63	41-7	2	34	.275	.354	.486	118	9	1-1	.990	-1	98	45	O59(53/0/6),1b29	0	0.3
1961	StL N★	123	372	46	107	22	4	15	70	52-17	1	35	.288	.371	.489	116	10	0-0	**.994**	2	95	130	O103L	0	0.7
1962	StL N★	135	433	57	143	18	1	19	82	64-4	3	46	.330	.416	.508	135	24	3-0	.977	-3	91	80	O119(97/0/23)	0	1.5
1963	StL N★	124	337	34	86	10	2	12	58	35-9	2	43	.255	.325	.404	100	1	2-0	.968	-3	99	22	O96L	0	-0.6
Total	22	3026	10972	1949	3630	725	177	475	1951	1599-127	53	696	.331	.417	.559	157	930	78-31	.984	-17	98	82	O1890(943/325/750),1b1016/P	0	76.0
Musser, Danny	William Daniel; B9.5.1905 Zion PA; D3.2.2000 Upper Sandusky OH; BL/TR/5´9.5˝/160; d9.18; Col Penn St.																								
1932	Was A	1	2	0	1	0	0	0	0	0	0	0	.500	.500	.500	162	0	0-0	ø	-0	0	0	/3	—	0.0
Myatt, George	George Edward "Mercury", "Stud","Foghorn"; B6.14.1914 Denver CO; D9.14.2000 Orlando FL; BL/TR/5´11˝/167; d8.16; M2/C23																								
1938	NY N	43	170	27	52	2	1	3	10	14	1	13	.306	.362	.382	104	1	10	.919	5	108	130	S24,3b19	—	0.9
1939	NY N	22	53	7	10	2	0	0	3	6	0	6	.189	.271	.226	35	-5	2	.907	0	108	124	3b14	—	-0.4
1943	Was A	42	53	11	13	3	0	0	3	13	0	7	.245	.394	.302	109	2	3-0	.930	-1	113	59	2b11,S2,3b2	0	0.2
1944	Was A	140	538	86	153	19	6	0	40	54	7	44	.284	.357	.342	105	5	26-10	.957	-20	87	93	2b121,S15,O3R	0	-0.6
1945	Was A	133	490	81	145	17	7	1	39	63	2	43	.296	.378	.365	127	19	30-11	.972	-15	88	88	2b94,O32(1/0/31),3b6/S	0	1.0
1946	Was A	15	34	7	8	1	0	0	4	2	1	3	.235	.297	.265	61	-2	1-1	.900	-2	85	68	3b7,2b2	0	-0.4
1947	Was A	12	7	1	0	0	0	0	0	4	0	4	.000	.364	.000	6	-1	0-0	1.000	0	152	0	/2	0	-0.1
Total	7	407	1345	220	381	44	14	4	99	156	11	120	.283	.362	.346	108	19	72-22	.962	-32	89	89	2b229,3b48,S42,O35(1/0/34)	0	0.6
Myatt, Glenn	Glenn Calvin; B7.9.1897 Argenta (now N.Little Rock) AR; D8.9.1969 Houston TX; BL/TR/5´11˝/165; d4.15																								
1920	Phi A	70	196	14	49	8	3	0	18	12	0	22	.250	.293	.321	62	-11	1-3	.900	-3	77	151	O37(1/0/36),C22	—	-1.5
1921	Phi A	44	69	6	14	2	0	0	5	6	0	7	.203	.267	.232	28	-8	1-0	.939	0	*97*	*139*	C27	—	-0.6
1923	Cle A	92	220	36	63	7	6	3	40	16	1	18	.286	.338	.414	97	-2	0-2	.934	-5	*122*	*53*	C69	—	-0.4
1924	Cle A	105	342	55	117	22	7	8	73	33	1	12	.342	.402	.518	134	17	6-1	.978	-9	*89*	*76*	C95	—	1.4
1925	Cle A	106	358	51	97	15	9	11	54	29	2	24	.271	.329	.455	97	-5	3-1	.973	-9	*120*	*66*	C98/lf	—	-0.7
1926	Cle A	56	117	14	29	5	2	0	13	13	0	13	.248	.323	.325	69	-5	1-0	1.000	1	*162*	*61*	C35	—	-0.2
1927	Cle A	55	94	15	23	6	0	2	8	12	1	7	.245	.336	.372	83	-2	1-1	.978	2	*118*	*153*	C26	—	0.1
1928	Cle A	58	125	9	36	7	2	1	15	13	0	13	.288	.355	.400	97	0	0-2	.967	-5	*88*	*82*	C30	—	-0.4
1929	Cle A	59	129	14	30	4	1	1	17	7	1	5	.233	.277	.302	47	-11	0-1	.976	-1	*87*	*129*	C41	—	-0.9
1930	Cle A	86	265	30	78	23	2	2	37	18	1	17	.294	.342	.419	88	-4	2-3	.977	-5	*81*	*97*	C71	—	-0.5
1931	Cle A	65	195	21	48	14	2	1	29	21	0	13	.246	.319	.354	73	-8	2-1	.991	-2	*103*	*127*	C53	—	-0.6
1932	Cle A	82	252	45	62	12	1	8	46	27	3	21	.246	.326	.397	81	-7	2-2	.988	-3	*116*	*75*	C65	—	-0.7
1933	Cle A	40	77	10	18	4	0	0	7	15	2	8	.234	.372	.286	73	-2	0-1	.965	0	*129*	*162*	C27	—	-0.1
1934	Cle A	36	107	18	34	6	1	0	12	13	0	5	.318	.392	.393	101	1	1-0	.980	-1	*114*	*64*	C34	—	0.2
1935	Cle A	10	36	1	3	1	0	0	2	4	0	3	.083	.175	.111	-24	-7	0-0	1.000	-1	*101*	*75*	C10	—	-0.7
	NY N	13	18	2	4	0	1	1	6	0	0	3	.222	.222	.500	90	-1	0	1.000	-1	*66*	*0*	C4	—	-0.1
1936	Det A	27	78	5	17	1	0	0	5	9	0	4	.218	.299	.231	32	-8	0-0	1.000	-1	*114*	*119*	C27	—	-0.7
Total	16	1004	2678	346	722	137	37	38	387	248	12	195	.270	.334	.391	85	-63	20-18	.974	-41	*107*	*90*	C734,O38(2/0/36)	—	-6.4
Myer, Buddy	Charles Solomon; B3.16.1904 Ellisville MS; D10.31.1974 Baton Rouge LA; BL/TR/5´10.5˝/163; d9.26; Col Mississippi St.																								
1925	†Was A	4	8	1	2	0	0	0	0	0	0	1	.250	.250	.250	28	-1	0-0	1.000	-1	66	0	S4	—	-0.2
1926	Was A	132	434	66	132	18	6	1	62	45	0	19	.304	.370	.380	98	-1	10-11	.928	-17	93	76	S118,3b8	—	-0.7
1927	Was A	15	51	7	11	1	0	0	7	8	0	3	.216	.322	.235	47	-4	3-1	.933	-2	90	115	S15	—	-0.4
	Bos A	133	469	59	135	22	11	2	47	48	4	15	.288	.359	.394	97	-2	9-5	.940	6	102	105	S101,3b14,O10L/2	—	1.4
	Year	148	520	66	146	23	11	2	54	56	4	18	.281	.355	.379	92	-6	12-6	.939	4	100	106	S116,3b14,O10L/2	—	1.0
1928	Bos A	147	536	78	168	26	6	1	44	53	4	28	.313	.379	.390	104	5	**30**-16	.967	6	108	**133**	3b144	—	2.0
1929	Was A	141	563	80	169	29	10	3	82	63	2	33	.300	.373	.403	99	0	19-7	.958	-12	93	92	2b88,3b53	—	-0.4
1930	Was A	138	541	97	164	18	8	2	61	58	2	31	.303	.373	.377	90	-7	14-11	.965	-14	92	**114**	2b134,O2(1/0/1)	—	-1.6
1931	Was A	139	591	114	173	33	11	4	56	58	4	42	.293	.360	.406	100	1	11-14	**.984**	-13	90	109	2b137	—	-0.6
1932	Was A	143	577	120	161	38	16	5	52	69	4	33	.279	.360	.426	104	4	12-7	.975	-17	92	**112**	2b139	—	-0.4
1933	†Was A	131	530	95	160	29	15	4	61	60	1	29	.302	.374	.436	115	12	6-8	.978	1	99	127	2b129	—	1.8
1934	Was A	139	524	103	160	33	8	3	57	102	1	32	.305	.419	.416	121	23	6-6	.975	-8	100	107	2b135	—	2.1
1935	Was A☆	151	616	115	215	36	11	5	100	96	4	40	**.349**	.440	.468	139	42	7-6	.979	7	95	**123**	2b151	—	5.3
1936	Was A	51	156	31	42	5	2	0	15	42	1	11	.269	.427	.327	94	2	7-2	.985	3	100	108	2b43	—	0.7
1937	Was A☆	125	430	54	126	16	10	1	65	78	5	41	.293	.407	.384	105	7	2-6	.966	-16	90	107	2b119/lf	—	-0.2
1938	Was A	127	437	79	147	22	8	6	71	93	1	32	.336	.454	.465	140	34	9-5	**.982**	-3	100	105	2b121	—	3.5
1939	Was A	83	258	33	78	10	3	1	32	40	0	18	.302	.396	.376	106	4	4-1	.968	3	100	113	2b65	—	1.1
1940	Was A	71	210	28	61	14	4	0	29	34	0	10	.290	.389	.395	111	5	6-3	.967	6	110	86	2b54	—	1.3
1941	Was A	53	107	14	27	3	1	0	9	18	0	10	.252	.360	.299	80	-2	2-0	.982	-3	87	83	2b24	0	-0.4
Total	17	1923	7038	1174	2131	353	130	38	850	965	33	428	.303	.389	.406	108	122	157-109	.974	-74	96	110	2b1340,S238,3b219,O13(12/0/1)	0	14.3
Myers, George	George D.; B11.13.1860 Buffalo NY; D12.14.1926 Buffalo NY; BR/TR/5´8˝/170; d5.2																								
1884	Buf N	78	325	34	59	9	2	2	32	13	—	33	.182	.213	.240	41	-22	—	.837	-14	—	—	C49,O34(16/18/0)	—	-3.0
1885	Buf N	89	326	40	67	7	2	0	19	23	—	40	.206	.258	.239	60	-14	—	.899	-4	—	—	C69,O23(0/21/1)	—	-1.3
1886	StL N	79	295	26	56	7	3	0	27	18	—	42	.190	.236	.234	46	-18	6	.928	-5	—	—	C72,O6(0/5/1)/3	—	-1.6
1887	Ind N	69	235	25	51	8	1	1	20	22	5	7	.217	.298	.272	61	-11	26	.929	-8	—	—	C50,O15(3/7/5),1b6/3	—	-1.3
1888	Ind N	66	248	36	59	9	0	2	16	16	3	14	.238	.292	.298	87	-3	28	.929	-4	—	—	C47,3b14,O10(2/1/7)/1	—	-0.3
1889	Ind N	43	149	22	29	3	0	0	12	17	4	13	.195	.294	.215	42	-11	12	.909	0	158	106	O23(6/17/0),C18/1	—	-0.9
Total	6	424	1578	183	321	43	8	5	126	109	12	149	.203	.260	.250	56	-79	72	.901	-34	—	—	C305,O111(27/69/14),3b16,1b8	—	-8.4
Myers, Greg	Gregory Richard; B4.14.1966 Riverside CA; BL/TR/6´2˝/(202–225); [TorA84 3/74]; d9.12																								
1987	Tor A	7	9	1	1	0	0	0	0	0-0	0	3	.111	.111	.111	-40	-2	0-0	1.000	2	0	0	C7	0	0.0
1989	Tor A	17	44	0	5	2	0	0	1	2-0	0	9	.114	.152	.159	-12	-7	0-1	1.000	3	103	84	C11,D6	63	-0.4
1990	Tor A	87	250	33	59	7	1	5	22	22-0	0	33	.236	.293	.332	74	-9	0-1	.993	1	118	105	C87	20	-0.4
1991	Tor A	107	309	25	81	22	0	8	36	21-4	0	45	.262	.306	.411	94	-3	0-0	.979	-8	77	89	C104	0	-0.6
1992	Tor A	22	61	4	14	6	0	1	13	5-0	0	5	.230	.279	.377	81	-2	0-0	.991	-1	61	110	C18/D	0	-0.2

YEAR	TM LG	G	AB	R	H	2B	3B	HR	RBI	BB-IB	HP	SO	AVG	OBP	SLG	AOPS	ABR	SB-CS	FA	FR	RNG	THR	GAMES AT POSITION	DL	BFW
	Cal A	8	17	0	4	1	0	0	0	0-0	0	6	.235	.235	.294	47	-1	0-0	1.000	0	51	57	C8	39	-0.1
	Year	30	78	4	18	7	0	1	13	5-0	0	11	.231	.271	.359	74	-3	0-0	.993	-1	59	98	C26/D	0	-0.3
1993	Cal A	108	290	27	74	10	0	7	40	17-2	2	47	.255	.298	.362	75	-11	3-3	.986	-7	71	102	C97,D2	0	-1.3
1994	Cal A	45	126	10	31	6	0	2	8	10-3	0	27	.246	.299	.341	64	-7	0-2	.991	1	123	161	C41/D	58	-0.4
1995	Cal A	85	273	35	71	12	2	9	38	17-3	1	49	.260	.304	.418	87	-7	0-1	.989	3	131	86	C61,D16	33	-0.1
1996	Min A	97	329	37	94	22	3	6	47	19-3	0	52	.286	.320	.426	86	-8	0-0	.985	-2	121	100	C90	19	-0.4
1997	Min A	62	165	24	44	11	1	5	28	16-2	0	29	.267	.328	.436	97	-1	0-0	.986	-2	103	111	C38,D10	15	-0.1
	Atl N	9	9	0	1	0	0	0	1	1-0	0	3	.111	.200	.111	-16	-2	0-0	1.000	1	40	273	C2	0	0.0
1998	†SD N	69	171	19	42	10	0	4	20	17-1	0	36	.246	.312	.374	86	-4	0-1	.987	-1	107	110	C52	50	-0.2
1999	SD N	50	128	9	37	4	0	3	15	13-2	0	14	.289	.355	.391	95	-1	0-0	.986	-6	89	73	C41	27	-0.5
	†Atl N	34	72	10	16	2	0	2	9	13-2	0	16	.222	.337	.333	72	-3	0-0	.994	6	196	110	C31	0	0.4
	Year	84	200	19	53	6	0	5	24	26-4	0	30	.265	.348	.370	86	-4	0-0	.990	-0	132	88	C72	0	-0.1
2000	Bal A	43	125	9	28	6	0	3	12	8-0	0	29	.224	.271	.344	57	-9	0-0	1.000	-3	59	110	C28,D8	13	-0.9
2001	Bal A	25	74	11	20	2	0	4	18	8-0	0	17	.270	.341	.459	114	1	0-0	1.000	-2	61	175	D11,C8	0	0.0
	†Oak A	33	87	13	16	1	0	7	13	13-1	0	21	.184	.290	.437	87	-2	0-0	1.000	1	114	120	C28,D2	0	0.0
	Year	58	161	24	36	3	0	11	31	21-1	0	38	.224	.313	.447	99	-1	0-0	1.000	-1	101	133	C36,D13	0	0.0
2002	†Oak A	65	144	15	32	5	0	6	21	26-3	0	36	.222	.341	.382	93	-1	0-0	.997	6	95	156	C53/D	0	0.8
2003	Tor A	121	329	51	101	19	0	15	52	37-2	0	57	.307	.374	.502	124	12	0-3	.982	-8	77	74	C81,D22	0	0.6
2004	Tor A	8	18	0	4	2	0	0	1	2-0	0	4	.222	.300	.333	61	-1	0-0	1.000	1	64	113	C4/D	160	0.0
2005	Tor A	6	12	0	1	0	0	0	1	1-0	0	1	.083	.154	.083	-33	-2	0-0	1.000	0	51	156	C4	0	-0.2
Total	18	1108	3042	333	776	150	7	87	396	268-28	3	539	.255	.313	.395	86	-70	3-12	.989	-14	99	104	C894,D81	497	-4.0
MYERS, HENRY	Henry C.; B5.1858 Philadelphia PA; D4.18.1895 Philadelphia PA; BR/TR/5´9˝/159; d8.20; M1; ▲																								
1881	Pro N	1	4	0	0	0	0	0	0	0	—	2	.000	.000	.000	-99	-1	—	1.000	-0	76	0	/S	—	-0.1
1882	Bal AA	69	294	43	53	3	0	0	—	12	—	—	.180	.212	.190	40	-17	—	.822	-6	**107**	76	S68,P6,M	—	-1.9
1884	Wil U	6	24	3	3	0	0	0	—	0	—	—	.125	.125	.125	-23	-4	—	.875	4	108	0	S5/2	—	-0.1
Total	3	76	322	46	56	3	0	0	0	12	—	2	.174	.204	.183	32	-22	—	.826	-3	107	70	S74,P6/2	—	-2.1
MYERS, HY	Henry Harrison; B4.27.1889 E.Liverpool OH; D5.1.1965 Minerva OH; BR/TR/5´9.5˝/175; d8.30; OF(5/1150/28)																								
1909	Bro N	6	22	1	5	1	0	0	6	2	0	—	.227	.292	.273	78	-1	1	1.000	-1	0	0	O6R	—	-0.1
1911	Bro N	13	43	2	7	1	0	0	0	2	0	3	.163	.200	.186	9	-5	1	.889	-1	88	124	O13(0/12/1)	—	-0.7
1914	Bro N	70	227	35	65	3	9	0	17	7	3	24	.286	.316	.379	104	-1	2	.964	-5	90	59	O60(4/45/12)	—	-1.0
1915	Bro N	153	605	69	150	21	7	2	46	17	6	51	.248	.275	.316	77	-19	19-22	.964	-2	93	119	O153C	—	-3.9
1916	†Bro N	113	412	54	108	12	14	3	36	21	6	35	.262	.308	.381	108	2	17	.969	-5	93	82	O106(0/105/1)	—	-1.2
1917	Bro N	120	471	37	126	15	10	1	41	18	0	25	.268	.294	.348	94	-5	5	.982	-6	104	67	O66(0/62/4),1b22,2b19,3b15	—	-1.7
1918	Bro N	107	407	36	104	9	8	4	40	20	1	26	.256	.292	.346	95	-4	17	.975	8	108	119	O107C	—	-0.5
1919	Bro N	133	512	62	157	23	**14**	5	**73**	23	2	34	.307	.339	**.436**	129	16	13	.979	4	109	76	O131C	—	1.1
1920	†Bro N	154	582	83	177	36	**22**	4	80	35	1	54	.304	.345	.462	126	18	9-13	.978	-1	101	78	O152C,3b2	—	0.4
1921	Bro N	144	549	51	158	14	4	4	68	22	2	51	.288	.318	.350	74	-21	8-6	.968	-4	85	136	O124C,2b21/3	—	-3.0
1922	Bro N	153	618	82	196	20	9	6	89	13	0	26	.317	.331	.408	90	-12	9-10	.974	-1	101	88	O152C/2	—	-1.9
1923	StL N	96	330	29	99	18	2	2	48	12	3	19	.300	.330	.385	90	-5	5-3	.977	7	108	138	O87C	—	-0.2
1924	StL N	43	124	12	26	5	1	1	15	3	0	10	.210	.228	.290	39	-11	1-2	.945	-2	107	100	O22(1/17/4),3b12,2b3	—	-1.4
1925	StL N	1	1	0	0	0	0	0	0	0	0	0	.000	.000	.000	-98	0	0-0	ø	0	—	—	/H	—	0.0
	Cin N	3	6	1	1	1	0	0	0	0	0	0	.167	.167	.333	25	-1	0-0	1.000	0	110	0	O3C	—	-0.1
	StL N	1	1	1	1	0	0	0	0	0	0	0	1.000	1.000	1.000	403	0	0-0	ø	0	—	—	/H	—	0.0
	Year	5	8	2	2	1	0	0	0	0	0	0	.250	.250	.375	58	-1	0-0	1.000	0	110	0	O3C	—	-0.1
Total	14	1310	4910	555	1380	179	100	32	559	195	24	358	.281	.312	.378	95	-49	107-56	.972	-7	99	98	O1182C,2b44,3b30,1b22	—	-14.2
MYERS, AL	James Albert "Cod"; B10.22.1863 Danville IL; D12.24.1927 Marshall IL; BR/TR/5´8.5˝/165; d9.27																								
1884	Mil U	**12**	46	6	15	6	0	0	—	0	—	—	.326	.326	.457	247	7	—	.848	3	93	48	2b12	—	0.9
1885	Phi N	93	357	25	73	13	2	1	28	11	—	41	.204	.228	.261	59	-16	—	.884	-16	98	85	2b93	—	-2.7
1886	KC N	118	473	69	131	22	9	4	51	22	—	42	.277	.309	.387	104	0	3	.913	2	**108**	88	2b118	—	0.6
1887	Was N	105	362	45	84	9	5	2	36	40	2	26	.232	.312	.301	76	-10	18	.909	-9	95	68	2b78,S27	—	-1.3
1888	Was N	132	502	46	104	12	7	2	46	37	6	46	.207	.270	.271	78	-11	20	.918	-22	95	71	2b132	—	-2.8
1889	Was N	46	176	24	46	3	0	0	20	22	1	7	.261	.347	.278	80	-3	10	.942	1	94	104	2b46	—	-0.1
	Phi N	75	305	52	82	14	2	0	28	36	4	9	.269	.354	.328	83	-7	8	.853	-14	101	88	2b75	—	-1.5
	Year	121	481	76	128	17	2	0	48	58	5	16	.266	.351	.310	82	-10	18	.886	-14	98	94	2b121	—	-1.6
1890	Phi N	117	487	95	135	29	7	2	81	57	10	46	.277	.365	.378	114	10	44	.948	6	94	129	2b117	—	1.8
1891	Phi N	135	514	67	118	27	2	2	69	69	9	46	.230	.331	.302	83	-9	8	.937	-12	98	111	2b135	—	-1.4
Total	8	833	3222	429	788	135	34	13	359	294	32	263	.245	.314	.320	88	-39	111	.914	-61	98	93	2b806,S27	—	-6.5
MYERS, BERT	James Albert; B4.8.1874 Frederick MD; D10.12.1915 Washington DC; BR/TR/5´10˝/?; d4.25																								
1896	StL N	122	454	47	116	12	8	0	37	40	3	32	.256	.320	.317	71	-19	8	.867	-6	96	82	3b121/S	—	-2.0
1898	Was N	31	110	14	29	1	4	0	13	13	0	—	.264	.341	.345	97	-1	2	.835	-3	94	123	3b31	—	-0.3
1900	Phi N	7	28	5	5	1	0	0	2	3	0	—	.179	.258	.214	31	-3	1	.909	1	128	260	3b7	—	-0.1
Total	3	160	592	66	150	14	12	0	52	56	3	32	.253	.321	.318	74	-23	11	.863	-8	97	99	3b159/S	—	-2.4
MYERS, LYNN	Lynnwood Lincoln; B2.23.1914 Enola PA; D1.19.2000 Harrisburg PA; BR/TR/5´6.5˝/145; d7.13; b–Billy																								
1938	StL N	70	227	18	55	10	2	1	19	9	0	25	.242	.271	.317	58	-13	9	.944	-1	101	94	S69	—	-1.0
1939	StL N	74	117	24	28	6	1	0	10	12	0	23	.239	.310	.308	63	-6	1	.897	-0	95	133	S36,3b13,2b5	—	-0.4
Total	2	144	344	42	83	16	3	1	29	21	0	48	.241	.285	.314	60	-19	10	.930	-2	99	105	S105,3b13,2b5	—	-1.4
MYERS, HAP	Ralph Edward; B4.8.1887 San Francisco CA; D6.30.1967 San Francisco CA; BR/TR/6´3˝/175; d4.16; Col California																								
1910	Bos A	3	6	0	2	0	0	0	0	0	0	—	.333	.333	.333	106	0	0	1.000	1	64	648	O2R	—	0.1
1911	StL A	11	37	4	11	1	0	0	1	1	0	—	.297	.316	.324	82	-1	0	.976	-2	43	93	1b11	—	-0.3
	Bos A	13	38	3	14	2	0	0	0	4	0	—	.368	.429	.421	139	2	4	.947	-1	87	103	1b12	—	0.1
	Year	24	75	7	25	3	0	0	1	5	0	—	.333	.375	.373	111	1	4	.963	-3	65	98	1b23	—	-0.2
1913	Bos N	140	524	74	143	20	1	2	50	38	9	48	.273	.333	.326	87	-8	57-18	.987	5	115	81	1b135	—	0.0
1914	Bro F	92	305	61	67	10	5	1	29	44	2	43	.220	.322	.295	69	-17	43	.989	1	102	101	1b88	—	-1.9
1915	Bro F	118	341	61	98	9	1	1	36	32	2	39	.287	.352	.328	93	-7	28	.990	1	105	93	1b107	—	-0.9
Total	5	377	1251	203	335	42	7	4	116	119	13	130	.268	.338	.322	85	-31	132-18	.987	5	106	90	1b353,O2R	—	-2.9
MYERS, RICHIE	Richard; B4.7.1930 Sacramento CA; BR/TR/5´6˝/150; d4.21																								
1956	Chi N	4	1	1	0	0	0	0	0	0-0	0	0	.000	.000	.000	-99	0	0-0	ø	0	—	—	/H	0	0.0
MYERS, ROD	Roderick Demond; B1.14.1973 Conroe TX; BL/TL/6´0˝/190; [KCA91 13/340]; d6.21; [DL 1998 KC A 82]																								
1996	KC A	22	63	9	18	7	0	1	11	7-0	0	16	.286	.357	.444	101	0	3-2	1.000	-2	80	0	O19(4/15/1)	0	-0.2
1997	KC A	31	101	14	26	7	0	2	9	17-0	1	22	.257	.370	.386	95	0	4-0	.982	-1	95	61	O26(12/9/10)	100	-0.1
Total	2	53	164	23	44	14	0	3	20	24-0	1	38	.268	.365	.409	97	0	7-2	.989	-4	89	38	O45(16/24/11)	182	-0.3
MYERS, BILLY	William Harrison; B8.14.1910 Enola PA; D4.10.1995 Carlisle PA; BR/TR/5´8˝/168; d4.16; b–Lynn																								
1935	Cin N	117	445	60	119	15	10	5	36	29	2	81	.267	.315	.380	89	-9	10	.939	2	101	125	S112	—	0.1
1936	Cin N	98	323	45	87	9	6	6	27	28	0	56	.269	.328	.390	99	-2	6	.938	4	101	118	S98	—	0.9
1937	Cin N	124	335	35	84	13	3	7	43	44	1	57	.251	.339	.370	97	-1	0	.948	7	107	99	S121,2b6	—	1.4
1938	Cin N	134	442	57	112	18	6	12	47	41	0	80	.253	.317	.403	99	-2	2	.939	-2	100	105	S123,2b11	—	0.6
1939	†Cin N	151	509	79	143	18	6	9	56	71	0	90	.281	.369	.393	104	5	4	.951	3	100	**113**	S151	—	1.9
1940	†Cin N	90	282	33	57	14	2	5	30	30	2	56	.202	.283	.319	65	-13	0	.961	-3	99	135	S88	—	-1.1
1941	Chi N	24	63	10	14	1	0	1	4	7	1	25	.222	.310	.286	71	-2	1	.939	2	108	113	S19/2	0	0.2
Total	7	738	2399	319	616	88	33	45	243	250	6	445	.257	.328	.377	93	-24	23	.946	13	101	115	S712,2b18	0	4.0
MYROW, BRIAN	Brian Shawn; B9.4.1976 Fort Worth TX; BL/TR/5´11˝/190; d9.6; Col Louisiana Tech																								
2005	LA N	19	20	2	4	1	0	0	0	5-0	0	8	.200	.360	.250	63	-1	0-0	1.000	-1	0	79	1b5	0	-0.2

YEAR	TM LG	G	AB	R	H	2B	3B	HR	RBI	BB-IB	HP	SO	AVG	OBP	SLG	AOPS	ABR	SB-CS	FA	FR	RNG	THR	GAMES AT POSITION	DL	BFW
NADY, XAVIER	Xavier Clifford; B11.14.1978 Salinas CA; BR/TR/6´4˝/(180–220); [SDN00 2/49]; d9.30; Col California																								
2000	SD N	1	1	1	1	0	0	0	0	0-0	0	0	1.000	1.000	1.000	435	1	0-0	ø	0	—	—	/H	0	0.0
2003	SD N	110	371	50	99	17	1	9	39	24-0	6	74	.267	.321	.391	93	-5	6-2	.968	1	93	193	O105R	0	-0.8
2004	SD N	34	77	7	19	4	0	3	9	5-0	1	13	.247	.301	.416	87	-2	0-0	.923	-2	71	108	O22(18/4/2),D2	0	-0.4
2005	†SD N	124	326	40	85	15	2	13	43	22-1	7	67	.261	.321	.439	101	-1	2-1	.976	-4	79	0	O68(26/30/13),1b44,3b3/D	0	-0.9
2006	NY N	75	265	37	70	15	1	14	40	19-4	6	51	.264	.326	.487	107	2	2-1	.973	1	98	145	O71R/1	19	-0.1
	Pit N	55	203	20	61	13	0	3	23	11-3	5	34	.300	.352	.409	92	-2	1-2	.993	6	215	118	1b34,O28R	0	0.0
	Year	130	468	57	131	28	1	17	63	30-7	11	85	.280	.337	.453	100	0	3-3	.980	7	97	126	O99R,1b35	0	-0.1
Total	5	399	1243	155	335	64	4	42	154	81-8	25	239	.270	.326	.429	98	-7	11-6	.972	2	90	126	O294(44/34/219),1b79,3b3,D3	19	-2.2
NAEHRING, TIM	Timothy James; B2.1.1967 Cincinnati OH; BR/TR/6´2˝/(190–205); [BosA88 8/199]; d7.15; Col Miami–Ohio; [DL 1998 Bos A 181]																								
1990	Bos A	24	85	10	23	6	0	2	12	8-1	0	15	.271	.333	.412	102	0	0-0	.918	2	105	96	S19,3b5/2	49	0.3
1991	Bos A	20	55	1	6	1	0	0	3	6-0	0	15	.109	.197	.127	-8	-8	0-0	.956	-0	107	86	S17,3b2/2	142	-0.7
1992	Bos A	72	186	12	43	8	0	3	14	18-0	3	31	.231	.308	.323	72	-7	0-0	.992	11	110	116	S30,2b23,3b10/lfD	40	0.7
1993	Bos A	39	127	14	42	10	0	1	17	10-0	0	26	.331	.377	.433	111	2	1-0	.973	-3	91	122	2b15,D10,3b9,S4	88	0.0
1994	Bos A	80	297	41	82	18	1	7	42	30-1	4	56	.276	.349	.414	92	-3	1-3	.981	5	108	106	2b49,3b11,1b8,S8,D7	29	0.3
1995	†Bos A	126	433	61	133	27	2	10	57	77-5	4	66	.307	.415	.448	121	18	0-2	.954	7	108	109	3b124/D	0	2.3
1996	Bos A	116	430	77	124	16	0	17	65	49-4	4	63	.288	.363	.444	102	1	2-1	.963	8	106	78	3b116/2	18	0.9
1997	Bos A	70	259	38	74	18	1	9	40	38-0	1	40	.286	.375	.467	117	8	1-1	.981	-9	88	87	3b68/D	97	-0.1
Total	8	547	1872	254	527	104	4	49	250	236-11	16	312	.282	.365	.420	102	11	5-7	.962	21	100	92	3b345,2b90,S78,D23,1b8/lf	644	3.7
NAGEL, BILL	William Taylor; B8.19.1915 Memphis TN; D10.8.1981 Freehold NJ; BR/TR/6´1˝/190; d4.20																								
1939	Phi A	105	341	39	86	19	4	12	39	25	2	86	.252	.307	.437	90	-7	2-1	.944	-12	96	82	2b56,3b43/P	—	-1.4
1941	Phi N	17	56	2	8	1	1	0	6	3	0	14	.143	.186	.196	8	-7	0	.935	2	123	100	2b12,O2L/3	0	-0.5
1945	Chi A	67	220	21	46	10	3	3	27	15	1	41	.209	.263	.323	71	-9	3-1	.984	-2	89	90	1b57/3	0	-1.5
Total	3	189	617	62	140	30	8	15	72	43	3	141	.227	.281	.374	77	-23	5-2	.942	-13	101	85	2b68,1b57,3b45,O2L/P	0	-3.4
NAGELSEN, LOU	Louis Marcellus (b Louis Marcellus Nageleisen); B6.29.1887 Piqua OH; D10.21.1965 Fort Wayne IN; BR/TR/6´2˝/180; d9.10; Col Notre Dame																								
1912	Cle A	2	3	0	0	0	0	0	0	0	0	—	.000	.000	.000	-97	-1	0	1.000	-0	*84*	*0*	C2	—	-0.1
NAGELSON, RUSS	Russell Charles; B9.19.1944 Cincinnati OH; BL/TR/6´0˝/(205–210); [CleA66 14/272]; d9.11; Col Ohio St.																								
1968	Cle A	5	3	0	1	0	0	0	0	2-0	0	2	.333	.600	.333	192	1	0-0	ø	0	—	—	/H	0	0.1
1969	Cle A	12	17	1	6	0	0	0	0	3-1	0	3	.353	.450	.353	123	1	0-0	1.000	-0	72	0	O3(1/0/2)/1	0	0.1
1970	Cle A	17	24	3	3	1	0	1	2	3-0	0	9	.125	.222	.292	39	-2	0-0	1.000	-0	84	0	O4(1/0/3)	0	-0.3
	Det A	28	32	5	6	0	0	0	2	5-0	0	6	.188	.297	.188	36	-3	0-0	1.000	-0	88	0	O4(3/0/2)/1	0	-0.3
	Year	45	56	8	9	1	0	1	4	8-0	0	15	.161	.266	.232	38	-5	0-0	1.000	-1	86	0	O8(4/0/5)/1	0	-0.6
Total	3	62	76	9	16	1	0	1	4	13-1	0	20	.211	.326	.263	64	-3	0-0	1.000	-1	83	0	O11(5/0/7),1b2	0	-0.4
NAGLE, TOM	Thomas Edward; B10.30.1865 Milwaukee WI; D3.9.1946 Milwaukee WI; BR/TR/5´10˝/150; d4.22																								
1890	Chi N	38	144	21	39	5	1	1	11	7	3	24	.271	.318	.340	88	-3	4	.939	-4	*111*	*62*	C33,O6R	—	-0.3
1891	Chi N	8	25	3	3	0	0	0	1	1	0	3	.120	.154	.120	-20	-4	0	.906	-2	*137*	*62*	C7/lf	—	-0.5
Total	2	46	169	24	42	5	1	1	12	8	3	27	.249	.294	.308	73	-7	4	.935	-5	*115*	*62*	C40,O7(1/0/6)	—	-0.8
NAHORODNY, BILL	William Gerard; B8.31.1953 Hamtramck MI; BR/TR/6´2˝/(190–200); [PhiN72 6/123]; d9.27; Col St. Clair Co. (MI) CC																								
1976	Phi N	3	5	0	1	1	0	0	0	0-0	0	0	.200	.200	.400	65	0	0-0	1.000	-0	31	0	C2	0	0.0
1977	Chi A	7	23	3	6	1	0	1	4	2-0	0	3	.261	.308	.435	103	0	0-0	1.000	-1	79	67	C7	0	-0.1
1978	Chi A	107	347	29	82	11	2	8	35	23-0	2	52	.236	.285	.349	77	-11	1-0	.980	-4	81	82	C104,1b4/D	0	-1.2
1979	Chi A	65	179	20	46	10	0	6	29	18-1	0	23	.257	.322	.413	97	-1	0-1	.973	-1	63	115	C60,D3	23	0.0
1980	Atl N	59	157	14	38	12	0	5	18	8-1	2	21	.242	.287	.414	93	-2	0-2	.990	-6	83	99	C54/1	14	-0.7
1981	Atl N	14	13	0	3	1	0	0	2	1-1	0	3	.231	.286	.308	68	-1	0-0	1.000	0	0	0	C3/1	0	-0.1
1982	Cle A	39	94	6	21	5	1	4	18	2-0	0	9	.223	.237	.426	78	-3	0-0	1.000	-5	92	62	C35	0	-0.7
1983	Det A	2	1	0	0	0	0	0	0	1-0	0	0	.000	.500	.000	53	0	0-0	ø	0	—	—	/H	0	0.0
1984	Sea A	12	25	2	6	0	0	1	3	1-0	2	7	.240	.310	.360	89	0	0-1	.976	-2	132	44	C10/1	0	-0.3
Total	9	308	844	74	203	41	3	25	109	56-3	6	118	.241	.290	.385	86	-18	1-4	.983	-19	80	87	C275,1b7,D4	37	-3.1
NAKAMURA, NORIHIRO	Norihiro; B7.24.1973 Osaka, Japan; BR/TR/5´10˝/200; d4.10																								
2005	LA N	17	39	1	5	2	0	0	3	2-0	0	7	.128	.171	.179	-8	-6	0-0	1.000	1	131	170	3b10,1b4,S2/2	0	-0.6
NALEWAY, FRANK	Frank "Chick"; B7.5.1902 Chicago IL; D1.28.1949 Chicago IL; BR/TR/5´9.5˝/165; d9.16																								
1924	Chi A	1	2	0	0	0	0	0	0	1	0	0	.000	.333	.000	-10	0	0-0	.750	-1	73	0	/S	—	-0.1
NANCE, DOC	William Gideon "Kid" (b Willie Gideon Cooper); B8.2.1876 Ft.Worth TX; D5.28.1958 Fort Worth TX; BR/TR/5´7˝/165; d8.19																								
1897	Lou N	35	120	25	29	5	3	3	17	20	1	—	.242	.355	.408	105	1	3	.986	3	161	386	O35(0/7/28)	—	0.2
1898	Lou N	22	76	13	24	5	0	1	16	12	1	—	.316	.416	.421	142	5	2	.946	2	235	274	O22R	—	0.6
1901	Det A	132	461	72	129	24	5	3	66	51	3	—	.280	.355	.373	98	0	9	.932	2	118	155	O132(130/0/2)	—	-0.5
Total	3	189	657	110	182	34	8	7	99	83	5	—	.277	.362	.385	104	6	14	.943	8	139	211	O189(130/7/52)	—	0.3
NAPLES, AL	Aloysius Francis; B8.28.1926 St.George NY; BR/TR/5´9˝/168; d6.25; Col Georgetown																								
1949	StL A	2	7	0	1	1	0	0	0	0	0	1	.143	.143	.286	12	-1	0-0	.875	-1	116	0	S2	0	-0.1
NAPOLEON, DANNY	Daniel; B1.11.1942 Claysburg PA; D4.26.2003 Trenton NJ; BR/TR/5´11˝/190; d4.14; Col Rider																								
1965	NY N	68	97	5	14	1	1	0	7	8-1	2	23	.144	.222	.175	15	-11	0-0	.941	-1	142	0	O15(14/0/1),3b7	0	-1.4
1966	NY N	12	33	2	7	2	0	0	0	1-0	0	10	.212	.235	.273	42	-3	0-1	.929	-0	79	168	O10L	0	-0.4
Total	2	80	130	7	21	3	1	0	7	9-1	2	33	.162	.225	.200	22	-14	0-1	.938	-1	117	66	O25(24/0/1),3b7	0	-1.8
NAPOLI, MIKE	Michael Anthony; B10.31.1981 Hollywood FL; BR/TR/6´0˝/205; [AnaA00 17/500]; d5.4																								
2006	LA A	99	268	47	61	13	0	16	42	51-0	5	90	.228	.360	.455	113	7	2-3	.987	4	109	96	C94/D	0	1.4
NARAGON, HAL	Harold Richard; B10.1.1928 Zanesville OH; BL/TR/6´0˝/(175–185); d9.23; Mil 1952–53; C7																								
1951	Cle A	3	8	0	2	0	0	0	0	1	1	0	.250	.400	.250	83	0	0-0	.929	-0	*82*	*0*	C2	0	0.0
1954	†Cle A	46	101	10	24	2	2	0	12	9	0	12	.238	.300	.297	63	-5	0-0	1.000	0	*108*	*120*	C45	0	-0.4
1955	Cle A	57	127	12	41	9	2	1	14	15-0	0	8	.323	.394	.449	122	4	1-0	.991	-1	*112*	*86*	C52	0	0.6
1956	Cle A	53	122	11	35	3	1	3	18	13-2	1	9	.287	.355	.402	99	0	0-0	.988	-6	*78*	*49*	C48	0	-0.5
1957	Cle A	57	121	12	31	1	1	0	8	12-1	1	9	.256	.326	.281	69	-5	0-0	.990	-1	128	92	C39	0	-0.4
1958	Cle A	9	9	2	3	0	1	0	0	0-0	0	0	.333	.333	.556	144	0	0-0	ø	0	—	—	/H	0	0.0
1959	Cle A	14	36	6	10	4	1	0	5	3-0	1	2	.278	.341	.444	121	1	0-0	1.000	0	148	160	C10	0	0.2
	Was A	71	195	12	47	3	2	0	11	8-0	1	9	.241	.272	.277	52	-13	0-1	.993	-3	61	66	C54	0	-1.4
	Year	85	231	18	57	7	3	0	16	11-0	2	11	.247	.283	.303	63	-12	0-1	.994	-2	74	80	C64	0	-1.2
1960	Was A	33	92	7	19	2	0	0	5	8-2	1	4	.207	.275	.228	39	-8	0-0	.978	-4	86	71	C29	0	-1.0
1961	Min A	57	139	10	42	2	1	2	11	4-0	1	8	.302	.326	.374	82	-4	0-0	.994	-8	57	83	C36	0	-1.0
1962	Min A	24	35	1	8	1	0	0	3	3-1	0	1	.229	.282	.257	47	-3	0-0	1.000	0	66	0	C9	0	-0.2
Total	10	424	985	83	262	27	11	6	87	76-6	7	62	.266	.321	.334	77	-33	1-1	.991	-20	*89*	*80*	C324	0	-4.1
NARLESKI, BILL	William Edward "Cap"; B3.9.1900 Perth Amboy NJ; D6.20.1964 Laurel Springs NJ; BR/TR/5´9˝/160; d4.18; s–Ray																								
1929	Bos A	96	260	30	72	16	1	0	25	21	1	22	.277	.333	.346	77	-8	4-4	.957	-9	97	98	S51,2b29,3b7	—	-1.2
1930	Bos A	39	98	11	23	9	0	0	7	7	3	5	.235	.306	.327	63	-5	0-0	.915	-6	84	121	S19,3b14,2b5	—	-0.8
Total	2	135	358	41	95	25	1	0	32	28	4	27	.265	.326	.341	73	-13	4-4	.949	-15	95	102	S70,2b34,3b21	—	-2.0
NARRON, JERRY	Jerry Austin; B1.15.1956 Goldsboro NC; BL/TR/6´3˝/(190–205); [NYA74 6/132]; d4.13; M4/C12																								
1979	NY A	61	123	17	21	3	1	4	18	9-0	0	26	.171	.226	.309	44	-10	0-0	.973	-4	108	66	C56/D	0	-1.2
1980	Sea A	48	107	7	21	3	0	4	18	13-2	0	18	.196	.279	.336	68	-5	0-0	.992	-6	96	82	C39/D	0	-1.0
1981	Sea A	76	203	13	45	5	0	3	17	16-3	2	35	.222	.285	.291	63	-10	0-0	.996	-13	70	70	C65	0	-2.1
1983	Cal A	10	22	1	3	0	0	1	4	1-0	0	3	.136	.174	.273	21	-3	0-0	.895	-1	90	156	C6/D	0	-0.3
1984	Cal A	69	150	9	37	5	0	3	17	8-1	1	12	.247	.286	.340	73	-6	0-0	.994	-4	95	89	C46,1b7	0	-0.9
1985	Cal A	67	132	12	29	4	0	5	14	11-2	0	17	.220	.280	.364	75	-5	0-0	1.000	3	78	130	C45/1D	0	-0.1
1986	†Cal A	57	95	5	21	3	1	1	8	9-0	1	14	.221	.292	.305	64	-5	0-0	.988	-0	114	132	C51,D2	0	-0.4

YEAR	TM LG	G	AB	R	H	2B	3B	HR	RBI	BB-IB	HP	SO	AVG	OBP	SLG	AOPS	ABR	SB-CS	FA	FR	RNG	THR	GAMES AT POSITION	DL	BFW
1987	Sea A	4	8	0	0	0	0	0	0	0-0	0	2	.000	.000	.000	-95	-2	0-0	1.000	-1	44	168	C3	0	-0.3
Total	8	392	840	64	177	23	2	21	96	67-8	4	127	.211	.270	.318	62	-46	0-0	.989	-26	91	92	C311,D12,1b8	0	-6.3
NARRON, SAM	Samuel Woody; B8.25.1913 Middlesex NC; D12.31.1996 Raleigh NC; BR/TR/5´10˝/180; d9.15; C13; gs–Sam																								
1935	StL N	4	7	0	3	0	0	0	0	0	0	0	.429	.429	.429	126	0	0	1.000	0	*0*	*0*	/C	—	0.0
1942	StL N	10	10	0	4	0	0	0	1	0	0	0	.400	.400	.400	125	0	0	1.000	-0	*0*	*0*	C2	0	0.0
1943	†StL N	10	11	0	1	0	0	0	0	1	0	2	.091	.167	.091	-24	-2	0	1.000	1	*0*	*0*	C3	0	-0.1
Total	3	24	28	0	8	0	0	0	1	1	0	2	.286	.310	.286	67	-2	0	1.000	0	*0*	*0*	C6	0	-0.1
NASH, COTTON	Charles Francis; B7.24.1942 Jersey City NJ; BR/TR/6´6˝/(215–220); d9.1; Col Kentucky; [DL 1965 Phi N 160]																								
1967	Chi A	3	3	1	0	0	0	0	0	1-0	0	0	.000	.250	.000	-21	0	0-0	.833	-1	0	393	1b3	0	-0.1
1969	Min A	6	9	0	2	0	0	0	0	1-0	0	2	.222	.300	.222	47	-1	0-0	1.000	1	272	0	1b6/lf	0	0.0
1970	Min A	4	4	1	1	0	0	0	2	1-0	0	1	.250	.400	.250	82	0	0-1	1.000	-0	0	251	1b2	0	-0.1
Total	3	13	16	2	3	0	0	0	2	3-0	0	3	.188	.316	.188	44	-1	0-1	.965	0	155	141	1b11/lf	160	-0.2
NASH, KEN	Kenneth Leland (Played One Game in 1912 Under Name of Costello); B7.14.1888 Weymouth MA; D2.16.1977 Epsom NH; BB/TR/5´8˝/140; d7.4; Col Brown																								
1912	Cle A	11	23	2	4	0	0	0	0	3	0	—	.174	.269	.174	27	-2	0	.826	-2	86	61	S8	—	-0.4
1914	StL N	24	51	4	14	3	1	0	6	6	0	10	.275	.351	.373	116	1	0	.875	-5	73	0	3b10,2b6,S3	—	-0.4
Total	2	35	74	6	18	3	1	0	6	9	0	10	.243	.325	.311	87	-1	0	.760	-7	79	56	S11,3b10,2b6	—	-0.8
NASH, BILLY	William Mitchell; B6.24.1865 Richmond VA; D11.15.1929 E.Orange NJ; BR/TR/5´8.5˝/167; d8.5; M1/U1																								
1884	Ric AA	**45**	166	31	33	8	8	1	—	12	7	—	.199	.281	.361	109	2	—	.828	9	114	158	3b45	—	1.1
1885	Bos N	26	94	9	24	4	0	0	11	2	—	9	.255	.271	.298	87	-1	—	.864	-2	83	139	3b19,2b8	—	-0.3
1886	Bos N	109	417	61	117	11	8	1	45	24	—	28	.281	.320	.353	107	3	16	.863	-6	96	84	3b90,S17,O2(1/1/0)	—	-0.1
1887	Bos N	121	475	100	140	24	12	6	94	60	2	30	.295	.376	.434	123	16	43	.884	7	103	96	3b117,O5(4/0/1)	—	2.1
1888	Bos N	135	526	71	149	18	15	4	75	50	4	46	.283	.350	.397	134	21	20	**.913**	18	**119**	**141**	3b105,2b31	—	4.1
1889	Bos N	128	481	84	132	20	2	3	76	79	2	44	.274	.379	.343	96	0	26	.905	11	102	117	3b128/P	—	1.2
1890	Bos P	129	488	103	130	28	6	5	90	88	4	43	.266	.383	.379	97	0	26	.866	19	**111**	**171**	3b129/P	—	1.6
1891	Bos N	**140**	537	92	148	24	9	5	95	74	5	50	.276	.369	.382	106	4	28	.900	-12	83	111	3b140	—	-0.5
1892	†Bos N	135	526	94	137	25	5	4	95	59	3	42	.260	.338	.350	99	-1	31	**.898**	25	117	**125**	3b135/lf	—	2.4
1893	Bos N	128	485	115	141	27	6	10	123	85	2	29	.291	.399	.433	112	9	30	**.923**	2	100	107	3b128	—	1.1
1894	Bos N	132	512	132	148	23	6	8	87	91	3	23	.289	.399	.404	87	-9	20	**.933**	4	98	116	3b132	—	-0.2
1895	Bos N	**133**	513	97	149	24	6	10	110	74	3	19	.290	.383	.419	99	-1	18	.881	-11	87	145	3b133	—	-0.8
1896	Phi N	65	227	29	56	9	1	3	30	34	4	21	.247	.355	.335	83	-4	3	.911	8	112	117	3b65,M	—	0.4
1897	Phi N	104	337	45	87	20	2	0	39	60	2	—	.258	.373	.329	89	-1	4	.919	-9	94	101	3b79,S19,2b4	—	-0.7
1898	Phi N	20	70	9	17	2	1	0	9	11	0	—	.243	.346	.300	89	0	0	.958	-1	77	203	3b20	—	-0.1
Total	15	1550	5854	1072	1608	267	87	60	979	803	41	384	.275	.366	.381	103	38	265	.897	62	101	123	3b1465,2b43,S36,O8(6/1/1),P2	—	11.3
NATAL, BOB	Robert Marcel; B11.13.1965 Long Beach CA; BR/TR/5´11˝/190; [MonN87 13/330]; d7.18; C4; Col California–San Diego																								
1992	Mon N	5	6	0	0	0	0	0	0	1-0	0	1	.000	.143	.000	-57	-1	0-0	.909	-1	40	0	C4	0	-0.2
1993	Fla N	41	117	3	25	4	1	1	6	6-0	4	22	.214	.273	.291	49	-9	1-0	1.000	2	104	100	C38	21	-0.5
1994	Fla N	10	29	2	8	2	0	0	2	5-0	0	5	.276	.382	.345	88	0	1-0	.983	2	74	145	C8	0	0.2
1995	Fla N	16	43	2	10	2	1	2	6	1-0	0	9	.233	.244	.465	82	-2	0-0	.988	0	167	86	C13	0	0.0
1996	Fla N	44	90	4	12	1	1	0	2	15-5	0	31	.133	.257	.167	15	-11	0-1	.976	-3	88	111	C43	0	-1.2
1997	Fla N	4	4	2	2	1	0	1	3	2-0	0	0	.500	.571	1.500	468	2	0-0	1.000	1	0	0	C4	0	0.3
Total	6	120	289	13	57	10	3	4	19	30-5	4	68	.197	.279	.294	52	-21	2-1	.986	1	100	103	C110	21	-1.4
NATON, PETE	Peter Alphonsus; B9.9.1931 Flushing NY; BR/TR/6´1˝/200; d6.16; Mil 1953–54; Col Holy Cross																								
1953	Pit N	6	12	2	2	0	0	0	1	2	0	1	.167	.286	.167	22	-1	0-0	1.000	-1	*75*	*0*	C4	0	-0.2
NAVA, SANDY	Vincent Irwin (b Vincent Irwin); B4.12.1850 San Francisco CA; D6.15.1906 Baltimore MD; 5´6˝/155; d5.5																								
1882	Pro N	28	97	15	20	2	0	0	7	1	—	13	.206	.214	.227	42	-6	—	.867	-6	—	—	C27/rf	—	-0.9
1883	Pro N	29	100	18	24	4	2	0	16	3	—	17	.240	.262	.320	74	-3	—	.813	-3	—	—	C27,O2(1/0/1)	—	-0.4
1884	Pro N	34	116	10	11	0	0	0	6	11	—	35	.095	.173	.095	-13	-15	—	.887	-0	—	—	C27,S6/2	—	-1.1
1885	Bal AA	8	27	2	5	1	0	0	4	1	0	—	.185	.214	.222	39	-2	—	.825	-4	—	—	C8	—	-0.4
1886	Bal AA	2	5	0	1	0	0	0	0	0	0	—	.200	.200	.200	26	0	1	.500	-1	54	0	/SC	—	-0.2
Total	5	101	345	45	61	7	2	0	33	16	0	65	.177	.213	.209	33	-26	1	.857	-14	—	—	C90,S7,O3(1/0/2)/2	—	-3.0
NAVARRO, DIONER	Dioner Favian (Vivas); B2.9.1984 Caracas, Distrito Capital, Venezuela; BB/TR/5´10˝/(190–215); d9.7																								
2004	NY A	5	7	2	3	0	0	0	1	0-0	0	0	.429	.429	.429	125	0	0-0	1.000	-0	0	0	C4	0	0.0
2005	LA N	50	176	21	48	9	0	3	14	20-1	2	21	.273	.354	.375	91	-2	0-0	.995	4	79	86	C50	0	0.5
2006	LA N	25	75	5	21	2	0	2	8	11-4	0	18	.280	.372	.387	95	0	1-0	.993	-4	79	0	C24	41	-0.3
	TB A	56	193	23	47	7	0	4	20	20-2	1	33	.244	.316	.342	72	-8	1-1	.981	4	84	174	C54	0	-0.1
Total	3	136	451	51	119	18	0	9	43	51-7	3	72	.264	.342	.364	84	-10	2-1	.989	3	80	106	C132	41	0.1
NAVARRO, TITO	Norberto (Rodriguez); B9.12.1970 Rio Piedras, PR; BB/TR/5´10˝/165; d9.6																								
1993	NY N	12	17	1	1	0	0	0	1	0-0	0	4	.059	.059	.059	-69	-4	0-0	1.000	1	118	0	S2	0	-0.3
NAVARRO, OSWALDO	Oswaldo Ramses; B10.2.1984 Villa de Cura, Aragua, Venezuela; BR/TR/6´0˝/155; d9.9																								
2006	Sea A	4	3	0	2	0	0	0	0	0-0	0	1	.667	.667	.667	264	1	0-0	.750	0	150	448	S2/D	0	0.1
NAYLOR, EARL	Earl Eugene; B5.19.1919 Kansas City MO; D1.16.1990 Winter Haven FL; BR/TR/6´0˝/190; d4.15; Mil 1944–45; ▲																								
1942	Phi N	76	168	9	33	4	1	0	14	11	0	18	.196	.246	.232	42	-13	1	.984	-4	87	37	O34(2/22/11),P20	0	-1.6
1943	Phi N	33	120	12	21	2	0	3	14	12	1	16	.175	.256	.267	53	-8	1	.964	3	107	176	O33C	0	-0.6
1946	Bro N	3	2	1	0	0	0	0	0	0	0	1	.000	.000	.000	-99	-1	0	ø	0	—	—	/H	0	-0.1
Total	3	112	290	22	54	6	1	3	28	23	1	35	.186	.248	.245	46	-22	2	.971	-0	98	113	O67(2/55/11),P20	0	-2.3
NEAGLE, JACK	John Henry; B1.2.1858 Syracuse NY; D9.20.1904 Syracuse NY; BR/TR/5´6˝/155; d7.8; ▲																								
1879	Cin N	3	12	1	2	0	0	0	2	0	—	0	.167	.167	.167	11	-1	—	ø	-0	0	0	O2(0/1/1),P2	—	0.0
1883	Phi N	18	73	6	12	1	0	0	4	1	—	9	.164	.176	.178	9	-8	—	.840	-2	39	0	O12(11/1/0),P8	—	-0.6
	Bal AA	9	35	3	10	4	0	0	—	2	—	—	.286	.324	.400	128	1	—	.769	-1	97	0	P6,O5(1/0/4)	—	-0.1
	Pit AA	27	101	14	19	0	1	0	—	5	—	—	.188	.226	.208	43	-6	—	.839	-2	87	0	P16,O15(0/8/7)	—	-0.4
	Year	36	136	17	29	4	1	0	—	7	—	—	.213	.252	.257	66	-5	—	.818	-3	90	0	P22,O20(1/8/11)	—	-0.5
1884	Pit AA	43	148	13	22	6	0	0	—	6	1	—	.149	.187	.189	23	-12	—	.760	-5	87	62	P38,O6(2/2/2)	—	-0.4
Total	3	100	369	37	65	11	1	0	6	14	1	9	.176	.208	.211	36	-26	—	.785	-11	85	36	P70,O40(14/12/14)	—	-1.5
NEAL, CHARLIE	Charles Lenard; B1.30.1931 Longview TX; D11.18.1996 Dallas TX; BR/TR/5´10˝/(155–165); d4.17; Negro Lg 1955																								
1956	†Bro N	62	136	22	39	5	1	2	14	14-1	0	19	.287	.353	.382	91	-1	2-2	.972	2	105	120	2b51/S	0	0.3
1957	Bro N	128	448	62	121	13	7	12	62	53-0	8	83	.270	.356	.411	96	-1	11-4	.949	-2	100	102	S100,3b23,2b3	0	0.6
1958	LA N	140	473	87	120	9	6	22	65	61-4	5	91	.254	.341	.438	102	1	7-6	.976	11	99	**124**	2b132,S9	0	2.2
1959	†LA N★	151	616	103	177	30	**11**	19	83	43-2	4	86	.287	.337	.464	103	2	17-6	**.989**	20	98	112	2b151/S	0	3.5
1960	LA N★	139	477	60	122	23	2	8	40	48-2	1	75	.256	.321	.363	83	-10	5-5	.977	-20	82	103	2b136,S3	0	-2.2
1961	LA N	108	341	40	80	6	1	10	48	30-6	1	49	.235	.297	.346	65	-18	3-2	.976	-2	90	92	2b104	0	-1.1
1962	NY N	136	508	59	132	14	9	11	58	56-1	0	90	.260	.330	.388	91	-7	2-8	.970	-7	104	91	2b85,S39,3b12	0	-0.6
1963	NY N	72	253	26	57	12	1	3	18	27-3	1	49	.225	.302	.316	77	-7	1-2	.961	6	109	96	3b66,S8	0	-0.1
	Cin N	34	64	2	10	1	0	0	3	5-0	0	15	.156	.217	.172	13	-7	0-1	.927	-4	55	0	3b19/2S	0	-1.3
	Year	106	317	28	67	13	1	3	21	32-3	1	64	.211	.286	.287	64	-14	1-3	.955	2	98	77	3b85,S9/2	0	-1.4
Total	8	970	3316	461	858	113	38	87	391	337-19	20	557	.259	.329	.394	90	-48	48-36	.978	4	95	107	2b663,S162,3b120	0	1.3
NEAL, OFFA	Theophilus Fountain; B6.5.1876 Benton IL; D4.11.1950 Mt.Vernon IL; BL/TR/6´0˝/185; d9.30																								
1905	NY N	4	13	0	0	0	0	0	0	0	0	—	.000	.000	.000	-98	-3	0	1.000	0	63	791	3b3/2	—	-0.3
NEALE, GREASY	Alfred Earle; B11.5.1891 Parkersburg WV; D11.2.1973 Lake Worth FL; BL/TR (BB 1916–18p)/6´0˝/170; d4.12; C1; Col West Virginia Wesleyan																								
1916	Cin N	138	530	53	139	13	5	0	20	19	6	79	.262	.295	.306	87	-10	17	.973	7	104	127	O133(79/55/2)	—	-1.2
1917	Cin N	121	385	40	113	14	9	3	33	24	5	36	.294	.343	.400	133	14	25	.979	2	103	100	O119(79/27/13)	—	1.2
1918	Cin N	107	371	57	100	11	11	1	32	24	6	38	.270	.324	.367	112	4	23	**.981**	7	117	90	O102(78/12/12)	—	0.7

THE BATTER REGISTER

YEAR	TM LG	G	AB	R	H	2B	3B	HR	RBI	BB-IB	HP	SO	AVG	OBP	SLG	AOPS	ABR	SB-CS	FA	FR	RNG	THR	GAMES AT POSITION	DL	BFW
1919	†Cin N	139	500	57	121	10	12	1	54	47	7	51	.242	.316	.316	93	-4	28	.959	-1	104	77	O138(24/5/109)	—	-1.5
1920	Cin N	150	530	55	135	10	7	3	46	45	8	48	.255	.322	.317	85	-9	29-12	.987	12	119	97	O150(0/3/148)	—	-0.4
1921	Phi N	22	57	7	12	1	0	0	1	14	0	9	.211	.366	.228	56	-3	3-4	.842	-3	68	0	O16R	—	-0.8
	Cin N	63	241	39	58	10	5	0	12	22	1	16	.241	.307	.324	70	-10	9-6	.964	-1	101	81	O60(1/8/53)	—	-1.6
	Year	85	298	46	70	11	5	0	13	36	1	25	.235	.319	.305	67	-13	12-10	.950	-4	96	68	O76(1/8/69)	—	-2.4
1922	Cin N	25	43	11	10	2	1	0	2	6	2	3	.233	.353	.326	77	-1	5-2	.864	-1	87	76	O16(5/0/11)	—	-0.3
1924	Cin N	3	4	0	0	0	0	0	0	0	0	1	.000	.000	.000	-99	-1	0-0	1.000	0	116	0	O2L	—	-0.1
Total	8	768	2661	319	688	71	50	8	200	201	35	281	.259	.319	.332	94	-20	139-24	.972	20	108	95	O736(268/110/364)	—	-4.0
Nealon, Jim	James Joseph; B12.15.1884 Sacramento CA; D4.2.1910 San Francisco CA; BR/TR/6´1.5˝/?; d4.12																								
1906	Pit N	**154**	556	82	142	21	12	3	**83**	53	6	—	.255	.327	.353	107	4	15	.987	1	102	**132**	1b154	—	0.3
1907	Pit N	105	381	29	98	10	8	0	47	23	1	—	.257	.301	.325	95	-4	11	.978	0	106	69	1b104	—	-0.6
Total	2	259	937	111	240	31	20	3	130	76	7	—	.256	.317	.342	102	0	26	.983	1	104	107	1b258	—	-0.3
Needham, Tom	Thomas Joseph "Deerfoot"; B4.17.1879 Steubenville OH; D12.14.1926 Steubenville OH; BR/TR/5´10˝/180; d5.12																								
1904	Bos N	84	269	18	70	12	3	4	19	11	1	—	.260	.292	.372	108	1	3	.945	-3	*88*	***124***	C77/cf	—	0.6
1905	Bos N	83	271	21	59	6	1	2	17	24	5	—	.218	.293	.269	70	-10	3	.949	-14	*73*	***121***	C77,O3C,1b2	—	-1.7
1906	Bos N	83	285	11	54	8	2	1	12	13	2	—	.189	.230	.242	49	-18	3	.962	-9	*81*	*115*	C76,2b5,1b2/3cf	—	-2.3
1907	Bos N	86	260	19	51	6	2	1	19	18	6	—	.196	.264	.246	60	-12	4	.967	-16	*73*	*107*	C78/1	—	-2.4
1908	NY N	54	91	8	19	3	0	0	11	12	6	—	.209	.339	.242	82	-1	0	.975	4	*147*	*84*	C47	—	0.7
1909	Chi N	13	28	3	4	0	0	0	0	0	0	—	.143	.143	.143	-11	-4	0	.980	1	*137*	*59*	C7	—	-0.3
1910	†Chi N	31	76	9	14	3	1	0	10	10	1	10	.184	.287	.250	57	-4	1	.982	4	*146*	*82*	C27/1	—	0.2
1911	Chi N	27	62	4	12	2	0	0	5	9	2	14	.194	.315	.226	52	-4	2	.984	6	*170*	*113*	C23	—	0.4
1912	Chi N	33	90	12	16	5	0	0	10	7	3	13	.178	.260	.233	36	-8	3	.994	2	*125*	*104*	C32	—	-0.4
1913	Chi N	20	42	5	10	4	1	0	11	4	0	8	.238	.304	.381	95	0	0	.962	3	123	158	C14/1	—	0.3
1914	Chi N	9	17	3	2	1	0	0	3	1	0	4	.118	.167	.176	2	-2	1	.943	0	*109*	*160*	C7	—	-0.1
Total	11	523	1491	113	311	50	10	8	117	109	26	49	.209	.274	.272	66	-62	20	.963	-24	*97*	*112*	C465,1b7,2b5,O5C/3	—	-5.0
Neel, Troy	Troy Lee; B9.14.1965 Freeport TX; BL/TR/6´4˝/(210–215); [CleA86*9/208]; d5.30; Col Texas A&M																								
1992	Oak A	24	53	8	14	3	0	3	9	5-0	1	15	.264	.339	.491	136	2	0-1	.846	-0	97	311	O9L,1b2,D9	0	0.2
1993	Oak A	123	427	59	124	21	0	19	63	49-5	4	101	.290	.367	.473	131	19	3-5	.981	-1	100	92	D85,1b34	0	1.0
1994	Oak A	83	278	43	74	13	0	15	48	38-5	2	61	.266	.357	.475	122	9	2-3	.994	-1	85	105	1b45,D35	21	0.2
Total	3	230	758	110	212	37	0	37	120	92-10	7	177	.280	.362	.475	128	30	5-9	.986	-2	90	98	D129,1b81,O9L	21	1.4
Neeman, Cal	Calvin Amandus; B2.18.1929 Valmeyer IL; BR/TR/6´1˝/(190–192); d4.16; Col Illinois Wesleyan																								
1957	Chi N	122	415	37	107	17	1	10	39	22-5	3	87	.258	.298	.376	81	-12	0-0	.990	5	82	**149**	C118	0	-0.1
1958	Chi N	76	201	30	52	7	0	12	29	21-2	3	41	.259	.336	.473	113	4	0-0	.992	-1	70	122	C71	0	0.6
1959	Chi N	44	105	7	17	2	0	3	9	11-2	0	23	.162	.241	.267	36	-10	0-0	.994	-5	56	29	C38	0	-1.4
1960	Chi N	9	13	0	2	1	0	0	0	0-0	0	5	.154	.154	.231	4	-2	0-0	1.000	2	35	169	C9	0	0.0
	Phi N	59	160	13	29	6	2	4	13	16-2	2	42	.181	.264	.319	59	-9	0-0	.979	0	73	152	C52	0	-0.7
	Year	68	173	13	31	7	2	4	13	16-2	2	47	.179	.257	.312	55	-11	0-0	.982	2	70	153	C61	0	-0.7
1961	Phi N	19	31	0	7	1	0	0	2	4-1	0	8	.226	.306	.258	55	-2	1-0	.986	-1	52	114	C19	0	-0.2
1962	Pit N	24	50	5	9	1	1	1	5	3-0	0	10	.180	.226	.300	40	-5	0-0	.983	4	119	95	C24	0	0.0
1963	Cle A	9	9	0	0	0	0	0	0	1-0	0	5	.000	.100	.000	-70	-2	0-0	1.000	1	143	297	C9	0	-0.1
	Was A	14	18	1	1	0	0	0	0	1-0	0	0	.056	.105	.056	-54	-4	0-0	.970	1	167	121	C12	0	-0.2
	Year	23	27	1	1	0	0	0	0	2-0	0	5	.037	.103	.037	-59	-6	0-0	.985	2	156	202	C21	0	-0.3
Total	7	376	1002	93	224	35	4	30	97	79-12	8	221	.224	.284	.356	72	-42	1-0	.988	6	78	129	C352	0	-2.1
Neff, Doug	Douglas Williams; B10.8.1891 Harrisonburg VA; D5.23.1932 Cape Charles VA; BR/TR/5´9˝/141; d6.26; Col Virginia																								
1914	Was A	3	2	0	0	0	0	0	0	0	0	0	.000	.000	.000	-96	0	0	.889	1	146	0	S3	—	0.0
1915	Was A	30	60	1	10	1	0	0	4	4	0	6	.167	.219	.183	20	-6	1-2	.867	-4	91	81	3b12,2b10,S7	—	-1.1
Total	2	33	62	1	10	1	0	0	4	4	0	6	.161	.212	.177	16	-6	1-2	.867	-4	91	81	3b12,2b10,S10	—	-1.1
Neighbors, Cy	Cecil Fleming; B9.23.1880 Fayetteville MO; D5.20.1964 Tacoma WA; BR/5´10˝/178; d4.29																								
1908	Pit N	1	0	0	0	0	0	0	0	0	0	—	ø	ø	ø	ø	0	0	ø	-0	0	0	/lf	—	0.0
Neighbors, Bob	Robert Otis; B11.9.1917 Talihina OK; D8.8.1952 , North Korea (MIA); BR/TR/5´11˝/165; d9.16																								
1939	StL A	7	11	3	2	0	0	1	1	0	0	1	.182	.182	.455	56	-1	0-0	.917	-0	90	64	S5	—	-0.1
Neill, Mike	Michael Robert; B4.27.1970 Martinsville VA; BL/TL/6´2˝/190; [OakA91 2/60]; d7.27; Col Villanova																								
1998	Oak A	6	15	2	4	1	0	0	0	2-0	0	4	.267	.353	.333	81	0	0-0	1.000	1	157	0	O6(4/2/0)	24	0.1
Neill, Tommy	Thomas White; B11.7.1919 Hartselle AL; D9.22.1980 Houston TX; BL/TR/6´2˝/200; d9.10																								
1946	Bos N	13	45	8	12	2	0	0	7	2	0	1	.267	.298	.311	72	-2	0	1.000	-0	91	115	O13L	0	-0.3
1947	Bos N	7	10	1	2	0	1	0	0	1	1	2	.200	.333	.400	96	0	0	1.000	-0	73	0	O2(1/0/1)	0	0.0
Total	2	20	55	9	14	2	1	0	7	3	1	3	.255	.305	.327	77	-2	0	1.000	-0	89	102	O15(14/0/1)	0	-0.3
Neis, Bernie	Bernard Edmund; B9.26.1895 Bloomington IL; D11.29.1972 Inverness FL; BB/TR (BR 1920–21)/5´7˝/160; d4.14																								
1920	†Bro N	95	249	38	63	11	2	2	22	26	2	35	.253	.329	.337	89	-3	9-9	.957	1	100	118	O83(11/7/65)	—	-0.7
1921	Bro N	102	230	34	59	5	4	4	34	25	1	41	.257	.332	.365	81	-6	9-7	.946	1	93	151	O77(11/24/45)/2	—	-1.0
1922	Bro N	61	70	15	16	4	1	1	9	13	0	8	.229	.349	.357	83	-1	3-2	.897	1	106	163	O27(7/3/17)	—	-0.2
1923	Bro N	126	445	78	122	17	4	5	37	36	1	38	.274	.330	.364	85	-10	8-8	.941	2	96	146	O111(13/87/11)	—	-1.4
1924	Bro N	80	211	43	64	8	3	4	26	27	1	17	.303	.385	.427	121	7	4-2	.937	-2	97	87	O62(19/22/22)	—	0.1
1925	Bos N	106	355	47	101	20	2	5	45	38	0	19	.285	.354	.394	100	1	8-10	.970	7	117	93	O87(9/76/2)	—	0.2
1926	Bos N	30	93	16	20	5	2	0	8	8	0	10	.215	.277	.312	64	-5	4	.925	0	110	87	O23(15/8/0)	—	-0.6
1927	Cle A	32	96	17	29	9	0	4	18	18	0	9	.302	.412	.521	140	6	0-1	.978	2	106	159	O29(5/24/0)	—	0.7
	Chi A	45	76	9	22	5	0	0	11	10	0	9	.289	.372	.355	92	0	1-0	.927	1	107	129	O21(6/9/7)	—	0.0
	Year	77	172	26	51	14	0	4	29	28	0	18	.297	.395	.448	120	6	1-1	.962	3	106	149	O50(11/33/7)	—	0.7
Total	8	677	1825	297	496	84	18	25	210	201	5	186	.272	.346	.379	94	-11	46-39	.950	13	102	124	O520(96/260/169)/2	—	-2.9
Neitzke, Ernie	Ernest Fredrich; B11.13.1894 Toledo OH; D4.27.1977 Sylvania OH; BR/TR/5´10˝/180; d6.2																								
1921	Bos A	11	25	3	6	0	0	0	2	4	0	4	.240	.345	.240	53	-2	0-0	.875	-0	89	109	O8(4/1/3),P2	—	-0.2
Nelson, Bry	Bryant Lawrence; B1.27.1974 Crossett AR; BB/TR/5´10˝/205; [HouN93 44/1230]; d5.14; Col Texarkana (TX) JC																								
2002	Bos A	25	34	6	9	3	0	0	2	4-0	0	1	.265	.342	.353	84	-1	1-1	.964	0	86	53	2b11,O11(7/2/2)/D	0	0.0
Nelson, Dave	David Earl; B6.20.1944 Fort Sill OK; BR/TR (BB 1968p)/5´10˝/(160–168); d4.11; C14; Col Cal St.–Los Angeles; OF(6/10/1)																								
1968	Cle A	88	189	26	44	4	5	0	19	17-0	1	35	.233	.295	.307	85	-4	23-7	.987	-5	81	95	2b59,S14	0	-0.1
1969	Cle A	52	123	11	25	0	0	0	6	9-1	1	26	.203	.259	.203	31	-11	4-3	.966	7	111	129	2b33,O2(1/0/1)	50	-0.2
1970	Was A	47	107	5	17	1	0	0	4	7-0	0	24	.159	.207	.168	6	-14	2-1	.986	4	113	117	2b33	0	-0.8
1971	Was A	85	329	47	92	11	3	5	33	23-2	1	29	.280	.328	.377	104	1	17-8	.938	-12	89	86	3b84/2	0	-1.2
1972	Tex A	145	499	68	113	16	3	2	28	67-3	5	81	.226	.324	.283	84	-7	51-17	.945	-5	95	99	3b119,O15(5/10/0)	0	-1.0
1973	Tex A★	142	576	71	165	24	4	7	48	34-3	0	78	.286	.325	.378	102	0	43-16	.984	-5	94	91	2b140	0	0.7
1974	Tex A	121	474	71	112	13	1	3	42	34-0	4	72	.236	.291	.287	69	-19	25-13	.969	2	97	86	2b120/D	29	-0.9
1975	Tex A	28	80	9	17	1	0	2	10	8-1	1	10	.213	.289	.300	68	-3	6-0	.959	0	97	113	2b23/D	110	0.0
1976	†KC A	78	153	24	36	4	2	1	17	14-0	0	26	.235	.298	.307	77	-5	15-5	.975	-2	98	74	2b46,D22,1b3	20	-0.4
1977	KC A	27	48	8	9	3	1	0	4	7-0	0	11	.188	.291	.292	59	-3	1-3	.926	-2	81	82	2b11,D7	63	-0.5
Total	10	813	2578	340	630	77	19	20	211	220-10	13	392	.244	.305	.312	80	-65	187-73	.976	-18	96	94	2b466,3b203,D31,O17C,S14,1b3	272	-4.4
Nelson, Rocky	Glenn Richard; B11.18.1924 Portsmouth OH; D10.31.2006 Portsmouth OH; BL/TL/5´11˝/(170–191); d4.27																								
1949	StL N	82	244	28	54	8	4	4	32	11	1	12	.221	.258	.336	55	-17	1	1.000	-3	70	101	1b70	0	-2.2
1950	StL N	76	235	27	58	10	4	1	20	26	1	9	.247	.324	.336	71	-10	4	.992	4	123	112	1b70	0	-0.8
1951	StL N	9	18	3	4	1	0	0	1	1	0	0	.222	.263	.278	45	-1	0-0	1.000	-1	47	167	1b4/lf	0	-0.2
	Pit N	71	195	29	52	7	4	1	14	10	0	7	.267	.302	.359	75	-8	1-1	.990	1	115	105	1b32,O12L	0	-0.9
	Year	80	213	32	56	8	4	1	15	11	0	7	.263	.299	.352	73	-9	1-1	.991	1	109	111	1b36,O13L	0	-1.1
	Chi A	6	5	0	0	0	0	0	0	1	0	0	.000	.167	.000	-53	-1	0-0	ø	0	—	—	/H	0	-0.1

YEAR	TM LG	G	AB	R	H	2B	3B	HR	RBI	BB-IB	HP	SO	AVG	OBP	SLG	AOPS	ABR	SB-CS	FA	FR	RNG	THR	GAMES AT POSITION	DL	BFW
1952	†Bro N	37	39	6	10	1	0	0	3	7	0	4	.256	.370	.282	82	-1	0-0	1.000	-1	0	89	1b5	0	-0.1
1954	Cle A	4	4	0	0	0	0	0	0	0	0	1	.000	.000	.000	-98	-1	0-0	1.000	-0	0	230	1b2	0	-0.1
1956	Bro N	31	96	7	20	2	0	4	15	4-1	0	10	.208	.235	.354	53	-7	0-0	.991	1	118	124	1b25	0	-0.7
	StL N	38	56	6	13	5	0	3	8	6-1	0	6	.232	.306	.482	108	1	0-0	1.000	1	165	127	1b14,O8L	0	0.1
	Year	69	152	13	33	7	0	7	23	10-2	0	16	.217	.262	.401	73	-6	0-0	.993	3	128	125	1b39,O8L	0	-0.6
1959	Pit N	98	175	31	51	11	0	6	32	23-4	3	19	.291	.379	.457	124	7	0-0	.994	-4	64	142	1b56,O2(1/0/1)	0	0.0
1960	†Pit N	93	200	34	60	11	1	7	35	24-5	5	15	.300	.382	.470	133	10	1-2	.996	0	98	120	1b73	0	0.7
1961	Pit N	75	127	15	25	5	1	5	13	17-2	2	11	.197	.301	.370	77	-4	0-0	.996	-1	84	116	1b35	0	-0.7
Total	9	620	1394	186	347	61	14	31	173	130-13	12	94	.249	.317	.379	84	-32	7-3	.995	-2	95	117	1b386,O23(22/0/1)	0	-5.0

NELSON, JAMIE James Victor; B9.5.1959 Clinton OK; BR/TR/5´11˝/180; [NYN78*8/166]; d7.21; Col Orange Coast (CA) JC

YEAR	TM LG	G	AB	R	H	2B	3B	HR	RBI	BB-IB	HP	SO	AVG	OBP	SLG	AOPS	ABR	SB-CS	FA	FR	RNG	THR	GAMES AT POSITION	DL	BFW
1983	Sea A	40	96	9	21	3	0	1	5	13-1	0	12	.219	.309	.281	62	-5	4-2	.978	1	71	156	C39	0	-0.2

NELSON, JOHN John Clark; B3.3.1979 Denton TX; BR/TR/6´1˝/190; [StLN01 8/254]; d9.7; Col Kansas

YEAR	TM LG	G	AB	R	H	2B	3B	HR	RBI	BB-IB	HP	SO	AVG	OBP	SLG	AOPS	ABR	SB-CS	FA	FR	RNG	THR	GAMES AT POSITION	DL	BFW
2006	StL N	8	5	2	0	0	0	0	0	0-0	0	4	.000	.000	.000	-99	-2	0-0	1.000	0	0	0	/1S	0	-0.1

NELSON, CANDY John W; B3.14.1849 Brooklyn NY; D9.4.1910 Brooklyn NY; BL/TR/5´6˝/145; d6.11

YEAR	TM LG	G	AB	R	H	2B	3B	HR	RBI	BB-IB	HP	SO	AVG	OBP	SLG	AOPS	ABR	SB-CS	FA	FR	RNG	THR	GAMES AT POSITION	DL	BFW
1872	Tro NA	4	20	2	7	0	0	0	4	0	—	2	.350	.350	.350	114	0	0-0	1.000	-1	0	0	O3C/S	—	0.0
	Eck NA	18	76	12	19	5	1	0	9	2	—	3	.250	.269	.342	102	2	1-0	.837	-0	120	93	2b8,O8C,3b4	—	0.1
	Year	22	96	14	26	5	1	0	13	2	—	5	.271	.286	.344	105	2	1-0	.813	-1	0	0	O11C,2b8,3b4/S	—	0.1
1873	Mut NA	36	168	28	55	4	1	0	22	1	—	2	.327	.331	.363	106	1	2-0	.867	-9	74	41	2b27,3b6,O6R/C1	—	-0.7
1874	Mut NA	**65**	297	55	73	7	5	0	31	**9**	—	5	.246	.268	.303	80	-7	6-0	.824	-18	77	57	2b51,S14/cf	—	-2.1
1875	Mut NA	70	276	28	55	7	1	0	23	9	—	0	.199	.225	.232	56	-12	4-2	.855	-1	97	93	2b49,3b23,S2/lf	—	-1.4
1878	Ind N	19	84	12	11	1	0	0	5	5	—	11	.131	.180	.143	8	-7	—	.841	-7	81	22	S19	—	-1.3
1879	Tro N	28	106	17	28	7	1	0	10	8	—	4	.264	.316	.349	127	4	—	.834	2	105	123	S24,O4L	—	0.6
1881	Wor N	24	103	13	29	1	0	1	15	5	—	6	.282	.315	.320	95	-1	—	.898	2	115	70	S24	—	0.2
1883	NY AA	**97**	417	75	127	19	6	0	—	31	—	—	.305	.353	.379	130	14	—	.875	-7	85	105	S97	—	0.9
1884	†NY AA	111	432	114	110	15	3	1	—	**74**	9	—	.255	.375	.310	129	21	—	.879	-16	84	71	S110/2	—	0.8
1885	NY AA	107	420	98	107	12	4	1	30	**61**	3	—	.255	.353	.310	115	13	—	.892	17	106	103	S107/3	—	2.9
1886	NY AA	109	413	89	93	7	2	0	23	64	2	—	.225	.332	.252	91	2	14	.855	-5	95	83	S73,O36(0/28/8)	—	-0.1
1887	NY AA	68	257	61	63	5	1	0	24	48	8	—	.245	.380	.272	88	1	29	.895	10	165	365	O37(0/1/36),S32/2	—	0.9
	NY N	1	2	0	0	0	0	0	0	0	0	1	.000	.000	.000	-99	-1	0	ø	-0	0	0	/3	—	-0.1
1890	Bro AA	60	223	44	56	3	2	0	12	35	5	—	.251	.365	.283	94	1	12	.866	-6	113	105	S57,O4R	—	-0.3
Total	4NA	193	837	125	209	23	8	0	89	21	—	12	.250	.268	.296	80	-16	13-2	.845	-28	86	69	2b135,3b33,O19(1/12/6),S17/1C	—	-4.1
Total	9	624	2457	523	624	70	19	3	119	331	27	22	.254	.349	.302	108	47	55	.875	-9	96	93	S543,O81(4/29/48),3b2,2b2	—	4.5

NELSON, RAY Raymond "Kell" (b Raymond Nelson Kellogg); B8.4.1875 Holyoke MA; D1.8.1961 Mt.Vernon NY; BR/TR/5´9˝/150; d5.6; Col Amherst

YEAR	TM LG	G	AB	R	H	2B	3B	HR	RBI	BB-IB	HP	SO	AVG	OBP	SLG	AOPS	ABR	SB-CS	FA	FR	RNG	THR	GAMES AT POSITION	DL	BFW
1901	NY N	39	130	12	26	2	0	0	7	10	1	—	.200	.262	.215	41	-10	3	.885	-4	113	70	2b39	—	-1.3

NELSON, RICKY Ricky Lee; B5.8.1959 Eloy AZ; BL/TR/6´0˝/200; [SeaA81 4/78]; d5.17; Col Arizona St.

YEAR	TM LG	G	AB	R	H	2B	3B	HR	RBI	BB-IB	HP	SO	AVG	OBP	SLG	AOPS	ABR	SB-CS	FA	FR	RNG	THR	GAMES AT POSITION	DL	BFW
1983	Sea A	98	291	32	74	13	3	5	36	17-3	0	50	.254	.294	.371	79	-9	7-4	.971	-3	81	179	O91(46/1/50)/D	0	-1.5
1984	Sea A	9	15	2	3	0	0	1	2	2-0	0	4	.200	.294	.400	90	0	0-0	1.000	0	147	0	O2R,D3	0	0.0
1985	Sea A	6	2	2	0	0	0	0	0	0-0	0	1	.000	.000	.000	-99	-1	0-0	1.000	-0	87	0	O3R	0	-0.1
1986	Sea A	10	12	2	2	0	0	0	1	0-0	0	4	.167	.167	.167	-9	-2	1-0	.667	-0	164	0	/cfD	0	-0.2
Total	4	123	320	38	79	13	3	6	39	19-3	0	59	.247	.288	.363	75	-12	8-4	.965	-3	82	175	O97(46/2/55),D9	0	-1.8

NELSON, ROB Robert Augustus; B5.17.1964 Pasadena CA; BL/TL/6´4˝/215; [OakA83 S1/7]; d9.9; Col Mt. San Antonio (CA) JC

YEAR	TM LG	G	AB	R	H	2B	3B	HR	RBI	BB-IB	HP	SO	AVG	OBP	SLG	AOPS	ABR	SB-CS	FA	FR	RNG	THR	GAMES AT POSITION	DL	BFW
1986	Oak A	5	9	1	2	1	0	0	0	1-0	0	4	.222	.300	.333	78	0	0-0	.800	-0	135	129	1b2/D	0	0.0
1987	Oak A	7	24	1	4	1	0	0	0	0-0	0	12	.167	.167	.208	-2	-4	0-0	.968	2	221	113	1b7	0	-0.2
	SD N	10	11	0	1	0	0	0	1	1-0	0	8	.091	.167	.091	-31	-2	0-0	1.000	-0	0	122	1b2	0	-0.3
1988	SD N	7	21	4	4	0	0	1	3	2-0	0	9	.190	.261	.333	71	-1	0-0	.981	0	129	141	1b5	0	-0.1
1989	SD N	42	82	6	16	0	1	3	7	20-1	0	29	.195	.353	.329	96	0	1-3	.991	3	151	110	1b31	0	0.1
1990	SD N	5	5	0	0	0	0	0	0	0-0	0	4	.000	.000	.000	-99	-1	0-0	ø	0	—	—	/H	0	-0.2
Total	5	76	152	12	27	2	1	4	11	24-1	0	66	.178	.290	.283	62	-8	1-3	.983	5	156	116	1b47/D	0	-0.7

NELSON, TEX Robert Sydney "Babe"; B8.7.1936 Dallas TX; BL/TL/6´3˝/(205–220); d6.22

YEAR	TM LG	G	AB	R	H	2B	3B	HR	RBI	BB-IB	HP	SO	AVG	OBP	SLG	AOPS	ABR	SB-CS	FA	FR	RNG	THR	GAMES AT POSITION	DL	BFW
1955	Bal A	25	31	4	6	0	0	0	1	7-0	0	13	.194	.342	.194	50	-2	0-0	.889	1	70	582	O6L,1b2	0	-0.2
1956	Bal A	39	68	5	14	2	0	0	5	7-0	0	22	.206	.276	.235	40	-6	0-0	.939	1	98	277	O24(9/0/16)	0	-0.5
1957	Bal A	15	23	2	5	0	2	0	5	1-0	1	5	.217	.280	.391	87	-1	0-0	1.000	-1	75	0	O8(2/0/6)	0	-0.2
Total	3	79	122	11	25	2	2	0	11	15-0	1	40	.205	.295	.254	52	-9	0-0	.938	1	89	276	O38(17/0/22),1b2	0	-0.9

NELSON, TOMMY Thomas Cousineau; B5.1.1917 Chicago IL; D9.24.1973 San Diego CA; BR/TR/5´11.5˝/180; d4.17

YEAR	TM LG	G	AB	R	H	2B	3B	HR	RBI	BB-IB	HP	SO	AVG	OBP	SLG	AOPS	ABR	SB-CS	FA	FR	RNG	THR	GAMES AT POSITION	DL	BFW
1945	Bos N	40	121	6	20	2	0	0	6	4	0	13	.165	.192	.182	4	-16	1	.910	-4	106	185	3b20,2b12	0	-2.0

NEN, DICK Richard Le Roy; B9.24.1939 South Gate CA; BL/TL/6´2˝/205; d9.18; s–Robb; Col Cal St.–Long Beach

YEAR	TM LG	G	AB	R	H	2B	3B	HR	RBI	BB-IB	HP	SO	AVG	OBP	SLG	AOPS	ABR	SB-CS	FA	FR	RNG	THR	GAMES AT POSITION	DL	BFW
1963	LA N	7	8	2	1	0	0	1	1	3-1	0	3	.125	.364	.500	157	1	0-0	1.000	-0	0	0	1b5	0	0.0
1965	Was A	69	246	18	64	7	1	6	31	19-1	1	47	.260	.312	.370	96	-2	1-2	.993	8	151	89	1b65	0	0.2
1966	Was A	94	235	20	50	8	0	6	30	28-2	0	46	.213	.294	.323	79	-6	0-2	.990	-1	95	93	1b76	0	-1.3
1967	Was A	110	238	21	52	7	1	6	29	21-4	0	39	.218	.280	.332	84	-5	0-1	.995	1	109	117	1b65/lf	0	-0.9
1968	Chi N	81	94	8	17	1	1	2	16	6-2	0	17	.181	.225	.277	48	-6	0-0	.987	-2	78	75	1b52	0	-1.0
1970	Was A	6	5	1	1	0	0	0	0	0-0	0	0	.200	.200	.200	11	-1	0-0	1.000	0	653	0	/1	0	0.0
Total	6	367	826	70	185	23	3	21	107	77-10	1	152	.224	.288	.335	82	-19	1-5	.992	7	114	96	1b264/lf	0	-3.0

NESS, JACK John Charles; B11.11.1884 Chicago IL; D12.4.1957 DeLand FL; BR/TR/6´2˝/165; d5.9

YEAR	TM LG	G	AB	R	H	2B	3B	HR	RBI	BB-IB	HP	SO	AVG	OBP	SLG	AOPS	ABR	SB-CS	FA	FR	RNG	THR	GAMES AT POSITION	DL	BFW
1911	Det A	12	39	6	6	0	0	0	2	2	0	—	.154	.195	.154	-2	-5	0	.977	1	122	72	1b12	—	-0.5
1916	Chi A	75	258	32	69	7	5	1	34	9	7	32	.267	.310	.345	96	-3	4	.979	-5	77	133	1b69	—	-1.0
Total	2	87	297	38	75	7	5	1	36	11	7	32	.253	.295	.320	82	-8	4	.978	-4	84	124	1b81	—	-1.5

NETTLES, GRAIG Graig; B8.20.1944 San Diego CA; BL/TR/6´0˝/(180–189); [MinA65 4/74]; d9.6; C2; b–Jim; Col San Diego St.; OF(58/2/13)

YEAR	TM LG	G	AB	R	H	2B	3B	HR	RBI	BB-IB	HP	SO	AVG	OBP	SLG	AOPS	ABR	SB-CS	FA	FR	RNG	THR	GAMES AT POSITION	DL	BFW
1967	Min A	3	3	0	1	1	0	0	0	0-0	0	0	.333	.333	.667	175	0	0-0	ø	0	—	—	/H	0	0.0
1968	Min A	22	76	13	17	2	1	5	8	7-1	1	20	.224	.298	.474	124	2	0-0	.968	1	112	245	O16(2/1/13),3b5,1b3	0	0.1
1969	†Min A	96	225	27	50	9	2	7	26	32-1	1	47	.222	.319	.373	91	-2	1-2	.987	1	99	62	O54(53/1/0),3b21	0	-0.4
1970	Cle A	157	549	81	129	13	1	26	62	81-3	3	77	.235	.336	.404	99	0	3-1	**.967**	26	112	126	3b154,O3L	0	2.6
1971	Cle A	158	598	78	156	18	1	28	86	82-6	3	56	.261	.350	.435	111	10	7-4	.973	**46**	**125**	**148**	3b158	0	**5.9**
1972	Cle A	150	557	65	141	28	0	17	70	57-5	4	50	.253	.325	.395	110	8	2-3	.956	8	**111**	90	3b150	0	1.6
1973	NY A	160	552	65	129	18	0	22	81	78-3	7	76	.234	.334	.386	105	5	0-0	.953	33	**128**	138	3b157,D2	0	3.7
1974	NY A	155	566	74	139	21	1	22	75	59-8	3	75	.246	.316	.403	108	5	1-0	.961	**20**	112	85	3b154/S	0	2.6
1975	NY A★	157	581	71	155	24	4	21	91	51-3	2	88	.267	.322	.430	114	9	1-3	.964	13	106	104	3b157	0	2.0
1976	†NY A	158	583	88	148	29	2	**32**	93	62-6	4	94	.254	.327	.475	134	24	11-6	.965	17	**115**	**122**	3b158/S	0	4.2
1977	†NY A★	158	589	99	150	23	4	37	107	68-8	3	79	.255	.333	.496	124	18	2-5	.974	-4	96	112	3b156/D	0	1.0
1978	†NY A★	159	587	81	162	23	2	27	93	59-6	6	69	.276	.343	.460	128	21	1-1	.975	-5	96	106	3b159,S2	0	1.4
1979	NY A★	145	521	71	132	15	1	20	73	59-6	0	53	.253	.325	.401	97	-2	1-2	.966	7	105	114	3b144	0	0.2
1980	†NY A★	89	324	52	79	14	0	16	45	42-5	1	42	.244	.331	.435	110	5	0-0	.960	-7	91	104	3b88/S	67	-0.4
1981	†NY A	103	349	46	85	7	1	15	46	47-4	1	49	.244	.333	.398	112	5	0-2	.972	4	98	91	3b97,D4	0	0.7
1982	NY A	122	405	47	94	11	2	18	55	51-4	1	49	.232	.317	.402	98	-1	1-5	.934	-2	97	101	3b113,D3	21	-0.6
1983	NY A	129	462	56	123	17	3	20	75	51-2	3	65	.266	.341	.446	119	12	0-1	.956	-9	93	69	3b126/D	0	0.1
1984	†SD N	124	395	56	90	11	1	20	65	58-4	5	55	.228	.329	.413	108	5	0-0	.936	-11	90	82	3b119	0	-0.8
1985	SD N★	137	440	66	115	23	1	15	61	72-5	0	59	.261	.363	.420	120	14	0-0	.959	-9	90	79	3b130	0	0.4
1986	SD N	126	354	36	77	9	0	16	55	41-8	2	62	.218	.300	.379	88	-7	0-1	.941	-3	93	86	3b114	0	-1.2
1987	Atl N	112	177	16	37	8	1	5	33	22-4	0	25	.209	.294	.350	68	-8	1-0	.951	-1	92	130	3b40,1b6	0	-0.9
1988	Mon N	80	93	5	16	4	0	1	14	9-2	0	19	.172	.240	.247	40	-7	0-0	.818	-1	95	177	3b12,1b5	0	-1.0
Total	22	2700	8986	1193	2225	328	28	390	1314	1088-94	50	1209	.248	.329	.421	110	116	32-36	.961	124	105	106	3b2412,O73L,1b14,D11,S5	88	21.2

THE BATTER REGISTER

YEAR	TM LG	G	AB	R	H	2B	3B	HR	RBI	BB-IB	HP	SO	AVG	OBP	SLG	AOPS	ABR	SB-CS	FA	FR	RNG	THR	GAMES AT POSITION	DL	BFW
NETTLES, JIM	James William; B3.2.1947 San Diego CA; BL/TL/6´0˝/(180–194); [MinA68 4/76]; d9.7; b–Graig; Col San Diego St.																								
1970	Min A	13	20	3	5	0	0	0	0	1-0	0	5	.250	.286	.250	48	-1	0-1	1.000	-1	83	0	O11(5/1/5)	0	-0.3
1971	Min A	70	168	17	42	5	1	6	24	19-2	0	24	.250	.321	.399	101	0	3-2	.986	5	120	101	O62(2/57/3)	0	0.3
1972	Min A	102	235	28	48	5	2	4	15	32-3	1	52	.204	.302	.294	74	-7	4-3	.982	-0	99	111	O78(12/58/8)/1	0	-1.1
1974	Det A	43	141	20	32	5	1	6	17	15-1	1	26	.227	.306	.404	99	0	3-4	1.000	-2	96	33	O41(8/4/30)	0	-0.5
1979	KC A	11	23	0	2	0	0	0	1	3-0	0	2	.087	.192	.087	-21	-4	0-0	1.000	1	139	0	O8(7/0/1)/1	0	-0.4
1981	Oak A	1	0	0	0	0	0	0	0	0-0	0	0	ø	ø	ø	ø	0	0-0	ø	-0	0	0	/rf	0	0.0
Total	6	240	587	68	129	15	4	16	57	70-6	2	109	.220	.304	.341	83	-12	10-10	.988	3	105	81	O201(34/120/48),1b2	0	-2.0
NETTLES, MORRIS	Morris; B1.26.1952 Los Angeles CA; BL/TL/6´1˝/168; [AnaA70*2/33]; d4.26																								
1974	Cal A	56	175	27	48	4	0	0	8	16-0	0	38	.274	.335	.297	88	-2	20-11	.990	-5	90	0	O54(3/37/14)	0	-0.9
1975	Cal A	112	294	50	68	11	0	0	23	26-2	1	57	.231	.295	.269	65	-13	22-15	.974	3	113	76	O90(39/38/17),D9	0	-1.4
Total	2	168	469	77	116	15	0	0	31	42-2	1	95	.247	.310	.279	73	-15	42-26	.980	-2	104	47	O144(42/75/31),D9	0	-2.3
NETZEL, MILO	Miles Albion; B5.12.1886 Eldred PA; D3.18.1938 Oxnard CA; BL/TL; d9.16																								
1909	Cle A	10	37	2	7	1	0	0	3	3	0	—	.189	.250	.216	46	-2	1	.800	-2	82	156	3b6,O2L	—	-0.5
NEU, OTTO	Otto Adam; B9.24.1894 Springfield OH; D9.19.1932 Kenton OH; BR/TR/5´11˝/170; d7.10																								
1917	StL A	1	0	0	0	0	0	0	0	0	0	0	ø	ø	ø	ø	0	0	ø	-0	0	0	/S	—	0.0
NEUN, JOHNNY	John Henry; B10.28.1900 Baltimore MD; D3.28.1990 Baltimore MD; BB/TL/5´10.5˝/175; d4.14; M3/C3																								
1925	Det A	60	75	15	20	3	3	0	4	9	0	12	.267	.345	.387	87	-2	2-3	.990	-1	66	67	1b13	—	-0.4
1926	Det A	97	242	47	72	14	4	0	15	27	1	26	.298	.370	.388	97	-1	4-7	.993	-2	78	95	1b49	—	-0.7
1927	Det A	79	204	38	66	9	4	0	27	35	2	13	.324	.427	.407	116	7	22-7	.980	-3	85	107	1b53	—	0.2
1928	Det A	36	108	15	23	3	1	0	5	7	0	10	.213	.261	.259	36	-10	2-2	.975	0	115	90	1b25	—	-1.1
1930	Bos N	81	212	39	69	12	2	2	23	21	1	18	.325	.389	.429	101	1	9	.991	0	101	101	1b55	—	-0.2
1931	Bos N	79	104	17	23	1	3	0	11	11	1	14	.221	.302	.288	62	-6	2	.994	0	99	106	1b36	—	-0.7
Total	6	432	945	171	273	42	17	2	85	110	5	93	.289	.366	.376	91	-11	41-19	.987	-6	91	99	1b231	—	-2.9
NEVIN, ALEXANDER	Alexander Brown; B10.3.1850 Allegheny City (now part of Pittsburgh) PA; D10.10.1921 Pensacola FL; d5.6																								
1873	Res NA	13	55	7	11	1	2	0	1	1	—	4	.200	.214	.291	52	-3	0-0	.561	-6	79	0	3b12/2rf	—	-0.7
NEVIN, PHIL	Phillip Joseph; B1.19.1971 Fullerton CA; BR/TR/6´2˝/(180–231); [HouN92 1/1]; d6.11; Col Cal St.–Fullerton; OF(89/0/40)																								
1995	Hou N	18	60	4	7	1	0	0	1	7-1	1	13	.117	.221	.133	-4	-9	1-0	.933	-1	95	146	3b16	0	-1.0
	Det A	29	96	9	21	3	1	2	12	11-0	3	27	.219	.318	.333	70	-4	0-0	.963	-1	90	108	O27L,D2	0	-0.6
1996	Det A	38	120	15	35	5	0	8	19	8-0	1	39	.292	.338	.533	116	2	1-0	.943	3	121	124	3b24,O9L,C4/D	0	0.5
1997	Det A	93	251	32	59	16	1	9	35	25-1	1	68	.235	.306	.414	86	-5	0-1	.986	-2	91	175	O40L,D30,3b17,1b7/C	15	-1.0
1998	Ana A	75	237	27	54	8	1	8	27	17-0	5	67	.228	.291	.371	70	-11	0-0	.989	-9	85	100	C69,1b2,D3	0	-1.5
1999	SD N	128	383	52	103	27	0	24	85	51-1	1	82	.269	.352	.527	129	17	1-0	.982	11	116	124	3b67,C31,O13(5/0/9),1b11/D	11	2.7
2000	SD N	143	538	87	163	34	1	31	107	59-9	4	121	.303	.374	.543	137	30	2-0	.929	-8	97	86	3b142	0	2.2
2001	SD N★	149	546	97	167	31	0	41	126	71-7	4	147	.306	.388	.588	160	49	4-4	.930	5	108	109	3b145/D	0	5.2
2002	SD N	107	407	53	116	16	0	12	57	38-4	1	87	.285	.344	.413	108	4	4-0	.928	2	103	119	3b71,1b36	58	0.4
2003	SD N	59	226	30	63	8	0	13	46	21-1	0	44	.279	.339	.487	123	7	2-0	.996	-1	104	101	1b31,O29R	115	0.2
2004	SD N	147	547	78	158	31	1	26	105	66-5	5	121	.289	.368	.492	127	22	0-0	.989	-2	97	103	1b144/CD	16	0.8
2005	SD N	73	281	31	72	11	1	9	47	19-0	1	67	.256	.301	.399	87	-7	1-0	.994	-3	82	87	1b71,C2	27	-1.6
	Tex A	29	99	15	18	5	0	3	8	8-0	1	30	.182	.250	.323	50	-7	2-0	1.000	0	151	104	D25,1b3/3	0	-0.8
2006	Tex A	46	176	26	38	8	0	9	31	21-0	2	39	.216	.307	.415	84	-4	0-0	1.000	-0	0	239	D44/1	0	-0.7
	Chi N	67	179	26	49	4	0	12	33	17-0	0	52	.274	.335	.497	108	1	0-0	1.000	-2	88	95	1b38,O10(8/0/2)/C	0	-0.4
	†Min A	16	42	2	8	1	0	1	4	10-1	0	15	.190	.340	.286	66	-2	0-0	1.000	-0	45	202	D10,1b5	0	-0.3
Total	12	1217	4188	584	1131	209	6	208	743	449-30	30	1019	.270	.343	.472	113	83	18-5	.938	-6	104	107	3b483,1b349,O128L,D119,C109	242	4.1
NEWELL, JOHN	John A.; B1.14.1868 Wilmington DE; D1.28.1919 Wilmington DE; BR/TL/5´9˝/170; d7.22																								
1891	Pit N	5	18	1	2	0	0	0	2	0	1	0	.111	.158	.111	-22	-3	0	.846	-1	114	0	3b5	—	-0.3
NEWELL, T. E.	T. E.; B St.Louis MO; d8.8																								
1877	StL N	1	3	0	0	0	0	0	0	0	—	0	.000	.000	.000	-99	-1	—	.833	0	96	0	/S	—	-0.1
NEWFIELD, MARC	Marc Alexander; B10.19.1972 Sacramento CA; BR/TR/6´4˝/(205–226); [SeaA90 1/6]; d7.6																								
1993	Sea A	22	66	5	15	3	0	1	7	2-0	1	8	.227	.257	.318	54	-5	0-1	ø	-1	0	0	D15,O5L	0	-0.7
1994	Sea A	12	38	3	7	1	0	1	4	2-0	0	4	.184	.225	.289	31	-4	0-0	1.000	-1	53	0	O3L,D9	0	-0.4
1995	Sea A	24	85	7	16	3	0	3	14	3-1	1	16	.188	.225	.329	41	-8	0-0	1.000	-0	110	0	O24(23/0/1)	0	-0.8
	SD N	21	55	6	17	5	1	1	7	2-0	0	8	.309	.333	.491	117	1	0-0	1.000	1	110	134	O19L	0	0.1
1996	SD N	84	191	27	48	11	0	5	26	16-1	2	44	.251	.311	.387	88	-3	1-1	.970	-4	89	0	O51(30/0/23),1b2	0	-0.9
	Mil A	49	179	21	55	15	0	7	31	11-1	4	26	.307	.354	.508	112	3	0-1	.990	-2	91	83	O49L	0	-0.1
1997	Mil A	50	157	14	36	8	0	1	18	14-0	2	27	.229	.295	.299	57	-10	0-0	.977	-2	93	0	O28L,D18	105	-1.3
1998	Mil N	93	186	15	44	7	0	3	25	19-1	1	29	.237	.306	.323	66	-9	0-1	.962	-1	94	108	O55L/D	0	-1.2
Total	6	355	957	98	238	53	1	22	132	69-4	11	162	.249	.303	.375	76	-35	1-4	.981	-8	93	54	O234(212/0/24),D43,1b2	105	-5.3
NEWHAN, DAVID	David Matthew; B9.7.1973 Fullerton CA; BL/TR/5´10˝/(170–180); [OakA95 17/456]; d6.4; Col Pepperdine; OF(56/51/62)																								
1999	SD N	32	43	7	6	1	0	2	6	1-0	0	11	.140	.159	.302	14	-6	2-1	.970	4	117	149	2b19/13	0	-0.2
2000	SD N	14	20	5	3	1	0	1	2	6-1	0	7	.150	.346	.350	82	0	0-0	1.000	-1	132	0	2b3,O5R,3b2	0	-0.1
	Phi N	10	17	3	3	0	0	0	0	2-0	0	6	.176	.263	.176	14	-2	0-0	1.000	3	158	221	2b5	0	0.1
	Year	24	37	8	6	1	0	1	2	8-1	0	13	.162	.311	.270	51	-3	0-0	1.000	2	153	180	2b8,O5R,3b2	0	0.0
2001	Phi N	7	6	2	2	1	0	0	1	1-0	0	0	.333	.375	.500	146	1	0-0	1.000	-1	0	0	/2	177	0.0
2004	Bal A	95	373	66	116	15	7	8	54	27-0	4	72	.311	.361	.453	112	6	11-1	1.000	-4	92	122	O42(19/0/24),D32,3b17,1b2	0	0.1
2005	Bal A	96	218	31	44	9	0	5	21	22-1	2	45	.202	.279	.312	58	-13	9-2	.990	-6	82	35	O73(20/32/30),3b8,D7	0	-1.9
2006	Bal A	39	131	14	33	4	0	4	18	7-1	2	22	.252	.294	.374	75	-5	4-2	.970	-4	85	0	O37(17/19/3)/1	133	-0.9
Total	6	293	808	128	207	31	7	20	102	66-3	8	163	.256	.315	.386	84	-19	26-6	.988	-8	85	51	O157R,D39,3b28,2b28,1b4	310	-2.9
NEWMAN, AL	Albert Dwayne; B6.30.1960 Kansas City MO; BB/TR/5´9˝/(175–198); [MonN81 S1/12]; d6.14; C4; Col San Diego St.; OF(11/1/0)																								
1985	Mon N	25	29	7	5	1	0	0	1	3-0	0	4	.172	.250	.207	31	-3	2-1	1.000	2	125	108	2b15,S2	0	0.0
1986	Mon N	95	185	23	37	3	0	1	8	21-2	0	20	.200	.279	.232	43	-14	11-11	.967	1	105	109	2b59,S22	0	-1.2
1987	†Min A	110	307	44	68	15	5	0	29	34-0	0	27	.221	.298	.303	58	-18	15-11	.982	-0	92	103	S55,2b47,3b12,O2L,D5	0	-1.3
1988	Min A	105	260	35	58	7	0	0	19	29-0	0	34	.223	.301	.250	54	-15	12-3	.966	-8	81	149	3b60,S28,2b23,D2	0	-2.0
1989	Min A	141	446	62	113	18	2	0	38	59-0	2	46	.253	.341	.303	78	-11	25-12	.980	-13	91	83	2b84,3b37,S31,O4(4/1/0),D2	0	-1.9
1990	Min A	144	388	43	94	14	0	0	30	33-0	2	34	.242	.304	.278	60	-20	13-6	.993	1	99	115	2b89,S48,3b28,O3L	0	-1.5
1991	†Min A	118	246	25	47	5	0	0	19	23-0	1	21	.191	.260	.211	31	-23	4-5	.987	-2	88	112	S55,2b35,3b35/1lfD	0	-2.3
1992	Tex A	116	246	25	54	5	0	0	12	34-0	1	26	.220	.317	.240	60	-12	9-6	.983	4	105	82	2b72,3b28,S20/lfD	0	-0.6
Total	8	854	2107	264	476	68	7	1	156	236-2	6	212	.226	.304	.266	58	-116	91-55	.984	-15	101	96	2b424,S261,3b200,D13,O11L/1	0	-10.8
NEWMAN, CHARLIE	Charles "Decker"; B11.5.1868 Juda WI; D11.23.1947 San Diego CA; BR/TR; d7.11																								
1892	NY N	3	12	1	4	0	0	0	1	2	0	0	.333	.429	.333	133	1	3	.750	-0	219	0	O3L	—	0.0
	Chi N	16	61	4	10	0	0	0	2	1	0	6	.164	.177	.164	3	-7	2	.950	-1	47	231	O16L	—	-0.9
	Year	19	73	5	14	0	0	0	3	3	0	6	.192	.224	.192	26	-7	5	.917	-2	77	190	O19L	—	-0.9
NEWMAN, JEFF	Jeffrey Lynn; B9.11.1948 Fort Worth TX; BR/TR/6´2˝/(210–218); [CleA70 26/608]; d6.30; M1/C11; Col TCU																								
1976	Oak A	43	77	5	15	4	0	0	4	4-0	0	12	.195	.235	.247	43	-6	0-0	.981	5	169	135	C43	0	0.1
1977	Oak A	94	162	17	36	9	0	4	15	4-1	1	24	.222	.244	.352	61	-9	2-0	.970	-3	118	**138**	C94/P	0	-0.9
1978	Oak A	105	268	25	64	7	1	9	32	18-2	1	40	.239	.288	.373	89	-5	0-3	.969	-2	95	84	C61,1b36,D2	15	-0.8
1979	Oak A☆	143	516	53	119	17	2	22	71	27-2	1	88	.231	.267	.399	82	-16	2-1	.977	2	124	**129**	C81,1b46,3b7,D7	0	-1.4
1980	Oak A	127	438	37	102	19	1	15	56	25-8	1	81	.233	.273	.384	84	-12	3-4	.982	-15	86	59	1b60,C55,3b2/2D	0	-2.9
1981	†Oak A	68	216	17	50	12	0	3	15	9-1	0	28	.231	.260	.329	72	-8	0-2	.995	1	136	102	C37,1b30	0	-0.9
1982	Oak A	72	251	19	50	11	0	6	30	14-1	0	49	.199	.240	.315	53	-17	0-1	.989	-4	73	84	C67,1b3/3D	0	-1.8
1983	Bos A	59	132	11	25	4	0	3	7	10-1	2	31	.189	.255	.288	46	-10	0-1	.990	0	88	135	C51,D6	0	-0.9
1984	Bos A	24	63	5	14	2	0	1	3	5-0	0	16	.222	.275	.302	58	-4	0-0	.992	0	92	80	C24	0	-0.2
Total	9	735	2123	189	475	85	4	63	233	116-16	6	369	.224	.264	.357	73	-87	7-12	.981	-15	108	108	C513,1b175,D25,3b10/2P	15	-9.7

YEAR	TM LG	G	AB	R	H	2B	3B	HR	RBI	BB-IB	HP	SO	AVG	OBP	SLG	AOPS	ABR	SB-CS	FA	FR	RNG	THR	GAMES AT POSITION	DL	BFW
NEWNAM, ROBERT	Robert Albert; B12.10.1880 Hempstead TX; D6.20.1938 San Antonio TX; BL/TR/6´0˝/180; d5.29																								
1910	StL A	103	384	45	83	3	8	2	26	29	2	—	.216	.275	.281	79	-11	16	.972	-3	97	100	1b103	—	-1.8
1911	StL A	20	62	11	12	4	0	0	5	12	3	—	.194	.351	.258	74	-1	4	.986	1	110	112	1b20	—	-0.1
Total	2	123	446	56	95	7	8	2	31	41	5	—	.213	.287	.278	78	-12	20	.974	-3	99	102	1b123	—	-1.9
NEWSOME, SKEETER	Lamar Ashby; B10.18.1910 Phenix City AL; D8.31.1989 Columbus GA; BR/TR/5´9˝/170; d4.19																								
1935	Phi A	59	145	18	30	7	1	1	10	5	0	9	.207	.233	.290	35	-15	2-1	.956	2	97	120	S24,2b13,3b4/rf	—	-1.0
1936	Phi A	127	471	41	106	15	2	0	46	25	1	27	.225	.266	.265	32	-52	13-4	.957	10	**108**	99	S123,2b2/3lf	—	-2.8
1937	Phi A	122	438	53	111	22	1	1	30	37	0	22	.253	.312	.315	59	-28	11-5	.954	10	106	97	S122	—	-0.8
1938	Phi A	17	48	7	13	4	0	0	7	1	0	4	.271	.286	.354	61	-3	1-1	.971	1	109	75	S15	—	-0.1
1939	Phi A	99	248	22	55	9	1	0	17	19	0	12	.222	.277	.266	40	-23	5-7	.950	0	100	91	S93,2b2	—	-1.7
1941	Bos A	93	227	28	51	6	0	2	17	22	1	11	.225	.296	.278	51	-16	10-4	.958	9	109	99	S69,2b23	0	-0.2
1942	Bos A	29	95	7	26	6	0	0	9	9	0	5	.274	.337	.337	87	-1	2-1	.925	1	118	194	3b12,2b10,S7	0	0.1
1943	Bos A	114	449	48	119	21	2	1	22	21	2	21	.265	.301	.327	82	-11	5-6	.962	9	105	103	S98,3b15	0	0.5
1944	Bos A	136	472	41	114	26	3	0	41	33	0	21	.242	.291	.309	72	-17	4-3	.963	9	104	90	S126,2b8/3	0	0.2
1945	Bos A	125	438	45	127	30	1	1	48	20	1	15	.290	.322	.370	98	-2	6-3	.963	16	103	100	2b82,S33,3b11	0	2.3
1946	Phi N	112	375	35	87	10	2	1	23	30	0	23	.232	.289	.277	63	-19	4	.955	-10	98	81	S107,2b3,3b2	0	-2.4
1947	Phi N	95	310	36	71	8	2	2	22	24	0	24	.229	.284	.287	54	-21	4	.969	3	105	130	S85,2b6,3b3	0	-1.3
Total	12	1128	3716	381	910	164	15	9	292	246	5	194	.245	.293	.304	62	-208	67-35	.959	59	105	99	S902,2b149,3b49,O2(1/0/1)	0	-7.2
NEWSON, WARREN	Warren Dale; B7.3.1964 Newnan GA; BL/TL/5´7˝/(190–202); [SDN86*4/90]; d5.29; Col Middle Georgia JC																								
1991	Chi A	71	132	20	39	5	0	4	25	28-1	0	34	.295	.419	.424	137	8	2-2	.962	-3	74	142	O50(16/1/34),D3	0	0.4
1992	Chi A	63	136	19	30	3	0	1	11	37-2	0	38	.221	.387	.265	86	0	3-0	1.000	1	87	199	O50(17/0/33),D4	0	0.0
1993	†Chi A	26	40	9	12	0	0	2	6	9-1	0	12	.300	.429	.450	139	3	0-0	1.000	-0	96	0	D10,O5(2/0/3)	0	0.2
1994	Chi A	63	102	16	26	5	0	2	7	14-1	0	23	.255	.345	.363	84	-2	1-0	.979	1	115	68	O34(9/0/26),D3	0	-0.2
1995	Chi A	51	85	19	20	0	2	3	9	23-0	1	27	.235	.404	.388	112	2	1-1	.978	2	128	86	O24(12/0/14),D7	0	0.3
	†Sea A	33	72	15	21	2	0	2	6	16-0	0	18	.292	.420	.403	114	2	1-0	.971	-0	101	93	O23(18/2/4)	0	0.2
	Year	84	157	34	41	2	2	5	15	39-0	1	45	.261	.411	.395	113	5	2-1	.975	2	115	89	O47(30/2/18),D7	0	0.5
1996	†Tex A	91	235	34	60	14	1	10	31	37-1	0	82	.255	.355	.451	96	-1	3-0	.992	4	111	130	O66(8/0/58),D9	0	0.1
1997	Tex A	81	169	23	36	10	1	10	23	31-2	0	53	.213	.333	.462	98	0	3-0	.949	-0	110	37	O58(20/0/44),D9	50	-0.2
1998	Tex A	10	21	1	4	1	0	0	2	1-1	0	5	.190	.227	.238	20	-2	0-0	1.000	0	125	0	O6L,D3	0	-0.2
Total	8	489	992	156	248	40	4	34	120	196-9	1	292	.250	.374	.401	102	10	14-3	.978	5	103	111	O316(108/3/216),D48	50	0.6
NIARHOS, GUS	Constantine Gregory; B12.6.1920 Birmingham AL; D12.29.2004 Harrisonburg VA; BR/TR/6´0˝/165; d6.9; C3																								
1946	NY A	37	40	11	9	1	1	0	2	11	0	2	.225	.392	.300	94	0	1-0	.989	4	*143*	*137*	C29	0	0.5
1948	NY A	83	228	41	61	12	2	0	19	52	0	15	.268	.404	.338	99	3	1-3	.990	6	*105*	*99*	C82	0	1.2
1949	†NY A	32	43	7	12	2	1	0	6	13	1	8	.279	.456	.372	120	2	0-0	1.000	3	*83*	*83*	C30	0	0.6
1950	NY A	1	0	0	0	0	0	0	0	0	0	0	ø	ø	ø	ø	0	0-0	ø	0	—	—	/R	0	0.0
	Chi A	41	105	17	34	4	0	0	16	14	1	6	.324	.408	.362	101	1	0-0	.978	4	*86*	*97*	C36	0	0.7
	Year	42	105	17	34	4	0	0	16	14	1	6	.324	.408	.362	101	1	0-0	.978	4	*86*	*97*	C36	0	0.7
1951	Chi A	66	168	27	43	6	0	1	10	47	0	9	.256	.419	.310	101	4	4-3	.985	3	*79*	*82*	C59	42	1.0
1952	Bos A	29	58	4	6	0	0	0	4	12	1	9	.103	.268	.103	6	-7	0-0	.992	4	*142*	*102*	C25	0	-0.2
1953	Bos A	16	35	6	7	1	1	0	2	4	1	4	.200	.300	.286	56	-2	0-1	.985	2	*100*	*76*	C16	0	0.0
1954	Phi N	3	5	0	1	0	0	0	0	0	0	1	.200	.200	.200	5	-1	0-0	1.000	1	*0*	*0*	C3	0	0.0
1955	Phi N	7	9	1	1	0	0	0	0	0-0	0	2	.111	.111	.111	-42	-2	0-0	1.000	1	*72*	*179*	C7	0	-0.1
Total	9	315	691	114	174	26	5	1	59	153-0	4	56	.252	.390	.308	89	-2	6-7	.988	27	*99*	*95*	C287	42	3.7
NICHOLAS, DON	Donald Leigh; B10.30.1930 Phoenix AZ; BL/TR/5´7˝/150; d4.16																								
1952	Chi A	3	2	0	0	0	0	0	0	0	0	0	.000	.000	.000	-99	-1	0-0	ø	0	—	—	/H	0	-0.1
1954	Chi A	7	0	3	0	0	0	0	0	1	0	0	ø	1.000	ø	185	0	0-1	ø	0	—	—	/H	0	0.0
Total	2	10	2	3	0	0	0	0	0	1	0	0	.000	.333	.000	-2	-1	0-1	ø	0	—	—	0	—	-0.1
NICHOLL, SAM	Samuel Anderson; B4.20.1869 Co. Antrim, Ireland; D4.19.1937 Steubenville OH; BR/TR/5´10˝/178; d10.5																								
1888	Pit N	8	22	3	1	0	0	0	0	2	0	2	.045	.125	.045	-48	-4	0	.952	1	90	0	O8C	—	-0.3
1890	Col AA	14	56	7	9	0	0	0	4	2	0	—	.161	.190	.161	4	-7	3	.903	2	178	375	O14L	—	-0.5
Total	2	22	78	10	10	0	0	0	4	4	0	2	.128	.171	.128	-10	-11	3	.923	2	152	266	O22(14/8/0)	—	-0.8
NICHOLLS, SIMON	Simon Burdette; B7.18.1882 Germantown MD; D3.12.1911 Baltimore MD; BL/TR/5´11.5˝/165; d9.18; Col Maryland																								
1903	Det A	2	8	0	3	0	0	0	0	0	0	—	.375	.375	.375	129	0	0	.600	-2	49	0	S2	—	-0.2
1906	Phi A	12	44	1	8	1	0	0	1	3	0	—	.182	.234	.205	36	-3	0	.965	-0	89	112	S12	—	-0.4
1907	Phi A	124	460	75	139	12	2	0	23	24	1	—	.302	.338	.337	113	6	13	.930	-13	93	50	S82,2b28,3b13	—	-0.4
1908	Phi A	150	550	58	119	17	3	4	31	35	1	—	.216	.265	.280	72	-17	14	.913	-20	89	69	S120,2b23,3b7	—	-3.8
1909	Phi A	21	71	10	15	2	1	0	3	3	0	—	.211	.243	.268	60	-3	0	.889	-2	81	80	S14,3b5/1	—	-0.6
1910	Cle A	3	0	0	0	0	0	0	0	0	0	—	ø	ø	ø	ø	0	0	.000	-1	0	0	S3	—	-0.1
Total	6	312	1133	144	284	32	6	4	58	65	2	—	.251	.292	.300	86	-17	27	.917	-38	90	64	S233,2b51,3b25/1	—	-5.5
NICHOLS, AL	Albert H.; B Brooklyn NY; 5´11˝/180; d4.24																								
1875	Atl NA	32	131	4	20	2	0	0	9	0	—	6	.153	.153	.168	13	-10	0-0	.785	8	122	194	3b32	—	-0.3
1876	NY N	**57**	212	20	38	4	0	0	9	2	—	3	.179	.187	.198	33	-13	—	.779	4	114	16	3b57	—	-0.7
1877	Lou N	6	19	1	4	0	1	0	0	0	—	2	.211	.211	.316	54	-1	—	.706	2	147	0	2b3/S31	—	0.1
Total	2	63	231	21	42	4	1	0	9	2	—	5	.182	.189	.208	35	-14	—	.785	6	115	16	3b58,2b3/1S	—	-0.6
NICHOLS, ART	Arthur Francis (b Arthur Francis Meikle); B7.14.1871 Manchester NH; D8.9.1945 Willimantic CT; BR/TR/5´10˝/175; d9.16																								
1898	Chi N	14	42	7	12	1	0	0	6	4	3	—	.286	.388	.310	101	1	6	.968	2	*146*	*94*	C14	—	0.3
1899	Chi N	17	47	5	12	2	0	1	11	0	2	—	.255	.286	.362	79	-2	3	.931	-1	*106*	*70*	C15	—	-0.1
1900	Chi N	8	25	1	5	0	0	0	0	3	0	—	.200	.286	.200	36	-2	1	.938	-1	*99*	*101*	C7	—	-0.2
1901	StL N	93	308	50	75	11	3	1	33	10	10	—	.244	.290	.308	77	-9	14	.960	-0	*94*	93	C47,O40(0/29/11)	—	-0.7
1902	StL N	73	251	36	67	12	0	1	31	21	4	—	.267	.333	.327	108	3	18	.984	-6	76	79	1b56,C11,O4(0/1/3)	—	-0.3
1903	StL N	36	120	13	23	2	0	0	9	12	3	—	.192	.281	.208	42	-9	9	.972	-5	21	82	1b25,O7L,C2	—	-1.4
Total	6	241	793	112	194	28	3	3	90	50	22	—	.245	.308	.299	81	-18	51	.952	-11	*103*	92	C96,1b81,O51(7/30/14)	—	-2.4
NICHOLS, CARL	Carl Edward; B10.14.1962 Los Angeles CA; BR/TR/6´0˝/(184–208); [BalA80 4/104]; d9.14																								
1986	Bal A	5	5	0	0	0	0	0	0	1-1	0	4	.000	.167	.000	-50	-1	0-0	1.000	-1	71	0	C5	0	-0.2
1987	Bal A	13	21	4	8	1	0	0	3	1-0	0	4	.381	.409	.429	126	1	0-0	1.000	-1	81	121	C13	0	0.0
1988	Bal A	18	47	2	9	1	0	0	1	3-0	0	10	.191	.235	.213	29	-5	0-0	.987	6	98	228	C13,O3R	0	0.2
1989	Hou N	8	13	0	1	0	0	0	2	0-0	0	3	.077	.077	.077	-58	-3	0-0	1.000	0	190	0	C6	0	-0.3
1990	Hou N	32	49	7	10	3	0	0	11	8-1	1	11	.204	.317	.265	67	-2	0-0	.986	3	114	110	C15,1b3/lf	22	0.2
1991	Hou N	20	51	3	10	3	0	0	1	5-1	0	17	.196	.268	.255	50	-3	0-0	.971	1	151	154	C17	0	-0.1
Total	6	96	186	16	38	8	0	0	18	18-3	1	49	.204	.274	.247	49	-13	0-0	.985	8	118	143	C69,O4(1/0/3),1b3	22	-0.2
NICHOLS, ROY	Roy; B3.3.1921 Little Rock AR; D4.3.2002 Hot Springs AR; BR/TR/5´11˝/155; d5.6																								
1944	NY N	11	9	3	2	1	0	0	0	2	0	2	.222	.364	.333	97	0	0	1.000	1	177	0	/23	0	0.1
NICHOLS, REID	Thomas Reid; B8.5.1958 Ocala FL; BR/TR/5´11˝/(165–175); [BosA76 12/286]; d9.16; C1																								
1980	Bos A	12	36	5	8	0	1	0	3	3-0	0	8	.222	.282	.278	51	-3	0-1	.962	-1	85	141	O9C/D	0	-0.4
1981	Bos A	39	48	13	9	0	1	0	3	2-0	0	6	.188	.216	.229	28	-5	0-1	1.000	-0	84	315	O27(1/25/1)/3D	0	-0.6
1982	Bos A	92	245	35	74	16	1	7	33	14-1	1	28	.302	.341	.461	111	4	5-3	.989	3	97	199	O82(30/57/2),D4	16	0.6
1983	Bos A	100	274	35	78	22	1	6	22	26-2	3	36	.285	.352	.438	108	4	7-5	.994	1	102	84	O72(11/32/30),D18/S	0	0.2
1984	Bos A	74	124	14	28	5	1	1	14	12-1	3	18	.226	.307	.306	68	-5	2-1	.988	0	93	138	O48(17/26/4)/D	0	-0.6
1985	Bos A	21	32	3	6	1	0	1	3	2-0	1	4	.188	.250	.313	53	-2	1-0	.933	-1	75	0	O10(2/7/1),2b3,D4	0	-0.3
	Chi A	51	118	20	35	7	1	1	15	15-1	0	13	.297	.373	.398	107	2	5-5	1.000	-1	97	52	O48(25/27/8)/D	0	-0.1
	Year	72	150	23	41	8	1	2	18	17-1	1	17	.273	.347	.380	96	0	6-5	.988	-2	93	42	O58(27/34/9),D5,2b3	0	-0.4
1986	Chi A	74	136	9	31	4	0	2	18	11-0	0	23	.228	.282	.301	58	-8	5-4	.989	2	107	128	O53(31/14/11),2b2,D3	22	-0.8
1987	Mon N	77	147	22	39	8	2	4	20	14-1	1	13	.265	.329	.429	96	-1	2-1	.990	3	112	188	O59(7/50/5),3b3	0	0.2
Total	8	540	1160	156	308	63	8	22	131	99-6	9	149	.266	.326	.391	91	-14	27-21	.990	7	99	142	O408(124/247/62),D39,2b5,3b4/S	38	-1.8

YEAR	TM LG	G	AB	R	H	2B	3B	HR	RBI	BB-IB	HP	SO	AVG	OBP	SLG	AOPS	ABR	SB-CS	FA	FR	RNG	THR	GAMES AT POSITION	DL	BFW
Nicholson, Dave	David Lawrence; B8.29.1939 St.Louis MO; BR/TR/6´2˝/215; d5.24																								
1960	Bal A	54	113	17	21	1	1	5	11	20-0	0	55	.186	.308	.345	77	-4	0-2	.982	-1	80	140	O44(34/0/11)	0	-0.7
1962	Bal A	97	173	25	30	4	1	9	15	27-0	1	76	.173	.289	.364	79	-6	3-4	.983	1	101	134	O80(34/20/27)	0	-0.8
1963	Chi A	126	449	53	103	11	4	22	70	63-0	0	175	.229	.319	.419	108	5	2-1	.970	0	92	117	O123L	0	-0.2
1964	Chi A	97	294	40	60	6	1	13	39	52-0	3	126	.204	.329	.364	95	-1	0-2	.972	-1	94	94	O92(91/0/1)	0	-0.8
1965	Chi A	54	85	11	13	2	1	2	12	9-0	0	40	.153	.234	.271	46	-6	0-0	1.000	-4	65	0	O36(25/12/1)	0	-1.3
1966	Hou N	100	280	36	69	8	4	10	31	46-6	3	92	.246	.356	.411	122	9	1-1	.968	5	104	210	O90(13/5/73)	0	1.0
1967	Atl N	10	25	2	5	0	0	0	1	2-1	0	9	.200	.250	.200	34	-2	0-0	1.000	-0	75	215	O7(7/1/0)	0	-0.3
Total	7	538	1419	184	301	32	12	61	179	219-7	7	573	.212	.318	.381	97	-5	6-10	.974	-0	93	129	O472(327/38/113)	0	-3.1
Nicholson, Fred	Fred "Shoemaker"; B9.1.1894 Honey Grove TX; D1.23.1972 Kilgore TX; BR/TR/5´10.5˝/173; d4.11; Mil 1918																								
1917	Det A	13	14	4	4	1	0	0	1	1	0	2	.286	.333	.357	111	0	0	1.000	-0	104	0	O3(1/0/2)	—	0.0
1919	Pit N	30	66	8	18	2	2	1	6	6	0	11	.273	.333	.409	118	1	2	.939	1	108	113	O17(13/1/3)/1	—	0.1
1920	Pit N	99	247	33	89	16	7	4	30	18	0	31	.360	.404	.530	162	19	9-6	.957	3	104	129	O58(28/18/13)	—	2.0
1921	Bos N	83	245	36	80	11	7	5	41	17	0	29	.327	.370	.490	133	11	5-4	.983	-1	105	65	O59(57/0/3),1b4,2b2	—	0.5
1922	Bos N	78	222	31	56	4	5	2	29	23	5	24	.252	.336	.342	79	-7	5-7	.915	-1	109	69	O63(20/0/44)	—	-1.4
Total	5	303	794	112	247	34	21	12	107	65	5	97	.311	.367	.452	124	24	21-17	.950	0	106	90	O200(119/19/65),1b5,2b2	—	1.2
Nicholson, Kevin	Kevin Ronald; B3.29.1976 Vancouver BC, Can.; BB/TR/5´10˝/190; [SDN97 1/27]; d6.23; Col Stetson																								
2000	SD N	37	97	7	21	6	1	1	8	4-0	1	31	.216	.255	.330	49	-8	1-0	.983	1	111	69	S30,2b4	26	-0.4
Nicholson, Ovid	Ovid Edward; B12.30.1888 Salem IN; D3.24.1968 Salem IN; BL/TR/5´9.5˝/155; d9.17																								
1912	Pit N	6	11	2	5	0	0	0	3	1	0	2	.455	.500	.455	164	1	0	1.000	0	125	0	O4L	—	0.1
Nicholson, Parson	Thomas Clark "Deacon"; B4.14.1863 Blaine OH; D2.28.1917 Bellaire OH; 5´9˝/148; d9.14																								
1888	Det N	24	85	11	22	2	3	1	9	2	1	7	.259	.284	.388	111	1	6	.935	-0	105	68	2b24	—	0.1
1890	Tol AA	**134**	523	78	140	16	11	4	72	42	9	—	.268	.333	.363	102	-1	46	.929	-7	102	83	2b134/C	—	-0.3
1895	Was N	10	38	7	7	2	1	0	5	7	0	4	.184	.311	.289	56	-2	6	.797	-2	101	88	S10	—	-0.3
Total	3	168	646	96	169	20	15	5	86	51	10	11	.262	.325	.362	100	-2	58	.930	-9	102	81	2b158,S10/C	—	-0.5
Nicholson, Bill	William Beck "Swish"; B12.11.1914 Chestertown MD; D3.8.1996 Chestertown MD; BL/TR/6´0˝/205; d6.13; Col Washington College																								
1936	Phi A	11	12	2	0	0	0	0	0	0	0	5	.000	.000	.000	-99	-4	0-0	1.000	0	106	0	/rf	—	-0.4
1939	Chi N	58	220	37	65	12	5	5	38	20	0	29	.295	.354	.464	116	4	0	.955	-1	101	89	O58R	—	0.0
1940	Chi N★	135	491	78	146	27	7	25	98	50	3	67	.297	.366	.534	148	31	2	.950	-6	91	101	O123(43/0/81)	—	1.8
1941	Chi N★	147	532	74	135	26	1	26	98	82	3	91	.254	.357	.453	132	23	1	.971	4	111	85	O143(3/0/140)	0	1.8
1942	Chi N	152	588	83	173	22	11	21	78	76	**8**	80	.294	.382	.476	156	42	8	.986	7	107	127	O151R	0	**4.1**
1943	Chi N★	**154**	608	95	188	30	9	**29**	**128**	71	5	86	.309	.386	.531	166	50	4	.978	3	107	96	O154R	0	4.5
1944	Chi N★	156	582	**116**	167	35	8	**33**	**122**	93	6	71	.287	.391	.545	162	49	3	.979	-2	96	105	O156R	0	3.8
1945	†Chi N✱	151	559	82	136	28	4	13	88	92	6	73	.243	.356	.377	106	8	4	.990	-2	99	86	O151R	0	-0.4
1946	Chi N	105	296	36	65	13	2	8	41	44	2	44	.220	.325	.358	95	-1	1	.973	2	120	51	O80R	0	-0.2
1947	Chi N	148	487	69	119	28	1	26	75	87	5	83	.244	.364	.466	124	18	1	**.990**	-5	99	57	O140R	0	0.9
1948	Chi N	143	494	68	129	24	5	19	67	81	5	60	.261	.371	.445	125	19	2	.980	-5	95	72	O136R	0	1.0
1949	Phi N	98	299	42	70	8	3	11	40	45	5	53	.234	.344	.391	99	0	1	.995	3	102	118	O91R	0	0.0
1950	Phi N	41	58	3	13	2	1	3	10	8	0	16	.224	.318	.448	101	0	0	.952	-1	109	0	O15R	30	-0.1
1951	Phi N	85	170	23	41	9	2	8	30	25	1	24	.241	.342	.459	115	4	0-1	.987	-1	105	29	O41R	0	0.1
1952	Phi N	55	88	17	24	3	0	6	19	14	3	26	.273	.390	.511	150	6	0-0	1.000	-1	109	0	O19R	0	0.5
1953	Phi N	38	62	12	13	5	1	2	16	12	0	20	.210	.338	.419	97	0	0-0	1.000	-1	77	0	O12R	0	-0.2
Total	16	1677	5546	837	1484	272	60	235	948	800	52	828	.268	.365	.465	133	249	27-1	.979	-4	102	87	O1471(46/0/1427)	30	17.2
Nicol, George	George Edward; B10.17.1870 Barry IL; D8.4.1924 Milwaukee WI; BR/TL/5´7˝/155; d9.23; ▲																								
1890	StL AA	3	7	4	2	1	0	0	1	4	0	—	.286	.545	.429	164	1	0	1.000	-0	0	0	P3	—	0.0
1891	Chi N	3	6	0	2	0	1	0	3	0	0	1	.333	.333	.667	189	1	0	.000	-1	0	0	P3	—	0.0
1894	Pit N	9	22	8	9	1	0	0	3	0	0	1	.409	.409	.455	109	2	0	.800	-1	48	0	P9	—	0.0
	Lou N	28	112	12	38	6	4	0	19	2	2	4	.339	.362	.464	105	0	4	.791	-4	52	102	O26R,P2	—	-0.4
	Year	37	134	20	47	7	4	0	22	2	2	5	.351	.370	.463	105	1	4	.791	-5	52	102	O26R,P11	—	-0.4
Total	3	43	147	24	51	8	5	0	26	6	2	6	.347	.381	.469	112	4	4	.791	-6	52	102	O26R,P17	—	-0.4
Nicol, Hugh	Hugh; B1.1.1858 Campsie, Scotland; D6.27.1921 Lafayette IN; BR/TR/5´4˝/145; d5.3; M1																								
1881	Chi N	26	108	13	22	2	0	0	7	4	—	12	.204	.232	.222	42	-7	—	.932	4	168	110	O26(2/12/12)/S	—	-0.4
1882	Chi N	47	186	19	37	9	1	1	16	7	—	29	.199	.228	.274	57	-9	—	.887	11	275	55	O47R,S8	—	0.1
1883	StL AA	94	368	73	105	13	3	0	39	18	—	—	.285	.319	.337	105	2	—	.916	10	181	247	O84(1/1/84),2b11	—	1.0
1884	StL AA	**110**	442	79	116	14	5	0	—	22	3	—	.262	.302	.317	99	-1	—	.873	17	**264**	113	O87R,2b23/S3	—	1.4
1885	†StL AA	**112**	425	59	88	11	1	0	45	34	3	—	.207	.271	.238	59	-19	—	.888	12	173	64	O111R/3	—	-0.8
1886	StL AA	67	253	44	52	6	3	0	19	26	0	—	.206	.280	.253	64	-11	38	.942	-4	116	0	O57(0/1/56),S8,2b4	—	-1.3
1887	Cin AA	125	475	122	102	18	2	1	34	86	5	—	.215	.341	.267	69	-16	**138**	.918	-3	98	24	O125(0/6/119)	—	-1.6
1888	Cin AA	135	548	112	131	10	2	1	35	67	7	—	.239	.330	.270	88	-5	103	.957	-3	71	69	O125R,2b12/S	—	-0.8
1889	Cin AA	122	474	82	121	7	8	2	58	54	5	35	.255	.338	.316	84	-10	80	.918	2	101	85	O115R,2b7,3b3	—	-0.7
1890	Cin N	50	186	28	39	1	4	0	19	19	0	12	.210	.283	.258	58	-10	24	.921	-6	95	188	O46R,S3/2	—	-1.5
Total	10	888	3465	631	813	91	29	5	272	337	23	88	.235	.307	.282	78	-86	383	.912	38	144	91	O823(3/20/802),2b58,S22,3b5	—	-4.6
Nicosia, Steve	Steven Richard; B8.6.1955 Paterson NJ; BR/TR/5´10˝/(183–185); [PitN73 1/24]; d7.8																								
1978	Pit N	3	5	0	0	0	0	0	0	1-0	0	0	.000	.167	.000	-47	-1	0-0	1.000	0	37	278	/C	0	-0.1
1979	†Pit N	70	191	22	55	16	0	4	13	23-7	0	17	.288	.364	.435	111	4	0-2	.991	1	130	74	C65	0	0.7
1980	Pit N	60	176	16	38	8	0	1	22	19-5	1	16	.216	.291	.278	59	-9	0-1	.984	-1	128	61	C58	0	-0.8
1981	Pit N	54	169	21	39	10	1	2	18	13-2	0	10	.231	.286	.337	73	-6	3-1	.982	-1	106	70	C52	0	-0.5
1982	Pit N	39	100	6	28	3	0	1	7	11-4	0	13	.280	.348	.340	90	-1	0-1	.990	2	104	112	C35,O3L	0	0.2
1983	Pit N	21	46	4	6	2	0	1	1	1-0	0	7	.130	.149	.239	6	-6	0-0	.988	-3	71	59	C15	26	-0.9
	SF N	15	33	4	11	0	0	0	6	3-1	0	2	.333	.389	.333	105	0	0-0	.984	2	107	28	C9	0	0.2
	Year	36	79	8	17	2	0	1	7	4-1	0	9	.215	.253	.278	47	-6	0-0	.986	-2	86	46	C24	0	-0.7
1984	SF N	48	132	9	40	11	2	2	19	8-0	0	14	.303	.336	.462	128	5	1-1	.985	-11	74	52	C41	15	-0.5
1985	Mon N	42	71	4	12	2	0	0	1	7-0	0	11	.169	.244	.197	26	-7	1-0	.988	-3	125	0	C23,1b2	26	-1.0
	Tor A	6	15	0	4	0	0	0	1	0-0	0	0	.267	.267	.267	45	-1	0-0	1.000	2	246	168	C6	0	0.0
Total	8	358	938	86	233	52	3	11	88	86-19	1	90	.248	.310	.345	81	-22	5-6	.987	-12	112	68	C305,O3L,1b2	67	-2.7
Niebergall, Charlie	Charles Arthur "Nig"; B5.23.1899 New York NY; D8.29.1982 Holiday FL; BR/TR/5´10˝/160; d6.17																								
1921	StL N	5	6	1	1	0	0	0	0	0	0	0	.167	.167	.167	-12	-1	0-0	1.000	-0	*52*	*203*	C3	—	-0.1
1923	StL N	9	28	2	3	1	0	0	1	2	0	2	.107	.167	.143	-18	-5	0-0	1.000	-0	*99*	*75*	C7	—	-0.5
1924	StL N	40	58	6	17	6	0	0	7	3	1	9	.293	.339	.397	98	0	0-0	.951	0	*111*	*117*	C34	—	0.1
Total	3	54	92	9	21	7	0	0	8	5	1	11	.228	.276	.304	55	-6	0-0	.966	-1	*105*	*107*	C44	—	-0.5
Niehaus, Al	Albert Bernard; B6.1.1899 Cincinnati OH; D10.14.1931 Cincinnati OH; BR/TR/5´11˝/175; d4.22																								
1925	Pit N	17	64	7	14	8	0	0	7	1	1	5	.219	.242	.344	45	-5	0-0	.962	-2	82	89	1b15	—	-0.7
	Cin N	51	147	16	44	10	2	0	14	13	1	10	.299	.360	.395	95	-1	1-4	.988	2	123	134	1b45	—	-0.2
	Year	68	211	23	58	18	2	0	21	14	2	15	.275	.326	.379	80	-6	1-4	.981	0	111	121	1b60	—	-0.9
Niehoff, Bert	John Albert; B5.13.1884 Louisville CO; D12.8.1974 Inglewood CA; BR/TR/5´10.5˝/170; d10.4; C1																								
1913	Cin N	2	8	0	0	0	0	0	0	0	0	2	.000	.000	.000	-99	-2	-0	.917	1	177	0	3b2	—	-0.1
1914	Cin N	142	484	46	117	16	9	4	49	38	1	77	.242	.298	.337	86	-10	20	.924	8	106	83	3b134,2b3	—	0.2
1915	†Phi N	148	529	61	126	27	2	2	49	30	1	63	.238	.280	.308	77	-15	21-11	.946	-5	97	103	2b148	—	-1.9
1916	Phi N	146	548	65	133	**42**	4	4	61	37	1	57	.243	.292	.356	95	-3	20-14	.936	1	102	120	2b144,3b2	—	0.0
1917	Phi N	114	361	30	92	17	4	2	42	23	2	29	.255	.303	.341	93	-3	8	.945	13	112	89	2b96,1b7,3b6	—	1.3
1918	StL N	22	84	5	15	2	0	0	5	3	0	10	.179	.207	.202	26	-8	2	.975	2	102	120	2b22	—	-0.6
	NY N	7	23	3	6	0	0	0	1	0	0	4	.261	.261	.261	60	-1	0	.871	-3	71	89	2b7	—	-0.4
	Year	29	107	8	21	2	0	0	6	3	0	14	.196	.218	.215	33	-9	2	.954	-1	95	113	2b29	—	-1.0
Total	6	581	2037	210	489	104	19	12	207	131	5	242	.240	.288	.327	84	-42	71-25	.943	16	102	106	2b420,3b144,1b7	—	-1.5

YEAR	TM LG	G	AB	R	H	2B	3B	HR	RBI	BB-IB	HP	SO	AVG	OBP	SLG	AOPS	ABR	SB-CS	FA	FR	RNG	THR	GAMES AT POSITION	DL	BFW
Niekro, Lance	Lance Joseph; B1.29.1979 Winter Haven FL; BR/TR/6´3˝/(210–215); [SFN00 2/61]; d9.5; f–Joe; Col Florida Southern; [DL 2004 SF N 6]																								
2003	SF N	5	5	2	1	1	0	0	2	0-0	0	1	.200	.200	.400	51	0	0-0	1.000	-0	0	156	1b3	0	-0.1
2005	SF N	113	278	32	70	16	3	12	46	17-0	2	53	.252	.295	.460	93	-4	0-2	.991	0	105	106	1b74/D	0	-1.0
2006	SF N	66	199	27	49	9	2	5	31	11-0	0	32	.246	.286	.387	70	-10	0-0	.989	2	117	91	1b58	32	-1.2
Total	3	184	482	61	120	26	5	17	79	28-0	2	86	.249	.290	.429	83	-14	0-2	.990	1	110	100	1b135/D	38	-2.3
Nielsen, Milt	Milton Robert; B2.8.1925 Tyler MN; D8.1.2005 Mankato MN; BL/TL/5´11˝/190; d9.27																								
1949	Cle A	3	9	1	1	0	0	0	0	2	0	4	.111	.273	.111	4	-1	0-0	1.000	-0	87	0	O3C	0	-0.2
1951	Cle A	16	6	1	0	0	0	0	0	1	0	1	.000	.143	.000	-63	-1	0-0	ø	0	—	—	/H	0	-0.1
Total	2	19	15	2	1	0	0	0	0	3	0	5	.067	.222	.067	-22	-2	0-0	1.000	-0	87	0	O3C	0	-0.3
Nieman, Butch	Elmer Le Roy; B2.8.1918 Herkimer KS; D11.2.1993 Topeka KS; BL/TL/6´2˝/195; d5.2; Col Kansas St.																								
1943	Bos N	101	335	39	84	15	8	7	46	39	1	39	.251	.331	.406	114	5	4	.963	1	99	131	O93(76/1/16)	0	0.1
1944	Bos N	134	468	65	124	16	6	16	65	47	0	47	.265	.332	.427	108	4	5	.975	-1	96	116	O126(86/0/46)	0	-0.5
1945	Bos N	97	247	43	61	15	0	14	56	43	1	33	.247	.361	.478	131	11	11	.932	-2	100	84	O57(43/0/14)	0	0.6
Total	3	332	1050	147	269	46	14	37	167	129	2	119	.256	.339	.432	116	20	20	.961	-1	98	114	O276(205/1/76)	0	0.2
Nieman, Bob	Robert Charles; B1.26.1927 Cincinnati OH; D3.10.1985 Corona CA; BR/TR/5´11˝/(185–205); d9.14; Col Kent St.																								
1951	StL A	12	43	6	16	3	1	2	8	3	0	5	.372	.413	.628	174	4	0-0	.962	-0	94	115	O11L	0	0.3
1952	StL A	131	478	66	138	22	2	18	74	46	1	73	.289	.352	.456	120	12	0-4	.976	1	101	107	O125(32/0/94)	0	0.7
1953	Det A	142	508	72	143	32	5	15	69	57	0	57	.281	.354	.453	118	12	0-3	.979	1	103	93	O135(74/0/64)	0	0.6
1954	Det A	91	251	24	66	14	1	8	35	22	0	32	.263	.319	.422	105	1	0-2	.984	-1	100	55	O62L	0	-0.4
1955	Chi A	99	272	36	77	11	2	11	53	36-1	2	37	.283	.366	.460	119	7	1-0	.976	-2	94	78	O78(29/0/52)	0	0.2
1956	Chi A	14	40	3	12	1	0	2	4	4-2	0	4	.300	.364	.475	118	1	0-1	1.000	0	119	0	O10R	0	0.0
	Bal A	114	388	60	125	20	6	12	64	86-3	0	59	.322	.442	.497	161	40	1-5	.980	3	112	49	O114L	0	3.3
	Year	128	428	63	137	21	6	14	68	90-5	0	63	.320	.436	.495	156	40	1-6	.982	3	**113**	45	O124(114/0/10)	0	3.3
1957	Bal A	129	445	61	123	17	6	13	70	63-3	2	86	.276	.363	.429	125	16	4-4	.980	4	105	97	O120(116/0/4)	0	1.3
1958	Bal A	105	366	56	119	20	2	16	60	44-5	0	57	.325	.395	.522	159	30	2-8	.961	-7	83	55	O100L	0	1.6
1959	Bal A	118	360	49	105	18	2	21	60	42-3	2	55	.292	.367	.528	146	23	1-2	.973	2	101	111	O97L	0	1.9
1960	StL N	81	188	19	54	13	5	4	31	24-1	2	31	.287	.372	.473	120	6	0-1	.940	-5	88	0	O55(53/0/2)	0	-0.2
1961	StL N	6	17	0	8	1	0	0	2	0-0	0	2	.471	.471	.529	150	1	0-0	1.000	-1	35	0	O4L	0	0.0
	Cle A	39	65	2	23	6	0	2	10	7-0	0	4	.354	.417	.538	157	6	1-0	.960	1	121	136	O12(7/0/5)	0	0.6
1962	Cle A	2	1	0	0	0	0	0	1	0-0	0	1	.000	.000	.000	-99	0	0-0	ø	0	—	—	/H	0	0.0
	†SF N	30	30	1	9	2	0	1	3	1-0	0	9	.300	.323	.467	111	0	0-0	1.000	0	127	0	O3L	0	0.0
Total	12	1113	3452	455	1018	180	32	125	544	435-18	9	512	.295	.373	.474	132	159	10-30	.975	-4	100	79	O926(702/0/231)	0	9.9
Niemiec, Al	Alfred Joseph; B5.18.1911 Meriden CT; D10.29.1995 Kirkland WA; BR/TR/5´11˝/158; d9.19; Col Holy Cross																								
1934	Bos A	9	32	2	7	0	0	0	3	3	0	4	.219	.286	.219	30	-3	0-0	1.000	3	121	131	2b9	—	0.0
1936	Phi A	69	203	22	40	3	2	1	20	26	1	16	.197	.291	.246	35	-22	2-2	.972	5	109	89	2b52,S5	—	-1.2
Total	2	78	235	24	47	3	2	1	23	29	1	20	.200	.291	.243	34	-25	2-2	.976	8	111	95	2b61,S5	—	-1.2
Nieto, Tom	Thomas Andrew; B10.27.1960 Downey CA; BR/TR/6´1˝/(193–210); [StLN81 3/60]; d5.10; Col Oral Roberts																								
1984	StL N	33	86	7	24	4	0	3	12	5-2	0	18	.279	.312	.430	111	1	0-0	.994	0	120	94	C32	0	0.3
1985	†StL N	95	253	15	57	10	2	0	34	26-8	3	37	.225	.305	.281	65	-11	0-2	.990	-6	115	45	C95	0	-1.5
1986	Mon N	30	65	5	13	3	1	1	7	6-1	1	21	.200	.278	.323	65	-3	0-1	.978	-9	48	46	C30	21	-1.2
1987	Min A	41	105	7	21	7	1	1	12	8-0	3	24	.200	.276	.314	54	-7	0-0	.996	-3	67	79	C40/D	65	-0.8
1988	Min A	24	60	1	4	0	0	0	0	1-0	1	17	.067	.097	.067	-52	-12	0-0	.991	0	123	55	C24	0	-1.2
1989	Phi N	11	20	1	3	0	0	0	0	6-0	1	7	.150	.370	.150	54	-1	0-0	1.000	1	85	31	C11	60	0.1
1990	Phi N	17	30	1	5	0	0	0	4	3-0	1	11	.167	.265	.167	21	-3	0-0	.984	-0	94	78	C17	11	-0.3
Total	7	251	619	37	127	24	4	5	69	55-11	10	135	.205	.280	.281	56	-36	0-3	.991	-16	99	60	C249/D	157	-4.6
Nieves, Jose	Jose Miguel (Pinto); B6.16.1975 Guacara, Carabobo, Venez.; BR/TR/6´1˝/(180–185); d8.7																								
1998	Chi N	2	1	0	0	0	0	0	0	0-0	0	0	.000	.000	.000	-97	0	0-0	ø	-0	0	0	/S	0	-0.1
1999	Chi N	54	181	16	45	9	1	2	18	8-0	4	25	.249	.291	.343	61	-11	0-2	.935	1	112	91	S52	0	-0.6
2000	Chi N	82	198	17	42	6	3	5	24	11-1	0	43	.212	.251	.348	51	-16	1-1	.949	-2	108	38	3b39,S24,2b7	17	-1.6
2001	Ana A	29	53	5	13	3	1	2	3	2-0	2	20	.245	.298	.453	92	-1	0-1	1.000	5	127	184	2b11,S10,3b2/1D	19	0.4
2002	Ana A	45	97	17	28	2	0	0	6	2-0	0	14	.289	.303	.309	64	-5	1-1	.938	-7	74	92	2b18,S13,3b5,1b3,O2(0/1/1)	0	-1.0
Total	5	212	530	55	128	20	5	9	51	23-1	6	102	.242	.278	.349	60	-33	2-5	.945	-3	101	91	S100,3b46,2b36,D4,1b4,O2(0/1/1)	36	-2.9
Nieves, Melvin	Melvin Ramos; B12.28.1971 San Juan, PR; BB/TR/6´2˝/(186–220); d9.1; b–Wilbert																								
1992	Atl N	12	19	0	4	1	0	0	1	2-0	0	7	.211	.286	.263	53	-1	0-0	.727	-1	99	0	O6(3/0/3)	0	-0.2
1993	SD N	19	47	4	9	0	0	2	3	3-0	1	21	.191	.255	.319	52	-3	0-0	.931	-0	116	0	O15R	0	-0.4
1994	SD N	10	19	2	5	1	0	1	4	3-0	0	10	.263	.364	.474	120	1	0-0	1.000	1	145	365	O6(2/0/4)	0	0.2
1995	SD N	98	234	32	48	6	1	14	38	19-0	5	88	.205	.276	.419	83	-7	2-3	.990	0	96	149	O79(62/6/15),1b2	0	-0.9
1996	Det A	120	431	71	106	23	4	24	60	44-2	6	158	.246	.322	.485	101	-1	1-2	.943	-1	98	122	O105(21/0/84),D11	32	-0.7
1997	Det A	116	359	46	82	18	1	20	64	39-6	5	157	.228	.311	.451	97	-3	1-7	.979	0	103	70	O99(0/2/99),D10	15	-0.9
1998	Cin N	83	119	8	30	4	0	2	17	26-1	0	42	.252	.381	.336	91	0	0-0	1.000	-1	89	82	O25(3/0/22),D3	44	-0.2
Total	7	458	1228	163	284	53	6	63	187	136-9	17	483	.231	.314	.438	93	-14	4-12	.962	-1	100	106	O335(91/8/242),D24,1b2	91	-3.1
Nieves, Wilbert	Wilbert; B9.25.1977 San Juan, PR; BR/TR/5´11˝/190; [SDN95 47/1286]; d7.21; b–Melvin																								
2002	SD N	28	72	2	13	3	1	0	3	4-4	0	15	.181	.224	.250	27	-8	1-0	.971	-0	121	54	C27	0	-0.7
2005	NY A	3	4	0	0	0	0	0	0	0-0	0	1	.000	.000	.000	-99	-1	0-0	1.000	1	0	0	C3	0	0.0
2006	NY A	6	6	0	0	0	0	0	0	0-0	0	1	.000	.000	.000	-99	-2	0-0	1.000	0	55	202	C6	0	-0.1
Total	3	37	82	2	13	3	1	0	3	4-4	0	17	.159	.198	.220	10	-11	1-0	.975	1	110	65	C36	0	-0.8
Niland, Tom	Thomas James "Honest Tom"; B4.14.1870 Brookfield MA; D4.30.1950 Lynn MA; BR/TR/5´11˝/160; d4.19																								
1896	StL N	18	68	3	12	0	1	0	3	5	1	4	.176	.243	.206	20	-8	0	.913	-2	117	210	O13(6/0/7),S5	—	-1.0
Niles, Harry	Herbert Clyde; B9.10.1880 Buchanan MI; D4.18.1953 Sturgis MI; BR/TR/5´8˝/175; d4.24																								
1906	StL A	142	541	71	124	14	4	2	31	46	6	—	.229	.297	.281	85	-9	30	.967	11	**256**	193	O108(0/6/102),3b34	—	-0.2
1907	StL A	120	492	65	142	9	5	2	35	28	3	—	.289	.331	.339	114	7	19	.949	-3	102	112	2b116/rf	—	0.6
1908	NY A	95	361	43	90	14	6	4	24	25	4	—	.249	.305	.355	113	5	18	.928	-17	89	52	2b85,O7(1/1/5)	—	-1.4
	Bos A	18	33	4	8	0	0	1	3	6	1	—	.242	.375	.333	127	1	3	1.000	-1	89	88	2b8,S2	—	0.1
	Year	113	394	47	98	14	6	5	27	31	5	—	.249	.312	.353	114	6	21	.934	-18	89	55	2b93,O7(1/1/5),S2	—	-1.3
1909	Bos A	145	546	65	134	12	5	1	38	39	13	—	.245	.311	.291	88	-7	27	.952	-2	127	85	O117(77/12/28),3b13,S9,2b5	—	-1.7
1910	Bos A	18	57	6	12	3	0	1	3	4	0	—	.211	.262	.316	79	-1	1	.920	0	105	108	O15(4/0/11)	—	-0.2
	Cle A	70	240	25	51	6	4	1	18	15	3	—	.213	.267	.283	72	-9	9	.975	-5	97	105	O50(13/0/37),S7,3b5	—	-1.7
	Year	88	297	31	63	9	4	2	21	19	3	—	.212	.266	.290	73	-10	10	.962	-5	99	106	O65(17/0/48),S7,3b5	—	-1.9
Total	5	608	2270	279	561	58	24	12	152	163	30	—	.247	.306	.310	95	-13	107	.960	-16	165	125	O298(95/19/184),2b214,3b52,S18	—	-4.5
Niles, Bill	William E.; B1.11.1867 Covington KY; D7.3.1936 Springfield OH; ?/160; d5.13																								
1895	Pit N	11	37	2	8	0	0	0	0	5	0	2	.216	.310	.216	39	-3	2	.930	0	94	68	3b10/2	—	-0.2
Nill, Rabbit	George Charles; B7.14.1881 Ft.Wayne IN; D5.24.1962 Fort Wayne IN; BR/TR/5´7˝/160; d9.27																								
1904	Was A	15	48	4	8	0	1	0	3	5	2	—	.167	.273	.208	54	-2	0	.878	-3	89	66	2b15	—	-0.6
1905	Was A	103	319	46	58	7	3	3	31	33	5	—	.182	.269	.251	68	-11	12	.897	-1	98	135	3b52,2b33,S6	—	-1.1
1906	Was A	89	315	37	74	8	2	0	15	47	3	—	.235	.340	.273	97	2	16	.882	2	97	112	S31,2b25,3b15,O15C	—	0.5
1907	Was A	66	215	21	47	7	3	0	25	15	4	—	.219	.282	.279	86	-3	6	.962	0	99	74	2b39,O18(17/0/1)/3	—	-0.4
	Cle A	12	43	5	12	1	0	0	2	3	0	—	.279	.326	.302	100	0	2	.815	-2	107	134	3b7,S4	—	-0.2
	Year	78	258	26	59	8	3	0	27	18	4	—	.229	.289	.283	88	-3	8	.962	-2	99	74	2b39,O18(17/0/1),3b8,S4	—	-0.6
1908	Cle A	11	23	3	5	0	0	0	1	0	0	—	.217	.217	.217	41	-2	0	.833	-1	109	120	S6,O3(2/0/2)/2	—	-0.2
Total	5	296	963	116	204	23	9	3	77	103	14	—	.212	.297	.264	82	-16	36	.943	-5	104	83	2b113,3b75,S47,O36(19/15/3)	—	-2.0

NILSSON, DAVE David Wayne; B12.14.1969 Brisbane, Queensland, Australia; BL/TR/6´3˝/(185–240); d5.18

YEAR	TM LG	G	AB	R	H	2B	3B	HR	RBI	BB-IB	HP	SO	AVG	OBP	SLG	AOPS	ABR	SB-CS	FA	FR	RNG	THR	GAMES AT POSITION	DL	BFW
1992	Mil A	51	164	15	38	8	0	4	25	17-1	0	18	.232	.304	.354	85	-3	2-2	.992	1	142	78	C46,1b3,D2	18	0.0
1993	Mil A	100	296	35	76	10	2	7	40	37-5	0	36	.257	.336	.375	93	-3	3-6	.981	-8	90	74	C91,1b4,D4	44	-0.7
1994	Mil A	109	397	51	109	28	3	12	69	34-9	0	61	.275	.326	.451	94	-4	1-0	.994	-5	72	58	C60,D43,1b5	0	-0.7
1995	Mil A	81	263	41	73	12	1	12	53	24-4	2	41	.278	.337	.468	102	0	2-0	.981	1	97	143	O58(15/0/47),D14,1b7,C2	60	-0.2
1996	Mil A	123	453	81	150	33	2	17	84	57-6	3	68	.331	.407	.525	129	22	2-3	.965	-1	88	121	O61(6/0/55),D40,1b24,C2	34	1.2
1997	Mil A	156	554	71	154	33	0	20	81	65-8	2	88	.278	.352	.446	106	6	2-3	.991	-3	84	129	1b74,D59,O22L	0	-0.7
1998	Mil N	102	309	39	83	14	1	12	56	33-1	1	48	.269	.339	.437	101	0	2-2	.984	-6	77	134	1b49,O37(37/0/3),C7	43	-1.0
1999	Mil N★	115	343	56	106	19	1	21	62	53-6	2	64	.309	.400	.554	139	21	1-2	.991	-16	63	100	C101/D	22	1.1
Total	8	837	2779	389	789	157	10	105	470	320-40	10	424	.284	.356	.461	109	39	15-18	.988	-37	86	78	C309,O178(80/0/105),1b166,D163	221	-1.0

NIVAR, RAMON Ramon A.; B2.22.1980 San Cristobal, D.R.; BR/TR/5´10˝/(170–185); d7.30

YEAR	TM LG	G	AB	R	H	2B	3B	HR	RBI	BB-IB	HP	SO	AVG	OBP	SLG	AOPS	ABR	SB-CS	FA	FR	RNG	THR	GAMES AT POSITION	DL	BFW
2003	Tex A	28	90	9	19	1	2	0	7	4-0	1	10	.211	.253	.267	35	-9	4-2	.961	2	108	267	O26C/D	0	-0.6
2004	Tex A	7	18	3	4	0	0	0	4	0-0	0	7	.222	.211	.222	16	-2	1-1	1.000	0	82	349	O6C	0	-0.2
2005	Bal A	7	13	1	4	0	0	0	1	0-0	1	2	.308	.357	.308	80	0	0-1	1.000	1	142	0	O4C	0	0.0
Total	3	42	121	13	27	1	2	0	12	4-0	2	19	.223	.258	.264	37	-11	5-4	.970	3	106	258	O36C/D	0	-0.8

NIX, LAYNCE Laynce Michael; B10.30.1980 Houston TX; BL/TL/6´0˝/(190–200); [TexA00 4/124]; d7.10

YEAR	TM LG	G	AB	R	H	2B	3B	HR	RBI	BB-IB	HP	SO	AVG	OBP	SLG	AOPS	ABR	SB-CS	FA	FR	RNG	THR	GAMES AT POSITION	DL	BFW
2003	Tex A	53	184	25	47	10	0	8	30	9-0	0	53	.255	.289	.440	83	-5	3-0	.963	3	123	39	O52(5/21/37)	0	-0.3
2004	Tex A	115	371	58	92	20	4	14	46	23-4	2	113	.248	.293	.437	84	-10	1-1	.996	-8	87	78	O114(0/111/3)	26	-1.6
2005	Tex A	63	229	28	55	12	3	6	32	9-3	0	45	.240	.267	.397	72	-10	2-0	.988	0	103	99	O61C	80	-0.8
2006	Tex A	9	32	1	3	1	0	0	4	0-0	1	17	.094	.118	.125	-36	-7	0-0	1.000	1	92	443	O9C	0	-0.5
	Mil N	10	35	2	8	1	0	1	6	0-0	1	11	.229	.250	.343	49	-3	0-0	1.000	-1	97	0	O9C	23	-0.3
Total	4	250	851	114	205	44	7	29	118	41-7	4	239	.241	.277	.411	75	-35	6-1	.986	-4	99	86	O245(5/211/40)	129	-3.5

NIXON, AL Albert Richard "Humpty Dumpty"; B4.11.1886 Atlantic City NJ; D11.9.1960 Opelousas LA; BR/TL/5´7.5˝/164; d9.4

YEAR	TM LG	G	AB	R	H	2B	3B	HR	RBI	BB-IB	HP	SO	AVG	OBP	SLG	AOPS	ABR	SB-CS	FA	FR	RNG	THR	GAMES AT POSITION	DL	BFW
1915	Bro N	14	26	3	6	1	0	0	2	2	0	4	.231	.286	.269	67	-1	1-1	1.000	0	85	130	O14(8/1/1)	—	-0.1
1916	Bro N	1	2	0	2	0	0	0	0	0	0	0	1.000	1.000	1.000	501	1	0	ø	-0	0	0	/lf	—	0.1
1918	Bro N	6	11	1	5	0	0	0	0	0	0	0	.455	.455	.455	178	1	0	1.000	0	123	0	O4(2/0/1)	—	0.1
1921	Bos N	55	138	25	33	6	3	1	9	7	1	11	.239	.281	.348	69	-7	3-2	.980	2	115	83	O43(22/10/13)	—	-0.7
1922	Bos N	86	318	35	84	14	4	2	22	9	0	19	.264	.284	.352	66	-17	6-6	.975	2	115	65	O79(48/22/11)	—	-2.0
1923	Bos N	88	321	53	88	12	4	0	19	24	5	14	.274	.334	.336	81	-9	2-3	.987	7	105	141	O80(14/62/4)	—	-0.6
1926	Phi N	93	311	38	91	18	2	4	41	13	1	20	.293	.323	.402	90	-5	5	.977	2	104	100	O88C	—	-0.6
1927	Phi N	54	154	18	48	7	0	0	18	5	0	5	.312	.333	.357	84	-4	1	.969	2	116	74	O44(0/43/1)	—	-0.3
1928	Phi N	25	64	7	15	2	0	0	7	6	0	4	.234	.300	.266	47	-5	1	1.000	1	113	66	O20(10/0/10)	—	-0.5
Total	9	422	1345	180	372	60	13	7	118	66	7	77	.277	.314	.356	78	-46	19-12	.980	16	110	95	O373(105/226/41)	—	-4.6

NIXON, TROT Christopher Trotman; B4.11.1974 Durham NC; BL/TL/6´2˝/(196–210); [BosA93 1/7]; d9.21

YEAR	TM LG	G	AB	R	H	2B	3B	HR	RBI	BB-IB	HP	SO	AVG	OBP	SLG	AOPS	ABR	SB-CS	FA	FR	RNG	THR	GAMES AT POSITION	DL	BFW
1996	Bos A	2	4	2	2	1	0	0	0	0-0	0	1	.500	.500	.750	207	1	1-0	1.000	0	134	0	O2R	0	0.1
1998	†Bos A	13	27	3	7	1	0	0	0	1-0	0	3	.259	.286	.296	51	-2	0-0	1.000	1	148	0	O7(1/0/6),D2	0	-0.1
1999	†Bos A	124	381	67	103	22	5	15	52	53-1	3	75	.270	.357	.472	108	5	3-1	.968	-7	95	38	O121R	0	-0.7
2000	Bos A	123	427	66	118	27	8	12	60	63-2	2	85	.276	.368	.461	106	5	8-1	.991	1	100	109	O118(0/6/115)/D	30	0.2
2001	Bos A	148	535	100	150	31	4	27	88	79-1	7	113	.280	.376	.505	130	25	7-4	.973	-5	95	85	O145(0/70/83)/D	0	1.6
2002	Bos A	152	532	81	136	36	3	24	94	65-2	5	109	.256	.338	.470	111	9	4-2	.984	-1	102	79	O152(0/13/145)	0	0.1
2003	†Bos A	134	441	81	135	24	6	28	87	65-4	3	96	.306	.396	.578	147	31	4-2	.983	-4	97	58	O130(0/1/129)	0	2.0
2004	†Bos A	48	149	24	47	9	1	6	23	15-1	1	24	.315	.377	.510	122	5	0-0	.985	-3	91	43	O40R,D3	117	0.1
2005	†Bos A	124	408	64	112	29	1	13	67	53-3	3	59	.275	.357	.446	109	7	2-1	.996	8	112	127	O118R,D2	27	0.9
2006	Bos A	114	381	59	102	24	0	8	52	60-1	7	56	.268	.373	.394	98	2	0-2	.995	2	105	95	O110R	34	-0.2
Total	10	982	3285	547	912	204	28	133	523	454-15	31	621	.278	.366	.478	116	88	29-13	.984	-9	100	81	O943(1/90/869),D9	208	4.0

NIXON, OTIS Otis Junior; B1.9.1959 Columbus Co. NC; BB/TR/6´2˝/180; [NYA79 S1/3]; d9.9; b–Donell; Col Louisburg (NC) JC

YEAR	TM LG	G	AB	R	H	2B	3B	HR	RBI	BB-IB	HP	SO	AVG	OBP	SLG	AOPS	ABR	SB-CS	FA	FR	RNG	THR	GAMES AT POSITION	DL	BFW
1983	NY A	13	14	2	2	0	0	0	0	1-0	0	5	.143	.200	.143	-4	-2	2-0	.938	1	129	303	O9(0/4/5)	0	-0.1
1984	Cle A	49	91	16	14	0	0	0	1	8-0	0	11	.154	.220	.154	6	-12	12-6	1.000	2	105	124	O46(43/4/0)	0	-1.1
1985	Cle A	104	162	34	38	4	0	3	9	8-0	0	27	.235	.271	.315	60	-9	20-11	.971	6	122	170	O80(53/26/0),D11	0	-0.4
1986	Cle A	105	95	33	25	4	1	0	8	13-0	0	12	.263	.352	.326	87	-1	23-6	.969	3	110	132	O95(84/14/0),D5	0	0.3
1987	Cle A	19	17	2	1	0	0	0	1	3-0	0	4	.059	.200	.059	-26	-3	2-3	1.000	1	121	0	O17(11/7/0),D2	0	-0.3
1988	Mon N	90	271	47	66	8	2	0	15	28-0	0	42	.244	.312	.288	70	-10	46-13	.994	-1	101	55	O82(25/61/0)	0	-0.6
1989	Mon N	126	258	41	56	7	2	0	21	33-1	0	36	.217	.306	.260	62	-12	37-12	.988	-1	102	61	O98(13/92/1)	0	-1.0
1990	Mon N	119	231	46	58	6	2	1	20	28-0	0	33	.251	.331	.307	80	-6	50-13	.994	2	102	145	O88(21/71/0)/S	0	0.2
1991	Atl N	124	401	81	119	10	1	0	26	47-3	2	40	.297	.371	.327	93	-2	72-21	.987	3	107	92	O115(55/17/48)	0	0.7
1992	†Atl N	120	456	79	134	14	2	2	22	39-0	0	54	.294	.348	.346	92	-4	41-18	.991	10	119	93	O111(2/102/16)	0	0.7
1993	†Atl N	134	461	77	124	12	3	1	24	61-2	0	63	.269	.351	.315	79	-12	47-13	.990	1	105	68	O116(0/115/2)	0	-0.4
1994	Bos A	103	398	60	109	15	1	0	25	55-1	0	65	.274	.360	.317	74	-14	42-10	.989	-2	98	76	O103C	0	-0.8
1995	Tex A	139	589	87	174	21	2	0	45	58-1	0	85	.295	.357	.338	80	-16	50-21	.989	-5	98	56	O138C	0	-1.5
1996	Tor A	125	496	87	142	15	1	1	29	71-1	1	68	.286	.377	.327	81	-12	54-13	.994	1	108	66	O125C	15	-0.2
1997	Tor A	103	401	54	105	12	1	1	26	52-0	0	54	.262	.343	.304	72	-15	47-10	.996	-3	102	20	O102C/D	0	-1.0
	LA N	42	175	30	48	6	2	1	18	13-0	0	24	.274	.323	.349	81	-5	12-2	.990	-1	103	51	O42C	0	-0.4
1998	Min A	110	448	71	133	6	6	1	20	44-0	2	56	.297	.361	.344	83	-11	37-7	.989	-3	100	59	O108C	30	-0.7
1999	†Atl N	84	151	31	31	2	1	0	8	23-1	0	15	.205	.309	.232	40	-14	26-7	.981	-5	77	0	O52(50/5/0)	34	-1.6
Total	17	1709	5115	878	1379	142	27	11	318	585-10	5	694	.270	.343	.314	76	-160	620-186	.989	8	104	74	O1527(357/1136/72),D19/S	79	-8.2

NIXON, DONELL Robert Donell; B12.31.1961 Evergreen NC; BR/TR/6´1˝/185; [SeaA80 10/240]; d4.7; b–Otis; Col Louisburg (NC) JC; [DL 1985 Sea A 182]

YEAR	TM LG	G	AB	R	H	2B	3B	HR	RBI	BB-IB	HP	SO	AVG	OBP	SLG	AOPS	ABR	SB-CS	FA	FR	RNG	THR	GAMES AT POSITION	DL	BFW
1987	Sea A	46	132	17	33	4	0	3	12	13-0	2	28	.250	.327	.348	75	-5	21-7	1.000	0	101	77	O32(1/32/0),D6	0	-0.2
1988	SF N	59	78	15	27	3	0	0	6	10-0	0	12	.346	.420	.385	138	4	11-8	.983	1	117	0	O46(32/15/0)	0	0.5
1989	†SF N	95	166	23	44	2	0	1	15	11-1	0	30	.265	.311	.295	76	-5	10-3	.967	-3	96	0	O64(15/29/26)	0	-0.9
1990	Bal A	8	20	1	5	2	0	0	2	1-0	0	7	.250	.286	.350	79	-1	5-0	1.000	-1	68	0	O4L,D3	0	0.0
Total	4	208	396	56	109	11	0	4	35	35-1	2	77	.275	.337	.333	88	-7	47-18	.983	-3	102	24	O146(52/76/26),D9	182	-0.6

NIXON, RUSS Russell Eugene; B2.19.1935 Cleves OH; BL/TR/6´1˝/(190–200); d4.20; M5/C12

YEAR	TM LG	G	AB	R	H	2B	3B	HR	RBI	BB-IB	HP	SO	AVG	OBP	SLG	AOPS	ABR	SB-CS	FA	FR	RNG	THR	GAMES AT POSITION	DL	BFW
1957	Cle A	62	185	15	52	7	1	2	18	12-7	0	12	.281	.323	.362	88	-3	0-1	.984	-4	61	117	C57	0	-0.5
1958	Cle A	113	376	42	113	17	4	9	46	13-4	0	38	.301	.322	.439	111	3	0-3	.991	-8	102	78	C101	0	0.0
1959	Cle A	82	258	23	62	10	3	1	29	15-1	0	28	.240	.277	.314	66	-13	0-0	.985	-5	74	67	C74	0	-1.4
1960	Cle A	25	82	6	20	5	0	1	6	6-2	2	6	.244	.308	.341	79	-2	0-1	.993	2	123	115	C25	0	0.0
	Bos A	80	272	24	81	17	3	5	33	13-3	0	23	.298	.329	.438	102	0	0-1	.987	-9	96	63	C74	0	-0.6
	Year	105	354	30	101	22	3	6	39	19-5	2	29	.285	.324	.415	97	-2	0-2	.989	-8	103	76	C99	0	-0.6
1961	Bos A	87	242	24	70	12	2	1	19	13-1	2	19	.289	.327	.368	84	-5	0-1	.975	-4	74	61	C66	0	-0.7
1962	Bos A	65	151	11	42	7	2	1	19	8-3	0	14	.278	.313	.371	81	-4	0-0	1.000	-4	76	0	C38	31	-0.6
1963	Bos A	98	287	27	77	18	1	5	30	22-5	4	32	.268	.327	.390	98	0	0-0	.992	-5	136	73	C76	0	-0.1
1964	Bos A	81	163	10	38	7	0	1	20	14-3	2	29	.233	.297	.294	64	-8	0-0	.990	-4	103	65	C45	0	-1.0
1965	Bos A	59	137	11	37	5	1	0	11	6-2	0	23	.270	.295	.321	72	-5	0-0	.981	-8	45	86	C38	0	-1.2
1966	Min A	51	96	5	25	2	1	0	7	7-3	1	13	.260	.314	.302	74	-3	0-0	.986	-4	75	85	C32	0	-0.7
1967	Min A	74	170	16	40	6	1	1	22	18-3	0	29	.235	.304	.300	74	-5	0-0	.994	-3	104	80	C69	0	-0.6
1968	Bos A	29	85	1	13	2	0	0	6	7-1	0	13	.153	.217	.176	19	-8	0-0	.994	-4	83	108	C27	0	-1.3
Total	12	906	2504	215	670	115	19	27	266	154-38	11	279	.268	.310	.361	84	-53	0-7	.988	-60	92	74	C722	31	-8.7

NOBLE, RAY Rafael Miguel (Magee); B3.15.1919 Central Hatillo, Cuba; D5.9.1998 Brooklyn NY; BR/TR/5´11˝/(185–210); d4.18; Negro Lg 1945–50

YEAR	TM LG	G	AB	R	H	2B	3B	HR	RBI	BB-IB	HP	SO	AVG	OBP	SLG	AOPS	ABR	SB-CS	FA	FR	RNG	THR	GAMES AT POSITION	DL	BFW
1951	†NY N	55	141	16	33	6	0	5	26	6	0	26	.234	.265	.383	72	-6	0-0	.974	-2	*142*	*54*	C41	0	-0.7
1952	NY N	6	5	0	0	0	0	0	0	0	0	1	.000	.000	.000	-99	-1	0-0	1.000	0	*0*	*0*	C5	0	-0.1
1953	NY N	46	97	15	20	0	1	4	14	19	3	14	.206	.353	.351	83	-2	1-0	.982	-0	*146*	*90*	C41	0	-0.1
Total	3	107	243	31	53	6	1	9	40	25	3	41	.218	.299	.362	74	-9	1-0	.979	-2	*142*	*71*	C87	0	-0.9

NOBOA, JUNIOR Milciades Arturo (Diaz); B11.10.1964 Azua, D.R.; BR/TR/5´10˝/(155–170); d8.22; OF(3/0/13)

YEAR	TM LG	G	AB	R	H	2B	3B	HR	RBI	BB-IB	HP	SO	AVG	OBP	SLG	AOPS	ABR	SB-CS	FA	FR	RNG	THR	GAMES AT POSITION	DL	BFW
1984	Cle A	23	11	3	4	0	0	0	0	0-0	0	2	.364	.364	.364	100	0	1-0	1.000	-3	74	103	2b19/D	0	-0.2
1987	Cle A	39	80	7	18	2	1	0	7	3-1	0	6	.225	.253	.275	40	-7	1-0	.983	-3	94	59	2b21,S8,3b5/D	0	-0.8
1988	Cal A	21	16	4	1	0	0	0	0	0-0	0	1	.063	.063	.063	-66	-4	0-0	.967	2	139	154	2b9,S3,3b2	0	-0.2

YEAR	TM LG	G	AB	R	H	2B	3B	HR	RBI	BB-IB	HP	SO	AVG	OBP	SLG	AOPS	ABR	SB-CS	FA	FR	RNG	THR	GAMES AT POSITION	DL	BFW
NOCE, PAUL	Paul David; B12.16.1959 San Francisco CA; BR/TR/5´10˝/175; [SDN81 14/343]; d6.1; Col Washington St.																								
1987	Chi N	70	180	17	41	9	2	3	14	6-1	2	49	.228	.261	.350	58	-12	5-3	.983	11	112	116	2b36,S35,3b2	0	0.3
1990	Cin N	1	1	0	1	0	0	0	0	0-0	0	0	1.000	1.000	1.000	434	0	0-0	ø	0	—	—	/H	0	0.0
Total	2	71	181	17	42	9	2	3	14	6-1	2	49	.232	.265	.354	60	-12	5-3	.983	11	112	116	2b36,S35,3b2	0	0.3
NOFTSKER, GEORGE	George Washington; B8.24.1859 Shippensburg PA; D5.8.1931 Shippensburg PA; BR/TR/5´8˝/135; d4.17																								
1884	Alt U	7	25	0	1	0	0	0	—	0	—	—	.040	.040	.040	-75	-6	—	.818	0	0	0	O5(0/1/4),C3	—	-0.5
NOKES, MATT	Matthew Dodge; B10.31.1963 San Diego CA; BL/TR/6´1˝/(185–210); [SFN81 20/503]; d9.3																								
1985	SF N	19	53	3	11	2	0	2	5	1-0	1	9	.208	.236	.358	67	-3	0-0	.977	-2	67	23	C14	0	-0.4
1986	Det A	7	24	2	8	1	0	1	2	1-1	0	1	.333	.360	.500	131	1	0-0	1.000	1	147	43	C7	0	0.2
1987	†Det A★	135	461	69	133	14	2	32	87	35-2	6	70	.289	.345	.536	134	21	2-1	.992	-6	103	55	C109,D19,O3(3/0/1),3b2	0	1.8
1988	Det A	122	382	53	96	18	0	16	53	34-3	1	58	.251	.313	.424	108	3	0-1	.989	5	135	101	C110,D4	0	1.4
1989	Det A	87	268	15	67	10	0	9	39	17-1	2	37	.250	.298	.388	94	-3	1-0	.978	-4	81	135	C51,D33	45	-0.5
1990	Det A	44	111	12	30	5	1	3	8	4-3	2	14	.270	.305	.414	99	-1	0-0	.984	-5	90	195	D24,C19	0	-0.5
	NY A	92	240	21	57	4	0	8	32	20-3	4	33	.237	.307	.354	84	-6	2-2	.995	-4	75	177	C46,D30,O2R	0	-0.9
	Year	136	351	33	87	9	1	11	40	24-6	6	47	.248	.306	.373	88	-6	2-2	.993	-9	79	182	C65,D54,O2R	0	-1.4
1991	NY A	135	456	52	122	20	0	24	77	25-5	5	49	.268	.308	.469	112	5	3-2	.992	-10	73	97	C130,D3	0	0.3
1992	NY A	121	384	42	86	9	1	22	59	37-11	3	62	.224	.293	.424	100	-2	0-1	.993	-14	72	84	C111	0	-1.0
1993	NY A	76	217	25	54	8	0	10	35	16-2	2	31	.249	.303	.424	97	-2	0-0	.992	-10	70	95	C56,D11	16	-0.9
1994	NY A	28	79	11	23	3	0	7	19	5-0	0	16	.291	.329	.595	138	4	0-0	.975	-2	116	50	C17,1b4,D5	64	0.3
1995	Bal A	26	49	4	6	1	0	2	6	4-0	0	11	.122	.185	.265	16	-6	0-0	.989	1	56	94	C16,D2	0	-0.5
	Col N	10	11	1	2	1	0	0	0	1-1	0	4	.182	.250	.273	29	-1	0-0	.909	0	0	0	C3	35	-0.1
Total	11	902	2735	310	695	96	4	136	422	200-32	26	395	.254	.308	.441	106	10	8-7	.990	-48	90	95	C689,D131,O5(3/0/3),1b4,3b2	160	-0.8
NOLAN, JOE	Joseph William; B5.12.1951 St.Louis MO; BL/TR/6´0˝/(175–203); [NYN69 2/28]; d9.21																								
1972	NY N	4	10	0	0	0	0	0	0	1-0	0	3	.000	.091	.000	-73	-2	0-0	.938	-1	130	133	C3	0	-0.3
1975	Atl N	4	4	0	1	0	0	0	0	1-0	0	0	.250	.400	.250	81	0	0-0	1.000	0	0	0	/C	0	0.0
1977	Atl N	62	82	13	23	3	0	3	9	13-1	0	12	.280	.375	.427	104	1	1-0	1.000	-3	55	68	C19	15	-0.2
1978	Atl N	95	213	22	49	7	3	4	22	34-5	1	28	.230	.339	.347	83	-4	3-2	.979	-9	78	46	C61	0	-1.1
1979	Atl N	89	230	28	57	9	3	4	21	27-3	3	28	.248	.333	.365	86	-4	1-3	.983	-9	62	71	C74	0	-1.2
1980	Atl N	17	22	2	6	1	0	0	2	2-0	0	4	.273	.333	.318	82	0	0-0	1.000	1	66	137	C6	0	0.1
	Cin N	53	154	14	48	7	0	3	24	13-0	0	8	.312	.353	.416	120	4	0-0	.982	-4	63	96	C51	0	0.2
	Year	70	176	16	54	8	0	3	26	15-0	0	12	.307	.350	.403	114	4	0-0	.983	-3	63	99	C57	0	0.3
1981	Cin N	81	236	25	73	18	1	1	26	24-6	1	19	.309	.371	.407	122	8	1-2	**.995**	-7	81	45	C81	0	0.4
1982	Bal A	77	219	24	51	7	1	6	35	16-1	0	35	.233	.278	.356	75	-8	1-1	.978	-3	72	116	C72	0	-0.8
1983	†Bal A	73	184	25	51	11	1	5	24	16-1	2	31	.277	.342	.429	112	3	0-0	.980	-7	96	56	C65	22	-0.1
1984	Bal A	35	62	2	18	1	1	1	9	12-4	0	10	.290	.400	.387	123	3	0-0	.962	-0	95	312	D11,C6	90	0.2
1985	Bal A	31	38	1	5	2	0	0	6	5-1	0	5	.132	.227	.184	16	-4	0-0	1.000	0	59	0	C5,D4	97	-0.4
Total	11	621	1454	156	382	66	10	27	178	164-22	7	183	.263	.336	.378	96	-3	7-8	.984	-41	75	74	C444,D15	224	-3.2
NONNENKAMP, RED	Leo William; B7.7.1910 St.Louis MO; D12.3.2000 Little Rock AR; BL/TL/5´11˝/165; d9.6																								
1933	Pit N	1	1	0	0	0	0	0	0	0	0	1	.000	.000	.000	-99	0	0	ø	0	—	—	/H	—	0.0
1938	Bos A	87	180	37	51	4	1	0	18	21	0	13	.283	.358	.317	67	-9	6-1	.968	3	111	152	O39(5/5/29),1b5	—	-0.7
1939	Bos A	58	75	12	18	2	1	0	5	12	0	6	.240	.345	.293	62	-4	0-1	.962	-1	99	0	O15(7/4/4)	—	-0.5
1940	Bos A	9	7	0	0	0	0	0	1	0	1	4	.000	.125	.000	-62	-2	0-0	ø	0	—	—	/H	—	-0.2
Total	4	155	263	49	69	6	2	0	24	33	1	24	.262	.347	.300	62	-15	6-2	.966	2	108	117	O54(12/9/33),1b5	—	-1.4
NOONAN, PETE	Peter John; B11.24.1881 W.Stockbridge MA; D2.11.1965 Great Barrington MA; BR/TR/6´0˝/180; d6.20; Col Holy Cross																								
1904	Phi A	39	114	13	23	3	1	2	13	1	0	—	.202	.209	.298	56	-6	1	.969	-2	*100*	*110*	C22,1b10	—	-0.7
1906	Chi N	5	3	0	1	0	0	0	0	0	0	—	.333	.333	.333	102	0	0	1.000	0	0	2150	/1	—	0.0
	StL N	44	125	8	21	1	3	1	9	11	0	—	.168	.235	.248	53	-7	1	.957	-2	*82*	*111*	C23,1b16	—	-0.8
	Year	49	128	8	22	1	3	1	9	11	0	—	.172	.237	.250	54	-8	1	.957	-2	*82*	*111*	C23,1b17	—	-0.8
1907	StL N	74	237	19	53	7	3	1	16	9	0	—	.224	.252	.291	73	-9	3	.951	-3	*83*	*95*	C70	—	-0.6
Total	3	162	479	40	98	11	7	4	38	21	0	—	.205	.238	.282	64	-22	5	.955	-7	*85*	*101*	C115,1b27	—	-2.1
NORDBROOK, TIM	Timothy Charles; B7.7.1949 Baltimore MD; BR/TR/6´1˝/170; [BalA70 9/222]; d9.13; Col Loyola–Maryland																								
1974	Bal A	6	15	4	4	0	0	0	1	2-0	0	2	.267	.353	.267	82	0	1-0	1.000	0	100	133	S5/2	0	0.1
1975	Bal A	40	34	6	4	1	0	0	0	7-0	0	7	.118	.268	.147	21	-3	0-0	.970	-2	110	90	S37,2b3	0	-0.4
1976	Bal A	27	22	4	5	0	0	0	0	3-0	0	5	.227	.320	.227	66	-1	0-0	1.000	-3	52	58	2b14,S12/D	0	-0.3
	Cal A	5	8	1	0	0	0	0	0	1-0	0	3	.000	.111	.000	-70	-2	1-0	.941	-1	89	0	S4/2	0	-0.2
	Year	32	30	5	5	0	0	0	0	4-0	0	8	.167	.265	.167	30	-3	1-0	.978	-4	94	90	S16,2b15/D	0	-0.5
1977	Chi A	15	20	2	5	0	0	0	1	7-0	0	4	.250	.429	.250	95	0	1-0	.850	-4	70	59	S11/3D	0	-0.2
	Tor A	24	63	9	11	0	1	0	1	4-0	0	11	.175	.224	.206	18	-7	1-0	.989	-3	89	71	S24	0	-0.8
	Year	39	83	11	16	0	1	0	2	11-0	0	15	.193	.284	.217	39	-7	2-0	.947	-7	84	68	S35,D2/3	0	-1.0
1978	Tor A	7	0	1	0	0	0	0	0	0-0	1	0	ø	1.000	ø	200	0	0-0	1.000	0	119	112	S7	0	0.1
	Mil A	2	5	0	0	0	0	0	0	1-0	0	1	.000	.167	.000	-49	-1	0-0	.909	0	158	0	S2	152	0.0
	Year	9	5	1	0	0	0	0	0	1-0	1	1	.000	.286	.000	-13	-1	0-0	.941	1	141	48	S9	0	0.1
1979	Mil A	2	2	0	1	0	0	0	0	0-0	0	0	.500	.500	.500	170	0	0-0	1.000	-1	0	0	S2	0	-0.1
Total	6	128	169	27	30	1	1	0	3	25-0	1	33	.178	.286	.195	38	-14	4-0	.961	-13	95	79	S104,2b19,D3/3	152	-1.8
NORDHAGEN, WAYNE	Wayne Oren; B7.4.1948 Thief River Falls MN; BR/TR/6´2˝/(195–210); [NYA68 7/136]; d7.16; Col Treasure Valley (OR) CC																								
1976	Chi A	22	53	6	10	2	0	0	5	4-0	0	12	.189	.233	.226	39	-4	0-0	1.000	1	118	167	O10R,C5,D6	0	-0.4
1977	Chi A	52	124	16	39	7	3	4	22	2-0	0	12	.315	.323	.516	125	3	1-0	.944	-4	83	45	O46(12/2/34),C3,D2	0	-0.2
1978	Chi A	68	206	28	62	16	0	5	35	5-0	0	18	.301	.310	.451	113	3	0-1	.941	-6	79	100	O36(19/0/18),D16,C12	44	-0.5
1979	Chi A	78	193	20	54	15	0	7	25	13-2	0	22	.280	.324	.466	110	3	0-0	1.000	1	98	562	D47,O12(6/0/7),C5,P2	0	0.1
1980	Chi A	123	415	45	115	22	4	15	59	10-3	1	45	.277	.294	.458	103	-1	0-1	.969	-3	88	120	O74(45/0/33),D32	0	-0.8
1981	Chi A	65	208	19	64	8	1	6	33	10-0	1	25	.308	.338	.442	127	6	0-1	.947	-4	81	111	O60(25/1/36)	0	-0.1
1982	Tor A	44	115	8	32	3	0	1	14	9-1	0	13	.278	.328	.330	76	-4	0-2	1.000	-0	73	175	D32,O10(10/0/1)	51	-0.6
	Pit N	1	4	0	2	0	0	0	2	0-0	0	1	.500	.500	.500	173	0	0-0	1.000	-0	100	0	/lf	0	0.0
	Tor A	28	70	4	18	3	0	0	6	1-0	0	9	.257	.264	.300	51	-5	0-0	ø	0	0	0	D28	0	-0.6
1983	Chi N	21	35	1	5	1	0	1	4	0-0	1	5	.143	.162	.257	15	-4	0-0	1.000	-1	65	0	O7L	0	-0.6
Total	8	502	1423	147	401	77	8	39	205	54-6	3	162	.282	.306	.429	101	-3	1-5	.962	-17	85	124	O256(125/3/139),D163,C25,P2	95	-3.7
NORDYKE, LOU	Louis Ellis; B8.7.1876 Brighton IA; D9.27.1945 Los Angeles CA; BR/TR/6´0˝/185; d4.18																								
1906	StL A	25	53	4	13	1	0	0	7	10	0	—	.245	.365	.264	102	1	3	.942	-3	53	261	1b12	—	-0.2
NOREN, IRV	Irving Arnold; B11.29.1924 Jamestown NY; BL/TL/6´0˝/(190–198); d4.18; C5; Col Pasadena (CA) City																								
1950	Was A	138	542	80	160	27	10	14	98	67	2	77	.295	.375	.459	118	14	5-2	.984	9	102	184	O121C,1b17	0	1.8
1951	Was A	129	509	82	142	33	5	8	86	51	0	35	.279	.345	.411	105	3	10-7	.978	12	117	113	O126C	0	1.2
1952	Was A	12	49	4	12	3	1	0	2	6	0	3	.245	.327	.347	91	-1	1-0	1.000	2	115	196	O12C	0	0.1
	†NY A	93	272	36	64	13	2	5	21	26	6	34	.235	.316	.353	91	-4	4-2	1.000	-3	91	83	O60(18/18/25),1b19	0	-0.9
	Year	105	321	40	76	16	3	5	23	32	6	37	.237	.318	.352	91	-4	5-2	1.000	-1	96	107	O72(18/30/25),1b19	0	-0.8
1953	†NY A	109	345	55	92	12	6	6	46	42	2	39	.267	.350	.388	103	1	3-3	.991	3	100	143	O96(21/44/38)	0	0.0
1954	NY A★	125	426	70	136	21	6	12	66	43	1	38	.319	.377	.481	140	23	4-6	.980	1	99	107	O116(55/23/49)/1	0	1.7
1955	†NY A	132	371	49	94	19	1	8	59	43-5	3	33	.253	.331	.375	92	-4	5-2	.980	4	108	104	O126(117/10/3)	0	-0.6
1956	NY A	29	37	4	8	1	0	0	6	12-2	0	7	.216	.408	.243	78	0	0-0	.875	-0	58	253	O10(4/0/6)/1	77	-0.1
1957	KC A	81	160	8	34	8	0	2	16	11-2	1	19	.213	.267	.300	54	-10	0-0	.990	-1	88	119	1b25,O6R	0	-1.3
	StL N	17	30	3	11	4	1	1	10	4-2	0	6	.367	.429	.667	189	4	0-1	1.000	-1	54	0	O8(1/0/7)	0	0.2
1958	StL N	117	178	24	47	9	1	4	22	13-2	4	21	.264	.327	.393	87	-3	0-1	.974	-2	95	34	O77(59/14/10)	0	-0.8
1959	StL N	8	8	0	1	1	0	0	0	0-0	0	2	.125	.125	.250	-3	-1	0-0	ø	-0	0	0	O2L/1	0	-0.1
	Chi N	65	156	27	50	6	2	4	19	13-1	3	24	.321	.384	.462	125	6	2-0	1.000	5	121	156	O40(16/6/18)/1	0	0.9
	Year	73	164	27	51	7	2	4	19	13-1	3	26	.311	.372	.451	118	4	2-0	1.000	4	119	154	O42(18/6/18),1b2	0	0.8
1960	Chi N	12	11	0	1	0	0	0	1	3-0	0	4	.091	.286	.091	9	-1	0-0	.833	-0	0	133	/1rf	0	-0.2
	LA N	26	25	1	5	0	0	1	1	1-0	0	8	.200	.231	.320	46	-2	0-0	ø	0	—	—	/H	0	-0.2
	Year	38	36	1	6	0	0	1	2	4-0	0	12	.167	.250	.250	36	-3	0-0	1.000	-0	0	133	/1rf	0	-0.4
Total	11	1093	3119	443	857	157	35	65	453	335-14	22	350	.275	.348	.410	106	25	34-24	.984	28	104	125	O801(293/374/163),1b66	77	1.7
NORMAN, DAN	Daniel Edmund; B1.11.1955 Los Angeles CA; BR/TR (BB 1908p)/6´2˝/(185–195); [CinN74 15/359]; d9.27; Col Barstow (CA) CC																								
1977	NY N	7	16	2	4	1	0	0	0	4-0	0	2	.250	.400	.313	97	0	0-0	1.000	-1	88	0	O6(0/1/6)	0	0.0
1978	NY N	19	64	7	17	0	1	4	10	2-0	0	14	.266	.284	.484	115	0	1-0	1.000	-0	99	70	O18(1/0/18)	0	-0.1
1979	NY N	44	110	9	27	3	1	3	11	10-2	1	26	.245	.311	.373	89	-2	2-0	.967	1	95	169	O33(8/0/25)	0	-0.3
1980	NY N	69	92	5	17	1	1	2	9	6-0	0	14	.185	.235	.283	44	-7	5-0	1.000	-1	78	99	O19(9/0/10)	0	-0.8

THE BATTER REGISTER

YEAR	TM LG	G	AB	R	H	2B	3B	HR	RBI	BB-IB	HP	SO	AVG	OBP	SLG	AOPS	ABR	SB-CS	FA	FR	RNG	THR	GAMES AT POSITION	DL	BFW
1982	Mon N	53	66	6	14	3	0	2	7	7-0	0	20	.212	.288	.348	74	-2	0-1	.969	-1	91	87	O31(17/6/8)	0	-0.4
Total	5	192	348	29	79	8	3	11	37	29-2	1	76	.227	.287	.362	80	-11	8-1	.981	-2	92	109	O107(35/7/67)	0	-1.6
NORMAN, BILL	Henry Willis Patrick; B7.16.1910 St.Louis MO; D4.21.1962 Milwaukee WI; BR/TR/6´2˝/190; d8.8; M2/C2; Col St. Louis																								
1931	Chi A	24	55	7	10	2	0	0	6	4	0	10	.182	.237	.218	22	-6	0-1	.933	1	117	96	O17(3/14/0)	—	-0.6
1932	Chi A	13	48	6	11	3	1	0	2	2	0	3	.229	.260	.333	56	-3	0-0	.917	-1	72	233	O13(1/11/1)	—	-0.4
Total	2	37	103	13	21	5	1	0	8	6	0	13	.204	.248	.272	38	-9	0-1	.928	-0	97	156	O30(4/25/1)	—	-1.0
NORMAN, LES	Leslie Eugene; B2.25.1969 Warren MI; BR/TR/6´1˝/185; [KCA91 25/652]; d5.29; Col St. Francis (IL)																								
1995	KC A	24	40	6	9	0	1	0	4	6-0	0	6	.225	.326	.275	57	-3	0-1	.958	-1	88	131	O17(4/5/8),D5	0	-0.4
1996	KC A	54	49	9	6	0	0	0	0	6-0	1	14	.122	.232	.122	-7	-8	1-1	1.000	2	129	89	O38(15/3/20),D7	57	-0.6
Total	2	78	89	15	15	0	1	0	4	12-0	1	20	.169	.275	.191	22	-11	1-2	.986	1	112	107	O55(19/8/28),D12	57	-1.0
NORMAN, NELSON	Nelson Augusto; B5.23.1958 San Pedro de Macoris, D.R.; BB/TR (BR 1978, 1979p)/6´2˝/160; d5.20; C1																								
1978	Tex A	23	34	1	9	2	0	0	1	0-0	0	5	.265	.265	.324	64	-2	0-0	.984	5	146	118	S18,3b6	0	0.4
1979	Tex A	147	343	36	76	9	3	0	21	19-0	0	41	.222	.260	.265	43	-28	4-1	.952	-29	83	86	S142/2	0	-4.4
1980	Tex A	17	32	4	7	0	0	0	1	1-0	0	1	.219	.242	.219	28	-3	0-1	.943	5	124	145	S17	0	0.3
1981	Tex A	7	13	1	3	1	0	0	2	1-0	0	2	.231	.267	.308	74	0	0-0	.963	3	153	186	S5	0	0.3
1982	Pit N	3	3	0	0	0	0	0	0	0-0	0	0	.000	.000	.000	-96	-1	0-0	ø	-1	0	0	2b2/S	0	-0.2
1987	Mon N	1	4	0	0	0	0	0	0	0-0	0	1	.000	.000	.000	-96	-1	0-0	.667	-1	37	0	/S	0	-0.2
Total	6	198	429	42	95	12	3	0	25	21-0	0	50	.221	.256	.263	42	-35	4-2	.954	-18	93	95	S184,3b6,2b3	0	-3.8
NORRIS, JIM	James Francis; B12.20.1948 Brooklyn NY; BL/TL/5´10˝/(175–190); [CleA71*A5/109]; d4.7; Col Maryland																								
1977	Cle A	133	440	59	119	23	6	2	37	64-4	0	57	.270	.360	.364	102	4	26-17	.982	8	116	108	O124(3/74/49),1b3	0	0.8
1978	Cle A	113	315	41	89	14	5	2	27	42-4	0	20	.283	.364	.378	111	6	12-7	.988	4	109	126	O78(26/5/51),D15,1b6	0	0.6
1979	Cle A	124	353	50	87	15	6	3	30	44-1	0	35	.246	.327	.348	83	-8	15-10	.982	3	117	34	O93(47/23/28),D13	0	-0.8
1980	Tex A	119	174	23	43	5	0	0	16	23-2	0	16	.247	.327	.276	71	-6	6-3	1.000	-3	84	101	O82(7/19/57),1b10/D	0	-1.1
Total	4	489	1282	173	338	57	17	7	110	173-11	0	128	.264	.348	.351	94	-4	59-37	.985	12	110	91	O377(83/121/185),D29,1b19	0	-0.5
NORRIS, LEO	Leo John; B5.17.1908 Bay St.Louis MS; D2.13.1987 Zachary LA; BR/TR/5´11˝/165; d4.14																								
1936	Phi N	**154**	581	64	154	27	4	11	76	39	3	79	.265	.315	.382	79	-18	4	.936	-3	93	84	S121,2b38	—	-1.0
1937	Phi N	116	381	45	98	24	3	9	36	21	0	53	.257	.296	.407	82	-10	3	.949	-8	94	83	2b74,3b24,S20	—	-1.2
Total	2	270	962	109	252	51	7	20	112	60	3	132	.262	.307	.392	80	-28	7	.940	-11	94	84	S141,2b112,3b24	—	-2.2
NORTH, BILLY	William Alex; B5.15.1948 Seattle WA; BB/TR (BR 1971)/5´11˝/185; [ChiN69 12/278]; d9.3; Col Central Washington																								
1971	Chi N	8	16	3	6	0	0	0	0	4-1	1	6	.375	.524	.375	138	1	1-1	1.000	-1	42	0	O6(1/0/5)	0	-0.1
1972	Chi N	66	127	22	23	2	3	0	4	13-1	1	33	.181	.262	.244	40	-10	6-0	.955	-1	89	146	O48(9/26/15)	0	-1.2
1973	Oak A	146	554	98	158	10	5	5	34	78-5	3	89	.285	.376	.348	110	10	53-20	.980	15	**120**	136	O138(0/136/2),D6	0	2.7
1974	†Oak A	149	543	79	141	20	5	4	33	69-1	5	86	.260	.347	.337	104	5	**54**-26	.991	11	119	92	O138C,D8	0	1.6
1975	†Oak A	140	524	74	143	17	5	1	43	81-3	4	80	.273	.373	.330	102	6	30-12	.975	11	120	106	O138(4/134/0)/D	0	1.6
1976	Oak A	154	590	91	163	20	5	2	31	73-3	2	95	.276	.356	.337	108	9	**75**-29	.978	-4	99	74	O144(0/137/7),D8	0	0.8
1977	Oak A	56	184	32	48	3	3	1	9	32-2	2	25	.261	.376	.326	95	0	17-13	.983	-4	93	31	O52C/D	81	-0.5
1978	Oak A	24	52	5	11	4	0	0	5	9-2	2	13	.212	.344	.288	85	0	3-2	1.000	-1	88	120	O17C	0	-0.1
	†LA N	110	304	54	71	10	0	0	10	65-2	2	48	.234	.371	.266	81	-4	27-8	.975	-3	101	40	O103(1/102/0)	0	-0.5
1979	SF N	142	460	87	119	15	4	5	30	96-3	1	84	.259	.386	.341	108	11	58-24	.987	1	105	98	O130C	0	1.6
1980	SF N	128	415	73	104	12	1	1	19	81-5	1	78	.251	.373	.292	91	0	45-19	.982	4	111	82	O115(1/114/0)	0	0.7
1981	SF N	46	131	22	29	7	0	1	12	26-0	1	28	.221	.354	.298	89	0	26-8	.966	-3	93	42	O37C	0	-0.1
Total	11	1169	3900	640	1016	120	31	20	230	627-28	25	665	.261	.365	.323	99	28	395-162	.981	26	108	90	O1066(16/1023/29),D24	81	6.5
NORTHEN, HUB	Hubbard Edwin; B8.16.1886 Atlanta TX; D10.1.1947 Shreveport LA; BL/TL/5´8˝/175; d9.10																								
1910	StL A	26	96	6	19	1	0	0	16	5	0	—	.198	.238	.208	42	-7	2	.926	-3	94	54	O26C	—	-1.2
1911	Cin N	1	0	0	0	0	0	0	0	0	0	0	ø	ø	ø	ø	0	0	ø	0	—	—	/H	—	0.0
	Bro N	19	76	16	24	2	2	0	1	14	1	9	.316	.429	.395	137	5	4	.911	0	96	164	O19C	—	0.4
	Year	20	76	16	24	2	2	0	1	14	1	9	.316	.429	.395	137	5	4	.911	0	96	164	O19C	—	0.4
1912	Bro N	118	412	54	116	26	6	3	46	41	4	46	.282	.352	.396	109	5	8	.950	-6	92	76	O102(10/43/49)	—	-0.7
Total	3	164	584	76	159	29	8	3	63	60	5	55	.272	.345	.365	103	3	14	.939	-8	93	85	O147(10/88/49)	—	-1.5
NORTHEY, RON	Ronald James; B4.26.1920 Mahanoy City PA; D4.16.1971 Pittsburgh PA; BL/TR/5´10˝/(195–215); d4.14; Mil 1945; C3; s–Scott; [DL 1951 Chi N 88]																								
1942	Phi N	127	402	31	101	13	2	5	31	28	0	33	.251	.300	.331	89	-7	2	.952	2	104	130	O109R	0	-1.2
1943	Phi N	147	586	72	163	31	5	16	68	51	3	52	.278	.339	.430	127	18	2	.978	1	97	122	O145R	0	1.0
1944	Phi N	152	570	72	164	35	9	22	104	67	4	51	.288	.367	.496	146	34	1	.981	1	90	141	O151R	0	2.5
1946	Phi N	128	438	55	109	24	6	16	62	39	2	59	.249	.313	.441	116	6	1	.971	-4	97	68	O111R	0	-0.1
1947	Phi N	13	47	7	12	3	0	0	3	6	0	3	.255	.340	.319	79	-1	1	1.000	-0	87	106	O13R	0	-0.2
	StL N	110	311	52	91	19	3	15	63	48	2	29	.293	.391	.518	133	16	0	.949	-3	87	137	O94(15/0/79),3b2	0	1.0
	Year	123	358	59	103	22	3	15	66	54	2	32	.288	.384	.492	127	15	1	.955	-3	87	133	O107(15/0/92),3b2	0	0.8
1948	StL N	96	246	40	79	10	1	13	64	38	4	25	.321	.420	.528	147	17	0	.989	-4	86	54	O67R	0	1.2
1949	StL N	90	265	28	69	18	2	7	50	31	0	15	.260	.338	.423	98	0	0	.980	-8	73	68	O73R	0	-1.1
1950	Cin N	27	77	11	20	5	0	5	9	15	0	6	.260	.380	.519	134	4	0	.955	-2	79	0	O24R	0	0.1
	Chi N	53	114	11	32	9	0	4	20	10	0	9	.281	.339	.465	110	2	0	.976	0	88	168	O27R	0	0.1
	Year	80	191	22	52	14	0	9	29	25	0	15	.272	.356	.487	120	6	0	.969	-2	84	102	O51R	0	0.2
1952	Chi N	1	1	0	0	0	0	0	0	0	0	0	.000	.000	.000	-99	0	0-0	ø	0	—	—	/H	0	0.0
1955	Chi A	14	14	1	5	2	0	1	4	3-0	0	3	.357	.471	.714	209	2	0-0	1.000	-0	66	0	O2R	0	0.2
1956	Chi A	53	48	4	17	2	0	3	23	8-2	0	1	.354	.417	.583	168	5	0-0	1.000	0	75	490	O4(3/0/3)	0	0.5
1957	Chi A	40	27	0	5	1	0	0	7	11-1	0	5	.185	.410	.222	80	0	0-0	ø	0	—	—	/H	0	0.0
	Phi N	33	26	1	7	0	0	1	5	6-1	0	6	.269	.406	.385	118	1	0-0	ø	0	—	—	/H	0	0.1
Total	12	1084	3172	385	874	172	28	108	513	361-4	15	297	.276	.352	.450	124	97	7-0	.972	-17	92	112	O820(18/0/804),3b2	88	4.1
NORTHEY, SCOTT	Scott Richard; B10.15.1946 Philadelphia PA; BR/TR/6´0˝/172; d9.2; f–Ron																								
1969	KC A	20	61	11	16	2	2	1	7	7-0	0	19	.262	.338	.410	107	0	6-3	.973	-0	99	104	O18C	0	0.0
NORTHRUP, JIM	James Thomas; B11.24.1939 Breckenridge MI; BL/TR/6´3˝/(190–205); d9.30; Col Alma																								
1964	Det A	5	12	1	1	1	0	0	0	0-0	0	3	.083	.083	.167	-32	-2	1-0	1.000	-0	93	0	O2(0/2/1)	0	-0.2
1965	Det A	80	219	20	45	12	3	2	16	12-1	2	50	.205	.253	.315	60	-12	1-1	.976	-5	90	0	O54(10/6/38)	0	-2.1
1966	Det A	123	419	53	111	24	6	16	58	33-4	4	52	.265	.322	.465	121	11	4-7	.980	10	**123**	132	O113(3/11/106)	0	1.3
1967	Det A	144	495	63	134	18	6	10	61	43-6	3	83	.271	.332	.392	110	6	7-1	.972	-2	106	37	O143(65/94/39)	0	-0.1
1968	†Det A	154	580	76	153	29	7	21	90	50-4	4	87	.264	.324	.447	129	19	4-5	.979	4	**113**	78	O151(12/47/103)	0	1.6
1969	Det A	148	543	79	160	31	5	25	66	52-1	3	83	.295	.358	.508	135	24	4-2	.985	5	111	83	O143(29/89/49)	0	2.4
1970	Det A	139	504	71	132	21	3	24	80	58-6	7	68	.262	.343	.458	119	13	3-6	.993	2	110	47	O136(34/39/78)	0	0.7
1971	Det A	136	459	72	124	27	2	16	71	60-9	2	43	.270	.355	.442	120	13	7-4	.981	-3	94	64	O108(42/68/39),1b32	0	0.5
1972	†Det A	134	426	40	111	15	2	8	42	38-6	2	47	.261	.324	.362	100	0	4-7	.978	-2	95	102	O127(50/42/72),1b2	0	-1.0
1973	Det A	119	404	55	124	14	7	12	44	38-6	1	41	.307	.366	.465	125	13	4-4	.982	2	105	90	O116(51/10/78)	0	0.9
1974	Det A	97	376	41	89	12	1	11	42	36-4	0	46	.237	.300	.362	87	-6	0-0	.973	-1	104	66	O97(0/2/97)	0	-1.3
	Mon N	21	54	3	13	1	0	2	8	5-1	0	9	.241	.305	.370	84	-1	0-0	1.000	-3	57	0	O13(7/0/6)	0	-0.5
	Bal A	8	7	2	4	0	0	1	3	2-1	0	1	.571	.667	1.000	383	3	0-0	1.000	1	95	644	O6(4/0/2)/D	0	0.3
1975	Bal A	84	194	27	53	13	0	5	29	22-1	2	22	.273	.348	.418	124	7	0-1	.979	-6	80	65	O58(3/56/0),D3	0	-0.1
Total	12	1392	4692	603	1254	218	42	153	610	449-50	30	635	.267	.333	.429	115	88	39-38	.981	3	105	73	O1267(310/466/708),1b34,D4	0	2.4
NORTON, FRANK	Frank Prescott; B7.9.1845 Port Jefferson NY; D8.1.1920 Greenwich CT; d5.5																								
1871	Oly NA	1	1	0	0	0	0	0	0	0	—	1	.000	.000	.000	-99	0	0-0	.000	-1	0	0	/3rf	—	0.0
NORTON, GREG	Gregory Blakemoor; B7.6.1972 San Leandro CA; BB/TR/6´1˝/(190–205); [ChiA93 2/59]; d8.18; Col Oklahoma; OF(33/0/35)																								
1996	Chi A	11	23	4	5	0	0	2	3	4-0	0	6	.217	.333	.478	106	0	0-1	.778	-3	35	0	S6,3b2,D2	0	-0.3
1997	Chi A	18	34	5	9	2	2	0	1	2-0	0	8	.265	.306	.441	95	-1	0-0	.864	-1	105	0	3b11,D2	0	-0.1
1998	Chi A	105	299	38	71	17	2	9	36	26-1	2	77	.237	.301	.398	82	-9	3-3	.994	-5	65	92	1b79,3b11/2D	0	-1.9
1999	Chi A	132	436	62	111	26	0	16	50	69-3	2	93	.255	.358	.424	97	0	4-4	.922	-6	95	88	3b120,1b26/D	0	-0.7
2000	Chi A	71	201	25	49	6	1	6	28	26-0	2	47	.244	.333	.373	77	-7	1-0	.926	-10	68	66	3b47,1b17,D3	0	-1.6

YEAR	TM LG	G	AB	R	H	2B	3B	HR	RBI	BB-IB	HP	SO	AVG	OBP	SLG	AOPS	ABR	SB-CS	FA	FR	RNG	THR	GAMES AT POSITION	DL	BFW
2001	Col N	117	225	30	60	13	2	13	40	19-2	0	65	.267	.321	.516	93	-3	1-0	1.000	-8	65	109	O25(22/0/4),3b24,1b13/D	0	-1.1
2002	Col N	113	168	19	37	8	1	7	37	24-0	0	52	.220	.314	.405	78	-5	2-3	.896	-4	77	108	3b22,1b15,O2L/D	18	-1.1
2003	Col N	114	179	19	47	15	0	6	31	16-0	1	47	.263	.325	.447	87	-3	2-1	.924	-2	94	56	3b34,1b9,O3R	0	-0.5
2004	Det A	41	86	9	15	1	0	2	2	12-1	0	21	.174	.276	.256	41	-8	0-0	.963	-4	75	0	3b18,1b7,O6L,D7	37	-1.2
2006	TB A	98	294	47	87	15	0	17	45	35-2	3	69	.296	.374	.520	130	14	1-5	.956	-4	81	62	O31(3/0/28),D31,1b25	0	0.4
Total	10	820	1945	258	491	103	8	78	273	233-9	10	485	.252	.333	.434	92	-22	14-17	.919	-47	86	72	3b289,1b191,O67R,D50,S6/2	55	-8.1
Norwood, Willie	Willie; B11.7.1950 Greene Co. AL; BR/TR/6´0˝/(185–190); [MinA72 3/56]; d4.21; Col La Verne																								
1977	Min A	39	83	15	19	3	0	3	9	6-0	0	17	.229	.281	.373	77	-3	6-1	.952	-0	113	0	O28(3/20/8),D5	0	-0.3
1978	Min A	125	428	56	109	22	3	8	46	28-0	3	64	.255	.301	.376	88	-7	25-10	.944	-4	94	94	O115(101/14/4),D6	0	-1.4
1979	Min A	96	270	32	67	13	3	6	30	20-2	0	51	.248	.299	.385	80	-8	9-5	.974	-3	91	90	O71(0/44/28),D14	0	-1.3
1980	Min A	34	73	6	12	2	0	1	8	3-0	0	13	.164	.197	.233	16	-9	1-1	1.000	1	129	0	O17(0/5/17),D9	0	-0.8
Total	4	294	854	109	207	40	6	18	93	57-2	3	145	.242	.290	.367	78	-27	41-17	.959	-6	97	77	O231(104/83/57),D34	0	-3.8
Nossek, Joe	Joseph Rudolph; B11.8.1940 Cleveland OH; BR/TR/6´0˝/(175–178); d4.18; C27; Col Ohio U.																								
1964	Min A	7	1	1	0	0	0	0	0	0-0	0	0	.000	.000	.000	-99	0	0-0	ø	-0	0	0	O2(1/1/0)	0	0.0
1965	†Min A	87	170	19	37	9	0	2	16	7-1	1	22	.218	.250	.306	55	-10	2-0	.970	1	93	73	O48(2/46/2),3b9	0	-1.1
1966	Min A	4	0	0	0	0	0	0	0	0-0	0	0	ø	ø	ø	ø	0	0-0	ø	-0	0	0	O2C	0	0.0
	KC A	87	230	13	60	10	3	1	27	8-1	0	21	.261	.285	.343	83	-6	4-2	.983	7	115	209	O78(12/65/3)/3	0	-0.2
	Year	91	230	13	60	10	3	1	27	8-1	0	21	.261	.285	.343	82	-6	4-2	.983	6	115	208	O80(12/67/3)/3	0	-0.2
1967	KC A	87	166	12	34	6	1	0	10	4-1	0	26	.205	.221	.253	42	-13	2-0	.982	4	126	76	O63(35/32/0)	0	-1.1
1969	Oak A	13	6	0	0	0	0	0	0	0-0	0	0	.000	.000	.000	-99	-2	0-0	1.000	-0	98	0	O12(9/3/0)	0	-0.2
	StL N	9	5	2	1	0	0	0	0	0-0	0	3	.200	.200	.200	12	-1	0-0	1.000	0	262	0	/cf	0	0.0
1970	StL N	1	1	0	0	0	0	0	0	0-0	0	0	.000	.000	.000	-97	0	0-0	ø	0	—	—	/H	0	0.0
Total	6	295	579	47	132	25	4	3	53	19-3	1	72	.228	.252	.301	60	-32	8-2	.980	11	113	132	O206(59/150/5),3b10	0	-2.6
Novikoff, Lou	Louis Alexander "The Mad Russian"; B10.12.1915 Glendale AZ; D9.30.1970 South Gate CA; BR/TR/5´10˝/185; d4.15; Mil 1945																								
1941	Chi N	62	203	22	49	8	0	5	24	11	1	15	.241	.284	.355	82	-6	0	1.000	-1	91	91	O54(51/0/3)	0	-1.0
1942	Chi N	128	483	48	145	25	5	7	64	24	3	28	.300	.337	.416	125	12	3	.964	-3	90	136	O120L	0	0.4
1943	Chi N	78	233	22	65	7	3	0	28	18	1	15	.279	.333	.335	95	-2	0	.980	-6	85	39	O61(60/1/0)	0	-1.1
1944	Chi N	71	139	15	39	4	2	3	19	10	0	11	.281	.329	.403	106	0	1	.976	-3	77	57	O29(28/1/0)	0	-0.4
1946	Phi N	17	23	0	7	1	0	0	3	1	0	2	.304	.333	.348	96	0	0	1.000	0	142	0	O3L	0	0.0
Total	5	356	1081	107	305	45	10	15	138	64	5	71	.282	.325	.384	107	4	4	.976	-12	89	97	O267(262/2/3)	0	-2.1
Novotney, Rube	Ralph Joseph; B8.5.1924 Streator IL; D7.16.1987 Redondo Beach CA; BR/TR/6´0˝/187; d4.29; Col Illinois																								
1949	Chi N	22	67	4	18	2	1	0	6	3	0	11	.269	.300	.328	70	-3	0	.958	-2	*64*	*101*	C20	0	-0.4
Nunamaker, Les	Leslie Grant; B1.25.1889 Aurora NE; D11.14.1938 Hastings NE; BR/TR/6´2˝/190; d4.28																								
1911	Bos A	62	183	18	47	4	3	0	19	12	0	—	.257	.303	.311	72	-7	1	.972	4	*100*	*101*	C59	—	0.1
1912	Bos A	35	103	15	26	5	2	0	6	6	3	—	.252	.313	.340	82	-3	2	.971	-1	*113*	*74*	C35	—	-0.1
1913	Bos A	29	65	9	14	5	2	0	9	8	1	8	.215	.311	.354	92	-1	2	.977	1	*100*	*66*	C27	—	0.3
1914	Bos A	5	5	0	1	0	0	0	0	1	0	0	.200	.333	.200	61	0	0	1.000	0	*120*	*306*	C3/1	—	0.0
	NY A	87	257	19	68	10	3	2	29	22	2	34	.265	.327	.350	104	1	11-9	.971	3	*92*	*116*	C70,1b5	—	1.0
	Year	92	262	19	69	10	3	2	29	23	2	34	.263	.328	.347	103	1	11-9	.971	3	*92*	*118*	C73,1b6	—	1.0
1915	NY A	87	249	24	56	6	3	0	17	23	1	24	.225	.293	.273	70	-10	3-2	.964	-4	*93*	*100*	C77,1b2	—	-0.8
1916	NY A	91	260	25	77	14	7	0	28	34	1	21	.296	.380	.404	133	11	4	.983	2	126	**99**	C79	—	2.1
1917	NY A	104	310	22	81	9	2	0	33	21	1	25	.261	.310	.303	86	-6	5	.976	3	*125*	*102*	C91	—	0.5
1918	StL A	85	274	22	71	9	2	0	22	28	5	16	.259	.339	.307	98	0	6	.979	-3	*81*	*111*	C81/1rf	—	0.4
1919	Cle A	26	56	6	14	1	1	0	7	2	0	6	.250	.276	.304	59	-3	0	.927	-3	*132*	*80*	C16	—	-0.5
1920	†Cle A	34	54	10	18	3	3	0	14	4	0	5	.333	.379	.500	128	2	1-0	.963	1	*124*	*89*	C17,1b6	—	0.4
1921	Cle A	46	131	16	47	7	2	0	25	11	0	8	.359	.408	.443	115	3	1-1	.970	2	*101*	*60*	C46	—	0.7
1922	Cle A	25	43	8	13	2	0	0	7	4	0	3	.302	.362	.349	85	-1	0-0	.936	-3	*88*	*48*	C13	—	-0.3
Total	12	716	1990	194	533	75	30	2	216	176	14	150	.268	.332	.339	95	-14	36-12	.972	3	*104*	*97*	C614,1b15/rf	—	3.8
Nunez, Abraham	Abraham; B2.5.1977 Haina, D.R.; BB/TR/6´3˝/210; d9.3; [DL 2003 Fla N 94]																								
2002	Fla N	19	17	2	2	0	0	0	1	0-0	0	5	.118	.118	.118	-39	-4	0-1	1.000	-0	101	0	O15(2/12/1)	0	-0.4
2004	Fla N	58	64	9	11	1	1	1	5	9-0	0	21	.172	.274	.266	43	-6	1-2	1.000	0	113	0	O48(28/0/20)	0	-0.7
	KC A	59	221	31	50	9	0	5	29	25-1	0	48	.226	.304	.335	67	-11	0-1	.993	3	111	79	O57(0/4/54),D2	0	-1.1
Total	2	136	302	42	63	10	1	6	35	34-1	0	74	.209	.288	.308	56	-21	1-4	.995	3	111	54	O120(30/16/75),D2	94	-2.2
Nunez, Abraham	Abraham Orlando (Adames); B3.16.1976 Santo Domingo, D.R.; BB/TR/5´11˝/(170–190); d8.27																								
1997	Pit N	19	40	3	9	2	2	0	6	3-0	1	10	.225	.289	.375	73	-2	1-0	1.000	1	103	97	S12,2b9	0	0.0
1998	Pit N	24	52	6	10	2	0	1	2	12-0	0	14	.192	.344	.288	68	-2	4-2	.930	3	110	108	S23	0	0.2
1999	Pit N	90	259	25	57	8	0	0	17	28-0	1	54	.220	.299	.251	41	-23	9-1	.953	11	108	104	S65,2b14	0	-0.6
2000	Pit N	40	91	10	20	1	0	1	8	8-1	0	14	.220	.283	.264	39	-9	0-0	.978	4	118	86	S21,2b6	0	-0.3
2001	Pit N	115	301	30	79	11	4	1	21	28-1	1	53	.262	.326	.336	70	-13	8-2	.990	17	114	119	2b48,S48/3lf	0	0.9
2002	Pit N	112	253	28	59	14	1	2	15	27-1	2	44	.233	.311	.320	66	-12	3-4	.991	15	127	133	2b46,S24/D	0	0.5
2003	Pit N	118	311	37	77	8	7	4	35	26-1	3	53	.248	.310	.357	73	-13	9-3	.979	0	109	101	2b71,S23/3	0	-0.8
2004	Pit N	112	182	17	43	9	0	2	13	10-0	0	36	.236	.275	.319	53	-13	1-3	.985	6	113	162	2b32,S13,3b6/PD	0	-0.6
2005	†StL N	139	421	64	120	13	2	5	44	37-4	0	63	.285	.343	.361	83	-10	0-1	.963	12	127	132	3b98,2b22,S21	0	0.3
2006	Phi N	123	322	42	68	10	2	2	32	41-8	2	58	.211	.303	.273	47	-25	1-0	.959	-3	107	74	3b74,2b6,S3	0	-2.7
Total	10	892	2232	262	542	78	18	18	193	220-16	10	399	.243	.313	.318	63	-122	36-16	.985	65	112	124	2b254,S253,3b180,D2/Plf	0	-3.1
Nunnally, Jon	Jonathan Keith; B11.9.1971 Pelham NC; BL/TR/5´10˝/190; [CleA92 3/70]; d4.26; Col Miami–Dade Kendall (FL) CC																								
1995	KC A	119	303	51	74	15	6	14	42	51-5	2	86	.244	.357	.472	111	5	6-4	.971	1	108	81	O107(16/7/92),D4	0	0.2
1996	KC A	35	90	16	19	5	1	5	17	13-2	0	25	.211	.308	.456	90	-2	0-0	.968	-0	112	0	O29(7/0/24),D4	0	-0.3
1997	KC A	13	29	8	7	0	1	1	4	5-0	0	7	.241	.353	.414	96	0	0-0	1.000	-1	74	0	O9(1/0/8)	0	-0.2
	Cin N	65	201	38	64	12	3	13	35	26-0	2	51	.318	.400	.602	156	16	7-3	.984	2	109	108	O60(14/46/11)	0	1.8
1998	Cin N	74	174	29	36	9	0	7	20	34-3	1	38	.207	.335	.379	88	-2	3-4	.956	5	122	151	O70(6/24/53)	0	0.0
1999	Bos A	10	14	4	4	1	0	0	1	0-0	0	6	.286	.286	.357	61	-1	0-0	ø	-0	0	0	O2(1/0/1),D3	0	-0.1
2000	NY N	48	74	16	14	5	1	2	6	17-0	0	26	.189	.337	.365	83	-2	3-1	.977	4	115	403	O34(25/11/4)	0	0.2
Total	6	364	885	162	218	47	12	42	125	146-10	5	239	.246	.354	.469	111	14	19-12	.971	10	111	112	O311(70/88/193),D11	0	1.6
Nunnari, Talmadge	Talmadge Raphael; B4.9.1975 Pensacola FL; BL/TL/6´1˝/200; [MonN97 9/286]; d9.7; Col Jacksonville																								
2000	Mon N	18	5	2	1	0	0	0	1	6-1	0	2	.200	.583	.200	124	1	0-0	1.000	-0	89	36	1b14	0	0.1
Nusz, Emory	Emory Moberly; B4.2.1866 Frederick MD; D8.3.1893 Point Of Rocks MD; d4.26																								
1884	Was U	1	4	1	0	0	0	0	—	0	—	—	.000	.000	.000	-99	-1	—	.500	-1	0	0	/lf	—	-0.2
Nutter, Dizzy	Everett Clarence; B8.27.1893 Roseville OH; D7.25.1958 Battle Creek MI; BL/TR/5´9˝/160; d9.7																								
1919	Bos N	18	52	4	11	0	0	0	3	4	0	5	.212	.268	.212	47	-3	1	1.000	1	97	191	O12C	—	-0.3
Nyce, Charlie	Charles Reiff (b Charles Reiff Nice); B7.1.1870 Philadelphia PA; D5.9.1908 Philadelphia PA; 5´8˝/160; d5.28																								
1895	Bos N	9	35	7	8	5	0	2	9	4	1	2	.229	.325	.543	113	0	0	.889	-1	99	120	S9	—	0.0
Nyman, Chris	Christopher Curtis; B6.6.1955 Pomona CA; BR/TR/6´4˝/200; d7.28; b–Nyls; Col Arizona St.																								
1982	Chi A	28	65	6	16	1	0	0	2	3-0	0	9	.246	.279	.262	49	-5	3-2	.994	1	111	108	1b24,O2(1/0/1)	0	-0.5
1983	Chi A	21	28	12	8	0	0	2	4	4-0	1	7	.286	.394	.500	138	2	2-2	1.000	-0	88	113	1b10,D10	0	0.0
Total	2	49	93	18	24	1	0	2	6	7-0	1	16	.258	.317	.333	78	-3	5-4	.996	1	103	110	1b34,D10,O2(1/0/1)	0	-0.5
Nyman, Nyls	Nyls Wallace Rex; B3.7.1954 Detroit MI; BL/TR/6´0˝/170; [ChiA72 16/372]; d9.6; b–Chris																								
1974	Chi A	5	14	5	9	2	1	0	4	0-0	1	1	.643	.667	.929	346	4	1-0	1.000	1	128	588	O3L	0	0.6
1975	Chi A	106	327	36	74	6	3	2	28	11-0	2	34	.226	.255	.281	51	-22	10-4	.958	-3	98	97	O94(62/26/8),D4	0	-2.9
1976	Chi A	8	15	2	2	1	0	0	1	0-0	0	3	.133	.133	.200	-3	-2	1-0	1.000	0	135	0	O7(6/1/0)	0	-0.2
1977	Chi A	1	1	0	0	0	0	0	0	0-0	0	0	.000	.000	.000	-99	0	0-0	ø	0	—	—	/H	0	0.0
Total	4	120	357	43	85	9	4	2	33	11-0	3	38	.238	.266	.303	60	-20	12-4	.962	-1	101	105	O104(71/27/8),D4	0	-2.5

YEAR	TM LG	G	AB	R	H	2B	3B	HR	RBI	BB-IB	HP	SO	AVG	OBP	SLG	AOPS	ABR	SB-CS	FA	FR	RNG	THR	GAMES AT POSITION	DL	BFW
OAKES, REBEL	Ennis Telfair; B12.17.1883 Arizona LA; D3.1.1948 Lisbon LA; BL/TR/5´8˝/170; d4.14; M2; Col Louisiana Tech																								
1909	Cin N	120	415	55	112	10	5	3	31	40	5	—	.270	.341	.340	112	6	23	.979	-1	101	87	O113(4/99/10)	—	0.0
1910	StL N	131	468	50	118	14	6	0	43	38	5	38	.252	.315	.308	85	-10	18	.939	-7	97	72	O127(3/118/6)	—	-2.4
1911	StL N	154	551	69	145	13	6	2	59	41	5	35	.263	.320	.319	81	-15	25	.961	6	104	117	O151(1/150/0)	—	-1.9
1912	StL N	136	495	57	139	19	5	3	58	31	4	24	.281	.328	.358	90	-8	26	.947	-5	102	72	O136C	—	-2.2
1913	StL N	147	539	60	158	14	5	0	49	43	4	32	.293	.350	.338	98	-1	22-26	.968	-9	91	77	O145C	—	-2.5
1914	Pit F	145	571	82	178	18	10	7	75	35	7	22	.312	.359	.415	111	-1	28	.960	-1	98	108	O145C,M	—	-1.1
1915	Pit F	153	580	55	161	24	5	0	82	37	2	19	.278	.323	.336	86	-20	21	.973	-6	104	55	O153(0/152/1),M	—	-3.9
Total	7	986	3619	428	1011	112	42	15	397	265	32	170	.279	.334	.346	95	-49	163-26	.961	-21	100	84	O970(8/945/17)	—	-14.0
OANA, PRINCE	Henry Kawaihoa; B1.22.1908 Waipahu HI; D6.19.1976 Austin TX; BR/TR/6´2˝/193; d4.22; ▲																								
1934	Phi N	6	21	3	5	1	0	0	3	0	0	1	.238	.238	.286	35	-2	0	1.000	0	129	0	O4L	—	-0.2
1943	Det A	20	26	5	10	2	1	1	7	1	0	2	.385	.407	.654	193	4	0-0	.750	-0	87	493	P10	0	0.0
1945	Det A	4	5	0	1	0	0	0	0	0	0	0	.200	.200	.200	15	0	0-0	1.000	-0	47	0	P3	0	0.0
Total	3	30	52	8	16	3	1	1	10	1	0	3	.308	.321	.462	108	2	0-0	.778	-0	77	372	P13,O4L	0	-0.2
OATES, JOHNNY	Johnny Lane; B1.21.1946 Sylva NC; D12.24.2004 Richmond VA; BL/TR/5´11˝/(185–190); [BalA67*S1/10]; d9.17; M11/C7; Col VPI																								
1970	Bal A	5	18	2	5	0	1	0	2	2-0	0	0	.278	.333	.389	102	0	0-0	.939	-1	229	65	C4	0	-0.1
1972	Bal A	85	253	20	66	12	1	4	21	28-8	0	31	.261	.332	.364	103	2	5-7	**.995**	4	133	87	C82	0	0.9
1973	Atl N	93	322	27	80	6	0	4	27	22-4	1	31	.248	.299	.304	63	-16	1-4	.981	-2	92	128	C86	47	-1.6
1974	Atl N	100	291	22	65	10	0	1	21	23-10	0	24	.223	.278	.268	52	-19	2-3	.992	12	107	102	C91	0	-0.3
1975	Atl N	8	18	0	4	1	0	0	0	1-0	0	4	.222	.263	.278	49	-1	0-0	1.000	-1	98	73	C6	0	-0.2
	Phi N	90	269	28	77	14	0	1	25	33-10	0	29	.286	.359	.349	94	-1	1-0	.990	9	163	109	C82	0	1.2
	Year	98	287	28	81	15	0	1	25	34-10	0	33	.282	.354	.345	91	-2	1-0	.990	8	159	107	C88	0	1.0
1976	†Phi N	37	99	10	25	2	0	0	8	8-0	0	12	.253	.308	.273	63	-5	0-1	.994	2	122	100	C33	48	-0.2
1977	†LA N	60	156	18	42	4	0	3	11	11-4	0	11	.269	.314	.353	79	-5	1-0	.987	3	87	106	C56	0	0.0
1978	†LA N	40	75	5	23	1	0	0	6	5-1	0	3	.307	.350	.320	88	-1	0-1	.956	-2	100	96	C24	0	-0.3
1979	LA N	26	46	4	6	2	0	0	2	4-1	0	1	.130	.200	.174	3	-6	0-1	.975	1	78	143	C20	0	-0.6
1980	NY A	39	64	6	12	3	0	1	3	2-0	1	3	.188	.224	.281	38	-6	1-2	.991	-3	126	160	C39	0	-0.8
1981	NY A	10	26	4	5	1	0	0	0	2-0	0	0	.192	.250	.231	40	-2	0-0	.963	-2	53	63	C10	0	-0.4
Total	11	593	1637	146	410	56	2	14	126	141-38	2	149	.250	.309	.313	72	-60	11-19	.987	21	117	108	C533	95	-2.4
OBANDO, SHERMAN	Sherman Omar (Gainor); B1.23.1970 Bocas Del Toro, Pan; BR/TR/6´4˝/(215–220); d4.10																								
1993	Bal A	31	92	8	25	2	0	3	15	4-0	1	26	.272	.309	.391	83	-3	0-0	.929	0	125	0	D21,O8(1/0/7)	45	-0.4
1995	Bal A	16	38	0	10	1	0	0	3	2-0	0	12	.263	.293	.289	53	-3	1-0	.923	0	143	0	O7R,D7	0	-0.2
1996	Mon N	89	178	30	44	9	0	8	22	22-1	1	48	.247	.332	.433	98	-1	2-0	.962	1	110	85	O47R	19	-0.1
1997	Mon N	41	47	3	6	1	0	2	9	6-0	1	14	.128	.241	.277	35	-5	0-0	1.000	-0	98	0	O15(1/0/14),D2	64	-0.5
Total	4	177	355	41	85	13	0	13	49	34-1	3	100	.239	.310	.386	81	-12	3-0	.957	1	113	60	O77(2/0/75),D30	128	-1.2
OBERBECK, HENRY	Henry A.; B5.17.1858 MO; D8.26.1921 St.Louis MO; d5.7; ▲																								
1883	Pit AA	2	9	1	2	1	0	0	—	0	—	—	.222	.222	.333	80	0	—	1.000	0	0	173	1b2	—	0.0
	StL AA	4	14	0	0	0	0	0	—	0	—	—	.000	.000	.000	-95	-3	—	.833	1	259	1371	O4(3/1/0)	—	-0.2
	Year	6	23	1	2	1	0	0	—	0	—	—	.087	.087	.130	-30	-3	—	.833	1	259	1371	O4(3/1/0),1b2	—	-0.2
1884	Bal U	33	125	19	23	4	0	0	—	3	—	—	.184	.203	.216	25	-15	—	.878	1	141	86	O28(1/0/27),3b8,P2	—	-1.2
	KC U	27	90	7	17	3	0	0	—	7	—	—	.189	.247	.222	50	-8	—	.823	6	149	115	3b15,O7(3/3/1),P6,1b3	—	-0.1
	Year	60	215	26	40	7	0	0	—	10	—	—	.186	.222	.219	34	-24	—	.908	7	115	70	O35(4/3/28),3b23,P8,1b3	—	-1.3
Total	2	66	238	27	42	8	0	0	—	10	—	—	.176	.210	.210	28	-26	—	.901	8	130	203	O39(7/4/28),3b23,P8,1b5	—	-1.5
OBERKFELL, KEN	Kenneth Ray; B5.4.1956 Highland IL; BL/TR/6´0˝/(175–210); d8.22; Col Southwestern Illinois CC																								
1977	StL N	9	9	0	1	0	0	0	1	0-0	0	3	.111	.111	.111	-40	-2	0-0	1.000	-0	94	114	2b6	0	-0.2
1978	StL N	24	50	7	6	1	0	0	0	3-0	0	1	.120	.170	.140	-13	-8	0-0	.987	2	116	97	2b17,3b4	0	-0.5
1979	StL N	135	369	53	111	19	5	1	35	57-9	4	35	.301	.396	.388	114	10	4-1	**.985**	0	105	105	2b117,3b17,S2	0	1.7
1980	StL N	116	422	58	128	27	6	3	46	51-8	1	23	.303	.377	.417	117	12	4-4	.989	-2	104	98	2b101,3b16	40	1.5
1981	StL N	102	376	43	110	12	6	2	45	37-6	0	28	.293	.353	.372	102	1	13-5	.956	9	116	**146**	3b102/S	0	1.0
1982	†StL N	137	470	55	136	22	5	2	34	40-6	1	31	.289	.345	.370	98	-1	11-9	**.972**	14	**121**	112	3b135/2	18	1.1
1983	StL N	151	488	62	143	26	5	3	38	61-5	1	27	.293	.371	.385	110	9	12-6	**.960**	6	**112**	**152**	3b127,2b32/S	0	1.5
1984	StL N	50	152	17	47	11	1	0	11	16-2	1	10	.309	.379	.395	120	5	1-2	.967	4	116	109	3b46,2b2/S	0	0.8
	Atl N	50	172	21	40	8	1	1	10	15-1	0	17	.233	.289	.308	65	-8	1-3	.964	-4	95	113	3b45,2b4	35	-1.4
	Year	100	324	38	87	19	2	1	21	31-3	1	27	.269	.331	.349	90	-3	2-5	.966	0	105	111	3b91,2b6/S	0	-0.6
1985	Atl N	134	412	30	112	19	4	3	35	51-6	6	38	.272	.359	.359	96	0	1-2	.963	1	108	93	3b117,2b16	0	0.0
1986	Atl N	151	503	62	136	24	3	5	48	83-6	2	40	.270	.373	.360	99	3	7-4	.976	18	**120**	118	3b130,2b41	0	2.2
1987	Atl N	135	508	59	142	29	2	3	48	48-5	2	29	.280	.342	.362	84	-10	3-3	.979	-2	105	92	3b126,2b11	15	-1.4
1988	Atl N	120	422	42	117	20	4	3	40	32-6	2	28	.277	.325	.365	96	-2	4-5	.951	-7	94	107	3b113/2	0	-1.0
	Pit N	20	54	7	12	2	0	0	2	5-1	0	6	.222	.288	.259	59	-3	0-0	1.000	-3	89	58	2b11,S3,3b2/1	0	-0.6
	Year	140	476	49	129	22	4	3	42	37-7	2	34	.271	.321	.353	92	-5	4-5	.952	-10	95	105	3b115,2b12,S3/1	0	-1.6
1989	Pit N	14	40	2	5	1	0	0	2	2-0	0	2	.125	.163	.150	-9	-6	0-0	.988	0	89	69	1b9,2b3	0	-0.7
	†SF N	83	116	17	37	5	1	2	15	8-0	2	8	.319	.367	.431	133	5	0-1	.971	-2	102	51	3b38,1b7,2b7	0	0.3
	Year	97	156	19	42	6	1	2	17	10-0	2	10	.269	.316	.359	97	-1	0-1	.971	-1	102	51	3b38,1b16,2b10	0	-0.4
1990	Hou N	77	150	10	31	6	1	1	12	15-1	1	17	.207	.281	.280	57	-9	1-1	.935	-3	104	129	3b24,1b11,2b11	15	-1.3
1991	Hou N	53	70	7	16	4	0	0	14	14-4	0	8	.229	.357	.286	88	0	0-0	1.000	-0	130	107	1b13,3b4	0	-0.1
1992	Cal A	41	91	6	24	1	0	0	10	8-2	0	5	.264	.317	.275	68	-4	0-1	.986	-7	74	35	2b21,1b2,D5	0	-1.1
Total	16	1602	4874	558	1354	237	44	29	446	546-68	23	356	.278	.351	.362	96	-8	62-47	.965	24	110	114	3b1046,2b402,1b43,S8,D5	123	1.8
O'BERRY, MIKE	Preston Michael; B4.20.1954 Birmingham AL; BR/TR/6´2˝/(190–195); [BosA75 22/516]; d4.8; Col South Alabama																								
1979	Bos A	43	59	8	10	1	0	1	4	5-0	1	16	.169	.242	.237	29	-6	0-0	.957	-3	120	58	C43	0	-0.8
1980	Chi N	19	48	7	10	1	0	0	5	5-0	0	13	.208	.273	.229	41	-4	0-0	.982	2	98	173	C19	0	-0.1
1981	Cin N	55	111	6	20	3	1	1	5	14-0	0	19	.180	.272	.252	50	-7	0-0	.983	-3	113	116	C55	0	-0.9
1982	Cin N	21	45	5	10	2	0	0	3	10-0	0	13	.222	.364	.267	79	-1	0-0	.990	-0	127	141	C21	0	0.0
1983	Cal A	26	60	7	10	1	0	1	5	3-0	0	11	.167	.206	.233	21	-7	0-0	1.000	-2	154	91	C26	0	-0.8
1984	NY A	13	32	3	8	2	0	0	5	2-0	0	2	.250	.294	.313	70	-1	0-0	1.000	-0	548	227	C12/3	0	-0.1
1985	Mon N	20	21	2	4	0	0	0	0	4-0	0	3	.190	.320	.190	49	-1	1-0	1.000	-1	57	202	C20	0	-0.1
Total	7	197	376	38	72	10	1	3	27	43-0	1	77	.191	.274	.247	46	-27	1-0	.984	-8	147	126	C196/3	0	-2.8
OBRADOVICH, JIM	James Thomas; B9.13.1949 Fort Campbell KY; BL/TL/6´2˝/200; [MinA67 24/472]; d9.12																								
1978	Hou N	10	17	3	3	0	1	0	2	1-1	0	3	.176	.222	.294	46	-1	0-0	1.000	-0	52	43	1b3	0	-0.2
O'BRIEN	; d8.2																								
1887	Was N	1	4	0	0	0	0	0	0	0	0	2	.000	.000	.000	-99	-1	0	.714	-0	131	0	/2	—	-0.1
O'BRIEN, CHARLIE	Charles Hugh; B5.1.1960 Tulsa OK; BR/TR/6´2˝/(190–215); [OakA82 5/132]; d6.2; Col Wichita St.																								
1985	Oak A	16	11	3	3	1	0	0	1	3-0	0	3	.273	.429	.364	128	1	0-0	.958	-1	0	71	C16	0	0.0
1987	Mil A	10	35	2	7	3	1	0	0	4-0	0	4	.200	.282	.343	63	-2	0-1	1.000	5	151	265	C10	0	0.3
1988	Mil A	40	118	12	26	6	0	2	9	5-0	0	16	.220	.252	.322	59	-7	0-1	.991	8	122	101	C40	0	0.3
1989	Mil A	62	188	22	44	10	0	6	35	21-1	9	11	.234	.339	.383	104	2	0-0	.986	5	125	96	C62	0	1.1
1990	Mil A	46	145	11	27	7	2	0	11	11-1	2	26	.186	.253	.262	44	-11	0-0	.992	2	130	97	C46	0	-0.6
	NY N	28	68	6	11	3	0	0	9	10-2	1	8	.162	.272	.206	35	-6	0-0	.986	6	117	174	C28	0	0.2
1991	NY N	69	168	16	31	6	0	2	14	17-1	4	25	.185	.272	.256	50	-11	0-2	.991	8	83	115	C67	0	0.0
1992	NY N	68	156	15	33	12	0	2	13	16-1	1	18	.212	.289	.327	75	-5	0-1	.979	1	106	164	C64	0	-0.1
1993	NY N	67	188	15	48	11	0	4	23	14-1	2	14	.255	.312	.378	85	-4	1-1	.986	6	102	119	C65	0	0.6
1994	Atl N	51	152	24	37	11	0	8	28	15-2	3	24	.243	.322	.474	101	0	0-0	.991	1	131	84	C48	0	0.4
1995	†Atl N	67	198	18	45	7	0	9	23	29-2	6	40	.227	.343	.399	91	-2	0-1	.992	-2	66	105	C64	0	-0.1
1996	Tor A	109	324	33	77	17	0	13	44	29-1	17	68	.238	.331	.410	87	-6	0-1	.995	13	142	95	C105	0	1.1
1997	Tor A	69	225	22	49	15	1	4	27	22-1	11	45	.218	.311	.347	73	-8	0-2	.995	27	177	142	C69	0	2.1
1998	Chi A	57	164	12	43	9	0	4	18	9-0	2	31	.262	.303	.390	82	-5	0-0	.988	-5	78	123	C57	11	-0.6
	Ana A	5	11	1	2	0	0	0	0	1-0	0	2	.182	.250	.182	15	-1	0-0	1.000	-0	128	172	C5	43	-0.1

YEAR	TM LG	G	AB	R	H	2B	3B	HR	RBI	BB-IB	HP	SO	AVG	OBP	SLG	AOPS	ABR	SB-CS	FA	FR	RNG	THR	GAMES AT POSITION	DL	BFW
	Year	62	175	13	45	9	0	4	18	10-0	2	33	.257	.300	.377	77	-6	0-0	.989	-5	81	126	C62	0	-0.7
1999	Ana A	27	62	3	6	0	0	1	4	1-0	2	12	.097	.136	.145	-28	-12	0-0	.993	8	159	114	C27	50	-0.3
2000	Mon N	9	19	1	4	1	0	1	2	2-1	0	7	.211	.286	.421	75	-1	0-0	1.000	-3	44	0	C9	0	-0.3
Total	15	800	2232	216	493	119	4	56	261	209-14	60	354	.221	.303	.353	75	-78	1-10	.990	81	117	117	C782	104	4.0
O'BRIEN, EDDIE	Edward Joseph; B12.11.1930 S.Amboy NJ; BR/TR/5´9˝/(165–170); d4.25; Mil 1954–55; C1; twb–Johnny; Col Seattle; ▲																								
1953	Pit N	89	261	21	62	5	3	0	14	17	2	30	.238	.289	.280	50	-20	6-1	.935	-12	96	78	S81	0	-2.4
1955	Pit N	75	236	26	55	3	1	0	8	18-0	1	13	.233	.290	.254	47	-18	4-5	.993	1	99	201	O56(1/56/0),3b7,S4	0	-2.1
1956	Pit N	63	53	17	14	2	0	0	3	2-0	0	2	.264	.291	.302	61	-3	1-1	.978	7	129	151	S23,O6(5/1/0),3b4,2b2/P	0	0.6
1957	Pit N	3	4	0	0	0	0	0	0	0-0	0	0	.000	.000	.000	-99	-1	0-0	1.000	0	103	695	P3	0	0.0
1958	Pit N	1	0	0	0	0	0	0	0	0-0	0	0	ø	ø	ø	ø	0	0-0	ø	-0	0	0	/P	0	0.0
Total	5	231	554	64	131	10	4	0	25	37-0	3	45	.236	.288	.269	48	-42	11-7	.942	-4	101	88	S108,O62(6/57/0),3b11,P5,2b2	0	-3.9
O'BRIEN, DINK	Frank Aloysius; B9.13.1894 San Francisco CA; D11.4.1971 Monterey Park CA; BR/TR/5´8˝/160; d4.26																								
1923	Phi N	15	21	3	7	2	0	0	0	2	0	1	.333	.391	.429	104	0	0-0	.909	-1	*80*	*162*	C9	—	0.0
O'BRIEN, GEORGE	George Joseph; B11.4.1889 Cleveland OH; D3.24.1966 Columbus OH; BR/TR/6´0˝/185; d8.16; Col Mount Union																								
1915	StL A	3	9	1	2	0	0	0	0	1	0	2	.222	.300	.222	59	0	0	.933	-1	*98*	*93*	C3	—	-0.1
O'BRIEN, JOHN	John E.; B10.22.1851 Columbus OH; D12.31.1914 Fall River MA; TR/5´11.5˝/187; d4.19																								
1884	Bal U	18	77	7	19	1	1	0	—	2	—	—	.247	.266	.286	61	-6	—	.865	-1	63	257	O18(3/14/1)	—	-0.7
O'BRIEN, JOHN	John Joseph "Chewing Gum"; B7.13.1866 St.John NB, Can.; D5.13.1913 Lewiston ME; BL/TR/5´9˝/175; d4.22																								
1891	Bro N	43	167	22	41	4	2	0	26	12	3	17	.246	.308	.293	76	-5	4	.854	-18	80	76	2b43	—	-2.0
1893	Chi N	4	14	3	5	0	1	0	1	2	1	2	.357	.471	.500	160	1	0	.900	-2	68	55	2b4	—	0.0
1895	Lou N	128	539	82	138	10	4	1	50	45	10	20	.256	.325	.295	65	-27	15	.938	7	105	95	2b125,1b3	—	-1.2
1896	Lou N	49	186	24	63	9	1	2	24	13	1	7	.339	.385	.430	119	5	4	.919	-3	96	81	2b49	—	0.4
	Was N	73	270	38	72	6	3	4	33	27	5	12	.267	.344	.356	85	-6	4	.952	6	104	103	2b73	—	0.2
	Year	122	456	62	135	15	4	6	57	40	6	19	.296	.361	.386	98	-1	8	.938	3	101	94	2b122	—	0.6
1897	Was N	86	320	37	78	12	2	3	45	19	11	—	.244	.309	.322	67	-16	6	.942	4	96	139	2b86	—	-0.6
1899	Bal N	39	135	14	26	4	0	1	17	15	2	—	.193	.283	.244	43	-10	4	.966	5	107	145	2b39	—	-0.3
	Pit N	79	279	26	63	2	4	1	33	21	2	—	.226	.285	.272	53	-19	8	.946	-2	98	106	2b79	—	-1.6
	Year	118	414	40	89	6	4	2	50	36	4	—	.215	.284	.263	50	-29	12	.953	3	101	119	2b118	—	-1.9
Total	6	501	1910	246	486	47	17	12	229	154	35	58	.254	.322	.316	72	-77	45	.936	-3	99	106	2b498,1b3	—	-5.1
O'BRIEN, JACK	John Joseph; B2.5.1873 Watervliet NY; D6.10.1933 Watervliet NY; BL/TR/6´1˝/165; d4.14																								
1899	Was N	127	468	68	132	11	5	6	51	31	3	—	.282	.331	.365	92	-6	17	.926	6	116	91	O121L,3b4	—	-1.0
1901	Was A	11	45	5	8	0	0	0	5	3	1	—	.178	.245	.178	19	-5	2	.929	-0	0	0	O11L	—	-0.5
	Cle A	92	375	54	106	14	5	0	39	22	4	—	.283	.329	.347	91	-4	13	.941	-0	81	143	O92(31/0/61)/3	—	-0.8
	Year	103	420	59	114	14	5	0	44	25	5	—	.271	.320	.329	83	-9	15	.939	-1	71	126	O103(42/0/61)/3	—	-1.3
1903	†Bos A	96	338	44	71	14	4	3	38	21	3	—	.210	.262	.302	65	-14	10	.958	-7	115	111	O71(2/68/1),3b11,2b4/S	—	-2.5
Total	3	326	1226	171	317	39	14	9	133	77	11	—	.259	.308	.335	82	-29	42	.937	-1	101	108	O295(165/68/62),3b16,2b4/S	—	-4.8
O'BRIEN, JACK	John K. (b John K. Bryne); B6.12.1860 Philadelphia PA; D11.20.1910 Philadelphia PA; BR/TR/5´10˝/184; d5.2; OF(5/36/31)																								
1882	Phi AA	62	241	44	73	13	3	3	37	13	—	—	.303	.339	.419	145	11	—	**.925**	10	—	—	C45,O18(0/6/12)/31	—	2.2
1883	Phi AA	94	390	74	113	14	10	0	70	25	—	—	.290	.333	.377	117	6	—	.876	-1	—	—	C58,O25C,3b19/S	—	0.7
1884	Phi AA	36	138	25	39	6	1	1	—	9	3	—	.283	.340	.362	121	3	—	.930	1	—	—	C30,O5C/1	—	0.6
1885	Phi AA	62	225	35	60	9	1	2	30	20	5	—	.267	.340	.342	109	3	—	.903	-4	—	—	C43,S9,1b7,O3R,3b2	—	0.2
1886	Phi AA	105	423	65	107	25	7	0	56	38	7	—	.253	.325	.345	109	5	23	.918	-12	—	—	C36,3b27,1b24,S10,2b7,O3R	—	-0.4
1887	Bro AA	30	123	18	28	4	1	1	17	6	0	—	.228	.264	.301	57	-8	8	.839	-5	—	—	C25,O4(1/0/3)/2	—	-0.9
1888	Bal AA	57	196	25	44	11	5	0	18	17	4	—	.224	.300	.332	105	2	14	.925	-11	—	—	C37,O13(4/0/9),1b7	—	-0.6
1890	Phi AA	109	433	80	113	24	14	4	80	52	12	—	.261	.356	.409	126	14	31	.976	4	122	92	1b109/rfC	—	0.8
Total	8	555	2169	366	577	106	42	11	308	180	31	—	.266	.331	.369	115	36	76	.903	-17	—	—	C275,1b149,O72C,3b49,S20,2b8	—	2.6
O'BRIEN, JOHNNY	John Thomas; B12.11.1930 S.Amboy NJ; BR/TR/5´9˝/(170–175); d4.19; Mil 1954–55; twb–Eddie; Col Seattle; ▲																								
1953	Pit N	89	279	28	69	13	2	2	22	21	4	36	.247	.309	.330	67	-13	1-1	.982	0	102	90	2b77/S	0	-0.8
1955	Pit N	84	278	22	83	15	2	1	25	20-1	1	19	.299	.346	.378	94	-2	1-1	.969	3	105	94	2b78	0	0.6
1956	Pit N	73	104	13	18	1	0	0	3	5-0	0	7	.173	.209	.183	7	-14	0-0	.959	1	112	84	2b53,P8/S	0	-0.9
1957	Pit N	34	35	7	11	2	1	0	1	1-0	2	4	.314	.368	.429	117	1	0-0	.857	-5	62	0	P16,S8,2b2	0	-0.4
1958	Pit N	3	1	1	0	0	0	0	0	0-0	0	1	.000	.000	.000	-99	0	0-0	ø	0	—	—	/H	0	0.0
	StL N	12	2	3	0	0	0	0	0	1-0	0	0	.000	.333	.000	-2	0	0-0	1.000	-1	41	0	S5/P2	0	-0.1
	Year	15	3	4	0	0	0	0	0	1-0	0	1	.000	.250	.000	-26	-1	0-0	1.000	-1	41	0	S5/P2	0	-0.1
1959	Mil N	44	116	16	23	4	0	1	8	11-1	1	15	.198	.271	.259	47	-9	0-0	.987	-6	89	116	2b37	0	-1.3
Total	6	339	815	90	204	35	5	4	59	59-2	8	82	.250	.306	.320	68	-37	2-2	.974	-8	102	94	2b248,P25,S15	0	-2.9
O'BRIEN, PETE	Peter J.; B6.17.1877 Binghamton NY; D1.31.1917 Jersey City NJ; BL/TR/5´7˝/170; d9.21																								
1901	Cin N	16	54	1	11	1	0	1	3	2	0	—	.204	.232	.278	51	-4	0	.889	-2	89	111	2b15	—	-0.6
1906	StL A	151	524	44	122	9	4	2	57	42	3	—	.233	.293	.277	82	-10	25	.933	-36	81	86	2b120,3b20,S11	—	-5.1
1907	Cle A	43	145	9	33	5	2	0	6	7	0	—	.228	.263	.290	76	-4	1	.949	-4	115	92	2b15,3b12,S12	—	-0.8
	Was A	39	134	6	25	3	1	0	12	12	1	—	.187	.259	.224	59	-6	4	.912	3	115	0	3b26,S13/2	—	-0.2
	Year	82	279	15	58	8	3	0	18	19	1	—	.208	.261	.258	68	-10	5	.911	-1	111	51	3b38,S25,2b16	—	-1.0
Total	3	249	857	60	191	18	7	3	78	63	4	—	.223	.279	.271	76	-24	30	.930	-39	85	89	2b151,3b58,S36	—	-6.7
O'BRIEN, PETE	Peter James; B6.16.1867 Chicago IL; D6.30.1937 York Twp. (Du Page Co.) IL; BR/TR/5´9.5˝/165; d4.29																								
1890	Chi N	27	106	15	30	7	0	3	16	5	0	10	.283	.315	.434	113	1	4	.929	-2	94	111	2b27	—	0.0
O'BRIEN, PETE	Peter Michael; B2.9.1958 Santa Monica CA; BL/TL/6´1˝/(185–205); [TexA79 15/381]; d9.3; Col Nebraska																								
1982	Tex A	20	67	13	16	4	1	4	13	6-0	0	8	.239	.297	.507	123	2	1-0	1.000	-0	76	155	O11L,1b3,D4	0	0.1
1983	Tex A	154	524	53	124	24	5	8	53	58-2	1	62	.237	.313	.347	83	-12	5-4	.993	13	**141**	100	1b133,O27(9/0/18)/D	0	-0.8
1984	Tex A	142	520	57	149	26	2	18	80	53-8	0	50	.287	.348	.448	115	11	3-5	.992	1	101	86	1b141/rf	0	0.3
1985	Tex A	159	573	69	153	34	3	22	92	69-4	1	53	.267	.342	.452	114	12	5-10	.995	-6	83	93	1b159	0	-0.6
1986	Tex A	156	551	86	160	23	3	23	90	87-11	0	66	.290	.385	.468	128	24	4-4	.992	1	98	95	1b155	0	1.4
1987	Tex A	159	569	84	163	26	1	23	88	59-6	0	61	.286	.348	.457	112	10	0-4	.992	15	**129**	90	1b158,O2R/D	0	1.3
1988	Tex A	156	547	57	149	24	1	16	71	72-9	0	73	.272	.352	.408	111	10	1-4	.995	13	129	95	1b155/D	0	1.1
1989	Cle A	155	554	75	144	24	1	12	55	83-17	2	48	.260	.356	.372	104	6	3-1	.994	5	113	88	1b154/D	0	0.0
1990	Sea A	108	366	32	82	18	0	5	27	44-1	2	33	.224	.308	.314	74	-12	0-0	.995	5	122	87	1b97,O6L,D6	45	-1.3
1991	Sea A	152	560	58	139	29	3	17	88	44-7	1	61	.248	.300	.402	93	-7	0-1	**.997**	2	103	118	1b132,D18,O13L	0	-1.5
1992	Sea A	134	396	40	88	15	1	14	52	40-8	0	27	.222	.289	.371	84	-9	2-1	.996	3	115	109	1b81,D36	0	-1.3
1993	Sea A	72	210	30	54	7	0	7	27	26-4	0	21	.257	.335	.390	93	-2	0-0	.988	2	202	197	D52,1b9/lf	0	-0.4
Total	12	1567	5437	654	1421	254	21	169	736	641-77	7	563	.261	.336	.409	104	33	24-34	.994	54	113	96	1b1377,D120,O61(40/0/21)	45	-1.7
O'BRIEN, RAY	Raymond Joseph; B10.31.1892 St.Louis MO; D3.31.1942 St.Louis MO; BL/TL/5´9˝/175; d6.27																								
1916	Pit N	16	57	5	12	3	2	0	3	1	0	14	.211	.224	.333	69	-2	0	.864	-0	70	204	O14(7/0/7)	—	-0.4
O'BRIEN, SYD	Sydney Lloyd; B2.18.1944 Compton CA; BR/TR/6´1˝/(185–195); d4.15; Col Long Beach (CA) City																								
1969	Bos A	100	263	47	64	10	5	9	29	15-0	1	37	.243	.287	.422	92	-5	2-3	.939	-0	111	115	3b53,S15,2b12	0	-0.4
1970	Chi A	121	441	48	109	13	2	8	44	22-1	2	62	.247	.285	.340	69	-20	3-3	.938	6	102	125	3b68,2b43,S5	0	-1.2
1971	Cal A	90	251	25	50	8	1	5	21	15-4	1	33	.199	.247	.299	58	-15	0-2	.961	-10	85	101	S52,2b7,3b6/1rf	0	-2.1
1972	Cal A	36	39	10	7	2	0	1	1	6-0	0	10	.179	.289	.308	82	-1	0-0	.889	-2	103	139	3b8,S4,2b3/1	0	-0.3
	Mil A	31	58	5	12	2	0	1	5	2-0	0	13	.207	.230	.293	57	-3	0-1	.852	-2	110	196	3b9,2b7	0	-0.7
	Year	67	97	15	19	4	0	2	6	8-0	0	23	.196	.255	.299	67	-4	0-1	.861	-5	108	178	3b17,2b10,S4/1	0	-1.0
Total	4	378	1052	135	242	35	8	24	100	60-5	4	155	.230	.273	.347	73	-44	5-9	.934	-8	106	121	3b144,S76,2b72,1b2/rf	0	-4.7

YEAR	TM LG	G	AB	R	H	2B	3B	HR	RBI	BB-IB	HP	SO	AVG	OBP	SLG	AOPS	ABR	SB-CS	FA	FR	RNG	THR	GAMES AT POSITION	DL	BFW
O'Brien, Tommy	Thomas Edward "Obie"; B12.19.1918 Anniston AL; D11.5.1978 Anniston AL; BR/TR/5´11˝/195; d4.24																								
1943	Pit N	89	232	35	72	12	7	2	26	15	0	24	.310	.352	.448	126	7	0	.964	-2	94	99	O48(17/0/31),3b9	0	0.2
1944	Pit N	85	156	27	39	6	2	3	20	21	1	12	.250	.343	.372	97	0	1	.965	-0	84	176	O48(15/0/33)/3	0	-0.2
1945	Pit N	58	161	23	54	6	5	0	18	9	1	13	.335	.374	.435	120	4	0	.961	-2	97	63	O45(12/0/33)	0	0.0
1949	Bos A	49	125	24	28	5	0	3	10	21	0	12	.224	.336	.336	73	-5	1-0	.984	-2	90	76	O32(0/8/25)	0	-0.7
1950	Bos A	9	31	0	4	1	0	0	3	3	0	5	.129	.206	.161	-5	-5	0-0	1.000	-0	84	175	O9(3/4/2)	0	-0.5
	Was A	3	9	1	1	0	0	0	1	1	0	0	.111	.200	.111	-20	-2	0-0	1.000	1	110	425	O3(2/0/1)	0	-0.1
	Year	12	40	1	5	1	0	0	4	4	0	5	.125	.205	.150	-8	-7	0-0	1.000	1	92	248	O12(5/4/3)	0	-0.6
Total	5	293	714	110	198	30	14	8	78	70	2	66	.277	.344	.392	100	-1	2-0	.970	-5	92	111	O185(49/12/125),3b10	0	-1.3
O'Brien, Tom	Thomas H.; B6.22.1860 Salem MA; D4.21.1921 Worcester MA; BR/TR/6´1˝/185; d6.14																								
1882	Wor N	22	89	9	18	1	1	0	7	1	—	10	.202	.211	.236	42	-6	—	.789	-3	81	0	O20(16/4/0),2b2/3	—	-0.9
1883	Bal AA	33	138	16	37	6	4	0	—	5	—	—	.268	.294	.370	109	1	—	.825	-4	105	60	2b29,O4C	—	-0.2
1884	Bos U	103	449	80	118	31	8	4	—	12	—	—	.263	.282	.394	104	-11	—	.853	0	100	82	2b99,O3(1/1/1),1b2/C	—	-0.7
1885	Bal AA	8	33	4	7	3	0	0	5	2	0	—	.212	.257	.303	78	-1	—	.932	1	235	38	1b6,2b2	—	0.0
1887	NY AA	31	129	13	25	3	2	0	18	2	1	—	.194	.212	.248	29	-13	10	.963	-3	87	90	1b20,O8(2/4/2),3b2,2b2/P	—	-1.4
1890	Roc AA	73	273	36	52	6	5	0	31	30	1	—	.190	.273	.249	58	-14	6	.971	-4	74	113	1b68,2b8	—	-2.1
Total	6	270	1111	158	257	50	20	4	61	52	2	10	.231	.267	.323	79	-44	16	.846	-13	102	79	2b142,1b96,O35(19/13/3),3b3/PC	—	-5.3
O'Brien, Tom	Thomas J.; B2.20.1873 Verona PA; D2.3.1901 Phoenix AZ; 5´11˝/170; d5.10; OF(169/61/32)																								
1897	†Bal N	50	147	25	37	6	0	0	32	20	2	—	.252	.349	.293	70	-5	7	.968	1	81	70	1b25,O24(13/1/10)	—	-0.5
1898	Bal N	18	60	9	13	0	0	0	14	10	1	—	.217	.338	.217	59	-3	0	.833	-0	130	831	O16R	—	-0.3
	Pit N	107	413	53	107	10	8	1	45	25	11	—	.259	.318	.329	87	-7	13	.924	-6	155	186	O69(10/59/0),1b21,3b8,2b7,S4	—	-1.6
	Year	125	473	62	120	10	8	1	59	35	12	—	.254	.321	.315	84	-10	13	.911	-6	150	310	O85(10/59/16),1b21,3b8,2b7,S4	—	-1.9
1899	NY N	151	577	101	171	22	10	6	77	44	4	—	.296	.350	.400	109	7	23	.933	-4	105	110	O128(125/0/3),3b21,S2/21	—	-0.7
1900	†Pit N	102	376	61	109	22	6	3	61	21	13	—	.290	.349	.404	107	3	12	.961	-10	69	111	1b65,O25(21/1/3),2b4,S2	—	-0.8
Total	4	428	1573	249	437	60	24	10	229	120	31	—	.278	.341	.366	97	-5	55	.928	-18	121	187	O262L,1b112,3b29,2b12,S8	—	-3.9
O'Brien, Darby	William D.; B9.1.1863 Peoria IL; D6.15.1893 Peoria IL; BR/TR/6´1˝/186; d4.16																								
1887	NY AA	127	522	97	157	30	13	5	73	40	4	—	.301	.355	.437	126	18	49	.913	7	102	83	O121(121/1/0),1b10,S2/3P	—	1.8
1888	Bro AA	136	532	105	149	27	6	2	65	30	7	—	.280	.327	.365	122	13	55	.932	1	66	23	O136L	—	0.9
1889	†Bro AA	136	567	146	170	30	11	5	80	61	16	76	.300	.384	.418	128	22	91	.906	-8	53	92	O136L	—	0.9
1890	†Bro N	85	350	78	110	28	6	2	63	32	4	43	.314	.378	.446	139	18	38	.960	0	90	67	O85(44/42/0)	—	1.3
1891	Bro N	103	395	79	100	18	6	5	57	39	7	53	.253	.331	.367	104	2	31	.951	2	67	35	O103L	—	0.1
1892	Bro N	122	490	72	119	14	5	1	56	29	3	52	.243	.289	.298	81	-12	57	.956	1	78	71	O122(115/3/4)	—	-2.1
Total	6	709	2856	577	805	147	47	20	394	231	41	224	.282	.344	.387	117	61	321	.934	3	75	62	O703(655/46/4),1b10,S2/P3	—	2.9
O'Brien, Billy	William Smith; B3.14.1860 Albany NY; D5.26.1911 Kansas City MO; BR/TR/6´0˝/185; d9.27; ▲																								
1884	StP U	8	30	1	7	3	0	0	—	0	—	—	.233	.233	.333	128	0	—	.840	2	138	0	3b8,P2	—	0.2
	KC U	4	17	2	4	0	0	0	—	0	—	—	.235	.235	.235	50	-2	—	.714	1	177	0	3b3/1	—	-0.1
	Year	12	47	3	11	3	0	0	—	0	—	—	.234	.234	.298	92	-2	—	.795	3	151	0	3b11,P2/1	—	0.1
1887	Was N	113	453	71	126	16	12	**19**	73	21	5	17	.278	.317	.492	130	16	11	.974	-4	69	91	1b104,O4(1/3/0),3b4,2b2	—	0.2
1888	Was N	133	528	42	119	15	2	9	66	9	0	70	.225	.238	.313	80	-13	10	.975	-4	81	82	1b132/3	—	-2.8
1889	Was N	2	8	1	0	0	0	0	0	1	0	1	.000	.111	.000	-72	-2	0	1.000	-0	0	0	1b2	—	-0.2
1890	Bro AA	96	388	47	108	25	8	4	67	28	3	—	.278	.332	.415	124	10	5	.973	-3	90	111	1b96	—	-0.1
Total	5	356	1424	164	364	59	22	32	206	59	8	88	.256	.289	.395	109	9	26	.974	-8	80	92	1b335,3b16,O4(1/3/0),2b2,P2	—	-2.8
Ochoa, Alex	Alex; B3.29.1972 Miami Lakes FL; BR/TR/6´0˝/(175–200); [BalA91 3/82]; d9.18																								
1995	NY N	11	37	7	11	1	0	0	0	2-0	0	10	.297	.333	.324	77	-1	1-0	1.000	1	120	160	O10R	0	0.0
1996	NY N	82	282	37	83	19	3	4	33	17-0	2	30	.294	.336	.426	105	2	4-3	.966	1	97	160	O76R	0	-0.1
1997	NY N	113	238	31	58	14	1	3	22	18-0	2	32	.244	.300	.349	73	-10	3-4	.982	-2	86	149	O88(0/4/84)/D	0	-1.5
1998	Min A	94	249	35	64	14	2	2	25	10-0	1	35	.257	.288	.353	64	-14	6-3	.969	-0	91	179	O74(21/4/52),D3	0	-1.6
1999	Mil N	119	277	47	83	16	3	8	40	45-2	5	43	.300	.404	.466	120	10	6-4	.979	-2	93	110	O85(50/9/31)/D	0	0.6
2000	Cin N	118	244	50	77	21	3	13	58	24-3	3	27	.316	.378	.586	136	13	9-4	.977	2	107	107	O95(74/3/37)	15	1.3
2001	Cin N	90	349	48	101	20	4	7	35	24-0	2	53	.289	.337	.430	92	-4	12-9	.989	1	100	102	O85(3/0/85)/D	0	-0.8
	Col N	58	187	25	47	10	3	1	17	21-0	2	23	.251	.330	.353	65	-9	5-4	.990	2	97	184	O52(33/2/21)	0	-0.9
	Year	148	536	73	148	30	7	8	52	45-0	4	76	.276	.334	.403	81	-15	17-13	.989	3	99	132	O137(36/2/106)/D	0	-1.7
2002	Mil N	85	215	32	55	9	0	6	21	32-2	2	30	.256	.357	.381	95	-1	8-5	.993	6	119	130	O72(18/2/61)	0	0.2
	†Ana A	37	65	8	18	7	0	2	10	10-0	0	5	.277	.373	.477	126	3	2-2	.975	-1	87	152	O36(7/0/31)	0	0.1
Total	8	807	2143	320	597	131	19	46	261	203-7	19	288	.279	.344	.422	96	-11	56-38	.981	10	98	139	O673(206/24/488),D6	15	-2.7
Ock, Whitey	Harold David; B3.17.1912 Brooklyn NY; D3.18.1975 Mt.Kisco NY; BR/TR/5´11˝/180; d9.29; Col Lehigh																								
1935	Bro N	1	3	0	0	0	0	0	0	1	0	2	.000	.250	.000	-27	-1	0	1.000	-0	*0*	*0*	/C	—	-0.1
O'Connell, Danny	Daniel Francis; B1.21.1927 Paterson NJ; D10.2.1969 Clifton NJ; BR/TR/6´0˝/(175–185); d7.14; Mil 1951–52; C2																								
1950	Pit N	79	315	39	92	16	1	8	32	24	0	33	.292	.342	.425	97	-1	7	.977	7	103	95	S65,3b12	0	0.9
1953	Pit N	149	588	88	173	26	8	7	55	57	4	42	.294	.361	.401	99	0	3-4	.958	7	**110**	66	3b104,2b47	0	0.9
1954	Mil N	146	541	61	151	28	4	2	37	38	2	46	.279	.326	.357	84	-13	2-2	.979	6	106	114	2b103,3b35,1b8/S	0	0.0
1955	Mil N	124	453	47	102	15	4	6	40	28-2	5	43	.225	.276	.316	60	-27	2-2	.981	14	**111**	92	2b114,3b7/S	0	-0.5
1956	Mil N	139	498	71	119	17	9	2	42	76-0	4	42	.239	.342	.321	86	-8	3-3	.985	-4	**104**	**119**	2b138,3b4/S	0	-0.2
1957	Mil N	48	183	29	43	9	1	1	8	19-0	2	20	.235	.312	.311	74	-6	1-0	.982	7	109	139	2b48	0	0.5
	NY N	95	364	57	97	18	3	7	28	33-0	2	30	.266	.330	.390	93	-3	8-3	.980	11	105	116	2b68,3b30	0	1.3
	Year	143	547	86	140	27	4	8	36	52-0	4	50	.256	.324	.364	87	-9	9-3	.981	18	107	**126**	2b116,3b30	0	1.8
1958	SF N	107	306	44	71	12	2	3	23	51-0	0	35	.232	.340	.314	77	-9	2-1	.986	6	107	103	2b104,3b3	0	0.4
1959	SF N	34	58	6	11	3	0	0	0	5-0	0	15	.190	.254	.241	34	-5	0-1	.927	2	131	144	3b26,2b8	0	-0.4
1961	Was A	138	493	61	128	30	1	1	37	77-0	3	62	.260	.361	.331	88	-4	15-5	.939	8	116	90	3b73,2b61	0	1.0
1962	Was A	84	236	24	62	7	2	2	18	23-1	0	28	.263	.327	.335	80	-7	5-1	.961	2	117	194	3b41,2b22	0	-0.3
Total	10	1143	4035	527	1049	181	35	39	320	431-3	22	396	.260	.333	.351	84	-83	48-22	.980	66	106	108	2b713,3b335,S68,1b8	0	3.6
O'Connell, Jimmy	James Joseph; B2.11.1901 Sacramento CA; D11.11.1976 Bakersfield CA; BL/TR/5´10.5˝/175; d4.17; Col Santa Clara																								
1923	†NY N	87	252	42	63	9	2	6	39	34	5	32	.250	.351	.373	92	-2	7-3	.980	-10	87	25	O64C,1b8	—	-1.4
1924	NY N	52	104	24	33	4	2	2	18	11	1	16	.317	.388	.452	128	4	2-1	.952	-2	88	95	O29(1/15/14)/2	—	0.2
Total	2	139	356	66	96	13	4	8	57	45	6	48	.270	.361	.396	102	2	9-4	.974	-11	87	41	O93(1/79/14),1b8/2	—	-1.2
O'Connell, John	John Charles; B6.13.1904 Verona PA; D10.17.1992 Canton OH; BR/TR/6´0˝/170; d8.16; Col Duquesne																								
1928	Pit N	1	1	0	0	0	0	0	0	0	0	0	.000	.000	.000	-96	0	0	1.000	1	*0*	*594*	/C	—	0.0
1929	Pit N	2	7	1	1	1	0	0	0	1	0	1	.143	.250	.286	32	-1	0	1.000	-0	*100*	0	C2	—	-0.1
Total	2	3	8	1	1	1	0	0	0	1	0	1	.125	.222	.250	17	-1	0	1.000	0	*80*	*119*	C3	—	-0.1
O'Connell, John	John Joseph; D5.14.1908 Derry NH; TR/5´9.5˝/170; d8.22																								
1891	Bal AA	8	29	2	5	1	0	0	7	3	0	6	.172	.250	.207	31	-3	2	.938	-2	99	0	S3,2b3,O2R	—	-0.4
1902	Det A	8	22	1	4	0	0	0	0	3	0	—	.182	.280	.182	29	-2	0	.919	0	113	79	2b6,1b2	—	-0.2
Total	2	16	51	3	9	1	0	0	7	6	0	6	.176	.263	.196	30	-5	2	.885	-2	99	85	2b9,S3,1b2,O2R	—	-0.6
O'Connell, Pat	Patrick H.; B6.10.1861 Bangor ME; D1.24.1943 Lewiston ME; BL/TR/5´10˝/175; d7.22																								
1886	Bal AA	42	166	20	30	3	2	0	8	11	1	—	.181	.236	.223	45	-10	10	.782	-6	58	0	O41C/1P	—	-1.6
O'Connor, Dan	Daniel Cornelius; B8.11.1868 Guelph ON, Can.; D3.3.1942 Guelph ON, Can.; BL/TR/6´2˝/185; d6.3																								
1890	Lou AA	6	26	3	12	1	1	0	5	1	0	—	.462	.481	.577	217	4	5	1.000	-1	0	117	1b6	—	0.2
O'Connor, Johnny	John Charles "Bucky"; B12.1.1891 Cahirciveen, Ireland; D5.30.1982 Bonner Springs KS; BR/TR/5´9˝/?; d9.16; Col Illinois																								
1916	Chi N	1	0	0	0	0	0	0	0	0	0	0	ø	ø	ø	ø	0	0	ø	0	0	0	/C	—	0.0

YEAR	TM LG	G	AB	R	H	2B	3B	HR	RBI	BB-IB	HP	SO	AVG	OBP	SLG	AOPS	ABR	SB-CS	FA	FR	RNG	THR	GAMES AT POSITION	DL	BFW
O'Connor, Jack	John Joseph "Rowdy Jack","Peach Pie"; B6.2.1869 St.Louis MO; D11.14.1937 St.Louis MO; BR/TR/5´10˝/170; d4.20; M1; OF(42/113/217)																								
1887	Cin AA	12	40	4	4	0	0	0	1	2	0	—	.100	.143	.100	-31	-7	3	.947	2	166	414	O7L,C5	—	-0.4
1888	Cin AA	36	137	14	28	3	1	1	17	6	1	—	.204	.243	.263	59	-7	12	.795	-2	141	0	O34(11/21/2),C2	—	-0.9
1889	Col AA	107	398	69	107	17	7	4	60	33	4	37	.269	.331	.377	107	3	26	**.955**	-1	—	—	C84,O19(3/0/16),2b4,1b3	—	0.7
1890	Col AA	121	457	89	148	14	10	2	66	38	1	—	.324	.377	.411	142	23	29	**.962**	11	105	99	C106,O9(3/4/2),S8,2b2/3	—	3.7
1891	Col AA	56	229	28	61	12	3	0	37	11	0	14	.266	.300	.345	90	-4	10	.878	0	113	205	O40(7/0/33),C21	—	-0.2
1892	†Cle N	140	572	71	142	22	5	1	58	25	2	48	.248	.282	.309	76	-19	17	.935	12	125	129	O106(6/0/100),C34	—	-0.9
1893	Cle N	96	384	72	110	23	1	4	75	29	3	12	.286	.341	.383	87	-8	29	.949	5	112	104	C56,O44(2/27/15)	—	0.0
1894	Cle N	86	330	67	104	23	7	2	51	15	0	7	.315	.345	.445	86	-9	15	.942	10	160	77	C45,O33(1/27/5),1b7	—	0.2
1895	Cle N	90	343	52	100	14	10	0	58	31	3	22	.292	.355	.391	87	-8	11	.927	0	119	96	C48,1b41/3	—	-0.3
1896	†Cle N	68	256	41	76	11	1	1	43	15	3	12	.297	.343	.359	81	-7	15	.966	2	149	82	C37,1b17,O12(0/3/9)	—	-0.2
1897	Cle N	103	397	49	115	21	4	2	69	26	3	—	.290	.338	.378	84	-10	20	.941	-8	46	0	O52(0/30/22),1b36,C13	—	-1.7
1898	Cle N	131	478	50	119	17	4	1	56	26	2	—	.249	.291	.308	72	-18	8	.983	9	122	99	1b69,C48,O15(2/1/12)	—	-0.6
1899	StL N	84	289	33	73	5	6	0	43	15	4	—	.253	.299	.311	66	-15	7	.943	6	125	87	C57,1b26	—	-0.4
1900	StL N	10	32	4	7	0	0	0	6	2	2	—	.219	.306	.219	46	-2	0	.957	-0	92	87	C10	—	-0.2
	†Pit N	43	147	15	35	4	1	0	19	3	2	—	.238	.263	.279	49	-11	5	.944	-4	130	96	C40,1b2	—	-1.0
	Year	53	179	19	42	4	1	0	25	5	4	—	.235	.271	.268	49	-13	5	.947	-4	122	94	C50,1b2	—	-1.2
1901	Pit N	61	202	16	39	7	3	0	22	10	2	—	.193	.238	.257	42	-15	2	.978	3	131	90	C59	—	-0.7
1902	Pit N	49	170	13	50	1	2	1	28	3	0	—	.294	.306	.341	96	-2	2	.979	0	140	100	C42,1b6/rf	—	0.2
1903	NY A	64	212	13	43	4	1	0	12	8	1	—	.203	.235	.231	38	-16	4	.988	2	110	80	C63/1	—	-0.9
1904	StL A	14	47	4	10	1	0	0	2	2	0	—	.213	.245	.234	55	-2	0	.943	-4	87	72	C14	—	-0.5
1906	StL A	55	174	8	33	0	0	0	11	2	0	—	.190	.199	.190	23	-16	4	.990	6	94	109	C51	—	-0.6
1907	StL A	25	89	2	14	2	0	0	4	0	2	—	.157	.176	.180	13	-9	0	.991	-2	87	97	C25	—	-0.9
1910	StL A	1	0	0	0	0	0	0	0	0	0	—	ø	ø	ø	ø	0	0	1.000	-0	30	0	/CM	—	0.0
Total	21	1452	5383	714	1418	201	66	19	738	302	35	152	.263	.307	.336	79	-159	219	.962	46	118	94	C861,O372R,1b208,S8,2b6,3b2	—	-5.6
O'Connor, Paddy	Patrick Francis; B8.4.1879 Co. Kerry, Ireland; D8.17.1950 Springfield MA; BR/TR/5´8˝/168; d4.17; C4																								
1908	Pit N	12	16	1	3	0	0	0	2	0	0	—	.188	.188	.188	20	-2	0	.889	-1	117	51	C4	—	-0.3
1909	†Pit N	9	16	1	5	1	0	0	3	0	0	—	.313	.313	.375	104	0	0	.700	-1	116	52	C3/3	—	-0.1
1910	Pit N	6	4	0	1	0	0	0	0	1	0	1	.250	.400	.250	85	0	0	1.000	-0	0	0	/C	—	0.0
1914	StL N	10	9	0	0	0	0	0	0	2	1	2	.000	.250	.000	-24	-1	0	1.000	-0	84	99	C7	—	-0.2
1915	Pit F	70	219	15	50	10	1	0	16	14	1	30	.228	.278	.283	58	-16	4	.987	7	118	108	C66	—	-0.3
1918	NY A	1	3	0	1	0	0	0	0	0	0	1	.333	.333	.333	99	0	0	1.000	-0	66	191	/C	—	0.0
Total	6	108	267	17	60	11	1	0	21	17	2	34	.225	.276	.273	57	-19	4	.979	4	116	105	C82/3	—	-0.9
O'Dea, Ken	James Kenneth; B3.16.1913 Lima NY; D12.17.1985 Lima NY; BL/TR/6´0˝/180; d4.21																								
1935	†Chi N	76	202	30	52	13	2	6	38	26	1	18	.257	.345	.431	106	2	0	.964	-1	107	101	C63	—	0.5
1936	Chi N	80	189	36	58	10	3	2	38	38	0	18	.307	.423	.423	126	9	0	.979	-1	117	90	C55	—	1.1
1937	Chi N	83	219	31	66	7	5	4	32	24	0	26	.301	.370	.434	113	4	1	.985	-4	117	80	C64	—	0.3
1938	†Chi N	86	247	22	65	12	1	3	33	12	0	18	.263	.297	.356	77	-8	1	.970	1	110	83	C71	—	-0.3
1939	NY N	52	97	7	17	1	0	3	11	10	0	16	.175	.252	.278	42	-8	0	.947	-2	86	99	C30	—	-0.9
1940	NY N	48	96	9	23	4	1	0	12	16	0	15	.240	.348	.302	80	-2	0	.992	3	143	172	C31	—	0.3
1941	NY N	59	89	13	19	5	1	3	17	8	0	20	.213	.278	.393	86	-2	0	1.000	1	110	106	C14	0	0.0
1942	†StL N	58	192	22	45	7	1	5	32	17	0	23	.234	.297	.359	85	-4	0	.979	9	159	134	C49	0	0.9
1943	†StL N	71	203	15	57	11	2	3	25	19	1	25	.281	.345	.399	110	3	0	.989	6	176	104	C56	0	1.2
1944	†StL N	85	265	35	66	11	2	6	37	37	1	29	.249	.343	.374	100	1	1	.994	7	141	89	C69	0	1.2
1945	StL N✳	100	307	36	78	18	2	4	43	50	0	31	.254	.359	.365	99	1	0	**.995**	4	99	**128**	C91	0	1.1
1946	StL N	22	57	2	7	2	0	1	3	8	0	8	.123	.231	.211	25	-6	0	.991	3	152	120	C22	0	-0.1
	Bos N	12	32	4	7	0	0	0	2	8	0	4	.219	.375	.219	70	-1	0	1.000	-1	72	108	C12	0	-0.1
	Year	34	89	6	14	2	0	1	5	16	0	12	.157	.286	.213	41	-7	0	.994	3	126	116	C34	0	-0.2
Total	12	832	2195	262	560	101	20	40	323	273	3	251	.255	.338	.374	95	-11	3	.983	27	125	106	C627	0	5.2
O'Dea, Paul	Paul "Lefty"; B7.3.1920 Cleveland OH; D12.11.1978 Cleveland OH; BL/TL/6´0˝/200; d4.19; Col Case Western Reserve																								
1944	Cle A	76	173	25	55	9	0	0	13	23	1	21	.318	.401	.370	126	7	2-2	.949	-2	93	68	O41(36/0/5),P3,1b3	0	0.3
1945	Cle A	87	221	21	52	2	2	1	21	20	0	26	.235	.299	.276	70	-9	3-0	.992	3	115	77	O53R/P	0	-1.0
Total	2	163	394	46	107	11	2	1	34	43	1	47	.272	.345	.317	95	-2	5-2	.975	0	106	73	O94(36/0/58),P4,1b3	0	-0.7
Odom, Heinie	Herman Boyd; B10.13.1900 Rusk TX; D8.31.1970 Rusk TX; BB/TR/6´0˝/170; d4.22; Col Texas																								
1925	NY A	1	1	0	1	0	0	0	0	0	0	0	1.000	1.000	1.000	416	0	0-0	1.000	0	148	0	/3	—	0.1
O'Donnell, Harry	Harry Herman "Butch"; B4.2.1894 Philadelphia PA; D1.31.1958 Philadelphia PA; BR/TR/5´8˝/175; d4.30																								
1927	Phi N	16	16	1	1	0	0	0	2	2	0	2	.063	.167	.063	-36	-3	0	1.000	-0	72	72	C12	—	-0.3
O'Donnell, John	John; B Littlestown PA; d7.16																								
1884	Phi U	1	4	0	1	0	0	0	—	0	—	—	.250	.250	.250	56	0	—	.545	-2	—	—	/C	—	-0.2
O'Doul, Lefty	Francis Joseph; B3.4.1897 San Francisco CA; D12.7.1969 San Francisco CA; BL/TL/6´0˝/180; d4.29; ▲																								
1919	NY A	19	16	2	4	0	0	0	1	1	0	2	.250	.294	.250	53	-1	1	.500	-0	75	0	P3/rf	—	-0.1
1920	NY A	13	12	2	2	1	0	0	1	1	0	1	.167	.231	.250	26	-1	0-0	ø	-0	0	0	P2/cf	—	-0.1
1922	NY A	8	9	0	3	1	0	0	4	0	0	2	.333	.333	.444	99	1	0-0	1.000	0	102	0	P6	—	0.0
1923	Bos A	36	35	2	5	0	0	0	4	2	0	3	.143	.189	.143	-12	-6	0-0	.958	1	153	0	P23/rf	—	0.0
1928	NY N	114	354	67	113	19	4	8	46	30	0	8	.319	.372	.463	117	8	9	.962	-7	86	62	O94L	—	-0.5
1929	Phi N	**154**	638	152	**254**	35	6	32	122	76	4	19	**.398**	**.465**	.622	157	59	2	.971	3	100	128	O154(139/0/15)	—	4.5
1930	Phi N	140	528	122	202	37	7	22	97	63	5	21	.383	.453	.604	142	39	3	.953	-5	102	33	O131L	—	2.1
1931	Bro N	134	512	85	172	32	11	7	75	48	3	16	.336	.396	.482	136	27	5	.954	-2	104	58	O132L	—	1.6
1932	Bro N	148	595	120	219	32	8	21	90	50	7	20	**.368**	.423	.555	164	54	11	.979	-5	99	44	O148L	—	4.0
1933	Bro N	43	159	14	40	5	1	5	21	15	1	6	.252	.320	.390	106	1	2	.947	-2	101	32	O41L	—	-0.3
	†NY N★	78	229	31	70	9	1	9	35	29	2	17	.306	.388	.472	147	15	1	.974	-3	91	82	O63(32/0/31)	—	0.9
	Year	121	388	45	110	14	2	14	56	44	3	23	.284	.361	.438	130	16	3	.962	-5	95	61	O104(73/0/31)	—	0.6
1934	NY N	83	177	27	56	4	3	9	46	18	1	7	.316	.383	.525	144	10	2	.968	-4	84	38	O38(27/0/11)	—	0.5
Total	11	970	3264	624	1140	175	41	113	542	333	23	122	.349	.413	.532	142	206	36-0	.964	-24	98	65	O804(744/1/59),P34	—	12.6
Odwell, Fred	Frederick William "Fritz"; B9.25.1872 Downsville NY; D8.19.1948 Downsville NY; BL/TR/5´9.5˝/160; d4.16																								
1904	Cin N	129	468	75	133	22	10	1	58	26	8	—	.284	.333	.380	110	5	30	.956	12	109	133	O126(107/14/5)/2	—	1.0
1905	Cin N	130	468	79	113	10	9	**9**	65	26	8	—	.241	.293	.359	85	-11	21	.967	2	106	114	O126(56/4/66)	—	-1.6
1906	Cin N	58	202	20	45	5	4	0	21	15	3	—	.223	.286	.287	76	-6	11	.963	2	134	0	O57R	—	-0.8
1907	Cin N	94	274	24	74	5	7	0	24	22	5	—	.270	.336	.339	107	2	10	.975	6	77	69	O84(77/0/8)/2	—	0.3
Total	4	411	1412	198	365	42	30	10	168	89	24	—	.258	.313	.352	96	-10	72	.964	22	105	94	O393(240/18/136),2b2	—	-1.1
Oertel, Chuck	Charles Frank "Ducky","Snuffy"; B3.12.1931 Coffeyville KS; D10.4.2000 Royal Oak MI; BL/TR/5´8˝/165; d9.1																								
1958	Bal A	14	12	4	2	0	0	1	1	1-1	0	1	.167	.231	.417	78	0	0-0	1.000	-0	44	0	O2(2/0/1)	0	-0.1
Oester, Ron	Ronald John; B5.5.1956 Cincinnati OH; BB/TR/6´2˝/(175–195); [CinN74 9/215]; d9.10; C7																								
1978	Cin N	6	8	1	3	0	0	0	1	0-0	0	2	.375	.375	.375	110	0	0-0	1.000	1	117	138	S6	0	0.1
1979	Cin N	6	3	0	0	0	0	0	0	0-0	0	1	.000	.000	.000	-99	-1	0-0	1.000	0	112	0	S2	0	-0.1
1980	Cin N	100	303	40	84	16	2	2	20	26-7	1	44	.277	.336	.363	97	-1	6-2	.980	-15	89	98	2b79,S17,3b3	0	-1.1
1981	Cin N	105	354	45	96	16	7	5	42	42-8	0	49	.271	.342	.398	112	6	2-5	.980	5	99	101	2b103,S9	0	1.7
1982	Cin N	151	549	63	143	19	4	9	47	35-8	0	82	.260	.303	.359	85	-13	5-6	.972	3	97	107	2b118,S29,3b13	0	-0.3
1983	Cin N	157	549	63	145	23	5	11	58	49-14	1	106	.264	.322	.384	93	-6	2-2	.977	-25	87	80	2b154	0	-2.4
1984	Cin N	150	553	54	134	26	3	3	38	41-7	1	97	.242	.295	.316	69	-23	7-2	.980	-15	89	80	2b147/S	0	-3.0
1985	Cin N	152	526	59	155	26	3	1	34	51-17	0	65	.295	.354	.361	96	-1	5-0	.989	9	100	103	2b149	0	1.8
1986	Cin N	153	523	52	135	23	2	8	44	52-16	1	84	.258	.325	.356	85	-10	9-2	.978	15	106	108	2b151	0	1.5
1987	Cin N	69	237	28	60	9	6	2	23	22-4	0	51	.253	.317	.367	77	-8	2-3	.974	1	96	88	2b69	91	-0.4
1988	Cin N	54	150	20	42	7	0	0	10	9-3	0	24	.280	.319	.327	83	-3	0-2	.995	-0	93	105	2b49,S5	0	-0.3
1989	Cin N	109	305	23	75	15	0	1	14	32-8	0	47	.246	.318	.305	76	-8	1-0	.985	3	97	82	2b102,S2	40	-0.2

YEAR	TM LG	G	AB	R	H	2B	3B	HR	RBI	BB-IB	HP	SO	AVG	OBP	SLG	AOPS	ABR	SB-CS	FA	FR	RNG	THR	GAMES AT POSITION	DL	BFW
1990	†Cin N	64	154	10	46	10	1	0	13	10-1	0	29	.299	.339	.377	93	-1	1-2	.982	-8	82	70	2b50,3b3	0	-0.9
Total	13	1276	4214	458	1118	190	33	42	344	369-93	4	681	.265	.323	.356	87	-69	40-26	.980	-27	95	94	2b1171,S71,3b19	131	-3.6
O'FARRELL, BOB	Robert Arthur; B10.19.1896 Waukegan IL; D2.20.1988 Waukegan IL; BR/TR/5´9.5˝/180; d9.5; M2																								
1915	Chi N	2	3	0	1	0	0	0	0	0	0	0	.333	.333	.333	102	0	0	.667	-1	*63*	*184*	C2	—	-0.1
1916	Chi N	1	0	0	0	0	0	0	0	0	0	0	ø	ø	ø	ø	0	0	ø	0	0	0	/C	—	0.0
1917	Chi N	3	8	1	3	2	0	0	1	1	0	0	.375	.444	.625	209	1	1	1.000	-1	*88*	*73*	C3	—	0.1
1918	†Chi N	52	113	9	32	7	3	1	14	10	1	15	.283	.347	.425	132	4	0	.974	-3	*98*	*108*	C45	—	0.4
1919	Chi N	49	125	11	27	4	2	0	9	7	0	10	.216	.258	.280	61	-6	2	.965	-1	*96*	*112*	C38	—	-0.5
1920	Chi N	94	270	29	67	11	4	3	19	34	0	23	.248	.332	.352	95	-1	1-0	.956	-2	*100*	*117*	C86	—	0.5
1921	Chi N	96	260	32	65	12	7	4	32	18	0	14	.250	.299	.396	82	-8	2-0	.967	-4	*95*	*112*	C90	—	-0.6
1922	Chi N	128	392	68	127	18	8	4	60	79	1	34	.324	.439	.441	125	20	5-3	.977	15	*121*	***143***	C125	—	4.1
1923	Chi N	131	452	73	144	25	4	12	84	67	1	38	.319	.408	.471	131	23	10-3	.976	9	*111*	*102*	C124	—	3.9
1924	Chi N	71	183	25	44	6	2	3	28	30	0	13	.240	.347	.344	85	-3	2-0	.984	1	*115*	*94*	C57	—	0.2
1925	Chi N	17	22	2	4	0	1	0	3	2	0	5	.182	.250	.273	33	-2	0-0	1.000	-1	*104*	*0*	C3	—	-0.3
	StL N	94	317	37	88	13	2	3	32	46	2	26	.278	.373	.360	86	-5	0-1	.975	1	*114*	*81*	C92	—	0.2
	Year	111	339	39	92	13	3	3	35	48	2	31	.271	.365	.354	83	-7	0-1	.975	0	*114*	*79*	C95	—	-0.1
1926	†StL N	147	492	63	144	30	9	7	68	61	0	44	.293	.371	.433	111	9	1	.983	13	*127*	*101*	C146	—	**3.2**
1927	StL N	61	178	19	47	10	1	0	18	23	0	22	.264	.348	.331	80	-4	3	.979	1	*91*	*146*	C53,M	—	0.0
1928	StL N	16	52	6	11	1	0	0	4	13	0	9	.212	.369	.231	59	-2	2	.985	0	*135*	*37*	C14	—	-0.1
	NY N	75	133	23	26	6	0	2	20	34	0	16	.195	.359	.286	70	-4	2	.988	1	*136*	*72*	C63	—	-0.1
	Year	91	185	29	37	7	0	2	24	47	0	25	.200	.362	.270	67	-7	4	.987	1	*136*	*63*	C77	—	-0.2
1929	NY N	91	248	35	76	14	3	4	42	28	3	30	.306	.384	.435	103	2	3	.979	-2	*138*	*28*	C84	—	0.4
1930	NY N	94	249	37	75	16	4	4	54	31	1	21	.301	.381	.446	101	1	1	.973	-1	*101*	*101*	C69	—	0.4
1931	NY N	85	174	11	39	8	3	1	19	21	1	23	.224	.311	.322	72	-7	0	.980	2	*142*	*90*	C80	—	-0.2
1932	NY N	50	67	7	16	3	0	0	8	11	1	10	.239	.354	.284	76	-2	0	.969	0	*101*	*88*	C41	—	0.0
1933	StL N	55	163	16	39	4	2	2	20	15	0	25	.239	.303	.325	76	-5	0	.970	-4	*89*	*94*	C50	—	-0.7
1934	Cin N	44	123	10	30	8	3	1	9	11	0	19	.244	.306	.382	85	-3	0	.993	0	*96*	*119*	C42,M	—	-0.1
	Chi N	22	67	3	15	3	0	0	5	3	0	11	.224	.257	.269	42	-6	0	1.000	2	*128*	*97*	C22	—	-0.3
	Year	66	190	13	45	11	3	1	14	14	0	30	.237	.289	.342	70	-8	0	.996	2	*107*	*111*	C64	—	-0.4
1935	StL N	14	10	0	0	0	0	0	0	2	0	0	.000	.167	.000	-49	-2	0	1.000	0	*59*	*0*	C8	—	-0.2
Total	21	1492	4101	517	1120	201	58	51	549	547	11	408	.273	.360	.388	97	0	35-7	.976	26	*113*	*101*	C1338	—	10.2
OFFERMAN, JOSE	Jose Antonio (Dono); B11.8.1968 San Pedro de Macoris, D.R.; BB/TR/6´0˝/(160–200); d8.19; OF(5/1/3)																								
1990	LA N	29	58	7	9	0	0	1	7	4-1	0	14	.155	.210	.207	15	-7	1-0	.946	-3	85	59	S27	0	-0.9
1991	LA N	52	113	10	22	2	0	0	3	25-2	1	32	.195	.345	.212	61	-4	3-2	.945	-1	106	89	S50	0	-0.2
1992	LA N	149	534	67	139	20	8	1	30	57-4	0	98	.260	.331	.333	90	-7	23-16	.935	-13	96	87	S149	0	-0.9
1993	LA N	158	590	77	159	21	6	1	62	71-7	2	75	.269	.346	.331	88	-8	30-13	.950	-7	98	99	S158	0	-0.1
1994	LA N	72	243	27	51	8	4	1	25	38-4	0	38	.210	.314	.288	63	-13	2-1	.967	4	98	104	S72	0	-0.4
1995	†LA N★	119	429	69	123	14	6	4	33	69-0	3	67	.287	.389	.375	111	10	2-7	.932	-4	95	99	S115	0	1.2
1996	KC A	151	561	85	170	33	8	5	47	74-3	1	98	.303	.384	.417	102	5	24-10	.994	4	121	116	1b96,2b38,S36/cf	0	0.6
1997	KC A	106	424	59	126	23	6	2	39	41-3	0	64	.297	.359	.394	93	-3	9-10	.981	-12	92	102	2b101/D	61	-1.2
1998	KC A	158	607	102	191	28	**13**	7	66	89-1	5	96	.315	.403	.438	115	17	45-12	.974	6	105	114	2b152,D6	0	3.3
1999	†Bos A★	149	586	107	172	37	**11**	8	69	96-5	2	79	.294	.391	.435	108	11	18-12	.975	-22	82	91	2b128,D17,1b8	0	-0.7
2000	Bos A	116	451	73	115	14	3	9	41	70-0	1	70	.255	.354	.359	80	-13	0-8	.981	6	97	96	2b80,1b38,D9	32	-0.8
2001	Bos A	128	524	76	140	23	3	9	49	61-2	1	97	.267	.342	.374	89	-7	5-2	.974	3	93	77	2b91,1b43	0	-0.3
2002	Bos A	72	237	39	55	10	0	4	27	33-0	1	29	.232	.325	.325	73	-8	8-5	.994	1	114	124	1b41,D24,O2R	0	-1.1
	Sea A	29	47	9	11	2	1	1	4	4-0	0	9	.234	.294	.383	81	-1	1-1	1.000	2	174	55	1b11,O6(5/0/1)/2D	0	0.0
	Year	101	284	48	66	12	1	5	31	37-0	1	38	.232	.320	.335	75	-10	9-6	.995	4	124	113	1b52,D28,O8(5/0/3)/2	0	-1.1
2004	†Min A	77	172	22	44	14	2	2	22	29-2	0	31	.256	.363	.395	95	0	1-1	.983	0	163	242	D39,1b7,2b3	0	-0.2
2005	Phi N	33	33	6	6	1	1	1	3	5-0	0	6	.182	.289	.364	67	-2	0-0	.938	-1	0	69	1b4	0	-0.3
	NY N	53	72	5	18	2	0	1	10	6-0	1	11	.250	.316	.319	69	-3	0-0	.988	-1	72	124	1b11/2	0	-0.5
	Year	86	105	11	24	3	1	2	13	11-0	1	17	.229	.308	.333	68	-5	0-0	.980	-2	60	115	1b15/2	0	-0.8
Total	15	1651	5681	840	1551	252	72	57	537	772-34	18	914	.273	.360	.373	93	-33	172-100	.943	-36	97	98	S607,2b595,1b259,D100,O9L	93	-2.5
OFFICE, ROWLAND	Rowland Johnie; B10.25.1952 Sacramento CA; BL/TL/6´0˝/(165–170); [AtlN70 4/94]; d8.5																								
1972	Atl N	2	5	1	2	0	0	0	0	1-0	0	2	.400	.500	.400	146	0	0-0	1.000	0	106	0	/cf	0	0.0
1974	Atl N	131	248	20	61	16	1	3	31	16-2	0	30	.246	.288	.355	77	-8	5-3	.994	-7	93	0	O119(1/118/0)	0	-1.8
1975	Atl N	126	355	30	103	14	1	3	30	23-4	3	41	.290	.337	.361	91	-4	2-2	.967	-5	93	98	O107(1/106/0)	0	-1.3
1976	Atl N	99	359	51	101	17	1	4	34	37-3	2	49	.281	.348	.368	99	0	2-8	.986	-8	91	55	O92C	16	-1.3
1977	Atl N	124	428	42	103	13	1	5	39	23-1	3	58	.241	.282	.311	53	-28	2-4	.988	2	104	126	O104(1/103/0)/1	18	-2.9
1978	Atl N	146	404	40	101	13	1	9	40	22-2	6	52	.250	.297	.354	74	-14	8-6	.990	2	108	68	O136C	0	-1.5
1979	Atl N	124	277	35	69	14	2	2	37	27-2	2	33	.249	.320	.336	75	-9	5-4	.988	-5	92	79	O97C	0	-1.5
1980	Mon N	116	292	36	78	13	4	6	30	36-1	0	39	.267	.343	.401	106	3	3-3	.987	-7	92	31	O97(3/27/68)	0	-0.8
1981	Mon N	26	40	4	7	0	0	0	0	4-0	0	6	.175	.250	.175	22	-4	0-0	.938	-1	84	0	O15(0/3/12)	111	-0.6
1982	Mon N	3	3	0	1	1	0	0	0	0-0	0	1	.333	.333	.667	167	0	0-0	1.000	0	436	0	/lf	0	0.1
1983	NY A	2	2	0	0	0	0	0	1	0-0	0	0	.000	.000	.000	-99	-1	0-0	1.000	-0	92	0	O2C	0	-0.1
Total	11	899	2413	259	626	101	11	32	242	189-15	16	311	.259	.315	.350	80	-65	27-30	.985	-29	97	67	O771(7/687/80)/1	145	-11.7
OGLESBY, JIM	James Dorn; B8.10.1905 Schofield MO; D9.1.1955 Tulsa OK; BL/TL/6´0˝/190; d4.14																								
1936	Phi A	3	11	0	2	0	0	0	2	2	0	0	.182	.308	.182	24	-1	0-0	1.000	0	143	83	1b3	—	-0.1
OGLIVIE, BEN	Benjamin Ambrosio (Palmer); B2.11.1949 Colon, Pan; BL/TL/6´2˝/(160–170); [BosA68 11/248]; d9.4; C1																								
1971	Bos A	14	38	2	10	3	0	0	4	0-0	0	5	.263	.263	.342	65	-2	0-0	.958	2	130	176	O11(10/0/1)	0	-0.1
1972	Bos A	94	253	27	61	10	2	8	30	18-2	1	61	.241	.293	.391	97	-2	1-1	.981	-2	87	113	O65(32/0/33)	0	-0.8
1973	Bos A	58	147	16	32	9	1	2	9	9-2	2	32	.218	.269	.333	66	-7	1-1	.983	-0	96	101	O32(4/0/28),D13	0	-0.9
1974	Det A	92	252	28	68	11	3	4	29	34-6	0	38	.270	.353	.385	109	4	12-3	.947	-3	85	82	O63(61/0/2),1b10,D4	0	-0.1
1975	Det A	100	332	45	95	14	1	9	36	16-0	2	62	.286	.319	.416	103	0	11-8	.975	4	111	65	O86(76/0/10),1b5,D2	0	-0.2
1976	Det A	115	305	36	87	12	3	15	47	11-3	3	44	.285	.313	.492	129	9	9-4	.986	1	104	160	O64(16/12/36),1b9/D	0	0.7
1977	Det A	132	450	63	118	24	2	21	61	40-2	3	80	.262	.325	.464	107	4	9-9	.976	2	100	118	O118R,D2	0	-0.1
1978	Mil A	128	469	71	142	29	4	18	72	52-10	0	69	.303	.370	.497	141	26	11-7	.980	-2	103	82	O89(65/0/25),D27,1b11	0	2.0
1979	Mil A	139	514	88	145	30	4	29	81	48-12	2	56	.282	.343	.525	131	21	12-5	.985	-2	101	76	O120(102/0/23),D13,1b9	0	1.3
1980	Mil A★	156	592	94	180	26	2	**41**	118	54-**19**	5	71	.304	.362	.563	155	42	11-9	.978	13	112	147	O152(150/1/2),D4	0	4.7
1981	†Mil A	107	400	53	97	15	2	14	72	37-10	6	49	.243	.310	.395	108	4	2-2	.982	-8	91	39	O101(99/2/0),D6	0	-1.0
1982	†Mil A★	159	602	92	147	22	1	34	102	70-13	4	81	.244	.326	.453	118	14	3-5	.982	6	102	147	O159L	0	1.1
1983	Mil A★	125	411	49	115	19	3	13	66	60-12	4	64	.280	.371	.436	132	20	4-6	.985	2	103	87	O113L,D8	0	1.6
1984	Mil A	131	461	49	121	16	2	12	60	44-5	1	56	.262	.327	.384	100	0	0-6	.970	-3	96	71	O125(113/0/23)/D	0	-1.1
1985	Mil A	101	341	40	99	17	2	10	61	37-3	2	51	.290	.354	.440	119	10	0-2	.965	-2	101	66	O91(48/0/54),D4	0	0.3
1986	Mil A	103	346	31	98	20	1	5	53	30-6	0	33	.283	.334	.390	95	-2	1-2	.991	4	118	141	O50(50/0/2),D42	0	-0.1
Total	16	1754	5913	784	1615	277	33	235	901	560-105	35	852	.273	.336	.450	118	141	87-70	.978	12	101	101	O1439(1098/15/357),D127,1b44	0	7.3
OGRODOWSKI, BRUCE	Ambrose Francis "Brusie"; B2.17.1912 Hoytville PA; D3.5.1956 San Francisco CA; BR/TR/5´11˝/175; d4.14																								
1936	StL N	94	237	28	54	15	1	1	20	10	0	20	.228	.259	.312	53	-16	0	.989	1	*120*	*78*	C85	—	-1.1
1937	StL N	90	279	37	65	10	3	3	31	11	2	17	.233	.267	.323	58	-17	2	.984	0	*90*	*88*	C87	—	-1.2
Total	2	184	516	65	119	25	4	4	51	21	2	37	.231	.263	.318	56	-33	2	.986	1	*103*	*84*	C172	—	-2.3
O'HAGEN, HAL	Patrick Henry; B9.30.1869 Washington DC; D1.14.1913 Newark NJ; TR/6´0˝/173; d9.24																								
1892	Was N	1	4	1	1	0	0	0	0	0	0	2	.250	.250	.250	53	0	0	1.000	0	*79*	*323*	/C	—	0.0
1902	Chi N	33	115	11	22	1	3	0	10	11	0	—	.191	.262	.252	60	-6	9	.983	3	147	128	1b33	—	-0.3
	NY N	4	11	0	1	0	0	0	0	0	0	—	.091	.091	.091	-44	-2	0	1.000	0	0	0	O4(0/3/1)	—	-0.2
	Cle A	3	13	2	5	2	0	0	1	0	0	—	.385	.385	.538	160	1	2	1.000	1	170	0	1b3	—	0.2
	NY N	22	73	5	11	2	1	0	8	2	2	—	.151	.195	.205	24	-7	3	.973	-0	109	115	1b18,O4R	—	-0.8
	Year	59	199	16	34	3	4	0	18	13	2	—	.171	.229	.226	52	-14	12	.980	3	133	123	1b51,O8(0/3/5)	—	-1.3
Total	2	63	216	19	40	5	4	0	19	13	2	2	.185	.238	.245	49	-14	14	.981	4	136	116	1b54,O8(0/3/5)/C	—	-1.1

YEAR	TM LG	G	AB	R	H	2B	3B	HR	RBI	BB-IB	HP	SO	AVG	OBP	SLG	AOPS	ABR	SB-CS	FA	FR	RNG	THR	GAMES AT POSITION	DL	BFW
O'Halloran, Greg	Gregory Joseph; B5.21.1968 Toronto ON, Can.; BL/TR/6´2˝/205; [TorA88 32/836]; d5.16; Col Orange Coast (CA) JC																								
1994	Fla N	12	11	1	2	0	0	0	1	0-0	0	1	.182	.167	.182	-5	-2	0-0	1.000	0	0	0	/C	0	-0.2
O'Hara, Kid	James Francis; B12.19.1875 Wilkes–Barre PA; D12.1.1954 Canton OH; BB/TR/5´7.5˝/152; d9.15; Col Georgetown																								
1904	Bos N	8	29	3	6	0	0	0	0	4	0	—	.207	.303	.207	60	-1	1	.923	0	196	0	O8R	—	-0.2
O'Hara, Tom	Thomas Francis; B7.13.1880 Waverly NY; D6.8.1954 Denver CO; d9.19; Col Manhattan																								
1906	StL N	14	53	8	16	1	0	0	0	3	0	—	.302	.339	.321	110	1	3	.889	-2	0	0	O14L	—	-0.2
1907	StL N	48	173	11	41	2	1	0	5	12	0	—	.237	.286	.260	74	-6	1	.943	-2	73	113	O47(24/0/23)	—	-1.2
Total	2	62	226	19	57	3	1	0	5	15	0	—	.252	.299	.274	82	-5	4	.930	-4	57	88	O61(38/0/23)	—	-1.4
O'Hara, Bill	William Alexander; B8.14.1883 Toronto ON, Can.; D6.13.1931 Jersey City NJ; BL/TR/5´10˝/165; d4.15																								
1909	NY N	115	360	48	85	9	3	1	30	41	2	—	.236	.318	.286	86	-5	31	.978	4	132	132	O111(11/89/11)	—	-0.6
1910	StL N	9	20	1	3	0	0	0	2	1	0	3	.150	.190	.150	-0	-3	0	1.000	0	86	208	O4C/P1	—	-0.3
Total	2	124	380	49	88	9	3	1	32	42	2	3	.232	.311	.279	82	-8	31	.979	4	130	135	O115(11/93/11)/1P	—	-0.9
Ojeda, Miguel	Miguel Arturo; B1.29.1975 Guaymas, Sonora, Mexico; BR/TR/6´2˝/(190–230); d5.17																								
2003	SD N	61	141	13	33	6	0	4	22	18-2	3	26	.234	.331	.362	89	-2	1-1	.981	-1	91	59	C48,1b2	0	0.0
2004	SD N	62	156	23	40	3	0	8	26	15-1	1	34	.256	.322	.429	98	-1	0-0	.996	-3	265	37	C50	16	-0.1
2005	SD N	43	73	6	10	3	1	0	6	9-2	0	21	.137	.232	.205	17	-9	1-1	1.000	-1	80	0	C25,O5(3/0/2)/D	0	-0.9
	Sea A	16	29	2	5	0	0	1	3	6-0	0	3	.172	.314	.276	64	-1	0-1	.986	1	94	210	C16	0	0.0
2006	Col N	25	74	5	17	3	0	2	11	8-2	0	16	.230	.305	.351	62	-4	0-0	.993	1	107	69	C24	0	-0.2
	Tex A	5	13	0	4	2	0	0	4	0-0	0	3	.308	.308	.462	95	0	0-0	1.000	-0	44	0	C5	0	0.0
Total	4	212	486	49	109	17	1	15	72	56-7	4	103	.224	.308	.356	75	-17	2-3	.990	-2	145	59	C168,O5(3/0/2),1b2/D	16	-1.2
Ojeda, Augie	Octavio Augie; B12.20.1974 Los Angeles CA; BB/TR/5´9˝/(165–175); [BalA96 13/381]; d6.4; Col Tennessee																								
2000	Chi N	28	77	10	17	3	1	2	8	10-1	0	9	.221	.307	.364	70	-4	0-1	.989	-1	106	83	S25,2b4	0	-0.3
2001	Chi N	78	144	16	29	5	1	1	12	12-1	2	20	.201	.269	.271	42	-13	1-0	.913	3	125	157	3b35,S31,2b10	0	-0.7
2002	Chi N	30	70	4	13	4	0	0	4	5-0	1	5	.186	.247	.243	31	-7	1-0	.966	0	106	45	S16,2b10,3b5	0	-0.5
2003	Chi N	12	25	2	3	0	0	0	0	1-1	1	5	.120	.185	.120	-18	-4	0-0	1.000	-1	91	95	S7,2b5/3	0	-0.4
2004	Min A	30	59	16	20	1	0	2	7	10-0	0	3	.339	.429	.458	130	3	1-1	.969	3	121	105	2b20,S7,3b4	0	0.6
Total	5	178	375	48	82	13	2	5	31	38-3	4	42	.219	.294	.304	57	-25	3-2	.982	4	97	76	S86,2b49,3b45	0	-1.3
Okrie, Len	Leonard Joseph; B7.16.1923 Detroit MI; BR/TR/6´0˝/185; d6.16; C5; f–Frank																								
1948	Was A	19	42	1	10	0	1	0	1	1	0	7	.238	.256	.286	45	-4	0-0	.981	1	*154*	*235*	C17	0	-0.2
1950	Was A	17	27	1	6	0	0	0	2	6	1	7	.222	.382	.222	61	-1	0-0	1.000	1	*66*	*176*	C17	0	-0.0
1951	Was A	5	8	1	1	1	0	0	0	2	0	1	.125	.300	.250	51	0	0-0	.850	-0	*125*	*216*	C5	0	0.0
1952	Bos A	1	1	0	0	0	0	0	0	0	0	1	.000	.000	.000	-93	0	0-0	1.000	-0	*0*	*0*	/C	0	0.0
Total	4	42	78	3	17	1	1	0	3	9	1	16	.218	.307	.256	51	-5	0-0	.965	1	*116*	*208*	C40	0	-0.2
Olander, Jim	James Bentley; B2.21.1963 Tucson AZ; BR/TR/6´1˝/185; [PhiN81 7/175]; d9.20																								
1991	Mil A	12	9	2	0	0	0	0	0	2-0	0	5	.000	.182	.000	-46	-2	0-0	1.000	0	115	0	O9(2/5/1),D2	0	-0.2
Oldfield, Dave	David; B12.18.1864 Philadelphia PA; D8.28.1939 Philadelphia PA; BB/TL/5´7˝/175; d6.28																								
1883	Bal AA	1	4	0	0	0	0	0	—	0	—	—	.000	.000	.000	-97	-1	—	.667	-1	—	—	/C	—	-0.2
1885	Bro AA	10	25	2	8	1	0	0	2	3	1	—	.320	.414	.360	145	2	—	.873	-1	—	—	C9,O2(0/1/1)	—	0.1
1886	Bro AA	14	55	7	13	1	0	0	5	2	0	—	.236	.263	.255	62	-3	1	.833	-3	—	—	C13/Srf	—	-0.4
	Was N	21	71	2	10	2	0	0	2	5	—	15	.141	.197	.169	13	-7	0	.899	-3	—	—	C12,O9(0/3/6)	—	-0.8
Total	3	46	155	11	31	4	0	0	9	10	—	15	.200	.253	.226	50	-9	1	.857	-7	—	—	C35,O12(0/4/8)/S	—	-1.3
Oldham, John	John Hardin; B11.6.1932 Salinas CA; BR/TL/6´3˝/198; d9.2; Col San Jose St.																								
1956	Cin N	1	0	0	0	0	0	0	0	0-0	0	0	ø	ø	ø	ø	0	0-0	ø	0	—	—	/R	0	0.0
Oldis, Bob	Robert Carl; B1.5.1928 Preston IA; BR/TR/6´1˝/(185–190); d4.28; C5																								
1953	Was A	7	16	0	4	0	0	0	3	1	0	2	.250	.294	.250	49	-1	0-0	1.000	1	*119*	*82*	C7	0	0.0
1954	Was A	11	24	1	8	1	0	0	0	1	0	3	.333	.360	.375	107	0	0-0	.941	-1	*99*	*61*	C8,3b2	0	-0.1
1955	Was A	6	6	1	0	0	0	0	0	1-0	0	0	.000	.143	.000	-62	-1	0-0	1.000	-0	*60*	*222*	C6	0	-0.1
1960	†Pit N	22	20	1	4	1	0	0	1	1-0	0	2	.200	.238	.250	34	-2	0-0	1.000	0	148	100	C22	0	-0.1
1961	Pit N	4	5	0	0	0	0	0	0	0-0	0	0	.000	.000	.000	-99	-1	0-0	1.000	1	21	796	C4	0	0.0
1962	Phi N	38	80	9	21	1	0	1	10	13-0	0	10	.262	.366	.313	87	-1	0-1	.987	-1	94	154	C30	0	-0.1
1963	Phi N	47	85	8	19	3	0	0	8	3-1	0	5	.224	.250	.259	47	-6	0-0	.979	1	52	70	C43	0	-0.5
Total	7	135	236	20	56	6	0	1	22	20-1	0	22	.237	.297	.275	60	-12	0-1	.983	1	*85*	*123*	C120,3b2	0	-0.9
Oldring, Rube	Reuben Henry; B5.30.1884 New York NY; D9.9.1961 Bridgeton NJ; BR/TR/5´10˝/186; d10.2; OF(455/627/48)																								
1905	NY A	8	30	2	9	0	1	1	6	2	0	—	.300	.344	.467	140	1	4	.967	4	120	136	S8	—	0.5
1906	Phi A	59	174	15	42	10	1	0	19	2	3	—	.241	.263	.310	77	-5	7	.897	1	99	119	3b49,S3,2b2/1	—	-0.3
1907	Phi A	117	441	48	126	27	8	1	40	7	5	—	.286	.305	.390	118	7	29	.974	-10	69	0	O117(0/116/1)	—	-0.9
1908	Phi A	116	434	38	96	14	2	1	39	18	9	—	.221	.267	.270	70	-14	13	.941	-2	65	79	O116(21/95/0)	—	-2.6
1909	Phi A	90	326	39	75	13	8	1	28	20	6	—	.230	.287	.328	92	-4	17	.963	-0	65	46	O89(32/56/1)/1	—	-0.9
1910	Phi A	134	546	79	168	27	14	4	57	23	4	—	.308	.340	.430	143	23	17	**.978**	-5	96	74	O134(1/130/3)	—	1.3
1911	†Phi A	121	495	84	147	11	14	3	59	21	5	—	.297	.332	.394	104	-1	21	**.979**	-8	92	71	O119C	—	-1.6
1912	Phi A	99	395	61	119	14	5	1	24	10	3	—	.301	.324	.370	102	-1	17	.974	-3	103	58	O98(11/87/0)	—	-1.1
1913	†Phi A	137	538	101	152	27	9	5	71	34	2	37	.283	.328	.394	113	7	40	.968	-3	109	57	O131L,S5	—	-0.1
1914	†Phi A	119	466	68	129	21	7	3	49	18	3	35	.277	.308	.371	108	1	14-16	.965	-3	104	46	O117(105/11/1)	—	-1.1
1915	Phi A	107	408	49	101	23	3	6	42	22	4	21	.248	.293	.363	100	-3	11-6	.982	4	114	74	O96(88/8/0),3b8	—	-0.3
1916	Phi A	40	146	10	36	8	3	0	14	9	0	9	.247	.290	.342	95	-2	1	.897	-3	80	118	O40L	—	-0.7
	NY A	43	158	17	37	8	0	1	12	12	0	13	.234	.288	.304	76	-5	6	.957	-3	102	20	O43(0/2/41)	—	-1.1
	Year	83	304	27	73	16	3	1	26	21	0	22	.240	.289	.322	85	-7	7	.926	-6	91	70	O83(40/2/41)	—	-1.8
1918	Phi A	49	133	5	31	2	1	0	11	8	1	10	.233	.282	.263	64	-6	0	.949	-4	75	66	O30(26/3/1),2b2,3b2	—	-1.2
Total	13	1239	4690	616	1268	205	76	27	471	206	45	125	.270	.307	.364	103	-2	197-22	.966	-35	91	58	O1130C,3b59,S16,2b4,1b2	—	-10.1
O'Leary, Charley	Charles Timothy; B10.15.1882 Chicago IL; D1.6.1941 Chicago IL; BR/TR/5´7˝/165; d4.14; C19																								
1904	Det A	135	456	39	97	10	3	1	16	21	4	—	.213	.254	.254	63	-20	9	.933	4	102	110	S135	—	-1.3
1905	Det A	148	512	47	109	13	1	0	33	29	3	—	.213	.259	.242	59	-24	13	.933	-4	94	83	S148	—	-2.6
1906	Det A	128	443	34	97	13	2	2	34	17	3	—	.219	.253	.271	62	-20	8	.926	-7	95	83	S127	—	-2.5
1907	†Det A	139	465	61	112	19	1	0	34	32	6	—	.241	.298	.286	83	-8	11	.943	-6	95	78	S138	—	-1.1
1908	†Det A	65	211	21	53	9	3	0	17	9	4	—	.251	.295	.322	96	-1	4	.920	-9	90	80	S64/2	—	-1.0
1909	†Det A	76	261	29	53	10	0	0	13	6	1	—	.203	.224	.241	45	-17	9	.922	-4	106	63	3b54,2b15,S4,O2(1/0/1)	—	-2.3
1910	Det A	65	211	23	51	7	1	0	9	9	1	—	.242	.276	.284	71	-8	7	.935	-0	94	78	2b38,S18,3b6	—	-0.7
1911	Det A	74	256	29	68	8	2	0	25	21	6	—	.266	.336	.313	77	-7	10	.966	3	105	78	2b67,3b6	—	-0.3
1912	Det A	3	10	1	2	0	0	0	1	0	0	—	.200	.200	.200	15	-1	0	1.000	1	158	0	2b3	—	0.0
1913	StL N	121	406	32	88	15	5	0	31	20	4	34	.217	.260	.278	55	-25	3-12	.951	-6	99	58	S103,2b15	—	-2.9
1934	StL A	1	1	1	1	0	0	0	0	0	0	0	1.000	1.000	1.000	385	0	0-0	ø	0	—	—	/H	—	0.0
Total	11	955	3232	317	731	104	18	3	213	164	32	34	.226	.270	.272	67	-131	74-12	.935	-29	97	83	S737,2b139,3b66,O2(1/0/1)	—	-14.7
O'Leary, Dan	Daniel "Hustling Dan"; B10.22.1856 Detroit MI; D6.24.1922 Chicago IL; BL/5´10˝/165; d9.3; M1																								
1879	Pro N	2	7	1	3	0	0	0	2	0	—	0	.429	.429	.429	187	1	—	ø	-0	0	0	O2R	—	0.1
1880	Bos N	3	12	1	3	2	0	0	1	0	—	3	.250	.250	.417	126	0	—	1.000	-1	0	0	O3R	—	0.0
1881	Det N	2	8	0	0	0	0	0	0	0	—	2	.000	.000	.000	-96	-2	—	.714	-1	0	0	O2C	—	-0.3
1882	Wor N	6	22	2	4	1	0	0	2	5	—	5	.182	.333	.227	82	0	—	.800	-2	0	0	O6C	—	-0.2
1884	Cin U	32	132	14	34	0	2	1	—	5	—	—	.258	.285	.311	74	-8	—	.862	1	99	0	O32(22/10/0),M	—	-0.8
Total	5	45	181	18	44	3	2	1	5	10	—	10	.243	.283	.298	75	-9	—	.843	-2	76	0	O45(22/18/5)	—	-1.2

O'Leary, Troy Troy Franklin; B8.4.1969 Compton CA; BL/TL/6´0˝/(175–200); [MilA87 13/331]; d5.9

YEAR	TM LG	G	AB	R	H	2B	3B	HR	RBI	BB-IB	HP	SO	AVG	OBP	SLG	AOPS	ABR	SB-CS	FA	FR	RNG	THR	GAMES AT POSITION	DL	BFW
1993	Mil A	19	41	3	12	3	0	0	3	5-0	0	9	.293	.370	.366	99	0	0-0	1.000	1	111	112	O19(15/0/5)	0	0.1
1994	Mil A	27	66	9	18	1	1	2	7	5-0	1	12	.273	.329	.409	86	-2	1-1	1.000	1	101	153	O21(13/0/10)/D	0	-0.1
1995	Bos A	112	399	60	123	31	6	10	49	29-4	1	64	.308	.355	.491	114	8	5-3	.976	-1	98	94	O105(16/13/91),D3	0	0.2
1996	Bos A	149	497	68	129	28	5	15	81	47-3	4	80	.260	.327	.427	87	-11	3-2	.971	-8	87	91	O146(66/17/110)	0	-2.2
1997	Bos A	146	499	65	154	32	4	15	80	39-7	2	70	.309	.358	.479	114	10	0-5	.979	-2	97	92	O142(24/0/119)/D	0	0.0
1998	†Bos A	156	611	95	165	36	8	23	83	36-2	5	108	.270	.314	.468	98	-4	2-2	.990	1	99	99	O155L	0	-0.8
1999	†Bos A	157	596	84	167	36	4	28	103	56-5	4	91	.280	.343	.495	108	6	1-2	.993	1	98	94	O157(157/0/2)	0	0.0
2000	Bos A	138	513	68	134	30	4	13	70	44-2	2	76	.261	.320	.411	82	-15	0-2	.988	-5	88	112	O137L	14	-2.4
2001	Bos A	104	341	50	82	16	6	13	50	25-2	5	73	.240	.298	.437	91	-6	1-3	.994	-1	100	58	O89(52/0/41),D4	0	-1.1
2002	Mon N	97	273	27	78	12	2	3	37	34-5	3	47	.286	.371	.377	93	-2	1-2	.977	-1	104	25	O70(69/0/1),D3	0	-0.5
2003	†Chi N	93	174	18	38	9	0	5	28	14-1	1	31	.218	.275	.356	63	-10	3-0	1.000	-0	90	139	O51(28/0/24)	0	-1.1
Total	11	1198	4010	547	1100	234	40	127	591	334-31	28	661	.274	.332	.448	97	-26	17-22	.985	-14	96	92	O1092(732/30/403),D12	14	-7.9

Olerud, John John Garrett; B8.5.1968 Seattle WA; BL/TL/6´5˝/(205–225); [TorA89 3/79]; d9.3; Col Washington St.

YEAR	TM LG	G	AB	R	H	2B	3B	HR	RBI	BB-IB	HP	SO	AVG	OBP	SLG	AOPS	ABR	SB-CS	FA	FR	RNG	THR	GAMES AT POSITION	DL	BFW
1989	Tor A	6	8	2	3	0	0	0	0	0-0	0	1	.375	.375	.375	114	0	0-0	1.000	0	168	0	1b5/D	0	0.0
1990	Tor A	111	358	43	95	15	1	14	48	57-6	1	75	.265	.364	.430	120	11	0-2	.986	-1	89	75	D90,1b18	0	0.6
1991	†Tor A	139	454	64	116	30	1	17	68	68-9	6	84	.256	.353	.438	115	11	0-2	.996	-3	88	76	1b135/D	0	-0.2
1992	†Tor A	138	458	68	130	28	0	16	66	70-11	1	61	.284	.375	.450	125	18	1-0	.994	-2	91	70	1b133/D	0	0.8
1993	†Tor A★	158	551	109	200	**54**	2	24	107	114-**33**	7	65	**.363**	**.473**	.599	**184**	**75**	0-2	.992	-2	94	90	1b137,D20	0	**5.7**
1994	Tor A	108	384	47	114	29	2	12	67	61-12	3	53	.297	.393	.477	123	16	1-2	.993	1	98	94	1b104,D3	0	0.7
1995	Tor A	135	492	72	143	32	0	8	54	84-10	4	54	.291	.398	.404	109	12	0-0	.997	-3	90	82	1b133	0	-0.3
1996	Tor A	125	398	59	109	25	0	18	61	60-6	10	37	.274	.382	.472	115	11	1-0	.998	-3	85	134	1b101,D15	0	0.0
1997	NY N	154	524	90	154	34	1	22	102	85-5	13	67	.294	.400	.489	139	35	0-0	.995	4	112	117	1b146	0	2.5
1998	NY N	160	557	91	197	36	4	22	93	96-11	4	73	.354	.447	.551	167	61	2-2	.996	3	104	101	1b157	0	4.8
1999	†NY N	162	581	107	173	39	0	19	96	125-5	11	66	.298	.427	.463	132	38	3-0	.994	3	105	107	1b160	0	2.6
2000	†Sea A	159	565	84	161	45	0	14	103	102-11	4	96	.285	.392	.439	114	17	0-2	**.996**	15	**134**	114	1b158	0	1.6
2001	†Sea A★	159	572	91	173	32	1	21	95	94-19	5	70	.302	.401	.472	138	36	3-1	.993	8	**119**	106	1b158	0	2.9
2002	Sea A	154	553	85	166	39	0	22	102	98-6	5	66	.300	.403	.490	143	40	0-0	.996	4	105	**107**	1b152,D2	0	2.8
2003	Sea A	152	539	64	145	35	0	10	83	84-7	6	67	.269	.372	.390	108	10	0-1	.998	10	**121**	115	1b152	0	0.7
2004	Sea A	78	261	29	64	13	1	5	22	40-3	6	41	.245	.354	.360	93	-1	0-0	.998	3	114	95	1b77	0	-0.4
	†NY A	49	164	16	46	7	0	4	26	21-1	2	20	.280	.367	.396	100	1	0-0	.997	-2	79	93	1b47	0	-0.5
	Year	127	425	45	110	20	1	9	48	61-4	8	61	.259	.359	.374	95	-1	0-0	**.998**	1	101	94	1b124	0	-0.9
2005	†Bos A	87	173	18	50	7	0	7	37	16-2	0	20	.289	.344	.451	106	2	0-0	.998	4	125	93	1b80	16	0.1
Total	17	2234	7592	1139	2239	500	13	255	1230	1275-157	88	1016	.295	.398	.465	129	393	11-14	.995	39	105	100	1b2053,D133	16	24.4

Olin, Frank Franklin Walter; B1.9.1860 Woodford VT; D5.21.1951 St.Louis MO; BL; d7.4; Col Cornell

YEAR	TM LG	G	AB	R	H	2B	3B	HR	RBI	BB-IB	HP	SO	AVG	OBP	SLG	AOPS	ABR	SB-CS	FA	FR	RNG	THR	GAMES AT POSITION	DL	BFW
1884	Was AA	21	83	12	32	4	1	0	—	7	0	—	.386	.433	.458	216	11	—	.775	-6	77	37	2b12,O11(1/7/3)	—	0.5
	Was U	1	4	0	0	0	0	0	—	0	—	—	.000	.000	.000	-99	-1	—	ø	0	0	0	/lf	—	-0.1
	Tol AA	26	86	16	22	0	1	1	—	5	1	—	.256	.304	.314	99	0	—	.875	2	141	0	O26L	—	0.1
1885	Det N	1	4	1	2	0	0	0	0	0	—	0	.500	.500	.500	224	1	—	.667	-0	80	0	/3	—	0.0
Total	2	49	177	29	56	4	2	1	0	12	—	0	.316	.363	.379	148	11	—	.849	-5	126	83	O38(28/7/3),2b12/3	—	0.5

Oliva, Jose Jose (Galvez); B3.3.1971 San Pedro de Macoris, D.R.; D12.22.1997 San Cristobal, D.R.; BR/TR/6´3˝/215; d7.1

YEAR	TM LG	G	AB	R	H	2B	3B	HR	RBI	BB-IB	HP	SO	AVG	OBP	SLG	AOPS	ABR	SB-CS	FA	FR	RNG	THR	GAMES AT POSITION	DL	BFW
1994	Atl N	19	59	9	17	5	0	6	11	7-0	0	10	.288	.364	.678	158	5	0-1	.932	0	99	84	3b16	0	0.5
1995	Atl N	48	109	7	17	4	0	5	12	7-0	0	22	.156	.207	.330	37	-11	0-0	.902	-3	84	88	3b25/1	0	-1.3
	StL N	22	74	8	9	1	0	2	8	5-0	2	24	.122	.195	.216	9	-10	0-0	.977	-2	86	142	3b18,1b2	0	-1.2
	Year	70	183	15	26	5	0	7	20	12-0	2	46	.142	.202	.284	26	-21	0-0	.933	-5	85	111	3b43,1b3	0	-2.5
Total	2	89	242	24	43	10	0	13	31	19-0	2	56	.178	.242	.380	59	-16	0-1	.932	-5	89	103	3b59,1b3	0	-2.0

Oliva, Tony Tony Pedro (b Antonio Oliva Lopez Hernandes Javique); B7.20.1938 Pinar Del Rio, Cuba; BL/TR/6´2˝/(180–190); d9.9; C10

YEAR	TM LG	G	AB	R	H	2B	3B	HR	RBI	BB-IB	HP	SO	AVG	OBP	SLG	AOPS	ABR	SB-CS	FA	FR	RNG	THR	GAMES AT POSITION	DL	BFW
1962	Min A	9	9	3	4	1	0	0	3	3-0	0	2	.444	.583	.556	201	2	0-0	1.000	0	143	0	O2R	0	0.2
1963	Min A	7	7	0	3	0	0	0	1	0-0	0	2	.429	.429	.429	138	0	0-0	ø	0	—	—	/H	0	0.0
1964	Min A★	161	672	**109**	**217**	**43**	9	32	94	34-8	6	68	**.323**	.359	.557	150	43	12-6	.981	0	109	51	O159(2/9/154)	0	3.3
1965	†Min A★	149	576	107	**185**	40	5	16	98	55-12	4	64	**.321**	.378	.491	141	32	19-9	.964	3	107	109	O147(0/8/143)	0	2.8
1966	Min A★	159	622	99	**191**	32	7	25	87	42-10	5	72	.307	.353	.502	135	27	13-7	.972	9	117	103	O159(0/19/140)	0	2.8
1967	Min A★	146	557	76	161	**34**	6	17	83	44-12	8	61	.289	.347	.463	128	20	11-3	.987	8	**119**	89	O146R	0	2.0
1968	Min A★	128	470	54	136	24	5	18	68	45-**16**	7	61	.289	.357	.477	144	25	10-9	.983	2	108	102	O126R	0	2.0
1969	†Min A✳	153	637	97	**197**	**39**	4	24	101	45-12	3	66	.309	.355	.496	133	26	10-13	.982	6	107	112	O152R	0	2.2
1970	†Min A★	157	628	96	**204**	**36**	7	23	107	38-12	3	67	.325	.364	.514	138	30	5-4	.968	13	**122**	116	O157(0/3/154)	0	3.6
1971	Min A✳	126	487	73	164	30	3	22	81	25-8	2	44	**.337**	.369	**.546**	153	32	4-1	.969	-2	98	78	O121R	0	2.6
1972	Min A	10	28	1	9	1	0	0	1	2-0	0	5	.321	.367	.357	110	0	0-0	.857	-2	50	0	O9(8/0/1)	147	-0.2
1973	Min A	146	571	63	166	20	0	16	92	45-14	4	44	.291	.345	.410	108	6	2-1	ø	0	0	0	D142	0	0.2
1974	Min A	127	459	43	131	16	2	13	57	27-11	2	31	.285	.325	.414	109	4	0-1	ø	0	0	0	D112	0	0.1
1975	Min A	131	455	46	123	10	0	13	58	41-15	**13**	45	.270	.344	.378	104	3	0-1	ø	0	0	0	D120	0	-0.1
1976	Min A	67	123	3	26	3	0	1	16	2-1	2	13	.211	.234	.260	44	-9	0-0	ø	0	0	0	D32	0	-1.0
Total	15	1676	6301	870	1917	329	48	220	947	448-131	59	645	.304	.353	.476	130	241	86-55	.975	37	111	94	O1178(10/39/1139),D406	147	20.5

Olivares, Ed Edward (Balzac); B11.5.1938 Mayaguez, PR; BR/TR/5´11˝/(160–165); d9.16; s–Omar; [DL 1962 Hou N 154]

YEAR	TM LG	G	AB	R	H	2B	3B	HR	RBI	BB-IB	HP	SO	AVG	OBP	SLG	AOPS	ABR	SB-CS	FA	FR	RNG	THR	GAMES AT POSITION	DL	BFW
1960	StL N	3	5	0	0	0	0	0	0	0-0	0	3	.000	.000	.000	-92	-1	0-0	.500	-1	57	0	/3	0	-0.2
1961	StL N	21	30	2	5	0	0	0	1	0-0	0	4	.167	.161	.167	-10	-5	1-0	1.000	-1	78	0	O10(5/0/5)	0	-0.6
Total	2	24	35	2	5	0	0	0	1	0-0	0	7	.143	.139	.143	-21	-6	1-0	1.000	-1	78	0	O10(5/0/5)/3	154	-0.8

Oliver, Al Albert; B10.14.1946 Portsmouth OH; BL/TL/6´0˝/(185–203); d9.23

YEAR	TM LG	G	AB	R	H	2B	3B	HR	RBI	BB-IB	HP	SO	AVG	OBP	SLG	AOPS	ABR	SB-CS	FA	FR	RNG	THR	GAMES AT POSITION	DL	BFW
1968	Pit N	4	8	1	1	0	0	0	0	0-0	0	4	.125	.125	.125	-25	-1	0-0	1.000	0	140	0	/rf	0	-0.1
1969	Pit N	129	463	55	132	19	2	17	70	21-11	13	38	.285	.333	.445	119	10	8-5	.991	-1	82	110	1b106,O21(13/0/8)	0	0.0
1970	†Pit N	151	551	63	149	33	5	12	83	35-8	14	35	.270	.326	.414	98	-2	1-1	.986	-1	96	74	O80(28/0/54),1b77	0	-1.2
1971	†Pit N	143	529	69	149	31	7	14	64	27-2	5	72	.282	.317	.446	115	9	4-3	.981	-1	107	61	O116C,1b25	0	0.3
1972	†Pit N★	140	565	88	176	27	4	12	89	34-4	5	44	.312	.352	.437	126	18	2-4	.985	-9	96	47	O138C,1b3	0	0.5
1973	Pit N	158	654	90	191	38	7	20	99	22-1	5	52	.292	.316	.463	117	11	6-0	.964	-11	90	72	O109C,1b50	0	-0.5
1974	†Pit N	147	617	96	198	38	12	11	85	33-1	5	58	.321	.358	.475	136	26	10-1	.986	-3	107	46	O98C,1b49	0	2.0
1975	†Pit N★	155	628	90	176	39	8	18	84	25-3	5	73	.280	.309	.454	110	5	4-2	.987	-6	98	52	O153C,1b4	0	-0.6
1976	Pit N★	121	443	62	143	22	5	12	61	26-7	5	29	.323	.363	.476	136	19	6-2	.984	-3	106	58	O106C,1b3	0	1.5
1977	Pit N	154	568	75	175	29	6	19	82	40-9	4	38	.308	.353	.481	118	14	13-16	.981	-1	105	62	O148(128/36/0)	0	0.5
1978	Tex A	133	525	65	170	35	5	14	89	31-6	2	41	.324	.358	.490	137	25	8-9	.987	0	96	112	O107(100/8/0),D26	28	1.8
1979	Tex A	136	492	69	159	28	4	12	76	34-8	4	34	.323	.367	.470	126	18	4-5	.975	-3	93	114	O119(49/71/0),D10	0	1.1
1980	Tex A★	**163**	656	96	209	43	3	19	117	39-9	5	47	.319	.357	.480	132	28	5-7	.973	-2	99	80	O157(141/0/16)/1D	0	1.8
1981	Tex A★	102	421	53	130	29	1	4	55	24-10	2	28	.309	.348	.411	124	13	3-0	1.000	-0	0	0	D101/1	0	1.1
1982	Mon N★	160	617	90	**204**	**43**	2	22	**109**	61-15	4	59	**.331**	.392	.514	147	40	5-2	.986	-12	76	87	1b159	0	2.0
1983	Mon N★	157	614	70	184	**38**	3	8	84	44-17	2	44	.300	.347	.410	110	8	1-3	.990	-0	101	83	1b153/rf	0	-0.2
1984	SF N	91	339	27	101	19	2	0	34	20-4	1	27	.298	.339	.366	101	0	2-2	.985	1	110	75	1b82	15	-0.5
	Phi N	28	93	9	29	7	0	0	14	7-2	0	9	.312	.360	.387	108	1	1-2	.987	-2	50	65	1b19,O5L	0	-0.3
	Year	119	432	36	130	26	2	0	48	27-6	1	36	.301	.343	.370	102	2	3-4	.985	-2	99	73	1b101,O5L	0	-0.8
1985	LA N	35	79	1	20	5	0	0	8	5-0	0	11	.253	.294	.316	73	-3	1-0	.882	-2	52	200	O17L	20	-0.5
	†Tor A	61	187	20	47	6	1	5	23	7-2	1	13	.251	.282	.374	76	-7	0-0	1.000	-0	0	0	D59/1	0	-0.9
Total	18	2368	9049	1189	2743	529	77	219	1326	535-119	82	756	.303	.344	.451	121	232	84-64	.980	-55	99	72	O1376(481/835/80),1b733,D200	63	7.8

Oliver, Dave David Jacob; B4.7.1951 Stockton CA; BL/TR/5´11˝/175; [CleA73 3/53]; d9.25; C10; Col Cal Poly–San Luis Obispo

YEAR	TM LG	G	AB	R	H	2B	3B	HR	RBI	BB-IB	HP	SO	AVG	OBP	SLG	AOPS	ABR	SB-CS	FA	FR	RNG	THR	GAMES AT POSITION	DL	BFW
1977	Cle A	7	22	2	7	0	1	0	3	4-0	1	0	.318	.444	.409	138	1	0-0	.949	0	84	165	2b7	0	0.2

Oliver, Gene Eugene George; B3.22.1935 Moline IL; BR/TR/6´2˝/(210–225); d6.6; Col Northwestern

YEAR	TM LG	G	AB	R	H	2B	3B	HR	RBI	BB-IB	HP	SO	AVG	OBP	SLG	AOPS	ABR	SB-CS	FA	FR	RNG	THR	GAMES AT POSITION	DL	BFW
1959	StL N	68	172	14	42	9	0	6	28	7-0	0	41	.244	.271	.401	72	-7	3-2	.955	-1	97	38	O42(41/0/3),C9,1b5	0	-1.1
1961	StL N	22	52	8	14	2	0	4	9	6-1	2	10	.269	.367	.538	124	2	0-0	1.000	3	74	36	C15/lf	0	0.5
1962	StL N	122	345	42	89	19	1	14	45	50-4	1	59	.258	.352	.441	102	2	5-2	.991	5	108	**108**	C98,O8(6/0/2),1b3	0	1.1
1963	StL N	39	102	10	23	4	0	6	18	13-3	0	19	.225	.308	.441	105	1	0-0	.981	0	60	107	C35	0	0.3

YEAR	TM LG	G	AB	R	H	2B	3B	HR	RBI	BB-IB	HP	SO	AVG	OBP	SLG	AOPS	ABR	SB-CS	FA	FR	RNG	THR	GAMES AT POSITION	DL	BFW
	Mil N	95	296	34	74	12	2	11	47	27-1	5	59	.250	.320	.416	112	5	4-4	.985	-10	63	110	1b55,O35L,C2	0	-1.1
	Year	134	398	44	97	16	2	17	65	40-4	5	78	.244	.317	.422	110	5	4-4	.985	-10	63	110	1b55,C37,O35L	0	-0.8
1964	Mil N	93	279	45	77	15	1	13	49	17-0	1	41	.276	.319	.477	120	7	3-7	.982	-5	80	98	1b76/C	0	-0.4
1965	Mil N	122	392	56	106	20	0	21	58	36-5	3	61	.270	.336	.482	127	14	5-4	.976	3	93	162	C64,1b52/lf	0	1.7
1966	Atl N	76	191	19	37	9	1	8	24	16-3	0	43	.194	.255	.377	72	-8	2-0	.990	6	84	149	C48,1b5,O2L	0	0.1
1967	Atl N	17	51	8	10	2	0	3	6	6-0	0	8	.196	.281	.412	97	0	0-0	.962	1	61	92	C13/1	0	0.1
	Phi N	85	263	29	59	16	0	7	34	29-3	1	56	.224	.300	.365	90	-3	2-2	.987	-6	91	46	C79,1b2	0	-0.7
	Year	102	314	37	69	18	0	10	40	35-3	1	64	.220	.297	.373	91	-3	2-2	.983	-5	87	52	C92,1b3	0	-0.6
1968	Bos A	16	35	2	5	0	0	0	1	4-1	1	12	.143	.250	.143	20	-3	0-0	.984	-1	51	88	C10/rf	0	-0.4
	Chi N	8	11	1	4	0	0	0	1	3-0	0	2	.364	.500	.364	152	1	0-0	1.000	1	0	0	1b2/Clf	63	0.2
1969	Chi N	23	27	0	6	3	0	0	0	1-1	1	9	.222	.276	.333	62	-1	0-0	1.000	2	153	0	C6	0	0.1
Total	10	786	2216	268	546	111	5	93	320	215-22	15	420	.246	.315	.427	103	10	24-21	.985	-3	89	105	C381,1b201,O91(87/0/6)	63	0.4

OLIVER, JOE Joseph Melton; B7.24.1965 Memphis TN; BR/TR/6´3″/(210–220); [CinN83 2/41]; d7.15

YEAR	TM LG	G	AB	R	H	2B	3B	HR	RBI	BB-IB	HP	SO	AVG	OBP	SLG	AOPS	ABR	SB-CS	FA	FR	RNG	THR	GAMES AT POSITION	DL	BFW
1989	Cin N	49	151	13	41	8	0	3	23	6-1	1	28	.272	.300	.384	92	-2	0-0	.986	4	121	79	C47	0	0.4
1990	†Cin N	121	364	34	84	23	0	8	52	37-15	2	75	.231	.304	.360	79	-10	1-1	**.992**	12	150	110	C118	0	0.9
1991	Cin N	94	269	21	58	11	0	11	41	18-5	0	53	.216	.265	.379	76	-10	0-0	.980	-1	92	88	C90	0	-0.6
1992	Cin N	143	485	42	131	25	1	10	57	35-19	1	75	.270	.316	.388	97	-2	2-3	.992	7	122	93	C141/1	0	1.3
1993	Cin N	139	482	40	115	28	0	14	75	27-2	1	91	.239	.276	.384	75	-18	0-0	.992	-6	92	117	C133,1b12/rf	0	-1.6
1994	Cin N	6	19	1	4	0	0	1	5	2-1	0	3	.211	.286	.368	69	-1	0-0	.980	1	75	171	C6	122	0.1
1995	Mil A	97	337	43	92	20	0	12	51	27-1	3	66	.273	.332	.439	93	-4	2-4	.982	-5	74	113	C91,1b2,D6	32	-0.4
1996	Cin N	106	289	31	70	12	1	11	46	28-6	2	54	.242	.311	.405	86	-6	2-0	.992	5	107	93	C97,1b3,O3(2/0/1)	0	0.4
1997	Cin N	111	349	28	90	13	0	14	43	25-1	5	58	.258	.313	.415	88	-7	1-3	.990	-3	108	92	C106,1b4	0	-0.4
1998	Det A	50	155	8	35	8	0	4	22	7-0	0	33	.226	.253	.355	57	-10	0-1	.982	-1	128	101	C48,1b2	0	-0.9
	Sea A	29	85	12	19	3	0	2	10	10-0	0	15	.224	.305	.329	65	-4	1-0	.984	-4	85	84	C29	0	-0.7
	Year	79	240	20	54	11	0	6	32	17-0	0	48	.225	.272	.346	60	-15	1-1	.983	-6	112	95	C77,1b2	0	-1.6
1999	Pit N	45	134	10	27	8	0	1	13	10-0	0	33	.201	.253	.284	36	-13	2-0	.993	-0	113	48	C44	0	-1.0
2000	†Sea A	69	200	33	53	13	1	10	35	14-1	0	38	.265	.313	.490	101	-1	2-1	.995	-2	98	71	C66/1D	0	0.1
2001	NY A	12	36	3	9	1	0	1	2	1-0	0	12	.250	.263	.361	64	-2	0-0	.991	1	65	61	C12	0	0.0
	Bos A	5	12	1	3	1	0	0	1	1-0	0	3	.250	.308	.333	69	-1	0-0	.971	-2	60	69	C5	0	-0.2
	Year	17	48	4	12	2	0	1	3	2-0	0	15	.250	.275	.354	65	-3	0-0	.986	-1	64	63	C17	0	-0.2
Total	13	1076	3367	320	831	174	3	102	476	248-52	15	637	.247	.299	.391	82	-91	13-13	.989	4	108	96	C1033,1b25,D7,O4(2/0/2)	154	-2.6

OLIVER, NATE Nathaniel "Peewee"; B12.13.1940 St.Petersburg FL; BR/TR/5´10″/160; d4.9

YEAR	TM LG	G	AB	R	H	2B	3B	HR	RBI	BB-IB	HP	SO	AVG	OBP	SLG	AOPS	ABR	SB-CS	FA	FR	RNG	THR	GAMES AT POSITION	DL	BFW
1963	LA N	65	163	23	39	2	3	1	9	13-0	1	25	.239	.298	.307	80	-5	3-4	.961	2	97	105	2b57,S2	0	0.0
1964	LA N	99	321	28	78	9	0	0	21	31-6	0	57	.243	.309	.271	70	-12	7-4	.967	-12	93	82	2b98/S	0	-1.6
1965	LA N	8	1	3	1	0	0	0	0	0-0	0	0	1.000	1.000	1.000	498	1	1-0	1.000	-0	65	0	2b2	0	0.1
1966	†LA N	80	119	17	23	2	0	0	3	13-2	1	17	.193	.276	.210	41	-9	3-3	.977	1	101	93	2b68,S2/3	21	-0.5
1967	LA N	77	232	18	55	6	2	0	7	13-0	2	50	.237	.283	.280	67	-10	3-2	.973	-3	94	75	2b39,S32/lf	0	-1.0
1968	SF N	36	73	3	13	2	0	0	1	1-0	0	13	.178	.189	.205	18	-7	0-1	.950	-1	131	169	2b14,S13/3	56	-0.8
1969	NY A	1	1	0	0	0	0	0	0	0-0	0	0	.000	.000	.000	-99	0	0-0	ø	0	—	—	/H	0	0.0
	Chi N	44	44	15	7	3	0	1	4	1-0	1	10	.159	.196	.295	32	-4	0-1	1.000	1	105	140	2b13	0	-0.3
Total	7	410	954	107	216	24	5	2	45	72-8	5	172	.226	.283	.268	62	-46	17-15	.969	-12	98	94	2b291,S50,3b2/lf	77	-4.1

OLIVER, BOB Robert Lee; B2.8.1943 Shreveport LA; BR/TR/6´2″/(205–215); d9.10; s–Darren; Col American River (CA) CC; OF(15/48/165)

YEAR	TM LG	G	AB	R	H	2B	3B	HR	RBI	BB-IB	HP	SO	AVG	OBP	SLG	AOPS	ABR	SB-CS	FA	FR	RNG	THR	GAMES AT POSITION	DL	BFW
1965	Pit N	3	2	1	0	0	0	0	0	0-0	0	0	.000	.000	.000	-99	-1	0-0	1.000	0	305	0	O3L	0	0.0
1969	KC A	118	394	43	100	8	4	13	43	21-2	2	74	.254	.294	.393	90	-8	5-5	.977	4	107	170	O98(9/48/45),1b12,3b8	0	-1.0
1970	KC A	160	612	83	159	24	6	27	99	42-4	3	126	.260	.309	.451	107	3	3-3	.993	-8	85	105	1b115,3b46	0	-1.6
1971	KC A	128	373	35	91	12	2	8	52	14-3	5	88	.244	.277	.351	79	-12	0-0	.988	1	96	129	1b68,O48(1/0/47),3b2	0	-1.9
1972	KC A	16	63	7	17	2	1	1	6	2-0	0	12	.270	.292	.381	100	0	1-0	.979	2	141	83	O16R	0	0.1
	Cal A	134	509	47	137	20	4	19	70	27-8	3	97	.269	.307	.436	127	13	4-3	.994	-6	74	88	1b127,O8(1/0/7)	0	-0.4
	Year	150	572	54	154	22	5	20	76	29-8	3	109	.269	.305	.430	124	13	5-3	.994	-4	74	88	1b127,O24(1/0/23)	0	-0.3
1973	Cal A	151	544	51	144	24	1	18	89	33-7	5	100	.265	.311	.412	110	5	1-1	.952	0	99	53	3b49,O47R,1b32,D12	0	0.0
1974	Cal A	110	359	22	89	9	1	8	55	16-2	1	51	.248	.277	.345	84	-9	2-1	.985	-12	66	96	1b57,3b46,O4(1/0/3)/D	0	-2.6
	Bal A	9	20	1	3	2	0	0	4	0-0	0	5	.150	.150	.250	14	-2	1-1	.974	1	258	33	1b4/D	0	-0.2
	Year	119	379	23	92	11	1	8	59	16-2	1	56	.243	.271	.340	80	-12	3-2	.984	-11	80	91	1b61,3b46,O4(1/0/3),D2	0	-2.8
1975	NY A	18	38	3	5	1	0	0	1	1-0	0	9	.132	.154	.158	-12	-6	0-0	1.000	-1	59	228	1b8/3D	0	-0.7
Total	8	847	2914	293	745	102	19	94	419	156-26	19	562	.256	.295	.400	100	-17	17-14	.991	-18	81	99	1b423,O224R,3b152,D17	0	-8.3

OLIVER, TOM Thomas Noble "Rebel"; B1.15.1903 Montgomery AL; D2.26.1988 Montgomery AL; BR/TR/6´0″/168; d4.14; C4

YEAR	TM LG	G	AB	R	H	2B	3B	HR	RBI	BB-IB	HP	SO	AVG	OBP	SLG	AOPS	ABR	SB-CS	FA	FR	RNG	THR	GAMES AT POSITION	DL	BFW
1930	Bos A	**154**	646	86	189	34	2	0	46	42	3	25	.293	.339	.351	78	-20	6-6	.982	6	107	75	O154C	—	-2.0
1931	Bos A	148	586	52	162	35	5	0	70	25	1	17	.276	.307	.353	77	-21	4-6	**.993**	6	102	122	O148C	—	-1.9
1932	Bos A	122	455	39	120	23	3	0	37	25	2	12	.264	.305	.327	66	-24	1-6	.983	3	101	121	O116C	—	-2.4
1933	Bos A	90	244	25	63	9	1	0	23	13	0	7	.258	.296	.303	60	-15	1-1	.985	8	113	196	O86C	—	-0.8
Total	4	514	1931	202	534	101	11	0	176	105	6	61	.277	.316	.340	73	-80	12-19	.986	22	105	117	O504C	—	-7.1

OLIVO, MIGUEL Miguel Eduardo (Pena); B7.15.1978 Villa Vasquez, D.R.; BR/TR/6´1″/(215–220); d9.15

YEAR	TM LG	G	AB	R	H	2B	3B	HR	RBI	BB-IB	HP	SO	AVG	OBP	SLG	AOPS	ABR	SB-CS	FA	FR	RNG	THR	GAMES AT POSITION	DL	BFW
2002	Chi A	6	19	2	4	1	0	1	5	2-0	0	5	.211	.286	.421	81	-1	0-0	1.000	-1	299	71	C6	0	-0.1
2003	Chi A	114	317	37	75	19	1	6	27	19-0	4	80	.237	.287	.360	67	-15	6-4	.988	15	158	82	C113	0	0.6
2004	Chi A	46	141	21	38	7	2	7	26	10-1	0	29	.270	.316	.496	104	0	5-4	.984	-9	108	102	C46	0	-0.6
	Sea A	50	160	25	32	8	2	6	14	10-1	3	55	.200	.260	.387	69	-8	2-2	.997	-4	188	65	C49	15	-0.9
	Year	96	301	46	70	15	4	13	40	20-2	3	84	.233	.286	.439	86	-8	7-6	.991	-13	149	83	C95	0	-1.5
2005	Sea A	54	152	14	23	4	0	5	18	4-0	0	49	.151	.172	.276	18	-19	1-1	.987	1	113	99	C54	0	-1.4
	†SD N	37	115	16	35	7	1	4	16	4-2	3	31	.304	.341	.487	120	3	6-1	.979	-3	152	59	C37	0	0.3
2006	Fla N	127	430	52	113	22	3	16	58	9-4	7	103	.263	.287	.440	87	-11	2-3	.991	6	133	126	C124,1b5	0	0.2
Total	5	434	1334	167	320	68	9	45	164	58-8	17	352	.240	.279	.406	77	-51	22-15	.989	6	145	95	C429,1b5	15	-1.9

OLMEDO, RAY Rainer Gustavo; B5.31.1981 Maracay, Zulia, Venezuela; BB/TR/5´11″/(150–155); d5.25

YEAR	TM LG	G	AB	R	H	2B	3B	HR	RBI	BB-IB	HP	SO	AVG	OBP	SLG	AOPS	ABR	SB-CS	FA	FR	RNG	THR	GAMES AT POSITION	DL	BFW
2003	Cin N	79	230	24	55	6	1	0	17	13-0	0	46	.239	.280	.274	48	-18	1-1	.929	-10	97	71	S51,2b18	0	-2.5
2004	Cin N	8	1	0	0	0	0	0	0	1-0	0	0	.000	.500	.000	46	0	0-0	1.000	1	136	149	S7	0	0.1
2005	Cin N	54	77	10	17	4	1	1	4	6-0	1	22	.221	.282	.338	62	-4	4-0	.975	-1	92	81	2b31,S5	75	-0.4
2006	Cin N	30	44	5	9	2	0	1	4	4-0	0	4	.205	.271	.318	48	-4	1-0	.900	-2	103	66	2b5,S4,3b3/rf	0	-0.5
Total	4	171	352	39	81	12	2	2	25	24-0	1	72	.230	.280	.293	51	-26	6-1	.933	-13	97	82	S67,2b54,3b3/rf	75	-3.3

OLMO, LUIS Luis Francisco (Rodriguez) (b Luis Francisco Rodriquez (Olmo)); B8.11.1919 Arecibo, PR; BR/TR/5´11.5″/190; d7.23

YEAR	TM LG	G	AB	R	H	2B	3B	HR	RBI	BB-IB	HP	SO	AVG	OBP	SLG	AOPS	ABR	SB-CS	FA	FR	RNG	THR	GAMES AT POSITION	DL	BFW
1943	Bro N	57	238	39	72	6	4	4	37	8	0	20	.303	.325	.412	112	2	3	.957	-1	96	122	O57(1/54/2)	0	-0.1
1944	Bro N	136	520	65	134	20	5	9	85	17	2	37	.258	.284	.367	84	-14	10	.971	-13	119	91	O64(3/61/1),2b42,3b31	0	-2.8
1945	Bro N	141	556	62	174	27	**13**	10	110	36	1	33	.313	.356	.462	127	17	15	.971	-8	98	105	O106(100/6/0),3b31/2	0	0.4
1949	†Bro N	38	105	15	32	4	1	1	14	5	0	11	.305	.336	.390	91	-2	2	.950	-1	91	157	O34(17/16/1)	0	-0.3
1950	Bos N	69	154	23	35	7	1	5	22	18	0	23	.227	.308	.383	86	-4	3	.974	-2	99	37	O55(18/11/24)/3	0	-0.7
1951	Bos N	21	56	4	11	1	1	0	4	4	0	4	.196	.250	.250	38	-5	0-1	1.000	-0	83	187	O16(10/6/2)	0	-0.6
Total	6	462	1629	208	458	65	25	29	272	88	3	128	.281	.319	.405	102	-6	33-1	.968	-25	101	105	O332(149/154/30),3b63,2b43	0	-4.1

OLSEN, BARNEY Bernard Charles; B9.11.1919 Everett MA; D3.30.1977 Everett MA; BR/TR/5´11″/179; d8.23

YEAR	TM LG	G	AB	R	H	2B	3B	HR	RBI	BB-IB	HP	SO	AVG	OBP	SLG	AOPS	ABR	SB-CS	FA	FR	RNG	THR	GAMES AT POSITION	DL	BFW
1941	Chi N	24	73	13	21	6	1	1	4	4	0	11	.288	.325	.438	118	1	0	.947	1	103	188	O23C	0	0.2

OLSON, GREG Gregory William; B9.6.1960 Marshall MN; BR/TR/6´0″/200; [NYN82 7/163]; d6.27; Col Minnesota

YEAR	TM LG	G	AB	R	H	2B	3B	HR	RBI	BB-IB	HP	SO	AVG	OBP	SLG	AOPS	ABR	SB-CS	FA	FR	RNG	THR	GAMES AT POSITION	DL	BFW
1989	Min A	3	2	0	1	0	0	0	0	0-0	0	0	.500	.500	.500	171	0	0-0	1.000	-0	39	0	C3	0	0.0
1990	Atl N★	100	298	36	78	12	1	7	36	30-4	2	51	.262	.332	.379	91	-3	1-1	.987	-5	102	76	C97/3	0	-0.3
1991	†Atl N	133	411	46	99	25	0	6	44	44-3	3	48	.241	.316	.345	82	-9	1-1	.995	1	99	80	C127	0	-0.1
1992	Atl N	95	302	27	72	14	2	3	27	34-4	1	31	.238	.316	.328	78	-8	2-1	.998	5	96	**140**	C94	16	0.2
1993	†Atl N	83	262	23	59	10	0	4	24	29-0	1	27	.225	.304	.309	63	-13	1-0	.988	-3	97	91	C81	23	-1.1
Total	5	414	1275	132	309	61	3	20	131	137-11	7	157	.242	.317	.342	79	-33	5-3	.992	-2	98	96	C402/3	39	-1.3

YEAR	TM LG	G	AB	R	H	2B	3B	HR	RBI	BB-IB	HP	SO	AVG	OBP	SLG	AOPS	ABR	SB-CS	FA	FR	RNG	THR	GAMES AT POSITION	DL	BFW
Olson, Ivy Ivan Massie; B10.14.1885 Kansas City MO; D9.1.1965 Inglewood CA; BR/TR/5´10.5˝/175; d4.12; C4; OF(8/0/2)																									
1911	Cle A	140	545	89	142	20	8	1	50	34	6	—	.261	.311	.332	79	-17	20	.909	-16	95	98	S139/3	—	-2.3
1912	Cle A	125	467	68	118	13	1	0	33	21	4	—	.253	.291	.285	63	-23	16	.917	2	101	52	S56,3b36,2b21,O3L	—	-1.6
1913	Cle A	104	370	47	92	13	3	0	32	22	3	28	.249	.296	.300	72	-14	7	.953	2	102	69	3b73,1b21/2	—	-1.1
1914	Cle A	89	310	22	75	6	2	1	20	13	1	24	.242	.275	.284	65	-14	15-9	.942	7	104	114	S31,2b23,3b19,O6(5/0/1),1b3	—	-0.5
1915	Cin N	63	207	18	48	5	4	0	14	12	0	13	.232	.274	.295	71	-8	10-6	.938	7	112	106	2b39,3b15,1b7	—	0.0
	Bro N	18	26	2	2	0	1	0	3	1	0	0	.077	.111	.154	-20	-4	0	.909	-2	80	85	S7/23rf	—	-0.6
	Year	81	233	20	50	5	5	0	17	13	0	13	.215	.256	.279	61	-12	10-6	.938	5	111	105	2b40,3b16,1b7,S7/rf	—	-0.6
1916	†Bro N	108	351	29	89	13	4	1	38	21	1	27	.254	.298	.322	88	-5	14	.920	-14	91	70	S103,2b3/1	—	-1.4
1917	Bro N	139	580	64	156	18	5	2	38	14	4	34	.269	.291	.328	87	-10	6	.941	-6	97	89	S133,3b6	—	-0.8
1918	Bro N	**126**	506	63	121	16	4	1	17	27	6	18	.239	.286	.292	77	-14	21	.918	-23	88	81	S126	—	-3.2
1919	Bro N	140	590	73	**164**	14	9	1	38	30	3	12	.278	.316	.337	94	-5	26	.947	-4	92	95	S140	—	0.2
1920	†Bro N	143	637	71	162	13	11	1	46	20	1	19	.254	.278	.314	68	-29	4-7	.935	-9	93	87	S125,2b21	—	-3.3
1921	Bro N	151	652	88	174	22	10	3	35	28	4	26	.267	.301	.345	68	-31	4-9	.943	7	100	97	S133,2b20	—	-1.1
1922	Bro N	136	551	63	150	26	6	1	47	25	2	10	.272	.306	.347	69	-27	8-5	.960	-4	101	88	2b85,S51	—	-2.1
1923	Bro N	82	292	33	76	11	1	1	35	14	1	10	.260	.296	.315	63	-16	5-0	.974	6	104	85	2b72,3b4,1b2,S2	—	-0.7
1924	Bro N	10	27	0	6	1	0	0	0	3	0	1	.222	.300	.259	53	-2	0-0	.941	-1	76	148	S8,2b2	—	-0.2
Total	14	1574	6111	730	1575	191	69	13	446	285	36	222	.258	.295	.318	74	-219	156-36	.932	-48	94	90	S1054,2b288,3b155,1b34,O10L	—	-18.7
Olson, Karl Karl Arthur "Ole"; B7.6.1930 Kentfield CA; BR/TR/6´3˝/205; d6.30; Mil 1952–54																									
1951	Bos A	5	10	0	1	0	0	0	0	0	0	3	.100	.100	.100	-42	-2	0-0	1.000	0	122	0	O5(2/0/3)	0	-0.2
1953	Bos A	25	57	5	7	2	0	1	6	1	0	9	.123	.138	.211	-7	-9	0-0	.970	0	103	93	O24(23/2/0)	0	-1.0
1954	Bos A	101	227	25	59	12	2	1	20	12	0	23	.260	.293	.344	68	-10	2-1	.957	2	93	225	O78(29/36/16)	0	-1.1
1955	Bos A	26	48	7	12	1	2	0	1	1-0	0	10	.250	.265	.354	60	-3	0-0	1.000	0	101	113	O21(11/8/5)	0	-0.3
1956	Was A	106	313	34	77	10	2	4	22	28-1	1	41	.246	.305	.329	69	-15	1-1	.990	-4	94	71	O101(16/84/3)	0	-2.3
1957	Was A	8	12	2	2	0	0	0	0	1-0	0	2	.167	.231	.167	10	-2	0-0	1.000	0	137	0	O6(2/4/0)	0	-0.1
	Det A	8	14	1	2	0	0	0	1	0-0	0	6	.143	.143	.143	-21	-2	0-0	1.000	-0	82	0	O5(4/1/0)	0	-0.3
	Year	16	26	3	4	0	0	0	1	1-0	0	8	.154	.185	.154	-6	-4	0-0	1.000	0	108	0	O11(6/5/0)	0	-0.4
Total	6	279	681	74	160	25	6	6	50	43-1	1	94	.235	.278	.316	57	-43	3-2	.979	-1	96	121	O240(87/135/27)	0	-5.3
Olson, Marv Marvin Clement "Sparky"; B5.28.1907 Gayville SD; D2.5.1998 Tyndall SD; BR/TR/5´7˝/160; d9.13; Col Luther																									
1931	Bos A	15	53	8	10	1	0	0	5	9	0	3	.189	.306	.208	40	-4	0-0	.963	1	103	87	2b15	—	-0.3
1932	Bos A	115	403	58	100	14	6	0	25	61	0	26	.248	.347	.313	74	-14	1-5	.955	-10	96	94	2b106/3	—	-1.8
1933	Bos A	3	1	1	0	0	0	0	0	0	0	1	.000	.000	.000	-99	0	0-0	ø	-0	0	0	/2	—	0.0
Total	3	133	457	67	110	15	6	0	30	70	0	30	.241	.342	.300	70	-18	1-5	.956	-10	97	93	2b122/3	—	-2.1
Olson, Tim Timothy Lane; B8.1.1978 Grand Forks ND; BR/TR/6´2˝/200; [AriN00 7/219]; d5.30; Col Florida																									
2004	Ari N	48	97	8	18	7	0	2	5	16-0	0	18	.186	.301	.320	57	-6	1-0	.963	6	151	89	3b19,S17,O4(1/2/1)	0	0.1
2005	Col N	3	2	0	0	0	0	0	0	1-0	0	2	.000	.333	.000	-2	0	0-0	ø	0	—	—	/D	0	0.0
Total	2	51	99	8	18	7	0	2	5	17-0	0	20	.182	.302	.313	56	-6	1-0	.963	6	151	89	3b19,S17,O4(1/2/1)/D	0	0.1
O'Malley, Tom Thomas Patrick; B12.25.1960 Orange NJ; BL/TR/6´0˝/(180–195); [SFN79 16/408]; d5.8																									
1982	SF N	92	291	26	80	12	4	2	27	33-9	1	39	.275	.350	.364	101	1	0-3	.965	-1	100	70	3b83/2S	21	-0.2
1983	SF N	135	410	40	106	16	1	5	45	52-4	4	47	.259	.345	.339	94	-2	2-4	.940	-2	101	67	3b117	0	-0.7
1984	SF N	13	25	2	3	0	0	0	0	2-0	0	2	.120	.185	.120	-13	-4	0-0	1.000	-1	77	105	3b7	0	-0.5
	Chi A	12	16	0	2	0	0	0	3	0-0	0	5	.125	.125	.125	-29	-3	0-0	1.000	-1	22	0	3b6	0	-0.4
1985	Bal A	8	14	1	1	0	0	1	2	0-0	0	2	.071	.071	.286	-8	-2	0-0	.833	-1	56	0	3b3	0	-0.4
1986	Bal A	56	181	19	46	9	0	1	18	17-1	0	21	.254	.317	.320	75	-6	0-1	.938	2	105	95	3b55	0	-0.5
1987	Tex A	45	117	10	32	8	0	1	12	15-1	0	9	.274	.351	.368	92	-1	0-0	.962	-1	97	47	3b40/2	0	-0.2
1988	Mon N	14	27	3	7	0	0	0	2	3-1	0	4	.259	.323	.259	69	-1	0-0	.905	1	130	0	3b7	0	0.0
1989	NY N	9	11	2	6	2	0	0	8	0-0	0	2	.545	.545	.727	272	2	0-0	1.000	-0	40	0	3b3	0	0.2
1990	NY N	82	121	14	27	7	0	3	14	11-1	0	20	.223	.286	.355	76	-4	0-0	.983	-0	76	134	3b38,1b3	0	-0.4
Total	9	466	1213	117	310	54	5	13	131	133-17	5	151	.256	.329	.340	87	-20	2-8	.951	-5	98	73	3b359,1b3,2b2/S	21	-3.1
O'Mara, Ollie Oliver Edward; B3.8.1891 St.Louis MO; D10.24.1989 Reno NV; BR/TR/5´9˝/155; d9.8																									
1912	Det A	1	4	0	0	0	0	0	0	0	0	—	.000	.000	.000	-99	-1	0	.857	-0	127	0	/S	—	-0.1
1914	Bro N	67	247	41	65	10	2	1	7	16	3	26	.263	.316	.332	91	-3	14	.918	-10	94	76	S63	—	-0.9
1915	Bro N	149	577	77	141	26	3	0	31	51	2	40	.244	.308	.300	83	-11	11-12	.906	-36	91	69	S149	—	-4.3
1916	†Bro N	72	193	18	39	5	2	0	15	12	0	20	.202	.249	.249	52	-11	10	.898	-7	89	149	S51	—	-1.6
1918	Bro N	121	450	29	96	8	1	1	24	7	10	18	.213	.242	.242	48	-29	11	.951	-1	100	76	3b121	—	-2.9
1919	Bro N	2	7	1	0	0	0	0	0	0	0	0	.000	.000	.000	-98	-2	0	.875	-1	62	0	3b2	—	-0.3
Total	6	412	1478	166	341	49	8	2	77	86	15	104	.231	.280	.279	69	-57	46-12	.907	-53	91	86	S264,3b123	—	-10.1
O'Meara, Ed Thomas Edward; B12.12.1872 Chicago IL; D2.16.1902 Fort Wayne IN; BR; d9.29																									
1895	Cle N	1	1	1	0	0	0	0	0	1	0	0	.000	.500	.000	34	0	0	.500	-0	*86*	*200*	/C	—	0.0
1896	Cle N	12	33	5	5	0	0	0	0	5	0	7	.152	.263	.152	10	-4	0	.914	-0	*144*	*75*	C9/1	—	-0.3
Total	2	13	34	6	5	0	0	0	0	6	0	7	.147	.275	.147	12	-4	0	.892	-0	*141*	*82*	C10/1	—	-0.3
O'Neal ; d10.23																									
1874	Har NA	1	3	0	0	0	0	0	0	0	—	1	.000	.000	.000	-95	-1	0-0	.667	1	1254	0	/rf	—	0.0
O'Neil, Mickey George Michael; B4.12.1900 St.Louis MO; D4.8.1964 St.Louis MO; BR/TR/5´10˝/185; d9.12; C1																									
1919	Bos N	11	28	3	6	0	0	0	1	1	0	7	.214	.241	.214	39	-2	0	.981	2	*107*	*144*	C11	—	0.1
1920	Bos N	112	304	19	86	5	4	0	28	21	5	20	.283	.339	.326	96	-2	4-4	.962	7	*112*	***135***	C105/2	—	1.4
1921	Bos N	98	277	26	69	9	4	2	29	23	0	21	.249	.307	.332	73	-11	2-2	.968	4	*114*	***138***	C95	—	-0.1
1922	Bos N	83	251	18	56	5	2	0	26	14	1	11	.223	.267	.259	38	-24	1-0	.978	-0	*101*	*126*	C79	—	-1.8
1923	Bos N	96	306	29	65	7	4	0	20	17	2	14	.212	.258	.261	39	-28	3-2	.973	6	*92*	***137***	C95	—	-1.5
1924	Bos N	106	362	32	89	4	1	0	22	14	1	27	.246	.276	.262	47	-28	4-3	.985	-2	*81*	*110*	C106	—	-2.3
1925	Bos N	70	222	29	57	6	5	2	30	21	2	16	.257	.327	.356	81	-7	1-2	.972	-6	*109*	*59*	C69	—	-0.8
1926	Bro N	75	201	19	42	5	3	0	20	23	1	8	.209	.293	.264	52	-14	3	.965	-3	*76*	*113*	C74	—	-1.2
1927	Was A	5	6	0	0	0	0	0	0	0	0	1	.000	.000	.000	-99	-2	0-0	1.000	-0	*75*	*0*	C4	—	-0.2
	NY N	16	38	2	5	0	0	0	3	5	0	2	.132	.233	.132	-0	-5	0	.969	2	*114*	*138*	C16	—	-0.3
Total	9	672	1995	177	475	41	23	4	179	139	12	127	.238	.292	.288	58	-123	18-13	.972	11	*98*	*120*	C654/2	—	-6.7
O'Neil, John John Francis; B4.19.1920 Shelbiana KY; BR/TR/5´9˝/155; d4.16																									
1946	Phi N	46	94	12	25	3	0	0	9	5	0	12	.266	.303	.298	73	-4	0	.940	0	100	97	S32	0	-0.2
O'Neill, Denny Dennis; B11.22.1866 Holyoke MA; D11.15.1922 Rushville IN; BL/TL/6´2.5˝/200; d6.18; Col Yale																									
1893	StL N	7	25	3	3	0	0	0	2	4	0	0	.120	.241	.120	-3	-4	3	.986	-1	0	75	1b7	—	-0.4
O'Neill, Fred Frederick James "Tip"; B1865 London ON, Can.; D3.7.1892 London ON, Can.; BR/5´7˝/142; d5.3																									
1887	NY AA	6	26	4	8	1	1	0	3	1	1	—	.308	.357	.423	123	1	3	.800	-1	142	0	O6(0/1/5)	—	0.0
O'Neill, Harry Harry Mink; B5.8.1917 Philadelphia PA; D3.6.1945 Iwo Jima, Marianas Islands; BR/TR/6´3˝/205; d7.23; Col Gettysburg																									
1939	Phi A	1	0	0	0	0	0	0	0	0	0	0	ø	ø	ø	ø	0	0-0	ø	0	*0*	*0*	/C	—	0.0
O'Neill, Tip James Edward; B5.25.1858 Springfield ON, Can.; D12.31.1915 Montreal QC, Can.; BR/TR/6´1.5˝/167; d5.5; ▲																									
1883	NY N	23	76	8	15	3	0	0	5	3	—	15	.197	.228	.237	42	-5	—	.917	-2	79	0	P19,O7(0/1/6)	—	-0.2
1884	StL AA	78	297	49	82	13	11	3	54	12	2	—	.276	.309	.424	132	9	—	.811	-5	51	59	O64(59/5/0),P17/1	—	0.0
1885	†StL AA	52	206	44	72	7	4	3	38	13	4	—	.350	.399	.466	165	15	—	.881	-2	66	67	O52L	—	1.1
1886	†StL AA	138	579	106	190	28	14	3	**107**	47	7	—	.328	.385	.440	151	33	9	.927	8	61	107	O138L	—	3.2
1887	†StL AA	124	517	**167**	**225**	**52**	**19**	**14**	**123**	50	5	—	**.435**	**.490**	**.691**	**205**	**71**	30	.895	-7	39	49	O124L	—	**4.8**
1888	†StL AA	130	529	96	**177**	24	10	5	98	44	4	—	**.335**	.390	.446	151	28	26	.937	-1	37	26	O130L	—	2.2
1889	StL AA	134	534	123	179	33	8	9	110	72	5	37	.335	.419	.478	137	25	28	.936	-4	46	57	O134L	—	1.5
1890	Chi P	137	577	112	174	20	16	3	75	65	5	36	.302	.377	.407	105	3	29	.926	-13	31	21	O137L	—	-1.0
1891	StL AA	127	514	111	166	28	4	10	95	61	9	33	.323	.404	.451	126	16	25	.935	-12	23	0	O127L	—	0.1

YEAR	TM LG	G	AB	R	H	2B	3B	HR	RBI	BB-IB	HP	SO	AVG	OBP	SLG	AOPS	ABR	SB-CS	FA	FR	RNG	THR	GAMES AT POSITION	DL	BFW
1892	Cin N	109	419	63	105	14	6	2	52	53	3	25	.251	.339	.327	103	3	14	.922	-4	73	82	O109L	—	-1.0
Total	10	1052	4248	879	1385	222	92	52	757	420	44	146	.326	.392	.458	140	198	161	.917	-41	46	50	O1022(1010/6/6),P36/1	—	10.7
O'NEILL, JIM	James Leo; B2.23.1893 Minooka PA; D9.5.1976 Chambersburg PA; BR/TR/5´10.5˝/165; d4.15; b–Jack b–Mike b–Steve																								
1920	Was A	86	294	27	85	17	7	1	40	13	2	30	.289	.324	.405	95	-4	7-3	.943	-9	100	68	S80,2b2	—	-0.6
1923	Was A	23	33	6	9	1	0	0	3	1	0	3	.273	.294	.303	60	-2	0-0	.946	2	110	115	2b8,3b4/Srf	—	0.0
Total	2	109	327	33	94	18	7	1	43	14	2	33	.287	.321	.394	91	-6	7-3	.943	-7	100	68	S81,2b10,3b4/rf	—	-0.6
O'NEILL, JOHN	John J.; B New York NY; TR; d9.6																								
1899	NY N	2	7	0	0	0	0	0	0	0	0	—	.000	.000	.000	-99	-2	0	.929	0	*79*	*159*	C2	—	-0.1
1902	NY N	2	8	0	0	0	0	0	0	0	0	—	.000	.000	.000	-99	-2	0	.933	0	*128*	*145*	C2	—	-0.2
Total	2	4	15	0	0	0	0	0	0	0	0	—	.000	.000	.000	-99	-4	0	.931	0	*104*	*152*	C4	—	-0.3
O'NEILL, JACK	John Joseph; B1.10.1873 Maam, Ireland; D6.29.1935 Minooka PA; BR/TR/5´10˝/165; d4.21; b–Jim b–Mike b–Steve																								
1902	StL N	63	192	13	27	1	1	0	12	13	5	—	.141	.214	.156	15	-19	2	.973	-2	*93*	*104*	C59	—	-1.6
1903	StL N	75	246	23	58	9	1	0	27	13	5	—	.236	.288	.280	64	-11	11	.972	9	*95*	*110*	C74	—	0.4
1904	Chi N	51	168	8	36	5	0	1	19	6	4	—	.214	.258	.262	61	-8	1	.981	5	*127*	*96*	C49	—	0.2
1905	Chi N	53	172	16	34	4	2	0	12	8	11	—	.198	.277	.244	54	-10	6	.974	7	*120*	*90*	C50	—	0.3
1906	Bos N	61	167	14	30	5	1	0	4	12	2	—	.180	.243	.222	46	-11	0	.971	4	*92*	*108*	C48,1b2/rf	—	-0.2
Total	5	303	945	74	185	24	5	1	74	52	27	—	.196	.258	.235	49	-59	20	.974	23	*104*	*102*	C280,1b2/rf	—	-0.9
O'NEILL, PAUL	Paul Andrew; B2.25.1963 Columbus OH; BL/TL/6´4˝/(200–215); [CinN81 4/93]; d9.3																								
1985	Cin N	5	12	1	4	1	0	0	1	0-0	0	2	.333	.333	.417	103	0	0-0	1.000	1	89	767	O2L	0	0.1
1986	Cin N	3	2	0	0	0	0	0	0	1-0	0	1	.000	.333	.000	-0	0	0-0	ø	0	—	—	/H	0	0.0
1987	Cin N	84	160	24	41	14	1	7	28	18-1	0	29	.256	.331	.488	109	2	2-1	.949	0	112	93	O42(14/10/22),1b2/P	0	0.1
1988	Cin N	145	485	58	122	25	3	16	73	38-5	2	65	.252	.306	.414	102	1	8-6	.984	1	103	90	O118(0/8/114),1b21	0	-0.4
1989	Cin N	117	428	49	118	24	2	15	74	46-8	2	64	.276	.346	.446	122	13	20-5	.983	-0	97	111	O115(0/4/115)	42	1.2
1990	†Cin N	145	503	59	136	28	0	16	78	53-13	2	103	.270	.339	.421	105	4	13-11	.993	3	99	128	O141(0/1/141)	0	0.2
1991	Cin N★	152	532	71	136	36	0	28	91	73-14	1	107	.256	.346	.481	125	19	12-7	.994	9	108	123	O150R	0	2.4
1992	Cin N	148	496	59	122	19	1	14	66	77-15	2	85	.246	.346	.373	102	4	6-3	**.997**	9	108	131	O143R	0	0.9
1993	NY A	141	498	71	155	34	1	20	75	44-5	2	69	.311	.367	.504	136	25	2-4	.992	-8	86	78	O138(46/0/103),D2	0	0.9
1994	NY A★	103	368	68	132	25	1	21	83	72-13	0	56	**.359**	.460	.603	179	48	5-4	.995	1	100	96	O99(12/0/90),D4	0	4.0
1995	†NY A★	127	460	82	138	30	4	22	96	71-8	1	76	.300	.387	.526	138	28	1-2	.987	-5	96	38	O121(25/0/107),D4	16	1.5
1996	†NY A	150	546	89	165	35	1	19	91	102-8	4	76	.302	.411	.474	124	26	0-1	**1.000**	3	104	72	O146R/1D	0	2.0
1997	†NY A★	149	553	89	179	42	0	21	117	75-8	0	92	.324	.399	.514	139	35	10-7	.984	-1	98	76	O146R,1b2,D2	0	2.5
1998	†NY A★	152	602	95	191	40	2	24	116	57-2	2	103	.317	.372	.510	134	30	15-1	.987	1	99	102	O150R/D	0	2.5
1999	†NY A	153	597	70	170	39	4	19	110	66-1	2	89	.285	.353	.459	108	8	11-9	.974	1	102	99	O151R	0	0.1
2000	†NY A	142	566	79	160	26	0	18	100	51-2	0	90	.283	.336	.424	94	-6	14-9	.993	4	112	56	O140R,D2	0	-0.7
2001	†NY A	137	510	77	136	33	1	21	70	48-4	2	59	.267	.330	.459	105	3	22-3	.981	-10	91	13	O130R,D6	0	-0.8
Total	17	2053	7318	1041	2105	451	21	281	1269	892-107	22	1166	.288	.363	.470	121	240	141-73	.988	9	101	88	O1932(99/23/1848),1b26,D24/P	58	16.5
O'NEILL, PEACHES	Philip Bernard; B8.30.1879 Anderson IN; D8.2.1955 Anderson IN; BR/TR/5´11˝/165; d4.16; Col Notre Dame																								
1904	Cin N	8	15	0	4	0	0	0	1	1	0	—	.267	.313	.267	73	0	0	.900	-2	*73*	*64*	C5/1	—	-0.3
O'NEILL, STEVE	Stephen Francis; B7.6.1891 Minooka PA; D1.26.1962 Cleveland OH; BR/TR/5´10˝/165; d9.18; M14/C4; b–Jim b–Jack b–Mike																								
1911	Cle A	9	27	1	4	1	0	0	1	4	1	—	.148	.281	.185	31	-2	2	.986	2	*100*	*123*	C9	—	0.0
1912	Cle A	69	215	17	49	4	0	0	14	12	1	—	.228	.272	.247	47	-15	2	.961	7	*97*	*108*	C68	—	-0.3
1913	Cle A	80	234	19	69	13	3	0	29	10	2	24	.295	.329	.376	103	0	5	.973	9	*119*	*100*	C80	—	1.6
1914	Cle A	87	269	28	68	12	2	0	20	15	0	35	.253	.292	.312	79	-8	1-3	.956	-2	*88*	***113***	C82/1	—	-0.4
1915	Cle A	121	386	32	91	14	2	2	34	26	5	41	.236	.293	.298	75	-13	2-3	.968	9	*107*	*103*	C115	—	0.6
1916	Cle A	130	378	30	89	23	0	0	29	24	4	33	.235	.288	.296	71	-13	2	.971	6	110	88	C128	—	0.4
1917	Cle A	129	370	21	68	10	2	0	29	41	4	55	.184	.272	.222	47	-22	2	.980	5	*105*	*103*	C127	—	-0.8
1918	Cle A	114	359	34	87	8	7	1	35	48	7	22	.242	.343	.312	89	-3	5	**.983**	9	*123*	*104*	C113	—	1.7
1919	Cle A	125	398	46	115	35	7	2	47	48	5	21	.289	.373	.427	117	11	4	.977	0	***139***	*84*	C123	—	2.2
1920	†Cle A	149	489	63	157	39	5	3	55	69	3	39	.321	.408	.440	121	19	3-5	.976	2	*114*	*79*	C148	—	3.1
1921	Cle A	106	335	39	108	22	1	1	50	57	2	22	.322	.424	.403	110	9	0-1	.982	4	*93*	*68*	C105	—	1.9
1922	Cle A	133	392	33	122	27	4	2	65	73	3	25	.311	.423	.416	118	16	2-2	.974	-15	*81*	*75*	C130	—	0.8
1923	Cle A	113	330	31	82	12	0	0	50	64	2	34	.248	.374	.285	75	-8	0-4	.968	-6	*118*	*56*	C111	—	-0.9
1924	Bos A	106	307	29	73	15	1	0	38	63	2	23	.238	.371	.293	73	-9	0-2	.970	-1	*99*	*98*	C92	—	-0.4
1925	NY A	35	91	7	26	5	0	1	13	10	1	3	.286	.363	.374	89	-1	0-0	.946	1	*101*	*108*	C31	—	0.2
1927	StL A	74	191	14	44	7	0	1	22	20	0	6	.230	.303	.283	51	-14	0-3	.983	1	*106*	*149*	C60	—	-1.0
1928	StL A	10	24	4	7	1	0	0	6	8	1	0	.292	.485	.333	115	1	0-0	.958	-3	*67*	*67*	C10	—	-0.1
Total	17	1590	4795	448	1259	248	34	13	537	592	43	383	.263	.349	.337	88	-52	30-23	.972	28	*108*	*92*	C1532/1	—	8.6
O'NEILL, BILL	William John; B1.22.1880 St.John NB, Can.; D7.20.1920 Woodhaven NY; BB/TR/5´11˝/175; d5.7																								
1904	Bos A	17	51	7	10	1	0	0	5	2	0	—	.196	.226	.216	38	-4	0	.933	-2	0	0	O9(8/1/0),S2	—	-0.7
	Was A	95	365	33	89	10	1	1	16	22	4	—	.244	.294	.285	85	-6	22	.893	-9	98	36	O93(14/79/0),2b3	—	-2.2
	Year	112	416	40	99	11	1	1	21	24	4	—	.238	.286	.276	79	-10	22	.896	-12	90	33	O102(22/80/0),2b3,S2	—	-2.9
1906	†Chi A	94	330	37	82	4	1	1	21	22	3	—	.248	.301	.276	83	-6	19	.949	-2	112	49	O93(0/7/87)	—	-1.4
Total	2	206	746	77	181	15	2	2	42	46	7	—	.243	.293	.276	81	-16	41	.919	-14	100	41	O195(22/87/87),2b3,S2	—	-4.3
ONIS, RALPH	Manuel Dominguez "Curly"; B10.24.1908 Tampa FL; D1.4.1995 Tampa FL; BR/TR/5´9˝/180; d4.27																								
1935	Bro N	1	1	0	1	0	0	0	0	0	0	0	1.000	1.000	1.000	449	0	0	.500	-0	*0*	*0*	/C	—	0.0
ONSLOW, EDDIE	Edward Joseph; B2.17.1893 Meadville PA; D5.8.1981 Dennison OH; BL/TL/6´0˝/170; d8.7; b–Jack																								
1912	Det A	36	128	11	29	1	2	1	13	3	1	—	.227	.250	.289	56	-8	3	.972	-4	75	108	1b35	—	-1.3
1913	Det A	17	55	7	14	1	0	0	8	5	1	9	.255	.328	.273	77	-1	1	.990	-1	70	95	1b17	—	-0.3
1918	Cle A	2	6	0	1	0	0	0	0	0	0	1	.167	.167	.167	1	-1	0	.000	-1	0	0	/lf	—	-0.2
1927	Was A	9	18	1	4	1	0	0	1	1	0	0	.222	.263	.278	41	-2	0-0	1.000	0	90	125	1b5	—	-0.2
Total	4	64	207	19	48	3	2	1	22	9	2	10	.232	.271	.280	59	-12	4-0	.979	-5	74	105	1b57/lf	—	-2.0
ONSLOW, JACK	John James; B10.13.1888 Scottdale PA; D12.22.1960 Concord MA; BR/TR/5´11˝/180; d5.2; M2/C7; b–Eddie																								
1912	Det A	36	69	7	11	1	0	0	4	10	2	—	.159	.284	.174	33	-6	1	.948	-4	*84*	*110*	C35/cf	—	-0.7
1917	NY N	9	8	1	2	1	0	0	0	0	1	1	.250	.333	.375	121	0	0	.929	-1	*110*	*59*	C9	—	0.0
Total	2	45	77	8	13	2	0	0	4	10	3	1	.169	.289	.195	41	-6	1	.947	-4	*86*	*105*	C44/cf	—	-0.7
ONTIVEROS, STEVE	Steven Robert; B10.26.1951 Bakersfield CA; BB/TR/6´0˝/(175–185); [SFN69 6/136]; d8.5																								
1973	SF N	24	33	3	8	0	0	1	5	4-0	0	7	.242	.324	.333	79	-1	0-0	1.000	1	200	53	1b5/rf	0	0.0
1974	SF N	120	343	45	91	15	1	4	33	57-4	3	41	.265	.375	.350	99	3	0-0	.929	-4	93	111	3b75,1b19,O2(1/0/1)	0	-0.3
1975	SF N	108	325	21	94	16	0	3	31	55-4	2	44	.289	.391	.366	109	7	2-0	.923	3	106	90	3b89,O8(2/0/7),1b4	0	1.0
1976	SF N	59	74	8	13	3	0	0	5	6-0	1	11	.176	.244	.216	31	-7	0-0	1.000	-1	113	192	3b7,O7(4/3/2),1b4	0	-0.8
1977	Chi N	156	546	54	163	32	3	10	68	81-4	3	69	.299	.390	.423	107	9	3-3	.955	3	106	97	3b155	0	1.0
1978	Chi N	82	276	34	67	14	4	1	22	34-3	0	33	.243	.321	.333	75	-8	0-2	.965	12	123	118	3b77/1	68	0.2
1979	Chi N	152	519	58	148	28	2	4	57	58-7	7	68	.285	.362	.370	92	-3	0-1	.941	2	101	104	3b142/1	0	-0.3
1980	Chi N	31	77	7	16	3	0	1	3	14-1	0	17	.208	.330	.286	67	-3	0-0	.929	-0	104	32	3b24	0	-0.3
Total	8	732	2193	230	600	111	10	24	224	309-23	16	290	.274	.365	.366	94	-3	5-6	.944	17	105	101	3b569,1b34,O18(7/3/11)	68	0.5
OQUENDO, JOSE	Jose Manuel (Contreras); B7.4.1963 Rio Piedras, PR; BB/TR (BR 1983p)/5´10˝/(156–171); d5.2; C8; OF(11/7/47)																								
1983	NY N	120	328	29	70	7	0	1	17	19-2	2	60	.213	.260	.244	41	-27	8-9	.960	0	106	103	S116	0	-1.8
1984	NY N	81	189	23	42	5	0	0	10	15-2	2	26	.222	.284	.249	52	-12	10-1	.972	0	92	102	S67	0	-0.4
1986	StL N	76	138	20	41	4	1	0	13	15-4	0	20	.297	.359	.341	96	0	2-3	.956	-9	90	109	S29,2b21/3lf	0	-0.7
1987	†StL N	116	248	43	71	9	0	1	24	54-6	0	29	.286	.408	.335	99	3	4-4	1.000	9	118	210	O46(8/3/37),2b32,S23,3b8,1b3/P	0	1.3
1988	StL N	148	451	36	125	10	1	7	46	52-7	0	40	.277	.350	.350	100	1	4-6	.997	8	106	116	2b69,3b47,S17,1b16,O15(2/4/9)/PC	0	1.1
1989	StL N	163	556	59	162	28	7	1	48	79-7	0	59	.291	.375	.372	112	12	3-5	**.994**	25	**110**	**124**	2b156,S7/1	0	4.3
1990	StL N	156	469	38	118	17	5	1	37	74-8	0	46	.252	.350	.316	85	-7	1-1	**.996**	-2	102	88	2b150,S4	0	-0.5
1991	StL N	127	366	37	88	11	4	1	26	67-13	1	48	.240	.357	.301	86	-4	1-2	.988	9	109	112	2b118,S22,1b3/P	0	0.9

YEAR	TM LG	G	AB	R	H	2B	3B	HR	RBI	BB-IB	HP	SO	AVG	OBP	SLG	AOPS	ABR	SB-CS	FA	FR	RNG	THR	GAMES AT POSITION	DL	BFW
1992	StL N	14	35	3	9	3	1	0	3	5-1	0	3	.257	.350	.400	115	1	0-0	1.000	1	121	147	2b9,S5	131	0.2
1993	StL N	46	73	7	15	0	0	0	4	12-1	0	8	.205	.314	.205	44	-6	0-0	.988	5	122	100	S22,2b16	56	0.1
1994	StL N	55	129	13	34	2	2	0	9	21-4	0	16	.264	.364	.310	79	-3	1-1	.945	-8	77	56	S28,2b16	0	-0.9
1995	StL N	88	220	31	46	8	3	2	17	35-3	0	21	.209	.316	.300	63	-11	1-1	.981	7	110	122	2b62,S24,3b2/rf	0	-0.1
Total	12	1190	3202	339	821	104	24	14	254	448-58	5	376	.256	.346	.317	85	-53	35-33	.992	46	107	114	2b649,S364,O63R,3b58,1b23,P3/C	187	3.5
Oran, Tom	Thomas; B1847 CA; D9.22.1886 St.Louis MO; d5.4																								
1875	RS NA	**19**	81	7	15	3	1	0	10	1	—	1	.185	.195	.247	58	-3	3-2	.633	-4	102	0	O19(0/2/17)/S	—	-0.5
Oravetz, Ernie	Ernest Eugene; B1.24.1932 Johnstown PA; BB/TL/5´4˝/145; d4.11																								
1955	Was A	100	263	24	71	5	1	0	25	26-0	1	19	.270	.336	.297	76	-9	1-2	.967	-5	94	24	O57(0/17/42)	0	-1.6
1956	Was A	88	137	20	34	3	2	0	11	27-0	0	20	.248	.370	.299	79	-3	1-0	.946	-1	97	103	O31(20/3/9)	0	-0.5
Total	2	188	400	44	105	8	3	0	36	53-0	1	39	.262	.348	.298	77	-12	2-2	.961	-5	95	48	O88(20/20/51)	0	-2.1
Ordaz, Luis	Luis Javier; B8.12.1975 Maracaibo, Venezuela; BR/TR/5´11˝/170; d9.3																								
1997	StL N	12	22	3	6	1	0	0	1	1-0	0	2	.273	.304	.318	63	-1	3-0	.964	-1	93	102	S11	0	-0.1
1998	StL N	57	153	9	31	5	0	0	8	12-1	0	18	.203	.261	.235	32	-15	2-0	.945	6	118	121	S54,3b2/2	0	-0.5
1999	StL N	10	9	3	1	0	0	0	2	1-0	0	2	.111	.200	.111	-18	-2	1-0	.786	-1	77	192	S8/23	0	-0.2
2000	KC A	65	104	17	23	2	0	0	11	5-0	1	10	.221	.257	.240	27	-12	4-2	.986	-10	72	117	S38,2b22	0	-1.8
2001	KC A	28	56	8	14	3	0	0	4	3-0	1	8	.250	.295	.304	54	-4	0-0	.987	5	129	177	2b19,S8/3D	44	0.2
2002	KC A	33	94	11	21	2	0	0	4	12-0	0	13	.223	.308	.245	45	-7	2-3	.982	-6	90	78	2b28,3b6,S2	0	-1.2
2006	TB A	1	2	0	0	0	0	0	0	0-0	0	0	.000	.000	.000	-99	-1	0-0	1.000	-0	61	0	/S	140	-0.1
Total	7	206	440	51	96	13	0	0	30	34-1	2	53	.218	.274	.248	37	-42	12-5	.948	-7	104	118	S122,2b71,3b10/D	184	-3.7
Ordenana, Tony	Antonio (Rodriguez) "Mosquito"; B10.30.1918 Guanabacoa, Cuba; D9.29.1988 Miami FL; BR/TR/5´9˝/158; d10.3																								
1943	Pit N	1	4	0	2	0	0	0	3	0	0	0	.500	.500	.500	183	0	0	1.000	1	136	150	/S	0	0.1
Ordonez, Magglio	Magglio (Delgado); B1.28.1974 Caracas, Distrito Capital, Venez.; BR/TR/6´0˝/(170–215); d8.29																								
1997	Chi A	21	69	12	22	6	0	4	11	2-0	0	8	.319	.338	.580	138	3	1-2	1.000	1	118	87	O19R	0	0.3
1998	Chi A	145	535	70	151	25	2	14	65	28-1	9	53	.282	.326	.415	93	-6	9-7	.985	5	108	97	O145(0/22/136)	0	-0.7
1999	Chi A★	157	624	100	188	34	3	30	117	47-4	1	64	.301	.349	.510	114	11	13-6	.991	7	107	111	O153R,D2	0	1.1
2000	†Chi A★	153	588	102	185	34	3	32	126	60-3	2	64	.315	.371	.546	126	23	18-4	.983	-3	91	114	O152R	0	1.4
2001	Chi A★	160	593	97	181	40	1	31	113	70-7	5	70	.305	.382	.533	130	27	25-7	.983	-3	94	108	O155(0/1/155),D3	0	1.9
2002	Chi A	153	590	116	189	47	1	38	135	53-2	7	77	.320	.381	.597	149	42	7-5	.986	-3	96	87	O150R/D	0	3.0
2003	Chi A★	160	606	95	192	46	3	29	99	57-1	7	73	.317	.380	.546	135	32	9-5	.994	4	106	82	O157(0/4/154),D2	0	2.7
2004	Chi A	52	202	32	59	8	2	9	37	16-2	3	22	.292	.351	.485	112	3	0-2	.990	1	110	36	O43R,D7	117	0.1
2005	Det A	82	305	38	92	17	0	8	46	30-1	1	35	.302	.359	.436	114	7	0-0	.993	-3	87	108	O81R/D	79	0.0
2006	†Det A★	155	593	82	177	32	1	24	104	45-3	4	87	.298	.350	.477	114	12	1-4	.974	-9	85	97	O148R,D6	0	-0.6
Total	10	1238	4705	744	1436	289	16	219	853	408-24	39	553	.305	.362	.513	123	154	83-42	.987	-4	98	98	O1203(0/27/1191),D22	196	9.2
Ordonez, Rey	Reynaldo; B1.11.1971 Havana, Cuba; BR/TR/5´9˝/(159–160); d4.1																								
1996	NY N	151	502	51	129	12	4	1	30	22-12	1	53	.257	.289	.303	59	-31	1-3	.962	10	**106**	109	S150	0	-1.2
1997	NY N	120	356	35	77	5	3	1	33	18-3	1	36	.216	.255	.256	36	-35	11-5	**.983**	10	112	113	S118	39	-1.6
1998	NY N	153	505	46	124	20	2	1	42	23-7	1	60	.246	.278	.299	54	-35	3-6	.975	-1	93	96	S151	0	-2.7
1999	†NY N	154	520	49	134	24	2	1	60	49-12	1	59	.258	.319	.317	66	-27	8-4	**.994**	6	98	106	S154	0	-0.9
2000	NY N	45	133	10	25	5	0	0	9	17-2	0	16	.188	.278	.226	32	-14	0-0	.965	-5	90	83	S44	124	-1.5
2001	NY N	149	461	31	114	24	4	3	44	34-17	1	43	.247	.299	.336	69	-22	3-2	.980	-3	93	100	S148	0	-1.5
2002	NY N	144	460	53	117	25	2	1	42	24-11	2	46	.254	.292	.324	66	-24	2-2	.969	1	99	96	S142	0	-1.3
2003	TB A	34	117	14	37	11	0	3	22	2-0	1	12	.316	.328	.487	115	2	0-2	.970	5	110	134	S34	143	0.9
2004	Chi N	23	61	2	10	3	0	1	5	2-0	0	14	.164	.190	.262	15	-8	0-0	.959	-2	78	88	S22	0	-0.9
Total	9	973	3115	291	767	129	17	12	287	191-64	8	339	.246	.289	.310	59	-194	28-24	.976	20	99	103	S963	306	-10.7
Orengo, Joe	Joseph Charles; B11.29.1914 San Francisco CA; D7.24.1988 San Francisco CA; BR/TR/6´0˝/185; d4.18																								
1939	StL N	7	3	0	0	0	0	0	0	0	0	1	.000	.000	.000	-94	-1	0	.667	-1	72	0	S7	—	-0.2
1940	StL N	129	415	58	119	23	4	7	56	65	0	90	.287	.383	.412	113	10	9	.952	-5	95	96	2b77,3b34,S19	—	1.2
1941	NY N	77	252	23	54	11	2	4	25	28	2	49	.214	.298	.321	73	-9	1	.958	10	105	108	3b59,S9,2b6	0	0.4
1943	NY N	83	266	28	58	8	2	6	29	36	0	46	.218	.311	.331	85	-5	1	.992	5	121	67	1b82	0	-0.5
	Bro N	7	15	1	3	2	0	0	1	4	0	2	.200	.368	.333	103	0	0	1.000	-0	100	0	3b6	0	0.0
	Year	90	281	29	61	10	2	6	30	40	0	48	.217	.315	.331	86	-5	1	.992	5	121	67	1b82,3b6	0	-0.5
1944	Det A	46	154	14	31	10	0	0	10	20	1	29	.201	.297	.266	58	-8	1-1	.903	3	104	123	S29,3b11,1b5,2b2	0	-0.3
1945	Chi A	17	15	5	1	0	0	0	1	3	0	2	.067	.222	.067	-15	-2	0-0	.923	-0	100	0	3b7/2	0	-0.3
Total	6	366	1120	129	266	54	8	17	122	156	3	219	.237	.332	.346	88	-15	12-1	.957	11	97	93	3b117,1b87,2b86,S64	0	0.3
Orie, Kevin	Kevin Leonard; B9.1.1972 West Chester PA; BR/TR/6´4˝/(210–215); [ChiN93 S1/29]; d4.1; Col Indiana																								
1997	Chi N	114	364	40	100	23	5	8	44	39-3	5	57	.275	.350	.431	101	1	2-2	.971	13	110	84	3b112,S3	30	1.3
1998	Chi N	64	204	24	37	14	0	2	21	18-0	3	35	.181	.253	.279	40	-18	1-1	.966	1	100	72	3b57	0	-1.7
	Fla N	48	175	23	46	8	1	6	17	14-2	5	24	.263	.335	.423	104	1	1-0	.939	5	113	51	3b48	0	0.6
	Year	112	379	47	83	22	1	8	38	32-2	8	59	.219	.291	.346	68	-18	2-1	.952	6	106	62	3b105	0	-1.1
1999	Fla N	77	240	26	61	16	0	6	29	22-1	3	43	.254	.322	.396	86	-5	1-0	.961	4	111	74	3b64/1	83	-0.1
2002	Chi N	13	32	4	9	3	0	0	5	1-0	1	4	.281	.306	.375	83	-1	0-0	.895	-2	77	55	3b12	0	-0.2
Total	4	316	1015	117	253	64	6	22	116	94-6	17	163	.249	.320	.389	85	-22	5-3	.960	21	108	73	3b293,S3/1	113	-0.1
Orme, George	George William; B9.16.1891 Lebanon IN; D3.16.1962 Indianapolis IN; BR/TR/5´10˝/160; d9.14																								
1920	Bos A	4	6	4	2	0	0	0	1	3	0	0	.333	.556	.333	146	1	0-0	1.000	0	146	0	O3(0/1/2)	—	0.1
Orndorff, Jess	Jesse Walworth Thayer; B1.15.1881 Chicago IL; D9.28.1960 Cardiff–By–The– Sea CA; BB/TR/6´0˝/168; d4.18																								
1907	Bos N	5	17	0	2	0	0	0	0	0	0	—	.118	.118	.118	-26	-3	0	.900	-2	*69*	*125*	C5	—	-0.5
O'Rourke, Frank	James Francis "Blackie"; B11.28.1894 Hamilton ON, Can.; D5.14.1986 Chatham NJ; BR/TR/5´10.5˝/165; d6.12																								
1912	Bos N	61	196	11	24	3	1	0	16	11	2	50	.122	.177	.148	-10	-31	1	.915	-10	97	67	S59/3	—	-3.7
1917	Bro N	64	198	18	47	7	1	0	15	14	2	25	.237	.294	.283	75	-5	11	.954	3	106	59	3b58	—	-0.1
1918	Bro N	4	12	0	2	0	0	0	2	1	0	3	.167	.231	.167	22	-1	0	.857	1	138	103	2b2/O	—	0.0
1920	Was A	14	54	8	16	1	0	0	5	2	0	5	.296	.321	.315	71	-2	2-1	.952	1	94	195	S13/3	—	0.0
1921	Was A	123	444	51	104	17	8	3	54	26	7	56	.234	.287	.329	60	-29	6-7	.922	-11	96	90	S122	—	-2.6
1922	Bos A	67	216	28	57	14	3	1	17	20	3	28	.264	.335	.370	84	-5	6-6	.909	-11	90	70	S49,3b20	—	-1.0
1924	Det A	47	181	28	50	11	2	0	19	12	3	19	.276	.332	.359	79	-6	7-4	.970	6	109	116	2b40,S7	—	0.2
1925	Det A	124	482	88	141	40	7	5	57	32	11	37	.293	.350	.436	100	-1	5-8	**.971**	15	107	98	2b118,3b6	—	1.4
1926	Det A	111	363	43	88	16	1	1	41	35	7	33	.242	.321	.300	62	-20	8-6	.936	4	95	176	3b60,2b41,S10	—	-1.1
1927	StL A	140	538	85	144	25	3	1	39	64	**12**	43	.268	.358	.331	77	-16	18-8	.955	11	99	101	3b121,2b16,1b3	—	0.4
1928	StL A	99	391	54	103	24	3	1	62	21	1	19	.263	.303	.348	68	-18	10-2	.954	-11	81	74	3b96,S2	—	-2.1
1929	StL A	**154**	585	81	147	23	9	2	62	41	5	28	.251	.306	.332	62	-35	14-7	.943	-17	87	113	3b151,2b3,S2	—	-3.9
1930	StL A	115	400	52	107	15	4	1	41	35	0	30	.268	.326	.333	65	-21	11-9	.950	6	97	111	3b84,S23,1b3	—	-0.8
1931	StL A	8	9	0	2	0	0	0	0	0	0	1	.222	.222	.222	17	-1	1-1	1.000	0	144	0	S2/1	—	-0.1
Total	14	1131	4069	547	1032	196	42	15	430	314	53	377	.254	.315	.333	68	-191	100-59	.949	-11	93	101	3b598,S289,2b220,1b7/O	—	-13.4
O'Rourke, Jim	James Henry "Orator Jim"; B9.1.1850 Bridgeport CT; D1.8.1919 Bridgeport CT; BR/TR/5´8˝/185; d4.26; M5/U1; HF1945; b–John s–Queenie; OF NA(0/44/22); OF(770/419/195); ▲																								
1872	Man NA	23	99	25	27	5	0	0	16	4	—	0	.273	.301	.323	98	1	1-0	.735	-2	118	27	S15,C9,3b2/1	—	-0.1
1873	Bos NA	57	280	79	98	21	2	1	49	15	—	3	.350	.383	.450	134	11	9-5	.912	1	139	**157**	1b34,O21R,C12	—	1.0
1874	Bos NA	70	331	82	104	15	8	**5**	61	4	—	5	.314	.322	.453	138	12	11-2	.943	1	90	**177**	1b70	—	1.2
1875	Bos NA	75	358	97	106	13	7	**6**	72	9	—	6	.296	.313	.422	148	16	17-5	.800	-5	109	79	O45(0/44/1),3b27,1b6/C	—	1.0
1876	Bos N	**70**	312	61	102	17	3	2	43	15	—	17	.327	.358	.420	156	19	—	.856	-3	61	38	O68(9/60/0),1b2/C	—	1.1
1877	Bos N	**61**	265	**68**	96	14	4	0	23	**20**	—	9	.362	**.407**	.445	162	20	—	.846	-2	74	0	O60(23/35/3)/1	—	1.2
1878	Bos N	**60**	255	44	71	17	7	1	29	5	—	21	.278	.292	.412	120	5	—	.860	1	100	189	O57C,1b2,C2	—	0.3
1879	Pro N	81	362	69	126	19	9	1	46	13	—	10	.348	**.371**	.459	174	29	—	.785	-10	85	149	O56(2/0/56),1b20,C5,3b3	—	1.7
1880	Bos N	**86**	363	71	100	20	11	**6**	45	21	—	8	.275	.315	.441	158	22	—	.907	-3	127	58	O37(15/4/19),1b19,S17,3b10,C9	—	1.9

YEAR	TM LG	G	AB	R	H	2B	3B	HR	RBI	BB-IB	HP	SO	AVG	OBP	SLG	AOPS	ABR	SB-CS	FA	FR	RNG	THR	GAMES AT POSITION	DL	BFW
1881	Buf N	**83**	348	71	105	21	7	0	30	27	—	18	.302	.352	.402	139	17	—	.821	-19	72	86	3b56,O18L,C8,S3/1M	—	-0.1
1882	Buf N	**84**	370	62	104	15	6	2	37	13	—	13	.281	.305	.370	114	5	—	.866	-1	87	83	O81(5/77/0),S2,C2/3M	—	0.1
1883	Buf N	94	436	102	143	29	8	1	38	15	—	13	.328	.350	.438	135	18	—	.866	-9	60	0	O61(60/1/0),C33,3b8,S3,P2,M	—	0.8
1884	Buf N	108	467	119	**162**	33	7	5	63	35	—	17	**.347**	.392	.480	167	36	—	.894	-7	36	77	O86L,1b18,C10,P4/3M	—	2.3
1885	NY N	**112**	477	119	143	21	**16**	5	42	40	—	21	.300	.354	.442	158	31	—	.940	-16	49	0	O112C,C8	—	1.0
1886	NY N	105	440	106	136	26	6	1	34	39	—	21	.309	.365	.402	132	18	14	.926	5	91	58	O63(1/62/0),C47,1b2	—	2.2
1887	NY N	103	397	73	113	15	13	3	88	36	5	11	.285	.352	.411	116	10	46	.890	-7	—	—	C40,3b38,O28(19/6/3),2b2	—	0.5
1888	†NY N	107	409	50	112	16	6	4	50	24	3	30	.274	.319	.372	121	10	25	.960	1	89	39	O87(75/3/9),C15,1b4,3b2	—	0.9
1889	†NY N	128	502	89	161	36	7	3	81	40	1	34	.321	.372	.438	125	16	33	.893	-7	75	47	O128L/C	—	0.6
1890	NY P	111	478	112	172	37	5	9	115	33	8	20	.360	.410	.515	135	22	23	.930	2	117	72	O111(10/1/100)	—	1.7
1891	NY N	**136**	555	92	164	28	7	5	95	26	6	29	.295	.334	.398	118	11	19	.906	-1	92	30	O126(126/1/0),C14	—	0.7
1892	NY N	115	448	62	136	28	5	0	56	30	5	30	.304	.354	.388	126	14	16	.913	-8	65	27	O111(106/0/5),C4/1	—	-0.2
1893	Was N	129	547	75	157	22	5	2	95	49	8	26	.287	.354	.356	92	-6	15	.927	5	110	56	O87L,1b33,C9,M	—	-0.6
1904	NY N	1	4	1	1	0	0	0	0	0	0	—	.250	.250	.250	52	0	0	.800	-1	*109*	*0*	/C	—	-0.1
Total	4NA	225	1068	283	335	54	17	12	198	32	—	14	.314	.334	.430	137	40	38-12	.931	-6	100	167	1b111,O66C,3b29,C22,S15	—	3.1
Total	19	1774	7435	1446	2304	414	132	50	1010	481	36	348	.310	.355	.421	133	297	191-0	.898	-79	82	53	O1377L,C209,3b119,1b103,S25,P6,2b2	—	16.0

O'Rourke, Charlie James Patrick; B6.22.1937 Walla Walla WA; BR/TR/6´2˝/195; d6.16; Col Santa Clara

YEAR	TM LG	G	AB	R	H	2B	3B	HR	RBI	BB-IB	HP	SO	AVG	OBP	SLG	AOPS	ABR	SB-CS	FA	FR	RNG	THR	GAMES AT POSITION	DL	BFW
1959	StL N	2	2	0	0	0	0	0	0	0-0	0	0	.000	.000	.000	-94	-1	0-0	ø	0	—	—	/H	0	-0.1

O'Rourke, Queenie James Stephen; B12.26.1883 Bridgeport CT; D12.22.1955 Sparrows Point MD; BR/TR/5´7˝/150; d8.15; f–Jim; Col Holy Cross

YEAR	TM LG	G	AB	R	H	2B	3B	HR	RBI	BB-IB	HP	SO	AVG	OBP	SLG	AOPS	ABR	SB-CS	FA	FR	RNG	THR	GAMES AT POSITION	DL	BFW
1908	NY A	34	108	5	25	1	0	0	3	4	0	—	.231	.259	.241	62	-5	4	1.000	-2	71	0	O14L,S11,2b4,3b3	—	-0.9

O'Rourke, John John W.; B8.23.1849 Bridgeport CT; D6.23.1911 Boston MA; BL/TL/6´0˝/190; d5.1; b–Jim

YEAR	TM LG	G	AB	R	H	2B	3B	HR	RBI	BB-IB	HP	SO	AVG	OBP	SLG	AOPS	ABR	SB-CS	FA	FR	RNG	THR	GAMES AT POSITION	DL	BFW
1879	Bos N	72	317	69	108	17	11	6	**62**	8	—	32	.341	.357	**.521**	181	26	—	.882	0	62	122	O71(0/70/1)	—	2.1
1880	Bos N	81	313	30	86	22	8	3	36	18	—	32	.275	.314	.425	153	18	—	.871	4	103	0	O81(3/78/1)	—	1.8
1883	NY AA	77	315	49	85	19	5	2	—	21	—	—	.270	.315	.381	118	7	—	.856	-7	79	139	O76C/1	—	-0.3
Total	3	230	945	148	279	58	24	11	98	47	—	64	.295	.329	.442	150	51	—	.871	-3	82	86	O228(3/224/2)/1	—	3.6

O'Rourke, Joe Joseph Leo Jr.; B10.28.1904 Philadelphia PA; D6.27.1990 Philadelphia PA; BL/TR/5´7˝/145; d4.19; f–Patsy

YEAR	TM LG	G	AB	R	H	2B	3B	HR	RBI	BB-IB	HP	SO	AVG	OBP	SLG	AOPS	ABR	SB-CS	FA	FR	RNG	THR	GAMES AT POSITION	DL	BFW
1929	Phi N	3	3	0	0	0	0	0	0	0	0	1	.000	.000	.000	-94	-1	0	ø	0	—	—	/H	—	-0.1

O'Rourke, Patsy Joseph Leo Sr.; B4.13.1881 Philadelphia PA; D4.18.1956 Philadelphia PA; BR/TR/5´7˝/160; d4.16; s–Joe

YEAR	TM LG	G	AB	R	H	2B	3B	HR	RBI	BB-IB	HP	SO	AVG	OBP	SLG	AOPS	ABR	SB-CS	FA	FR	RNG	THR	GAMES AT POSITION	DL	BFW
1908	StL N	53	164	8	32	4	2	0	16	14	1	—	.195	.263	.244	65	-6	2	.860	-8	101	59	S53	—	-1.5

O'Rourke, Tom Thomas Joseph; B10.1865 New York NY; D7.19.1929 New York NY; TR/5´9˝/158; d5.11

YEAR	TM LG	G	AB	R	H	2B	3B	HR	RBI	BB-IB	HP	SO	AVG	OBP	SLG	AOPS	ABR	SB-CS	FA	FR	RNG	THR	GAMES AT POSITION	DL	BFW
1887	Bos N	22	78	12	12	3	0	0	10	7	1	6	.154	.233	.192	19	-8	4	.777	-7	—	—	C21/rf3	—	-1.2
1888	Bos N	20	74	3	13	0	0	0	4	1	0	9	.176	.187	.176	16	-7	2	.881	1	—	—	C20/rf	—	-0.5
1890	NY N	2	7	1	0	0	0	0	0	1	0	0	.000	.125	.000	-63	-1	0	.864	0	*95*	*180*	C2	—	-0.1
	Syr AA	41	153	16	33	8	0	0	12	12	1	—	.216	.277	.268	68	-6	2	.907	-15	*79*	*77*	C40/1	—	-1.6
Total	3	85	312	32	58	11	0	0	26	21	2	15	.186	.242	.221	39	-22	8	.867	-21	*80*	*83*	C83,O2R/13	—	-3.4

O'Rourke, Tim Timothy Patrick "Voiceless Tim"; B5.18.1864 Chicago IL; D4.20.1938 Seattle WA; BL/TR/5´10˝/170; d5.27; OF(32/1/40)

YEAR	TM LG	G	AB	R	H	2B	3B	HR	RBI	BB-IB	HP	SO	AVG	OBP	SLG	AOPS	ABR	SB-CS	FA	FR	RNG	THR	GAMES AT POSITION	DL	BFW
1890	Syr AA	87	332	48	94	13	6	1	46	36	4	—	.283	.360	.367	128	13	22	.866	-8	92	65	3b87	—	0.6
1891	Col AA	34	136	22	38	1	3	0	12	15	2	7	.279	.359	.331	104	1	9	.879	0	101	129	3b34	—	0.2
1892	Bal N	63	239	40	74	8	4	0	35	24	0	19	.310	.373	.377	123	7	12	.869	-8	95	72	S58,O4(2/1/1)/3	—	0.1
1893	Bal N	31	135	22	49	4	1	0	19	12	2	4	.363	.423	.407	119	4	5	.980	-2	26	0	O25L,3b5/S	—	0.0
	Lou N	92	352	80	99	8	4	0	53	77	8	15	.281	.421	.327	108	13	22	.865	-11	90	101	S60,O26(4/0/22),3b6	—	0.3
	Year	123	487	102	148	12	5	0	72	89	10	19	.304	.422	.349	112	17	27	.861	-13	89	99	S61,O51(29/0/22),3b11	—	0.3
1894	Lou N	55	220	46	61	3	3	0	27	23	2	9	.277	.351	.318	67	-11	9	.977	-1	145	144	1b30,O18(1/0/17),S3,3b3/2	—	-1.0
	StL N	18	71	10	20	4	1	0	10	8	0	3	.282	.354	.366	74	-3	2	.861	-2	85	99	3b18	—	-0.4
	Was N	7	25	4	5	2	1	0	2	2	0	1	.200	.259	.360	49	-2	0	.909	0	105	0	2b4,S3	—	-0.2
	Year	80	316	60	86	9	5	0	39	33	2	13	.272	.345	.332	67	-16	11	.977	-3	145	144	1b30,3b21,O18(1/0/17),S6,2b5	—	-1.6
Total	5	387	1510	272	440	43	23	1	204	197	18	58	.291	.380	.352	105	22	81	.861	-31	93	85	3b154,S125,O73R,1b30,2b5	—	-0.4

Orr, Dave David L.; B9.29.1859 New York NY; D6.2.1915 Richmond Hill NY; BR/TR/5´11˝/250; d5.17; M1; ▲

YEAR	TM LG	G	AB	R	H	2B	3B	HR	RBI	BB-IB	HP	SO	AVG	OBP	SLG	AOPS	ABR	SB-CS	FA	FR	RNG	THR	GAMES AT POSITION	DL	BFW
1883	NY AA	1	4	1	1	1	0	0	—	0	—	—	.250	.250	.500	130	0	—	1.000	0	0	0	/1	—	0.0
	NY N	1	3	0	0	0	0	0	0	0	—	1	.000	.000	.000	-99	-1	—	1.000	0	0	0	/lf	—	-0.1
	NY AA	12	46	5	15	3	3	2	11	0	—	—	.326	.326	.652	198	5	—	.938	-2	0	0	1b12	—	0.2
1884	†NY AA	110	458	82	**162**	32	13	9	112	5	1	—	**.354**	.362	.539	**195**	**46**	—	.960	-5	64	69	1b110,O3R	—	2.8
1885	NY AA	107	444	76	152	29	**21**	6	77	8	3	—	.342	.358	**.543**	189	42	—	.966	-3	73	86	1b107,P3	—	2.6
1886	NY AA	136	571	93	**193**	25	**31**	7	91	17	5	—	.338	.363	**.527**	**193**	**56**	16	**.981**	0	79	95	1b136	—	3.8
1887	NY AA	84	345	63	127	25	10	2	66	22	1	—	.368	.408	.516	164	29	17	.969	-1	107	90	1b81,O3C,M	—	1.7
1888	Bro AA	99	394	57	120	20	5	1	59	7	8	—	.305	.330	.388	130	12	11	.979	4	121	106	1b99	—	0.6
1889	Col AA	134	560	70	183	31	12	4	87	9	2	38	.327	.340	.446	129	18	12	.983	9	**130**	81	1b134	—	1.3
1890	Bro P	107	464	89	172	32	13	6	124	30	4	11	.371	.414	.534	144	26	10	.972	-5	78	100	1b107	—	0.9
Total	8	791	3289	536	1125	198	108	37	627	98	24	50	.342	.366	.502	163	233	66	.973	-1	92	89	1b787,O7(1/3/3),P3	—	13.8

Orr, Pete Peterson Thomas Gordon; B6.8.1979 Richmond Hill ON, Can.; BL/TR/6´1˝/(175–185); d4.5; Col Galveston (TX) JC

YEAR	TM LG	G	AB	R	H	2B	3B	HR	RBI	BB-IB	HP	SO	AVG	OBP	SLG	AOPS	ABR	SB-CS	FA	FR	RNG	THR	GAMES AT POSITION	DL	BFW
2005	†Atl N	112	150	32	45	8	1	1	8	6-0	1	23	.300	.331	.387	87	-3	7-1	.948	0	108	91	2b25,3b12,O3L/SD	0	-0.1
2006	Atl N	102	154	22	39	3	4	1	8	5-1	0	30	.253	.277	.344	57	-11	2-4	1.000	3	119	95	2b32,3b10	0	-0.7
Total	2	214	304	54	84	11	5	2	16	11-1	1	53	.276	.304	.365	72	-14	9-5	.974	4	114	93	2b57,3b22,O3L/DS	0	-0.8

Orr, Billy William John; B4.22.1891 San Francisco CA; D3.10.1967 St.Helena CA; BR/TR/5´11˝/168; d5.3

YEAR	TM LG	G	AB	R	H	2B	3B	HR	RBI	BB-IB	HP	SO	AVG	OBP	SLG	AOPS	ABR	SB-CS	FA	FR	RNG	THR	GAMES AT POSITION	DL	BFW
1913	Phi A	30	67	6	13	1	1	0	7	4	0	10	.194	.239	.239	41	-5	1	.967	-2	98	22	S16,1b3,3b3,2b2	—	-0.7
1914	Phi A	10	24	3	4	1	1	0	1	2	0	5	.167	.231	.292	59	-1	1-1	.810	-3	93	0	S6/3	—	-0.5
Total	2	40	91	9	17	2	2	0	8	6	0	15	.187	.237	.253	46	-6	2-1	.927	-5	97	16	S22,3b4,1b3,2b2	—	-1.2

Orsatti, Ernie Ernest Ralph; B9.8.1902 Los Angeles CA; D9.4.1968 Canoga Park CA; BL/TL/5´7.5˝/154; d9.4

YEAR	TM LG	G	AB	R	H	2B	3B	HR	RBI	BB-IB	HP	SO	AVG	OBP	SLG	AOPS	ABR	SB-CS	FA	FR	RNG	THR	GAMES AT POSITION	DL	BFW
1927	StL N	27	92	15	29	7	3	0	12	11	0	12	.315	.388	.457	122	3	2	.922	-1	97	98	O26(0/6/20)	—	0.1
1928	†StL N	27	69	10	21	6	0	3	15	10	1	11	.304	.400	.522	137	4	0	1.000	-1	92	136	O17(2/0/15),1b5	—	0.2
1929	StL N	113	346	64	115	21	7	3	39	33	2	43	.332	.394	.460	110	6	7	.974	6	108	159	O77(9/2/67),1b10	—	0.4
1930	†StL N	48	131	24	42	8	4	1	15	12	1	18	.321	.382	.466	100	0	1	.985	3	120	93	1b22,O11R	—	0.1
1931	†StL N	70	158	27	46	16	6	0	19	14	0	16	.291	.349	.468	113	3	1	.988	-1	104	0	O45(30/6/9)/1	—	-0.1
1932	StL N	101	375	44	126	27	6	2	44	18	1	29	.336	.368	.456	117	9	5	.976	-7	92	45	O96(40/55/1)/1	—	-0.2
1933	StL N	120	436	55	130	21	6	0	38	33	0	33	.298	.348	.374	101	1	14	.986	-2	103	68	O107(6/96/5),1b3	—	-0.4
1934	†StL N	105	337	39	101	14	4	0	31	27	1	31	.300	.353	.365	87	-5	6	.986	-3	96	84	O90C	—	-1.0
1935	StL N	90	221	28	53	9	3	1	24	18	0	25	.240	.297	.321	64	-11	10	.975	-1	100	66	O60(6/26/28)	—	-1.4
Total	9	701	2165	306	663	129	39	10	237	176	6	218	.306	.360	.416	102	10	46	.979	-7	99	84	O529(93/281/156),1b42	—	-2.3

Orsino, John John Joseph "Horse"; B4.22.1938 Teaneck NJ; BR/TR/6´3˝/(207–215); d7.14

YEAR	TM LG	G	AB	R	H	2B	3B	HR	RBI	BB-IB	HP	SO	AVG	OBP	SLG	AOPS	ABR	SB-CS	FA	FR	RNG	THR	GAMES AT POSITION	DL	BFW
1961	SF N	25	83	5	23	3	2	4	12	3-0	1	13	.277	.310	.506	116	1	0-0	.959	-3	111	85	C25	0	0.0
1962	†SF N	18	48	4	13	2	0	0	4	5-0	0	11	.271	.333	.313	78	-1	0-0	.963	-2	78	96	C16	0	-0.3
1963	Bal A	116	379	53	103	18	1	19	56	38-6	9	53	.272	.349	.475	134	18	2-3	.990	-2	101	97	C109,1b3	0	2.1
1964	Bal A	81	248	21	55	10	0	8	23	23-3	2	55	.222	.290	.359	81	-7	0-0	.976	2	67	87	C66,1b5	0	-0.2
1965	Bal A	77	232	30	54	10	2	9	28	23-2	5	51	.233	.313	.409	102	1	1-0	.987	-4	86	94	C62,1b5	0	-0.1
1966	Was A	14	23	1	4	1	0	0	0	0-0	0	7	.174	.174	.217	12	-3	0-0	1.000	-0	90	114	1b5,C2	81	-0.3
1967	Was A	1	1	0	0	0	0	0	0	0-0	0	1	.000	.000	.000	-99	0	0-0	ø	0	—	—	/H	0	0.0
Total	7	332	1014	114	252	44	5	40	123	92-11	17	191	.249	.319	.420	106	9	3-3	.982	-9	89	93	C280,1b18	81	1.2

Orsulak, Joe Joseph Michael; B5.31.1962 Glen Ridge NJ; BL/TL/6´1˝/(185–210); [PitN80 6/153]; d9.1; [DL 1987 Pit N 46]

YEAR	TM LG	G	AB	R	H	2B	3B	HR	RBI	BB-IB	HP	SO	AVG	OBP	SLG	AOPS	ABR	SB-CS	FA	FR	RNG	THR	GAMES AT POSITION	DL	BFW
1983	Pit N	7	11	0	2	0	0	0	1	0-0	0	2	.182	.167	.182	1	-2	0-1	1.000	1	37	1952	O4C	0	-0.1
1984	Pit N	32	67	12	17	1	2	0	3	1-0	1	7	.254	.271	.328	69	-3	3-1	1.000	1	112	98	O25(7/12/5)	0	-0.2
1985	Pit N	121	397	54	119	14	6	0	21	26-3	1	27	.300	.342	.365	99	-1	24-11	.976	4	103	157	O115(41/72/16)	15	0.2
1986	Pit N	138	401	60	100	19	6	2	19	28-2	1	38	.249	.299	.342	75	-15	24-11	.981	2	97	**159**	O120(9/46/73)	0	-1.6
1988	Bal A	125	379	48	109	21	3	8	27	23-2	3	30	.288	.331	.422	113	6	9-8	.979	4	108	105	O117(36/14/76)	0	0.6

YEAR	TM LG	G	AB	R	H	2B	3B	HR	RBI	BB-IB	HP	SO	AVG	OBP	SLG	AOPS	ABR	SB-CS	FA	FR	RNG	THR	GAMES AT POSITION	DL	BFW
1989	Bal A	123	390	59	111	22	5	7	55	41-6	2	35	.285	.351	.421	121	11	5-3	.985	6	109	124	O109(20/0/91),D5	0	1.4
1990	Bal A	124	413	49	111	14	3	11	57	46-9	1	48	.269	.343	.397	109	5	6-8	.989	9	**124**	68	O109(30/0/80),D5	0	0.9
1991	Bal A	143	486	57	135	22	1	5	43	28-1	4	45	.278	.321	.358	91	-6	6-2	.997	17	108	**286**	O132(85/1/68),D2	0	0.8
1992	Bal A	117	391	45	113	18	3	4	39	28-5	4	34	.289	.342	.381	99	0	5-4	.983	2	102	122	O110(14/0/98)/D	16	-0.2
1993	NY N	134	409	59	116	15	4	8	35	28-1	2	25	.284	.331	.399	96	-3	5-4	.978	1	99	132	O114(66/40/23),1b4	0	-0.5
1994	NY N	96	292	39	76	3	0	8	42	16-2	3	21	.260	.299	.353	72	-13	4-2	.979	-4	81	146	O90(18/13/63),1b6	0	-2.0
1995	NY N	108	290	41	82	19	2	1	37	19-2	1	35	.283	.323	.372	87	-5	1-3	.965	-4	88	69	O86(56/0/31)/1	0	-1.3
1996	Fla N	120	217	23	48	6	1	2	19	16-1	0	38	.221	.274	.286	49	-16	1-1	.956	3	99	255	O59(30/14/19),1b2	0	-1.5
1997	Mon N	106	150	13	34	12	1	1	7	18-0	0	17	.227	.310	.340	71	-6	0-1	1.000	-1	80	156	O63(37/0/26),1b15/D	0	-0.9
Total	14	1494	4293	559	1173	186	37	57	405	318-34	23	402	.273	.324	.374	93	-48	93-60	.982	41	102	150	O1253(449/216/669),1b28,D14	77	-4.4
ORTA, JORGE	Jorge (Nunez); B11.26.1950 Mazatlan, Sinaloa, Mexico; BL/TR/5´10˝/(165–175); d4.15; OF(96/3/246)																								
1972	Chi A	51	124	20	25	3	1	3	11	6-0	1	37	.202	.244	.315	64	-6	3-3	.958	0	86	147	S18,2b14,3b9	0	-0.4
1973	Chi A	128	425	46	113	9	10	6	40	37-3	1	87	.266	.323	.376	94	-5	8-8	.969	-23	91	85	2b122/S	0	-2.1
1974	Chi A	139	525	73	166	31	2	10	67	40-1	3	88	.316	.365	.440	128	20	9-5	.971	-4	100	99	2b123,D10,S3	0	2.4
1975	Chi A✷	140	542	64	165	26	10	11	83	48-7	4	67	.304	.363	.450	128	19	16-9	.978	-3	99	94	2b135,D2	0	2.6
1976	Chi A	158	636	74	174	29	8	14	72	38-2	5	77	.274	.316	.410	112	7	24-8	.971	0	100	164	O77(76/0/2),3b49,D31	0	0.5
1977	Chi A	144	564	71	159	27	8	11	84	46-3	2	49	.282	.334	.417	104	3	4-4	.970	-40	80	67	2b139	0	-3.0
1978	Chi A	117	420	45	115	19	2	13	53	42-3	4	39	.274	.340	.421	113	8	1-2	.984	-12	87	81	2b114,D2	0	0.1
1979	Chi A	113	325	49	85	18	3	11	46	44-2	1	33	.262	.348	.437	111	6	1-5	.978	-11	85	72	D62,2b41	0	-0.7
1980	Cle A☆	129	481	78	140	18	3	10	64	71-2	2	44	.291	.379	.403	115	13	6-5	.982	9	118	116	O120(0/2/118),D7	0	1.5
1981	Cle A	88	338	50	92	14	3	5	34	21-3	1	43	.272	.312	.376	99	-1	4-3	.994	1	88	181	O86(0/1/86)	0	-0.5
1982	LA N	86	115	13	25	5	0	2	8	12-3	1	13	.217	.295	.313	73	-4	0-1	.947	2	135	102	O17(1/0/16)	0	-0.4
1983	Tor A	103	245	30	58	6	3	10	38	19-0	0	29	.237	.287	.408	85	-6	1-2	1.000	0	88	148	D70,O17(5/0/12)	0	-0.9
1984	†KC A	122	403	50	120	23	7	9	50	28-8	2	39	.298	.343	.457	119	10	0-1	.980	-3	91	0	D83,O26(14/0/12)/2	0	0.3
1985	†KC A	110	300	32	80	21	1	4	45	22-5	2	28	.267	.317	.383	91	-3	2-1	ø	0	0	0	D85	0	-0.6
1986	KC A	106	336	35	93	14	2	9	46	23-3	0	34	.277	.321	.411	96	-3	0-3	ø	0	0	0	D87	0	-0.6
1987	KC A	21	50	3	9	4	0	2	4	3-1	0	8	.180	.226	.380	55	-3	0-0	ø	0	0	0	D12	14	-0.4
Total	16	1755	5829	733	1619	267	63	130	745	500-46	29	715	.278	.334	.412	107	55	79-60	.974	-85	91	85	2b689,D451,O343R,3b58,S22	14	-2.2
ORTEGA, BILL	William (Bobadilla); B7.24.1975 Havana, Cuba; BR/TR/6´4˝/205; d9.7																								
2001	StL N	5	5	0	1	0	0	0	0	0-0	0	1	.200	.200	.200	4	-1	0-0	ø	0	—	—	/H	0	-0.1
ORTENZIO, FRANK	Frank Joseph; B2.24.1951 Fresno CA; BR/TR/6´2˝/205; [KCA69 47/956]; d9.9																								
1973	KC A	9	25	1	7	2	0	1	6	2-0	0	6	.280	.333	.480	118	1	0-0	.983	1	161	73	1b7/D	0	0.1
ORTH, AL	Albert Lewis "Smiling Al","The Curveless Wonder"; B9.5.1872 Tipton IN; D10.8.1948 Lynchburg VA; BL/TR/6´0˝/200; d8.15; U6; Col DePauw; ▲																								
1895	Phi N	11	45	8	16	4	0	1	13	1	0	6	.356	.370	.511	125	4	0	.842	-2	70	0	P11	—	0.0
1896	Phi N	25	82	12	21	3	3	1	13	3	0	11	.256	.282	.402	80	3	2	.901	1	111	109	P25	—	0.0
1897	Phi N	53	152	26	50	7	4	1	17	3	0	—	.329	.342	.447	110	1	5	.929	0	107	46	P36,O6(3/3/0)	—	0.0
1898	Phi N	39	123	17	36	6	4	1	14	3	0	—	.293	.310	.431	117	1	1	.959	0	100	49	P32/rf	—	0.0
1899	Phi N	22	62	5	13	3	1	1	5	1	0	—	.210	.222	.339	55	-4	2	.793	-4	52	0	P21/lf	—	-0.2
1900	Phi N	39	129	6	40	4	1	1	21	2	1	—	.310	.326	.380	95	-1	2	.943	1	103	156	P33,O3C	—	0.0
1901	Phi N	41	128	14	36	6	0	1	15	3	1	—	.281	.303	.352	88	-2	3	.945	2	116	102	P35,O4C	—	0.1
1902	Was A	56	175	20	38	3	2	2	10	9	0	—	.217	.255	.291	51	-12	2	.923	0	100	86	P38,O13(1/4/8)/1S	—	-0.3
1903	Was A	55	162	19	49	9	7	0	11	4	1	—	.302	.323	.444	126	4	3	.920	-2	102	0	P36,S7,O4(2/0/2),1b2	—	-0.1
1904	Was A	31	102	7	22	3	1	0	11	1	2	—	.216	.238	.265	60	-5	2	.816	-2	50	0	O18(12/6/0),P10	—	-0.8
	NY A	24	64	6	19	1	1	0	7	0	1	—	.297	.308	.344	101	0	2	.968	0	107	82	P20,O2(0/1/1)	—	0.0
	Year	55	166	13	41	4	2	0	18	1	3	—	.247	.265	.295	76	-5	4	.969	-2	106	53	P30,O20(12/7/1)	—	-0.8
1905	NY A	55	131	13	24	3	1	1	8	4	1	—	.183	.213	.244	40	-9	2	.940	-1	103	38	P40/1rf	—	-0.1
1906	NY A	47	135	12	37	2	2	1	17	6	0	—	.274	.305	.341	93	-2	2	.934	-1	99	38	P45/rf	—	0.0
1907	NY A	44	105	11	34	6	0	1	13	4	1	—	.324	.355	.410	133	4	1	.920	2	122	41	P36/lf	—	0.1
1908	NY A	38	69	4	20	1	2	0	4	2	0	—	.290	.310	.362	117	5	0	.980	-1	99	154	P21	—	0.0
1909	NY A	22	34	3	9	0	1	0	5	5	0	—	.265	.359	.324	115	1	1	1.000	-1	92	0	2b6/P	—	-0.1
Total	15	602	1698	183	464	61	30	12	184	51	8	17	.273	.298	.366	91	-12	30	.932	-8	102	63	P440,O55(20/21/14),S8,2b6,1b4	—	-1.4
ORTIZ, JUNIOR	Adalberto Colon; B10.24.1959 Humacao, PR; BR/TR/5´11˝/(174–185); d9.20																								
1982	Pit N	7	15	1	3	1	0	0	0	1-0	0	3	.200	.250	.267	43	-1	0-0	1.000	-0	227	48	C7	0	-0.1
1983	Pit N	5	8	1	1	0	0	0	0	1-0	0	0	.125	.222	.125	-1	-1	0-0	1.000	1	0	0	C4	0	0.0
	NY N	68	185	10	47	5	0	0	12	3-0	1	34	.254	.270	.281	53	-12	1-0	.965	-6	70	95	C67	0	-1.6
	Year	73	193	11	48	5	0	0	12	4-0	1	34	.249	.268	.275	51	-13	1-0	.967	-5	67	91	C71	0	-1.6
1984	NY N	40	91	6	18	3	0	0	11	5-0	0	15	.198	.235	.231	33	-8	1-0	.980	-5	97	93	C32	0	-1.3
1985	Pit N	23	72	4	21	2	0	1	5	3-1	0	17	.292	.320	.361	91	-1	1-0	.985	-1	94	137	C23	0	-0.1
1986	Pit N	49	110	11	37	6	0	0	14	9-0	0	13	.336	.380	.391	112	2	0-1	.983	-3	99	81	C36	0	0.0
1987	Pit N	75	192	16	52	8	1	1	22	15-1	0	23	.271	.322	.339	75	-7	0-2	.975	-1	93	121	C72	0	-0.6
1988	Pit N	49	118	8	33	6	0	2	18	9-0	2	9	.280	.336	.381	108	1	1-4	.983	-3	92	41	C40	39	-0.1
1989	Pit N	91	230	16	50	6	1	1	22	20-4	2	20	.217	.282	.265	60	-12	2-2	.995	-12	69	96	C84	0	-2.2
1990	Min A	71	170	18	57	7	1	0	18	12-0	2	16	.335	.384	.388	110	3	0-4	1.000	-1	154	89	C68,D3	0	0.3
1991	†Min A	61	134	9	28	5	1	0	11	15-0	1	12	.209	.293	.261	52	-9	0-1	.995	-2	177	96	C60	15	-0.8
1992	Cle A	86	244	20	61	7	0	0	24	12-0	4	23	.250	.296	.279	63	-12	1-3	.989	-7	92	98	C86	0	-1.6
1993	Cle A	95	249	19	55	13	0	0	20	11-1	5	26	.221	.267	.273	46	-19	1-0	.990	4	112	127	C95	0	-1.0
1994	Tex A	29	76	3	21	2	0	0	9	5-0	1	11	.276	.329	.303	64	-4	0-1	.992	-2	145	153	C28	0	-0.4
Total	13	749	1894	142	484	71	4	5	186	121-7	18	222	.256	.305	.305	69	-80	8-18	.986	-38	105	101	C702,D3	54	-9.5
ORTIZ, DAVID	David Americo (Arias) "Big Papi"; B11.18.1975 Santo Domingo, D.R.; BL/TL/6´4˝/(190–230); d9.2																								
1997	Min A	15	49	10	16	3	0	1	6	2-0	0	19	.327	.353	.449	106	0	0-0	.989	1	155	119	1b11/D	0	0.1
1998	Min A	86	278	47	77	20	0	9	46	39-3	5	72	.277	.371	.446	110	6	1-0	.989	-0	102	92	1b70,D10	60	-0.1
1999	Min A	10	20	1	0	0	0	0	0	5-0	0	12	.000	.200	.000	-41	-4	0-0	1.000	-0	0	204	/1D	0	-0.4
2000	Min A	130	415	59	117	36	1	10	63	57-2	0	81	.282	.364	.446	98	1	1-0	.996	-1	82	78	D88,1b27	0	-0.6
2001	Min A	89	303	46	71	17	1	18	48	40-8	1	68	.234	.324	.475	102	1	1-0	1.000	-1	49	40	D80,1b8	77	-0.5
2002	†Min A	125	412	52	112	32	1	20	75	43-0	3	87	.272	.339	.500	117	10	1-2	.990	-1	80	89	D95,1b15	23	0.3
2003	†Bos A	128	448	79	129	39	2	31	101	58-8	1	83	.288	.369	.592	142	28	0-0	.992	-0	96	55	D74,1b45	0	1.9
2004	†Bos A★	150	582	94	175	47	3	41	139	75-8	4	133	.301	.380	.603	143	38	0-0	.986	-0	102	99	D115,1b34	0	2.7
2005	†Bos A★	159	601	119	180	40	1	47	**148**	102-9	1	124	.300	.397	.604	156	51	1-0	.976	2	190	100	D148,1b10	0	4.2
2006	Bos A★	151	558	115	160	29	2	**54**	**137**	**119**-23	4	117	.287	.413	.636	163	56	1-0	.971	0	125	114	D138,1b10	0	4.5
Total	10	1043	3666	622	1037	263	11	231	763	540-61	19	796	.283	.374	.550	133	187	6-2	.989	0	102	85	D754,1b231	160	12.1
ORTIZ, HECTOR	Hector (Montanez); B10.14.1969 Rio Piedras, PR; BR/TR/6´0˝/205; [LAN88 35/894]; d9.14; Col Ranger (TX) JC																								
1998	KC A	4	4	1	0	0	0	0	0	0-0	0	0	.000	.000	.000	-96	-1	0-0	1.000	-1	0	0	C3/1	0	-0.2
2000	KC A	26	88	15	34	6	0	0	5	8-1	1	8	.386	.443	.455	121	4	0-0	.993	-2	85	107	C26	0	0.3
2001	KC A	56	154	12	38	6	1	0	11	9-0	1	24	.247	.293	.299	51	-11	1-3	.990	6	126	121	C55/D	0	-0.2
2002	Tex A	7	14	1	3	1	0	1	2	1-0	0	1	.214	.267	.500	95	0	0-0	.957	-2	0	0	C7	0	-0.2
Total	4	93	260	29	75	13	1	1	18	18-1	2	33	.288	.339	.358	75	-8	1-3	.990	1	103	108	C91/D1	0	-0.3
ORTIZ, JAVIER	Javier Victor; B1.22.1963 Boston MA; BR/TR/6´4˝/220; [TexA83*1/4]; d6.15; Col Florida																								
1990	Hou N	30	77	7	21	5	1	1	10	12-0	0	11	.273	.367	.403	116	2	1-1	.978	-1	98	65	O25(20/1/9)	69	0.1
1991	Hou N	47	83	7	23	4	1	1	5	14-0	0	14	.277	.381	.386	123	3	0-0	1.000	-0	77	177	O24(15/0/11)	0	0.2
Total	2	77	160	14	44	9	2	2	15	26-0	0	25	.275	.374	.394	119	5	1-1	.987	-1	88	116	O49(35/1/20)	69	0.3
ORTIZ, JOSE	Jose Daniel (Santos); B6.13.1977 Santo Domingo, D.R.; BR/TR/5´9˝/(177–182); d9.15																								
2000	Oak A	7	11	4	2	0	0	0	1	2-0	0	3	.182	.308	.182	29	-1	0-0	.857	-1	70	71	2b3,D4	0	-0.2
2001	Oak A	11	42	4	7	0	0	0	3	3-0	0	5	.167	.217	.167	5	-6	1-0	.951	-2	84	124	2b10/D	31	-0.7
	Col N	53	204	38	52	8	1	13	35	14-0	4	36	.255	.314	.495	87	-4	3-1	.965	1	111	97	2b51	0	-0.1
2002	Col N	65	192	22	48	7	1	1	12	16-0	3	30	.250	.315	.313	59	-11	2-0	.987	-5	100	70	2b53/3	77	-1.3
Total	3	136	449	68	109	15	2	14	51	35-0	7	74	.243	.305	.379	68	-22	6-1	.973	-7	103	87	2b117,D5/3	108	-2.3

YEAR	TM LG	G	AB	R	H	2B	3B	HR	RBI	BB-IB	HP	SO	AVG	OBP	SLG	AOPS	ABR	SB-CS	FA	FR	RNG	THR	GAMES AT POSITION	DL	BFW
ORTIZ, JOSE	Jose Luis (Irizarry); B6.25.1947 Ponce, PR; BR/TR/5´9.5˝/(155–165); d9.4																								
1969	Chi A	16	11	0	3	1	0	0	2	1-1	0	0	.273	.333	.364	90	0	0-0	1.000	0	58	420	O8(2/5/2)	0	0.0
1970	Chi A	15	24	4	8	1	0	0	1	2-0	1	2	.333	.407	.375	113	1	1-0	1.000	1	66	706	O8(1/5/2)	0	0.2
1971	Chi N	36	88	10	26	7	1	0	3	4-0	3	10	.295	.347	.398	96	0	2-2	1.000	-2	88	72	O30(0/29/1)	0	-0.3
Total	3	67	123	14	37	9	1	0	6	7-1	4	12	.301	.358	.390	99	1	3-2	1.000	-0	81	222	O46(3/39/5)	0	-0.1
ORTIZ, LUIS	Luis Alberto (Galarza); B5.25.1970 Santo Domingo, D.R.; BR/TR/6´0˝/195; [BosA91 8/226]; d8.31; Col Union (TN)																								
1993	Bos A	9	12	0	3	0	0	0	1	0-0	0	2	.250	.250	.250	33	-1	0-0	1.000	-1	50	272	3b5,D3	0	-0.2
1994	Bos A	7	18	3	3	2	0	0	6	1-0	0	5	.167	.182	.278	23	-2	0-0	ø	0	—	—	D6	0	-0.2
1995	Tex A	41	108	10	25	5	2	1	18	6-0	0	18	.231	.270	.343	57	-7	0-1	.867	-8	83	40	3b35,D3	0	-1.4
1996	Tex A	3	7	1	2	0	1	1	1	0-0	0	1	.286	.286	1.000	194	1	0-0	ø	0	—	—	/D	0	0.1
Total	4	60	145	14	33	7	3	2	26	7-0	0	26	.228	.256	.359	58	-9	0-1	.875	-8	81	57	3b40,D13	0	-1.7
ORTIZ, ROBERTO	Roberto Gonzalo (Nunez); B6.30.1915 Camaguey, Cuba; D9.15.1971 Miami FL; BR/TR/6´4˝/200; d9.6; b–Baby																								
1941	Was A	22	79	10	26	1	2	1	17	3	0	10	.329	.354	.430	112	1	0-1	.860	-0	97	178	O21R	0	-0.1
1942	Was A	20	42	4	7	1	3	1	4	5	1	11	.167	.271	.405	89	-1	0-0	.941	0	97	174	O9(1/0/8)	0	-0.2
1943	Was A	1	4	0	1	0	0	0	0	0	0	0	.250	.250	.250	48	0	0-1	1.000	0	126	0	/rf	0	-0.1
1944	Was A	85	316	36	80	11	4	5	35	19	**8**	47	.253	.312	.361	96	-3	4-1	.949	-2	106	37	O80(10/0/71)	0	-1.0
1949	Was A	40	129	12	36	3	0	1	11	9	0	12	.279	.326	.326	74	-5	0-0	.946	1	90	204	O32(4/0/28)	0	-0.5
1950	Was A	39	75	4	17	2	1	0	8	7	1	12	.227	.301	.280	52	-6	0-0	1.000	-0	86	170	O19R	0	-0.6
	Phi A	6	14	1	1	0	0	0	3	0	0	3	.071	.071	.071	-65	-4	0-0	1.000	-0	98	0	O3(1/0/3)	0	-0.4
	Year	45	89	5	18	2	1	0	11	7	1	15	.202	.268	.247	34	-9	0-0	1.000	-0	88	144	O22(1/0/22)	0	-1.0
Total	6	213	659	67	168	18	10	8	78	43	10	95	.255	.310	.349	84	-18	4-3	.942	-2	100	103	O165(16/0/151)	0	-2.9
ORTMEIER, DAN	Daniel D.; B5.11.1981 Chattanooga TN; BB/TL/6´4˝/(215–220); [SFN02 3/97]; d9.5; Col Texas–Arlington																								
2005	SF N	15	22	1	3	0	0	0	1	3-0	1	5	.136	.269	.136	11	-3	1-0	1.000	0	120	0	O7R	0	-0.3
2006	SF N	9	12	0	3	1	0	0	2	0-0	0	4	.250	.250	.333	47	-1	0-0	1.000	0	146	0	O3R,D2	0	-0.1
Total	2	24	34	1	6	1	0	0	3	3-0	1	9	.176	.263	.206	24	-4	1-0	1.000	0	125	0	O10R,D2	0	-0.4
ORTON, JOHN	John Andrew; B12.8.1965 Santa Cruz CA; BR/TR/6´1˝/(192–195); [CalA87 1/25]; d8.20; Col Cal Poly–San Luis Obispo																								
1989	Cal A	16	39	4	7	1	0	0	4	2-0	0	17	.179	.220	.205	21	-4	0-0	.988	2	135	116	C16	0	-0.2
1990	Cal A	31	84	8	16	5	0	1	6	5-0	1	31	.190	.244	.286	49	-6	0-1	.987	-1	113	91	C31	0	-0.6
1991	Cal A	29	69	7	14	4	0	0	3	10-0	1	17	.203	.313	.261	60	-3	0-1	.994	6	93	144	C28/D	0	0.3
1992	Cal A	43	114	11	25	3	0	2	12	7-0	2	32	.219	.276	.298	60	-6	1-1	.981	7	128	130	C43	93	0.3
1993	Cal A	37	95	5	18	5	0	1	4	7-0	1	24	.189	.252	.274	40	-8	1-2	.980	6	116	82	C35/lf	84	-0.1
Total	5	156	401	35	80	18	0	4	29	31-0	5	121	.200	.265	.274	49	-27	2-5	.985	19	117	112	C153/lfD	177	-0.3
ORWOLL, OSSIE	Oswald Christian; B11.17.1900 Portland OR; D5.8.1967 Decorah IA; BL/TL/6´0˝/174; d4.13; Col Luther; ▲																								
1928	Phi A	64	170	28	52	13	2	0	22	16	0	24	.306	.366	.406	100	0	3-1	.983	-1	96	131	1b34,P27	—	-0.2
1929	Phi A	30	51	6	13	2	1	0	6	2	0	11	.255	.283	.333	56	-4	0-0	1.000	-1	93	328	P12,O9(1/8/0)	—	-0.3
Total	2	94	221	34	65	15	3	0	28	18	0	35	.294	.347	.389	90	-4	3-1	.970	-2	85	72	P39,1b34,O9(1/8/0)	—	-0.5
OSBORN, FRED	Wilferd Pearl "Ossie"; B11.28.1883 Nevada OH; D9.2.1954 Upper Sandusky OH; BL/TR/5´9˝/178; d6.8																								
1907	Phi N	56	163	22	45	2	3	0	9	3	2	—	.276	.298	.325	97	-2	4	1.000	-2	48	0	O36(8/26/1)/1	—	-0.6
1908	Phi N	152	555	62	148	19	12	2	44	30	1	—	.267	.305	.355	107	2	16	.969	-5	71	67	O152(0/146/6)	—	-1.1
1909	Phi N	58	189	14	35	4	1	0	19	12	1	—	.185	.238	.217	41	-13	6	.979	7	175	172	O54C	—	-1.0
Total	3	266	907	98	228	25	16	2	72	45	4	—	.251	.290	.321	91	-13	26	.975	1	93	84	O242(8/226/7)/1	—	-2.7
OSBORNE, FRED	Frederick W.; B Alberta, Can; BL/TL; d7.14; ▲																								
1890	Pit N	41	168	24	40	8	3	1	14	6	1	18	.238	.269	.339	87	-4	0	.828	-1	125	0	O35(28/1/6),P8	—	-0.4
OSBORNE, BOBO	Lawrence Sidney; B10.12.1935 Chattahoochee GA; BL/TR/6´1˝/205; d6.27; f–Tiny																								
1957	Det A	11	27	4	4	1	0	0	1	3-0	0	7	.148	.233	.185	15	-3	0-0	1.000	-0	104	0	O5R,1b4	0	-0.4
1958	Det A	2	2	0	0	0	0	0	0	0-0	0	0	.000	.000	.000	-93	-1	0-0	ø	0	—	—	/H	0	-0.1
1959	Det A	86	209	27	40	7	1	3	21	16-0	2	41	.191	.254	.278	44	-16	1-0	.983	-1	96	101	1b56/rf	0	-2.0
1961	Det A	71	93	8	20	7	0	2	13	20-0	0	15	.215	.354	.355	88	-1	1-0	.957	-2	79	145	3b8,1b11	0	-0.3
1962	Det A	64	74	12	17	1	0	0	7	16-0	1	25	.230	.374	.243	68	-2	0-0	.857	-3	83	0	3b13,1b7/C	0	-0.5
1963	Was A	125	358	42	76	14	1	12	44	49-7	3	83	.212	.308	.358	87	-5	0-0	.988	-5	103	102	1b81,3b16	0	-1.6
Total	6	359	763	93	157	30	2	17	86	104-7	6	171	.206	.304	.317	71	-28	2-0	.987	-11	98	97	1b159,3b37,O6R/C	0	-4.9
OSIK, KEITH	Keith Richard; B10.22.1968 Port Jefferson NY; BR/TR/6´0˝/(185–215); [PitN90 24/641]; d4.5; Col Louisiana St.; OF(3/0/1)																								
1996	Pit N	48	140	18	41	14	1	1	14	14-1	1	22	.293	.361	.429	104	1	1-0	.977	-5	69	127	C41,3b2,O2L	28	0.0
1997	Pit N	49	105	10	27	9	1	0	7	9-1	1	21	.257	.322	.362	77	-3	0-1	.989	-1	133	112	C32,2b4/13	0	-0.3
1998	Pit N	39	98	8	21	4	0	0	7	13-2	2	16	.214	.316	.255	53	-6	1-2	1.000	3	109	113	C26,3b7	0	-0.2
1999	Pit N	66	167	12	31	3	1	2	13	11-0	1	30	.186	.239	.251	24	-20	0-0	.997	2	121	89	C50/P	22	-1.5
2000	Pit N	46	123	11	36	6	1	4	22	14-0	5	11	.293	.387	.455	112	3	3-0	.992	-5	83	73	C26,3b12,1b5/PD	0	-0.1
2001	Pit N	56	120	9	25	4	0	2	13	13-0	3	24	.208	.299	.292	53	-8	1-0	.995	-0	83	101	C39,1b5,3b3,2b2/rf	15	-0.6
2002	Pit N	55	100	6	16	3	0	2	11	6-0	1	25	.160	.211	.250	21	-12	0-0	.993	6	75	77	C27,3b4,1b3/2lf	0	-0.5
2003	Mil N	80	241	22	60	12	0	2	21	31-0	3	44	.249	.342	.324	75	-8	0-1	.991	1	90	113	C78	0	-0.2
2004	Bal A	11	25	0	2	0	0	0	0	0-0	0	7	.080	.080	.080	-59	-6	0-0	1.000	-0	113	62	C11	0	-0.6
2005	Was N	6	4	0	0	0	0	0	0	0-0	0	2	.000	.000	.000	-99	-1	0-0	1.000	-0	16	0	C5	0	-0.2
Total	10	456	1123	96	259	55	4	13	108	111-4	17	202	.231	.308	.321	63	-60	6-4	.991	-1	95	103	C335,3b29,1b14,2b7,O4L,P2/D	65	-4.2
OSTDIEK, HARRY	Henry Girard; B4.12.1881 Ottumwa IA; D5.6.1956 Minneapolis MN; BR/TR/5´11˝/185; d9.10																								
1904	Cle A	7	18	1	3	0	1	0	3	3	1	—	.167	.318	.278	90	0	1	.946	-0	*110*	*91*	C7	—	0.0
1908	Bos A	1	3	0	0	0	0	0	0	0	0	—	.000	.000	.000	-97	-1	0	.889	-0	*123*	*98*	/C	—	-0.1
Total	2	8	21	1	3	0	1	0	3	3	1	—	.143	.280	.238	65	-1	1	.935	-0	*112*	92	C8	—	-0.1
OSTEEN, CHAMP	James Champlin; B2.24.1877 Hendersonville NC; D12.14.1962 Greenville SC; BL/TR/5´8˝/150; d9.18; Col Erskine																								
1903	Was A	10	40	4	8	0	2	0	4	2	1	—	.200	.256	.300	65	-2	0	.938	1	96	102	S10	—	-0.1
1904	NY A	28	107	15	21	1	4	2	9	1	2	—	.196	.218	.336	71	-4	0	.930	-0	114	71	3b17,S8,1b4	—	-0.5
1908	StL N	29	112	2	22	4	0	0	11	0	1	—	.196	.204	.232	41	-8	0	.847	-4	80	114	S17,3b12	—	-1.4
1909	StL N	16	45	6	9	1	0	0	7	7	0	—	.200	.308	.222	69	-1	1	.879	-4	101	0	S16	—	-0.6
Total	4	83	304	27	60	6	6	2	31	10	4	—	.197	.233	.276	60	-15	1	.890	-8	91	72	S51,3b29,1b4	—	-2.6
OSTERGARD, RED	Roy Lund; B5.16.1896 Denmark WI; D1.13.1977 Hemet CA; BR/TR/5´10.5˝/175; d6.14; Col Southwestern (TX)																								
1921	Chi A	12	11	2	4	0	0	0	0	0	0	2	.364	.364	.364	87	0	0-0	ø	0	—	—	/H	—	0.0
OSTERHOUT, CHARLIE	Charles H.; B6.1856 Syracuse NY; D5.21.1933 Syracuse NY; TR; d6.23																								
1879	Syr N	2	8	0	0	0	0	0	0	0	—	0	.000	.000	.000	-99	-2	—	1.000	-0	0	0	/cfC	—	-0.2
OSTROSSER, BRIAN	Brian Leonard; B6.17.1949 Hamilton ON, Can.; BL/TR/6´0˝/180; d8.5																								
1973	NY N	4	5	0	0	0	0	0	0	0-0	0	2	.000	.000	.000	-99	-1	0-0	1.000	-1	71	0	S4	0	-0.2
OSTROWSKI, JOHNNY	John Thaddeus; B10.17.1917 Chicago IL; D11.13.1992 Chicago IL; BR/TR/5´10.5˝/170; d9.24																								
1943	Chi N	10	29	2	6	0	1	0	3	3	1	8	.207	.303	.276	69	-1	0	1.000	-1	89	0	O5L,3b4	0	-0.3
1944	Chi N	8	13	2	2	1	0	0	2	1	0	4	.154	.214	.231	25	-1	0	.500	-1	31	0	O2L	0	-0.2
1945	Chi N	7	10	4	3	2	0	0	1	0	0	0	.300	.300	.500	123	0	0	.750	-1	63	0	3b4	0	0.0
1946	Chi N	64	160	20	34	4	2	3	12	20	0	31	.213	.300	.319	77	-5	1	.934	0	111	89	3b50/2	0	-0.5
1948	Bos A	1	1	0	0	0	0	0	0	0	0	1	.000	.000	.000	-95	0	0-0	ø	0	—	—	/H	0	0.0
1949	Chi A	49	158	19	42	9	4	5	31	15	1	41	.266	.333	.468	115	2	4-3	.944	-1	100	106	O41(40/0/3),3b8	0	-0.2
1950	Chi A	21	45	9	10	1	1	2	2	9	1	8	.222	.364	.422	104	0	0-0	1.000	0	106	106	O14(6/1/8)	0	0.0
	Was A	55	141	16	32	2	1	4	23	20	1	31	.227	.327	.340	75	-6	2-0	.947	1	111	92	O45(34/7/4)	0	-0.6
	Chi A	1	4	1	2	1	0	0	0	0	0	1	.500	.500	.750	223	1	0-0	1.000	-0	106	106	/cf	0	0.0
	Year	77	190	26	44	4	2	6	25	29	2	40	.232	.339	.368	85	-5	2-0	.958	2	109	94	O60(40/9/12)	0	-0.6
Total	7	216	561	73	131	20	9	14	74	68	4	125	.234	.321	.376	89	-10	7-3	.950	-2	103	93	O108(87/9/15),3b66/2	0	-1.8

YEAR	TM LG	G	AB	R	H	2B	3B	HR	RBI	BB-IB	HP	SO	AVG	OBP	SLG	AOPS	ABR	SB-CS	FA	FR	RNG	THR	GAMES AT POSITION	DL	BFW
OTANEZ, WILLIS	Willis Alexander; B4.19.1973 Las Vega Baja, D.R.; BR/TR/6´1˝/(200–213); d8.25																								
1998	Bal A	3	5	0	1	0	0	0	0	0-0	0	2	.200	.200	.200	5	-1	0-0	1.000	-0	56	0	O2R	31	-0.1
1999	Bal A	29	80	7	17	3	0	2	11	6-0	1	16	.213	.273	.325	54	-6	0-0	.917	-3	80	62	3b22,1b5,D3	0	-0.8
	Tor A	42	127	21	32	8	0	5	13	9-0	1	30	.252	.307	.433	84	-3	0-0	.953	-3	71	191	3b24,1b13,D2	21	-0.6
	Year	71	207	28	49	11	0	7	24	15-0	2	46	.237	.293	.391	73	-9	0-0	.934	-6	76	125	3b46,1b18,D5	0	-1.4
Total	2	74	212	28	50	11	0	7	24	15-0	2	48	.236	.291	.387	72	-10	0-0	.934	-6	76	125	3b46,1b18,D5,O2R	52	-1.5
OTERO, REGGIE	Regino Jose (Gomez); B9.7.1915 Havana, Cuba; D10.21.1988 Hialeah FL; BL/TR/6´0˝/165; d9.2; C8																								
1945	Chi N	14	23	1	9	0	0	0	5	2	0	2	.391	.440	.391	135	1	0	.967	-0	110	116	1b8	0	0.1
OTERO, RICKY	Ricardo (Figueroa); B4.15.1972 Vega Baja, PR; BB/TR/5´7˝/(150–155); [NYN90 45/1173]; d4.26																								
1995	NY N	35	51	5	7	2	0	0	1	3-0	0	10	.137	.185	.176	-4	-8	2-1	1.000	2	130	145	O23(15/9/0)	0	-0.6
1996	Phi N	104	411	54	112	11	7	2	32	34-0	2	30	.273	.330	.348	79	-13	16-10	.985	7	111	165	O100C	0	-0.5
1997	Phi N	50	151	20	38	6	2	0	3	19-0	1	15	.252	.339	.318	74	-5	0-3	1.000	6	124	247	O42(1/40/1)	0	-0.1
Total	3	189	613	79	157	19	9	2	36	56-0	3	55	.256	.320	.326	71	-26	18-14	.990	14	116	184	O165(16/149/1)	0	-1.2
OTIS, AMOS	Amos Joseph; B4.26.1947 Mobile AL; BR/TR/5´11˝/(165–186); [BosA65 5/95]; d9.6; C4																								
1967	NY N	19	59	6	13	2	0	0	1	5-0	1	13	.220	.292	.254	59	-3	0-4	1.000	-1	66	214	O16(2/14/3)/3	0	-0.7
1969	NY N	48	93	6	14	3	1	0	4	6-1	0	27	.151	.202	.204	14	-11	1-0	1.000	1	104	233	O35(16/18/1),3b3	0	-1.1
1970	KC A★	159	620	91	176	**36**	9	11	58	68-3	1	67	.284	.353	.424	114	12	33-2	.990	0	98	141	O159C	0	1.5
1971	KC A★	147	555	80	167	26	4	15	79	40-2	2	74	.301	.345	.443	124	16	**52**-8	.990	8	112	109	O144C	0	3.1
1972	KC A✳	143	540	75	158	28	2	11	54	50-3	3	59	.293	.352	.413	129	20	28-12	.992	-2	103	66	O137C	0	1.8
1973	KC A★	148	583	89	175	21	4	26	93	63-5	1	47	.300	.368	.484	129	22	13-9	.986	-4	96	102	O135C,D14	0	1.4
1974	KC A	146	552	87	157	31	9	12	73	58-4	2	67	.284	.348	.438	120	15	18-5	.986	-2	104	73	O143C,D2	0	1.2
1975	KC A	132	470	87	116	26	6	9	46	66-1	4	48	.247	.342	.385	103	4	39-11	.988	-5	94	102	O130C	19	0.0
1976	†KC A★	153	592	93	165	**40**	2	18	86	55-7	5	100	.279	.341	.444	129	22	26-7	.992	-17	87	43	O152C	0	0.5
1977	†KC A	142	478	85	120	20	8	17	78	71-5	0	88	.251	.342	.433	110	7	23-7	.991	-7	91	103	O140C	0	0.2
1978	†KC A	141	486	74	145	30	7	22	96	66-7	4	54	.298	.380	.525	149	33	32-8	**.995**	2	103	103	O136C/D	0	3.9
1979	KC A	151	577	100	170	28	2	18	90	68-8	3	92	.295	.369	.444	116	15	30-5	**.992**	-4	93	110	O146C,D4	0	1.4
1980	†KC A	107	394	56	99	16	3	10	53	39-0	3	70	.251	.316	.383	91	-5	16-1	.988	-0	103	79	O105C	43	-0.3
1981	†KC A	99	372	49	100	22	3	9	57	31-1	2	59	.269	.321	.417	114	6	16-7	.993	4	109	94	O97(13/86/1)/D	0	1.1
1982	KC A	125	475	73	136	25	3	11	88	37-3	2	65	.286	.335	.421	107	4	9-5	.997	-8	92	61	O125C	0	-0.4
1983	KC A	98	356	35	93	16	3	4	41	27-3	0	63	.261	.313	.357	83	-8	5-2	.996	-1	97	90	O96(0/55/41)/D	0	-1.2
1984	Pit N	40	97	6	16	4	0	0	10	7-0	0	15	.165	.213	.206	21	-10	0-0	.964	3	103	248	O32L	48	-0.9
Total	17	1998	7299	1092	2020	374	66	193	1007	757-53	33	1008	.277	.343	.425	114	139	341-93	.991	-31	98	97	O1928(63/1825/46),D23,3b4	110	11.5
OTIS, BILL	Paul Franklin; B12.24.1889 Scituate MA; D12.15.1990 Duluth MN; BL/TR/5´10.5˝/150; d7.4; Col Williams																								
1912	NY A	4	17	1	1	0	0	0	2	3	0	—	.059	.200	.059	-24	-3	0	.917	0	97	147	O4C	—	-0.3
OTT, MEL	Melvin Thomas "Master Melvin"; B3.2.1909 Gretna LA; D11.21.1958 New Orleans LA; BL/TR/5´9˝/170; d4.27; M7; HF1951																								
1926	NY N	35	60	7	23	2	0	0	4	1	0	9	.383	.393	.417	120	2	1	.913	1	92	329	O10L	—	0.2
1927	NY N	82	163	23	46	7	3	1	19	13	0	9	.282	.335	.380	91	-2	2	.982	-3	79	75	O32(13/21/0)	—	-0.7
1928	NY N	124	435	69	140	26	4	18	77	52	2	36	.322	.397	.524	138	25	3	.970	-1	92	127	O115(5/1/108),2b5/3	—	1.5
1929	NY N	150	545	138	179	37	2	42	151	**113**	6	38	.328	.449	.635	166	61	6	.973	7	97	156	O149R/2	—	5.0
1930	NY N	148	521	122	182	34	5	25	119	103	2	35	.349	**.458**	.578	152	50	9	.969	4	99	126	O146R	—	3.7
1931	NY N	138	497	104	145	23	8	29	115	**80**	2	44	.292	.392	.545	**153**	38	10	.981	3	96	140	O137(0/71/66)	—	3.4
1932	NY N	**154**	566	119	180	30	8	**38**	123	**100**	4	39	.318	**.424**	.601	**175**	**64**	6	.984	-1	103	70	O154R	—	**5.2**
1933	†NY N	152	580	98	164	36	1	23	103	**75**	2	48	.283	.367	.467	139	32	1	.983	-8	89	89	O152(0/19/143)	—	1.6
1934	NY N★	**153**	582	119	190	29	10	**35**	**135**	85	3	43	.326	.415	.591	**170**	**59**	0	.974	-13	84	84	O153(0/16/137)	—	3.6
1935	NY N★	152	593	113	191	33	6	31	114	82	3	58	.322	.407	.555	159	51	7	**.990**	1	98	113	O137R,3b15	—	4.2
1936	†NY N★	150	534	120	175	28	6	**33**	135	111	5	41	.328	.448	**.588**	**179**	**65**	6	.985	-5	85	122	O148R	—	4.8
1937	†NY N★	151	545	99	160	28	2	**31**	95	**102**	3	69	.294	.408	.523	149	41	7	.939	-2	105	75	3b60,O91R	—	3.5
1938	NY N★	150	527	**116**	164	23	6	**36**	116	118	5	47	.311	**.442**	.583	**178**	**62**	2	.957	2	106	78	3b113,O37R	—	**6.4**
1939	NY N★	125	396	85	122	23	2	27	80	100	1	50	.308	**.449**	.581	173	47	2	.973	-7	91	68	O96R,3b20	—	3.4
1940	NY N★	151	536	89	155	27	3	19	79	100	6	50	.289	.407	.457	137	32	6	.982	-0	99	104	O111R,3b42	—	2.6
1941	NY N★	148	525	89	150	29	0	27	90	100	3	68	.286	.403	.495	149	38	5	.968	0	93	153	O145(1/0/144)	0	3.0
1942	NY N★	152	549	**118**	162	21	0	**30**	93	**109**	3	61	.295	.415	.497	**165**	**50**	6	.990	-4	91	110	O152R,M	0	3.9
1943	NY N★	125	380	65	89	12	2	18	47	95	3	48	.234	.391	.418	133	21	7	.975	-2	98	103	O111R/3M	0	1.3
1944	NY N★	120	399	91	115	16	4	26	82	90	3	47	.288	.423	.544	171	42	2	.986	-3	102	57	O103R,3b4,M	0	3.3
1945	NY N✳	135	451	73	139	23	0	21	79	71	**8**	41	.308	.411	.499	150	33	1	.983	-4	92	100	O118R,M	0	2.1
1946	NY N	31	68	2	5	1	0	1	4	8	0	15	.074	.171	.132	-13	-10	0	1.000	0	88	149	O16R,M	0	-1.2
1947	NY N	4	4	0	0	0	0	0	0	0	0	0	.000	.000	.000	-99	-1	0	ø	0	—	—	/HM	0	-0.1
Total	22	2730	9456	1859	2876	488	72	511	1860	1708	64	896	.304	.414	.533	155	800	89	.980	-34	94	111	O2313(29/128/2167),3b256,2b6	0	60.7
OTT, ED	Nathan Edward; B7.11.1951 Muncy PA; BL/TR/5´10˝/(190–196); [PitN70 23/548]; d6.10; C7; [DL 1982 Cal A 182, 1983 Cal A 182]																								
1974	Pit N	7	5	1	0	0	0	0	0	0-0	0	1	.000	.000	.000	-99	-1	0-0	1.000	0	216	0	O2R	0	-0.1
1975	Pit N	5	5	0	1	0	0	0	0	0-0	0	0	.200	.200	.200	11	-1	0-0	1.000	-0	0	0	C2	0	-0.1
1976	Pit N	27	39	2	12	2	0	0	5	3-1	0	5	.308	.349	.359	102	0	0-0	1.000	-0	139	187	C8	22	0.0
1977	Pit N	104	311	40	82	14	3	7	38	32-6	2	41	.264	.334	.395	92	-3	7-7	.982	4	144	90	C90	0	0.3
1978	Pit N	112	379	49	102	18	4	9	38	27-6	0	56	.269	.315	.409	97	-2	4-1	.975	-4	104	78	C97,O4L	0	-0.2
1979	†Pit N	117	403	49	110	20	2	7	51	26-8	0	62	.273	.314	.385	86	-8	0-1	.994	-0	109	78	C116	0	-0.4
1980	Pit N	120	392	35	102	14	0	8	41	33-8	0	47	.260	.317	.357	85	-8	1-6	.983	7	117	114	C117,O3L	0	0.2
1981	Cal A	75	258	20	56	8	1	2	22	17-1	1	42	.217	.266	.279	57	-14	2-1	.979	-2	93	123	C72	0	-1.4
Total	8	567	1792	196	465	76	10	33	195	138-30	3	254	.259	.311	.368	85	-37	14-16	.983	4	114	96	C502,O9(7/0/2)	386	-1.7
OTT, BILLY	William Joseph; B11.23.1940 New York NY; BB/TR/6´1˝/190; d9.4; Col St. Johns																								
1962	Chi N	12	28	3	4	0	0	1	2	2-0	0	10	.143	.200	.250	19	-3	0-0	1.000	0	87	200	O7R	0	-0.4
1964	Chi N	20	39	4	7	3	0	0	1	3-0	0	10	.179	.238	.256	38	-3	0-1	1.000	-1	85	0	O10R	0	-0.5
Total	2	32	67	7	11	3	0	1	3	5-0	0	20	.164	.222	.254	30	-6	0-1	1.000	-1	86	86	O17R	0	-0.9
OTTEN, JOHN	John G.; B8.1870 , Netherlands; D10.17.1905 Chicago IL; TR/?/175; d7.5																								
1895	StL N	26	87	8	21	0	0	0	8	5	0	8	.241	.283	.241	36	-8	2	.947	-5	*77*	*75*	C24,O2(1/1/0)	—	-0.9
OTTERSON, BILLY	William John; B5.4.1862 Pittsburgh PA; D9.21.1940 Pittsburgh PA; BR/TR/5´7˝/124; d9.4																								
1887	Bro AA	30	100	16	20	4	1	2	15	8	0	—	.200	.259	.320	60	-6	8	.859	3	108	147	S30	—	-0.1
OUELLETTE, PHIL	Philip Roland; B11.10.1961 Salem OR; BB/TR/6´0˝/190; d9.10; Col Citrus (CA) JC; [DL 1987 SF N 96]																								
1986	SF N	10	23	1	4	0	0	0	0	3-0	0	3	.174	.269	.174	26	-2	0-0	1.000	0	85	75	C9	0	-0.2
OULLIBER, JOHNNY	John Andrew; B2.24.1911 New Orleans LA; D12.26.1980 New Orleans LA; BR/TR/5´11˝/165; d7.25																								
1933	Cle A	22	75	9	20	1	0	0	3	4	1	5	.267	.313	.280	55	-5	0-0	1.000	-2	80	0	O18(12/0/6)	—	-0.8
OUTEN, CHINK	William Austin; B6.17.1905 Mt.Holly NC; D9.11.1961 Durham NC; BL/TR/6´0˝/200; d4.16; Col North Carolina St.																								
1933	Bro N	93	153	20	38	10	0	4	17	20	0	15	.248	.335	.392	112	3	1	.982	-6	*92*	*64*	C56	—	-0.1
OUTLAW, JIMMY	James Paulus; B1.20.1913 Orme TN; D4.9.2006 Jackson AL; BR/TR/5´8˝/168; d4.20; Col Auburn																								
1937	Cin N	49	165	18	45	7	3	0	11	3	1	31	.273	.290	.352	77	-6	2	.914	4	117	74	3b41	—	-0.1
1938	Cin N	4	0	1	0	0	0	0	0	0	0	0	ø	ø	ø	ø	0	0	ø	0	—	—	/R	—	0.0
1939	Bos N	65	133	15	35	2	0	0	5	10	0	14	.263	.315	.278	65	-7	1	.964	0	111	43	O39(15/22/2),3b2	—	-0.8
1943	Det A	20	67	8	18	1	0	1	6	8	0	4	.269	.347	.328	91	-1	0-0	1.000	-0	87	162	O16(4/3/9)	0	-0.2
1944	Det A	139	535	69	146	20	6	3	57	41	2	40	.273	.327	.350	88	-8	7-8	.964	-4	89	133	O137(71/6/60)	0	-2.3
1945	†Det A	132	446	56	121	16	5	0	34	45	0	33	.271	.338	.330	88	-6	6-7	.967	-2	87	143	O105(82/17/8),3b21	0	-1.6
1946	Det A	92	299	36	78	14	2	2	31	29	1	24	.261	.328	.341	82	-7	5-4	1.000	-5	87	189	O43(26/10/9),3b38	0	-1.5
1947	Det A	70	127	20	29	7	1	0	15	21	0	14	.228	.338	.299	76	-3	3-1	.983	-2	107	0	O37(21/3/13),3b9	0	-0.6
1948	Det A	74	198	33	56	12	0	0	25	31	1	15	.283	.383	.343	91	-1	0-1	.920	-0	101	101	3b47,O13(10/0/3)	0	-0.2

YEAR	TM LG	G	AB	R	H	2B	3B	HR	RBI	BB-IB	HP	SO	AVG	OBP	SLG	AOPS	ABR	SB-CS	FA	FR	RNG	THR	GAMES AT POSITION	DL	BFW
1949	Det A	5	4	1	1	0	0	0	0	0	0	1	.250	.250	.250	32	0	0-0	ø	0	—	—	/H	0	0.0
Total	10	650	1974	257	529	79	17	6	184	188	5	176	.268	.333	.334	85	-39	24-21	.972	-9	92	127	O390(229/61/104),3b158	0	-7.3
OVERBAY, LYLE	Lyle Stefan; B1.28.1977 Centralia WA; BL/TL/6´2˝/(215–235); [AriN99 18/538]; d9.19; Col Nevada–Reno																								
2001	Ari N	2	2	0	1	0	0	0	0	0-0	0	1	.500	.500	.500	150	0	0-0	ø	0	—	—	/H	0	0.0
2002	Ari N	10	10	0	1	0	0	0	1	0-0	0	5	.100	.100	.100	-43	-2	0-0	ø	0	—	—	/H	0	-0.3
2003	Ari N	86	254	23	70	20	0	4	28	35-7	2	67	.276	.365	.402	93	-1	1-0	.997	6	125	86	1b75	0	-0.1
2004	Mil N	159	579	83	174	**53**	1	16	87	81-9	2	128	.301	.385	.478	121	22	2-1	.992	3	108	90	1b158	0	1.1
2005	Mil N	158	537	80	148	34	1	19	72	78-8	2	98	.276	.367	.449	113	12	1-0	.992	5	111	86	1b154	0	0.4
2006	Tor A	157	581	82	181	46	1	22	92	55-7	2	96	.312	.372	.508	120	18	5-3	.994	6	116	103	1b145,D11	0	1.0
Total	6	572	1963	268	575	153	3	61	280	249-31	8	395	.293	.372	.467	114	49	9-4	.993	20	113	92	1b532,D11	0	2.1
OWEN, MICKEY	Arnold Malcolm; B4.4.1916 Nixa MO; D7.13.2005 Mount Vernon MO; BR/TR/5´10˝/190; d5.2; Mil 1945; C2																								
1937	StL N	80	234	17	54	4	2	0	20	15	0	13	.231	.277	.265	47	-18	1	.974	-2	*89*	*109*	C78	—	-1.5
1938	StL N	122	397	45	106	25	2	4	36	32	2	14	.267	.325	.370	86	-7	2	.980	1	*91*	*113*	C116	—	0.1
1939	StL N	131	344	32	89	18	2	3	35	43	2	28	.259	.344	.349	82	-8	6	.982	6	*120*	*91*	C126	—	0.4
1940	StL N	117	307	27	81	16	2	0	27	34	2	13	.264	.341	.329	81	-7	4	.980	1	*86*	*118*	C113	—	0.0
1941	†Bro N★	128	386	32	89	15	2	1	44	34	2	14	.231	.296	.288	62	-19	1	.995	9	***160***	*87*	C128	0	-0.3
1942	Bro N★	133	421	53	109	16	3	0	44	44	1	17	.259	.330	.311	87	-6	10	.987	8	*144*	*94*	C133	0	1.1
1943	Bro N☆	106	365	31	95	11	2	0	54	25	1	15	.260	.309	.301	77	-11	4	.987	-5	*97*	*96*	C100,3b3/S	0	-1.1
1944	Bro N☆	130	461	43	126	20	3	1	42	36	0	17	.273	.326	.336	88	-7	4	.979	-8	*87*	*98*	C125/2	0	-0.8
1945	Bro N	24	84	5	24	9	0	0	11	10	1	2	.286	.368	.393	113	2	0	.963	-2	*105*	*96*	C24	0	0.2
1949	Chi N	62	198	15	54	9	3	2	18	12	1	13	.273	.318	.379	88	-4	1	.969	-3	*65*	*148*	C59	0	-0.4
1950	Chi N	86	259	22	63	11	0	2	21	13	1	16	.243	.282	.309	56	-17	2	.978	-1	*66*	***119***	C86	0	-1.4
1951	Chi N	58	125	10	23	6	0	0	15	19	0	13	.184	.292	.232	42	-10	1-0	.969	2	*66*	*133*	C57	0	-0.6
1954	Bos A	32	68	6	16	3	0	1	11	9	0	6	.235	.309	.324	70	-3	0-1	.989	-1	*70*	*73*	C30	0	-0.3
Total	13	1209	3649	338	929	163	21	14	378	326	13	181	.255	.318	.322	76	-115	36-1	.982	4	*103*	*105*	C1175,3b3/2S	0	-4.6
OWEN, DAVE	Dave; B4.25.1958 Cleburne TX; BB/TR/6´2˝/(170–175); [ChiN79 10/246]; d9.6; b–Spike; Col Texas–Arlington																								
1983	Chi N	16	22	1	2	0	1	0	2	2-0	0	7	.091	.160	.182	-3	-3	1-0	1.000	1	119	105	S14,3b3	0	-0.1
1984	Chi N	47	93	8	18	2	2	1	10	8-1	2	15	.194	.269	.290	54	-6	1-2	.969	1	111	127	S35,3b6,2b4	0	-0.3
1985	Chi N	22	19	6	7	0	0	0	4	1-0	0	5	.368	.400	.368	106	0	1-1	.917	-1	132	166	S7,3b7,2b4	0	-0.1
1988	KC A	7	5	0	0	0	0	0	0	0-0	0	3	.000	.000	.000	-99	-1	0-0	.941	2	110	343	S7	0	0.0
Total	4	92	139	15	27	2	3	1	16	11-1	2	30	.194	.260	.273	47	-10	3-3	.969	3	114	140	S63,3b16,2b8	0	-0.5
OWEN, LARRY	Lawrence Thomas; B5.31.1955 Cleveland OH; BR/TR/5´11˝/(185–190); [AtlN77 17/420]; d8.14; Col Bowling Green																								
1981	Atl N	13	16	0	0	0	0	0	0	1-0	0	4	.000	.059	.000	-82	-4	0-0	.964	0	57	50	C10	0	-0.4
1982	Atl N	2	3	1	1	1	0	0	0	0-0	0	1	.333	.333	.667	170	0	0-0	1.000	-0	61	360	C2	0	0.0
1983	Atl N	17	17	0	2	0	0	0	1	0-0	0	2	.118	.118	.118	-32	-3	0-1	.970	-1	120	0	C16	0	-0.4
1985	Atl N	26	71	7	17	3	0	2	12	8-3	0	17	.239	.313	.366	85	-1	0-0	.966	1	78	75	C25	0	0.0
1987	KC A	76	164	17	31	6	0	5	14	16-0	0	51	.189	.260	.317	51	-12	0-0	.983	17	122	136	C75	0	0.7
1988	KC A	37	81	5	17	1	0	1	3	9-0	2	23	.210	.304	.259	59	-4	0-0	.989	2	127	91	C37	0	0.0
Total	6	171	352	30	68	11	0	8	30	34-3	2	98	.193	.267	.293	51	-24	0-1	.980	19	112	106	C165	0	-0.1
OWEN, MARV	Marvin James "Freck"; B3.22.1906 Agnew CA; D6.22.1991 Mountain View CA; BR/TR/6´1˝/175; d4.16; Col Santa Clara																								
1931	Det A	105	377	35	84	11	6	3	39	29	2	38	.223	.282	.308	53	-27	2-2	.937	-1	95	94	S37,3b37,1b27,2b4	—	-2.4
1933	Det A	138	550	77	144	24	9	2	65	44	4	56	.262	.321	.349	76	-20	2-2	.944	-10	90	83	3b136	—	-2.4
1934	†Det A	**154**	565	79	179	34	9	8	96	59	4	37	.317	.385	.451	115	13	3-3	.956	-6	84	**118**	3b154	—	1.1
1935	†Det A	134	483	52	127	24	5	2	71	43	2	37	.263	.326	.346	76	-17	1-4	.958	-9	87	112	3b131	—	-2.1
1936	Det A	**154**	583	72	172	20	4	9	105	53	7	41	.295	.361	.389	85	-14	9-6	.952	-2	93	**112**	3b153,1b2	—	-1.0
1937	Det A	107	396	48	114	22	5	1	45	41	2	24	.288	.358	.376	83	-10	3-4	**.970**	-2	102	78	3b106	—	-0.8
1938	Chi A	141	577	84	162	23	6	6	55	45	4	31	.281	.337	.373	76	-23	6-4	.948	-1	**106**	**112**	3b140	—	-1.7
1939	Chi A	58	194	22	46	9	0	0	15	16	2	15	.237	.302	.284	49	-15	4-5	.953	-3	90	116	3b55	—	-1.6
1940	Bos A	20	57	4	12	0	0	0	6	8	0	4	.211	.308	.211	36	-5	0-0	.962	2	99	191	3b9,1b8	—	-0.4
Total	9	1011	3782	473	1040	167	44	31	497	338	27	283	.275	.339	.367	80	-118	30-30	.953	-32	94	106	3b921,1b37,S37,2b4	—	-11.3
OWEN, SPIKE	Spike Dee; B4.19.1961 Cleburne TX; BB/TR/5´10˝/(160–170); [SeaA82 1/6]; d6.25; b–Dave; Col Texas																								
1983	Sea A	80	306	36	60	11	3	2	21	24-0	2	44	.196	.257	.271	44	-24	10-6	.970	6	99	92	S80	0	-1.0
1984	Sea A	152	530	67	130	18	8	3	43	46-0	3	63	.245	.308	.326	76	-17	16-8	.977	16	102	86	S151	0	1.5
1985	Sea A	118	352	41	91	10	6	6	37	34-0	0	27	.259	.322	.372	89	-6	11-5	.975	25	113	102	S117	17	3.0
1986	Sea A	112	402	46	99	22	6	0	35	34-1	1	42	.246	.305	.331	73	-15	1-3	.972	36	121	128	S112	0	3.1
	†Bos A	42	126	21	23	2	1	1	10	17-0	1	9	.183	.283	.238	44	-10	3-1	.976	-0	87	139	S42	0	-0.6
	Year	154	528	67	122	24	7	1	45	51-1	2	51	.231	.300	.309	66	-25	4-4	.973	**36**	**112**	131	S154	0	2.5
1987	Bos A	132	437	50	113	17	7	2	48	53-2	1	43	.259	.337	.343	80	-12	11-8	.975	-12	92	88	S130	0	-1.1
1988	†Bos A	89	257	40	64	14	1	5	18	27-0	2	27	.249	.324	.370	90	-3	0-1	.967	-2	94	76	S76,D7	0	0.0
1989	Mon N	142	437	52	102	17	4	6	41	76-25	3	44	.233	.349	.332	94	0	3-2	**.979**	10	101	96	S142	15	2.1
1990	Mon N	149	453	55	106	24	5	5	35	70-12	0	60	.234	.333	.342	90	-4	8-6	**.989**	-19	89	77	S148	0	-1.3
1991	Mon N	139	424	39	108	22	8	3	26	42-11	1	61	.255	.321	.366	94	-3	2-6	.986	7	105	105	S133	0	1.2
1992	Mon N	122	386	52	104	16	3	7	40	50-3	0	30	.269	.348	.381	108	5	9-4	.982	-4	95	76	S116	15	1.1
1993	NY A	103	334	41	78	16	2	2	20	29-2	0	30	.234	.294	.311	65	-17	3-2	.968	6	113	78	S96,D2	0	-0.4
1994	Cal A	82	268	30	83	17	2	3	37	49-0	1	17	.310	.418	.422	115	9	2-8	.956	-6	93	140	3b70,S5,1b4/2D	0	0.2
1995	Cal A	82	218	17	50	9	3	1	28	18-1	0	22	.229	.288	.312	57	-15	3-2	.945	-7	75	75	3b29,S25,2b16	26	-1.9
Total	13	1544	4930	587	1211	215	59	46	439	569-57	15	519	.246	.324	.341	83	-112	82-62	.977	55	101	93	S1373,3b99,2b17,D11,1b4	73	5.9
OWENS, JAYHAWK	Claude Jayhawk; B2.10.1969 Cincinnati OH; BR/TR/6´1˝/(200–213); [MinA90 2/52]; d6.6; Col Middle Tennessee																								
1993	Col N	33	86	12	18	5	0	3	6	6-1	2	30	.209	.277	.372	61	-5	1-0	.957	-2	103	134	C32	0	-0.5
1994	Col N	6	12	4	3	0	1	0	1	3-0	0	3	.250	.400	.417	97	0	0-0	1.000	0	150	221	C6	0	0.0
1995	†Col N	18	45	7	11	2	0	4	12	2-0	1	15	.244	.286	.556	91	-1	0-0	.988	3	302	133	C16	0	0.3
1996	Col N	73	180	31	43	9	1	4	17	27-0	1	56	.239	.338	.367	70	-7	4-1	.974	-2	97	134	C68	24	-0.5
Total	4	130	323	54	75	16	2	11	36	38-1	4	104	.232	.318	.396	72	-13	5-1	.973	-1	127	138	C122	24	-0.7
OWENS, ERIC	Eric Blake; B2.3.1971 Danville VA; BR/TR/6´0˝/(185–198); [CinN92 4/101]; d6.6; Col Ferrum; OF(291/201/251)																								
1995	Cin N	2	2	0	2	0	0	0	1	0-0	0	0	1.000	1.000	1.000	425	1	0-0	ø	-1	0	0	3b2	1	0.0
1996	Cin N	88	205	26	41	6	0	0	9	23-1	1	38	.200	.281	.229	37	-19	16-2	.986	-1	95	137	O52L,2b6,3b5	0	-1.8
1997	Cin N	27	57	8	15	0	0	0	3	4-0	0	11	.263	.311	.263	51	-4	3-2	.938	-5	69	0	O18(9/8/1),2b2	0	-0.9
1998	Mil N	34	40	5	5	2	0	1	4	2-0	0	6	.125	.167	.250	8	-6	0-0	1.000	-1	73	369	O16(10/5/2),2b4	0	-0.7
1999	SD N	149	440	55	117	22	3	9	61	38-2	3	50	.266	.327	.391	87	-9	33-7	.990	-1	104	74	O116(69/47/27),1b12,3b4/2	0	-0.8
2000	SD N	145	583	87	171	19	7	6	51	45-4	4	63	.293	.346	.381	90	-11	29-14	**1.000**	3	105	67	O144(65/34/68)/2	0	-1.0
2001	Fla N	119	400	51	101	16	1	5	28	29-2	0	59	.253	.302	.335	67	-20	8-6	.984	-5	89	100	O106(1/37/72)/D	19	-2.8
2002	Fla N	131	385	44	104	15	5	4	37	31-1	0	33	.270	.324	.366	85	-10	26-9	.975	9	114	163	O121(75/22/39)	0	-0.2
2003	Ana A	111	241	29	65	6	0	1	20	10-0	1	24	.270	.300	.307	64	-13	11-8	.971	2	108	89	O97(10/48/42),D3	0	-1.2
Total	9	806	2353	305	621	86	16	26	214	182-10	9	284	.264	.318	.347	75	-91	126-48	.985	-1	102	102	O670L,2b14,1b12,3b11,D4	20	-9.4
OWENS, FRANK	Frank Walter "Yip"; B1.26.1886 Toronto ON, Can.; D7.2.1958 Minneapolis MN; BR/TR/6´0˝/170; d9.11																								
1905	Bos A	1	2	0	0	0	0	0	0	0	0	—	.000	.000	.000	-99	0	0	1.000	-0	*0*	*198*	/C	—	-0.1
1909	Chi A	64	174	12	35	4	1	0	17	8	2	—	.201	.245	.236	54	-9	3	.959	-6	*94*	*85*	C57	—	-1.2
1914	Bro F	58	184	15	51	7	3	2	20	9	1	16	.277	.314	.380	89	-6	2	.967	-11	*78*	*96*	C58	—	-1.4
1915	Bal F	99	334	32	84	14	7	3	28	17	1	34	.251	.290	.362	80	-15	4	.976	-2	*107*	*105*	C99	—	-0.9
Total	4	222	694	59	170	25	11	5	65	34	4	50	.245	.284	.334	77	-30	9	.969	-20	*96*	*98*	C215	—	-3.6
OWENS, JACK	Furman Lee; B5.6.1908 Converse SC; D11.14.1958 Greenville SC; BR/TR/6´1˝/186; d9.21																								
1935	Phi A	2	8	0	2	0	0	0	1	0	0	1	.250	.250	.250	30	-1	0-0	.900	-0	*82*	*180*	C2	—	-0.1
OWENS, JERRY	Jerry Lee; B2.16.1981 Hollywood CA; BL/TL/6´3˝/195; [MonN03 2/57]; d9.11; Col The Master's College																								
2006	Chi A	12	9	4	3	1	0	0	0	0-0	0	2	.333	.333	.444	96	0	1-0	1.000	0	159	0	O5(0/4/1),D6	15	0.1

YEAR	TM LG	G	AB	R	H	2B	3B	HR	RBI	BB-IB	HP	SO	AVG	OBP	SLG	AOPS	ABR	SB-CS	FA	FR	RNG	THR	GAMES AT POSITION	DL	BFW
OWENS, RED	Thomas Llewellyn; B11.1.1874 Pottsville PA; D8.20.1952 Harrisburg PA; BR/TR/5´10˝/175; d7.28																								
1899	Phi N	8	21	0	1	0	0	0	1	2	0	—	.048	.130	.048	-52	-4	0	.914	-0	104	91	2b8	—	-0.4
1905	Bro N	43	168	14	36	6	2	1	20	6	0	—	.214	.241	.292	63	-8	1	.929	2	98	118	2b43	—	-0.6
Total	2	51	189	14	37	6	2	1	21	8	0	—	.196	.228	.265	49	-12	1	.927	2	99	115	2b51	—	-1.0
OXLEY, HENRY	Henry Havelock; B1.4.1858 Covehead PE (now Canada); D10.12.1945 Somerville MA; BR/5´11˝/163; d7.30																								
1884	NY N	2	4	0	0	0	0	0	0	1	—	2	.000	.200	.000	-31	-1	—	.900	0	—	—	C2	—	0.0
	NY AA	1	3	0	0	0	0	0	—	0	0	—	.000	.000	.000	-99	-1	—	.889	-0	—	—	/C	—	-0.1
Total	1	3	7	0	0	0	0	0	0	1	0	2	.000	.125	.000	-56	-2	—	.895	0	—	—	C3	—	-0.1
OYLER, ANDY	Andrew Paul "Pepper"; B5.5.1880 Newville PA; D10.24.1970 E.Pennsboro Twp. PA; BR/TR/5´6.5˝/138; d5.8; Col Washington & Jefferson																								
1902	Bal A	27	77	9	17	1	0	1	6	8	3	—	.221	.318	.273	62	-4	3	.947	-4	67	36	3b20,O3(0/2/1),S2/2	—	-0.7
OYLER, RAY	Raymond Francis; B8.4.1938 Indianapolis IN; D1.26.1981 Seattle WA; BR/TR/5´11˝/165; d4.18																								
1965	Det A	82	194	22	36	6	0	5	13	21-3	0	61	.186	.265	.294	58	-11	1-0	.955	-4	102	59	S57,2b11/13	0	-1.0
1966	Det A	71	210	16	36	8	3	1	9	23-4	3	62	.171	.263	.252	48	-14	0-0	.965	5	103	111	S69	0	-0.4
1967	Det A	148	367	33	76	14	2	1	29	37-3	2	91	.207	.281	.264	61	-17	0-2	.964	14	107	99	S146	0	0.7
1968	†Det A	111	215	13	29	6	1	1	12	20-0	2	59	.135	.213	.186	22	-20	0-2	.977	-6	89	82	S111	0	-2.4
1969	Sea A	106	255	24	42	5	0	7	22	31-0	2	80	.165	.260	.267	48	-18	1-2	.965	3	104	87	S106	0	-0.6
1970	Cal A	24	24	2	2	0	0	0	1	3-0	0	6	.083	.185	.083	-24	-4	0-0	1.000	-4	60	33	S13,3b2	0	-0.8
Total	6	542	1265	110	221	39	6	15	86	135-10	9	359	.175	.258	.251	48	-84	2-6	.966	7	101	89	S502,2b11,3b3/1	0	-4.5
OZUNA, PABLO	Pablo Jose; B8.25.1974 Santo Domingo, D.R.; BR/TR/6´0˝/(160–195); d4.23; OF(47/6/2); [DL 2001 Fla N 190]																								
2000	Fla N	14	24	2	8	1	0	0	0	0-0	0	2	.333	.333	.375	83	-1	1-0	.967	-1	96	70	2b7	0	-0.1
2002	Fla N	34	47	4	13	2	2	0	3	1-0	1	3	.277	.300	.404	88	-1	1-1	.967	-2	85	65	2b10/cf	0	-0.3
2003	Col N	17	40	5	8	1	0	0	2	2-0	2	6	.200	.273	.225	28	-4	3-0	.981	4	140	155	2b8,O5C,S3	68	0.1
2005	†Chi A	70	203	27	56	7	2	0	11	7-0	4	26	.276	.313	.330	69	-9	14-7	.941	3	116	83	3b32,S15,O10(9/0/1),2b6,1b2,D4	0	-0.5
2006	Chi A	79	189	25	62	12	2	2	17	7-0	4	16	.328	.365	.444	105	2	6-6	1.000	-6	71	131	O39(38/0/1),3b17,2b6,D9	0	-0.5
Total	5	214	503	63	147	23	6	2	33	17-0	11	53	.292	.329	.374	81	-13	25-14	1.000	-1	68	101	O55L,3b49,2b37,S18,D13,1b2	258	-1.3
PABOR, CHARLIE	Charles Henry; B9.24.1846 New York NY; D4.23.1913 New Haven CT; BL/TL/5´8˝/155; d5.4; M2; ▲																								
1871	Cle NA	**29**	142	24	42	2	4	0	18	1	—	3	.296	.301	.366	96	0	1-0	.773	-4	103	0	O28L,P7,M	—	-0.2
1872	Cle NA	21	92	12	19	0	0	0	7	0	—	0	.207	.207	.207	29	-7	0-0	.863	-0	47	209	O19L,P2	—	-0.4
1873	Atl NA	**55**	228	36	82	9	3	0	41	6	—	3	.360	.376	.425	153	17	2-0	.811	-3	51	62	O55L	—	1.2
1874	Phi NA	17	77	11	17	0	1	0	1	0	—	0	.221	.221	.247	48	-5	0-1	.553	-2	196	210	O17(2/3/13)	—	-0.5
1875	Atl NA	42	153	14	36	2	2	0	11	1	—	1	.235	.240	.275	90	0	0-0	.803	1	71	60	O42L/PM	—	0.1
	NH NA	6	23	4	8	0	2	0	2	0	—	1	.348	.348	.522	227	3	0-0	.818	-1	0	0	O6L,M	—	0.2
	Year	**48**	176	18	44	2	4	0	13	1	—	2	.250	.254	.307	108	2	0-0	.804	-0	63	53	O48L/P	—	0.3
Total	5NA	170	715	101	204	13	12	0	80	8	—	8	.285	.293	.337	103	8	3-1	.789	-10	77	83	O167(152/3/13),P10	—	0.4
PABST, ED	Edward D. A.; B1868 St.Louis MO; D6.19.1940 St.Louis MO; TR/5´11˝/170; d9.26																								
1890	Phi AA	8	25	7	10	2	0	0	3	5	0	—	.400	.500	.480	190	3	3	.963	3	232	0	O8L	—	0.5
	StL AA	4	14	1	2	0	1	0	0	0	0	—	.143	.143	.286	23	-2	0	1.000	1	259	0	O4L	—	0.0
	Year	12	39	8	12	2	1	0	3	5	0	—	.308	.386	.410	129	1	3	.972	4	240	0	O12L	—	0.5
PACIOREK, JIM	James Joseph; B6.7.1960 Detroit MI; BR/TR/6´3˝/205; [MilA82 8/209]; d4.9; b–John b–Tom; Col Michigan																								
1987	Mil A	48	101	16	23	5	0	2	10	12-0	0	20	.228	.302	.337	69	-4	1-0	.980	-3	75	84	1b21,3b15,O5(4/0/1),D2	0	-0.8
PACIOREK, JOHN	John Francis; B2.11.1945 Detroit MI; BR/TR/6´2˝/200; d9.29; b–Jim b–Tom																								
1963	Hou N	1	3	4	3	0	0	0	3	2-0	0	0	1.000	1.000	1.000	509	2	0-0	1.000	0	116	0	/rf	0	0.2
PACIOREK, TOM	Thomas Marian; B11.2.1946 Detroit MI; BR/TR/6´4˝/(204–215); [LAN68 5/89]; d9.12; b–Jim b–John; Col Houston; OF(476/73/281)																								
1970	LA N	8	9	2	2	1	0	0	0	0-0	1	3	.222	.300	.333	72	0	0-0	1.000	-0	45	0	O3(1/0/2)	0	-0.1
1971	LA N	2	2	0	1	0	0	0	1	0-0	0	0	.500	.500	.500	194	0	0-0	1.000	0	243	0	/lf	0	0.0
1972	LA N	11	47	4	12	4	0	1	6	1-0	0	7	.255	.271	.404	91	-1	1-0	.979	1	97	92	1b6,O6(1/0/5)	0	0.0
1973	LA N	96	195	26	51	8	0	5	18	11-2	1	35	.262	.304	.379	91	-3	3-3	.979	-3	90	54	O77(36/22/25),1b4	0	-1.0
1974	†LA N	85	175	23	42	8	6	1	24	10-1	1	32	.240	.282	.371	86	-5	1-3	.944	-4	92	33	O77(44/23/15)/1	0	-1.2
1975	LA N	62	145	14	28	8	0	1	5	11-1	0	29	.193	.250	.269	46	-11	4-3	.972	-3	93	0	O54(30/2/25)	0	-1.7
1976	Atl N	111	324	39	94	10	4	4	36	19-2	3	57	.290	.333	.383	98	-2	2-3	.983	-7	82	56	O84(38/7/44),1b12/3	0	-1.5
1977	Atl N	72	155	20	37	8	0	3	15	6-2	0	46	.239	.262	.348	57	-9	1-0	.984	-1	88	82	1b32,O9(4/2/3)/3	0	-1.2
1978	Atl N	5	9	2	3	0	0	0	0	0-0	0	1	.333	.333	.333	78	0	0-0	1.000	-0	0	82	1b2	0	-0.1
	Sea A	70	251	32	75	20	3	4	30	15-0	0	39	.299	.336	.450	120	6	2-2	.980	-2	88	88	O54(53/4/0),D12,1b3	0	0.1
1979	Sea A	103	310	38	89	23	4	6	42	28-1	5	62	.287	.353	.445	112	6	6-4	1.000	-1	101	40	O75(47/0/29),1b15	0	0.1
1980	Sea A	126	418	44	114	19	1	15	59	17-1	1	67	.273	.301	.431	97	-3	3-2	1.000	-2	95	73	O60(19/1/41),1b36,D23	0	-1.0
1981	Sea A★	104	405	50	132	28	2	14	66	35-3	4	50	.326	.379	.509	149	26	13-10	.974	3	104	128	O103(84/12/14)	0	2.5
1982	Chi A	104	382	49	119	27	4	11	55	24-3	9	53	.312	.361	.490	132	17	3-3	.993	3	116	109	1b102,O6L	35	1.4
1983	†Chi A	115	420	65	129	32	3	9	63	25-4	3	58	.307	.347	.462	116	10	6-1	1.000	-3	97	91	1b67,O55(30/0/27),D2	0	0.2
1984	Chi A	111	363	35	93	21	2	4	29	25-4	4	69	.256	.308	.358	81	-9	6-0	.993	-9	57	115	1b67,O41(25/0/17)	28	-2.2
1985	Chi A	46	122	14	30	2	0	0	9	8-0	1	22	.246	.293	.262	53	-8	2-0	.970	0	94	97	O23(21/0/2),D12,1b6	0	-0.9
	NY N	46	116	14	33	3	1	1	11	6-1	1	14	.284	.325	.353	92	-2	1-0	1.000	-2	89	0	O29(6/0/24),1b8	0	-0.5
1986	Tex A	88	213	17	61	7	0	4	22	3-0	3	41	.286	.305	.376	82	-6	1-3	.967	3	74	271	O25(22/0/3),1b23,3b21/SD	0	-0.5
1987	Tex A	27	60	6	17	3	0	3	12	1-0	1	19	.283	.302	.483	104	0	0-1	1.000	1	139	155	1b12,O12(8/0/5),D3	118	0.0
Total	18	1392	4121	494	1162	232	30	86	503	245-25	38	704	.282	.325	.415	102	6	55-38	.979	-26	93	75	O794L,1b396,D61,3b23/S	181	-7.6
PACK, FRANKIE	Frank; B4.10.1928 Morristown TN; D1.26.2000 Hendersonville NC; BL/TR/6´0˝/190; d6.5																								
1949	StL A	1	1	0	0	0	0	0	0	0	0	1	.000	.000	.000	-96	0	0-0	ø	0	—	—	/H	0	0.0
PADDEN, DICK	Richard Joseph "Brains"; B9.17.1870 Wheeling WV; D10.31.1922 Martins Ferry OH; BR/TR/5´10˝/165; d7.15																								
1896	Pit N	61	219	33	53	4	8	2	24	14	2	9	.242	.294	.361	75	-10	8	.931	-14	78	56	2b61	—	-1.8
1897	Pit N	**134**	517	84	146	16	10	2	58	38	16	—	.282	.350	.364	92	-5	18	.941	4	95	78	2b134	—	0.4
1898	Pit N	128	463	61	119	7	6	2	43	35	19	—	.257	.335	.311	87	-7	11	.947	-1	103	97	2b128	—	-0.2
1899	Was N	134	451	66	125	20	7	2	61	24	17	—	.277	.337	.366	94	-4	27	.913	5	103	96	S85,2b48	—	0.7
1901	StL N	123	489	71	125	17	7	2	62	31	11	—	.256	.315	.331	92	-5	26	.950	-1	**101**	121	2b115,S8	—	-0.4
1902	StL A	117	413	54	109	26	3	1	40	30	9	—	.264	.327	.349	89	-5	11	**.967**	12	105	**141**	2b117	—	0.8
1903	StL A	29	94	7	19	3	0	0	6	9	5	—	.202	.306	.234	65	-3	5	.955	2	104	164	2b29	—	-0.1
1904	StL A	132	453	42	108	19	4	0	36	40	**18**	—	.238	.325	.298	104	5	23	.959	-16	95	80	2b132	—	-1.1
1905	StL A	16	58	5	10	1	1	0	4	3	0	—	.172	.213	.224	41	-4	3	.950	-0	104	50	2b16	—	-0.5
Total	9	874	3157	423	814	113	46	11	334	224	97	9	.258	.326	.333	90	-38	132	.950	-8	97	97	2b780,S93	—	-2.2
PADDEN, TOM	Thomas Francis; B10.6.1908 Manchester NH; D6.10.1973 Manchester NH; BR/TR/5´11.5˝/170; d5.29; Col Holy Cross																								
1932	Pit N	47	118	13	31	6	1	0	10	9	0	7	.263	.315	.331	75	-4	0	.985	-1	*81*	*88*	C43	—	-0.3
1933	Pit N	30	90	5	19	2	0	0	8	2	1	6	.211	.237	.233	35	-8	0	.984	3	*76*	*129*	C27	—	-0.3
1934	Pit N	82	237	27	76	12	2	0	22	30	1	23	.321	.399	.388	109	5	3	.978	-7	*69*	*61*	C76	—	0.3
1935	Pit N	97	302	35	82	9	1	1	30	48	0	26	.272	.371	.318	84	-4	1	.966	8	*83*	*124*	C94	—	0.9
1936	Pit N	88	281	22	70	9	2	1	31	22	0	41	.249	.304	.306	63	-15	0	.976	1	*77*	***127***	C87	—	-0.9
1937	Pit N	35	98	14	28	2	0	0	8	13	0	11	.286	.369	.306	85	-1	1	.983	2	*62*	*145*	C34	—	0.2
1943	Phi N	17	41	5	12	0	0	0	1	2	1	6	.293	.341	.293	87	-1	0	1.000	2	*84*	*60*	C16	0	0.2
	Was A	3	3	1	0	0	0	0	0	1	0	1	.000	.250	.000	-25	0	0-0	1.000	0	*0*	*0*	C2	0	0.0
Total	7	399	1170	122	318	40	6	2	110	127	3	121	.272	.345	.321	80	-28	5-0	.977	9	*76*	*108*	C379	0	0.1
PADDOCK, DEL	Delmar Harold; B6.8.1887 Volga SD; D2.6.1952 Remer MN; BL/TR/5´9˝/165; d4.14																								
1912	Chi A	1	1	0	0	0	0	0	0	0	0	—	.000	.000	.000	-99	0	0	ø	0	—	—	/H	—	0.0
	NY A	46	156	26	45	5	3	1	14	23	4	—	.288	.393	.378	114	4	9	.894	-5	90	71	3b41,2b2/rf	—	0.0
	Year	47	157	26	45	5	3	1	14	23	4	—	.287	.391	.376	113	4	9	.894	-5	90	71	3b41,2b2/rf	—	0.0

PADGETT, DON Don Wilson; B12.5.1911 Caroleen NC; D12.9.1980 High Point NC; BL/TR/6´0˝/190; d4.23; Mil 1942–45; Col Lenoir–Rhyne

YEAR	TM LG	G	AB	R	H	2B	3B	HR	RBI	BB-IB	HP	SO	AVG	OBP	SLG	AOPS	ABR	SB-CS	FA	FR	RNG	THR	GAMES AT POSITION	DL	BFW
1937	StL N	123	446	62	140	22	6	10	74	30	0	43	.314	.357	.457	117	10	4	.955	1	108	81	O109(0/6/102)	—	0.4
1938	StL N	110	388	59	105	26	5	8	65	18	0	28	.271	.303	.425	93	-5	0	.962	6	102	231	O71(3/5/63),1b16,C6	—	-0.4
1939	StL N	92	233	38	93	15	3	5	53	18	1	11	.399	.444	.554	157	19	1	.978	-1	*120*	*61*	C61,1b6	—	2.1
1940	StL N	93	240	24	58	15	1	6	41	26	2	14	.242	.321	.387	89	-3	1	.962	-6	*86*	*107*	C72,1b2	—	-0.5
1941	StL N	107	324	39	80	18	0	5	44	21	0	16	.247	.293	.349	75	-11	0	.959	-6	96	25	O62(59/0/3),C18,1b2	0	-2.0
1946	Bro N	19	30	2	5	1	0	1	9	4	0	4	.167	.265	.300	59	-2	0	1.000	0	*195*	*67*	C10	0	-0.1
	Bos N	44	98	6	25	3	0	2	21	5	0	7	.255	.291	.347	80	-3	0	.939	-5	*80*	*109*	C26	0	-0.7
	Year	63	128	8	30	4	0	3	30	9	0	11	.234	.285	.336	75	-5	0	.954	-5	*106*	*99*	C36	0	-0.8
1947	Phi N	75	158	14	50	8	1	0	24	16	1	5	.316	.383	.380	107	2	0	.962	-5	*71*	*117*	C39	0	-0.1
1948	Phi N	36	74	3	17	3	0	0	7	3	0	2	.230	.260	.270	44	-6	0	.957	-3	*63*	*30*	C19	0	-0.8
Total	8	699	1991	247	573	111	16	37	338	141	4	130	.288	.336	.415	101	1	6	.962	-18	*96*	*86*	C251,O242(62/11/168),1b26	0	-2.1

PADGETT, ERNIE Ernest Kitchen "Red"; B3.1.1899 Philadelphia PA; D4.15.1957 E.Orange NJ; BR/TR/5´8˝/155; d10.3

YEAR	TM LG	G	AB	R	H	2B	3B	HR	RBI	BB-IB	HP	SO	AVG	OBP	SLG	AOPS	ABR	SB-CS	FA	FR	RNG	THR	GAMES AT POSITION	DL	BFW
1923	Bos N	4	11	3	2	0	0	0	0	2	0	0	.182	.308	.182	33	-1	0-0	.947	1	92	190	S2/2	—	0.0
1924	Bos N	138	502	42	128	25	9	1	46	37	3	56	.255	.310	.347	79	-15	4-9	.967	-9	102	108	3b113,2b29	—	-1.9
1925	Bos N	86	256	31	78	9	7	0	29	14	0	14	.305	.341	.395	96	-3	3-5	.964	-15	85	76	2b47,S18,3b7	—	-1.6
1926	Cle A	36	62	7	13	0	1	0	6	8	0	3	.210	.300	.242	42	-5	1-0	.930	1	116	158	3b29,S2	—	-0.3
1927	Cle A	7	7	1	2	0	0	0	0	0	0	2	.286	.286	.286	48	-1	0-0	1.000	-0	60	0	2b4	—	-0.1
Total	5	271	838	84	223	34	17	1	81	61	3	75	.266	.318	.351	80	-25	8-14	.957	-23	102	113	3b149,2b81,S22	—	-3.9

PAEPKE, DENNIS Dennis Ray; B4.17.1945 Long Beach CA; BR/TR/6´0˝/(200–202); d6.2; Col Fullerton (CA) JC/Orange Coast (CA) JC

YEAR	TM LG	G	AB	R	H	2B	3B	HR	RBI	BB-IB	HP	SO	AVG	OBP	SLG	AOPS	ABR	SB-CS	FA	FR	RNG	THR	GAMES AT POSITION	DL	BFW
1969	KC A	12	27	2	3	1	0	0	0	2-0	0	3	.111	.172	.148	-10	-4	0-0	1.000	2	72	99	C8	0	-0.2
1971	KC A	60	152	11	31	6	0	2	14	8-1	0	29	.204	.242	.283	49	-11	0-0	.994	0	83	82	C32,O17(1/0/16)	0	-1.1
1972	KC A	2	6	0	0	0	0	0	0	1-1	0	2	.000	.143	.000	-55	-1	0-0	.842	-0	30	172	C2	0	-0.1
1974	KC A	6	12	0	2	0	0	0	0	1-0	0	2	.167	.231	.167	15	-1	0-1	1.000	-1	45	352	C4/rf	0	-0.2
Total	4	80	197	13	36	7	0	2	14	12-2	0	36	.183	.229	.249	36	-17	0-1	.984	1	76	106	C46,O18(1/0/17)	0	-1.6

PAFKO, ANDY Andrew "Handy Andy","Pruschka"; B2.25.1921 Boyceville WI; BR/TR/6´0˝/(185–190); d9.24; C3

YEAR	TM LG	G	AB	R	H	2B	3B	HR	RBI	BB-IB	HP	SO	AVG	OBP	SLG	AOPS	ABR	SB-CS	FA	FR	RNG	THR	GAMES AT POSITION	DL	BFW
1943	Chi N	13	58	7	22	3	0	0	10	2	0	5	.379	.400	.431	142	3	1	1.000	-2	87	0	O13C	0	0.1
1944	Chi N	128	469	47	126	16	2	6	62	28	4	23	.269	.315	.350	87	-9	2	.983	10	100	**215**	O123(0/123/1)	0	-0.2
1945	†Chi N✳	144	534	64	159	24	12	12	110	45	**8**	36	.298	.361	.455	129	19	5	**.995**	-0	100	98	O140C	0	1.4
1946	Chi N	65	234	18	66	6	4	3	39	27	4	15	.282	.366	.380	114	5	4	.978	3	93	211	O64C	0	0.6
1947	Chi N★	129	513	68	155	25	7	13	66	31	3	39	.302	.346	.454	115	9	4	.985	-1	99	102	O127C	0	0.5
1948	Chi N★	142	548	82	171	30	2	26	101	50	5	50	.312	.375	.516	145	33	3	.938	10	109	**121**	3b139	0	4.2
1949	Chi N★	144	519	79	146	29	2	18	69	63	**9**	33	.281	.369	.449	121	17	4	.987	-6	90	120	O98(1/89/9),3b49	0	0.8
1950	Chi N★	146	514	95	156	24	8	36	92	69	11	32	.304	.397	.591	158	43	4	.978	-4	94	104	O144(0/138/6)	0	3.4
1951	Chi N	49	178	26	47	5	3	12	35	17	4	10	.264	.342	.528	128	6	1-1	.992	-1	91	142	O48C	0	0.4
	Bro N	84	277	42	69	11	0	18	58	35	8	27	.249	.350	.484	120	8	1-4	.993	-0	92	128	O76(70/9/0)	0	0.1
	Year	133	455	68	116	16	3	30	93	52	**12**	37	.255	.347	.501	123	14	2-5	.993	-1	92	134	O124(70/57/0)	0	0.5
1952	†Bro N	150	551	76	158	17	5	19	85	64	5	48	.287	.366	.439	121	16	4-3	.988	0	90	**175**	O139(105/12/38),3b13	0	0.9
1953	Mil N	140	516	70	153	23	4	17	72	37	3	33	.297	.347	.455	114	10	2-1	.976	-8	92	49	O139R	0	-0.4
1954	Mil N	138	510	61	146	22	4	14	69	37	4	36	.286	.335	.427	105	2	1-2	.969	-6	93	75	O138(0/7/131)	0	-0.9
1955	Mil N	86	252	29	67	3	5	5	34	7-1	4	23	.266	.293	.377	81	-9	1-2	.980	-3	101	25	O58(1/7/52),3b12	0	-1.4
1956	Mil N	45	93	15	24	5	0	2	9	10-0	0	13	.258	.330	.376	95	0	0-0	.978	-0	94	125	O37(33/0/5)	0	-0.2
1957	†Mil N	83	220	31	61	6	1	8	27	10-2	1	22	.277	.308	.423	102	-1	1-0	.982	-1	104	26	O69(32/1/36)	0	-0.4
1958	†Mil N	95	164	17	39	7	1	3	23	15-3	2	17	.238	.306	.348	80	-5	0-0	1.000	1	109	52	O93(80/3/17)	0	-0.7
1959	Mil N	71	142	17	31	8	2	1	15	14-1	1	15	.218	.293	.324	70	-6	0-0	.978	-1	105	34	O64(40/22/9)	0	-0.9
Total	17	1852	6292	844	1796	264	62	213	976	561-7	76	477	.285	.350	.449	118	141	38-13	.984	-7	96	110	O1570(362/803/443),3b213	0	7.3

PAGAN, ANGEL Angel Anthony; B7.2.1981 Rio Piedras, PR; BB/TR/6´1˝/180; [NYN99 4/136]; d4.3; Col Indian River (FL) CC

YEAR	TM LG	G	AB	R	H	2B	3B	HR	RBI	BB-IB	HP	SO	AVG	OBP	SLG	AOPS	ABR	SB-CS	FA	FR	RNG	THR	GAMES AT POSITION	DL	BFW
2006	Chi N	77	170	28	42	6	2	5	18	15-0	0	28	.247	.306	.394	77	-7	4-2	.989	3	118	103	O58(39/1/21)	75	-0.5

PAGAN, JOSE Jose Antonio (Rodriguez); B5.5.1935 Barceloneta, PR; BR/TR/5´9˝/(165–170); d8.4; C5; OF(83/0/10)

YEAR	TM LG	G	AB	R	H	2B	3B	HR	RBI	BB-IB	HP	SO	AVG	OBP	SLG	AOPS	ABR	SB-CS	FA	FR	RNG	THR	GAMES AT POSITION	DL	BFW
1959	SF N	31	46	7	8	1	0	0	1	2-0	0	8	.174	.208	.196	9	-6	1-0	.900	1	108	124	3b18,S5,2b3	0	-0.5
1960	SF N	18	49	8	14	2	2	0	2	1-0	0	6	.286	.300	.408	97	-1	2-2	.917	-6	58	36	S11/3	0	-0.6
1961	SF N	134	434	38	110	15	2	5	46	31-7	2	45	.253	.306	.332	72	-18	8-5	.964	-16	89	72	S132,O4(3/0/2)	0	-2.3
1962	†SF N	164	580	73	150	25	6	7	57	47-4	1	77	.259	.312	.359	82	-15	13-9	**.973**	-22	90	86	S164	0	-2.4
1963	SF N	148	483	46	113	12	1	6	39	26-5	4	67	.234	.277	.300	67	-21	10-7	.970	-10	94	87	S143/2lf	0	-2.1
1964	SF N	134	367	33	82	10	1	1	28	35-10	1	66	.223	.289	.264	57	-20	5-4	.958	-21	87	80	S132,O8(6/0/2)	0	-3.3
1965	SF N	26	83	10	17	4	0	0	5	8-2	0	9	.205	.272	.253	48	-5	1-0	.941	-6	92	52	S26	0	-1.0
	Pit N	42	38	6	9	1	0	0	1	1-0	1	7	.237	.275	.263	52	-2	1-0	.923	1	112	150	3b15,S7	0	-0.1
	Year	68	121	16	26	5	0	0	6	9-2	1	16	.215	.273	.256	50	-8	2-0	.923	-5	96	64	S33,3b15	0	-1.1
1966	Pit N	109	368	44	97	15	6	4	54	13-3	4	38	.264	.292	.370	84	-9	0-2	.949	4	111	128	3b83,S18,2b3,O3L	0	-0.5
1967	Pit N	81	211	17	61	6	2	1	19	10-3	3	28	.289	.323	.351	95	-2	1-1	.938	6	119	84	3b25,O23L,S16,2b2/C	0	0.4
1968	Pit N	80	163	24	36	7	1	4	21	11-3	3	32	.221	.278	.350	90	-2	2-3	.924	-4	99	70	3b30,O19L,S8,2b2/1	0	-0.9
1969	Pit N	108	274	29	78	11	4	9	42	17-2	1	46	.285	.325	.453	120	6	1-0	.954	-2	92	99	3b44,O23(21/0/2)/2	0	0.3
1970	†Pit N	95	230	21	61	14	1	7	29	20-1	0	24	.265	.321	.426	99	-1	1-1	.957	1	98	154	3b53,O4(1/0/3)/12	0	0.0
1971	†Pit N	57	158	16	38	1	0	5	15	16-2	1	25	.241	.311	.342	85	-3	0-0	.980	-1	94	135	3b41,O3L,1b2	39	-0.5
1972	Pit N	53	127	11	32	9	0	3	8	5-0	1	17	.252	.284	.394	93	-2	0-0	.899	-8	69	67	3b32,O2L	0	-1.0
1973	Phi N	46	78	4	16	5	0	0	5	1-1	0	15	.205	.213	.269	33	-7	0-1	.958	-1	76	48	3b16,1b5,O2(1/0/1)/2	0	-0.9
Total	15	1326	3689	387	922	138	26	52	372	244-43	22	510	.250	.298	.344	79	-108	46-35	.963	-84	91	81	S662,3b358,O92L,2b14,1b9/C	39	-15.4

PAGE, MIKE Michael Randy; B7.12.1940 Woodruff SC; BL/TR/6´2.5˝/210; d6.30

YEAR	TM LG	G	AB	R	H	2B	3B	HR	RBI	BB-IB	HP	SO	AVG	OBP	SLG	AOPS	ABR	SB-CS	FA	FR	RNG	THR	GAMES AT POSITION	DL	BFW
1968	Atl N	20	28	1	5	0	0	0	1	1-0	0	9	.179	.207	.179	16	-3	0-0	1.000	-1	69	0	O6(1/0/5)	0	-0.5

PAGE, MITCHELL Mitchell Otis; B10.15.1951 Los Angeles CA; BL/TR/6´2˝/205; [PitN73 3/72]; d4.9; C8; Col Cal Poly–Pomona

YEAR	TM LG	G	AB	R	H	2B	3B	HR	RBI	BB-IB	HP	SO	AVG	OBP	SLG	AOPS	ABR	SB-CS	FA	FR	RNG	THR	GAMES AT POSITION	DL	BFW
1977	Oak A	145	501	85	154	28	8	21	75	78-6	6	95	.307	.405	.521	153	40	42-5	.954	5	111	116	O133(131/0/5),D8	0	4.5
1978	Oak A	147	516	62	147	25	7	17	70	53-6	4	95	.285	.355	.459	134	23	23-19	.973	-0	102	61	O114(112/0/2),D33	16	1.6
1979	Oak A	133	478	51	118	11	2	9	42	52-5	3	93	.247	.323	.335	82	-12	17-16	1.000	-1	59	0	D126,O4L	0	-1.8
1980	Oak A	110	348	58	85	10	4	17	51	35-3	1	87	.244	.311	.443	112	4	14-7	ø	0	0	0	D101	0	0.2
1981	Oak A	34	92	9	13	1	0	4	13	7-0	0	29	.141	.200	.283	40	-8	2-1	ø	0	0	0	D29	0	-0.9
1982	Oak A	31	78	14	20	5	0	4	7	7-1	2	24	.256	.333	.474	123	2	3-4	ø	0	0	0	D24	0	0.1
1983	Oak A	57	79	16	19	3	0	0	1	10-0	2	22	.241	.341	.278	77	-2	3-3	1.000	0	128	0	D34,O10(7/0/3)	0	-0.3
1984	Pit N	16	12	2	4	1	0	0	0	3-0	0	4	.333	.467	.417	150	1	0-0	ø	0	—	—	/H	0	0.1
Total	8	673	2104	297	560	84	21	72	259	245-21	18	449	.266	.346	.429	117	48	104-55	.963	4	106	89	D355,O261(254/0/10)	16	3.5

PAGEL, KARL Karl Douglas; B3.29.1955 Madison WI; BL/TL/6´2˝/(185–190); [ChiN76 S1/20]; d9.21; Col Texas

YEAR	TM LG	G	AB	R	H	2B	3B	HR	RBI	BB-IB	HP	SO	AVG	OBP	SLG	AOPS	ABR	SB-CS	FA	FR	RNG	THR	GAMES AT POSITION	DL	BFW
1978	Chi N	2	2	0	0	0	0	0	0	0-0	0	2	.000	.000	.000	-89	-1	0-0	ø	0	—	—	/H	0	-0.1
1979	Chi N	1	1	0	0	0	0	0	0	0-0	0	1	.000	.000	.000	-91	0	0-0	ø	0	—	—	/H	18	0.0
1981	Cle A	14	15	3	4	0	2	1	4	4-1	0	1	.267	.421	.733	228	2	0-0	1.000	1	225	142	1b6/D	0	0.4
1982	Cle A	23	18	3	3	0	0	0	2	7-1	0	11	.167	.400	.167	62	0	0-0	.970	-0	81	66	1b10/D	0	-0.1
1983	Cle A	8	20	1	6	0	0	0	1	0-0	0	5	.300	.300	.300	63	-1	0-0	.000	-0	0	0	/lfD	0	-0.1
Total	5	48	56	7	13	0	2	1	7	11-2	0	20	.232	.358	.357	98	0	0-0	.985	1	155	105	1b16,D7/lf	18	0.1

PAGLIARONI, JIM James Vincent "Pag"; B12.8.1937 Dearborn MI; BR/TR/6´4˝/(200–210); d8.13; Mil 1956–57

YEAR	TM LG	G	AB	R	H	2B	3B	HR	RBI	BB-IB	HP	SO	AVG	OBP	SLG	AOPS	ABR	SB-CS	FA	FR	RNG	THR	GAMES AT POSITION	DL	BFW
1955	Bos A	1	0	0	0	0	0	0	0	1	0-0	0	ø	.000	ø	ø	0	0-0	ø	0	*0*	*0*	/C	0	0.0
1960	Bos A	28	62	7	19	5	2	2	9	13-0	1	11	.306	.434	.548	158	6	0-0	.990	0	106	58	C18	0	0.7
1961	Bos A	120	376	50	91	17	0	16	58	55-0	4	74	.242	.342	.415	100	1	1-1	.984	-2	98	80	C108	0	0.4
1962	Bos A	90	260	39	67	14	0	11	37	36-0	5	55	.258	.359	.438	110	5	2-1	.987	-1	88	92	C73	0	0.7
1963	Pit N	92	252	27	58	5	0	11	26	36-8	2	57	.230	.330	.381	104	2	0-0	.988	-1	87	112	C85	0	0.5
1964	Pit N	97	302	33	89	12	3	10	36	41-4	2	56	.295	.383	.454	135	15	1-0	.992	-1	102	97	C96	0	2.0
1965	Pit N	134	403	42	108	15	0	17	65	41-11	3	84	.268	.337	.432	115	8	0-0	.994	3	127	63	C131	0	1.8
1966	Pit N	123	374	37	88	20	0	11	49	50-9	4	71	.235	.329	.377	96	0	0-5	**.997**	-9	100	55	C118	0	-0.5
1967	Pit N	44	100	4	20	1	1	0	9	16-5	1	26	.200	.314	.230	59	-5	0-0	.984	2	134	70	C38	27	-0.2

YEAR	TM LG	G	AB	R	H	2B	3B	HR	RBI	BB-IB	HP	SO	AVG	OBP	SLG	AOPS	ABR	SB-CS	FA	FR	RNG	THR	GAMES AT POSITION	DL	BFW
1968	Oak A	66	199	19	49	4	0	6	20	24-1	2	42	.246	.330	.357	114	4	0-0	.997	-7	82	76	C63	50	0.0
1969	Oak A	14	27	1	4	1	0	1	2	5-0	1	2	.148	.303	.296	71	-1	0-0	.981	3	64	217	C7	0	0.2
	Sea A	40	110	10	29	4	1	5	14	13-1	0	16	.264	.333	.455	122	3	0-0	.988	-7	45	96	C29,1b2/rf	22	-0.3
	Year	54	137	11	33	5	1	6	16	18-1	1	18	.241	.327	.423	112	2	0-0	.987	-5	49	120	C36,1b2/rf	0	-0.1
Total	11	849	2465	269	622	98	7	90	326	330-39	25	494	.252	.344	.407	109	38	4-7	.991	-19	*100*	*81*	C767,1b2/rf	99	5.3
PAGLIARULO, MIKE	Michael Timothy; B3.15.1960 Medford MA; BL/TR/6´2˝/(195–201); [NYA81 6/155]; d7.7; Col Miami																								
1984	NY A	67	201	24	48	15	3	7	34	15-0	0	46	.239	.288	.448	105	1	0-0	.955	-2	90	147	3b67	0	-0.2
1985	NY A	138	380	55	91	16	2	19	62	45-4	4	86	.239	.324	.442	110	5	0-0	.951	-17	84	76	3b134	0	-1.4
1986	NY A	149	504	71	120	24	3	28	71	54-10	4	120	.238	.316	.464	110	6	4-1	.953	-3	99	106	3b143,S2	0	0.1
1987	NY A	150	522	76	122	26	3	32	87	53-9	2	111	.234	.305	.479	105	2	1-3	.959	-2	101	**130**	3b147/1	0	-0.3
1988	NY A	125	444	46	96	20	1	15	67	37-9	2	104	.216	.276	.367	80	-13	1-0	.943	-5	100	79	3b124	17	-1.8
1989	NY A	74	223	19	44	10	0	4	16	19-0	2	43	.197	.266	.296	59	-12	1-1	.936	-2	106	58	3b69/D	0	-1.4
	SD N	50	148	12	29	7	0	3	14	18-4	1	39	.196	.287	.304	69	-6	2-0	.936	-5	96	44	3b49	0	-1.0
1990	SD N	128	398	29	101	23	2	7	38	39-3	3	66	.254	.322	.374	91	-4	1-3	.955	-5	95	103	3b116	0	-1.1
1991	†Min A	121	365	38	102	20	0	6	36	21-3	3	55	.279	.322	.384	91	-5	1-2	.965	15	**120**	**158**	3b118/2	0	0.9
1992	Min A	42	105	10	21	4	0	0	9	1-0	1	17	.200	.213	.238	26	-11	1-0	.962	2	116	70	3b37/D	100	-0.8
1993	Min A	83	253	31	74	16	4	3	23	18-2	5	34	.292	.350	.423	106	2	6-6	.984	-0	102	85	3b79	0	0.2
	Bal A	33	117	24	38	9	0	6	21	8-0	1	15	.325	.373	.556	139	6	0-0	.937	-1	88	126	3b28,1b4	0	0.5
	Year	116	370	55	112	25	4	9	44	26-2	6	49	.303	.357	.465	117	9	6-6	.969	-1	98	96	3b107,1b4	0	0.7
1995	Tex A	86	241	27	56	16	0	4	27	15-2	1	49	.232	.277	.349	60	-14	0-0	.963	6	111	124	3b68,1b11	16	-0.8
Total	11	1246	3901	462	942	206	18	134	505	343-46	29	785	.241	.306	.407	93	-43	18-16	.955	-18	100	104	3b1179,1b16,D2,S2/2	133	-7.1
PAGNOZZI, TOM	Thomas Alan; B7.30.1962 Tucson AZ; BR/TR/6´1˝/(190–195); [StLN83 8/208]; d4.12; Col Arkansas																								
1987	†StL N	27	48	8	9	1	0	2	9	4-2	0	13	.188	.250	.333	52	-4	1-0	1.000	-2	353	66	C25/1	0	-0.5
1988	StL N	81	195	17	55	9	0	0	15	11-1	0	32	.282	.319	.328	85	-4	0-0	.971	-1	85	157	C28,1b28,3b5	0	-0.6
1989	StL N	52	80	3	12	2	0	0	3	6-2	1	19	.150	.216	.175	13	-9	0-0	.982	-6	61	91	C38,1b2/3	0	-1.5
1990	StL N	69	220	20	61	15	0	2	23	14-1	1	37	.277	.321	.373	90	-3	1-1	.989	12	128	155	C63,1b2	0	1.2
1991	StL N	140	459	38	121	24	5	2	57	36-6	4	63	.264	.319	.351	88	-7	9-13	.991	9	122	**138**	C139,1b3	0	0.8
1992	StL N★	139	485	33	121	26	3	7	44	28-9	1	64	.249	.290	.359	85	-11	2-5	**.999**	-9	115	78	C138	0	-1.4
1993	StL N	92	330	31	85	15	1	7	41	19-6	1	30	.258	.296	.373	79	-10	1-0	.991	-5	112	100	C92	40	-0.9
1994	StL N	70	243	21	66	12	1	7	40	21-5	0	39	.272	.327	.416	93	-3	0-0	**.998**	2	**189**	116	C70/1	32	0.3
1995	StL N	62	219	17	47	14	1	2	15	11-0	1	31	.215	.254	.315	49	-17	0-1	.995	3	98	145	C61	39	-1.0
1996	†StL N	119	407	48	110	23	0	13	55	24-2	2	78	.270	.311	.423	92	-6	4-1	.990	0	126	104	C116/1	14	0.2
1997	StL N	25	50	4	11	3	0	1	8	1-0	0	7	.220	.235	.340	48	-4	0-0	1.000	-3	142	59	C13,1b2/3	128	-0.6
1998	StL N	51	160	7	35	9	0	1	10	14-0	0	37	.219	.280	.294	52	-11	0-0	.982	-3	86	98	C44	24	-1.1
Total	12	927	2896	247	733	153	11	44	320	189-34	11	450	.253	.299	.359	79	-89	18-21	.992	-4	124	113	C827,1b40,3b7	277	-5.1
PALACIOS, REY	Robert Rey; B11.8.1962 Brooklyn NY; BR/TR/5´10˝/190; d9.8; Col Kingsborough (NY) CC																								
1988	KC A	5	11	2	1	0	0	0	0	0-0	0	4	.091	.091	.091	-48	-2	0-0	1.000	1	77	0	C3/3D	0	-0.2
1989	KC A	55	47	12	8	2	0	1	8	2-0	1	14	.170	.216	.277	39	-4	0-1	.958	-1	68	0	3b21,1b18,C13/rfD	0	-0.5
1990	KC A	41	56	8	13	3	0	2	9	5-0	0	24	.232	.295	.393	92	-1	2-2	.992	1	104	56	C27,1b7,3b3/rf	48	0.1
Total	3	101	114	22	22	5	0	3	17	7-0	1	42	.193	.244	.316	57	-7	2-3	.994	1	103	55	C43,1b25,3b25,D3,O2R	48	-0.6
PALMEIRO, ORLANDO	Orlando; B1.19.1969 Hoboken NJ; BL/TL/5´11˝/(155–185); [CalA91 33/870]; d7.1; Col Miami																								
1995	Cal A	15	20	3	7	0	0	0	1	1-0	0	1	.350	.381	.350	93	0	0-0	1.000	-0	93	0	O7(3/4/0)/D	0	0.0
1996	Cal A	50	87	6	25	6	1	0	6	8-1	2	13	.287	.361	.379	86	-2	0-1	1.000	-3	80	0	O31(7/17/8),D4	0	-0.4
1997	Ana A	74	134	19	29	2	2	0	8	17-1	1	11	.216	.307	.261	51	-10	2-2	.975	-1	101	60	O52(4/45/4),D11	15	-1.1
1998	Ana A	75	165	28	53	7	2	0	21	20-1	0	11	.321	.395	.388	103	1	5-4	1.000	1	118	0	O54(46/6/4),D3	0	0.1
1999	Ana A	109	317	46	88	12	1	1	23	39-1	6	30	.278	.364	.331	80	-8	5-5	.994	1	101	118	O92(60/1/35),D10	0	-1.0
2000	Ana A	108	243	38	73	20	2	0	25	38-0	2	20	.300	.395	.399	100	2	4-1	.984	3	103	167	O72(40/2/31),D19	0	0.2
2001	Ana A	104	230	29	56	10	1	2	23	25-2	3	24	.243	.319	.322	70	-9	6-6	.989	-0	102	74	O59(26/7/28),D30	0	-1.3
2002	†Ana A	110	263	35	79	12	1	0	31	30-1	0	22	.300	.368	.354	96	0	7-2	.993	1	104	74	O86(33/11/47),D6	0	-0.1
2003	StL N	141	317	37	86	13	1	3	33	32-3	2	31	.271	.336	.347	81	-8	3-3	**1.000**	5	112	129	O112(42/17/62)	0	-0.6
2004	†Hou N	102	133	19	32	5	0	3	12	18-1	3	19	.241	.344	.346	77	-4	2-1	1.000	-0	105	0	O37(20/4/13)	0	-0.5
2005	†Hou N	114	204	22	58	17	2	3	20	15-1	4	23	.284	.341	.431	100	0	3-1	.986	-2	87	87	O71(47/5/26)	0	-0.3
2006	Hou N	103	119	12	30	6	1	0	17	6-0	1	17	.252	.294	.319	56	-8	0-1	1.000	-1	77	0	O23(12/0/11)	0	-1.0
Total	12	1105	2232	294	616	110	14	12	220	249-12	24	222	.276	.352	.354	84	-46	37-27	.992	4	102	86	O696(340/119/269),D84	15	-6.0
PALMEIRO, RAFAEL	Rafael (Corrales); B9.24.1964 Havana, Cuba; BL/TL/6´0˝/(180–215); [ChiN85 1/22]; d9.8; Col Mississippi St.																								
1986	Chi N	22	73	9	18	4	0	3	12	4-0	1	6	.247	.295	.425	89	-1	1-1	.900	1	102	166	O20(19/0/3)	0	-0.2
1987	Chi N	84	221	32	61	15	1	14	30	20-1	1	26	.276	.336	.543	124	7	2-2	1.000	-2	95	41	O45(44/0/2),1b18	0	0.3
1988	Chi N★	152	580	75	178	41	5	8	53	38-6	3	34	.307	.349	.436	120	15	12-2	.983	-0	100	67	O147(145/2/3),1b5	0	1.3
1989	Tex A	156	559	76	154	23	4	8	64	63-3	6	48	.275	.354	.374	104	4	4-3	.991	9	117	85	1b147,D6	0	0.3
1990	Tex A	154	598	72	**191**	35	6	14	89	40-6	3	59	.319	.361	.468	131	24	3-3	.995	-3	89	98	1b146,D6	0	1.0
1991	Tex A★	159	631	115	203	**49**	3	26	88	68-10	6	72	.322	.389	.532	156	49	4-3	.992	-6	86	84	1b157,D2	0	3.2
1992	Tex A	159	608	84	163	27	4	22	85	72-8	10	83	.268	.352	.434	124	20	2-3	.995	13	122	92	1b156,D2	0	2.1
1993	Tex A	160	597	**124**	176	40	2	37	105	73-22	5	85	.295	.371	.554	151	43	22-3	.997	18	138	96	1b160	0	4.9
1994	Bal A	111	436	82	139	32	0	23	76	54-1	2	63	.319	.392	.550	133	23	7-3	.996	-1	93	102	1b111	0	1.1
1995	Bal A	143	554	89	172	30	2	39	104	62-5	3	65	.310	.380	.583	144	35	3-1	.997	10	118	108	1b142	0	3.0
1996	†Bal A	162	626	110	181	40	2	39	142	95-12	3	96	.289	.381	.546	133	33	8-0	.995	6	113	111	1b159,D3	0	2.4
1997	†Bal A	158	614	95	156	24	2	38	110	67-7	5	109	.254	.329	.485	113	10	5-2	.993	6	111	102	1b155,D3	0	0.2
1998	Bal A★	**162**	619	98	183	36	1	43	121	79-8	7	91	.296	.379	.565	144	41	11-7	.994	8	114	98	1b159,D3	0	3.2
1999	†Tex A★	158	565	96	183	30	1	47	148	97-14	3	69	.324	.420	.630	155	49	2-4	.996	-2	74	91	D128,1b28	0	3.4
2000	Tex A	158	565	102	163	29	3	39	120	103-17	3	77	.288	.397	.558	137	34	2-1	.995	-3	88	82	1b108,D46	0	1.8
2001	Tex A	160	600	98	164	33	0	47	123	101-8	7	90	.273	.381	.563	141	38	1-1	.992	4	116	107	1b113,D46	0	2.8
2002	Tex A	155	546	99	149	34	0	43	105	104-16	6	94	.273	.391	.571	148	41	2-0	.994	10	138	96	1b97,D55	0	3.8
2003	Tex A	154	561	92	146	21	2	38	112	84-9	5	77	.260	.359	.508	118	15	2-0	.996	5	133	108	D97,1b55	0	1.0
2004	Bal A	154	550	68	142	29	0	23	88	86-15	6	61	.258	.359	.436	109	9	2-1	.993	5	**115**	98	1b130,D20	0	0.2
2005	Bal A	110	369	47	98	13	0	18	60	43-4	2	43	.266	.339	.447	109	5	2-0	.995	3	109	89	1b93,D15	0	0.0
Total	20	2831	10472	1663	3020	585	38	569	1835	1353-172	87	1348	.288	.371	.515	132	494	97-40	.994	80	111	97	1b2139,D432,O212(208/2/8)	0	35.8
PALMER, DEAN	Dean William; B12.27.1968 Tallahassee FL; BR/TR/6´1˝/(175–210); [TexA86 3/59]; d9.1																								
1989	Tex A	16	19	0	2	2	0	0	1	0-0	0	12	.105	.100	.211	-13	-3	0-0	.667	-0	82	0	3b6/SlfD	0	-0.3
1991	Tex A	81	268	38	50	9	2	15	37	32-0	3	98	.187	.281	.403	88	-6	0-2	.944	-9	82	53	3b50,O29L,D5	0	-1.5
1992	Tex A	152	541	74	124	25	0	26	72	62-2	4	154	.229	.311	.420	107	4	10-4	.945	-1	92	90	3b150	0	0.4
1993	Tex A	148	519	88	127	31	2	33	96	53-4	8	154	.245	.321	.503	123	14	11-10	.922	-14	91	82	3b148/S	0	0.0
1994	Tex A	93	342	50	84	14	2	19	59	26-0	2	89	.246	.302	.465	93	-6	3-4	.912	-3	105	54	3b91	15	-0.8
1995	Tex A	36	119	30	40	6	0	9	24	21-1	4	21	.336	.448	.613	168	13	1-1	.948	2	113	148	3b36	110	1.4
1996	†Tex A	154	582	98	163	26	2	38	107	59-4	5	145	.280	.348	.527	111	8	2-0	.953	-19	84	63	3b154/D	0	-0.9
1997	Tex A	94	355	47	87	21	0	14	55	26-2	1	84	.245	.296	.423	80	-11	1-0	.959	-4	97	61	3b93	0	-1.4
	KC A	49	187	23	52	10	1	9	31	15-0	2	50	.278	.335	.487	109	2	1-2	.924	-8	87	97	3b48/D	0	-0.6
	Year	143	542	70	139	31	1	23	86	41-2	3	134	.256	.310	.445	90	-10	2-2	.948	-12	94	74	3b141/D	0	-2.0
1998	KC A★	152	572	84	159	27	2	34	119	48-3	6	134	.278	.333	.510	113	9	8-2	.921	-24	81	80	3b129,D22	0	-1.4
1999	Det A	150	560	92	147	25	2	38	100	57-3	10	153	.262	.339	.518	113	9	3-3	.945	-5	96	**105**	3b141,D9	0	0.5
2000	Det A	145	524	73	134	22	2	29	102	66-2	4	146	.256	.338	.471	104	2	4-2	.914	-15	92	72	3b115,1b20,D14	0	-1.2
2001	Det A	57	216	34	48	11	0	11	40	27-0	3	59	.222	.317	.426	96	-1	4-1	ø	0	0	0	D57	119	-0.4
2002	Det A	4	12	0	0	0	0	0	0	1-0	0	5	.000	.077	.000	-80	-3	0-0	ø	0	—	—	D4	176	-0.3
2003	Det A	26	86	3	12	2	0	0	6	9-0	2	28	.140	.235	.163	9	-11	0-0	1.000	1	162	0	D22/13	142	-1.2
Total	14	1357	4902	734	1229	231	15	275	849	502-21	54	1332	.251	.324	.472	105	20	48-31	.935	-98	92	80	3b1162,D141,O30L,1b21,S2	562	-7.7
PALMER, EDDIE	Edwin Henry "Baldy"; B6.1.1893 Petty TX; D1.9.1983 Marlow OK; BR/TR/5´9.5˝/175; d9.6																								
1917	Phi A	16	52	7	11	1	0	0	5	7	0	7	.212	.305	.231	65	-2	1	.898	0	106	49	3b13/S	—	-0.1

YEAR	TM LG	G	AB	R	H	2B	3B	HR	RBI	BB-IB	HP	SO	AVG	OBP	SLG	AOPS	ABR	SB-CS	FA	FR	RNG	THR	GAMES AT POSITION	DL	BFW
PALMISANO, JOE	Joseph; B11.19.1902 West Point GA; D11.5.1971 Albuquerque NM; BR/TR/5´8˝/160; d5.31; Col Georgia Tech																								
1931	Phi A	19	44	5	10	2	0	0	4	6	0	3	.227	.320	.273	54	-3	0-0	.960	-1	*109*	77	C16/2	—	-0.3
PALYS, STAN	Stanley Francis; B5.1.1930 Blakely PA; BR/TR/6´2˝/(187–190); d9.20																								
1953	Phi N	2	2	0	0	0	0	0	0	1	0	0	.000	.333	.000	-4	0	0-0	ø	-0	0	0	/rf	0	0.0
1954	Phi N	2	4	0	1	0	0	0	0	1	0	1	.250	.400	.250	74	0	0-0	1.000	0	113	0	/rf	0	0.0
1955	Phi N	15	52	8	15	3	0	1	8	6-0	0	5	.288	.362	.404	105	1	1-0	1.000	0	103	93	O15(3/4/8)	0	0.0
	Cin N	79	222	29	51	14	0	7	30	12-0	1	35	.230	.271	.387	69	-10	1-1	.992	2	113	78	O55L/1	0	-1.1
	Year	94	274	37	66	17	0	8	38	18-0	1	40	.241	.289	.391	75	-10	2-1	.993	3	111	81	O70(58/4/8)/1	0	-1.1
1956	Cin N	40	53	5	12	0	0	2	5	6-0	0	13	.226	.300	.340	69	-2	0-0	.929	-1	97	0	O10(7/0/4)	0	-0.3
Total	4	138	333	42	79	17	0	10	43	26-0	1	54	.237	.293	.378	74	-11	2-1	.988	2	109	72	O82(65/4/14)/1	0	-1.4
PANKOVITS, JIM	James Franklin; B8.6.1955 Pennington Gap VA; BR/TR/5´10˝/(174–175); [HouN76 4/73]; d5.27; Col South Carolina; OF(28/0/20)																								
1984	Hou N	53	81	6	23	7	0	1	14	2-0	0	20	.284	.298	.407	104	0	2-1	.925	-3	80	138	2b15,S4,O3L	0	-0.2
1985	Hou N	75	172	24	42	3	0	4	14	17-1	1	29	.244	.316	.331	83	-4	1-0	.983	2	112	108	O33(14/0/20),2b21/S3	41	-0.2
1986	†Hou N	70	113	12	32	6	1	1	7	11-1	0	25	.283	.347	.381	103	1	1-1	.969	2	102	99	2b26,O5L/C	0	0.4
1987	Hou N	50	61	7	14	2	0	1	8	6-1	0	13	.230	.299	.311	64	-3	2-0	1.000	3	95	140	2b9,O6L,3b4	0	0.0
1988	Hou N	68	140	13	31	7	1	2	12	8-0	2	28	.221	.272	.329	75	-5	2-1	.939	-5	93	128	2b31,3b11,1b2	0	-1.0
1990	Bos A	2	0	0	0	0	0	0	0	0-0	0	0	ø	ø	ø	ø	0	0-0	ø	-1	0	0	2b2	0	-0.1
Total	6	318	567	62	142	25	2	9	55	44-3	3	115	.250	.307	.349	86	-11	8-3	.961	-1	96	116	2b104,O47L,3b16,S5,1b2/C	41	-1.1
PAPE, KEN	Kenneth Wayne; B10.1.1951 San Antonio TX; BR/TR/5´11˝/185; [TexA73 5/97]; d5.17; Col Texas																								
1976	Tex A	21	23	7	5	1	0	1	4	3-1	2	2	.217	.357	.391	117	1	0-1	.968	3	167	161	S6,3b4/2D	44	0.4
PAPI, STAN	Stanley Gerard; B2.4.1951 Fresno CA; BR/TR/6´0˝/(165–180); [HouN69 2/26]; d4.11																								
1974	StL N	8	4	0	1	0	0	0	1	0-0	0	0	.250	.250	.250	40	0	0-0	1.000	1	83	443	S7/2	0	0.0
1977	Mon N	13	43	5	10	2	1	0	4	1-0	0	9	.233	.250	.326	54	-3	1-0	.952	-4	66	0	3b10,S2/2	0	-0.7
1978	Mon N	67	152	15	35	11	0	0	11	10-1	2	28	.230	.285	.303	65	-7	0-0	.976	-2	93	84	S22,3b15,2b5	0	-0.8
1979	Bos A	50	117	9	22	8	0	1	6	5-0	0	20	.188	.221	.282	33	-11	0-0	.982	7	118	119	2b26,S21/D	47	-0.2
1980	Bos A	1	0	0	0	0	0	0	0	0-0	0	0	ø	ø	ø	ø	0	0-0	ø	-0	0	0	/3	0	0.0
	Det A	46	114	12	27	3	4	3	17	5-0	0	24	.237	.267	.412	82	-4	0-0	.973	-6	80	88	2b31,3b11,S5/1	0	-0.8
	Year	47	114	12	27	3	4	3	17	5-0	0	24	.237	.267	.412	82	-4	0-0	.973	-6	80	88	2b31,3b12,S5/1	0	-0.8
1981	Det A	40	93	8	19	2	1	3	12	3-0	0	18	.204	.224	.344	61	-5	1-0	.941	-0	106	74	3b32/12lfD	0	-0.6
Total	6	225	523	49	114	26	6	7	51	24-1	2	99	.218	.253	.331	59	-30	2-0	.931	-4	93	74	3b69,2b65,S57,D4,1b2/lf	47	-3.1
PAPPAS, ERIK	Erik Daniel; B4.25.1966 Chicago IL; BR/TR/6´0˝/190; [CalA84 1/6]; d4.19																								
1991	Chi N	7	17	1	3	0	0	0	2	1-0	0	5	.176	.222	.176	13	-2	0-0	1.000	1	89	116	C6	0	-0.1
1993	StL N	82	228	25	63	12	0	1	28	35-2	0	35	.276	.368	.342	93	0	1-3	.982	7	110	102	C63,O16(1/0/15),1b2	0	0.9
1994	StL N	15	44	8	4	1	0	0	5	10-0	1	13	.091	.259	.114	6	-6	0-0	.955	-5	69	21	C15	0	-1.0
Total	3	104	289	34	70	13	0	1	35	46-2	1	53	.242	.342	.298	75	-8	1-3	.978	3	101	87	C84,O16(1/0/15),1b2	0	-0.2
PAQUETTE, CRAIG	Craig Harold; B3.28.1969 Long Beach CA; BR/TR/6´0˝/190; [OakA89 8/218]; d6.1; Col Golden West (CA) JC; OF(131/0/75)																								
1993	Oak A	105	393	35	86	20	4	12	46	14-2	0	108	.219	.245	.382	69	-20	4-2	.950	-8	91	87	3b104/lfD	0	-2.6
1994	Oak A	14	49	0	7	2	0	0	0	0-0	0	14	.143	.143	.184	-18	-9	1-0	1.000	1	95	139	3b14	0	-0.7
1995	Oak A	105	283	42	64	13	1	13	49	12-0	1	88	.226	.256	.417	76	-12	5-2	.935	-11	73	103	3b75,O20(18/0/2),S8,1b3	0	-2.2
1996	KC A	118	429	61	111	15	1	22	67	23-2	2	101	.259	.296	.452	86	-12	5-3	.891	-8	99	60	3b51,O47L,1b19,S11,D6	0	-2.0
1997	KC A	77	252	26	58	15	1	8	33	10-0	2	57	.230	.263	.393	67	-13	2-2	.935	-0	100	133	3b72,O4L	0	-1.3
1998	NY N	7	19	3	5	2	0	0	0	0-0	0	6	.263	.263	.368	66	-1	1-0	1.000	-2	34	198	3b4,1b2/lf	144	-0.3
1999	StL N	48	157	21	45	6	0	10	37	6-0	0	38	.287	.309	.516	103	0	1-0	.955	3	90	0	O27(3/0/25),3b10,2b7,1b6	0	0.1
2000	†StL N	134	384	47	94	24	2	15	61	27-1	2	83	.245	.294	.435	80	-13	4-3	.942	-7	84	88	3b86,O31(18/0/16),1b28,2b13	0	-2.1
2001	†StL N	123	340	47	96	17	0	15	64	18-1	5	67	.282	.326	.465	99	-1	3-1	1.000	-5	80	66	O56(32/0/26),3b33,1b23,2b4	0	-0.8
2002	Det A	72	252	20	49	14	1	4	20	10-0	0	53	.194	.223	.306	41	-22	1-0	.936	-2	99	63	3b49,1b14,O8(4/0/4),D5	0	-2.4
2003	Det A	11	33	2	5	0	0	0	0	0-0	0	5	.152	.152	.152	-21	-6	0-0	1.000	-1	38	113	1b5,O5(3/0/2)	0	-0.7
Total	11	814	2591	304	620	128	10	99	377	120-6	12	620	.239	.274	.411	75	-109	27-13	.941	-39	91	95	3b498,O200L,1b100,2b24,S19,D12	144	-15.0
PARDO, AL	Alberto Judas; B9.8.1962 Oviedo, Spain; BB/TR/6´2˝/(187–196); [BalA80 2/52]; d7.3																								
1985	Bal A	34	75	3	10	1	0	0	1	3-0	0	15	.133	.167	.147	-14	-12	0-0	.979	-3	50	43	C29	0	-1.4
1986	Bal A	16	51	3	7	1	0	1	3	0-0	0	14	.137	.137	.216	-6	-8	0-0	.987	-2	103	94	C14/D	0	-0.9
1988	Phi N	2	2	0	0	0	0	0	0	0-0	0	2	.000	.000	.000	-98	-1	0-0	1.000	-0	0	0	C2	0	-0.1
1989	Phi N	1	1	0	0	0	0	0	0	0-0	0	0	.000	.000	.000	-99	0	0-0	1.000	0	0	0	/C	0	0.0
Total	4	53	129	6	17	2	0	1	4	3-0	0	31	.132	.152	.171	-12	-21	0-0	.982	-5	68	60	C46/D	0	-2.4
PAREDES, JOHNNY	Johnny Alfonso (Isambert); B9.2.1962 Maracaibo, Zulia, Venez.; BR/TR/5´11˝/(165–175); d4.29; [DL 1989 Mon N 178]																								
1988	Mon N	35	91	6	17	2	0	1	10	9-0	3	17	.187	.282	.242	49	-6	5-2	.976	-1	100	131	2b28/rf	0	-0.6
1990	Det A	6	8	2	1	0	0	0	0	1-0	0	0	.125	.222	.125	-0	-1	0-0	.917	-0	98	115	2b4	0	-0.1
	Mon N	3	6	0	2	1	0	0	1	1-1	0	0	.333	.429	.500	160	1	0-0	.889	-0	116	192	2b2	0	0.0
1991	Det A	16	18	4	6	0	0	0	0	0-0	0	1	.333	.333	.333	83	0	1-1	.958	-1	91	150	2b7/3SD	0	-0.1
Total	3	60	123	12	26	3	0	1	11	11-1	3	18	.211	.292	.260	56	-6	6-3	.965	-2	100	136	2b41,D2/S3rf	178	-0.8
PARENT, FREDDY	Frederick Alfred; B11.25.1875 Biddeford ME; D11.2.1972 Sanford ME; BR/TR/5´7˝/154; d7.14																								
1899	StL N	2	8	0	1	0	0	0	1	0	0	—	.125	.125	.125	-31	-1	0	.889	-0	93	157	2b2	—	-0.2
1901	Bos A	**138**	517	87	158	23	9	4	59	41	9	—	.306	.367	.408	117	13	16	.918	-2	100	115	S138	—	1.4
1902	Bos A	**138**	567	91	156	31	8	3	62	24	4	—	.275	.309	.374	86	-12	16	.932	0	102	108	S138	—	-0.7
1903	†Bos A	139	560	83	170	31	17	4	80	13	6	—	.304	.326	.441	122	13	24	.930	8	103	82	S139	—	2.6
1904	Bos A	155	591	85	172	22	9	6	77	28	6	—	.291	.330	.389	120	12	20	.929	-10	98	107	S155	—	0.9
1905	Bos A	**153**	602	55	141	16	5	0	33	47	6	—	.234	.296	.277	81	-12	25	.920	-11	99	109	S153	—	-2.0
1906	Bos A	149	600	67	141	14	10	1	49	31	4	—	.235	.277	.297	80	-16	16	.933	-4	99	104	S143,2b6	—	-1.7
1907	Bos A	114	409	51	113	19	5	1	26	22	5	—	.276	.321	.355	116	7	12	.978	-1	186	73	O47(26/13/9),S43,3b7,2b5	—	0.6
1908	Chi A	119	391	28	81	7	5	0	35	50	2	—	.207	.300	.251	81	-6	9	.930	2	107	100	S118	—	-0.1
1909	Chi A	136	472	61	123	10	5	0	30	46	7	—	.261	.335	.303	106	5	32	.929	14	114	115	S98,O38(7/30/1)/2	—	2.3
1910	Chi A	81	258	23	46	6	1	1	16	29	2	—	.178	.266	.221	55	-13	14	.970	-3	87	65	O62(1/59/2),2b11,S4/3	—	-2.0
1911	Chi A	3	9	2	4	1	0	0	3	2	0	—	.444	.545	.556	214	2	0	1.000	1	123	0	2b3	—	0.2
Total	12	1327	4984	633	1306	180	74	20	471	333	51	—	.262	.315	.340	99	-8	184	.927	-7	102	106	S1129,O147(34/102/12),2b28,3b8	—	1.3
PARENT, MARK	Mark Alan; B9.16.1961 Ashland OR; BR/TR/6´5˝/(215–245); [SDN79 4/92]; d9.20																								
1986	SD N	8	14	1	2	0	0	0	0	1-0	0	3	.143	.200	.143	-4	-2	0-0	.889	-2	38	0	C3	0	-0.4
1987	SD N	12	25	0	2	0	0	0	2	0-0	0	9	.080	.080	.080	-60	-6	0-0	1.000	-0	190	0	C10	0	-0.6
1988	SD N	41	118	9	23	3	0	6	15	6-0	0	23	.195	.232	.373	73	-5	0-0	.986	6	172	84	C36	0	0.3
1989	SD N	52	141	12	27	4	0	7	21	8-2	0	34	.191	.229	.369	70	-6	1-0	1.000	6	143	90	C41/1	0	0.2
1990	SD N	65	189	13	42	11	0	3	16	16-3	0	29	.222	.283	.328	67	-9	1-0	.992	2	94	90	C60	0	-0.3
1991	Tex A	3	1	0	0	0	0	0	0	0-0	0	1	.000	.000	.000	-99	0	0-0	1.000	0	0	0	C3	151	0.0
1992	Bal A	17	34	4	8	1	0	2	4	3-0	1	7	.235	.316	.441	107	0	0-0	.988	3	122	93	C16	0	0.4
1993	Bal A	22	54	7	14	2	0	4	12	3-0	0	14	.259	.293	.519	110	0	0-0	.989	-3	161	16	C21/D	0	-0.1
1994	Chi N	44	99	8	26	4	0	3	16	13-1	1	24	.263	.348	.394	95	-1	0-1	.976	-1	88	170	C37	0	0.0
1995	Pit N	69	233	25	54	9	0	15	33	23-2	0	62	.232	.301	.464	96	-3	0-0	.990	-4	101	151	C67	0	-0.2
	Chi N	12	32	5	8	2	0	3	5	3-0	0	7	.250	.314	.594	133	1	0-0	1.000	3	165	143	C10	0	0.5
	Year	81	265	30	62	11	0	18	38	26-2	0	69	.234	.302	.479	100	-1	0-0	.992	-1	108	**150**	C77	0	0.3
1996	Det A	38	104	13	25	6	0	7	17	3-0	0	27	.240	.259	.500	86	-3	0-0	.994	-4	121	142	C33/1	0	-0.4
	†Bal A	18	33	4	6	1	0	2	6	2-0	0	10	.182	.229	.394	54	-3	0-0	.987	0	172	67	C18	0	-0.2
	Year	56	137	17	31	7	0	9	23	5-0	0	37	.226	.252	.474	78	-6	0-0	.992	-4	135	122	C51/1	0	-0.6
1997	Phi N	39	113	4	17	3	0	0	8	7-0	0	39	.150	.198	.177	-0	-17	0-1	.996	-5	89	136	C38	0	-2.1
1998	Phi N	34	113	7	25	4	0	1	13	10-0	0	30	.221	.278	.283	50	-8	1-1	.987	-6	119	86	C34	0	-1.2
Total	13	474	1303	112	279	50	0	53	168	98-8	2	319	.214	.268	.375	71	-62	3-3	.990	-3	119	110	C427,1b2/D	151	-4.1

YEAR	TM LG	G	AB	R	H	2B	3B	HR	RBI	BB-IB	HP	SO	AVG	OBP	SLG	AOPS	ABR	SB-CS	FA	FR	RNG	THR	GAMES AT POSITION	DL	BFW
PARIS, KELLY	Kelly Jay; B10.17.1957 Encino CA; BR/TR/6´0˝/(175–180); [StLN75 2/40]; d9.1																								
1982	StL N	12	29	1	3	0	0	0	1	0-0	0	7	.103	.100	.103	-41	-6	0-0	.867	2	125	382	3b5,S4	0	-0.3
1983	Cin N	56	120	13	30	6	0	0	7	15-1	1	22	.250	.336	.300	75	-3	8-2	1.000	-4	116	0	3b16,2b10,S7,1b3	0	-0.6
1985	Bal A	5	9	0	0	0	0	0	0	0-0	0	1	.000	.000	.000	-99	-3	0-0	.857	-1	61	0	2b2,D2	0	-0.4
1986	Bal A	5	10	0	2	0	0	0	0	0-0	0	3	.200	.200	.200	9	-1	0-1	.857	0	130	240	3b3,D2	0	-0.1
1988	Chi A	14	44	6	11	0	0	3	6	0-0	0	6	.250	.250	.455	93	-1	0-0	1.000	-0	75	136	1b9,3b4/D	45	-0.2
Total	5	92	212	20	46	6	0	3	14	15-1	1	39	.217	.270	.288	54	-14	8-3	.944	-4	121	85	3b28,1b12,2b12,S11,D5	45	-1.6
PARISSE, TONY	Louis Peter; B6.25.1911 Philadelphia PA; D6.2.1956 Philadelphia PA; BR/TR/5´10˝/165; d9.22																								
1943	Phi A	6	17	0	3	0	0	0	1	2	0	2	.176	.263	.176	30	-1	0-0	1.000	0	*81*	*173*	C5	0	-0.1
1944	Phi A	4	4	0	0	0	0	0	0	0	0	1	.000	.000	.000	-99	-1	0-0	.500	-1	*0*	*0*	C2	0	-0.2
Total	2	10	21	0	3	0	0	0	1	2	0	3	.143	.217	.143	6	-2	0-0	.960	-0	*74*	*158*	C7	0	-0.3
PARKER, ACE	Clarence McKay; B5.17.1912 Portsmouth VA; BR/TR/6´0˝/180; d4.24; Col Duke																								
1937	Phi A	38	94	8	11	0	1	2	13	4	0	17	.117	.153	.202	-11	-17	0-0	.905	-3	93	91	S19,2b9,O5(2/3/0)	—	-1.8
1938	Phi A	56	113	12	26	5	0	0	12	10	0	16	.230	.293	.274	44	-10	1-2	.972	-3	91	57	S26,2b9,3b9	—	-1.1
Total	2	94	207	20	37	5	1	2	25	14	0	33	.179	.231	.242	19	-27	1-2	.934	-6	92	75	S45,2b18,3b9,O5(2/3/0)	—	-2.9
PARKER, PAT	Clarence Perkins; B5.22.1893 Somerville MA; D3.21.1967 Claremont NH; BR/TR/5´7˝/160; d8.10; Col Dubuque																								
1915	StL A	3	6	0	1	0	0	0	1	0	0	3	.167	.167	.167	-0	-1	0-1	1.000	0	133	0	O2R	—	-0.1
PARKER, DAVE	David Gene; B6.9.1951 Grenada MS; BL/TR/6´5˝/(220–250); [PitN70 14/332]; d7.12; C2																								
1973	Pit N	54	139	17	40	9	1	4	14	2-1	2	27	.288	.308	.453	110	1	1-1	.964	3	122	130	O39(4/16/19)	0	0.3
1974	†Pit N	73	220	27	62	10	3	4	29	10-1	3	53	.282	.322	.409	106	1	3-3	.964	2	104	158	O49(11/14/27),1b6	47	-0.1
1975	†Pit N	148	558	75	172	35	10	25	101	38-4	5	89	.308	.357	**.541**	146	31	8-6	.972	5	110	71	O141R	0	2.9
1976	Pit N	138	537	82	168	28	10	13	90	30-6	2	80	.313	.349	.475	131	19	19-7	.956	1	104	102	O134R	0	1.6
1977	Pit N★	159	637	107	**215**	**44**	8	21	88	58-13	7	107	**.338**	.397	.531	142	39	17-19	.965	23	**118**	**203**	O158R/2	0	5.0
1978	Pit N	148	581	102	194	32	12	30	117	57-**23**	2	92	**.334**	.394	**.585**	162	**47**	20-7	.960	1	105	98	O147R	15	**4.4**
1979	†Pit N★	158	622	109	193	45	7	25	94	67-14	9	101	.310	.380	.526	138	34	20-4	.960	0	104	108	O158R	0	2.9
1980	Pit N★	139	518	71	153	31	1	17	79	25-5	2	69	.295	.327	.458	114	8	10-7	.965	1	100	130	O130R	0	0.3
1981	Pit N★	67	240	29	62	14	3	9	48	9-3	2	25	.258	.287	.454	104	0	6-2	.941	-4	99	21	O60R	15	-0.7
1982	Pit N	73	244	41	66	19	3	6	29	22-2	1	45	.270	.330	.447	111	4	7-5	.957	-3	97	47	O63R	66	-0.3
1983	Pit N	144	552	68	154	29	4	12	69	28-6	0	89	.279	.311	.411	96	-4	12-9	.973	0	111	32	O142R	0	-1.3
1984	Cin N	156	607	73	173	28	0	16	94	41-10	1	89	.285	.328	.410	102	1	11-10	.974	-2	104	60	O151R	0	-1.0
1985	Cin N★	160	635	88	198	**42**	4	34	**125**	52-**24**	3	80	.312	.365	.551	146	38	5-13	.972	6	109	110	O159R	0	3.3
1986	Cin N★	**162**	637	89	174	31	3	31	116	56-16	1	126	.273	.330	.477	116	12	1-6	.970	-9	91	68	O159R	0	-0.7
1987	Cin N	153	589	77	149	28	0	26	97	44-13	8	104	.253	.311	.433	92	-8	7-3	.967	4	103	134	O142R,1b9	0	-1.2
1988	†Oak A	101	377	43	97	18	1	12	55	32-2	0	70	.257	.314	.406	104	1	0-1	.953	-0	88	164	D61,O34L/1	47	-0.2
1989	†Oak A	144	553	56	146	27	0	22	97	38-13	1	91	.264	.308	.432	111	6	0-0	1.000	0	104	0	D140/rf	0	0.2
1990	Mil A☆	157	610	71	176	30	3	21	92	41-11	4	102	.289	.330	.451	119	14	4-7	.960	-1	0	168	D153,1b3	0	0.6
1991	Cal A	119	466	45	108	22	2	11	56	29-3	3	91	.232	.279	.358	76	-17	3-2	ø	0	0	0	D119	0	-2.1
	Tor A	13	36	2	12	4	0	0	3	4-0	0	7	.333	.400	.444	128	2	0-1	ø	0	0	0	D11	0	0.1
	Year	132	502	47	120	26	2	11	59	33-3	3	98	.239	.288	.365	79	-15	3-3	ø	0	0	0	D130	0	-2.0
Total	19	2466	9358	1272	2712	526	75	339	1493	683-170	56	1537	.290	.339	.471	120	229	154-113	.965	27	105	101	O1867(49/30/1791),D484,1b19/2	190	14.0
PARKER, DIXIE	Douglas Woolley; B4.24.1895 Forest Home AL; D5.15.1972 Tuscaloosa AL; BL/TR/5´11˝/160; d7.28																								
1923	Phi N	4	5	0	1	0	0	0	1	0	0	1	.200	.200	.200	5	-1	0-0	.500	-1	*47*	*0*	C2	—	-0.2
PARKER, SALTY	Francis James; B7.8.1912 E.St.Louis IL; D7.27.1992 Houston TX; BR/TR/6´0˝/173; d8.13; M2/C16																								
1936	Det A	11	25	6	7	2	0	0	4	2	0	3	.280	.333	.360	71	-1	0-2	.906	2	111	151	S7,1b2	—	0.0
PARKER, WES	Maurice Wesley; B11.13.1939 Evanston IL; BB/TL/6´1˝/(180–190); d4.19; Col Claremont McKenna																								
1964	LA N	124	214	29	55	7	1	3	10	14-3	1	45	.257	.303	.341	88	-4	5-4	.971	4	116	92	O69(9/15/49),1b31	0	-0.4
1965	†LA N	154	542	80	129	24	7	8	51	75-1	5	95	.238	.334	.352	101	3	13-7	**.997**	4	104	105	1b154/cf	0	-0.2
1966	†LA N	156	475	67	120	17	5	12	51	69-9	5	83	.253	.351	.385	114	11	7-3	.992	2	95	83	1b140,O14(2/7/5)	0	0.6
1967	LA N	139	413	56	102	16	5	5	31	65-10	7	83	.247	.358	.346	112	9	10-5	**.996**	5	114	94	1b112,O18C	0	0.9
1968	LA N	135	468	42	112	22	2	3	27	49-6	2	87	.239	.312	.314	96	-1	4-6	**.999**	3	105	96	1b114,O28(22/6/1)	0	-0.8
1969	LA N	132	471	76	131	23	4	13	68	56-6	2	46	.278	.353	.427	127	17	4-1	.995	1	100	95	1b128,O2(0/1/1)	22	0.9
1970	LA N	**161**	614	84	196	**47**	4	10	111	79-18	0	70	.319	.392	.458	133	32	8-2	**.996**	4	109	92	1b161	0	2.4
1971	LA N	157	533	69	146	24	1	6	62	63-5	1	63	.274	.347	.356	106	6	6-1	.996	5	116	**111**	1b148,O18(1/0/18)	0	0.1
1972	LA N	130	427	45	119	14	3	4	59	62-5	1	43	.279	.367	.354	109	7	3-5	**.997**	4	**113**	108	1b120,O5(0/3/2)	0	0.1
Total	9	1288	4157	548	1110	194	32	64	470	532-63	24	615	.267	.351	.375	112	80	60-34	.996	32	108	98	1b1108,O155(34/51/76)	22	3.6
PARKER, RICK	Richard Alan; B3.20.1963 Kansas City MO; BR/TR/6´0˝/185; [PhiN85 16/408]; d5.4; Col Texas																								
1990	SF N	54	107	19	26	5	0	2	14	10-0	1	15	.243	.314	.346	84	-2	6-1	.978	-2	90	63	O35(13/5/23),2b2/3S	0	-0.4
1991	SF N	13	14	0	1	0	0	0	1	1-0	0	5	.071	.133	.071	-42	-3	0-0	1.000	0	140	0	O4(4/1/0)	38	-0.3
1993	Hou N	45	45	11	15	3	0	0	4	3-0	0	8	.333	.375	.400	111	1	1-2	1.000	-1	89	0	O16(3/13/1)/2S	0	-0.1
1994	NY N	8	16	1	1	0	0	0	0	0-0	0	2	.063	.063	.063	-68	-4	0-0	1.000	1	139	282	O6(4/1/3)	26	-0.3
1995	LA N	27	29	3	8	0	0	0	4	2-0	0	4	.276	.323	.276	64	-2	1-1	1.000	1	130	201	O21(19/1/1),3b2,S2	0	-0.1
1996	LA N	16	14	2	4	1	0	0	1	0-0	1	2	.286	.333	.357	87	0	1-0	1.000	-1	30	0	O4(1/3/0)	0	-0.1
Total	6	163	225	36	55	9	0	2	24	16-0	2	36	.244	.300	.311	68	-10	9-4	.990	-0	102	96	O86(44/24/28),S4,3b3,2b3	64	-1.3
PARKER, BILLY	William David; B1.14.1947 Hayneville AL; D2.9.2003 Sun City West AZ; BR/TR/5´8˝/168; d9.9																								
1971	Cal A	20	70	4	16	0	1	1	6	2-0	0	20	.229	.250	.300	59	-4	1-1	.958	-4	97	100	2b20	0	-0.8
1972	Cal A	36	80	11	17	2	0	2	8	9-0	0	17	.213	.286	.313	84	-2	0-2	.951	-0	77	108	3b21,2b9,O5L/S	0	-0.3
1973	Cal A	38	102	14	23	2	1	0	7	8-1	1	23	.225	.286	.265	61	-5	0-1	.959	-8	71	72	2b32,S3/D	0	-1.2
Total	3	94	252	29	56	4	2	3	21	19-1	1	60	.222	.276	.290	68	-11	1-4	.963	-12	85	89	2b61,3b21,O5L,S4/D	0	-2.3
PARKINSON, FRANK	Frank Joseph "Parky"; B3.23.1895 Dickson City PA; D7.4.1960 Trenton NJ; BR/TR/5´11˝/175; d4.13																								
1921	Phi N	108	391	36	99	20	2	5	32	13	0	81	.253	.277	.353	61	-22	3-4	.931	9	**111**	89	S105/3	—	-0.2
1922	Phi N	141	545	86	150	18	6	15	70	55	2	93	.275	.344	.413	86	-12	3-4	.963	**28**	**117**	98	2b139	—	1.8
1923	Phi N	67	219	21	53	12	0	3	28	13	1	31	.242	.288	.338	58	-13	0-4	.950	2	105	99	2b37,S15,3b11	—	-1.0
1924	Phi N	62	156	14	33	7	0	1	19	14	1	28	.212	.281	.276	44	-12	3-1	.952	6	109	128	3b28,S21,2b10	—	-0.3
Total	4	378	1311	157	335	57	8	24	149	95	4	233	.256	.308	.366	69	-59	9-13	.962	44	115	99	2b186,S141,3b40	—	0.3
PARKS, ART	Artie William; B11.1.1911 Paris AR; D12.6.1989 Little Rock AR; BL/TR/5´9˝/170; d9.25																								
1937	Bro N	7	16	2	5	2	0	0	0	2	0	2	.313	.389	.438	122	1	0	1.000	1	67	469	O4L	—	0.1
1939	Bro N	71	239	27	65	13	2	1	19	28	0	14	.272	.348	.356	86	-4	2	.977	-3	97	41	O65(32/0/34)	—	-1.1
Total	2	78	255	29	70	15	2	1	19	30	0	16	.275	.351	.361	89	-3	2	.978	-3	96	61	O69(36/0/34)	—	-1.0
PARKS, DEREK	Derek Gavin; B9.29.1968 Covina CA; BR/TR/6´0˝/(205–217); [MinA86 1/10]; d9.11																								
1992	Min A	7	6	1	2	0	0	0	0	1-0	1	1	.333	.500	.333	133	0	0-0	1.000	-0	40	100	C7	0	0.0
1993	Min A	7	20	3	4	0	0	0	1	1-0	0	2	.200	.238	.200	19	-2	0-0	.970	-1	98	0	C7	0	-0.3
1994	Min A	31	89	6	17	6	0	1	9	4-0	2	20	.191	.242	.292	37	-9	0-1	.993	-3	84	141	C31	0	-1.0
Total	3	45	115	10	23	6	0	1	10	6-0	3	23	.200	.258	.278	40	-11	0-1	.989	-4	83	113	C45	0	-1.3
PARKS, BILL	William Robert; B6.4.1849 Easton PA; D10.10.1911 Easton PA; BR/TR/5´8˝/150; d4.26; M1; ▲																								
1875	Was NA	27	111	13	20	0	0	0	6	1	—	1	.180	.188	.180	29	-7	1-1	.836	3	137	0	O17(16/1/0),P14,M	—	-0.1
	Phi NA	2	6	0	1	0	0	0	0	0	—	1	.167	.167	.167	16	-1	0-0	.500	-0	0	0	P2,O2L	—	0.0
	Year	29	117	13	21	0	0	0	6	1	—	2	.179	.186	.179	29	-8	1-1	.833	2	125	0	O19(18/1/0),P16	—	-0.1
1876	Bos N	1	4	0	0	0	0	0	0	0	—	0	.000	.000	.000	-98	-1	—	.750	-0	0	0	/lf	—	-0.1
PARRILLA, SAM	Samuel (Monge); B6.12.1943 Santurce, PR; D2.9.1994 Brooklyn NY; BR/TR/5´11˝/185; d4.11																								
1970	Phi N	11	16	0	2	1	0	0	0	1-0	0	4	.125	.176	.188	-2	-2	0-0	1.000	0	125	0	O3L	0	-0.2

YEAR	TM LG	G	AB	R	H	2B	3B	HR	RBI	BB-IB	HP	SO	AVG	OBP	SLG	AOPS	ABR	SB-CS	FA	FR	RNG	THR	GAMES AT POSITION	DL	BFW
PARRISH, LANCE	Lance Michael; B6.15.1956 Clairton PA; BR/TR/6´3˝/(195–224); [DetA74 1/16]; d9.5; C6																								
1977	Det A	12	46	10	9	2	0	3	7	5-0	0	12	.196	.275	.435	85	-1	0-0	1.000	4	388	101	C12	0	0.3
1978	Det A	85	288	37	63	11	3	14	41	11-0	3	71	.219	.254	.424	85	-8	0-0	.987	7	161	81	C79	0	0.3
1979	Det A	143	493	65	136	26	3	19	65	49-2	2	105	.276	.343	.456	110	7	6-7	.989	7	121	121	C142	0	1.8
1980	Det A★	144	553	79	158	34	6	24	82	31-3	3	109	.286	.325	.499	120	13	6-4	.990	5	128	95	C121,D16,1b5,O5(1/0/4)	0	2.1
1981	Det A	96	348	39	85	18	2	10	46	34-6	0	52	.244	.311	.394	98	-1	2-3	.993	4	124	104	C90,D5	0	0.6
1982	Det A★	133	486	75	138	19	2	32	87	40-5	1	99	.284	.338	.529	133	20	3-4	.989	17	142	107	C132/lf	0	4.2
1983	Det A★	155	605	80	163	42	3	27	114	44-7	1	106	.269	.314	.483	120	15	1-3	.995	11	**150**	131	C131,D27	0	3.0
1984	†Det A★	147	578	75	137	16	2	33	98	41-6	2	120	.237	.287	.443	100	-3	2-3	.991	16	**156**	99	C127,D22	0	1.7
1985	Det A✳	140	549	64	150	27	1	28	98	41-5	2	90	.273	.323	.479	117	12	2-6	.993	3	128	99	C120,D22	0	1.7
1986	Det A★	91	327	53	84	6	1	22	62	38-3	5	83	.257	.340	.483	122	9	0-0	.989	11	131	115	C85,D6	60	2.3
1987	Phi N	130	466	42	114	21	0	17	67	47-2	1	104	.245	.313	.399	85	-11	0-1	.989	-2	85	110	C127	0	-0.7
1988	Phi N★	123	424	44	91	17	2	15	60	47-7	2	93	.215	.293	.370	88	-7	0-0	.988	1	83	119	C117/1	15	0.1
1989	Cal A	124	433	48	103	12	1	17	50	42-6	2	104	.238	.306	.388	97	-3	1-1	.993	0	114	75	C122,D2	0	0.4
1990	Cal A★	133	470	54	126	14	0	24	70	46-4	5	107	.268	.338	.451	121	12	2-2	.993	19	**136**	127	C131,1b4/D	0	3.8
1991	Cal A	119	402	38	87	12	0	19	51	35-2	5	117	.216	.285	.388	85	-10	0-1	.997	12	125	115	C111,1b3,D5	15	0.8
1992	Cal A	24	83	7	19	2	0	4	11	5-1	0	22	.229	.270	.398	85	-2	0-0	.975	-4	66	141	C22,D2	38	-0.5
	Sea A	69	192	19	45	11	1	8	21	19-2	1	48	.234	.304	.427	102	0	1-1	.995	-1	55	128	C34,1b16,D14	0	-0.1
	Year	93	275	26	64	13	1	12	32	24-3	1	70	.233	.294	.418	97	-2	1-1	.987	-5	60	134	C56,D16,1b16	0	-0.6
1993	Cle A	10	20	2	4	1	0	1	2	4-0	0	5	.200	.333	.400	96	0	1-0	.950	1	38	222	C10	0	0.2
1994	Pit N	40	126	10	34	5	0	3	16	18-1	1	28	.270	.363	.381	93	-1	1-1	.988	1	118	92	C38/1	0	0.2
1995	Tor A	70	178	15	36	9	0	4	22	15-0	1	52	.202	.265	.320	52	-13	0-0	1.000	10	93	169	C67/D	0	0.1
Total	19	1988	7067	856	1782	305	27	324	1070	612-62	37	1527	.252	.313	.440	105	28	28-37	.991	123	125	110	C1818,D123,1b30,O6(2/0/4)	128	22.3
PARRISH, LARRY	Larry Alton; B11.10.1953 Winter Haven FL; BR/TR/6´3˝/(190–215); d9.6; M2/C2; Col Seminole (FL) CC; OF(3/0/405)																								
1974	Mon N	25	69	9	14	5	0	0	4	6-2	2	19	.203	.286	.275	54	-4	0-0	.986	5	125	74	3b24	0	0.1
1975	Mon N	145	532	50	146	32	5	10	65	28-5	4	74	.274	.314	.410	95	-5	4-5	.919	-8	98	126	3b143/2S	0	-1.5
1976	Mon N	154	543	65	126	28	5	11	61	41-2	2	91	.232	.285	.363	80	-15	2-6	.945	7	105	116	3b153	0	-1.2
1977	Mon N	123	402	50	99	19	2	11	46	37-9	4	71	.246	.314	.386	89	-7	2-4	.936	-5	103	63	3b115	0	-1.5
1978	Mon N	144	520	68	144	39	4	15	70	32-9	2	103	.277	.321	.454	115	9	2-3	.947	-12	92	86	3b139	0	-0.6
1979	Mon N★	153	544	83	167	39	2	30	82	41-11	2	101	.307	.357	.551	144	31	5-1	.947	-16	89	98	3b153	0	1.4
1980	Mon N	126	452	55	115	27	3	15	72	36-6	4	80	.254	.310	.427	103	1	2-6	.949	-6	92	80	3b124	28	-0.8
1981	†Mon N	97	349	41	85	19	3	8	44	28-2	0	73	.244	.297	.384	90	-5	0-0	.935	-17	75	51	3b95	0	-2.6
1982	Tex A	128	440	59	116	15	0	17	62	30-0	4	84	.264	.314	.414	103	1	5-2	.962	-9	78	142	O124R,3b3,D2	0	-1.4
1983	Tex A	145	555	76	151	26	4	26	88	46-8	3	91	.272	.326	.474	120	14	0-0	.962	-13	79	107	O132R,D13	0	-0.7
1984	Tex A	156	613	72	175	42	1	22	101	42-7	6	116	.285	.336	.465	115	13	2-4	.982	-0	90	156	O81(2/0/80),D63,3b12	0	0.5
1985	Tex A	94	346	44	86	11	1	17	51	33-2	1	77	.249	.314	.434	101	-1	0-2	.991	-4	84	90	O69R,D22,3b2	57	-1.0
1986	Tex A	129	464	67	128	22	1	28	94	52-7	2	114	.276	.347	.509	127	17	3-1	.935	-6	69	39	D98,3b30	29	0.8
1987	Tex A★	152	557	79	149	22	1	32	100	49-7	3	154	.268	.328	.483	111	7	3-1	.918	-7	57	119	D122,3b28/lf	0	-0.3
1988	Tex A	68	248	22	47	9	1	7	26	20-2	2	79	.190	.253	.319	58	-14	0-0	ø	0	0	0	D67	0	-1.7
	†Bos A	52	158	10	41	5	0	7	26	8-0	1	32	.259	.298	.424	96	-2	0-1	.988	3	129	86	1b36,D14	0	-0.2
	Year	120	406	32	88	14	1	14	52	28-2	3	111	.217	.270	.360	73	-16	0-1	.988	3	129	86	D81,1b36	0	-1.9
Total	15	1891	6792	850	1789	360	33	256	992	529-79	42	1359	.263	.318	.439	106	40	30-36	.941	-88	93	91	3b1021,O407R,D401,1b36/S2	114	-10.7
PARROTT, TOM	Thomas William "Tacky Tom"; B4.10.1868 Portland OR; D1.1.1932 Dundee OR; BR/TR/5´10.5˝/170; d6.18; b–Jiggs; OF(15/88/28); ▲																								
1893	Chi N	7	27	4	7	1	0	0	3	1	0	2	.259	.286	.296	56	-2	0	.800	-1	17	0	P4,3b2/2	—	-0.1
	Cin N	24	68	5	13	1	1	1	9	1	0	9	.191	.203	.279	27	-8	0	.915	1	117	90	P22/lf	—	0.0
	Year	31	95	9	20	2	1	1	12	2	0	11	.211	.227	.284	35	-10	0	.906	0	102	77	P26,3b2/2lf	—	-0.1
1894	Cin N	68	229	51	74	12	6	4	40	17	1	10	.323	.372	.480	101	-1	4	.929	2	113	92	P41,O13(9/2/2),1b12/S32	—	0.0
1895	Cin N	64	201	35	69	13	7	3	41	11	0	8	.343	.377	.522	126	6	10	.922	1	107	100	P41,1b14,O9(1/8/0)	—	0.1
1896	StL N	118	474	62	138	13	12	7	70	11	0	24	.291	.307	.414	93	-9	12	.951	7	99	156	O108(4/78/26),P7,1b6	—	-0.7
Total	4	281	999	157	301	40	26	15	163	41	1	53	.301	.329	.438	96	-14	26	.940	11	109	147	O131C,P115,1b32,3b3,2b2/S	—	-0.7
PARROTT, JIGGS	Walter Edward; B7.14.1871 Portland OR; D4.14.1898 Phoenix AZ; 5´11˝/160; d7.11; b–Tom																								
1892	Chi N	78	333	38	67	8	5	2	22	8	1	30	.201	.222	.273	49	-23	7	.891	-1	96	63	3b78	—	-2.1
1893	Chi N	110	455	54	111	10	9	1	65	13	1	25	.244	.267	.312	54	-33	25	.904	10	**108**	109	3b99,2b7,O4R	—	-1.8
1894	Chi N	126	525	82	130	17	9	3	65	16	3	35	.248	.274	.331	43	-53	30	.932	-3	100	91	2b125/3	—	-3.9
1895	Chi N	3	4	0	1	0	0	0	0	0	0	0	.250	.250	.250	27	0	0	ø	-1	0	0	/lfS1	—	-0.1
Total	4	317	1317	174	309	35	23	6	152	37	5	90	.235	.258	.310	48	-109	62	.899	6	103	89	3b178,2b132,O5(1/0/4)/1S	—	-7.9
PARSONS, CASEY	Casey Robert; B4.14.1954 Wenatchee WA; BL/TR/6´1˝/(180–187); d5.31; Col Gonzaga																								
1981	Sea A	36	22	6	5	1	0	1	5	1-0	2	4	.227	.308	.409	104	0	0-0	1.000	2	134	387	O24(3/2/19)/1	0	0.2
1983	Chi A	8	5	1	1	0	0	0	0	2-1	0	1	.200	.429	.200	76	0	0-0	1.000	0	194	0	O3(0/1/2),D2	0	0.0
1984	Chi A	1	1	0	0	0	0	0	0	0-0	0	1	.000	.000	.000	-95	0	0-0	ø	0	—	—	/H	0	0.0
1987	Cle A	18	25	2	4	0	0	1	5	0-0	0	5	.160	.160	.280	13	-3	0-0	1.000	0	189	0	O2(0/1/1)/1D	0	-0.3
Total	4	63	53	9	10	1	0	2	10	3-1	2	11	.189	.254	.321	57	-3	0-0	1.000	3	141	341	O29(3/4/22),D7,1b2	0	-0.1
PARSONS, DIXIE	Edward Dixon; B5.12.1916 Talladega AL; D10.31.1991 Longview TX; BR/TR/6´2˝/180; d8.16																								
1939	Det A	5	1	0	0	0	0	0	0	1	0	1	.000	.500	.000	36	0	0-0	1.000	0	*0*	*0*	C4	—	0.0
1942	Det A	63	188	8	37	4	0	2	11	13	0	22	.197	.249	.250	37	-16	1-0	.981	8	*106*	*112*	C62	0	-0.5
1943	Det A	40	106	2	15	3	0	0	4	6	0	16	.142	.188	.170	4	-13	0-0	.975	4	*99*	*154*	C40	0	-0.8
Total	3	108	295	10	52	7	0	2	15	20	0	39	.176	.229	.220	26	-29	1-0	.979	11	*103*	*127*	C106	0	-1.3
PARTEE, ROY	Roy Robert; B9.7.1917 Los Angeles CA; D12.27.2000 Eureka CA; BR/TR/5´10˝/180; d4.23; Mil 1945																								
1943	Bos A	96	299	30	84	14	2	0	31	39	2	33	.281	.368	.341	106	4	0-0	.983	-5	*95*	*100*	C91	0	0.5
1944	Bos A	89	280	18	68	12	0	2	41	37	1	29	.243	.333	.307	85	-4	0-1	.989	-3	*95*	*93*	C85	0	-0.3
1946	†Bos A	40	111	13	35	5	2	0	9	13	0	14	.315	.387	.396	113	2	0-0	.974	-4	*126*	*71*	C38	0	0.0
1947	Bos A	60	169	14	39	2	0	0	16	18	0	23	.231	.305	.243	50	-11	0-0	.975	-0	*90*	*62*	C54	0	-0.9
1948	StL A	82	231	14	47	8	1	0	17	25	1	21	.203	.284	.247	41	-20	2-2	.982	-4	*67*	*62*	C76	0	-2.0
Total	5	367	1090	89	273	41	5	2	114	132	4	120	.250	.334	.303	78	-29	2-3	.982	-17	*91*	*82*	C344	0	-2.7
PARTENHEIMER, STEVE	Harold Philip; B8.30.1891 Greenfield MA; D6.16.1971 Mansfield OH; BR/TR/5´8.5˝/145; d6.28; s–Stan; Col Amherst																								
1913	Det A	1	2	0	0	0	0	0	0	0	1	0	.000	.333	.000	-1	0	0	.750	-0	156	0	/3	—	0.0
PARTRIDGE, JAY	James Bugg; B11.15.1902 Mountville GA; D1.14.1974 Nashville TN; BL/TR/5´11˝/160; d4.12; Col Oglethorpe																								
1927	Bro N	146	572	72	149	17	6	7	40	20	3	36	.260	.289	.348	70	-27	9	.938	-13	93	80	2b140	—	-3.6
1928	Bro N	37	73	18	18	0	1	0	12	13	1	6	.247	.368	.274	71	-3	2	.908	-4	86	76	2b18,3b2	—	-0.6
Total	2	183	645	90	167	17	7	7	52	33	4	42	.259	.299	.340	70	-30	11	.935	-17	92	80	2b158,3b2	—	-4.2
PASCHAL, BEN	Benjamin Edwin; B10.13.1895 Enterprise AL; D11.10.1974 Charlotte NC; BR/TR/5´11˝/185; d8.16																								
1915	Cle A	9	9	0	1	0	0	0	0	0	0	3	.111	.111	.111	-33	-2	0	ø	0	—	—	/H	—	-0.2
1920	Bos A	9	28	5	10	0	0	0	5	5	0	2	.357	.455	.357	122	1	1-0	1.000	0	94	123	O7R	—	0.1
1924	NY A	4	12	2	3	1	0	0	3	1	0	0	.250	.308	.333	65	-1	0-0	1.000	0	66	470	O4C	—	0.0
1925	NY A	89	247	49	89	16	5	12	56	22	2	29	.360	.417	.611	161	22	14-9	.953	-1	98	100	O66(16/14/36)	—	1.5
1926	†NY A	96	258	46	74	12	3	7	32	26	1	35	.287	.354	.438	108	2	7-6	.935	1	101	147	O74(12/17/47)	—	-0.2
1927	NY A	50	82	16	26	9	2	2	16	4	0	10	.317	.349	.549	134	4	0-2	.976	0	113	59	O27(11/4/12)	—	0.2
1928	†NY A	65	79	12	25	6	1	1	15	8	0	11	.316	.379	.456	122	3	1-0	1.000	0	103	84	O25(16/1/8)	—	0.2
1929	NY A	42	72	13	15	3	0	2	11	6	0	3	.208	.269	.333	58	-5	1-2	.951	1	113	134	O20(12/4/4)	—	-0.5
Total	8	364	787	143	243	47	11	24	138	72	3	93	.309	.369	.488	123	24	24-19	.953	3	102	121	O223(67/44/114)	—	1.1
PASCUCCI, VAL	Valentino Martin; B11.17.1978 Bellflower CA; BR/TR/6´6˝/235; [MonN99 15/450]; d4.26; Col Oklahoma																								
2004	Mon N	32	62	6	11	1	0	2	6	10-1	1	22	.177	.297	.290	52	-4	1-0	1.000	-1	111	0	O17(4/0/13),1b5	0	-0.6

YEAR	TM LG	G	AB	R	H	2B	3B	HR	RBI	BB-IB	HP	SO	AVG	OBP	SLG	AOPS	ABR	SB-CS	FA	FR	RNG	THR	GAMES AT POSITION	DL	BFW
Pasek, Johnny	John Paul; B6.25.1905 Niagara Falls NY; D3.13.1976 Niagara Falls NY; BR/TR/5´10˝/175; d7.28																								
1933	Det A	28	61	6	15	4	0	0	4	7	0	7	.246	.324	.311	68	-3	2-0	.989	-1	*58*	*129*	C28	—	-0.2
1934	Chi A	4	9	1	3	0	0	0	0	1	0	1	.333	.400	.333	88	0	0-0	1.000	-0	*61*	*144*	C4	—	0.0
Total	2	32	70	7	18	4	0	0	4	8	0	8	.257	.333	.314	70	-3	2-0	.990	-2	*58*	*131*	C32	—	-0.2
Paskert, Dode	George Henry; B8.28.1881 Cleveland OH; D2.12.1959 Cleveland OH; BR/TR/5´11˝/165; d9.21; OF(146/1461/35)																								
1907	Cin N	16	50	10	14	4	0	1	8	2	2	—	.280	.333	.420	130	2	2	.973	1	149	0	O16C	—	0.2
1908	Cin N	118	395	40	96	14	4	1	36	27	4	—	.243	.298	.306	96	-2	25	.953	5	103	84	O116(77/34/5)	—	-0.4
1909	Cin N	104	322	49	81	7	4	0	33	34	2	—	.252	.327	.298	95	-1	23	.968	1	98	115	O82(36/46/1),1b6	—	-0.5
1910	Cin N	144	506	63	152	21	5	2	46	70	3	60	.300	.389	.374	128	21	51	.957	9	110	128	O139(6/126/8),1b2	—	2.4
1911	Phi N	**153**	560	96	153	18	5	4	47	70	4	70	.273	.358	.345	96	-1	28	.979	1	102	88	O153(2/146/7)	—	-1.1
1912	Phi N	145	540	102	170	37	5	2	43	91	7	67	.315	.420	.413	120	21	36	.967	-0	103	89	O141C,2b2/3	—	1.1
1913	Phi N	124	454	83	119	21	9	4	29	65	3	69	.262	.358	.374	105	5	12-17	.972	11	114	111	O120(1/119/0)	—	0.5
1914	Phi N	132	451	59	119	25	6	3	44	56	3	68	.264	.349	.366	106	5	23	.958	8	112	133	O128C,S4	—	0.5
1915	†Phi N	109	328	51	80	17	4	3	39	35	1	38	.244	.319	.348	100	1	9-6	.970	-3	91	95	O92(19/74/1),1b5	—	-0.9
1916	Phi N	149	555	82	155	30	7	8	46	54	3	76	.279	.346	.402	125	18	22-21	.983	-5	96	78	O146(2/145/0)/S	—	0.0
1917	Phi N	141	546	78	137	27	11	4	43	62	3	63	.251	.331	.363	108	7	19	**.984**	-11	83	98	O138C	—	-1.7
1918	†Chi N	127	461	69	132	24	3	3	59	53	2	49	.286	.362	.371	121	14	20	.980	-8	92	74	O121C,3b6	—	-0.3
1919	Chi N	88	270	21	53	11	3	2	29	28	1	33	.196	.274	.281	67	-10	7	.969	-5	82	126	O80(3/76/3)	—	-2.3
1920	Chi N	139	487	57	136	22	10	5	71	64	3	58	.279	.366	.396	117	13	16-14	.956	-2	92	122	O137(0/136/1)	—	0.1
1921	Cin N	27	92	8	16	1	1	0	4	4	0	8	.174	.208	.207	11	-12	0-2	.984	1	112	61	O24(0/15/9)	—	-1.4
Total	15	1716	6017	868	1613	279	77	42	577	715	41	659	.268	.350	.361	108	81	293-60	.969	2	100	100	O1633C,1b13,3b7,S5,2b2	—	-3.8
Pasley, Kevin	Kevin Patrick; B7.22.1953 Bronx NY; BR/TR/6´0˝/185; [LAN71 29/657]; d10.2																								
1974	LA N	1	0	0	0	0	0	0	0	0-0	0	0	ø	ø	ø	ø	0	0-0	1.000	0	0	0	/C	0	0.0
1976	LA N	23	52	4	12	2	0	0	2	3-1	0	7	.231	.273	.269	55	-3	0-0	.971	1	81	112	C23	0	-0.2
1977	LA N	2	3	0	1	0	0	0	0	0-0	0	0	.333	.333	.333	79	0	0-0	1.000	-1	30	0	C2	0	-0.1
	Sea A	4	13	1	5	0	0	0	2	1-0	0	2	.385	.429	.385	124	0	0-0	1.000	-1	252	0	C4	0	-0.1
1978	Sea A	25	54	3	13	5	0	1	5	2-0	0	4	.241	.268	.389	83	-1	0-0	1.000	-1	108	0	C25	0	-0.1
Total	4	55	122	8	31	7	0	1	9	6-1	0	13	.254	.289	.336	76	-4	0-0	.986	-2	107	50	C55	0	-0.5
Pasqua, Dan	Daniel Anthony; B10.17.1961 Yonkers NY; BL/TL/6´0˝/(203–218); [NYA82 3/76]; d5.30; Col William Paterson																								
1985	NY A	60	148	17	31	3	1	9	25	16-4	1	38	.209	.289	.426	95	-2	0-0	1.000	4	129	114	O37(31/0/6),D14	0	0.0
1986	NY A	102	280	44	82	17	0	16	45	47-3	3	78	.293	.399	.525	150	22	2-0	.987	-1	102	84	O81(71/0/12),1b5,D3	0	1.7
1987	NY A	113	318	42	74	7	1	17	42	40-3	1	99	.233	.319	.421	95	-3	0-2	.985	0	107	46	O74(61/0/14),D20,1b12	0	-0.7
1988	Chi A	129	422	48	96	16	2	20	50	46-5	3	100	.227	.307	.417	101	0	1-0	**.996**	6	110	90	O112(65/0/52),1b7,D2	0	0.2
1989	Chi A	73	246	26	61	9	1	11	47	25-1	1	58	.248	.315	.427	111	3	1-2	.993	3	110	72	O66(52/0/20),D5	80	0.3
1990	Chi A	112	325	43	89	27	3	13	58	37-7	2	66	.274	.347	.495	137	16	1-1	.962	3	108	228	D57,O43(21/0/22)	0	1.7
1991	Chi A	134	417	71	108	22	5	18	66	62-4	3	86	.259	.358	.465	129	17	0-2	.991	-3	99	92	1b83,O59(9/0/51),D8	0	0.7
1992	Chi A	93	265	26	56	16	1	6	33	36-1	1	57	.211	.305	.347	84	-5	0-1	.963	-2	100	79	O81R,1b5/D	36	-1.0
1993	†Chi A	78	176	22	36	10	1	5	20	26-1	0	51	.205	.302	.358	79	-5	2-2	.984	-2	89	137	O37(11/0/26),1b32,D6	0	-1.0
1994	Chi A	11	23	2	5	2	0	2	4	0-0	0	9	.217	.217	.565	94	0	0-0	.867	-0	148	0	O5(1/0/5),1b3	102	-0.1
Total	10	905	2620	341	638	129	15	117	390	335-29	15	642	.244	.330	.438	112	43	7-10	.984	8	105	92	O595(322/0/289),1b147,D116	218	1.8
Pasquella, Mike	Michael John "Toney" (b Michael John Pasquariello); B11.7.1898 Philadelphia PA; D4.5.1965 Bridgeport CT; BR/TR/5´11˝/167; d7.9; Col Villanova																								
1919	Phi N	1	1	1	1	0	0	0	0	0	0	0	1.000	1.000	1.000	469	0	0	ø	0	0	0	/1	—	0.0
	StL N	1	1	0	0	0	0	0	0	0	0	1	.000	.000	.000	-99	0	0	ø	0	—	—	/H	—	0.0
	Year	2	2	1	1	0	0	0	0	0	0	1	.500	.500	.500	200	0	0	ø	0	0	0	/1	—	0.0
Pastornicky, Cliff	Clifford Scott; B11.18.1958 Seattle WA; BR/TR/5´10˝/170; [KCA80 8/198]; d6.14; Col Brigham Young																								
1983	KC A	10	32	4	4	0	0	2	5	0-0	0	3	.125	.125	.313	16	-4	0-0	.929	-0	111	0	3b10	0	-0.4
Pate, Bob	Robert Wayne; B12.3.1953 Los Angeles CA; BR/TR/6´3.5˝/(196–200); [MonN76 4/81]; d6.2; Col Arizona St.																								
1980	Mon N	23	39	3	10	2	0	0	5	3-0	0	6	.256	.295	.308	71	-1	0-1	1.000	-1	86	0	O18(2/0/16)	0	-0.4
1981	Mon N	8	6	0	2	0	0	0	0	1-0	0	0	.333	.429	.333	115	0	0-0	1.000	-0	97	0	O5(1/2/2)	0	0.0
Total	2	31	45	3	12	2	0	0	5	4-0	0	6	.267	.314	.311	77	-1	0-1	1.000	-1	87	0	O23(3/2/18)	0	-0.4
Patek, Freddie	Frederick Joseph "The Flea"; B10.9.1944 Seguin TX; BR/TR/5´5˝/(140–165); [PitN65 12/434]; d6.3																								
1968	Pit N	61	208	31	53	4	2	2	18	12-0	2	37	.255	.298	.322	89	-3	18-7	.976	-0	104	83	S52,O5(2/0/3)/3	27	0.2
1969	Pit N	147	460	48	110	9	1	5	32	53-15	1	86	.239	.318	.296	75	-15	15-8	.954	-10	90	96	S146	0	-0.8
1970	†Pit N	84	237	42	58	10	5	1	19	29-1	0	46	.245	.322	.342	80	-7	8-2	.971	13	109	111	S65	0	1.4
1971	KC A	147	591	86	158	21	**11**	6	36	44-3	5	80	.267	.323	.371	97	-4	49-14	.968	22	105	**126**	S147	0	4.3
1972	KC A✷	136	518	59	110	25	4	0	32	47-4	3	64	.212	.280	.276	67	-21	33-7	.971	**38**	**120**	**140**	S136	10	4.2
1973	KC A	135	501	82	117	19	5	5	45	54-0	3	63	.234	.311	.321	73	-17	36-14	.966	**40**	**119**	**125**	S135	15	4.1
1974	KC A	149	537	72	121	18	6	3	38	77-1	3	69	.225	.324	.298	76	-14	33-15	.967	8	**106**	**119**	S149	0	1.4
1975	KC A	136	483	58	110	14	5	5	45	42-0	2	65	.228	.291	.308	68	-21	32-7	.959	4	102	101	S136/D	0	0.3
1976	†KC A★	144	432	58	104	19	3	1	43	50-5	2	63	.241	.318	.306	84	-7	51-15	.962	-7	98	111	S143/D	0	0.8
1977	†KC A	154	497	72	130	26	6	5	60	41-2	5	84	.262	.320	.368	87	-8	**53**-13	.958	-17	92	84	S154	0	-0.3
1978	†KC A★	138	440	54	109	23	1	2	46	42-1	1	56	.248	.312	.318	76	-13	38-11	.949	-21	87	113	S137	0	-1.6
1979	KC A	106	306	30	77	17	0	1	37	16-0	3	42	.252	.293	.317	64	-15	11-12	.955	-24	85	88	S104	15	-3.2
1980	Cal A	86	273	41	72	10	5	5	34	15-1	1	26	.264	.302	.392	91	-5	7-6	.953	-18	84	78	S81	0	-1.5
1981	Cal A	27	47	3	11	1	1	0	5	1-0	0	6	.234	.250	.298	57	-3	1-0	.983	-2	84	96	2b16,3b7,S3	0	-0.4
Total	14	1650	5530	736	1340	216	55	41	490	523-33	31	787	.242	.309	.324	78	-153	385-131	.962	24	100	108	S1588,2b16,3b8,O5(2/0/3),D2	67	8.9
Patrick, Bob	Robert Lee; B10.27.1917 Ft.Smith AR; D10.6.1999 Ft.Smith AR; BR/TR/6´2˝/190; d9.20; Mil 1943–45																								
1941	Det A	5	7	2	2	0	0	0	0	0	0	1	.286	.286	.286	47	-1	0-0	.750	-0	90	0	O3L	0	-0.1
1942	Det A	4	8	1	2	1	0	1	3	1	0	0	.250	.333	.750	185	1	0-0	1.000	0	116	0	O3R	0	0.1
Total	2	9	15	3	4	1	0	1	3	1	0	1	.267	.313	.533	118	0	0-0	.889	-0	105	0	O6(3/0/3)	0	0.0
Pattee, Harry	Harry Ernest; B1.17.1882 Charlestown MA; D7.17.1971 Lynchburg VA; BL/TR/5´8˝/149; d4.14; Col Brown																								
1908	Bro N	80	264	19	57	5	2	0	9	25	1	—	.216	.286	.250	74	-7	24	.964	11	111	70	2b74	—	0.5
Patterson, Corey	Donald Corey; B8.13.1979 Atlanta GA; BL/TR/5´10˝/(175–180); [ChiN98 1/3]; d9.18																								
2000	Chi N	11	42	9	7	1	0	2	2	3-0	1	14	.167	.239	.333	43	-4	1-1	.963	-0	109	0	O11C	0	-0.4
2001	Chi N	59	131	26	29	3	0	4	14	6-0	3	33	.221	.266	.336	58	-9	4-0	.976	1	117	0	O54(13/45/1)	0	-0.7
2002	Chi N	153	592	71	150	30	5	14	54	19-1	8	142	.253	.284	.392	76	-23	18-3	.990	-4	99	71	O147C	0	-2.3
2003	Chi N	83	329	49	98	17	7	13	55	15-2	1	77	.298	.329	.511	112	4	16-5	.975	-6	87	74	O82C	84	0.1
2004	Chi N	157	631	91	168	33	6	24	72	45-7	5	168	.266	.320	.452	94	-8	32-9	**.997**	-4	93	110	O157C	0	-0.6
2005	Chi N	126	451	47	97	15	3	13	34	23-3	1	118	.215	.254	.348	54	-32	15-5	.980	-3	95	110	O122C	0	-3.3
2006	Bal A	135	463	75	128	19	5	16	53	21-5	5	94	.276	.314	.443	96	-5	45-9	.989	7	112	115	O134C	0	1.0
Total	7	724	2639	368	677	118	26	86	284	132-18	24	646	.257	.297	.419	83	-77	131-32	.987	-10	99	91	O707(13/698/1)	84	-6.2
Patterson, George	George; d4.24																								
1884	Phi U	2	7	0	1	0	0	0	—	0	—	—	.143	.143	.143	-14	-1	—	.500	-0	221	0	O2(1/0/1)	—	-0.1
Patterson, Ham	Hamilton; B10.13.1877 Belleville IL; D11.25.1945 Swansea IL; BR/TR/6´2˝/185; d5.18; b–Pat																								
1909	StL A	17	49	2	10	1	0	0	5	0	0	—	.204	.204	.224	38	-4	1	1.000	-1	54	66	1b6,O6L	—	-0.6
	Chi A	1	3	2	0	0	0	0	0	1	0	—	.000	.250	.000	-21	0	0	1.000	1	416	0	/1	—	0.0
	Year	18	52	4	10	1	0	0	5	1	0	—	.192	.208	.212	35	-4	1	1.000	0	96	58	1b7,O6L	—	-0.6
Patterson, Hank	Henry Joseph Colquit; B7.17.1907 San Francisco CA; D9.30.1970 Los Angeles CA; BR/TR/5´11.5˝/170; d9.5; C1																								
1932	Bos A	1	1	0	0	0	0	0	0	0	0	0	.000	.000	.000	-99	0	0-0	ø	0	*0*	*0*	/C	—	0.0

YEAR	TM LG	G	AB	R	H	2B	3B	HR	RBI	BB-IB	HP	SO	AVG	OBP	SLG	AOPS	ABR	SB-CS	FA	FR	RNG	THR	GAMES AT POSITION	DL	BFW
PATTERSON, JARROD Jarrod Lane; B9.7.1973 Montgomery AL; BL/TR/6´1˝/195; [NYN93 20/556]; d6.16; Col Jefferson Davis (AL) CC																									
2001	Det A	13	41	6	11	1	1	2	4	0-0	2	4	.268	.302	.488	106	0	0-1	.923	-4	69	0	3b13	0	-0.4
2003	KC A	13	22	3	4	0	0	0	0	3-1	0	6	.182	.280	.182	24	-2	0-0	.000	-1	0	0	3b4,1b2,D4	0	-0.3
Total	2	26	63	9	15	1	1	2	4	3-1	2	10	.238	.294	.381	75	-2	0-1	.889	-5	63	0	3b17,D4,1b2	0	-0.7
PATTERSON, JOHN John Allen; B2.11.1967 Key West FL; BB/TR/5´9˝/(160–168); [SFN88 23/594]; d4.6; Col Grand Canyon																									
1992	SF N	32	103	10	19	1	1	0	4	5-0	1	24	.184	.229	.214	27	-10	5-1	.960	2	98	144	2b22,O5C	16	-0.8
1993	SF N	16	16	1	3	0	0	1	2	0-0	0	5	.188	.188	.375	48	-1	0-1	ø	0	—	—	/H	149	-0.3
1994	SF N	85	240	36	57	10	1	3	32	16-0	11	43	.237	.315	.325	70	-11	13-3	.979	-6	94	93	2b63	0	-1.2
1995	SF N	95	205	27	42	5	3	1	14	14-1	12	41	.205	.294	.273	52	-14	4-2	.983	-5	89	117	2b53	0	-1.7
Total	4	228	564	74	121	16	5	5	52	35-1	24	113	.215	.289	.287	56	-36	22-7	.977	-10	93	110	2b138,O5C	165	-4.0
PATTERSON, CLARE Lorenzo Clare; B10.5.1887 Arkansas City KS; D3.28.1913 Mojave CA; BL/TR/6´0˝/180; d9.5																									
1909	Cin N	4	8	0	1	0	0	0	1	0	0	—	.125	.125	.125	-23	-1	0	1.000	0	0	0	O2L	—	-0.1
PATTERSON, MIKE Michael Lee; B1.26.1958 Santa Monica CA; BL/TR/5´10˝/(170–190); d4.15																									
1981	Oak A	12	23	4	8	1	1	0	1	2-1	0	5	.348	.400	.478	158	2	0-1	1.000	-0	94	0	O5(2/0/3),D2	0	0.1
	NY A	4	9	2	2	0	2	0	0	0-0	0	0	.222	.222	.667	149	0	0-0	1.000	0	120	0	O4(3/0/1)	0	0.0
	Year	16	32	6	10	1	3	0	1	2-1	0	5	.313	.353	.531	156	2	0-1	1.000	-0	105	0	O9(5/0/4),D2	0	0.1
1982	NY A	11	16	3	3	1	0	1	1	2-0	0	6	.188	.278	.438	94	0	1-0	1.000	-2	42	0	O9(2/7/0)/D	0	-0.2
Total	2	27	48	9	13	2	3	1	2	4-1	0	11	.271	.327	.500	134	2	1-1	1.000	-2	77	0	O18(7/7/4),D3	0	-0.1
PATTERSON, TOM Thomas W. H.; B1845 New York NY; D5.31.1900 New York NY; TL/5´9˝/143; d5.18																									
1871	Mut NA	32	151	31	31	2	0	0	13	1	—	0	.205	.211	.219	26	-13	2-1	.824	-2	58	0	O31(9/0/22),2b2	—	-0.8
1872	Eck NA	12	47	6	10	1	0	0	3	0	—	2	.213	.213	.234	44	-2	0-3	.861	3	272	321	O11(2/9/0)/1	—	0.0
1874	Mut NA	1	5	1	2	0	0	0	2	0	—	0	.400	.400	.400	153	0	0-0	1.000	0	0	0	/1lf	—	0.0
1875	Atl NA	12	45	4	9	0	0	0	4	0	—	0	.200	.200	.200	45	-2	1-0	.636	-5	67	0	2b7,O7R	—	-0.6
Total	4NA	57	248	42	52	3	0	0	22	1	—	2	.210	.213	.222	35	-17	3-4	.827	-4	99	72	O50(12/9/29),2b9,1b2	—	-1.4
PATTERSON, PAT William Jennings Bryan; B1.29.1897 Belleville IL; D10.1.1977 St.Louis MO; BR/TR/6´0˝/175; d4.14; b–Ham																									
1921	NY N	23	35	5	14	0	0	1	5	2	0	5	.400	.432	.486	142	2	0-1	.970	2	156	0	3b14,S7	—	0.5
PATTON, GENE Gene Tunney; B7.8.1926 Coatesville PA; BL/TR/5´10˝/165; d6.17; Mil 1945																									
1944	Bos N	1	0	0	0	0	0	0	0	0	0	0	ø	ø	ø	ø	0	0	ø	0	—	—	/R	0	0.0
PATTON, BILL George William; B10.12.1912 Cornwall PA; D3.15.1986 Philadelphia PA; BR/TR/6´2˝/180; d6.29; Col Temple																									
1935	Phi A	9	10	1	3	1	0	0	2	2	0	3	.300	.417	.400	113	0	0-0	1.000	0	*59*	*499*	C3	—	0.1
PATTON, TOM Tommy Allen; B9.5.1935 Honey Brook PA; BR/TR/5´9.5˝/175; d4.30																									
1957	Bal A	1	2	0	0	0	0	0	0	0-0	0	0	.000	.000	.000	-99	-1	0-0	1.000	1	16	668	/C	0	0.0
PAUL, JOSH Joshua William; B5.19.1975 Evanston IL; BR/TR/6´1˝/(185–220); [ChiA96 2/47]; d9.7; Col Vanderbilt																									
1999	Chi A	6	18	2	4	1	0	0	1	0-0	0	4	.222	.222	.278	26	-2	0-0	1.000	1	67	0	C6	0	-0.1
2000	†Chi A	36	71	15	20	3	2	1	8	5-0	1	17	.282	.338	.423	88	-2	1-0	.974	2	114	179	C34/lf	0	0.2
2001	Chi A	57	139	20	37	11	0	3	18	13-0	0	25	.266	.327	.410	88	-2	6-2	.980	-1	73	69	C56	0	0.0
2002	Chi A	33	104	11	25	4	0	0	11	9-0	1	22	.240	.302	.279	55	-7	2-0	.990	-0	82	39	C32/lf	0	-0.4
2003	Chi A	13	17	6	6	0	0	0	4	3-0	0	3	.353	.450	.353	111	0	0-0	1.000	-2	171	270	C11/D	0	-0.1
	Chi N	3	6	0	0	0	0	0	0	0-0	0	3	.000	.000	.000	-98	-2	0-0	1.000	1	108	410	C3	0	0.0
2004	Ana A	46	70	11	17	3	0	2	10	7-0	0	17	.243	.308	.371	80	-2	2-1	.993	-1	72	88	C37,O4L,D2	0	-0.2
2005	†LA A	34	37	4	7	1	0	2	4	2-0	0	9	.189	.231	.378	60	-2	0-0	.989	-0	119	77	C29,O2L	24	-0.2
2006	TB A	58	146	15	38	9	0	1	8	14-0	1	39	.260	.327	.342	75	-5	1-2	1.000	2	54	120	C52/lfD	0	0.0
Total	8	286	608	84	154	32	2	9	64	53-0	3	139	.253	.314	.357	74	-24	12-5	.989	1	81	101	C260,O9L,D4	24	-0.8
PAUL, LOU Louis; BR/TR; d9.5																									
1876	Phi N	3	12	2	2	1	0	0	0	0	—	0	.167	.167	.250	37	-1	—	.643	-2	—	—	C3	—	-0.2
PAULA, CARLOS Carlos (Conill); B11.28.1927 Havana, Cuba; D4.25.1983 Miami FL; BR/TR/6´3˝/195; d9.6																									
1954	Was A	9	24	2	4	1	0	0	2	2	0	4	.167	.231	.208	22	-3	0-0	1.000	1	118	266	O6L	0	-0.2
1955	Was A	115	351	34	105	20	7	6	45	17-3	2	43	.299	.332	.447	115	5	2-3	.941	-4	96	77	O85(6/0/80)	0	-0.2
1956	Was A	33	82	8	15	2	1	3	13	8-0	0	15	.183	.250	.341	56	-6	0-2	.974	-1	104	0	O20(9/0/11)	0	-0.8
Total	3	157	457	44	124	23	8	9	60	27-3	2	62	.271	.311	.416	99	-4	2-5	.950	-4	99	74	O111(21/0/91)	0	-1.2
PAULETTE, GENE Eugene Edward; B5.26.1891 Centralia IL; D2.8.1966 Little Rock AR; BR/TR/6´0˝/150; d6.16; OF(1/3/10)																									
1911	NY N	10	12	1	2	0	0	0	1	0	0	1	.167	.167	.167	-6	-2	0	.938	-1	63	0	1b7/S3	—	-0.3
1916	StL A	5	4	1	2	0	0	0	0	1	0	1	.500	.600	.500	242	1	0	ø	0	—	—	/H	—	0.1
1917	StL A	12	22	3	4	0	0	0	0	3	0	3	.182	.280	.182	43	-1	0	.982	-0	108	36	1b5,2b3/3	—	-0.2
	StL N	95	332	32	88	21	7	0	34	16	2	16	.265	.303	.370	109	3	9	.993	-2	88	142	1b93	—	-0.2
1918	StL N	125	461	33	126	15	3	0	52	27	2	16	.273	.316	.319	97	-2	11	.983	1	97	**108**	1b97,S12,2b7,O6(1/1/3),3b2/P	—	-0.4
1919	StL N	43	144	11	31	6	0	0	11	9	0	6	.215	.261	.257	60	-7	4	.990	2	116	114	1b35,S3	—	-0.6
	Phi N	67	243	20	63	8	3	1	31	19	1	10	.259	.316	.329	88	-3	10	.957	-2	95	100	2b58,O10(0/2/7)/1	—	-0.5
	Year	110	387	31	94	14	3	1	42	28	1	16	.243	.296	.302	78	-10	14	.957	0	95	100	2b58,1b36,O10(0/2/7),S3	—	-1.1
1920	Phi N	143	562	59	162	16	6	1	36	33	4	16	.288	.332	.343	90	-7	9-8	.988	6	**120**	95	1b139,S2	—	-0.5
Total	6	500	1780	160	478	66	19	2	165	108	9	69	.269	.314	.330	92	-18	43-8	.988	4	105	111	1b377,2b68,S18,O16R,3b4/P	—	-2.6
PAULINO, RONNY Ronny Leonel; B4.21.1981 Santo Domingo, D.R.; BR/TR/6´3˝/240; d9.25																									
2005	Pit N	2	4	1	2	0	0	0	0	1-0	0	0	.500	.600	.500	192	1	0-0	1.000	0	65	0	C2	0	0.1
2006	Pit N	129	442	37	137	19	0	6	55	34-5	2	79	.310	.360	.394	92	-5	0-0	.988	9	106	**139**	C124	0	1.2
Total	2	131	446	38	139	19	0	6	55	35-5	2	79	.312	.363	.395	93	-4	0-0	.988	10	106	138	C126	0	1.3
PAUXTIS, SI Simon Francis; B7.20.1885 Pittston PA; D3.13.1961 Philadelphia PA; BR/TR/6´0˝/175; d9.18; Col Penn																									
1909	Cin N	4	8	2	1	0	0	0	0	0	1	—	.125	.222	.125	8	-1	0	1.000	-1	*85*	*47*	C4	—	-0.1
PAVLETICH, DON Donald Stephen; B7.13.1938 Milwaukee WI; BR/TR/5´11˝/(190–214); d4.20; Mil 1957–58																									
1957	Cin N	1	1	0	0	0	0	0	0	0-0	0	0	.000	.000	.000	-93	0	0-0	ø	0	—	—	/H	0	0.0
1959	Cin N	1	0	1	0	0	0	0	0	0-0	0	0	ø	ø	ø	ø	0	0-0	ø	0	—	—	/R	0	0.0
1962	Cin N	34	63	7	14	3	0	1	7	8-1	0	18	.222	.310	.317	67	-3	0-0	1.000	0	90	82	1b25,C2	0	-0.4
1963	Cin N	71	183	18	38	11	0	5	18	17-3	0	12	.208	.274	.350	76	-5	0-0	.991	-1	61	68	1b57,C13	0	-0.9
1964	Cin N	34	91	12	22	4	0	5	11	10-1	0	17	.242	.314	.451	109	1	0-0	.983	-3	71	34	C27/1	0	-0.1
1965	Cin N	68	191	25	61	11	1	8	32	23-5	1	27	.319	.394	.513	144	12	1-1	.986	-7	66	67	C54,1b9	0	0.7
1966	Cin N	83	235	29	69	13	2	12	38	18-3	1	37	.294	.344	.519	126	8	1-0	.975	-7	63	116	C55,1b10	0	0.3
1967	Cin N	74	231	25	55	14	3	6	34	21-7	4	38	.238	.310	.403	93	-2	2-1	.986	-3	59	95	C66,1b6/3	0	-0.2
1968	Cin N	46	98	11	28	3	1	2	11	8-2	2	23	.286	.352	.398	117	2	0-0	1.000	-1	88	93	1b22,C5	0	0.1
1969	Chi A	78	188	26	46	12	0	6	33	28-4	0	45	.245	.338	.404	103	2	0-0	.974	-3	49	124	C51,1b13	31	-0.1
1970	Bos A	32	65	4	9	1	1	0	6	10-0	0	15	.138	.250	.185	21	-7	1-0	1.000	-3	125	123	1b16,C10	0	-1.1
1971	Bos A	14	27	5	7	1	0	1	3	5-0	0	5	.259	.375	.407	113	1	0-0	.973	-1	43	62	C8	0	0.0
Total	12	536	1373	163	349	73	8	46	193	148-26	8	237	.254	.328	.420	103	9	5-2	.983	-29	60	85	C291,1b159/3	31	-1.7
PAWELEK, TED Theodore John "Porky"; B8.15.1919 Chicago Heights IL; D2.12.1964 Chicago Heights IL; BL/TR/5´10.5˝/202; d9.13																									
1946	Chi N	4	4	0	1	1	0	0	0	0	0	0	.250	.250	.500	112	0	0	ø	-0	*0*	*0*	/C	0	0.0
PAWLOSKI, STAN Stanley Walter; B9.6.1931 Wanamie PA; BR/TR/6´1˝/175; d9.24; Col Temple																									
1955	Cle A	2	8	0	1	0	0	0	0	0-0	0	2	.125	.125	.125	-31	-2	0-0	1.000	1	154	0	2b2	0	-0.1

YEAR	TM LG	G	AB	R	H	2B	3B	HR	RBI	BB-IB	HP	SO	AVG	OBP	SLG	AOPS	ABR	SB-CS	FA	FR	RNG	THR	GAMES AT POSITION	DL	BFW
PAYNE, FRED	Frederick Thomas; B9.2.1880 Camden NY; D1.16.1954 Camden NY; BR/TR/5´10˝/162; d4.21																								
1906	Det A	72	222	23	60	5	5	0	20	13	2	—	.270	.316	.338	102	0	4	.966	2	*106*	*81*	C47,O17(1/12/4)	—	0.6
1907	†Det A	53	169	17	28	2	2	0	14	7	5	—	.166	.221	.201	34	-13	4	.981	5	*106*	*98*	C46,O5(3/1/1)	—	-0.4
1908	Det A	20	45	3	3	0	0	0	2	3	3	—	.067	.176	.067	-20	-6	1	.954	-2	*86*	*70*	C17/rf	—	-0.8
1909	Chi A	32	82	8	20	2	0	0	12	5	1	—	.244	.295	.268	82	-2	0	.987	-1	*90*	*113*	C27,O3R	—	0.0
1910	Chi A	91	252	17	56	5	4	0	19	11	2	—	.222	.260	.274	70	-15	6	.974	2	***118***	*87*	C78,O2R	—	-0.1
1911	Chi A	66	133	14	27	2	1	1	19	8	2	—	.203	.259	.256	45	-10	6	.963	0	*144*	*81*	C56	—	-0.7
Total	6	334	903	82	194	16	12	1	86	47	15	—	.215	.265	.262	64	-41	21	.972	7	*113*	*89*	C271,O28(4/13/11)	—	-1.4
PAYNTER, GEORGE	George Washington (b George Washington Paner); B7.6.1871 Cincinnati OH; D10.1.1950 Cincinnati OH; BR/TR/5´9˝/125; d8.12																								
1894	StL N	1	4	0	0	0	0	0	0	1	0	0	.000	.200	.000	-48	-1	1	1.000	1	854	0	/cf	—	0.0
PAYTON, JAY	Jason Lee; B11.22.1972 Zanesville OH; BR/TR/5´10˝/185; [NYN94 S1/29]; d9.1; Col Georgia Tech																								
1998	NY N	15	22	2	7	1	0	0	0	1-0	0	4	.318	.348	.364	90	0	0-0	1.000	0	75	354	O10(8/0/1)	0	0.0
1999	NY N	13	8	1	2	1	0	0	1	0-0	1	2	.250	.333	.375	83	0	1-2	1.000	0	106	0	O6(5/2/0)	64	-0.1
2000	†NY N	149	488	63	142	23	1	17	62	30-0	3	60	.291	.331	.447	101	-1	5-11	.981	-1	103	93	O146(4/143/0)	0	-0.4
2001	NY N	104	361	44	92	16	1	8	34	18-1	5	52	.255	.298	.371	77	-14	4-3	.984	1	107	118	O103C	49	-1.1
2002	NY N	87	275	33	78	6	3	8	31	21-0	1	34	.284	.336	.415	102	-1	4-1	.994	-1	96	152	O82C	0	0.0
	Col N	47	170	36	57	14	4	8	28	8-0	3	20	.335	.376	.606	135	8	3-3	1.000	2	106	122	O44(32/16/2)	0	0.9
	Year	134	445	69	135	20	7	16	59	29-0	4	54	.303	.351	.488	117	9	7-4	.996	1	100	141	O126(32/98/2)	0	0.9
2003	Col N	157	600	93	181	32	5	28	89	43-3	7	77	.302	.354	.512	108	6	6-4	.987	3	109	64	O151(149/8/3)	0	0.4
2004	SD N	143	458	57	119	17	4	8	55	43-2	4	56	.260	.326	.367	84	-12	2-0	.989	14	118	179	O137(9/128/0)/D	0	0.4
2005	Bos A	55	133	24	35	7	0	5	21	10-0	0	14	.263	.313	.429	91	-2	0-0	1.000	2	107	151	O53(13/16/31)	0	-0.1
	Oak A	69	275	38	74	9	1	13	42	14-2	0	33	.269	.302	.451	98	-2	0-1	1.000	-1	100	54	O69(47/25/0)	0	-0.5
	Year	124	408	62	109	16	1	18	63	24-2	0	47	.267	.306	.444	95	-4	0-1	**1.000**	1	102	86	O122(60/41/31)	0	-0.6
2006	†Oak A	142	557	78	165	32	3	10	59	22-1	4	52	.296	.325	.418	93	-7	8-4	.978	-3	102	57	O137(62/46/45),D4	0	-1.2
Total	9	981	3347	469	952	158	22	105	422	210-9	28	404	.284	.330	.439	98	-25	33-29	.987	17	106	104	O938(329/569/82),D5	113	-1.7
PEACOCK, JOHNNY	John Gaston; B1.10.1910 Fremont NC; D10.17.1981 Wilson NC; BL/TR/5´11˝/165; d9.23; Col North Carolina																								
1937	Bos A	9	32	3	10	2	1	0	6	1	0	0	.313	.333	.438	89	-1	0-0	.980	1	*126*	*138*	C9	—	0.1
1938	Bos A	72	195	29	59	7	1	1	39	17	0	4	.303	.358	.364	78	-7	4-1	.984	-5	*101*	*52*	C57/1lf	—	-0.8
1939	Bos A	92	274	33	76	11	4	0	36	29	0	11	.277	.347	.347	75	-10	1-1	.972	-6	*87*	*77*	C84	—	-1.0
1940	Bos A	63	131	20	37	4	1	0	13	23	0	10	.282	.390	.328	85	-2	1-1	.994	-6	*90*	*77*	C48	—	-0.6
1941	Bos A	79	261	28	74	20	1	0	27	21	1	3	.284	.339	.368	85	-5	2-1	.988	-2	*102*	*90*	C70	0	-0.2
1942	Bos A	88	286	17	76	7	3	0	25	21	0	11	.266	.316	.311	74	-10	1-1	.988	-2	*103*	*112*	C82	0	-0.8
1943	Bos A	48	114	7	23	3	1	0	7	10	0	9	.202	.266	.246	49	-7	1-1	.972	-1	*102*	*97*	C32	0	-0.8
1944	Bos A	4	4	0	0	0	0	0	0	0	0	0	.000	.000	.000	-99	-1	0-0	1.000	0	*0*	*0*	C2	0	-0.1
	Phi N	83	253	21	57	9	3	0	21	31	0	15	.225	.310	.285	70	-10	1	.990	1	*103*	*106*	C73/2	0	-0.5
1945	Phi N	33	74	6	15	6	0	0	6	6	0	0	.203	.262	.284	53	-5	1	.969	-4	*70*	*87*	C23	0	-0.7
	Bro N	48	110	11	28	5	1	0	14	24	0	10	.255	.388	.318	98	1	2	.975	0	*107*	*71*	C38	0	0.3
	Year	81	184	17	43	11	1	0	20	30	0	10	.234	.341	.304	82	-3	3	.973	-3	*94*	*76*	C61	0	-0.4
Total	9	619	1734	175	455	74	16	1	194	183	1	73	.262	.333	.325	76	-57	14-6	.983	-24	*98*	*89*	C518/2lf1	0	-5.1
PEAK, ELIAS	Elias; B5.23.1859 Philadelphia PA; D12.17.1916 Philadelphia PA; d4.19																								
1884	Bos U	1	3	2	2	0	0	0	—	1	—	—	.667	.750	.667	338	1	—	1.000	-0	0	0	/rf	—	0.1
	Phi U	54	215	35	42	6	4	0	—	7	—	—	.195	.221	.260	49	-20	—	.825	-8	106	78	2b47,O5(4/0/1),S2	—	-2.4
	Year	55	218	37	44	6	4	0	—	8	—	—	.202	.230	.266	54	-19	—	.825	-8	106	78	2b47,O6(4/0/2),S2	—	-2.3
PEARCE, HARRY	Harry James; B7.12.1889 Philadelphia PA; D1.8.1942 Philadelphia PA; BR/TR/5´9˝/158; d10.2																								
1917	Phi N	7	16	2	4	3	0	0	2	0	1	4	.250	.294	.438	118	0	0	.967	3	166	59	S4	—	0.4
1918	Phi N	60	164	16	40	3	2	0	18	9	3	31	.244	.295	.287	73	-5	5	.944	-0	110	89	2b46,S2/13	—	-0.5
1919	Phi N	68	244	24	44	3	3	0	9	8	1	27	.180	.209	.217	26	-22	6	.948	-0	101	107	2b43,S23,3b2	—	-2.3
Total	3	135	424	42	88	9	5	0	29	17	5	62	.208	.247	.252	48	-27	11	.946	3	106	97	2b89,S29,3b3/1	—	-2.4
PEARCE, DICKEY	Richard J.; B2.29.1836 Brooklyn NY; D9.18.1908 Wareham MA; BR/TR/5´3.5˝/161; d5.18; M2/U2																								
1871	Mut NA	**33**	163	31	44	5	0	0	20	4	—	1	.270	.287	.301	76	-3	0-0	.793	-7	92	114	S33	—	-0.7
1872	Mut NA	44	206	32	39	2	1	1	22	4	—	1	.189	.205	.223	34	-14	1-1	**.844**	2	103	162	S42,O2(1/0/1),M	—	-1.0
1873	Atl NA	**55**	262	42	72	6	0	1	23	8	—	2	.275	.296	.309	89	0	3-0	.777	2	116	96	S55/12	—	0.1
1874	Atl NA	**56**	255	48	75	1	0	0	26	6	—	1	.294	.310	.298	109	5	1-0	**.845**	8	**109**	69	S56,3b2/2	—	0.9
1875	StL NA	**70**	311	51	77	6	3	0	29	7	—	7	.248	.264	.286	100	2	8-3	.830	11	**113**	150	S70,P2,M	—	1.0
1876	StL N	25	102	12	21	1	0	0	10	3	—	5	.206	.229	.216	51	-5	—	.902	3	109	170	S23/lf2	—	-0.1
1877	StL N	8	29	1	5	0	0	0	4	1	—	4	.172	.200	.172	19	-3	—	.950	3	126	169	S8	—	0.0
Total	5NA	258	1197	204	307	20	4	2	120	29	—	12	.256	.274	.285	84	-10	13-4	.818	17	108	118	S256,P2,3b2,2b2,O2(1/0/1)/1	—	0.3
Total	2	33	131	13	26	1	0	0	14	4	—	9	.198	.222	.206	44	-8	—	.914	6	113	170	S31/2lf	—	-0.1
PEARCE, BUNNY	William Charles; B3.17.1885 Corning OH; D5.22.1933 Brownstown IN; BR/TR/6´1˝/185; d7.1																								
1908	Cin N	2	2	0	0	0	0	0	0	0	0	—	.000	.000	.000	-99	0	0	1.000	1	*121*	*195*	C2	—	0.0
1909	Cin N	2	2	0	0	0	0	0	0	0	0	—	.000	.000	.000	-99	0	0	1.000	-0	*63*	*0*	C2	—	-0.1
Total	2	4	4	0	0	0	0	0	0	0	0	—	.000	.000	.000	-99	0	0	1.000	1	*102*	*130*	C4	—	-0.1
PEARSON, ALBIE	Albert Gregory; B9.12.1934 Alhambra CA; BL/TL/5´5˝/(141–160); d4.14																								
1958	Was A	146	530	63	146	25	5	3	33	64-1	2	31	.275	.354	.358	99	1	7-8	.980	-3	102	77	O141(0/136/6)	0	-1.0
1959	Was A	25	80	9	15	1	0	0	2	14-0	0	3	.188	.309	.200	43	-6	1-1	.974	-3	80	0	O21(0/11/10)	0	-1.0
	Bal A	80	138	22	32	4	2	0	6	13-0	0	5	.232	.296	.290	64	-7	4-0	.987	2	113	100	O50(22/16/16)	0	-0.6
	Year	105	218	31	47	5	2	0	8	27-0	0	8	.216	.301	.257	56	-13	5-1	.983	-2	100	59	O71(22/27/26)	0	-1.6
1960	Bal A	48	82	17	20	2	0	1	6	17-0	0	3	.244	.370	.305	87	-1	4-0	.975	-1	96	79	O32(11/7/15)	0	-0.1
1961	LA A	144	427	92	123	21	3	7	41	96-1	3	40	.288	.420	.400	109	11	11-3	.956	-1	103	98	O113(1/46/76)	0	0.6
1962	LA A	160	614	**115**	160	29	6	5	42	95-3	1	36	.261	.360	.352	96	0	15-6	.989	-3	100	102	O160(0/143/17)	0	-0.8
1963	LA A★	154	578	92	176	26	5	6	47	92-5	3	37	.304	.402	.398	133	31	17-10	.983	-5	98	103	O148(2/135/15)	0	2.3
1964	LA A	107	265	34	59	5	1	2	16	35-2	1	22	.223	.316	.272	72	-9	6-4	.978	-2	102	25	O66(10/52/7)	0	-1.5
1965	Cal A	122	360	41	100	17	2	4	21	51-0	2	17	.278	.370	.369	114	9	12-1	.988	-1	98	88	O101(7/12/87)	0	0.4
1966	Cal A	2	3	0	0	0	0	0	0	0-0	0	1	.000	.000	.000	-99	-1	0-0	ø	-0	0	0	/lf	95	-0.1
Total	9	988	3077	485	831	130	24	28	214	477-12	12	195	.270	.369	.355	102	28	77-33	.980	-18	100	86	O833(54/558/249)	95	-1.8
PECHOUS, CHARLIE	Charles Edward; B10.5.1896 Chicago IL; D9.13.1980 Kenosha WI; BR/TR/6´0˝/170; d9.14; Col Loyola–Chicago																								
1915	Chi F	18	51	4	9	3	0	0	4	4	0	15	.176	.236	.235	35	-5	1	.938	-0	113	0	3b18	—	-0.6
1916	Chi N	22	69	5	10	1	1	0	4	3	0	21	.145	.181	.188	12	-7	1	.940	6	137	70	3b22	—	-0.1
1917	Chi N	13	41	2	10	0	0	0	1	2	1	9	.244	.295	.244	61	-2	1	1.000	-2	67	0	3b7,S5	—	-0.4
Total	3	53	161	11	29	4	1	0	9	9	1	45	.180	.228	.217	32	-14	3	.947	3	118	35	3b47,S5	—	-1.1
PECK, HAL	Harold Arthur; B4.20.1917 Big Bend WI; D4.13.1995 Milwaukee WI; BL/TL/5´11˝/175; d5.13																								
1943	Bro N	1	1	0	0	0	0	0	0	0	0	0	.000	.000	.000	-99	0	0	ø	0	—	—	/H	0	0.0
1944	Phi A	2	8	0	2	0	0	0	1	0	0	2	.250	.250	.250	44	-1	0-2	1.000	-0	89	0	O2R	0	-0.2
1945	Phi A	112	449	51	124	22	9	5	39	37	0	28	.276	.331	.399	112	5	5-3	.943	-10	85	80	O110R	0	-1.3
1946	Phi A	48	150	14	37	8	2	2	11	16	0	14	.247	.319	.367	92	-2	1-2	.981	-0	85	158	O35R	0	-0.4
1947	Cle A	114	392	58	115	18	2	8	44	27	2	31	.293	.342	.411	112	5	3-3	.983	-2	97	80	O97(3/0/95)	0	-0.1
1948	†Cle A	45	63	12	18	3	0	0	8	4	0	8	.286	.328	.333	78	-2	1-0	1.000	-1	93	0	O9(1/0/9)	0	-0.3
1949	Cle A	33	29	1	9	1	0	0	9	3	0	3	.310	.375	.345	93	0	0-0	1.000	0	147	0	O2R	0	0.0
Total	7	355	1092	136	305	52	13	15	112	87	2	86	.279	.334	.392	106	5	10-10	.965	-13	90	87	O255(4/0/253)	0	-2.3
PECKINPAUGH, ROGER	Roger Thorpe; B2.5.1891 Wooster OH; D11.17.1977 Cleveland OH; BR/TR/5´10.5˝/165; d9.15; M8																								
1910	Cle A	15	45	1	9	0	0	0	6	1	1	—	.200	.234	.200	36	-3	3	.906	-5	89	60	S14	—	-0.9
1912	Cle A	70	236	18	50	4	1	1	22	16	0	—	.212	.262	.250	45	-17	11	.924	-1	98	77	S68	—	-1.5
1913	Cle A	1	0	1	0	0	0	0	0	0	0	0	ø	ø	ø	ø	0	0	ø	0	—	—	/H	—	0.0
	NY A	95	340	35	91	10	7	1	32	24	0	47	.268	.316	.347	94	-4	19	.931	-3	103	79	S93	—	-0.1

YEAR	TM LG	G	AB	R	H	2B	3B	HR	RBI	BB-IB	HP	SO	AVG	OBP	SLG	AOPS	ABR	SB-CS	FA	FR	RNG	THR	GAMES AT POSITION	DL	BFW
	Year	96	340	36	91	10	7	1	32	24	0	47	.268	.316	.347	94	-4	19	.931	-3	103	79	S93	—	-0.1
1914	NY A	**157**	570	55	127	14	6	3	51	51	1	73	.223	.288	.284	72	-20	38-17	.956	5	105	82	S157,M	—	-0.2
1915	NY A	142	540	67	119	18	7	5	44	49	3	72	.220	.289	.307	79	-16	19-12	.942	5	**106**	114	S142	—	0.0
1916	NY A	145	552	65	141	22	8	4	58	62	1	50	.255	.332	.346	101	1	18	.946	-0	102	96	S145	—	1.2
1917	NY A	148	543	63	141	24	7	0	41	64	2	46	.260	.340	.330	103	4	17	.934	7	102	133	S148	—	2.3
1918	NY A	122	446	59	103	15	3	0	43	43	3	41	.231	.303	.278	74	-14	12	.961	**22**	**113**	**148**	S122	—	1.9
1919	NY A	122	453	89	138	20	2	7	33	59	4	37	.305	.390	.404	122	16	10	.943	**26**	**116**	**139**	S121	—	5.1
1920	NY A	139	534	109	144	26	6	8	54	72	0	47	.270	.356	.386	93	-4	8-12	.962	8	102	113	S137	—	1.1
1921	†NY A	149	577	128	166	25	7	8	71	84	2	44	.288	.380	.397	96	-1	2-2	.948	-3	96	111	S149	—	1.1
1922	Was A	147	520	62	132	14	4	2	48	55	3	36	.254	.329	.308	70	-22	11-6	.951	18	**109**	120	S147	—	1.2
1923	Was A	154	568	73	150	18	4	2	62	64	1	30	.264	.340	.320	78	-17	10-8	.948	**22**	**107**	**127**	S154	—	2.0
1924	†Was A	155	523	72	142	20	5	2	73	72	0	45	.272	.360	.340	84	-11	9-6	.963	11	105	**119**	S155	—	1.5
1925	†Was A	126	422	67	124	16	4	4	64	49	0	23	.294	.367	.379	91	-5	13-4	.952	-14	92	102	S124/1	—	-0.4
1926	Was A	57	147	19	35	4	1	1	14	28	0	12	.238	.360	.299	75	-4	3-0	.960	-1	96	96	S46/1	—	-0.1
1927	Chi A	68	217	23	64	6	3	0	23	21	1	6	.295	.360	.350	87	-4	2-3	.964	0	104	106	S60	—	0.1
Total	17	2012	7233	1006	1876	256	75	48	739	814	22	609	.259	.336	.335	87	-121	205-70	.949	97	104	112	S1982,1b2	—	14.3
PECOTA, BILL	William Joseph; B2.16.1960 Redwood City CA; BR/TR/6´2˝/(190–195); [KCA81*10/234]; d9.19; Col De Anza (CA) JC; OF(13/2/19)																								
1986	KC A	12	29	3	6	2	0	0	2	3-0	1	3	.207	.294	.276	58	-2	0-2	.974	4	163	62	3b12,S2,D4	0	0.2
1987	KC A	66	156	22	43	5	1	3	14	15-0	1	25	.276	.343	.378	89	-2	5-0	.977	9	113	129	S36,3b17,2b15/D	0	1.0
1988	KC A	90	178	25	37	3	3	1	15	18-0	2	34	.208	.286	.275	58	-10	7-2	.976	7	110	96	S41,3b21,1b11,O9(3/0/6),D4,2b3/C	0	0.0
1989	KC A	65	83	21	17	4	2	3	5	7-1	1	9	.205	.275	.410	91	-2	5-0	.988	1	104	75	S29,O15(4/2/9),2b12,3b7,1b4/D	0	0.2
1990	KC A	87	240	43	58	15	2	5	20	33-0	1	39	.242	.336	.383	102	1	8-5	.986	10	97	73	2b50,S21,3b11,O6(4/0/3),1b4,D2	0	1.4
1991	KC A	125	398	53	114	23	2	6	45	41-6	2	45	.286	.356	.399	108	5	16-7	.983	-3	97	82	3b102,2b34,S9,1b8,D2/lfP	0	0.4
1992	NY N	117	269	28	61	13	0	2	26	25-3	1	40	.227	.293	.297	69	-11	9-3	.926	8	102	140	3b48,S39,2b38/P1	15	0.1
1993	†Atl N	72	62	17	20	2	1	0	5	2-0	0	5	.323	.344	.387	93	-1	1-1	1.000	-1	86	0	3b23,2b4/rf	0	-0.2
1994	Atl N	64	112	11	24	5	0	2	16	16-1	0	16	.214	.310	.313	61	-6	1-0	.974	6	122	112	3b31/2lf	0	0.1
Total	9	698	1527	223	380	72	11	22	148	160-11	9	216	.249	.323	.354	86	-28	52-20	.968	43	109	99	3b272,S177,2b157,O33R,1b28,D14,P2/C15		3.2
PEDEN, LES	Leslie Earl "Gooch"; B9.17.1923 Azle TX; D2.11.2002 Jacksonville FL; BR/TR/6´1.5˝/212; d4.17; C1; Col Texas A&M																								
1953	Was A	9	28	4	7	1	0	1	1	4	0	3	.250	.344	.393	101	0	0-0	1.000	0	*89*	*110*	C8	0	0.0
PEDERSON, STU	Stuart Russell; B1.28.1960 Palo Alto CA; BL/TL/6´0˝/185; [LAN81 9/229]; d9.8; Col USC																								
1985	LA N	8	4	1	0	0	0	0	1	0-0	0	2	.000	.000	.000	-99	-1	0-0	1.000	0	120	0	O5(3/0/2)	0	-0.1
PEDRE, JORGE	Jorge Enrique; B10.12.1966 Culver City CA; BR/TR/5´11˝/(205–210); [KCA87 33/846]; d9.7; Col Los Angeles Harbor (CA) JC																								
1991	KC A	10	19	2	5	1	1	0	3	3-0	0	5	.263	.364	.421	115	0	0-0	.971	-2	51	110	C9/1	0	-0.1
1992	Chi N	4	4	0	0	0	0	0	0	0-0	0	1	.000	.000	.000	-97	-1	0-0	1.000	-1	0	0	C4	0	-0.2
Total	2	14	23	2	5	1	1	0	3	3-0	0	6	.217	.308	.348	81	-1	0-0	.973	-2	44	95	C13/1	0	-0.3
PEDRIQUE, AL	Alfredo Jose (Garcia); B8.11.1960 Valencia, Carabobo, Venez.; BR/TR/6´0˝/(155–165); d4.14; M1/C1																								
1987	NY N	5	6	1	0	0	0	0	0	1-0	0	2	.000	.143	.000	-61	-1	0-0	1.000	1	147	0	S4/2	0	0.0
	Pit N	88	246	23	74	10	1	1	27	18-4	3	27	.301	.354	.362	90	-3	5-4	.968	-5	93	114	S76,3b3,2b2	0	-0.1
	Year	93	252	24	74	10	1	1	27	19-4	3	29	.294	.349	.353	86	-5	5-4	.969	-3	94	111	S80,2b3,3b3	0	-0.1
1988	Pit N	50	128	7	23	5	0	0	4	8-2	1	17	.180	.234	.219	31	-11	0-0	.974	5	112	115	S46,3b5	0	-0.4
1989	Det A	31	69	1	14	3	0	0	5	2-0	0	15	.203	.225	.246	34	-6	0-0	.960	4	104	63	3b12,S12,2b8	0	-0.1
Total	3	174	449	32	111	18	1	1	36	29-6	4	61	.247	.298	.298	64	-21	5-4	.971	6	100	112	S138,3b20,2b11	0	-0.6
PEDROES, CHICK	Charles P. (b Charles F. Pedro); B10.27.1869 Havana, Cuba; D8.6.1927 Chicago IL; d8.21																								
1902	Chi N	2	6	0	0	0	0	0	0	0	0	—	.000	.000	.000	-99	-1	0	1.000	-0	0	0	O2R	—	-0.2
PEDROIA, DUSTIN	Dustin Luis; B8.17.1983 Woodland CA; BR/TR/5´9˝/180; [BosA04 2/65]; d8.22; Col Arizona St.																								
2006	Bos A	31	89	5	17	4	0	2	7	7-0	1	7	.191	.258	.303	44	-8	0-1	.975	8	125	121	2b27,S6	0	0.1
PEEL, HOMER	Homer Hefner; B10.10.1902 Port Sullivan TX; D4.8.1997 Shreveport LA; BR/TR/5´9.5˝/170; d9.13																								
1927	StL N	2	2	0	0	0	0	0	0	0	0	1	.000	.000	.000	-97	-1	0	ø	-0	0	0	/rf	—	-0.1
1929	Phi N	53	156	16	42	12	1	0	19	12	2	7	.269	.329	.359	66	-8	1	.990	0	103	61	O39(1/36/2)/1	—	-0.8
1930	StL N	26	73	9	12	2	0	0	10	3	0	4	.164	.197	.192	-5	-13	0	.968	-2	92	0	O21(6/0/15)	—	-1.4
1933	†NY N	84	148	16	38	1	1	1	12	14	1	10	.257	.325	.297	80	-4	0	.962	-3	81	48	O45(35/9/1)	—	-0.9
1934	NY N	21	41	7	8	0	0	1	3	1	0	2	.195	.214	.268	29	-4	0	.929	-1	76	0	O10(0/8/2)	—	-0.6
Total	5	186	420	48	100	15	2	2	44	30	3	24	.238	.294	.298	53	-30	1	.974	-6	91	40	O116(42/53/21)/1	—	-3.8
PEERSON, JACK	Jack Chiles; B8.28.1910 Brunswick GA; D10.23.1966 Ft.Walton Beach FL; BR/TR/5´11˝/175; d9.7																								
1935	Phi A	10	19	3	6	1	0	0	1	1	0	1	.316	.350	.368	87	0	0-0	.952	-1	105	0	S4	—	-0.1
1936	Phi A	8	34	7	11	1	1	0	5	0	0	3	.324	.324	.412	82	-1	0-1	.942	2	127	87	S7/2	—	0.1
Total	2	18	53	10	17	2	1	0	6	1	0	4	.321	.333	.396	84	-1	0-1	.945	2	120	59	S11/2	—	0.0
PEETE, CHARLIE	Charles "Mule"; B2.22.1929 Franklin VA; D11.27.1956 Caracas, Distrito Capital, Venez.; BL/TR/5´9.5˝/190; d7.17; Negro Lg 1950																								
1956	StL N	23	52	3	10	2	2	0	6	6-0	1	10	.192	.288	.308	60	-3	0-2	1.000	1	88	256	O21C	0	-0.4
PEFFER, MONTE	Monte (b Montague Pfeiffer); B10.8.1891 New York NY; D9.27.1941 New York NY; BR/TR/5´4.5˝/147; d9.29																								
1913	Phi A	1	3	0	0	0	0	0	0	0	1	1	.000	.250	.000	-26	0	0	.800	-0	123	0	/S	—	-0.1
PEGUERO, JULIO	Julio Cesar; B9.7.1968 San Isidro, D.R.; BB/TR/6´0˝/160; d4.8																								
1992	Phi N	14	9	3	2	0	0	0	0	3-0	0	3	.222	.417	.222	86	0	0-0	1.000	0	104	0	O14(0/9/5)	0	0.0
PEGUES, STEVE	Steven Antone; B5.21.1968 Pontotoc MS; BR/TR/6´2˝/190; [DetA87 1/21]; d7.6																								
1994	Cin N	11	10	1	3	0	0	0	0	1-0	0	3	.300	.364	.300	76	0	0-0	.833	0	195	0	O4(3/0/1)	0	0.0
	Pit N	7	26	1	10	2	0	0	2	1-0	0	2	.385	.407	.462	124	1	1-0	1.000	-2	57	0	O7(5/2/0)	0	0.0
	Year	18	36	2	13	2	0	0	2	2-0	0	5	.361	.395	.417	111	1	1-0	.929	-1	80	0	O11(8/2/1)	0	0.0
1995	Pit N	82	171	17	42	8	0	6	16	4-0	1	36	.246	.263	.398	71	-8	1-2	.954	1	113	80	O53(31/4/25)	0	-0.9
Total	2	100	207	19	55	10	0	6	18	6-0	1	41	.266	.286	.401	78	-7	2-2	.950	-0	107	66	O64(39/6/26)	0	-0.9
PEITZ, HEINIE	Henry Clement; B11.28.1870 St.Louis MO; D10.23.1943 Cincinnati OH; BR/TR/5´11˝/165; d10.15; C3; b–Joe; OF(4/0/7); ▲																								
1892	StL N	1	3	0	0	0	0	0	0	0	0	0	.000	.000	.000	-99	-1	0	1.000	-0	*101*	*0*	/C	—	-0.1
1893	StL N	96	362	53	92	12	9	1	45	54	1	20	.254	.353	.345	86	-7	12	.948	3	*87*	*110*	C74,S11,O10(4/0/6),1b5	—	0.2
1894	StL N	99	338	52	89	19	9	3	49	43	1	21	.263	.348	.399	80	-12	14	.897	3	86	61	3b47,C39,1b14/P	—	-0.3
1895	StL N	90	334	44	95	14	12	2	65	29	2	20	.284	.345	.416	97	-3	9	.937	-10	*77*	*111*	C71,1b11,3b10	—	-0.5
1896	Cin N	68	211	33	63	12	5	2	34	30	0	15	.299	.386	.431	108	3	7	.968	11	*142*	*68*	C67	—	1.6
1897	Cin N	77	266	35	78	11	7	1	44	18	1	—	.293	.340	.398	89	-6	3	***.979***	16	*156*	*85*	C71,P2	—	1.4
1898	Cin N	105	330	49	90	15	5	1	43	35	3	—	.273	.348	.358	96	-2	9	.945	10	***166***	*78*	C101	—	1.6
1899	Cin N	94	293	45	79	13	2	1	43	46	2	—	.270	.372	.338	94	0	11	.977	7	***130***	*84*	C92/P	—	1.3
1900	Cin N	91	294	34	75	14	1	2	34	20	7	—	.255	.318	.330	81	-7	5	.958	7	*116*	*99*	C80,1b8	—	0.7
1901	Cin N	82	269	24	82	13	5	1	24	23	2	—	.305	.364	.401	130	11	3	.982	3	*112*	*90*	C49,2b21,3b6,1b2	—	1.9
1902	Cin N	112	387	54	122	22	5	1	60	24	9	—	.315	.369	.406	127	13	7	.919	3	90	129	2b48,C47,1b6,3b6	—	2.1
1903	Cin N	105	358	45	93	15	3	0	42	37	1	—	.260	.331	.318	77	-10	7	.970	3	*122*	*82*	C78,1b11,3b9,2b4	—	0.0
1904	Cin N	84	272	32	66	13	2	1	30	14	1	—	.243	.282	.316	78	-7	1	.975	5	*104*	*104*	C64,1b18/3	—	0.4
1905	Pit N	88	278	18	62	10	0	0	27	24	2	—	.223	.289	.259	62	-12	2	.965	-2	*118*	*93*	C87/2	—	-0.6
1906	Pit N	40	125	13	30	8	0	0	20	13	2	—	.240	.321	.304	91	-1	1	.979	1	*122*	*87*	C38	—	0.5
1913	StL N	3	4	1	1	0	1	0	0	0	0	0	.250	.250	.750	182	0	0	.625	-1	86	77	C2/rf	—	-0.1
Total	16	1235	4124	532	1117	191	66	16	560	410	34	76	.271	.342	.361	92	-41	91	.963	58	*122*	*93*	C961,3b79,1b75,2b74,O11R,S11,P4	—	10.1
PEITZ, JOE	Joseph; B11.8.1869 St.Louis MO; D12.4.1919 St.Louis MO; d6.28; b–Heinie																								
1894	StL N	7	26	10	11	2	3	0	3	6	0	1	.423	.531	.731	202	5	2	.818	-1	67	283	O7R	—	0.3
PELAEZ, ALEX	Alejandro; B4.6.1976 San Diego CA; BR/TR/5´9˝/190; [SDN98 42/1252]; d5.16; Col San Diego St.																								
2002	SD N	3	8	0	2	0	0	0	0	0-0	0	0	.250	.250	.250	35	-1	0-0	1.000	-0	148	325	/123	0	-0.1

YE R	TM LG	G	AB	R	H	2B	3B	HR	RBI	BB-IB	HP	SO	AVG	OBP	SLG	AOPS	ABR	SB-CS	FA	FR	RNG	THR	GAMES AT POSITION	DL	BFW
P LLAGRINI, EDDIE	Edward Charles; B3.13.1918 Boston MA; D10.11.2006 Weymouth MA; BR/TR/5´9″/(160–165); d4.22; Col Boston College																								
1(6	Bos A	22	71	7	15	3	1	2	4	3	1	18	.211	.253	.366	68	-3	1-0	.891	-2	88	140	3b14,S9	0	-0.6
1 '	Bos A	74	231	29	47	8	1	4	19	23	2	35	.203	.281	.299	57	-14	2-2	.926	-7	93	107	3b42,S26	0	-2.0
1 3	StL A	105	290	31	69	8	3	2	27	34	1	40	.238	.320	.307	65	-15	1-2	.964	18	110	123	S98	0	0.8
1(9	StL A	79	235	26	56	8	1	2	15	14	1	24	.238	.284	.306	54	-17	2-1	.961	3	104	84	S76	0	-0.9
19 1	Phi N	86	197	31	46	4	5	5	30	23	4	25	.234	.326	.381	91	-3	5-1	.990	-12	95	64	2b53,S8,3b6	0	-1.2
19 2	Cin N	46	100	15	17	2	0	1	3	8	0	18	.170	.231	.220	26	-10	1-0	.983	4	116	106	2b22,1b8/S3	0	-0.5
19 3	Pit N	78	174	16	44	3	2	4	19	14	0	20	.253	.309	.362	75	-7	1-1	.972	-2	93	60	2b31,3b12,S3	0	-0.7
19 4	Pit N	73	125	12	27	6	0	0	16	9	4	21	.216	.288	.264	46	-10	0-0	.968	2	113	129	3b31,2b7/S	0	-0.8
To al	8	563	1423	167	321	42	13	20	133	128	13	201	.226	.295	.316	62	-79	13-7	.956	4	104	99	S222,2b113,3b106,1b8	0	-5.9
P LLOW, KIT	Kit Donovan; B8.28.1973 Kansas City MO; BR/TR/6´1″/205; [KCA96 22/649]; d8.14; Col Arkansas																								
20 2	KC A	29	63	6	15	1	0	1	5	9-0	1	21	.238	.342	.302	65	-3	1-1	.844	1	135	185	3b12,1b10,D5	0	-0.2
20 3	Col N	11	18	6	8	3	1	1	4	0-0	2	4	.444	.476	.889	222	3	0-0	1.000	-1	69	0	C7/1lf	0	0.2
20 4	Col N	59	121	15	29	5	1	2	10	8-1	4	43	.240	.308	.347	61	-7	1-0	1.000	-2	67	145	O36(11/0/27),1b5,C4,3b4	0	-0.9
To al	3	99	202	27	52	9	2	4	19	17-1	7	68	.257	.335	.381	77	-7	2-1	1.000	-2	68	141	O37(12/0/27),1b16,3b16,C11,D5	0	-0.9
P LOUZE, LOUIS	Louis Henri; B9.10.1863 Fort Monroe VA; D1.9.1939 New York NY; BL/TL/6´0″/175; d7.24																								
18 6	StL N	1	3	0	0	0	0	0	0	0	—	2	.000	.000	.000	-99	-1	0	1.000	0	0	0	/cf	—	-0.1
P LTIER, DAN	Daniel Edward; B6.30.1968 Clifton Park NY; BL/TL/6´1″/(200–205); [TexA89 3/65]; d6.26; Col Notre Dame																								
1 ?	Tex A	12	24	1	4	0	0	0	2	0-0	0	3	.167	.167	.167	-7	-4	0-0	.857	-2	53	0	O10(1/0/9)	0	-0.5
1. 3	Tex A	65	160	23	43	7	1	1	17	20-0	1	27	.269	.352	.344	91	-1	0-4	.950	-2	83	130	O55(2/0/54),1b5	0	-0.7
19 6	SF N	31	59	3	15	2	0	0	9	7-1	0	9	.254	.328	.288	67	-3	0-0	1.000	-1	72	113	1b13/lf	0	-0.5
To al	3	108	243	27	62	9	1	1	28	27-1	1	39	.255	.330	.313	77	-8	0-4	.943	-5	79	113	O66(4/0/63),1b18	0	-1.7
P LTZ, JOHN	John; B4.23.1861 New Orleans LA; D2.27.1906 New Orleans LA; BR/TR/5´8″/175; d5.1																								
18 4	Ind AA	106	393	40	86	13	17	3	—	7	2	—	.219	.236	.361	95	-4	—	.818	5	81	30	O106L	—	-0.1
18 8	Bal AA	1	4	1	1	0	0	0	0	0	0	—	.250	.250	.250	62	0	1	.500	-0	0	0	/lf	—	-0.1
18 0	Bro AA	98	384	55	87	9	6	1	33	32	2	—	.227	.289	.289	73	-14	10	.904	1	107	137	O98C	—	-1.4
	Syr AA	5	17	2	3	1	1	0	2	3	0	—	.176	.300	.353	103	0	0	.857	1	316	665	O5C	—	0.1
	Tol AA	20	73	8	18	2	2	0	13	3	1	—	.247	.286	.329	79	-3	7	.886	-0	108	171	O20C	—	-0.3
	Year	123	474	65	108	12	9	1	48	38	3	—	.228	.289	.297	75	-16	17	.900	1	114	158	O123C	—	-1.6
To al	3	230	871	106	195	25	26	4	48	45	5	—	.224	.266	.326	84	-21	18	.865	6	98	98	O230(107/123/0)	—	-1.8
MBERTON, BROCK	Brock; B11.5.1953 Tulsa OK; BB/TL/6´3″/(185–190); [NYN72 6/133]; d9.10																								
19 4	NY N	11	22	0	4	0	0	0	1	0-0	0	3	.182	.182	.182	2	-3	0-1	1.000	1	193	138	1b4	0	-0.3
1975	NY N	2	2	0	0	0	0	0	0	0-0	0	1	.000	.000	.000	-99	-1	0-0	ø	0	—	—	/H	0	-0.1
To al	2	13	24	0	4	0	0	0	1	0-0	0	4	.167	.167	.167	-7	-4	0-1	1.000	1	193	138	1b4	0	-0.4
P EMBERTON, RUDY	Rudy Hector (Perez); B12.17.1969 San Pedro de Macoris, D.R.; BR/TR/6´1″/185; d4.26																								
19 5	Det A	12	30	3	9	3	1	0	3	1-0	1	5	.300	.344	.467	108	0	0-0	1.000	-1	95	0	O8(6/0/2),D3	0	0.0
19 6	Bos A	13	41	11	21	8	0	1	10	2-0	2	4	.512	.556	.780	229	9	3-1	1.000	-3	42	0	O13(1/0/12)	0	0.5
19 7	Bos A	27	63	8	15	2	0	2	10	4-0	3	13	.238	.314	.365	75	-2	0-0	.949	0	94	170	O23R	0	-0.3
Tc al	3	52	134	22	45	13	1	3	23	7-0	6	22	.336	.395	.515	130	7	3-1	.968	-3	79	84	O44(7/0/37),D3	0	0.2
P ENA, BERT	Adalberto (Rivera); B7.11.1959 Santurce, PR; BR/TR/5´11″/165; d9.14																								
19 1	Hou N	4	2	0	1	0	0	0	0	0-0	0	0	.500	.500	.500	195	0	0-0	1.000	-0	55	325	S3	0	0.0
19 3	Hou N	4	8	0	1	0	0	0	0	2-0	0	2	.125	.300	.125	23	-1	0-0	1.000	-2	72	110	S4	0	-0.2
19 4	Hou N	24	39	3	8	1	0	1	4	3-1	0	8	.205	.262	.308	63	-2	0-0	.956	1	101	71	S21	15	0.0
19 5	Hou N	20	29	7	8	2	0	0	4	1-0	0	6	.276	.290	.345	82	-1	0-0	1.000	-2	98	0	3b7,S6,2b2	83	-0.3
1 6	Hou N	15	29	3	6	1	0	0	2	5-2	0	5	.207	.324	.241	60	-1	1-0	.907	1	96	51	S10,3b2/2	0	0.0
1	Hou N	21	46	5	7	0	0	0	0	2-0	1	7	.152	.204	.152	-4	-7	0-0	.982	-4	81	37	S19/3	0	-0.9
Total	6	88	153	18	31	4	0	1	10	13-3	1	28	.203	.268	.248	45	-12	1-0	.953	-6	88	64	S63,3b10,2b3	98	-1.4
PENA, ANGEL	Angel Maria; B2.16.1975 San Pedro de Macoris, D.R.; BR/TR/5´10″/228; d9.8																								
1998	LA N	6	13	1	3	0	0	0	0	0-0	0	6	.231	.231	.231	23	-2	0-0	1.000	1	200	107	C4	0	-0.1
1999	LA N	43	120	14	25	6	0	4	21	12-0	0	24	.208	.276	.358	63	-7	0-1	.989	-0	92	128	C43	0	-0.5
2001	LA N	22	54	3	11	1	0	1	2	1-0	0	17	.204	.214	.278	29	-6	0-0	1.000	6	107	107	C15	0	0.1
Total	3	71	187	18	39	7	0	5	23	13-0	0	47	.209	.256	.326	51	-15	0-1	.993	6	102	121	C62	0	-0.5
PENA, TONY	Antonio Francisco (Padilla); B6.4.1957 Monte Cristi, D.R.; BR/TR/6´0″/(175–190); d9.1; M4/C2; b–Ramon s–Tony																								
1980	Pit N	8	21	1	9	1	1	0	1	0-0	0	4	.429	.429	.571	171	2	0-1	.952	1	78	95	C6	0	0.3
1981	Pit N	66	210	16	63	9	1	2	17	8-2	1	23	.300	.326	.381	96	-1	1-2	.985	8	**173**	86	C64	0	0.9
1982	Pit N★	138	497	53	147	28	4	11	63	17-3	4	57	.296	.323	.435	106	2	2-5	.982	7	**145**	106	C137	0	1.5
1983	Pit N	151	542	51	163	22	3	15	70	31-8	0	73	.301	.338	.435	110	6	6-7	.992	6	128	90	C149	0	1.8
1984	Pit N★	147	546	77	156	27	2	15	78	36-5	4	79	.286	.333	.425	112	8	12-8	.991	23	**137**	111	C146	0	3.8
1985	Pit N★	147	546	53	136	27	2	10	59	29-4	0	67	.249	.284	.361	81	-16	12-8	.988	22	**139**	120	C146/1	0	1.3
1986	Pit N★	144	510	56	147	26	2	10	52	53-6	1	69	.288	.356	.406	107	6	9-10	.981	17	115	122	C139,1b4	0	2.8
1987	†StL N	116	384	40	82	13	4	5	44	36-9	1	54	.214	.281	.307	55	-26	6-1	.988	7	131	68	C112,1b4,O2R	41	-1.3
1988	StL N	149	505	55	133	23	1	10	51	33-11	1	60	.263	.308	.372	93	-5	6-2	**.994**	11	130	91	C142,1b3	0	1.6
1989	StL N★	141	424	36	110	17	2	4	37	35-19	2	33	.259	.318	.337	85	-8	5-3	**.997**	13	103	103	C134/rf	0	1.3
1990	†Bos A	143	491	62	129	19	1	7	56	43-3	1	71	.263	.322	.348	84	-11	8-6	.995	10	93	100	C142/1	0	0.8
1 '	Bos A	141	464	45	107	23	2	5	48	37-1	4	53	.231	.291	.321	66	-21	8-3	.995	12	107	91	C140	0	-0.1
'	Bos A	133	410	39	99	21	1	1	38	24-0	1	61	.241	.284	.305	61	-22	3-2	.993	19	121	84	C132	0	0.5
1993	Bos A	126	304	20	55	11	0	4	19	25-0	2	46	.181	.246	.257	34	-29	1-3	.995	21	138	76	C125/D	0	-0.2
1994	Cle A	40	112	18	33	8	1	2	10	9-0	0	11	.295	.341	.438	100	0	0-1	.996	2	90	106	C40	0	0.3
1995	†Cle A	91	263	25	69	15	0	5	28	14-1	1	44	.262	.302	.376	74	-11	1-0	.987	-1	74	80	C91	0	-0.5
1996	†Cle A	67	174	14	34	4	0	1	27	15-0	0	25	.195	.255	.236	26	-20	0-1	.992	6	112	120	C67	0	-1.0
1997	Chi A	31	67	4	11	1	0	0	8	8-0	0	13	.164	.250	.179	16	-8	0-0	1.000	-2	58	43	C30/3	17	-0.9
	†Hou N	9	19	2	4	3	0	0	2	2-0	0	3	.211	.273	.368	72	-1	0-0	1.000	2	55	48	C8	0	0.2
Total	18	1988	6489	667	1687	298	27	107	708	455-72	23	846	.260	.309	.364	83	-155	80-63	.991	184	121	97	C1950,1b13,O3R/3D	58	13.1
PENA, BRAYAN	Brayan Eduardo; B1.7.1982 Havana, Cuba; BB/TR/5´11″/(210–220); d5.23																								
2005	Atl N	18	39	2	7	2	0	0	4	1-1	0	7	.179	.200	.231	12	-5	0-0	1.000	-2	59	102	C15	0	-0.6
2006	Atl N	23	41	9	11	2	0	1	5	2-0	0	5	.268	.302	.390	75	-2	0-0	1.000	-5	162	0	C15/3	0	-0.6
Total	2	41	80	11	18	4	0	1	9	3-1	0	12	.225	.253	.313	45	-7	0-0	1.000	-7	107	54	C30/3	0	-1.2
PENA, CARLOS	Carlos Felipe; B5.17.1978 Santo Domingo, D.R.; BL/TL/6´2″/(210–215); [TexA98 1/10]; d9.5; Col Northeastern																								
2001	Tex A	22	62	6	16	4	1	3	12	10-0	0	17	.258	.361	.500	120	2	0-0	.987	2	147	87	1b16/D	0	0.2
2002	Oak A	40	124	12	27	4	0	7	16	15-0	1	38	.218	.305	.419	91	-2	0-0	.997	8	177	83	1b40	0	0.2
	Det A	75	273	31	69	13	4	12	36	26-0	2	73	.253	.321	.462	109	3	2-2	.996	-7	62	110	1b73,D2	0	-1.1
	'ear	115	397	43	96	17	4	19	52	41-0	3	111	.242	.316	.448	103	1	2-2	.996	0	102	101	1b113,D2	0	-0.9
	t A	131	452	51	112	21	6	18	50	53-1	6	123	.248	.332	.440	107	4	4-5	.990	-0	108	114	1b128/D	25	-0.8
	A	142	481	89	116	22	4	27	82	70-2	3	146	.241	.338	.472	113	9	7-1	.995	-2	94	114	1b135,D5	0	-0.3
	A	79	260	37	61	9	0	18	44	31-2	4	95	.235	.325	.477	112	4	0-1	.993	2	117	111	1b51,D24	0	0.0
	A	18	33	3	9	2	0	1	3	4-0	0	10	.273	.351	.424	97	0	0-0	.989	-1	88	182	1b17/lf	0	-0.1
		507	1685	229	410	75	15	86	243	209-5	16	502	.243	.331	.459	109	20	13-9	.993	1	104	111	1b460,D33/lf	25	-1.9
VIS	Elvis (Mendez); B9.15.1976 San Pedro de Macoris, D.R.; BB/TR/5´11″/(155–165); d9.2																								
	Col N	10	9	1	3	1	0	0	1	1-0	0	1	.333	.400	.444	92	0	1-0	1.000	-0	103	228	S3/2	0	0.0
	Mil N	15	40	5	9	2	0	0	6	6-0	1	6	.225	.333	.275	63	-2	2-0	.980	3	136	116	2b11	0	0.2
Total	2	25	49	6	12	3	0	0	7	7-0	1	7	.245	.345	.306	70	-2	3-0	.980	3	134	115	2b12,S3	0	0.2

YEAR	TM LG	G	AB	R	H	2B	3B	HR	RBI	BB-IB	HP	SO	AVG	OBP	SLG	AOPS	ABR	SB-CS	FA	FR	RNG	THR	GAMES AT POSITION	DL	BFW
PENA, GERONIMO	Geronimo (Martinez); B3.29.1967 Distrito Nacional, D.R.; BB/TR/6´1˝/(170–195); d9.5; [DL 1989 StL N 63]																								
1990	StL N	18	45	5	11	2	0	0	2	4-0	1	14	.244	.314	.289	68	-2	1-1	.982	2	111	135	2b11	0	0.0
1991	StL N	104	185	38	45	8	3	5	17	18-1	5	45	.243	.322	.400	102	0	15-5	.976	-7	94	107	2b83,O4L	0	-0.4
1992	StL N	62	203	31	62	12	1	7	31	24-0	5	37	.305	.386	.478	149	14	13-8	.984	11	116	136	2b57	100	2.7
1993	StL N	74	254	34	65	19	2	5	30	25-0	4	71	.256	.330	.406	97	-1	13-5	.966	3	112	121	2b64	59	0.6
1994	StL N	83	213	33	54	13	1	11	34	24-1	6	54	.254	.344	.479	112	4	9-1	.990	3	105	124	2b59/3	9	1.1
1995	StL N	32	101	20	27	6	1	1	8	16-1	1	30	.267	.367	.376	96	0	3-2	.976	-1	102	112	2b25	101	0.0
1996	Cle A	5	9	1	1	0	0	1	2	1-0	0	4	.111	.200	.444	57	-1	0-0	ø	-1	0	0	3b3/2	0	-0.1
Total	7	378	1010	162	265	60	8	30	124	112-3	22	255	.262	.345	.427	109	14	54-22	.978	9	107	122	2b300,3b4,O4L	332	3.9
PENA, ROBERTO	Roberto Cesar "Baby" (b Roberto Cesar Zapata (Pena)); B4.17.1937 Santo Domingo, D.R.; D7.23.1982 Santiago, D.R.; BR/TR/5´8˝/(163–175); d4.12																								
1965	Chi N	51	170	17	37	5	1	2	12	16-4	2	19	.218	.291	.294	64	-8	1-2	.930	-5	102	97	S50	0	-1.0
1966	Chi N	6	17	0	3	2	0	0	1	0-0	0	4	.176	.176	.294	28	-2	0-0	.957	1	99	86	S5	0	-0.1
1968	Phi N	138	500	56	130	13	2	1	38	34-2	2	63	.260	.307	.300	84	-10	3-5	.954	9	101	121	S133	0	1.1
1969	SD N	139	472	44	118	16	3	4	30	21-0	3	63	.250	.286	.322	72	-19	0-3	.977	-2	104	89	S65,2b33,3b27,1b12	0	-1.6
1970	Oak A	19	58	4	15	1	0	0	3	3-0	0	4	.259	.295	.276	60	-3	1-1	.961	-3	89	48	S12,3b5	0	-0.5
	Mil A	121	416	36	99	19	1	3	42	25-4	2	45	.238	.282	.310	64	-21	3-5	.981	-13	94	95	S99,2b15,1b7	0	-2.4
	Year	140	474	40	114	20	1	3	45	28-4	2	49	.241	.283	.306	63	-24	4-6	**.979**	-16	93	90	S111,2b15,1b7,3b5	0	-2.9
1971	Mil A	113	274	17	65	9	3	3	28	15-3	1	37	.237	.279	.325	71	-11	2-1	.996	1	88	87	1b50,3b37,S23/2	0	-1.2
Total	6	587	1907	174	467	65	10	13	154	114-13	10	235	.245	.290	.310	72	-74	10-17	.962	-13	100	103	S387,1b69,3b69,2b49	0	-5.7
PENA, TONY	Tony Francisco; B3.23.1981 Santiago, D.R.; BR/TR/6´1˝/180; d4.13; f–Tony																								
2006	Atl N	40	44	12	10	2	0	1	3	2-1	0	10	.227	.261	.341	52	-3	0-0	.977	0	103	114	S22/3	0	-0.2
PENA, WILY MO	Wily Modesto; B1.23.1982.Laguna Salada, D.R.; BR/TR/6´3˝/(215–245); d9.10; [DL 2000 NY A 80]																								
2002	Cin N	13	18	1	4	0	0	1	1	0-0	0	11	.222	.222	.389	55	-1	0-0	1.000	-1	68	0	O4(3/0/1)	0	-0.2
2003	Cin N	80	165	20	36	6	1	5	16	12-2	3	53	.218	.283	.358	69	-8	3-2	.977	-2	95	41	O47(8/26/14)/3	25	-1.1
2004	Cin N	110	336	45	87	10	1	26	66	22-1	6	108	.259	.316	.527	115	5	5-2	.969	6	116	127	O91(1/46/51)	0	0.9
2005	Cin N	99	311	42	79	17	0	19	51	20-0	3	116	.254	.304	.492	104	0	2-1	.976	-2	100	46	O83(10/25/50)	35	-0.4
2006	Bos A	84	276	36	83	15	2	11	42	20-0	3	90	.301	.349	.489	113	5	0-1	.981	1	100	124	O76(18/27/39),D5	52	0.3
Total	5	386	1106	144	289	48	4	62	176	74-3	15	378	.261	.315	.480	104	1	10-6	.975	2	104	89	O301(40/124/155),D5/3	192	-0.5
PENCE, ELMER	Elmer Clair; B8.17.1900 Valley Springs CA; D9.17.1968 San Francisco CA; BR/TR/6´0˝/185; d8.23																								
1922	Chi A	1	0	0	0	0	0	0	0	0	0	0	ø	ø	ø	ø	0	0-0	1.000	0	164	0	/rf	—	0.0
PENDLETON, JIM	James Edward; B1.7.1924 St.Charles MO; D3.20.1996 Houston TX; BR/TR/6´0˝/(180–190); d4.17; Negro Lg 1948																								
1953	Mil N	120	251	48	75	12	4	7	27	7	2	36	.299	.323	.462	108	2	6-5	.961	7	114	138	O105(75/15/25),S7	0	0.5
1954	Mil N	71	173	20	38	3	1	1	16	4	0	21	.220	.236	.266	33	-18	2-1	.950	1	98	167	O50(23/18/11)	0	-1.9
1955	Mil N	8	10	0	0	0	0	0	0	0-0	0	2	.000	.000	.000	-99	-3	0-0	1.000	-1	0	0	/S3cf	0	-0.4
1956	Mil N	14	11	0	0	0	0	0	0	1-0	0	3	.000	.083	.000	-80	-3	0-0	1.000	-0	99	0	S3,3b2/12	0	-0.3
1957	Pit N	46	59	9	18	1	1	0	9	9-1	1	14	.305	.394	.356	110	1	0-0	.917	-2	64	173	O9(2/1/6),3b2/S	0	-0.1
1958	Pit N	3	3	0	1	0	0	0	0	0-0	0	0	.333	.333	.333	79	0	0-0	ø	0	—	—	/H	0	0.0
1959	Cin N	65	113	13	29	2	0	3	9	8-2	1	18	.257	.309	.354	75	-4	3-0	.971	2	137	216	O24L,3b16,S3	0	-0.3
1962	Hou N	117	321	30	79	12	2	8	36	14-2	2	57	.246	.279	.371	79	-11	0-0	.963	-3	100	79	O90(65/7/21),1b8,3b3,S2	0	-1.9
Total	8	444	941	120	240	30	8	19	97	43-5	6	151	.255	.290	.365	76	-36	11-6	.959	3	105	127	O279(189/42/63),3b24,S17,1b9/2	0	-4.4
PENDLETON, TERRY	Terry Lee; B7.16.1960 Los Angeles CA; BB/TR/5´9˝/(180–195); [StLN82 7/179]; d7.18; C5; Col Cal St.–Fresno																								
1984	StL N	67	262	37	85	16	3	1	33	16-3	0	32	.324	.357	.420	122	7	20-5	.943	9	117	91	3b66	0	1.9
1985	†StL N	149	559	56	134	16	3	5	69	37-4	0	75	.240	.285	.306	66	-26	17-12	.965	26	121	111	3b149	15	-0.4
1986	StL N	159	578	56	138	26	5	1	59	34-10	1	59	.239	.279	.306	62	-31	24-6	.962	19	118	**150**	3b156/rf	0	-1.2
1987	†StL N	159	583	82	167	29	4	12	96	70-6	2	74	.286	.360	.412	103	4	19-12	.949	5	108	100	3b158	0	0.6
1988	StL N	110	391	44	99	20	2	6	53	21-4	2	51	.253	.293	.361	86	-8	3-3	.963	14	118	81	3b101	27	0.6
1989	StL N	162	613	83	162	28	5	13	74	44-3	0	81	.264	.313	.390	97	-4	9-5	**.971**	**35**	**129**	101	3b161	0	3.3
1990	StL N	121	447	46	103	20	2	6	58	30-8	1	58	.230	.277	.324	65	-22	7-5	.947	8	111	106	3b117	15	-1.4
1991	†Atl N	153	586	94	**187**	34	8	22	86	43-8	1	70	**.319**	.363	.517	138	28	10-2	.950	20	**114**	**139**	3b148	0	5.1
1992	†Atl N★	160	640	98	**199**	39	1	21	105	37-8	0	67	.311	.345	.473	123	18	5-2	.960	7	101	109	3b158	0	2.8
1993	†Atl N	161	633	81	172	33	1	17	84	36-5	3	97	.272	.311	.408	89	-11	5-1	.959	11	102	138	3b161	0	0.2
1994	Atl N	77	309	25	78	18	3	7	30	12-3	0	57	.252	.280	.398	72	-14	2-0	.950	3	96	113	3b77	33	-1.0
1995	Fla N	133	513	70	149	32	1	14	78	38-7	2	84	.290	.339	.439	102	2	1-2	.952	3	97	107	3b129	0	0.5
1996	Fla N	111	406	30	102	20	1	7	58	26-5	3	75	.251	.298	.357	75	-16	0-2	.961	6	103	126	3b108	0	-1.0
	†Atl N	42	162	21	33	6	0	4	17	15-1	0	36	.204	.271	.315	51	-12	2-1	.939	1	99	88	3b41	0	-1.1
	Year	153	568	51	135	26	1	11	75	41-6	3	111	.238	.290	.345	68	-28	2-3	.955	6	102	116	3b149	0	-2.1
1997	Cin N	50	113	11	28	9	0	1	17	12-1	0	14	.248	.320	.354	75	-4	2-1	.942	-7	70	24	3b32	44	-1.0
1998	KC A	79	237	17	61	10	0	3	29	15-1	0	49	.257	.299	.338	63	-13	1-0	.957	1	105	74	D40,3b23	40	-1.4
Total	15	1893	7032	851	1897	356	39	140	946	486-77	15	979	.270	.316	.391	91	-102	127-59	.957	159	110	113	3b1785,D40/rf	174	6.5
PENN, SHANNON	Shannon Dion; B9.11.1969 Cincinnati OH; BB/TR/5´10˝/163; [TexA88 58/1350]; d4.28; Col Lakeland (OH) CC																								
1995	Det A	3	9	0	3	0	0	0	0	1-0	0	2	.333	.400	.333	93	0	0-0	.864	2	138	248	2b3	0	0.2
1996	Det A	6	14	0	1	0	0	0	1	0-0	0	3	.071	.071	.071	-64	-4	0-0	ø	-0	0	0	/lfD	0	-0.3
Total	2	9	23	0	4	0	0	0	1	1-0	0	5	.174	.208	.174	-1	-4	0-0	.864	2	138	248	D4,2b3/lf	0	-0.1
PENNYFEATHER, WILL	William Nathaniel; B5.25.1968 Perth Amboy NJ; BR/TR/6´2˝/(195–215); d6.27																								
1992	Pit N	15	9	2	2	0	0	0	0	0-0	0	0	.222	.222	.222	26	-1	0-0	1.000	0	113	0	O10(1/6/5)	0	-0.1
1993	Pit N	21	34	4	7	1	0	0	2	0-0	0	6	.206	.206	.235	18	-4	0-1	1.000	-1	94	0	O17(1/15/2)	0	-0.5
1994	Pit N	4	3	0	0	0	0	0	0	0-0	0	0	.000	.000	.000	-98	-1	0-0	ø	-0	0	0	/lf	0	-0.1
Total	3	40	46	6	9	1	0	0	2	0-0	0	6	.196	.196	.217	11	-6	0-1	1.000	-1	98	0	O28(3/21/7)	0	-0.7
PEOPLES, JIMMY	James Elsworth; B10.8.1863 Big Beaver MI; D8.29.1920 Detroit MI; TR/5´8˝/200; d5.29; U1; OF(5/6/24); ▲																								
1884	Cin AA	69	267	28	45	2	2	1	16	6	0	—	.169	.187	.202	26	-22	—	.829	-2	93	160	S47,C14,O10(0/4/6)/31	—	-2.1
1885	Cin AA	7	22	1	4	0	0	0	1	1	0	—	.182	.217	.182	27	-2	—	.826	-1	—	—	C5,P2/rf	—	-0.2
	Bro AA	41	151	21	30	4	1	1	15	5	1	—	.199	.229	.258	53	-8	—	.902	-0	—	—	C37,S2/13cf	—	-0.5
	Year	48	173	22	34	4	1	1	16	6	1	—	.197	.228	.249	50	-10	—	.896	-1	—	—	C42,P2,O2(0/1/1),S2/13	—	-0.7
1886	Bro AA	93	340	43	74	7	3	3	38	20	0	—	.218	.261	.282	70	-13	20	.879	14	—	—	C76,S14,O8(4/1/3)/3	—	0.6
1887	Bro AA	73	268	36	68	14	2	1	38	16	4	—	.254	.306	.332	77	-9	22	.853	-4	—	—	C57,O8(1/0/7),S4,1b4/2	—	-0.6
1888	Bro AA	32	103	15	20	5	3	0	17	8	1	—	.194	.259	.301	79	-2	10	.904	4	—	—	C25,S5,O2R	—	0.4
1889	Col AA	29	100	13	23	6	2	1	16	6	0	8	.230	.274	.360	84	-2	3	.922	-4	—	—	C22,O5R,2b2/S	—	-0.4
Total	6	344	1251	157	264	38	13	7	141	62	6	8	.211	.252	.279	62	-58	55	.887	7	—	—	C236,S73,O35R,1b6,2b3,3b3,P2	—	-2.8
PEPITONE, JOE	Joseph Anthony "Pepi"; B10.9.1940 Brooklyn NY; BL/TL/6´2˝/(170–200); d4.10; C1																								
1962	NY A	63	138	14	33	3	2	7	17	3-0	0	21	.239	.255	.442	86	-4	1-1	1.000	-3	66	0	O32(14/7/13),1b16	0	-0.9
1963	†NY A★	157	580	79	157	16	3	27	89	23-2	7	63	.271	.304	.448	109	4	3-5	.995	5	113	**114**	1b143,O16(0/7/9)	0	-0.1
1964	†NY A★	160	613	71	154	12	3	28	100	24-7	3	63	.251	.281	.418	90	-11	2-1	.988	6	**124**	112	1b155,O30(0/28/3)	0	-1.6
1965	NY A★	143	531	51	131	18	3	18	62	43-11	2	59	.247	.305	.394	98	-3	4-2	**.997**	1	100	**119**	1b115,O41(2/3/36)	0	-1.1
1966	NY A	152	585	85	149	21	4	31	83	29-6	2	58	.255	.290	.463	118	10	4-3	**.995**	10	**129**	**106**	1b119,O55(0/49/9)	0	1.2
1967	NY A	133	501	45	126	18	3	13	64	34-4	3	62	.251	.301	.377	104	1	1-3	.976	-7	94	90	O123C,1b6	0	-1.2
1968	NY A	108	380	41	93	9	3	15	56	37-9	1	45	.245	.311	.403	120	8	8-2	.980	-10	85	62	O92(4/88/0),1b12	22	-0.6
1969	NY A	135	513	49	124	16	3	27	70	30-11	1	42	.242	.284	.442	104	-1	8-6	**.995**	-4	88	118	1b132	0	-1.7
1970	Hou N	75	279	44	70	9	5	14	35	18-9	1	28	.251	.298	.470	107	0	5-2	.995	-1	90	116	1b50,O28(15/3/13)	0	-0.5
	Chi N	56	213	38	57	9	2	12	44	15-2	0	15	.268	.313	.498	102	0	0-2	.992	-1	107	35	O56C,1b13	0	-0.3
	Year	131	492	82	127	18	7	26	79	33-11	1	43	.258	.304	.482	104	0	5-4	.989	-1	109	42	O84(15/59/13),1b63	0	-0.8
1971	Chi N	115	427	50	131	19	4	16	61	24-8	4	41	.307	.347	.482	116	9	1-2	.990	-4	104	102	1b95,O23(1/22/0)	15	-0.3
1972	Chi N	66	214	23	56	5	0	8	21	13-4	3	22	.262	.309	.397	91	-3	1-2	.997	-1	89	120	1b66	0	-1.0
1973	Chi N	31	112	16	30	3	0	3	18	8-0	1	6	.268	.320	.375	86	-2	3-1	.985	-0	100	122	1b28	0	-0.5
	Atl N	3	11	0	4	0	0	0	1	1-0	0	1	.364	.417	.364	110	0	0-0	.963	-1	0	192	1b3	0	-0.1

YEAR	TM LG	G	AB	R	H	2B	3B	HR	RBI	BB-IB	HP	SO	AVG	OBP	SLG	AOPS	ABR	SB-CS	FA	FR	RNG	THR	GAMES AT POSITION	DL	BFW
	Year	34	123	16	34	3	0	3	19	9-0	1	7	.276	.328	.374	88	-2	3-1	.983	-1	90	129	1b31	0	-0.6
Total	12	1397	5097	606	1315	158	35	219	721	302-73	28	526	.258	.301	.432	105	8	41-32	.993	-9	107	113	1b953,O496(36/386/83)	37	-8.7
PEPLOSKI, HENRY	Henry Stephen "Pep"; B9.15.1905 Garlin, Prussia (now Poland); D1.28.1982 Dover NJ; BL/TR/5´9˝/155; d9.19; b–Pepper																								
1929	Bos N	6	10	1	2	0	0	0	1	1	0	3	.200	.273	.200	20	-1	0	1.000	-0	82	0	3b2	—	-0.1
PEPLOSKI, PEPPER	Joseph Aloysius; B9.12.1891 Brooklyn NY; D7.13.1972 New York NY; BR/TR/5´8˝/155; d6.24; b–Henry; Col Seton Hall																								
1913	Det A	2	4	1	2	0	0	0	0	0	0	0	.500	.500	.500	196	0	0	1.000	-0	78	0	3b2	—	0.0
PEPPER, DON	Donald Hoyte; B10.8.1943 Saratoga Sprgs. NY; BL/TR/6´4.5˝/210; d9.10																								
1966	Det A	4	3	0	0	0	0	0	0	0-0	0	1	.000	.000	.000	-98	-1	0-0	1.000	0	0	0	/1	0	-0.1
PEPPER, RAY	Raymond Watson; B8.5.1905 Decatur AL; D3.24.1996 Belle Mina AL; BR/TR/6´2˝/195; d4.15; Col Alabama																								
1932	StL N	21	57	3	14	2	1	0	7	5	0	13	.246	.306	.316	66	-3	1	.971	0	104	108	O17(16/0/1)	—	-0.3
1933	StL N	3	9	2	2	0	0	1	2	0	0	1	.222	.222	.556	110	0	0	1.000	-0	86	0	O2L	—	0.0
1934	StL A	148	564	71	168	24	6	7	101	29	1	67	.298	.333	.399	81	-17	1-4	.963	3	100	133	O136(101/37/1)	—	-2.1
1935	StL A	92	261	20	66	15	3	4	37	20	0	32	.253	.306	.379	73	-11	0-2	.982	-1	92	113	O57(27/4/26)	—	-1.5
1936	StL A	75	124	13	35	5	0	2	23	5	0	23	.282	.310	.371	66	-7	0-2	.941	-1	93	73	O18(2/5/11)	—	-0.9
Total	5	339	1015	109	285	46	10	14	170	59	1	136	.281	.321	.387	77	-38	2-8	.967	1	98	121	O230(148/46/39)	—	-4.8
PERALTA, JHONNY	Jhonny Antonio; B5.28.1982 Santiago, D.R.; BR/TR/6´1˝/(180–210); d6.12																								
2003	Cle A	77	242	24	55	10	1	4	21	20-0	4	65	.227	.295	.326	65	-13	1-3	.976	1	108	94	S72,3b6	0	-0.7
2004	Cle A	8	25	2	6	1	0	0	2	3-0	0	6	.240	.321	.280	61	-1	0-1	.889	-2	94	49	S7,3b2	0	-0.3
2005	Cle A	141	504	82	147	35	4	24	78	58-3	3	128	.292	.366	.520	137	28	0-2	.970	5	101	**129**	S141	0	4.1
2006	Cle A	149	569	84	146	28	3	13	68	56-0	1	152	.257	.323	.385	86	-12	0-1	.977	16	109	99	S147/D	0	1.4
Total	4	375	1340	192	354	74	8	41	169	137-3	8	351	.264	.334	.423	101	2	1-7	.973	21	105	109	S367,3b8/D	0	4.5
PERCONTE, JACK	John Patrick; B8.31.1954 Joliet IL; BL/TR/5´10˝/(160–165); [LAN76 16/379]; d9.13; Col Murray St.																								
1980	LA N	14	17	2	4	0	0	0	2	2-0	0	1	.235	.316	.235	57	-1	3-0	1.000	2	122	107	2b9	0	0.2
1981	LA N	8	9	2	2	0	1	0	1	2-0	0	2	.222	.364	.444	134	0	1-1	1.000	4	291	355	2b2	0	0.5
1982	Cle A	93	219	27	52	4	4	0	15	22-1	0	25	.237	.303	.292	65	-11	9-3	.976	-6	100	51	2b82,D2	0	-1.2
1983	Cle A	14	26	1	7	1	0	0	0	5-0	0	2	.269	.387	.308	90	0	3-1	.950	7	161	215	2b13	0	0.8
1984	Sea A	155	612	93	180	24	4	0	31	57-1	5	47	.294	.357	.346	97	-1	29-6	.981	5	100	85	2b150	0	1.7
1985	Sea A	125	485	60	128	17	7	2	23	50-0	3	36	.264	.335	.340	85	-9	31-2	.986	16	108	105	2b125	0	1.9
1986	Chi A	24	73	6	16	1	0	0	4	11-1	0	10	.219	.321	.233	52	-5	2-0	.990	-8	76	79	2b24	0	-1.1
Total	7	433	1441	191	389	47	16	2	76	149-3	8	123	.270	.340	.329	85	-27	78-13	.982	21	103	89	2b405,D2	0	2.8
PEREZ, ANTONIO	Antonio Miguel; B1.26.1980 Bani, D.R.; BR/TR/5´11˝/(170–175); d5.14																								
2003	TB A	48	125	19	31	6	1	2	12	18-0	1	34	.248	.345	.360	89	-1	4-1	.990	-13	77	56	2b31,3b6,S6,D3	0	-1.2
2004	LA N	13	13	5	3	1	0	0	0	0-0	1	5	.231	.286	.308	54	-1	1-0	.750	-0	40	185	2b2/S	0	-0.1
2005	LA N	98	259	28	77	13	2	3	23	21-1	5	61	.297	.360	.398	98	0	11-4	.946	2	120	89	3b35,2b29,S9/lfD	39	0.4
2006	Oak A	57	98	10	10	5	1	1	8	10-0	0	44	.102	.185	.204	1	-15	0-1	.944	1	107	89	3b27,D21,S4,2b2	0	-1.5
Total	4	216	495	62	121	25	4	6	43	49-1	7	144	.244	.320	.347	76	-17	16-6	.942	-11	114	83	3b68,2b64,D25,S20/lf	39	-2.4
PEREZ, TONY	Atanasio (Rigal); B5.14.1942 Ciego de Avila, Cuba; BR/TR/6´2˝/(175–215); d7.26; M2/C6; HF2000; s–Eduardo																								
1964	Cin N	12	25	1	2	1	0	0	1	3-0	0	9	.080	.179	.120	-14	-4	0-0	.981	-1	0	59	1b6	0	-0.6
1965	Cin N	104	281	40	73	14	4	12	47	21-5	2	67	.260	.315	.466	110	3	0-2	.989	-2	86	95	1b93	0	-0.4
1966	Cin N	99	257	25	68	10	4	4	39	14-2	2	44	.265	.304	.381	83	-6	1-0	.989	-5	63	96	1b75	0	-1.5
1967	Cin N★	156	600	78	174	28	7	26	102	33-10	4	102	.290	.328	.490	119	13	0-3	.963	-18	82	56	3b139,1b18/2	0	-0.8
1968	Cin N★	160	625	93	176	25	7	18	92	51-13	6	92	.282	.338	.430	123	17	3-2	.952	6	106	100	3b160	0	2.6
1969	Cin N★	160	629	103	185	31	2	37	122	63-7	2	131	.294	.357	.526	138	31	4-2	.937	-3	105	114	3b160	0	2.9
1970	†Cin N★	158	587	107	186	28	6	40	129	83-13	4	134	.317	.401	.589	162	52	8-3	.923	-5	99	122	3b153,1b8	0	4.6
1971	Cin N	158	609	72	164	22	3	25	91	51-5	1	120	.269	.325	.438	116	11	4-1	.959	5	108	117	3b148,1b44	0	1.6
1972	†Cin N	136	515	64	146	33	7	21	90	55-15	0	121	.283	.349	.497	146	30	4-2	.993	-5	86	**110**	1b136	0	1.5
1973	†Cin N	151	564	73	177	33	3	27	101	74-10	3	117	.314	.393	.527	160	47	3-1	.991	-2	99	**110**	1b151	0	3.5
1974	Cin N★	158	596	81	158	28	2	28	101	61-7	2	112	.265	.331	.460	123	16	1-3	**.996**	-5	83	99	1b157	0	-0.1
1975	†Cin N★	137	511	74	144	28	3	20	109	54-6	3	101	.282	.350	.466	124	16	1-2	.993	-6	86	113	1b132	0	0.0
1976	†Cin N★	139	527	77	137	32	6	19	91	50-9	5	88	.260	.328	.452	117	11	10-5	.996	-6	82	104	1b136	0	-0.6
1977	Mon N	154	559	71	158	32	6	19	91	63-15	2	111	.283	.352	.463	121	16	4-3	.992	5	115	79	1b148	0	1.2
1978	Mon N	148	544	63	158	38	3	14	78	38-9	2	104	.290	.336	.449	119	13	2-0	.991	2	108	114	1b145	0	0.7
1979	Mon N	132	489	58	132	29	4	13	73	38-4	3	82	.270	.322	.425	103	1	2-1	.991	-4	88	87	1b129	0	-1.1
1980	Bos A	151	585	73	161	31	3	25	105	41-11	1	93	.275	.320	.467	108	5	1-0	.993	-4	90	115	1b137,D13	0	-0.8
1981	Bos A	84	306	35	77	11	3	9	39	27-0	0	66	.252	.310	.395	96	-2	0-0	.993	-1	94	119	1b56,D23	0	-0.8
1982	Bos A	69	196	18	51	14	2	6	31	19-3	0	48	.260	.326	.444	103	1	0-1	.857	0	169	0	D46,1b2	0	-0.1
1983	†Phi N	91	253	18	61	11	2	6	43	28-1	1	57	.241	.316	.372	91	-3	1-0	.998	1	98	81	1b69	0	-0.5
1984	Cin N	71	137	9	33	6	1	2	15	11-2	0	21	.241	.295	.343	76	-4	0-0	.990	-2	73	85	1b31	0	-0.8
1985	Cin N	72	183	25	60	8	0	6	33	22-1	0	22	.328	.396	.470	136	9	0-2	.995	-3	76	102	1b50	0	0.4
1986	Cin N	77	200	14	51	12	1	2	29	25-2	0	25	.255	.333	.355	88	-3	0-0	.984	-3	87	127	1b55	0	-0.9
Total	23	2777	9778	1272	2732	505	79	379	1652	925-150	43	1867	.279	.341	.463	121	270	49-33	.992	-53	90	103	1b1778,3b760,D82/2	0	10.0
PEREZ, DANNY	Daniel; B2.26.1971 El Paso TX; BR/TR/5´10˝/188; [MilA92 21/584]; d6.30; Col Oklahoma St.																								
1996	Mil A	4	4	0	0	0	0	0	0	0-0	0	0	.000	.000	.000	-96	-1	0-0	1.000	0	155	0	O3(2/1/0)	0	-0.1
PEREZ, EDUARDO	Eduardo Atanasio; B9.11.1969 Cincinnati OH; BR/TR/6´4˝/(215–240); [CalA91 1/17]; d7.27; f–Tony; Col Florida St.																								
1993	Cal A	52	180	16	45	6	2	4	30	9-0	2	39	.250	.292	.372	75	-7	5-4	.962	2	110	88	3b45,D3	0	-0.5
1994	Cal A	38	129	10	27	7	0	5	16	12-1	0	29	.209	.275	.380	66	-7	3-0	.997	-2	74	97	1b38	0	-1.1
1995	Cal A	29	71	9	12	4	1	1	7	12-0	2	9	.169	.302	.296	58	-4	0-2	.883	-2	88	85	3b23/D	0	-0.7
1996	Cin N	18	36	8	8	0	0	3	5	5-1	0	9	.222	.317	.472	103	0	0-0	1.000	1	147	111	1b8,3b3	0	0.0
1997	Cin N	106	297	44	75	18	0	16	52	29-1	2	76	.253	.321	.475	104	1	5-1	.996	-2	83	80	1b67,O12(11/0/1),3b8/D	0	-0.6
1998	Cin N	84	172	20	41	4	0	4	30	21-2	2	45	.238	.325	.331	73	-6	0-1	.985	7	157	113	1b51/3lf	0	-0.4
1999	StL N	21	32	6	11	2	0	1	9	7-0	0	6	.344	.462	.500	141	3	0-0	1.000	1	125	350	O6L,1b5	0	0.3
2000	StL N	35	91	9	27	4	0	3	10	5-0	3	19	.297	.350	.440	97	-1	1-0	1.000	1	100	122	1b24,O4L,3b2	35	-0.1
2002	†StL N	96	154	22	31	9	0	10	26	17-0	3	36	.201	.290	.455	92	-2	0-0	.982	2	125	294	O35(7/0/29),1b10,3b6/D	0	-0.2
2003	StL N	105	253	47	72	16	0	11	41	29-1	4	53	.285	.365	.478	120	8	5-2	.966	-2	114	30	O71(10/0/64),3b12,1b5/D	0	0.4
2004	TB A	13	38	2	8	2	0	1	7	4-0	0	9	.211	.286	.342	64	-2	0-0	1.000	-1	62	139	1b5,O3(2/0/1)/3D	147	-0.3
2005	TB A	77	161	23	41	6	0	11	28	26-0	3	30	.255	.368	.497	130	7	0-2	.993	-2	82	62	1b49,O4(3/0/1),3b3,D7	0	0.1
2006	Cle A	37	99	16	30	9	0	8	22	5-0	2	11	.303	.343	.636	154	7	0-0	.991	1	109	115	1b29,O5R	0	0.6
	Sea A	43	87	6	17	1	0	1	11	13-2	1	22	.195	.304	.241	48	-7	0-1	1.000	0	206	131	D36,1b5	0	-0.8
	Year	80	186	22	47	10	0	9	33	18-2	3	33	.253	.324	.452	105	1	0-1	.992	2	116	116	D36,1b34,O5R	0	-0.2
Total	13	754	1800	238	445	88	3	79	294	194-8	24	393	.247	.326	.431	97	-10	19-13	.994	5	100	96	1b296,O141(44/0/101),3b104,D53	182	-3.3
PEREZ, EDDIE	Eduardo Rafael; B5.4.1968 Ciudad Ojeda, Zulia, Venez.; BR/TR/6´1˝/(175–220); d9.10																								
1995	Atl N	7	13	1	4	1	0	1	4	0-0	0	2	.308	.308	.615	130	0	0-0	1.000	3	0	0	C5/1	0	0.3
1996	†Atl N	68	156	19	40	9	1	4	17	8-0	1	19	.256	.293	.404	78	-5	0-0	.993	-4	160	67	C54,1b7	15	-0.7
1997	†Atl N	73	191	20	41	5	0	6	18	10-0	2	35	.215	.259	.335	54	-14	0-1	.988	-2	87	84	C64,1b6	0	-1.3
1998	†Atl N	61	149	18	50	12	0	6	32	15-0	2	28	.336	.404	.537	146	10	1-1	.997	0	76	115	C45,1b8/D	0	1.3
1999	†Atl N	104	309	30	77	17	0	7	30	17-4	6	40	.249	.299	.372	70	-15	0-1	.993	6	122	89	C98,1b2	0	-0.4
2000	Atl N	7	22	0	4	1	0	0	3	0-0	0	2	.182	.182	.227	2	-3	0-0	.976	-1	71	60	C7	150	-0.4
2001	Atl N	5	10	0	3	0	0	0	0	0-0	0	2	.300	.300	.300	55	-1	0-0	1.000	-1	66	0	C5	153	-0.2
2002	Cle A	42	117	6	25	9	0	0	4	5-0	1	25	.214	.252	.291	43	-10	0-0	.988	-1	83	154	C42	0	-0.8
2003	Mil N	107	350	26	95	17	1	11	45	17-3	0	47	.271	.304	.420	87	-8	0-1	.991	-14	75	91	C102	0	-1.6
2004	†Atl N	74	170	14	39	12	0	3	13	11-1	3	29	.229	.286	.353	64	-9	0-0	.990	2	118	134	C66/1	0	-0.4
2005	Atl N	16	38	3	8	2	0	2	6	1-0	0	5	.211	.231	.421	65	-2	0-0	1.000	-3	509	143	C13	112	-0.4
Total	11	564	1525	137	386	85	2	40	172	84-8	15	234	.253	.297	.390	77	-57	1-4	.991	-16	110	100	C501,1b25/D	430	-4.6

YEAR	TM LG	G	AB	R	H	2B	3B	HR	RBI	BB-IB	HP	SO	AVG	OBP	SLG	AOPS	ABR	SB-CS	FA	FR	RNG	THR	GAMES AT POSITION	DL	BFW
PEREZ, MARTY	Martin Roman; B2.28.1946 Visalia CA; BR/TR/5´11˝/160; d9.9																								
1969	Cal A	13	13	3	3	0	0	0	0	2-0	0	1	.231	.333	.231	63	-1	0-0	1.000	4	145	278	S7,2b2,3b2	0	0.4
1970	Cal A	3	3	0	0	0	0	0	1	0-0	0	0	.000	.000	.000	-99	-1	0-0	.833	-1	57	155	S2	0	-0.1
1971	Atl N	130	410	28	93	15	3	4	32	25-5	1	44	.227	.272	.307	60	-22	1-2	.955	-13	97	**115**	S126/2	0	-2.3
1972	Atl N	141	479	33	109	13	1	1	28	30-1	3	55	.228	.276	.265	50	-31	0-3	.957	-34	87	84	S141	0	-5.4
1973	Atl N	141	501	66	125	15	5	8	57	49-1	2	66	.250	.316	.347	79	-14	2-3	.962	-6	102	91	S139	0	-0.6
1974	Atl N	127	447	51	116	20	5	2	34	35-1	1	51	.260	.314	.340	80	-12	2-0	.985	-4	100	108	2b102,S14,3b6	0	-0.9
1975	Atl N	120	461	50	127	14	2	2	34	37-2	0	44	.275	.327	.328	80	-12	2-2	.985	-4	100	94	2b116,S7	32	-0.9
1976	Atl N	31	96	12	24	4	0	1	6	8-0	0	9	.250	.305	.323	75	-3	0-0	.976	0	98	99	2b18,S17,3b2	0	-0.1
	SF N	93	332	37	86	13	1	2	26	30-0	0	28	.259	.318	.322	80	-8	3-4	.979	1	107	89	2b89,S5	0	-0.2
	Year	124	428	49	110	17	1	3	32	38-0	0	37	.257	.315	.322	79	-11	3-4	.978	1	106	90	2b107,S22,3b2	0	-0.3
1977	NY A	1	4	0	2	0	0	0	0	0-0	0	1	.500	.500	.500	175	0	0-0	1.000	1	207	621	/3	0	0.1
	Oak A	115	373	32	86	14	5	2	23	29-0	3	65	.231	.290	.311	65	-18	1-3	.974	4	109	80	2b105,3b12,S4	0	-1.0
	Year	116	377	32	88	14	5	2	23	29-0	3	66	.233	.292	.313	66	-18	1-3	.974	5	109	80	2b105,3b13,S4	0	-0.9
1978	Oak A	16	12	1	0	0	0	0	0	0-0	0	5	.000	.000	.000	-99	-3	0-0	1.000	0	99	112	3b11,S3/2	0	-0.3
Total	10	931	3131	313	771	108	22	22	241	245-10	10	369	.246	.301	.316	70	-125	11-17	.958	-51	96	98	S465,2b434,3b34	32	-11.3
PEREZ, MIGUEL	Miguel Antonio; B9.25.1983 Caracas, Distrito Capital, Venezuela; BR/TR/6´3˝/190; d9.7																								
2005	Cin N	2	3	0	0	0	0	0	0	0-0	0	1	.000	.000	.000	-99	-1	0-0	1.000	0	0	0	/C	0	-0.1
PEREZ, NEIFI	Neifi Neftali (Diaz); B6.2.1973 Villa Mella, D.R.; BB/TR/6´0˝/(173–195); d8.31																								
1996	Col N	17	45	4	7	2	0	0	3	0-0	0	8	.156	.156	.200	-6	-7	2-2	.972	-1	86	146	S14,2b4	0	-0.7
1997	Col N	83	313	46	91	13	10	5	31	21-4	1	43	.291	.333	.444	84	-8	4-3	.975	26	131	123	S45,2b41,3b2	0	2.2
1998	Col N	**162**	647	80	177	25	9	9	59	38-0	1	70	.274	.313	.382	68	-30	5-6	.975	**29**	**113**	**123**	S162/C	0	1.0
1999	Col N	157	690	108	193	27	**11**	12	70	28-0	1	54	.280	.307	.403	62	-40	13-5	.981	27	**109**	**112**	S157	0	-0.1
2000	Col N	**162**	651	92	187	39	11	10	71	30-6	0	63	.287	.314	.427	70	-30	3-6	.978	**37**	**115**	117	S162	0	1.6
2001	Col N	87	382	65	114	19	8	7	47	16-1	0	49	.298	.326	.445	80	-11	6-2	.976	7	102	114	S87	15	0.3
	KC A	49	199	18	48	7	1	1	12	10-0	1	19	.241	.277	.302	49	-15	3-4	.978	8	107	130	S46,2b4	0	-0.4
2002	KC A	145	554	65	131	20	4	3	37	20-2	0	53	.236	.260	.303	44	-45	8-9	.972	6	102	113	S139,2b5	0	-2.8
2003	†SF N	120	328	27	84	19	4	1	31	14-3	0	23	.256	.285	.348	63	-18	3-2	.987	22	109	130	2b57,S45,3b2	0	0.8
2004	SF N	103	319	28	74	12	1	2	33	21-3	0	35	.232	.276	.295	47	-25	0-1	.978	11	108	93	S57,2b39,3b2	0	-0.9
	Chi N	23	62	12	23	5	0	2	6	3-0	0	6	.371	.400	.548	138	3	1-0	.968	4	105	125	S19,2b2	0	0.8
	Year	126	381	40	97	17	1	4	39	24-3	0	41	.255	.296	.336	62	-22	1-1	.976	15	107	100	S76,2b41,3b2	0	-0.1
2005	Chi N	154	572	59	157	33	1	9	54	18-3	3	47	.274	.298	.383	75	-22	8-4	.982	25	111	108	S130,2b26,3b4	0	1.4
2006	Chi N	87	236	27	60	13	1	2	24	5-2	0	21	.254	.266	.343	55	-17	0-1	.973	1	103	95	2b53,S21,3b10	0	-1.3
	†Det A	21	65	4	13	1	0	0	5	3-0	0	4	.200	.235	.215	18	-8	1-0	1.000	6	112	134	2b14,S7/3D	0	-0.1
Total	11	1370	5063	635	1359	235	61	63	483	227-24	7	495	.268	.298	.376	64	-273	57-45	.978	208	110	117	S1091,2b245,3b21/DC	15	1.8
PEREZ, ROBERT	Robert Alexander (Jimenez); B6.4.1969 Bolivar, Venezuela; BR/TR/6´3˝/(190–230); d7.20																								
1994	Tor A	4	8	0	1	0	0	0	0	0-0	0	1	.125	.125	.125	-35	-2	0-0	1.000	0	60	555	O4(2/0/2)	0	-0.1
1995	Tor A	17	48	2	9	2	0	1	3	0-0	0	5	.188	.188	.292	22	-6	0-0	1.000	0	119	0	O15(5/0/11)	0	-0.6
1996	Tor A	86	202	30	66	10	0	2	21	8-0	1	17	.327	.354	.406	93	-2	3-0	.983	1	102	80	O79(59/0/25),D2	0	-0.3
1997	Tor A	37	78	4	15	4	1	2	6	0-0	0	16	.192	.192	.346	37	-8	0-0	1.000	-1	102	0	O25(17/0/9),D7	0	-0.9
1998	Sea A	17	35	3	6	1	0	2	6	0-0	0	5	.171	.171	.371	36	-4	0-0	1.000	1	112	158	O17(2/0/15)	0	-0.3
	Mon N	52	106	9	25	1	0	1	8	2-0	1	23	.236	.255	.274	41	-10	0-0	.852	-2	56	239	O29L	22	-1.2
2001	NY A	6	15	1	4	1	0	0	0	1-0	0	7	.267	.313	.333	70	-1	0-1	1.000	-0	94	0	O5(0/3/2)/D	0	-0.1
	Mil N	2	5	0	0	0	0	0	0	0-0	0	0	.000	.000	.000	-99	-2	0-0	1.000	0	146	0	/rf	0	-0.1
Total	6	221	497	49	126	19	1	8	44	11-0	2	74	.254	.271	.354	58	-35	3-1	.976	-1	96	99	O175(114/3/65),D10	22	-3.6
PEREZ, SANTIAGO	Santiago Alberto; B12.30.1975 Santo Domingo, D.R.; BB/TR/6´2˝/150; d6.3																								
2000	Mil N	24	52	8	9	2	0	0	2	8-2	1	9	.173	.290	.212	31	-5	4-0	.917	-2	105	108	S20	0	-0.5
2001	SD N	43	81	13	16	1	0	0	4	15-0	0	29	.198	.320	.210	46	-6	5-1	.947	-3	110	108	O26(9/10/8),S8,2b2	18	-0.8
Total	2	67	133	21	25	3	0	0	6	23-2	1	38	.188	.308	.211	40	-11	9-1	.913	-5	93	87	S28,O26(9/10/8),2b2	18	-1.3
PEREZ, TIMO	Timoniel; B4.8.1975 Bani, D.R.; BL/TL/5´9˝/(165–180); d9.1																								
2000	†NY N	24	49	11	14	4	1	1	3	3-0	1	5	.286	.333	.469	107	0	1-1	.970	2	120	272	O19(8/7/8)	0	0.2
2001	NY N	85	239	26	59	9	1	5	22	12-0	2	25	.247	.287	.356	70	-12	1-6	1.000	4	108	133	O73(6/8/62)	18	-1.2
2002	NY N	136	444	52	131	27	6	8	47	23-2	2	36	.295	.331	.437	106	2	10-6	.979	7	111	148	O122(24/93/17)	0	0.9
2003	NY N	127	346	32	93	21	0	4	42	18-1	2	29	.269	.301	.364	78	-12	5-6	.989	1	100	117	O104(58/49/14)	15	-1.3
2004	Chi A	103	293	38	72	12	0	5	40	15-0	2	29	.246	.285	.338	60	-18	3-1	.986	0	88	186	O80(12/25/49),D6	0	-1.8
2005	†Chi A	76	179	13	39	8	0	2	15	12-1	0	25	.218	.266	.296	48	-13	2-2	.964	1	92	223	O50(27/2/21),D11,1b2	0	-1.5
2006	StL N	23	31	3	6	1	0	1	3	3-1	1	4	.194	.286	.323	55	-2	0-0	1.000	-1	75	0	O7(3/0/4)/D	0	-0.3
Total	7	574	1581	175	414	82	8	26	172	86-5	10	153	.262	.301	.373	78	-55	22-22	.984	14	102	156	O455(138/184/175),D18,1b2	33	-5.0
PEREZ, TOMAS	Tomas Orlando; B12.29.1973 Barquisimeto, Lara, Venez.; BB/TR/5´11˝/(165–190); d5.3; OF(1/0/5)																								
1995	Tor A	41	98	12	24	3	1	1	8	7-0	0	18	.245	.292	.327	61	-6	0-1	.954	-2	99	88	S31,2b7/3	0	-0.6
1996	Tor A	91	295	24	74	13	4	1	19	25-0	1	29	.251	.311	.332	63	-17	1-2	.970	6	105	133	2b75,3b11,S5	0	-0.7
1997	Tor A	40	123	9	24	3	2	0	9	11-0	1	28	.195	.267	.252	36	-12	1-1	.993	8	105	119	S32,2b8	28	-0.1
1998	Tor A	6	9	1	1	0	0	0	0	1-0	0	3	.111	.200	.111	-16	-2	0-0	1.000	-1	56	52	S4/2	0	-0.2
2000	Phi N	45	140	17	31	7	1	1	13	11-2	0	30	.221	.278	.307	48	-12	1-1	.976	-6	79	83	S44	0	-1.4
2001	Phi N	62	135	11	41	7	1	3	19	7-1	2	22	.304	.347	.437	106	1	0-1	1.000	7	110	108	2b29,3b9,S8/rf	0	0.8
2002	Phi N	92	212	22	53	13	1	5	20	21-6	1	40	.250	.319	.392	92	-3	1-0	.994	9	113	119	2b50,3b14,S13,1b3/P	16	0.8
2003	Phi N	125	298	39	79	18	1	5	33	23-11	0	54	.265	.316	.383	88	-6	0-1	.953	1	99	150	3b58,2b26,1b9,S4	0	-0.4
2004	Phi N	86	176	22	38	13	2	6	21	9-2	1	44	.216	.257	.415	68	-9	0-0	.944	-3	98	51	3b22,2b17,1b10,S10	0	-1.1
2005	Phi N	94	159	17	37	7	0	0	22	11-2	2	27	.233	.289	.277	48	-12	1-0	1.000	-2	94	128	1b24,3b15,S14	0	-1.4
2006	TB A	99	241	31	51	12	0	2	16	5-0	0	44	.212	.224	.286	32	-25	1-0	.963	1	96	93	3b40,S36,2b22,O5(1/0/4)/1	0	-2.0
Total	11	781	1886	205	453	96	13	24	180	131-24	8	339	.240	.291	.343	65	-103	6-7	.982	18	107	112	2b235,S201,3b170,1b47,O6R/P	44	-6.3
PEREZCHICA, TONY	Antonio Llamas (Gonzales); B4.20.1966 Mexicali, Baja California, Mexico; BR/TR/5´11˝/(165–175); [SFN84 3/63]; d9.7																								
1988	SF N	7	8	1	1	0	0	0	1	2-0	0	1	.125	.273	.125	27	-1	0-0	1.000	-2	59	0	2b6	0	-0.3
1990	SF N	4	3	1	1	0	0	0	0	1-0	0	2	.333	.500	.333	139	0	0-0	1.000	-1	0	0	2b2,S2	0	-0.1
1991	SF N	23	48	2	11	4	1	0	3	2-0	0	12	.229	.260	.354	73	-2	0-1	.947	-3	90	72	S13,2b6	0	-0.4
	Cle A	17	22	4	8	2	0	0	0	3-0	0	5	.364	.440	.455	147	2	0-0	1.000	-3	43	50	S6,3b3,2b2/D	0	-0.1
1992	Cle A	18	20	2	2	1	0	0	1	2-0	0	6	.100	.182	.150	-6	-3	0-0	.875	-3	131	0	3b9,2b4,S4/D	0	-0.6
Total	4	69	101	10	23	7	1	0	5	10-0	0	26	.228	.295	.317	74	-4	0-1	.944	-11	73	53	S25,2b20,3b12,D2	0	-1.5
PERKINS, BRODERICK	Broderick Phillip; B11.23.1954 Pittsburg CA; BL/TL/5´10˝/180; [SDN76 15/341]; d7.7; Col St. Marys (CA)																								
1978	SD N	62	217	14	52	14	1	2	33	5-2	0	29	.240	.253	.341	71	-10	4-0	.993	4	135	138	1b59	0	-0.8
1979	SD N	57	87	8	23	0	0	0	8	8-2	0	12	.264	.323	.264	67	-4	0-0	.982	-0	105	124	1b28	17	-0.5
1980	SD N	43	100	18	37	9	0	2	14	11-1	0	10	.370	.432	.520	176	11	2-1	.988	-2	94	110	1b20,O10R	0	0.8
1981	SD N	92	254	27	71	18	3	2	40	14-4	0	16	.280	.314	.398	111	3	0-4	.997	-1	94	104	1b80,O3(1/0/2)	0	-0.5
1982	SD N	125	347	32	94	10	4	2	34	26-10	3	20	.271	.325	.340	92	-4	2-1	.994	2	110	99	1b98,O11(4/0/7)	0	-0.9
1983	Cle A	79	184	23	50	10	0	0	24	9-3	0	19	.272	.299	.326	71	-7	1-5	.991	-1	33	101	1b19,O17(5/0/12),D16	0	-1.2
1984	Cle A	58	66	5	13	1	0	0	4	7-1	1	10	.197	.276	.212	39	-5	0-0	1.000	-0	0	220	D10,1b2	0	-0.6
Total	7	516	1255	127	340	62	8	8	157	80-23	4	116	.271	.313	.352	91	-16	9-11	.993	1	106	111	1b306,O41(10/0/31),D26	17	-3.7
PERKINS, CY	Ralph Foster; B2.27.1896 Gloucester MA; D10.2.1963 Philadelphia PA; BR/TR/5´10.5˝/158; d9.25; M1/C17																								
1915	Phi A	7	20	2	4	1	0	0	0	3	0	3	.200	.304	.250	68	-1	0	.920	-1	*69*	*89*	C6	—	-0.1
1917	Phi A	6	18	1	3	0	0	0	2	2	0	1	.167	.250	.167	28	-2	0	.978	2	*97*	*164*	C6	—	0.1
1918	Phi A	68	218	9	41	4	1	1	14	8	0	15	.188	.217	.229	34	-18	1	.990	9	*89*	*126*	C60	—	-0.5
1919	Phi A	101	305	22	77	12	7	2	29	27	0	22	.252	.313	.357	87	-6	2	.971	0	*79*	***135***	C87,S8	—	0.2
1920	Phi A	148	492	40	128	24	6	5	52	28	2	35	.260	.303	.364	75	-19	5-6	.979	15	*98*	***145***	C146/2	—	0.6
1921	Phi A	141	538	58	155	31	4	12	73	32	1	32	.288	.329	.428	91	-9	5-9	.971	0	*88*	*118*	C141	—	-0.1
1922	Phi A	148	505	58	135	20	6	6	69	40	1	30	.267	.322	.366	77	-18	1-7	.984	0	*107*	*115*	C141	—	-1.1
1923	Phi A	143	500	53	135	34	5	2	65	65	2	30	.270	.356	.370	90	-5	1-3	.971	-5	*104*	*93*	C137	—	-0.2

YEAR	TM LG	G	AB	R	H	2B	3B	HR	RBI	BB-IB	HP	SO	AVG	OBP	SLG	AOPS	ABR	SB-CS	FA	FR	RNG	THR	GAMES AT POSITION	DL	BFW
1924	Phi A	128	392	31	95	19	4	0	32	31	4	20	.242	.304	.311	58	-25	3-4	.983	0	*105*	*85*	C128	—	-1.7
1925	Phi A	65	140	21	43	10	0	1	18	26	3	6	.307	.426	.400	104	3	0-0	.980	6	*115*	*84*	C58/3	—	1.1
1926	Phi A	63	148	14	43	6	0	0	19	18	1	7	.291	.371	.331	80	-4	0-2	.984	8	*113*	*102*	C55	—	0.6
1927	Phi A	59	137	11	35	7	2	1	15	12	0	8	.255	.315	.358	70	-6	0-2	.979	1	*118*	*83*	C54/1	—	-0.3
1928	Phi A	19	29	1	5	0	0	0	1	1	0	1	.172	.200	.172	-1	-4	0-1	.982	2	*122*	*88*	C19	—	-0.2
1929	Phi A	38	76	4	16	4	0	0	9	5	0	4	.211	.259	.263	34	-8	0-0	.990	1	*89*	*88*	C38	—	-0.5
1930	Phi A	20	38	1	6	2	0	0	4	2	0	3	.158	.200	.211	4	-6	0-0	.964	-0	*114*	*31*	C19/1	—	-0.5
1931	NY A	16	47	3	12	1	0	0	7	1	1	4	.255	.286	.277	51	-3	0-0	1.000	-3	*90*	*0*	C16	—	-0.5
1934	Det A	1	1	0	0	0	0	0	0	0	0	0	.000	.000	.000	-99	0	0-0	ø	0	—	—	/H	—	0.0
Total	17	1171	3604	329	933	175	35	30	409	301	15	221	.259	.319	.352	75	-131	18-34	.978	35	*99*	*110*	C1111,S8,1b2/32	—	-3.1
PERLOZZO, SAM	Samuel Benedict; B3.4.1951 Cumberland MD; BR/TR/5´9˝/170; d9.13; M2/C19; Col George Washington																								
1977	Min A	10	24	6	7	0	2	0	0	2-0	0	3	.292	.346	.458	118	0	0-0	1.000	-3	76	43	2b10/3	0	-0.2
1979	SD N	2	2	0	0	0	0	0	0	1-0	0	0	.000	.333	.000	-1	0	0-0	.500	-1	0	0	2b2	0	-0.1
Total	2	12	26	6	7	0	2	0	0	3-0	0	3	.269	.345	.423	110	0	0-0	.967	-4	70	40	2b12/3	0	-0.3
PERRIN, JOHN	John Stephenson; B2.4.1898 Escanaba MI; D6.24.1969 Detroit MI; BL/TR/5´9˝/160; d7.11; Col Michigan																								
1921	Bos A	4	13	3	3	0	0	0	1	0	0	3	.231	.231	.231	19	-2	0-0	1.000	-1	33	0	O4R	—	-0.2
PERRINE, NIG	John Grover; B1.14.1885 Clinton WI; D8.13.1948 Kansas City MO; BR/TR/5´9˝/160; d4.11																								
1907	Was A	44	146	13	25	4	1	0	15	13	3	—	.171	.253	.212	53	-7	10	.946	-4	86	152	2b24,S18,3b2	—	-1.1
PERRING, GEORGE	George Wilson; B8.13.1884 Sharon WI; D8.20.1960 Beloit WI; BR/TR/6´0˝/190; d4.25; Col Beloit																								
1908	Cle A	89	310	23	67	8	5	0	19	16	0	—	.216	.255	.274	72	-11	8	.928	-11	100	114	S48,3b41	—	-2.2
1909	Cle A	88	283	26	63	10	9	0	20	19	5	—	.223	.283	.322	87	-5	6	.932	2	105	71	3b67,S11,2b4	—	-0.1
1910	Cle A	39	122	14	27	6	3	0	8	3	0	—	.221	.240	.320	74	-4	3	.931	1	106	96	3b33,1b4	—	-0.4
1914	KC F	144	496	68	138	28	10	2	69	59	0	39	.278	.355	.387	106	-3	7	.934	9	118	127	3b101,1b41/PS	—	0.8
1915	KC F	**153**	553	67	143	23	7	7	67	55	1	30	.259	.327	.363	98	-11	10	.958	11	108	98	3b102,1b31,2b31/S	—	0.3
Total	5	513	1764	198	438	75	34	9	183	152	6	69	.248	.310	.345	93	-34	34	.939	11	108	92	3b344,1b76,S61,2b35/P	—	-1.6
PERRY, BOYD	Boyd Glenn; B3.21.1914 Snow Camp NC; D6.29.1990 Burlington NC; BR/TR/5´10˝/158; d5.23; Col Guilford																								
1941	Det A	36	83	9	15	5	0	0	11	10	0	9	.181	.269	.241	32	-8	1-0	.974	0	103	95	S25,2b11	0	-0.6
PERRY, CHAN	Chan Everett; B9.13.1972 Live Oak FL; BR/TR/6´2˝/200; [CleA94 44/1212]; d8.5; Col Florida																								
2000	Cle A	13	14	1	1	0	0	0	0	0-0	0	5	.071	.071	.071	-61	-3	0-0	1.000	0	110	0	O7(1/0/6)/1D	0	-0.3
2002	KC A	5	11	0	1	0	0	0	3	0-0	0	1	.091	.091	.091	-46	-2	0-0	1.000	0	98	74	1b5	0	-0.3
Total	2	18	25	1	2	0	0	0	3	0-0	0	6	.080	.080	.080	-54	-5	0-0	1.000	0	110	0	O7(1/0/6),1b6,D4	0	-0.6
PERRY, CLAY	Clayton Shields; B12.18.1881 Clayton WI; D1.13.1954 Rice Lake WI; BR/TR/5´10.5˝/175; d9.2; Col Wisconsin–Madison																								
1908	Det A	7	17	0	2	0	0	0	0	0	1	—	.118	.167	.118	-7	-2	0	.850	-1	91	160	3b7	—	-0.3
PERRY, GERALD	Gerald June; B10.30.1960 Savannah GA; BL/TR/6´0˝/(172–201); [AtlN78 11/261]; d8.11; C7																								
1983	Atl N	27	39	5	14	2	0	1	6	5-0	0	4	.359	.422	.487	144	3	0-1	.982	-2	0	102	1b7/lf	0	0.0
1984	Atl N	122	347	52	92	12	2	7	47	61-5	2	38	.265	.372	.372	104	5	15-12	.988	-8	78	112	1b64,O53L	0	-1.0
1985	Atl N	110	238	22	51	5	0	3	13	23-1	0	28	.214	.282	.273	53	-15	9-5	.985	-2	101	104	1b55/lf	0	-2.1
1986	Atl N	29	70	6	19	2	0	2	11	8-1	0	4	.271	.342	.386	97	0	0-1	.889	-3	53	0	O21(21/0/1)/1	0	-0.5
1987	Atl N	142	533	77	144	35	2	12	74	48-1	1	63	.270	.329	.411	92	-6	42-16	.990	-11	77	110	1b136,O7L	0	-2.2
1988	Atl N★	141	547	61	164	29	1	8	74	36-9	1	49	.300	.338	.400	109	6	29-14	.988	1	106	91	1b141	15	-0.2
1989	Atl N	72	266	24	67	11	0	4	21	32-5	3	28	.252	.337	.338	92	-2	10-6	.987	1	108	103	1b72	99	-0.6
1990	KC A	133	465	57	118	22	2	8	57	39-4	3	56	.254	.313	.361	90	-7	17-4	.986	1	109	94	D68,1b51	0	-0.9
1991	StL N	109	242	29	58	8	4	6	36	22-1	0	34	.240	.300	.380	90	-4	15-8	.989	-5	72	93	1b61,O5(4/0/1)	0	-1.3
1992	StL N	87	143	13	34	8	0	1	18	15-4	1	23	.238	.311	.315	81	-3	3-6	.987	-4	60	142	1b29	0	-1.1
1993	StL N	96	98	21	33	5	0	4	16	18-2	0	23	.337	.440	.510	154	9	1-1	.976	-1	56	82	1b15/rf	0	0.7
1994	StL N	60	77	12	25	7	0	3	18	15-1	0	12	.325	.435	.532	150	7	1-1	.990	-2	54	99	1b13	0	0.4
1995	StL N	65	79	4	13	4	0	0	5	6-0	0	12	.165	.224	.215	16	-10	0-0	1.000	-1	54	63	1b11	0	-1.1
Total	13	1193	3144	383	832	150	11	59	396	328-34	11	374	.265	.333	.376	95	-17	142-75	.988	-35	90	102	1b656,O89(87/0/3),D68	114	-9.9
PERRY, HERBERT	Herbert Edward; B9.15.1969 Live Oak FL; BR/TR/6´2˝/(210–235); [CleA91 2/57]; d5.3; Col Florida; [DL 1998 TB A 181]																								
1994	Cle A	4	9	1	1	0	0	0	1	3-1	1	1	.111	.357	.111	36	-1	0-0	1.000	1	176	48	1b2,3b2	0	0.0
1995	†Cle A	52	162	23	51	13	1	3	23	13-0	4	28	.315	.376	.463	116	4	1-3	1.000	-1	91	87	1b45/3D	0	-0.1
1996	Cle A	7	12	1	1	1	0	0	0	1-0	0	2	.083	.154	.167	-19	-2	1-0	1.000	-0	85	109	1b5/3	19	-0.2
1999	TB A	66	209	29	53	10	1	6	32	16-1	10	42	.254	.331	.397	85	-5	0-0	.955	5	111	162	3b42,1b14,D10,O6L	41	-0.1
2000	TB A	7	28	2	6	1	0	0	1	2-0	0	7	.214	.267	.250	32	-3	0-0	.938	-1	86	85	3b7/1	0	-0.4
	†Chi A	109	383	69	118	29	1	12	61	22-1	9	68	.308	.356	.483	107	4	4-1	.969	6	103	95	3b104,1b3,D3	0	1.0
	Year	116	411	71	124	30	1	12	62	24-1	9	75	.302	.350	.467	102	1	4-1	.967	5	102	94	3b111,1b4,D3	0	0.6
2001	Chi A	92	285	38	73	21	1	7	32	23-1	7	55	.256	.326	.411	87	-5	2-2	.940	-6	93	48	3b68,1b12,D10	15	-1.2
2002	Tex A	132	450	64	124	24	1	22	77	34-1	6	66	.276	.333	.480	110	6	4-2	.951	-1	96	87	3b112,1b12/lfD	0	0.5
2003	Tex A	11	24	1	4	1	0	0	2	0-0	0	3	.167	.167	.208	-2	-4	0-0	1.000	0	145	73	1b5,3b2	164	-0.3
2004	Tex A	49	134	13	30	2	1	5	17	14-0	3	19	.224	.307	.366	73	-6	0-0	1.000	-2	38	114	D21,1b15,3b6	60	-0.9
Total	9	529	1696	241	461	102	6	55	246	128-5	40	291	.272	.335	.436	96	-12	12-8	.953	1	99	90	3b345,1b114,D56,O7L	480	-1.7
PERRY, BOB	Melvin Gray; B9.14.1934 New Bern NC; BR/TR/6´2˝/180; d5.17																								
1963	LA A	61	166	16	42	9	0	3	14	9-2	3	31	.253	.300	.361	91	-2	1-1	.946	-5	90	33	O55(7/23/26)	0	-1.0
1964	LA A	70	221	19	61	8	1	3	16	14-0	0	52	.276	.318	.362	99	-1	1-1	.975	-6	87	50	O62(0/62/1)	0	-0.9
Total	2	131	387	35	103	17	1	6	30	23-2	3	83	.266	.310	.362	95	-3	2-2	.962	-11	88	42	O117(7/85/27)	0	-1.9
PERRY, HANK	William Henry "Socks"; B7.28.1886 Howell MI; D7.18.1956 Pontiac MI; BL/TR/5´11˝/190; d4.12																								
1912	Det A	13	36	3	6	1	0	0	0	3	0	—	.167	.231	.194	23	-4	0	1.000	1	108	163	O7C	—	-0.3
PESKY, JOHNNY	John Michael (b John Michael Paveskovich); B9.27.1919 Portland OR; BL/TR/5´9˝/(165–168); d4.14; Mil 1943–45; M3/C13																								
1942	Bos A	147	620	105	**205**	29	9	2	51	42	2	36	.331	.375	.416	118	14	12-7	.955	20	**110**	109	S147	0	4.5
1946	†Bos A★	153	621	115	**208**	43	4	2	55	65	3	29	.335	.401	.427	124	23	9-8	.969	12	106	104	S153	0	4.6
1947	Bos A	155	638	106	**207**	27	8	0	39	72	0	22	.324	.393	.392	110	11	12-9	.976	-10	95	95	S133,3b22	0	0.9
1948	Bos A	143	565	124	159	26	6	3	55	99	6	32	.281	.394	.365	98	3	3-5	.951	7	**113**	**136**	3b141	0	0.8
1949	Bos A	148	604	111	185	27	7	2	69	100	4	19	.306	.408	.384	103	7	8-4	.970	19	108	**139**	3b148	0	2.5
1950	Bos A	127	490	112	153	22	6	1	49	104	5	31	.312	.437	.388	103	9	2-1	.974	16	105	112	3b116,S8	0	2.3
1951	Bos A	131	480	93	150	20	6	3	41	84	2	15	.313	.417	.398	110	11	2-2	.961	2	105	95	S106,3b11,2b5	0	2.0
1952	Bos A	25	67	10	10	2	0	0	2	15	1	5	.149	.313	.179	36	-5	0-3	.917	-4	82	0	3b19,S2	0	-1.1
	Det A	69	177	26	45	4	0	1	9	41	0	11	.254	.394	.294	93	1	1-2	.952	-2	89	100	S41,2b22,3b3	0	0.1
	Year	94	244	36	55	6	0	1	11	56	1	16	.225	.372	.262	77	-4	1-5	.953	-6	88	101	S43,3b22,2b22	0	-1.0
1953	Det A	103	308	43	90	22	1	2	24	27	2	10	.292	.353	.390	102	1	3-7	.991	-7	96	83	2b73	0	-0.2
1954	Det A	20	17	5	3	0	0	1	1	3	0	1	.176	.300	.353	80	-1	0-0	ø	0	—	—	/H	0	-0.1
	Was A	49	158	17	40	4	3	0	9	10	0	7	.253	.296	.316	72	-7	1-1	.979	-4	101	81	2b37/S	0	-0.8
	Year	69	175	22	43	4	3	1	10	13	0	8	.246	.296	.320	72	-8	1-1	.979	-4	101	81	2b37/S	0	-0.9
Total	10	1270	4745	867	1455	226	50	17	404	662	25	218	.307	.394	.386	106	67	53-49	.964	50	103	101	S591,3b460,2b137	0	15.5
PETAGINE, ROBERTO	Roberto Antonio (Guerra); B6.7.1971 Nueva Esparta, Venezuela; BL/TL/6´1˝/(170–172); d4.4																								
1994	Hou N	8	7	0	0	0	0	0	0	1-0	0	3	.000	.125	.000	-67	-2	0-0	1.000	-0	0	0	1b2	0	-0.2
1995	SD N	89	124	15	29	8	0	3	17	26-2	0	41	.234	.367	.371	98	1	0-0	.996	-0	98	89	1b51,O2(1/0/1)	0	-0.2
1996	NY N	50	99	10	23	3	0	4	17	9-1	3	27	.232	.313	.384	88	-2	0-2	.996	1	113	91	1b40	0	-0.4
1997	NY N	12	15	2	1	0	0	0	2	3-0	0	6	.067	.222	.067	-21	-3	0-0	1.000	1	193	0	1b6/lf	0	-0.2
1998	Cin N	34	62	14	16	2	1	3	7	16-0	0	11	.258	.405	.468	129	3	1-0	1.000	2	110	102	1b15,O15(1/0/15)	0	0.4
2005	Bos A	18	32	4	9	2	0	1	9	4-0	0	5	.281	.361	.438	107	0	0-0	.983	0	150	72	1b10,O2L,D3	0	0.0
2006	Sea A	31	27	3	5	2	0	1	2	4-0	1	10	.185	.313	.370	81	-1	0-0	1.000	1	248	118	1b9	0	0.0
Total	7	242	366	48	83	17	1	12	54	63-3	4	103	.227	.345	.377	93	-4	1-2	.996	5	117	87	1b133,O20(5/0/16),D3	0	-0.6

YEAR	TM LG	G	AB	R	H	2B	3B	HR	RBI	BB-IB	HP	SO	AVG	OBP	SLG	AOPS	ABR	SB-CS	FA	FR	RNG	THR	GAMES AT POSITION		
Peterman, Bill	William David; B3.20.1921 Philadelphia PA; D3.13.1999 Philadelphia PA; BR/TR/6´2˝/185; d4.26; Mil 1943–45																								
1942	Phi N	1	1	0	1	0	0	0	0	0	0	0	1.000	1.000	1.000	512	1	0	ø	0	*0*	*0*	/C		
Peters, John	John Paul; B4.8.1850 New Orleans LA; D1.4.1924 St.Louis MO; BR/TR/5´7˝/180; d5.23																								
1874	Chi NA	55	239	39	69	10	0	1	25	2	—	11	.289	.295	.343	103	1	2-2	.799	2	104	75	S36,2b19	—	
1875	Chi NA	**69**	297	40	85	16	2	0	34	0	—	3	.286	.286	.354	120	6	12-6	.871	9	109	158	S65,2b6	—	1.1
1876	Chi N	**66**	316	70	111	14	2	1	47	3	—	2	.351	.357	.418	141	12	—	**.932**	1	91	**146**	S66/P	—	1.3
1877	Chi N	**60**	265	45	84	10	3	0	41	1	—	7	.317	.320	.377	106	1	—	.883	**20**	**116**	**164**	S60	—	2.0
1878	Mil N	55	246	33	76	6	1	0	22	5	—	8	.309	.323	.341	111	2	—	.853	2	114	96	2b34,S22	—	0.6
1879	Chi N	**83**	379	45	93	13	2	1	31	1	—	19	.245	.247	.298	74	-11	—	.837	-7	99	79	S83	—	-1.4
1880	Pro N	86	359	30	82	5	0	0	24	5	—	15	.228	.239	.242	66	-13	—	**.900**	-4	94	**139**	S86	—	-1.2
1881	Buf N	54	229	21	49	8	1	0	25	3	—	12	.214	.224	.258	52	-13	—	.869	2	100	88	S53/rf	—	-0.7
1882	Pit AA	78	333	46	96	10	1	0	—	4	—	—	.288	.297	.324	115	5	—	.883	6	103	**114**	S77/2	—	1.2
1883	Pit AA	8	28	3	3	0	0	0	—	0	—	—	.107	.107	.107	-32	-4	—	.818	2	121	150	S8	—	-0.2
1884	Pit AA	1	4	0	0	0	0	0	—	0	0	—	.000	.000	.000	-99	-1	—	.667	-1	40	0	/S	—	-0.2
Total	2NA	124	536	79	154	26	2	1	59	2	—	14	.287	.290	.349	112	7	14-8	.846	11	107	129	S101,2b25	—	1.1
Total	9	491	2159	293	594	66	10	2	190	22	0	63	.275	.282	.318	94	-22	—	.881	20	100	119	S456,2b35/rfP	—	1.4
Peters, John	John William "Big Pete","Shotgun"; B7.14.1893 Kansas City KS; D2.21.1932 Kansas City MO; BR/TR/6´0˝/192; d5.1																								
1915	Det A	1	3	0	0	0	0	0	0	0	0	1	.000	.000	.000	-95	-1	0	1.000	1	*136*	*191*	/C	—	0.0
1918	Cle A	1	1	0	0	0	0	0	0	1	0	1	.000	.500	.000	46	0	0	.500	-1	*0*	*140*	/C	—	-0.1
1921	Phi N	55	155	7	45	4	0	3	23	6	3	13	.290	.329	.374	79	-5	1-0	.933	-11	*65*	*69*	C44	—	-1.3
1922	Phi N	55	143	15	35	9	1	4	24	9	4	18	.245	.308	.406	75	-5	0-1	.953	-5	*81*	*73*	C39	—	-0.8
Total	4	112	302	22	80	13	1	7	47	16	7	33	.265	.317	.384	76	-11	1-1	.934	-16	*73*	*74*	C85	—	-2.2
Peters, Rick	Richard Devin; B11.21.1955 Lynwood CA; BB/TR/5´9˝/(160–170); [DetA77 7/161]; d9.8; Col Arizona St.; [DL 1982 Det A 182]																								
1979	Det A	12	19	3	5	0	0	0	2	5-0	0	3	.263	.417	.263	85	0	0-0	.000	-2	0	0	3b3,2b2/lfD	0	-0.2
1980	Det A	133	477	79	139	19	7	2	42	54-2	6	48	.291	.369	.373	102	3	13-7	.977	-4	103	13	O109(8/97/5),D11	0	-0.2
1981	Det A	63	207	26	53	7	3	0	15	29-2	2	28	.256	.351	.319	91	-1	1-6	.991	3	114	141	O38(5/33/0),D19	0	-0.1
1983	Oak A	55	178	20	51	7	0	0	20	12-0	1	21	.287	.327	.326	87	-3	4-9	.986	7	131	100	O47(6/30/16),D8	0	0.0
1986	Oak A	44	38	7	7	1	0	0	1	7-1	0	7	.184	.311	.211	49	-2	2-2	1.000	1	120	0	O27(19/7/1)/2	22	-0.2
Total	5	307	919	135	255	34	10	2	80	107-5	9	107	.277	.356	.343	94	-3	20-24	.983	4	112	54	O222(39/167/22),D41,2b3,3b3	204	-0.7
Peters, Rusty	Russell Dixon; B12.14.1914 Roanoke VA; D2.21.2003 Harrisonburg VA; BR/TR/5´11˝/170; d4.14; Mil 1945–46; Col Washington and Lee																								
1936	Phi A	45	119	12	26	3	2	3	16	4	0	28	.218	.244	.353	47	-11	1-1	.898	-1	96	95	S25,3b10,O2L/2	—	-1.0
1937	Phi A	116	339	39	88	17	6	3	43	41	0	59	.260	.339	.372	80	-10	4-4	.966	-9	96	84	2b70,3b31,S13	—	-1.3
1938	Phi A	2	7	0	0	0	0	0	0	0	0	1	.000	.000	.000	-99	-2	0-0	.714	-2	41	0	S2	—	-0.4
1940	Cle A	30	71	5	17	3	2	0	7	4	0	14	.239	.280	.338	61	-4	1-0	.922	-2	82	119	2b9,S6,3b6/1	—	-0.5
1941	Cle A	29	63	6	13	2	0	0	2	7	0	10	.206	.286	.238	42	-5	0-1	.891	0	115	92	S11,3b9,2b3	0	-0.5
1942	Cle A	34	58	6	13	5	1	0	2	2	0	14	.224	.250	.345	70	-3	0-0	.944	0	119	101	S24/23	0	-0.1
1943	Cle A	79	215	22	47	6	2	1	19	18	1	29	.219	.282	.279	69	-9	1-1	.913	-5	92	119	3b46,S14,2b6,O2L	0	-1.4
1944	Cle A	88	282	23	63	13	3	1	24	15	2	35	.223	.268	.301	65	-14	2-1	.976	-2	103	97	2b63,S13,3b8	0	-1.2
1946	Cle A	9	21	0	6	0	0	0	2	1	0	1	.286	.318	.286	74	-1	0-1	1.000	1	94	99	S7	0	0.0
1947	StL A	39	47	10	16	4	0	0	2	6	0	8	.340	.415	.426	131	2	0-0	.955	3	108	118	2b13,S2	0	0.6
Total	10	471	1222	123	289	53	16	8	117	98	3	199	.236	.295	.326	69	-57	9-9	.966	-15	98	95	2b166,S117,3b111,O4L/1	0	-5.8
Petersen, Chris	Christopher Ronald; B11.6.1970 Boston MA; BR/TR/5´11˝/180; [ChiN92 9/247]; d5.25; Col Georgia Southern																								
1999	Col N	7	13	1	2	0	0	0	2	2-0	0	3	.154	.267	.154	8	-2	0-0	.955	3	136	208	2b6/S	0	0.1
Peterson, Buddy	Carl Francis; B4.23.1925 Portland OR; D9.19.2006 Sacramento CA; BR/TR/5´9.5˝/170; d9.14																								
1955	Chi A	6	21	7	6	1	0	0	2	3-0	1	2	.286	.400	.333	96	0	0-0	.962	-1	88	124	S6	0	0.0
1957	Bal A	7	17	1	3	2	0	0	0	2-0	0	2	.176	.263	.294	55	-1	0-0	.963	-1	85	91	S7	0	-0.1
Total	2	13	38	8	9	3	0	0	2	5-0	1	4	.237	.341	.316	80	-1	0-0	.962	-1	87	108	S13	0	-0.1
Peterson, Cap	Charles Andrew; B8.15.1942 Tacoma WA; D5.16.1980 Tacoma WA; BR/TR/6´2˝/(190–195); d9.12; OF(142/0/139)																								
1962	SF N	4	6	1	1	0	0	0	0	1-0	0	4	.167	.286	.167	25	-1	0-0	1.000	-1	51	134	S2	0	-0.1
1963	SF N	22	54	7	14	2	0	1	2	2-0	0	13	.259	.286	.352	83	-1	0-0	.917	-2	110	0	2b8,3b5,O3(2/0/1)/S	0	-0.4
1964	SF N	66	74	8	15	1	1	1	8	3-1	0	20	.203	.234	.284	44	-6	0-0	1.000	-1	101	0	O10(10/0/1),1b2/23	0	-0.7
1965	SF N	63	105	14	26	7	0	3	15	10-2	0	16	.248	.310	.400	97	0	0-0	1.000	-2	66	91	O27(23/0/4)	0	-0.4
1966	SF N	89	190	13	45	6	1	2	19	11-1	1	32	.237	.279	.311	63	-10	2-0	1.000	-1	89	74	O51(50/0/1),1b2	0	-1.3
1967	Was A	122	405	35	97	17	2	8	46	32-1	3	61	.240	.299	.351	95	-3	0-3	.970	-1	103	72	O101(18/0/88)	0	-1.3
1968	Was A	94	226	20	46	8	1	3	18	18-3	1	31	.204	.262	.288	70	-9	2-1	1.000	-2	95	68	O53(14/0/39)	0	-1.5
1969	Cle A	76	110	8	25	3	0	1	14	24-3	1	18	.227	.365	.282	82	-1	0-0	.977	-0	106	125	O30(25/0/5),3b4	0	-0.3
Total	8	536	1170	106	269	44	5	19	122	101-11	6	195	.230	.292	.325	80	-31	4-4	.983	-10	96	76	O275L,3b10,2b9,1b4,S3	0	-6.0
Peterson, Hardy	Harding William; B10.17.1929 Perth Amboy NJ; BR/TR/6´0˝/(183–205); d5.5; Col Rutgers; [DL 1956 Pit N 144]																								
1955	Pit N	32	81	7	20	6	0	1	10	7-1	1	7	.247	.311	.358	79	-2	0-0	.965	3	*87*	*220*	C31	0	0.1
1957	Pit N	30	73	10	22	2	1	2	11	9-2	0	10	.301	.378	.438	122	2	0-1	.985	1	85	182	C30	0	0.4
1958	Pit N	2	6	0	2	0	0	0	0	1-0	0	0	.333	.429	.333	108	0	0-0	1.000	0	0	282	C2	0	0.0
1959	Pit N	2	1	0	0	0	0	0	0	0-0	0	0	.000	.000	.000	-99	0	0-0	1.000	0	0	0	C2	0	0.0
Total	4	66	161	17	44	8	1	3	21	17-3	1	17	.273	.344	.391	99	0	0-1	.976	4	*82*	*201*	C65	144	0.5
Peterson, Bob	Robert Andrew; B6.16.1884 Philadelphia PA; D11.27.1962 Evesham Twp. NJ; BR/TR/6´1˝/160; d4.18																								
1906	Bos A	39	118	10	24	1	1	1	9	11	1	—	.203	.277	.254	67	-4	1	.899	-9	*81*	*101*	C30,2b3,1b2/lf	—	-1.2
1907	Bos A	4	13	1	1	0	0	0	0	0	0	—	.077	.077	.077	-51	-2	0	1.000	0	*113*	*84*	C4	—	-0.2
Total	2	43	131	11	25	1	1	1	9	11	1	—	.191	.259	.237	56	-6	1	.910	-9	*85*	*99*	C34,2b3,1b2/lf	—	-1.4
Petoskey, Ted	Frederick Lee; B1.5.1911 St.Charles MI; D11.30.1996 Elgin SC; BR/TR/5´11.5˝/183; d9.9; Col Michigan																								
1934	Cin N	6	7	0	0	0	0	0	1	0	0	5	.000	.000	.000	-99	-2	0	1.000	1	164	992	O2C	—	-0.1
1935	Cin N	4	5	0	2	0	0	0	0	0	0	1	.400	.400	.400	119	0	1	1.000	-0	52	0	O2(1/1/0)	—	0.0
Total	2	10	12	0	2	0	0	0	1	0	0	6	.167	.167	.167	-11	-2	1	1.000	1	123	627	O4(1/3/0)	—	-0.1
Petralli, Geno	Eugene James; B9.25.1959 Sacramento CA; BL/TR (BB 1982–86, 87p)/6´2˝/(180–200); [TorA78*3/53]; d9.4; Col Sacramento (CA) City; OF(1/0/2)																								
1982	Tor A	16	44	3	16	2	0	0	1	4-0	0	6	.364	.417	.409	117	1	0-0	.981	-1	77	66	C12,3b3	0	0.0
1983	Tor A	6	4	0	0	0	0	0	0	1-0	0	1	.000	.200	.000	-37	-1	0-0	1.000	-0	0	0	C5/D	0	-0.1
1984	Tor A	3	3	0	0	0	0	0	0	0-0	0	0	.000	.000	.000	-96	-1	0-0	1.000	0	0	0	/CD	0	0.0
1985	Tex A	42	100	7	27	2	0	0	11	8-0	1	12	.270	.319	.290	70	-4	1-0	.990	-2	64	105	C41	0	-0.4
1986	Tex A	69	137	17	35	9	3	2	18	5-0	0	14	.255	.282	.409	83	-4	3-0	.988	-7	87	39	C41,3b15,2b2,D2	0	-0.9
1987	Tex A	101	202	28	61	11	2	7	31	27-2	2	29	.302	.388	.480	128	9	0-2	.995	-4	59	144	C63,3b17,1b5,2b4,O3(1/0/2),D2	0	0.6
1988	Tex A	129	351	35	99	14	2	7	36	41-5	2	52	.282	.356	.393	108	5	0-1	.981	1	79	142	C85,D23,3b9,1b2,2b2	0	0.9
1989	Tex A	70	184	18	56	7	0	4	23	17-1	2	24	.304	.368	.408	117	4	0-0	.989	-1	74	116	C49,D16	68	0.6
1990	Tex A	133	325	28	83	13	1	0	21	50-3	3	49	.255	.357	.302	86	-3	0-2	.991	-2	106	108	C118,3b7,2b3	0	0.0
1991	Tex A	87	199	21	54	8	1	2	20	21-1	0	25	.271	.339	.352	93	-1	2-1	.972	-7	81	113	C66,3b7,D5	40	-0.6
1992	Tex A	94	192	11	38	12	0	1	18	20-2	0	34	.198	.274	.276	56	-11	0-0	.990	-1	143	126	C54,D14,3b4,2b2	0	-1.0
1993	Tex A	59	133	16	32	5	0	1	13	22-3	0	17	.241	.348	.301	79	-3	2-0	.990	-9	73	122	C39/23D	39	-0.9
Total	12	809	1874	184	501	83	9	24	192	216-17	10	263	.267	.344	.360	95	-9	8-6	.987	-32	87	116	C574,D66,3b63,2b14,1b7,O3R	147	-1.8
Petrick, Ben	Benjamin Wayne; B4.7.1977 Salem OR; BR/TR/6´0˝/(199–205); [ColN95 2/38]; d9.1																								
1999	Col N	19	62	13	20	3	0	4	12	10-0	0	13	.323	.417	.565	116	2	1-0	.982	-7	65	36	C19	0	-0.4
2000	Col N	52	146	32	47	10	1	3	20	20-2	2	33	.322	.401	.466	98	0	1-2	.985	-3	96	60	C48	0	0.0
2001	Col N	85	244	41	58	15	3	11	39	31-3	3	67	.238	.327	.459	84	-6	3-3	.984	-6	81	74	C77,1b2	30	-0.8
2002	Col N	38	95	10	20	3	1	5	11	9-0	1	33	.211	.283	.421	73	-4	0-1	.952	-1	88	0	O16(15/2/0),C14	0	-0.5
2003	Col N	3	2	0	0	0	0	0	0	0-0	0	1	.000	.000	.000	-88	-1	0-0	1.000	1	201	3625	O2(1/1/0)/C	0	0.0
	Det A	43	120	18	27	6	0	4	12	8-0	0	30	.225	.273	.375	72	-5	0-0	.969	-1	91	126	O32(18/14/3),C6,1b2	0	-0.6
Total	5	240	669	114	172	37	5	27	94	78-5	6	177	.257	.336	.448	87	-14	5-6	.984	-18	85	62	C165,O50(34/17/3),1b4	30	-2.3

YEAR	TM LG	G	AB	R	H	2B	3B	HR	RBI	BB-IB	HP	SO	AVG	OBP	SLG	AOPS	ABR	SB-CS	FA	FR	RNG	THR	GAMES AT POSITION	DL	BFW
Petrocelli, Rico	Americo Peter; B6.27.1943 Brooklyn NY; BR/TR/6´0˝/(175–185); d9.21																								
1963	Bos A	1	4	0	1	1	0	0	1	0-0	0	1	.250	.250	.500	101	0	0-0	.833	-0	69	0	/S	0	0.0
1965	Bos A	103	323	38	75	15	2	13	33	36-4	1	71	.232	.309	.412	98	-1	0-2	.958	9	110	83	S93	0	1.6
1966	Bos A	139	522	58	124	20	1	18	59	41-2	3	99	.238	.295	.383	85	-10	1-1	.954	5	107	88	S127,3b5	18	0.6
1967	†Bos A★	142	491	53	127	24	2	17	66	49-9	5	93	.259	.330	.420	112	8	2-4	.970	5	103	98	S141	0	2.6
1968	Bos A	123	406	41	95	17	2	12	46	31-2	4	73	.234	.292	.374	96	-2	0-1	**.978**	11	109	106	S117/1	0	2.1
1969	Bos A★	154	535	92	159	32	2	40	97	98-13	1	68	.297	.403	.589	168	51	3-5	**.981**	6	102	107	S153/3	0	**7.6**
1970	Bos A	157	583	82	152	31	3	29	103	67-6	2	82	.261	.334	.473	114	11	1-1	.970	-0	94	89	S141,3b18	0	2.7
1971	Bos A	158	553	82	139	24	4	28	89	91-5	2	108	.251	.354	.461	122	18	2-0	**.976**	-1	99	111	3b156	0	1.7
1972	Bos A	147	521	62	125	15	2	15	75	78-9	2	91	.240	.339	.363	103	4	0-1	.970	5	94	**126**	3b146	0	1.0
1973	Bos A	100	356	44	87	13	1	13	45	47-3	1	64	.244	.333	.396	99	0	0-0	.980	6	105	125	3b99	29	0.6
1974	Bos A	129	454	53	121	23	1	15	76	48-4	2	74	.267	.336	.421	110	6	1-0	.962	-13	90	96	3b116,D9	0	-0.7
1975	†Bos A	115	402	31	96	15	1	7	59	41-1	3	66	.239	.310	.333	77	-12	0-2	.960	-13	92	60	3b113/D	15	-2.7
1976	Bos A	85	240	17	51	7	1	3	24	34-3	0	36	.213	.307	.287	68	-9	0-5	.967	-3	95	104	3b73,2b5/1SD	0	-1.5
Total	13	1553	5390	653	1352	237	22	210	773	661-61	26	926	.251	.332	.420	108	64	10-22	.969	17	104	96	S774,3b727,D14,2b5,1b2	62	15.6
Pettee, Pat	Patrick E.; B1.10.1863 Natick MA; D10.9.1934 Natick MA; BR/TR/5´10˝/170; d4.8																								
1891	Lou AA	2	5	1	0	0	0	0	0	3	0	1	.000	.375	.000	9	0	1	.818	-1	98	116	2b2	—	-0.1
Pettigrew, Ned	Jim Ned; B8.25.1881 Honey Grove TX; D8.20.1952 Duncan OK; BR/TR/5´11˝/175; d4.23																								
1914	Buf F	2	2	0	0	0	0	0	0	0	0	0	.000	.000	.000	-98	-1	0	ø	0	—	—	/H	—	-0.1
Pettini, Joe	Joseph Paul; B1.26.1955 Wheeling WV; BR/TR/5´9˝/165; d7.10; C5; Col Mercer																								
1980	SF N	63	190	19	44	3	1	1	9	17-1	0	33	.232	.295	.274	62	-10	5-2	.955	-13	81	72	S42,3b18,2b8	0	-2.0
1981	SF N	35	29	3	2	1	0	0	2	4-0	0	5	.069	.182	.103	-18	-5	1-0	.920	-2	102	31	2b12,S12,3b9	0	-0.6
1982	SF N	29	39	5	8	1	0	0	2	3-0	0	4	.205	.262	.231	39	-3	0-1	.934	-3	87	72	S26/3	0	-0.5
1983	SF N	61	86	11	16	0	1	0	7	9-1	0	11	.186	.260	.209	33	-8	4-1	.949	1	89	119	S26,2b14,3b12	0	-0.4
Total	4	188	344	38	70	5	2	1	20	33-2	0	53	.203	.272	.238	45	-26	10-4	.943	-16	84	85	S106,3b40,2b34	0	-3.5
Pettis, Gary	Gary George; B4.3.1958 Oakland CA; BB/TR/6´1˝/(159–165); [CalA79*6/141]; d9.13; C4; Col Laney (CA) JC																								
1982	Cal A	10	5	5	1	0	0	1	1	0-0	0	2	.200	.200	.800	158	0	0-0	1.000	1	99	798	O8(1/6/1)	0	0.1
1983	Cal A	22	85	19	25	2	3	3	6	7-0	0	15	.294	.348	.494	129	3	8-3	.982	1	82	362	O21(0/20/1)	0	0.4
1984	Cal A	140	397	63	90	11	6	2	29	60-1	3	115	.227	.332	.300	77	-11	48-17	.983	6	106	145	O134C	0	-0.2
1985	Cal A	125	443	67	114	10	8	1	32	62-0	0	125	.257	.347	.323	85	-8	56-9	.990	9	108	162	O122C	26	0.9
1986	†Cal A	154	539	93	139	23	4	5	58	69-2	0	132	.258	.339	.343	88	-7	50-13	.985	11	**113**	109	O153C/D	0	0.8
1987	Cal A	133	394	49	82	13	2	1	17	52-0	1	124	.208	.302	.259	52	-26	24-5	.980	6	115	39	O131C	0	-1.7
1988	Det A	129	458	65	96	14	4	3	36	47-0	1	85	.210	.285	.277	60	-25	44-10	.987	6	110	90	O126C,D2	16	-1.4
1989	Det A	119	444	77	114	8	6	1	18	84-0	0	106	.257	.375	.309	97	2	43-15	.988	-2	105	16	O119C	42	0.3
1990	Tex A	136	423	66	101	16	8	3	31	57-0	4	118	.239	.333	.336	88	-6	38-15	.993	1	95	170	O128C,D2	0	-0.3
1991	Tex A	137	282	37	61	7	5	0	19	54-0	0	91	.216	.341	.277	74	-8	29-13	.977	1	107	87	O126C,D3	0	-0.6
1992	SD N	30	30	0	6	1	0	0	0	2-0	0	11	.200	.250	.233	37	-2	1-0	.952	0	134	0	O14(0/13/1)	0	-0.2
	Det A	48	129	27	26	4	3	1	12	27-0	0	34	.202	.338	.302	80	-3	13-4	.993	3	113	76	O46C	0	0.1
Total	11	1183	3629	568	855	109	49	21	259	521-3	9	958	.236	.332	.310	80	-91	354-104	.986	41	107	108	O1128(1/1125/3),D8	84	-1.8
Pettit, Bob	Robert Henry; B7.19.1861 Williamstown MA; D11.1.1910 Derby CT; BL/TR/5´9˝/160; d9.3																								
1887	Chi N	32	138	29	36	3	3	2	12	8	0	15	.261	.301	.370	76	-6	16	.894	-1	145	0	O32R/CP	—	-0.6
1888	Chi N	43	169	23	43	1	4	4	23	7	1	9	.254	.288	.379	104	0	7	.931	-0	133	246	O43(0/2/42)	—	-0.1
1891	Mil AA	21	80	10	14	4	0	1	5	7	3	7	.175	.267	.262	43	-6	2	.932	-3	116	32	2b9,O7(3/2/2),3b6	—	-0.8
Total	3	96	387	62	93	8	7	7	40	22	4	31	.240	.288	.351	79	-12	25	.919	-4	131	126	O82(3/4/76),2b9,3b6/PC	—	-1.5
Pevey, Marty	Marty Ashley; B12.25.1962 Savannah GA; BL/TR/6´1˝/185; [MinA82 19/474]; d5.16; C3; Col Georgia Southern																								
1989	Mon N	13	41	2	9	1	1	0	3	0-0	0	8	.220	.220	.293	44	-3	0-0	.985	-4	50	107	C11/rf	0	-0.7
Pezold, Larry	Lorenz Johannes; B6.22.1893 New Orleans LA; D10.22.1957 Baton Rouge LA; BR/TR/5´9.5˝/175; d7.27																								
1914	Cle A	23	71	4	16	0	1	0	5	9	0	6	.225	.313	.254	68	-3	2-3	.827	-1	105	63	3b20/rf	—	-0.5
Pfeffer, Fred	Nathaniel Frederick "Fritz","Dandelion"; B3.17.1860 Louisville KY; D4.10.1932 Chicago IL; BR/TR/5´10.5˝/184; d5.1; M1; ▲																								
1882	Tro N	**85**	330	26	72	7	4	1	43	1	—	24	.218	.221	.273	60	-15	—	.857	10	105	133	S83,2b2	—	-0.2
1883	Chi N	96	371	41	87	22	7	1	45	8	—	50	.235	.251	.340	71	-14	—	.887	16	108	**141**	2b79,S18/31	—	0.5
1884	Chi N	**112**	467	105	135	10	10	25	101	25	—	47	.289	.325	.514	148	22	—	.903	**43**	**117**	**185**	2b112/P	—	**6.0**
1885	†Chi N	112	469	90	113	12	7	5	73	26	—	47	.241	.281	.328	85	-10	—	.893	22	112	**159**	2b109,P5/rf	—	1.5
1886	†Chi N	118	474	88	125	17	8	7	95	36	—	46	.264	.316	.378	96	-5	30	.903	8	94	**148**	2b118/1	—	0.7
1887	Chi N	123	479	95	133	21	6	16	89	34	1	20	.278	.327	.447	100	-3	57	.917	23	98	**133**	2b123,O2C	—	2.0
1888	Chi N	**135**	517	90	129	22	10	8	57	32	3	38	.250	.297	.377	106	2	64	.931	**38**	**104**	**151**	2b135	—	**4.4**
1889	Chi N	134	531	85	128	15	7	7	77	53	3	51	.241	.313	.335	77	-19	45	.943	10	104	113	2b134	—	-0.3
1890	Chi P	124	499	86	128	21	8	5	80	44	2	23	.257	.319	.361	78	-18	27	.916	20	98	**129**	2b124	—	0.5
1891	Chi N	**137**	498	93	123	12	9	7	77	79	3	60	.247	.353	.349	105	5	40	.921	24	105	**137**	2b137	—	3.0
1892	Lou N	124	470	78	121	14	9	2	76	67	2	36	.257	.353	.338	119	14	27	.932	8	104	**149**	2b116,1b10/PM	—	2.5
1893	Lou N	125	508	85	129	29	12	3	75	51	0	18	.254	.322	.376	93	-6	32	.939	12	101	118	2b125	—	0.9
1894	Lou N	105	414	70	128	12	15	5	61	30	1	14	.309	.357	.447	100	-2	32	.939	15	103	134	2b91,S15/P	—	1.4
1895	Lou N	11	45	8	13	1	0	0	5	5	0	3	.289	.360	.311	79	-1	2	.742	-3	67	122	S5,2b3,1b3	—	-0.3
1896	NY N	4	14	1	2	0	0	0	4	1	1	1	.143	.250	.143	5	-2	0	.760	-2	82	0	2b4	—	-0.3
	Chi N	94	360	45	88	16	7	2	52	23	2	20	.244	.294	.344	65	-20	22	.947	7	105	107	2b94	—	-0.7
	Year	98	374	46	90	16	7	2	56	24	3	21	.241	.292	.337	63	-22	22	.939	5	104	103	2b98	—	-1.0
1897	Chi N	32	114	10	26	0	1	0	11	12	3	—	.228	.318	.246	48	-8	5	.883	-4	94	104	2b32	—	-1.0
Total	16	1671	6560	1096	1680	231	120	94	1021	527	21	498	.256	.313	.371	93	-80	383	.920	246	104	137	2b1538,S121,1b15,P8,O3(0/2/1)/3	—	20.6
Pfeil, Bobby	Robert Raymond; B11.13.1943 Passaic NJ; BR/TR/6´1˝/(176–185); d6.26; Col Los Angeles Pierce (CA) JC																								
1969	NY N	62	211	20	49	9	0	0	10	7-0	1	27	.232	.260	.275	49	-15	0-1	.976	-3	101	120	3b49,2b11,O2L	0	-1.8
1971	Phi N	44	70	5	19	3	0	2	9	6-1	0	9	.271	.329	.400	105	0	1-1	1.000	-2	101	292	3b15,C4,O3(2/0/1)/12S	0	-0.1
Total	2	106	281	25	68	12	0	2	19	13-1	1	36	.242	.278	.306	63	-15	1-2	.980	-4	101	158	3b64,2b12,O5(4/0/1),C4/S1	0	-1.9
Pfister, George	George Edward; B9.4.1918 Bound Brook NJ; D8.14.1997 Somerset NJ; BR/TR/6´0˝/200; d9.27; C1																								
1941	Bro N	1	2	0	0	0	0	0	0	0	0	0	.000	.000	.000	-96	-1	0	ø	0	*0*	0	/C	0	-0.1
Pfyl, Monte	Meinhard Charles; B5.11.1886 St.Louis MO; D10.18.1945 San Francisco CA; BL/TL/6´3˝/190; d7.30																								
1907	NY N	1	0	0	0	0	0	0	0	0	0	—	ø	ø	ø	ø	0	0	ø	0	0	0	/1	—	0.0
Phelan, Art	Arthur Thomas "Dugan"; B8.14.1887 Niantic IL; D12.27.1964 Ft.Worth TX; BR/TR/5´8˝/160; d6.25																								
1910	Cin N	23	42	7	9	0	0	0	4	7	0	6	.214	.327	.214	61	-2	5	1.000	-0	112	0	3b8,2b5,O3L/S	—	-0.2
1912	Cin N	130	461	56	112	9	11	3	54	46	2	37	.243	.314	.330	79	-15	25	.924	-1	102	103	3b127,2b3	—	-1.2
1913	Chi N	91	261	41	65	11	6	2	35	29	3	26	.249	.331	.360	97	-1	8-8	.931	-2	100	82	2b46,3b38/S	—	-0.3
1914	Chi N	25	46	5	13	2	1	0	3	4	0	3	.283	.340	.370	111	1	0	.905	-1	110	0	3b7,2b3,S2	—	0.0
1915	Chi N	133	448	41	98	16	7	3	35	55	2	42	.219	.307	.306	86	-7	12-9	.939	-2	94	92	3b110,2b24	—	-0.6
Total	5	402	1258	150	297	38	25	8	131	141	7	114	.236	.317	.325	86	-24	50-17	.931	-6	99	89	3b290,2b81,S4,O3L	—	-2.3
Phelan, Dan	Daniel T.; B7.23.1864 Thomaston CT; D12.7.1945 West Haven CT; BL/5´10˝/175; d4.18																								
1890	Lou AA	8	32	4	8	1	1	0	4	0	0	—	.250	.250	.344	77	-1	1	.975	0	99	0	1b8	—	-0.2
Phelan, Dick	James Dickson; B12.10.1854 Towanda PA; D2.13.1931 San Antonio TX; BR; d4.17																								
1884	Bal U	101	402	63	99	13	3	3	—	12	—	—	.246	.268	.316	69	-28	—	.872	-12	94	104	2b100,3b5/cf	—	-3.2
1885	Buf N	4	16	2	2	0	0	1	3	0	—	3	.125	.125	.313	37	-1	—	.808	-1	120	102	2b4	—	-0.1
	StL N	2	4	1	1	1	0	0	1	0	—	2	.250	.250	.500	147	0	—	1.000	-0	0	0	3b2	—	0.0
	Year	6	20	3	3	1	0	1	4	0	—	5	.150	.150	.350	58	-1	—	.808	-1	120	102	2b4,3b2	—	-0.1
Total	2	107	422	66	102	14	3	4	4	12	—	5	.242	.263	.318	69	-29	—	.869	-13	95	104	2b104,3b7/cf	—	-3.3

YEAR	TM LG	G	AB	R	H	2B	3B	HR	RBI	BB-IB	HP	SO	AVG	OBP	SLG	AOPS	ABR	SB-CS	FA	FR	RNG	THR	GAMES AT POSITION	DL	BFW
Phelps, Nealy	Cornelius Carman; B11.19.1840 New York NY; D2.12.1885 New York NY; d7.1																								
1871	Kek NA	1	3	0	0	0	0	0	0	1	—	0	.000	.250	.000	-20	0	0-0	.889	-0	0	205	/1	—	0.0
1873	Mut NA	1	6	0	0	0	0	0	0	0	—	0	.000	.000	.000	-99	-1	0-0	1.000	0	0	0	/1rf	—	-0.1
1874	Mut NA	6	24	5	3	0	0	0	2	0	—	0	.125	.125	.125	-19	-3	0-0	.818	1	196	610	O6R	—	-0.1
1875	Mut NA	2	6	1	2	1	0	0	0	0	—	1	.333	.333	.500	176	0	0-0	1.000	1	389	0	O2R	—	0.1
1876	NY N	1	3	0	0	0	0	0	0	0	—	1	.000	.000	.000	-99	-1	—	.667	-0	0	0	/cf	—	-0.1
	Phi N	1	4	0	0	0	0	0	0	0	—	0	.000	.000	.000	-99	-1	—	.571	-1	—	—	/C	—	-0.2
	Year	2	7	0	0	0	0	0	0	0	—	1	.000	.000	.000	-99	-1	—	.667	-2	0	0	/cfC	—	-0.3
Total	4NA	10	39	6	5	1	0	0	2	1	—	1	.128	.150	.154	-3	-4	0-0	.857	1	—	—	O9R,1b2	—	-0.1
Phelps, Ed	Edward Jaykill "Yaller"; B3.3.1879 Albany NY; D1.31.1942 E.Greenbush NY; BR/TR/5´11˝/185; d9.3																								
1902	Pit N	18	61	5	13	1	0	0	6	4	2	—	.213	.284	.230	57	-3	2	.968	-3	120	66	C13,1b5	—	-0.5
1903	†Pit N	81	273	32	77	7	3	2	31	17	6	—	.282	.338	.352	94	-3	2	.980	0	**133**	81	C76,1b3	—	0.4
1904	Pit N	94	302	29	73	5	3	0	28	15	5	—	.242	.289	.278	73	-10	2	.964	-6	106	84	C91/1	—	-0.7
1905	Cin N	44	156	18	36	5	3	0	18	12	5	—	.231	.306	.301	73	-5	4	.949	-3	94	85	C44	—	-0.4
1906	Cin N	12	40	3	11	0	2	1	5	3	0	—	.275	.326	.450	136	1	2	.987	-0	95	85	C12	—	0.3
	Pit N	43	118	9	28	3	1	0	12	9	2	—	.237	.302	.280	78	-3	1	.971	-1	121	66	C40	—	0.0
	Year	55	158	12	39	3	3	1	17	12	2	—	.247	.308	.323	93	-2	3	.975	-1	114	71	C52	—	0.3
1907	Pit N	43	113	11	24	1	0	0	12	9	2	—	.212	.282	.221	57	-5	1	.979	1	126	92	C35/1	—	-0.1
1908	Pit N	34	64	3	15	2	2	0	11	2	1	—	.234	.269	.328	90	-1	0	.977	0	127	71	C20	—	0.1
1909	StL N	104	306	43	76	13	1	0	22	39	9	—	.248	.350	.297	108	6	7	.954	-14	75	92	C83	—	-0.1
1910	StL N	93	270	25	71	4	2	0	37	36	3	29	.263	.356	.293	93	-1	9	.976	-18	73	81	C80	—	-1.2
1912	Bro N	52	111	8	32	4	3	0	23	16	2	15	.288	.388	.378	114	3	1	.976	-2	86	93	C32	—	0.3
1913	Bro N	15	18	0	4	0	0	0	0	1	0	2	.222	.263	.222	38	-1	0	.875	-1	71	60	C4	—	-0.3
Total	11	633	1832	186	460	45	20	3	205	163	37	46	.251	.325	.302	88	-22	31	.968	-46	101	83	C530,1b10	—	-2.2
Phelps, Babe	Ernest Gordon "Blimp"; B4.19.1908 Odenton MD; D12.10.1992 Odenton MD; BL/TR/6´2˝/225; d9.17																								
1931	Was A	3	3	0	1	0	0	0	0	0	0	0	.333	.333	.333	75	0	0-0	ø	0	—	—	/H	—	0.0
1933	Chi N	3	7	0	2	0	0	0	2	0	0	1	.286	.286	.286	64	0	0	1.000	1	0	228	C2	—	0.0
1934	Chi N	44	70	7	20	5	2	2	12	1	0	8	.286	.296	.500	111	1	0	.981	-1	145	129	C18	—	0.0
1935	Bro N	47	121	17	44	7	2	5	22	9	0	10	.364	.408	.579	165	11	0	.957	-0	114	97	C34	—	1.2
1936	Bro N	115	319	36	117	23	2	5	57	27	3	18	.367	.421	.498	145	22	1	.977	-10	65	112	C98/rf	—	1.6
1937	Bro N	121	409	42	128	37	3	7	58	25	3	28	.313	.357	.469	121	12	2	.971	-3	85	104	C111	—	1.5
1938	Bro N✳	66	208	33	64	12	2	5	46	23	1	15	.308	.379	.457	126	8	2	.980	-2	82	87	C55	—	0.9
1939	Bro N★	98	323	33	92	21	2	6	42	24	1	24	.285	.336	.418	98	-1	0	.980	3	110	93	C92	—	0.7
1940	Bro N★	118	370	47	109	24	5	13	61	30	1	27	.295	.349	.492	122	11	2	.977	-4	121	55	C99/1	—	1.2
1941	Bro N	16	30	3	7	3	0	2	4	1	0	2	.233	.258	.533	114	0	0	.971	-0	227	0	C11	0	0.1
1942	Pit N	95	257	21	73	11	1	9	41	20	4	24	.284	.345	.440	126	8	2	.959	-3	87	99	C72	0	1.0
Total	11	726	2117	239	657	143	19	54	345	160	13	157	.310	.362	.472	124	72	9-0	.974	-19	97	92	C592/1rf	0	8.2
Phelps, Josh	Joshua Lee; B5.12.1978 Anchorage AK; BR/TR/6´3˝/(215–225); [TorA96 10/279]; d6.13																								
2000	Tor A	1	1	0	0	0	0	0	0	0-0	0	1	.000	.000	.000	-97	0	0-0	1.000	-0	0	0	/C	0	0.0
2001	Tor A	8	12	3	0	0	0	0	1	2-0	0	5	.000	.143	.000	-56	-3	1-0	1.000	0	74	161	C7	0	-0.2
2002	Tor A	74	265	41	82	20	1	15	58	19-0	3	82	.309	.362	.562	136	13	0-0	1.000	-0	0	112	D71,1b2	0	0.9
2003	Tor A	119	396	57	106	18	1	20	66	39-3	17	115	.268	.358	.470	112	7	1-2	.967	-1	83	33	D106,1b8	18	0.0
2004	Tor A	79	295	38	70	13	2	12	51	18-2	7	73	.237	.296	.417	79	-10	0-0	.981	-3	26	70	D65,1b12	0	-1.6
	Cle A	24	76	13	23	6	0	5	10	4-0	0	20	.303	.338	.579	138	4	0-0	.978	-1	49	18	D16,1b8	0	0.1
	Year	103	371	51	93	19	2	17	61	22-2	7	93	.251	.304	.450	90	-7	0-0	.980	-4	34	51	D81,1b20	0	-1.5
2005	TB A	47	158	21	42	10	0	5	26	12-1	4	48	.266	.328	.424	102	1	0-0	1.000	-0	0	302	D42/1	0	-0.2
Total	6	352	1203	173	323	67	4	57	212	94-6	31	344	.268	.336	.473	107	12	2-2	.978	-5	45	55	D300,1b31,C8	18	-1.0
Phelps, Ken	Kenneth Allen; B8.6.1954 Seattle WA; BL/TL/6´1˝/(200–209); [KCA76 15/354]; d9.20; Col Arizona St.																								
1980	KC A	3	4	0	0	0	0	0	0	0-0	0	2	.000	.000	.000	-99	-1	0-0	1.000	-0	0	243	1b2	0	-0.1
1981	KC A	21	22	1	3	0	1	0	1	1-0	0	13	.136	.174	.227	15	-3	0-0	1.000	0	451	0	1b2,D4	0	-0.2
1982	Mon N	10	8	0	2	0	0	0	0	0-0	1	3	.250	.333	.250	63	0	0-0	ø	0	—	—	/H	0	-0.1
1983	Sea A	50	127	10	30	4	1	7	16	13-0	0	25	.236	.301	.449	101	0	0-0	1.000	2	116	60	1b22,D19	0	-0.1
1984	Sea A	101	290	52	70	9	0	24	51	61-5	5	73	.241	.378	.521	148	21	3-3	.987	-1	62	84	D84,1b9	41	1.7
1985	Sea A	61	116	18	24	3	0	9	24	24-2	0	33	.207	.343	.466	118	3	2-0	1.000	-1	58	116	D25,1b8	0	0.2
1986	Sea A	125	344	69	85	16	4	24	64	88-6	6	96	.247	.406	.526	150	28	2-3	.983	-4	82	118	1b55,D52	0	1.9
1987	Sea A	120	332	68	86	13	1	27	68	80-5	8	75	.259	.410	.548	145	25	1-1	1.000	-0	0	0	D114/1	0	2.0
1988	Sea A	72	190	37	54	8	0	14	32	51-2	1	35	.284	.434	.547	166	20	1-0	.952	-0	105	89	D68,1b3	0	1.8
	NY A	45	107	17	24	5	0	10	22	19-3	0	26	.224	.339	.551	146	7	0-0	ø	0	0	0	D24/1	0	0.6
	Year	117	297	54	78	13	0	24	54	70-5	1	61	.263	.402	.549	160	27	1-0	.952	-0	101	85	D92,1b4	0	2.4
1989	NY A	86	185	26	46	3	0	7	29	27-2	0	47	.249	.340	.378	104	1	0-0	.980	-1	35	99	D55,1b8	0	-0.2
	†Oak A	11	9	0	1	1	0	0	0	4-0	0	0	.111	.385	.222	78	0	0-0	ø	-0	0	0	/1D	0	0.0
	Year	97	194	26	47	4	0	7	29	31-2	0	47	.242	.342	.371	103	2	0-0	.980	-1	28	80	D56,1b9	0	-0.2
1990	Oak A	32	59	6	11	2	0	1	6	12-1	0	10	.186	.319	.271	71	-2	0-0	.964	0	176	171	D15,1b5	0	-0.2
	Cle A	24	61	4	7	0	0	0	0	10-2	0	11	.115	.239	.115	2	-8	1-0	1.000	-0	92	41	1b14,D6	0	-0.9
	Year	56	120	10	18	2	0	1	6	22-3	0	21	.150	.280	.192	36	-10	1-0	.992	0	106	63	D21,1b19	0	-1.1
Total	11	761	1854	308	443	64	7	123	313	390-28	21	449	.239	.374	.480	131	91	10-7	.987	-5	86	95	D467,1b131	41	6.4
Philley, Dave	David Earl; B5.16.1920 Paris TX; BB/TR/6´0˝/(185–195); d9.6; Mil 1943–45																								
1941	Chi A	7	9	4	2	1	0	0	0	3	0	3	.222	.417	.333	102	0	0-0	ø	-0	0	0	O2L	0	0.0
1946	Chi A	17	68	10	24	2	3	0	17	4	0	4	.353	.389	.471	145	4	5-0	.983	3	113	197	O17(16/1/0)	0	0.6
1947	Chi A	143	551	55	142	25	11	2	45	35	1	39	.258	.303	.354	85	-14	21-16	.986	-1	97	97	O133(39/95/0),3b4	0	-2.2
1948	Chi A	137	488	51	140	28	3	5	42	50	0	33	.287	.353	.387	100	0	8-10	.978	10	100	**200**	O128(6/123/0)	0	0.4
1949	Chi A	146	598	84	171	20	8	0	44	54	2	51	.286	.347	.346	86	-13	13-4	.977	-2	95	115	O145(0/3/143)	0	-1.7
1950	Chi A	**156**	619	69	150	21	5	14	80	52	1	57	.242	.302	.360	71	-31	6-3	.980	5	100	141	O154(0/70/103)	0	-2.9
1951	Chi A	7	25	0	6	2	0	0	2	2	0	3	.240	.296	.320	68	-1	0-0	.938	-1	100	0	O6L	0	-0.2
	Phi A	125	468	71	123	18	7	7	59	63	3	38	.263	.354	.376	95	-2	9-6	.978	-3	92	125	O120(2/116/2),3b2	0	-0.9
	Year	132	493	71	129	20	7	7	61	65	3	41	.262	.351	.373	94	-4	9-6	.976	-4	92	118	O126(8/116/2),3b2	0	-1.1
1952	Phi A	151	586	80	154	25	4	7	71	59	4	35	.263	.334	.355	86	-10	11-4	.991	7	106	112	O149C,3b2	0	-0.7
1953	Phi A	**157**	620	80	188	30	9	9	59	51	2	35	.303	.358	.424	106	5	13-5	.981	-4	92	128	O157(0/31/129)/3	0	-0.4
1954	†Cle A	133	452	48	102	13	3	12	60	57	0	48	.226	.308	.347	79	-14	2-4	.984	-4	99	64	O129(1/0/129)	0	-2.4
1955	Cle A	43	104	15	31	4	2	2	9	12-2	0	10	.298	.368	.433	111	2	0-2	1.000	0	98	108	O34(2/0/32)	0	0.0
	Bal A	83	311	50	93	13	3	6	41	34-2	0	38	.299	.367	.418	119	8	1-2	.970	-3	95	92	O82(46/2/48),3b2	0	0.1
	Year	126	415	65	124	17	5	8	50	46-4	0	48	.299	.367	.422	116	9	1-4	.976	-2	96	96	O116(48/2/80),3b2	0	0.1
1956	Bal A	32	117	13	24	4	2	1	17	18-3	0	13	.205	.309	.299	67	-6	3-1	.935	-1	101	95	O31(23/0/16),3b5	0	-0.7
	Chi A	86	279	44	74	14	2	4	47	28-0	1	27	.265	.328	.373	85	-6	1-3	.978	-4	69	88	1b51,O30(17/0/19)	0	-1.4
	Year	118	396	57	98	18	4	5	64	46-3	1	40	.247	.322	.351	80	-12	4-4	.965	-5	99	98	O61(40/0/35),1b51,3b5	0	-2.1
1957	Chi A	22	71	9	23	4	0	0	9	4-0	0	10	.324	.360	.380	102	0	1-1	.975	0	126	0	O17R,1b2	0	-0.1
	Det A	65	173	15	49	8	1	2	16	7-0	0	16	.283	.309	.376	85	-4	3-1	.996	2	153	84	1b27,O12(4/0/8)/3	0	-0.4
	Year	87	244	24	72	12	1	2	25	11-0	0	26	.295	.324	.377	90	-4	4-2	.965	2	105	0	O29(4/0/25),1b29/3	0	-0.5
1958	Phi N	91	207	30	64	11	4	3	31	15-3	1	20	.309	.357	.444	113	4	1-1	1.000	-4	74	0	O24R,1b18	0	-0.2
1959	Phi N	99	254	32	74	18	2	7	37	18-3	1	27	.291	.339	.461	109	3	0-0	1.000	-0	103	152	O34R,1b24	0	0.1
1960	Phi N	14	15	2	5	2	0	0	4	3-1	0	2	.333	.444	.467	149	1	0-0	ø	-1	0	0	O3(2/0/1),1b2	0	0.1
	SF N	39	61	5	10	0	0	1	7	6-0	0	14	.164	.239	.213	26	-6	0-0	.941	-1	105	0	O10L,3b3	0	-0.8
	Year	53	76	7	15	2	0	1	11	9-1	0	16	.197	.282	.263	53	-5	0-0	.941	-2	113	0	O13(12/0/1),3b3,1b2	0	-0.7
	Bal A	14	34	6	9	2	1	1	5	4-0	0	5	.265	.342	.471	119	1	1-0	1.000	0	113	0	O8(6/0/2)/3	0	0.1
1961	Bal A	99	144	13	36	9	2	1	23	10-0	0	20	.250	.293	.361	78	-5	2-0	1.000	-3	65	0	O25(22/0/3)/1	0	-0.8
1962	Bos A	38	42	3	6	2	0	0	4	5-0	1	3	.143	.250	.190	20	-5	0-0	1.000	0	123	0	O4R	0	-0.5
Total	18	1904	6296	789	1700	276	72	84	729	594-14	17	551	.270	.334	.377	91	-89	101-63	.981	-4	97	114	O1454(204/590/714),1b125,3b21	0	-14.9

YEAR	TM LG	G	AB	R	H	2B	3B	HR	RBI	BB-IB	HP	SO	AVG	OBP	SLG	AOPS	ABR	SB-CS	FA	FR	RNG	THR	GAMES AT POSITION	DL	BFW
Phillips, Adolfo	Adolfo Emilio (Lopez); B12.16.1941 Bethania, Pan; BR/TR/6´0˝/(173–177); d9.2																								
1964	Phi N	13	13	4	3	0	0	0	0	3-0	0	3	.231	.375	.231	76	0	0-0	1.000	1	92	528	O4(3/2/1)	0	0.0
1965	Phi N	41	87	14	20	4	0	3	5	5-0	0	34	.230	.272	.379	83	-2	3-3	1.000	-1	98	0	O32(2/30/0)	0	-0.5
1966	Phi N	2	3	1	0	0	0	0	0	0-0	0	0	.000	.000	.000	-99	-1	0-0	1.000	0	156	0	/cf	0	-0.1
	Chi N	116	416	68	109	29	1	16	36	43-3	12	135	.262	.348	.452	119	12	32-15	.978	7	106	189	O111C	0	1.9
	Year	118	419	69	109	29	1	16	36	43-3	12	135	.260	.346	.449	118	12	32-15	.979	7	106	**188**	O112C	0	1.8
1967	Chi N	144	448	66	120	20	7	17	70	80-**29**	6	93	.268	.384	.458	134	23	24-10	.981	7	106	**163**	O141C	0	3.0
1968	Chi N	143	439	49	106	20	5	13	33	47-20	5	90	.241	.320	.399	108	5	9-7	.979	4	103	134	O141C	0	0.6
1969	Chi N	28	49	5	11	3	1	0	1	16-3	1	15	.224	.424	.327	100	1	1-3	.956	-0	112	0	O25(1/24/0)	0	-0.1
	Mon N	58	199	25	43	4	4	4	7	19-1	1	62	.216	.286	.337	74	-8	6-5	.981	-1	97	106	O53C	0	-1.1
	Year	86	248	30	54	7	5	4	8	35-4	2	77	.218	.318	.335	80	-6	7-8	.973	-2	101	77	O78(1/77/0)	0	-1.2
1970	Mon N	92	214	36	51	6	3	6	21	36-1	2	51	.238	.352	.379	96	-1	7-1	.985	-1	106	32	O75(6/71/0)	0	-0.1
1972	Cle A	12	7	2	0	0	0	0	0	2-0	0	2	.000	.222	.000	-29	-1	0-0	1.000	0	129	0	O10(6/2/2)	0	-0.1
Total	8	649	1875	270	463	86	21	59	173	251-57	27	485	.247	.343	.410	110	28	82-44	.980	16	104	131	O593(18/576/3)	0	3.5
Phillips, Brandon	Brandon Emil; B6.28.1981 Raleigh NC; BR/TR/5´11˝/(185–195); [MonN99 2/57]; d9.13																								
2002	Cle A	11	31	5	8	3	1	0	4	3-0	1	6	.258	.343	.419	99	0	0-0	.957	0	108	61	2b11	0	0.1
2003	Cle A	112	370	36	77	18	1	6	33	14-0	3	77	.208	.242	.311	45	-31	4-5	.981	16	112	112	2b109	0	-1.0
2004	Cle A	6	22	1	4	2	0	0	1	2-0	0	5	.182	.250	.273	38	-2	0-2	.973	1	102	94	2b6	0	-0.1
2005	Cle A	6	9	1	0	0	0	0	0	0-0	0	4	.000	.000	.000	-99	-3	0-0	1.000	0	68	163	2b2/SD	0	-0.2
2006	Cin N	149	536	65	148	28	1	17	75	35-3	6	88	.276	.324	.427	86	-11	25-2	.977	-19	87	90	2b142,S3	0	-1.8
Total	5	284	968	108	237	51	3	23	113	54-3	10	180	.245	.290	.375	69	-47	29-9	.978	-2	98	99	2b270,S4/D	0	-3.0
Phillips, J. R.	Charles Gene; B4.29.1970 West Covina CA; BL/TL/6´1˝/(185–205); [CalA88 4/91]; d9.3																								
1993	SF N	11	16	1	5	1	1	1	4	0-0	0	5	.313	.313	.688	164	1	0-0	.971	-0	88	45	1b5	0	0.1
1994	SF N	15	38	1	5	0	0	1	3	1-0	0	13	.132	.150	.211	-7	-6	1-0	.989	1	154	103	1b10	0	-0.6
1995	SF N	92	231	27	45	9	0	9	28	19-2	0	69	.195	.256	.351	59	-15	1-1	.993	-3	85	95	1b79/lf	0	-2.4
1996	SF N	15	25	3	5	0	0	2	5	1-0	0	13	.200	.231	.440	73	-1	0-0	.981	-1	51	87	1b10	0	-0.3
	Phi N	35	79	9	12	5	0	5	10	10-1	1	38	.152	.256	.405	70	-4	0-0	.957	3	178	119	O15R,1b11	0	-0.2
	Year	50	104	12	17	5	0	7	15	11-1	1	51	.163	.250	.413	71	-5	0-0	.992	2	54	102	1b21,O15R	0	-0.5
1997	Hou N	13	15	2	2	0	0	1	4	0-0	0	7	.133	.125	.333	18	-2	0-0	1.000	-0	0	106	1b3,O3R	0	-0.2
1998	Hou N	36	58	4	11	0	0	2	9	7-1	0	22	.190	.277	.293	51	-4	0-0	.962	-1	101	107	1b12,O6L	0	-0.6
1999	Col N	25	39	5	9	4	0	2	4	0-0	1	13	.231	.250	.487	64	-2	0-0	.933	2	103	848	O7(1/0/6),1b4	0	0.0
Total	7	242	501	52	94	19	1	23	67	38-4	2	180	.188	.247	.367	59	-33	2-1	.989	1	87	97	1b134,O32(8/0/24)	0	-4.2
Phillips, Damon	Damon Roswell "Dee"; B6.8.1919 Corsicana TX; D11.4.2004 Fort Worth TX; BR/TR/6´0˝/176; d7.19; Mil 1945																								
1942	Cin N	28	84	4	17	2	0	0	6	7	0	5	.202	.264	.226	44	-6	0	.964	3	110	124	S27	0	-0.1
1944	Bos N	140	489	35	126	30	1	1	53	28	2	34	.258	.301	.329	74	-17	1	.932	2	109	155	3b90,S60	0	-1.0
1946	Bos N	2	2	0	1	0	0	0	0	0	0	0	.500	.500	.500	182	0	0	ø	0	—	—	/H	0	0.0
Total	3	170	575	39	144	32	1	1	59	35	2	39	.250	.296	.315	70	-23	1	.932	5	109	155	3b90,S87	0	-1.1
Phillips, Eddie	Edward David; B2.17.1901 Worcester MA; D1.26.1968 Buffalo NY; BR/TR/6´0˝/178; d5.4; Col Boston College																								
1924	Bos N	3	3	0	0	0	0	0	0	0	0	2	.000	.000	.000	-99	-1	0-0	1.000	-0	*0*	*817*	/C	—	-0.1
1929	Det A	68	221	24	52	13	1	2	21	20	1	16	.235	.302	.330	62	-13	0-1	.967	-8	*74*	*87*	C63	—	-1.6
1931	Pit N	106	353	30	82	18	3	7	44	41	3	49	.232	.317	.360	82	-8	1	.986	-5	*99*	*74*	C103	—	-0.7
1932	NY A	9	31	4	9	1	0	2	4	2	0	3	.290	.333	.516	123	1	1-0	1.000	1	*113*	*122*	C9	—	0.2
1934	Was A	56	169	6	33	6	1	2	16	26	1	24	.195	.306	.278	54	-12	1-0	.984	-5	*148*	*98*	C53	—	-1.2
1935	Cle A	70	220	18	60	16	1	1	41	15	0	21	.273	.319	.368	76	-8	0-0	.980	-7	*111*	*71*	C69	—	-1.0
Total	6	312	997	82	236	54	6	14	126	104	5	115	.237	.312	.345	72	-41	3-1	.980	-24	*105*	*82*	C298	—	-4.4
Phillips, Andy	George Andrew; B4.6.1977 Tuscaloosa AL; BR/TR/6´0˝/205; [NYA99 7/231]; d9.14; Col Alabama																								
2004	NY A	5	8	1	2	0	0	1	2	0-0	0	1	.250	.250	.625	117	0	0-0	1.000	0	118	0	3b4	0	0.0
2005	NY A	27	40	7	6	4	0	1	4	1-0	0	13	.150	.171	.325	28	-4	0-0	.987	-2	41	105	1b19/3lfD	0	-0.6
2006	†NY A	110	246	30	59	11	3	7	29	15-0	0	56	.240	.281	.394	73	-11	3-2	.988	-5	74	107	1b94,3b10/2D	15	-2.0
Total	3	142	294	38	67	15	3	9	35	16-0	0	70	.228	.266	.391	68	-15	3-2	.988	-6	70	107	1b113,3b15,D10/2lf	15	-2.6
Phillips, Eddie	Howard Edward; B7.8.1931 St.Louis MO; BB/TR/6´1˝/180; d9.10																								
1953	StL N	9	0	4	0	0	0	0	0	0	0	0	ø	ø	ø	ø	0	0-0	ø	0	—	—	/R	0	0.0
Phillips, Jack	Jack Dorn "Stretch"; B9.6.1921 Clarence NY; BR/TR/6´4˝/(190–193); d8.22; Col Clarkson																								
1947	†NY A	16	36	5	10	0	1	1	2	3	0	5	.278	.333	.417	109	0	0-0	.986	-2	17	118	1b10	0	-0.2
1948	NY A	1	2	0	0	0	0	0	0	0	0	1	.000	.000	.000	-99	-1	0-0	.889	-0	0	0	/1	0	-0.1
1949	NY A	45	91	16	28	4	1	1	10	12	0	9	.308	.388	.407	110	2	1-0	.977	-2	73	110	1b38	0	-0.2
	Pit N	18	56	6	13	3	1	0	3	4	0	6	.232	.283	.321	60	-3	1	1.000	-0	94	91	1b16/3	0	-0.4
1950	Pit N	69	208	25	61	7	6	5	34	20	0	17	.293	.355	.457	108	2	1	.986	1	119	96	1b54,3b3/P	0	0.1
1951	Pit N	70	156	12	37	7	3	0	12	15	0	17	.237	.304	.321	66	-7	1-2	.991	-1	88	107	1b53,3b4	0	-1.0
1952	Pit N	1	1	0	0	0	0	0	0	0	0	0	.000	.000	.000	-97	0	0-0	1.000	-0	0	451	/1	0	0.0
1955	Det A	55	117	15	37	8	2	1	20	10-0	0	12	.316	.364	.444	121	3	0-0	.992	-2	77	71	1b35,3b3	0	0.0
1956	Det A	67	224	31	66	13	2	1	20	21-0	0	19	.295	.354	.384	95	-1	1-1	.981	-2	97	99	1b56/2lf	0	-0.6
1957	Det A	1	1	1	0	0	0	0	0	0-0	0	0	.000	.000	.000	-97	0	0-0	ø	0	—	—	/H	0	0.0
Total	9	343	892	111	252	42	16	9	101	85-0	0	86	.283	.344	.396	95	-5	5-3	.986	-8	92	98	1b264,3b11/lf2P	0	-2.4
Phillips, Jason	Jason Lloyd; B9.27.1976 LaMesa CA; BR/TR/6´1˝/(177–210); [NYN97 24/720]; d9.19; Col San Diego St.																								
2001	NY N	6	7	2	1	1	0	0	0	0-0	0	1	.143	.143	.286	7	-1	0-0	1.000	0	96	0	C5	0	-0.1
2002	NY N	11	19	4	7	0	0	1	3	1-0	1	1	.368	.409	.526	159	2	0-0	1.000	-0	0	89	C7	0	0.2
2003	NY N	119	403	45	120	25	0	11	58	39-3	10	50	.298	.373	.442	116	11	0-1	.990	-5	91	104	1b84,C29	0	0.0
2004	NY N	128	362	34	79	18	0	7	34	35-4	8	42	.218	.298	.326	64	-20	0-1	.998	7	93	121	C87,1b38	0	-1.0
2005	LA N	121	399	38	95	20	0	10	55	25-4	4	50	.238	.287	.363	69	-19	0-1	.992	-10	60	102	C93,1b21	0	-2.5
2006	Tor A	25	48	4	12	6	0	0	6	1-0	1	5	.250	.275	.375	65	-2	0-1	1.000	-1	40	0	C9,1b6,D9	0	-0.3
Total	6	410	1238	127	314	70	0	29	156	101-11	24	149	.254	.319	.380	84	-29	0-4	.995	-10	84	101	C230,1b149,D9	0	-3.7
Phillips, Bubba	John Melvin; B2.24.1928 West Point MS; D6.22.1993 Hattiesburg MS; BR/TR/5´9˝/(170–180); d4.30; Col Southern Mississippi																								
1955	Det A	95	184	18	43	4	0	3	23	14-1	2	20	.234	.289	.304	63	-10	2-1	.992	3	120	47	O65(61/2/4),3b4	0	-1.0
1956	Chi A	67	99	16	27	6	0	2	11	6-0	1	12	.273	.321	.394	87	-2	1-2	1.000	3	128	124	O35(6/7/22),3b2	0	0.0
1957	Chi A	121	393	38	106	13	3	7	42	28-3	3	32	.270	.322	.372	89	-7	5-3	.958	14	115	111	3b97,O20(1/13/8)	0	0.6
1958	Chi A	84	260	26	71	10	0	5	30	15-3	1	14	.273	.310	.369	89	-4	3-0	.954	3	104	151	3b47,O37(19/15/4)	37	-0.2
1959	†Chi A	117	379	43	100	27	1	5	40	27-7	4	28	.264	.319	.380	92	-4	1-1	.951	-1	107	83	3b100,O23(8/14/1)	0	-0.6
1960	Cle A	113	304	34	63	14	1	4	33	14-3	4	37	.207	.249	.299	50	-22	1-0	.953	-6	87	109	3b85,O25(15/3/7)/S	0	-3.0
1961	Cle A	143	546	64	144	23	1	18	72	29-4	5	61	.264	.305	.408	92	-9	1-0	.958	-15	83	77	3b143	0	-2.4
1962	Cle A	148	562	53	145	26	0	10	54	20-0	7	55	.258	.289	.358	76	-20	4-0	.977	-10	88	60	3b145,O3C/2	0	-3.1
1963	Det A	128	464	42	114	11	2	5	45	19-1	4	42	.246	.276	.310	63	-23	6-2	.961	1	97	126	3b117,O5C	0	-2.4
1964	Det A	46	87	14	22	1	0	3	6	10-2	0	13	.253	.327	.368	92	-1	1-2	.983	0	100	142	3b22/lf	0	-0.1
Total	10	1062	3278	348	835	135	8	62	356	182-24	31	314	.255	.297	.358	79	-102	25-11	.960	-7	95	97	3b762,O214(111/62/46)/2S	37	-12.2
Phillips, Tony	Keith Anthony; B4.25.1959 Atlanta GA; BB/TR/5´10˝/(160–175); [MonN78*S1/10]; d5.10; Col New Mexico Mil. Inst. [JC]; OF(566/97/169)																								
1982	Oak A	40	81	11	17	2	2	0	8	12-0	2	26	.210	.326	.284	72	-3	2-3	.953	-0	107	90	S39	0	-0.1
1983	Oak A	148	412	54	102	12	3	4	35	48-1	2	70	.248	.327	.320	84	-8	16-5	.941	-20	101	110	S101,2b63,3b4/D	0	-1.5
1984	Oak A	154	451	62	120	24	3	4	37	42-1	0	86	.266	.325	.359	96	-2	10-6	.941	-8	106	107	S91,2b90/lf	0	0.1
1985	Oak A	42	161	23	45	12	2	4	17	13-0	0	34	.280	.331	.453	121	5	3-2	.980	3	108	108	3b31,2b24	136	0.7
1986	Oak A	118	441	76	113	14	5	5	52	76-0	3	82	.256	.367	.345	103	5	15-10	.976	7	115	71	2b88,3b30,O4C/SD	50	1.6
1987	Oak A	111	379	48	91	20	0	10	46	57-1	0	76	.240	.337	.372	95	-1	7-6	.974	1	103	73	2b87,3b11,S9,O2(1/0/1)/D	47	0.4
1988	†Oak A	79	212	32	43	8	4	2	17	36-0	1	50	.203	.320	.307	79	-5	0-2	.913	-13	78	99	3b32,O31(24/6/3),2b27,S10,1b3,D2	51	-1.9
1989	†Oak A	143	451	48	118	15	6	4	47	58-2	3	66	.262	.345	.348	100	2	3-8	.985	-8	104	96	2b84,3b49,S17,O16(13/0/4)/1	0	-0.6
1990	Det A	152	573	97	144	23	5	8	55	99-0	4	85	.251	.364	.351	100	4	19-9	.931	15	112	92	3b104,2b47,S11,O8(4/1/4),D4	0	2.2
1991	Det A	146	564	87	160	28	4	17	72	79-5	3	95	.284	.371	.438	122	19	10-5	.992	23	123	111	O56(25/9/23),3b46,2b36,D18,S13	0	4.1

YEAR	TM LG	G	AB	R	H	2B	3B	HR	RBI	BB-IB	HP	SO	AVG	OBP	SLG	AOPS	ABR	SB-CS	FA	FR	RNG	THR	GAMES AT POSITION	DL	BFW
1992	Det A	159	606	**114**	167	32	3	10	64	114-2	1	93	.276	.387	.388	117	20	12-10	.968	11	122	72	O69(14/24/35),2b57,D34,3b20/S	0	2.9
1993	Det A	151	566	113	177	27	0	7	57	**132**-5	4	102	.313	.443	.398	128	34	16-11	.969	10	106	80	O108(70/9/34),2b51/3D	0	4.1
1994	Det A	114	438	91	123	19	3	19	61	95-3	2	105	.281	.409	.468	124	20	13-5	.980	8	112	83	O104L,2b12,D6	0	2.4
1995	Cal A	139	525	119	137	21	1	27	61	113-6	3	135	.261	.394	.459	122	22	13-10	.924	7	107	122	3b88,O48(47/8/0),D2	0	2.5
1996	Chi A	153	581	119	161	29	3	12	63	**125**-9	4	132	.277	.404	.399	110	17	13-8	.981	10	110	122	O150(150/2/0),2b2/1	0	1.9
1997	Chi A	36	129	23	40	6	0	2	9	29-0	1	29	.310	.440	.403	126	7	4-1	.972	3	129	183	O28R,3b9	0	0.9
	Ana A	105	405	73	107	28	2	6	48	73-5	2	89	.264	.376	.388	100	4	9-9	.968	-12	88	78	2b43,O35(31/2/3),D26/3	0	-0.9
	Year	141	534	96	147	34	2	8	57	102-5	3	118	.275	.392	.391	107	11	13-10	.970	-9	108	107	O63(31/2/31),2b43,D26,3b10	0	0.0
1998	Tor A	13	48	9	17	5	0	1	7	9-1	2	6	.354	.467	.521	158	5	0-0	.960	-1	98	0	O13(11/0/4)	0	0.4
	NY N	52	188	25	42	11	0	3	14	38-0	0	44	.223	.351	.330	84	-3	1-1	.967	-2	95	62	O51(43/0/15)	0	-0.6
1999	Oak A	106	406	76	99	24	4	15	49	71-3	5	94	.244	.362	.433	105	5	11-3	.974	-7	97	107	2b66,O62(28/32/15),3b2/SD	49	0.1
Total	18	2161	7617	1300	2023	360	50	160	819	1319-44	42	1499	.266	.374	.389	108	147	177-114	.973	25	108	92	O786L,2b777,3b428,S294,D101,1b5	333	18.7

PHILLIPS, MARR Marr B.; B6.16.1857 Pittsburgh PA; D4.1.1928 Pittsburgh PA; BR/5´6.5˝/164; d5.1

YEAR	TM LG	G	AB	R	H	2B	3B	HR	RBI	BB-IB	HP	SO	AVG	OBP	SLG	AOPS	ABR	SB-CS	FA	FR	RNG	THR	GAMES AT POSITION	DL	BFW
1884	Ind AA	97	413	41	111	18	8	0	—	5	1	—	.269	.279	.351	107	3	—	.862	16	**112**	62	S97	—	1.9
1885	Det N	33	139	13	29	5	0	0	17	0	—	13	.209	.209	.245	46	-8	—	.881	0	105	54	S33	—	-0.7
	Pit AA	4	15	1	4	0	0	0	2	2	0	—	.267	.353	.267	99	0	—	.875	-1	94	193	S4	—	0.0
1890	Roc AA	64	257	18	53	8	0	0	34	16	3	—	.206	.261	.237	51	-16	10	.918	5	106	123	S64	—	-0.8
Total	3	198	824	73	197	31	8	0	53	23	4	13	.239	.263	.296	79	-21	10	.884	20	108	83	S198	—	0.4

PHILLIPS, MIKE Michael Dwaine; B8.19.1950 Beaumont TX; BL/TR/6´1˝/(168–185); [SFN69 1/18]; d4.15

YEAR	TM LG	G	AB	R	H	2B	3B	HR	RBI	BB-IB	HP	SO	AVG	OBP	SLG	AOPS	ABR	SB-CS	FA	FR	RNG	THR	GAMES AT POSITION	DL	BFW
1973	SF N	63	104	18	25	3	4	1	9	6-0	1	17	.240	.288	.375	79	-4	0-3	.931	-7	83	50	3b28,S20,2b7	0	-1.0
1974	SF N	100	283	19	62	6	1	2	20	14-0	1	37	.219	.258	.269	46	-21	4-5	.909	3	116	95	3b34,2b30,S23	0	-1.7
1975	SF N	10	31	3	6	0	0	0	1	6-0	0	4	.194	.324	.194	45	-2	1-0	.969	3	106	108	2b6,3b6	0	0.1
	NY N	116	383	31	98	10	7	1	28	25-5	1	47	.256	.300	.326	77	-14	3-0	.944	-4	95	82	S115/2	0	-0.4
	Year	126	414	34	104	10	7	1	29	31-5	1	51	.251	.302	.316	75	-16	4-0	.944	-1	95	82	S115,2b7,3b6	0	-0.3
1976	NY N	87	262	30	67	4	6	4	29	25-8	0	29	.256	.315	.363	98	-2	2-2	.955	-1	88	71	S53,2b19,3b10	0	0.3
1977	NY N	38	86	5	18	2	1	1	3	2-0	2	15	.209	.244	.291	44	-7	0-1	1.000	-2	84	64	S24,3b9,2b4	0	-0.8
	StL N	48	87	17	21	3	2	0	9	9-1	1	13	.241	.320	.322	73	-3	1-0	.971	3	105	134	2b31,S5,3b5	0	0.1
	Year	86	173	22	39	5	3	1	12	11-1	3	28	.225	.283	.306	59	-11	1-1	.973	1	98	116	2b35,S29,3b14	0	-0.7
1978	StL N	76	164	14	44	8	1	1	28	13-2	2	25	.268	.317	.348	90	-2	0-0	.971	3	98	107	2b55,S10/3	0	0.4
1979	StL N	44	97	10	22	3	1	1	6	10-0	1	9	.227	.306	.309	67	-4	0-0	.973	4	126	101	S25,2b16/3	0	0.2
1980	StL N	63	128	13	30	5	0	0	7	9-3	0	17	.234	.283	.273	54	-8	0-0	.971	7	126	153	S37,2b9,3b8	0	0.2
1981	SD N	14	29	1	6	0	1	0	0	0-0	0	3	.207	.207	.276	39	-3	1-0	.979	2	105	122	2b9/S	0	0.0
	†Mon N	34	55	5	12	2	0	0	4	5-0	0	15	.218	.279	.255	52	-3	0-1	.974	-3	88	92	S26,2b6	0	-0.5
	Year	48	84	6	18	2	1	0	4	5-0	0	18	.214	.256	.262	48	-6	1-1	.974	-1	89	101	S27,2b15	0	-0.5
1982	Mon N	14	8	0	1	0	0	0	1	0-0	0	3	.125	.111	.125	-29	-1	0-0	1.000	-0	88	55	2b10,S2	0	-0.2
1983	Mon N	5	2	0	0	0	0	0	0	0-0	0	0	.000	.000	.000	-99	-1	0-0	.000	-2	0	0	S3,3b2	0	-0.2
Total	11	712	1719	166	412	46	24	11	145	124-19	9	234	.240	.291	.314	69	-75	12-12	.956	5	100	94	S344,2b203,3b104	0	-3.5

PHILLIPS, PAUL Paul Anthony; B4.15.1977 Demopolis AL; BR/TR/6´1˝/(200–210); [KCA98 9/257]; d9.9; Col Alabama

YEAR	TM LG	G	AB	R	H	2B	3B	HR	RBI	BB-IB	HP	SO	AVG	OBP	SLG	AOPS	ABR	SB-CS	FA	FR	RNG	THR	GAMES AT POSITION	DL	BFW
2004	KC A	4	5	2	1	0	0	0	0	0-0	1	1	.200	.333	.200	44	0	0-0	1.000	1	0	0	C4	0	0.0
2005	KC A	23	67	6	18	4	1	1	9	0-0	0	5	.269	.269	.403	78	-2	0-0	.990	-3	247	170	C20,D2	0	-0.4
2006	KC A	23	65	8	18	3	0	1	5	1-0	0	8	.277	.284	.369	70	-3	0-0	.988	1	129	148	C13,1b5,D2	0	-0.1
Total	3	50	137	16	37	7	1	2	14	1-0	1	14	.270	.279	.380	73	-5	0-0	.990	-1	190	153	C37,1b5,D4	0	-0.5

PHILLIPS, DICK Richard Eugene; B11.24.1931 Racine WI; D3.29.1998 Burnaby BC, Can.; BL/TR/6´0˝/180; d4.15; C1; Col Valparaiso

YEAR	TM LG	G	AB	R	H	2B	3B	HR	RBI	BB-IB	HP	SO	AVG	OBP	SLG	AOPS	ABR	SB-CS	FA	FR	RNG	THR	GAMES AT POSITION	DL	BFW
1962	SF N	5	3	1	0	0	0	0	1	1-0	0	1	.000	.250	.000	-27	-1	0-0	1.000	0	0	0	/1	0	-0.1
1963	Was A	124	321	33	76	8	0	10	32	29-0	2	35	.237	.300	.355	84	-7	1-0	.994	3	129	128	1b68,2b5,3b4	0	-0.8
1964	Was A	109	234	17	54	6	1	2	23	27-0	1	22	.231	.307	.291	70	-9	1-2	.994	1	111	115	1b61,3b4	0	-1.3
1966	Was A	25	37	3	6	0	0	0	4	2-1	1	5	.162	.225	.162	13	-4	0-0	1.000	-0	62	52	1b5	0	-0.5
Total	4	263	595	54	136	14	1	12	60	59-1	4	63	.229	.298	.316	74	-21	2-2	.995	3	119	119	1b135,3b8,2b5	0	-2.7

PHILLIPS, BILL William B.; B4.1857 St.John NB (now Canada); D10.7.1900 Chicago IL; BR/TR/6´0˝/202; d5.1

YEAR	TM LG	G	AB	R	H	2B	3B	HR	RBI	BB-IB	HP	SO	AVG	OBP	SLG	AOPS	ABR	SB-CS	FA	FR	RNG	THR	GAMES AT POSITION	DL	BFW
1879	Cle N	81	365	58	99	15	4	0	29	2	—	20	.271	.275	.334	101	0	—	.954	-4	120	66	1b75,C11,O2(0/1/1)	—	-0.6
1880	Cle N	**85**	334	41	85	14	10	1	36	6	—	29	.254	.268	.365	115	4	—	.963	2	**110**	**101**	1b85	—	0.3
1881	Cle N	**85**	357	51	97	18	10	1	44	5	—	19	.272	.282	.387	114	5	—	.966	-1	78	**113**	1b85	—	0.0
1882	Cle N	78	335	40	87	17	7	4	47	7	—	18	.260	.275	.388	114	5	—	.971	3	112	142	1b78/C	—	0.1
1883	Cle N	97	382	42	94	29	8	2	40	8	—	49	.246	.262	.380	93	-3	—	.967	-2	68	116	1b97	—	-1.2
1884	Cle N	111	464	58	128	25	12	3	46	18	—	80	.276	.303	.401	115	7	—	.959	-2	93	110	1b111	—	-0.4
1885	Bro AA	99	391	65	118	16	11	3	63	27	11	—	.302	.364	.422	147	21	—	**.973**	0	91	82	1b99	—	1.1
1886	Bro AA	**141**	585	68	160	26	15	0	72	33	1	—	.274	.313	.369	113	6	13	.978	-2	73	90	1b141	—	-0.7
1887	Bro AA	132	533	82	142	34	11	2	101	45	6	—	.266	.330	.383	97	-2	16	**.982**	4	107	91	1b132	—	-0.8
1888	KC AA	129	509	57	120	20	10	1	56	27	7	—	.236	.284	.320	88	-9	10	.980	3	117	97	1b129	—	-1.6
Total	10	1038	4255	562	1130	214	98	17	534	178	25	215	.266	.299	.374	109	34	39	.971	2	96	100	1b1032,C12,O2(0/1/1)	—	-3.8

PHYLE, BILL William Joseph; B6.25.1875 Duluth MN; D8.6.1953 Los Angeles CA; TR; d9.17; ▲

YEAR	TM LG	G	AB	R	H	2B	3B	HR	RBI	BB-IB	HP	SO	AVG	OBP	SLG	AOPS	ABR	SB-CS	FA	FR	RNG	THR	GAMES AT POSITION	DL	BFW
1898	Chi N	4	9	1	1	0	0	0	0	2	0	—	.111	.273	.111	11	0	0	.800	-1	70	0	P3	—	0.0
1899	Chi N	10	34	2	6	0	0	0	1	0	0	—	.176	.176	.176	-3	-2	0	.935	0	108	167	P10	—	0.0
1901	NY N	25	66	8	12	2	0	0	3	2	0	—	.182	.206	.212	22	-7	0	.903	1	112	0	P24/S	—	0.0
1906	StL N	22	73	6	13	3	1	0	4	5	0	—	.178	.231	.247	51	-4	2	.935	1	102	84	3b21	—	-0.3
Total	4	61	182	17	32	5	1	0	8	9	0	—	.176	.215	.214	28	-13	2	.907	2	107	51	P37,3b21/S	—	-0.3

PIATT, ADAM Adam David; B2.8.1976 Chicago IL; BR/TR/6´2˝/(195–218); [OakA97 8/245]; d4.24; Col Mississippi St.

YEAR	TM LG	G	AB	R	H	2B	3B	HR	RBI	BB-IB	HP	SO	AVG	OBP	SLG	AOPS	ABR	SB-CS	FA	FR	RNG	THR	GAMES AT POSITION	DL	BFW
2000	†Oak A	60	157	24	47	5	5	5	23	23-0	1	44	.299	.392	.490	123	6	0-1	.950	-6	79	65	O29(8/0/22),3b13,D13,1b3	0	-0.2
2001	Oak A	36	95	9	20	5	1	0	6	13-0	0	26	.211	.300	.284	57	-6	0-0	.962	0	92	172	O32R/D	87	-0.7
2002	†Oak A	55	137	18	32	8	0	5	18	12-0	2	33	.234	.303	.401	86	-3	2-1	1.000	-4	84	43	O50(40/0/12)/1	0	-0.8
2003	Oak A	47	100	6	24	10	0	4	15	6-0	0	30	.240	.280	.460	91	-1	1-2	.978	-2	79	119	O38(32/0/7)/1D	0	-0.5
	TB A	14	32	5	6	3	0	2	3	3-0	0	16	.188	.250	.469	88	-1	0-0	1.000	-1	55	0	O7(1/0/6),D4	0	-0.2
	Year	61	132	11	30	13	0	6	18	9-0	0	46	.227	.273	.462	90	-2	1-2	.981	-4	75	98	O45(33/0/13),D6/1	0	-0.7
Total	4	212	521	62	129	31	6	16	65	57-0	3	149	.248	.323	.422	94	-5	3-4	.977	-13	82	91	O156(81/0/79),D20,3b13,1b5	87	-2.4

PIAZZA, MIKE Michael Joseph; B9.4.1968 Norristown PA; BR/TR/6´3˝/(197–223); [LAN88 62/1390]; d9.1; Col Miami–Dade North (FL) CC

YEAR	TM LG	G	AB	R	H	2B	3B	HR	RBI	BB-IB	HP	SO	AVG	OBP	SLG	AOPS	ABR	SB-CS	FA	FR	RNG	THR	GAMES AT POSITION	DL	BFW
1992	LA N	21	69	5	16	3	0	1	7	4-0	1	12	.232	.284	.319	71	-3	0-0	.990	-1	123	70	C16	0	-0.3
1993	LA N★	149	547	81	174	24	2	35	112	46-6	3	86	.318	.370	.561	155	40	3-4	.989	6	97	123	C146/1	0	5.3
1994	LA N★	107	405	64	129	18	0	24	92	33-10	1	65	.319	.370	.541	142	23	1-3	.985	-10	91	82	C104	0	1.9
1995	†LA N★	112	434	82	150	17	0	32	93	39-10	1	80	.346	.400	.606	**173**	44	1-0	.990	-1	94	83	C112	24	4.9
1996	†LA N★	148	547	87	184	16	0	36	105	81-21	1	93	.336	.422	.563	167	55	0-3	.992	-12	72	76	C146	0	4.9
1997	LA N★	152	556	104	201	32	1	40	124	69-11	3	77	.362	.431	.638	**189**	**73**	5-1	.986	-2	93	89	C139,D7	0	7.7
1998	LA N	37	149	20	42	5	0	9	30	11-4	0	27	.282	.329	.497	120	3	0-0	.993	4	56	120	C37	0	0.9
	Fla N	5	18	1	5	0	1	0	5	0-0	0	0	.278	.263	.389	78	-1	0-0	.968	0	82	89	C4	0	0.0
	NY N★	109	394	67	137	33	0	23	76	47-10	2	53	.348	.417	.607	171	42	1-0	.989	4	83	102	C99,D4	0	5.1
	Year	151	561	88	184	38	1	32	111	58-14	2	80	.328	.390	.570	155	45	1-0	.990	8	76	106	C140,D4	0	6.0
1999	†NY N★	141	534	100	162	25	0	40	124	51-11	1	70	.303	.361	.575	139	29	2-2	.989	-14	84	93	C137/D	15	2.3
2000	†NY N✱	136	482	90	156	26	0	38	113	58-10	3	69	.324	.398	.614	160	44	4-2	**.997**	-10	66	97	C124,D5	0	3.9
2001	NY N★	141	503	81	151	29	0	36	94	67-19	2	87	.300	.384	.573	153	40	0-2	.991	-13	61	97	C131,D5	0	3.3
2002	NY N★	135	478	69	134	23	2	33	98	57-9	3	82	.280	.359	.544	142	27	0-3	.986	-19	53	88	C121,D6	0	1.6
2003	NY N	68	234	37	67	13	0	11	34	35-3	1	40	.286	.377	.483	129	11	0-0	.982	-7	51	169	C64/1	88	0.8
2004	NY N★	129	455	47	121	21	0	20	54	68-14	2	78	.266	.362	.444	110	8	0-0	.985	-10	93	88	1b68,C50,D8	23	-0.5
2005	NY N★	113	398	41	100	23	0	19	62	41-6	3	67	.251	.326	.452	104	1	0-0	.997	-1	55	68	C101,D5	24	0.7
2006	†SD N	126	399	39	113	19	1	22	68	34-2	3	66	.283	.342	.501	119	10	0-0	.987	-14	48	70	C99,D8	0	0.1
Total	15	1829	6602	1015	2042	327	7	419	1291	741-146	30	1052	.309	.379	.551	147	446	17-20	.989	-99	75	94	C1630,1b70,D49	174	42.6

YEAR	TM LG	G	AB	R	H	2B	3B	HR	RBI	BB-IB	HP	SO	AVG	OBP	SLG	AOPS	ABR	SB-CS	FA	FR	RNG	THR	GAMES AT POSITION	DL	BFW
PICCIOLO, ROB	Robert Michael; B2.4.1953 Santa Monica CA; BR/TR/6´2˝/(180–185); [OakA75*S1/4]; d4.9; C16; Col Pepperdine; OF(2/0/1)																								
1977	Oak A	148	419	35	84	12	3	2	22	9-0	1	55	.200	.218	.258	30	-42	1-4	.966	-8	97	88	S148	0	-3.8
1978	Oak A	78	93	16	21	1	0	2	7	2-0	0	13	.226	.242	.301	54	-6	1-1	.958	-5	83	108	S41,2b19,3b13	0	-0.9
1979	Oak A	115	348	37	88	16	2	2	27	3-1	1	45	.253	.261	.328	61	-21	2-1	.964	-14	88	68	S105,2b6,3b4/lf	0	-2.4
1980	Oak A	95	271	32	65	9	2	5	18	2-0	0	63	.240	.245	.343	63	-15	1-1	.977	-25	75	79	S49,2b47/lf	0	-3.4
1981	†Oak A	82	179	23	48	5	3	4	13	5-0	1	22	.268	.290	.397	100	-1	0-1	.981	-16	84	78	S82	0	-1.1
1982	Oak A	18	49	3	11	1	0	0	3	1-0	0	10	.224	.240	.245	35	-5	1-0	.979	4	117	104	S18	0	0.2
	Mil A	22	21	7	6	1	0	0	1	1-0	0	4	.286	.318	.333	83	0	0-0	1.000	-2	44	60	2b11,S6/D	0	-0.2
	Year	40	70	10	17	2	0	0	4	2-0	0	14	.243	.264	.271	49	-5	1-0	.973	2	113	102	S24,2b11/D	0	0.0
1983	Mil A	14	27	2	6	3	0	0	1	0-0	0	4	.222	.214	.333	54	-2	0-0	1.000	1	106	227	S7,2b2,3b2/1D	0	0.0
1984	Cal A	87	119	18	24	6	0	1	9	0-0	0	21	.202	.200	.277	31	-11	0-1	.974	0	101	83	S66,3b13,2b9/rf	0	-0.8
1985	Oak A	71	102	19	28	2	0	1	8	2-0	0	17	.275	.288	.324	72	-4	3-2	.889	-3	100	111	3b19,2b17,1b13,D10,S9	22	-0.7
Total	9	730	1628	192	381	56	10	17	109	25-1	3	254	.234	.246	.312	55	-107	9-11	.970	-66	91	84	S531,2b111,3b51,1b14,D12,O3L	22	-13.1
PICCIUTO, NICK	Nicholas Thomas; B8.27.1921 Newark NJ; D1.10.1997 Winchester VA; BR/TR/5´8.5˝/165; d5.11; Col Michigan St.																								
1945	Phi N	36	89	7	12	6	0	0	6	6	0	17	.135	.189	.202	9	-11	0	.839	-5	89	55	3b30,2b4	0	-1.6
PICINICH, VAL	Valentine John; B9.8.1896 New York NY; D12.5.1942 Nobleboro ME; BR/TR/5´9˝/165; d7.25; Mil 1918; C1																								
1916	Phi A	40	118	8	23	3	1	0	5	6	0	33	.195	.234	.237	44	-9	1	.967	-5	60	102	C37	—	-1.2
1917	Phi A	2	6	0	2	0	0	0	0	1	0	2	.333	.429	.333	135	0	0	.786	-1	78	53	C2	—	-0.1
1918	Was A	47	148	13	34	3	3	0	12	9	0	25	.230	.274	.291	72	-6	0	.960	-3	103	79	C46	—	-0.5
1919	Was A	80	212	18	58	12	3	3	22	17	1	43	.274	.330	.401	106	1	6	.978	10	96	123	C69	—	1.7
1920	Was A	48	133	14	27	6	2	3	14	9	1	33	.203	.259	.346	61	-8	0-0	.978	6	103	96	C45	—	0.1
1921	Was A	45	141	10	39	9	0	0	12	16	1	21	.277	.354	.340	82	-3	0-3	.966	2	154	70	C45	—	0.1
1922	Was A	76	210	16	48	12	2	0	19	23	2	33	.229	.311	.305	64	-11	1-0	.976	5	102	92	C76	—	-0.1
1923	Bos A	87	268	33	74	21	1	2	31	46	2	32	.276	.386	.384	103	4	3-5	.957	-2	80	128	C81	—	0.5
1924	Bos A	69	161	25	44	6	3	1	24	29	3	19	.273	.394	.366	97	0	5-1	.951	-3	94	96	C52	—	0.1
1925	Bos A	90	251	31	64	21	0	1	25	33	1	21	.255	.344	.351	77	-8	2-0	.968	-9	70	75	C74,1b2	—	-1.1
1926	Cin N	89	240	33	63	16	1	2	31	29	0	22	.262	.342	.363	92	-2	4	.967	-3	108	78	C86	—	0.0
1927	Cin N	65	173	16	44	8	3	0	12	24	0	15	.254	.345	.335	85	-3	3	.980	0	83	51	C61	—	0.1
1928	Cin N	96	324	29	98	15	1	7	35	20	0	25	.302	.343	.420	100	-1	1	.983	-1	103	108	C93	—	0.5
1929	Bro N	93	273	28	71	16	6	4	31	34	0	24	.260	.342	.407	86	-6	3	.979	-8	59	**137**	C85	—	-0.9
1930	Bro N	23	46	4	10	3	0	0	3	5	0	6	.217	.294	.283	41	-4	1	.944	-1	94	109	C22	—	-0.4
1931	Bro N	24	45	5	12	4	0	1	4	4	0	9	.267	.327	.422	100	0	1	.967	-0	107	55	C15	—	0.1
1932	Bro N	41	70	8	18	6	0	1	11	4	0	8	.257	.297	.386	84	-2	0	.985	-1	99	75	C24	—	-0.2
1933	Bro N	6	6	1	1	1	0	0	0	0	0	1	.167	.167	.333	42	0	0	.889	-0	54	217	C6	—	-0.1
	Pit N	16	52	6	13	4	0	1	7	5	0	10	.250	.316	.385	99	0	0	.982	-2	81	72	C16	—	-0.1
	Year	22	58	7	14	5	0	1	7	5	0	11	.241	.302	.379	95	0	0	.969	-2	78	88	C22	—	-0.2
Total	18	1037	2877	298	743	166	26	26	298	314	11	382	.258	.334	.361	86	-58	31-9	.970	-15	92	96	C935,1b2	—	-1.5
PICK, CHARLIE	Charles Thomas; B4.10.1888 Brookneal VA; D6.26.1954 Lynchburg VA; BL/TR/5´10˝/160; d9.20																								
1914	Was A	10	23	0	9	0	0	0	1	4	0	4	.391	.481	.391	157	2	1-2	.833	0	73	237	O7(6/0/1)	—	0.1
1915	Was A	3	2	0	0	0	0	0	0	0	0	0	.000	.000	.000	-98	0	0	ø	0	—	—	/H	—	-0.1
1916	Phi A	121	398	29	96	10	3	0	20	40	3	24	.241	.315	.281	83	-8	25-16	.899	5	102	103	3b108,O8(5/3/0)	—	-0.1
1918	†Chi N	29	89	13	29	4	1	0	12	14	0	4	.326	.417	.393	144	6	7	.964	-0	104	74	2b20,3b8	—	0.7
1919	Chi N	75	269	27	65	8	6	0	18	14	5	12	.242	.292	.316	82	-6	17	.946	5	109	109	2b71,3b3	—	0.0
	Bos N	34	114	12	29	1	1	1	7	7	5	5	.254	.325	.307	94	-1	4	.924	-5	86	130	2b21,3b5,O3(2/1/0),1b2	—	-0.6
	Year	109	383	39	94	9	7	1	25	21	10	17	.245	.302	.313	86	-7	21	.942	-0	104	113	2b92,3b8,O3(2/1/0),1b2	—	-0.6
1920	Bos N	95	383	34	105	16	6	2	28	23	3	11	.274	.320	.363	100	0	10-16	.952	0	105	92	2b94	—	-0.2
Total	6	367	1278	115	333	39	17	3	86	102	16	60	.261	.323	.325	95	-7	64-34	.949	5	105	100	2b206,3b124,O18(13/4/1),1b2	—	-0.2
PICK, EDDIE	Edgar Everett; B5.7.1899 Attleboro MA; D5.13.1967 Santa Monica CA; BB/TR/6´0˝/185; d9.13																								
1923	Cin N	9	8	2	3	0	0	0	2	3	0	3	.375	.545	.375	150	1	0-0	1.000	-0	71	0	O4L	—	0.1
1924	Cin N	3	2	0	0	0	0	0	0	0	0	1	.000	.000	.000	-99	-1	0-0	1.000	0	142	0	/lf	—	-0.1
1927	Chi N	54	181	23	31	5	2	2	15	20	0	26	.171	.254	.254	36	-17	0	.910	-5	83	124	3b49/2rf	—	-1.9
Total	3	66	191	25	34	5	2	2	17	23	0	30	.178	.266	.257	40	-17	0-0	.910	-5	83	124	3b49,O6(5/0/1)/2	—	-1.9
PICKERING, CALVIN	Calvin Elroy; B9.29.1976 St.Thomas, V.I.; BL/TL/6´5˝/(260–295); [BalA95 35/976]; d9.12; [DL 2002 Bos A 183]																								
1998	Bal A	9	21	4	5	0	0	2	3	3-0	0	4	.238	.333	.524	120	0	1-0	.969	-1	0	114	1b5,D3	0	-0.1
1999	Bal A	23	40	4	5	1	0	1	5	11-0	0	16	.125	.314	.225	42	-3	0-0	.960	-1	59	166	1b8,D7	0	-0.4
2001	Cin N	4	4	0	1	0	0	0	1	0-0	0	2	.250	.250	.250	28	0	0-0	ø	0	—	—	/H	0	-0.1
	Bos A	17	50	4	14	1	0	3	7	8-0	0	13	.280	.379	.480	124	2	0-0	1.000	-1	71	82	1b12,D2	0	0.0
2004	KC A	35	122	21	30	8	1	7	26	18-1	0	42	.246	.338	.500	116	3	0-0	1.000	-0	75	97	D27,1b8	0	0.0
2005	KC A	7	27	4	4	0	0	1	3	3-0	0	14	.148	.226	.259	32	-3	0-0	ø	0	—	—	D7	0	-0.3
Total	5	95	264	37	59	10	1	14	45	43-1	0	91	.223	.329	.428	97	-1	1-0	.988	-3	61	106	D46,1b33	183	-0.9
PICKERING, OLLIE	Oliver Daniel; B4.9.1870 Olney IL; D1.20.1952 Vincennes IN; BL/TR/5´10˝/175; d8.9																								
1896	Lou N	45	165	28	50	6	4	1	22	12	0	11	.303	.350	.406	103	0	13	.901	3	190	217	O45(3/44/0)	—	0.0
1897	Lou N	64	249	34	62	5	2	1	21	26	2	—	.249	.325	.297	67	-11	20	.938	4	170	109	O63(0/62/1)	—	-1.0
	Cle N	46	182	33	64	5	2	1	22	11	1	—	.352	.392	.418	108	2	18	.950	-1	76	86	O46(1/45/1)/2	—	-0.1
	Year	110	431	67	126	10	4	2	43	37	3	—	.292	.352	.348	85	-9	38	.943	3	130	99	O109(1/107/2)/2	—	-1.1
1901	Cle A	137	547	102	169	25	6	0	40	58	8	—	.309	.383	.377	116	16	36	.949	13	125	**204**	O137(2/110/25)	—	2.0
1902	Cle A	69	293	46	75	5	2	3	26	19	2	—	.256	.306	.317	76	-10	22	.979	-3	62	61	O64(3/57/4),1b2	—	-1.5
1903	Phi A	**137**	512	93	144	18	6	1	36	53	4	—	.281	.353	.346	105	5	40	.970	3	114	135	O135(0/134/1)	—	0.2
1904	Phi A	124	455	56	103	10	3	0	30	45	2	—	.226	.299	.262	74	-12	17	.939	-2	99	61	O121(10/111/0)	—	-2.2
1907	StL A	151	576	63	159	15	10	0	60	35	3	—	.276	.321	.337	110	5	15	.949	-9	75	120	O151(0/22/128)	—	-1.1
1908	Was A	113	373	45	84	7	4	2	30	28	3	—	.225	.285	.282	92	-4	13	.940	-6	57	35	O98(0/27/71)	—	-1.6
Total	8	886	3352	500	910	96	39	9	287	287	25	11	.271	.334	.331	97	-9	194	.949	2	103	116	O860(19/612/231),1b2/2	—	-5.3
PICKERING, URBANE	Urbane Henry "Pick"; B6.3.1899 Hoxie KS; D5.13.1970 Modesto CA; BR/TR/5´10˝/180; d4.18																								
1931	Bos A	103	341	48	86	13	4	9	52	33	0	53	.252	.318	.393	91	-6	3-4	.967	-1	108	64	3b74,2b16	—	-0.4
1932	Bos A	132	457	47	119	28	5	2	40	39	1	71	.260	.320	.357	77	-16	3-4	.941	-5	101	103	3b126/C	—	-1.6
Total	2	235	798	95	205	41	9	11	92	72	1	124	.257	.319	.372	83	-22	6-8	.951	-6	104	88	3b200,2b16/C	—	-2.0
PICKETT, DAVE	David; B5.26.1874 Brookline MA; D4.22.1950 Easton MA; TR/5´7.5˝/170; d7.21																								
1898	Bos N	14	43	3	12	1	0	0	3	6	1	—	.279	.380	.302	91	0	2	.955	-1	67	0	O14L	—	-0.1
PICKETT, JOHN	John Thomas; B2.20.1866 Chicago IL; D7.4.1922 Chicago IL; BR/TR/5´10.5˝/186; d6.6																								
1889	KC AA	53	201	20	45	7	0	0	12	11	2	21	.224	.271	.259	48	-14	7	.900	-11	43	89	O28(23/4/1),3b14,2b11	—	-2.2
1890	Phi P	100	407	82	114	7	9	4	64	40	2	17	.280	.347	.371	90	-7	12	.893	-23	91	94	2b100	—	-2.1
1892	Bal N	36	141	13	30	2	3	1	12	7	2	10	.213	.260	.291	65	-7	2	.915	-1	103	53	2b36	—	-0.5
Total	3	189	749	115	189	16	12	5	88	58	6	48	.252	.311	.326	74	-28	21	.900	-34	93	81	2b147,O28(23/4/1),3b14	—	-4.8
PICKUP, TY	Clarence William; B10.29.1897 Philadelphia PA; D8.2.1974 Philadelphia PA; BR/TR/6´0˝/180; d4.30																								
1918	Phi N	1	1	0	1	0	0	0	0	0	0	0	1.000	1.000	1.000	478	0	0	1.000	0	125	0	/rf	—	0.0
PIEDRA, JORGE	Jorge Moises; B4.19.1979 Sun Valley CA; BL/TL/6´0˝/(190–200); d8.7																								
2004	Col N	38	91	15	27	8	0	3	10	5-0	1	19	.297	.340	.484	97	0	0-1	1.000	-0	96	77	O34(14/18/7)	0	-0.1
2005	Col N	61	112	19	35	8	1	6	16	10-0	1	15	.313	.371	.563	126	4	2-1	1.000	-2	72	90	O26(9/0/17)/D	0	0.2
2006	Col N	43	59	4	10	2	0	3	10	3-0	1	22	.169	.222	.356	41	-6	1-0	1.000	0	117	0	O5(2/1/2),D5	29	-0.5
Total	3	142	262	38	72	18	1	12	36	18-0	3	56	.275	.327	.489	97	-2	3-2	1.000	-2	87	78	O65(25/19/26),D6	29	-0.4
PIERCE, GRACIE	Grayson S.; B New York NY; D8.28.1894 New York NY; BL/TR; d5.2; U3																								
1882	Lou AA	9	33	3	10	1	0	0	—	1	—	—	.303	.324	.333	129	1	—	.864	1	113	131	2b9	—	0.2
	Bal AA	41	151	8	30	2	1	0	—	3	—	—	.199	.214	.225	52	-7	—	.796	-10	92	95	2b38,O3R/S	—	-1.4
	Year	50	184	11	40	3	1	0	—	4	—	—	.217	.234	.245	66	-6	—	.808	-8	96	101	2b47,O3R/S	—	-1.2

YEAR	TM LG	G	AB	R	H	2B	3B	HR	RBI	BB-IB	HP	SO	AVG	OBP	SLG	AOPS	ABR	SB-CS	FA	FR	RNG	THR	GAMES AT POSITION	DL	BFW
1883	Col AA	11	41	5	7	0	0	0	—	0	—	—	.171	.171	.171	11	-4	—	.744	-2	71	141	2b6,O5(0/4/1)	—	-0.5
	NY N	18	62	3	5	0	1	0	2	1	—	9	.081	.095	.113	-37	-10	—	.850	-1	30	183	O18(0/17/1)/2	—	-1.1
1884	NY AA	5	20	2	5	1	0	0	—	0	0	—	.250	.250	.300	81	0	—	1.000	-4	0	0	O3(0/2/1),2b3	—	-0.4
Total	3	84	307	21	57	4	2	0	2	5	0	9	.186	.199	.212	36	-20	—	.795	-15	88	98	2b57,O29(0/23/6)/S	—	-3.2
PIERCE, JACK	Lavern Jack; B6.2.1948 Laurel MS; BL/TR/6´0˝/(210–215); [AtlN69*S3/63]; d4.27; Col San Jose (CA) City																								
1973	Atl N	11	20	0	1	0	0	0	0	1-0	0	8	.050	.095	.050	-55	-4	0-0	1.000	0	133	26	1b6	0	-0.4
1974	Atl N	6	9	1	1	0	0	0	0	1-0	0	0	.111	.200	.111	-11	-1	0-0	.958	0	160	74	1b2	0	-0.1
1975	Det A	53	170	19	40	6	1	8	22	20-1	2	40	.235	.320	.424	105	1	0-0	.971	-4	80	92	1b49	0	-0.7
Total	3	70	199	20	42	6	1	8	22	22-1	2	48	.211	.293	.372	83	-4	0-0	.973	-4	87	86	1b57	0	-1.2
PIERCE, MAURY	Preston Maurice; B3.1859 MD; d4.23																								
1884	Was U	2	7	0	1	0	0	0	—	0	—	—	.143	.143	.143	-14	-1	—	.778	-0	52	0	3b2	—	-0.1
PIERCY, ANDY	Andrew J.; B8.1856 San Jose CA; D12.27.1932 San Jose CA; TR; d5.12																								
1881	Chi N	2	8	1	2	0	0	0	0	0	—	1	.250	.250	.250	55	0	—	.750	-1	0	0	/32	—	-0.2
PIERRE, JUAN	Juan D'Vaughn; B8.14.1977 Mobile AL; BL/TL/6´0˝/(170–180); [ColN98 13/390]; d8.7; Col South Alabama																								
2000	Col N	51	200	26	62	2	0	0	20	13-0	1	15	.310	.353	.320	59	-12	7-6	.975	-2	100	70	O50C	0	-1.4
2001	Col N	156	617	108	202	26	11	2	55	41-1	10	29	.327	.378	.415	87	-10	**46**-17	.979	-5	104	38	O154C	0	-0.9
2002	Col N	152	592	90	170	20	5	1	35	31-0	9	52	.287	.332	.343	69	-26	47-12	.995	-2	108	26	O149C	0	-2.0
2003	†Fla N	**162**	668	100	204	28	7	1	41	55-1	5	35	.305	.361	.373	96	-3	**65**-20	.993	2	106	68	O161C	0	0.8
2004	Fla N	**162**	678	100	**221**	22	**12**	3	49	45-1	8	35	.326	.374	.407	107	7	45-24	.995	-9	94	37	O162C	0	0.1
2005	Fla N	**162**	656	96	181	19	13	2	47	41-1	9	45	.276	.326	.354	83	-19	57-17	.988	-9	90	88	O160C	0	-2.0
2006	Chi N	**162**	699	87	**204**	32	13	3	40	32-0	8	38	.292	.330	.388	82	-21	58-20	**1.000**	-2	102	67	O162C	0	-1.5
Total	7	1007	4110	607	1244	149	61	12	287	258-4	50	249	.303	.350	.377	86	-84	325-116	.991	-28	100	56	O998C	0	-6.9
PIERSALL, JIM	James Anthony; B11.14.1929 Waterbury CT; BR/TR/6´0˝/(175–190); d9.7; C1																								
1950	Bos A	6	7	4	2	0	0	0	0	4	0	0	.286	.545	.286	107	1	0-0	1.000	1	152	0	O2C	0	0.1
1952	Bos A	56	161	28	43	8	0	1	16	28	1	26	.267	.379	.335	93	0	3-3	.928	-2	100	77	S30,O22(0/1/21)/3	0	-0.2
1953	Bos A	151	585	76	159	21	9	3	52	41	9	52	.272	.329	.354	80	-17	11-10	.987	11	**117**	106	O151(1/2/150)	0	-1.3
1954	Bos A★	133	474	77	135	24	2	8	38	36	3	42	.285	.338	.395	90	-6	5-1	.985	-2	96	102	O126(0/30/96)	0	-1.3
1955	Bos A	149	515	68	146	25	5	13	62	67-7	2	52	.283	.364	.427	104	4	6-1	.993	1	103	76	O147C	0	-0.2
1956	Bos A★	**155**	601	91	176	**40**	6	14	87	58-2	1	48	.293	.350	.449	99	-1	7-7	**.991**	7	111	94	O155C	0	-0.2
1957	Bos A	151	609	103	159	27	5	19	63	62-1	4	54	.261	.331	.415	98	-2	14-6	.990	2	104	114	O151C	0	-0.6
1958	Bos A	130	417	55	99	13	5	8	48	42-2	0	43	.237	.303	.350	75	-14	12-2	.985	3	108	120	O125C	0	-1.5
1959	Cle A	100	317	42	78	13	2	4	30	25-1	2	31	.246	.303	.338	79	-9	6-3	.982	1	108	56	O91C/3	0	-1.2
1960	Cle A	138	486	70	137	12	4	18	66	24-3	0	38	.282	.313	.434	104	-1	18-5	.992	9	**122**	68	O134(8/127/2)	0	0.4
1961	Cle A	121	484	81	156	26	7	6	40	43-1	2	46	.322	.378	.442	122	16	8-2	**.991**	8	112	142	O120C	0	2.0
1962	Was A	135	471	38	115	20	4	4	31	39-3	0	53	.244	.301	.329	70	-20	12-7	**.997**	-1	104	83	O132C	0	-2.4
1963	Was A	29	94	9	23	1	0	1	5	6-0	0	11	.245	.284	.287	63	-5	4-0	1.000	0	118	0	O25C	0	-0.5
	NY N	40	124	13	24	4	1	1	10	10-1	0	14	.194	.250	.266	49	-8	1-2	1.000	-2	85	139	O38C	0	-1.2
	LA A	20	52	4	16	1	0	0	4	5-0	0	5	.308	.368	.327	103	0	0-1	1.000	-2	81	0	O18(1/12/5)	0	-0.3
1964	LA A	87	255	28	80	11	0	2	13	16-1	0	32	.314	.353	.380	116	5	5-3	1.000	-2	93	55	O72(48/32/0)	0	0.0
1965	Cal A	53	112	10	30	5	2	2	12	5-1	1	15	.268	.305	.402	101	0	2-2	.984	1	120	0	O41(29/10/4)	55	-0.1
1966	Cal A	75	123	14	26	5	0	0	14	13-0	0	19	.211	.283	.252	58	-6	1-2	.973	-1	93	129	O63(25/14/27)	0	-1.0
1967	Cal A	5	3	0	0	0	0	0	0	0-0	0	2	.000	.000	.000	-99	-1	0-0	1.000	0	474	0	/lf	0	-0.1
Total	17	1734	5890	811	1604	256	52	104	591	524-23	25	583	.272	.332	.386	92	-64	115-57	.990	32	107	94	O1614(113/1214/305),S30,3b2	55	-9.6
PIERSON, DAVE	David P.; B8.20.1855 Wilkes–Barre PA; D11.11.1922 Newark NJ; BR/TR/5´7˝/142; d4.25; b–Dick																								
1876	Cin N	57	233	33	55	4	1	0	13	1	—	9	.236	.239	.262	78	-4	—	.760	-1	—	—	C31,O30(1/0/29)/S32P	—	-0.3
PIERSON, DICK	Edmund Dana; B10.24.1857 Wilkes–Barre PA; D7.20.1922 Newark NJ; TR; d6.23; b–Dave																								
1885	NY AA	3	9	1	1	0	0	0	0	2	0	—	.111	.273	.111	26	-1	—	.682	-3	61	70	2b3	—	-0.3
PIERZYNSKI, A.J.	Anthony John; B12.30.1976 Bridgehampton NY; BL/TR/6´3˝/(218–245); [MinA94 3/71]; d9.9																								
1998	Min A	7	10	1	3	0	0	0	1	1-0	1	2	.300	.385	.300	89	0	0-0	1.000	2	76	73	C6	0	0.2
1999	Min A	9	22	3	6	2	0	0	3	1-0	1	4	.273	.333	.364	74	-1	0-0	1.000	-1	417	49	C9	0	-0.1
2000	Min A	33	88	12	27	5	1	2	11	5-0	2	14	.307	.354	.455	97	0	1-0	1.000	-2	157	88	C32	0	0.0
2001	Min A	114	381	51	110	33	2	7	55	16-4	4	57	.289	.322	.441	94	-3	1-7	.985	3	165	71	C110/D	0	0.4
2002	†Min A★	130	440	54	132	31	6	6	49	13-1	11	61	.300	.334	.439	100	0	1-2	.996	2	143	66	C124	0	0.9
2003	†Min A	137	487	63	152	35	3	11	74	24-12	15	55	.312	.360	.464	112	9	3-1	.993	3	159	64	C135	0	2.1
2004	SF N	131	471	45	128	28	2	11	77	19-4	15	27	.272	.319	.410	84	-11	0-1	.999	-8	126	61	C118	0	-1.2
2005	†Chi A	128	460	61	118	21	0	18	56	23-5	12	68	.257	.308	.420	88	-9	0-2	**.999**	1	81	86	C128	0	0.1
2006	Chi A☆	140	509	65	150	24	0	16	64	22-6	8	72	.295	.333	.436	95	-5	1-0	.997	-7	76	88	C132	0	-0.3
Total	9	829	2868	355	826	179	14	71	390	124-32	69	360	.288	.331	.434	95	-20	7-13	.995	-7	127	73	C794/D	0	2.1
PIET, TONY	Anthony Francis (b Anthony Francis Pietruszka); B12.7.1906 Berwick PA; D12.1.1981 Hinsdale IL; BR/TR/6´0˝/175; d8.15																								
1931	Pit N	44	167	22	50	12	4	0	24	13	1	24	.299	.354	.419	108	2	10	.987	-5	99	62	2b44/S	—	0.0
1932	Pit N	**154**	574	66	162	25	8	7	85	46	7	56	.282	.343	.390	98	-1	19	.970	-26	92	90	2b154	—	-1.7
1933	Pit N	107	362	45	117	21	5	1	42	19	6	28	.323	.367	.417	124	11	12	.955	-8	98	109	2b97	—	1.0
1934	Cin N	106	421	58	109	20	5	1	38	23	6	44	.259	.307	.337	74	-16	6	.934	-9	98	92	3b51,2b49	—	-2.0
1935	Cin N	6	5	2	1	1	0	0	2	0	0	0	.200	.200	.400	59	0	0	1.000	0	145	0	/rf	—	0.0
	Chi A	77	292	47	87	17	5	3	27	33	3	27	.298	.375	.421	103	2	2-1	.975	2	111	85	2b59,3b17	—	0.8
1936	Chi A	109	352	69	96	15	2	7	42	66	9	48	.273	.400	.386	92	-2	15-5	.966	5	120	108	2b68,3b32	—	0.9
1937	Chi A	100	332	34	78	15	1	4	38	32	6	36	.235	.314	.322	61	-20	14-6	.939	1	98	77	3b86,2b13	—	-1.4
1938	Det A	41	80	9	17	6	0	0	14	15	2	11	.213	.351	.287	58	-5	2-4	.919	1	125	90	3b18/2	—	-0.4
Total	8	744	2585	352	717	132	30	23	312	247	40	274	.277	.350	.378	91	-29	80-16	.967	-39	101	95	2b485,3b204/rfS	—	-2.8
PIEZ, SANDY	Charles William; B10.13.1888 New York NY; D12.29.1930 Absecon NJ; BR/TR/5´10˝/170; d4.17; Col Bucknell																								
1914	NY N	37	8	9	3	0	1	0	3	0	0	1	.375	.375	.625	202	1	4	1.000	1	217	0	O5(2/2/1)	—	0.2
PIGNATANO, JOE	Joseph Benjamin; B8.4.1929 Brooklyn NY; BR/TR/5´10˝/(178–183); d4.28; C20																								
1957	Bro N	8	14	0	3	1	0	0	1	0-0	0	5	.214	.214	.286	30	-1	0-0	1.000	1	69	107	C6	0	0.0
1958	LA N	63	142	18	31	4	0	9	17	16-1	2	26	.218	.306	.437	91	-2	4-1	1.000	2	222	145	C57	0	0.2
1959	†LA N	52	139	17	33	4	1	1	11	21-2	2	15	.237	.346	.302	69	-5	1-0	.997	5	201	70	C49	0	0.2
1960	LA N	58	90	11	21	4	0	2	9	15-2	0	17	.233	.343	.344	83	-1	1-1	.984	5	158	155	C40	0	0.5
1961	KC A	92	243	31	59	10	3	4	22	36-2	4	42	.243	.347	.358	88	-3	2-2	.979	4	115	89	C83,3b2	0	0.4
1962	SF N	7	5	2	1	0	0	0	0	4-0	0	0	.200	.556	.200	114	1	0-0	1.000	-1	33	202	C7	0	0.0
	NY N	27	56	2	13	2	0	0	2	2-0	0	11	.232	.259	.268	41	-5	0-0	.991	0	63	99	C25	0	-0.3
	Year	34	61	4	14	2	0	0	2	6-0	0	11	.230	.299	.262	51	-4	0-0	.992	-0	60	110	C32	0	-0.3
Total	6	307	689	81	161	25	4	16	62	94-7	8	116	.234	.332	.351	80	-16	8-4	.990	17	156	109	C267,3b2	0	1.0
PIKE, JAY	Jacob Emanuel; B Brooklyn NY; d8.27; b–Lip																								
1877	Har N	1	4	0	1	0	0	0	0	0	—	0	.250	.250	.250	65	0	—	.000	-1	0	0	/rf	—	-0.1
PIKE, JESS	Jess Willard; B7.31.1915 Dustin OK; D3.28.1984 San Diego CA; BL/TL/6´3˝/175; d4.18																								
1946	NY N	16	41	4	7	1	1	1	6	6	0	9	.171	.277	.317	68	-2	0	.929	-2	71	0	O10(0/6/4)	0	-0.4
PIKE, LIP	Lipman Emanuel; B5.25.1845 New York NY; D10.10.1893 Brooklyn NY; BL/TL/5´8˝/158; d5.9; M3; b–Jay; OF NA(7/98/88)																								
1871	Tro NA	28	130	43	49	10	7	**4**	39	5	—	7	.377	.400	.654	194	15	3-2	.850	2	161	0	O18R,2b7,1b4,M	—	1.1
1872	Bal NA	56	285	68	85	15	5	**7**	**60**	4	—	6	.298	.308	.460	127	7	10-1	.875	-10	0	0	O25(6/5/16),2b24,3b9	—	-0.1
1873	Bal NA	56	285	71	90	15	8	**4**	51	8	—	4	.316	.334	.467	135	12	8-1	.747	-3	114	291	O56(0/2/54),2b2	—	1.0
1874	Har NA	52	234	58	83	**22**	5	1	50	5	—	1	.355	.368	**.504**	168	17	4-1	.856	7	166	118	O27C,S20,2b7/3M	—	1.8
1875	StL NA	**70**	312	61	108	22	12	0	44	3	—	8	.346	.352	.494	**210**	**35**	25-10	.885	-3	51	120	O64(1/64/0),2b10,3b2/S	—	2.8
1876	StL N	63	282	55	91	19	10	1	50	8	—	9	.323	.341	.472	178	24	—	.896	-5	125	**312**	O62C,2b2	—	1.4

YEAR	TM LG	G	AB	R	H	2B	3B	HR	RBI	BB-IB	HP	SO	AVG	OBP	SLG	AOPS	ABR	SB-CS	FA	FR	RNG	THR	GAMES AT POSITION	DL	BFW
1877	Cin N	**58**	262	45	78	12	4	**4**	23	9	—	7	.298	.321	.420	148	16	—	.802	-4	141	67	O38C,2b22,S2,M	—	0.9
1878	Cin N	31	145	28	47	5	1	0	11	4	—	9	.324	.342	.372	149	8	—	.824	-3	56	100	O31C	—	0.3
	Pro N	5	22	4	5	0	1	0	4	1	—	1	.227	.261	.318	90	0	—	.788	-3	78	0	2b5	—	-0.3
	Year	36	167	32	52	5	2	0	15	5	—	10	.311	.331	.365	140	8	—	.824	-6	56	100	O31C,2b5	—	0.0
1881	Wor N	5	18	1	2	0	0	0	0	4	—	3	.111	.273	.111	24	-1	—	.647	-2	65	394	O5C	—	-0.3
1887	NY AA	1	4	0	0	0	0	0	0	0	0	—	.000	.000	.000	-99	-1	0	1.000	-0	0	0	/cf	—	-0.1
Total	5NA	262	1246	301	415	84	37	16	244	25	—	26	.333	.346	.498	162	86	50-15	.846	-7	91	146	O190C,2b50,S21,3b12,1b4	—	6.6
Total	5	163	733	133	223	36	16	5	88	26	0	29	.304	.328	.417	152	46	0	.833	-17	112	201	O137C,2b29,S2	—	1.9

PILARCIK, AL Alfred James; B7.3.1930 Whiting IN; BL/TL/5´10˝/(170–180); d7.13

YEAR	TM LG	G	AB	R	H	2B	3B	HR	RBI	BB-IB	HP	SO	AVG	OBP	SLG	AOPS	ABR	SB-CS	FA	FR	RNG	THR	GAMES AT POSITION	DL	BFW
1956	KC A	69	239	28	60	10	1	4	22	30-1	0	32	.251	.333	.351	81	-6	9-2	.976	-4	83	185	O67(0/64/3)	0	-1.2
1957	Bal A	142	407	52	113	16	3	9	49	53-6	4	28	.278	.359	.398	116	10	14-7	.996	4	97	**181**	O126(2/54/79)	0	1.0
1958	Bal A	141	379	40	92	21	0	1	24	42-1	2	37	.243	.320	.306	78	-10	7-3	.986	-1	105	64	O119(4/32/104)	0	-1.5
1959	Bal A	130	273	37	77	12	1	3	16	30-1	1	25	.282	.355	.366	101	1	9-3	.978	-3	96	70	O106(3/8/102)	0	-0.4
1960	Bal A	104	194	30	48	5	1	4	17	15-2	4	16	.247	.313	.345	79	-6	0-2	1.000	-2	88	135	O75(0/2/74)	0	-1.0
1961	KC A	35	60	9	12	1	1	0	9	6-0	0	7	.200	.269	.250	40	-5	1-0	1.000	2	116	204	O21(0/2/19)	0	-0.4
	Chi A	47	62	9	11	1	0	1	6	9-0	0	5	.177	.282	.242	42	-5	1-1	.944	1	100	257	O17(2/14/1)	0	-0.5
	Year	82	122	18	23	2	1	1	15	15-0	0	12	.189	.275	.246	41	-10	2-1	.971	3	108	231	O38(2/16/20)	0	-0.9
Total	6	668	1614	205	413	66	7	22	143	185-11	11	150	.256	.334	.346	89	-21	41-18	.986	-3	96	134	O531(11/176/382)	0	-4.0

PILNEY, ANDY Antone James; B1.19.1913 Frontenac KS; D9.15.1996 Kenner LA; BR/TR/5´11˝/174; d6.12; Col Notre Dame

YEAR	TM LG	G	AB	R	H	2B	3B	HR	RBI	BB-IB	HP	SO	AVG	OBP	SLG	AOPS	ABR	SB-CS	FA	FR	RNG	THR	GAMES AT POSITION	DL	BFW
1936	Bos N	3	2	0	0	0	0	0	0	0	0	1	.000	.000	.000	-99	-1	0	ø	0	—	—	/H	—	-0.1

PINELLI, BABE Ralph Arthur (b Rinaldo Angelo Paolinelli); B10.18.1895 San Francisco CA; D10.22.1984 Daly City CA; BR/TR/5´9˝/165; d8.3; U22

YEAR	TM LG	G	AB	R	H	2B	3B	HR	RBI	BB-IB	HP	SO	AVG	OBP	SLG	AOPS	ABR	SB-CS	FA	FR	RNG	THR	GAMES AT POSITION	DL	BFW
1918	Chi A	24	78	7	18	1	1	1	7	7	1	8	.231	.302	.308	83	-2	3	.847	-7	72	99	3b24	—	-0.9
1920	Det A	102	284	33	65	9	3	0	21	25	2	16	.229	.296	.282	55	-19	6-8	.954	12	112	167	3b74,S18/2	—	-0.5
1922	Cin N	**156**	547	77	167	19	7	1	72	48	6	37	.305	.368	.371	93	-4	17-22	.945	22	**117**	83	3b156	—	2.2
1923	Cin N	117	423	44	117	14	5	0	51	27	0	29	.277	.320	.333	74	-16	10-14	.938	7	**109**	88	3b116	—	-0.5
1924	Cin N	144	510	61	156	16	7	0	70	32	5	32	.306	.353	.365	94	-4	23-17	.956	24	**119**	94	3b143	—	2.8
1925	Cin N	130	492	68	139	33	6	2	49	22	2	28	.283	.316	.386	80	-15	8-19	.945	17	**124**	113	3b109,S17	—	0.5
1926	Cin N	71	207	26	46	7	4	0	24	15	3	5	.222	.284	.295	58	-13	2	.978	2	127	82	3b40,S27,2b3	—	-0.7
1927	Cin N	30	76	11	15	2	0	1	4	6	1	7	.197	.265	.263	43	-6	2	.968	-1	107	73	3b15,S9,2b5	—	-0.5
Total	8	774	2617	327	723	101	33	5	298	182	20	162	.276	.328	.346	79	-79	71-80	.947	77	116	100	3b677,S71,2b9	—	2.4

PINIELLA, LOU Louis Victor; B8.28.1943 Tampa FL; BR/TR/6´2˝/(182–200); d9.4; M19/C2; Col Tampa

YEAR	TM LG	G	AB	R	H	2B	3B	HR	RBI	BB-IB	HP	SO	AVG	OBP	SLG	AOPS	ABR	SB-CS	FA	FR	RNG	THR	GAMES AT POSITION	DL	BFW
1964	Bal A	4	1	0	0	0	0	0	0	0-0	0	0	.000	.000	.000	-99	0	0-0	ø	0	—	—	/H	0	0.0
1968	Cle A	6	5	1	0	0	0	0	1	0-0	0	0	.000	.000	.000	-99	-1	0-0	1.000	-0	85	0	O2L	0	-0.2
1969	KC A	135	493	43	139	21	6	11	68	33-2	3	56	.282	.325	.416	106	3	2-4	.977	10	112	128	O129(126/3/0)	0	0.4
1970	KC A	144	542	54	163	24	5	11	88	35-6	2	42	.301	.342	.424	111	7	3-6	.984	-1	98	68	O139L/1	0	-0.4
1971	KC A	126	448	43	125	21	5	3	51	21-4	2	43	.279	.311	.368	93	-5	5-3	.986	-2	93	85	O115L	34	-1.5
1972	KC A★	151	574	65	179	**33**	4	11	72	34-9	8	59	.312	.356	.441	138	26	7-2	.976	-2	99	69	O150L	0	1.8
1973	KC A	144	513	53	128	28	1	9	69	30-7	2	65	.250	.291	.361	77	-16	5-7	.986	-7	80	104	O128L,D9	0	-3.2
1974	NY A	140	518	71	158	26	0	9	70	32-7	2	58	.305	.341	.407	118	11	1-8	.989	9	104	176	O130(99/0/34)/1D	0	1.1
1975	NY A	74	199	7	39	4	1	0	22	16-3	3	22	.196	.262	.226	41	-16	0-0	.986	-1	84	162	O46(15/0/31),D12	19	-2.0
1976	†NY A	100	327	36	92	16	6	3	38	18-8	2	34	.281	.322	.394	110	3	0-1	.982	2	106	113	O49(10/0/39),D38	0	0.1
1977	†NY A	103	339	47	112	19	3	12	45	20-3	1	31	.330	.365	.510	138	17	2-2	.975	-4	82	58	O51(24/0/27),D43/1	0	0.9
1978	†NY A	130	472	67	148	34	5	6	69	34-8	2	36	.314	.361	.445	128	18	3-1	.969	-2	103	58	O103(78/2/25),D23	0	1.1
1979	NY A	130	461	49	137	22	2	11	69	17-6	2	31	.297	.320	.425	102	0	3-2	.982	1	93	161	O112(84/0/29),D16	0	-0.5
1980	†NY A	116	321	39	92	18	0	2	27	29-5	0	20	.287	.343	.361	95	-1	0-2	.971	-1	97	134	O104(102/1/1),D7	0	-0.6
1981	†NY A	60	159	16	44	9	0	5	18	13-4	0	9	.277	.331	.428	119	4	0-1	.986	2	118	99	O36(11/0/25),D19	15	0.4
1982	NY A	102	261	33	80	17	1	6	37	18-6	1	18	.307	.352	.448	120	7	0-1	1.000	-0	98	87	D55,O40(13/0/27)	0	0.4
1983	NY A	53	148	19	43	9	1	2	16	11-3	1	12	.291	.344	.405	109	2	1-1	.959	-1	87	139	O43(15/0/28)/D	18	-0.1
1984	NY A	29	86	8	26	4	1	1	6	7-1	0	5	.302	.355	.407	114	2	0-0	1.000	1	90	210	O24(15/0/9),D2	0	0.1
Total	18	1747	5867	651	1705	305	41	102	766	368-82	31	541	.291	.333	.409	108	61	32-41	.981	4	97	109	O1401(1126/6/275),D231,1b3	86	-2.2

PINKHAM, ED Edward; B1846 Brooklyn NY; D12.19.1906 Brooklyn NY; BL/TL/5´7˝/142; d5.8; ▲

YEAR	TM LG	G	AB	R	H	2B	3B	HR	RBI	BB-IB	HP	SO	AVG	OBP	SLG	AOPS	ABR	SB-CS	FA	FR	RNG	THR	GAMES AT POSITION	DL	BFW
1871	Chi NA	24	95	27	25	5	5	1	17	**18**	—	3	.263	.381	.453	125	2	5-2	.754	9	159	57	3b18,O8R,P3	—	0.7

PINKNEY, GEORGE George Burton; B1.11.1859 Orange Prairie IL; D11.10.1926 Peoria IL; BR/TR/5´7˝/160; d8.16

YEAR	TM LG	G	AB	R	H	2B	3B	HR	RBI	BB-IB	HP	SO	AVG	OBP	SLG	AOPS	ABR	SB-CS	FA	FR	RNG	THR	GAMES AT POSITION	DL	BFW
1884	Cle N	36	144	18	45	9	0	0	16	10	—	7	.313	.357	.375	126	5	—	.848	-6	83	93	2b25,S11	—	0.0
1885	Bro AA	110	447	77	124	16	5	0	42	27	7	—	.277	.328	.336	109	6	—	.904	-6	101	66	2b57,3b51,S3	—	0.2
1886	Bro AA	**141**	597	119	156	22	7	0	37	**70**	0	—	.261	.339	.322	106	7	32	.858	-16	84	83	3b141/P	—	-0.6
1887	Bro AA	**138**	580	133	155	26	6	3	69	61	6	—	.267	.343	.348	92	-5	59	**.890**	15	107	122	3b136,S2	—	1.0
1888	Bro AA	**143**	575	**134**	156	18	8	4	52	66	12	—	.271	.358	.351	128	21	51	.898	-27	76	78	3b143	—	-0.3
1889	†Bro AA	**138**	545	103	134	25	7	4	82	59	7	43	.246	.327	.339	90	-7	47	**.897**	-9	95	83	3b138	—	-1.1
1890	†Bro N	126	485	115	150	20	9	7	83	80	4	19	.309	.411	.431	145	31	47	.933	-16	84	78	3b126	—	1.5
1891	Bro N	135	501	80	137	19	6	2	71	67	7	32	.273	.367	.347	109	9	44	.904	-18	89	52	3b130,S5	—	-0.6
1892	StL N	78	290	31	50	3	2	0	25	36	2	26	.172	.268	.197	43	-19	4	.888	-8	92	93	3b78	—	-2.4
1893	Lou N	118	446	64	105	12	6	1	62	50	8	8	.235	.323	.296	71	-17	12	.923	2	105	**114**	3b118	—	-1.1
Total	10	1163	4610	874	1212	170	56	21	539	526	53	135	.263	.345	.338	103	31	296	.897	-90	91	86	3b1061,2b82,S21/P	—	-3.4

PINSON, VADA Vada Edward; B8.11.1938 Memphis TN; D10.21.1995 Oakland CA; BL/TL/5´11˝/(170–187); d4.15; C16

YEAR	TM LG	G	AB	R	H	2B	3B	HR	RBI	BB-IB	HP	SO	AVG	OBP	SLG	AOPS	ABR	SB-CS	FA	FR	RNG	THR	GAMES AT POSITION	DL	BFW
1958	Cin N	27	96	20	26	7	0	1	8	11-0	1	18	.271	.352	.375	88	-1	2-1	1.000	1	96	189	O27(4/5/18)	0	-0.1
1959	Cin N★	**154**	648	**131**	205	**47**	9	20	84	55-3	1	98	.316	.371	.509	128	26	21-6	.984	6	111	122	O154C	0	2.7
1960	Cin N★	**154**	652	107	187	**37**	12	20	61	47-3	5	96	.287	.339	.472	117	14	32-12	.981	-2	100	91	O154C	0	0.8
1961	†Cin N	**154**	607	101	**208**	34	8	16	87	39-1	1	63	.343	.379	.504	131	27	23-10	.976	8	106	169	O153C	0	3.1
1962	Cin N	155	619	107	181	31	7	23	100	45-7	4	68	.292	.341	.477	114	11	26-8	.989	-2	96	129	O152C	0	0.8
1963	Cin N	**162**	652	96	**204**	37	**14**	22	106	36-3	1	80	.313	.347	.514	141	32	27-8	.979	0	104	89	O162(0/147/17)	0	3.2
1964	Cin N	156	625	99	166	23	11	23	84	42-2	5	99	.266	.316	.448	109	6	8-2	.972	-6	91	148	O156C	0	-0.4
1965	Cin N	159	669	97	204	34	10	22	94	43-3	7	81	.305	.352	.484	125	21	21-8	**.992**	2	105	103	O159C	0	2.2
1966	Cin N	156	618	70	178	35	6	16	76	33-6	5	83	.288	.326	.442	103	3	18-10	.964	0	106	88	O154(0/139/24)	0	-0.3
1967	Cin N	158	650	90	187	28	**13**	18	66	26-1	3	86	.288	.318	.454	106	4	26-8	.986	-5	98	46	O157C	0	-0.3
1968	Cin N	130	499	60	135	29	6	5	48	32-8	0	59	.271	.311	.383	102	1	17-11	.978	-5	92	90	O123(1/120/3)	0	-0.9
1969	StL N	132	495	58	126	22	6	10	70	35-2	3	63	.255	.303	.384	92	-7	4-4	**.996**	-3	99	64	O124(0/1/124)	0	-1.7
1970	Cle A	148	574	74	164	28	6	24	82	28-7	3	69	.286	.319	.481	113	8	7-6	.982	4	109	94	O141(15/14/120),1b7	0	0.4
1971	Cle A	146	566	60	149	23	4	11	35	21-0	6	58	.263	.295	.376	82	-15	25-6	.978	1	99	130	O141(9/100/39),1b3	0	-1.7
1972	Cal A	136	484	56	133	24	2	7	49	30-12	5	54	.275	.321	.376	114	7	17-6	.991	-2	90	124	O134(104/15/29)/1	0	0.0
1973	Cal A	124	466	56	121	14	6	8	57	20-3	0	55	.260	.286	.367	90	-9	5-5	.965	-1	92	144	O120(75/32/25)	0	-1.7
1974	KC A	115	406	46	112	18	2	6	41	21-4	2	45	.276	.312	.374	92	-5	21-5	.980	-3	91	115	O110(14/6/91)/1D	0	-1.1
1975	KC A	103	319	38	71	14	5	4	22	10-4	2	21	.223	.248	.335	63	-17	5-6	.993	-1	96	104	O82(12/12/59),1b4,D5	0	-2.4
Total	18	2469	9645	1366	2757	485	127	256	1170	574-69	54	1196	.286	.327	.442	110	106	305-122	.981	-7	100	109	O2403(234/1676/549),1b16,D7	0	2.6

PIPP, WALLY Walter Clement; B2.17.1893 Chicago IL; D1.11.1965 Grand Rapids MI; BL/TL/6´1˝/180; d6.29; Mil 1918; Col Catholic America

YEAR	TM LG	G	AB	R	H	2B	3B	HR	RBI	BB-IB	HP	SO	AVG	OBP	SLG	AOPS	ABR	SB-CS	FA	FR	RNG	THR	GAMES AT POSITION	DL	BFW
1913	Det A	12	31	3	5	0	3	0	5	2	1	6	.161	.235	.355	73	-2	0	.977	-1	85	136	1b10	—	-0.2
1915	NY A	136	479	59	118	20	13	4	60	66	1	81	.246	.339	.367	112	7	18-7	**.992**	2	104	**125**	1b134	—	0.8
1916	NY A	151	545	70	143	20	14	**12**	93	54	2	82	.262	.331	.417	122	12	16	.992	5	111	**112**	1b148	—	1.4
1917	NY A	**155**	587	82	143	29	12	**9**	70	60	6	66	.244	.320	.380	112	7	11	.990	4	109	110	1b155	—	0.8
1918	NY A	91	349	48	106	15	9	2	44	22	0	34	.304	.345	.415	127	9	11	.988	1	101	130	1b91	—	0.8
1919	NY A	138	523	74	144	23	10	7	50	39	4	42	.275	.330	.398	103	0	9	.991	0	99	112	1b138	—	-0.3
1920	NY A	153	610	109	171	30	14	11	76	48	6	54	.280	.339	.430	99	-3	4-10	.991	0	99	**121**	1b153	—	-0.9
1921	†NY A	**153**	588	96	174	35	9	8	97	45	1	28	.296	.347	.427	94	-6	17-10	.991	-5	88	**114**	1b153	—	-2.0
1922	†NY A	152	577	96	190	32	10	9	90	56	4	32	.329	.392	.466	120	18	7-12	.993	-6	85	107	1b152	—	-0.1
1923	†NY A	144	569	79	173	19	8	6	108	36	6	28	.304	.352	.397	95	-6	6-13	.992	-4	87	99	1b144	—	-2.2
1924	NY A	**153**	589	88	174	30	**19**	9	114	51	0	36	.295	.352	.457	108	3	12-5	**.994**	1	98	96	1b153	—	-0.5
1925	NY A	62	178	19	41	6	3	3	24	13	1	12	.230	.286	.348	61	-12	3-3	.991	4	131	119	1b47	—	-1.0

YEAR	TM LG	G	AB	R	H	2B	3B	HR	RBI	BB-IB	HP	SO	AVG	OBP	SLG	AOPS	ABR	SB-CS	FA	FR	RNG	THR	GAMES AT POSITION	DL	BFW
1926	Cin N	155	574	72	167	22	15	6	99	49	5	26	.291	.352	.413	108	5	8	.992	2	104	**123**	1b155	—	-0.3
1927	Cin N	122	443	49	115	19	6	2	41	32	0	11	.260	.309	.343	77	-15	2	**.996**	1	97	104	1b114	—	-2.2
1928	Cin N	95	272	30	77	11	3	2	26	23	1	13	.283	.341	.368	87	-5	1	.989	1	109	124	1b72	—	-0.8
Total	15	1872	6914	974	1941	311	148	90	997	596	38	551	.281	.341	.408	104	12	125-60	.992	6	100	113	1b1819	—	-6.7
PIRIE, JIM	James Moir; B3.31.1853 Ontario, Can; D6.2.1934 Dundas ON, Can.; BB/5´8˝/169; d9.25																								
1883	Phi N	5	19	1	3	0	0	0	0	0	—	2	.158	.158	.158	-4	-2	—	.577	-4	66	65	S5	—	-0.5
PIRKL, GREG	Gregory Daniel; B8.7.1970 Long Beach CA; BR/TR/6´5˝/(225–240); [SeaA88 2/44]; d8.13																								
1993	Sea A	7	23	1	4	0	0	1	4	0-0	0	4	.174	.174	.304	25	-3	0-0	1.000	1	149	186	1b5,D2	0	-0.2
1994	Sea A	19	53	7	14	3	0	6	11	1-1	1	12	.264	.286	.660	133	2	0-0	.983	-1	24	48	D10,1b7	0	0.0
1995	Sea A	10	17	2	4	0	0	0	0	1-0	0	7	.235	.278	.235	35	-2	0-0	1.000	0	109	28	1b6/D	71	-0.2
1996	Sea A	7	21	2	4	1	0	1	1	0-0	0	3	.190	.190	.381	39	-2	0-0	1.000	0	160	115	1b2,D3	0	-0.2
	Bos A	2	2	0	0	0	0	0	0	0-0	0	1	.000	.000	.000	-98	-1	0-0	ø	0	—	—	/H	0	-0.1
	Year	9	23	2	4	1	0	1	1	0-0	0	4	.174	.174	.348	27	-3	0-0	1.000	0	160	115	D3,1b2	0	-0.3
Total	4	45	116	12	26	4	0	8	16	2-1	1	27	.224	.242	.466	77	-6	0-0	.994	0	93	90	1b20,D16	71	-0.7
PISONI, JIM	James Pete; B8.14.1929 St.Louis MO; BR/TR/5´10˝/(169–172); d9.25																								
1953	StL A	3	12	1	1	0	0	1	1	0	0	5	.083	.083	.333	8	-2	0-0	1.000	-0	106	0	O3(0/2/1)	0	-0.2
1956	KC A	10	30	4	8	0	0	2	5	2-0	0	8	.267	.303	.467	103	0	0-0	.966	3	117	517	O9L	0	0.3
1957	KC A	44	97	14	23	2	2	3	12	10-1	2	17	.237	.318	.392	92	-1	0-0	.989	2	108	132	O44(0/44/1)	0	-0.1
1959	Mil N	9	24	4	4	1	0	0	0	2-0	0	6	.167	.231	.208	20	-3	0-0	.941	0	105	263	O9(2/8/0)	0	-0.3
	NY A	17	17	2	3	0	1	0	1	1-0	0	9	.176	.222	.294	42	-2	0-0	1.000	1	128	0	O15(9/3/3)	0	-0.1
1960	NY A	20	9	1	1	0	0	0	1	1-0	0	2	.111	.200	.111	-14	-1	0-0	.938	0	124	0	O18(12/6/0)	0	-0.2
Total	5	103	189	26	40	3	3	6	20	16-1	2	47	.212	.278	.354	71	-9	0-0	.978	6	112	175	O98(32/63/5)	0	-0.6
PITKO, ALEX	Alexander "Spunk"; B11.22.1914 Burlington NJ; BR/TR/5´10˝/180; d9.11																								
1938	Phi N	7	19	2	6	1	0	0	2	3	0	3	.316	.409	.368	118	1	1	.889	-1	86	0	O7R	—	0.0
1939	Was A	4	8	0	1	0	0	0	1	1	0	3	.125	.222	.125	-10	-1	0-0	1.000	-0	87	0	O3(2/0/1)	—	-0.2
Total	2	11	27	2	7	1	0	0	3	4	0	6	.259	.355	.296	80	0	1-0	.917	-1	86	0	O10(2/0/8)	—	-0.2
PITLER, JAKE	Jacob Albert; B4.22.1894 New York NY; D2.3.1968 Binghamton NY; BR/TR/5´8˝/150; d5.30; C11																								
1917	Pit N	109	382	39	89	8	5	0	23	30	5	24	.233	.297	.280	75	-11	6	**.966**	-15	85	90	2b106,O3(1/0/1)	—	-2.8
1918	Pit N	2	1	1	0	0	0	0	0	1	0	0	.000	.500	.000	55	0	2	.667	-0	97	0	/2	—	0.0
Total	2	111	383	40	89	8	5	0	23	31	5	24	.232	.298	.279	75	-11	8	.962	-16	85	89	2b107,O3(1/0/1)	—	-2.8
PITTARO, CHRIS	Christopher Francis; B9.16.1961 Trenton NJ; BB/TR/5´11˝/(161–170); [DetA82 6/152]; d4.8; Col North Carolina																								
1985	Det A	28	62	10	15	3	1	0	7	5-0	0	13	.242	.299	.323	70	-3	1-1	.881	-2	92	37	3b22,2b4/D	18	-0.5
1986	Min A	11	21	0	2	0	0	0	0	0-0	0	8	.095	.095	.095	-47	-4	0-0	.969	0	92	180	2b8,S4	0	-0.4
1987	Min A	14	12	6	4	0	0	0	0	1-0	0	0	.333	.385	.333	89	0	1-0	1.000	-2	48	108	2b8,D2	0	-0.2
Total	3	53	95	16	21	3	1	0	7	6-0	0	21	.221	.267	.274	47	-7	2-1	.881	-4	92	37	3b22,2b20,S4,D3	18	-1.1
PITTINGER, PINKY	Clarke Alonzo; B2.24.1899 Hudson MI; D11.4.1977 Ft.Lauderdale FL; BR/TR/5´10˝/160; d4.15; Col Ohio St.																								
1921	Bos A	40	91	6	18	1	0	0	5	4	0	13	.198	.232	.209	13	-12	3-2	.985	3	117	132	O27(19/4/4),3b3,S2/2	—	-1.0
1922	Bos A	66	186	16	48	3	0	0	7	9	2	10	.258	.299	.274	51	-14	2-5	.920	-2	97	136	3b33,S29	—	-1.2
1923	Bos A	60	177	15	38	5	0	0	15	5	0	10	.215	.236	.243	26	-20	3-1	.959	-8	87	61	2b42,S10,3b3	—	-2.5
1925	Chi N	59	173	21	54	7	2	0	15	12	2	7	.312	.364	.376	88	-3	5-4	.940	2	100	69	S24,3b24	—	0.2
1927	Cin N	31	84	17	23	5	0	1	10	2	0	5	.274	.291	.369	78	-3	4	.963	1	111	158	2b20,S9,3b2	—	-0.1
1928	Cin N	40	38	12	9	0	1	0	4	0	0	1	.237	.237	.289	37	-4	2	.892	4	145	221	S12,2b4,3b4	—	0.1
1929	Cin N	77	210	31	62	11	0	0	27	5	2	4	.295	.318	.348	68	-11	8	.956	2	99	130	S50,3b8,2b4	—	-0.3
Total	7	373	959	118	252	32	3	1	83	37	6	50	.263	.294	.306	55	-67	27-12	.938	1	102	103	S136,3b77,2b71,O27(19/4/4)	—	-4.8
PITTMAN, JOE	Joseph Wayne; B1.1.1954 Houston TX; BR/TR/6´1˝/180; [HouN75 5/110]; d4.25; Col Southern A&M																								
1981	†Hou N	52	135	11	38	4	2	0	7	11-3	0	16	.281	.333	.341	98	-1	4-4	.980	-6	90	82	2b35,3b4	0	-0.6
1982	Hou N	15	10	0	2	1	0	0	0	0-0	0	2	.200	.200	.300	41	-1	0-0	1.000	0	76	0	3b3/rf	0	-0.1
	SD N	55	118	16	30	2	0	0	7	9-2	0	13	.254	.307	.271	67	-5	8-3	.964	-6	101	106	2b30,S13	0	-0.9
	Year	70	128	16	32	3	0	0	7	9-2	0	15	.250	.299	.273	65	-6	8-3	.964	-6	101	106	2b30,S13,3b3/rf	0	-1.0
1984	SF N	17	22	2	5	0	0	0	2	0-0	0	6	.227	.217	.227	29	-2	1-1	.900	-4	89	0	S6,2b5,3b2	0	-0.6
Total	3	139	285	29	75	7	2	0	16	20-5	0	37	.263	.309	.302	78	-9	13-8	.974	-16	94	91	2b70,S19,3b9/rf	0	-2.2
PITTS, GAYLEN	Gaylen Richard; B6.6.1946 Wichita KS; BR/TR/6´1˝/175; d5.12; C5																								
1974	Oak A	18	41	4	10	3	0	0	3	5-0	0	4	.244	.326	.317	91	0	0-0	.909	-1	96	57	3b11,2b6/1	0	-0.1
1975	Oak A	10	3	1	1	1	0	0	1	0-0	0	0	.333	.333	.667	180	0	0-0	.800	1	124	0	3b6,S2/2	0	0.1
Total	2	28	44	5	11	4	0	0	4	5-0	0	4	.250	.327	.341	97	0	0-0	.895	-0	99	51	3b17,2b7,S2/1	0	0.0
PITZ, HERMAN	Herman; B7.18.1865 Brooklyn NY; D9.3.1924 Far Rockaway NY; 5´6˝/140; d4.18																								
1890	Bro AA	61	189	26	26	0	0	0	6	45	3	—	.138	.312	.138	34	-12	25	.885	-11	*82*	*96*	C34,3b16,O9(5/0/4),S2/2	—	-1.8
	Syr AA	29	95	17	21	0	0	0	3	13	1	—	.221	.321	.221	67	-3	14	.929	-7	*79*	*108*	C27/Scf	—	-0.7
	Year	90	284	43	47	0	0	0	9	58	4	—	.165	.315	.165	44	-15	39	.906	-17	*81*	*101*	C61,3b16,O10(5/1/4),S3/2	—	-2.5
PLANTIER, PHIL	Phillip Alan; B1.27.1969 Manchester NH; BL/TR/5´11˝/(175–205); [BosA87 11/292]; d8.21																								
1990	Bos A	14	15	1	2	1	0	0	3	4-0	1	6	.133	.333	.200	55	-1	0-0	ø	-0	0	0	/lfD	0	-0.1
1991	Bos A	53	148	27	49	7	1	11	35	23-2	1	38	.331	.420	.615	174	15	1-0	.976	2	120	46	O40(16/0/27),D5	0	1.6
1992	Bos A	108	349	46	86	19	0	7	30	44-8	2	83	.246	.332	.361	88	-4	2-3	.975	1	100	125	O76(13/0/63),D23	0	-0.7
1993	SD N	138	462	67	111	20	1	34	100	61-7	7	124	.240	.335	.509	122	14	4-5	.990	10	106	147	O134L	15	1.8
1994	SD N	96	341	44	75	21	0	18	41	36-6	5	91	.220	.302	.440	94	-4	3-1	.988	1	97	97	O91L	0	-0.6
1995	Hou N	22	68	12	17	2	0	4	15	11-1	1	19	.250	.349	.456	122	2	0-0	.962	-2	80	0	O20(8/0/12)	51	-0.1
	SD N	54	148	21	38	4	0	5	19	17-2	0	29	.257	.333	.385	91	-2	1-1	.958	3	104	238	O39L	0	-0.1
	Year	76	216	33	55	6	0	9	34	28-3	1	48	.255	.339	.407	101	0	1-1	.959	1	96	162	O59(47/0/12)	0	-0.2
1996	Oak A	73	231	29	49	8	1	7	31	28-0	3	56	.212	.304	.346	65	-13	2-2	.973	4	102	175	O68(67/1/1)/D	0	-1.1
1997	SD N	10	8	0	1	0	0	0	0	2-0	0	3	.125	.300	.125	17	-1	0-0	1.000	0	125	0	O3L	36	-0.1
	StL N	42	113	13	29	8	0	5	18	11-1	3	27	.257	.333	.460	106	1	0-3	.981	-1	96	48	O32(10/0/23)	51	-0.2
	Year	52	121	13	30	8	0	5	18	13-1	3	30	.248	.331	.438	102	0	0-3	.982	-1	97	46	O35(13/0/23)	0	-0.3
Total	8	610	1883	260	457	90	3	91	292	237-27	23	476	.243	.332	.439	103	7	13-15	.980	17	102	126	O504(382/1/126),D33	153	0.4
PLARSKI, DON	Donald Joseph; B11.9.1929 Chicago IL; D12.29.1981 St.Louis MO; BR/TR/5´6˝/160; d7.20																								
1955	KC A	8	11	0	1	0	0	0	0	0-0	0	2	.091	.091	.091	-50	-2	1-0	1.000	-0	105	0	O6C	0	-0.2
PLASKETT, ELMO	Elmo Alexander; B6.27.1938 Frederiksted, V.I.; D11.2.1998 Christiansted, V.I.; BR/TR/5´10˝/190; d9.8																								
1962	Pit N	7	14	2	4	0	0	1	3	1-0	0	3	.286	.333	.500	120	0	0-0	1.000	-1	76	0	C4	0	-0.1
1963	Pit N	10	21	1	3	0	0	0	2	0-0	0	5	.143	.143	.143	-17	-3	0-0	1.000	-1	0	0	C5/3	0	-0.5
Total	2	17	35	3	7	0	0	1	5	1-0	0	8	.200	.222	.286	41	-3	0-0	1.000	-3	34	0	C9/3	0	-0.6
PLATT, WHITEY	Mizell George; B8.21.1920 W.Palm Beach FL; D7.27.1970 W.Palm Beach FL; BR/TR/6´2˝/195; d9.16; Mil 1944–45																								
1942	Chi N	4	16	1	1	0	0	0	2	0	0	3	.063	.063	.063	-66	-3	0	1.000	0	87	352	O4(2/2/0)	0	-0.4
1943	Chi N	20	41	2	7	3	0	0	2	1	0	7	.171	.190	.244	25	-4	0	.952	-1	98	0	O14(7/7/0)	0	-0.6
1946	Chi A	84	247	28	62	8	5	3	32	17	3	34	.251	.307	.360	89	-5	1-7	.971	-1	96	93	O61(25/23/14)	0	-1.2
1948	StL A	123	454	57	123	22	10	7	82	39	2	51	.271	.331	.410	94	-6	1-4	.948	-7	92	60	O114L	0	-2.3
1949	StL A	102	244	29	63	8	2	3	29	24	0	27	.258	.325	.344	74	-10	0-1	.986	1	108	73	O59L,1b2	0	-1.3
Total	5	333	1002	117	256	41	17	13	147	81	5	122	.255	.314	.369	83	-28	2-12	.964	-8	97	73	O252(207/32/14),1b2	0	-5.8
PLATTE, AL	Alfred Frederick Joseph; B4.13.1890 Grand Rapids MI; D8.29.1976 Grand Rapids MI; BL/TL/5´7˝/160; d9.1																								
1913	Det A	9	18	1	2	1	0	0	0	1	0	1	.111	.158	.167	-5	-2	0	.800	-1	96	0	O5L	—	-0.4
PLESS, RANCE	Rance; B12.6.1925 Greeneville TN; BR/TR/6´0˝/195; d4.21																								
1956	KC A	48	85	4	23	3	1	0	9	10-0	1	13	.271	.354	.329	81	-2	0-1	1.000	2	83	141	1b15,3b5	0	-0.2

YEAR	TM LG	G	AB	R	H	2B	3B	HR	RBI	BB-IB	HP	SO	AVG	OBP	SLG	AOPS	ABR	SB-CS	FA	FR	RNG	THR	GAMES AT POSITION	DL	BFW
PLEWS, HERB	Herbert Eugene; B6.14.1928 Helena MT; BL/TR/5´11˝/(160–165); d4.18; Col Illinois																								
1956	Was A	91	256	24	69	10	7	1	25	26-3	1	40	.270	.337	.375	88	-5	1-2	.947	-2	110	77	2b66,S5,3b2	0	-0.3
1957	Was A	104	329	51	89	19	4	1	26	28-1	2	39	.271	.326	.362	90	-4	0-3	.979	-7	94	76	2b79,3b11,S4	0	-0.7
1958	Was A	111	380	46	98	12	6	2	29	17-1	1	45	.258	.291	.337	74	-15	2-3	.976	-6	102	91	2b64,3b36	0	-1.8
1959	Was A	27	40	4	9	0	0	0	2	3-0	0	5	.225	.279	.225	40	-3	0-1	.971	1	108	55	2b6	0	-0.2
	Bos A	13	12	0	1	1	0	0	0	0-0	0	4	.083	.083	.167	-32	-2	0-0	.833	1	211	400	2b2	0	-0.1
	Year	40	52	4	10	1	0	0	2	3-0	0	9	.192	.236	.212	24	-6	0-1	.951	2	114	76	2b8	0	-0.3
Total	4	346	1017	125	266	42	17	4	82	74-5	4	133	.262	.312	.348	80	-29	3-9	.967	-12	102	81	2b217,3b49,S9	0	-3.1
PLOCK, WALTER	Walter S.; B7.2.1869 Philadelphia PA; D4.28.1900 Richmond VA; 6´3˝/180; d8.21																								
1891	Phi N	2	5	2	2	0	0	0	0	0	1	1	.400	.500	.400	159	0	0	.000	-1	0	0	O2C	—	0.0
PLUMMER, BILL	William Francis; B3.21.1947 Oakland CA; BR/TR/6´1˝/(190–210); d4.19; M1/C7																								
1968	Chi N	2	2	0	0	0	0	0	0	0-0	0	1	.000	.000	.000	-94	0	0-0	1.000	0	0	0	/C	0	0.0
1970	Cin N	4	8	0	1	0	0	0	0	0-0	1	2	.125	.222	.125	-4	-1	0-0	.857	-2	35	0	C4	0	-0.3
1971	Cin N	10	19	0	0	0	0	0	0	0-0	0	4	.000	.000	.000	-99	-5	0-0	1.000	-1	0	172	C4,3b2	0	-0.6
1972	Cin N	38	102	8	19	4	0	2	9	4-2	0	20	.186	.211	.284	43	-8	0-0	.994	-4	224	84	C36/13	20	-1.1
1973	Cin N	50	119	8	18	3	0	2	11	18-5	1	26	.151	.268	.227	40	-10	1-0	.994	-5	119	65	C42,3b5	0	-1.3
1974	Cin N	50	120	7	27	7	0	2	10	6-0	0	21	.225	.258	.333	67	-6	1-0	.974	-2	116	44	C49/3	0	-0.6
1975	Cin N	65	159	17	29	7	0	1	19	24-2	2	28	.182	.291	.245	51	-10	1-0	.990	-8	117	14	C63	0	-1.6
1976	Cin N	56	153	16	38	6	1	4	19	14-0	0	36	.248	.311	.379	93	-2	0-2	.977	-2	79	60	C54	0	-0.2
1977	Cin N	51	117	10	16	5	0	1	7	17-1	0	34	.137	.244	.205	22	-13	1-1	.986	-3	158	66	C50	0	-1.5
1978	Sea A	41	93	6	20	5	0	2	7	12-0	0	19	.215	.305	.333	79	-2	0-0	.978	-10	68	24	C40	0	-1.2
Total	10	367	892	72	168	37	1	14	82	95-10	4	191	.188	.267	.279	53	-57	4-3	.984	-36	120	50	C343,3b9/1	20	-8.4
POCOROBA, BIFF	Biff; B7.25.1953 Burbank CA; BB/TR (BL 1975p, 77p, 80p, 81–84)/5´10˝/(170–184); [AtlN71 17/399]; d4.25																								
1975	Atl N	67	188	15	48	7	1	1	22	20-2	0	11	.255	.325	.319	77	-5	0-0	.970	-11	55	79	C62	0	-1.4
1976	Atl N	54	174	16	42	7	0	0	14	19-2	0	12	.241	.313	.282	67	-7	1-0	.978	5	114	95	C54	90	0.1
1977	Atl N	113	321	46	93	24	1	8	44	57-15	1	27	.290	.394	.445	113	9	3-4	.989	-3	71	**133**	C100	0	0.9
1978	Atl N★	92	289	21	70	8	0	6	34	29-6	2	14	.242	.312	.332	73	-10	0-3	.990	-3	76	88	C79	48	-1.1
1979	Atl N	28	38	6	12	4	0	0	4	7-1	0	0	.316	.422	.421	123	2	1-1	.933	0	55	132	C7	106	0.2
1980	Atl N	70	83	7	22	4	0	2	8	11-0	0	11	.265	.347	.386	104	1	1-0	.934	-1	51	27	C10	51	0.0
1981	Atl N	57	122	4	22	4	0	0	8	12-1	2	15	.180	.265	.213	37	-10	0-0	.938	-2	80	130	3b21,C9	23	-1.3
1982	†Atl N	56	120	5	33	7	0	2	22	13-2	1	12	.275	.351	.383	103	1	0-0	.988	-7	58	112	C36,3b2	15	-0.5
1983	Atl N	55	120	11	32	6	0	2	16	12-4	0	7	.267	.331	.367	87	-2	0-0	.983	-5	65	74	C34	0	-0.5
1984	Atl N	4	2	1	0	0	0	0	0	2-0	0	0	.000	.500	.000	48	0	0-0	ø	-0	—	—	/H	0	0.0
Total	10	596	1457	132	374	71	2	21	172	182-33	6	109	.257	.339	.351	87	-21	6-8	.982	-27	74	100	C391,3b23	333	-3.6
PODSEDNIK, SCOTT	Scott Eric; B3.18.1976 West TX; BL/TL/6´0˝/(170–190); [TexA94 3/85]; d7.6																								
2001	Sea A	5	6	1	1	0	1	0	3	0-0	0	1	.167	.167	.500	70	0	0-0	1.000	-0	63	0	O5(3/1/1)	0	-0.1
2002	Sea A	14	20	2	4	0	0	1	5	4-0	0	6	.200	.320	.350	85	0	0-0	.938	0	127	0	O11(9/1/2),D2	0	0.0
2003	Mil N	154	558	100	175	29	8	9	58	56-2	4	91	.314	.379	.443	114	13	43-10	.992	2	107	65	O139(3/123/13)	0	2.1
2004	Mil N	154	640	85	156	27	7	12	39	58-2	7	105	.244	.313	.364	74	-26	**70**-13	.990	1	106	65	O153C	0	-1.1
2005	†Chi A★	129	507	80	147	28	1	0	25	47-0	3	75	.290	.351	.349	85	-9	59-23	.989	-0	105	43	O127(124/7/0)	16	-0.9
2006	Chi A	139	524	86	137	27	6	3	45	54-1	2	96	.261	.330	.353	76	-18	40-19	.969	-5	98	44	O135L,D2	0	-2.4
Total	6	595	2255	354	620	111	23	25	175	219-5	16	374	.275	.342	.378	87	-40	212-65	.985	-2	104	54	O570(274/285/16),D4	16	-2.4
POEPPING, MIKE	Michael Harold; B8.7.1950 Little Falls MN; BR/TR/6´6˝/230; d9.6; Col St. Cloud St.																								
1975	Min A	14	37	0	5	1	0	0	1	5-0	0	7	.135	.238	.162	15	-4	0-0	.950	-1	82	107	O13R	0	-0.6
POFAHL, JIMMY	James Willard; B6.18.1917 Faribault MN; D9.14.1984 Owatonna MN; BR/TR/5´11˝/185; d4.16																								
1940	Was A	119	406	34	95	23	5	2	36	37	0	55	.234	.298	.330	67	-21	2-0	.952	-3	96	98	S112,2b4	—	-1.4
1941	Was A	22	75	9	14	3	2	0	6	10	0	11	.187	.282	.280	52	-5	1-0	.934	-3	101	61	S21	0	-0.6
1942	Was A	84	283	22	59	7	2	0	28	29	0	30	.208	.282	.247	50	-19	4-3	.956	-1	96	108	S49,2b15,3b14	0	-1.6
Total	3	225	764	65	168	33	9	2	70	76	0	96	.220	.290	.295	59	-45	7-3	.951	-7	97	97	S182,2b19,3b14	0	-3.6
POFF, JOHN	John William; B10.23.1952 Chillicothe OH; BL/TL/6´2˝/200; d9.8; Col Duke																								
1979	Phi N	12	19	2	2	1	0	0	1	1-0	0	4	.105	.150	.158	-15	-3	0-0	.875	-0	107	0	O4L/1	0	-0.4
1980	Mil A	19	68	7	17	1	2	1	7	3-2	0	7	.250	.282	.368	78	-3	0-0	1.000	-1	104	0	O7R,1b3,D7	0	-0.4
Total	2	31	87	9	19	2	2	1	8	4-2	0	11	.218	.253	.322	57	-6	0-0	.957	-2	105	0	O11(4/0/7),D7,1b4	0	-0.8
POINTER, AARON	Aaron Elton "Hawk"; B4.19.1942 Little Rock AR; BR/TR/6´2˝/185; d9.22; Col San Francisco																								
1963	Hou N	2	5	0	1	0	0	0	0	0-0	0	1	.200	.200	.200	17	-1	0-0	1.000	-0	58	0	/rf	0	-0.1
1966	Hou N	11	26	5	9	1	0	1	5	5-0	1	6	.346	.469	.500	182	3	1-1	1.000	2	95	564	O11L	0	0.5
1967	Hou N	27	70	6	11	4	0	1	10	13-1	1	26	.157	.291	.257	62	-3	1-0	.951	1	109	158	O22L	0	-0.3
Total	3	40	101	11	21	5	0	2	15	18-1	2	33	.208	.333	.317	91	-1	2-1	.966	3	104	258	O34(33/0/1)	0	0.1
POLANCO, PLACIDO	Placido Enrique; B10.10.1975 Santo Domingo, D.R.; BR/TR/5´10˝/(168–195); [StLN94 19/530]; d7.3; Col Miami–Dade Wolfson (FL) CC																								
1998	StL N	45	114	10	29	3	2	1	11	5-0	1	9	.254	.292	.342	66	-6	2-0	.952	5	124	129	S28,2b14	0	0.2
1999	StL N	88	220	24	61	9	3	1	19	15-1	0	24	.277	.321	.359	71	-10	1-3	.979	0	99	102	2b66,3b9,S9	0	-0.7
2000	†StL N	118	323	50	102	12	3	5	39	16-0	1	26	.316	.347	.418	91	-5	4-4	.984	4	95	72	2b51,3b35,S29/1	14	0.2
2001	†StL N	144	564	87	173	26	4	3	38	25-0	6	43	.307	.342	.383	85	-12	12-3	.985	24	117	104	3b103,S42,2b15/D	0	1.6
2002	StL N	94	342	47	97	19	1	5	27	12-1	4	27	.284	.316	.389	84	-9	3-1	.974	6	110	141	3b78,S13,2b6	0	-0.1
	Phi N	53	206	28	61	13	1	4	22	14-0	4	14	.296	.353	.427	111	3	2-2	.983	12	126	141	3b53	0	1.5
	Year	147	548	75	158	32	2	9	49	26-1	8	41	.288	.330	.403	93	-6	5-3	.978	18	117	141	3b131,S13,2b6	0	1.4
2003	Phi N	122	492	87	142	30	3	14	63	42-1	8	38	.289	.352	.447	116	11	14-2	.992	5	103	103	2b99,3b21	15	2.2
2004	Phi N	126	503	74	150	21	0	17	55	27-0	12	39	.298	.345	.441	99	-1	7-4	**.995**	14	102	116	2b109,3b13	30	1.8
2005	Phi N	43	158	26	50	7	0	3	20	12-0	3	9	.316	.376	.418	104	1	0-0	1.000	9	97	161	2b29,3b8,O5L/S	0	1.1
	Det A	86	343	58	116	20	2	6	36	21-0	8	16	.338	.386	.461	128	14	4-3	.993	14	108	128	2b84/3	15	3.0
2006	†Det A	110	461	58	136	18	1	4	52	17-0	7	27	.295	.329	.364	81	-13	1-2	.989	12	109	114	2b108	37	0.3
Total	9	1029	3726	549	1117	178	20	63	382	206-3	54	272	.300	.344	.409	95	-27	50-24	.991	105	103	115	2b581,3b321,S122,O5L/D1	111	11.1
POLAND, HUGH	Hugh Reid; B1.19.1913 Tompkinsville KY; D3.29.1984 Guthrie KY; BL/TR/5´11.5˝/185; d4.22; Mil 1945; Col Western Kentucky																								
1943	NY N	4	12	1	1	0	1	0	2	1	0	0	.083	.154	.250	16	-1	0	.889	-1	*78*	*162*	C4	0	-0.3
	Bos N	44	141	5	27	7	0	0	13	4	0	11	.191	.214	.241	32	-13	0	.973	-5	*58*	*46*	C38	0	-1.7
	Year	48	153	6	28	7	1	0	15	5	0	11	.183	.209	.242	30	-14	0	.969	-6	*59*	*53*	C42	0	-2.0
1944	Bos N	8	23	1	3	1	0	0	2	0	0	1	.130	.130	.174	-14	-4	0	.939	-0	*67*	*0*	C6	0	-0.4
1946	Bos N	4	6	0	1	1	0	0	0	0	0	0	.167	.167	.333	40	0	0	1.000	-0	*43*	*0*	C2	0	-0.1
1947	Phi N	4	8	0	0	0	0	0	0	0	0	0	.000	.000	.000	-99	-2	0	1.000	0	*47*	*267*	C2	0	-0.2
	Cin N	16	18	1	6	1	0	0	2	1	0	4	.333	.368	.389	102	0	0	.667	-1	*0*	*0*	C3	0	-0.1
	Year	20	26	1	6	1	0	0	2	1	0	4	.231	.259	.269	41	-2	0	.867	-1	*27*	*154*	C5	0	-0.3
1948	Cin N	3	3	0	1	0	0	0	0	0	0	0	.333	.333	.333	84	0	0	ø	0	—	—	/H	0	0.0
Total	5	83	211	8	39	10	1	0	19	6	0	16	.185	.207	.242	28	-20	0	.958	-7	*58*	*51*	C55	0	-2.8
POLCOVICH, KEVIN	Kevin Michael; B6.28.1970 Auburn NY; BR/TR/5´9˝/(168–182); [PitN92 30/847]; d5.17; Col Florida																								
1997	Pit N	84	245	37	67	16	1	4	21	21-4	9	45	.273	.350	.396	94	-1	2-2	.969	13	116	83	S80,2b2/3	16	1.6
1998	Pit N	81	212	18	40	12	0	0	14	15-2	5	33	.189	.255	.245	33	-21	4-3	.916	14	115	113	S54,2b15,3b8	0	-0.3
Total	2	165	457	55	107	28	1	4	35	36-6	14	78	.234	.307	.326	66	-22	6-5	.948	27	116	95	S134,2b17,3b9	16	1.3
POLHEMUS, MARK	Mark S. "Humpty Dumpty"; B10.4.1860 Brooklyn NY; D11.12.1923 Lynn MA; 5´6.5˝/185; d7.13																								
1887	Ind N	20	75	6	18	1	0	0	8	2	0	9	.240	.260	.253	45	-6	4	.744	0	236	0	O20R	—	-0.5
POLIDOR, GUS	Gustavo Adolfo (Gonzalez); B10.26.1961 Caracas, Distrito Capital, Venezuela; D4.28.1995 Caracas, Distrito Capital, Venezuela; BR/TR/6´0˝/(170–180); d9.7																								
1985	Cal A	2	1	1	1	0	0	0	0	0-0	0	0	1.000	1.000	1.000	450	0	0-0	1.000	-0	207	0	/Srf	0	0.1
1986	Cal A	6	19	1	5	1	0	0	1	1-0	0	0	.263	.300	.316	68	-1	0-0	1.000	-2	71	89	2b4/S3	0	-0.2
1987	Cal A	63	137	12	36	3	0	2	15	2-0	1	15	.263	.277	.328	62	-8	0-0	.983	-12	83	60	S46,3b11,2b3	0	-1.6

YEAR	TM LG	G	AB	R	H	2B	3B	HR	RBI	BB-IB	HP	SO	AVG	OBP	SLG	AOPS	ABR	SB-CS	FA	FR	RNG	THR	GAMES AT POSITION	DL	BFW
1988	Cal A	54	81	4	12	3	0	0	4	3-0	0	11	.148	.179	.185	2	-11	0-0	.984	-2	109	64	S25,3b22,2b3/D	17	-1.2
1989	Mil A	79	175	15	34	7	0	0	14	6-0	2	18	.194	.230	.234	31	-16	3-0	.923	-5	105	105	3b30,2b29,S21,D2	0	-2.0
1990	Mil A	18	15	0	1	0	0	0	1	0-0	0	1	.067	.067	.067	-63	-3	0-0	1.000	-1	105	0	3b14,2b2,S2	0	-0.5
1993	Fla N	7	6	0	1	1	0	0	0	0-0	0	2	.167	.167	.333	28	-1	0-0	ø	-0	0	0	/23	0	-0.1
Total	7	229	434	33	90	15	0	2	35	12-0	3	47	.207	.233	.256	35	-40	3-0	.970	-22	93	75	S96,3b79,2b42,D3/rf	17	-5.5
Polly, Nick	Nicholas (b Nicholas Joseph Polachanin); B4.18.1917 Chicago IL; D1.17.1993 Chicago IL; BR/TR/5´11˝/190; d9.11																								
1937	Bro N	10	18	2	4	0	0	0	2	0	0	1	.222	.222	.222	21	-2	0	.850	1	142	0	3b7	—	-0.1
1945	Bos A	4	7	0	1	0	0	0	1	0	0	1	.143	.143	.143	-17	-1	0-0	1.000	0	99	0	3b2	0	-0.1
Total	2	14	25	2	5	0	0	0	3	0	0	2	.200	.200	.200	11	-3	0-0	.870	1	135	0	3b9	0	-0.2
Polonia, Luis	Luis Andrew (Almonte); B10.12.1963 Santiago, D.R.; BL/TL/5´8˝/(150–160); d4.24																								
1987	Oak A	125	435	78	125	16	10	4	49	32-1	0	64	.287	.335	.398	100	-1	29-7	.979	0	105	40	O104(35/69/8),D18	0	0.0
1988	†Oak A	84	288	51	84	11	4	2	27	21-0	0	40	.292	.338	.378	104	1	24-9	.988	1	104	73	O76(76/0/1),D2	0	0.2
1989	Oak A	59	206	31	59	6	4	1	17	9-0	0	15	.286	.315	.369	96	-2	13-4	.985	6	123	104	O55L	0	0.3
	NY A	66	227	39	71	11	2	2	29	16-1	2	29	.313	.359	.405	117	5	9-4	.982	3	105	203	O53L,D9	0	0.8
	Year	125	433	70	130	17	6	3	46	25-1	2	44	.300	.338	.388	107	3	22-8	.984	9	114	154	O108L,D9	0	1.1
1990	NY A	11	22	2	7	0	0	0	3	0-0	0	1	.318	.304	.318	78	-1	1-0	ø	0	—	—	D4	0	-0.1
	Cal A	109	381	50	128	7	9	2	32	25-1	1	42	.336	.376	.417	124	11	20-14	.980	-6	86	61	O85(73/13/0),D11	0	0.2
	Year	120	403	52	135	7	9	2	35	25-1	1	43	.335	.372	.412	122	10	21-14	.980	-6	86	61	O85(73/13/0),D15	0	0.1
1991	Cal A	150	604	92	179	28	8	2	50	52-4	1	74	.296	.352	.379	102	2	48-23	.981	-6	91	116	O143(143/1/0),D4	0	-0.6
1992	Cal A	149	577	83	165	17	4	0	35	45-6	1	64	.286	.337	.329	87	-10	51-21	.980	-1	100	123	O99L,D47	0	-1.2
1993	Cal A	152	576	75	156	17	6	1	32	48-7	2	53	.271	.328	.326	74	-21	55-24	.983	4	105	143	O141L,D4	0	-1.8
1994	NY A	95	350	62	109	21	6	1	36	37-1	4	36	.311	.383	.414	110	6	20-12	.976	-1	94	149	O84L,D2	0	0.2
1995	NY A	67	238	37	62	9	3	2	15	25-1	0	29	.261	.326	.349	78	-8	10-4	1.000	6	118	132	O64L/D	0	-0.4
	†Atl N	28	53	6	14	7	0	0	2	3-0	0	9	.264	.304	.396	79	-1	3-0	1.000	-2	51	0	O15(11/4/1)	0	-0.3
1996	Bal A	58	175	25	42	4	1	2	14	10-0	1	20	.240	.285	.309	50	-14	8-6	.983	-2	94	49	O34(32/0/2),D18	0	-1.6
	†Atl N	22	31	3	13	0	0	0	2	1-0	0	3	.419	.424	.419	120	1	1-1	.800	-1	53	0	O7L	0	0.0
1999	Det A	87	333	46	108	21	8	10	32	16-0	2	32	.324	.357	.526	120	9	17-9	.986	2	101	181	D43,O40(31/0/10)	0	0.7
2000	Det A	80	267	37	73	10	5	6	25	22-1	1	25	.273	.325	.416	88	-6	8-5	1.000	2	119	156	D44,O27(1/0/26)	0	-0.6
	†NY A	37	77	11	22	4	0	1	5	7-0	0	7	.286	.341	.377	84	-2	4-2	.970	-2	91	0	O28(22/0/6),D7	0	-0.4
	Year	117	344	48	95	14	5	7	30	29-1	1	32	.276	.329	.407	87	-8	12-7	.987	0	105	80	O55(23/0/32),D51	0	-1.0
Total	12	1379	4840	728	1417	189	70	36	405	369-23	15	543	.293	.342	.383	96	-31	321-145	.983	3	100	110	O1055(927/87/54),D214	0	-4.6
Ponce, Carlos	Carlos Antonio (Diaz); B2.7.1959 Rio Piedras, PR; BR/TR/5´10˝/170; d8.14; Col Abraham Baldwin (GA) JC																								
1985	Mil A	21	62	4	10	2	0	1	5	1-0	0	9	.161	.169	.242	13	-8	0-0	1.000	-1	60	121	1b10,O6(5/0/1),D3	0	-0.9
Pond, Ralph	Ralph Benjamin; B5.4.1890 Eau Claire WI; D9.8.1947 Cleveland OH; TR/5´9˝/?; d6.8; Col Maine																								
1910	Bos A	1	4	0	1	0	0	0	0	0	0	—	.250	.250	.250	55	0	1	.000	-1	0	0	/cf	—	-0.1
Pond, Simon	Simon Emilio; B10.27.1976 North Vancouver BC, Can.; BL/TR/6´1˝/205; [MonN94 8/224]; d4.7																								
2004	Tor A	16	49	4	8	2	0	1	6	5-0	1	12	.163	.250	.265	34	-5	0-0	1.000	-0	101	0	O9(6/0/3),D6	0	-0.5
Pool, Harlin	Harlin Welty "Samson"; B3.13.1908 Lakeport CA; D2.15.1963 Rodeo CA; BL/TR/5´10˝/195; d5.30																								
1934	Cin N	99	358	38	117	22	5	2	50	17	7	18	.327	.369	.433	117	9	3	.953	0	99	115	O94(76/0/18)	—	0.3
1935	Cin N	28	68	8	12	6	2	0	11	2	0	2	.176	.200	.324	39	-6	0	.962	-1	89	103	O18(15/0/3)	—	-0.7
Total	2	127	426	46	129	28	7	2	61	19	7	20	.303	.343	.415	105	3	3	.954	-1	98	114	O112(91/0/21)	—	-0.4
Poole, Jim	James Robert "Easy"; B5.12.1895 Taylorsville NC; D1.2.1975 Hickory NC; BL/TR/6´0˝/175; d4.14																								
1925	Phi A	133	480	65	143	29	8	5	67	27	2	37	.298	.338	.423	86	-12	5-4	.982	-8	80	106	1b123	—	-2.6
1926	Phi A	112	361	49	106	23	5	8	63	23	2	25	.294	.339	.452	99	-2	4-3	.992	1	99	113	1b101/rf	—	-0.7
1927	Phi A	38	99	4	22	2	0	0	10	9	0	6	.222	.287	.242	36	-9	0-0	.993	0	99	75	1b31	—	-1.0
Total	3	283	940	118	271	54	13	13	140	59	4	68	.288	.333	.415	86	-23	9-7	.987	-7	89	105	1b255/rf	—	-4.3
Poole, Ray	Raymond Herman; B1.16.1920 Salisbury NC; D3.1.2006 Burlington NC; BL/TR/6´0˝/180; d9.9; Mil 1942–45; Col Catawba																								
1941	Phi A	2	2	0	0	0	0	0	0	0	0	1	.000	.000	.000	-99	-1	0-0	ø	0	—	—	/H	0	-0.1
1947	Phi A	13	13	1	3	0	0	0	1	1	0	4	.231	.286	.231	44	-1	0-0	ø	0	—	—	/H	0	-0.1
Total	2	15	15	1	3	0	0	0	1	1	0	5	.200	.250	.200	25	-2	0-0	ø	0	—	—	0	—	-0.2
Poorman, Tom	Thomas Iverson; B10.14.1857 Lock Haven PA; D2.18.1905 Lock Haven PA; BL/TR/5´7˝/135; d5.5; ▲																								
1880	Buf N	19	70	5	11	1	0	0	1	0	—	13	.157	.157	.171	11	-6	—	.879	-0	141	0	P11,O10C	—	-0.3
	Chi N	7	25	3	5	1	2	0	0	0	—	2	.200	.200	.400	92	0	—	.778	-2	77	0	O7R,P2	—	-0.1
	Year	26	95	8	16	2	2	0	1	0	—	15	.168	.168	.232	33	-7	—	.750	-2	40	0	O17(0/10/7),P13	—	-0.4
1884	Tol AA	94	382	56	89	8	7	0	—	10	1	—	.233	.254	.291	75	-12	—	.845	3	162	183	O93R/P	—	-0.8
1885	Bos N	56	227	44	54	5	3	3	25	7	—	32	.238	.261	.326	92	-2	—	.867	-3	83	65	O56R	—	-0.6
1886	Bos N	88	371	72	97	16	6	3	41	19	—	52	.261	.297	.361	102	1	31	.902	3	115	211	O88R	—	0.3
1887	Phi AA	135	585	140	155	18	**19**	4	61	35	10	—	.265	.317	.381	94	-7	88	.911	2	82	130	O135R,2b2/P	—	-0.5
1888	Phi AA	97	383	76	87	16	6	2	44	31	5	—	.227	.294	.316	96	-1	46	.898	-10	52	32	O97R	—	-1.1
Total	6	496	2043	396	498	65	43	12	172	102	16	99	.244	.285	.335	90	-27	165	.885	-6	97	125	O486(0/10/476),P15,2b2	—	-3.1
Pope, Dave	David; B6.17.1921 Talladega AL; D8.28.1999 Cleveland OH; BL/TR/5´10.5˝/170; d7.1; Negro Lg 1946; Col Pittsburgh																								
1952	Cle A	12	34	9	10	1	1	1	4	1	0	7	.294	.314	.471	124	1	0-0	1.000	-1	100	0	O10R	0	0.0
1954	†Cle A	60	102	21	30	2	1	4	13	10	0	22	.294	.354	.451	118	2	2-1	1.000	-0	101	69	O29(18/6/5)	0	0.1
1955	Cle A	35	104	17	31	5	0	6	22	12-0	1	31	.298	.373	.519	134	5	0-0	.954	-2	100	0	O31(12/14/7)	0	0.1
	Bal A	86	222	21	55	8	4	1	30	16-3	2	34	.248	.302	.333	77	-8	5-2	1.000	2	110	70	O73(19/37/31)	0	-0.9
	Year	121	326	38	86	13	4	7	52	28-3	3	65	.264	.325	.393	97	-3	5-2	.986	0	107	47	O104(31/51/38)	0	-0.8
1956	Bal A	12	19	1	3	0	0	0	1	0-0	1	7	.158	.200	.158	-5	-3	0-0	1.000	-0	69	0	O4(2/0/3)	0	-0.3
	Cle A	25	70	6	17	3	1	0	3	1-0	0	12	.243	.250	.314	48	-6	0-0	1.000	0	103	104	O18(4/12/2)	0	-0.6
	Year	37	89	7	20	3	1	0	4	1-0	1	19	.225	.239	.281	38	-8	0-0	1.000	-0	99	90	O22(6/12/5)	0	-0.9
Total	4	230	551	75	146	19	7	12	73	40-3	4	113	.265	.317	.390	92	-9	7-3	.990	-0	104	53	O165(55/69/58)	0	-1.6
Popovich, Paul	Paul Edward; B8.18.1940 Flemington WV; BB/TR (BR 1964, 66–67)/6´0˝/(170–175); d4.19; Col West Virginia																								
1964	Chi N	1	1	0	1	0	0	0	0	0-0	0	0	1.000	1.000	1.000	447	0	0-0	ø	0	—	—	/H	0	0.0
1966	Chi N	2	6	0	0	0	0	0	0	0-0	0	2	.000	.000	.000	-99	-2	0-0	.889	-0	75	101	2b2	0	-0.2
1967	Chi N	49	159	18	34	4	0	0	2	9-0	2	12	.214	.265	.239	43	-12	0-1	.967	1	95	84	S31,2b17,3b2	0	-0.9
1968	LA N	134	418	35	97	8	1	2	25	29-2	1	37	.232	.280	.270	72	-15	1-3	.983	4	102	101	2b89,S45,3b7	0	-0.1
1969	LA N	28	50	5	10	0	0	0	4	1-0	0	4	.200	.212	.200	18	-6	0-0	.985	-4	93	107	2b23,S3	0	-0.9
	Chi N	60	154	26	48	6	0	1	14	18-0	1	14	.312	.387	.370	100	1	0-1	.974	1	97	91	2b25,S7,3b6/cf	0	0.4
	Year	88	204	31	58	6	0	1	18	19-0	1	18	.284	.347	.328	85	-4	0-1	.978	-2	95	97	2b48,S10,3b6/cf	0	-0.5
1970	Chi N	78	186	22	47	5	1	4	20	18-4	2	18	.253	.324	.355	73	-7	0-1	.990	-2	105	151	2b22,S17,3b16	0	-0.7
1971	Chi N	89	226	24	49	7	1	4	28	14-0	0	17	.217	.260	.310	54	-14	0-1	.985	3	111	108	2b40,3b16/S	0	-0.9
1972	Chi N	58	129	8	25	3	2	1	11	12-2	0	8	.194	.261	.271	47	-9	0-1	.981	12	126	141	2b36,S8/3	15	0.6
1973	Chi N	99	280	24	66	6	3	2	24	18-5	1	27	.236	.280	.300	58	-16	3-2	.981	16	113	115	2b84,S9/3	0	0.5
1974	†Pit N	59	83	9	18	2	1	0	5	5-1	0	10	.217	.256	.265	49	-6	0-0	.962	-0	109	76	2b12,S10	0	-0.6
1975	Pit N	25	40	5	8	1	0	0	1	3-0	1	2	.200	.273	.225	39	-3	0-0	1.000	-2	76	48	2b8,S8	0	-0.4
Total	11	682	1732	176	403	42	9	14	134	127-14	8	151	.233	.286	.292	62	-89	4-10	.982	31	108	112	2b358,S139,3b49/cf	15	-3.2
Popplein, George	George J.; B8.1840 Baltimore MD; D3.31.1901 Baltimore MD; d7.11																								
1873	Mar NA	1	4	0	0	0	0	0	0	0	—	0	.000	.000	.000	-99	-1	0-0	.500	-0	118	0	/3cf	—	-0.1
Poquette, Tom	Thomas Arthur; B10.30.1951 Eau Claire WI; BL/TR/5´10˝/175; [KCA70 4/81]; d9.1; C2; [DL 1980 Bos A 180]																								
1973	KC A	21	28	4	6	1	0	0	3	1-0	1	4	.214	.258	.250	43	-2	1-1	.870	-0	100	155	O20(0/2/18)	0	-0.3
1976	†KC A	104	344	43	104	18	10	2	34	29-3	4	31	.302	.361	.430	131	13	6-5	.979	-5	100	15	O98(84/0/17),D2	22	0.3
1977	†KC A	106	342	43	100	23	6	2	33	19-2	5	21	.292	.337	.412	102	1	1-4	1.000	1	106	65	O96(72/1/28)	13	-0.3
1978	†KC A	80	204	16	44	9	2	4	30	14-1	0	9	.216	.259	.338	67	-10	2-0	.955	9	142	147	O63(48/1/17)/D	0	-0.3
1979	KC A	21	26	1	5	0	0	0	3	1-0	0	4	.192	.214	.192	13	-3	0-0	1.000	-0	60	237	O10(2/0/8)	0	-0.4

YEAR	TM LG	G	AB	R	H	2B	3B	HR	RBI	BB-IB	HP	SO	AVG	OBP	SLG	AOPS	ABR	SB-CS	FA	FR	RNG	THR	GAMES AT POSITION	DL	BFW
	Bos A	63	154	14	51	9	0	2	23	8-1	3	7	.331	.365	.429	110	3	2-2	.949	-4	83	81	O43(3/30/11),D4	0	-0.3
	Year	84	180	15	56	9	0	2	26	9-1	3	11	.311	.343	.394	97	-1	2-2	.954	-4	80	102	O53(5/30/19),D4	0	-0.7
1981	Bos A	3	2	0	0	0	0	0	0	0-0	0	0	.000	.000	.000	-94	0	0-0	ø	-0	0	0	O2L	0	-0.1
	Tex A	30	64	2	10	1	0	0	7	5-0	1	1	.156	.225	.172	18	-7	0-1	.963	-3	73	0	O18(10/5/3)	0	-1.1
	Year	33	66	2	10	1	0	0	7	5-0	1	1	.152	.219	.167	14	-7	0-1	.963	-3	71	0	O20(12/5/3)	0	-1.2
1982	KC A	24	62	4	9	1	0	0	3	4-0	1	5	.145	.206	.161	3	-8	1-0	.957	1	125	95	O23(20/0/3)	0	-0.8
Total	7	452	1226	127	329	62	18	10	136	81-7	15	82	.268	.317	.373	92	-13	13-13	.971	-1	106	70	O373(241/39/105),D7	215	-3.3
Porter, Colin	Colin Frederick; B11.23.1975 Tucson AZ; BL/TL/6´2˝/(200–210); [HouN98 17/512]; d5.30; Col Arizona																								
2003	Hou N	24	32	5	6	0	0	0	0	1-0	0	17	.188	.212	.188	5	-5	1-0	1.000	-0	100	0	O14(1/7/6)	0	-0.5
2004	StL N	23	35	3	11	1	0	1	2	0-0	0	13	.314	.314	.429	88	-1	0-0	1.000	-0	94	0	O14(6/2/8)	0	-0.1
Total	2	47	67	8	17	1	0	1	2	1-0	0	30	.254	.265	.313	48	-6	1-0	1.000	-1	97	0	O28(7/9/14)	0	-0.6
Porter, Dan	Daniel Edward; B10.17.1931 Decatur IL; BL/TL/6´0˝/164; d8.16; Mil 1952–53																								
1951	Was A	13	19	2	4	0	0	0	0	2	0	4	.211	.286	.211	36	-2	0-0	1.000	-0	94	0	O3R	0	-0.2
Porter, Darrell	Darrell Ray; B1.17.1952 Joplin MO; D2.27.2002 Sugar Creek MO; BL/TR/6´0˝/(190–202); [MilA70 1/4]; d9.2																								
1971	Mil A	22	70	4	15	2	0	2	9	9-0	0	20	.214	.300	.329	80	-2	2-2	.977	2	81	229	C22	0	0.1
1972	Mil A	18	56	2	7	1	0	1	2	5-0	1	21	.125	.210	.196	22	-6	0-0	.976	3	167	78	C18	0	-0.2
1973	Mil A	117	350	50	89	19	2	16	67	57-6	4	85	.254	.363	.457	132	16	5-2	.977	0	101	125	C90,D19	0	2.1
1974	Mil A☆	131	432	59	104	15	4	12	56	50-7	5	88	.241	.326	.377	102	2	8-7	.978	1	114	103	C117,D9	0	0.7
1975	Mil A	130	409	66	95	12	5	18	60	89-10	5	77	.232	.371	.418	123	16	2-5	.979	-3	96	114	C124,D2	0	1.7
1976	Mil A	119	389	43	81	14	1	5	32	51-3	1	61	.208	.298	.288	74	-11	2-0	.975	-5	106	74	C111,D2	0	-1.2
1977	†KC A	130	425	61	117	21	3	16	60	53-6	1	70	.275	.353	.452	117	11	1-0	.982	6	127	88	C125/D	0	2.2
1978	†KC A★	150	520	77	138	27	6	18	78	75-14	2	75	.265	.358	.444	121	16	0-5	.988	2	111	83	C145,D4	0	2.3
1979	KC A★	157	533	101	155	23	10	20	112	**121**-8	8	65	.291	.421	.484	142	39	3-4	.982	9	133	114	C141,D15	0	5.0
1980	†KC A★	118	418	51	104	14	2	7	51	69-5	2	50	.249	.354	.342	91	-2	1-1	.978	1	125	106	C81,D34	23	0.1
1981	StL N	61	174	22	39	10	2	6	31	39-7	1	32	.224	.364	.408	115	5	1-2	.979	1	108	107	C52	93	0.9
1982	†StL N	120	373	46	86	18	5	12	48	66-6	2	66	.231	.347	.402	107	5	1-1	.983	3	98	106	C111	21	1.3
1983	StL N	145	443	57	116	24	3	15	66	68-12	4	94	.262	.363	.431	119	14	1-3	.989	9	**167**	92	C133	0	2.7
1984	StL N	127	422	56	98	16	3	11	68	60-12	5	79	.232	.331	.363	98	0	5-3	.984	0	105	102	C122	0	0.6
1985	†StL N	84	240	30	53	12	2	10	36	41-6	1	48	.221	.335	.412	109	4	6-1	.990	5	111	96	C82	58	1.4
1986	Tex A	68	155	21	41	6	0	12	29	22-0	1	51	.265	.360	.535	136	8	1-1	.994	-2	46	111	C25,D19	42	0.6
1987	Tex A	85	130	19	31	3	0	7	21	30-4	2	43	.238	.387	.423	115	4	0-0	1.000	-0	69	167	D35,C7,1b5	0	0.2
Total	17	1782	5539	765	1369	237	48	188	826	905-106	45	1025	.247	.354	.409	113	119	39-37	.982	32	116	102	C1506,D140,1b5	237	20.5
Porter, Irv	Irving Marble; B5.17.1888 Lynn MA; D2.20.1971 Lynn MA; BB/TR/5´9˝/155; d8.20																								
1914	Chi A	1	4	1	1	0	0	0	0	0	0	1	.250	.250	.250	51	0	0	1.000	-0	88	0	/rf	—	0.0
Porter, Jay	J W "J W"; B1.17.1933 Shawnee OK; BR/TR/6´2˝/(180–185); d7.30; Mil 1953																								
1952	StL A	33	104	12	26	4	1	0	7	10	0	10	.250	.316	.308	72	-4	4-0	.973	0	105	160	O29(3/26/0),3b2	0	-0.4
1955	Det A	24	55	6	13	2	0	0	3	8-0	0	15	.236	.333	.273	66	-2	0-0	1.000	-2	25	94	1b6,C4,O4L	0	-0.5
1956	Det A	14	21	0	2	0	0	0	3	0-0	0	8	.095	.091	.095	-49	-5	0-0	1.000	-1	*0*	*0*	C2,O2L	0	-0.5
1957	Det A	58	140	14	35	8	0	2	18	14-1	1	20	.250	.323	.350	82	-3	0-0	.953	1	105	68	O27(5/0/22),C12,1b3	0	-0.3
1958	Cle A	40	85	13	17	1	0	4	19	9-0	1	23	.200	.284	.353	76	-3	0-0	1.000	-2	110	106	C20,1b4/3	0	-0.5
1959	Was A	37	106	8	24	4	0	1	10	11-1	1	16	.226	.300	.292	65	-5	0-0	.993	-3	52	159	C34,1b2	0	-0.6
	StL N	23	33	5	7	3	0	1	2	1-0	1	4	.212	.257	.394	66	-2	0-0	1.000	-2	63	219	C19/1	0	-0.3
Total	6	229	544	58	124	22	1	8	62	53-2	4	96	.228	.300	.316	68	-24	4-0	.990	-8	*80*	*146*	C91,O62(14/26/22),1b16,3b3	0	-3.1
Porter, Bo	Marquis Donnell; B7.5.1972 Newark NJ; BR/TR/6´2˝/195; [ChiN93 40/1118]; d5.9; Col Iowa																								
1999	Chi N	24	26	2	5	1	0	0	0	2-0	0	13	.192	.250	.231	23	-3	0-0	.941	-0	96	0	O21(16/5/3)	0	-0.4
2000	†Oak A	17	13	3	2	0	0	1	2	2-0	0	5	.154	.267	.385	63	-1	0-0	1.000	0	115	0	O16(1/2/14)	0	-0.1
2001	Tex A	48	87	18	20	4	2	1	6	9-0	0	34	.230	.296	.356	71	-4	3-2	.969	0	109	63	O40(18/10/12),D2	0	-0.4
Total	3	89	126	23	27	5	2	2	8	13-0	0	52	.214	.284	.333	60	-8	3-2	.968	0	107	42	O77(35/17/29),D2	0	-0.9
Porter, Matthew	Matthew Sheldon; B Kansas City MO; d6.27; M1																								
1884	KC U	3	12	1	1	1	0	0	—	0	—	—	.083	.083	.167	-30	-2	—	.750	1	272	731	O3C,M	—	-0.1
Porter, Dick	Richard Twilley "Wiggles","Twitches"; B12.30.1901 Princess Anne MD; D9.24.1974 Philadelphia PA; BL/TR/5´10˝/170; d4.16																								
1929	Cle A	71	192	26	63	16	5	1	24	17	1	14	.328	.386	.479	117	5	3-5	.941	-2	86	146	O28(4/0/24),2b20	—	0.1
1930	Cle A	119	480	100	168	43	8	4	57	55	3	31	.350	.420	.498	127	22	3-3	.962	-6	85	110	O118R	—	0.6
1931	Cle A	114	414	82	129	24	3	1	38	56	1	36	.312	.395	.391	102	4	6-9	.970	-5	93	72	O109R/2	—	-0.8
1932	Cle A	146	621	106	191	42	8	4	60	64	1	43	.308	.373	.420	99	0	2-4	.982	-13	90	17	O145R	—	-2.2
1933	Cle A	132	499	73	133	19	6	0	41	51	0	42	.267	.335	.329	73	-19	4-4	**.996**	-2	96	78	O124(7/0/119)	—	-2.8
1934	Cle A	13	44	9	10	2	1	1	6	4	0	5	.227	.292	.386	73	-2	0-0	1.000	-1	84	0	O10R	—	-0.3
	Bos A	80	265	30	80	13	6	0	56	21	1	15	.302	.355	.396	87	-5	5-2	.940	-5	92	21	O65(1/0/64)	—	-1.3
	Year	93	309	39	90	15	7	1	62	25	1	20	.291	.346	.395	85	-7	5-2	.947	-6	91	18	O75(1/0/74)	—	-1.6
Total	6	675	2515	426	774	159	37	11	282	268	7	186	.308	.376	.414	99	5	23-27	.973	-34	91	64	O599(12/0/589),2b21	—	-6.7
Porter, Bob	Robert Lee; B7.22.1959 Yuma AZ; BL/TL/5´10˝/180; [AtlN77 3/56]; d5.13																								
1981	Atl N	17	14	2	4	1	0	0	4	2-0	0	1	.286	.375	.357	108	0	0-0	ø	0	—	—	/H	0	0.0
1982	Atl N	24	27	1	3	0	0	0	0	1-0	0	9	.111	.143	.111	-28	-5	0-0	1.000	-1	62	0	O4L/1	0	-0.6
Total	2	41	41	3	7	1	0	0	4	3-0	0	10	.171	.227	.195	19	-5	0-0	1.000	-1	62	0	O4L/1	0	-0.6
Posada, Jorge	Jorge Rafael (Villeta); B8.17.1971 Santurce, PR; BB/TR/6´2˝/205; [NYA90 24/646]; d9.4; Col Calhoun (AL) CC																								
1995	†NY A	1	0	0	0	0	0	0	0	0-0	0	0	ø	ø	ø	ø	0	0-0	1.000	0	0	0	/C	0	0.0
1996	NY A	8	14	1	1	0	0	0	0	1-0	0	6	.071	.133	.071	-46	-3	0-0	1.000	0	0	0	C4,D3	0	-0.3
1997	†NY A	60	188	29	47	12	0	6	25	30-2	3	33	.250	.359	.410	102	2	1-2	.992	-6	92	57	C60	0	-0.1
1998	†NY A	111	358	56	96	23	0	17	63	47-7	0	92	.268	.350	.475	118	10	0-1	.994	4	131	110	C99/1D	0	1.9
1999	†NY A	112	379	50	93	19	2	12	57	53-2	3	91	.245	.341	.401	90	-5	1-0	.993	0	86	93	C109/1D	0	0.2
2000	†NY A★	151	505	92	145	35	1	28	86	107-10	8	151	.287	.417	.527	139	36	2-2	.993	3	111	101	C142,1b12,D4	0	4.3
2001	†NY A★	138	484	59	134	28	1	22	95	62-10	6	132	.277	.363	.475	118	14	2-6	.990	-3	94	99	C131,1b2,D6	0	1.7
2002	†NY A★	143	511	79	137	40	1	20	99	81-9	3	143	.268	.370	.468	122	19	1-0	.988	4	96	90	C138,D5	0	3.1
2003	†NY A★	142	481	83	135	24	0	30	101	93-6	10	110	.281	.405	.518	144	35	2-4	.994	11	101	88	C137,D2	0	5.1
2004	†NY A★	137	449	72	122	31	0	21	81	88-5	9	92	.272	.400	.481	129	24	1-3	.990	-2	96	82	C134	0	2.8
2005	†NY A	142	474	67	124	23	0	19	71	66-5	2	94	.262	.352	.430	108	7	1-0	.996	-6	72	**139**	C133,D3	0	0.9
2006	†NY A	143	465	65	129	27	2	23	93	64-1	11	97	.277	.374	.492	123	18	3-0	.990	10	96	139	C134/1D	0	3.4
Total	12	1288	4308	653	1163	262	7	198	771	692-57	55	1041	.270	.375	.472	121	157	14-18	.992	17	97	102	C1222,D32,1b17	0	23.0
Posada, Leo	Leopoldo Jesus (Hernandez); B4.15.1936 Havana, Cuba; BR/TR/5´11˝/175; d9.21																								
1960	KC A	10	36	8	13	0	2	1	2	3-0	0	7	.361	.410	.556	158	3	1-0	1.000	-1	62	165	O9(4/0/8)	0	0.1
1961	KC A	116	344	37	87	10	4	7	53	36-1	4	84	.253	.321	.366	85	-8	0-0	.973	4	108	119	O102(69/20/29)	0	-0.9
1962	KC A	29	46	6	9	1	1	0	3	7-1	0	14	.196	.302	.261	51	-3	0-0	1.000	0	85	199	O11(10/0/1)	0	-0.3
Total	3	155	426	51	109	11	7	8	58	46-2	4	105	.256	.326	.371	87	-8	1-0	.976	4	102	129	O122(83/20/38)	0	-1.1
Pose, Scott	Scott Vernon; B2.11.1967 Davenport IA; BL/TR/5´11˝/(165–190); [CinN89 34/888]; d4.5; Col Arkansas																								
1993	Fla N	15	41	0	8	2	0	0	3	2-0	0	4	.195	.233	.244	26	-4	0-2	1.000	-2	66	0	O10(6/8/0)	0	-0.7
1997	†NY A	54	87	19	19	2	1	0	5	9-0	0	11	.218	.292	.264	47	-7	3-1	1.000	-1	88	126	O45(28/3/17),D5	0	-0.8
1999	KC A	86	137	27	39	3	0	0	12	21-1	0	22	.285	.377	.307	75	-4	6-2	.970	2	96	307	O25(18/1/6),D18	0	-0.3
2000	KC A	47	48	6	9	0	0	0	1	6-0	0	13	.188	.278	.188	20	-6	0-1	1.000	-1	55	0	O11(3/2/7),D4	0	-0.7
Total	4	202	313	52	75	7	1	0	21	38-1	0	50	.240	.321	.268	53	-21	9-6	.990	-2	84	143	O91(55/14/30),D27	0	-2.5
Post, Lew	Lewis George; B4.12.1875 Woodland MI; D8.21.1944 Chicago IL; d9.21																								
1902	Det A	3	12	2	1	0	0	0	2	0	0	—	.083	.083	.083	-53	-2	0	.800	-1	0	0	O3R	—	-0.3

YEAR	TM LG	G	AB	R	H	2B	3B	HR	RBI	BB-IB	HP	SO	AVG	OBP	SLG	AOPS	ABR	SB-CS	FA	FR	RNG	THR	GAMES AT POSITION	DL	BFW
Post, Sam	Samuel Gilbert; B11.17.1896 Richmond VA; D3.31.1971 Portsmouth VA; BL/TL/6´1.5˝/170; d4.22																								
1922	Bro N	9	25	3	7	0	0	0	4	1	0	4	.280	.308	.280	53	-2	1-0	.982	-1	32	22	1b8	—	-0.3
Post, Wally	Walter Charles; B7.9.1929 St.Wendelin OH; D1.6.1982 St.Henry OH; BR/TR/6´1˝/(190–205); d9.18																								
1949	Cin N	6	8	1	2	0	0	0	1	0	0	3	.250	.250	.250	34	-1	0	.750	-0	91	0	O3(1/1/1)	0	-0.1
1951	Cin N	15	41	6	9	3	0	1	7	3	0	4	.220	.273	.366	69	-2	0-0	.963	0	102	126	O9C	0	-0.2
1952	Cin N	19	58	5	9	1	0	2	7	4	1	20	.155	.222	.276	37	-5	0-0	1.000	2	126	86	O16(15/1/0)	0	-0.5
1953	Cin N	11	33	3	8	1	0	1	4	4	0	6	.242	.324	.364	78	-1	1-0	.960	1	98	249	O11(0/4/7)	0	0.0
1954	Cin N	130	451	46	115	21	3	18	83	26	3	70	.255	.297	.435	86	-11	2-2	.957	2	102	123	O116(0/1/115)	0	-1.4
1955	Cin N	**154**	601	116	186	33	3	40	109	60-5	2	102	.309	.372	.574	139	33	7-4	.978	-1	100	98	O154R	0	2.6
1956	Cin N	143	539	94	134	25	3	36	83	37-2	4	124	.249	.301	.506	105	2	6-0	.969	6	109	124	O136R	0	0.5
1957	Cin N	134	467	68	114	26	2	20	74	33-5	0	84	.244	.291	.437	87	-9	2-2	.985	10	115	137	O124(1/0/123)	0	-0.4
1958	Phi N	110	379	51	107	21	3	12	62	32-5	3	74	.282	.340	.449	109	5	0-2	.952	4	108	156	O91(2/0/90)	0	0.5
1959	Phi N	132	468	62	119	17	6	22	94	36-4	3	101	.254	.310	.457	100	-2	0-0	.992	6	105	131	O120(2/0/118)	0	0.0
1960	Phi N	34	84	11	24	6	1	2	12	9-1	0	24	.286	.351	.452	119	2	0-0	1.000	2	130	68	O22(18/0/5)	0	0.3
	Cin N	77	249	36	70	14	0	17	38	28-3	0	51	.281	.350	.542	139	13	0-2	.985	2	98	136	O67(44/0/23)	0	1.1
	Year	111	333	47	94	20	1	19	50	37-4	0	75	.282	.350	.520	134	16	0-2	.989	3	105	122	O89(62/0/28)	0	1.4
1961	†Cin N	99	282	44	83	16	3	20	57	22-1	1	61	.294	.346	.585	140	15	0-1	.959	3	106	118	O81(41/0/40)	0	1.3
1962	Cin N	109	285	43	75	10	3	17	62	32-2	2	67	.263	.341	.498	118	7	1-0	.935	-4	86	97	O90(88/0/2)	0	-0.1
1963	Cin N	5	7	1	0	0	0	0	0	0-0	1	1	.000	.125	.000	-59	-1	0-0	1.000	0	201	0	/lf	0	-0.1
	Min A	21	47	6	9	0	1	2	6	2-0	0	17	.191	.224	.362	60	-3	0-0	1.000	-1	86	0	O12(2/0/10)	0	-0.5
1964	Cle A	5	8	1	0	0	0	0	0	3-0	0	4	.000	.273	.000	-16	-1	0-0	.667	-0	75	0	O2R	0	-0.2
Total	15	1204	4007	594	1064	194	28	210	699	331-28	20	813	.266	.323	.485	109	41	19-13	.970	30	105	122	O1055(215/16/826)	0	2.8
Potter, Mike	Michael Gary; B5.16.1951 Montebello CA; BR/TR/6´1˝/195; [StLN71*A6/116]; d9.6; Col Mt. San Antonio (CA) JC																								
1976	StL N	9	16	0	0	0	0	0	0	1-0	0	6	.000	.059	.000	-81	-4	0-0	1.000	1	150	0	O4L	0	-0.4
1977	StL N	5	7	0	0	0	0	0	0	0-0	0	2	.000	.000	.000	-99	-2	0-0	ø	-0	0	0	/rf	0	-0.2
Total	2	14	23	0	0	0	0	0	0	1-0	0	8	.000	.042	.000	-87	-6	0-0	1.000	0	130	0	O5(4/0/1)	0	-0.6
Potts, John	John Frederick "Fred"; B2.6.1887 Tipp City OH; D9.5.1962 Cleveland OH; BL/TR/5´7˝/165; d4.18; Col Case Western Reserve																								
1914	KC F	41	102	14	27	4	0	1	9	25	1	13	.265	.414	.333	110	2	7	.933	-3	91	45	O31(1/5/25)	—	-0.2
Potts, Dan	Vivian; B1.1869 Bristol PA; D8.17.1934 Bristol PA; d10.3																								
1892	Was N	1	4	0	1	0	0	0	0	0	0	1	.250	.250	.250	53	0	0	1.000	0	*59*	*287*	/C	—	0.0
Poulsen, Ken	Ken Sterling; B8.4.1947 Van Nuys CA; BL/TR/6´1˝/190; [BosA65 3/45]; d7.3																								
1967	Bos A	5	5	0	1	1	0	0	0	0-0	0	2	.200	.200	.400	68	0	0-0	.667	-0	175	0	3b2/S	0	0.0
Powell, Abner	Abner Charles "Ab"; B12.15.1860 Shenandoah PA; D8.7.1953 New Orleans LA; BL/TR/5´7˝/160; d8.4; ▲																								
1884	Was U	48	191	36	54	10	5	0	—	3	—	—	.283	.294	.387	109	-4	—	.875	-0	51	0	O30(0/12/18),P18,3b2/S2	—	-0.3
1886	Bal AA	11	39	4	7	2	1	0	7	1	0	—	.179	.200	.282	52	-2	4	.917	1	175	628	P7,O4(3/0/1)	—	-0.1
	Cin AA	19	74	13	17	1	1	0	8	4	0	—	.230	.269	.270	67	-3	0	.760	-0	144	0	O13(5/6/2),S6,P4	—	-0.3
	Year	30	113	17	24	3	2	0	15	5	0	—	.212	.246	.274	62	-5	4	.735	0	106	0	O17(8/6/3),P11,S6	—	-0.4
Total	2	78	304	53	78	13	7	0	15	8	0	—	.257	.276	.345	91	-9	4	.817	0	74	0	O47(8/18/21),P29,S7,3b2/2	—	-0.7
Powell, Alonzo	Alonzo Sidney; B12.12.1964 San Francisco CA; BR/TR/6´2˝/190; d4.6																								
1987	Mon N	14	41	3	8	3	0	0	4	5-0	0	17	.195	.283	.268	45	-3	0-0	1.000	-1	70	0	O11(10/0/1)	0	-0.5
1991	Sea A	57	111	16	24	6	1	3	12	11-0	1	24	.216	.288	.369	82	-3	0-2	.960	-4	82	0	O40(24/6/15),1b7,D7	0	-0.8
Total	2	71	152	19	32	9	1	3	16	16-0	1	41	.211	.287	.342	71	-6	0-2	.968	-5	79	0	O51(34/6/16),D7,1b7	0	-1.3
Powell, Jake	Alvin Jacob; B7.15.1908 Silver Spring MD; D11.4.1948 Washington DC; BR/TR/5´11.5˝/180; d8.3																								
1930	Was A	3	4	1	0	0	0	0	0	0	0	1	.000	.000	.000	-99	-1	0-0	1.000	0	113	0	O2(1/0/1)	—	-0.1
1934	Was A	9	35	6	10	2	0	0	1	4	0	2	.286	.359	.343	85	-1	1-1	.955	1	81	434	O9C	—	0.0
1935	Was A	139	551	88	172	26	10	6	98	37	4	37	.312	.360	.428	107	4	15-7	.976	-2	97	94	O136(0/136/1),2b2	—	-0.1
1936	Was A	53	210	40	62	11	5	1	30	18	2	21	.295	.357	.410	94	-3	10-4	.951	-5	89	48	O53C	—	-0.7
	†NY A	87	328	62	99	13	3	7	48	33	0	30	.302	.366	.424	98	-2	16-7	.976	1	104	87	O84(42/42/0)	—	-0.3
	Year	140	538	102	161	24	8	8	78	51	2	51	.299	.362	.418	96	-4	26-11	.967	-4	99	73	O137(42/95/0)	—	-1.0
1937	†NY A	97	365	54	96	22	3	3	45	25	2	36	.263	.314	.364	70	-18	7-5	.981	-1	99	67	O94L	—	-2.3
1938	†NY A	45	164	27	42	12	1	2	20	15	2	20	.256	.326	.378	76	-6	3-1	.978	-2	97	31	O43(37/1/6)	—	-1.0
1939	NY A	31	86	12	21	4	1	1	9	3	0	8	.244	.270	.349	58	-6	1-2	.983	1	112	64	O23(19/2/3)	—	-0.6
1940	NY A	12	27	3	5	0	0	0	2	1	0	4	.185	.214	.185	5	-4	0-0	1.000	1	109	219	O7(3/2/2)	—	-0.3
1943	Was A	37	132	14	35	10	2	0	20	5	1	13	.265	.297	.371	99	-1	3-5	.978	2	105	150	O33(25/8/0)	0	-0.2
1944	Was A	96	367	29	88	9	1	1	37	16	0	26	.240	.272	.278	60	-21	7-2	.980	0	105	72	O90(58/0/32)/3	0	-2.7
1945	Was A	31	98	4	19	2	0	0	3	8	0	8	.194	.255	.214	40	-8	1-1	.950	-0	108	44	O27(21/0/6)	0	-1.1
	Phi N	48	173	13	40	5	0	1	14	8	0	13	.231	.265	.277	52	-12	1	.986	-0	87	152	O44(4/5/35)	0	-1.4
Total	11	688	2540	353	689	116	26	22	327	173	11	219	.271	.320	.363	81	-79	65-35	.975	-5	100	87	O645(304/258/86),2b2/3	0	-10.8
Powell, Hosken	Hosken; B5.14.1955 Selma AL; BL/TL/6´1˝/(180–185); [MinA75 S1/3]; d4.5; Col Chipola (FL) JC																								
1978	Min A	121	381	55	94	20	2	3	31	45-1	0	31	.247	.323	.333	84	-7	11-5	.983	0	99	113	O117R	0	-1.2
1979	Min A	104	338	49	99	17	3	2	36	33-1	3	25	.293	.360	.379	96	-1	5-1	.977	-2	95	95	O93(8/0/85),D5	33	-0.6
1980	Min A	137	485	58	127	17	5	6	35	32-2	3	46	.262	.312	.355	77	-16	14-3	.968	3	104	115	O129R	0	-1.8
1981	Min A	80	264	30	63	11	3	2	25	17-0	1	31	.239	.286	.326	72	-10	7-4	.970	2	102	143	O64(12/0/52),D8	0	-1.2
1982	Tor A	112	265	43	73	13	4	3	26	12-2	0	23	.275	.304	.389	82	-7	4-4	.974	-3	99	51	O75(8/0/68),D19	0	-1.4
1983	Tor A	40	83	6	14	0	0	1	7	5-0	0	8	.169	.213	.205	15	-10	2-0	.981	1	127	0	O33(5/0/29)/1D	0	-1.0
Total	6	594	1816	241	470	78	17	17	160	144-6	7	164	.259	.314	.349	79	-51	43-17	.975	1	101	101	O511(33/0/480),D33/1	33	-7.2
Powell, Jim	James Edwin; B8.30.1859 Richmond VA; D11.20.1929 Butte MT; 5´10˝/170; d8.5																								
1884	Ric AA	41	151	23	37	8	4	0	—	7	4	—	.245	.296	.351	112	2	—	.943	1	136	76	1b41	—	0.0
1885	Phi AA	19	75	5	12	0	3	0	5	1	2	—	.160	.192	.240	34	-6	—	.973	-0	64	63	1b19	—	-0.7
Total	2	60	226	28	49	8	7	0	5	8	6	—	.217	.262	.314	84	-4	—	.952	1	113	72	1b60	—	-0.7
Powell, Boog	John Wesley; B8.17.1941 Lakeland FL; BL/TR/6´4˝/(230–250); d9.26																								
1961	Bal A	4	13	0	1	0	0	0	1	0-0	0	2	.077	.077	.077	-61	-3	0-0	1.000	-1	53	0	O3L	0	-0.4
1962	Bal A	124	400	44	97	13	2	15	53	38-5	2	79	.243	.311	.398	95	-4	1-1	.969	-6	91	17	O112L/1	0	-1.6
1963	Bal A	140	491	67	130	22	2	25	82	49-8	0	87	.265	.328	.470	126	16	1-2	.969	-4	87	77	O121(121/0/1),1b23	0	0.5
1964	Bal A	134	424	74	123	17	0	39	99	76-6	2	91	.290	.399	**.606**	176	45	0-0	.974	6	93	235	O124L,1b5	0	4.6
1965	Bal A	144	472	54	117	20	2	17	72	71-13	4	93	.248	.347	.407	112	10	1-1	.992	3	127	106	1b78,O71L	0	0.5
1966	†Bal A	140	491	78	141	18	0	34	109	67-9	1	125	.287	.372	.532	159	39	0-4	.989	-8	77	97	1b136	0	2.3
1967	Bal A	125	415	53	97	14	1	13	55	55-5	2	94	.234	.324	.366	105	4	1-3	.986	-6	83	104	1b114	0	-1.1
1968	Bal A★	154	550	60	137	21	1	22	85	73-12	3	97	.249	.338	.411	127	19	7-1	.990	-5	83	100	1b149	0	0.7
1969	†Bal A★	152	533	83	162	25	0	37	121	72-10	1	76	.304	.383	.559	160	43	1-1	.995	-1	97	107	1b144	0	3.2
1970	†Bal A★	154	526	82	156	28	0	35	114	104-18	5	80	.297	.412	.549	162	49	1-1	.992	-1	98	100	1b145	0	3.7
1971	†Bal A✳	128	418	59	107	19	0	22	92	82-11	4	64	.256	.379	.459	137	24	1-0	.995	-2	94	110	1b124	0	1.4
1972	Bal A	140	465	53	117	20	1	21	81	65-14	4	92	.252	.346	.434	127	17	4-0	.988	-2	97	**120**	1b133	0	0.6
1973	†Bal A	114	370	52	98	13	1	11	54	85-10	0	64	.265	.398	.395	124	17	0-2	.989	4	**121**	**118**	1b111	0	1.2
1974	†Bal A	110	344	37	91	13	1	12	45	52-10	0	58	.265	.358	.413	125	13	0-1	.996	4	121	129	1b102/D	0	0.9
1975	Cle A	134	435	64	129	18	0	27	86	59-5	1	72	.297	.377	.524	153	31	1-3	**.997**	-2	89	96	1b121,D5	0	1.9
1976	Cle A	95	293	29	63	9	0	9	33	41-3	0	43	.215	.305	.338	91	-3	1-1	.987	1	102	111	1b89	41	-1.0
1977	LA N	50	41	0	10	0	0	0	5	12-1	0	9	.244	.415	.244	81	0	0-0	.938	-1	0	84	1b4	0	-0.1
Total	17	2042	6681	889	1776	270	11	339	1187	1001-140	29	1226	.266	.361	.462	134	317	20-21	.991	-20	97	107	1b1479,O431(431/0/1),D6	41	17.3
Powell, Dante	Le Jon Dante; B8.25.1973 Long Beach CA; BR/TR/6´2˝/(182–185); [SFN94 1/22]; d4.15; Col Cal St.–Fullerton																								
1997	†SF N	27	39	8	12	1	0	1	3	4-0	0	11	.308	.372	.410	107	0	1-1	1.000	-0	107	0	O22(0/20/2)	0	0.0
1998	SF N	8	4	2	2	0	0	1	1	3-0	0	0	.500	.714	1.250	425	2	0-0	1.000	-1	49	0	O8C	0	0.2
1999	Ari N	22	25	4	4	3	0	0	1	2-0	0	6	.160	.222	.280	26	-3	2-1	.929	-1	80	0	O15(0/8/7)	0	-0.4

THE BATTER REGISTER

YEAR	TM LG	G	AB	R	H	2B	3B	HR	RBI	BB-IB	HP	SO	AVG	OBP	SLG	AOPS	ABR	SB-CS	FA	FR	RNG	THR	GAMES AT POSITION	DL	BFW
2001	SF N	13	6	5	2	0	0	0	0	0-0	0	0	.333	.333	.333	78	0	0-0	1.000	1	172	0	O9(5/1/3)	0	0.0
Total	4	70	74	19	20	4	0	2	5	9-0	0	17	.270	.349	.405	96	-1	3-2	.980	-1	100	0	O54(5/37/12)	0	-0.2
Powell, Martin	Martin J.; B3.25.1856 Fitchburg MA; D2.5.1888 Fitchburg MA; BL/TL/6´0˝/170; d6.18																								
1881	Det N	55	219	47	74	9	4	1	38	15	—	9	.338	.380	.429	148	12	—	.947	-3	85	150	1b55/C	—	0.6
1882	Det N	80	338	44	81	13	0	0	29	19	—	27	.240	.280	.278	80	-7	—	.940	-5	62	64	1b80	—	-1.7
1883	Det N	**101**	421	76	115	17	5	1	48	28	—	23	.273	.318	.344	106	5	—	.950	-3	97	115	1b101	—	-0.6
1884	Cin U	43	185	46	59	4	2	1	—	13	—	—	.319	.364	.378	116	-2	—	.940	-2	81	136	1b43	—	-0.7
Total	4	279	1163	213	329	43	11	3	115	75	—	59	.283	.326	.347	109	8	—	.945	-12	82	110	1b279/C	—	-2.4
Powell, Paul	Paul Ray; B3.19.1948 San Angelo TX; BR/TR/5´11˝/185; [MinA69 1/7]; d4.7; Col Arizona St.																								
1971	Min A	20	31	7	5	0	0	1	2	3-0	0	12	.161	.235	.258	38	-3	0-0	1.000	0	117	0	O15C	0	-0.3
1973	LA N	2	1	0	0	0	0	0	0	0-0	0	1	.000	.000	.000	-99	0	0-0	ø	-0	0	0	/lf	0	0.0
1975	LA N	8	10	2	2	1	0	0	0	1-0	0	2	.200	.273	.300	61	-1	0-0	.955	0	39	395	C7/lf	0	0.0
Total	3	30	42	9	7	1	0	1	2	4-0	0	15	.167	.239	.262	41	-4	0-0	1.000	0	107	0	O17(2/15/0),C7	0	-0.3
Powell, Ray	Raymond Reath "Rabbit"; B11.20.1888 Siloam Springs AR; D10.16.1962 Chillicothe MO; BL/TR/5´9˝/160; d4.16; Mil 1918																								
1913	Det A	2	0	0	0	0	0	0	0	0	0	0	ø	ø	ø	ø	0	0	ø	-0	0	0	/cf	—	0.0
1917	Bos N	88	357	42	97	10	4	4	30	24	0	54	.272	.318	.356	113	4	12	.976	3	104	112	O88C	—	0.1
1918	Bos N	53	188	31	40	7	5	0	20	29	1	30	.213	.321	.303	95	0	2	.949	-1	94	118	O53C	—	-0.5
1919	Bos N	123	470	51	111	12	12	2	33	41	4	79	.236	.303	.326	93	-5	16	.951	-1	92	114	O122(0/1/120)	—	-1.4
1920	Bos N	147	609	69	137	12	12	6	29	44	4	83	.225	.282	.314	74	-22	10-18	.956	3	100	118	O147(0/147/1)	—	-3.6
1921	Bos N	149	624	114	191	25	**18**	12	74	58	4	85	.306	.369	.462	125	22	6-17	.954	-9	93	91	O149C	—	0.2
1922	Bos N	142	550	82	163	22	11	6	37	59	4	66	.296	.369	.409	105	5	3-12	.980	6	106	110	O136C	—	0.1
1923	Bos N	97	338	57	102	20	4	4	38	45	1	36	.302	.385	.420	117	10	1-6	.941	-5	97	74	O84(1/83/0)	—	0.0
1924	Bos N	74	188	21	49	9	1	1	15	21	1	28	.261	.338	.335	85	-3	1-3	.947	4	104	191	O46(7/36/3)	—	-0.2
Total	9	875	3324	467	890	117	67	35	276	321	19	461	.268	.336	.375	102	11	51-56	.959	0	98	110	O826(8/694/124)	—	-5.3
Powell, Leroy	Robert Leroy; B10.17.1933 Flint MI; BR/TR/6´1˝/190; d9.16; Mil 1956; Col Michigan St.																								
1955	Chi A	1	0	0	0	0	0	0	0	0-0	0	0	ø	ø	ø	ø	0	0-0	ø	0	—	—	/R	38	0.0
1957	Chi A	1	0	1	0	0	0	0	0	0-0	0	0	ø	ø	ø	ø	0	0-0	ø	0	—	—	/R	0	0.0
Total	2	2	0	1	0	0	0	0	0	0-0	0	0	ø	ø	ø	ø	0	0-0	ø	0	—	—	0	—	0.0
Power, Tom	Thomas E.; B San Francisco CA; D2.25.1898 San Francisco CA; 5´11˝/164; d8.27																								
1890	Bal AA	**38**	125	11	26	3	1	0	6	13	2	—	.208	.293	.248	57	-7	6	.960	-3	68	60	1b26,2b12	—	-1.0
Power, Vic	Victor Pellot (b Victor Felipe Pellot (Pove)); B11.1.1927 Arecibo, PR; D11.29.2005 Bayamon, PR; BR/TR/5´11˝/(170–195); d4.13; OF(41/56/18)																								
1954	Phi A	127	462	36	118	17	5	8	38	19	2	19	.255	.287	.366	78	-17	2-1	.985	8	107	161	O101(33/56/12),1b21/S3	0	-1.5
1955	KC A★	147	596	91	190	34	10	19	76	35-6	0	27	.319	.354	.505	128	20	0-2	.993	14	**140**	97	1b144	0	2.5
1956	KC A★	127	530	77	164	21	5	14	63	24-2	1	16	.309	.340	.447	106	2	2-2	.993	8	130	101	1b76,2b47,O7L	0	0.8
1957	KC A	129	467	48	121	15	1	14	42	19-3	3	21	.259	.291	.385	82	-13	3-2	**.998**	13	**147**	95	1b113,O6R,2b4	0	-0.7
1958	KC A	52	205	35	62	13	4	4	27	7-0	0	3	.302	.325	.463	112	3	1-1	.992	6	150	123	1b50/2	0	0.5
	Cle A	93	385	63	122	24	6	12	53	13-2	1	11	.317	.336	.504	133	15	2-1	.977	6	100	150	3b42,1b41,2b27,S2/lf	0	2.1
	Year	145	590	98	184	37	**10**	16	80	20-2	1	14	.312	.332	.490	125	17	3-2	.992	11	149	121	1b91,3b42,2b28,S2/lf	0	2.6
1959	Cle A★	147	595	102	172	31	6	10	60	40-2	2	22	.289	.334	.412	108	5	9-13	**.995**	12	**145**	97	1b121,2b21,3b7	0	0.9
1960	Cle A★	147	580	69	167	26	3	10	84	24-5	0	20	.288	.313	.395	94	-7	9-5	**.996**	21	**146**	106	1b147,S5,3b4	0	0.6
1961	Cle A	147	563	64	151	34	4	5	63	38-5	1	16	.268	.309	.369	85	-13	4-3	.994	17	**133**	83	1b141,2b7	0	-0.5
1962	Min A	144	611	80	177	28	2	16	63	22-0	3	35	.290	.316	.421	93	-7	7-1	.993	17	**143**	**122**	1b142,2b2	0	0.2
1963	Min A	138	541	65	146	28	2	10	52	22-0	0	24	.270	.297	.384	88	-10	3-1	.992	5	110	112	1b124,2b18,3b5	0	-1.0
1964	Min A	19	45	6	10	2	0	0	1	1-0	0	3	.222	.239	.267	40	-4	0-0	.990	2	162	113	1b12/2	0	-0.3
	LA A	68	221	17	55	6	0	3	13	8-0	1	14	.249	.275	.317	72	-9	1-1	1.000	3	133	84	1b48,3b28,2b5	0	-0.9
	Year	87	266	23	65	8	0	3	14	9-0	1	17	.244	.269	.308	66	-13	1-1	.998	4	125	89	1b60,3b28,2b6	0	-1.2
	Phi N	18	48	1	10	4	0	0	3	2-0	0	3	.208	.240	.292	50	-3	0-0	.993	1	125	89	1b17	0	-0.3
1965	Cal A	124	197	11	51	7	1	1	20	5-1	1	13	.259	.281	.320	72	-8	2-2	.996	4	135	92	1b107,2b6,3b2	0	-0.8
Total	12	1627	6046	765	1716	290	49	126	658	279-26	15	247	.284	.315	.411	97	-46	45-35	.994	135	138	102	1b1304,2b139,O115C,3b89,S8	0	1.6
Powers, Mike	Ellis Foree; B3.2.1906 Toddspoint KY; D12.2.1983 Louisville KY; BL/TL/6´1˝/185; d8.19																								
1932	Cle A	14	33	4	6	4	0	0	5	2	0	2	.182	.229	.303	34	-3	0-0	.917	-1	81	0	O8R	—	-0.4
1933	Cle A	24	47	6	13	2	1	0	2	6	0	6	.277	.358	.362	87	-1	2-1	.952	-1	102	0	O11(4/0/8)	—	-0.2
Total	2	38	80	10	19	6	1	0	7	8	0	8	.237	.307	.338	65	-4	2-1	.939	-2	93	0	O19(4/0/16)	—	-0.6
Powers, John	John Calvin; B7.8.1929 Birmingham AL; D9.25.2001 Birmingham AL; BL/TR/6´0˝/(185–195); d9.24																								
1955	Pit N	2	4	0	1	0	0	0	0	0-0	0	0	.250	.250	.250	34	0	0-0	1.000	0	155	0	O2R	0	0.0
1956	Pit N	11	21	0	1	0	0	0	0	1-0	0	4	.048	.091	.048	-63	-5	0-0	1.000	0	115	0	O5(4/0/1)	0	-0.5
1957	Pit N	20	35	7	10	3	0	2	8	5-0	3	9	.286	.409	.543	161	4	0-0	1.000	0	95	183	O9(4/0/4)	0	0.3
1958	Pit N	57	82	6	15	1	0	2	2	8-0	0	19	.183	.256	.268	40	-7	0-0	1.000	1	120	102	O14(3/0/12)	0	-0.7
1959	Cin N	43	43	8	11	2	1	2	4	3-0	1	13	.256	.319	.488	108	0	0-0	1.000	-0	80	0	O5(4/0/1)	0	0.0
1960	Bal A	10	18	3	2	0	0	0	0	3-0	0	1	.111	.238	.111	-2	-3	0-0	.833	-1	88	0	O4R	0	-0.3
	Cle A	8	12	2	2	1	1	0	0	2-0	0	2	.167	.286	.417	90	0	0-0	1.000	1	180	0	O5(3/0/3)	0	0.0
	Year	18	30	5	4	1	1	0	0	5-0	0	3	.133	.257	.233	34	-3	0-0	.929	0	126	0	O9(3/0/7)	0	-0.3
Total	6	151	215	26	42	7	2	6	14	22-0	4	48	.195	.281	.330	64	-11	0-0	.986	1	113	79	O44(18/0/27)	0	-1.2
Powers, Les	Leslie Edwin; B11.5.1909 Seattle WA; D11.13.1978 Santa Monica CA; BL/TL/6´0˝/175; d9.17; Col Loyola Marymount																								
1938	NY N	2	3	0	0	0	0	0	0	0	0	1	.000	.000	.000	-99	-1	0	ø	0	—	—	/H	—	-0.1
1939	Phi N	19	52	7	18	1	1	0	2	4	0	6	.346	.393	.404	118	1	0	.983	-2	48	82	1b13	—	-0.2
Total	2	21	55	7	18	1	1	0	2	4	0	7	.327	.373	.382	106	0	0	.983	-2	48	82	1b13	—	-0.3
Powers, Doc	Michael Riley; B9.22.1870 Pittsfield MA; D4.26.1909 Philadelphia PA; BR/TR; d6.12; Col Notre Dame																								
1898	Lou N	34	99	13	27	4	3	1	19	5	0	—	.273	.308	.404	105	0	1	.962	-3	*81*	*93*	C22,1b6/lf	—	-0.1
1899	Lou N	49	169	15	35	8	2	0	22	6	1	—	.207	.239	.278	42	-14	1	.942	-2	*115*	*59*	C38,1b7	—	-1.2
	Was N	14	38	3	10	2	0	0	3	1	0	—	.263	.282	.316	65	-2	0	.942	-2	*76*	*97*	C12/1	—	-0.3
	Year	63	207	18	45	10	2	0	25	7	1	—	.217	.247	.285	46	-16	1	.942	-4	*107*	*67*	C50,1b8	—	-1.5
1901	Phi A	116	431	53	108	26	5	1	47	18	7	—	.251	.292	.341	72	-17	10	.952	-6	*98*	*98*	C111,1b3	—	-1.1
1902	Phi A	71	246	35	65	7	1	2	39	14	3	—	.264	.312	.325	74	-9	3	.950	7	*95*	*132*	C68,1b3	—	0.3
1903	Phi A	75	247	19	56	11	1	0	23	5	0	—	.227	.242	.279	54	-14	1	.982	1	*97*	*111*	C66,1b7	—	-0.7
1904	Phi A	57	184	11	35	3	0	0	11	6	1	—	.190	.220	.207	33	-14	3	.965	-3	*104*	*89*	C56/rf	—	-1.3
1905	†Phi A	21	60	6	10	0	0	0	5	0	1	—	.167	.180	.167	10	-6	2	.928	1	*126*	*126*	C21	—	-0.4
	NY A	11	33	3	6	1	0	0	2	1	0	—	.182	.206	.212	29	-3	0	.975	-0	110	68	1b7,C4	—	-0.3
	†Phi A	19	61	2	8	0	0	0	5	3	0	—	.131	.172	.131	-3	-7	2	.991	-2	*126*	*126*	C19	—	-0.9
	Year	51	154	11	24	1	0	0	12	4	1	—	.156	.182	.162	9	-16	4	.957	-2	*114*	*111*	C44,1b7	—	-1.6
1906	Phi A	58	185	5	29	1	0	0	7	1	2	—	.157	.170	.162	4	-21	2	.974	7	*99*	*112*	C57/1	—	-1.0
1907	Phi A	59	159	9	29	3	0	0	9	7	0	—	.182	.217	.201	33	-12	1	.983	9	*99*	*116*	C59	—	0.2
1908	Phi A	62	172	8	31	6	1	0	7	5	3	—	.180	.217	.227	41	-11	1	.967	0	*75*	*106*	C60,1b2	—	-0.7
1909	Phi A	1	4	1	1	0	0	0	0	0	0	—	.250	.250	.250	57	0	0	1.000	0	*153*	*79*	/C	—	0.0
Total	11	647	2088	183	450	72	13	4	199	72	18	—	.216	.248	.268	51	-130	27	.965	7	*97*	*104*	C594,1b37,O2(1/0/1)	—	-7.5
Powers, Phil	Phillip J. "Grandmother"; B7.26.1854 New York NY; D12.22.1914 New York NY; BR/TR/5´7˝/166; d8.31; U8																								
1878	Chi N	8	31	2	5	1	1	0	2	1	—	5	.161	.188	.258	42	-2	—	.930	3	—	—	C8	—	0.1
1880	Bos N	37	126	11	18	5	0	0	10	5	—	15	.143	.176	.183	22	-10	—	.851	-2	—	—	C37,O2(1/1/1)	—	-1.1
1881	Cle N	5	15	1	1	0	0	0	0	1	—	2	.067	.125	.067	-40	-2	—	.955	-0	—	—	C4/3	—	-0.2
1882	Cin AA	16	60	4	13	1	1	0	5	3	—	—	.217	.254	.267	72	-2	—	.921	3	—	—	C10,1b5/rf	—	0.1
1883	Cin AA	30	114	16	28	1	4	0	8	3	—	—	.246	.265	.325	84	-3	—	.893	1	—	—	C17,O13(0/2/11)	—	-0.1
1884	Cin AA	35	133	10	18	1	0	0	8	5	0	—	.135	.167	.143	2	-14	—	.891	6	—	—	C31,O3R,1b2	—	-0.5
1885	Cin AA	15	60	6	16	2	0	0	7	0	0	—	.267	.267	.300	77	-2	—	.833	-3	—	—	C15	—	-0.3
	Bal AA	9	34	6	4	1	0	0	2	1	0	—	.118	.143	.147	-8	-4	—	.844	-3	—	—	C8/rf	—	-0.6

YEAR	TM LG	G	AB	R	H	2B	3B	HR	RBI	BB-IB	HP	SO	AVG	OBP	SLG	AOPS	ABR	SB-CS	FA	FR	RNG	THR	GAMES AT POSITION	DL	BFW
	Year	24	94	12	20	3	0	0	9	1	0	—	.213	.221	.245	47	-6	—	.837	-6	—	—	C23/rf	—	-0.9
Total	7	155	573	56	103	12	6	0	42	19	0	22	.180	.206	.222	39	-39	—	.877	5	—	—	C130,O20(1/3/17),1b7/3	—	-2.6
Powis, Carl	Carl Edgar "Jug"; B1.11.1928 Philadelphia PA; D5.10.1999 Houston TX; BR/TR/6´0˝/185; d4.15; Col Murray St.																								
1957	Bal A	15	41	4	8	3	1	0	2	7-0	1	9	.195	.314	.317	82	-1	2-0	.909	-0	96	122	O13R	0	-0.1
Pozo, Arquimedez	Arquimedez (Ortiz); B8.24.1973 Santo Domingo, D.R.; BR/TR/5´10˝/160; d9.12																								
1995	Sea A	1	1	0	0	0	0	0	0	0-0	0	0	.000	.000	.000	-99	0	0-0	1.000	0	148	0	/2	0	0.0
1996	Bos A	21	58	4	10	3	1	1	11	2-0	1	10	.172	.210	.310	30	-7	1-0	.930	0	95	51	2b10,3b10	0	-0.5
1997	Bos A	4	15	0	4	1	0	0	3	0-0	0	5	.267	.250	.333	54	-1	0-0	.947	3	191	136	3b4	0	0.2
Total	3	26	74	4	14	4	1	1	14	2-0	1	15	.189	.215	.311	33	-8	1-0	.952	3	139	84	3b14,2b11	0	-0.3
Prado, Martin	Martin Manuel; B10.27.1983 Maracay, Venezuela; BR/TR/6´1˝/170; d4.23																								
2006	Atl N	24	42	3	11	1	1	1	9	5-0	0	7	.262	.340	.405	89	-1	0-0	.976	0	130	84	2b11,3b8	0	0.0
Pramesa, Johnny	John Steven; B8.28.1925 Barton OH; D9.9.1996 Los Angeles CA; BR/TR/6´2˝/(210–225); d4.24																								
1949	Cin N	17	25	2	6	1	0	1	2	3	0	5	.240	.321	.400	91	0	0	.966	-1	*92*	*0*	C13	0	-0.1
1950	Cin N	74	228	14	70	10	1	5	30	19	1	15	.307	.363	.425	106	2	0	.981	-3	*72*	*116*	C73	0	0.2
1951	Cin N	72	227	12	52	5	2	6	22	5	0	17	.229	.246	.348	57	-15	0-0	.968	-6	*74*	*83*	C63	0	-1.9
1952	Chi N	22	46	1	13	1	0	1	5	4	0	4	.283	.340	.370	96	0	0-0	.958	0	*63*	*68*	C17	0	0.1
Total	4	185	526	29	141	17	3	13	59	31	1	41	.268	.310	.386	84	-13	0-0	.973	-10	*73*	*93*	C166	0	-1.7
Pratt, Del	Derrill Burnham; B1.10.1888 Walhalla SC; D9.30.1977 Texas City TX; BR/TR/5´11˝/175; d4.11; Col Alabama; OF(3/3/8)																								
1912	StL A	152	570	76	172	26	15	5	69	36	4	—	.302	.348	.426	125	16	24	.943	13	106	122	2b122,S21,O8(0/3/5)/3	—	3.1
1913	StL A	**155**	592	60	175	31	13	2	87	40	1	57	.296	.341	.402	121	13	37	.951	3	101	104	2b146,1b9	—	1.9
1914	StL A	158	584	85	165	34	13	5	65	50	2	45	.283	.341	.411	131	20	37-28	.944	-1	100	95	2b152,O5(2/0/3)/S	—	2.2
1915	StL A	**159**	602	61	175	31	11	3	78	26	3	43	.291	.323	.394	119	10	32-23	.965	16	96	130	2b158	—	2.9
1916	StL A	**158**	596	64	159	35	12	5	**103**	54	3	56	.267	.331	.391	123	14	26-17	.966	20	105	114	2b158	—	4.0
1917	StL A	123	450	40	111	22	8	1	53	33	2	36	.247	.301	.338	98	-2	18	.959	18	103	119	2b119,1b2	—	1.9
1918	NY A	**126**	477	65	131	19	7	2	55	35	2	26	.275	.327	.356	104	1	12	.969	10	100	**143**	2b126	—	1.5
1919	NY A	140	527	69	154	27	7	4	56	36	4	24	.292	.342	.393	105	3	22	.969	25	**115**	122	2b140	—	3.1
1920	NY A	**154**	574	84	180	37	8	4	97	50	3	24	.314	.372	.427	107	7	12-10	.971	13	107	**118**	2b154	—	2.1
1921	Bos A	135	521	80	169	36	10	5	102	44	1	10	.324	.378	.461	116	12	8-10	.961	0	101	**137**	2b134	—	1.4
1922	Bos A	**154**	607	73	183	44	7	6	86	53	4	20	.301	.361	.427	106	6	7-10	.966	-14	100	91	2b154	—	-0.6
1923	Det A	101	297	43	92	18	3	0	40	25	6	9	.310	.375	.391	104	2	6-1	.947	-7	96	77	2b60,1b17,3b12	—	-0.2
1924	Det A	121	429	56	130	32	3	1	77	31	2	10	.303	.353	.399	95	-3	6-9	.948	-2	108	118	2b65,1b51,3b4/lf	—	-0.8
Total	13	1836	6826	856	1996	392	117	43	968	513	37	360	.292	.345	.403	112	99	247-108	.960	94	103	116	2b1688,1b79,S22,3b17,O14R	—	22.5
Pratt, Frank	Francis Bruce "Truckhorse"; B8.24.1897 Blocton AL; D3.8.1974 Centreville AL; BL/TR/5´9.5˝/155; d5.13; Col Alabama																								
1921	Chi A	1	1	0	0	0	0	0	0	0	0	0	.000	.000	.000	-99	0	0-0	ø	0	—	—	/H	—	0.0
Pratt, Larry	Lester John; B10.8.1887 Gibson City IL; D1.8.1969 Peoria IL; BR/TR/6´0˝/183; d9.19																								
1914	Bos A	5	4	0	0	0	0	0	0	0	0	4	.000	.000	.000	-99	-1	0	.923	1	*210*	*233*	C5	—	0.0
1915	Bro F	20	49	5	9	1	0	1	2	2	0	18	.184	.216	.265	35	-5	2	.949	-2	*82*	*117*	C17	—	-0.6
	New F	5	4	2	2	2	0	0	0	3	0	1	.500	.714	1.000	403	2	2	1.000	-0	*133*	*93*	C3	—	0.2
	Year	25	53	7	11	3	0	1	2	5	0	19	.208	.276	.321	69	-3	4	.953	-2	*86*	*115*	C20	—	-0.4
Total	2	30	57	7	11	3	0	1	2	5	0	23	.193	.258	.298	58	-4	4	.949	-1	*98*	*127*	C25	—	-0.4
Pratt, Tom	Thomas Jefferson; B1.26.1844 Chelsea MA; D9.28.1908 Philadelphia PA; TL/5´7.5˝/150; d10.18; U1																								
1871	Ath NA	1	6	2	2	0	0	0	1	0	—	0	.333	.333	.333	93	0	0-0	.786	-1	0	0	/1	—	0.0
Pratt, Todd	Todd Alan; B2.9.1967 Bellevue NE; BR/TR/6´3˝/(195–240); [BosA85 6/153]; d7.29																								
1992	Phi N	16	46	6	13	1	0	2	10	4-0	0	12	.283	.340	.435	118	1	0-0	.972	-1	97	0	C11	0	0.1
1993	†Phi N	33	87	8	25	6	0	5	13	5-0	1	19	.287	.330	.529	128	3	0-0	.989	2	138	52	C26	29	0.7
1994	Phi N	28	102	10	20	6	1	2	9	12-0	0	29	.196	.281	.333	58	-6	0-1	1.000	0	168	63	C28	0	-0.5
1995	Chi N	25	60	3	8	2	0	0	4	6-1	0	21	.133	.209	.167	2	-9	0-0	.981	1	81	73	C25	0	-0.7
1997	NY N	39	106	12	30	6	0	2	19	13-0	2	32	.283	.372	.396	106	2	0-1	.990	3	142	148	C36/D	0	0.6
1998	NY N	41	69	9	19	9	1	2	18	2-0	0	20	.275	.296	.522	113	1	0-0	.973	-2	132	135	C16,1b3	47	0.0
1999	†NY N	71	140	18	41	4	0	3	21	15-0	3	32	.293	.369	.386	97	0	2-0	.996	2	131	69	C52/1lf	0	0.4
2000	†NY N	80	160	33	44	6	0	8	25	22-1	5	31	.275	.378	.463	118	5	0-0	.997	-2	131	106	C71/D	0	0.6
2001	NY N	45	80	6	13	5	0	2	4	15-1	2	36	.162	.306	.300	63	-4	1-0	.994	-7	116	16	C31	0	-0.9
	Phi N	35	93	12	19	3	0	2	7	19-2	1	25	.204	.345	.301	73	-3	0-0	.985	-3	190	50	C34/1	0	-0.5
	Year	80	173	18	32	8	0	4	11	34-3	3	61	.185	.327	.301	68	-7	1-0	.989	-10	157	35	C65/1	0	-1.4
2002	Phi N	39	106	14	33	11	0	3	16	24-6	4	28	.311	.449	.500	162	12	2-0	1.000	1	102	70	C34,1b2	0	1.5
2003	Phi N	43	125	16	34	10	1	4	20	22-0	6	38	.272	.400	.464	136	8	0-0	.996	-4	60	66	C35,1b6	0	0.6
2004	Phi N	45	128	16	33	5	0	3	16	18-0	1	38	.258	.351	.367	84	-3	0-0	1.000	-5	72	50	C43	0	-0.5
2005	Phi N	60	175	17	44	4	0	7	23	19-5	2	50	.251	.332	.394	86	-4	0-0	.997	3	132	85	C57	0	0.3
2006	Atl N	62	135	14	28	6	0	4	19	12-0	1	43	.207	.272	.341	56	-9	1-0	.986	-2	87	100	C54	0	-0.8
Total	14	662	1612	194	404	84	3	49	224	208-16	28	454	.251	.344	.398	95	-6	6-2	.993	-14	118	76	C553,1b13,D2/lf	76	0.9
Preibisch, Mel	Melvin Adolphus "Primo"; B11.23.1914 Sealy TX; D4.12.1980 Sealy TX; BR/TR/5´11˝/185; d9.17; Col Texas																								
1940	Bos N	11	40	3	9	2	0	0	5	2	0	4	.225	.262	.275	51	-3	0	1.000	0	107	111	O11C	—	-0.3
1941	Bos N	5	4	0	0	0	0	0	0	1	0	2	.000	.200	.000	-42	-1	0	1.000	0	392	0	O2(1/1/1)	0	-0.1
Total	2	16	44	3	9	2	0	0	5	3	0	6	.205	.255	.250	42	-4	0	1.000	1	110	110	O13(1/12/1)	0	-0.4
Prescott, Bobby	George Bertrand; B3.27.1931 Colon, Pan; BR/TR/5´11˝/180; d6.17																								
1961	KC A	10	12	0	1	0	0	0	0	2-0	0	5	.083	.214	.083	-17	-2	0-0	ø	-1	0	0	O2L	0	-0.3
Presley, Jim	James Arthur; B10.23.1961 Pensacola FL; BR/TR/6´1˝/(180–200); [SeaA79 4/79]; d6.24; C4																								
1984	Sea A	70	251	27	57	12	1	10	36	6-1	1	63	.227	.247	.402	77	-9	1-1	.958	-5	85	88	3b69/D	0	-1.6
1985	Sea A	155	570	71	157	33	1	28	84	44-9	1	100	.275	.324	.484	118	13	2-2	.961	5	109	76	3b154	0	1.5
1986	Sea A☆	155	616	83	163	33	4	27	107	32-3	4	172	.265	.303	.463	104	1	0-4	.965	6	105	103	3b155	0	0.3
1987	Sea A	152	575	78	142	23	6	24	88	38-1	4	157	.247	.296	.433	86	-14	2-0	.953	11	110	103	3b148,S4/D	0	-0.4
1988	Sea A	150	544	50	125	26	0	14	62	36-1	4	114	.230	.280	.355	74	-20	3-5	.940	-12	85	102	3b146,D4	0	-3.3
1989	Sea A	117	390	42	92	20	1	12	41	21-2	1	107	.236	.275	.385	82	-11	0-0	.924	-3	99	89	3b90,1b30/D	0	-1.5
1990	Atl N	140	541	59	131	34	1	19	72	29-0	3	130	.242	.282	.414	85	-12	1-1	.930	-2	93	94	3b133,1b17	0	-1.6
1991	SD N	20	59	3	8	0	0	1	5	4-1	1	16	.136	.200	.186	10	-7	0-1	.923	-4	73	0	3b16	0	-1.2
Total	8	959	3546	413	875	181	14	135	495	210-18	19	859	.247	.290	.420	90	-59	9-14	.949	-3	99	93	3b911,1b47,D7,S4	0	-7.8
Preston, Walt	Walter B.; B4.6.1868 Richmond VA; D12.23.1937 New Orleans LA; BL/TR/6´0˝/175; d4.18																								
1895	Lou N	50	197	42	55	6	4	1	24	17	10	17	.279	.366	.365	95	0	11	.893	-5	142	221	O26(0/19/7),3b25	—	-0.5
Price, Jim	Jimmie William; B10.13.1941 Harrisburg PA; BR/TR/6´0˝/(190–195); d4.11																								
1967	Det A	44	92	9	24	4	0	0	8	4-1	0	10	.261	.292	.304	74	-3	0-0	.974	-2	67	82	C24	0	-0.5
1968	†Det A	64	132	12	23	4	0	3	13	13-1	1	14	.174	.253	.273	58	-7	0-0	.996	-5	132	19	C42	0	-1.2
1969	Det A	72	192	21	45	8	0	9	28	18-1	0	20	.234	.294	.417	95	-2	0-0	.989	-2	67	82	C51	0	-0.2
1970	Det A	52	132	12	24	4	0	5	15	21-0	0	23	.182	.290	.326	70	-5	0-0	.979	-4	89	65	C38	0	-0.7
1971	Det A	29	54	4	13	2	0	1	7	6-1	1	3	.241	.323	.333	84	-1	0-0	.981	-2	60	113	C25	21	-0.2
Total	5	261	602	58	129	22	0	18	71	62-4	2	70	.214	.287	.341	78	-18	0-0	.985	-15	86	67	C180	21	-2.8
Price, Jackie	John Thomas Reid "Johnny"; B11.13.1912 Winborn MS; D10.2.1967 San Francisco CA; BL/TR/5´10.5˝/150; d8.18																								
1946	Cle A	7	13	1	3	0	0	0	0	0	0	0	.231	.231	.231	31	-1	0-0	.947	1	119	50	S4	0	0.0
Price, Joe	Joseph Preston "Lumber"; B4.10.1897 Milligan College TN; D1.15.1961 Washington DC; BR/TR/6´1.5˝/187; d9.5; Col Milligan																								
1928	NY N	1	1	0	0	0	0	0	0	0	0	1	.000	.000	.000	-99	0	0	ø	-0	0	0	/cf	—	0.0

YEAR	TM LG	G	AB	R	H	2B	3B	HR	RBI	BB-IB	HP	SO	AVG	OBP	SLG	AOPS	ABR	SB-CS	FA	FR	RNG	THR	GAMES AT POSITION	DL	BFW
PRICHARD, BOB	Robert Alexander; B10.21.1917 Paris TX; D9.25.1991 Abilene TX; BL/TL/6´1˝/195; d6.14																								
1939	Was A	26	85	8	20	5	0	0	8	19	0	16	.235	.375	.294	79	-1	0-2	.992	-1	84	135	1b26	—	-0.5
PRIDDY, JERRY	Gerald Edward; B11.9.1919 Los Angeles CA; D3.3.1980 N.Hollywood CA; BR/TR/5´11.5˝/(180–186); d4.17; Mil 1944–45																								
1941	NY A	56	174	18	37	7	0	1	26	18	1	16	.213	.290	.270	50	-13	4-2	.968	6	102	160	2b31,3b14,1b10	0	-0.5
1942	†NY A	59	189	23	53	9	2	2	28	31	1	27	.280	.385	.381	118	6	0-1	.944	3	101	37	3b35,1b11,2b8,S3	0	0.9
1943	Was A	149	560	68	152	31	3	4	62	67	1	76	.271	.350	.359	112	10	5-5	.971	5	103	111	2b134,S15/3	0	2.4
1946	Was A	138	511	54	130	22	8	6	58	57	2	73	.254	.332	.364	100	-1	9-3	.962	-1	104	101	2b138	0	0.7
1947	Was A	147	505	42	108	20	3	3	49	62	1	79	.214	.301	.283	65	-24	7-6	.980	-1	98	84	2b146	0	-1.8
1948	StL A	151	560	96	166	40	9	8	79	86	1	71	.296	.391	.443	118	17	6-5	.968	**23**	**108**	111	2b146	0	4.5
1949	StL A	145	544	83	158	26	4	11	63	80	1	81	.290	.382	.414	106	6	5-3	.968	-2	99	75	2b145	0	1.2
1950	Det A	**157**	618	104	171	26	6	13	75	95	3	95	.277	.376	.401	96	-2	2-7	.981	**28**	**114**	**120**	2b157	0	3.0
1951	Det A	**154**	584	73	152	22	6	8	57	69	0	73	.260	.338	.360	88	-10	4-3	.980	11	102	99	2b154/S	0	1.0
1952	Det A	75	279	37	79	23	3	4	20	42	1	29	.283	.379	.430	124	11	1-8	.968	-2	96	80	2b75	74	1.1
1953	Det A	65	196	14	46	6	2	1	24	17	1	19	.235	.299	.301	63	-10	1-1	.977	1	97	83	2b45,1b11,3b2	0	-0.8
Total	11	1296	4720	612	1252	232	46	61	541	624	13	639	.265	.353	.373	97	-10	44-44	.973	70	104	100	2b1179,3b52,1b32,S19	74	11.7
PRIDE, CURTIS	Curtis John; B12.17.1968 Washington DC; BL/TR/6´0˝/(195–210); [NYN86 10/258]; d9.14																								
1993	Mon N	10	9	3	4	1	1	1	5	0-0	0	3	.444	.444	1.111	288	2	1-0	1.000	0	439	0	O2L	0	0.3
1995	Mon N	48	63	10	11	1	0	0	2	5-0	0	16	.175	.235	.190	13	-8	3-2	.920	-1	100	0	O24(24/1/0)	0	-1.0
1996	Det A	95	267	52	80	17	5	10	31	31-1	0	63	.300	.372	.513	121	8	11-6	.967	1	116	0	O48(45/0/5),D31	27	0.5
1997	Det A	79	162	21	34	4	4	2	19	24-1	1	45	.210	.314	.321	67	-8	6-4	.980	-2	96	0	O35(34/0/3),D23	0	-1.2
	Bos A	2	2	1	1	0	0	1	1	0-0	0	1	.500	.500	2.000	501	1	0-0	ø	0	—	—	/H	0	0.1
	Year	81	164	22	35	4	4	3	20	24-1	1	46	.213	.316	.341	72	-7	6-4	.980	-2	96	0	O35(34/0/3),D23	0	-1.1
1998	Atl N	70	107	19	27	6	1	3	9	9-0	3	29	.252	.325	.411	93	-1	4-0	1.000	2	140	0	O22(8/0/14),D2	16	0.1
2000	Bos A	9	20	4	5	1	0	0	0	1-0	0	7	.250	.286	.300	47	-2	0-0	1.000	0	121	0	O9(7/2/0)/D	0	-0.1
2001	Mon N	36	76	8	19	3	1	1	9	9-0	2	22	.250	.345	.355	82	-2	3-2	1.000	1	107	94	O23(19/1/3),D2	64	-0.2
2003	NY A	4	12	1	1	0	0	1	1	0-0	0	2	.083	.083	.333	3	-2	0-0	1.000	-0	86	0	O3(1/0/2)	0	-0.2
2004	†Ana A	35	40	5	10	3	0	0	3	0-0	1	11	.250	.268	.325	56	-3	1-0	1.000	2	155	0	O24(15/2/7),D2	0	-0.1
2005	LA A	11	11	2	1	1	0	0	0	0-0	0	4	.091	.091	.182	-31	-2	0-0	1.000	0	177	0	O4L,D3	24	-0.2
2006	LA A	22	27	6	6	2	0	1	2	6-0	0	8	.222	.364	.407	103	0	0-0	1.000	0	111	0	O11(8/0/3),D4	12	0.0
Total	11	421	796	132	199	39	12	20	82	85-2	7	211	.250	.327	.405	88	-17	29-14	.980	2	115	11	O205(167/6/37),D68	143	-2.0
PRIEST, JOHNNY	John Gooding; B6.23.1891 St.Joseph MO; D11.4.1979 Washington DC; BR/TR/5´11˝/170; d5.30																								
1911	NY A	8	21	2	3	0	0	0	2	2	1	—	.143	.250	.143	10	-3	3	.824	-2	65	0	2b5,3b2	—	-0.5
1912	NY A	2	2	1	1	0	0	0	1	0	0	—	.500	.500	.500	176	0	0	ø	0	—	—	/H	—	0.0
Total	2	10	23	3	4	0	0	0	3	2	1	—	.174	.269	.174	23	-3	3	.824	-2	65	0	2b5,3b2	—	-0.5
PRIETO, ALEX	Alejandro Antonio; B6.19.1976 Caracas, Distrito Capital, Venezuela; BR/TR/5´10˝/(200–205); d7.26																								
2003	Min A	8	11	1	1	0	0	0	0	0-0	0	4	.091	.091	.091	-50	-2	0-0	1.000	-0	97	75	2b5/S	0	-0.2
2004	Min A	16	32	4	8	1	0	1	4	3-0	0	9	.250	.306	.375	77	-1	0-1	1.000	1	118	158	2b8,3b5,S3/D	0	0.0
Total	2	24	43	5	9	1	0	1	4	3-0	0	13	.209	.255	.302	45	-3	0-1	1.000	0	113	137	2b13,3b5,S4/D	0	-0.2
PRIETO, CHRIS	Christian Michael; B8.24.1972 Carmel CA; BL/TL/5´11˝/180; [SDN93 24/674]; d5.14; Col Nevada–Reno																								
2005	LA A	2	2	0	0	0	0	0	0	0-0	0	0	.000	.000	.000	-99	-1	0-0	1.000	0	195	0	O2C	0	0.0
PRINCE, TOM	Thomas Albert; B8.13.1964 Kankakee IL; BR/TR/5´11˝/(185–206); [PitN84*S4/64]; d9.22; Col Kankakee (IL) CC																								
1987	Pit N	4	9	1	2	1	0	1	2	0-0	0	2	.222	.222	.667	123	0	0-0	1.000	-0	70	88	C4	0	0.0
1988	Pit N	29	74	3	13	2	0	0	6	4-0	0	15	.176	.218	.203	22	-8	0-0	.983	-4	98	61	C28	0	-1.1
1989	Pit N	21	52	1	7	4	0	0	5	6-1	0	12	.135	.220	.212	26	-5	1-1	.960	-2	49	122	C21	0	-0.7
1990	Pit N	4	10	1	1	0	0	0	0	1-0	0	2	.100	.182	.100	-21	-2	0-1	1.000	0	79	0	C3	0	-0.2
1991	Pit N	26	34	4	9	3	0	1	2	7-0	1	3	.265	.405	.441	139	2	0-0	.984	0	105	190	C19/1	19	0.3
1992	Pit N	27	44	1	4	2	0	0	5	6-0	0	9	.091	.192	.136	-3	-6	1-1	.977	2	128	82	C19/3	0	-0.4
1993	Pit N	66	179	14	35	14	0	2	24	13-2	7	38	.196	.272	.307	56	-11	1-1	.984	-7	73	96	C59	0	-1.4
1994	LA N	3	6	2	2	0	0	0	1	1-0	0	3	.333	.429	.333	108	0	0-0	1.000	1	0	0	C3	0	0.1
1995	LA N	18	40	3	8	2	1	1	4	4-0	0	10	.200	.273	.375	74	-2	0-0	.988	-3	119	99	C17	36	-0.4
1996	LA N	40	64	6	19	6	0	1	11	6-2	2	15	.297	.365	.438	121	2	0-0	.994	2	105	63	C35	0	0.6
1997	LA N	47	100	17	22	5	0	3	14	5-0	3	15	.220	.275	.360	70	-5	0-0	.996	8	377	143	C45	0	0.5
1998	LA N	37	81	7	15	5	1	0	5	7-1	2	24	.185	.267	.272	44	-7	0-0	1.000	3	113	174	C32	0	-0.2
1999	Phi N	4	6	1	1	0	0	0	0	1-0	0	1	.167	.286	.167	18	-1	0-0	1.000	0	135	0	C4	151	0.0
2000	Phi N	46	122	14	29	9	0	2	16	13-0	2	31	.238	.321	.361	72	-5	1-0	.996	-1	124	84	C46	0	-0.3
2001	Min A	64	196	19	43	4	1	7	23	12-0	6	39	.219	.284	.357	64	-11	3-1	1.000	14	152	120	C64	0	0.7
2002	†Min A	51	125	14	28	7	1	4	16	14-0	4	26	.224	.317	.392	86	-2	1-3	.997	2	192	78	C50	0	0.1
2003	Min A	24	40	5	8	2	0	2	5	5-0	2	7	.200	.319	.400	85	-1	1-0	1.000	1	360	98	C22,D2	0	0.1
	KC A	8	8	0	2	0	0	0	1	0-0	0	0	.250	.250	.250	31	-1	0-0	1.000	-2	64	0	C7/D	0	-0.2
	Year	32	48	5	10	2	0	2	6	5-0	2	7	.208	.309	.375	76	-2	1-0	1.000	-0	314	83	C29,D3	0	-0.1
Total	17	519	1190	113	248	66	4	24	140	105-6	29	252	.208	.286	.331	65	-63	9-8	.992	15	149	103	C478,D3/31	206	-2.5
PRINCE, WALTER	Walter Farr; B5.9.1861 Amherst NH; D3.2.1938 Bristol NH; BL/TR/5´9˝/150; d8.7																								
1883	Lou AA	4	11	1	2	0	0	0	—	0	—	—	.182	.182	.182	19	-1	—	.500	-2	0	0	O2R,1b2/S	—	-0.3
1884	Det N	7	21	0	3	0	0	0	1	3	—	4	.143	.250	.143	29	-2	—	.375	-3	0	0	O7R	—	-0.4
	Was AA	43	166	22	36	3	2	1	—	13	3	—	.217	.286	.277	95	1	—	.940	-5	28	78	1b43	—	-0.8
	Was U	1	4	0	1	0	0	0	—	0	—	—	.250	.250	.250	54	0	—	.818	-0	0	0	/1	—	-0.1
Total	2	55	202	23	42	3	2	1	1	16	—	4	.208	.276	.257	83	-2	—	.935	-11	34	74	1b46,O9R/S	—	-1.6
PRITCHARD, BUDDY	Harold William; B1.25.1936 South Gate CA; BR/TR/6´1˝/165; d4.21; Col USC																								
1957	Pit N	23	11	1	1	0	0	0	0	0-0	0	4	.091	.091	.091	-53	-2	0-0	.947	-1	74	143	S10,2b3	0	-0.3
PRITCHETT, CHRIS	Christopher Davis; B1.31.1970 Merced CA; BL/TR/6´4˝/(185–212); [CalA91 2/61]; d9.6; Col UCLA																								
1996	Cal A	5	13	1	2	0	0	0	1	0-0	0	3	.154	.154	.154	-22	-2	0-0	1.000	-0	53	110	1b5	0	-0.3
1998	Ana A	31	80	12	23	2	1	2	8	4-0	0	16	.287	.321	.412	88	-2	2-0	.995	2	139	65	1b29/D	16	-0.1
1999	Ana A	20	45	3	7	1	0	1	2	2-0	0	9	.156	.188	.244	10	-6	1-1	.990	1	129	85	1b15,D5	0	-0.6
2000	Phi N	5	11	0	1	0	0	0	0	1-0	0	3	.091	.167	.091	-33	-2	0-0	1.000	1	217	43	1b3	0	-0.2
Total	4	61	149	16	33	3	1	3	11	7-0	0	31	.221	.255	.315	46	-12	3-1	.995	4	135	72	1b52,D6	16	-1.2
PROESER, GEORGE	George "Yatz"; B5.30.1864 Cincinnati OH; D10.13.1941 New Burlington OH; BL/TL/5´10˝/190; d9.15; ▲																								
1888	Cle AA	7	23	5	7	2	0	0	1	1	0	—	.304	.333	.391	136	2	0	.846	-1	84	0	P7	—	0.0
1890	Syr AA	13	53	11	13	1	1	1	6	10	0	—	.245	.365	.358	126	2	1	.895	-2	47	0	O13R	—	0.1
Total	2	20	76	16	20	3	1	1	7	11	0	—	.263	.356	.368	129	4	1	.895	-2	47	0	O13R,P7	—	0.1
PROPST, JAKE	William Jacob; B3.10.1895 Kennedy AL; D2.24.1967 Columbus MS; BL/TR/5´10˝/165; d8.7																								
1923	Was A	1	1	0	0	0	0	0	0	0	0	0	.000	.000	.000	-99	0	0-0	ø	0	—	—	/H	—	0.0
PROTHRO, DOC	James Thompson; B7.16.1893 Memphis TN; D10.14.1971 Memphis TN; BR/TR/5´10.5˝/170; d9.26; M3																								
1920	Was A	6	13	2	5	0	0	0	2	0	0	4	.385	.385	.385	107	0	0-0	1.000	0	56	290	S2,3b2	—	0.0
1923	Was A	6	8	2	2	0	1	0	3	1	0	3	.250	.333	.500	124	0	0-0	1.000	2	148	0	3b6	—	0.2
1924	Was A	46	159	17	53	11	5	0	24	15	1	11	.333	.394	.465	125	6	4-4	.915	-9	80	96	3b45	—	-0.1
1925	Bos A	119	415	44	130	23	3	0	51	52	0	21	.313	.390	.383	97	0	9-11	.945	-2	**103**	73	3b108,S3	—	0.3
1926	Cin N	3	5	1	1	0	1	0	1	1	0	1	.200	.333	.600	151	0	0	1.000	-0	114	0	3b2	—	0.0
Total	5	180	600	66	191	34	10	0	81	69	1	40	.318	.390	.408	105	6	13-15	.940	-9	98	85	3b163,S5	—	-0.4
PRUESS, EARL	Earl Henry "Gibby"; B4.2.1895 Chicago IL; D8.28.1979 Branson MO; BR/TR/5´10.5˝/170; d9.15																								
1920	StL A	1	0	1	0	0	0	0	0	1	0	0	ø	1.000	ø	176	0	1-0	1.000	0	197	0	/rf	—	0.1

YEAR	TM LG	G	AB	R	H	2B	3B	HR	RBI	BB-IB	HP	SO	AVG	OBP	SLG	AOPS	ABR	SB-CS	FA	FR	RNG	THR	GAMES AT POSITION	DL	BFW
Pruett, Jim	James Calvin; B12.16.1917 Nashville TN; D7.29.2003 Waukesha WI; BR/TR/5´10˝/178; d9.26																								
1944	Phi A	3	4	1	1	0	0	0	0	1	1	0	.250	.500	.250	119	0	0-0	1.000	0	*61*	*269*	C2	0	0.1
1945	Phi A	6	9	1	2	0	0	0	0	1	0	2	.222	.300	.222	53	-1	0-1	1.000	0	*94*	*0*	C4	0	-0.1
Total	2	9	13	2	3	0	0	0	0	2	1	2	.231	.375	.231	77	-1	0-1	1.000	1	*82*	*98*	C6	0	0.0
Pruitt, Ron	Ronald Ralph; B10.21.1951 Flint MI; BR/TR/6´0˝/(185–191); [TexA72 2/28]; d6.25; Col Michigan St.																								
1975	Tex A	14	17	2	3	0	0	0	0	1-0	0	3	.176	.222	.176	14	-2	0-0	1.000	-1	71	93	C13/lf	0	-0.3
1976	Cle A	47	86	7	23	1	1	0	5	16-1	0	8	.267	.375	.302	103	1	2-3	1.000	3	119	251	O26(12/1/13),C6,3b6/1D	0	0.3
1977	Cle A	78	219	29	63	10	2	2	32	28-0	2	22	.288	.369	.379	109	4	2-3	.972	-4	88	47	O69(27/3/42),C4/3D	0	-0.4
1978	Cle A	71	187	17	44	6	1	6	17	16-3	0	20	.235	.296	.374	88	-4	2-1	.984	-11	55	69	C48,O16(12/0/4),3b2,D5	0	-1.4
1979	Cle A	64	166	23	47	7	0	2	21	19-1	0	21	.283	.355	.361	94	-1	2-0	.957	-4	80	51	O29(19/0/11),D14,C11,3b3	0	-0.6
1980	Cle A	23	36	1	11	1	0	0	4	4-0	0	6	.306	.366	.333	95	0	0-0	1.000	0	87	267	O6(0/1/5),3b2,D2	0	0.0
	Chi A	33	70	8	21	2	0	2	11	8-1	0	7	.300	.372	.414	115	2	0-0	1.000	-2	111	0	O11(10/1/0),C5,3b3/1D	0	-0.1
	Year	56	106	9	32	3	0	2	15	12-1	0	13	.302	.370	.387	108	2	0-0	1.000	-2	102	102	O17(10/2/5),D9,3b5,C5/1	0	-0.1
1981	Cle A	5	9	0	0	0	0	0	0	1-0	0	2	.000	.100	.000	-69	-2	0-0	1.000	-1	69	0	O3(2/0/1)/CD	0	-0.3
1982	SF N	5	4	1	2	1	0	0	2	1-1	0	1	.500	.600	.750	278	1	0-0	1.000	1	0	0	/Crf	0	0.2
1983	SF N	1	1	0	0	0	0	0	0	0-0	0	0	.000	.000	.000	-99	0	0-0	ø	0	—	—	/H	0	0.0
Total	9	341	795	88	214	28	4	12	92	94-7	2	90	.269	.345	.360	97	-1	8-7	.977	-19	94	75	O162(83/6/77),C89,D37,3b17,1b2	0	-2.6
Pryor, Greg	Gregory Russell; B10.2.1949 Marietta OH; BR/TR/6´0˝/(175–186); [TexA71 6/128]; d6.4; Col Florida Southern																								
1976	Tex A	5	8	2	3	0	0	0	1	0-0	0	1	.375	.375	.375	118	0	0-0	1.000	0	92	72	2b3/S3	0	0.0
1978	Chi A	82	222	27	58	11	0	2	15	11-0	1	18	.261	.298	.338	78	-7	3-1	.966	2	95	74	2b35,S28,3b20	0	-0.1
1979	Chi A	143	476	60	131	23	3	3	34	35-1	2	41	.275	.324	.355	84	-11	3-4	.961	-2	103	72	S119,2b25,3b22	0	-0.1
1980	Chi A	122	338	32	81	18	4	1	29	12-0	2	35	.240	.265	.325	62	-18	2-2	.975	15	115	99	S76,3b41,2b5/D	0	0.3
1981	Chi A	47	76	4	17	1	0	0	6	6-0	2	8	.224	.298	.237	56	-4	0-0	.931	-0	101	29	3b27,S13,2b5	0	-0.4
1982	KC A	73	152	23	41	10	1	2	12	10-0	0	20	.270	.315	.388	91	-2	2-0	.951	-3	97	109	3b40,2b15,1b14,S7	0	-0.4
1983	KC A	68	115	9	25	4	0	1	14	7-0	0	8	.217	.260	.278	48	-8	0-0	.958	1	109	96	3b60,1b6,2b3	0	-0.8
1984	†KC A	123	270	32	71	11	1	4	25	12-0	3	28	.263	.301	.356	80	-8	0-3	.970	2	100	110	3b105,2b22,S2/1D	0	-0.7
1985	†KC A	63	114	8	25	3	0	1	3	8-0	0	12	.219	.270	.272	49	-8	0-1	.946	-3	111	84	3b26,2b20,S13/1D	0	-1.0
1986	KC A	63	112	7	19	4	0	0	7	3-0	0	14	.170	.191	.205	8	-14	1-1	.935	1	118	188	3b35,S17,2b12/1	0	-1.3
Total	10	789	1883	204	471	85	9	14	146	104-1	10	185	.250	.291	.327	70	-80	11-12	.952	12	107	108	3b377,S276,2b145,1b23,D3	0	-4.5
Puccinelli, George	George Lawrence "Pooch","Count"; B6.22.1907 San Francisco CA; D4.16.1956 San Francisco CA; BR/TR/6´0.5˝/190; d7.17																								
1930	†StL N	11	16	5	9	1	0	3	8	0	0	1	.563	.563	1.188	298	5	0	1.000	-0	59	0	O3(3/0/1)	—	0.4
1932	StL N	31	108	17	30	8	0	3	11	12	0	13	.278	.350	.435	107	1	1	.942	2	94	298	O30(24/0/6)	—	0.2
1934	StL A	10	26	4	6	1	0	2	5	1	1	8	.231	.286	.500	92	-1	0-0	.941	0	108	176	O6L	—	0.0
1936	Phi A	135	457	83	127	30	3	11	78	65	1	70	.278	.369	.429	98	0	2-3	.948	0	104	101	O117(1/0/116)	—	-0.7
Total	4	187	607	109	172	40	3	19	102	78	2	92	.283	.367	.453	105	5	3-3	.947	2	102	143	O156(34/0/123)	—	-0.1
Puckett, Kirby	Kirby; B3.14.1960 Chicago IL; D3.6.2006 Phoenix AZ; BR/TR/5´8˝/(175–223); [MinA82*1/3]; d5.8; HF2001; Col Bradley; OF(10/1432/276); [DL 1996 Min A 182, 1997 Min A 181]																								
1984	Min A	128	557	63	165	12	5	0	31	16-1	4	69	.296	.320	.336	78	-18	14-7	.993	18	117	**179**	O128C	0	0.0
1985	Min A	161	691	80	199	29	13	4	74	41-0	4	87	.288	.330	.385	90	-10	21-12	.984	10	105	182	O161C	0	-0.2
1986	Min A★	161	680	119	223	37	6	31	96	34-4	7	99	.328	.366	.537	138	33	20-12	.986	1	102	94	O160C	0	3.2
1987	†Min A★	157	624	96	**207**	32	5	28	99	32-7	6	91	.332	.367	.534	131	26	12-7	.986	-4	93	126	O147C,D8	0	2.0
1988	Min A★	158	657	109	**234**	42	5	24	121	23-4	2	83	.356	.375	.545	151	42	6-7	.994	9	106	166	O158C	0	4.9
1989	Min A★	159	635	75	**215**	45	4	9	85	41-9	3	59	**.339**	.379	.465	129	25	11-4	.991	11	109	159	O157C,D2	0	3.5
1990	Min A★	146	551	82	164	40	3	12	80	57-11	3	73	.298	.365	.446	119	15	5-4	.989	2	102	123	O141(9/125/9)/23SD	0	1.6
1991	†Min A★	152	611	92	195	29	6	15	89	31-4	4	78	.319	.352	.460	118	13	11-5	.985	1	96	161	O152(0/144/19)	0	1.3
1992	Min A★	160	639	104	**210**	38	4	19	110	44-13	6	97	.329	.374	.490	136	30	17-7	.993	-1	99	110	O149C,2b2,3b2/SD	0	2.9
1993	Min A★	156	622	89	184	39	3	22	89	47-7	7	93	.296	.349	.474	119	15	8-6	.994	-3	90	149	O139(1/95/47),D17	0	1.0
1994	Min A★	108	439	79	139	32	3	20	**112**	28-7	7	47	.317	.362	.540	129	18	6-3	.986	6	103	181	O95(0/3/95),D13	0	1.8
1995	Min A★	137	538	83	169	39	0	23	99	56-18	3	89	.314	.379	.515	130	24	3-2	.981	-2	92	125	O109(0/5/106),D28/23S	0	1.4
Total	12	1783	7244	1071	2304	414	57	207	1085	450-85	56	965	.318	.360	.477	122	213	134-76	.989	46	101	146	O1696C,D81,3b4,2b4,S3	363	23.4
Puhl, John	John G.; B1.10.1876 Brooklyn NY; D8.24.1900 Bayonne NJ; d10.13																								
1898	NY N	2	9	1	2	0	0	0	1	0	0	—	.222	.222	.222	28	-1	0	.667	-1	102	288	3b2	—	-0.1
1899	NY N	1	2	0	0	0	0	0	0	0	1	—	.000	.333	.000	-6	0	0	.667	-0	110	0	/3	—	0.0
Total	2	3	11	1	2	0	0	0	1	0	1	—	.182	.250	.182	24	-1	0	.667	-1	104	213	3b3	—	-0.1
Puhl, Terry	Terry Stephen; B7.8.1956 Melville SK, Can.; BL/TR/6´2˝/(190–200); d7.12																								
1977	Hou N	60	229	40	69	13	5	0	10	30-0	1	31	.301	.385	.402	121	8	10-1	.992	0	98	77	O59(48/11/1)	0	0.7
1978	Hou N☆	149	585	87	169	25	6	3	35	48-5	4	46	.289	.343	.368	107	5	32-14	.992	7	112	66	O148(43/109/4)	0	1.1
1979	Hou N	157	600	87	172	22	4	8	49	58-8	4	46	.287	.352	.377	105	5	30-22	**1.000**	-6	97	61	O152(6/109/40)	0	-0.6
1980	†Hou N	141	535	75	151	24	5	13	55	60-3	4	52	.282	.357	.419	127	20	27-11	.991	10	114	126	O135(4/30/107)	0	2.6
1981	†Hou N	96	350	43	88	19	4	3	28	31-5	4	49	.251	.315	.354	96	-2	22-4	**1.000**	0	103	72	O88(0/20/71)	0	-0.2
1982	Hou N	145	507	64	133	17	9	8	50	51-2	2	49	.262	.331	.379	107	3	17-9	.989	-4	101	45	O138(0/32/122)	0	-0.6
1983	Hou N	137	465	66	136	25	7	8	44	36-2	2	48	.292	.343	.428	120	11	24-11	.991	-4	100	51	O124(0/13/118)	0	0.4
1984	Hou N	132	449	66	135	19	7	9	55	59-12	1	45	.301	.380	.434	138	24	13-8	.986	-6	91	73	O126(8/0/123)	17	1.2
1985	Hou N	57	194	34	55	14	3	2	23	18-4	1	23	.284	.343	.418	116	4	6-2	1.000	0	100	90	O53(1/0/53)	99	0.3
1986	†Hou N	81	172	17	42	10	0	3	14	15-1	0	24	.244	.302	.355	84	-4	3-2	1.000	-2	97	0	O47(5/0/42)	29	-0.9
1987	Hou N	90	122	9	28	5	0	2	15	11-0	0	16	.230	.293	.320	65	-6	1-1	.980	1	128	0	O40(28/5/9)	0	-0.6
1988	Hou N	113	234	42	71	7	2	3	19	35-3	1	30	.303	.395	.389	131	11	22-4	.983	-0	103	61	O78(48/1/33)	0	1.3
1989	Hou N	121	354	41	96	25	4	0	27	45-3	1	39	.271	.353	.364	110	6	9-8	1.000	-1	100	55	O103(37/11/64),1b3	0	0.1
1990	Hou N	37	41	5	12	1	0	0	8	5-0	1	7	.293	.375	.317	97	0	1-2	1.000	-1	62	0	O8(6/2/0)/1	107	-0.2
1991	KC A	15	18	0	4	0	0	0	3	3-1	0	2	.222	.333	.222	56	-1	0-0	ø	-0	0	0	/lfD	0	-0.1
Total	15	1531	4855	676	1361	226	56	62	435	505-49	26	507	.280	.349	.388	112	84	217-99	.993	-7	102	66	O1300(235/343/787),1b4,D2	252	4.5
Puig, Rich	Richard Gerald; B3.16.1953 Tampa FL; BL/TR/5´10˝/170; d9.13																								
1974	NY N	4	10	0	0	0	0	0	0	1-0	0	2	.000	.091	.000	-73	-2	0-0	.923	-0	97	139	2b3/3	0	-0.2
Pujols, Albert	Jose Alberto; B1.16.1980 Santo Domingo, D.R.; BR/TR/6´3˝/(210–225); [StLN99 13/402]; d4.2; Col Maple Woods (MO) CC																								
2001	†StL N★	161	590	112	194	47	4	37	130	69-6	9	93	.329	.403	.610	155	50	1-3	.964	9	95	128	O78(39/0/39),3b55,1b42,D2	0	5.0
2002	†StL N	157	590	118	185	40	2	34	127	72-13	9	69	.314	.394	.561	147	42	2-4	.978	-4	91	63	O118(117/0/1),3b41,1b21/SD	0	3.2
2003	StL N★	157	591	**137**	**212**	**51**	1	43	124	79-12	10	65	**.359**	.439	.667	186	78	5-1	.986	2	98	106	O113L,1b62/D	0	7.1
2004	†StL N★	154	592	**133**	196	51	2	46	123	84-12	7	52	.331	.415	.657	171	65	5-5	.994	2	106	**120**	1b150,D3	0	5.0
2005	†StL N★	161	591	**129**	195	38	2	41	117	97-**27**	9	65	.330	.430	.609	166	61	16-2	.992	-3	98	**142**	1b157	0	4.6
2006	†StL N★	143	535	119	177	33	1	49	137	92-28	4	50	.331	.431	**.671**	**175**	**63**	7-2	.996	7	**120**	**124**	1b143	18	**5.5**
Total	6	933	3489	748	1159	260	12	250	758	493-98	48	394	.332	.419	.629	166	359	36-17	.993	13	107	127	1b575,O309(269/0/40),3b96,D8/S	18	30.4
Pujols, Luis	Luis Bienvenido (Toribio); B11.18.1955 Santiago Rodriguez, D.R.; BR/TR/6´1˝/(175–205); d9.22; M1/C13																								
1977	Hou N	6	15	0	1	0	0	0	0	0-0	0	5	.067	.067	.067	-70	-4	0-0	1.000	-1	79	225	C6	0	-0.5
1978	Hou N	56	153	11	20	8	1	1	11	12-1	1	45	.131	.198	.216	17	-18	0-0	.981	-6	67	76	C55/1	0	-2.4
1979	Hou N	26	75	7	17	2	1	0	8	2-0	0	14	.227	.247	.280	46	-6	0-0	.993	-0	77	13	C26	0	-0.5
1980	†Hou N	78	221	15	44	6	1	0	20	13-3	1	29	.199	.245	.235	38	-19	0-0	.990	-5	89	78	C75/3	0	-2.3
1981	†Hou N	40	117	5	28	3	1	1	14	10-3	0	17	.239	.297	.308	77	-4	1-0	.995	-1	122	77	C39	0	-0.3
1982	Hou N	65	176	8	35	6	2	4	15	10-2	0	40	.199	.242	.324	62	-10	0-3	.991	-5	91	104	C64	0	-1.5
1983	Hou N	40	87	4	17	2	0	0	12	5-2	0	14	.195	.234	.218	29	-9	0-0	.971	-4	61	24	C39	0	-1.2
1984	KC A	4	5	0	1	0	0	0	1	0-0	0	0	.200	.200	.200	11	-1	0-0	1.000	0	0	0	C4	0	0.0
1985	Tex A	1	1	0	1	0	0	0	0	0-0	0	0	1.000	1.000	1.000	441	0	0-0	1.000	-1	7	0	/C	158	0.0
Total	9	316	850	50	164	27	6	6	81	52-11	2	164	.193	.240	.260	43	-71	1-3	.987	-23	85	73	C309/31	158	-8.7

YEAR	TM LG	G	AB	R	H	2B	3B	HR	RBI	BB-IB	HP	SO	AVG	OBP	SLG	AOPS	ABR	SB-CS	FA	FR	RNG	THR	GAMES AT POSITION	DL	BFW
PULLIAM, HARVEY	Harvey Jerome; B10.20.1967 San Francisco CA; BR/TR/6´0˝/(205–218); [KCA86 3/79]; d8.10																								
1991	KC A	18	33	4	9	1	0	3	4	3-1	0	9	.273	.333	.576	145	2	0-0	.917	0	100	155	O15(11/0/5)	0	0.1
1992	KC A	4	5	2	1	1	0	0	0	1-0	0	3	.200	.333	.400	101	0	0-0	1.000	0	305	0	/lfD	0	0.0
1993	KC A	27	62	7	16	5	0	1	6	2-0	1	14	.258	.292	.387	76	-2	0-0	.971	-1	100	0	O26(12/0/16)	0	-0.4
1995	Col N	5	5	1	2	1	0	1	3	0-0	0	2	.400	.400	1.200	235	1	0-0	ø	-0	0	0	/lf	0	0.1
1996	Col N	10	15	2	2	0	0	0	0	2-0	0	6	.133	.235	.133	0	-2	0-0	1.000	-0	100	0	O3L	43	-0.2
1997	Col N	59	67	15	19	3	0	3	9	5-0	0	15	.284	.333	.463	86	-1	0-1	.962	0	87	208	O33(24/1/10)	0	-0.2
Total	6	123	187	31	49	11	0	8	22	13-1	1	49	.262	.313	.449	89	-2	0-1	.956	-1	98	103	O79(52/1/31),D2	43	-0.6
PUNTO, NICK	Nicholas Paul; B11.8.1977 San Diego CA; BB/TR/5´9˝/(170–190); [PhiN98 21/614]; d9.9; Col Saddleback (CA) CC																								
2001	Phi N	4	5	0	2	0	0	0	0	0-0	0	0	.400	.400	.400	113	0	0-0	1.000	-1	67	0	/S	0	0.0
2002	Phi N	9	6	0	1	0	0	0	0	0-0	0	3	.167	.167	.167	-13	-1	0-0	1.000	0	314	1350	/2S	0	-0.1
2003	Phi N	64	92	14	20	2	0	1	4	7-1	0	22	.217	.273	.272	46	-8	2-1	.985	2	101	95	2b16,3b9,S7	0	-0.4
2004	Min A	38	91	17	23	0	0	2	12	12-0	0	19	.253	.340	.319	71	-4	6-0	.982	1	95	131	2b19,S11,3b2,O2C,D3	121	0.0
2005	Min A	112	394	45	94	18	4	4	26	36-0	0	86	.239	.301	.335	68	-18	13-8	.979	2	103	114	2b73,S34,3b12,O3(0/2/1),D4	30	-1.0
2006	†Min A	135	459	73	133	21	7	1	45	47-0	1	68	.290	.352	.373	89	-7	17-5	.962	4	97	110	3b89,S26,2b17,O3(1/2/0),D2	0	0.2
Total	6	362	1047	149	273	41	11	8	87	102-1	1	198	.261	.324	.344	76	-38	38-14	.979	9	106	115	2b126,3b112,S80,D9,O8(1/6/1)	151	-1.3
PURCELL, BLONDIE	William Aloysius; B Paterson NJ; BR/TR/5´9.5˝/159; d5.1; M1; OF(480/92/430); ▲																								
1879	Syr N	63	277	32	72	6	3	0	25	3	—	13	.260	.268	.303	99	0	—	.773	-11	44	0	O47(0/10/37),P22/C	—	-0.9
	Cin N	12	50	10	11	0	0	0	4	0	—	3	.220	.220	.220	48	-3	—	.750	0	128	0	O10(0/7/3),P2	—	-0.2
	Year	75	327	42	83	6	3	0	29	3	—	16	.254	.261	.291	91	-3	—	.767	-10	61	0	O57(0/17/40),P24/C	—	-1.1
1880	Cin N	77	325	48	95	13	6	1	24	5	—	13	.292	.303	.378	131	10	—	.814	-2	117	42	O55(0/54/2),P25/S		0.3
1881	Cle N	20	80	3	14	2	1	0	4	5	—	8	.175	.224	.225	44	-5	—	.786	-3	73	0	O20(7/13/0)	—	-0.8
	Buf N	30	113	15	33	7	2	0	17	8	—	8	.292	.339	.389	130	4	—	.706	-5	65	0	O25L,P9	—	-0.3
	Year	50	193	18	47	9	3	0	21	13	—	16	.244	.291	.321	95	0	—	.748	-7	69	0	O45(32/13/0),P9	—	-1.1
1882	Buf N	**84**	380	79	105	18	6	2	40	14	—	27	.276	.302	.371	113	5	—	.820	-4	60	0	O82(78/5/0),P6	—	-0.2
1883	Phi N	97	425	70	114	20	5	1	32	13	—	26	.268	.290	.346	101	2	—	.777	3	114	83	3b46,O44L,P11,M	—	0.4
1884	Phi N	103	428	67	108	11	7	1	31	29	—	30	.252	.300	.318	99	1	—	.874	1	58	27	O103L/P	—	-0.1
1885	Phi AA	66	304	71	90	15	5	0	22	16	3	—	.296	.337	.378	119	6	—	.858	0	122	48	O66(66/1/0)/P	—	0.4
	Bos N	21	87	9	19	1	1	0	3	3	—	15	.218	.244	.253	63	-4	—	.840	-2	61	0	O21L	—	-0.6
1886	Bal AA	26	85	17	19	0	1	0	8	17	2	—	.224	.365	.247	96	1	13	.867	-0	96	0	O26(25/1/0)/SP	—	0.0
1887	Bal AA	140	567	101	142	25	8	4	96	46	10	—	.250	.318	.344	90	-6	88	.932	-5	74	103	O140R/P	—	-1.0
1888	Bal AA	101	406	53	96	9	4	2	39	27	3	—	.236	.289	.293	89	-5	16	.906	-6	54	78	O100(7/1/95),S2/1	—	-1.1
	Phi AA	18	66	10	11	3	1	0	6	5	1	—	.167	.236	.242	54	-3	10	.903	-1	96	160	O17R/3	—	-0.4
	Year	119	472	63	107	12	5	2	45	32	4	—	.227	.281	.286	84	-8	26	.905	-7	61	91	O117(7/1/112),S2/13	—	-1.5
1889	Phi AA	129	507	72	160	19	7	0	85	50	5	27	.316	.383	.381	119	14	22	.903	-11	60	54	O129R	—	0.2
1890	Phi AA	110	463	110	128	28	3	2	59	43	4	—	.276	.343	.363	109	5	48	.949	0	93	42	O110(104/0/7)	—	0.3
Total	12	1097	4563	767	1217	177	60	13	495	284	28	170	.267	.314	.340	103	22	197	.870	-45	78	50	O995L,P79,3b47,S4/1C	—	-4.0
PURDY, PID	Everett Virgil; B6.15.1904 Beatrice NE; D1.16.1951 Beatrice NE; BL/TR/5´6˝/150; d9.7; Col Beloit																								
1926	Chi A	11	33	5	6	2	1	0	6	2	0	1	.182	.229	.303	39	-3	0-1	1.000	0	105	104	O9R	—	-0.4
1927	Cin N	18	62	15	22	2	4	1	12	4	2	3	.355	.412	.565	164	5	0	.946	-3	81	0	O16C	—	0.1
1928	Cin N	70	223	32	69	11	1	0	25	23	1	13	.309	.377	.368	97	0	1	.966	-0	106	62	O61(56/1/4)	—	-0.5
1929	Cin N	82	181	22	49	7	5	1	16	19	3	8	.271	.350	.381	85	-4	2	.978	1	103	103	O42(34/0/8)	—	-0.6
Total	4	181	499	74	146	22	11	2	59	48	6	25	.293	.362	.393	97	-2	3-1	.969	-3	102	70	O128(90/17/21)	—	-1.4
PURNELL, JESSE	Jesse Rhoades; B5.11.1881 Glenside PA; D7.4.1966 Philadelphia PA; BL/TR/5´5.5˝/140; d10.1																								
1904	Phi N	7	19	2	2	0	0	0	1	4	1	—	.105	.292	.105	25	-1	1	.864	-1	93	0	3b7	—	-0.2
PURTELL, BILLY	William Patrick; B1.6.1886 Columbus OH; D3.17.1962 Bradenton FL; BR/TR/5´9˝/170; d4.16																								
1908	Chi A	26	69	3	9	2	0	0	3	2	0	—	.130	.155	.159	2	-7	2	.940	5	138	241	3b25	—	-0.2
1909	Chi A	103	361	34	93	9	3	0	40	19	4	—	.258	.302	.299	94	-3	14	.929	-1	100	130	3b71,2b32	—	-0.2
1910	Chi A	102	368	21	82	5	3	1	36	21	4	—	.223	.272	.261	70	-14	5	.907	-1	102	117	3b102	—	-1.3
	Bos A	49	168	15	35	1	2	1	15	18	1	—	.208	.289	.256	69	-6	2	.908	-4	102	37	3b41,S8	—	-1.0
	Year	151	536	36	117	6	5	2	51	39	5	—	.218	.278	.259	70	-19	7	.907	-4	102	95	3b143,S8	—	-2.3
1911	Bos A	27	82	5	23	5	3	0	7	1	1	—	.280	.298	.415	99	-1	1	.867	-1	96	47	3b15,2b3,S3/cf	—	-0.1
1914	Det A	28	76	4	13	4	0	0	3	2	1	7	.171	.203	.224	27	-7	0-2	.946	-1	107	89	3b16,S2/2	—	-0.9
Total	5	335	1124	82	255	26	11	2	104	63	11	7	.227	.275	.275	73	-38	24-2	.915	-2	104	113	3b270,2b36,S13/cf	—	-3.7
PUTMAN, ED	Eddy William; B9.25.1953 Los Angeles CA; BR/TR/6´1˝/190; [ChiN75*S1/3]; d9.7; Col USC																								
1976	Chi N	5	7	0	3	0	0	0	0	0-0	0	0	.429	.429	.429	132	0	0-0	1.000	0	0	0	C3/1	0	0.0
1978	Chi N	17	25	2	5	0	0	0	3	4-0	0	6	.200	.310	.200	40	-2	0-0	.950	0	124	111	3b8,1b3,C2	0	-0.2
1979	Det A	21	39	4	9	3	0	2	4	4-0	0	12	.231	.302	.462	99	0	0-1	1.000	-1	102	69	C16,1b5	0	-0.1
Total	3	43	71	6	17	3	0	2	7	8-0	0	18	.239	.316	.366	81	-2	0-1	1.000	-0	92	62	C21,1b9,3b8	0	-0.3
PUTNAM, PAT	Patrick Edward; B12.3.1953 Bethel VT; BL/TR/6´1˝/(195–214); [TexA75 S1/22]; d9.2; Col South Alabama																								
1977	Tex A	11	26	3	8	4	0	0	3	1-1	0	4	.308	.333	.462	113	1	0-1	1.000	-1	33	94	1b7,D3	0	-0.1
1978	Tex A	20	46	4	7	1	0	1	2	2-1	0	5	.152	.188	.239	19	-5	0-0	1.000	0	107	94	D12,1b4	0	-0.6
1979	Tex A	139	426	57	118	19	2	18	64	23-6	6	50	.277	.319	.458	109	4	1-6	.994	-0	96	86	1b96,D32	0	-0.5
1980	Tex A	147	410	42	108	16	2	13	55	36-6	0	49	.263	.319	.407	101	0	0-2	.992	4	108	101	1b137/3D	0	-0.4
1981	Tex A	95	297	33	79	17	2	8	35	17-3	0	38	.266	.304	.418	112	3	4-2	.993	3	116	99	1b94,O3(3/0/1)	0	0.1
1982	Tex A	43	122	14	28	8	0	2	9	10-1	1	18	.230	.293	.344	78	-4	0-2	.990	2	119	91	1b39/3lf	0	-0.5
1983	Sea A	144	469	58	126	23	2	19	67	39-8	3	57	.269	.326	.448	107	4	2-1	.994	4	107	99	1b125,D11	0	0.1
1984	Sea A	64	155	11	31	6	0	2	16	12-1	0	27	.200	.254	.277	48	-11	3-0	1.000	1	97	0	D30,O13L,1b6	0	-1.2
	Min A	14	38	1	3	1	0	0	4	4-0	0	12	.079	.163	.105	-22	-6	0-0	ø	0	0	0	D11	0	-0.7
	Year	78	193	12	34	7	0	2	20	16-1	0	39	.176	.236	.244	34	-17	3-0	1.000	1	97	0	D41,O13L,1b6	0	-1.9
Total	8	677	1989	223	508	95	8	63	255	144-27	10	260	.255	.306	.406	96	-14	10-14	.993	12	108	97	1b508,D100,O17(17/0/1),3b2	0	-3.8
PYBURN, JIM	James Edward; B11.1.1932 Fairfield AL; BR/TR/6´0˝/190; d4.17; Col Auburn																								
1955	Bal A	39	98	5	20	2	2	0	7	8-0	1	24	.204	.271	.265	48	-8	1-1	1.000	-3	83	22	3b33/rf	62	-1.1
1956	Bal A	84	156	23	27	3	3	2	11	17-0	0	26	.173	.251	.269	41	-14	4-1	.975	3	106	169	O77(11/64/3)	0	-1.3
1957	Bal A	35	40	8	9	0	0	1	2	9-0	0	6	.225	.367	.300	90	0	1-0	1.000	4	133	313	O28(7/13/9)/C	0	0.3
Total	3	158	294	36	56	5	5	3	20	34-0	1	56	.190	.275	.272	51	-22	6-2	.982	4	113	202	O106(18/77/13),3b33/C	62	-2.1
PYE, EDDIE	Robert Edward; B2.13.1967 Columbia TN; BR/TR/5´10˝/(175–183); [LAN88 10/244]; d6.3; Col Middle Tennessee																								
1994	LA N	7	10	2	1	0	0	0	0	1-0	0	4	.100	.182	.100	-25	-2	0-0	1.000	2	181	227	2b3,S3	0	0.0
1995	LA N	7	8	0	0	0	0	0	0	0-0	0	4	.000	.000	.000	-99	-2	0-0	ø	-1	0	0	3b2	0	-0.3
Total	2	14	18	2	1	0	0	0	0	1-0	0	8	.056	.105	.056	-60	-4	0-0	1.000	1	131	201	S3,2b3,3b2	0	-0.3
PYTLAK, FRANKIE	Frank Anthony; B7.30.1908 Buffalo NY; D5.8.1977 Buffalo NY; BR/TR/5´7.5˝/160; d4.22; Mil 1942–45																								
1932	Cle A	12	29	5	7	1	1	0	4	3	1	2	.241	.333	.345	71	-1	0-0	1.000	2	*149*	*94*	C12	—	0.1
1933	Cle A	80	248	36	77	10	6	2	33	17	0	10	.310	.355	.423	101	-1	3-4	1.000	10	*136*	*155*	C69	—	1.2
1934	Cle A	91	289	46	75	12	4	0	35	36	**5**	11	.260	.352	.329	75	-10	11-2	.989	-6	*105*	*73*	C88	—	-0.8
1935	Cle A	55	149	14	44	6	1	1	12	11	1	4	.295	.348	.369	84	-4	3-2	.984	-1	*117*	*110*	C48	—	-0.2
1936	Cle A	75	224	35	72	15	4	0	31	24	3	11	.321	.394	.424	101	1	5-2	.996	-2	*88*	*133*	C58	—	0.3
1937	Cle A	125	397	60	125	15	6	1	44	52	7	15	.315	.404	.390	100	3	16-5	.986	6	*87*	***132***	C115	—	1.7
1938	Cle A	113	364	46	112	14	7	1	43	36	4	15	.308	.376	.393	95	-3	9-5	.987	-6	*76*	*112*	C99	—	-0.2
1939	Cle A	63	183	20	49	2	5	0	14	20	1	5	.268	.343	.333	76	-7	4-1	1.000	4	*111*	*93*	C51	—	-0.0
1940	Cle A	62	149	16	21	2	1	0	16	17	1	5	.141	.234	.168	6	-21	0-1	.996	7	*143*	*124*	C58/rf	—	-1.1
1941	Bos A	106	336	36	91	23	1	2	39	28	1	19	.271	.329	.363	81	-9	5-7	.991	1	*109*	*86*	C91	0	-0.4
1945	Bos A	9	17	1	2	0	0	0	0	3	0	0	.118	.250	.118	8	-2	0-0	1.000	0	*86*	*208*	C6	0	-0.1
1946	Bos A	4	14	1	2	0	0	0	1	0	0	0	.143	.143	.143	-19	-2	0-0	1.000	1	*150*	*0*	C4	0	-0.1
Total	12	795	2399	316	677	100	36	7	272	247	24	97	.282	.355	.363	84	-56	56-29	.991	17	*105*	*112*	C699/rf	0	0.4

YEAR	TM LG	G	AB	R	H	2B	3B	HR	RBI	BB-IB	HP	SO	AVG	OBP	SLG	AOPS	ABR	SB-CS	FA	FR	RNG	THR	GAMES AT POSITION	DL	BFW
PYZNARSKI, TIM Timothy Matthew; B2.4.1960 Chicago IL; BR/TR/6´2˝/195; [OakA81 1/15]; d9.14; Col Eastern Illinois																									
1986	SD N	15	42	3	10	1	0	0	0	4-0	1	11	.238	.319	.262	63	-2	2-0	.977	-1	93	117	1b13	0	-0.3
QUALLS, JIM James Robert; B10.9.1946 Exeter CA; BB/TR/5´10˝/(155–158); d4.10																									
1969	Chi N	43	120	12	30	5	3	0	9	2-0	1	14	.250	.266	.342	62	-6	2-1	1.000	-3	87	57	O35C,2b4	20	-1.1
1970	Mon N	9	9	1	1	0	0	0	1	0-0	0	0	.111	.111	.111	-40	-2	0-0	1.000	-0	120	0	2b2,O2L	0	-0.2
1972	Chi A	11	10	0	0	0	0	0	0	0-0	0	2	.000	.000	.000	-98	-2	0-0	1.000	0	121	0	/cf	0	-0.3
Total	3	63	139	13	31	5	3	0	10	2-0	1	16	.223	.238	.302	46	-10	2-1	1.000	-3	86	54	O38(2/36/0),2b6	20	-1.6
QUEEN, MEL Melvin Douglas; B3.26.1942 Johnson City NY; BL/TR/6´1˝/(190–197); d4.13; M1/C5; s–Mel; ▲																									
1964	Cin N	48	95	7	19	2	0	2	12	4-0	0	19	.200	.232	.284	43	-7	0-1	.977	1	139	0	O20R	0	-0.8
1965	Cin N	5	3	0	0	0	0	0	0	0-0	0	1	.000	.000	.000	-94	-1	0-0	1.000	0	507	0	/rf	0	-0.1
1966	Cin N	56	55	4	7	1	0	0	5	10-1	0	12	.127	.250	.145	16	-6	0-0	1.000	2	137	98	O32(2/0/31),P7	28	-0.5
1967	Cin N	49	81	6	17	4	0	0	5	4-0	0	10	.210	.244	.259	40	3	2-0	.941	-3	52	106	P31	0	0.0
1968	Cin N	10	8	2	1	0	0	0	0	1-0	0	3	.125	.222	.125	6	0	0-0	1.000	0	136	0	P5	84	0.0
1969	Cin N	2	6	0	1	0	0	0	1	0-0	0	2	.167	.167	.167	-6	0	0-0	1.000	-0	52	0	P2	0	0.0
1970	Cal A	37	16	1	4	0	0	0	1	0-0	0	2	.250	.250	.250	39	1	0-0	1.000	-1	57	0	P34	21	0.0
1971	Cal A	45	8	0	0	0	0	0	1	1-0	0	0	.000	.100	.000	-71	-1	0-0	.900	-1	76	0	P44	0	0.0
1972	Cal A	17	2	0	0	0	0	0	0	1-0	0	1	.000	.333	.000	5	0	0-0	1.000	-0	83	0	P17	0	0.0
Total	9	269	274	20	49	7	0	2	25	21-1	0	50	.179	.233	.226	30	-11	2-1	.951	-1	64	53	P140,O53(2/0/52)	133	-1.4
QUEEN, BILLY William Eddleman "Doc"; B11.28.1928 Gastonia NC; D4.23.2006 Gastonia NC; BR/TR/6´1˝/190; d4.13																									
1954	Mil N	3	2	0	0	0	0	0	0	0	0	2	.000	.000	.000	-99	-1	0-0	1.000	0	115	0	/rf	0	-0.1
QUELLICH, GEORGE George William; B2.10.1906 Johnsville CA; D8.31.1958 Johnsville CA; BR/TR/6´1˝/180; d8.1																									
1931	Det A	13	54	6	12	5	0	1	11	3	0	4	.222	.263	.370	63	-3	1-0	1.000	1	107	227	O13L	—	-0.2
QUENTIN, CARLOS Carlos Jose; B8.28.1982 Bellflower CA; BR/TR/6´1˝/225; [AriN03 1/29]; d7.20; Col Stanford																									
2006	Ari N	57	166	23	42	13	3	9	32	15-2	8	34	.253	.342	.530	113	3	1-0	.980	2	110	133	O46(2/0/44)	0	0.3
QUEST, JOE Joseph L.; B11.16.1852 New Castle PA; D11.14.1924 San Diego CA; BR/TR/5´6˝/150; d8.30; U2																									
1871	Cle NA	3	13	1	3	1	0	0	2	1	—	0	.231	.286	.308	75	0	0-0	.571	-2	114	0	2b2/S	—	-0.2
1878	Ind N	62	278	45	57	3	2	0	13	12	—	24	.205	.238	.230	63	-9	—	.876	-0	92	106	2b62	—	-0.6
1879	Chi N	**83**	334	38	69	16	1	0	22	9	—	33	.207	.227	.260	57	-15	—	**.925**	16	112	97	2b83	—	0.4
1880	Chi N	82	300	37	71	12	1	0	27	8	—	16	.237	.256	.283	78	-7	—	.895	0	101	89	2b80,S2/3	—	-0.3
1881	Chi N	78	293	35	72	6	0	1	26	2	—	29	.246	.251	.276	63	-13	—	**.929**	8	**103**	80	2b77/S	—	-0.2
1882	Chi N	42	159	24	32	5	2	0	15	8	—	16	.201	.240	.258	57	-8	—	.879	-5	96	106	2b41/S	—	-1.1
1883	Det N	37	137	22	32	8	2	0	15	10	—	18	.234	.286	.321	88	-1	—	.897	-3	92	140	2b37	—	-0.2
	StL AA	19	78	12	20	3	1	0	10	1	—	—	.256	.266	.321	83	-2	—	.890	-3	92	71	2b19	—	-0.4
1884	StL AA	81	310	46	64	9	5	0	—	19	2	—	.206	.257	.268	69	-11	—	.893	-11	93	117	2b81	—	-1.7
	Pit AA	12	43	2	9	3	0	0	—	0	1	—	.209	.227	.279	65	-1	—	.938	1	110	111	2b7,S5	—	0.0
	Year	93	353	48	73	12	5	0	—	19	3	—	.207	.253	.269	69	-12	—	.897	-10	94	117	2b88,S5	—	-1.7
1885	Det N	55	200	24	39	8	2	0	21	14	—	25	.195	.248	.255	63	-8	—	.898	-4	96	57	2b39,S15/lf	—	-0.9
1886	Phi AA	42	150	14	31	4	1	0	10	20	0	—	.207	.300	.247	71	-4	5	.847	0	104	115	S41,2b2	—	-0.2
Total	9	593	2282	299	496	77	17	1	159	103	3	161	.217	.252	.267	67	-79	5	.901	-1	99	97	2b528,S65/lf3	—	-5.2
QUICK, HAL James Harold "Blondie"; B10.4.1917 Rome GA; D3.9.1974 Swansea IL; BR/TR/5´10.5˝/163; d9.7																									
1939	Was A	12	41	3	10	1	0	0	2	1	1	1	.244	.279	.268	44	-4	1-0	.927	-0	106	98	S10	—	-0.3
QUILICI, FRANK Francis Ralph "Guido"; B5.11.1939 Chicago IL; BR/TR/6´0˝/(170–177); d7.18; M4/C2; Col Western Michigan																									
1965	†Min A	56	149	16	31	5	1	0	7	15-0	0	33	.208	.280	.255	51	-9	1-1	.990	2	105	133	2b52,S4	0	-0.4
1967	Min A	23	19	2	2	1	0	0	0	3-0	0	4	.105	.227	.158	14	-2	0-0	1.000	-2	82	169	2b13,3b8/S	0	-0.3
1968	Min A	97	229	22	56	11	4	1	22	21-0	1	45	.245	.305	.341	92	-2	0-0	1.000	11	106	104	2b48,3b40,S6/1	0	1.4
1969	Min A	118	144	19	25	3	1	2	12	12-0	0	22	.174	.236	.250	35	-13	2-0	.935	7	104	39	3b84,2b36/S	0	-0.4
1970	†Min A	111	141	19	32	3	0	2	12	15-3	0	16	.227	.297	.291	63	-7	0-2	.987	-4	93	88	2b73,3b27/S	0	-0.9
Total	5	405	682	78	146	23	6	5	53	66-3	1	120	.214	.281	.287	62	-33	3-3	.993	14	104	108	2b222,3b159,S13/1	0	-0.6
QUILLEN, LEE Leon Abner; B5.5.1882 North Branch MN; D5.14.1965 St.Paul MN; BR/TR/5´10˝/165; d9.30																									
1906	Chi A	4	9	1	3	0	0	0	0	0	0	—	.333	.333	.333	112	0	1	.600	-2	66	155	S3	—	-0.2
1907	Chi A	49	151	17	29	5	0	0	14	10	3	—	.192	.256	.225	56	-7	8	.871	-1	105	87	3b48	—	-0.8
Total	2	53	160	18	32	5	0	0	14	10	3	—	.200	.260	.231	59	-7	9	.871	-4	105	87	3b48,S3	—	-1.0
QUINLAN ; d9.7																									
1874	Phi NA	1	4	0	1	0	0	0	1	0	—	0	.250	.250	.250	59	0	0-0	1.000	0	132	0	/S	—	0.0
QUINLAN, FRANK Francis Patrick; B3.9.1869 Marlborough MA; D5.4.1904 Brockton MA; 5´9˝/180; d10.5																									
1891	Bos AA	2	5	0	0	0	0	0	0	0	0	2	.000	.000	.000	-99	-1	0	1.000	0	*181*	*91*	/Clf	—	-0.1
QUINLAN, ROBB Robb William; B3.17.1977 St.Paul MN; BR/TR/6´1˝/200; [AnaA99 10/311]; d7.28; b–Tom; Col Minnesota																									
2003	Ana A	38	94	13	27	4	2	0	4	6-0	0	16	.287	.330	.372	88	-2	1-2	.988	-0	87	87	1b33/lfD	0	-0.4
2004	Ana A	56	160	23	55	14	0	5	23	14-0	2	26	.344	.401	.525	145	11	3-1	.983	-0	104	26	3b32,1b13,O9(6/0/3),D4	49	1.0
2005	†LA A	54	134	17	31	8	0	5	14	7-0	1	26	.231	.273	.403	79	-4	0-1	.913	-2	98	87	3b33,1b9,O6L	53	-0.6
2006	LA A	86	234	28	75	11	1	9	32	7-1	2	28	.321	.344	.491	117	5	2-1	.992	-2	86	111	1b54,3b18,O16(11/0/5),D2	0	-0.1
Total	4	234	622	81	188	37	3	19	73	34-1	5	96	.302	.342	.463	112	10	6-5	.993	-5	84	102	1b109,3b83,O32(24/0/8),D9	102	-0.1
QUINLAN, FINNERS Thomas Finners; B10.21.1887 Scranton PA; D2.17.1966 Scranton PA; BL/TL/5´8˝/154; d9.6																									
1913	StL N	13	50	1	8	0	0	0	1	1	0	9	.160	.176	.160	-4	-7	0	.897	1	99	169	O12(1/0/11)	—	-0.7
1915	Chi A	42	114	11	22	3	0	0	7	4	8	11	.193	.270	.219	45	-8	3-4	1.000	1	90	151	O32(9/10/13)	—	-0.9
Total	2	55	164	12	30	3	0	0	8	5	8	20	.183	.243	.201	31	-15	3-4	.961	2	93	157	O44(10/10/24)	—	-1.6
QUINLAN, TOM Thomas Raymond; B3.27.1968 St.Paul MN; BR/TR/6´3˝/(200–214); [TorA86 27/686]; d9.4; b–Robb																									
1990	Tor A	1	2	0	1	0	0	0	0	0-0	1	1	.500	.667	.500	226	1	0-0	1.000	-1	55	0	/3	0	0.0
1992	Tor A	13	15	2	1	1	0	0	2	2-0	0	9	.067	.176	.133	-12	-2	0-0	.909	-1	64	0	3b13	0	-0.4
1994	Phi N	24	35	6	7	2	0	1	3	3-1	0	13	.200	.263	.343	55	-2	0-0	.966	-1	89	57	3b20	0	-0.3
1996	Min A	4	6	0	0	0	0	0	0	0-0	0	3	.000	.000	.000	-98	-2	0-0	.667	-1	51	0	3b4	0	-0.3
Total	4	42	58	8	9	3	0	1	5	5-1	1	26	.155	.234	.259	30	-5	0-0	.932	-4	77	34	3b38	0	-1.0
QUINN ; d5.4																									
1875	Atl NA	2	8	2	1	0	0	0	0	0	—	0	.125	.125	.125	-15	-1	0-0	.800	-2	0	0	O2(0/1/1)/S	—	-0.3
QUINN, FRANK Frank Cady; B8.24.1876 Sheffield PA; D2.2.1920 Camden NJ; 5´8˝/157; d8.9																									
1899	Chi N	12	34	6	6	0	1	0	1	6	0	—	.176	.300	.235	49	-2	1	.909	-2	0	0	O10(4/6/0)/2	—	-0.5
QUINN, JOHN John Edward "Pick"; B9.12.1885 Framingham MA; D4.9.1956 Marlboro MA; BR/TR/5´11˝/150; d10.9																									
1911	Phi N	1	2	0	0	0	0	0	0	0	0	0	.000	.000	.000	-99	-1	0	1.000	-0	*79*	*158*	/C	—	-0.1
QUINN, JOE Joseph; B Boston MA; D3.1893; 5´8˝/162; d9.7																									
1881	Bos N	1	4	0	0	0	0	0	0	0	—	0	.000	.000	.000	-99	-1	—	1.000	-0	0	0	/1	—	-0.1
	Wor N	2	7	0	1	0	0	0	1	1	—	2	.143	.250	.143	25	-1	—	.714	-2	—	—	C2	—	-0.3
	Year	3	11	0	1	0	0	0	1	1	—	2	.091	.167	.091	-16	-1	—	.714	-2	—	—	C2/1	—	-0.4
QUINN, JOE Joseph J.; B12.25.1864 Sydney, New South Wales (now Australia); D11.12.1940 St.Louis MO; BR/TR/5´7˝/158; d4.26; M2; OF(31/66/27)																									
1884	StL U	103	429	74	116	21	1	0	—	9	—	—	.270	.285	.324	81	-22	—	.945	-1	**109**	**186**	1b100,O3(1/0/2)/S	—	-2.9
1885	StL N	97	343	27	73	8	2	0	15	9	—	38	.213	.233	.248	59	-15	—	.875	-3	86	0	O57(27/13/17),3b31,1b11	—	-1.9
1886	StL N	75	271	33	63	11	3	1	21	8	—	31	.232	.254	.306	75	-8	12	.895	-3	131	64	O48(0/47/1),2b15,1b7,3b4,S2	—	-1.2
1888	Bos N	38	156	19	47	8	3	4	29	2	0	5	.301	.310	.468	142	6	12	.914	-5	93	78	2b38	—	0.3
1889	Bos N	112	444	57	116	13	5	2	69	25	5	21	.261	.308	.327	72	-19	24	.860	-17	89	97	S63,2b47,3b2	—	-2.8

YEAR	TM LG	G	AB	R	H	2B	3B	HR	RBI	BB-IB	HP	SO	AVG	OBP	SLG	AOPS	ABR	SB-CS	FA	FR	RNG	THR	GAMES AT POSITION	DL	BFW
1890	Bos P	**130**	509	87	153	19	8	7	82	44	2	24	.301	.359	.411	99	-4	29	**.942**	16	98	113	2b130	—	1.3
1891	Bos N	124	508	70	122	8	10	3	63	28	6	28	.240	.288	.313	67	-25	24	.938	-24	89	93	2b124	—	-4.0
1892	†Bos N	143	532	63	116	14	1	1	59	35	7	40	.218	.275	.254	55	-30	17	**.951**	5	98	143	2b143	—	-1.8
1893	StL N	**135**	547	68	126	18	6	0	71	33	4	7	.230	.279	.285	50	-41	24	.942	-33	83	101	2b135	—	-5.7
1894	StL N	106	405	59	116	18	1	4	61	24	1	8	.286	.328	.365	67	-23	25	.952	18	99	**148**	2b106	—	0.0
1895	StL N	135	547	86	172	19	9	3	76	37	2	7	.314	.360	.399	97	-3	22	.945	1	96	104	2b135,M	—	0.3
1896	StL N	48	191	19	40	6	1	1	17	9	2	5	.209	.252	.267	39	-17	8	.956	2	114	33	2b48	—	-1.2
	†Bal N	24	82	22	27	1	1	0	5	6	0	1	.329	.375	.366	94	-1	6	.951	-2	84	99	2b8,O8(1/1/6),3b5/S	—	-0.2
	Year	72	273	41	67	7	2	1	22	15	2	6	.245	.290	.297	56	-18	14	.955	-0	110	43	2b56,O8(1/1/6),3b5/S	—	-1.4
1897	Bal N	75	285	33	74	11	4	1	45	13	3	—	.260	.299	.337	68	-14	12	.946	8	114	142	3b37,S21,2b11,O6(1/5/0),1b2	—	-0.4
1898	Bal N	12	32	5	8	1	0	0	5	1	0	—	.250	.273	.281	58	-2	0	.893	-0	88	114	3b8/2lf	—	-0.2
	StL N	103	375	35	94	10	5	0	36	24	3	—	.251	.301	.304	72	-15	13	.962	-1	105	78	2b62,S41/rf	—	-1.0
	Year	115	407	40	102	11	5	0	41	25	3	—	.251	.299	.302	71	-16	13	.960	-1	105	77	2b63,S41,3b8,O2(1/0/1)	—	-1.2
1899	Cle N	147	615	73	176	24	6	0	72	21	2	—	.286	.312	.345	86	-13	22	**.962**	11	101	86	2b147,M	—	0.3
1900	StL N	22	80	12	21	2	0	1	11	10	0	—	.262	.344	.325	86	-1	4	.933	-6	81	60	2b14,S6/3	—	-0.6
	Cin N	74	266	18	73	5	2	0	25	16	0	—	.274	.316	.308	74	-10	7	.950	-10	89	90	2b74	—	-1.5
	Year	96	346	30	94	7	2	1	36	26	0	—	.272	.323	.312	77	-11	11	.947	-15	88	85	2b88,S6/3	—	-2.1
1901	Was A	66	266	33	67	11	2	2	34	11	2	—	.252	.287	.331	72	-11	7	.954	-6	92	64	2b66	—	-1.5
Total	17	1769	6883	893	1800	228	70	30	796	365	39	215	.262	.302	.328	74	-268	268	.946	-52	95	101	2b1304,S135,O124C,1b120,3b88	—	-24.7

QUINN, MARK Mark David; B5.21.1974 LaMirada CA; BR/TR/6´1˝/(175–195); [KCA95 11/302]; d9.14; Col Rice

YEAR	TM LG	G	AB	R	H	2B	3B	HR	RBI	BB-IB	HP	SO	AVG	OBP	SLG	AOPS	ABR	SB-CS	FA	FR	RNG	THR	GAMES AT POSITION	DL	BFW
1999	KC A	17	60	11	20	4	1	6	18	4-0	1	11	.333	.385	.733	170	6	1-0	.964	-1	81	200	O15(15/0/1)/D	0	0.5
2000	KC A	135	500	76	147	33	2	20	78	35-1	3	91	.294	.342	.488	102	0	5-2	.988	1	90	180	O81(78/1/4),D48	0	-0.3
2001	KC A	118	453	57	122	31	2	17	60	12-1	7	69	.269	.298	.459	87	-9	9-5	.976	1	97	124	O99(49/0/50),D18	27	-1.3
2002	KC A	23	76	9	18	4	0	2	11	5-0	2	15	.237	.301	.368	68	-3	2-1	1.000	-1	88	0	O15R,D7	156	-0.5
Total	4	293	1089	153	307	72	5	45	167	56-2	13	186	.282	.324	.481	97	-6	17-8	.981	0	93	143	O210(142/1/70),D74	183	-1.6

QUINN, PADDY Patrick J.; B8.1849 Chicago IL; D1.2.1909 Chicago IL; 5´8.5˝/148; d7.26

YEAR	TM LG	G	AB	R	H	2B	3B	HR	RBI	BB-IB	HP	SO	AVG	OBP	SLG	AOPS	ABR	SB-CS	FA	FR	RNG	THR	GAMES AT POSITION	DL	BFW
1871	Kek NA	5	17	8	4	0	0	0	2	4	—	0	.235	.381	.235	81	0	3-1	.964	2	—	—	C5	—	0.1
1875	Wes NA	11	43	4	14	1	0	0	5	0	—	1	.326	.326	.349	127	1	0-1	.861	1	—	—	C10/cf	—	0.1
	Har NA	5	13	1	3	0	0	0	1	1	—	3	.231	.286	.231	78	0	0-1	.833	-1	—	—	C3,O3(0/1/2)	—	-0.1
	Chi NA	17	61	12	14	0	0	0	1	0	—	2	.230	.230	.230	59	-3	1-1	.778	-4	—	—	C11,O10(0/9/1)	—	-0.6
	Year	33	117	17	31	1	0	0	7	1	—	6	.265	.271	.274	87	-2	1-3	.826	-4	—	—	C24,O14(0/11/3)	—	-0.6
1877	Chi N	4	14	1	1	0	0	0	0	1	—	0	.071	.133	.071	-30	-2	—	.667	-0	114	0	O4R	—	-0.2
Total	2NA	38	134	25	35	1	0	0	9	5	—	6	.261	.288	.269	87	-2	4-4	.849	-2	—	—	C29,O14(0/11/3)	—	-0.5

QUINN, TOM Thomas Oscar; B4.25.1864 Annapolis MD; D7.24.1932 Pittsburgh PA; BR/TR/5´8˝/180; d9.2

YEAR	TM LG	G	AB	R	H	2B	3B	HR	RBI	BB-IB	HP	SO	AVG	OBP	SLG	AOPS	ABR	SB-CS	FA	FR	RNG	THR	GAMES AT POSITION	DL	BFW
1886	Pit AA	3	11	1	0	0	0	0	0	0	0	—	.000	.000	.000	-99	-3	1	.929	-1	—	—	C3	—	-0.3
1889	Bal AA	55	194	18	34	2	1	1	15	19	1	22	.175	.252	.211	32	-18	6	.925	7	—	—	C55	—	-0.5
1890	Pit P	55	207	23	44	4	3	1	15	17	3	8	.213	.282	.275	54	-14	1	.888	-3	*103*	*84*	C55	—	-1.0
Total	3	113	412	42	78	6	4	2	30	36	4	30	.189	.261	.238	40	-35	8	.910	2	*103*	*84*	C113	—	-1.8

QUINONES, LUIS Luis Raul; B4.28.1962 Ponce, PR; BB/TR/5´11˝/(155–185); d5.27

YEAR	TM LG	G	AB	R	H	2B	3B	HR	RBI	BB-IB	HP	SO	AVG	OBP	SLG	AOPS	ABR	SB-CS	FA	FR	RNG	THR	GAMES AT POSITION	DL	BFW
1983	Oak A	19	42	5	8	2	1	0	4	1-0	0	4	.190	.205	.286	37	-4	1-1	1.000	2	129	99	2b6,3b4,O4R,S3,D4	0	-0.2
1986	SF N	71	106	13	19	1	3	0	11	3-1	1	17	.179	.207	.245	26	-12	3-1	.922	-6	100	101	S33,3b31,2b8	0	-1.7
1987	Chi N	49	101	12	22	6	0	0	8	10-0	0	16	.218	.288	.277	49	-7	0-0	.965	-1	89	74	S28,2b4/3	0	-0.6
1988	Cin N	23	52	4	12	3	0	1	11	2-1	0	11	.231	.255	.346	70	-2	1-1	.974	1	121	103	S10,2b4,3b4	0	-0.1
1989	Cin N	97	340	43	83	13	4	12	34	25-0	3	46	.244	.300	.412	99	-2	2-4	.979	-2	94	85	2b53,3b50,S5	0	-0.4
1990	†Cin N	83	145	10	35	7	0	2	17	13-3	1	29	.241	.301	.331	73	-5	1-0	.981	6	122	0	3b22,2b13,S9/1	0	0.2
1991	Cin N	97	212	15	47	4	3	4	20	21-3	2	31	.222	.297	.325	72	-8	1-2	.975	-7	101	115	2b33,3b19,S5	0	-1.6
1992	Min A	3	5	0	1	0	0	0	1	0-0	0	0	.200	.167	.200	12	-1	0-0	.714	0	120	0	/3SD	0	-0.1
Total	8	442	1003	102	227	36	11	19	106	75-8	7	154	.226	.282	.341	72	-41	9-9	.937	-8	94	55	3b132,2b121,S94,D5,O4R/1	0	-4.5

QUINONES, REY Rey Francisco (Santiago); B11.11.1963 Rio Piedras, PR; BR/TR/5´11˝/185; d5.17

YEAR	TM LG	G	AB	R	H	2B	3B	HR	RBI	BB-IB	HP	SO	AVG	OBP	SLG	AOPS	ABR	SB-CS	FA	FR	RNG	THR	GAMES AT POSITION	DL	BFW
1986	Bos A	62	190	26	45	12	1	2	15	19-0	3	26	.237	.315	.342	79	-5	3-2	.940	-8	92	71	S62	0	-0.7
	Sea A	36	122	6	23	4	0	0	7	5-0	0	31	.189	.219	.221	20	-14	1-1	.945	0	99	115	S36	0	-1.0
	Year	98	312	32	68	16	1	2	22	24-0	3	57	.218	.279	.295	56	-19	4-3	.942	-8	95	87	S98	0	-1.7
1987	Sea A	135	478	55	132	18	2	12	56	26-0	4	71	.276	.317	.397	84	-12	1-3	.959	-4	100	98	S135	0	-0.2
1988	Sea A	140	499	63	124	30	3	12	52	23-1	3	71	.248	.284	.393	84	-12	0-3	.963	8	100	119	S135,D4	0	0.5
1989	Sea A	7	19	2	2	0	0	0	0	1-0	0	1	.105	.150	.105	-26	-3	0-0	.889	-2	98	70	S7	9	-0.5
	Pit N	71	225	21	47	11	0	3	29	15-2	1	40	.209	.253	.298	61	-12	0-2	.934	-14	95	73	S69	0	-2.3
Total	4	451	1533	173	373	75	6	29	159	89-3	11	240	.243	.287	.357	74	-58	5-11	.952	-19	98	98	S444,D4	9	-4.2

QUINTANA, CARLOS Carlos Narcis (Hernandez); B8.26.1965 Estado Miranda, Venezuela; BR/TR/6´2˝/(195–220); d9.16; [DL 1992 Bos A 182]

YEAR	TM LG	G	AB	R	H	2B	3B	HR	RBI	BB-IB	HP	SO	AVG	OBP	SLG	AOPS	ABR	SB-CS	FA	FR	RNG	THR	GAMES AT POSITION	DL	BFW
1988	Bos A	5	6	1	2	0	0	0	2	2-0	0	3	.333	.500	.333	132	0	0-0	1.000	0	106	0	O3R/D	0	0.0
1989	Bos A	34	77	6	16	5	0	0	6	7-0	0	12	.208	.274	.273	51	-5	0-0	.926	-2	90	0	O21(4/1/17)/1D	15	-0.7
1990	†Bos A	149	512	56	147	28	0	7	67	52-0	2	74	.287	.354	.383	101	2	1-2	.987	13	**133**	96	1b148,O3R	0	0.5
1991	Bos A	149	478	69	141	21	1	11	71	61-2	2	66	.295	.375	.412	112	10	1-0	.993	9	**124**	102	1b138,O13(1/0/12)/D	0	0.9
1993	Bos A	101	303	31	74	5	0	1	19	31-2	2	52	.244	.317	.271	56	-18	1-0	.991	-1	80	102	1b53,O51(1/0/50)	0	-2.4
Total	5	438	1376	163	380	59	1	19	165	153-4	6	207	.276	.350	.362	92	-11	3-2	.990	19	123	99	1b340,O91(6/1/85),D9	197	-1.7

QUINTANILLA, OMAR Omar; B10.24.1981 El Paso TX; BL/TR/5´9˝/190; [OakA03 1/33]; d7.31; Col Texas

YEAR	TM LG	G	AB	R	H	2B	3B	HR	RBI	BB-IB	HP	SO	AVG	OBP	SLG	AOPS	ABR	SB-CS	FA	FR	RNG	THR	GAMES AT POSITION	DL	BFW
2005	Col N	39	128	16	28	1	1	0	7	9-0	0	15	.219	.270	.242	32	-13	2-1	.992	-1	100	71	S31,2b6	0	-1.1
2006	Col N	11	34	3	6	1	1	0	3	3-1	0	9	.176	.243	.265	28	-4	1-1	1.000	2	125	150	S8,2b3	19	-0.1
Total	2	50	162	19	34	2	2	0	10	12-1	0	24	.210	.264	.247	31	-17	3-2	.994	1	105	86	S39,2b9	19	-1.2

QUINTERO, HUMBERTO Humberto; B8.2.1979 Maracaibo, Zulia, Venezuela; BR/TR/5´9˝/(190–215); d9.3

YEAR	TM LG	G	AB	R	H	2B	3B	HR	RBI	BB-IB	HP	SO	AVG	OBP	SLG	AOPS	ABR	SB-CS	FA	FR	RNG	THR	GAMES AT POSITION	DL	BFW
2003	SD N	12	23	1	5	0	0	0	2	1-1	0	6	.217	.250	.217	26	-3	0-0	.982	0	164	68	C11	0	-0.2
2004	SD N	23	72	7	18	3	0	2	10	5-0	0	16	.250	.295	.375	76	-3	0-2	1.000	-0	134	24	C21	0	-0.2
2005	Hou N	18	54	6	10	1	0	1	8	1-1	0	10	.185	.200	.259	19	-7	0-0	.989	-3	102	68	C16/1	27	-0.9
2006	Hou N	11	21	2	7	2	0	0	2	1-0	0	3	.333	.364	.429	99	0	0-0	1.000	2	192	206	C10	0	0.2
Total	4	64	170	16	40	6	0	3	22	8-2	0	35	.235	.268	.324	55	-13	0-2	.994	-1	137	69	C58/1	27	-1.1

QUINTON, MARSHALL Marshall J.; B Philadelphia PA; 5´11˝/190; d8.7

YEAR	TM LG	G	AB	R	H	2B	3B	HR	RBI	BB-IB	HP	SO	AVG	OBP	SLG	AOPS	ABR	SB-CS	FA	FR	RNG	THR	GAMES AT POSITION	DL	BFW
1884	Ric AA	26	94	12	22	5	0	0	—	0	1	—	.234	.242	.287	73	-3	—	.878	-4	—	—	C14,O10R,S2	—	-0.5
1885	Phi AA	7	29	6	6	1	0	0	4	1	1	—	.207	.258	.241	55	-1	—	.869	-2	—	—	C7	—	-0.3
Total	2	33	123	18	28	6	0	0	4	1	2	—	.228	.246	.276	68	-4	—	.874	-6	—	—	C21,O10R,S2	—	-0.8

QUIRK, JAMIE James Patrick; B10.22.1954 Whittier CA; BL/TR/6´4˝/(185–200); [KCA72 1/18]; d9.4; C14; OF(24/0/8)

YEAR	TM LG	G	AB	R	H	2B	3B	HR	RBI	BB-IB	HP	SO	AVG	OBP	SLG	AOPS	ABR	SB-CS	FA	FR	RNG	THR	GAMES AT POSITION	DL	BFW
1975	KC A	14	39	2	10	0	0	1	5	2-1	0	7	.256	.293	.333	75	-1	0-0	.909	0	106	161	O10L,3b2/D	0	-0.2
1976	†KC A	64	114	11	28	6	0	1	15	2-0	0	22	.246	.252	.325	69	-5	0-0	1.000	-2	56	77	D19,S12,3b11,1b2	0	-0.7
1977	Mil A	93	221	16	48	14	1	3	13	8-2	2	47	.217	.251	.330	57	-14	0-1	.950	1	147	218	D53,O10L,3b8	0	-1.4
1978	KC A	17	29	3	6	2	0	0	2	5-0	0	4	.207	.324	.276	68	-1	0-0	.926	0	96	77	3b10,S2/D	22	-0.1
1979	KC A	51	79	8	24	6	1	1	11	5-0	1	13	.304	.353	.443	111	1	0-0	.944	-1	277	0	C9,S5,3b3,D9	0	0.1
1980	KC A	62	163	13	45	5	0	5	21	7-2	1	24	.276	.305	.399	91	-2	3-2	.929	-1	111	41	3b28,C15,O7(2/0/5)/1D	0	-0.3
1981	KC A	46	100	8	25	7	0	0	10	6-1	1	17	.250	.299	.320	78	-3	0-2	.985	-3	67	74	C22,3b8/2rf	0	-0.7
1982	KC A	36	78	8	18	3	0	1	5	3-0	0	15	.231	.256	.308	55	-5	0-0	1.000	1	91	84	C29,1b6/3lf	22	-0.3
1983	StL N	48	86	3	18	2	1	2	11	6-0	1	27	.209	.269	.326	64	-5	0-0	.929	-7	66	106	C22,3b7/S	0	-1.1
1984	Chi A	3	2	0	0	0	0	0	1	0-0	0	2	.000	.000	.000	-95	-1	0-0	1.000	0	0	0	/3	0	0.0
	Cle A	1	1	1	1	0	0	1	1	0-0	0	0	1.000	1.000	4.000	1186	1	0-0	ø	-0	6	0	/C	0	0.1
	Year	4	3	1	1	0	0	1	2	0-0	0	2	.333	.250	1.333	323	1	0-0	1.000	-0	0	0	/3C	0	0.1
1985	†KC A	19	57	3	16	3	1	0	4	2-0	0	9	.281	.305	.368	83	-1	0-0	.986	-2	83	196	C17/1	0	-0.3
1986	KC A	80	219	24	47	10	0	8	26	17-3	1	41	.215	.273	.370	72	-9	0-1	.989	18	148	186	C41,3b24,1b6/lf	0	0.9
1987	KC A	109	296	24	70	17	0	5	33	28-1	4	56	.236	.307	.345	72	-12	1-0	.986	5	89	107	C108/S	15	-0.3
1988	KC A	84	196	22	47	7	1	8	25	28-2	1	41	.240	.333	.408	106	2	1-5	.982	14	75	109	C79/13	0	1.8
1989	NY A	13	24	0	2	0	0	0	0	3-0	0	5	.083	.185	.083	-22	-4	0-1	1.000	0	51	123	C6/SD	0	-0.4

YEAR	TM LG	G	AB	R	H	2B	3B	HR	RBI	BB-IB	HP	SO	AVG	OBP	SLG	AOPS	ABR	SB-CS	FA	FR	RNG	THR	GAMES AT POSITION	DL	BFW
	Oak A	9	10	1	2	0	0	1	1	0-0	0	4	.200	.200	.500	94	0	0-0	.500	0	119	0	3b3,C2/1rf	0	0.0
	Bal A	25	51	5	11	2	0	0	9	9-0	0	11	.216	.328	.255	70	-2	0-1	1.000	4	154	160	C24	0	0.3
	Year	47	85	6	15	2	0	1	10	12-0	0	20	.176	.276	.235	47	-6	0-2	1.000	5	129	150	C32,3b3/SD1rf	0	-0.1
1990	†Oak A	56	121	12	34	5	1	3	26	14-1	1	34	.281	.353	.413	120	3	0-0	.977	2	183	112	C37,1b8,3b8/rfD	0	0.7
1991	Oak A	76	203	16	53	4	0	1	17	16-1	2	28	.261	.321	.296	76	-7	0-3	.982	1	80	150	C54,1b8/3D	0	-0.5
1992	†Oak A	78	177	13	39	7	1	2	11	16-3	3	28	.220	.294	.305	72	-7	0-0	.973	3	78	122	C59,1b9,3b2/D	0	-0.2
Total	18	984	2266	193	544	100	7	43	247	177-17	18	435	.240	.298	.347	78	-72	5-16	.982	33	98	125	C525,3b118,D88,1b43,O32L,S22/2	59	-2.6
Quiroz, Guillermo	Guillermo Antonio; B11.29.1981 Maracaibo, Zulia, Venezuela; BR/TR/6´1˝/200; d9.4																								
2004	Tor A	17	52	2	11	2	0	0	6	2-0	2	8	.212	.263	.250	34	-5	1-0	.976	-0	138	63	C15,D2	0	-0.4
2005	Tor A	12	36	3	7	2	0	0	4	2-0	1	13	.194	.256	.250	34	-3	0-0	1.000	-0	47	137	C10,D2	0	-0.3
2006	Sea A	1	2	0	0	0	0	0	0	0-0	0	2	.000	.000	.000	-99	-1	0-0	1.000	-0	0	0	/C	0	-0.1
Total	3	30	90	5	18	4	0	0	10	4-0	3	23	.200	.255	.244	31	-9	1-0	.987	-1	96	91	C26,D4	0	-0.8
Raabe, Brian	Brian Charles; B11.5.1967 New Ulm MN; BR/TR/5´9˝/(176–177); [MinA90 41/1081]; d9.17; Col Minnesota																								
1995	Min A	6	14	4	3	0	0	0	1	1-0	0	0	.214	.267	.214	27	-2	0-0	1.000	-0	114	187	2b4,3b2	0	-0.2
1996	Min A	7	9	0	2	0	0	0	1	0-0	0	1	.222	.200	.222	13	-1	0-0	.857	-0	97	253	3b6/2	0	-0.1
1997	Sea A	2	3	0	0	0	0	0	0	1-0	0	2	.000	.250	.000	-27	-1	0-0	1.000	-1	72	0	3b2/2	0	-0.1
	Col N	2	3	0	1	0	0	0	0	0-0	0	1	.333	.333	.333	61	0	0-0	1.000	-0	144	0	/2	0	0.0
Total	3	17	29	4	6	0	0	0	2	2-0	0	4	.207	.250	.207	21	-4	0-0	.889	-1	66	141	3b10,2b7	0	-0.4
Rabb, John	John Andrew; B6.23.1960 Los Angeles CA; BR/TR/6´1˝/(179–180); [SFN78 11/267]; d9.4																								
1982	SF N	2	2	0	1	0	1	0	0	0-0	0	1	.500	.500	1.500	444	1	0-0	1.000	0	217	0	/lf	0	0.1
1983	SF N	40	104	10	24	9	0	1	14	9-1	0	17	.231	.292	.346	78	-3	1-0	.973	-2	73	58	C31,O2R	0	-0.4
1984	SF N	54	82	10	16	1	0	3	9	10-0	0	33	.195	.283	.317	70	-3	1-1	.988	-2	98	37	1b13,O8(3/0/6),C6	0	-0.6
1985	Atl N	3	2	0	0	0	0	0	0	0-0	0	1	.000	.000	.000	-94	-1	0-0	ø	-0	0	0	/lf	0	-0.1
1988	Sea A	9	14	2	5	2	0	0	4	0-0	0	1	.357	.357	.500	131	1	0-0	1.000	0	194	0	O2R/1D	0	0.1
Total	5	108	204	22	46	12	1	4	27	19-1	0	53	.225	.291	.353	81	-5	2-1	.966	-4	72	59	C37,1b14,O14(5/0/10),D5	0	-0.9
Rabbitt, Joe	Joseph Patrick; B1.16.1900 Frontenac KS; D12.5.1969 Norwalk CT; BL/TR/5´10˝/165; d9.15																								
1922	Cle A	2	3	1	1	0	0	0	0	0	0	0	.333	.333	.333	74	0	0-0	ø	-0	0	0	/lf	—	0.0
Rabe, Josh	Joshua Wayne; B10.15.1978 Quincy IL; BR/TR/6´3˝/215; [MinA00 11/312]; d7.17; Col Quincy																								
2006	Min A	24	49	8	14	1	0	3	7	2-0	0	11	.286	.314	.490	103	0	0-1	.917	1	182	0	D12,O11(10/0/1)	0	0.0
Rabelo, Mike	Michael Gregory; B1.17.1980 New Port Richey FL; BB/TR/6´1˝/200; [DetA01 4/117]; d9.23; Col Tampa																								
2006	Det A	1	1	0	0	0	0	0	0	0-0	0	1	.000	.000	.000	-99	0	0-0	ø	0	—	—	/D	0	0.0
Raburn, Ryan	Ryan N.; B4.17.1981 Tampa FL; BR/TR/6´0˝/185; [DetA01 5/147]; d9.12; Col South Florida JC																								
2004	Det A	12	29	4	4	1	0	0	1	2-0	0	15	.138	.194	.172	-4	-5	1-0	.969	-1	106	102	2b11	0	-0.5
Rackley, Marv	Marvin Eugene; B7.25.1921 Seneca SC; BL/TL/5´10˝/170; d4.15																								
1947	Bro N	18	9	2	2	0	0	0	2	1	0	0	.222	.300	.222	39	-1	0	1.000	0	153	0	O2(0/1/1)	0	0.0
1948	Bro N	88	281	55	92	13	5	0	15	19	0	25	.327	.370	.409	107	3	8	.949	-2	91	137	O74(43/33/1)	0	-0.3
1949	†Bro N	9	9	2	4	1	0	0	1	1	0	0	.444	.500	.556	175	1	0	1.000	-0	90	0	O3L	0	0.1
	Pit N	11	35	5	11	2	0	0	2	2	0	3	.314	.351	.371	92	0	1	1.000	-0	101	0	O8C	0	-0.1
	†Bro N	54	141	23	41	4	1	1	14	13	0	8	.291	.351	.355	86	-3	1	.986	-2	90	0	O44(41/3/0)	0	-0.7
	Year	74	185	30	56	7	1	1	17	16	0	11	.303	.358	.368	91	-2	2	.990	-3	99	0	O55(44/11/0)	0	-0.7
1950	Cin N	5	2	0	1	0	0	0	1	0	0	0	.500	.500	.500	163	0	0	ø	0	—	—	/H	0	0.0
Total	4	185	477	87	151	20	6	1	35	36	0	36	.317	.365	.390	100	0	10	.966	-4	95	82	O131(87/45/2)	0	-1.0
Radcliff, John	John Y.; B6.29.1846 Philadelphia PA; D7.26.1911 Ocean City NJ; 5´6˝/140; d5.20																								
1871	Ath NA	**28**	145	47	44	7	5	0	22	6	—	1	.303	.331	.421	116	3	5-1	.804	3	110	79	S28	—	0.4
1872	Bal NA	56	297	70	86	13	4	1	44	0	—	2	.290	.290	.370	97	-3	3-3	.771	-5	92	96	S50,3b6/2	—	-0.6
1873	Bal NA	45	244	59	70	5	0	0	33	4	—	2	.287	.298	.307	80	-6	0-0	.772	-1	125	60	3b24,S23/2	—	-0.5
1874	Phi NA	23	103	20	25	7	0	1	14	2	—	0	.243	.257	.340	87	-1	1-1	.800	-1	57	0	O15(0/1/14),2b4,S3,3b3,1b2	—	-0.2
1875	Cen NA	5	23	2	4	0	0	0	0	1	—	0	.174	.208	.174	37	-1	0-0	.651	-1	121	0	S5	—	-0.2
Total	5NA	157	812	198	229	32	9	2	113	13	—	5	.282	.293	.351	93	-8	9-5	.765	-4	97	85	S109,3b33,O15(0/1/14),2b6,1b2	—	-1.1
Radcliff, Rip	Raymond Allen; B1.19.1906 Kiowa OK; D5.23.1962 Enid OK; BL/TL/5´10˝/170; d9.17; Mil 1944–46																								
1934	Chi A	14	56	7	15	2	1	0	5	0	0	2	.268	.268	.339	54	-4	1-0	.946	-0	118	0	O14R	—	-0.5
1935	Chi A	146	623	95	178	28	8	10	68	53	4	21	.286	.346	.404	91	-9	4-4	.968	-17	75	68	O142L	—	-3.3
1936	Chi A★	138	618	120	207	31	7	8	82	44	2	12	.335	.381	.447	100	-1	6-3	.936	-17	79	52	O132L	—	-2.2
1937	Chi A	144	584	105	190	38	10	4	79	53	2	25	.325	.383	.445	108	8	6-1	.966	-3	96	87	O139L	—	-0.1
1938	Chi A	129	503	64	166	23	6	5	81	36	1	17	.330	.376	.429	99	-1	5-7	.979	-3	104	65	O99L,1b23	—	-1.3
1939	Chi A	113	397	49	105	25	2	2	53	26	2	21	.264	.313	.353	68	-19	6-4	.970	-8	88	18	O78(10/0/69),1b20	—	-3.1
1940	StL A	150	584	83	**200**	33	9	7	81	47	1	20	.342	.392	.466	119	17	6-4	.973	-5	93	77	O139(116/0/23),1b4	—	0.3
1941	StL A	19	71	12	20	2	2	2	14	10	0	1	.282	.370	.451	112	1	1-1	1.000	-2	87	0	O14L,1b3	0	-0.2
	Det A	96	379	47	120	14	5	3	40	19	1	13	.317	.351	.404	90	-6	4-4	.970	-5	88	87	O87(85/0/2)	0	-1.6
	Year	115	450	59	140	16	7	5	54	29	1	14	.311	.354	.411	94	-5	5-5	.974	-7	88	75	O101(99/0/2),1b3	0	-1.8
1942	Det A	62	144	13	36	5	0	1	20	9	0	6	.250	.294	.306	64	-7	0-1	.978	0	95	60	O24(6/0/18),1b4	0	-1.0
1943	Det A	70	115	3	30	4	0	0	10	13	1	3	.261	.341	.296	81	-2	1-1	1.000	1	97	75	O19(2/0/17)/1	0	-0.3
Total	10	1081	4074	598	1267	205	50	42	533	310	14	141	.311	.362	.417	96	-23	40-30	.967	-59	89	65	O887(745/0/143),1b55	0	-13.3
Rader, Dave	David Martin; B12.26.1948 Claremore OK; BL/TR/5´11˝/(160–176); [SFN67 1/18]; d9.5																								
1971	SF N	3	4	0	0	0	0	0	0	0-0	0	0	.000	.000	.000	-99	-1	0-0	1.000	0	0	0	/C	0	-0.1
1972	SF N	133	459	44	119	14	1	6	41	29-4	3	31	.259	.306	.333	81	-12	1-2	.985	-8	85	99	C127	0	-1.6
1973	SF N	148	462	59	106	15	4	9	41	63-23	6	22	.229	.326	.338	82	-10	0-0	.991	-13	75	77	C148	0	-1.7
1974	SF N	113	323	26	94	16	2	1	26	31-9	0	21	.291	.351	.362	96	-1	1-0	.984	-5	97	76	C109	0	-0.2
1975	SF N	98	292	39	85	15	0	5	31	32-12	1	30	.291	.360	.394	106	3	1-0	.984	-3	85	96	C94	0	0.5
1976	SF N	88	255	25	67	15	0	1	22	27-8	0	21	.263	.332	.333	87	-3	2-0	.984	-4	89	74	C81	0	-0.4
1977	StL N	66	114	15	30	7	1	1	16	9-0	0	10	.263	.310	.368	84	-3	1-0	.976	3	96	81	C38	0	0.2
1978	Chi N	116	305	29	62	13	3	3	36	34-7	1	26	.203	.281	.295	56	-18	1-1	.977	-6	116	126	C114	0	-2.1
1979	Phi N	31	54	3	11	1	1	1	5	6-0	0	7	.204	.283	.315	60	-3	0-0	.932	-5	70	151	C25	0	-0.7
1980	Bos A	50	137	14	45	11	0	3	17	14-1	0	12	.328	.388	.474	129	6	1-1	.981	1	93	112	C34,D9	0	0.8
Total	10	846	2405	254	619	107	12	30	235	245-64	11	180	.257	.326	.349	86	-42	8-4	.983	-40	90	98	C771,D9	0	-5.3
Rader, Don	Donald Russell; B9.5.1893 Wolcott IN; D6.26.1983 Walla Walla WA; BL/TR/5´10˝/164; d7.25; Col Oregon																								
1913	Chi A	4	3	1	1	1	0	0	0	0	0	0	.333	.333	.667	193	0	0	.000	-1	0	0	/3lf	—	0.0
1921	Phi N	9	32	4	9	2	0	0	3	3	0	5	.281	.343	.344	76	-1	0-0	1.000	-2	84	67	S9	—	-0.2
Total	2	13	35	5	10	3	0	0	3	3	0	5	.286	.342	.371	84	-1	0-0	1.000	-3	84	67	S9/lf3	—	-0.2
Rader, Doug	Douglas Lee "Rojo","The Red Rooster"; B7.30.1944 Chicago IL; BR/TR/6´3˝/(208–210); d7.31; M7/C8; Col Illinois Wesleyan																								
1967	Hou N	47	162	24	54	10	4	2	26	7-2	2	31	.333	.360	.481	146	9	0-3	.972	-1	91	96	1b36,3b7	0	0.5
1968	Hou N	98	333	42	89	16	4	6	43	31-3	1	51	.267	.328	.393	119	8	2-2	.930	-0	96	83	3b86,1b5	0	0.8
1969	Hou N	155	569	62	140	25	3	11	83	62-7	6	103	.246	.325	.359	93	-5	1-5	.945	13	100	126	3b154,1b4	0	0.7
1970	Hou N	156	576	90	145	25	3	25	87	57-7	4	102	.252	.322	.436	106	3	3-2	**.966**	25	**118**	128	3b154/1	0	2.7
1971	Hou N	135	484	51	118	21	4	12	56	40-2	3	112	.244	.303	.378	95	-4	5-1	.946	7	**110**	**129**	3b135	0	0.4
1972	Hou N	152	553	70	131	24	7	22	90	57-8	5	120	.237	.309	.425	111	7	5-5	.958	18	110	119	3b152	0	2.4
1973	Hou N	154	574	79	146	26	0	21	89	46-6	3	97	.254	.310	.409	99	-2	4-3	.945	-9	91	80	3b152	0	-1.2
1974	Hou N	152	533	61	137	27	3	17	78	60-7	4	131	.257	.334	.415	114	10	7-2	.965	3	104	91	3b152	0	1.3
1975	Hou N	129	448	41	100	23	2	12	48	42-3	5	101	.223	.296	.364	89	-8	5-4	**.971**	7	102	106	3b124,S2	0	-0.2
1976	SD N	139	471	45	121	22	4	9	55	55-3	3	102	.257	.335	.378	112	8	3-4	.955	6	108	88	3b137	0	1.3
1977	SD N	52	170	19	46	8	3	5	27	33-1	1	40	.271	.392	.441	136	10	0-1	.961	-1	97	104	3b51	0	0.8
	Tor A	96	313	47	75	18	2	13	40	38-2	3	65	.240	.323	.435	104	2	2-1	.966	4	114	22	3b45,D34,1b7/rf	0	0.4
Total	11	1465	5186	631	1302	245	39	155	722	528-51	40	1055	.251	.322	.403	106	38	37-33	.956	73	105	104	3b1349,1b53,D34,S2/rf	0	9.9

YEAR	TM LG	G	AB	R	H	2B	3B	HR	RBI	BB-IB	HP	SO	AVG	OBP	SLG	AOPS	ABR	SB-CS	FA	FR	RNG	THR	GAMES AT POSITION	DL	BFW
RADFORD, PAUL	Paul Revere "Shorty"; B10.14.1861 Roxbury MA; D2.21.1945 Boston MA; BR/TR/5´6˝/148; d5.1; OF(33/153/724); ▲																								
1883	Bos N	72	258	46	53	6	3	0	14	9	—	26	.205	.232	.252	46	-17	—	.836	-3	105	93	O72(1/24/50)	—	-1.9
1884	†Pro N	97	355	56	70	11	2	1	29	25	—	43	.197	.250	.248	58	-16	—	.882	2	125	155	O96R,P2	—	-1.4
1885	Pro N	105	371	55	90	12	5	0	32	33	—	43	.243	.304	.302	99	1	—	.852	3	**155**	**306**	O88(2/8/80),S16,P3/2	—	0.3
1886	KC N	122	493	78	113	17	5	0	20	58	—	48	.229	.310	.284	77	-13	39	.890	6	**155**	151	O92R,S30/2	—	-0.6
1887	NY AA	128	486	127	129	15	5	4	45	**106**	6	—	.265	.403	.342	114	19	73	.833	0	98	127	S76,O37(1/1/36),2b18,P2	—	1.7
1888	Bro AA	90	308	48	67	9	3	2	29	35	4	—	.218	.305	.286	90	-2	33	.944	6	151	72	O88(0/83/5),2b2	—	0.1
1889	Cle N	**136**	487	94	116	21	5	1	46	91	6	37	.238	.365	.308	90	-1	30	.942	-1	92	129	O136(0/2/136)/3	—	-0.3
1890	Cle P	122	466	98	136	24	12	2	62	82	8	28	.292	.406	.408	128	26	25	.895	10	113	160	O80(6/35/39),S36,3b7,2b4/P	—	2.7
1891	Bos AA	133	456	102	118	11	5	0	65	96	5	36	.259	.393	.305	102	8	55	.906	19	**111**	128	S131,O4L/P	—	2.6
1892	Was N	137	510	93	130	19	4	1	37	86	3	47	.255	.366	.314	109	11	35	.933	-2	136	352	O62(2/0/60),3b54,S20,2b2	—	0.8
1893	Was N	124	464	87	106	18	3	2	34	104	8	42	.228	.378	.293	82	-5	32	.901	7	142	79	O123(7/0/116)/2P	—	-0.3
1894	Was N	95	325	61	78	13	5	0	49	65	7	23	.240	.378	.311	70	-13	24	.852	1	109	65	S47,2b25,O24(10/0/14)	—	-0.8
Total	12	1361	4979	945	1206	176	57	13	462	790	47	373	.242	.351	.308	92	-2	346	.901	46	132	151	O902R,S356,3b62,2b54,P10	—	2.9
RADMANOVICH, RYAN	Ryan Ashley; B8.9.1971 Calgary AL, Can.; BL/TR/6´2˝/200; [MinA93 14/401]; d4.13; Col Pepperdine																								
1998	Sea A	25	69	5	15	4	0	2	10	4-1	0	25	.217	.260	.362	59	-4	1-1	1.000	-0	87	148	O24R/1	0	-0.5
RADTKE, JACK	Jack William; B4.14.1913 Denver CO; D10.24.2006 Twin Falls ID; BB/TR/5´7˝/160; d8.1																								
1936	Bro N	33	31	8	3	0	0	0	2	4	0	9	.097	.200	.097	-18	-5	3	1.000	2	150	0	2b14,3b5,S4	—	-0.3
RAFTER, JACK	John Cornelius; B2.20.1875 Troy NY; D1.5.1943 Troy NY; BR/TR/5´8˝/165; d9.24; Col Fordham																								
1904	Pit N	1	3	0	0	0	0	0	0	0	0	—	.000	.000	.000	-97	-1	0	1.000	0	*103*	*114*	/C	—	-0.1
RAFTERY, TOM	Thomas Francis; B10.5.1881 Boston MA; D12.31.1954 Boston MA; BR/TR/5´10.5˝/175; d4.18																								
1909	Cle A	8	32	6	7	2	1	0	0	4	0	—	.219	.306	.344	101	0	1	1.000	-1	0	0	O8(1/1/6)	—	-0.1
RAGLAND, TOM	Thomas; B6.16.1946 Talladega AL; BR/TR/5´10˝/155; [TexA65 11/358]; d4.5																								
1971	Was A	10	23	1	4	0	0	0	0	0-0	1	5	.174	.208	.174	10	-3	0-0	1.000	-2	80	64	2b10	0	-0.4
1972	Tex A	25	58	3	10	2	0	0	2	5-0	0	11	.172	.238	.207	34	-5	0-1	.982	-3	104	68	2b13,3b5,S3	0	-0.8
1973	Cle A	67	183	16	47	7	1	0	12	8-0	1	31	.257	.292	.306	67	-8	2-3	.984	3	101	104	2b65,S2	0	-0.3
Total	3	102	264	20	61	9	1	0	14	13-0	2	47	.231	.272	.273	56	-16	2-4	.985	-2	99	95	2b88,S5,3b5	0	-1.5
RAINES, LARRY	Lawrence Glenn Hope; B3.9.1930 St.Albans WV; D1.28.1978 Lansing MI; BR/TR/5´10˝/165; d4.16																								
1957	Cle A	96	244	39	64	14	0	2	16	19-1	1	40	.262	.318	.344	82	-6	5-2	.922	-5	117	137	3b27,S25,2b10,O8L	0	-0.9
1958	Cle A	7	9	1	0	0	0	0	0	0-0	0	5	.000	.000	.000	-99	-3	0-1	.933	2	177	291	2b2	0	-0.1
Total	2	103	253	40	64	14	0	2	16	19-1	1	45	.253	.308	.332	76	-9	5-3	.922	-3	117	137	3b27,S25,2b12,O8L	0	-1.0
RAINES, TIM	Timothy Jr.; B8.31.1979 Memphis TN; BB/TR (BR 2001)/5´10˝/(183–190); [BalA98 6/189]; d10.1; f–Tim																								
2001	Bal A	7	23	6	4	2	0	0	0	3-0	0	8	.174	.269	.261	43	-2	3-0	1.000	-1	73	0	O7C	0	-0.2
2003	Bal A	20	43	4	6	1	1	0	2	2-0	1	12	.140	.196	.209	7	-6	0-0	.974	2	125	185	O18(1/17/0)/D	0	-0.4
2004	Bal A	48	94	14	24	6	0	0	5	4-0	1	16	.255	.293	.319	60	-5	7-3	1.000	1	103	148	O38(1/27/10),D4	0	-0.4
Total	3	75	160	24	34	9	1	0	7	9-0	2	36	.213	.263	.281	43	-13	10-3	.991	1	104	136	O63(2/51/10),D5	0	-1.0
RAINES, TIM	Timothy Sr. "Rock"; B9.16.1959 Sanford FL; BB/TR/5´8˝/(165–195); [MonN77 5/106]; d9.11; C3; s–Tim																								
1979	Mon N	6	0	3	0	0	0	0	0	0-0	0	0	ø	ø	ø	ø	0	2-0	ø	0	—	—	/R	0	0.0
1980	Mon N	15	20	5	1	0	0	0	0	6-0	0	3	.050	.269	.050	-6	-3	5-0	1.000	-1	87	54	2b7/lf	0	-0.3
1981	†Mon N★	88	313	61	95	13	7	5	37	45-5	2	31	.304	.391	.438	132	14	**71**-11	.976	-1	98	83	O81L/2	0	2.3
1982	Mon N★	156	647	90	179	32	8	4	43	75-9	2	83	.277	.353	.369	99	1	**78**-16	.992	-6	95	72	O120L,2b36	0	0.4
1983	Mon N★	156	615	**133**	183	32	8	11	71	97-9	2	70	.298	.393	.429	128	28	**90**-14	.988	9	97	174	O154(153/2/0),2b7	0	4.6
1984	Mon N★	160	622	106	192	**38**	9	8	60	87-7	2	69	.309	.393	.437	139	36	**75**-10	.988	-1	102	88	O160C,2b2	0	4.8
1985	Mon N★	150	575	115	184	30	13	11	41	81-13	3	60	.320	.405	.475	154	44	70-9	.993	2	101	74	O146L	0	5.3
1986	Mon N★	151	580	91	194	35	10	9	62	78-9	2	60	**.334**	**.413**	.476	146	39	70-9	.979	2	93	129	O147L	0	4.8
1987	Mon N★	139	530	**123**	175	34	8	18	68	90-26	4	52	.330	.429	.526	147	40	50-5	.987	7	108	93	O139L	0	4.9
1988	Mon N	109	429	66	116	19	7	12	48	53-14	2	44	.270	.350	.431	118	11	33-7	.988	2	102	72	O108L	15	1.5
1989	Mon N	145	517	76	148	29	6	9	60	93-18	3	48	.286	.395	.418	131	26	41-9	.996	-5	89	90	O139L	0	2.4
1990	Mon N	130	457	65	131	11	5	9	62	70-8	3	43	.287	.379	.392	118	14	49-16	.976	-8	91	33	O123L	15	0.8
1991	Chi A	155	609	102	163	20	6	5	50	83-9	5	68	.268	.359	.345	98	1	51-15	.990	3	97	157	O133(134/1/0),D19	0	0.5
1992	Chi A	144	551	102	162	22	9	7	54	81-4	0	48	.294	.380	.405	122	19	45-6	.994	10	112	134	O129(129/1/0),D14	0	3.2
1993	†Chi A	115	415	75	127	16	4	16	54	64-4	3	35	.306	.401	.480	138	24	21-7	**1.000**	-3	91	78	O112L	42	1.9
1994	Chi A	101	384	80	102	15	5	10	52	61-3	1	43	.266	.365	.409	101	2	13-0	.981	1	107	45	O96L	0	0.1
1995	Chi A	133	502	81	143	25	4	12	67	70-3	3	52	.285	.374	.422	112	11	13-2	.980	-2	96	102	O107(107/0/1),D22	0	0.6
1996	†NY A	59	201	45	57	10	0	9	33	34-1	1	29	.284	.383	.468	116	6	10-1	.988	-2	87	96	O50L,D2	96	0.3
1997	†NY A	74	271	56	87	20	2	4	38	41-0	0	34	.321	.403	.454	126	13	8-5	.988	-6	82	31	O57L,D13	81	0.4
1998	†NY A	109	321	53	93	13	1	5	47	55-1	3	49	.290	.395	.383	109	7	8-3	.985	-3	78	125	D56,O47L	0	0.1
1999	Oak A	58	135	20	29	5	0	4	17	26-1	0	17	.215	.337	.341	77	-4	4-1	1.000	-1	101	0	O38(38/1/0),D3	77	-0.5
2001	Mon N	47	78	13	24	8	1	0	4	18-0	0	6	.308	.433	.436	128	5	1-0	1.000	-2	79	0	O20L	110	0.3
	Bal A	4	11	1	3	0	0	1	5	0-0	0	3	.273	.250	.545	114	0	0-0	1.000	0	151	0	O2L/D	0	0.0
2002	Fla N	98	89	9	17	3	0	1	7	22-4	1	19	.191	.351	.258	68	-3	0-0	.917	1	107	319	O14L/D	0	-0.3
Total	23	2502	8872	1571	2605	430	113	170	980	1330-148	42	966	.294	.385	.425	123	331	808-146	.988	-4	98	95	O2123(1965/165/1),D131,2b53	436	38.1
RAINEY, JOHN	John Paul; B7.26.1864 Birmingham MI; D11.11.1912 Detroit MI; BL/TR/5´10˝/164; d8.25																								
1887	NY N	17	58	6	17	3	0	0	12	5	0	6	.293	.349	.345	98	0	0	.818	-2	84	128	3b17	—	-0.2
1890	Buf P	42	166	29	39	5	1	1	20	24	5	15	.235	.349	.295	79	-3	12	.870	0	123	87	O28R,S7,3b6,2b2	—	-0.2
Total	2	59	224	35	56	8	1	1	32	29	5	21	.250	.349	.308	84	-3	12	.870	-2	123	87	O28R,3b23,S7,2b2	—	-0.4
RAJSICH, GARY	Gary Louis; B10.28.1954 Youngstown OH; BL/TL/6´2˝/(200–206); [HouN76 11/241]; d4.9; b–Dave; Col Arizona St.																								
1982	NY N	80	162	17	42	8	3	2	12	17-3	1	40	.259	.333	.383	99	0	1-3	1.000	-2	95	0	O35(10/0/26),1b2	0	-0.5
1983	NY N	11	36	5	12	3	0	1	3	3-1	1	1	.333	.400	.500	149	3	0-0	1.000	-1	79	111	1b10	0	0.1
1984	StL N	7	7	1	1	0	0	0	2	2-0	0	1	.143	.300	.143	39	0	0-0	1.000	-0	0	171	1b3	0	-0.1
1985	SF N	51	91	5	15	6	0	0	10	17-4	0	22	.165	.296	.231	52	-5	0-1	.990	-1	86	105	1b23	0	-0.8
Total	4	149	296	28	70	17	3	3	27	39-8	2	64	.236	.328	.345	90	-2	1-4	.994	-4	82	111	1b38,O35(10/0/26)	0	-1.3
RALSTON, DOC	Samuel Beryl; B8.3.1885 Pierpont OH; D8.29.1950 Lancaster PA; BR/TR/6´0˝/185; d9.8; Col Pittsburgh																								
1910	Was A	21	73	4	15	1	0	0	3	3	2	—	.205	.256	.219	52	-4	2	.976	2	119	122	O21L	—	-0.4
RAMAZZOTTI, BOB	Robert Louis; B1.16.1917 Eleanora PA; D2.15.2000 Altoona PA; BR/TR/5´8.5˝/(175–182); d4.20																								
1946	Bro N	62	120	10	25	4	0	0	7	9	0	13	.208	.264	.242	43	-9	0	.939	2	97	99	3b30,2b16	0	-0.7
1948	Bro N	4	3	0	0	0	0	0	0	0	0	1	.000	.000	.000	-97	-1	0	1.000	-0	0	0	3b2/2	0	-0.1
1949	Bro N	5	13	1	2	0	0	1	3	0	0	3	.154	.154	.385	38	-1	0	.833	-1	63	0	3b3	0	-0.2
	Chi N	65	190	14	34	3	1	0	6	5	0	33	.179	.200	.205	9	-25	9	.972	6	111	106	3b36,S12,2b4	0	-1.8
	Year	70	203	15	36	3	1	1	9	5	0	36	.177	.197	.217	11	-27	9	.965	5	108	99	3b39,S12,2b4	0	-2.0
1950	Chi N	61	145	19	38	3	3	1	6	4	1	16	.262	.287	.345	66	-8	3	.961	-3	108	79	2b31,3b10,S3	0	-0.9
1951	Chi N	73	158	13	39	5	2	1	15	10	0	23	.247	.292	.323	64	-8	0-0	.950	6	111	115	S51,2b6/3	0	0.1
1952	Chi N	50	183	26	52	5	3	1	12	14	1	14	.284	.338	.361	93	-2	3-1	.979	-1	108	93	2b50	50	0.0
1953	Chi N	26	39	3	6	2	0	0	4	3	0	4	.154	.214	.205	10	-5	0-0	.911	-2	81	81	2b18	82	-0.7
Total	7	346	851	86	196	22	9	4	53	45	2	107	.230	.271	.291	52	-59	15-1	.966	8	107	91	2b126,3b82,S66	132	-4.3
RAMIREZ, ALEX	Alexander Ramon; B10.3.1974 Caracas, Distrito Capital, Venez.; BR/TR/5´11˝/176; d9.19; [DL 1997 Cle A 27]																								
1998	Cle A	3	8	1	1	0	0	0	0	0-0	0	3	.125	.125	.125	-33	-2	0-0	.833	-0	127	0	O3(2/0/1)	0	-0.2
1999	Cle A	48	97	11	29	6	1	3	18	3-0	1	26	.299	.327	.474	96	-1	1-1	.920	-1	92	122	O29(5/1/23),D14	0	-0.3
2000	Cle A	41	112	13	32	5	1	5	12	5-0	0	17	.286	.316	.482	95	-1	1-0	.978	-1	95	69	O31(15/1/16),D6	0	-0.3
	Pit N	43	115	13	24	6	1	4	18	7-2	0	32	.209	.254	.383	58	-8	1-0	.949	-1	101	58	O31R/1	0	-1.0
Total	3	135	332	38	86	17	3	12	48	15-2	1	78	.259	.293	.437	80	-12	3-1	.949	-2	98	73	O94(22/2/71),D20/1	27	-1.8

YEAR	TM LG	G	AB	R	H	2B	3B	HR	RBI	BB-IB	HP	SO	AVG	OBP	SLG	AOPS	ABR	SB-CS	FA	FR	RNG	THR	GAMES AT POSITION	DL	BFW
Ramirez, Aramis	Aramis (Nin); B6.25.1978 Santo Domingo, D.R.; BR/TR/6´1˝/(190–219); d5.26																								
1998	Pit N	72	251	23	59	9	1	6	24	18-0	4	72	.235	.296	.351	69	-12	0-1	.941	-11	85	107	3b71	25	-2.3
1999	Pit N	18	56	2	10	2	1	0	7	6-0	0	9	.179	.254	.250	29	-6	0-0	.930	0	103	79	3b17	0	-0.6
2000	Pit N	73	254	19	65	15	2	6	35	10-0	5	36	.256	.293	.402	74	-11	0-0	.917	-6	101	52	3b72	33	-1.6
2001	Pit N	158	603	83	181	40	0	34	112	40-4	8	100	.300	.350	.536	121	18	5-4	.945	7	112	117	3b157	0	2.5
2002	Pit N	142	522	51	122	26	0	18	71	29-3	8	95	.234	.279	.387	73	-22	2-0	.946	2	106	128	3b131,D3	0	-1.9
2003	Pit N	96	375	44	105	25	1	12	67	25-3	7	68	.280	.330	.448	101	0	1-1	.924	5	119	55	3b96	0	0.6
	†Chi N	63	232	31	60	7	1	15	39	17-0	3	31	.259	.314	.491	104	0	1-1	.939	3	98	124	3b63	0	0.3
	Year	159	607	75	165	32	2	27	106	42-3	10	99	.272	.324	.465	102	1	2-2	.929	8	**111**	82	3b159	0	0.9
2004	Chi N	145	547	99	174	32	1	36	103	49-6	3	62	.318	.373	.578	138	30	0-2	.969	-14	82	61	3b144	0	1.5
2005	Chi N★	123	463	72	140	30	0	31	92	35-4	6	60	.302	.358	.568	134	22	0-1	.947	-1	97	67	3b119	39	2.1
2006	Chi N	157	594	93	173	38	4	38	119	50-4	9	63	.291	.352	.561	127	23	2-1	**.965**	-12	83	57	3b156	0	1.1
Total	9	1047	3897	517	1089	224	11	196	669	279-24	53	596	.279	.332	.493	109	42	11-11	.946	-28	98	84	3b1026,D3	97	1.7
Ramirez, Hanley	Hanley; B12.23.1983 Samana, D.R.; BR/TR/6´3˝/195; d9.20																								
2005	Bos A	2	2	0	0	0	0	0	0	0-0	0	2	.000	.000	.000	-96	-1	0-0	1.000	-1	51	0	S2	0	-0.1
2006	Fla N	158	633	119	185	46	11	17	59	56-0	4	128	.292	.353	.480	116	15	51-15	.963	2	93	112	S154	0	3.3
Total	2	160	635	119	185	46	11	17	59	56-0	4	130	.291	.352	.479	116	14	51-15	.963	1	93	111	S156	0	3.2
Ramirez, Julio	Julio Cesar (Figueroa); B8.10.1977 San Juan de la Maguana, D.R.; BR/TR/5´11˝/(170–195); d9.10																								
1999	Fla N	15	21	3	3	1	0	0	2	1-0	0	6	.143	.182	.190	-6	-4	0-1	.950	0	131	0	O11C	0	-0.3
2001	Chi A	22	37	2	3	0	0	0	1	2-0	0	15	.081	.128	.081	-41	-8	2-0	.978	3	123	255	O21(1/21/0)	0	-0.4
2002	Ana A	29	32	6	9	0	1	1	7	2-0	1	14	.281	.343	.438	107	0	0-2	1.000	0	105	161	O23(0/15/9)	77	0.0
2003	Ana A	6	2	1	0	0	0	0	0	0-0	0	0	.000	.000	.000	-99	-1	0-0	.750	0	161	0	O5(0/3/2)/D	0	-0.1
2005	SF N	12	4	3	1	0	0	0	1	0-0	0	1	.250	.250	.250	31	0	0-0	1.000	0	117	0	O6(0/2/4)	0	0.0
Total	5	84	96	15	16	1	1	1	11	5-0	1	36	.167	.216	.229	17	-13	2-3	.970	3	119	162	O66(1/52/15)/D	77	-0.8
Ramirez, Manny	Manuel Aristides (Onelcida); B5.30.1972 Santo Domingo, D.R.; BR/TR/6´0˝/(190–215); [CleA91 1/13]; d9.2																								
1993	Cle A	22	53	5	9	1	0	2	5	2-0	0	8	.170	.200	.302	33	-5	0-0	1.000	0	155	0	D20/rf	0	-0.6
1994	Cle A	91	290	51	78	22	0	17	60	42-4	0	72	.269	.357	.521	123	10	4-2	.994	-1	96	119	O84R,D5	0	0.5
1995	†Cle A★	137	484	85	149	26	1	31	107	75-6	5	112	.308	.402	.558	145	34	6-6	.978	-11	88	35	O131R,D5	0	1.5
1996	†Cle A	152	550	94	170	45	3	33	112	85-8	3	104	.309	.399	.582	145	41	8-5	.970	1	90	178	O149R,D3	0	3.1
1997	†Cle A	150	561	99	184	40	0	26	88	79-5	7	115	.328	.415	.538	142	38	2-3	.975	-5	90	109	O146R,D4	0	2.4
1998	†Cle A★	150	571	108	168	35	2	45	145	76-6	6	121	.294	.377	.599	145	38	5-3	.977	-4	97	90	O148R,D2	0	2.4
1999	†Cle A★	147	522	131	174	34	3	44	**165**	96-9	13	131	.333	.442	**.663**	**170**	**59**	2-4	.975	-2	100	74	O146R,D2	0	4.4
2000	Cle A✳	118	439	92	154	34	2	38	122	86-9	3	117	.351	.457	**.697**	181	58	1-1	.986	-7	78	118	O93R,D25	43	4.1
2001	Bos A★	142	529	93	162	33	2	41	125	81-**25**	8	147	.306	.405	.609	162	50	0-1	1.000	-3	90	31	D87,O55L	0	3.8
2002	Bos A★	120	436	84	152	31	0	33	107	73-14	8	85	**.349**	**.450**	.647	184	57	0-0	.959	-3	83	157	O68(64/0/7),D51	42	4.6
2003	†Bos A✳	154	569	117	185	36	1	37	104	97-**28**	8	94	.325	**.427**	.587	158	53	3-1	.982	-4	83	150	O128L,D26	0	4.1
2004	†Bos A★	152	568	108	175	44	0	**43**	130	82-15	6	124	.308	.397	**.613**	150	44	2-4	.967	-10	81	60	O132L,D19	0	2.5
2005	†Bos A★	152	554	112	162	30	1	45	144	80-9	10	119	.292	.388	.594	151	42	1-0	.974	0	87	**225**	O149L,D2	0	3.5
2006	Bos A✳	130	449	79	144	27	1	35	102	100-16	1	102	.321	**.439**	.619	168	50	0-1	.989	-11	75	83	O123L,D5	0	3.2
Total	14	1817	6575	1258	2066	438	16	470	1516	1054-154	78	1451	.314	.411	.600	155	569	34-31	.977	-59	88	113	O1553(651/0/904),D256	85	39.5
Ramirez, Mario	Mario (Torres); B9.12.1957 Yauco, PR; BR/TR/5´9˝/(153–173); d4.25																								
1980	NY N	18	24	2	5	0	0	0	0	1-0	0	7	.208	.240	.208	27	-2	0-0	1.000	-1	82	128	S7,2b4,3b3	0	-0.3
1981	SD N	13	13	1	1	0	0	0	1	2-1	0	5	.077	.200	.077	-21	-2	0-0	1.000	1	146	0	S2,3b2	0	-0.1
1982	SD N	13	23	1	4	1	0	0	1	2-0	0	4	.174	.240	.217	31	-2	0-0	.963	1	106	115	S8/23	0	-0.1
1983	SD N	55	107	11	21	6	3	0	12	20-1	1	23	.196	.326	.308	80	-2	0-0	.985	-10	81	74	S38/3	0	-0.9
1984	†SD N	48	59	12	7	1	0	2	9	13-1	0	14	.119	.278	.237	46	-4	0-0	.971	-9	69	111	S33,3b6,2b2	0	-1.2
1985	SD N	37	60	6	17	0	0	2	5	3-0	0	11	.283	.317	.383	96	-1	0-0	.918	-9	72	105	S27,2b7	0	-0.9
Total	6	184	286	33	55	8	3	4	28	41-3	1	64	.192	.295	.283	64	-13	0-0	.970	-27	79	94	S115,2b14,3b13	0	-3.5
Ramirez, Milt	Milton (Barboza); B4.2.1950 Mayaguez, PR; BR/TR/5´9˝/150; d4.11																								
1970	StL N	62	79	8	15	2	1	0	3	8-1	0	9	.190	.264	.241	35	-7	0-1	.923	3	104	141	S59/3	0	-0.1
1971	StL N	4	11	2	3	0	0	0	0	2-0	0	1	.273	.385	.273	85	0	0-0	.947	-0	68	47	S4	0	0.0
1979	Oak A	28	62	4	10	1	1	0	3	3-0	0	8	.161	.200	.210	11	-8	0-0	.923	-8	72	0	3b12,2b11,S8	0	-1.5
Total	3	94	152	14	28	3	2	0	6	13-1	0	18	.184	.248	.230	30	-15	0-1	.920	-5	102	114	S71,3b13,2b11	0	-1.6
Ramirez, Orlando	Orlando (Leal); B12.18.1951 Cartagena, Colombia; BR/TR/5´10˝/(168–175); d7.6																								
1974	Cal A	31	86	4	14	0	0	0	7	6-0	0	23	.163	.215	.163	11	-10	2-1	.956	2	98	109	S31	0	-0.5
1975	Cal A	44	100	10	24	4	1	0	4	11-0	0	22	.240	.315	.300	80	-2	9-6	.905	-2	88	134	S40	0	0.0
1976	Cal A	30	70	3	14	1	0	0	5	6-0	0	11	.200	.263	.214	44	-5	3-2	.966	-3	97	72	S30	0	-0.5
1977	Cal A	25	13	6	1	0	0	0	0	0-0	0	3	.077	.077	.077	-60	-3	1-0	1.000	0	98	49	2b5,S3/D	56	-0.2
1979	Cal A	13	12	1	0	0	0	0	0	1-0	1	6	.000	.143	.000	-59	-3	1-0	.844	-2	99	66	S10/D	0	-0.3
Total	5	143	281	24	53	5	1	0	16	24-0	1	65	.189	.254	.214	37	-23	16-9	.931	-4	95	104	S114,2b5,D2	56	-1.5
Ramirez, Rafael	Rafael Emilio (Peguero); B2.18.1958 San Pedro de Macoris, D.R.; BR/TR/6´0˝/(168–190); d8.4																								
1980	Atl N	50	165	17	44	6	1	2	11	2-0	4	33	.267	.292	.352	78	-5	2-1	.949	1	107	106	S46	0	0.0
1981	Atl N	95	307	30	67	16	2	2	20	24-3	1	47	.218	.276	.303	64	-15	7-3	.942	2	105	98	S95	0	-0.3
1982	†Atl N	157	609	74	169	24	4	10	52	36-7	3	49	.278	.319	.379	93	-7	27-14	.956	18	106	**140**	S157	0	3.0
1983	Atl N	152	622	82	185	13	5	7	58	36-4	2	48	.297	.337	.368	89	-10	16-12	.949	12	106	**128**	S152	0	1.8
1984	Atl N☆	145	591	51	157	22	4	2	48	26-1	1	70	.266	.295	.327	70	-24	14-17	.959	5	102	113	S145	0	-0.8
1985	Atl N	138	568	54	141	25	4	5	58	20-1	0	63	.248	.272	.333	65	-28	2-6	.954	15	**112**	**130**	S133	0	-0.1
1986	Atl N	134	496	57	119	21	1	8	33	21-1	3	60	.240	.273	.335	64	-25	19-8	.952	23	118	125	S86,3b57,O3(2/0/1)	0	0.7
1987	Atl N	56	179	22	47	12	0	1	21	8-0	2	16	.263	.300	.346	68	-8	6-3	.946	1	106	153	S38,3b12	85	-0.4
1988	Hou N	155	566	51	156	30	5	6	59	18-6	3	61	.276	.298	.378	98	-4	3-2	.965	-17	90	85	S154	0	-1.0
1989	Hou N	151	537	46	132	20	2	6	54	29-3	0	64	.246	.283	.324	76	-18	3-1	.945	-41	82	84	S149	0	-5.3
1990	Hou N	132	445	44	116	19	3	2	37	24-9	1	46	.261	.299	.330	75	-16	10-5	.953	-15	95	91	S129	15	-2.2
1991	Hou N	101	233	17	55	10	0	1	20	13-1	0	40	.236	.274	.292	63	-12	3-3	.953	-8	81	81	S45,2b27,3b2	0	-1.8
1992	Hou N	73	176	17	44	6	0	1	13	7-1	1	24	.250	.283	.301	68	-8	0-0	.961	-3	98	77	S57/3	23	-0.8
Total	13	1539	5494	562	1432	224	31	53	484	264-37	21	621	.261	.295	.342	77	-180	112-75	.953	-7	101	110	S1386,3b72,2b27,O3(2/0/1)	123	-7.2
Ramos, Domingo	Domingo Antonio (De Ramos); B3.29.1958 Santiago, D.R.; BR/TR/5´10˝/(154–170); d9.8																								
1978	NY A	1	0	0	0	0	0	0	0	0-0	0	0	ø	ø	ø	ø	0	0-0	ø	-0	0	0	/S	0	0.0
1980	Tor A	5	16	0	2	0	0	0	0	2-0	0	5	.125	.222	.125	-2	-2	0-0	1.000	-0	124	86	2b2,S2/D	0	-0.2
1982	Sea A	8	26	3	4	2	0	0	1	3-0	0	2	.154	.241	.231	29	-2	0-0	.920	-5	57	0	S8	0	-0.7
1983	Sea A	53	127	14	36	4	0	2	10	7-0	1	12	.283	.326	.362	86	-3	3-1	.948	7	112	137	S28,2b8,3b8,D2	0	0.8
1984	Sea A	59	81	6	15	2	0	0	2	5-0	0	12	.185	.233	.210	24	-8	2-2	.911	-2	74	126	3b38,S13,1b5,2b3	0	-1.0
1985	Sea A	75	168	19	33	6	0	1	15	17-0	0	23	.196	.267	.250	43	-13	0-1	.951	-5	86	75	S36,2b20,1b14,3b7	0	-1.5
1986	Sea A	49	99	8	18	2	0	0	5	8-0	1	13	.182	.250	.202	25	-10	0-1	.966	8	125	75	S21,2b16,3b8,D2	0	-0.1
1987	Sea A	42	103	9	32	6	0	2	11	3-0	1	12	.311	.336	.427	96	-1	0-1	.953	4	109	131	S25,3b7,2b6,D2	0	0.5
1988	Cle A	22	46	7	12	1	0	0	5	3-0	1	7	.261	.308	.283	68	-2	0-0	1.000	1	120	139	2b11,1b5,S4,3b2	0	0.0
	Cal A	10	15	3	2	0	0	0	0	0-0	0	0	.133	.133	.133	-26	-3	0-0	1.000	0	117	0	3b8/lf	0	-0.3
	Year	32	61	10	14	1	0	0	5	3-0	1	7	.230	.269	.246	47	-4	0-0	1.000	1	120	139	2b11,3b10,1b5,S4/lf	0	-0.3
1989	†Chi N	85	179	18	47	6	2	1	19	17-4	2	23	.263	.333	.335	86	-3	1-1	.959	3	129	120	S42,3b30	0	0.3
1990	Chi N	98	226	22	60	5	0	2	17	27-1	1	29	.265	.342	.314	78	-6	0-2	.932	-12	55	27	3b66,S21/2	0	-1.8
Total	11	507	1086	109	261	34	2	8	85	92-5	7	138	.240	.302	.297	64	-53	6-9	.955	-1	108	109	S201,3b174,2b67,1b24,D7/lf	0	-4.0
Ramos, Chucho	Jesus Manuel (Garcia); B4.12.1918 Maturin, Monagas, Venez.; D9.2.1977 Caracas, Distrito Capital, Venez.; BR/TL/5´10.5˝/167; d5.7																								
1944	Cin N	4	10	1	5	1	0	0	0	0	0	0	.500	.500	.600	217	1	0	1.000	-0	106	0	O3(1/0/3)	0	0.1
Ramos, John	John Joseph; B8.6.1965 Tampa FL; BR/TR/6´0˝/190; [NYA86 5/132]; d9.18; Col Stanford; [DL 1992 NY A 90]																								
1991	NY A	10	26	4	8	1	0	0	3	1-0	0	3	.308	.310	.346	88	0	0-0	1.000	-2	98	0	C5,D4	0	-0.2

YEAR	TM LG	G	AB	R	H	2B	3B	HR	RBI	BB-IB	HP	SO	AVG	OBP	SLG	AOPS	ABR	SB-CS	FA	FR	RNG	THR	GAMES AT POSITION	DL	BFW
Ramos, Ken	Kenneth Cecil; B6.6.1967 Sidney NE; BL/TL/6´1˝/185; d5.16; Col Nebraska																								
1997	Hou N	14	12	0	0	0	0	0	1	2-0	0	0	.000	.133	.000	-61	-3	0-0	ø	-0	0	0	O2(1/0/1)	0	-0.3
Ramos, Bobby	Roberto; B11.5.1955 Havana, Cuba; BR/TR/5´11˝/(190–208); [MonN74 7/153]; d9.26; C4																								
1978	Mon N	2	4	0	0	0	0	0	0	0-0	0	1	.000	.000	.000	-99	-1	0-0	1.000	-0	73	0	/C	0	-0.1
1980	Mon N	13	32	5	5	2	0	0	2	5-0	0	5	.156	.270	.219	37	-3	0-0	.964	-1	113	141	C12	0	-0.3
1981	Mon N	26	41	4	8	1	0	1	3	3-0	0	5	.195	.250	.293	52	-3	0-0	.974	0	84	76	C23	0	-0.2
1982	NY A	4	11	1	1	0	0	1	2	0-0	0	3	.091	.091	.364	18	-1	0-0	1.000	1	190	93	C4	0	-0.1
1983	Mon N	27	61	2	14	3	1	0	5	8-1	1	11	.230	.329	.311	78	-2	0-0	.984	0	93	125	C25	0	-0.1
1984	Mon N	31	83	8	16	1	0	2	5	6-1	0	13	.193	.244	.277	49	-6	0-0	.982	2	74	167	C31	0	-0.3
Total	6	103	232	20	44	7	1	4	17	22-2	1	38	.190	.262	.280	52	-16	0-0	.980	2	92	131	C96	0	-1.1
Ramsey, Fernando	Fernando David (Ramsey); B12.20.1965 Rainbow City, Pan; BR/TR/6´1˝/175; [ChiN87 33/841]; d9.7																								
1992	Chi N	18	25	0	3	0	0	0	2	0-0	0	6	.120	.120	.120	-31	-4	0-0	1.000	-1	91	0	O15C	0	-0.6
Ramsey, Mike	Michael James; B7.8.1960 Thomson GA; BB/TL/6´0˝/173; d4.6; Col Gulf Coast (FL) CC																								
1987	LA N	48	125	18	29	4	2	0	12	10-0	0	32	.232	.287	.296	57	-8	2-4	.973	-4	85	51	O43(4/38/1)	0	-1.3
Ramsey, Mike	Michael Jeffrey; B3.29.1954 Roanoke VA; BB/TR/6´1˝/(170–175); [StLN75 3/64]; d9.4; Col Appalachian St.																								
1978	StL N	12	5	4	1	0	0	0	0	0-0	0	1	.200	.200	.200	12	-1	0-0	.909	1	108	291	S4	0	0.0
1980	StL N	59	126	11	33	8	1	0	8	3-2	0	17	.262	.279	.341	69	-5	0-0	.960	-3	114	118	2b24,S20,3b8	0	-0.6
1981	StL N	47	124	19	32	3	0	0	9	8-1	0	16	.258	.303	.282	64	-6	4-0	.966	5	119	111	S35,3b5/2lf	61	0.3
1982	†StL N	112	256	18	59	8	2	1	21	22-3	1	34	.230	.294	.289	62	-13	6-5	.963	-1	96	109	2b43,3b28,S22,O2L	0	-1.1
1983	StL N	97	175	25	46	4	3	1	16	12-2	1	23	.263	.309	.337	80	-5	4-2	.968	-10	88	110	2b66,S20,3b8/lf	15	-1.3
1984	StL N	21	15	1	1	1	0	0	0	1-0	0	3	.067	.125	.133	-28	-3	0-0	1.000	1	119	47	2b7,S7/3	0	-0.2
	Mon N	37	70	2	15	1	0	0	3	0-0	0	13	.214	.214	.229	25	-7	0-0	.975	-4	102	132	S26,2b12	0	-0.9
	Year	58	85	3	16	2	0	0	3	1-0	0	16	.188	.198	.212	16	-10	0-0	.978	-3	103	148	S33,2b19/3	0	-1.1
1985	LA N	9	15	1	2	1	0	0	0	2-0	0	4	.133	.235	.200	23	-2	0-0	.923	-1	121	89	S4,2b2	0	-0.2
Total	7	394	786	81	189	26	6	2	57	48-8	2	111	.240	.285	.296	62	-42	14-7	.964	-12	94	106	2b155,S138,3b50,O4L	76	-4.0
Ramsey, Bill	William Thrace "Square Jaw"; B10.20.1920 Osceola AR; BR/TR/6´0˝/175; d4.19; Col Florida																								
1945	Bos N	78	137	16	40	8	0	1	12	4	3	22	.292	.326	.372	93	-1	1	.963	1	116	46	O43(30/13/0)	0	-0.2
Rand, Dick	Richard Hilton; B3.7.1931 South Gate CA; D1.22.1996 Moreno Valley CA; BR/TR/6´2˝/(175–185); d9.16																								
1953	StL N	9	31	3	9	1	0	0	1	2	0	6	.290	.333	.323	72	-1	0-0	.984	1	*99*	*111*	C9	0	0.0
1955	StL N	3	10	1	3	0	0	1	3	1-0	0	1	.300	.364	.600	150	1	0-1	1.000	-1	*65*	*209*	C3	0	-0.1
1957	Pit N	60	105	7	23	2	1	1	9	11-1	0	24	.219	.288	.286	58	-6	0-0	.973	-2	115	54	C57	0	-0.7
Total	3	72	146	11	35	3	1	2	13	14-1	0	31	.240	.302	.315	68	-6	0-1	.977	-2	*109*	*73*	C69	0	-0.8
Randa, Joe	Joseph Gregory; B12.18.1969 Milwaukee WI; BR/TR/5´11˝/(185–190); [KCA91 11/288]; d4.30; Col Tennessee																								
1995	KC A	34	70	6	12	2	0	1	5	6-0	0	17	.171	.237	.243	25	-8	0-1	.949	-4	104	38	3b22,2b9,D2	0	-1.1
1996	KC A	110	337	36	102	24	1	6	47	26-4	1	47	.303	.351	.433	97	-1	13-4	.951	-9	91	81	3b92,2b15,1b7/D	22	-0.7
1997	Pit N	126	443	58	134	27	9	7	60	41-1	6	64	.302	.366	.451	112	8	4-2	.937	19	117	119	3b120,2b13	29	2.7
1998	Det A	138	460	56	117	21	2	9	50	41-1	7	70	.254	.323	.367	79	-14	8-7	.976	8	**112**	107	3b118,2b20/1D	0	-0.6
1999	KC A	156	628	92	197	36	8	16	84	50-4	3	80	.314	.363	.473	108	7	5-4	.952	9	**110**	102	3b156	0	1.5
2000	KC A	158	612	88	186	29	4	15	106	36-3	6	66	.304	.343	.438	92	-8	6-3	.957	9	108	102	3b156/D	0	0.2
2001	KC A	151	581	59	147	34	2	13	83	42-2	6	80	.253	.307	.386	74	-22	3-2	.966	4	104	**129**	3b137,D14/2	0	-1.7
2002	KC A	151	549	63	155	36	5	11	80	46-1	9	69	.282	.341	.426	93	-5	2-1	.972	0	102	53	3b129,D19	0	-0.5
2003	KC A	131	502	80	146	31	1	16	72	41-0	7	61	.291	.348	.452	103	3	1-0	**.980**	-0	101	54	3b129,D2	15	0.4
2004	KC A	128	485	65	139	31	2	8	56	40-1	6	77	.287	.343	.408	96	-2	0-1	.967	4	105	107	3b119,1b3,D6	26	0.2
2005	Cin N	92	332	44	96	26	1	13	48	33-2	2	52	.289	.356	.491	119	9	0-0	.974	-5	89	79	3b84	0	0.5
	†SD N	58	223	27	57	17	1	4	20	14-1	2	29	.256	.303	.395	86	-5	0-1	.955	-10	73	77	3b58,D2	0	-1.5
	Year	150	555	71	153	43	2	17	68	47-3	4	81	.276	.335	.452	106	5	0-1	.967	-15	82	78	3b142,D2	0	-1.0
2006	Pit N	89	206	23	55	13	0	4	28	16-2	0	26	.267	.316	.388	79	-7	0-0	.962	-0	94	109	3b42,1b15,D3	42	-0.7
Total	12	1522	5428	697	1543	327	36	123	739	432-22	55	738	.284	.339	.426	94	-45	42-26	.962	25	103	93	3b1362,2b58,D51,1b26	134	-1.3
Randall, Sap	James Odell; B8.19.1960 Mobile AL; BB/TR/5´11˝/195; [CalA81 10/236]; d8.2; Col Grambling St.																								
1988	Chi A	4	12	1	0	0	0	0	1	2-0	0	3	.000	.133	.000	-56	-3	0-0	1.000	0	155	124	1b2/rfD	0	-0.3
Randall, Newt	Newton John; B2.3.1880 New Lowell ON, Can.; D5.3.1955 Duluth MN; BR/TR/5´10˝/181; d4.18																								
1907	Chi N	22	78	6	16	4	2	0	4	8	0	—	.205	.279	.308	79	-2	2	.904	-0	85	134	O21(1/1/21)	—	-0.4
	Bos N	75	258	16	55	6	3	0	15	19	7	—	.213	.285	.260	71	-8	4	.920	-6	92	38	O73(59/3/12)	—	-2.1
	Year	97	336	22	71	10	5	0	19	27	7	—	.211	.284	.271	73	-10	6	.915	-6	90	63	O94(60/4/33)	—	-2.5
Randall, Bob	Robert Lee; B6.10.1948 Norton KS; BR/TR/6´3˝/180; [LAN69 S2/32]; d4.13; C1; Col Kansas St.																								
1976	Min A	153	475	55	127	18	4	1	34	28-0	8	38	.267	.317	.328	88	-7	3-5	.969	-4	96	**123**	2b153	0	-0.2
1977	Min A	103	306	36	73	13	2	0	22	15-0	7	25	.239	.289	.294	60	-17	1-4	.985	12	107	120	2b101/13D	16	-0.1
1978	Min A	119	330	36	89	11	3	0	21	24-0	6	22	.270	.329	.321	82	-8	5-3	.983	17	**113**	122	2b116,3b2/D	0	1.5
1979	Min A	80	199	25	49	7	0	0	14	15-0	0	17	.246	.299	.281	55	-12	2-2	.983	10	110	131	2b71,3b7/Slf	0	0.1
1980	Min A	5	15	2	3	1	0	0	0	1-0	0	0	.200	.250	.267	39	-1	0-0	.909	-0	116	138	3b4/2	0	-0.1
Total	5	460	1325	154	341	50	9	1	91	83-0	21	102	.257	.310	.311	74	-45	11-14	.979	36	105	123	2b442,3b14,D2/lfS1	16	1.2
Randle, Len	Leonard Shenoff; B2.12.1949 Long Beach CA; BB/TR (BR 1971)/5´10˝/(169–175); [TexA70 S1/10]; d6.16; Col Arizona St.; OF(62/85/6)																								
1971	Was A	75	215	27	47	11	0	2	13	24-2	1	56	.219	.298	.298	73	-7	1-1	.967	8	106	118	2b66	0	0.5
1972	Tex A	74	249	23	48	13	0	2	21	13-2	1	51	.193	.235	.269	52	-15	4-5	.952	-0	99	86	2b65,S4,O2C	0	-1.4
1973	Tex A	10	29	3	6	1	1	1	1	0-0	0	2	.207	.207	.414	74	-1	0-2	.964	-3	58	69	2b5,O2C	0	-0.5
1974	Tex A	151	520	65	157	17	4	1	49	29-2	2	43	.302	.338	.356	103	1	26-17	.935	11	96	125	3b89,2b40,O21(13/5/3)/SD	0	1.4
1975	Tex A	156	601	85	166	24	7	4	57	57-3	4	80	.276	.341	.359	100	0	16-19	.973	11	104	120	2b79,O66(7/61/0),3b17/CSD	0	1.2
1976	Tex A	142	539	53	121	11	6	1	51	46-2	2	63	.224	.286	.273	63	-25	30-15	.971	0	95	89	2b113,O30(28/1/1),3b2/D	0	-1.9
1977	NY N	136	513	78	156	22	7	5	27	65-3	2	70	.304	.383	.404	116	13	33-21	.961	2	96	**152**	3b110,2b20,O6(4/4/0)/S	0	1.4
1978	NY N	132	437	53	102	16	8	2	35	64-7	1	57	.233	.330	.320	85	-7	14-11	.967	-7	91	108	3b124,2b5	0	-1.8
1979	NY A	20	39	2	7	0	0	0	3	3-0	0	2	.179	.238	.179	15	-5	0-0	1.000	1	94	377	O11(4/7/0),D2	0	-0.4
1980	Chi N	130	489	67	135	19	6	5	39	50-2	1	55	.276	.343	.370	92	-4	19-13	.929	6	109	40	3b111,2b17,O6(4/2/0)	0	0.0
1981	Sea A	82	273	22	63	9	1	4	25	17-4	1	22	.231	.276	.315	67	-12	11-6	.986	7	111	92	3b59,2b21,O5(2/1/2),S3	0	-0.4
1982	Sea A	30	46	10	8	2	0	0	1	4-0	0	4	.174	.240	.217	26	-5	2-2	.964	0	112	59	D13,3b9,2b6	0	-0.5
Total	12	1138	3950	488	1016	145	40	27	322	372-27	15	505	.257	.321	.335	86	-67	156-112	.953	36	99	103	3b521,2b437,O149C,D21,S10/C	0	-2.4
Randolph, Willie	Willie Larry; B7.6.1954 Holly Hill SC; BR/TR/5´11˝/(161–170); [PitN72 7/167]; d7.29; M2/C11																								
1975	†Pit N	30	61	9	10	1	0	0	3	7-1	0	6	.164	.246	.180	21	-7	1-0	.962	2	115	97	2b14/3	0	-0.4
1976	†NY A✶	125	430	59	115	15	4	1	40	58-5	3	39	.267	.356	.328	102	4	37-12	.974	11	110	117	2b124	0	2.9
1977	†NY A★	147	551	91	151	28	11	4	40	64-1	1	53	.274	.347	.387	101	2	28-12	.980	14	106	**121**	2b147	0	2.4
1978	NY A	134	499	87	139	18	6	3	42	82-1	4	51	.279	.381	.357	112	12	36-7	.978	3	99	102	2b134	21	2.8
1979	NY A	153	574	98	155	15	13	5	61	95-5	3	39	.270	.374	.368	103	6	33-12	.985	17	108	123	2b153	0	3.3
1980	†NY A★	138	513	99	151	23	7	7	46	**119**-4	2	45	.294	.427	.407	132	32	30-5	.976	7	99	100	2b138	0	5.0
1981	†NY A★	93	357	59	83	14	3	2	24	57-0	0	24	.232	.336	.305	88	-4	14-5	.977	9	100	**127**	2b93	0	1.2
1982	NY A	144	553	85	155	21	4	3	36	75-3	3	35	.280	.368	.349	100	3	16-9	.981	11	100	103	2b142/D	0	2.2
1983	NY A	104	420	73	117	21	1	2	38	53-0	1	32	.279	.361	.348	99	2	12-4	.979	15	106	109	2b104	38	2.3
1984	NY A	142	564	86	162	24	2	2	31	86-4	0	42	.287	.377	.348	107	10	10-6	.983	22	103	119	2b142	0	3.9
1985	NY A	143	497	75	137	21	2	5	40	85-3	4	39	.276	.382	.356	107	9	16-9	.985	5	100	110	2b143	0	2.2
1986	NY A	141	492	76	136	15	2	5	50	94-0	3	49	.276	.393	.346	104	9	15-2	.972	3	103	107	2b139/D	0	2.1
1987	NY A★	120	449	96	137	24	2	7	67	82-1	2	25	.305	.411	.414	122	19	11-1	.981	9	104	115	2b119/D	30	3.4
1988	NY A	110	404	43	93	20	1	2	34	55-2	2	39	.230	.322	.300	76	-11	8-4	.988	14	109	**111**	2b110	40	0.7
1989	LA N★	145	549	62	155	18	0	2	36	71-2	4	51	.282	.366	.326	101	4	7-6	.987	-5	96	112	2b140	0	0.3
1990	LA N	26	96	15	26	4	0	1	9	13-0	1	9	.271	.364	.344	98	0	1-0	.969	-1	96	77	2b26	0	0.1
	†Oak A	93	292	37	75	9	3	1	21	32-1	1	25	.257	.331	.318	86	-5	6-1	.982	-8	97	128	2b84,D6	17	-1.0
1991	Mil A	124	431	60	141	14	3	0	54	75-3	0	38	.327	.424	.374	126	20	4-2	.969	9	**108**	**123**	2b121,D2	0	3.2

YEAR	TM LG	G	AB	R	H	2B	3B	HR	RBI	BB-IB	HP	SO	AVG	OBP	SLG	AOPS	ABR	SB-CS	FA	FR	RNG	THR	GAMES AT POSITION	DL	BFW
1992	NY N	90	286	29	72	11	1	2	15	40-1	4	34	.252	.352	.318	92	-1	1-3	.977	-5	90	118	2b79	50	-0.6
Total	18	2202	8018	1239	2210	316	65	54	687	1243-37	38	675	.276	.373	.351	104	104	271-94	.980	132	103	113	2b2152,D11/3	196	36.0

RANEW, MERRITT Merritt Thomas; B5.10.1938 Albany GA; BL/TR/5´10˝/(178–180); d4.13

YEAR	TM LG	G	AB	R	H	2B	3B	HR	RBI	BB-IB	HP	SO	AVG	OBP	SLG	AOPS	ABR	SB-CS	FA	FR	RNG	THR	GAMES AT POSITION	DL	BFW
1962	Hou N	71	218	26	51	6	8	4	24	14-5	3	43	.234	.287	.390	87	-6	2-2	.980	-7	63	87	C58	0	-1.0
1963	Chi N	78	154	18	52	8	1	3	15	9-1	2	32	.338	.380	.461	134	7	1-0	.980	-1	97	67	C37,1b9	0	0.7
1964	Chi N	16	33	0	3	0	0	0	1	2-0	1	6	.091	.167	.091	-24	-5	0-0	1.000	1	37	155	C9	0	-0.5
	Mil N	9	17	1	2	0	0	0	0	0-0	0	3	.118	.118	.118	-33	-3	0-1	1.000	-1	0	303	C3	0	-0.4
	Year	25	50	1	5	0	0	0	1	2-0	1	9	.100	.151	.100	-27	-8	0-1	1.000	0	28	192	C12	0	-0.9
1965	Cal A	41	91	12	19	4	0	1	10	7-0	0	22	.209	.260	.286	58	-5	0-0	.988	-5	189	131	C24	0	-1.0
1969	Sea A	54	81	11	20	2	0	0	4	10-3	0	14	.247	.330	.272	70	-3	0-0	.969	-4	78	0	C13,O3L/3	0	-0.7
Total	5	269	594	68	147	20	9	8	54	42-9	6	120	.247	.301	.352	83	-15	3-3	.982	-17	89	92	C144,1b9,O3L/3	0	-2.9

RANSOM, CODY Bryan Cody; B2.17.1976 Mesa AZ; BR/TR/6´2˝/(190–210); [SFN98 9/278]; d9.5; Col Grand Canyon

YEAR	TM LG	G	AB	R	H	2B	3B	HR	RBI	BB-IB	HP	SO	AVG	OBP	SLG	AOPS	ABR	SB-CS	FA	FR	RNG	THR	GAMES AT POSITION	DL	BFW
2001	SF N	9	7	1	0	0	0	0	0	0-0	0	5	.000	.000	.000	-99	-2	0-0	1.000	-0	134	0	S6	0	-0.2
2002	SF N	7	3	2	2	0	0	0	1	1-1	0	1	.667	.750	.667	287	1	0-0	1.000	-0	76	0	S3	0	0.1
2003	SF N	20	27	7	6	1	0	1	1	1-0	0	11	.222	.250	.370	58	-2	0-0	.963	-2	82	164	S12	0	-0.3
2004	SF N	78	68	13	17	6	0	1	11	6-0	1	20	.250	.320	.382	78	-2	2-2	.948	1	109	160	S45,2b16/3lf	0	0.0
Total	4	114	105	23	25	7	0	2	13	8-1	1	37	.238	.298	.362	69	-5	2-2	.958	-1	99	143	S66,2b16/lf3	0	-0.4

RANSOM, JEFF Jeffrey Dean; B11.11.1960 Fresno CA; BR/TR/5´11˝/185; [SFN78 5/111]; d9.5

YEAR	TM LG	G	AB	R	H	2B	3B	HR	RBI	BB-IB	HP	SO	AVG	OBP	SLG	AOPS	ABR	SB-CS	FA	FR	RNG	THR	GAMES AT POSITION	DL	BFW
1981	SF N	5	15	2	4	1	0	0	0	1-1	0	1	.267	.313	.333	86	0	0-0	1.000	2	65	63	C5	0	0.2
1982	SF N	15	44	5	7	0	0	0	3	6-0	0	7	.159	.255	.159	20	-5	0-0	.988	-1	79	72	C14	0	-0.5
1983	SF N	6	20	3	4	0	0	1	3	4-0	0	7	.200	.333	.350	92	0	0-0	.946	-4	33	39	C6	0	-0.4
Total	3	26	79	10	15	1	0	1	6	11-1	0	15	.190	.286	.241	50	-5	0-0	.980	-2	65	62	C25	0	-0.7

RAPP, EARL Earl Wellington; B5.20.1921 Corunna MI; D2.13.1992 Swedesboro NJ; BL/TR/6´2˝/185; d4.28

YEAR	TM LG	G	AB	R	H	2B	3B	HR	RBI	BB-IB	HP	SO	AVG	OBP	SLG	AOPS	ABR	SB-CS	FA	FR	RNG	THR	GAMES AT POSITION	DL	BFW
1949	Det A	1	0	0	0	0	0	0	0	1	0	0	ø	1.000	ø	175	0	0-0	ø	0	—	—	/H	0	0.0
	Chi A	19	54	3	14	1	1	0	11	5	0	6	.259	.322	.315	71	-2	1-1	.974	2	115	178	O13(11/0/2)	0	-0.2
	Year	20	54	3	14	1	1	0	11	6	0	6	.259	.333	.315	74	-2	1-1	.974	2	115	178	O13(11/0/2)	0	-0.2
1951	NY N	13	11	0	1	0	0	0	1	2	0	3	.091	.231	.091	-10	-2	0-0	ø	0	—	—	/H	0	-0.2
	StL A	26	98	14	32	5	3	2	14	11	0	11	.327	.394	.500	137	5	1-0	.979	-0	97	119	O25R	0	0.4
1952	StL A	30	49	3	7	4	0	0	4	0	0	8	.143	.143	.224	1	-7	0-0	1.000	-0	112	0	O7R	0	-0.7
	Was A	46	67	7	19	6	0	0	9	6	1	13	.284	.351	.373	105	1	0-0	.917	-1	82	0	O10R	0	-0.1
	Year	76	116	10	26	10	0	0	13	6	1	21	.224	.268	.310	61	-6	0-0	.958	-1	95	0	O17R	0	-0.8
Total	3	135	279	27	73	16	4	2	39	25	1	41	.262	.325	.369	89	-5	2-1	.973	-0	102	105	O55(11/0/44)	0	-0.8

RAPP, GOLDIE Joseph Aloysius; B2.6.1894 Cincinnati OH; D7.1.1966 LaMesa CA; BB/TR/5´10˝/165; d4.13

YEAR	TM LG	G	AB	R	H	2B	3B	HR	RBI	BB-IB	HP	SO	AVG	OBP	SLG	AOPS	ABR	SB-CS	FA	FR	RNG	THR	GAMES AT POSITION	DL	BFW
1921	NY N	58	181	21	39	9	1	0	15	15	0	13	.215	.276	.276	46	-14	3-11	.941	9	124	130	3b56	—	-0.4
	Phi N	52	202	28	56	7	1	1	10	14	0	8	.277	.324	.337	70	-8	6-7	.950	1	97	73	3b50/2	—	-0.5
	Year	110	383	49	95	16	2	1	25	29	0	21	.248	.301	.308	59	-22	9-18	.945	10	**112**	104	3b106/2	—	-0.9
1922	Phi N	119	502	58	127	26	3	0	38	32	1	29	.253	.299	.317	54	-34	6-12	.948	3	110	97	3b117,S2	—	-2.5
1923	Phi N	47	179	27	47	5	0	1	10	14	1	14	.263	.320	.307	59	-10	1-1	.947	-0	96	95	3b45	—	-0.8
Total	3	276	1064	134	269	47	5	2	73	75	2	64	.253	.303	.312	57	-66	16-31	.947	13	108	99	3b268,S2/2	—	-4.2

RARIDEN, BILL William Angel "Bedford Bill"; B2.4.1888 Bedford IN; D8.28.1942 Bedford IN; BR/TR/5´10˝/168; d8.12

YEAR	TM LG	G	AB	R	H	2B	3B	HR	RBI	BB-IB	HP	SO	AVG	OBP	SLG	AOPS	ABR	SB-CS	FA	FR	RNG	THR	GAMES AT POSITION	DL	BFW
1909	Bos N	13	42	1	6	1	0	0	1	4	0	—	.143	.217	.167	18	-4	1	.912	-3	*80*	*95*	C13	—	-0.6
1910	Bos N	49	137	15	31	5	1	1	14	12	1	22	.226	.293	.299	70	-5	1	.962	-2	*87*	*119*	C49	—	-0.3
1911	Bos N	70	246	22	56	9	0	0	21	21	0	18	.228	.288	.264	51	-16	3	.952	-8	*77*	*124*	C65,3b3/2	—	-1.8
1912	Bos N	79	247	27	55	3	1	1	14	18	2	35	.223	.281	.255	46	-19	3	.964	-6	*91*	*105*	C73	—	-1.9
1913	Bos N	95	246	31	58	9	2	3	30	30	2	21	.236	.324	.325	84	-4	5-1	.976	-0	102	99	C87	—	0.3
1914	Ind F	131	396	44	93	15	5	0	47	61	0	43	.235	.337	.298	67	-22	12	.981	15	*89*	***112***	C130	—	0.4
1915	New F	142	444	49	120	30	7	0	40	60	3	29	.270	.361	.369	112	3	8	.978	25	***123***	*103*	C142	—	4.3
1916	NY N	120	351	23	78	9	3	1	29	55	3	32	.222	.333	.274	92	0	4	.972	-4	113	85	C119	—	0.7
1917	†NY N	101	266	20	72	10	1	0	25	42	1	17	.271	.372	.316	116	8	3	.971	-10	*102*	57	C100	—	0.6
1918	NY N	69	183	15	41	5	1	0	17	15	0	15	.224	.283	.262	68	-7	1	**.984**	-6	*93*	*63*	C63	—	-0.9
1919	†Cin N	74	218	16	47	6	3	1	24	17	1	19	.216	.275	.284	70	-8	4	.983	6	*113*	*80*	C70	—	0.4
1920	Cin N	39	101	9	25	3	0	0	10	5	0	0	.248	.283	.277	62	-5	2-0	.972	0	*104*	*106*	C37	—	-0.2
Total	12	982	2877	272	682	105	24	7	272	340	13	251	.237	.320	.298	78	-79	47-1	.973	7	*102*	*96*	C948,3b3/2	—	1.0

RATH, MORRIE Morris Charles; B12.25.1886 Mobeetie TX; D11.18.1945 Upper Darby PA; BL/TR/5´8.5˝/160; d9.28; Mil 1918

YEAR	TM LG	G	AB	R	H	2B	3B	HR	RBI	BB-IB	HP	SO	AVG	OBP	SLG	AOPS	ABR	SB-CS	FA	FR	RNG	THR	GAMES AT POSITION	DL	BFW
1909	Phi A	7	26	4	7	1	0	0	3	2	3	—	.269	.387	.308	117	1	1	.846	-1	77	108	S4,3b2	—	0.0
1910	Phi A	18	26	3	4	0	0	0	1	5	0	—	.154	.290	.154	40	-2	0	.950	-1	87	0	3b11,2b3	—	-0.3
	Cle A	24	67	5	13	3	0	0	0	10	0	—	.194	.299	.239	68	-2	2	.950	1	104	127	3b22/S	—	-0.1
	Year	42	93	8	17	3	0	0	1	15	0	—	.183	.296	.215	60	-3	2	.950	-0	100	97	3b33,2b3/S	—	-0.4
1912	Chi A	157	591	104	161	10	2	1	19	95	7	—	.272	.380	.301	98	5	31	**.963**	16	**108**	91	2b157	—	2.4
1913	Chi A	92	295	37	59	2	0	0	12	46	1	22	.200	.310	.207	52	-16	22	.962	-0	102	114	2b86	—	-1.6
1919	†Cin N	138	537	77	142	13	1	1	29	64	0	24	.264	.343	.298	96	1	17	.974	13	103	114	2b138	—	1.7
1920	Cin N	129	506	61	135	7	4	2	28	36	3	24	.267	.319	.308	82	-12	10-11	**.977**	-2	95	101	2b126/3rf	—	-1.4
Total	6	565	2048	291	521	36	7	4	92	258	14	70	.254	.342	.285	86	-25	83-11	.970	25	102	104	2b510,3b36,S5/rf	—	0.7

RATLIFF, GENE Kelly Eugene; B9.28.1945 Macon GA; BR/TR/6´5˝/185; d5.15

YEAR	TM LG	G	AB	R	H	2B	3B	HR	RBI	BB-IB	HP	SO	AVG	OBP	SLG	AOPS	ABR	SB-CS	FA	FR	RNG	THR	GAMES AT POSITION	DL	BFW
1965	Hou N	4	4	0	0	0	0	0	0	0-0	0	4	.000	.000	.000	-99	-1	0-0	ø	0	—	—	/H	0	-0.1

RATLIFF, PAUL Paul Hawthorne; B1.23.1944 San Diego CA; BL/TR/6´2˝/(190–210); d4.14

YEAR	TM LG	G	AB	R	H	2B	3B	HR	RBI	BB-IB	HP	SO	AVG	OBP	SLG	AOPS	ABR	SB-CS	FA	FR	RNG	THR	GAMES AT POSITION	DL	BFW
1963	Min A	10	21	2	4	1	0	1	3	2-0	1	7	.190	.292	.381	85	0	0-0	.976	2	87	235	C7	0	0.2
1970	†Min A	69	149	19	40	7	2	5	22	15-2	7	51	.268	.363	.443	119	4	0-0	.980	-10	129	28	C53	0	-0.4
1971	Min A	21	44	3	7	1	0	2	6	4-1	0	17	.159	.224	.318	52	-3	0-0	1.000	1	126	63	C15	0	-0.1
	Mil A	23	41	3	7	1	0	3	7	5-1	1	21	.171	.277	.415	94	-1	0-0	.966	-0	48	123	C13	0	0.0
	Year	44	85	6	14	2	0	5	13	9-2	1	38	.165	.250	.365	72	-4	0-0	.985	1	92	89	C28	0	-0.1
1972	Mil A	22	42	1	3	0	0	1	4	2-1	0	23	.071	.114	.143	-24	-7	0-0	1.000	-4	66	106	C13	0	-1.2
Total	4	145	297	28	61	10	2	12	42	28-5	9	119	.205	.293	.374	85	-7	0-0	.983	-11	107	70	C101	0	-1.5

RAUB, TOMMY Thomas Jefferson; B12.1.1870 Raubsville PA; D2.15.1949 Phillipsburg NJ; BR/TR/5´10˝/155; d5.3

YEAR	TM LG	G	AB	R	H	2B	3B	HR	RBI	BB-IB	HP	SO	AVG	OBP	SLG	AOPS	ABR	SB-CS	FA	FR	RNG	THR	GAMES AT POSITION	DL	BFW
1903	Chi N	36	84	6	19	3	2	0	7	5	1	—	.226	.278	.310	69	-4	3	.900	-3	*122*	*67*	C12,1b6,O5R,3b4	—	-0.6
1906	StL N	24	78	9	22	2	4	0	2	4	1	—	.282	.325	.410	135	2	2	.957	-4	*73*	*111*	C22	—	0.0
Total	2	60	162	15	41	5	6	0	9	9	2	—	.253	.301	.358	99	-2	5	.940	-7	*88*	*98*	C34,1b6,O5R,3b4	—	-0.6

RAUDMAN, BOB Robert Joyce "Shorty"; B3.14.1942 Erie PA; BL/TL/5´9.5˝/(185–186); d9.13

YEAR	TM LG	G	AB	R	H	2B	3B	HR	RBI	BB-IB	HP	SO	AVG	OBP	SLG	AOPS	ABR	SB-CS	FA	FR	RNG	THR	GAMES AT POSITION	DL	BFW
1966	Chi N	8	29	1	7	2	0	0	2	1-0	0	4	.241	.267	.310	59	-2	0-0	.909	0	61	372	O8L	0	-0.2
1967	Chi N	8	26	0	4	0	0	0	1	1-1	0	4	.154	.185	.154	-2	-3	0-0	.875	0	101	196	O8R	0	-0.4
Total	2	16	55	1	11	2	0	0	3	2-1	0	8	.200	.228	.236	30	-5	0-0	.889	1	80	290	O16(8/0/8)	0	-0.6

RAWLINGS, JOHNNY John William "Red"; B8.17.1892 Bloomfield IA; D10.16.1972 Inglewood CA; BR/TR/5´8˝/158; d4.14

YEAR	TM LG	G	AB	R	H	2B	3B	HR	RBI	BB-IB	HP	SO	AVG	OBP	SLG	AOPS	ABR	SB-CS	FA	FR	RNG	THR	GAMES AT POSITION	DL	BFW
1914	Cin N	33	60	9	13	1	0	0	8	6	0	8	.217	.288	.233	54	-3	1	.885	0	115	96	3b10,2b7,S5	—	-0.3
	KC F	61	193	19	41	3	0	0	15	22	1	25	.212	.296	.228	46	-17	6	.937	10	118	106	S61	—	-0.3
1915	KC F	120	399	40	86	9	2	2	24	27	2	40	.216	.269	.263	52	-33	17	.926	-5	104	86	S120	—	-3.2
1917	Bos N	122	371	37	95	9	4	2	31	38	7	32	.256	.337	.318	107	5	12	.977	3	104	95	2b96,S17/3lf	—	1.2
1918	Bos N	111	410	32	85	7	3	0	21	30	2	31	.207	.265	.239	56	-21	10	.956	8	106	91	S71,2b20,O18R	—	-1.1
1919	Bos N	77	275	30	70	8	2	1	16	16	1	20	.255	.298	.309	86	-5	10	.961	-9	95	82	2b58,O10(7/1/5),S5	—	-1.5
1920	Bos N	5	3	0	0	0	0	0	2	0	0	1	.000	.000	.000	-99	-1	0-0	1.000	-0	67	0	/2	—	-0.1
	Phi N	98	384	39	90	19	2	3	30	22	1	25	.234	.278	.318	67	-16	9-6	.970	-2	98	101	2b97	—	-1.8
	Year	103	387	39	90	19	2	3	32	22	1	26	.233	.276	.315	67	-17	9-6	.970	-3	98	101	2b98	—	-1.9
1921	Phi N	60	254	20	74	14	2	1	16	8	2	12	.291	.318	.374	76	-8	4-5	.954	7	109	103	2b60	—	0.0
	†NY N	86	307	40	82	8	1	1	30	18	4	19	.267	.316	.309	66	-15	4-4	.970	3	99	163	2b86/S	—	-1.0
	Year	146	561	60	156	22	3	2	46	26	6	31	.278	.317	.339	71	-23	8-9	.963	10	103	**138**	2b146/S	—	-1.0

YEAR	TM LG	G	AB	R	H	2B	3B	HR	RBI	BB-IB	HP	SO	AVG	OBP	SLG	AOPS	ABR	SB-CS	FA	FR	RNG	THR	GAMES AT POSITION	DL	BFW
1922	NY N	88	308	46	87	13	8	1	30	23	5	15	.282	.342	.386	87	-6	7-6	.984	-1	99	126	2b77,3b5	—	-0.5
1923	Pit N	119	461	53	131	18	4	1	45	25	1	29	.284	.322	.347	75	-17	9-0	.958	-8	95	97	2b119	—	-1.9
1924	Pit N	3	3	0	1	0	0	0	2	0	0	0	.333	.333	.333	78	0	0-0	ø	0	—	—	/H	—	0.0
1925	Pit N	36	110	17	31	7	0	2	13	8	1	8	.282	.336	.400	82	-3	0-1	.981	2	106	86	2b29	—	-0.1
1926	Pit N	61	181	27	42	6	0	0	20	14	0	10	.232	.287	.265	47	-13	3	.970	-1	96	87	2b59	—	-1.3
Total	12	1080	3719	409	928	122	28	14	303	257	27	275	.250	.303	.309	71	-153	92-22	.968	7	100	106	2b709,S280,O29(8/1/23),3b16	—	-11.9
Ray, Irv	Irving Burton "Stubby"; B1.22.1864 Harrington ME; D2.21.1948 Harrington ME; BL/TR/5´6˝/165; d7.7; Col Maine																								
1888	Bos N	50	206	26	51	2	3	2	26	6	1	11	.248	.272	.316	85	-4	7	.879	-7	99	49	S48,2b3	—	-1.0
1889	Bos N	9	33	8	10	1	0	0	2	4	0	0	.303	.378	.333	93	0	1	.875	-3	83	72	S5,3b4	—	-0.2
	Bal AA	26	106	20	36	4	1	0	17	7	3	6	.340	.397	.396	124	3	12	.784	-8	79	110	S20,O6R	—	-0.4
1890	Bal AA	**38**	139	28	50	6	2	1	20	15	3	—	.360	.433	.453	154	10	11	.894	-7	88	65	S38	—	0.3
1891	Bal AA	103	418	72	116	17	5	0	58	54	4	18	.278	.366	.342	102	2	28	.885	-14	99	43	O64R,S40	—	-0.9
Total	4	226	902	154	263	30	11	3	123	86	11	35	.292	.360	.359	109	11	59	.863	-39	89	68	S151,O70R,3b4,2b3	—	-2.2
Ray, Johnny	John Cornelius; B3.1.1957 Chouteau OK; BB/TR/5´11˝/(170–189); [HouN79 12/294]; d9.2; Col Arkansas																								
1981	Pit N	31	102	10	25	11	0	0	6	6-2	0	9	.245	.284	.353	77	-3	0-0	.987	2	109	126	2b31	0	0.1
1982	Pit N	**162**	647	79	182	30	7	7	63	36-1	1	34	.281	.318	.382	91	-8	16-7	.977	9	102	88	2b162	0	1.1
1983	Pit N	151	576	68	163	**38**	7	5	53	35-3	0	26	.283	.323	.399	96	-3	18-9	.983	21	105	111	2b151	0	2.8
1984	Pit N	155	555	75	173	**38**	6	6	67	37-2	3	31	.312	.354	.434	121	16	11-6	.984	-3	96	105	2b149	0	2.2
1985	Pit N	154	594	67	163	33	3	7	70	46-10	1	24	.274	.325	.375	97	-3	13-9	.976	-19	92	85	2b151	0	-1.4
1986	Pit N	155	579	67	174	33	0	7	78	58-10	3	47	.301	.363	.394	107	8	6-9	.993	8	107	98	2b151	0	2.3
1987	Pit N	123	472	48	129	19	3	5	54	41-4	0	36	.273	.328	.358	82	-12	4-2	.981	2	100	117	2b119	0	-0.4
	Cal A	30	127	16	44	11	0	0	15	3-0	0	10	.346	.359	.433	113	2	0-0	.986	0	106	106	2b29/D	0	0.4
1988	Cal A★	153	602	75	184	42	7	6	83	36-2	4	38	.306	.345	.429	119	15	4-1	.972	-5	107	89	2b104,O40L,D6	0	1.2
1989	Cal A	134	530	52	153	16	3	5	62	36-3	0	30	.289	.327	.358	97	-3	6-3	.984	5	101	120	2b130	15	0.6
1990	Cal A	105	404	47	112	23	0	5	43	19-2	0	44	.277	.308	.371	91	-6	2-3	.987	15	106	117	2b100/D	21	1.2
Total	10	1353	5188	604	1502	294	36	53	594	353-39	12	329	.290	.333	.391	100	3	80-49	.982	36	102	103	2b1277,O40L,D8	36	10.1
Ray, Larry	Larry Dale; B3.11.1958 Madison IN; BL/TR/6´1˝/195; [HouN79 4/86]; d9.10; Col Kentucky Wesleyan																								
1982	Hou N	5	6	0	1	0	0	0	1	0-0	0	4	.167	.143	.167	-7	-1	0-0	1.000	-0	81	0	/lf	0	-0.1
Rayford, Floyd	Floyd Kinnard; B7.27.1957 Memphis TN; BR/TR/5´10˝/(195–220); [AnaA75 4/73]; d4.17																								
1980	Bal A	8	18	1	4	0	0	0	1	0-0	0	5	.222	.222	.222	23	-2	0-0	.900	-0	106	0	3b4/2D	0	-0.2
1982	Bal A	34	53	7	7	0	0	3	5	6-0	0	14	.132	.220	.302	42	-5	0-1	.898	1	114	61	3b27,C2,D2	0	-0.5
1983	StL N	56	104	5	22	4	0	3	14	10-1	0	27	.212	.278	.337	70	-4	1-0	.883	-3	96	83	3b33	0	-0.8
1984	Bal A	86	250	24	64	14	0	4	27	12-0	3	51	.256	.296	.360	83	-6	0-3	.991	12	87	108	C66,3b22/1	0	0.7
1985	Bal A	105	359	55	110	21	1	18	48	10-0	0	69	.306	.324	.521	130	13	3-1	.972	2	107	93	3b78,C29/D	0	1.5
1986	Bal A	81	210	15	37	4	0	8	19	15-0	0	50	.176	.231	.310	46	-17	0-0	.912	-1	101	146	3b72,C10/D	14	-1.8
1987	Bal A	20	50	5	11	0	0	2	3	2-0	0	9	.220	.250	.340	56	-4	0-0	.980	2	67	107	C17/3D	0	-0.1
Total	7	390	1044	112	255	43	1	38	117	55-1	3	225	.244	.283	.397	85	-25	4-5	.931	12	105	105	3b237,C124,D6/12	14	-1.2
Raymer, Fred	Frederick Charles; B11.12.1875 Leavenworth KS; D6.11.1957 Los Angeles CA; BR/TR/5´11˝/185; d4.24																								
1901	Chi N	120	463	41	108	14	2	0	43	11	4	—	.233	.257	.272	56	-27	18	.881	-11	94	59	3b82,S29,1b5,2b3	—	-3.5
1904	Bos N	114	419	28	88	12	3	1	27	13	1	—	.210	.236	.260	55	-23	17	**.958**	5	98	94	2b114	—	-1.9
1905	Bos N	137	498	26	105	14	2	0	31	8	6	—	.211	.232	.247	44	-36	15	.949	-16	94	80	2b134/1lf	—	-5.4
Total	3	371	1380	95	301	40	7	1	101	32	11	—	.218	.242	.259	51	-86	50	.954	-22	96	85	2b251,3b82,S29,1b6/lf	—	-10.8
Raymond, Harry	Harry H. "Jack"; B2.20.1862 Utica NY; D3.21.1925 San Diego CA; 5´9˝/179; d9.9; ▲																								
1888	Lou AA	32	123	8	26	2	0	0	13	1	0	—	.211	.218	.228	44	-8	7	.884	-2	81	21	3b31/rf	—	-0.9
1889	Lou AA	130	515	58	123	12	9	0	47	19	3	45	.239	.270	.297	63	-28	19	.886	-3	96	87	3b129/lfP	—	-2.4
1890	†Lou AA	123	521	91	135	7	4	2	51	22	3	—	.259	.293	.299	76	-18	18	.874	-9	88	113	3b119,S4	—	-2.2
1891	Lou AA	14	59	4	12	2	0	0	2	5	2	6	.203	.288	.237	51	-4	3	.898	4	110	179	S14	—	0.1
1892	Pit N	12	49	4	4	0	1	0	2	4	0	8	.082	.151	.122	-17	-7	1	.867	-1	95	55	3b12	—	-0.8
	Was N	4	15	2	1	0	0	0	0	3	0	2	.067	.222	.067	-12	-2	1	.783	0	125	0	3b4	—	-0.2
	Year	16	64	6	5	0	1	0	2	7	0	10	.078	.169	.109	-16	-9	2	.838	-1	104	39	3b16	—	-1.0
Total	5	315	1282	167	301	23	14	2	115	54	8	61	.235	.270	.279	62	-67	49	.878	-11	92	88	3b295,S18,O2(1/0/1)/P	—	-6.4
Raymond, Lou	Louis Anthony (b Louis Anthony Raymondjack); B12.11.1894 Buffalo NY; D5.2.1979 Rochester NY; BR/TR/5´10.5˝/187; d5.2																								
1919	Phi N	1	2	0	1	0	0	0	0	0	0	0	.500	.500	.500	188	0	0	ø	-0	0	0	/2		0.0
Reach, Al	Alfred James; B5.25.1840 London, England; D1.14.1928 Atlantic City NJ; BL/TL/5´6˝/155; d5.20; M1; b–Bob																								
1871	Ath NA	26	133	43	47	7	6	0	34	5	—	6	.353	.377	.496	150	8	2-0	.844	-1	93	119	2b26	—	0.4
1872	Ath NA	24	118	21	23	0	0	0	10	4	—	0	.195	.221	.195	29	-10	1-1	.943	4	207	567	O20R,1b4	—	-0.3
1873	Ath NA	16	73	13	16	5	1	0	9	0	—	0	.219	.219	.315	52	-5	2-0	.875	4	140	85	2b8,O8(0/5/3)	—	0.0
1874	Ath NA	14	55	8	7	2	0	0	2	0	—	4	.127	.127	.164	-7	-7	0-0	.732	4	277	296	O14R	—	-0.2
1875	Ath NA	3	14	4	4	1	0	0	1	0	—	0	.286	.286	.357	110	0	2-1	1.000	-1	0	0	O2R/2	—	-0.1
Total	5NA	83	393	89	97	15	7	0	56	9	—	10	.247	.264	.321	73	-14	7-2	.860	10	235	342	O44(0/5/39),2b35,1b4	—	-0.2
Reach, Bob	Robert; B8.28.1843 Williamsburg NY; D5.19.1922 Springfield MA; 5´5˝/155; d4.18; b–Al																								
1872	Oly NA	2	8	1	2	0	0	0	0	0	—	0	.250	.250	.250	57	0	0-0	.727	-1	93	0	S2	—	-0.1
1873	Was NA	1	5	1	1	0	0	0	0	0	—	0	.200	.200	.200	19	0	0-0	.500	-1	67	0	/S	—	-0.1
Total	2NA	3	13	2	3	0	0	0	0	0	—	0	.231	.231	.231	42	0	0-0	.632	-2	83	0	S3	—	-0.2
Ready, Randy	Randy Max; B1.8.1960 Fremont CA; BR/TR/5´11˝/(180–184); [MilA80 6/155]; d9.4; Col Mesa St.; OF(167/0/6)																								
1983	Mil A	12	37	8	15	3	2	1	6	6-1	0	3	.405	.488	.676	232	7	0-1	1.000	0	91	112	3b4,D6	0	0.6
1984	Mil A	37	123	13	23	6	1	3	13	14-0	0	18	.187	.270	.325	66	-6	0-0	.946	5	121	63	3b36	0	-0.1
1985	Mil A	48	181	29	48	9	5	1	21	14-0	1	23	.265	.318	.387	93	-2	0-0	.989	-1	107	205	O37(36/0/3),3b7,2b3,D2	50	-0.5
1986	Mil A	23	79	8	15	4	0	1	4	9-0	0	9	.190	.273	.278	49	-6	2-0	.950	-1	92	0	O11L,2b7,3b3/D	0	-0.6
	SD N	1	3	0	0	0	0	0	0	0-0	0	1	.000	.000	.000	-99	-1	0-0	.667	-0	129	0	/3	18	-0.1
1987	SD N	124	350	69	108	26	6	12	54	67-2	3	44	.309	.423	.520	154	31	7-3	.912	9	117	153	3b52,2b51,O16L	0	4.0
1988	SD N	114	331	43	88	16	2	7	39	39-1	3	38	.266	.346	.390	114	7	6-2	.952	-2	99	150	3b57,2b26,O16(15/0/1)	0	0.6
1989	SD N	28	67	4	17	2	1	0	5	11-0	0	6	.254	.354	.313	94	0	0-0	.963	3	121	172	3b18,2b2/lf	0	0.4
	Phi N	72	187	33	50	11	1	8	21	31-0	2	31	.267	.372	.465	140	11	4-3	.962	-3	81	244	O36L,3b14,2b7	0	0.8
	Year	100	254	37	67	13	2	8	26	42-0	2	37	.264	.368	.425	127	11	4-3	.962	1	81	243	O37L,3b32,2b9	0	1.2
1990	Phi N	101	217	26	53	9	1	1	26	29-0	1	35	.244	.332	.309	79	-5	3-2	1.000	4	67	117	O30L,2b28	0	-0.1
1991	Phi N	76	205	32	51	10	1	1	20	47-3	1	25	.249	.385	.322	104	4	2-1	.989	-3	93	72	2b66	34	0.3
1992	†Oak A	61	125	17	25	2	0	3	17	25-1	0	23	.200	.329	.288	79	-3	1-0	1.000	2	102	96	O24(22/0/2),D24,3b7,1b4,2b4	37	-0.2
1993	Mon N	40	134	22	34	8	1	1	10	23-0	1	8	.254	.367	.351	89	-1	2-1	.968	-0	103	113	2b28,1b13,3b3	0	-0.1
1994	Phi N	17	42	5	16	1	0	1	3	8-0	0	6	.381	.480	.476	148	4	0-1	1.000	-4	83	43	2b11/3	0	0.0
1995	Phi N	23	29	3	4	0	0	0	0	3-0	0	6	.138	.219	.138	-3	-4	0-1	.967	-2	52	143	1b3/2	0	-0.7
Total	13	777	2110	312	547	107	21	40	239	326-8	12	276	.259	.359	.387	108	36	27-15	.979	8	100	92	2b234,3b203,O171L,D33,1b20	139	4.3
Reams, Leroy	Leroy; B8.11.1943 Pine Bluff AR; BL/TR/6´2˝/175; d5.7																								
1969	Phi N	1	1	0	0	0	0	0	0	0-0	0	1	.000	.000	.000	-99	0	0-0	ø	0	—	—	/H	0	0.0
Reardon, Phil	Philip Michael; B10.3.1883 Brooklyn NY; D9.28.1920 Brooklyn NY; BR/TR/5´9˝/160; d9.19																								
1906	Bro N	5	14	0	1	0	0	0	0	0	1	—	.071	.133	.071	-39	-2	0	.917	1	176	713	O4(0/1/3)	—	-0.2
Rebel, Art	Arthur Anthony; B3.4.1914 Cincinnati OH; D7.10.2004 Tampa FL; BL/TL/5´8˝/180; d4.19																								
1938	Phi N	7	9	2	2	0	0	0	1	1	0	1	.222	.300	.222	47	-1	0	1.000	-0	103	0	O3(0/1/2)	—	-0.1
1945	StL N	26	72	12	25	4	0	0	5	6	0	4	.347	.397	.403	120	2	1	.976	3	110	259	O18R	0	0.4
Total	2	33	81	14	27	4	0	0	6	7	0	5	.333	.386	.383	112	1	1	.978	2	109	239	O21(0/1/20)	0	0.3

YEAR	TM LG	G	AB	R	H	2B	3B	HR	RBI	BB-IB	HP	SO	AVG	OBP	SLG	AOPS	ABR	SB-CS	FA	FR	RNG	THR	GAMES AT POSITION	DL	BFW
1989	Mon N	21	44	3	10	0	0	0	1	1-0	0	3	.227	.244	.227	35	-4	0-0	1.000	4	143	118	2b13,S4/3	0	0.1
1990	Mon N	81	158	15	42	7	2	0	14	7-2	1	14	.266	.294	.335	78	-5	4-1	1.000	-15	63	73	2b31,O9(2/0/7),3b8,S7/P	0	-2.0
1991	Mon N	67	95	5	23	3	0	1	2	1-1	0	8	.242	.250	.305	56	-6	2-3	1.000	-1	71	0	O7(1/0/6),2b6,3b2,S2/1	0	-0.8
1992	NY N	46	47	7	7	0	0	0	3	3-0	1	8	.149	.212	.149	5	-6	0-0	.977	3	133	139	2b16,3b3,S2	0	-0.3
1994	Oak A	17	40	3	13	1	1	0	6	2-0	0	5	.325	.357	.400	103	0	1-0	.943	-1	92	98	2b14/S	0	0.0
	Pit N	2	2	0	0	0	0	0	0	0-0	0	0	.000	.000	.000	-98	-1	0-0	1.000	0	286	0	/S	0	0.0
Total	8	317	493	47	118	13	4	1	33	17-4	2	47	.239	.265	.288	54	-33	9-4	.981	-14	95	95	2b129,S28,3b21,O16R,D2/1P	0	-4.2
Reboulet, Jeff	Jeffrey Allen; B4.30.1964 Dayton OH; BR/TR/6´0˝/(165–175); [MinA86 10/247]; d5.12; Col Louisiana St.; OF(7/3/15)																								
1992	Min A	73	137	15	26	7	1	1	16	23-0	1	26	.190	.311	.277	63	-6	3-2	.971	16	126	131	S36,3b22,2b13,O7(1/1/5)/D	0	1.2
1993	Min A	109	240	33	62	8	0	1	15	35-0	2	37	.258	.356	.304	79	-6	5-5	.982	10	99	91	S62,3b35,2b11,O3(1/2/0)/D	0	0.7
1994	Min A	74	189	28	49	11	1	3	23	18-0	1	23	.259	.327	.376	80	-6	0-0	.963	-4	101	53	S42,2b14,1b10,3b6,O4(1/0/3)/D	0	-0.7
1995	Min A	87	216	39	63	11	0	4	23	27-0	1	34	.292	.373	.398	100	1	1-2	.993	9	101	113	S39,3b22,1b17,2b15/C	0	1.0
1996	Min A	107	234	20	52	9	0	0	23	25-1	1	34	.222	.298	.261	43	-20	4-2	.987	-11	72	102	S37,3b36,2b22,1b13,O7(2/0/6),D3	0	-2.7
1997	†Bal A	99	228	26	54	9	0	4	27	23-0	1	44	.237	.307	.329	69	-10	3-0	.977	-7	98	99	2b63,S22,3b12/rfD	0	-1.3
1998	Bal A	79	126	20	31	6	0	1	8	19-0	2	34	.246	.351	.317	78	-3	0-1	.974	0	95	117	2b28,S28,3b23	0	-0.1
1999	Bal A	99	154	25	25	4	0	0	4	33-0	2	29	.162	.317	.188	35	-14	1-0	.987	11	136	106	3b56,2b36,S10	0	-0.1
2000	KC A	66	182	29	44	7	0	0	14	23-0	0	32	.242	.325	.280	53	-13	3-1	.982	5	114	122	2b50,3b11,S5/D	0	-0.5
2001	LA N	94	214	35	57	15	2	3	22	33-1	1	48	.266	.367	.397	104	3	0-1	.961	-6	83	135	S56,2b22,3b7,O2L	0	0.0
2002	LA N	38	48	3	10	3	0	0	2	6-0	0	13	.208	.291	.271	54	-3	0-0	.933	-1	148	59	2b11,S5,3b3/D	42	-0.4
2003	Pit N	93	261	37	63	10	2	3	25	27-3	4	47	.241	.321	.330	70	-12	2-1	.989	6	110	114	2b76,3b7	0	-0.2
Total	12	1018	2229	310	536	100	6	20	202	292-5	16	401	.240	.332	.318	71	-89	22-15	.984	29	105	110	2b361,S342,3b240,1b40,O24R,D9/C	42	-3.1
Reccius, John	John; B10.29.1859 Louisville KY; D9.1.1930 Louisville KY; 5´6.5˝/168; d5.2; b–Phil; ▲																								
1882	Lou AA	74	266	46	63	12	3	1	—	23	—	—	.237	.298	.316	113	6	—	.857	-3	104	**222**	O65(0/55/11),P13	—	0.1
1883	Lou AA	18	63	10	9	2	0	0	3	7	—	—	.143	.229	.175	34	-4	—	.833	-1	31	264	O18(0/15/4)/P	—	-0.4
Total	2	92	329	56	72	14	3	1	3	30	—	—	.219	.284	.289	98	2	—	.851	-3	88	231	O83(0/70/15),P14	—	-0.3
Reccius, Phil	Phillip; B6.7.1862 Louisville KY; D2.15.1903 Louisville KY; 5´9˝/163; d9.25; b–John; ▲																								
1882	Lou AA	4	15	0	2	0	0	0	—	0	—	—	.133	.133	.133	-10	-2	—	.778	-0	104	0	O4C	—	-0.2
1883	Lou AA	1	3	1	1	1	0	0	—	0	—	—	.333	.333	.667	231	0	—	1.000	-0	0	0	/rf	—	0.0
1884	Lou AA	73	263	23	63	9	2	3	21	5	5	—	.240	.267	.323	96	-1	—	.845	-3	102	91	3b51,P18,S10	—	-0.2
1885	Lou AA	102	402	57	97	8	10	1	38	13	1	—	.241	.267	.318	84	-8	—	.829	-1	99	**130**	3b97,P7	—	-0.7
1886	Lou AA	5	13	4	4	1	1	0	2	3	1	—	.308	.471	.538	204	2	0	.889	1	278	0	O5(2/0/3)/P	—	0.2
1887	Lou AA	11	37	9	9	2	0	0	4	8	1	—	.243	.391	.297	92	0	3	.926	1	102	0	O10(2/0/8)/S	—	0.1
	Cle AA	62	229	23	47	6	3	0	29	24	5	—	.205	.295	.258	56	-13	9	.877	10	113	165	3b62/P	—	-0.1
	Year	73	266	32	56	8	3	0	33	32	6	—	.211	.309	.263	62	-12	12	.877	11	113	165	3b62,O10(2/0/8)/SP	—	0.0
1888	Lou AA	2	9	0	2	1	0	0	4	1	0	—	.222	.300	.333	105	0	0	.750	-1	78	0	3b2	—	-0.1
1890	Roc AA	1	4	0	0	0	0	0	1	0	0	—	.000	.000	.000	-99	-1	0	ø	-0	0	0	/rf	—	-0.1
Total	8	261	975	117	225	28	16	4	99	54	13	—	.231	.280	.305	81	-23	12	.848	6	104	130	3b212,P27,O21(4/4/13),S11	—	-1.1
Reder, Johnny	John Anthony; B9.24.1909 Lublin, Poland; D4.12.1990 Fall River MA; BR/TR/6´0˝/184; d4.16																								
1932	Bos A	17	37	4	5	1	0	0	3	6	0	6	.135	.256	.162	11	-5	0-0	.990	0	152	141	1b10/3	—	-0.5
Redfern, Buck	George Howard; B4.7.1902 Asheville NC; D9.8.1964 Asheville NC; BR/TR/5´11˝/165; d4.11; Col North Carolina St.																								
1928	Chi A	86	261	22	61	6	3	0	35	12	0	19	.234	.267	.280	44	-22	8-4	.953	-2	108	83	2b45,S33/3	—	-1.8
1929	Chi A	21	46	0	6	0	0	0	3	3	0	3	.130	.184	.130	-18	-8	1-1	.967	-3	82	29	2b11,3b5,S4	—	-1.1
Total	2	107	307	22	67	6	3	0	38	15	0	22	.218	.255	.257	35	-30	9-5	.955	-5	105	77	2b56,S37,3b6	—	-2.9
Redfield, Joe	Joseph Randall; B1.14.1961 Doylestown PA; BR/TR/6´2˝/185; [NYN82 9/215]; d6.4; Col California–Santa Barbara																								
1988	Cal A	1	2	0	0	0	0	0	0	0-0	0	0	.000	.000	.000	-99	-1	0-0	1.000	-0	61	614	/3	0	-0.1
1991	Pit N	11	18	1	2	0	0	0	0	4-0	0	1	.111	.273	.111	12	-2	0-1	.917	-1	64	373	3b9	0	-0.4
Total	2	12	20	1	2	0	0	0	0	4-0	0	1	.100	.250	.100	2	-3	0-1	.923	-1	64	409	3b10	0	-0.5
Redman, Tike	Julian Jawonn; B3.10.1977 Tuscaloosa AL; BL/TL/5´11˝/(166–180); [PitN96 5/126]; d6.30; b–Prentice																								
2000	Pit N	9	18	2	6	1	0	1	1	1-0	0	7	.333	.368	.556	129	1	1-0	1.000	2	169	442	O6(2/0/4)	0	0.2
2001	Pit N	37	125	8	28	4	1	1	4	4-0	0	25	.224	.246	.296	39	-12	3-5	.980	6	126	285	O35(0/28/7)	0	-0.7
2003	Pit N	56	230	36	76	16	5	3	19	14-0	2	18	.330	.374	.483	120	7	7-3	.985	-2	100	34	O54C	0	0.5
2004	Pit N	155	546	65	153	19	4	8	51	23-2	3	52	.280	.310	.374	77	-21	18-6	.986	-2	104	44	O147C	0	-1.9
2005	Pit N	135	319	33	80	12	4	2	26	19-0	1	27	.251	.292	.332	64	-18	4-1	.962	2	109	144	O85(2/75/8)	0	-1.4
Total	5	392	1238	144	343	52	14	15	101	61-2	6	129	.277	.312	.378	78	-43	33-15	.979	6	107	95	O327(4/304/19)	0	-3.3
Redman, Prentice	Prentice Montezz; B8.23.1979 Tuscaloosa AL; BR/TR/6´3˝/180; [NYN99 10/316]; d8.24; b–Tike; Col Bevill St. (AL) JC																								
2003	NY N	15	24	3	3	1	0	1	2	1-0	1	9	.125	.192	.292	25	-3	2-0	1.000	-0	97	0	O10(0/9/2)	0	-0.3
Redmon, Glenn	Glenn Vincent; B1.11.1948 Detroit MI; BR/TR/5´11˝/175; d9.8; Col Michigan																								
1974	SF N	7	17	0	4	3	0	0	4	1-0	0	3	.235	.278	.412	87	0	0-0	.955	-1	79	79	2b4	0	-0.1
Redmon, Billy	William T.; B Brooklyn NY; BL/TL; d5.4																								
1875	RS NA	**19**	82	12	16	2	0	0	1	2	—	7	.195	.214	.220	56	-3	3-0	.837	5	130	0	S19,C2	—	0.2
1877	Cin N	3	12	1	3	1	0	0	3	1	—	1	.250	.308	.333	115	0	—	.833	1	122	0	S3	—	0.1
1878	Mil N	48	187	16	43	8	0	0	21	8	—	13	.230	.262	.273	71	-6	—	.785	-16	83	57	S39,O7(0/4/3),3b3/C	—	-1.9
Total	2	51	199	17	46	9	0	0	24	9	—	14	.231	.264	.276	73	-6	—	.791	-16	87	52	S42,O7(0/4/3),3b3/C	—	-1.8
Redmond, Harry	Harry John; B9.13.1887 Cleveland OH; D7.10.1960 Cleveland OH; BR/TR/5´8˝/170; d9.7																								
1909	Bro N	6	19	3	0	0	0	0	1	0	0	—	.000	.000	.000	-99	-5	0	.892	2	134	99	2b5	—	-0.3
Redmond, Wayne	Howard Wayne; B11.25.1945 Athens AL; BR/TR/5´10˝/(160–165); d9.7																								
1965	Det A	4	4	1	0	0	0	0	0	1-0	0	1	.000	.200	.000	-38	-1	0-0	1.000	0	168	0	O2(1/1/0)	0	-0.1
1969	Det A	5	3	0	0	0	0	0	0	0-0	0	2	.000	.000	.000	-96	-1	0-0	ø	0	—	—	/H	0	-0.1
Total	2	9	7	1	0	0	0	0	0	1-0	0	3	.000	.125	.000	-60	-2	0-0	1.000	0	168	0	O2(1/1/0)	0	-0.2
Redmond, Jack	John McKittrick "Red" (b Jackson Mc Kittrick Redmond); B9.3.1910 Florence AZ; D7.27.1968 Garland TX; BL/TR/5´11˝/185; d4.22; Col Arizona																								
1935	Was A	22	34	8	6	1	0	1	7	3	0	1	.176	.243	.294	40	-3	0-0	.978	0	*88*	*82*	C15	—	-0.2
Redmond, Mike	Michael Patrick; B5.5.1971 Seattle WA; BR/TR/6´1˝/(185–200); d5.31; Col Gonzaga																								
1998	Fla N	37	118	10	39	9	0	2	12	5-2	2	16	.331	.368	.458	123	4	0-0	.992	-3	95	171	C37	15	0.4
1999	Fla N	84	242	22	73	9	0	1	27	26-2	5	34	.302	.381	.351	92	-2	0-0	.992	2	122	123	C82	0	0.5
2000	Fla N	87	210	17	53	8	1	0	15	13-3	8	19	.252	.316	.300	61	-13	0-0	.996	2	88	124	C85	0	-0.6
2001	Fla N	48	141	19	44	4	0	4	14	13-4	2	13	.312	.376	.426	111	2	0-0	.994	1	104	123	C47	0	0.6
2002	Fla N	89	256	19	78	15	0	2	28	21-8	8	34	.305	.372	.387	105	3	0-2	.993	5	95	162	C80,1b2	0	1.2
2003	†Fla N	59	125	12	30	7	1	0	11	7-0	5	16	.240	.302	.312	64	-7	0-0	.995	-5	47	85	C37/13	0	-0.9
2004	Fla N	81	246	19	63	15	0	2	25	14-0	8	28	.256	.315	.341	74	-9	1-0	.996	-0	71	100	C79	0	-0.5
2005	Min A	45	148	17	46	9	0	1	26	6-0	3	14	.311	.350	.392	96	-1	0-0	1.000	-2	247	105	C45	0	0.0
2006	Min A	47	179	20	61	13	0	0	23	4-0	4	18	.341	.365	.413	102	1	0-0	1.000	6	127	93	C43,D2	0	0.9
Total	9	577	1665	155	487	89	2	12	181	109-19	45	192	.292	.350	.370	91	-22	1-2	.995	7	109	123	C535,1b3,D2/3	15	1.6
Redus, Gary	Gary Eugene; B11.1.1956 Athens AL; BR/TR/6´1˝/(180–195); [CinN78 15/381]; d9.7; Col Athens St.																								
1982	Cin N	20	83	12	18	3	2	1	7	5-0	0	21	.217	.258	.337	66	-4	11-2	.970	-1	75	190	O20L	0	-0.4
1983	Cin N	125	453	90	112	20	9	17	51	71-4	3	111	.247	.352	.444	115	10	39-14	.972	4	102	123	O120L	0	1.3
1984	Cin N	123	394	69	100	21	3	7	22	52-3	1	71	.254	.338	.376	97	0	48-11	.967	-1	97	80	O114(93/24/1)	0	0.1
1985	Cin N	101	246	51	62	14	4	6	28	44-2	1	52	.252	.366	.415	113	6	48-12	.986	1	106	71	O85(63/37/0)	0	1.2
1986	Phi N	90	340	62	84	22	4	11	33	47-4	3	78	.247	.343	.432	109	5	25-7	.980	6	110	132	O89L	64	1.0
1987	Chi A	130	475	78	112	26	6	12	48	69-0	0	90	.236	.328	.392	89	-7	52-11	.979	3	98	152	O123(97/19/20),D4	0	-0.1

THE BATTER REGISTER

YEAR	TM LG	G	AB	R	H	2B	3B	HR	RBI	BB-IB	HP	SO	AVG	OBP	SLG	AOPS	ABR	SB-CS	FA	FR	RNG	THR	GAMES AT POSITION	DL	BFW
1988	Chi A	77	262	42	69	10	4	6	34	33-1	2	52	.263	.342	.401	110	4	26-2	.987	0	92	182	O68(54/16/2),D2	0	0.7
	Pit N	30	71	12	14	2	0	2	4	15-0	1	19	.197	.341	.310	90	0	5-2	.957	2	124	206	O19(11/1/7)	0	0.2
1989	Pit N	98	279	42	79	18	7	6	33	40-3	1	51	.283	.372	.462	143	16	25-6	.987	2	123	93	1b72,O16(2/1/12)	23	1.8
1990	†Pit N	96	227	32	56	15	3	6	23	33-0	2	38	.247	.341	.419	113	5	11-5	.988	0	102	94	1b72,O7(4/1/2)	0	0.2
1991	†Pit N	98	252	45	62	12	2	7	24	28-2	3	39	.246	.324	.393	103	1	17-3	.990	-3	89	130	1b47,O33(11/12/11)	0	-0.2
1992	†Pit N	76	176	26	45	7	3	3	12	17-0	0	25	.256	.321	.381	98	-1	11-4	1.000	-3	79	72	1b36,O15(2/1/12)	33	-0.5
1993	Tex A	77	222	28	64	12	4	6	31	23-1	0	35	.288	.351	.459	121	6	4-4	.981	-2	96	87	O61(5/17/46),1b5/2D	17	0.2
1994	Tex A	18	33	2	9	1	0	0	2	4-1	0	6	.273	.351	.303	70	-1	0-0	1.000	0	108	0	O7(0/3/4),1b5	80	-0.2
Total	13	1159	3513	591	886	183	51	90	352	481-21	17	688	.252	.342	.410	107	40	322-83	.974	9	100	124	O777(571/132/117),1b237,D7/2	217	5.3
Reece, Bob	Robert Scott; B1.5.1951 Sacramento CA; BR/TR/6´1˝/190; d4.22; Col Stanford																								
1978	Mon N	9	11	2	2	1	0	0	3	0-0	0	4	.182	.182	.273	26	-1	0-0	.947	-1	94	0	C9	0	-0.2
Reed, Darren	Darren A. Douglas; B10.16.1965 Ojai CA; BR/TR/6´1˝/(190–205); [NYA84 S3/63]; d5.1; Col Ventura (CA) JC; [DL 1991 Mon N 182, 1993 NY N 157]																								
1990	NY N	26	39	5	8	4	1	1	2	3-0	0	11	.205	.262	.436	88	-1	1-0	.955	0	100	188	O14(2/7/6)	0	-0.1
1992	Mon N	42	81	10	14	2	0	5	10	6-2	1	23	.173	.239	.383	74	-3	0-0	1.000	-0	95	81	O29(8/0/21)	36	-0.5
	Min A	14	33	2	6	2	0	0	4	2-0	0	11	.182	.216	.242	31	-3	0-0	1.000	-0	81	175	O13(10/0/4)/D	0	-0.4
Total	2	82	153	17	28	8	1	6	16	11-2	1	45	.183	.240	.366	68	-7	1-0	.987	-0	93	129	O56(20/7/31)/D	375	-1.0
Reed, Eric	Eric Shane; B12.2.1980 Little Rock AR; BL/TL/5´11˝/170; [FlaN02 9/263]; d4.3; Col Texas A&M																								
2006	Fla N	42	41	6	4	0	0	0	0	2-1	2	10	.098	.178	.098	-28	-8	3-1	1.000	1	106	161	O32(1/31/0)	0	-0.7
Reed, Jeff	Jeffrey Scott; B11.12.1962 Joliet IL; BL/TR/6´2˝/(185–204); [MinA80 1/12]; d4.5																								
1984	Min A	18	21	3	3	3	0	0	1	2-0	0	6	.143	.217	.286	36	-2	0-0	.977	-1	61	73	C18	0	-0.2
1985	Min A	7	10	2	2	0	0	0	0	0-0	0	3	.200	.200	.200	9	-1	0-0	1.000	-0	89	116	C7	0	-0.1
1986	Min A	68	165	13	39	6	1	2	9	16-0	1	19	.236	.308	.321	69	-7	1-0	.994	2	83	67	C64	0	-0.3
1987	Mon N	75	207	15	44	11	0	1	21	12-1	1	20	.213	.254	.280	41	-18	0-1	.970	-9	85	85	C74	35	-2.5
1988	Mon N	43	123	10	27	3	2	0	9	13-1	0	22	.220	.292	.276	61	-6	1-0	.995	-1	72	106	C39	0	-0.5
	Cin N	49	142	10	33	6	0	1	7	15-0	0	19	.232	.306	.296	71	-5	0-0	.993	4	112	101	C49	0	0.1
	Year	92	265	20	60	9	2	1	16	28-1	0	41	.226	.299	.287	66	-11	1-0	.994	3	94	103	C88	0	-0.4
1989	Cin N	102	287	16	64	11	0	3	23	34-5	2	46	.223	.306	.293	71	-10	0-0	.988	-9	81	**149**	C99	0	-1.5
1990	†Cin N	72	175	12	44	8	1	3	16	24-5	0	26	.251	.340	.360	90	-2	0-0	.987	-4	74	74	C70	0	-0.3
1991	Cin N	91	270	20	72	15	2	3	31	23-3	1	38	.267	.321	.370	92	-3	0-1	.991	3	116	86	C89	18	0.5
1992	Cin N	15	25	2	4	0	0	0	2	1-1	0	4	.160	.192	.160	1	-3	0-0	1.000	-0	85	62	C6	127	-0.4
1993	SF N	66	119	10	31	3	0	6	12	16-4	0	22	.261	.346	.437	112	2	0-1	1.000	4	127	130	C37	34	0.8
1994	SF N	50	103	11	18	3	0	1	7	11-4	0	21	.175	.254	.233	29	-11	0-0	.993	0	89	56	C33	0	-0.9
1995	SF N	66	113	12	30	2	0	0	9	20-3	0	17	.265	.376	.283	79	-2	0-0	.995	5	134	142	C42	0	0.4
1996	Col N	116	341	34	97	20	1	8	37	43-8	2	65	.284	.365	.419	87	-5	2-2	.982	-10	95	107	C111	0	-0.9
1997	Col N	90	256	43	76	10	0	17	47	35-1	2	55	.297	.386	.535	113	5	2-1	.987	10	111	107	C78	0	1.9
1998	Col N	113	259	43	75	17	1	9	39	37-4	1	57	.290	.377	.467	100	1	0-0	.986	3	105	108	C99	0	0.9
1999	Col N	46	106	11	27	5	0	2	11	17-1	1	24	.255	.360	.358	66	-5	0-1	.983	-7	50	146	C36	0	-1.0
	Chi N	57	150	18	39	11	2	1	17	28-0	2	34	.260	.381	.380	94	0	1-1	.987	-2	86	92	C49/3D	0	0.1
	Year	103	256	29	66	16	2	3	28	45-1	3	58	.258	.373	.371	81	-6	1-2	.985	-9	72	113	C85/3D	0	-0.9
2000	Chi N	90	229	26	49	10	0	4	25	44-2	1	68	.214	.342	.310	68	-10	0-1	.990	-6	131	87	C71	0	-1.2
Total	17	1234	3101	311	774	144	10	61	323	391-43	14	566	.250	.334	.361	80	-82	7-9	.988	-20	97	102	C1071/D3	214	-5.1
Reed, Jeremy	Jeremy Thomas; B6.15.1981 San Dimas CA; BL/TL/6´0˝/(180–200); [ChiA02 2/59]; d9.8; Col Cal St.–Long Beach																								
2004	Sea A	18	58	11	23	4	0	0	5	7-1	1	4	.397	.470	.466	152	5	3-1	.981	2	139	0	O16(1/16/0)	0	0.7
2005	Sea A	141	488	61	124	33	3	3	45	48-1	2	74	.254	.322	.352	86	-9	12-11	.992	8	112	106	O137C	0	0.0
2006	Sea A	67	212	27	46	6	5	6	17	11-1	2	31	.217	.260	.377	67	-12	2-3	.992	-4	88	104	O64C	91	-1.5
Total	3	226	758	99	193	43	8	9	67	66-3	5	109	.255	.317	.368	86	-16	17-15	.991	6	107	98	O217(1/217/0)	91	-0.8
Reed, Jody	Jody Eric; B7.26.1962 Tampa FL; BR/TR/5´9˝/(160–170); [BosA84 8/198]; d9.12; Col Florida St.																								
1987	Bos A	9	30	4	9	1	1	0	8	4-0	0	0	.300	.382	.400	105	0	1-1	1.000	3	97	195	S4,2b2/3	0	0.3
1988	†Bos A	109	338	60	99	23	1	1	28	45-1	4	21	.293	.380	.376	108	6	1-3	.971	8	98	92	S94,2b11,3b4/D	0	2.0
1989	Bos A	146	524	76	151	42	2	3	40	73-0	4	44	.288	.376	.393	111	12	4-5	.967	3	94	85	S77,2b70,3b4/rfD	0	2.1
1990	†Bos A	155	598	70	173	**45**	0	5	51	75-4	4	65	.289	.371	.390	108	10	4-4	.990	7	**106**	103	2b119,S50/D	0	2.3
1991	Bos A	153	618	87	175	42	2	5	60	60-2	4	53	.283	.349	.382	97	0	6-5	.982	11	100	110	2b152,S6	0	1.4
1992	Bos A	143	550	64	136	27	1	3	40	62-2	0	44	.247	.321	.316	74	-17	7-8	.982	**30**	**115**	116	2b142/D	0	1.6
1993	LA N	132	445	48	123	21	2	2	31	38-10	1	40	.276	.333	.346	87	-8	1-3	**.993**	10	102	96	2b132	29	0.8
1994	Mil A	108	399	48	108	22	0	2	37	57-1	2	34	.271	.362	.341	79	-10	5-4	**.995**	7	109	106	2b106	0	0.2
1995	SD N	131	445	58	114	18	1	4	40	59-1	5	38	.256	.348	.328	82	-9	6-4	.994	18	100	102	2b130,S5	0	1.4
1996	†SD N	146	495	45	121	20	0	2	49	59-8	3	53	.244	.325	.297	69	-20	2-5	.987	-5	99	103	2b145	0	-1.9
1997	Det A	52	112	6	22	2	0	0	8	10-0	3	15	.196	.278	.214	32	-11	3-2	.987	8	131	102	2b41,D5	0	-0.2
Total	11	1284	4554	566	1231	263	10	27	392	542-29	30	407	.270	.349	.350	90	-47	40-44	.988	100	105	105	2b1050,S236,D9,3b9/rf	29	10.0
Reed, Jack	John Burwell; B2.2.1933 Silver City MS; BR/TR/6´0˝/(175–185); d4.23; Col U. of Mississippi																								
1961	†NY A	28	13	4	2	0	0	0	1	1-0	0	1	.154	.214	.154	0	-2	0-0	.933	-1	93	0	O27(12/14/1)	0	-0.3
1962	NY A	88	43	17	13	2	1	1	4	4-1	0	7	.302	.362	.465	125	1	2-1	.941	-1	106	0	O75(20/39/16)	0	0.0
1963	NY A	106	73	18	15	3	1	0	1	9-0	0	14	.205	.293	.274	60	-4	5-1	1.000	2	119	101	O89(14/30/46)	0	-0.3
Total	3	222	129	39	30	5	2	1	6	14-1	0	22	.233	.308	.326	76	-5	7-2	.972	1	111	53	O191(46/83/63)	0	-0.6
Reed, Keith	Keith A.; B10.8.1978 Yarmouthport MA; BR/TR/6´4˝/205; [BalA99 1/23]; d5.11; Col Providence																								
2005	Bal A	6	5	1	1	0	0	0	1	1-0	0	2	.200	.333	.200	47	0	0-0	1.000	-0	63	0	O6(0/1/5)	0	-0.1
Reed, Milt	Milton D.; B7.4.1890 Atlanta GA; D7.27.1938 Atlanta GA; BL/TR/5´9.5˝/150; d9.9																								
1911	StL N	1	1	0	0	0	0	0	0	0	0	0	.000	.000	.000	-99	0	0	ø	0	—	—	/H	—	0.0
1913	Phi N	13	24	4	6	1	0	0	0	1	0	5	.250	.280	.292	61	-1	1	.900	-3	85	0	S9,2b3	—	-0.3
1914	Phi N	44	107	10	22	2	1	0	2	10	1	13	.206	.280	.243	52	-6	4	.887	-10	76	32	S22,2b11/3	—	-1.7
1915	Bro F	10	31	2	9	1	1	0	8	2	1	0	.290	.353	.387	109	0	2	.864	-4	76	56	S10	—	-0.4
Total	4	68	163	16	37	4	2	0	10	13	2	18	.227	.292	.276	63	-7	7	.880	-17	77	37	S41,2b14/3	—	-2.4
Reed, Ted	Ralph Edwin; B10.18.1890 Beaver PA; D2.16.1959 Beaver PA; BR/TR/5´11˝/190; d9.10; Col Princeton																								
1915	New F	20	77	5	20	1	2	0	4	2	1	7	.260	.287	.325	76	-4	1	.863	-4	77	127	3b20	—	-0.8
Reed, Billy	William Joseph; B11.12.1922 Shawano WI; D12.5.2005 Houston TX; BL/TR/5´10.5˝/175; d4.15; Col Notre Dame																								
1952	Bos N	15	52	4	13	0	0	0	0	0	1	5	.250	.264	.250	45	-4	0-0	.931	-4	90	70	2b14	0	-0.8
Reeder, Icicle	Julius Edward; B1858 Cincinnati OH; D1.15.1913 Cincinnati OH; BR/6´0˝/?; d6.24																								
1884	Cin AA	3	14	0	2	0	0	0	—	0	0	—	.143	.143	.143	-6	-2	—	1.000	-0	0	0	O3L	—	-0.2
	Was U	3	12	0	2	0	0	0	—	0	—	—	.167	.167	.167	1	-2	—	.500	-1	0	0	O3(0/1/2)	—	-0.3
Total	1	6	26	0	4	0	0	0	—	0	—	—	.154	.154	.154	-3	-4	—	.714	-1	0	0	O6(3/1/2)	—	-0.5
Reeder, Nick	Nicholas (b Nicholas Herchenroeder); B3.22.1867 Louisville KY; D9.26.1894 Louisville KY; BR/TR/5´9˝/189; d4.11																								
1891	Lou AA	1	2	0	0	0	0	0	0	0	0	1	.000	.000	.000	-99	-1	0	1.000	0	131	0	/3	—	0.0
Reese, Randy	Andrew Jackson; B2.7.1904 Tupelo MS; D1.10.1966 Tupelo MS; BR/TR/5´11˝/180; d4.15; Col Vanderbilt; OF(81/26/15)																								
1927	NY N	97	355	43	94	14	2	4	21	13	4	52	.265	.298	.349	73	-14	5	.912	-1	107	141	3b64,O16(7/0/9)/1	—	-1.3
1928	NY N	109	406	61	125	18	4	6	44	13	1	24	.308	.331	.416	94	-5	7	.941	-4	89	65	O64(59/2/4),2b26,1b6,S6,3b6	—	-1.2
1929	NY N	58	209	36	55	11	3	0	21	15	1	19	.263	.316	.344	64	-12	8	.960	2	110	96	2b44,O8(7/1/0),3b4	—	-0.8
1930	NY N	67	172	26	47	4	2	4	25	10	0	12	.273	.313	.390	70	-9	1	.957	-4	86	39	O32(8/23/2),3b10/1	—	-1.3
Total	4	331	1142	166	321	47	11	14	111	51	6	107	.281	.315	.378	78	-40	21	.954	-7	88	60	O120L,3b84,2b70,1b8,S6	—	-4.6

YEAR	TM LG	G	AB	R	H	2B	3B	HR	RBI	BB-IB	HP	SO	AVG	OBP	SLG	AOPS	ABR	SB-CS	FA	FR	RNG	THR	GAMES AT POSITION	DL	BFW
Reese, Pokey	Calvin; B6.10.1973 Columbia SC; BR/TR/5´11˝/(180–190); [CinN91 1/20]; d4.1; [DL 1996 Cin N 13, 2005 Sea A 183]																								
1997	Cin N	128	397	48	87	15	0	4	26	31-2	5	82	.219	.284	.287	49	-30	25-7	.966	-6	90	99	S110,2b8,3b8	0	-2.5
1998	Cin N	59	133	20	34	2	2	1	16	14-1	0	28	.256	.322	.323	71	-6	3-2	.985	-3	96	165	3b32,S18,2b3	59	-0.7
1999	Cin N	149	585	85	167	37	5	10	52	35-3	6	81	.285	.330	.417	85	-14	38-7	.991	17	**107**	111	2b146,S16	0	1.5
2000	Cin N	135	518	76	132	20	6	12	46	45-5	6	86	.255	.319	.386	75	-21	29-3	.980	14	110	107	2b133	0	0.4
2001	Cin N	133	428	50	96	20	2	9	40	34-4	3	82	.224	.284	.343	58	-27	25-4	.972	5	111	75	S78,2b51	0	-1.0
2002	Pit N	119	421	46	111	25	0	4	50	41-4	3	81	.264	.330	.352	79	-12	12-1	.988	**28**	**117**	108	2b117	15	2.3
2003	Pit N	37	107	9	23	2	0	1	12	9-1	0	31	.215	.271	.262	41	-10	6-0	.969	11	133	117	2b33	138	0.4
2004	†Bos A	96	244	32	54	7	2	3	29	17-1	0	60	.221	.271	.303	47	-20	6-2	.979	22	117	106	S71,2b30	49	0.8
Total	8	856	2833	366	704	128	17	44	271	226-21	23	531	.248	.307	.352	68	-140	144-26	.985	88	113	109	2b521,S293,3b40	457	1.2
Reese, Pee Wee	Harold Henry; B7.23.1918 Ekron KY; D8.14.1999 Louisville KY; BR/TR/5´9˝/(175–177); d4.23; Mil 1943–45; C1; HF1984																								
1940	Bro N	84	312	58	85	8	4	5	28	45	1	42	.272	.366	.372	98	0	15	.960	-13	87	87	S83	—	-0.6
1941	†Bro N	152	595	76	136	23	5	2	46	68	3	56	.229	.311	.294	68	-24	10	.946	8	102	97	S151	0	-0.5
1942	Bro N★	151	564	87	144	24	5	3	53	82	0	55	.255	.350	.332	98	2	15	.959	18	103	**122**	S151	0	3.3
1946	Bro N✳	152	542	79	154	16	10	5	60	87	1	71	.284	.384	.378	116	14	10	.966	-4	97	109	S152	0	2.0
1947	†Bro N★	142	476	81	135	24	4	12	73	**104**	2	67	.284	.414	.426	119	19	7	.966	-0	99	115	S142	0	2.7
1948	Bro N★	151	566	96	155	31	4	9	75	79	0	63	.274	.363	.390	100	3	25	.962	6	97	108	S149	0	1.8
1949	†Bro N★	155	617	**132**	172	27	3	16	73	116	4	59	.279	.396	.410	112	16	26	**.977**	1	92	105	S155	0	2.6
1950	Bro N★	141	531	97	138	21	5	11	52	91	1	62	.260	.369	.380	96	-1	17	.963	2	94	105	S134,3b7	0	0.9
1951	Bro N★	154	616	94	176	20	8	10	84	81	2	57	.286	.371	.393	103	5	20-14	.953	-7	92	113	S154	0	0.7
1952	†Bro N★	149	559	94	152	18	8	6	58	86	0	59	.272	.369	.365	103	5	**30**-5	.969	-12	90	99	S145	0	0.7
1953	†Bro N★	140	524	108	142	25	7	13	61	82	4	61	.271	.374	.420	104	6	22-6	.966	1	94	105	S135	0	2.0
1954	Bro N☆	141	554	98	171	35	8	10	69	90	3	62	.309	.404	.455	121	21	8-5	.965	-3	98	81	S140	0	2.9
1955	†Bro N	145	553	99	156	29	4	10	61	78-1	3	60	.282	.371	.403	103	6	8-7	.965	-11	94	101	S142	0	0.6
1956	†Bro N	147	572	85	147	19	2	9	46	56-1	1	69	.257	.322	.344	74	-20	13-4	.965	-2	94	103	S136,3b12	0	-0.9
1957	Bro N	103	330	33	74	3	1	1	29	39-1	1	32	.224	.306	.248	47	-24	5-2	.943	15	129	45	3b75,S23	0	-0.7
1958	LA N	59	147	21	33	7	2	4	17	26-0	0	15	.224	.337	.381	88	-2	1-2	.929	-6	89	101	S22,3b21	0	-0.7
Total	16	2166	8058	1338	2170	330	80	126	885	1210-3	26	890	.269	.366	.377	98	26	232-45	.962	-6	95	104	S2014,3b115	0	16.8
Reese, Jimmie	James Herman (b James Herman Soloman); B10.1.1901 New York NY; D7.13.1994 Santa Ana CA; BL/TR/5´11.5˝/165; d4.19; C22																								
1930	NY A	77	188	44	65	14	2	3	18	11	0	8	.346	.382	.489	125	7	1-1	.974	-5	86	115	2b48,3b5	—	0.3
1931	NY A	65	245	41	59	10	2	3	26	17	1	10	.241	.293	.335	68	-12	2-3	.972	2	90	125	2b61	—	-0.7
1932	StL N	90	309	38	82	15	0	2	26	20	2	19	.265	.314	.333	72	-12	4	.979	11	96	107	2b77	—	0.4
Total	3	232	742	123	206	39	4	8	70	48	3	37	.278	.324	.373	84	-17	7-4	.975	8	92	115	2b186,3b5	—	0.0
Reese, Kevin	Kevin Patrick; B3.11.1978 San Diego CA; BL/TL/5´11˝/195; [SDN00 27/799]; d6.26; Col San Diego																								
2005	NY A	2	1	0	0	0	0	0	0	1-0	0	1	.000	.500	.000	50	0	0-0	1.000	-0	93	0	O2(1/1/0)	0	0.0
2006	NY A	10	12	2	5	0	0	0	1	1-0	1	1	.417	.500	.417	141	1	1-0	.667	-1	43	0	O4(2/0/2),D2	0	0.0
Total	2	12	13	2	5	0	0	0	1	2-0	1	2	.385	.500	.385	135	1	1-0	.800	-1	59	0	O6(3/1/2),D2	0	0.0
Reese, Rich	Richard Benjamin; B9.29.1941 Leipsic OH; BL/TL/6´3˝/(185–200); d9.4																								
1964	Min A	10	7	0	0	0	0	0	0	0-0	0	1	.000	.000	.000	-99	-2	0-0	1.000	0	0	0	/1	0	-0.2
1965	Min A	14	7	0	2	1	0	0	0	2-1	0	2	.286	.444	.429	143	1	0-0	1.000	0	118	0	1b6/lf	0	0.1
1966	Min A	3	2	0	0	0	0	0	0	1-0	0	2	.000	.333	.000	5	0	0-0	ø	0	—	—	/H	0	0.0
1967	Min A	95	101	13	25	5	0	4	20	8-2	0	17	.248	.300	.416	102	0	0-0	.990	-1	44	69	1b36,O10L	0	-0.2
1968	Min A	126	332	40	86	15	2	4	28	18-4	3	36	.259	.301	.352	93	-3	3-1	.991	-0	97	76	1b87,O15L	0	-0.9
1969	†Min A	132	419	52	135	24	4	16	69	23-3	5	57	.322	.362	.513	139	21	1-5	.993	-4	87	**122**	1b117,O5L	0	0.7
1970	†Min A	153	501	63	131	15	5	10	56	48-5	7	70	.261	.332	.371	93	-5	5-4	.992	-2	92	90	1b146	0	-1.9
1971	Min A	120	329	40	72	8	3	10	39	20-2	5	35	.219	.270	.353	74	-13	7-4	.994	-3	85	103	1b95,O9(8/0/1)	0	-2.4
1972	Min A	132	197	23	43	3	2	5	26	25-4	0	27	.218	.305	.330	85	-4	0-1	.988	1	109	100	1b98,O13L	0	-0.8
1973	Det A	59	102	10	14	1	0	2	4	7-1	0	17	.137	.193	.206	12	-12	0-0	1.000	-1	93	66	1b37,O21(21/0/1)	0	-1.6
	Min A	22	23	7	4	1	1	1	3	6-0	0	6	.174	.345	.435	113	0	0-0	1.000	1	133	136	1b17	0	0.1
	Year	81	125	17	18	2	1	3	7	13-1	0	23	.144	.225	.248	31	-12	0-0	1.000	-1	107	90	1b54,O21(21/0/1)	0	-1.5
Total	10	866	2020	248	512	73	17	52	245	158-22	20	270	.253	.312	.384	95	-17	16-15	.992	-10	92	97	1b640,O74(73/0/2)	0	-7.1
Reeves, Bobby	Robert Edwin "Gunner"; B6.24.1904 Hill City TN; D6.4.1993 Chattanooga TN; BR/TR/5´11˝/170; d6.9; Col Georgia Tech																								
1926	Was A	20	49	4	11	0	1	0	7	6	1	9	.224	.321	.265	56	-3	1-1	.940	-1	87	122	3b16/2S	—	-0.3
1927	Was A	112	380	37	97	11	5	1	39	21	1	53	.255	.296	.318	60	-24	3-1	.923	-10	98	69	S96,3b12,2b2	—	-2.2
1928	Was A	102	353	44	107	16	8	3	42	24	2	47	.303	.351	.419	102	0	4-8	.908	-6	98	85	S66,2b22,3b8/rf	—	0.0
1929	Bos A	140	460	66	114	19	2	2	28	60	**7**	57	.248	.343	.311	71	-18	7-8	.912	5	108	**115**	3b131,2b2,S2/1	—	-0.6
1930	Bos A	92	272	41	59	7	4	2	18	50	3	36	.217	.345	.294	66	-13	6-2	.895	0	111	198	3b62,S15,2b11	—	-0.6
1931	Bos A	36	84	11	14	2	2	0	1	14	1	16	.167	.293	.238	43	-7	0-1	.912	-7	84	77	2b29/P	—	-1.2
Total	6	502	1598	203	402	55	22	8	135	175	15	218	.252	.331	.329	73	-65	21-21	.906	-20	107	136	3b229,S180,2b67/P1rf	—	-4.9
Regalado, Rudy	Rudolph Valentino; B5.21.1930 Los Angeles CA; BR/TR/6´1˝/185; d4.13; Col USC																								
1954	†Cle A	65	180	21	45	5	0	2	24	19	4	16	.250	.333	.311	76	-5	0-2	.967	-6	83	86	3b50,2b2	0	-1.3
1955	Cle A	10	26	2	7	2	0	0	5	2-0	0	4	.269	.321	.346	77	-1	0-0	.955	1	101	158	3b8/2	0	0.0
1956	Cle A	16	47	4	11	1	0	0	2	4-0	1	1	.234	.308	.255	49	-3	0-0	.783	-5	44	161	3b14/1	0	-0.8
Total	3	91	253	27	63	8	0	2	31	25-0	5	21	.249	.327	.304	71	-9	0-2	.944	-10	79	105	3b72,2b3/1	0	-2.1
Regan, Joe	Joseph Charles; B7.12.1872 Seymour CT; D11.18.1948 Hartford CT; BR/TR/6´1˝/?; d9.21																								
1898	NY N	2	5	1	1	0	0	0	2	0	0	—	.200	.200	.200	15	-1	0	1.000	-0	0	0	O2R	—	-0.1
Regan, Bill	William Wright; B1.23.1899 Pittsburgh PA; D6.11.1968 Pittsburgh PA; BR/TR/5´10˝/155; d6.2																								
1926	Bos A	108	403	40	106	21	3	4	34	23	4	37	.263	.309	.360	77	-15	6-3	.965	16	**112**	105	2b106	—	0.3
1927	Bos A	129	468	43	128	37	10	2	66	26	2	51	.274	.315	.408	88	-10	10-10	.960	0	101	99	2b121	—	-0.8
1928	Bos A	138	511	53	135	30	6	7	75	21	2	40	.264	.296	.387	80	-17	9-6	.963	15	**109**	110	2b137/rf	—	0.1
1929	Bos A	104	371	38	107	27	7	1	54	22	0	38	.288	.328	.407	90	-6	7-5	.962	-13	92	112	2b91,3b10/1	—	-1.6
1930	Bos A	134	507	54	135	35	10	3	53	25	2	60	.266	.303	.393	78	-19	4-2	.963	-10	100	113	2b127,3b2	—	-2.2
1931	Pit N	28	104	8	21	8	0	1	10	5	0	19	.202	.239	.308	46	-8	2	.944	-3	103	79	2b28	—	-1.0
Total	6	641	2364	236	632	158	36	18	292	122	10	245	.267	.306	.387	81	-75	38-26	.962	5	103	106	2b610,3b12/1rf	—	-5.2
Rego, Tony	Antone (b Antone De Rego); B10.31.1897 Wailuku HI; D1.6.1978 Tulsa OK; BR/TR/5´4˝/165; d6.21																								
1924	StL A	24	59	5	13	1	0	0	5	1	0	3	.220	.233	.237	20	-7	0-0	.972	-1	*95*	*110*	C23	—	-0.6
1925	StL A	20	32	5	13	2	1	0	3	3	1	2	.406	.472	.531	147	2	0-0	.979	1	*90*	*183*	C19	—	0.4
Total	2	44	91	10	26	3	1	0	8	4	1	5	.286	.323	.341	66	-5	0-0	.975	0	*93*	*137*	C42	—	-0.2
Rehg, Wally	Walter Phillip; B8.31.1888 Summerfield IL; D4.5.1946 Burbank CA; BR/TR/5´8˝/160; d4.14; Mil 1918																								
1912	Pit N	8	9	1	0	0	0	0	0	0	0	1	.000	.000	.000	-99	-3	0	1.000	0	125	0	O2(0/1/1)	—	-0.3
1913	Bos A	30	101	13	28	3	2	0	9	2	0	7	.277	.291	.347	84	-3	4	.943	-1	91	105	O26(8/3/15)	—	-0.5
1914	Bos A	88	151	14	33	4	2	0	11	18	1	11	.219	.306	.272	74	-5	5-8	.980	1	99	106	O43(16/0/28)	—	-0.8
1915	Bos A	5	5	2	1	0	0	0	0	0	0	1	.200	.200	.200	20	-1	1	1.000	0	144	0	/rf	—	0.0
1917	Bos N	87	341	48	92	12	6	1	31	24	1	32	.270	.320	.349	111	4	13	.956	-5	87	84	O86R	—	-0.6
1918	Bos N	40	133	6	32	5	1	1	12	5	0	14	.241	.268	.316	81	-4	3	.988	3	108	143	O38(30/1/7)	—	-0.2
1919	Cin N	5	12	1	2	0	0	0	3	1	0	0	.167	.231	.167	21	-1	0	.875	1	69	384	O5(0/1/3)	—	-0.1
Total	7	263	752	85	188	24	11	2	66	50	2	66	.250	.299	.319	90	-13	26-8	.965	-1	94	108	O201(54/6/141)	—	-2.5
Reiber, Frank	Frank Bernard "Tubby"; B9.19.1909 Huntington WV; D12.26.2002 Bradenton FL; BR/TR/5´8.5˝/169; d4.13																								
1933	Det A	13	18	3	5	0	1	1	3	2	0	3	.278	.350	.556	134	1	0-0	.929	-1	*57*	*0*	C6	—	0.0
1934	Det A	3	1	0	0	0	0	0	0	2	0	0	.000	.667	.000	84	0	0-0	ø	0	—	—	/H	—	0.0
1935	Det A	8	11	3	3	0	0	0	1	3	0	3	.273	.429	.273	88	0	0-0	1.000	-0	*82*	*0*	C5	—	0.0
1936	Det A	20	55	7	15	2	0	1	5	5	0	7	.273	.333	.364	72	-3	0-1	.982	-2	*116*	*93*	C17/rf	—	-0.4
Total	4	44	85	13	23	2	1	2	9	12	0	13	.271	.361	.388	89	-2	0-1	.975	-4	*102*	*66*	C28/rf	—	-0.4

YEAR	TM LG	G	AB	R	H	2B	3B	HR	RBI	BB-IB	HP	SO	AVG	OBP	SLG	AOPS	ABR	SB-CS	FA	FR	RNG	THR	GAMES AT POSITION	DL	BFW
REICH, HERMAN	Herman Charles; B11.23.1917 Bell CA; BR/TL/6´2″/200; d5.3; Col Loyola Marymount																								
1949	Was A	2	2	0	0	0	0	0	0	0	0	1	.000	.000	.000	-99	-1	0-0	ø	0	—	—	/H	0	-0.1
	Cle A	1	2	0	1	0	0	0	0	1	0	0	.500	.667	.500	215	1	0-0	ø	-0	0	0	/rf	0	0.0
	Year	3	4	0	1	0	0	0	0	1	0	1	.250	.400	.250	75	0	0-0	ø	-0	83	262	/rf	0	-0.1
	Chi N	108	386	43	108	18	2	3	34	13	1	32	.280	.305	.360	80	-12	4	.989	13	160	75	1b85,O16R	0	-0.2
Total	1	111	390	43	109	18	2	3	34	14	1	33	.279	.306	.359	80	-12	4-0	.989	13	160	75	1b85,O17R	0	-0.3
REICHARDT, RICK	Frederic Carl; B3.16.1943 Madison WI; BR/TR/6´3″/(213–215); d9.1; Col Wisconsin–Madison																								
1964	LA A	11	37	0	6	0	0	0	0	1-1	0	12	.162	.184	.162	-3	-5	1-0	1.000	-1	103	0	O11C	0	-0.6
1965	Cal A	20	75	8	20	4	0	1	6	5-0	1	12	.267	.321	.360	95	0	4-1	.975	0	103	88	O20(17/4/0)	0	-0.1
1966	Cal A	89	319	48	92	5	4	16	44	27-3	**13**	61	.288	.367	.480	145	18	8-4	.976	-1	89	142	O87(77/20/0)	51	1.4
1967	Cal A	146	498	56	132	14	2	17	69	35-4	7	90	.265	.320	.404	118	9	5-3	.974	7	106	108	O138L	0	1.0
1968	Cal A	151	534	62	136	20	3	21	73	42-2	18	118	.255	.328	.421	130	19	8-7	.989	4	103	95	O148L	0	1.6
1969	Cal A	137	493	60	125	11	4	13	68	43-5	8	100	.254	.319	.371	98	-3	3-6	.981	6	99	128	O136L,1b3	0	-0.7
1970	Cal A	9	6	1	1	0	0	0	1	3-1	0	0	.167	.400	.167	78	0	0-0	1.000	0	117	0	/rf	0	0.0
	Was A	107	277	42	70	14	2	15	46	23-2	9	69	.253	.328	.480	126	9	2-4	.985	-2	103	0	O79(38/18/31)/3	0	0.2
	Year	116	283	43	71	14	2	15	47	26-3	9	69	.251	.330	.473	125	9	2-4	.985	-2	103	0	O80(38/18/32)/3	0	0.2
1971	Chi A	138	496	53	138	14	2	19	62	37-0	6	90	.278	.335	.429	112	7	5-10	.981	-8	91	55	O128(117/15/0),1b9	0	-1.2
1972	Chi A	101	291	31	73	14	4	8	43	28-1	3	63	.251	.321	.409	114	5	2-2	.981	-7	90	41	O90(11/84/0)	0	-0.5
1973	Chi A	46	153	15	42	8	1	3	16	8-0	1	29	.275	.315	.399	96	-1	2-3	1.000	-2	90	42	O37(30/6/1),D6	0	-0.6
	KC A	41	127	15	28	5	2	3	17	11-1	0	28	.220	.279	.362	75	-5	0-1	1.000	0	79	326	D31,O7(1/0/6)	0	-0.6
	Year	87	280	30	70	13	3	6	33	19-1	1	57	.250	.298	.382	86	-6	2-4	1.000	-2	89	76	O44(31/6/7),D37	0	-1.2
1974	KC A	1	1	0	1	0	0	0	0	0-0	0	0	1.000	1.000	1.000	451	0	0-0	ø	0	—	—	/H	0	0.0
Total	11	997	3307	391	864	109	24	116	445	263-20	66	672	.261	.326	.414	114	53	40-41	.982	-4	98	87	O882(713/158/39),D37,1b12/3	51	-0.1
REICHLE, DICK	Richard Wendell; B11.23.1896 Lincoln IL; D6.13.1967 Richmond Heights MO; BL/TR/6´0″/185; d9.19; Col Illinois																								
1922	Bos A	6	24	3	6	1	0	0	0	0	1	2	.250	.280	.292	50	-2	0-0	1.000	-0	100	0	O6C	—	-0.2
1923	Bos A	122	361	40	93	17	3	1	39	22	8	34	.258	.315	.330	69	-17	3-6	.976	-2	94	108	O93(3/87/4),1b2	—	-2.3
Total	2	128	385	43	99	18	3	1	39	22	9	36	.257	.313	.327	68	-19	3-6	.977	-2	94	101	O99(3/93/4),1b2	—	-2.5
REID, HUGH	Hugh A.; B5.10.1852 Cleveland OH; D12.22.1928 Chicago IL; d8.26																								
1874	Bal NA	1	4	0	0	0	0	0	0	0	—	0	.000	.000	.000	-99	-1	0-0	1.000	-0	0	0	/rf	—	-0.1
REID, JESSIE	Jessie Thomas; B6.1.1962 Honolulu HI; BL/TL/6´1″/200; [SFN80 1/7]; d9.9																								
1987	SF N	6	8	1	1	0	0	1	1	1-0	0	5	.125	.222	.500	89	0	0-0	1.000	0	116	0	O3(1/0/2)	0	0.0
1988	SF N	2	2	0	0	0	0	0	0	0-0	0	1	.000	.000	.000	-99	-1	0-0	ø	0	—	—	/H	0	-0.1
Total	2	8	10	1	1	0	0	1	1	1-0	0	6	.100	.182	.400	54	-1	0-0	1.000	0	116	0	O3(1/0/2)	0	-0.1
REID, SCOTT	Scott Donald; B1.7.1947 Chicago IL; BL/TR/6´1″/(190–195); [PhiN67 S2/38]; d9.10; Col Arizona St.																								
1969	Phi N	13	19	5	4	0	0	0	0	7-1	0	5	.211	.423	.211	84	0	0-1	1.000	-0	83	0	O5(2/4/0)	0	-0.1
1970	Phi N	25	49	5	6	1	0	0	1	11-0	0	22	.122	.283	.143	18	-5	0-0	1.000	5	98	759	O18(3/12/5)	0	-0.1
Total	2	38	68	10	10	1	0	0	1	18-1	0	27	.147	.326	.162	37	-5	0-1	1.000	4	95	588	O23(5/16/5)	0	-0.2
REID, BILLY	William Alexander; B5.17.1857 London ON, Can.; D6.26.1940 London ON, Can.; BL/TR/6´0″/170; d5.1																								
1883	Bal AA	24	97	14	27	3	0	0	—	4	—	—	.278	.307	.309	96	0	—	.842	-5	92	69	2b23/S	—	-0.4
1884	Pit AA	19	70	11	17	2	0	0	—	4	1	—	.243	.293	.271	86	-1	—	.724	-4	0	0	O17L/32	—	-0.5
Total	2	43	167	25	44	5	0	0	—	8	1	—	.263	.301	.293	92	-1	—	.839	-9	91	67	2b24,O17L/3S	—	-0.9
REILLEY, DUKE	Alexander Aloysius "Midget"; B8.25.1884 Chicago IL; D3.4.1968 Indianapolis IN; BB/TR/5´4.5″/148; d8.28																								
1909	Cle A	20	62	10	13	0	0	0	0	4	0	—	.210	.258	.210	46	-4	5	.979	1	39	178	O18(13/5/0)	—	-0.4
REILLEY, CHARLIE	Charles Augustine (b Charles Augustine O'Reilly); B1856 Providence RI; D11.4.1904 Providence RI; BR/TR/5´10″/165; d5.1																								
1879	Tro N	62	236	17	54	5	1	0	19	1	—	20	.229	.232	.258	66	-8	—	.867	-16	—	—	C49,1b11,O2(1/0/1)	—	-2.2
1880	Cin N	30	103	8	21	1	0	0	9	0	—	5	.204	.204	.214	42	-6	—	.759	-2	132	0	O16(1/14/1),C13,3b4	—	-0.8
1881	Det N	19	70	8	12	2	0	0	3	0	—	10	.171	.171	.200	16	-7	—	.889	-3	—	—	C10,O4(1/1/2),S3,3b3/1	—	-0.9
	Wor N	2	8	2	3	0	0	0	1	0	—	1	.375	.375	.375	129	0	—	1.000	-1	—	—	C2	—	-0.1
	Year	21	78	10	15	2	0	0	4	0	—	11	.192	.192	.218	28	-6	—	.897	-4	—	—	C12,O4(1/1/2),S3,3b3/1	—	-1.0
1882	Pro N	3	11	0	2	0	0	0	2	1	—	2	.182	.250	.182	41	-1	—	.714	-2	—	—	C3	—	-0.3
1884	Bos U	3	11	1	0	0	0	0	—	1	—	—	.000	.083	.000	-74	-3	—	1.000	-1	0	0	O2R/3	—	-0.3
Total	5	119	439	36	92	8	1	0	34	3	—	38	.210	.215	.232	48	-25	—	.867	-25	—	—	C77,O24(3/15/6),1b12,3b8,S3	—	-4.6
REILLY, ARCH	Archer Edwin; B8.17.1891 Alton IL; D11.29.1963 Columbus OH; BR/TR/5´10″/163; d6.1; Col Ohio St.																								
1917	Pit N	1	0	0	0	0	0	0	0	0	0	0	ø	ø	ø	ø	0	0	1.000	-0	0	0	/3	—	0.0
REILLY, BARNEY	Bernard Eugene; B2.7.1885 Brockton MA; D11.15.1934 St.Joseph MO; BR/TR/6´0″/175; d7.2; Col Yale																								
1909	Chi A	12	25	3	5	0	0	0	3	3	0	—	.200	.286	.200	56	-1	2	.962	2	124	0	2b11/rf	—	0.0
REILLY, CHARLIE	Charles Thomas "Princeton Charlie" (b Charles Thomas O'Reilly); B2.15.1867 Princeton NJ; D12.16.1937 Los Angeles CA; BB/TR/5´11″/190; d10.9																								
1889	Col AA	6	23	5	11	1	0	3	6	2	1	2	.478	.538	.913	326	7	9	.923	2	135	0	3b6	—	0.7
1890	Col AA	137	530	75	141	23	3	4	77	35	6	—	.266	.319	.343	102	1	43	**.893**	29	**117**	**143**	3b137	—	2.8
1891	Pit N	114	415	43	91	8	5	3	44	29	4	58	.219	.277	.284	65	-19	20	.857	0	104	57	3b99,S11,O4(1/3/0)	—	-1.6
1892	Phi N	91	331	42	65	7	3	1	24	18	2	43	.196	.242	.245	47	-22	13	.905	9	111	132	3b70,O15(5/8/2),2b4	—	-1.2
1893	Phi N	104	416	64	102	16	7	4	56	33	9	36	.245	.314	.346	76	-16	13	.895	1	99	**114**	3b104	—	-1.1
1894	Phi N	40	136	21	40	1	2	0	19	16	3	10	.294	.381	.331	74	-5	9	.874	3	121	81	3b28,O6(5/0/1),2b4/S1	—	-0.1
1895	Phi N	49	179	28	48	6	1	0	25	13	5	12	.268	.335	.313	67	-8	7	.900	-2	100	92	S34,3b11,2b3/rf	—	-0.7
1897	Was N	101	351	64	97	18	3	2	60	34	11	—	.276	.359	.362	91	-3	18	.905	16	114	129	3b101	—	1.3
Total	8	642	2381	342	595	80	24	17	311	180	41	161	.250	.314	.325	80	-65	132	.890	58	110	113	3b556,S46,O26(11/11/4),2b11/1	—	0.1
REILLY, HAL	Harold John; B4.1.1894 Oshkosh WI; D12.24.1957 Chicago IL; BL/TL/6´0″/180; d6.19																								
1919	Chi N	1	3	0	0	0	0	0	0	0	0	1	.000	.000	.000	-99	-1	0	ø	-0	0	0	/lf	—	-0.1
REILLY, JOHN	John Good "Long John"; B10.5.1858 Cincinnati OH; D5.31.1937 Cincinnati OH; BR/TR/6´3″/178; d5.18																								
1880	Cin N	73	272	21	56	8	4	0	16	3	—	36	.206	.215	.265	62	-11	—	.947	-3	70	100	1b72,O3R	—	-1.7
1883	Cin AA	**98**	437	103	136	21	14	9	79	9	—	—	.311	.325	.485	149	21	—	.961	-1	67	131	1b98/rf	—	1.0
1884	Cin AA	105	448	114	152	24	19	**11**	91	5	14	—	.339	.366	**.551**	186	39	—	.971	-1	74	125	1b103,O3R/S	—	2.6
1885	Cin AA	111	482	92	143	18	11	5	60	11	7	—	.297	.322	.411	128	13	—	.963	-3	78	105	1b107,O7(0/2/5)	—	0.0
1886	Cin AA	115	441	92	117	12	11	6	79	31	5	—	.265	.321	.383	116	6	19	.967	-0	104	**136**	1b110,O6(0/5/1)	—	-0.4
1887	Cin AA	134	551	106	170	35	14	10	96	22	15	—	.309	.352	.477	127	17	50	.980	-1	79	**142**	1b127,O9(1/6/2)	—	0.4
1888	Cin AA	127	527	112	169	28	14	**13**	**103**	17	18	—	.321	.363	**.501**	**167**	36	82	.977	0	95	**144**	1b117,O10(0/2/8)	—	2.3
1889	Cin AA	111	427	84	111	24	13	5	66	34	18	37	.260	.340	.412	110	5	43	**.984**	-1	75	**124**	1b109,O2(1/1/0)	—	-0.6
1890	Cin N	133	553	114	166	25	**26**	6	86	16	7	41	.300	.328	.472	133	16	29	.977	-3	82	**122**	1b132/cf	—	0.1
1891	Cin N	135	546	60	132	20	13	4	64	9	10	42	.242	.267	.348	78	-19	22	.982	-7	59	116	1b100,O36(25/10/1)	—	-3.3
Total	10	1142	4684	898	1352	215	139	69	740	157	94	156	.289	.325	.438	128	123	245	.972	-22	79	126	1b1075,O78(27/27/24)/S	—	0.4
REILLY, JOE	Joseph J.; B1861 New York NY; 5´10″/140; d6.8																								
1885	NY AA	10	40	6	7	3	0	0	3	2	0	—	.175	.214	.250	48	-2	—	.848	-1	85	73	2b8,3b2	—	-0.2
REILLY, TOM	Thomas Henry; B8.3.1884 St.Louis MO; D10.18.1918 New Orleans LA; BR/TR/5´10″/?; d7.27																								
1908	StL N	29	81	5	14	1	0	1	3	2	0	—	.173	.193	.222	34	-6	4	.866	-4	94	136	S29	—	-1.1
1909	StL N	5	7	0	2	0	1	0	2	0	0	—	.286	.286	.571	176	0	0	1.000	0	125	0	S5	—	0.1
1914	Cle A	1	1	0	0	0	0	0	0	0	0	0	.000	.000	.000	-96	0	0	ø	0	—	—	/H	—	0.0
Total	3	35	89	5	16	1	1	1	5	2	0	0	.180	.198	.247	44	-6	4	.875	-4	96	126	S34	—	-1.0
REILLY, JOSH	William Henry; B5.9.1868 San Francisco CA; D6.12.1938 San Francisco CA; BR/TR/5´8″/160; d5.2																								
1896	Chi N	9	42	6	9	1	0	0	2	1	0	1	.214	.233	.238	23	-5	2	.857	-2	103	27	2b8/S	—	-0.6

YEAR	TM LG	G	AB	R	H	2B	3B	HR	RBI	BB-IB	HP	SO	AVG	OBP	SLG	AOPS	ABR	SB-CS	FA	FR	RNG	THR	GAMES AT POSITION	DL	BFW
REIMER, KEVIN	Kevin Michael; B6.28.1964 Macon GA; BL/TR/6´2˝/(215–230); [TexA85 11/265]; d9.13; Col Cal St.–Fullerton																								
1988	Tex A	12	25	2	3	0	0	1	2	0-0	0	6	.120	.115	.240	-2	-4	0-0	ø	-0	0	0	/lfD	0	-0.4
1989	Tex A	3	5	0	0	0	0	0	0	0-0	0	1	.000	.000	.000	-98	-1	0-0	ø	0	—	—	/D	0	-0.1
1990	Tex A	64	100	5	26	9	1	2	15	10-0	1	22	.260	.333	.430	111	2	0-1	.857	-1	97	0	D21,O9(5/0/5)	0	0.0
1991	Tex A	136	394	46	106	22	0	20	69	33-6	7	93	.269	.332	.477	124	12	0-3	.948	-3	101	0	O66(61/0/6),D56	0	0.5
1992	Tex A	148	494	56	132	32	2	16	58	42-5	10	103	.267	.336	.437	119	12	2-4	.949	-0	99	111	O110L,D32	0	0.7
1993	Mil A	125	437	53	109	22	1	13	60	30-4	5	72	.249	.303	.394	87	-9	5-4	.962	1	115	50	D83,O37(28/0/10)	0	-1.4
Total	6	488	1455	162	376	85	4	52	204	115-15	23	297	.258	.320	.430	107	12	7-12	.948	-3	102	66	O223(205/0/21),D200	0	-0.7
REINBACH, MIKE	Michael Wayne; B8.6.1949 San Diego CA; D5.20.1989 Palm Desert CA; BL/TR/6´2˝/195; d4.7; Col UCLA																								
1974	Bal A	12	20	2	5	1	0	0	2	2-1	0	5	.250	.304	.300	80	0	0-0	1.000	0	123	0	O3(1/0/2),D3	0	0.0
REINECKER, WALLY	Walter (b Walter Joseph Smith); B4.21.1890 Pittsburgh PA; D4.18.1957 Pittsburgh PA; BR/TR/5´6˝/150; d9.17																								
1915	Bal F	3	8	0	1	0	0	0	0	0	1	0	.125	.222	.125	-1	-1	0	.571	-2	24	0	3b3	—	-0.3
REINHOLZ, ART	Arthur August; B1.27.1903 Detroit MI; D12.29.1980 New Port Richey FL; BR/TR/5´10.5˝/175; d9.27																								
1928	Cle A	2	3	0	1	0	0	0	0	1	0	0	.333	.500	.333	122	0	0-0	.833	0	153	0	3b2	—	0.0
REIPSCHLAGER, CHARLIE	Charles W.; B2.1854; D3.16.1910 Atlantic City NJ; BR/TR/5´6.5˝/160; d5.2																								
1883	NY AA	37	145	8	27	4	2	0	—	4	—	—	.186	.208	.241	42	-9	—	.936	7	—	—	C29,O8(0/7/1)	—	-0.1
1884	†NY AA	59	233	21	56	13	2	0	—	1	2	—	.240	.250	.313	85	-4	—	.925	16	—	—	C51,O8(5/2/1)	—	1.5
1885	NY AA	72	268	29	65	11	1	0	21	9	1	—	.243	.270	.291	80	-5	—	.879	1	—	—	C59,O6(2/3/1),3b6/S2	—	0.0
1886	NY AA	65	232	21	49	4	6	0	25	9	1	—	.211	.244	.280	70	-9	2	.884	-2	—	—	C57,O9(1/6/2)	—	-0.5
1887	Cle AA	63	231	20	49	8	3	0	17	11	1	—	.212	.251	.273	47	-17	7	.888	5	—	—	C48,1b16	—	-0.7
Total	5	296	1109	99	246	40	14	0	63	34	5	—	.222	.248	.283	66	-44	9	.901	26	—	—	C244,O31(8/18/5),1b16,3b6/2S	—	0.2
REIS, BOBBY	Robert Joseph Thomas; B1.2.1909 Woodside NY; D5.1.1973 St.Paul MN; BR/TR/6´1˝/175; d9.19; OF(19/17/15); ▲																								
1931	Bro N	6	17	3	5	0	0	0	2	2	0	0	.294	.368	.294	81	0	0	.933	-1	74	0	3b6	—	-0.1
1932	Bro N	1	4	0	1	0	0	0	0	0	0	1	.250	.250	.250	36	0	0	.500	-1	67	0	/3	—	-0.1
1935	Bro N	52	85	10	21	3	2	0	4	6	0	13	.247	.297	.329	70	-4	2	.950	5	103	274	O21(4/3/14),P14,2b4/13	—	0.0
1936	Bos N	37	60	3	13	2	0	0	5	3	0	6	.217	.254	.250	39	-5	0	1.000	4	160	103	P35,O2C	—	0.1
1937	Bos N	45	86	10	21	5	0	0	6	13	0	12	.244	.343	.302	84	-1	2	1.000	-2	101	0	O18(6/12/0),P4,1b4	—	-0.4
1938	Bos N	34	49	6	9	0	0	0	4	1	0	3	.184	.200	.184	7	-6	1	1.000	-1	128	0	P16,O10(9/0/1),S3/C2	—	-0.5
Total	6	175	301	32	70	10	2	0	21	25	0	35	.233	.291	.279	59	-16	5	1.000	4	147	95	P69,O51L,3b8,1b5,2b5,S3/C	—	-1.0
REISER, PETE	Harold Patrick; B3.17.1919 St.Louis MO; D10.25.1981 Palm Springs CA; BL/TR (BB 1940p,1948–52p)/5´10.5˝/185; d7.23; Mil 1943–45; C14																								
1940	Bro N	58	225	34	66	11	4	3	20	15	0	33	.293	.338	.418	101	0	2	.960	-3	95	160	3b30,O17(5/1/9),S5	—	-0.2
1941	†Bro N★	137	536	**117**	184	**39**	**17**	14	76	46	**11**	71	**.343**	.406	**.558**	**163**	44	4	.981	4	104	127	O133(0/133/2)	0	**4.5**
1942	Bro N★	125	480	89	149	33	5	10	64	48	2	45	.310	.375	.463	142	26	**20**	.969	-8	92	78	O125C	0	1.5
1946	Bro N☆	122	423	75	117	21	5	11	73	55	1	58	.277	.361	.428	122	13	**34**	.978	5	98	168	O97(69/28/0),3b15	0	1.2
1947	†Bro N	110	388	68	120	23	2	5	46	68	2	41	.309	.415	.418	117	14	14	.988	-5	97	41	O108(51/62/0)	0	0.4
1948	Bro N	64	127	17	30	8	2	1	19	29	1	21	.236	.382	.354	97	1	4	.981	-2	94	54	O30(17/10/5),3b4	0	-0.2
1949	Bos N	84	221	32	60	8	3	8	40	33	1	42	.271	.369	.443	123	8	3	.980	0	98	115	O63(27/36/0),3b4	0	0.5
1950	Bos N	53	78	12	16	2	0	1	10	18	2	22	.205	.367	.269	75	-2	1	.979	0	116	0	O24(16/6/0)/3	0	-0.3
1951	Pit N	74	140	22	38	9	3	2	13	27	0	20	.271	.389	.421	115	4	4-2	.982	-2	91	44	O27(20/6/1),3b5	0	0.1
1952	Cle A	34	44	7	6	1	0	3	7	4	0	16	.136	.208	.364	61	-3	1-1	1.000	0	110	0	O10(4/6/0)	0	-0.3
Total	10	861	2662	473	786	155	41	58	368	343	20	369	.295	.380	.450	127	105	87-3	.979	-10	98	93	O634(209/413/17),3b59,S5	0	7.2
REISING, CHARLIE	Charles "Pop"; B8.28.1861 Lanesville IN; D7.26.1915 Louisville KY; d7.19																								
1884	Ind AA	2	8	0	0	0	0	0	—	1	0	—	.000	.111	.000	-62	-1	—	.400	-1	0	0	O2(1/1/1)	—	-0.3
REISS, AL	Albert Allen; B1.8.1909 Elizabeth NJ; D5.13.1989 Red Bank NJ; BB/TR/5´10.5˝/165; d6.22																								
1932	Phi A	9	5	0	1	0	0	0	1	1	0	1	.200	.333	.200	40	0	0-0	1.000	0	107	0	S6	—	0.0
REITZ, HEINIE	Henry P.; B6.29.1867 Chicago IL; D11.10.1914 Sacramento CA; BL/TR/5´7˝/158; d4.27																								
1893	Bal N	**130**	490	90	140	17	13	1	76	65	7	32	.286	.377	.380	100	1	24	.939	4	102	99	2b130	—	0.8
1894	†Bal N	108	446	86	135	22	**31**	2	105	42	7	24	.303	.372	.504	105	-1	18	**.968**	21	109	114	2b97,3b12	—	1.8
1895	Bal N	71	245	45	72	15	5	0	29	18	3	11	.294	.350	.396	89	-4	15	.938	-3	95	140	2b48,3b18/S	—	-0.4
1896	†Bal N	120	464	76	133	15	6	4	106	49	2	32	.287	.357	.371	91	-6	28	.952	-22	90	120	2b118,S3	—	-1.9
1897	†Bal N	128	477	76	138	15	6	2	84	50	11	—	.289	.370	.358	93	-3	23	**.962**	19	**111**	**151**	2b128	—	1.8
1898	Was N	132	489	62	148	20	2	2	47	32	9	—	.303	.357	.364	107	5	11	**.959**	11	101	99	2b132	—	2.0
1899	Pit N	35	133	12	35	4	2	0	16	10	0	—	.263	.315	.323	75	-5	3	.976	0	104	59	2b35	—	-0.3
Total	7	724	2744	447	801	108	65	11	463	266	39	99	.292	.363	.391	97	-13	122	.955	30	102	115	2b688,3b30,S4	—	3.8
REITZ, KEN	Kenneth John; B6.24.1951 San Francisco CA; BR/TR/6´0˝/(175–185); [StLN69 31/730]; d9.5																								
1972	StL N	21	78	5	28	4	0	0	10	2-0	0	4	.359	.370	.410	124	2	0-1	.956	-4	71	90	3b20	0	-0.2
1973	StL N	147	426	40	100	20	2	6	42	9-2	4	25	.235	.256	.333	62	-23	0-1	**.974**	-1	99	90	3b135/S	0	-2.7
1974	StL N	154	579	48	157	28	2	7	54	23-7	2	63	.271	.299	.363	85	-14	0-0	**.974**	-20	86	96	3b151,S2/2	0	-3.6
1975	StL N	161	592	43	159	25	1	5	63	22-9	5	54	.269	.298	.340	74	-22	1-1	.946	-15	89	75	3b160	0	-4.0
1976	SF N	155	577	40	154	21	1	5	66	24-5	1	48	.267	.293	.333	76	-19	5-4	.959	2	101	109	3b155/S	0	-2.0
1977	StL N	157	587	58	153	36	1	17	79	19-4	7	74	.261	.291	.412	87	-13	2-6	**.980**	-0	99	143	3b157	0	-1.7
1978	StL N	150	540	41	133	26	2	10	75	23-5	5	61	.246	.280	.357	78	-17	1-0	**.973**	10	**108**	72	3b150	0	-1.1
1979	StL N	159	605	42	162	41	2	8	73	25-7	4	85	.268	.299	.382	83	-14	1-0	.972	-11	95	95	3b158	0	-2.8
1980	StL N★	151	523	39	141	33	0	8	58	22-5	3	44	.270	.300	.379	85	-11	0-1	**.979**	-7	99	113	3b150	0	-2.1
1981	Chi N	82	260	10	56	9	1	2	28	15-3	3	56	.215	.261	.281	52	-16	0-0	**.977**	4	105	83	3b81	0	-1.5
1982	Pit N	7	10	0	0	0	0	0	0	0-0	1	4	.000	.091	.000	-69	-2	0-0	1.000	0	130	0	3b4	0	-0.2
Total	11	1344	4777	366	1243	243	12	68	548	184-47	35	518	.260	.290	.359	78	-149	10-14	.970	-41	97	98	3b1321,S4/2	0	-21.9
RELAFORD, DESI	Desmond Lamont; B9.16.1973 Valdosta GA; BB/TR (BL 2003p)/5´9˝/(155–180); [SeaA91 4/110]; d8.1; OF(48/9/37)																								
1996	Phi N	15	40	2	7	2	0	0	1	3-0	0	9	.175	.233	.225	21	-5	1-0	.933	1	80	52	S9,2b4	0	-0.3
1997	Phi N	15	38	3	7	1	2	0	6	5-0	0	6	.184	.279	.316	56	-3	3-0	.977	-1	100	46	S12	0	-0.2
1998	Phi N	142	494	45	121	25	3	5	41	33-4	3	87	.245	.293	.338	66	-25	9-5	.960	-7	98	89	S137	0	-2.1
1999	Phi N	65	211	31	51	11	2	1	26	19-2	6	34	.242	.322	.327	64	-11	4-3	.952	8	111	119	S63	88	0.1
2000	Phi N	83	253	29	56	12	3	3	30	48-7	9	45	.221	.363	.328	77	-7	5-0	.930	-12	89	94	S81	0	-1.1
	SD N	45	157	26	32	2	0	2	16	27-0	3	26	.204	.330	.255	54	-11	8-0	.965	-1	98	120	S45	0	-0.6
	Year	128	410	55	88	14	3	5	46	75-7	12	71	.215	.351	.300	69	-17	13-0	.943	-13	92	103	S126	0	-1.7
2001	NY N	120	301	43	91	27	0	8	36	27-1	5	65	.302	.364	.472	124	12	13-5	.969	-9	87	94	2b54,S25,3b20/P	0	0.7
2002	Sea A	112	329	55	88	13	2	6	43	33-2	6	51	.267	.339	.374	94	-2	10-3	.964	-5	88	118	S40,3b38,O35(25/0/10),2b11,D4	0	-0.4
2003	KC A	141	500	70	127	27	5	8	59	40-1	6	70	.254	.315	.376	77	-17	20-4	.981	1	98	89	2b89,3b33,O20(1/5/15),S6,D5	0	-0.8
2004	KC A	114	380	45	84	14	0	6	34	34-3	8	56	.221	.296	.305	58	-24	5-4	.927	3	110	79	3b42,2b36,O32(22/3/9),S12	23	-1.8
2005	Col N	73	210	24	47	13	2	1	16	22-2	4	42	.224	.308	.319	58	-12	3-3	.960	-2	108	68	S37,3b21,2b11,O4(0/1/3)	9	-1.1
Total	10	925	2913	373	711	147	19	40	308	291-22	50	491	.244	.321	.349	75	-105	81-27	.955	-22	98	96	S467,2b205,3b154,O91L,D9/P	120	-7.6
REMENTER, BUTCH	Willis J. H.; B3.14.1878 Philadelphia PA; D9.23.1922 Philadelphia PA; BR/TR/5´6.5˝/180; d10.8																								
1904	Phi N	1	2	0	0	0	0	0	0	0	0	—	.000	.000	.000	-99	0	0	1.000	-0	*74*	*0*	/C	—	-0.1
REMSEN, JACK	John Jay; B4.1850 Brooklyn NY; BR/TR/5´11˝/189; d5.2																								
1872	Atl NA	**37**	165	25	39	3	5	1	14	2	—	6	.236	.246	.333	65	-10	1-2	.797	2	123	**192**	O37C	—	-0.6
1873	Atl NA	50	207	29	61	5	6	1	29	2	—	6	.295	.301	.391	115	5	1-2	.793	-2	70	136	O50C	—	0.2
1874	Mut NA	64	284	52	65	9	3	2	38	0	—	5	.229	.229	.303	67	-11	6-0	.864	4	134	139	O63(8/57/0),1b3	—	-0.4
1875	Har NA	**86**	358	70	96	10	4	0	34	5	—	4	.268	.278	.318	102	-1	6-3	.887	2	71	48	O86(0/81/5)	—	0.1
1876	Har N	**69**	324	62	89	12	5	1	30	1	—	15	.275	.277	.352	100	-2	—	.887	7	102	250	O69(3/66/0)	—	0.2
1877	StL N	33	123	14	32	3	4	0	13	4	—	3	.260	.283	.350	104	1	—	.906	0	61	0	O33C	—	0.0
1878	Chi N	56	224	32	52	11	1	1	19	**17**	—	33	.232	.286	.304	88	-2	—	**.944**	4	95	237	O56C	—	-0.1
1879	Chi N	42	152	14	33	4	2	0	8	2	—	23	.217	.227	.270	60	-7	—	.862	-1	64	149	O31(5/26/0),1b11	—	-0.9
1881	Cle N	48	172	14	30	4	3	0	13	9	—	31	.174	.215	.233	43	-11	—	.873	-2	54	55	O48C	—	-1.4

YEAR	TM LG	G	AB	R	H	2B	3B	HR	RBI	BB-IB	HP	SO	AVG	OBP	SLG	AOPS	ABR	SB-CS	FA	FR	RNG	THR	GAMES AT POSITION	DL	BFW
1884	Phi N	12	43	9	9	2	0	0	3	6	—	9	.209	.306	.256	83	0	—	.952	1	160	0	O12C	—	0.0
	Bro AA	81	301	45	67	6	6	3	—	23	0	—	.223	.278	.312	91	-3	—	.914	3	45	79	O81(32/49/0)	—	-0.2
Total	4NA	237	1014	176	261	27	18	4	115	9	—	17	.257	.264	.331	87	-17	14-7	.842	5	96	114	O236(8/225/5),1b3	—	-0.7
Total	6	341	1339	190	312	42	21	5	86	62	0	114	.233	.267	.307	84	-24	—	.900	12	74	135	O330(40/290/0),1b11	—	-2.4
Remy, Jerry	Gerald Peter; B11.8.1952 Fall River MA; BL/TR/5´9˝/(155–165); [AnaA71*A8/130]; d4.7; [DL 1985 Bos A 182]																								
1975	Cal A	147	569	82	147	17	5	1	46	45-1	0	55	.258	.311	.311	82	-14	34-21	.982	16	103	109	2b147	0	1.1
1976	Cal A	143	502	64	132	14	3	0	28	38-1	0	43	.263	.313	.303	87	-9	35-16	.977	19	109	96	2b133,D5	0	2.2
1977	Cal A	154	575	74	145	19	10	4	44	59-2	2	59	.252	.322	.341	84	-12	41-17	.975	-3	95	92	2b152/3	0	-0.4
1978	Bos A☆	148	583	87	162	24	6	2	44	40-0	0	55	.278	.321	.350	81	-15	30-13	.983	1	99	**123**	2b140/SD	0	-0.4
1979	Bos A	80	306	49	91	11	2	0	29	26-1	0	25	.297	.350	.346	85	-6	14-9	.970	-18	87	83	2b76	52	-1.9
1980	Bos A	63	230	24	72	7	2	0	9	10-0	0	14	.313	.339	.361	88	-4	14-6	.977	-2	106	73	2b60/rf	83	-0.2
1981	Bos A	88	358	55	110	9	1	0	31	36-2	0	30	.307	.368	.338	99	1	9-2	.984	-11	99	91	2b87	0	-0.4
1982	Bos A	155	636	89	178	22	3	0	47	55-1	2	77	.280	.337	.324	78	-17	16-9	.982	-16	97	96	2b154	0	-2.5
1983	Bos A	146	592	73	163	16	5	0	43	40-2	0	35	.275	.320	.319	72	-23	11-3	.990	-17	93	100	2b144	11	-3.1
1984	Bos A	30	104	8	26	1	1	0	8	7-0	0	11	.250	.297	.279	58	-6	4-3	.973	-1	101	82	2b24	135	-0.6
Total	10	1154	4455	605	1226	140	38	7	329	356-10	4	404	.275	.327	.328	82	-105	208-99	.981	-31	99	98	2b1117,D9/rfS3	463	-6.2
Renick, Rick	Warren Richard; B3.16.1944 London OH; BR/TR/6´0˝/(185–190); d7.11; C13; Col Ohio St.																								
1968	Min A	42	97	16	21	5	2	3	13	9-1	0	42	.216	.283	.402	100	0	0-0	.946	0	100	84	S40	0	0.3
1969	†Min A	71	139	21	34	3	0	5	17	12-1	1	32	.245	.307	.374	88	-3	0-1	.913	-6	82	104	3b30,O10(8/0/2),S6	21	-0.9
1970	†Min A	81	179	20	41	8	0	7	25	22-0	1	29	.229	.317	.391	93	-2	0-2	.987	1	95	99	3b30,O25(25/1/0)/S	0	-0.2
1971	Min A	27	45	4	10	2	0	1	8	5-2	1	14	.222	.308	.333	81	-1	0-0	.846	-2	75	0	3b7,O7L	65	-0.3
1972	Min A	55	93	10	16	2	0	4	8	15-0	0	25	.172	.282	.323	77	-2	0-1	1.000	-2	87	0	O21(19/0/2),1b6,3b4/S	0	-0.6
Total	5	276	553	71	122	20	2	20	71	63-4	3	142	.221	.302	.373	89	-8	0-4	.940	-8	90	86	3b71,O63(59/1/4),S48,1b6	86	-1.7
Renna, Bill	William Beneditto "Big Bill"; B10.14.1924 Hanford CA; BR/TR/6´3˝/(218–230); d4.14; Col Santa Clara																								
1953	NY A	61	121	19	38	6	3	2	13	13	1	31	.314	.385	.463	133	5	0-1	.983	-1	101	0	O40(32/5/3)	0	0.2
1954	Phi A	123	422	52	98	15	4	13	53	41	3	60	.232	.302	.379	86	-10	1-3	.972	6	106	156	O115(1/114)	0	-0.9
1955	KC A	100	249	33	53	7	3	7	28	31-0	2	42	.213	.305	.349	75	-10	0-3	.992	0	99	102	O79(8/0/72)	0	-1.3
1956	KC A	33	48	12	13	3	0	2	5	3-0	0	10	.271	.314	.458	101	0	1-0	.950	-0	93	138	O25(22/0/3)	0	-0.1
1958	Bos A	39	56	5	15	5	0	4	18	6-1	0	14	.268	.339	.571	136	3	0-0	1.000	0	109	0	O11L	0	0.2
1959	Bos A	14	22	2	2	0	0	0	2	5-0	0	9	.091	.259	.091	0	-3	0-0	1.000	-1	55	0	O7L	0	-0.4
Total	6	370	918	123	219	36	10	28	119	99-1	6	166	.239	.315	.391	91	-15	2-7	.979	4	102	113	O277(81/6/192)	0	-2.3
Rensa, Tony	George Anthony "Pug"; B9.29.1901 Parsons PA; D1.4.1987 Wilkes-Barre PA; BR/TR/5´10˝/180; d5.5																								
1930	Det A	20	37	6	10	2	1	1	3	6	1	7	.270	.386	.459	111	1	1-0	.964	-1	*63*	*141*	C18	—	0.0
	Phi N	54	172	31	49	11	2	3	31	10	1	18	.285	.328	.424	75	-7	0	.932	-11	*74*	*91*	C49	—	-1.3
1931	Phi N	19	29	2	3	1	0	0	2	6	0	2	.103	.257	.138	8	-4	0	.958	1	*69*	*206*	C17	—	-0.2
1933	NY A	8	29	4	9	2	1	0	3	1	0	3	.310	.333	.448	112	0	0-1	.977	-1	*125*	*96*	C8	—	0.0
1937	Chi A	26	57	10	17	5	1	0	5	8	0	6	.298	.385	.421	103	1	3-0	.975	1	*119*	*90*	C23	—	0.3
1938	Chi A	59	165	15	41	5	0	0	19	25	1	16	.248	.351	.333	71	-7	1-1	.982	6	*125*	*105*	C57	—	0.1
1939	Chi A	14	25	3	5	0	0	0	2	1	0	2	.200	.231	.200	11	-3	0-0	.972	0	*105*	*158*	C13	—	-0.2
Total	6	200	514	71	134	26	5	7	65	57	3	54	.261	.338	.372	74	-19	5-2	.965	-5	*100*	*111*	C185	—	-1.3
Renteria, Edgar	Edgar Enrique; B8.7.1976 Barranquilla, Colombia; BR/TR/6´1˝/(172–200); d5.10																								
1996	Fla N	106	431	68	133	18	3	5	31	33-0	2	68	.309	.358	.399	103	2	16-2	.979	14	108	115	S106	17	2.6
1997	†Fla N	154	617	90	171	21	3	4	52	45-1	4	108	.277	.327	.340	80	-19	32-15	.975	-4	92	104	S153	0	-1.0
1998	Fla N★	133	517	79	146	18	2	3	31	48-1	4	78	.282	.347	.342	88	-9	41-22	.966	-7	98	102	S129	15	-0.4
1999	StL N	154	585	92	161	36	2	11	63	53-0	2	82	.275	.334	.400	84	-14	37-8	.959	-11	96	94	S151	0	-0.8
2000	†StL N★	150	562	94	156	32	1	16	76	63-3	1	77	.278	.346	.423	93	-6	21-13	.958	-8	94	92	S149	0	-0.2
2001	†StL N	141	493	54	128	19	3	10	57	39-4	3	73	.260	.314	.371	76	-18	17-4	.961	7	104	109	S137/1D	0	0.1
2002	†StL N	152	544	77	166	36	2	11	83	49-7	4	57	.305	.364	.439	110	9	22-7	.970	-18	97	79	S149	0	0.5
2003	StL N★	157	587	96	194	47	1	13	100	65-12	1	54	.330	.394	.480	129	28	34-7	.975	-26	98	85	S156	0	1.9
2004	†StL N★	149	586	84	168	37	0	10	72	39-5	1	78	.287	.327	.401	87	-11	17-11	.983	-2	99	110	S149	0	-0.1
2005	†Bos A	153	623	100	172	36	4	8	70	55-0	3	100	.276	.335	.385	88	-10	9-4	.954	-15	94	91	S153	0	-1.2
2006	Atl N★	149	598	100	175	40	2	14	70	62-0	3	89	.293	.361	.436	102	3	17-6	.978	-12	97	82	S146/D	0	0.3
Total	11	1598	6143	934	1770	340	23	105	705	551-33	28	864	.288	.346	.402	94	-45	263-99	.969	-81	98	96	S1578,D2/1	32	1.7
Renteria, Rich	Richard Avina; B12.25.1961 Harbor City CA; BR/TR/5´9˝/(172–175); [PitN80 1/20]; d9.14; [DL 1989 Sea A 88]																								
1986	Pit N	10	12	2	3	1	0	0	1	0-0	0	4	.250	.250	.333	58	-1	0-0	.600	-0	134	0	/3	0	-0.1
1987	Sea A	12	10	2	1	1	0	0	0	1-0	0	2	.100	.182	.200	1	-1	1-0	.833	0	91	0	2b4/SD	12	-0.1
1988	Sea A	31	88	6	18	9	0	0	6	2-0	0	8	.205	.222	.307	44	-6	1-3	.958	1	90	103	D12,S11,3b5,2b4	0	-0.6
1993	Fla N	103	263	27	67	9	2	2	30	21-1	2	31	.255	.314	.327	68	-12	0-2	.989	-3	99	65	2b45,3b25/lf	0	-1.3
1994	Fla N	28	49	5	11	0	0	2	4	1-0	2	4	.224	.269	.347	57	-3	0-1	.929	2	115	285	3b14,2b6,O2L	74	-0.2
Total	5	184	422	42	100	20	2	4	41	25-1	4	49	.237	.285	.322	60	-23	2-6	.986	0	99	73	2b59,3b45,D16,S12,O3L	174	-2.3
Repass, Bob	Robert Willis; B11.6.1917 W.Pittston PA; D1.16.2006 Wethersfield CT; BR/TR/6´1˝/185; d9.18																								
1939	StL N	3	6	0	2	1	0	0	1	0	0	2	.333	.333	.500	114	0	0	1.000	0	142	137	2b2	—	0.1
1942	Was A	81	259	30	62	11	1	2	23	33	1	30	.239	.328	.313	81	-6	6-1	.973	-4	89	70	2b33,3b29,S11	0	-0.5
Total	2	84	265	30	64	12	1	2	24	33	1	32	.242	.328	.317	82	-6	6-1	.973	-4	91	72	2b35,3b29,S11	0	-0.4
Repko, Jason	Jason Edward; B12.27.1980 East Chicago IN; BR/TR/5´11˝/175; [LAN99 1/37]; d4.6																								
2005	LA N	129	276	43	61	15	3	8	30	16-1	7	80	.221	.281	.384	72	-12	5-0	.968	2	99	159	O118(24/58/42)	0	-1.1
2006	†LA N	69	130	21	33	5	1	3	16	15-1	3	24	.254	.345	.377	85	-3	10-4	.977	1	95	213	O62(13/40/14)	75	-0.1
Total	2	198	406	64	94	20	4	11	46	31-2	10	104	.232	.302	.382	76	-15	15-4	.971	3	98	176	O180(37/98/56)	75	-1.2
Repoz, Roger	Roger Allen; B8.3.1940 Bellingham WA; BL/TL/6´3˝/(175–195); d9.11; Col Western Washington																								
1964	NY A	11	1	1	0	0	0	0	0	1-0	0	1	.000	.500	.000	52	0	0-0	1.000	-1	35	0	O9R	0	-0.1
1965	NY A	79	218	34	48	7	4	12	28	25-4	0	57	.220	.298	.454	112	2	1-1	.993	-3	97	36	O69(0/65/7)	0	-0.3
1966	NY A	37	43	4	15	4	1	0	9	4-0	0	8	.349	.396	.488	161	4	0-0	1.000	-3	69	0	O30(0/28/5)	0	0.0
	KC A	101	319	40	69	10	3	11	34	44-4	2	80	.216	.314	.370	99	0	3-3	.991	-5	104	35	O52(8/41/3),1b45	0	-1.0
	Year	138	362	44	84	14	4	11	43	48-4	2	88	.232	.324	.384	106	4	3-3	.992	-8	96	27	O82(8/69/8),1b45	0	-1.0
1967	KC A	40	87	9	21	6	1	2	8	12-1	1	20	.241	.340	.402	122	3	4-2	1.000	3	119	203	O31(16/9/6)	0	0.5
	Cal A	74	176	25	44	9	1	5	20	19-1	0	37	.250	.318	.398	116	4	2-2	.959	0	109	102	O63(6/54/4)	0	0.2
	Year	114	263	34	65	15	2	7	28	31-2	1	57	.247	.326	.399	118	6	6-4	.972	4	112	135	O94(22/63/10)	0	0.7
1968	Cal A	133	375	30	90	8	1	13	54	38-3	3	83	.240	.309	.371	111	4	8-7	.987	1	107	63	O114(0/71/52)	0	-0.1
1969	Cal A	103	219	25	36	1	1	8	19	32-2	0	52	.164	.270	.288	59	-13	1-3	.985	2	98	144	O48(13/22/16),1b31	0	-1.6
1970	Cal A	137	407	50	97	17	6	18	47	45-6	3	90	.238	.317	.442	111	5	4-2	.995	-1	103	95	O110(6/42/68),1b18	0	-0.2
1971	Cal A	113	297	39	59	11	1	13	41	60-6	1	69	.199	.333	.374	108	5	3-5	1.000	-1	96	104	O97(5/25/72),1b13	0	-0.2
1972	Cal A	3	3	0	1	0	0	0	0	0-0	0	2	.333	.333	.333	104	0	0-0	ø	0	—	—	/H	0	0.0
Total	9	831	2145	257	480	73	19	82	260	280-27	10	499	.224	.314	.390	105	14	26-25	.989	-7	102	83	O623(54/357/242),1b107	0	-2.8
Repulski, Rip	Eldon John; B10.4.1928 Sauk Rapids MN; D2.10.1993 Waite Park MN; BR/TR/6´0˝/(195–201); d4.14; Col St. Cloud St.																								
1953	StL N	153	567	75	156	25	4	15	66	33	9	71	.275	.325	.413	91	-9	3-6	.987	-10	92	54	O153C	0	-2.6
1954	StL N	152	619	99	175	39	5	19	79	43	4	75	.283	.329	.454	102	1	8-10	.975	-9	94	40	O152(137/12/3)	0	-1.9
1955	StL N	147	512	64	138	28	2	23	73	49-3	4	66	.270	.333	.467	111	8	5-7	.974	-4	100	50	O141(110/1/32)	0	-0.5
1956	StL N★	112	376	44	104	18	3	11	55	24-3	7	46	.277	.330	.428	102	1	2-2	.974	-3	99	48	O100(99/1/1)	0	-0.8
1957	Phi N	134	516	65	134	23	4	20	68	19-0	5	74	.260	.290	.436	95	-6	7-1	.968	2	109	66	O130(54/0/84)	0	-0.9
1958	Phi N	85	238	33	58	9	4	13	40	15-1	4	47	.244	.296	.479	103	0	0-0	.949	-3	89	73	O56(35/0/21)	0	-0.7
1959	†LA N	53	94	11	24	4	0	2	14	13-2	0	23	.255	.343	.362	83	-2	0-1	1.000	-2	84	0	O31(16/2/13)	0	-0.5
1960	LA N	4	5	0	1	0	0	0	0	0-0	0	1	.200	.200	.200	9	-1	0-0	1.000	0	51	0	O2R	0	-0.1
	Bos A	73	136	14	33	6	1	3	20	10-0	0	25	.243	.289	.368	75	-5	0-0	1.000	0	106	0	O33L	0	-0.7
1961	Bos A	15	25	2	7	1	0	0	1	1-0	0	5	.280	.308	.320	66	-1	0-2	1.000	-1	61	0	O4L	0	-0.3
Total	9	928	3088	407	830	153	23	106	416	207-9	33	433	.269	.319	.436	98	-14	25-29	.976	-30	97	50	O802(488/169/156)	0	-9.0

YEAR	TM LG	G	AB	R	H	2B	3B	HR	RBI	BB-IB	HP	SO	AVG	OBP	SLG	AOPS	ABR	SB-CS	FA	FR	RNG	THR	GAMES AT POSITION	DL	BFW
Ressler, Larry	Lawrence P.; B8.10.1848 , France; D6.12.1918 Reading PA; d4.26																								
1875	Was NA	27	108	17	21	1	0	0	5	0	—	4	.194	.194	.204	40	-6	4-0	.831	3	281	210	O20(0/3/17),2b7	—	-0.2
Restelli, Dino	Dino Paolo "Dingo"; B9.23.1924 St.Louis MO; D8.8.2006 San Carlos CA; BR/TR/6´1.5˝/191; d6.14; Col Santa Clara																								
1949	Pit N	72	232	41	58	11	0	12	40	35	4	26	.250	.358	.453	113	5	3	.961	-0	103	83	O61(0/47/14)/1	0	0.3
1951	Pit N	21	38	1	7	1	0	1	3	2	0	4	.184	.225	.289	36	-4	0-0	.920	0	104	124	O11(8/4/0)	0	-0.4
Total	2	93	270	42	65	12	0	13	43	37	4	30	.241	.341	.430	103	1	3-0	.956	-0	103	88	O72(8/51/14)/1	0	-0.1
Restovich, Michael	Michael Jerome; B1.3.1979 Rochester MN; BR/TR/6´4˝/(233–250); [MinA97 2/61]; d9.18																								
2002	Min A	8	13	3	4	0	0	1	1	1-0	0	4	.308	.357	.538	129	0	1-0	1.000	0	111	0	O5(4/0/1),D2	0	0.1
2003	Min A	24	53	10	15	3	2	0	4	10-0	1	12	.283	.406	.415	113	2	0-0	1.000	-0	95	113	O17(3/0/14),D7	0	0.1
2004	Min A	29	47	9	12	3	0	2	6	4-0	0	10	.255	.314	.447	92	-1	0-0	1.000	-1	91	0	O19(12/0/7),D5	0	-0.2
2005	Col N	14	31	5	9	2	0	1	3	3-0	0	5	.290	.353	.452	97	0	0-0	1.000	1	131	0	O8(1/0/7)	0	0.0
	Pit N	52	84	10	18	3	1	2	5	8-0	0	24	.214	.283	.345	63	-5	0-0	.976	0	107	91	O31(14/0/20)	0	-0.5
	Year	66	115	15	27	5	1	3	8	11-0	0	29	.235	.302	.374	74	-5	0-0	.983	1	114	66	O39(15/0/27)	0	-0.5
2006	Chi N	10	12	0	2	1	0	0	1	1-0	0	5	.167	.231	.250	23	-1	0-0	1.000	-0	48	0	O3(1/0/2)	0	-0.2
Total	5	137	240	37	60	12	3	6	20	27-0	1	60	.250	.328	.400	87	-5	1-0	.991	-0	103	61	O83(35/0/51),D14	0	-0.7
Rettenmund, Merv	Mervin Weldon; B6.6.1943 Flint MI; BR/TR/5´10˝/(190–195); d4.14; C21; Col Ball St.																								
1968	Bal A	31	64	10	19	5	0	2	7	18-0	1	20	.297	.452	.469	181	8	1-1	1.000	-2	78	87	O23(4/13/13)	0	0.6
1969	†Bal A	95	190	27	47	10	3	4	25	28-1	0	28	.247	.338	.395	105	2	6-1	.991	-0	100	74	O78(45/18/21)	0	0.0
1970	†Bal A	106	338	60	109	17	2	18	58	38-1	3	59	.322	.394	.544	154	25	13-7	.976	5	111	107	O93(30/44/36)	0	2.7
1971	†Bal A	141	491	81	156	23	4	11	75	87-2	4	60	.318	.422	.448	146	35	15-6	.977	1	104	79	O134(46/40/72)	0	3.3
1972	Bal A	102	301	40	70	10	2	6	21	41-0	0	37	.233	.325	.339	94	-1	6-4	.989	2	104	102	O98(6/23/79)	15	-0.4
1973	†Bal A	95	321	59	84	17	2	9	44	57-4	4	38	.262	.378	.411	122	12	11-2	.985	5	116	70	O90(11/2/81)	0	1.4
1974	Cin N	80	208	30	45	6	0	6	28	37-1	2	39	.216	.337	.332	90	-2	5-1	1.000	-3	92	77	O69(0/9/60)	0	-0.7
1975	†Cin N	93	188	24	45	6	1	2	19	35-3	0	22	.239	.356	.314	87	-2	5-0	1.000	-1	101	28	O61(20/4/38)/3	0	-0.5
1976	SD N	86	140	16	32	7	0	2	11	29-0	0	23	.229	.361	.321	103	2	4-1	.977	6	127	261	O43(34/1/11)	0	0.8
1977	SD N	107	126	23	36	6	1	4	17	33-2	1	28	.286	.432	.444	152	12	1-2	1.000	-2	81	0	O27(23/1/3)/3	0	0.8
1978	Cal A	50	108	16	29	5	1	1	14	30-0	2	13	.269	.433	.361	130	7	0-3	.968	-2	89	0	O22(5/0/17),D18	0	0.3
1979	†Cal A	35	76	7	20	2	0	1	10	11-1	1	14	.263	.360	.329	91	0	1-0	1.000	-2	46	0	D17,O9(4/0/5)	0	-0.3
1980	Cal A	2	4	0	1	0	0	0	0	1-0	0	1	.250	.400	.250	84	0	0-0	ø	0	—	—	/D	0	0.0
Total	13	1023	2555	393	693	114	16	66	329	445-15	18	382	.271	.381	.406	123	98	68-28	.985	6	104	84	O747(228/155/436),D36,3b2	15	8.0
Retzer, Ken	Kenneth Leo; B4.30.1934 Wood River IL; BL/TR/6´0˝/(175–185); d9.9; Col Jefferson City (MO) JC																								
1961	Was A	16	53	7	18	4	0	1	3	4-0	0	5	.340	.386	.472	130	2	1-0	.988	0	73	211	C16	0	0.3
1962	Was A	109	340	36	97	11	2	8	37	26-4	0	21	.285	.334	.400	98	-2	2-0	.985	5	97	117	C99	0	0.9
1963	Was A	95	265	21	64	10	0	5	31	17-2	2	20	.242	.290	.336	76	-9	2-0	.981	-15	61	131	C81	0	-2.1
1964	Was A	17	32	1	3	0	0	0	1	5-1	1	4	.094	.237	.094	-4	-4	0-0	.971	2	84	407	C13	0	-0.2
Total	4	237	690	65	182	25	2	14	72	52-7	3	50	.264	.316	.367	87	-13	5-0	.983	-7	81	146	C209	0	-1.1
Revering, Dave	David Alvin; B2.12.1953 Roseville CA; BL/TR/6´4˝/205; [CinN71 7/170]; d4.8																								
1978	Oak A	152	521	49	141	21	3	16	46	26-5	0	55	.271	.303	.415	106	1	0-1	.989	7	120	88	1b138,D3	0	0.0
1979	Oak A	125	472	63	136	25	5	19	77	34-5	1	65	.288	.334	.483	124	14	1-4	.986	1	106	72	1b104,D18	15	0.7
1980	Oak A	106	376	48	109	21	5	15	62	32-6	0	37	.290	.344	.492	135	17	1-0	.989	0	102	74	1b95,D5	0	1.1
1981	Oak A	31	87	12	20	1	1	2	10	11-2	1	12	.230	.320	.333	93	-1	0-1	.995	-2	74	60	1b29,D2	0	-0.5
	†NY A	45	119	8	28	4	1	2	7	11-5	0	20	.235	.300	.336	84	-3	0-1	.994	5	153	94	1b44	0	0.0
	Year	76	206	20	48	5	2	4	17	22-7	1	32	.233	.309	.335	88	-3	0-2	.994	3	120	80	1b73,D2	0	-0.5
1982	NY A	14	40	2	6	2	0	0	2	3-2	0	4	.150	.205	.200	13	-5	0-0	1.000	-2	30	72	1b13/D	0	-0.7
	Tor A	55	135	15	29	6	0	5	18	22-1	0	30	.215	.321	.370	83	-3	0-3	1.000	-0	67	118	D49,1b4	0	-0.6
	Sea A	29	82	8	17	3	1	3	12	9-0	0	17	.207	.283	.378	78	-3	0-0	.986	-2	71	114	1b27	0	-0.6
	Year	98	257	25	52	11	1	8	32	34-3	0	51	.202	.292	.346	71	-10	0-3	.992	-4	59	102	D50,1b44	0	-1.9
Total	5	557	1832	205	486	83	16	62	234	148-26	2	240	.265	.318	.430	109	17	2-10	.989	8	107	81	1b454,D78	15	-0.6
Reville, Henry	Henry; B Baltimore MD; d10.14																								
1874	Bal NA	1	4	0	0	0	0	0	0	0	—	0	.000	.000	.000	-99	-1	0-0	1.000	1	627	0	/rf	—	0.0
Rexter, William	William H.; B1850 Brooklyn NY; D6.23.1898 Staten Island NY; d9.25																								
1875	Atl NA	1	4	0	0	0	0	0	0	0	—	0	.000	.000	.000	-99	-1	0-0	1.000	0	0	0	/rf	—	-0.1
Reyes, Gil	Gilberto Rolando (Polanco); B12.10.1963 Santo Domingo, D.R.; BR/TR/6´2˝/(175–205); d6.11; [DL 1992 Mon N 28]																								
1983	LA N	19	31	1	5	2	0	0	0	0-0	1	5	.161	.188	.226	14	-4	0-0	.944	0	111	137	C19	0	-0.3
1984	LA N	4	5	0	0	0	0	0	0	0-0	0	3	.000	.000	.000	-99	-1	0-0	1.000	-0	0	0	C2	0	-0.2
1985	LA N	6	1	0	0	0	0	0	0	1-0	1	1	.000	.667	.000	104	0	0-0	1.000	1	0	203	C6	0	0.2
1987	LA N	1	0	0	0	0	0	0	0	0-0	0	0	ø	ø	ø	ø	0	0-0	1.000	0	0	0	/C	0	0.0
1988	LA N	5	9	1	1	0	0	0	0	0-0	0	3	.111	.111	.111	-37	-2	0-0	1.000	0	207	0	C5	0	-0.1
1989	Mon N	4	5	0	1	0	0	0	1	0-0	0	1	.200	.200	.200	14	-1	0-0	1.000	0	102	0	C4	0	0.0
1991	Mon N	83	207	11	45	9	0	0	13	19-2	1	51	.217	.285	.261	56	-12	2-4	.975	13	134	171	C80	0	0.4
Total	7	122	258	13	52	11	0	0	14	20-2	3	64	.202	.266	.244	45	-20	2-4	.973	15	129	157	C117	28	0.0
Reyes, Jose	Jose Ariel (Ramirez); B2.26.1983 Barahona, D.R.; BB/TR/5´11˝/180; d9.13																								
2006	Chi N	4	5	0	1	0	0	0	2	0-0	0	3	.200	.200	.200	3	-1	0-0	1.000	1	0	0	C2	0	0.0
Reyes, Jose	Jose Bernabe; B6.11.1983 Villa Gonzalez, D.R.; BB/TR/6´0˝/(160–175); d6.10																								
2003	NY N	69	274	47	84	12	4	5	32	13-0	0	36	.307	.334	.434	104	0	13-3	.973	3	106	92	S69	28	1.0
2004	NY N	53	220	33	56	16	2	2	14	5-0	0	31	.255	.271	.373	66	-12	19-2	.980	-0	107	99	2b43,S10	119	-0.6
2005	NY N	161	696	99	190	24	**17**	7	58	27-0	2	78	.273	.300	.386	81	-24	**60**-15	.974	-15	93	106	S161	0	-1.9
2006	†NY N∗	153	647	122	194	30	**17**	19	81	53-6	1	81	.300	.354	.487	115	12	**64**-17	.971	-26	89	82	S149	0	0.5
Total	4	436	1837	301	524	82	40	33	185	98-6	3	226	.285	.321	.427	95	-24	156-37	.972	-38	94	94	S389,2b43	147	-1.0
Reyes, Nap	Napoleon Aguilera; B11.24.1919 Santiago de Cuba, Cuba; D9.15.1995 Miami FL; BR/TR/6´1˝/205; d5.19																								
1943	NY N	40	125	13	32	4	2	0	13	4	2	12	.256	.290	.320	76	-4	2	.994	-5	41	78	1b38/3	0	-1.2
1944	NY N	116	374	38	108	16	5	8	53	15	5	24	.289	.325	.422	109	3	2	.990	2	67	93	1b63,3b37,O3L	0	0.3
1945	NY N	122	431	39	124	15	4	5	44	25	**8**	26	.288	.338	.376	97	-3	1	.961	1	105	59	3b115,1b5	0	-0.1
1950	NY N	1	1	0	0	0	0	0	0	0	0	0	.000	.000	.000	-99	0	0	.667	-0	0	0	/1	0	-0.1
Total	4	279	931	90	264	35	11	13	110	44	15	62	.284	.326	.387	99	-4	5	.960	-2	110	67	3b153,1b107,O3L	0	-1.1
Reyes, Rene	Rene; B2.21.1978 Margarita, Venezuela; BB/TR/5´11˝/(210–215); d7.22																								
2003	Col N	53	116	13	30	7	1	2	7	5-0	0	19	.259	.287	.388	65	-6	2-1	.964	0	95	176	O36(11/5/24)	0	-0.6
2004	Col N	28	61	5	9	2	0	0	1	5-2	0	17	.148	.212	.180	3	-9	0-0	1.000	-1	88	120	O21(1/16/4)	0	-0.9
Total	2	81	177	18	39	9	1	2	8	10-2	0	36	.220	.261	.316	44	-15	2-1	.977	-0	92	155	O57(12/21/28)	0	-1.5
Reynolds, Carl	Carl Nettles; B2.1.1903 Larue TX; D5.29.1978 Houston TX; BR/TR/6´0˝/194; d9.1; Col Southwestern (TX)																								
1927	Chi A	14	42	5	9	3	0	1	7	5	1	7	.214	.313	.357	75	-2	1-2	1.000	2	134	75	O13(11/0/2)	—	-0.1
1928	Chi A	84	291	51	94	21	11	2	36	17	5	13	.323	.371	.491	126	10	15-3	.979	-0	102	85	O74(15/1/58)	—	0.6
1929	Chi A	131	517	81	164	24	12	11	67	20	4	37	.317	.348	.474	111	5	19-9	.949	-2	100	96	O130(13/21/98)	—	-0.5
1930	Chi A	138	563	103	202	25	18	22	104	20	7	39	.359	.388	.584	148	36	16-4	.975	4	105	97	O132(35/54/47)	—	2.9
1931	Chi A	118	462	71	134	24	14	6	77	24	6	26	.290	.333	.442	108	3	17-6	.949	-4	95	93	O109(11/18/90)	—	-0.5
1932	Was A	102	406	53	124	28	7	9	63	13	3	19	.305	.332	.475	108	2	8-4	.983	2	114	38	O95R	—	-0.1
1933	StL A	135	475	81	136	26	14	8	71	49	3	25	.286	.357	.451	106	3	5-4	.965	-2	101	64	O124(123/2/0)	—	-0.6
1934	Bos A	113	413	61	125	26	9	4	86	27	3	28	.303	.350	.438	95	-4	5-3	.977	-1	101	74	O100(2/66/33)	—	-0.8
1935	Bos A	78	244	33	66	13	4	6	35	24	0	20	.270	.336	.430	91	-4	4-1	.975	4	113	127	O64(3/1/60)	—	-0.3
1936	Was A	89	293	41	81	18	2	4	41	21	2	22	.276	.329	.392	82	-9	8-4	.968	1	100	124	O72(0/4/69)	—	-1.1
1937	Chi N	7	11	0	3	1	0	0	1	2	0	2	.273	.385	.364	100	0	0	.800	-0	99	0	O2L	—	0.0
1938	†Chi N	125	497	59	150	28	10	3	67	22	3	32	.302	.335	.416	103	1	9	.983	2	104	90	O125(63/83/4)	—	-0.3

YEAR	TM LG	G	AB	R	H	2B	3B	HR	RBI	BB-IB	HP	SO	AVG	OBP	SLG	AOPS	ABR	SB-CS	FA	FR	RNG	THR	GAMES AT POSITION	DL	BFW
1939	Chi N	88	281	33	69	10	6	4	44	16	5	38	.246	.298	.367	76	-11	5	.972	-1	100	85	O72(3/51/18)	—	-1.4
Total	13	1222	4495	672	1357	247	107	80	699	260	42	308	.302	.346	.458	107	30	112-40	.970	5	103	86	O1112(281/301/574)	—	-2.2
REYNOLDS, CHARLIE	Charles Lawrence; B5.1.1865 Williamsburg IN; D7.3.1944 Denver CO; BR/5´9˝/175; d5.8																								
1889	KC AA	1	4	1	1	0	0	0	1	0	0	1	.250	.250	.250	40	0	0	1.000	-1	—	—	/C	—	-0.1
	Bro AA	12	42	5	9	1	1	0	3	1	0	6	.214	.233	.286	47	-3	2	.892	0	—	—	C12	—	-0.2
	Year	13	46	6	10	1	1	0	4	1	0	7	.217	.234	.283	46	-4	2	.893	-1	—	—	C13	—	-0.3
REYNOLDS, DANNY	Daniel Vance "Squirrel"; B11.27.1919 Stony Point NC; BR/TR/5´11˝/158; d5.26																								
1945	Chi A	29	72	6	12	2	1	0	4	3	0	8	.167	.200	.222	23	-7	1-2	.947	2	109	94	S14,2b11	0	-0.5
REYNOLDS, DON	Donald Edward; B4.16.1953 Arkadelphia AR; BR/TR/5´8˝/180; [SDN75 18/410]; d4.7; b–Harold; Col Oregon																								
1978	SD N	57	87	8	22	2	0	0	10	15-2	0	14	.253	.363	.276	87	-1	1-0	.923	-1	77	159	O25(22/0/3)	16	-0.2
1979	SD N	30	45	6	10	1	2	0	6	7-1	0	6	.222	.321	.333	86	-1	0-1	.950	1	86	283	O14(7/5/2)	0	-0.1
Total	2	87	132	14	32	3	2	0	16	22-3	0	20	.242	.348	.295	87	-2	1-1	.935	-0	80	206	O39(29/5/5)	16	-0.3
REYNOLDS, CRAIG	Gordon Craig; B12.27.1952 Houston TX; BL/TR/6´1˝/175; [PitN71 1/22]; d8.1; OF(3/0/1)																								
1975	†Pit N	31	76	8	17	3	0	0	4	3-1	0	5	.224	.253	.263	43	-6	0-1	.969	3	107	90	S30	0	-0.1
1976	Pit N	7	4	1	1	0	0	1	1	0-0	0	0	.250	.250	1.000	238	1	0-0	.889	-0	106	100	S4/2	0	0.0
1977	Sea A	135	420	41	104	12	3	4	28	15-1	3	23	.248	.277	.319	63	-23	6-6	.955	8	107	110	S134	0	-0.2
1978	Sea A☆	148	548	57	160	16	7	5	44	36-1	3	41	.292	.336	.374	100	-1	9-6	.960	8	108	110	S146	0	2.3
1979	Hou N★	146	555	63	147	20	9	0	39	21-0	2	49	.265	.292	.333	75	-21	12-6	.965	-5	98	115	S143	0	-1.1
1980	†Hou N	137	381	34	86	9	6	3	28	20-1	0	39	.226	.262	.304	64	-21	2-1	.969	5	104	96	S135	0	-0.5
1981	†Hou N	87	323	43	84	10	**12**	4	31	12-2	0	31	.260	.286	.402	99	-4	3-3	.973	1	98	80	S85	0	0.6
1982	Hou N	54	118	16	30	2	3	1	7	11-3	1	9	.254	.321	.347	95	-1	3-1	.958	-4	95	86	S35,3b7	24	-0.2
1983	Hou N	65	98	10	21	3	0	1	6	6-1	0	10	.214	.260	.276	51	-7	0-1	.956	-7	91	79	2b26,3b15,S8/lf	0	-1.4
1984	Hou N	146	527	61	137	15	11	6	60	22-2	0	53	.260	.286	.364	88	-12	7-1	.965	24	112	118	S143/3	0	2.9
1985	Hou N	107	379	43	103	18	8	4	32	12-2	0	30	.272	.293	.393	93	-6	4-4	.977	16	109	115	S102/2	0	2.0
1986	†Hou N	114	313	32	78	7	3	6	41	12-5	0	31	.249	.274	.348	73	-13	3-1	.978	-8	88	87	S98,1b5,3b4,O2(1/0/1)/P	0	-1.3
1987	Hou N	135	374	35	95	17	3	4	28	30-8	0	44	.254	.303	.348	77	-13	5-1	.970	-9	90	71	S129,3b2	0	-1.0
1988	Hou N	78	161	20	41	7	0	1	14	8-2	0	23	.255	.290	.317	77	-5	3-0	.970	-3	100	122	S22,3b19,2b11,1b10	0	-0.7
1989	Hou N	101	189	16	38	4	0	2	14	19-5	0	18	.201	.274	.254	54	-12	1-0	.979	7	119	110	2b29,S26,3b10,1b5/Plf	0	-0.2
Total	15	1491	4466	480	1142	143	65	42	377	227-34	9	406	.256	.291	.345	80	-144	58-32	.966	36	102	102	S1240,2b68,3b58,1b20,O4L,P2	24	1.1
REYNOLDS, HAROLD	Harold Craig; B11.26.1960 Eugene OR; BB/TR/5´11˝/165; [SeaA80 S1/2]; d9.2; b–Don; Col Canada (CA) JC																								
1983	Sea A	20	59	8	12	4	1	0	1	2-0	0	9	.203	.226	.305	44	-5	0-2	.975	-1	94	112	2b18	0	-0.5
1984	Sea A	10	10	3	3	0	0	0	0	0-0	1	1	.300	.364	.300	86	0	1-1	1.000	2	127	132	2b6	0	0.2
1985	Sea A	67	104	15	15	3	1	0	6	17-0	0	14	.144	.264	.192	27	-10	3-2	.960	5	116	84	2b61	0	-0.3
1986	Sea A	126	445	46	99	19	4	1	24	29-0	3	42	.222	.275	.290	53	-29	30-12	.977	30	**115**	**122**	2b126	0	1.0
1987	Sea A★	160	530	73	146	31	8	1	35	39-0	2	34	.275	.325	.370	80	-15	**60**-20	.977	24	111	108	2b160	0	2.3
1988	Sea A★	158	598	61	169	26	**11**	4	41	51-1	2	51	.283	.340	.383	98	-2	35-29	.977	8	102	104	2b158	0	0.8
1989	Sea A	153	613	87	184	24	9	0	43	55-1	3	45	.300	.359	.369	103	3	25-18	.980	**25**	**111**	107	2b151/D	0	3.1
1990	Sea A	160	642	100	162	36	5	5	55	81-3	3	52	.252	.336	.347	91	-5	31-16	.978	20	**106**	100	2b160	0	2.1
1991	Sea A	161	631	95	160	34	6	3	57	72-2	5	63	.254	.332	.341	87	-9	28-8	.978	8	98	121	2b159/D	0	0.7
1992	Sea A	140	458	55	113	23	3	3	33	45-1	3	41	.247	.316	.330	81	-11	15-12	.982	8	102	94	2b134/lfD	0	-0.1
1993	Bal A	145	485	64	122	20	4	4	47	66-3	4	47	.252	.343	.334	80	-12	12-11	.986	3	99	**121**	2b141/D	0	-0.3
1994	Cal A	74	207	33	48	10	1	0	11	23-0	1	18	.232	.310	.290	55	-13	10-7	.996	-11	85	69	2b65,D3	0	-2.1
Total	12	1374	4782	640	1233	230	53	21	353	480-11	27	417	.258	.327	.341	82	-108	250-138	.979	122	105	107	2b1339,D7/lf	0	6.9
REYNOLDS, R. J.	Robert James; B4.19.1959 Sacramento CA; BB/TR/6´0˝/(175–190); [LAN80*2/36]; d9.1; Col Sacramento (CA) City																								
1983	LA N	24	55	5	13	0	0	2	11	3-1	0	11	.236	.267	.345	71	-2	5-0	.931	0	87	222	O18(9/5/7)	0	-0.2
1984	LA N	73	240	24	62	12	2	2	24	14-0	1	38	.258	.300	.350	83	-6	7-5	.973	-2	90	104	O63(25/19/34)	15	-1.1
1985	LA N	73	207	22	55	10	4	0	25	13-0	1	31	.266	.308	.353	87	-4	6-3	.970	-1	99	87	O54(31/5/24)	30	-0.7
	Pit N	31	130	22	40	5	3	3	17	9-1	1	18	.308	.357	.462	128	4	12-2	.958	1	105	137	O31(29/8/0)	0	0.6
	Year	104	337	44	95	15	7	3	42	22-1	2	49	.282	.327	.395	104	1	18-5	.965	0	101	106	O85(60/13/24)	0	-0.1
1986	Pit N	118	402	63	108	30	2	9	48	40-4	1	78	.269	.335	.420	105	3	16-9	.955	-7	94	27	O112(84/12/44)	0	-0.8
1987	Pit N	117	335	47	87	24	1	7	51	34-8	0	80	.260	.323	.400	91	-4	14-1	.993	-4	83	118	O99(29/0/72)	0	-0.9
1988	Pit N	130	323	35	80	14	2	6	51	20-3	0	62	.248	.288	.359	87	-6	15-2	.974	1	94	177	O95(19/1/79)	0	-0.6
1989	Pit N	125	363	45	98	16	2	6	48	34-8	1	66	.270	.331	.375	106	3	22-5	.990	2	100	119	O98(5/30/72)	0	0.6
1990	†Pit N	95	215	25	62	10	1	0	19	23-1	0	35	.288	.354	.344	97	0	12-2	.972	-3	88	93	O59(13/24/26)	15	-0.2
Total	8	786	2270	288	605	121	17	35	294	190-26	5	419	.267	.321	.381	96	-12	109-29	.973	-13	93	106	O629(244/104/358)	60	-3.3
REYNOLDS, RONN	Ronn Dwayne; B9.28.1958 Wichita KS; BR/TR/6´0˝/(200–205); [NYN80 5/105]; d9.29; Col Arkansas																								
1982	NY N	2	4	0	0	0	0	0	0	1-0	0	1	.000	.200	.000	-39	-1	0-0	1.000	-2	153	0	C2	0	-0.2
1983	NY N	24	66	4	13	1	0	0	2	8-1	0	12	.197	.280	.212	40	-5	0-0	.942	-5	76	109	C24	0	-0.9
1985	NY N	28	43	4	9	2	0	0	1	0-0	1	18	.209	.227	.256	36	-4	0-0	.990	1	116	178	C25	0	-0.3
1986	Phi N	43	126	8	27	4	0	3	10	5-0	0	30	.214	.242	.317	52	-9	0-0	.991	-5	71	84	C42	0	-1.2
1987	Hou N	38	102	5	17	4	0	1	7	3-0	0	29	.167	.189	.235	12	-13	0-1	.975	-2	77	103	C38	0	-1.4
1990	SD N	8	15	1	1	1	0	0	1	1-0	0	6	.067	.125	.133	-29	-3	0-0	1.000	-1	73	113	C8	0	-0.4
Total	6	143	356	22	67	12	0	4	21	18-1	1	96	.188	.228	.256	32	-35	0-1	.977	-13	81	106	C139	0	-4.4
REYNOLDS, TOMMIE	Tommie D; B8.15.1941 Arizona LA; BR/TR (BB 1967p)/6´2˝/(190–195); d9.5; C8; Col San Diego (CA) City																								
1963	KC A	8	19	1	1	1	0	0	0	1-0	1	7	.053	.143	.105	-28	-3	0-0	.800	-1	83	0	O5L	0	-0.5
1964	KC A	31	94	11	19	1	0	2	9	10-0	2	22	.202	.292	.277	58	-5	0-0	.976	-0	95	171	O25L,3b3	0	-0.7
1965	KC A	90	270	34	64	11	3	1	22	36-1	0	41	.237	.327	.311	83	-5	9-2	.982	6	108	168	O83(77/0/6)/3	0	-0.3
1967	NY N	101	136	16	28	1	0	2	9	11-3	3	26	.206	.278	.257	56	-8	1-1	.971	1	108	142	O72(42/13/21),3b5/C	0	-1.0
1969	Oak A	107	315	51	81	10	0	2	20	34-1	8	29	.257	.343	.308	87	-4	1-3	.979	5	112	75	O89(81/0/8)	26	-0.5
1970	Cal A	59	120	11	30	3	1	1	6	6-0	1	10	.250	.291	.317	70	-5	1-1	.969	1	123	56	O32(4/1/28)/3	0	-0.6
1971	Cal A	45	86	4	16	3	0	2	8	9-1	3	6	.186	.286	.291	68	-4	0-1	.978	2	106	143	O26(6/0/23)/3	0	-0.4
1972	Mil A	72	130	13	26	5	1	2	13	10-0	1	25	.200	.262	.300	68	-5	0-0	.961	4	134	92	O41(36/0/6)/13	0	-0.4
Total	8	513	1170	141	265	35	5	12	87	117-6	19	166	.226	.306	.296	73	-39	12-8	.973	16	111	118	O373(276/14/92),3b12/1C	26	-4.4
REYNOLDS, BILL	William Dee; B8.14.1884 Eastland TX; D6.5.1924 Carnegie OK; BR/TR/6´0˝/185; d9.15																								
1913	NY A	5	5	0	0	0	0	0	0	0	0	1	.000	.000	.000	-99	-1	0	.917	-0	*72*	*57*	C5	—	-0.1
1914	NY A	4	5	0	2	0	0	0	0	0	0	3	.400	.400	.400	141	0	0	1.000	0	*85*	*138*	/C	—	0.1
Total	2	9	10	0	2	0	0	0	0	0	0	4	.200	.200	.200	19	-1	0	.941	0	*76*	*81*	C6	—	0.0
RHAWN, BOBBY	Robert John "Rocky"; B2.13.1919 Catawissa PA; D6.9.1984 Danville PA; BR/TR/5´8˝/180; d9.17																								
1947	NY N	13	45	7	14	3	0	1	3	8	0	1	.311	.415	.444	128	2	0	.913	1	119	76	2b8,3b5	0	0.3
1948	NY N	36	44	11	12	2	1	1	8	8	0	6	.273	.385	.432	120	1	3	.872	-1	104	75	S14,3b7	0	0.1
1949	NY N	14	29	8	5	0	0	0	2	7	0	2	.172	.333	.172	40	-2	1	.959	2	127	134	2b8	0	0.0
	Pit N	3	7	0	1	0	0	0	0	0	0	0	.143	.143	.143	-23	-1	0	.889	0	108	0	3b2	0	-0.1
	Year	17	36	8	6	0	0	0	2	7	0	2	.167	.302	.167	29	-3	1	.959	2	127	134	2b8,3b2	0	-0.1
	Chi A	24	73	12	15	4	1	0	5	12	0	8	.205	.318	.288	63	-4	0-1	.959	1	101	84	3b19,S3	0	-0.3
Total	3	90	198	38	47	9	2	2	18	35	0	17	.237	.352	.333	84	-4	4-1	.963	3	103	111	3b33,S17,2b16	0	0.0
RHEAM, CY	Kenneth Johnston; B9.28.1893 Pittsburgh PA; D10.23.1947 Pittsburgh PA; BR/TR/6´0˝/175; d5.20; Col Indiana (PA)																								
1914	Pit F	73	214	15	45	5	3	0	20	9	0	33	.210	.242	.262	38	-23	6	.976	-6	59	53	1b43,3b13,2b11/lf	—	-3.1
1915	Pit F	34	69	10	12	0	0	1	5	1	0	7	.174	.186	.217	13	-9	4	.959	1	129	81	O22(12/4/6)/1	—	-1.0
Total	2	107	283	25	57	5	3	1	25	10	0	40	.201	.229	.251	32	-32	10	.976	-4	58	52	1b44,O23(13/4/6),3b13,2b11	—	-4.1
RHIEL, BILLY	William Joseph; B8.16.1900 Youngstown OH; D8.16.1946 Youngstown OH; BR/TR/5´11˝/175; d4.20; Col Newberry																								
1929	Bro N	76	205	27	57	9	4	4	25	19	0	25	.278	.339	.420	89	-4	0	.979	-2	95	59	2b47,3b7,S2	—	-0.4
1930	Bos N	20	47	3	8	4	0	0	4	2	0	5	.170	.204	.255	11	-7	0	.947	-2	70	67	3b13,2b2	—	-0.8
1932	Det A	85	250	30	70	13	3	3	38	17	1	23	.280	.328	.392	82	-7	2-0	.956	-2	85	147	3b37,1b12,O8L/2	—	-0.8

YEAR	TM LG	G	AB	R	H	2B	3B	HR	RBI	BB-IB	HP	SO	AVG	OBP	SLG	AOPS	ABR	SB-CS	FA	FR	RNG	THR	GAMES AT POSITION	DL	BFW
1933	Det A	19	17	1	3	0	1	0	1	5	0	4	.176	.364	.294	75	-1	0-0	1.000	0	137	0	/lf	—	0.0
Total	4	200	519	61	138	26	8	7	68	43	1	57	.266	.323	.387	78	-19	2-0	.949	-6	88	136	3b57,2b50,1b12,O9L,S2	—	-2.0
RHODES, DUSTY	James Lamar; B5.13.1927 Mathews AL; BL/TR/6´0˝/180; d7.15																								
1952	NY N	67	176	34	44	8	1	10	36	23	1	33	.250	.340	.477	123	5	1-0	.917	-2	98	79	O56(55/2/0)	0	0.0
1953	NY N	76	163	18	38	7	0	11	30	10	0	28	.233	.277	.479	91	-3	0-1	.965	2	95	182	O47(25/0/22)	0	-0.4
1954	†NY N	82	164	31	56	7	3	15	50	18	1	25	.341	.410	.695	181	19	1-0	.984	-1	96	49	O37(33/2/1)	0	1.5
1955	NY N	94	187	22	57	5	2	6	32	27-2	0	26	.305	.389	.449	122	7	1-1	.986	-1	94	74	O45L	0	0.3
1956	NY N	111	244	20	53	10	3	8	33	30-2	0	41	.217	.301	.381	83	-6	0-0	.958	-0	87	178	O68(64/0/5)	0	-1.0
1957	NY N	92	190	20	39	5	1	4	19	18-3	1	34	.205	.276	.305	57	-12	0-0	1.000	-5	82	0	O44(22/0/23)	0	-1.9
1959	SF N	54	48	1	9	2	0	0	7	5-3	0	9	.188	.259	.229	34	-5	0-0	ø	0	—	—	/H	0	-0.5
Total	7	576	1172	146	296	44	10	54	207	131-10	3	196	.253	.328	.445	104	5	3-2	.963	-8	92	99	O297(244/4/51)	0	-2.0
RHODES, KARL	Karl Derrick "Tuffy"; B8.21.1968 Cincinnati OH; BL/TL/5´11˝/(170–195); [HouN86 3/68]; d8.7																								
1990	Hou N	38	86	12	21	6	1	1	3	13-3	0	12	.244	.340	.372	99	0	4-1	.955	1	107	119	O30(19/9/5)	0	0.1
1991	Hou N	44	136	7	29	3	1	1	12	14-3	1	26	.213	.289	.272	63	-7	2-2	.958	3	115	135	O44R	0	-0.6
1992	Hou N	5	4	0	0	0	0	0	0	0-0	0	2	.000	.000	.000	-99	-1	0-0	ø	-0	0	0	/O(1/0/1)	0	-0.1
1993	Hou N	5	2	0	0	0	0	0	0	0-0	0	0	.000	.000	.000	-99	-1	0-0	1.000	0	110	0	O4(1/2/1)	0	-0.1
	Chi N	15	52	12	15	2	1	3	7	11-0	0	9	.288	.413	.538	153	4	2-0	.970	-0	93	140	O14(6/14/1)	0	0.5
	Year	20	54	12	15	2	1	3	7	11-0	0	9	.278	.400	.519	146	4	2-0	.971	-0	94	132	O18(7/16/2)	0	0.4
1994	Chi N	95	269	39	63	17	0	8	19	33-1	1	64	.234	.318	.387	83	-6	6-4	.967	-3	90	113	O76(15/67/1)	0	-0.9
1995	Chi N	13	16	2	2	0	0	0	2	0-0	0	4	.125	.118	.125	-34	-3	0-0	.889	-0	118	0	O11L	0	-0.3
	Bos A	10	25	2	2	1	0	0	1	3-0	0	4	.080	.179	.120	-20	-5	0-0	.947	-1	101	0	O9C	0	-0.5
Total	6	225	590	74	132	29	3	13	44	74-7	2	121	.224	.310	.349	78	-19	14-7	.960	0	101	114	O189(53/101/53)	0	-1.9
RHOMBERG, KEVIN	Kevin Jay; B11.22.1955 Dubuque IA; BR/TR/6´0˝/175; [CleA77 14/349]; d9.1; Col St. Francis (IL)																								
1982	Cle A	16	18	3	6	0	0	1	1	2-0	0	4	.333	.400	.500	145	1	0-2	.900	1	113	508	O7L/3D	0	0.1
1983	Cle A	12	21	2	10	0	0	0	2	2-0	0	4	.476	.500	.476	170	2	1-1	1.000	-1	82	0	O9(8/1/0)/D	0	0.1
1984	Cle A	13	8	0	2	0	0	0	0	0-0	0	3	.250	.250	.250	38	-1	0-0	1.000	0	129	0	O7L/12D	0	0.0
Total	3	41	47	5	18	0	0	1	3	4-0	0	11	.383	.423	.447	139	2	1-3	.963	1	101	148	O23(22/1/0),D6/213	0	0.2
RHYNE, HAL	Harold J.; B3.30.1899 Paso Robles CA; D1.7.1971 Orangevale CA; BR/TR/5´8.5˝/163; d4.18																								
1926	Pit N	109	366	46	92	14	3	2	39	35	6	21	.251	.327	.322	71	-14	1	.967	5	99	123	2b66,S44/3	—	-0.3
1927	†Pit N	62	168	21	46	5	0	0	17	14	0	9	.274	.330	.304	66	-8	0	.963	-8	79	95	2b45,3b10,S7	—	-1.3
1929	Bos A	120	346	41	87	24	5	0	38	25	4	14	.251	.309	.350	71	-15	4-1	.935	-2	97	112	S113/3rf	—	-0.5
1930	Bos A	107	296	34	60	8	5	0	23	25	2	19	.203	.269	.264	37	-29	1-4	.944	3	107	**117**	S107	—	-1.6
1931	Bos A	147	565	75	154	34	3	0	51	57	2	41	.273	.341	.343	85	-11	3-3	**.963**	18	**115**	88	S147	—	1.6
1932	Bos A	71	207	26	47	12	5	0	14	23	2	14	.227	.310	.333	69	-10	3-2	.966	5	113	96	S55,3b4/2	—	-0.1
1933	Chi A	39	83	9	22	1	1	0	10	5	1	9	.265	.315	.301	67	-4	1-1	.955	2	108	125	2b19,3b13,S2	—	-0.2
Total	7	655	2031	252	508	98	22	2	192	184	17	127	.250	.318	.323	69	-91	13-11	.950	23	107	104	S475,2b131,3b29/rf	—	-2.4
RICE, DEL	Delbert; B10.27.1922 Portsmouth OH; D1.26.1983 Buena Park CA; BR/TR/6´2˝/(190–195); d5.2; M1/C7																								
1945	StL N	83	253	27	66	17	3	1	28	16	3	33	.261	.313	.364	86	-5	0	.994	5	*97*	*120*	C77	0	0.4
1946	†StL N	55	139	10	38	8	1	1	12	8	0	16	.273	.313	.367	89	-2	0	.977	1	*152*	*51*	C53	0	0.1
1947	StL N	97	261	28	57	7	3	12	44	36	1	40	.218	.315	.406	87	-6	1	.981	3	*126*	*74*	C94	0	0.2
1948	StL N	100	290	24	57	10	1	4	34	37	5	46	.197	.298	.279	54	-18	1	**.996**	11	***292***	*73*	C99	0	-0.2
1949	StL N	92	284	25	67	16	1	4	29	30	5	40	.236	.320	.342	74	-10	0	.992	1	*127*	*66*	C92	0	-0.5
1950	StL N	130	414	39	101	20	3	9	54	43	5	65	.244	.323	.372	78	-13	0	.984	7	*134*	*91*	C130	0	0.1
1951	StL N	122	374	34	94	13	1	9	47	34	3	26	.251	.319	.364	83	-9	0-0	.985	4	*124*	*90*	C120	0	0.1
1952	StL N	147	495	43	128	27	2	11	65	33	6	38	.259	.313	.388	93	-5	0-1	.992	2	*139*	*95*	C147	0	0.4
1953	StL N✱	135	419	32	99	22	1	6	37	48	6	49	.236	.323	.337	72	-16	0-0	.988	-5	*87*	*91*	C135	0	-1.4
1954	StL N	56	147	13	37	10	1	2	16	16	0	21	.252	.321	.374	81	-4	0-1	.985	1	*165*	*87*	C52	0	-0.1
1955	StL N	20	59	6	12	3	0	1	7	7-0	0	6	.203	.284	.305	58	-4	0-0	.964	-4	*89*	*92*	C18	0	-0.7
	Mil N	27	71	5	14	0	1	2	7	6-2	0	12	.197	.260	.310	53	-5	0-0	.981	0	*117*	*152*	C22	0	-0.4
	Year	47	130	11	26	3	1	3	14	13-2	0	18	.200	.271	.308	55	-9	0-0	.973	-4	*104*	*125*	C40	0	-1.1
1956	Mil N	71	188	15	40	9	1	3	17	18-7	0	34	.213	.282	.319	65	-9	0-0	.983	2	*156*	*81*	C65	0	-0.5
1957	†Mil N	54	144	15	33	1	1	9	20	17-7	0	37	.229	.309	.438	106	0	0-0	.992	3	100	85	C48	0	0.6
1958	Mil N	43	121	10	27	7	0	1	8	8-1	0	30	.223	.271	.306	57	-8	0-0	.995	0	135	43	C38	0	-0.6
1959	Mil N	13	29	3	6	0	0	0	1	2-0	0	3	.207	.250	.207	28	-3	0-0	.956	-0	265	0	C9	57	-0.3
1960	Chi N	18	52	2	12	3	0	0	4	2-1	0	7	.231	.255	.288	50	-4	0-0	.968	-5	55	134	C18	0	-0.8
	StL N	1	2	0	0	0	0	0	0	1-0	0	0	.000	.333	.000	1	0	0-0	1.000	-0	0	0	/C	0	-0.1
	Year	19	54	2	12	3	0	0	4	3-1	0	7	.222	.259	.278	49	-4	0-0	.970	-5	0	0	C19	0	-0.9
	Bal A	1	1	0	0	0	0	0	0	0-0	0	0	.000	.000	.000	-99	0	0-0	1.000	-0	0	0	/C	0	-0.1
1961	LA A	44	83	11	20	4	0	4	11	20-5	0	19	.241	.385	.434	107	2	0-1	.994	-1	80	208	C30	0	0.2
Total	17	1309	3826	342	908	177	20	79	441	382-23	34	522	.237	.312	.356	78	-119	2-3	.987	26	*137*	*88*	C1249	57	-3.6
RICE, SAM	Edgar Charles; B2.20.1890 Morocco IN; D10.13.1974 Rossmoor MD; BL/TR/5´9˝/150; d8.7; Mil 1918; HF1963; ▲																								
1915	Was A	4	8	0	3	0	0	0	0	0	0	1	.375	.375	.375	122	1	0	.889	0	131	592	P4	—	0.0
1916	Was A	58	197	26	59	8	3	1	17	15	1	13	.299	.352	.386	123	5	4	.957	2	117	94	O46(4/0/42),P5	—	0.4
1917	Was A	155	586	77	177	25	7	0	69	50	3	41	.302	.360	.369	124	17	35	.960	5	103	124	O155R	—	1.5
1918	Was A	7	23	3	8	1	0	0	3	2	0	0	.348	.400	.391	141	1	1	1.000	3	94	446	O6R	—	0.4
1919	Was A	141	557	80	179	23	9	3	71	42	7	26	.321	.376	.411	122	16	26	.962	5	113	92	O141R	—	1.4
1920	Was A	**153**	624	83	211	29	9	3	80	39	4	23	.338	.381	.428	117	15	**63**-30	.960	**17**	**121**	124	O153C	—	2.3
1921	Was A	143	561	83	185	39	13	4	79	38	9	10	.330	.382	.467	121	17	26-12	.964	6	109	101	O141(0/137/4)	—	1.7
1922	Was A	**154**	633	91	187	37	13	6	69	48	2	13	.295	.347	.423	105	3	20-9	.951	2	98	143	O154C	—	0.0
1923	Was A	148	595	117	188	35	**18**	3	75	57	6	12	.316	.381	.450	125	20	20-8	.970	7	107	108	O147R	—	1.6
1924	†Was A	154	646	106	**216**	39	14	1	76	46	4	24	.334	.382	.443	116	14	24-13	.967	1	106	89	O154(0/34/123)	—	0.4
1925	†Was A	**152**	649	111	227	31	13	1	87	37	4	10	.350	.388	.442	113	11	26-11	.968	7	106	122	O152(0/29/133)	—	0.7
1926	Was A	**152**	641	98	**216**	32	14	3	76	42	2	20	.337	.380	.445	117	14	24-23	.961	9	106	148	O152(0/44/120)	—	1.0
1927	Was A	142	603	98	179	33	14	2	65	36	0	11	.297	.336	.408	93	-8	19-6	.975	-2	100	81	O139(1/0/138)	—	-1.8
1928	Was A	148	616	95	202	32	15	2	55	49	2	15	.328	.379	.438	115	13	16-3	.973	-10	88	73	O147(1/0/147)	—	-0.6
1929	Was A	150	616	119	199	39	10	1	62	55	4	9	.323	.382	.424	106	7	16-8	.970	3	99	132	O147R	—	-0.1
1930	Was A	147	593	121	207	35	13	1	73	55	3	14	.349	.407	.457	118	18	13-8	.963	3	106	101	O145(0/15/133)	—	0.9
1931	Was A	120	413	81	128	21	8	0	42	35	1	11	.310	.365	.400	100	0	6-5	.970	2	107	76	O105(10/11/85)	—	-0.4
1932	Was A	106	288	58	93	16	7	1	34	32	0	6	.323	.391	.438	116	7	7-4	.972	2	98	143	O69(10/14/48)	—	0.5
1933	†Was A	73	85	19	25	4	3	1	12	2	2	7	.294	.326	.447	104	0	0-2	1.000	4	120	285	O39(8/10/23)	—	0.2
1934	Cle A	97	335	48	98	19	1	1	33	28	2	9	.293	.351	.364	83	-8	5-1	.963	-6	90	35	O78(13/0/65)	—	-1.7
Total	20	2404	9269	1514	2987	498	184	34	1078	708	56	275	.322	.374	.427	113	163	351-143	.965	58	105	110	O2270(47/601/1657),P9	—	8.4
RICE, HAL	Harold Housten "Hoot"; B2.11.1924 Morganette WV; D12.22.1997 Bloomington IN; BL/TR/6´1˝/195; d9.25																								
1948	StL N	8	31	3	10	1	2	0	3	2	0	4	.323	.364	.484	121	1	0	1.000	-0	105	0	O8L	0	0.0
1949	StL N	40	46	3	9	2	1	1	9	3	0	7	.196	.245	.348	55	-3	0	1.000	0	89	286	O10L	0	-0.3
1950	StL N	44	128	12	27	3	1	2	11	10	0	10	.211	.268	.297	46	-10	0	.972	1	100	124	O37(33/0/4)	0	-1.2
1951	StL N	69	236	20	60	12	1	4	38	24	0	22	.254	.323	.364	84	-5	0-1	.953	-0	98	118	O63(48/0/16)	0	-1.0
1952	StL N	98	295	37	85	14	5	7	45	16	0	26	.288	.325	.441	110	3	1-3	.972	-2	96	92	O81(77/4/5)	0	-0.5
1953	StL N	8	8	0	2	0	0	0	0	0	0	3	.250	.250	.250	31	-1	0-0	ø	0	—	—	/H	0	-0.1
	Pit N	78	286	39	89	16	1	4	42	17	0	22	.311	.350	.416	99	0	0-1	.973	8	109	213	O70(68/0/2)	0	0.3
	Year	86	294	39	91	16	1	4	42	17	0	25	.310	.347	.412	97	-1	0-1	.973	8	109	213	O70(68/0/2)	0	0.2
1954	Pit N	28	81	10	14	4	1	1	9	14	0	24	.173	.295	.284	52	-6	0-2	1.000	3	112	190	O24(24/0/2)	0	-0.5
	Chi N	51	72	5	11	0	0	0	5	8	0	15	.153	.235	.153	4	-10	0-0	.897	-0	94	176	O24(3/0/21)	0	-1.1
	Year	79	153	15	25	4	1	1	14	22	0	39	.163	.267	.222	29	-16	0-2	.966	3	106	185	O48(27/0/23)	0	-1.6
Total	7	424	1183	129	307	52	12	19	162	94	0	133	.260	.314	.372	82	-31	1-7	.969	10	102	145	O317(271/4/50)	0	-4.4

RICE, HARRY Harry Francis; B11.22.1901 Ware Station IL; D1.1.1971 Portland OR; BL/TR/5´9˝/185; d4.18; OF(28/465/421)

YEAR	TM LG	G	AB	R	H	2B	3B	HR	RBI	BB-IB	HP	SO	AVG	OBP	SLG	AOPS	ABR	SB-CS	FA	FR	RNG	THR	GAMES AT POSITION	DL	BFW
1923	StL A	4	3	0	0	0	0	0	0	0	0	0	.000	.000	.000	-95	-1	0-0	ø	0	—	—	/H	—	-0.1
1924	StL A	54	93	19	26	7	0	0	15	7	3	5	.280	.350	.355	77	-3	1-3	.917	-1	94	125	3b15,2b4,1b2,S2,O2(1/0/1)	—	-0.3
1925	StL A	103	354	87	127	25	8	11	47	54	5	15	.359	.450	.568	149	28	8-7	.984	3	102	142	O85(3/6/76),1b3/C23	—	2.2
1926	StL A	148	578	86	181	27	10	9	59	63	4	40	.313	.384	.441	110	9	10-11	.970	5	102	149	O133(0/47/87),3b8,2b4,S2	—	0.3
1927	StL A	137	520	90	149	26	9	7	68	50	2	21	.287	.351	.412	94	-5	5-4	.938	11	104	**196**	O130(0/44/87),3b7	—	-0.3
1928	Det A	131	510	87	154	21	12	6	81	44	2	27	.302	.360	.425	104	2	20-12	.962	-5	101	70	O129C,3b2	—	-0.8
1929	Det A	130	536	97	163	33	7	6	69	61	4	23	.304	.379	.425	106	7	6-11	.960	1	98	119	O127C,3b3	—	0.0
1930	Det A	37	128	16	39	6	0	2	24	19	2	8	.305	.403	.398	102	1	0-3	.944	-1	101	72	O35(19/0/16)	—	-0.3
	NY A	100	346	62	103	17	5	7	74	31	3	21	.298	.361	.436	106	3	3-3	.969	2	103	109	O87(4/83/0),1b6/3	—	0.1
	Year	137	474	78	142	23	5	9	98	50	5	29	.300	.372	.426	105	4	3-6	.964	1	102	99	O122(23/83/16),1b6/3	—	-0.2
1931	Was A	47	162	32	43	5	6	0	15	12	1	10	.265	.320	.370	81	-5	2-1	.968	0	102	90	O42(1/19/23)	—	-0.7
1933	Cin N	143	510	44	133	19	6	0	54	35	6	24	.261	.316	.322	84	-11	4	**.991**	4	104	106	O141(0/10/131)/3	—	-1.6
Total	10	1034	3740	620	1118	186	63	48	506	376	32	194	.299	.368	.421	104	25	59-55	.966	19	102	124	O911C,3b38,1b11,2b9,S4/C	—	-1.5

RICE, JIM James Edward; B3.8.1953 Anderson SC; BR/TR/6´2˝/(200–217); [BosA71 1/15]; d8.19; C7

YEAR	TM LG	G	AB	R	H	2B	3B	HR	RBI	BB-IB	HP	SO	AVG	OBP	SLG	AOPS	ABR	SB-CS	FA	FR	RNG	THR	GAMES AT POSITION	DL	BFW
1974	Bos A	24	67	6	18	2	1	1	13	4-0	1	12	.269	.307	.373	92	-1	0-0	.800	-0	85	0	D16,O3L	0	-0.2
1975	Bos A	144	564	92	174	29	4	22	102	36-7	4	122	.309	.350	.491	126	18	10-5	1.000	-4	87	91	O90L,D54	0	0.8
1976	Bos A	153	581	75	164	25	8	25	85	28-2	4	123	.282	.315	.482	119	11	8-5	.967	-2	93	109	O98L,D54	0	0.1
1977	Bos A★	160	644	104	206	29	15	**39**	114	53-10	8	120	.320	.376	**.593**	144	37	5-4	.956	-1	94	124	D116,O44(19/0/27)	0	3.0
1978	Bos A★	**163**	677	121	**213**	25	**15**	**46**	**139**	58-7	5	126	.315	.370	**.600**	153	**45**	7-5	.989	4	95	158	O114(101/1/15),D49	0	4.2
1979	Bos A★	158	619	117	201	39	6	39	130	57-4	4	97	.325	.381	.596	152	44	9-4	.984	-6	87	83	O125(124/0/1),D33	0	3.1
1980	Bos A✱	124	504	81	148	22	6	24	86	30-5	4	87	.294	.336	.504	121	12	8-3	.988	-1	92	115	O109L,D15	35	0.7
1981	Bos A	**108**	451	51	128	18	1	17	62	34-3	3	76	.284	.333	.441	115	8	2-2	.988	-2	95	110	O108L	0	0.1
1982	Bos A	145	573	86	177	24	5	24	97	55-6	7	98	.309	.375	.494	129	23	0-1	.969	-6	88	112	O145L	0	1.0
1983	Bos A★	155	626	90	191	34	1	**39**	**126**	52-10	6	102	.305	.361	.550	137	31	0-2	.984	10	103	170	O151L,D4	0	3.3
1984	Bos A★	159	657	98	184	25	7	28	122	44-8	1	102	.280	.323	.467	111	8	4-0	.989	4	101	110	O157L,D2	0	0.5
1985	Bos A★	140	546	85	159	20	3	27	103	51-5	2	75	.291	.349	.487	122	16	2-0	.964	-8	86	95	O130L,D7	0	0.3
1986	†Bos A★	157	618	98	200	39	2	20	110	62-5	4	78	.324	.384	.490	137	33	0-1	.977	8	103	162	O156L/D	0	3.3
1987	Bos A	108	404	66	112	14	0	13	62	45-3	7	77	.277	.357	.408	100	1	1-1	.977	1	85	197	O94L,D12	0	-0.3
1988	†Bos A	135	485	57	128	18	3	15	72	48-2	3	89	.264	.330	.406	102	1	1-1	.968	-2	88	0	D112,O19L	0	-0.5
1989	Bos A	56	209	22	49	10	2	3	28	13-0	1	39	.234	.276	.344	71	-8	1-0	ø	0	0	0	D55	82	-1.0
Total	16	2089	8225	1249	2452	373	79	382	1451	670-77	64	1423	.298	.352	.502	126	279	58-34	.980	-4	94	125	O1543(1504/1/43),D530	117	18.4

RICE, LEN Leonard Oliver; B9.2.1918 Lead SD; D6.13.1992 Sonora CA; BR/TR/6´0˝/175; d4.26

YEAR	TM LG	G	AB	R	H	2B	3B	HR	RBI	BB-IB	HP	SO	AVG	OBP	SLG	AOPS	ABR	SB-CS	FA	FR	RNG	THR	GAMES AT POSITION	DL	BFW
1944	Cin N	10	4	1	0	0	0	0	0	0	0	0	.000	.000	.000	-99	-1	0	1.000	0	*0*	*0*	C5	0	-0.1
1945	Chi N	32	99	10	23	3	0	0	7	5	0	8	.232	.269	.263	49	-7	2	.976	1	*157*	*55*	C29	0	-0.5
Total	2	42	103	11	23	3	0	0	7	5	0	8	.223	.259	.252	44	-8	2	.977	1	*153*	*54*	C34	0	-0.6

RICE, BOB Robert Turnbull; B5.28.1899 Philadelphia PA; D2.20.1986 Elizabethtown PA; BR/TR/5´10˝/170; d9.1

YEAR	TM LG	G	AB	R	H	2B	3B	HR	RBI	BB-IB	HP	SO	AVG	OBP	SLG	AOPS	ABR	SB-CS	FA	FR	RNG	THR	GAMES AT POSITION	DL	BFW
1926	Phi N	19	54	3	8	0	1	0	10	3	0	4	.148	.193	.185	2	-8	0	.864	0	100	242	3b15,2b2,S2	—	-0.7

RICHARD, CHRIS Christopher Robert; B6.7.1974 San Diego CA; BL/TL/6´2˝/(185–190); [StLN95 19/519]; d7.17; Col Oklahoma St.

YEAR	TM LG	G	AB	R	H	2B	3B	HR	RBI	BB-IB	HP	SO	AVG	OBP	SLG	AOPS	ABR	SB-CS	FA	FR	RNG	THR	GAMES AT POSITION	DL	BFW
2000	StL N	6	16	1	2	0	0	1	1	2-0	0	2	.125	.222	.313	32	-2	0-0	1.000	0	121	0	O3(1/0/2),1b2	0	-0.2
	Bal A	56	199	38	55	14	2	13	36	15-3	4	38	.276	.335	.563	129	8	7-5	.989	-7	50	106	1b53/rfD	0	-0.4
2001	Bal A	136	483	74	128	31	3	15	61	45-4	8	100	.265	.335	.435	107	5	11-9	1.000	5	115	102	O96(0/36/69),D20,1b18	15	0.5
2002	Bal A	50	155	15	36	11	0	4	21	12-0	2	30	.232	.292	.381	82	-4	0-3	1.000	-1	63	0	D36,1b9	122	-0.8
2003	Col N	19	27	3	6	1	1	1	3	3-0	0	6	.222	.300	.444	80	-1	0-1	1.000	0	110	0	O3L/1	151	-0.1
Total	4	267	880	131	227	57	6	34	122	77-7	14	176	.258	.324	.452	106	6	18-18	1.000	-2	115	95	O103(4/36/72),1b83,D57	288	-1.0

RICHARD, LEE Lee Edward "Bee Bee"; B9.18.1948 Lafayette LA; BR/TR (BB 1975)/5´11˝/165; [ChiA70 1/6]; d4.7; Col Southern A&M

YEAR	TM LG	G	AB	R	H	2B	3B	HR	RBI	BB-IB	HP	SO	AVG	OBP	SLG	AOPS	ABR	SB-CS	FA	FR	RNG	THR	GAMES AT POSITION	DL	BFW
1971	Chi A	87	260	38	60	7	3	2	17	20-0	1	46	.231	.286	.304	66	-12	8-9	.920	13	119	92	S68,O16C	0	0.6
1972	Chi A	11	29	5	7	0	0	0	1	0-0	0	7	.241	.241	.241	43	-2	1-0	1.000	-0	57	268	O6C/S	0	-0.3
1974	Chi A	32	67	5	11	1	0	0	1	5-1	0	8	.164	.222	.179	16	-7	0-0	.821	-2	95	104	3b12,S6,2b3/rfD	0	-0.9
1975	Chi A	43	45	11	9	0	1	0	5	4-0	0	7	.200	.265	.244	44	-3	2-3	1.000	-1	97	0	3b12,S9,2b5,D5	0	-0.4
1976	StL N	66	91	12	16	4	2	0	5	4-1	0	9	.176	.211	.264	33	-8	1-0	.975	-3	100	101	2b26,S12/3	0	-1.0
Total	5	239	492	71	103	12	6	2	29	33-2	1	77	.209	.259	.270	50	-32	12-12	.923	6	113	102	S96,2b34,3b25,O23(0/22/1),D10	0	-2.0

RICHARDS, GENE Eugene; B9.29.1953 Monticello SC; BL/TL/6´0˝/175; [SDN75*1/1]; d4.6; Col South Carolina St.

YEAR	TM LG	G	AB	R	H	2B	3B	HR	RBI	BB-IB	HP	SO	AVG	OBP	SLG	AOPS	ABR	SB-CS	FA	FR	RNG	THR	GAMES AT POSITION	DL	BFW
1977	SD N	146	525	79	152	16	11	5	32	60-12	2	80	.290	.363	.390	114	10	56-12	.963	3	93	200	O109(72/41/1),1b32	0	1.7
1978	SD N	154	555	90	171	26	12	4	45	64-7	4	80	.308	.381	.420	134	26	37-17	.965	-8	91	88	O124(113/26/0),1b26	0	1.6
1979	SD N	150	545	77	152	17	9	4	41	47-6	8	62	.279	.343	.365	100	0	24-8	.973	-4	97	73	O132(20/102/10)	0	-0.4
1980	SD N	158	642	91	193	26	8	4	41	61-7	2	73	.301	.363	.385	117	15	61-16	.979	7	100	174	O156(156/0/1)	0	2.3
1981	SD N	104	393	47	113	14	**12**	3	42	53-3	1	44	.288	.373	.407	132	17	20-8	.975	-2	88	148	O102L	0	1.3
1982	SD N	132	521	63	149	13	8	3	28	36-1	2	52	.286	.333	.359	100	-2	30-20	.977	-1	104	98	O103L,1b25	27	-0.9
1983	SD N	95	233	37	64	11	3	3	22	17-1	1	17	.275	.325	.386	100	-1	14-5	.980	1	110	57	O54L	0	-0.1
1984	SF N	87	135	18	34	4	0	0	4	18-2	0	28	.252	.340	.281	78	-3	5-3	.940	-1	103	59	O26(15/1/11)	0	-0.5
Total	8	1026	3549	502	1028	127	63	26	255	356-39	20	436	.290	.357	.383	113	62	247-89	.972	-5	97	124	O806(634/170/23),1b83	27	5.0

RICHARDS, FRED Fred Charles "Fuzzy"; B11.3.1927 Warren OH; BL/TL/6´1.5˝/185; d9.15

YEAR	TM LG	G	AB	R	H	2B	3B	HR	RBI	BB-IB	HP	SO	AVG	OBP	SLG	AOPS	ABR	SB-CS	FA	FR	RNG	THR	GAMES AT POSITION	DL	BFW
1951	Chi N	10	27	1	8	2	0	0	4	2	0	3	.296	.345	.370	91	0	0-0	1.000	1	162	44	1b9	0	0.1

RICHARDS, PAUL Paul Rapier; B11.21.1908 Waxahachie TX; D5.4.1986 Waxahachie TX; BR/TR/6´1.5˝/180; d4.17; M12

YEAR	TM LG	G	AB	R	H	2B	3B	HR	RBI	BB-IB	HP	SO	AVG	OBP	SLG	AOPS	ABR	SB-CS	FA	FR	RNG	THR	GAMES AT POSITION	DL	BFW
1932	Bro N	3	8	0	0	0	0	0	0	0	0	2	.000	.000	.000	-99	-2	0	1.000	2	*122*	*102*	C3	—	0.0
1933	NY N	51	87	4	17	3	0	0	10	3	0	12	.195	.222	.230	30	-8	0	.989	1	*112*	*157*	C36	—	-0.6
1934	NY N	42	75	10	12	1	0	0	3	13	0	8	.160	.284	.173	26	-8	0	1.000	2	*118*	*125*	C37	—	-0.4
1935	NY N	7	4	0	1	0	0	0	0	2	0	1	.250	.500	.250	110	0	0	1.000	1	*0*	*272*	C4	—	0.1
	Phi A	85	257	31	63	10	1	4	29	24	0	12	.245	.310	.339	68	-13	0-0	.977	-6	*72*	*105*	C79	—	-1.3
1943	Det A	100	313	32	69	7	1	5	33	38	1	35	.220	.307	.297	71	-11	1-0	**.986**	16	*102*	***139***	C100	0	1.3
1944	Det A	95	300	24	71	13	0	3	37	35	1	30	.237	.318	.310	76	-9	8-3	.979	17	***191***	***147***	C90	0	1.5
1945	†Det A	83	234	26	60	12	1	3	32	19	1	31	.256	.315	.355	88	-4	4-0	**.995**	9	*122*	*102*	C83	0	1.2
1946	Det A	57	139	13	28	5	2	0	11	23	0	18	.201	.315	.266	60	-7	2-0	.997	10	*112*	*102*	C54	0	0.6
Total	8	523	1417	140	321	51	5	15	155	157	3	149	.227	.305	.301	68	-62	15-3	.987	52	*121*	*125*	C486	0	2.4

RICHARDSON B Boston MA; 5´4˝/136; d7.10

YEAR	TM LG	G	AB	R	H	2B	3B	HR	RBI	BB-IB	HP	SO	AVG	OBP	SLG	AOPS	ABR	SB-CS	FA	FR	RNG	THR	GAMES AT POSITION	DL	BFW
1884	CP U	1	4	0	0	0	0	0	—	0	—	—	.000	.000	.000	-99	-1	—	.667	-1	46	0	/2	—	-0.2

RICHARDSON, HARDY Abram Harding "Old True Blue"; B4.21.1855 Clarksboro NJ; D1.14.1931 Utica NY; BR/TR/5´9.5˝/170; d5.1; OF(375/158/11); ▲

YEAR	TM LG	G	AB	R	H	2B	3B	HR	RBI	BB-IB	HP	SO	AVG	OBP	SLG	AOPS	ABR	SB-CS	FA	FR	RNG	THR	GAMES AT POSITION	DL	BFW
1879	Buf N	**79**	336	54	95	18	10	0	37	16	—	30	.283	.315	.396	130	11	—	.843	-7	93	150	3b78/C	—	0.6
1880	Buf N	83	343	48	89	18	8	0	17	14	—	37	.259	.289	.359	116	5	—	.848	-5	98	64	3b81,C5	—	0.3
1881	Buf N	**83**	344	62	100	18	9	2	53	12	—	27	.291	.315	.413	129	11	—	.914	23	**217**	88	O79C,2b5/S3	—	2.8
1882	Buf N	83	354	61	96	20	8	2	57	11	—	33	.271	.293	.390	115	5	—	.898	19	109	75	2b83	—	2.5
1883	Buf N	92	399	73	124	34	7	1	56	22	—	20	.311	.347	.439	134	17	—	.903	16	113	80	2b92	—	3.1
1884	Buf N	102	439	85	132	27	9	6	60	22	—	41	.301	.334	.444	138	18	—	.897	6	106	65	2b71,O24C,3b5,1b3	—	2.3
1885	Buf N	96	426	90	136	19	11	6	44	20	—	22	.319	.350	.458	154	24	—	.905	9	107	69	2b50,O48(1/47/0)/SP	—	3.0
1886	Det N	125	538	125	**189**	27	11	**11**	61	46	—	27	.351	.402	.504	168	43	42	.899	8	123	43	O80L,2b42,P4,S3,3b2	—	4.5
1887	†Det N	120	543	131	178	25	18	8	94	31	2	40	.328	.366	.484	129	19	29	.941	20	104	105	2b64,O59(58/1/0)	—	3.3
1888	Det N	58	266	60	77	18	2	6	32	17	1	23	.289	.335	.440	144	13	13	.925	-0	94	99	2b58	—	1.5
1889	Bos N	132	536	122	163	33	10	6	79	48	5	44	.304	.367	.437	116	10	47	.924	10	105	115	2b86,O46L	—	1.9
1890	Bos P	**130**	555	126	181	26	14	13	**146**	52	0	46	.326	.384	.494	125	16	42	.950	2	56	66	O124L,S6/1	—	1.2
1891	Bos AA	74	278	45	71	9	4	7	52	40	1	26	.255	.351	.392	114	5	16	.955	-1	48	98	O60(57/1/2),3b9,S4,1b3	—	0.3
1892	Was N	10	37	2	4	0	0	0	0	5	0	3	.108	.214	.108	-2	-4	2	.941	0	0	0	O7L,3b2/2	—	-0.5
	NY N	64	248	36	53	11	5	2	34	21	1	26	.214	.278	.323	83	-6	14	.931	3	105	77	2b33,O17(2/6/9),1b9,S6	—	-0.1
	Year	74	285	38	57	11	5	2	34	26	1	29	.200	.269	.295	72	-10	16	.933	3	104	75	2b34,O24(9/6/9),1b9,S6,3b2	—	-0.6
Total	14	1331	5642	1120	1688	303	126	70	822	377	10	445	.299	.344	.435	129	187	205	.915	102	106	86	2b585,O544L,3b178,S21,1b16,C6,P5	—	26.7

YEAR	TM LG	G	AB	R	H	2B	3B	HR	RBI	BB-IB	HP	SO	AVG	OBP	SLG	AOPS	ABR	SB-CS	FA	FR	RNG	THR	GAMES AT POSITION	DL	BFW
RICHARDSON, NOLEN	Clifford Nolen; B1.18.1903 Chattanooga TN; D9.25.1951 Athens GA; BR/TR/6´1.5˝/170; d4.16; Col Georgia																								
1929	Det A	13	21	2	4	0	0	0	2	2	0	1	.190	.261	.190	18	-3	1-1	.839	-4	58	46	S13	—	-0.6
1931	Det A	38	148	13	40	9	2	0	16	6	0	3	.270	.299	.358	70	-7	2-1	.946	-1	109	30	3b38	—	-0.6
1932	Det A	69	155	13	34	5	2	0	12	9	0	13	.219	.262	.277	38	-15	5-2	.986	7	111	110	3b65,S4	—	-0.5
1935	NY A	12	46	3	10	1	1	0	5	3	0	1	.217	.265	.283	44	-4	0-0	.922	-5	67	65	S12	—	-0.8
1938	Cin N	35	100	8	29	4	0	0	10	3	0	4	.290	.311	.330	78	-3	0	.966	0	101	81	S35	—	-0.1
1939	Cin N	1	3	0	0	0	0	0	0	0	0	0	.000	.000	.000	-99	-1	0	1.000	0	89	155	/S	—	0.0
Total	6	168	473	39	117	19	5	0	45	23	0	22	.247	.282	.309	55	-33	8-4	.969	-2	110	74	3b103,S65	—	-2.6
RICHARDSON, DANNY	Daniel; B1.25.1863 Elmira NY; D9.12.1926 New York NY; BR/TR/5´8˝/165; d5.22; M1; OF(41/51/51); ▲																								
1884	NY N	74	277	36	70	8	1	1	27	16	—	17	.253	.294	.300	85	-5	—	.907	2	176	153	O55(11/7/37),S19	—	-0.3
1885	NY N	49	198	26	52	9	3	0	25	10	—	14	.263	.298	.338	107	2	—	.950	0	69	0	O22(10/2/12),3b21,P9	—	0.2
1886	NY N	68	237	43	55	9	1	1	27	17	—	21	.232	.283	.291	74	-7	12	.953	1	64	0	O64(20/42/2),P5/S32	—	-0.7
1887	NY N	122	450	79	125	19	10	3	62	36	4	25	.278	.337	.384	105	4	41	.928	18	109	106	2b108,3b14/P	—	2.1
1888	†NY N	135	561	82	127	16	7	8	61	15	1	35	.226	.248	.323	82	-13	35	**.942**	9	96	97	2b135	—	0.1
1889	†NY N	125	497	88	139	22	8	7	100	46	1	37	.280	.342	.398	105	2	32	.934	15	102	108	2b125	—	1.9
1890	NY P	123	528	102	135	12	9	4	80	37	2	19	.256	.307	.335	66	-30	37	.900	14	107	112	S68,2b56	—	-1.0
1891	NY N	123	516	85	139	18	5	4	51	33	0	27	.269	.313	.347	96	-4	28	.952	**45**	**114**	122	2b114,S9	—	4.0
1892	Was N	142	551	48	132	13	4	3	58	25	1	45	.240	.274	.294	74	-19	25	.931	**45**	111	126	S93,2b49/3M	—	3.0
1893	Bro N	54	206	36	46	6	2	0	27	13	3	18	.223	.279	.272	49	-15	7	.949	-12	77	90	2b46,3b5,S3	—	-2.1
1894	Lou N	116	430	51	109	17	2	1	40	35	5	31	.253	.317	.309	55	-31	8	.916	5	98	121	S107,2b10	—	-1.5
Total	11	1131	4451	676	1129	149	52	32	558	283	17	289	.254	.301	.332	81	-116	225	.940	142	103	104	2b644,S300,O141C,3b42,P15	—	5.7
RICHARDSON, JEFF	Jeffrey Scott; B8.26.1965 Grand Island NE; BR/TR/6´2˝/(175–180); [CinN86 7/176]; d7.14; Col Louisiana Tech																								
1989	Cin N	53	125	10	21	4	0	2	11	10-0	1	23	.168	.234	.248	37	-10	1-0	.969	-11	76	83	S39,3b8	0	-2.0
1991	Pit N	6	4	0	1	0	0	0	0	0-0	0	3	.250	.250	.250	41	0	0-0	ø	-1	0	0	3b3,S2	0	-0.1
1993	Bos A	15	24	3	5	2	0	0	2	1-0	0	3	.208	.240	.292	40	-2	0-0	1.000	4	164	96	2b8,S5/3D	127	0.2
Total	3	74	153	13	27	6	0	2	13	11-0	1	29	.176	.235	.255	38	-12	1-0	.971	-8	77	86	S46,3b12,2b8,D2	127	-1.9
RICHARDSON, KEN	Kenneth Franklin; B5.2.1915 Orleans IN; D12.7.1987 Woodland Hills CA; BR/TR/5´10.5˝/187; d4.14																								
1942	Phi A	6	15	1	1	0	0	0	0	2	0	0	.067	.176	.067	-30	-3	0-0	1.000	0	88	596	O3(1/0/2)/13	0	-0.3
1946	Phi N	6	20	1	3	1	0	0	2	0	0	2	.150	.150	.200	-1	-3	0	.939	-1	95	29	2b6	0	-0.4
Total	2	12	35	2	4	1	0	0	2	2	0	2	.114	.162	.143	-14	-6	0-0	.939	-1	95	29	2b6,O3(1/0/2)/31	0	-0.7
RICHARDSON, BOBBY	Robert Clinton; B8.19.1935 Sumter SC; BR/TR/5´9˝/(160–173); d8.5																								
1955	NY A	11	26	2	4	0	0	0	3	2-0	0	0	.154	.214	.154	0	-4	1-1	.864	-3	59	30	2b6,S4	0	-0.7
1956	NY A	5	7	1	1	0	0	0	0	0-0	0	1	.143	.143	.143	-25	-1	0-0	1.000	1	57	102	2b5	0	-0.1
1957	†NY A☆	97	305	36	78	11	1	0	19	9-3	0	26	.256	.274	.298	58	-18	1-3	.979	2	101	103	2b93	0	-1.2
1958	†NY A	73	182	18	45	6	2	0	14	8-0	0	5	.247	.276	.302	62	-10	1-3	.973	3	96	108	2b51,3b13,S2	0	-0.5
1959	NY A☆	134	469	53	141	18	6	2	33	26-3	0	20	.301	.335	.377	99	-2	5-5	.970	-2	98	115	2b109,S14,3b12	0	0.5
1960	†NY A	150	460	45	116	12	3	1	26	35-6	0	19	.252	.303	.298	68	-22	6-6	.973	-13	94	111	2b141,3b11	0	-2.7
1961	†NY A	162	662	80	173	17	5	3	49	30-1	2	23	.261	.295	.316	67	-34	9-7	.978	-4	91	**135**	2b161	0	-2.4
1962	†NY A★	161	692	99	**209**	38	5	8	59	37-1	1	24	.302	.337	.406	103	1	11-9	.982	-3	101	116	2b161	0	1.2
1963	†NY A★	151	630	72	167	20	6	3	48	25-0	2	22	.265	.294	.330	76	-22	15-1	.984	13	**105**	**123**	2b150	0	0.7
1964	†NY A★	159	679	90	181	25	4	4	50	28-1	0	36	.267	.294	.333	73	-25	11-2	.982	-13	94	110	2b157/S	0	-2.4
1965	NY A★	160	664	76	164	28	2	6	47	37-4	1	39	.247	.287	.322	74	-24	7-5	.981	1	97	121	2b158	0	-1.0
1966	NY A★	149	610	71	153	21	3	7	42	25-1	1	28	.251	.280	.330	78	-19	6-6	.980	7	108	101	2b147,3b2	0	-0.1
Total	12	1412	5386	643	1432	196	37	34	390	262-20	7	243	.266	.299	.335	77	-180	73-48	.979	-12	98	115	2b1339,3b38,S21	0	-8.7
RICHARDSON, TOM	Thomas Mitchell; B8.7.1883 Louisville IL; D11.15.1939 Onawa IA; BR/TR/6´0˝/190; d8.2																								
1917	StL A	1	1	0	0	0	0	0	0	0	0	0	.000	.000	.000	-99	0	0	ø	0	—	—	/H	—	0.0
RICHARDSON, BILL	William Henry; B1.24.1878 Salem IN; D11.6.1949 Sullivan IN; BR/TR/5´11˝/200; d9.20																								
1901	StL N	15	52	7	11	2	0	2	7	6	0	—	.212	.293	.365	95	0	1	.981	-1	58	95	1b15	—	-0.2
RICHARDT, MIKE	Michael Anthony; B5.24.1958 Los Angeles CA; BR/TR/6´0˝/(160–170); [TexA78 S1/10]; d8.30; Col Fresno (CA) City; [DL 1985 Hou N 182]																								
1980	Tex A	22	71	2	16	2	0	0	8	1-0	0	7	.225	.236	.254	35	-7	0-0	.978	-3	92	75	2b20/D	0	-0.9
1982	Tex A	119	402	34	97	10	0	3	43	23-1	1	42	.241	.281	.289	60	-23	9-1	.988	11	105	101	2b98,D15,O6L	15	-0.5
1983	Tex A	22	83	9	13	2	1	1	7	2-0	0	11	.157	.174	.241	14	-10	2-1	.992	3	99	116	2b20	83	-0.6
1984	Tex A	6	9	0	1	0	0	0	0	1-0	0	1	.111	.200	.111	-11	-1	0-1	1.000	0	87	267	2b4	0	-0.1
	Hou N	16	15	1	4	1	0	0	2	0-0	0	1	.267	.267	.333	72	-1	0-0	ø	0	—	—	/H	15	-0.1
Total	4	185	580	46	131	15	1	4	60	27-1	1	62	.226	.259	.276	50	-42	11-3	.988	11	102	102	2b142,D16,O6L	295	-2.2
RICHBOURG, LANCE	Lance Clayton; B12.18.1897 DeFuniak Springs FL; D9.10.1975 Crestview FL; BL/TR/5´10.5˝/160; d7.4; Col Florida																								
1921	Phi N	10	5	2	1	1	0	0	0	0	0	3	.200	.200	.400	51	0	1-1	1.000	1	175	0	2b4	—	0.0
1924	Was A	15	32	3	9	2	1	0	1	2	0	6	.281	.324	.406	90	-1	0-0	1.000	1	100	240	O7R	—	0.0
1927	Bos N	115	450	57	139	12	9	2	34	22	1	30	.309	.342	.389	104	0	24	.953	-4	100	74	O110(0/3/107)	—	-1.3
1928	Bos N	148	612	105	206	26	12	2	52	62	2	39	.337	.399	.428	123	22	11	.972	4	114	52	O148R	—	1.3
1929	Bos N	139	557	76	170	24	13	3	56	42	1	26	.305	.355	.411	93	-7	7	.971	5	**108**	97	O134(2/0/132)	—	-1.3
1930	Bos N	130	529	81	161	23	8	3	54	19	2	31	.304	.331	.395	77	-21	13	.971	-2	105	56	O128R	—	-3.0
1931	Bos N	97	286	32	82	11	6	2	29	19	0	14	.287	.331	.388	96	-3	9	.981	-2	102	40	O71(15/0/56)	—	-0.9
1932	Chi N	44	148	22	38	2	2	1	21	8	0	4	.257	.295	.318	65	-8	0	.986	-2	91	58	O33(1/3/29)	—	-1.2
Total	8	698	2619	378	806	101	51	13	247	174	6	153	.308	.352	.400	97	-18	65-1	.970	-1	106	67	O631(18/6/607),2b4	—	-6.4
RICHIE, ROB	Robert Eugene; B9.5.1965 Reno NV; BL/TR/6´2˝/190; [DetA87 2/53]; d8.19; Col Nevada–Reno																								
1989	Det A	19	49	6	13	4	2	1	10	5-1	0	10	.265	.333	.490	132	2	0-1	.917	-1	88	139	O13(11/0/2),D4	0	0.1
RICHMOND, DON	Donald Lester; B10.27.1919 Gillett PA; D5.24.1981 Elmira NY; BL/TR/6´1˝/175; d9.16; Mil 1942–45																								
1941	Phi A	9	35	3	7	1	1	0	5	0	0	1	.200	.200	.286	28	-4	0-2	.957	-1	98	195	3b9	0	-0.5
1946	Phi A	16	62	3	18	3	0	1	9	0	0	10	.290	.290	.387	89	-1	1-0	.940	-1	90	27	3b16	0	-0.2
1947	Phi A	19	21	2	4	1	1	0	4	3	0	3	.190	.292	.333	72	-1	0-0	.500	-2	53	0	3b4/2	0	-0.3
1951	StL N	12	34	3	3	1	0	1	4	3	0	3	.088	.162	.206	-2	-5	0-1	1.000	3	119	116	3b11	0	-0.3
Total	4	56	152	11	32	6	2	2	22	6	0	17	.211	.241	.316	51	-11	1-3	.957	-2	99	91	3b40/2	0	-1.3
RICHMOND, LEE	J Lee; B5.5.1857 Sheffield OH; D10.1.1929 Toledo OH; TL/5´10˝/155; d9.27; Col Brown; ▲																								
1879	Bos N	1	6	0	2	0	0	0	1	0	—	1	.333	.333	.333	118	0	—	1.000	0	106	0	/P	—	0.0
1880	Wor N	77	309	44	70	8	4	0	34	9	—	32	.227	.248	.278	72	-10	—	.827	-8	82	49	P74,O20(1/1/18)	—	-0.5
1881	Wor N	61	252	31	63	5	1	0	28	10	—	10	.250	.279	.278	71	-9	—	.937	1	113	79	P53,O11(0/2/9)	—	-0.2
1882	Wor N	55	228	50	64	8	9	2	28	9	—	11	.281	.308	.421	128	6	—	.889	3	124	66	P48,O11(1/1/9)	—	0.2
1883	Pro N	49	194	41	55	8	6	1	19	15	—	19	.284	.335	.402	120	4	—	.714	-8	37	0	O41(33/3/5),P12	—	-0.5
1886	Cin AA	8	29	3	8	0	0	0	3	3	0	—	.276	.344	.276	92	0	0	.400	-3	0	0	O7C,P3	—	-0.3
Total	6	251	1018	169	262	29	20	3	113	46	0	73	.257	.289	.334	94	-9	0	.886	-15	103	58	P191,O90(35/14/41)	—	-1.3
RICHMOND, JOHN	John H.; B3.5.1854 PA; TR/5´9˝/170; d4.22																								
1875	Ath NA	29	125	29	25	2	0	0	12	1	—	4	.200	.206	.216	42	-8	1-0	.814	-3	79	136	2b17,O11(2/3/6),C3	—	-1.0
1879	Syr N	62	254	31	54	8	4	1	23	4	—	24	.213	.225	.287	76	-5	—	.875	-7	90	102	O35(4/29/2),S28,C2	—	-1.1
1880	Bos N	32	129	12	32	3	1	0	9	2	—	18	.248	.260	.287	88	-2	—	.844	-7	81	178	S31/cf	—	-0.7
1881	Bos N	27	98	13	27	2	2	1	12	6	—	7	.276	.317	.367	120	2	—	.969	-0	61	100	O25(0/24/1),S2	—	0.1
1882	Cle N	41	140	12	24	6	2	0	11	11	—	27	.171	.232	.243	54	-6	—	.917	3	143	0	O41C	—	-0.4
	Phi AA	18	65	8	12	2	2	0	4	11	—	—	.185	.303	.277	91	0	—	.892	-0	94	0	O18(0/17/1)	—	-0.1
1883	Col AA	92	385	63	109	7	8	0	—	25	—	—	.283	.327	.343	126	13	—	**.877**	28	**123**	88	S91,O2C	—	**3.8**
1884	Col AA	105	398	57	100	13	7	3	—	35	3	—	.251	.317	.342	125	14	—	.866	-8	93	114	S105	—	0.8
1885	Pit AA	34	131	14	27	2	2	0	12	8	2	—	.206	.262	.252	64	-5	—	.849	-9	89	102	S23,O11(0/8/3)	—	-1.2
Total	7	411	1600	210	385	43	28	5	71	102	5	76	.241	.288	.312	101	11	—	.866	0	99	104	S280,O133(4/122/7),C2	—	1.2

YEAR	TM LG	G	AB	R	H	2B	3B	HR	RBI	BB-IB	HP	SO	AVG	OBP	SLG	AOPS	ABR	SB-CS	FA	FR	RNG	THR	GAMES AT POSITION	DL	BFW
RICHTER, AL	Allen Gordon; B2.7.1927 Norfolk VA; BR/TR/5´11˝/(165–175); d9.23																								
1951	Bos A	5	11	1	1	0	0	0	0	3	0	0	.091	.286	.091	5	-1	0-0	1.000	2	112	232	S3	0	0.0
1953	Bos A	1	0	0	0	0	0	0	0	0	0	0	ø	ø	ø	ø	0	0-0	1.000	0	93	443	/S	0	0.0
Total	2	6	11	1	1	0	0	0	0	3	0	0	.091	.286	.091	5	-1	0-0	1.000	2	110	254	S4	0	0.0
RICHTER, JOHN	John Marcellus; B2.8.1873 Louisville KY; D10.4.1927 Louisville KY; 6´0˝/178; d10.6																								
1898	Lou N	3	13	1	2	0	0	0	0	0	0	—	.154	.154	.154	-12	-2	0	.929	0	108	195	3b3	—	-0.1
RICKERT, JOE	Joseph Francis "Diamond Joe"; B12.12.1876 London OH; D10.15.1943 Springfield OH; BR/TR/5´10.5˝/165; d10.12																								
1898	Pit N	2	6	0	1	0	0	0	0	0	0	—	.167	.167	.167	-5	-1	0	1.000	1	0	0	O2L	—	-0.1
1901	Bos N	13	60	6	10	1	2	0	1	3	0	—	.167	.206	.250	29	-6	1	.974	2	107	231	O13L	—	-0.5
Total	2	15	66	6	11	1	2	0	1	3	0	—	.167	.203	.242	27	-7	1	.979	2	89	193	O15L	—	-0.6
RICKERT, MARV	Marvin August "Twitch"; B1.8.1921 Longbranch WA; D6.3.1978 Oakville WA; BL/TR/6´2˝/195; d9.10; Mil 1943–45																								
1942	Chi N	8	26	5	7	0	0	0	1	1	0	5	.269	.296	.269	69	-1	0	1.000	1	106	154	O6C	0	-0.1
1946	Chi N	111	392	44	103	18	3	7	47	28	1	54	.263	.314	.378	98	-3	3	.972	-4	97	59	O104(75/19/10)	0	-1.4
1947	Chi N	71	137	7	20	0	0	2	15	15	0	17	.146	.230	.190	13	-18	0	.982	1	99	106	O30(18/3/9),1b7	0	-1.8
1948	Cin N	8	6	0	1	0	0	0	0	0	0	0	.167	.167	.167	-10	-1	0	ø	0	—	—	/H	0	-0.1
	†Bos N	3	13	1	3	0	1	0	2	0	1	1	.231	.286	.385	81	-1	0	1.000	1	109	324	O3L	0	0.0
	Year	11	19	1	4	0	1	0	2	0	1	1	.211	.250	.316	54	-1	0	1.000	1	109	324	O3L	0	-0.1
1949	Bos N	100	277	44	81	18	3	6	49	23	0	38	.292	.347	.444	117	6	1	.981	5	107	162	O75(50/3/25),1b12	0	0.7
1950	Pit N	17	20	0	3	0	0	0	4	0	0	4	.150	.150	.150	-20	-4	0	ø	-0	0	0	O3R	0	-0.4
	Chi A	84	278	38	66	9	2	4	27	21	0	42	.237	.291	.327	60	-18	0-1	.968	-2	105	52	O78(18/0/63)/1	0	-2.2
Total	6	402	1149	139	284	45	9	19	145	88	2	161	.247	.302	.352	79	-40	4-1	.976	1	102	93	O299(164/31/110),1b20	0	-5.3
RICKETTS, DAVE	David William; B7.12.1935 Pottstown PA; BB/TR/6´2˝/(190–195); d9.25; C19; b–Dick; Col Duquesne																								
1963	StL N	3	8	0	2	0	0	0	0	0-0	0	2	.250	.250	.250	41	-1	0-0	1.000	-1	102	0	C3	0	-0.2
1965	StL N	11	29	1	7	0	0	0	0	1-0	0	3	.241	.267	.241	40	-2	0-0	.977	-4	51	0	C11	0	-0.6
1967	†StL N	52	99	11	27	8	0	1	14	4-0	0	7	.273	.295	.384	96	-1	0-0	1.000	-2	75	190	C21	0	-0.2
1968	†StL N	20	22	1	3	0	0	0	1	0-0	0	3	.136	.136	.136	-18	-3	0-0	1.000	0	23	0	/C	0	-0.4
1969	StL N	30	44	2	12	1	0	0	5	4-0	0	5	.273	.320	.295	77	-1	0-0	.983	0	36	104	C8	0	-0.1
1970	Pit N	14	11	0	2	0	0	0	0	1-0	0	3	.182	.250	.182	18	-1	0-0	.909	-0	92	221	C7	0	-0.1
Total	6	130	213	15	53	9	0	1	20	10-0	0	23	.249	.278	.305	67	-9	0-0	.988	-7	65	120	C51	0	-1.6
RICKEY, BRANCH	Wesley Branch "The Mahatma"; B12.20.1881 Flat OH; D12.9.1965 Columbia MO; BL/TR/5´9˝/175; d6.16; M10; HF1967; Col Ohio Wesleyan																								
1905	StL A	1	3	0	0	0	0	0	0	0	0	—	.000	.000	.000	-99	-1	0	1.000	-0	75	166	/C	—	-0.1
1906	StL A	65	201	22	57	7	3	3	24	16	3	—	.284	.345	.393	137	8	4	.954	-6	86	93	C55/rf	—	0.8
1907	NY A	52	137	16	25	1	3	0	15	11	2	—	.182	.253	.234	51	-8	4	.846	-4	40	0	O22(20/1/1),C11,1b9	—	-1.4
1914	StL A	2	2	0	0	0	0	0	0	0	0	1	.000	.000	.000	-99	-1	0	ø	0	—	—	/HM	—	-0.1
Total	4	120	343	38	82	8	6	3	39	27	5	1	.239	.304	.324	97	-2	8	.940	-11	88	90	C67,O23(20/1/2),1b9	—	-0.8
RICKLEY, CHRIS	Christian; B10.7.1859 Philadelphia PA; D10.25.1911 Philadelphia PA; 5´8˝/160; d6.9																								
1884	Phi U	6	25	5	5	2	0	0	—	2	—	—	.200	.259	.280	69	-2	—	.757	-0	111	156	S6	—	-0.1
RICKS, JOHN	John; B9.26.1867 St.Louis MO; D8.30.1920 St.Louis MO; d9.21																								
1891	StL AA	5	18	3	3	0	0	0	0	0	0	2	.167	.167	.167	-4	-3	0	.810	-1	55	0	3b5	—	-0.3
1894	StL N	1	1	0	0	0	0	0	0	0	0	0	.000	.000	.000	-99	0	0	.250	-1	0	0	/3	—	-0.1
Total	2	6	19	3	3	0	0	0	0	0	0	2	.158	.158	.158	-9	-3	0	.720	-3	48	0	3b6	—	-0.4
RICO, FRED	Alfredo (Cruz); B7.4.1944 Jerome AZ; BR/TR/5´10˝/180; d9.1; Col Arizona St.																								
1969	KC A	12	26	2	6	2	0	0	2	9-1	0	10	.231	.429	.308	107	1	0-1	1.000	4	167	319	O9(0/2/7)/3	0	0.4
RICO, ART	Arthur Ramon; B7.23.1895 Roxbury MA; D1.3.1919 Boston MA; BR/TR/5´9.5˝/185; d7.31; Mil 1918																								
1916	Bos N	4	4	0	0	0	0	0	0	0	0	0	.000	.000	.000	-99	-1	0	1.000	-0	109	118	C4	—	-0.1
1917	Bos N	13	14	1	4	1	0	0	2	0	0	2	.286	.286	.357	102	0	0	.950	-1	104	82	C11,O2L	—	0.0
Total	2	17	18	1	4	1	0	0	2	0	0	2	.222	.222	.278	56	-1	0	.962	-1	105	90	C15,O2L	—	-0.1
RICONDA, HARRY	Henry Paul; B3.17.1897 New York NY; D11.15.1958 Mahopac NY; BR/TR/5´10˝/175; d4.19																								
1923	Phi A	55	175	23	46	11	4	0	12	12	2	18	.263	.317	.371	80	-6	4-2	.911	-1	108	98	3b47,S2	—	-0.3
1924	Phi A	83	281	34	71	16	3	1	21	27	2	43	.253	.323	.342	71	-13	3-4	.927	-3	97	108	3b73,S2	—	-1.1
1926	Bos N	4	12	1	2	0	0	0	0	2	0	2	.167	.286	.167	27	-1	0	.818	-1	46	0	3b4	—	-0.2
1928	Bro N	92	281	22	63	15	4	3	35	20	4	28	.224	.285	.338	63	-16	6	.957	0	94	64	2b53,3b21,S16	—	-1.3
1929	Pit N	8	15	3	7	2	0	0	2	0	0	0	.467	.467	.600	158	1	0	.840	-2	67	124	S4	—	0.0
1930	Cin N	1	1	0	0	0	0	0	0	0	0	0	.000	.000	.000	-99	0	0	ø	0	—	—	/H	—	0.0
Total	6	243	765	83	189	44	11	4	70	61	8	91	.247	.309	.349	71	-35	13-6	.922	-7	101	95	3b145,2b53,S24	—	-2.9
RIDDLE, JOHN	John H.; B2.1864 PA; D5.5.1931 Camden NJ; BR/TR; d9.18																								
1889	Was N	11	37	3	8	3	0	0	3	2	0	8	.216	.256	.297	57	-2	0	.841	1	—	—	C9,O2R	—	-0.1
1890	Phi AA	27	85	7	7	0	1	0	2	17	1	—	.082	.243	.106	3	-10	4	.914	-3	84	88	C13,O12(9/3/0),2b2/3	—	-1.1
Total	2	38	122	10	15	3	1	0	5	19	1	8	.123	.246	.164	20	-12	4	.880	-3	84	88	C22,O14(9/3/2),2b2/3	—	-1.2
RIDDLE, JOHNNY	John Ludy "Mutt"; B10.3.1905 Clinton SC; D12.15.1998 Indianapolis IN; BR/TR/5´11˝/190; d4.17; C11; b–Elmer																								
1930	Chi A	25	58	7	14	3	1	0	4	3	1	6	.241	.290	.328	58	-4	0-0	1.000	-1	91	132	C25	—	-0.4
1937	Was A	8	26	2	7	0	0	0	3	0	1	2	.269	.296	.269	46	-2	0-0	.971	0	110	150	C8	—	-0.2
	Bos N	2	3	0	0	0	0	0	0	1	0	0	.000	.250	.000	-29	-1	0	1.000	1	0	243	C2	—	0.0
1938	Bos N	19	57	6	16	1	0	0	2	4	0	2	.281	.328	.298	81	-2	0	.951	3	162	125	C19	—	0.2
1941	Cin N	10	10	2	3	0	0	0	0	0	0	1	.300	.300	.300	69	0	0	1.000	1	95	0	C10	0	0.0
1944	Cin N	1	0	0	0	0	0	0	0	0	0	0	ø	ø	ø	ø	0	0	ø	0	0	0	/C	0	0.0
1945	Cin N	23	45	0	8	0	0	0	2	4	0	6	.178	.245	.178	19	-5	0	1.000	2	85	127	C23	0	-0.2
1948	Pit N	10	15	1	3	0	0	0	0	1	0	2	.200	.250	.200	23	-2	0	1.000	1	151	99	C10	0	-0.1
Total	7	98	214	18	51	4	1	0	11	13	2	19	.238	.288	.266	51	-16	0-0	.983	5	114	124	C98	0	-0.7
RIEBE, HANK	Harvey Donald; B10.10.1921 Cleveland OH; D4.16.2001 Cleveland OH; BR/TR/5´9.5˝/175; d8.26; Mil 1943–45																								
1942	Det A	11	35	1	11	2	0	0	2	0	0	6	.314	.314	.371	85	-1	0-0	1.000	0	101	71	C11	0	0.0
1947	Det A	8	7	0	0	0	0	0	2	0	0	2	.000	.000	.000	-97	-2	0-0	1.000	-0	0	0	C3	0	-0.2
1948	Det A	25	62	0	12	0	0	0	5	3	0	5	.194	.231	.194	13	-8	0-1	1.000	0	108	50	C24	0	-0.7
1949	Det A	17	33	1	6	2	0	0	2	0	0	5	.182	.182	.242	12	-4	1-0	.960	-1	88	152	C11	0	-0.5
Total	4	61	137	2	29	4	0	0	11	3	0	18	.212	.229	.241	26	-15	1-1	.994	-1	101	73	C49	0	-1.4
RIESGO, NIKCO	Damon Nikco; B1.11.1967 Long Beach CA; BR/TR/6´2˝/185; [SDN88 8/188]; d4.20; Col San Diego St.																								
1991	Mon N	4	7	1	1	0	0	0	0	3-0	0	1	.143	.400	.143	60	0	0-0	.500	-0	0	638	O2R	10	-0.1
RIGGANS, SHAWN	Shawn Willis; B7.25.1980 Fort Lauderdale FL; BR/TR/6´2˝/190; [TBA00 24/706]; d9.5; Col Indian River (FL) JC																								
2006	TB A	10	29	3	5	1	0	0	1	4-0	0	7	.172	.273	.207	27	-3	0-0	1.000	3	0	179	C8/D	0	0.0
RIGGERT, JOE	Joseph Aloysius; B12.11.1886 Janesville WI; D12.10.1973 Kansas City MO; BR/TR/5´9.5˝/170; d5.12																								
1911	Bos A	50	146	19	31	4	4	2	13	12	4	—	.212	.290	.336	75	-6	5	.929	-3	99	37	O39(21/11/6)	—	-1.0
1914	Bro N	27	83	6	16	1	3	2	6	4	0	20	.193	.230	.349	70	-4	2	.972	-1	93	92	O20(1/0/20)	—	-0.6
	StL N	34	89	9	19	5	2	0	8	5	0	14	.213	.255	.315	70	-4	4	.961	-1	92	103	O30(9/19/2)	—	-0.6
	Year	61	172	15	35	6	5	2	14	9	0	34	.203	.243	.331	70	-8	6	.966	-1	92	98	O50(10/19/22)	—	-1.2
1919	Bos N	63	240	34	68	8	5	4	17	25	2	30	.283	.356	.408	135	10	9	.950	-2	103	72	O61C	—	0.5
Total	3	174	558	68	134	18	14	8	44	46	6	64	.240	.305	.366	98	-4	20	.950	-6	99	71	O150(31/91/28)	—	-1.7

YEAR	TM LG	G	AB	R	H	2B	3B	HR	RBI	BB-IB	HP	SO	AVG	OBP	SLG	AOPS	ABR	SB-CS	FA	FR	RNG	THR	GAMES AT POSITION	DL	BFW
RIGGS, ADAM	Adam David; B10.4.1972 Steubenville OH; BR/TR/6´0˝/(190–194); [LAN94 22/608]; d8.7; Col South Carolina–Aiken; [DL 1998 LA N 115]																								
1997	LA N	9	20	3	4	1	0	0	1	4-1	0	3	.200	.333	.250	59	-1	1-0	1.000	-1	98	81	2b8	0	-0.2
2001	SD N	12	36	2	7	1	0	0	1	2-0	0	8	.194	.237	.222	21	-4	1-1	1.000	-1	86	100	2b11/3	0	-0.5
2003	Ana A	24	61	11	15	4	1	3	5	9-0	0	9	.246	.343	.492	121	2	3-1	.976	2	170	74	1b10,O8L,2b3,D3	0	0.3
2004	†Ana A	16	36	2	7	3	0	0	3	1-0	0	10	.194	.216	.278	29	-4	1-0	1.000	2	138	454	O8L/12D	0	-0.2
Total	4	61	153	18	33	9	1	3	10	16-1	0	30	.216	.290	.346	69	-7	6-2	1.000	2	92	84	2b23,O16L,1b11,D7/3	115	-0.6
RIGGS, LEW	Lewis Sidney; B4.22.1910 Mebane NC; D8.12.1975 Durham NC; BL/TR/6´0˝/175; d4.28; Mil 1943–45																								
1934	StL N	2	1	0	0	0	0	0	0	0	0	1	.000	.000	.000	-94	0	0	ø	0	—	—	/H	—	0.0
1935	Cin N	142	532	73	148	26	8	5	46	43	2	32	.278	.334	.385	96	-3	8	.928	8	110	99	3b135	—	0.9
1936	Cin N★	141	538	69	138	20	12	6	57	38	7	33	.257	.314	.372	90	-10	5	.968	13	116	**108**	3b140	—	0.7
1937	Cin N	122	384	43	93	17	5	6	45	24	1	17	.242	.289	.359	79	-13	4	.941	18	121	119	3b100,2b4/S	—	0.9
1938	Cin N	142	531	53	134	21	13	2	55	40	5	28	.252	.311	.352	84	-13	3	.947	-1	100	78	3b140	—	-0.9
1939	Cin N	22	38	5	6	1	0	0	1	5	0	4	.158	.256	.184	20	-4	1	.957	-0	102	75	3b11	—	-0.4
1940	†Cin N	41	72	8	21	7	1	1	9	2	0	4	.292	.311	.458	109	1	0	.943	1	118	145	3b11	—	0.2
1941	†Bro N	77	197	27	60	13	4	5	36	16	0	12	.305	.357	.487	131	7	1	.932	-8	83	56	3b43/12	0	0.1
1942	Bro N	70	180	20	50	5	0	3	22	13	2	9	.278	.333	.356	100	0	0	.944	-5	86	107	3b46/1	0	-0.4
1946	Bro N	1	4	0	0	0	0	0	0	0	0	0	.000	.000	.000	-99	-1	0	1.000	0	93	0	/3	0	-0.1
Total	10	760	2477	298	650	110	43	28	271	181	17	140	.262	.317	.375	91	-36	22	.945	26	107	97	3b627,2b5,1b2/S	0	1.0
RIGNEY, TOPPER	Emory Elmo; B1.7.1897 Groveton TX; D6.6.1972 San Antonio TX; BR/TR/5´9˝/150; d4.12; Col Texas A&M																								
1922	Det A	**155**	536	68	161	17	7	2	63	68	1	44	.300	.380	.369	99	2	17-8	.938	-15	98	89	S155	—	0.5
1923	Det A	129	470	63	148	24	11	1	74	55	2	35	.315	.389	.419	115	11	7-5	.944	-10	99	73	S129	—	1.4
1924	Det A	147	499	81	144	29	9	4	94	102	1	39	.289	.410	.407	113	15	11-11	**.967**	8	106	103	S146	—	3.5
1925	Det A	62	146	21	36	5	2	2	18	21	0	15	.247	.341	.349	77	-5	2-2	.934	-9	91	36	S51,3b4	—	-1.0
1926	Bos A	148	525	71	142	32	6	4	53	108	0	31	.270	.395	.377	105	10	6-8	**.969**	**21**	**114**	97	S146	—	4.3
1927	Bos A	8	18	0	2	1	0	0	0	1	0	2	.111	.158	.167	-16	-3	0-0	1.000	-1	62	190	3b4/S	—	-0.4
	Was A	45	132	20	36	5	4	0	13	22	1	10	.273	.381	.371	97	0	1-2	.929	-2	93	123	S32,3b6	—	0.1
	Year	53	150	20	38	6	4	0	13	23	1	12	.253	.356	.347	84	-3	1-2	.932	-3	91	123	S33,3b10	—	-0.3
Total	6	694	2326	324	669	113	39	13	315	377	5	176	.288	.388	.387	104	30	44-36	.953	-8	103	90	S660,3b14	—	8.4
RIGNEY, BILL	William Joseph "Specs","The Cricket"; B1.29.1918 Alameda CA; D2.20.2001 Walnut Creek CA; BR/TR/6´1˝/(165–178); d4.16; M18/C1																								
1946	NY N	110	360	38	85	9	1	3	31	36	1	29	.236	.307	.292	70	-14	9	.965	3	107	76	3b73,S33	0	-1.1
1947	NY N	130	531	84	142	24	3	17	59	51	5	54	.267	.337	.420	99	-1	7	.974	4	112	84	2b72,3b41,S24	0	0.7
1948	NY N★	113	424	72	112	17	3	10	43	47	3	54	.264	.342	.389	97	-2	4	.967	-7	99	80	2b105,S7	0	-0.3
1949	NY N	122	389	53	108	19	6	6	47	47	0	38	.278	.356	.404	103	2	3	.928	-11	95	80	S81,2b26,3b14	0	-0.3
1950	NY N	56	83	8	15	2	0	0	8	8	0	13	.181	.253	.205	22	-9	0	.966	3	107	130	2b23,3b11	0	-0.6
1951	†NY N	44	69	9	16	2	0	4	9	8	1	7	.232	.321	.435	100	0	0-1	.953	3	115	193	3b12,2b9	0	0.2
1952	NY N	60	90	15	27	5	1	1	14	11	2	6	.300	.388	.411	121	3	2-3	.889	-2	83	220	3b10,2b9,S4/1	0	0.2
1953	NY N	19	20	2	5	0	0	0	1	0	0	5	.250	.250	.250	30	-2	0-0	1.000	-0	52	0	3b2/2	0	-0.2
Total	8	654	1966	281	510	78	14	41	212	208	12	206	.259	.334	.376	91	-23	25-4	.971	-7	106	84	2b245,3b163,S149/1	0	-1.4
RIKARD, CULLEY	Culley; B5.9.1914 Oxford MS; D2.25.2000 Memphis TN; BL/TR/5´11˝/183; d9.20; Mil 1943–45																								
1941	Pit N	6	20	1	4	1	0	0	0	1	0	1	.200	.238	.250	38	-2	0	1.000	1	129	0	O5(3/3/0)	0	-0.1
1942	Pit N	38	52	6	10	2	1	0	5	7	0	8	.192	.288	.269	62	-2	0	.958	-1	107	0	O16(2/14/0)	0	-0.3
1947	Pit N	109	324	57	93	16	4	4	32	50	1	39	.287	.384	.398	105	4	1	.978	-3	103	33	O79(5/28/45)	0	-0.1
Total	3	153	396	64	107	19	5	4	37	58	1	48	.270	.365	.374	97	0	1	.978	-3	105	28	O100(10/45/45)	0	-0.5
RILES, ERNEST	Ernest; B10.2.1960 Cairo GA; BL/TR/6´1˝/180; [MilA81*S3/63]; d5.14; Col Middle Georgia JC; OF(2/0/3)																								
1985	Mil A	116	448	54	128	12	7	5	45	36-0	2	54	.286	.339	.377	97	-3	2-2	.957	-16	94	83	S115/D	0	-0.7
1986	Mil A	145	524	69	132	24	2	9	47	54-0	1	80	.252	.321	.357	82	-12	7-7	.964	-32	82	86	S142	0	-3.0
1987	Mil A	83	276	38	72	11	1	4	38	30-1	1	47	.261	.329	.351	80	-7	3-4	.935	-8	88	96	3b65,S21	83	-1.4
1988	Mil A	41	127	7	32	6	1	1	9	7-0	0	26	.252	.291	.339	75	-4	2-2	.958	-1	96	51	3b28,S9,D5	0	-0.6
	SF N	79	187	26	55	7	2	3	28	10-2	0	33	.294	.323	.401	114	2	1-2	.975	10	142	116	3b30,2b17,S16	0	1.3
1989	†SF N	122	302	43	84	13	2	7	40	28-3	2	50	.278	.339	.404	116	6	0-6	.962	-2	91	136	3b83,2b18,S7,O5(2/0/3)	0	0.2
1990	SF N	92	155	22	31	2	1	8	21	26-3	0	26	.200	.313	.381	93	-2	0-0	.986	2	129	106	S26,2b24,3b10	0	0.1
1991	Oak A	108	281	30	60	8	4	5	32	31-3	1	42	.214	.290	.324	75	-10	3-2	.939	0	97	126	3b69,S20,2b7,1b5	0	-1.0
1992	Hou N	39	61	5	16	1	0	1	4	2-0	0	11	.262	.281	.328	76	-2	1-0	1.000	-1	77	134	S6,3b5,1b4,2b2	0	-0.4
1993	Bos A	94	143	15	27	8	0	5	20	20-3	2	40	.189	.292	.350	69	-6	1-3	1.000	1	119	99	2b20,D15,3b11/1	0	-0.6
Total	9	919	2504	309	637	92	20	48	284	244-15	9	409	.254	.319	.365	89	-38	20-28	.964	-49	90	91	S362,3b301,2b88,D21,1b10,O5R	83	-6.1
RILEY, JIM	James Joseph; B11.10.1886 Buffalo NY; D3.25.1949 Buffalo NY; BR/TR/6´0˝/165; d8.2																								
1910	Bos N	1	1	0	0	0	0	0	0	1	0	1	.000	.500	.000	46	0	0	.600	-0	116	0	/lf	—	0.0
RILEY, JIM	James Norman; B5.25.1895 Bayfield NB, Can.; D5.25.1969 Seguin TX; BL/TR/5´10.5˝/185; d7.3																								
1921	StL A	4	11	0	0	0	0	0	0	1	0	3	.000	.083	.000	-73	-3	0-0	.818	-2	63	0	2b4	—	-0.5
1923	Was A	2	3	1	0	0	0	0	0	2	0	0	.000	.400	.000	12	0	0-0	.882	-1	0	191	1b2	—	-0.1
Total	2	6	14	1	0	0	0	0	0	3	0	3	.000	.176	.000	-50	-3	0-0	.818	-3	63	0	2b4,1b2	—	-0.6
RILEY, LEE	Leon Francis; B8.20.1906 Princeton NE; D9.13.1970 Schenectady NY; BL/TR/6´1˝/185; d4.19																								
1944	Phi N	4	12	1	1	1	0	0	1	0	0	0	.083	.083	.167	-32	-2	0	1.000	-1	50	0	O3L	0	-0.3
RILEY, BILLY	William James "Pigtail Billy"; B1855 Cincinnati OH; D11.9.1887 Cincinnati OH; BR/TR/5´10˝/160; d5.4																								
1875	Wes NA	8	33	4	5	1	0	0	1	1	—	1	.152	.176	.182	23	-2	0-0	.667	-0	151	0	O8R	—	-0.2
1879	Cle N	43	161	14	23	2	0	0	9	2	—	26	.143	.153	.155	2	-17	—	.850	5	120	82	O43L	—	-1.4
RINGO, FRANK	Frank C.; B10.12.1860 Parkville MO; D4.12.1889 Kansas City MO; BR/5´11˝/175; d5.1																								
1883	Phi N	60	221	24	42	10	1	0	12	6	—	34	.190	.211	.244	42	-14	—	.847	-8	—	—	C39,O11(3/8/0),S6,3b5,2b2	—	-1.6
1884	Phi N	26	91	4	12	2	0	0	6	3	—	19	.132	.160	.154	-1	-10	—	.783	-14	—	—	C26	—	-2.1
	Phi AA	2	6	0	0	0	0	0	—	0	0	—	.000	.000	.000	-94	-1	—	.762	-1	—	—	C2	—	-0.2
1885	Det N	17	65	12	16	3	0	0	2	0	—	7	.246	.246	.292	73	-2	—	.852	0	—	—	C8,3b8/cf	—	-0.1
	Pit AA	3	11	0	2	0	0	0	0	0	0	—	.182	.182	.182	15	-1	—	.941	1	—	—	C3	—	0.1
1886	Pit AA	15	56	3	12	2	2	0	5	1	0	—	.214	.228	.321	72	-2	0	.934	0	87	190	1b9,C6	—	-0.2
	KC N	16	56	6	13	7	0	0	7	5	—	10	.232	.295	.357	92	0	0	.904	-4	—	—	C13,O2C/3	—	-0.3
Total	4	139	506	49	97	24	3	0	32	15	—	70	.192	.215	.251	46	-30	0	.844	-25	—	—	C97,3b14,O14(3/11/0),1b9,S6,2b2	—	-4.4
RINKER, BOB	Robert John; B4.21.1921 Audenried PA; D12.19.2002 Hazleton PA; BR/TR/6´0˝/190; d9.6																								
1950	Phi A	3	3	0	1	0	0	0	0	0	0	0	.333	.333	.333	72	0	0-0	ø	0	*0*	*0*	/C	0	0.0
RIOS, ALEX	Alexis Israel; B2.18.1981 Coffee Co. AL; BR/TR/6´5˝/195; [TorA99 1/19]; d5.27																								
2004	Tor A	111	426	55	122	24	7	1	28	31-0	2	84	.286	.338	.383	83	-11	15-3	.991	1	96	147	O111(0/3/108)	0	-1.2
2005	Tor A	146	481	71	126	23	6	10	59	28-1	5	101	.262	.306	.397	82	-13	14-9	.992	0	99	94	O142(0/5/138)/D	0	-1.8
2006	Tor A✱	128	450	68	136	33	6	17	82	35-1	3	89	.302	.349	.516	117	11	15-6	.996	1	99	117	O125(0/6/124)	30	0.8
Total	3	385	1357	194	384	80	19	28	169	94-2	10	274	.283	.331	.432	94	-13	44-18	.993	3	98	118	O378(0/14/370)/D	30	-2.2
RIOS, ARMANDO	Armando; B9.13.1971 Santurce, PR; BL/TL/5´9˝/(185–190); d9.1; Col Louisiana St.																								
1998	SF N	12	7	3	4	0	0	2	3	3-0	0	2	.571	.700	1.429	465	4	0-0	1.000	0	167	0	O5(2/1/2)	0	0.4
1999	SF N	72	150	32	49	9	0	7	29	24-1	1	35	.327	.420	.527	148	12	7-4	.978	4	114	210	O53(14/2/39)	72	1.4
2000	†SF N	115	233	38	62	15	5	10	50	31-4	0	43	.266	.347	.502	120	7	3-2	.959	5	113	161	O93(19/0/76)/1	0	0.8
2001	SF N	93	316	38	82	17	3	14	49	34-6	0	73	.259	.330	.465	109	3	3-2	.971	7	114	125	O87(13/3/76)	0	0.6
	Pit N	2	3	0	1	0	0	0	1	2-0	0	1	.333	.500	.333	147	0	0-0	ø	-1	0	0	O2R	67	0.0
	Year	95	319	38	83	17	3	14	50	36-6	0	74	.260	.332	.464	110	4	3-2	.971	6	112	123	O89(13/3/78)	0	0.6
2002	Pit N	76	208	20	55	11	0	1	24	16-1	1	39	.264	.319	.332	71	-9	1-1	1.000	1	92	153	O56(11/0/47)	77	-1.1
2003	Chi A	49	104	4	22	3	0	2	11	5-0	0	13	.212	.245	.298	41	-9	0-1	.981	-1	92	91	O32(9/23/6),D4	0	-1.0
Total	6	419	1021	135	275	55	8	36	167	115-12	2	206	.269	.341	.445	105	8	14-10	.975	15	107	146	O328(68/29/248),D4/1	216	1.1

YEAR	TM LG	G	AB	R	H	2B	3B	HR	RBI	BB-IB	HP	SO	AVG	OBP	SLG	AOPS	ABR	SB-CS	FA	FR	RNG	THR	GAMES AT POSITION	DL	BFW
Rios, Juan	Juan Onofre Velez (b Juan Onofre Velez (Rios)); B6.14.1942 Mayaguez, PR; D8.28.1995 Mayaguez, PR; BR/TR/6´3˝/185; d4.9																								
1969	KC A	87	196	20	44	5	1	1	5	7-2	3	19	.224	.262	.276	50	-14	1-3	.967	-19	76	77	2b46,S32,3b4	0	-3.1
Ripken, Cal	Calvin Edwin Jr.; B8.24.1960 Havre de Grace MD; BR/TR/6´4˝/(200–225); [BalA78 2/48]; d8.10; b–Billy; HF2006																								
1981	Bal A	23	39	1	5	0	0	0	0	1-0	0	8	.128	.150	.128	-19	-6	0-0	.946	-0	95	96	S12,3b6	0	-0.6
1982	Bal A	160	598	90	158	32	5	28	93	46-3	3	95	.264	.317	.475	116	11	3-3	.972	-3	99	89	S94,3b71	0	1.6
1983	†Bal A★	**162**	663	**121**	**211**	**47**	2	27	102	58-0	0	97	.318	.371	.517	144	40	0-4	.970	16	**105**	**118**	S162	0	**7.0**
1984	Bal A★	**162**	641	103	195	37	7	27	86	71-1	2	89	.304	.374	.510	145	40	2-1	.971	**39**	**117**	**125**	S162	0	**9.4**
1985	Bal A★	**161**	642	116	181	32	5	26	110	67-1	1	68	.282	.347	.469	125	22	2-3	.967	9	102	115	S161	0	4.5
1986	Bal A★	**162**	627	98	177	35	1	25	81	70-5	4	60	.282	.355	.461	122	20	4-2	.982	10	105	103	S162	0	4.6
1987	Bal A★	**162**	624	97	157	28	3	27	98	81-0	1	77	.252	.333	.436	106	6	3-5	.973	-5	102	104	S162	0	1.6
1988	Bal A★	**161**	575	87	152	25	1	23	81	102-7	2	69	.264	.372	.431	129	26	2-2	.973	4	103	109	S161	0	4.2
1989	Bal A★	**162**	646	80	166	30	0	21	93	57-5	3	72	.257	.317	.401	105	3	3-2	.990	5	107	112	S162	0	2.1
1990	Bal A★	**161**	600	78	150	28	4	21	84	82-18	5	66	.250	.341	.415	115	13	3-1	**.996**	-26	93	91	S161	0	0.0
1991	Bal A★	**162**	650	99	210	46	5	34	114	53-15	5	46	.323	.374	.566	163	54	6-1	**.986**	20	**109**	111	S162	0	**8.5**
1992	Bal A★	**162**	637	73	160	29	1	14	72	64-14	7	50	.251	.323	.366	91	-7	4-3	.984	-10	91	**117**	S162	0	-0.5
1993	Bal A★	**162**	641	87	165	26	3	24	90	65-19	6	58	.257	.329	.420	96	-5	1-4	.977	-5	101	100	S162	0	0.2
1994	Bal A★	**112**	444	71	140	19	3	13	75	32-3	4	41	.315	.364	.459	105	3	1-0	**.985**	-12	95	111	S112	0	0.0
1995	Bal A★	**144**	550	71	144	33	2	17	88	52-6	2	59	.262	.324	.422	92	-7	0-1	**.989**	3	97	118	S144	0	0.6
1996	†Bal A★	**163**	640	94	178	40	1	26	102	59-3	4	78	.278	.341	.466	102	2	1-2	.980	2	101	104	S158,3b6	0	1.3
1997	†Bal A★	**162**	615	79	166	30	0	17	84	56-3	5	73	.270	.331	.402	94	-5	1-0	.949	2	103	98	3b162,S3	0	-0.2
1998	Bal A★	161	601	65	163	27	1	14	61	51-0	4	68	.271	.331	.389	88	-11	0-2	**.979**	-0	97	95	3b161	0	-1.0
1999	Bal A★	86	332	51	113	27	0	18	57	13-3	3	31	.340	.368	.584	143	21	0-1	.932	-5	100	85	3b85	56	1.5
2000	Bal A✳	83	309	43	79	16	0	15	56	23-0	3	37	.256	.310	.453	96	-3	0-0	.974	7	107	131	3b73,D10	64	0.3
2001	Bal A	128	477	43	114	16	0	14	68	26-1	2	63	.239	.276	.361	71	-22	0-2	.956	4	102	119	3b111,D14	0	-1.8
Total	21	3001	11551	1647	3184	603	44	431	1695	1129-107	66	1305	.276	.340	.447	112	195	36-39	.979	54	102	109	S2302,3b675,D24	120	43.3
Ripken, Billy	William Oliver; B12.16.1964 Havre de Grace MD; BR/TR/6´1˝/(178–190); [BalA82 11/286]; d7.11; b–Cal																								
1987	Bal A	58	234	27	72	9	0	2	20	21-0	0	23	.308	.363	.372	98	0	4-1	.990	2	97	138	2b58	0	0.6
1988	Bal A	150	512	52	106	18	1	2	34	33-0	5	63	.207	.260	.258	47	-37	8-2	.984	-0	101	108	2b149,3b2/D	0	-3.3
1989	Bal A	115	318	31	76	11	2	2	26	22-0	0	53	.239	.284	.305	69	-14	1-2	.985	7	106	118	2b114/D	26	-0.4
1990	Bal A	129	406	48	118	28	1	3	38	28-2	4	43	.291	.342	.387	106	4	5-2	.987	-8	98	104	2b127	15	-0.1
1991	Bal A	104	287	24	62	11	1	0	14	15-0	0	31	.216	.253	.261	45	-22	0-1	.986	1	100	117	2b103	31	-1.9
1992	Bal A	111	330	35	76	15	0	4	36	18-1	3	26	.230	.275	.312	63	-17	2-3	**.993**	0	102	99	2b108,D2	0	-1.5
1993	Tex A	50	132	12	25	4	0	0	11	11-0	4	19	.189	.270	.220	35	-12	0-2	.992	0	92	84	2b34,S18/3	87	-1.0
1994	Tex A	32	81	9	25	5	0	0	6	3-0	0	11	.309	.333	.370	80	-2	2-0	.970	1	95	182	3b18,2b12,S2/1	42	-0.1
1995	Cle A	8	17	4	7	0	0	2	3	0-0	0	3	.412	.412	.765	194	2	0-0	1.000	-3	50	42	2b7/3	0	-0.1
1996	Bal A	57	135	19	31	8	0	2	12	9-0	1	18	.230	.281	.333	55	-9	0-0	.968	1	105	113	2b30,3b25/1	0	-0.7
1997	Tex A	71	203	18	56	9	1	3	24	9-0	0	32	.276	.300	.374	72	-9	0-1	.971	1	93	92	S31,2b25,3b13,1b9	34	-0.5
1998	Det A	27	74	8	20	3	0	0	5	5-0	1	10	.270	.321	.311	66	-4	3-2	.926	-4	100	95	S21,1b2,2b2,3b2/D	54	-0.6
Total	12	912	2729	287	674	121	6	20	229	174-3	18	332	.247	.294	.318	69	-120	25-16	.987	-1	101	110	2b769,S72,3b62,1b13,D5	289	-9.6
Ripple, Jimmy	James Albert; B10.14.1909 Export PA; D7.16.1959 Greensburg PA; BL/TR/5´10˝/170; d4.20																								
1936	†NY N	96	311	42	95	17	2	7	47	28	1	15	.305	.365	.441	117	8	1	.980	-5	89	86	O76(0/75/1)	—	0.0
1937	†NY N	121	426	70	135	23	3	5	66	29	1	20	.317	.362	.420	110	6	3	.980	-9	86	63	O111(0/54/57)	—	-0.7
1938	NY N	134	501	68	131	21	3	10	60	49	5	21	.261	.333	.375	94	-4	2	.976	-4	90	112	O131(0/17/115)	—	-1.6
1939	NY N	66	123	10	28	4	0	1	12	8	2	7	.228	.286	.285	53	-8	0	1.000	-1	86	130	O23(9/4/10)	—	-1.0
	Bro N	28	106	18	35	8	4	0	22	11	1	8	.330	.398	.481	131	5	0	1.000	-2	95	0	O28(12/1/15)	—	0.1
	Year	94	229	28	63	12	4	1	34	19	3	15	.275	.339	.376	90	-3	0	1.000	-3	91	54	O51(21/5/25)	—	-0.9
1940	Bro N	7	13	0	3	0	0	0	0	2	0	2	.231	.333	.231	55	-1	0	1.000	0	135	0	O3(1/0/2)	—	-0.1
	†Cin N	32	101	15	31	10	0	4	20	13	2	5	.307	.397	.525	151	8	1	1.000	-3	85	0	O30(27/0/3)	—	0.4
	Year	39	114	15	34	10	0	4	20	15	2	7	.298	.389	.491	139	7	1	1.000	-2	92	0	O33(28/0/5)	—	0.3
1941	Cin N	38	102	10	22	6	1	1	9	9	0	4	.216	.279	.324	69	-4	0	1.000	-1	88	60	O25(7/0/18)	0	-0.7
1943	Phi A	32	126	8	30	3	1	0	15	7	1	7	.238	.284	.278	65	-6	0-0	1.000	-2	92	0	O31(10/0/21)	0	-1.1
Total	7	554	1809	241	510	92	14	28	251	156	13	89	.282	.343	.395	101	4	7-0	.984	-27	89	72	O458(66/151/242)	0	-4.7
Risberg, Swede	Charles August; B10.13.1894 San Francisco CA; D10.13.1975 Red Bluff CA; BR/TR/6´0˝/175; d4.11; Mil 1918																								
1917	†Chi A	149	474	59	96	20	8	1	45	59	5	65	.203	.297	.285	76	-13	16	.913	-40	80	97	S146	—	-4.8
1918	Chi A	82	273	36	70	12	3	1	27	23	3	32	.256	.321	.333	96	-1	5	.944	-7	93	122	S30,3b24,2b12,1b7,O3R	—	-0.7
1919	†Chi A	119	414	48	106	19	6	2	38	35	2	38	.256	.317	.345	86	-8	19	.934	-12	95	119	S97,1b22	—	-1.5
1920	Chi A	126	458	53	122	21	10	2	65	31	2	45	.266	.316	.369	81	-14	12-10	.934	-7	99	**127**	S124	—	-1.3
Total	4	476	1619	196	394	72	27	6	175	148	12	180	.243	.311	.332	83	-36	52-10	.928	-66	91	114	S397,1b29,3b24,2b12,O3R	—	-8.3
Rising, Pop	Percival Sumner; B1.2.1872 Industry PA; D1.28.1938 Rochester PA; TR; d8.10																								
1905	Bos A	11	29	2	3	1	1	0	2	2	0	—	.103	.161	.207	16	-3	0	1.000	0	152	0	O6R/3	—	-0.3
Ritchey, Claude	Claude Cassius "Little All Right"; B10.5.1873 Emlenton PA; D11.8.1951 Emlenton PA; BB/TR/5´6.5˝/167; d4.22																								
1897	Cin N	101	337	58	95	12	4	0	41	42	5	—	.282	.370	.341	83	-7	11	.897	-11	92	87	S70,O22(10/1/11),2b8	—	-1.4
1898	Lou N	151	551	65	140	10	4	5	51	46	9	—	.254	.322	.314	84	-12	19	.919	-16	87	95	S80,2b71	—	-1.9
1899	Lou N	148	540	66	162	16	7	4	73	49	10	—	.300	.369	.378	105	5	21	.938	-9	97	108	2b138,S11	—	0.3
1900	†Pit N	123	476	62	139	17	8	1	67	29	5	—	.292	.339	.368	94	-4	18	.952	6	100	113	2b123	—	0.7
1901	Pit N	**140**	540	66	160	20	4	1	74	47	5	—	.296	.358	.354	104	4	15	.941	4	99	**127**	2b139/S	—	0.9
1902	Pit N	115	405	54	112	13	1	2	55	53	7	—	.277	.370	.328	112	9	10	**.966**	6	100	128	2b114/rf	—	1.7
1903	†Pit N	138	506	66	145	28	10	0	59	55	3	—	.287	.360	.381	108	6	15	**.961**	17	**115**	106	2b137	—	2.3
1904	Pit N	**156**	544	79	143	22	12	0	51	59	3	—	.263	.338	.347	109	7	12	.958	1	101	103	2b156,S2	—	1.0
1905	Pit N	153	533	54	136	29	6	0	52	51	3	—	.255	.324	.332	93	-3	12	**.961**	-6	101	125	2b153,S2	—	-0.8
1906	Pit N	152	484	46	130	21	5	1	62	68	9	—	.269	.369	.339	116	13	6	**.966**	-1	98	**130**	2b151	—	1.4
1907	Bos N	144	499	45	127	17	4	2	51	50	5	—	.255	.329	.317	103	3	8	**.971**	13	109	100	2b144	—	1.9
1908	Bos N	121	421	44	115	10	3	2	36	50	8	—	.273	.361	.325	121	13	7	.967	13	101	**129**	2b120	—	3.1
1909	Bos N	30	87	4	15	1	0	0	3	8	0	—	.172	.242	.184	31	-7	1	.959	-0	84	118	2b25	—	-0.8
Total	13	1672	5923	709	1619	216	68	18	675	607	72	—	.273	.348	.342	101	27	155	.957	18	101	116	2b1479,S166,O23(10/1/12)	—	8.4
Ritter, Charlie	Charles J.; d9.21																								
1885	Buf N	2	6	0	1	0	0	0	0	0	—	2	.167	.167	.167	8	-1	—	.813	-0	82	105	2b2	—	-0.1
Ritter, Floyd	Floyd Alexander; B6.1.1870 Dorset OH; D2.7.1943 Stevenson WA; BR/TR/5´8˝/155; d6.4																								
1890	Tol AA	1	3	0	0	0	0	0	0	0	0	—	.000	.000	.000	-97	-1	0	.778	-0	*120*	*207*	/C	—	-0.1
Ritter, Lew	Lewis Elmer "Old Dog"; B9.7.1875 Liverpool PA; D5.27.1952 Harrisburg PA; BR/TR/5´9˝/150; d9.10																								
1902	Bro N	16	57	5	12	1	0	0	2	1	1	—	.211	.237	.228	43	-4	2	.973	0	*87*	*87*	C16	—	-0.2
1903	Bro N	78	259	26	61	9	6	0	37	19	1	—	.236	.290	.317	75	-9	9	.940	-22	*67*	*88*	C74,O2(1/1/0)	—	-2.3
1904	Bro N	72	214	23	53	4	1	0	19	20	2	—	.248	.318	.276	86	-3	17	.966	7	*99*	*107*	C57,2b5/3	—	1.0
1905	Bro N	92	311	32	68	10	5	1	28	15	0	—	.219	.255	.293	68	-14	16	.951	-15	*75*	*98*	C84,O4(0/1/3),3b2	—	-2.1
1906	Bro N	73	226	22	47	1	3	0	15	16	1	—	.208	.263	.239	61	-11	6	.978	-5	*91*	*93*	C53,O9(5/0/5),1b3,3b2	—	-1.3
1907	Bro N	93	271	15	55	6	1	0	17	18	1	—	.203	.255	.232	57	-14	5	.969	-6	*88*	*91*	C89	—	-1.2
1908	Bro N	38	99	6	19	2	1	0	2	7	0	—	.192	.245	.232	55	-5	0	.961	-3	*81*	*100*	C37	—	-0.6
Total	7	462	1437	129	315	33	17	1	120	96	6	—	.219	.271	.268	67	-60	55	.960	-43	*83*	*95*	C410,O15(6/2/8),3b5,2b5,1b3	—	-6.7
Ritterson, Whitey	Edward West; B4.26.1855 Philadelphia PA; D7.28.1917 Sellersville PA; BR/TR/5´8˝/?; d5.2																								
1876	Phi N	16	52	8	13	3	0	0	4	0	—	2	.250	.250	.308	86	-1	—	.671	-6	—	—	C14,O4(0/2/2)/3	—	-0.6
Ritz, Jim	James L.; B1874 Pittsburgh PA; D11.10.1896 Pittsburgh PA; 5´8˝/160; d7.20																								
1894	Pit N	1	4	1	0	0	0	0	0	0	1	0	.000	.200	.000	-49	-1	1	.750	-0	85	537	/3	—	-0.1

YEAR	TM LG	G	AB	R	H	2B	3B	HR	RBI	BB-IB	HP	SO	AVG	OBP	SLG	AOPS	ABR	SB-CS	FA	FR	RNG	THR	GAMES AT POSITION	DL	BFW
RIVAS, LUIS	Luis Wilfredo; B8.30.1979 LaGuaira, Vargas, Venez.; BR/TR/5´10˝/(175–190); d9.16																								
2000	Min A	16	58	8	18	4	1	0	6	2-0	0	4	.310	.323	.414	82	-2	2-0	.983	-3	75	86	2b14,S2	0	-0.3
2001	Min A	153	563	70	150	21	6	7	47	40-0	6	99	.266	.319	.362	76	-20	31-11	.974	-52	81	72	2b150	0	-6.1
2002	†Min A	93	316	46	81	23	4	4	35	19-2	3	51	.256	.305	.392	81	-9	9-4	.986	-29	79	92	2b93	61	-3.2
2003	†Min A	135	475	69	123	16	9	8	43	30-0	5	65	.259	.308	.381	78	-16	17-7	.982	-31	87	80	2b134/D	0	-3.9
2004	†Min A	109	336	44	86	19	5	10	34	13-0	1	53	.256	.283	.432	81	-11	15-1	.994	16	114	**126**	2b109	20	1.2
2005	Min A	59	136	21	35	3	1	1	12	9-0	2	17	.257	.311	.316	67	-7	4-0	.995	-6	94	106	2b53,S6	16	-0.9
Total	6	565	1884	258	493	86	26	30	177	113-2	17	289	.262	.307	.383	78	-65	78-23	.984	-105	89	91	2b553,S8/D	97	-13.2
RIVERA, CARLOS	Carlos Alberto; B6.10.1978 Fajardo, PR; BL/TL/5´11˝/(230–235); [PitN96 10/276]; d6.22																								
2003	Pit N	78	95	12	21	5	0	3	10	8-2	1	28	.221	.283	.368	69	-5	0-0	.984	-1	91	109	1b60	0	-0.8
2004	Pit N	7	15	1	3	0	0	0	1	1-1	0	3	.200	.250	.200	18	-2	0-0	1.000	-0	69	158	1b7	0	-0.3
Total	2	85	110	13	24	5	0	3	11	9-3	1	31	.218	.279	.345	62	-7	0-0	.986	-2	87	117	1b67	0	-1.1
RIVERA, GERMAN	German (Diaz); B7.6.1960 Santurce, PR; BR/TR/6´2˝/(170–195); d9.2																								
1983	LA N	13	17	1	6	1	0	0	0	2-0	0	2	.353	.421	.412	132	1	0-1	.929	1	130	0	3b8	0	0.1
1984	LA N	94	227	20	59	12	2	2	17	21-5	1	30	.260	.321	.357	92	-2	1-0	.937	10	113	102	3b90	0	0.7
1985	Hou N	13	36	3	7	2	1	0	2	4-1	0	8	.194	.275	.306	64	-2	0-0	.941	3	140	195	3b11	0	0.1
Total	3	120	280	24	72	15	3	2	19	27-6	1	40	.257	.322	.354	91	-3	1-1	.937	13	117	107	3b109	0	0.9
RIVERA, BOMBO	Jesus Manuel (Torres); B8.2.1952 Ponce, PR; BR/TR/5´10˝/(170–195); d4.17																								
1975	Mon N	5	9	1	1	0	0	0	0	2-0	0	3	.111	.273	.111	9	-1	0-0	.889	-0	121	0	O5(4/0/2)	0	-0.1
1976	Mon N	68	185	22	51	11	4	2	19	13-1	0	32	.276	.323	.411	102	0	1-0	.950	3	99	215	O56(44/0/15)	0	0.1
1978	Min A	101	251	35	68	8	2	3	23	35-1	2	47	.271	.362	.355	100	1	5-3	.982	2	108	95	O94(32/0/72)/D	0	0.0
1979	Min A	112	263	37	74	13	5	2	31	17-0	0	40	.281	.324	.392	88	-5	5-5	.989	9	114	222	O105(61/1/50),D2	0	0.1
1980	Min A	44	113	13	25	7	0	3	10	4-0	0	20	.221	.248	.363	61	-6	0-0	.922	-2	98	45	O37(10/0/28)/D	76	-1.0
1982	KC A	5	10	1	1	0	0	0	0	0-0	0	2	.100	.100	.100	-45	-2	0-0	1.000	-0	78	0	O3(2/0/1)	0	-0.3
Total	6	335	831	109	220	39	11	10	83	71-2	2	144	.265	.323	.374	89	-13	11-8	.970	13	107	151	O300(153/1/168),D4	76	-1.2
RIVERA, JUAN	Juan Luis; B7.3.1978 Guarenas, Miranda, Venez.; BR/TR/6´2˝/(170–205); d9.4																								
2001	NY A	3	4	0	0	0	0	0	0	0-0	0	0	.000	.000	.000	-99	-1	0-0	1.000	-0	37	0	O3(0/1/2)	0	-0.2
2002	†NY A	28	83	9	22	5	0	1	6	6-0	0	10	.265	.311	.361	80	-2	1-1	.966	1	102	125	O28(15/0/15)	72	-0.3
2003	†NY A	57	173	22	46	14	0	7	26	10-1	0	27	.266	.304	.468	101	0	0-0	.979	-1	97	108	O56(34/0/22)	0	-0.2
2004	Mon N	134	391	48	120	24	1	12	49	34-7	1	45	.307	.364	.465	108	5	6-2	.986	4	95	**222**	O121(10/13/104)/D	0	0.6
2005	†LA A	106	350	46	95	17	1	15	59	23-0	0	44	.271	.316	.454	105	1	1-9	.992	1	98	141	O74(33/4/38),D28	0	-0.4
2006	LA A	124	448	65	139	27	0	23	85	33-0	7	59	.310	.362	.525	132	21	0-4	.974	7	104	206	O103(56/20/33),D18	21	2.1
Total	6	452	1449	190	422	87	2	58	225	106-8	8	185	.291	.341	.474	111	24	8-16	.981	12	99	178	O385(148/38/214),D47	93	1.6
RIVERA, LUIS	Luis Antonio (Pedraza); B1.3.1964 Cidra, PR; BR/TR/5´9˝/(165–175); d8.3; C1																								
1986	Mon N	55	166	20	34	11	1	0	13	17-0	2	33	.205	.285	.283	58	-9	1-1	.953	-10	87	90	S55	0	-1.5
1987	Mon N	18	32	0	5	2	0	0	1	1-0	0	8	.156	.182	.219	5	-4	0-0	.923	-0	109	86	S15	0	-0.4
1988	Mon N	123	371	35	83	17	3	4	30	24-4	1	69	.224	.271	.318	66	-17	3-4	.962	-2	99	**128**	S116	0	-1.2
1989	Bos A	93	323	35	83	17	1	5	29	20-1	1	60	.257	.301	.362	81	-8	2-3	.958	-8	92	104	S90/2D	0	-1.0
1990	†Bos A	118	346	38	78	20	0	7	45	25-0	1	58	.225	.279	.344	70	-14	4-3	.965	5	101	97	S112,2b3/3	0	-0.1
1991	Bos A	129	414	64	107	22	3	8	40	35-0	3	86	.258	.318	.384	89	-6	4-4	.959	7	102	113	S129	0	1.0
1992	Bos A	102	288	17	62	11	1	0	29	26-0	3	56	.215	.287	.260	51	-19	4-3	.966	13	112	105	S93/23lfD	0	0.0
1993	Bos A	62	130	13	27	8	1	1	7	11-0	1	36	.208	.273	.308	53	-9	1-2	.969	-4	102	108	2b27,S27,3b2,D7	42	-1.1
1994	NY N	32	43	11	12	2	1	3	5	4-0	2	14	.279	.367	.581	144	3	0-1	.971	4	124	192	S11,2b5	0	0.6
1997	Hou N	7	13	2	3	0	1	0	3	1-0	0	6	.231	.286	.385	76	-1	0-0	.875	-1	70	182	S6/2	0	-0.2
1998	KC A	42	89	14	22	4	0	0	7	7-0	0	17	.247	.302	.292	53	-6	1-1	.961	4	115	126	S30,2b6,3b6	0	-0.1
Total	11	781	2215	249	516	114	12	28	209	171-5	14	443	.233	.291	.333	70	-90	20-22	.961	7	100	110	S684,2b44,3b10,D10/lf	42	-4.0
RIVERA, JIM	Manuel Joseph "Jungle Jim"; B7.22.1922 New York NY; BL/TL/6´0˝/(195–196); d4.15																								
1952	StL A	97	336	45	86	13	6	4	30	29	2	59	.256	.319	.366	88	-6	8-7	.976	6	112	103	O88(8/81/0)	0	-0.4
	Chi A	53	201	27	50	7	3	3	18	21	0	27	.249	.320	.358	88	-4	13-2	.988	-1	102	47	O53C	0	-0.4
	Year	150	537	72	136	20	9	7	48	50	2	86	.253	.319	.363	88	-10	21-9	.980	5	108	81	O141(8/134/0)	0	-0.8
1953	Chi A	**156**	567	79	147	26	**16**	11	78	53	6	70	.259	.329	.420	98	-4	22-15	.976	-8	90	110	O156(0/153/3)	0	-2.0
1954	Chi A	145	490	62	140	16	8	13	61	49	6	68	.286	.356	.431	111	7	18-10	.959	-9	94	49	O143(3/28/128)	0	-0.7
1955	Chi A	147	454	71	120	24	4	10	52	62-6	1	59	.264	.352	.401	100	1	**25**-16	.981	11	102	**230**	O143(2/50/115)	0	0.7
1956	Chi A	139	491	76	125	23	5	12	66	49-2	3	75	.255	.322	.395	88	-9	20-9	.976	2	104	96	O134(0/14/122)	0	-1.0
1957	Chi A	125	402	51	103	21	6	14	52	40-6	3	80	.256	.326	.443	108	4	18-2	.974	-7	94	99	O86(1/4/83),1b31	0	-0.5
1958	Chi A	116	276	37	62	8	4	9	35	24-5	1	49	.225	.282	.380	84	-7	21-3	.994	1	96	119	O99(54/1/45)	0	-0.7
1959	†Chi A	80	177	18	39	9	4	4	19	11-3	1	19	.220	.266	.384	78	-6	5-3	.976	-2	79	168	O69(21/0/48)	0	-1.1
1960	Chi A	48	17	17	5	0	0	1	1	3-0	0	3	.294	.400	.471	136	1	4-0	1.000	-0	109	0	O24(9/1/14)	0	0.1
1961	Chi A	1	0	0	0	0	0	0	0	0-0	0	0	ø	ø	ø	ø	0	0-1	ø	0	—	—	/H	44	0.0
	KC A	64	141	20	34	8	0	2	10	24-0	0	14	.241	.352	.340	84	-2	6-2	.981	-6	71	0	O43(0/7/36)	0	-1.0
	Year	65	141	20	34	8	0	2	10	24-0	0	14	.241	.352	.340	84	-2	6-3	.981	-6	71	0	O43(0/7/36)	0	-1.0
Total	10	1171	3552	503	911	155	56	83	422	365-22	23	523	.256	.328	.402	96	-25	160-70	.977	-13	97	110	O1038(98/392/594),1b31	44	-7.0
RIVERA, MIKE	Michael R.; B9.8.1976 Rio Piedras, PR; BR/TR/6´0˝/(190–210); d9.18; Col Troy St.																								
2001	Det A	4	12	2	4	2	0	0	1	0-0	0	2	.333	.333	.500	118	0	0-0	.929	1	70	347	C4	0	0.2
2002	Det A	39	132	11	30	8	1	1	11	4-0	1	35	.227	.254	.326	55	-9	0-0	.990	1	95	138	C37/D	0	-0.5
2003	SD N	19	53	2	9	1	0	1	2	5-0	0	11	.170	.241	.245	30	-6	0-0	.986	3	79	85	C19/1	0	-0.2
2006	Mil N	46	142	16	38	9	0	6	24	10-5	3	21	.268	.325	.458	98	-1	0-0	.988	3	61	89	C44	0	0.4
Total	4	108	339	31	81	20	1	8	38	19-5	4	69	.239	.285	.375	73	-16	0-0	.986	7	77	115	C104/1D	0	-0.1
RIVERA, RENE	Rene; B7.31.1983 Bayamon, PR; BR/TR/5´10˝/(190–210); [SeaA01 2/49]; d9.22																								
2004	Sea A	2	3	0	0	0	0	0	0	0-0	0	1	.000	.000	.000	-99	-1	0-0	1.000	0	0	0	C2	0	-0.1
2005	Sea A	16	48	3	19	3	0	1	6	1-0	0	11	.396	.408	.521	156	4	0-0	.961	-1	164	72	C15	0	0.3
2006	Sea A	35	99	8	15	4	0	2	4	3-0	1	29	.152	.184	.253	12	-13	1-0	.987	3	106	131	C35	0	-0.8
Total	3	53	150	11	34	7	0	3	10	4-0	1	41	.227	.252	.333	55	-10	1-0	.981	2	122	113	C52	0	-0.6
RIVERA, RUBEN	Ruben (Moreno); B11.14.1973 Chorrera, Pan; BR/TR/6´3˝/(200–208); d9.3; [DL 1997 NY A 59]																								
1995	NY A	5	1	0	0	0	0	0	0	0-0	0	1	.000	.000	.000	-99	0	0-0	1.000	0	174	0	O4L	0	0.0
1996	†NY A	46	88	17	25	6	1	2	16	13-0	2	26	.284	.381	.443	110	2	6-2	1.000	4	125	112	O45(13/14/19)	0	0.5
1997	SD N	17	20	2	5	1	0	0	1	2-0	0	9	.250	.318	.300	67	-1	2-1	1.000	1	140	0	O7(2/4/4)	75	0.0
1998	†SD N	95	172	31	36	7	2	6	29	28-0	2	52	.209	.325	.378	91	-2	5-1	.973	-0	100	86	O91(13/13/73)	0	-0.4
1999	SD N	147	411	65	80	16	1	23	48	55-1	5	143	.195	.295	.406	82	-14	18-7	.976	5	111	128	O143C	0	-0.6
2000	SD N	135	423	62	88	18	6	17	57	44-1	10	137	.208	.296	.400	79	-16	8-4	.984	1	102	136	O132(1/131/0)	22	-1.3
2001	Cin N	117	263	37	67	13	1	10	34	21-1	5	83	.255	.321	.426	86	-6	6-3	.983	1	107	97	O99(10/70/21)	0	-0.4
2002	Tex A	69	158	17	33	4	0	4	14	17-0	5	45	.209	.302	.310	63	-8	4-2	.983	4	120	71	O67C,D2	0	-0.3
2003	SF N	31	50	6	9	2	0	2	4	5-1	0	14	.180	.255	.340	52	-4	1-0	1.000	2	151	0	O27(9/13/6)	0	-0.1
Total	9	662	1586	237	343	67	11	64	203	185-4	29	510	.216	.307	.393	81	-49	50-20	.982	18	110	108	O615(52/455/123),D2	156	-2.6
RIVERS, MICKEY	John Milton; B10.31.1948 Miami FL; BL/TL/5´10˝/(160–165); [AtlN69 S2/40]; d8.4; Mil 1971; Col Miami–Dade North (FL) CC																								
1970	Cal A	17	25	6	8	2	0	0	3	3-0	1	5	.320	.414	.400	129	1	1-0	1.000	0	107	0	O5R	0	0.1
1971	Cal A	79	268	31	71	12	2	1	12	19-1	1	38	.265	.316	.336	91	-4	13-1	.976	-2	94	110	O76(4/61/18)	0	-0.5
1972	Cal A	58	159	18	34	6	2	0	7	8-1	1	26	.214	.256	.277	62	-8	4-3	.981	1	116	0	O48(6/38/7)	0	-1.0
1973	Cal A	30	129	26	45	6	4	0	16	8-0	1	11	.349	.391	.457	149	8	8-3	.909	-6	81	0	O29C	0	0.2
1974	Cal A	118	466	69	133	19	**11**	3	31	39-0	1	47	.285	.341	.393	117	9	30-13	.994	3	106	115	O116C	43	1.2
1975	Cal A	155	616	70	175	17	**13**	1	53	43-5	2	42	.284	.331	.359	102	0	**70**-14	.977	1	100	125	O152(27/125/0)/D	0	0.6
1976	†NY A★	137	590	95	184	31	8	8	67	13-0	3	51	.312	.327	.432	123	13	43-7	.986	-1	104	57	O136C	0	1.6
1977	†NY A	138	565	79	184	18	5	12	69	18-4	4	45	.326	.350	.439	114	9	22-14	.982	7	110	118	O136C/D	0	1.4
1978	†NY A	141	559	78	148	25	8	11	48	29-3	3	51	.265	.302	.397	98	-4	25-5	.980	4	108	96	O138C	15	0.3
1979	NY A	74	286	37	82	18	5	3	25	13-2	1	21	.287	.315	.416	98	-1	3-7	.974	-7	82	92	O69C/D	20	-1.1

YEAR	TM LG	G	AB	R	H	2B	3B	HR	RBI	BB-IB	HP	SO	AVG	OBP	SLG	AOPS	ABR	SB-CS	FA	FR	RNG	THR	GAMES AT POSITION	DL	BFW
	Tex A	58	247	35	74	9	3	6	25	9-0	1	18	.300	.323	.433	104	0	7-2	.981	1	102	109	O57C	0	0.1
	Year	132	533	72	156	27	8	9	50	22-2	2	39	.293	.319	.424	101	-1	10-9	.978	-7	91	100	O126C/D	0	-1.0
1980	Tex A	147	630	96	210	32	6	7	60	20-1	1	34	.333	.353	.437	119	14	18-7	.978	3	94	**208**	O141C,D4	0	1.7
1981	Tex A	99	399	62	114	21	2	3	26	24-2	1	31	.286	.327	.371	106	3	9-5	.996	-1	88	**207**	O97C	0	0.1
1982	Tex A	19	68	6	16	1	1	1	4	0-0	0	7	.235	.232	.324	54	-5	0-0	ø	0	0	0	D16	146	-0.5
1983	Tex A	96	309	37	88	17	0	1	20	11-0	1	21	.285	.309	.350	82	-8	9-4	.980	0	110	62	D53,O23(15/0/8)	0	-0.9
1984	Tex A	102	313	40	94	13	1	4	33	9-1	0	23	.300	.320	.387	91	-4	5-5	1.000	1	92	177	D48,O30(26/2/2)	0	-0.7
Total	15	1468	5629	785	1660	247	71	61	499	266-20	22	471	.295	.327	.397	106	23	267-90	.982	3	100	117	O1253(78/1145/40),D124	224	2.6
RIZZO, JOHNNY	John Costa; B7.30.1912 Houston TX; D12.4.1977 Houston TX; BR/TR/6´0˝/190; d4.19; Mil 1943–46																								
1938	Pit N	143	555	97	167	31	9	23	111	54	5	61	.301	.368	.514	139	29	1	.951	-11	90	43	O140L	—	0.9
1939	Pit N	94	330	49	86	23	3	6	55	42	3	27	.261	.349	.403	103	3	0	.974	-3	99	36	O86L	—	-0.6
1940	Pit N	9	28	1	5	1	0	0	2	5	1	5	.179	.324	.214	51	-2	0	.818	-2	65	0	O7L	—	-0.4
	Cin N	31	110	17	31	6	0	4	17	14	0	14	.282	.363	.445	121	3	1	.974	4	99	260	O30L	—	0.5
	Phi N	103	367	53	107	12	2	20	53	37	1	31	.292	.358	.499	139	18	2	.968	5	104	88	O91(56/23/15),3b7	—	1.9
	Year	143	505	71	143	19	2	24	72	56	2	50	.283	.357	.471	130	20	3	.964	7	101	126	O128(93/23/15),3b7	—	2.0
1941	Phi N	99	235	20	51	9	2	4	24	24	2	34	.217	.295	.323	77	-8	1	.968	2	103	170	O62(3/8/53),3b2	0	-0.9
1942	Bro N	78	217	31	50	8	0	4	27	24	0	25	.230	.307	.323	83	-5	2	.977	2	108	118	O70(9/0/62)	0	-0.6
Total	5	557	1842	268	497	90	16	61	289	200	12	197	.270	.345	.435	116	38	7	.964	-3	98	89	O486(331/31/130),3b9	0	0.8
RIZZUTO, PHIL	Philip Francis "Scooter" (b Fiero Francis Rizzuto); B9.25.1917 Brooklyn NY; BR/TR/5´6˝/160; d4.14; Mil 1943–45; HF1994																								
1941	†NY A	133	515	65	158	20	9	3	46	27	1	36	.307	.343	.398	97	-5	14-5	.957	19	**108**	**141**	S128	0	2.4
1942	†NY A☆	144	553	79	157	24	7	4	68	44	6	40	.284	.343	.374	104	2	22-6	.962	**30**	108	**149**	S144	0	4.6
1946	NY A	126	471	53	121	17	1	2	38	34	6	39	.257	.315	.310	74	-16	14-7	.961	17	104	**129**	S125	0	0.9
1947	†NY A	153	549	78	150	26	9	2	60	57	**8**	31	.273	.350	.364	100	0	11-6	.969	18	99	111	S151	0	2.8
1948	NY A	128	464	65	117	13	2	6	50	60	2	24	.252	.340	.328	79	-14	6-5	.973	-13	87	95	S128	0	-1.8
1949	†NY A	153	614	110	169	22	7	5	65	72	1	34	.275	.352	.358	88	-11	18-6	**.971**	3	94	101	S152	0	0.3
1950	†NY A★	**155**	617	125	200	36	7	7	66	92	7	39	.324	.418	.439	123	26	12-8	**.982**	8	95	108	S155	0	**4.0**
1951	†NY A★	144	540	87	148	21	6	2	43	58	5	27	.274	.350	.346	92	-5	18-3	.968	11	97	**116**	S144	0	1.7
1952	†NY A★	152	578	89	147	24	10	2	43	67	5	42	.254	.337	.341	95	-4	17-6	.976	21	**105**	**127**	S152	0	2.9
1953	†NY A★	134	413	54	112	21	3	2	54	71	4	39	.271	.383	.351	103	6	4-3	.963	3	103	127	S133	0	1.9
1954	NY A	127	307	47	60	11	0	2	15	41	1	23	.195	.291	.251	51	-20	3-2	.968	6	98	**137**	S126/2	0	-0.6
1955	†NY A	81	143	19	37	4	1	1	9	22-1	3	18	.259	.369	.322	88	-1	7-1	.957	-8	84	97	S79/2	0	-0.4
1956	NY A	31	52	6	12	0	0	0	6	6-0	0	6	.231	.310	.231	46	-4	3-0	.934	2	106	156	S30	0	0.0
Total	13	1661	5816	877	1588	239	62	38	563	651-<u>1</u>	49	398	.273	.351	.355	93	-46	149-58	.968	117	99	121	S1647,2b2	0	18.7
ROACH, MEL	Melvin Earl; B1.25.1933 Richmond VA; BR/TR/6´1˝/(190–195); d7.31; Mil 1955–56; Col Virginia																								
1953	Mil N	5	2	1	0	0	0	0	0	0	0	1	.000	.000	.000	-99	-1	0-0	ø	-0	0	0	/2	0	-0.1
1954	Mil N	3	4	0	0	0	0	0	0	0	0	1	.000	.000	.000	-99	-1	0-0	1.000	-0	0	511	/1	0	-0.1
1957	Mil N	7	6	1	1	0	0	0	0	0-0	0	3	.167	.167	.167	-11	-1	0-0	1.000	-1	63	0	2b5	0	-0.2
1958	Mil N	44	136	14	42	7	0	3	10	6-0	0	15	.309	.336	.426	110	2	0-0	.993	2	115	80	2b27,O7(4/0/3)/1	52	0.5
1959	Mil N	19	31	1	3	0	0	0	0	2-0	0	4	.097	.152	.097	-35	-6	0-0	.880	0	114	74	2b8,O4L/3	96	-0.6
1960	Mil N	48	140	12	42	12	0	3	18	6-1	1	19	.300	.329	.450	121	4	0-0	.975	-8	111	0	O21L,2b20/13	0	-0.4
1961	Mil N	13	36	3	6	0	0	1	6	2-0	2	4	.167	.244	.250	35	-3	0-0	1.000	-2	76	0	O9L,1b2	0	-0.6
	Chi N	23	39	1	5	2	0	0	1	3-0	0	9	.128	.190	.179	-1	-6	1-0	.981	-4	83	178	1b7,2b7	0	-1.0
	Year	36	75	4	11	2	0	1	7	5-0	2	13	.147	.217	.213	16	-9	1-0	1.000	-6	76	0	O9L,1b9,2b7	0	-1.6
1962	Phi N	65	105	9	20	4	0	0	8	5-0	0	19	.190	.225	.229	23	-11	0-0	.951	-2	98	77	3b26,2b9,1b4,O3L	0	-1.3
Total	8	227	499	42	119	25	0	7	43	24-1	3	75	.238	.275	.331	66	-23	1-0	.969	-14	95	67	2b77,O44(41/0/3),3b28,1b16	148	-3.8
ROACH, MIKE	Michael Stephen; B12.23.1869 Driftwood PA; D11.12.1916 New York NY; 5´7˝/145; d8.10; b–John																								
1899	Was N	24	78	7	17	1	0	0	7	3	2	—	.218	.265	.231	37	-7	3	.964	-4	76	73	C20,1b3	—	-0.9
ROACH, ROXEY	Wilbur Charles; B11.28.1882 Anita PA; D12.26.1947 Bay City MI; BR/TR/5´11˝/160; d5.2																								
1910	NY A	70	220	27	47	9	2	0	20	29	3	—	.214	.313	.273	79	-4	15	.913	-4	96	139	S58,O9L	—	-0.7
1911	NY A	13	40	4	10	2	1	0	2	6	0	—	.250	.348	.350	89	0	0	.891	-2	86	179	S8,2b5	—	-0.1
1912	Was A	2	2	1	1	0	0	1	1	0	0	—	.500	.500	2.000	600	1	0	.500	-1	71	0	S2	—	0.1
1915	Buf F	92	346	35	93	20	3	2	31	17	0	34	.269	.303	.361	85	-13	11	.959	17	108	104	S92	—	1.1
Total	4	177	608	67	151	31	6	3	54	52	3	<u>34</u>	.248	.311	.334	85	-16	26	.938	11	102	120	S160,O9L,2b5	—	0.4
ROARKE, MIKE	Michael Thomas; B11.8.1930 West Warwick RI; BR/TR/6´2˝/195; d4.19; C20; Col Boston College																								
1961	Det A	86	229	21	51	6	1	2	22	20-3	0	31	.223	.283	.284	51	-16	0-0	.988	1	132	104	C85	0	-1.2
1962	Det A	56	136	11	29	4	1	4	14	13-2	1	17	.213	.287	.346	67	-7	0-0	.982	3	87	143	C53	0	-0.2
1963	Det A	23	44	5	14	0	0	0	1	2-1	1	3	.318	.362	.318	89	-1	0-0	.986	0	116	117	C16	0	0.0
1964	Det A	29	82	4	19	1	0	0	7	10-0	0	10	.232	.315	.244	57	-4	0-0	.994	1	269	82	C27	0	-0.2
Total	4	194	491	41	113	11	2	6	44	45-6	2	61	.230	.296	.297	60	-28	0-0	.987	5	141	112	C181	0	-1.6
ROAT, FRED	Frederick R.; B11.10.1867 Oregon IL; D9.24.1913 Oregon IL; TR; d5.10																								
1890	Pit N	57	215	18	48	2	0	2	17	16	3	22	.223	.286	.260	67	-8	7	.847	4	119	103	3b44,1b9,O4R	—	-0.4
1892	Chi N	8	31	4	6	0	1	0	2	2	0	3	.194	.242	.258	51	-2	2	.897	-3	97	32	2b8	—	-0.4
Total	2	65	246	22	54	2	1	2	19	18	3	25	.220	.281	.260	65	-10	9	.847	1	119	103	3b44,1b9,2b8,O4R	—	-0.8
ROBELLO, TONY	Thomas Vardasco; B2.9.1913 San Leandro CA; D12.25.1994 Fort Worth TX; BR/TR/5´10.5˝/175; d8.13																								
1933	Cin N	14	30	1	7	3	0	0	3	1	0	5	.233	.258	.333	69	-1	0	1.000	1	121	88	2b11,3b2	—	0.0
1934	Cin N	2	2	0	0	0	0	0	0	0	0	1	.000	.000	.000	-99	-1	0	ø	0	—	—	/H	—	-0.1
Total	2	16	32	1	7	3	0	0	3	1	0	6	.219	.242	.313	58	-2	0	1.000	1	121	88	2b11,3b2	—	-0.1
ROBERGE, SKIPPY	Joseph Albert Armand; B5.19.1917 Lowell MA; D6.7.1993 Lowell MA; BR/TR/5´11˝/185; d7.18; Mil 1943–45																								
1941	Bos N	55	167	12	36	6	0	0	15	9	0	18	.216	.256	.251	45	-13	0	.978	4	111	123	2b46,3b5,S2	0	-0.6
1942	Bos N	74	172	10	37	7	0	1	12	9	1	19	.215	.258	.273	57	-10	1	.977	5	103	96	2b29,3b27,S6	0	-0.2
1946	Bos N	48	169	13	39	6	2	2	20	7	2	12	.231	.270	.325	68	-8	1	.973	2	95	174	3b48	0	-0.7
Total	3	177	508	35	112	19	2	3	47	25	3	49	.220	.261	.283	57	-31	2	.967	12	105	154	3b80,2b75,S8	0	-1.5
ROBERSON, CHRIS	Christopher William; B8.23.1979 Oakland CA; BB/TR/6´2˝/180; [PhiN01 9/260]; d5.12; Col Feather River (CA) JC																								
2006	Phi N	57	41	9	8	0	1	0	1	0-0	1	9	.195	.214	.244	16	-5	3-0	1.000	-1	83	0	O45(30/0/21)	0	-0.6
ROBERSON, KEVIN	Kevin Lynn; B1.29.1968 Decatur IL; BB/TR/6´4˝/210; [ChiN88 16/404]; d7.15; Col Parkland (IL) JC																								
1993	Chi N	62	180	23	34	4	1	9	27	12-0	3	48	.189	.251	.372	65	-10	0-1	.963	-5	83	56	O51(14/0/42)	0	-1.8
1994	Chi N	44	55	8	12	4	0	4	9	2-0	2	14	.218	.271	.509	97	-1	0-0	.800	-1	65	242	O9R	38	-0.1
1995	Chi N	32	38	5	7	1	0	4	6	6-0	1	14	.184	.311	.526	116	1	0-1	1.000	-1	78	0	O11(10/0/1)	0	-0.1
1996	NY N	27	36	8	8	1	0	3	9	7-0	1	17	.222	.348	.500	131	2	0-0	1.000	-1	93	0	O10(1/0/9)	0	0.1
Total	4	165	309	44	61	10	1	20	51	27-0	7	93	.197	.275	.430	85	-8	0-2	.955	-6	82	61	O81(25/0/61)	38	-1.9
ROBERTS, BRIAN	Brian Michael; B10.9.1977 Durham NC; BB/TR/5´9˝/(170–180); [BalA99 1/50]; d6.14; Col South Carolina																								
2001	Bal A	75	273	42	69	12	3	2	17	13-0	0	36	.253	.284	.341	68	-14	12-3	.939	-4	102	84	S51,2b12,D7	0	-1.1
2002	Bal A	38	128	18	29	6	0	1	11	15-0	1	21	.227	.308	.297	67	-6	9-2	.976	1	105	117	2b25,D8	0	-0.3
2003	Bal A	112	460	65	124	22	4	5	41	46-1	1	58	.270	.337	.367	86	-9	23-6	.987	4	103	94	2b107,S2,D4	0	0.4
2004	Bal A	159	641	107	175	**50**	2	4	53	71-1	1	95	.273	.344	.376	89	-8	29-12	.988	-13	99	88	2b150,D6	0	-1.1
2005	Bal A★	143	561	92	176	45	7	18	73	67-5	3	83	.314	.387	.515	139	33	27-10	.988	9	105	97	2b141	0	4.9
2006	Bal A	138	563	85	161	34	3	10	55	55-4	0	66	.286	.347	.410	99	0	36-7	.985	-7	100	97	2b137/D	24	0.4
Total	6	665	2626	409	734	169	19	40	250	267-11	6	359	.280	.345	.404	98	-4	136-40	.986	-10	102	95	2b572,S53,D26	24	3.2
ROBERTS, RED	Charles Emory; B8.8.1918 Carrollton GA; D12.2.1998 Atlanta GA; BR/TR/6´0˝/170; d9.3; Mil 1944–45																								
1943	Was A	9	23	1	6	1	0	1	3	4	0	2	.261	.370	.435	140	1	0-0	.778	-4	59	39	S6/3	0	-0.2

YEAR	TM LG	G	AB	R	H	2B	3B	HR	RBI	BB-IB	HP	SO	AVG	OBP	SLG	AOPS	ABR	SB-CS	FA	FR	RNG	THR	GAMES AT POSITION	DL	BFW
Roberts, Skipper	Clarence Ashley; B1.11.1888 Wardner ID; D12.24.1963 Long Beach CA; BL/TR/5´10.5˝/175; d6.12																								
1913	StL N	26	41	4	6	2	0	0	3	3	0	13	.146	.205	.195	15	-5	1-2	.859	-3	84	53	C16	—	-0.8
1914	Pit F	33	55	7	12	2	1	0	4	1	1	11	.218	.246	.291	46	-5	2	.941	-1	*107*	*77*	C14	—	-0.6
	Chi F	4	3	0	1	0	0	0	1	1	0	1	.333	.500	.333	138	0	0	ø	0	—	—	/H	—	0.0
	Pit F	19	39	5	10	2	1	1	4	1	1	8	.256	.293	.436	98	-1	1	.923	-2	*107*	*77*	C9/rf	—	-0.3
	Year	56	97	12	23	4	2	1	9	3	2	20	.237	.275	.351	70	-6	3	.935	-4	*102*	*87*	C23/rf	—	-0.9
Total	2	82	138	16	29	6	2	1	12	6	2	33	.210	.253	.304	54	-11	4-2	.906	-7	*95*	*75*	C39/rf	—	-1.7
Roberts, Curt	Curtis Benjamin; B8.16.1929 Pineland TX; D11.14.1969 Oakland CA; BR/TR/5´8˝/165; d4.13; Negro Lg 1947–50																								
1954	Pit N	134	496	47	115	18	7	1	36	55	2	49	.232	.309	.302	62	-28	6-3	.969	5	105	77	2b131	0	-1.3
1955	Pit N	6	17	1	2	1	0	0	0	2-0	0	1	.118	.211	.176	4	-2	0-0	.913	-0	112	120	2b6	0	-0.2
1956	Pit N	31	62	6	11	5	2	0	4	5-0	0	12	.177	.239	.323	50	-5	1-0	.988	-0	95	108	2b27	0	-0.4
Total	3	171	575	54	128	24	9	1	40	62-0	2	62	.223	.299	.301	59	-35	7-3	.969	4	104	82	2b164	0	-1.9
Roberts, Dave	David Leonard; B6.30.1933 Panama City, Pan; BL/TL/6´0˝/(172–175); d9.5																								
1962	Hou N	16	53	3	13	3	0	1	10	8-0	1	8	.245	.349	.358	99	0	0-0	1.000	-0	115	0	O12(6/0/6),1b6	0	-0.1
1964	Hou N	61	125	9	23	4	1	1	7	14-1	1	28	.184	.270	.256	52	-8	0-1	.983	3	138	89	1b34,O4L	0	-0.7
1966	Pit N	14	16	3	2	1	0	0	0	0-0	0	7	.125	.125	.188	-15	-2	0-0	.950	0	168	126	1b2	0	-0.3
Total	3	91	194	15	38	8	1	2	17	22-1	2	43	.196	.282	.278	60	-10	0-1	.983	3	130	86	1b42,O16(10/0/6)	0	-1.1
Roberts, Dave	David Ray; B5.31.1972 Okinawa, Japan; BL/TL/5´10˝/(172–180); [DetA94 28/781]; d8.7; Col UCLA																								
1999	†Cle A	41	143	26	34	4	0	2	12	9-0	0	16	.238	.281	.308	48	-12	11-3	1.000	-1	105	0	O39(1/38/0)	0	-1.0
2000	Cle A	19	10	1	2	0	0	0	0	2-0	0	2	.200	.333	.200	38	-1	1-1	1.000	-0	86	0	O17(12/5/1)	0	-0.1
2001	Cle A	15	12	3	4	1	0	0	2	1-0	0	2	.333	.385	.417	107	0	0-1	1.000	-0	102	0	O13(9/2/2),D2	83	0.0
2002	LA N	127	422	63	117	14	7	3	34	48-0	2	51	.277	.353	.365	95	-3	45-10	**1.000**	-3	99	68	O117(3/115/0)	0	0.2
2003	LA N	107	388	56	97	6	5	2	16	43-1	4	39	.250	.331	.307	70	-17	40-14	.976	-6	91	78	O105C	39	-1.8
2004	LA N	68	233	45	59	4	7	2	21	28-0	4	31	.253	.340	.356	82	-6	33-1	.976	-1	104	63	O62(48/19/0)	23	-0.1
	†Bos A	45	86	19	22	10	0	2	14	10-0	1	17	.256	.330	.442	96	0	5-2	.982	0	103	73	O38(18/16/14)/D	0	0.0
2005	†SD N	115	411	65	113	19	10	8	38	53-3	1	59	.275	.356	.428	110	6	23-12	.992	-4	97	76	O109C	15	0.5
2006	†SD N	129	499	80	146	18	13	2	44	51-2	4	61	.293	.360	.393	99	-1	49-6	**1.000**	3	109	15	O127(116/13/0)	17	0.6
Total	8	666	2204	358	594	76	42	21	181	245-6	16	278	.270	.344	.371	89	-34	207-50	.991	-11	100	54	O627(207/422/17),D3	177	-1.7
Roberts, Dave	David Wayne; B2.17.1951 Lebanon OR; BR/TR/6´3˝/(200–215); [SDN72 1/1]; d6.7; C1; Col Oregon; OF(3/6/10)																								
1972	SD N	100	418	38	102	17	0	5	33	18-1	0	64	.244	.275	.321	74	-16	7-2	.931	-13	97	130	3b84,2b20,S3/C	0	-3.0
1973	SD N	127	479	56	137	20	3	21	64	17-3	1	83	.286	.310	.472	124	11	11-2	.942	7	106	111	3b111,2b12	0	2.0
1974	SD N	113	318	26	53	10	1	5	18	32-6	2	69	.167	.246	.252	42	-26	2-0	.955	-8	88	72	3b103,S3/lf	0	-3.5
1975	SD N	33	113	7	32	2	0	2	12	13-3	2	19	.283	.367	.354	108	2	3-1	.925	-4	102	98	3b30,2b5	0	-0.2
1977	SD N	82	186	15	41	14	1	1	23	11-1	1	32	.220	.268	.323	64	-10	2-1	.982	-8	104	104	C63,2b2,3b2/S	0	-1.6
1978	SD N	54	97	7	21	4	1	1	7	12-6	1	25	.216	.309	.309	79	-3	0-0	.980	-3	122	87	C41,1b8,O2(1/1/0)	14	-0.5
1979	Tex A	44	84	12	22	2	1	3	14	7-0	0	17	.262	.319	.417	97	-1	1-0	.980	1	169	107	C14,O11(1/5/5),2b8,1b6/3D	21	0.1
1980	Tex A	101	235	27	56	4	0	10	30	13-2	1	38	.238	.280	.383	82	-7	0-1	.930	-8	76	31	3b37,S33,C22,O5R,1b4,2b4	0	-1.4
1981	†Hou N	27	54	4	13	3	0	1	5	3-0	0	6	.241	.271	.352	83	-1	1-0	.958	-0	135	101	1b10,3b7,2b3/C	0	-0.2
1982	Phi N	28	33	2	6	1	0	0	2	2-0	0	8	.182	.229	.212	23	-3	0-1	.818	-2	102	0	3b11,C10,2b7	0	-0.6
Total	10	709	2017	194	483	77	7	49	208	128-22	8	361	.239	.286	.357	83	-54	27-8	.939	-36	96	97	3b386,C152,2b61,S40,1b28,O19R,D4	35	-8.9
Roberts, Bip	Leon Joseph; B10.27.1963 Berkeley CA; BB/TR/5´7˝/(160–165); [PitN82 S1/13]; d4.7; Col Chabot (CA) JC; OF(382/72/25)																								
1986	SD N	101	241	34	61	5	2	1	12	14-1	0	29	.253	.293	.303	66	-12	14-12	.971	-3	90	82	2b87	15	-1.3
1988	SD N	5	9	1	3	0	0	0	0	1-0	0	2	.333	.400	.333	115	0	0-2	.500	-1	33	0	3b2/2	0	-0.1
1989	SD N	117	329	81	99	15	8	3	25	49-0	1	45	.301	.391	.422	133	16	21-11	.976	5	104	147	O54(34/1/21),3b37,S14,2b9	0	2.3
1990	SD N	149	556	104	172	36	3	9	44	55-1	6	65	.309	.375	.433	121	18	46-12	.982	5	108	153	O75L,3b56,S18,2b8	0	2.9
1991	SD N	117	424	66	119	13	3	3	32	37-0	4	71	.281	.342	.347	92	-4	26-11	.978	-1	100	109	2b68,O46(19/29/0)	23	-0.2
1992	Cin N★	147	532	92	172	34	6	4	45	62-4	2	54	.323	.393	.432	131	24	44-16	.993	-3	106	33	O79(69/16/0),2b42,3b36	0	2.6
1993	Cin N	83	292	46	70	13	0	1	18	38-1	3	46	.240	.330	.295	69	-11	26-6	.984	1	96	83	2b64,O11(11/1/0),3b3/S	76	-0.4
1994	SD N	105	403	52	129	15	5	2	31	39-1	3	57	.320	.383	.397	108	5	21-7	.976	-12	86	82	2b90,O20(16/5/0)	0	-0.1
1995	SD N	73	296	40	90	14	0	2	25	17-1	2	36	.304	.346	.372	92	-3	20-2	.989	6	128	85	O50(48/4/0),2b25,S7	54	0.6
1996	KC A	90	339	39	96	21	2	0	52	25-8	2	38	.283	.331	.357	75	-12	12-9	.986	6	117	114	2b63,D16,O11(8/2/1)	64	-0.5
1997	KC A	97	346	44	107	17	2	1	36	21-2	1	53	.309	.348	.379	88	-6	15-3	.981	-2	101	108	O84(82/2/0),3b10	25	-0.8
	†Cle A	23	85	19	23	3	0	3	8	7-0	2	14	.271	.333	.412	92	-1	3-0	.932	1	100	129	2b13,O10L	0	0.1
	Year	120	431	63	130	20	2	4	44	28-2	3	67	.302	.345	.385	88	-7	18-3	.982	-0	98	136	O94(92/2/0),2b13,3b10	0	-0.7
1998	Det A	34	113	17	28	6	0	0	9	16-0	2	14	.248	.351	.301	71	-4	6-1	1.000	0	33	0	D29,O2L/2	36	-0.4
	Oak A	61	182	28	51	11	0	1	15	15-0	2	24	.280	.340	.357	83	-4	10-3	.970	-4	89	123	2b30,O22(8/12/3),3b3	0	-0.6
	Year	95	295	45	79	17	0	1	24	31-0	4	38	.268	.344	.336	79	-8	16-4	.971	-4	90	139	2b31,D29,O24(10/12/3),3b3	0	-1.0
Total	12	1202	4147	663	1220	203	31	30	352	396-19	30	548	.294	.358	.380	99	6	264-95	.977	-1	98	95	2b501,O464L,3b147,D45,S40	293	4.1
Roberts, Leon	Leon Kauffman; B1.22.1951 Vicksburg MI; BR/TR/6´3˝/(198–200); [DetA72 10/236]; d9.3; C2; Col Michigan																								
1974	Det A	17	63	5	17	3	2	0	7	3-1	0	10	.270	.303	.381	92	-1	0-2	.926	-3	76	0	O17(0/1/16)	0	-0.6
1975	Det A	129	447	51	115	17	5	10	38	36-1	4	94	.257	.316	.385	94	-5	3-7	.982	5	112	97	O127R/D	0	-0.9
1976	Hou N	87	235	31	68	11	2	7	33	19-1	3	43	.289	.347	.443	135	10	1-0	.980	-4	89	25	O60(49/0/12)	0	0.4
1977	Hou N	19	27	1	2	0	0	0	2	1-0	0	8	.074	.107	.074	-55	-6	0-0	1.000	-0	28	491	O9(4/0/6)	0	-0.7
1978	Sea A	134	472	78	142	21	7	22	92	41-2	8	52	.301	.364	.515	145	27	6-3	.975	6	112	105	O128R,D2	0	2.8
1979	Sea A	140	450	61	122	24	6	15	54	56-6	2	64	.271	.352	.451	113	9	3-3	.983	5	114	65	O136(67/0/69)/D	0	0.7
1980	Sea A	119	374	48	94	18	3	10	33	43-1	1	59	.251	.325	.396	96	-2	8-4	.984	3	111	81	O104(20/20/70),D4	0	-0.2
1981	Tex A	72	233	26	65	17	2	4	31	25-2	1	38	.279	.345	.421	128	9	3-4	.992	-5	91	41	O71(25/3/46)	0	0.0
1982	Tex A	31	73	7	17	3	0	1	6	4-1	1	14	.233	.278	.315	67	-3	0-0	1.000	-2	95	0	O28(11/2/17)/D	0	-0.6
	Tor A	40	105	6	24	4	0	1	5	7-0	0	16	.229	.274	.295	53	-7	1-1	1.000	-2	74	0	D21,O16L	0	-1.0
	Year	71	178	13	41	7	0	2	11	11-1	1	30	.230	.276	.303	58	-10	1-1	1.000	-4	86	0	O44(27/2/17),D22	0	-1.6
1983	KC A	84	213	24	55	7	0	8	24	17-1	1	27	.258	.313	.404	96	-2	1-1	.979	0	107	63	O76(41/3/35)/D	0	-0.4
1984	KC A	29	45	4	10	1	1	0	3	4-0	1	3	.222	.300	.289	63	-2	0-0	1.000	-0	107	0	O16(10/0/7)/PD	16	-0.3
Total	11	901	2737	342	731	126	28	78	328	256-16	22	428	.267	.332	.419	108	27	26-25	.982	4	105	72	O788(243/29/533),D34/P	16	-0.8
Roberts, Ryan	Ryan Alan; B9.19.1980 Fort Worth TX; BR/TR/5´11˝/190; [TorA03 18/530]; d7.30; Col Texas–Arlington																								
2006	Tor A	9	13	1	1	0	0	1	1	1-0	0	4	.077	.143	.308	11	-2	0-0	1.000	0	101	114	2b8	0	-0.1
Robertson, Jim	Alfred James; B1.29.1928 Chicago IL; BR/TR/5´9˝/183; d4.15; Col Bradley																								
1954	Phi A	63	147	9	27	8	0	0	8	23	1	25	.184	.298	.238	48	-10	0-0	.974	-3	*94*	*68*	C50	0	-1.1
1955	KC A	6	8	1	2	0	0	0	0	1-0	0	2	.250	.333	.250	58	0	0-0	1.000	0	*0*	*251*	C4	0	0.0
Total	2	69	155	10	29	8	0	0	8	24-0	1	27	.187	.300	.239	49	-10	0-0	.975	-3	*90*	*76*	C54	0	-1.1
Robertson, Andre	Andre Levett; B10.2.1957 Orange TX; BR/TR/5´10˝/(155–162); [TorA79 4/81]; d9.3; Col Texas																								
1981	†NY A	10	19	1	5	1	0	0	0	0-0	0	3	.263	.263	.316	67	-1	1-1	1.000	0	98	65	S8,2b3	0	0.0
1982	NY A	44	118	16	26	5	0	2	9	8-0	0	19	.220	.270	.314	60	-7	0-0	.966	4	98	153	S27,2b15,3b2	0	0.0
1983	NY A	98	322	37	80	16	3	1	22	8-0	3	54	.248	.271	.326	66	-16	2-4	.960	11	115	126	S78,2b29	46	0.2
1984	NY A	52	140	10	30	5	1	0	6	4-0	0	20	.214	.236	.264	40	-12	0-1	.930	3	105	130	S49,2b6	0	-0.5
1985	NY A	50	125	16	41	5	0	2	17	6-0	1	24	.328	.358	.416	115	2	1-2	.867	-6	82	136	3b33,S14,2b2	51	-0.4
Total	5	254	724	80	182	32	4	5	54	26-0	4	120	.251	.279	.327	69	-34	4-8	.953	11	107	131	S176,2b55,3b35	97	-0.7
Robertson, Daryl	Daryl Berdene; B1.5.1936 Cripple Creek CO; BR/TR/6´0˝/184; d5.4																								
1962	Chi N	9	19	0	2	0	0	0	2	2-0	0	10	.105	.182	.105	-18	-3	0-0	1.000	-1	98	32	S6/3	0	-0.4
Robertson, Dave	Davis Aydelotte; B9.25.1889 Portsmouth VA; D11.5.1970 Virginia Beach VA; BL/TL/6´0˝/186; d6.5; Def 1918; Col North Carolina St.																								
1912	NY N	3	2	0	1	0	0	0	1	0	0	1	.500	.500	.500	169	0	1	1.000	-0	0	0	/1lf	—	0.0
1914	NY N	82	256	25	68	12	3	2	32	10	2	26	.266	.299	.359	99	-2	9	.950	2	97	141	O71(15/0/56)	—	-0.3
1915	NY N	141	544	72	160	17	10	3	58	22	4	52	.294	.326	.379	120	10	22-10	.956	-1	102	86	O138(16/0/123)	—	0.4
1916	NY N	150	587	88	180	18	8	**12**	69	14	3	56	.307	.326	.426	137	21	21-17	.960	-0	101	92	O144R	—	1.3
1917	†NY N	142	532	64	138	16	9	**12**	54	10	2	47	.259	.276	.391	107	0	17	.942	-1	112	66	O140(0/1/140)	—	-0.9

YEAR	TM LG	G	AB	R	H	2B	3B	HR	RBI	BB-IB	HP	SO	AVG	OBP	SLG	AOPS	ABR	SB-CS	FA	FR	RNG	THR	GAMES AT POSITION	DL	BFW
1919	NY N	1	0	0	0	0	0	0	0	0	0	0	ø	ø	ø	ø	0	0	ø	0	—	—	/R	—	0.0
	Chi N	27	96	8	20	2	0	1	10	1	1	10	.208	.224	.260	45	-7	3	.932	-3	86	61	O25(1/24/0)	—	-1.3
	Year	28	96	8	20	2	0	1	10	1	1	10	.208	.224	.260	45	-7	3	.932	-3	86	61	O25(1/24/0)	—	-1.3
1920	Chi N	134	500	68	150	29	11	10	75	40	1	44	.300	.353	.462	130	19	17-23	.968	-11	87	69	O134L	—	-0.2
1921	Chi N	22	36	7	8	3	0	0	14	1	0	3	.222	.243	.306	44	-3	0-2	1.000	-1	81	0	O7(1/6/0)	—	-0.5
	Pit N	60	230	29	74	18	3	6	48	12	2	16	.322	.361	.504	123	8	4-5	.960	-4	107	26	O58(2/1/55)	—	-0.1
	Year	82	266	36	82	21	3	6	62	13	2	19	.308	.345	.477	113	5	4-7	.962	-5	105	24	O65(3/7/55)	—	-0.6
1922	NY N	42	47	5	13	2	0	1	3	3	0	7	.277	.320	.383	80	-1	0-0	.909	0	86	193	O8(1/6/1)	—	-0.1
Total	9	804	2830	366	812	117	44	47	364	113	15	262	.287	.318	.409	117	45	94-57	.955	-18	100	79	O726(171/38/519)/1	—	-1.7
Robertson, Don	Donald Alexander; B10.15.1930 Harvey IL; BL/TL/5´10˝/180; d4.13																								
1954	Chi N	14	6	2	0	0	0	0	0	0	0	2	.000	.000	.000	-99	-2	0-0	1.000	0	152	0	O6R	0	-0.2
Robertson, Gene	Eugene Edward; B12.25.1898 St.Louis MO; D10.21.1981 Fallon NV; BL/TR/5´7˝/152; d7.4; Col St. Louis																								
1919	StL A	5	7	1	1	0	0	0	0	1	0	2	.143	.250	.143	11	-1	0	.750	-1	33	0	S2	—	-0.2
1922	StL A	18	27	2	8	2	1	0	1	1	0	1	.296	.321	.444	95	0	1-0	.875	0	126	0	3b7,S6/2	—	0.1
1923	StL A	78	251	36	62	10	1	0	17	21	2	7	.247	.310	.295	57	-16	4-2	.935	-12	79	50	3b74/2	—	-2.3
1924	StL A	121	439	70	140	25	4	4	52	36	2	14	.319	.373	.421	99	-1	3-5	.958	-9	91	122	3b111,2b2	—	-0.4
1925	StL A	**154**	582	97	158	26	5	14	76	81	4	30	.271	.364	.405	90	-8	10-7	.939	-4	94	**127**	3b154/S	—	-0.2
1926	StL A	78	247	23	62	12	6	1	19	17	1	10	.251	.302	.360	69	-12	5-1	.924	-3	102	98	3b55,S10,2b3	—	-1.0
1928	†NY A	83	251	29	73	9	0	1	36	14	0	6	.291	.328	.339	78	-8	2-4	.926	-11	83	42	3b70,2b3	—	-1.6
1929	NY A	90	309	45	92	15	6	0	35	28	1	6	.298	.358	.385	98	-1	3-3	.966	-10	83	45	3b77	—	-0.7
	Bos N	8	28	1	8	0	0	0	6	1	0	0	.286	.310	.286	51	-2	1	.875	-2	67	0	3b6/S	—	-0.3
1930	Bos N	21	59	7	11	1	0	0	7	5	0	3	.186	.250	.203	12	-9	0	.949	-2	83	119	3b17	—	-0.8
Total	9	656	2200	311	615	100	23	20	249	205	10	79	.280	.344	.373	83	-58	29-22	.941	-52	89	90	3b571,S20,2b10	—	-7.4
Robertson, Mike	Michael Francis; B10.9.1970 Norwich CT; BL/TL/6´0˝/(180–189); [ChiA91 3/98]; d9.6; Col USC																								
1996	Chi A	6	7	0	1	1	0	0	0	0-0	0	1	.143	.143	.286	5	-1	0-0	1.000	0	118	182	1b2,D2	0	-0.1
1997	Phi N	22	38	3	8	2	1	0	4	0-0	3	6	.211	.268	.316	53	-3	1-0	1.000	-1	61	56	1b5,O5(4/0/1)/D	0	-0.3
1998	Ari N	11	13	0	2	0	0	0	0	0-0	0	2	.154	.154	.154	-19	-2	0-0	ø	0	—	—	D2	0	-0.2
Total	3	39	58	3	11	3	1	0	4	0-0	3	9	.190	.230	.276	32	-6	1-0	1.000	-1	82	102	1b7,O5(4/0/1),D5	0	-0.6
Robertson, Bob	Robert Eugene; B10.2.1946 Frostburg MD; BR/TR/6´1˝/(195–210); d9.18																								
1967	Pit N	9	35	4	6	0	0	2	4	3-0	0	12	.171	.237	.343	64	-2	0-0	.990	-0	90	115	1b9	0	-0.3
1969	Pit N	32	96	7	20	4	1	1	9	8-0	0	30	.208	.267	.302	61	-5	1-0	.996	1	108	97	1b26	0	-0.6
1970	†Pit N	117	390	69	112	19	4	27	82	51-2	2	98	.287	.367	.564	148	26	4-1	.995	2	115	131	1b99,3b5,O3L	0	2.0
1971	†Pit N	131	469	65	127	18	2	26	72	60-8	4	101	.271	.356	.484	136	22	1-2	.993	14	**139**	100	1b126	0	2.7
1972	†Pit N	115	306	25	59	11	0	12	41	41-2	3	84	.193	.291	.346	83	-7	1-1	.993	8	157	124	1b89,O23L,3b11	0	-0.6
1973	Pit N	119	397	43	95	16	0	14	40	55-4	1	77	.239	.332	.385	101	1	0-4	.995	4	113	96	1b107	0	-0.5
1974	†Pit N	91	236	25	54	11	0	16	48	33-1	0	48	.229	.320	.479	126	7	0-0	.991	1	113	93	1b63	0	0.4
1975	†Pit N	75	124	17	34	4	0	6	18	23-0	2	25	.274	.388	.452	134	7	0-0	.996	2	129	54	1b27	0	0.7
1976	Pit N	61	129	10	28	5	1	2	25	16-0	0	23	.217	.299	.318	75	-4	0-1	.996	-0	96	126	1b29	19	-0.7
1978	Sea A	64	174	17	40	5	2	8	28	24-1	1	39	.230	.325	.420	108	2	0-0	1.000	-1	74	115	D29,1b18	17	-0.1
1979	Tor A	15	29	1	3	0	0	1	1	3-0	0	9	.103	.188	.207	6	-4	0-0	1.000	1	168	106	1b9,D4	0	-0.3
Total	11	829	2385	283	578	93	10	115	368	317-18	13	546	.242	.331	.434	113	43	7-9	.994	32	123	106	1b602,D33,O26L,3b16	36	2.7
Robertson, Sherry	Sherrard Alexander; B1.1.1919 Montreal QC, Can.; D10.23.1970 Houghton SD; BL/TR/6´0˝/(175–180); d9.8; Mil 1944–45; C1; Col Maryland																								
1940	Was A	10	33	4	7	0	1	0	0	5	0	6	.212	.316	.273	58	-2	0-0	.940	1	103	137	S10	—	-0.1
1941	Was A	1	3	0	0	0	0	0	0	0	0	3	.000	.000	.000	-99	-1	0-0	.750	-0	95	0	/3	0	-0.1
1943	Was A	59	120	22	26	4	1	3	14	17	1	19	.217	.319	.342	97	0	0-2	.897	-3	92	23	3b27/S	0	-0.5
1946	Was A	74	230	30	46	6	3	6	19	30	0	42	.200	.292	.330	78	-8	6-2	.902	-7	97	108	3b38,2b14,S12/rf	0	-1.3
1947	Was A	95	266	25	62	9	3	1	23	32	1	52	.233	.318	.301	74	-9	4-5	.949	0	101	131	O55L,3b10,2b4	0	-1.4
1948	Was A	71	187	19	46	11	3	2	22	24	1	26	.246	.335	.369	90	-3	8-0	.939	-0	106	86	O51(1/1/49)	0	-0.3
1949	Was A	110	374	59	94	17	3	11	42	42	1	35	.251	.329	.401	95	-5	10-3	.947	-6	106	68	2b71,3b19,O13R	0	-0.6
1950	Was A	71	123	19	32	3	3	2	16	22	0	18	.260	.372	.382	98	0	1-1	.952	-4	85	106	O14R,2b12/3	0	-0.4
1951	Was A	62	111	14	21	2	1	1	10	9	1	22	.189	.256	.252	38	-10	2-1	.949	2	122	125	O22(1/0/21)	0	-0.9
1952	Was A	1	0	0	0	0	0	0	0	0	0	0	ø	ø	ø	ø	0	0-0	ø	0	—	—	/R	0	0.0
	Phi A	43	60	8	12	3	0	0	5	21	0	15	.200	.407	.250	81	0	1-2	.958	-2	89	56	2b8,O7R,3b2	0	-0.3
	Year	44	60	8	12	3	0	0	5	21	0	15	.200	.407	.250	81	0	1-2	.958	-2	89	56	2b8,O7R,3b2	0	-0.3
Total	10	597	1507	200	346	55	18	26	151	202	5	238	.230	.323	.342	83	-38	32-16	.946	-20	105	107	O163(57/1/105),2b109,3b98,S23	0	-5.9
Robidoux, Billy Jo	William Joseph; B1.13.1964 Ware MA; BL/TR/6´1˝/200; [MilA82 6/157]; d9.11																								
1985	Mil A	18	51	5	9	2	0	3	8	12-0	0	16	.176	.333	.392	98	0	0-0	1.000	1	83	182	O11L,1b6/D	0	0.0
1986	Mil A	56	181	15	41	8	0	1	21	33-1	0	36	.227	.344	.287	72	-6	0-0	.986	-1	96	102	1b43,D10	72	-0.9
1987	Mil A	23	62	9	12	0	0	0	4	8-1	0	17	.194	.286	.194	30	-6	0-1	.983	-0	91	171	1b10,D10	0	-0.7
1988	Mil A	33	91	9	23	5	0	0	5	8-3	0	14	.253	.307	.308	74	-3	1-1	.983	2	130	102	1b30/D	0	-0.3
1989	Chi A	16	39	2	5	2	0	0	1	4-0	0	9	.128	.209	.179	11	-5	0-0	.990	-1	88	164	1b15/lf	0	-0.6
1990	Bos A	27	44	3	8	4	0	1	4	6-1	1	14	.182	.288	.341	73	-1	0-0	.981	-1	74	63	1b11,D4	62	-0.3
Total	6	173	468	43	98	21	0	5	43	71-6	1	106	.209	.313	.286	65	-21	1-2	.986	0	104	113	1b115,D26,O12L	134	-2.8
Robinson, Aaron	Aaron Andrew; B6.23.1915 Lancaster SC; D3.9.1966 Lancaster SC; BL/TR/6´2˝/205; d5.6; Mil 1943–45																								
1943	NY A	1	1	0	0	0	0	0	0	0	0	1	.000	.000	.000	-99	0	0-0	ø	0	—	—	/H	0	0.0
1945	NY A	50	160	19	45	6	1	8	24	21	1	23	.281	.368	.481	139	8	0-0	1.000	-4	*74*	*73*	C45	0	0.7
1946	NY A	100	330	32	98	17	2	16	64	48	1	39	.297	.388	.506	146	21	0-1	.983	-3	*112*	*101*	C95	0	2.4
1947	†NY A☆	82	252	23	68	11	5	5	36	40	0	26	.270	.370	.413	119	7	0-1	.997	-1	*86*	*87*	C74	0	1.0
1948	Chi A	98	326	47	82	14	2	8	39	46	0	30	.252	.344	.380	96	-2	0-1	.989	-5	*83*	*112*	C92	0	-0.3
1949	Det A	110	331	38	89	12	0	13	56	73	1	21	.269	.402	.423	118	11	0-2	.986	-3	*105*	*96*	C108	0	1.3
1950	Det A	107	283	37	64	7	0	9	37	75	0	35	.226	.388	.346	86	-3	0-1	.993	-0	*140*	*96*	C103	0	0.2
1951	Det A	36	82	3	17	6	0	0	9	17	0	9	.207	.343	.280	70	-3	0-0	1.000	-2	*75*	*116*	C35	0	-0.3
	Bos A	26	74	9	15	1	1	2	7	17	0	10	.203	.352	.324	76	-2	0-0	.983	-0	*116*	*84*	C25	0	-0.1
	Year	62	156	12	32	7	1	2	16	34	0	19	.205	.347	.301	73	-5	0-0	.991	-2	*95*	*100*	C60	0	-0.4
Total	8	610	1839	208	478	74	11	61	272	337	3	194	.260	.375	.412	112	37	0-6	.990	-17	*102*	*97*	C577	0	4.9
Robinson, Val	Alfred Valentine; B8.31.1848 Washington DC; D8.2.1898 Washington DC; d5.1																								
1872	Oly NA	7	30	6	6	0	0	0	4	1	—	1	.200	.226	.200	34	-2	0-0	.750	-0	135	0	O7R	—	-0.1
Robinson, Brooks	Brooks Calbert; B5.18.1937 Little Rock AR; BR/TR/6´1˝/(180–190); d9.17; C1; HF1983																								
1955	Bal A	6	22	0	2	0	0	0	1	0-0	0	10	.091	.091	.091	-55	-5	0-0	.833	-1	89	106	3b6	0	-0.7
1956	Bal A	15	44	5	10	4	0	1	1	1-0	0	5	.227	.244	.386	70	-2	0-0	.944	0	109	131	3b14/2	0	-0.2
1957	Bal A	50	117	13	28	6	1	2	14	7-0	1	10	.239	.286	.359	81	-4	1-0	.971	-1	96	86	3b47	58	-0.5
1958	Bal A	145	463	31	110	16	3	3	32	31-1	5	51	.238	.292	.305	68	-21	1-2	.953	7	100	**123**	3b140,2b16	0	-1.5
1959	Bal A	88	313	29	89	15	2	4	24	17-5	2	37	.284	.325	.383	96	-2	2-2	.955	7	108	174	3b87/2	0	0.4
1960	Bal A★	152	595	74	175	27	9	14	88	35-0	0	49	.294	.329	.440	109	5	2-2	**.977**	17	107	110	3b152,2b3	0	2.1
1961	Bal A★	**163**	668	89	192	38	7	7	61	47-2	4	57	.287	.334	.397	99	-2	1-3	**.972**	-6	94	108	3b163,2b2/S	0	-0.9
1962	Bal A★	**162**	634	77	192	29	9	23	86	42-3	1	70	.303	.342	.486	129	23	3-1	**.979**	8	104	111	3b162,S3,2b2	0	3.1
1963	Bal A★	161	589	67	148	26	4	11	67	46-4	1	84	.251	.305	.365	91	-8	2-3	**.976**	7	101	**148**	3b160/S	0	-0.2
1964	Bal A★	**163**	612	82	194	35	3	28	**118**	51-10	4	64	.317	.368	.521	146	38	1-0	**.972**	-1	98	**147**	3b163	0	3.8
1965	Bal A★	144	559	81	166	25	2	18	80	47-9	2	47	.297	.351	.445	123	17	3-0	.967	-8	95	129	3b143	0	0.9
1966	†Bal A★	157	620	91	167	35	2	23	100	56-11	5	36	.269	.333	.444	123	19	2-3	**.976**	1	94	93	3b157	0	2.0
1967	Bal A★	158	610	88	164	25	5	22	77	54-9	4	54	.269	.328	.434	126	19	1-3	**.980**	**32**	**120**	142	3b158	0	5.3
1968	Bal A★	**162**	608	65	154	36	6	17	75	44-11	4	55	.253	.304	.416	118	12	1-1	**.970**	19	**107**	115	3b162	0	3.3
1969	†Bal A★	156	598	73	140	21	3	23	84	56-10	3	55	.234	.298	.395	93	-8	2-1	**.976**	11	104	131	3b156	0	0.2
1970	†Bal A★	158	608	84	168	31	4	18	94	53-5	4	53	.276	.335	.429	108	6	1-1	.966	-7	93	104	3b156	0	-0.2
1971	†Bal A★	156	589	67	160	21	1	20	92	63-8	3	50	.272	.341	.413	113	10	0-0	.968	4	103	123	3b156	0	1.4
1972	Bal A★	153	556	48	139	23	2	8	64	43-4	2	45	.250	.303	.342	89	-8	1-0	**.977**	6	103	104	3b152	0	-0.2
1973	†Bal A★	155	549	53	141	17	2	9	72	55-5	3	50	.257	.326	.344	89	-8	2-0	.970	5	107	98	3b154	0	-0.3

YEAR	TM LG	G	AB	R	H	2B	3B	HR	RBI	BB-IB	HP	SO	AVG	OBP	SLG	AOPS	ABR	SB-CS	FA	FR	RNG	THR	GAMES AT POSITION	DL	BFW
1974	†Bal A★	153	553	46	159	27	0	7	59	56-13	3	47	.288	.353	.374	113	11	2-0	.967	8	109	**137**	3b153	0	1.9
1975	Bal A	144	482	50	97	15	1	6	53	44-10	1	33	.201	.267	.274	57	-28	0-0	**.979**	-3	104	122	3b143	0	-3.2
1976	Bal A	71	218	16	46	8	2	3	11	8-0	1	24	.211	.240	.307	64	-11	0-0	.969	-3	94	108	3b71	0	-1.5
1977	Bal A	24	47	3	7	2	0	1	4	4-0	0	4	.149	.212	.255	29	-5	0-0	1.000	0	109	98	3b15	0	-0.5
Total	23	2896	10654	1232	2848	482	68	268	1357	860-120	53	990	.267	.322	.401	105	48	28-22	.971	103	102	121	3b2870,2b25,S5	58	14.5
Robinson, Bruce	Bruce Philip; B4.16.1954 LaJolla CA; BL/TR/6´1˝/(194–195); [OakA75 1/21]; d8.19; b–Dave; Col Stanford; [DL 1981 NY A 151]																								
1978	Oak A	28	84	5	21	3	1	0	8	3-0	0	8	.250	.276	.310	68	-4	0-0	.965	8	94	158	C28	0	0.5
1979	NY A	6	12	0	2	0	0	0	2	1-0	0	0	.167	.231	.167	9	-2	0-0	.943	1	75	61	C6	0	0.0
1980	NY A	4	5	0	0	0	0	0	0	0-0	0	4	.000	.000	.000	-99	-1	0-0	1.000	-0	0	0	C3	0	-0.1
Total	3	38	101	5	23	3	1	0	10	4-0	0	12	.228	.257	.277	51	-7	0-0	.962	9	88	137	C37	151	0.4
Robinson, Charlie	Charles Henry; B7.27.1856 Westerly RI; D5.18.1913; BL/TR; d8.2																								
1884	Ind AA	20	80	11	23	2	0	0	—	3	0	—	.287	.313	.313	108	1	—	.967	1	—	—	C17,S3/rf	—	0.3
1885	Bro AA	11	40	5	6	2	1	0	4	3	0	—	.150	.209	.250	44	-2	—	.840	-3	—	—	C11	—	-0.4
Total	2	31	120	16	29	4	1	0	4	6	0	—	.242	.278	.292	85	-1	—	.919	-2	—	—	C28,S3/rf	—	-0.1
Robinson, Rabbit	Clyde; B3.5.1882 Wellsburg WV; D4.9.1915 Waterbury CT; BR/TR/5´6˝/148; d4.22																								
1903	Was A	103	373	41	79	10	8	1	20	33	2	—	.212	.279	.290	69	-14	16	.917	4	113	112	2b45,O30(0/14/16),S24,3b5	—	-1.0
1904	Det A	101	320	30	77	13	6	0	37	29	5	—	.241	.314	.319	103	2	14	.925	2	106	78	S30,3b26,O20(7/0/13),2b19	—	0.6
1910	Cin N	2	7	0	0	0	0	0	1	1	0	0	.000	.125	.000	-66	-1	0	1.000	-0	78	0	3b2	—	-0.2
Total	3	206	700	71	156	23	14	1	58	63	7	0	.223	.294	.300	83	-13	30	.940	6	114	108	2b64,S54,O50(7/14/29),3b33	—	-0.6
Robinson, Craig	Craig George; B8.21.1948 Abington PA; BR/TR/5´10˝/165; [PhiN70 11/252]; d9.9; Col Wake Forest																								
1972	Phi N	5	15	0	3	1	0	0	0	1-0	0	2	.200	.250	.267	46	-1	0-0	1.000	2	147	199	S4	0	0.2
1973	Phi N	46	146	11	33	7	0	0	7	0-0	0	25	.226	.226	.274	37	-13	1-1	.945	-5	89	100	S42,2b4	0	-1.4
1974	Atl N	145	452	52	104	4	6	0	29	30-4	3	57	.230	.280	.265	52	-30	11-2	.956	-11	95	101	S142	0	-2.5
1975	Atl N	10	17	1	1	0	0	0	0	0-0	0	5	.059	.059	.059	-65	-4	0-0	1.000	-1	75	61	S7	0	-0.4
	SF N	29	29	4	2	1	0	0	0	2-0	0	6	.069	.129	.103	-34	-5	0-0	.941	-1	91	122	S12,2b9	0	-0.6
	Year	39	46	5	3	1	0	0	0	2-0	0	11	.065	.104	.087	-45	-9	0-0	.967	-2	84	95	S19,2b9	0	-1.0
1976	SF N	15	13	4	4	1	0	0	2	3-0	0	4	.308	.438	.385	131	1	0-1	.952	-0	132	98	2b7,3b2/S	0	0.0
	Atl N	15	17	4	4	0	0	0	3	5-0	0	2	.235	.391	.235	81	0	0-0	.952	0	107	43	2b5,S2/3	0	0.0
	Year	30	30	8	8	1	0	0	5	8-0	0	6	.267	.410	.300	103	1	0-1	.952	-0	121	75	2b12,3b3,S3	0	0.0
1977	Atl N	27	29	4	6	1	0	0	1	1-0	0	6	.207	.233	.241	25	-3	0-0	1.000	0	83	87	S23	42	-0.2
Total	6	292	718	80	157	15	6	0	42	42-4	3	107	.219	.263	.256	44	-55	12-4	.956	-16	93	101	S233,2b25,3b3	42	-4.9
Robinson, Dave	David Tanner; B5.22.1946 Minneapolis MN; BB/TL/6´1˝/(180–186); [SDN68 7/155]; d9.10; b–Bruce; Col San Diego St.																								
1970	SD N	15	38	5	12	2	0	2	6	5-1	0	4	.316	.395	.526	150	3	2-0	1.000	1	123	140	O13(12/1/0)	0	0.4
1971	SD N	7	6	0	0	0	0	0	0	1-0	0	3	.000	.143	.000	-60	-1	0-0	ø	0	—	—	/H	0	-0.1
Total	2	22	44	5	12	2	0	2	6	6-1	0	7	.273	.360	.455	123	2	2-0	1.000	1	123	140	O13(12/1/0)	0	0.3
Robinson, Earl	Earl John; B11.3.1936 New Orleans LA; BR/TR/6´1˝/(187–190); d9.10; Col California																								
1958	LA N	8	15	3	3	0	0	0	0	1-0	0	4	.200	.250	.200	20	-2	0-0	1.000	0	101	0	3b6	0	-0.2
1961	Bal A	96	222	37	59	12	3	8	30	31-1	0	54	.266	.354	.455	119	6	4-3	.973	5	115	132	O82(6/1/78)	0	0.7
1962	Bal A	29	63	12	18	3	1	1	4	8-0	0	10	.286	.361	.413	116	2	2-0	1.000	0	119	0	O17(1/0/16)	0	0.1
1964	Bal A	37	121	11	33	5	1	3	10	7-0	0	24	.273	.310	.405	98	-1	1-2	.986	1	100	151	O34(16/20/0)	0	-0.2
Total	4	170	421	63	113	20	5	12	44	47-1	0	92	.268	.340	.425	109	5	7-5	.980	7	111	118	O133(23/21/94),3b6	0	0.4
Robinson, Floyd	Floyd Andrew; B5.9.1936 Prescott AR; BL/TR/5´9˝/(170–175); d8.10																								
1960	Chi A	22	46	7	13	0	0	0	1	11-0	1	8	.283	.431	.283	98	1	2-3	.960	-2	90	0	O17(1/4/12)	0	-0.2
1961	Chi A	132	432	69	134	20	7	11	59	52-3	4	32	.310	.389	.465	129	19	7-4	.991	2	104	88	O106R	0	1.3
1962	Chi A	156	600	89	187	**45**	10	11	109	72-7	2	47	.312	.384	.475	131	29	4-2	.973	-1	90	141	O155(114/0/75)	0	1.8
1963	Chi A	146	527	71	149	21	6	13	71	62-4	4	43	.283	.361	.419	120	16	4-3	.984	-2	96	88	O137(36/0/119)	0	0.5
1964	Chi A	141	525	83	158	17	3	11	59	70-7	5	41	.301	.388	.408	125	21	9-5	.987	-6	93	63	O138(54/0/112)	0	0.7
1965	Chi A	156	577	70	153	15	6	14	66	76-6	5	51	.265	.352	.385	117	15	4-1	.985	-8	92	61	O153(6/1/148)	0	-0.4
1966	Chi A	127	342	44	81	11	2	5	35	44-4	5	32	.237	.330	.325	96	0	8-2	.962	-9	85	37	O113(4/0/111)	0	-1.6
1967	Cin N	55	130	19	31	6	2	1	10	14-1	0	14	.238	.310	.338	77	-3	3-1	.981	-2	100	0	O39(4/0/35)	42	-0.8
1968	Oak A	53	81	5	20	5	0	1	14	4-1	0	10	.247	.276	.346	93	-1	0-0	1.000	-1	81	117	O18L	0	-0.2
	Bos A	23	24	1	3	0	0	0	2	3-0	1	4	.125	.250	.125	15	-2	1-0	.833	-1	72	0	O10(5/0/5)	0	-0.4
	Year	76	105	6	23	5	0	1	16	7-1	1	14	.219	.270	.295	73	-3	1-0	.963	-1	79	90	O28(23/0/5)	0	-0.6
Total	9	1011	3284	458	929	140	36	67	426	408-33	27	282	.283	.365	.409	118	95	42-21	.981	-28	93	79	O886(242/5/723)	42	0.7
Robinson, Frank	Frank; B8.31.1935 Beaumont TX; BR/TR/6´1˝/(185–195); d4.17; M16/C7; HF1982; OF(820/99/1281)																								
1956	Cin N★	152	572	**122**	166	27	6	38	83	64-7	**20**	95	.290	.379	.558	139	33	8-4	.976	-4	100	48	O152(143/10/0)	0	2.0
1957	Cin N★	150	611	97	197	29	5	29	75	44-5	12	92	.322	.376	.529	131	27	10-2	.989	17	117	118	O136(106/32/1),1b24	0	3.7
1958	Cin N	148	554	90	149	25	6	31	83	62-5	7	80	.269	.350	.504	116	13	10-1	.991	-0	102	112	O138(83/53/0),3b11	0	0.7
1959	Cin N★	146	540	106	168	31	4	36	125	69-9	**8**	93	.311	.391	.583	152	42	18-8	.984	-4	89	**112**	1b125,O40L	0	3.0
1960	Cin N	139	464	86	138	33	6	31	83	82-6	**9**	67	.297	.407	**.595**	169	48	13-6	.993	5	101	100	1b78,O51L/3	0	4.6
1961	†Cin N★	153	545	117	176	32	7	37	124	71-**23**	10	64	.323	.404	**.611**	164	52	22-3	.990	6	105	116	O150(52/3/99)/3	0	5.1
1962	Cin N★	**162**	609	**134**	208	**51**	2	39	136	76-**16**	**11**	62	.342	**.421**	**.624**	**172**	**65**	18-9	.994	4	111	74	O161(9/0/155)	0	5.7
1963	Cin N	140	482	79	125	19	3	21	91	81-**20**	**14**	69	.259	.379	.442	132	24	26-10	.984	7	105	149	O139(116/1/31)/1	0	2.7
1964	Cin N	156	568	103	174	38	6	29	96	79-**20**	9	67	.306	.396	.548	158	47	23-5	.986	3	108	67	O156(77/0/102)	0	4.5
1965	Cin N★	156	582	109	172	33	5	33	113	70-18	**18**	100	.296	.386	.540	148	40	13-9	.990	-1	104	49	O155(7/0/152)	0	2.9
1966	†Bal A★	155	576	**122**	182	34	2	**49**	**122**	87-11	10	90	**.316**	**.410**	**.637**	**200**	**78**	8-5	.985	-7	93	46	O151(20/0/135),1b3	0	**6.3**
1967	Bal A✳	129	479	83	149	23	7	30	94	71-14	7	84	.311	.403	.576	189	55	2-3	.990	-6	87	84	O126(31/0/95),1b2	0	4.3
1968	Bal A	130	421	69	113	27	1	15	52	73-4	12	84	.268	.390	.444	153	32	11-2	.962	-6	90	76	O117(55/0/78),1b3	0	2.2
1969	†Bal A★	148	539	111	166	19	5	32	100	88-11	**13**	62	.308	.415	.540	164	49	9-3	.987	-2	97	90	O134(1/0/134),1b19	0	4.2
1970	†Bal A★	132	471	88	144	24	1	25	78	69-9	7	70	.306	.398	.520	150	34	2-1	.987	1	99	113	O120R,1b7	0	2.9
1971	†Bal A★	133	455	82	128	16	2	28	99	72-11	9	62	.281	.384	.510	152	33	3-0	.973	-4	103	51	O92(1/0/91),1b37	0	2.4
1972	LA N	103	342	41	86	6	1	19	59	55-0	2	76	.251	.353	.442	128	13	2-3	.967	-2	95	88	O95(9/0/88)	0	0.6
1973	Cal A	147	534	85	142	29	0	30	97	82-12	10	93	.266	.372	.489	152	39	1-1	.976	3	121	265	D127,O17L	0	3.8
1974	Cal A★	129	427	75	107	26	2	20	63	75-14	10	85	.251	.371	.461	147	30	5-1	ø	-0	0	0	D123/lf	0	2.8
	Cle A	15	50	6	10	1	1	2	5	10-0	0	10	.200	.328	.380	105	1	0-1	.958	-1	0	39	D11,1b4	0	-0.1
	Year	144	477	81	117	27	3	22	68	85-14	10	95	.245	.367	.453	143	30	5-2	.958	-1	0	39	D134,1b4/lf	0	2.7
1975	Cle A	49	118	19	28	5	0	9	24	29-3	0	15	.237	.385	.508	151	9	0-0	ø	0	0	0	D42,M	19	0.8
1976	Cle A	36	67	5	15	0	0	3	10	11-0	0	12	.224	.329	.358	103	0	0-0	1.000	-0	0	119	D18,1b2/lfM	18	-0.1
Total	21	2808	10006	1829	2943	528	72	586	1812	1420-218	198	1532	.294	.389	.537	153	764	204-77	.984	7	102	89	O2132R,D321,1b305,3b13	37	65.0
Robinson, Fred	Frederic Henry; B7.6.1856 South Acton MA; D12.18.1933 Hudson MA; BR/TR; d4.17; b–Wilbert																								
1884	Cin U	3	13	1	3	0	0	0	—	0	—	—	.231	.231	.231	37	-1	—	.727	-2	84	0	2b3	—	-0.3
Robinson, Jackie	Jack Roosevelt; B1.31.1919 Cairo GA; D10.24.1972 Stamford CT; BR/TR/5´11˝/(204–210); d4.15; HF1962; Negro Lg 1945; Col UCLA; OF(161/0/1)																								
1947	†Bro N	151	590	125	175	31	5	12	48	74	9	36	.297	.383	.427	111	11	**29**	.989	-3	94	**119**	1b151	0	0.3
1948	Bro N	147	574	108	170	38	8	12	85	57	**7**	37	.296	.367	.453	117	14	22	**.980**	0	97	**115**	2b116,1b30,3b6	0	2.0
1949	†Bro N★	**156**	593	122	203	38	12	16	124	86	8	27	**.342**	.432	.528	150	46	**37**	.981	-4	95	**117**	2b156	0	5.0
1950	Bro N★	144	518	99	170	39	4	14	81	80	5	24	.328	.423	.500	139	34	12	**.986**	11	98	**128**	2b144	0	**5.0**
1951	Bro N★	153	548	106	185	33	7	19	88	79	9	27	.338	.429	.527	153	45	25-8	**.992**	19	104	**130**	2b150	0	**7.3**
1952	†Bro N★	149	510	104	157	17	3	19	75	106	14	40	.308	**.440**	.465	149	42	24-7	.974	4	97	**122**	2b146	0	**5.7**
1953	†Bro N★	136	484	109	159	34	7	12	95	74	7	30	.329	.425	.502	137	31	17-4	.981	5	99	144	O76L,3b44,2b9,1b6/S	0	3.2
1954	Bro N★	124	386	62	120	22	4	15	59	63	7	20	.311	.413	.505	135	23	7-3	1.000	-1	93	109	O74(73/0/1),3b50,2b4	0	1.9
1955	†Bro N	105	317	51	81	6	2	8	36	61-5	3	18	.256	.378	.363	96	1	12-3	.966	11	116	132	3b84,O10L/12	0	1.3
1956	†Bro N	117	357	61	98	15	2	10	43	60-2	3	32	.275	.382	.412	106	6	12-5	.967	19	132	141	3b72,2b22,1b9,O2L	0	2.6
Total	10	1382	4877	947	1518	273	54	137	734	740-7	72	291	.311	.409	.474	131	253	197-30	.983	62	98	123	2b748,3b256,1b197,O162L/S	0	34.3
Robinson, Jack	John W. "Bridgeport"; B7.15.1880 Portland ME; D7.22.1921 Macon GA; TR; d9.6; Col Harvard																								
1902	NY N	4	9	0	0	0	0	0	0	0	0	—	.000	.000	.000	-99	-2	0	1.000	0	*135*	92	C3	—	-0.2

YEAR	TM LG	G	AB	R	H	2B	3B	HR	RBI	BB-IB	HP	SO	AVG	OBP	SLG	AOPS	ABR	SB-CS	FA	FR	RNG	THR	GAMES AT POSITION	DL	BFW
Robinson, Kerry	Kerry Keith; B10.3.1973 St.Louis MO; BL/TL/6´0˝/175; [StLN95 34/939]; d9.22; Col Southeast Missouri																								
1998	TB A	2	3	0	0	0	0	0	0	0-0	0	1	.000	.000	.000	-98	-1	0-0	1.000	1	294	0	O2L	0	0.0
1999	Cin N	9	1	4	0	0	0	0	0	0-0	0	1	.000	.000	.000	-97	0	0-1	ø	-0	0	0	O2L	0	-0.1
2001	†StL N	114	186	34	53	6	1	1	15	12-0	2	20	.285	.330	.344	75	-7	11-2	.981	3	121	77	O74(42/22/17)	0	-0.3
2002	†StL N	124	181	27	47	7	4	1	15	11-3	0	29	.260	.301	.359	73	-8	7-4	.977	1	121	0	O76(52/10/17)/D	0	-0.8
2003	StL N	116	208	19	52	6	3	1	16	8-3	1	27	.250	.281	.322	57	-14	6-1	1.000	-2	102	0	O88(36/20/39)	0	-1.6
2004	SD N	80	92	20	27	4	0	0	5	5-0	1	8	.293	.330	.337	79	-3	11-4	1.000	2	124	95	O49(39/9/2),D2	0	0.0
2006	KC A	18	64	8	17	2	1	0	5	1-0	0	7	.266	.277	.328	57	-4	1-1	1.000	1	106	131	O16(1/15/1)	0	-0.4
Total	7	463	735	112	196	25	9	3	56	37-6	4	93	.267	.303	.337	67	-37	36-13	.989	6	115	45	O307(174/76/76),D3	0	-3.2
Robinson, Wilbert	Wilbert "Uncle Robby"; B6.29.1863 Bolton MA; D8.8.1934 Atlanta GA; BR/TR/5´8.5˝/215; d4.19; M19/C3; HF1945; b–Fred																								
1886	Phi AA	87	342	57	69	11	3	1	30	21	3	—	.202	.254	.260	61	-16	33	.893	-7	—	—	C61,1b22,O5(0/4/1)	—	-1.8
1887	Phi AA	68	264	28	60	6	2	1	24	14	1	—	.227	.269	.277	52	-18	15	.901	2	—	—	C67,1b3/cf	—	-0.8
1888	Phi AA	66	254	32	62	7	2	1	31	9	0	—	.244	.270	.299	83	-6	11	.938	21	—	—	C65/1	—	1.9
1889	Phi AA	69	264	31	61	13	2	0	28	6	1	34	.231	.251	.295	56	-16	9	.943	7	—	—	C69	—	-0.3
1890	Phi AA	82	329	32	78	13	4	4	42	16	3	—	.237	.279	.337	82	-10	20	.930	-15	*84*	*80*	C82	—	-1.6
	Bal AA	14	48	7	13	1	0	0	4	3	0	—	.271	.314	.292	75	-2	1	.989	6	*119*	*64*	C11,1b3	—	0.4
	Year	96	377	39	91	14	4	4	46	19	3	—	.241	.283	.332	81	-11	21	.938	-9	*88*	*78*	C93,1b3	—	-1.2
1891	Bal AA	93	334	25	72	8	5	2	46	16	0	37	.216	.251	.287	54	-23	18	.954	14	***140***	*67*	C92/rf	—	-0.1
1892	Bal N	90	330	36	88	14	4	2	57	15	2	35	.267	.303	.352	95	-4	5	.921	-14	*95*	*84*	C87,1b2/rf	—	-1.0
1893	Bal N	95	359	49	120	21	3	3	57	26	2	22	.334	.382	.435	115	7	17	.942	-9	*90*	*68*	C93/1	—	0.6
1894	†Bal N	109	414	69	146	21	4	1	98	46	3	18	.353	.421	.430	101	2	12	.944	6	*123*	*77*	C109	—	1.3
1895	†Bal N	77	282	38	74	19	1	0	48	12	1	19	.262	.295	.337	61	-17	11	**.979**	24	***148***	*107*	C75	—	1.1
1896	†Bal N	67	245	43	85	9	6	2	38	14	1	13	.347	.385	.457	120	6	9	.948	4	*111*	*73*	C67	—	1.3
1897	Bal N	48	181	25	57	9	0	0	23	8	1	—	.315	.347	.365	88	-3	0	.965	-1	*102*	*72*	C48	—	0.0
1898	Bal N	79	289	29	80	12	2	0	38	16	1	—	.277	.317	.332	84	-6	3	.965	1	*112*	*93*	C77	—	0.1
1899	Bal N	108	356	40	101	15	2	0	47	31	2	—	.284	.344	.337	83	-8	5	.949	-7	*117*	*79*	C105	—	-0.5
1900	StL N	60	210	26	52	5	1	0	28	11	2	—	.248	.291	.281	59	-12	7	.974	1	*94*	*103*	C54	—	-0.6
1901	Bal A	68	239	32	72	12	3	0	26	10	2	—	.301	.335	.377	93	-3	9	.949	-0	*107*	*81*	C67	—	0.3
1902	Bal A	91	335	38	98	16	7	1	57	12	2	—	.293	.321	.391	93	-5	11	.949	-15	*80*	*86*	C87,M	—	-1.1
Total	17	1371	5075	637	1388	212	51	18	722	286	27	178	.273	.316	.346	83	-134	196	.941	16	*109*	*81*	C1316,1b32,O8(0/5/3)	—	-0.8
Robinson, Eddie	William Edward; B12.15.1920 Paris TX; BL/TR/6´2.5˝/(205–215); d9.9; Mil 1943–45; C3; Col Paris (TX) JC																								
1942	Cle A	8	8	1	1	0	0	0	2	1	0	0	.125	.222	.125	-1	-1	0-0	1.000	-0	0	0	/1	0	-0.1
1946	Cle A	8	30	6	12	1	0	3	4	2	0	4	.400	.438	.733	238	5	0-0	.988	-2	17	53	1b8	0	0.3
1947	Cle A	95	318	52	78	10	1	14	52	30	2	18	.245	.314	.415	105	0	1-0	.994	-3	88	109	1b87	0	-0.5
1948	†Cle A	134	493	53	125	18	5	16	83	36	2	42	.254	.307	.408	91	-10	1-0	**.995**	-1	94	**114**	1b131	0	-1.5
1949	Was A★	143	527	66	155	27	3	18	78	67	**7**	30	.294	.381	.459	125	18	3-4	.987	-2	97	82	1b143	0	1.0
1950	Was A	36	129	21	30	4	2	1	13	25	2	4	.233	.365	.318	80	-3	0-0	1.000	0	96	96	1b36	0	-0.4
	Chi A	119	424	62	133	11	2	20	73	60	5	28	.314	.405	.491	132	21	0-0	.987	-5	84	88	1b119	0	1.1
	Year	**155**	553	83	163	15	4	21	86	85	7	32	.295	.395	.450	120	18	0-0	.990	-5	87	90	1b155	0	0.7
1951	Chi A★	151	564	85	159	23	5	29	117	77	3	54	.282	.371	.495	135	27	2-5	.988	-8	85	107	1b147	0	1.2
1952	Chi A★	155	594	79	176	33	1	22	104	70	12	49	.296	.382	.466	134	29	2-0	.990	-8	78	106	1b155	0	1.6
1953	Phi A★	156	615	64	152	28	4	22	102	63	5	56	.247	.322	.413	94	-7	1-2	.988	-13	70	86	1b155	0	-3.0
1954	NY A	85	142	11	37	9	0	3	27	19	0	21	.261	.344	.387	105	1	0-0	.980	1	118	97	1b29	0	0.1
1955	†NY A	88	173	25	36	1	0	16	42	36-7	5	26	.208	.358	.491	129	7	0-0	.995	-2	74	94	1b46	0	0.2
1956	NY A	26	54	7	12	1	0	5	11	5-1	3	3	.222	.323	.519	123	1	0-1	1.000	-1	76	112	1b14	0	0.0
	KC A	75	172	13	34	5	1	2	12	26-1	2	20	.198	.308	.273	55	-11	0-0	.977	-4	75	113	1b47	0	-1.7
	Year	101	226	20	46	6	1	7	23	31-2	5	23	.204	.312	.332	71	-10	0-1	.983	-4	75	113	1b61	0	-1.7
1957	Det A	13	9	0	0	0	0	0	0	3-1	1	0	.000	.308	.000	-9	-1	0-0	1.000	0	348	0	/1	0	-0.1
	Cle A	19	27	1	6	1	0	1	3	0-0	1	3	.222	.241	.370	68	-1	0-0	1.000	0	106	66	1b7	0	-0.2
	Bal A	4	3	0	0	0	0	0	0	1-0	0	1	.000	.250	.000	-28	-1	0-0	ø	0	—	—	/H	0	-0.1
	Year	36	39	1	6	1	0	1	3	4-1	2	4	.154	.261	.256	44	-3	0-0	1.000	1	128	60	1b8	0	-0.4
Total	13	1315	4282	546	1146	172	24	172	723	521-10	50	359	.268	.353	.440	113	74	10-12	.990	-48	84	98	1b1126	0	-2.1
Robinson, Yank	William H.; B9.19.1859 Philadelphia PA; D8.25.1894 St.Louis MO; BR/TR/5´6.5˝/170; d8.24; OF(52/2/2); ▲																								
1882	Det N	11	39	1	7	1	0	0	2	1	—	13	.179	.200	.205	30	-3	—	.800	-3	78	79	S10/cfP	—	-0.5
1884	Bal U	102	415	101	111	24	4	3	—	**37**	—	—	.267	.327	.366	100	-11	—	.831	10	122	128	3b71,S14,C11,P11,2b3	—	0.3
1885	†StL AA	78	287	63	75	8	8	0	35	29	7	—	.261	.344	.345	113	5	—	.862	-2	121	74	O52L,2b19,C5,3b2/1	—	0.2
1886	†StL AA	133	481	89	132	26	9	3	71	64	15	—	.274	.377	.385	132	21	51	.888	-6	102	**133**	2b125,3b6/cfSP	—	1.7
1887	†StL AA	125	430	102	131	32	4	1	74	92	17	—	.305	.445	.405	125	20	75	.899	-12	101	117	2b117,3b6,O2R,S2/CP	—	1.0
1888	†StL AA	134	455	111	105	17	6	3	53	**116**	12	—	.231	**.400**	.314	117	16	56	.895	-37	87	61	2b102,S34	—	-1.5
1889	StL AA	132	452	97	94	17	3	5	70	**118**	6	55	.208	.378	.292	81	-7	39	.887	-37	85	92	2b132	—	-3.4
1890	Pit P	98	306	59	70	10	3	0	38	101	10	33	.229	.434	.281	101	14	17	.887	-19	95	104	2b98	—	-0.1
1891	Cin AA	97	342	48	61	9	4	1	37	68	8	51	.178	.328	.237	57	-18	23	.867	-14	101	79	2b97	—	-2.5
	StL AA	1	3	0	0	0	0	0	0	0	0	0	.000	.000	.000	-87	-1	0	.750	-1	0	0	/2	—	-0.1
	Year	98	345	48	61	9	4	1	37	68	8	51	.177	.325	.235	56	-18	23	.866	-15	100	78	2b98	—	-2.6
1892	Was N	67	218	26	39	4	3	0	19	38	0	29	.179	.301	.225	61	-9	11	.852	-3	100	121	3b58,S5,2b4	—	-0.9
Total	10	978	3428	697	825	148	44	16	399	664	75	181	.241	.375	.324	101	27	272	.887	-124	95	99	2b698,3b143,S66,O56L,C17,P14/1	—	-5.8
Robinson, Bill	William Henry; B6.26.1943 McKeesport PA; BR/TR/6´3˝/(175–200); d9.20; C10																								
1966	Atl N	6	11	1	3	0	1	0	3	0-0	0	1	.273	.273	.455	96	0	0-0	.800	-1	79	0	O5(2/0/3)	0	-0.1
1967	NY A	116	342	31	67	6	1	7	29	28-4	2	56	.196	.259	.281	62	-17	2-2	.968	-2	90	159	O102(20/33/53)	0	-2.7
1968	NY A	107	342	34	82	16	7	6	40	26-3	2	54	.240	.294	.380	108	2	7-6	.985	-4	97	49	O98(6/51/44)	0	-0.9
1969	NY A	87	222	23	38	11	2	3	21	16-3	0	39	.171	.226	.279	42	-18	3-1	.963	-1	94	126	O62(17/19/29)/1	0	-2.3
1972	Phi N	82	188	19	45	9	1	8	21	5-0	0	30	.239	.258	.426	89	-4	2-3	.982	1	104	63	O72(13/30/32)	0	-0.6
1973	Phi N	124	452	62	130	32	1	25	65	27-1	1	91	.288	.326	.529	130	17	5-4	.979	-0	110	104	O113(13/44/75),3b14	23	1.2
1974	Phi N	100	280	32	66	14	1	5	29	17-4	1	61	.236	.280	.346	72	-11	5-3	.971	4	105	174	O87(40/40/19)	0	-1.0
1975	†Pit N	92	200	26	56	12	2	6	33	11-4	0	36	.280	.313	.450	111	2	3-1	.991	2	112	93	O57(31/15/13)	0	0.2
1976	Pit N	122	393	55	119	22	3	21	64	16-1	1	73	.303	.329	.534	140	18	2-4	.993	-12	95	141	O78(24/27/29),3b37,1b3	0	0.2
1977	Pit N	137	507	74	154	32	1	26	104	25-3	3	92	.304	.337	.525	124	15	12-6	.992	-9	78	110	1b86,O43(41/2/1),3b17	0	0.1
1978	Pit N	136	499	70	123	36	2	14	80	35-8	5	105	.246	.296	.411	93	-5	14-11	.988	4	105	90	O127(111/19/10),3b29,1b3	15	-0.7
1979	†Pit N	148	421	59	111	17	6	24	75	24-11	1	81	.264	.302	.504	110	3	13-2	.982	-2	97	91	O125(119/0/6),1b28,3b3	0	-0.2
1980	Pit N	100	272	28	78	10	1	12	36	15-2	0	45	.287	.320	.463	113	4	1-4	.985	-4	67	92	1b49,O41(28/0/14)	23	-0.6
1981	Pit N	39	88	8	19	3	0	2	8	5-1	0	18	.216	.258	.318	60	-5	1-0	1.000	0	98	77	1b23,O7(1/0/6)/3	108	-0.6
1982	Pit N	31	71	8	17	3	0	4	12	5-3	0	19	.239	.286	.451	100	0	0-1	1.000	0	117	0	O22(12/0/11)	0	-0.1
	Phi N	35	69	6	18	6	0	3	19	7-1	0	15	.261	.321	.478	119	2	1-1	.960	1	85	316	O19R,1b5	0	0.2
	Year	66	140	14	35	9	0	7	31	12-4	0	34	.250	.303	.464	109	1	1-2	.984	1	103	140	O41(12/0/30),1b5	0	0.1
1983	Phi N	10	7	0	1	0	0	0	2	1-0	0	4	.143	.250	.143	12	-1	0-0	1.000	-1	0	0	1b3,3b2/lf	0	-0.2
Total	16	1472	4364	536	1127	229	29	166	641	263-49	16	820	.258	.300	.438	103	2	71-49	.979	-23	100	106	O1059(479/280/364),1b201,3b103	169	-8.1
Robles, Oscar	Oscar Manuel (Arenas); B4.9.1976 Tijuana, Baja California, Mexico; BL/TR/5´11˝/(155–185); d5.10																								
2005	LA N	110	364	44	99	18	1	5	34	31-0	2	33	.272	.332	.368	83	-9	0-8	.981	-3	93	91	S54,3b40/2	0	-1.1
2006	LA N	29	33	6	5	0	1	0	0	5-0	0	5	.152	.263	.212	24	-4	0-0	1.000	-2	68	118	2b13,3b6	0	-0.5
Total	2	139	397	50	104	18	2	5	34	36-0	2	38	.262	.326	.355	78	-13	0-8	.981	-4	93	91	S54,3b46,2b14	0	-1.6
Robles, Rafael	Rafael Orlando (Natera); B10.20.1947 San Pedro de Macoris, D.R.; D8.13.1998 New York NY; BR/TR/6´0˝/(160–170); d4.8																								
1969	SD N	6	20	1	2	0	0	0	0	1-0	0	3	.100	.143	.100	-32	-4	1-1	.895	-4	59	28	S6	0	-0.8
1970	SD N	23	89	5	19	1	0	0	3	5-0	1	11	.213	.263	.225	33	-9	3-0	.968	6	122	101	S23	0	0.0
1972	SD N	18	24	1	4	0	0	0	0	0-0	0	3	.167	.167	.167	-5	-3	0-0	.952	-3	89	0	S15/3	0	-0.6
Total	3	47	133	7	25	1	0	0	3	6-0	1	17	.188	.229	.195	17	-16	4-1	.958	-1	106	71	S44/3	0	-1.4

YEAR TM LG	G	AB	R	H	2B	3B	HR	RBI	BB-IB	HP	SO	AVG	OBP	SLG	AOPS	ABR	SB-CS	FA	FR	RNG	THR	GAMES AT POSITION	DL	BFW
ROBLES, SERGIO	Sergio (Valenzuela); B4.16.1946 Magdalena de Kino, Sonora, Mexico; BR/TR/6´2˝/190; d8.27																							
1972 Bal A	2	5	0	1	0	0	0	0	0-0	0	0	.200	.200	.200	19	-1	0-0	1.000	-1	0	0	/C	0	-0.1
1973 Bal A	8	13	0	1	0	0	0	0	3-0	0	1	.077	.250	.077	-4	-2	0-0	1.000	2	0	0	C8	0	0.1
1976 LA N	6	3	0	0	0	0	0	0	0-0	0	2	.000	.000	.000	-99	-1	0-0	1.000	-0	122	0	C6	0	-0.1
Total 3	16	21	0	2	0	0	0	0	3-0	0	3	.095	.208	.095	-11	-4	0-0	1.000	1	28	0	C15	0	-0.1
ROBSON, TOM	Thomas James; B1.15.1946 Rochester NY; BR/TR/6´3˝/220; [NYN67 50/859]; d9.14; C13; Col Utah St.; [DL 1976 NY A 23]																							
1974 Tex A	6	13	2	3	1	0	0	2	4-0	0	3	.231	.412	.308	112	1	0-0	1.000	0	0	1016	/1D	0	0.1
1975 Tex A	17	35	3	7	0	0	0	2	1-0	0	3	.200	.216	.200	20	-4	0-0	1.000	-0	79	202	1b5,D4	15	-0.4
Total 2	23	48	5	10	1	0	0	4	5-0	0	6	.208	.278	.229	48	-3	0-0	1.000	-0	77	227	D9,1b6	38	-0.3
ROCAP, ADAM	Adam; B1854 Philadelphia PA; D3.29.1892 Philadelphia PA; 5´9˝/170; d5.5																							
1875 Ath NA	16	69	13	12	1	0	0	4	1	—	7	.174	.186	.188	27	-5	3-2	.839	-2	154	0	O12(0/5/7),2b4	—	-0.6
ROCCO, MICKEY	Michael Dominick; B3.2.1916 St.Paul MN; D6.1.1997 St.Paul MN; BL/TL/5´11˝/188; d6.5																							
1943 Cle A	108	405	43	97	14	4	5	46	51	2	40	.240	.328	.331	99	0	1-2	**.995**	-5	81	118	1b108	0	-1.2
1944 Cle A	**155**	653	87	174	29	7	13	70	56	1	51	.266	.325	.392	108	5	4-8	.993	17	**142**	105	1b155	0	1.2
1945 Cle A	143	565	81	149	28	6	10	56	52	0	40	.264	.326	.388	111	6	0-4	**.992**	4	105	93	1b141	0	0.1
1946 Cle A	34	98	8	24	2	0	2	14	15	0	15	.245	.345	.327	94	0	1-1	.996	5	155	79	1b27	0	0.3
Total 4	440	1721	219	444	73	17	30	186	174	3	146	.258	.327	.372	106	11	6-15	.994	20	115	103	1b431	0	0.4
ROCHE, JACK	John Joseph "Red"; B11.22.1890 Los Angeles CA; D3.30.1983 Peoria AZ; BR/TR/6´1˝/178; d5.24																							
1914 StL N	12	9	1	6	2	1	0	3	0	1	1	.667	.700	1.111	441	4	1	.667	-1	*63*	*0*	C9	—	0.3
1915 StL N	46	39	2	8	0	1	0	6	4	1	8	.205	.295	.256	68	-2	1	1.000	0	*74*	*323*	C4	—	-0.1
1917 StL N	1	1	0	0	0	0	0	0	0	0	0	.000	.000	.000	-99	0	0	.000	-1	*0*	*0*	/C	—	-0.1
Total 3	59	49	3	14	2	2	0	9	4	2	9	.286	.364	.408	133	2	2	.750	-2	*60*	*119*	C14	—	0.1
ROCHEFORT, BEN	Bennett Harold (b Bennett Harold Rochefort Gilbert); B8.15.1896 Camden NJ; D4.2.1981 Red Bank NJ; BL/TR/6´2˝/185; d10.3; Col Temple																							
1914 Phi A	1	2	0	1	0	0	0	0	0	0	1	.500	.500	.500	209	0	0	1.000	0	352	0	/1	—	0.1
ROCHELLI, LOU	Louis Joseph; B1.11.1919 Staunton IL; D10.23.1992 Victoria TX; BR/TR/6´1˝/175; d8.25; Mil 1944–46																							
1944 Bro N	5	17	0	3	0	1	0	2	2	0	6	.176	.263	.294	58	-1	0	.964	-1	100	30	2b5	0	-0.1
ROCK, LES	Lester Henry (b Lester Henry Schwarzrock); B8.19.1912 Springfield MN; D9.9.1991 Davis CA; BL/TR/6´2˝/184; d9.11																							
1936 Chi A	2	1	0	0	0	0	0	1	0	0	0	.000	.000	.000	-97	0	0-0	ø	0	0	0	1b2	—	0.0
ROCKENFIELD, IKE	Isaac Broc; B11.3.1876 Omaha NE; D2.21.1927 San Diego CA; BR/TR/5´7˝/150; d5.5																							
1905 StL A	95	322	40	70	12	0	0	16	46	14	—	.217	.340	.255	95	3	11	.926	-9	96	76	2b95	—	-0.6
1906 StL A	27	89	3	21	4	0	0	8	1	4	—	.236	.277	.281	78	-2	0	.956	-6	81	60	2b26	—	-0.9
Total 2	122	411	43	91	16	0	0	24	47	18	—	.221	.328	.260	91	1	11	.933	-15	93	72	2b121	—	-1.5
ROCKETT, PAT	Patrick Edward; B1.9.1955 San Antonio TX; BR/TR/5´11˝/165; [AtlN73 1/10]; d9.17																							
1976 Atl N	4	5	0	1	0	0	0	0	0-0	0	1	.200	.200	.200	13	-1	0-0	1.000	-1	55	0	S2	0	-0.1
1977 Atl N	93	264	27	67	10	0	1	24	27-2	3	32	.254	.330	.303	64	-12	1-2	.940	-14	85	72	S84	42	-1.8
1978 Atl N	55	142	6	20	2	0	0	4	13-3	0	12	.141	.212	.155	4	-18	1-2	.970	-18	71	61	S51	0	-3.5
Total 3	152	411	33	88	12	0	1	28	40-5	3	45	.214	.288	.251	43	-31	2-4	.949	-32	80	68	S137	42	-5.4
RODGERS, ANDRE	Kenneth Andre Ian "Andy"; B12.2.1934 Nassau, Bahamas; D12.13.2004 Nassau, Bahamas; BR/TR/6´3˝/(180–200); d4.16																							
1957 NY N	32	86	8	21	2	1	3	9	9-0	1	21	.244	.320	.395	92	-1	0-0	.950	2	102	116	S20,3b8	0	0.3
1958 SF N	22	63	7	13	3	1	2	11	4-0	0	14	.206	.243	.381	67	-3	0-0	.972	-4	89	74	S18	0	-0.6
1959 SF N	71	228	32	57	12	1	6	24	32-1	1	50	.250	.342	.390	98	0	2-1	.933	-8	95	91	S66	0	-0.2
1960 SF N	81	217	22	53	8	5	2	22	24-4	3	44	.244	.325	.355	92	-2	1-1	.953	-4	92	105	S41,3b21,1b6,O2L	0	-0.4
1961 Chi N	73	214	27	57	17	0	6	23	25-1	1	54	.266	.343	.430	103	2	1-1	.983	-2	93	97	1b42,S24,O2R/2	0	-0.1
1962 Chi N	138	461	40	128	20	8	5	44	44-4	3	93	.278	.343	.388	93	-4	5-6	.960	12	**111**	105	S133/1	0	1.8
1963 Chi N	150	516	51	118	17	4	5	33	65-6	9	90	.229	.324	.306	79	-12	5-7	.954	-2	102	119	S150	0	-0.1
1964 Chi N	129	448	50	107	17	3	12	46	53-5	0	88	.239	.317	.371	90	-5	5-1	.965	9	**113**	92	S126	0	1.6
1965 Pit N	75	178	17	51	12	0	2	25	18-3	0	28	.287	.350	.388	108	3	2-1	.950	-1	101	137	S33,3b15,1b6/2	0	0.4
1966 Pit N	36	49	6	9	1	0	0	4	8-0	0	7	.184	.293	.204	43	-4	0-1	.913	-1	101	201	S5,3b3,O3L,1b2	18	-0.5
1967 Pit N	47	61	8	14	3	0	2	4	8-2	0	18	.230	.314	.377	98	0	1-1	1.000	1	158	84	1b9,3b5,S3,2b2	0	0.1
Total 11	854	2521	268	628	112	23	45	245	290-26	18	507	.249	.328	.365	90	-26	22-20	.956	3	105	105	S619,1b66,3b52,O7(5/0/2),2b4	18	2.3
RODGERS, BUCK	Robert Leroy; B8.16.1938 Delaware OH; BB/TR/6´2˝/(190–195); d9.8; M13/C9																							
1961 LA A	16	56	8	18	2	0	2	13	1-0	0	6	.321	.333	.464	99	0	0-0	.965	-1	60	228	C14	0	-0.1
1962 LA A	155	565	65	146	34	6	6	61	45-6	0	68	.258	.309	.372	86	-12	1-8	.989	5	129	116	C150	0	-0.1
1963 LA A	100	300	24	70	6	0	4	23	29-2	2	35	.233	.303	.293	73	-11	2-2	.979	-6	118	127	C85	0	-1.3
1964 LA A	148	514	38	125	18	3	4	54	40-11	4	71	.243	.299	.313	80	-15	4-3	.987	16	130	**124**	C146	0	0.8
1965 Cal A	132	411	33	86	14	3	1	32	35-9	3	61	.209	.271	.265	56	-24	4-5	.991	8	116	85	C128	0	-1.1
1966 Cal A	133	454	45	107	20	3	7	48	29-8	2	57	.236	.281	.339	81	-12	3-4	.992	-3	114	106	C133	0	-1.1
1967 Cal A	139	429	29	94	13	3	6	41	34-5	2	55	.219	.277	.305	76	-14	1-4	.991	2	133	122	C134/lf	0	-0.8
1968 Cal A	91	258	13	49	6	0	1	14	16-3	3	48	.190	.244	.225	45	-18	2-1	.985	-2	117	113	C87	0	-1.9
1969 Cal A	18	46	4	9	1	0	0	2	5-1	1	8	.196	.288	.217	45	-3	0-0	1.000	-4	47	91	C18	0	-0.7
Total 9	932	3033	259	704	114	18	31	288	234-45	17	409	.232	.288	.312	74	-109	17-27	.988	15	121	115	C895/lf	0	-6.3
RODGERS, BILL	Wilbur Kincaid "Rawmeat Bill"; B4.18.1887 Pleasant Ridge OH; D12.24.1978 Goliad TX; BL/TR/5´9.5˝/170; d4.15																							
1915 Cle A	16	45	8	14	2	0	0	7	8	0	7	.311	.415	.356	128	2	3-3	.945	-3	93	22	2b13	—	-0.1
Bos A	11	6	2	0	0	0	0	0	3	0	2	.000	.333	.000	-0	0	0	.900	1	162	0	2b6	—	0.0
Year	27	51	10	14	2	0	0	7	11	0	9	.275	.403	.314	115	2	3-3	.938	-2	114	141	2b19	—	-0.1
Cin N	72	213	20	51	13	4	0	12	11	7	29	.239	.299	.338	91	-2	8-5	.947	6	114	141	2b56,S6/3rf	—	0.5
1916 Cin N	3	4	0	0	0	0	0	0	0	0	2	.000	.000	.000	-99	-1	0	1.000	-0	68	0	/S	—	-0.1
Total 2	102	268	30	65	15	4	0	19	22	7	40	.243	.316	.328	93	-1	11-8	.945	3	111	116	2b75,S7/rf3	—	0.3
RODGERS, BILL	William Sherman; B12.5.1922 Harrisburg PA; D5.13.2002 Worcester MA; BL/TL/6´0˝/162; d9.27; Mil 1945																							
1944 Pit N	2	4	1	1	0	0	0	0	0	0	1	.250	.250	.250	39	0	0	ø	-0	0	0	/rf	0	0.0
1945 Pit N	1	1	0	1	0	0	0	0	0	0	0	1.000	1.000	1.000	440	0	0	ø	0	—	—	/H	0	0.0
Total 2	3	5	1	2	0	0	0	0	0	0	1	.400	.400	.400	120	0	0	.000	-0	0	0	/rf	0	0.0
RODIN, ERIC	Eric Chapman; B2.5.1930 Orange NJ; D1.4.1991 Somerville NJ; BR/TR/6´2˝/215; d9.7; Col Penn																							
1954 NY N	5	6	0	0	0	0	0	0	0	0	2	.000	.000	.000	-99	-2	0-0	1.000	0	109	0	O3(0/2/1)	0	-0.2
RODRIGUEZ, ALEX	Alexander Emmanuel "A-Rod"; B7.27.1975 New York NY; BR/TR/6´3˝/(190–225); [SeaA93 1/1]; d7.8																							
1994 Sea A	17	54	4	11	0	0	0	2	3-0	0	20	.204	.241	.204	17	-7	3-0	.915	-2	91	81	S17	0	-0.7
1995 †Sea A	48	142	15	33	6	2	5	19	6-0	0	42	.232	.264	.408	71	-7	4-2	.953	-4	92	52	S46/D	0	-0.8
1996 Sea A★	146	601	**141**	215	**54**	1	36	123	59-1	4	104	**.358**	.414	.631	160	56	15-4	.977	-6	95	94	S146	15	5.6
1997 †Sea A★	141	587	100	176	40	3	23	84	41-1	5	99	.300	.350	.496	118	15	29-6	.962	-3	94	90	S140/D	15	2.5
1998 Sea A★	**161**	686	123	**213**	35	5	42	124	45-0	10	121	.310	.360	.560	134	32	46-13	.975	-1	92	88	S160/D	0	4.4
1999 Sea A	129	502	110	143	25	0	42	111	56-2	5	109	.285	.357	.586	138	27	21-7	.977	1	99	107	S129	37	3.6
2000 †Sea A✳	148	554	134	175	34	2	41	132	100-5	7	121	.316	.420	.606	160	55	15-4	.986	6	99	**125**	S148	15	**6.6**
2001 Tex A	**162**	632	**133**	201	34	1	**52**	135	75-6	16	131	.318	.399	.622	160	56	18-3	.976	3	100	107	S161/D	0	**6.9**
2002 Tex A★	**162**	624	125	187	27	2	**57**	**142**	87-12	10	122	.300	.392	.623	160	54	9-4	.987	12	104	96	S162	0	**7.4**
2003 Tex A★	161	607	**124**	181	30	6	**47**	118	87-10	15	126	.298	.396	**.600**	148	44	17-3	**.989**	13	**106**	98	S158/D	0	**6.7**
2004 †NY A★	155	601	112	172	24	2	36	106	80-6	10	131	.286	.375	.512	129	27	28-4	.965	-2	100	101	3b155,S2	0	2.9
2005 †NY A★	**162**	605	**124**	194	29	1	**48**	130	91-8	16	139	.321	.421	**.610**	**171**	**66**	21-6	.971	-6	93	91	3b161,S3/D	0	**6.0**
2006 †NY A★	154	572	113	166	26	1	35	121	90-8	8	139	.290	.392	.523	134	32	15-4	.937	-20	88	80	3b151,D3	0	1.4
Total 13	1746	6767	1358	2067	364	26	464	1347	820-59	106	1404	.305	.386	.573	144	450	241-60	.977	-10	98	99	S1272,3b467,D9	82	52.5

YEAR	TM LG	G	AB	R	H	2B	3B	HR	RBI	BB-IB	HP	SO	AVG	OBP	SLG	AOPS	ABR	SB-CS	FA	FR	RNG	THR	GAMES AT POSITION	DL	BFW
Rodriguez, Aurelio	Aurelio (Ituarte); B12.28.1947 Cananea, Sonora, Mexico; D9.23.2000 Detroit MI; BR/TR/5´10˝/(175–180); d9.1																								
1967	Cal A	29	130	14	31	3	1	1	8	2-0	0	21	.238	.250	.300	64	-7	1-0	.989	4	117	224	3b29	0	-0.2
1968	Cal A	76	223	14	54	10	1	1	16	17-2	1	36	.242	.299	.309	87	-3	0-2	.921	-8	87	162	3b70,2b2	26	-1.5
1969	Cal A	159	561	47	130	17	2	7	49	32-11	2	88	.232	.272	.307	66	-28	5-3	.954	15	109	**135**	3b159	0	-1.5
1970	Cal A	17	63	6	17	2	2	0	7	3-0	1	6	.270	.313	.365	89	-1	0-1	1.000	3	109	209	3b17	0	0.1
	Was A	142	547	64	135	31	5	19	76	37-5	7	81	.247	.300	.426	103	0	15-5	.961	13	117	118	3b136,S7	0	1.5
	Year	159	610	70	152	33	7	19	83	40-5	8	87	.249	.302	.420	102	-1	15-6	.965	16	116	128	3b153,S7	0	1.6
1971	Det A	154	604	68	153	30	7	15	39	27-6	3	93	.253	.288	.401	90	-11	4-6	.953	6	100	105	3b153/S	0	-0.8
1972	†Det A	153	601	65	142	23	5	13	56	28-4	2	104	.236	.272	.356	83	-15	2-3	.969	20	105	114	3b153,S2	0	0.5
1973	Det A	160	555	46	123	27	3	9	58	31-0	3	85	.222	.266	.330	63	-28	3-1	.971	5	97	102	3b160/S	0	-2.5
1974	Det A	159	571	54	127	23	5	5	49	26-2	1	70	.222	.255	.306	60	-31	2-0	.961	15	107	110	3b159	0	-1.7
1975	Det A	151	507	47	124	20	6	13	60	30-1	0	63	.245	.286	.385	85	-13	1-1	.953	27	**116**	105	3b151	0	1.3
1976	Det A	128	480	40	115	13	2	8	50	19-3	1	61	.240	.267	.325	71	-19	0-4	**.978**	8	102	92	3b128	35	-1.4
1977	Det A	96	306	30	67	14	1	10	32	16-1	0	36	.219	.257	.369	65	-16	1-1	.972	15	124	120	3b95/S	34	-0.2
1978	Det A	134	385	40	102	25	2	7	43	19-1	3	37	.265	.303	.395	92	-4	0-1	**.987**	6	109	101	3b131	0	-0.1
1979	Det A	106	343	27	87	18	0	5	36	11-0	1	40	.254	.277	.350	66	-17	0-2	.956	6	105	124	3b106/1	0	-1.3
1980	SD N	89	175	7	35	7	2	2	13	6-0	0	26	.200	.227	.297	48	-13	1-1	.965	2	106	139	3b88,S2	0	-1.3
	†NY A	52	164	14	36	6	1	3	14	7-1	0	35	.220	.251	.323	57	-10	0-0	.954	-11	75	57	3b49,2b6	0	-2.2
1981	†NY A	27	52	4	18	2	0	2	8	2-0	0	10	.346	.370	.500	150	3	0-0	.951	2	104	53	3b20,2b3/1D	0	0.5
1982	Chi A	118	257	24	62	15	1	3	31	11-0	1	35	.241	.275	.342	68	-12	0-0	.969	9	107	103	3b112,2b3,S2	0	-0.3
1983	Bal A	45	67	0	8	0	0	0	2	0-0	1	13	.119	.130	.119	-31	-12	0-0	.969	-3	86	41	3b45	0	-1.6
	†Chi A	22	20	1	4	1	0	1	1	0-0	0	3	.200	.200	.400	58	-1	0-0	1.000	2	117	299	3b22	0	0.1
	Year	67	87	1	12	1	0	1	3	0-0	1	16	.138	.146	.184	-9	-13	0-0	.978	-1	94	108	3b67	0	-1.5
Total	17	2017	6611	612	1570	287	46	124	648	324-37	27	943	.237	.275	.351	75	-238	35-31	.964	134	106	114	3b1983,S16,2b14,D2,1b2	95	-12.6
Rodriguez, Carlos	Carlos (Marquez); B11.1.1967 Mexico City, Distrito Federal, Mexico; BB/TR/5´9˝/160; d6.16																								
1991	NY A	15	37	1	7	0	0	0	2	1-0	0	2	.189	.211	.189	11	-5	0-0	.957	1	117	148	S11,2b3	0	-0.3
1994	Bos A	57	174	15	50	14	1	1	13	11-0	0	13	.287	.330	.397	82	-4	1-0	.973	0	80	94	S32,2b20,3b4	0	-0.1
1995	Bos A	13	30	5	10	2	0	0	5	2-0	1	2	.333	.394	.400	104	0	0-0	.960	0	94	84	2b7,S6/3	0	0.1
Total	3	85	241	21	67	16	1	1	20	14-0	1	17	.278	.320	.365	75	-9	1-0	.972	1	91	110	S49,2b30,3b5	0	-0.3
Rodriguez, Edwin	Edwin (Morales); B8.14.1960 Ponce, PR; BR/TR/5´11˝/175; d9.28																								
1982	NY A	3	9	2	3	0	0	0	1	1-0	0	1	.333	.400	.333	105	0	0-0	.875	2	205	67	2b3	0	0.2
1983	SD N	7	12	1	2	1	0	0	0	1-0	0	3	.167	.231	.250	34	-1	0-0	1.000	-2	79	92	2b5,S2/3	0	-0.3
1985	SD N	1	1	0	0	0	0	0	0	0-0	0	0	.000	.000	.000	-99	0	0-0	ø	0	—	—	/H	0	0.0
Total	3	11	22	3	5	1	0	0	1	2-0	0	4	.227	.292	.273	58	-1	0-0	.935	-0	127	83	2b8,S2/3	0	-0.1
Rodriguez, Ellie	Eliseo (Delgado); B5.24.1946 Fajardo, PR; BR/TR/5´11˝/(175–185); d5.26; [DL 1977 LA N 26]																								
1968	NY A	9	24	1	5	0	0	1	3-0	0	3	.208	.296	.208	57	-1	0-0	1.000	-1	128	133	C9	0	-0.2
1969	KC A☆	95	267	27	63	10	0	2	20	31-6	8	26	.236	.333	.296	76	-7	3-2	.990	-7	136	108	C90	0	-1.1
1970	KC A	80	231	25	52	8	2	1	15	27-2	4	35	.225	.312	.290	68	-9	2-1	.988	3	73	83	C75	0	-0.3
1971	Mil A	115	319	28	67	10	1	1	30	41-5	8	51	.210	.311	.257	64	-13	1-1	.992	10	144	**150**	C114	0	0.1
1972	Mil A☆	116	355	31	101	14	2	2	35	52-5	7	43	.285	.382	.352	123	13	1-4	.983	-4	107	105	C114	0	1.5
1973	Mil A	94	290	30	78	8	1	0	30	41-3	10	28	.269	.376	.303	95	1	4-3	.986	3	123	143	C75,D14	0	0.7
1974	Cal A	140	395	48	100	20	0	7	36	69-6	9	56	.253	.373	.357	118	14	4-5	.992	3	**127**	**119**	C137/D	0	2.2
1975	Cal A	90	226	20	53	6	0	3	27	49-0	6	37	.235	.380	.301	103	5	2-2	.991	-8	71	81	C90	29	0.0
1976	LA N	36	66	10	14	0	0	0	9	19-2	3	12	.212	.400	.212	81	0	0-0	.986	2	54	87	C33	17	0.3
Total	9	775	2173	220	533	76	6	16	203	332-29	55	291	.245	.356	.308	94	3	17-18	.989	1	112	114	C737,D15	72	3.2
Rodriguez, Hector	Hector Antonio (Ordenana); B6.13.1920 Alquizar, Cuba; D9.1.2003 Cancun, Quintana Roo, Mexico; BR/TR/5´8˝/165; d4.15; Negro Lg 1939–44																								
1952	Chi A	124	407	55	108	14	0	1	40	47	3	22	.265	.346	.307	82	-8	7-6	.959	5	98	106	3b113	0	-0.4
Rodriguez, Henry	Henry Anderson (Lorenzo); B11.8.1967 Santo Domingo, D.R.; BL/TL/6´1˝/(180–225); d7.5																								
1992	LA N	53	146	11	32	7	0	3	14	8-0	0	30	.219	.258	.329	66	-7	0-0	.960	2	84	290	O48(17/0/31)/1	0	-0.7
1993	LA N	76	176	20	39	10	0	8	23	11-2	0	39	.222	.266	.415	84	-5	1-0	.984	-2	78	108	O48(26/0/23),1b13	0	-0.9
1994	LA N	104	306	33	82	14	2	8	49	17-2	2	58	.268	.307	.405	90	-6	0-1	.986	3	105	95	O86(85/0/6),1b17	0	-0.7
1995	LA N	21	80	6	21	4	1	1	10	5-2	0	17	.262	.306	.375	84	-2	0-1	1.000	-1	103	0	O20R/1	0	-0.4
	Mon N	24	58	7	12	0	0	1	5	6-0	0	11	.207	.277	.259	42	-5	0-0	1.000	-1	117	116	1b10,O8(4/0/4)	75	-0.7
	Year	45	138	13	33	4	1	2	15	11-2	0	28	.239	.293	.326	65	-7	0-1	.977	-1	94	0	O28(4/0/24),1b11	0	-1.1
1996	Mon N★	145	532	81	147	42	1	36	103	37-7	3	160	.276	.325	.562	126	18	2-0	.947	-9	76	113	O89(88/0/2),1b51	0	0.2
1997	Mon N	132	476	55	116	28	3	26	83	42-5	2	149	.244	.306	.479	103	0	3-3	.985	-4	92	53	O126(126/0/1),1b3	0	-0.9
1998	†Chi N	128	415	56	104	21	1	31	85	54-7	0	113	.251	.334	.530	119	10	1-3	.996	9	115	109	O114L,D5	15	1.5
1999	Chi N	130	447	72	136	29	0	26	87	56-6	0	113	.304	.381	.544	131	21	2-4	.974	1	100	98	O122L,D2	0	1.6
2000	Chi N	76	259	37	65	15	1	18	51	22-2	3	76	.251	.314	.525	109	2	1-2	.983	-0	90	126	O70(70/0/1)	0	-0.1
	Fla N	36	108	10	29	6	0	2	10	14-0	1	23	.269	.358	.380	91	-1	0-0	1.000	-2	82	63	O29(24/0/6)	0	-0.4
	Year	112	367	47	94	21	1	20	61	36-2	4	99	.256	.327	.482	104	1	1-2	.987	-2	88	108	O99(94/0/7)	0	-0.5
2001	NY A	5	8	0	0	0	0	0	0	0-0	0	6	.000	.000	.000	-99	-2	0-0	ø	0	—	—	/D	52	-0.2
2002	Mon N	20	20	1	1	0	0	0	3	4-0	0	8	.050	.200	.050	-26	-4	0-0	ø	-1	0	0	O5(4/0/1)	0	-0.5
Total	11	950	3031	389	784	176	9	160	523	276-33	11	803	.259	.321	.481	107	19	10-14	.980	-4	94	103	O765(680/0/95),1b96,D8	142	-2.2
Rodriguez, Ivan	Ivan (Torres) "Pudge"; B11.27.1971 Manati, PR; BR/TR/5´9˝/(165–220); d6.20																								
1991	Tex A	88	280	24	74	16	0	3	27	5-0	0	42	.264	.276	.354	74	-11	0-1	.983	11	138	**132**	C88	0	0.5
1992	Tex A★	123	420	39	109	16	1	8	37	24-2	1	73	.260	.300	.360	87	-9	0-0	.983	20	**160**	**134**	C116,D2	21	1.8
1993	Tex A★	137	473	56	129	28	4	10	66	29-3	4	70	.273	.315	.412	98	-2	8-7	.991	11	133	107	C134/D	0	1.6
1994	Tex A★	99	363	56	108	19	1	16	57	31-5	7	42	.298	.360	.488	116	8	6-3	.992	2	**177**	77	C99	0	1.6
1995	Tex A★	130	492	56	149	32	2	12	67	16-2	4	48	.303	.327	.449	97	-3	0-2	.990	13	**198**	108	C127/D	0	1.6
1996	†Tex A★	153	639	116	192	47	3	19	86	38-7	4	55	.300	.342	.473	97	-3	5-0	.989	26	**194**	**122**	C146,D6	0	3.0
1997	Tex A★	150	597	98	187	34	4	20	77	38-7	8	89	.313	.360	.484	111	9	7-3	.992	24	**253**	109	C143,D5	0	4.0
1998	†Tex A★	145	579	88	186	40	4	21	91	32-4	3	88	.321	.358	.513	117	14	9-0	.994	17	**262**	109	C139,D6	0	3.9
1999	†Tex A★	144	600	116	199	29	1	35	113	24-2	1	64	.332	.356	.558	122	17	25-12	.993	19	**257**	96	C141/D	0	4.2
2000	Tex A★	91	363	66	126	27	4	27	83	19-5	1	48	.347	.375	.667	156	29	5-5	**.996**	8	**248**	90	C87/D	68	3.7
2001	Tex A	111	442	70	136	24	2	25	65	23-3	4	73	.308	.347	.541	125	15	10-3	.990	14	**308**	118	C106,D5	53	3.4
2002	Tex A	108	408	67	128	32	2	19	60	25-2	2	71	.314	.353	.542	130	17	5-4	.990	5	**203**	61	C100,D6	51	2.7
2003	†Fla N	144	511	90	152	36	3	16	85	55-6	6	92	.297	.369	.474	124	19	10-6	.992	1	151	75	C138/D	0	2.8
2004	Det A★	135	527	72	176	32	2	19	86	41-6	3	91	.334	.383	.510	136	28	7-4	.987	3	153	68	C124,D8	0	3.6
2005	Det A★	129	504	71	139	33	5	14	50	11-2	2	93	.276	.290	.444	94	-6	7-3	.995	14	**191**	130	C123,D3	0	1.6
2006	†Det A★	136	547	74	164	28	4	13	69	26-4	1	86	.300	.332	.437	99	-2	8-3	**.998**	16	**264**	96	C123,1b7/2D	0	2.1
Total	16	2023	7745	1159	2354	473	42	277	1119	437-60	51	1125	.304	.342	.483	112	120	112-56	.991	203	206	102	C1934,D51,1b7/2	193	42.1
Rodriguez, John	John Joseph; B1.20.1978 New York NY; BL/TL/6´0˝/205; d7.18																								
2005	†StL N	56	149	15	44	6	0	5	24	19-4	3	45	.295	.382	.436	113	3	2-0	.973	0	96	138	O45(40/0/9)	0	0.2
2006	†StL N	102	183	31	55	12	3	2	19	21-1	3	45	.301	.374	.432	107	3	0-0	.986	-1	98	54	O51(41/0/15)/D	0	0.1
Total	2	158	332	46	99	18	3	7	43	40-5	6	90	.298	.378	.434	110	6	2-0	.979	-0	97	97	O96(81/0/24)/D	0	0.3
Rodriguez, Jose	Jose "El Hombre Goma"; B2.23.1894 Havana, Cuba; D1.21.1953 Havana, Cuba; BR/TR/5´8˝/150; d10.5																								
1916	NY N	1	0	0	0	0	0	0	0	0	0	0	ø	ø	ø	ø	0	0	ø	0	—	—	/R	—	0.0
1917	NY N	7	20	2	4	0	1	0	2	2	0	1	.200	.273	.300	78	-1	2	1.000	-1	36	71	1b7	—	-0.2
1918	NY N	50	125	15	20	0	2	0	15	12	1	3	.160	.239	.192	33	-10	6	.978	0	91	104	2b40,1b8,3b2	—	-1.1
Total	3	58	145	17	24	0	3	0	17	14	1	4	.166	.244	.207	39	-11	8	.978	-0	91	104	2b40,1b15,3b2	—	-1.3
Rodriguez, Liu	Liubiemithz; B11.5.1976 Caracas, Distrito Capital, Venez.; BB/TR/5´9˝/170; d6.9																								
1999	Chi A	39	93	8	22	2	2	1	12	12-0	3	11	.237	.343	.333	72	-4	0-0	.985	-8	84	50	2b22,S14/3	0	-0.9
Rodriguez, Tony	Luis Antonio; B8.15.1970 Rio Piedras, PR; BR/TR/5´11˝/178; [BosA91 10/278]; d7.6; Col Charleston (WV)																								
1996	Bos A	27	67	7	16	1	0	1	9	4-0	1	8	.239	.292	.299	49	-5	0-0	.979	2	112	78	S21,3b5	0	-0.2

YEAR	TM LG	G	AB	R	H	2B	3B	HR	RBI	BB-IB	HP	SO	AVG	OBP	SLG	AOPS	ABR	SB-CS	FA	FR	RNG	THR	GAMES AT POSITION	DL	BFW
RODRIGUEZ, LUIS	Luis Orlando; B6.27.1980 San Carlos, Venezuela; BB/TR/5´9˝/(180–190); d5.21																								
2005	Min A	79	175	21	47	10	2	2	20	18-0	1	23	.269	.335	.383	91	-2	2-2	1.000	1	102	149	2b40,3b27,S10,D3	0	0.0
2006	Min A	59	115	11	27	4	0	2	6	14-1	0	16	.235	.315	.322	66	-6	0-0	1.000	2	93	225	3b29,2b14,S2/1D	0	-0.3
Total	2	138	290	32	74	14	2	4	26	32-1	1	39	.255	.327	.359	81	-8	2-2	.975	3	96	167	3b56,2b54,S12,D6/1	0	-0.3
RODRIGUEZ, RUBEN	Ruben Dario (Martinez); B8.4.1964 Cabrera, D.R.; BR/TR/6´3˝/(170–175); d9.15																								
1986	Pit N	2	3	0	0	0	0	0	0	0-0	0	1	.000	.000	.000	-97	-1	0-0	1.000	0	95	0	C2	0	-0.1
1988	Pit N	2	5	1	1	0	1	0	1	0-0	0	2	.200	.200	.600	123	0	0-0	1.000	1	0	0	C2	0	0.1
Total	2	4	8	1	1	0	1	0	1	0-0	0	3	.125	.125	.375	36	-1	0-0	1.000	1	45	0	C4	0	0.0
RODRIGUEZ, STEVE	Steven James; B11.29.1970 Las Vegas NV; BR/TR/5´8˝/170; [BosA92 5/142]; d4.30; Col Pepperdine																								
1995	Bos A	6	8	1	1	0	0	0	0	1-0	0	1	.125	.222	.125	-6	-1	1-0	.667	-1	85	0	S4/2D	0	-0.2
	Det A	12	31	4	6	1	0	0	0	5-0	0	9	.194	.306	.226	41	-3	1-2	.982	-2	100	71	2b12/S	0	-0.4
	Year	18	39	5	7	1	0	0	0	6-0	0	10	.179	.289	.205	31	-4	2-2	.983	-3	98	66	2b13,S5/D	0	-0.6
RODRIGUEZ, VIC	Victor Manuel (Rivera); B7.14.1961 New York NY; BR/TR/5´11˝/173; d9.5																								
1984	Bal A	11	17	4	7	3	0	0	2	0-0	0	2	.412	.412	.588	176	2	0-0	.958	-0	112	35	2b7/D	0	0.2
1989	Min A	6	11	2	5	2	0	0	0	0-0	0	1	.455	.455	.636	192	1	0-0	.900	0	103	202	3b5/D	0	0.2
Total	2	17	28	6	12	5	0	0	2	0-0	0	3	.429	.429	.607	182	3	0-0	.958	-0	112	35	2b7,3b5,D2	0	0.4
ROENICKE, GARY	Gary Steven; B12.5.1954 Covina CA; BR/TR/6´3˝/(198–203); [MonN73 1/8]; d6.8; b–Ron																								
1976	Mon N	29	90	9	20	3	1	2	5	4-0	1	18	.222	.260	.344	68	-4	0-0	.955	0	92	170	O25(3/0/22)	0	-0.6
1978	Bal A	27	58	5	15	3	0	3	15	8-0	1	3	.259	.348	.466	138	3	0-1	1.000	-1	74	104	O20L	0	0.1
1979	†Bal A	133	376	60	98	16	1	25	64	61-4	12	74	.261	.378	.508	142	24	1-3	.981	0	98	118	O130(114/26/8),D2	0	1.9
1980	Bal A	118	297	40	71	13	0	10	28	41-5	6	49	.239	.340	.384	100	1	2-0	**1.000**	3	103	119	O113(86/13/38)	35	0.1
1981	Bal A	85	219	31	59	16	0	3	20	23-1	2	29	.269	.340	.384	110	4	1-2	.983	5	123	43	O83(45/13/54)	0	0.5
1982	Bal A	137	393	58	106	25	1	21	74	70-2	9	73	.270	.392	.499	144	27	6-7	.990	9	118	98	O125(80/34/42),1b10	0	3.0
1983	†Bal A	115	323	45	84	13	0	19	64	30-2	4	35	.260	.326	.477	121	8	2-2	.982	-3	93	115	O100(79/8/23),1b7,3b2,D2	0	0.2
1984	Bal A	121	326	36	73	19	1	10	44	58-1	4	43	.224	.346	.380	103	4	1-2	.995	-3	93	89	O117(85/6/32)	0	-0.4
1985	Bal A	114	225	36	49	9	0	15	43	44-1	0	36	.218	.342	.458	120	7	2-2	.993	3	104	155	O89(76/9/9),D17	0	0.7
1986	NY A	69	136	11	36	5	0	3	18	27-0	1	30	.265	.388	.368	108	3	1-1	1.000	-2	72	172	O37(33/3/2),D15,3b3,1b2	0	0.0
1987	Atl N	67	151	25	33	8	0	9	28	32-0	1	23	.219	.353	.450	108	3	0-0	.968	-2	88	0	O44(40/0/4),1b9	0	-0.1
1988	Atl N	49	114	11	26	5	0	1	7	8-0	0	15	.228	.279	.298	63	-5	0-0	1.000	-2	92	0	O35(32/1/2)/1	0	-0.9
Total	12	1064	2708	367	670	135	4	121	410	406-16	41	428	.247	.351	.434	117	75	16-20	.988	7	101	101	O918(693/113/236),D36,1b29,3b5	35	4.5
ROENICKE, RON	Ronald Jon; B8.19.1956 Covina CA; BB/TL/6´0˝/180; [LAN77 S1/17]; d9.2; C7; b–Gary; Col UCLA																								
1981	LA N	22	47	6	11	0	0	0	0	6-0	0	8	.234	.321	.234	62	-2	1-1	1.000	2	133	98	O20(5/6/10)	0	-0.1
1982	LA N	109	143	18	37	8	0	1	12	21-3	2	32	.259	.359	.336	99	1	5-0	.984	-3	84	43	O72(21/18/39)	0	-0.2
1983	LA N	81	145	12	32	4	0	2	12	14-1	0	26	.221	.287	.290	61	-8	3-2	.987	-1	98	43	O62(9/17/44)	0	-1.1
	Sea A	59	198	23	50	12	0	4	23	33-1	2	22	.253	.362	.374	100	2	6-2	.993	7	98	362	O54(16/38/4),1b8/D	0	0.7
1984	†SD N	12	20	4	6	1	0	1	2	2-1	0	5	.300	.364	.500	140	1	0-0	1.000	-1	86	0	O10(7/2/2)	0	0.0
1985	SF N	65	133	23	34	9	1	3	13	35-3	0	27	.256	.408	.406	135	9	6-2	.984	-1	106	0	O35(9/6/20)	0	0.7
1986	Phi N	102	275	42	68	13	1	5	42	61-4	0	52	.247	.381	.356	102	4	2-2	.989	-0	105	63	O83(24/63/8)	0	0.2
1987	Phi N	63	78	9	13	3	1	1	4	14-1	0	15	.167	.293	.269	49	-6	1-0	.964	0	102	138	O26(9/15/4)	0	-0.6
1988	Cin N	14	37	4	5	1	0	0	5	4-0	1	8	.135	.238	.162	16	-4	0-0	1.000	-1	82	0	O14(0/4/10)	0	-0.6
Total	8	527	1076	141	256	51	3	17	113	190-14	5	195	.238	.353	.338	92	-3	24-9	.989	2	100	109	O376(100/169/141),1b8/D	0	-1.0
ROETTGER, OSCAR	Oscar Frederick Louis "Okkie"; B2.19.1900 St.Louis MO; D7.4.1986 St.Louis MO; BR/TR/6´0˝/170; d7.7; b–Wally; ▲																								
1923	NY A	5	2	0	0	0	0	0	0	0	0	0	.000	.000	.000	-98	0	0-0	1.000	0	64	0	P5	—	0.0
1924	NY A	1	0	0	0	0	0	0	0	0	0	0	ø	ø	ø	ø	0	0-0	ø	0	0	0	/P	—	0.0
1927	Bro N	5	4	0	0	0	0	0	0	1	1	1	.000	.333	.000	-4	0	0	ø	-0	0	0	/rf	—	-0.1
1932	Phi A	26	60	7	14	1	0	0	6	5	0	4	.233	.292	.250	40	-5	0-0	.978	-1	63	57	1b15	—	-0.8
Total	4	37	66	7	14	1	0	0	6	6	1	5	.212	.288	.227	34	-5	0-0	.978	-1	63	57	1b15,P6/rf	—	-0.9
ROETTGER, WALLY	Walter Henry; B8.28.1902 St.Louis MO; D9.14.1951 Champaign IL; BR/TR/6´1.5˝/190; d5.1; b–Oscar; Col Illinois																								
1927	StL N	5	1	0	0	0	0	0	0	1	0	0	.000	.500	.000	42	0	0	.500	-1	83	0	O3L	—	-0.1
1928	StL N	68	261	27	89	17	4	6	44	10	3	22	.341	.372	.506	125	9	2	.981	-3	101	31	O66(33/0/34)	—	0.1
1929	StL N	79	269	27	68	11	3	3	42	13	0	27	.253	.287	.349	56	-20	0	.993	0	105	66	O69(7/0/62)	—	-2.2
1930	NY N	121	420	51	119	15	5	5	51	25	4	29	.283	.330	.379	72	-20	1	**.992**	-3	91	109	O114(28/85/4)	—	-2.5
1931	Cin N	44	185	25	65	11	4	1	20	7	1	9	.351	.378	.470	135	8	1	.990	-0	101	75	O44(18/2/24)	—	0.6
	†StL N	45	151	16	43	12	2	0	17	9	3	14	.285	.337	.391	92	-2	0	.974	-3	92	28	O42(8/7/27)	—	-0.7
	Year	89	336	41	108	23	6	1	37	16	4	23	.321	.360	.435	114	6	1	.983	-4	97	53	O86(26/9/51)	—	-0.1
1932	Cin N	106	347	26	96	18	3	3	43	23	1	24	.277	.323	.372	89	-5	0	.991	2	108	53	O94(89/5/0)	—	-0.8
1933	Cin N	84	209	13	50	7	1	1	17	8	0	10	.239	.267	.297	62	-11	0	.977	2	111	88	O55(26/1/28)	—	-1.2
1934	Pit N	47	106	7	26	5	1	0	11	3	0	8	.245	.266	.311	53	-7	0	1.000	1	115	64	O23(19/0/4)	—	-0.7
Total	8	599	1949	192	556	96	23	19	245	99	12	143	.285	.324	.387	85	-48	4	.986	-4	102	68	O510(231/100/183)	—	-7.5
ROETZ, ED	Edward Bernard; B8.6.1905 Philadelphia PA; D3.16.1965 Philadelphia PA; BR/TR/5´10˝/160; d5.26																								
1929	StL A	16	45	7	11	4	1	0	5	4	0	6	.244	.306	.378	72	-2	0-0	.909	-2	84	140	S8,1b5,2b2/3	—	-0.3
ROGELL, BILLY	William George; B11.24.1904 Springfield IL; D8.9.2003 Sterling Heights MI; BB/TR/5´10.5˝/163; d4.14																								
1925	Bos A	58	169	12	33	5	1	0	17	11	0	17	.195	.244	.237	22	-21	0-3	.935	6	113	114	2b49,S6	—	-1.3
1927	Bos A	82	207	35	55	14	6	2	28	24	0	28	.266	.342	.420	99	-1	3-1	.966	6	123	73	3b53,2b2,O2(1/0/1)	—	0.8
1928	Bos A	102	296	33	69	10	4	0	29	22	4	47	.233	.295	.294	56	-19	2-6	.935	-2	104	84	S67,2b22,O6(1/2/3),3b3	—	-1.6
1930	Det A	54	144	20	24	4	2	0	9	15	1	23	.167	.250	.222	20	-18	1-2	.938	3	105	85	S33,3b13/lf	—	-1.1
1931	Det A	48	185	21	56	12	3	2	24	24	0	17	.303	.383	.432	110	3	8-8	.958	7	116	84	S48	—	1.2
1932	Det A	144	554	88	150	29	6	9	61	50	1	38	.271	.332	.394	84	-14	14-6	.944	11	105	104	S139,3b4	—	0.8
1933	Det A	**155**	587	67	173	42	11	0	57	79	3	33	.295	.381	.404	106	8	6-9	.944	19	104	**133**	S155	—	3.4
1934	†Det A	**154**	592	114	175	32	8	3	100	74	0	36	.296	.374	.392	97	-1	13-3	.962	10	104	108	S154	—	2.1
1935	†Det A	150	560	88	154	23	11	6	71	80	1	29	.275	.367	.387	99	0	3-6	**.971**	11	104	**114**	S150	—	1.9
1936	Det A	146	585	85	160	27	5	6	68	73	3	41	.274	.357	.368	79	-19	14-10	**.965**	2	101	104	S146/3	—	-0.5
1937	Det A	146	536	85	148	30	7	8	64	83	3	48	.276	.376	.403	94	-3	5-5	**.967**	1	99	112	S146	—	0.7
1938	Det A	136	501	76	130	22	8	3	55	86	5	37	.259	.373	.353	78	-14	9-2	.959	10	**106**	109	S134	—	0.6
1939	Det A	74	174	24	40	6	3	2	23	26	0	14	.230	.330	.333	65	-9	3-1	.931	0	95	115	S43,3b21,2b2	—	-0.5
1940	Chi N	33	59	7	8	0	0	1	3	2	0	8	.136	.164	.186	-4	-9	1	.900	-4	84	83	S14,3b9,2b3	—	-1.2
Total	14	1482	5149	755	1375	256	75	42	609	649	21	416	.267	.351	.370	84	-117	82-62	.956	80	104	109	S1235,3b104,2b78,O9(3/2/4)	—	5.3
ROGERS, EDDIE	Edward Antonio; B8.29.1978 San Pedro de Macoris, D.R.; BR/TR/6´1˝/(165–190); d9.5																								
2002	Bal A	5	3	0	0	0	0	0	0	0-0	0	0	.000	.000	.000	-99	-1	0-0	1.000	1	226	196	S4	0	0.0
2005	Bal A	8	1	4	1	0	0	1	2	0-0	0	0	1.000	1.000	4.000	1144	1	0-2	ø	-0	0	0	/SD	0	0.0
2006	Bal A	17	25	1	5	0	0	0	2	0-0	0	3	.200	.192	.200	4	-4	0-0	1.000	-3	70	106	2b4,3b4,O4(3/0/1)/S	0	-0.7
Total	3	30	29	5	6	0	0	1	4	0-0	0	3	.207	.200	.310	33	-4	0-2	1.000	-2	158	137	S6,O4(3/0/1),3b4,2b4,D2	0	-0.7
ROGERS, EMMETT	Emmett E.; B10.11.1870 Hot Springs AR; D10.24.1941 Fort Smith AR; BB/5´10˝/165; d4.19																								
1890	Tol AA	35	110	18	19	3	3	0	7	14	0	—	.173	.266	.255	52	-7	2	.924	5	*115*	*96*	C34/lf	—	0.1
ROGERS, FRALEY	Fraley W.; B1850 Brooklyn NY; D5.10.1881 New York NY; 5´8˝/184; d4.30																								
1872	Bos NA	45	204	39	56	7	1	1	28	1	—	4	.275	.278	.333	83	-5	2-0	.790	-3	89	138	O41(4/0/38),1b6	—	-0.3
1873	Bos NA	2	11	2	4	1	0	0	3	0	—	2	.364	.364	.455	130	0	0-0	.893	-0	0	96	1b2	—	0.0
Total	2NA	47	215	41	60	8	1	1	31	1	—	6	.279	.282	.340	85	-5	2-0	.790	-3	89	138	O41(4/0/38),1b8	—	-0.3
ROGERS, JIM	James F.; B4.9.1872 Hartford CT; 5´7.5˝/180; d4.17; M1																								
1896	Was N	38	154	21	43	6	4	1	30	10	0	9	.279	.323	.390	87	-4	3	.882	-2	111	40	3b32,2b6/cf	—	-0.4
	Lou N	72	290	39	75	8	6	0	38	15	1	14	.259	.297	.328	67	-15	13	.971	-1	115	100	1b60,S12	—	-1.3
	Year	110	444	60	118	14	10	1	68	25	1	23	.266	.306	.349	74	-18	16	.971	-3	115	100	1b60,3b32,S12,2b6/cf	—	-1.7

YEAR	TM LG	G	AB	R	H	2B	3B	HR	RBI	BB-IB	HP	SO	AVG	OBP	SLG	AOPS	ABR	SB-CS	FA	FR	RNG	THR	GAMES AT POSITION	DL	BFW
1897	Lou N	42	153	22	22	3	2	2	22	23	1	—	.144	.260	.229	31	-16	4	.929	-3	98	89	2b40,1b3,M	—	-1.5
Total	2	152	597	82	140	17	12	3	90	48	2	23	.235	.294	.318	63	-35	20	.970	-6	114	97	1b63,2b46,3b32,S12/cf	—	-3.2
Rogers, Jay	Jay Lewis; B8.3.1888 Sandusky NY; D7.1.1964 Carlisle NY; BR/TR/5´11.5˝/178; d5.22																								
1914	NY A	5	8	0	0	0	0	0	0	0	0	4	.000	.000	.000	-99	-2	0	.923	-0	*121*	*49*	C4	—	-0.2
Rogers, Packy	Stanley Frank (b Stanley Frank Hazinski); B4.26.1913 Swoyersville PA; D5.15.1998 Elmira NY; BR/TR/5´8˝/175; d7.12; Col Fordham																								
1938	Bro N	23	37	3	7	1	1	0	5	6	0	6	.189	.302	.270	57	-2	0	1.000	-1	94	42	S9,3b8,2b3/lf	—	-0.3
Rogodzinski, Mike	Michael George; B2.22.1948 Evanston IL; BL/TR/6´0˝/(180–185); [PhiN69 2/30]; d5.4; Col Southern Illinois																								
1973	Phi N	66	80	13	19	3	0	2	7	12-1	0	19	.237	.333	.350	88	-1	0-0	.947	0	89	244	O16(5/0/13)	0	-0.1
1974	Phi N	17	15	1	1	0	0	0	1	2-0	0	3	.067	.176	.067	-29	-3	0-0	ø	-0	0	0	/rf	12	-0.3
1975	Phi N	16	19	3	5	1	0	0	4	3-0	0	2	.263	.364	.316	85	0	0-1	.667	-1	51	0	O2L	0	-0.1
Total	3	99	114	17	25	4	0	2	12	17-1	0	24	.219	.318	.307	72	-4	0-1	.909	-0	82	199	O19(7/0/14)	12	-0.5
Rohde, Dave	David Grant; B5.8.1964 Los Altos CA; BB/TR/6´2˝/182; [HouN86 5/120]; d4.9; Col Arizona																								
1990	Hou N	59	98	8	18	4	0	0	5	9-2	5	20	.184	.283	.224	43	-7	0-0	1.000	-1	108	105	2b32,3b4,S2	0	-0.8
1991	Hou N	29	41	3	5	0	0	0	0	5-0	0	8	.122	.217	.122	-2	-6	0-0	1.000	2	123	56	2b4,3b3,S3/1	0	-0.4
1992	Cle A	5	7	0	0	0	0	0	0	2-1	0	3	.000	.222	.000	-33	-1	0-0	.900	1	131	248	3b5	0	0.0
Total	3	93	146	11	23	4	0	0	5	16-3	5	31	.158	.262	.185	27	-14	0-0	1.000	1	110	98	2b36,3b12,S5/1	0	-1.2
Rohe, George	George Anthony "Whitey"; B9.15.1874 Cincinnati OH; D6.10.1957 Cincinnati OH; BR/TR/5´9˝/165; d5.7																								
1901	Bal A	14	36	7	10	2	0	0	4	5	1	—	.278	.381	.333	95	0	1	.912	-2	27	94	1b8,3b6	—	-0.2
1905	Chi A	34	113	14	24	1	0	1	12	12	4	—	.212	.310	.248	81	-2	2	.934	-1	89	191	2b17,3b17	—	-0.3
1906	†Chi A	77	225	14	58	5	1	0	25	16	3	—	.258	.316	.289	92	-2	8	.926	5	114	133	3b57,2b5/lf	—	0.5
1907	Chi A	144	494	46	105	11	2	2	51	39	3	—	.213	.274	.255	71	-15	16	.898	-2	108	199	3b76,2b39,S30	—	-1.6
Total	4	269	868	81	197	19	3	3	92	72	11	—	.227	.294	.266	79	-19	27	.917	-1	110	189	3b156,2b61,S30,1b8/lf	—	-1.6
Rohn, Dan	Daniel Jay; B1.10.1956 Alpena MI; BL/TR/5´7˝/(165–166); [ChiN77 4/90]; d9.2; Col Central Michigan																								
1983	Chi N	23	31	3	12	3	2	0	6	2-0	0	2	.387	.424	.613	176	3	1-0	.923	-0	95	73	2b6/S		0.3
1984	Chi N	25	31	1	4	0	0	1	3	1-0	0	6	.129	.152	.226	6	-4	0-0	1.000	-1	121	173	3b7,2b5,S5	0	-0.5
1986	Cle A	6	10	1	2	0	0	0	2	1-0	0	1	.200	.273	.200	32	-1	0-0	.900	0	178	121	2b2,3b2/S	20	0.0
Total	3	54	72	5	18	3	2	1	11	4-0	0	9	.250	.286	.389	82	-2	1-0	.930	-1	103	63	2b13,3b9,S7	20	-0.2
Rohrmeier, Dan	Daniel; B9.27.1965 Cincinnati OH; BR/TR/6´0˝/195; [ChiA87 5/115]; d9.3; Col St. Thomas (FL)																								
1997	Sea A	7	9	4	3	0	0	0	2	2-0	0	4	.333	.455	.333	110	0	0-0	1.000	0	295	0	1b3,D4	0	0.0
Rohwer, Ray	Ray; B6.5.1895 Dixon CA; D1.24.1988 Davis CA; BL/TL/5´10˝/155; d4.13; Col California																								
1921	Pit N	30	40	6	10	3	2	0	6	4	0	8	.250	.318	.425	93	-1	0-1	.842	0	100	218	O10(0/3/7)	—	-0.1
1922	Pit N	53	129	19	38	6	3	3	22	10	1	17	.295	.350	.457	105	1	1-0	.938	1	97	137	O30(0/2/28)	—	-0.1
Total	2	83	169	25	48	9	5	3	28	14	1	25	.284	.342	.450	102	0	1-1	.917	1	98	152	O40(0/5/35)	—	-0.2
Roig, Tony	Anton Ambrose; B12.23.1927 New Orleans LA; BR/TR/6´1˝/(180–184); d9.13																								
1953	Was A	3	8	0	1	1	0	0	0	0	0	1	.125	.125	.250	-1	-1	0-0	1.000	1	114	126	2b2	0	0.0
1955	Was A	29	57	3	13	1	1	0	4	2-0	0	15	.228	.254	.281	46	-5	0-0	.932	0	114	126	S21,3b8/2	0	-0.4
1956	Was A	44	119	11	25	5	2	0	7	20-0	0	29	.210	.321	.286	62	-6	2-0	.973	5	119	114	2b27,S19	0	0.1
Total	3	76	184	14	39	7	3	0	11	22-0	0	45	.212	.295	.283	55	-12	2-0	.927	5	108	99	S40,2b30,3b8	0	-0.3
Rojas, Cookie	Octavio Victor (Rivas); B3.6.1939 Havana, Cuba; BR/TR/5´10˝/(160–170); d4.10; M2/C14; OF(79/124/10)																								
1962	Cin N	39	86	9	19	2	0	0	6	9-1	1	4	.221	.302	.244	47	-6	1-1	.949	-7	76	84	2b30/3	0	-1.1
1963	Phi N	64	77	18	17	0	1	1	2	3-0	1	8	.221	.259	.286	57	-5	4-1	.991	7	127	116	2b25/lf	0	0.5
1964	Phi N	109	340	58	99	19	5	2	31	22-0	2	17	.291	.334	.394	107	3	1-3	.967	-2	95	193	O70(23/54/1),2b20,S18/C3	0	0.0
1965	Phi N★	142	521	78	158	25	3	3	42	42-3	3	33	.303	.356	.380	110	8	5-5	.986	6	96	108	2b84,O55(11/41/5),S11,C2/1	0	2.0
1966	Phi N	156	626	77	168	18	1	6	55	35-3	4	46	.268	.310	.329	78	-18	4-6	.983	-5	99	106	2b106,O56(30/28/3),S2	0	-1.9
1967	Phi N	147	528	60	137	21	2	4	45	30-3	0	58	.259	.297	.330	79	-15	8-4	.977	-1	98	114	2b137,O9(8/1/1),C3,S2/P3	0	-0.5
1968	Phi N	152	621	53	144	19	0	9	48	16-2	0	55	.232	.248	.306	67	-27	4-8	**.987**	16	103	118	2b150/C	0	0.0
1969	Phi N	110	391	35	89	11	1	4	30	23-1	1	28	.228	.269	.292	59	-22	1-6	.980	1	91	107	2b95,O2L	0	-1.8
1970	StL N	23	47	2	5	0	0	0	2	3-0	1	4	.106	.176	.106	-22	-8	0-0	1.000	2	125	150	2b10,O3L,S2	0	-0.6
	KC A	98	384	36	100	13	3	2	28	20-0	0	29	.260	.296	.326	71	-16	3-7	.982	4	105	109	2b97	0	-0.8
1971	KC A★	115	414	56	124	22	2	6	59	39-3	2	35	.300	.357	.406	118	11	8-3	**.991**	-4	98	107	2b111,S2/lf	22	1.5
1972	KC A★	137	487	49	127	25	0	3	53	41-5	1	35	.261	.315	.331	94	-3	2-8	.986	-1	105	102	2b131,3b6,S2	0	0.3
1973	KC A★	139	551	78	152	29	3	6	69	37-1	1	38	.276	.320	.372	88	-8	18-4	.982	13	111	110	2b137	0	1.6
1974	KC A☆	144	542	52	147	17	1	6	60	30-4	3	43	.271	.309	.339	83	-12	8-4	**.987**	-18	97	94	2b141	0	-2.2
1975	KC A	120	406	34	103	18	2	2	37	30-2	0	24	.254	.304	.323	76	-13	4-5	.980	-10	95	92	2b116,D2	0	-1.7
1976	†KC A	63	132	11	32	6	0	0	16	8-0	0	15	.242	.280	.288	68	-5	2-0	1.000	-6	76	88	2b40,3b6/1D	0	-1.1
1977	†KC A	64	156	8	39	9	1	0	10	8-2	0	17	.250	.285	.321	64	-8	1-3	.944	3	106	121	3b31,2b16,D6	0	-0.5
Total	16	1822	6309	714	1660	254	25	54	593	396-30	20	489	.263	.306	.337	83	-144	74-68	.984	-1	100	106	2b1446,O197C,3b46,S39,D17,C7,1b2/P22	0	-6.3
Rojek, Stan	Stanley Andrew; B4.21.1919 N.Tonawanda NY; D7.9.1997 N.Tonawanda NY; BR/TR/5´10˝/(165–170); d9.22; Mil 1943–45																								
1942	Bro N	1	0	1	0	0	0	0	0	0	0	0	ø	ø	ø	ø	0	0	ø	0	—	—	/R	0	0.0
1946	Bro N	45	47	11	13	2	1	0	2	4	0	1	.277	.333	.362	96	0	1	.974	2	114	100	S15,2b6,3b4	0	0.3
1947	Bro N	32	80	7	21	0	1	0	7	7	0	3	.262	.322	.287	61	-5	1	.971	5	111	131	S17,3b9,2b7	0	0.1
1948	Pit N	**156**	641	85	186	27	5	4	51	61	3	41	.290	.355	.367	94	-5	24	.962	-4	102	105	S156	0	0.1
1949	Pit N	144	557	72	136	19	2	0	31	50	2	31	.244	.309	.285	59	-32	4	.966	1	101	103	S144	0	-2.2
1950	Pit N	76	230	28	59	12	1	0	17	18	1	13	.257	.313	.317	64	-12	2	.967	-10	91	99	S68,2b3	0	-1.8
1951	Pit N	8	16	0	3	0	0	0	0	0	0	1	.188	.188	.188	1	-2	0-0	.900	-1	107	0	S8	0	-0.3
	StL N	51	186	21	51	7	3	0	14	10	2	10	.274	.318	.344	78	-6	0-3	.974	2	96	123	S51	0	-0.3
	Year	59	202	21	54	7	3	0	14	10	2	11	.267	.308	.332	72	-8	0-3	.968	1	97	113	S59	0	-0.6
1952	StL A	9	7	0	1	0	0	0	0	2	0	0	.143	.333	.143	35	-1	0-0	1.000	1	141	79	S4/2	0	0.0
Total	8	522	1764	225	470	67	13	4	122	152	8	100	.266	.327	.326	74	-63	32-3	.965	-4	100	105	S463,2b17,3b13	0	-4.1
Rolen, Scott	Scott Bruce; B4.4.1975 Evansville IN; BR/TR/6´4˝/(195–240); [PhiN93 2/46]; d8.1																								
1996	Phi N	37	130	10	33	7	0	4	18	13-0	1	27	.254	.322	.400	90	-2	0-2	.954	-7	72	68	3b37		-0.9
1997	Phi N	156	561	93	159	35	3	21	92	76-4	13	138	.283	.377	.469	123	21	16-6	.948	19	103	110	3b155	0	4.1
1998	Phi N	160	601	120	174	45	4	31	110	93-6	11	141	.290	.391	.532	141	39	14-7	.970	13	105	98	3b159	0	5.1
1999	Phi N	112	421	74	113	28	1	26	77	67-2	3	114	.268	.368	.525	122	15	12-2	.960	16	**112**	114	3b112	0	3.1
2000	Phi N	128	483	88	144	32	6	26	89	51-9	5	99	.298	.370	.551	129	21	8-1	.971	5	102	63	3b128	15	2.6
2001	Phi N	151	554	96	160	39	1	25	107	74-6	13	127	.289	.378	.498	132	29	16-5	.973	13	111	86	3b151	0	4.3
2002	Phi N★	100	375	52	97	21	4	17	66	52-2	8	68	.259	.358	.472	125	14	5-2	.973	8	107	119	3b100	0	2.3
	†StL N	55	205	37	57	8	4	14	44	20-2	4	34	.278	.354	.561	135	9	3-2	.958	12	123	170	3b55	0	2.1
	Year	155	580	89	154	29	8	31	110	72-4	12	102	.266	.357	.503	129	23	8-4	.967	20	113	137	3b155	0	4.4
2003	StL N★	154	559	98	160	49	1	28	104	82-5	9	104	.286	.382	.528	137	33	13-3	.969	-3	102	83	3b153	0	3.2
2004	†StL N★	142	500	109	157	32	4	34	124	72-5	13	92	.314	.409	.598	155	43	4-3	.977	22	**125**	99	3b141	0	6.4
2005	StL N✳	56	196	28	46	12	1	5	28	25-1	1	28	.235	.323	.383	83	-5	1-2	.966	13	140	176	3b56	111	0.8
2006	†StL N☆	142	521	94	154	48	1	22	95	56-7	9	69	.296	.369	.518	124	21	7-4	.965	23	**125**	124	3b142	0	4.3
Total	11	1393	5106	899	1454	356	30	253	954	681-49	90	1041	.285	.375	.515	130	238	99-39	.966	134	111	104	3b1389	126	37.4
Rolfe, Red	Robert Abial; B10.17.1908 Penacook NH; D7.8.1969 Gilford NH; BL/TR/5´11.5˝/170; d6.29; M4/C1; Col Dartmouth																								
1931	NY A	1	0	0	0	0	0	0	0	0	0	0	ø	ø	ø	ø	0	0-0	1.000	-0	0	0	/S	—	0.0
1934	NY A	89	279	54	80	13	2	0	18	26	0	16	.287	.348	.348	86	-6	2-3	.944	-3	87	124	S46,3b26	—	-0.5
1935	NY A	**149**	639	108	192	33	9	5	67	57	3	39	.300	.361	.404	103	2	7-3	**.964**	-7	91	96	3b136,S17	—	0.2
1936	†NY A	135	568	116	181	39	**15**	10	70	68	0	38	.319	.392	.493	121	19	3-0	**.957**	1	98	91	3b133	—	2.2
1937	†NY A★	154	648	143	179	34	10	4	62	90	1	53	.276	.365	.378	87	-11	4-2	.962	3	96	95	3b154	—	-0.2
1938	†NY A☆	151	631	132	196	36	8	10	80	74	3	44	.311	.386	.441	107	8	13-1	.959	-6	96	99	3b151	—	0.9
1939	†NY A★	**152**	648	**139**	**213**	**46**	10	14	80	81	1	41	.329	.404	.495	131	32	7-6	.958	-15	89	86	3b152	—	2.0
1940	NY A✳	139	588	102	147	26	6	10	53	50	2	48	.250	.311	.366	78	-21	4-2	.949	0	99	96	3b138	—	-1.5

YEAR	TM LG	G	AB	R	H	2B	3B	HR	RBI	BB-IB	HP	SO	AVG	OBP	SLG	AOPS	ABR	SB-CS	FA	FR	RNG	THR	GAMES AT POSITION	DL	BFW
1941	†NY A	136	561	106	148	22	5	8	42	57	0	38	.264	.332	.364	85	-13	3-2	.946	-8	94	121	3b134	0	-1.5
1942	†NY A	69	265	42	58	8	2	8	25	23	0	18	.219	.281	.355	80	-9	1-1	.959	5	109	159	3b60	0	-0.2
Total	10	1175	4827	942	1394	257	67	69	497	526	10	335	.289	.360	.413	100	1	44-20	.956	-28	95	101	3b1084,S64	0	1.4
Rolison, Nate	Nathan Mardis; B3.27.1977 Hattiesburg MS; BL/TR/6´6˝/240; [FlaN95 2/36]; d9.5; [DL 2001 Fla N 190]																								
2000	Fla N	8	13	0	1	0	0	0	2	1-0	0	4	.077	.125	.077	-45	-3	0-0	1.000	0	113	45	1b4	0	-0.3
Rolling, Ray	Raymond Copeland; B9.8.1886 Martinsburg MO; D8.25.1966 St.Paul MN; BR/TR/5´10.5˝/160; d9.6																								
1912	StL N	5	15	0	3	0	0	0	0	0	0	5	.200	.200	.200	10	-2	0	.947	-1	92	0	2b4	—	-0.2
Rollings, Red	William Russell; B3.21.1904 Mobile AL; D12.31.1964 Mobile AL; BL/TR/5´11˝/167; d4.17																								
1927	Bos A	82	184	19	49	4	1	0	9	12	4	10	.266	.325	.299	64	-10	3-1	.938	-3	98	27	3b44,1b10,2b2	—	-1.0
1928	Bos A	50	48	7	11	3	1	0	9	6	0	8	.229	.315	.333	72	-2	0-0	1.000	-2	0	222	1b5,2b4,O4(2/0/2)/3	—	-0.4
1930	Bos N	52	123	10	29	6	0	0	10	9	0	5	.236	.288	.285	40	-12	2	.973	1	113	119	3b28,2b10	—	-0.9
Total	3	184	355	36	89	13	2	0	28	27	4	23	.251	.311	.299	57	-24	5-1	.947	-5	103	64	3b73,2b16,1b15,O4(2/0/2)	—	-2.3
Rollins, Jimmy	James Calvin "J-Roll"; B11.27.1978 Oakland CA; BB/TR/5´8˝/(154–175); [PhiN96 2/46]; d9.17																								
2000	Phi N	14	53	5	17	1	1	0	5	2-0	0	7	.321	.345	.377	83	-2	3-0	.978	-3	66	125	S13	0	-0.3
2001	Phi N★	158	656	97	180	29	**12**	14	54	48-2	2	108	.274	.323	.419	95	-7	**46**-8	.979	-19	92	104	S157	0	-0.7
2002	Phi N★	154	637	82	156	33	**10**	11	60	54-3	4	103	.245	.306	.380	85	-16	31-13	.980	1	103	93	S152/2	0	-0.2
2003	Phi N	156	628	85	165	42	6	8	62	54-4	0	113	.263	.320	.387	90	-10	20-12	.979	-1	103	95	S154	0	0.1
2004	Phi N	154	657	119	190	43	**12**	14	73	57-3	3	73	.289	.348	.455	102	2	30-9	.986	-30	87	94	S154	0	-1.2
2005	Phi N★	158	677	115	196	38	11	12	54	47-8	4	71	.290	.338	.431	97	-4	41-6	.981	-11	92	86	S157	0	0.3
2006	Phi N	158	689	127	191	45	9	25	83	57-2	5	80	.277	.334	.478	100	0	36-4	.984	-3	98	99	S157	0	1.5
Total	7	952	3997	630	1095	231	61	84	391	319-22	18	555	.274	.329	.425	95	-37	207-52	.981	-66	95	96	S944/2	0	-0.5
Rollins, Rich	Richard John "Red"; B4.16.1938 Mount Pleasant PA; BR/TR/5´10˝/(175–185); d6.16; Col Kent St.																								
1961	Min A	13	17	3	5	1	0	0	3	2-0	1	2	.294	.400	.353	98	0	0-0	1.000	-1	80	74	2b5,3b4	0	-0.1
1962	Min A★	159	624	96	186	23	5	16	96	75-2	6	61	.298	.374	.428	112	13	3-1	.943	-8	94	118	3b159/S	0	0.5
1963	Min A	136	531	75	163	23	1	16	61	36-4	8	59	.307	.359	.444	122	16	2-0	.935	-8	94	96	3b132/2	0	0.8
1964	Min A	148	596	87	161	25	**10**	12	68	53-3	5	80	.270	.334	.406	104	3	2-5	.947	-7	95	66	3b146	0	-0.6
1965	†Min A	140	469	59	117	22	1	5	32	37-7	4	54	.249	.309	.333	79	-12	4-0	.958	-2	97	102	3b112,2b16	0	-1.4
1966	Min A	90	269	30	66	7	1	10	40	13-1	4	34	.245	.286	.390	88	-5	0-2	.953	-6	89	138	3b65,2b2/lf	0	-1.3
1967	Min A	109	339	31	83	11	2	6	39	27-4	3	58	.245	.305	.342	84	-6	1-1	.963	-6	84	99	3b97	0	-1.4
1968	Min A	93	203	14	49	5	0	6	30	10-2	3	34	.241	.287	.355	89	-3	3-1	.931	-0	105	56	3b56	0	-0.4
1969	Sea A	58	187	15	42	7	0	4	21	7-0	5	19	.225	.270	.326	67	-9	2-0	.948	5	115	60	3b47/S	76	-0.4
1970	Mil A	14	25	3	5	1	0	0	5	3-0	0	4	.200	.276	.240	46	-2	0-0	1.000	2	150	213	3b7	0	0.0
	Cle A	42	43	6	10	0	0	2	4	3-0	0	5	.233	.283	.372	75	-2	0-0	.600	-2	41	207	3b5	0	-0.3
	Year	56	68	9	15	1	0	2	9	6-0	0	9	.221	.280	.324	65	-3	0-0	.900	0	113	211	3b12	0	-0.3
Total	10	1002	3303	419	887	125	20	77	399	266-23	39	410	.269	.328	.388	98	-7	17-10	.947	-32	95	96	3b830,2b24,S2/lf	76	-4.6
Rollinson, Bill	William (b William Henry Winslow); B6.10.1856 Fairfield ME; D9.28.1938 Bristow VA; d6.17																								
1884	Was U	1	3	0	0	0	0	0	—	0	—	—	.000	.000	.000	-99	-1	—	.714	-0	—	—	/C	—	-0.1
Rolls, Damian	Damian Michael; B9.15.1977 Manhattan KS; BR/TR/6´2˝/(205–215); [LAN96 1/23]; d9.3																								
2000	TB A	4	3	0	1	0	0	0	0	0-0	0	1	.333	.333	.333	71	0	0-0	ø	-0	0	0	/3D	150	0.0
2001	TB A	81	237	33	62	11	1	2	12	10-0	0	47	.262	.291	.342	67	-12	12-4	.968	-2	99	79	2b42,O25(7/18/0)/3D	0	-1.0
2002	TB A	21	89	15	26	6	1	0	6	3-0	2	16	.292	.330	.382	90	-1	2-5	.947	1	115	76	O21(4/4/13)	0	-0.2
2003	TB A	107	373	43	95	20	0	7	46	19-1	7	84	.255	.301	.365	77	-13	11-3	.972	7	109	128	3b73,O37(6/0/33),2b2	34	-0.5
2004	TB A	53	117	12	19	5	0	0	9	10-0	1	36	.162	.231	.205	16	-15	2-1	1.000	0	100	107	O24(16/5/5),3b19,2b2/1D	39	-1.4
Total	5	266	819	103	203	42	2	9	73	42-1	10	184	.248	.291	.337	67	-41	27-13	.980	7	102	81	O107(33/27/51),3b94,2b46,D12/1	223	-3.1
Roman, Bill	William Anthony; B10.11.1938 Detroit MI; BL/TL/6´4˝/(190–205); d9.30; Col Michigan																								
1964	Det A	3	8	2	3	0	0	1	1	0-0	0	2	.375	.375	.750	201	1	0-0	1.000	0	103	169	1b2	0	0.1
1965	Det A	21	27	0	2	0	0	0	0	2-0	0	7	.074	.138	.074	-38	-5	0-0	1.000	-1	37	63	1b6	0	-0.6
Total	2	24	35	2	5	0	0	1	1	2-0	0	9	.143	.189	.229	17	-4	0-0	1.000	-1	54	91	1b8	0	-0.5
Romano, Jason	Jason Anthony; B6.24.1979 Tampa FL; BR/TR/6´0˝/185; [TexA97 1/39]; d4.17																								
2002	Tex A	29	54	8	11	4	0	0	4	4-0	0	13	.204	.254	.278	42	-4	2-0	1.000	1	131	0	O18(11/8/0),2b8/3D	0	-0.3
	Col N	18	37	9	12	0	1	0	1	3-0	0	11	.324	.375	.378	87	-1	4-1	.952	-2	119	66	2b12,S5,O3C/3	0	-0.2
2003	LA N	37	36	3	3	0	0	0	0	1-0	0	8	.083	.108	.083	-51	-8	2-0	1.000	-1	93	0	O28(9/17/2)/2	0	-0.9
2004	TB A	4	8	0	1	0	0	0	1	0-0	0	2	.125	.125	.125	-35	-2	0-0	.500	-0	0	0	/2lf	0	-0.2
	Cin N	22	26	3	4	0	0	1	3	2-0	0	10	.154	.214	.269	24	-3	0-0	1.000	0	77	344	O11(0/5/6)	70	-0.3
2005	Cin N	19	30	3	8	2	0	1	3	3-0	1	9	.267	.353	.433	104	0	0-0	.941	0	92	229	O14(7/5/2)	0	0.0
Total	4	129	191	26	39	6	1	2	12	13-0	1	53	.204	.257	.277	40	-18	8-1	.989	-2	104	196	O75(28/38/10),2b22,S5,D4,3b2	70	-1.9
Romano, Johnny	John Anthony "Honey"; B8.23.1934 Hoboken NJ; BR/TR/5´11˝/(200–205); d9.12																								
1958	Chi A	4	7	1	2	0	0	0	1	1-0	0	0	.286	.375	.286	86	0	0-0	1.000	1	0	0	C2	0	0.1
1959	†Chi A	53	126	20	37	5	1	5	25	23-0	1	18	.294	.407	.468	141	8	0-1	.979	-1	64	90	C38	0	0.9
1960	Cle A	108	316	40	86	12	2	16	52	37-4	3	50	.272	.349	.475	126	11	0-0	.988	-9	81	97	C99	0	0.6
1961	Cle A★	142	509	76	152	29	1	21	80	61-3	5	60	.299	.377	.483	132	25	0-0	.989	-8	108	104	C141	0	2.3
1962	Cle A★	135	459	71	120	19	3	25	81	73-0	5	64	.261	.363	.479	130	21	0-1	.990	-4	99	115	C130	0	2.3
1963	Cle A	89	255	28	55	5	2	10	34	38-4	2	49	.216	.317	.369	94	-2	4-3	.993	-8	111	115	C71,O4L	37	-0.7
1964	Cle A	106	352	46	85	18	1	19	47	51-6	7	83	.241	.346	.460	124	13	2-2	.991	-4	80	99	C96/1	0	1.4
1965	Chi A	122	356	39	86	11	0	18	48	59-3	5	74	.242	.355	.424	129	15	0-2	.992	7	87	108	C111,O4L,1b2	0	2.7
1966	Chi A	122	329	33	76	12	0	15	47	58-7	1	72	.231	.344	.404	124	12	0-0	.993	10	80	83	C102	0	2.8
1967	StL N	24	58	1	7	1	0	0	2	13-0	0	15	.121	.282	.138	24	-5	1-0	.983	-2	139	20	C20	0	-0.6
Total	10	905	2767	355	706	112	10	129	417	414-27	29	485	.255	.354	.443	123	98	7-9	.990	-17	93	101	C810,O8L,1b3	37	11.8
Romano, Tom	Thomas Michael; B10.25.1958 Syracuse NY; BR/TR/5´10˝/170; [KCA80 17/432]; d9.1; Col Coastal Carolina																								
1987	Mon N	7	3	1	0	0	0	0	0	0-0	0	1	.000	.000	.000	-96	-1	0-0	ø	-0	0	0	O3L	0	-0.1
Romero, Mandy	Armando; B10.29.1967 Miami FL; BB/TR/5´11˝/(180–190); [PitN88 19/486]; d7.15; Col Brevard (FL) CC																								
1997	SD N	21	48	7	10	0	0	2	4	2-0	0	18	.208	.240	.333	51	-4	1-0	1.000	2	67	49	C19	0	-0.1
1998	SD N	6	9	1	0	0	0	0	0	1-0	0	3	.000	.100	.000	-76	-2	0-0	.963	1	86	127	C6	0	-0.2
	Bos A	12	13	2	3	1	0	0	1	3-0	0	3	.231	.375	.308	79	0	0-0	1.000	1	0	0	C4,D3	0	0.1
2003	Col N	3	7	2	3	1	0	0	0	0-0	2	1	.429	.556	.571	171	1	0-0	.938	1	49	232	C2	0	0.2
Total	3	42	77	12	16	2	0	2	5	6-0	2	25	.208	.282	.312	57	-5	1-0	.987	4	64	80	C31,D3	0	-0.0
Romero, Ed	Edgardo Ralph (Rivera); B12.9.1957 Santurce, PR; BR/TR/5´11˝/(150–180); d7.16; OF(17/1/14)																								
1977	Mil A	10	25	4	7	1	0	0	2	4-0	0	3	.280	.379	.320	93	0	0-0	.971	-3	91	56	S10	0	-0.2
1980	Mil A	42	104	20	27	7	0	1	10	9-0	0	11	.260	.319	.356	87	-2	2-0	.894	-2	102	115	S22,2b15,3b3	0	-0.1
1981	†Mil A	44	91	6	18	3	0	1	10	4-0	0	9	.198	.227	.264	44	-7	0-2	.949	5	92	122	S22,2b18,3b3	0	0.0
1982	Mil A	52	144	18	36	8	0	1	7	8-0	0	16	.250	.289	.326	72	-6	0-0	.975	-2	96	123	2b39,S10,3b2/lf	0	-0.5
1983	Mil A	59	145	17	46	7	0	1	18	8-0	0	8	.317	.348	.386	111	2	1-0	.962	-11	73	103	S22,O15(14/0/1),3b5,2b3,D5	0	-0.7
1984	Mil A	116	357	36	90	12	0	1	31	29-2	1	25	.252	.307	.294	71	-14	3-3	.943	5	131	151	3b59,S39,2b11,1b4/rfD	0	-0.5
1985	Mil A	88	251	24	63	11	1	0	21	26-0	0	20	.251	.321	.303	72	-9	1-1	.977	6	108	113	S43,2b31,O14(2/0/12)/3	0	0.2
1986	†Bos A	100	233	41	49	11	0	2	23	18-0	2	16	.210	.270	.283	51	-16	2-0	.959	-8	85	84	S75,3b18,2b4/cf	0	-1.8
1987	Bos A	88	235	23	64	5	0	0	14	18-0	0	22	.272	.322	.294	64	-12	0-2	.973	-0	106	108	2b29,S24,3b24,1b8	0	-1.0
1988	†Bos A	31	75	3	18	3	0	0	5	3-0	1	8	.240	.272	.280	54	-5	0-0	1.000	-2	66	66	3b15,S8,2b5/1D	45	-0.6
1989	Bos A	46	113	14	24	4	0	0	6	7-1	1	7	.212	.260	.248	42	-9	0-2	.983	7	105	126	2b22,3b14,S10,D2	0	-0.2
	Atl N	7	19	1	5	1	0	1	1	0-0	0	0	.263	.263	.474	104	0	0-0	.947	4	141	121	2b4,S2/3	0	0.4
	Mil A	15	50	3	10	3	0	0	3	0-0	0	10	.200	.200	.260	29	-5	0-0	1.000	-3	86	75	2b11,3b4/S	0	-0.8
1990	Det A	32	70	8	16	3	0	0	4	6-1	0	4	.229	.286	.271	57	-4	0-0	.982	0	95	216	3b27,D3	0	-0.4
Total	12	730	1912	218	473	79	1	8	155	140-4	5	159	.247	.298	.302	67	-87	9-10	.958	-4	94	92	S288,2b192,3b176,O32L,1b13,D13	45	-6.2

YEAR	TM LG	G	AB	R	H	2B	3B	HR	RBI	BB-IB	HP	SO	AVG	OBP	SLG	AOPS	ABR	SB-CS	FA	FR	RNG	THR	GAMES AT POSITION	DL	BFW
ROMINE, KEVIN	Kevin Andrew; B5.23.1961 Exeter NH; BR/TR/5´11˝/(171–204); [BosA82 1/29]; d9.5; Col Arizona St.																								
1985	Bos A	24	28	3	6	2	0	0	1	1-0	0	4	.214	.241	.286	42	-2	1-0	1.000	1	114	179	O23(12/1/12)/D	0	-0.2
1986	Bos A	35	35	6	9	2	0	0	2	3-0	0	9	.257	.316	.314	72	-1	2-0	1.000	2	123	130	O33(0/28/5)	0	0.1
1987	Bos A	9	24	5	7	2	0	0	2	2-0	0	6	.292	.346	.375	89	0	0-0	1.000	0	74	294	O7(1/4/3),D2	0	0.0
1988	†Bos A	57	78	17	15	2	1	1	6	7-0	0	15	.192	.259	.282	49	-5	2-0	.957	-3	84	0	O45(5/9/38),D5	0	-0.9
1989	Bos A	92	274	30	75	13	0	1	23	21-1	2	53	.274	.327	.332	82	-6	1-1	.982	1	89	204	O89(9/48/32),D2	0	-0.7
1990	Bos A	70	136	21	37	7	0	2	14	12-0	1	27	.272	.331	.368	92	-1	4-0	.976	-3	92	0	O64(16/18/30)/D	0	-0.5
1991	Bos A	44	55	7	9	2	0	1	7	3-0	0	10	.164	.207	.255	25	-6	1-1	.964	-1	95	0	O23(10/4/10),D14	0	-0.8
Total	7	331	630	89	158	30	1	5	55	49-1	3	124	.251	.306	.325	73	-21	11-2	.980	-3	93	112	O284(53/112/130),D25	0	-3.0
RONAN, MARC	Edward Marcus; B9.19.1969 Ozark AL; BL/TR/6´2˝/190; [StLN90 3/86]; d9.21; Col Florida St.																								
1993	StL N	6	12	0	1	0	0	0	0	0-0	0	5	.083	.083	.083	-56	-3	0-0	1.000	2	0	0	C6	0	-0.1
RONDEAU, HENRI	Henri Joseph; B5.7.1887 Danielson CT; D5.28.1943 Woonsocket RI; BL/TR/5´11˝/175; d4.11																								
1913	Det A	36	70	5	13	2	0	0	5	14	0	16	.186	.321	.214	58	-3	1	1.000	-2	*77*	*124*	C16,1b6	—	-0.4
1915	Was A	14	40	3	7	0	0	0	4	4	0	3	.175	.250	.175	27	-4	1-2	1.000	2	131	136	O11L	—	-0.3
1916	Was A	50	162	20	36	5	3	1	28	18	3	18	.222	.311	.309	87	-3	7	.958	3	126	68	O48(31/0/17)	—	-0.2
Total	3	100	272	28	56	7	3	1	37	36	3	37	.206	.305	.265	71	-10	9-2	.967	3	127	82	O59(42/0/17),C16,1b6	—	-0.9
ROOF, GENE	Eugene Lawrence; B1.13.1958 Paducah KY; BB/TR/6´2˝/(180–195); [StLN76 12/279]; d9.3; C4; b–Phil																								
1981	StL N	23	60	11	18	6	0	0	3	12-2	0	16	.300	.411	.400	127	3	5-1	.950	-1	109	0	O20L	0	0.2
1982	StL N	11	15	3	4	0	0	0	2	1-0	0	4	.267	.313	.267	62	-1	2-0	1.000	-0	102	0	O5(4/0/2)	0	-0.1
1983	StL N	6	3	1	0	0	0	0	0	0-0	0	0	.000	.000	.000	-99	-1	0-0	ø	-0	0	0	/lf	0	-0.1
	Mon N	8	12	2	2	2	0	0	1	1-0	0	3	.167	.231	.333	55	-1	0-0	1.000	-0	81	0	O5(0/1/4)	0	-0.1
	Year	14	15	3	2	2	0	0	1	1-0	0	3	.133	.188	.267	24	-2	0-0	1.000	-0	77	0	O6(1/1/4)	0	-0.2
Total	3	48	90	17	24	8	0	0	6	14-2	0	23	.267	.362	.356	100	0	7-1	.958	-1	105	0	O31(25/1/6)	0	-0.1
ROOF, PHIL	Phillip Anthony; B3.5.1941 Paducah KY; BR/TR/6´3˝/(195–210); d4.29; C9; b–Gene																								
1961	Mil N	1	0	0	0	0	0	0	0	0-0	0	0	ø	ø	ø	ø	0	0-0	1.000	0	0	0	/C	0	0.0
1964	Mil N	1	2	0	0	0	0	0	0	0-0	0	1	.000	.000	.000	-99	-1	0-0	1.000	-1	0	0	/C	0	0.0
1965	Cal A	9	22	1	3	0	0	0	0	0-0	0	6	.136	.136	.136	-23	-4	0-0	.983	4	286	69	C9	0	0.1
	Cle A	43	52	3	9	1	0	0	3	5-1	1	13	.173	.259	.192	30	-5	0-0	.994	8	153	174	C41	0	0.5
	Year	52	74	4	12	1	0	0	3	5-1	1	19	.162	.225	.176	15	-8	0-0	.992	12	189	145	C50	0	0.6
1966	KC A	127	369	33	77	14	3	7	44	37-6	3	95	.209	.285	.320	76	-11	2-5	.985	-1	89	100	C123,1b2	0	-0.9
1967	KC A	114	327	23	67	14	5	6	24	23-5	5	85	.205	.266	.333	79	-9	4-1	.991	-4	94	67	C113	0	-0.9
1968	Oak A	34	64	5	12	0	0	1	2	2-0	0	15	.188	.212	.234	37	-5	1-0	.968	-5	71	57	C32	45	-1.0
1969	Oak A	106	247	19	58	6	1	2	19	33-3	5	55	.235	.337	.291	80	-5	1-0	.983	-1	127	83	C106	0	-0.2
1970	Mil A	110	321	39	73	7	1	13	37	32-1	5	72	.227	.306	.377	88	-6	3-2	.988	-2	69	108	C107/1	0	-0.4
1971	Mil A	41	114	6	22	2	1	1	10	8-1	1	28	.193	.252	.254	44	-9	0-0	.975	5	196	161	C39	0	-0.2
	Min A	31	87	6	21	4	0	0	6	8-0	0	18	.241	.305	.287	67	-4	0-1	.985	6	118	81	C29	0	0.4
	Year	72	201	12	43	6	1	1	16	16-1	1	46	.214	.275	.269	54	-12	0-1	.980	11	160	125	C68	0	0.2
1972	Min A	61	146	16	30	11	1	3	12	6-0	0	27	.205	.235	.356	71	-6	0-1	.978	-5	133	75	C61	0	-1.0
1973	Min A	47	117	10	23	4	1	1	15	13-0	0	27	.197	.277	.274	53	-7	0-0	.992	1	91	95	C47	0	-0.5
1974	Min A	44	97	10	19	1	0	2	13	6-0	2	24	.196	.257	.268	50	-7	0-0	1.000	3	96	162	C44	0	-0.2
1975	Min A	63	126	18	38	2	0	7	21	9-1	1	28	.302	.353	.484	133	5	0-0	.989	2	95	106	C63	37	0.9
1976	Min A	18	46	1	10	3	0	0	4	2-0	0	6	.217	.250	.283	55	-3	0-0	.962	3	50	184	C12/D	0	0.1
	Chi A	4	9	0	1	0	0	0	0	0-0	0	3	.111	.111	.111	-35	-2	0-0	1.000	-0	0	164	C4	0	-0.2
	Year	22	55	1	11	3	0	0	4	2-0	0	9	.200	.228	.255	41	-4	0-0	.967	3	39	180	C16/D	0	-0.1
1977	Tor A	3	5	0	0	0	0	0	0	0-0	0	1	.000	.000	.000	-99	-1	0-0	1.000	-1	33	237	C3	63	-0.2
Total	15	857	2151	190	463	69	13	43	210	184-18	23	504	.215	.283	.319	73	-80	11-10	.986	15	104	100	C835,1b3/D	145	-3.7
ROOKS, GEORGE	George Brinton McClellan (b George Brinton Mc Clellan Ruckser); B10.21.1863 Chicago IL; D3.11.1935 Chicago IL; BR/TR/5´11˝/170; d5.12; gs–Lou Possehl																								
1891	Bos N	5	16	1	2	0	0	0	0	4	0	1	.125	.300	.125	23	-1	0	1.000	1	121	0	O5L	—	-0.1
ROOMES, ROLANDO	Rolando Audley; B2.15.1962 Kingston, Jamaica; BR/TR/6´3˝/180; d4.12																								
1988	Chi N	17	16	3	3	0	0	0	0	0-0	0	4	.188	.188	.188	8	-2	0-1	.833	-1	67	0	O5(4/0/1)	0	-0.4
1989	Cin N	107	315	36	83	18	5	7	34	13-0	3	100	.263	.296	.419	100	-1	12-8	.981	5	117	90	O100(45/29/37)	0	0.1
1990	Cin N	30	61	5	13	0	0	2	7	0-0	0	20	.213	.213	.311	41	-5	0-0	1.000	1	115	99	O19(12/0/7)	0	-0.5
	Mon N	16	14	1	4	0	1	0	1	1-1	0	6	.286	.333	.429	112	0	0-2	1.000	-0	85	0	O6(3/2/1)	0	-0.1
	Year	46	75	6	17	0	1	2	8	1-1	0	26	.227	.237	.333	54	-5	0-2	1.000	1	110	81	O25(15/2/8)	0	-0.6
Total	3	170	406	45	103	18	6	9	42	14-1	3	130	.254	.282	.394	88	-8	12-11	.980	5	114	85	O130(64/31/46)	0	-0.9
ROONEY, FRANK	Frank (b Frank Rovny); B10.12.1884 Podebrady, Bohemia (Austria–Hungary); D4.6.1977 Bessemer MI; d4.18																								
1914	Ind F	12	35	1	7	0	1	1	8	1	0	0	.200	.222	.343	47	-3	2	.980	-1	41	122	1b9	—	-0.5
ROONEY, PAT	Patrick Eugene; B11.28.1957 Chicago IL; BR/TR/6´1˝/190; [MonN78 20/500]; d9.9; Col Eastern Illinois																								
1981	Mon N	4	5	0	0	0	0	0	0	0-0	0	3	.000	.000	.000	-97	-1	0-0	1.000	-0	57	0	O2R	0	-0.2
ROQUE, JORGE	Jorge (Vargas); B4.28.1950 Ponce, PR; BR/TR/5´10˝/158; d9.4																								
1970	StL N	5	1	2	0	0	0	0	0	0-0	1	1	.000	.500	.000	45	0	0-0	ø	-0	0	0	/lf	0	0.0
1971	StL N	3	10	2	3	0	0	0	1	0-0	0	3	.300	.300	.300	67	0	1-0	1.000	-0	86	0	O3C	0	-0.1
1972	StL N	32	67	3	7	2	1	1	5	6-0	0	19	.104	.176	.209	10	-8	1-1	.980	-0	112	0	O24(0/21/3)	0	-1.0
1973	Mon N	25	61	7	9	2	0	1	6	4-0	1	17	.148	.212	.230	22	-7	2-2	.878	-1	96	180	O24(1/23/0)	0	-0.9
Total	4	65	139	14	19	4	1	2	12	10-0	2	40	.137	.204	.223	20	-15	4-3	.934	-2	103	80	O52(2/47/3)	0	-2.0
ROSADO, LUIS	Luis (Robles); B12.6.1955 Santurce, PR; BR/TR/6´0˝/(180–189); d9.8																								
1977	NY N	9	24	1	5	1	0	0	3	1-0	1	3	.208	.250	.250	42	-2	0-0	.980	-2	109	88	1b7/C	0	-0.4
1980	NY N	2	4	0	0	0	0	0	0	0-0	0	1	.000	.000	.000	-99	-1	0-0	1.000	-0	0	141	/1	0	-0.2
Total	2	11	28	1	5	1	0	0	3	1-0	1	4	.179	.219	.214	22	-3	0-0	.983	-2	95	95	1b8/C	0	-0.6
ROSAR, BUDDY	Warren Vincent; B7.3.1914 Buffalo NY; D3.13.1994 Rochester NY; BR/TR/5´9˝/190; d4.29; Def 1944–45																								
1939	NY A	43	105	18	29	5	1	0	12	13	0	10	.276	.356	.343	81	-3	4-0	.980	4	*165*	*63*	C35	—	0.3
1940	NY A	73	228	34	68	11	3	4	37	19	2	11	.298	.357	.425	106	2	7-1	.983	2	*140*	*94*	C63	—	0.8
1941	†NY A	67	209	25	60	17	2	1	36	22	0	10	.287	.355	.402	101	1	0-0	.996	1	*138*	*83*	C60	0	0.5
1942	†NY A☆	69	209	18	48	10	0	2	34	17	0	20	.230	.288	.306	68	-9	1-2	.996	6	*177*	*86*	C58	0	0.0
1943	Cle A☆	115	382	53	108	17	1	1	41	33	0	12	.283	.340	.340	106	3	0-4	.983	9	***146***	*123*	C114	0	1.8
1944	Cle A	99	331	29	87	9	3	0	30	34	4	17	.263	.339	.308	89	-4	1-2	**.989**	-0	*93*	*113*	C98	0	0.1
1945	Phi A	92	300	23	63	12	1	1	25	20	1	16	.210	.262	.267	54	-18	2-1	.987	-3	*88*	*108*	C85	0	-1.7
1946	Phi A★	121	424	34	120	22	2	2	47	36	0	17	.283	.339	.358	96	-2	1-3	**1.000**	10	*123*	*115*	C117	0	1.4
1947	Phi A★	102	359	40	93	20	2	1	33	40	1	13	.259	.335	.334	85	-7	1-3	**.996**	13	*139*	***129***	C102	0	1.2
1948	Phi A★	90	302	30	77	13	0	4	41	39	2	12	.255	.344	.338	82	-7	0-2	**.997**	0	*115*	*85*	C90	0	-0.3
1949	Phi A	32	95	7	19	2	0	0	6	16	0	5	.200	.315	.221	45	-7	0-0	.992	-1	*107*	*57*	C31	0	-0.7
1950	Bos A	27	84	13	25	2	0	1	12	7	0	4	.298	.352	.357	75	-3	0-0	.991	-1	*125*	*46*	C25	0	-0.3
1951	Bos A	58	170	11	39	7	0	1	13	19	0	14	.229	.307	.288	56	-10	0-0	.996	0	*124*	*55*	C56	0	-0.7
Total	13	988	3198	335	836	147	15	18	367	315	10	161	.261	.330	.334	84	-64	17-18	.992	41	*127*	*100*	C934	0	2.4
ROSARIO, JIMMY	Angel Ramon (Ferrer); B5.5.1945 Bayamon, PR; BB/TR/5´10˝/(155–170); [SFN65 8/180]; d4.8																								
1971	†SF N	92	192	26	43	6	1	0	13	33-4	1	35	.224	.338	.266	75	-5	7-4	1.000	1	110	30	O67(9/60/1)	0	-0.6
1972	SF N	7	2	1	0	0	0	0	0	0-0	0	0	.000	.000	.000	-98	-1	0-1	ø	-0	0	0	/cf	0	-0.1
1976	Mil A	15	37	4	7	0	0	1	5	3-0	0	8	.189	.250	.270	53	-2	1-3	1.000	-1	96	0	O12(11/2/0),D2	0	-0.5
Total	3	114	231	31	50	6	1	1	18	36-4	1	43	.216	.322	.264	70	-8	8-8	1.000	0	108	25	O80(20/63/1),D2	0	-1.2
ROSARIO, MEL	Melvin Gregorio; B5.25.1973 Santo Domingo, D.R.; BB/TR/6´0˝/191; d9.11																								
1997	Bal A	4	3	0	0	0	0	0	0	0-0	0	1	.000	.000	.000	-99	-1	0-0	.875	-1	87	0	C4	0	-0.2

YEAR	TM LG	G	AB	R	H	2B	3B	HR	RBI	BB-IB	HP	SO	AVG	OBP	SLG	AOPS	ABR	SB-CS	FA	FR	RNG	THR	GAMES AT POSITION	DL	BFW
ROSARIO, SANTIAGO	Santiago; B7.25.1939 Guayanilla, PR; BL/TL/5´11˝/165; d6.23																								
1965	KC A	81	85	8	20	3	0	2	8	6-0	1	16	.235	.287	.341	81	-2	0-0	.991	-1	81	47	1b31,O3(2/0/1)	0	-0.4
ROSARIO, VICTOR	Victor Manuel (Rivera); B8.26.1966 Hato Mayor Del Rey, D.R.; BR/TR/5´11˝/155; d9.6																								
1990	Atl N	9	7	3	1	0	0	0	0	1-0	0	1	.143	.250	.143	10	-1	0-0	1.000	-1	71	0	S3/2	0	-0.2
ROSE, MIKE	Michael John-Ferrero; B8.25.1976 Sacramento CA; BB/TR/6´1˝/(185–225); [HouN95 5/137]; d10.1																								
2004	Oak A	2	2	1	0	0	0	0	0	0-0	0	2	.000	.000	.000	-99	-1	0-0	1.000	-0	18	1179	C2	0	-0.1
2005	LA N	15	43	2	9	2	0	1	1	3-0	0	6	.209	.261	.326	52	-3	0-0	.978	-3	37	113	C13	0	-0.5
2006	StL N	10	9	0	2	0	0	0	1	0-0	0	4	.222	.222	.222	14	-1	0-0	1.000	1	0	0	C4	0	0.0
Total	3	27	54	3	11	2	0	1	2	3-0	0	12	.204	.246	.296	40	-5	0-0	.980	-2	34	133	C19	0	-0.6
ROSE, PETE	Peter Edward Jr.; B11.16.1969 Cincinnati OH; BL/TR/6´1˝/180; [BalA88 12/295]; d9.1; f–Pete																								
1997	Cin N	11	14	2	2	0	0	0	0	2-0	0	9	.143	.250	.143	6	-2	0-0	.600	-1	102	0	3b2/1	0	-0.3
ROSE, PETE	Peter Edward Sr. "Charlie Hustle"; B4.14.1941 Cincinnati OH; BB/TR/5´11˝/(185–203); d4.8; M6; s–Pete; OF(671/70/594)																								
1963	Cin N	157	623	101	170	25	9	6	41	55-0	5	72	.273	.334	.371	101	1	13-15	.971	-16	86	88	2b157/lf	0	-0.4
1964	Cin N	136	516	64	139	13	2	4	34	36-0	2	51	.269	.319	.326	79	-14	4-10	.979	-9	88	94	2b128	0	-1.6
1965	Cin N★	**162**	670	117	**209**	35	11	11	81	69-2	8	76	.312	.382	.446	124	24	8-3	.975	-18	84	86	2b162	0	2.2
1966	Cin N	156	654	97	205	38	5	16	70	37-3	1	61	.313	.351	.460	113	12	4-9	.981	-8	84	84	2b140,3b16	0	1.5
1967	Cin N★	148	585	86	176	32	8	12	76	56-9	3	66	.301	.364	.444	117	15	11-6	.982	3	103	68	O123(123/1/0),2b35	0	1.4
1968	Cin N✳	149	626	94	**210**	42	6	10	49	56-15	4	76	**.335**	**.391**	.470	149	39	3-7	.990	3	94	156	O148(0/7/144),2b3/1	21	3.4
1969	Cin N★	156	627	**120**	218	33	11	16	82	88-18	5	65	**.348**	.428	.512	155	50	7-10	.988	-3	97	85	O156(0/56/101),2b2	0	4.0
1970	†Cin N★	159	649	120	**205**	37	9	15	52	73-10	2	64	.316	.385	.470	128	27	12-7	**.997**	-1	100	72	O159(1/5/155)	0	1.8
1971	Cin N★	160	632	86	192	27	4	13	44	68-15	3	50	.304	.373	.421	126	23	13-9	.994	-0	94	108	O158(0/1/158)	0	1.5
1972	†Cin N	**154**	645	107	**198**	31	11	6	57	73-4	7	46	.307	.382	.417	134	30	10-3	.994	10	103	129	O154L	0	3.4
1973	†Cin N★	160	680	115	**230**	36	8	5	64	65-6	6	42	**.338**	.401	.437	138	37	10-7	.992	8	102	127	O159L	0	3.5
1974	Cin N★	**163**	652	**110**	185	**45**	7	3	51	106-14	5	54	.284	.385	.388	119	23	2-4	**.997**	9	109	94	O163L	0	2.2
1975	†Cin N★	**162**	662	**112**	210	**47**	4	7	74	89-8	11	50	.317	.406	.432	131	33	0-1	.963	-22	86	99	3b137,O35L	0	0.9
1976	†Cin N★	**162**	665	**130**	**215**	**42**	6	10	63	86-7	6	54	.323	.404	.450	139	38	9-5	**.969**	-11	94	91	3b159/rf	0	2.8
1977	Cin N★	**162**	655	95	204	38	7	9	64	66-7	5	42	.311	.377	.432	114	15	16-4	.958	-19	86	76	3b161	0	-0.4
1978	Cin N★	159	655	103	198	**51**	3	7	52	62-6	3	30	.302	.362	.421	119	18	13-9	.961	-14	88	91	3b156,O7L,1b2	0	0.2
1979	Phi N★	**163**	628	90	208	40	5	4	59	95-10	2	32	.331	**.418**	.430	127	30	20-11	.995	-2	94	104	1b159,3b5/2	0	1.9
1980	†Phi N★	**162**	655	95	185	**42**	1	1	64	66-5	**6**	33	.282	.352	.354	92	-3	12-8	**.997**	12	**127**	92	1b162	0	-0.2
1981	†Phi N★	**107**	431	73	**140**	18	5	0	33	46-5	3	26	.325	.391	.390	116	11	4-4	.996	11	132	82	1b107	0	1.6
1982	Phi N★	**162**	634	80	172	25	4	3	54	66-9	7	32	.271	.345	.338	89	-7	8-8	.995	6	107	97	1b162	0	-1.2
1983	†Phi N	151	493	52	121	14	3	0	45	52-5	2	28	.245	.316	.286	70	-19	7-7	.990	2	115	81	1b112,O35R	0	-2.7
1984	Mon N	95	278	34	72	6	2	0	23	31-3	1	20	.259	.334	.295	82	-6	1-1	.988	8	171	84	1b40,O28L	0	-0.1
	Cin N	26	96	9	35	9	0	0	11	9-1	2	7	.365	.430	.458	143	6	0-0	.990	-2	62	79	1b23,M	0	0.3
	Year	121	374	43	107	15	2	0	34	40-4	3	27	.286	.359	.337	99	1	1-1	.989	6	129	82	1b63,O28L	0	0.2
1985	Cin N★	119	405	60	107	12	2	2	46	86-5	4	35	.264	.395	.319	98	4	8-1	.995	1	99	94	1b110,M	0	0.0
1986	Cin N	72	237	15	52	8	2	0	25	30-0	4	31	.219	.316	.270	61	-12	3-0	.990	-1	101	117	1b61,M	16	-1.6
Total	24	3562	14053	2165	4256	746	135	160	1314	1566-167	107	1143	.303	.375	.409	117	375	198-149	.991	-55	100	101	O1327L,1b939,3b634,2b628	37	24.4
ROSE, BOBBY	Robert Richard; B3.15.1967 Covina CA; BR/TR/5´11˝/(170–187); [CalA85 5/121]; d8.12																								
1989	Cal A	14	38	4	8	1	2	1	3	2-0	1	10	.211	.268	.421	93	-1	0-0	.920	-2	91	69	3b10,2b3	0	-0.2
1990	Cal A	7	13	5	5	0	0	1	2	2-0	0	1	.385	.467	.615	204	2	0-0	1.000	-1	77	0	2b4,3b3	0	0.1
1991	Cal A	22	65	5	18	5	1	1	8	3-0	0	13	.277	.304	.431	102	0	0-0	1.000	1	118	116	2b8,O7(6/0/1),3b4,1b3	44	0.1
1992	Cal A	30	84	10	18	5	0	2	10	8-1	2	9	.214	.295	.345	79	-2	1-1	.953	9	142	115	2b28,1b2	38	0.7
Total	4	73	200	24	49	11	3	5	23	15-1	3	33	.245	.305	.405	97	-1	1-1	.965	8	132	106	2b43,3b17,O7(6/0/1),1b5	82	0.7
ROSEBORO, JOHNNY	John Junior; B5.13.1933 Ashland OH; D8.16.2002 Los Angeles CA; BL/TR/5´11.5˝/(189–200); d6.14; C5																								
1957	Bro N	35	69	6	10	2	0	2	6	10-2	0	20	.145	.253	.261	35	-6	0-0	.972	0	96	62	C19,1b5	0	-0.6
1958	LA N☆	114	384	52	104	11	9	14	43	36-2	2	56	.271	.333	.456	104	1	11-8	.987	-2	105	88	C104,O5(4/1/0)	0	0.3
1959	†LA N	118	397	39	92	14	7	10	38	52-11	3	69	.232	.322	.378	81	-11	7-5	.991	10	**222**	108	C117	0	0.5
1960	LA N	103	287	22	61	15	3	8	42	44-6	4	53	.213	.323	.369	84	-5	7-6	.993	14	130	91	C87/13	0	1.3
1961	LA N★	128	394	59	99	16	6	18	59	56-8	4	62	.251	.346	.459	104	2	6-4	.986	10	130	105	C125	0	1.8
1962	LA N★	128	389	45	97	16	7	7	55	50-11	7	60	.249	.341	.380	101	1	12-3	.985	1	123	83	C128	0	0.9
1963	†LA N	135	470	50	111	13	7	9	49	36-3	3	50	.236	.291	.351	91	-7	7-6	.992	-1	136	73	C134	0	-0.2
1964	LA N	134	414	42	119	24	1	3	45	44-9	4	61	.287	.357	.372	115	11	3-3	.993	12	**204**	104	C128	0	3.0
1965	†LA N	136	437	42	102	10	0	8	57	34-7	2	51	.233	.289	.311	75	-15	1-6	.994	2	141	91	C131/3	0	-1.0
1966	†LA N	142	445	47	123	23	2	9	53	44-13	3	51	.276	.343	.398	115	10	3-2	.993	13	132	83	C138	0	3.0
1967	LA N	116	334	37	91	18	2	4	24	38-12	2	33	.272	.348	.374	117	8	2-4	.984	-3	124	102	C107	0	1.0
1968	Min A	135	380	31	82	12	0	8	39	46-9	2	57	.216	.300	.311	82	-7	2-3	.991	4	108	75	C117	0	0.2
1969	†Min A★	115	361	33	95	12	0	3	32	39-12	0	44	.263	.333	.321	82	-8	5-5	.980	3	112	76	C111	0	-0.1
1970	Was A	46	86	7	20	4	0	1	6	18-5	0	10	.233	.365	.314	93	0	1-1	1.000	-2	71	33	C30	0	-0.1
Total	14	1585	4847	512	1206	190	44	104	548	547-110	36	677	.249	.326	.371	95	-26	67-56	.989	62	139	89	C1476,1b6,O5(4/1/0),3b2	0	10.0
ROSELLI, BOB	Robert Edward; B12.10.1931 San Francisco CA; BR/TR/5´11˝/(170–185); d8.16																								
1955	Mil N	6	9	1	2	1	0	0	0	1-0	1	4	.222	.364	.333	91	0	0-0	.917	-0	*0*	*204*	C2	0	0.0
1956	Mil N	4	2	1	1	0	0	1	1	0-0	0	1	.500	.500	2.000	564	1	0-0	1.000	1	*0*	*0*	C3	0	0.2
1958	Mil N	1	1	0	0	0	0	0	0	0-0	0	0	.000	.000	.000	-99	0	0-0	ø	0	—	—	/H	0	0.0
1961	Chi A	22	38	2	10	3	0	0	4	0-0	0	11	.263	.263	.342	61	-2	0-0	1.000	-1	0	140	C10	0	-0.3
1962	Chi A	35	64	4	12	3	1	1	5	11-1	1	15	.188	.316	.313	70	-2	1-0	.988	-2	45	139	C20	0	-0.4
Total	5	68	114	8	25	7	1	2	10	12-1	2	31	.219	.305	.351	76	-3	1-0	.986	-3	*27*	*139*	C35	0	-0.5
ROSELLO, DAVE	David (Rodriguez); B6.26.1950 Mayaguez, PR; BR/TR/5´11˝/(160–191); d9.10																								
1972	Chi N	5	12	2	3	0	0	1	3	3-0	0	2	.250	.400	.500	139	1	0-0	.846	-0	88	173	S5	0	0.1
1973	Chi N	16	38	4	10	2	0	0	2	2-0	0	4	.263	.300	.316	66	-2	2-2	.964	-1	85	78	2b13/S	0	-0.2
1974	Chi N	62	148	9	30	7	0	0	10	10-1	0	28	.203	.252	.250	39	-12	1-1	.972	-5	91	130	2b49,S12	0	-1.5
1975	Chi N	19	58	7	15	2	0	1	8	9-2	0	8	.259	.348	.345	91	0	0-1	.952	-3	92	58	S19	0	-0.2
1976	Chi N	91	227	27	55	5	1	1	11	41-8	1	33	.242	.359	.286	78	-4	1-2	.966	-5	95	100	S86/2	0	-0.1
1977	Chi N	56	82	18	18	2	1	1	9	12-1	0	12	.220	.319	.305	62	-4	0-0	.938	-3	108	103	3b21,S10,2b3	0	-0.7
1979	Cle A	59	107	20	26	6	1	3	14	15-0	0	27	.243	.328	.402	98	0	1-0	.976	-8	105	61	2b33,3b14,S11	0	-0.7
1980	Cle A	71	117	16	29	3	0	2	12	9-0	0	19	.248	.295	.325	71	-5	0-0	.980	-8	80	74	2b43,3b22,S3/D	0	-1.1
1981	Cle A	43	84	11	20	4	0	1	7	7-0	0	12	.238	.297	.321	79	-2	0-1	.979	-2	81	92	2b26,3b8,S4,D4	0	-0.3
Total	9	422	873	114	206	31	3	10	76	108-12	1	145	.236	.318	.313	73	-28	5-7	.975	-35	89	90	2b168,S151,3b65,D5	0	-4.7
ROSEMAN, CHIEF	James John; B1856 New York NY; D7.4.1938 Brooklyn NY; BR/TR/5´7˝/167; d5.1; M1; ▲																								
1882	Tro N	82	331	41	78	21	6	1	29	3	—	41	.236	.243	.344	90	-3	—	.853	-5	114	139	O82(1/0/81)	—	-0.8
1883	NY AA	93	398	48	100	13	6	0	—	11	—	—	.251	.271	.314	84	-8	—	.855	-6	102	169	O91(3/8/80),1b2	—	-1.3
1884	†NY AA	107	436	97	130	16	11	4	—	21	6	—	.298	.339	.413	148	23	—	.885	-4	58	0	O107(4/103/0)	—	1.4
1885	NY AA	101	410	72	114	13	14	4	46	25	10	—	.278	.335	.407	139	19	—	.865	-7	53	30	O101(1/99/1)/P	—	0.7
1886	NY AA	134	559	90	127	19	10	5	53	24	8	—	.227	.269	.324	93	-4	6	.891	-4	80	148	O134(88/44/3)/P	—	-1.1
1887	Phi AA	21	73	16	16	2	1	0	8	10	5	—	.219	.352	.274	76	-2	3	.821	-1	147	140	O21C	—	-0.2
	NY AA	60	241	30	55	10	1	1	27	9	3	—	.228	.265	.290	57	-14	3	.868	-5	69	93	O59(9/36/14),1b3,P2	—	-1.7
	Bro AA	1	3	2	1	0	0	0	1	0	1	—	.333	.500	.333	133	0	0	1.000	0	0	0	/rf	—	0.0
	Year	82	317	48	72	12	2	1	36	19	9	—	.227	.290	.287	63	-15	6	.856	-6	89	104	O81(9/57/15),1b3,P2	—	-1.9
1890	StL AA	80	302	47	103	26	0	2	58	30	29	—	.341	.449	.447	144	19	7	.819	-6	82	112	O58(17/40/1),1b22,M	—	0.9
	Lou AA	2	8	0	2	0	0	0	0	0	0	—	.250	.250	.250	48	-1	0	.864	-1	0	351	1b2	—	-0.1
	Year	82	310	47	105	26	0	2	58	30	29	—	.339	.444	.442	142	19	7	.819	-7	82	112	O58(17/40/1),1b24	—	0.8
Total	7	681	2761	443	726	120	49	17	222	133	62	41	.263	.312	.360	110	29	19	.866	-38	81	99	O654(123/351/181),1b29,P4	—	-2.2

Rosen, Al Albert Leonard "Flip"; B2.29.1924 Spartanburg SC; BR/TR/5´10.5˝/(180–185); d9.10; Col Florida

YEAR	TM LG	G	AB	R	H	2B	3B	HR	RBI	BB-IB	HP	SO	AVG	OBP	SLG	AOPS	ABR	SB-CS	FA	FR	RNG	THR	GAMES AT POSITION	DL	BFW
1947	Cle A	7	9	1	1	0	0	0	0	0	0	3	.111	.111	.111	-39	-2	0-0	ø	1	0	0	3b2/lf	0	-0.1
1948	†Cle A	5	5	0	1	0	0	0	0	0	0	2	.200	.200	.200	7	-1	0-0	1.000	0	93	0	3b2	0	-0.1
1949	Cle A	23	44	3	7	2	0	0	5	7	0	4	.159	.275	.205	28	-5	0-1	1.000	-1	89	51	3b10	0	-0.6
1950	Cle A	**155**	554	100	159	23	4	**37**	116	100	**10**	72	.287	.405	.543	146	39	5-7	.969	6	**107**	79	3b154	0	4.0
1951	Cle A	154	573	82	152	30	1	24	102	85	2	71	.265	.362	.447	125	20	7-5	.958	-10	95	66	3b154	0	1.0
1952	Cle A★	148	567	101	171	32	5	28	**105**	75	4	54	.302	.387	.524	162	47	8-6	.958	-15	88	78	3b147,1b4,S3	0	3.3
1953	Cle A★	**155**	599	**115**	201	27	5	**43**	**145**	85	4	48	.336	.422	**.613**	**181**	**68**	8-7	.964	9	**108**	107	3b154/1S	0	**7.4**
1954	†Cle A★	137	466	76	140	20	2	24	102	85	3	43	.300	.404	.506	148	34	6-2	.959	-13	81	94	3b87,1b46/2S	0	1.9
1955	Cle A★	139	492	61	120	13	1	21	81	92-5	4	44	.244	.362	.402	103	4	4-2	.963	-1	89	84	3b106,1b41	0	0.1
1956	Cle A	121	416	64	111	18	2	15	61	58-4	0	44	.267	.351	.428	104	3	1-3	.945	-9	93	94	3b116	0	-0.7
Total	10	1044	3725	603	1063	165	20	192	717	587-9	27	385	.285	.384	.495	138	207	39-33	.961	-32	96	85	3b932,1b92,S5/2lf	0	16.2

Rosen, Goody Goodwin George; B8.28.1912 Toronto ON, Can.; D4.6.1994 Toronto ON, Can.; BL/TL/5´10˝/155; d9.14

YEAR	TM LG	G	AB	R	H	2B	3B	HR	RBI	BB-IB	HP	SO	AVG	OBP	SLG	AOPS	ABR	SB-CS	FA	FR	RNG	THR	GAMES AT POSITION	DL	BFW
1937	Bro N	22	77	10	24	5	1	0	6	6	0	6	.312	.361	.403	106	1	2	.981	1	111	66	O21(8/13/0)	—	0.1
1938	Bro N	138	473	75	133	17	11	4	51	65	0	43	.281	.368	.389	106	5	0	**.989**	9	103	**187**	O113(13/43/59)	—	0.9
1939	Bro N	54	183	22	46	6	4	1	12	23	0	21	.251	.335	.344	80	-5	4	1.000	-3	97	0	O47(1/40/7)	—	-1.0
1944	Bro N	89	264	38	69	8	3	0	23	26	1	27	.261	.330	.314	83	-6	0	.991	11	119	210	O65(1/62/3)	0	0.4
1945	Bro N✱	145	606	126	197	24	11	12	75	50	3	36	.325	.379	.460	134	26	6	.993	-4	101	59	O141C	0	1.8
1946	Bro N	3	3	0	1	0	0	0	0	0	0	1	.333	.333	.333	89	0	0	ø	-0	0	0	/cf	0	0.0
	NY N	100	310	39	87	11	4	5	30	48	0	32	.281	.377	.390	117	8	2	.976	-3	106	36	O84(0/30/52)	0	0.3
	Year	103	313	39	88	11	4	5	30	48	0	33	.281	.377	.390	117	8	2	.976	-3	106	36	O85(0/31/52)	0	0.3
Total	6	551	1916	310	557	71	34	22	197	218	4	166	.291	.364	.398	111	29	14	.989	11	105	101	O472(23/330/121)	0	2.5

Rosenberg, Harry Harry; B6.22.1908 San Francisco CA; D4.13.1997 San Mateo CA; BR/TR/5´9.5˝/160; d7.15; b–Lou

YEAR	TM LG	G	AB	R	H	2B	3B	HR	RBI	BB-IB	HP	SO	AVG	OBP	SLG	AOPS	ABR	SB-CS	FA	FR	RNG	THR	GAMES AT POSITION	DL	BFW
1930	NY N	9	5	1	0	0	0	0	0	1	0	4	.000	.167	.000	-56	-1	0	1.000	0	118	0	O3(0/2/1)	—	-0.1

Rosenberg, Lou Louis; B3.5.1904 San Francisco CA; D9.8.1991 Daly City CA; BR/TR/5´7˝/155; d5.22; b–Harry

YEAR	TM LG	G	AB	R	H	2B	3B	HR	RBI	BB-IB	HP	SO	AVG	OBP	SLG	AOPS	ABR	SB-CS	FA	FR	RNG	THR	GAMES AT POSITION	DL	BFW
1923	Chi A	3	4	0	1	0	0	0	0	0	0	1	.250	.250	.250	32	0	0-1	1.000	-1	0	0	2b2	—	-0.1

Rosenfeld, Max Max; B12.23.1902 New York NY; D3.10.1969 Miami FL; BR/TR/5´8˝/175; d4.21; Col Alabama

YEAR	TM LG	G	AB	R	H	2B	3B	HR	RBI	BB-IB	HP	SO	AVG	OBP	SLG	AOPS	ABR	SB-CS	FA	FR	RNG	THR	GAMES AT POSITION	DL	BFW
1931	Bro N	3	9	0	2	1	0	0	0	1	0	1	.222	.300	.333	70	0	0	1.000	-0	100	0	O3C	—	-0.1
1932	Bro N	34	39	8	14	3	0	2	7	0	0	10	.359	.359	.590	153	3	2	.970	1	119	95	O30(1/10/19)	—	0.3
1933	Bro N	5	9	0	1	0	0	0	0	1	0	1	.111	.200	.111	-10	-1	0	1.000	0	110	0	O2(1/1/0)	—	-0.2
Total	3	42	57	8	17	4	0	2	7	2	0	12	.298	.322	.474	115	2	2	.978	1	115	66	O35(2/14/19)	—	0.0

Rosenthal, Larry Lawrence John; B5.21.1910 St.Paul MN; D3.4.1992 Woodbury MN; BL/TL/6´0.5˝/190; d6.20

YEAR	TM LG	G	AB	R	H	2B	3B	HR	RBI	BB-IB	HP	SO	AVG	OBP	SLG	AOPS	ABR	SB-CS	FA	FR	RNG	THR	GAMES AT POSITION	DL	BFW
1936	Chi A	85	317	71	89	15	8	3	46	59	0	37	.281	.394	.407	95	-1	2-0	.977	2	103	92	O80C	—	-0.1
1937	Chi A	58	97	20	28	5	3	0	9	9	1	20	.289	.355	.402	90	-2	1-0	.980	1	100	188	O25C	—	0.0
1938	Chi A	61	105	14	30	5	1	1	12	12	0	13	.286	.359	.381	83	-3	0-1	.959	0	93	176	O22(0/22/2)	—	-0.3
1939	Chi A	107	324	50	86	21	5	10	51	53	0	46	.265	.369	.454	106	4	6-4	.990	-2	97	68	O93(0/20/75)	—	-0.3
1940	Chi A	107	276	46	83	14	5	6	42	64	0	32	.301	.432	.453	128	15	2-3	.977	4	116	67	O92(68/15/11)	—	1.4
1941	Chi A	20	59	9	14	4	0	0	1	12	0	5	.237	.366	.305	80	-1	0-0	.938	-0	82	203	O18(0/2/16)	0	-0.2
	Cle A	45	75	10	14	3	1	1	8	9	0	10	.187	.274	.293	53	-5	1-0	1.000	0	106	87	O14(5/8/1)/1	0	-0.5
	Year	65	134	19	28	7	1	1	9	21	0	15	.209	.316	.299	66	-6	1-0	.971	0	93	148	O32(5/10/17)/1	0	-0.7
1944	NY A	36	101	9	20	3	0	0	9	19	0	15	.198	.325	.228	57	-5	1-0	.986	2	111	91	O26(10/5/11)	0	-0.5
	Phi A	32	54	5	11	2	0	1	6	5	0	9	.204	.271	.296	63	-3	0-0	.960	-1	106	0	O19(5/0/15)	0	-0.4
	Year	68	155	14	31	5	0	1	15	24	0	24	.200	.307	.252	60	-7	1-0	.979	1	110	65	O45(15/5/26)	0	-0.9
1945	Phi A	28	75	6	15	3	2	0	5	9	0	8	.200	.286	.293	68	-3	0-1	1.000	-1	90	61	O21L	0	-0.6
Total	8	579	1483	240	390	75	25	22	189	251	1	195	.263	.370	.392	96	-4	13-9	.979	5	103	89	O410(109/177/131)/1	0	-1.5

Rosenthal, Si Simon; B11.13.1903 Boston MA; D4.7.1969 Boston MA; BL/TL/5´9˝/165; d9.8

YEAR	TM LG	G	AB	R	H	2B	3B	HR	RBI	BB-IB	HP	SO	AVG	OBP	SLG	AOPS	ABR	SB-CS	FA	FR	RNG	THR	GAMES AT POSITION	DL	BFW
1925	Bos A	19	72	6	19	5	2	0	8	7	0	3	.264	.329	.389	82	-2	1-0	.919	-1	86	155	O17(7/0/10)	—	-0.4
1926	Bos A	104	285	34	76	12	3	4	34	19	2	18	.267	.317	.372	82	-9	4-1	.962	-10	81	0	O67(48/0/19)	—	-2.3
Total	2	123	357	40	95	17	5	4	42	26	2	21	.266	.319	.375	82	-11	5-1	.950	-10	82	35	O84(55/0/29)	—	-2.7

Roser, Bunny John William Joseph "Jack"; B11.15.1901 St.Louis MO; D5.6.1979 Rocky Hill CT; BL/TL/5´11˝/175; d8.24

YEAR	TM LG	G	AB	R	H	2B	3B	HR	RBI	BB-IB	HP	SO	AVG	OBP	SLG	AOPS	ABR	SB-CS	FA	FR	RNG	THR	GAMES AT POSITION	DL	BFW
1922	Bos N	32	113	13	27	3	4	0	16	10	1	19	.239	.306	.336	69	-6	2-1	.915	-2	105	55	O32L	—	-0.9

Roskos, John John Edward; B11.19.1974 Victorville CA; BR/TR/5´11˝/195; [FlaN93 2/69]; d4.20

YEAR	TM LG	G	AB	R	H	2B	3B	HR	RBI	BB-IB	HP	SO	AVG	OBP	SLG	AOPS	ABR	SB-CS	FA	FR	RNG	THR	GAMES AT POSITION	DL	BFW
1998	Fla N	10	10	1	1	0	0	0	0	0-0	0	5	.100	.100	.100	-50	-2	0-0	1.000	0	0	0	/1	0	-0.2
1999	Fla N	13	12	0	2	2	0	0	1	1-0	0	7	.167	.231	.333	43	-1	0-0	1.000	0	0	0	/C	0	-0.1
2000	SD N	14	27	0	1	1	0	0	1	3-0	0	7	.037	.133	.074	-49	-6	0-0	.875	-1	72	0	O6(4/0/2),1b2	0	-0.7
Total	3	37	49	1	4	3	0	0	2	4-0	0	19	.082	.151	.143	-26	-9	0-0	.875	-0	72	0	O6(4/0/2),1b3/C	0	-1.0

Ross, Chet Chester James; B4.1.1917 Buffalo NY; D2.21.1989 Buffalo NY; BR/TR/6´1˝/195; d9.15; Mil 1945

YEAR	TM LG	G	AB	R	H	2B	3B	HR	RBI	BB-IB	HP	SO	AVG	OBP	SLG	AOPS	ABR	SB-CS	FA	FR	RNG	THR	GAMES AT POSITION	DL	BFW
1939	Bos N	11	31	4	10	1	1	0	0	2	0	10	.323	.364	.419	118	1	0	1.000	1	111	137	O8(1/1/7)	—	0.1
1940	Bos N	149	569	84	160	23	14	17	89	59	3	127	.281	.352	.460	130	21	4	.962	5	106	108	O149L	—	1.8
1941	Bos N	29	50	1	6	1	0	0	4	9	0	17	.120	.254	.140	14	-6	0	1.000	0	97	145	O12L	0	-0.6
1942	Bos N	76	220	20	43	7	2	5	19	16	0	37	.195	.250	.314	66	-11	0	.992	0	105	52	O57(52/0/6)	0	-1.5
1943	Bos N	94	285	27	62	12	2	7	32	26	1	67	.218	.285	.347	84	-7	1	.977	2	104	111	O73L	0	-1.0
1944	Bos N	54	154	20	35	9	2	5	26	12	1	23	.227	.287	.409	91	-3	1	1.000	3	93	238	O38(25/0/15)	0	-0.2
Total	6	413	1309	156	316	53	21	34	170	124	5	281	.241	.309	.392	100	-5	6	.976	12	104	116	O337(312/1/28)	0	-1.4

Ross, Cody Cody Joseph; B12.23.1980 Portales NM; BR/TL/5´11˝/(180–205); [DetA99 4/117]; d7.4

YEAR	TM LG	G	AB	R	H	2B	3B	HR	RBI	BB-IB	HP	SO	AVG	OBP	SLG	AOPS	ABR	SB-CS	FA	FR	RNG	THR	GAMES AT POSITION	DL	BFW
2003	Det A	6	19	1	4	1	0	1	5	1-0	1	3	.211	.286	.421	87	0	0-0	.882	0	126	0	O6R	0	-0.1
2005	LA N	14	25	1	4	1	0	0	1	1-0	0	10	.160	.192	.200	3	-4	0-0	.933	1	105	585	O9R	0	-0.2
2006	LA N	8	14	4	7	1	1	2	9	0-0	0	2	.500	.500	1.143	302	4	1-0	1.000	-0	92	0	O3(1/0/2)	0	0.4
	Cin N	2	5	0	1	0	0	0	0	0-0	0	2	.200	.200	.200	3	-1	0-0	1.000	-0	51	0	/lf	24	-0.1
	Fla N	91	250	30	53	11	1	11	37	22-0	4	61	.212	.284	.396	76	-10	0-1	.985	-1	95	93	O79(39/21/32)	0	-1.4
	Year	101	269	34	61	12	2	13	46	22-0	4	65	.227	.293	.431	86	-7	1-1	.985	-2	94	89	O83(41/21/34)	0	-1.1
Total	3	121	313	36	69	14	2	14	52	24-0	5	78	.220	.285	.412	80	-11	1-1	.970	-0	97	119	O98(41/21/49)	24	-1.4

Ross, David David Wade; B3.19.1977 Bainbridge GA; BR/TR/6´2˝/(205–215); [LAN98 7/216]; d6.29; Col Florida

YEAR	TM LG	G	AB	R	H	2B	3B	HR	RBI	BB-IB	HP	SO	AVG	OBP	SLG	AOPS	ABR	SB-CS	FA	FR	RNG	THR	GAMES AT POSITION	DL	BFW
2002	LA N	8	10	2	2	1	0	1	2	2-0	1	4	.200	.385	.600	163	1	0-0	1.000	0	0	125	C6	0	0.2
2003	LA N	40	124	19	32	7	0	10	18	13-0	2	42	.258	.336	.556	131	5	0-0	.986	-0	61	200	C38	0	0.7
2004	†LA N	70	165	13	28	3	1	5	15	15-1	5	62	.170	.253	.291	43	-15	0-0	.992	1	101	114	C67	0	-1.1
2005	Pit N	40	108	9	24	8	0	3	15	6-0	1	24	.222	.263	.380	68	-5	0-0	.986	4	324	136	C35	0	0.1
	SD N	11	17	2	6	0	1	0	0	0-0	1	4	.353	.389	.471	130	1	0-0	1.000	0	180	0	C7	0	0.1
	Year	51	125	11	30	8	1	3	15	6-0	2	28	.240	.279	.392	76	-5	0-0	.987	5	309	122	C42	0	0.2
2006	Cin N	90	247	37	63	15	1	21	52	37-7	3	75	.255	.353	.579	127	10	0-0	.985	8	238	88	C75	18	2.2
Total	5	259	671	82	155	34	3	40	102	73-8	13	211	.231	.313	.469	99	-3	0-0	.988	13	179	122	C228	18	2.2

Ross, Don Donald Raymond; B7.16.1914 Pasadena CA; D3.28.1996 Arcadia CA; BR/TR/6´2˝/200; d4.19

YEAR	TM LG	G	AB	R	H	2B	3B	HR	RBI	BB-IB	HP	SO	AVG	OBP	SLG	AOPS	ABR	SB-CS	FA	FR	RNG	THR	GAMES AT POSITION	DL	BFW
1938	Det A	77	265	22	69	7	1	1	30	29	0	11	.260	.333	.306	58	-17	1-0	.946	5	107	111	3b75	—	-0.8
1940	Bro N	10	38	4	11	2	0	1	8	3	0	3	.289	.341	.421	103	0	1	.879	-1	97	0	3b10	—	-0.1
1942	Det A	87	226	29	62	10	2	3	30	36	2	16	.274	.379	.376	104	3	2-1	.964	-4	96	135	O38(5/0/33),3b20	0	-0.3
1943	Det A	89	247	19	66	13	0	0	18	20	1	3	.267	.325	.320	82	-5	2-0	.985	-3	92	126	O38(6/0/32),S18,2b7/3	0	-0.9
1944	Det A	66	167	14	35	5	0	2	15	14	1	9	.210	.275	.275	54	-10	2-1	.958	-1	94	83	O37R,S2/1	0	-1.4
1945	Det A	8	29	3	11	4	0	0	4	5	0	1	.379	.471	.517	175	3	2-0	.960	-0	104	0	3b8	0	0.4
	Cle A	106	363	26	95	15	1	2	43	42	1	15	.262	.340	.325	97	0	0-4	.958	-11	84	71	3b106	0	-1.2
	Year	114	392	29	106	19	1	2	47	47	1	16	.270	.350	.339	104	3	2-4	.958	-11	85	66	3b114	0	-0.8
1946	Cle A	55	153	12	41	7	0	3	14	17	0	12	.268	.341	.373	106	1	0-0	.944	-7	73	66	3b41,O2R	0	-0.6
Total	7	498	1488	129	390	63	4	12	162	166	5	70	.262	.338	.334	86	-25	10-6	.946	-22	90	75	3b261,O115(11/0/104),S20,2b7/1	0	-4.9

YEAR	TM LG	G	AB	R	H	2B	3B	HR	RBI	BB-IB	HP	SO	AVG	OBP	SLG	AOPS	ABR	SB-CS	FA	FR	RNG	THR	GAMES AT POSITION	DL	BFW
ROSSI, JOE	Joseph Anthony (b Giuseppe Rossi); B3.13.1921 Oakland CA; D2.20.1999 Oakland CA; BR/TR/6´1˝/205; d4.20																								
1952	Cin N	55	145	14	32	0	1	1	6	20	1	20	.221	.319	.255	61	-7	1-0	.982	1	96	101	C46	0	-0.4
ROSSMAN, CLAUD	Claud; B6.17.1881 Philmont NY; D1.16.1928 Poughkeepsie NY; BL/TL/6´0˝/188; d9.16																								
1904	Cle A	18	62	5	13	5	0	0	6	0	0	—	.210	.210	.290	58	-3	0	.933	-2	0	0	O17(0/1/16)	—	-0.6
1906	Cle A	118	396	49	122	13	2	1	53	17	1	—	.308	.338	.359	120	8	11	.984	-9	69	**120**	1b105/cf	—	-0.3
1907	†Det A	**153**	571	60	158	21	8	0	69	33	2	—	.277	.318	.342	107	3	20	.981	-14	64	81	1b153	—	-1.5
1908	†Det A	138	524	45	154	33	13	2	71	27	1	—	.294	.330	.418	137	19	8	.981	6	**120**	110	1b138	—	2.5
1909	Det A	82	287	16	75	8	3	0	39	13	0	—	.261	.293	.310	87	-5	10	.981	-6	77	84	1b75	—	-1.5
	StL A	2	8	0	1	0	0	0	0	0	0	—	.125	.125	.125	-23	-1	0	1.000	-0	0	0	O2R	—	-0.2
	Year	84	295	16	76	8	3	0	39	13	0	—	.258	.289	.305	84	-6	10	.981	-6	77	84	1b75,O2R	—	-1.7
Total	5	511	1848	175	523	80	26	3	238	90	4	—	.283	.318	.359	113	21	49	.982	-26	84	99	1b471,O20(0/2/18)	—	-1.6
ROSSY, RICO	Elam Jose (Ramos); B2.16.1964 San Juan, PR; BR/TR/5´10˝/175; [BalA85 33/803]; d9.11; Col Purdue																								
1991	Atl N	5	1	0	0	0	0	0	0	0-0	0	1	.000	.000	.000	-95	0	0-0	ø	-0	0	0	/S	0	0.0
1992	KC A	59	149	21	32	8	1	1	12	20-1	1	20	.215	.310	.302	70	-5	0-3	.961	1	104	137	S51,3b9,2b3	0	-0.2
1993	KC A	46	86	10	19	4	0	2	12	9-0	1	11	.221	.302	.337	67	-4	0-0	.987	-2	103	109	2b24,3b16,S11	15	-0.5
1998	Sea A	37	81	12	16	6	0	1	4	6-0	0	13	.198	.253	.309	45	-7	0-0	1.000	5	110	159	3b25,2b6,S4/D	0	-0.2
Total	4	147	317	43	67	18	1	4	28	35-1	2	45	.211	.293	.312	62	-16	0-3	.967	4	100	132	S67,3b50,2b33/D	15	-0.9
ROTH, FRANK	Francis Charles; B10.11.1878 Chicago IL; D3.27.1955 Burlington WI; BR/TR/5´10˝/160; d4.18; C7; b–Braggo																								
1903	Phi N	68	220	27	60	11	4	0	22	9	1	—	.273	.304	.359	92	-3	3	.935	-8	*85*	*96*	C60/3	—	-0.6
1904	Phi N	81	229	28	59	8	1	1	20	12	1	—	.258	.298	.314	92	-2	8	.958	-10	*77*	*94*	C67/12	—	-0.7
1905	StL A	35	107	9	25	3	0	0	7	6	0	—	.234	.274	.262	74	-3	1	.962	-6	*69*	*110*	C29	—	-0.7
1906	Chi A	16	51	4	10	1	1	0	7	3	0	—	.196	.241	.255	57	-3	1	.990	3	*152*	*95*	C15	—	0.2
1909	Cin N	56	147	12	35	7	2	0	16	6	4	—	.238	.287	.313	87	-3	5	.967	-2	*92*	*90*	C54	—	0.0
1910	Cin N	26	29	3	7	2	0	0	3	0	1	2	.241	.267	.310	71	-1	1	.938	-0	*146*	*129*	C4/lf	—	-0.1
Total	6	282	783	83	196	32	8	1	75	36	7	2	.250	.289	.315	86	-15	19	.956	-23	*88*	*96*	C229/lf213	—	-1.9
ROTH, BRAGGO	Robert Frank; B8.28.1892 Burlington WI; D9.11.1936 Chicago IL; BR/TR/5´7.5˝/170; d9.1; b–Frank																								
1914	Chi A	34	126	14	37	4	6	1	10	8	4	25	.294	.355	.444	142	6	3-3	.924	1	92	159	O34(0/12/22)	—	0.4
1915	Chi A	70	240	44	60	6	10	3	35	29	3	50	.250	.338	.396	116	4	12-6	.837	-12	68	22	3b35,O30(29/1/0)	—	-0.9
	Cle A	39	144	23	43	4	7	4	20	22	2	22	.299	.399	.507	168	12	14-4	.878	-4	78	105	O39C	—	0.7
	Year	109	384	67	103	10	17	**7**	55	51	5	72	.268	.361	.438	135	15	26-10	.906	-17	81	122	O69(29/40/0),3b35	—	-0.2
1916	Cle A	125	409	50	117	19	7	4	72	38	2	48	.286	.350	.396	117	8	29-14	.954	2	92	**148**	O112(0/9/103)	—	0.6
1917	Cle A	145	495	69	141	30	9	1	72	52	2	73	.285	.355	.388	118	11	51	.957	2	105	101	O135R	—	0.7
1918	Cle A	106	375	53	106	21	12	1	59	53	**8**	41	.283	.383	.411	127	14	36	.936	-4	91	109	O106(2/0/104)	—	0.6
1919	Phi A	48	195	33	63	13	8	5	29	15	2	21	.323	.377	.549	156	13	11	.975	-5	95	15	O48R	—	0.6
	Bos A	63	227	32	58	9	4	0	23	24	4	32	.256	.337	.330	93	-2	9	.943	-5	87	85	O58(1/57/0)	—	-1.1
	Year	111	422	65	121	22	12	5	52	39	6	53	.287	.355	.431	124	12	20	.955	-10	91	54	O106(1/57/48)	—	-0.5
1920	Was A	138	468	80	136	23	8	9	92	75	6	57	.291	.395	.432	122	18	24-12	.952	-8	85	92	O128(7/0/121)	—	0.5
1921	NY A	43	152	29	43	9	2	2	10	19	2	20	.283	.370	.408	96	0	1-2	.923	-4	88	63	O37(3/17/17)	—	-0.7
Total	8	811	2831	427	804	138	73	30	422	335	35	389	.284	.367	.416	122	84	190-41	.944	-37	92	104	O727(42/135/550),3b35	—	1.4
ROTHEL, BOB	Robert Burton; B9.17.1923 Columbia Station OH; D3.21.1984 Huron OH; BR/TR/5´10.5˝/170; d4.22																								
1945	Cle A	4	10	0	2	0	0	0	0	3	0	1	.200	.385	.200	75	0	0-0	.875	-1	81	0	3b4	0	-0.1
ROTHERMEL, BOBBY	Edward Hill; B12.18.1870 Fleetwood PA; D2.11.1927 Detroit MI; BR/5´6.5˝/148; d6.18																								
1899	Bal N	10	21	1	2	0	0	0	3	1	0	—	.095	.136	.095	-34	-4	0	.867	-2	93	0	2b5,3b2/S	—	-0.6
ROTHFUSS, JACK	John Albert; B4.18.1872 Newark NJ; D4.20.1947 Basking Ridge NJ; BR/TR/5´11.5˝/195; d8.2																								
1897	Pit N	35	115	20	36	3	1	2	18	5	2	—	.313	.352	.409	105	0	3	.984	-1	82	56	1b32	—	0.0
ROTHGEB, CLAUDE	Claude James; B1.1.1880 Milford IL; D7.6.1944 Manitowoc WI; BB/6´0.5˝/200; d6.17; Col Illinois																								
1905	Was A	7	16	2	2	0	0	0	0	0	0	—	.125	.125	.125	-22	-2	1	.833	0	259	0	O4R	—	-0.3
ROTHROCK, JACK	John Huston; B3.14.1905 Long Beach CA; D2.2.1980 San Bernardino CA; BB/TR/5´11.5˝/165; d7.28; OF(138/194/311)																								
1925	Bos A	22	55	6	19	3	3	0	7	3	0	7	.345	.379	.509	124	2	0-0	.893	-3	86	64	S22	—	0.0
1926	Bos A	15	17	3	5	1	0	0	2	3	0	1	.294	.400	.353	101	0	0-0	.692	-2	86	0	S2	—	-0.1
1927	Bos A	117	428	61	111	24	8	1	36	24	2	46	.259	.302	.360	73	-19	5-5	.953	4	100	115	S40,2b36,3b20,1b13	—	-1.0
1928	Bos A	117	344	52	92	9	4	3	22	33	1	40	.267	.333	.343	79	-11	12-6	.979	-8	93	22	O53(26/12/19),3b17,1b16,S13,2b2/PC	—	-2.0
1929	Bos A	143	473	70	142	19	7	6	59	43	2	47	.300	.361	.408	100	0	24-13	.970	3	104	95	O128(0/126/2)	—	-0.2
1930	Bos A	45	65	4	18	3	1	0	4	2	0	9	.277	.299	.354	67	-3	0-2	.947	1	105	129	O9(1/0/8)/3	—	-0.4
1931	Bos A	133	475	81	132	32	3	4	42	47	0	48	.278	.343	.383	96	-2	13-7	.982	-3	87	149	O79(75/2/2),2b23,1b8,3b2/S	—	-0.8
1932	Bos A	12	48	3	10	1	0	0	0	5	0	5	.208	.283	.229	35	-5	3-0	.973	1	112	91	O12L	—	-0.4
	Chi A	39	64	8	12	2	1	0	6	5	0	9	.188	.246	.250	31	-7	1-0	.929	-3	100	0	O19(12/1/6),3b8/1	—	-0.9
	Year	51	112	11	22	3	1	0	6	10	0	14	.196	.262	.241	33	-11	4-0	.961	-2	108	64	O31(24/1/6),3b8/1	—	-1.3
1934	†StL N	**154**	647	106	184	35	3	11	72	49	1	56	.284	.336	.399	90	-9	10	.975	3	109	72	O154(5/0/149)/2	—	-1.5
1935	StL N	129	502	76	137	18	5	3	56	57	0	29	.273	.347	.347	84	-10	7	.980	-2	109	38	O127(1/1/125)	—	-2.0
1937	Phi A	88	232	28	62	15	0	0	21	28	0	15	.267	.346	.332	73	-9	1-0	.992	-2	99	44	O58(6/52/0)/2	—	-1.1
Total	11	1014	3350	498	924	162	35	28	327	299	6	312	.276	.336	.370	85	-73	76-33	.976	-13	103	74	O639R,S78,2b63,3b48,1b38/CP	—	-10.4
ROTTINO, VINNY	Vincent Anthony; B4.7.1980 Racine WI; BR/TR/6´0˝/195; d9.1; Col Wisconsin–LaCrosse																								
2006	Mil N	9	14	1	3	1	0	0	1	1-0	0	2	.214	.267	.286	41	-1	1-0	1.000	0	93	0	3b3,O2L/C	0	-0.1
ROUSE, MIKE	Michael Gregory; B4.25.1980 San Jose CA; BL/TR/5´11˝/200; [TorA01 5/151]; d6.9; Col Cal St.–Fullerton																								
2006	Oak A	8	24	2	7	3	0	0	2	1-0	1	4	.292	.346	.417	98	0	1-0	1.000	-3	81	83	2b7	0	-0.2
ROUSH, EDD	Edd J; B5.8.1893 Oakland City IN; D3.21.1988 Bradenton FL; BL/TL/5´11˝/170; d8.20; C1; HF1962																								
1913	Chi A	9	10	2	1	0	0	0	0	0	0	2	.100	.100	.100	-42	-2	0	1.000	-0	109	0	O2C	—	-0.2
1914	Ind F	74	166	26	54	8	4	1	30	6	1	20	.325	.353	.440	104	-2	12	.989	3	124	86	O43(38/4/1),1b2	—	-0.1
1915	New F	145	551	73	164	20	11	3	60	38	6	25	.298	.350	.390	115	1	28	.972	-3	99	92	O144(0/143/1)	—	-1.3
1916	NY N	39	69	4	13	0	1	0	5	1	0	4	.188	.200	.217	30	-6	4	.952	0	86	145	O15(0/5/10)	—	-0.8
	Cin N	69	272	34	78	7	14	0	15	13	7	19	.287	.336	.415	133	9	15	.971	2	112	79	O69C	—	0.7
	Year	108	341	38	91	7	15	0	20	14	7	23	.267	.309	.375	114	3	19	.969	2	108	88	O84(0/74/10)	—	-0.1
1917	Cin N	136	522	82	178	19	14	4	67	27	5	24	**.341**	.379	.454	162	36	21	.962	-2	104	83	O134C	—	2.8
1918	Cin N	113	435	61	145	18	10	5	62	22	2	10	.333	.368	**.455**	**153**	25	24	.960	5	113	87	O113C	—	2.5
1919	†Cin N	133	504	73	162	19	12	4	71	42	6	19	**.321**	.380	.431	147	29	20	.989	5	100	126	O133C	—	2.8
1920	Cin N	149	579	81	196	22	16	4	90	42	3	22	.339	.386	.453	142	31	36-24	.975	10	114	88	O139C,1b11/2	—	3.1
1921	Cin N	112	418	68	147	27	12	4	71	31	5	8	.352	.403	.502	145	27	19-17	.980	-2	105	59	O108C	—	1.8
1922	Cin N	49	165	29	58	7	4	1	24	19	3	5	.352	.428	.461	132	9	5-3	.990	1	89	162	O43C	—	0.7
1923	Cin N	138	527	88	185	**41**	18	6	88	46	3	16	.351	.406	.531	149	37	10-15	.970	-10	91	77	O137C	—	1.8
1924	Cin N	121	483	67	168	23	**21**	3	72	22	0	11	.348	.376	.501	135	21	17-13	.959	-10	84	102	O119C	—	0.5
1925	Cin N	134	540	91	183	28	16	8	83	35	4	14	.339	.383	.494	125	19	22-20	.978	-5	90	115	O134C	—	0.6
1926	Cin N	144	563	95	182	37	10	7	79	38	0	17	.323	.366	.462	125	19	8	.955	-18	79	89	O143C/1	—	-0.5
1927	NY N	140	570	83	173	27	4	7	58	26	1	15	.304	.335	.402	97	-4	18	.975	-6	87	130	O138(0/137/1)	—	-1.6
1928	NY N	46	163	20	41	5	3	2	13	14	1	8	.252	.315	.356	75	-7	1	.955	0	93	198	O39C	—	-0.8
1929	NY N	115	450	76	146	19	7	8	52	45	3	16	.324	.390	.451	108	6	6	.982	-6	80	**165**	O107C	—	-0.4
1931	Cin N	101	376	46	102	12	5	1	41	17	3	5	.271	.308	.338	78	-13	2	.981	-3	95	86	O88(43/45/0)	—	-1.9
Total	18	1967	7363	1099	2376	339	182	68	981	484	53	260	.323	.369	.446	126	235	268-92	.972	-38	97	102	O1848(81/1754/13),1b14/2	—	9.7
ROUTCLIFFE, PHIL	Philip John "Chicken"; B10.24.1870 Oswego NY; D10.4.1918 Oswego NY; BR/TR/6´0˝/175; d4.21																								
1890	Pit N	1	4	1	1	0	0	0	1	0	1	0	.250	.400	.250	102	0	1	1.000	0	0	0	/lf	—	0.0
ROWAN, DAVE	David (b David Drohan); B12.6.1882 Elora ON, Can.; D7.30.1955 Toronto ON, Can.; BL/TL/5´11˝/175; d5.27																								
1911	StL A	18	65	7	25	1	1	0	11	4	0	—	.385	.420	.431	143	4	0	.945	-1	99	59	1b18	—	0.2

YEAR	TM LG	G	AB	R	H	2B	3B	HR	RBI	BB-IB	HP	SO	AVG	OBP	SLG	AOPS	ABR	SB-CS	FA	FR	RNG	THR	GAMES AT POSITION	DL	BFW
ROWAND, AARON	Aaron Ryan; B8.29.1977 Portland OR; BR/TR/6´1˝/(200–205); [ChiA98 1/35]; d6.16; Col Cal St.–Fullerton																								
2001	Chi A	63	123	21	36	5	0	4	20	15-0	4	28	.293	.385	.431	109	2	5-1	.991	3	109	127	O61(34/32/11)	0	0.5
2002	Chi A	126	302	41	78	16	2	7	29	12-1	6	54	.258	.298	.394	79	-10	0-1	.983	6	108	112	O120(40/76/7)	0	-0.5
2003	Chi A	93	157	22	45	8	0	6	24	7-0	3	21	.287	.327	.452	99	0	0-0	1.000	3	94	268	O87(24/65/12)	0	0.2
2004	Chi A	140	487	94	151	38	2	24	69	30-1	10	91	.310	.361	.544	128	20	17-5	.975	1	98	158	O137(0/126/12)	0	2.2
2005	†Chi A	157	578	77	156	30	5	13	69	32-3	21	116	.270	.329	.407	91	-7	16-5	.992	-8	96	38	O157C	0	-1.1
2006	Phi N	109	405	59	106	24	3	12	47	18-2	18	76	.262	.321	.425	85	-10	10-4	.981	-0	101	121	O107C	56	-0.8
Total	6	688	2052	314	572	121	12	66	258	114-7	62	386	.279	.334	.446	99	-5	48-16	.985	4	100	118	O669(98/563/42)	56	0.5
ROWDON, WADE	Wade Lee; B9.7.1960 Riverhead NY; BR/TR/6´2˝/(170–180); [ChiA81 8/188]; d9.8; Col Stetson																								
1984	Cin N	4	7	0	2	0	0	0	0	0-0	0	1	.286	.286	.286	58	0	0-0	1.000	0	125	161	/S3	0	0.0
1985	Cin N	5	9	2	2	0	0	0	2	2-0	0	1	.222	.364	.222	64	0	0-0	.667	-1	64	0	3b4	0	-0.2
1986	Cin N	38	80	9	20	5	1	0	10	9-0	1	17	.250	.330	.338	82	-2	2-0	.889	-4	117	107	3b7,S6,O5L,2b3	0	-0.5
1987	Chi N	11	31	2	7	1	1	1	4	3-0	0	10	.226	.294	.419	83	-1	0-2	.818	-1	97	0	3b9	0	-0.3
1988	Bal A	20	30	1	3	0	0	0	0	0-0	0	6	.100	.100	.100	-45	-6	1-1	.947	3	179	141	3b8,O5L,D5	0	-0.3
Total	5	78	157	14	34	6	2	1	16	14-0	1	35	.217	.283	.299	59	-9	3-3	.866	-4	112	57	3b29,O10L,S7,D5,2b3	0	-1.3
ROWE, DAVE	David Elwood; B10.9.1854 Harrisburg PA; D12.9.1930 Glendale CA; BR/TR/5´9˝/180; d5.30; M2; b–Jack; ▲																								
1877	Chi N	2	7	0	2	0	0	0	0	0	—	3	.286	.286	.286	72	0	—	.667	-0	0	0	O2R/P	—	-0.1
1882	Cle N	24	97	13	25	4	3	1	17	4	—	9	.258	.287	.392	119	2	—	.837	-3	63	103	O23(3/20/1)/P	—	-0.1
1883	Bal AA	59	256	40	80	11	6	0	—	2	—	—	.313	.318	.402	127	6	—	.798	-6	54	0	O50(2/0/48),S7,1b3/P	—	0.0
1884	StL U	109	485	95	142	32	11	4	—	10	—	—	.293	.307	.429	116	-6	—	**.947**	-4	69	**175**	O92C,S14,2b2,1b2/P	—	-1.1
1885	StL N	16	62	8	10	3	0	0	3	5	—	8	.161	.224	.210	44	-3	—	.906	-2	35	251	O16C	—	-0.5
1886	KC N	105	429	53	103	24	8	3	57	15	—	43	.240	.266	.354	82	-11	2	.851	-9	61	63	O90(4/86/0),S11,2b4,M	—	-2.1
1888	KC AA	32	122	14	21	3	4	0	13	6	1	—	.172	.217	.262	50	-8	2	.914	2	209	81	O32C,M	—	-0.6
Total	7	347	1458	223	383	77	32	8	90	42	1	63	.263	.284	.376	99	-20	4	.878	-23	76	101	O305(9/246/51),S32,2b6,1b5,P4	—	-4.5
ROWE, HARLAND	Harland Stimson "Hypie"; B4.20.1896 Springvale ME; D5.26.1969 Springvale ME; BL/TR/6´1˝/170; d6.23; Col Maine																								
1916	Phi A	17	36	2	5	1	0	0	3	2	0	8	.139	.184	.167	6	-4	0	.842	-1	96	0	3b8/rf	—	-0.6
ROWE, JACK	John Charles; B12.8.1856 Hamburg PA; D4.25.1911 St.Louis MO; BL/TR/5´8˝/170; d9.6; M1; b–Dave																								
1879	Buf N	8	34	8	12	1	0	0	8	0	—	1	.353	.353	.382	139	1	—	.905	0	—	—	C6,O2R	—	0.2
1880	Buf N	79	326	43	82	10	6	1	36	6	—	17	.252	.265	.328	98	-1	—	.897	-14	—	—	C60,O25(2/6/19),3b3	—	-1.4
1881	Buf N	64	246	30	82	11	**11**	1	43	1	—	12	.333	.336	.480	156	14	—	.900	-9	—	—	C46,S7,3b7,O5(0/1/4)	—	0.6
1882	Buf N	75	308	43	82	14	5	1	42	12	—	0	.266	.294	.354	105	1	—	.950	-6	—	—	C46,S22,3b7/cf	—	0.0
1883	Buf N	87	374	65	104	18	7	1	38	15	—	14	.278	.306	.372	102	1	—	.899	-16	—	—	C49,O28L,S18,3b3	—	-1.0
1884	Buf N	93	400	85	126	14	14	4	61	23	—	14	.315	.352	.450	146	19	—	**.943**	-5	—	—	C65,O30(17/12/1),S6	—	1.7
1885	Buf N	98	421	62	122	28	8	2	51	13	—	19	.290	.311	.409	127	11	—	.834	-12	91	115	S65,C23,O12C	—	0.3
1886	Det N	111	468	97	142	21	9	6	87	26	—	27	.303	.340	.425	127	14	12	.880	-21	91	95	S110,C3	—	-0.4
1887	†Det N	124	537	135	171	30	10	6	96	39	3	11	.318	.368	.445	120	14	22	.907	-24	92	95	S124	—	-0.5
1888	Det N	105	451	62	125	19	8	2	74	19	3	28	.277	.311	.368	114	7	10	.861	-9	100	87	S105	—	0.1
1889	Pit N	75	317	57	82	14	3	2	32	22	3	16	.259	.313	.341	90	-4	5	.896	-6	100	105	S75	—	-0.6
1890	Buf P	125	504	77	126	22	7	2	76	48	7	18	.250	.324	.333	83	-11	10	**.901**	4	95	96	S125,M	—	-0.3
Total	12	1044	4386	764	1256	202	88	28	644	224	16	177	.286	.323	.392	114	66	59	.882	-117	—	—	S657,C298,O103(47/32/26),3b20	—	-1.3
ROWELL, BAMA	Carvel William; B1.13.1916 Citronelle AL; D8.16.1993 Citronelle AL; BL/TR/5´11˝/185; d9.4; Mil 1942–45; Col Louisiana St.																								
1939	Bos N	21	59	5	11	2	2	0	6	1	0	4	.186	.200	.288	32	-6	0	.853	-1	82	177	O16(0/13/3)	—	-0.8
1940	Bos N	130	486	46	148	19	8	3	58	18	1	22	.305	.331	.395	105	1	12	.953	-2	105	108	2b115,O7(0/1/6)	—	0.6
1941	Bos N	138	483	49	129	23	6	7	60	39	0	36	.267	.322	.383	102	0	11	.935	-8	98	**120**	2b112,O14(7/2/6),3b2	0	-0.2
1946	Bos N	95	293	37	82	12	6	3	31	29	0	15	.280	.345	.392	108	2	5	.978	3	104	123	O85(71/14/0)	0	0.0
1947	Bos N	113	384	48	106	23	2	5	40	18	1	14	.276	.310	.385	86	-9	7	.945	-5	100	58	O100(99/2/0),2b7,3b4	0	-2.1
1948	Phi N	77	196	15	47	16	2	1	22	8	0	14	.240	.270	.357	70	-9	2	.821	-8	72	149	3b18,O17(14/0/3),2b12	0	-1.8
Total	6	574	1901	200	523	95	26	19	217	113	2	105	.275	.316	.382	95	-21	37	.945	-22	101	110	2b246,O239(191/32/18),3b24	0	-4.3
ROWEN, ED	W. Edward; B10.22.1857 Bridgeport CT; D2.22.1892 Bridgeport CT; 5´6˝/155; d5.1																								
1882	Bos N	83	327	36	81	7	4	1	43	19	—	18	.248	.289	.303	90	-4	—	.885	-9	71	108	O48R,C34,S6/3	—	-0.9
1883	Phi AA	49	196	28	43	10	1	0	21	11	—	—	.219	.261	.281	68	-7	—	.855	-2	—	—	C44,O8(0/5/3)/32	—	-0.5
1884	Phi AA	4	15	4	6	1	0	0	1	1	1	—	.400	.471	.467	194	2	—	.806	-2	—	—	C4	—	0.0
Total	3	136	538	68	130	18	5	1	65	31	1	18	.242	.284	.299	85	-9	—	.866	-14	—	—	C82,O56(0/5/51),S6,3b2/2	—	-1.4
ROWLAND, CHUCK	Charlie Leland; B7.23.1899 Warrenton NC; D1.21.1992 Raleigh NC; BR/TR/6´1˝/185; d5.11																								
1923	Phi A	5	6	0	0	0	0	0	0	0	0	2	.000	.000	.000	-99	-2	0-0	1.000	0	*77*	*160*	C4	—	-0.2
ROWLAND, RICH	Richard Garnet; B2.25.1964 Cloverdale CA; BR/TR/6´1˝/(210–215); [DetA88 17/447]; d9.7; Col Mendocino (CA) CC																								
1990	Det A	7	19	3	3	1	0	0	0	2-1	0	4	.158	.238	.211	26	-2	0-0	.967	-1	47	70	C5,D2	0	-0.2
1991	Det A	4	4	0	1	0	0	0	1	1-0	0	2	.250	.333	.250	82	0	0-0	1.000	1	0	0	C2/D	0	0.1
1992	Det A	6	14	2	3	0	0	0	0	3-0	0	3	.214	.353	.214	61	-1	0-0	1.000	-1	74	0	C3/13D	0	-0.2
1993	Det A	21	46	2	10	3	0	0	4	5-0	0	16	.217	.294	.283	56	-3	0-0	.988	1	94	63	C17,D3	0	0.0
1994	Bos A	46	118	14	27	3	0	9	20	11-0	0	35	.229	.295	.483	92	-2	0-0	.972	-5	105	121	C39/1D	0	-0.4
1995	Bos A	14	29	1	5	1	0	0	1	0-0	0	11	.172	.172	.207	-2	-4	0-0	.977	1	140	54	C11,D3	0	-0.3
Total	6	98	230	22	49	8	0	9	26	22-1	0	71	.213	.281	.365	67	-12	0-0	.976	-4	101	92	C77,D15,1b2/3	0	-1.0
ROXBURGH, JIM	James A.; B1.17.1858 San Francisco CA; D2.21.1934 San Francisco CA; BR/TR/5´10˝/170; d5.30																								
1884	Bal AA	2	4	1	2	0	0	0	—	1	1	—	.500	.667	.500	275	1	—	.824	-1	—	—	C2	—	0.0
1887	Phi AA	2	8	0	1	0	0	0	0	0	0	—	.125	.125	.125	-30	-1	0	.875	-2	—	—	C2/2	—	-0.2
Total	2	4	12	1	3	0	0	0	0	1	1	—	.250	.357	.250	81	0	0	.840	-2	—	—	C4/2	—	-0.2
ROYER, STAN	Stanley Dean; B8.31.1967 Olney IL; BR/TR/6´3˝/(195–221); [OakA88 1/16]; d9.11; Col Eastern Illinois																								
1991	StL N	9	21	1	6	1	0	0	1	1-0	0	2	.286	.318	.333	82	0	0-0	1.000	-1	51	0	3b5	0	-0.2
1992	StL N	13	31	6	10	2	0	2	9	1-0	0	4	.323	.333	.581	161	2	0-0	.900	0	127	400	3b5,1b4	0	0.3
1993	StL N	24	46	4	14	2	0	1	8	2-0	0	14	.304	.333	.413	99	0	0-1	.857	-1	99	85	3b10,1b2	0	-0.2
1994	StL N	39	57	3	10	5	0	1	2	0-0	0	18	.175	.175	.316	25	-6	0-0	.972	-1	105	57	1b11,3b5	0	-0.7
	Bos A	4	9	0	1	0	0	0	1	0-0	0	3	.111	.111	.111	-41	-2	0-0	.833	-1	74	0	3b3/1	0	-0.2
Total	4	89	164	14	41	10	0	4	21	4-0	0	41	.250	.266	.384	73	-6	0-1	.895	-3	92	92	3b28,1b18	0	-1.0
ROYSTER, JERRY	Jeron Kennis; B10.18.1952 Sacramento CA; BR/TR/6´0˝/(160–170); d8.14; M1/C4; OF(123/21/9)																								
1973	LA N	10	19	1	4	0	0	0	2	0-0	0	5	.211	.211	.211	18	-2	1-0	.842	0	121	115	3b6/2	0	-0.2
1974	LA N	6	0	2	0	0	0	0	0	0-0	0	0	ø	ø	ø	ø	0	0-0	1.000	1	618	0	/23rf	0	0.1
1975	LA N	13	36	2	9	2	1	0	1	1-0	0	3	.250	.270	.361	77	-1	1-0	1.000	0	81	0	O7(1/0/6),2b4,3b3/S	0	-0.1
1976	Atl N	149	533	65	132	13	1	5	45	52-4	1	53	.248	.313	.304	72	-19	24-13	.962	**25**	**113**	**127**	3b148,S2	0	0.7
1977	Atl N	140	445	64	96	10	2	6	28	38-3	1	67	.216	.278	.288	47	-33	28-10	.953	-12	94	79	3b56,S51,2b38/cf	0	-3.9
1978	Atl N	140	529	67	137	17	8	2	35	56-2	3	49	.259	.331	.333	78	-14	27-17	.974	-4	91	84	2b75,S60/3	0	-0.9
1979	Atl N	154	601	103	164	25	6	3	51	62-0	0	59	.273	.337	.349	84	-12	35-8	.948	**29**	124	83	3b80,2b77	0	2.5
1980	Atl N	123	392	42	95	17	5	1	20	37-1	1	48	.242	.309	.319	75	-13	22-13	.948	-7	90	107	2b49,3b48,O41L	0	-2.1
1981	Atl N	64	93	13	19	4	1	0	9	7-0	0	14	.204	.257	.269	50	-6	7-5	.950	1	99	105	3b24,2b13	0	-0.5
1982	†Atl N	108	261	43	77	13	2	2	25	22-1	2	36	.295	.351	.383	104	2	14-6	.943	0	89	61	3b62,O25L,2b16,S10	0	0.3
1983	Atl N	91	268	32	63	10	3	3	30	28-2	0	35	.235	.305	.328	71	-10	11-7	.940	8	123	104	3b47,2b26,O18L,S13	21	-0.1
1984	Atl N	81	227	22	47	13	2	1	21	15-1	1	41	.207	.257	.295	52	-15	6-4	.973	10	128	101	2b29,3b17,S16,O11L	0	-0.3
1985	SD N	90	249	31	70	13	2	5	31	32-1	1	31	.281	.363	.410	117	7	6-5	.975	9	116	111	2b58,3b29,S7,O2(0/1/1)	0	1.9
1986	SD N	118	257	31	66	12	0	5	26	32-3	0	45	.257	.336	.362	95	-1	3-5	.931	4	113	140	3b59,S24,2b21,O7L	0	0.4
1987	Chi A	55	154	25	37	11	0	7	23	19-1	1	28	.240	.324	.448	100	0	2-1	.969	-4	87	88	3b30,O13L,2b5,D4	0	-0.4
	NY A	18	42	1	15	2	0	0	4	4-0	0	4	.357	.413	.405	119	1	2-1	.909	1	88	121	3b13/2Slf	0	0.2
	Year	73	196	26	52	13	0	7	27	23-1	1	32	.265	.342	.439	104	2	4-2	.954	-3	87	97	3b43,O14L,2b6,D4/S	0	-0.2
1988	Atl N	68	102	8	18	3	0	0	1	6-1	0	16	.176	.222	.206	23	-10	0-0	1.000	0	111	249	O26(7/19/1),3b10,2b2,S2	0	-1.1
Total	16	1428	4208	552	1049	165	33	40	352	411-20	11	534	.249	.315	.333	76	-126	189-95	.951	63	108	100	3b634,2b416,S187,O153L,D4	21	-3.5

YEAR	TM LG	G	AB	R	H	2B	3B	HR	RBI	BB-IB	HP	SO	AVG	OBP	SLG	AOPS	ABR	SB-CS	FA	FR	RNG	THR	GAMES AT POSITION	DL	BFW
ROYSTER, WILLIE	Willie Arthur; B4.11.1954 Clarksville VA; BR/TR/5´11˝/180; [BalA72 22/525]; d9.3																								
1981	Bal A	4	4	0	0	0	0	0	0	0-0	0	2	.000	.000	.000	-99	-1	0-0	1.000	-0	0	0	C4	0	-0.1
ROZNOVSKY, VIC	Victor Joseph; B10.19.1938 Shiner TX; BL/TR/6´1˝/(171–180); d6.28																								
1964	Chi N	35	76	2	15	1	0	0	2	5-0	0	18	.197	.244	.211	29	-7	0-1	.976	-4	115	201	C26	0	-1.1
1965	Chi N	71	172	9	38	4	1	3	15	16-1	3	30	.221	.295	.308	70	-7	1-0	.984	2	110	98	C63	0	-0.2
1966	Bal A	41	97	4	23	5	0	1	10	9-4	1	11	.237	.308	.320	82	-2	0-0	.995	-4	82	96	C34	0	-0.5
1967	Bal A	45	97	7	20	5	0	0	10	1-0	0	20	.206	.212	.258	39	-8	0-0	.993	-0	100	144	C23	0	-0.8
1969	Phi N	13	13	0	3	0	0	0	1	1-0	0	4	.231	.286	.231	47	-1	0-0	1.000	1	0	0	C2	0	0.0
Total	5	205	455	22	99	15	1	4	38	32-5	4	83	.218	.273	.281	59	-25	1-1	.988	-5	102	121	C148	0	-2.6
RUAN, WILKIN	Wilkin Chal; B11.18.1978 Guaymate, D.R.; BR/TR/6´0˝/170; d9.1																								
2002	LA N	12	11	2	3	1	0	0	3	0-0	0	2	.273	.273	.364	70	-1	0-0	1.000	-0	92	0	O5C	0	-0.1
2003	LA N	21	41	2	9	2	1	0	2	0-0	0	7	.220	.220	.317	39	-4	1-0	1.000	-0	91	178	O20C	0	-0.4
Total	2	33	52	4	12	3	1	0	5	0-0	0	9	.231	.231	.327	45	-5	1-0	1.000	-0	91	147	O25C	0	-0.5
RUBELING, AL	Albert William; B5.10.1913 Baltimore MD; D1.28.1988 Baltimore MD; BR/TR/6´0˝/185; d4.16; Col Towson																								
1940	Phi A	108	376	49	92	16	6	4	38	48	0	58	.245	.330	.351	78	-12	4-5	.933	-7	96	71	3b98,2b10	—	-1.5
1941	Phi A	6	19	0	5	0	0	0	2	2	0	1	.263	.333	.263	61	-1	0-0	.833	-2	74	98	3b6	0	-0.2
1943	Pit N	47	168	23	44	8	4	0	9	8	0	17	.262	.295	.357	85	-4	0	.974	0	109	106	2b44/3	0	-0.2
1944	Pit N	92	184	22	45	7	2	4	30	19	2	19	.245	.322	.370	90	-2	4	1.000	1	106	72	O18(9/0/9),2b17,3b16	0	-0.2
Total	4	253	747	94	186	31	12	8	79	77	2	95	.249	.321	.355	82	-19	8-5	.939	-7	97	88	3b121,2b71,O18(9/0/9)	0	-2.1
RUBERTO, SONNY	John Edward; B1.2.1946 Staten Island NY; BR/TR/5´11˝/175; d5.25; C2																								
1969	SD N	19	21	3	3	0	0	0	0	1-0	0	7	.143	.182	.143	-8	-3	0-0	1.000	1	105	98	C15	0	-0.2
1972	Cin N	2	3	0	0	0	0	0	0	0-0	1	1	.000	.250	.000	-25	0	0-0	1.000	-0	47	0	C2	0	-0.1
Total	2	21	24	3	3	0	0	0	0	1-0	1	8	.125	.192	.125	-10	-3	0-0	1.000	1	98	86	C17	0	-0.3
RUBLE, ART	William Arthur "Speedy"; B3.11.1903 Knoxville TN; D11.1.1983 Maryville TN; BL/TR/5´10.5˝/168; d4.18; Col Maryville																								
1927	Det A	56	91	16	15	4	2	0	11	14	1	15	.165	.283	.253	39	-8	2-2	.970	1	104	110	O43(24/13/7)	—	-0.9
1934	Phi N	19	54	7	15	4	0	0	8	7	0	3	.278	.361	.352	81	-1	0	.839	-1	86	179	O14(4/1/10)	—	-0.3
Total	2	75	145	23	30	8	2	0	19	21	1	18	.207	.311	.290	55	-9	2-2	.929	0	98	133	O57(28/14/17)	—	-1.2
RUCKER, JOHNNY	John Joel; B1.15.1917 Crabapple GA; D8.7.1985 Moultrie GA; BL/TR/6´2˝/175; d4.16; Col Georgia																								
1940	NY N	86	277	38	82	7	5	4	23	7	0	32	.296	.313	.401	95	-4	4	.954	-7	85	64	O57C	—	-1.2
1941	NY N	143	622	95	179	38	9	1	42	29	0	61	.288	.320	.383	95	-6	8	.967	-2	97	113	O142C	0	-1.2
1943	NY N	132	505	56	138	19	4	2	46	22	0	44	.273	.304	.339	85	-12	4	.969	-4	98	81	O117C	0	-2.1
1944	NY N	144	587	79	143	14	8	6	39	24	1	48	.244	.275	.325	69	-28	8	.985	-12	82	111	O139C	0	-4.6
1945	NY N	105	429	58	117	19	11	7	51	20	0	36	.273	.305	.417	98	-4	7	.978	-5	95	73	O98C	0	-1.3
1946	NY N	95	197	28	52	8	2	1	13	7	3	27	.264	.300	.340	81	-6	4	.948	-5	90	28	O54(0/50/6)	0	-1.3
Total	6	705	2617	354	711	105	39	21	214	109	4	248	.272	.302	.366	87	-60	35	.971	-35	92	89	O607(0/603/6)	0	-11.7
RUDDERHAM, JOHN	John Edmund; B8.30.1863 Quincy MA; D4.3.1942 Randolph MA; BR/TR/5´8˝/170; d9.18																								
1884	Bos U	1	4	0	1	0	0	0	—	0	—	—	.250	.250	.250	53	0	—	.000	-1	0	0	/lf	—	-0.1
RUDI, JOE	Joseph Oden; B9.7.1946 Modesto CA; BR/TR/6´2˝/200; d4.11; C2; [DL 1983 Oak A 182]																								
1967	KC A	19	43	4	8	2	0	0	1	3-0	0	7	.186	.239	.233	41	-3	0-0	.984	-1	0	19	1b9,O6L	0	-0.6
1968	Oak A	68	181	10	32	5	1	1	12	12-3	2	32	.177	.236	.232	44	-13	1-1	.987	-2	91	34	O56(55/1/1)	0	-2.1
1969	Oak A	35	122	10	23	3	1	2	6	5-1	0	16	.189	.220	.279	40	-11	1-1	1.000	1	112	139	O18L,1b11	0	-1.2
1970	Oak A	106	350	40	108	23	2	11	42	16-1	2	61	.309	.341	.480	128	12	3-1	.982	1	100	138	O63(58/1/12),1b28	0	0.8
1971	†Oak A	127	513	62	137	23	4	10	52	28-2	1	62	.267	.304	.386	97	-4	3-2	.996	4	111	68	O121(115/0/9),1b5	0	-0.8
1972	†Oak A★	147	593	94	**181**	32	**9**	19	75	37-6	2	62	.305	.345	.486	153	35	3-4	.992	-8	88	76	O147L/3	0	2.0
1973	†Oak A	120	437	53	118	25	1	12	66	30-4	2	72	.270	.315	.414	110	5	0-0	.992	2	106	75	O117L/1D	16	0.0
1974	†Oak A★	158	593	73	174	**39**	4	22	99	34-6	5	92	.293	.334	.484	142	30	2-3	.984	-6	92	76	O140L,1b27,D2	0	1.4
1975	†Oak A★	126	468	66	130	26	6	21	75	40-12	3	56	.278	.338	.494	135	20	2-1	.991	-7	69	102	1b91,O44L,D2	31	0.4
1976	Oak A	130	500	54	135	32	3	13	94	41-10	3	71	.270	.323	.424	124	15	6-1	.989	-4	95	64	O126(126/0/1),1b2,D2	0	0.4
1977	Cal A	64	242	48	64	13	2	13	53	22-4	4	48	.264	.333	.496	128	9	1-0	1.000	3	114	70	O61L,D3	99	0.9
1978	Cal A	133	497	58	127	27	1	17	79	28-4	2	82	.256	.295	.416	102	-1	2-1	.992	2	105	57	O111L,D11,1b10	0	-0.5
1979	Cal A	90	330	35	80	11	3	11	61	24-3	1	61	.242	.294	.394	87	-8	0-0	.989	2	106	85	O80(69/0/12),1b5,D3	43	-0.9
1980	Cal A	104	372	42	88	17	1	16	53	17-2	5	84	.237	.277	.417	89	-7	1-0	.991	5	115	74	O90(89/0/1),1b6,D3	47	-0.6
1981	Bos A	49	122	14	22	3	0	6	24	8-1	2	29	.180	.239	.352	65	-6	0-0	1.000	-1	30	44	D21,1b5/rf	0	-0.8
1982	Oak A	71	193	21	41	6	1	5	18	24-0	1	35	.212	.301	.332	77	-6	0-0	.991	-5	65	90	1b49,O14(4/0/10),D3	0	-1.5
Total	16	1547	5556	684	1468	287	39	179	810	369-59	35	870	.264	.311	.427	112	67	25-15	.991	-16	101	74	O1195(1160/2/47),1b249,D51/3	418	-3.1
RUDOLPH, DUTCH	John Herman; B7.10.1882 Natrona PA; D4.17.1967 Natrona PA; BL/TL/5´10˝/160; d7.3																								
1903	Phi N	1	1	0	0	0	0	0	0	0	0	—	.000	.000	.000	-99	0	0	ø	0	—	—	/H	—	0.0
1904	Chi N	2	3	0	1	0	0	0	0	0	0	—	.333	.333	.333	106	0	0	1.000	-0	0	0	O2R	—	0.0
Total	2	3	4	0	1	0	0	0	0	0	0	—	.250	.250	.250	52	0	0	1.000	-0	0	0	O2R	—	0.0
RUDOLPH, KEN	Kenneth Victor; B12.29.1946 Rockford IL; BR/TR/6´1˝/(180–190); [ChiN65 2/26]; d4.20; Col Los Angeles (CA) City																								
1969	Chi N	27	34	7	7	1	0	1	6	6-0	0	11	.206	.325	.324	73	-1	0-0	.977	-1	99	0	C11,O3L	0	-0.2
1970	Chi N	20	40	1	4	1	0	0	2	1-1	0	12	.100	.122	.125	-30	-7	0-0	1.000	2	294	172	C16	0	-0.5
1971	Chi N	25	76	5	15	3	0	0	7	6-0	1	20	.197	.265	.237	38	-6	0-0	1.000	7	371	219	C25	0	0.2
1972	Chi N	42	106	10	25	1	1	2	9	6-0	1	14	.236	.283	.321	64	-5	1-2	.966	3	125	157	C41	0	-0.1
1973	Chi N	64	170	12	35	8	1	2	17	7-0	1	25	.206	.239	.300	46	-13	1-4	.970	-5	89	148	C64	15	-1.8
1974	SF N	57	158	11	41	3	0	0	10	21-5	1	15	.259	.350	.278	74	-5	0-0	.996	-1	91	69	C56	0	-0.3
1975	StL N	44	80	5	16	2	0	1	6	3-0	0	10	.200	.229	.262	35	-7	0-0	.972	-1	77	116	C31	0	-0.8
1976	StL N	27	50	1	8	3	0	0	5	1-0	0	7	.160	.176	.220	12	-6	0-0	.940	0	103	111	C14	0	-0.6
1977	SF N	11	15	1	3	0	0	0	0	1-1	0	3	.200	.250	.200	22	-2	0-0	.946	2	214	131	C11	0	0.0
	Bal A	11	14	2	4	1	0	0	2	0-0	0	4	.286	.286	.357	78	0	0-0	1.000	3	67	138	C11	0	0.2
Total	9	328	743	55	158	23	2	6	64	52-7	4	121	.213	.267	.273	48	-52	2-6	.980	9	140	130	C280,O3L	15	-3.9
RUEL, MUDDY	Herold Dominic; B2.20.1896 St.Louis MO; D11.13.1963 Palo Alto CA; BR/TR/5´9˝/150; d5.29; Mil 1918; M1/C14																								
1915	StL A	10	14	0	0	0	0	0	1	5	0	5	.000	.263	.000	-22	-2	0	.958	-1	*89*	*61*	C6	—	-0.3
1917	NY A	6	17	1	2	0	0	0	1	2	0	2	.118	.211	.118	0	-2	1	1.000	0	*130*	*96*	C6	—	-0.2
1918	NY A	3	6	0	2	0	0	0	0	2	0	1	.333	.500	.333	148	1	1	1.000	0	*176*	*71*	C2	—	0.1
1919	NY A	79	233	18	56	6	0	0	31	34	1	26	.240	.340	.266	71	-7	4	.975	-1	*110*	*98*	C79	—	-0.2
1920	NY A	82	261	30	70	14	1	1	15	15	1	18	.268	.310	.341	70	-11	4-2	.984	3	*114*	*66*	C80	—	-0.2
1921	Bos A	113	358	41	99	21	1	1	45	41	1	15	.277	.352	.349	82	-8	2-7	.977	-2	*111*	*95*	C109	—	-0.5
1922	Bos A	116	361	34	92	15	1	0	28	41	1	26	.255	.333	.302	67	-16	4-2	.978	-1	*86*	*84*	C112	—	-1.0
1923	Was A	136	449	63	142	24	3	0	54	55	3	21	.316	.394	.383	111	10	4-6	.980	15	*102*	*123*	C133	—	3.1
1924	†Was A	149	501	50	142	20	2	0	57	62	7	20	.283	.370	.331	84	-9	7-11	.980	21	***147***	*77*	C147	—	1.9
1925	†Was A	127	393	55	122	9	2	0	54	63	4	16	.310	.411	.344	95	1	4-5	.982	15	*109*	*97*	C126/1	—	2.1
1926	Was A	117	368	42	110	22	4	1	53	61	2	14	.299	.401	.389	109	8	7-6	**.989**	1	*98*	*93*	C117	—	1.6
1927	Was A	131	428	61	132	16	5	1	52	63	5	18	.308	.403	.376	104	6	9-6	.988	1	*109*	*87*	C128	—	1.4
1928	Was A	108	350	31	90	18	2	0	55	44	1	14	.257	.342	.320	75	-11	12-10	**.989**	8	***120***	*94*	C101,1b2	—	0.3
1929	Was A	69	188	16	46	4	2	0	20	31	0	7	.245	.352	.287	66	-9	0-5	.990	7	*123*	*140*	C62	—	0.1
1930	Was A	66	198	18	50	3	4	0	26	24	3	13	.253	.342	.308	66	-10	1-0	.986	5	*128*	*115*	C60	—	-0.1
1931	Bos A	33	83	6	25	5	0	0	6	9	0	6	.301	.370	.361	98	0	0-0	.945	0	*122*	*106*	C30	—	0.2
	Det A	14	50	1	6	1	0	0	3	5	0	1	.120	.200	.140	-9	-8	0-0	.975	1	*78*	*173*	C14	—	-0.5
	Year	47	133	7	31	6	0	0	9	14	0	7	.233	.306	.278	56	-8	0-0	.958	1	*106*	*131*	C44	—	-0.3
1932	Det A	51	136	10	32	4	2	0	18	17	0	6	.235	.320	.294	58	-8	1-0	.989	-1	*88*	*107*	C49	—	-0.6
1933	StL A	36	63	13	12	2	0	0	8	24	0	4	.190	.414	.222	68	-1	0-0	1.000	3	*118*	*154*	C28	—	0.3
1934	Chi A	22	57	4	12	3	0	0	7	8	0	5	.211	.308	.263	47	-4	0-0	.976	-2	*60*	*90*	C21	—	-0.5
Total	19	1468	4514	494	1242	187	29	4	534	606	29	238	.275	.365	.332	84	-80	61-60	.982	72	*111*	*97*	C1410,1b3	—	7.0

RUETHER, DUTCH Walter Henry; B9.13.1893 Alameda CA; D5.16.1970 Phoenix AZ; BL/TL/6´1.5˝/180; d4.13; Mil 1918; ▲

YEAR	TM LG	G	AB	R	H	2B	3B	HR	RBI	BB-IB	HP	SO	AVG	OBP	SLG	AOPS	ABR	SB-CS	FA	FR	RNG	THR	GAMES AT POSITION	DL	BFW
1917	Chi N	31	44	3	12	1	3	0	11	8	0	11	.273	.385	.432	139	2	0	1.000	1	108	297	P10,1b5	—	0.1
	Cin N	19	24	1	5	2	0	0	1	3	0	6	.208	.296	.292	84	2	1	.833	-0	98	0	P7	—	0.0
	Year	50	68	4	17	3	3	0	12	11	0	17	.250	.354	.382	122	2	1	.920	0	103	149	P17,1b5	—	0.1
1918	Cin N	2	3	0	0	0	0	0	0	0	0	2	.000	.000	.000	-99	0	0	1.000	-0	69	0	P2	—	0.0
1919	†Cin N	42	92	8	24	2	3	0	6	4	0	18	.261	.292	.348	94	5	1	.971	-3	82	57	P33	—	0.0
1920	Cin N	45	104	3	20	4	0	0	10	5	0	24	.192	.229	.231	33	-9	0-0	.952	0	102	227	P37/1	—	0.0
1921	Bro N	49	97	12	34	5	2	2	13	4	0	9	.351	.376	.505	127	11	1-0	.966	-1	93	126	P36	—	0.0
1922	Bro N	67	125	12	26	6	1	2	20	12	1	11	.208	.283	.320	56	6	0-0	**1.000**	-0	90	227	P35	—	0.0
1923	Bro N	49	117	6	32	1	0	0	10	12	0	12	.274	.341	.282	68	-5	0-0	.968	-2	82	143	P34/1	—	-0.1
1924	Bro N	34	62	5	15	1	1	0	4	5	0	2	.242	.299	.290	60	2	0-0	.981	1	112	154	P30	—	0.0
1925	†Was A	55	108	18	36	3	2	1	15	10	0	8	.333	.390	.426	109	1	0-1	.962	-3	83	40	P30/1	—	-0.1
1926	Was A	47	92	6	23	2	0	1	11	6	0	10	.250	.296	.304	58	4	0-0	.974	-2	84	86	P23	—	0.0
	†NY A	13	21	2	2	0	0	0	0	0	1	1	.095	.136	.095	-39	-2	0-0	.875	-1	55	0	P5	—	0.0
	Year	60	113	8	25	2	0	1	11	6	1	11	.221	.267	.265	40	2	0-0	.957	-3	79	71	P28	—	0.0
1927	NY A	35	80	7	21	3	0	1	10	8	0	15	.262	.330	.338	76	5	0-0	**1.000**	0	104	103	P27	—	0.0
Total	11	488	969	83	250	30	12	7	111	77	2	129	.258	.314	.335	76	22	3-1	.970	-9	91	132	P309,1b8	—	-0.1

RUFER, RUDY Rudolph Joseph; B10.28.1926 Ridgewood NY; BR/TR/6´0.5˝/165; d9.22; Col Oklahoma

YEAR	TM LG	G	AB	R	H	2B	3B	HR	RBI	BB-IB	HP	SO	AVG	OBP	SLG	AOPS	ABR	SB-CS	FA	FR	RNG	THR	GAMES AT POSITION	DL	BFW
1949	NY N	7	15	1	1	0	0	0	2	2	0	0	.067	.176	.067	-32	-3	0	.957	-0	94	79	S7	0	-0.3
1950	NY N	15	11	1	1	0	0	0	0	0	0	1	.091	.091	.091	-52	-2	1	.889	1	165	120	S8	0	-0.2
Total	2	22	26	2	2	0	0	0	2	2	0	1	.077	.143	.077	-40	-5	1	.938	0	111	89	S15	0	-0.5

RUFFING, RED Charles Herbert; B5.3.1905 Granville IL; D2.17.1986 Mayfield Hts. OH; BR/TR/6´1.5˝/205; d5.31; Mil 1943–44; C1; HF1967; ▲

YEAR	TM LG	G	AB	R	H	2B	3B	HR	RBI	BB-IB	HP	SO	AVG	OBP	SLG	AOPS	ABR	SB-CS	FA	FR	RNG	THR	GAMES AT POSITION	DL	BFW
1924	Bos A	8	7	0	1	0	1	0	0	0	0	1	.143	.143	.429	44	0	0-0	1.000	-1	56	0	P8	—	0.0
1925	Bos A	37	79	6	17	4	2	0	11	1	1	22	.215	.235	.316	39	0	0-0	.983	-1	92	111	P37	—	0.0
1926	Bos A	37	51	8	10	1	0	1	5	2	0	12	.196	.226	.275	31	1	0-1	.978	-1	81	88	P37	—	0.0
1927	Bos A	29	55	5	14	3	1	0	4	0	1	6	.255	.268	.345	59	2	0-0	.978	0	93	49	P26	—	0.0
1928	Bos A	60	121	12	38	13	1	2	19	3	0	12	.314	.331	.488	115	13	0-0	.951	-3	78	102	P42	—	0.0
1929	Bos A	60	114	9	35	9	0	2	17	2	1	13	.307	.325	.439	97	-1	0-0	.946	-1	88	36	P35,O2L	—	-0.1
1930	Bos A	6	11	2	3	2	0	0	1	0	0	1	.273	.273	.455	84	1	0-0	.667	-1	41	0	P4	—	0.0
	NY A	52	99	15	37	6	2	4	21	7	0	7	.374	.415	.596	160	17	0-0	.938	-3	67	0	P34	—	0.0
	Year	58	110	17	40	8	2	4	22	7	0	8	.364	.402	.582	153	17	0-0	.914	-3	64	0	P38	—	0.0
1931	NY A	48	109	14	36	8	1	3	12	1	0	13	.330	.336	.505	125	3	0-0	**1.000**	-3	66	42	P37/rf	—	-0.1
1932	†NY A	55	124	20	38	6	1	3	19	6	0	10	.306	.338	.444	106	13	0-0	.955	-2	72	133	P35	—	0.0
1933	NY A	55	115	10	29	3	1	2	13	7	0	15	.252	.295	.348	74	8	0-0	.964	-0	89	178	P35	—	0.0
1934	NY A★	45	113	11	28	3	0	2	13	3	1	17	.248	.274	.327	58	6	0-0	.933	-3	63	83	P36	—	0.0
1935	NY A	50	109	13	37	10	0	2	18	3	1	9	.339	.363	.486	125	13	0-0	**1.000**	-2	59	144	P30	—	0.0
1936	†NY A	53	127	14	37	5	0	5	22	11	0	12	.291	.348	.449	99	15	0-0	.986	2	113	222	P33	—	0.0
1937	†NY A	54	129	11	26	3	0	1	10	13	0	24	.202	.275	.248	32	2	0-0	.974	-4	58	91	P31	—	0.0
1938	†NY A☆	45	107	12	24	4	1	3	17	17	0	21	.224	.331	.364	74	9	0-0	**1.000**	-2	73	72	P31	—	0.0
1939	†NY A★	44	114	12	35	1	0	1	20	7	0	18	.307	.347	.342	78	8	1-0	.952	-2	81	83	P28	—	0.0
1940	NY A★	33	89	8	11	4	0	1	7	3	0	9	.124	.152	.202	-9	-3	0-0	.947	-3	73	86	P30	—	0.0
1941	†NY A☆	38	89	10	27	8	1	2	22	4	0	12	.303	.333	.483	115	11	0-0	**1.000**	-3	62	130	P23	0	0.0
1942	†NY A☆	30	80	8	20	4	0	1	13	5	1	13	.250	.302	.338	81	6	0-0	.974	-2	77	191	P24	0	0.0
1945	NY A	21	46	4	10	0	1	1	5	0	0	8	.217	.217	.326	54	0	0-0	.929	-2	65	94	P11	0	0.0
1946	NY A	8	25	1	3	1	0	0	1	1	0	8	.120	.154	.160	-12	-1	0-0	1.000	-1	57	157	P8	73	0.0
1947	Chi A	14	24	2	5	0	0	0	3	1	0	3	.208	.240	.208	26	0	0-0	1.000	-1	82	174	P9	65	0.0
Total	22	882	1937	207	521	98	13	36	273	97	6	266	.269	.306	.389	81	123	1-1	.968	-37	76	104	P624,O3(2/0/1)	138	-0.2

RUIZ, CARLOS Carlos Joaquin; B1.22.1979 David, Pan; BR/TR/5´10˝/200; d5.6

YEAR	TM LG	G	AB	R	H	2B	3B	HR	RBI	BB-IB	HP	SO	AVG	OBP	SLG	AOPS	ABR	SB-CS	FA	FR	RNG	THR	GAMES AT POSITION	DL	BFW
2006	Phi N	27	69	5	18	1	1	3	10	5-2	1	8	.261	.316	.435	87	-2	0-0	.981	1	107	66	C24	0	0.1

RUIZ, CHICO Hiraldo (Sablon) (b (Hiraldo Sablon (Ruiz)); B12.5.1938 Santo Domingo, Cuba; D2.9.1972 San Diego CA; BB/TR/6´0˝/(168–175); d4.13; OF(11/0/3)

YEAR	TM LG	G	AB	R	H	2B	3B	HR	RBI	BB-IB	HP	SO	AVG	OBP	SLG	AOPS	ABR	SB-CS	FA	FR	RNG	THR	GAMES AT POSITION	DL	BFW
1964	Cin N	77	311	33	76	13	2	2	16	7-1	4	41	.244	.269	.318	63	-16	11-3	.942	-6	73	136	3b49,2b30	0	-2.0
1965	Cin N	29	18	7	2	1	0	0	1	0-0	0	5	.111	.111	.167	-21	-3	1-2	.875	-0	96	0	3b4,S3	39	-0.4
1966	Cin N	82	110	13	28	2	1	0	5	5-0	0	14	.255	.287	.291	56	-6	1-2	.927	-2	88	56	3b27,O8(7/0/1),S6	0	-0.9
1967	Cin N	105	250	32	55	12	4	0	13	11-0	2	35	.220	.258	.300	53	-15	9-4	.969	-2	100	90	2b56,3b13,S11,O5(3/0/2)	0	-1.3
1968	Cin N	85	139	15	36	2	1	0	9	12-0	0	18	.259	.316	.288	78	-4	4-3	.979	7	133	115	2b34,1b16,3b5,S3	0	0.6
1969	Cin N	88	196	19	48	4	1	0	13	14-3	0	28	.245	.292	.276	58	-11	4-2	.949	-6	99	115	2b39,S29,3b7,1b2/lf	0	-1.3
1970	Cal A	68	107	10	26	3	1	0	12	7-1	1	16	.243	.293	.290	64	-5	3-0	.985	-2	100	105	3b27,2b3,S3,1b2/C	0	-0.7
1971	Cal A	31	19	4	5	0	0	0	0	2-0	0	7	.263	.333	.263	76	-1	1-0	1.000	-2	45	0	3b3,2b2	0	-0.2
Total	8	565	1150	133	276	37	10	2	69	58-5	7	164	.240	.279	.295	60	-61	34-16	.966	-13	105	104	2b164,3b135,S55,1b20,O14L/C	39	-6.2

RUIZ, CHICO Manuel (Cruz); B11.1.1951 Santurce, PR; BR/TR/5´11.5˝/170; d7.29

YEAR	TM LG	G	AB	R	H	2B	3B	HR	RBI	BB-IB	HP	SO	AVG	OBP	SLG	AOPS	ABR	SB-CS	FA	FR	RNG	THR	GAMES AT POSITION	DL	BFW
1978	Atl N	18	46	3	13	3	0	0	2	2-1	0	4	.283	.313	.348	76	-1	0-0	.984	1	99	73	2b14/3	0	0.0
1980	Atl N	25	26	3	8	2	1	0	2	3-0	0	7	.308	.379	.462	132	1	0-1	.875	-0	146	0	3b16,S4,2b2	0	0.1
Total	2	43	72	6	21	5	1	0	4	5-1	0	11	.292	.338	.389	96	0	0-1	.880	0	133	0	3b17,2b16,S4	0	0.1

RULLO, JOE Joseph Vincent; B6.16.1916 New York NY; D10.28.1969 Philadelphia PA; BR/TR/5´11˝/168; d9.22

YEAR	TM LG	G	AB	R	H	2B	3B	HR	RBI	BB-IB	HP	SO	AVG	OBP	SLG	AOPS	ABR	SB-CS	FA	FR	RNG	THR	GAMES AT POSITION	DL	BFW
1943	Phi A	16	55	2	16	3	0	0	6	8	0	7	.291	.381	.345	114	1	0-0	.963	-1	111	89	2b16	0	0.2
1944	Phi A	35	96	5	16	0	0	0	5	6	1	19	.167	.223	.167	12	-11	1-0	.954	0	101	113	2b33/1cf	0	-1.0
Total	2	51	151	7	32	3	0	0	11	14	1	26	.212	.283	.232	50	-10	1-0	.957	-0	104	105	2b49/cf1	0	-0.8

RUMLER, WILLIAM William George; B3.27.1891 Milford NE; D5.26.1966 Lincoln NE; BR/TR/6´1˝/190; d5.4; Mil 1918

YEAR	TM LG	G	AB	R	H	2B	3B	HR	RBI	BB-IB	HP	SO	AVG	OBP	SLG	AOPS	ABR	SB-CS	FA	FR	RNG	THR	GAMES AT POSITION	DL	BFW
1914	StL A	34	46	2	8	1	0	0	6	3	1	12	.174	.240	.196	32	-4	2-2	1.000	-1	*81*	*118*	C10,O6R	—	-0.5
1916	StL A	27	37	6	12	3	0	0	10	3	0	7	.324	.375	.405	141	2	0	.971	0	83	61	C9	—	0.3
1917	StL A	78	88	7	23	3	4	1	16	8	0	9	.261	.323	.420	132	3	2	.938	1	97	194	O9(3/0/6)	—	0.3
Total	3	139	171	15	43	7	4	1	32	14	1	28	.251	.312	.357	107	1	4-2	.986	-0	*82*	*90*	C19,O15(3/0/12)	—	0.1

RUNGE, PAUL Paul William; B5.21.1958 Kingston NY; BR/TR/6´0˝/(165–175); [AtlN79 9/212]; d9.25; Col Jacksonville

YEAR	TM LG	G	AB	R	H	2B	3B	HR	RBI	BB-IB	HP	SO	AVG	OBP	SLG	AOPS	ABR	SB-CS	FA	FR	RNG	THR	GAMES AT POSITION	DL	BFW
1981	Atl N	10	27	2	7	1	0	0	2	4-0	0	4	.259	.355	.296	86	0	0-0	.911	-2	95	91	S10	0	-0.1
1982	Atl N	4	2	0	0	0	0	0	0	0-0	0	0	.000	.000	.000	-98	-1	0-0	ø	0	—	—	/H	0	-0.1
1983	Atl N	5	8	0	2	0	0	0	1	1-0	0	4	.250	.333	.250	60	0	0-0	1.000	-1	48	76	2b2	0	-0.2
1984	Atl N	28	90	5	24	3	1	0	3	10-0	0	14	.267	.340	.322	81	-2	5-3	.970	7	125	115	2b22,S7,3b3	0	0.7
1985	Atl N	50	87	15	19	3	0	1	5	18-0	0	18	.218	.349	.287	76	-2	0-1	.929	2	133	72	3b28,S5,2b2	0	0.0
1986	Atl N	7	8	1	2	0	0	0	0	2-0	0	4	.250	.400	.250	80	0	0-0	1.000	-0	114	0	2b5	0	0.0
1987	Atl N	27	47	9	10	1	0	3	8	5-0	0	10	.213	.288	.426	83	-1	0-1	.923	-1	94	205	3b10,S9,2b2	0	-0.2
1988	Atl N	52	76	11	16	5	0	0	7	14-0	0	21	.211	.330	.276	74	-2	0-0	1.000	-6	84	89	3b19,2b7,S6	0	-0.8
Total	8	183	345	43	80	13	1	4	26	54-0	0	75	.232	.334	.310	78	-8	5-5	.941	-2	111	101	3b60,2b40,S37	0	-0.7

RUNNELLS, TOM Thomas William; B4.17.1955 Greeley CO; BB/TR/6´0˝/175; d8.10; M2/C2; Col Northern Colorado

YEAR	TM LG	G	AB	R	H	2B	3B	HR	RBI	BB-IB	HP	SO	AVG	OBP	SLG	AOPS	ABR	SB-CS	FA	FR	RNG	THR	GAMES AT POSITION	DL	BFW
1985	Cin N	28	35	3	7	1	0	0	0	3-0	0	4	.200	.263	.229	37	-3	0-0	1.000	-1	95	103	S11/2	0	-0.3
1986	Cin N	12	11	1	1	1	0	0	0	0-0	0	2	.091	.091	.182	-26	-2	0-0	1.000	0	165	160	2b4,3b3	0	-0.2
Total	2	40	46	4	8	2	0	0	0	3-0	0	6	.174	.224	.217	23	-5	0-0	1.000	-1	95	103	S11,2b5,3b3	0	-0.5

RUNNELS, PETE James Edward (b James Edward Runnells); B1.28.1928 Lufkin TX; D5.20.1991 Pasadena TX; BL/TR/6´0˝/170; d7.1; M1/C2

YEAR	TM LG	G	AB	R	H	2B	3B	HR	RBI	BB-IB	HP	SO	AVG	OBP	SLG	AOPS	ABR	SB-CS	FA	FR	RNG	THR	GAMES AT POSITION	DL	BFW
1951	Was A	78	273	31	76	12	2	0	25	31	1	24	.278	.354	.337	89	-3	0-3	.949	-15	86	77	S73	0	-1.5
1952	Was A	152	555	70	158	18	3	1	64	72	1	55	.285	.368	.333	99	2	0-10	.966	-13	95	100	S147/2	0	-0.5
1953	Was A	137	486	64	125	15	5	2	50	64	3	36	.257	.347	.321	83	-10	3-4	.958	-20	90	122	S121,2b11	0	-2.1
1954	Was A	139	488	75	131	17	15	3	56	78	0	60	.268	.368	.383	112	9	2-3	.953	-17	95	97	S107,2b27/lf	0	0.3
1955	Was A	134	503	66	143	16	4	2	49	55-2	1	51	.284	.353	.344	94	-4	3-9	.976	4	103	97	2b132,S2	0	0.7
1956	Was A	147	578	72	179	29	9	8	76	58-2	2	64	.310	.372	.433	113	11	5-5	.995	3	103	88	1b81,2b69,S3	0	1.3
1957	Was A	134	473	53	109	18	4	2	35	55-5	2	51	.230	.310	.298	69	-20	2-3	.995	1	100	84	1b72,3b32,2b23	0	-2.3
1958	Bos A	147	568	103	183	32	5	8	59	87-0	6	49	.322	.416	.438	127	27	1-2	.985	8	**111**	101	2b106,1b42	0	4.1
1959	Bos A★	147	560	95	176	33	6	6	57	95-1	1	48	.314	.415	.427	126	25	6-5	.982	9	99	113	2b101,1b44,S9	0	**3.9**
1960	Bos A★	143	528	80	169	29	2	2	35	71-2	2	51	**.320**	.401	.394	112	13	5-2	**.986**	14	107	103	2b129,1b57,3b3	0	3.5

YEAR	TM LG	G	AB	R	H	2B	3B	HR	RBI	BB-IB	HP	SO	AVG	OBP	SLG	AOPS	ABR	SB-CS	FA	FR	RNG	THR	GAMES AT POSITION	DL	BFW
1961	Bos A	143	360	49	114	20	3	3	38	46-2	3	32	.317	.396	.414	115	10	5-1	**.995**	0	78	120	1b113,3b11,2b7/S	0	0.6
1962	Bos A★	152	562	80	183	33	5	10	60	79-11	3	57	**.326**	.408	.456	129	27	3-4	.993	-3	89	95	1b151	0	1.3
1963	Hou N	124	388	35	98	9	1	2	23	45-2	3	42	.253	.332	.296	89	-4	2-0	.993	-11	88	66	1b70,2b36,3b3	0	-1.8
1964	Hou N	22	51	3	10	1	0	0	3	8-1	0	7	.196	.305	.216	53	-3	0-0	.986	-2	53	82	1b14	0	-0.6
Total	14	1799	6373	876	1854	282	64	49	630	844-28	28	627	.291	.375	.378	106	80	37-51	.994	-41	89	96	1b644,2b642,S463,3b49/lf	0	6.9
RUSHFORD, JIM	James Thomas; B3.24.1974 Chicago IL; BL/TL/6´1˝/225; d9.3; Col San Diego St.																								
2002	Mil N	23	77	8	11	2	0	1	6	6-0	1	9	.143	.214	.208	12	-10	0-0	.956	-1	105	0	O22(1/0/21)	0	-1.2
RUSS, JOHN	John; B4.1.1858 Cannelton IN; D1.18.1912 Louisville KY; d7.4																								
1882	Bal AA	1	3	0	1	0	0	0	—	0	—	—	.333	.333	.333	136	0	—	ø	-0	0	0	/cfP	—	0.0
RUSSELL, REB	Ewell Albert; B3.12.1889 Jackson MS; D9.30.1973 Indianapolis IN; BL/TL/5´11˝/185; d4.18; ▲																								
1913	Chi A	54	106	9	20	5	3	1	7	1	1	29	.189	.204	.321	54	3	0	.953	-5	76	108	P52	—	0.0
1914	Chi A	46	64	6	17	1	1	0	7	1	0	14	.266	.277	.313	78	3	0	.946	0	104	0	P38	—	0.0
1915	Chi A	45	86	11	21	2	3	0	7	4	2	14	.244	.293	.337	86	4	1	.971	-2	83	48	P41	—	0.0
1916	Chi A	56	91	9	13	2	0	0	6	0	1	18	.143	.152	.165	-5	-4	1	.974	-2	95	75	P56	—	0.0
1917	†Chi A	39	68	4	19	3	3	0	9	2	0	10	.279	.300	.412	115	0	0	.984	-1	93	110	P35/lf	—	0.0
1918	Chi A	27	50	2	7	3	0	0	3	0	1	6	.140	.157	.200	8	-6	0	1.000	-1	83	75	P19/rf	—	-0.1
1919	Chi A	1	0	0	0	0	0	0	0	0	0	0	ø	ø	ø	ø	0	0	ø	0	0	0	/P	—	0.0
1922	Pit N	60	220	51	81	14	8	12	75	14	7	18	.368	.423	.668	175	23	4-2	.968	-1	101	68	O60R	—	1.6
1923	Pit N	94	291	49	84	18	7	9	58	20	3	21	.289	.341	.491	115	5	3-1	.970	-0	110	50	O76(4/0/72)	—	-0.1
Total	9	422	976	141	262	48	25	22	172	42	15	130	.268	.309	.436	104	28	9-3	.968	-12	88	74	P242,O138(5/0/133)	—	1.4
RUSSELL, RIP	Glen David; B1.26.1915 Los Angeles CA; D9.26.1976 Los Alamitos CA; BR/TR/6´1˝/180; d5.5																								
1939	Chi N	143	542	55	148	24	5	9	79	36	0	56	.273	.318	.386	87	-11	2	.988	-5	87	85	1b143	—	-3.0
1940	Chi N	68	215	15	53	7	2	5	33	8	1	23	.247	.277	.367	78	-8	1	.982	-6	59	55	1b51,3b3	—	-1.9
1941	Chi N	6	17	1	5	1	0	0	1	1	0	5	.294	.333	.353	97	0	0	.975	0	119	118	1b5	0	0.0
1942	Chi N	102	302	32	73	9	0	8	41	17	0	21	.242	.282	.351	88	-6	0	.974	-9	60	107	1b35,2b24,3b10,O3L	0	-1.8
1946	†Bos A	80	274	22	57	10	1	6	35	13	1	30	.208	.247	.318	54	-18	1-1	.942	-0	99	172	3b70,2b3	0	-2.0
1947	Bos A	26	52	8	8	1	0	1	3	8	0	7	.154	.267	.231	36	-4	0-0	.923	1	121	90	3b13	0	-0.4
Total	6	425	1402	133	344	52	8	29	192	83	2	142	.245	.289	.356	77	-47	4-1	.984	-19	78	82	1b234,3b96,2b27,O3L	0	-9.1
RUSSELL, HARVEY	Harvey Holmes; B1.10.1887 Marshall VA; D1.8.1980 Alexandria VA; BL/TR/5´9.5˝/163; d4.17																								
1914	Bal F	81	168	18	39	3	2	0	13	18	1	17	.232	.310	.274	58	-12	2	.956	-10	*99*	*76*	C47/SO(1/1/0)	—	-2.0
1915	Bal F	53	73	5	19	1	2	0	11	14	4	5	.260	.407	.329	105	1	1	.989	-2	*101*	*85*	C21	—	0.0
Total	2	134	241	23	58	4	4	0	24	32	5	22	.241	.342	.290	73	-11	3	.965	-12	*100*	*79*	C68/O(1/1/0)S	—	-2.0
RUSSELL, JIM	James William; B10.1.1918 Fayette City PA; D11.24.1987 Orlando FL; BB/TR/6´1˝/181; d9.12																								
1942	Pit N	5	14	2	1	0	0	0	0	1	0	4	.071	.133	.071	-38	-2	0	1.000	0	129	0	O3C	0	-0.3
1943	Pit N	146	533	79	138	19	11	4	44	77	1	67	.259	.354	.358	102	3	12	.990	4	101	124	O134(133/2/2),1b6	0	-0.1
1944	Pit N	152	580	109	181	34	14	8	66	79	5	63	.312	.399	.460	136	30	6	.986	9	102	164	O149(139/6/4)	0	3.1
1945	Pit N	146	510	88	145	24	8	12	77	71	5	40	.284	.377	.433	120	15	15	.973	5	109	93	O140(139/1/0)	0	1.2
1946	Pit N	146	516	68	143	29	6	8	50	67	2	54	.277	.362	.403	114	11	11	.966	-7	98	58	O134(67/68/0),1b5	0	-0.3
1947	Pit N	128	478	68	121	21	8	8	51	63	2	58	.253	.343	.381	89	-7	7	.980	3	109	67	O119(1/102/19)	0	-0.7
1948	Bos N	89	322	44	85	18	1	9	54	46	3	31	.264	.361	.410	110	6	4	.992	-2	103	46	O84(2/82/0)	0	0.2
1949	Bos N	130	415	57	96	22	1	8	54	64	2	68	.231	.337	.347	88	-5	3	.975	-8	93	36	O120(30/93/0)	0	-1.8
1950	Bro N	77	214	37	49	8	2	10	32	31	1	36	.229	.329	.425	95	-2	1	.993	4	119	80	O55(53/3/0)	0	-0.1
1951	Bro N	16	13	2	0	0	0	0	0	4	1	6	.000	.278	.000	-18	-2	0-0	1.000	-0	96	0	O4L	0	-0.2
Total	10	1035	3595	554	959	175	51	67	428	503	22	427	.267	.360	.400	108	47	59-0	.981	8	103	88	O942(568/360/25),1b11	0	1.0
RUSSELL, JOHN	John William; B1.5.1961 Oklahoma City OK; BR/TR/6´0˝/(190–200); [PhiN82 1/13]; d6.22; C3; Col Oklahoma; OF(88/0/36)																								
1984	Phi N	39	99	11	28	8	1	2	11	12-2	0	33	.283	.351	.444	123	3	0-1	1.000	-1	100	53	O29(14/0/18),C2	0	0.1
1985	Phi N	81	216	22	47	12	0	9	23	18-0	0	72	.218	.278	.398	85	-5	2-0	1.000	-5	72	131	O49L,1b18	0	-1.3
1986	Phi N	93	315	35	76	21	2	13	60	25-2	3	103	.241	.300	.444	100	-1	0-1	.976	-11	67	98	C89	0	-0.8
1987	Phi N	24	62	5	9	1	0	3	8	3-0	0	17	.145	.185	.306	26	-7	0-1	.955	-3	114	153	O10L,C7	0	-1.0
1988	Phi N	22	49	5	12	1	0	2	4	3-0	1	15	.245	.302	.388	94	0	0-0	.945	1	49	161	C15	0	0.1
1989	Atl N	74	159	14	29	2	0	2	9	8-1	1	53	.182	.225	.233	31	-15	0-0	.990	-1	122	153	C45,O14(1/0/15),1b2,3b2/P	0	-1.6
1990	Tex A	68	128	16	35	4	0	2	8	11-2	0	41	.273	.331	.352	91	-2	1-0	.980	-1	49	30	C31,D19,O6L,1b3/3	0	-0.2
1991	Tex A	22	27	3	3	0	0	0	1	1-0	0	7	.111	.138	.111	-29	-5	0-0	1.000	-1	68	0	O8(6/0/2),C5,D5	70	-0.6
1992	Tex A	7	10	1	1	0	0	0	2	1-0	1	4	.100	.231	.100	2	-1	0-0	1.000	-1	54	243	C4,O2(1/0/1)/D	102	-0.2
1993	Tex A	18	22	1	5	1	0	1	3	2-0	0	10	.227	.292	.409	89	0	0-0	1.000	-2	252	71	C11/13lf	0	-0.2
Total	10	448	1087	113	245	50	3	34	129	84-7	6	355	.225	.282	.371	79	-33	3-3	.979	-24	80	101	C209,O119L,D25,1b24,3b4/P	172	-5.7
RUSSELL, LLOYD	Lloyd Opal; B4.10.1913 Atoka OK; D5.24.1968 Waco TX; BR/TR/5´11˝/166; d4.26; Col Baylor																								
1938	Cle A	2	0	0	0	0	0	0	0	0	0	0	ø	ø	ø	ø	0	0-0	ø	0	—	—	/R	—	0.0
RUSSELL, PAUL	Paul A. (b Benjamin Paul Sheeder); B3.23.1871 Reading PA; D10.8.1957 Norristown PA; d7.29																								
1894	StL N	3	10	1	1	0	0	0	0	0	0	2	.100	.100	.100	-52	-3	0	1.000	-0	513	0	/cf32	—	-0.2
RUSSELL, BILL	William Ellis; B10.21.1948 Pittsburg KS; BR/TR (BB 1971)/6´0˝/(170–187); [LAN66 9/179]; d4.7; M3/C9																								
1969	LA N	98	212	35	48	6	2	5	15	22-1	1	45	.226	.301	.344	86	-4	4-1	.978	5	121	101	O86(7/24/62)	0	-0.2
1970	LA N	81	278	30	72	11	9	0	28	16-1	3	28	.259	.303	.363	82	-9	9-1	.983	7	115	169	O79(2/23/57)/S	0	-0.4
1971	LA N	91	211	29	48	7	4	2	15	11-2	0	39	.227	.265	.327	71	-9	6-3	.964	-0	108	94	2b41,O40(3/8/35),S6	0	-0.8
1972	LA N	129	434	47	118	19	5	4	34	34-9	2	64	.272	.326	.366	98	-1	14-7	.949	10	109	104	S121,O6(1/1/4)	0	2.5
1973	LA N★	**162**	615	55	163	26	3	4	56	34-20	1	63	.265	.301	.337	80	-18	15-7	.963	-1	101	**118**	S162	0	0.2
1974	†LA N	160	553	61	149	18	6	5	65	53-**25**	4	53	.269	.336	.351	96	-3	14-5	.946	-17	97	84	S160/rf	0	0.0
1975	LA N	84	252	24	52	9	2	0	14	23-6	2	28	.206	.277	.258	51	-17	5-0	.967	-14	93	70	S83	73	-2.1
1976	LA N★	149	554	53	152	17	3	5	65	21-9	3	46	.274	.301	.343	84	-13	15-5	.963	-9	98	108	S149	0	-0.4
1977	†LA N	153	634	84	176	28	6	4	51	24-1	2	43	.278	.304	.360	77	-22	16-7	.963	17	108	**130**	S153	0	1.2
1978	†LA N	155	625	72	179	32	4	3	46	30-8	2	34	.286	.320	.365	91	-8	10-6	.962	21	111	113	S155	0	3.0
1979	LA N	153	627	72	170	26	4	7	56	24-2	1	43	.271	.297	.359	80	-19	6-9	.957	-15	98	79	S150	0	-2.1
1980	LA N★	130	466	38	123	23	2	3	34	18-0	3	44	.264	.295	.341	79	-14	13-2	.968	-11	97	84	S129	0	-1.0
1981	†LA N	82	262	20	61	9	2	0	22	19-3	1	20	.233	.284	.282	65	-12	2-1	.965	8	105	115	S80	0	0.4
1982	LA N	153	497	64	136	20	2	3	46	63-11	4	30	.274	.357	.340	100	2	10-2	.961	-2	104	82	S150	0	1.8
1983	†LA N	131	451	47	111	13	1	1	30	33-4	4	31	.246	.302	.286	64	-22	13-9	.964	9	104	90	S127	0	-0.1
1984	LA N	89	262	25	70	12	1	0	19	25-1	0	24	.267	.329	.321	84	-5	4-4	.965	-3	96	91	S65,O18C,2b5	36	-0.3
1985	LA N	76	169	19	44	6	1	0	13	18-1	1	9	.260	.333	.308	83	-3	4-0	.919	-3	103	104	S23,O21L,2b8,3b5	0	-0.4
1986	LA N	105	216	21	54	11	0	0	18	15-2	2	23	.250	.302	.301	72	-8	7-0	1.000	2	101	111	O48(28/1/20),S32,2b8/3	0	-0.3
Total	18	2181	7318	796	1926	293	57	46	627	483-106	36	667	.263	.310	.338	82	-185	167-69	.960	4	102	99	S1746,O299(62/75/179),2b62,3b6	109	1.0
RUSZKOWSKI, HANK	Henry Alexander; B11.10.1925 Cleveland OH; D5.31.2000 Cleveland OH; BR/TR/6´0˝/190; d9.26; Mil 1945–46; Col Dayton																								
1944	Cle A	3	8	1	3	0	0	0	1	0	0	1	.375	.375	.375	119	0	0-0	1.000	-0	*75*	*222*	C2	0	0.0
1945	Cle A	14	49	2	10	0	0	0	5	4	0	9	.204	.264	.204	38	-4	0-0	.975	2	*95*	*158*	C14	0	-0.1
1947	Cle A	23	27	5	7	2	0	3	4	2	0	6	.259	.310	.667	172	2	0-0	1.000	-1	*167*	*213*	C16	0	0.2
Total	3	40	84	8	20	2	0	3	10	6	0	16	.238	.289	.369	91	-2	0-0	.981	1	*111*	*176*	C32	0	0.1
RUTH, BABE	George Herman "The Bambino","The Sultan of Swat"; B2.6.1895 Baltimore MD; D8.16.1948 New York NY; BL/TL/6´2˝/215; d7.11; C1; HF1936; ▲																								
1914	Bos A	5	10	1	2	1	0	0	2	0	0	4	.200	.200	.300	50	0	0	1.000	-0	106	0	P4	—	0.0
1915	†Bos A	42	92	16	29	10	1	4	21	9	0	23	.315	.376	.576	191	16	0	.976	1	98	148	P32	—	0.0
1916	†Bos A	67	136	18	37	5	3	3	15	10	0	23	.272	.322	.419	122	13	0	.973	1	90	172	P44	—	0.0
1917	Bos A	52	123	14	40	6	3	2	12	12	0	18	.325	.385	.472	163	17	0	.984	2	107	131	P41	—	0.0
1918	†Bos A	95	317	50	95	26	11	**11**	66	58	2	58	.300	.411	**.555**	195	38	6	.949	0	92	95	O59(47/12/0),P20,1b13	—	2.7
1919	Bos A	130	432	**103**	139	34	12	**29**	**114**	101	6	58	.322	**.456**	**.657**	**224**	**76**	7	**.996**	10	111	137	O111L,P17,1b5	—	**7.3**
1920	NY A	142	458	**158**	172	36	9	**54**	**137**	**150**	3	80	.376	**.532**	**.847**	**252**	**110**	14-14	.936	-2	96	114	O141(36/20/85),1b2/P	—	**9.3**
1921	†NY A	152	540	**177**	204	44	16	**59**	**171**	**145**	4	81	.378	**.512**	**.846**	**236**	**118**	17-13	.966	-0	100	87	O152(134/18/0),P2,1b2	—	**9.4**

YEAR	TM LG	G	AB	R	H	2B	3B	HR	RBI	BB-IB	HP	SO	AVG	OBP	SLG	AOPS	ABR	SB-CS	FA	FR	RNG	THR	GAMES AT POSITION	DL	BFW
1922	†NY A	110	406	94	128	24	8	35	99	84	1	80	.315	.434	**.672**	**181**	49	2-5	.964	-2	96	99	O110(71/0/40)/1	—	3.5
1923	†NY A	**152**	522	**151**	205	45	13	**41**	**131**	**170**	4	93	.393	**.545**	**.764**	**238**	**119**	17-21	.973	6	110	95	O148(68/7/73),1b4	—	**10.1**
1924	NY A	**153**	529	**143**	200	39	7	**46**	121	**142**	4	81	**.378**	**.513**	**.739**	**221**	**104**	9-13	.962	3	109	90	O152(50/7/99)	—	**8.4**
1925	NY A	98	359	61	104	12	2	25	66	59	2	68	.290	.393	.543	138	20	2-4	.974	6	105	140	O98(33/0/66)	—	1.5
1926	†NY A	152	495	**139**	184	30	5	**47**	**146**	**144**	3	76	.372	**.516**	**.737**	**228**	**103**	11-9	.979	0	105	72	O149(82/0/68),1b2	—	**8.5**
1927	†NY A	151	540	**158**	192	29	8	**60**	164	**137**	0	89	.356	**.486**	**.772**	**229**	108	7-6	.963	1	104	83	O151(56/0/95)	—	**8.8**
1928	†NY A	**154**	536	**163**	173	29	8	**54**	**142**	**137**	3	87	.323	.463	**.709**	**211**	**92**	4-5	.975	-4	102	59	O154(55/0/99)	—	**7.1**
1929	NY A	135	499	121	172	26	6	**46**	154	72	3	60	.345	.430	**.697**	**199**	**72**	5-3	.984	-5	101	41	O133(55/0/78)	—	**5.4**
1930	NY A	145	518	150	186	28	9	**49**	153	**136**	1	61	.359	**.493**	**.732**	**216**	**100**	10-10	.965	-1	102	86	O144(53/0/91)/P	—	7.6
1931	NY A	145	534	149	199	31	3	**46**	163	**128**	1	51	.373	**.495**	**.700**	**223**	**104**	5-4	.972	-7	95	46	O142(51/0/91)/1	—	**8.1**
1932	†NY A	133	457	120	156	13	5	41	137	**130**	2	62	.341	**.489**	.661	**206**	81	2-2	.961	-1	95	121	O128(44/0/87)/1	—	6.5
1933	NY A★	137	459	97	138	21	3	34	103	**114**	2	90	.301	.442	.582	180	59	4-5	.970	0	101	91	O132(55/0/78)/P1	—	4.7
1934	NY A★	125	365	78	105	17	4	22	84	104	2	63	.288	.448	.537	164	42	1-3	.962	-3	104	40	O111(34/0/77)	—	3.0
1935	Bos N	28	72	13	13	0	0	6	12	20	0	24	.181	.359	.431	121	3	0	.952	-1	96	69	O26(22/0/4)	—	0.1
Total	22	2503	8399	2174	2873	506	136	714	2213	2062	43	1330	.342	.474	.690	209	1444	123-117	.968	5	102	87	O2241(1057/64/1131),P163,1b32	—	112.0
RUTHERFORD, JIM James Hollis; B9.26.1886 Stillwater MN; D9.18.1956 Cleveland OH; BL/TR/6´1˝/180; d7.12; Col Cornell																									
1910	Cle A	1	2	0	1	0	0	0	0	0	0	—	.500	.500	.500	210	0	0	1.000	0	109	0	/cf	—	0.0
RUTNER, MICKEY Milton; B3.18.1920 Hempstead NY; BR/TR/5´11˝/190; d9.11; Col St. Johns																									
1947	Phi A	12	48	4	12	1	0	1	4	3	0	2	.250	.294	.333	73	-2	0-0	.885	-2	99	118	3b11	0	-0.4
RYAL, MARK Mark Dwayne; B4.28.1960 Henryetta OK; BL/TL/6´1˝/(180–197); [KCA78 3/77]; d9.7																									
1982	KC A	6	13	0	1	0	0	0	0	1-0	0	3	.077	.143	.077	-37	-2	0-0	.900	-0	100	0	O5(4/1/0)	0	-0.3
1985	Chi A	12	33	4	5	3	0	0	3	3-0	0	3	.152	.222	.242	26	-3	0-0	1.000	-0	105	0	O12(12/1/0)	0	-0.4
1986	Cal A	13	32	6	12	0	0	2	5	2-1	0	4	.375	.412	.563	164	3	1-0	.900	-0	117	0	O6R,1b4,D2	0	0.2
1987	Cal A	58	100	7	20	6	0	5	18	3-1	0	15	.200	.223	.410	65	-6	0-0	.955	-2	94	0	O21(6/0/15),1b4,D5	0	-0.8
1989	Phi N	29	33	2	8	2	0	0	5	1-0	0	6	.242	.265	.303	62	-2	0-0	1.000	-0	0	0	1b4,O4(2/0/2)	0	-0.2
1990	Pit N	9	12	0	1	0	0	0	0	0-0	0	3	.083	.083	.083	-56	-3	0-0	1.000	0	109	0	O4(3/0/2)	0	-0.3
Total	6	127	223	19	47	11	0	7	31	10-2	0	34	.211	.245	.354	61	-13	1-0	.957	-3	104	0	O52(27/2/25),1b12,D7	0	-1.8
RYAN, CONNIE Cornelius Joseph; B2.27.1920 New Orleans LA; D1.3.1996 Metairie LA; BR/TR/5´11˝/175; d4.14; Mil 1944–45; M2/C8; Col Louisiana St.																									
1942	NY N	11	27	4	5	0	0	0	2	4	0	3	.185	.290	.185	40	-2	1	.944	3	122	102	2b11	0	0.2
1943	Bos N	132	457	52	97	10	2	1	24	58	0	56	.212	.301	.249	61	-22	7	.962	-20	95	67	2b100,3b30	0	-3.9
1944	Bos N★	88	332	56	98	18	5	4	25	36	0	40	.295	.364	.416	114	7	13	.974	12	110	117	2b80,3b14	0	2.3
1946	Bos N	143	502	55	121	28	8	1	48	55	1	63	.241	.317	.335	84	-10	7	.968	-6	95	85	2b120,3b24	0	-1.1
1947	Bos N	150	544	60	144	33	5	5	69	71	1	60	.265	.351	.371	94	-3	5	.973	-6	101	95	2b150/S	0	0.0
1948	†Bos N	51	122	14	26	3	0	0	10	21	1	16	.213	.333	.238	58	-6	0	.966	1	111	97	2b40,3b4	0	-0.3
1949	Bos N	85	208	28	52	13	1	6	20	21	0	30	.250	.319	.409	99	-1	1	.973	3	113	161	3b25,S18,2b16,1b3	0	0.3
1950	Bos N	20	72	12	14	2	0	3	6	12	2	9	.194	.326	.347	82	-2	0	1.000	1	101	99	2b20	0	0.0
	Cin N	106	367	45	95	18	5	3	43	52	1	46	.259	.352	.360	87	-5	4	.973	5	95	97	2b103	0	0.5
	Year	126	439	57	109	20	5	6	49	64	3	55	.248	.348	.358	87	-7	4	.978	6	96	97	2b123	0	0.5
1951	Cin N	136	473	75	112	17	4	16	53	79	3	72	.237	.350	.391	97	0	11-6	.970	-4	99	82	2b121,3b3,1b2/rf	0	0.3
1952	Phi N	**154**	577	81	139	24	6	12	49	69	5	72	.241	.327	.366	93	-5	13-5	.972	-7	103	101	2b154	0	-0.2
1953	Phi N	90	247	47	73	14	6	5	26	30	0	35	.296	.372	.462	116	6	5-1	.958	-3	97	101	2b65,1b2	0	0.8
	Chi A	17	54	6	12	1	0	0	6	9	0	12	.222	.333	.241	55	-3	2-0	.927	-2	91	27	3b16	0	-0.4
1954	Cin N	1	0	0	0	0	0	0	0	1	0	0	ø	1.000	ø	182	0	0-0	ø	0	—	—	/H	0	0.0
Total	12	1184	3982	535	988	181	42	56	381	518	14	514	.248	.337	.357	90	-46	69-12	.970	-22	100	93	2b980,3b116,S19,1b7/rf	0	-1.5
RYAN, CYCLONE Daniel R.; B1866 Cappagh White, Ireland; D1.30.1917 Medfield MA; TR/6´0˝/200; d8.8																									
1887	NY AA	8	32	4	7	1	0	0	3	3	0	—	.219	.286	.250	52	-2	1	.938	0	161	162	1b8,P2	—	-0.2
1891	Bos N	1	1	0	0	0	0	0	0	0	0	0	.000	.000	.000	-89	0	0	1.000	0	162	0	/P	—	0.0
Total	2	9	33	4	7	1	0	0	3	3	0	0	.212	.278	.242	48	-2	1	.938	0	161	162	1b8,P3	—	-0.2
RYAN, MIKE J.; B St.Louis MO; d7.25																									
1895	StL N	2	2	0	0	0	0	0	0	0	0	0	.000	.000	.000	-99	-1	0	.000	-1	0	0	3b2	—	-0.1
RYAN, JIMMY James Edward "Pony"; B2.11.1863 Clinton MA; D10.26.1923 Chicago IL; BR/TL/5´9˝/162; d10.8; Col Boston College; OF(393/956/609); ▲																									
1885	Chi N	3	13	2	6	1	0	0	2	1	—	1	.462	.500	.538	207	2	—	.737	-1	129	0	S2/cf	—	0.0
1886	†Chi N	84	327	58	100	17	6	4	53	12	—	28	.306	.330	.431	113	3	10	.828	-1	123	149	O70(38/8/24),S6,3b6,2b5,P5	—	0.0
1887	Chi N	126	508	117	145	23	10	11	74	53	6	19	.285	.360	.435	106	2	50	.857	-3	156	190	O122(1/97/24),P8,2b3	—	-0.4
1888	Chi N	129	549	115	**182**	**33**	10	**16**	64	35	5	50	.332	.377	**.515**	170	42	60	.878	3	**162**	117	O128(0/127/1),P8	—	3.8
1889	Chi N	135	576	140	187	31	14	17	72	70	6	62	.325	.403	.516	147	36	45	.926	-4	168	**243**	O106(0/105/1),S29	—	2.5
1890	Chi P	118	486	99	165	32	5	6	89	60	4	36	.340	.416	.463	129	22	30	.919	-1	114	123	O118C	—	1.3
1891	Chi N	118	505	110	140	22	15	9	66	53	8	38	.277	.355	.434	129	18	27	.905	1	134	99	O117(43/74/0),S2,P2	—	1.3
1892	Chi N	128	505	105	148	21	11	10	65	61	5	41	.293	.375	.438	144	27	27	.921	-0	130	124	O120C,S9	—	1.8
1893	Chi N	83	341	82	102	21	7	3	30	59	3	25	.299	.407	.428	124	15	8	.908	-1	130	72	O73(1/73/1),S10/P	—	0.7
1894	Chi N	110	482	133	172	37	7	3	62	51	3	24	.357	.422	.481	111	10	12	.908	6	116	60	O110(0/5/106)	—	0.8
1895	Chi N	108	438	83	139	22	8	6	49	48	6	22	.317	.392	.445	109	5	18	.937	2	113	163	O108R	—	0.1
1896	Chi N	128	489	83	149	24	10	3	86	46	4	16	.305	.369	.413	102	1	29	.912	-1	116	85	O128R	—	-0.6
1897	Chi N	136	520	103	156	33	17	5	85	50	7	—	.300	.369	.458	113	9	27	.945	7	146	177	O136R	—	0.8
1898	Chi N	144	572	122	185	32	13	4	79	73	5	—	.323	.405	.446	144	35	29	.914	-8	96	43	O144(134/0/10)	—	1.4
1899	Chi N	125	525	91	158	20	10	3	68	43	3	—	.301	.357	.394	109	6	9	.956	-2	91	116	O125L	—	-0.7
1900	Chi N	105	415	66	115	25	4	5	59	29	3	—	.277	.329	.393	102	1	19	.913	-5	87	83	O105(49/9/57)	—	-1.0
1902	Was A	120	484	92	155	32	6	6	44	43	7	—	.320	.384	.448	129	20	10	.949	1	102	0	O120(2/105/13)	—	1.5
1903	Was A	114	437	42	109	25	4	7	46	17	8	—	.249	.290	.373	96	-2	9	.970	3	56	30	O114C	—	-0.5
Total	18	2014	8172	1643	2513	451	157	118	1093	804	83	362	.308	.375	.444	123	252	419	.918	-6	120	109	O1945C,S58,P24,2b8,3b6	—	12.8
RYAN, JACK John Bernard; B11.12.1868 Haverhill MA; D8.21.1952 Boston MA; BR/TR/5´10.5˝/165; d9.2; C7; OF(4/4/7)																									
1889	Lou AA	21	79	8	14	1	0	0	2	3	0	17	.177	.207	.190	14	-9	2	.864	-5	—	—	C15,O4(0/3/1),3b2	—	-1.1
1890	†Lou AA	93	337	43	73	16	4	0	35	12	0	—	.217	.244	.288	58	-20	6	.932	15	**136**	*110*	C89,O3(1/0/2)/S1	—	0.2
1891	Lou AA	75	253	24	57	5	4	2	25	15	1	40	.225	.271	.300	64	-13	3	.930	-9	*82*	*131*	C56,1b11,3b6,O4(3/1/0),2b3	—	-1.6
1894	Bos N	53	201	39	54	12	7	1	29	13	1	16	.269	.316	.413	69	-12	3	.911	4	*121*	*91*	C51,1b2	—	-0.3
1895	Bos N	49	189	22	55	7	0	0	18	6	0	6	.291	.313	.328	61	-12	3	.951	5	*129*	*106*	C43,2b5/rf	—	-0.3
1896	Bos N	8	32	2	3	1	0	0	0	0	0	1	.094	.094	.125	-40	-7	0	.911	2	*112*	*108*	C8	—	-0.3
1898	Bro N	87	301	39	57	11	4	0	24	15	2	—	.189	.233	.252	39	-25	5	.960	-1	*94*	*100*	C84,3b4/1	—	-1.7
1899	Bal N	2	4	0	2	1	0	0	1	0	0	—	.500	.500	.750	229	1	1	1.000	1	*103*	*245*	C2	—	0.1
1901	StL N	83	300	27	59	6	5	0	31	7	1	—	.197	.218	.250	37	-25	5	.982	3	*97*	*102*	C65,2b9,1b5,O3R	—	-1.6
1902	StL N	76	267	23	48	4	4	0	14	4	1	—	.180	.195	.225	31	-23	2	.966	-6	*88*	*100*	C66,1b4,3b4,2b2/S	—	-2.4
1903	StL N	67	227	18	54	5	1	1	10	10	1	—	.238	.273	.282	60	-12	2	.971	-5	*82*	*96*	C47,1b18,S2	—	-1.3
1912	Was A	1	1	0	0	0	0	0	0	0	0	—	.000	.000	.000	-99	0	0	1.000	0	107	0	/3	—	0.0
1913	Was A	1	1	0	0	0	0	0	0	0	0	0	.000	.000	.000	-98	0	0	1.000	0	*0*	*424*	/C	—	0.0
Total	13	616	2192	245	476	69	29	4	189	85	7	80	.217	.249	.281	50	-157	32	.947	3	*105*	*105*	C527,1b42,2b19,3b17,O15R,S4	—	-10.3
RYAN, BUDDY John Budd; B10.6.1885 Denver CO; D7.9.1956 Sacramento CA; BL/TR/5´9.5˝/172; d4.11																									
1912	Cle A	93	328	53	89	12	9	1	31	30	6	—	.271	.343	.372	101	0	12	.963	6	112	124	O90(56/0/34)	—	0.2
1913	Cle A	73	243	26	72	6	1	0	32	11	2	13	.296	.332	.329	91	-3	9	.986	-1	101	71	O68(3/65/0)/1	—	-0.9
Total	2	166	571	79	161	18	10	1	63	41	8	13	.282	.339	.354	97	-3	21	.973	6	107	101	O158(59/65/34)/1	—	-0.7
RYAN, BLONDY John Collins; B1.4.1906 Lynn MA; D11.28.1959 Swampscott MA; BR/TR/6´1˝/178; d7.13; Col Holy Cross																									
1930	Chi A	28	87	9	18	0	4	1	10	6	0	13	.207	.258	.333	50	-8	2-0	.875	-1	105	140	3b23,S2/2	—	-0.6
1933	†NY N	146	525	47	125	10	5	3	48	15	0	62	.238	.259	.293	58	-30	0	.950	17	107	**117**	S146	—	-0.4
1934	NY N	110	385	35	93	19	0	2	41	19	0	68	.242	.277	.306	57	-23	3	.953	10	120	91	3b65,S30,2b25	—	-0.8
1935	Phi N	39	129	13	34	3	0	1	10	7	2	20	.264	.312	.310	61	-7	1	.912	0	101	108	S35/23	—	-0.4
	NY A	30	105	12	25	1	3	0	11	3	0	10	.238	.259	.305	48	-9	0-0	.908	-6	90	79	S30	—	-1.2
1937	†NY N	21	75	10	18	3	1	1	13	6	0	8	.240	.296	.347	73	-3	0	.941	2	100	138	S19/23	—	0.0

YEAR	TM LG	G	AB	R	H	2B	3B	HR	RBI	BB-IB	HP	SO	AVG	OBP	SLG	AOPS	ABR	SB-CS	FA	FR	RNG	THR	GAMES AT POSITION	DL	BFW
1938	NY N	12	24	1	5	0	0	0	0	1	0	3	.208	.240	.208	24	-3	0	1.000	-1	118	72	2b5,3b3,S2	—	-0.3
Total	6	386	1330	127	318	36	13	8	133	57	2	184	.239	.271	.304	57	-83	6-0	.936	21	103	114	S264,3b93,2b33	—	-3.7
Ryan, Jack	John Francis; B5.5.1905 West Mineral KS; D9.2.1967 Rochester MN; BR/TR/6´0˝/185; d6.18																								
1929	Bos A	2	3	0	0	0	0	0	0	0	0	0	.000	.000	.000	-99	-1	0-0	1.000	-0	61	0	O2(1/0/1)	—	-0.1
Ryan, Johnny	John Joseph; B10.1853 Philadelphia PA; D3.22.1902 Philadelphia PA; 5´7.5˝/150; d8.19; ▲																								
1873	Phi NA	2	8	1	2	0	0	0	1	0	—	0	.250	.250	.250	47	-1	0-0	.727	-0	488	247	/1cf	—	0.0
1874	Bal NA	**47**	181	29	35	8	1	0	19	5	—	13	.193	.215	.249	49	-10	3-0	.862	13	105	69	O47L/P	—	0.5
1875	NH NA	37	146	17	23	2	2	0	8	3	—	12	.158	.174	.199	34	-8	10-4	.796	-8	21	97	O30L,P10,C4/S	—	-1.1
1876	Lou N	64	241	32	61	5	1	1	18	6	—	23	.253	.271	.295	75	-8	—	.886	-8	9	50	O64(63/1/0)/P	—	-1.7
1877	Cin N	6	26	2	4	0	1	0	2	1	—	5	.154	.185	.231	34	-2	—	.769	-1	0	0	O6(1/5/0)	—	-0.3
Total	3NA	86	335	47	60	10	3	0	28	8	—	25	.179	.198	.227	43	-19	13-4	.850	5	72	79	O78(77/1/0),P11,C4/S1	—	-0.6
Total	2	70	267	34	65	5	2	1	20	7	—	28	.243	.263	.288	72	-10	—	.877	-9	8	46	O70(64/6/0)/P	—	-2.0
Ryan, John	John M. (Played 1 Game For Washington Under Real Name of Daniel Sheehan); B Washington DC; d6.11																								
1884	Was U	7	28	2	4	0	1	0	—	1	—	—	.143	.172	.214	17	-4	—	.667	-1	64	0	O7(2/3/2)/3	—	-0.5
	Wil U	2	6	0	1	0	0	0	—	1	—	—	.167	.286	.167	39	-1	—	.800	-0	0	0	O2(1/1/0)	—	-0.1
	Year	9	34	2	5	0	1	0	—	2	—	—	.147	.194	.206	22	-4	—	.706	-1	47	0	O9(3/4/2)/3	—	-0.6
Ryan, Mike	Michael James; B11.25.1941 Haverhill MA; BR/TR/6´2˝/(200–215); d10.3; C16																								
1964	Bos A	1	3	0	1	0	0	0	2	1-1	0	0	.333	.500	.333	131	0	0-0	1.000	-0	0	0	/C	0	0.0
1965	Bos A	33	107	7	17	0	1	3	9	5-1	0	19	.159	.193	.262	27	-11	0-0	.981	-2	69	149	C33	0	-1.2
1966	Bos A	116	369	27	79	15	3	2	32	29-3	0	68	.214	.271	.287	55	-21	1-0	.992	-5	76	115	C114	0	-2.2
1967	†Bos A	79	226	21	45	4	2	2	27	26-5	1	42	.199	.282	.261	58	-12	2-0	.988	3	132	87	C79	0	-0.5
1968	Phi N	96	296	12	53	6	1	1	15	15-3	0	59	.179	.218	.216	31	-25	0-3	.991	-2	**151**	**143**	C96	0	-2.8
1969	Phi N	133	446	41	91	17	2	12	44	30-4	2	66	.204	.256	.332	65	-22	1-1	.991	3	106	103	C132	0	-1.4
1970	Phi N	46	134	14	24	8	0	2	11	16-3	0	24	.179	.265	.284	49	-10	0-0	.992	-10	118	97	C46	98	-1.9
1971	Phi N	43	134	9	22	5	1	3	6	10-1	0	32	.164	.222	.284	42	-11	0-0	1.000	7	138	218	C43	0	-0.2
1972	Phi N	46	106	6	19	4	0	2	10	10-2	1	25	.179	.254	.274	49	-7	0-0	.992	3	111	110	C46	0	-0.2
1973	Phi N	28	69	7	16	1	2	1	5	6-0	0	19	.232	.289	.348	75	-3	0-0	.992	-0	213	103	C27	0	-0.2
1974	Pit N	15	30	2	3	0	0	0	0	4-0	0	16	.100	.206	.100	-13	-5	0-0	1.000	1	348	87	C15	28	-0.3
Total	11	636	1920	146	370	60	12	28	161	152-23	4	370	.193	.252	.280	51	-127	4-4	.991	-2	120	120	C632	126	-10.9
Ryan, Mike	Michael Sean; B7.6.1977 Indiana PA; BL/TR/5´10˝/(182–215); [MinA96 5/127]; d9.20																								
2002	Min A	7	11	3	1	0	0	0	0	0-0	0	2	.091	.091	.091	-50	-2	0-0	1.000	-1	51	0	O5(4/3/0)	0	-0.3
2003	†Min A	27	61	13	24	7	0	5	13	6-0	0	12	.393	.441	.754	202	9	2-1	1.000	3	132	277	O16(4/0/12),D4	0	1.1
2004	Min A	36	71	9	17	2	1	0	7	4-1	0	16	.239	.280	.296	49	-6	1-1	.947	-1	94	0	O15(10/2/3),D11	36	-0.7
2005	Min A	57	117	7	27	5	0	2	13	9-1	0	22	.231	.283	.325	61	-7	1-2	1.000	-1	73	173	O25(16/0/10),D13/3	0	-1.0
Total	4	127	260	32	69	14	1	7	33	19-2	0	52	.265	.313	.408	87	-6	4-4	.989	0	92	155	O61(34/5/25),D28/3	36	-0.9
Ryan, Rob	Robert James; B6.24.1973 Havre MT; BL/TL/5´11˝/(190–192); [AriN96 26/785]; d8.20; Col Washington St.																								
1999	Ari N	20	29	4	7	1	0	2	5	1-0	0	8	.241	.267	.483	84	-1	0-0	1.000	-0	103	0	O5(1/0/4)	0	-0.1
2000	Ari N	27	27	4	8	1	1	0	2	4-0	1	7	.296	.406	.407	103	0	0-0	1.000	-0	44	0	O2R/D	0	0.0
2001	Ari N	1	1	0	0	0	0	0	0	0-0	0	1	.000	.000	.000	-94	0	0-0	ø	0	—	—	/H	0	0.0
	Oak A	7	7	0	0	0	0	0	0	0-0	0	5	.000	.000	.000	-99	-2	0-0	1.000	-0	71	0	O5(0/4/1)/D	0	-0.2
Total	3	55	64	8	15	2	1	2	7	5-0	1	21	.234	.300	.391	72	-3	0-0	1.000	-1	85	0	O12(1/4/7),D2	0	-0.3
Ryder, Tom	Thomas; B5.9.1863 Dubuque IA; D7.18.1935 Dubuque IA; BL; d7.22																								
1884	StL U	8	28	4	7	1	0	0	—	2	—	—	.250	.300	.286	76	-2	—	.650	-1	140	0	O8(5/3/0)	—	-0.2
Rye, Gene	Eugene Rudolph "Half-Pint" (b Eugene Rudolph Mercantelli); B11.15.1906 Chicago IL; D1.21.1980 Park Ridge IL; BL/TR/5´6˝/165; d4.22																								
1931	Bos A	17	39	3	7	0	0	0	1	2	0	5	.179	.220	.179	6	-5	0-0	.944	-1	94	0	O10L	—	-0.6
Sabo, Alex	Alexander "Giz" (b Alexsander Szabo); B2.14.1910 New Brunswick NJ; D1.3.2001 Tuckerton NJ; BR/TR/6´0˝/192; d8.1; Col Fordham																								
1936	Was A	4	8	1	3	0	0	0	1	0	0	2	.375	.375	.375	91	0	0-0	.923	0	*100*	*164*	C4	—	0.0
1937	Was A	1	0	0	0	0	0	0	0	0	0	0	ø	ø	ø	ø	0	0-0	1.000	-0	*0*	*0*	/C	—	0.0
Total	2	5	8	1	3	0	0	0	1	0	0	2	.375	.375	.375	91	0	0-0	.929	0	*91*	*150*	C5	—	0.0
Sabo, Chris	Christopher Andrew; B1.19.1962 Detroit MI; BR/TR/6´0˝/185; [CinN83 2/30]; d4.4; Col Michigan																								
1988	Cin N★	137	538	74	146	40	2	11	44	29-1	6	52	.271	.314	.414	104	3	46-14	**.966**	10	108	**149**	3b135,S2	0	2.0
1989	Cin N	82	304	40	79	21	1	6	29	25-2	1	33	.260	.316	.395	99	0	14-9	.943	-5	97	96	3b76	66	-0.5
1990	†Cin N★	148	567	95	153	38	2	25	71	61-7	4	58	.270	.343	.476	119	15	25-10	**.966**	-8	96	83	3b146	0	1.0
1991	Cin N★	153	582	91	175	35	3	26	88	44-3	6	79	.301	.354	.505	134	26	19-6	.966	-16	86	98	3b151	0	1.2
1992	Cin N	96	344	42	84	19	3	12	43	30-1	1	54	.244	.302	.422	102	0	4-5	.961	-4	90	92	3b93	15	-0.5
1993	Cin N	148	552	86	143	33	2	21	82	43-5	6	105	.259	.315	.440	100	-1	6-4	.967	-12	91	67	3b148	15	-1.2
1994	Bal A	68	258	41	66	15	3	11	42	20-2	5	38	.256	.320	.465	94	-3	1-1	.958	-8	74	82	3b37,O22(9/0/13),D10	15	-1.2
1995	Chi A	20	71	10	18	5	0	1	8	3-1	2	12	.254	.295	.366	76	-3	2-0	.909	-1	0	118	D15/13	0	-0.4
	StL N	5	13	0	2	1	0	0	3	1-0	0	2	.154	.214	.231	17	-2	1-0	.929	-1	148	65	1b2/3	77	-0.2
1996	Cin N	54	125	15	32	7	1	3	16	18-0	1	27	.256	.354	.400	97	0	2-0	.961	5	112	112	3b43	27	0.5
Total	9	911	3354	494	898	214	17	116	426	274-22	32	460	.268	.326	.445	108	35	120-49	.963	-38	94	97	3b831,D25,O22(9/0/13),1b3,S2	215	0.7
Sacka, Frank	Frank; B8.30.1924 Romulus MI; D12.7.1994 Dearborn MI; BR/TR/6´0˝/195; d4.29																								
1951	Was A	7	16	1	4	0	0	0	3	0	0	5	.250	.250	.250	36	-2	0-0	.962	1	*163*	*166*	C6	0	-0.1
1953	Was A	7	18	2	5	0	0	0	3	3	0	1	.278	.381	.278	82	0	0-0	1.000	1	*141*	*138*	C6	0	0.1
Total	2	14	34	3	9	0	0	0	6	3	0	6	.265	.324	.265	62	-2	0-0	.982	2	*151*	*151*	C12	0	0.0
Sadek, Mike	Michael George; B5.30.1946 Minneapolis MN; BR/TR (BB 1979p)/5´9˝/(165–170); [MinA67 S5/83]; d4.13; Col Minnesota																								
1973	SF N	39	66	6	11	1	1	0	4	11-0	0	8	.167	.282	.212	38	-5	1-0	.981	3	89	80	C35	15	-0.1
1975	SF N	42	106	14	25	5	2	0	9	14-1	0	14	.236	.322	.321	77	-3	1-0	.995	5	92	69	C38	0	0.3
1976	SF N	55	93	8	19	2	0	0	7	11-2	1	10	.204	.295	.226	48	-6	0-0	.985	3	95	108	C51	0	-0.2
1977	SF N	61	126	12	29	7	0	1	15	12-0	0	5	.230	.297	.310	63	-6	2-1	.992	6	96	151	C57	0	0.2
1978	SF N	40	109	15	26	3	0	2	9	10-2	0	11	.239	.303	.321	77	-4	1-0	.975	-3	67	68	C37	37	-0.5
1979	SF N	63	126	14	30	5	0	1	11	15-2	1	24	.238	.322	.302	77	-4	1-0	.993	-0	94	80	C60/rf	0	-0.2
1980	SF N	64	151	14	38	4	1	1	16	27-6	0	18	.252	.363	.311	94	0	0-0	.974	-1	108	103	C59	15	0.1
1981	SF N	19	36	5	6	3	0	0	3	8-0	0	7	.167	.318	.250	65	-1	0-0	.979	3	79	123	C19	0	0.3
Total	8	383	813	88	184	30	4	5	74	108-13	2	97	.226	.317	.292	71	-29	6-1	.985	16	92	98	C356/rf	67	-0.1
Sadler, Donnie	Donnie Lamont; B6.17.1975 Clifton TX; BR/TR/5´6˝/(165–175); [BosA94 11/299]; d4.1; OF(50/64/26)																								
1998	†Bos A	58	124	21	28	4	4	3	15	6-0	3	28	.226	.276	.395	71	-6	4-0	.972	-5	85	72	2b50,S4,D4	0	-0.8
1999	†Bos A	49	107	18	30	5	1	0	4	5-0	0	20	.280	.313	.346	66	-6	2-1	.930	-5	76	80	S14,2b10,3b9,O8(1/6/1),D3	0	-0.9
2000	Bos A	49	99	14	22	5	0	1	10	5-0	1	18	.222	.262	.303	43	-9	3-1	.958	1	116	78	S19,O17(3/13/1),2b12,3b3,D2	0	-0.6
2001	Cin N	39	84	9	17	3	0	1	3	9-0	0	20	.202	.280	.274	42	-7	3-3	.947	-1	105	109	2b15,S12,O8(6/2/2)/D	0	-0.8
	KC A	54	101	19	13	3	0	0	2	9-0	2	17	.129	.212	.158	0	-15	4-1	1.000	15	128	311	O16(5/4/7),3b15,2b13,S6	0	0.1
2002	KC A	35	68	10	13	1	1	0	5	4-0	0	12	.191	.233	.235	23	-8	3-1	.957	-3	108	0	O15(11/0/4),3b11,2b4,S4,D3	24	-1.0
	Tex A	38	30	6	3	1	0	0	2	3-0	2	7	.100	.229	.133	-0	-4	2-2	1.000	1	126	327	O18(2/14/3),S12,3b4,2b2/D	0	-0.3
	Year	73	98	16	16	2	1	0	7	7-0	2	19	.163	.231	.204	17	-12	5-3	.976	-2	115	122	O33(13/14/7),S16,3b15,2b6,D4	0	-1.3
2003	Tex A	77	131	27	26	5	2	1	5	13-0	2	34	.198	.277	.290	48	-10	4-3	1.000	-1	95	215	O41(19/22/7),3b23,S19/2	0	-1.0
2004	Ari N	18	23	1	3	2	0	0	0	1-0	0	7	.130	.167	.217	-2	-3	0-0	1.000	-2	50	0	O6(3/3/1),S3,2b2,3b2	0	-0.5
Total	7	417	767	125	155	29	8	6	46	55-0	10	163	.202	.262	.284	40	-68	25-12	.982	-1	100	208	O129C,2b109,S93,3b67,D14	24	-5.8
Sadler, Ray	Raymond Lee; B9.19.1980 Clifton TX; BR/TR/6´1˝/200; [ChiN99 30/920]; d5.8; Col Hill (TX) JC																								
2005	Pit N	3	8	1	2	0	0	1	1	0-0	0	1	.250	.250	.625	119	0	0-0	1.000	-0	89	0	O3L	0	0.0

YEAR	TM LG	G	AB	R	H	2B	3B	HR	RBI	BB-IB	HP	SO	AVG	OBP	SLG	AOPS	ABR	SB-CS	FA	FR	RNG	THR	GAMES AT POSITION	DL	BFW
SADOWSKI, ED	Edward Roman; B1.19.1931 Pittsburgh PA; D11.6.1993 Garden Grove CA; BR/TR/5´11˝/175; d4.20; b–Bob b–Ted																								
1960	Bos A	38	93	10	20	2	0	3	8	8-2	1	13	.215	.284	.333	64	-5	0-0	.995	5	242	125	C36	30	0.1
1961	LA A	69	164	16	38	13	0	4	12	11-1	0	33	.232	.278	.384	68	-7	2-3	.987	-1	106	54	C56	0	-0.6
1962	LA A	27	55	4	11	4	0	1	3	2-0	0	14	.200	.228	.327	49	-4	1-0	.968	-1	43	112	C18	0	-0.4
1963	LA A	80	174	24	30	1	1	4	15	17-5	0	33	.172	.245	.259	44	-14	2-1	.997	12	144	183	C68	0	0.1
1966	Atl N	3	9	1	1	0	0	0	1	1-0	0	1	.111	.200	.111	-10	-1	0-0	1.000	-0	62	366	C3	0	-0.1
Total	5	217	495	55	100	20	1	12	39	39-8	1	94	.202	.261	.319	56	-31	5-4	.991	15	140	128	C181	30	-0.9
SADOWSKI, BOB	Robert Frank "Sid"; B1.15.1937 St.Louis MO; BL/TR/6´0˝/(170–175); d9.16																								
1960	StL N	1	1	0	0	0	0	0	0	1-0	0	0	.000	.500	.000	47	0	0-0	.000	-1	0	0	/2	0	-0.1
1961	Phi N	16	54	4	7	0	0	0	0	4-0	1	7	.130	.203	.130	-9	-9	1-0	.971	0	102	125	3b14	0	-0.9
1962	Chi A	79	130	22	30	3	3	6	24	13-2	0	22	.231	.299	.438	97	-1	0-0	.955	4	120	0	3b16,2b12	0	0.3
1963	LA A	88	144	12	36	6	0	1	22	15-2	0	34	.250	.317	.313	83	-3	2-1	1.000	-2	111	0	O25(1/0/24),3b6,2b4	0	-0.6
Total	4	184	329	38	73	9	3	7	46	33-4	1	63	.222	.292	.331	73	-13	3-1	.953	1	100	50	3b36,O25(1/0/24),2b17	0	-1.3
SAENZ, OLMEDO	Olmedo (Sanchez); B10.8.1970 Chitre, Pan; BR/TR/6´0˝/(175–220); d5.28																								
1994	Chi A	5	14	2	2	0	1	0	0	0-0	0	5	.143	.143	.286	7	-2	0-0	1.000	-1	66	0	3b5	0	-0.3
1999	Oak A	97	255	41	70	18	0	11	41	22-1	15	47	.275	.363	.475	116	7	1-1	.938	1	102	165	3b56,1b28,D8	21	0.6
2000	†Oak A	76	214	40	67	12	2	9	33	25-2	7	40	.313	.401	.514	132	11	1-0	.923	-2	90	72	D27,3b18,1b17	48	0.6
2001	†Oak A	106	305	33	67	21	1	9	32	19-1	13	64	.220	.291	.384	76	-11	0-1	.986	-0	131	91	D58,1b28,3b14	0	-1.5
2002	†Oak A	68	156	15	43	10	1	6	18	13-1	7	31	.276	.354	.468	118	4	1-1	1.000	2	84	94	1b34,3b15,D7	0	0.4
2004	LA N	77	111	17	31	1	0	8	22	12-1	2	33	.279	.352	.505	122	3	0-0	.986	1	132	146	1b25,3b2,D4	0	0.3
2005	LA N	109	319	39	84	24	0	15	63	27-1	3	63	.263	.325	.480	107	3	0-1	.998	-6	53	81	1b66,3b17,D8	0	-0.9
2006	†LA N	103	179	30	53	15	0	11	48	14-1	7	47	.296	.363	.564	134	9	0-0	.989	0	60	175	1b30,3b16,D3	0	0.7
Total	8	641	1553	217	417	101	5	69	257	132-8	54	330	.269	.343	.473	110	24	3-4	.993	-5	85	103	1b228,3b143,D115	69	-0.1
SAFFELL, TOM	Thomas Judson; B7.26.1921 Etowah TN; BL/TR/5´11˝/170; d7.2; Col Maryville																								
1949	Pit N	73	205	36	66	7	1	2	25	21	0	27	.322	.385	.395	107	3	5	.992	-2	96	59	O53(0/52/2)	0	-0.1
1950	Pit N	67	182	18	37	7	0	2	6	14	1	34	.203	.264	.275	41	-16	1	.993	4	110	135	O43(0/42/2)	0	-1.3
1951	Pit N	49	65	11	13	0	0	1	5	5	0	18	.200	.257	.246	35	-6	1-1	.929	-1	97	112	O17(1/13/3)	0	-0.7
1955	Pit N	73	113	21	19	1	0	1	3	15-3	0	22	.168	.266	.204	27	-12	1-0	.964	1	111	91	O47(6/37/4)	0	-1.2
	KC A	9	37	5	8	0	0	0	1	4-0	0	7	.216	.293	.216	38	-3	1-0	.962	-1	98	0	O9C	0	-0.4
Total	4	271	602	91	143	15	1	6	40	59-3	1	108	.238	.307	.296	60	-34	9-1	.980	2	104	90	O169(7/153/11)	0	-3.7
SAGE, HARRY	Harry "Doc"; B3.16.1864 Rock Island IL; D5.27.1947 Rock Island IL; BR/TR/5´10˝/185; d4.17																								
1890	Tol AA	81	275	40	41	8	4	2	25	29	2	—	.149	.235	.229	36	-23	10	.948	18	*115*	***129***	C80/cf	—	0.1
SAGER, PONY	Samuel B.; B1847 Marshalltown IA; ?/140; d5.6																								
1871	Rok NA	8	39	9	11	0	0	0	5	2	—	2	.282	.317	.282	78	-1	5-1	.643	-3	90	0	S4,O4L	—	-0.2
SAGMOEN, MARC	Marc Richard; B4.16.1971 Seattle WA; BL/TL/5´11˝/185; [TexA93 13/367]; d4.15; Col Nebraska																								
1997	Tex A	21	43	2	6	2	0	1	4	2-0	0	13	.140	.174	.256	11	-6	0-0	1.000	-1	99	0	O17(2/0/16)/1D	0	-0.7
SAIER, VIC	Victor Sylvester; B5.4.1891 Lansing MI; D5.14.1967 E.Lansing MI; BL/TR/5´11˝/185; d5.3																								
1911	Chi N	86	259	42	67	15	1	1	37	25	7	37	.259	.340	.336	89	-3	11	.980	-4	81	115	1b73	—	-0.9
1912	Chi N	122	451	74	130	25	14	2	61	34	1	65	.288	.340	.419	107	3	11	.992	-5	77	105	1b120	—	-0.6
1913	Chi N	149	519	94	150	15	**21**	14	92	62	5	62	.289	.370	.480	141	27	26-20	.983	-5	87	101	1b149	—	1.7
1914	Chi N	153	537	87	129	24	8	18	72	94	4	61	.240	.357	.415	130	22	19	.986	-11	69	78	1b153	—	0.9
1915	Chi N	144	497	74	131	35	11	11	64	64	2	62	.264	.350	.445	140	25	29-9	.985	-5	87	88	1b139	—	2.1
1916	Chi N	147	498	60	126	25	3	7	50	79	1	68	.253	.356	.357	108	9	20-17	.984	-1	103	97	1b147	—	0.4
1917	Chi N	6	21	5	5	1	0	0	2	2	0	1	.238	.304	.286	75	-1	0	1.000	2	224	85	1b6	—	0.1
1919	Pit N	58	166	19	37	3	3	2	17	18	2	13	.223	.306	.313	83	-3	5	.985	-5	61	77	1b51	—	-1.0
Total	8	865	2948	455	775	143	61	55	395	378	22	369	.263	.351	.409	119	79	121-46	.986	-33	84	94	1b838	—	2.7
ST.CLAIRE, EBBA	Edward Joseph; B8.5.1921 Whitehall NY; D8.22.1982 Whitehall NY; BB/TR/6´1˝/219; d4.17; s–Randy; Col Colgate																								
1951	Bos N	72	220	22	62	17	2	1	25	12	1	24	.282	.322	.391	98	-1	2-0	.977	-0	*82*	*100*	C62	31	0.2
1952	Bos N	39	108	5	23	2	0	2	4	8	0	12	.213	.267	.287	56	-7	0-1	.972	1	*101*	*135*	C34	0	-0.5
1953	Mil N	33	80	7	16	3	0	2	5	3	0	9	.200	.229	.313	42	-7	0-0	.992	2	*90*	*144*	C27	0	-0.4
1954	NY N	20	42	5	11	1	0	2	6	12	1	7	.262	.436	.429	126	2	0-0	.975	1	*134*	*107*	C16	0	0.4
Total	4	164	450	39	112	23	2	7	40	35	2	52	.249	.306	.356	81	-13	2-1	.978	4	*94*	*117*	C139	31	-0.3
SAKATA, LENN	Lenn Haruki; B6.8.1954 Honolulu HI; BR/TR/5´9˝/(160–174); [MilA75*S1/10]; d7.21; Col Gonzaga																								
1977	Mil A	53	154	13	25	2	0	2	12	9-0	0	22	.162	.209	.214	15	-18	1-3	.985	6	110	132	2b53	0	-1.0
1978	Mil A	30	78	8	15	4	0	0	3	8-1	0	11	.192	.267	.244	44	-6	1-0	.975	-5	94	79	2b29	0	-0.9
1979	Mil A	4	14	1	7	2	0	0	1	0-0	0	1	.500	.500	.643	205	2	0-0	1.000	1	110	184	2b4	0	0.3
1980	Bal A	43	83	12	16	3	2	1	9	6-0	0	10	.193	.244	.313	53	-6	2-1	.984	1	101	112	2b34,S4/D	0	-0.4
1981	Bal A	61	150	19	34	4	0	5	15	11-0	1	18	.227	.282	.353	83	-4	4-0	.963	5	102	107	S42,2b20	18	0.6
1982	Bal A	136	343	40	89	18	1	6	31	30-2	4	39	.259	.323	.370	91	-4	7-4	.977	-13	93	95	2b83,S56	0	-0.8
1983	†Bal A	66	134	23	34	7	0	3	12	16-0	1	17	.254	.338	.373	97	0	8-4	.990	-3	95	128	2b60/CD	0	-0.1
1984	Bal A	81	157	23	30	1	0	3	11	6-2	0	15	.191	.221	.255	32	-15	4-1	.988	5	117	112	2b76/lf	0	-0.8
1985	Bal A	55	97	15	22	3	0	3	6	6-0	1	15	.227	.279	.351	73	-4	3-2	.960	-5	94	83	2b50/D	0	-0.7
1986	Oak A	17	34	4	12	2	0	0	5	3-0	0	6	.353	.395	.412	132	2	0-1	.984	2	119	55	2b16/D	0	0.4
1987	NY A	19	45	5	12	0	1	2	4	2-0	1	4	.267	.313	.444	98	0	0-1	.929	-0	113	54	3b12,2b6	64	-0.1
Total	11	565	1289	163	296	46	4	25	109	97-5	8	158	.230	.286	.330	71	-53	30-17	.982	-8	103	109	2b431,S102,3b12,D4/lfC	82	-3.5
SALAS, MARK	Mark Bruce; B3.8.1961 Montebello CA; BL/TR/6´0˝/(180–205); [StLN79 18/448]; d6.19																								
1984	StL N	14	20	1	2	1	0	0	1	0-0	0	3	.100	.100	.150	-31	-4	0-0	1.000	-1	50	108	C4,O3(2/0/1)	0	-0.4
1985	Min A	120	360	51	108	20	5	9	41	18-5	1	37	.300	.332	.458	108	3	0-1	.991	8	100	121	C115,D3	0	1.5
1986	Min A	91	258	28	60	7	4	8	33	18-2	1	32	.233	.282	.384	78	-9	3-1	.980	1	92	110	C69,D8	24	-0.6
1987	Min A	22	45	8	17	2	0	3	9	5-1	0	6	.378	.431	.622	171	5	0-1	.989	-0	41	28	C14	0	0.4
	NY A	50	115	13	23	4	0	3	12	10-0	3	17	.200	.279	.313	58	-7	0-0	1.000	0	102	120	C41/lfD	0	-0.5
	Year	72	160	21	40	6	0	6	21	15-1	3	23	.250	.322	.400	90	-2	0-1	.996	-0	85	95	C55,D4/lf	0	-0.1
1988	Chi A	75	196	17	49	7	0	3	9	12-2	3	17	.250	.303	.332	78	-6	0-0	.979	-1	98	121	C69/D	0	-0.3
1989	Cle A	30	77	4	17	4	1	2	7	5-1	1	13	.221	.277	.377	81	-2	0-0	1.000	0	57	396	D20,C5	0	-0.3
1990	Det A	74	164	18	38	3	0	9	24	21-2	1	28	.232	.323	.415	103	0	0-0	.988	-6	81	107	C57/3D	0	-0.3
1991	Det A	33	57	2	5	1	0	1	7	0-0	2	10	.088	.117	.158	-24	-10	0-0	1.000	-0	68	140	C11,1b5,D8	0	-1.0
Total	8	509	1292	142	319	49	10	38	143	89-13	12	163	.247	.300	.389	86	-30	3-3	.987	1	92	114	C385,D47,1b5,O4(3/0/1)/3	24	-1.5
SALAZAR, ANGEL	Argenis Antonio (Yepez); B11.4.1961 Anaco, Anzoategui, Venez.; BR/TR/6´0˝/(170–180); d8.10																								
1983	Mon N	36	37	5	8	1	1	0	1	1-0	0	8	.216	.231	.297	47	-3	0-0	.966	-4	69	117	S34	0	-0.6
1984	Mon N	80	174	12	27	4	2	0	12	4-0	1	38	.155	.178	.201	7	-22	1-1	.960	-7	91	113	S80	0	-2.5
1986	KC A	117	298	24	73	20	2	0	24	7-0	2	47	.245	.266	.326	59	-17	1-1	.978	-2	107	87	S115/2	0	-0.9
1987	KC A	116	317	24	65	7	0	2	21	6-0	0	46	.205	.219	.246	23	-36	4-4	.981	20	**120**	98	S116	22	-0.6
1988	Chi N	34	60	4	15	1	1	0	1	1-1	0	11	.250	.262	.300	58	-3	0-0	.966	1	95	106	S29,2b2/3	0	-0.1
Total	5	383	886	69	188	33	6	2	59	19-1	3	150	.212	.230	.270	35	-81	6-6	.974	9	106	99	S374,2b3/3	22	-4.7
SALAZAR, JEFF	Jeffrey Dewan; B11.24.1980 Oklahoma City OK; BL/TL/6´0˝/190; [ColN02 8/231]; d9.7; Col Oklahoma St.																								
2006	Col N	19	53	13	15	4	0	1	8	11-2	1	16	.283	.409	.415	105	1	2-0	1.000	-2	78	0	O14(0/14/1)	0	0.0
SALAZAR, LUIS	Luis Ernesto (Garcia); B5.19.1956 Barcelona, Anzoategui, Venez.; BR/TR/5´9˝/(180–190); d8.15; C1; OF(161/114/36)																								
1980	SD N	44	169	28	57	4	7	1	25	9-1	1	25	.337	.372	.462	141	8	11-2	.944	-1	99	111	3b42,O4(0/3/1)	0	0.8
1981	SD N	109	400	37	121	19	6	3	38	16-2	1	72	.303	.329	.403	117	6	11-8	.955	-1	101	106	3b94,O23(1/10/14)	0	0.3
1982	SD N	145	524	55	127	15	5	8	62	23-10	2	80	.242	.274	.336	75	-20	32-9	.938	-2	107	**147**	3b129,S18/cf	0	-2.0
1983	SD N	134	481	52	124	16	2	14	45	17-8	2	80	.258	.285	.387	87	-11	24-9	.949	4	110	98	3b118,S19	0	-0.6
1984	†SD N	93	228	20	55	7	2	3	17	6-1	0	38	.241	.261	.329	64	-12	11-7	.970	4	105	77	3b58,O24(4/19/2),S4	27	-0.9
1985	Chi A	122	327	39	80	18	2	10	45	12-2	0	60	.245	.267	.404	78	-11	14-4	.968	-6	83	87	O84(26/68/1),3b39,1b6,D8	0	-1.

YEAR	TM LG	G	AB	R	H	2B	3B	HR	RBI	BB-IB	HP	SO	AVG	OBP	SLG	AOPS	ABR	SB-CS	FA	FR	RNG	THR	GAMES AT POSITION	DL	BFW
1986	Chi A	4	7	1	1	0	0	0	0	1-0	0	3	.143	.250	.143	10	-1	0-0	ø	0	—	—	D2	167	-0.1
1987	SD N	84	189	13	48	5	0	3	17	14-2	0	30	.254	.302	.328	70	-8	3-3	.957	-6	101	93	3b38,S22,O10(4/6/2),P2/1	0	-1.3
1988	Det A	130	452	61	122	14	1	12	62	21-2	3	70	.270	.305	.385	96	-4	6-0	.992	-1	107	127	O68(60/5/5),S37,3b31,2b5,1b4	0	-0.3
1989	SD N	95	246	27	66	7	2	8	22	11-3	1	44	.268	.302	.411	102	-1	1-3	.968	4	112	123	3b72,O14(2/2/10),S9,1b2	0	0.2
	†Chi N	26	80	7	26	5	0	1	12	4-0	0	13	.325	.357	.425	115	2	0-1	.921	-4	81	35	3b25,O2L	0	-0.3
	Year	121	326	34	92	12	2	9	34	15-3	1	57	.282	.316	.414	105	1	1-4	.959	0	104	101	3b97,O16(4/2/10),S9,1b2	0	-0.1
1990	Chi N	115	410	44	104	13	3	12	47	19-3	4	59	.254	.293	.388	80	-12	3-1	.950	-9	90	91	3b91,O28L	0	-2.2
1991	Chi N	103	333	34	86	14	1	14	38	15-1	1	45	.258	.292	.432	97	-3	0-3	.956	-3	106	39	3b86,1b7/lf	0	-0.7
1992	Chi N	98	255	20	53	7	2	5	25	11-2	0	34	.208	.237	.310	53	-17	1-1	.935	5	126	144	3b40,O34(33/0/1),S12,1b5	0	-1.3
Total	13	1302	4101	438	1070	144	33	94	455	179-37	15	653	.261	.293	.381	88	-84	117-51	.950	-14	104	100	3b863,O293L,S121,1b25,D10,2b5,P2	194	-10.1
Salazar, Oscar	Oscar Enrique; B6.27.1978 Maracay, Aragua, Venezuela; BR/TR/5´11˝/175; d4.10																								
2002	Det A	8	21	2	4	1	0	1	3	1-0	0	2	.190	.227	.381	60	-1	0-0	.938	-2	69	105	2b6/3S	0	-0.3
Sales, Ed	Edward A.; B1861 Harrisburg PA; D8.10.1912 New Haven CT; BL/TR; d7.15																								
1890	Pit N	51	189	19	43	7	3	1	23	16	3	15	.228	.298	.312	88	-2	3	.871	-12	91	44	S51	—	-1.1
Salkeld, Bill	William Franklin; B3.8.1917 Pocatello ID; D4.22.1967 Los Angeles CA; BL/TR/5´10˝/190; d4.18; gs–Roger																								
1945	Pit N	95	267	45	83	16	1	15	52	50	0	16	.311	.420	.547	161	24	2	.973	-6	*84*	*100*	C86	0	2.2
1946	Pit N	69	160	18	47	8	0	3	19	39	0	16	.294	.432	.400	133	10	2	.972	-3	*68*	*128*	C51	0	1.0
1947	Pit N	47	61	5	13	2	0	0	8	6	0	8	.213	.284	.246	41	-5	0	.971	-2	*82*	*101*	C15	0	-0.7
1948	†Bos N	78	198	26	48	8	1	8	28	42	1	37	.242	.378	.414	116	6	1	.990	3	*91*	*114*	C59	0	1.2
1949	Bos N	66	161	17	41	5	0	5	25	44	1	24	.255	.417	.379	121	8	1	.980	-2	*97*	*75*	C63	0	0.8
1950	Chi A	1	3	0	0	0	0	0	0	1	0	0	.000	.250	.000	-33	-1	0-0	1.000	0	*0*	*0*	/C	0	-0.1
Total	6	356	850	111	232	39	2	31	132	182	2	101	.273	.402	.433	129	42	6-0	.979	-10	*85*	*103*	C275	0	4.4
Salmon, Chico	Ruthford Eduardo; B12.3.1940 Colon, Pan; D9.17.2000 Bocas Del Toro, Pan; BR/TR/5´10˝/(155–170); d6.28; OF(56/5/64)																								
1964	Cle A	86	283	43	87	17	2	4	25	13-0	2	37	.307	.340	.424	113	5	10-6	1.000	0	104	43	O53(1/0/52),2b32,1b13	0	0.4
1965	Cle A	79	120	20	29	8	0	3	12	5-0	2	19	.242	.281	.383	87	-2	7-4	.985	-3	65	83	1b28,O17(10/1/6),2b5,3b5	0	-0.7
1966	Cle A	126	422	46	108	13	2	7	40	21-2	0	41	.256	.289	.346	82	-11	10-1	.958	-7	88	100	S61,2b28,1b24,O10(9/0/1),3b6	0	-1.1
1967	Cle A	90	203	19	46	13	1	2	19	17-1	1	29	.227	.288	.330	82	-4	10-4	1.000	9	139	123	O28(24/4/3),1b24,2b24,S14,3b4	0	0.7
1968	Cle A	103	276	24	59	8	1	3	12	12-0	3	30	.214	.253	.283	64	-13	7-7	.971	-8	87	87	2b45,3b18,S15,O13(11/0/2),1b11	21	-2.1
1969	†Bal A	52	91	18	27	5	0	3	12	10-1	2	22	.297	.375	.451	130	4	0-0	1.000	-6	60	106	1b17,2b9,S9,3b3/lf	0	-0.1
1970	†Bal A	63	172	19	43	4	0	7	22	8-0	1	30	.250	.287	.395	85	-4	2-2	.946	-14	79	79	S33,2b12,3b11,1b2	0	-1.6
1971	Bal A	42	84	11	15	1	0	2	7	3-0	0	21	.179	.205	.262	32	-8	0-0	1.000	-1	57	93	1b9,2b9,3b6,S5	0	-1.0
1972	Bal A	17	16	2	1	1	0	0	0	0-0	0	4	.063	.063	.125	-43	-3	0-0	1.000	-0	0	601	1b2/3	0	-0.3
Total	9	658	1667	202	415	70	6	31	149	89-4	11	233	.249	.290	.354	84	-36	46-24	.959	-29	96	80	2b164,S137,1b130,O122R,3b54	21	-5.8
Salmon, Tim	Timothy James; B8.24.1968 Long Beach CA; BR/TR/6´3˝/(200–241); [CalA89 3/69]; d8.21; Col Grand Canyon; [DL 2005 Ala A 183]																								
1992	Cal A	23	79	8	14	1	0	2	6	11-1	1	23	.177	.283	.266	55	-5	1-1	.953	-2	86	67	O21R	0	-0.7
1993	Cal A	142	515	93	146	35	1	31	95	82-5	5	135	.283	.382	.536	141	31	5-6	.980	9	110	113	O140(0/1/140)/D	0	3.1
1994	Cal A	100	373	67	107	18	2	23	70	54-2	5	102	.287	.382	.531	131	18	1-3	.966	4	105	121	O99R	16	1.4
1995	Cal A	143	537	111	177	34	3	34	105	91-2	6	111	.330	.429	.594	165	55	5-5	.988	7	113	74	O142R/D	0	5.0
1996	Cal A	156	581	90	166	27	4	30	98	93-7	4	125	.286	.386	.501	121	20	4-2	.975	0	96	121	O153R,D3	0	1.2
1997	Ana A	157	582	95	172	28	1	33	129	95-5	7	142	.296	.394	.517	137	34	9-12	.971	10	107	147	O153R,D4	0	3.2
1998	Ana A	136	463	84	139	28	1	26	88	90-5	3	100	.300	.410	.533	142	33	0-1	.959	1	126	75	D111,O19R	16	2.5
1999	Ana A	98	353	60	94	24	2	17	69	63-2	0	82	.266	.372	.490	119	12	4-1	.981	5	110	108	O89R,D7	74	1.2
2000	Ana A	158	568	108	165	36	2	34	97	104-5	6	139	.290	.404	.540	133	32	0-2	.979	6	105	134	O124R,D33	0	2.7
2001	Ana A	137	475	63	108	21	1	17	49	96-4	8	121	.227	.365	.383	96	1	9-3	.989	6	102	156	O125R,D12	19	0.1
2002	†Ana A	138	483	84	138	37	1	22	88	71-3	7	102	.286	.380	.503	136	28	6-3	.986	-4	95	60	O111R,D25	18	1.6
2003	Ana A	148	528	78	145	35	4	19	72	77-3	10	93	.275	.374	.464	125	22	3-1	.958	-1	98	102	O78R,D68	0	1.4
2004	Ana A	60	186	15	47	7	0	2	23	14-0	2	41	.253	.306	.323	69	-9	1-0	1.000	1	126	264	D39,O8(3/0/6)	41	-0.9
2006	LA A	76	211	30	56	8	2	9	27	29-1	3	44	.265	.361	.450	113	4	0-2	1.000	-1	52	0	D54,O4(1/0/3)	0	0.0
Total	14	1672	5934	986	1674	339	24	299	1016	970-45	67	1360	.282	.385	.498	128	276	48-42	.978	41	104	114	O1266(4/1/1263),D358	367	21.8
Saltzgaver, Jack	Otto Hamlin; B1.23.1903 Croton IA; D2.1.1978 Keokuk IA; BL/TR/5´11˝/165; d4.12																								
1932	NY A	20	47	10	6	2	1	0	5	10	0	10	.128	.281	.213	31	-5	1-1	.958	-3	72	64	2b16	—	-0.6
1934	NY A	94	350	64	95	8	1	6	36	48	0	28	.271	.359	.351	90	-4	8-1	.953	-11	84	74	3b84,1b4	—	-1.1
1935	NY A	61	149	17	39	6	0	3	18	23	2	12	.262	.368	.362	95	0	0-2	.937	-9	86	60	2b25,3b18,1b6	—	-0.8
1936	NY A	34	90	14	19	5	0	1	13	13	0	18	.211	.311	.300	53	-7	0-0	.972	-4	90	53	3b16,2b6,1b4	—	-0.8
1937	NY A	17	11	6	2	0	0	0	0	3	0	4	.182	.357	.182	40	-1	0-0	1.000	0	98	281	1b4	—	-0.1
1945	Pit N	52	117	20	38	5	3	0	10	8	0	8	.325	.368	.419	114	2	0	.963	-2	95	83	2b31/3	0	0.2
Total	6	278	764	131	199	26	5	10	82	105	2	80	.260	.351	.347	85	-15	9-4	.957	-28	83	79	3b119,2b78,1b18	0	-3.2
Samcoff, Ed	Edward William; B9.1.1924 Sacramento CA; BR/TR/5´10˝/165; d4.21																								
1951	Phi A	4	11	0	0	0	0	0	0	1	0	2	.000	.083	.000	-75	-3	0-0	1.000	-0	80	178	2b3	0	-0.3
Samford, Ron	Ronald Edward; B2.28.1930 Dallas TX; BR/TR/5´11˝/(156–165); d4.15																								
1954	NY N	12	5	2	0	0	0	0	0	0	0	1	.000	.000	.000	-99	-1	0-1	1.000	0	124	0	2b3	0	-0.1
1955	Det A	1	1	0	0	0	0	0	0	0-0	0	1	.000	.000	.000	-99	0	0-0	1.000	0	193	0	/S	0	0.0
1957	Det A	54	91	6	20	1	2	0	5	6-0	1	15	.220	.276	.275	49	-7	1-0	.964	-1	99	121	S35,2b11,3b4	0	-0.5
1959	Was A	91	237	23	53	13	0	5	22	11-0	2	29	.224	.262	.342	65	-12	1-0	.947	-1	105	95	S64,2b23	0	-0.6
Total	4	158	334	31	73	14	2	5	27	17-0	3	46	.219	.261	.317	58	-20	2-1	.952	-0	104	102	S100,2b37,3b4	0	-1.2
Sample, Bill	William Amos; B4.2.1955 Roanoke VA; BR/TR/5´9˝/175; [TexA76 10/228]; d9.2; Col James Madison																								
1978	Tex A	8	15	2	7	2	0	0	3	0-0	0	3	.467	.467	.600	197	2	0-0	ø	-0	0	0	O2L,D3	0	0.2
1979	Tex A	128	325	60	95	21	2	5	35	37-1	2	28	.292	.365	.415	112	7	8-6	1.000	1	96	113	O103(91/10/5),D9	0	0.4
1980	Tex A	99	204	29	53	10	0	4	19	18-2	6	15	.260	.335	.368	96	-1	8-5	.973	-4	91	53	O72(15/18/40),D4	0	-0.6
1981	Tex A	66	230	36	65	16	0	3	25	17-1	7	21	.283	.346	.391	119	6	4-1	.993	-2	92	87	O64(62/5/0)	27	0.2
1982	Tex A	97	360	56	94	14	2	10	29	27-0	3	35	.261	.318	.394	99	-1	10-2	.981	-1	98	105	O91(85/9/0)/D	0	-0.4
1983	Tex A	147	554	80	152	28	3	12	57	44-2	5	46	.274	.331	.401	102	2	44-8	.988	2	103	70	O146(144/2/1)	0	0.4
1984	Tex A	130	489	67	121	20	2	5	33	29-1	0	46	.247	.286	.327	68	-22	18-6	.986	-4	99	37	O122(72/51/3),D2	0	-2.8
1985	NY A	59	139	18	40	5	0	1	15	9-0	2	10	.288	.336	.345	90	-2	2-1	.989	-1	104	39	O55(51/4/0)	0	-0.4
1986	Atl N	92	200	23	57	11	0	6	14	14-1	3	26	.285	.338	.430	106	2	4-2	.986	-4	88	30	O56(10/0/48)/2	0	-0.4
Total	9	826	2516	371	684	127	9	46	230	195-8	28	230	.272	.329	.384	97	-7	98-31	.987	-12	97	70	O711(532/99/97),D19/2	27	-3.4
Samuel, Amado	Amado Ruperto; B12.6.1938 San Pedro de Macoris, D.R.; BR/TR/6´1˝/170; d4.10																								
1962	Mil N	76	209	16	43	10	0	3	20	12-1	0	54	.206	.248	.297	47	-16	0-2	.958	-10	84	81	S36,2b28,3b3	0	-2.3
1963	Mil N	15	17	0	3	1	0	0	0	0-0	0	4	.176	.176	.235	18	-2	0-1	.786	-2	76	118	S7,2b4	0	-0.4
1964	NY N	53	142	7	33	7	0	0	5	4-0	2	24	.232	.264	.282	55	-8	0-1	.945	1	105	144	S34,3b17,2b3	0	-0.6
Total	3	144	368	23	79	18	0	3	25	16-1	2	82	.215	.251	.288	49	-26	0-4	.942	-11	92	109	S77,2b35,3b20	0	-3.3
Samuel, Juan	Juan Milton; B12.9.1960 San Pedro de Macoris, D.R.; BR/TR/5´11˝/(163–190); d8.24; C7; OF(34/197/40)																								
1983	†Phi N	18	65	14	18	1	2	2	5	4-1	1	16	.277	.324	.446	114	1	3-2	.916	3	110	87	2b18	0	0.5
1984	Phi N☆	160	701	105	191	36	**19**	15	69	28-2	7	168	.272	.307	.442	107	2	72-15	.962	-15	95	78	2b160	0	0.7
1985	Phi N	161	663	101	175	31	13	19	74	33-2	6	141	.264	.303	.436	102	-1	53-19	.983	1	99	79	2b159	0	1.4
1986	Phi N	145	591	90	157	36	12	16	78	26-3	8	142	.266	.302	.448	102	-2	42-14	.967	-5	105	92	2b143	19	0.6
1987	Phi N★	160	655	113	178	37	**15**	28	100	60-5	5	162	.272	.335	.502	115	12	35-15	.978	-12	97	94	2b160	0	1.1
1988	Phi N	157	629	68	153	32	9	12	67	39-6	12	151	.243	.298	.380	92	-8	33-10	.978	-21	87	90	2b152,O3(0/2/1)/3	0	-2.3
1989	Phi N	51	199	32	49	3	1	8	20	18-1	1	45	.246	.311	.392	100	-1	11-3	.993	1	109	80	O50C	16	0.2
	NY N	86	333	37	76	13	1	3	28	24-1	10	75	.228	.299	.300	75	-11	31-9	.986	1	103	98	O84C	0	-0.8
	Year	137	532	69	125	16	2	11	48	42-2	11	120	.235	.303	.335	85	-11	42-12	.989	2	105	91	O134C	0	-0.6
1990	LA N	143	492	62	119	24	3	13	52	51-5	5	126	.242	.316	.382	94	-4	38-20	.972	-12	86	92	2b108,O31C	0	-1.2
1991	LA N★	153	594	74	161	22	6	12	58	49-4	3	133	.271	.328	.389	103	1	23-8	.978	-5	96	95	2b152	0	0.3
1992	LA N	47	122	7	32	3	1	0	15	7-3	1	22	.262	.303	.303	74	-4	2-2	.974	-2	86	70	2b38/rf	44	-0.6
	KC A	29	102	15	29	5	3	0	8	7-1	1	27	.284	.336	.392	100	0	6-1	.903	-1	78	183	O18R,2b10	0	-0.1

YEAR	TM LG	G	AB	R	H	2B	3B	HR	RBI	BB-IB	HP	SO	AVG	OBP	SLG	AOPS	ABR	SB-CS	FA	FR	RNG	THR	GAMES AT POSITION	DL	BFW
1993	Cin N	103	261	31	60	10	4	4	26	23-3	3	53	.230	.298	.345	72	-11	9-7	.971	-2	91	87	2b70,1b6,3b4,O3(2/0/1)	0	-1.0
1994	Det A	59	136	32	42	9	5	5	21	10-0	3	26	.309	.364	.559	133	6	5-2	1.000	1	92	76	O27(2/25/0),D10,2b8,1b2	0	0.7
1995	Det A	76	171	28	48	10	1	10	34	24-0	2	38	.281	.376	.526	132	8	5-4	.983	-1	109	93	1b37,D16,O9L,2b6	0	0.3
	KC A	15	34	3	6	0	0	2	5	5-1	0	11	.176	.282	.353	63	-2	1-0	1.000	-1	39	0	O5L/1D	0	-0.3
	Year	91	205	31	54	10	1	12	39	29-1	2	49	.263	.360	.498	120	6	6-4	.984	-2	105	90	1b38,D23,O14L,2b6	0	0.0
1996	Tor A	69	188	34	48	8	3	8	26	15-0	3	65	.255	.319	.457	94	-3	9-1	1.000	-5	77	0	O24(8/5/15),D24,1b17	15	-0.8
1997	Tor A	45	95	13	27	5	4	3	15	10-0	2	28	.284	.364	.516	126	3	5-3	1.000	-3	49	155	D15,3b9,1b7,2b4,O2R	0	0.0
1998	Tor A	43	50	14	9	2	0	1	2	7-0	1	13	.180	.293	.280	50	-4	13-8	.882	-1	98	0	D11,O10(8/0/2),1b3,2b2	0	-0.5
Total	16	1720	6081	873	1578	287	102	161	703	440-38	74	1442	.259	.315	.420	100	-18	396-143	.973	-76	95	88	2b1190,O267C,D83,1b73,3b14	94	-1.8
Samuels, Ike Samuel Earl; B2.20.1874 Quincy IL; D2.22.1964 New York NY; BR/TR/5´7˝/?; d8.3																									
1895	StL N	24	74	5	17	2	0	0	5	5	0	7	.230	.278	.257	39	-7	5	.750	-6	92	32	3b21,S3	—	-1.0
Sanchez, Alejandro Alejandro (Pimentel); B2.14.1959 San Pedro de Macoris, D.R.; BR/TR/6´0˝/(175–185); d9.6																									
1982	Phi N	7	14	3	4	1	0	2	4	0-0	0	4	.286	.286	.786	184	1	0-0	1.000	-0	107	0	O4R	0	0.1
1983	Phi N	8	7	2	2	0	0	0	2	0-0	0	2	.286	.286	.286	59	0	0-0	.500	-0	62	0	O2R	0	-0.1
1984	SF N	13	41	3	8	0	1	0	2	0-0	0	12	.195	.195	.244	23	-5	2-3	.952	1	91	280	O11(3/0/9)	0	-0.5
1985	Det A	71	133	19	33	6	2	6	12	0-0	0	39	.248	.248	.459	89	-3	2-2	.923	-1	93	82	O31(5/2/24),D28	0	-0.6
1986	Min A	8	16	1	2	0	0	0	1	1-0	0	8	.125	.176	.125	-16	-3	0-0	ø	-0	0	0	/lfD	0	-0.3
1987	Oak A	2	3	0	0	0	0	0	0	0-0	0	1	.000	.000	.000	-99	-1	0-0	1.000	-0	91	0	/rfD	0	-0.1
Total	6	109	214	28	49	7	3	8	21	1-0	0	66	.229	.233	.402	71	-11	4-5	.929	-2	92	128	O50(9/2/40),D32	0	-1.5
Sanchez, Alex Alexis; B8.26.1976 Havana, Cuba; BL/TL/5´10˝/180; [TBA96 5/154]; d6.15; Col Miami–Dade Wolfson (FL) CC																									
2001	Mil N	30	68	7	14	3	2	0	4	5-0	0	13	.206	.260	.309	47	-6	6-2	.963	-1	72	237	O19(3/14/3)	15	-0.6
2002	Mil N	112	394	55	114	10	7	1	33	31-0	2	62	.289	.343	.358	86	-9	37-14	.982	6	126	19	O100(16/86/0)	28	0.1
2003	Mil N	43	163	15	46	10	3	0	10	7-0	2	28	.282	.316	.380	82	-5	8-6	.990	3	116	152	O36C	0	-0.1
	Det A	101	394	43	114	13	5	1	22	18-0	1	46	.289	.320	.355	82	-11	44-18	.979	-1	107	22	O99C	0	-0.7
2004	Det A	79	332	41	107	9	3	2	26	7-0	0	50	.322	.335	.386	91	-6	19-13	.952	-6	92	53	O78C	77	-1.1
2005	TB A	43	133	28	46	8	1	2	13	7-1	0	25	.346	.373	.466	125	5	6-3	.957	-1	99	66	O31(0/18/14),D7	0	0.3
	SF N	19	43	4	11	3	0	0	3	1-0	1	9	.256	.289	.326	59	-3	2-2	.870	0	105	215	O10(0/4/6)/D	15	-0.3
Total	5	427	1527	193	452	56	21	6	111	76-1	6	233	.296	.330	.372	86	-35	122-58	.971	0	108	58	O373(19/335/23),D8	135	-2.4
Sanchez, Angel Angel Luis; B9.20.1983 Humacao, PR; BR/TR/6´2˝/185; [KCA01 11/325]; d9.23																									
2006	KC A	8	27	2	6	0	0	0	1	0-0	0	4	.222	.214	.222	16	-3	0-0	1.000	5	180	88	2b4,S4	0	0.2
Sanchez, Celerino Celerino (Perez); B2.3.1944 El Guayabal, Veracruz, Mexico; D5.1.1992 Leon, Guanajuato, Mexico; BR/TR/5´11˝/160; d6.13																									
1972	NY A	71	250	18	62	8	3	0	22	12-1	4	30	.248	.292	.304	80	-7	0-0	.939	2	114	98	3b68	0	-0.6
1973	NY A	34	64	12	14	3	0	1	9	2-0	0	12	.219	.239	.313	57	-4	1-1	1.000	-0	99	0	3b11,D11,S2,O2R	0	-0.5
Total	2	105	314	30	76	11	3	1	31	14-1	4	42	.242	.281	.306	75	-11	1-1	.943	2	113	89	3b79,D11,O2R,S2	0	-1.1
Sanchez, Freddy Frederick Philip; B12.21.1977 Hollywood CA; BR/TR/5´11˝/(185–190); d9.10; Col Oklahoma City																									
2002	Bos A	12	16	3	3	0	0	0	2	2-0	0	3	.188	.278	.188	27	-2	0-0	1.000	-1	93	51	2b5,S5	0	-0.2
2003	Bos A	20	34	6	8	2	0	0	2	0-0	0	8	.235	.235	.294	37	-3	0-0	1.000	2	158	0	3b7,S6,2b3	0	0.0
2004	Pit N	9	19	2	3	0	0	0	2	0-0	0	3	.158	.158	.158	-18	-3	0-0	.800	-3	75	0	S4,2b3/3	96	-0.7
2005	Pit N	132	453	54	132	26	4	5	35	27-1	5	36	.291	.336	.400	92	-5	2-2	.977	10	114	176	3b65,2b58,S11	0	0.7
2006	Pit N★	157	582	85	200	**53**	2	6	85	31-6	7	52	**.344**	.378	.473	115	15	3-2	.981	23	123	124	3b99,S28,2b23	0	4.0
Total	5	330	1104	150	346	81	6	11	126	60-7	12	102	.313	.352	.428	100	2	5-4	.980	31	121	139	3b172,2b92,S54	96	3.8
Sanchez, Orlando Orlando (Marquez); B9.7.1956 Canovanas, PR; BL/TR/6´1˝/185; d5.6																									
1981	StL N	27	49	5	14	2	1	0	6	2-1	0	6	.286	.308	.367	89	-1	1-0	.926	-3	71	44	C18	0	-0.4
1982	StL N	26	37	6	7	0	1	0	3	5-0	0	5	.189	.286	.243	48	-3	0-0	1.000	-3	49	0	C15	0	-0.5
1983	StL N	6	6	0	0	0	0	0	0	0-0	0	4	.000	.000	.000	-99	-2	0-0	1.000	0	0	0	/C	0	-0.2
1984	KC A	10	10	0	1	1	0	0	2	0-0	0	2	.100	.100	.200	-19	-2	0-0	1.000	0	0	0	/C	0	-0.1
	Bal A	4	8	0	2	0	0	0	1	0-0	0	2	.250	.250	.250	40	-1	0-0	1.000	0	113	158	C4	0	0.0
	Year	14	18	0	3	1	0	0	3	0-0	0	4	.167	.167	.222	6	-2	0-0	1.000	0	107	149	C5	0	-0.1
Total	4	73	110	11	24	3	2	0	12	7-1	0	19	.218	.263	.282	52	-9	1-0	.962	-5	65	36	C39	0	-1.2
Sanchez, Rey Rey Francisco (Guadalupe); B10.5.1967 Rio Piedras, PR; BR/TR/5´9˝/(165–175); [TexA86 13/319]; d9.8																									
1991	Chi N	13	23	1	6	0	0	0	2	4-0	0	3	.261	.370	.261	77	-1	0-0	1.000	-1	80	27	S10,2b2	0	-0.1
1992	Chi N	74	255	24	64	14	3	1	19	10-1	3	17	.251	.285	.341	75	-9	2-1	.974	10	104	142	S68,2b4	15	0.7
1993	Chi N	105	344	35	97	11	2	0	28	15-7	3	22	.282	.316	.326	73	-13	1-1	.969	27	122	116	S98	0	2.0
1994	Chi N	96	291	26	83	13	1	0	24	20-4	7	29	.285	.345	.337	79	-8	2-5	.993	**20**	108	84	2b50,S30,3b17	0	1.4
1995	Chi N	114	428	57	119	22	2	3	27	14-2	1	48	.278	.301	.360	74	-17	6-4	.987	2	**109**	87	2b111,S4	16	-0.9
1996	Chi N	95	289	28	61	9	0	1	12	22-6	3	42	.211	.272	.253	39	-26	7-1	.977	21	119	103	S92	66	0.3
1997	Chi N	97	205	14	51	9	0	1	12	11-2	0	26	.249	.287	.307	54	-14	4-2	.964	-7	91	63	S63,2b32/3	0	-1.7
	†NY A	38	138	21	43	12	0	1	15	5-0	1	21	.312	.338	.420	98	0	0-4	.976	2	108	98	2b37,S6	0	0.2
1998	SF N	109	316	44	90	14	2	2	30	16-0	4	47	.285	.325	.361	85	-7	0-0	.977	12	109	97	S76,2b36	0	1.0
1999	KC A	134	479	66	141	18	6	2	56	22-2	4	48	.294	.329	.370	75	-19	11-5	.982	29	**119**	115	S134	0	1.9
2000	KC A	143	509	68	139	18	2	1	38	28-0	4	55	.273	.314	.322	59	-32	7-3	.994	19	**112**	108	S143	0	-0.2
2001	KC A	100	390	46	118	14	5	0	28	11-0	2	34	.303	.322	.364	74	-15	9-1	.994	32	126	158	S100	0	2.4
	†Atl N	49	154	10	35	4	1	0	9	4-1	0	15	.227	.245	.266	32	-16	2-0	.986	8	113	122	S48	0	-0.4
2002	Bos A	107	357	46	102	12	3	1	38	17-1	2	31	.286	.318	.345	76	-13	2-2	.991	4	100	111	2b100,S10	37	-0.3
2003	NY N	56	174	11	36	3	1	0	12	8-2	0	18	.207	.240	.236	26	-20	1-1	.989	-1	99	87	S42,2b12	41	-1.7
	Sea A	46	170	22	50	5	1	0	11	8-1	2	21	.294	.330	.335	82	-5	1-0	.979	-3	88	128	S46	0	-0.4
2004	TB A	91	285	23	70	14	3	2	26	12-0	3	28	.246	.281	.337	62	-17	0-1	.987	4	103	104	2b87,S4	0	-0.8
2005	NY A	23	43	7	12	1	0	0	2	2-0	1	3	.279	.326	.302	69	-2	0-1	.955	3	112	141	S10,2b9/3D	115	0.1
Total	15	1490	4850	549	1317	193	32	15	389	229-29	40	508	.272	.308	.334	68	-234	55-32	.981	183	113	117	S984,2b480,3b19,D2	290	3.5
Sand, Heinie John Henry; B7.3.1897 San Francisco CA; D11.3.1958 San Francisco CA; BR/TR/5´8˝/160; d4.17																									
1923	Phi N	132	470	85	107	16	5	4	32	82	4	56	.228	.347	.309	67	-20	7-3	.934	-3	98	106	S120,3b11	—	-0.9
1924	Phi N	137	539	79	132	21	6	6	40	52	4	57	.245	.316	.340	67	-24	5-4	**.959**	2	100	97	S137	—	-0.7
1925	Phi N	148	496	69	138	30	7	3	55	64	3	65	.278	.364	.385	84	-10	1-1	.928	-6	94	100	S143	—	-0.2
1926	Phi N	149	567	99	154	30	5	4	37	66	2	56	.272	.350	.363	88	-8	2	.939	-0	102	85	S149	—	0.7
1927	Phi N	141	535	87	160	22	8	1	49	58	1	59	.299	.369	.376	98	0	5	.949	-4	92	65	S86,3b58	—	0.8
1928	Phi N	141	426	38	90	26	1	0	38	60	1	47	.211	.310	.277	53	-28	1	.951	-0	98	95	S137	—	-1.4
Total	6	848	3033	457	781	145	32	18	251	382	15	340	.258	.343	.344	77	-90	21-8	.943	-12	98	93	S772,3b69	—	-1.7
Sandberg, Gus Gustave E.; B2.23.1895 Long Island City NY; D2.3.1930 Los Angeles CA; BR/TR/6´1˝/189; d5.11																									
1923	Cin N	7	17	1	3	1	0	0	1	1	0	1	.176	.222	.235	21	-2	0-0	1.000	-0	*117*	*113*	C5	—	-0.2
1924	Cin N	24	52	1	9	0	0	0	3	2	0	7	.173	.204	.173	2	-7	0-0	1.000	0	*94*	*83*	C24	—	-0.6
Total	2	31	69	2	12	1	0	0	4	3	0	8	.174	.208	.188	7	-9	0-0	1.000	-0	*99*	*89*	C29	—	-0.8
Sandberg, Jared Jared Lawrence; B3.2.1978 Olympia WA; BR/TR/6´3˝/212; [TBA96 16/484]; d8.7																									
2001	TB A	39	136	13	28	7	0	1	15	10-0	1	45	.206	.265	.279	45	-11	1-0	.944	-1	93	101	3b38/1	0	-1.1
2002	TB A	102	358	55	82	21	1	18	54	39-3	1	139	.229	.305	.444	98	-2	3-2	.948	-2	98	107	3b97,1b3,D2	0	-0.3
2003	TB A	55	136	15	29	10	1	6	23	16-1	2	52	.213	.305	.434	94	-1	0-0	.956	1	106	56	3b50/1S	0	0.0
Total	3	196	630	83	139	38	2	25	92	65-4	4	236	.221	.297	.406	86	-14	4-2	.949	-2	99	94	3b185,1b5,D2/S	0	-1.4
Sandberg, Ryne Ryne Dee; B9.18.1959 Spokane WA; BR/TR/6´2˝/(175–190); [PhiN78 20/511]; d9.2; HF2005																									
1981	Phi N	13	6	2	1	0	0	0	0	0-0	0	1	.167	.167	.167	-5	-1	0-0	1.000	1	85	0	S5/2	0	0.0
1982	Chi N	156	635	103	172	33	5	7	54	36-3	4	90	.271	.312	.372	88	-11	32-12	.970	15	112	88	3b133,2b24	0	0.7
1983	Chi N	158	633	94	165	25	4	8	48	51-3	3	79	.261	.316	.351	81	-16	37-11	**.986**	**44**	**121**	**123**	2b157/S	0	4.2
1984	†Chi N★	156	636	**114**	200	36	**19**	19	84	52-3	3	101	.314	.367	.520	136	29	32-7	**.993**	22	**112**	103	2b156	0	**6.6**
1985	Chi N★	153	609	113	186	31	6	26	83	57-5	1	97	.305	.364	.504	128	23	54-11	.986	13	108	95	2b153/S	0	5.4
1986	Chi N★	154	627	68	178	28	5	14	76	46-6	0	79	.284	.330	.411	97	-3	34-11	**.994**	4	104	84	2b153	0	1.3
1987	Chi N★	132	523	81	154	25	2	16	59	59-4	2	79	.294	.367	.442	109	8	21-2	.985	5	98	93	2b131	27	2.4

YEAR	TM LG	G	AB	R	H	2B	3B	HR	RBI	BB-IB	HP	SO	AVG	OBP	SLG	AOPS	ABR	SB-CS	FA	FR	RNG	THR	GAMES AT POSITION	DL	BFW
1988	Chi N★	155	618	77	163	23	8	19	69	54-3	1	91	.264	.322	.419	107	4	25-10	.987	12	**111**	82	2b153	0	2.3
1989	†Chi N★	157	606	**104**	176	25	5	30	76	59-8	4	85	.290	.356	.497	132	25	15-5	.992	-1	103	92	2b155	0	3.1
1990	Chi N★	155	615	**116**	188	30	3	**40**	100	50-8	1	84	.306	.354	.559	139	31	25-7	.989	4	106	93	2b154	0	4.3
1991	Chi N★	158	585	104	170	32	2	26	100	87-4	2	89	.291	.379	.485	137	31	22-8	**.995**	-3	108	77	2b157	0	3.6
1992	Chi N★	158	612	100	186	32	8	26	87	68-4	1	73	.304	.371	.510	144	35	17-6	.990	12	**112**	100	2b157	0	5.6
1993	Chi N★	117	456	67	141	20	0	9	45	37-1	2	62	.309	.359	.412	108	6	9-2	.988	1	105	111	2b115	25	1.4
1994	Chi N	57	223	36	53	9	5	5	24	23-0	1	40	.238	.312	.390	81	-7	2-3	.987	6	115	98	2b57	0	0.1
1996	Chi N	150	554	85	135	28	4	25	92	54-4	7	116	.244	.316	.444	95	-5	12-8	.991	-16	101	94	2b146	0	-1.5
1997	Chi N	135	447	54	118	26	0	12	64	28-3	2	94	.264	.308	.403	82	-12	7-4	.984	-20	90	81	2b126/D	0	-2.7
Total	16	2164	8385	1318	2386	403	76	282	1061	761-59	34	1260	.285	.344	.452	113	137	344-107	.989	99	107	94	2b1995,3b133,S7/D	52	36.8
SANDERS, BEN	Alexander Bennett; B2.16.1865 Catharpin VA; D8.29.1930 Memphis TN; BR/TR/6´0˝/210; d6.6; Col Roanoke; ▲																								
1888	Phi N	57	236	26	58	11	2	1	25	8	2	12	.246	.276	.322	86	-4	13	.929	3	125	81	P31,O25(13/6/7)/3	—	-0.1
1889	Phi N	44	169	21	47	8	2	0	21	6	1	11	.278	.307	.349	76	-6	4	.879	-2	84	36	P44,O3(1/2/0)	—	-0.1
1890	Phi P	52	189	31	59	6	6	0	30	10	0	10	.312	.347	.407	99	-2	2	.924	1	103	171	P43,O10(0/3/7)	—	0.0
1891	Phi AA	40	156	24	39	6	4	1	19	7	2	12	.250	.291	.359	86	-4	2	.839	-4	0	0	O22(10/0/13),P19	—	-0.6
1892	Lou N	54	198	30	54	12	2	3	18	16	1	17	.273	.330	.399	131	7	6	.930	-3	90	150	P31,1b15,O9R	—	0.1
Total	5	247	948	132	257	43	16	5	113	47	6	62	.271	.310	.366	95	-9	27	.916	-5	99	107	P168,O69(24/11/36),1b15/3	—	-0.7
SANDERS, ANTHONY	Anthony Marcus; B3.2.1974 Tucson AZ; BR/TR/6´2˝/(200–205); [TorA92 7/205]; d4.26																								
1999	Tor A	3	7	1	2	1	0	0	2	0-0	0	2	.286	.286	.429	78	0	0-0	1.000	-0	49	0	/lfD	0	0.0
2000	Sea A	1	1	1	1	0	0	0	0	0-0	0	0	1.000	1.000	1.000	416	0	0-0	1.000	0	431	0	/rf	0	0.1
2001	Sea A	9	17	1	3	2	0	0	2	2-0	0	3	.176	.263	.294	49	-1	0-0	1.000	0	121	0	O9(8/0/1)	0	-0.1
Total	3	13	25	3	6	3	0	0	4	2-0	0	5	.240	.296	.360	73	-1	0-0	1.000	0	115	0	O11(9/0/2),D2	0	0.0
SANDERS, DEION	Deion Luwynn; B8.9.1967 Ft.Myers FL; BL/TL/6´1˝/(195–196); [NYA88 30/781]; d5.31; Col Florida St.; [DL 2000 Cin N 59]																								
1989	NY A	14	47	7	11	2	0	2	7	3-1	0	8	.234	.280	.404	91	-1	1-0	.969	-0	95	144	O14(3/11/0)	0	-0.1
1990	NY A	57	133	24	21	2	2	3	9	13-0	1	27	.158	.236	.271	42	-11	8-2	.973	-3	83	92	O42(29/15/0),D4	0	-1.4
1991	Atl N	54	110	16	21	1	2	4	13	12-0	0	23	.191	.270	.345	68	-5	11-3	.952	-1	93	169	O44(41/5/1)	0	-0.6
1992	†Atl N	97	303	54	92	6	**14**	8	28	18-0	2	52	.304	.346	.495	128	9	26-9	.983	-1	99	100	O75(12/60/9)	0	1.0
1993	†Atl N	95	272	42	75	18	6	6	28	16-3	3	42	.276	.321	.452	102	0	19-7	.986	-3	95	33	O60(5/55/0)	15	-0.1
1994	Atl N	46	191	32	55	10	0	4	21	16-1	1	28	.288	.343	.403	91	-2	19-7	.980	-4	91	0	O46C	0	-0.4
	Cin N	46	184	26	51	7	4	0	7	16-0	2	35	.277	.342	.359	83	-5	19-9	1.000	1	104	86	O45C	0	-0.2
	Year	92	375	58	106	17	4	4	28	32-1	3	63	.283	.342	.381	87	-7	38-16	.991	-4	97	42	O91C	0	-0.6
1995	Cin N	33	129	19	31	2	3	1	10	9-0	2	18	.240	.296	.326	64	-7	16-3	.968	2	117	117	O33C	45	-0.2
	SF N	52	214	29	61	9	5	5	18	18-0	2	42	.285	.346	.444	109	2	8-6	.984	-3	101	0	O52C	0	0.0
	Year	85	343	48	92	11	8	6	28	27-0	4	60	.268	.327	.399	92	-5	24-9	.977	-0	107	45	O85C	0	-0.2
1997	Cin N	115	465	53	127	13	7	5	23	34-2	6	67	.273	.329	.363	80	-14	56-13	.984	-2	102	52	O113(37/77/0)	0	-0.9
2001	Cin N	32	75	6	13	2	0	1	4	4-0	2	10	.173	.235	.240	22	-9	3-4	1.000	3	109	404	O16(12/4/1),D2	0	-0.7
Total	9	641	2123	308	558	72	43	39	168	159-7	21	352	.263	.319	.392	88	-43	186-63	.982	-11	99	76	O540(139/403/11),D6	119	-3.6
SANDERS, JOHN	John Frank; B11.20.1945 Grand Island NE; BR/TR/6´2˝/200; d4.13																								
1965	KC A	1	0	0	0	0	0	0	0	0-0	0	0	ø	ø	ø	ø	0	0-0	ø	0	—	—	/R	0	0.0
SANDERS, RAY	Raymond Floyd; B12.4.1916 Bonne Terre MO; D10.28.1983 Washington MO; BL/TR/6´2˝/185; d4.14; [DL 1947 Bos N 114]																								
1942	†StL N	95	282	37	71	17	2	5	39	42	1	31	.252	.351	.379	106	3	2	.991	-3	79	107	1b77	0	-0.7
1943	†StL N	144	478	69	134	21	5	11	73	77	1	33	.280	.381	.414	124	17	1	.995	-5	80	**130**	1b141	0	0.5
1944	†StL N	154	601	87	177	34	9	12	102	71	2	50	.295	.371	.441	126	21	2	**.994**	-12	64	**136**	1b152	0	0.1
1945	StL N	143	537	85	148	29	3	8	78	83	2	55	.276	.375	.385	109	10	3	.986	-5	92	**113**	1b142	0	-0.2
1946	Bos N	80	259	43	63	12	0	6	35	50	1	38	.243	.368	.359	105	4	0	.988	3	116	106	1b77	0	0.5
1948	†Bos N	5	4	0	1	0	0	0	2	1	0	0	.250	.400	.250	81	0	0	ø	0	—	—	/H	0	0.0
1949	Bos N	9	21	0	3	1	0	0	0	4	0	9	.143	.280	.190	30	-2	0	.984	2	250	40	1b7	136	0.0
Total	7	630	2182	321	597	114	19	42	329	328	7	216	.274	.370	.401	115	53	8	.991	-20	85	121	1b596	250	0.2
SANDERS, REGGIE	Reginald Jerome; B9.9.1949 Birmingham AL; BR/TR/6´2˝/194; d9.1																								
1974	Det A	26	99	12	27	7	0	3	10	5-2	0	20	.273	.308	.434	108	1	1-0	.987	1	119	82	1b25/D	0	0.0
SANDERS, REGGIE	Reginald Laverne; B12.1.1967 Florence SC; BR/TR/6´1˝/(180–205); [CinN87 7/180]; d8.22; Col Spartanburg Methodist (SC) JC																								
1991	Cin N	9	40	6	8	0	0	1	3	0-0	0	9	.200	.200	.275	31	-4	1-1	1.000	-0	105	0	O9C	27	-0.5
1992	Cin N	116	385	62	104	26	6	12	36	48-2	4	98	.270	.356	.462	127	15	16-7	.978	11	112	**212**	O110(53/77/0)	32	2.6
1993	Cin N	138	496	90	136	16	4	20	83	51-7	5	118	.274	.343	.444	109	6	27-10	.975	2	117	29	O137(0/4/135)	0	0.4
1994	Cin N	107	400	66	105	20	8	17	62	41-1	2	114	.262	.332	.480	109	4	21-9	.975	6	107	155	O104R	0	0.6
1995	†Cin N★	133	484	91	148	36	6	28	99	69-4	8	122	.306	.397	.579	153	39	36-12	.983	4	101	128	O130(0/16/125)	0	4.0
1996	Cin N	81	287	49	72	17	1	14	33	44-4	2	86	.251	.353	.463	112	6	24-8	.988	4	106	131	O80R	60	0.8
1997	Cin N	86	312	52	79	19	2	19	56	42-3	3	93	.253	.347	.510	119	8	13-7	.974	3	113	63	O85R	76	0.7
1998	Cin N	135	481	83	129	18	6	14	59	51-2	7	137	.268	.346	.418	99	-1	20-9	.978	-4	102	53	O131(0/88/57)	0	-0.5
1999	SD N	133	478	92	136	24	7	26	72	65-1	6	108	.285	.376	.527	136	25	36-13	.975	-3	98	54	O129(97/15/41)/D	15	2.0
2000	†Atl N	103	340	43	79	23	1	11	37	32-2	2	78	.232	.302	.403	77	-13	21-4	.964	-1	92	127	O96(69/1/27)	39	-1.4
2001	†Ari N	126	441	84	116	21	3	33	90	46-7	5	126	.263	.337	.549	116	9	14-10	.996	1	102	67	O119R	7	0.4
2002	†SF N	140	505	75	126	23	6	23	85	47-3	12	121	.250	.324	.455	107	3	18-6	.984	9	112	136	O137R	0	0.7
2003	Pit N	130	453	74	129	27	4	31	87	38-4	5	110	.285	.345	.567	132	19	15-5	.983	-1	100	80	O120(39/0/91),D2	0	1.4
2004	†StL N	135	446	64	116	27	3	22	67	33-5	4	118	.260	.315	.482	101	-1	21-5	.981	-3	95	90	O119(38/0/81)/D	0	-0.5
2005	†StL N	93	295	49	80	14	2	21	54	28-1	4	75	.271	.340	.546	125	10	14-1	.983	-5	75	138	O81(80/0/1)/D	58	0.5
2006	KC A	88	325	45	80	23	1	11	49	28-3	1	86	.246	.304	.425	88	-6	7-7	.989	5	118	90	O73R,D13	53	-0.6
Total	16	1753	6168	1025	1643	334	60	303	972	663-49	70	1599	.266	.342	.487	114	119	304-114	.980	28	104	100	O1660(376/210/1156),D18	367	10.6
SANDLOCK, MIKE	Michael Joseph; B10.17.1915 Old Greenwich CT; BB/TR (BL 1944)/6´1˝/185; d9.19																								
1942	Bos N	2	1	1	1	0	0	0	0	0	0	0	1.000	1.000	1.000	496	0	0	ø	-0	0	0	S2	0	0.0
1944	Bos N	30	30	1	3	0	0	0	2	5	1	3	.100	.250	.100	1	-4	0	.956	4	143	55	3b22,S7	0	0.0
1945	Bro N	80	195	21	55	14	2	2	17	18	1	19	.282	.346	.405	109	2	2	.991	-1	*108*	*79*	C47,S22,2b4,3b2	0	0.5
1946	Bro N	19	34	1	5	0	0	0	0	3	0	4	.147	.216	.147	4	-4	0	.973	4	*130*	*167*	C17/3	0	0.0
1953	Pit N	64	186	10	43	5	0	0	12	12	1	19	.231	.281	.258	42	-16	0-0	.991	7	*76*	*170*	C64	0	-0.5
Total	5	195	446	34	107	19	2	2	31	38	3	45	.240	.304	.305	66	-22	2-0	.989	14	*94*	*135*	C128,S31,3b25,2b4	0	0.0
SANDOVAL, DANNY	Danny E.; B4.7.1979 Lara, Venezuela; BB/TR/5´11˝/(190–200); d7.17																								
2005	Phi N	3	2	1	0	0	0	0	0	0-0	0	1	.000	.000	.000	-97	-1	0-0	1.000	0	305	0	/S	0	0.0
2006	Phi N	28	38	1	8	1	0	0	4	4-0	0	3	.211	.279	.237	34	-4	0-0	1.000	-2	67	40	2b8,S6	0	-0.5
Total	2	31	40	2	8	1	0	0	4	4-0	0	4	.200	.267	.225	29	-5	0-0	1.000	-2	67	40	2b8,S7	0	-0.5
SANDS, CHARLIE	Charles Duane; B12.17.1947 Newport News VA; BL/TR/6´2˝/(200–215); [BalA65 11/380]; d6.21																								
1967	NY A	1	1	0	0	0	0	0	0	0-0	0	1	.000	.000	.000	-99	0	0-0	ø	0	—	—	/H	0	0.0
1971	†Pit N	28	25	4	5	2	0	1	5	7-1	0	6	.200	.375	.400	119	1	0-0	1.000	-0	41	225	C3	0	0.1
1972	Pit N	1	1	0	0	0	0	0	0	0-0	0	0	.000	.000	.000	-99	0	0-0	ø	0	—	—	/H	0	0.0
1973	Cal A	17	33	5	9	2	1	1	5	5-1	0	10	.273	.368	.485	149	2	0-0	.917	-5	83	0	C10	0	-0.3
1974	Cal A	43	83	6	16	2	0	4	13	23-2	1	17	.193	.370	.361	118	3	0-0	1.000	-0	174	0	D21,C5	64	0.3
1975	Oak A	3	2	0	1	0	0	0	0	1-0	0	1	.500	.667	.500	238	1	0-0	ø	0	—	—	/D	0	0.1
Total	6	93	145	15	31	6	1	6	23	36-4	1	35	.214	.372	.393	125	7	0-0	.955	-5	98	34	D22,C18	64	0.2
SANDT, TOMMY	Thomas James; B12.22.1950 Brooklyn NY; BR/TR/5´11˝/175; [OakA69 2/33]; d6.29; C16																								
1975	Oak A	1	0	0	0	0	0	0	0	0-0	0	0	ø	ø	ø	ø	0	0-0	ø	-0	0	0	/2	0	0.0
1976	Oak A	41	67	6	14	1	0	0	3	7-0	0	9	.209	.284	.224	52	-4	0-0	.966	-4	88	100	S29,2b9,3b2	0	-0.6
Total	2	42	67	6	14	1	0	0	3	7-0	0	9	.209	.284	.224	52	-4	0-0	.966	-4	88	100	S29,2b10,3b2	0	-0.6

YEAR	TM LG	G	AB	R	H	2B	3B	HR	RBI	BB-IB	HP	SO	AVG	OBP	SLG	AOPS	ABR	SB-CS	FA	FR	RNG	THR	GAMES AT POSITION	DL	BFW
Sanford, Chance	Chance Steven; B6.2.1972 Houston TX; BL/TR/5´10˝/175; [PitN92 27/763]; d4.30; Col San Jacinto North (TX) JC																								
1998	Pit N	14	28	3	4	1	1	0	3	1-0	0	6	.143	.172	.250	9	-4	0-0	.900	-3	49	217	3b5/2S	0	-0.7
1999	LA N	5	8	1	2	0	0	0	2	0-0	0	1	.250	.250	.250	28	-1	0-0	1.000	-1	34	0	2b2	0	-0.2
Total	2	19	36	4	6	1	1	0	5	1-0	0	7	.167	.189	.250	13	-5	0-0	.900	-4	49	217	3b5,2b3/S	0	-0.9
Sanford, Jack	John Doward; B6.23.1917 Chatham VA; D1.4.2005 Greensboro NC; BR/TR/6´3˝/195; d8.24; Mil 1942–45; Col Richmond																								
1940	Was A	34	122	5	24	4	2	0	10	6	0	17	.197	.234	.262	30	-13	0-0	.993	-2	76	132	1b34	—	-1.7
1941	Was A	3	5	1	2	0	1	0	0	1	0	1	.400	.500	.800	251	1	0-0	1.000	-0	0	97	/1	0	0.1
1946	Was A	10	26	7	6	0	1	0	1	2	0	6	.231	.286	.308	70	-1	0-0	.971	-2	23	116	1b6	0	-0.3
Total	3	47	153	13	32	4	4	0	11	9	0	24	.209	.253	.288	44	-13	0-0	.989	-4	65	128	1b41	0	-1.9
Sanguillen, Manny	Manuel De Jesus (Magan); B3.21.1944 Colon, Pan; BR/TR/6´0˝/(189–193); d7.23																								
1967	Pit N	30	96	6	26	4	0	0	8	4-3	0	12	.271	.300	.313	75	-3	0-1	.986	-3	179	106	C28	0	-0.5
1969	Pit N	129	459	62	139	21	6	5	57	12-4	3	48	.303	.324	.407	106	2	8-4	.981	6	99	115	C113	0	1.3
1970	†Pit N	128	486	63	158	19	9	7	61	17-9	0	45	.325	.344	.444	111	5	2-3	.988	10	155	101	C125	0	2.0
1971	†Pit N☆	138	533	60	170	26	5	7	81	19-13	3	32	.319	.345	.426	117	10	6-4	.994	12	**172**	112	C135	0	2.9
1972	†Pit N★	136	520	55	155	18	8	7	71	21-11	0	38	.298	.322	.404	108	2	1-2	.988	4	157	74	C127,O2L	0	1.2
1973	Pit N	149	589	64	166	26	7	12	65	17-8	3	29	.282	.301	.411	99	-4	2-5	.983	4	100	73	C89,O59R	0	-0.1
1974	†Pit N	151	596	77	171	21	4	7	68	21-9	5	27	.287	.313	.371	94	-7	2-2	.985	2	128	105	C151	0	0.1
1975	†Pit N☆	133	481	60	158	24	4	9	58	48-15	3	31	.328	.391	.451	133	22	5-4	.987	1	114	67	C132	0	3.0
1976	Pit N	114	389	52	113	16	6	2	36	28-14	2	18	.290	.338	.378	102	1	2-4	.978	-1	119	103	C111	0	0.3
1977	Oak A	152	571	42	157	17	5	6	58	22-4	2	35	.275	.302	.354	80	-18	2-5	.985	-3	68	139	C77,D58,O9R,1b7	0	-2.1
1978	Pit N	85	220	15	58	5	1	3	16	9-2	2	10	.264	.296	.336	73	-8	2-2	1.000	-4	68	93	1b40,C18	0	-1.5
1979	†Pit N	56	74	8	17	5	2	0	4	2-2	0	5	.230	.247	.351	59	-4	0-0	.947	1	72	155	C8,1b5	0	-0.4
1980	Pit N	47	48	2	12	3	0	0	2	3-2	0	1	.250	.294	.313	67	-2	3-2	.956	-0	127	111	1b5	0	-0.3
Total	13	1448	5062	566	1500	205	57	65	585	223-96	23	331	.296	.326	.398	102	-4	35-38	.986	27	129	97	C1114,O70(2/0/68),D58,1b57	0	5.9
Sanicki, Ed	Edward Robert "Butch"; B7.7.1923 Wallington NJ; D7.6.1998 Old Bridge NJ; BR/TR/5´9˝/175; d9.14																								
1949	Phi N	7	13	4	3	0	0	3	7	1	0	4	.231	.286	.923	217	2	0	1.000	0	121	0	O6(0/1/5)	0	0.2
1951	Phi N	13	4	1	2	1	0	0	1	1	0	1	.500	.600	.750	265	1	1-0	1.000	0	101	0	O10L	0	0.1
Total	2	20	17	5	5	1	0	3	8	2	0	5	.294	.368	.882	231	3	1-0	1.000	0	119	0	O16(10/1/5)	0	0.3
Sankey, Ben	Benjamin Turner; B9.2.1907 Nauvoo AL; D10.14.2001 Washington GA; BR/TR/5´10˝/155; d10.5; Col Auburn																								
1929	Pit N	2	7	1	1	0	0	0	0	0	0	1	.143	.143	.143	-28	-1	0	.909	-0	101	81	S2	—	-0.2
1930	Pit N	13	30	6	5	0	0	0	0	2	0	3	.167	.219	.167	-5	-5	0	.871	-1	104	56	S6,2b4	—	-0.5
1931	Pit N	57	132	14	30	2	5	0	14	14	0	10	.227	.301	.318	67	-7	0	.920	-8	100	95	S49,2b2,3b2	—	-1.1
Total	3	72	169	21	36	2	5	0	14	16	0	14	.213	.281	.284	49	-13	0	.914	-9	100	90	S57,2b6,3b2	—	-1.8
Santana, Andres	Andres Confesor (Belonis); B2.5.1968 San Pedro de Macoris, D.R.; BB/TR/5´11˝/150; d9.16; [DL 1992 SF N 182]																								
1990	SF N	6	2	0	0	0	0	0	1	0-0	0	0	.000	.000	.000	-99	-1	0-0	1.000	-1	35	177	S3	0	-0.1
Santana, Pedro	Pedro; B9.21.1976 San Pedro de Macoris, D.R.; BR/TR/5´11˝/160; d7.16																								
2001	Det A	1	0	0	0	0	0	0	0	0-0	0	0	ø	ø	ø	ø	0	0-0	1.000	0	0	0	/2	0	0.0
Santana, Rafael	Rafael Francisco (De La Cruz); B1.31.1958 LaRomana, D.R.; BR/TR/6´1˝/(160–165); d4.5; C2; [DL 1989 NY A 182]																								
1983	StL N	30	14	1	3	0	0	0	2	2-0	1	2	.214	.353	.214	60	-1	0-1	.857	-3	61	70	2b9,S6,3b4	0	-0.4
1984	NY N	51	152	14	42	11	1	1	12	9-0	0	17	.276	.317	.382	97	-1	0-3	.970	-2	79	132	S50	15	0.1
1985	NY N	154	529	41	136	19	1	1	29	29-12	0	54	.257	.295	.302	69	-23	1-0	.965	-16	84	96	S153	0	-2.4
1986	†NY N	139	394	38	86	11	0	1	28	36-12	2	43	.218	.285	.254	51	-26	0-0	.973	10	103	107	S137/2	0	-0.4
1987	NY N	139	439	41	112	21	2	5	44	29-10	1	57	.255	.302	.346	74	-17	1-1	.973	13	104	113	S138	0	0.9
1988	NY A	148	480	50	115	12	1	4	38	33-0	1	61	.240	.289	.294	64	-24	1-2	.966	-14	98	102	S148	0	-2.8
1990	Cle A	7	13	3	3	0	0	1	3	0-0	0	0	.231	.231	.462	89	0	0-0	1.000	-2	78	77	S7	0	-0.2
Total	7	668	2021	188	497	74	5	13	156	138-34	5	234	.246	.295	.307	68	-92	3-7	.969	-14	95	106	S639,2b10,3b4	197	-5.2
Santangelo, F. P.	Frank-Paul; B10.24.1967 Livonia MI; BB/TR/5´10˝/(165–180); [MonN89 20/514]; d8.2; Col Miami; OF(217/195/88)																								
1995	Mon N	35	98	11	29	5	1	1	9	12-0	2	9	.296	.384	.398	103	1	1-1	.979	-2	115	0	O25(20/2/7),2b5	0	-0.2
1996	Mon N	152	393	54	109	20	5	7	56	49-4	11	61	.277	.369	.407	103	4	5-2	.983	10	119	83	O124(33/76/18),3b23,2b5/S	0	1.3
1997	Mon N	130	350	56	87	19	5	5	31	50-1	25	73	.249	.379	.374	100	3	8-5	1.000	1	111	83	O99(40/13/51),3b32,2b7/S	0	0.2
1998	Mon N	122	383	53	82	18	0	4	23	44-1	23	72	.214	.330	.292	68	-16	7-3	.983	-2	110	124	O92(72/23/1),2b35/3	15	-1.8
1999	SF N	113	254	49	66	17	3	3	26	53-0	11	54	.260	.406	.386	110	8	12-4	.993	-2	99	123	O81(26/49/9),2b11,3b3/S	0	0.7
2000	LA N	81	142	19	28	4	0	1	9	21-0	6	33	.197	.322	.246	50	-10	3-2	.983	-3	90	0	O50(26/27/1),2b7	44	-1.3
2001	†Oak A	32	71	16	14	4	0	0	8	11-0	5	17	.197	.341	.254	61	-3	1-1	1.000	-2	96	81	2b20,O6(0/5/1),3b3,D2	0	-0.4
Total	7	665	1691	258	415	87	14	21	162	240-6	83	319	.245	.364	.351	89	-13	37-18	.988	1	109	85	O477L,2b90,3b62,S3,D2	59	-1.5
Santiago, Benito	Benito (Rivera); B3.9.1965 Ponce, PR; BR/TR/6´1˝/(180–200); d9.14																								
1986	SD N	17	62	10	18	2	0	3	6	2-0	0	12	.290	.308	.468	115	1	0-1	.946	-5	107	44	C17	0	-0.4
1987	SD N	146	546	64	164	33	2	18	79	16-2	5	112	.300	.324	.467	111	6	21-12	.976	2	122	98	C146	0	1.4
1988	SD N	139	492	49	122	22	2	10	46	24-2	1	82	.248	.282	.362	86	-11	15-7	.985	10	**213**	93	C136	0	0.8
1989	SD N★	129	462	50	109	16	3	16	62	26-6	1	89	.236	.277	.387	88	-9	11-6	.975	5	**205**	73	C127	0	0.4
1990	SD N✳	100	344	42	93	8	5	11	53	27-2	3	55	.270	.323	.419	103	0	5-5	.980	5	138	92	C98	56	1.0
1991	SD N★	152	580	60	155	22	3	17	87	23-5	4	114	.267	.296	.403	93	-8	8-10	.985	8	137	95	C151/lf	0	0.8
1992	SD N★	106	386	37	97	21	0	10	42	21-1	0	52	.251	.287	.383	88	-7	2-5	.982	-7	113	110	C103	41	-1.0
1993	Fla N	139	469	49	108	19	6	13	50	37-2	5	88	.230	.291	.380	74	-18	10-7	.987	-4	103	92	C136/lf	0	-1.4
1994	Fla N	101	337	35	92	14	2	11	41	25-1	1	57	.273	.322	.424	90	-6	1-2	.991	10	141	**135**	C97	0	1.0
1995	†Cin N	81	266	40	76	20	0	11	44	24-1	4	48	.286	.351	.485	117	7	2-2	**.996**	8	**150**	60	C75,1b8	57	1.8
1996	Phi N	136	481	71	127	21	2	30	85	49-7	1	104	.264	.332	.503	116	9	2-0	.987	2	136	81	C114,1b14	0	1.7
1997	Tor A	97	341	31	83	10	0	13	42	17-1	2	80	.243	.279	.387	72	-15	1-0	.997	0	128	103	C95/D	15	-0.8
1998	Tor A	15	29	3	9	5	0	0	4	1-0	0	6	.310	.333	.483	108	0	0-0	1.000	-4	53	0	C15	156	-0.3
1999	Chi N	109	350	28	87	18	3	7	36	32-6	2	71	.249	.313	.377	74	-14	1-1	.990	-9	**175**	85	C107/1	0	-1.6
2000	Cin N	89	252	22	66	11	1	8	45	19-8	1	45	.262	.310	.409	79	-9	2-2	.994	6	**221**	71	C84	0	0.2
2001	SF N	133	477	39	125	25	4	6	45	23-0	2	78	.262	.295	.369	76	-19	5-4	.994	-1	105	103	C130,1b2	0	-1.2
2002	†SF N★	126	478	56	133	24	5	16	74	27-8	2	73	.278	.315	.450	103	0	4-2	.995	-1	122	75	C125	0	0.7
2003	†SF N	108	401	53	112	21	2	11	56	29-0	2	69	.279	.329	.424	94	-4	0-1	.993	-5	118	44	C106	15	-0.3
2004	KC A	49	175	15	48	10	0	6	23	8-0	2	32	.274	.312	.434	92	-2	1-2	.996	-12	88	72	C49	107	-1.1
2005	Pit N	6	23	1	6	1	1	0	0	0-0	0	3	.261	.261	.391	68	-1	0-0	1.000	1	95	0	C6	23	0.0
Total	20	1978	6951	755	1830	323	41	217	920	430-52	38	1270	.263	.307	.415	92	-100	91-69	.987	9	142	87	C1917,1b25,O2L/D	470	1.7
Santiago, Ramon	Ramon D.; B8.31.1979 Las Matas de Farfan, D.R.; BB/TR/5´11˝/(150–175); d5.17																								
2002	Det A	65	222	33	54	5	5	4	20	13-0	8	48	.243	.306	.365	81	-7	8-5	.977	5	114	95	S63/D	39	0.3
2003	Det A	141	444	41	100	18	1	2	29	33-0	10	66	.225	.292	.284	56	-28	10-4	.975	-2	106	116	S85,2b53	0	-2.0
2004	Sea A	19	39	8	7	1	0	0	2	3-0	1	3	.179	.256	.205	23	-4	0-0	.946	-1	89	105	S16,D2	0	-0.5
2005	Sea A	8	8	2	1	0	0	0	0	1-0	3	2	.125	.417	.125	59	0	0-0	1.000	-2	71	77	2b2,S2	0	-0.2
2006	†Det A	43	80	9	18	1	1	0	3	1-0	1	14	.225	.244	.262	32	-8	2-0	1.000	-2	108	65	S27,2b12/3	0	-0.8
Total	5	276	793	93	180	25	7	6	54	51-0	23	133	.227	.292	.299	59	-47	20-9	.975	-2	108	103	S193,2b67,D3/3	39	-3.2
Santo, Ron	Ronald Edward; B2.25.1940 Seattle WA; BR/TR/6´0˝/(185–195); d6.26; OF(7/0/1)																								
1960	Chi N	95	347	44	87	24	2	9	44	31-5	0	44	.251	.311	.409	97	-2	0-3	.945	-22	79	35	3b94	0	-2.6
1961	Chi N	154	578	84	164	32	6	23	83	73-7	0	77	.284	.362	.479	120	18	2-3	.937	4	103	**133**	3b153	0	2.0
1962	Chi N	**162**	604	44	137	20	4	17	83	65-5	2	94	.227	.302	.358	74	-22	4-1	.955	13	**114**	107	3b157,S8	0	-0.9
1963	Chi N★	**162**	630	79	187	29	6	25	99	42-7	4	92	.297	.339	.481	128	22	6-4	.951	14	**116**	106	3b162	0	3.8
1964	Chi N☆	161	592	94	185	33	**13**	30	114	**86**-5	2	96	.313	**.398**	.564	162	51	3-4	.963	20	**119**	117	3b161	0	**7.1**
1965	Chi N★	**164**	608	88	173	30	4	33	101	88-7	5	109	.285	.378	.510	144	38	3-1	.957	22	**119**	97	3b164	0	6.2
1966	Chi N★	155	561	93	175	21	8	30	94	**95**-7	6	78	.312	**.412**	.538	161	51	4-5	.956	25	115	116	3b152,S8	0	**7.6**
1967	Chi N	161	586	107	176	23	4	31	98	**96**-9	3	103	.300	.395	.512	153	44	1-5	.957	**31**	**117**	**126**	3b161	0	**7.7**
1968	Chi N★	162	577	86	142	17	3	26	98	**96**-7	3	106	.246	.354	.421	125	21	3-4	**.971**	20	**115**	**112**	3b162	0	4.4

YEAR	TM LG	G	AB	R	H	2B	3B	HR	RBI	BB-IB	HP	SO	AVG	OBP	SLG	AOPS	ABR	SB-CS	FA	FR	RNG	THR	GAMES AT POSITION	DL	BFW
1969	Chi N★	160	575	97	166	18	4	29	123	96-7	2	97	.289	.384	.485	128	24	1-3	.947	7	103	85	3b160	0	3.0
1970	Chi N	154	555	83	148	30	4	26	114	92-6	1	108	.267	.369	.476	112	11	2-0	.945	18	109	**135**	3b152/rf	0	2.8
1971	Chi N★	154	555	77	148	22	1	21	88	79-8	0	95	.267	.354	.423	105	6	4-0	.958	1	97	120	3b149,O6L	0	0.7
1972	Chi N★	133	464	68	140	25	5	17	74	69-5	4	75	.302	.391	.487	135	24	1-4	.948	14	**116**	94	3b129,2b3/Slf	0	3.9
1973	Chi N★	149	536	65	143	29	2	20	77	63-8	4	97	.267	.348	.440	109	7	1-2	.950	-3	99	61	3b146	0	0.4
1974	Chi A	117	375	29	83	12	1	5	41	37-1	2	72	.221	.293	.299	69	-15	0-2	.970	1	101	136	D47,2b39,3b28,1b3/S	0	-1.4
Total	15	2243	8143	1138	2254	365	67	342	1331	1108-94	38	1343	.277	.362	.464	123	278	35-41	.954	165	109	105	3b2130,D47,2b42,S18,O8L,1b3	0	44.7

Santo Domingo, Rafael Rafael (Molina); B11.24.1955 Orocovis, PR; BB/TR/6´0˝/160; d9.7

YEAR	TM LG	G	AB	R	H	2B	3B	HR	RBI	BB-IB	HP	SO	AVG	OBP	SLG	AOPS	ABR	SB-CS	FA	FR	RNG	THR	GAMES AT POSITION	DL	BFW
1979	Cin N	7	6	0	1	0	0	0	0	1-0	0	3	.167	.286	.167	27	-1	0-0	ø	0	—	—	/H	0	-0.1

Santos, Angel Angel Ramon; B8.14.1979 Rio Piedras, PR; BB/TR/5´11˝/185; [BosA97 4/131]; d9.8

YEAR	TM LG	G	AB	R	H	2B	3B	HR	RBI	BB-IB	HP	SO	AVG	OBP	SLG	AOPS	ABR	SB-CS	FA	FR	RNG	THR	GAMES AT POSITION	DL	BFW
2001	Bos A	9	16	2	2	1	0	0	1	2-0	0	7	.125	.211	.188	10	-2	0-0	.905	-1	90	0	2b6	0	-0.3
2003	Cle A	32	76	9	17	3	1	3	6	3-0	0	18	.224	.253	.408	71	-4	1-1	.981	1	108	123	2b28,3b4	0	-0.2
Total	2	41	92	11	19	4	1	3	7	5-0	0	25	.207	.245	.370	60	-6	1-1	.968	-1	105	102	2b34,3b4	0	-0.5

Santos, Chad Chad Roque; B4.28.1981 Honolulu HI; BL/TL/5´11˝/220; [KCA99 22/661]; d7.16

YEAR	TM LG	G	AB	R	H	2B	3B	HR	RBI	BB-IB	HP	SO	AVG	OBP	SLG	AOPS	ABR	SB-CS	FA	FR	RNG	THR	GAMES AT POSITION	DL	BFW
2006	SF N	3	7	2	3	0	0	1	2	1-0	0	2	.429	.500	.857	237	1	0-0	.947	-0	70	52	1b3	0	0.1

Santos, Francisco Francisco Alejandro; B3.9.1974 Santo Domingo, D.R.; BL/TL/6´1˝/175; d6.18

YEAR	TM LG	G	AB	R	H	2B	3B	HR	RBI	BB-IB	HP	SO	AVG	OBP	SLG	AOPS	ABR	SB-CS	FA	FR	RNG	THR	GAMES AT POSITION	DL	BFW
2003	SF N	8	15	2	3	2	0	1	1	0-0	0	3	.200	.200	.533	81	0	0-0	1.000	-0	102	0	O3R/1	0	-0.1

Santovenia, Nelson Nelson Gil (Mayol); B7.27.1961 Pinar Del Rio, Cuba; BR/TR/6´3˝/(205–220); [MonN82 S1/19]; d9.16; Col Miami

YEAR	TM LG	G	AB	R	H	2B	3B	HR	RBI	BB-IB	HP	SO	AVG	OBP	SLG	AOPS	ABR	SB-CS	FA	FR	RNG	THR	GAMES AT POSITION	DL	BFW
1987	Mon N	2	1	0	0	0	0	0	0	0-0	0	0	.000	.000	.000	-96	0	0-0	1.000	0	0	0	/C	0	0.0
1988	Mon N	92	309	26	73	20	2	8	41	24-3	3	77	.236	.294	.392	92	-3	2-3	.983	2	93	108	C86/1	16	0.3
1989	Mon N	97	304	30	76	14	1	5	31	24-2	3	37	.250	.307	.352	88	-5	2-1	.981	8	84	135	C89/1	31	0.9
1990	Mon N	59	163	13	31	3	1	6	28	8-0	0	31	.190	.222	.331	54	-12	0-3	.980	-3	73	74	C51	50	-1.3
1991	Mon N	41	96	7	24	5	0	2	14	2-2	0	18	.250	.255	.365	76	-3	0-0	.976	-1	93	102	C30,1b7	0	-0.4
1992	Chi A	2	3	1	1	0	0	1	2	0-0	0	0	.333	.333	1.333	349	1	0-0	1.000	-1	0	261	C2	0	0.0
1993	KC A	4	8	0	1	0	0	0	0	1-0	0	2	.125	.222	.125	-4	-1	0-0	1.000	-1	177	0	C4	0	-0.2
Total	7	297	884	77	206	42	4	22	116	59-7	6	165	.233	.281	.364	82	-23	4-7	.981	5	87	110	C263,1b9	97	-0.7

Santry, Edward Edward; B Chicago IL; D3.6.1899 Chicago IL; d8.7

YEAR	TM LG	G	AB	R	H	2B	3B	HR	RBI	BB-IB	HP	SO	AVG	OBP	SLG	AOPS	ABR	SB-CS	FA	FR	RNG	THR	GAMES AT POSITION	DL	BFW
1884	Det N	6	22	1	4	0	0	0	0	1	—	2	.182	.217	.182	29	-2	—	.821	-1	82	77	S5/2	—	-0.2

Sardinha, Dane Dane K.; B4.8.1969 Honolulu HI; BR/TR/6´0˝/(210–215); [CinN00 2/46]; d9.6; Col Pepperdine

YEAR	TM LG	G	AB	R	H	2B	3B	HR	RBI	BB-IB	HP	SO	AVG	OBP	SLG	AOPS	ABR	SB-CS	FA	FR	RNG	THR	GAMES AT POSITION	DL	BFW
2003	Cin N	1	2	0	0	0	0	0	0	0-0	0	1	.000	.000	.000	-99	-1	0-0	1.000	-0	0	0	/C	0	-0.1
2005	Cin N	1	3	0	0	0	0	0	0	0-0	0	1	.000	.000	.000	-99	-1	0-0	1.000	0	0	0	/C	0	-0.1
Total	2	2	5	0	0	0	0	0	0	0-0	0	2	.000	.000	.000	-99	-2	0-0	1.000	-0	0	0	C2	0	-0.2

Sargent, Joe Joseph Alexander "Horse Belly"; B9.24.1893 Rochester NY; D7.5.1950 Rochester NY; BR/TR/5´10˝/165; d4.27

YEAR	TM LG	G	AB	R	H	2B	3B	HR	RBI	BB-IB	HP	SO	AVG	OBP	SLG	AOPS	ABR	SB-CS	FA	FR	RNG	THR	GAMES AT POSITION	DL	BFW
1921	Det A	66	178	21	45	8	5	2	22	24	0	26	.253	.342	.388	86	-4	2-3	.927	-2	91	102	2b24,3b23,S19	—	-0.3

Sarni, Bill William Florine; B9.19.1927 Los Angeles CA; D4.15.1983 Creve Coeur MO; BR/TR/5´11˝/187; d5.9; C1

YEAR	TM LG	G	AB	R	H	2B	3B	HR	RBI	BB-IB	HP	SO	AVG	OBP	SLG	AOPS	ABR	SB-CS	FA	FR	RNG	THR	GAMES AT POSITION	DL	BFW
1951	StL N	36	86	7	15	1	0	0	2	9	0	13	.174	.253	.186	20	-10	1-0	.984	1	*119*	*68*	C35	0	-0.7
1952	StL N	3	5	0	1	0	0	0	0	0	0	1	.200	.200	.200	11	-1	0-0	1.000	1	*0*	*0*	C3	0	0.1
1954	StL N	123	380	40	114	18	4	9	70	25	0	42	.300	.337	.439	101	0	3-3	**.996**	-8	*141*	*79*	C118	0	-0.3
1955	StL N	107	325	32	83	15	2	3	34	27-0	1	33	.255	.313	.342	74	-12	1-1	.987	-6	*107*	*105*	C99	0	-1.3
1956	StL N	43	148	12	43	7	2	5	22	8-2	1	15	.291	.329	.466	111	2	1-0	.992	1	*97*	*102*	C41	0	0.6
	NY N	78	238	16	55	9	3	5	23	20-2	1	31	.231	.290	.357	74	-9	0-1	.993	-0	*118*	*101*	C78	0	-0.6
	Year	121	386	28	98	16	5	10	45	28-4	2	46	.254	.305	.399	88	-7	1-1	.992	1	*110*	*101*	C119	0	0.0
Total	5	390	1182	107	311	50	11	22	151	89-4	3	135	.263	.313	.380	84	-30	6-5	.991	-10	*119*	*92*	C374	0	-2.2

Sasser, Mackey Mack Daniel; B8.3.1962 Fort Gaines GA; BL/TR/6´1˝/(190–210); [SFN84*5/114]; d7.17; Col Troy St.

YEAR	TM LG	G	AB	R	H	2B	3B	HR	RBI	BB-IB	HP	SO	AVG	OBP	SLG	AOPS	ABR	SB-CS	FA	FR	RNG	THR	GAMES AT POSITION	DL	BFW
1987	SF N	2	4	0	0	0	0	0	0	0-0	0	0	.000	.000	.000	-99	-1	0-0	1.000	0	0	0	/C	0	-0.1
	Pit N	12	23	2	5	0	0	0	2	0-0	0	2	.217	.217	.217	15	-3	0-0	1.000	-0	104	0	C5	0	-0.3
	Year	14	27	2	5	0	0	0	2	0-0	0	2	.185	.185	.185	-1	-4	0-0	1.000	-0	79	0	C6	0	-0.4
1988	†NY N	60	123	9	35	10	1	1	17	6-4	0	9	.285	.313	.407	111	2	0-0	.977	1	61	116	C42/3rf	0	0.5
1989	NY N	72	182	17	53	14	2	1	22	7-4	0	15	.291	.316	.407	110	2	0-1	.992	-3	89	93	C62/3	0	0.2
1990	NY N	100	270	31	83	14	0	6	41	15-9	1	19	.307	.344	.426	111	4	0-0	.975	-5	67	**150**	C87/1	0	0.3
1991	NY N	96	228	18	62	14	2	5	35	9-2	1	19	.272	.298	.417	101	-1	0-2	.994	-2	88	95	C43,O21(7/0/14),1b10	0	-0.3
1992	NY N	92	141	7	34	6	0	2	18	3-0	0	10	.241	.248	.326	65	-7	0-0	.989	-8	49	73	C27,1b12,O9(7/0/2)	0	-1.6
1993	Sea A	83	188	18	41	10	2	1	21	15-6	1	30	.218	.274	.309	57	-12	1-0	.946	-2	83	156	O37(26/0/11),D19,C4/1	16	-1.5
1994	Sea A	3	4	0	0	0	0	0	0	0-0	0	0	.000	.000	.000	-98	-1	0-0	ø	-1	0	0	/Clf	22	-0.2
1995	Pit N	14	26	1	4	1	0	0	0	0-0	0	0	.154	.154	.192	-9	-4	0-0	1.000	-0	118	157	C11	0	-0.4
Total	9	534	1189	103	317	69	7	16	156	55-25	3	104	.267	.296	.377	88	-21	1-3	.983	-18	74	115	C283,O69(41/0/28),1b24,D19,3b2	38	-3.4

Sasser, Rob Robert Doffell; B3.9.1975 Philadelphia PA; BR/TR/6´3˝/205; [AtlN93 10/292]; d7.31

YEAR	TM LG	G	AB	R	H	2B	3B	HR	RBI	BB-IB	HP	SO	AVG	OBP	SLG	AOPS	ABR	SB-CS	FA	FR	RNG	THR	GAMES AT POSITION	DL	BFW
1998	Tex A	1	1	0	0	0	0	0	0	0-0	0	0	.000	.000	.000	-95	0	0-0	ø	0	—	—	/H	0	0.0

Satriano, Tom Thomas Victor Nicholas; B8.28.1940 Pittsburgh PA; BL/TR/6´1˝/(185–195); d7.23; Col USC

YEAR	TM LG	G	AB	R	H	2B	3B	HR	RBI	BB-IB	HP	SO	AVG	OBP	SLG	AOPS	ABR	SB-CS	FA	FR	RNG	THR	GAMES AT POSITION	DL	BFW
1961	LA A	35	96	15	19	5	1	1	8	12-0	1	16	.198	.294	.302	53	-6	2-0	.915	1	113	135	3b23,2b10/S	0	-0.4
1962	LA A	10	19	4	8	2	0	2	6	0-0	0	1	.421	.421	.842	238	3	0-0	.833	0	125	163	3b5	0	0.4
1963	LA A	23	50	1	9	1	0	0	2	9-2	0	10	.180	.305	.200	48	-3	0-0	.952	4	159	98	3b13,C2/1	0	0.0
1964	LA A	108	255	18	51	9	0	1	17	30-3	0	37	.200	.282	.247	55	-15	0-2	.917	-3	114	86	3b38,1b32,C25,S2/2	0	-2.1
1965	Cal A	47	79	8	13	2	0	1	4	10-1	0	10	.165	.258	.228	40	-6	1-1	1.000	-1	80	78	3b15,C12,2b12,1b3	0	-0.7
1966	Cal A	103	226	16	54	5	3	0	24	27-2	0	32	.239	.320	.288	78	-6	3-3	.991	-9	64	73	C43,1b36,3b25,2b4	0	-1.5
1967	Cal A	90	201	13	45	7	0	4	21	28-3	0	25	.224	.319	.318	92	-1	1-0	.962	-2	95	89	3b38,C23,2b15,1b5	0	-0.2
1968	Cal A	111	297	20	75	9	0	8	35	37-5	1	44	.253	.337	.364	116	6	0-0	.989	-4	109	**142**	C85,2b14,3b11/1	0	0.8
1969	Cal A	41	108	5	28	2	0	1	16	18-1	1	15	.259	.364	.306	95	0	0-2	1.000	2	107	97	C36,1b5,2b2	0	0.3
	Bos A	47	127	9	24	2	0	0	11	22-7	2	12	.189	.310	.205	47	-8	0-0	.978	0	104	81	C44	0	-0.7
	Year	88	235	14	52	4	0	1	27	40-8	3	27	.221	.335	.251	68	-8	0-2	.987	2	105	88	C80,1b5,2b2	0	-0.4
1970	Bos A	59	165	21	39	9	1	3	13	21-3	1	23	.236	.326	.358	83	-3	0-0	.985	1	105	68	C51	0	0.0
Total	10	674	1623	130	365	53	5	21	157	214-27	6	225	.225	.316	.303	79	-39	7-8	.987	-11	100	107	C321,3b168,1b83,2b58,S3	0	-4.1

Saturria, Luis Luis Arturo; B7.21.1976 San Pedro de Macoris, D.R.; BR/TR/6´2˝/165; d9.11

YEAR	TM LG	G	AB	R	H	2B	3B	HR	RBI	BB-IB	HP	SO	AVG	OBP	SLG	AOPS	ABR	SB-CS	FA	FR	RNG	THR	GAMES AT POSITION	DL	BFW
2000	StL N	12	5	1	0	0	0	0	0	1-0	0	3	.000	.167	.000	-52	-1	0-0	1.000	-1	59	0	O9(0/5/4)	0	-0.2
2001	StL N	13	5	0	1	1	0	0	1	0-0	0	1	.200	.200	.400	48	0	1-0	1.000	-0	75	0	O9(3/3/3)	0	0.0
Total	2	25	10	1	1	1	0	0	1	1-0	0	4	.100	.182	.200	-3	-1	1-0	1.000	-1	65	0	O18(3/8/7)	0	-0.2

Saucier, Frank Francis Field; B5.28.1926 Leslie MO; BL/TR/6´1˝/180; d7.21; Mil 1952–54; Col Westminster (MO)

YEAR	TM LG	G	AB	R	H	2B	3B	HR	RBI	BB-IB	HP	SO	AVG	OBP	SLG	AOPS	ABR	SB-CS	FA	FR	RNG	THR	GAMES AT POSITION	DL	BFW
1951	StL A	18	14	4	1	1	0	0	1	3	1	4	.071	.278	.143	16	-2	0-0	.714	-0	126	0	O3(1/0/2)	0	-0.2

Sauer, Ed Edward "Horn"; B1.3.1919 Pittsburgh PA; D7.1.1988 Thousand Oaks CA; BR/TR/6´1˝/188; d9.17; b–Hank; Col Elon

YEAR	TM LG	G	AB	R	H	2B	3B	HR	RBI	BB-IB	HP	SO	AVG	OBP	SLG	AOPS	ABR	SB-CS	FA	FR	RNG	THR	GAMES AT POSITION	DL	BFW
1943	Chi N	14	55	3	15	3	0	0	9	3	1	6	.273	.322	.327	89	-1	1	1.000	0	108	64	O13L	0	-0.2
1944	Chi N	23	50	3	11	4	0	0	5	2	0	6	.220	.250	.300	55	-3	0	.960	-0	96	119	O12L	0	-0.4
1945	†Chi N	49	93	8	24	4	1	2	11	8	0	23	.258	.317	.387	97	-1	2	1.000	1	106	70	O26(21/2/3)	0	-0.1
1949	StL N	24	45	5	10	2	1	0	1	3	0	8	.222	.271	.311	53	-3	0	1.000	-0	76	146	O10(4/0/7)	0	-0.4
	Bos N	79	214	26	57	12	0	3	31	17	1	34	.266	.323	.364	89	-3	0	.972	0	106	64	O71(29/20/25)	0	-0.6
	Year	103	259	31	67	14	1	3	32	20	1	42	.259	.314	.355	82	-7	0	.974	-0	102	74	O81(33/20/32)	0	-1.0
Total	4	189	457	45	117	25	2	5	57	33	2	77	.256	.309	.352	83	-11	3	.981	0	103	76	O132(79/22/35)	0	-1.7

Sauer, Hank Henry John; B3.17.1917 Pittsburgh PA; D8.24.2001 Burlingame CA; BR/TR/6´4˝/(194–200); d9.9; Mil 1944–45; C1; b–Ed

YEAR	TM LG	G	AB	R	H	2B	3B	HR	RBI	BB-IB	HP	SO	AVG	OBP	SLG	AOPS	ABR	SB-CS	FA	FR	RNG	THR	GAMES AT POSITION	DL	BFW
1941	Cin N	9	33	4	10	4	0	0	5	1	0	4	.303	.324	.424	109	0	0	.957	1	102	152	O8L	0	0.0
1942	Cin N	7	20	4	5	0	0	2	4	2	0	2	.250	.318	.550	152	1	0	.976	0	149	254	1b4	0	0.1
1945	Cin N	31	116	18	34	1	0	5	20	6	0	16	.293	.328	.431	112	1	2	.972	0	109	0	O28L,1b3	0	-0.1
1948	Cin N	145	530	78	138	22	1	35	97	60	4	85	.260	.340	.504	130	20	2	.973	5	100	137	O132L,1b12	0	1.5

YEAR	TM LG	G	AB	R	H	2B	3B	HR	RBI	BB-IB	HP	SO	AVG	OBP	SLG	AOPS	ABR	SB-CS	FA	FR	RNG	THR	GAMES AT POSITION	DL	BFW
1949	Cin N	42	152	22	36	6	0	4	16	18	0	19	.237	.318	.355	79	-4	0	.956	4	110	169	O39L/1	0	-0.4
	Chi N	96	357	59	104	17	1	27	83	37	3	47	.291	.363	.571	151	24	0	.981	1	95	127	O96L	0	1.7
	Year	138	509	81	140	23	1	31	99	55	3	66	.275	.349	.507	129	19	0	.972	4	100	**140**	O135L/1	0	1.3
1950	Chi N★	145	540	85	148	32	2	32	103	60	3	67	.274	.350	.519	127	20	1	.965	-4	85	125	O125L,1b18	0	0.6
1951	Chi N	141	525	77	138	19	4	30	89	45	3	77	.263	.325	.486	113	7	2-1	.981	8	102	**165**	O132(131/0/1)	0	0.6
1952	Chi N★	151	567	89	153	31	3	**37**	**121**	77	4	92	.270	.361	.531	143	33	1-2	.983	10	107	147	O151L	0	3.1
1953	Chi N	108	395	61	104	16	5	19	60	50	2	56	.263	.349	.473	109	5	0-0	.970	-1	106	59	O105(42/0/64)	0	0.0
1954	Chi N	142	520	98	150	18	1	41	103	70	6	68	.288	.375	.563	140	30	2-1	.963	-3	103	64	O141(9/0/140)	0	2.2
1955	Chi N	79	261	29	55	8	1	12	28	26-0	2	47	.211	.286	.387	77	-9	0-0	.984	0	100	88	O68(67/0/1)	0	-1.3
1956	StL N	75	151	11	45	4	0	5	24	25-3	3	31	.298	.403	.424	124	7	0-0	1.000	-1	90	97	O37(35/0/2)	0	0.4
1957	NY N	127	378	46	98	14	1	26	76	49-2	0	59	.259	.343	.508	126	13	1-0	.992	-11	70	65	O98L	0	-0.3
1958	SF N	88	236	27	59	8	0	12	46	35-2	4	37	.250	.354	.436	111	4	0-0	.950	-3	86	72	O67L	0	-0.2
1959	SF N	13	15	1	1	0	0	1	1	0-0	0	7	.067	.067	.267	-17	-3	0-0	ø	-0	0	0	/lf	0	-0.3
Total	15	1399	4796	709	1278	200	19	288	876	561-7	34	714	.266	.347	.496	123	149	11-4	.974	7	97	109	O1228(1029/0/208),1b38	0	7.6
SAUNDERS, DOUG	Douglas Long; B12.13.1969 Yorba Linda CA; BR/TR/6´0˝/172; [NYN88 3/78]; d6.13																								
1993	NY N	28	67	8	14	2	0	0	0	3-0	0	4	.209	.243	.239	30	-7	0-0	.956	2	107	178	2b22,3b4/S	0	-0.4
SAUNDERS, RUSTY	Russell Collier; B3.12.1906 Trenton NJ; D11.24.1967 Trenton NJ; BR/TR/6´2˝/205; d9.24																								
1927	Phi A	5	15	2	2	1	0	0	2	3	0	2	.133	.278	.200	24	-2	0-0	.818	-0	78	205	O4L	—	-0.2
SAUTER, AL	Albert C.; B9.2.1868 Philadelphia PA; D7.15.1928 Ocean City NJ; d9.8																								
1890	Phi AA	14	41	1	4	0	0	0	0	11	0	—	.098	.288	.098	14	-4	0	.850	-3	87	0	3b11,O2C,2b2	—	-0.6
SAVAGE, DON	Donald Anthony; B3.5.1919 Bloomfield NJ; D12.25.1961 Montclair NJ; BR/TR/6´0˝/180; d4.18; Col Rutgers																								
1944	NY A	71	239	31	63	7	5	4	24	20	1	41	.264	.323	.385	98	-1	1-1	.946	-8	84	100	3b60	0	-1.0
1945	NY A	34	58	5	13	1	0	0	3	3	0	14	.224	.262	.241	44	-4	1-0	.891	0	103	135	3b14,O2L	0	-0.4
Total	2	105	297	36	76	8	5	4	27	23	1	55	.256	.312	.357	88	-5	2-1	.935	-8	87	106	3b74,O2L	0	-1.4
SAVAGE, JIMMIE	James Harold; B8.29.1883 Southington CT; D6.26.1940 New Castle PA; BB/TR/5´5˝/150; d9.3; Col Villanova																								
1912	Phi N	2	3	1	0	0	0	0	0	1	0	0	.000	.250	.000	-27	-1	0	.750	-0	99	0	/2	—	-0.1
1914	Pit F	132	479	81	136	9	9	1	26	67	0	32	.284	.372	.347	97	-7	17	.963	-4	103	108	O93(22/5/66),3b29,S11,2b3	—	-1.4
1915	Pit F	14	21	0	3	0	0	0	0	1	0	0	.143	.182	.143	-8	-3	0	1.000	-1	113	0	O3R/3	—	-0.5
Total	3	148	503	82	139	9	9	1	26	69	0	32	.276	.364	.336	92	-11	17	.964	-5	103	105	O96(22/5/69),3b30,S11,2b4	—	-2.0
SAVAGE, TED	Theodore Edmund (b Ephesian Savage); B2.21.1936 Venice IL; BR/TR/6´1˝/185; d4.9; Col Lincoln Missouri																								
1962	Phi N	127	335	54	89	11	2	7	39	40-0	2	66	.266	.345	.373	96	-1	16-5	.974	4	114	63	O109(92/12/10)	0	-0.1
1963	Pit N	85	149	22	29	2	1	5	14	14-1	1	31	.195	.268	.322	69	-6	4-3	.943	-1	81	147	O47(36/9/2)	30	-1.0
1965	StL N	30	63	7	10	3	0	1	4	6-1	0	9	.159	.232	.254	34	-5	1-1	.938	-1	96	88	O20R	0	-0.8
1966	StL N	16	29	4	5	2	1	0	3	4-0	0	7	.172	.273	.310	61	-1	4-0	1.000	-1	80	0	O7(0/2/5)	0	-0.2
1967	StL N	9	8	1	1	0	0	0	0	1-0	0	3	.125	.222	.125	2	-1	0-0	ø	0	—	—	/H	0	-0.1
	Chi N	96	225	40	49	10	1	5	33	40-6	5	54	.218	.346	.338	93	0	7-6	.979	-0	98	104	O86(0/23/66)/3	0	-0.5
	Year	105	233	41	50	10	1	5	33	41-6	5	57	.215	.342	.330	90	-1	7-6	.979	-0	98	104	O86(0/23/66)/3	0	-0.6
1968	Chi N	3	8	0	2	0	0	0	0	0-0	0	1	.250	.250	.250	47	-1	0-1	1.000	-0	79	0	O2(0/1/2)	0	-0.2
	LA N	61	126	7	26	6	1	2	7	10-0	1	20	.206	.270	.317	82	-3	1-2	.985	4	122	185	O39(18/0/24)	0	-0.2
	Year	64	134	7	28	6	1	2	7	10-0	1	21	.209	.269	.313	80	-4	1-3	.986	4	119	174	O41(18/1/26)	0	-0.4
1969	Cin N	68	110	20	25	7	0	2	11	20-0	0	27	.227	.344	.345	90	-1	3-0	.983	1	116	0	O42(28/12/4)/2	0	0.0
1970	Mil A	114	276	43	77	10	5	12	50	57-1	2	44	.279	.402	.482	144	19	10-6	.953	-6	87	66	O82(34/22/33)/1	0	1.0
1971	Mil A	14	17	2	3	0	0	0	1	5-0	0	4	.176	.364	.176	58	-1	1-0	1.000	-0	87	0	O6(6/0/1)	0	-0.1
	KC A	19	29	2	5	0	0	0	1	3-0	0	6	.172	.250	.172	22	-3	2-0	1.000	0	36	539	O9(5/0/5)	37	-0.3
	Year	33	46	4	8	0	0	0	2	8-0	0	10	.174	.296	.174	36	-4	3-0	1.000	-0	51	380	O15(11/0/6)	0	-0.4
Total	9	642	1375	202	321	51	11	34	163	200-9	11	272	.233	.334	.361	95	-4	49-24	.970	-1	100	93	O449(219/81/172)/123	67	-2.5
SAVERINE, BOB	Robert Paul “Rabbit”; B6.2.1941 Norwalk CT; BB/TR/5´9˝/(160–165); d9.12																								
1959	Bal A	1	0	1	0	0	0	0	0	0-0	0	0	ø	ø	ø	ø	0	0-0	ø	0	—	—	/R	0	0.0
1962	Bal A	8	21	2	5	2	0	0	3	1-0	0	3	.238	.273	.333	66	-1	0-2	1.000	0	113	79	2b7	0	-0.1
1963	Bal A	115	167	21	39	1	2	1	12	25-0	0	44	.234	.332	.281	77	-5	8-3	.976	0	91	86	O59(1/58/0),2b19,S13	0	-0.1
1964	Bal A	46	34	14	5	1	0	0	0	3-0	0	6	.147	.216	.176	11	-4	3-1	1.000	-4	77	26	S15,O2C	0	-0.7
1966	Was A	120	406	54	102	10	4	5	24	27-1	2	62	.251	.300	.333	83	-10	4-3	.972	-5	98	87	2b70,3b26,S11,O9(5/0/4)	0	-1.0
1967	Was A	89	233	22	55	13	0	0	8	17-1	0	34	.236	.287	.292	75	-7	8-0	.957	-12	94	95	2b48,S10,3b8,O2L	0	-1.5
Total	6	379	861	114	206	27	6	6	47	73-2	2	149	.239	.299	.305	76	-27	23-9	.971	-19	97	88	2b144,O72(8/60/4),S49,3b34	0	-3.4
SAWATSKI, CARL	Carl Ernest “Swats”; B11.4.1927 Shickshinny PA; D11.24.1991 Little Rock AR; BL/TR/5´10˝/(205–220); d9.29; Mil 1951–52																								
1948	Chi N	2	2	0	0	0	0	0	0	0	0	0	.000	.000	.000	-99	-1	0	ø	0	—	—	/H	0	-0.1
1950	Chi N	38	103	4	18	1	0	1	7	11	0	19	.175	.254	.214	25	-11	0	.983	-1	*64*	*165*	C32	0	-1.1
1953	Chi N	43	59	5	13	3	0	1	5	7	0	7	.220	.303	.322	62	-3	0-0	.943	-1	*88*	*114*	C15	0	-0.4
1954	Chi A	43	109	6	20	3	3	1	12	15	0	20	.183	.276	.294	56	-7	0-0	.987	1	*108*	*123*	C33	0	-0.5
1957	†Mil N	58	105	13	25	4	0	6	17	10-2	2	15	.238	.316	.448	110	1	0-0	.986	7	101	167	C28	0	0.9
1958	Mil N	10	10	1	1	0	0	0	1	2-0	0	5	.100	.231	.100	-3	-1	0-0	1.000	1	45	342	C3	0	-0.1
	Phi N	60	183	12	42	4	1	5	12	16-4	3	42	.230	.300	.344	72	-8	0-0	.986	-5	80	95	C53	0	-1.1
	Year	70	193	13	43	4	1	5	13	18-4	3	47	.223	.296	.332	68	-9	0-0	.987	-5	79	102	C56	0	-1.2
1959	Phi N	74	198	15	58	10	0	9	43	32-11	1	36	.293	.392	.480	129	10	0-0	.979	-5	67	87	C69	0	0.7
1960	StL N	78	179	16	41	4	0	6	27	22-2	0	24	.229	.310	.352	75	-6	0-0	.993	6	128	92	C67	0	0.2
1961	StL N	86	174	23	52	8	0	10	33	25-7	0	17	.299	.385	.517	125	7	0-0	.996	-3	56	83	C60/cf	0	0.6
1962	StL N	85	222	26	56	9	1	13	42	36-5	0	38	.252	.351	.477	111	4	0-0	.997	1	102	69	C70	0	0.8
1963	StL N	56	105	12	25	0	0	6	14	15-7	0	28	.238	.333	.410	103	1	2-0	.986	-4	53	112	C27	0	-0.2
Total	11	633	1449	133	351	46	5	58	213	191-38	6	251	.242	.330	.401	92	-14	2-0	.988	-4	*86*	*102*	C457/cf	0	-0.3
SAWYER, CARL	Carl Everett “Huck”; B10.19.1890 Seattle WA; D1.17.1957 Los Angeles CA; BR/TR/5´11˝/160; d9.11																								
1915	Was A	10	32	8	8	1	0	0	3	4	1	5	.250	.351	.281	88	0	2	.964	-2	96	0	2b6,S4	—	-0.2
1916	Was A	16	31	3	6	1	0	0	2	4	1	4	.194	.306	.226	60	-1	3	.963	0	91	151	2b6,S5/3	—	-0.1
Total	2	26	63	11	14	2	0	0	5	8	2	9	.222	.329	.254	74	-1	5	.964	-2	94	71	2b12,S9/3	—	-0.3
SAX, DAVE	David John; B9.22.1958 Sacramento CA; BR/TR/6´0˝/(175–185); d9.1; b–Steve																								
1982	LA N	2	2	0	0	0	0	0	0	0-0	0	0	.000	.000	.000	-99	-1	0-0	1.000	0	454	0	/lf	0	0.0
1983	LA N	7	8	0	0	0	0	0	1	0-0	0	0	.000	.000	.000	-99	-2	0-0	.917	-1	30	0	C4	0	-0.3
1985	Bos A	22	36	2	11	3	0	0	6	3-0	0	3	.306	.350	.389	100	0	0-1	.985	-4	52	28	C16,O4(2/0/2)	0	-0.3
1986	Bos A	4	11	1	5	1	0	1	1	0-0	0	1	.455	.455	.818	236	2	0-0	1.000	-0	114	172	C2/1	0	0.2
1987	Bos A	2	3	0	0	0	0	0	0	0-0	0	1	.000	.000	.000	-97	-1	0-0	1.000	1	0	0	C2	0	0.0
Total	5	37	60	3	16	4	0	1	8	3-0	0	5	.267	.297	.383	84	-2	0-1	.980	-4	55	41	C24,O5(3/0/2)/1	0	-0.4
SAX, OLLIE	Erik Oliver; B11.5.1904 Branford CT; D3.21.1982 Newark NJ; BR/TR/5´8˝/164; d4.13																								
1928	StL A	16	17	4	3	0	0	0	0	5	0	3	.176	.364	.176	45	-1	0-0	.955	2	138	210	3b9	—	0.1
SAX, STEVE	Stephen Louis; B1.29.1960 Sacramento CA; BR/TR/5´11˝/(175–189); [LAN78 9/229]; d8.18; b–Dave																								
1981	†LA N	31	119	15	33	2	0	2	9	7-1	0	14	.277	.317	.345	92	-2	5-7	.975	4	108	135	2b29	0	0.3
1982	LA N★	150	638	88	180	23	7	4	47	49-1	2	53	.282	.335	.359	97	-3	49-19	.977	3	103	96	2b149	0	1.3
1983	†LA N★	155	623	94	175	18	5	5	41	58-3	1	73	.281	.342	.350	92	-6	56-30	.961	-19	90	80	2b152	0	-1.5
1984	LA N	145	569	70	138	24	4	1	35	47-3	1	53	.243	.300	.304	71	-22	34-19	.973	23	109	112	2b141	0	1.0
1985	†LA N	136	488	62	136	8	4	1	42	54-12	3	43	.279	.352	.318	91	-5	27-11	.969	-5	94	103	2b135/3	15	0.0
1986	LA N★	157	633	91	210	43	4	6	56	59-5	3	58	.332	.390	.441	138	35	40-17	.980	2	96	74	2b154	0	**4.9**
1987	LA N	157	610	84	171	22	7	6	46	44-5	3	61	.280	.331	.369	88	-12	37-11	.982	4	95	96	2b152/3lf	0	0.5
1988	†LA N	160	632	70	175	19	4	5	57	45-6	1	51	.277	.325	.343	95	-5	42-12	.981	-19	92	81	2b158	0	-1.6
1989	NY A★	158	651	88	205	26	3	5	63	52-2	1	44	.315	.364	.387	113	12	43-17	**.987**	1	103	107	2b158	0	2.1
1990	NY A★	155	615	70	160	24	2	4	42	49-3	4	46	.260	.316	.325	80	-16	43-9	.987	-7	101	93	2b154	0	-1.3
1991	NY A	158	652	85	198	38	2	10	56	41-2	3	38	.304	.345	.414	109	8	31-11	.990	-2	100	104	2b149,3b5,D4	0	1.3

YEAR	TM LG	G	AB	R	H	2B	3B	HR	RBI	BB-IB	HP	SO	AVG	OBP	SLG	AOPS	ABR	SB-CS	FA	FR	RNG	THR	GAMES AT POSITION	DL	BFW
1992	Chi A	143	567	74	134	26	4	4	47	43-4	2	42	.236	.290	.317	71	-22	30-12	.972	-26	92	78	2b141/D	0	-4.4
1993	Chi A	57	119	20	28	5	0	1	8	8-0	0	6	.235	.283	.303	58	-7	7-3	1.000	-2	78	0	O32(26/0/6),D21/2	0	-1.1
1994	Oak A	7	24	2	6	0	1	0	1	0-0	0	2	.250	.250	.333	53	-2	0-0	1.000	2	111	79	2b6	95	0.0
Total	14	1769	6940	913	1949	278	47	54	550	556-47	24	584	.281	.335	.358	95	-47	444-178	.978	-39	98	94	2b1679,O33(27/0/6),D26,3b7	110	1.5
Say, Jimmy	James I.; B1862 Baltimore MD; D6.23.1894 Baltimore MD; d7.22; b–Lou																								
1882	Lou AA	1	4	1	1	0	0	0	—	0	—	—	.250	.250	.250	73	0	—	.333	-1	0	0	/3	—	-0.1
	Phi AA	22	82	12	17	2	0	1	—	1	—	—	.207	.217	.268	59	-4	—	.884	4	105	200	S22	—	0.1
	Year	23	86	13	18	2	0	1	—	1	—	—	.209	.218	.267	59	-4	—	.884	3	105	200	S22/3	—	0.0
1884	Wil U	16	59	3	13	1	2	0	—	1	—	—	.220	.233	.305	60	-5	—	.733	-3	75	116	3b16	—	-0.7
	KC U	2	8	0	2	0	0	0	—	0	—	—	.250	.250	.250	60	-1	—	.200	-2	38	0	3b2	—	-0.2
	Year	18	67	3	15	1	2	0	—	1	—	—	.224	.235	.299	60	-6	—	.680	-4	72	106	3b18	—	-0.9
1887	Cle AA	16	64	9	24	5	3	0	12	1	0	—	.375	.385	.547	163	5	0	.714	-4	85	109	3b16	—	0.1
Total	3	57	217	25	57	8	5	1	12	3	0	—	.263	.273	.359	91	-5	0	.690	-6	76	104	3b35,S22	—	-0.8
Say, Lou	Louis I.; B2.4.1854 Baltimore MD; D6.5.1930 Fallston MD; BR/TR/5´7˝/145; d4.14; b–Jimmy																								
1873	Mar NA	3	12	1	2	0	0	0	2	0	—	0	.167	.167	.167	-1	-1	0-0	.667	0	107	0	S2/rf	—	-0.1
1874	Bal NA	18	66	4	14	3	0	0	5	0	—	1	.212	.212	.258	50	-3	0-0	.786	6	140	0	S18	—	0.2
1875	Was NA	11	38	4	10	0	0	0	2	0	—	7	.263	.263	.263	87	0	0-0	.698	-3	104	0	S8,2b2/cf	—	-0.3
1880	Cin N	48	191	14	38	8	1	0	15	4	—	31	.199	.215	.251	58	-8	—	.832	-4	101	76	S48	—	-0.9
1882	Phi AA	49	199	35	45	4	3	1	28	8	—	—	.226	.256	.291	79	-5	—	.867	4	107	56	S49	—	0.0
1883	Bal AA	74	324	52	83	13	2	1	—	10	—	—	.256	.278	.318	89	-4	—	.794	3	113	70	S74	—	0.1
1884	Bal U	78	339	65	81	14	2	2	—	11	—	—	.239	.263	.310	66	-24	—	.795	-2	100	119	S78	—	-2.1
	KC U	17	70	6	14	2	0	1	—	2	—	—	.200	.222	.271	56	-6	—	.860	7	134	91	S16/2	—	0.1
	Year	95	409	71	95	16	2	3	—	13	—	—	.232	.256	.303	65	-30	—	.808	5	**106**	114	S94/2	—	-2.0
Total	3NA	32	116	9	26	3	0	0	9	0	—	8	.224	.224	.250	57	-4	0-0	.750	3	127	0	S28,2b2,O2(0/1/1)	—	-0.2
Total	4	266	1123	172	261	41	8	5	43	35	—	31	.232	.256	.297	73	-47	—	.820	8	107	84	S265/2	—	-2.8
Scala, Jerry	Gerard Michael; B9.27.1924 Bayonne NJ; D12.14.1993 Fallston MD; BL/TR/5´11˝/178; d4.22																								
1948	Chi A	3	6	1	0	0	0	0	0	0	0	3	.000	.000	.000	-99	-2	0-0	1.000	0	135	0	O2C	0	-0.2
1949	Chi A	37	120	17	30	7	1	1	13	17	1	19	.250	.348	.350	88	-2	3-3	.988	-2	96	45	O37(2/35/0)	0	-0.5
1950	Chi A	40	67	8	13	2	1	0	6	10	0	10	.194	.299	.254	44	-6	0-0	1.000	1	109	81	O23(1/22/0)	0	-0.5
Total	3	80	193	26	43	9	2	1	19	27	1	32	.223	.321	.306	67	-10	3-3	.993	-1	101	55	O62(3/59/0)	0	-1.2
Scalzi, Skeeter	Frank John; B6.16.1913 Lafferty OH; D8.25.1984 Pittsburgh PA; BR/TR/5´6˝/160; d7.21; Col Alabama																								
1939	NY N	11	18	3	6	0	0	0	0	3	0	2	.333	.429	.333	106	0	1	.875	1	119	96	S5/3	—	0.1
Scalzi, Johnny	John Anthony; B3.22.1907 Stamford CT; D9.27.1962 Port Chester NY; BR/TR/5´7˝/170; d6.19; Col Georgetown																								
1931	Bos N	2	1	0	0	0	0	0	0	0	0	1	.000	.000	.000	-99	0	0	ø	0	—	—	/H	—	0.0
Scanlan, Mort	Mortimer J.; B3.18.1861 Chicago IL; D12.29.1928 Chicago IL; 6´1˝/186; d4.21																								
1890	NY N	3	10	0	0	0	0	0	0	2	0	5	.000	.167	.000	-50	-2	1	1.000	-0	0	135	1b3	—	-0.2
Scanlan, Patrick	Patrick J.; B3.25.1861 Halifiax NS (now Canada); D7.17.1913 Springfield MA; BL/6´0˝/180; d7.4																								
1884	Bos U	6	24	2	7	1	0	0	—	0	—	—	.292	.292	.333	90	-1	—	.800	0	129	0	O6L	—	-0.1
Scanlon, Pat	James Patrick; B9.23.1952 Minneapolis MN; BL/TR/6´0˝/170; [MonN70 5/101]; d9.27																								
1974	Mon N	2	4	1	1	0	0	0	0	0-0	0	1	.250	.250	.250	38	0	0-0	1.000	0	195	0	/3	0	0.0
1975	Mon N	60	109	5	20	3	1	2	15	17-3	0	25	.183	.294	.284	58	-6	0-1	.957	1	118	94	3b28/1	0	-0.5
1976	Mon N	11	27	2	5	1	0	1	2	2-0	0	5	.185	.241	.333	59	-2	0-0	.842	-0	112	0	3b7/1	0	-0.2
1977	SD N	47	79	9	15	3	0	1	11	12-3	0	20	.190	.297	.266	58	-5	0-0	.957	-2	99	62	2b15,3b11/lf	0	-0.6
Total	4	120	219	17	41	7	1	4	28	31-6	0	51	.187	.288	.283	58	-13	0-1	.938	-0	118	77	3b47,2b15,1b2/lf	0	-1.3
Scarritt, Russ	Stephen Russell Mallory; B1.14.1903 Pensacola FL; D12.4.1994 Pensacola FL; BL/TR/5´10.5˝/165; d4.18; Col Florida																								
1929	Bos A	151	540	69	159	26	17	1	71	34	1	38	.294	.337	.411	94	-7	13-11	.944	-2	96	111	O145(134/1/10)	—	-2.0
1930	Bos A	113	447	48	129	17	8	2	48	12	3	49	.289	.312	.376	76	-18	4-7	.967	-0	107	56	O110L	—	-2.6
1931	Bos A	10	39	2	6	1	0	0	1	2	0	2	.154	.195	.179	-1	-6	0-0	1.000	0	98	135	O9L	—	-0.6
1932	Phi N	11	11	0	2	0	0	0	0	1	0	2	.182	.250	.182	16	-1	0	1.000	0	135	0	/lf	—	-0.1
Total	4	285	1037	119	296	44	25	3	120	49	4	91	.285	.320	.385	82	-32	17-18	.956	-2	101	88	O265(254/1/10)	—	-5.3
Scarsella, Les	Leslie George; B11.23.1913 Santa Cruz CA; D12.16.1958 San Francisco CA; BL/TL/5´11˝/185; d9.15; Col St. Marys (CA)																								
1935	Cin N	6	10	4	2	1	0	0	0	3	0	1	.200	.385	.300	89	0	0	1.000	1	238	130	1b2	—	0.1
1936	Cin N	115	485	63	152	21	9	3	65	14	2	36	.313	.335	.412	107	2	6	.989	2	108	94	1b115	—	-0.7
1937	Cin N	110	329	35	81	11	4	3	34	17	1	26	.246	.285	.331	70	-15	5	.984	-3	89	106	1b65,O14(12/0/2)	—	-2.4
1939	Cin N	16	14	0	2	0	0	0	2	0	0	2	.143	.143	.143	-23	-2	0	ø	0	—	—	/H	—	-0.2
1940	Bos N	18	60	7	18	1	3	0	8	3	1	5	.300	.344	.417	115	1	2	.986	-1	78	137	1b15	—	-0.2
Total	5	265	898	109	255	34	16	6	109	37	4	70	.284	.315	.378	92	-14	13	.988	-1	101	101	1b197,O14(12/0/2)	—	-3.4
Scarsone, Steve	Steven Wayne; B4.11.1966 Anaheim CA; BR/TR/6´2˝/(170–195); [PhiN86*2/34]; d5.15; Col Santa Ana (CA) JC; OF(1/1/0)																								
1992	Phi N	7	13	1	2	0	0	0	0	1-0	0	6	.154	.214	.154	6	-2	0-0	1.000	-2	48	74	2b3	0	-0.4
	Bal A	11	17	2	3	0	0	0	0	1-0	0	6	.176	.222	.176	13	-2	0-0	.889	-1	54	251	2b5,3b2/S	0	-0.3
1993	SF N	44	103	16	26	9	0	2	15	4-0	0	32	.252	.278	.398	82	-3	0-1	1.000	-4	73	110	2b20,3b8,1b6	57	-0.7
1994	SF N	52	103	21	28	8	0	2	13	10-1	0	20	.272	.330	.408	96	0	0-2	.990	8	118	176	2b22,3b8,1b6/S	0	0.7
1995	SF N	80	233	33	62	10	3	11	29	18-0	6	82	.266	.333	.476	113	4	3-2	.927	-6	84	113	3b50,2b13,1b11	0	-0.3
1996	SF N	105	283	28	62	12	1	5	23	25-0	2	91	.219	.286	.322	62	-16	2-3	.973	-4	91	106	2b74,3b14/1S	0	-1.7
1997	StL N	5	10	0	1	0	0	0	0	2-0	0	5	.100	.250	.100	-4	-2	1-0	1.000	-3	33	0	2b2,O2(1/1/0)/3	0	-0.4
1999	KC A	46	68	2	14	5	0	0	6	9-0	0	24	.206	.295	.279	47	-5	1-0	.977	2	123	126	S16,1b12,2b9,3b3,D2	0	-0.2
Total	7	350	830	103	198	44	4	20	86	70-1	8	266	.239	.302	.373	79	-26	7-8	.975	-10	91	120	2b148,3b86,1b36,S19,D2,O2L	57	-3.3
Schaal, Paul	Paul; B3.3.1943 Pittsburgh PA; BR/TR/5´11˝/(165–185); d9.3																								
1964	LA A	17	32	3	4	0	0	0	0	2-0	0	5	.125	.176	.125	-16	-5	0-1	1.000	-0	155	151	2b9,3b9	0	-0.6
1965	Cal A	155	483	48	108	12	2	9	45	61-8	1	88	.224	.310	.313	80	-12	6-3	.970	-12	100	67	3b153/2	0	-2.6
1966	Cal A	138	386	59	94	15	7	6	24	68-0	5	56	.244	.362	.365	113	10	6-4	.948	-3	104	99	3b131	0	0.7
1967	Cal A	99	272	31	51	9	1	6	20	38-3	1	39	.188	.286	.294	76	-8	2-2	.970	-1	98	74	3b88,S2/2	0	-1.0
1968	Cal A	60	219	22	46	7	1	2	16	29-0	2	25	.210	.307	.279	81	-4	5-7	.958	12	123	132	3b58	94	0.7
1969	KC A	61	205	22	54	6	0	1	13	25-2	2	27	.263	.346	.307	84	-3	2-1	.897	-16	81	33	3b49,2b6,S6	0	-2.0
1970	KC A	124	380	50	102	12	3	5	35	43-1	1	39	.268	.343	.355	93	-3	7-4	.938	-17	87	64	3b97,S10,2b6	0	-2.0
1971	KC A	**161**	548	80	150	31	6	11	63	103-5	2	51	.274	.387	.412	129	26	7-5	.940	-8	101	95	3b161	0	1.8
1972	KC A	127	435	47	99	19	3	6	41	61-1	2	59	.228	.323	.326	95	-1	1-3	.947	-11	97	67	3b123/S	0	-1.6
1973	KC A	121	396	61	114	14	3	8	42	63-0	5	45	.288	.389	.399	115	11	5-6	.913	-10	100	57	3b121	17	-0.1
1974	KC A	12	34	3	6	2	0	1	4	5-0	1	5	.176	.286	.324	75	-1	0-0	.949	1	109	161	3b12	0	0.0
	Cal A	53	165	10	41	5	0	2	20	18-1	0	27	.248	.322	.315	89	-2	2-2	.903	-9	79	87	3b51	0	-1.2
	Year	65	199	13	47	7	0	3	24	23-1	1	32	.236	.316	.317	86	-3	2-2	.914	-8	85	102	3b63	0	-1.2
Total	11	1128	3555	436	869	132	26	57	323	516-21	22	466	.244	.341	.344	98	8	43-38	.943	-75	99	78	3b1053,2b23,S19	111	-7.9
Schaefer, Jeff	Jeffrey Scott; B5.31.1960 Patchogue NY; BR/TR/5´10˝/170; [BalA81 12/310]; d4.7; Col Maryland																								
1989	Chi A	15	10	2	1	0	0	0	0	0-0	0	2	.100	.100	.100	-44	-2	1-1	.900	0	130	353	S5,2b4,3b4/D	0	-0.2
1990	Sea A	55	107	11	22	3	0	0	6	3-0	2	11	.206	.239	.234	33	-10	4-1	.933	6	127	218	3b26,S24,2b3	0	-0.2
1991	Sea A	84	164	19	41	7	1	1	11	5-0	0	25	.250	.272	.323	64	-9	3-1	.968	-7	81	102	S46,3b30,2b11/D	0	-1.2
1992	Sea A	65	70	5	8	2	0	1	3	2-0	0	10	.114	.139	.186	-10	-11	0-1	.922	1	107	50	S33,3b21,2b7,D2	0	-0.9
1994	Oak A	6	8	0	1	0	0	0	0	0-0	0	1	.125	.125	.125	-38	-2	0-0	.800	-1	56	0	3b3,S2/1	0	-0.3
Total	5	225	359	37	73	12	1	2	20	10-0	2	49	.203	.228	.259	35	-34	8-4	.957	-1	91	95	S110,3b84,2b25,D4/1	0	-2.8

THE BATTER REGISTER

YEAR	TM LG	G	AB	R	H	2B	3B	HR	RBI	BB-IB	HP	SO	AVG	OBP	SLG	AOPS	ABR	SB-CS	FA	FR	RNG	THR	GAMES AT POSITION	DL	BFW
SCHAEFER, GERMANY	William Herman; B2.4.1876 Chicago IL; D5.16.1919 Saranac Lake NY; BR/TR/5'9"/175; d10.5; C1; OF(18/13/46)																								
1901	Chi N	2	5	0	3	1	0	0	0	2	0	—	.600	.714	.800	352	2	0	1.000	0	77	318	/23	—	0.2
1902	Chi N	81	291	32	57	2	3	0	14	19	2	—	.196	.250	.223	48	-18	12	.864	-12	93	116	3b75,1b3,O2R/S	—	-3.0
1905	Det A	153	554	64	135	17	9	2	47	45	1	—	.244	.302	.318	96	-3	19	.955	9	96	87	2b151,S3	—	0.8
1906	Det A	124	446	48	106	14	3	2	42	32	1	—	.238	.290	.296	81	-10	31	.948	7	101	100	2b114,S7	—	-0.1
1907	†Det A	109	372	44	96	12	3	1	32	30	0	—	.258	.313	.315	97	-1	21	.961	-10	90	92	2b74,S18,3b14/rf	—	-1.1
1908	†Det A	153	584	96	151	20	10	3	52	37	1	—	.259	.304	.342	106	2	40	.918	-2	103	150	S68,2b58,3b29	—	0.5
1909	Det A	87	280	26	70	12	0	0	22	14	0	—	.250	.286	.293	79	-7	12	.966	8	114	92	2b86/rf	—	0.2
	Was A	37	128	13	31	5	1	1	4	6	1	—	.242	.281	.320	94	-1	2	.941	1	107	144	2b32/3	—	0.0
	Year	124	408	39	101	17	1	1	26	20	1	—	.248	.284	.301	84	-8	14	.960	9	**112**	106	2b118/rf3	—	0.2
1910	Was A	74	229	27	63	6	5	0	14	25	2	—	.275	.352	.345	124	7	17	.953	3	108	130	2b35,O26(8/13/5),3b2	—	1.0
1911	Was A	125	440	73	147	14	7	0	45	57	1	—	.334	.412	.398	129	20	22	.980	2	105	**116**	1b108,O7L	—	1.8
1912	Was A	60	166	21	41	7	3	0	19	23	1	—	.247	.342	.325	90	-1	11	.900	-7	74	221	O19R,1b15,2b15/P	—	-0.9
1913	Was A	54	100	17	32	1	1	0	7	15	2	12	.320	.419	.350	123	4	6	.926	-3	91	110	2b16,1b6,3b2/Prf	—	0.1
1914	Was A	30	29	6	7	1	0	0	2	3	0	5	.241	.313	.276	74	-1	4-1	1.000	0	45	0	2b3,O3R	—	0.0
1915	New F	59	154	26	33	5	3	0	8	25	1	11	.214	.328	.286	78	-6	3	.952	-0	76	172	O17(3/0/14),1b13,3b9,2b2	—	-0.8
1916	NY A	1	1	0	0	0	0	0	0	0	0	0	.000	.000	.000	-98	0	0	ø	0	0	0	/O	—	0.0
1918	Cle A	1	5	2	0	0	0	0	0	0	0	0	.000	.000	.000	-91	-1	1	1.000	-0	87	0	/2	—	-0.2
Total	15	1150	3784	495	972	117	48	9	308	333	13	28	.257	.319	.320	96	-14	201-1	.954	-3	99	100	2b588,1b145,3b133,S97,O78R,P2	—	-1.5
SCHAFER, HARRY	Harry C. "Silk Stocking"; B8.14.1846 Philadelphia PA; D2.28.1935 Philadelphia PA; BR/TR/5'9.5"/143; d5.5																								
1871	Bos NA	**31**	149	38	42	7	5	0	28	3	—	1	.282	.296	.396	94	-2	13-4	.684	3	116	190	3b31	—	0.1
1872	Bos NA	**48**	226	51	65	10	4	1	35	0	—	8	.288	.288	.381	99	-2	3-0	.792	4	111	**145**	3b43,O5L,C2	—	0.1
1873	Bos NA	**60**	296	65	79	12	2	2	42	3	—	4	.267	.274	.341	75	-11	14-7	.703	-15	67	**169**	3b47,O13L	—	-1.9
1874	Bos NA	**71**	327	69	87	10	2	1	45	1	—	5	.266	.268	.318	83	-7	2-4	.785	6	105	**188**	3b71/S	—	-0.4
1875	Bos NA	52	222	49	64	9	0	0	17	1	—	8	.288	.291	.329	111	2	3-2	.795	3	105	87	3b51/cf	—	0.3
1876	Bos N	**70**	286	47	72	11	0	0	35	4	—	11	.252	.262	.290	82	-5	—	.810	4	104	122	3b70	—	0.1
1877	Bos N	33	141	20	39	5	2	0	13	0	—	7	.277	.277	.340	90	-2	—	.621	-11	26	0	O23(1/0/22),3b9/S	—	-1.1
1878	Bos N	2	8	0	1	0	0	0	0	0	—	1	.125	.125	.125	-16	-1	—	1.000	-0	0	0	O2R	—	-0.1
Total	5NA	262	1220	272	337	48	13	4	167	8	—	26	.276	.281	.347	90	-20	35-17	.758	0	100	156	3b243,O19(18/1/0),C2/S	—	-1.8
Total	3	105	435	67	112	16	2	0	48	4	—	19	.257	.264	.303	83	-8	—	.810	-8	95	120	3b79,O25(1/0/24)/S	—	-1.1
SCHAFFER, JIMMIE	Jimmie Ronald; B4.5.1936 Limeport PA; BR/TR/5'9"/185; d5.20; C10																								
1961	StL N	68	153	15	39	7	0	1	16	9-1	1	29	.255	.301	.320	59	-9	0-0	.996	0	129	126	C68	0	-0.6
1962	StL N	70	66	7	16	2	1	0	6	6-0	0	16	.242	.301	.303	58	-4	1-0	.993	-4	122	109	C69	0	-0.6
1963	Chi N	57	142	17	34	7	0	7	19	11-2	0	35	.239	.294	.437	102	0	0-0	.996	-0	224	127	C54	0	0.2
1964	Chi N	54	122	9	25	6	1	2	9	17-4	1	17	.205	.307	.320	74	-4	2-4	.970	-6	144	48	C43	30	-1.0
1965	Chi A	17	31	2	6	3	1	0	1	3-0	0	4	.194	.265	.355	79	-1	0-0	1.000	2	177	170	C14	0	0.2
	NY N	24	37	0	5	2	0	0	0	1-0	0	15	.135	.158	.189	-3	-5	0-0	.968	-2	103	0	C21	0	-0.7
1966	Phi N	8	15	2	2	1	0	1	4	1-0	0	7	.133	.188	.400	58	-1	0-0	.952	-2	64	157	C6	0	-0.3
1967	Phi N	2	2	1	0	0	0	0	0	1-1	0	1	.000	.333	.000	3	0	0-0	1.000	0	0	0	/C	0	0.0
1968	Cin N	4	6	0	1	0	0	0	1	0-0	0	3	.167	.167	.167	0	-1	0-0	1.000	-1	17	0	C2	0	-0.2
Total	8	304	574	53	128	28	3	11	56	49-8	2	127	.223	.286	.340	69	-25	3-4	.989	-12	153	103	C278	30	-3.0
SCHAIVE, JOHNNY	John Edward; B2.25.1934 Springfield IL; BR/TR/5'8"/175; d9.19																								
1958	Was A	7	24	1	6	0	0	0	1	1-0	0	4	.250	.280	.250	48	-2	0-0	1.000	0	84	86	2b6	0	-0.1
1959	Was A	16	59	3	9	2	0	0	2	0-0	1	7	.153	.167	.186	-3	-8	0-0	.977	2	118	92	2b16	0	-0.6
1960	Was A	6	12	1	3	1	0	0	0	0-0	0	3	.250	.250	.333	57	-1	0-0	.917	-1	91	109	2b4	0	-0.1
1962	Was A	82	225	20	57	15	1	6	29	6-1	0	25	.253	.270	.409	81	-7	0-1	.967	2	108	82	3b49,2b6	0	-0.5
1963	Was A	3	3	0	0	0	0	0	0	0-0	0	1	.000	.000	.000	-99	-1	0-0	ø	0	—	—	/H	0	-0.1
Total	5	114	323	25	75	18	1	6	32	7-1	1	40	.232	.249	.350	61	-19	0-1	.967	3	108	82	3b49,2b32	0	-1.4
SCHALK, ROY	Le Roy John; B11.9.1908 Chicago IL; D3.11.1990 Gainesville TX; BR/TR/5'10"/168; d9.17; Mil 1943																								
1932	NY A	3	12	3	3	1	0	0	0	2	0	2	.250	.357	.333	84	0	0-0	.867	-1	92	55	2b3	—	-0.1
1944	Chi A	146	587	47	129	14	4	1	44	45	1	52	.220	.276	.262	55	-35	5-4	.964	-10	97	111	2b142,S5	0	-3.9
1945	Chi A	133	513	50	127	23	1	1	65	32	1	41	.248	.293	.302	75	-17	3-6	.977	10	105	100	2b133	0	-0.1
Total	3	282	1112	100	259	38	5	2	109	79	2	95	.233	.285	.281	64	-52	8-10	.970	-0	101	105	2b278,S5	0	-4.1
SCHALK, RAY	Raymond William "Cracker"; B8.12.1892 Harvel IL; D5.19.1970 Chicago IL; BR/TR/5'9"/165; d8.11; M2/C2; HF1955																								
1912	Chi A	23	63	7	18	2	0	0	8	3	4	—	.286	.357	.317	96	0	2	.917	1	107	109	C23	—	0.3
1913	Chi A	129	401	38	98	15	5	1	38	27	3	36	.244	.297	.314	80	-11	14	.980	10	**129**	82	C125	—	1.0
1914	Chi A	136	392	30	106	13	2	0	36	38	8	24	.270	.347	.314	100	1	24-11	.974	14	**128**	94	C125	—	3.0
1915	Chi A	135	413	46	110	14	4	1	54	62	3	21	.266	.366	.327	104	5	15-18	**.984**	13	**173**	85	C134	—	2.8
1916	Chi A	129	410	36	95	12	9	0	41	41	6	31	.232	.311	.305	84	-8	30-13	**.988**	23	**154**	73	C124	—	3.0
1917	†Chi A	140	424	48	96	12	5	2	51	59	7	27	.226	.331	.292	88	-4	19	.981	16	**140**	95	C139	—	2.7
1918	Chi A	108	333	35	73	6	3	0	22	36	3	22	.219	.301	.255	67	-13	12	.978	1	**124**	77	C106	—	-0.3
1919	†Chi A	131	394	57	111	9	3	0	34	51	2	25	.282	.367	.320	93	-1	11	.981	4	118	95	C129	—	1.4
1920	Chi A	151	485	64	131	25	5	1	61	68	2	19	.270	.362	.348	89	-5	10-4	**.986**	6	**150**	93	C151	—	1.4
1921	Chi A	128	416	32	105	24	4	0	47	40	7	36	.252	.328	.329	69	-19	3-4	**.985**	4	87	**121**	C126	—	-0.7
1922	Chi A	142	442	57	124	22	3	4	60	67	3	36	.281	.379	.371	97	1	12-4	**.989**	19	114	121	C142	—	2.9
1923	Chi A	123	382	42	87	12	2	1	44	39	4	28	.228	.306	.277	55	-25	7-4	.983	1	78	91	C121	—	-1.5
1924	Chi A	57	153	15	30	4	2	1	11	21	2	10	.196	.301	.268	49	-12	1-5	.959	3	83	128	C56	—	-0.7
1925	Chi A	125	343	44	94	18	1	0	52	57	3	27	.274	.382	.332	87	-3	11-5	.983	7	**186**	**119**	C125	—	1.1
1926	Chi A	82	226	26	60	9	1	0	32	27	2	11	.265	.349	.314	77	-7	5-1	.977	-2	133	85	C80	—	-0.4
1927	Chi A	16	26	2	6	2	0	0	2	2	0	1	.231	.286	.308	55	-2	0-0	1.000	1	117	139	C15,M	—	0.0
1928	Chi A	2	1	0	1	0	0	0	1	0	0	0	1.000	1.000	1.000	433	0	1-0	1.000	0	0	0	/CM	—	0.1
1929	NY N	5	2	0	0	0	0	0	0	0	0	1	.000	.000	.000	-99	-1	0	1.000	1	0	0	C5	—	0.0
Total	18	1762	5306	579	1345	199	49	11	594	638	59	355	.253	.340	.316	83	-104	177-69	.981	121	130	96	C1727	—	16.1
SCHALL, GENE	Eugene David; B6.5.1970 Abington PA; BR/TR/6'3"/(190–206); [PhiN91 4/109]; d6.16; Col Villanova																								
1995	Phi N	24	65	2	15	2	0	0	5	6-1	1	16	.231	.306	.262	51	-4	0-0	.984	-1	105	87	1b14,O4L	0	-0.6
1996	Phi N	28	66	7	18	5	1	2	10	12-0	1	15	.273	.392	.470	125	3	0-0	.986	-2	68	118	1b19	0	0.0
Total	2	52	131	9	33	7	1	2	15	18-1	2	31	.252	.351	.366	89	-1	0-0	.985	-2	84	105	1b33,O4L	0	-0.6
SCHALLER, BIFF	Walter; B9.23.1889 Chicago IL; D10.9.1939 Emeryville CA; BL/TR/5'11"/168; d4.30																								
1911	Det A	40	60	8	8	0	1	1	7	4	1	—	.133	.200	.217	15	-7	1	1.000	2	126	114	O16(7/9/0)/1	—	-0.6
1913	Chi A	36	96	12	21	3	0	0	4	20	0	16	.219	.353	.250	78	-1	5	.918	-5	88	0	O32L	—	-0.8
Total	2	76	156	20	29	3	1	1	11	24	1	16	.186	.298	.237	54	-8	6	.949	-2	98	31	O48(39/9/0)/1	—	-1.4
SCHANG, BOBBY	Robert Martin; B12.7.1886 Wales Center NY; D8.29.1966 Sacramento CA; BR/TR/5'7"/165; d9.23; b–Wally																								
1914	Pit N	11	35	0	8	1	1	0	1	0	0	10	.229	.229	.314	64	-2	0	.964	-1	107	74	C10	—	-0.2
1915	Pit N	56	125	13	23	6	3	0	4	14	1	32	.184	.271	.280	68	-5	2-2	.974	-4	81	104	C45	—	-0.7
	NY N	12	21	1	3	0	0	0	1	4	0	5	.143	.280	.143	31	-2	1	.875	-3	82	73	C6	—	-0.4
	Year	68	146	14	26	6	3	0	5	18	1	37	.178	.273	.260	63	-6	3-2	.960	-7	81	100	C51	—	-1.1
1927	StL N	3	5	0	1	0	0	0	0	0	0	0	.200	.200	.200	7	-1	0	1.000	-0	56	0	C3	—	-0.1
Total	3	82	186	14	35	7	4	0	6	18	1	47	.188	.263	.269	62	-10	3-2	.962	-8	86	93	C64	—	-1.4
SCHANG, WALLY	Walter Henry; B8.22.1889 S.Wales NY; D3.6.1965 St.Louis MO; BB/TR/5'10"/180; d5.9; C3; b–Bobby																								
1913	†Phi A	79	207	32	55	16	3	3	30	34	9	44	.266	.392	.415	139	13	4	.967	-3	111	95	C72	—	1.6
1914	†Phi A	107	307	44	88	11	8	3	45	32	9	33	.287	.371	.404	138	14	7-7	.956	-6	90	110	C100	—	1.7
1915	Phi A	116	359	64	89	9	11	1	44	66	14	47	.248	.385	.343	122	14	18-3	.890	-2	99	104	3b43,O41(20/21/0),C26	—	1.6
1916	Phi A	110	338	41	90	15	8	7	38	38	10	44	.266	.358	.420	140	16	14	.966	-3	100	121	O61(58/3/0),C36	—	1.4
1917	Phi A	118	316	41	90	14	9	3	36	29	**9**	24	.285	.362	.415	139	14	6	.956	-10	72	**120**	C80,3b12,O6(2/0/4)	—	1.1
1918	†Bos A	88	225	36	55	7	1	0	20	46	2	35	.244	.377	.284	101	4	4	.962	-7	101	73	C57,O16(14/2/0),3b5/S	—	0.0
1919	Bos A	113	330	43	101	16	3	0	55	71	5	42	.306	.436	.373	136	23	15	.972	-1	98	108	C103	—	3.1

YEAR	TM LG	G	AB	R	H	2B	3B	HR	RBI	BB-IB	HP	SO	AVG	OBP	SLG	AOPS	ABR	SB-CS	FA	FR	RNG	THR	GAMES AT POSITION	DL	BFW
1920	Bos A	122	387	58	118	30	7	4	51	64	7	37	.305	.413	.450	134	23	7-7	.958	-7	76	92	C73,O40(0/39/1)	—	1.8
1921	†NY A	134	424	77	134	30	5	6	55	78	5	35	.316	.428	.453	122	19	7-4	.969	-4	101	88	C132	—	2.3
1922	†NY A	124	408	46	130	21	7	1	53	53	6	36	.319	.405	.412	111	9	12-6	.976	2	**135**	112	C119	—	1.9
1923	†NY A	84	272	39	75	8	2	2	29	27	9	17	.276	.360	.342	84	-6	5-2	.970	-5	**120**	86	C81	—	-0.5
1924	NY A	114	356	46	104	19	7	5	52	48	4	43	.292	.382	.427	109	5	2-6	.972	-1	108	96	C108	—	1.0
1925	NY A	73	167	17	40	8	1	2	24	17	0	9	.240	.310	.335	65	-9	2-1	.974	2	96	135	C58	—	-0.4
1926	StL A	103	285	36	94	19	5	8	50	32	4	20	.330	.405	.516	133	14	5-5	.968	1	126	**144**	C82,O3L	—	1.8
1927	StL A	97	264	40	84	15	2	5	42	41	2	33	.318	.414	.447	119	9	3-2	.976	-5	98	147	C75	—	0.9
1928	StL A	91	245	41	70	10	5	3	39	68	4	26	.286	.448	.404	121	13	8-2	.984	-9	84	74	C82	—	1.0
1929	StL A	94	249	43	59	10	5	5	36	74	**7**	22	.237	.424	.378	104	6	1-4	**.988**	-0	**134**	89	C85	—	1.0
1930	Phi A	45	92	16	16	4	1	1	9	17	1	15	.174	.309	.272	47	-7	0-0	.973	1	103	103	C36	—	-0.4
1931	Det A	30	76	9	14	2	0	0	2	14	0	11	.184	.311	.211	38	-6	1-0	.965	-1	72	137	C30	—	-0.5
Total	19	1842	5307	769	1506	264	90	59	710	849	107	573	.284	.393	.401	117	168	121-49	.967	-57	102	107	C1435,O167(97/65/5),3b60/S	—	20.4
SCHAREIN, ART	Arthur Otto "Scoop"; B6.30.1905 Decatur IL; D7.2.1969 San Antonio TX; BR/TR/5´11˝/155; d7.6; b–George																								
1932	StL A	81	303	43	92	19	2	0	42	25	3	10	.304	.363	.380	87	-5	4-8	.965	15	114	160	3b77,S3,2b2	—	1.0
1933	StL A	123	471	49	96	13	3	0	26	41	1	21	.204	.269	.244	35	-45	7-9	.949	16	117	181	3b95,S24,2b7	—	-2.4
1934	StL A	1	2	0	1	0	0	0	2	0	0	0	.500	.500	.500	146	0	0-0	ø	0	—	—	/H	—	0.0
Total	3	205	776	92	189	32	5	0	70	66	4	31	.244	.306	.298	56	-50	11-17	.956	31	116	171	3b172,S27,2b9	—	-1.4
SCHAREIN, GEORGE	George Albert "Tom"; B11.21.1914 Decatur IL; D12.23.1981 Decatur IL; BR/TR/6´1˝/174; d4.19; b–Art																								
1937	Phi N	146	511	44	123	20	1	0	57	36	2	47	.241	.293	.284	53	-33	13	.947	8	102	104	S146	—	-1.4
1938	Phi N	117	390	47	93	16	4	1	29	16	0	33	.238	.268	.308	60	-23	11	.921	-5	96	80	S77,2b39/3	—	-2.1
1939	Phi N	118	399	35	95	17	1	1	33	13	0	40	.238	.262	.293	50	-29	4	.958	-11	91	83	S117	—	-3.3
1940	Phi N	7	17	0	5	0	0	0	0	0	0	3	.294	.294	.294	65	-1	0	.839	-2	82	64	S7	—	-0.2
Total	4	388	1317	126	316	53	6	2	119	65	2	123	.240	.277	.294	54	-86	28	.943	-10	97	91	S347,2b39/3	—	-7.0
SCHARF, NICK	Edward T.; B7.18.1858 Baltimore MD; D5.11.1937 Baltimore MD; TR; d5.18																								
1882	Bal AA	10	39	4	8	1	1	1	—	0	—	—	.205	.205	.359	94	0	—	.727	-2	44	0	O9(1/7/1)/3	—	-0.2
1883	Bal AA	3	13	1	2	1	0	0	—	1	—	—	.154	.214	.231	42	-1	—	.643	-2	62	118	S3	—	-0.3
Total	2	13	52	5	10	2	1	1	—	1	—	—	.192	.208	.327	79	-1	—	.727	-4	44	0	O9(1/7/1),S3/3	—	-0.5
SCHEER, AL	Allen George; B10.27.1888 Groveport OH; D5.6.1959 Logansport IN; BL/TR/5´9˝/165; d8.2																								
1913	Bro N	6	22	3	5	0	0	0	0	2	0	4	.227	.292	.227	48	-1	1	.800	-1	45	192	O6R	—	-0.2
1914	Ind F	120	363	63	111	23	6	3	45	49	5	39	.306	.396	.427	112	4	9	.926	-1	103	91	O102(46/2/54),2b4/S	—	-0.2
1915	New F	**155**	546	75	146	25	14	2	60	65	7	38	.267	.353	.375	111	0	31	.971	-4	97	77	O155L	—	-1.1
Total	3	281	931	141	262	48	20	5	105	116	12	81	.281	.368	.392	110	3	41	.953	-5	98	84	O263(201/2/60),2b4/S	—	-1.5
SCHEER, HEINIE	Henry; B7.31.1900 New York NY; D3.21.1976 New Haven CT; BR/TR/5´8˝/146; d4.20																								
1922	Phi A	51	135	10	23	3	0	4	12	3	0	25	.170	.188	.281	21	-17	1-0	.976	6	126	55	2b30,3b10	—	-0.9
1923	Phi A	69	210	26	50	8	1	2	21	17	2	41	.238	.301	.314	61	-12	3-4	.971	-5	93	92	2b61	—	-1.6
Total	2	120	345	36	73	11	1	6	33	20	2	66	.212	.259	.301	46	-29	4-4	.973	1	103	80	2b91,3b10	—	-2.5
SCHEEREN, FRITZ	Frederick "Dutch"; B9.8.1891 Kokomo IN; D6.17.1973 Kittaning PA; BR/TR/6´0˝/180; d9.14; Col Lafayette																								
1914	Pit N	11	31	4	9	0	1	1	2	1	0	6	.290	.313	.452	132	1	1	.824	-2	95	0	O10(0/4/7)	—	-0.1
1915	Pit N	4	3	0	0	0	0	0	0	0	0	0	.000	.000	.000	-99	-1	0	ø	-0	0	0	/cf	—	-0.1
Total	2	15	34	4	9	0	1	1	2	1	0	6	.265	.286	.412	111	0	1	.824	-2	94	0	O11(0/5/7)	—	-0.2
SCHEFFING, BOB	Robert Boden; B8.11.1913 Overland MO; D10.26.1985 Phoenix AZ; BR/TR/6´2˝/189; d4.27; Mil 1943–45; M6/C5																								
1941	Chi N	51	132	9	32	8	0	1	20	5	0	19	.242	.270	.326	70	-6	2	.966	-3	91	93	C34	0	-0.7
1942	Chi N	44	102	7	20	3	0	2	12	7	0	11	.196	.248	.284	58	-6	2	.986	2	111	94	C32	0	-0.2
1946	Chi N	63	115	8	32	4	1	0	18	12	0	18	.278	.346	.330	94	-1	0	1.000	-3	117	69	C40	0	-0.3
1947	Chi N	110	363	33	96	11	5	5	50	25	0	25	.264	.312	.364	82	-11	2	.984	-2	111	104	C97	0	-0.8
1948	Chi N	102	293	23	88	18	2	5	45	22	1	27	.300	.351	.427	114	5	0	.989	-3	94	113	C78	0	0.7
1949	Chi N	55	149	12	40	6	1	3	19	9	1	9	.268	.314	.383	88	-3	0	.977	-3	63	115	C40	0	-0.4
1950	Chi N	12	16	0	3	1	0	0	1	0	0	2	.188	.188	.250	14	-2	0	.917	-0	64	0	C3	0	-0.2
	Cin N	21	47	4	13	0	0	2	6	4	0	2	.277	.333	.404	93	-1	0	1.000	-2	70	45	C11	0	-0.2
	Year	33	63	4	16	1	0	2	7	4	0	4	.254	.299	.365	74	-3	0	.982	-3	69	36	C14	0	-0.4
1951	Cin N	47	122	9	31	2	0	2	14	16	1	9	.254	.345	.320	79	-3	0-0	.976	-4	76	63	C41	0	-0.5
	StL N	12	18	0	2	0	0	0	2	3	0	5	.111	.238	.111	-3	-3	0-0	1.000	1	119	68	C11	0	-0.2
	Year	59	140	9	33	2	0	2	16	19	1	14	.236	.331	.293	68	-6	0-0	.980	-3	83	64	C52	0	-0.7
Total	8	517	1357	105	357	53	9	20	187	103	3	127	.263	.316	.360	86	-31	6-0	.984	-18	96	95	C387	0	-2.8
SCHEFFLER, TED	Theodore J.; B4.5.1864 New York NY; D2.24.1949 Jamaica NY; BR/TR/5´10˝/160; d8.7																								
1888	Det N	27	94	17	19	3	1	0	4	9	2	9	.202	.286	.255	73	-2	4	.847	-4	22	120	O27(4/23/0)	—	-0.8
1890	Roc AA	119	445	111	109	12	6	3	34	78	14	—	.245	.374	.319	113	14	77	.911	8	**140**	131	O119(2/0/117)/C	—	1.8
Total	2	146	539	128	128	15	7	3	38	87	16	9	.237	.360	.308	106	12	81	.899	4	118	129	O146(6/23/117)/C	—	1.0
SCHEIBECK, FRANK	Frank S.; B6.28.1865 Detroit MI; D10.22.1956 Detroit MI; BR/TR/5´7˝/145; d5.9; ▲																								
1887	Cle AA	3	9	2	2	0	0	0	0	2	0	—	.222	.364	.222	67	0	0	.500	-2	84	0	/S3P	—	-0.1
1888	Det N	1	4	0	0	0	0	0	0	0	0	0	.000	.000	.000	-99	-1	0	.500	-1	0	0	/S	—	-0.2
1890	Tol AA	**134**	485	72	117	13	5	1	49	76	5	—	.241	.350	.295	88	-5	57	.883	2	95	91	S134	—	0.1
1894	Pit N	28	102	20	36	2	3	1	10	11	0	9	.353	.416	.461	112	2	7	.891	-6	71	87	S11,O9(8/1/0),3b3,2b2	—	-0.3
	Was N	52	196	49	45	2	4	0	17	45	4	24	.230	.384	.281	64	-9	11	.876	9	119	63	S52	—	0.2
	Year	80	298	69	81	4	7	1	27	56	4	33	.272	.394	.342	81	-7	18	.878	3	111	67	S63,O9(8/1/0),3b3,2b2	—	-0.1
1895	Was N	49	172	18	31	5	2	0	25	17	1	23	.180	.258	.233	27	-19	5	.889	1	101	92	S45,3b2,2b2	—	-1.3
1899	Was N	27	94	19	27	4	1	0	9	11	1	—	.287	.368	.351	99	0	5	.877	-6	91	29	S27	—	-0.4
1901	Cle A	93	329	33	70	11	3	0	38	18	2	—	.213	.258	.264	47	-24	3	.897	-11	92	70	S92	—	-2.9
1906	Det A	3	10	1	1	0	0	0	0	2	0	—	.100	.250	.100	11	-1	0	.889	-0	92	178	2b3	—	-0.1
Total	8	390	1401	214	329	37	18	2	148	182	13	56	.235	.328	.291	69	-57	88	.884	-14	97	77	S363,O9(8/1/0),2b7,3b6/P	—	-5.0
SCHEINBLUM, RICHIE	Richard Alan; B11.5.1942 New York NY; BB/TR/6´1˝/(175–180); d9.1; Col Long Island–C.W.Post																								
1965	Cle A	4	1	1	0	0	0	0	0	0-0	0	0	.000	.000	.000	-99	0	0-0	ø	0	—	—	/H	0	0.0
1967	Cle A	18	66	8	21	4	2	0	6	5-1	0	10	.318	.361	.439	136	3	0-2	.943	-1	109	0	O18R	0	0.0
1968	Cle A	19	55	3	12	5	0	0	5	5-0	1	8	.218	.281	.309	85	-1	0-0	1.000	1	140	0	O16(6/0/11)	0	0.0
1969	Cle A	102	199	13	37	5	1	1	13	19-0	0	30	.186	.253	.236	38	-17	0-2	.974	1	98	132	O50(32/3/15)	0	-2.0
1971	Was A	27	49	5	7	3	0	0	4	8-0	0	5	.143	.263	.204	35	-4	0-0	.933	4	112	720	O13(7/0/6)	0	-0.1
1972	KC A★	134	450	60	135	21	4	8	66	58-3	4	40	.300	.383	.418	139	24	0-1	.965	-5	96	71	O119(2/0/119)	0	1.5
1973	Cin N	29	54	5	12	2	0	1	8	10-1	0	4	.222	.338	.315	87	-1	0-0	.960	0	90	178	O19(1/0/18)	0	-0.1
	Cal A	77	229	28	75	10	2	3	21	35-6	1	27	.328	.417	.428	149	17	0-0	.969	-1	97	93	O54(6/0/49),D7	0	1.4
1974	Cal A	10	26	1	4	0	0	0	2	1-0	0	2	.154	.185	.154	-2	-4	0-0	.929	0	132	0	O8(4/0/5)/D	0	-0.4
	KC A	36	83	7	15	2	0	0	2	8-0	0	8	.181	.253	.205	31	-7	0-1	ø	-0	0	0	D17,O2L	0	-0.9
	Year	46	109	8	19	2	0	0	4	9-0	0	10	.174	.237	.193	24	-11	0-1	.929	0	127	0	D18,O10(6/0/5)	0	-1.3
	StL N	6	6	0	2	0	0	0	0	0-0	0	1	.333	.333	.333	87	0	0-0	ø	0	—	—	/H	0	0.0
Total	8	462	1218	131	320	52	9	13	127	149-11	6	135	.263	.343	.352	103	10	0-6	.965	-0	101	104	O299(60/3/241),D25	0	-0.6
SCHELL, DANNY	Clyde Daniel; B12.26.1927 Fostoria MI; D5.11.1972 Mayville MI; BR/TR/6´1˝/195; d4.13																								
1954	Phi N	92	272	25	77	14	3	7	33	17	2	31	.283	.327	.434	97	-2	0-3	.974	0	103	89	O69(60/3/6)	0	-0.6
1955	Phi N	2	2	0	0	0	0	0	0	0-0	0	1	.000	.000	.000	-99	-1	0-0	ø	0	—	—	/H	0	-0.1
Total	2	94	274	25	77	14	3	7	33	17-0	2	32	.281	.324	.431	96	-3	0-3	.974	0	103	89	O69(60/3/6)	0	-0.7
SCHELLHASE, AL	Albert Herman "Schelley"; B9.13.1864 Evansville IN; D1.3.1919 Evansville IN; BR/TR/5´8˝/148; d5.7																								
1890	Bos N	9	29	1	4	0	0	0	1	1	0	10	.138	.167	.138	-10	-4	0	.778	-1	253	0	O5R,C2/S3	—	-0.4
1891	Lou AA	6	16	3	2	0	0	0	0	1	0	1	.125	.176	.125	-14	-2	2	.929	-1	83	127	C6	—	-0.3
Total	2	15	45	4	6	0	0	0	1	2	0	11	.133	.170	.133	-11	-6	2	.909	-2	95	121	C8,O5R/3S	—	-0.7

Schemer, Mike Michael "Lefty"; B11.20.1917 Baltimore MD; D4.22.1983 Miami FL; BL/TL/6´0˝/180; d8.8

YEAR	TM LG	G	AB	R	H	2B	3B	HR	RBI	BB-IB	HP	SO	AVG	OBP	SLG	AOPS	ABR	SB-CS	FA	FR	RNG	THR	GAMES AT POSITION	DL	BFW
1945	NY N	31	108	10	36	3	1	1	10	6	0	1	.333	.368	.407	114	2	2	.993	4	145	104	1b27	0	0.4
1946	NY N	1	1	0	0	0	0	0	0	0	0	0	.000	.000	.000	-99	0	0	ø	0	—	—	/H	0	0.0
Total	2	32	109	10	36	3	1	1	10	6	0	1	.330	.365	.404	112	2	2	.993	4	145	104	1b27	0	0.4

Schenck, Bill William G.; B7.1854 Brooklyn NY; D1.29.1934 Brooklyn NY; 5´7˝/171; d5.29; ▲

YEAR	TM LG	G	AB	R	H	2B	3B	HR	RBI	BB-IB	HP	SO	AVG	OBP	SLG	AOPS	ABR	SB-CS	FA	FR	RNG	THR	GAMES AT POSITION	DL	BFW
1882	Lou AA	60	231	37	60	11	3	0	—	8	—	—	.260	.285	.333	114	4	—	.814	-5	91	73	3b58,S2,P2	—	0.0
1884	Ric AA	42	151	14	31	4	0	3	—	1	1	—	.205	.216	.291	65	-6	—	.836	-2	104	79	S40,2b2	—	-0.6
1885	Bro AA	1	4	0	0	0	0	0	0	0	0	—	.000	.000	.000	-99	-1	—	1.000	0	59	0	/3	—	-0.1
Total	3	103	386	51	91	15	3	3	0	9	1	—	.236	.255	.313	92	-3	—	.817	-7	90	72	3b59,S42,2b2,P2	—	-0.7

Schenz, Hank Henry Leonard; B4.11.1919 New Richmond OH; D5.12.1988 Cincinnati OH; BR/TR/5´9.5˝/175; d9.18

YEAR	TM LG	G	AB	R	H	2B	3B	HR	RBI	BB-IB	HP	SO	AVG	OBP	SLG	AOPS	ABR	SB-CS	FA	FR	RNG	THR	GAMES AT POSITION	DL	BFW
1946	Chi N	6	11	0	2	0	0	0	1	0	0	0	.182	.182	.182	3	-1	1	1.000	0	98	317	3b5	0	-0.1
1947	Chi N	7	14	2	1	0	0	0	0	2	1	1	.071	.235	.071	-16	-2	0	.917	0	130	0	3b5	0	-0.2
1948	Chi N	96	337	43	88	17	1	1	14	18	4	15	.261	.306	.326	74	-13	3	.974	-1	96	100	2b78,3b5	0	-1.0
1949	Chi N	7	14	2	6	0	0	0	1	1	0	0	.429	.467	.429	146	1	2	1.000	1	132	405	3b5	0	0.2
1950	Pit N	58	101	17	23	4	2	1	5	6	0	7	.228	.271	.337	57	-7	0	.987	3	107	150	2b21,3b12,S4	0	-0.3
1951	Pit N	25	61	5	13	1	0	0	3	0	1	2	.213	.226	.230	22	-7	0-2	.961	-1	87	146	2b19,3b2	0	-0.8
	†NY N	8	0	1	0	0	0	0	0	0	0	0	ø	ø	ø	ø	0	0-0	ø	0	—	—	/R	0	0.0
	Year	33	61	6	13	1	0	0	3	0	1	2	.213	.226	.230	22	-7	0-2	.961	-1	87	146	2b19,3b2	0	-0.8
Total	6	207	538	70	133	22	3	2	24	27	6	25	.247	.291	.310	63	-29	6-2	.974	2	96	113	2b118,3b34,S4	0	-2.2

Schepner, Joe Joseph Maurice "Gentleman Joe"; B8.10.1895 Aliquippa PA; D7.25.1959 Mobile AL; BR/TR/5´10˝/160; d9.11

YEAR	TM LG	G	AB	R	H	2B	3B	HR	RBI	BB-IB	HP	SO	AVG	OBP	SLG	AOPS	ABR	SB-CS	FA	FR	RNG	THR	GAMES AT POSITION	DL	BFW
1919	StL A	14	48	2	10	4	0	0	6	1	0	5	.208	.224	.292	43	-4	0	.947	-0	84	121	3b13	—	-0.4

Scherbarth, Bob Robert Elmer; B1.18.1926 Milwaukee WI; BR/TR/6´0˝/180; d4.23

YEAR	TM LG	G	AB	R	H	2B	3B	HR	RBI	BB-IB	HP	SO	AVG	OBP	SLG	AOPS	ABR	SB-CS	FA	FR	RNG	THR	GAMES AT POSITION	DL	BFW
1950	Bos A	1	0	0	0	0	0	0	0	0	0	0	ø	ø	ø	ø	0	0-0	ø	0	*0*	*0*	/C	0	0.0

Scherer, Harry Harry; d7.24

YEAR	TM LG	G	AB	R	H	2B	3B	HR	RBI	BB-IB	HP	SO	AVG	OBP	SLG	AOPS	ABR	SB-CS	FA	FR	RNG	THR	GAMES AT POSITION	DL	BFW
1889	Lou AA	1	3	0	1	0	0	0	0	0	0	0	.333	.333	.333	92	0	0	.500	-1	0	0	/cf	—	-0.1

Schiappacasse, Lou Louis Joseph; B3.29.1881 Ann Arbor MI; D9.20.1910 Ann Arbor MI; BR/TR; d9.7

YEAR	TM LG	G	AB	R	H	2B	3B	HR	RBI	BB-IB	HP	SO	AVG	OBP	SLG	AOPS	ABR	SB-CS	FA	FR	RNG	THR	GAMES AT POSITION	DL	BFW
1902	Det A	2	5	0	0	0	0	0	1	1	0	—	.000	.167	.000	-50	-1	0	.000	-1	0	0	O2R	—	-0.2

Schick, Morrie Maurice Francis; B4.17.1892 Chicago IL; D10.25.1979 Hazel Crest IL; BR/TR/5´11˝/170; d4.15; Mil 1918

YEAR	TM LG	G	AB	R	H	2B	3B	HR	RBI	BB-IB	HP	SO	AVG	OBP	SLG	AOPS	ABR	SB-CS	FA	FR	RNG	THR	GAMES AT POSITION	DL	BFW
1917	Chi N	14	34	3	5	0	0	0	3	3	0	10	.147	.216	.147	11	-4	0	.960	2	103	257	O12(2/10/0)	—	-0.3

Schilling, Chuck Charles Thomas; B10.25.1937 Brooklyn NY; BR/TR/5´11˝/(165–170); d4.11; Col Manhattan

YEAR	TM LG	G	AB	R	H	2B	3B	HR	RBI	BB-IB	HP	SO	AVG	OBP	SLG	AOPS	ABR	SB-CS	FA	FR	RNG	THR	GAMES AT POSITION	DL	BFW
1961	Bos A	158	646	87	167	25	2	5	62	78-0	2	77	.259	.340	.327	77	-19	7-6	**.991**	15	103	105	2b158	0	0.9
1962	Bos A	119	413	48	95	17	1	7	35	29-5	4	48	.230	.286	.327	63	-22	1-0	.985	7	100	107	2b118	30	-0.5
1963	Bos A	146	576	63	135	25	0	8	33	41-0	5	72	.234	.291	.319	69	-24	3-2	.985	-13	93	85	2b143	0	-2.5
1964	Bos A	47	163	18	32	6	0	0	7	15-0	0	22	.196	.263	.233	38	-13	0-1	.974	-1	92	73	2b42	0	-1.2
1965	Bos A	71	171	14	41	3	2	3	9	13-0	0	17	.240	.292	.333	73	-6	0-1	.976	10	118	91	2b41	0	0.7
Total	5	541	1969	230	470	76	5	23	146	176-5	11	236	.239	.304	.317	68	-84	11-10	.985	18	100	96	2b502	30	-2.6

Schindler, Bill William Gibbons; B7.10.1896 Perryville MO; D2.6.1979 Perryville MO; BR/TR/5´11˝/160; d9.3

YEAR	TM LG	G	AB	R	H	2B	3B	HR	RBI	BB-IB	HP	SO	AVG	OBP	SLG	AOPS	ABR	SB-CS	FA	FR	RNG	THR	GAMES AT POSITION	DL	BFW
1920	StL N	1	2	0	0	0	0	0	0	0	0	1	.000	.000	.000	-99	-1	0-0	1.000	-0	*0*	*0*	/C	—	-0.1

Schirick, Dutch Harry Ernest; B6.15.1890 Ruby NY; D11.12.1968 Kingston NY; BR/TR/5´8˝/160; d9.17

YEAR	TM LG	G	AB	R	H	2B	3B	HR	RBI	BB-IB	HP	SO	AVG	OBP	SLG	AOPS	ABR	SB-CS	FA	FR	RNG	THR	GAMES AT POSITION	DL	BFW
1914	StL A	1	0	0	0	0	0	0	0	1	0	0	ø	1.000	ø	212	0	2	ø	0	—	—	/H	—	0.1

Schlafly, Larry Harry Fenton; B9.19.1878 Port Washington OH; D6.27.1919 Beach City OH; BR/TR/5´11˝/182; d9.18; M2

YEAR	TM LG	G	AB	R	H	2B	3B	HR	RBI	BB-IB	HP	SO	AVG	OBP	SLG	AOPS	ABR	SB-CS	FA	FR	RNG	THR	GAMES AT POSITION	DL	BFW
1902	Chi N	10	31	5	10	0	3	0	5	6	0	—	.323	.432	.516	198	4	2	1.000	-2	0	0	O5R,2b4,3b2	—	0.2
1906	Was A	123	426	60	105	13	8	2	30	50	**14**	—	.246	.345	.329	117	11	29	.961	16	103	93	2b123	—	3.1
1907	Was A	24	74	10	10	0	0	1	4	22	3	—	.135	.354	.176	75	0	7	.928	-8	68	60	2b24	—	-0.8
1914	Buf F	51	127	16	33	7	1	2	19	12	3	22	.260	.338	.378	93	-3	3	.951	1	106	89	2b23,1b7/C3lfM	—	-0.2
Total	4	208	658	91	158	20	12	5	58	90	20	22	.240	.349	.330	111	12	41	.954	8	98	86	2b174,1b7,O6(1/0/5),3b3/C	—	2.3

Schlei, Admiral George Henry; B1.12.1878 Cincinnati OH; D1.24.1958 Huntington WV; BR/TR/5´8.5˝/179; d4.24

YEAR	TM LG	G	AB	R	H	2B	3B	HR	RBI	BB-IB	HP	SO	AVG	OBP	SLG	AOPS	ABR	SB-CS	FA	FR	RNG	THR	GAMES AT POSITION	DL	BFW
1904	Cin N	97	291	25	69	8	3	0	32	17	8	—	.237	.297	.285	74	-9	7	.977	9	*107*	*101*	C88	—	0.9
1905	Cin N	99	314	32	71	8	3	1	36	22	4	—	.226	.285	.280	62	-15	9	.962	11	*101*	*113*	C89,1b6	—	0.5
1906	Cin N	116	388	44	95	13	8	4	54	29	4	—	.245	.304	.351	100	-1	7	.961	7	*102*	*108*	C91,1b21	—	1.6
1907	Cin N	84	246	28	67	3	2	0	27	28	0	—	.272	.347	.301	99	1	5	.980	6	*103*	*117*	C67,1b3,O2(1/0/1)	—	1.4
1908	Cin N	92	300	31	66	6	4	1	22	22	2	—	.220	.278	.277	79	-7	2	.962	-3	*106*	*94*	C88	—	-0.2
1909	NY N	92	279	25	68	12	0	0	30	40	2	—	.244	.343	.287	94	0	4	.963	3	*113*	*109*	C89	—	1.3
1910	NY N	55	99	10	19	2	1	0	8	14	2	10	.192	.304	.232	57	-5	4	.986	0	*96*	*106*	C49	—	-0.2
1911	NY N	1	1	0	0	0	0	0	0	0	0	1	.000	.000	.000	-97	0	0	ø	0	—	—	/H	—	0.0
Total	8	636	1918	195	455	52	21	6	209	172	22	11	.237	.307	.296	83	-36	38	.968	33	*105*	*107*	C561,1b30,O2(1/0/1)	—	5.3

Schlesinger, Rudy William Cordes; B11.5.1941 Cincinnati OH; BR/TR/6´2˝/175; d5.4; Col Cincinnati

YEAR	TM LG	G	AB	R	H	2B	3B	HR	RBI	BB-IB	HP	SO	AVG	OBP	SLG	AOPS	ABR	SB-CS	FA	FR	RNG	THR	GAMES AT POSITION	DL	BFW
1965	Bos A	1	1	0	0	0	0	0	0	0-0	0	0	.000	.000	.000	-94	0	0-0	ø	0	—	—	/H	0	0.0

Schliebner, Dutch Frederick Paul; B5.19.1891 Berlin, Germany; D4.15.1975 Toledo OH; BR/TR/5´10˝/180; d4.17

YEAR	TM LG	G	AB	R	H	2B	3B	HR	RBI	BB-IB	HP	SO	AVG	OBP	SLG	AOPS	ABR	SB-CS	FA	FR	RNG	THR	GAMES AT POSITION	DL	BFW
1923	Bro N	19	76	11	19	4	0	0	4	5	0	7	.250	.296	.303	60	-4	1-0	.981	2	165	118	1b19	—	-0.3
	StL A	127	444	50	122	19	6	4	52	39	4	60	.275	.339	.372	82	-12	3-2	.989	-0	98	110	1b127	—	-2.0
Total	1	146	520	61	141	23	6	4	56	44	4	67	.271	.333	.362	79	-16	4-2	.988	2	107	111	1b146	—	-2.3

Schlueter, Jay Jay D; B7.31.1949 Phoenix AZ; BR/TR/6´0˝/182; d6.18

YEAR	TM LG	G	AB	R	H	2B	3B	HR	RBI	BB-IB	HP	SO	AVG	OBP	SLG	AOPS	ABR	SB-CS	FA	FR	RNG	THR	GAMES AT POSITION	DL	BFW
1971	Hou N	7	3	1	1	0	0	0	0	0-0	0	1	.333	.333	.333	92	0	0-0	1.000	0	278	0	O2L	0	0.0

Schlueter, Norm Norman John "Duke"; B9.25.1916 Belleville IL; D10.6.2004 Belleville IL; BR/TR/5´10˝/175; d5.28

YEAR	TM LG	G	AB	R	H	2B	3B	HR	RBI	BB-IB	HP	SO	AVG	OBP	SLG	AOPS	ABR	SB-CS	FA	FR	RNG	THR	GAMES AT POSITION	DL	BFW
1938	Chi A	35	118	11	27	5	1	0	7	4	0	15	.229	.254	.288	35	-12	1-0	.952	-2	*112*	*62*	C34	—	-1.1
1939	Chi A	34	56	5	13	2	1	0	8	1	0	11	.232	.246	.304	39	-5	2-0	.988	0	*103*	*23*	C32	—	-0.4
1944	Cle A	49	122	2	15	4	0	0	11	12	0	22	.123	.201	.156	3	-16	0-2	.985	-6	*84*	*50*	C43	0	-2.1
Total	3	118	296	18	55	11	2	0	26	17	0	48	.186	.230	.236	24	-33	3-2	.974	-7	*99*	*49*	C109	0	-3.6

Schmandt, Ray Raymond Henry; B1.25.1896 St.Louis MO; D2.2.1969 St.Louis MO; BR/TR/6´1˝/175; d6.24; Mil 1918; Col St. Louis

YEAR	TM LG	G	AB	R	H	2B	3B	HR	RBI	BB-IB	HP	SO	AVG	OBP	SLG	AOPS	ABR	SB-CS	FA	FR	RNG	THR	GAMES AT POSITION	DL	BFW
1915	StL A	3	4	0	0	0	0	0	0	0	0	1	.000	.000	.000	-99	-1	0	1.000	-0	0	0	/1	—	-0.1
1918	Bro N	34	114	11	35	5	4	0	18	7	0	7	.307	.347	.421	134	4	1	.934	-3	92	61	2b34	—	0.2
1919	Bro N	47	127	8	21	4	0	0	10	4	0	13	.165	.191	.197	16	-13	0	.911	-1	102	93	2b18,1b12,3b6	—	-1.6
1920	†Bro N	28	63	7	15	2	1	0	7	3	0	4	.238	.273	.302	63	-3	1-1	.995	3	175	159	1b20	—	-0.1
1921	Bro N	95	350	42	107	8	5	1	43	11	1	22	.306	.329	.366	81	-10	3-4	.989	0	103	112	1b92	—	-1.7
1922	Bro N	110	396	54	106	17	3	2	44	21	1	28	.268	.306	.341	67	-20	6-6	.989	4	119	106	1b110	—	-2.2
Total	6	317	1054	122	284	36	13	3	122	46	2	75	.269	.301	.337	72	-43	11-11	.990	4	116	113	1b235,2b52,3b6	—	-5.5

Schmees, George George Edward "Rocky"; B9.6.1924 Cincinnati OH; D10.30.1998 San Jose CA; BL/TL/6´0˝/195; d4.15

YEAR	TM LG	G	AB	R	H	2B	3B	HR	RBI	BB-IB	HP	SO	AVG	OBP	SLG	AOPS	ABR	SB-CS	FA	FR	RNG	THR	GAMES AT POSITION	DL	BFW
1952	StL A	34	61	9	8	1	1	0	3	2	0	18	.131	.159	.180	-6	-9	0-0	.932	1	127	90	O19(9/2/8),1b2	0	-0.9
	Bos A	42	64	8	13	3	0	0	3	10	0	11	.203	.311	.250	53	-4	0-1	1.000	0	97	98	O29(0/18/11),P2,1b2	0	-0.5
	Year	76	125	17	21	4	1	0	6	12	0	29	.168	.241	.216	26	-13	0-1	.960	1	113	94	O48(9/20/19),1b4,P2	0	-1.4

Schmidt, Boss Charles; B9.12.1880 Coal Hill AR; D11.14.1932 Altus AR; BB/TR/5´11˝/200; d4.30; b–Walter

YEAR	TM LG	G	AB	R	H	2B	3B	HR	RBI	BB-IB	HP	SO	AVG	OBP	SLG	AOPS	ABR	SB-CS	FA	FR	RNG	THR	GAMES AT POSITION	DL	BFW
1906	Det A	68	216	13	47	4	3	0	10	6	1	—	.218	.242	.264	57	-11	1	.958	8	*111*	*116*	C67	—	0.3
1907	†Det A	104	349	32	85	6	6	0	23	5	7	—	.244	.269	.295	77	-11	8	.944	5	*107*	***103***	C103	—	0.4
1908	†Det A	122	419	45	111	14	3	1	38	16	3	—	.265	.297	.320	96	-3	5	.951	2	97	***119***	C121	—	1.3
1909	†Det A	84	253	21	53	8	2	1	28	7	3	—	.209	.240	.269	58	-13	7	.955	-6	*99*	***111***	C81/rf	—	-1.2
1910	Det A	71	197	22	51	7	7	1	23	2	3	—	.259	.277	.381	99	-2	2	.973	-3	*99*	*94*	C66	—	0.0

YEAR	TM LG	G	AB	R	H	2B	3B	HR	RBI	BB-IB	HP	SO	AVG	OBP	SLG	AOPS	ABR	SB-CS	FA	FR	RNG	THR	GAMES AT POSITION	DL	BFW
1911	Det A	28	46	4	13	2	1	0	2	0	1	—	.283	.298	.370	82	-1	0	1.000	-1	90	95	C9/rf	—	-0.2
Total	6	477	1480	137	360	41	22	3	124	36	18	—	.243	.270	.307	79	-41	23	.955	4	102	110	C447,O2R	—	0.6
SCHMIDT, BUTCH Charles John "Butcher Boy"; B7.19.1886 Baltimore MD; D9.4.1952 Baltimore MD; BL/TL/6´1.5˝/200; d5.11																									
1909	NY A	1	2	0	0	0	0	0	0	0	0	—	.000	.000	.000	-99	0	0	.500	-0	65	0	/P	—	0.0
1913	Bos N	22	78	6	24	2	2	1	14	2	1	5	.308	.333	.423	113	1	1	.983	1	123	54	1b22	—	0.1
1914	†Bos N	147	537	67	153	17	9	1	71	43	11	55	.285	.350	.356	111	7	14	.990	2	106	144	1b147	—	0.6
1915	Bos N	127	458	46	115	26	7	2	60	36	9	59	.251	.318	.352	107	4	3-10	.987	-4	87	119	1b127	—	-0.6
Total	4	297	1075	119	292	45	18	4	145	81	21	119	.272	.335	.358	109	12	18-10	.988	-1	99	128	1b296/P	—	0.1
SCHMIDT, DAVE David Frederick; B12.22.1956 Mesa AZ; BR/TR/6´1˝/205; [BosA75 2/39]; d4.28																									
1981	Bos A	15	42	6	10	1	0	2	3	7-0	0	17	.238	.347	.405	109	1	0-0	1.000	-3	109	66	C15	0	-0.2
SCHMIDT, MIKE Michael Jack; B9.27.1949 Dayton OH; BR/TR/6´2˝/(195–203); [PhiN71 2/30]; d9.12; HF1995; Col Ohio U.																									
1972	Phi N	13	34	2	7	0	0	1	3	5-0	1	15	.206	.325	.294	75	-1	0-0	.964	2	114	208	3b11/2	0	0.1
1973	Phi N	132	367	43	72	11	0	18	52	62-3	9	136	.196	.324	.373	91	-3	8-2	.954	18	112	136	3b125,2b4,1b2,S2	16	1.6
1974	Phi N★	162	568	108	160	28	7	36	116	106-14	4	138	.282	.395	.546	155	44	23-12	.954	28	117	118	3b162	0	7.3
1975	Phi N	158	562	93	140	34	3	38	95	101-10	4	180	.249	.367	.523	138	30	29-12	.954	19	110	119	3b151,S10	0	5.2
1976	†Phi N★	160	584	112	153	31	4	38	107	100-8	11	149	.262	.376	.524	149	40	14-9	.961	18	107	109	3b160	0	5.9
1977	†Phi N★	154	544	114	149	27	11	38	101	104-4	9	122	.274	.393	.574	149	40	15-8	.964	27	119	144	3b149,S2/2	0	6.4
1978	†Phi N	145	513	93	129	27	2	21	78	91-12	4	103	.251	.364	.435	121	18	19-6	.963	9	106	162	3b139/S	0	2.8
1979	Phi N★	160	541	109	137	25	4	45	114	120-12	3	115	.253	.386	.564	151	41	9-5	.954	17	113	134	3b157,S2	0	5.6
1980	†Phi N✳	150	548	104	157	25	8	48	121	89-10	2	119	.286	.380	.624	167	49	12-5	.946	19	115	135	3b149	0	6.8
1981	†Phi N✳	102	354	78	112	19	2	31	91	73-18	4	71	.316	.435	.644	193	46	12-4	.956	23	123	127	3b101	0	7.1
1982	Phi N★	148	514	108	144	26	3	35	87	107-17	3	131	.280	.403	.547	159	45	14-7	.950	19	109	122	3b148	15	6.3
1983	†Phi N★	154	534	104	136	16	4	40	109	128-17	3	148	.255	.399	.524	156	45	7-8	.959	22	110	122	3b153,S2	0	6.4
1984	Phi N★	151	528	93	146	23	3	36	106	92-14	4	116	.277	.383	.536	155	40	5-7	.941	9	112	85	3b145,1b2/S	0	4.7
1985	Phi N	158	549	89	152	31	5	33	93	87-8	3	117	.277	.375	.532	148	37	1-3	.993	7	122	100	1b106,3b54/S	0	3.7
1986	Phi N★	160	552	97	160	29	1	37	119	89-25	7	84	.290	.390	.547	151	41	1-2	.980	-8	95	134	3b124,1b35	0	3.0
1987	Phi N★	147	522	88	153	28	0	35	113	83-15	2	80	.293	.388	.548	141	32	2-1	.971	8	110	122	3b138,1b9,S3	15	3.7
1988	Phi N	108	390	52	97	21	2	12	62	49-10	6	42	.249	.337	.405	111	7	3-0	.939	5	106	89	3b104,1b3	51	1.3
1989	Phi N✳	42	148	19	30	7	0	6	28	21-4	0	17	.203	.297	.372	91	-2	0-1	.918	-4	91	118	3b42	0	-0.6
Total	18	2404	8352	1506	2234	408	59	548	1595	1507-201	79	1883	.267	.380	.527	146	549	174-92	.955	237	111	123	3b2212,1b157,S24,2b6	97	77.3
SCHMIDT, BOB Robert Benjamin; B4.22.1933 St.Louis MO; BR/TR/6´2˝/(190–205); d4.16																									
1958	SF N☆	127	393	46	96	20	2	14	54	33-5	3	59	.244	.306	.412	90	-6	0-1	.982	2	102	125	C123	0	0.1
1959	SF N	71	181	17	44	7	1	5	20	13-4	1	24	.243	.296	.376	80	-6	0-2	1.000	-3	82	68	C70	0	-0.6
1960	SF N	110	344	31	92	12	1	8	37	26-4	0	51	.267	.317	.378	96	-3	0-3	.981	-2	81	51	C108	0	-0.1
1961	SF N	2	6	0	1	0	0	0	1	0-0	0	1	.167	.143	.167	-12	-1	0-0	1.000	1	0	227	C2	0	0.0
	Cin N	27	70	4	9	0	0	1	4	8-1	0	14	.129	.218	.171	5	-10	0-0	.993	-1	55	76	C27	0	-1.0
	Year	29	76	4	10	0	0	1	5	8-1	0	15	.132	.212	.171	4	-11	0-0	.994	-0	50	89	C29	0	-1.0
1962	Was A	88	256	28	62	14	0	10	31	14-2	1	37	.242	.281	.414	86	-6	0-0	.997	-1	162	123	C88	0	-0.4
1963	Was A	9	15	3	3	1	0	0	0	3-0	0	5	.200	.333	.267	71	0	0-0	1.000	-1	118	0	C6	0	-0.1
1965	NY A	20	40	4	10	1	0	1	3	3-1	0	8	.250	.302	.350	85	-1	0-0	.990	0	118	0	C20	0	0.0
Total	7	454	1305	133	317	55	4	39	150	100-17	5	199	.243	.297	.381	84	-33	0-6	.988	-4	103	89	C444	0	-2.1
SCHMIDT, WALTER Walter Joseph; B3.20.1887 Coal Hill AR; D7.4.1973 Modesto CA; BR/TR/5´9˝/159; d4.13; b–Boss																									
1916	Pit N	64	184	16	35	1	2	2	15	10	1	13	.190	.236	.250	49	-12	3	.976	-0	84	115	C57	—	-0.8
1917	Pit N	72	183	9	45	7	0	0	17	11	2	11	.246	.296	.284	76	-5	4	.978	1	77	132	C61	—	0.1
1918	Pit N	105	323	31	77	6	3	0	27	17	2	19	.238	.281	.276	68	-13	7	.981	24	160	116	C104	—	2.2
1919	Pit N	85	267	23	67	9	2	0	29	23	0	9	.251	.310	.300	81	-6	5	.982	5	129	102	C85	—	0.8
1920	Pit N	94	310	22	86	8	4	0	20	24	4	15	.277	.337	.329	89	-4	9-3	.971	-4	94	94	C92	—	0.2
1921	Pit N	114	393	30	111	9	3	0	38	12	2	13	.282	.307	.321	65	-20	10-6	.986	8	138	88	C111	—	-0.4
1922	Pit N	40	152	21	50	11	1	0	22	1	0	5	.329	.333	.414	91	-2	2-1	.995	-3	92	50	C40	—	-0.3
1923	Pit N	97	335	39	83	7	2	0	37	22	3	12	.248	.300	.281	53	-23	10-5	.981	-2	117	86	C96	—	-1.7
1924	Pit N	58	177	16	43	3	2	1	20	13	0	5	.243	.295	.299	59	-11	6-1	.986	4	145	92	C57	—	-0.2
1925	StL N	37	87	9	22	2	1	0	9	4	1	3	.253	.293	.299	51	-7	1-0	.967	5	122	144	C31	—	0.0
Total	10	766	2411	216	619	63	20	3	234	137	15	105	.257	.301	.303	68	-103	57-16	.980	38	120	100	C734	—	-0.1
SCHMULBACH, HANK Henry Alrives; B1.17.1925 E.St.Louis IL; D5.3.2001 Belleville IL; BL/TR/5´11˝/165; d9.27; Mil 1944–46; Col Washington–St. Louis																									
1943	StL A	1	0	1	0	0	0	0	0	0	0	0	ø	ø	ø	ø	0	0-0	ø	0	—	—	/R	0	0.0
SCHNECK, DAVE David Lee; B6.18.1949 Allentown PA; BL/TL/5´10˝/200; d7.14																									
1972	NY N	37	123	7	23	3	2	3	10	10-2	1	26	.187	.254	.317	62	-7	0-1	.985	-2	97	49	O33(1/17/16)	0	-1.1
1973	NY N	13	36	2	7	0	1	0	0	1-1	0	4	.194	.216	.250	29	-4	0-0	1.000	1	137	0	O12C	0	-0.3
1974	NY N	93	254	23	52	11	1	5	25	16-2	1	43	.205	.254	.315	59	-15	4-1	.974	5	109	161	O84(23/59/9)	0	-1.2
Total	3	143	413	32	82	14	4	8	35	27-5	2	73	.199	.251	.310	57	-26	4-2	.979	5	108	115	O129(24/88/25)	0	-2.6
SCHNEIDER, BRIAN Brian Duncan; B11.26.1976 Jacksonville FL; BL/TR/6´1˝/(195–200); [MonN95 5/143]; d5.26																									
2000	Mon N	45	115	6	27	6	0	0	11	7-2	0	24	.235	.276	.287	43	-10	0-1	.974	-2	71	111	C43	0	-1.0
2001	Mon N	27	41	4	13	3	0	1	6	6-1	0	3	.317	.396	.463	125	2	0-0	1.000	3	136	148	C14	0	0.5
2002	Mon N	73	207	21	57	19	2	5	29	21-8	0	41	.275	.339	.459	103	1	1-2	.993	2	129	130	C65,O2(1/0/1)	0	0.7
2003	Mon N	108	335	34	77	26	1	9	46	37-8	2	75	.230	.309	.394	80	-10	0-2	.996	22	195	127	C98,D2	0	1.8
2004	Mon N	135	436	40	112	20	3	12	49	42-10	3	63	.257	.325	.399	83	-11	0-1	.998	14	185	138	C133	0	1.1
2005	Was N	116	369	38	99	20	1	10	44	29-7	6	48	.268	.330	.409	97	-2	1-0	.993	6	117	147	C113	0	1.1
2006	Was N	124	410	30	105	18	0	4	55	38-10	2	67	.256	.320	.329	71	-18	2-2	.993	-2	111	104	C123/1	15	-1.2
Total	7	628	1913	173	490	112	7	41	240	180-46	13	321	.256	.322	.386	83	-48	4-8	.994	43	144	128	C589,D2,O2(1/0/1)/1	15	3.0
SCHOENDIENST, RED Albert Fred; B2.2.1923 Germantown IL; BB/TR/6´0˝/(168–175); d4.17; M14/C17; HF1989																									
1945	StL N	137	565	89	157	22	6	1	47	21	1	17	.278	.305	.343	78	-19	26	.983	1	105	110	O118L,S10/2	0	-2.5
1946	†StL N★	142	606	94	170	28	5	0	34	37	0	27	.281	.322	.343	85	-13	12	.984	2	98	121	2b128,3b12,S4	0	-0.3
1947	StL N	151	659	91	167	25	9	3	48	48	0	27	.253	.304	.332	66	-33	6	.976	-2	99	118	2b142,3b5/lf	0	-2.7
1948	StL N★	119	408	64	111	21	4	4	36	28	0	16	.272	.319	.373	82	-11	1	.980	7	106	108	2b96	0	0.1
1949	StL N★	151	640	102	190	25	2	3	54	51	2	18	.297	.351	.356	86	-12	8	.987	27	114	116	2b138,S14,3b6,O2C	0	2.4
1950	StL N★	153	642	81	177	43	9	7	63	33	2	32	.276	.313	.403	83	-17	3	.985	12	104	114	2b143,S10/3	0	0.3
1951	StL N★	135	553	88	160	32	7	6	54	35	3	23	.289	.335	.405	98	-3	0-1	.990	17	110	116	2b124,S8	0	2.1
1952	StL N☆	152	620	91	188	40	7	7	67	42	0	30	.303	.347	.424	113	10	9-6	.977	36	109	119	2b142,3b11,S3	0	5.4
1953	StL N★	146	564	107	193	35	5	15	79	60	0	23	.342	.405	.502	135	31	3-3	.983	29	111	112	2b140	0	6.5
1954	StL N★	148	610	98	192	38	8	5	79	54	1	22	.315	.366	.428	107	7	4-2	.980	28	113	123	2b144	0	4.5
1955	StL N★	145	553	68	148	21	3	11	51	54-5	4	28	.268	.335	.376	89	-8	7-7	.985	-14	97	95	2b142	0	-1.2
1956	StL N	40	153	22	48	9	0	0	15	13-0	0	5	.314	.365	.373	100	1	0-1	.995	1	93	114	2b36	0	0.4
	NY N	92	334	39	99	12	3	2	14	28-1	2	10	.296	.352	.368	95	-2	1-2	.993	-6	94	93	2b85	0	-0.2
	Year	132	487	61	147	21	3	2	29	41-1	2	15	.302	.356	.370	97	-1	1-3	.993	-5	94	99	2b121	0	0.2
1957	NY N	57	254	35	78	8	4	9	33	10-0	2	8	.307	.337	.476	116	5	2-1	.984	-2	100	105	2b57	0	0.7
	†Mil N★	93	394	56	122	23	4	6	32	23-1	1	7	.310	.348	.434	117	9	2-3	.987	11	110	121	2b92,O2C	0	2.6
	Year	150	648	91	200	31	8	15	65	33-1	3	15	.309	.344	.451	117	14	4-4	.986	9	106	115	2b149,O2C	0	3.3
1958	†Mil N	106	427	47	112	23	1	1	24	31-0	1	21	.262	.313	.328	77	-14	3-1	.987	6	105	115	2b105	0	-0.1
1959	Mil N	5	3	0	0	0	0	0	0	0-0	0	0	.000	.000	.000	-99	-1	0-0	.667	-1	53	0	2b4	119	-0.2
1960	Mil N	68	226	21	58	9	1	1	19	17-4	1	13	.257	.311	.319	79	-7	1-0	.964	-5	98	100	2b62	0	-0.8
1961	StL N	72	120	9	36	9	0	1	12	12-2	0	6	.300	.364	.400	93	0	1-0	.955	-7	76	71	2b32	0	-0.5
1962	StL N	98	143	21	43	4	0	2	12	9-2	1	12	.301	.346	.371	84	-3	0-0	.986	3	118	130	2b21,3b4	0	0.1
1963	StL N	6	5	0	0	0	0	0	0	0-0	0	1	.000	.000	.000	-91	-1	0-0	ø	0	—	—	/H	0	-0.1
Total	19	2216	8479	1223	2449	427	78	84	773	606-15	21	346	.289	.337	.387	93	-81	89-27	.983	143	105	113	2b1834,O123(119/4/0),S49,3b39	119	16.5

YEAR	TM LG	G	AB	R	H	2B	3B	HR	RBI	BB-IB	HP	SO	AVG	OBP	SLG	AOPS	ABR	SB-CS	FA	FR	RNG	THR	GAMES AT POSITION	DL	BFW
SCHOENECK, JUMBO	Louis N.; B3.3.1862 Chicago IL; D1.20.1930 Chicago IL; BR/TR/6´3˝/223; d4.20																								
1884	CP U	90	366	56	116	22	2	2	—	8	—	—	.317	.332	.404	123	0	—	.956	0	90	93	1b90	—	-0.7
	Bal U	16	60	5	15	2	0	0	—	0	—	—	.250	.250	.283	56	-5	—	.962	2	152	53	1b16	—	-0.4
	Year	106	426	61	131	24	2	2	—	8	—	—	.308	.320	.387	113	-6	—	**.957**	2	99	87	1b106	—	-1.1
1888	Ind N	48	169	15	40	4	0	0	20	9	2	24	.237	.283	.260	73	-5	11	.974	-1	93	75	1b48,P2	—	-1.0
1889	Ind N	16	62	3	15	2	2	0	8	3	2	3	.242	.299	.339	76	-2	1	.978	2	174	79	1b16	—	-0.1
Total	3	170	657	79	186	30	4	2	28	20	4	27	.283	.308	.350	99	-12	12	.964	3	104	83	1b170,P2	—	-2.2
SCHOFIELD, DICK	John Richard "Ducky"; B1.7.1935 Springfield IL; BB/TR/5´9˝/(155–170); d7.3; s–Dick gs–Jayson Werth																								
1953	StL N	33	39	9	7	0	0	2	4	2	0	11	.179	.220	.333	42	-4	0-0	.917	5	137	147	S15	0	0.2
1954	StL N	43	7	17	1	0	1	0	1	0	0	3	.143	.143	.429	42	-1	1-1	1.000	1	144	217	S11	0	0.0
1955	StL N	12	4	3	0	0	0	0	0	0-0	0	1	.000	.000	.000	-99	-1	0-0	1.000	0	145	0	S3	0	-0.1
1956	StL N	16	30	3	3	2	0	0	1	0-0	0	6	.100	.100	.167	-30	-5	0-0	.923	-1	85	120	S9	0	-0.6
1957	StL N	65	56	10	9	0	0	0	1	7-0	0	13	.161	.254	.161	14	-7	1-3	.948	-4	83	90	S23	0	-1.1
1958	StL N	39	108	16	23	4	0	1	8	23-0	0	15	.213	.348	.278	67	-4	0-2	.932	-4	99	67	S27	0	-0.7
	Pit N	26	27	4	4	0	1	0	2	3-0	0	6	.148	.226	.222	22	-3	0-1	1.000	0	98	145	S5,3b2	0	-0.3
	Year	65	135	20	27	4	1	1	10	26-0	0	21	.200	.325	.267	59	-7	0-3	.943	-4	99	79	S32,3b2	0	-1.0
1959	Pit N	81	145	21	34	10	1	1	9	16-0	0	22	.234	.311	.338	73	-5	1-1	.980	3	112	132	2b28,S8,O3R	0	0.0
1960	†Pit N	65	102	9	34	4	1	0	10	16-4	1	20	.333	.429	.392	126	5	0-1	.947	1	108	147	S23,2b10/3	0	0.8
1961	Pit N	60	78	16	15	2	1	0	2	10-0	0	19	.192	.284	.244	42	-7	0-1	.923	4	149	77	3b11,S9,2b5,O3(2/0/2)	0	-0.2
1962	Pit N	54	104	19	30	3	0	2	10	17-0	0	22	.288	.382	.375	106	2	0-1	.933	-4	77	58	3b20,2b2/S	0	-0.3
1963	Pit N	138	541	54	133	18	2	3	32	69-1	3	83	.246	.333	.303	84	-8	2-4	.966	17	**108**	**138**	S117,2b20/3	0	2.1
1964	Pit N	121	398	50	98	22	5	3	36	54-3	7	60	.246	.345	.349	97	1	1-2	.950	12	108	**122**	S111	0	2.3
1965	Pit N	31	109	13	25	5	0	0	6	15-1	0	19	.229	.317	.275	70	-4	1-0	.974	5	113	155	S28	0	0.4
	SF N	101	379	39	77	10	1	2	19	33-0	3	50	.203	.272	.251	47	-26	2-4	.984	1	98	101	S93	0	-1.9
	Year	132	488	52	102	15	1	2	25	48-1	3	69	.209	.282	.256	52	-30	3-4	**.981**	6	102	114	S121	0	-1.5
1966	SF N	11	16	4	1	0	0	0	0	2-0	0	2	.063	.167	.063	-32	-3	0-0	1.000	0	91	118	S8	0	-0.3
	NY A	25	58	5	9	2	0	0	2	9-0	0	8	.155	.265	.190	36	-5	0-0	.909	2	118	103	S19	0	-0.2
	LA N	20	70	10	18	0	0	0	4	8-0	2	8	.257	.350	.257	78	-2	1-1	.923	-2	100	0	3b19,S3	0	-0.3
1967	LA N	84	232	23	50	10	1	2	15	31-4	0	40	.216	.307	.293	79	-5	1-2	.976	8	110	106	S69,2b4,3b2	0	0.8
1968	†StL N	69	127	14	28	7	1	1	8	13-2	2	31	.220	.303	.315	87	-2	1-2	.973	5	96	64	S43,2b23	0	0.7
1969	Bos A	94	226	30	58	9	3	2	20	29-1	4	44	.257	.349	.350	92	-1	0-2	.981	5	120	97	2b37,S11,3b9,O5(3/0/2)	0	0.6
1970	Bos A	76	139	16	26	1	2	1	14	21-2	1	26	.187	.294	.245	48	-10	0-1	.969	-2	97	70	2b15,3b15,S3	0	-1.1
1971	Mil A	23	28	2	3	2	0	0	1	2-0	1	8	.107	.194	.179	6	-3	0-0	1.000	-1	96	203	3b12,S4,2b2	0	-0.5
	StL N	34	60	7	13	2	0	1	6	10-0	2	9	.217	.347	.300	81	-1	0-0	.935	4	110	103	S17,2b13,3b3	0	0.4
Total	19	1321	3083	394	699	113	20	21	211	390-18	26	526	.227	.317	.297	73	-99	12-29	.961	56	105	116	S660,2b159,3b95,O11(5/0/7)	0	0.7
SCHOFIELD, DICK	Richard Craig; B11.21.1962 Springfield IL; BR/TR/5´10˝/(175–180); [CalA81 1/3]; d9.8; f–Dick																								
1983	Cal A	21	54	4	11	2	0	3	4	6-0	1	8	.204	.295	.407	91	-1	0-0	.929	-2	111	78	S21	0	0.0
1984	Cal A	140	400	39	77	10	3	4	21	33-0	6	79	.192	.264	.262	46	-30	5-2	**.982**	10	107	117	S140	23	-0.5
1985	Cal A	147	438	50	96	19	3	8	41	35-0	8	70	.219	.287	.331	69	-19	11-4	.963	11	104	**130**	S147	0	0.7
1986	†Cal A	139	458	67	114	17	6	13	57	48-2	5	55	.249	.321	.397	97	-2	23-5	.972	17	105	**134**	S137	0	3.1
1987	Cal A	134	479	52	120	17	3	9	46	37-0	2	63	.251	.305	.355	77	-16	19-3	**.984**	-18	92	101	S131,2b2/D	29	-1.6
1988	Cal A	155	527	61	126	11	6	6	34	40-0	9	57	.239	.303	.317	76	-18	20-5	**.983**	22	110	118	S155	0	1.8
1989	Cal A	91	302	42	69	11	2	4	26	28-0	3	47	.228	.299	.318	75	-10	9-3	.983	-2	102	105	S90	65	-0.4
1990	Cal A	99	310	41	79	8	1	1	18	52-3	2	61	.255	.363	.297	89	-2	3-4	.966	10	106	114	S99	58	1.5
1991	Cal A	134	427	44	96	9	3	0	31	50-2	3	69	.225	.310	.260	59	-23	8-4	.975	4	99	107	S133	0	-0.9
1992	Cal A	1	3	0	1	0	0	0	0	1-0	0	0	.333	.500	.333	136	0	0-0	1.000	-1	31	0	/S	0	0.0
	NY N	142	420	52	86	18	2	4	36	60-4	5	82	.205	.309	.286	71	-14	11-4	**.988**	15	104	110	S141	0	1.3
1993	Tor A	36	110	11	21	1	2	0	5	16-0	0	25	.191	.294	.236	44	-9	3-0	.977	5	104	102	S36	111	-0.1
1994	Tor A	95	325	38	83	14	1	4	32	34-0	4	62	.255	.332	.342	74	-12	7-7	.972	-8	84	97	S95	0	-1.3
1995	LA N	9	10	0	1	0	0	0	0	1-0	0	3	.100	.182	.100	-25	-2	0-0	1.000	3	227	401	S3/3	0	0.1
	Cal A	12	20	1	5	0	0	0	2	4-0	0	2	.250	.375	.250	67	-1	0-0	1.000	-4	83	35	S12	0	-0.3
1996	Cal A	13	16	3	4	0	0	0	0	1-0	0	1	.250	.294	.250	39	-2	1-0	.889	-2	36	50	S7,2b2/3D	133	-0.3
Total	14	1368	4299	505	989	137	32	56	353	446-11	48	684	.230	.308	.316	73	-161	120-41	.976	59	102	113	S1348,2b4,3b2,D2	419	3.1
SCHOMBERG, OTTO	Otto H. (b Otto H. Shambrick); B11.14.1864 Milwaukee WI; D5.3.1927 Ottawa KS; BL/TL/5´11˝/175; d7.7																								
1886	Pit AA	72	246	53	67	6	6	1	29	57	4	—	.272	.417	.358	144	17	7	.966	-7	26	109	1b72	—	0.4
1887	Ind N	112	419	91	129	18	16	5	83	56	6	32	.308	.397	.463	143	27	21	.958	-10	70	111	1b112/rf	—	0.6
1888	Ind N	30	112	11	24	5	1	1	10	10	2	12	.214	.290	.304	88	-1	6	.857	-3	144	0	O15R,1b15	—	-0.6
Total	3	214	777	155	220	29	23	7	122	123	12	44	.283	.389	.407	136	43	34	.961	-20	49	110	1b199,O16R	—	0.4
SCHOONMAKER, JERRY	Jerald Lee; B12.14.1933 Seymour MO; BR/TR/5´11˝/190; d6.11; Mil 1956; Col Missouri																								
1955	Was A	20	46	5	7	0	1	1	4	5-0	0	11	.152	.235	.261	35	-5	1-0	.960	0	92	231	O15(5/3/7)	0	-0.5
1957	Was A	30	23	5	2	1	0	0	0	2-0	0	11	.087	.160	.130	-20	-4	0-0	1.000	0	108	0	O13(5/8/0)	0	-0.4
Total	2	50	69	10	9	1	1	1	4	7-0	0	22	.130	.211	.217	16	-9	1-0	.975	0	98	150	O28(10/11/7)	0	-0.9
SCHRAMKA, PAUL	Paul Edward; B3.22.1928 Milwaukee WI; BL/TL/6´0˝/185; d4.14; Col San Francisco																								
1953	Chi N	2	0	0	0	0	0	0	0	0	0	0	ø	ø	ø	ø	0	0-0	ø	-0	0	0	/lf	0	0.0
SCHRECKENGOST, OSSEE	Ossee Freeman (aka Ossee Schreck) (b Schrecongost); B4.11.1875 New Bethlehem PA; D7.9.1914 Philadelphia PA; BR/TR/5´10˝/180; d9.8																								
1897	Lou N	1	3	0	0	0	0	0	0	0	0	—	.000	.000	.000	-99	-1	0	1.000	0	*117*	*147*	/C	—	-0.1
1898	Cle N	10	35	5	11	2	3	0	10	0	0	—	.314	.314	.543	146	1	1	.860	0	*116*	*84*	C9	—	0.2
1899	StL N	6	8	0	0	0	0	0	0	1	0	—	.000	.111	.000	-67	-2	0	1.000	-0	0	0	/1rf	—	-0.2
	Cle N	43	150	15	47	8	3	0	10	6	2	—	.313	.348	.407	115	3	4	.911	-14	*59*	*124*	C39/1Srf	—	-0.7
	StL N	66	269	42	77	12	2	2	37	14	1	—	.286	.324	.368	88	-5	14	.963	-3	0	0	1b41,C25/2	—	-0.5
	Year	115	427	57	124	20	5	2	47	21	3	—	.290	.328	.375	94	-5	18	.927	-17	*87*	122	C64,1b43,O2R/S2	—	-1.4
1901	Bos A	86	280	37	85	13	5	0	38	19	4	—	.304	.356	.386	108	3	6	.926	4	*105*	*100*	C72,1b4	—	1.3
1902	Cle A	18	74	5	25	0	0	0	9	0	0	—	.338	.338	.338	91	-1	2	.975	-1	86	62	1b17	—	-0.2
	Phi A	79	284	45	92	17	2	2	43	9	1	—	.324	.347	.419	107	2	3	.960	17	*108*	*105*	C71,1b7/cf	—	2.4
	Year	97	358	50	117	17	2	2	52	9	1	—	.327	.345	.402	104	1	5	.960	16	*108*	*105*	C71,1b24/cf	—	2.2
1903	Phi A	92	306	26	78	13	4	3	30	11	2	—	.255	.285	.353	87	-6	0	.975	12	*107*	*105*	C77,1b10	—	1.4
1904	Phi A	95	311	23	58	9	1	1	21	5	0	—	.186	.199	.232	34	-24	3	.979	3	*109*	*81*	C84,1b9	—	-1.3
1905	†Phi A	123	420	30	114	19	6	0	45	3	1	—	.271	.278	.345	96	-4	9	**.984**	9	*117*	*84*	C114,1b2	—	1.7
1906	Phi A	98	338	29	96	20	1	1	41	10	0	—	.284	.305	.358	104	1	5	.971	8	*97*	*90*	C89,1b4	—	1.9
1907	Phi A	101	356	30	97	16	3	0	38	17	0	—	.272	.306	.334	102	0	4	**.985**	10	*97*	***103***	C99,1b2	—	2.2
1908	Phi A	71	207	16	46	7	1	0	16	6	1	—	.222	.248	.266	63	-9	1	.978	1	*74*	*112*	C65/1	—	-0.2
	Chi A	6	16	1	3	0	0	0	0	1	0	—	.188	.235	.188	38	-1	0	.982	2	*155*	*46*	C6	—	0.2
	Year	77	223	17	49	7	1	0	16	7	1	—	.220	.247	.260	61	-10	1	.978	3	*83*	*105*	C71/1	—	0.0
Total	11	895	3057	304	829	136	31	9	338	102	12	—	.271	.297	.345	90	-43	52	.970	49	*102*	*98*	C751,1b99,O3(0/1/2)/2S	—	8.1
SCHREIBER, HANK	Henry Walter; B7.12.1891 Cleveland OH; D2.23.1968 Indianapolis IN; BR/TR/5´11˝/165; d4.14; Mil 1918																								
1914	Chi A	1	2	0	0	0	0	0	0	0	0	1	.000	.000	.000	-99	0	0	ø	-0	0	0	/lf	—	-0.1
1917	Bos N	2	7	1	2	0	0	0	0	0	0	1	.286	.286	.286	80	0	0	1.000	-1	39	0	/S3	—	-0.1
1919	Cin N	19	58	5	13	4	0	0	4	0	0	12	.224	.224	.293	56	-3	0	.984	5	134	281	3b17,S2	—	0.2
1921	NY N	4	6	2	2	0	0	0	2	1	0	1	.333	.429	.333	104	0	0-0	.500	-1	0	0	2b2,S2/3	—	-0.1
1926	Chi N	10	18	2	1	1	0	0	0	0	0	1	.056	.056	.111	-55	-4	0	1.000	0	148	0	S3,3b3/2	—	-0.3
Total	5	36	91	10	18	5	0	0	6	1	0	16	.198	.207	.253	34	-7	0-0	.986	4	126	233	3b22,S8,2b3/lf	—	-0.4
SCHREIBER, TED	Theodore Henry; B7.11.1938 Brooklyn NY; BR/TR/5´11˝/175; d4.14; Col St. Johns																								
1963	NY N	39	50	1	8	0	0	0	2	4-0	1	14	.160	.236	.160	16	-5	0-1	.977	5	138	158	3b17,S9,2b3	0	-0.1

YEAR	TM LG	G	AB	R	H	2B	3B	HR	RBI	BB-IB	HP	SO	AVG	OBP	SLG	AOPS	ABR	SB-CS	FA	FR	RNG	THR	GAMES AT POSITION	DL	BFW
SCHRIVER, POP	William Frederick; B7.11.1865 Brooklyn NY; D12.27.1932 New York NY; BR/TR/5´9.5˝/172; d4.29; OF(8/10/5)																								
1886	Bro AA	8	21	2	1	0	0	0	0	2	0	—	.048	.130	.048	-43	-3	0	.667	1	264	0	O5(2/0/3),C3	—	-0.2
1888	Phi N	40	134	15	26	5	2	1	23	7	3	21	.194	.250	.284	66	-5	2	.870	-7	—	—	C27,S6,3b6/rf	—	-1.0
1889	Phi N	55	211	24	56	10	0	1	19	16	2	8	.265	.323	.327	75	-8	5	.920	1	—	—	C48,2b6/3	—	-0.2
1890	Phi N	57	223	37	61	9	6	0	35	22	0	15	.274	.339	.368	103	0	9	.916	-2	*105*	*98*	C34,1b10,3b8,2b3,O2L	—	0.0
1891	Chi N	27	90	15	30	1	4	1	21	10	2	9	.333	.412	.467	156	6	1	.964	3	*132*	*84*	C27,1b2	—	1.0
1892	Chi N	92	326	40	73	10	6	1	34	27	7	25	.224	.297	.301	80	-8	4	.929	-3	*105*	*100*	C82,O10C	—	-0.4
1893	Chi N	64	229	49	65	8	3	4	34	14	4	9	.284	.336	.397	96	-2	4	.926	1	*90*	*108*	C56,O5(4/0/1)	—	0.3
1894	Chi N	98	354	56	97	12	3	3	49	32	6	21	.274	.344	.350	64	-22	9	.920	-5	*80*	*109*	C90,S3,3b3,1b2	—	-1.5
1895	NY N	24	92	16	29	2	1	1	16	9	1	10	.315	.382	.391	102	1	3	.898	-3	*94*	*126*	C18,1b6	—	-0.1
1897	Cin N	61	178	29	54	12	4	1	30	19	1	—	.303	.374	.433	106	1	3	.959	5	*155*	*84*	C53	—	0.9
1898	Pit N	95	315	25	72	15	3	0	32	23	3	—	.229	.287	.295	68	-13	0	.957	-2	*105*	*90*	C92/1	—	-0.6
1899	Pit N	92	302	31	85	19	5	1	49	24	5	—	.281	.344	.387	101	1	4	.958	9	*121*	*88*	C78,1b9	—	1.5
1900	†Pit N	37	92	12	27	7	0	1	12	10	3	—	.293	.381	.402	115	3	0	.959	-1	*127*	*67*	C24/1	—	0.3
1901	StL N	53	166	17	45	7	3	1	23	12	4	—	.271	.335	.367	109	2	2	.971	2	*95*	*139*	C24,1b19	—	0.6
Total	14	803	2733	368	721	117	40	16	377	227	41	118	.264	.330	.353	88	-47	46	.934	-2	*107*	*98*	C656,1b50,O23C,3b18,2b9,S9	—	0.6
SCHRODER, BOB	Robert James; B12.30.1944 Ridgefield NJ; BL/TR/6´0˝/175; d4.20; Col Loyola–New Orleans																								
1965	SF N	31	9	4	2	0	0	0	1	1-0	0	1	.222	.300	.222	48	-1	0-0	1.000	1	172	151	2b4/3	0	0.1
1966	SF N	10	33	0	8	0	0	0	2	0-0	0	2	.242	.242	.242	34	-3	0-0	.963	-5	69	45	S9	0	-0.8
1967	SF N	62	135	20	31	4	0	0	7	15-3	0	15	.230	.307	.259	64	-6	1-0	.993	-6	95	64	2b45,3b4	0	-0.9
1968	SF N	35	44	5	7	1	1	0	2	7-0	1	3	.159	.283	.227	56	-2	0-0	.960	-5	80	50	2b12,S4,3b2	0	-0.7
Total	4	138	221	29	48	5	1	0	12	23-3	1	21	.217	.293	.249	58	-12	1-0	.989	-14	95	64	2b61,S13,3b7	0	-2.3
SCHROEDER, BILL	Alfred William; B9.7.1958 Baltimore MD; BR/TR/6´2˝/200; [MilA79 8/205]; d7.13; Col Clemson																								
1983	Mil A	23	73	7	13	2	1	3	7	3-0	1	23	.178	.221	.356	60	-5	0-1	.980	-4	97	71	C23	0	-0.8
1984	Mil A	61	210	29	54	6	0	14	25	8-2	2	54	.257	.288	.486	115	3	0-1	.987	-9	67	90	C58/1D	0	-0.4
1985	Mil A	53	194	18	47	8	0	8	25	12-1	2	61	.242	.290	.407	89	-3	0-1	.987	-7	78	88	C48/1D	57	-0.9
1986	Mil A	64	217	32	46	14	0	7	19	9-0	6	59	.212	.262	.373	68	-10	1-0	.995	-3	84	74	C35,1b19,D10	27	-1.2
1987	Mil A	75	250	35	83	12	0	14	42	16-0	3	56	.332	.379	.548	137	13	5-2	.995	-11	94	64	C67,1b4,D2	0	0.5
1988	Mil A	41	122	9	19	2	0	5	10	6-0	2	36	.156	.208	.295	39	-11	0-0	1.000	4	89	89	C30,1b10/D	19	-0.6
1989	Cal A	41	138	16	28	2	0	6	15	3-0	0	44	.203	.220	.348	59	-9	0-0	.991	9	80	81	C33,1b8	18	0.2
1990	Cal A	18	58	7	13	3	0	4	9	1-0	0	10	.224	.237	.483	98	-1	0-0	1.000	-1	64	130	C15,1b3	84	-0.1
Total	8	376	1262	153	303	49	1	61	152	58-3	16	343	.240	.281	.426	91	-23	6-5	.992	-21	82	82	C309,1b46,D20	205	-3.3
SCHU, RICK	Richard Spencer; B1.26.1962 Philadelphia PA; BR/TR/6´0˝/(170–194); d9.1; C1; Col Sacramento (CA) City																								
1984	Phi N	17	29	12	8	2	1	2	5	6-0	0	6	.276	.389	.621	180	3	0-0	.952	-2	68	209	3b15	0	0.1
1985	Phi N	112	416	54	105	21	4	7	24	38-3	2	78	.252	.318	.373	90	-5	8-6	.933	-15	82	94	3b111	0	-2.4
1986	Phi N	92	208	32	57	10	1	8	25	18-1	2	44	.274	.335	.447	110	3	2-2	.913	-1	101	75	3b58	0	0.1
1987	Phi N	92	196	24	46	6	3	7	23	20-1	2	36	.235	.311	.403	85	-5	0-2	.905	-6	93	37	3b45,1b28	15	-1.3
1988	Bal A	89	270	22	69	9	4	4	20	21-0	3	49	.256	.316	.363	92	-4	6-4	.937	-8	89	59	3b72,1b4,D9	47	-1.2
1989	Bal A	1	0	0	0	0	0	0	0	0-0	0	0	ø	ø	ø	ø	0	0-0	1.000	-0	0	0	/2	0	0.0
	Det A	98	266	25	57	11	0	7	21	24-0	0	37	.214	.278	.335	74	-10	1-2	.934	-3	94	89	3b83,2b5,1b3,S3,D9	0	-1.3
	Year	99	266	25	57	11	0	7	21	24-0	0	37	.214	.278	.335	74	-10	1-2	.934	-3	94	89	3b83,D9,2b6,1b3,S3	0	-1.3
1990	Cal A	61	157	19	42	8	0	6	14	11-0	0	25	.268	.314	.433	109	1	0-0	.918	1	115	154	3b38,1b15,O4L/2	0	0.2
1991	Phi N	17	22	1	2	0	0	0	2	1-0	0	7	.091	.125	.091	-37	-4	0-0	.667	-1	0	0	3b3/1	0	-0.6
1996	Mon N	1	4	0	0	0	0	0	0	0-0	0	0	.000	.000	.000	-98	-1	0-0	.667	-0	94	0	/3	0	-0.2
Total	9	580	1568	189	386	67	13	41	134	139-5	9	282	.246	.310	.384	91	-22	17-16	.926	-35	91	87	3b426,1b51,D18,2b7,O4L,S3	62	-6.6
SCHUBLE, HEINIE	Henry George; B11.1.1906 Houston TX; D10.2.1990 Baytown TX; BR/TR/5´9˝/152; d7.8																								
1927	StL N	65	218	29	56	6	2	4	28	7	1	27	.257	.283	.358	69	-11	0	.915	-5	100	110	S65	—	-1.0
1929	Det A	92	258	35	60	11	7	2	28	19	1	23	.233	.288	.353	64	-15	3-2	.886	-16	94	82	S86,3b2	—	-2.2
1932	Det A	102	340	58	92	20	6	5	52	24	0	37	.271	.319	.409	84	-9	14-5	.941	5	106	80	3b76,S16	—	0.1
1933	Det A	49	96	12	21	4	1	0	6	5	0	17	.219	.257	.281	42	-8	2-0	.951	0	113	29	3b23,S2/2	—	-0.7
1934	Det A	11	15	2	4	2	0	0	2	1	0	4	.267	.313	.400	83	0	0-0	1.000	0	98	0	S3,3b2/2	—	0.0
1935	Det A	11	8	3	2	0	0	0	0	1	0	0	.250	.333	.250	55	-1	0-0	.714	0	158	1142	3b2/2	—	0.0
1936	StL N	2	0	0	0	0	0	0	0	0	0	0	ø	ø	ø	ø	0	0	ø	-0	0	0	/3	—	0.0
Total	7	332	935	139	235	43	16	11	116	57	2	108	.251	.296	.367	70	-44	19-7	.906	-16	97	97	S172,3b106,2b3	—	-3.8
SCHULMERICH, WES	Edward Wesley; B8.21.1901 Hillsboro OR; D6.26.1985 Corvallis OR; BR/TR/5´11˝/210; d5.1; Col Oregon St.																								
1931	Bos N	95	327	36	101	17	7	2	43	28	0	30	.309	.363	.422	115	6	0	.966	-4	101	56	O87R	—	-0.2
1932	Bos N	119	404	47	105	22	5	11	57	27	5	61	.260	.314	.421	99	-1	5	.968	1	100	101	O101R	—	-0.7
1933	Bos N	29	85	10	21	6	1	1	13	5	0	10	.247	.289	.376	97	-1	0	.980	1	102	148	O21R	—	-0.1
	Phi N	97	365	53	122	19	4	8	59	32	4	45	.334	.394	.474	130	16	1	.977	-1	100	78	O97L	—	1.0
	Year	126	450	63	143	25	5	9	72	37	4	55	.318	.375	.456	126	16	1	.978	0	100	90	O118(97/0/21)	—	0.9
1934	Phi N	15	52	2	13	1	0	0	1	4	1	8	.250	.316	.269	51	-3	0	.963	-0	100	96	O13(3/0/10)	—	-0.4
	Cin N	74	209	21	55	8	3	5	19	22	0	43	.263	.333	.402	98	-1	1	.976	-2	105	21	O56(13/0/43)	—	-0.6
	Year	89	261	23	68	9	3	5	20	26	1	51	.261	.330	.375	88	-4	1	.974	-2	104	35	O69(16/0/53)	—	-1.0
Total	4	429	1442	169	417	73	20	27	192	118	10	197	.289	.347	.424	109	16	7	.971	-5	101	75	O375(113/0/262)	—	-1.0
SCHULT, ART	Arthur William "Dutch"; B6.20.1928 Brooklyn NY; BR/TR/6´4˝/(210–220); d5.17; Col Georgetown																								
1953	NY A	7	0	3	0	0	0	0	0	0	0	0	ø	ø	ø	ø	0	0-0	ø	0	—	—	/R	0	0.0
1956	Cin N	5	7	3	3	0	0	0	2	1-0	0	1	.429	.500	.429	144	1	0-0	ø	-0	0	0	/lf	0	0.0
1957	Cin N	21	34	4	9	2	0	0	4	0-0	1	2	.265	.286	.324	59	-2	0-0	1.000	1	170	0	O5L	0	-0.1
	Was A	77	247	30	65	14	0	4	35	14-0	1	30	.263	.303	.368	84	-6	0-1	.987	-2	57	104	1b35,O31(14/1/17)	0	-1.1
1959	Chi N	42	118	17	32	7	0	2	14	7-0	2	14	.271	.320	.381	88	-2	0-0	.985	-3	56	127	1b23,O15(12/0/6)	0	-0.7
1960	Chi N	12	15	1	2	1	0	0	1	1-1	0	3	.133	.188	.200	6	-2	0-0	1.000	-0	80	0	O4L/1	0	-0.2
Total	5	164	421	58	111	24	0	6	56	23-1	4	50	.264	.306	.363	81	-11	0-1	.987	-4	57	111	1b59,O56(36/1/23)	0	-2.1
SCHULTE, FRANK	Frank M. "Wildfire"; B9.17.1882 Cohocton NY; D10.2.1949 Oakland CA; BL/TR/5´11˝/170; d9.21																								
1904	Chi N	20	84	16	24	4	3	2	13	2	1	—	.286	.310	.476	141	3	1	.949	-0	111	0	O20L	—	0.2
1905	Chi N	123	493	67	135	15	14	1	47	32	6	—	.274	.326	.367	102	0	16	.981	-6	86	0	O123(107/0/16)	—	-1.4
1906	†Chi N	146	563	77	158	18	**13**	7	60	31	5	—	.281	.324	.396	118	8	25	.975	-2	96	**183**	O146R	—	-0.1
1907	†Chi N	97	342	44	98	14	7	2	32	22	5	—	.287	.339	.386	120	7	7	.973	-3	89	38	O92(1/0/91)	—	0.1
1908	†Chi N	102	386	42	91	20	2	1	43	29	3	—	.236	.294	.306	88	-5	15	.994	-6	63	71	O102(12/1/89)	—	-1.8
1909	Chi N	140	538	57	142	16	11	4	60	24	2	—	.264	.298	.357	101	-3	23	.968	-12	73	27	O140R	—	-2.4
1910	†Chi N	151	559	93	168	29	15	**10**	68	39	3	57	.301	.349	.460	137	22	22	.968	-6	91	87	O150R	—	1.0
1911	Chi N	154	577	105	173	30	21	**21**	**107**	76	3	71	.300	.384	**.534**	**156**	**40**	23	.971	-7	92	86	O154R	—	2.5
1912	Chi N	139	553	90	146	27	11	12	64	53	7	70	.264	.336	.418	106	3	17	.952	-5	94	92	O139R	—	-0.9
1913	Chi N	132	497	85	138	28	6	9	68	39	5	68	.278	.336	.412	113	8	21-19	.956	-6	92	84	O130(1/0/129)	—	-0.7
1914	Chi N	137	465	54	112	22	7	5	61	39	5	55	.241	.306	.351	95	-3	16	.954	-9	92	58	O134(134/0/2)	—	-1.9
1915	Chi N	151	550	66	137	20	6	12	62	49	2	68	.249	.313	.373	107	4	19-17	.962	5	97	139	O147(146/0/4)	—	0.0
1916	Chi N	72	230	31	68	11	1	5	27	20	0	35	.296	.352	.417	123	7	9	.951	-1	94	127	O67(66/0/1)	—	0.4
	Pit N	55	177	12	45	5	3	0	14	17	1	19	.254	.323	.316	96	-1	5	.968	-2	109	37	O48(20/0/28)	—	-0.5
	Year	127	407	43	113	16	4	5	41	37	1	54	.278	.339	.373	111	6	14	.958	-2	101	88	O115(86/0/29)	—	-0.1
1917	Pit N	30	103	11	22	5	1	0	7	10	0	14	.214	.283	.282	71	-3	5	.963	0	105	87	O28(3/0/25)	—	-0.5
	Phi N	64	149	21	32	10	0	1	15	16	2	22	.215	.299	.302	81	-2	4	.923	-6	74	24	O42(20/7/15)	—	-1.2
	Year	94	252	32	54	15	1	1	22	26	2	36	.214	.293	.294	77	-6	9	.943	-6	88	52	O70(23/7/40)	—	-1.7
1918	Was A	93	267	35	77	14	3	0	44	47	6	36	.288	.406	.363	135	15	5	.969	2	105	98	O75(14/1/60)	—	1.4
Total	15	1806	6533	906	1766	288	124	92	792	545	56	515	.270	.332	.395	114	100	233-36	.966	-64	90	82	O1737(544/9/1189)	—	-5.8
SCHULTE, FRED	Fred William "Fritz" (b Fred William Schult); B1.13.1901 Belvidere IL; D5.20.1983 Belvidere IL; BR/TR/6´1˝/183; d4.15																								
1927	StL A	60	189	32	60	16	5	3	34	20	0	14	.317	.383	.503	124	7	5-3	.916	-3	102	67	O49C	—	0.2
1928	StL A	146	556	90	159	44	6	7	85	51	1	60	.286	.347	.424	99	-1	6-5	.973	10	108	130	O143C	—	0.2
1929	StL A	121	446	63	137	24	5	3	71	59	1	44	.307	.389	.404	101	3	8-3	**.989**	6	107	93	O116C	—	0.4

YEAR	TM LG	G	AB	R	H	2B	3B	HR	RBI	BB-IB	HP	SO	AVG	OBP	SLG	AOPS	ABR	SB-CS	FA	FR	RNG	THR	GAMES AT POSITION	DL	BFW
1930	StL A	113	392	59	109	23	5	5	62	41	1	44	.278	.348	.401	86	-8	12-8	.966	-5	94	70	O98C,1b5	—	-1.6
1931	StL A	134	553	100	168	32	7	9	65	56	1	49	.304	.369	.436	107	6	6-8	.971	-1	96	119	O134C	—	0.0
1932	StL A	146	565	106	166	35	6	9	73	71	0	44	.294	.373	.425	100	2	5-9	.986	-4	96	85	O129(3/126/0),1b5	—	-0.8
1933	†Was A	144	550	98	162	30	7	5	87	61	1	27	.295	.366	.402	104	4	10-12	.980	8	**112**	94	O142C	—	0.6
1934	Was A	136	524	72	156	32	6	3	73	53	1	34	.298	.363	.399	100	1	3-7	.986	-4	101	46	O134C	—	-0.8
1935	Was A	76	226	33	60	6	4	2	23	26	1	22	.265	.344	.354	83	-6	0-3	.980	-2	97	55	O56(12/19/26)	—	-1.0
1936	Pit N	74	238	28	62	7	3	1	17	20	1	20	.261	.320	.328	73	-9	1	.977	-3	96	28	O55(1/54/0)	—	-1.3
1937	Pit N	29	20	5	2	0	0	0	3	4	1	3	.100	.280	.100	7	-2	0	.800	-0	116	0	O4(1/1/2)	—	-0.3
Total	11	1179	4259	686	1241	249	54	47	593	462	9	361	.291	.362	.408	98	-3	56-58	.976	2	102	87	O1060(17/1016/28),1b10	—	-4.4
SCHULTE, HAM	Herman Joseph (b Herman Joseph Schultehenrich); B9.1.1912 St.Louis MO; D12.21.1993 St.Charles MO; BR/TR/5´8.5˝/158; d4.16; b–Len																								
1940	Phi N	120	436	44	103	18	2	1	21	32	0	30	.236	.288	.294	63	-22	3	**.980**	-9	91	98	2b119/S	—	-2.4
SCHULTE, JOHNNY	John Clement; B9.8.1896 Fredericktown MO; D6.28.1978 St.Louis MO; BL/TR/5´11˝/190; d4.18; C18																								
1923	StL A	7	3	1	0	0	0	0	1	4	0	0	.000	.571	.000	56	0	0-0	1.000	1	*0*	*289*	/C1	—	0.1
1927	StL N	64	156	35	45	8	2	9	32	47	1	19	.288	.456	.538	160	17	1	.956	0	*91*	*131*	C59	—	2.0
1928	Phi N	65	113	14	28	2	2	4	17	15	0	12	.248	.336	.407	90	-2	0	.949	-4	*77*	*137*	C34	—	-0.4
1929	Chi N	31	69	6	18	3	0	0	9	7	0	11	.261	.329	.304	58	-4	0	.978	1	*129*	*133*	C30	—	-0.2
1932	StL A	15	24	2	5	2	0	0	3	1	0	6	.208	.240	.292	35	-2	0-0	.864	-1	*176*	*0*	C6	—	-0.2
	Bos N	10	9	1	2	0	0	1	2	2	0	1	.222	.364	.556	149	1	0	1.000	1	*135*	*0*	C10	—	0.1
Total	5	192	374	59	98	15	4	14	64	76	1	49	.262	.388	.436	112	10	1-0	.957	-3	*99*	*124*	C140/1	—	1.4
SCHULTE, JACK	John Herman Frank; B11.15.1881 Cincinnati OH; D8.17.1975 Roseville MI; BR/TR/5´9˝/180; d8.19																								
1906	Bos N	2	7	0	0	0	0	0	0	0	0	—	.000	.000	.000	-99	-2	0	1.000	-1	69	0	S2	—	-0.3
SCHULTE, LEN	Leonard Bernard (b Leonard Bernard Schultehenrich); B12.5.1916 St.Charles MO; D5.6.1986 Orlando FL; BR/TR/5´10˝/160; d9.27; b–Herman; Col Iowa																								
1944	StL A	1	0	0	0	0	0	0	0	1	0	0	ø	1.000	ø	188	0	0-0	ø	0	—	—	/H	0	0.0
1945	StL A	119	430	37	106	16	1	0	36	24	0	35	.247	.286	.288	64	-20	0-3	.961	-10	101	69	3b71,2b37,S14	0	-3.0
1946	StL A	4	5	1	2	0	0	0	2	0	0	0	.400	.400	.400	118	0	0-0	1.000	0	75	0	/23	0	0.0
Total	3	124	435	38	108	16	1	0	38	25	0	35	.248	.289	.290	65	-20	0-3	.962	-9	102	68	3b72,2b38,S14	0	-3.0
SCHULTZ, HOWIE	Howard Henry "Stretch","Steeple"; B7.3.1922 St.Paul MN; BR/TR/6´6˝/200; d8.16; Col Hamline																								
1943	Bro N	45	182	20	49	12	0	1	34	6	2	24	.269	.300	.352	88	-3	3	.986	1	113	69	1b45	0	-0.4
1944	Bro N	138	526	59	134	32	3	11	83	24	2	67	.255	.290	.390	92	-8	6	.988	-0	98	77	1b136	0	-1.6
1945	Bro N	39	142	18	34	8	2	1	19	10	1	14	.239	.294	.345	78	-5	2	.984	2	126	123	1b38	0	-0.4
1946	Bro N	90	249	27	63	14	1	3	27	16	0	34	.253	.298	.353	84	-6	2	.989	5	124	122	1b87	0	-0.4
1947	Bro N	2	1	0	0	0	0	0	0	0	0	0	.000	.000	.000	-96	0	0	1.000	-0	0	0	/1	0	0.0
	Phi N	114	403	30	90	19	1	6	35	21	1	70	.223	.264	.320	56	-27	0	.993	-1	95	105	1b114	0	-3.2
	Year	116	404	30	90	19	1	6	35	21	1	70	.223	.263	.319	56	-27	0	.993	-1	95	105	1b115	0	-3.2
1948	Phi N	6	13	0	1	0	0	0	1	1	0	2	.077	.143	.077	-40	-3	0	1.000	0	118	153	1b3	0	-0.3
	Cin N	36	72	9	12	0	0	2	9	4	0	7	.167	.211	.250	25	-8	2	.982	-3	45	103	1b26	0	-1.1
	Year	42	85	9	13	0	0	2	10	5	0	9	.153	.200	.224	15	-11	2	.984	-3	54	109	1b29	0	-1.4
Total	6	470	1588	163	383	85	7	24	208	82	6	218	.241	.281	.349	75	-60	15	.989	4	103	97	1b450	0	-7.4
SCHULTZ, JOE	Joseph Charles Jr. "Dode"; B8.29.1918 Chicago IL; D1.10.1996 St.Louis MO; BL/TR/5´11˝/184; d9.27; M2/C14; f–Joe																								
1939	Pit N	4	14	3	4	2	0	0	2	2	0	0	.286	.375	.429	117	0	0	1.000	0	*148*	*0*	C4	—	0.1
1940	Pit N	16	36	2	7	0	1	0	4	2	0	1	.194	.237	.250	35	-3	0	.917	-2	*75*	*82*	C13	—	-0.5
1941	Pit N	2	2	1	1	0	0	0	0	0	0	0	.500	.500	.500	183	0	0	ø	0	*0*	*0*	C2	0	0.0
1943	StL A	46	92	6	22	5	0	0	8	9	0	8	.239	.307	.293	74	-3	0-1	.979	-4	*61*	*70*	C26	0	-0.7
1944	StL A	3	8	1	2	0	0	0	0	0	0	1	.250	.250	.250	41	-1	0-0	.818	-1	*101*	*0*	C3	0	-0.1
1945	StL A	41	44	1	13	2	0	0	8	3	0	1	.295	.340	.341	93	0	0-0	.941	0	*121*	*0*	C4	0	0.0
1946	StL A	42	57	1	22	4	0	0	14	11	0	2	.386	.485	.456	156	5	0-0	1.000	-3	*59*	*0*	C17	0	0.3
1947	StL A	43	38	3	7	0	0	1	1	4	0	5	.184	.262	.263	45	-3	0-0	ø	0	—	—	/H	0	-0.3
1948	StL A	43	37	0	7	0	0	0	9	6	0	3	.189	.302	.189	32	-4	0-0	ø	0	—	—	/H	0	-0.3
Total	9	240	328	18	85	13	1	1	46	37	0	21	.259	.334	.314	81	-9	0-1	.964	-10	*77*	*42*	C69	0	-1.5
SCHULTZ, JOE	Joseph Charles Sr. "Germany"; B7.24.1893 Pittsburgh PA; D4.13.1941 Columbia SC; BR/TR/5´11.5˝/172; d9.28; s–Joe; OF(104/9/307)																								
1912	Bos N	4	12	1	3	1	0	0	4	0	0	2	.250	.250	.333	58	-1	0	.824	-1	99	80	2b4	—	-0.1
1913	Bos N	9	18	2	4	0	0	0	1	2	1	7	.222	.333	.222	59	-1	0	1.000	-0	121	0	O5(0/2/3)/2	—	-0.1
1915	Bro N	56	120	13	35	3	2	0	4	10	0	18	.292	.346	.350	109	1	3-4	.894	-4	77	80	3b27/S	—	-0.3
	Chi N	7	8	1	2	0	0	0	3	0	0	2	.250	.250	.250	51	-1	0	.857	-0	93	0	2b2	—	-0.1
	Year	63	128	14	37	3	2	0	7	10	0	20	.289	.341	.344	106	1	3-4	.894	-5	77	80	3b27,2b2/S	—	-0.4
1916	Pit N	77	204	18	53	8	2	0	22	7	4	14	.260	.298	.319	88	-3	6	.840	-15	89	24	2b24,3b24,O6(4/0/3)/S	—	-2.0
1919	StL N	88	229	24	58	9	1	2	21	11	0	7	.253	.287	.328	90	-3	4	1.000	-3	95	97	O49(2/2/46),2b6/3	—	-0.9
1920	StL N	99	320	38	84	5	5	0	32	21	0	11	.262	.308	.309	81	-9	5-4	.945	-3	101	72	O80(2/0/79)	—	-1.7
1921	StL N	92	275	37	85	20	3	6	45	15	1	11	.309	.347	.469	116	6	4-3	.977	1	109	90	O67R,3b3,1b2	—	0.2
1922	StL N	112	344	50	108	13	4	2	64	19	0	10	.314	.350	.392	96	-3	3-1	.976	2	113	65	O89(33/3/53)	—	-0.7
1923	StL N	2	7	0	2	0	0	0	1	1	0	0	.286	.375	.286	78	0	0-0	1.000	0	117	0	O2R	—	0.0
1924	StL N	12	12	0	2	0	0	0	2	3	0	0	.167	.333	.167	39	-1	0-0	1.000	-0	41	0	O2(1/1/0)	—	-0.1
	Phi N	88	284	35	80	15	1	5	29	20	0	18	.282	.329	.394	83	-7	6-2	.960	-3	94	92	O76(54/1/25)	—	-1.4
	Year	100	296	35	82	15	1	5	31	23	0	18	.277	.329	.385	82	-7	6-2	.960	-3	93	91	O78(55/2/25)	—	-1.5
1925	Phi N	24	64	10	22	6	0	0	8	4	0	1	.344	.382	.438	100	0	1-1	.923	0	106	95	O20(3/0/17)	—	-0.1
	Cin N	33	62	6	20	3	1	0	13	3	0	1	.323	.354	.403	95	-1	3-1	.950	-1	79	150	O15(5/0/12)/2	—	-0.2
	Year	57	126	16	42	9	1	0	21	7	0	2	.333	.368	.421	99	0	4-2	.932	-1	95	117	O35(8/0/29)/2	—	-0.3
Total	11	703	1959	235	558	83	19	15	249	116	6	102	.285	.327	.370	93	-23	35-16	.966	-26	103	83	O411R,3b55,2b38,1b2,S2	—	-7.5
SCHULZ, JEFF	Jeffrey Alan; B6.2.1961 Evansville IN; BL/TR/6´1˝/190; [KCA83 23/586]; d9.2; Col Southern Indiana																								
1989	KC A	7	9	0	2	0	0	0	1	0-0	0	2	.222	.222	.222	26	-1	0-0	1.000	0	150	0	O5L	0	-0.1
1990	KC A	30	66	5	17	5	1	0	6	6-2	0	13	.258	.319	.364	92	-1	0-0	.943	-1	98	0	O22(8/0/16)/D	29	-0.3
1991	Pit N	3	3	0	0	0	0	0	0	0-0	0	2	.000	.000	.000	-99	-1	0-0	ø	0	—	—	/H	0	-0.1
Total	3	40	78	5	19	5	1	0	7	6-2	0	17	.244	.298	.333	77	-3	0-0	.951	-1	103	0	O27(12/0/16)/D	29	-0.5
SCHULZE, JOHN	John H.; B4.1866 St.Louis MO; D5.19.1941 St.Louis MO; d8.7																								
1891	StL AA	1	2	0	0	0	0	0	0	0	0	0	.000	.000	.000	-87	0	0	1.000	-0	*88*	*186*	/C	—	0.0
SCHUMAKER, SKIP	Jared Michael; B2.3.1980 Torrance CA; BL/TR/5´10˝/175; [StLN01 5/164]; d6.8; Col California–Santa Barbara																								
2005	StL N	27	24	9	6	1	0	0	1	2-0	0	2	.250	.308	.292	57	-1	1-0	1.000	0	121	0	O21(14/4/7)	0	-0.1
2006	StL N	28	54	3	10	1	0	1	2	5-1	0	6	.185	.254	.259	32	-6	2-1	1.000	-1	98	0	O25(13/5/9)	0	-0.6
Total	2	55	78	12	16	2	0	1	3	7-1	0	8	.205	.271	.269	40	-7	3-1	1.000	-0	105	0	O46(27/9/16)	0	-0.7
SCHUSTER, BILL	William Charles "Broadway Bill"; B8.4.1912 Buffalo NY; D6.28.1987 El Monte CA; BR/TR/5´9˝/164; d9.29																								
1937	Pit N	3	6	2	3	0	0	0	1	1	0	0	.500	.571	.500	193	1	0	1.000	1	120	216	S2	—	0.2
1939	Bos N	2	3	0	0	0	0	0	0	0	0	1	.000	.000	.000	-99	-1	0	.833	-1	100	0	/S3	—	-0.1
1943	Chi N	13	51	3	15	2	1	0	0	3	0	2	.294	.333	.373	105	0	0	.977	4	109	165	S13	0	0.6
1944	Chi N	60	154	14	34	7	1	1	14	12	0	16	.221	.277	.299	62	-8	4	.946	-1	101	100	S38,2b6	0	-0.6
1945	†Chi N	45	47	8	9	2	1	0	2	7	0	4	.191	.296	.277	61	-2	2	.949	4	99	142	S22,2b3/3	0	0.2
Total	5	123	261	27	61	11	3	1	17	23	0	23	.234	.296	.310	72	-10	6	.954	7	103	126	S76,2b9,3b2	0	0.3
SCHWARTZ, RANDY	Douglas Randall; B2.9.1944 Los Angeles CA; BL/TL/6´3˝/(220–230); d9.8; Col UCLA																								
1965	KC A	6	7	0	2	0	0	0	1	0-0	0	4	.286	.286	.286	64	0	0-0	1.000	1	237	0	1b2	0	0.0
1966	KC A	10	11	0	1	0	0	0	1	1-0	0	3	.091	.167	.091	-24	-2	0-0	1.000	-0	0	148	1b2	0	-0.2
Total	2	16	18	0	3	0	0	0	2	1-0	0	7	.167	.211	.167	10	-2	0-0	1.000	0	145	58	1b4	0	-0.2

YEAR	TM LG	G	AB	R	H	2B	3B	HR	RBI	BB-IB	HP	SO	AVG	OBP	SLG	AOPS	ABR	SB-CS	FA	FR	RNG	THR	GAMES AT POSITION	DL	BFW
Schwartz, Bill	William August "Pop","Scooper Bill"; B4.3.1864 Jamestown KY; D12.22.1940 Newport KY; BR/TR/6´1˝/195; d5.3																								
1883	Col AA	2	4	0	1	0	0	0	—	0	—	—	.250	.250	.250	67	0	—	.600	-2	0	0	/1C	—	-0.1
1884	Cin U	29	106	14	25	4	0	1	—	3	—	—	.236	.257	.302	64	-8	—	.837	-6	—	—	C25,O3(2/1/1)/3	—	-1.0
Total	2	31	110	14	26	4	0	1	—	3	—	—	.236	.257	.300	64	-8	—	.828	-7	—	—	C26,O3(2/1/1)/31	—	-1.1
Schwartz, Bill	William Charles "Blab"; B4.22.1884 Cleveland OH; D8.29.1961 Nashville TN; BR/TR/6´2˝/185; d5.2																								
1904	Cle A	24	86	5	13	2	0	0	0	0	0	—	.151	.151	.174	3	-10	4	.980	-4	36	43	1b22/3	—	-1.7
Schweitzer, Al	Albert Caspar "Cheese"; B12.23.1882 Cleveland OH; D1.27.1969 Newark OH; BR/TR/5´6˝/170; d4.30																								
1908	StL A	64	182	22	53	4	2	1	14	20	4	—	.291	.374	.352	135	8	6	.952	6	247	202	O55(0/28/27)	—	1.4
1909	StL A	27	76	7	17	2	0	0	2	5	3	—	.224	.298	.250	79	-2	3	.933	-1	88	0	O22(6/7/9)	—	-0.4
1910	StL A	113	379	37	87	11	2	2	37	36	4	—	.230	.303	.285	90	-4	26	.937	-2	93	106	O109(1/32/76)	—	-1.2
1911	StL A	76	237	31	51	11	4	0	34	43	1	—	.215	.338	.295	80	-4	12	.934	1	97	118	O68(9/8/51)	—	-0.7
Total	4	280	874	97	208	28	8	3	87	104	12	—	.238	.327	.299	95	-2	47	.940	4	127	122	O254(16/75/163)	—	-0.9
Schwert, Pi	Pius Louis; B11.22.1892 Angola NY; D3.11.1941 Washington DC; BR/TR/5´10.5˝/160; d8.20; Col Penn																								
1914	NY A	3	6	0	0	0	0	0	0	2	0	3	.000	.250	.000	-24	-1	0	.923	0	*85*	*231*	C3	—	0.0
1915	NY A	9	18	6	5	3	0	0	6	1	0	6	.278	.316	.444	128	1	0	.972	0	*102*	*108*	C9	—	0.1
Total	2	12	24	6	5	3	0	0	6	3	0	9	.208	.296	.333	89	0	0	.959	0	*97*	*142*	C12	—	0.1
Schwind, Art	Arthur Edwin; B11.4.1889 Ft.Wayne IN; D1.13.1968 Sullivan IL; BB/TR/5´8˝/150; d10.3																								
1912	Bos N	1	2	0	1	0	0	0	0	0	0	0	.500	.500	.500	171	0	0	ø	-0	0	0	/3	—	0.0
Schypinski, Jerry	Gerald Albert; B9.16.1931 Detroit MI; BL/TR/5´10˝/170; d8.31; Col Detroit Mercy																								
1955	KC A	22	69	7	15	2	0	0	5	1-0	0	6	.217	.229	.246	27	-7	0-0	.932	-2	99	95	S21,2b2	0	-0.8
Scioscia, Mike	Michael Lorri; B11.27.1958 Upper Darby PA; BL/TR/6´2˝/(200–229); [LAN76 1/19]; d4.20; M7/C2; [DL 1993 SD N 182]																								
1980	LA N	54	134	8	34	5	1	1	8	12-2	0	9	.254	.313	.328	82	-3	1-0	.992	-1	84	112	C54	0	-0.3
1981	†LA N	93	290	27	80	10	0	2	29	36-8	1	18	.276	.353	.331	101	2	0-2	.987	1	114	101	C91	0	0.6
1982	LA N	129	365	31	80	11	1	5	38	44-11	1	31	.219	.302	.296	71	-14	2-0	.986	-3	112	88	C123	0	-1.2
1983	LA N	12	35	3	11	3	0	1	7	5-1	0	2	.314	.400	.486	144	2	0-0	1.000	0	277	123	C11	141	0.3
1984	LA N	114	341	29	93	18	0	5	38	52-10	1	26	.273	.367	.370	109	7	2-1	.985	15	118	127	C112	15	2.7
1985	†LA N	141	429	47	127	26	3	7	53	77-9	5	21	.296	.407	.420	135	25	3-3	.986	10	138	91	C139	0	4.3
1986	LA N	122	374	36	94	18	1	5	26	62-4	3	23	.251	.359	.345	103	4	3-3	.982	4	125	84	C119	35	1.3
1987	LA N	142	461	44	122	26	1	6	38	55-9	1	23	.265	.343	.364	90	-5	7-4	.989	16	132	104	C138	15	1.6
1988	†LA N	130	408	29	105	18	0	3	35	38-12	0	31	.257	.318	.324	88	-6	0-3	.991	15	132	130	C123	0	1.6
1989	LA N★	133	408	40	102	16	0	10	44	52-14	3	29	.250	.338	.363	102	2	0-2	.988	20	131	107	C130	0	3.0
1990	LA N★	135	435	46	115	25	0	12	66	55-14	3	31	.264	.348	.405	110	7	4-1	.989	9	112	86	C132	0	2.4
1991	LA N	119	345	39	91	16	2	8	40	47-3	3	32	.264	.353	.391	112	7	4-3	.990	5	106	71	C115	15	1.9
1992	LA N	117	348	19	77	6	3	3	24	32-4	1	31	.221	.286	.282	63	-18	3-2	.988	12	88	120	C108	0	0.0
Total	13	1441	4373	398	1131	198	12	68	446	567-101	22	307	.259	.344	.356	99	10	29-24	.988	101	120	101	C1395	403	18.2
Scoffic, Lou	Louis "Weaser"; B5.20.1913 Herrin IL; D8.28.1997 Herrin IL; BR/TR/5´10˝/182; d4.16																								
1936	StL N	4	7	2	3	0	0	0	2	1	0	2	.429	.500	.429	153	1	0	.875	-0	129	0	O3R	—	0.0
Sconiers, Daryl	Daryl Anthony; B10.3.1958 San Bernardino CA; BL/TL/6´2˝/(185–199); [AnaA77*3/59]; d9.13; Col Orange Coast (CA) JC																								
1981	Cal A	15	52	6	14	1	1	1	7	1-0	0	10	.269	.283	.385	90	-1	0-0	1.000	1	116	124	1b12,D3	0	-0.1
1982	Cal A	12	13	0	2	0	0	0	2	2-0	0	1	.154	.267	.154	19	-1	0-0	1.000	-0	82	332	1b3/D	0	-0.2
1983	Cal A	106	314	49	86	19	3	8	46	17-2	0	41	.274	.310	.430	102	0	4-2	.986	-6	72	99	1b57,D27/lf	0	-0.9
1984	Cal A	57	160	14	39	4	0	4	17	13-2	0	17	.244	.301	.344	78	-5	1-2	.990	-2	90	82	1b41/D	92	-1.0
1985	Cal A	44	98	14	28	6	1	2	12	15-0	0	18	.286	.371	.429	121	3	2-1	.973	-1	30	57	D20,1b6	48	0.2
Total	5	234	637	83	169	30	5	15	84	48-4	0	87	.265	.315	.399	96	-4	7-5	.989	-8	81	98	1b119,D52/lf	140	-2.0
Scott	; d7.16																								
1884	Bal U	13	53	10	12	1	1	1	—	2	—	—	.226	.255	.340	71	-4	—	.909	-1	42	257	O13R/3	—	-0.4
Scott, Tony	Anthony; B9.18.1951 Cincinnati OH; BB/TR/6´0˝/(163–195); [MonN69 71/1017]; d9.1; C3																								
1973	Mon N	11	1	2	0	0	0	0	0	0-0	0	1	.000	.000	.000	-96	0	0-0	.000	-1	0	0	O3(1/1/1)	0	-0.1
1974	Mon N	19	7	2	2	0	0	0	1	1-0	0	3	.286	.375	.286	82	0	1-1	1.000	-0	101	0	O16(2/1/14)	0	-0.1
1975	Mon N	92	143	19	26	4	2	0	11	12-2	3	38	.182	.258	.238	37	-12	5-6	.962	4	110	194	O71(45/4/28)	0	-1.3
1977	StL N	95	292	38	85	16	3	3	41	33-4	3	48	.291	.368	.397	106	4	13-10	.996	5	115	95	O89(3/82/6)	45	0.7
1978	StL N	96	219	28	50	5	2	1	14	14-1	2	41	.228	.278	.283	58	-13	5-6	.946	-0	93	166	O77(38/31/10)	0	-1.7
1979	StL N	153	587	69	152	22	10	6	68	34-4	5	92	.259	.301	.361	80	-18	37-17	.984	6	107	120	O151(0/140/14)	0	-1.3
1980	StL N	143	415	51	104	19	3	0	28	35-9	1	68	.251	.308	.311	70	-16	22-10	**.997**	1	105	63	O134C	0	-1.5
1981	StL N	45	176	21	40	5	2	2	17	5-0	1	22	.227	.253	.313	57	-11	10-7	1.000	-1	100	63	O44C	0	-1.3
	†Hou N	55	225	28	66	13	2	2	22	15-1	0	32	.293	.338	.396	114	4	8-3	.985	-2	92	138	O55C	0	0.2
	Year	100	401	49	106	18	4	4	39	20-1	1	54	.264	.301	.359	87	-8	18-10	.992	-3	96	105	O99C	0	-1.1
1982	Hou N	132	460	43	110	16	3	1	29	15-4	1	56	.239	.262	.293	61	-26	18-4	.982	-5	95	103	O129(2/125/3)	0	-3.2
1983	Hou N	80	186	20	42	6	1	2	17	11-0	0	39	.226	.264	.301	61	-11	5-4	1.000	-1	99	79	O61(7/30/28)	0	-1.3
1984	Hou N	25	21	2	4	1	0	0	0	4-1	0	3	.190	.320	.238	63	-1	0-0	1.000	-0	98	0	O6(1/5/0)	0	-0.1
	Mon N	45	71	8	18	4	0	0	5	7-1	0	21	.254	.316	.310	81	-2	1-1	1.000	-0	91	106	O17(16/1/2)	0	-0.2
	Year	70	92	10	22	5	0	0	5	11-2	0	24	.239	.317	.293	77	-2	1-1	1.000	-0	93	83	O23(17/6/2)	0	-0.3
Total	11	991	2803	331	699	111	28	17	253	186-27	16	464	.249	.297	.327	74	-102	125-69	.986	6	102	107	O853(115/653/106)	45	-11.2
Scott, Donnie	Donald Malcolm; B8.16.1961 Dunedin FL; BB/TR/5´11˝/(185–200); [TexA79 2/43]; d9.30																								
1983	Tex A	2	4	0	0	0	0	0	0	0-0	0	0	.000	.000	.000	-99	-1	0-0	1.000	1	0	273	C2	0	0.0
1984	Tex A	81	235	16	52	9	0	3	20	20-1	0	44	.221	.280	.298	58	-13	0-1	.974	4	117	100	C80	0	-0.7
1985	Sea A	80	185	18	41	13	0	4	23	15-0	0	41	.222	.275	.357	72	-7	1-1	.981	-2	82	125	C74	0	-0.7
1991	Cin N	10	19	0	3	0	0	0	0	0-0	0	2	.158	.158	.158	-11	-3	0-0	1.000	-4	49	0	C8	0	-0.7
Total	4	173	443	34	96	22	0	7	43	35-1	0	87	.217	.271	.314	60	-24	1-2	.977	-1	100	108	C164	0	-2.1
Scott, Pete	Floyd John; B12.21.1897 Woodland CA; D5.3.1953 Daly City CA; BR/TR/5´11.5˝/175; d4.13; Col St. Marys (CA)																								
1926	Chi N	77	189	34	54	13	1	3	34	22	1	31	.286	.363	.413	107	3	3	.968	2	108	118	O59(34/0/29)/3	—	0.1
1927	Chi N	71	156	28	49	18	1	0	21	19	1	18	.314	.392	.442	123	6	1	.986	-1	98	73	O36(1/1/35)	—	0.3
1928	Pit N	60	177	33	55	10	4	5	33	18	1	14	.311	.378	.497	122	5	1	.979	3	112	155	O42(29/0/13),1b8	—	0.5
Total	3	208	522	95	158	41	6	8	88	59	3	63	.303	.377	.450	117	14	5	.976	5	107	117	O137(64/1/77),1b8/3	—	0.9
Scott, Gary	Gary Thomas; B8.22.1968 New Rochelle NY; BR/TR/6´0˝/175; [ChiN89 2/38]; d4.9; Col Villanova																								
1991	Chi N	31	79	8	13	3	0	1	5	13-4	3	14	.165	.305	.241	53	-4	0-1	.969	-1	101	136	3b31	0	-0.6
1992	Chi N	36	96	8	15	2	0	2	11	5-1	0	14	.156	.198	.240	23	-10	0-1	.922	-4	85	68	3b29,S2	0	-1.6
Total	2	67	175	16	28	5	0	3	16	18-5	3	28	.160	.250	.240	38	-14	0-2	.946	-5	93	102	3b60,S2	0	-2.2
Scott, George	George Charles "Boomer"; B3.23.1944 Greenville MS; BR/TR/6´2˝/(205–225); d4.12																								
1966	Bos A★	**162**	601	73	147	18	7	27	90	65-13	8	152	.245	.324	.433	105	4	4-0	.991	-1	98	98	1b158,3b5	0	-0.7
1967	†Bos A	159	565	74	171	21	7	19	82	63-10	4	119	.303	.373	.465	136	27	10-8	.987	-8	86	107	1b152,3b2	0	1.0
1968	Bos A	124	350	23	60	14	0	3	25	26-3	5	88	.171	.236	.237	42	-24	3-5	.987	-1	95	95	1b112,3b6	0	-3.7
1969	Bos A	152	549	63	139	14	5	16	52	61-12	4	74	.253	.331	.384	95	-4	4-3	.954	-8	93	121	3b109,1b53	0	-1.7
1970	Bos A	127	480	50	142	24	5	16	63	44-5	2	95	.296	.355	.467	118	11	4-11	.934	-9	80	90	3b68,1b59	30	-0.6
1971	Bos A	146	537	72	141	16	4	24	78	41-5	5	102	.263	.317	.441	106	3	0-3	.992	-6	82	96	1b143	0	-1.8
1972	Mil A	152	578	71	154	24	4	20	88	43-4	4	130	.266	.321	.426	123	14	16-4	.992	-3	92	96	1b139,3b23	0	0.3
1973	Mil A	158	604	98	185	30	4	24	107	61-6	2	94	.306	.370	.488	142	34	9-5	.994	3	110	100	1b157/D	0	2.5
1974	Mil A	158	604	74	170	36	2	17	82	59-5	3	90	.281	.345	.432	124	19	9-9	**.992**	7	**125**	105	1b148,D9	0	1.4
1975	Mil A★	158	617	86	176	26	4	**36**	**109**	51-7	3	97	.285	.341	.515	139	28	6-5	.989	2	109	92	1b144,D12,3b5	0	1.9
1976	Mil A	156	606	73	166	21	5	18	77	53-6	5	118	.274	.334	.414	121	15	0-1	.991	-1	99	100	1b155	0	0.1
1977	Bos A★	157	584	103	157	26	5	33	95	57-4	6	112	.269	.337	.500	113	10	1-1	.985	-3	97	118	1b157	0	-0.4
1978	Bos A	120	412	51	96	16	4	12	54	44-3	0	86	.233	.305	.379	83	-10	1-1	.991	-11	68	107	1b113,D7	0	-2.9

YEAR	TM LG	G	AB	R	H	2B	3B	HR	RBI	BB-IB	HP	SO	AVG	OBP	SLG	AOPS	ABR	SB-CS	FA	FR	RNG	THR	GAMES AT POSITION	DL	BFW
1979	Bos A	45	156	18	35	9	1	4	23	17-1	0	22	.224	.299	.372	76	-5	0-0	.986	-4	77	107	1b41	0	-1.1
	KC A	44	146	19	39	8	2	1	20	12-1	2	32	.267	.329	.370	87	-3	1-1	.989	-3	82	81	1b41/3D	0	-0.7
	NY A	16	44	9	14	3	1	1	6	2-0	0	7	.318	.340	.500	128	2	1-0	1.000	0	0	0	D15/1	0	0.1
	Year	105	346	46	88	20	4	6	49	31-2	2	61	.254	.317	.387	87	-6	2-1	.987	-6	79	95	1b83,D17/3	0	-1.7
Total	14	2034	7433	957	1992	306	60	271	1051	699-85	53	1418	.268	.333	.435	113	121	69-57	.990	-46	96	101	1b1773,3b219,D46	30	-6.3

SCOTT, JIM James Walter; B9.22.1888 Shenandoah PA; D5.12.1972 S.Pasadena FL; BR/TR/5´9.5˝/165; d4.22

YEAR	TM LG	G	AB	R	H	2B	3B	HR	RBI	BB-IB	HP	SO	AVG	OBP	SLG	AOPS	ABR	SB-CS	FA	FR	RNG	THR	GAMES AT POSITION	DL	BFW
1914	Pit F	8	24	2	6	1	0	0	1	5	0	0	.250	.379	.292	85	-1	1	.800	-3	88	150	S8	—	-0.3

SCOTT, JOHN John Henry; B1.24.1952 Jackson MS; BR/TR/6´2˝/(160–165); [SDN70*1/2]; d9.7

YEAR	TM LG	G	AB	R	H	2B	3B	HR	RBI	BB-IB	HP	SO	AVG	OBP	SLG	AOPS	ABR	SB-CS	FA	FR	RNG	THR	GAMES AT POSITION	DL	BFW
1974	SD N	14	15	3	1	0	0	0	0	0-0	0	4	.067	.067	.067	-66	-3	1-0	1.000	1	86	361	O8(5/2/1)	0	-0.3
1975	SD N	25	9	6	0	0	0	0	0	0-0	0	2	.000	.000	.000	-99	-3	2-0	ø	-0	0	0	/cf	0	-0.2
1977	Tor A	79	233	26	56	9	0	2	15	8-0	0	39	.240	.266	.305	54	-15	10-8	.963	-4	90	72	O67(27/41/0),D2	0	-2.1
Total	3	118	257	35	57	9	0	2	15	8-0	0	45	.222	.245	.280	43	-21	13-8	.965	-3	89	91	O76(32/44/1),D2	0	-2.6

SCOTT, LE GRANT Le Grant Edward; B7.25.1910 Cleveland OH; D11.12.1993 Birmingham AL; BL/TL/5´8.5˝/170; d4.19; Col Alabama

YEAR	TM LG	G	AB	R	H	2B	3B	HR	RBI	BB-IB	HP	SO	AVG	OBP	SLG	AOPS	ABR	SB-CS	FA	FR	RNG	THR	GAMES AT POSITION	DL	BFW
1939	Phi N	76	232	31	65	15	1	1	26	22	0	14	.280	.343	.366	93	-2	5	.959	1	99	139	O55(1/1/54)	—	-0.4

SCOTT, EVERETT Lewis Everett "Deacon"; B11.19.1892 Bluffton IN; D11.2.1960 Fort Wayne IN; BR/TR/5´8˝/148; d4.14

YEAR	TM LG	G	AB	R	H	2B	3B	HR	RBI	BB-IB	HP	SO	AVG	OBP	SLG	AOPS	ABR	SB-CS	FA	FR	RNG	THR	GAMES AT POSITION	DL	BFW
1914	Bos A	144	539	66	129	15	6	2	37	32	3	43	.239	.286	.301	76	-18	9-14	.949	-11	95	106	S143	—	-2.4
1915	†Bos A	100	359	25	72	11	0	0	28	17	0	21	.201	.237	.231	41	-27	4-7	.961	0	99	96	S100	—	-2.3
1916	†Bos A	123	366	37	85	19	2	0	27	23	3	24	.232	.283	.295	73	-13	8	**.967**	5	102	96	S121/23	—	0.0
1917	Bos A	**157**	528	40	127	24	7	0	50	20	0	46	.241	.268	.313	78	-17	12	**.953**	8	103	105	S157	—	0.3
1918	†Bos A	**126**	443	40	98	11	5	0	43	12	0	16	.221	.242	.269	55	-27	11	**.976**	21	108	79	S126	—	0.2
1919	Bos A	**138**	507	41	141	19	0	0	38	19	1	26	.278	.306	.316	79	-16	8	**.976**	11	104	128	S138	—	0.4
1920	Bos A	**154**	569	41	153	21	12	4	61	21	4	15	.269	.300	.369	80	-20	4-11	**.973**	14	102	112	S154	—	0.1
1921	Bos A	**154**	576	65	151	21	9	1	62	27	0	21	.262	.295	.335	62	-36	5-9	**.972**	**41**	110	**135**	S154	—	1.9
1922	†NY A	**154**	557	64	150	23	5	3	45	23	5	22	.269	.304	.345	67	-28	2-3	**.966**	17	107	104	S154	—	0.5
1923	†NY A	**152**	533	48	131	16	4	6	60	13	2	19	.246	.266	.325	54	-39	1-3	**.961**	-13	95	99	S152	—	-3.6
1924	NY A	**153**	548	56	137	12	6	4	64	21	0	15	.250	.278	.316	53	-42	3-7	.966	10	99	110	S153	—	-1.6
1925	NY A	22	60	3	13	0	0	0	4	2	0	2	.217	.242	.217	17	-8	0-1	.988	2	92	173	S18	—	-0.4
	Was A	33	103	10	28	6	1	0	18	4	0	4	.272	.299	.350	65	-6	1-2	.932	-1	95	112	S30,3b2	—	-0.4
	Year	55	163	13	41	6	1	0	22	6	0	6	.252	.278	.301	48	-14	1-3	.952	1	94	134	S48,3b2	—	-0.8
1926	Chi A	40	143	15	36	10	1	0	13	9	0	8	.252	.296	.336	67	-7	1-3	.955	5	111	105	S39	—	0.0
	Cin N	4	6	1	4	0	0	0	1	0	0	0	.667	.667	.667	267	1	0	.875	-1	77	0	S4	—	0.1
Total	13	1654	5837	552	1455	208	58	20	551	243	18	282	.249	.281	.315	65	-303	69-60	.965	108	102	108	S1643,3b3/2	—	-7.2

SCOTT, LUKE Luke Brandon; B6.25.1978 DeLeon Springs FL; BL/TR/6´0˝/210; [CleA01 9/277]; d4.5; Col Oklahoma St.

YEAR	TM LG	G	AB	R	H	2B	3B	HR	RBI	BB-IB	HP	SO	AVG	OBP	SLG	AOPS	ABR	SB-CS	FA	FR	RNG	THR	GAMES AT POSITION	DL	BFW
2005	†Hou N	34	80	6	15	4	2	0	4	9-1	0	23	.188	.270	.287	45	-7	1-1	.963	-2	68	186	O24(21/1/4)	0	-0.9
2006	Hou N	65	214	31	72	19	6	10	37	30-4	4	43	.336	.426	.621	160	20	2-1	1.000	-3	88	34	O60(50/1/13)	0	1.4
Total	2	99	294	37	87	23	8	10	41	39-5	4	66	.296	.385	.531	130	13	3-2	.992	-5	83	73	O84(71/2/17)	0	0.5

SCOTT, MILT Milton Parker "Mikado Milt"; B1.17.1861 Chicago IL; D11.3.1938 Baltimore MD; BR/5´9˝/160; d9.30

YEAR	TM LG	G	AB	R	H	2B	3B	HR	RBI	BB-IB	HP	SO	AVG	OBP	SLG	AOPS	ABR	SB-CS	FA	FR	RNG	THR	GAMES AT POSITION	DL	BFW
1882	Chi N	1	5	1	2	0	0	0	0	0	—	0	.400	.400	.400	150	0	—	1.000	0	0	0	/1	—	0.0
1884	Det N	110	438	29	108	17	5	3	50	9	—	62	.247	.262	.329	90	-5	—	.968	-1	82	68	1b110	—	-1.4
1885	Det N	38	148	14	39	7	0	0	12	4	—	16	.264	.283	.311	92	-1	—	.967	2	136	82	1b38	—	-0.3
	Pit AA	55	210	15	52	7	1	0	18	5	2	—	.248	.272	.290	79	-5	—	.986	3	108	106	1b55	—	-0.7
1886	Bal AA	137	484	48	92	11	4	2	52	22	9	—	.190	.239	.242	52	-27	11	.974	8	**137**	57	1b137/P	—	-2.7
Total	4	341	1285	107	293	42	10	5	132	40	11	78	.228	.257	.288	74	-38	11	.973	12	114	71	1b341/P	—	-5.1

SCOTT, DICKIE Richard Edward; B7.19.1962 Ellsworth ME; BR/TR/6´1˝/170; [NYA81 17/441]; d5.19

YEAR	TM LG	G	AB	R	H	2B	3B	HR	RBI	BB-IB	HP	SO	AVG	OBP	SLG	AOPS	ABR	SB-CS	FA	FR	RNG	THR	GAMES AT POSITION	DL	BFW
1989	Oak A	3	2	0	0	0	0	0	1	0-0	0	0	.000	.000	.000	-99	-1	0-0	ø	-0	0	0	S3	0	-0.1

SCOTT, RODNEY Rodney Darrell; B10.16.1953 Indianapolis IN; BB/TR (BR 1975)/6´0˝/(155–160); [KCA72 11/258]; d4.11; OF(0/10/1)

YEAR	TM LG	G	AB	R	H	2B	3B	HR	RBI	BB-IB	HP	SO	AVG	OBP	SLG	AOPS	ABR	SB-CS	FA	FR	RNG	THR	GAMES AT POSITION	DL	BFW
1975	KC A	48	15	13	1	0	0	0	0	1-0	0	3	.067	.125	.067	-43	-3	4-2	1.000	-2	39	88	D22,2b9,S8/R	0	-0.5
1976	Mon N	7	10	3	4	0	0	0	0	1-0	0	1	.400	.455	.400	137	1	2-0	1.000	-1	63	86	2b6,S3	0	0.0
1977	Oak A	133	364	56	95	4	4	0	20	43-0	3	50	.261	.342	.294	77	-11	33-18	.963	-10	96	75	2b71,S70,3b5/rfD	0	-1.3
1978	Chi N	78	227	41	64	5	1	0	15	43-0	3	41	.282	.403	.313	91	0	27-10	.929	-3	102	176	3b59,O10C,2b6,S6	0	-0.1
1979	Mon N	151	562	69	134	12	5	3	42	66-2	2	82	.238	.319	.294	69	-24	39-12	.980	-5	102	105	2b113,S39	0	-1.4
1980	Mon N	154	567	84	127	13	**13**	0	46	70-0	1	75	.224	.307	.293	68	-24	63-13	.982	-8	96	92	2b129,S21	0	-1.5
1981	†Mon N	95	336	43	69	9	3	0	26	50-1	1	35	.205	.308	.250	58	-17	30-7	.983	-12	94	79	2b93	0	-2.2
1982	Mon N	14	25	2	5	0	0	0	1	3-0	0	2	.200	.286	.200	37	-2	5-0	.971	-2	74	74	2b12	0	-0.3
	NY A	10	26	5	5	0	0	0	0	4-0	0	2	.192	.300	.192	39	-2	2-0	.963	-0	100	159	S6,2b4	0	-0.1
Total	8	690	2132	316	504	43	26	3	150	281-2	10	291	.236	.326	.285	70	-82	205-62	.979	-42	96	88	2b443,S153,3b64,D23,O11C	0	-7.4

SCRANTON, JIM James Dean; B4.5.1960 Torrance CA; BR/TR/6´0˝/175; d9.5; Col Arizona

YEAR	TM LG	G	AB	R	H	2B	3B	HR	RBI	BB-IB	HP	SO	AVG	OBP	SLG	AOPS	ABR	SB-CS	FA	FR	RNG	THR	GAMES AT POSITION	DL	BFW
1984	KC A	2	2	0	0	0	0	0	0	0-0	0	0	.000	.000	.000	-99	-1	0-0	1.000	0	142	753	/S3	0	0.0
1985	KC A	6	4	1	0	0	0	0	0	0-0	0	0	.000	.000	.000	-99	-1	0-0	1.000	1	148	89	S5	0	0.0
Total	2	8	6	1	0	0	0	0	0	0-0	0	0	.000	.000	.000	-99	-2	0-0	1.000	1	147	163	S6/3	0	0.0

SCRIVENER, CHUCK Wayne Allison; B10.3.1947 Alexandria VA; BR/TR/5´9˝/170; [DetA68*S2/23]; d9.18; Col CC of Baltimore (MD)

YEAR	TM LG	G	AB	R	H	2B	3B	HR	RBI	BB-IB	HP	SO	AVG	OBP	SLG	AOPS	ABR	SB-CS	FA	FR	RNG	THR	GAMES AT POSITION	DL	BFW
1975	Det A	4	16	0	4	1	0	0	0	0-0	0	1	.250	.250	.313	56	-1	1-0	1.000	-1	81	0	3b3,S2	0	-0.2
1976	Det A	80	222	28	49	7	1	2	16	19-0	0	34	.221	.282	.288	65	-10	1-0	.976	13	116	89	2b43,S37,3b5	0	1.0
1977	Det A	61	72	10	6	0	0	0	2	5-0	0	9	.083	.143	.083	-35	-14	0-0	.981	0	98	102	S50,2b8,3b3	0	-1.1
Total	3	145	310	38	59	8	1	2	18	24-0	0	44	.190	.249	.242	40	-25	2-0	.970	12	103	116	S89,2b51,3b11	0	-0.3

SCRUGGS, TONY Anthony Raymond; B3.19.1966 Riverside CA; BR/TR/6´1˝/210; [TexA87 7/181]; d4.8; Col UCLA

YEAR	TM LG	G	AB	R	H	2B	3B	HR	RBI	BB-IB	HP	SO	AVG	OBP	SLG	AOPS	ABR	SB-CS	FA	FR	RNG	THR	GAMES AT POSITION	DL	BFW
1991	Tex A	5	6	1	0	0	0	0	0	0-0	0	1	.000	.000	.000	-99	-2	0-0	1.000	0	111	0	O5(5/1/0)	0	-0.2

SCUTARO, MARCO Marcos; B10.30.1975 San Felipe, Yaracuy, Venezuela; BR/TR/5´10˝/(170–190); d7.21

YEAR	TM LG	G	AB	R	H	2B	3B	HR	RBI	BB-IB	HP	SO	AVG	OBP	SLG	AOPS	ABR	SB-CS	FA	FR	RNG	THR	GAMES AT POSITION	DL	BFW
2002	NY N	27	36	2	8	0	1	1	6	0-0	0	11	.222	.216	.361	53	-3	0-1	1.000	-2	84	0	2b12,S6,3b3/lf	0	-0.5
2003	NY N	48	75	10	16	4	0	2	6	13-2	1	14	.213	.333	.347	82	-2	2-0	.981	-5	83	81	2b39/S	0	-0.5
2004	Oak A	137	455	50	124	32	1	7	43	16-1	0	58	.273	.297	.393	78	-15	0-0	**.995**	7	104	112	2b123,S16/3	0	-0.1
2005	Oak A	118	381	48	94	22	3	9	37	36-1	0	48	.247	.310	.391	86	-8	5-2	.976	4	98	112	S81,2b30,3b5,O2L	0	0.4
2006	†Oak A	117	365	52	97	21	6	5	41	50-0	0	66	.266	.350	.397	96	-1	5-1	.966	-14	89	89	S69,2b37,3b12,O2L	0	-0.8
Total	5	447	1312	162	339	79	11	24	133	115-4	1	197	.258	.316	.390	86	-29	12-4	.993	-9	99	108	2b241,S173,3b21,O5L	0	-1.5

SEABOL, SCOTT Scott Anthony; B5.17.1975 McKeesport PA; BR/TR/6´4˝/200; [NYA96 88/1718]; d4.8; Col West Virginia; [DL 1998 NY A 28]

YEAR	TM LG	G	AB	R	H	2B	3B	HR	RBI	BB-IB	HP	SO	AVG	OBP	SLG	AOPS	ABR	SB-CS	FA	FR	RNG	THR	GAMES AT POSITION	DL	BFW
2001	NY A	1	1	0	0	0	0	0	0	0-0	0	0	.000	.000	.000	-99	0	0-0	ø	0	—	—	/D	0	0.0
2005	StL N	59	105	11	23	5	0	1	10	8-0	0	23	.219	.272	.295	48	-8	0-0	.929	3	132	244	3b20,2b8,1b5,O4(2/0/2),D3	0	-0.5
Total	2	60	106	11	23	5	0	1	10	8-0	0	23	.217	.270	.292	47	-8	0-0	.929	3	132	244	3b20,2b8,1b5,O4(2/0/2),D4	28	-0.5

SEARS, KEN Kenneth Eugene "Ziggy"; B7.6.1917 Streator IL; D7.17.1968 Bridgeport TX; BL/TR/6´1˝/200; d5.2; Mil 1944–45; Col Alabama

YEAR	TM LG	G	AB	R	H	2B	3B	HR	RBI	BB-IB	HP	SO	AVG	OBP	SLG	AOPS	ABR	SB-CS	FA	FR	RNG	THR	GAMES AT POSITION	DL	BFW
1943	NY A	60	187	22	52	7	0	2	22	11	3	18	.278	.328	.348	97	-1	1-3	.974	2	*177*	*96*	C50	0	0.4
1946	StL A	7	15	1	5	0	0	0	1	3	0	0	.333	.444	.333	114	1	0-0	1.000	-2	*54*	*0*	C4	0	-0.1
Total	2	67	202	23	57	7	0	2	23	14	3	18	.282	.338	.347	99	0	1-3	.975	1	*170*	*90*	C54	0	0.3

SEARS, TODD Todd Andrew; B10.23.1975 Des Moines IA; BL/TR/6´5˝/215; [ColN97 3/102]; d9.17; Col Nebraska

YEAR	TM LG	G	AB	R	H	2B	3B	HR	RBI	BB-IB	HP	SO	AVG	OBP	SLG	AOPS	ABR	SB-CS	FA	FR	RNG	THR	GAMES AT POSITION	DL	BFW
2002	Min A	7	12	2	4	2	0	0	0	0-0	0	1	.333	.333	.500	113	0	0-0	1.000	0	102	128	1b6	0	0.0
2003	Min A	24	65	7	16	2	0	2	11	7-0	1	15	.246	.324	.369	81	-2	0-0	.990	-0	96	81	1b14,D6	0	-0.3
	SD N	9	8	2	2	1	0	0	0	0-0	0	3	.250	.250	.375	66	0	0-0	1.000	0	0	1013	/1	0	0.0
Total	2	40	85	11	22	5	0	2	11	7-0	1	19	.259	.319	.388	84	-2	0-0	.992	-0	97	99	1b21,D6	0	-0.3

SEBRING, JIMMY James Dennison; B3.22.1882 Liberty PA; D12.22.1909 Williamsport PA; BL/TR/6´0˝/180; d9.8; Col Bucknell

YEAR	TM LG	G	AB	R	H	2B	3B	HR	RBI	BB-IB	HP	SO	AVG	OBP	SLG	AOPS	ABR	SB-CS	FA	FR	RNG	THR	GAMES AT POSITION	DL	BFW
1902	Pit N	19	80	15	26	4	4	0	15	5	0	—	.325	.365	.475	154	4	2	.974	2	173	312	O19R	—	0.6
1903	†Pit N	124	506	71	140	16	13	4	64	32	4	—	.277	.325	.383	98	-4	20	.927	5	114	**279**	O124R	—	-0.4
1904	Pit N	80	305	28	82	11	7	0	32	17	0	—	.269	.307	.351	100	-1	8	.959	6	150	162	O80R	—	0.2

YEAR	TM LG	G	AB	R	H	2B	3B	HR	RBI	BB-IB	HP	SO	AVG	OBP	SLG	AOPS	ABR	SB-CS	FA	FR	RNG	THR	GAMES AT POSITION	DL	BFW
	Cin N	56	222	22	50	9	2	0	24	14	0	—	.225	.271	.284	65	-9	8	1.000	4	159	158	O56R	—	-0.8
	Year	136	527	50	132	20	9	0	56	31	0	—	.250	.292	.323	85	-10	16	.974	10	**154**	160	O136R	—	-0.6
1905	Cin N	58	217	31	62	10	5	2	28	14	0	—	.286	.329	.406	107	1	11	.885	-4	90	116	O56R	—	-0.6
1909	Bro N	25	81	11	8	1	1	0	5	11	0	—	.099	.207	.136	7	-9	3	.951	0	144	150	O25(0/21/4)	—	-1.1
	Was A	1	0	0	0	0	0	0	0	0	0	—	ø	ø	ø	ø	0	0	ø	-0	0	0	/cf	—	0.0
Total	5	363	1411	178	368	51	32	6	168	93	4	—	.261	.308	.355	93	-18	52	.945	13	131	204	O361(0/22/339)	—	-2.1

SECORY, FRANK Frank Edward; B8.24.1912 Mason City IA; D4.7.1995 Port Huron MI; BR/TR/6´1˝/200; d4.28; U19; Col Western Michigan

YEAR	TM LG	G	AB	R	H	2B	3B	HR	RBI	BB-IB	HP	SO	AVG	OBP	SLG	AOPS	ABR	SB-CS	FA	FR	RNG	THR	GAMES AT POSITION	DL	BFW
1940	Det A	1	1	0	0	0	0	0	0	0	0	1	.000	.000	.000	-91	0	0-0	ø	0	—	—	/H	—	0.0
1942	Cin N	2	5	1	0	0	0	0	1	3	0	2	.000	.375	.000	14	0	0	.857	-0	106	0	O2L	0	-0.1
1944	Chi N	22	56	10	18	1	0	4	17	6	0	8	.321	.387	.554	163	4	1	1.000	-0	112	0	O17(17/1/0)	0	0.3
1945	†Chi N	35	57	4	9	1	0	0	6	2	0	7	.158	.186	.175	1	-8	0	1.000	-0	104	0	O12(10/0/2)	0	-0.9
1946	Chi N	33	43	6	10	3	0	3	12	6	0	6	.233	.327	.512	139	2	0	.833	-1	84	0	O9L	0	0.0
Total	5	93	162	21	37	5	0	7	36	17	0	24	.228	.302	.389	95	-2	1-0	.964	-2	105	0	O40(38/1/2)	0	-0.7

SEE, CHARLIE Charles Henry "Chad"; B10.13.1896 Pleasantville NY; D7.19.1948 Bridgeport CT; BL/TR/5´10.5˝/175; d8.6

YEAR	TM LG	G	AB	R	H	2B	3B	HR	RBI	BB-IB	HP	SO	AVG	OBP	SLG	AOPS	ABR	SB-CS	FA	FR	RNG	THR	GAMES AT POSITION	DL	BFW
1919	Cin N	8	14	1	4	0	0	0	1	1	0	0	.286	.333	.286	89	0	0	.833	-1	90	0	O4(2/2/0)	—	-0.1
1920	Cin N	47	82	9	25	4	0	0	15	1	2	7	.305	.329	.354	97	0	2-4	1.000	3	125	130	O17(0/14/4)/P	—	0.1
1921	Cin N	37	106	11	26	5	1	1	7	7	1	5	.245	.298	.340	72	-4	3-2	.954	0	101	108	O30(0/11/18)	—	-0.6
Total	3	92	202	21	55	9	1	1	23	9	3	12	.272	.313	.342	83	-4	5-6	.967	3	109	110	O51(2/27/22)/P	—	-0.6

SEE, LARRY Ralph Laurence; B6.20.1960 Norwalk CA; BR/TR/6´1˝/(195–204); [LAN80*3/62]; d9.3; Col Cerritos (CA) JC

YEAR	TM LG	G	AB	R	H	2B	3B	HR	RBI	BB-IB	HP	SO	AVG	OBP	SLG	AOPS	ABR	SB-CS	FA	FR	RNG	THR	GAMES AT POSITION	DL	BFW
1986	LA N	13	20	1	5	2	0	0	2	2-0	0	7	.250	.318	.350	90	0	0-0	.979	1	171	76	1b9	0	0.0
1988	Tex A	13	23	0	3	0	0	0	0	1-0	0	8	.130	.167	.130	-15	-4	0-0	1.000	-1	0	0	C2,1b2/3D	0	-0.4
Total	2	26	43	1	8	2	0	0	2	3-0	0	15	.186	.239	.233	32	-4	0-0	.967	0	178	109	1b11,D7,C2/3	0	-0.4

SEEDS, BOB Ira Robert "Suitcase Bob"; B2.24.1907 Ringgold TX; D10.28.1993 Erick OK; BR/TR/6´0˝/180; d4.19

YEAR	TM LG	G	AB	R	H	2B	3B	HR	RBI	BB-IB	HP	SO	AVG	OBP	SLG	AOPS	ABR	SB-CS	FA	FR	RNG	THR	GAMES AT POSITION	DL	BFW
1930	Cle A	85	277	37	79	11	3	3	32	12	0	22	.285	.315	.379	72	-12	1-3	.953	1	102	117	O70(48/21/1)	—	-1.6
1931	Cle A	48	134	26	41	4	1	1	10	11	0	11	.306	.359	.373	88	-2	1-0	.966	-1	98	37	O33(3/1/29),1b2	—	-0.4
1932	Cle A	2	4	0	0	0	0	0	0	0	0	0	.000	.000	.000	-94	-1	0-0	ø	-0	0	0	/rf	—	-0.1
	Chi A	116	434	53	126	18	6	2	45	31	3	37	.290	.342	.373	91	-6	5-7	.964	-4	96	82	O112(34/34/53)	—	-1.5
	Year	118	438	53	126	18	6	2	45	31	3	37	.288	.339	.370	89	-8	5-7	.964	-4	96	82	O113(34/34/54)	—	-1.6
1933	Bos A	82	230	26	56	13	4	0	23	21	1	20	.243	.310	.335	71	-10	1-3	.985	0	89	107	1b41,O32(17/0/16)	—	-1.4
1934	Bos A	8	6	0	1	0	0	0	1	0	1	1	.167	.167	.167	-13	-1	0-0	ø	-0	0	0	/rf	—	-0.1
	Cle A	61	186	28	46	8	1	0	18	21	1	13	.247	.327	.301	62	-10	2-1	.977	-2	93	56	O48(26/2/21)	—	-1.4
	Year	69	192	28	47	8	1	0	19	21	1	14	.245	.322	.297	59	-11	2-1	.977	-3	93	56	O49(26/2/22)	—	-1.5
1936	†NY A	13	42	12	11	1	0	4	10	5	0	3	.262	.340	.571	126	1	3-1	1.000	1	115	125	O9(1/0/8),3b3	—	0.1
1938	NY N	81	296	35	86	12	3	9	52	20	1	33	.291	.338	.443	112	4	0	.987	-4	87	100	O76(37/40/1)	—	-0.3
1939	NY N	63	173	33	46	5	1	5	26	22	1	31	.266	.352	.393	99	0	1	.975	-4	81	66	O50(12/38/0)	—	-0.6
1940	NY N	56	155	18	45	5	2	4	16	17	3	19	.290	.371	.426	118	4	0	.985	-2	82	116	O40(16/24/0)	—	0.1
Total	9	615	1937	268	537	77	21	28	233	160	10	190	.277	.336	.382	89	-33	14-15	.970	-16	93	93	O472(194/160/131),1b43,3b3	—	-7.2

SEEREY, PAT James Patrick; B3.17.1923 Wilburton OK; D4.28.1986 Jennings MO; BR/TR/5´10˝/200; d6.9

YEAR	TM LG	G	AB	R	H	2B	3B	HR	RBI	BB-IB	HP	SO	AVG	OBP	SLG	AOPS	ABR	SB-CS	FA	FR	RNG	THR	GAMES AT POSITION	DL	BFW
1943	Cle A	26	72	8	16	3	0	1	5	4	0	19	.222	.263	.306	70	-3	0-0	.974	1	99	235	O16L	0	-0.3
1944	Cle A	101	342	39	80	16	0	15	39	19	1	99	.234	.276	.412	99	-3	0-2	.986	1	100	109	O86(63/19/4)	0	-0.7
1945	Cle A	126	414	56	98	22	2	14	56	66	0	97	.237	.342	.401	120	12	1-2	.975	-4	97	69	O117(38/28/68)	0	0.1
1946	Cle A	117	404	57	91	17	2	26	62	65	1	101	.225	.334	.470	131	16	2-3	.981	-2	103	50	O115(39/40/43)	0	0.9
1947	Cle A	82	216	24	37	4	1	11	29	34	0	66	.171	.284	.352	78	-7	0-1	.957	-1	85	181	O68(53/1/16)	0	-1.3
1948	Cle A	10	23	7	6	0	0	1	6	7	0	8	.261	.433	.391	123	1	0-0	1.000	-1	62	0	O7R	0	0.0
	Chi A	95	340	44	78	11	0	18	64	61	0	94	.229	.347	.421	107	3	0-0	.981	0	93	130	O93(82/12/0)	0	-0.3
	Year	105	363	51	84	11	0	19	70	68	0	102	.231	.353	.419	108	4	0-0	.982	-1	92	124	O100(82/12/7)	0	-0.3
1949	Chi A	4	4	1	0	0	0	0	0	3	0	1	.000	.429	.000	19	0	0-0	1.000	-0	61	0	O2R	0	0.0
Total	7	561	1815	236	406	73	5	86	261	259	2	485	.224	.321	.412	109	19	3-8	.978	-5	96	101	O504(291/100/140)	0	-1.6

SEERY, EMMETT John Emmett; B2.13.1861 Princeville IL; D8.7.1930 Saranac Lake NY; BL/TR/5´7˝/145; d4.17

YEAR	TM LG	G	AB	R	H	2B	3B	HR	RBI	BB-IB	HP	SO	AVG	OBP	SLG	AOPS	ABR	SB-CS	FA	FR	RNG	THR	GAMES AT POSITION	DL	BFW
1884	Bal U	**105**	463	113	144	25	7	2	—	20	—	—	.311	.340	.408	114	-6	—	.828	3	96	68	O103(99/0/5),C3,3b2	—	-0.4
	KC U	1	4	2	2	1	0	0	—	1	—	—	.500	.600	.750	353	1	—	ø	-0	0	0	/lf	—	0.1
	Year	106	467	115	146	26	7	2	—	21	—	—	.313	.342	.411	116	-5	—	.828	3	96	68	O104(100/0/5),C3,3b2	—	-0.3
1885	StL N	59	216	20	35	7	0	1	14	16	—	37	.162	.220	.208	42	-13	—	.874	4	139	63	O59(49/0/10)/3	—	-1.0
1886	StL N	**126**	453	73	108	22	6	2	48	57	—	82	.238	.324	.327	105	7	24	.883	-4	82	51	O126L,P2	—	0.0
1887	Ind N	122	465	104	104	18	15	4	28	71	4	68	.224	.331	.353	93	-2	48	.891	7	114	45	O122(122/1/1)/S	—	0.1
1888	Ind N	133	500	87	110	20	10	5	50	64	6	73	.220	.316	.330	104	5	80	.939	9	87	126	O133L/S	—	1.1
1889	Ind N	127	526	123	165	26	12	8	59	67	10	59	.314	.401	.454	135	26	19	.909	2	83	88	O127L	—	2.2
1890	Bro P	104	394	78	88	12	7	1	50	70	5	36	.223	.348	.297	69	-17	44	.894	6	105	71	O104L	—	-1.1
1891	Cin AA	97	372	77	106	15	10	4	36	81	8	52	.285	.423	.411	128	17	19	.898	1	98	77	O97(17/1/80)	—	1.4
1892	Lou N	42	154	18	31	6	1	0	15	24	0	19	.201	.309	.253	76	-3	6	.962	4	149	72	O42R	—	-0.1
Total	9	916	3547	695	893	152	68	27	300	471	33	426	.252	.345	.356	103	15	240	.896	31	100	75	O914(778/2/138),3b3,C3,S2,P2	—	2.3

SEFCIK, KEVIN Kevin John; B2.10.1971 Tinley Park IL; BR/TR/5´10˝/(175–182); [PhiN93 33/916]; d9.8; Col St. Xavier

YEAR	TM LG	G	AB	R	H	2B	3B	HR	RBI	BB-IB	HP	SO	AVG	OBP	SLG	AOPS	ABR	SB-CS	FA	FR	RNG	THR	GAMES AT POSITION	DL	BFW
1995	Phi N	5	4	1	0	0	0	0	0	0-0	0	2	.000	.000	.000	-99	-1	0-0	1.000	0	86	1057	3b2	0	-0.1
1996	Phi N	44	116	10	33	5	3	0	9	9-3	2	16	.284	.341	.379	91	-2	3-0	.986	-2	109	101	S21,3b20/2	0	-0.2
1997	Phi N	61	119	11	32	3	0	2	6	4-0	1	9	.269	.298	.345	69	-6	1-2	.961	-4	97	59	2b22,S10,3b4	0	-0.9
1998	Phi N	104	169	27	53	7	2	3	20	25-0	7	32	.314	.421	.432	125	8	4-2	.989	1	114	39	O60(35/8/20),3b2/2	0	0.8
1999	Phi N	111	209	28	58	15	3	1	11	29-0	1	24	.278	.368	.392	91	-2	9-4	.986	-4	90	46	O64(31/19/17),2b15	0	-0.5
2000	Phi N	99	153	15	36	6	2	0	10	13-0	2	19	.235	.300	.301	54	-11	4-2	1.000	1	116	0	O50(25/20/9)/D	0	-1.0
2001	Col N	1	1	0	0	0	0	0	0	0-0	0	0	.000	.000	.000	-83	0	0-0	ø	0	—	—	/H	0	0.0
Total	7	425	771	92	212	36	10	6	56	80-3	13	102	.275	.351	.371	87	-14	21-10	.991	-7	106	30	O174(91/47/46),2b39,S31,3b28/D	0	-1.9

SEGRIST, KAL Kal Hill; B4.14.1931 Greenville TX; BR/TR/6´0˝/180; d7.16; Col Texas

YEAR	TM LG	G	AB	R	H	2B	3B	HR	RBI	BB-IB	HP	SO	AVG	OBP	SLG	AOPS	ABR	SB-CS	FA	FR	RNG	THR	GAMES AT POSITION	DL	BFW
1952	NY A	13	23	3	1	0	0	0	1	3	0	1	.043	.154	.043	-46	-5	0-0	.971	0	107	115	2b11/3	0	-0.4
1955	Bal A	7	9	1	3	0	0	0	0	2-0	0	0	.333	.455	.333	123	0	0-0	1.000	0	162	0	3b3/12	0	0.1
Total	2	20	32	4	4	0	0	0	1	5-0	0	1	.125	.243	.125	4	-5	0-0	.971	1	109	111	2b12,3b4/1	0	-0.3

SEGUI, DAVID David Vincent; B7.19.1966 Kansas City KS; BB/TL/6´1˝/(170–220); [BalA87 18/455]; d5.8; f–Diego; Col Louisiana Tech

YEAR	TM LG	G	AB	R	H	2B	3B	HR	RBI	BB-IB	HP	SO	AVG	OBP	SLG	AOPS	ABR	SB-CS	FA	FR	RNG	THR	GAMES AT POSITION	DL	BFW
1990	Bal A	40	123	14	30	7	0	2	15	11-2	1	15	.244	.311	.350	87	-2	0-0	.990	0	105	85	1b36,D4	0	-0.5
1991	Bal A	86	212	15	59	7	0	2	22	12-2	0	19	.278	.316	.340	85	-5	1-1	.996	1	125	104	1b42,O33(28/0/5),D4	0	-0.6
1992	Bal A	115	189	21	44	9	0	1	17	20-3	0	23	.233	.306	.296	67	-8	1-0	.998	1	104	117	1b95,O18(3/0/15)	0	-1.1
1993	Bal A	146	450	54	123	27	0	10	60	58-4	0	53	.273	.351	.400	98	0	2-1	.996	4	109	111	1b144/D	0	-0.7
1994	NY N	92	336	46	81	17	1	10	43	33-6	1	43	.241	.308	.387	81	-10	0-0	**.996**	-4	95	**115**	1b78,O21(19/0/2)	15	-2.0
1995	NY N	33	73	9	24	3	1	2	11	12-1	1	9	.329	.420	.479	144	5	1-3	1.000	-2	57	224	O18L,1b7	0	0.2
	Mon N	97	383	59	117	22	3	10	57	28-4	2	38	.305	.355	.457	108	4	1-4	.997	3	109	92	1b97,O2L	0	-0.2
	Year	130	456	68	141	25	4	12	68	40-5	3	47	.309	.367	.461	115	10	2-7	.997	2	107	93	1b104,O20L	0	0.0
1996	Mon N	115	416	69	119	30	1	11	58	60-4	0	54	.286	.375	.442	112	10	4-4	.993	7	**119**	94	1b113	43	0.6
1997	Mon N	125	459	75	141	22	3	21	68	57-12	1	66	.307	.380	.505	132	22	1-0	.995	-1	96	111	1b125	17	1.0
1998	Sea A	143	522	79	159	36	1	19	84	49-4	0	80	.305	.359	.487	118	14	3-1	**.999**	17	**145**	98	1b134/lf	0	1.9
1999	Sea A	90	345	43	101	22	3	9	39	32-4	1	43	.293	.352	.452	105	3	1-2	.996	6	130	102	1b90	0	0.0
	Tor A	31	95	14	30	5	0	5	13	8-0	0	17	.316	.365	.526	123	3	0-0	.955	-0	111	108	D25,1b4	25	0.1
	Year	121	440	57	131	27	3	14	52	40-4	1	60	.298	.355	.468	109	6	1-2	.995	6	129	102	1b94,D25	0	0.1
2000	Tex A	93	351	52	118	29	1	11	57	34-1	0	51	.336	.391	.519	127	15	0-1	1.000	2	121	99	D52,1b38	0	1.0
	Cle A	57	223	41	74	13	0	8	46	19-1	1	33	.332	.384	.498	118	6	0-0	1.000	4	148	68	1b35,D16,O7R	0	0.5
	Year	150	574	93	192	42	1	19	103	53-2	1	84	.334	.388	.510	123	22	0-1	1.000	6	134	84	1b73,D68,O7R	0	1.5
2001	Bal A	82	292	48	88	18	1	10	46	49-5	4	61	.301	.406	.473	139	19	1-1	.983	-6	74	93	1b65,D16	41	0.7
2002	Bal A	26	95	10	25	4	0	2	16	11-0	0	22	.263	.336	.368	93	-1	0-0	1.000	0	110	225	D19,1b7	135	-0.2
2003	Bal A	67	224	26	59	10	1	5	25	26-2	1	47	.263	.341	.384	92	-2	1-0	1.000	1	130	121	D53,1b8	86	-0.5
2004	Bal A	18	59	8	20	3	0	1	7	5-1	1	13	.339	.400	.441	120	2	0-1	1.000	-1	0	55	D15,1b2	154	0.0
Total	15	1456	4847	683	1412	284	16	139	684	524-56	14	687	.291	.359	.443	110	75	17-19	.995	34	113	102	1b1120,D205,O100(71/0/29)	516	0.2

YEAR	TM LG	G	AB	R	H	2B	3B	HR	RBI	BB-IB	HP	SO	AVG	OBP	SLG	AOPS	ABR	SB-CS	FA	FR	RNG	THR	GAMES AT POSITION	DL	BFW
SEGUIGNOL, FERNANDO	Fernando Alfredo; B1.19.1975 Bocas Del Toro, Pan; BB/TR/6´5˝/(190–230); d9.5																								
1998	Mon N	16	42	6	11	4	0	2	3	3-0	0	15	.262	.304	.500	112	1	0-0	1.000	3	189	0	O9(8/0/1),1b7	0	0.2
1999	Mon N	35	105	14	27	9	0	5	10	5-1	7	33	.257	.328	.486	108	1	0-0	.989	-2	79	121	1b23,O8(6/0/3)	58	-0.3
2000	Mon N	76	162	22	45	8	0	10	22	9-0	3	46	.278	.326	.512	107	1	0-1	.987	-3	87	103	1b30,O30(17/0/14)/D	0	-0.5
2001	Mon N	46	50	0	7	2	0	0	5	2-1	1	17	.140	.185	.180	-4	-8	0-0	1.000	1	100	356	O13(7/0/7),1b7	0	-0.7
2003	NY A	5	7	0	1	0	0	0	0	1-0	0	3	.143	.250	.143	8	-1	0-0	1.000	1	290	0	1b3/D	0	0.0
Total	5	178	366	42	91	23	0	17	40	20-2	11	114	.249	.303	.451	91	-6	0-1	.986	-1	101	106	1b70,O60(38/0/25),D2	58	-1.3
SEIBERT, KURT	Kurt Elliott; B10.16.1955 Cheverly MD; BB/TR/6´0˝/190; [ChiN76 3/55]; d9.3; Col Clemson																								
1979	Chi N	7	2	2	0	0	0	0	0	0-0	0	1	.000	.000	.000	-91	-1	0-0	1.000	0	0	0	/2	0	-0.1
SEIBOLD, SOCKS	Harry; B5.31.1896 Philadelphia PA; D9.21.1965 Philadelphia PA; BR/TR/5´8.5˝/162; d9.18; Mil 1918; ▲																								
1915	Phi A	10	26	3	3	1	0	0	2	4	0	4	.115	.233	.154	16	-3	0	.714	-4	94	33	S7	—	-0.6
1916	Phi A	5	12	0	2	1	0	0	1	0	0	4	.167	.167	.250	26	-1	0	1.000	1	160	0	P3/cf	—	0.1
1917	Phi A	36	59	6	13	1	1	0	5	4	1	8	.220	.281	.271	70	-2	1	.978	-1	89	111	P33,O2L	—	-0.1
1919	Phi A	15	13	1	2	0	0	0	1	0	0	4	.154	.154	.154	-13	-1	0	.941	0	90	159	P14	—	0.0
1929	Bos N	33	70	6	20	2	0	0	9	6	0	6	.286	.342	.314	67	5	0	**1.000**	-1	87	107	P33	—	0.0
1930	Bos N	36	90	6	19	2	0	1	5	6	0	6	.211	.260	.267	29	0	0	.941	-3	75	88	P36	—	0.0
1931	Bos N	33	70	3	9	0	0	0	2	1	0	9	.129	.141	.129	-28	-4	0	**1.000**	-0	102	183	P33	—	0.0
1932	Bos N	28	46	2	7	0	0	0	2	2	0	0	.152	.188	.152	-8	-2	0	1.000	2	123	235	P28	—	0.0
1933	Bos N	11	9	0	1	0	0	0	0	2	0	2	.111	.273	.111	14	0	0	1.000	0	123	0	P11	—	0.0
Total	9	207	395	27	76	7	1	1	27	25	1	43	.192	.242	.223	25	-8	1	.982	-5	95	131	P191,S7,O3(2/1/0)	—	-0.6
SEILHEIMER, RICKY	Ricky Allen; B8.30.1960 Brenham TX; BL/TR/5´11˝/185; [ChiA79 1/19]; d7.5																								
1980	Chi A	21	52	4	11	3	1	1	3	4-1	0	15	.212	.268	.365	72	-2	1-0	.946	-8	40	71	C21	0	-0.9
SEITZER, KEVIN	Kevin Lee; B3.26.1962 Springfield IL; BR/TR/5´11˝/(180–195); [KCA83 11/283]; d9.3; Col Eastern Illinois; OF(14/1/1)																								
1986	KC A	28	96	16	31	4	1	2	11	19-0	1	14	.323	.440	.448	139	7	0-0	.987	1	102	94	1b22,O5L,3b3	0	0.5
1987	KC A★	161	641	105	**207**	33	8	15	83	80-0	2	85	.323	.399	.470	126	26	12-7	.947	10	105	120	3b141,1b25,O3L/D	0	3.2
1988	KC A	149	559	90	170	32	5	5	60	72-4	6	64	.304	.387	.406	121	20	10-8	.938	4	104	135	3b147/lfD	0	2.3
1989	KC A	160	597	78	168	17	2	4	48	102-7	5	76	.281	.387	.337	107	12	17-8	.950	-3	95	111	3b159,S6,O3(2/1/0),1b2	0	1.0
1990	KC A	158	622	91	171	31	5	6	38	67-2	2	66	.275	.346	.370	102	3	7-5	.953	7	101	113	3b152,2b10	0	1.0
1991	KC A	85	234	28	62	11	3	1	25	29-3	2	21	.265	.350	.350	94	-1	4-1	.940	6	115	69	3b68,D3	34	0.6
1992	Mil A	148	540	74	146	35	1	5	71	57-4	2	44	.270	.337	.367	100	2	13-11	**.969**	-5	100	81	3b146,2b2/1	0	-0.4
1993	Oak A	73	255	24	65	10	2	4	27	27-1	1	33	.255	.324	.357	89	-4	4-7	.933	-6	85	71	3b46,1b24,O3L,2b2/PDS	0	-1.3
	Mil A	47	162	21	47	6	0	7	30	17-0	1	15	.290	.359	.457	119	4	3-0	.942	-1	100	124	3b33,1b7/2rfD	0	0.3
	Year	120	417	45	112	16	2	11	57	44-1	2	48	.269	.338	.396	101	0	7-7	.937	-7	91	93	3b79,1b31,D6,O4(3/0/1),2b3/PS	0	-1.0
1994	Mil A	80	309	44	97	24	2	5	49	30-1	2	38	.314	.375	.453	108	4	2-1	.924	-1	99	95	3b43,1b35,D4	35	0.1
1995	Mil A★	132	492	56	153	33	3	5	69	64-2	6	57	.311	.395	.421	107	8	2-0	.968	4	114	128	3b88,1b36,D14	0	0.9
1996	Mil A	132	490	74	155	25	3	12	62	73-6	4	68	.316	.406	.453	113	13	6-1	.996	2	118	102	1b65,D56,3b12	0	0.7
	†Cle A	22	83	11	32	10	0	1	16	14-1	1	11	.386	.480	.542	158	9	0-0	1.000	2	252	24	D17,1b5	0	0.9
	Year	154	573	85	187	35	3	13	78	87-7	5	79	.326	.416	.466	119	21	6-1	.990	4	128	96	D73,1b70,3b12	0	1.6
1997	†Cle A	64	198	27	53	14	0	2	24	18-0	0	25	.268	.326	.369	79	-6	0-0	1.000	1	112	118	D24,1b19,3b13	0	-0.7
Total	12	1439	5278	739	1557	285	35	74	613	669-31	35	617	.295	.375	.404	110	97	80-49	.949	21	102	107	3b1051,1b241,D126,O16L,2b15,S7/P	69	9.1
SELBACH, KIP	Albert Karl; B3.24.1872 Columbus OH; D2.17.1956 Columbus OH; BR/TR/5´7˝/190; d4.24																								
1894	Was N	97	372	69	114	21	17	7	71	51	0	20	.306	.390	.511	119	11	21	.915	-6	62	59	O80(45/2/33),S19	—	0.0
1895	Was N	130	519	116	168	22	**22**	6	55	71	1	28	.324	.406	.486	131	24	31	.913	16	119	88	O119(118/0/1),S6,2b5	—	2.4
1896	Was N	127	487	100	148	17	13	5	100	76	7	28	.304	.405	.423	118	16	49	.946	8	74	61	O126(124/0/2)	—	1.1
1897	Was N	124	486	113	152	25	16	5	59	80	4	—	.313	.414	.461	131	25	46	.955	12	79	55	O124L	—	2.2
1898	Was N	132	515	88	156	28	11	3	60	64	3	—	.303	.383	.417	130	22	25	.948	20	130	123	O131(127/4/0)/S	—	2.8
1899	Cin N	141	525	105	156	28	11	3	87	70	6	—	.297	.386	.410	116	14	38	.953	11	116	166	O141(101/40/0)	—	1.2
1900	NY N	**141**	523	98	176	29	12	4	68	72	8	—	.337	.425	.461	151	41	36	.951	12	132	**141**	O141L	—	3.7
1901	NY N	125	502	89	145	29	6	1	56	45	2	—	.289	.350	.376	115	11	8	.942	-9	70	46	O125L	—	-0.4
1902	Bal A	128	503	86	161	27	9	3	60	58	2	—	.320	.393	.427	122	17	22	.941	10	105	79	O127L	—	1.9
1903	Was A	**140**	533	68	134	23	12	3	49	41	0	—	.251	.305	.356	96	-3	20	.956	-1	66	49	O140(120/0/20)/3	—	-1.2
1904	Was A	48	178	15	49	8	4	0	14	24	0	—	.275	.361	.365	132	8	9	.931	1	86	57	O48L	—	0.7
	Bos A	98	376	50	97	19	8	0	30	48	3	—	.258	.347	.351	114	8	10	.961	1	72	81	O98L	—	0.4
	Year	146	554	65	146	27	12	0	44	72	3	—	.264	.351	.356	120	16	19	.950	2	77	73	O146L	—	1.1
1905	Bos A	121	418	54	103	16	6	4	47	67	3	—	.246	.355	.342	120	13	12	.928	-6	60	35	O112(0/20/92)	—	0.2
1906	Bos A	60	228	15	48	9	2	0	23	18	3	—	.211	.277	.268	71	-7	7	.966	0	79	122	O58L	—	-1.1
Total	13	1612	6165	1066	1807	301	149	44	779	785	42	76	.293	.377	.412	121	200	334	.944	72	92	85	O1570(1356/66/148),S26,2b5/3	—	13.9
SELBY, BILL	William Frank; B6.11.1970 Monroeville AL; BL/TR/5´9˝/(190–195); [BosA92 13/366]; d4.19; Col Southern Mississippi																								
1996	Bos A	40	95	12	26	4	0	3	6	9-1	0	11	.274	.337	.411	86	-2	1-1	.980	-6	80	56	2b14,3b14,O6L	0	-0.7
2000	Cle A	30	46	8	11	1	0	0	4	1-0	1	9	.239	.271	.261	34	-5	0-0	1.000	-1	119	0	O10(4/0/6),2b6,3b4,D6	0	-0.5
2001	Cin N	36	92	7	21	7	1	2	12	5-1	1	13	.228	.273	.391	66	-5	0-0	1.000	-2	99	114	2b21,3b8,1b2	0	-0.6
2002	Cle A	65	159	15	34	7	2	6	21	15-2	0	27	.214	.278	.396	76	-6	0-1	.933	-2	95	59	3b33,O18(13/0/5),2b6	0	-0.8
2003	Cle A	27	39	3	4	1	0	0	5	3-0	0	11	.103	.163	.128	-21	-7	0-0	.926	3	159	197	3b10/12lfD	0	-0.4
Total	5	198	431	45	96	20	3	11	48	33-4	2	71	.223	.279	.360	63	-25	1-2	.917	-7	96	87	3b69,2b48,O35(24/0/11),D8,1b3	0	-3.0
SELF, TODD	Todd Douglas; B11.9.1978 Shreveport LA; BL/TR/6´5˝/215; [HouN00 15/457]; d5.12; Col Louisiana–Monroe																								
2005	Hou N	21	45	7	9	2	0	1	4	3-0	0	9	.200	.250	.311	45	-4	0-0	1.000	0	118	0	O15(5/0/10)	0	-0.4
SELKIRK, GEORGE	George Alexander "Twinkletoes"; B1.4.1908 Huntsville ON, Can.; D1.19.1987 Ft.Lauderdale FL; BL/TR/6´1˝/182; d8.12; Mil 1943–45																								
1934	NY A	46	176	23	55	7	1	5	38	15	1	17	.313	.370	.449	118	4	1-1	.989	1	105	86	O46(43/0/7)	—	0.3
1935	NY A	128	491	64	153	29	12	11	94	44	3	36	.312	.372	.487	128	18	2-7	.975	5	114	88	O127R	—	1.3
1936	†NY A★	137	493	93	152	28	9	18	107	94	1	60	.308	.420	.511	133	29	13-7	.974	2	106	80	O135(18/0/118)	—	2.0
1937	†NY A	78	256	49	84	13	5	18	68	34	2	24	.328	.411	.629	157	22	8-2	.987	4	104	138	O69R	—	2.0
1938	†NY A	99	335	58	85	12	5	10	62	68	3	52	.254	.384	.409	99	1	9-4	.973	-3	91	104	O95L	—	-0.6
1939	†NY A★	128	418	103	128	17	4	21	101	103	8	49	.306	.452	.517	149	38	12-5	**.989**	-4	98	47	O124(86/0/38)	—	2.6
1940	NY A	118	379	68	102	17	5	19	71	84	3	43	.269	.406	.491	137	24	3-6	.962	-0	95	111	O111(79/2/31)	—	1.5
1941	†NY A	70	164	30	36	5	0	6	25	28	2	30	.220	.340	.360	86	-3	1-0	.967	0	99	107	O47(19/0/28)	0	-0.5
1942	†NY A	42	78	15	15	3	0	0	10	16	0	8	.192	.330	.231	60	-3	0-0	1.000	-0	109	0	O19R	0	-0.5
Total	9	846	2790	503	810	131	41	108	576	486	23	319	.290	.400	.483	128	130	49-32	.977	4	102	89	O773(340/2/437)	0	8.1
SELLERS, RUBE	Oliver; B3.7.1881 Duquesne PA; D1.14.1952 Pittsburgh PA; BR/TR/5´10˝/180; d8.12																								
1910	Bos N	12	32	3	5	0	0	0	2	6	0	5	.156	.289	.156	29	-3	1	1.000	-1	86	0	O9(8/0/1)	—	-0.4
SELLMAN, FRANK	Charles Francis (aka Frank C. Williams 1871-75); B1852 Baltimore MD; D5.6.1907 Baltimore MD; d5.4; ▲																								
1871	Kek NA	14	65	14	15	3	0	1	10	4	—	0	.231	.275	.323	70	-2	1-0	.711	-2	38	157	3b14,C5,S2	—	-0.3
1872	Oly NA	**9**	42	3	10	2	0	0	1	0	—	1	.238	.238	.286	64	-1	0-2	.788	-3	—	—	C7,3b2	—	-0.3
1873	Mar NA	1	3	1	1	0	0	0	0	0	—	0	.333	.333	.333	127	0	0-0	.000	-0	0	0	/P	—	0.0
1874	Bal NA	12	54	9	16	3	2	0	7	0	—	2	.296	.296	.426	130	2	2-0	.304	-15	—	—	C6,S6,2b2,3b2,O2(0/1/1)	—	-1.0
1875	Was NA	1	3	0	1	0	0	0	0	0	—	0	.333	.333	.333	137	0	0-0	1.000	0	0	0	/1	—	0.0
Total	5NA	37	167	27	43	8	2	1	18	4	—	3	.257	.275	.347	88	-1	3-2	.657	-20	—	—	C18,3b18,S8,O2(0/1/1),2b2/1P	—	-1.6
SELPH, CAREY	Carey Isom; B12.5.1901 Donaldson AR; D2.24.1976 Houston TX; BR/TR/5´9.5˝/175; d5.25; Col Ouachita Baptist																								
1929	StL N	25	51	8	12	1	1	0	7	6	0	4	.235	.316	.294	52	-4	1	.981	-3	85	47	2b16	—	-0.6
1932	Chi A	116	396	50	112	19	8	0	51	31	4	9	.283	.341	.371	90	-6	7-6	.910	-4	91	109	3b71,2b26	—	-0.7
Total	2	141	447	58	124	20	9	0	58	37	4	13	.277	.338	.362	85	-10	8-6	.910	-7	91	109	3b71,2b42	—	-1.3
SEMBER, MIKE	Michael David; B2.24.1953 Hammond IN; BR/TR/6´0˝/(183–185); [ChiN74 2/31]; d8.18; Col Tulsa																								
1977	Chi N	3	4	0	1	0	0	0	0	0-0	0	2	.250	.250	.250	31	0	0-0	1.000	0	84	209	/2	0	0.0
1978	Chi N	9	3	2	1	0	0	0	0	1-0	0	1	.333	.500	.333	122	0	0-0	.667	-0	86	0	3b7/S	0	0.0
Total	2	12	7	2	2	0	0	0	0	1-0	0	3	.286	.375	.286	75	0	0-0	.667	-0	86	0	3b7/S2	0	0.0

YEAR	TM LG	G	AB	R	H	2B	3B	HR	RBI	BB-IB	HP	SO	AVG	OBP	SLG	AOPS	ABR	SB-CS	FA	FR	RNG	THR	GAMES AT POSITION	DL	BFW
Seminick, Andy	Andrew Wasal; B9.12.1920 Pierce WV; D2.22.2004 Melbourne FL; BR/TR/5´11˝/(187–198); d9.14; C5																								
1943	Phi N	22	72	9	13	2	0	2	5	7	0	22	.181	.253	.292	60	-4	0	.930	-0	96	113	C22/lf	0	-0.3
1944	Phi N	22	63	9	14	2	1	0	4	6	1	17	.222	.300	.286	68	-3	2	.963	1	118	114	C11,O7L	0	-0.2
1945	Phi N	80	188	18	45	7	2	6	26	18	2	38	.239	.313	.394	98	-1	3	.979	-4	69	121	C70,3b4/lf	0	-0.2
1946	Phi N	124	406	55	107	15	5	12	52	39	4	86	.264	.334	.414	115	6	2	.974	-3	93	93	C118	0	1.0
1947	Phi N	111	337	48	85	16	2	13	50	58	5	69	.252	.370	.427	115	9	4	.978	1	72	**120**	C107	0	1.6
1948	Phi N	125	391	49	88	11	3	13	44	58	2	68	.225	.328	.368	90	-6	4	.965	-2	63	153	C124	0	0.0
1949	Phi N★	109	334	52	81	11	2	24	68	69	5	74	.243	.380	.503	138	20	0	.975	3	86	**120**	C98	0	2.7
1950	†Phi N	130	393	55	113	15	3	24	68	68	6	50	.288	.400	.524	143	27	0	.976	4	104	80	C124	0	3.6
1951	Phi N	101	291	42	66	8	1	11	37	63	3	67	.227	.370	.375	102	3	1-0	.979	-1	109	92	C91	0	0.8
1952	Cin N	108	336	38	86	16	1	14	50	35	2	65	.256	.330	.435	111	4	1-3	.973	-3	92	103	C99	0	0.6
1953	Cin N	119	387	46	91	12	0	19	64	49	1	82	.235	.323	.413	90	-6	2-2	.982	-3	130	67	C112	0	-0.4
1954	Cin N	86	247	25	58	9	4	7	30	48	2	39	.235	.362	.389	93	-1	0-0	.989	4	**172**	115	C82	0	0.7
1955	Cin N	6	15	1	2	0	0	1	1	0-0	0	3	.133	.133	.333	18	-2	0-0	1.000	1	128	0	C5	0	-0.1
	Phi N	93	289	32	71	12	1	11	34	32-2	6	59	.246	.333	.408	97	-1	1-2	.994	11	112	79	C88	0	1.4
	Year	99	304	33	73	12	1	12	35	32-2	6	62	.240	.325	.405	93	-3	1-2	**.994**	12	113	75	C93	0	1.3
1956	Phi N	60	161	16	32	3	1	7	23	31-7	1	38	.199	.332	.360	88	-2	3-0	.976	-8	72	109	C54	0	-0.7
1957	Phi N	8	11	0	1	0	0	0	0	1-0	0	3	.091	.167	.091	-29	-2	0-0	1.000	0	112	0	C8	0	-0.2
Total	15	1304	3921	495	953	139	26	164	556	582-9	40	780	.243	.347	.417	107	41	23-7	.977	2	98	103	C1213,O9L,3b4	0	10.3
Senerchia, Sonny	Emanuel Robert; B4.6.1931 Newark NJ; D11.1.2003 Freehold NJ; BR/TR/6´1˝/195; d8.22; Col Montclair St.																								
1952	Pit N	29	100	5	22	5	0	3	11	4	0	21	.220	.250	.360	66	-5	0-3	.953	-5	70	72	3b28	0	-1.1
Sensenderfer, Count	John Phillips Jenkins; B12.28.1847 Philadelphia PA; D5.3.1903 Philadelphia PA; 5´9˝/170; d5.20																								
1871	Ath NA	25	127	38	41	5	2	0	23	0	—	1	.323	.323	.394	106	1	5-3	.814	-2	68	196	O25C	—	-0.1
1872	Ath NA	1	5	2	2	0	0	0	1	0	—	0	.400	.400	.400	146	0	0-1	ø	0	0	0	/rf	—	0.0
1873	Ath NA	20	86	12	24	1	0	0	8	0	—	2	.279	.279	.291	64	-4	0-2	.827	-0	38	0	O19C/1	—	-0.4
1874	Ath NA	5	16	3	3	0	0	0	2	0	—	0	.188	.188	.188	19	-2	0-0	.625	-1	0	0	O5(0/1/4)	—	-0.2
Total	4NA	51	234	55	70	6	2	0	34	0	—	3	.299	.299	.342	85	-5	5-6	.807	-3	51	103	O50(0/45/5)/1	—	-0.7
Sentell, Paul	Leopold Theodore; B8.27.1879 New Orleans LA; D4.27.1923 Cincinnati OH; BR/TR/5´9˝/176; d4.12; U2																								
1906	Phi N	63	192	19	44	5	1	1	14	14	3	—	.229	.292	.281	79	-5	15	.887	-9	99	26	3b33,2b19,O2R/S	—	-1.5
1907	Phi N	3	3	0	0	0	0	0	0	1	0	—	.000	.250	.000	-22	0	0	1.000	-1	57	0	S2/rf	—	-0.1
Total	2	66	195	19	44	5	1	1	14	15	3	—	.226	.291	.277	77	-5	15	.887	-10	99	26	3b33,2b19,S3,O3R	—	-1.6
Sepkowski, Ted	Theodore Walter (b Theodore Walter Sczepkowski); B11.9.1923 Baltimore MD; D3.8.2002 Severna Park MD; BL/TR/5´11˝/190; d9.9; Mil 1944–45																								
1942	Cle A	5	10	0	1	0	0	0	0	0	0	3	.100	.100	.100	-46	-2	0-0	.824	-1	113	0	2b2	0	-0.3
1946	Cle A	2	8	2	4	1	0	0	1	0	0	0	.500	.500	.625	228	1	0-0	.833	-1	49	225	3b2	0	0.1
1947	Cle A	10	8	0	1	1	0	0	0	1	0	1	.125	.222	.250	32	-1	0-0	ø	-0	0	0	/rf	0	-0.1
	NY A	2	0	1	0	0	0	0	0	0	0	0	ø	ø	ø	ø	0	0-1	ø	0	—	—	/R	0	0.0
	Year	12	8	1	1	1	0	0	0	1	0	1	.125	.222	.250	32	-1	0-1	ø	-0	0	0	/rf	0	-0.1
Total	3	19	26	3	6	2	0	0	1	1	0	4	.231	.259	.308	61	-2	0-1	.833	-1	49	225	3b2,2b2/rf	0	-0.3
Serena, Bill	William Robert; B10.2.1924 Alameda CA; D4.17.1996 Hayward CA; BR/TR/5´9.5˝/(175–185); d9.16																								
1949	Chi N	12	37	3	8	3	0	1	7	7	0	9	.216	.341	.378	95	0	0	.923	-3	76	0	3b11	0	-0.3
1950	Chi N	127	435	56	104	20	4	17	61	65	1	75	.239	.339	.421	100	0	1	.945	-3	102	86	3b125	0	-0.4
1951	Chi N	13	39	8	13	3	1	1	4	11	1	4	.333	.490	.538	173	5	0-2	.941	-2	75	37	3b12	40	0.2
1952	Chi N	122	390	49	107	21	5	15	61	39	3	83	.274	.345	.469	122	11	1-0	.971	-5	90	53	3b58,2b49	0	1.0
1953	Chi N	93	275	30	69	10	5	10	52	41	1	46	.251	.350	.433	100	0	0-0	.983	-11	88	68	2b49,3b28	0	-0.7
1954	Chi N	41	63	8	10	0	1	4	13	14	1	18	.159	.316	.381	81	-2	0-0	.933	-2	107	0	3b12,2b2	0	-0.4
Total	6	408	1239	154	311	57	16	48	198	177	7	235	.251	.348	.439	108	14	2-2	.951	-25	96	73	3b246,2b100	40	-0.6
Serna, Paul	Paul David; B11.16.1958 El Centro CA; BR/TR/5´8˝/170; d9.1; Col Azusa Pacific																								
1981	Sea A	30	94	11	24	2	0	4	9	3-0	2	11	.255	.293	.404	95	-1	2-3	.954	-3	105	45	S23,2b7	0	-0.2
1982	Sea A	65	169	15	38	3	0	3	8	4-0	1	13	.225	.246	.296	47	-13	0-5	.936	-3	101	100	S31,2b18,3b15,D2	0	-1.5
Total	2	95	263	26	62	5	0	7	17	7-0	3	24	.236	.263	.335	63	-14	2-8	.945	-6	103	73	S54,2b25,3b15,D2	0	-1.7
Servais, Scott	Scott Daniel; B6.4.1967 LaCrosse WI; BR/TR/6´2˝/(195–210); [HouN88 3/64]; d7.12; Col Creighton																								
1991	Hou N	16	37	0	6	3	0	0	6	4-0	0	8	.162	.244	.243	39	-3	0-0	.988	1	180	91	C14	34	-0.1
1992	Hou N	77	205	12	49	9	0	0	15	11-2	5	25	.239	.294	.283	67	-9	0-0	.995	-0	97	67	C73	0	-0.6
1993	Hou N	85	258	24	63	11	0	11	32	22-2	5	45	.244	.313	.415	97	-2	0-0	.996	4	100	71	C82	0	0.7
1994	Hou N	78	251	27	49	15	1	9	41	10-0	4	44	.195	.235	.371	58	-17	0-0	.996	-2	92	61	C78	0	-1.4
1995	Hou N	28	89	7	20	10	0	1	12	9-2	1	15	.225	.300	.371	82	-2	0-1	.977	-1	73	71	C28	0	-0.1
	Chi N	52	175	31	50	12	0	12	35	23-6	2	37	.286	.371	.560	143	11	2-1	.981	-0	85	120	C52	24	1.4
	Year	80	264	38	70	22	0	13	47	32-8	3	52	.265	.348	.496	123	9	2-2	.980	-1	81	103	C80	0	1.3
1996	Chi N	129	445	42	118	20	0	11	63	30-1	14	75	.265	.327	.384	85	-9	0-2	.988	1	99	102	C128/1	0	-0.1
1997	Chi N	122	385	36	100	21	0	6	45	24-7	6	56	.260	.311	.361	73	-15	0-1	.990	0	92	117	C118/1D	0	-0.7
1998	†Chi N	113	325	35	72	15	1	7	36	26-6	5	51	.222	.289	.338	62	-18	1-0	.994	-8	92	94	C110/1	0	-2.0
1999	SF N	69	198	21	54	10	0	5	21	13-2	3	31	.273	.327	.399	88	-4	0-0	.992	-4	88	75	C62/1	22	-0.5
2000	Col N	33	101	6	22	4	0	1	13	7-2	1	16	.218	.273	.287	34	-10	0-1	.987	6	80	102	C32	57	-0.2
	SF N	7	8	1	2	0	0	0	0	2-1	0	1	.250	.400	.250	74	0	0-0	1.000	0	0	0	C6	0	0.0
	Year	40	109	7	24	4	0	1	13	9-3	1	17	.220	.283	.284	38	-10	0-1	.988	7	74	94	C38	0	-0.2
2001	Hou N	11	16	1	6	0	0	0	0	2-0	0	3	.375	.444	.375	107	0	0-0	1.000	2	212	0	C9	20	0.2
Total	11	820	2493	243	611	130	2	63	319	183-31	46	407	.245	.306	.375	79	-78	3-6	.991	-1	94	90	C792,1b4,D2	157	-3.4
Sessi, Walter	Walter Anthony "Watsie"; B7.23.1918 Finleyville PA; D4.18.1998 Mobile AL; BL/TL/6´3˝/225; d9.18; Mil 1942–45																								
1941	StL N	5	13	2	0	0	0	0	0	1	0	2	.000	.071	.000	-74	-3	0	.750	-1	65	0	O3R	0	-0.4
1946	StL N	15	14	2	2	0	0	1	2	1	0	4	.143	.200	.357	54	-1	0	ø	0	—	—	/H	0	-0.1
Total	2	20	27	4	2	0	0	1	2	2	0	6	.074	.138	.185	-9	-4	0	.750	-1	65	0	O3R	0	-0.5
Sevcik, John	John Joseph; B7.11.1942 Oak Park IL; BR/TR/6´2˝/205; d4.24; Col Missouri																								
1965	Min A	12	16	1	1	1	0	0	0	1-0	0	5	.063	.118	.125	-30	-3	0-0	1.000	2	29	218	C11	0	-0.1
Severeid, Hank	Henry Levai; B6.1.1891 Story City IA; D12.17.1968 San Antonio TX; BR/TR/6´0˝/175; d5.15; Mil 1918																								
1911	Cin N	37	56	5	17	6	1	0	10	3	1	6	.304	.350	.446	127	2	0	.913	-1	129	79	C22	—	0.2
1912	Cin N	50	114	10	27	0	3	0	13	8	0	11	.237	.287	.289	60	-7	0	.943	-6	88	63	C20,1b7,O6(5/1/0)	—	-1.1
1913	Cin N	8	6	0	0	0	0	0	0	1	0	1	.000	.143	.000	-58	-1	0	1.000	-0	56	0	C2/lf	—	-0.2
1915	StL A	80	203	12	45	6	1	1	22	16	0	25	.222	.279	.276	69	-8	2-1	.966	-7	87	91	C64	—	-1.1
1916	StL A	100	293	23	80	8	2	0	34	26	4	17	.273	.341	.314	102	1	3	.976	-15	80	85	C89/13	—	-0.8
1917	StL A	143	501	45	133	23	4	1	57	28	1	20	.265	.306	.333	99	-3	6	.966	-20	81	100	C139/1	—	-1.2
1918	StL A	51	133	8	34	4	0	0	11	18	3	4	.256	.357	.286	97	1	4	.946	-6	80	95	C42	—	-0.2
1919	StL A	112	351	16	87	12	2	0	36	21	4	13	.248	.298	.293	65	-17	2	.983	-2	96	85	C103	—	-1.0
1920	StL A	123	422	46	117	14	5	2	49	33	4	11	.277	.336	.348	79	-13	5-3	.983	-1	95	98	C117	—	-0.3
1921	StL A	143	472	66	153	23	7	2	78	42	0	9	.324	.379	.415	97	-2	7-2	.972	-1	106	97	C126	—	0.6
1922	StL A	137	517	49	166	32	7	3	78	28	0	12	.321	.356	.427	100	-1	1-4	.984	9	119	120	C133	—	1.6
1923	StL A	122	432	50	133	27	6	3	51	31	1	11	.308	.356	.419	98	-2	3-0	**.993**	8	99	98	C116	—	1.4
1924	StL A	137	432	37	133	23	2	4	48	36	1	15	.308	.362	.398	90	-6	1-6	**.989**	-3	93	118	C130	—	-0.2
1925	StL A	34	109	15	40	9	0	1	21	11	0	2	.367	.425	.477	122	4	0-2	.993	-1	85	109	C31	—	0.4
	†Was A	50	110	11	39	8	1	0	14	13	0	6	.355	.423	.445	123	5	0-0	.986	3	114	63	C35	—	0.8
	Year	84	219	26	79	17	1	1	35	24	0	8	.361	.424	.461	123	9	0-2	.990	2	99	87	C66	—	1.2
1926	Was A	22	34	2	7	1	0	0	4	3	0	2	.206	.270	.235	34	-3	0-0	.977	-0	104	96	C16	—	-0.3
	†NY A	41	127	13	34	8	1	0	13	13	0	4	.268	.336	.346	79	-4	1-1	.988	-2	82	96	C40	—	-0.3
	Year	63	161	15	41	9	1	0	17	16	0	6	.255	.322	.323	70	-7	1-1	.985	-2	86	96	C56	—	-0.6
Total	15	1390	4312	408	1245	204	42	17	539	331	19	169	.289	.342	.367	91	-54	35-19	.978	-43	96	99	C1225,1b9,O7(6/1/0)/3	—	-1.7

THE BATTER REGISTER

SEVERSON, RICH Richard Allen; B1.18.1945 Artesia CA; BR/TR/6´0˝/(160–170); d4.10

YEAR	TM LG	G	AB	R	H	2B	3B	HR	RBI	BB-IB	HP	SO	AVG	OBP	SLG	AOPS	ABR	SB-CS	FA	FR	RNG	THR	GAMES AT POSITION	DL	BFW
1970	KC A	77	240	22	60	11	1	1	22	16-2	1	33	.250	.300	.317	70	-10	0-0	.962	0	107	120	S50,2b25	0	-0.3
1971	KC A	16	30	4	9	0	2	0	1	3-0	0	5	.300	.364	.433	126	1	0-0	1.000	4	154	225	2b6,S6/3	0	0.5
Total	2	93	270	26	69	11	3	1	23	19-2	1	38	.256	.307	.330	76	-9	0-0	.958	4	108	124	S56,2b31/3	0	0.2

SEWARD, GEORGE George T.; B St.Louis MO; D3.28.1904 St.Louis MO; 5´7.5˝/145; d5.19

YEAR	TM LG	G	AB	R	H	2B	3B	HR	RBI	BB-IB	HP	SO	AVG	OBP	SLG	AOPS	ABR	SB-CS	FA	FR	RNG	THR	GAMES AT POSITION	DL	BFW
1875	StL NA	25	96	12	24	2	0	0	8	1	—	1	.250	.258	.271	92	0	1-0	.817	-2	—	—	C18,O7(3/1/3),2b2	—	-0.2
1876	NY N	1	3	0	0	0	0	0	0	0	—	0	.000	.000	.000	-99	-1	—	1.000	0	118	0	/2	—	0.0
1882	StL AA	38	144	23	31	1	1	0	—	12	—	—	.215	.276	.236	71	-4	—	.776	0	150	118	O35(6/2/27),C5	—	-0.4
Total	2	39	147	23	31	1	1	0	0	12	—	0	.211	.270	.231	68	-5	—	.817	0	—	—	O35(6/2/27),C5/2	—	-0.4

SEWELL, LUKE James Luther; B1.5.1901 Titus AL; D5.14.1987 Akron OH; BR/TR/5´9˝/160; d6.30; M10/C4; b–Joe b–Tommy; Col Alabama

YEAR	TM LG	G	AB	R	H	2B	3B	HR	RBI	BB-IB	HP	SO	AVG	OBP	SLG	AOPS	ABR	SB-CS	FA	FR	RNG	THR	GAMES AT POSITION	DL	BFW
1921	Cle A	3	6	0	0	0	0	0	1	0	0	3	.000	.000	.000	-99	-2	0-0	1.000	1	112	109	C3	—	-0.1
1922	Cle A	41	87	14	23	5	0	0	10	5	1	8	.264	.312	.322	65	-4	1-1	.963	-2	88	63	C39	—	-0.5
1923	Cle A	10	10	2	2	0	1	0	1	1	0	0	.200	.273	.400	76	-1	0-0	.833	0	145	173	C7	—	0.0
1924	Cle A	63	165	27	48	9	1	0	17	22	4	13	.291	.387	.358	92	-1	1-0	.959	1	103	87	C57	—	0.4
1925	Cle A	74	220	30	51	10	2	0	18	33	2	18	.232	.337	.295	61	-12	6-2	.971	4	135	90	C66,O2L	—	-0.3
1926	Cle A	126	433	41	103	16	4	0	46	36	4	27	.238	.302	.293	55	-29	9-3	.983	9	**173**	63	C125	—	-1.0
1927	Cle A	128	470	52	138	27	6	0	53	20	4	23	.294	.328	.377	82	-14	4-8	.963	3	**117**	**146**	C126	—	-0.4
1928	Cle A	122	411	52	111	16	9	3	52	26	3	27	.270	.318	.375	81	-13	4-4	.972	8	106	**124**	C118	—	0.3
1929	Cle A	124	406	41	96	16	3	1	39	29	0	26	.236	.287	.298	49	-31	6-6	.966	2	92	**111**	C124	—	-2.1
1930	Cle A	76	292	40	75	21	2	1	43	14	1	9	.257	.293	.353	61	-18	5-2	.974	-4	86	91	C76	—	-1.4
1931	Cle A	108	375	45	103	30	4	1	53	36	2	17	.275	.341	.384	86	-7	1-1	.980	-6	103	108	C104	—	-0.7
1932	Cle A	87	300	36	76	20	2	2	52	38	0	24	.253	.337	.353	74	-11	4-5	.978	3	125	85	C84	—	-0.3
1933	†Was A	141	474	65	125	30	4	2	61	48	3	24	.264	.335	.357	84	-10	7-2	.990	1	**181**	61	C141	—	0.0
1934	Was A	72	207	21	49	7	3	2	21	22	1	10	.237	.313	.329	68	-10	0-1	.994	0	150	121	C50,O7(2/0/5),1b6/23	—	-0.8
1935	Chi A	118	421	52	120	19	3	2	67	32	0	18	.285	.336	.359	78	-14	3-2	.988	7	85	99	C112	—	0.0
1936	Chi A	128	451	59	113	20	5	5	73	54	1	16	.251	.332	.350	66	-25	11-2	.984	13	122	113	C126	—	-0.2
1937	Chi A☆	122	412	51	111	21	6	1	61	46	0	18	.269	.343	.357	77	-15	4-5	.985	9	118	93	C118	—	0.1
1938	Chi A	65	211	23	45	4	1	0	27	20	1	20	.213	.284	.242	32	-23	0-0	.985	8	118	130	C65	—	-1.0
1939	Cle A	16	20	1	3	1	0	0	1	3	0	1	.150	.261	.200	20	-2	0-0	.966	-1	90	126	C15/1	—	-0.2
1942	StL A	6	12	1	1	0	0	0	0	1	0	5	.083	.154	.083	-32	-2	0-0	.944	0	84	170	C6,M	0	-0.2
Total	20	1630	5383	653	1393	272	56	20	696	486	27	307	.259	.323	.341	70	-244	66-44	.978	56	121	100	C1562,O9(4/0/5),1b7/32	0	-8.4

SEWELL, JOE Joseph Wheeler; B10.9.1898 Titus AL; D3.6.1990 Mobile AL; BL/TR/5´6.5˝/155; d9.10; C2; HF1977; b–Luke b–Tommy; Col Alabama

YEAR	TM LG	G	AB	R	H	2B	3B	HR	RBI	BB-IB	HP	SO	AVG	OBP	SLG	AOPS	ABR	SB-CS	FA	FR	RNG	THR	GAMES AT POSITION	DL	BFW
1920	†Cle A	22	70	14	23	4	1	0	12	9	1	4	.329	.412	.414	116	2	1-0	.884	1	106	144	S22	—	0.4
1921	Cle A	**154**	572	101	182	36	12	4	93	80	11	17	.318	.412	.444	116	18	7-6	.944	-2	99	107	S154	—	3.0
1922	Cle A	153	558	80	167	28	7	2	83	73	6	20	.299	.386	.385	101	4	10-12	.939	9	102	96	S139,2b12	—	2.6
1923	Cle A	**153**	553	98	195	41	10	3	109	98	7	12	.353	.456	.479	147	45	9-6	.930	5	106	104	S151	—	6.2
1924	Cle A	**153**	594	99	188	**45**	5	4	106	67	2	13	.316	.388	.429	109	10	3-3	.960	**22**	**110**	95	S153	—	4.5
1925	Cle A	**155**	608	78	204	37	7	1	98	64	4	4	.336	.402	.424	109	11	7-6	**.967**	**16**	**111**	85	S153,2b3	—	3.9
1926	Cle A	**154**	578	91	187	41	5	4	85	65	8	6	.324	.399	.433	116	16	17-7	.955	1	101	110	S154	—	3.4
1927	Cle A	**153**	569	83	180	48	5	1	92	51	9	7	.316	.382	.424	108	9	3-16	**.962**	5	100	88	S153	—	2.4
1928	Cle A	**155**	588	79	190	40	2	4	70	58	7	9	.323	.391	.418	111	13	7-1	**.963**	26	109	**119**	S137,3b19	—	5.3
1929	Cle A	**152**	578	90	182	38	3	7	73	48	5	4	.315	.372	.427	102	3	6-6	.975	14	**115**	92	3b152	—	2.4
1930	Cle A	109	353	44	102	17	6	0	48	41	7	3	.289	.374	.371	86	-6	1-4	.950	0	109	92	3b97	—	-0.1
1931	NY A	130	484	102	146	22	1	6	64	61	9	8	.302	.390	.388	111	12	1-1	.952	-6	92	66	3b121/2	—	0.9
1932	†NY A	125	503	95	137	21	3	11	68	56	3	3	.272	.349	.392	96	-2	0-2	.974	1	93	76	3b123	—	0.2
1933	NY A	135	524	87	143	18	1	2	54	71	1	4	.273	.361	.323	87	-6	2-2	.964	4	95	**120**	3b131	—	0.1
Total	14	1903	7132	1141	2226	436	68	49	1055	842	80	114	.312	.391	.413	109	129	74-72	.951	94	105	101	S1216,3b643,2b16	—	35.2

SEWELL, TOMMY Thomas Wesley; B4.16.1906 Titus AL; D7.30.1956 Montgomery AL; BL/TR/5´7.5˝/155; d6.21; b–Luke b–Joe; Col Alabama

YEAR	TM LG	G	AB	R	H	2B	3B	HR	RBI	BB-IB	HP	SO	AVG	OBP	SLG	AOPS	ABR	SB-CS	FA	FR	RNG	THR	GAMES AT POSITION	DL	BFW
1927	Chi N	1	1	0	0	0	0	0	0	0	0	0	.000	.000	.000	-99	0	0	ø	0	—	—	/H	—	0.0

SEXSON, RICHIE Richmond Lockwood; B12.29.1974 Portland OR; BR/TR/6´7˝/(206–235); [CleA93 24/671]; d9.14

YEAR	TM LG	G	AB	R	H	2B	3B	HR	RBI	BB-IB	HP	SO	AVG	OBP	SLG	AOPS	ABR	SB-CS	FA	FR	RNG	THR	GAMES AT POSITION	DL	BFW
1997	Cle A	5	11	1	3	0	0	0	0	0-0	0	2	.273	.273	.273	41	-1	0-0	1.000	-0	74	0	1b2/D	0	-0.1
1998	†Cle A	49	174	28	54	14	1	11	35	6-0	3	42	.310	.344	.592	132	8	1-1	.984	2	126	102	1b45,O3L,D2	0	0.6
1999	†Cle A	134	479	72	122	17	7	31	116	34-0	4	117	.255	.305	.514	100	-4	3-3	.988	3	146	96	1b61,O49(48/0/3),D24	0	-0.9
2000	Cle A	91	324	45	83	16	1	16	44	25-0	4	96	.256	.315	.460	90	-6	1-0	1.000	-0	76	99	O58L,1b27,D10	0	-1.0
	Mil N	57	213	44	63	14	0	14	47	34-2	3	63	.296	.398	.559	140	14	1-0	.991	9	164	102	1b57	0	1.7
2001	Mil N	158	598	94	162	24	3	45	125	60-5	6	178	.271	.342	.547	128	22	2-4	.995	9	121	95	1b158	0	1.5
2002	Mil N★	157	570	86	159	37	2	29	102	70-7	8	136	.279	.363	.504	127	23	0-0	.995	10	125	99	1b154/D	0	1.9
2003	Mil N★	**162**	606	97	165	28	2	45	124	98-7	9	151	.272	.379	.548	139	36	2-3	.993	9	124	89	1b162	0	3.0
2004	Ari N	23	90	20	21	4	0	9	23	14-0	0	21	.233	.337	.578	122	3	0-0	.996	5	185	91	1b23	156	0.6
2005	Sea A	156	558	99	147	36	1	39	121	89-4	6	167	.263	.369	.541	149	42	1-1	.995	10	126	94	1b151,D5	0	3.6
2006	Sea A	158	591	75	156	40	0	34	107	64-5	4	154	.264	.338	.504	122	19	1-1	.997	11	**130**	86	1b150,D8	0	1.6
Total	10	1150	4214	661	1135	230	17	273	844	494-30	47	1127	.269	.350	.526	125	156	12-13	.994	68	131	92	1b990,O110(109/0/3),D51	156	12.5

SEXTON, CHRIS Christopher Philip; B8.3.1971 Cincinnati OH; BR/TR/5´11˝/(178–180); [CinN93 10/288]; d5.3; Col Miami–Ohio

YEAR	TM LG	G	AB	R	H	2B	3B	HR	RBI	BB-IB	HP	SO	AVG	OBP	SLG	AOPS	ABR	SB-CS	FA	FR	RNG	THR	GAMES AT POSITION	DL	BFW
1999	Col N	35	59	9	14	0	1	1	7	11-1	0	10	.237	.357	.322	59	-4	4-2	1.000	0	72	264	O13(3/9/1),2b10,S6	0	-0.3
2000	Cin N	35	100	9	21	4	0	0	10	13-1	2	12	.210	.310	.250	43	-8	4-2	.954	-5	97	72	S14,2b12,3b3	0	-1.1
Total	2	70	159	18	35	4	1	1	17	24-2	2	22	.220	.328	.277	50	-12	8-4	.976	-4	93	78	2b22,S20,O13(3/9/1),3b3	0	-1.4

SEXTON, JIMMY Jimmy Dale; B12.15.1951 Mobile AL; BR/TR/5´10˝/(160–175); d9.2

YEAR	TM LG	G	AB	R	H	2B	3B	HR	RBI	BB-IB	HP	SO	AVG	OBP	SLG	AOPS	ABR	SB-CS	FA	FR	RNG	THR	GAMES AT POSITION	DL	BFW
1977	Sea A	14	37	5	8	1	1	1	3	2-0	0	6	.216	.256	.378	71	-2	1-1	.929	2	124	147	S12	0	0.1
1978	Hou N	88	141	17	29	3	2	2	6	13-1	0	28	.206	.273	.298	63	-8	16-2	.981	-10	80	82	S58,3b8,2b3	0	-1.1
1979	Hou N	52	43	8	9	0	0	0	1	7-0	0	7	.209	.320	.209	50	-3	1-3	.943	0	107	159	S11,3b4,2b2	0	-0.3
1981	Oak A	7	3	3	0	0	0	0	0	0-0	0	2	.000	.000	.000	-99	-1	2-0	1.000	1	344	0	/3D	0	0.0
1982	Oak A	69	139	19	34	4	0	2	14	9-0	1	24	.245	.289	.317	70	-6	16-0	.957	-10	86	68	S47,3b8,D5	0	-0.9
1983	StL N	6	9	1	1	0	0	0	0	1-1	0	4	.111	.200	.222	17	-1	0-0	1.000	1	143	205	S4,3b2	0	0.1
Total	6	236	372	53	81	9	3	5	24	32-2	1	71	.218	.279	.298	63	-21	36-6	.962	-16	90	91	S132,3b23,D6,2b5	0	-2.1

SEXTON, TOM Thomas William; B3.14.1865 Rock Island IL; D2.8.1934 Rock Island IL; BL; d9.27

YEAR	TM LG	G	AB	R	H	2B	3B	HR	RBI	BB-IB	HP	SO	AVG	OBP	SLG	AOPS	ABR	SB-CS	FA	FR	RNG	THR	GAMES AT POSITION	DL	BFW
1884	Mil U	**12**	47	9	11	2	0	0	—	4	—	—	.234	.294	.277	136	2	—	.853	-1	61	91	S12	—	0.1

SEYBOLD, SOCKS Ralph Orlando; B11.23.1870 Washingtonville OH; D12.22.1921 Greensburg PA; BR/TR/5´11˝/175; d8.20

YEAR	TM LG	G	AB	R	H	2B	3B	HR	RBI	BB-IB	HP	SO	AVG	OBP	SLG	AOPS	ABR	SB-CS	FA	FR	RNG	THR	GAMES AT POSITION	DL	BFW
1899	Cin N	22	85	13	19	5	1	0	8	6	1	—	.224	.283	.306	60	-5	2	.917	1	120	0	O22(3/0/19)	—	-0.5
1901	Phi A	114	449	74	150	24	14	8	90	40	7	—	.334	.397	.503	142	25	15	.954	-5	79	68	O100(2/25/74),1b14	—	1.4
1902	Phi A	**137**	522	91	165	27	12	**16**	97	43	6	—	.316	.375	.506	137	24	6	.963	-1	61	81	O136(0/16/120)	—	1.6
1903	Phi A	**137**	522	76	156	**45**	8	8	84	38	6	—	.299	.353	.462	137	24	5	.964	-1	70	126	O120(0/1/119),1b18	—	1.8
1904	Phi A	143	510	56	149	26	9	3	64	42	4	—	.292	.351	.396	129	18	12	.975	2	87	145	O129R,1b13	—	1.6
1905	†Phi A	133	492	64	135	37	4	6	59	42	8	—	.274	.341	.402	133	20	5	.983	8	87	153	O133R	—	2.4
1906	Phi A	116	411	41	130	23	2	5	59	30	3	—	.316	.367	.418	141	20	9	.925	-3	73	102	O114R	—	1.3
1907	Phi A	147	564	58	153	29	4	5	92	40	4	—	.271	.324	.363	116	10	10	.973	0	100	171	O147R	—	0.5
1908	Phi A	48	130	5	28	2	0	0	3	12	1	—	.215	.287	.231	64	-5	2	.921	-1	96	0	O34R	—	-0.8
Total	9	997	3685	478	1085	218	54	51	556	293	40	—	.294	.353	.424	129	131	66	.961	-1	82	117	O935(5/42/889),1b45	—	9.3

SEYMOUR, CY James Bentley; B12.9.1872 Albany NY; D9.20.1919 New York NY; BL/TL/6´0˝/200; d4.22; OF(20/1094/224); ▲

YEAR	TM LG	G	AB	R	H	2B	3B	HR	RBI	BB-IB	HP	SO	AVG	OBP	SLG	AOPS	ABR	SB-CS	FA	FR	RNG	THR	GAMES AT POSITION	DL	BFW
1896	NY N	12	32	2	7	0	0	0	0	0	0	7	.219	.219	.219	16	-4	0	.857	1	109	164	P11/cf	—	0.0
1897	NY N	45	141	13	34	5	1	2	14	4	0	—	.241	.262	.333	58	-9	3	.853	7	**158**	241	P39,O6(2/4/0)	—	0.2
1898	NY N	80	297	41	82	5	2	4	23	9	1	—	.276	.300	.347	88	-6	8	.887	6	127	233	P45,O35(10/12/15)/2	—	-0.3
1899	NY N	50	159	25	52	3	2	2	27	4	0	—	.327	.344	.409	110	1	2	.839	2	130	43	P32,O8(2/1/5),1b3/3	—	0.0
1900	NY N	23	40	9	12	0	0	0	2	3	0	—	.300	.349	.300	84	-1	0	.828	-0	150	0	P13,O3(1/1/2)/1	—	-0.1
1901	Bal A	**134**	547	84	166	19	8	1	77	28	0	—	.303	.337	.373	93	-7	38	.945	14	135	99	O133(4/0/131)/1	—	0.1
1902	Bal A	72	280	38	75	8	8	3	41	18	2	—	.268	.317	.386	90	-5	12	.956	2	99	94	O72(0/3/70)	—	-0.6

YEAR	TM LG	G	AB	R	H	2B	3B	HR	RBI	BB-IB	HP	SO	AVG	OBP	SLG	AOPS	ABR	SB-CS	FA	FR	RNG	THR	GAMES AT POSITION	DL	BFW
	Cin N	62	244	27	83	8	2	2	37	12	3	—	.340	.378	.414	132	9	8	.920	2	118	137	O61C/P3	—	0.8
1903	Cin N	135	558	85	191	25	15	7	72	33	3	—	.342	.382	.478	130	19	25	.902	3	76	46	O135C	—	1.5
1904	Cin N	131	531	71	166	26	13	5	58	29	3	—	.313	.352	.439	132	18	11	.951	9	121	88	O130C	—	2.1
1905	Cin N	149	581	95	**219**	**40**	**21**	8	**121**	51	2	—	**.377**	.429	**.559**	**175**	**52**	21	.947	10	128	**237**	O149C	—	5.6
1906	Cin N	79	307	35	79	7	2	4	38	24	3	—	.257	.317	.332	98	-1	9	.968	7	97	118	O79C	—	0.2
	NY N	72	269	35	86	12	3	4	42	18	1	—	.320	.365	.431	145	13	20	.978	-2	81	150	O72C	—	0.9
	Year	151	576	70	165	19	5	8	80	42	4	—	.286	.339	.378	120	12	29	.972	5	90	133	O151C	—	1.1
1907	NY N	131	473	46	139	25	8	3	75	36	5	—	.294	.350	.400	131	16	21	.975	-0	4	59	O126C	—	1.1
1908	NY N	156	587	60	157	23	2	5	92	30	3	—	.267	.306	.339	101	0	18	.949	5	145	**208**	O155C	—	-0.3
1909	NY N	80	280	37	87	12	5	1	30	25	1	—	.311	.369	.400	137	12	14	.968	-1	107	138	O74(1/71/1)	—	0.8
1910	NY N	79	287	32	76	9	4	1	40	23	2	18	.265	.324	.334	92	-4	10	.936	-7	84	93	O76C	—	-1.5
1913	Bos N	39	73	2	13	2	0	0	10	7	1	7	.178	.259	.205	33	-6	2-1	.950	1	95	189	O18C	—	-0.6
Total	16	1529	5686	737	1724	229	96	52	799	354	30	32	.303	.347	.405	117	97	222-1	.945	58	102	126	O1333C,P141,1b5,3b2/2	—	9.9
SHABALA, ADAM	Adam Jason; B2.6.1978 Streator IL; BL/TR/6´1˝/190; [SFN00 10/301]; d6.16; Col Nebraska																								
2005	SF N	6	15	1	3	0	0	0	4	1-0	0	5	.200	.235	.200	20	-2	0-0	.875	-0	107	0	O5(4/0/1)	0	-0.2
SHAFER, TILLIE	Arthur Joseph; B3.22.1889 Los Angeles CA; D1.10.1962 Los Angeles CA; BB/TR/5´10˝/165; d4.24; Col Santa Clara																								
1909	NY N	38	84	11	15	2	1	0	7	14	0	—	.179	.296	.226	61	-3	6	.750	-3	91	82	3b16,2b13,O2(0/1/1)	—	-0.6
1910	NY N	29	21	5	4	1	0	0	1	0	0	6	.190	.190	.238	25	-2	0	.889	2	183	478	3b8,2b2,S2	—	0.0
1912	†NY N	78	163	48	47	4	1	0	23	30	3	19	.288	.408	.325	99	2	22	.879	-5	81	81	S31,3b16,2b15	—	0.0
1913	†NY N	138	508	74	146	17	12	5	52	61	5	55	.287	.369	.398	118	13	32-29	.923	-10	89	118	3b79,2b25,S16,O15(4/12/0)	—	0.4
Total	4	283	776	138	212	24	14	5	83	105	8	80	.273	.366	.360	106	10	60-29	.903	-14	95	110	3b119,2b55,S49,O17(4/13/1)	—	-0.2
SHAFER, ORATOR	George W.; B10.1851 Philadelphia PA; D1.21.1922 Philadelphia PA; BL/TR/5´9˝/165; d5.23; b–Taylor																								
1874	Har NA	9	35	6	8	0	0	1	3	0	—	4	.229	.229	.314	69	-1	0-0	.710	-2	0	0	O9(8/0/1)	—	-0.2
	Mut NA	1	5	1	1	0	0	0	0	0	—	0	.200	.200	.200	28	0	0-0	ø	0	0	0	/rf	—	0.0
	Year	10	40	7	9	0	0	1	3	0	—	4	.225	.225	.300	64	-2	0-0	.710	-2	0	0	O10(8/0/2)	—	-0.2
1875	Phi NA	19	70	10	17	2	1	0	6	0	—	4	.243	.243	.300	84	-1	2-0	.769	-2	55	307	O12(3/8/1),3b5,1b2	—	-0.2
1877	Lou N	**61**	260	38	74	9	5	3	34	9	—	17	.285	.309	.392	101	-1	—	.835	13	179	56	O60(0/1/60)/1	—	1.0
1878	Ind N	**63**	266	48	90	19	6	0	30	13	—	20	.338	.369	.455	**196**	**29**	—	.842	8	172	80	O63(1/0/63)	—	**3.3**
1879	Chi N	73	316	53	96	13	0	0	35	6	—	28	.304	.317	.345	111	3	—	.801	19	**304**	169	O72R/3	—	2.0
1880	Cle N	83	338	62	90	14	9	0	21	17	—	36	.266	.301	.361	126	9	—	.901	15	180	156	O83R	—	2.3
1881	Cle N	**85**	343	48	88	13	6	1	34	23	—	20	.257	.303	.338	107	4	—	.880	-0	105	124	O85R	—	0.3
1882	Cle N	**84**	313	37	67	14	2	3	28	27	—	27	.214	.276	.300	88	-2	—	.805	-10	90	52	O84(2/1/83)	—	-1.2
1883	Buf N	95	401	67	117	11	3	0	41	27	—	39	.292	.336	.334	103	1	—	.861	16	186	87	O95R	—	1.5
1884	StL U	106	467	130	168	**40**	10	2	—	30	—	—	.360	.398	.501	165	25	—	.870	-3	99	95	O100(6/0/96),2b7/1	—	1.9
1885	StL N	69	257	30	50	11	2	0	18	19	—	31	.195	.250	.253	67	-8	—	.918	10	213	0	O69(0/1/68)	—	0.1
	Phi AA	2	9	1	2	0	1	0	1	1	0	—	.222	.300	.444	125	0	—	1.000	-0	0	0	O2C	—	0.0
1886	Phi AA	21	82	15	22	3	3	0	8	8	0	—	.268	.333	.378	121	2	3	.815	0	114	286	O21(0/18/4)	—	0.1
1890	Phi AA	100	390	55	110	15	5	1	58	47	5	—	.282	.367	.354	113	8	29	**.958**	2	102	137	O98R,1b3	—	0.7
Total	2NA	29	110	17	26	2	1	1	9	0	—	8	.236	.236	.300	76	-2	2-0	.737	-4	29	161	O22(11/8/3),3b5,1b2	—	-0.4
Total	11	842	3442	584	974	162	52	10	308	227	5	218	.283	.328	.369	119	70	32	.865	70	157	103	O832(9/23/807),2b7,1b5/3	—	12.0
SHAFER, RALPH	Ralph Newton; B3.17.1894 Cincinnati OH; D2.5.1950 Akron OH; 5´11˝/?; d7.25; Col Cincinnati																								
1914	Pit N	1	0	0	0	0	0	0	0	0	0	0	ø	ø	ø	ø	0	0	ø	0	—	—	/H	—	0.0
SHAFER, TAYLOR	Zachary Taylor; B7.13.1866 Philadelphia PA; D10.27.1945 Glendale CA; BL/5´7˝/155; d4.24; b–Orator																								
1884	Alt U	19	74	11	21	2	0	0	—	3	—	—	.284	.312	.311	88	-3	—	.889	-2	54	0	O17(9/7/1),C2/3	—	-0.5
	KC U	44	164	18	28	3	2	0	—	15	—	—	.171	.240	.213	44	-16	—	.768	-3	115	0	O41R,C2/2S3	—	-1.7
	Bal U	3	13	1	1	0	0	0	—	0	—	—	.077	.077	.077	-48	-3	—	.750	-0	148	0	O3(1/0/3)	—	-0.3
	Year	66	251	30	50	5	2	0	—	18	—	—	.199	.253	.235	53	-22	—	.796	-6	101	0	O61(10/7/45),C4,3b2/2S	—	-2.5
1890	Phi AA	69	261	28	45	3	4	0	21	28	2	—	.172	.258	.215	40	-20	19	.921	-3	93	103	2b69	—	-1.8
Total	2	135	512	58	95	8	6	0	21	46	2	—	.186	.255	.225	46	-42	19	.920	-8	92	102	2b70,O61(10/7/45),C4,3b2/S	—	-4.3
SHAFFER	; d9.15																								
1875	Atl NA	1	4	0	0	0	0	0	0	0	—	0	.000	.000	.000	-99	-1	0-0	.500	-0	0	0	/rf	—	-0.1
SHAMSKY, ART	Arthur Louis; B10.14.1941 St.Louis MO; BL/TL/6´1˝/(168–180); d4.17; Col Missouri																								
1965	Cin N	64	96	13	25	4	3	2	10	10-0	0	29	.260	.330	.427	104	0	1-0	.966	2	120	251	O18(3/0/15)/1	0	0.1
1966	Cin N	96	234	41	54	5	0	21	47	32-1	0	45	.231	.321	.521	120	6	0-2	.973	-0	101	73	O74(42/0/33)	0	0.1
1967	Cin N	76	147	6	29	3	1	3	13	15-5	1	34	.197	.274	.293	56	-8	0-1	.984	1	111	97	O40(18/0/25)	0	-1.0
1968	NY N	116	345	30	82	14	4	12	48	21-6	7	58	.238	.292	.406	108	2	1-0	.993	3	111	129	O82(71/0/12),1b17	0	0.1
1969	†NY N	100	303	42	91	9	3	14	47	36-2	3	32	.300	.375	.488	138	16	1-2	.992	-4	96	41	O78(16/0/63),1b9	22	0.7
1970	NY N	122	403	48	118	19	2	11	49	49-13	3	33	.293	.371	.432	114	9	1-1	1.000	3	115	60	O58(4/0/54),1b56	0	0.5
1971	NY N	68	135	13	25	6	2	5	18	21-2	1	18	.185	.299	.370	89	-2	1-1	.984	5	112	320	O38(12/0/27)/1	27	0.1
1972	Chi N	15	16	1	2	0	0	0	1	3-0	0	3	.125	.263	.125	12	-2	0-0	1.000	-0	66	54	1b4	0	-0.2
	Oak A	8	7	0	0	0	0	0	0	1-0	0	2	.000	.125	.000	-64	-1	0-0	ø	0	—	—	/H	0	-0.2
Total	8	665	1686	194	426	60	15	68	233	188-29	15	254	.253	.330	.427	109	20	5-7	.987	9	107	108	O388(166/0/229),1b88	49	0.2
SHANABROOK, WARREN	Warren Hilton; B11.30.1880 Massillon OH; D3.10.1964 N.Canton OH; BR/TR/6´0˝/170; d8.13																								
1906	Was A	1	2	0	0	0	0	0	0	0	0	—	.000	.000	.000	-99	0	0	1.000	-0	88	0	/3	—	-0.1
SHANDLEY, JIM	James H.; B NY; D11.4.1904 Brooklyn NY; d5.3																								
1876	NY N	2	8	0	1	0	0	0	0	0	—	0	.125	.125	.125	-19	-1	—	.600	-1	0	0	O2(0/1/1)	—	-0.2
SHANER, WALLY	Walter Dedaker "Skinny"; B5.24.1900 Lynchburg VA; D11.13.1992 Las Vegas NV; BR/TR/6´2˝/195; d5.4; Col VPI																								
1923	Cle A	3	4	1	1	0	0	0	0	1	0	1	.250	.400	.250	74	0	0-0	1.000	-0	102	0	O2L/3	—	0.0
1926	Bos A	69	191	20	54	12	2	0	21	17	2	13	.283	.348	.366	89	-3	1-0	.965	-2	97	58	O48L	—	-0.9
1927	Bos A	122	406	54	111	33	6	3	49	21	1	35	.273	.311	.406	87	-10	11-4	.955	-1	94	121	O108(85/25/10)/1	—	-1.6
1929	Cin N	13	28	5	9	0	0	1	4	4	0	5	.321	.406	.429	112	1	1	1.000	-1	26	187	1b8,O2L	—	-0.1
Total	4	207	629	80	175	45	8	4	74	43	3	54	.278	.327	.394	89	-12	13-4	.959	-4	95	98	O160(137/25/10),1b9/3	—	-2.6
SHANKS, HOWIE	Howard Samuel "Hank"; B7.21.1890 Chicago IL; D7.30.1941 Monaca PA; BR/TR/5´11˝/170; d5.9; C5; OF(603/55/44)																								
1912	Was A	116	399	52	92	14	7	1	48	40	3	—	.231	.305	.308	75	-13	21	.962	-2	91	101	O114(112/0/2)	—	-2.1
1913	Was A	109	390	38	99	11	5	1	37	15	3	40	.254	.287	.315	75	-14	24	.978	2	104	89	O109L	—	-1.9
1914	Was A	143	500	44	112	22	10	4	64	29	2	51	.224	.269	.332	78	-16	18-16	.954	-2	102	74	O139(94/43/2)	—	-3.1
1915	Was A	141	492	52	123	19	8	0	47	30	3	42	.250	.297	.321	83	-12	12-14	.982	7	110	141	O80(75/1/4),3b49,2b10	—	-0.9
1916	Was A	140	471	51	119	15	7	1	48	41	3	34	.253	.317	.321	92	-5	23-12	.987	7	117	167	O88(72/3/13),3b31,S8,1b7	—	0.0
1917	Was A	126	430	45	87	15	5	0	28	33	6	37	.202	.269	.260	62	-20	15	.929	7	92	110	S90,O26(21/5/0),1b2	—	-0.9
1918	Was A	120	436	42	112	19	4	1	56	31	4	21	.257	.312	.326	94	-4	23	.957	-6	114	80	O64(54/2/8),2b48,3b3	—	-1.3
1919	Was A	135	491	33	122	8	7	1	54	25	3	48	.248	.289	.299	66	-24	13	.922	-16	88	70	S94,2b34,O6L	—	-3.6
1920	Was A	128	444	56	119	16	7	4	37	29	2	43	.268	.316	.363	82	-13	11-6	.951	-4	90	37	3b63,O35(32/0/3),1b14,2b5/S	—	-1.6
1921	Was A	**154**	562	81	170	24	**18**	7	69	57	3	38	.302	.370	.447	113	9	11-10	**.960**	3	96	**124**	3b154/2	—	1.9
1922	Was A	84	272	35	77	10	9	1	32	25	4	25	.283	.352	.397	100	-1	6-0	.920	5	106	151	3b54,O27(21/0/6)	—	0.6
1923	Bos A	131	464	38	118	19	5	3	57	19	1	37	.254	.285	.336	63	-27	6-6	.939	-11	99	103	3b83,2b38,O6(4/1/1)/S	—	-3.3
1924	Bos A	72	193	22	50	16	3	0	25	21	0	12	.259	.332	.373	81	-5	1-0	.972	6	96	114	S41,3b22,O4R,1b2,2b2	—	0.5
1925	NY A	66	155	15	40	3	1	1	18	20	0	15	.258	.343	.310	68	-7	1-0	.938	-4	70	51	3b26,2b21,O4(3/0/1)	—	-0.9
Total	14	1665	5699	604	1440	211	96	25	620	415	37	443	.253	.308	.337	82	-152	185-64	.971	-8	115	109	O702L,3b485,S235,2b159,1b25	—	-16.6
SHANLEY, DOC	Harry Root; B1890 Granbury TX; D12.13.1934 St.Petersburg FL; BR/TR/6´0˝/174; d9.15; Col Washington–St. Louis																								
1912	StL A	5	8	1	0	0	0	0	1	2	0	—	.000	.200	.000	-43	-1	0	.833	-1	43	130	S4	—	-0.3

THE BATTER REGISTER

YEAR	TM LG	G	AB	R	H	2B	3B	HR	RBI	BB-IB	HP	SO	AVG	OBP	SLG	AOPS	ABR	SB-CS	FA	FR	RNG	THR	GAMES AT POSITION	DL	BFW
Shannon, Dan	Daniel Webster; B3.23.1865 Bridgeport CT; D10.24.1913 Bridgeport CT; 5´9˝/175; d4.17; M2																								
1889	Lou AA	121	498	90	128	22	12	4	48	42	0	52	.257	.315	.373	97	-3	26	.910	5	**113**	90	2b121,M	—	0.5
1890	Phi P	19	75	15	18	5	1	1	16	4	0	12	.240	.278	.373	72	-4	4	.926	-3	96	48	2b19	—	-0.5
	NY P	83	324	59	70	7	8	3	44	25	1	34	.216	.274	.315	53	-25	21	.908	0	111	98	2b77,S6	—	-1.8
	Year	102	399	74	88	12	9	4	60	29	1	46	.221	.275	.326	56	-29	25	.911	-3	108	89	2b96,S6	—	-2.3
1891	Was AA	19	67	7	9	2	0	0	3	6	0	9	.134	.205	.164	6	-8	3	.878	1	101	114	S14,2b5,M	—	-0.6
Total	3	242	964	171	225	36	21	8	111	77	1	107	.233	.291	.339	73	-40	54	.911	2	110	88	2b222,S20	—	-2.4
Shannon, Frank	John Francis; B12.3.1873 San Francisco CA; D2.27.1934 Boston MA; 5´3˝/155; d10.1																								
1892	Was N	1	4	0	1	0	0	0	2	0	0	2	.250	.250	.250	53	0	0	.625	-1	52	0	/S	—	-0.1
1896	Lou N	31	115	14	18	1	1	1	15	13	1	15	.157	.248	.209	22	-13	3	.830	-12	79	52	S28,3b3	—	-2.1
Total	2	32	119	14	19	1	1	1	17	13	1	17	.160	.248	.210	23	-13	3	.820	-13	78	50	S29,3b3	—	-2.2
Shannon, Joe	Joseph Aloysius; B2.11.1897 Jersey City NJ; D7.28.1955 Jersey City NJ; BR/TR/5´11˝/170; d7.7; twb–Red; Col Seton Hall																								
1915	Bos N	5	10	3	2	0	0	0	1	0	0	3	.200	.200	.200	22	-1	0	.750	-1	68	0	O4(1/1/0)/2	—	-0.2
Shannon, Red	Maurice Joseph; B2.11.1897 Jersey City NJ; D4.12.1970 Jersey City NJ; BB/TR/5´11˝/170; d10.7; twb–Joe; Col Seton Hall																								
1915	Bos N	1	3	0	0	0	0	0	0	0	0	0	.000	.000	.000	-99	-1	0	.857	0	104	260	/2	—	-0.1
1917	Phi A	11	35	8	10	0	0	0	7	6	0	9	.286	.390	.286	108	1	2	.875	-1	103	43	S10	—	0.1
1918	Phi A	72	225	23	54	6	5	0	16	42	3	52	.240	.367	.311	103	3	5	.898	1	97	139	S45,2b26	—	0.8
1919	Phi A	39	155	14	42	7	2	0	14	12	2	28	.271	.331	.342	88	-2	4	.948	-2	106	60	2b37	—	-0.4
	Bos A	80	290	36	75	11	7	0	17	17	6	42	.259	.313	.345	90	-5	7	.973	-1	98	126	2b79	—	-0.5
	Year	119	445	50	117	18	9	0	31	29	8	70	.263	.320	.344	89	-7	11	.965	-3	101	105	2b116	—	-0.9
1920	Was A	62	222	30	64	8	7	0	30	22	0	32	.288	.352	.387	98	-1	2-5	.919	-13	83	118	S31,2b16,3b15	—	-1.3
	Phi A	25	88	4	15	1	1	0	3	4	0	12	.170	.207	.205	9	-12	1-1	.945	1	106	95	S24	—	-0.9
	Year	87	310	34	79	9	8	0	33	26	0	44	.255	.313	.335	73	-13	3-6	.931	-12	93	108	S55,2b16,3b15	—	-2.2
1921	Phi A	1	1	0	0	0	0	0	0	0	0	0	.000	.000	.000	-99	0	0-0	ø	0	—	—	/H	—	0.0
1926	Chi N	19	51	9	17	5	0	0	4	6	1	3	.333	.414	.431	126	2	0	.957	-1	100	77	S13	—	0.3
Total	7	310	1070	124	277	38	22	0	91	109	12	178	.259	.334	.336	89	-15	21-6	.957	-16	103	99	2b159,S123,3b15	—	-2.0
Shannon, Owen	Owen Dennis Ignatius; B12.22.1879 Omaha NE; D4.10.1918 Omaha NE; BR/TR; d9.6																								
1903	StL A	9	28	1	6	2	0	0	3	1	0	—	.214	.241	.286	59	-1	0	.957	-0	*133*	*63*	C8/1	—	-0.1
1907	Was A	4	7	0	1	0	0	0	0	0	0	—	.143	.143	.143	-10	-1	0	1.000	2	*134*	*235*	C4	—	0.1
Total	2	13	35	1	7	2	0	0	3	1	0	—	.200	.222	.257	47	-2	0	.970	1	*133*	*107*	C12/1	—	0.0
Shannon, Mike	Thomas Michael "Moonman"; B7.5.1939 St.Louis MO; BR/TR/6´3˝/(195–200); d9.11; Col Missouri																								
1962	StL N	10	15	3	2	0	0	0	0	1-0	0	3	.133	.188	.133	-11	-2	0-0	1.000	0	87	296	O7(5/0/2)	0	-0.2
1963	StL N	32	26	3	8	0	0	1	2	0-0	1	6	.308	.333	.423	106	0	0-1	.944	1	99	329	O26(13/1/12)	0	0.0
1964	†StL N	88	253	30	66	8	2	9	43	19-1	0	54	.261	.310	.415	95	-2	4-0	.983	-1	88	138	O88(9/6/76)	0	-0.8
1965	StL N	124	244	32	54	17	3	3	25	28-1	2	46	.221	.305	.352	78	-6	2-1	.994	9	132	108	O101(1/14/87),C4	0	-0.1
1966	StL N	137	459	61	132	20	6	16	64	37-0	0	106	.288	.339	.462	120	12	8-4	.985	5	109	114	O129(14/7/112)/C	0	1.0
1967	†StL N	130	482	53	118	18	3	12	77	37-6	4	89	.245	.302	.369	93	-5	2-4	.919	-13	93	92	3b122,O6(2/2/5)	0	-2.2
1968	†StL N	156	576	62	153	29	2	15	79	37-5	2	114	.266	.309	.401	114	9	1-2	.952	-13	95	92	3b156	0	-0.6
1969	StL N	150	551	51	140	15	5	12	55	49-7	1	87	.254	.315	.365	90	-9	1-4	.945	-18	86	88	3b149	0	-3.0
1970	StL N	55	174	18	37	9	2	0	22	16-4	0	20	.213	.275	.287	51	-12	1-1	.919	-19	61	42	3b51	82	-3.2
Total	9	882	2780	313	710	116	23	68	367	224-24	10	525	.255	.311	.387	96	-15	19-17	.938	-48	88	86	3b478,O357(44/30/294),C5	82	-9.1
Shannon, Wally	Walter Charles; B1.23.1933 Cleveland OH; D2.8.1992 Creve Coeur MO; BL/TR/6´0˝/(170–178); d7.9																								
1959	StL N	47	95	5	27	5	0	0	5	0-0	1	12	.284	.292	.337	63	-5	0-0	1.000	-5	55	107	S21,2b10	0	-0.9
1960	StL N	18	23	2	4	0	0	0	1	3-1	1	6	.174	.296	.174	30	-2	0-0	1.000	3	157	122	2b15/S	0	0.2
Total	2	65	118	7	31	5	0	0	6	3-1	2	18	.263	.293	.305	56	-7	0-0	.955	-2	123	79	2b25,S22	0	-0.7
Shannon, Spike	William Porter; B2.7.1878 Pittsburgh PA; D5.16.1940 Minneapolis MN; BB/TR/5´11˝/180; d4.15; U2; Col Grove City																								
1904	StL N	134	500	84	140	10	3	1	26	50	3	—	.280	.349	.318	111	9	34	**.978**	5	101	**203**	O133(13/3/117)	—	0.7
1905	StL N	140	544	73	146	16	3	0	41	47	0	—	.268	.327	.309	92	-4	27	**.984**	1	38	65	O140L	—	-1.2
1906	StL N	80	302	36	78	4	0	0	25	36	0	—	.258	.337	.272	94	-1	15	.972	4	84	113	O80L	—	-0.2
	NY N	76	287	42	73	5	1	0	25	34	4	—	.254	.342	.279	92	-1	18	.958	-5	44	96	O76L	—	-1.2
	Year	156	589	78	151	9	1	0	50	70	4	—	.256	.339	.275	93	-2	33	.966	-2	66	105	O156L	—	-1.4
1907	NY N	**155**	585	**104**	155	12	5	1	33	82	8	—	.265	.363	.308	107	9	33	.977	2	84	60	O155L	—	0.3
1908	NY N	77	268	34	60	2	1	1	21	28	7	—	.224	.314	.250	77	-6	13	.976	-3	84	146	O74(60/0/15)	—	-1.5
	Pit N	32	127	10	25	0	2	0	12	9	0	—	.197	.250	.228	53	-7	5	.947	-1	43	0	O32(8/20/7)	—	-1.1
	Year	109	395	44	85	2	3	1	33	37	7	—	.215	.294	.243	69	-13	18	.964	-4	71	98	O106(68/20/22)	—	-2.6
Total	5	694	2613	383	677	49	15	3	183	286	22	—	.259	.337	.293	96	-1	145	.974	2	72	106	O690(532/23/139)	—	-4.2
Shantz, Billy	Wilmer Ebert; B7.31.1927 Pottstown PA; D12.13.1993 Lauderhill FL; BR/TR/6´1˝/160; d4.13; b–Bobby																								
1954	Phi A	51	164	13	42	9	3	1	17	17	0	23	.256	.326	.366	89	-3	0-0	.975	-9	*83*	*106*	C51	0	-1.0
1955	KC A	79	217	18	56	4	1	1	12	11-1	0	14	.258	.293	.300	59	-13	0-0	.990	-7	*117*	*67*	C78	0	-1.7
1960	NY A	1	0	0	0	0	0	0	0	0-0	0	0	ø	ø	ø	ø	0	0-0	1.000	0	0	0	/C	0	0.0
Total	3	131	381	31	98	13	4	2	29	28-1	0	37	.257	.307	.328	72	-16	0-0	.984	-15	*103*	*83*	C130	0	-2.7
Sharman, Ralph	Ralph Edward "Bally"; B4.11.1895 Cleveland OH; D5.24.1918 Camp Sheridan AL; BR/TR/5´11˝/176; d9.10																								
1917	Phi A	13	37	2	11	2	1	0	2	3	1	2	.297	.366	.405	137	2	1	.941	-2	72	68	O10(2/3/5)	—	-0.1
Sharon, Dick	Richard Louis; B4.15.1950 San Mateo CA; BR/TR/6´2˝/(185–195); [PitN68 1/9]; d5.13																								
1973	Det A	91	178	20	43	9	0	7	16	10-0	0	31	.242	.280	.410	87	-4	2-0	.970	4	115	137	O91(19/7/71)	0	-0.2
1974	Det A	60	129	12	28	4	0	2	10	14-0	0	29	.217	.292	.295	67	-5	4-4	.989	1	103	109	O56(23/14/19)	0	-0.7
1975	SD N	91	160	14	31	7	0	4	20	26-0	0	35	.194	.306	.313	77	-5	0-2	.948	-2	102	32	O57(39/12/7)	0	-1.0
Total	3	242	467	46	102	20	0	13	46	50-0	0	95	.218	.293	.345	79	-14	6-6	.969	3	108	97	O204(81/33/97)	0	-1.9
Sharp, Bill	William Howard; B1.18.1950 Lima OH; BL/TL/5´10˝/178; [ChiA71 2/25]; d5.26; Col Ohio St.																								
1973	Chi A	77	196	23	54	8	3	4	22	19-2	3	28	.276	.345	.408	109	2	2-3	.981	5	101	238	O70(11/59/0)/D	0	0.5
1974	Chi A	100	320	45	81	13	2	4	24	25-2	2	37	.253	.309	.344	86	-6	0-3	.986	1	110	43	O99(13/7/85)	0	-1.1
1975	Chi A	18	35	1	7	0	0	0	4	2-0	0	3	.200	.243	.200	26	-3	0-0	.941	-2	76	0	O14(2/1/11)	0	-0.6
	Mil A	125	373	37	95	27	3	1	34	19-2	1	26	.255	.289	.351	81	-10	0-3	.994	13	113	157	O124(43/82/23)	0	-0.2
	Year	143	408	38	102	27	3	1	38	21-2	1	29	.250	.285	.338	76	-13	0-3	.991	11	110	143	O138(45/83/34)	0	-0.8
1976	Mil A	78	180	16	44	4	0	0	11	10-0	1	15	.244	.288	.267	64	-8	1-3	.975	6	117	224	O56(11/10/37),D7	0	-0.5
Total	4	398	1104	122	281	52	8	9	95	75-6	7	109	.255	.304	.341	83	-25	3-12	.985	23	109	142	O363(80/159/156),D8	0	-1.9
Sharpe, Bud	Bayard Heston; B8.6.1881 West Chester PA; D5.31.1916 Haddock GA; BR/TR/6´1˝/170; d4.14; Col Penn St.																								
1905	Bos N	46	170	8	31	3	2	0	11	7	0	—	.182	.215	.224	31	-15	0	.904	2	205	223	O42R,C3/1	—	-1.6
1910	Pit N	4	16	2	3	0	1	0	1	0	0	2	.188	.188	.313	43	-1	0	1.000	0	131	0	1b4	—	-0.1
	Bos N	115	439	30	105	14	3	0	29	14	1	31	.239	.264	.285	58	-25	4	.987	8	128	103	1b113	—	-2.1
	Year	119	455	32	108	14	4	0	30	14	1	33	.237	.262	.286	57	-27	4	.987	8	**128**	99	1b117	—	-2.2
Total	2	165	625	40	139	17	6	0	41	21	1	33	.222	.249	.269	50	-41	4	.987	10	127	99	1b118,O42R,C3	—	-3.8
Sharperson, Mike	Michael Tyrone; B10.4.1961 Orangeburg SC; D5.26.1996 Las Vegas NV; BR/TR/6´3˝/(185–205); [TorA81 S1/11]; d4.6; Col Georgia Perimeter JC																								
1987	Tor A	32	96	4	20	4	1	0	9	7-0	1	15	.208	.269	.271	43	-8	2-1	.971	-4	85	91	2b32	0	-1.0
	LA N	10	33	7	9	2	0	0	1	4-1	0	5	.273	.351	.333	85	-1	0-0	1.000	1	131	0	3b7,2b6	0	0.0
1988	†LA N	46	59	8	16	1	0	0	4	1-0	1	12	.271	.290	.288	70	-2	0-1	.949	-2	102	128	2b20,3b6,S4	0	-0.5
1989	LA N	27	28	2	7	3	0	0	5	4-1	0	7	.250	.333	.357	102	0	0-1	1.000	-1	50	142	2b4,1b2,3b2/S	0	-0.1
1990	LA N	129	357	42	106	14	2	3	36	46-6	1	39	.297	.376	.373	110	7	15-6	.949	11	107	91	3b106,S15,2b9,1b6	0	1.9
1991	LA N	105	216	24	60	11	2	2	20	25-0	1	24	.278	.355	.375	107	3	1-3	.981	-2	85	70	3b68,S16,1b10,2b5	22	0.1
1992	LA N★	128	317	48	95	21	0	3	36	47-1	0	33	.300	.387	.394	124	13	2-2	.979	18	114	107	2b63,3b60,S2	0	3.4
1993	LA N	73	90	13	23	4	0	2	10	5-0	1	17	.256	.299	.367	82	-2	2-0	.945	-0	87	127	2b17,3b6,S3/1rf	0	-0.2
1995	Atl N	7	7	1	1	1	0	0	2	0-0	0	2	.143	.143	.286	9	-1	0-0	ø	-0	0	0	/3	0	-0.1
Total	8	557	1203	149	337	61	5	10	123	139-9	5	154	.280	.355	.364	102	9	22-14	.952	21	104	77	3b256,2b156,S41,1b19/rf	22	3.5

YEAR	TM LG	G	AB	R	H	2B	3B	HR	RBI	BB-IB	HP	SO	AVG	OBP	SLG	AOPS	ABR	SB-CS	FA	FR	RNG	THR	GAMES AT POSITION	DL	BFW
SHARROTT, JACK	John Henry; B8.13.1869 Staten Island NY; D12.31.1927 Los Angeles CA; BR/TR/5´9˝/165; d4.22; ▲																								
1890	NY N	32	109	16	22	3	2	0	14	0	0	14	.202	.202	.266	36	-10	6	.932	-1	129	0	P25,O9(5/0/4)	—	-0.3
1891	NY N	10	30	5	10	2	0	1	7	1	0	2	.333	.355	.500	154	4	3	.950	1	105	0	P10	—	0.0
1892	NY N	4	8	1	1	0	0	0	0	0	0	1	.125	.125	.125	-25	-1	0	.333	-1	0	0	O3R/P	—	-0.2
1893	Phi N	50	152	25	38	4	3	1	22	8	0	14	.250	.287	.336	65	-9	6	.824	-1	114	0	O33(24/9/5),P12	—	-0.9
Total	4	96	299	47	71	9	5	2	43	9	0	31	.237	.260	.321	61	-16	15	.927	-2	120	0	P48,O45(29/9/12)	—	-1.4
SHAUGHNESSY, SHAG	Francis Joseph; B4.8.1883 Amboy IL; D5.15.1969 Montreal QC, Can.; BR/TR/6´1.5˝/185; d4.17; C1; Col Notre Dame																								
1905	Was A	1	3	0	0	0	0	0	0	0	1	—	.000	.250	.000	-19	0	0	.667	-0	0	0	/rf	—	-0.1
1908	Phi A	8	29	2	9	0	0	0	1	2	0	—	.310	.355	.310	109	0	3	1.000	-1	0	0	O8C	—	-0.1
Total	2	9	32	2	9	0	0	0	1	2	1	—	.281	.343	.281	97	0	3	.938	-1	0	0	O9(0/8/1)	—	-0.2
SHAVE, JON	Jonathan Taylor; B11.4.1967 Waycross GA; BR/TR/6´0˝/(180–185); [TexA90 5/144]; d5.15; Col Mississippi St.; [DL 1994 Tex A 16]																								
1993	Tex A	17	47	3	15	2	0	0	7	0-0	0	8	.319	.306	.362	85	-1	1-3	.917	-2	93	131	S9,2b8	0	-0.3
1998	Min A	19	40	7	10	3	0	1	5	3-0	0	10	.250	.302	.400	79	-1	1-2	1.000	-0	103	124	3b15/1SD	0	-0.2
1999	Tex A	43	73	10	21	4	0	0	9	5-0	2	17	.288	.350	.342	73	-3	1-0	.953	2	112	118	S24,1b9,3b6/2D	0	0.1
Total	3	79	160	20	46	9	0	1	21	8-0	2	35	.287	.326	.363	78	-5	3-5	.942	-0	106	121	S34,3b21,1b10,2b9,D4	16	-0.4
SHAW, AL	Albert Simpson; B3.1.1881 Toledo IL; D12.30.1974 Danville IL; BL/TR/5´8.5˝/165; d9.28																								
1907	StL N	9	25	2	7	0	0	0	1	3	1	—	.280	.379	.280	110	1	1	.947	-1	84	0	O9C	—	0.0
1908	StL N	107	367	40	97	13	4	1	19	25	0	—	.264	.311	.330	110	3	9	.931	5	200	237	O91(2/67/22),S4/3	—	0.4
1909	StL N	114	331	45	82	12	7	2	34	55	0	—	.248	.355	.344	125	12	15	.940	-4	106	30	O92(0/90/2)	—	0.3
1914	Bro F	112	376	81	122	27	7	5	49	44	0	59	.324	.395	.473	137	15	24	.955	2	102	109	O102C	—	1.1
1915	KC F	132	448	67	126	22	10	6	67	46	0	45	.281	.348	.415	119	4	15	.942	-12	83	71	O124(120/4/0)	—	-1.4
Total	5	474	1547	235	434	74	28	14	170	173	1	104	.281	.353	.392	123	35	64	.942	-9	119	106	O418(122/272/24),S4/3	—	0.4
SHAW, AL	Alfred Louis "Shoddy"; B5.22.1873 Burslem, England; D3.25.1958 Uhrichsville OH; BR/TR/5´8˝/170; d6.8																								
1901	Det A	55	171	20	46	7	0	1	23	10	3	—	.269	.321	.327	76	-5	2	.938	1	*119*	*96*	C42,1b9,3b2/S	—	-0.1
1907	Bos A	76	198	10	38	1	3	0	7	18	3	—	.192	.269	.227	59	-9	4	.971	11	*124*	*105*	C73/1	—	1.0
1908	Chi A	32	49	0	4	1	0	0	2	2	0	—	.082	.118	.102	-29	-7	0	.953	0	*129*	*72*	C29	—	-0.6
1909	Bos N	18	41	1	4	0	0	0	0	5	1	—	.098	.213	.098	-3	-5	0	.975	2	*92*	*123*	C14	—	-0.2
Total	4	181	459	31	92	9	3	1	32	35	7	—	.200	.267	.240	53	-26	6	.961	14	*120*	*100*	C158,1b10,3b2/S	—	0.1
SHAW, BEN	Benjamin Nathaniel; B6.18.1893 LaCenter KY; D3.16.1959 Cleveland OH; BR/TR/5´11.5˝/190; d4.11; Mil 1918; Col Rhodes																								
1917	Pit N	2	2	0	0	0	0	0	0	0	0	0	.000	.000	.000	-97	0	0	ø	0	—	—	/H	—	-0.1
1918	Pit N	21	36	5	7	1	0	0	2	2	2	2	.194	.275	.222	51	-2	0	.981	-1	31	108	1b9,C5	—	-0.3
Total	2	23	38	5	7	1	0	0	2	2	2	2	.184	.262	.211	43	-2	0	.981	-1	31	108	1b9,C5	—	-0.4
SHAW, HUNKY	Royal N; B9.29.1884 Yakima WA; D7.3.1969 Yakima WA; BB/TR/5´8˝/165; d5.16; Col Washington																								
1908	Pit N	1	1	0	0	0	0	0	0	0	0	—	.000	.000	.000	-99	0	0	ø	0	—	—	/H	—	0.0
SHAY, MARTY	Arthur Joseph; B4.25.1896 Boston MA; D2.20.1951 Worcester MA; BR/TR/5´7.5˝/148; d9.16																								
1916	Chi N	2	7	0	2	0	0	0	0	0	0	1	.286	.286	.286	68	0	0	.917	-0	76	237	S2	—	0.0
1924	Bos N	19	68	4	16	3	1	0	2	5	1	5	.235	.297	.309	65	-3	2-1	.950	-8	69	96	2b19/S	—	-1.1
Total	2	21	75	4	18	3	1	0	2	5	1	6	.240	.296	.307	66	-3	2-1	.950	-8	69	96	2b19,S3	—	-1.1
SHAY, DANNY	Daniel Charles; B11.8.1876 Springfield OH; D12.1.1927 Kansas City MO; BR/TR/5´10˝/?; d4.30																								
1901	Cle A	19	75	4	17	2	2	0	10	2	2	—	.227	.266	.307	61	-4	0	.901	-3	89	39	S19	—	-0.6
1904	StL N	99	340	45	87	11	1	1	18	39	3	—	.256	.338	.303	103	3	36	.911	-8	105	93	S97,2b2	—	-0.2
1905	StL N	78	281	30	67	12	1	0	28	35	4	—	.238	.331	.288	88	-2	11	.953	-15	99	106	2b39,S39	—	-1.6
1907	NY N	35	79	10	15	1	1	1	6	12	1	—	.190	.304	.266	76	-2	5	.931	-6	70	24	2b13,S9,O2C	—	-0.9
Total	4	231	775	89	186	26	5	2	62	88	10	—	.240	.325	.294	90	-5	52	.902	-33	98	75	S164,2b54,O2C	—	-3.3
SHEA, GERRY	Gerald Joseph; B10.26.1881 St.Louis MO; D5.3.1964 Berkeley MO; TR/5´7˝/160; d10.1; Col Creighton																								
1905	StL N	2	6	0	2	0	0	0	0	0	0	—	.333	.333	.333	102	0	0	.917	0	*85*	*144*	C2	—	0.0
SHEA, NAP	John Edward "Napoleon"; B5.23.1874 Ware MA; D7.8.1968 Bloomfield Hills MI; BR/TR/5´5˝/155; d9.11																								
1902	Phi N	3	8	1	1	0	0	0	0	1	1	—	.125	.300	.125	32	-1	0	1.000	-1	*75*	*82*	C3	—	-0.1
SHEA, MERV	Mervyn John; B9.5.1900 San Francisco CA; D1.27.1953 Sacramento CA; BR/TR/5´11˝/175; d4.23; C8																								
1927	Det A	34	85	5	15	6	3	0	9	7	0	15	.176	.239	.318	43	-8	0-0	.949	-2	*97*	*72*	C31	—	-0.7
1928	Det A	39	85	8	20	2	3	0	9	9	1	11	.235	.316	.329	69	-4	2-1	.951	1	*107*	*183*	C30	—	-0.1
1929	Det A	50	162	23	47	6	0	3	24	19	0	18	.290	.365	.383	92	-1	2-1	.964	-7	*70*	*120*	C46	—	-0.5
1933	Bos A	16	56	1	8	3	0	0	8	4	0	7	.143	.200	.196	5	-8	0-0	1.000	-1	*69*	*145*	C16	—	-0.7
	StL A	94	279	26	73	11	1	1	27	43	0	26	.262	.360	.319	76	-8	2-0	.995	9	*121*	*113*	C85	—	0.7
	Year	110	335	27	81	14	1	1	35	47	0	33	.242	.335	.299	65	-15	2-0	**.996**	9	*114*	*117*	C101	—	0.0
1934	Chi A	62	176	8	28	3	0	0	5	24	0	19	.159	.260	.176	14	-23	0-1	.972	-3	*64*	*128*	C60	—	-2.1
1935	Chi A	46	122	8	28	2	0	0	13	30	0	9	.230	.382	.246	64	-5	0-0	.990	6	*93*	*100*	C43	—	0.3
1936	Chi A	14	24	3	3	0	0	0	2	6	0	5	.125	.300	.125	8	-3	0-0	1.000	1	*116*	*49*	C14	—	-0.2
1937	Chi A	25	71	7	15	1	0	0	5	15	0	10	.211	.349	.225	48	-5	1-0	.966	3	*126*	*144*	C25	—	-0.1
1938	Bro N	48	120	14	22	5	0	0	12	28	0	20	.183	.338	.225	56	-6	1	.977	-0	*86*	*90*	C47	—	-0.4
1939	Det A	4	2	0	0	0	0	0	0	0	0	1	.000	.000	.000	-93	-1	0-0	.500	-1	*0*	*0*	C4	—	-0.1
1944	Phi N	7	15	2	4	0	0	1	1	4	0	4	.267	.421	.467	155	1	0	.952	-0	*143*	*94*	C6	0	0.1
Total	11	439	1197	105	263	39	7	5	115	189	1	145	.220	.327	.277	58	-71	8-3	.976	7	*95*	*116*	C407	0	-3.8
SHEAFFER, DANNY	Danny Todd; B8.2.1961 Jacksonville FL; BR/TR/6´0˝/(185–202); [BosA81*1/20]; d4.9; Col Clemson; OF(20/2/9)																								
1987	Bos A	25	66	5	8	1	0	1	5	0-0	0	14	.121	.119	.182	-21	-12	0-0	.977	-5	104	88	C25	0	-1.5
1989	Cle A	7	16	1	1	0	0	0	0	2-0	0	2	.063	.167	.063	-32	-3	0-0	ø	-0	0	0	3b2/lfD	0	-0.3
1993	Col N	82	216	26	60	9	1	4	32	8-0	1	15	.278	.299	.384	72	-9	2-3	.994	-1	114	82	C65,1b7,O2L/3	0	-0.7
1994	Col N	44	110	11	24	4	0	1	12	10-0	0	11	.218	.283	.282	41	-9	0-2	.995	2	77	107	C30,1b2/lf	0	-0.6
1995	StL N	76	208	24	48	10	1	5	30	23-2	0	38	.231	.306	.361	74	-8	0-0	.993	9	74	99	C67,1b3/3	0	0.5
1996	†StL N	79	198	10	45	9	3	2	20	9-0	3	25	.227	.271	.333	58	-13	3-3	.983	4	100	107	C47,3b17,1b6,O3L	0	-0.6
1997	StL N	76	132	10	33	5	0	0	11	8-0	1	17	.250	.296	.288	54	-9	1-0	.957	-2	102	62	3b30,O22(13/2/9),C9,2b3	0	-1.0
Total	7	389	946	87	219	38	5	13	110	60-2	5	122	.232	.278	.323	56	-63	6-8	.990	8	93	94	C243,3b51,O29L,1b18,2b3,D3	0	-4.2
SHEALY, RYAN	Ryan Nelson; B8.29.1979 Fort Lauderdale FL; BR/TR/6´5˝/(240–250); [ColN02 11/321]; d6.14; Col Florida																								
2005	Col N	36	91	14	30	7	0	2	16	13-0	0	22	.330	.413	.473	118	3	1-0	1.000	-1	73	47	1b19,D5	0	0.1
2006	Col N	5	9	2	2	2	0	0	1	0-0	0	4	.222	.222	.444	59	0	0-0	1.000	-0	0	100	1b2	39	-0.1
	KC A	51	193	29	54	10	1	7	36	15-1	2	50	.280	.338	.451	104	1	1-1	.993	-1	91	114	1b51	0	-0.5
Total	2	92	293	45	86	19	1	9	53	28-1	2	76	.294	.359	.457	107	4	2-1	.995	-3	85	97	1b72,D5	39	-0.5
SHEAN, DAVE	David William; B7.9.1883 Arlington MA; D5.22.1963 Boston MA; BR/TR/5´11˝/175; d9.10; Col Fordham																								
1906	Phi A	22	75	7	16	3	2	0	3	5	2	—	.213	.280	.307	81	-2	6	.980	-1	94	70	2b22	—	-0.3
1908	Phi N	14	48	4	7	2	0	0	2	1	1	—	.146	.180	.188	17	-4	1	.871	-5	80	52	S14	—	-1.1
1909	Phi N	36	112	14	26	2	2	0	4	14	1	—	.232	.323	.286	88	-1	3	.982	-2	95	78	2b14,1b11,O3C/S	—	-0.3
	Bos N	75	267	32	66	11	4	1	29	17	2	—	.247	.297	.330	90	-4	14	.956	7	106	125	2b72	—	0.5
	Year	111	379	46	92	13	6	1	33	31	3	—	.243	.305	.317	90	-5	17	.960	6	104	118	2b86,1b11,O3C/S	—	0.2
1910	Bos N	150	543	52	130	12	7	3	36	42	0	45	.239	.294	.304	71	-22	16	.953	**43**	**116**	**132**	2b148	—	2.4
1911	Chi N	54	145	17	28	4	0	0	15	8	1	15	.193	.240	.221	29	-14	4	.947	1	106	59	2b23,S19/3	—	-1.2
1912	Bos N	4	10	1	3	0	0	0	0	1	1	2	.300	.417	.300	96	0	0	.917	-0	106	170	S4	—	0.0
1917	Cin N	131	442	36	93	9	5	2	35	22	1	39	.210	.249	.267	61	-22	10	.961	17	**106**	112	2b131	—	-0.3
1918	†Bos A	115	425	58	112	16	3	0	34	40	3	25	.264	.331	.315	97	-1	11	.967	-4	97	85	2b115	—	-0.4
1919	Bos A	29	100	4	14	0	0	0	8	5	1	7	.140	.189	.140	-7	-15	1	.981	3	100	155	2b29	—	-1.2
Total	9	630	2167	225	495	59	23	6	166	155	13	133	.228	.284	.285	70	-85	66	.961	59	106	111	2b554,S38,1b11,O3C/3	—	-1.9

YEAR	TM LG	G	AB	R	H	2B	3B	HR	RBI	BB-IB	HP	SO	AVG	OBP	SLG	AOPS	ABR	SB-CS	FA	FR	RNG	THR	GAMES AT POSITION	DL	BFW
Shearer, Ray	Ray Solomon; B9.19.1929 Jacobus PA; D2.21.1982 York PA; BR/TR/6´0˝/200; d9.18																								
1957	Mil N	2	2	1	1	0	0	0	0	1-0	0	1	.500	.667	.500	237	1	0-0	ø	-0	0	0	/lf	0	0.0
Shearon, John	John; B1871 PA; D2.12.1932 Chicago IL; d7.28; ▲																								
1891	Cle N	30	124	10	30	1	1	0	13	1	0	15	.242	.248	.266	48	-9	6	.814	-1	160	0	O25(4/14/10),P6	—	-0.8
1896	Cle N	16	64	6	11	0	1	0	3	4	0	6	.172	.221	.203	11	-9	3	.818	-4	0	0	O16R	—	-1.1
Total	2	46	188	16	41	1	2	0	16	5	0	21	.218	.238	.245	34	-18	9	.815	-5	94	0	O41(4/14/26),P6	—	-1.9
Sheckard, Jimmy	Samuel James Tilden; B11.23.1878 Upper Chanceford PA; D1.15.1947 Lancaster PA; BL/TR/5´9˝/175; d9.14; OF(1843/22/214)																								
1897	Bro N	13	49	12	14	3	2	3	14	6	0	—	.286	.364	.612	164	4	5	.753	-6	100	108	S11,O2R	—	-0.1
1898	Bro N	105	408	51	113	17	9	4	64	37	8	—	.277	.349	.392	113	6	8	.926	-7	76	52	O105(101/4/0)/3	—	-0.9
1899	Bal N	147	536	104	158	18	10	3	75	56	18	—	.295	.380	.382	104	5	**77**	.943	19	147	244	O146(0/1/146)/1	—	1.5
1900	Bro N	85	273	74	82	19	10	1	39	42	12	—	.300	.416	.454	132	14	30	.925	3	125	108	O78(67/6/5)	—	1.0
1901	Bro N	133	554	116	196	29	**19**	11	104	47	5	—	.354	.409	**.534**	168	47	35	.944	5	96	121	O121(120/1/0),3b12	—	4.3
1902	Bal A	4	15	3	4	1	0	0	0	1	0	—	.267	.313	.333	76	0	2	1.000	-1	0	0	O4C	—	-0.1
	Bro N	123	486	86	129	20	10	4	37	57	5	—	.265	.349	.372	122	14	23	.964	9	71	128	O123(122/1/0)	—	1.6
1903	Bro N	**139**	515	99	171	29	9	**9**	75	75	6	—	.332	.423	.476	161	**45**	**67**	.951	**25**	**190**	154	O139L	—	**5.8**
1904	Bro N	143	507	70	121	23	6	1	46	56	2	—	.239	.317	.314	97	0	21	.956	9	92	95	O141L,2b2	—	0.1
1905	Bro N	130	480	58	140	20	11	3	41	61	7	—	.292	.380	.398	142	28	23	.967	17	144	130	O129L	—	3.8
1906	†Chi N	149	549	90	144	27	10	1	45	67	6	—	.262	.349	.353	112	10	30	.986	-2	68	26	O149L	—	0.0
1907	†Chi N	143	484	76	129	23	1	1	36	76	6	—	.267	.373	.324	112	12	31	.975	-8	68	49	O142L	—	-0.5
1908	†Chi N	115	403	54	93	18	3	2	22	62	2	—	.231	.336	.305	101	4	18	.955	-4	85	89	O115L	—	-0.9
1909	Chi N	148	525	81	134	29	5	1	43	72	1	—	.255	.346	.335	109	8	15	.967	-5	84	122	O148L	—	-0.5
1910	†Chi N	144	507	82	130	27	6	5	51	83	5	53	.256	.366	.363	114	12	22	.976	8	107	117	O143L	—	1.3
1911	Chi N	156	539	**121**	149	26	11	4	50	**147**	3	58	.276	**.434**	.388	130	34	32	.963	15	107	144	O156L	—	**4.1**
1912	Chi N	146	523	85	128	22	10	3	47	**122**	5	81	.245	.392	.342	102	9	15	.962	9	107	119	O146L	—	1.2
1913	StL N	52	136	18	27	2	1	0	17	41	1	25	.199	.388	.228	79	0	5-7	.953	0	98	105	O46(16/0/36)	—	-0.4
	Cin N	47	116	16	22	1	3	0	7	27	0	16	.190	.343	.250	71	-3	6-5	.969	-0	99	96	O38(9/5/25)	—	-0.6
	Year	99	252	34	49	3	4	0	24	68	1	41	.194	.368	.238	76	-4	11-12	.960	-0	98	101	O84(25/5/61)	—	-1.0
Total	17	2122	7605	1296	2084	354	136	56	813	1135	92	233	.274	.375	.378	120	249	465-12	.958	87	104	113	O2071L,3b13,S11,2b2/1	—	20.7
Sheehan, Jim	James Thomas "Big Jim"; B6.3.1913 New Haven CT; D12.2.2003 New Haven CT; BR/TR/6´2˝/196; d9.26; Col Alabama																								
1936	NY N	1	4	0	0	0	0	0	0	0	0	2	.000	.000	.000	-99	-1	0	.833	-0	*0*	*0*	/C	—	-0.1
Sheehan, Jack	John Thomas; B4.15.1893 Chicago IL; D5.29.1987 W.Palm Beach FL; BB/TR/5´8.5˝/165; d9.11; Col Fordham																								
1920	†Bro N	3	5	0	2	1	0	0	0	1	0	0	.400	.500	.600	208	1	0-0	.875	-0	120	0	S2/3	—	0.1
1921	Bro N	5	12	2	0	0	0	0	0	0	0	1	.000	.000	.000	-97	-3	0-0	.900	-0	84	112	2b2/S3	—	-0.4
Total	2	8	17	2	2	1	0	0	0	1	0	1	.118	.167	.176	-7	-2	0-0	.909	-1	105	0	S3,2b2,3b2	—	-0.3
Sheehan, Tommy	Thomas H.; B11.6.1877 Sacramento CA; D5.22.1959 Ancon, Canal Zone; BR/TR/5´8˝/160; d8.2																								
1900	NY N	1	2	0	0	0	0	0	0	0	0	—	.000	.000	.000	-99	-1	0	ø	-0	0	0	/S	—	-0.1
1906	Pit N	95	315	28	76	6	3	1	34	18	1	—	.241	.284	.289	75	-10	13	.947	-4	97	122	3b90	—	-1.2
1907	Pit N	75	226	23	62	2	3	0	25	23	0	—	.274	.341	.310	103	1	10	.941	1	115	42	3b57,S10	—	0.4
1908	Bro N	146	468	45	100	18	2	0	29	53	6	—	.214	.302	.261	83	-6	9	.930	-4	97	73	3b145	—	-0.8
Total	4	317	1011	96	238	26	8	1	88	94	7	—	.235	.305	.280	85	-16	32	.938	-7	101	82	3b292,S11	—	-1.7
Sheehan, Biff	Timothy James; B2.13.1868 Hartford CT; D10.21.1923 Hartford CT; BL/TR/5´9˝/165; d7.22																								
1895	StL N	52	180	24	57	3	6	1	18	20	3	6	.317	.394	.417	111	3	7	.940	-0	135	80	O41(0/2/39),1b11	—	0.1
1896	StL N	6	19	0	3	0	0	0	1	4	0	0	.158	.304	.158	25	-2	0	1.000	-0	0	0	O6(1/0/5)	—	-0.2
Total	2	58	199	24	60	3	6	1	19	24	3	6	.302	.385	.392	103	1	7	.948	-1	117	69	O47(1/2/44),1b11	—	-0.1
Sheely, Earl	Earl Homer "Whitey"; B2.12.1893 Bushnell IL; D9.16.1952 Seattle WA; BR/TR/6´3.5˝/195; d4.14; s–Bud																								
1921	Chi A	**154**	563	68	171	25	6	11	95	57	7	34	.304	.375	.428	106	5	4-9	.988	6	**119**	108	1b154	—	-0.1
1922	Chi A	149	526	72	167	37	4	6	80	60	5	27	.317	.393	.437	117	15	4-6	.993	2	102	96	1b149	—	0.6
1923	Chi A	**156**	570	74	169	25	3	4	88	79	5	30	.296	.387	.372	102	5	5-5	.992	-1	95	97	1b156	—	-0.7
1924	Chi A	146	535	84	171	34	3	3	103	95	4	28	.320	.426	.411	120	23	7-4	.991	-11	75	85	1b146	—	0.3
1925	Chi A	153	600	93	189	43	3	9	111	68	5	23	.315	.389	.442	117	17	3-3	.988	-6	88	109	1b153	—	0.1
1926	Chi A	145	525	77	157	40	2	6	89	75	7	13	.299	.394	.417	116	16	3-1	**.995**	-1	93	86	1b144	—	0.6
1927	Chi A	45	129	11	27	3	0	2	16	20	1	5	.209	.320	.279	58	-8	1-3	.982	-4	65	101	1b36	—	-1.4
1929	Pit N	139	485	63	142	22	4	6	88	75	4	24	.293	.392	.392	93	-3	6	**.996**	-1	93	94	1b139	—	-1.2
1931	Bos N	147	538	30	147	15	2	1	77	34	2	21	.273	.319	.314	73	-21	0	.992	-2	93	93	1b143	—	-3.6
Total	9	1234	4471	572	1340	244	27	48	747	563	40	205	.300	.383	.399	104	49	33-31	.991	-18	94	96	1b1220	—	-5.4
Sheely, Bud	Hollis Kimball; B11.26.1920 Spokane WA; D10.17.1985 Sacramento CA; BL/TR/6´1˝/200; d7.26; f–Earl; Col St. Marys (CA)																								
1951	Chi A	34	89	2	16	2	0	0	7	6	1	7	.180	.240	.202	21	-10	0-0	.986	2	*86*	*68*	C33	0	-0.6
1952	Chi A	36	75	1	18	2	0	0	3	12	1	7	.240	.352	.267	73	-2	0-1	.992	-1	*72*	*97*	C31	0	-0.3
1953	Chi A	31	46	4	10	1	0	0	2	9	0	8	.217	.345	.239	58	-2	0-0	1.000	0	*84*	*41*	C17	0	-0.1
Total	3	101	210	7	44	5	0	0	12	27	2	22	.210	.305	.233	49	-14	0-1	.991	2	*81*	*73*	C81	0	-1.0
Sheerin, Chuck	Charles Joseph; B4.17.1909 Brooklyn NY; D9.27.1986 Valley Stream NY; BR/TR/5´11.5˝/198; d4.21; Col Fordham																								
1936	Phi N	39	72	4	19	4	0	0	4	7	0	18	.264	.329	.319	68	-3	0	.942	-1	103	33	2b17,3b13,S5	—	-0.3
Sheets, Andy	Andrew Mark; B11.19.1971 Baton Rouge LA; BR/TR/6´2˝/180; [SeaA92 4/110]; d4.22; Col Louisiana St.																								
1996	Sea A	47	110	18	21	8	0	0	9	10-0	1	41	.191	.262	.264	34	-11	2-0	.947	3	99	186	3b25,2b18,S7	0	-0.7
1997	†Sea A	32	89	18	22	3	0	4	9	7-0	0	34	.247	.299	.416	85	-2	2-0	.872	-5	84	120	3b21,S9,2b2	0	-0.5
1998	†SD N	88	194	31	47	5	3	7	29	21-3	1	62	.242	.318	.407	96	-2	7-2	.964	1	109	106	S39,3b23,2b22,1b2	0	0.2
1999	Ana A	87	244	22	48	10	0	3	29	14-0	0	59	.197	.236	.275	31	-26	1-2	.966	-22	85	77	S76,2b7/3	0	-4.1
2000	Bos A	12	21	1	2	0	0	0	1	0-0	0	3	.095	.095	.095	-50	-5	0-0	1.000	1	108	122	S10/1D	0	-0.3
2001	TB A	49	153	10	30	8	0	1	14	12-0	0	35	.196	.251	.268	39	-14	2-0	.990	0	94	96	S49	0	-0.9
2002	TB A	41	149	18	37	4	0	4	22	12-0	0	41	.248	.301	.356	76	-5	2-3	.992	3	96	137	2b26,S11,3b4	0	-0.1
Total	7	356	960	118	207	38	3	19	113	76-3	2	275	.216	.271	.321	55	-65	16-7	.975	-19	95	88	S201,2b75,3b74,1b3,D2	0	-6.4
Sheets, Larry	Larry Kent; B12.6.1959 Staunton VA; BL/TR/6´3˝/(215–236); [BalA78 2/29]; d9.18; OF(192/0/144)																								
1984	Bal A	8	16	3	7	1	0	1	2	1-0	0	3	.438	.471	.688	220	3	0-0	1.000	1	126	350	O7R	0	0.3
1985	Bal A	113	328	43	86	8	0	17	50	28-2	2	52	.262	.323	.442	110	3	0-1	.875	-1	63	0	D93,O9(1/0/8)/1	0	-0.1
1986	Bal A	112	338	42	92	17	1	18	60	21-3	2	56	.272	.317	.488	117	7	2-0	.984	-1	111	57	D58,O32(21/0/11),C6,1b4,3b2	17	0.3
1987	Bal A	135	469	74	148	23	0	31	94	31-1	3	67	.316	.358	.563	143	28	1-1	.975	-5	95	60	O124(72/0/58),1b3,D7	0	1.6
1988	Bal A	136	452	38	104	19	1	10	47	42-4	6	72	.230	.302	.343	83	-10	1-6	.974	3	94	215	O76(42/0/36),D50,1b3	0	-1.4
1989	Bal A	102	304	33	74	12	1	7	33	26-10	3	58	.243	.305	.359	90	-4	1-1	ø	0	0	0	D88	0	-0.7
1990	Det A	131	360	40	94	17	2	10	52	24-2	2	42	.261	.308	.403	97	-2	1-3	.981	-2	80	178	O79(56/0/23),D44	0	-0.9
1993	Sea A	11	17	0	2	1	0	0	1	2-0	1	1	.118	.250	.176	16	-2	0-0	1.000	-0	86	0	/rfD	0	-0.2
Total	8	748	2284	273	607	98	5	94	339	175-22	19	351	.266	.321	.437	108	23	6-12	.976	-5	93	125	D345,O328L,1b11,C6,3b2	17	-1.1
Sheffield, Gary	Gary Antonian; B11.18.1968 Tampa FL; BR/TR/5´11˝/(190–215); [MilA86 1/6]; d9.3; OF(428/0/1135)																								
1988	Mil A	24	80	12	19	1	0	4	12	7-0	0	7	.237	.295	.400	93	-1	3-1	.967	-11	67	64	S24	0	-1.0
1989	Mil A	95	368	34	91	18	0	5	32	27-0	4	33	.247	.303	.337	81	-9	10-6	.959	-11	93	91	S70,3b21,D4	57	-1.5
1990	Mil A	125	487	67	143	30	1	10	67	44-1	3	41	.294	.350	.421	117	12	25-10	.934	-1	105	69	3b125	0	1.3
1991	Mil A	50	175	25	34	12	2	2	22	19-1	3	15	.194	.277	.320	68	-7	5-5	.922	-9	80	85	3b43,D5	95	-1.7
1992	SD N★	146	557	87	184	34	3	33	100	48-5	6	40	**.330**	.385	.580	168	49	5-6	.961	9	106	109	3b144	0	6.0
1993	SD N	68	258	34	76	12	2	10	36	18-0	3	30	.295	.344	.473	116	5	5-1	.905	-7	89	102	3b67	0	-0.1
	Fla N★	72	236	33	69	8	3	10	37	29-6	6	34	.292	.378	.479	122	8	12-4	.894	-3	103	37	3b66	0	0.6
	Year	140	494	67	145	20	5	20	73	47-6	9	64	.294	.361	.476	119	13	17-5	.899	-10	96	70	3b133	0	0.5
1994	Fla N	87	322	61	89	16	1	27	78	51-11	6	50	.276	.380	.584	142	21	12-6	.970	-3	91	107	O87R	30	1.4
1995	Fla N	63	213	46	69	8	0	16	46	55-8	4	45	.324	.467	.587	174	27	19-4	.942	-1	95	116	O61(3/0/59)	82	2.4
1996	Fla N★	161	519	118	163	33	1	42	120	142-19	10	66	.314	**.465**	.624	**190**	**79**	16-9	.976	-14	80	77	O161R	0	5.6
1997	†Fla N	135	444	86	111	22	1	21	71	121-11	15	79	.250	.424	.446	135	32	11-7	.980	2	96	152	O132R/D	15	2.7

YEAR	TM LG	G	AB	R	H	2B	3B	HR	RBI	BB-IB	HP	SO	AVG	OBP	SLG	AOPS	ABR	SB-CS	FA	FR	RNG	THR	GAMES AT POSITION	DL	BFW
1998	Fla N	40	136	21	37	11	1	6	28	26-1	2	16	.272	.392	.500	142	10	4-2	.986	0	94	118	O37R	0	0.8
	LA N★	90	301	52	95	16	1	16	57	69-11	6	30	.316	.444	.535	166	34	18-5	.994	-2	91	103	O89R	0	2.9
	Year	130	437	73	132	27	2	22	85	95-12	8	46	.302	.428	.524	159	44	22-7	.991	-2	92	107	O126R	0	3.7
1999	LA N★	152	549	103	165	20	0	34	101	101-4	4	64	.301	.407	.523	142	38	11-5	.972	-8	84	79	O145L,D3	0	2.4
2000	LA N★	141	501	105	163	24	3	43	109	101-7	4	71	.325	.438	.643	178	64	4-6	.954	-8	83	64	O139L,D2	0	4.6
2001	LA N	143	515	98	160	28	2	36	100	94-13	4	67	.311	.417	.583	166	54	10-4	.972	-3	77	189	O141(141/0/2),D2	15	4.5
2002	†Atl N	135	492	82	151	26	0	25	84	72-2	11	53	.307	.404	.512	140	32	12-2	.984	-6	90	81	O127R,D4	0	2.2
2003	†Atl N★	155	576	126	190	37	2	39	132	86-6	8	55	.330	.419	.604	165	58	18-4	.986	-5	95	70	O153R	0	4.7
2004	†NY A★	154	573	117	166	30	1	36	121	92-7	11	83	.290	.393	.534	140	37	5-6	.983	1	100	122	O136R,D18,3b2	0	2.7
2005	†NY A★	154	584	104	170	27	0	34	123	78-7	8	76	.291	.379	.512	136	32	10-2	.988	-4	95	68	O131R,D23	0	2.1
2006	†NY A	39	151	22	45	5	0	6	25	13-2	1	16	.298	.355	.450	107	2	5-1	.976	-1	102	84	O21R,1b9,D9	129	0.0
Total	19	2229	8037	1433	2390	418	24	455	1501	1293-122	119	971	.297	.398	.525	145	577	220-96	.977	-83	90	101	O1560R,3b468,S94,D71,1b9	423	42.6
SHELBY, JOHN	John T.; B2.23.1958 Lexington KY; BB/TR/6´1″/(175–180); [BalA77*1/19]; d9.15; C9; Col Columbia St. (TN) CC																								
1981	Bal A	7	2	2	0	0	0	0	0	0-0	0	1	.000	.000	.000	-99	-1	2-0	1.000	-0	46	0	O4C	0	0.0
1982	Bal A	26	35	8	11	3	0	1	2	0-0	0	5	.314	.314	.486	117	1	0-1	1.000	-1	75	152	O24C	0	-0.1
1983	†Bal A	126	325	52	84	15	2	5	27	18-2	0	64	.258	.297	.363	82	-9	15-2	.981	0	93	185	O115C/D	0	-0.7
1984	Bal A	128	383	44	80	12	5	6	30	20-0	0	71	.209	.248	.313	55	-25	12-4	.993	-1	96	136	O124(0/118/9)	0	-2.6
1985	Bal A	69	205	28	58	6	2	7	27	7-0	0	44	.283	.307	.434	102	-1	5-1	.981	4	117	95	O59(9/43/10)/2D	0	0.4
1986	Bal A	135	404	54	92	14	4	11	49	18-0	2	75	.228	.263	.364	70	-19	18-6	.978	-2	97	84	O121(49/56/31),D2	0	-2.2
1987	Bal A	21	32	4	6	0	0	1	3	1-0	0	13	.188	.212	.281	30	-3	0-1	1.000	0	113	0	O19(0/4/15)/D	0	-0.4
	LA N	120	476	61	132	26	0	21	69	31-2	1	97	.277	.317	.464	108	4	16-6	.972	-1	98	138	O117C	0	0.3
1988	†LA N	140	494	65	130	23	6	10	64	44-5	0	128	.263	.320	.395	108	4	16-5	.982	-3	96	116	O140C	20	0.2
1989	LA N	108	345	28	63	11	1	1	12	25-5	0	92	.183	.237	.229	34	-30	10-7	.991	-6	92	61	O98C	0	-4.0
1990	LA N	25	24	2	6	1	0	0	2	0-0	0	7	.250	.250	.292	50	-2	1-0	1.000	0	121	0	O12(7/1/4)	0	-0.2
	Det A	78	222	22	55	9	3	4	20	10-0	0	51	.248	.280	.369	79	-7	3-5	.973	2	100	146	O68(24/35/13),D5	0	-0.8
1991	Det A	53	143	19	22	8	1	3	8	8-1	1	23	.154	.204	.287	34	-13	0-2	.982	4	120	183	O47(25/26/3),D4	0	-1.1
Total	11	1036	3090	389	739	128	24	70	313	182-15	4	671	.239	.281	.364	78	-101	98-40	.982	-3	98	120	O948(114/781/85),D16/2	20	-11.2
SHELDON, BOB	Bob Mitchell; B11.27.1950 Montebello CA; BL/TR/6´0″/170; [MilA72 22/507]; d4.10; Col Loyola Marymount																								
1974	Mil A	10	17	4	2	1	1	0	0	4-0	0	2	.118	.286	.294	67	-1	0-1	1.000	-1	97	0	2b3,D4	0	-0.2
1975	Mil A	53	181	17	52	3	3	0	14	13-0	2	14	.287	.338	.337	92	-2	0-3	.977	1	104	113	2b44,D6	0	0.0
1977	Mil A	31	64	9	13	4	1	0	3	6-0	0	9	.203	.268	.297	55	-4	0-0	1.000	-1	80	78	D17,2b5	0	-0.6
Total	3	94	262	30	67	8	5	0	17	23-0	2	25	.256	.317	.324	81	-7	0-4	.979	-2	102	106	2b52,D27	0	-0.8
SHELDON, SCOTT	Scott Patrick; B11.28.1968 Hammond IN; BR/TR/6´3″/(185–215); [OakA91 8/229]; d5.18; Col Houston; OF(4/1/2)																								
1997	Oak A	13	24	2	6	0	0	1	2	1-0	1	6	.250	.308	.375	77	-1	0-0	.939	-3	71	68	S12/23	0	-0.3
1998	Tex A	7	16	0	2	0	0	0	1	1-0	0	6	.125	.176	.125	-19	-3	0-0	1.000	2	157	849	3b3,S2/1D	0	0.0
1999	Tex A	2	1	0	0	0	0	0	0	0-0	0	0	.000	.000	.000	-94	0	0-0	1.000	1	497	0	3b2	0	0.1
2000	Tex A	58	124	21	35	11	0	4	19	10-0	1	37	.282	.336	.468	101	0	0-0	.970	-0	94	56	S22,3b15,2b12,1b10,C3,O2(2/1/1)/P	0	0.1
2001	Tex A	61	120	11	24	5	0	3	11	3-0	0	35	.200	.216	.317	38	-11	1-1	.951	4	102	18	3b38,S16,O3(2/0/1)/C	0	-0.7
Total	5	141	285	34	67	16	0	8	33	15-0	2	84	.235	.275	.375	65	-15	1-1	.961	4	114	112	3b59,S52,2b13,1b11,O5L,C4/PD	0	-0.8
SHELLEY, HUGH	Hubert Leneirre; B10.26.1910 Rogers TX; D6.16.1978 Beaumont TX; BR/TR/6´0″/170; d6.25																								
1935	Det A	7	8	1	2	0	0	0	1	2	0	1	.250	.400	.250	74	0	0-0	1.000	0	119	0	O5(3/1/1)	—	0.0
SHELTON, SKEETER	Andrew Kemper; B6.29.1888 Huntington WV; D1.9.1954 Huntington WV; BR/TR/5´11″/175; d8.25; Col West Virginia																								
1915	NY A	10	40	1	1	0	0	0	0	2	0	10	.025	.071	.025	-71	-9	0	1.000	0	87	141	O10C	—	-1.0
SHELTON, BEN	Benjamin Davis; B9.21.1969 Chicago IL; BR/TL/6´3″/210; [PitN87 2/34]; d6.16																								
1993	Pit N	15	24	3	6	1	0	2	7	3-0	0	3	.250	.333	.542	130	1	0-0	.889	0	90	326	O6L,1b2	0	0.1
SHELTON, CHRIS	Christopher Bob; B6.26.1980 Salt Lake City UT; BR/TR/6´0″/(215–220); [PitN01 33/984]; d4.15; Col Utah																								
2004	Det A	27	46	6	9	1	0	1	3	9-0	0	14	.196	.321	.283	64	-2	0-0	1.000	0	219	119	D11,1b8,C6/rf	40	-0.3
2005	Det A	107	388	61	116	22	3	18	59	34-0	5	87	.299	.360	.510	131	17	0-0	.993	3	116	122	1b84,D15/lf	0	1.1
2006	Det A	115	373	50	102	16	4	16	47	34-1	4	107	.273	.340	.466	108	4	1-2	.994	-2	94	107	1b115	0	-0.7
Total	3	249	807	117	227	39	7	35	109	77-1	9	208	.281	.348	.477	116	19	1-2	.994	1	106	114	1b207,D26,C6,O2(1/0/1)	40	0.1
SHEMO, STEVE	Stephen Michael; B4.9.1915 Swoyersville PA; D4.13.1992 Eden NC; BR/TR/5´11″/175; d4.18																								
1944	Bos N	18	31	3	9	2	0	0	1	1	0	3	.290	.313	.355	84	-1	0	.966	2	124	74	2b16,3b2	0	0.2
1945	Bos N	17	46	4	11	1	0	0	7	1	0	3	.239	.255	.261	43	-4	0	.921	-5	67	23	2b12,3b3/S	0	-0.8
Total	2	35	77	7	20	3	0	0	8	2	0	6	.260	.278	.299	60	-5	0	.948	-3	98	51	2b28,3b5/S	0	-0.6
SHEPARD, JACK	Jack Leroy; B5.13.1932 Clovis CA; D12.31.1994 Atherton CA; BR/TR/6´2″/195; d6.19; Col Stanford																								
1953	Pit N	2	4	0	1	0	0	0	0	0	0	2	.250	.250	.250	31	0	0-0	.750	-1	*0*	*0*	C2	0	-0.1
1954	Pit N	82	227	24	69	8	2	3	22	26	0	33	.304	.370	.396	103	2	0-0	.977	-2	*56*	*166*	C67	0	0.3
1955	Pit N	94	264	24	63	10	2	2	23	33-3	0	25	.239	.321	.314	71	-10	1-0	.982	-7	*72*	*127*	C77	0	-1.4
1956	Pit N	100	256	24	62	11	2	7	30	25-5	0	37	.242	.309	.383	87	-5	1-1	.990	3	*102*	*118*	C86,1b2	0	0.1
Total	4	278	751	72	195	29	6	12	75	84-8	0	97	.260	.331	.362	86	-13	2-1	.982	-7	*77*	*135*	C232,1b2	0	-1.1
SHEPARDSON, RAY	Raymond Francis; B5.3.1897 Little Falls NY; D11.8.1975 Little Falls NY; BR/TR/5´11.5″/170; d9.19																								
1924	StL N	3	6	1	0	0	0	0	0	0	0	3	.000	.000	.000	-99	-2	0-0	1.000	0	*97*	*121*	C3	—	-0.2
SHEPHERD, RON	Ronald Wayne; B10.27.1960 Longview TX; BR/TR/6´4″/175; [TorA79 2/29]; d9.5; [DL 1988 Mon N 131]																								
1984	Tor A	12	4	0	0	0	0	0	0	0-0	0	3	.000	.000	.000	-96	-1	0-1	1.000	1	86	1367	O5L,D4	0	-0.1
1985	Tor A	38	35	7	4	2	0	0	1	2-0	0	12	.114	.162	.171	-8	-5	3-0	1.000	-0	107	0	O16(3/13/1),D15	14	-0.5
1986	Tor A	65	69	16	14	4	0	2	4	3-0	0	22	.203	.236	.348	55	-5	0-0	1.000	-3	71	0	O32(12/10/11),D16	0	-0.9
Total	3	115	108	23	18	6	0	2	5	5-0	0	37	.167	.204	.278	29	-11	3-1	1.000	-3	83	50	O53(20/23/12),D35	145	-1.5
SHEPPARD, JOHN	John; B Baltimore MD; d6.27																								
1873	Mar NA	3	11	1	0	0	0	0	0	0	—	1	.000	.000	.000	-99	-3	0-0	.500	-2	0	0	O2(1/0/1)/C	—	-0.3
SHERIDAN	; d10.9																								
1875	Atl NA	1	4	0	0	0	0	0	0	0	—	1	.000	.000	.000	-99	-1	0-0	ø	-0	0	0	/lf	—	-0.1
SHERIDAN, RED	Eugene Anthony; B11.14.1896 Brooklyn NY; D11.25.1975 Queens Village NY; BR/TR/5´10.5″/160; d7.3; Mil 1918																								
1918	Bro N	2	4	0	1	0	0	0	0	1	0	0	.250	.400	.250	100	0	1	1.000	-1	58	0	2b2	—	0.0
1920	Bro N	3	2	0	0	0	0	0	0	0	0	1	.000	.000	.000	-97	-1	0-0	1.000	1	113	591	S3	—	0.0
Total	2	5	6	0	1	0	0	0	0	1	0	1	.167	.286	.167	37	-1	1-0	1.000	0	113	591	S3,2b2	—	0.0
SHERIDAN, NEILL	Neill Rawlins "Wild Horse"; B11.20.1921 Sacramento CA; BR/TR/6´1.5″/195; d9.19; Col San Francisco																								
1948	Bos A	2	1	0	0	0	0	0	0	0	0	1	.000	.000	.000	-95	0	0-0	ø	0	—	—	/H	0	0.0
SHERIDAN, PAT	Patrick Arthur; B12.4.1957 Ann Arbor MI; BL/TR/6´3″/(175–195); [KCA79 3/73]; d9.16; Col Eastern Michigan																								
1981	KC A	3	1	0	0	0	0	0	0	0-0	0	1	.000	.000	.000	-99	0	0-0	1.000	0	158	0	O3(1/0/2)	0	0.0
1983	KC A	109	333	43	90	12	2	7	36	20-0	0	64	.270	.312	.381	89	-6	12-3	.988	6	115	93	O100(28/36/48)	0	-0.1
1984	†KC A	138	481	64	136	24	4	8	53	41-3	1	91	.283	.338	.399	103	2	19-6	.986	-4	93	98	O134(0/35/101)	0	-0.5
1985	†KC A	78	206	18	47	9	2	3	17	23-2	1	38	.228	.307	.335	76	-7	11-3	.983	-1	97	76	O69R/D	44	-1.0
1986	Det A	98	236	41	56	9	1	6	19	21-4	1	57	.237	.300	.360	79	-7	9-2	.977	-3	99	23	O90(11/51/32),D5	0	-1.1
1987	†Det A	141	421	57	109	19	3	6	49	44-4	1	90	.259	.327	.361	87	-8	18-13	.976	-2	102	78	O137(0/26/124)	0	-1.5
1988	Det A	127	347	47	88	9	5	11	47	44-4	2	64	.254	.339	.403	111	5	8-6	.981	-2	103	38	O111(92/9/12),D3	0	0.1
1989	Det A	50	120	16	29	3	0	3	15	17-0	0	21	.242	.333	.342	93	-1	4-0	.982	-1	88	119	O35(19/7/9),D8	0	-0.1
	†SF N	70	161	20	33	3	4	3	14	13-1	0	45	.205	.264	.329	71	-7	4-1	.983	3	118	77	O66(8/3/58)	0	-0.6
1991	NY A	62	113	13	23	3	0	4	7	13-1	0	30	.204	.286	.336	71	-5	1-1	1.000	0	90	183	O34(3/6/26),D2	0	-0.5
Total	9	876	2419	319	611	91	21	51	257	236-19	6	501	.253	.319	.371	90	-34	86-35	.983	-3	101	77	O779(162/173/481),D19	44	-5.3

YEAR	TM LG	G	AB	R	H	2B	3B	HR	RBI	BB-IB	HP	SO	AVG	OBP	SLG	AOPS	ABR	SB-CS	FA	FR	RNG	THR	GAMES AT POSITION	DL	BFW
Sherling, Ed	Edward Creech "Shine"; B7.18.1897 Coalburg AL; D11.16.1965 Enterprise AL; BR/TR/6´1˝/185; d8.13; Col Auburn																								
1924	Phi A	4	2	2	1	1	0	0	0	0	0	0	.500	.500	1.000	278	1	0-0	ø	0	—	—	/H	—	0.1
Sherlock, Monk	John Clinton; B10.26.1904 Buffalo NY; D11.26.1985 Buffalo NY; BR/TR/5´10˝/175; d4.20; b–Vince																								
1930	Phi N	92	299	51	97	18	2	0	38	27	0	28	.324	.380	.398	83	-7	0	.990	3	123	77	1b70,2b5/cf	—	-0.7
Sherlock, Vince	Vincent Thomas "Baldy"; B3.27.1910 Buffalo NY; D5.11.1997 Cheektowaga NY; BR/TR/6´0˝/180; d9.18; b–Monk																								
1935	Bro N	9	26	4	12	1	0	0	6	1	0	2	.462	.481	.500	168	3	1	.907	-2	76	27	2b8	—	0.1
Sherman, Darrell	Darrell Edward; B12.4.1967 Los Angeles CA; BL/TL/5´9˝/160; [SDN89 6/156]; d4.8; Col Cal St.–Long Beach																								
1993	SD N	37	63	8	14	1	0	0	2	6-0	3	8	.222	.315	.238	51	-4	2-1	1.000	2	143	0	O26(24/6/1)	0	-0.2
Sherrill, Dennis	Dennis Lee; B3.3.1956 Miami FL; BR/TR/6´0˝/165; [NYA74 1/12]; d9.4																								
1978	NY A	2	1	1	0	0	0	0	0	0-0	0	1	.000	.000	.000	-99	0	0-0	ø	-0	0	0	/3D	0	-0.1
1980	NY A	3	4	0	1	0	0	0	0	0-0	0	1	.250	.250	.250	38	0	0-0	1.000	-1	0	0	S2/2	0	-0.1
Total	2	5	5	1	1	0	0	0	0	0-0	0	2	.200	.200	.200	11	0	0-0	1.000	-1	0	0	S2/2D3	0	-0.2
Sherry, Norm	Norman Burt; B7.16.1931 New York NY; BR/TR/5´11˝/(180–181); d4.12; M2/C16; b–Larry																								
1959	LA N	2	3	0	1	0	0	0	2	0-0	1	0	.333	.500	.333	119	0	0-0	1.000	-1	0	0	C2	0	-0.1
1960	LA N	47	138	22	39	4	1	8	19	12-3	3	29	.283	.353	.500	122	4	0-0	.993	-3	148	48	C44	0	0.3
1961	LA N	47	121	10	31	2	0	5	21	9-2	0	30	.256	.308	.397	78	-4	0-0	.993	0	62	67	C45	33	-0.2
1962	LA N	35	88	7	16	2	0	3	16	6-0	1	17	.182	.240	.307	49	-7	0-0	.992	5	120	89	C34	0	0.0
1963	NY N	63	147	6	20	1	0	2	11	10-1	3	26	.136	.205	.184	13	-17	1-0	.980	-2	120	129	C61	0	-1.7
Total	5	194	497	45	107	9	1	18	69	37-6	8	102	.215	.279	.346	69	-24	1-0	.989	-0	114	85	C186	33	-1.7
Shetrone, Barry	Barry Stevan; B7.6.1938 Baltimore MD; D7.18.2001 Bowie MD; BL/TR/6´2˝/(185–190); d7.27																								
1959	Bal A	33	79	8	16	1	1	0	5	5-1	0	9	.203	.247	.241	36	-7	3-0	.947	-4	74	0	O23(5/17/1)	0	-1.2
1960	Bal A	1	0	1	0	0	0	0	0	0-0	0	0	ø	ø	ø	ø	0	0-0	ø	0	—	—	/R	0	0.0
1961	Bal A	3	7	0	1	0	0	0	1	0-0	0	2	.143	.143	.143	-24	-1	0-0	1.000	-0	91	0	O2C	0	-0.1
1962	Bal A	21	24	3	6	1	0	1	1	0-0	0	5	.250	.250	.417	81	-1	0-0	1.000	1	153	0	O6(3/2/1)	0	0.0
1963	Was A	2	2	0	0	0	0	0	0	0-0	0	0	.000	.000	.000	-99	-1	0-0	ø	0	—	—	/H	0	-0.1
Total	5	60	112	12	23	2	1	1	7	5-1	0	16	.205	.237	.268	39	-10	3-0	.962	-3	86	0	O31(8/21/2)	0	-1.4
Shetzline, John	John Henry; B1852 Philadelphia PA; D12.15.1892 Philadelphia PA; 5´11.5˝/190; d5.2																								
1882	Bal AA	73	282	23	62	8	3	0	—	-5	—	—	.220	.233	.270	75	-7	—	.800	4	106	138	3b52,2b20/rfS	—	-0.1
Shevlin, Jimmy	James Cornelius; B7.9.1909 Cincinnati OH; D10.30.1974 Ft.Lauderdale FL; BL/TL/5´10.5˝/155; d6.29; Col Holy Cross																								
1930	Det A	28	14	4	2	0	0	0	2	2	0	3	.143	.250	.143	2	-2	0-0	1.000	0	115	0	1b25	—	-0.2
1932	Cin N	7	24	3	5	2	0	0	4	4	1	0	.208	.345	.292	76	-1	4	.985	-0	85	58	1b7	—	-0.2
1934	Cin N	18	39	6	12	2	0	0	6	6	0	5	.308	.400	.359	107	1	0	1.000	1	124	119	1b10	—	0.1
Total	3	53	77	13	19	4	0	0	12	12	1	8	.247	.356	.299	77	-2	4-0	.995	1	108	70	1b42	—	-0.3
Shields, Pete	Francis Leroy; B9.21.1891 Swiftwater MS; D2.11.1961 Jackson MS; BR/TR/6´0˝/175; d4.14; Col U. of Mississippi																								
1915	Cle A	23	72	4	15	6	0	0	6	4	0	14	.208	.250	.292	61	-4	3-3	.974	-0	107	47	1b23	—	-0.5
Shields, Tommy	Thomas Charles; B8.14.1964 Fairfax VA; BL/TR/6´0˝/(180–185); [PitN86 15/368]; d7.25; Col Notre Dame																								
1992	Bal A	2	0	0	0	0	0	0	0	0-0	0	0	ø	ø	ø	ø	0	0-0	ø	0	—	—	/R	0	0.0
1993	Chi N	20	34	4	6	1	0	0	1	2-0	0	10	.176	.222	.206	16	-4	0-0	1.000	2	143	173	2b7,3b7/1lf	0	-0.2
Total	2	22	34	4	6	1	0	0	1	2-0	0	10	.176	.222	.206	16	-4	0-0	1.000	2	104	136	3b7,2b7/lf1	0	-0.2
Shilling, Jim	James Robert; B5.14.1914 Tulsa OK; D9.12.1986 Tulsa OK; BR/TR/5´11˝/175; d4.21																								
1939	Cle A	31	98	8	27	7	2	0	12	7	0	9	.276	.324	.388	84	-3	1-0	.935	0	105	105	2b27,S3	—	0.0
	Phi N	11	33	3	10	1	3	0	4	1	0	4	.303	.324	.515	126	1	0	.944	-2	79	85	2b5,S3,3b3/lf	—	-0.1
Total	1	42	131	11	37	8	5	0	16	8	0	13	.282	.324	.420	94	-2	1-0	.936	-2	102	103	2b32,S6,3b3/lf	—	-0.1
Shinault, Ginger	Enoch Erskine; B9.7.1892 Benton AR; D12.29.1930 Denver CO; BR/TR/5´11˝/170; d7.4																								
1921	Cle A	22	29	5	11	1	0	0	4	6	0	5	.379	.486	.414	129	2	1-0	.917	1	*103*	*142*	C20	—	0.3
1922	Cle A	13	15	1	2	1	0	0	0	0	0	2	.133	.133	.200	-14	-3	0-0	.400	-3	*60*	*0*	C11	—	-0.5
Total	2	35	44	6	13	2	0	0	4	6	0	7	.295	.380	.341	85	-1	1-0	.868	-2	*95*	*114*	C31	—	-0.2
Shindle, Billy	William D.; B12.5.1860 Gloucester NJ; D6.3.1936 Lakeland NJ; BR/TR/5´8.5˝/155; d10.5																								
1886	Det N	7	26	4	7	0	0	0	4	0	—	5	.269	.269	.269	62	-1	2	.900	0	118	61	S7	—	-0.1
1887	Det N	22	84	17	24	3	2	0	12	7	0	10	.286	.341	.369	93	-1	13	.818	-3	83	180	3b21/lf	—	-0.3
1888	Bal AA	135	514	61	107	14	8	1	53	20	8	—	.208	.249	.272	69	-19	52	**.922**	**38**	120	128	3b135	—	2.0
1889	Bal AA	138	567	122	178	24	7	3	64	42	7	37	.314	.369	.397	116	11	56	.862	23	**113**	105	3b138	—	3.0
1890	Phi P	**132**	584	127	189	21	21	10	90	40	4	30	.324	.371	.483	124	15	51	.856	8	103	**125**	S130,3b2	—	2.2
1891	Phi N	103	415	68	87	13	1	0	38	33	6	39	.210	.278	.246	51	-26	17	.874	4	106	**156**	3b100,S3	—	-1.7
1892	Bal N	143	619	100	156	20	18	3	50	35	8	34	.252	.301	.357	96	-7	24	.882	37	**130**	114	3b134,S9	—	3.0
1893	Bal N	125	521	100	136	22	11	1	75	66	8	17	.261	.353	.351	86	-10	17	.885	10	**108**	103	3b125	—	0.1
1894	Bro N	117	480	94	142	22	9	4	96	29	6	21	.296	.344	.404	86	-12	19	.896	1	96	62	3b117	—	-0.7
1895	Bro N	117	481	92	135	21	2	3	70	47	11	28	.281	.358	.351	91	-3	17	.895	-0	106	98	3b117	—	-0.1
1896	Bro N	131	516	75	144	24	9	1	61	24	4	20	.279	.316	.366	84	-13	24	.912	-11	93	105	3b131	—	-1.8
1897	Bro N	134	542	83	154	32	6	4	105	35	7	—	.284	.336	.387	96	-3	23	.904	-14	90	76	3b134	—	-1.3
1898	Bro N	120	466	50	105	10	3	1	41	10	5	—	.225	.249	.266	48	-33	3	.911	4	107	128	3b120	—	-2.6
Total	13	1424	5815	993	1564	226	97	31	759	388	74	241	.269	.323	.357	88	-102	318	.892	96	107	108	3b1274,S149/lf	—	1.7
Shines, Razor	Anthony Raymond "Ray"; B7.18.1956 Durham NC; BB/TR/6´1˝/210; [MonN78 18/451]; d9.9; Col St. Augustines																								
1983	Mon N	3	2	0	1	0	0	0	0	0-0	0	0	.500	.500	.500	178	0	0-0	ø	-0	0	0	/lf	0	0.0
1984	Mon N	12	20	0	6	1	0	0	2	0-0	0	3	.300	.286	.350	86	0	0-0	1.000	-1	0	91	1b3/3	0	-0.2
1985	Mon N	47	50	0	6	0	0	0	3	4-0	0	9	.120	.185	.120	-14	-8	0-1	.950	0	167	37	1b5/P	0	-0.8
1987	Mon N	6	9	0	2	0	0	0	0	1-0	1	0	.222	.364	.222	58	0	1-0	1.000	-0	82	169	1b2	0	0.0
Total	4	68	81	0	15	1	0	0	5	5-0	1	12	.185	.239	.198	24	-8	1-1	.975	-1	88	83	1b10/P3lf	0	-1.0
Shinjo, Tsuyoshi	Tsuyoshi; B1.28.1972 Fukuoka, Japan; BR/TR/6´1˝/185; d4.3																								
2001	NY N	123	400	46	107	23	1	10	56	25-3	7	70	.268	.320	.405	93	-5	4-5	.989	13	**117**	**190**	O119(46/53/39)	28	0.4
2002	†SF N	118	362	42	86	15	3	9	37	24-2	6	46	.238	.294	.370	77	-14	5-0	.980	12	**121**	179	O117(1/108/10)	18	0.0
2003	NY N	62	114	10	22	3	0	1	7	6-1	1	12	.193	.238	.246	28	-13	0-1	.972	7	129	275	O54(7/50/1)	0	-0.6
Total	3	303	876	98	215	41	4	20	100	55-6	14	128	.245	.299	.370	77	-32	9-6	.982	31	120	197	O290(54/211/50)	46	-0.2
Shinners, Ralph	Ralph Peter; B10.4.1895 Monches WI; D7.23.1962 Milwaukee WI; BR/TR/6´0˝/180; d4.12; Col Marquette																								
1922	NY N	56	135	16	34	4	2	0	15	5	6	22	.252	.308	.311	60	-8	3-5	.915	-4	94	46	O37(1/30/6)	—	-1.4
1923	NY N	33	13	5	2	1	0	0	0	2	0	1	.154	.267	.231	33	-1	0-0	1.000	1	171	0	O6(2/1/3)	—	-0.1
1925	StL N	74	251	39	74	9	2	7	36	12	1	19	.295	.330	.430	90	-5	8-5	.982	-2	103	34	O66(3/56/7)	—	-0.9
Total	3	163	399	60	110	14	4	7	51	19	7	42	.276	.320	.383	78	-14	11-10	.959	-5	101	38	O109(6/87/16)	—	-2.4
Shinnick, Tim	Timothy James "Dandy","Good Eye"; B11.6.1867 Exeter NH; D5.18.1944 Exeter NH; BB/TR/5´9˝/150; d4.19																								
1890	†Lou AA	133	493	87	126	16	11	1	82	62	8	—	.256	.348	.339	105	4	62	.925	-31	92	87	2b130,3b3	—	-1.9
1891	Lou AA	126	436	77	96	9	11	1	52	54	5	46	.220	.313	.298	76	-14	36	.913	-21	95	94	2b118,3b7/S	—	-2.7
Total	2	259	929	164	222	25	22	2	134	116	13	46	.239	.332	.320	91	-10	98	.919	-52	93	90	2b248,3b10/S	—	-4.6
Shipke, Bill	William Martin "Skipper Bill","Muskrat Bill" (b William Martin Shipkrethaver); B11.18.1882 St.Louis MO; D9.10.1940 Omaha NE; BR/TR/5´7˝/145; d4.23																								
1906	Cle A	2	6	0	0	0	0	0	0	0	0	—	.000	.000	.000	-99	-1	0	.933	1	124	294	2b2	—	-0.1
1907	Was A	64	189	17	37	3	2	1	9	15	2	—	.196	.262	.249	68	-7	6	.944	8	117	33	3b63	—	0.3
1908	Was A	111	341	40	71	7	8	0	20	38	5	—	.208	.297	.276	94	-1	15	.932	-4	96	103	3b110/2	—	-0.3
1909	Was A	9	16	2	2	1	0	0	0	2	0	—	.125	.222	.188	31	-1	0	.905	1	137	154	3b6,S2	—	0.0
Total	4	186	552	59	110	11	10	1	29	55	7	—	.199	.280	.261	81	-10	21	.935	6	105	80	3b179,2b3,S2	—	-0.1

YEAR	TM LG	G	AB	R	H	2B	3B	HR	RBI	BB-IB	HP	SO	AVG	OBP	SLG	AOPS	ABR	SB-CS	FA	FR	RNG	THR	GAMES AT POSITION	DL	BFW
SHIPLEY, CRAIG	Craig Barry; B1.7.1963 Parramatta, New South Wales, Australia; BR/TR/6´1˝/(168–190); d6.22; Col Alabama; OF(4/4/4)																								
1986	LA N	12	27	3	3	1	0	0	4	2-1	1	5	.111	.200	.148	-3	-4	0-0	.914	-3	61	80	S10/23	0	-0.7
1987	LA N	26	35	3	9	1	0	0	2	0-0	0	6	.257	.257	.286	45	-3	0-0	.949	-2	95	39	S18,3b6	0	-0.4
1989	NY N	4	7	3	1	0	0	0	0	0-0	0	1	.143	.143	.143	-19	-1	0-0	1.000	-1	47	0	S3,3b2	0	-0.2
1991	SD N	37	91	6	25	3	0	1	6	2-0	1	14	.275	.298	.341	77	-3	0-1	.902	-4	75	83	S19,2b14	0	-0.6
1992	SD N	52	105	7	26	6	0	0	7	2-1	0	21	.248	.262	.305	59	-6	1-1	.986	5	113	183	S23,2b11,3b8	0	0.1
1993	SD N	105	230	25	54	9	0	4	22	10-0	3	31	.235	.275	.326	60	-14	12-3	.964	-6	89	51	S38,3b37,2b12,O5(2/3/0)	17	-1.5
1994	SD N	81	240	32	80	14	4	4	30	9-1	3	28	.333	.362	.475	121	7	6-6	.936	-3	96	88	3b53,S14,2b13,O2(1/1/0)/1	25	0.4
1995	Hou N	92	232	23	61	8	1	3	24	8-3	2	28	.263	.291	.345	72	-10	6-1	.982	-3	90	67	3b65,S11,2b4/1	0	-1.1
1996	SD N	33	92	13	29	5	0	1	7	2-1	2	15	.315	.337	.402	100	0	7-0	.985	3	114	87	2b17,S7,3b4,O3R	90	0.5
1997	SD N	63	139	22	38	9	0	5	19	7-0	0	20	.273	.306	.446	101	-1	1-1	.947	-4	96	59	S21,2b16,1b4,3b2	66	-0.3
1998	Ana A	77	147	18	38	7	1	2	17	5-0	5	22	.259	.304	.361	71	-6	0-4	.963	2	80	26	3b48,2b11,1b8,S5,O2(1/0/1)	33	-0.5
Total	11	582	1345	155	364	63	6	20	138	47-7	17	191	.271	.302	.371	80	-41	33-17	.963	-14	90	76	3b226,S169,2b99,1b14,O12L	231	-4.3
SHIRES, ART	Charles Arthur "Art the Great"; B8.13.1907 Italy TX; D7.13.1967 Italy TX; BL/TR/6´1˝/195; d8.20																								
1928	Chi A	33	123	20	42	6	1	1	11	13	1	10	.341	.409	.431	122	5	0-3	.990	3	138	90	1b32	—	0.4
1929	Chi A	100	353	41	110	20	7	3	41	32	1	20	.312	.370	.433	108	4	4-5	.991	-0	107	110	1b90,2b3	—	-0.3
1930	Chi A	37	128	14	33	5	1	1	18	6	0	6	.258	.291	.336	61	-8	2-0	.979	-2	81	67	1b33	—	-1.1
	Was A	38	84	11	31	5	0	1	19	5	0	5	.369	.404	.464	119	3	1-3	.982	0	113	151	1b21	—	0.1
	Year	75	212	25	64	10	1	2	37	11	0	11	.302	.336	.387	84	-5	3-3	.980	-2	92	96	1b54	—	-1.0
1932	Bos N	82	298	32	71	9	3	5	30	25	1	21	.238	.299	.339	74	-11	1	.988	-2	95	100	1b80	—	-2.1
Total	4	290	986	118	287	45	12	11	119	81	3	62	.291	.347	.395	95	-7	8-11	.988	-1	104	101	1b256,2b3	—	-3.0
SHIRLEY, BART	Barton Arvin; B1.4.1940 Corpus Christi TX; BR/TR/5´10˝/(183–189); d9.14; Col Texas																								
1964	LA N	18	62	6	17	1	1	0	7	4-2	0	8	.274	.318	.323	87	-1	0-0	.900	-2	51	0	3b10,S8	0	-0.3
1966	LA N	12	5	2	1	0	0	0	0	0-0	0	2	.200	.200	.200	13	-1	0-0	1.000	-0	61	0	S5	0	-0.1
1967	NY N	6	12	1	0	0	0	0	0	0-0	0	5	.000	.000	.000	-99	-3	0-0	.917	-1	108	53	2b3	0	-0.4
1968	LA N	39	83	6	15	3	0	0	4	10-1	0	13	.181	.269	.217	51	-5	0-1	.903	-0	94	180	S21,2b18	0	-0.3
Total	4	75	162	15	33	4	1	0	11	14-3	0	28	.204	.267	.241	52	-10	0-1	.936	-4	105	153	S34,2b21,3b10	0	-1.1
SHIRLEY, MULE	Ernest Raeford; B5.24.1901 Snow Hill NC; D8.3.1955 Goldsboro NC; BL/TL/5´11˝/180; d5.6; Col North Carolina																								
1924	†Was A	30	77	12	18	2	2	0	16	3	0	7	.234	.262	.312	49	-6	0-0	.984	0	103	133	1b25	—	-0.7
1925	Was A	14	23	2	3	1	0	0	2	1	0	7	.130	.167	.174	-14	-4	0-0	1.000	0	92	104	1b9	—	-0.4
Total	2	44	100	14	21	3	2	0	18	4	0	14	.210	.240	.280	34	-10	0-0	.988	0	101	127	1b34	—	-1.1
SHIVER, IVEY	Ivey Merwin "Chick"; B1.22.1906 Sylvester GA; D8.31.1972 Savannah GA; BR/TR/6´1.5˝/190; d4.14; Col Georgia																								
1931	Det A	2	9	2	1	0	0	0	0	0	0	3	.111	.111	.111	-40	-2	0-0	1.000	-0	64	0	O2C	—	-0.2
1934	Cin N	19	59	6	12	1	0	2	6	3	0	15	.203	.242	.322	51	-4	1	1.000	-1	94	0	O15R	—	-0.6
Total	2	21	68	8	13	1	0	2	6	3	0	18	.191	.225	.294	38	-6	1-0	1.000	-2	91	0	O17(0/2/15)	—	-0.8
SHOCH, GEORGE	George Quintus; B1.6.1859 Philadelphia PA; D9.30.1937 Philadelphia PA; BR/TR/5´6˝/158; d9.10; OF(99/41/159)																								
1886	Was N	26	95	11	28	2	1	1	18	2	—	13	.295	.309	.368	114	1	2	.882	-3	47	0	O25(1/0/24)/S	—	-0.2
1887	Was N	70	264	47	63	9	1	1	18	21	4	16	.239	.304	.292	71	-9	29	.897	4	124	137	O63(11/3/49),S6/2	—	-0.5
1888	Was N	90	317	46	58	6	3	2	24	25	9	22	.183	.262	.240	65	-11	23	.900	6	111	39	S52,O35(9/0/26)/2P	—	-0.4
1889	Was N	30	109	12	26	2	0	0	11	20	6	5	.239	.385	.257	85	0	9	.905	3	145	86	O29(16/0/13)/S	—	0.2
1891	Mil AA	34	127	29	40	7	1	1	16	18	9	5	.315	.435	.409	118	4	12	.932	3	107	52	S25,3b9	—	0.6
1892	Bal N	76	308	42	85	15	3	1	50	24	6	19	.276	.340	.354	107	3	14	.872	-1	105	73	S57,O12(8/4/0),3b7	—	0.3
1893	Bro N	94	327	53	86	17	1	2	54	48	5	13	.263	.366	.339	92	-1	9	.892	-3	87	0	O46(32/0/15),3b37,S11,2b3	—	-0.5
1894	Bro N	65	243	47	77	6	5	1	37	26	5	6	.317	.394	.395	97	1	16	.926	0	86	70	O35(1/28/6),3b14,2b9,S7	—	0.0
1895	Bro N	61	216	49	56	9	7	0	29	32	5	6	.259	.368	.366	97	1	7	.952	-4	81	77	O39(16/2/21),2b13,S6,3b3	—	-0.4
1896	Bro N	76	250	36	73	7	4	1	28	33	3	10	.292	.381	.364	103	3	11	.941	-6	105	69	2b62,O10(2/3/5),3b3/S	—	0.0
1897	Bro N	85	284	42	79	9	2	0	38	49	5	—	.278	.393	.324	96	3	6	.941	-3	104	98	2b68,S13,O4(3/1/0)	—	0.3
Total	11	707	2540	414	671	89	28	10	323	298	57	115	.264	.354	.333	93	-5	138	.912	-4	96	67	O298R,S180,2b157,3b73/P	—	-0.6
SHOCKLEY, COSTEN	John Costen; B2.8.1942 Georgetown DE; BL/TL/6´2˝/195; d7.17																								
1964	Phi N	11	35	4	8	0	0	1	2	2-0	0	8	.229	.263	.314	65	-2	0-0	.968	-1	78	119	1b9	0	-0.3
1965	Cal A	40	107	5	20	2	0	2	17	9-0	1	16	.187	.252	.262	49	-7	0-0	.996	1	106	124	1b31/rf	0	-0.9
Total	2	51	142	9	28	2	0	3	19	11-0	1	24	.197	.255	.275	53	-9	0-0	.991	-0	100	123	1b40/rf	0	-1.2
SHOEMAKER, CHARLIE	Charles Landis; B8.10.1939 Los Angeles CA; D5.31.1990 Mount Penn PA; BL/TR/5´10˝/(155–160); d9.9; Col Arizona																								
1961	KC A	7	26	5	10	2	0	0	1	2-0	0	2	.385	.429	.462	135	1	0-0	1.000	1	112	64	2b6	0	0.3
1962	KC A	5	11	1	2	0	0	0	0	0-0	0	2	.182	.182	.182	-2	-2	0-0	1.000	1	144	67	2b4	0	0.0
1964	KC A	16	52	6	11	2	2	0	3	0-0	0	9	.212	.212	.327	46	-4	0-0	.964	-8	63	39	2b14	0	-1.2
Total	3	28	89	12	23	4	2	0	4	2-0	0	13	.258	.275	.348	67	-5	0-0	.981	-6	84	48	2b24	0	-0.9
SHOFNER, STRICK	Frank Strickland; B7.23.1919 Crawford TX; D10.10.1998 Crawford TX; BL/TR/5´10.5˝/187; d4.19																								
1947	Bos A	5	13	1	2	0	1	0	0	0	0	3	.154	.154	.308	25	-2	0-0	1.000	1	118	182	3b4	0	-0.1
SHOKES, EDDIE	Edward Christopher; B1.27.1920 Charleston SC; D9.14.2002 Winchester VA; BL/TL/6´0˝/170; d6.9; Mil 1943–45; Col Duke																								
1941	Cin N	1	1	0	0	0	0	0	0	0	0	1	.000	.000	.000	-99	0	0	ø	0	—	—	/H	0	0.0
1946	Cin N	31	83	3	10	1	0	0	5	18	0	21	.120	.277	.133	19	-8	1	.996	-2	76	138	1b29	0	-1.2
Total	2	32	84	3	10	1	0	0	5	18	0	22	.119	.275	.131	18	-8	1	.996	-2	76	138	1b29	0	-1.2
SHOOK, RAY	Raymond Curtis; B11.18.1889 Perry OH; D9.16.1970 South Bend IN; BR/TR/5´7.5˝/155; d4.16																								
1916	Chi A	1	0	0	0	0	0	0	0	0	0	0	ø	ø	ø	ø	0	0	ø	0	—	—	/R	—	0.0
SHOOP, RON	Ronald Lee; B9.19.1931 Rural Valley PA; D3.14.2003 Rural Valley PA; BR/TR/5´11˝/185; d8.22																								
1959	Det A	3	7	1	1	0	0	0	1	0-0	0	1	.143	.143	.143	-20	-1	0-0	1.000	-2	37	0	C3	0	-0.3
SHOPAY, TOM	Thomas Michael; B2.21.1945 Bristol CT; BL/TR/5´9.5˝/160; [NYA65 16/633]; d9.17; Col Dean (MA) JC																								
1967	NY A	8	27	2	8	1	0	2	6	1-1	0	5	.296	.310	.556	161	2	2-0	.917	0	69	393	O7L	0	0.2
1969	NY A	28	48	2	4	0	1	0	0	2-1	0	10	.083	.120	.125	-33	-9	0-1	1.000	1	137	0	O11(7/0/5)	0	-1.0
1971	†Bal A	47	74	10	19	2	0	0	5	3-1	0	7	.257	.286	.284	61	-4	2-1	1.000	-0	90	146	O13(4/0/9)	43	-0.5
1972	Bal A	49	40	3	9	0	0	0	2	5-0	0	12	.225	.311	.225	59	-2	0-0	1.000	-0	100	0	O3L	0	-0.2
1975	Bal A	40	31	4	5	1	0	0	2	4-0	0	7	.161	.257	.194	31	-3	3-0	1.000	1	109	0	O13(1/6/6)/CD	0	-0.1
1976	Bal A	14	20	4	4	0	0	0	1	3-0	0	3	.200	.304	.200	53	-1	1-0	1.000	-1	75	0	O11(6/2/3)/C	0	-0.2
1977	Bal A	67	69	15	13	3	0	1	4	8-0	0	7	.188	.273	.275	53	-4	3-3	1.000	2	111	134	O52(25/28/14),D2	0	-0.3
Total	7	253	309	40	62	7	1	3	20	26-3	0	51	.201	.262	.259	49	-21	11-5	.993	4	104	121	O110(53/36/37),D5,C2	43	-2.1
SHOPPACH, KELLY	Kelly Brian; B4.29.1980 Fort Worth TX; BR/TR/6´1˝/210; [BosA01 2/48]; d5.28; Col Baylor																								
2005	Bos A	9	15	1	0	0	0	0	0	0-0	1	7	.000	.063	.000	-78	-4	0-0	1.000	-2	90	0	C7,D2	0	-0.6
2006	Cle A	41	110	7	27	6	0	3	16	8-0	0	45	.245	.297	.382	77	-4	0-0	.991	6	92	147	C40	0	0.4
Total	2	50	125	8	27	6	0	3	16	8-0	1	52	.216	.269	.336	57	-8	0-0	.992	4	92	133	C47,D2	0	-0.2
SHORT, DAVE	David Orvis; B5.11.1917 Magnolia AR; D11.22.1983 Shreveport LA; BL/TR/5´11.5˝/162; d9.16; Mil 1941–45; Col Louisiana Tech																								
1940	Chi A	4	3	1	1	0	0	0	0	1	0	2	.333	.500	.333	119	0	0-0	ø	0	—	—	/H	—	0.0
1941	Chi A	3	8	0	0	0	0	0	0	2	0	1	.000	.200	.000	-44	-2	0-0	.800	-1	80	0	O2L	0	-0.2
Total	2	7	11	1	1	0	0	0	0	3	0	3	.091	.286	.091	3	-2	0-0	.800	-1	80	0	O2L	0	-0.2
SHORT, RICK	Richard Ryan; B12.6.1972 Elgin IL; BR/TR/6´0˝/200; [BalA94 33/923]; d6.10; Col Western Illinois																								
2005	Was N	11	15	4	6	2	0	2	4	1-0	1	1	.400	.471	.933	268	4	0-0	.938	-1	78	88	2b6/1	9	0.3
SHORTEN, CHICK	Charles Henry; B4.19.1892 Scranton PA; D10.23.1965 Scranton PA; BL/TL/6´0˝/175; d9.22; Mil 1918																								
1915	Bos A	6	14	1	3	1	0	0	0	0	0	2	.214	.214	.286	51	-1	0	1.000	1	98	254	O5(0/4/1)	—	-0.1
1916	†Bos A	53	112	14	33	2	1	0	11	10	0	8	.295	.352	.330	105	1	1	1.000	-3	95	0	O33(13/19/1)	—	-0.4
1917	Bos A	69	168	12	30	4	2	0	16	10	1	10	.179	.229	.226	39	-13	2	.977	-3	100	37	O43(16/20/7)	—	-2.0

YEAR	TM LG	G	AB	R	H	2B	3B	HR	RBI	BB-IB	HP	SO	AVG	OBP	SLG	AOPS	ABR	SB-CS	FA	FR	RNG	THR	GAMES AT POSITION	DL	BFW
1919	Det A	95	270	37	85	9	3	0	22	22	0	13	.315	.366	.370	110	4	5	.973	-6	100	19	O75(0/18/57)	—	-0.7
1920	Det A	116	364	35	105	9	6	1	40	28	0	14	.288	.339	.354	86	-8	2-4	.989	-0	92	115	O99(0/31/68)	—	-1.4
1921	Det A	92	217	33	59	11	3	0	23	20	0	11	.272	.333	.350	75	-8	2-3	.981	-2	98	52	O51(3/36/12)	—	-1.2
1922	StL A	55	131	22	36	12	5	2	16	16	0	8	.275	.354	.489	114	2	0-1	1.000	-0	98	69	O31(4/16/12)	—	0.0
1924	Cin N	41	69	7	19	3	0	0	6	4	0	2	.275	.315	.319	71	-3	0-0	1.000	-1	71	104	O15(11/0/4)	—	-0.4
Total	8	527	1345	161	370	51	20	3	134	110	1	68	.275	.330	.349	87	-26	12-8	.985	-14	96	62	O352(47/144/162)	—	-6.2
SHOTTON, BURT	Burton Edwin "Barney"; B10.18.1884 Brownhelm OH; D7.29.1962 Lake Wales FL; BL/TR/5´11˝/175; d9.13; M11/C8																								
1909	StL A	17	61	5	16	0	1	0	0	5	1	—	.262	.328	.295	104	0	3	.915	0	85	0	O17(2/15/0)	—	-0.1
1911	StL A	139	572	84	146	11	8	0	36	51	1	—	.255	.317	.302	76	-19	26	.950	3	111	87	O139(18/121/0)	—	-2.5
1912	StL A	154	580	87	168	15	8	2	40	86	9	—	.290	.390	.353	117	18	35	.941	4	112	89	O154C	—	1.2
1913	StL A	147	549	105	163	23	8	1	28	**99**	1	63	.297	.405	.373	132	28	43	.951	7	104	118	O146C	—	2.7
1914	StL A	154	579	82	156	19	9	0	38	64	2	66	.269	.344	.333	108	6	40-29	.940	-4	103	74	O152C	—	-1.1
1915	StL A	156	559	93	158	18	11	1	30	118	2	62	.283	.409	.360	135	32	43-32	.931	-3	103	78	O154(138/5/11)	—	2.2
1916	StL A	156	614	97	174	23	6	1	36	**110**	0	65	.283	.392	.345	128	27	41-28	.950	8	107	117	O156L	—	3.0
1917	StL A	118	398	48	89	9	1	1	20	62	1	47	.224	.330	.259	83	-5	16	.923	-12	28	36	O107L	—	-2.5
1918	Was A	126	505	68	132	16	7	0	21	67	1	28	.261	.349	.321	104	4	25	.942	-1	105	81	O122(67/1/54)	—	-0.4
1919	StL N	85	270	35	77	13	5	1	20	22	1	25	.285	.341	.381	125	8	16	.927	-4	83	124	O67L	—	0.2
1920	StL N	62	180	28	41	5	0	1	12	18	2	14	.228	.305	.272	69	-7	5-1	.959	2	93	175	O51(41/2/6)	—	-0.6
1921	StL N	38	48	9	12	1	1	1	7	7	1	4	.250	.357	.375	96	0	0-2	.958	1	107	181	O11(1/10/0)	—	0.0
1922	StL N	34	30	5	6	1	0	0	2	4	0	6	.200	.294	.233	39	-3	0-1	1.000	0	398	0	O3(1/1/1)	—	-0.3
1923	StL N	1	0	1	0	0	0	0	0	0	0	0	ø	ø	ø	ø	0	0-0	ø	0	—	—	/R	—	0.0
Total	14	1387	4945	747	1338	154	65	9	290	713	22	380	.271	.365	.333	110	89	293-93	.942	2	98	91	O1279(598/607/72)	—	1.8
SHOUPE, JOHN	John F.; B9.30.1851 Cincinnati OH; D2.13.1920 Cincinnati OH; BL/TL/5´7˝/140; d5.3																								
1879	Tro N	11	44	5	4	0	0	0	1	0	—	3	.091	.091	.091	-43	-6	—	.820	-3	101	0	S10/2	—	-0.8
1882	StL AA	2	7	1	0	0	0	0	—	0	—	—	.000	.000	.000	-96	-1	—	1.000	1	130	0	2b2	—	-0.1
1884	Was U	1	4	1	3	0	0	0	—	0	—	—	.750	.750	.750	368	1	—	.857	2	354	1092	/cf	—	0.2
Total	3	14	55	7	7	0	0	0	1	0	—	3	.127	.127	.127	-17	-6	—	.820	-0	101	0	S10,2b3/cf	—	-0.7
SHOVLIN, JOHN	John Joseph "Brode"; B1.14.1891 Drifton PA; D2.16.1976 Bethesda MD; BR/TR/5´7˝/163; d6.21																								
1911	Pit N	2	1	1	0	0	0	0	0	0	0	1	.000	.000	.000	-96	0	0	ø	0	—	—	/H	—	0.0
1919	StL A	9	35	4	7	0	0	0	1	5	0	2	.200	.300	.200	41	-3	0	.936	-1	92	134	2b9	—	-0.4
1920	StL A	7	7	2	2	0	0	0	2	0	0	0	.286	.286	.286	50	-1	0-0	1.000	0	117	0	S5	—	0.0
Total	3	18	43	7	9	0	0	0	3	5	0	3	.209	.292	.209	39	-4	0-0	.936	-1	92	134	2b9,S5	—	-0.4
SHUBA, GEORGE	George Thomas "Shotgun"; B12.13.1924 Youngstown OH; BL/TR/5´11˝/180; d7.2																								
1948	Bro N	63	161	21	43	6	0	4	32	34	0	31	.267	.395	.379	107	3	1	.936	-4	91	28	O56(55/2/1)	0	-0.4
1949	Bro N	1	1	0	0	0	0	0	0	0	0	0	.000	.000	.000	-96	0	0	ø	0	—	—	/H	0	0.0
1950	Bro N	34	111	15	23	8	2	3	12	13	2	22	.207	.302	.396	80	-3	2	.984	3	105	219	O27L	0	-0.2
1952	†Bro N	94	256	40	78	12	1	9	40	38	0	29	.305	.395	.465	136	14	1-3	.992	-2	98	44	O67(66/0/1)	0	0.7
1953	†Bro N	74	169	19	43	12	1	5	23	17	1	20	.254	.326	.426	92	-2	1-2	.984	-3	92	36	O44(43/0/1)	0	-0.7
1954	Bro N	45	65	3	10	5	0	2	10	7	1	10	.154	.240	.323	46	-5	0-0	.913	-1	100	0	O13(7/0/5)	0	-0.7
1955	†Bro N	44	51	8	14	2	0	1	8	11-1	2	10	.275	.422	.373	110	2	0-0	.909	-1	80	0	O9(7/1/2)	0	0.0
Total	7	355	814	106	211	45	4	24	125	120-1	6	122	.259	.358	.413	104	9	5-5	.967	-8	96	59	O216(205/3/10)	0	-1.3
SHUGART, FRANK	Frank Harry (b Frank Harry Shugarts); B12.10.1866 Luthersburg PA; D9.9.1944 Clearfield PA; BL/TR (BB 1897)/5´8˝/170; d8.23																								
1890	Chi P	29	106	8	20	5	5	0	15	5	1	13	.189	.232	.330	47	-9	5	.881	-3	87	110	S25,O5(0/1/4)	—	-0.9
1891	Pit N	75	320	57	88	19	8	3	33	20	3	26	.275	.324	.412	117	5	21	.902	2	92	131	S75	—	0.8
1892	Pit N	137	554	94	148	19	14	0	62	47	4	48	.267	.329	.352	105	2	28	.886	6	104	89	S134,C2/rf	—	1.4
1893	Pit N	52	210	37	55	7	3	1	32	19	3	15	.262	.332	.338	80	-6	12	.882	-3	103	77	S51/O(2/1/0)	—	-0.5
	StL N	59	246	41	69	10	4	0	28	22	6	10	.280	.354	.354	88	-4	13	.907	-6	183	99	O28(0/19/9),S23,3b9	—	-0.8
	Year	111	456	78	124	17	7	1	60	41	9	25	.272	.344	.346	84	-10	25	.868	-8	100	80	S74,O29(2/20/9),3b9	—	-1.3
1894	StL N	**133**	527	103	154	19	18	7	72	38	9	37	.292	.350	.436	89	-13	21	.912	-9	125	41	O122C,S7,3b7	—	-2.3
1895	Lou N	113	473	61	125	14	13	4	70	31	4	25	.264	.315	.374	83	-14	14	.874	-18	88	97	S88,O27(0/22/5)	—	-2.4
1897	Phi N	40	163	20	41	8	2	5	25	8	0	—	.252	.287	.417	87	-4	5	.872	-10	88	92	S40	—	-1.0
1901	Chi A	107	415	62	104	9	12	2	47	28	2	—	.251	.301	.345	81	-12	12	.885	-11	96	85	S107	—	-1.8
Total	8	745	3014	483	804	110	79	22	384	218	32	174	.267	.323	.378	90	-55	131	.883	-51	95	95	S550,O184(2/165/19),3b16,C2	—	-7.5
SHUMPERT, TERRY	Terrance Darnell; B8.16.1966 Paducah KY; BR/TR/5´11˝/(185–200); [KCA87 2/41]; d5.1; Col Kentucky; OF(84/9/15)																								
1990	KC A	32	91	7	25	6	1	0	8	2-0	1	17	.275	.292	.363	85	-2	3-3	.977	-2	89	79	2b27,D3	99	-0.4
1991	KC A	144	369	45	80	16	4	5	34	30-0	5	75	.217	.283	.322	67	-17	17-11	.975	-8	93	94	2b144	0	-2.2
1992	KC A	36	94	6	14	5	1	1	11	3-0	0	17	.149	.175	.255	19	-11	2-2	.969	-9	87	85	2b33/SD	31	-2.0
1993	KC A	8	10	0	1	0	0	0	0	2-0	0	2	.100	.250	.100	-2	-1	1-0	1.000	1	95	119	2b8	0	0.0
1994	KC A	64	183	28	44	6	2	8	24	13-0	0	39	.240	.289	.426	78	-7	18-3	.964	-5	102	71	2b38,3b24/SD	0	-0.7
1995	Bos A	21	47	6	11	3	0	0	3	4-0	0	13	.234	.294	.298	53	-3	3-1	1.000	2	82	97	2b8,3b5,S3/D	0	0.0
1996	Chi N	27	31	5	7	1	0	2	6	2-0	1	11	.226	.286	.452	90	-1	0-1	.923	-1	48	0	3b10,2b4/S	15	-0.2
1997	SD N	13	33	4	9	3	0	1	6	3-0	0	4	.273	.324	.455	111	1	0-0	.973	-1	78	89	2b7,O3(2/0/1),3b2	70	0.0
1998	Col N	23	26	3	6	1	0	1	2	2-0	0	8	.231	.286	.385	61	-1	0-0	1.000	3	211	188	2b6	0	0.1
1999	Col N	92	262	58	91	26	3	10	37	31-2	2	41	.347	.413	.584	120	9	14-0	.988	8	116	99	2b54,O19(6/9/4),3b14,S2	0	2.1
2000	Col N	115	263	52	68	11	7	9	40	28-1	6	40	.259	.340	.456	81	-8	8-4	.967	-2	104	114	O40L,2b23,3b15,S7,1b6/D	0	-0.9
2001	Col N	114	242	37	70	14	5	4	24	15-2	3	44	.289	.337	.438	82	-6	14-3	.968	2	108	122	2b41,O24L,3b12,S4	0	-0.1
2002	Col N	106	234	30	55	12	1	6	21	21-0	4	41	.235	.304	.372	69	-10	4-1	.974	-1	104	93	2b60,O8(7/0/1),S3/3	0	-0.9
2003	TB A	59	84	14	16	5	2	2	7	10-0	2	17	.190	.289	.369	74	-3	1-0	.978	-3	89	48	D17,2b14,O14(5/0/9),3b11/S	33	-0.7
Total	14	854	1969	295	497	109	26	49	223	166-5	24	369	.252	.315	.409	80	-60	85-29	.977	-17	98	93	2b467,O108L,3b94,D25,S23,1b6	248	-5.9
SHUPE, VINCE	Vincent William; B9.5.1921 E.Canton OH; D4.5.1962 Canton OH; BL/TL/5´11˝/180; d7.7																								
1945	Bos N	78	283	22	76	8	0	0	15	17	1	16	.269	.312	.297	69	-12	3	.989	1	107	147	1b77	0	-1.5
SICKING, ED	Edward Joseph; B3.30.1897 St.Bernard OH; D8.30.1978 Madeira OH; BR/TR/5´9.5˝/165; d8.26; Mil 1918																								
1916	Chi N	1	1	0	0	0	0	0	0	0	0	0	.000	.000	.000	-90	0	0	ø	0	—	—	/H	—	0.0
1918	NY N	46	132	9	33	4	0	0	12	6	0	11	.250	.283	.280	73	-4	2	.917	-7	83	0	3b24,2b18,S3	—	-1.2
1919	NY N	6	15	2	5	0	0	0	3	1	1	0	.333	.412	.333	127	1	0	.971	2	133	147	S6	—	0.3
	Phi N	61	185	16	40	2	1	0	15	8	1	17	.216	.253	.238	45	-12	4	.925	3	101	167	S35,2b22	—	-0.8
	Year	67	200	18	45	2	1	0	18	9	2	17	.225	.265	.245	51	-12	4	.933	5	106	164	S41,2b22	—	-0.5
1920	NY N	46	134	11	23	3	1	0	9	10	1	10	.172	.234	.209	28	-12	6-2	.915	-1	101	25	3b28,2b15,S3	—	-1.2
	Cin N	37	123	12	33	3	0	0	17	13	0	5	.268	.338	.293	83	-2	2-3	.955	-2	105	77	2b25,S9,3b2	—	-0.4
	Year	83	257	23	56	6	1	0	26	23	1	15	.218	.285	.249	55	-14	8-5	.952	-2	103	122	2b40,3b30,S12	—	-1.6
1927	Pit N	6	7	1	1	1	0	0	3	1	0	0	.143	.250	.286	40	-1	0	1.000	1	112	89	2b5	—	0.0
Total	5	203	597	51	135	13	2	0	59	39	3	43	.226	.277	.255	57	-30	14-5	.965	-3	97	113	2b85,S56,3b54	—	-3.3
SIDDALL, JOE	Joseph Todd; B10.25.1967 Windsor ON, Can.; BL/TR/6´1˝/(197–200); d7.28																								
1993	Mon N	19	20	0	2	1	0	0	1	1-1	0	5	.100	.143	.150	-21	-3	0-0	1.000	-1	75	135	C15/1lf	0	-0.4
1995	Mon N	7	10	4	3	0	0	0	1	3-0	1	3	.300	.500	.300	113	1	0-0	.882	-4	35	0	C7	0	-0.3
1996	Fla N	18	47	0	7	1	0	0	3	2-0	0	8	.149	.184	.170	-6	-7	0-0	.977	-1	86	147	C18	0	-0.8
1998	Det A	29	65	3	12	3	0	1	6	7-0	0	25	.185	.264	.277	40	-6	0-0	.994	6	116	162	C27/rf	0	0.2
Total	4	73	142	7	24	5	0	1	11	13-1	1	41	.169	.244	.225	24	-15	0-0	.983	1	95	142	C67,O2(1/0/1)/1	0	-1.3
SIEBERN, NORM	Norman Leroy; B7.26.1933 St.Louis MO; BL/TR/6´3˝/(200–205); d6.15																								
1956	†NY A	54	162	27	33	1	4	4	21	19-0	0	38	.204	.286	.333	66	-9	1-1	.971	-1	104	27	O51L	0	-1.4
1958	†NY A	134	460	79	138	19	5	14	55	66-3	1	87	.300	.388	.454	136	25	5-8	.982	3	101	103	O133(127/11/0)	0	1.8
1959	NY A	120	380	52	103	17	0	11	53	41-2	2	71	.271	.341	.403	108	5	3-1	.989	-4	95	17	O93(82/5/9),1b2	0	-0.4
1960	KC A	144	520	69	145	31	6	19	69	72-6	2	68	.279	.366	.471	125	19	0-0	.987	-2	100	78	O75L,1b69	0	0.9
1961	KC A	153	560	68	166	36	5	18	98	82-3	1	91	.296	.384	.475	127	24	2-4	.989	1	100	86	1b109,O47L	0	1.5
1962	KC A★	**162**	600	114	185	25	6	25	117	110-9	1	88	.308	.412	.495	138	36	3-1	.994	2	101	87	1b162	0	2.9
1963	KC A☆	152	556	80	151	25	2	16	83	79-6	0	82	.272	.358	.410	110	10	1-4	.991	1	103	88	1b131,O16(16/0/1)	0	0.1

YEAR	TM LG	G	AB	R	H	2B	3B	HR	RBI	BB-IB	HP	SO	AVG	OBP	SLG	AOPS	ABR	SB-CS	FA	FR	RNG	THR	GAMES AT POSITION	DL	BFW
1964	Bal A★	150	478	92	117	24	2	12	56	**106**-3	2	87	.245	.379	.379	114	15	2-3	.995	4	108	**114**	1b149	0	0.9
1965	Bal A	106	297	44	76	13	4	8	32	50-7	1	49	.256	.362	.407	117	8	1-2	.991	0	104	121	1b76	0	0.4
1966	Cal A	125	336	29	83	14	1	5	41	63-7	0	61	.247	.361	.339	107	6	0-1	.992	3	115	138	1b99	0	0.4
1967	SF N	46	58	6	9	1	1	0	4	14-0	0	13	.155	.319	.207	54	-3	0-0	1.000	-0	85	98	1b15,O2L	0	-0.4
	†Bos A	33	44	2	9	0	2	0	7	6-1	0	8	.205	.300	.295	71	-2	0-0	.981	1	105	43	1b13/lf	0	-0.2
1968	Bos A	27	30	0	2	0	0	0	0	0-0	0	5	.067	.067	.067	-56	-6	0-0	1.000	0	141	114	1b2,O2(1/0/1)	0	-0.7
Total	12	1406	4481	662	1217	206	38	132	636	708-47	10	748	.272	.369	.423	117	128	18-25	.992	6	103	101	1b827,O420(402/16/11)	0	5.8
Siebert, Dick	Richard Walther; B2.19.1912 Fall River MA; D12.9.1978 Minneapolis MN; BL/TL/6´0˝/170; d9.7; s–Paul; Col Concordia (TX)																								
1932	Bro N	6	7	1	2	0	0	0	0	2	0	2	.286	.444	.286	104	0	0	1.000	-0	0	0	1b2	—	0.0
1936	Bro N	2	2	0	0	0	0	0	0	0	0	0	.000	.000	.000	-99	-1	0	1.000	1	0	2806	/rf	—	0.0
1937	StL N	22	38	3	7	2	0	0	2	4	1	8	.184	.279	.237	41	-3	1	.979	-1	75	44	1b7	—	-0.4
1938	StL N	1	1	0	1	0	0	0	0	0	0	0	1.000	1.000	1.000	427	0	0	ø	0	—	—	/H	—	0.0
	Phi A	48	194	24	55	8	3	0	28	10	3	9	.284	.329	.356	73	-9	2-3	1.000	5	136	81	1b46	—	-0.7
1939	Phi A	101	402	58	118	28	3	6	47	21	0	22	.294	.329	.423	93	-6	4-1	.991	5	123	81	1b99	—	-0.9
1940	Phi A	**154**	595	69	170	31	6	5	77	33	2	34	.286	.325	.383	85	-15	8-6	.985	8	125	84	1b154	—	-2.0
1941	Phi A	123	467	63	156	28	8	5	79	37	2	22	.334	.385	.460	126	17	1-3	.990	5	119	91	1b123	0	1.0
1942	Phi A	153	612	57	159	25	7	2	74	24	3	17	.260	.291	.333	76	-23	4-5	.989	-2	94	80	1b152	0	-4.1
1943	Phi A★	146	558	50	140	26	7	1	72	33	2	21	.251	.295	.328	83	-14	6-7	.990	3	108	89	1b145	0	-2.2
1944	Phi A	132	468	52	143	27	5	6	52	62	0	17	.306	.387	.423	133	22	2-0	.993	2	102	99	1b74,O58(42/0/17)	0	1.9
1945	Phi A	147	573	62	153	29	1	7	51	50	2	33	.267	.328	.358	99	-1	2-7	.991	8	**117**	98	1b147	0	-0.3
Total	11	1035	3917	439	1104	204	40	32	482	276	15	185	.282	.332	.379	96	-33	30-32	.990	33	113	88	1b949,O59(42/0/18)	0	-7.7
Siefke, Ed	Frederick Edwin; B3.27.1870 New York NY; D4.18.1893 New York NY; 5´11˝/168; d5.2																								
1890	Bro AA	16	58	1	8	2	0	0	3	5	0	—	.138	.206	.172	12	-6	2	.811	-1	124	69	3b16	—	-0.6
Siegel, John	John; B York PA; d6.9																								
1884	Phi U	8	31	4	7	2	0	0	—	1	—	—	.226	.250	.290	69	-2	—	.533	-4	61	0	3b8	—	-0.6
Siegle, Johnny	John Herbert; B7.8.1874 Urbana OH; D2.12.1968 Urbana OH; BR/TR/5´10˝/165; d9.15																								
1905	Cin N	17	56	9	17	1	2	1	8	7	1	—	.304	.391	.446	135	2	0	.960	-1	51	0	O16R	—	0.1
1906	Cin N	22	68	4	8	2	2	0	7	3	2	—	.118	.178	.206	19	-7	0	.959	0	39	157	O21(7/14/0)	—	-0.9
Total	2	39	124	13	25	3	4	1	15	10	3	—	.202	.277	.315	75	-5	0	.959	-1	44	91	O37(7/14/16)	—	-0.8
Siemer, Oscar	Oscar Sylvester "Cotton"; B8.14.1901 St.Louis MO; D12.5.1959 St.Louis MO; BR/TR/5´9˝/162; d5.20																								
1925	Bos N	16	46	5	14	0	1	1	6	1	0	0	.304	.319	.413	94	-1	0-0	.900	-2	*112*	*99*	C16	—	-0.2
1926	Bos N	31	73	3	15	1	0	0	5	2	0	7	.205	.227	.219	22	-8	0	.920	-3	*83*	*65*	C30	—	-1.0
Total	2	47	119	8	29	1	1	1	11	3	0	7	.244	.262	.294	51	-9	0-0	.913	-5	*94*	*78*	C46	—	-1.2
Sierra, Ruben	Ruben Angel (Garcia); B10.6.1965 Rio Piedras, PR; BB/TR/6´1˝/(175–220); d6.1																								
1986	Tex A	113	382	50	101	13	10	16	55	22-3	1	65	.264	.302	.476	106	1	7-8	.972	-2	95	109	O107(44/21/68),D3	0	-0.6
1987	Tex A	158	643	97	169	35	4	30	109	39-4	2	114	.263	.302	.470	101	-1	16-11	.963	-1	92	159	O157(0/4/156)	0	-1.0
1988	Tex A	156	615	77	156	32	2	23	91	44-10	1	91	.254	.301	.424	99	-2	18-4	.979	-0	96	118	O153R/D	0	-0.5
1989	Tex A★	**162**	634	101	194	35	**14**	29	**119**	43-2	2	82	.306	.347	**.543**	146	35	8-2	.973	-1	98	112	O162(0/2/161)	0	3.0
1990	Tex A	159	608	70	170	37	2	16	96	49-13	1	86	.280	.330	.426	111	8	9-0	.967	-8	94	65	O151R,D7	0	-0.3
1991	Tex A★	161	661	110	203	44	5	25	116	56-7	0	91	.307	.357	.502	138	33	16-4	.979	-3	92	126	O161(0/3/161)	0	2.7
1992	Tex A★	124	500	66	139	30	6	14	70	31-6	0	59	.278	.315	.446	116	8	12-4	.970	-6	93	75	O119R,D4	0	-0.1
	†Oak A	27	101	17	28	4	1	3	17	14-6	0	9	.277	.359	.426	127	4	2-0	1.000	0	116	0	O25R,D2	0	0.4
	Year	151	601	83	167	34	7	17	87	45-12	0	68	.278	.323	.443	118	12	14-4	.976	-6	97	62	O144R,D6	0	0.3
1993	Oak A	158	630	77	147	23	5	22	101	52-16	0	97	.233	.288	.390	86	-16	25-5	.977	1	105	89	O133R,D25	0	-1.9
1994	Oak A★	110	426	71	114	21	1	23	92	23-4	0	64	.268	.298	.484	107	2	8-5	.948	-6	85	119	O98(0/1/97),D10	0	-0.9
1995	Oak A	70	264	40	70	17	0	12	42	24-2	0	42	.265	.323	.466	108	3	4-4	.957	-7	82	27	O62R,D7	15	-0.7
	†NY A	56	215	33	56	15	0	7	44	22-2	0	34	.260	.322	.428	96	-1	1-0	.950	0	104	170	D46,O10R	0	-0.3
	Year	126	479	73	126	32	0	19	86	46-4	0	76	.263	.323	.449	103	1	5-4	.956	-6	85	46	O72R,D53	0	-1.0
1996	NY A	96	360	39	93	17	1	11	52	40-11	0	58	.258	.327	.403	85	-9	1-3	.984	2	95	243	D61,O33(32/0/1)	0	-1.1
	Det A	46	158	22	35	9	1	1	20	20-1	0	25	.222	.306	.310	57	-10	3-1	.914	-0	109	60	O23(4/0/19),D20	0	-1.1
	Year	142	518	61	128	26	2	12	72	60-12	0	83	.247	.320	.375	76	-19	4-4	.950	2	101	164	D81,O56(36/0/20)	0	-2.2
1997	Cin N	25	90	6	22	5	1	2	7	6-1	0	21	.244	.292	.389	75	-4	0-0	1.000	0	87	203	O24(12/0/12)	0	-0.4
	Tor A	14	48	4	10	0	2	1	5	3-1	0	13	.208	.250	.354	57	-4	0-0	.929	-1	90	0	O7(6/0/2),D6	0	-0.4
1998	Chi A	27	74	7	16	4	1	4	11	3-0	0	11	.216	.247	.459	80	-3	2-0	1.000	-1	82	122	O14(2/0/12),D5	0	-0.3
2000	Tex A	20	60	5	14	0	0	1	7	4-0	0	9	.233	.281	.283	43	-5	1-0	ø	0	0	0	D14	0	-0.6
2001	Tex A	94	344	55	100	22	1	23	67	19-0	0	52	.291	.322	.561	124	11	2-0	.937	-3	92	0	D50,O36(1/0/35)	15	0.3
2002	Sea A	122	419	47	113	23	0	13	60	31-5	0	66	.270	.319	.418	97	-2	4-0	.979	-3	94	35	O60(59/0/1),D52	0	-0.8
2003	Tex A	43	133	14	35	9	0	3	12	14-1	0	27	.263	.333	.398	86	-2	1-1	.962	-3	66	92	O23(20/0/4),D15	0	-0.6
	†NY A	63	174	19	48	8	1	6	31	13-2	0	20	.276	.323	.437	100	0	1-0	1.000	-1	84	0	D32,O17(6/0/11)	0	-0.3
	Year	106	307	33	83	17	1	9	43	27-3	0	47	.270	.327	.420	94	-3	2-1	.978	-4	73	55	D47,O40(26/0/15)	0	-0.9
2004	†NY A	107	307	40	75	12	1	17	65	25-4	0	55	.244	.296	.456	94	-4	1-0	.977	-1	99	74	D56,O29(8/0/22)	0	-0.8
2005	†NY A	61	170	14	39	12	0	4	29	9-1	0	41	.229	.265	.371	68	-8	0-0	.958	-2	86	0	D30,O18(8/0/10)	73	-1.1
2006	Min A	14	28	3	5	1	0	0	4	4-0	0	7	.179	.273	.214	31	-3	0-0	ø	0	—	—	D7	47	-0.3
Total	20	2186	8044	1084	2152	428	59	306	1322	610-102	7	1239	.268	.315	.450	105	31	142-52	.970	-43	94	100	O1622(202/31/1425),D453	150	-7.7
Sievers, Roy	Roy Edward "Squirrel"; B11.18.1926 St.Louis MO; BR/TR/6´1˝/(195–200); d4.21; C1																								
1949	StL A	140	471	84	144	28	1	16	91	70	2	75	.306	.398	.471	124	18	1-5	.973	5	101	162	O125(51/76/0),3b7	0	1.4
1950	StL A	113	370	46	88	20	4	10	57	34	2	42	.238	.305	.395	75	-16	1-3	.983	4	106	183	O78(10/68/0),3b21	0	-1.4
1951	StL A	31	89	10	20	2	1	1	11	9	1	21	.225	.303	.303	62	-5	0-0	.985	0	111	48	O25(9/19/0)	0	-0.5
1952	StL A	11	30	3	6	3	0	0	5	1	0	4	.200	.226	.300	44	-2	0-0	.968	-1	63	123	1b7	139	-0.4
1953	StL A	92	285	37	77	15	0	8	35	32	0	47	.270	.344	.407	100	0	0-1	.992	-6	66	87	1b76	0	-1.0
1954	Was A	145	514	75	119	26	6	24	102	80	2	77	.232	.331	.446	120	13	2-1	.971	8	110	117	O133L,1b8	0	1.3
1955	Was A	144	509	74	138	20	8	25	106	73-3	4	66	.271	.364	.489	136	25	1-2	.988	-3	101	49	O129L,1b17,3b2	0	1.3
1956	Was A★	152	550	92	139	27	2	29	95	100-10	5	88	.253	.370	.467	121	18	0-0	.987	1	98	52	O78L,1b76	0	0.9
1957	Was A☆	152	572	99	172	23	5	**42**	**114**	76-11	7	55	.301	.388	.579	163	49	1-1	.985	-1	97	86	O130L,1b21	0	4.0
1958	Was A	148	550	85	162	18	1	39	108	53-2	4	63	.295	.357	.544	148	34	3-1	.991	-2	94	72	O114L,1b33	0	2.5
1959	Was A★	115	385	55	93	19	0	21	49	53-6	2	62	.242	.333	.455	116	8	1-1	.989	4	124	94	1b93,O13L	0	0.7
1960	Chi A	127	444	87	131	22	0	28	93	74-**8**	3	69	.295	.396	.534	152	34	1-1	.993	-4	87	**114**	1b114,O6L	0	2.3
1961	Chi A★	141	492	76	145	26	6	27	92	61-4	6	62	.295	.377	.537	144	31	1-0	.993	4	109	89	1b132	0	2.7
1962	Phi N	144	477	61	125	19	5	21	80	56-3	7	80	.262	.346	.455	117	11	2-1	.991	4	114	98	1b130,O7(3/0/4)	0	0.8
1963	Phi N	138	450	46	108	19	2	19	82	43-5	5	72	.240	.308	.418	110	6	0-2	.989	-0	97	106	1b126	0	-0.3
1964	Phi N	49	120	7	22	3	1	4	16	13-1	1	20	.183	.265	.325	67	-5	0-0	.992	-1	80	101	1b33	0	-0.9
	Was A	33	58	5	10	1	0	4	11	9-2	0	14	.172	.284	.397	87	-1	0-0	1.000	2	151	166	1b15	0	0.0
1965	Was A	12	21	3	4	1	0	0	0	4-0	0	3	.190	.320	.238	62	-1	0-0	1.000	-1	35	155	1b7	0	-0.2
Total	17	1887	6387	945	1703	292	42	318	1147	841-55	51	920	.267	.354	.475	124	217	14-19	.991	12	101	102	1b888,O838(676/163/4),3b30	139	13.2
Siffell, Frank	Frank; B1860 , Germany; D10.26.1909 Philadelphia PA; d6.14																								
1884	Phi AA	7	17	3	3	1	0	0	3	0	1	—	.176	.222	.235	46	-1	—	.875	-2	—	—	C7	—	-0.2
1885	Phi AA	3	10	0	1	1	0	0	0	0	0	—	.100	.100	.100	-35	-2	—	.750	-2	—	—	C2/rf	—	-0.3
Total	2	10	27	3	4	1	0	0	3	0	1	—	.148	.179	.185	16	-3	—	.841	-4	—	—	C9/rf	—	-0.5
Sigafoos, Frank	Francis Leonard; B3.21.1904 Easton PA; D4.12.1968 Indianapolis IN; BR/TR/5´9˝/170; d9.3; Col Purdue																								
1926	Phi A	13	43	4	11	0	0	0	2	0	0	3	.256	.256	.256	32	-4	0-0	.915	-2	99	95	S12	—	-0.5
1929	Det A	14	23	3	4	1	0	0	2	5	0	4	.174	.321	.217	41	-2	0-2	.909	-2	66	0	3b6,S5	—	-0.4
	Chi A	7	3	1	1	0	0	0	1	2	0	1	.333	.600	.333	148	1	0-0	1.000	1	172	114	2b6	—	0.1
	Year	21	26	4	5	1	0	0	3	7	0	5	.192	.364	.231	56	-1	0-2	.909	-1	66	0	3b6,2b6,S5	—	-0.3
1931	Cin N	21	65	6	11	2	0	0	8	0	1	6	.169	.182	.200	3	-9	0	.881	-2	89	79	3b15,S2	—	-1.1
Total	3	55	134	14	27	3	0	0	13	7	1	14	.201	.246	.224	25	-14	0-2	.887	-5	85	64	3b21,S19,2b6	—	-1.9

YEAR	TM LG	G	AB	R	H	2B	3B	HR	RBI	BB-IB	HP	SO	AVG	OBP	SLG	AOPS	ABR	SB-CS	FA	FR	RNG	THR	GAMES AT POSITION	DL	BFW
Siglin, Paddy	Wesley Peter; B9.24.1891 Aurelia IA; D8.5.1956 Oakland CA; BR/TR/5´10˝/160; d9.12																								
1914	Pit N	14	39	4	6	0	0	0	2	4	0	6	.154	.233	.154	16	-4	1	.911	-5	61	30	2b11	—	-1.0
1915	Pit N	6	7	1	2	0	0	0	0	1	0	2	.286	.375	.286	103	0	1	.800	-0	117	0	/2	—	0.0
1916	Pit N	3	4	0	1	0	0	0	0	0	0	2	.250	.250	.250	53	0	0	.857	0	55	596	2b3	—	0.0
Total	3	23	50	5	9	0	0	0	2	5	0	10	.180	.255	.180	32	-4	2	.895	-5	65	89	2b15	—	-1.0
Sigman, Tripp	Wesley Triplett; B1.17.1899 Mooresville NC; D3.8.1971 Augusta GA; BL/TR/6´0˝/180; d9.18																								
1929	Phi N	10	29	8	15	1	0	2	9	3	0	1	.517	.563	.759	210	5	0	.944	-1	102	0	O10(5/5/0)	—	0.4
1930	Phi N	52	100	15	27	4	1	4	6	6	2	9	.270	.324	.450	79	-4	1	.932	-0	95	156	O19(3/16/0)	—	-0.4
Total	2	62	129	23	42	5	1	6	15	9	2	10	.326	.379	.519	108	1	1	.935	-1	97	109	O29(8/21/0)	—	0.0
Silber, Eddie	Edward James; B6.6.1914 Philadelphia PA; D10.26.1976 Dunedin FL; BR/TR/5´11˝/170; d9.3; Col Temple																								
1937	StL A	22	83	10	26	2	0	0	4	5	0	13	.313	.352	.337	74	-3	0-2	.871	-4	73	0	O21(2/6/15)	—	-0.8
1939	StL A	1	1	0	0	0	0	0	0	0	0	1	.000	.000	.000	-98	0	0-0	ø	0	—	—	/H	—	0.0
Total	2	23	84	10	26	2	0	0	4	5	0	14	.310	.348	.333	72	-3	0-2	.871	-4	73	0	O21(2/6/15)	—	-0.8
Silch, Ed	Edward "Baldy"; B2.22.1865 St.Louis MO; D1.15.1895 St.Louis MO; TR/6´2˝/180; d4.29																								
1888	Bro AA	14	48	5	13	4	0	0	3	4	0	—	.271	.327	.354	118	1	4	.870	-1	51	0	O14(0/6/8)	—	0.0
Silva, Danny	Daniel James; B10.5.1896 Everett MA; D4.4.1974 Hyannis MA; BR/TR/6´0˝/170; d8.11																								
1919	Was A	1	4	0	1	0	0	0	0	0	0	0	.250	.250	.250	41	0	0	1.000	1	155	0	/3	—	0.0
Silvera, Al	Aaron Albert; B8.26.1935 San Diego CA; D7.24.2002 Los Angeles CA; BR/TR/6´0˝/180; d6.12; Col USC																								
1955	Cin N	13	7	3	1	0	0	0	2	0-0	0	1	.143	.143	.143	-23	-1	0-0	ø	-0	0	0	/lf	0	-0.1
1956	Cin N	1	0	0	0	0	0	0	0	0-0	0	0	ø	ø	ø	ø	0	0-0	ø	0	—	—	/R	0	0.0
Total	2	14	7	3	1	0	0	0	2	0-0	0	1	.143	.143	.143	-23	-1	0-0	.000	-0	0	0	/lf	0	-0.1
Silvera, Charlie	Charles Anthony Ryan "Swede"; B10.13.1924 San Francisco CA; BR/TR/5´10˝/175; d9.29; C6																								
1948	NY A	4	14	1	8	0	1	0	1	0	0	1	.571	.571	.714	243	3	0-0	1.000	-0	*102*	*126*	C4	0	0.3
1949	†NY A	58	130	8	41	2	0	0	13	18	1	5	.315	.403	.331	95	0	2-1	.985	4	*82*	*117*	C51	0	0.5
1950	NY A	18	25	2	4	0	0	0	1	1	0	2	.160	.192	.160	-9	-4	0-0	.959	2	*148*	*0*	C15	0	-0.2
1951	NY A	18	51	5	14	3	0	1	7	5	0	3	.275	.339	.392	101	0	0-0	1.000	1	*132*	*93*	C18	0	0.2
1952	NY A	20	55	4	18	3	0	0	11	5	0	2	.327	.383	.382	121	2	0-3	1.000	-1	*92*	*126*	C20	0	0.0
1953	NY A	42	82	11	23	3	1	0	12	9	0	5	.280	.352	.341	91	-1	0-1	.992	4	*121*	*112*	C39/3	0	0.4
1954	NY A	20	37	1	10	1	0	0	4	3	1	2	.270	.341	.297	79	-1	0-1	.962	3	*172*	*77*	C18	0	0.2
1955	NY A	14	26	1	5	0	0	0	1	6-0	0	4	.192	.344	.192	48	-2	0-0	1.000	2	*184*	*126*	C11	0	0.1
1956	NY A	7	9	0	2	0	0	0	0	2-0	0	3	.222	.364	.222	60	0	0-0	.909	-1	*58*	*0*	C7	0	-0.1
1957	Chi N	26	53	1	11	3	0	0	2	4-0	0	5	.208	.263	.264	43	-4	0-0	.982	-2	75	130	C26	0	-0.5
Total	10	227	482	34	136	15	2	1	52	53-0	2	32	.282	.356	.328	86	-7	2-6	.985	11	*111*	*106*	C209/3	0	0.9
Silverio, Luis	Luis Pascual (Delmonte); B10.23.1956 Villa Gonzalez, D.R.; BR/TR/5´11˝/150; d9.9; C4																								
1978	KC A	8	11	7	6	2	1	0	3	2-0	0	3	.545	.615	.909	314	3	1-1	.833	-1	71	0	O6(4/0/2),D2	0	0.2
Silverio, Tom	Tomas Roberto (Veloz); B10.14.1945 Santiago, D.R.; BL/TL/5´10˝/170; d4.30																								
1970	Cal A	15	15	1	0	0	0	0	0	2-1	0	4	.000	.118	.000	-67	-4	0-1	1.000	-1	30	0	O5(1/4/0)/1	0	-0.5
1971	Cal A	3	3	0	1	0	0	0	0	0-0	0	0	.333	.333	.333	96	0	0-0	ø	-0	0	0	/cf	0	0.0
1972	Cal A	13	12	1	2	0	0	0	0	0-0	0	5	.167	.167	.167	-1	-2	0-0	1.000	-0	36	0	O4(2/1/1)	0	-0.2
Total	3	31	30	2	3	0	0	0	0	2-1	0	9	.100	.156	.100	-27	-6	0-1	1.000	-1	32	0	O10(3/6/1)/1	0	-0.7
Silvestri, Dave	David Joseph; B9.29.1967 St.Louis MO; BR/TR/6´0˝/(180–196); [HouN88 2/52]; d4.27; Col Missouri																								
1992	NY A	7	13	3	4	0	2	0	1	0-0	0	3	.308	.308	.615	153	1	0-0	.889	0	113	127	S6	0	0.1
1993	NY A	7	21	4	6	1	0	1	4	5-0	0	3	.286	.423	.476	145	2	0-0	.955	0	93	153	S4,3b3	0	0.2
1994	NY A	12	18	3	2	0	1	1	2	4-0	0	9	.111	.261	.389	70	-1	0-1	1.000	-0	84	74	2b9,3b2/S	0	-0.1
1995	NY A	17	21	4	2	0	0	1	4	4-0	1	9	.095	.259	.238	34	-2	0-0	1.000	1	150	61	2b7,1b4/SD	17	-0.1
	Mon N	39	72	12	19	6	0	2	7	9-0	0	27	.264	.341	.431	99	0	2-0	1.000	-3	81	22	S9,3b8,1b4,2b3,O3L	0	-0.1
1996	Mon N	86	162	16	33	4	0	1	17	34-6	0	41	.204	.340	.247	57	-9	2-1	.913	-2	102	83	3b47,S10,O2(1/1/0)/12	0	-1.0
1997	Tex A	2	4	0	0	0	0	0	0	0-0	0	1	.000	.000	.000	-94	-1	0-0	ø	-1	0	0	/3S	0	-0.2
1998	TB A	8	14	0	1	0	0	0	0	0-0	0	2	.071	.071	.071	-61	-3	0-0	1.000	-0	61	0	3b3,2b2/SD	0	-0.3
1999	Ana A	3	11	0	1	1	0	0	1	0-0	0	1	.091	.091	.182	-33	-2	0-0	1.000	-1	127	0	/2Slf	0	-0.3
Total	8	181	336	42	68	12	3	6	36	56-6	1	96	.202	.315	.310	65	-15	4-2	.912	-5	106	67	3b64,S34,2b23,1b9,O6(5/1/0),D6	17	-1.8
Silvestri, Ken	Kenneth Joseph "Hawk"; B5.3.1916 Chicago IL; D3.31.1992 Tallahassee FL; BB/TR/6´1˝/200; d4.18; Mil 1942–45; M1/C17																								
1939	Chi A	22	75	6	13	3	0	2	5	6	1	13	.173	.244	.293	36	-8	0-1	.947	0	*96*	*152*	C20	—	-0.6
1940	Chi A	28	24	5	6	2	0	2	10	4	0	7	.250	.357	.583	138	1	0-0	1.000	-0	*0*	*0*	/C	—	0.1
1941	NY A	17	40	6	10	5	0	1	4	7	0	6	.250	.362	.450	115	1	0-0	1.000	0	*129*	*112*	C13	0	0.2
1946	NY A	13	21	4	6	1	0	0	1	3	0	7	.286	.375	.333	98	0	0-0	.977	1	*111*	*53*	C12	0	0.2
1947	NY A	3	10	0	2	0	0	0	0	2	0	2	.200	.333	.200	51	-1	0-0	1.000	-1	*76*	*0*	C3	0	-0.1
1949	Phi N	4	4	1	0	0	0	0	0	2	0	1	.000	.333	.000	-3	0	0	1.000	-0	*48*	*268*	/C2S	0	-0.1
1950	†Phi N	11	20	2	5	0	1	0	4	4	1	3	.250	.400	.350	101	0	0	1.000	-1	*86*	*0*	C9	0	0.0
1951	Phi N	4	9	2	2	0	0	0	1	3	0	2	.222	.417	.222	78	0	0-0	1.000	-2	*68*	*0*	C3/2	0	-0.2
Total	8	102	203	26	44	11	1	5	25	31	2	41	.217	.326	.355	78	-7	0-1	.974	-2	*100*	*102*	C62,2b2/S	0	-0.5
Simmons, Al	Aloysius Harry "Bucketfoot Al" (b Aloys Szymanski); B5.22.1902 Milwaukee WI; D5.26.1956 Milwaukee WI; BR/TR/5´11˝/190; d4.15; C11; HF1953																								
1924	Phi A	**152**	594	69	183	31	9	8	102	30	2	60	.308	.343	.431	98	-5	16-15	.976	-2	95	106	O152(51/101/0)	—	-1.7
1925	Phi A	**153**	654	122	**253**	43	12	24	129	35	1	41	.387	.419	.599	146	43	7-14	.966	-6	103	47	O153C	—	2.5
1926	Phi A	147	583	90	199	53	10	19	109	48	1	49	.341	.392	.564	139	32	11-3	.975	-10	88	76	O147C	—	1.6
1927	Phi A	106	406	86	159	36	11	15	108	31	1	30	.392	.436	.645	168	39	10-2	.985	-1	98	99	O105(10/94/1)	—	3.3
1928	Phi A	119	464	78	163	33	9	15	107	31	3	30	.351	.396	.558	144	28	1-4	.988	-0	97	94	O114L	—	1.7
1929	†Phi A	143	581	114	212	41	9	34	**157**	31	1	38	.365	.398	.642	158	46	4-3	.989	20	**124**	145	O142L	—	5.1
1930	†Phi A	138	554	**152**	211	41	16	36	165	39	1	34	**.381**	.423	.708	173	58	9-2	**.990**	2	101	100	O136(129/7/0)	—	4.5
1931	†Phi A	128	513	105	200	37	13	22	128	47	3	45	**.390**	.444	.641	172	52	3-3	.987	6	108	108	O128(125/3/0)	—	4.6
1932	Phi A	**154**	670	144	**216**	28	9	35	151	47	1	76	.322	.368	.548	129	25	4-2	.980	-6	91	79	O154(154/1/0)	—	1.0
1933	Chi A★	146	605	85	200	29	10	14	119	39	2	49	.331	.373	.481	130	24	5-1	.990	9	111	97	O145(144/1/0)	—	2.4
1934	Chi A★	138	558	102	192	36	7	18	104	53	2	58	.344	.403	.530	135	28	3-2	.987	4	100	122	O138(136/2/0)	—	2.3
1935	Chi A★	128	525	68	140	22	7	16	79	33	2	43	.267	.313	.427	87	-13	4-6	.981	-4	100	49	O126(11/115/0)	—	-2.1
1936	Det A	143	568	96	186	38	6	13	112	49	2	35	.327	.383	.484	112	10	6-4	**.986**	-5	97	68	O138(7/134/0)/1	—	0.2
1937	Was A	103	419	60	117	21	10	8	84	27	4	35	.279	.329	.434	95	-6	3-2	.984	4	109	86	O102(98/4/0)	—	-0.7
1938	Was A	125	470	79	142	23	6	21	95	38	2	40	.302	.357	.511	123	14	2-1	.983	-5	96	47	O117(112/8/0)	—	0.3
1939	Bos N	93	330	39	93	17	5	7	43	22	2	40	.282	.331	.427	110	3	0	.982	1	95	141	O82(81/1/0)	—	-0.1
	†Cin N	9	21	0	3	0	0	0	1	2	0	3	.143	.217	.143	-1	-3	0	.938	0	97	233	O5L	—	-0.3
	Year	102	351	39	96	17	5	7	44	24	2	43	.274	.324	.410	103	0	0	.978	1	95	149	O87(86/1/0)	—	-0.4
1940	Phi A	37	81	7	25	4	0	1	19	4	0	8	.309	.341	.395	92	-1	0-0	.963	2	125	73	O18L	—	0.0
1941	Phi A	9	24	1	3	1	0	0	1	1	0	2	.125	.160	.167	-14	-4	0-0	1.000	0	128	0	O5L	0	-0.4
1943	Bos A	40	133	9	27	5	0	1	12	8	0	21	.203	.248	.263	49	-9	0-1	.986	-1	91	117	O33L	0	-1.3
1944	Phi A	4	6	1	3	0	0	0	2	0	0	0	.500	.500	.500	189	1	0-0	1.000	0	120	0	O2L	0	0.1
Total	20	2215	8759	1507	2927	539	149	307	1827	615	30	737	.334	.380	.535	132	362	88-65	.982	9	101	91	O2142(1377/771/1)/1	0	23.0
Simmons, Brian	Brian Lee; B9.4.1973 Lebanon PA; BB/TR/6´2˝/(185–190); [ChiA95 2/55]; d9.21; Col Michigan; [DL 2000 Chi A 181]																								
1998	Chi A	5	19	4	7	0	0	2	6	0-0	0	2	.368	.368	.684	168	2	0-1	1.000	0	111	0	O5(2/4/0)	0	0.1
1999	Chi A	54	126	14	29	3	3	4	17	9-0	0	30	.230	.281	.397	69	-7	4-0	.976	2	113	93	O46(28/11/9),D3	23	-0.5
2001	Tor A	60	107	8	19	5	0	2	8	8-0	1	26	.178	.239	.280	36	-10	1-0	1.000	1	110	69	O37(19/12/7),D2	0	-0.9
Total	3	119	252	26	55	8	3	8	31	17-0	1	58	.218	.269	.369	62	-15	5-1	.987	3	112	77	O88(49/27/16),D5	204	-1.3

SIMMONS, HACK George Washington; B1.29.1885 Brooklyn NY; D4.26.1942 Arverne NY; BR/TR/5´8˝/179; d4.15

YEAR	TM LG	G	AB	R	H	2B	3B	HR	RBI	BB-IB	HP	SO	AVG	OBP	SLG	AOPS	ABR	SB-CS	FA	FR	RNG	THR	GAMES AT POSITION	DL	BFW
1910	Det A	42	110	12	25	3	1	0	9	10	2	—	.227	.303	.273	75	-3	1	.984	-0	104	97	1b22,3b7,O2(0/1/1)	—	-0.4
1912	NY A	110	401	45	96	17	2	0	41	33	7	—	.239	.308	.292	68	-16	19	.946	-17	90	75	2b88,1b13,S4	—	-3.2
1914	Bal F	114	352	50	95	16	5	1	38	32	6	26	.270	.341	.352	86	-11	7	.894	-3	84	103	O73(61/0/12),2b26,1b4,S2/3	—	-1.7
1915	Bal F	39	88	8	18	7	1	1	14	10	1	9	.205	.293	.341	76	-4	1	1.000	-2	103	0	2b13,O13L	—	-0.7
Total	4	305	951	115	234	43	9	2	102	85	16	35	.246	.318	.317	76	-34	28	.953	-21	93	68	2b127,O88(74/1/13),1b39,3b8,S6	—	-6.0

SIMMONS, JOHN John Earl; B7.7.1924 Birmingham AL; BR/TR/6´1.5˝/192; d4.22; Col NYU

YEAR	TM LG	G	AB	R	H	2B	3B	HR	RBI	BB-IB	HP	SO	AVG	OBP	SLG	AOPS	ABR	SB-CS	FA	FR	RNG	THR	GAMES AT POSITION	DL	BFW
1949	Was A	62	93	12	20	0	0	0	5	11	0	6	.215	.298	.215	38	-8	0-0	1.000	-1	95	75	O26(18/0/8)	0	-1.0

SIMMONS, JOE Joseph S. (b Joseph S. Chabriel); B6.13.1845 New York NY; D7.24.1901 Jersey City NJ; 5´9˝/166; d5.8; M2

YEAR	TM LG	G	AB	R	H	2B	3B	HR	RBI	BB-IB	HP	SO	AVG	OBP	SLG	AOPS	ABR	SB-CS	FA	FR	RNG	THR	GAMES AT POSITION	DL	BFW
1871	Chi NA	27	129	29	28	6	1	0	17	1	—	0	.217	.223	.279	39	-11	4-1	.894	-1	34	0	O25(0/9/17),1b2	—	-0.7
1872	Cle NA	18	90	11	23	5	1	0	9	1	—	2	.256	.264	.333	87	-1	1-0	.938	1	164	168	1b15,O3(1/0/2)	—	0.1
1875	Wes NA	**13**	53	5	9	1	0	0	4	0	—	2	.170	.170	.189	23	-4	1-2	.733	-0	75	0	O10(0/9/1),1b3,M	—	-0.4
Total	3NA	58	272	45	60	12	2	0	30	2	—	4	.221	.226	.279	51	-16	6-3	.855	-0	44	0	O38(1/18/20),1b20	—	-1.0

SIMMONS, NELSON Nelson Bernard; B6.27.1963 Washington DC; BB/TR/6´1˝/195; [DetA81 2/43]; d9.4

YEAR	TM LG	G	AB	R	H	2B	3B	HR	RBI	BB-IB	HP	SO	AVG	OBP	SLG	AOPS	ABR	SB-CS	FA	FR	RNG	THR	GAMES AT POSITION	DL	BFW
1984	Det A	9	30	4	13	2	0	0	3	2-1	0	5	.433	.469	.500	168	3	1-0	1.000	-0	92	0	O5(2/0/4),D4	0	0.3
1985	Det A	75	251	31	60	11	0	10	33	26-5	0	41	.239	.306	.402	94	-2	1-0	.945	-2	92	88	O38(25/0/13),D31	21	-0.6
1987	Bal A	16	49	3	13	1	1	1	4	3-0	0	8	.265	.296	.388	85	-1	0-1	1.000	1	104	239	O13R/D	0	-0.1
Total	3	100	330	38	86	14	1	11	40	31-6	0	54	.261	.319	.409	99	0	2-1	.963	-1	95	115	O56(27/0/30),D36	21	-0.4

SIMMONS, TED Ted Lyle; B8.9.1949 Highland Park MI; BB/TR/6´0˝/(187–200); [StLN67 1/10]; d9.21; Mil 1970; OF(37/0/3)

YEAR	TM LG	G	AB	R	H	2B	3B	HR	RBI	BB-IB	HP	SO	AVG	OBP	SLG	AOPS	ABR	SB-CS	FA	FR	RNG	THR	GAMES AT POSITION	DL	BFW
1968	StL N	2	3	0	1	0	0	0	0	1-0	0	1	.333	.500	.333	156	0	0-0	1.000	-1	0	0	C2	0	0.0
1969	StL N	5	14	0	3	0	1	0	3	1-0	0	1	.214	.250	.357	73	-1	0-0	.957	-0	64	0	C4	0	-0.1
1970	StL N	82	284	29	69	8	2	3	24	37-5	2	37	.243	.333	.317	73	-10	2-2	.990	-4	109	118	C79	0	-1.0
1971	StL N	133	510	64	155	32	4	7	77	36-3	3	50	.304	.347	.424	114	10	1-3	.989	-6	135	96	C130	0	1.0
1972	StL N☆	152	594	70	180	36	6	16	96	29-8	2	57	.303	.336	.465	127	18	1-3	.991	4	79	97	C135,1b15	0	2.8
1973	StL N★	161	619	62	192	36	2	13	91	61-15	2	47	.310	.370	.438	124	21	2-2	.987	12	115	118	C153,1b6,O2R	0	4.1
1974	StL N☆	152	599	66	163	33	6	20	103	47-8	6	35	.272	.327	.447	116	11	0-0	.986	-6	85	112	C141,1b12	0	1.1
1975	StL N	157	581	80	193	32	3	18	100	63-16	1	35	.332	.396	.491	139	32	1-3	.983	-4	90	80	C154,1b2,O2L	0	3.5
1976	StL N	150	546	60	159	35	3	5	75	73-**19**	0	35	.291	.371	.394	116	15	0-7	.993	-1	122	**129**	C113,1b30,O7L,3b2	0	1.4
1977	StL N★	150	516	82	164	25	3	21	95	79-**25**	2	37	.318	.408	.500	144	35	2-6	.987	-5	112	97	C143/rf	0	3.4
1978	StL N★	152	516	71	148	40	5	22	80	77-17	3	39	.287	.377	.512	149	36	1-1	.988	-1	77	**142**	C134,O23L	0	4.1
1979	StL N✳	123	448	68	127	22	0	26	87	61-22	4	34	.283	.369	.507	135	23	0-1	.985	-2	92	87	C122	29	2.6
1980	StL N	145	495	84	150	33	2	21	98	59-13	2	45	.303	.375	.505	138	27	1-0	.985	-6	98	102	C129,O5L	0	2.8
1981	†Mil A★	100	380	45	82	13	3	14	61	23-2	3	32	.216	.262	.376	87	-9	0-1	.980	-8	95	102	C75,D22,1b4	0	-1.5
1982	†Mil A	137	539	73	145	29	0	23	97	32-5	2	40	.269	.309	.451	112	7	0-0	**.995**	-4	77	129	C121,D15	0	0.8
1983	Mil A★	153	600	76	185	39	3	13	108	41-6	2	51	.308	.351	.448	128	23	4-2	.975	-6	69	123	C86,D66	0	1.9
1984	Mil A	132	497	44	110	23	2	4	52	30-3	3	40	.221	.269	.300	59	-28	3-0	.995	-3	93	104	D77,1b37,3b14	0	-3.6
1985	Mil A	143	528	60	144	28	2	12	76	57-9	1	32	.273	.342	.402	104	4	1-1	.992	-2	82	92	D99,1b28,C15,3b2	0	-0.2
1986	Atl N	76	127	14	32	5	0	4	25	12-5	1	14	.252	.313	.386	90	-2	1-0	.964	-3	112	135	1b14,C10,3b9	0	-0.6
1987	Atl N	73	177	20	49	8	0	4	30	21-5	0	23	.277	.350	.390	93	-1	1-1	.984	-1	138	125	1b28,C15,3b2	0	-0.3
1988	Atl N	78	107	6	21	6	0	2	11	15-2	0	9	.196	.293	.308	71	-4	0-0	.993	-0	130	71	1b19,C10	16	-0.5
Total	21	2456	8680	1074	2472	483	47	248	1389	855-188	39	694	.285	.348	.437	117	207	21-33	.987	-46	97	107	C1771,D279,1b195,O40L,3b29	45	21.7

SIMMS, MIKE Michael Howard; B1.12.1967 Orange CA; BR/TR/6´4˝/(185–230); [HouN85 6/144]; d9.5; [DL 2000 Tex A 165]

YEAR	TM LG	G	AB	R	H	2B	3B	HR	RBI	BB-IB	HP	SO	AVG	OBP	SLG	AOPS	ABR	SB-CS	FA	FR	RNG	THR	GAMES AT POSITION	DL	BFW
1990	Hou N	12	13	3	4	1	0	1	2	0-0	0	4	.308	.308	.615	151	1	0-0	1.000	-0	55	123	1b6	0	0.0
1991	Hou N	49	123	18	25	5	0	3	16	18-0	0	38	.203	.301	.317	79	-3	1-0	.889	-2	75	176	O41(1/0/41)	0	-0.7
1992	Hou N	15	24	1	6	1	0	1	3	2-0	1	9	.250	.333	.417	116	0	0-0	1.000	0	58	556	O9R/1	0	0.1
1994	Hou N	6	12	1	1	1	0	0	0	0-0	0	5	.083	.083	.167	-39	-2	1-0	.857	-0	111	0	O3R	0	-0.3
1995	Hou N	50	121	14	31	4	0	9	24	13-0	3	28	.256	.341	.512	130	5	1-2	.995	-1	105	93	1b25,O12R	0	0.1
1996	Hou N	49	68	6	12	2	1	1	8	4-0	1	16	.176	.233	.279	37	-7	1-0	1.000	0	115	0	O12(9/0/3),1b5	0	-0.7
1997	Tex A	59	111	13	28	8	0	5	22	8-1	0	27	.252	.298	.459	89	-2	0-1	.958	-0	115	0	D28,O19(2/0/17),1b2	0	-0.4
1998	†Tex A	86	186	36	55	11	0	16	46	24-0	3	47	.296	.381	.613	146	13	0-1	1.000	-2	86	52	O43(3/0/40),D26,1b16	0	0.6
1999	Tex A	4	2	0	1	0	0	0	0	0-0	0	1	.500	.500	.500	147	0	0-0	1.000	0	1401	0	/1rfD	155	0.0
Total	9	330	660	92	163	33	1	36	121	69-1	8	175	.247	.323	.464	108	5	4-4	.954	-5	87	104	O140(15/0/126),D56,1b56	320	-1.3

SIMON, HANK Henry Joseph; B8.25.1862 Hawkinsville NY; D1.1.1925 Albany NY; BR/TR/5´6˝/155; d10.7

YEAR	TM LG	G	AB	R	H	2B	3B	HR	RBI	BB-IB	HP	SO	AVG	OBP	SLG	AOPS	ABR	SB-CS	FA	FR	RNG	THR	GAMES AT POSITION	DL	BFW
1887	Cle AA	3	10	1	1	0	0	0	0	0	0	—	.100	.100	.100	-45	-2	0	1.000	-0	0	0	O3L	—	-0.2
1890	Bro AA	89	373	66	96	17	11	0	38	34	2	—	.257	.323	.362	105	1	23	.951	5	108	99	O89L	—	0.4
	Syr AA	38	156	33	47	5	3	2	23	17	0	—	.301	.370	.410	145	9	12	.941	-2	33	70	O38(36/2/0)	—	0.6
	Year	127	529	99	143	22	14	2	61	51	2	—	.270	.337	.376	116	10	35	.948	3	87	91	O127(125/2/0)	—	1.0
Total	2	130	539	100	144	22	14	2	61	51	2	—	.267	.333	.371	113	8	35	.949	3	86	90	O130(128/2/0)	—	0.8

SIMON, MIKE Michael Edward; B4.13.1883 Hayden IN; D6.10.1963 Los Angeles CA; BR/TR/5´11˝/188; d6.27; Col Indiana

YEAR	TM LG	G	AB	R	H	2B	3B	HR	RBI	BB-IB	HP	SO	AVG	OBP	SLG	AOPS	ABR	SB-CS	FA	FR	RNG	THR	GAMES AT POSITION	DL	BFW
1909	Pit N	12	18	2	3	0	0	0	2	1	0	—	.167	.211	.167	16	-2	0	.917	0	*171*	*71*	C9	—	-0.1
1910	Pit N	22	50	3	10	0	1	0	5	1	0	2	.200	.216	.240	31	-5	1	1.000	-1	*104*	*74*	C14	—	-0.5
1911	Pit N	71	215	19	49	4	3	0	22	10	4	14	.228	.275	.274	52	-15	1	.968	3	*118*	*86*	C68	—	-0.6
1912	Pit N	42	113	10	34	2	1	0	11	5	0	9	.301	.331	.336	84	-3	1	.991	3	*135*	*102*	C40	—	0.3
1913	Pit N	92	255	23	63	6	2	1	17	10	2	15	.247	.281	.298	68	-11	3-2	.975	9	94	**117**	C92	—	0.5
1914	StL F	93	276	21	57	11	2	0	21	18	3	21	.207	.263	.261	41	-27	2	.984	2	*88*	*102*	C78	—	-1.9
1915	Bro F	47	142	7	25	5	1	0	12	9	0	12	.176	.225	.225	27	-16	1	.992	-2	*82*	*110*	C45	—	-1.6
Total	7	379	1069	85	241	28	10	1	90	54	9	73	.225	.269	.273	51	-79	9-2	.979	14	*102*	*102*	C346	—	-3.9

SIMON, RANDALL Randall Carlito; B5.25.1975 Willemstad, Curacao; BL/TL/6´0˝/(180–240); d9.1

YEAR	TM LG	G	AB	R	H	2B	3B	HR	RBI	BB-IB	HP	SO	AVG	OBP	SLG	AOPS	ABR	SB-CS	FA	FR	RNG	THR	GAMES AT POSITION	DL	BFW
1997	Atl N	13	14	2	6	1	0	0	1	1-0	0	2	.429	.467	.500	151	1	0-0	1.000	0	109	110	1b6	0	0.1
1998	Atl N	7	16	2	3	0	0	0	4	0-0	0	1	.188	.176	.188	-1	-2	0-0	1.000	-1	42	122	1b4	0	-0.3
1999	Atl N	90	218	26	69	16	0	5	25	17-6	1	25	.317	.367	.459	109	3	2-2	.994	-2	80	96	1b70	0	-0.4
2001	Det A	81	256	28	78	14	2	6	37	15-2	0	28	.305	.341	.445	108	3	0-1	.992	-1	96	109	1b43,D29	0	-0.4
2002	Det A	130	482	51	145	17	1	19	82	13-5	4	30	.301	.320	.459	109	4	0-1	.988	-5	76	97	D65,1b59	0	-1.0
2003	Pit N	91	307	34	84	14	0	10	51	12-1	2	30	.274	.305	.417	85	-8	0-0	.994	1	109	94	1b80	16	-1.3
	†Chi N	33	103	13	29	3	0	6	21	4-1	2	7	.282	.318	.485	104	0	0-0	.991	2	120	80	1b29	0	0.0
	Year	124	410	47	113	17	0	16	72	16-2	4	37	.276	.309	.434	90	-8	0-0	.994	3	112	90	1b109	0	-1.3
2004	Pit N	61	175	14	34	6	0	3	14	15-5	2	17	.194	.264	.280	41	-16	0-0	.992	0	101	113	1b46,D4	33	-1.9
	TB A	8	17	2	2	0	0	0	0	3-0	1	2	.118	.286	.118	11	-2	0-0	ø	0	0	0	/1D	0	-0.2
2006	Phi N	23	21	0	5	0	0	0	2	2-0	0	6	.238	.304	.238	40	-2	0-0	ø	0	—	—	/H	0	-0.3
Total	8	537	1609	172	455	71	3	49	237	82-20	12	148	.283	.320	.422	93	-19	2-4	.992	-5	94	99	1b338,D104	49	-5.7

SIMON, SYL Sylvester Adam "Sammy"; B12.14.1897 Evansville IN; D2.28.1973 Chandler IN; BR/TR/5´10.5˝/170; d10.1

YEAR	TM LG	G	AB	R	H	2B	3B	HR	RBI	BB-IB	HP	SO	AVG	OBP	SLG	AOPS	ABR	SB-CS	FA	FR	RNG	THR	GAMES AT POSITION	DL	BFW
1923	StL A	1	1	0	0	0	0	0	0	0	0	0	.000	.000	.000	-95	0	0-0	ø	0	—	—	/H	—	0.0
1924	StL A	23	32	5	8	1	1	0	6	3	0	5	.250	.314	.344	66	-2	0-0	.889	-1	55	228	3b6,S5	—	-0.2
Total	2	24	33	5	8	1	1	0	6	3	0	5	.242	.306	.333	61	-2	0-0	.889	-1	55	228	3b6,S5	—	-0.2

SIMONS, MEL Melbern Ellis "Butch"; B7.1.1900 Carlyle IL; D11.10.1974 Paducah KY; BL/TR/5´10˝/175; d4.14

YEAR	TM LG	G	AB	R	H	2B	3B	HR	RBI	BB-IB	HP	SO	AVG	OBP	SLG	AOPS	ABR	SB-CS	FA	FR	RNG	THR	GAMES AT POSITION	DL	BFW
1931	Chi A	68	189	24	52	9	0	0	12	12	0	17	.275	.318	.323	73	-7	1-1	.950	-1	101	89	O59(15/45/0)	—	-0.9
1932	Chi A	7	5	0	0	0	0	0	0	0	0	1	.000	.000	.000	-99	-2	0-0	1.000	-0	91	0	O6(4/2/0)	—	-0.2
Total	2	75	194	24	52	9	0	0	12	12	0	18	.268	.311	.314	69	-9	1-1	.951	-1	101	87	O65(19/47/0)	—	-1.1

SIMPSON, HARRY Harry Leon "Suitcase","Goody"; B12.3.1925 Atlanta GA; D4.3.1979 Akron OH; BL/TR/6´1˝/(170–180); d4.21; Negro Lg 1946–48

YEAR	TM LG	G	AB	R	H	2B	3B	HR	RBI	BB-IB	HP	SO	AVG	OBP	SLG	AOPS	ABR	SB-CS	FA	FR	RNG	THR	GAMES AT POSITION	DL	BFW
1951	Cle A	122	332	51	76	7	0	7	24	45	2	48	.229	.325	.313	77	-10	6-4	.971	-4	105	65	O68(5/8/58),1b50	0	-1.7
1952	Cle A	146	545	66	145	21	10	10	65	56	2	82	.266	.337	.396	111	6	5-3	.988	-4	101	112	O127(0/11/117),1b28	0	-0.3
1953	Cle A	82	242	25	55	3	1	7	22	18	1	27	.227	.284	.335	68	-12	0-0	.968	-2	100	74	O69(1/7/62),1b2	0	-1.7
1955	Cle A	3	1	1	0	0	0	0	0	2-0	0	0	.000	.667	.000	88	0	0-0	ø	0	—	—	/H	0	0.0
	KC A	112	396	42	119	16	7	5	52	34-4	2	61	.301	.356	.414	106	3	3-5	.978	-5	94	75	O100(4/91/10),1b3	0	-0.8

YEAR	TM LG	G	AB	R	H	2B	3B	HR	RBI	BB-IB	HP	SO	AVG	OBP	SLG	AOPS	ABR	SB-CS	FA	FR	RNG	THR	GAMES AT POSITION	DL	BFW
	Year	115	397	43	119	16	7	5	52	36-4	2	61	.300	.358	.413	106	3	3-5	.978	-5	94	75	O100(4/91/10),1b3	0	-0.8
1956	KC A★	141	543	76	159	22	**11**	21	105	47-8	1	82	.293	.347	.490	119	12	2-3	.965	-13	85	38	O111(0/19/96),1b32	0	-0.7
1957	KC A	50	179	24	53	9	6	6	24	12-2	0	28	.296	.339	.514	128	6	0-1	.996	1	136	84	1b27,O21R	0	0.4
	†NY A	75	224	27	56	7	3	7	39	19-0	0	36	.250	.307	.402	94	-3	1-0	.952	-1	82	210	O42(16/0/26),1b21	0	-0.7
	Year	125	403	51	109	16	**9**	13	63	31-2	0	64	.270	.321	.452	110	3	1-1	.957	-1	82	160	O63(16/0/47),1b48	0	-0.3
1958	NY A	24	51	1	11	2	1	0	6	6-0	1	12	.216	.310	.294	70	-2	0-0	1.000	-1	98	0	O15(8/0/9)	0	-0.3
	KC A	78	212	21	56	7	1	7	27	26-3	0	33	.264	.345	.406	104	1	0-2	.990	-2	68	114	1b43,O11(9/0/2)	0	-0.5
	Year	102	263	22	67	9	2	7	33	32-3	1	45	.255	.338	.384	98	-1	0-2	.990	-3	68	114	1b43,O26(17/0/11)	0	-0.8
1959	KC A	8	14	1	4	0	0	1	2	2-0	1	4	.286	.389	.500	146	1	0-0	1.000	0	91	63	1b4	0	0.1
	Chi A	38	75	5	14	5	1	2	13	4-0	0	14	.187	.228	.360	59	-5	0-0	.947	-2	82	0	O12R/1	0	-0.7
	Year	46	89	6	18	5	1	3	15	6-0	1	18	.202	.258	.382	75	-4	0-0	.947	-2	123	0	O12R,1b5	0	-0.6
	Pit N	9	15	3	4	2	0	0	2	0-0	0	2	.267	.267	.400	75	-1	0-0	1.000	0	123	0	O3(1/0/2)	0	-0.1
Total	8	888	2829	343	752	101	41	73	381	271-17	10	429	.266	.331	.408	102	-4	17-18	.974	-33	95	82	O579(44/136/415),1b211	0	-7.0

SIMPSON, JOE Joe Allen; B12.31.1951 Purcell OK; BL/TL/6´3˝/(175–190); [LAN73 3/66]; d9.2; Col Oklahoma

YEAR	TM LG	G	AB	R	H	2B	3B	HR	RBI	BB-IB	HP	SO	AVG	OBP	SLG	AOPS	ABR	SB-CS	FA	FR	RNG	THR	GAMES AT POSITION	DL	BFW
1975	LA N	9	6	3	2	0	0	0	0	0-0	0	2	.333	.333	.333	89	0	0-0	1.000	-0	89	0	O6C	0	0.0
1976	LA N	23	30	2	4	1	0	0	0	1-0	0	6	.133	.161	.167	-7	-4	0-1	1.000	-0	102	0	O20(5/6/9)	0	-0.6
1977	LA N	29	23	2	4	0	0	0	1	2-0	0	6	.174	.240	.174	13	-3	1-1	.957	0	92	131	O28(5/7/16)/1	0	-0.3
1978	LA N	10	5	1	2	0	0	0	1	0-0	0	2	.400	.400	.400	124	0	0-0	1.000	0	133	0	O10(3/2/6)	0	0.0
1979	Sea A	120	265	29	75	11	0	2	27	11-1	1	21	.283	.312	.347	77	-9	6-3	.966	5	106	183	O105(27/5/73),D3	0	-0.7
1980	Sea A	129	365	42	91	15	3	3	34	28-3	1	43	.249	.302	.332	73	-14	17-4	.977	-1	92	139	O119(24/36/63),1b3	0	-1.6
1981	Sea A	91	288	32	64	11	3	2	30	15-0	1	41	.222	.261	.302	60	-16	12-3	.978	2	105	106	O88(0/86/2)	0	-1.4
1982	Sea A	105	296	39	76	14	4	2	23	22-4	2	48	.257	.312	.351	79	-9	8-14	.984	-2	90	136	O97(32/59/10)	0	-1.5
1983	KC A	91	119	16	20	2	2	0	8	11-2	2	21	.168	.248	.218	30	-12	1-1	.995	6	128	115	1b54,O38(4/19/19),P2/D	0	-0.8
Total	9	607	1397	166	338	54	12	9	124	90-10	7	190	.242	.289	.317	66	-67	45-27	.978	10	100	140	O511(100/226/198),1b58,D4,P2	0	-6.9

SIMPSON, MARTY Martin; B Baltimore MD; d5.14

YEAR	TM LG	G	AB	R	H	2B	3B	HR	RBI	BB-IB	HP	SO	AVG	OBP	SLG	AOPS	ABR	SB-CS	FA	FR	RNG	THR	GAMES AT POSITION	DL	BFW
1873	Mar NA	4	15	4	2	0	0	0	2	0	—	0	.133	.133	.133	-27	-2	0-0	.792	1	181	0	2b3/C	—	-0.1

SIMPSON, DICK Richard Charles; B7.28.1943 Washington DC; BR/TR/6´4˝/(170–176); d9.21

YEAR	TM LG	G	AB	R	H	2B	3B	HR	RBI	BB-IB	HP	SO	AVG	OBP	SLG	AOPS	ABR	SB-CS	FA	FR	RNG	THR	GAMES AT POSITION	DL	BFW
1962	LA A	6	8	1	2	1	0	0	1	2-0	0	3	.250	.400	.375	114	0	0-0	1.000	1	162	0	O4(4/0/1)	0	0.1
1964	LA A	21	50	11	7	1	0	2	4	8-0	0	15	.140	.259	.280	55	-3	2-2	1.000	-2	80	0	O16C	0	-0.7
1965	Cal A	8	27	2	6	1	0	0	3	2-0	0	8	.222	.267	.259	54	-2	1-0	.875	-2	72	0	O8C	0	-0.4
1966	Cin N	92	84	26	20	2	0	4	14	10-0	2	32	.238	.333	.405	96	0	0-1	.921	-4	74	0	O64(9/10/46)	0	-0.7
1967	Cin N	44	54	8	14	3	0	1	6	7-1	0	11	.259	.339	.370	94	0	0-1	.973	2	118	186	O26(1/4/21)	0	0.0
1968	StL N	26	56	11	13	0	0	3	8	8-2	0	21	.232	.323	.393	117	1	0-1	1.000	-1	84	71	O22R	0	-0.2
	Hou N	59	177	25	33	7	2	3	11	20-2	4	61	.186	.282	.299	77	-5	4-4	.970	-6	71	60	O49(13/16/23)	0	-1.6
	Year	85	233	36	46	7	2	6	19	28-4	4	82	.197	.292	.322	86	-4	4-5	.979	-7	74	63	O71(13/16/45)	0	-1.8
1969	NY A	6	11	2	3	2	0	0	4	3-0	0	6	.273	.429	.455	152	1	0-0	1.000	-0	53	386	O5(3/2/0)	0	0.1
	Sea A	26	51	8	9	2	0	2	5	4-0	0	17	.176	.236	.333	58	-3	3-1	1.000	-1	86	0	O17(1/16/0)	76	-0.5
	Year	32	62	10	12	4	0	2	9	7-0	0	23	.194	.275	.355	76	-2	3-1	1.000	-1	78	92	O22(4/18/0)	0	-0.4
Total	7	288	518	94	107	19	2	15	56	64-5	6	174	.207	.299	.338	84	-11	10-10	.967	-15	81	57	O211(31/72/113)	76	-3.9

SIMS, DUKE Duane B; B6.5.1941 Salt Lake City UT; BL/TR/6´2˝/(197–209); d9.22

YEAR	TM LG	G	AB	R	H	2B	3B	HR	RBI	BB-IB	HP	SO	AVG	OBP	SLG	AOPS	ABR	SB-CS	FA	FR	RNG	THR	GAMES AT POSITION	DL	BFW
1964	Cle A	2	6	0	0	0	0	0	0	0-0	0	2	.000	.000	.000	-99	-2	0-0	1.000	0	0	0	/C	0	-0.1
1965	Cle A	48	118	9	21	0	0	6	15	15-2	0	33	.178	.271	.331	69	-5	0-0	.980	-0	120	145	C40	0	-0.4
1966	Cle A	52	133	12	35	2	2	6	19	11-1	4	31	.263	.338	.444	122	4	0-1	.975	1	123	53	C48	44	0.6
1967	Cle A	88	272	25	55	8	2	12	37	30-2	6	64	.202	.294	.379	97	-1	3-3	.989	-6	77	102	C85	0	-0.4
1968	Cle A	122	361	48	90	21	0	11	44	62-11	5	68	.249	.366	.399	134	18	1-3	.983	-1	92	105	C84,1b31,O4(2/0/2)	0	2.1
1969	Cle A	114	326	40	77	8	0	18	45	66-5	6	80	.236	.374	.426	120	11	1-2	.991	8	123	96	C102,O3(2/0/1)/1	0	2.4
1970	Cle A	110	345	46	91	12	0	23	56	46-1	6	59	.264	.360	.499	128	13	0-4	.993	1	120	62	C39,O36(26/0/10),1b29	0	1.1
1971	LA N	90	230	23	63	7	2	6	25	30-7	1	39	.274	.357	.400	121	7	0-1	.992	3	105	94	C74	0	1.3
1972	LA N	51	151	7	29	7	0	2	11	17-3	1	23	.192	.278	.278	59	-8	0-0	.989	1	100	71	C48	0	-0.6
	†Det A	38	98	11	31	4	0	4	19	19-0	1	18	.316	.432	.480	165	9	0-0	.994	-5	70	41	C25,O4R	0	0.6
1973	Det A	80	252	31	61	10	0	8	30	30-1	2	36	.242	.324	.377	92	-2	1-2	.979	-1	79	121	C68,O6(5/0/1)	0	-0.1
	NY A	4	9	3	3	0	0	1	1	3-0	0	1	.333	.500	.667	231	2	0-0	1.000	1	0	288	/CD	0	0.3
	Year	84	261	34	64	10	0	9	31	33-1	2	37	.245	.331	.387	97	-1	1-2	.979	-0	78	124	C69,O6(5/0/1),D2	0	0.2
1974	NY A	5	15	1	2	1	0	0	2	1-0	0	5	.133	.188	.200	12	-2	0-0	1.000	0	52	0	/CD	0	-0.2
	Tex A	39	106	7	22	0	0	3	6	8-1	3	24	.208	.280	.292	67	-5	0-0	.970	-1	55	139	C30/rfD	0	-0.4
	Year	44	121	8	24	1	0	3	8	9-1	3	29	.198	.269	.281	60	-6	0-0	.971	-0	55	135	C31,D5/rf	0	-0.6
Total	11	843	2422	263	580	80	6	100	310	338-34	35	483	.239	.340	.401	111	39	6-16	.986	0	98	96	C646,1b61,O54(35/0/19),D7	44	6.2

SIMS, GREG Gregory Emmett; B6.28.1946 San Francisco CA; BB/TR/6´0˝/190; d4.15; Col Sacramento (CA) City

YEAR	TM LG	G	AB	R	H	2B	3B	HR	RBI	BB-IB	HP	SO	AVG	OBP	SLG	AOPS	ABR	SB-CS	FA	FR	RNG	THR	GAMES AT POSITION	DL	BFW
1966	Hou N	7	6	1	1	0	0	0	0	1-0	0	3	.167	.286	.167	32	-1	0-0	.500	-0	126	0	/lf	0	-0.1

SINATRO, MATT Matthew Stephen; B3.22.1960 Hartford CT; BR/TR/5´9˝/(174–179); [AtlN78 2/27]; d9.22; C11

YEAR	TM LG	G	AB	R	H	2B	3B	HR	RBI	BB-IB	HP	SO	AVG	OBP	SLG	AOPS	ABR	SB-CS	FA	FR	RNG	THR	GAMES AT POSITION	DL	BFW
1981	Atl N	12	32	4	9	1	1	0	4	5-1	0	4	.281	.378	.375	114	1	1-0	1.000	4	215	140	C12	0	0.6
1982	Atl N	37	81	10	11	2	0	1	4	4-0	0	9	.136	.176	.198	4	-11	0-1	1.000	-1	72	101	C35	0	-1.2
1983	Atl N	7	12	0	2	0	0	0	2	2-0	0	1	.167	.286	.167	26	-1	0-0	.967	0	67	210	C7	0	-0.1
1984	Atl N	2	4	0	0	0	0	0	0	0-0	0	0	.000	.000	.000	-93	-1	0-0	1.000	-1	33	0	C2	0	-0.2
1987	Oak A	6	3	0	0	0	0	0	0	0-0	0	1	.000	.000	.000	-99	-1	0-0	1.000	-1	60	0	C6	0	-0.1
1988	Oak A	10	9	1	3	2	0	0	5	0-0	0	1	.333	.300	.556	149	1	0-0	1.000	1	0	0	C9	15	0.2
1989	Det A	13	25	2	3	0	0	0	1	1-0	1	3	.120	.185	.120	-13	-4	0-0	1.000	-4	63	104	C13	0	-0.7
1990	Sea A	30	50	2	15	1	0	0	4	4-0	0	10	.300	.352	.320	88	-1	1-0	.992	3	94	186	C28	0	0.4
1991	Sea A	5	8	1	2	0	0	0	1	1-0	0	1	.250	.333	.250	64	0	0-0	1.000	1	181	0	C5	0	0.1
1992	Sea A	18	28	0	3	0	0	0	0	0-0	0	5	.107	.107	.107	-39	-5	0-0	1.000	-2	183	82	C18	141	-0.7
Total	10	140	252	20	48	6	1	1	21	17-1	1	35	.190	.244	.234	34	-22	2-1	.996	1	106	117	C135	156	-1.7

SINER, HOSEA Hosea John; B3.20.1885 Shelburn IN; D6.10.1948 Sullivan IN; BR/TR/5´10.5˝/185; d7.28

YEAR	TM LG	G	AB	R	H	2B	3B	HR	RBI	BB-IB	HP	SO	AVG	OBP	SLG	AOPS	ABR	SB-CS	FA	FR	RNG	THR	GAMES AT POSITION	DL	BFW
1909	Bos N	10	23	1	3	0	0	0	1	2	0	—	.130	.200	.130	3	-3	0	.909	-1	83	238	3b5/2S	—	-0.4

SINGLETON, CHRIS Christopher Verdell; B8.15.1972 Martinez CA; BL/TL/6´2˝/(195–210); [SFN93 2/48]; d4.10; Col Nevada–Reno

YEAR	TM LG	G	AB	R	H	2B	3B	HR	RBI	BB-IB	HP	SO	AVG	OBP	SLG	AOPS	ABR	SB-CS	FA	FR	RNG	THR	GAMES AT POSITION	DL	BFW
1999	Chi A	133	496	72	149	31	6	17	72	22-1	1	45	.300	.328	.490	104	1	20-5	.990	12	**118**	113	O127(11/121/1),D2	0	1.5
2000	†Chi A	147	511	83	130	22	5	11	62	35-2	1	85	.254	.301	.382	69	-25	22-7	.992	5	106	129	O145(19/143/0)	0	-1.5
2001	Chi A	140	392	57	117	21	5	7	45	20-2	1	61	.298	.331	.431	94	-4	12-11	.991	7	111	124	O133(19/121/3),D2	0	0.2
2002	Bal A	136	466	67	122	30	6	9	50	21-0	4	83	.262	.296	.410	91	-8	20-2	.986	-11	88	48	O126C/D	0	-1.3
2003	†Oak A	120	306	38	75	24	1	1	36	26-4	1	55	.245	.301	.340	70	-13	7-2	.969	-12	81	24	O113(4/102/8)	0	-2.3
2005	TB A	28	59	9	16	5	0	0	11	6-0	1	14	.271	.348	.356	90	0	0-0	.973	2	126	144	O19(2/6/11),D4	0	0.1
Total	6	704	2230	326	609	133	23	45	276	130-9	9	343	.273	.312	.414	86	-49	81-27	.987	3	103	93	O663(55/619/23),D9	0	-3.3

SINGLETON, DUANE Duane Earl; B8.6.1972 Staten Island NY; BL/TR/6´1˝/(170–177); [MilA90 5/142]; d8.4

YEAR	TM LG	G	AB	R	H	2B	3B	HR	RBI	BB-IB	HP	SO	AVG	OBP	SLG	AOPS	ABR	SB-CS	FA	FR	RNG	THR	GAMES AT POSITION	DL	BFW
1994	Mil A	2	0	0	0	0	0	0	0	0-0	0	0	ø	ø	ø	ø	0	0-0	1.000	0	155	0	O2C	0	0.0
1995	Mil A	13	31	0	2	0	0	0	0	1-0	0	10	.065	.094	.065	-55	-7	1-0	1.000	-0	86	193	O11(3/9/0)	0	-0.7
1996	Det A	18	56	5	9	1	0	0	3	4-0	1	15	.161	.230	.179	5	-8	0-2	1.000	1	85	354	O15(3/15/0)	0	-0.7
Total	3	33	87	5	11	1	0	0	3	5-0	1	25	.126	.183	.138	-16	-15	1-2	1.000	1	87	281	O28(6/26/0)	0	-1.4

SINGLETON, KEN Kenneth Wayne; B6.10.1947 New York NY; BB/TR/6´4˝/(205–213); [NYN67*1/3]; d6.24; Col Hofstra

YEAR	TM LG	G	AB	R	H	2B	3B	HR	RBI	BB-IB	HP	SO	AVG	OBP	SLG	AOPS	ABR	SB-CS	FA	FR	RNG	THR	GAMES AT POSITION	DL	BFW
1970	NY N	69	198	22	52	8	0	5	26	30-1	1	48	.263	.361	.379	98	0	1-1	.968	-1	107	30	O51(26/0/26)	0	-0.3
1971	NY N	115	298	34	73	5	0	13	46	61-9	2	64	.245	.374	.393	118	10	0-1	.974	-3	93	89	O96(10/3/85)	0	0.2
1972	Mon N	142	507	77	139	23	2	14	50	70-5	2	99	.274	.363	.410	118	14	5-10	.972	-4	86	91	O137(111/0/29)	0	0.0
1973	Mon N	**162**	560	100	169	26	2	23	103	123-13	2	91	.302	**.425**	.479	146	42	2-8	.983	-0	89	133	O161(2/0/161)	0	3.2
1974	Mon N	148	511	68	141	20	2	9	74	93-12	0	84	.276	.385	.376	108	10	5-2	.955	-13	86	71	O143R	0	-1.1
1975	Bal A	155	586	88	176	37	4	15	55	118-12	1	82	.300	.415	.454	155	51	3-5	.990	-12	87	65	O155R	0	2.9
1976	Bal A	154	544	62	151	25	2	13	70	79-6	0	76	.278	.366	.403	133	26	2-2	.983	-1	99	91	O134(80/0/63),D19	0	1.7
1977	Bal A★	152	536	90	176	24	0	24	99	107-13	2	101	.328	.438	.507	167	58	0-1	.986	-3	93	76	O150R/D	0	4.6
1978	Bal A	149	502	67	147	21	2	20	81	98-5	2	94	.293	.409	.462	**154**	41	0-0	.976	-11	93	11	O140(4/0/139),D5	0	2.4

YEAR	TM LG	G	AB	R	H	2B	3B	HR	RBI	BB-IB	HP	SO	AVG	OBP	SLG	AOPS	ABR	SB-CS	FA	FR	RNG	THR	GAMES AT POSITION	DL	BFW
1979	†Bal A★	**159**	570	93	168	29	1	35	111	109-**16**	1	118	.295	.405	.533	157	51	3-1	.981	-9	88	78	O143(7/0/136),D16	0	3.4
1980	Bal A	156	583	85	177	28	3	24	104	92-1	1	94	.304	.397	.485	143	38	0-2	.984	-12	88	28	O151R,D5	0	1.8
1981	Bal A★	103	363	48	101	16	1	13	49	61-6	0	59	.278	.380	.435	136	19	0-0	**1.000**	-3	95	43	O72(0/1/72),D30	0	1.3
1982	Bal A	156	561	71	141	27	2	14	77	86-2	2	93	.251	.349	.381	102	5	0-1	1.000	1	149	0	D148,O5(2/0/3)	0	0.0
1983	†Bal A	151	507	52	140	21	3	18	84	99-**19**	1	83	.276	.393	.436	130	26	0-2	ø	0	0	0	D150	0	2.0
1984	Bal A	111	363	28	78	7	1	6	36	37-5	0	60	.215	.286	.289	61	-19	0-0	ø	0	0	0	D103	16	-2.3
Total	15	2082	7189	985	2029	317	25	246	1065	1263-125	17	1246	.282	.388	.436	132	372	21-36	.980	-71	91	71	O1538(242/4/1313),D477	16	19.8

Sington, Fred Frederic William; B2.24.1910 Birmingham AL; D8.20.1998 Birmingham AL; BR/TR/6´2˝/215; d9.23; Col Alabama

YEAR	TM LG	G	AB	R	H	2B	3B	HR	RBI	BB-IB	HP	SO	AVG	OBP	SLG	AOPS	ABR	SB-CS	FA	FR	RNG	THR	GAMES AT POSITION	DL	BFW
1934	Was A	9	35	2	10	2	0	0	6	4	0	3	.286	.359	.343	85	-1	0-1	.933	-0	81	155	O9(3/0/6)	—	-0.2
1935	Was A	20	22	1	4	0	0	0	3	5	0	1	.182	.333	.182	38	-2	0-0	.889	0	96	335	O4(2/0/2)	—	-0.2
1936	Was A	25	94	13	30	8	0	1	28	15	0	9	.319	.413	.436	116	3	0-0	.946	-1	102	43	O25R	—	0.1
1937	Was A	78	228	27	54	15	4	3	36	37	2	33	.237	.348	.377	87	-4	1-1	.961	-0	106	77	O64(14/0/50)	—	-0.7
1938	Bro N	17	53	10	19	6	1	2	5	13	1	5	.358	.493	.623	200	9	1	1.000	-1	104	0	O17R	—	0.7
1939	Bro N	32	84	13	23	5	0	1	7	15	0	15	.274	.384	.369	100	1	0	.978	-1	98	55	O22(7/0/15)	—	-0.1
Total	6	181	516	66	140	36	5	7	85	89	3	66	.271	.382	.401	104	6	2-2	.961	-3	102	70	O141(26/0/115)	—	-0.4

Sipek, Dick Richard Francis; B1.16.1923 Chicago IL; D7.17.2005 Quincy IL; BL/TR/5´9˝/170; d4.28

YEAR	TM LG	G	AB	R	H	2B	3B	HR	RBI	BB-IB	HP	SO	AVG	OBP	SLG	AOPS	ABR	SB-CS	FA	FR	RNG	THR	GAMES AT POSITION	DL	BFW
1945	Cin N	82	156	14	38	6	2	0	13	9	4	15	.244	.302	.308	71	-6	0	.972	0	105	78	O31(14/0/17)	0	-0.8

Sipin, John John White; B8.29.1946 Watsonville CA; BR/TR/6´1.5˝/175; [StLN65 23/782]; d5.24

YEAR	TM LG	G	AB	R	H	2B	3B	HR	RBI	BB-IB	HP	SO	AVG	OBP	SLG	AOPS	ABR	SB-CS	FA	FR	RNG	THR	GAMES AT POSITION	DL	BFW
1969	SD N	68	229	22	51	12	2	2	9	8-1	1	44	.223	.251	.319	61	-13	2-0	.976	2	113	108	2b60	0	-0.7

Sisco, Steve Steven Michael; B12.2.1969 Thousand Oaks CA; BR/TR/5´10˝/190; [KCA92 16/442]; d5.6; Col Cal St.–Fullerton

YEAR	TM LG	G	AB	R	H	2B	3B	HR	RBI	BB-IB	HP	SO	AVG	OBP	SLG	AOPS	ABR	SB-CS	FA	FR	RNG	THR	GAMES AT POSITION	DL	BFW
2000	Atl N	25	27	4	5	0	0	1	2	3-0	0	4	.185	.267	.296	42	-3	0-0	1.000	0	140	1423	O6(5/0/1),2b5,3b2/D	0	-0.2

Sisler, George George Harold "Georgeous George"; B3.24.1893 Manchester OH; D3.26.1973 Richmond Heights MO; BL/TL/5´11˝/170; d6.28; M3/C1; HF1939; s–Dave s–Dick; Col Michigan; OF(12/10/15); ▲

YEAR	TM LG	G	AB	R	H	2B	3B	HR	RBI	BB-IB	HP	SO	AVG	OBP	SLG	AOPS	ABR	SB-CS	FA	FR	RNG	THR	GAMES AT POSITION	DL	BFW
1915	StL A	81	274	28	78	10	2	3	29	7	2	27	.285	.307	.369	106	0	10-9	.989	-2	84	102	1b36,O29(6/8/15),P15	—	-0.6
1916	StL A	151	580	83	177	21	11	4	76	40	5	37	.305	.355	.400	133	20	34-26	.985	-2	97	107	1b141,P3,O3(1/2/0),3b2	—	1.4
1917	StL A	135	539	60	190	30	9	2	52	30	3	19	.353	.390	.453	163	38	37	.985	5	**121**	**117**	1b133,2b2	—	4.3
1918	StL A	114	452	69	154	21	9	2	41	40	5	17	.341	.400	.440	159	32	**45**	.990	8	**124**	94	1b114,P2	—	4.0
1919	StL A	132	511	96	180	31	15	10	83	27	5	20	.352	.390	.530	153	33	28	.991	13	**135**	88	1b131	—	4.4
1920	StL A	**154**	631	137	**257**	49	18	19	122	46	2	19	**.407**	.449	.632	179	69	42-17	.990	15	**137**	91	1b154/P	—	7.9
1921	StL A	138	582	125	216	38	**18**	12	104	34	5	27	.371	.411	.560	137	31	**35**-11	.993	8	**119**	89	1b138	—	3.1
1922	StL A	142	586	**134**	**246**	42	**18**	8	105	49	3	14	**.420**	.467	.594	169	**60**	**51**-19	.988	12	**131**	**122**	1b141	—	**6.3**
1924	StL A	151	636	94	194	27	10	9	74	31	3	29	.305	.340	.421	90	-12	19-17	.984	1	106	103	1b151,M	—	-2.2
1925	StL A	150	649	100	224	21	15	12	105	27	0	24	.345	.371	.479	109	5	11-12	.983	11	**129**	91	1b150/PM	—	0.3
1926	StL A	150	613	78	178	21	12	7	71	30	3	30	.290	.327	.398	84	-17	12-8	.987	-3	97	**116**	1b149/PM	—	-2.9
1927	StL A	149	614	87	201	32	8	5	97	24	4	15	.327	.357	.430	100	-2	**27**-7	.984	12	**132**	110	1b149	—	0.4
1928	Was A	20	49	1	12	1	0	0	2	1	0	2	.245	.260	.265	39	-5	0-1	1.000	-1	0	80	1b5,O5L	—	-0.7
	Bos N	118	491	71	167	26	4	4	68	30	2	15	.340	.380	.434	119	13	11	.988	7	**129**	90	1b118/P	—	1.2
1929	Bos N	**154**	629	67	205	40	8	2	79	33	4	17	.326	.363	.424	98	-2	6	.982	4	116	100	1b154	—	-0.8
1930	Bos N	116	431	54	133	15	7	3	67	23	2	15	.309	.346	.397	82	-13	7	.987	5	123	105	1b107	—	-1.3
Total	15	2055	8267	1284	2812	425	164	102	1175	472	48	327	.340	.379	.468	124	250	375-127	.987	93	120	102	1b1971,O37R,P24,2b2,3b2	—	24.8

Sisler, Dick Richard Allan; B11.2.1920 St.Louis MO; D11.20.1998 Nashville TN; BL/TR/6´2˝/205; d4.16; M2/C13; b–Dave f–George

YEAR	TM LG	G	AB	R	H	2B	3B	HR	RBI	BB-IB	HP	SO	AVG	OBP	SLG	AOPS	ABR	SB-CS	FA	FR	RNG	THR	GAMES AT POSITION	DL	BFW
1946	†StL N	83	235	17	61	11	2	3	42	14	2	28	.260	.307	.362	86	-5	0	.988	2	119	117	1b37,O29L	0	-0.7
1947	StL N	46	74	4	15	2	1	0	9	3	0	8	.203	.234	.257	29	-8	0	.976	0	119	49	1b10,O5L	0	-0.8
1948	Phi N	121	446	60	122	21	3	11	56	47	1	46	.274	.344	.408	105	3	1	.983	-4	93	96	1b120	0	-0.5
1949	Phi N	121	412	42	119	19	6	7	50	25	2	38	.289	.333	.415	102	0	0	.987	-9	67	92	1b96	0	-1.3
1950	†Phi N★	141	523	79	155	29	4	13	83	64	0	50	.296	.373	.442	115	13	1	.987	1	100	89	O137L	0	0.3
1951	Phi N	125	428	46	123	20	5	8	52	40	2	39	.287	.351	.414	107	4	1-0	.968	-1	99	83	O111L	0	-0.5
1952	Cin N	11	27	3	5	1	1	0	4	3	0	5	.185	.267	.296	56	-2	0-0	1.000	-0	103	0	O7(3/0/4)	0	-0.2
	StL N	119	418	48	109	14	5	13	60	29	2	35	.261	.312	.411	99	-3	3-3	.985	4	**115**	**122**	1b114	0	-0.3
	Year	130	445	51	114	15	6	13	64	32	2	40	.256	.309	.404	96	-4	3-3	.985	3	**115**	**122**	1b114,O7(3/0/4)	0	-0.5
1953	StL N	32	43	3	11	1	1	0	4	1	0	4	.256	.273	.326	55	-3	0-0	1.000	1	179	112	1b10	0	-0.2
Total	8	799	2606	302	720	118	28	55	360	226	9	253	.276	.336	.406	101	-1	6-3	.985	-7	97	104	1b387,O289(285/0/4)	0	-4.2

Sisti, Sibby Sebastian Daniel; B7.26.1920 Buffalo NY; D4.24.2006 Amherst NY; BR/TR/5´11˝/(175–185); d7.21; Mil 1943–45; C2; OF(29/14/35)

YEAR	TM LG	G	AB	R	H	2B	3B	HR	RBI	BB-IB	HP	SO	AVG	OBP	SLG	AOPS	ABR	SB-CS	FA	FR	RNG	THR	GAMES AT POSITION	DL	BFW
1939	Bos N	63	215	19	49	7	1	1	11	12	0	38	.228	.269	.284	52	-15	4	.994	-1	88	118	2b34,3b17,S10	—	-1.3
1940	Bos N	123	459	73	115	19	5	6	34	36	4	64	.251	.311	.353	87	-9	4	.936	-1	99	124	3b102,2b16	—	-0.5
1941	Bos N	140	541	72	140	24	3	1	45	38	1	76	.259	.309	.320	81	-15	7	.916	-6	101	105	3b137,2b2,S2	—	-1.6
1942	Bos N	129	407	50	86	11	4	4	35	45	4	55	.211	.296	.287	73	-14	5	.970	-2	101	90	2b124/cf	—	-1.0
1946	Bos N	1	0	0	0	0	0	0	0	0	0	0	ø	ø	ø	ø	0	0	ø	-0	0	0	/3	0	0.0
1947	Bos N	56	153	22	43	8	0	2	15	20	2	17	.281	.371	.373	100	1	2	.947	-8	88	96	S51/2	57	-0.4
1948	†Bos N	83	221	30	54	6	2	0	21	31	1	34	.244	.340	.290	73	-7	0	.972	-6	96	88	2b44,S26	0	-1.0
1949	Bos N	101	268	39	69	12	0	5	22	34	1	42	.257	.343	.358	93	-2	1	.989	-6	101	64	O48(21/13/17),2b21,S18/3	0	-0.8
1950	Bos N	69	105	21	18	3	1	2	11	16	1	19	.171	.287	.276	52	-7	1	.931	-3	79	85	S23,2b19,3b13/1rf	0	-1.0
1951	Bos N	114	362	46	101	20	2	2	38	32	2	50	.279	.341	.362	96	-2	4-5	.944	-16	81	77	S55,2b52,3b6/1rf	0	-1.3
1952	Bos N	90	245	19	52	10	1	4	24	14	0	43	.212	.255	.310	58	-15	2-0	.966	-9	90	75	2b33,O23(8/0/16),S18,3b9	0	-2.3
1953	Mil N	38	23	8	5	1	0	0	4	5	0	2	.217	.357	.261	69	-1	0-0	1.000	2	107	51	2b13,S6,3b4	0	0.1
1954	Mil N	9	0	2	0	0	0	0	0	0	0	0	ø	ø	ø	ø	0	0-0	ø	0	—	—	/R	0	0.0
Total	13	1016	2999	401	732	121	19	27	260	283	16	440	.244	.313	.324	79	-86	30-5	.973	-56	96	86	2b359,3b290,S209,O74R,1b2	57	-11.1

Sixsmith, Ed Edward; B2.26.1863 Philadelphia PA; D12.12.1926 Philadelphia PA; BR/TR; d9.11

YEAR	TM LG	G	AB	R	H	2B	3B	HR	RBI	BB-IB	HP	SO	AVG	OBP	SLG	AOPS	ABR	SB-CS	FA	FR	RNG	THR	GAMES AT POSITION	DL	BFW
1884	Phi N	1	2	0	0	0	0	0	0	0	—	0	.000	.000	.000	-99	0	—	1.000	-1	—	—	/C	—	-0.1

Sizemore, Grady Grady; B8.2.1982 Seattle WA; BL/TL/6´2˝/(200–210); [MonN00 3/75]; d7.21

YEAR	TM LG	G	AB	R	H	2B	3B	HR	RBI	BB-IB	HP	SO	AVG	OBP	SLG	AOPS	ABR	SB-CS	FA	FR	RNG	THR	GAMES AT POSITION	DL	BFW
2004	Cle A	43	138	15	34	6	2	4	24	14-0	5	34	.246	.333	.406	96	-1	2-0	.991	-1	105	0	O42C	0	-0.1
2005	Cle A	158	640	111	185	37	11	22	81	52-1	7	132	.289	.348	.484	123	20	22-10	.992	-9	94	39	O155C	0	1.4
2006	Cle A★	**162**	655	**134**	190	**53**	11	28	76	78-8	13	153	.290	.375	.533	137	38	22-6	.993	-1	101	88	O160C/D	0	3.9
Total	3	363	1433	260	409	96	24	54	181	144-9	25	319	.285	.359	.499	127	57	46-16	.992	-11	98	56	O357C/D	0	5.2

Sizemore, Ted Theodore Crawford; B4.15.1945 Gadsden AL; BR/TR/5´10˝/(155–170); [LAN66 15/299]; d4.7; Col Michigan

YEAR	TM LG	G	AB	R	H	2B	3B	HR	RBI	BB-IB	HP	SO	AVG	OBP	SLG	AOPS	ABR	SB-CS	FA	FR	RNG	THR	GAMES AT POSITION	DL	BFW
1969	LA N	159	590	69	160	20	5	4	46	45-7	5	40	.271	.328	.342	94	-6	5-5	.979	1	101	112	2b118,S46/lf	0	0.8
1970	LA N	96	340	40	104	10	1	1	34	34-6	0	19	.306	.367	.350	97	0	5-1	.984	-3	101	95	2b86,O9(8/0/1),S2	29	0.3
1971	StL N	135	478	53	126	14	5	3	42	42-5	1	26	.264	.322	.333	82	-11	4-6	.976	17	102	92	2b93,S39,O15(7/0/8)/3	0	1.5
1972	StL N	120	439	53	116	17	4	2	38	37-1	4	36	.264	.324	.335	89	-6	8-3	.976	5	104	99	2b111	0	0.7
1973	StL N	142	521	69	147	22	1	1	54	68-0	2	34	.282	.365	.334	95	0	6-4	.981	7	**106**	93	2b139,3b3	19	1.7
1974	StL N	129	504	68	126	17	0	2	47	70-2	0	37	.250	.339	.296	79	-11	8-4	.980	15	108	**129**	2b128/Srf	16	1.3
1975	StL N	153	562	56	135	23	1	3	49	45-2	2	37	.240	.296	.301	64	-27	1-5	.972	-21	90	83	2b153	0	-4.3
1976	LA N	84	266	18	64	8	1	0	18	15-1	0	22	.241	.280	.278	60	-15	2-3	.986	5	103	133	2b71,3b3,C2	0	-0.6
1977	†Phi N	152	519	64	146	20	3	4	47	52-21	1	40	.281	.345	.355	84	-10	8-11	.986	15	107	121	2b152	0	1.1
1978	†Phi N	108	351	38	77	12	0	0	25	25-8	1	29	.219	.270	.254	47	-25	8-1	.978	10	108	113	2b107	52	-0.9
1979	Chi N	98	330	36	82	17	0	2	24	32-7	3	25	.248	.319	.318	68	-13	3-3	.973	23	111	109	2b96	0	1.4
	Bos A	26	88	12	23	7	0	1	6	4-0	1	5	.261	.301	.375	77	-3	1-0	.993	8	117	150	2b26,C2	0	0.6
1980	Bos A	9	23	1	5	1	0	0	0	0-0	0	0	.217	.217	.261	29	-2	0-0	.927	-1	96	132	2b8	0	-0.2
Total	12	1411	5011	577	1311	188	21	23	430	469-60	20	350	.262	.325	.321	79	-129	59-46	.979	81	104	108	2b1288,S88,O26(16/0/10),3b7,C4	116	3.4

Skaff, Frank Francis Michael; B9.30.1910 LaCrosse WI; D4.12.1988 Towson MD; BR/TR/5´10˝/185; d9.11; M1/C4; Col Villanova

YEAR	TM LG	G	AB	R	H	2B	3B	HR	RBI	BB-IB	HP	SO	AVG	OBP	SLG	AOPS	ABR	SB-CS	FA	FR	RNG	THR	GAMES AT POSITION	DL	BFW
1935	Bro N	6	11	4	6	1	1	0	3	0	0	2	.545	.545	.818	267	2	0	.857	-1	54	0	3b3	—	0.2
1943	Phi A	32	64	8	18	2	1	1	8	6	0	11	.281	.343	.391	115	1	0-0	.976	1	142	111	1b18,3b3/S	0	0.1
Total	2	38	75	12	24	3	2	1	11	6	0	13	.320	.370	.453	138	3	0-0	.976	0	142	111	1b18,3b6/S	0	0.3

YEAR	TM LG	G	AB	R	H	2B	3B	HR	RBI	BB-IB	HP	SO	AVG	OBP	SLG	AOPS	ABR	SB-CS	FA	FR	RNG	THR	GAMES AT POSITION	DL	BFW
Skaggs, Dave	David Lindsey; B6.12.1951 Santa Monica CA; BR/TR/6´2˝/(190–205); [BalA69 6/135]; d4.17																								
1977	Bal A	80	216	22	62	9	1	1	24	20-0	0	34	.287	.345	.352	97	-1	0-0	.995	-3	116	93	C80	0	0.0
1978	Bal A	36	86	6	13	1	1	0	2	9-1	0	14	.151	.232	.186	20	-9	0-1	.988	2	112	106	C35	0	-0.7
1979	†Bal A	63	137	9	34	8	0	1	14	13-0	0	14	.248	.313	.328	76	-4	0-0	.984	-4	82	74	C63	0	-0.6
1980	Bal A	2	5	0	1	0	0	0	0	0-0	0	1	.200	.200	.200	10	-1	0-0	1.000	0	53	0	C2	0	-0.1
	Cal A	24	66	7	13	0	0	1	9	9-0	0	13	.197	.289	.242	49	-5	0-0	.968	-8	87	28	C24	105	-1.2
	Year	26	71	7	14	0	0	1	9	9-0	0	14	.197	.284	.239	47	-5	0-0	.971	-8	85	26	C26	0	-1.3
Total	4	205	510	44	123	18	2	3	49	51-1	0	76	.241	.309	.302	71	-20	0-1	.988	-13	102	81	C204	105	-2.6
Sketchley, Bud	Harry Clement; B3.30.1919 Virden MB, Can.; D12.19.1979 Los Angeles CA; BL/TL/5´10˝/180; d4.14; Col UCLA																								
1942	Chi A	13	36	1	7	1	0	0	3	7	0	4	.194	.326	.222	57	-2	0-1	.952	0	98	141	O12R	0	-0.3
Skidmore, Roe	Robert Roe; B10.30.1945 Decatur IL; BR/TR/6´3˝/188; [AtlN66 47/780]; d9.17; Col Millikin																								
1970	Chi N	1	1	0	1	0	0	0	0	0-0	0	0	1.000	1.000	1.000	390	0	0-0	ø	0	—	—	/H	0	0.0
Skiff, Bill	William Franklin; B10.16.1895 New Rochelle NY; D12.25.1976 Bronxville NY; BR/TR/5´10˝/170; d5.17																								
1921	Pit N	16	45	7	13	2	0	0	11	0	0	4	.289	.289	.333	63	-2	1-1	.982	-0	*140*	*56*	C13	—	-0.2
1926	NY A	6	11	0	1	0	0	0	0	0	0	1	.091	.091	.091	-53	-3	0-0	1.000	-0	*61*	*0*	C6	—	-0.3
Total	2	22	56	7	14	2	0	0	11	0	0	5	.250	.250	.286	40	-5	1-1	.984	-1	*127*	*47*	C19	—	-0.5
Skinner, Alexander	Alexander; B8.14.1856 Chicago IL; D3.5.1901 Washington MA; d7.12																								
1884	Bal U	1	3	0	1	0	0	0	—	0	—	—	.333	.333	.333	93	0	—	1.000	0	0	0	/rf	—	0.0
	CP U	1	3	1	1	0	0	0	—	0	—	—	.333	.333	.333	104	0	—	ø	-0	0	0	/cf	—	0.0
	Year	2	6	1	2	0	0	0	—	0	—	—	.333	.333	.333	98	0	—	1.000	-0	0	0	O2(0/1/1)	—	0.0
Skinner, Camp	Elisha Harrison; B6.25.1897 Douglasville GA; D8.4.1944 Douglasville GA; BL/TR/5´11˝/165; d5.2																								
1922	NY A	27	33	1	6	0	0	0	2	0	1	4	.182	.206	.182	2	-5	1-0	1.000	0	118	0	O4(1/3/0)	—	-0.5
1923	Bos A	7	13	1	3	2	0	0	1	0	0	0	.231	.231	.385	60	-1	0-0	ø	-0	0	0	O2C	—	-0.1
Total	2	34	46	2	9	2	0	0	3	0	1	4	.196	.213	.239	18	-6	1-0	1.000	-0	114	0	O6(1/5/0)	—	-0.6
Skinner, Joel	Joel Patrick; B2.21.1961 LaJolla CA; BR/TR/6´4˝/(198–208); [PitN79 37/842]; d6.12; M1/C6; f–Bob; [DL 1992 Cle A 182, 1993 Cle A 182]																								
1983	Chi A	6	11	2	3	0	0	0	1	0-0	0	1	.273	.273	.273	49	-1	0-0	.960	1	113	174	C6	0	0.1
1984	Chi A	43	80	4	17	2	0	0	3	7-0	0	19	.213	.273	.237	41	-6	1-0	.989	4	78	70	C43	0	-0.1
1985	Chi A	22	44	9	15	4	1	1	5	5-0	0	13	.341	.408	.545	151	3	0-0	.971	-0	95	130	C21	0	0.4
1986	Chi A	60	149	17	30	5	1	4	20	9-0	1	43	.201	.250	.329	54	-10	1-0	.988	-11	115	68	C60	0	-1.9
	NY A	54	166	6	43	4	0	1	17	7-0	0	40	.259	.287	.301	61	-9	0-4	.981	2	147	97	C54	0	-0.7
	Year	114	315	23	73	9	1	5	37	16-0	1	83	.232	.269	.314	58	-19	1-4	.984	-10	131	83	C114	0	-2.6
1987	NY A	64	139	9	19	4	0	3	14	8-0	1	46	.137	.187	.230	11	-18	0-0	.984	-8	97	108	C64	0	-2.3
1988	NY A	88	251	23	57	15	0	4	23	14-0	0	72	.227	.267	.335	68	-11	0-0	.990	-8	**217**	53	C85,O2(1/0/1)/1	0	-1.5
1989	Cle A	79	178	10	41	10	0	1	13	9-0	1	42	.230	.271	.303	60	-9	1-1	.990	-8	100	92	C79	0	-1.4
1990	Cle A	49	139	16	35	4	1	2	16	7-0	0	44	.252	.288	.338	74	-5	0-0	.996	-4	140	89	C49	0	-0.7
1991	Cle A	99	284	23	69	14	0	1	24	14-1	1	67	.243	.279	.303	61	-15	0-2	.991	-0	107	96	C99	0	-1.1
Total	9	564	1441	119	329	62	3	17	136	80-1	4	387	.228	.269	.311	59	-81	3-7	.988	-32	129	86	C560,O2(1/0/1)/1	364	-9.2
Skinner, Bob	Robert Ralph; B10.3.1931 LaJolla CA; BL/TR/6´4˝/(185–195); d4.13; M3/C19; s–Joel																								
1954	Pit N	132	470	67	117	15	9	8	46	47	0	59	.249	.316	.370	80	-15	4-0	.986	-2	98	76	1b118,O2R	0	-2.4
1956	Pit N	113	233	29	47	8	3	5	29	26-1	1	50	.202	.282	.326	65	-12	1-1	.977	-5	91	125	O36(26/0/10),1b23/3	0	-2.0
1957	Pit N	126	387	58	118	12	6	13	45	38-6	2	50	.305	.370	.468	127	14	10-4	.963	3	100	154	O93L,1b9/3	0	1.3
1958	Pit N★	144	529	93	170	33	9	13	70	58-7	2	55	.321	.387	.491	135	28	12-4	.977	1	84	183	O141L	0	2.2
1959	Pit N	143	547	78	153	18	4	13	61	67-8	0	65	.280	.357	.399	102	3	10-7	.964	-2	97	75	O142L/1	0	-0.9
1960	†Pit N★	145	571	83	156	33	6	15	86	59-11	1	86	.273	.340	.431	109	8	11-8	.981	-2	93	109	O141L	0	-0.3
1961	Pit N	119	381	61	102	20	3	3	42	51-9	4	49	.268	.358	.360	91	-2	3-5	.973	-0	101	65	O97L	0	-0.9
1962	Pit N	144	510	87	154	29	7	20	75	76-5	4	89	.302	.395	.504	140	31	10-4	.960	-6	89	64	O139L	0	1.8
1963	Pit N	34	122	18	33	5	5	0	8	13-1	0	22	.270	.341	.393	110	2	4-1	.983	0	103	49	O32L	0	0.0
	Cin N	72	194	25	49	10	2	3	17	21-1	2	42	.253	.332	.371	99	0	1-2	1.000	1	97	105	O51L	0	-0.2
	Year	106	316	43	82	15	7	3	25	34-2	2	64	.259	.335	.380	103	2	5-3	.993	1	99	82	O83L	0	-0.2
1964	Cin N	25	59	6	13	3	0	3	5	4-0	0	12	.220	.270	.424	89	-1	0-0	.913	1	109	144	O12L	0	-0.1
	†StL N	55	118	10	32	5	0	1	16	11-2	0	20	.271	.333	.339	83	-2	0-0	.938	1	103	177	O31(4/0/27)	0	-0.3
	Year	80	177	16	45	8	0	4	21	15-2	0	32	.254	.313	.367	85	-3	0-0	.930	1	105	166	O43(16/0/27)	0	-0.4
1965	StL N	80	152	25	47	5	4	5	26	12-2	0	30	.309	.360	.493	126	5	1-0	.935	-2	93	0	O33(15/0/19)	0	0.1
1966	StL N	49	45	2	7	1	0	1	5	2-0	1	17	.156	.208	.244	25	-5	0-0	ø	0	—	—	/H	0	-0.5
Total	12	1381	4318	642	1198	197	58	103	531	485-53	17	646	.277	.351	.421	108	54	67-36	.969	-14	94	105	O950(893/0/58),1b151,3b2	0	-2.2
Skizas, Lou	Louis Peter "The Nervous Greek"; B6.2.1932 Chicago IL; BR/TR/5´11˝/(170–175); d4.19																								
1956	NY A	6	6	0	1	0	0	0	1	0-0	0	2	.167	.167	.167	-12	-1	0-0	ø	0	—	—	/H	0	-0.1
	KC A	83	297	39	94	11	3	11	39	15-1	0	17	.316	.346	.485	118	6	3-1	.975	3	100	161	O74(57/0/18)	0	0.5
	Year	89	303	39	95	11	3	11	40	15-1	0	19	.314	.343	.479	116	5	3-1	.975	3	100	161	O74(57/0/18)	0	0.4
1957	KC A	119	376	34	92	14	1	18	44	27-1	2	15	.245	.297	.431	95	-4	5-2	.976	0	98	106	O76(14/0/69),3b32	0	-0.7
1958	Det A	23	33	4	8	2	0	1	2	5-1	0	1	.242	.342	.394	95	0	0-0	.750	-2	61	0	O5(4/0/1),3b4	0	-0.2
1959	Chi A	8	13	3	1	0	0	0	0	3-0	0	2	.077	.250	.077	-6	-2	0-0	1.000	1	100	522	O6(5/0/1)	0	-0.1
Total	4	239	725	80	196	27	4	30	86	50-3	2	37	.270	.317	.443	102	-1	8-3	.973	2	98	140	O161(80/0/89),3b36	0	-0.6
Skowron, Bill	William Joseph "Moose"; B12.18.1930 Chicago IL; BR/TR/5´11˝/(191–200); d4.13; Col Purdue																								
1954	NY A	87	215	37	73	12	9	7	41	19	1	18	.340	.392	.577	170	19	2-1	.986	-0	98	126	1b61,3b5,2b2	0	1.7
1955	†NY A	108	288	46	92	17	3	12	61	21-4	3	32	.319	.369	.524	141	15	1-1	.989	-2	94	115	1b74,3b3	0	1.0
1956	†NY A	134	464	78	143	21	6	23	90	50-3	6	60	.308	.382	.528	143	27	4-4	.993	4	**112**	**131**	1b120,3b2	0	2.3
1957	†NY A★	122	457	54	139	15	5	17	88	31-6	3	60	.304	.347	.470	125	14	3-2	.992	6	120	**114**	1b115	0	1.4
1958	†NY A★	126	465	61	127	22	3	14	73	28-1	4	69	.273	.317	.424	107	3	1-1	**.993**	-2	100	**107**	1b118,3b2	0	-0.6
1959	NY A★	74	282	39	84	13	5	15	59	20-0	3	47	.298	.349	.539	145	16	1-0	.991	0	99	117	1b72	65	1.2
1960	†NY A★	146	538	63	166	34	3	26	91	38-2	2	95	.309	.353	.528	144	31	2-3	.991	10	128	107	1b142	0	3.1
1961	†NY A☆	150	561	76	150	23	4	28	89	35-9	8	108	.267	.318	.472	115	8	0-0	.993	1	100	**126**	1b149	0	0.0
1962	†NY A	140	478	63	129	16	6	23	80	36-4	5	99	.270	.325	.473	116	8	0-1	.991	-5	86	104	1b135	0	-0.5
1963	†LA N	89	237	19	48	8	0	4	19	13-4	3	49	.203	.252	.287	59	-13	0-1	.991	-0	95	104	1b66/3	0	-1.9
1964	Was A	73	262	28	71	10	0	13	41	11-2	3	56	.271	.306	.458	110	3	0-0	.994	-1	95	79	1b66	0	-0.3
	Chi A	73	273	19	80	11	3	4	38	19-4	1	36	.293	.337	.399	108	3	0-0	.998	-1	93	112	1b70	0	-0.2
	Year	146	535	47	151	21	3	17	79	30-6	4	92	.282	.322	.428	109	5	0-0	.996	-2	94	96	1b136	0	-0.5
1965	Chi A✳	146	559	63	153	24	3	18	78	32-4	5	77	.274	.316	.424	116	9	1-3	.994	-6	83	117	1b145	0	-0.7
1966	Chi A	120	337	27	84	15	2	6	29	26-4	3	45	.249	.308	.359	98	-1	1-1	.991	3	116	135	1b98	0	-0.4
1967	Chi A	8	8	0	0	0	0	0	0	1-0	0	1	.000	.000	.000	-99	-2	0-0	ø	0	—	—	/H	0	-0.2
	Cal A	62	123	8	27	2	1	1	10	4-1	4	18	.220	.267	.276	63	-6	0-0	.988	-1	93	82	1b32	0	-0.9
	Year	70	131	8	27	2	1	1	11	4-1	4	19	.206	.252	.260	53	-8	0-0	.988	-1	93	82	1b32	0	-1.1
Total	14	1658	5547	681	1566	243	53	211	888	383-48	54	870	.282	.332	.459	121	134	16-18	.992	6	102	114	1b1463,3b13,2b2	65	5.0
Skube, Bob	Robert Jacob; B10.8.1957 Northridge CA; BL/TL/6´0˝/182; [MilA79 13/335]; d9.17; Col USC																								
1982	Mil A	4	3	0	2	0	0	0	0	0-0	0	0	.667	.667	.667	282	1	0-0	ø	-0	0	0	/cfD	0	0.1
1983	Mil A	12	25	2	5	1	1	0	9	4-0	0	7	.200	.310	.320	79	-1	0-0	1.000	-0	111	0	O8(0/4/4)/1D	0	-0.1
Total	2	16	28	2	7	1	1	0	9	4-0	0	7	.250	.344	.357	100	0	0-0	1.000	-0	109	0	O9(0/5/4),D3/1	0	0.0
Slade, Gordon	Gordon Leigh "Oskie"; B10.9.1904 Salt Lake City UT; D1.2.1974 Long Beach CA; BR/TR/5´10.5˝/160; d4.21; Col Oregon																								
1930	Bro N	25	37	8	8	2	0	1	2	3	0	5	.216	.275	.351	51	-3	0	.938	6	137	183	S21	—	0.4
1931	Bro N	85	272	27	65	13	2	1	29	23	5	28	.239	.310	.313	68	-12	2	.947	10	107	105	S82,3b2	—	0.4
1932	Bro N	79	250	23	60	15	1	1	23	11	3	26	.240	.280	.320	62	-13	3	.943	8	100	108	S55,3b23	—	-0.1
1933	StL N	39	62	6	7	1	0	0	3	6	0	7	.113	.191	.129	-7	-9	1	.941	0	102	95	S31/2	—	-0.8
1934	Cin N	138	555	61	158	19	8	4	52	25	4	34	.285	.320	.369	86	-12	6	.952	5	105	103	S97,2b39	—	0.2

YEAR	TM LG	G	AB	R	H	2B	3B	HR	RBI	BB-IB	HP	SO	AVG	OBP	SLG	AOPS	ABR	SB-CS	FA	FR	RNG	THR	GAMES AT POSITION	DL	BFW
1935	Cin N	71	196	22	55	10	0	1	14	16	2	16	.281	.341	.347	88	-3	0	.927	-5	91	94	S30,2b19,O8L,3b7	—	-0.5
Total	6	437	1372	147	353	60	11	8	123	84	14	116	.257	.307	.335	73	-52	12	.945	25	104	106	S316,2b59,3b32,O8L	—	-0.4
SLADEN, ART	Arthur; B10.28.1860 Dracut MA; D2.28.1914 Dracut MA; d4.22																								
1884	Bos U	2	7	0	0	0	0	0	—	0	—	—	.000	.000	.000	-99	-2	—	1.000	-0	0	0	O2R	—	-0.2
SLAGLE, JIMMY	James Franklin "Rabbit","Shorty"; B7.11.1873 Worthville PA; D5.10.1956 Chicago IL; BL/TR/5´10.5˝/144; d4.17																								
1899	Was N	147	599	92	163	15	8	0	41	55	5	—	.272	.338	.324	83	-13	22	.953	18	91	120	O146C	—	-0.4
1900	Phi N	**141**	574	115	165	16	9	0	45	60	3	—	.287	.358	.347	96	-2	34	.922	0	112	90	O141L	—	-1.3
1901	Phi N	48	183	20	37	6	2	1	20	16	3	—	.202	.277	.273	59	-9	5	.930	5	187	206	O48L	—	-0.7
	Bos N	66	255	35	69	7	0	0	7	34	1	—	.271	.359	.298	84	-4	14	.935	-2	133	157	O66(0/5/61)	—	-0.8
	Year	114	438	55	106	13	2	1	27	50	4	—	.242	.325	.288	74	-13	19	.932	3	**157**	178	O114(48/5/61)	—	-1.5
1902	Chi N	117	463	66	146	11	4	0	28	53	0	—	.315	.386	.356	133	20	41	.965	4	90	125	O115(94/22/0)	—	1.8
1903	Chi N	**139**	543	104	162	20	6	0	44	81	4	—	.298	.393	.357	117	18	33	.936	-3	78	176	O139(115/24/0)	—	0.7
1904	Chi N	120	481	73	125	12	10	1	31	41	3	—	.260	.322	.333	102	1	28	.921	-5	94	166	O120(102/18/0)	—	-1.2
1905	Chi N	**155**	568	96	153	19	4	0	37	97	3	—	.269	.379	.317	104	9	27	.962	-1	129	137	O155(33/123/0)	—	0.1
1906	Chi N	127	498	71	119	8	6	0	33	63	0	—	.239	.324	.279	83	-8	25	.976	-3	54	147	O127(4/123/0)	—	-1.9
1907	†Chi N	136	489	71	126	6	6	0	32	76	1	—	.258	.359	.294	99	3	28	.962	-10	83	131	O136(4/132/0)	—	-1.5
1908	Chi N	104	352	38	78	4	1	0	26	43	0	—	.222	.306	.239	71	-10	17	.976	-6	48	73	O101(26/75/0)	—	-2.5
Total	10	1300	5005	781	1343	124	56	2	344	619	23	—	.268	.352	.317	97	5	274	.950	-2	95	135	O1294(567/668/61)	—	-7.7
SLATTERY, JACK	John Thomas; B1.6.1878 S.Boston MA; D7.17.1949 Boston MA; BR/TR/6´2˝/191; d9.28; M1/C2; Col Fordham																								
1901	Bos A	1	3	1	1	0	0	0	1	1	0	—	.333	.500	.333	137	0	0	1.000	0	*124*	*102*	/C	—	0.1
1903	Cle A	4	11	1	0	0	0	0	0	0	0	—	.000	.000	.000	-99	-3	0	.885	-1	71	280	1b2	—	-0.4
	Chi A	63	211	8	46	3	2	0	20	2	2	—	.218	.233	.251	47	-14	2	.974	-4	*109*	*80*	C56,1b5	—	-1.4
	Year	67	222	9	46	3	2	0	20	2	2	—	.207	.221	.239	40	-17	2	.974	-5	*109*	*80*	C56,1b7	—	-1.8
1906	StL N	3	7	0	2	0	0	0	0	1	0	—	.286	.375	.286	111	0	0	1.000	-1	*68*	*45*	C2	—	0.0
1909	Was A	32	56	4	12	2	0	0	6	2	1	—	.214	.254	.250	62	-2	1	.953	-1	128	51	1b11,C6	—	-0.4
Total	4	103	288	14	61	5	2	0	27	6	3	—	.212	.236	.243	47	-19	3	.974	-6	*106*	*79*	C65,1b18	—	-2.1
SLATTERY, MIKE	Michael J.; B11.26.1866 Boston MA; D10.16.1904 Boston MA; BL/TL/6´2˝/210; d4.17																								
1884	Bos U	106	413	60	86	6	2	0	—	4	—	—	.208	.216	.232	36	-45	—	.802	4	112	89	O96(1/96/0),1b11	—	-4.1
1888	†NY N	103	391	50	96	12	6	1	35	13	1	28	.246	.272	.315	87	-6	26	.919	-0	93	101	O103(4/90/9)	—	-1.0
1889	†NY N	12	48	7	14	2	0	1	12	4	0	3	.292	.346	.396	106	0	2	.852	-1	86	241	O12(4/7/1)	—	-0.1
1890	NY P	97	411	80	126	20	11	5	67	27	2	25	.307	.352	.445	103	-2	18	.905	-12	28	29	O97(53/39/9)	—	-1.3
1891	Cin N	41	158	24	33	3	2	1	16	10	0	10	.209	.256	.272	53	-10	1	.941	-2	62	92	O41(4/37/0)	—	-1.2
	Was AA	15	60	8	17	1	0	0	5	4	3	5	.283	.358	.300	93	0	6	.862	-2	41	163	O15(3/12/0)	—	-0.2
Total	5	374	1481	229	372	44	21	8	135	62	6	71	.251	.284	.325	77	-63	53	.883	-13	75	85	O364(69/281/19),1b11	—	-7.9
SLAUGHT, DON	Donald Martin; B9.11.1958 Long Beach CA; BR/TR/6´1˝/(185–190); [KCA80 7/172]; d7.6; C1; Col UCLA																								
1982	KC A	43	115	14	32	6	0	3	8	9-0	0	12	.278	.331	.409	101	0	0-0	.994	2	147	70	C43	0	0.3
1983	KC A	83	276	21	86	13	4	0	28	11-0	0	27	.312	.336	.388	98	-1	3-1	.964	-7	90	95	C79/D	16	-0.4
1984	†KC A	124	409	48	108	27	4	4	42	20-4	2	55	.264	.297	.379	86	-8	0-0	.982	-1	99	105	C123/D	0	-0.4
1985	Tex A	102	343	34	96	17	4	8	35	20-1	6	41	.280	.331	.423	102	1	5-4	.990	-4	97	95	C102	17	0.0
1986	Tex A	95	314	39	83	17	1	13	46	16-0	5	59	.264	.308	.449	101	-1	3-2	.993	-11	60	104	C91,D2	47	-0.7
1987	Tex A	95	237	25	53	15	2	8	16	24-3	1	51	.224	.298	.405	83	-6	0-3	.985	-5	71	111	C85,D5	0	-0.9
1988	NY A	97	322	33	91	25	1	9	43	24-3	3	54	.283	.334	.450	119	8	1-0	.979	-9	92	64	C94/D	36	0.5
1989	NY A	117	350	34	88	21	3	5	38	30-3	5	57	.251	.315	.371	95	-2	1-1	.991	0	123	112	C105,D3	0	0.4
1990	†Pit N	84	230	27	69	18	3	4	29	27-2	3	27	.300	.375	.457	134	12	0-1	.979	2	100	109	C78	16	1.7
1991	†Pit N	77	220	19	65	17	1	1	29	21-1	3	32	.295	.363	.395	115	5	1-0	.987	2	116	107	C69/3	22	1.1
1992	†Pit N	87	255	26	88	17	3	4	37	17-5	2	23	.345	.384	.482	146	16	2-2	.988	1	120	97	C79	17	2.2
1993	Pit N	116	377	34	113	19	2	10	55	29-2	6	56	.300	.356	.440	113	7	2-1	.993	-7	88	88	C105	0	0.7
1994	Pit N	76	240	21	69	7	0	2	21	34-2	3	31	.287	.381	.342	89	-2	0-0	.994	1	98	76	C74	0	0.3
1995	Pit N	35	112	13	34	6	0	0	13	9-2	1	8	.304	.361	.357	88	-2	0-0	.996	1	72	62	C33	89	0.2
1996	Cal A	62	207	23	67	9	0	6	32	13-0	2	20	.324	.366	.454	105	2	0-0	.992	-5	62	126	C59/D	15	0.1
	Chi A	14	36	2	9	1	0	0	4	2-0	0	2	.250	.289	.278	46	-3	0-0	.986	-3	56	34	C12/D	0	-0.5
	Year	76	243	25	76	10	0	6	36	15-0	2	22	.313	.355	.428	97	-1	0-0	.991	-7	61	110	C71,D2	0	-0.4
1997	SD N	20	20	2	0	0	0	0	0	5-0	0	4	.000	.200	.000	-45	-4	0-0	1.000	-1	104	0	C6	0	-0.5
Total	16	1327	4063	415	1151	235	28	77	476	311-28	42	559	.283	.338	.412	104	22	18-15	.987	-42	95	95	C1237,D15/3	275	4.1
SLAUGHTER, ENOS	Enos Bradsher "Country"; B4.27.1916 Roxboro NC; D8.12.2002 Durham NC; BL/TR/5´9˝/(188–195); d4.19; Mil 1943–45; HF1985																								
1938	StL N	112	395	59	109	20	10	8	58	32	0	38	.276	.330	.438	104	1	1	.970	-0	103	90	O92(1/20/75)	—	-0.4
1939	StL N	149	604	95	193	**52**	5	12	86	44	5	53	.320	.371	.482	120	18	2	.968	13	118	132	O149R	—	2.2
1940	StL N	140	516	96	158	25	13	17	73	50	2	35	.306	.370	.504	131	21	8	.989	5	111	81	O132R	—	1.8
1941	StL N★	113	425	71	132	22	9	13	76	53	2	28	.311	.390	.496	139	22	4	.947	-11	86	55	O108R	0	0.5
1942	†StL N★	152	591	100	**188**	31	**17**	13	98	88	6	30	.318	.412	.494	153	42	9	.987	0	98	112	O151R	0	3.5
1946	†StL N★	**156**	609	100	183	30	8	18	**130**	69	2	41	.300	.374	.465	131	25	9	.981	2	92	**146**	O156R	0	2.2
1947	StL N★	147	551	100	162	31	13	10	86	59	4	27	.294	.366	.452	111	9	4	.982	2	96	129	O142(110/0/32)	0	0.1
1948	StL N★	146	549	91	176	27	11	11	90	81	1	29	.321	.409	.470	130	25	4	.971	2	107	77	O146(107/0/39)	0	1.8
1949	StL N★	151	568	92	191	34	**13**	13	96	79	1	37	.336	.418	.511	141	36	3	.983	-1	100	78	O150L	0	2.3
1950	StL N★	148	556	82	161	26	7	10	101	66	2	33	.290	.367	.415	100	2	3	.978	-6	94	81	O145(20/0/125)	0	-1.0
1951	StL N★	123	409	48	115	17	8	4	64	67	3	25	.281	.386	.391	109	8	7-2	.995	1	101	109	O106R	0	0.7
1952	StL N★	140	510	73	153	17	12	11	101	70	1	25	.300	.386	.445	130	21	6-1	.989	-2	98	89	O137R	0	1.7
1953	StL N★	143	492	64	143	34	9	6	89	80	5	28	.291	.395	.433	116	16	4-4	**.996**	-8	95	21	O137R	0	0.3
1954	NY A	69	125	19	31	4	2	1	19	28	0	8	.248	.386	.336	102	2	0-2	.974	-3	84	0	O30(3/0/29)	45	-0.3
1955	NY A	10	9	1	1	0	0	0	1	1-0	0	1	.111	.200	.111	-15	-1	0-0	ø	0	—	—	/H	0	-0.2
	KC A	108	267	49	86	12	4	5	34	40-4	2	17	.322	.408	.453	132	13	2-3	.985	-1	98	95	O77R	0	1.0
	Year	118	276	50	87	12	4	5	35	41-4	2	18	.315	.401	.442	127	12	2-3	.985	-1	98	95	O77R	0	0.8
1956	KC A	91	223	37	62	14	3	2	23	29-1	1	20	.278	.362	.395	100	1	1-0	.981	-3	98	25	O56(19/1/37)	0	-0.4
	†NY A	24	83	15	24	4	2	0	4	5-0	0	6	.289	.330	.386	91	-1	1-1	1.000	-1	80	75	O20(17/0/4)	0	-0.4
	Year	115	306	52	86	18	5	2	27	34-1	1	26	.281	.354	.392	97	-1	2-1	.985	-4	93	38	O76(36/1/41)	0	-0.8
1957	†NY A	96	209	24	53	7	1	5	34	40-5	0	19	.254	.369	.368	105	3	0-2	1.000	1	102	73	O64(56/0/9)	0	0.0
1958	†NY A	77	138	21	42	4	1	4	19	21-0	0	16	.304	.396	.435	133	7	2-0	.957	-3	83	50	O35(16/0/20)	0	0.4
1959	NY A	74	99	10	17	2	0	6	21	13-1	0	19	.172	.265	.374	77	-4	1-0	.964	-1	95	0	O26(9/0/18)	0	-0.5
	Mil N	11	18	0	3	0	0	0	1	3-0	0	3	.167	.286	.167	27	-2	0-0	1.000	-0	82	0	O5L	0	-0.2
Total	19	2380	7946	1247	2383	413	148	169	1304	1018-11	37	538	.300	.382	.453	122	264	71-15	.980	-13	99	89	O2064(513/21/1541)	45	15.1
SLAYBACK, SCOTTIE	Elbert; B10.5.1901 Paducah KY; D11.30.1979 Cincinnati OH; BR/TR/5´8˝/165; d9.26																								
1926	NY N	2	8	0	0	0	0	0	0	0	0	0	.000	.000	.000	-99	-2	0	.889	-1	68	0	2b2	—	-0.4
SLEDGE, TERRMEL	Terrmel; B3.18.1977 Fayetteville NC; BL/TL/6´0˝/185; [SeaA99 8/245]; d4.6; Col Cal St.–Long Beach																								
2004	Mon N	133	398	45	107	20	6	15	62	40-4	1	66	.269	.336	.462	100	-1	3-3	.987	5	112	84	O114(79/4/43),1b10	0	-0.1
2005	Was N	20	37	7	9	0	1	1	8	7-1	0	8	.243	.348	.378	99	0	2-1	1.000	1	113	181	O13(12/0/1)	153	0.1
2006	SD N	38	70	7	16	3	0	2	7	8-0	0	17	.229	.308	.357	74	-3	0-0	.971	1	113	134	O22(12/0/10)	0	-0.2
Total	3	191	505	59	132	23	7	18	77	55-5	1	91	.261	.333	.442	96	-4	5-4	.986	7	112	97	O149(103/4/54),1b10	153	-0.2
SLOAN, BRUCE	Bruce Adams "Fatso"; B10.4.1914 McAlester OK; D9.24.1973 Oklahoma City OK; BL/TL/5´9˝/195; d4.29; Col Oklahoma City																								
1944	NY N	59	104	7	28	4	1	1	9	13	0	8	.269	.350	.356	99	0	0	.935	-2	91	0	O21(3/0/18)	0	-0.3
SLOAN, TOD	Yale Yeastman; B12.24.1890 Madisonville TN; D9.12.1956 Akron OH; BL/TR/6´0˝/175; d9.22; Mil 1918																								
1913	StL A	7	26	2	7	1	0	0	2	1	1	9	.269	.321	.308	87	0	1	.950	1	125	147	O7R	—	0.0
1917	StL A	109	313	32	72	6	2	2	25	28	7	34	.230	.307	.281	83	-6	8	.963	-1	93	99	O77(16/1/60)	—	-1.3
1919	StL A	27	63	9	15	1	3	0	6	12	1	3	.238	.368	.349	99	0	0	.933	1	79	221	O20R	—	0.0
Total	3	143	402	43	94	8	5	2	33	41	9	46	.234	.319	.294	86	-6	9	.957	1	94	123	O104(16/1/87)	—	-1.3

YEAR	TM LG	G	AB	R	H	2B	3B	HR	RBI	BB-IB	HP	SO	AVG	OBP	SLG	AOPS	ABR	SB-CS	FA	FR	RNG	THR	GAMES AT POSITION	DL	BFW
SLOCUM, RON	Ronald Reece; B7.2.1945 Modesto CA; BR/TR/6´2˝/185; d9.8																								
1969	SD N	13	24	6	7	1	0	1	5	0-0	0	5	.292	.280	.458	111	0	0-0	.938	-1	133	0	2b4,3b4/S	0	0.0
1970	SD N	60	71	8	10	2	2	1	11	8-1	1	24	.141	.237	.268	36	-7	0-1	.978	6	75	111	C19,S17,3b11,2b9	0	0.0
1971	SD N	7	18	1	0	0	0	0	0	0-0	1	8	.000	.053	.000	-90	-5	0-0	.905	0	103	0	3b6	0	-0.5
Total	3	80	113	15	17	3	2	2	16	8-1	2	37	.150	.218	.265	33	-12	0-1	.887	6	119	123	3b21,C19,S18,2b13	0	-0.5
SMAJSTRLA, CRAIG	Craig Lee; B6.19.1962 Houston TX; BB/TR/5´9˝/160; [ChiA81 4/84]; d9.6																								
1988	Hou N	8	3	2	0	0	0	0	0	0-0	0	1	.000	.000	.000	-99	-1	0-0	1.000	-0	0	0	2b2	0	-0.1
SMALL, CHARLIE	Charles Albert; B10.24.1905 Auburn ME; D1.14.1953 Auburn ME; BL/TR/5´11˝/180; d7.7; Col Bates																								
1930	Bos A	25	18	1	3	1	0	0	0	2	0	5	.167	.250	.222	22	-2	1-0	1.000	0	153	0	/cf	—	-0.2
SMALL, HANK	George Henry; B7.31.1953 Atlanta GA; BR/TR/6´3˝/205; [AtlN75 4/90]; d9.27; Col South Carolina																								
1978	Atl N	1	4	0	0	0	0	0	0	0-0	0	0	.000	.000	.000	-90	-1	0-0	1.000	0	156	119	/1	0	-0.1
SMALL, JIM	James Arthur Patrick; B3.8.1937 Portland OR; BL/TL/6´1.5˝/180; d6.22																								
1955	Det A	12	4	2	0	0	0	0	0	1-0	0	1	.000	.200	.000	-44	-1	0-0	1.000	1	117	1449	O4(3/0/1)	0	0.0
1956	Det A	58	91	13	29	4	2	0	10	6-0	0	10	.319	.361	.407	102	0	0-0	.940	0	121	0	O26(4/12/10)	0	-0.1
1957	Det A	36	42	7	9	2	0	0	0	2-0	0	11	.214	.250	.262	39	-4	0-2	1.000	-1	90	0	O14(8/1/5)	0	-0.6
1958	KC A	2	4	0	0	0	0	0	0	1-0	0	0	.000	.200	.000	-39	-1	0-0	1.000	0	111	0	/rf	0	-0.1
Total	4	108	141	22	38	6	2	0	10	10-0	0	22	.270	.318	.340	75	-6	0-2	.957	0	111	42	O45(15/13/17)	0	-0.8
SMALLEY, ROY	Roy Frederick III; B10.25.1952 Los Angeles CA; BB/TR/6´1˝/(180–190); [TexA74*1/1]; d4.30; f–Roy; Col USC																								
1975	Tex A	78	250	22	57	8	0	3	33	30-1	0	42	.228	.309	.296	73	-8	4-0	.941	1	112	96	S59,2b19/C	0	0.1
1976	Tex A	41	129	15	29	2	0	1	8	29-3	0	27	.225	.363	.264	85	-1	2-0	.963	-11	86	77	2b38,S5	0	-0.9
	Min A	103	384	46	104	16	3	2	36	47-1	2	79	.271	.353	.344	103	3	0-4	.967	10	105	106	S103	0	2.5
	Year	144	513	61	133	18	3	3	44	76-4	2	106	.259	.356	.324	98	2	2-4	.966	-1	104	104	S108,2b38	0	1.6
1977	Min A	150	584	93	135	21	5	6	56	74-1	1	89	.231	.316	.315	74	-19	5-5	.958	20	112	**125**	S150	0	1.5
1978	Min A	158	586	80	160	31	3	19	77	85-3	1	70	.273	.362	.433	121	19	2-8	.970	18	108	**123**	S157	0	**5.1**
1979	Min A★	**162**	621	94	168	28	3	24	95	80-8	4	80	.271	.353	.441	109	9	2-3	.968	**33**	111	**130**	S161/1	0	**5.6**
1980	Min A	133	486	64	135	24	1	12	63	65-4	2	63	.278	.359	.405	103	4	3-3	.975	26	**113**	122	S125,1b3,D3	0	4.2
1981	Min A	56	167	24	44	7	1	7	22	31-5	0	24	.263	.375	.443	128	7	0-0	.946	-13	81	56	S37,D15/1	0	-0.2
1982	Min A	4	13	2	2	1	0	0	0	3-1	0	4	.154	.313	.231	50	-1	0-0	1.000	1	124	78	S4	0	0.1
	NY A	142	486	55	125	14	2	20	67	68-7	0	100	.257	.346	.418	111	8	0-1	.977	-15	89	85	S89,3b53/2D	0	0.1
	Year	146	499	57	127	15	2	20	67	71-8	0	104	.255	.345	.413	109	7	0-1	.979	-14	91	85	S93,3b53,D4/2	0	0.2
1983	NY A	130	451	70	124	24	1	18	62	58-2	2	68	.275	.357	.452	126	17	3-3	.959	-14	87	82	S91,3b26,1b22	0	1.0
1984	NY A	67	209	17	50	8	1	7	26	15-2	0	35	.239	.286	.388	89	-4	2-1	.905	-2	108	120	3b35,S13,1b5,D5	0	-0.6
	Chi A	47	135	15	23	4	0	4	13	22-1	0	30	.170	.285	.289	57	-8	1-1	.947	-4	93	105	3b38,S3/1D	0	-1.2
	Year	114	344	32	73	12	1	11	39	37-3	0	65	.212	.286	.349	75	-12	3-2	.923	-5	101	113	3b73,S16,D7,1b6	0	-1.8
1985	Min A	129	388	57	100	20	0	12	45	60-3	1	65	.258	.357	.402	102	3	0-2	.987	-3	82	67	D56,S49,3b14/1	0	0.1
1986	Min A	143	459	59	113	20	4	20	57	68-4	0	80	.246	.342	.438	108	5	1-3	.963	-1	73	84	D114,S19,3b8	0	0.1
1987	†Min A	110	309	32	85	16	1	8	34	36-1	1	52	.275	.352	.411	98	0	2-0	.850	-5	52	0	D73,3b14,S4	0	-0.6
Total	13	1653	5657	745	1454	244	25	163	694	771-47	14	908	.257	.345	.395	102	34	27-34	.966	43	104	109	S1069,D272,3b188,2b58,1b34/C	0	16.9
SMALLEY, ROY	Roy Frederick Jr.; B6.9.1926 Springfield MO; BR/TR/6´3˝/(185–190); d4.20; s–Roy																								
1948	Chi N	124	361	25	78	11	4	4	36	23	1	76	.216	.265	.302	55	-24	0	.941	11	**107**	**112**	S124	0	-0.7
1949	Chi N	135	477	57	117	21	10	8	35	36	4	77	.245	.304	.382	85	-12	2	.947	18	**108**	107	S132	0	1.3
1950	Chi N	**154**	557	58	128	21	9	21	85	49	4	114	.230	.297	.413	85	-15	2	.945	**20**	**111**	104	S154	0	1.4
1951	Chi N	79	238	24	55	7	4	8	31	25	0	53	.231	.304	.395	85	-6	0-0	.953	-8	94	92	S74	53	-1.0
1952	Chi N	87	261	36	58	14	1	5	30	29	2	58	.222	.305	.341	78	-8	0-0	.952	-13	91	69	S82	0	-1.7
1953	Chi N	82	253	20	63	9	0	6	25	28	2	57	.249	.329	.356	77	-8	0-0	.932	-8	92	81	S77	0	-1.0
1954	Mil N	25	36	5	8	0	0	1	7	4	1	9	.222	.310	.306	67	-2	0-0	.950	2	99	242	S9,2b7,1b2	0	0.1
1955	Phi N	92	260	33	51	11	1	7	39	39-2	2	58	.196	.304	.327	69	-11	0-0	.974	-12	91	70	S87/23	0	-1.7
1956	Phi N	65	168	14	38	9	3	0	16	23-4	1	29	.226	.323	.315	74	-6	0-0	.949	-3	99	104	S60	0	-0.4
1957	Phi N	28	31	5	5	0	1	1	1	1-0	1	9	.161	.212	.323	42	-3	0-0	.941	-4	76	90	S20	0	-0.6
1958	Phi N	1	2	0	0	0	0	0	0	0-0	0	1	.000	.000	.000	-99	-1	0-0	.714	0	97	213	/S	0	-0.1
Total	11	872	2644	277	601	103	33	61	305	257-6	18	541	.227	.300	.360	77	-96	4-0	.947	4	101	96	S820,2b8,1b2/3	53	-4.4
SMALLEY, WILL	William Darwin "Deacon"; B6.27.1871 Oakland CA; D10.11.1891 Bay City MI; BR/TR; d4.19																								
1890	Cle N	**136**	502	62	107	11	1	0	42	60	5	44	.213	.303	.239	60	-23	10	.895	20	**118**	116	3b136	—	-0.1
1891	Was AA	11	38	5	6	0	1	0	3	5	0	2	.158	.256	.211	35	-3	0	.762	-1	102	58	3b9,2b2	—	-0.4
Total	2	147	540	67	113	11	2	0	45	65	5	46	.209	.300	.237	58	-26	10	.887	19	117	112	3b145,2b2	—	-0.5
SMAZA, JOE	Joseph Paul; B7.7.1923 Detroit MI; D5.30.1979 Royal Oak MI; BL/TL/5´11˝/175; d9.18; Col Western Michigan																								
1946	Chi A	2	5	2	1	0	0	0	0	0	0	0	.200	.200	.200	12	-1	0-0	ø	-0	0	0	/rf	0	-0.1
SMILEY, BILL	William B.; B1856 Baltimore MD; D7.11.1884 Baltimore MD; d10.13																								
1874	Bal NA	2	7	0	0	0	0	0	0	0	—	0	.000	.000	.000	-99	-2	0-0	.786	0	75	0	3b2	—	-0.1
1882	StL AA	59	240	30	51	4	2	0	—	6	—	—	.213	.232	.246	59	-11	—	.885	-8	94	81	2b57,O2(1/0/1)	—	-1.6
	Bal AA	16	61	3	9	0	0	0	—	0	—	—	.148	.148	.148	-0	-6	—	.843	1	123	96	2b16,S2	—	-0.4
	Year	75	301	33	60	4	2	0	—	6	—	—	.199	.215	.226	48	-16	—	.874	-7	100	84	2b73,O2(1/0/1),S2	—	-2.0
SMITH, EDGAR	Albert Edgar; B10.15.1860 North Haven CT; TR/6´0˝/200; d6.20; Col Yale																								
1883	Bos N	30	115	10	25	5	3	0	16	5	—	11	.217	.250	.313	68	-5	—	.905	-0	46	325	O30C/C	—	-0.5
SMITH, ALECK	Alexander Benjamin "Broadway Aleck"; B1871 New York NY; D7.9.1919 New York NY; TR; d4.23; OF(35/13/10)																								
1897	Bro N	66	237	36	71	13	1	1	39	4	2	—	.300	.317	.376	87	-5	12	.903	-6	*89*	*118*	C43,O18(14/2/2),1b6	—	-0.7
1898	Bro N	52	199	25	52	6	5	0	23	3	1	—	.261	.276	.342	77	-7	7	.909	-8	0	135	O26(17/5/5),C20,3b2,2b2/1	—	-1.4
1899	Bro N	17	61	6	11	0	1	0	6	2	0	—	.180	.206	.213	15	-7	0	.917	-2	*92*	*69*	C17	—	-0.7
	Bal N	41	120	17	46	6	4	0	25	4	3	—	.383	.417	.500	144	7	7	.951	-1	*118*	*71*	C36,O2R/1	—	0.8
	Year	58	181	23	57	6	5	0	31	6	3	—	.315	.347	.403	101	-1	7	.939	-3	*110*	*70*	C53,O2R/1	—	0.1
1900	Bro N	7	25	2	6	0	0	0	3	1	0	—	.240	.269	.240	39	-2	2	.875	-2	74	0	3b6/C	—	-0.4
1901	NY N	26	78	5	11	0	0	0	6	0	0	—	.141	.141	.141	-19	-12	2	.962	-2	*86*	*85*	C24	—	-1.2
1902	Bal A	41	145	10	34	3	0	0	21	8	0	—	.234	.275	.255	45	-11	5	.947	-6	*78*	*100*	C27,1b7,O4L,2b3/3	—	-1.4
1903	Bos A	11	33	4	10	1	0	0	4	0	0	—	.303	.303	.333	86	-1	0	.932	0	*131*	*96*	C10	—	0.1
1904	Chi N	10	29	2	6	1	0	0	1	3	0	—	.207	.281	.241	62	-1	1	.778	-2	0	0	O6C/C3	—	-0.3
1906	NY N	16	28	0	5	0	0	0	2	1	0	—	.179	.207	.179	20	-3	1	1.000	1	*104*	*70*	C8,1b3/rf	—	-0.2
Total	9	287	955	107	252	30	11	1	130	26	6	—	.264	.288	.321	69	-42	37	.933	-27	*96*	94	C187,O57L,1b18,3b10,2b5	—	-5.4
SMITH, AL	Alphonse Eugene "Fuzzy"; B2.7.1928 Kirkwood MO; D1.3.2002 Hammond IN; BR/TR/6´0˝/(189–196); d7.10; Negro Lg 1946–48																								
1953	Cle A	47	150	28	36	9	0	3	14	20	3	25	.240	.341	.360	92	-1	2-0	.920	-4	92	59	O39(4/0/35),3b2	0	-0.6
1954	†Cle A	131	481	101	135	29	6	11	50	88	7	65	.281	.398	.435	126	22	2-9	.984	-8	94	100	O109(98/0/17),3b21,S4	0	0.5
1955	Cle A★	**154**	607	**123**	186	27	4	22	77	93-1	15	77	.306	.407	.473	132	32	11-6	.977	-13	92	57	O120(7/9/111),3b45,S5/2	0	1.4
1956	Cle A	141	526	87	144	26	5	16	71	84-7	8	72	.274	.378	.433	112	12	6-3	.981	-7	101	69	O122(50/23/58),3b28/2	0	0.0
1957	Cle A	135	507	78	125	23	5	11	49	79-3	4	70	.247	.348	.377	100	2	12-6	.913	-10	89	93	3b84,O58(18/41/6)	0	-1.0
1958	Chi A	139	480	61	121	23	5	12	58	48-2	5	77	.252	.323	.396	100	0	3-3	.970	-3	96	94	O138(77/2/63)/3	0	-1.0
1959	†Chi A	129	472	65	112	16	4	17	55	46-3	5	74	.237	.311	.396	94	-5	7-5	.980	5	108	97	O128(84/3/45)/3	0	-0.7
1960	Chi A★	142	536	80	169	31	3	12	72	50-3	3	65	.315	.374	.451	124	19	8-3	.966	-9	94	55	O141(3/5/139)	0	0.6
1961	Chi A	147	532	88	148	29	4	28	93	56-2	5	67	.278	.348	.506	128	20	4-4	.948	-6	101	83	3b80,O71(10/3/59)	0	1.0
1962	Chi A	142	511	62	149	23	8	16	82	57-7	3	60	.292	.363	.462	122	16	3-3	.935	-11	96	47	3b105,O39(38/0/2)	0	0.2
1963	Bal A	120	368	45	100	17	1	10	39	32-1	3	74	.272	.335	.405	110	5	9-0	.971	-1	97	104	O97(7/0/92)	0	0.0
1964	Cle A	61	136	15	22	1	1	4	9	8-1	1	32	.162	.214	.272	34	-13	0-1	1.000	1	114	104	O48(1/1/46)/3	0	-1.5
	Bos A	29	51	10	11	4	0	2	7	13-0	1	10	.216	.385	.412	116	2	0-0	.917	0	105	74	3b10,O8(2/0/6)	0	0.2
	Year	90	187	25	33	5	1	6	16	21-1	2	42	.176	.267	.310	59	-11	0-1	.987	2	113	89	O56(3/1/52),3b11	0	-1.3
Total	12	1517	5357	843	1458	258	46	164	676	674-30	63	768	.272	.358	.429	113	111	67-43	.974	-63	96	87	O1118(399/87/679),3b378,S9,2b2	0	-0.9

YEAR	TM LG	G	AB	R	H	2B	3B	HR	RBI	BB-IB	HP	SO	AVG	OBP	SLG	AOPS	ABR	SB-CS	FA	FR	RNG	THR	GAMES AT POSITION	DL	BFW
Smith, Tony	Anthony; B5.14.1884 Chicago IL; D2.27.1964 Galveston TX; BR/TR/5´9˝/150; d8.12																								
1907	Was A	51	139	12	26	1	1	0	8	18	1	—	.187	.285	.209	63	-5	3	.920	-5	92	71	S51	—	-0.9
1910	Bro N	106	321	31	58	10	1	1	16	69	2	53	.181	.329	.227	65	-10	9	.941	9	101	136	S101,3b6	—	0.2
1911	Bro N	13	40	3	6	1	0	0	2	8	0	7	.150	.292	.175	33	-3	1	.870	-1	114	133	S10,2b3	—	-0.3
Total	3	170	500	46	90	12	2	1	26	95	3	60	.180	.314	.218	62	-18	13	.931	3	99	117	S162,3b6,2b3	—	-1.0
Smith, Klondike	Armstrong Frederick; B1.4.1887 London, England; D11.15.1959 Springfield MA; BL/TL/5´9˝/160; d9.28																								
1912	NY A	7	27	0	5	1	0	0	0	0	0	—	.185	.185	.222	15	-3	1	1.000	-1	93	0	O7(0/5/2)	—	-0.4
Smith, Billy	Billy Edward; B7.14.1953 Jonesboro LA; BB/TR/6´2.5˝/(165–185); d4.13																								
1975	Cal A	59	143	10	29	5	1	0	14	12-0	0	27	.203	.263	.252	50	-10	1-3	.932	-12	75	73	S50,1b6,3b2,D4	0	-1.8
1976	Cal A	13	8	0	3	0	0	0	0	0-0	0	2	.375	.375	.375	128	0	0-0	.625	-2	81	90	S10/D	0	-0.1
1977	Bal A	109	367	44	79	12	2	5	29	33-2	1	71	.215	.281	.300	62	-20	3-2	.991	9	102	130	2b104,S5,1b2/3	0	-0.5
1978	Bal A	85	250	29	65	12	2	5	30	27-3	1	40	.260	.333	.384	108	3	3-0	.986	-1	99	99	2b83,S2	19	0.7
1979	†Bal A	68	189	18	47	9	4	6	33	15-1	2	33	.249	.309	.434	102	0	1-0	.980	-5	95	106	2b63,S5	0	-0.2
1981	SF N	36	61	6	11	0	0	1	5	9-0	0	16	.180	.282	.230	49	-4	0-0	.971	1	101	118	S21,2b5,3b3	0	-0.1
Total	6	370	1018	107	234	38	9	17	111	96-6	4	189	.230	.297	.335	79	-31	8-5	.987	-8	100	114	2b255,S93,1b8,3b6,D5	19	-2.0
Smith, Bobby Gene	Bobby Gene; B5.28.1934 Hood River OR; BR/TR/5´11˝/(180–185); d4.16																								
1957	StL N	93	185	24	39	7	1	3	18	13-3	0	35	.211	.260	.308	52	-13	1-1	.973	2	101	149	O79(0/61/18)	0	-1.4
1958	StL N	28	88	8	25	3	0	2	5	2-0	1	18	.284	.304	.386	79	-3	1-0	1.000	-0	99	110	O27(0/25/2)	0	-0.4
1959	StL N	43	60	11	13	1	1	1	7	1-0	0	9	.217	.230	.317	41	-5	0-0	.971	2	103	265	O32(11/6/15)	0	-0.4
1960	Phi N	98	217	24	62	5	2	4	27	10-1	0	28	.286	.317	.382	90	-4	2-3	1.000	5	121	93	O70(65/6/0)/3	0	-0.2
1961	Phi N	79	174	16	44	7	0	2	18	15-2	1	32	.253	.313	.328	72	-7	0-1	.971	8	126	250	O47(33/3/12)	0	-0.2
1962	NY N	8	22	1	3	0	1	0	2	3-0	0	2	.136	.240	.227	26	-2	0-1	1.000	-0	106	0	O6(0/3/4)	0	-0.3
	Chi N	13	29	3	5	0	0	1	2	2-0	0	6	.172	.219	.276	33	-3	0-1	1.000	-1	58	211	O7(0/6/1)	0	-0.4
	StL N	91	130	13	30	9	0	0	12	7-0	0	14	.231	.270	.300	48	-9	1-1	1.000	0	89	144	O80(66/13/7)	0	-1.1
	Year	112	181	17	38	9	1	1	16	12-0	0	22	.210	.258	.287	43	-15	1-3	1.000	-1	87	137	O93(66/22/12)	0	-1.8
1965	Cal A	23	57	1	13	3	0	0	5	2-0	1	10	.228	.262	.281	57	-3	0-1	1.000	0	99	132	O15(14/0/1)	0	-0.4
Total	7	476	962	101	234	35	5	13	96	55-6	3	154	.243	.284	.331	64	-49	5-9	.986	16	106	153	O363(189/123/60)/3	0	-4.8
Smith, Brick	Brick Dudley; B5.2.1959 Charlotte NC; BR/TR/6´4˝/225; [SeaA81 5/104]; d9.13; Col Wake Forest																								
1987	Sea A	5	8	1	1	0	0	0	0	2-0	0	4	.125	.300	.125	18	-1	0-0	.963	-0	117	52	1b3/D	0	-0.1
1988	Sea A	4	10	1	1	0	0	0	1	0-0	0	1	.100	.100	.100	-42	-2	0-0	1.000	1	172	110	1b4	0	-0.1
Total	2	9	18	2	2	0	0	0	1	2-0	0	5	.111	.200	.111	-12	-3	0-0	.983	1	148	85	1b7/D	0	-0.2
Smith, Bernie	Calvin Bernard; B9.4.1941 Ponchatoula LA; BR/TR/5´9˝/164; d7.31; Col Southern A&M																								
1970	Mil A	44	76	8	21	3	1	1	6	11-1	2	12	.276	.382	.382	111	2	1-3	.979	0	119	0	O39(2/11/27)	0	0.0
1971	Mil A	15	36	1	5	1	0	1	3	0-0	1	5	.139	.162	.250	15	-4	0-0	.923	-1	68	178	O12(3/1/9)	0	-0.6
Total	2	59	112	9	26	4	1	2	9	11-1	3	17	.232	.317	.339	83	-2	1-3	.967	-1	104	54	O51(5/12/36)	0	-0.6
Smith, Reggie	Carl Reginald; B4.2.1945 Shreveport LA; BB/TR/6´0˝/(170–195); d9.18; Mil 1963; C5; OF(3/808/874)																								
1966	Bos A	6	26	1	4	1	0	0	0	0-0	0	5	.154	.154	.192	-1	-3	0-0	.944	0	121	0	O6C	0	-0.4
1967	†Bos A	158	565	78	139	24	6	15	61	57-11	1	95	.246	.315	.389	99	0	16-6	.983	3	103	117	O144C,2b6	0	0.1
1968	Bos A	155	558	78	148	**37**	5	15	69	64-13	4	77	.265	.342	.430	126	19	22-18	.985	2	107	77	O155C	0	1.7
1969	Bos A★	143	543	87	168	29	7	25	93	54-7	1	67	.309	.368	.527	142	30	7-13	.959	-4	100	91	O139(3/136/0)	0	1.9
1970	Bos A	147	580	109	176	32	7	22	74	51-1	4	60	.303	.361	.497	126	20	10-7	.977	7	108	**167**	O145C	0	2.4
1971	Bos A	159	618	85	175	**33**	2	30	96	63-4	5	82	.283	.352	.489	127	22	11-3	.966	7	108	144	O159(0/87/74)	0	2.6
1972	Bos A★	131	467	75	126	25	4	21	74	68-12	4	63	.270	.365	.475	141	25	15-4	.981	0	103	89	O129(0/4/125)	0	2.3
1973	Bos A	115	423	79	128	23	2	21	69	68-7	1	49	.303	.398	.515	147	29	3-2	.983	4	110	112	O104C/1D	0	3.0
1974	StL N★	143	517	79	160	26	9	23	100	71-10	1	70	.309	.389	.528	156	39	4-3	.976	2	107	95	O132R/1	0	3.4
1975	StL N★	135	477	67	144	26	3	19	76	63-9	3	59	.302	.382	.488	136	24	9-7	.963	-5	103	69	O69(0/1/68),1b66/3	0	1.1
1976	StL N	47	170	20	37	7	1	8	23	14-2	1	28	.218	.281	.412	93	-2	1-2	.986	7	104	127	1b17,O16(0/3/13),3b13	0	0.2
	LA N	65	225	35	63	8	4	10	26	18-4	1	42	.280	.335	.484	132	8	2-0	.985	1	112	62	O58(0/1/57)/3	0	0.7
	Year	112	395	55	100	15	5	18	49	32-6	2	70	.253	.312	.453	115	5	3-2	.989	8	113	131	O74(0/4/70),1b17,3b14	0	0.9
1977	†LA N★	148	488	104	150	27	4	32	87	104-11	3	76	.307	**.427**	.576	**167**	51	7-5	.980	-7	93	69	O140(0/9/138)	0	3.7
1978	†LA N★	128	447	82	132	27	2	29	93	70-8	1	90	.295	.382	.559	**163**	39	12-5	.950	-5	95	82	O126(0/1/126)	0	3.0
1979	LA N	68	234	41	64	13	1	10	32	31-3	2	50	.274	.359	.466	127	9	6-5	.988	8	137	104	O62(0/5/59)	42	1.4
1980	LA N★	92	311	47	100	13	0	15	55	41-1	1	63	.322	.392	.508	157	25	5-6	.994	6	98	216	O84(0/7/82)	42	2.7
1981	†LA N	41	35	5	7	1	0	1	8	7-3	0	8	.200	.318	.314	88	0	0-0	1.000	0	104	92	1b2	0	0.0
1982	SF N	106	349	51	99	11	0	18	56	46-9	0	46	.284	.364	.470	134	16	7-0	.982	5	128	92	1b99	15	1.7
Total	17	1987	7033	1123	2020	363	57	314	1092	890-115	33	1030	.287	.366	.489	136	351	137-86	.976	32	105	110	O1668R,1b186,3b15,D8,2b6	99	31.5
Smith, Charlie	Charles J.; B12.11.1840 Brooklyn NY; D11.15.1897 Great Neck NY; 5´10.5˝/150; d5.18																								
1871	Mut NA	14	72	15	19	2	1	0	5	1	—	1	.264	.274	.319	77	-1	6-0	.688	-1	96	73	3b12,2b3	—	-0.1
Smith, Pop	Charles Marvin; B10.12.1856 Digby NS (now Canada); D4.18.1927 Boston MA; BR/TR/5´11˝/170; d5.1; U1																								
1880	Cin N	**83**	334	35	69	10	9	0	27	6	—	36	.207	.221	.290	72	-10	—	.855	-9	92	85	2b83	—	-1.4
1881	Cle N	10	34	1	4	0	0	0	3	0	—	8	.118	.118	.118	-27	-5	—	.838	-3	73	0	3b10	—	-0.7
	Buf N	3	11	3	0	0	0	0	1	3	—	5	.000	.214	.000	-27	-1	—	.840	-1	64	215	2b3	—	-0.2
	Wor N	11	41	1	3	0	0	0	2	3	—	5	.073	.136	.073	-31	-6	—	.955	2	176	265	O8(1/4/3),2b3	—	-0.4
	Year	24	86	5	7	0	0	0	6	6	—	18	.081	.141	.081	-28	-12	—	.838	-2	73	0	3b10,O8(1/4/3),2b6	—	-1.3
1882	Phi AA	20	65	10	6	0	0	0	2	12	—	—	.092	.234	.092	13	-6	—	.732	-0	93	0	3b11,S4,O3(0/2/1),2b2	—	-0.5
	Lou AA	3	11	1	2	0	0	0	—	0	—	—	.182	.182	.182	24	-1	—	.778	-1	91	0	S3	—	-0.1
	Year	23	76	11	8	0	0	0	2	12	—	—	.105	.227	.105	15	-6	—	.732	-1	93	0	3b11,S7,O3(0/2/1),2b2	—	-0.6
1883	Col AA	**97**	405	82	106	14	**17**	4	—	22	—	—	.262	.300	.410	137	17	—	.889	19	**117**	119	2b73,3b24,P3	—	3.4
1884	Col AA	108	445	78	106	18	10	6	—	20	12	—	.238	.289	.364	122	12	—	.905	30	**115**	135	2b108	—	4.1
1885	Pit AA	106	453	85	113	11	13	0	35	25	3	—	.249	.293	.331	98	-1	—	.922	29	**114**	**123**	2b106	—	2.8
1886	Pit AA	126	483	75	105	20	9	2	57	42	6	—	.217	.288	.308	87	-7	38	**.895**	18	112	108	S98,2b28/C	—	1.3
1887	Pit N	122	456	69	98	12	7	2	54	30	**13**	48	.215	.283	.285	63	-22	30	.914	-12	100	85	2b89,S33	—	-2.5
1888	Pit N	131	481	61	99	15	2	4	52	22	5	78	.206	.248	.270	71	-14	37	.901	1	110	85	S75,2b56	—	-0.9
1889	Pit N	72	258	26	54	10	2	5	27	24	6	38	.209	.292	.322	78	-7	12	.897	-1	103	107	S58,2b9,3b3,O3(1/0/2)	—	-0.5
	Bos N	59	208	21	54	13	4	0	32	23	4	30	.260	.345	.361	91	-2	11	.890	-6	86	112	S59	—	-0.6
	Year	131	466	47	108	23	6	5	59	47	10	68	.232	.315	.339	84	-9	23	.894	-7	94	110	S117,2b9,3b3,O3(1/0/2)	—	-1.1
1890	Bos N	**134**	463	82	106	16	12	1	53	80	9	81	.229	.353	.322	90	-5	39	.918	-21	97	88	2b134/S	—	-1.8
1891	Was AA	27	90	13	16	2	2	0	13	13	2	16	.178	.295	.244	57	-5	2	.919	4	103	112	2b19,S5,3b4	—	0.0
Total	12	1112	4238	643	941	141	87	24	358	325	60	345	.222	.287	.313	86	-63	169	.903	50	105	106	2b713,S336,3b52,O14(2/6/6),P3/C	—	2.0
Smith, Charley	Charles William; B9.15.1937 Charleston SC; D11.29.1994 Reno NV; BR/TR/6´0˝/(175–177); d9.8																								
1960	LA N	18	60	2	10	1	1	0	5	1-0	0	15	.167	.172	.217	8	-8	0-0	.953	-1	87	77	3b18	0	-0.9
1961	LA N	9	24	4	6	1	0	2	3	1-0	0	6	.250	.280	.542	103	0	0-0	1.000	-1	40	138	3b4,S3	0	-0.1
	Phi N	112	411	43	102	13	4	9	47	23-3	5	76	.248	.294	.365	75	-16	3-4	.924	-3	110	101	3b94,S14	0	-1.9
	Year	121	435	47	108	14	4	11	50	24-3	5	82	.248	.293	.375	77	-16	3-4	.926	-5	107	102	3b98,S17	0	-2.0
1962	Chi A	65	145	11	30	4	0	2	17	9-0	1	32	.207	.256	.276	44	-12	0-1	.944	-3	97	173	3b54	0	-1.5
1963	Chi A	4	7	0	2	0	1	0	1	0-0	0	2	.286	.286	.571	136	0	0-0	1.000	2	168	724	/S	0	0.2
1964	Chi A	2	7	1	1	0	1	0	0	1-0	0	1	.143	.250	.429	87	0	0-0	1.000	3	234	640	3b2	0	0.2
	NY N	127	443	44	106	12	0	20	58	19-1	3	101	.239	.275	.402	90	-8	2-2	.917	-5	109	65	3b85,S36,O13L	0	-1.3
1965	NY N	135	499	49	122	20	3	16	62	17-3	4	123	.244	.273	.393	89	-10	2-1	.957	15	114	**125**	3b131,S6/2	0	0.5
1966	StL N	116	391	34	104	13	4	10	43	22-4	0	81	.266	.301	.396	93	-5	0-2	.964	-5	94	134	3b107/S	0	-1.2
1967	NY A	135	425	38	95	15	3	9	38	32-6	1	110	.224	.278	.336	84	-9	0-2	.947	8	115	116	3b115	0	-0.3
1968	NY A	46	70	2	16	4	1	1	7	5-2	0	18	.229	.280	.357	95	-1	0-0	.961	3	120	141	3b13	32	0.3
1969	Chi N	2	2	0	0	0	0	0	0	0-0	0	0	.000	.000	.000	-89	0	0-0	ø	0	—	—	/H	0	-0.1
Total	10	771	2484	228	594	83	18	69	281	130-19	14	565	.239	.279	.370	82	-69	7-12	.945	12	108	117	3b623,S61,O13L/2	32	-6.1

YEAR	TM LG	G	AB	R	H	2B	3B	HR	RBI	BB-IB	HP	SO	AVG	OBP	SLG	AOPS	ABR	SB-CS	FA	FR	RNG	THR	GAMES AT POSITION	DL	BFW
Smith, Chris	Christopher William; B7.18.1957 Torrance CA; BB/TR/6´0˝/185; [TexA78 11/280]; d5.14; Col USC																								
1981	Mon N	7	7	0	0	0	0	0	0	0-0	0	2	.000	.000	.000	-97	-2	0-0	1.000	0	270	0	/2	0	-0.2
1982	Mon N	2	2	0	0	0	0	0	0	0-0	0	1	.000	.000	.000	-97	-1	0-0	ø	0	—	—	/H	0	-0.1
1983	SF N	22	67	13	22	6	1	1	11	7-1	2	12	.328	.403	.493	153	5	0-0	.976	-2	81	56	1b15,O4L/3	0	0.3
Total	3	31	76	13	22	6	1	1	11	7-1	2	15	.289	.360	.434	124	2	0-0	.976	-1	81	56	1b15,O4L/32	0	0.0
Smith, Earl	Earl Calvin; B3.14.1928 Sunnyside WA; BR/TR/6´0˝/185; d4.14; Col Cal St.–Fresno																								
1955	Pit N	5	16	1	1	0	0	0	0	4-0	1	2	.063	.286	.063	-1	-2	0-0	1.000	-0	99	0	O5C	0	-0.3
Smith, Earl	Earl Leonard "Sheriff"; B1.20.1891 Oak Hill OH; D3.14.1943 Portsmouth OH; BB/TR/5´11˝/170; d9.10																								
1916	Chi N	14	27	2	7	1	1	0	4	2	0	5	.259	.310	.370	98	0	1	.800	-1	52	0	O7(6/0/1)	—	-0.2
1917	StL A	52	199	31	56	7	7	0	10	15	0	21	.281	.332	.387	124	4	5	.977	3	93	155	O51(22/29/0)	—	0.4
1918	StL A	89	286	28	77	10	5	0	32	13	1	16	.269	.303	.339	97	-3	13	.952	1	95	127	O81(54/25/2)	—	-0.8
1919	StL A	88	252	21	63	12	5	1	36	18	0	27	.250	.300	.349	80	-7	1	.971	7	116	127	O68(0/4/64)	—	-0.4
1920	StL A	103	353	45	108	21	8	3	55	13	3	18	.306	.336	.436	100	-1	11-4	.916	-4	98	18	3b70,O15(4/2/9)	—	-0.4
1921	StL A	25	78	7	26	4	2	2	14	3	1	4	.333	.366	.513	115	1	0-0	.878	-3	80	0	3b13,O4C	—	-0.1
	Was A	59	180	20	39	5	2	2	12	10	2	19	.217	.266	.300	46	-16	1-0	.949	4	108	180	O43(3/4/36)/3	—	-1.4
	Year	84	258	27	65	9	4	4	26	13	3	23	.252	.296	.364	69	-14	1-0	.944	1	107	166	O47(3/8/36),3b14	—	-1.5
1922	Was A	65	205	22	53	12	2	1	23	8	2	17	.259	.293	.351	71	-10	4-4	.917	3	91	208	O49(47/0/2),3b2	—	-1.0
Total	7	495	1580	176	429	72	32	9	186	82	9	127	.272	.311	.375	90	-32	36-8	.952	8	100	150	O318(136/68/114),3b86	—	-3.9
Smith, Earl	Earl Sutton "Oil"; B2.14.1897 Sheridan AR; D6.8.1963 Little Rock AR; BL/TR/5´10.5˝/180; d4.24																								
1919	NY N	21	36	5	9	2	1	0	8	3	0	3	.250	.308	.361	102	0	1	.973	-2	*88*	*86*	C14/2	—	-0.1
1920	NY N	91	262	20	77	7	1	1	30	18	2	16	.294	.344	.340	98	0	5-2	.976	1	*124*	*76*	C82	—	0.8
1921	†NY N	89	229	35	77	8	4	10	51	27	1	8	.336	.409	.537	148	16	4-3	.965	-5	*114*	*92*	C78	—	1.5
1922	†NY N	90	234	29	65	11	4	9	39	37	3	12	.278	.383	.474	119	7	1-1	.978	1	*133*	*72*	C75	—	1.2
1923	NY N	24	34	2	7	1	1	1	4	4	0	1	.206	.289	.382	77	-1	0-0	.975	1	*164*	*100*	C12	—	0.0
	Bos N	72	191	22	55	15	1	3	19	22	1	10	.288	.364	.424	112	4	0-1	.975	-2	*82*	*125*	C54	—	0.5
	Year	96	225	24	62	16	2	4	23	26	1	11	.276	.353	.418	106	3	0-1	.975	-1	*93*	*122*	C66	—	0.5
1924	Bos N	33	59	1	16	3	0	0	8	6	0	3	.271	.338	.322	81	-1	0-1	.946	-2	*83*	*109*	C13	—	-0.2
	Pit N	39	111	12	41	10	1	4	21	13	0	4	.369	.435	.586	168	11	2-0	.974	2	*154*	*60*	C35	—	1.5
	Year	72	170	13	57	13	1	4	29	19	0	7	.335	.402	.494	140	11	2-1	.967	0	*136*	*72*	C48	—	1.3
1925	†Pit N	109	329	34	103	22	3	8	64	31	1	13	.313	.374	.471	107	4	4-1	.968	11	*142*	*87*	C96	—	2.0
1926	Pit N	105	292	29	101	17	2	2	46	28	2	7	.346	.407	.438	121	10	1	.964	5	*119*	*84*	C98	—	2.0
1927	†Pit N	66	189	16	51	3	1	5	25	21	1	11	.270	.346	.376	87	-3	0	.986	-0	*135*	*61*	C61	—	0.0
1928	Pit N	32	85	8	21	6	0	2	11	11	0	7	.247	.333	.388	85	-2	0	.967	-3	*80*	*71*	C28	—	-0.3
	†StL N	24	58	3	13	2	0	0	7	5	0	4	.224	.286	.259	42	-5	0	1.000	-0	*127*	*58*	C18	—	-0.4
	Year	56	143	11	34	8	0	2	18	16	0	11	.238	.314	.336	68	-6	0	.980	-3	*98*	*66*	C46	—	-0.7
1929	StL N	57	145	9	50	8	0	1	22	18	0	6	.345	.417	.421	107	3	0	.962	-3	*115*	*80*	C50	—	0.2
1930	StL N	8	10	0	0	0	0	0	0	3	0	1	.000	.231	.000	-36	-2	0	.913	0	*128*	*200*	C6	—	-0.1
Total	12	860	2264	225	686	115	19	46	355	247	11	106	.303	.374	.432	111	41	18-9	.971	5	*123*	*83*	C720/2	—	8.6
Smith, Edgar	Edgar Eugene; B6.12.1862 Providence RI; D11.3.1892 Providence RI; BR/TR/5´10˝/160; d5.25; ▲																								
1883	Pro N	2	9	2	2	1	0	0	1	0	—	2	.222	.222	.333	64	0	—	1.000	-0	0	0	1b2,O2L	—	-0.1
	Phi N	1	4	1	3	0	0	0	1	0	—	0	.750	.750	.750	393	1	—	.000	-1	0	0	/Plf	—	0.0
	Year	3	13	3	5	1	0	0	2	0	—	2	.385	.385	.462	158	1	—	1.000	-1	0	0	O3L,1b2/P	—	-0.1
1884	Was AA	14	57	5	5	0	1	0	—	1	0	—	.088	.103	.123	-30	-8	—	.794	4	350	814	O12R,P3	—	-0.2
1885	Pro N	1	4	0	1	0	0	0	0	0	—	0	.250	.250	.250	64	0	—	.750	0	148	0	/P	—	0.0
1890	Cle N	8	24	2	7	0	1	0	4	4	0	1	.292	.393	.375	126	1	0	.900	2	202	0	P6,O2R	—	0.1
Total	4	26	98	10	18	1	2	0	6	5	0	3	.184	.223	.235	47	-6	0	.816	5	286	828	O17(3/0/14),P11,1b2	—	-0.2
Smith, Mayo	Edward Mayo; B1.17.1915 New London MO; D11.24.1977 Boynton Beach FL; BL/TR/6´0˝/183; d6.24; M9																								
1945	Phi A	73	203	18	43	5	0	0	11	36	1	13	.212	.333	.236	67	-7	0-1	.976	-3	91	80	O65(33/27/7)	0	-1.4
Smith, Elmer	Elmer Ellsworth; B3.23.1868 Pittsburgh PA; D11.3.1945 Pittsburgh PA; BL/TL/5´11˝/178; d9.10; ▲																								
1886	Cin AA	9	28	6	8	1	1	0	2	9	0	—	.286	.459	.393	163	3	0	.600	-2	24	0	P9/lf	—	-0.1
1887	Cin AA	52	186	26	47	10	6	0	23	11	1	—	.253	.298	.371	84	-5	5	.851	-6	74	105	P52,O2C	—	-0.2
1888	Cin AA	40	129	15	29	4	1	0	9	20	0	—	.225	.329	.271	88	-1	2	.838	-6	76	0	P40,O2C	—	-0.3
1889	Cin AA	29	83	12	23	3	1	2	17	7	2	18	.277	.348	.410	112	5	1	.821	-4	52	0	P29	—	0.0
1892	Pit N	138	511	86	140	16	14	4	63	82	1	43	.274	.375	.384	129	20	22	.885	-7	73	0	O124(115/2/7),P17	—	0.0
1893	Pit N	128	518	121	179	26	23	7	103	77	5	23	.346	.435	.525	158	44	26	.921	4	92	160	O128L	—	2.9
1894	Pit N	126	490	128	175	33	19	6	74	68	5	12	.357	.440	.539	136	31	34	.933	2	83	154	O126(121/5/0)/P	—	1.7
1895	Pit N	125	484	89	146	15	12	1	81	55	6	25	.302	.380	.388	104	5	34	.897	-3	85	48	O124L	—	-0.7
1896	Pit N	122	484	121	175	21	14	6	94	74	8	18	.362	.454	.500	158	46	33	.946	8	80	137	O122L	—	3.6
1897	Pit N	123	467	99	145	19	17	6	54	70	7	—	.310	.408	.463	135	26	25	.904	3	110	30	O123L	—	1.6
1898	Cin N	123	486	79	166	21	10	1	66	69	2	—	.342	.425	.432	136	26	20	.949	2	84	120	O123L/P	—	1.6
1899	Cin N	88	343	65	101	13	6	1	24	47	1	—	.294	.381	.376	106	4	10	.923	-2	89	85	O88(38/28/22)	—	-0.3
1900	Cin N	29	111	14	31	4	4	1	18	18	2	—	.279	.389	.414	125	4	5	.930	-1	74	95	O27L	—	0.1
	NY N	85	312	47	81	9	7	2	34	24	2	—	.260	.317	.353	89	-6	14	.953	-6	95	63	O83R	—	-1.4
	Year	114	423	61	112	13	11	3	52	42	4	—	.265	.337	.369	99	-1	19	.944	-7	89	72	O110(27/0/83)	—	-1.3
1901	Pit N	4	4	0	0	0	0	0	0	2	0	—	.000	.333	.000	1	0	0	1.000	0	0	0	/lf	—	0.0
	Bos N	16	57	5	10	2	1	0	3	6	0	—	.175	.254	.246	41	-4	2	.833	-2	55	0	O15(4/0/11)	—	-0.7
	Year	20	61	5	10	2	1	0	3	8	0	—	.164	.261	.230	40	-5	2	.846	-2	52	0	O16(5/0/11)	—	-0.7
Total	14	1237	4693	913	1456	197	136	37	665	639	42	139	.310	.398	.434	126	198	233	.922	-21	86	89	O1089(927/39/123),P149	—	7.8
Smith, Elmer	Elmer John; B9.21.1892 Sandusky OH; D8.3.1984 Columbia KY; BL/TR/5´10˝/165; d9.20; Mil 1918																								
1914	Cle A	13	53	5	17	3	0	0	8	2	0	11	.321	.345	.377	113	1	1-1	1.000	1	103	122	O13C	—	0.0
1915	Cle A	144	476	37	118	23	12	3	67	36	0	75	.248	.301	.366	97	-4	10-11	.923	-0	105	101	O123(21/0/102)	—	-1.3
1916	Cle A	79	213	25	59	15	3	3	40	18	1	35	.277	.336	.418	119	5	3	.966	-0	94	111	O57(1/0/56)	—	0.2
	Was A	45	168	12	36	10	3	2	27	18	2	28	.214	.298	.345	94	-2	4	.988	2	111	101	O45(10/0/35)	—	-0.2
	Year	124	381	37	95	25	6	5	67	36	3	63	.249	.319	.386	108	3	7	.976	2	102	107	O102(11/0/91)	—	0.0
1917	Was A	35	117	8	26	4	3	0	17	5	1	14	.222	.260	.308	74	-4	1	.901	-0	107	103	O29(27/0/2)	—	-0.7
	Cle A	64	161	21	42	5	1	3	22	13	0	18	.261	.316	.360	99	-1	6	.986	0	100	99	O40(8/0/32)	—	-0.2
	Year	99	278	29	68	9	4	3	39	18	1	32	.245	.293	.338	89	-5	7	.943	0	103	101	O69(35/0/34)	—	-0.9
1919	Cle A	114	395	60	110	24	6	9	54	41	5	30	.278	.354	.438	115	8	15	.957	-4	90	83	O111R	—	-0.2
1920	†Cle A	129	456	82	144	37	10	12	103	53	3	35	.316	.391	.520	135	23	5-4	.970	-6	101	48	O129R	—	1.0
1921	Cle A	129	431	98	125	28	9	16	85	56	2	46	.290	.374	.508	121	13	0-2	.971	-3	90	104	O127(1/0/126)	—	0.0
1922	Bos A	73	231	43	66	13	6	6	32	25	1	21	.286	.358	.472	116	5	0-3	.947	3	112	109	O58(0/1/57)	—	0.2
	†NY A	21	27	1	5	0	0	1	5	3	0	5	.185	.267	.296	46	-2	0-0	.933	1	116	145	O11(2/0/9)	—	-0.2
	Year	94	258	44	71	13	6	7	37	28	1	26	.275	.348	.453	108	2	0-3	.945	3	112	112	O69(2/1/66)	—	0.0
1923	NY A	70	183	30	56	6	2	7	35	21	0	21	.306	.377	.475	121	5	3-1	.948	1	107	91	O47R	—	0.3
1925	Cin N	96	284	47	77	13	7	8	46	28	1	20	.271	.339	.451	102	0	6-5	.967	-1	94	105	O80(53/2/26)	—	-0.6
Total	10	1012	3195	469	881	181	62	70	541	319	16	359	.276	.344	.437	112	47	54-27	.957	-9	100	93	O870(123/16/732)	—	-1.7
Smith, Mike	Elwood Hope; B11.16.1904 Norfolk VA; D5.31.1981 Chesapeake VA; BL/TR/5´11.5˝/170; d9.4; Col William and Mary																								
1926	NY N	4	7	0	1	0	0	0	0	0	0	2	.143	.143	.143	-23	-1	0	1.000	0	129	0	/lf	—	-0.1
Smith, Carr	Emanuel Carr; B4.8.1901 Kernersville NC; D4.14.1989 Miami FL; BR/TR/6´1˝/175; d9.23																								
1923	Was A	5	9	0	1	1	0	0	1	0	0	0	.111	.111	.222	-14	-2	0-0	1.000	-0	86	0	O4C	—	-0.2
1924	Was A	5	10	1	2	0	0	0	0	0	0	3	.200	.200	.200	3	-1	0-0	1.000	-0	97	0	O4R	—	-0.2
Total	2	10	19	1	3	1	0	0	1	0	0	3	.158	.158	.211	-5	-3	0-0	1.000	-1	91	0	O8(0/4/4)	—	-0.4
Smith, Ernie	Ernest Henry "Kansas City Kid"; B10.11.1899 Totowa NJ; D4.6.1973 Brooklyn NY; BR/TR/5´8˝/155; d4.17																								
1930	Chi A	24	79	5	19	3	0	0	3	5	0	6	.241	.286	.278	45	-7	2-0	.920	-2	95	64	S21	—	-0.6

YEAR	TM LG	G	AB	R	H	2B	3B	HR	RBI	BB-IB	HP	SO	AVG	OBP	SLG	AOPS	ABR	SB-CS	FA	FR	RNG	THR	GAMES AT POSITION	DL	BFW
SMITH, FRANK	Frank L.; B11.24.1857 Fonthill ON, Can.; D10.11.1928 Canandaigua NY; BR/5´10˝/175; d8.6																								
1884	Pit AA	10	36	3	9	0	1	0	—	0	0	—	.250	.250	.306	81	-1	—	.930	-1	—	—	C7,O3(1/1/1)	—	-0.2
SMITH, FRED	Fred Vincent; B7.29.1886 Cleveland OH; D5.28.1961 Cleveland OH; BR/TR/5´11.5˝/185; d4.17; b–Charlie																								
1913	Bos N	92	285	35	65	9	3	0	27	29	1	55	.228	.302	.281	65	-12	7-11	.920	-10	82	55	3b59,2b14,S11,O4(2/1/1)	—	-2.3
1914	Buf F	145	473	48	104	12	10	2	45	49	3	78	.220	.297	.300	62	-34	24	.930	-3	95	75	3b127,S19/1	—	-3.4
1915	Buf F	35	114	8	27	2	4	0	11	13	1	15	.237	.320	.325	80	-5	2	.920	3	101	111	S32/3	—	0.0
	Bro F	110	385	41	95	16	6	5	58	25	3	49	.247	.298	.358	85	-15	21	.920	-2	101	63	S94,3b15	—	-1.1
	Year	145	499	49	122	18	10	5	69	38	4	64	.244	.303	.351	84	-20	23	.920	1	101	75	S126,3b16	—	-1.1
1917	StL N	56	165	11	30	0	2	1	17	17	1	22	.182	.262	.224	51	-9	4	.950	6	112	63	3b51,2b2/S	—	-0.3
Total	4	438	1422	143	321	39	25	8	158	133	9	219	.226	.296	.305	69	-75	58-11	.932	-7	98	76	3b253,S157,2b16,O4(2/1/1)/1	—	-7.1
SMITH, GEORGE	George Cornelius; B7.7.1937 St.Petersburg FL; D6.15.1987 St.Petersburg FL; BR/TR/5´10˝/168; d8.4; Col Michigan St.																								
1963	Det A	52	171	16	37	8	2	0	17	18-1	2	34	.216	.298	.287	63	-8	4-0	.982	7	112	89	2b52	0	0.4
1964	Det A	5	7	1	2	0	0	0	2	1-0	0	4	.286	.375	.286	86	0	1-0	1.000	-0	94	160	2b3	0	0.0
1965	Det A	32	53	6	5	0	0	1	1	3-0	0	18	.094	.143	.151	-16	-8	0-0	.984	-2	88	123	2b22,S3,3b3	0	-1.0
1966	Bos A	128	403	41	86	19	4	8	37	37-6	3	86	.213	.283	.340	71	-15	4-0	.969	2	99	110	2b109,S19	0	-0.2
Total	4	217	634	64	130	27	6	9	57	59-7	5	142	.205	.277	.309	62	-31	9-0	.974	6	102	105	2b186,S22,3b3	0	-0.8
SMITH, HEINIE	George Henry; B10.24.1871 Pittsburgh PA; D6.25.1939 Buffalo NY; BR/TR/5´9.5˝/160; d9.8; M1; ▲																								
1897	Lou N	21	76	7	20	3	0	1	7	3	1	—	.263	.300	.342	72	-3	1	.928	-2	93	111	2b21	—	-0.4
1898	Lou N	35	121	14	23	4	0	0	13	6	3	—	.190	.246	.223	35	-10	6	.910	-7	92	64	2b33	—	-1.5
1899	Pit N	15	53	9	15	3	1	0	12	5	0	—	.283	.345	.377	98	0	2	.851	-5	96	51	2b15/S	—	-0.4
1901	NY N	9	29	5	6	2	1	1	4	1	0	—	.207	.233	.448	99	0	1	.969	-1	93	0	2b7,P2	—	-0.1
1902	NY N	140	517	48	129	19	2	0	34	17	3	—	.250	.277	.294	77	-15	32	.954	5	98	113	2b140,M	—	-0.9
1903	Det A	93	336	36	75	11	3	1	22	19	3	—	.223	.271	.283	68	-13	12	.928	-1	98	89	2b93	—	-1.3
Total	6	313	1132	119	268	42	7	3	92	51	10	—	.237	.276	.294	71	-41	54	.935	-11	97	95	2b309,P2/S	—	-4.6
SMITH, GERMANY	George J.; B4.21.1863 Pittsburgh PA; D12.1.1927 Altoona PA; BR/TR/6´0˝/175; d4.17																								
1884	Alt U	**25**	108	9	34	8	1	0	—	1	—	—	.315	.321	.407	118	-1	—	.871	5	122	20	S25/P	—	0.5
	Cle N	72	291	31	74	14	4	4	26	2	—	45	.254	.259	.371	93	-3	—	.879	6	96	123	2b42,S30	—	0.5
1885	Bro AA	108	419	63	108	17	11	4	62	10	0	—	.258	.275	.379	105	0	—	.884	**40**	**127**	77	S108	—	3.9
1886	Bro AA	105	426	66	105	17	6	2	45	19	0	—	.246	.279	.329	89	-7	22	.860	12	112	94	S105/lfC	—	0.8
1887	Bro AA	103	435	79	128	19	16	4	72	13	1	—	.294	.316	.439	108	1	26	**.886**	**30**	**123**	84	S101,3b2	—	2.7
1888	Bro AA	103	402	47	86	10	7	3	61	22	0	—	.214	.255	.296	76	-12	27	.844	1	103	130	S103/2	—	-0.7
1889	†Bro AA	121	446	89	103	22	3	3	53	40	1	42	.231	.296	.314	73	-16	35	.899	-6	99	92	S120/rf	—	-1.6
1890	†Bro N	**129**	481	76	92	6	5	1	47	42	3	23	.191	.260	.231	43	-36	24	.904	1	106	114	S129	—	-2.7
1891	Cin N	**138**	512	50	103	11	5	3	53	38	1	32	.201	.258	.260	50	-34	16	.909	12	110	85	S138	—	-1.6
1892	Cin N	139	506	58	123	13	6	8	63	42	0	52	.243	.301	.340	95	-5	19	.920	23	**119**	113	S139	—	2.4
1893	Cin N	130	500	63	118	18	6	4	56	38	2	20	.236	.293	.320	61	-30	14	**.934**	16	110	124	S130	—	-0.6
1894	Cin N	129	492	73	130	34	6	3	79	41	2	28	.264	.323	.376	66	-29	15	.910	19	**116**	**130**	S129	—	-0.3
1895	Cin N	127	503	75	151	23	6	4	74	34	0	24	.300	.345	.394	87	-12	13	.923	1	104	110	S127	—	-0.3
1896	Cin N	120	456	65	131	21	9	3	71	28	1	22	.287	.330	.393	84	-13	22	.926	-10	100	102	S120	—	-1.4
1897	Bro N	112	428	47	86	17	3	0	29	14	4	—	.201	.233	.255	30	-44	1	.908	-11	106	84	S112	—	-4.3
1898	StL N	51	157	16	25	2	1	1	9	24	1	—	.159	.275	.204	37	-12	1	.904	-6	105	67	S51	—	-1.5
Total	15	1712	6562	907	1597	252	95	47	800	408	16	288	.243	.289	.332	74	-253	235	.902	135	111	100	S1667,2b43,3b2,O2(1/0/1)/CP	—	-4.2
SMITH, JUD	Grant Judson; B1.13.1869 Green Oak MI; D12.7.1947 Los Angeles CA; BR/TR/6´0˝/185; d5.21; Col Ohio St.																								
1893	Cin N	17	43	7	10	1	0	1	5	9	0	5	.233	.365	.326	82	-1	1	.750	-1	82	0	O9(1/0/8),3b6/S	—	-0.2
	StL N	4	13	1	1	0	0	0	0	1	1	2	.077	.200	.077	-25	-2	0	.889	1	100	296	3b4	—	-0.2
	Year	21	56	8	11	1	0	1	5	10	1	7	.196	.328	.268	58	-3	1	.844	-1	117	381	3b10,O9(1/0/8)/S	—	-0.4
1896	Pit N	10	35	6	12	2	1	0	4	2	1	2	.343	.395	.457	129	2	3	.909	0	88	178	3b10	—	0.1
1898	Was N	66	234	33	71	7	5	3	28	22	6	—	.303	.378	.415	127	8	11	.903	-6	79	85	3b47,S10,1b7/2	—	0.3
1901	Pit N	6	21	1	3	1	0	0	0	3	0	—	.143	.250	.190	28	-2	0	.947	0	106	0	3b6	—	-0.1
Total	4	103	346	48	97	11	6	4	37	37	8	9	.280	.363	.382	109	5	15	.900	-7	87	126	3b73,S11,O9(1/0/8),1b7/2	—	-0.1
SMITH, GREG	Gregory Alan; B4.5.1967 Baltimore MD; BB/TR/5´11˝/170; [ChiN85 2/52]; d9.2																								
1989	Chi N	4	5	1	2	0	0	0	2	0-0	1	0	.400	.500	.400	150	0	0-0	.778	-1	68	118	2b2	0	0.0
1990	Chi N	18	44	4	9	2	1	0	5	2-0	0	5	.205	.234	.295	43	-4	1-0	1.000	3	118	105	2b7,S7	0	0.0
1991	LA N	5	3	1	0	0	0	0	0	0-0	0	2	.000	.000	.000	-99	-1	0-0	ø	-0	0	0	/2	0	-0.1
Total	3	27	52	6	11	2	1	0	7	2-0	1	7	.212	.250	.288	47	-5	1-0	.944	2	105	106	2b10,S7	0	-0.1
SMITH, HAL	Harold Raymond "Cura"; B6.1.1931 Barling AR; BR/TR/5´11˝/(185–189); d5.2; C8																								
1956	StL N	75	227	27	64	12	0	5	23	15-4	0	22	.282	.326	.401	94	-2	1-0	.982	-2	*90*	*98*	C66	0	-0.1
1957	StL N☆	100	333	25	93	12	3	2	37	18-2	0	18	.279	.314	.351	78	-11	2-2	.990	-3	99	84	C97	0	-1.0
1958	StL N	77	220	13	50	4	1	1	24	14-4	0	14	.227	.272	.268	42	-18	0-0	.989	-6	79	78	C71	0	-2.2
1959	StL N★	142	452	35	122	15	3	13	50	15-6	1	28	.270	.295	.403	78	-15	2-6	.989	3	97	**130**	C141	0	-0.7
1960	StL N	127	337	20	77	16	0	2	28	29-13	1	33	.228	.291	.294	56	-20	1-0	.990	15	133	**120**	C124	0	0.0
1961	StL N	45	125	6	31	4	1	0	10	11-4	1	12	.248	.309	.296	57	-7	0-0	.993	15	126	118	C45	104	1.0
1965	Pit N	4	3	0	0	0	0	0	0	0-0	0	1	.000	.000	.000	-99	-1	0-0	1.000	1	0	0	C4	0	0.0
Total	7	570	1697	126	437	63	8	23	172	102-33	3	128	.258	.300	.345	69	-74	6-8	.989	23	*104*	*107*	C548	104	-3.0
SMITH, HAL	Harold Wayne; B12.7.1930 W.Frankfort IL; BR/TR/6´0˝/(190–195); d4.11																								
1955	Bal A	135	424	41	115	23	4	4	52	30-2	2	21	.271	.318	.373	93	-6	1-3	.986	-4	*77*	***141***	C125	0	-0.5
1956	Bal A	77	229	16	60	14	0	3	18	17-3	1	22	.262	.315	.362	85	-5	1-0	.994	3	*74*	*108*	C71	0	0.1
	KC A	37	142	15	39	9	2	2	24	3-0	0	12	.275	.284	.408	82	-4	1-1	.986	1	*86*	*121*	C37	0	-0.2
	Year	114	371	31	99	23	2	5	42	20-3	1	34	.267	.303	.380	85	-10	2-1	.991	4	*79*	*113*	C108	0	-0.1
1957	KC A	107	360	41	109	26	0	13	41	14-0	1	44	.303	.328	.483	118	8	2-2	.983	1	91	73	C103	0	1.3
1958	KC A	99	315	32	86	19	2	5	46	25-2	2	47	.273	.323	.394	97	-1	0-0	.949	-1	98	101	3b43,C31,1b14	0	-0.1
1959	KC A	108	292	36	84	12	0	5	31	34-0	3	39	.288	.367	.380	104	3	0-3	.953	3	89	81	3b77,C22	0	0.6
1960	†Pit N	77	258	37	76	18	2	11	45	22-0	2	48	.295	.351	.508	132	11	1-1	.985	-4	150	52	C71	0	1.1
1961	Pit N	67	193	12	43	10	0	3	26	11-1	1	38	.223	.267	.321	55	-12	0-0	.990	-2	157	46	C65	0	-1.2
1962	Hou N	109	345	32	81	14	0	12	35	24-1	2	55	.235	.286	.380	84	-9	0-0	.986	-4	75	107	C92,3b6,1b2	0	-0.9
1963	Hou N	31	58	1	14	2	0	0	2	4-1	0	15	.241	.290	.276	68	-2	0-0	.985	-2	149	62	C11	0	-0.4
1964	Cin N	32	66	6	8	1	0	0	3	12-2	0	20	.121	.256	.136	14	-7	1-0	.983	-6	96	106	C20	0	-1.3
Total	10	879	2682	269	715	148	10	58	323	196-12	14	361	.267	.317	.394	94	-24	7-10	.986	-14	*110*	*96*	C648,3b126,1b16	0	-1.5
SMITH, HARRY	Harry Thomas; B10.31.1874 Yorkshire, England; D2.17.1933 Salem NJ; BR/TR/5´8.5˝/165; d7.11; M1																								
1901	Phi A	11	34	3	11	1	0	0	3	2	1	—	.324	.378	.353	99	0	1	.969	-2	*83*	*110*	C9/rf	—	-0.1
1902	Pit N	50	185	14	35	4	1	0	12	4	1	—	.189	.211	.222	32	-15	4	.972	2	*146*	*77*	C50	—	-0.9
1903	†Pit N	61	212	15	37	3	2	0	19	12	1	—	.175	.222	.208	22	-22	2	.974	1	*136*	*90*	C60/rf	—	-1.5
1904	Pit N	47	141	17	35	3	1	0	18	16	5	—	.248	.346	.284	92	0	5	.964	-1	*104*	*111*	C44,O3(2/0/1)	—	0.3
1905	Pit N	1	3	0	0	0	0	0	1	0	0	—	.000	.000	.000	-98	-1	1	1.000	0	*117*	*105*	/C	—	-0.1
1906	Pit N	1	1	0	0	0	0	0	0	0	0	—	.000	.000	.000	-96	0	0	.800	0	*0*	*0*	/C	—	0.0
1907	Pit N	18	38	4	10	1	0	0	1	4	2	—	.263	.364	.289	103	1	0	.939	-1	*124*	*106*	C18	—	0.1
1908	Bos N	41	130	13	32	2	2	1	16	7	2	—	.246	.295	.315	96	-1	2	.975	-2	*89*	*112*	C38	—	0.1
1909	Bos N	43	113	9	19	4	1	0	4	5	0	—	.168	.203	.221	30	-10	3	.972	1	*87*	*98*	C31,M	—	-0.6
1910	Bos N	70	147	8	35	4	0	1	15	5	0	14	.238	.263	.286	57	-8	5	.949	-2	*87*	*127*	C38	—	-0.8
Total	10	343	1004	83	214	22	7	2	89	55	12	14	.213	.262	.255	54	-56	23	.967	-4	*113*	*100*	C290,O5(2/0/3)	—	-3.5
SMITH, HARRY	Harry W.; B2.5.1856 N.Vernon IN; D6.4.1898 Queensville IN; BR/TR/6´0˝/175; d5.8																								
1877	Chi N	24	94	7	19	1	0	0	3	4	—	6	.202	.235	.213	37	-7	—	.853	-7	80	45	2b14,O10(0/7/3)	—	-1.2
	Cin N	10	36	4	9	2	1	0	3	1	—	5	.250	.270	.361	109	1	—	.879	-1	—	—	C8,2b3,O3C	—	0.0
	Year	34	130	11	28	3	1	0	6	5	—	11	.215	.244	.254	54	-7	—	.837	-8	78	40	2b17,O13(0/10/3),C8	—	-1.2

YEAR	TM LG	G	AB	R	H	2B	3B	HR	RBI	BB-IB	HP	SO	AVG	OBP	SLG	AOPS	ABR	SB-CS	FA	FR	RNG	THR	GAMES AT POSITION	DL	BFW
1889	Lou AA	1	2	0	1	0	0	0	1	0	0	1	.500	.500	.500	189	0	0	ø	-1	0	0	/cfC	—	-0.1
Total	2	35	132	11	29	3	1	0	7	5	0	12	.220	.248	.258	56	-6	0	.837	-9	78	40	2b17,O14(0/11/3),C9	—	-1.3
SMITH, HARVEY	Harvey Fetterhoff; B7.24.1871 Union Deposit PA; D11.12.1962 Harrisburg PA; BL/TR/5´8˝/160; d8.19; Col Bucknell																								
1896	Was N	36	131	21	36	7	2	0	17	12	2	7	.275	.345	.359	86	-3	9	.861	1	117	85	3b36	—	-0.1
SMITH, HAPPY	Henry Joseph; B7.14.1883 Coquille OR; D2.26.1961 San Jose CA; BL/TR/6´0˝/185; d4.15																								
1910	Bro N	35	76	6	18	2	0	0	5	4	0	14	.237	.275	.263	59	-4	4	.974	2	106	172	O16(0/5/11)	—	-0.3
SMITH, JACK	Jack; B6.23.1895 Chicago IL; D5.2.1972 Westchester IL; BL/TL/5´8˝/165; d9.30; Mil 1918																								
1915	StL N	4	16	2	3	0	1	0	0	1	0	5	.188	.235	.313	65	-1	0	1.000	-1	70	0	O4(3/1/0)	—	-0.2
1916	StL N	130	357	43	87	6	5	6	34	20	4	50	.244	.291	.339	94	-4	24-16	.949	-4	92	98	O120(1/109/11)	—	-1.8
1917	StL N	137	462	64	137	16	11	3	34	38	1	65	.297	.351	.398	133	18	25	.961	-11	86	72	O128(27/65/37)	—	-0.1
1918	StL N	42	166	24	35	2	1	0	4	7	4	21	.211	.260	.235	53	-9	5	.941	0	85	167	O42C	—	-1.4
1919	StL N	119	408	47	91	16	3	0	15	26	1	29	.223	.271	.277	69	-15	30	.960	2	95	132	O111(1/36/76)	—	-2.2
1920	StL N	91	313	53	104	22	5	1	28	25	2	23	.332	.385	.444	143	18	14-9	.963	-2	89	128	O83(18/57/14)	—	1.3
1921	StL N	116	411	86	135	22	9	7	33	21	0	24	.328	.361	.477	122	12	11-6	.955	-2	98	89	O103(0/19/84)	—	0.3
1922	StL N	143	510	117	158	23	12	8	46	50	3	30	.310	.375	.449	117	13	18-7	.951	-5	98	73	O136(17/79/40)	—	0.2
1923	StL N	124	407	98	126	16	6	5	41	27	2	20	.310	.356	.415	105	2	32-11	.974	7	**113**	106	O109(77/10/23)	—	0.4
1924	StL N	124	459	91	130	18	6	2	33	33	1	27	.283	.333	.362	88	-8	24-16	.968	9	108	140	O114(25/14/77)	—	-0.8
1925	StL N	80	243	53	61	11	4	4	31	19	1	13	.251	.308	.379	73	-11	20-2	.958	1	105	104	O64(5/38/28)	—	-0.9
1926	StL N	1	1	0	0	0	0	0	0	0	0	1	.000	.000	.000	-96	0	0	ø	0	—	—	/H	—	0.0
	Bos N	96	322	46	100	15	2	2	25	28	2	12	.311	.369	.388	114	7	11	.973	2	105	99	O83(10/59/15)	—	0.5
	Year	97	323	46	100	15	2	2	25	28	2	13	.310	.368	.387	113	7	11	.973	2	105	99	O83(10/59/15)	—	0.5
1927	Bos N	84	183	27	58	6	4	1	24	16	1	12	.317	.375	.410	119	5	8	.950	2	106	137	O48(3/14/32)	—	0.4
1928	Bos N	96	254	30	71	9	2	1	32	21	0	14	.280	.335	.343	82	-7	6	.988	2	109	75	O65(18/40/7)	—	-0.9
1929	Bos N	19	20	2	5	0	0	0	2	2	0	2	.250	.318	.250	45	-2	0	.833	-1	108	0	O9(2/4/3)	—	-0.2
Total	15	1406	4532	783	1301	182	71	40	382	334	22	348	.287	.339	.385	103	18	228-67	.961	-1	99	104	O1219(207/587/447)	—	-5.4
SMITH, STUB	James Abner; B11.24.1873 Elmwood IL; D11.14.1947 Fall River MA; BL/TR/5´6˝/145; d9.10																								
1898	Bos N	3	10	1	1	0	0	0	0	0	0	—	.100	.100	.100	-41	-2	0	.933	0	111	0	S3	—	-0.2
SMITH, RED	James Carlisle; B4.6.1890 Greenville SC; D10.11.1966 Atlanta GA; BR/TR/5´11˝/165; d9.5; Col Auburn																								
1911	Bro N	28	111	10	29	6	1	0	19	5	1	13	.261	.299	.333	80	-3	5	.900	-2	99	178	3b28	—	-0.4
1912	Bro N	128	486	75	139	28	6	4	57	54	4	51	.286	.362	.393	111	8	22	.938	7	106	95	3b125	—	1.8
1913	Bro N	151	540	70	160	**40**	10	6	76	45	7	67	.296	.358	.441	124	17	22-19	.933	-2	103	65	3b151	—	1.8
1914	Bro N	90	330	39	81	10	8	4	48	30	1	26	.245	.310	.361	97	-2	11	.937	13	108	129	3b90	—	1.4
	Bos N	60	207	30	65	17	1	3	37	28	2	24	.314	.401	.449	153	15	4	.937	6	108	139	3b60	—	2.4
	Year	150	537	69	146	27	9	7	85	58	3	50	.272	.346	.395	119	13	15	.937	18	108	133	3b150	—	3.8
1915	Bos N	**157**	549	66	145	34	4	2	65	67	1	49	.264	.345	.352	116	14	10-5	.947	-6	94	129	3b157	—	1.4
1916	Bos N	150	509	48	132	16	10	3	60	53	3	55	.259	.333	.348	114	9	13	.928	-5	97	75	3b150	—	1.0
1917	Bos N	147	505	60	149	31	6	2	62	53	6	61	.295	.369	.392	142	27	16	.925	-23	85	111	3b147	—	1.0
1918	Bos N	119	429	55	128	20	3	2	65	45	6	47	.298	.373	.373	133	19	8	.922	3	**110**	78	3b119	—	2.9
1919	Bos N	87	241	24	59	6	0	1	25	40	3	22	.245	.359	.282	98	2	6	.981	2	104	55	O48(17/30/3),3b23	—	0.2
Total	9	1117	3907	477	1087	208	49	27	514	420	34	415	.278	.353	.377	120	106	117-24	.932	-6	100	101	3b1050,O48(17/30/3)	—	13.5
SMITH, HARRY	James Harry; B5.15.1890 Brooklyn NY; D4.1.1922 Charlotte NC; BR/TR/5´10˝/180; d9.21																								
1914	NY N	5	7	0	3	0	0	0	2	3	0	1	.429	.600	.429	215	1	1	1.000	1	*166*	*76*	C4	—	0.3
1915	NY N	21	32	1	4	0	1	0	3	6	0	12	.125	.263	.188	40	-2	0-1	.967	-2	*87*	*69*	C18	—	-0.4
	Bro F	28	65	5	13	0	0	1	4	7	0	16	.200	.278	.246	48	-6	2	.967	-4	*77*	*95*	C19/rf	—	-0.9
1917	Cin N	8	17	0	2	0	0	0	1	2	0	7	.118	.211	.118	2	-2	0	.978	2	*119*	*130*	C7	—	0.1
1918	Cin N	13	27	4	5	1	2	0	4	3	0	6	.185	.267	.370	95	0	1	1.000	-1	*105*	*49*	C6/cf	—	-0.1
Total	4	75	148	10	27	1	3	1	14	21	0	42	.182	.284	.250	59	-9	4-1	.975	-4	*96*	*87*	C54,O2(0/1/1)	—	-1.0
SMITH, JIMMY	James Lawrence "Greenfield Jimmy"; B5.15.1895 Pittsburgh PA; D1.1.1974 Pittsburgh PA; BB/TR (BR 1914)/5´9˝/152; d9.26; Col Duquesne																								
1914	Chi F	3	6	1	3	1	0	0	1	0	0	0	.500	.500	.667	229	1	0	1.000	1	113	434	S3	—	0.2
1915	Chi F	95	318	32	69	11	4	4	30	14	0	65	.217	.250	.314	62	-24	4	.904	-15	91	89	S92/2	—	-3.6
	Bal F	33	108	9	19	1	1	1	11	11	1	23	.176	.258	.231	37	-11	3	.883	-3	90	66	S33	—	-1.3
	Year	128	426	41	88	12	5	5	41	25	1	88	.207	.252	.293	55	-35	7	.898	-18	91	83	S125/2	—	-4.9
1916	Pit N	36	96	4	18	1	1	0	5	6	3	22	.188	.257	.219	46	-6	0	.929	-2	96	66	S27,3b6	—	-0.7
1917	NY N	36	96	12	22	5	1	0	9	9	0	18	.229	.295	.302	86	-1	6	.971	-1	105	60	2b29,S7	—	-0.2
1918	Bos N	34	102	8	23	3	4	1	14	3	1	13	.225	.255	.363	91	-2	1	1.000	-3	73	47	2b10,S9,O6(2/3/1),3b5	—	-0.5
1919	†Cin N	28	40	9	11	1	3	1	10	4	0	8	.275	.341	.525	163	3	1	1.000	-1	114	0	3b6,S5,2b4,O4(1/0/3)	—	0.2
1921	Phi N	67	247	31	57	8	1	4	22	11	1	28	.231	.266	.320	50	-18	2-8	.971	11	119	60	2b66	—	-0.8
1922	Phi N	38	114	13	25	1	0	1	6	5	1	9	.219	.258	.254	30	-12	1-3	.952	-1	93	120	S23,2b13/3	—	-1.2
Total	8	370	1127	119	247	32	15	12	108	63	7	186	.219	.265	.306	60	-70	18-11	.910	-15	92	89	S199,2b123,3b18,O10(3/3/4)	—	-7.9
SMITH, JIM	James Lorne; B9.8.1954 Santa Monica CA; BR/TR/6´3˝/185; [BalA76 6/140]; d4.12; Col Cal St.–Long Beach																								
1982	Pit N	42	42	5	10	2	1	0	4	5-0	0	7	.238	.313	.333	79	-1	0-1	.929	0	94	101	S29,2b3/3	0	0.0
SMITH, JASON	Jason William; B7.24.1977 Meridian MS; BL/TR/6´3˝/(195–200); [ChiN96 23/682]; d6.17; Col Meridian (MS) CC																								
2001	Chi N	2	1	0	0	0	0	0	0	0-0	0	1	.000	.000	.000	-99	0	0-0	1.000	0	0	0	/S	0	0.0
2002	TB A	26	65	9	13	1	2	1	6	2-0	0	24	.200	.224	.323	44	-6	3-0	.962	-3	102	169	3b12,S9/2	0	-0.7
2003	TB A	1	4	0	1	0	0	0	0	0-0	0	0	.250	.250	.250	33	0	0-0	.500	-0	123	607	/3	0	-0.1
2004	Det A	61	155	20	37	7	4	5	19	8-0	1	37	.239	.280	.432	85	-4	1-2	.987	5	107	110	2b34,S20,3b5,D2	0	0.2
2005	Det A	27	58	4	11	1	2	0	2	0-0	1	16	.190	.203	.276	26	-7	2-1	1.000	4	129	131	S15,2b6,3b3/1D	0	-0.1
2006	Col N	49	99	9	26	1	0	5	13	7-1	2	29	.263	.324	.424	82	-3	3-0	.975	4	124	141	2b18,1b6,3b3/S	0	0.2
Total	6	166	382	42	88	10	8	11	40	17-1	4	107	.230	.270	.385	68	-20	9-3	.981	11	110	118	2b59,S46,3b24,1b7,D3	0	-0.5
SMITH, JOHN	John; B Baltimore MD; d4.14																								
1873	Mar NA	5	19	2	2	0	0	0	1	0	—	1	.105	.105	.105	-49	-3	0-0	.773	-1	91	0	S3,O2L	—	-0.3
1874	Bal NA	6	21	2	4	1	0	0	1	0	—	1	.190	.190	.238	37	-1	0-0	.731	-2	64	0	S6	—	-0.3
1875	NH NA	1	3	0	0	0	0	0	0	1	—	0	.000	.250	.000	-6	0	0-0	.500	-1	58	0	/S	—	-0.1
Total	3NA	12	43	4	6	1	0	0	2	1	—	2	.140	.159	.163	0	-4	0-0	.722	-4	73	0	S10,O2L	—	-0.7
SMITH, DWIGHT	John Dwight; B11.8.1963 Tallahassee FL; BL/TR/5´11˝/(175–195); [ChiN84 S3/62]; d5.1; Col Spartanburg Methodist (SC) JC																								
1989	†Chi N	109	343	52	111	19	6	9	52	31-0	2	51	.324	.382	.493	139	17	9-4	.975	4	104	141	O102(75/0/32)	0	2.0
1990	Chi N	117	290	34	76	15	0	6	27	28-2	2	46	.262	.329	.376	88	-4	11-6	.986	-0	98	82	O81(59/3/22)	0	-0.6
1991	Chi N	90	167	16	38	7	2	3	21	11-2	1	32	.228	.279	.347	72	-7	2-3	.962	0	100	126	O42(5/13/28)	0	-0.8
1992	Chi N	109	217	28	60	10	3	3	24	13-0	1	40	.276	.318	.392	98	-1	9-8	.979	-3	86	76	O63(20/27/22)	0	-0.7
1993	Chi N	111	310	51	93	17	5	11	35	25-1	3	51	.300	.355	.494	126	11	8-6	.955	-2	95	115	O89(14/53/28)	28	0.8
1994	Cal A	45	122	19	32	5	1	5	18	7-0	0	20	.262	.300	.443	87	-3	2-3	.912	-1	98	107	O31L,D2	0	-0.5
	Bal A	28	74	12	23	2	1	3	12	5-1	1	17	.311	.363	.486	110	1	0-1	.939	-3	81	0	O22(20/2/1),D3	0	-0.3
	Year	73	196	31	55	7	2	8	30	12-1	1	37	.281	.324	.459	96	-2	2-4	.922	-4	91	63	O53(51/2/1),D5	0	-0.8
1995	†Atl N	103	131	16	33	8	2	3	21	13-1	2	35	.252	.327	.412	90	-2	0-3	.923	-2	80	0	O25(11/0/14)	0	-0.6
1996	Atl N	101	153	16	31	5	0	3	16	17-1	1	42	.203	.285	.294	50	-11	1-3	.962	2	124	73	O29(3/0/26)	0	-1.1
Total	8	813	1807	244	497	88	20	46	226	150-8	13	334	.275	.333	.422	101	1	42-37	.964	-5	97	98	O484(238/98/173),D5	28	-1.8
SMITH, JACK	John Joseph "Big"; B1858 New York NY; D1.6.1899 San Francisco CA; 5´11˝/210; d5.1																								
1882	Tro N	35	149	27	36	4	3	0	14	3	—	24	.242	.257	.309	84	-3	—	.960	-0	95	95	1b35	—	-0.5
	Wor N	19	70	10	17	3	2	0	5	5	—	10	.243	.293	.343	101	0	—	.939	1	199	101	1b19	—	-0.1
	Year	54	219	37	53	7	5	0	19	8	—	34	.242	.269	.320	90	-3	—	.952	1	131	97	1b54	—	-0.6
SMITH, JACK	John Joseph (b John Joseph Coffey); B8.8.1893 Oswayo PA; D12.4.1962 New York NY; BR/TR/5´9˝/?; d5.18																								
1912	Det A	1	0	0	0	0	0	0	0	0	0	—	ø	ø	ø	ø	0	0	1.000	0	86	1159	/3	—	0.0

YEAR	TM LG	G	AB	R	H	2B	3B	HR	RBI	BB-IB	HP	SO	AVG	OBP	SLG	AOPS	ABR	SB-CS	FA	FR	RNG	THR	GAMES AT POSITION	DL	BFW
Smith, John	John Marshall; B9.27.1906 Washington DC; D5.9.1982 Silver Spring MD; BB/TR/6´1˝/180; d9.17																								
1931	Bos A	4	15	2	2	0	0	0	1	2	0	1	.133	.235	.133	-1	-2	1-0	1.000	-1	0	31	1b4	—	-0.3
Smith, Keith	Keith Lavarne; B5.3.1953 Palmetto FL; BR/TR/5´9˝/175; [TexA72 S4/48]; d8.2; Col Manatee (FL) CC																								
1977	Tex A	23	67	13	16	4	0	2	6	4-0	2	7	.239	.301	.388	85	-1	2-0	.975	-0	97	70	O22L	0	-0.2
1979	StL N	6	13	1	3	0	0	0	0	0-0	0	1	.231	.231	.231	26	-1	0-1	1.000	2	197	365	O5L	0	0.0
1980	StL N	24	31	3	4	1	0	0	2	2-1	0	2	.129	.182	.161	-3	-4	0-0	1.000	-0	109	0	O7(4/1/2)	0	-0.5
Total	3	53	111	17	23	5	0	2	8	6-1	2	10	.207	.261	.306	54	-6	2-1	.985	2	112	96	O34(31/1/2)	0	-0.7
Smith, Ken	Kenneth Earl; B2.12.1958 Youngstown OH; BL/TR/6´1˝/(195–213); [AtlN76 1/3]; d9.22																								
1981	Atl N	5	3	0	1	1	0	0	0	0-0	0	1	.333	.333	.667	178	0	0-0	1.000	0	118	0	1b4	0	0.0
1982	Atl N	48	41	6	12	1	0	0	3	6-0	0	13	.293	.383	.317	96	0	0-0	1.000	-1	88	0	1b6,O3L	0	-0.1
1983	Atl N	30	12	2	2	0	0	1	2	1-0	0	5	.167	.231	.417	71	-1	1-0	1.000	2	277	132	1b13	0	0.1
Total	3	83	56	8	15	2	0	1	5	7-0	0	19	.268	.349	.357	95	-1	1-0	1.000	1	193	69	1b23,O3L	0	0.0
Smith, L.	L.; d9.7																								
1882	Bal AA	1	3	0	0	0	0	0	—	0	—	—	.000	.000	.000	-99	-1	—	.500	-1	0	0	/cf	—	-0.1
Smith, Paddy	Lawrence Patrick; B5.16.1894 Pelham NY; D12.2.1990 New Rochelle NY; BL/TR/6´0˝/195; d7.6; Col Fordham																								
1920	Bos A	2	2	0	0	0	0	0	0	0	0	1	.000	.000	.000	-99	-1	0-0	ø	-0	*0*	*0*	/C	—	-0.1
Smith, Bull	Lewis Oscar; B8.20.1880 Plum WV; D5.1.1928 Charleston WV; BR/TR/6´0˝/180; d8.30; Col West Virginia																								
1904	Pit N	13	42	2	6	0	1	0	0	1	0	—	.143	.163	.190	9	-5	0	.857	-0	123	0	O13(11/0/2)	—	-0.6
1906	Chi N	1	1	0	0	0	0	0	0	0	0	—	.000	.000	.000	-95	0	0	ø	0	—	—	/H	—	0.0
1911	Was A	1	0	0	0	0	0	0	0	0	0	—	ø	ø	ø	ø	0	0	ø	0	—	—	/R	—	0.0
Total	3	15	43	2	6	0	1	0	0	1	0	—	.140	.159	.186	6	-5	0	.857	-0	123	0	O13(11/0/2)	—	-0.6
Smith, Leo	Lionel H.; B5.13.1859 Brooklyn NY; D8.30.1935 Brooklyn NY; 5´6˝/142; d8.28																								
1890	Roc AA	35	112	11	21	1	3	0	11	14	1	—	.188	.283	.250	62	-5	1	.948	6	104	146	S35	—	0.2
Smith, Lonnie	Lonnie "Skates"; B12.22.1955 Chicago IL; BR/TR/5´9˝/(170–195); [PhiN74 1/3]; d9.2																								
1978	Phi N	17	4	6	0	0	0	0	0	4-0	0	3	.000	.500	.000	49	0	4-0	1.000	1	94	529	O11(10/1/1)	0	0.2
1979	Phi N	17	30	4	5	2	0	0	3	1-0	0	7	.167	.194	.233	15	-4	2-1	1.000	1	113	180	O11(3/5/4)	0	-0.3
1980	†Phi N	100	298	69	101	14	4	3	20	26-2	4	48	.339	.397	.443	126	12	33-13	.969	-7	88	37	O82(52/9/23)	0	0.5
1981	†Phi N	62	176	40	57	14	3	2	11	18-1	5	14	.324	.402	.472	139	10	21-10	.971	6	104	338	O51(8/23/24)	0	1.7
1982	†StL N★	156	592	**120**	182	35	8	8	69	64-2	**9**	74	.307	.381	.434	125	22	68-26	.970	2	95	135	O149(135/36/0)	0	2.5
1983	StL N	130	492	83	158	31	5	8	45	41-2	**9**	55	.321	.381	.453	130	21	43-18	.941	1	93	148	O126L	27	2.1
1984	StL N	145	504	77	126	20	4	6	49	70-0	**9**	90	.250	.349	.341	98	1	50-13	.948	-5	76	**179**	O140L	0	-0.3
1985	StL N	28	96	15	25	2	2	0	7	15-0	3	20	.260	.377	.323	98	1	12-6	1.000	-1	94	57	O28L	0	0.0
	†KC A	120	448	77	115	23	4	6	41	41-0	4	69	.257	.321	.366	88	-7	40-7	.958	-4	88	143	O119L	0	-0.9
1986	KC A	134	508	80	146	25	7	8	44	46-0	10	78	.287	.357	.411	106	5	26-9	.965	-0	105	68	O118L,D10	21	0.2
1987	KC A	48	167	26	42	7	1	3	8	24-0	4	31	.251	.355	.359	89	-2	9-4	.915	-3	85	94	O32L,D15	0	-0.6
1988	Atl N	43	114	14	27	3	0	3	9	10-0	0	25	.237	.296	.342	80	-3	4-2	.968	1	104	113	O35L	0	-0.3
1989	Atl N	134	482	89	152	34	4	21	79	76-3	11	95	.315	**.415**	.533	167	46	25-12	.993	3	110	41	O132L	24	4.8
1990	Atl N	135	466	72	142	27	9	9	42	58-3	6	69	.305	.384	.459	125	18	10-10	.956	2	110	73	O122L	0	1.5
1991	†Atl N	122	353	58	97	19	1	7	44	50-3	9	64	.275	.377	.394	111	8	9-5	.965	-7	81	103	O99L	20	-0.1
1992	†Atl N	84	158	23	39	8	2	6	33	17-1	3	37	.247	.324	.437	109	2	4-0	.954	1	110	153	O35L	0	0.3
1993	Pit N	94	199	35	57	5	4	6	24	43-2	5	42	.286	.422	.442	133	12	9-4	.981	-0	112	28	O60(58/3/0)	0	1.1
	Bal A	9	24	8	5	1	0	2	3	8-0	0	10	.208	.406	.500	136	2	0-0	1.000	0	66	442	O4L,D5	0	0.1
1994	Bal A	35	59	13	12	3	0	0	2	11-0	1	18	.203	.333	.254	53	-4	1-0	1.000	1	61	839	D30,O2R	23	-0.4
Total	17	1613	5170	909	1488	273	58	98	533	623-19	92	849	.288	.371	.420	117	140	370-140	.964	-9	96	114	O1356(1257/77/54),D60	115	12.1
Smith, Mark	Mark Edward; B5.7.1970 Pasadena CA; BR/TR/6´3˝/(195–235); [BalA91 1/9]; d5.14; Col USC																								
1994	Bal A	3	7	0	1	0	0	0	2	0-0	0	2	.143	.143	.143	-25	-1	0-0	1.000	1	190	0	O3R	0	-0.1
1995	Bal A	37	104	11	24	5	0	3	15	12-2	1	22	.231	.314	.365	75	-4	3-0	1.000	1	107	105	O32(15/0/17),D3	0	-0.3
1996	Bal A	27	78	9	19	2	0	4	10	3-0	3	20	.244	.298	.423	80	-3	0-2	.980	2	137	0	O20(12/0/8),D6	69	-0.2
1997	Pit N	71	193	29	55	13	1	9	35	28-1	0	36	.285	.374	.503	125	8	3-1	1.000	-0	83	169	O42(21/0/22),1b9,D5	23	0.6
1998	Pit N	59	128	18	25	6	0	2	13	10-0	3	26	.195	.264	.289	47	-10	7-0	.977	0	110	0	O24(16/0/9),1b6,D3	15	-0.9
2000	Fla N	104	192	22	47	8	1	5	27	17-1	2	54	.245	.310	.375	77	-8	2-0	1.000	2	95	183	O49(29/0/25)/D	24	-0.6
2001	Mon N	80	194	28	47	13	1	6	18	23-0	2	38	.242	.326	.412	91	-3	0-2	1.000	1	105	62	O60(54/6/4)/1	0	-0.4
2003	Mil N	33	63	8	15	4	0	3	10	4-0	0	13	.238	.275	.444	86	-2	0-0	.960	-1	104	0	O15(12/0/3)	0	-0.3
Total	8	414	959	125	233	51	3	32	130	97-4	11	211	.243	.316	.403	85	-23	15-5	.993	6	104	91	O245(159/6/91),D18,1b16	131	-2.2
Smith, Red	Marvin Harold; B7.17.1899 Ashley IL; D2.19.1961 Los Angeles CA; BL/TR/5´7˝/165; d4.14																								
1925	Phi A	20	14	1	4	0	0	0	1	2	0	5	.286	.375	.286	65	-1	0-0	.864	-1	113	0	S16,3b2	—	-0.1
Smith, Milt	Milton; B3.27.1929 Columbus GA; D4.11.1997 San Diego CA; BR/TR/5´10˝/165; d7.21; Negro Lg 1949–50																								
1955	Cin N	36	102	15	20	3	1	3	8	13-0	1	24	.196	.293	.333	62	-6	2-2	.915	-1	105	87	3b28,2b5	0	-0.7
Smith, Nate	Nathaniel Beverly; B4.26.1935 Chicago IL; BR/TR/5´11˝/170; d9.19; Col Tennessee St.																								
1962	Bal A	5	9	3	2	1	0	0	0	1-0	1	4	.222	.364	.333	95	0	0-0	1.000	-0	48	0	C3	0	0.0
Smith, Ollie	Orlin Hudson; B10.19.1865 Mt.Vernon OH; D2.4.1954 Torrance CA; BL/TL; d7.11																								
1894	Lou N	39	137	27	41	6	1	3	20	29	3	15	.299	.432	.423	115	6	13	.883	-3	78	0	O39R	—	0.1
Smith, Ozzie	Osborne Earl "The Wizard of Oz"; B12.26.1954 Mobile AL; BB/TR/5´11˝/(150–180); [SDN77 4/86]; d4.7; HF2002; Col Cal Poly–San Luis Obispo																								
1978	SD N	159	590	69	152	17	6	1	46	47-0	0	43	.258	.311	.312	81	-17	40-12	.970	30	**113**	115	S159	0	3.5
1979	SD N	156	587	77	124	18	6	0	27	37-5	2	37	.211	.260	.262	46	-46	28-7	.976	20	112	96	S155	0	-0.7
1980	SD N	158	609	67	140	18	5	0	35	71-1	5	49	.230	.313	.276	71	-22	57-15	.974	**39**	117	117	S158	0	4.2
1981	SD N★	**110**	450	53	100	11	2	0	21	41-1	5	37	.222	.294	.256	62	-22	22-12	**.976**	22	**115**	98	S110	0	1.3
1982	†StL N★	140	488	58	121	24	1	2	43	68-12	2	32	.248	.339	.314	82	-8	25-5	**.984**	**36**	**119**	125	S139	0	4.7
1983	StL N★	159	552	69	134	30	6	3	50	64-9	1	36	.243	.321	.335	82	-12	34-7	.975	16	110	107	S158	0	2.6
1984	StL N★	124	412	53	106	20	5	1	44	56-5	2	17	.257	.347	.337	96	0	35-7	**.982**	**32**	**116**	**132**	S124	36	5.0
1985	†StL N★	158	537	70	148	22	3	6	54	65-11	2	27	.276	.355	.361	102	3	31-8	**.983**	18	109	124	S158	0	4.3
1986	StL N★	153	514	67	144	19	4	0	54	79-13	2	27	.280	.376	.333	98	2	31-7	**.978**	-12	101	**122**	S144	0	1.1
1987	†StL N★	158	600	104	182	40	4	0	75	89-3	1	36	.303	.392	.383	104	9	43-9	**.987**	12	**108**	**122**	S158	0	4.3
1988	StL N★	153	575	80	155	27	1	3	51	74-2	1	43	.270	.350	.336	97	1	57-9	.972	**21**	**115**	96	S150	0	4.6
1989	StL N★	155	593	82	162	30	8	2	50	55-3	2	37	.273	.335	.361	96	-2	29-7	.976	12	112	99	S153	12	2.7
1990	StL N★	143	512	61	130	21	1	1	50	61-4	2	33	.254	.330	.305	77	-14	32-6	.980	-12	96	90	S140	0	-1.2
1991	StL N★	150	550	96	157	30	3	3	50	83-2	1	36	.285	.380	.367	110	12	35-9	**.987**	-7	95	114	S150	0	2.1
1992	StL N★	132	518	73	153	20	2	0	31	59-4	0	34	.295	.367	.342	104	5	43-9	.985	16	111	**125**	S132	15	3.9
1993	StL N	141	545	75	157	22	6	1	53	43-1	1	18	.288	.337	.356	87	-9	21-8	.974	**23**	**113**	**129**	S134	0	2.5
1994	StL N★	98	381	51	100	18	3	3	30	38-3	0	26	.262	.326	.349	77	-13	6-3	**.982**	2	103	110	S96	0	-0.3
1995	StL N✳	44	156	16	31	5	1	0	11	17-0	2	12	.199	.282	.244	41	-13	4-3	.964	5	109	123	S41	92	-0.5
1996	†StL N★	82	227	36	64	10	2	2	18	25-0	2	9	.282	.358	.370	92	-2	7-5	.969	7	106	121	S52	20	0.8
Total	19	2573	9396	1257	2460	402	69	28	793	1072-79	33	589	.262	.337	.328	87	-148	580-148	.978	279	110	113	S2511	175	44.9
Smith, Keith	Patrick Keith; B10.20.1961 Los Angeles CA; BB/TR/6´1˝/(175–185); [NYA79 15/389]; d4.12																								
1984	NY A	2	4	0	0	0	0	0	0	0-0	1	2	.000	.200	.000	-41	-1	0-0	.923	1	167	83	S2	0	0.1
1985	NY A	4	0	1	0	0	0	0	0	0-0	0	0	ø	ø	ø	ø	0	0-0	1.000	-0	100	0	S3	0	0.0
Total	2	6	4	1	0	0	0	0	0	0-0	1	2	.000	.200	.000	-41	-1	0-0	.929	1	157	71	S5	0	0.1
Smith, Paul	Paul Leslie; B3.19.1931 New Castle PA; BL/TL/5´8˝/(160–165); d4.14; Mil 1955–56																								
1953	Pit N	118	389	41	110	12	7	4	44	24	3	23	.283	.329	.380	85	-9	3-0	.985	-1	100	75	1b74,O19L	0	-1.4
1957	Pit N	81	150	12	38	4	0	3	11	12-1	1	17	.253	.313	.340	78	-5	0-2	1.000	1	105	109	O33(16/1/20)/1	0	-0.6
1958	Pit N	6	3	0	1	0	0	0	0	3-0	0	0	.333	.667	.333	180	1	0-0	ø	0	—	—	/H	0	0.1

YEAR	TM LG	G	AB	R	H	2B	3B	HR	RBI	BB-IB	HP	SO	AVG	OBP	SLG	AOPS	ABR	SB-CS	FA	FR	RNG	THR	GAMES AT POSITION	DL	BFW
	Chi N	18	20	1	3	0	0	0	1	3-0	0	4	.150	.261	.150	13	-3	0-0	.941	0	127	0	1b4	0	-0.3
	Year	24	23	1	4	0	0	0	1	6-0	0	4	.174	.345	.174	44	-2	0-0	.941	0	127	0	1b4	0	-0.2
Total	3	223	562	54	152	16	7	7	56	42-1	4	44	.270	.326	.361	81	-16	3-2	.984	0	101	72	1b79,O52(35/1/20)	0	-2.2
SMITH, PAUL	Paul Stoner; B5.7.1888 Mt.Zion IL; D7.3.1958 Decatur IL; BL/TR/6´1˝/190; d9.19; Col Millikin																								
1916	Cin N	10	44	5	10	0	1	0	1	1	0	8	.227	.244	.273	60	-2	3	1.000	-1	79	111	O10L	—	-0.4
SMITH, RAY	Raymond Edward; B9.18.1955 Glendale CA; BR/TR/6´1˝/185; d4.9; Col Oregon																								
1981	Min A	15	40	4	8	1	0	1	1	0-0	0	3	.200	.200	.300	40	-3	0-0	1.000	-0	158	63	C15	150	-0.3
1982	Min A	9	23	1	5	0	1	0	1	1-0	0	3	.217	.250	.304	50	-2	0-0	1.000	-0	167	71	C9	0	-0.1
1983	Min A	59	152	11	34	5	0	0	8	10-0	1	12	.224	.274	.257	46	-11	1-0	.984	9	92	150	C59	0	0.0
Total	3	83	215	16	47	6	1	1	10	11-0	1	18	.219	.259	.270	45	-16	1-0	.988	8	113	125	C83	150	-0.4
SMITH, DICK	Richard Arthur; B5.17.1939 Lebanon OR; BR/TR/6´2˝/205; d7.20																								
1963	NY N	20	42	4	10	0	1	0	3	5-2	0	10	.238	.319	.286	74	-1	3-2	1.000	-1	79	0	O10(3/7/0),1b2	0	-0.4
1964	NY N	46	94	14	21	6	1	0	3	1-0	2	29	.223	.247	.309	57	-5	6-2	.987	-1	103	85	1b18,O13(12/1/1)	0	-0.7
1965	LA N	10	6	0	0	0	0	0	1	0-0	0	3	.000	.000	.000	-99	-2	0-0	1.000	-1	19	0	O9(5/4/1)	0	-0.3
Total	3	76	142	18	31	6	2	0	7	6-2	2	42	.218	.260	.289	56	-8	9-4	1.000	-3	72	0	O32(20/12/2),1b20	0	-1.4
SMITH, DICK	Richard Harrison; B7.21.1927 Blandburg PA; BR/TR/5´8˝/160; d9.14; Col Lock Haven																								
1951	Pit N	12	46	2	8	0	0	0	4	8	0	8	.174	.296	.174	29	-4	0-2	.936	2	115	188	3b12	0	-0.3
1952	Pit N	29	66	8	7	1	0	0	5	9	0	3	.106	.213	.121	-5	-9	0-0	.958	3	111	118	3b16,2b4,S4	0	-0.6
1953	Pit N	13	43	4	7	0	1	0	2	6	0	6	.163	.265	.209	26	-5	0-1	.961	3	131	101	S13	0	-0.1
1954	Pit N	12	31	2	3	1	1	0	0	6	0	5	.097	.243	.194	16	-4	0-0	.933	1	121	171	3b9	0	-0.3
1955	Pit N	4	0	1	0	0	0	0	0	1-0	0	0	ø	1.000	ø	198	0	0-0	ø	-0	0	0	/S	0	0.0
Total	5	70	186	17	25	2	2	0	11	30-0	0	22	.134	.255	.167	15	-22	0-3	.944	10	115	156	3b37,S18,2b4	0	-1.3
SMITH, DICK	Richard Kelly; B8.25.1944 Lincolnton NC; BR/TR/6´5˝/200; d8.20; Col Lenoir–Rhyne																								
1969	Was A	21	28	2	3	0	0	0	0	4-1	1	7	.107	.242	.107	1	-4	0-0	.909	-1	82	0	O9L	0	-0.5
SMITH, RED	Richard Paul; B5.18.1904 Brokaw WI; D3.8.1978 Sylvania OH; BR/TR/5´10˝/185; d5.31; C4; Col Notre Dame																								
1927	NY N	1	0	0	0	0	0	0	0	0	0	0	ø	ø	ø	ø	0	0	1.000	-0	*0*	*0*	/C	—	0.0
SMITH, BOB	Robert Eldridge; B4.22.1895 Rogersville TN; D7.19.1987 Waycross GA; BR/TR/5´10˝/175; d4.19; ▲																								
1923	Bos N	115	375	30	94	16	3	0	40	17	1	35	.251	.285	.309	59	-23	4-9	.944	12	106	110	S101,2b8	—	-0.3
1924	Bos N	106	347	32	79	12	3	2	38	15	0	26	.228	.260	.297	51	-25	5-2	.958	4	103	103	S80,3b23	—	-1.1
1925	Bos N	58	174	17	49	9	4	0	23	5	0	6	.282	.302	.379	80	-6	2-2	.906	-1	111	110	S21,2b15,P13/cf	—	-0.3
1926	Bos N	40	84	10	25	6	2	0	13	2	0	4	.298	.314	.417	105	8	0	.972	2	120	207	P33	—	0.0
1927	Bos N	54	109	10	27	3	1	1	10	2	0	4	.248	.261	.321	60	5	0	.966	2	110	101	P41	—	0.0
1928	Bos N	39	92	11	23	2	0	1	8	1	0	6	.250	.258	.304	49	3	2	.965	2	116	142	P38	—	0.0
1929	Bos N	39	99	12	17	4	2	1	8	2	0	8	.172	.188	.283	16	-14	1	.986	3	109	96	P34,S5	—	0.1
1930	Bos N	39	81	7	19	2	0	0	4	0	0	5	.235	.235	.259	20	-1	0	.984	1	106	100	P38	—	0.0
1931	Chi N	36	87	7	19	2	0	0	4	5	0	2	.218	.261	.241	35	1	0	**1.000**	1	109	118	P36	—	0.0
1932	†Chi N	36	42	5	10	4	1	0	4	0	0	2	.238	.238	.381	64	-2	1	1.000	2	105	206	P34,2b2	—	0.2
1933	Cin N	23	25	2	5	1	0	0	1	1	0	0	.200	.231	.240	35	-2	1	.882	-1	92	471	P16/S	—	-0.1
	Bos N	14	20	1	4	0	1	0	2	0	0	1	.200	.200	.300	45	0	0	1.000	1	146	0	P14	—	0.0
	Year	37	45	3	9	1	1	0	3	1	0	1	.200	.217	.267	39	-4	1	.946	0	116	262	P30/S	—	-0.1
1934	Bos N	42	36	5	9	1	0	0	3	0	0	1	.250	.250	.278	44	1	0	1.000	1	119	139	P39	—	0.0
1935	Bos N	47	63	3	17	0	0	0	4	1	0	5	.270	.281	.270	53	3	0	.980	-1	91	40	P46	—	0.0
1936	Bos N	35	45	1	10	2	0	0	4	0	0	4	.222	.222	.267	33	0	0	1.000	1	118	105	P35	—	0.0
1937	Bos N	19	10	1	2	0	0	0	0	1	0	1	.200	.273	.200	33	0	0	1.000	-1	63	0	P18	—	0.0
Total	15	742	1689	154	409	64	17	5	166	52	1	110	.242	.265	.309	53	-52	16-13	.981	29	109	125	P435,S208,2b25,3b23/cf	—	-1.5
SMITH, BOBBY	Robert Eugene; B4.10.1974 Oakland CA; BR/TR/6´3˝/190; [AtlN92 11/313]; d3.31																								
1998	TB A	117	370	44	102	15	3	11	55	34-0	6	110	.276	.343	.422	96	-2	5-3	.963	10	109	85	3b97,S7,2b6,D7	15	0.8
1999	TB A	68	199	18	36	4	1	3	19	16-0	1	64	.181	.244	.256	28	-23	4-4	.933	5	115	149	3b59,2b13	0	-1.6
2000	TB A	49	175	21	41	8	0	6	26	14-1	1	59	.234	.293	.383	71	-8	2-2	.970	2	107	86	2b45,3b5	43	-0.4
2001	TB A	6	19	1	2	0	0	0	1	3-0	0	10	.105	.227	.105	-8	-3	0-0	.958	-2	66	77	2b6	0	-0.5
2002	TB A	18	63	4	11	2	0	1	6	3-0	0	25	.175	.212	.254	24	-7	0-0	.897	1	101	159	3b10,1b6,O2(1/0/1)/D	0	-0.6
Total	5	258	826	88	192	29	4	21	107	70-1	8	268	.232	.297	.354	67	-43	11-9	.947	15	111	110	3b171,2b70,D8,S7,1b6,O2(1/0/1)	58	-2.3
SMITH, JOE	Salvatore Joseph (b Salvatore Persico); B12.29.1893 New York NY; D1.12.1974 Yonkers NY; BR/TR/5´7˝/170; d7.7; Col California																								
1913	NY A	14	32	1	5	0	0	0	2	1	0	14	.156	.182	.156	-1	-4	1	.952	-1	*71*	*126*	C14	—	-0.5
SMITH, SKYROCKET	Samuel J.; B3.19.1868 St.Louis MO; D4.26.1916 St.Louis MO; BR/6´2˝/170; d4.18																								
1888	Lou AA	58	206	27	49	9	4	1	31	24	11	—	.238	.349	.335	122	7	5	.970	-0	105	56	1b58	—	0.2
SMITH, SYD	Sydney A.; B8.31.1883 Smithville SC; D6.5.1961 Orangeburg SC; BR/TR/5´10˝/190; d4.14; Col South Carolina																								
1908	Phi A	46	128	8	26	8	0	1	10	4	1	—	.203	.233	.289	65	-5	0	.975	-2	*70*	*102*	C31,1b6/cf	—	-0.5
	StL A	27	76	6	14	4	0	0	5	4	0	—	.184	.225	.237	50	-4	2	.977	6	*142*	*89*	C24	—	0.4
	Year	73	204	14	40	12	0	1	15	8	1	—	.196	.230	.270	60	-9	2	.976	4	*103*	*96*	C55,1b6/cf	—	-0.1
1910	Cle A	9	27	1	9	1	0	0	3	3	0	—	.333	.400	.370	140	1	0	.958	-1	*82*	*114*	C9	—	0.2
1911	Cle A	58	154	8	46	8	1	1	21	11	2	—	.299	.353	.383	104	1	0	.979	5	*93*	*94*	C48/13	—	0.9
1914	Pit N	5	11	1	3	0	0	0	1	0	0	1	.273	.273	.273	65	-1	0	1.000	-0	*101*	*82*	C3	—	0.0
1915	Pit N	1	1	0	0	0	0	0	0	0	0	0	.000	.000	.000	-99	0	0	ø	0	—	—	/H	—	0.0
Total	5	146	397	24	98	21	1	2	40	22	3	1	.247	.291	.320	83	-8	2	.977	8	*97*	*96*	C115,1b7/3cf	—	1.0
SMITH, TOM	Thomas N.; B1851 Guelph ON, Can.; D3.28.1889 Detroit MI; BR/5´8˝/141; d9.15																								
1875	Atl NA	3	13	0	1	0	0	0	1	0	—	0	.077	.077	.077	-53	-2	0-0	.783	-0	116	0	2b3	—	-0.2
SMITH, TOMMY	Tommy Alexander; B8.1.1948 Albemarle NC; BL/TR/6´3˝/(210–215); [CleA70 5/100]; d9.6; Col North Carolina St.																								
1973	Cle A	14	41	6	10	2	0	2	3	1-0	0	2	.244	.262	.439	92	-1	1-0	1.000	-1	93	0	O13(1/11/1)	0	-0.2
1974	Cle A	23	31	4	3	1	0	0	0	2-1	1	7	.097	.176	.129	-11	-4	0-0	.938	2	133	141	O17(9/4/4)/D	0	-0.4
1975	Cle A	8	8	0	1	0	0	0	2	0-0	0	1	.125	.111	.125	-29	-1	0-0	1.000	0	135	0	O3(1/0/2),D3	0	-0.1
1976	Cle A	55	164	17	42	3	1	2	12	8-2	0	8	.256	.289	.323	80	-5	8-0	.979	1	104	131	O50(12/0/38),D2	0	-0.4
1977	Sea A	21	27	1	7	1	1	0	4	0-0	0	6	.259	.259	.370	70	-1	0-1	1.000	2	86	711	O14(1/0/14)	0	0.0
Total	5	121	271	28	63	7	2	4	21	11-3	1	24	.232	.263	.317	67	-12	9-1	.977	4	105	156	O97(24/15/59),D6	0	-1.1
SMITH, VINNIE	Vincent Ambrose; B12.7.1915 Richmond VA; D12.14.1979 Virginia Beach VA; BR/TR/6´1˝/176; d9.10; Mil 1942–45; U9; [DL 1947 Pit N 162]																								
1941	Pit N	9	33	3	10	1	0	0	5	1	0	5	.303	.324	.333	86	-1	0	.941	-1	*92*	*84*	C9	0	-0.1
1946	Pit N	7	21	2	4	0	0	0	0	1	0	5	.190	.227	.190	19	-2	0	.967	0	*80*	*109*	C7	115	-0.2
Total	2	16	54	5	14	1	0	0	5	2	0	10	.259	.286	.278	59	-3	0	.953	-1	*87*	*94*	C16	277	-0.3
SMITH, WALLY	Wallace Henry; B3.13.1888 Philadelphia PA; D6.10.1930 Florence AZ; BR/TR/5´11.5˝/180; d4.17																								
1911	StL N	81	194	23	42	6	5	2	19	21	3	33	.216	.303	.330	79	-6	5	.936	2	108	30	3b26,S25,2b8/cf	—	-0.2
1912	StL N	75	219	22	56	5	5	0	26	29	3	27	.256	.351	.324	87	-3	4	.949	1	106	69	3b32,S22,1b6	—	-0.1
1914	Was A	45	97	11	19	4	1	0	8	3	2	12	.196	.235	.258	46	-7	3-4	.955	-3	57	99	2b12,1b7,S7,3b5/rf	—	-1.2
Total	3	201	510	56	117	15	11	2	53	53	8	72	.229	.312	.314	77	-16	12-4	.947	-1	107	63	3b63,S54,2b20,1b13,O2(0/1/1)	—	-1.5
SMITH, WIB	Wilbur Floyd; B8.30.1886 Evart MI; D11.18.1959 Fargo ND; BL/TR/5´10.5˝/165; d5.31; Col Albion																								
1909	StL A	17	42	3	8	0	0	0	2	0	0	—	.190	.190	.190	22	-4	0	.836	-7	*82*	*78*	C13/1	—	-1.1
SMITH, RED	Willard Jehu; B4.11.1892 Logansport IN; D7.17.1972 Noblesville IN; BR/TR/5´8˝/165; d9.17																								
1917	Pit N	11	21	1	3	1	0	0	2	3	0	4	.143	.250	.190	35	-1	1	1.000	1	*79*	*163*	C6	—	0.0
1918	Pit N	15	24	1	4	1	0	0	3	3	0	0	.167	.259	.208	42	-2	0	.939	0	*142*	*45*	C10	—	-0.1
Total	2	26	45	2	7	2	0	0	5	6	0	4	.156	.255	.200	39	-3	1	.969	1	*113*	*99*	C16	—	-0.1

YEAR	TM LG	G	AB	R	H	2B	3B	HR	RBI	BB-IB	HP	SO	AVG	OBP	SLG	AOPS	ABR	SB-CS	FA	FR	RNG	THR	GAMES AT POSITION	DL	BFW
SMITH, BILL	William E.; B3.1860 E.Liverpool OH; D8.9.1886 Toronto ON, Can.; 5´11˝/178; d9.17																								
1884	Cle N	1	3	0	0	0	0	0	0	0	—	2	.000	.000	.000	-97	-1	—	ø	0	0	0	/lf	—	-0.1
SMITH, BILL	William J.; B Baltimore MD; D8.9.1886; d4.14; M1																								
1873	Mar NA	**6**	23	2	4	0	0	0	1	0	—	0	.174	.174	.174	4	-2	0-0	.500	-3	0	0	O3C,C2/2M	—	-0.3
SMITH, WILLIE	Willie; B2.11.1939 Anniston AL; D1.16.2006 Anniston AL; BL/TL/6´0˝/(178–190); d6.18; ▲																								
1963	Det A	17	8	2	1	0	0	0	0	0-0	0	1	.125	.125	.125	-29	0	0-0	1.000	0	118	0	P11	0	0.0
1964	LA A	118	359	46	108	14	6	11	51	8-1	2	39	.301	.317	.465	128	10	7-5	.977	-5	88	45	O87(58/3/31),P15	0	0.0
1965	Cal A	136	459	52	120	14	9	14	57	32-10	1	60	.261	.308	.423	109	3	9-8	.980	2	92	145	O123(123/0/1),1b2	0	-0.3
1966	Cal A	90	195	18	36	3	2	1	20	12-2	3	37	.185	.239	.236	39	-16	1-0	.974	1	98	164	O52(32/0/22)	0	-1.8
1967	Cle A	21	32	0	7	2	0	0	2	1-0	0	10	.219	.242	.281	54	-2	0-2	.800	-1	74	0	O4L,1b3	0	-0.4
1968	Cle A	33	42	1	6	2	0	0	3	3-2	1	14	.143	.213	.190	25	-4	0-0	1.000	-0	65	149	1b7,P2/lf	0	-0.5
	Chi N	55	142	13	39	8	2	5	25	12-2	1	33	.275	.333	.465	130	5	0-0	1.000	-2	81	49	O38L,1b4/P	0	0.1
1969	Chi N	103	195	21	48	9	1	9	25	25-3	0	49	.246	.330	.441	102	1	1-0	.929	-5	64	0	O33(32/0/1),1b24	0	-0.7
1970	Chi N	87	167	15	36	9	1	5	24	11-0	1	32	.216	.267	.371	62	-9	2-1	.994	-5	45	120	1b43/rf	0	-1.7
1971	Cin N	31	55	3	9	2	0	1	4	3-0	0	9	.164	.207	.255	30	-5	0-0	1.000	1	150	138	1b10	0	-0.5
Total	9	691	1654	171	410	63	21	46	211	107-20	9	284	.248	.295	.395	94	-17	20-16	.975	-13	88	95	O339(288/3/56),1b93,P29	0	-5.8
SMITHERMAN, STEPHEN	Stephen Lydell; B9.1.1978 McAlester OK; BR/TR/6´4˝/230; [CinN00 23/693]; d7.1; Col Arkansas–Little Rock																								
2003	Cin N	21	44	3	7	2	0	1	6	3-0	0	9	.159	.213	.273	27	-5	1-0	1.000	-1	83	0	O14L	0	-0.6
SMOOT, HOMER	Homer Vernon "Doc"; B3.23.1878 Galestown MD; D3.25.1928 Salisbury MD; BL/TR/5´10˝/180; d4.17; Col Washington College																								
1902	StL N	129	518	58	161	19	4	3	48	23	8	—	.311	.350	.380	131	18	20	.931	-2	80	102	O129C	—	1.0
1903	StL N	129	500	67	148	22	8	4	49	32	3	—	.296	.342	.396	114	8	17	.942	-7	82	67	O129C	—	-0.5
1904	StL N	137	520	58	146	23	6	3	66	37	2	—	.281	.331	.365	120	12	23	.966	-2	98	125	O137C	—	0.4
1905	StL N	139	534	73	166	21	16	4	58	33	7	—	.311	.359	.433	140	24	21	.975	-0	101	134	O138C	—	1.8
1906	StL N	86	343	41	85	9	10	0	31	11	9	—	.248	.289	.332	98	-3	3	.953	-2	70	140	O86(0/55/31)	—	-1.1
	Cin N	60	220	11	57	8	1	1	17	13	5	—	.259	.315	.318	93	-2	0	.944	1	145	0	O59(4/55/0)	—	-0.3
	Year	146	563	52	142	17	11	1	48	24	14	—	.252	.300	.327	96	-5	3	.950	-1	98	87	O145(4/110/31)	—	-1.4
Total	5	680	2635	308	763	102	45	15	269	149	34	—	.290	.336	.380	120	57	84	.953	-12	92	103	O678(4/643/31)	—	1.3
SMOYER, HENRY	Henry Neitz "Hennie" (b Henry Neitz Smowery); B4.24.1890 Fredericksburg PA; D2.28.1958 DuBois PA; BR/TR/5´6˝/?; d8.14; Col Albright																								
1912	StL A	6	14	1	3	0	0	0	0	2	0	—	.214	.313	.214	53	-1	0	1.000	0	125	0	S4,3b2	—	0.0
SMYKAL, FRANK	Frank John (b Frank John Smejkal); B10.13.1889 Chicago IL; D8.11.1950 Chicago IL; BR/TR/5´7˝/150; d8.30; Col Illinois																								
1916	Pit N	6	10	1	3	0	0	0	2	3	1	1	.300	.500	.300	147	1	1	.842	-1	114	66	S5/3	—	0.1
SMYRES, CLANCY	Clarence Melvin; B5.24.1922 Culver City CA; BB/TR/5´11.5˝/175; d4.18																								
1944	Bro N	5	2	1	0	0	0	0	0	0	0	0	.000	.000	.000	-99	-1	0	ø	0	—	—	/H	0	-0.1
SMYTH, RED	James Daniel; B1.30.1891 Holly Springs MS; D4.14.1958 Inglewood CA; BL/TR/5´9˝/152; d8.11																								
1915	Bro N	19	22	3	3	1	0	0	3	4	0	2	.136	.269	.182	37	-1	1-2	1.000	1	126	154	O9(6/2/1)	—	-0.1
1916	Bro N	2	5	0	0	0	0	0	0	0	0	3	.000	.000	.000	-97	-1	0	1.000	-0	60	240	2b2	—	-0.2
1917	Bro N	29	24	5	3	0	0	0	1	4	0	6	.125	.250	.125	16	-2	0	.667	-1	47	297	3b4,O2C	—	-0.4
	StL N	38	72	5	15	0	2	0	4	4	2	9	.208	.269	.264	66	-3	3	.889	-3	73	50	O23(12/4/5)	—	-0.8
	Year	67	96	10	18	0	2	0	5	8	2	15	.188	.264	.229	52	-5	3	.871	-4	77	48	O25(12/6/5),3b4	—	-1.2
1918	StL N	40	113	19	24	1	2	0	4	16	1	11	.212	.315	.257	78	-2	3	.956	-1	86	99	O25(2/0/22),2b11	—	-0.5
Total	4	128	236	32	45	2	4	0	12	28	3	31	.191	.285	.233	60	-9	7-2	.934	-4	87	88	O59(20/8/28),2b13,3b4	—	-2.0
SNEAD, ESIX	Esix; B6.7.1976 Fort Myers FL; BB/TR/5´10˝/(170–175); [StLN98 18/528]; d9.3; Col Central Florida																								
2002	NY N	17	13	3	4	0	0	1	3	1-0	0	4	.308	.357	.538	139	1	4-3	1.000	-0	88	0	O6(1/5/0)	0	0.0
2004	NY N	1	0	1	0	0	0	0	0	0-0	0	0	ø	ø	ø	ø	0	0-0	ø	-0	0	0	/lf	0	0.0
Total	2	18	13	4	4	0	0	1	3	1-0	0	4	.308	.357	.538	139	1	4-3	1.000	-0	84	0	O7(2/5/0)	0	0.0
SNEED, JOHN	John Law; B1861 Shelby Co. TN; D1.4.1899 Memphis TN; BL/5´8˝/160; d5.1																								
1884	Ind AA	27	102	14	22	4	0	1	—	6	0	—	.216	.259	.284	79	-2	—	.817	-1	79	0	O27(0/21/6)	—	-0.3
1890	Tol AA	9	30	3	6	0	0	0	4	8	0	—	.200	.368	.200	66	-1	5	.889	2	332	315	O9R	—	0.1
	Col AA	128	484	114	141	13	15	2	65	63	9	—	.291	.383	.393	138	26	39	.883	-9	92	121	O126(26/3/97),S2	—	1.3
	Year	137	514	117	147	13	15	2	69	71	9	—	.286	.382	.381	133	25	44	.883	-7	108	134	O135(26/3/106),S2	—	1.4
1891	Col AA	99	366	66	94	9	6	1	61	55	8	29	.257	.366	.322	103	5	24	.894	-5	59	114	O99R	—	-0.1
Total	3	263	982	197	263	26	21	4	130	132	17	29	.268	.364	.349	117	28	68	.879	-13	86	113	O261(26/24/211),S2	—	1.0
SNELL, CHARLIE	Charles Anthony (b Charles Anthony Schnell); B11.29.1893 Hampstead MD; D4.4.1988 Reading PA; BR/TR/5´11˝/160; d7.19																								
1912	StL A	8	19	0	4	1	0	0	0	3	1	—	.211	.348	.263	78	0	0	.941	0	*98*	*116*	C8	—	0.1
SNELL, WALLY	Walter Henry "Doc"; B5.19.1889 W.Bridgewater MA; D7.23.1980 Providence RI; BR/TR/5´10˝/170; d8.1; Col Brown																								
1913	Bos A	6	12	1	3	0	0	0	0	0	0	1	.250	.250	.250	45	-1	1	.923	-0	*140*	*88*	C2	—	-0.1
SNELLING, CHRIS	Christopher Doyle; B12.3.1981 North Miami FL; BL/TL/5´10˝/(165–205); d5.25; [DL 2003 Sea A 30, 2004 Sea A 183]																								
2002	Sea A	8	27	2	4	0	0	1	3	2-0	0	4	.148	.207	.259	24	-3	0-0	1.000	0	113	0	O8(6/0/2)	117	-0.3
2005	Sea A	15	29	4	8	2	0	1	1	5-0	0	2	.276	.382	.448	129	1	0-2	1.000	2	111	402	O10(7/0/3)	63	0.2
2006	Sea A	36	96	14	24	6	1	3	8	13-0	4	38	.250	.360	.427	110	2	2-1	.979	-3	79	57	O34(1/1/33)	68	-0.2
Total	3	59	152	20	36	8	1	5	12	20-0	4	44	.237	.339	.401	99	0	2-3	.988	-1	91	118	O52(14/1/38)	461	-0.3
SNIDER, DUKE	Edwin Donald "The Silver Fox"; B9.19.1926 Los Angeles CA; BL/TR/6´0˝/(185–206); d4.17; C2; HF1980																								
1947	Bro N	40	83	6	20	3	1	0	5	3	1	24	.241	.276	.301	51	-6	2	.980	-1	108	0	O25(4/13/7)	0	-0.7
1948	Bro N	53	160	22	39	6	6	5	21	12	0	27	.244	.297	.450	96	-2	4	.989	1	93	188	O47(0/41/7)	0	-0.3
1949	†Bro N	146	552	100	161	28	7	23	92	56	4	92	.292	.361	.493	122	16	12	.984	-4	93	120	O145C	0	0.8
1950	Bro N★	152	620	109	**199**	31	10	31	107	58	0	79	.321	.379	.553	139	33	16	.983	-1	96	121	O151C	0	2.7
1951	Bro N★	150	606	96	168	26	6	29	101	62	0	97	.277	.344	.483	118	14	14-10	.987	-6	95	92	O150C	0	0.3
1952	†Bro N☆	144	534	80	162	25	7	21	92	55	0	77	.303	.368	.494	136	25	7-4	.992	-5	94	95	O141C	0	1.7
1953	†Bro N★	153	590	**132**	198	38	4	42	126	82	3	90	.336	.419	**.627**	165	58	16-7	.987	-11	91	52	O151C	0	3.9
1954	Bro N★	149	584	**120**	199	39	10	40	130	84	4	96	.341	.423	.647	170	**61**	6-6	.981	-10	91	72	O148C	0	4.3
1955	†Bro N★	148	538	**126**	166	34	6	42	**136**	104-19	1	87	.309	.418	.628	169	57	9-7	.989	-3	97	85	O146C	0	4.5
1956	†Bro N★	151	542	112	158	33	2	**43**	101	**99-26**	1	101	.292	**.399**	**.598**	152	**43**	3-3	.984	-4	94	104	O150C	0	3.2
1957	Bro N	139	508	91	139	25	7	40	92	77-12	1	104	.274	.368	.587	139	28	3-4	.990	-12	87	63	O136C	0	0.9
1958	LA N	106	327	45	102	12	3	15	58	32-4	1	49	.312	.371	.505	126	12	2-2	.987	-10	79	65	O92(6/78/11)	0	-0.2
1959	†LA N	126	370	59	114	11	2	23	88	58-13	0	71	.308	.400	.535	137	21	1-5	.975	-12	80	31	O107(0/53/71)	0	0.3
1960	LA N	101	235	38	57	13	5	14	36	46-8	1	54	.243	.366	.519	131	11	1-0	.965	-6	83	63	O75(0/48/35)	0	0.2
1961	LA N	85	233	35	69	8	3	16	56	29-3	1	43	.296	.375	.562	133	11	1-1	.975	3	107	133	O66(0/24/51)	30	1.0
1962	LA N	80	158	28	44	11	3	5	30	36-6	2	32	.278	.418	.481	150	14	2-0	.967	-1	92	113	O39(15/2/24)	0	1.1
1963	NY N★	129	354	44	86	8	3	14	45	56-9	1	74	.243	.345	.401	113	7	0-1	.986	-6	84	76	O106(34/13/62)	0	-0.5
1964	SF N	91	167	16	35	7	0	4	17	22-4	0	40	.210	.302	.323	74	-5	0-0	.979	-2	78	88	O43(19/0/25)	0	-1.0
Total	18	2143	7161	1259	2116	358	85	407	1333	971-104	21	1237	.295	.380	.540	138	398	99-50	.985	-92	91	86	O1918(78/1590/293)	30	22.2
SNIDER, VAN	Van Voorhees; B8.11.1963 Birmingham AL; BL/TR/6´3˝/(185–205); d9.2																								
1988	Cin N	11	28	4	6	1	0	1	6	0-0	0	13	.214	.207	.357	59	-2	0-1	1.000	0	111	0	O8(6/0/3)	0	-0.2
1989	Cin N	8	7	1	1	0	0	0	0	0-0	0	5	.143	.143	.143	-18	-1	0-0	1.000	0	138	0	O6(5/0/2)	0	-0.1
Total	2	19	35	5	7	1	0	1	6	0-0	0	18	.200	.194	.314	44	-3	0-1	1.000	0	117	0	O14(11/0/5)	0	-0.3
SNIPES, ROXY	Wyatt Eure "Rock"; B10.28.1896 Marion SC; D5.1.1941 Fayetteville NC; BL/TR/6´0˝/185; d7.15; Col South Carolina																								
1923	Chi A	1	1	0	0	0	0	0	0	0	0	0	.000	.000	.000	-99	0	0-0	ø	0	—	—	/H	—	0.0
SNODGRASS, CHAPPIE	Amzie Beal; B3.18.1870 Springfield OH; D9.9.1951 New York NY; BR/TR/5´10˝/165; d5.15																								
1901	Bal A	3	10	0	1	0	0	0	1	0	0	—	.100	.100	.100	-43	-2	0	.500	-1	0	0	O2L	—	-0.3

YEAR	TM LG	G	AB	R	H	2B	3B	HR	RBI	BB-IB	HP	SO	AVG	OBP	SLG	AOPS	ABR	SB-CS	FA	FR	RNG	THR	GAMES AT POSITION	DL	BFW
Snodgrass, Fred	Frederick Carlisle "Snow"; B10.19.1887 Ventura CA; D4.5.1974 Ventura CA; BR/TR/5´11.5˝/175; d6.4; OF(108/666/73)																								
1908	NY N	6	4	2	1	0	0	0	1	0	0	—	.250	.250	.250	57	0	1	1.000	1	0	192	C3	—	0.0
1909	NY N	28	70	10	21	5	0	1	6	7	3	—	.300	.387	.414	146	4	7	.921	0	153	181	O20(15/3/1),C2/1	—	0.4
1910	NY N	123	396	69	127	22	8	2	44	71	13	52	.321	.440	.432	154	33	33	.970	-2	97	85	O101(31/70/22),1b9/C3	—	2.7
1911	†NY N	151	534	83	157	27	10	1	77	72	15	59	.294	.393	.388	115	14	51	.973	6	91	**153**	O149(1/149/0)/13	—	1.0
1912	†NY N	146	535	91	144	24	9	3	69	70	8	65	.269	.362	.364	96	-1	43	.948	-3	88	140	O116(52/66/5),1b27/2	—	-1.2
1913	†NY N	141	457	65	133	21	6	3	49	53	7	44	.291	.373	.383	115	11	27-18	.968	-2	97	100	O133C,1b3/2	—	-0.1
1914	NY N	113	392	54	103	20	4	0	44	37	6	43	.263	.336	.334	103	2	25	.977	4	109	87	O96(9/47/40),1b14/23	—	0.0
1915	NY N	80	252	36	49	9	0	0	20	35	6	33	.194	.307	.230	68	-8	11-12	.935	-0	94	136	O75(0/68/5)	—	-1.7
	Bos N	23	79	10	22	2	0	0	9	7	2	9	.278	.352	.304	104	1	0-4	.938	-2	104	46	O18C,1b5	—	-0.4
	Year	103	331	46	71	11	0	0	29	42	8	42	.215	.318	.248	76	-7	11-16	.935	-2	96	118	O93(0/88/5),1b5	—	-2.1
1916	Bos N	112	382	33	95	13	5	1	32	34	5	54	.249	.318	.317	100	0	14	.983	9	106	142	O110C	—	0.2
Total	9	923	3101	453	852	143	42	11	351	386	65	359	.275	.367	.359	110	56	212-34	.965	10	98	121	O818C,1b60,C6,2b3,3b3	—	0.9
Snopek, Chris	Christopher Charles; B9.20.1970 Cynthiana KY; BR/TR/6´1˝/185; [ChiA92 6/176]; d7.31; Col U. of Mississippi																								
1995	Chi A	22	68	12	22	4	0	1	7	9-0	0	12	.324	.403	.426	121	3	1-0	1.000	-3	50	0	3b17,S6	0	0.1
1996	Chi A	46	104	18	27	6	1	6	18	6-0	1	16	.260	.304	.510	106	0	0-1	.939	2	103	152	3b27,S12,D3	0	0.2
1997	Chi A	86	298	27	65	15	0	5	35	18-0	1	51	.218	.263	.319	53	-21	3-2	.915	-15	79	80	3b82,S4	0	-3.5
1998	Chi A	53	125	17	26	2	0	1	4	14-0	1	24	.208	.291	.248	43	-10	3-0	.972	1	111	87	S33,2b12,3b3/1rfD	0	-0.6
	Bos A	8	12	2	2	0	0	0	2	2-0	0	5	.167	.286	.167	21	-1	0-0	.750	-1	120	0	2b3,3b3,D2	0	-0.2
	Year	61	137	19	28	2	0	1	6	16-0	1	29	.204	.290	.241	41	-12	3-0	.972	0	111	87	S33,2b15,3b6,D4/1rf	0	-0.8
Total	4	215	607	76	142	27	1	13	66	49-0	3	108	.234	.293	.346	67	-29	7-3	.928	-15	79	81	3b132,S55,2b15,D6/rf1	0	-4.0
Snow, Charlie	Charles M.; B8.3.1849 Lowell MA; D8.27.1929 Brooklyn NY; d10.1																								
1874	Atl NA	1	1	0	1	0	0	0	0	0	—	0	1.000	1.000	1.000	615	1	0-0	.000	-1	—	—	/C	—	0.0
Snow, J.T.	Jack Thomas; B2.26.1968 Long Beach CA; BL/TL (BB 1992–98)/6´2˝/(202–210); [NYA89 5/129]; d9.20; Col Arizona																								
1992	NY A	7	14	1	2	1	0	0	2	5-1	0	5	.143	.368	.214	67	0	0-0	1.000	-0	62	177	1b6/D	0	-0.1
1993	Cal A	129	419	60	101	18	2	16	57	55-4	2	88	.241	.328	.408	95	-3	3-0	.995	2	106	98	1b129	0	-1.1
1994	Cal A	61	223	22	49	4	0	8	30	19-1	3	48	.220	.289	.345	62	-14	0-1	.996	1	103	105	1b61	0	-1.7
1995	Cal A	143	544	80	157	22	1	24	102	52-4	3	91	.289	.353	.465	112	9	2-1	.997	-13	61	88	1b143	0	-1.6
1996	Cal A	155	575	69	148	20	1	17	67	56-6	5	96	.257	.327	.384	78	-20	1-6	.993	3	106	95	1b154	0	-3.0
1997	†SF N	157	531	81	149	36	1	28	104	96-13	1	124	.281	.387	.510	137	32	6-4	.995	1	104	108	1b156	0	1.9
1998	SF N	138	435	65	108	29	1	15	79	58-3	0	84	.248	.332	.423	103	3	1-2	**.999**	4	110	105	1b136	0	-0.4
1999	SF N	161	570	93	156	25	2	24	98	86-7	5	121	.274	.370	.451	115	14	0-4	.996	11	**127**	99	1b160	0	0.9
2000	†SF N	155	536	82	152	33	2	19	96	66-6	11	129	.284	.365	.459	116	15	1-3	.995	-0	98	**114**	1b153	0	0.1
2001	SF N	101	285	43	70	12	1	8	34	55-10	4	81	.246	.371	.379	102	3	0-0	.999	-0	98	120	1b92	54	-0.4
2002	†SF N	143	422	47	104	26	2	6	53	59-5	7	90	.246	.344	.360	90	-4	0-0	.993	1	105	**112**	1b135	0	-1.3
2003	†SF N	103	330	48	90	18	3	8	51	55-0	8	55	.273	.387	.418	109	7	1-2	.994	5	122	110	1b97	30	0.3
2004	SF N	107	346	62	113	32	1	12	60	58-0	7	61	.327	.429	.529	142	26	4-0	.995	-2	93	92	1b100	34	1.6
2005	SF N	117	367	40	101	17	2	4	40	32-1	7	61	.275	.343	.365	84	-8	1-0	.997	0	101	75	1b108	0	-1.6
2006	Bos A	38	44	5	9	0	0	0	4	8-0	1	8	.205	.340	.205	45	-3	0-0	.990	1	125	86	1b26/D	0	-0.4
Total	15	1715	5641	798	1509	293	19	189	877	760-61	64	1142	.268	.357	.427	105	57	20-23	.995	14	103	101	1b1656,D2	118	-6.8
Snyder, Bernie	Bernard Austin; B8.25.1913 Philadelphia PA; D4.15.1999 Havertown PA; BR/TR/6´0˝/165; d9.15																								
1935	Phi A	10	32	5	11	1	0	0	3	1	0	2	.344	.364	.375	92	0	0-0	.880	-3	66	33	2b5,S4	—	-0.3
Snyder, Charles	Charles; B Camden NJ; D3.3.1901 Philadelphia PA; BR/TR; d9.19																								
1890	Phi AA	9	33	5	9	1	0	0	4	2	0	—	.273	.314	.303	82	-1	0	.583	-4	95	0	O5(1/0/4),C5	—	-0.4
Snyder, Pop	Charles N.; B10.6.1854 Washington DC; D10.29.1924 Washington DC; BR/TR/5´11.5˝/184; d6.16; M4/U7																								
1873	Was NA	28	107	16	21	2	0	0	3	3	—	4	.196	.218	.215	30	-9	0-1	.819	-2	—	—	C28,O3C	—	-0.8
1874	Bal NA	39	151	24	33	4	0	1	17	1	—	2	.219	.224	.265	56	-7	0-0	.789	-2	—	—	C39	—	-0.7
1875	Phi NA	66	263	38	64	8	2	1	25	4	—	4	.243	.255	.300	89	-3	3-8	.825	4	—	—	C66/1	—	-0.1
1876	Lou N	56	224	21	44	4	1	1	9	2	—	7	.196	.204	.237	39	-16	—	.833	12	—	—	C55,O4(0/3/1)	—	-0.2
1877	Lou N	**61**	248	23	64	7	2	2	28	3	—	14	.258	.267	.327	73	-9	—	**.910**	15	—	—	C61/rfS	—	0.6
1878	Bos N	**60**	226	21	48	5	0	0	14	1	—	19	.212	.216	.235	44	-14	—	**.912**	7	—	—	C58,O2R	—	-0.5
1879	Bos N	81	329	42	78	16	3	2	35	5	—	31	.237	.249	.322	85	-5	—	**.925**	**25**	—	—	C80,O2R	—	2.0
1881	Bos N	62	219	14	50	8	0	0	16	3	—	23	.228	.239	.265	61	-9	—	.897	3	—	—	C60/rfS2	—	-0.5
1882	Cin AA	72	309	49	90	12	2	1	50	9	—	—	.291	.311	.353	117	5	—	.916	18	—	—	C70,1b2/rfM	—	2.5
1883	Cin AA	58	250	38	64	14	6	0	34	8	—	—	.256	.279	.360	99	-1	—	.919	13	—	—	C57,S2,M	—	1.5
1884	Cin AA	67	268	32	69	9	9	0	39	7	0	—	.257	.276	.358	101	-1	—	.922	26	—	—	C65,1b2/rfM	—	2.7
1885	Cin AA	39	152	13	36	4	3	1	19	6	1	—	.237	.270	.322	85	-3	—	.880	2	—	—	C38/1	—	0.2
1886	Cin AA	60	220	33	41	8	3	0	28	13	3	—	.186	.242	.250	52	-13	11	.874	-4	—	—	C41,1b19/cf	—	-1.3
1887	Cle AA	74	282	33	72	12	6	0	27	9	1	—	.255	.281	.340	75	-11	5	.905	16	—	—	C63,1b13	—	0.8
1888	Cle AA	64	237	22	51	7	3	0	14	6	1	—	.215	.238	.270	64	-10	9	.901	10	—	—	C58,1b4,O3R	—	0.4
1889	Cle N	22	83	5	16	3	0	0	12	2	1	12	.193	.221	.229	26	-9	4	.907	3	—	—	C22	—	-0.3
1890	Cle P	13	48	5	5	1	0	0	12	1	1	9	.188	.220	.208	16	-6	1	.958	-1	71	108	C13	—	-0.4
1891	Was AA	8	27	4	5	0	1	0	2	0	2	3	.185	.241	.259	45	-2	0	1.000	0	73	0	1b4,C3/rfM	—	-0.2
Total	3NA	133	521	78	118	14	2	2	45	8	—	10	.226	.238	.273	66	-19	3-9	.814	-0	—	—	C133,O3C/1	—	-1.6
Total	15	797	3122	355	737	110	39	7	339	75	10	118	.236	.256	.303	73	-104	30	.904	144	74	111	C744,1b45,O17(0/4/13),S4/2	—	7.3
Snyder, Chris	Christopher Ryan; B2.12.1981 Houston TX; BR/TR/6´3˝/(220–230); [AriN02 2/68]; d8.21; Col Houston																								
2004	Ari N	29	96	10	23	6	0	5	15	13-1	0	25	.240	.327	.458	95	-1	0-0	1.000	4	118	102	C29	0	0.5
2005	Ari N	115	326	24	66	14	0	6	28	40-5	4	87	.202	.297	.301	55	-21	0-1	.997	-7	119	76	C113	0	-2.2
2006	Ari N	61	184	19	51	9	0	6	32	22-4	1	39	.277	.349	.424	94	-1	0-0	.995	9	159	133	C60	0	1.1
Total	3	205	606	53	140	29	0	17	75	75-10	5	151	.231	.318	.363	73	-23	0-1	.997	6	131	97	C202	0	-0.6
Snyder, Earl	Earl Clifford; B5.6.1976 New Britain CT; BR/TR/6´0˝/(200–207); [NYN98 36/1084]; d4.28; Col Hartford																								
2002	Cle A	18	55	5	11	2	0	1	4	6-0	0	21	.200	.279	.291	51	-4	0-0	.981	0	119	31	1b12,3b2/D	0	-0.5
2004	Bos A	1	4	0	1	0	0	0	0	0-0	0	1	.250	.250	.250	29	0	0-0	1.000	1	172	0	/3	0	0.0
Total	2	19	59	5	12	2	0	1	4	6-0	0	22	.203	.277	.288	49	-4	0-0	.981	1	119	31	1b12,3b3/D	0	-0.5
Snyder, Redleg	Emanuel Sebastian (b Emanuel Sebastian Schneider); B12.12.1854 Camden NJ; D11.24.1932 Camden NJ; BR/TR/5´10˝/175; d4.25																								
1876	Cin N	55	205	10	31	3	1	0	12	1	—	19	.151	.155	.176	12	-17	—	.825	4	62	39	O55(54/0/1)	—	-1.5
1884	Wil U	**17**	52	4	10	0	0	0	—	1	—	—	.192	.208	.192	21	-7	—	.976	1	111	136	1b16/lf	—	-0.6
Total	2	72	257	14	41	3	1	0	12	2	—	19	.160	.166	.179	14	-24	—	.825	5	62	39	O56(55/0/1),1b16	—	-2.1
Snyder, Cooney	Frank C.; B1872 Toronto ON, Can.; D3.9.1917 Toronto ON, Can.; BR/6´3˝/180; d5.19																								
1898	Lou N	17	61	4	10	0	0	0	6	3	1	—	.164	.215	.164	9	-7	0	.935	-5	83	100	C17	—	-1.0
Snyder, Frank	Frank Elton "Pancho"; B5.27.1894 San Antonio TX; D1.5.1962 San Antonio TX; BR/TR/6´2˝/185; d8.25; Mil 1918; C9																								
1912	StL N	11	18	2	2	0	0	0	0	2	0	7	.111	.200	.111	-14	-3	1	.919	-1	80	122	C11	—	-0.3
1913	StL N	7	21	1	4	0	1	0	2	0	0	4	.190	.190	.286	35	-2	0	.956	0	85	126	C7	—	-0.1
1914	StL N	100	326	19	75	15	4	1	25	13	1	28	.230	.262	.310	71	-13	1	**.979**	4	104	96	C98	—	-0.1
1915	StL N	144	473	41	141	22	7	2	55	39	1	49	.298	.353	.387	124	13	3-6	.983	11	111	109	C142	—	3.8
1916	StL N	132	406	23	105	12	4	0	39	18	0	31	.259	.290	.308	84	-9	7	.973	7	83	100	C72,1b46/S	—	0.4
1917	StL N	115	313	18	74	9	2	1	33	27	2	43	.236	.301	.288	83	-6	4	.975	3	**121**	**117**	C94/2	—	0.5
1918	StL N	39	112	5	28	7	1	0	10	6	0	13	.250	.288	.330	92	-1	4	.959	-1	86	112	C27,1b3	—	0.1
1919	StL N	50	154	7	28	4	2	0	14	5	1	13	.182	.213	.234	36	-12	2	.983	4	103	143	C48/1	—	-0.5
	NY N	32	92	7	21	6	0	0	11	8	1	9	.228	.297	.293	79	-2	1	.983	-3	93	93	C31	—	-0.3
	Year	82	246	14	49	10	2	0	25	13	2	22	.199	.245	.256	53	-14	3	.983	1	99	**123**	C79/1	—	-0.8
1920	NY N	87	264	26	66	13	4	3	27	17	0	18	.250	.295	.364	89	-4	2-2	.978	4	**128**	90	C84	—	0.7
1921	†NY N	108	309	36	99	13	2	8	45	27	4	24	.320	.382	.453	120	10	3-4	.985	4	121	112	C101	—	1.9
1922	†NY N	104	318	34	109	21	5	5	51	23	0	25	.343	.387	.487	123	11	1-5	.980	2	**129**	74	C97	—	1.6

YEAR	TM LG	G	AB	R	H	2B	3B	HR	RBI	BB-IB	HP	SO	AVG	OBP	SLG	AOPS	ABR	SB-CS	FA	FR	RNG	THR	GAMES AT POSITION	DL	BFW
1923	†NY N	120	402	37	103	13	6	5	63	24	0	29	.256	.298	.356	73	-17	5-3	**.990**	7	***164***	*85*	C112	—	-0.3
1924	†NY N	118	354	37	107	18	3	5	53	30	0	43	.302	.357	.412	109	5	3-0	.987	-11	*95*	*84*	C110	—	0.1
1925	NY N	107	325	21	78	9	1	11	51	20	1	49	.240	.286	.375	70	-16	0-0	**.985**	2	*93*	*108*	C96	—	-0.8
1926	NY N	55	148	10	32	3	2	5	16	13	0	13	.216	.280	.365	73	-6	0	.981	-1	*85*	*105*	C55	—	-0.4
1927	StL N	63	194	7	50	5	0	1	30	9	0	18	.258	.291	.299	56	-12	0	.981	-0	*90*	*108*	C62	—	-0.9
Total	16	1392	4229	331	1122	170	44	47	525	281	11	416	.265	.313	.360	90	-64	37-20	.981	32	*111*	*101*	C1247,1b50/2S	—	5.4

SNYDER, JERRY Gerald George; B7.21.1929 Jenks OK; BR/TR/6´0˝/170; d5.8

YEAR	TM LG	G	AB	R	H	2B	3B	HR	RBI	BB-IB	HP	SO	AVG	OBP	SLG	AOPS	ABR	SB-CS	FA	FR	RNG	THR	GAMES AT POSITION	DL	BFW
1952	Was A	36	57	5	9	2	0	0	2	5	0	8	.158	.226	.193	18	-6	1-0	.965	2	118	117	2b19,S4	0	-0.4
1953	Was A	29	62	10	21	4	0	0	4	5	0	8	.339	.388	.403	117	2	1-1	.988	3	117	109	S17,2b4	0	0.5
1954	Was A	64	154	17	36	3	1	0	17	15	0	18	.234	.298	.266	60	-9	3-0	.978	3	107	106	S48,2b3	0	-0.1
1955	Was A	46	107	7	24	5	0	0	5	6-0	0	6	.224	.265	.271	47	-8	1-1	.977	1	108	122	2b22,S20	0	-0.5
1956	Was A	43	148	14	40	3	1	2	14	10-0	1	9	.270	.321	.345	76	-6	1-0	.968	-1	106	93	S35,2b7	112	-0.3
1957	Was A	42	93	6	14	1	0	1	4	4-0	0	9	.151	.186	.194	4	-13	0-1	.966	1	100	86	S15,2b13/3	0	-1.1
1958	Was A	6	9	1	1	0	0	0	1	1-0	0	1	.111	.200	.111	-12	-1	0-0	1.000	-1	35	59	2b2/S	0	-0.2
Total	7	266	630	60	145	18	2	3	47	46-0	1	59	.230	.283	.279	54	-41	7-3	.971	7	105	95	S140,2b70/3	112	-2.1

SNYDER, JIM James C. A.; B9.15.1847 Brooklyn NY; D12.1.1922 Rockaway Beach NY; 5´7˝/130; d5.7

YEAR	TM LG	G	AB	R	H	2B	3B	HR	RBI	BB-IB	HP	SO	AVG	OBP	SLG	AOPS	ABR	SB-CS	FA	FR	RNG	THR	GAMES AT POSITION	DL	BFW
1872	Eck NA	25	103	16	30	2	3	0	11	0	—	1	.291	.291	.369	120	4	0-2	.755	3	123	62	S24/Crf	—	0.4

SNYDER, CORY James Cory; B11.11.1962 Inglewood CA; BR/TR/6´3˝/(175–206); [CleA84 1/4]; d6.13; Col Brigham Young; OF(99/17/793)

YEAR	TM LG	G	AB	R	H	2B	3B	HR	RBI	BB-IB	HP	SO	AVG	OBP	SLG	AOPS	ABR	SB-CS	FA	FR	RNG	THR	GAMES AT POSITION	DL	BFW
1986	Cle A	103	416	58	113	21	1	24	69	16-0	0	123	.272	.299	.500	114	6	2-3	.987	-5	106	82	O74(6/0/70),S34,3b11/D	0	-0.1
1987	Cle A	157	577	74	136	24	2	33	82	31-4	1	166	.236	.273	.456	88	-13	5-1	.971	3	105	165	O139(15/0/134),S18	0	-1.4
1988	Cle A	142	511	71	139	24	3	26	75	42-7	1	101	.272	.326	.483	121	12	5-1	.985	10	105	**187**	O141(1/3/139)/D	0	1.9
1989	Cle A	132	489	49	105	17	0	18	59	23-1	2	134	.215	.251	.360	69	-22	6-5	**.997**	16	107	**184**	O125R,S7,D2	16	-1.1
1990	Cle A	123	438	46	102	27	3	14	55	21-3	2	118	.233	.268	.404	86	-10	1-4	.975	-2	96	133	O120R,S5	0	-1.7
1991	Chi A	50	117	10	22	4	0	3	11	6-1	0	41	.188	.228	.299	45	-9	0-0	.981	-1	104	65	O29(13/0/17),1b18	0	-1.2
	Tor A	21	49	4	7	0	1	0	6	3-0	0	19	.143	.189	.184	4	-7	0-0	1.000	-0	62	145	O14R,1b4,3b3,D3	0	-0.8
	Year	71	166	14	29	4	1	3	17	9-1	0	60	.175	.216	.265	33	-16	0-0	.985	-1	92	88	O43(13/0/31),1b22,3b3,D3	0	-2.0
1992	SF N	124	390	48	105	22	2	14	57	23-2	2	96	.269	.311	.444	118	7	4-4	.992	-0	93	181	O70(22/13/48),1b27,3b14,2b4,S3	0	0.4
1993	LA N	143	516	61	137	33	1	11	56	47-3	4	147	.266	.331	.397	99	0	4-1	.979	-11	81	170	O115(2/1/113),3b23,1b12,S2	0	-1.6
1994	LA N	73	153	18	36	6	0	6	18	14-4	1	47	.235	.300	.392	84	-4	1-0	.967	-2	94	50	O50(40/0/13),1b9,3b6,S4,2b3	11	-0.6
Total	9	1068	3656	439	902	178	13	149	488	226-25	13	992	.247	.291	.425	95	-40	28-19	.983	7	99	155	O877R,S73,1b70,3b57,2b7,D7	27	-6.2

SNYDER, JIM James Robert; B8.15.1932 Dearborn MI; BR/TR/6´1˝/185; d9.15; M1/C4; Col Eastern Michigan

YEAR	TM LG	G	AB	R	H	2B	3B	HR	RBI	BB-IB	HP	SO	AVG	OBP	SLG	AOPS	ABR	SB-CS	FA	FR	RNG	THR	GAMES AT POSITION	DL	BFW
1961	Min A	3	5	0	0	0	0	0	0	0-0	0	1	.000	.000	.000	-95	-1	0-0	1.000	-0	79	97	2b3	0	-0.1
1962	Min A	12	10	1	1	0	0	0	1	0-0	0	0	.100	.100	.100	-44	-2	0-1	.941	0	96	152	2b5/1	0	-0.2
1964	Min A	26	71	3	11	2	0	1	9	4-0	1	11	.155	.208	.225	21	-8	0-0	.990	-4	84	109	2b25	0	-1.0
Total	3	41	86	4	12	2	0	1	10	4-0	1	12	.140	.185	.198	6	-11	0-1	.984	-4	85	113	2b33/1	0	-1.3

SNYDER, JACK John William; B10.6.1886 Lincoln PA; D12.13.1981 Brownsville PA; BR/TR/5´9˝/168; d6.13

YEAR	TM LG	G	AB	R	H	2B	3B	HR	RBI	BB-IB	HP	SO	AVG	OBP	SLG	AOPS	ABR	SB-CS	FA	FR	RNG	THR	GAMES AT POSITION	DL	BFW
1914	Buf F	1	0	0	0	0	0	0	0	1	0	0	ø	1.000	ø	183	0	0	ø	-0	*0*	*0*	/C	—	0.0
1917	Bro N	7	11	1	3	0	0	0	1	0	0	2	.273	.273	.273	66	0	0	1.000	0	*114*	*113*	C5	—	0.0
Total	2	8	11	1	3	0	0	0	1	1	0	2	.273	.333	.273	84	0	0	1.000	0	*109*	*108*	C6	—	0.0

SNYDER, JOSH Joshua M.; B3.1844 Brooklyn NY; D4.21.1881 Brooklyn NY; d5.18

YEAR	TM LG	G	AB	R	H	2B	3B	HR	RBI	BB-IB	HP	SO	AVG	OBP	SLG	AOPS	ABR	SB-CS	FA	FR	RNG	THR	GAMES AT POSITION	DL	BFW
1872	Eck NA	9	37	4	6	2	0	0	1	1	—	3	.162	.184	.216	27	-2	0-0	.788	2	291	0	O9L	—	0.0

SNYDER, RUSS Russell Henry; B6.22.1934 Oak NE; BL/TR/6´1˝/(189–195); d4.18

YEAR	TM LG	G	AB	R	H	2B	3B	HR	RBI	BB-IB	HP	SO	AVG	OBP	SLG	AOPS	ABR	SB-CS	FA	FR	RNG	THR	GAMES AT POSITION	DL	BFW
1959	KC A	73	243	41	76	13	2	3	21	19-0	2	29	.313	.367	.420	113	5	6-2	.986	5	101	243	O64(27/30/12)	0	0.8
1960	KC A	125	304	45	79	10	5	4	26	20-1	1	28	.260	.306	.365	81	-9	7-3	.986	-2	96	87	O91(21/16/62)	0	-1.4
1961	Bal A	115	312	46	91	13	5	1	13	20-0	0	32	.292	.333	.375	92	-4	5-3	.966	-2	101	53	O108(75/28/22)	0	-1.0
1962	Bal A	139	416	47	127	19	4	9	40	17-0	2	46	.305	.335	.435	113	5	7-4	.974	4	105	146	O121(43/41/45)	0	0.4
1963	Bal A	148	429	51	110	21	2	7	36	40-1	2	48	.256	.321	.364	95	-2	18-5	.988	0	106	71	O130(32/74/57)	0	-0.5
1964	Bal A	56	93	11	27	3	0	1	7	11-1	0	22	.290	.362	.355	102	1	0-2	.971	-3	80	0	O40(31/8/3)	76	-0.4
1965	Bal A	132	345	49	93	11	2	1	29	27-1	1	38	.270	.323	.322	83	-8	3-4	1.000	5	114	82	O106(36/36/52)	0	-0.9
1966	†Bal A	117	373	66	114	21	5	3	41	38-1	0	37	.306	.368	.413	127	14	2-1	.986	3	108	106	O104(59/86/4)	0	1.4
1967	Bal A	108	275	40	65	8	2	4	23	32-0	1	48	.236	.314	.324	91	-3	5-2	.985	-0	103	73	O69(24/25/27)	0	-0.7
1968	Chi A	38	82	2	11	2	0	1	5	4-1	0	16	.134	.172	.195	12	-9	0-0	1.000	-3	71	0	O22(9/1/16)	0	-1.5
	Cle A	68	217	30	61	8	2	2	23	25-0	0	21	.281	.354	.364	120	6	1-1	.991	5	121	142	O54(5/11/43)/1	0	0.8
	Year	106	299	32	72	10	2	3	28	29-1	0	37	.241	.306	.318	90	-3	1-1	.992	2	108	106	O76(14/12/59)/1	0	-0.7
1969	Cle A	122	266	26	66	10	0	2	24	25-3	0	33	.248	.312	.308	72	-10	3-2	.961	2	120	46	O84(37/28/21)	0	-1.1
1970	Mil A	124	276	34	64	11	0	4	31	16-1	0	40	.232	.270	.315	62	-15	1-3	.966	-3	99	23	O106(43/40/26)	0	-2.3
Total	12	1365	3631	488	984	150	29	42	319	294-10	9	438	.271	.325	.363	94	-29	58-32	.981	13	105	91	O1099(442/424/390)/1	76	-6.4

SOCKALEXIS, CHIEF Louis Francis; B10.24.1871 Old Town ME; D12.24.1913 Burlington ME; BL/TR/5´11˝/185; d4.22; Col Holy Cross

YEAR	TM LG	G	AB	R	H	2B	3B	HR	RBI	BB-IB	HP	SO	AVG	OBP	SLG	AOPS	ABR	SB-CS	FA	FR	RNG	THR	GAMES AT POSITION	DL	BFW
1897	Cle N	66	278	43	94	9	8	3	42	18	3	—	.338	.385	.460	116	5	16	.888	-0	103	173	O66(0/1/66)	—	0.1
1898	Cle N	21	67	11	15	2	0	0	10	1	1	—	.224	.246	.254	44	-5	0	.964	3	299	693	O16(4/4/8)	—	-0.3
1899	Cle N	7	22	0	6	1	0	0	3	1	0	—	.273	.304	.318	76	-1	0	.818	0	229	323	O5R	—	-0.1
Total	3	94	367	54	115	12	8	3	55	20	4	—	.313	.355	.414	103	-1	16	.896	3	143	267	O87(4/5/79)	—	-0.3

SODD, BILL William; B9.18.1914 Ft.Worth TX; D5.14.1998 Fort Worth TX; BR/TR/6´2˝/210; d9.27; Col Texas A&M

YEAR	TM LG	G	AB	R	H	2B	3B	HR	RBI	BB-IB	HP	SO	AVG	OBP	SLG	AOPS	ABR	SB-CS	FA	FR	RNG	THR	GAMES AT POSITION	DL	BFW
1937	Cle A	1	1	0	0	0	0	0	0	0	0	1	.000	.000	.000	-99	0	0-0	ø	0	—	—	/H	—	0.0

SODERHOLM, ERIC Eric Thane; B9.24.1948 Cortland NY; BR/TR/5´11˝/(187–202); [MinA68*S1/1]; d9.3; Col South Georgia JC; [DL 1976 Min A 179, 1981 NY A 180]

YEAR	TM LG	G	AB	R	H	2B	3B	HR	RBI	BB-IB	HP	SO	AVG	OBP	SLG	AOPS	ABR	SB-CS	FA	FR	RNG	THR	GAMES AT POSITION	DL	BFW
1971	Min A	21	64	9	10	4	0	1	4	10-1	3	17	.156	.299	.266	59	-3	0-1	.942	2	112	47	3b20	0	-0.2
1972	Min A	93	287	28	54	10	0	13	39	19-2	3	48	.188	.245	.359	75	-10	3-3	.942	1	104	116	3b79	0	-1.1
1973	Min A	35	111	22	33	7	2	1	9	21-0	1	16	.297	.414	.423	130	6	1-2	.921	2	110	86	3b33/S	0	0.7
1974	Min A	141	464	63	128	18	3	10	51	48-1	5	68	.276	.349	.392	110	7	7-3	.956	4	101	68	3b130/S	0	1.1
1975	Min A	117	419	62	120	17	2	11	58	53-1	0	66	.286	.365	.415	119	12	3-5	.969	15	114	61	3b113,D3	39	2.5
1977	Chi A	130	460	77	129	20	3	25	67	47-5	4	47	.280	.350	.500	129	18	2-4	**.978**	-1	98	73	3b126,D3	0	1.4
1978	Chi A	143	457	57	118	17	1	20	67	39-2	4	44	.258	.318	.431	109	4	2-2	.964	5	96	73	3b128,D11/2	0	0.6
1979	Chi A	56	210	31	53	8	2	6	34	19-1	0	19	.252	.313	.395	90	-4	0-1	.986	13	118	109	3b56	0	0.8
	Tex A	63	147	15	40	6	0	4	19	12-0	1	9	.272	.325	.395	96	-1	0-0	.944	0	99	116	3b37,D14,1b2	0	-0.2
	Year	119	357	46	93	14	2	10	53	31-1	1	28	.261	.318	.395	92	-4	0-1	.975	13	112	111	3b93,D14,1b2	0	0.6
1980	†NY A	95	275	38	79	13	1	11	35	27-2	1	25	.287	.353	.462	123	9	0-0	.952	-1	100	71	D51,3b37	0	0.6
Total	9	894	2894	402	764	120	14	102	383	295-15	22	359	.264	.335	.421	110	38	18-21	.962	39	104	79	3b759,D82,1b2,S2/2	398	6.2

SOFIELD, RICK Richard Michael; B12.16.1956 Cheyenne WY; BL/TR/6´1˝/193; [MinA75 1/13]; d4.6

YEAR	TM LG	G	AB	R	H	2B	3B	HR	RBI	BB-IB	HP	SO	AVG	OBP	SLG	AOPS	ABR	SB-CS	FA	FR	RNG	THR	GAMES AT POSITION	DL	BFW
1979	Min A	35	93	8	28	5	0	0	12	12-0	0	27	.301	.381	.355	96	0	2-3	.954	-1	99	48	O35(7/6/22)	0	-0.3
1980	Min A	131	417	52	103	18	4	9	49	24-2	2	92	.247	.287	.374	75	-15	4-5	.979	-2	100	84	O126(74/49/9),D2	0	-2.1
1981	Min A	41	102	9	18	2	0	0	5	8-0	0	22	.176	.234	.196	24	-10	3-2	.983	1	85	242	O34(33/0/1)	0	-1.1
Total	3	207	612	69	149	25	4	9	66	44-2	2	141	.243	.293	.342	71	-25	9-10	.975	-2	97	105	O195(114/55/32),D2	0	-3.5

SOJO, LUIS Luis Beltran (Sojo); B1.3.1965 Caracas, Distrito Capital, Venez.; BR/TR/5´11˝/(165–185); d7.14; C2

YEAR	TM LG	G	AB	R	H	2B	3B	HR	RBI	BB-IB	HP	SO	AVG	OBP	SLG	AOPS	ABR	SB-CS	FA	FR	RNG	THR	GAMES AT POSITION	DL	BFW
1990	Tor A	33	80	14	18	3	0	1	9	5-0	0	5	.225	.271	.300	58	-5	1-1	.969	-4	62	57	2b15,S5,O5L,3b4,D3	0	-0.9
1991	Cal A	113	364	38	94	14	1	3	20	14-0	5	26	.258	.295	.327	72	-15	4-2	.981	**27**	115	118	2b107,S2/3lfD	0	1.5
1992	Cal A	106	368	37	100	12	3	7	43	14-0	1	24	.272	.299	.378	88	-8	7-11	.985	14	112	121	2b96,3b9,S5	0	0.7
1993	Tor A	19	47	5	8	2	0	0	6	4-0	0	2	.170	.231	.213	21	-5	0-0	1.000	-0	81	67	2b8,S8,3b3	20	-0.5
1994	Sea A	63	213	32	59	9	2	6	22	8-0	2	25	.277	.308	.423	84	-6	2-1	.973	18	117	97	2b40,S24/3D	0	1.4
1995	†Sea A	102	339	50	98	18	2	7	39	23-0	1	19	.289	.335	.416	93	-4	4-2	.983	-14	82	70	S80,2b19,O6L	16	-1.1
1996	Sea A	77	247	20	52	8	1	1	16	10-0	1	13	.211	.244	.263	28	-28	2-2	.940	5	113	147	3b33,2b27,S19	0	-2.0
	†NY A	18	40	3	11	2	0	0	5	1-0	0	4	.275	.286	.325	56	-3	0-0	1.000	3	127	147	2b14,S4/3	0	0.0
	Year	95	287	23	63	10	1	1	21	11-0	1	17	.220	.250	.272	32	-31	2-2	.986	7	104	111	2b41,3b34,S23	0	-2.0
1997	NY A	77	215	27	66	6	1	2	25	16-0	1	14	.307	.355	.372	92	-3	3-1	.982	4	101	104	2b72,S4,3b3,1b2	45	0.5
1998	†NY A	54	147	16	34	3	1	0	14	4-0	0	15	.231	.250	.265	36	-14	1-0	.973	0	91	132	S20,1b19,2b8,3b6,D2	27	-1.3

YEAR	TM LG	G	AB	R	H	2B	3B	HR	RBI	BB-IB	HP	SO	AVG	OBP	SLG	AOPS	ABR	SB-CS	FA	FR	RNG	THR	GAMES AT POSITION	DL	BFW
1999	†NY A	49	127	20	32	6	0	2	16	4-0	0	17	.252	.275	.346	58	-8	1-0	.974	1	71	108	3b20,2b16,S6,1b4,D2	0	-0.6
2000	Pit N	61	176	14	50	11	0	5	20	11-3	1	16	.284	.328	.432	90	-3	1-0	.960	4	120	58	3b50/2	21	0.1
	†NY A	34	125	19	36	7	1	2	17	6-0	0	6	.288	.321	.408	84	-3	1-0	.989	-3	100	51	2b25,3b10,1b7,S2	0	-0.4
2001	†NY A	39	79	5	13	2	0	0	9	4-0	1	12	.165	.214	.190	8	-11	1-0	.933	-0	100	119	3b17,1b8,2b7,S5/D	0	-1.0
2003	NY A	3	4	0	0	0	0	0	0	0-0	0	0	.000	.000	.000	-99	-1	0-0	ø	-0	0	0	/12D	0	-0.1
Total	13	848	2571	300	671	103	12	36	261	124-3	13	198	.261	.297	.352	71	-117	28-20	.982	53	108	106	2b456,S184,3b158,1b41,D12,O12L	129	-3.7
Solaita, Tony	Tolia; B1.15.1947 Nuuuli, American Samoa; D2.10.1990 Tafuna, American Samoa; BL/TL/6´0˝/(210–215); d9.16																								
1968	NY A	1	1	0	0	0	0	0	0	0-0	0	1	.000	.000	.000	-99	0	0-0	1.000	-0	0	407	/1	0	0.0
1974	KC A	96	239	31	64	12	0	7	30	35-5	1	70	.268	.361	.406	115	6	0-3	.991	1	113	72	1b65,D14/rf	0	0.1
1975	KC A	93	231	35	60	11	0	16	44	39-1	2	79	.260	.369	.515	145	14	0-1	.994	3	130	99	D37,1b35	0	1.4
1976	KC A	31	68	4	16	4	0	0	9	6-0	0	17	.235	.286	.294	73	-2	0-0	.974	0	126	38	D14,1b5	0	-0.3
	Cal A	63	215	25	58	9	0	9	33	34-3	0	44	.270	.367	.437	144	13	1-1	.998	8	147	76	1b54,D7	0	1.8
	Year	94	283	29	74	13	0	9	42	40-3	0	61	.261	.348	.403	126	10	1-1	.996	8	146	74	1b59,D21	0	1.5
1977	Cal A	116	324	40	78	15	0	14	53	56-6	0	77	.241	.349	.417	113	7	1-3	.990	3	108	77	1b91,D6	0	0.4
1978	Cal A	60	94	10	21	3	0	1	14	16-3	0	25	.223	.336	.287	79	-2	0-0	1.000	1	127	106	D18,1b11	0	-0.2
1979	Mon N	29	42	5	12	4	0	1	7	11-0	0	16	.286	.434	.452	142	3	0-0	.989	0	108	100	1b13	0	0.3
	Tor A	36	102	14	27	8	1	2	13	17-0	0	16	.265	.364	.422	112	2	0-0	1.000	0	133	195	D26,1b6	0	0.2
Total	7	525	1316	164	336	66	1	50	203	214-18	3	345	.255	.357	.421	120	41	2-8	.993	16	122	82	1b281,D122/rf	0	3.7
Solomon, Mose	Mose Hirsch "The Rabbi of Swat"; B12.8.1900 New York NY; D6.25.1966 Miami FL; BL/TL/5´9.5˝/180; d9.30																								
1923	NY N	2	8	0	3	1	0	0	1	0	0	1	.375	.375	.500	131	0	0-0	.833	-1	70	0	O2R	—	-0.1
Solters, Moose	Julius Joseph (b Julius Joseph Soltesz); B3.22.1906 Pittsburgh PA; D9.28.1975 Pittsburgh PA; BR/TR/6´0˝/190; d4.17																								
1934	Bos A	101	365	61	109	25	4	7	58	18	1	50	.299	.333	.447	93	-5	9-4	.933	-1	94	155	O89(6/57/26)	—	-0.9
1935	Bos A	24	79	15	19	6	1	0	8	2	1	7	.241	.268	.342	53	-6	1-1	.966	2	120	108	O21(10/0/11)	—	-0.5
	StL A	127	552	79	182	39	6	18	104	34	0	35	.330	.369	.520	122	16	10-1	.989	12	107	158	O127(116/12/0)	—	2.0
	Year	151	631	94	201	45	7	18	112	36	1	42	.319	.356	.498	113	10	11-2	.985	13	109	151	O148(126/12/11)	—	1.5
1936	StL A	152	628	100	183	45	7	17	134	41	1	76	.291	.336	.467	93	-10	3-0	.956	13	**118**	125	O147(145/6/0)	—	-0.4
1937	Cle A	152	589	90	190	42	11	20	109	42	4	56	.323	.372	.533	125	20	6-9	.953	2	93	171	O149L	—	1.0
1938	Cle A	67	199	30	40	6	3	2	22	13	0	28	.201	.250	.291	36	-21	4-1	.969	2	104	126	O46(40/0/6)	—	-2.0
1939	Cle A	41	102	19	28	7	2	2	19	9	0	15	.275	.333	.441	100	0	2-1	.915	-2	93	67	O25(17/0/8)	—	-0.3
	StL A	40	131	14	27	6	1	0	14	10	0	20	.206	.262	.267	35	-13	1-0	.935	-1	101	89	O30(22/1/7)	—	-1.4
	Year	81	233	33	55	13	3	2	33	19	0	35	.236	.294	.343	63	-14	3-1	.927	-2	98	80	O55(39/1/15)	—	-1.7
1940	Chi A	116	428	65	132	28	3	12	80	27	1	54	.308	.351	.472	110	5	3-3	.971	6	**115**	77	O107L	—	0.5
1941	Chi A	76	251	24	65	9	4	4	43	18	1	31	.259	.311	.375	82	-8	3-2	.966	-0	95	123	O63(62/0/1)	0	-1.2
1943	Chi A	42	97	6	15	0	0	1	8	7	0	5	.155	.212	.186	17	-11	0-1	.941	-1	81	152	O21(13/0/8)	0	-1.4
Total	9	938	3421	503	990	213	42	83	599	221	9	377	.289	.334	.449	96	-33	42-23	.960	31	104	133	O825(687/76/67)	0	-4.6
Somerlott, Jock	John Wesley; B10.26.1882 Flint IN; D4.21.1965 Butler IN; BR/TR/6´0˝/160; d9.19																								
1910	Was A	16	63	6	14	0	0	0	2	3	0	—	.222	.258	.222	53	-4	2	.994	0	91	59	1b16	—	-0.4
1911	Was A	13	40	2	7	0	0	0	2	0	1	—	.175	.195	.175	4	-5	2	.992	2	140	135	1b12	—	-0.4
Total	2	29	103	8	21	0	0	0	4	3	1	—	.204	.234	.204	32	-9	4	.993	2	111	91	1b28	—	-0.8
Somerville, Ed	Edward G.; B3.1.1853 Philadelphia PA; D10.1.1877 London ON, Can.; BR/TR/5´7˝/158; d4.21																								
1875	Cen NA	**14**	57	6	13	3	0	0	6	1	—	3	.228	.241	.281	88	0	1-0	.771	-6	84	34	2b14/S	—	-0.6
	NH NA	33	136	14	29	5	0	0	7	1	—	3	.213	.219	.250	72	-2	1-2	.802	13	139	123	2b29,3b2/1S	—	0.7
	Year	47	193	20	42	8	0	0	13	2	—	6	.218	.226	.259	77	-2	2-2	.794	7	121	94	2b43,S2,3b2/1	—	0.1
1876	Lou N	64	256	29	48	5	1	0	14	1	—	6	.188	.191	.215	30	-20	—	.870	**28**	**131**	115	2b64	—	0.9
Sommer, Joe	Joseph John; B11.20.1858 Covington KY; D1.16.1938 Cincinnati OH; BR/TR; d7.8; OF(567/15/132); ▲																								
1880	Cin N	24	88	10	16	1	0	0	6	0	—	2	.182	.182	.193	28	-7	—	.913	1	88	110	O22(14/8/0)/S3C	—	-0.7
1882	Cin AA	**80**	354	82	102	12	6	1	29	24	—	—	.288	.333	.364	128	10	—	**.925**	3	47	121	O80L	—	1.0
1883	Cin AA	97	413	79	115	5	7	3	52	20	—	—	.278	.312	.346	106	1	—	.854	-3	58	53	O94(82/0/12),3b3/P	—	-0.3
1884	Bal AA	107	479	96	129	11	10	4	—	8	8	—	.269	.293	.359	107	2	—	.841	3	94	95	3b97,O9(0/2/7)/2	—	0.6
1885	Bal AA	**110**	471	84	118	23	6	1	44	24	3	—	.251	.291	.331	98	0	—	.920	12	77	54	O107(105/2/0),S2,3b2,P2/1	—	0.8
1886	Bal AA	**139**	560	79	117	18	4	1	52	24	3	—	.209	.245	.261	60	-26	31	.900	7	73	131	O95L,2b32,3b11,S3/P	—	-1.8
1887	Bal AA	131	463	88	123	11	5	0	65	63	4	—	.266	.358	.311	93	0	29	.902	-3	81	102	O110L,2b13,3b10,S2/P	—	-0.4
1888	Bal AA	79	297	31	65	10	0	0	35	18	1	—	.219	.266	.253	68	-10	13	.871	-2	106	65	O44(30/0/14),S34,2b2/1	—	-1.1
1889	Bal AA	106	386	51	85	13	2	1	36	42	1	49	.220	.298	.272	62	-19	18	.929	9	119	157	O105(4/3/99)/S	—	-0.9
1890	Cle N	9	35	4	8	1	0	0	0	2	0	2	.229	.270	.257	55	-2	0	.789	-2	0	0	O9L/P	—	-0.3
	Bal AA	**38**	129	13	33	4	2	0	23	13	0	—	.256	.324	.318	85	-3	10	.892	2	80	221	O38L	—	-0.2
Total	10	920	3675	617	911	109	42	11	<u>342</u>	238	20	<u>53</u>	.248	.297	.309	88	-54	101	.901	27	83	108	O713L,3b124,2b48,S43,P6,1b2/C	—	-3.3
Sommers, Pete	Joseph Andrews; B10.26.1866 Cleveland OH; D7.22.1908 Cleveland OH; BR/TR/5´11.5˝/181; d4.27																								
1887	NY AA	33	116	9	21	3	0	1	12	7	1	—	.181	.234	.233	32	-11	6	.830	-7	—	—	C31/rf1	—	-1.3
1888	Bos N	4	13	1	3	1	0	0	0	0	0	3	.231	.231	.308	69	0	0	.880	-1	—	—	C4	—	-0.1
1889	Chi N	12	45	5	10	5	0	0	8	2	1	8	.222	.271	.333	64	-2	0	.836	-4	—	—	C11/rf	—	-0.5
	Ind N	23	84	12	21	2	2	2	14	1	1	16	.250	.267	.393	81	-3	2	.905	-4	—	—	C21,O2C	—	-0.4
	Year	35	129	17	31	7	2	2	22	3	2	24	.240	.269	.372	75	-5	2	.882	-8	*0*	*0*	C32,O3(0/2/1)	—	-0.9
1890	NY N	17	47	4	5	1	1	0	1	4	1	13	.106	.192	.170	6	-6	0	.837	-1	*98*	*148*	C11,1b5,O2R	—	-0.5
	Cle N	9	34	4	7	1	1	0	1	2	0	3	.206	.250	.294	60	-2	0	.906	1	*119*	*117*	C8/cf	—	0.0
	Year	26	81	8	12	2	2	0	2	6	1	16	.148	.216	.222	28	-8	0	.865	1	*108*	*133*	C19,1b5,O3(0/1/2)	—	-0.5
Total	4	98	339	35	67	13	4	3	36	16	4	<u>43</u>	.198	.242	.286	49	-24	8	.860	-15	*<u>108</u>*	*<u>133</u>*	C86,O7(0/3/4),1b6	—	-2.8
Sommers, Bill	William Dunn; B2.17.1923 Brooklyn NY; D9.22.2000 Palm City FL; BR/TR/6´0˝/180; d4.25																								
1950	StL A	65	137	24	35	5	1	0	14	25	0	14	.255	.370	.307	72	-5	0-1	.917	-7	95	76	3b37,2b21	0	-1.1
Sorensen, Zach	Zach Hart; B1.3.1977 Salt Lake City UT; BB/TR/6´0˝/190; [CleA98 2/63]; d6.3; Col Wichita St.																								
2003	Cle A	36	37	2	5	1	0	1	2	7-0	0	13	.135	.273	.243	38	-3	0-3	.944	-1	90	96	2b14,S3/3lfD	0	-0.5
2005	LA A	12	12	3	2	1	0	0	0	0-0	0	2	.167	.167	.250	9	-2	0-0	1.000	-1	61	59	2b5/3	0	-0.2
Total	2	48	49	5	7	2	0	1	2	7-0	0	15	.143	.250	.245	32	-5	0-3	.955	-3	83	87	2b19,S3,3b2/Dlf	0	-0.7
Soriano, Alfonso	Alfonso Guilleard; B1.7.1976 San Pedro de Macoris, D.R.; BR/TR/6´1˝/(160–180); d9.14																								
1999	NY A	9	8	2	1	0	0	1	1	0-0	0	3	.125	.125	.500	50	-1	0-1	.500	-1	37	166	/SD	0	-0.2
2000	NY A	22	50	5	9	3	0	2	3	1-0	0	15	.180	.196	.360	37	-5	2-0	.846	-6	77	153	3b10,S9/2D	0	-0.9
2001	†NY A	158	574	77	154	34	3	18	73	29-0	3	125	.268	.304	.432	91	-9	43-14	.973	-12	84	99	2b156,D2	0	-0.8
2002	†NY A★	156	696	**128**	**209**	51	2	39	102	23-1	14	157	.300	.332	.547	130	28	**41**-13	.968	-13	92	90	2b155/D	0	2.6
2003	†NY A★	156	682	114	198	36	5	38	91	38-7	12	130	.290	.338	.525	125	22	35-8	.975	3	100	91	2b155	0	3.5
2004	Tex A★	145	608	77	170	32	4	28	91	33-4	10	121	.280	.324	.484	103	1	18-5	.969	7	102	109	2b142,D3	0	1.6
2005	Tex A★	156	637	102	171	43	2	36	104	33-3	7	125	.268	.309	.512	111	8	30-2	.972	-11	100	90	2b153,D2	0	1.1
2006	Was N★	159	647	119	179	41	2	46	95	67-16	9	160	.277	.351	.560	135	32	41-17	.969	16	104	**256**	O158L	0	4.3
Total	8	961	3902	624	1091	240	18	208	560	224-31	55	836	.280	.325	.510	115	76	210-60	.971	-16	95	96	2b762,O158L,D15,3b10,S10	0	11.2
Sorrell, Bill	William; B10.14.1940 Morehead KY; BL/TR/6´0˝/(180–190); d9.2																								
1965	Phi N	10	13	2	5	0	0	1	2	2-0	0	1	.385	.467	.615	206	2	0-0	ø	-1	0	0	/3	0	0.1
1967	SF N	18	17	1	3	1	0	0	1	3-0	0	2	.176	.300	.235	56	-1	0-0	1.000	-1	28	0	O5L	0	-0.2
1970	KC A	57	135	12	36	2	0	4	14	10-4	0	13	.267	.317	.370	89	-2	1-0	.873	-6	87	57	3b29,O4(2/0/2),1b3	0	-0.9
Total	3	85	165	15	44	3	0	5	17	15-4	0	16	.267	.328	.376	95	-1	1-0	.873	-8	82	54	3b30,O9(7/0/2),1b3	0	-1.0
Sorrells, Chick	Raymond Edwin; B7.31.1896 Stringtown OK; D7.20.1983 Terrell TX; BR/TR/5´9˝/155; d9.18; Col St. Edwards																								
1922	Cle A	2	1	0	0	0	0	0	0	0	0	0	.000	.000	.000	-99	0	0-0	1.000	0	205	0	/S	—	0.0

SORRENTO, PAUL Paul Anthony; B11.17.1965 Somerville MA; BL/TR/6´2˝/(210–223); [CalA86 4/103]; d9.8; Col Florida St.

YEAR	TM LG	G	AB	R	H	2B	3B	HR	RBI	BB-IB	HP	SO	AVG	OBP	SLG	AOPS	ABR	SB-CS	FA	FR	RNG	THR	GAMES AT POSITION	DL	BFW
1989	Min A	14	21	2	5	0	0	0	1	5-1	0	4	.238	.370	.238	74	0	0-0	1.000	-0	0	82	1b5,D5	0	-0.1
1990	Min A	41	121	11	25	4	1	5	13	12-0	1	31	.207	.281	.380	79	-4	1-1	.992	-1	71	109	D23,1b15	0	-0.7
1991	†Min A	26	47	6	12	2	0	4	13	4-2	0	11	.255	.314	.553	129	2	0-0	1.000	1	119	106	1b13,D2	0	0.1
1992	Cle A	140	458	52	123	24	1	18	60	51-7	1	89	.269	.341	.443	120	12	0-3	.993	-2	96	107	1b121,D11	0	0.1
1993	Cle A	148	463	75	119	26	1	18	65	58-11	2	121	.257	.340	.434	107	5	3-1	.995	-1	98	95	1b144,O3R/D	0	-0.7
1994	Cle A	95	322	43	90	14	0	14	62	34-6	0	68	.280	.345	.453	104	1	0-1	.995	-1	95	104	1b86,D8	0	-0.7
1995	†Cle A	104	323	50	76	14	0	25	79	51-6	0	71	.235	.336	.511	115	6	1-1	.992	-4	88	128	1b91,D11	0	-0.5
1996	Sea A	143	471	67	136	32	1	23	93	57-10	7	103	.289	.370	.507	119	15	0-2	.990	-0	100	100	1b138	0	0.2
1997	†Sea A	146	457	68	123	19	0	31	80	51-9	3	112	.269	.345	.514	121	13	0-2	.996	8	120	86	1b139/D	0	0.9
1998	TB A	137	435	40	98	27	0	17	57	54-1	3	133	.225	.313	.405	83	-11	2-3	1.000	3	138	102	D86,1b27,O18(4/0/14)	0	-1.5
1999	TB A	99	294	40	69	14	1	11	42	49-1	4	101	.235	.351	.401	90	-4	1-1	.957	-5	89	63	O57L,1b27,D9	15	-1.2
Total	11	1093	3412	454	876	176	5	166	565	426-54	21	844	.257	.340	.457	107	35	8-15	.994	-2	100	102	1b806,D157,O78(61/0/17)	15	-4.1

SOSA, JUAN Juan Luis (Encarnacion); B8.19.1975 San Francisco de Macoris, D.R.; BR/TR/6´1˝/175; d9.10

YEAR	TM LG	G	AB	R	H	2B	3B	HR	RBI	BB-IB	HP	SO	AVG	OBP	SLG	AOPS	ABR	SB-CS	FA	FR	RNG	THR	GAMES AT POSITION	DL	BFW
1999	Col N	11	9	3	2	0	0	0	0	2-0	0	2	.222	.364	.222	42	-1	0-0	1.000	0	81	0	O6(1/5/0),S2	0	0.0
2001	Ari N	2	1	0	0	0	0	0	0	0-0	0	1	.000	.000	.000	-94	0	0-0	1.000	0	454	0	/3	0	0.0
Total	2	13	10	3	2	0	0	0	0	2-0	0	3	.200	.333	.200	32	-1	0-0	1.000	1	81	0	O6(1/5/0),S2/3	0	0.0

SOSA, SAMMY Samuel Peralta "Slammin' Sammy"; B11.12.1968 San Pedro de Macoris, D.R.; BR/TR/6´0˝/(165–230); d6.16

YEAR	TM LG	G	AB	R	H	2B	3B	HR	RBI	BB-IB	HP	SO	AVG	OBP	SLG	AOPS	ABR	SB-CS	FA	FR	RNG	THR	GAMES AT POSITION	DL	BFW
1989	Tex A	25	84	8	20	3	0	1	3	0-0	0	20	.238	.238	.310	52	-6	0-2	.944	-1	96	116	O19(12/8/1),D6	0	-0.7
	Chi A	33	99	19	27	5	0	3	10	11-2	2	27	.273	.351	.414	119	3	7-3	.969	-4	81	55	O33(1/25/9)	0	-0.1
	Year	58	183	27	47	8	0	4	13	11-2	2	47	.257	.303	.366	89	-3	7-5	.960	-4	86	77	O52(13/33/10),D6	0	-0.8
1990	Chi A	153	532	72	124	26	10	15	70	33-4	6	150	.233	.282	.404	93	-8	32-16	.962	4	106	133	O152(0/1/152)	0	-0.7
1991	Chi A	116	316	39	64	10	1	10	33	14-2	2	98	.203	.240	.335	59	-19	13-6	.973	3	110	92	O111(0/13/102),D2	0	-1.8
1992	Chi N	67	262	41	68	7	2	8	25	19-1	4	63	.260	.317	.393	98	-1	15-7	.961	-8	83	105	O67C	84	-0.9
1993	Chi N	159	598	92	156	25	5	33	93	38-6	4	135	.261	.309	.485	110	5	36-11	.976	3	97	160	O158(0/70/114)	0	0.7
1994	Chi N	105	426	59	128	17	6	25	70	25-1	2	92	.300	.339	.545	126	14	22-13	.973	3	114	63	O105(0/15/98)	0	1.2
1995	Chi N★	**144**	564	89	151	17	3	36	119	58-11	5	134	.268	.340	.500	119	13	34-7	.962	8	113	121	O143R	0	1.9
1996	Chi N	124	498	84	136	21	2	40	100	34-6	5	134	.273	.323	.564	125	14	18-5	.964	6	105	174	O124R	40	1.6
1997	Chi N	**162**	642	90	161	31	4	36	119	45-9	2	174	.251	.300	.480	97	-6	22-12	.977	7	108	134	O161R	0	-0.6
1998	†Chi N✳	159	643	**134**	198	20	0	66	**158**	73-14	1	171	.308	.377	.647	158	51	18-9	.975	7	110	130	O159(0/7/156)	0	5.0
1999	Chi N★	**162**	625	114	180	24	2	63	141	78-8	3	171	.288	.367	.635	148	43	7-8	.978	9	118	75	O162(0/25/146)	0	4.1
2000	Chi N★	156	604	106	193	38	1	**50**	138	91-19	2	168	.320	.406	.634	161	57	7-4	.970	-6	100	30	O156(0/2/156)	0	4.1
2001	Chi N★	160	577	**146**	189	34	5	64	**160**	116-**37**	6	153	.328	.437	.737	204	94	0-2	.982	6	112	82	O160R	0	8.6
2002	Chi N★	150	556	**122**	160	19	2	**49**	108	103-15	3	144	.288	.399	.594	158	48	2-0	.980	2	108	77	O150R	0	4.3
2003	†Chi N	137	517	99	144	22	0	40	103	62-9	5	143	.279	.358	.553	131	23	0-1	.977	-10	90	25	O137R	20	0.5
2004	Chi N★	126	478	69	121	21	0	35	80	56-4	2	133	.253	.332	.517	112	7	0-0	.984	1	105	67	O124R,D2	33	0.1
2005	Bal A	102	380	39	84	15	1	14	45	39-3	2	84	.221	.295	.376	78	-13	1-1	.976	-2	93	80	O66R,D35	57	-2.0
Total	17	2240	8401	1422	2304	355	44	588	1575	895-151	56	2194	.274	.345	.537	128	319	234-107	.973	29	105	97	O2187(13/233/1999),D45	234	25.3

SOTHERN, DENNY Dennis Elwood (b Dennis Elwood Southern); B1.20.1904 Washington DC; D12.7.1977 Durham NC; BR/TR/5´11˝/175; d9.10

YEAR	TM LG	G	AB	R	H	2B	3B	HR	RBI	BB-IB	HP	SO	AVG	OBP	SLG	AOPS	ABR	SB-CS	FA	FR	RNG	THR	GAMES AT POSITION	DL	BFW
1926	Phi N	14	53	5	13	1	0	3	10	4	1	10	.245	.310	.434	94	-1	0	.975	1	117	70	O13(11/3/0)	—	-0.1
1928	Phi N	141	579	82	165	27	5	5	38	34	2	53	.285	.327	.375	80	-17	17	.964	5	101	**161**	O136(8/127/1)	—	-1.8
1929	Phi N	76	294	52	90	21	3	5	27	16	2	24	.306	.346	.449	90	-5	13	.967	2	102	132	O71(2/63/6)	—	-0.6
1930	Phi N	90	347	66	97	26	1	5	36	22	2	37	.280	.326	.403	70	-17	6	.967	7	100	226	O84(3/81/0)	—	-1.2
	Pit N	17	51	4	9	4	0	1	4	3	0	4	.176	.222	.314	28	-6	2	.971	0	114	0	O13(0/12/1)	—	-0.6
	Year	107	398	70	106	30	1	6	40	25	2	41	.266	.313	.392	65	-23	8	.967	7	102	199	O97(3/93/1)	—	-1.8
1931	Bro N	19	31	10	5	1	0	0	0	4	0	8	.161	.257	.194	23	-3	0	.958	0	120	0	O10(3/7/0)	—	-0.3
Total	5	357	1355	219	379	80	9	19	115	83	7	136	.280	.325	.394	77	-49	38	.966	15	103	158	O327(27/293/8)	—	-4.6

SOTO, GEOVANY Geovany; B1.20.1983 San Juan, PR; BR/TR/6´1˝/230; [ChiN01 11/318]; d9.23

YEAR	TM LG	G	AB	R	H	2B	3B	HR	RBI	BB-IB	HP	SO	AVG	OBP	SLG	AOPS	ABR	SB-CS	FA	FR	RNG	THR	GAMES AT POSITION	DL	BFW
2005	Chi N	1	1	0	0	0	0	0	0	0-0	0	0	.000	.000	.000	-97	0	0-0	ø	0	—	—	/H	0	0.0
2006	Chi N	11	25	1	5	1	0	0	2	0-0	1	5	.200	.231	.240	21	-3	0-0	.986	3	72	0	C7	0	0.0
Total	2	12	26	1	5	1	0	0	2	0-0	1	5	.192	.222	.231	16	-3	0-0	.986	3	72	0	C7	0	0.0

SOUCHOCK, STEVE Stephen "Bud"; B3.3.1919 Yatesboro PA; D7.28.2002 Westland MI; BR/TR/6´2.5˝/(200–203); d5.25

YEAR	TM LG	G	AB	R	H	2B	3B	HR	RBI	BB-IB	HP	SO	AVG	OBP	SLG	AOPS	ABR	SB-CS	FA	FR	RNG	THR	GAMES AT POSITION	DL	BFW
1946	NY A	47	86	15	26	3	3	2	10	7	1	13	.302	.362	.477	131	3	0-3	.964	-2	71	123	1b20	0	-0.1
1948	NY A	44	118	11	24	3	1	3	11	7	0	13	.203	.248	.322	51	-9	3-0	.988	-2	73	101	1b32	0	-1.1
1949	Chi A	84	252	29	59	13	5	7	37	25	0	38	.234	.303	.409	90	-6	5-2	.951	1	109	33	O39L,1b30	0	-0.8
1951	Det A	91	188	33	46	10	3	11	28	18	1	27	.245	.314	.505	118	3	0-2	.941	-1	101	94	O59(30/0/29),3b3/12	0	-0.1
1952	Det A	92	265	40	66	16	4	13	45	21	0	28	.249	.304	.487	117	4	1-0	.964	2	110	106	O56(16/1/41),3b13,1b9	0	0.4
1953	Det A	89	278	29	84	13	3	11	46	8	2	35	.302	.326	.489	119	5	5-1	.962	2	105	122	O80(39/0/44)/1	0	0.5
1954	Det A	25	39	6	7	0	1	3	8	2	0	10	.179	.220	.462	84	-2	1-1	1.000	0	115	0	O9L,3b2	34	-0.2
1955	Det A	1	1	0	1	0	0	0	1	0-0	0	0	1.000	1.000	1.000	449	0	0-0	ø	0	—	—	/H	0	0.0
Total	8	473	1227	163	313	58	20	50	186	88-0	4	164	.255	.307	.457	106	-2	15-9	.957	0	106	92	O243(133/1/114),1b93,3b18/2	34	-1.4

SOUTHWICK, CLYDE Clyde Aubra; B11.3.1886 Maxwell IA; D10.14.1961 Freeport IL; BL/TR/6´0˝/180; d8.22; Col Iowa St.

YEAR	TM LG	G	AB	R	H	2B	3B	HR	RBI	BB-IB	HP	SO	AVG	OBP	SLG	AOPS	ABR	SB-CS	FA	FR	RNG	THR	GAMES AT POSITION	DL	BFW
1911	StL A	4	12	3	3	0	0	0	0	1	0	—	.250	.308	.250	58	-1	0	.938	-1	*75*	*82*	C4	—	-0.1

SOUTHWORTH, BILL William Frederick; B11.10.1945 Madison WI; BR/TR/6´2˝/205; d10.2

YEAR	TM LG	G	AB	R	H	2B	3B	HR	RBI	BB-IB	HP	SO	AVG	OBP	SLG	AOPS	ABR	SB-CS	FA	FR	RNG	THR	GAMES AT POSITION	DL	BFW
1964	Mil N	3	7	2	2	0	0	1	2	0-0	2	3	.286	.444	.714	219	1	0-0	1.000	-1	48	0	3b2	0	0.0

SOUTHWORTH, BILLY William Harrison; B3.9.1893 Harvard NE; D11.15.1969 Columbus OH; BL/TR/5´9˝/170; d8.4; M13/C1

YEAR	TM LG	G	AB	R	H	2B	3B	HR	RBI	BB-IB	HP	SO	AVG	OBP	SLG	AOPS	ABR	SB-CS	FA	FR	RNG	THR	GAMES AT POSITION	DL	BFW
1913	Cle A	1	0	0	0	0	0	0	0	0	0	0	ø	ø	ø	ø	0	0	ø	0	0	0	/O	—	0.0
1915	Cle A	60	177	25	39	2	5	0	8	36	0	12	.220	.352	.288	90	-1	2-4	.942	0	96	117	O44(10/30/4)	—	-0.5
1918	Pit N	64	246	37	84	5	7	2	43	26	2	9	.341	.409	.443	154	16	19	.980	6	119	112	O64R	—	2.1
1919	Pit N	121	453	56	127	14	**14**	4	61	32	1	22	.280	.329	.400	114	6	23	.968	6	110	105	O121(75/0/46)	—	0.7
1920	Pit N	146	546	64	155	17	13	2	53	52	2	20	.284	.348	.374	104	3	23-25	**.991**	7	121	64	O142R	—	-0.1
1921	Bos N	141	569	86	175	25	15	7	79	36	2	13	.308	.351	.441	115	10	22-20	.975	5	101	123	O141R	—	0.2
1922	Bos N	43	158	27	51	4	4	4	18	18	0	1	.323	.392	.475	128	7	4-1	.955	4	118	126	O41R	—	0.7
1923	Bos N	153	611	95	195	29	16	6	78	61	2	23	.319	.383	.448	124	21	14-16	.943	3	103	122	O151R,2b2	—	0.9
1924	†NY N	94	281	40	72	13	0	3	36	32	0	16	.256	.332	.335	81	-6	1-6	.935	-6	94	63	O75(1/51/19)	—	-1.8
1925	NY N	123	473	79	138	19	5	6	44	51	2	11	.292	.363	.391	97	-1	6-13	.964	-15	85	59	O119(0/117/2)	—	-2.3
1926	NY N	36	116	23	38	6	1	5	30	7	0	1	.328	.366	.526	139	6	1	.970	-2	93	67	O29(7/16/8)	—	0.3
	†StL N	99	391	76	124	22	6	11	69	26	3	9	.317	.364	.488	123	12	13	.971	-3	109	36	O99R	—	0.1
	Year	135	507	99	162	28	7	16	99	33	3	10	.320	.365	.497	127	18	14	.971	-5	105	43	O128(7/16/107)	—	0.4
1927	StL N	92	306	52	92	15	5	2	39	23	0	7	.301	.350	.402	98	-1	10	.970	-4	95	64	O83R	—	-1.1
1929	StL N	19	32	1	6	2	0	0	3	2	0	4	.188	.235	.250	20	-4	0	1.000	0	118	0	O5R,M	—	-0.4
Total	13	1192	4359	661	1296	173	91	52	561	402	14	148	.297	.359	.415	111	68	138-85	.965	3	104	88	O1115(93/214/805),2b2	—	-1.2

SOWDERS, LEN Leonard; B6.29.1861 Louisville KY; D11.19.1888 Indianapolis IN; 5´11.5˝/172; d9.10; b–John b–Bill

YEAR	TM LG	G	AB	R	H	2B	3B	HR	RBI	BB-IB	HP	SO	AVG	OBP	SLG	AOPS	ABR	SB-CS	FA	FR	RNG	THR	GAMES AT POSITION	DL	BFW
1886	Bal AA	23	76	10	20	3	1	0	14	12	0	—	.263	.364	.329	121	3	6	.889	0	121	0	O23C/1	—	0.2

SPALDING, AL Albert Goodwill; B9.2.1850 Byron IL; D9.9.1915 San Diego CA; BR/TR/6´1˝/170; d5.5; M2; HF1939; ▲

YEAR	TM LG	G	AB	R	H	2B	3B	HR	RBI	BB-IB	HP	SO	AVG	OBP	SLG	AOPS	ABR	SB-CS	FA	FR	RNG	THR	GAMES AT POSITION	DL	BFW
1871	Bos NA	**31**	144	43	39	10	1	1	31	8	—	1	.271	.309	.375	93	-1	2-0	.776	-1	108	105	P31,O9C	—	0.0
1872	Bos NA	**48**	237	60	84	12	5	0	47	3	—	1	.354	.363	.447	140	10	3-0	.902	8	**148**	111	P48,O7C	—	0.3
1873	Bos NA	**60**	323	83	106	15	1	1	71	3	—	2	.328	.334	.390	105	0	9-0	**.885**	10	154	197	P60,O14C	—	0.3
1874	Bos NA	**71**	362	80	119	13	1	0	54	3	—	0	.329	.334	.370	119	6	2-1	**.854**	5	124	144	P71,O6C	—	0.2
1875	Bos NA	74	343	68	107	15	3	0	56	3	—	3	.312	.318	.373	134	11	2-2	.906	3	112	**223**	P72,O18(1/9/9),1b4	—	0.2
1876	Chi N	**66**	292	54	91	14	2	0	44	6	—	3	.312	.326	.373	118	4	—	.951	4	110	**306**	P61,O10(9/1/0),1b3/SM	—	0.2
1877	Chi N	**60**	254	29	65	7	6	0	35	3	—	16	.256	.265	.331	77	-8	—	.959	5	**155**	**116**	1b45,2b13,P4,3b2,M	—	-0.4
1878	Chi N	1	4	0	2	0	0	0	0	0	—	0	.500	.500	.500	215	0	—	.429	-2	0	0	/2	—	-0.2
Total	5NA	284	1409	334	455	65	11	2	259	20	—	7	.323	.332	.389	120	26	18-3	.875	25	130	164	P282,O54(1/45/9),1b4	—	1.0
Total	3	127	550	83	158	21	8	0	79	9	—	19	.287	.299	.355	99	-4	—	.948	7	114	300	P65,1b48,2b14,O10(9/1/0),3b2/S	—	-0.4

SPALDING, DICK Charles Harry; B10.13.1893 Philadelphia PA; D2.3.1950 Philadelphia PA; BL/TL/5´11˝/185; d4.18; C6

YEAR	TM LG	G	AB	R	H	2B	3B	HR	RBI	BB-IB	HP	SO	AVG	OBP	SLG	AOPS	ABR	SB-CS	FA	FR	RNG	THR	GAMES AT POSITION	DL	BFW
1927	Phi N	115	442	68	131	16	3	0	25	38	0	40	.296	.352	.346	86	-8	5	**.992**	2	109	68	O113L	—	-1.4
1928	Was A	16	23	1	8	0	0	0	0	0	0	4	.348	.348	.348	84	-1	0-2	1.000	-0	105	0	O11(8/0/3)	—	-0.2
Total	2	131	465	69	139	16	3	0	25	38	0	44	.299	.352	.346	86	-9	5-2	.993	2	109	66	O124(121/0/3)	—	-1.6

SPANGLER, AL Albert Donald; B7.8.1933 Philadelphia PA; BL/TL/6´0˝/(175–180); d9.16; C3; Col Duke

YEAR	TM LG	G	AB	R	H	2B	3B	HR	RBI	BB-IB	HP	SO	AVG	OBP	SLG	AOPS	ABR	SB-CS	FA	FR	RNG	THR	GAMES AT POSITION	DL	BFW
1959	Mil N	6	12	3	5	0	1	0	0	1-0	0	1	.417	.462	.583	192	1	1-0	1.000	-0	94	0	O4(1/3/0)	0	0.1
1960	Mil N	101	105	26	28	5	2	0	6	14-1	1	17	.267	.355	.352	103	1	6-2	.989	5	126	129	O92(90/1/1)	0	0.4
1961	Mil N	68	97	23	26	2	0	0	6	28-2	0	9	.268	.432	.289	102	3	4-2	1.000	-0	98	95	O44(23/21/1)	0	0.2
1962	Hou N	129	418	51	119	10	9	5	35	70-6	3	46	.285	.389	.388	119	14	7-6	.960	-3	91	96	O121(93/28/0)	0	0.5
1963	Hou N	120	430	52	121	25	4	4	27	50-5	1	38	.281	.355	.386	122	14	5-8	.987	0	102	70	O113(87/33/3)	0	0.8
1964	Hou N	135	449	51	110	18	5	4	38	41-1	4	43	.245	.311	.334	88	-7	7-8	.964	-6	89	41	O127(113/18/0)	0	-2.2
1965	Hou N	38	112	18	24	1	1	1	7	14-2	0	8	.214	.299	.268	66	-5	1-1	.956	-1	81	192	O33(31/1/1)	0	-0.8
	Cal A	51	96	17	25	1	0	0	1	8-0	0	9	.260	.317	.271	70	-4	4-0	.973	-2	91	0	O24(4/17/6)	0	-0.6
1966	Cal A	6	9	2	6	0	0	0	0	2-0	0	2	.667	.727	.667	312	3	0-0	1.000	-0	71	0	O3R	0	0.2
1967	Chi N	62	130	18	33	7	0	0	13	23-4	0	17	.254	.361	.308	91	0	2-2	.986	-1	104	0	O41(0/7/34)	0	-0.4
1968	Chi N	88	177	21	48	9	3	2	18	20-2	1	24	.271	.343	.390	114	4	0-1	.973	-2	93	62	O48(1/7/42)	0	-0.2
1969	Chi N	82	213	23	45	8	1	4	23	21-0	1	16	.211	.284	.315	60	-11	0-2	.950	-6	84	26	O58(0/1/57)	0	-2.1
1970	Chi N	21	14	2	2	1	0	1	1	3-0	0	3	.143	.294	.429	81	0	0-0	1.000	0	164	0	O6(3/0/3)	0	0.0
1971	Chi N	5	5	0	2	0	0	0	0	0-0	0	1	.400	.400	.400	111	0	0-0	ø	0	—	—	/H	0	0.0
Total	13	912	2267	307	594	87	26	21	175	295-23	11	234	.262	.347	.351	100	13	37-32	.973	-16	95	68	O714(446/137/151)	0	-4.1

SPEAKE, BOB Robert Charles "Spook"; B8.22.1930 Springfield MO; BL/TL/6´1˝/(178–185); d4.16

YEAR	TM LG	G	AB	R	H	2B	3B	HR	RBI	BB-IB	HP	SO	AVG	OBP	SLG	AOPS	ABR	SB-CS	FA	FR	RNG	THR	GAMES AT POSITION	DL	BFW
1955	Chi N	95	261	36	57	9	5	12	43	28-4	3	71	.218	.300	.429	91	-4	3-4	.959	-1	94	110	O55(49/0/8),1b8	0	-0.9
1957	Chi N	129	418	65	97	14	5	16	50	38-1	3	68	.232	.299	.404	89	-8	5-6	.974	3	103	124	O60(20/40/0),1b39	0	-1.2
1958	SF N	66	71	9	15	3	0	3	10	13-1	0	15	.211	.333	.380	90	-1	0-1	.938	1	87	347	O10L	0	-0.1
1959	SF N	15	11	0	1	0	0	0	1	1-0	0	4	.091	.167	.091	-30	-2	0-0	ø	0	—	—	/H	0	-0.2
Total	4	305	761	110	170	26	10	31	104	80-6	6	158	.223	.301	.406	88	-15	8-11	.966	3	98	133	O125(79/40/8),1b47	0	-2.4

SPEAKER, TRIS Tristram E "The Grey Eagle"; B4.4.1888 Hubbard TX; D12.8.1958 Lake Whitney TX; BL/TL/5´11.5˝/193; d9.12; M8; HF1937; Col Texas Wesleyan

YEAR	TM LG	G	AB	R	H	2B	3B	HR	RBI	BB-IB	HP	SO	AVG	OBP	SLG	AOPS	ABR	SB-CS	FA	FR	RNG	THR	GAMES AT POSITION	DL	BFW
1907	Bos A	7	19	0	3	0	0	0	1	1	0	—	.158	.200	.158	14	-2	0	1.000	1	394	930	O4R	—	-0.1
1908	Bos A	31	116	12	26	2	2	0	9	4	2	—	.224	.262	.276	73	-4	3	1.000	4	254	314	O31(1/30/0)	—	-0.1
1909	Bos A	143	544	73	168	26	13	7	77	38	7	—	.309	.362	.443	151	30	35	.973	19	**195**	**298**	O142C	—	4.6
1910	Bos A	141	538	92	183	20	14	7	65	52	6	—	.340	.404	.468	169	43	35	.957	9	**117**	96	O140C	—	4.8
1911	Bos A	141	500	88	167	34	13	8	70	59	13	—	.334	.418	.502	158	41	25	.956	3	100	118	O138C	—	3.3
1912	†Bos A	153	580	136	222	**53**	12	**10**	90	82	6	—	.383	**.464**	.567	185	68	52	.958	16	110	**156**	O153C	—	**7.2**
1913	Bos A	141	520	94	189	35	22	3	71	65	7	22	.363	.441	.533	180	54	46	.942	19	**122**	137	O139C	—	6.5
1914	Bos A	158	571	101	**193**	**46**	18	4	90	77	7	25	.338	.423	.503	178	57	42-29	.968	23	**121**	142	O156C/P1	—	**7.3**
1915	†Bos A	150	547	108	176	25	12	0	69	81	7	14	.322	.416	.411	152	39	29-25	.976	8	108	97	O150C	—	3.6
1916	Cle A	151	546	102	**211**	**41**	8	2	79	82	4	20	**.386**	**.470**	**.502**	**181**	**60**	35-27	.975	6	103	117	O151C	—	**5.7**
1917	Cle A	142	523	90	184	42	11	2	60	67	7	14	.352	.432	.486	168	45	30	.980	2	101	107	O142C	—	4.1
1918	Cle A	127	471	73	150	**33**	11	0	61	64	3	9	.318	.403	.435	140	25	27	.973	8	**118**	83	O127C	—	2.7
1919	Cle A	134	494	83	146	38	12	2	63	73	8	12	.296	.395	.433	125	20	19	.983	15	112	130	O134C,M	—	2.6
1920	†Cle A	150	552	137	214	**50**	11	8	107	97	5	13	.388	.483	.562	171	64	10-13	.977	6	102	130	O148C,M	—	5.4
1921	Cle A	132	506	107	183	**52**	14	3	75	68	2	12	.362	.439	.538	146	38	2-4	**.984**	9	**115**	98	O128C,M	—	3.8
1922	Cle A	131	426	85	161	**48**	8	11	71	77	1	11	.378	**.474**	.606	178	55	8-3	**.983**	3	101	114	O109C,M	—	5.1
1923	Cle A	150	574	133	218	**59**	11	17	130	93	4	15	.380	.469	.610	183	74	8-9	.968	3	94	**148**	O150C,M	—	6.5
1924	Cle A	135	486	94	167	36	9	9	65	72	4	13	.344	.432	.510	141	32	5-7	.963	1	94	164	O128(0/127/1),M	—	2.5
1925	Cle A	117	429	79	167	35	5	12	87	70	4	12	.389	**.479**	.578	166	48	5-2	.967	4	99	130	O109C,M	—	**4.3**
1926	Cle A	150	539	96	164	52	8	7	86	94	0	15	.304	.408	.469	127	26	6-1	.981	4	98	130	O149C,M	—	2.4
1927	Was A	141	523	71	171	43	6	2	73	55	4	8	.327	.395	.444	119	17	9-8	.967	-3	94	103	O120(0/119/1),1b17	—	0.7
1928	Phi A	64	191	28	51	22	2	3	30	10	2	5	.267	.310	.450	95	-2	5-1	.975	1	94	162	O50(1/49/0)	—	-0.2
Total	22	2789	10195	1882	3514	792	222	117	1529	1381	103	220	.345	.428	.500	156	828	436-129	.970	161	113	136	O2698(2/2690/6),1b18/P	—	82.7

SPEED, HORACE Horace Arthur; B10.4.1951 Los Angeles CA; BR/TR/6´1˝/(172–180); [SFN69 3/66]; d4.10

YEAR	TM LG	G	AB	R	H	2B	3B	HR	RBI	BB-IB	HP	SO	AVG	OBP	SLG	AOPS	ABR	SB-CS	FA	FR	RNG	THR	GAMES AT POSITION	DL	BFW
1975	SF N	17	15	2	2	1	0	0	1	1-0	1	8	.133	.235	.200	21	-2	0-0	.900	-0	105	0	O9(5/0/5)	0	-0.2
1978	Cle A	70	106	13	24	4	1	0	4	14-1	1	31	.226	.320	.283	72	-3	2-4	.977	-1	99	39	O61(12/23/30),D3	26	-0.7
1979	Cle A	26	14	6	2	0	0	0	1	5-0	0	7	.143	.368	.143	44	-1	2-1	.875	-1	102	0	O16(10/3/3),D4	0	-0.2
Total	3	113	135	21	28	5	1	0	6	20-1	2	46	.207	.316	.259	63	-6	4-5	.956	-2	100	30	O86(27/26/38),D7	26	-1.1

SPEHR, TIM Timothy Joseph; B7.2.1966 Excelsior Springs MO; BR/TR/6´2˝/(195–205); [KCA88 5/127]; d7.18; Col Arizona St.

YEAR	TM LG	G	AB	R	H	2B	3B	HR	RBI	BB-IB	HP	SO	AVG	OBP	SLG	AOPS	ABR	SB-CS	FA	FR	RNG	THR	GAMES AT POSITION	DL	BFW
1991	KC A	37	74	7	14	5	0	3	14	9-0	1	18	.189	.282	.378	81	-2	1-0	.986	9	126	167	C37	0	0.9
1993	Mon N	53	87	14	20	6	0	2	10	6-1	1	20	.230	.281	.368	71	-4	2-0	.954	1	49	170	C49	0	-0.1
1994	Mon N	52	36	8	9	3	1	0	5	4-0	0	11	.250	.325	.389	84	-1	2-0	1.000	5	108	27	C46,O2L	0	0.6
1995	Mon N	41	35	4	9	5	0	1	3	6-0	0	7	.257	.366	.486	118	1	0-0	.990	4	69	147	C38	63	0.6
1996	Mon N	63	44	4	4	1	0	1	3	3-0	1	15	.091	.167	.182	-8	-7	1-0	.985	-1	79	39	C58/rf	19	-0.7
1997	KC A	17	35	3	6	0	0	1	2	2-0	1	12	.171	.237	.257	28	-4	0-0	1.000	3	59	118	C17	0	-0.1
	Atl N	8	14	2	3	1	0	1	4	0-0	0	4	.214	.214	.500	79	-1	1-0	.947	1	159	273	C7	0	0.1
1998	NY N	21	51	3	7	1	0	0	3	7-1	2	16	.137	.267	.157	15	-6	1-0	1.000	1	89	147	C21/1	114	-0.3
	KC A	11	25	5	6	2	0	1	2	8-0	2	3	.240	.457	.440	130	2	0-0	1.000	-2	150	58	C11	0	0.0
1999	KC A	60	155	26	32	7	0	9	26	22-0	6	47	.206	.324	.426	87	-3	1-0	.990	-9	93	49	C59	0	-0.8
Total	8	363	556	76	110	31	1	19	72	67-2	14	153	.198	.298	.360	71	-25	9-0	.985	12	92	106	C343,O3(2/0/1)/1	196	0.2

SPEIER, CHRIS Chris Edward; B6.28.1950 Alameda CA; BR/TR (BB 1972p)/6´1˝/(175–182); [SFN70*S1/2]; d4.7; C5; s–Justin; Col California–Santa Barbara

YEAR	TM LG	G	AB	R	H	2B	3B	HR	RBI	BB-IB	HP	SO	AVG	OBP	SLG	AOPS	ABR	SB-CS	FA	FR	RNG	THR	GAMES AT POSITION	DL	BFW
1971	†SF N	157	601	74	141	17	6	8	46	56-6	7	90	.235	.307	.323	79	-16	4-7	.958	-4	103	102	S156	0	-0.4
1972	SF N★	150	562	74	151	25	2	15	71	82-2	3	92	.269	.361	.400	115	14	9-4	.974	3	107	76	S150	0	3.7
1973	SF N★	153	542	58	135	17	4	11	71	66-4	2	69	.249	.332	.356	87	-9	4-5	.956	0	102	103	S150/2	0	0.9
1974	SF N☆	141	501	55	125	19	5	9	53	62-8	4	64	.250	.336	.361	91	-5	3-2	.969	10	107	105	S135,2b4	0	2.1
1975	SF N	141	487	60	132	30	5	10	69	70-7	1	50	.271	.362	.415	112	10	4-5	**.982**	9	98	96	S136/3	0	3.5
1976	SF N	145	495	51	112	18	4	3	40	60-1	4	52	.226	.311	.297	72	-17	2-2	.974	3	104	95	S135,2b7,3b5/1	0	0.2
1977	SF N	6	17	1	3	1	0	0	0	0-0	0	3	.176	.176	.235	9	-2	0-0	.920	2	153	82	S5	0	0.0
	Mon N	139	531	58	125	30	6	5	38	67-3	1	78	.235	.321	.343	80	-14	1-2	.970	-8	99	94	S138	0	-0.8
	Year	145	548	59	128	31	6	5	38	67-3	1	81	.234	.317	.339	78	-16	1-2	.968	-6	101	94	S143	0	-0.8
1978	Mon N	150	501	47	126	18	3	5	51	60-10	1	75	.251	.329	.329	86	-8	1-0	.975	-2	99	114	S148	0	0.6
1979	Mon N	113	344	31	78	13	1	7	26	43-10	3	45	.227	.317	.331	77	-10	0-0	.970	1	101	88	S112	19	0.2
1980	Mon N	128	388	35	103	14	4	1	32	52-18	0	38	.265	.351	.330	90	-4	0-3	.965	0	102	88	S127/3	0	0.9
1981	†Mon N	96	307	33	69	10	2	2	25	38-10	0	29	.225	.310	.290	69	-12	1-2	.964	-6	94	108	S96	0	-0.9
1982	Mon N	156	530	41	136	26	4	7	60	47-12	1	67	.257	.316	.360	86	-9	1-6	.982	-14	86	94	S155	0	-1.0
1983	Mon N	88	261	31	67	12	2	2	22	29-4	2	37	.257	.332	.341	88	-4	2-1	.962	-6	99	83	S74,3b12,2b2	15	-0.3
1984	Mon N	25	40	1	6	0	0	0	1	1-0	0	8	.150	.171	.150	-10	-6	0-0	.960	1	98	126	S13,3b4	0	-0.5
	StL N	38	118	9	21	7	1	3	8	9-1	1	19	.178	.242	.331	61	-7	0-0	.983	7	121	129	S34,3b2	0	0.4
	Year	63	158	10	27	7	1	3	9	10-1	1	27	.171	.225	.285	44	-12	0-0	.980	8	85	93	S47,3b6	0	-0.1
	Min A	12	33	2	7	0	0	0	1	3-0	0	7	.212	.278	.212	36	-3	0-0	.977	-3	85	93	S12	16	-0.5
1985	Chi N	106	218	16	53	11	0	4	24	17-0	0	34	.243	.295	.349	73	-8	1-3	.964	5	113	151	S58,3b31,2b13	0	0.0
1986	Chi N	95	155	21	44	8	0	6	23	15-3	1	32	.284	.349	.452	111	2	2-2	.984	3	92	71	3b53,S23,2b7	0	0.7
1987	†SF N	111	317	39	79	13	0	11	39	42-5	3	51	.249	.342	.394	99	0	4-7	.989	4	90	94	2b55,3b44,S22	0	0.5
1988	SF N	82	171	26	37	9	1	3	18	23-2	1	39	.216	.311	.333	89	-2	3-3	.985	4	105	117	2b45,3b22,S12	0	0.3
1989	SF N	28	37	7	9	4	0	0	2	5-0	0	9	.243	.333	.351	99	0	0-0	1.000	-1	82	0	3b9,S9,2b4/1	119	0.0
Total	19	2260	7156	770	1759	302	50	112	720	847-106	35	988	.246	.327	.349	87	-110	42-54	.970	6	101	99	S1900,3b184,2b138,1b2	169	9.6

SPENCE, BOB John Robert; B2.10.1946 San Diego CA; BL/TR/6´4˝/(205–215); [ChiA67*S1/4]; d9.5; Col Santa Clara

YEAR	TM LG	G	AB	R	H	2B	3B	HR	RBI	BB-IB	HP	SO	AVG	OBP	SLG	AOPS	ABR	SB-CS	FA	FR	RNG	THR	GAMES AT POSITION	DL	BFW
1969	Chi A	12	26	0	4	1	0	0	3	0-0	0	9	.154	.148	.192	-4	-4	0-0	1.000	-0	73	130	1b6	0	-0.5
1970	Chi A	46	130	11	29	4	1	4	15	11-0	1	32	.223	.285	.362	75	-5	0-0	.994	3	133	122	1b37	0	-0.5
1971	Chi A	14	27	2	4	0	0	0	1	5-0	0	6	.148	.273	.148	24	-3	0-0	.986	-1	50	109	1b7	0	-0.4
Total	3	72	183	13	37	5	1	4	19	16-0	1	47	.202	.265	.306	57	-12	0-0	.993	2	114	121	1b50	0	-1.4

YEAR	TM LG	G	AB	R	H	2B	3B	HR	RBI	BB-IB	HP	SO	AVG	OBP	SLG	AOPS	ABR	SB-CS	FA	FR	RNG	THR	GAMES AT POSITION	DL	BFW
SPENCE, STAN	Stanley Orville; B3.20.1915 S.Portsmouth KY; D1.9.1983 Kinston NC; BL/TL/5´10.5˝/180; d6.8; Mil 1945																								
1940	Bos A	51	68	5	19	2	1	2	13	4	0	9	.279	.319	.426	88	-2	0-1	1.000	-1	97	0	O15(6/0/9)	—	-0.3
1941	Bos A	86	203	22	47	10	3	2	28	18	3	14	.232	.304	.340	68	-10	1-0	1.000	3	103	161	O52(27/10/16)/1	0	-0.8
1942	Was A☆	149	629	94	203	27	**15**	4	79	62	1	16	.323	.384	.432	131	25	5-2	.973	-7	97	63	O149C	0	1.5
1943	Was A	149	570	72	152	23	10	12	88	84	5	39	.267	.366	.405	130	23	8-1	.983	-1	99	104	O148C	0	2.1
1944	Was A★	153	592	83	187	31	8	18	100	69	4	28	.316	.391	.486	157	44	3-7	.989	15	103	197	O150C,1b3	0	5.4
1946	Was A★	152	578	83	169	50	10	16	87	62	4	31	.292	.365	.497	148	36	1-7	.982	2	99	142	O150C	0	3.3
1947	Was A★	147	506	62	141	22	6	16	73	81	0	41	.279	.378	.441	131	22	2-2	.984	6	105	131	O142C	0	2.5
1948	Bos A	114	391	71	92	17	4	12	61	82	0	33	.235	.368	.391	97	0	0-2	.977	-3	101	57	O92(24/0/70),1b14	0	-0.8
1949	Bos A	7	20	3	3	1	0	0	1	6	0	1	.150	.346	.200	43	-1	0-0	1.000	1	101	196	O5(0/2/3)	0	-0.1
	StL A	104	314	46	77	13	3	13	45	52	2	36	.245	.356	.430	103	1	1-1	.995	4	100	168	O87(33/50/6)/1	0	0.1
	Year	111	334	49	80	14	3	13	46	58	2	37	.240	.355	.416	99	-1	1-1	.996	4	100	170	O92(33/52/9)/1	0	0.0
Total	9	1112	3871	541	1090	196	60	95	575	520	19	248	.282	.369	.437	126	138	21-23	.984	19	101	125	O990(90/801/104),1b19	0	12.9
SPENCER	; d6.3																								
1872	Nat NA	1	4	1	0	0	0	0	0	0	—	0	.000	.000	.000	-86	-1	0-0	.429	-1	99	0	/S	—	-0.1
SPENCER, CHET	Chester Arthur; B3.4.1883 S.Webster OH; D11.10.1938 Portsmouth OH; BL/TR/6´0˝/180; d8.22																								
1906	Bos N	8	27	1	4	1	0	0	0	0	0	—	.148	.148	.185	4	-3	0	.875	-1	144	0	O8(1/3/3)	—	-0.5
SPENCER, DARYL	Daryl Dean "Big Dee"; B7.13.1929 Wichita KS; BR/TR/6´2˝/(185–197); d9.17; Mil 1954–55; Col Wichita St.																								
1952	NY N	7	17	0	5	0	1	0	3	1	0	4	.294	.333	.412	105	0	0-0	1.000	1	116	59	S3,3b3	0	0.1
1953	NY N	118	408	55	85	18	5	20	56	42	3	74	.208	.287	.424	81	-13	0-1	.927	-8	103	86	S53,3b36,2b32	0	-1.6
1956	NY N	146	489	46	108	13	2	14	42	35-2	3	65	.221	.275	.342	66	-25	1-3	.974	-8	95	80	2b70,S66,3b12	0	-2.5
1957	NY N	148	534	65	133	31	2	11	50	50-0	1	50	.249	.313	.376	85	-11	3-1	.950	18	107	**135**	S110,2b36,3b6	0	1.9
1958	SF N	148	539	71	138	20	5	17	74	73-4	3	60	.256	.343	.406	101	2	1-0	.955	-2	106	102	S134,2b17	0	1.3
1959	SF N	152	555	59	147	20	1	12	62	58-4	0	67	.265	.332	.369	89	-8	5-0	.970	2	101	90	2b151,S4	0	0.6
1960	StL N	148	507	70	131	20	3	16	58	81-7	5	74	.258	.365	.404	102	4	1-1	.946	-18	87	90	S138,2b16	0	-0.2
1961	StL N	37	130	19	33	4	0	4	21	23-3	0	17	.254	.366	.377	89	-1	1-0	.956	1	100	108	S37	0	0.3
	LA N	60	189	27	46	7	0	8	27	20-1	4	35	.243	.327	.407	86	-3	0-1	.964	1	91	141	3b57,S3	0	-0.3
	Year	97	319	46	79	11	0	12	48	43-4	4	52	.248	.343	.395	88	-5	1-1	.964	2	91	141	3b57,S40	0	0.0
1962	LA N	77	157	24	37	5	1	2	12	32-4	0	31	.236	.365	.318	91	0	0-0	.925	-2	98	49	3b57,S10	0	-0.2
1963	LA N	7	9	0	1	0	0	0	0	3-0	0	2	.111	.333	.111	37	-1	0-0	1.000	-1	60	0	3b3	0	-0.1
	Cin N	50	155	21	37	7	0	1	23	31-0	1	37	.239	.359	.303	93	1	1-0	.979	4	99	135	3b48	0	0.5
	Year	57	164	21	38	7	0	1	23	34-0	1	39	.232	.358	.293	91	0	1-0	.979	3	97	128	3b51	0	0.4
Total	10	1098	3689	457	901	145	20	105	428	449-25	20	516	.244	.327	.380	88	-55	13-7	.953	-12	99	103	S558,2b322,3b222	0	-0.2
SPENCER, TUBBY	Edward Russell; B1.26.1884 Oil City PA; D2.1.1945 San Francisco CA; BR/TR/5´10˝/215; d7.23																								
1905	StL A	35	115	6	27	1	2	0	11	7	1	—	.235	.285	.278	83	-3	2	.962	-6	*71*	*107*	C34	—	-0.6
1906	StL A	58	188	15	33	6	1	0	17	7	0	—	.176	.205	.218	34	-15	4	.935	-6	*88*	*100*	C54	—	-1.7
1907	StL A	71	230	27	61	11	1	1	25	7	4	—	.265	.299	.335	102	0	1	.957	-5	*93*	*99*	C63	—	0.2
1908	StL A	91	286	19	60	6	1	0	28	17	0	—	.210	.254	.238	60	-13	1	.983	5	*121*	*91*	C88	—	0.1
1909	Bos A	28	74	6	12	1	0	0	9	6	0	—	.162	.225	.176	26	-6	2	.992	-1	*108*	*82*	C26	—	-0.6
1911	Phi N	11	32	2	5	1	0	1	3	3	0	7	.156	.229	.281	42	-3	0	.925	-2	*88*	*114*	C11	—	-0.4
1916	Det A	19	54	7	20	1	1	1	10	6	1	6	.370	.443	.481	172	5	2	.988	-5	77	114	C19	—	0.1
1917	Det A	70	192	13	46	8	3	0	22	15	**9**	15	.240	.324	.313	95	-1	0	.978	-4	*89*	*89*	C62	—	0.1
1918	Det A	66	155	11	34	8	1	0	8	19	2	18	.219	.313	.284	83	-3	1	.966	-11	*73*	*91*	C48/1	—	-1.1
Total	9	449	1326	106	298	43	10	3	133	87	17	46	.225	.281	.279	76	-39	13	.966	-33	*94*	*96*	C405/1	—	-3.9
SPENCER, TOM	Hubert Thomas; B2.28.1951 Gallipolis OH; BR/TR/6´0˝/170; [CinN69 20/468]; d7.17; C5																								
1978	Chi A	29	65	3	12	1	0	0	4	2-0	0	9	.185	.209	.200	15	-7	0-1	1.000	2	115	173	O27(6/19/2),D2	0	-0.6
SPENCER, JIM	James Lloyd; B7.30.1947 Hanover PA; D2.10.2002 Ft.Lauderdale FL; BL/TL/6´2˝/(190–206); [AnaA65 1/11]; d9.7; gf–Ben																								
1968	Cal A	19	68	2	13	1	0	0	5	3-0	1	10	.191	.233	.206	36	-5	0-0	.994	3	155	107	1b19	0	-0.5
1969	Cal A	113	386	39	98	14	3	10	31	26-6	2	53	.254	.304	.383	95	-4	1-0	.991	-1	94	100	1b107	0	-1.4
1970	Cal A	146	511	61	140	20	4	12	68	28-6	0	61	.274	.309	.399	98	-4	0-2	**.995**	-0	97	**123**	1b142	0	-1.7
1971	Cal A	148	510	50	121	21	2	18	59	48-7	3	63	.237	.304	.392	104	1	0-1	**.996**	2	104	99	1b145	0	-1.0
1972	Cal A	82	212	13	47	5	0	1	14	12-1	0	25	.222	.262	.259	59	-11	0-1	.990	0	126	98	1b35,O24L	0	-1.8
1973	Cal A	29	87	10	21	4	2	2	11	9-1	1	9	.241	.316	.402	110	1	0-0	1.000	-3	46	109	1b26,D2	0	-0.4
	Tex A★	102	352	35	94	12	3	4	43	34-6	1	41	.267	.332	.352	97	-2	0-3	.999	5	113	93	1b99/D	0	-0.5
	Year	131	439	45	115	16	5	6	54	43-7	2	50	.262	.329	.362	99	-1	0-3	**.999**	2	99	96	1b125,D3	0	-0.9
1974	Tex A	118	352	36	98	11	4	7	44	22-3	3	27	.278	.323	.392	108	3	1-2	.998	0	93	94	1b60,D54	0	-0.3
1975	Tex A	132	403	50	107	18	1	11	47	35-6	2	43	.266	.327	.397	105	2	0-1	.995	3	111	124	1b99,D25	0	-0.3
1976	Chi A	150	518	53	131	13	2	14	70	49-**19**	1	52	.253	.315	.367	100	-1	6-4	**.998**	9	119	96	1b143,D2	0	-0.3
1977	Chi A	128	470	56	116	16	1	18	69	36-11	2	50	.247	.300	.400	90	-8	1-2	.991	2	105	70	1b125	15	-1.4
1978	†NY A	71	150	12	34	9	1	7	24	15-3	0	32	.227	.295	.440	107	1	0-1	1.000	0	106	55	D35,1b15	16	-0.1
1979	NY A	106	295	60	85	15	3	23	53	38-11	0	25	.288	.367	.593	157	23	0-2	.992	-0	96	155	D71,1b26	0	1.8
1980	†NY A	97	259	38	61	9	0	13	43	30-2	1	44	.236	.313	.421	102	0	1-0	.990	2	109	91	1b75,D15	0	-0.2
1981	NY A	25	63	6	9	2	0	2	4	9-2	0	7	.143	.250	.270	50	-4	0-0	1.000	3	140	107	1b25	0	-0.3
	†Oak A	54	171	14	35	6	0	2	9	10-1	0	20	.205	.246	.275	53	-11	1-0	.997	1	107	79	1b48	0	-1.3
	Year	79	234	20	44	8	0	4	13	19-3	0	27	.188	.247	.274	52	-15	1-0	.998	4	117	88	1b73	0	-1.6
1982	Oak A	33	101	6	17	3	1	2	5	3-1	0	20	.168	.190	.277	28	-11	0-0	.992	1	120	82	1b32	21	-1.1
Total	15	1553	4908	541	1227	179	27	146	599	407-86	17	582	.250	.307	.387	98	-30	11-19	.995	26	106	100	1b1221,D205,O24L	52	-10.8
SPENCER, BEN	Lloyd Benjamin; B5.15.1890 Patapsco MD; D9.1.1970 Finksburg MD; BL/TL/5´8˝/160; d9.8; gs–Jim																								
1913	Was A	8	21	2	6	1	1	0	2	2	0	4	.286	.348	.429	124	1	0	.917	-0	87	120	O8(7/1/0)	—	0.0
SPENCER, SHANE	Michael Shane; B2.20.1972 Key West FL; BR/TR/5´11˝/(210–225); [NYA90 28/750]; d4.10																								
1998	†NY A	27	67	18	25	6	0	10	27	5-0	0	12	.373	.411	.910	242	13	0-1	1.000	-1	83	94	O22(9/0/15)/1D	0	1.1
1999	†NY A	71	205	25	48	8	0	8	20	18-0	2	51	.234	.301	.390	76	-8	0-4	1.000	3	104	146	O64(46/0/22),D3	24	-0.8
2000	NY A	73	248	33	70	11	3	9	40	19-0	2	45	.282	.330	.460	101	-1	1-2	.989	4	118	142	O40(33/0/7),D33	81	-0.1
2001	†NY A	80	283	40	73	14	2	10	46	21-0	4	58	.258	.315	.428	93	-3	4-1	.993	7	117	183	O68(44/0/28),D14	28	0.1
2002	†NY A	94	288	32	71	15	2	6	34	31-4	4	62	.247	.324	.375	87	-5	0-3	.975	-1	97	105	O91(40/0/55)/D	0	-1.0
2003	Cle A	64	210	23	57	10	0	8	26	18-0	1	52	.271	.328	.433	100	0	2-0	.987	-3	92	84	O43(16/0/30),1b11,D7	0	-0.5
	Tex A	55	185	16	42	10	0	4	23	27-0	2	40	.227	.329	.346	74	-6	0-0	.982	0	102	65	O54(50/0/12)/D	0	-0.8
	Year	119	395	39	99	20	0	12	49	45-0	3	92	.251	.328	.392	88	-7	2-0	.984	-3	98	73	O97(66/0/42),1b11,D8	0	-1.3
2004	NY N	74	185	21	52	10	1	4	26	13-0	2	37	.281	.332	.411	94	-2	6-0	.974	4	127	77	O62(43/6/19)/1	8	0.1
Total	7	538	1671	208	438	84	8	59	242	152-4	17	357	.262	.326	.428	96	-12	13-11	.986	13	106	116	O444(281/6/188),D63,1b13	141	-1.9
SPENCER, ROY	Roy Hampton; B2.22.1900 Scranton NC; D2.8.1973 Port Charlotte FL; BR/TR/5´10˝/168; d4.19																								
1925	Pit N	14	28	1	6	1	0	0	2	1	0	3	.214	.241	.250	24	-3	1-0	.905	-1	*138*	*0*	C11	—	-0.3
1926	Pit N	28	43	5	17	3	0	0	4	1	0	0	.395	.409	.465	128	2	0	.970	-0	*125*	*34*	C12	—	0.2
1927	†Pit N	38	92	9	26	3	1	0	13	3	0	3	.283	.305	.337	67	-4	0	.974	2	*134*	*58*	C34	—	-0.1
1929	Was A	50	116	18	18	4	0	1	9	8	2	15	.155	.222	.216	13	-15	0-0	.967	-0	*116*	*99*	C41	—	-1.3
1930	Was A	93	321	32	82	11	4	0	36	18	4	27	.255	.303	.315	57	-22	3-0	.989	6	*127*	*97*	C93	—	-0.8
1931	Was A	145	483	48	133	16	3	1	60	35	2	21	.275	.327	.327	72	-20	0-0	.985	7	*126*	*82*	C145	—	-0.4
1932	Was A	102	317	28	78	9	0	1	41	24	1	17	.246	.301	.284	53	-22	0-1	.978	-4	***152***	*87*	C98	—	-2.0
1933	Cle A	75	227	26	46	5	2	0	23	23	2	17	.203	.282	.242	38	-20	0-0	.990	6	*136*	*116*	C72	—	-1.0
1934	Cle A	5	7	0	1	1	0	0	2	0	0	1	.143	.143	.286	8	-1	0-0	1.000	0	*78*	*224*	C4	—	-0.1
1936	NY N	19	18	3	5	1	0	0	3	2	0	3	.278	.350	.333	86	0	0	1.000	1	*141*	*82*	C14	—	0.1
1937	Bro N	51	117	5	24	2	2	0	4	8	0	17	.205	.256	.256	39	-10	0	1.000	6	*85*	*115*	C45	—	-0.2
1938	Bro N	16	45	2	12	1	1	0	6	5	0	6	.267	.340	.333	84	-1	0	.968	-1	*84*	*73*	C16	—	-0.1
Total	12	636	1814	177	448	57	13	3	203	128	11	130	.247	.301	.298	56	-116	4-1	.984	21	*128*	*91*	C585	—	-6.0

YEAR	TM LG	G	AB	R	H	2B	3B	HR	RBI	BB-IB	HP	SO	AVG	OBP	SLG	AOPS	ABR	SB-CS	FA	FR	RNG	THR	GAMES AT POSITION	DL	BFW
SPENCER, VERN	Vernon Murray; B2.4.1894 Wixom MI; D6.3.1971 Wixom MI; BL/TR/5´7˝/165; d7.4																								
1920	NY N	45	140	15	28	2	3	0	19	11	0	17	.200	.258	.257	49	-10	4-3	.932	4	119	169	O40(38/1/2)	—	-0.8
SPERAW, PAUL	Paul Bachman "Polly","Birdie"; B10.5.1893 Annville PA; D2.22.1962 Cedar Rapids IA; BR/TR/5´8.5˝/145; d9.15																								
1920	StL A	1	2	0	0	0	0	0	0	0	0	0	.000	.000	.000	-97	-1	0-0	1.000	-0	76	0	/3	—	-0.1
SPERBER, ED	Edwin George; B1.21.1895 Cincinnati OH; D1.5.1976 Cincinnati OH; BL/TL/5´11˝/175; d4.16																								
1924	Bos N	24	59	8	17	2	0	1	12	10	1	9	.288	.400	.373	113	2	3-1	.897	-2	82	56	O17(2/1/14)	—	-0.1
1925	Bos N	2	2	0	0	0	0	0	0	0	0	0	.000	.000	.000	-99	-1	0-0	ø	0	—	—	/H	—	-0.1
Total	2	26	61	8	17	2	0	1	12	10	1	9	.279	.389	.361	106	1	3-1	.897	-2	82	56	O17(2/1/14)	—	-0.2
SPERRING, ROB	Robert Walter; B10.10.1949 San Francisco CA; BR/TR/6´1˝/175; [ChiN71 5/112]; d8.11; Col Pacific (CA)																								
1974	Chi N	42	107	9	22	3	0	1	5	9-1	0	28	.206	.267	.262	46	-8	1-2	.952	-4	104	83	2b35,S8	0	-1.0
1975	Chi N	65	144	25	30	4	1	1	9	16-3	1	31	.208	.288	.271	54	-9	0-2	.946	4	124	60	3b22,2b17,S16,O8(2/0/6)	0	-0.4
1976	Chi N	43	93	8	24	3	0	0	7	9-0	0	25	.258	.320	.290	69	-4	0-2	.955	-11	36	34	3b20,S15,2b4,O3L	0	-1.5
1977	Hou N	58	129	6	24	3	0	1	9	12-2	0	23	.186	.254	.233	35	-12	0-0	.940	-5	65	113	S22,2b20,3b11	0	-1.5
Total	4	208	473	48	100	13	1	3	30	46-6	1	107	.211	.281	.262	50	-33	1-6	.964	-15	102	66	2b76,S61,3b53,O11(5/0/6)	0	-4.4
SPERRY, STAN	Stanley Kenneth; B2.19.1914 Evansville WI; D9.27.1962 Evansville WI; BL/TR/5´10.5˝/164; d7.28																								
1936	Phi N	20	37	2	5	3	0	0	4	3	0	5	.135	.200	.216	11	-5	0	.900	-3	78	72	2b15	—	-0.7
1938	Phi A	60	253	28	69	6	3	0	27	15	0	9	.273	.313	.320	61	-16	1-2	.959	-5	105	60	2b60	—	-1.6
Total	2	80	290	30	74	9	3	0	31	18	0	14	.255	.299	.307	54	-21	1-2	.951	-8	102	62	2b75	—	-2.3
SPIERS, BILL	William James; B6.5.1966 Orangeburg SC; BL/TR/6´2˝/190; [MilA87 1/13]; d4.7; Col Clemson; OF(33/11/20)																								
1989	Mil A	114	345	44	88	9	3	4	33	21-1	1	63	.255	.298	.333	79	-11	10-2	.962	10	107	110	S89,3b12,2b4,1b2,D4	0	0.7
1990	Mil A	112	363	44	88	15	3	2	36	16-0	1	45	.242	.274	.317	66	-18	11-6	.976	-7	103	99	S111	36	-1.6
1991	Mil A	133	414	71	117	13	6	8	54	34-0	2	55	.283	.337	.401	106	3	14-8	.970	-12	93	116	S128/cfD	0	0.0
1992	Mil A	12	16	2	5	2	0	0	2	1-0	0	4	.313	.353	.438	122	1	1-1	1.000	-4	19	0	S5,2b4/3D	149	-0.3
1993	Mil A	113	340	43	81	8	4	2	36	29-2	4	51	.238	.302	.303	65	-17	9-8	.971	-23	83	86	2b104,O7(2/2/4),S4/D	0	-3.6
1994	Mil A	73	214	27	54	10	1	0	17	19-1	1	42	.252	.316	.308	59	-13	7-1	.947	4	104	96	3b35,S35,O2R/1D	0	-0.5
1995	NY N	63	72	5	15	2	1	0	11	12-1	0	15	.208	.314	.264	58	-4	0-1	.794	3	128	180	3b11,2b6	41	-0.1
1996	Hou N	122	218	27	55	10	1	6	26	20-4	2	34	.252	.320	.390	93	-3	7-0	.959	-0	109	119	3b77,2b7,1b4,S4,O2(0/1/1)	0	-0.1
1997	†Hou N	132	291	51	93	27	4	4	48	61-6	1	42	.320	.438	.481	145	24	10-5	.935	18	119	130	3b84,S28,1b8,2b4	0	4.2
1998	†Hou N	123	384	66	105	27	4	4	43	45-0	5	62	.273	.356	.396	100	2	11-2	.966	-5	97	64	3b99,2b9,1b7,S2	0	-0.1
1999	†Hou N	127	393	56	113	18	5	4	39	47-2	0	45	.288	.363	.389	92	-4	10-5	.958	13	128	118	3b71,O31(25/7/9),S13,2b4/1	0	0.9
2000	Hou N	124	355	41	107	17	3	3	43	49-3	1	38	.301	.386	.392	91	-3	7-4	.959	9	124	108	3b51,S27,2b26,O10(6/0/4)	0	0.8
2001	Hou N	4	3	0	1	0	0	0	0	1-1	0	0	.333	.500	.333	114	0	0-0	ø	0	—	—	/H	182	0.0
Total	13	1252	3408	477	922	158	35	37	388	355-21	18	496	.271	.341	.370	90	-43	97-43	.970	7	101	113	S446,3b441,2b168,O53L,1b23,D11	408	0.3
SPIES, HARRY	Henry; B6.12.1866 New Orleans LA; D7.7.1942 Los Angeles CA; BL/TR/5´9˝/170; d4.20																								
1895	Cin N	14	50	2	11	0	1	0	5	3	0	2	.220	.264	.260	34	-5	0	.867	2	*103*	*165*	C12,1b2	—	-0.2
	Lou N	72	276	42	74	14	7	2	35	11	7	19	.268	.313	.391	86	-7	4	.981	-6	90	98	1b47,C26/S	—	-0.8
	Year	86	326	44	85	14	8	2	40	14	7	21	.261	.305	.371	78	-12	4	.979	-4	96	106	1b49,C38/S	—	-1.0
SPIEZIO, ED	Edward Wayne; B10.31.1941 Joliet IL; BR/TR/5´11˝/180; d7.23; s–Scott; Col Lewis																								
1964	StL N	12	12	0	4	0	0	0	0	0-0	0	1	.333	.333	.333	81	0	0-0	ø	0	—	—	/H	0	0.0
1965	StL N	10	18	0	3	0	0	0	5	1-0	1	4	.167	.250	.167	18	-2	0-0	1.000	0	128	0	3b3	0	-0.2
1966	StL N	26	73	4	16	5	1	2	10	5-1	0	11	.219	.269	.397	82	-2	1-0	.885	-5	80	87	3b19	0	-0.7
1967	†StL N	55	105	9	22	2	0	3	10	7-0	1	18	.210	.265	.314	66	-5	2-1	.962	1	103	156	3b19,O7(2/0/6)	0	-0.5
1968	†StL N	29	51	1	8	0	0	0	2	5-0	0	6	.157	.228	.157	19	-5	1-1	1.000	1	107	127	O11(3/0/9),3b2	0	-0.5
1969	SD N	121	355	29	83	9	0	13	43	38-3	4	64	.234	.313	.369	94	-3	1-2	.939	0	105	55	3b98/lf	0	-0.5
1970	SD N	110	316	45	90	18	1	12	42	43-2	4	42	.285	.373	.462	128	14	4-0	.953	2	108	59	3b93	0	1.6
1971	SD N	97	308	16	71	10	1	7	36	22-3	4	50	.231	.286	.338	83	-8	6-5	.962	1	101	83	3b91/lf	0	-0.8
1972	SD N	20	29	2	4	2	0	0	4	1-0	0	6	.138	.161	.207	6	-4	1-0	1.000	-1	57	158	3b5	0	-0.5
	Chi A	74	277	20	66	10	1	2	22	13-3	2	43	.238	.276	.303	71	-10	0-1	.952	6	106	75	3b74	0	-0.6
Total	9	554	1544	126	367	56	4	39	174	135-12	16	245	.238	.303	.355	88	-25	16-10	.949	5	104	72	3b404,O20(7/0/15)	0	-2.7
SPIEZIO, SCOTT	Scott Edward; B9.21.1972 Joliet IL; BB/TR/6´2˝/(195–225); [OakA93 6/181]; d9.14; f–Ed; Col Illinois; OF(64/0/19)																								
1996	Oak A	9	29	6	9	2	0	2	8	4-1	0	4	.310	.394	.586	145	2	0-1	.846	-1	67	0	3b5,D4	0	0.1
1997	Oak A	147	538	58	131	28	4	14	65	44-2	1	75	.243	.300	.388	79	-18	9-3	**.990**	-8	99	88	2b146/3	17	-1.8
1998	Oak A	114	406	54	105	19	1	9	50	44-3	2	56	.259	.333	.377	85	-8	1-3	.975	-3	101	103	2b112/D	46	-0.7
1999	Oak A	89	247	31	60	24	0	8	33	29-3	2	36	.243	.324	.437	95	-1	0-0	.984	5	127	111	2b42,3b31,1b10,D6	0	0.4
2000	Ana A	123	297	47	72	11	2	17	49	40-2	3	56	.242	.334	.465	98	-2	1-2	.993	-2	35	74	D50,1b29,3b15,O10(8/0/2),2b2	0	-0.8
2001	Ana A	139	457	57	124	29	4	13	54	34-4	5	65	.271	.326	.438	98	-2	5-2	.999	6	125	86	1b105,D20,O18(10/0/8),3b10	0	-0.5
2002	†Ana A	153	491	80	140	34	2	12	82	67-7	4	52	.285	.371	.436	117	15	6-7	**.997**	-8	72	106	1b143,3b20,O10(8/0/2)/2	0	-0.6
2003	Ana A	158	521	69	138	36	7	16	83	46-8	5	66	.265	.326	.453	108	6	6-3	.994	-10	89	83	1b114,3b52,O10(3/0/7)	0	-1.2
2004	Sea A	112	367	38	79	12	3	10	41	36-2	4	60	.215	.288	.346	69	-18	4-1	.964	5	104	136	3b66,1b42,D2	13	-1.4
2005	Sea A	29	47	2	3	1	0	1	1	4-0	0	18	.064	.137	.149	-26	-9	0-0	1.000	-2	32	350	3b6,1b4/2D	73	-1.1
2006	†StL N	119	276	44	75	15	4	13	52	37-1	5	66	.272	.366	.496	118	8	1-0	.932	-3	105	93	3b38,O35L,1b13,2b8,D5	0	0.4
Total	11	1192	3676	486	936	211	27	115	518	385-33	31	554	.255	.327	.421	95	-27	33-22	.996	-22	90	91	1b460,2b312,3b244,D93,O83L	149	-7.2
SPIKES, CHARLIE	Leslie Charles; B1.23.1951 Bogalusa LA; BR/TR/6´3˝/(205–220); [NYA69 1/11]; d9.1																								
1972	NY A	14	34	2	5	1	0	0	3	1-0	0	13	.147	.171	.176	4	-4	0-1	1.000	0	91	175	O9R	0	-0.5
1973	Cle A	140	506	68	120	12	3	23	73	45-1	5	103	.237	.303	.409	98	-4	5-3	.964	3	94	**174**	O111(90/0/22),D26	0	-0.8
1974	Cle A	155	568	63	154	23	1	22	80	34-2	7	100	.271	.319	.431	115	9	10-7	.968	-2	94	135	O154R	0	0.0
1975	Cle A	111	345	41	79	13	3	11	33	30-3	0	51	.229	.291	.380	88	-7	7-6	.974	4	96	176	O103(31/0/72),D2	0	-0.9
1976	Cle A	101	334	34	79	11	5	3	31	23-3	5	50	.237	.294	.326	82	-8	5-6	.985	1	102	108	O98(2/0/96),D2	0	-1.4
1977	Cle A	32	95	13	22	2	0	3	11	11-0	2	17	.232	.321	.347	85	-2	0-2	.972	-3	74	60	O27R,D2	0	-0.6
1978	Det A	10	28	1	7	1	0	0	2	2-1	2	6	.250	.344	.286	76	-1	0-0	.909	-1	58	178	O9R	0	-0.2
1979	Atl N	66	93	12	26	8	0	3	21	5-1	0	30	.280	.310	.462	104	0	0-0	.842	-2	72	0	O15(12/0/3)	0	-0.2
1980	Atl N	41	36	6	10	1	0	0	2	3-2	1	18	.278	.350	.306	84	-1	0-0	1.000	-0	91	0	O7(1/0/6)	0	-0.1
Total	9	670	2039	240	502	72	12	65	256	154-13	22	388	.246	.304	.389	96	-18	27-25	.969	0	94	140	O533(136/0/398),D32	0	-4.7
SPILBORGHS, RYAN	Ryan Adam; B9.5.1979 Santa Barbara CA; BR/TR/6´1˝/190; [ColN02 7/201]; d7.16; Col California–Santa Barbara																								
2005	Col N	1	4	0	2	0	0	0	1	0-0	0	1	.500	.500	.500	146	0	0-0	1.000	2	337	1904	/rf	0	0.2
2006	Col N	67	167	26	48	6	3	4	21	14-0	0	30	.287	.337	.431	89	-3	5-2	.988	0	91	216	O46(10/24/15)/D	0	-0.3
Total	2	68	171	26	50	6	3	4	22	14-0	0	31	.292	.340	.433	90	-3	5-2	.989	2	97	258	O47(10/24/16)/D	0	-0.1
SPILMAN, HARRY	William Harry; B7.18.1954 Albany GA; BL/TR/6´1˝/(180–190); d9.11; C6																								
1978	Cin N	4	4	1	1	0	0	0	0	0-0	0	1	.250	.250	.250	40	0	0-0	ø	0	—	—	/H	0	0.0
1979	†Cin N	43	56	7	12	3	0	0	5	7-2	2	5	.214	.323	.268	63	-2	0-0	1.000	-0	42	54	1b12,3b4	0	-0.3
1980	Cin N	65	101	14	27	4	0	4	19	9-1	1	19	.267	.327	.426	113	2	0-0	.986	1	131	99	1b18,O2L/C3	0	0.1
1981	Cin N	23	24	4	4	1	0	0	3	3-0	0	7	.167	.259	.208	34	-2	0-0	1.000	-0	58	0	3b3,1b2	0	-0.2
	†Hou N	28	34	5	10	0	0	0	1	2-0	0	3	.294	.333	.294	84	-1	0-1	1.000	-1	54	81	1b13	0	-0.2
	Year	51	58	9	14	1	0	0	4	5-0	0	10	.241	.302	.259	62	-3	0-1	.984	-1	64	65	1b15,3b3	0	-0.4
1982	Hou N	38	61	7	17	2	0	3	11	5-0	0	10	.279	.333	.459	130	2	0-0	.989	-1	71	73	1b11	0	0.1
1983	Hou N	42	78	7	13	3	0	1	9	5-0	0	12	.167	.212	.244	29	-8	0-0	1.000	-2	75	52	1b19,C6	0	-1.1
1984	Hou N	32	72	14	19	2	0	2	15	12-0	0	10	.264	.356	.375	117	2	0-0	.978	-4	62	127	1b18,C8	77	-0.3
1985	Hou N	44	66	3	9	1	0	1	4	3-0	0	7	.136	.174	.197	4	-9	0-0	1.000	-1	45	141	1b19,C2	0	-1.2
1986	Det A	24	49	6	12	2	0	3	8	3-0	0	8	.245	.288	.469	102	0	0-0	1.000	-0	66	0	D11,3b2/C1	0	-0.1
	SF N	58	94	12	27	7	0	2	22	12-3	0	13	.287	.368	.426	124	3	0-0	.994	1	126	70	1b19,3b5/C2lf	0	0.3
1987	†SF N	83	90	5	24	5	0	1	14	9-0	0	20	.267	.327	.356	87	-2	1-1	.875	-2	75	152	3b10,1b9/C	0	-0.4
1988	SF N	40	40	4	7	1	1	1	3	4-1	0	6	.175	.250	.325	67	-2	0-0	1.000	0	68	218	1b6,C2/lf	0	-0.2
	Hou N	7	5	0	0	0	0	0	0	0-0	0	3	.000	.000	.000	-99	-1	0-0	1.000	-0	0	0	/1	0	-0.2
	Year	47	45	4	7	1	1	1	3	4-1	0	9	.156	.224	.289	48	-3	0-0	1.000	0	56	178	1b7,C2/lf	0	-0.4

YEAR	TM LG	G	AB	R	H	2B	3B	HR	RBI	BB-IB	HP	SO	AVG	OBP	SLG	AOPS	ABR	SB-CS	FA	FR	RNG	THR	GAMES AT POSITION	DL	BFW
1989	Hou N	32	36	7	10	3	0	0	3	7-1	0	2	.278	.395	.361	122	2	0-0	1.000	0	120	58	1b9/C	0	0.1
Total	12	563	810	96	192	34	1	18	117	81-8	3	126	.237	.306	.348	85	-16	1-2	.991	-11	82	91	1b157,3b25,C23,D11,O4L/2	77	-3.6
Spindel, Hal	Harold Stewart; B5.27.1913 Chandler OK; D7.28.2002 San Clemente CA; BR/TR/6´0˝/185; d4.23; Col UCLA																								
1939	StL A	48	119	13	32	3	1	0	11	8	0	7	.269	.315	.311	59	-7	0-2	.993	-2	*82*	*100*	C32	—	-0.8
1945	Phi N	36	87	7	20	3	0	0	8	6	0	7	.230	.280	.264	53	-6	0	.964	-1	*68*	*119*	C31	0	-0.5
1946	Phi N	1	3	0	1	0	0	0	1	0	0	0	.333	.333	.333	92	0	0	1.000	0	*0*	*0*	/C	0	0.0
Total	3	85	209	20	53	6	1	0	20	14	0	14	.254	.300	.292	57	-13	0-2	.980	-3	*75*	*107*	C64	0	-1.3
Spivey, Junior	Ernest Lee; B1.28.1975 Oklahoma City OK; BR/TR/6´0˝/(185–200); [AriN96 36/1085]; d6.2; Col Cowley Co. (KS) CC; [DL 2000 Ari N 98]																								
2001	Ari N	72	163	33	42	6	3	5	21	23-0	2	47	.258	.354	.423	94	-1	3-0	.985	-2	88	112	2b66/S	0	0.0
2002	†Ari N★	143	538	103	162	34	6	16	78	65-5	16	100	.301	.389	.476	116	15	11-6	.977	1	94	78	2b143	16	2.3
2003	Ari N	106	365	52	93	22	2	13	50	33-1	7	95	.255	.326	.433	89	-6	4-3	.982	2	98	89	2b98/cf	36	0.1
2004	Mil N	59	228	33	62	13	0	7	28	25-0	7	48	.272	.359	.421	101	1	5-3	.963	2	106	114	2b58/S	93	0.6
2005	Mil N	49	182	22	43	8	1	5	17	18-1	1	57	.236	.308	.374	77	-6	7-3	.968	-3	92	91	2b48	0	-0.6
	Was N	28	77	15	17	7	0	2	7	11-1	2	26	.221	.330	.390	93	0	2-0	1.000	-4	95	97	2b22	70	-0.3
	Year	77	259	37	60	15	1	7	24	29-2	3	83	.232	.315	.378	82	-7	9-3	.978	-6	93	93	2b70	0	-0.9
Total	5	457	1553	258	419	90	12	48	201	175-8	35	373	.270	.354	.436	100	3	32-15	.977	-3	96	92	2b435,S2/cf	313	2.1
Spognardi, Andy	Andrea Ettore; B10.18.1908 Boston MA; D1.1.2000 Dedham MA; BR/TR/5´9.5˝/160; d9.2; Col Boston College																								
1932	Bos A	17	34	9	10	1	0	0	1	6	0	6	.294	.400	.324	92	0	0-0	.979	2	130	110	2b9,S3,3b2	—	0.3
Spohrer, Al	Alfred Ray; B12.3.1902 Philadelphia PA; D7.17.1972 Plymouth NH; BR/TR/5´10.5˝/175; d4.13																								
1928	NY N	2	2	0	0	0	0	0	0	0	0	0	.000	.000	.000	-99	-1	0	1.000	0	*0*	*0*	C2	—	0.0
	Bos N	51	124	15	27	3	0	0	9	5	1	11	.218	.254	.242	32	-13	1	.976	-5	*90*	*89*	C48	—	-1.5
	Year	53	126	15	27	3	0	0	9	5	1	11	.214	.250	.238	30	-13	1	.977	-5	*89*	*88*	C50	—	-1.5
1929	Bos N	114	342	42	93	21	8	2	48	26	2	35	.272	.327	.398	82	-11	1	.954	-5	*105*	*90*	C109	—	-0.9
1930	Bos N	112	356	44	113	22	8	2	37	22	2	24	.317	.361	.441	96	-3	3	.957	-10	*115*	*61*	C108	—	-0.6
1931	Bos N	114	350	23	84	17	5	0	27	22	0	27	.240	.285	.317	64	-19	2	.982	1	*106*	*79*	C111	—	-1.1
1932	Bos N	104	335	31	90	12	2	0	33	15	0	26	.269	.300	.316	69	-15	2	.991	8	*138*	*101*	C100	—	-0.1
1933	Bos N	67	184	11	46	6	1	1	12	11	0	13	.250	.292	.310	78	-6	3	.972	-3	*196*	*73*	C65	—	-0.6
1934	Bos N	100	265	25	59	15	0	0	17	14	0	18	.223	.262	.279	49	-20	1	.977	-1	*112*	*96*	C98	—	-1.5
1935	Bos N	92	260	22	63	7	1	1	16	9	2	12	.242	.273	.288	55	-17	0	.958	-10	*88*	*100*	C90	—	-2.2
Total	8	756	2218	213	575	103	25	6	199	124	7	166	.259	.301	.336	70	-105	13	.972	-25	*117*	*86*	C731	—	-8.5
Spotts, Jim	James Russell; B4.10.1909 Honey Brook PA; D6.15.1964 Medford NJ; BR/TR/5´10.5˝/175; d4.23; Col Marshall																								
1930	Phi N	3	2	1	0	0	0	0	0	0	0	1	.000	.000	.000	-93	-1	0	1.000	0	*0*	*0*	C2	—	0.0
Sprague, Charlie	Charles Wellington; B10.10.1864 Cleveland OH; D12.31.1912 Des Moines IA; BL/TL/5´11˝/150; d9.17; ▲																								
1887	Chi N	3	13	0	2	0	0	0	0	0	0	2	.154	.154	.154	-13	-2	0	.667	-1	48	0	P3/cf	—	0.0
1889	Cle N	2	7	2	1	0	0	0	1	1	0	0	.143	.250	.143	11	0	1	.857	1	180	780	P2	—	0.0
1890	Tol AA	55	199	25	47	5	6	1	19	16	3	—	.236	.303	.337	86	-5	10	.892	-4	84	79	O40(24/10/6),P19	—	-0.6
Total	3	60	219	27	50	5	6	1	20	17	3	2	.228	.293	.320	77	-7	11	.892	-4	83	78	O41(24/11/6),P24	—	-0.6
Sprague, Ed	Edward Nelson Jr.; B7.25.1967 Castro Valley CA; BR/TR/6´2˝/(205–215); [TorA88 1/25]; d5.7; f–Ed; Col Stanford; OF(14/0/2)																								
1991	Tor A	61	160	17	44	7	0	4	20	19-2	3	43	.275	.361	.394	105	2	0-3	.870	-2	101	38	3b35,1b22,C2,D2	0	-0.3
1992	†Tor A	22	47	6	11	2	0	1	7	3-0	0	7	.234	.280	.340	70	-2	0-0	.985	0	104	26	C15,1b4/3D	0	-0.1
1993	†Tor A	150	546	50	142	31	1	12	73	32-1	10	85	.260	.310	.386	85	-12	1-0	.955	-6	88	79	3b150	0	-1.6
1994	Tor A	109	405	38	97	19	1	11	44	23-1	11	95	.240	.296	.373	71	-19	1-0	.946	-10	74	107	3b107,1b3	0	-2.6
1995	Tor A	**144**	521	77	127	27	2	18	74	58-3	**15**	96	.244	.333	.407	92	-6	0-0	.958	-1	94	78	3b139,1b7,D2	0	-0.6
1996	Tor A	159	591	88	146	35	2	36	101	60-3	12	146	.247	.325	.496	105	3	0-0	.956	-10	87	115	3b148,D10	0	-0.7
1997	Tor A	138	504	63	115	29	4	14	48	51-0	6	102	.228	.306	.385	79	-16	0-1	.945	-4	90	93	3b129,D8	25	-1.9
1998	Tor A	105	382	49	91	20	0	17	51	24-1	11	73	.238	.301	.424	86	-9	0-2	.924	-6	90	52	3b105	0	-1.4
	Oak A	27	87	8	13	5	0	3	7	2-1	2	17	.149	.187	.310	27	-10	1-0	.909	-1	95	59	3b23/1	0	-1.0
	Year	132	469	57	104	25	0	20	58	26-2	13	90	.222	.280	.403	75	-19	1-2	.921	-6	91	53	3b128/1	0	-2.4
1999	Pit N★	137	490	71	131	27	2	22	81	50-6	**17**	93	.267	.352	.465	105	4	3-6	.920	-1	103	99	3b134	14	0.2
2000	SD N	53	117	17	32	10	0	10	25	10-2	2	28	.274	.336	.615	144	7	0-0	.964	-8	69	83	1b24,3b5,O5(4/0/1)	0	-0.2
	Bos A	33	111	11	24	4	0	2	9	12-0	0	18	.216	.293	.306	51	-9	0-0	.972	0	96	22	3b30,1b3/D	0	-0.8
	SD N	20	40	2	9	2	0	0	2	3-0	1	12	.225	.295	.275	48	-3	0-0	1.000	-9	27	0	3b5,O2L/12	0	-1.4
2001	†Sea A	45	94	9	28	7	0	2	16	11-1	1	18	.298	.374	.436	120	3	0-0	.981	-2	43	79	1b12,O9(8/0/1),3b8/CD	24	0.0
Total	11	1203	4095	506	1010	225	12	152	558	358-21	91	833	.247	.318	.419	90	-67	6-12	.942	-59	90	85	3b1019,1b77,D34,C18,O16L/2	63	-12.4
Spratt, Harry	Henry Lee; B7.10.1887 Broadford VA; D7.3.1969 Washington DC; BL/TR/5´8.5˝/175; d4.13; Col Emory & Henry																								
1911	Bos N	62	154	22	37	4	4	2	13	13	0	25	.240	.299	.357	77	-6	1	.892	-9	82	70	S26,2b5,3b4,O4(0/3/1)	—	-1.3
1912	Bos N	27	89	6	23	3	2	3	15	7	0	11	.258	.313	.438	102	0	2	.842	-10	88	65	S23	—	-0.9
Total	2	89	243	28	60	7	6	5	28	20	0	36	.247	.304	.387	86	-6	3	.871	-18	85	68	S49,2b5,O4(0/3/1),3b4	—	-2.2
Spriggs, George	George Herman; B5.22.1941 Jewell MD; BL/TR/5´11˝/(175–180); d9.15																								
1965	Pit N	9	2	5	1	0	0	0	0	0-0	0	0	.500	.500	.500	182	0	2-0	ø	-0	0	0	/rf	0	0.1
1966	Pit N	9	7	0	1	0	0	0	0	0-0	0	3	.143	.143	.143	-20	-1	0-0	ø	0	—	—	/H	0	-0.1
1967	Pit N	38	57	14	10	1	1	0	5	6-0	0	20	.175	.246	.228	39	-5	3-0	1.000	-1	85	0	O13(10/0/3)	0	-0.6
1969	KC A	23	29	4	4	2	1	0	0	3-0	1	8	.138	.242	.276	44	-2	0-0	1.000	-1	82	0	O6(4/1/1)	0	-0.3
1970	KC A	51	130	12	27	2	3	1	7	14-0	0	32	.208	.283	.292	59	-8	4-3	.953	1	98	188	O36R	0	-0.9
Total	5	130	225	35	43	5	5	1	12	23-0	1	63	.191	.266	.271	51	-16	9-3	.965	-1	93	128	O56(14/1/41)	0	-1.8
Springer, Steve	Steven Michael; B2.11.1961 Long Beach CA; BR/TR/6´0˝/190; [NYN82 20/501]; d5.22; Col Utah																								
1990	Cle A	4	12	1	2	0	0	0	1	0-0	0	6	.167	.154	.167	-7	-2	0-0	1.000	-1	57	0	3b3/D	0	-0.3
1992	NY N	4	5	0	2	1	0	0	0	0-0	0	1	.400	.400	.600	181	1	0-0	1.000	-0	37	182	/23	0	0.0
Total	2	8	17	1	4	1	0	0	1	0-0	0	7	.235	.222	.294	48	-1	0-0	1.000	-1	55	0	3b4/2D	0	-0.3
Sprinz, Joe	Joseph Conrad "Mule"; B8.3.1902 St.Louis MO; D1.11.1994 Fremont CA; BR/TR/5´11˝/185; d7.16																								
1930	Cle A	17	45	5	8	1	0	0	2	4	0	4	.178	.245	.200	14	-6	0-0	1.000	4	*108*	*116*	C17	—	-0.1
1931	Cle A	1	3	0	0	0	0	0	0	0	0	0	.000	.000	.000	-95	-1	0-0	1.000	0	*0*	*411*	/C	—	-0.1
1933	StL N	3	5	1	1	0	0	0	0	1	0	1	.200	.333	.200	53	0	0	1.000	1	*74*	*159*	C3	—	0.1
Total	3	21	53	6	9	1	0	0	2	5	0	5	.170	.241	.189	12	-7	0-0	1.000	4	*99*	*133*	C21	—	-0.1
Spurgeon, Freddy	Fred; B10.9.1900 Wabash IN; D11.5.1970 Kalamazoo MI; BR/TR/5´11.5˝/160; d9.19; Col Valparaiso																								
1924	Cle A	3	7	0	1	1	0	0	0	0	1	0	.143	.250	.286	37	-1	0-0	.882	-0	125	0	2b3	—	-0.1
1925	Cle A	107	376	50	108	9	3	0	32	15	0	21	.287	.315	.327	62	-23	8-5	.927	-3	110	119	3b56,2b46,S3	—	-2.0
1926	Cle A	149	614	101	181	31	3	0	49	27	2	36	.295	.327	.355	77	-22	7-2	.962	-6	100	**119**	2b149	—	-2.3
1927	Cle A	57	179	30	45	6	1	1	19	18	1	14	.251	.323	.313	65	-9	8-1	.938	-6	93	91	2b52	—	-1.2
Total	4	316	1176	181	335	47	7	1	100	60	4	71	.285	.322	.339	70	-55	23-8	.958	-16	99	104	2b250,3b56,S3	—	-5.6
Spurney, Ed	Edward Frederick; B1.19.1872 Cleveland OH; D10.12.1932 Cleveland OH; d6.26																								
1891	Pit N	3	7	2	2	1	0	0	0	2	0	1	.286	.444	.429	158	1	0	.889	-0	109	0	S3	—	0.0
Squires, Mike	Michael Lynn; B3.5.1952 Kalamazoo MI; BL/TL/5´11˝/(185–198); [ChiA73 18/429]; d9.1; C4; Col Western Michigan																								
1975	Chi A	20	65	5	15	0	0	0	4	8-2	0	5	.231	.311	.231	56	-4	3-0	.988	0	108	82	1b20	0	-0.4
1977	Chi A	3	3	0	0	0	0	0	0	0-0	0	1	.000	.000	.000	-99	-1	0-0	1.000	0	418	0	/1	0	-0.1
1978	Chi A	46	150	25	42	9	2	0	19	16-0	0	21	.280	.343	.367	100	1	4-4	.997	-2	75	83	1b45	0	-0.5
1979	Chi A	122	295	44	78	10	1	2	22	22-3	2	9	.264	.318	.325	74	-11	15-5	.995	5	123	84	1b110/lf	0	-0.9
1980	Chi A	131	343	38	97	11	3	2	33	33-1	1	24	.283	.347	.350	92	-3	8-9	.995	6	123	90	1b114,C2	0	-0.5
1981	Chi A	92	294	35	78	9	0	0	25	22-0	0	17	.265	.312	.296	78	-8	7-2	.992	4	118	101	1b88/lf	0	-0.9
1982	Chi A	116	195	33	52	9	3	1	21	14-3	0	13	.267	.316	.359	84	-4	3-3	.995	5	**134**	**119**	1b109	0	-0.3
1983	†Chi A	143	153	21	34	4	1	1	11	22-3	2	11	.222	.326	.281	67	-6	3-3	**.996**	3	119	**131**	1b124/3D	0	-0.7
1984	Chi A	104	82	9	15	1	0	0	6	6-1	0	7	.183	.239	.195	21	-9	2-2	1.000	1	93	155	1b77,3b13,O3(0/1/1)/P	0	-1.0

YEAR	TM LG	G	AB	R	H	2B	3B	HR	RBI	BB-IB	HP	SO	AVG	OBP	SLG	AOPS	ABR	SB-CS	FA	FR	RNG	THR	GAMES AT POSITION	DL	BFW
1985	Chi A	2	0	1	0	0	0	0	0	0-0	0	0	ø	ø	ø	ø	0	0-0	ø	0	—	—	/R	0	0.0
Total	10	779	1580	211	411	53	10	6	141	143-13	5	108	.260	.321	.318	78	-45	45-28	.995	23	117	102	1b688,3b14,D5,O5(2/1/1),C2/P	0	-5.3
STABELL, JOE Joseph F.; B Buffalo NY; D7.10.1923 Buffalo NY; 5´11.5˝/?; d9.19																									
1885	Buf N	7	22	0	1	0	0	0	0	0	—	9	.045	.045	.045	-68	-4	—	.545	-2	0	0	O6(0/6/1)/2	—	-0.6
STAEHLE, MARV Marvin Gustave; B3.13.1942 Oak Park IL; BL/TR/5´10˝/(165–176); d9.15																									
1964	Chi A	6	5	0	2	0	0	0	2	0-0	0	0	.400	.400	.400	127	0	1-0	ø	0	—	—	/H	0	0.0
1965	Chi A	7	7	0	3	0	0	0	2	0-0	0	0	.429	.429	.429	154	0	0-0	ø	0	—	—	/H	0	0.0
1966	Chi A	8	15	2	2	0	0	0	0	4-0	0	2	.133	.316	.133	37	-1	1-0	1.000	1	121	202	2b6	0	0.1
1967	Chi A	32	54	1	6	1	0	0	1	4-0	0	8	.111	.172	.130	-10	-7	1-1	1.000	-3	107	48	2b17,S5	0	-1.0
1969	Mon N	6	17	4	7	2	0	1	1	2-0	0	0	.412	.474	.706	225	3	0-0	.944	-1	103	73	2b4	0	0.3
1970	Mon N	104	321	41	70	9	1	0	26	39-1	3	21	.218	.306	.252	52	-21	1-3	.963	-17	89	94	2b91/S	0	-3.4
1971	Atl N	22	36	5	4	0	0	0	1	5-0	1	4	.111	.238	.111	2	-5	0-0	1.000	4	132	113	2b7/3	0	0.0
Total	7	185	455	53	94	12	1	1	33	54-1	4	35	.207	.295	.244	49	-31	4-4	.971	-15	95	94	2b125,S6/3	0	-4.0
STAFFORD, HEINIE Henry Alexander; B11.1.1891 Orleans VT; D1.29.1972 Lake Worth FL; BR/TR/5´7˝/160; d10.5; Col Tufts																									
1916	NY N	1	1	0	0	0	0	0	0	0	0	0	.000	.000	.000	-99	0	0	ø	0	—	—	/H	—	0.0
STAFFORD, GENERAL James Joseph "Jamsey"; B7.9.1868 Webster MA; D9.18.1923 Worcester MA; BR/TR/5´8˝/165; d8.27; b–John; OF(96/111/44); ▲																									
1890	Buf P	15	49	11	7	1	0	0	3	7	0	8	.143	.250	.163	13	-6	2	.893	-2	82	207	P12,O4(1/1/2)	—	-0.2
1893	NY N	67	281	58	79	7	4	5	27	25	2	31	.281	.344	.388	94	-4	19	.901	-7	72	173	O67C	—	-1.3
1894	NY N	14	46	10	10	1	1	0	4	10	1	7	.217	.368	.283	59	-3	2	.750	-4	75	104	3b6,O5R/21	—	-0.5
1895	NY N	124	463	79	129	12	5	3	73	40	6	32	.279	.344	.346	80	-14	42	.911	-7	99	97	2b110,O12L,3b2	—	-1.4
1896	NY N	59	230	28	66	9	1	0	40	13	3	18	.287	.333	.335	79	-7	15	.897	-2	133	116	O53L,S6	—	-1.1
1897	NY N	7	23	0	2	0	0	0	3	3	0	—	.087	.192	.087	-26	-4	0	1.000	-3	0	0	O5L,S2	—	-0.6
	Lou N	113	441	68	122	16	5	7	54	31	3	—	.277	.328	.383	91	-7	15	.886	-10	101	82	S105,O7(4/2/1)/3	—	-1.1
	Year	120	464	68	124	16	5	7	57	34	3	—	.267	.321	.369	85	-11	15	.881	-12	100	83	S107,O12(9/2/1)/3	—	-1.7
1898	Lou N	49	181	26	54	3	0	1	25	19	1	—	.298	.368	.331	102	1	7	.901	-5	95	56	2b28,O22(6/7/9)/3	—	-0.4
	Bos N	37	123	21	32	2	0	1	8	4	1	—	.260	.289	.301	66	-6	3	.909	-3	22	0	O35(9/1/25)/1	—	-1.0
	Year	86	304	47	86	5	0	2	33	23	2	—	.283	.337	.319	87	-5	10	.924	-8	69	170	O57(15/8/34),2b28/31	—	-1.4
1899	Bos N	55	182	29	55	4	2	3	40	7	0	—	.302	.328	.396	89	-4	9	.956	-8	0	0	O41(6/33/2),2b5,S5	—	-1.3
	Was N	31	118	11	29	5	1	1	14	5	0	—	.246	.276	.331	67	-6	4	.951	-4	85	39	2b17,S13,3b2	—	-0.8
	Year	86	300	40	84	9	3	4	54	12	0	—	.280	.308	.370	81	-10	13	.956	-12	0	0	O41(6/33/2),2b22,S18,3b2	—	-2.1
Total	8	571	2137	341	585	60	19	21	291	164	17	96	.274	.330	.349	82	-60	118	.911	-54	69	111	O251C,2b161,S131,3b12,P12,1b2	—	-9.7
STAFFORD, BOB Robert M.; B6.26.1872 Oak Ridge NC; D8.20.1916 Moores Springs NC; 6´0˝/180; d10.12																									
1890	Phi AA	1	2	0	0	0	0	0	0	0	0	—	.000	.000	.000	-99	-1	0	ø	-0	0	0	/rf	—	-0.1
STAGGS, STEVE Stephen Robert; B5.6.1951 Anchorage AK; BR/TR/5´9˝/155; [KCA71 A2/33]; d7.1; Col Cerritos (CA) JC																									
1977	Tor A	72	290	37	75	11	6	2	28	36-0	0	38	.259	.339	.359	90	-4	5-9	.965	-13	88	67	2b72	0	-1.5
1978	Oak A	47	78	10	19	2	2	0	0	19-0	0	17	.244	.392	.321	108	2	2-3	.976	-3	90	64	2b40,S2,3b2,D2	0	0.0
Total	2	119	368	47	94	13	8	2	28	55-0	0	55	.255	.351	.351	94	-2	7-12	.968	-16	88	66	2b112,D2,3b2,S2	0	-1.5
STAHL, CHICK Charles Sylvester; B1.10.1873 Avilla IN; D3.28.1907 W.Baden IN; BL/TL/5´10˝/160; d4.19; M1																									
1897	†Bos N	114	469	112	166	30	13	4	97	38	3	—	.354	.406	.499	130	19	18	.928	-5	104	141	O111(1/0/110)	—	0.8
1898	Bos N	125	467	72	144	21	8	3	52	46	4	—	.308	.375	.407	118	11	6	.968	-3	79	110	O125(8/0/118)	—	0.2
1899	Bos N	148	576	122	202	23	19	7	52	72	4	—	.351	.426	.493	138	31	33	.969	3	113	110	O148(1/1/146)/P	—	2.4
1900	Bos N	136	553	88	163	23	16	5	82	34	0	—	.295	.336	.421	96	-6	27	**.968**	5	110	80	O135(64/1/71)	—	-1.0
1901	Bos A	131	515	105	156	20	16	6	72	54	7	—	.303	.377	.439	128	20	29	.957	-5	70	89	O131(0/130/1)	—	0.8
1902	Bos A	127	508	92	164	22	11	2	58	37	5	—	.323	.375	.421	117	12	24	.953	-6	119	68	O125C	—	0.0
1903	†Bos A	77	299	60	82	12	6	2	44	28	1	—	.274	.338	.375	108	3	10	.961	-3	134	106	O74C	—	-0.3
1904	Bos A	**157**	587	83	170	27	**19**	3	67	64	7	—	.290	.366	.416	139	28	11	.961	-18	34	0	O157C	—	0.2
1905	Bos A	134	500	61	129	17	4	0	47	50	5	—	.258	.332	.308	102	3	18	.977	-6	77	133	O134C	—	-1.1
1906	Bos A	**155**	595	63	170	24	6	4	51	47	8	—	.286	.346	.366	123	17	13	.961	7	124	**216**	O155C,M	—	1.8
Total	10	1304	5069	858	1546	219	118	36	622	470	44	—	.305	.369	.416	121	138	189	.961	-31	94	104	O1295(74/777/446)/P	—	3.8
STAHL, JAKE Garland; B4.13.1879 Elkhart IL; D9.18.1922 Monrovia CA; BR/TR/6´2˝/195; d4.20; M4; Col Illinois																									
1903	Bos A	40	92	14	22	3	5	2	8	4	2	—	.239	.286	.446	111	1	1	.956	0	*119*	*89*	C28/lf	—	0.3
1904	Was A	142	520	54	136	29	12	3	50	21	15	—	.262	.309	.381	119	11	25	.978	4	115	90	1b119,O23C	—	1.3
1905	Was A	141	501	66	125	22	12	5	66	28	**17**	—	.250	.311	.371	121	11	41	.986	2	104	86	1b140,M	—	1.1
1906	Was A	137	482	38	107	9	8	0	51	21	8	—	.222	.266	.274	73	-17	30	.983	-2	93	82	1b136,M	—	-2.3
1908	NY A	75	274	34	70	18	5	2	42	11	8	—	.255	.304	.380	120	6	17	.933	4	177	123	O68(64/4/0),1b6	—	0.7
	Bos A	78	262	29	64	9	11	0	23	20	15	—	.244	.333	.363	123	7	13	.984	-2	88	98	1b78	—	0.4
	Year	153	536	63	134	27	16	2	65	31	**23**	—	.250	.319	.371	122	13	30	.984	2	87	91	1b84,O68(64/4/0)	—	1.1
1909	Bos A	127	435	62	128	19	12	6	60	43	8	—	.294	.377	.434	153	27	16	.986	-12	64	93	1b126	—	1.5
1910	Bos A	144	531	68	144	19	16	**10**	77	42	8	—	.271	.334	.424	134	18	22	.985	-7	75	75	1b142	—	0.9
1912	†Bos A	95	326	40	98	21	6	3	60	31	6	—	.301	.372	.429	123	10	13	.980	-2	92	96	1b92,M	—	0.6
1913	Bos A	2	2	0	0	0	0	0	0	0	0	1	.000	.000	.000	-98	-1	0	ø	0	—	—	/HM	—	-0.1
Total	9	981	3425	405	894	149	87	31	437	221	94	1	.261	.323	.382	120	73	178	.983	-13	90	87	1b839,O92(65/27/0),C28	—	4.4
STAHL, LARRY Larry Floyd; B6.29.1941 Belleville IL; BL/TL/6´1˝/(175–185); d9.11																									
1964	KC A	15	46	7	12	1	0	3	6	1-0	0	10	.261	.277	.478	102	0	0-0	.955	1	102	171	O10(5/4/1)	0	0.0
1965	KC A	28	81	9	16	2	1	4	14	5-0	1	16	.198	.250	.395	82	-2	1-0	1.000	2	119	98	O21(8/12/4)	0	-0.2
1966	KC A	119	312	37	78	11	5	5	34	17-3	1	63	.250	.289	.365	90	-5	5-3	.980	1	98	123	O94(69/2/27)	0	-1.0
1967	NY N	71	155	9	37	5	0	1	18	8-0	2	25	.239	.283	.290	66	-7	2-2	.969	5	129	204	O43(3/32/8)	0	-0.3
1968	NY N	53	183	15	43	7	2	3	10	21-1	0	38	.235	.314	.344	97	0	3-0	.983	7	128	168	O47(13/30/19),1b9	0	0.5
1969	SD N	95	162	10	32	6	2	3	10	17-3	1	31	.198	.278	.315	68	-7	3-3	.981	4	99	192	O37(27/4/5),1b13	0	-0.6
1970	SD N	52	66	5	12	2	0	0	3	2-0	0	14	.182	.206	.212	13	-8	2-2	1.000	-0	82	129	O20(17/0/4)	0	-1.0
1971	SD N	114	308	27	78	13	4	8	36	26-4	0	59	.253	.310	.399	107	1	4-3	.987	7	94	208	O75(46/8/26),1b7	0	0.4
1972	SD N	107	297	31	67	9	3	7	20	31-3	0	67	.226	.298	.347	89	-5	1-3	.986	-1	98	78	O76(26/10/42)/1	0	-1.2
1973	†Cin N	76	111	17	25	2	2	2	12	14-3	1	34	.225	.315	.333	84	-3	1-0	1.000	-1	68	176	O29(3/4/24),1b2	0	-0.4
Total	10	730	1721	167	400	58	19	36	163	142-17	6	357	.232	.292	.351	86	-36	22-16	.983	23	103	150	O452(217/106/160),1b32	0	-3.8
STAHOVIAK, SCOTT Scott Edmund; B3.6.1970 Waukegan IL; BL/TR/6´5˝/(210–230); [MinA91 1/27]; d9.10; Col Creighton																									
1993	Min A	20	57	1	11	4	0	0	1	3-0	0	22	.193	.233	.263	33	-5	0-2	.922	2	129	35	3b19	0	-0.4
1995	Min A	94	263	28	70	19	0	3	23	30-1	1	61	.266	.341	.373	86	-5	5-1	.998	7	144	94	1b69,3b22/D	0	-0.2
1996	Min A	130	405	72	115	30	3	13	61	59-7	2	114	.284	.376	.469	111	8	3-3	.994	10	**134**	89	1b114,D9	0	0.7
1997	Min A	91	275	33	63	17	0	10	33	24-1	6	73	.229	.301	.400	81	-8	5-2	.990	4	124	110	1b81,D5	44	-1.0
1998	Min A	9	19	1	2	0	0	1	1	0-0	0	7	.105	.105	.263	-8	-3	0-0	.975	0	145	117	1b4/rf	0	-0.3
Total	5	344	1019	135	261	70	3	27	119	116-9	9	277	.256	.335	.410	90	-13	13-8	.994	23	134	97	1b268,3b41,D15/rf	44	-1.2
STAIGER, ROY Roy Joseph; B1.6.1950 Tulsa OK; BR/TR/6´0˝/195; [NYN70*S1/24]; d9.12; Col Bacone																									
1975	NY N	13	19	2	3	1	0	0	0	0-0	0	4	.158	.158	.211	2	-3	0-0	1.000	-1	79	0	3b13	0	-0.4
1976	NY N	95	304	23	67	8	1	2	26	25-6	1	35	.220	.278	.273	61	-16	3-3	.967	13	111	132	3b93/S	0	-0.4
1977	NY N	40	123	16	31	9	0	2	11	4-0	0	20	.252	.276	.374	75	-5	1-0	.934	4	116	85	3b36/S	0	-0.1
1979	NY A	4	11	1	3	1	0	0	1	1-0	0	0	.273	.308	.364	89	0	0-0	1.000	-0	90	158	3b4	0	0.0
Total	4	152	457	42	104	19	1	4	38	30-6	1	59	.228	.274	.300	63	-24	4-3	.960	16	110	115	3b146,S2	0	-0.9
STAINBACK, TUCK George Tucker; B8.4.1911 Los Angeles CA; D11.29.1992 Camarillo CA; BR/TR/5´11.5˝/175; d4.17																									
1934	Chi N	104	359	47	110	14	3	2	46	8	3	42	.306	.327	.379	90	-6	7	.955	-3	97	64	O96(60/22/15)/3	—	-1.3
1935	Chi N	47	94	16	24	4	0	3	11	0	2	13	.255	.271	.394	76	-4	1	.932	-1	99	49	O28(1/1/26)	—	-0.6
1936	Chi N	44	75	13	13	3	0	1	5	6	0	14	.173	.235	.253	31	-7	1	1.000	1	110	79	O26(15/6/5)	—	-0.7
1937	Chi N	72	160	18	37	7	1	0	14	7	1	16	.231	.268	.287	49	-11	3	.981	2	105	126	O49(9/39/1)	—	-1.1
1938	StL N	6	10	2	0	0	0	0	0	0	0	3	.000	.000	.000	-95	-3	0	1.000	0	133	0	O2(1/1/0)	—	-0.3
	Phi N	30	81	9	21	3	0	1	11	3	1	3	.259	.294	.333	74	-3	1	.980	1	117	63	O25(13/4/9)	—	-0.3

YEAR	TM LG	G	AB	R	H	2B	3B	HR	RBI	BB-IB	HP	SO	AVG	OBP	SLG	AOPS	ABR	SB-CS	FA	FR	RNG	THR	GAMES AT POSITION	DL	BFW
	Bro N	35	104	15	34	6	3	0	20	2	1	4	.327	.346	.442	113	1	1	.981	-1	99	56	O23(2/21/0)	—	0.0
	Year	71	195	26	55	9	3	1	31	5	2	10	.282	.307	.374	86	-4	2	.982	0	109	56	O50(16/26/9)	—	-0.6
1939	Bro N	68	201	22	54	7	0	3	19	4	2	23	.269	.290	.348	68	-10	0	.938	-4	103	0	O55(10/39/7)	—	-1.5
1940	Det A	15	40	4	9	2	0	0	1	1	1	9	.225	.262	.275	36	-4	0-0	.968	2	99	542	O9(1/8/0)	—	-0.2
1941	Det A	94	200	19	49	8	1	2	10	3	1	21	.245	.260	.325	49	-15	6-3	.948	-1	103	69	O80(39/6/36)	0	-1.9
1942	†NY A	15	10	0	2	0	0	0	0	0	0	2	.200	.200	.200	13	-1	0-0	1.000	0	122	0	O3(2/0/1)	0	-0.1
1943	†NY A	71	231	31	60	11	2	0	10	7	1	16	.260	.285	.325	77	-8	3-3	.993	-0	101	71	O60(12/43/5)	0	-1.1
1944	NY A	30	78	13	17	3	0	0	5	3	0	7	.218	.247	.256	42	-6	1-0	.957	-0	104	68	O24(4/4/17)	0	-0.8
1945	NY A	95	327	40	84	12	2	5	32	13	2	20	.257	.289	.352	82	-9	0-4	.968	5	107	137	O83(2/72/9)	0	-0.9
1946	Phi A	91	291	35	71	10	2	0	20	7	1	20	.244	.264	.292	56	-19	3-2	.963	2	110	98	O66(11/18/37)	0	-2.0
Total	13	817	2261	284	585	90	14	17	204	64	16	213	.259	.284	.333	68	-105	27-12	.965	3	104	88	O629(182/284/168)/3	0	-12.8
Stairs, Matt	Matthew Wade; B2.27.1968 St.John NB, Can.; BL/TR/5´9˝/(175–217); d5.29																								
1992	Mon N	13	30	2	5	2	0	0	5	7-0	0	7	.167	.316	.233	61	-1	0-0	.933	-1	93	0	O10L	0	-0.2
1993	Mon N	6	8	1	3	1	0	0	2	0-0	0	1	.375	.375	.500	126	0	0-0	1.000	-0	88	0	/lf	0	0.0
1995	†Bos A	39	88	8	23	7	1	1	17	4-0	1	14	.261	.298	.398	78	-3	0-1	.913	-4	48	150	O23(17/0/6),D2	0	-0.8
1996	Oak A	61	137	21	38	5	1	10	23	19-2	1	23	.277	.367	.547	129	6	1-1	.985	4	86	339	O44(16/0/29)/1D	0	0.8
1997	Oak A	133	352	62	105	19	0	27	73	50-1	3	60	.298	.386	.582	150	26	3-2	.977	-3	83	129	O89(28/0/63),D16,1b7	0	1.7
1998	Oak A	149	523	88	154	33	1	26	106	59-4	6	93	.294	.370	.511	128	22	8-3	1.000	4	102	449	D120,O12(11/0/2),1b6	0	1.8
1999	Oak A	146	531	94	137	26	3	38	102	89-6	2	124	.258	.366	.533	129	24	2-7	.981	-4	89	133	O139(0/1/139)/1D	0	1.0
2000	†Oak A	143	476	74	108	26	0	21	81	78-4	1	122	.227	.333	.414	90	-7	5-2	.979	-4	94	73	O103(0/1/102),D37/1	0	-1.6
2001	Chi N	128	340	48	85	21	0	17	61	52-7	7	76	.250	.358	.462	114	8	2-3	.993	3	105	69	1b89,O22(22/0/1)/2D	0	0.4
2002	Mil N	107	270	41	66	15	0	16	41	36-4	8	50	.244	.349	.478	116	7	2-0	.993	1	98	134	O84(35/0/51)	18	0.5
2003	Pit N	121	305	49	89	20	1	20	57	45-3	5	64	.292	.389	.561	143	20	0-1	.987	-6	81	131	O55(8/0/47),1b31,D2	22	1.0
2004	KC A	126	439	48	117	21	3	18	66	49-2	5	92	.267	.345	.451	106	4	1-0	.986	-2	96	116	O71(14/0/57),1b30,D22	15	-0.4
2005	KC A	127	396	55	109	26	1	13	66	60-4	5	69	.275	.373	.444	122	15	1-2	.993	-2	97	103	1b64,D40,O15(2/0/13)	0	0.5
2006	KC A	77	226	31	59	14	0	8	32	31-2	2	52	.261	.352	.429	104	2	0-0	1.000	-2	20	81	D54,1b11,O2L	0	-0.3
	Tex A	26	81	6	17	4	0	3	11	6-1	1	22	.210	.273	.370	64	-5	0-0	1.000	-0	0	319	D19/1rf	0	-0.6
	Det A	14	41	5	10	3	0	2	8	3-0	0	12	.244	.295	.463	94	0	0-0	ø	0	0	0	D14	0	-0.1
	Year	117	348	42	86	21	0	13	51	40-3	3	86	.247	.328	.420	93	-3	0-0	.969	-2	19	90	D87,1b12,O3(2/0/1)	0	-1.0
Total	14	1416	4243	633	1125	243	11	220	751	588-40	47	881	.265	.358	.483	118	118	25-22	.982	-14	89	132	O671(166/2/511),D338,1b242/2	55	3.7
Staley, Gale	George Gaylord; B5.2.1899 DePere WI; D4.19.1989 Walnut Creek CA; BL/TR/5´8.5˝/167; d9.16																								
1925	Chi N	7	26	2	11	2	0	0	3	2	0	1	.423	.464	.500	144	2	0-1	.979	3	117	171	2b7	—	0.4
Stallcup, Virgil	Thomas Virgil "Red"; B1.3.1922 Ravensford NC; D5.2.1989 Greenville SC; BR/TR/6´3˝/185; d4.18																								
1947	Cin N	8	1	1	0	0	0	0	0	0	0	1	.000	.000	.000	-99	0	0	ø	-0	0	0	/S	0	0.0
1948	Cin N	149	539	40	123	30	4	3	65	18	0	52	.228	.253	.315	55	-36	2	.956	-0	98	99	S148	0	-2.8
1949	Cin N	141	575	49	146	28	5	3	45	9	2	44	.254	.268	.336	60	-34	1	.962	-14	96	97	S141	0	-3.9
1950	Cin N	136	483	44	121	23	2	8	54	17	0	39	.251	.276	.356	65	-26	4	**.973**	-5	95	89	S136	0	-2.3
1951	Cin N	121	428	33	103	17	2	8	49	6	0	40	.241	.251	.346	58	-27	2-4	**.969**	-6	99	87	S117	0	-2.7
1952	Cin N	2	1	0	0	0	0	0	0	0	0	0	.000	.000	.000	-99	0	0-0	ø	-0	0	0	/S	0	0.0
	StL N	29	31	4	4	1	0	0	1	1	0	5	.129	.156	.161	-12	-5	0-0	1.000	2	134	159	S12	0	-0.3
	Year	31	32	4	4	1	0	0	1	1	0	5	.125	.152	.156	-15	-5	0-0	1.000	2	130	155	S13	0	-0.3
1953	StL N	1	1	0	0	0	0	0	0	0	0	0	.000	.000	.000	-99	0	0-0	ø	0	—	—	/H	0	0.0
Total	7	587	2059	171	497	99	13	22	214	51	2	181	.241	.260	.334	58	-128	9-4	.965	-23	97	94	S556	0	-12.0
Staller, George	George Walborn "Stopper"; B4.1.1916 Rutherford Heights PA; D7.3.1992 Harrisburg PA; BL/TL/5´11˝/190; d9.14; Mil 1944–45; C9																								
1943	Phi A	21	85	14	23	1	3	3	12	5	2	6	.271	.326	.459	129	2	1-0	.977	-0	101	68	O20R	0	0.1
Stallings, George	George Tweedy "Gentleman George"; B11.17.1867 Augusta GA; D5.13.1929 Haddock GA; BR/TR/6´1˝/187; d5.22; M13																								
1890	Bro N	4	11	1	0	0	0	0	0	1	1	3	.000	.154	.000	-54	-2	0	.933	-1	*85*	*29*	C4	—	-0.3
1897	Phi N	2	9	1	2	1	0	0	0	0	0	—	.222	.222	.333	47	-1	0	1.000	0	431	0	/rf1M	—	0.0
1898	Phi N	1	0	1	0	0	0	0	0	0	0	—	ø	ø	ø	ø	0	0	ø	0	—	—	/HM	—	0.0
Total	3	7	20	3	2	1	0	0	0	1	1	3	.100	.182	.150	-7	-3	0	.933	-1	*85*	*29*	C4/1rf	—	-0.3
Stanage, Oscar	Oscar Harland; B3.17.1883 Tulare CA; D11.11.1964 Detroit MI; BR/TR/5´9.5˝/185; d5.19; C5																								
1906	Cin N	1	1	0	0	0	0	0	0	0	0	—	.000	.000	.000	-96	0	0	1.000	-0	*0*	*0*	/C	—	0.0
1909	†Det A	77	252	17	66	8	6	0	21	11	2	—	.262	.298	.341	98	-2	2	.964	-5	*98*	*88*	C77	—	0.1
1910	Det A	88	275	24	57	7	4	2	25	20	2	—	.207	.266	.284	68	-11	1	.952	-1	*103*	***113***	C84	—	-0.4
1911	Det A	141	503	45	133	13	7	3	51	20	3	—	.264	.297	.336	73	-21	3	.952	-10	*103*	*105*	C141	—	-1.8
1912	Det A	121	394	35	103	9	4	0	41	34	4	—	.261	.326	.305	83	-8	3	.950	-34	*75*	*106*	C120	—	-3.3
1913	Det A	80	241	19	54	13	2	0	21	21	2	35	.224	.292	.295	73	-8	5	.960	-12	*81*	*108*	C77	—	-1.5
1914	Det A	122	400	16	77	8	4	0	25	24	2	58	.192	.242	.233	41	-30	2-1	.960	-13	*91*	*104*	C122	—	-3.6
1915	Det A	100	300	27	67	9	2	1	31	20	1	41	.223	.274	.277	62	-15	5-1	.964	-9	*97*	*92*	C100	—	-1.7
1916	Det A	94	291	16	69	17	3	0	30	17	3	48	.237	.286	.316	78	-8	3	.969	-13	88	87	C94	—	-1.5
1917	Det A	99	297	19	61	14	1	0	30	20	3	35	.205	.262	.259	59	-15	3	.977	-6	*88*	*88*	C95	—	-1.5
1918	Det A	54	186	9	47	4	0	1	14	11	0	18	.253	.294	.290	80	-5	2	.980	-9	*76*	*90*	C47,1b5/S	—	-1.2
1919	Det A	38	120	9	29	4	1	1	15	7	2	12	.242	.295	.317	73	-5	1	.974	-0	*89*	*90*	C36/1	—	-0.2
1920	Det A	78	238	12	55	17	0	0	17	14	1	21	.231	.277	.303	55	-16	0-0	.958	-9	*87*	*105*	C77	—	-1.9
1925	Det A	3	5	0	1	0	0	0	0	0	0	0	.200	.200	.200	2	-1	0-0	1.000	-1	*52*	*0*	C3	—	-0.1
Total	14	1096	3503	248	819	123	34	8	321	219	25	268	.234	.284	.295	69	-145	30-2	.961	-123	*91*	*99*	C1074,1b6/S	—	-18.6
Standaert, Jerry	Jerome John; B11.2.1901 Chicago IL; D8.4.1964 Chicago IL; BR/TR/5´10˝/168; d4.16																								
1925	Bro N	1	1	0	0	0	0	0	0	0	0	1	.000	.000	.000	-99	0	0-0	ø	0	—	—	/H	—	0.0
1926	Bro N	66	113	13	39	8	2	0	14	5	1	7	.345	.378	.451	124	4	0	.918	-7	72	57	2b21,3b14,S6	—	-0.3
1929	Bos A	19	18	1	3	2	0	0	4	3	0	2	.167	.286	.278	47	-1	0-0	.958	0	121	90	1b10	—	-0.1
Total	3	86	132	14	42	10	2	0	18	8	1	10	.318	.362	.424	111	3	0-0	.918	-7	72	57	2b21,3b14,1b10,S6	—	-0.4
Stanicek, Pete	Peter Louis; B4.18.1963 Harvey IL; BB/TR/5´11˝/185; [BalA85 9/229]; d9.1; b–Steve; Col Stanford; [DL 1989 Bal A 34]																								
1987	Bal A	30	113	9	31	3	0	0	9	8-1	2	19	.274	.333	.301	72	-4	8-1	.975	-4	83	129	2b19,D10,3b2	0	-0.6
1988	Bal A	83	261	29	60	7	1	4	17	28-0	4	45	.230	.313	.310	77	-8	12-6	.985	-1	100	114	O65L,2b16/D	8	-1.0
Total	2	113	374	38	91	10	1	4	26	36-1	6	64	.243	.319	.307	75	-12	20-7	.985	-5	100	114	O65L,2b35,D11,3b2	42	-1.6
Stanicek, Steve	Stephen Blair; B6.19.1961 Lake Forest IL; BR/TR/6´0˝/190; [SFN82 1/11]; d9.16; b–Pete; Col Nebraska; [DL 1988 Mil A 66]																								
1987	Mil A	4	7	2	2	0	0	0	0	0-0	0	2	.286	.286	.286	51	-1	0-0	ø	0	—	—	/D	0	-0.1
1989	Phi N	9	9	0	1	0	0	0	1	0-0	0	3	.111	.111	.111	-36	-2	0-0	ø	0	—	—	/H	0	-0.2
Total	2	13	16	2	3	0	0	0	1	0-0	0	5	.188	.188	.188	4	-3	0-0	ø	0	0	0	/D	66	-0.3
Stankard, Tom	Thomas Francis; B3.20.1882 Waltham MA; D6.13.1958 Waltham MA; BR/TR/6´0˝/190; d7.2; Col Holy Cross																								
1904	Pit N	2	2	0	0	0	0	0	0	0	0	—	.000	.000	.000	-97	0	0	1.000	-0	69	0	/S3	—	-0.1
Stankiewicz, Andy	Andrew Neal; B8.10.1964 Inglewood CA; BR/TR/5´9˝/165; [NYA86 12/314]; d4.11; Col Pepperdine																								
1992	NY A	116	400	52	107	22	2	2	25	38-0	5	42	.268	.338	.348	93	-3	9-5	.973	11	108	102	S81,2b34/D	15	1.5
1993	NY A	16	9	5	0	0	0	0	0	1-0	0	1	.000	.100	.000	-73	-2	0-0	1.000	2	143	245	2b6,3b4/SD	0	0.0
1994	Hou N	37	54	10	14	3	0	1	5	12-0	1	12	.259	.403	.370	109	2	1-1	1.000	-2	107	77	S17,2b6/3	32	0.1
1995	Hou N	43	52	6	6	1	0	0	7	12-2	0	19	.115	.281	.135	15	-6	4-2	.985	4	137	81	S14,2b6,3b3	28	-0.1
1996	Mon N	64	77	12	22	5	1	0	9	6-1	3	12	.286	.356	.377	93	-1	1-0	.969	-2	111	54	2b19,S13/3	20	-0.1
1997	Mon N	76	107	11	24	9	0	1	5	4-0	0	22	.224	.250	.336	53	-8	1-1	.957	1	118	109	2b25,S14,3b3,D2	0	-0.5
1998	Ari N	77	145	9	30	5	0	0	8	7-0	2	33	.207	.252	.241	31	-15	1-0	.994	-6	98	80	2b61	31	-1.9
Total	7	429	844	105	203	45	3	4	59	80-3	11	141	.241	.313	.315	72	-33	17-9	.986	9	107	93	2b157,S140,3b12,D4	126	-1.0
Stanky, Eddie	Edward Raymond "The Brat","Muggsy"; B9.3.1916 Philadelphia PA; D6.6.1999 Fairhope AL; BR/TR/5´8˝/(165–170); d4.21; M8/C2																								
1943	Chi N	142	510	92	125	15	1	0	47	92	2	42	.245	.363	.278	88	-3	4	.966	12	104	102	2b131,S12,3b2	0	1.8
1944	Chi N	13	25	4	6	0	1	0	0	2	0	2	.240	.296	.320	74	-1	1	.875	1	67	344	2b3,S3,3b3	0	0.0
	Bro N	89	261	32	72	9	2	0	16	44	1	13	.276	.382	.326	102	3	3	.961	-16	89	81	2b58,S35/3	0	-0.7

YEAR	TM LG	G	AB	R	H	2B	3B	HR	RBI	BB-IB	HP	SO	AVG	OBP	SLG	AOPS	ABR	SB-CS	FA	FR	RNG	THR	GAMES AT POSITION	DL	BFW
	Year	102	286	36	78	9	3	0	16	46	1	15	.273	.375	.325	100	2	4	.958	-15	88	88	2b61,S38,3b4	0	-0.7
1945	Bro N	153	555	**128**	143	29	5	1	39	**148**	4	42	.258	.417	.333	111	21	6	.962	9	97	117	2b153/S	0	3.7
1946	Bro N	144	483	98	132	24	7	0	36	**137**	2	56	.273	**.436**	.352	124	27	8	.977	-6	92	110	2b141	0	2.9
1947	†Bro N★	146	559	97	141	24	5	3	53	103	5	39	.252	.373	.329	85	-7	3	**.985**	8	98	**130**	2b146	0	0.9
1948	†Bos N✻	67	247	49	79	14	2	2	29	61	0	13	.320	.455	.417	140	19	3	.981	3	106	123	2b66	60	2.5
1949	Bos N	138	506	90	144	24	5	1	42	113	2	41	.285	.417	.358	116	20	3	.979	-7	95	100	2b135	0	2.0
1950	NY N☆	152	527	115	158	25	5	8	51	**144**	**12**	50	.300	**.460**	.412	131	37	9	.976	4	99	124	2b151	0	4.6
1951	†NY N	145	515	88	127	17	2	14	43	127	6	63	.247	.401	.369	108	13	8-5	.977	0	100	118	2b140	0	2.1
1952	StL N	53	83	13	19	4	0	0	7	19	0	9	.229	.373	.277	83	-1	0-0	1.000	2	103	90	2b20,M	0	0.2
1953	StL N	17	30	5	8	0	0	0	1	6	1	4	.267	.405	.267	80	0	0-0	1.000	1	117	85	2b8,M	30	0.1
Total	11	1259	4301	811	1154	185	35	29	364	996	35	374	.268	.410	.348	109	128	48-5	.975	11	98	114	2b1152,S51,3b6	90	20.1
STANLEY, FRED	Frederick Blair; B8.13.1947 Farnhamville IA; BR/TR (BB 1969–71)/5´10˝/(155–170); [HouN66 8/143]; d9.11; C1																								
1969	Sea A	17	43	2	12	2	1	0	4	3-0	0	8	.279	.319	.372	96	0	1-0	.962	-6	70	94	S15/2	0	-0.5
1970	Mil A	6	0	1	0	0	0	0	0	0-0	0	0	ø	ø	ø	ø	0	0-0	1.000	0	147	0	2b2	0	0.0
1971	Cle A	60	129	14	29	4	0	2	12	27-3	1	25	.225	.361	.302	82	-2	1-0	.971	4	110	99	S55,2b3	0	0.9
1972	Cle A	6	12	1	2	1	0	0	0	2-0	0	3	.167	.286	.250	58	-1	0-0	.917	-2	56	0	S5/2	0	-0.3
	SD N	39	85	15	17	2	0	0	2	12-1	1	19	.200	.306	.224	57	-4	1-0	.989	0	106	124	2b21,S17,3b4	0	-0.2
1973	NY A	26	66	6	14	0	1	1	5	7-0	0	16	.212	.288	.288	64	-3	0-0	.981	2	107	95	S21,2b3	0	0.1
1974	NY A	33	38	2	7	0	0	0	3	3-0	0	2	.184	.244	.184	25	-4	1-2	.973	6	117	90	S19,2b15	0	0.3
1975	NY A	117	252	34	56	5	1	0	15	21-0	1	27	.222	.283	.250	53	-16	3-1	.977	-3	91	95	S83,2b33/3	0	-1.0
1976	†NY A	110	260	32	62	2	2	1	20	34-0	1	29	.238	.329	.273	78	-6	1-0	.983	-23	88	74	S110,2b3	0	-2.0
1977	†NY A	48	46	6	12	0	0	1	7	8-0	0	6	.261	.370	.326	92	0	1-1	.958	-3	91	65	S42,3b3,2b2	0	-0.2
1978	†NY A	81	160	14	35	7	0	1	9	25-0	0	31	.219	.324	.281	73	-5	0-0	.959	-8	89	84	S71,2b11,3b4	0	-0.7
1979	NY A	57	100	9	20	1	0	2	14	5-0	0	17	.200	.236	.270	37	-9	0-1	.978	4	114	152	S31,3b16,2b8/1lf	0	-0.4
1980	NY A	49	86	13	18	3	0	0	5	5-0	2	5	.209	.266	.244	42	-7	0-0	.923	-0	105	110	S19,2b17,3b12	37	-0.5
1981	†Oak A	66	145	15	28	4	0	0	7	15-0	0	23	.193	.269	.221	44	-10	2-0	.986	-18	75	78	S62,2b6	0	-2.4
1982	Oak A	101	228	33	44	7	0	2	17	29-0	1	32	.193	.287	.250	51	-15	0-1	.963	-19	91	81	S98,2b2	0	-2.6
Total	14	816	1650	197	356	38	5	10	120	196-4	7	243	.216	.301	.263	61	-82	11-6	.971	-66	91	87	S648,2b128,3b40/lf1	37	-9.5
STANLEY, JIM	James F.; B1889; BB/TR/5´6˝/148; d4.19																								
1914	Chi F	54	98	13	19	3	0	0	4	19	4	14	.194	.347	.224	61	-6	2	.878	-8	85	110	S40,3b3/2lf	—	-1.2
STANLEY, JOE	Joseph; B NJ; d4.24																								
1884	Bal U	6	21	3	5	1	0	0	—	0	—	—	.238	.238	.286	53	-2	—	.444	-2	77	0	O6(0/4/2)	—	-0.3
STANLEY, JOE	Joseph Bernard; B4.2.1881 Washington DC; D9.13.1967 Detroit MI; BB/TR/5´9.5˝/150; d9.11; b–Buck																								
1897	Was N	1	1	0	0	0	0	0	0	0	0	—	.000	.000	.000	-99	0	0	ø	-0	0	0	/P	—	0.0
1902	Was A	3	12	2	4	0	0	0	1	0	0	—	.333	.333	.333	84	0	0	.833	-1	0	0	O3L	—	-0.1
1903	Bos N	86	308	40	77	12	5	1	47	18	7	—	.250	.306	.331	85	-7	10	.902	2	197	74	O77(11/32/34)/PS	—	-0.8
1904	Bos N	3	8	0	0	0	0	0	0	0	0	—	.000	.000	.000	-99	-2	0	.800	1	633	0	O3(1/0/2)	—	-0.1
1905	Was A	28	92	13	24	2	1	1	17	7	0	—	.261	.313	.337	111	1	4	.944	1	140	0	O27(13/9/5)	—	0.0
1906	Was A	73	221	18	36	0	4	0	9	20	1	—	.163	.236	.199	38	-16	6	.934	-3	97	0	O63(0/7/56)/P	—	-2.4
1909	Chi N	22	52	4	7	1	0	0	2	6	0	—	.135	.224	.154	17	-5	0	.947	-1	60	0	O16(5/4/9)	—	-0.8
Total	7	216	694	77	148	15	10	2	76	51	8	—	.213	.275	.272	66	-29	20	.918	-2	150	32	O189(33/52/106),P3/S	—	-4.2
STANLEY, MICKEY	Mitchell Jack; B7.20.1942 Grand Rapids MI; BR/TR/6´1˝/(180–195); d9.13; Col Grand Rapids (MI) CC; OF(44/1171/82)																								
1964	Det A	4	11	3	3	0	0	0	1	0-0	0	1	.273	.273	.273	52	-1	0-0	1.000	-0	89	0	O4(3/1/1)	0	-0.1
1965	Det A	30	117	14	28	6	0	3	13	3-0	0	12	.239	.256	.368	75	-4	1-0	.986	0	106	81	O29C	0	-0.5
1966	Det A	92	235	28	68	15	4	3	19	17-4	0	20	.289	.336	.426	115	5	2-1	1.000	4	108	153	O82C	33	0.7
1967	Det A	145	333	38	70	7	3	7	24	29-2	0	46	.210	.273	.312	71	-13	9-2	.982	2	114	59	O129(2/126/2),1b8	0	-1.4
1968	†Det A	153	583	88	151	16	6	11	60	42-1	4	57	.259	.311	.364	102	0	4-3	**1.000**	-1	101	83	O130C,1b15,S9/2	0	-0.6
1969	Det A	149	592	73	139	28	1	16	70	52-1	2	56	.235	.299	.367	82	-15	8-4	.985	-13	103	39	O101(0/98/3),S59,1b4	0	-2.5
1970	Det A	142	568	83	143	21	11	13	47	45-1	0	56	.252	.305	.396	92	-9	10-1	**1.000**	-2	106	37	O132C,1b9	0	-1.3
1971	Det A	139	401	43	117	14	5	7	41	24-5	0	44	.292	.329	.404	103	0	1-3	.988	9	114	142	O139C	0	0.6
1972	†Det A	142	435	45	102	16	6	14	55	29-8	0	49	.234	.278	.395	97	-4	1-0	.994	2	103	114	O139C	0	-0.6
1973	Det A	157	602	81	147	23	5	17	57	48-4	0	65	.244	.297	.384	86	-13	0-4	.993	5	109	91	O157C	0	-1.4
1974	Det A	99	394	40	87	13	2	8	34	26-1	1	63	.221	.270	.325	68	-17	5-3	.992	2	107	63	O91(1/90/0),1b12/2	44	-1.9
1975	Det A	52	164	26	42	7	3	3	19	15-2	1	27	.256	.320	.390	96	-1	1-1	.983	0	102	58	O28(14/15/0),1b14,3b7/D	59	-0.3
1976	Det A	84	214	34	55	17	1	4	29	14-1	0	19	.257	.301	.402	101	0	2-0	.969	3	90	101	O38(15/19/4),1b17,3b11,S3,2b2,D2	0	0.2
1977	Det A	75	222	30	51	9	1	8	23	18-2	0	30	.230	.284	.387	78	-7	0-0	.972	-5	89	51	O57(7/10/44),1b3,S3,D2	0	-1.5
1978	Det A	53	151	15	40	9	0	3	8	9-0	0	19	.265	.306	.384	90	-2	0-1	.960	-4	79	49	O34(2/4/28),1b12	0	-0.8
Total	15	1516	5022	641	1243	201	48	117	500	371-32	8	564	.248	.298	.377	89	-81	44-23	.991	2	105	83	O1290C,1b94,S74,3b18,D5,2b4	136	-11.4
STANLEY, MIKE	Robert Michael; B6.25.1963 Ft.Lauderdale FL; BR/TR/6´1˝/(185–205); [TexA85 16/395]; d6.24; C1; Col Florida																								
1986	Tex A	15	30	4	10	3	0	1	1	3-0	0	7	.333	.394	.533	145	2	1-0	.857	-2	86	143	3b7,C4/lfD	0	0.1
1987	Tex A	78	216	34	59	8	1	6	37	31-0	1	48	.273	.361	.403	103	2	3-0	.980	-21	53	57	C61,1b12/lfD	0	-1.6
1988	Tex A	94	249	21	57	8	0	3	27	37-0	0	62	.229	.323	.297	75	-7	0-0	.991	-8	58	73	C64,D18,1b6,3b2	21	-1.3
1989	Tex A	67	122	9	30	3	1	1	11	12-1	2	29	.246	.324	.311	78	-3	1-0	.978	-8	122	60	C25,D21,1b7,3b3	15	-1.1
1990	Tex A	103	189	21	47	8	1	2	19	30-2	0	25	.249	.350	.333	92	-1	1-0	.985	-8	65	85	C63,D14,3b8,1b6	0	-0.7
1991	Tex A	95	181	25	45	13	1	3	25	34-0	2	44	.249	.372	.381	111	5	0-0	.980	-13	75	53	C58,1b12,3b6/lfD	0	-0.6
1992	NY A	68	173	24	43	7	0	8	27	33-0	1	45	.249	.372	.428	124	7	0-0	.980	-2	90	102	C55,1b4,D6	0	0.8
1993	NY A	130	423	70	129	17	1	26	84	57-4	5	85	.305	.389	.534	151	31	1-1	**.996**	-5	124	65	C122,D2	0	3.3
1994	NY A	82	290	54	87	20	0	17	57	39-2	2	56	.300	.384	.545	142	19	0-0	.993	4	162	102	C72,1b7,D4	15	2.4
1995	†NY A★	118	399	63	107	29	1	18	83	57-1	5	106	.268	.360	.481	119	13	1-1	.993	-4	93	101	C107,D10	0	1.4
1996	Bos A	121	397	73	107	20	1	24	69	69-3	5	62	.270	.383	.506	120	14	2-0	.985	-28	65	72	C105,D10	0	-0.7
1997	Bos A	97	260	45	78	17	0	13	53	39-0	6	50	.300	.394	.515	135	15	0-1	.996	-3	103	110	D53,1b31,C15	0	0.7
	†NY A	28	87	16	25	8	0	3	12	15-4	0	22	.287	.388	.483	128	4	0-0	1.000	-1	55	110	D16,1b12	0	0.2
	Year	125	347	61	103	25	0	16	65	54-4	6	72	.297	.393	.507	133	19	0-1	.997	-4	91	110	D69,1b43,C15	0	0.9
1998	Tor A	98	341	49	82	13	0	22	47	56-3	5	86	.240	.353	.472	112	7	2-1	.995	-2	74	78	D73,1b22/lf	0	-0.1
	†Bos A	47	156	25	45	12	0	7	32	26-2	2	43	.288	.388	.500	128	8	1-0	1.000	-1	70	150	D34,1b13	0	0.4
	Year	145	497	74	127	25	0	29	79	82-5	7	129	.256	.364	.481	117	14	3-1	.997	-2	73	103	D107,1b35/lf	0	0.3
1999	†Bos A	136	427	59	120	22	0	19	72	70-3	11	94	.281	.393	.466	115	13	0-0	.988	-1	94	88	1b111,D20	0	0.1
2000	Bos A	58	185	22	41	5	0	10	28	30-0	0	44	.222	.327	.411	84	-5	0-0	.997	4	138	93	1b39,D18	20	-0.5
	Oak A	32	97	11	26	7	0	4	18	14-0	1	21	.268	.363	.464	110	2	0-0	.988	0	111	109	1b19,D8	0	0.0
	Year	90	282	33	67	12	0	14	46	44-0	1	65	.238	.339	.429	93	-3	0-0	.993	4	129	98	1b58,D26	0	-0.5
Total	15	1467	4222	625	1138	220	7	187	702	652-25	48	929	.270	.370	.458	117	126	13-4	.988	-97	93	80	C751,D321,1b301,3b26,O4L	71	2.8
STANSBURY, JACK	John James; B12.6.1885 Phillipsburg NJ; D12.26.1970 Easton PA; BR/TR/5´9˝/165; d6.30																								
1918	Bos A	20	47	3	6	1	0	0	2	6	1	3	.128	.241	.149	18	-5	0	.980	2	118	192	3b18,O2C	—	-0.2
STANTON, BUCK	George Washington; B6.19.1906 Stantonsburg NC; D1.1.1992 San Antonio TX; BL/TL/5´10˝/150; d9.5; Col North Carolina																								
1931	StL A	13	15	3	3	2	0	0	0	0	0	6	.200	.200	.333	37	-1	0-0	.750	-0	100	0	/rf	—	-0.2
STANTON, HARRY	Harry Andrew; B St.Louis MO; TR; d10.14																								
1900	StL N	1	0	0	0	0	0	0	0	0	0	—	ø	ø	ø	ø	0	0	ø	0	*0*	*0*	/C	—	0.0
STANTON, LEROY	Leroy Bobby; B4.10.1946 Latta SC; BR/TR/6´1˝/(195–200); d9.10																								
1970	NY N	4	4	0	1	0	1	0	0	0-0	0	0	.250	.250	.750	155	0	0-0	1.000	0	404	0	/cf	0	0.0
1971	NY N	5	21	2	4	1	0	0	2	2-1	0	4	.190	.261	.238	42	-2	0-0	1.000	-1	90	0	O5R	0	-0.3
1972	Cal A	127	402	44	101	15	3	12	39	22-4	4	100	.251	.295	.393	110	2	2-3	.983	2	109	77	O124(0/2/123)	0	-0.2
1973	Cal A	119	306	41	72	9	2	8	34	27-2	2	88	.235	.300	.356	91	-5	3-3	.965	-1	99	89	O107(36/0/76)	0	-1.1
1974	Cal A	118	415	48	111	21	2	11	62	33-3	5	107	.267	.325	.407	117	9	10-8	.975	5	107	139	O114(0/10/110)	35	0.7
1975	Cal A	137	440	67	115	20	3	14	82	52-4	6	85	.261	.345	.416	123	14	18-6	.961	3	98	**165**	O131(0/5/127)/D	0	1.3
1976	Cal A	93	231	12	44	13	1	2	25	24-1	1	57	.190	.266	.281	65	-10	2-6	.985	-6	90	22	O79(33/31/27),D4	0	-2.2
1977	Sea A	133	454	56	125	24	1	27	90	42-2	5	115	.275	.341	.511	130	18	0-1	.953	4	105	148	O91(8/0/84),D33	0	1.6

YEAR	TM LG	G	AB	R	H	2B	3B	HR	RBI	BB-IB	HP	SO	AVG	OBP	SLG	AOPS	ABR	SB-CS	FA	FR	RNG	THR	GAMES AT POSITION	DL	BFW
1978	Sea A	93	302	24	55	11	0	3	24	34-1	1	80	.182	.265	.248	46	-21	1-0	1.000	2	117	62	D59,O30(30/0/1)	0	-2.3
Total	9	829	2575	294	628	114	13	77	358	236-18	24	636	.244	.311	.388	103	5	36-27	.972	8	103	110	O682(107/49/553),D97	35	-2.5
STANTON, TOM	Thomas Patrick; B10.25.1874 St.Louis MO; D1.17.1957 St.Louis MO; BB/TR/5´10˝/175; d4.19																								
1904	Chi N	1	3	0	0	0	0	0	0	0	0	—	.000	.000	.000	-99	-1	0	1.000	-0	*99*	*118*	/C	—	-0.1
STAPLETON, DAVE	David Leslie; B1.16.1954 Fairhope AL; BR/TR/6´1˝/(170–185); [BosA75 10/231]; d5.30; Col South Alabama; OF(5/0/2)																								
1980	Bos A	106	449	61	144	33	5	7	45	13-1	1	32	.321	.338	.463	112	7	3-2	.979	11	111	132	2b94,1b8,O6(4/0/2),3b2,D3	0	2.2
1981	Bos A	93	355	45	101	17	1	10	42	21-1	1	22	.285	.325	.423	107	3	0-4	.948	-7	89	82	S33,3b25,2b23,1b12,D3	0	-0.2
1982	Bos A	150	538	66	142	28	1	14	65	31-5	3	40	.264	.305	.398	87	-10	2-4	.991	5	113	108	1b106,S27,2b9,3b5/lfD	0	-1.0
1983	Bos A	151	542	54	134	31	1	10	66	40-2	2	44	.247	.297	.363	76	-17	1-1	.993	-0	102	97	1b145,2b5	0	-2.7
1984	Bos A	13	39	4	9	2	0	0	1	3-1	0	3	.231	.286	.282	55	-2	0-0	1.000	1	111	57	1b10/D	0	-0.2
1985	Bos A	30	66	4	15	6	0	0	2	4-0	0	11	.227	.271	.318	58	-4	0-0	1.000	-1	91	88	2b14,1b8,D5	22	-0.4
1986	†Bos A	39	39	4	5	1	0	0	3	2-0	0	10	.128	.171	.154	-11	-6	0-0	1.000	0	89	126	1b29,2b6,3b2	0	-0.7
Total	7	582	2028	238	550	118	8	41	224	114-10	7	162	.271	.310	.398	90	-29	6-11	.993	9	105	102	1b318,2b151,S60,3b34,D16,O7L	22	-3.0
STARGELL, WILLIE	Wilver Dornel "Pops"; B3.6.1940 Earlsboro OK; D4.9.2001 Wilmington NC; BL/TL/6´2.5˝/(190–228); d9.16; C4; HF1988																								
1962	Pit N	10	31	1	9	3	1	0	4	3-1	0	10	.290	.353	.452	114	1	0-1	.929	-0	86	165	O9(2/1/6)	0	0.0
1963	Pit N	108	304	34	74	11	6	11	47	19-0	2	85	.243	.290	.428	104	0	0-2	.953	-8	74	74	O65(35/6/24),1b16	0	-1.4
1964	Pit N★	117	421	53	115	19	7	21	78	17-2	2	92	.273	.304	.501	123	10	1-1	.900	-6	90	60	O59(57/1/2),1b50	0	-0.2
1965	Pit N★	144	533	68	145	25	8	27	107	39-13	7	127	.272	.328	.501	130	19	1-1	.965	-1	90	156	O137(125/0/19),1b7	0	1.1
1966	Pit N★	140	485	84	153	30	0	33	102	48-16	6	109	.315	.381	.581	164	42	2-3	.945	-5	88	110	O127(121/0/7),1b15	0	3.0
1967	Pit N	134	462	54	125	18	6	20	73	67-25	3	103	.271	.365	.465	136	23	1-0	.938	-2	86	198	O98(92/0/6),1b37	0	1.5
1968	Pit N	128	435	57	103	15	1	24	67	47-11	6	105	.237	.315	.441	129	15	5-0	.945	-5	78	165	O113(108/0/5),1b13	0	0.5
1969	Pit N	145	522	89	160	31	6	29	92	61-14	6	120	.307	.382	.556	164	45	1-0	.970	-5	90	69	O116(115/0/1),1b23	0	3.3
1970	†Pit N	136	474	70	125	18	3	31	85	44-11	5	119	.264	.329	.511	123	13	0-1	.976	3	90	**187**	O125(123/0/2)/1	0	0.8
1971	†Pit N★	141	511	104	151	26	0	**48**	125	83-20	7	154	.295	.398	.628	186	**59**	0-0	.984	-4	88	85	O138L	0	**4.9**
1972	†Pit N★	138	495	75	145	28	2	33	112	65-15	2	129	.293	.373	.558	165	42	1-1	.984	-12	67	133	1b101,O32L	0	2.1
1973	Pit N★	148	522	106	156	**43**	3	**44**	**119**	80-22	3	129	.299	.392	**.646**	**187**	**63**	0-0	.975	2	91	145	O142L	0	5.7
1974	†Pit N	140	508	90	153	37	4	25	96	87-21	6	106	.301	.407	.537	**168**	**49**	0-2	.967	-4	95	80	O135L/1	0	3.7
1975	†Pit N	124	461	71	136	32	2	22	90	58-6	3	109	.295	.375	.516	145	29	0-0	.992	-7	75	**116**	1b122	0	1.2
1976	Pit N	117	428	54	110	20	3	20	65	50-6	5	101	.257	.339	.458	123	13	2-0	.988	-8	76	86	1b111	0	-0.4
1977	Pit N	63	186	29	51	12	0	13	35	31-10	3	55	.274	.383	.548	143	12	0-1	.986	-1	98	73	1b55	75	0.8
1978	Pit N★	122	390	60	115	18	2	28	97	50-10	7	93	.295	.382	.567	155	29	3-2	.994	-2	91	95	1b112	0	2.2
1979	†Pit N	126	424	60	119	19	0	32	82	47-12	3	105	.281	.352	.552	136	20	0-1	**.997**	-8	68	**124**	1b113	0	0.6
1980	Pit N	67	202	28	53	10	1	11	38	26-10	2	52	.262	.351	.485	127	8	0-0	.992	0	100	143	1b54	71	0.5
1981	Pit N	38	60	2	17	4	0	0	9	5-1	0	9	.283	.333	.350	91	-1	0-0	1.000	-2	0	143	1b9	0	-0.4
1982	Pit N	74	73	6	17	4	0	3	17	10-1	0	24	.233	.318	.411	100	0	0-0	1.000	0	104	65	1b8	0	0.0
Total	21	2360	7927	1195	2232	423	55	475	1540	937-227	78	1936	.282	.360	.529	147	491	17-16	.961	-73	88	123	O1296(1225/8/72),1b848	146	29.5
STARK, MATT	Matthew Scott; B1.21.1965 Whittier CA; BR/TR/6´4˝/225; [TorA83 1/9]; d4.8; [DL 1988 Tor A 74]																								
1987	Tor A	5	12	0	1	0	0	0	0	0-0	0	0	.083	.083	.083	-54	-3	0-0	1.000	-0	41	89	C5	20	-0.3
1990	Chi A	8	16	0	4	1	0	0	3	1-0	0	6	.250	.294	.313	71	-1	0-0	ø	0	—	—	D6	0	-0.1
Total	2	13	28	0	5	1	0	0	3	1-0	0	6	.179	.207	.214	15	-4	0-0	1.000	-0	41	89	D6,C5	94	-0.4
STARK, DOLLY	Monroe Randolph; B1.19.1885 Ripley MS; D12.1.1924 Memphis TN; BR/TR/5´9˝/160; d9.12																								
1909	Cle A	19	60	4	12	0	0	0	1	6	0	—	.200	.273	.200	48	-3	4	.875	-7	73	52	S19	—	-1.2
1910	Bro N	30	103	7	17	3	0	0	8	7	1	19	.165	.225	.194	23	-10	2	.893	-2	98	106	S30	—	-1.2
1911	Bro N	70	193	25	57	4	1	0	19	20	3	24	.295	.370	.326	100	1	6	.910	-4	96	101	S34,2b18,3b3	—	-0.1
1912	Bro N	8	22	2	4	0	0	0	2	1	0	3	.182	.217	.182	10	-3	2	.892	-1	98	113	S7	—	-0.3
Total	4	127	378	38	90	7	1	0	30	34	4	46	.238	.308	.262	66	-15	14	.896	-14	92	94	S90,2b18,3b3	—	-2.8
STARNAGLE, GEORGE	George Henry (b George Henry Steuernagel); B10.6.1873 Belleville IL; D2.15.1946 Belleville IL; BR/TR/5´11˝/175; d9.14																								
1902	Cle A	1	3	0	0	0	0	0	0	0	0	—	.000	.000	.000	-99	-1	0	.667	-1	*83*	*0*	/C	—	-0.1
STARR, CHARLIE	Charles Watkin; B8.30.1878 Pike Co. OH; D10.18.1937 Pasadena CA; TR/5´10.5˝/165; d4.29																								
1905	StL A	26	97	9	20	0	0	0	6	7	0	—	.206	.260	.206	51	-5	0	.938	-2	109	27	2b18,3b6	—	-0.8
1908	Pit N	20	59	8	11	2	0	0	8	13	1	—	.186	.342	.220	80	0	6	.926	-4	99	95	2b12,S5,3b2	—	-0.5
1909	Bos N	61	216	16	48	2	3	0	6	31	5	—	.222	.333	.259	80	-4	7	.931	-4	100	99	2b54,S6,3b3	—	-0.8
	Phi N	3	3	0	0	0	0	0	0	0	0	—	.000	.000	.000	-99	-1	0	ø	0	—	—	/H	—	-0.1
	Year	64	219	16	48	2	3	0	6	31	5	—	.219	.329	.256	78	-4	7	.931	-4	100	99	2b54,S6,3b3	—	-0.9
Total	3	110	375	33	79	4	3	0	20	51	6	—	.211	.315	.237	72	-10	13	.931	-10	102	85	2b84,S11,3b11	—	-2.2
STARR, BILL	William; B2.26.1911 Brooklyn NY; D8.12.1991 LaJolla CA; BR/TR/6´1˝/175; d8.23																								
1935	Was A	12	24	1	5	0	0	0	1	0	0	1	.208	.208	.208	8	-3	0-0	.971	0	*92*	*157*	C12	—	-0.3
1936	Was A	1	0	0	0	0	0	0	0	0	0	0	ø	ø	ø	ø	0	0-0	ø	0	*0*	*0*	/C	—	0.0
Total	2	13	24	1	5	0	0	0	1	0	0	1	.208	.208	.208	8	-3	0-0	.971	0	*91*	*155*	C13	—	-0.3
START, JOE	Joseph "Old Reliable","Rocks"; B10.14.1842 New York NY; D3.27.1927 Providence RI; BL/TL/5´9˝/165; d5.18; M1																								
1871	Mut NA	**33**	161	35	58	5	1	1	34	3	—	0	.360	.372	.422	140	10	4-2	.921	-2	38	82	1b33	—	0.6
1872	Mut NA	54	277	60	75	5	0	0	48	0	—	0	.271	.271	.289	77	-6	3-3	**.958**	2	0	139	1b54	—	-0.2
1873	Mut NA	**53**	252	42	67	8	3	1	29	4	—	0	.266	.277	.333	80	-6	1-0	.943	6	**150**	88	1b53,O2R,M	—	0.1
1874	Mut NA	63	306	67	96	13	3	2	46	4	—	0	.314	.323	.395	125	8	5-0	**.961**	5	**108**	67	1b63,O2(1/1/0)	—	1.2
1875	Mut NA	69	314	58	90	10	5	4	30	3	—	0	.287	.293	.389	128	7	1-4	.948	2	88	72	1b69	—	0.8
1876	NY N	56	264	40	73	6	0	0	21	1	—	2	.277	.279	.299	107	3	—	**.964**	3	99	48	1b56	—	0.4
1877	Har N	**60**	271	55	90	3	6	1	21	6	—	2	.332	.347	.399	150	16	—	**.964**	-2	52	98	1b60	—	0.9
1878	Chi N	**61**	285	58	**100**	12	5	1	27	2	—	3	.351	.355	.439	150	14	—	.957	-2	75	103	1b61	—	0.8
1879	Pro N	66	317	70	101	11	5	2	37	7	—	4	.319	.333	.404	144	14	—	**.973**	0	65	88	1b65/rf	—	1.1
1880	Pro N	82	345	53	96	14	6	0	27	13	—	20	.278	.304	.354	126	10	—	.971	-3	45	93	1b82	—	0.3
1881	Pro N	79	348	56	114	12	6	0	29	9	—	7	.328	.345	.397	135	13	—	.963	-4	59	111	1b79	—	0.5
1882	Pro N	82	356	58	117	8	10	0	48	11	—	7	.329	.349	.407	142	15	—	.974	2	92	**144**	1b82	—	0.9
1883	Pro N	87	370	63	105	16	7	1	57	22	—	16	.284	.324	.373	108	3	—	.957	-1	102	**126**	1b87	—	-0.5
1884	†Pro N	93	381	80	105	10	5	2	32	35	—	25	.276	.337	.344	117	9	—	**.980**	1	75	91	1b93	—	0.1
1885	Pro N	101	374	47	103	11	4	0	41	39	—	10	.275	.344	.326	121	11	—	.972	1	104	83	1b101	—	0.3
1886	Was N	31	122	10	27	4	1	0	17	5	—	13	.221	.252	.270	64	-5	4	.973	-2	58	92	1b31	—	-0.9
Total	5NA	272	1310	262	386	41	12	8	187	14	—	0	.295	.302	.363	108	13	14-9	.948	13	81	89	1b272,O4(1/1/2)	—	2.5
Total	11	798	3433	590	1031	107	55	7	357	150	—	109	.300	.330	.370	127	103	4	.968	-7	77	100	1b797/rf	—	3.9
STATON, DAVE	David Alan; B4.12.1968 Seattle WA; BR/TR/6´5˝/(215–225); [SDN89 5/130]; d9.8; Col Cal St.–Fullerton																								
1993	SD N	17	42	7	11	3	0	5	9	3-0	1	12	.262	.326	.690	162	3	0-0	1.000	3	200	137	1b12	0	0.5
1994	SD N	29	66	6	12	2	0	4	6	10-0	0	18	.182	.289	.394	78	-2	0-0	1.000	3	150	65	1b20	0	-0.1
Total	2	46	108	13	23	5	0	9	15	13-0	1	30	.213	.303	.509	111	1	0-0	1.000	6	167	90	1b32	0	0.4
STATON, JOE	Joseph; B3.8.1948 Seattle WA; BL/TL/6´3˝/(175–180); d9.5																								
1972	Det A	6	2	1	0	0	0	0	0	0-0	0	1	.000	.000	.000	-97	0	0-1	1.000	-0	0	0	1b2	0	-0.1
1973	Det A	9	17	2	4	0	0	0	3	0-0	0	3	.235	.235	.235	31	-2	1-0	.969	1	257	30	1b5	0	0.0
Total	2	15	19	3	4	0	0	0	3	0-0	0	4	.211	.211	.211	18	-2	1-1	.973	1	213	25	1b7	0	-0.1
STATZ, JIGGER	Arnold John; B10.20.1897 Waukegan IL; D3.16.1988 Corona Del Mar CA; BR/TR (BB 1922p)/5´7.5˝/150; d7.30; Col Holy Cross																								
1919	NY N	21	60	7	18	2	1	0	6	3	0	8	.300	.333	.367	112	1	2	.977	-1	115	0	O18(3/7/8),2b5	—	-0.1
1920	NY N	16	30	0	4	0	1	0	5	2	0	9	.133	.188	.200	11	-4	0-1	.944	-2	69	76	O12C	—	-0.7
	Bos A	2	3	0	0	0	0	0	0	0	0	0	.000	.000	.000	-99	-1	0-0	1.000	-0	98	0	O2R	—	-0.1
1922	Chi N	110	462	77	137	19	5	1	34	41	1	31	.297	.355	.366	85	-10	16-13	.959	1	100	113	O110C	—	-1.4
1923	Chi N	**154**	655	110	209	33	8	10	70	56	3	42	.319	.375	.440	114	14	29-23	.975	11	106	128	O154C	—	1.6
1924	Chi N	135	549	69	152	22	5	3	49	37	2	50	.277	.325	.352	80	-15	13-9	.961	8	104	**154**	O131C/2	—	-1.3
1925	Chi N	38	148	21	38	6	3	2	14	11	2	16	.257	.317	.378	76	-6	4-0	.943	-1	104	82	O37C	—	-0.7

YEAR	TM LG	G	AB	R	H	2B	3B	HR	RBI	BB-IB	HP	SO	AVG	OBP	SLG	AOPS	ABR	SB-CS	FA	FR	RNG	THR	GAMES AT POSITION	DL	BFW
1927	Bro N	130	507	64	139	24	7	1	21	26	0	43	.274	.310	.355	77	-17	10	.990	10	**111**	108	O122(3/118/1)/2	—	-1.3
1928	Bro N	77	171	28	40	8	1	0	16	18	1	12	.234	.311	.292	59	-10	3	.965	-1	99	83	O52(2/49/1)/2	—	-1.3
Total	8	683	2585	376	737	114	31	17	215	194	9	211	.285	.337	.373	87	-48	77-<u>46</u>	.969	25	105	117	O638(8/618/12),2b8	—	-5.3
STAUB, RUSTY Daniel Joseph; B4.1.1944 New Orleans LA; BL/TR/6´2˝/(190–230); d4.9; C1																									
1963	Hou N	150	513	43	115	17	4	6	45	59-8	5	58	.224	.309	.308	84	-10	0-0	.989	-3	81	71	1b109,O49(0/1/48)	0	-2.3
1964	Hou N	89	292	26	63	10	2	8	35	21-4	3	31	.216	.272	.346	78	-9	1-1	.992	-2	79	95	1b49,O38(0/7/31)	0	-1.8
1965	Hou N	131	410	43	105	20	1	14	63	52-5	2	57	.256	.339	.412	120	12	3-0	.951	2	100	157	O112(1/2/110)/1	0	0.7
1966	Hou N	153	554	60	155	28	3	13	81	58-13	1	61	.280	.345	.412	119	15	2-1	.962	8	112	127	O148(55/1/105)/1	0	1.4
1967	Hou N★	149	546	71	182	**44**	1	10	74	60-21	3	47	.333	.398	.473	155	42	0-4	.962	1	105	98	O144R	0	3.4
1968	Hou N★	161	591	54	172	37	1	6	72	73-24	7	57	.291	.373	.387	132	27	2-0	.992	0	100	84	1b147,O15R	0	2.1
1969	Mon N☆	158	549	89	166	26	5	29	79	110-11	9	61	.302	.426	.526	165	54	3-4	.966	2	99	140	O156R	0	4.8
1970	Mon N★	160	569	98	156	23	7	30	94	112-11	3	93	.274	.394	.497	138	34	12-11	.985	6	105	130	O160R	0	3.0
1971	Mon N☆	**162**	599	94	186	34	6	19	97	74-13	9	42	.311	.392	.482	145	38	9-5	.945	2	96	173	O162(1/0/162)	0	3.4
1972	NY N	66	239	32	70	11	0	9	38	31-7	2	13	.293	.372	.452	137	13	0-1	.982	-3	91	86	O65R	42	0.7
1973	†NY N	152	585	77	163	36	1	15	76	74-10	3	52	.279	.361	.421	117	16	1-1	.978	5	102	126	O152R	0	1.3
1974	NY N	151	561	65	145	22	2	19	78	77-12	3	39	.258	.347	.406	112	10	2-1	.983	3	92	**185**	O147R	0	0.6
1975	NY N	155	574	93	162	30	4	19	105	77-14	9	55	.282	.371	.448	132	26	2-0	.986	1	92	146	O153R	0	2.0
1976	Det A★	**161**	589	73	176	28	3	15	96	83-11	7	49	.299	.386	.433	136	30	3-1	.970	-10	82	86	O126R,D36	0	1.4
1977	Det A	158	623	84	173	34	3	22	101	59-4	1	47	.278	.336	.448	107	7	1-1	ø	0	0	0	D156	0	0.2
1978	Det A	162	642	75	175	30	1	24	121	76-5	3	35	.273	.347	.435	116	15	3-1	ø	0	0	0	D162	0	1.1
1979	Det A	68	246	32	58	12	1	9	40	32-1	5	18	.236	.331	.402	95	-1	1-0	ø	0	0	0	D66	0	-0.3
	Mon N	38	86	9	23	3	0	3	14	14-3	0	10	.267	.366	.407	111	2	0-0	.994	-2	64	79	1b22/rf	0	-0.1
1980	Tex A	109	340	42	102	23	2	9	55	39-3	2	18	.300	.370	.459	131	16	1-1	.977	-0	58	109	D57,1b30,O14(3/0/11)	35	1.1
1981	NY N	70	161	9	51	9	0	5	21	22-3	1	12	.317	.398	.466	146	11	1-0	.989	-2	77	87	1b41	0	0.7
1982	NY N	112	219	11	53	9	0	3	27	24-1	0	10	.242	.309	.324	79	-6	0-0	.959	2	91	212	O27(12/0/15),1b18	0	-0.6
1983	NY N	104	115	5	34	6	0	3	28	14-3	1	10	.296	.371	.426	123	4	0-0	.976	-1	132	148	1b5,O5(3/0/2)	0	0.3
1984	NY N	78	72	2	19	4	0	1	18	4-3	0	9	.264	.291	.361	87	-1	0-0	1.000	-0	0	168	1b3	0	-0.2
1985	NY N	54	45	2	12	3	0	1	8	10-3	0	4	.267	.400	.400	127	2	0-0	1.000	-0	68	0	/rf	0	0.2
Total	23	2951	9720	1189	2716	499	47	292	1466	1255-193	79	888	.279	.362	.431	124	347	47-33	.969	12	99	138	O1675(75/11/1604),D477,1b426	77	23.1
STEARNS, ECKY Daniel Eckford; B10.17.1861 Buffalo NY; D6.28.1944 Glendale CA; BL/TR/6´1˝/185; d8.17; U1; OF(7/3/28)																									
1880	Buf N	28	104	8	19	6	1	0	13	3	—	23	.183	.206	.260	55	-5	—	.774	-5	88	142	O20(6/1/15),C8,3b5/S	—	-1.0
1881	Det N	3	11	1	1	1	0	0	0	0	—	2	.091	.091	.182	-16	-1	—	.714	-1	100	115	S3	—	-0.2
1882	Cin AA	49	214	28	55	10	2	0	35	6	—	—	.257	.277	.322	96	-1	—	.931	-3	57	126	1b35,O12R,2b2/S	—	-0.7
1883	Bal AA	93	382	54	94	10	9	1	—	**34**	—	—	.246	.308	.327	101	1	—	.947	3	**141**	79	1b92/lf	—	-0.4
1884	Bal AA	100	396	61	94	12	3	3	—	28	6	—	.237	.298	.306	94	-2	—	.949	4	139	78	1b100/2	—	-0.7
1885	Bal AA	67	253	40	47	3	8	1	29	38	6	—	.186	.306	.273	85	-2	—	.973	2	115	102	1b63,O3(0/2/1),C2	—	-0.5
	Buf N	30	105	7	21	6	1	0	9	8	—	23	.200	.257	.276	70	-3	—	.821	-7	75	59	S19,1b12,C2	—	-1.0
1889	KC AA	**139**	560	96	160	24	12	3	87	56	0	69	.286	.351	.387	104	1	67	.967	0	117	91	1b135,3b4	—	-0.9
Total	7	509	2025	295	491	72	36	8	<u>173</u>	173	12	<u>117</u>	.242	.306	.325	94	-12	67	.956	-7	122	89	1b437,O36R,S24,C12,3b9,2b3	—	-5.4
STEARNS, JOHN John Hardin; B8.21.1951 Denver CO; BR/TR/6´0˝/(180–185); [PhiN73 1/2]; d9.22; C5; Col Colorado																									
1974	Phi N	1	2	0	1	0	0	0	0	0-0	0	0	.500	.500	.500	172	0	0-0	1.000	0	0	0	/C	0	0.0
1975	NY N	59	169	25	32	5	1	3	10	17-4	2	15	.189	.268	.284	56	-11	4-1	.994	3	76	167	C54	0	-0.5
1976	NY N	32	103	13	27	6	0	2	10	16-0	1	11	.262	.364	.379	117	3	1-2	.987	6	138	172	C30	0	1.0
1977	NY N★	139	431	52	108	25	1	12	55	77-7	7	76	.251	.370	.397	110	10	9-8	.982	11	117	103	C127,1b6	0	2.5
1978	NY N	143	477	65	126	24	1	15	73	70-4	8	57	.264	.364	.413	121	16	25-13	.985	4	126	106	C141/3	0	2.8
1979	NY N☆	155	538	58	131	29	2	9	66	52-5	4	57	.243	.312	.355	84	-11	15-15	.983	1	87	117	C121,1b16,3b11,O6L	0	-0.9
1980	NY N★	91	319	42	91	25	1	0	45	33-1	1	24	.285	.346	.370	104	3	7-3	.985	9	108	92	C74,1b16/3	71	1.6
1981	NY N	80	273	25	74	12	1	1	24	24-2	0	17	.271	.329	.333	89	-4	12-2	.983	1	123	93	C66,1b9,3b4	0	0.2
1982	NY N★	98	352	46	103	25	3	4	28	30-2	2	35	.293	.349	.415	113	7	17-7	.987	-4	100	**146**	C81,3b12	17	0.8
1983	NY N	4	0	2	0	0	0	0	0	0-0	0	0	ø	ø	ø	ø	0	0-0	ø	0	—	—	/R	147	0.0
1984	NY N	8	17	6	3	1	0	0	1	4-0	0	2	.176	.333	.235	63	-1	1-0	1.000	-0	89	0	C4,1b2	144	-0.1
Total	11	810	2681	334	696	152	10	46	312	323-25	25	294	.260	.341	.375	101	12	91-51	.985	30	109	116	C699,1b49,3b29,O6L	379	7.4
STEDRONSKY, JOHN John; B Troy NY; d9.26																									
1879	Chi N	4	12	0	1	0	0	0	0	0	—	3	.083	.083	.083	-42	-2	—	.789	1	144	233	3b4	—	-0.1
STEELMAN, FARMER Morris James; B6.29.1875 Millville NJ; D9.16.1944 Merchantville NJ; TR/5´11˝/?; d9.15																									
1899	Lou N	4	15	2	1	0	1	0	2	2	0	—	.067	.176	.200	3	-2	0	.929	-1	*111*	*46*	C4	—	-0.3
1900	Bro N	1	4	0	0	0	0	0	0	0	0	—	.000	.000	.000	-94	-1	0	1.000	0	*81*	*153*	/C	—	-0.1
1901	Bro N	1	3	0	1	0	0	0	0	0	0	—	.333	.333	.333	91	0	0	.875	0	*126*	*199*	/C	—	0.0
	Phi A	27	88	5	23	2	0	0	7	10	2	—	.261	.350	.284	74	-3	4	1.000	3	*100*	*132*	C14,O12R	—	0.1
1902	Phi A	10	32	1	6	1	0	0	6	2	0	—	.188	.235	.219	25	-3	2	1.000	1	*94*	*80*	C5,O5R	—	-0.2
Total	4	43	142	8	31	3	1	0	15	14	2	—	.218	.297	.254	52	-9	6	.985	3	*101*	*114*	C25,O17R	—	-0.5
STEELS, JAMES James Earl; B5.30.1961 Jackson MS; BL/TL/5´10˝/(180–190); [SDN79 8/196]; d4.6																									
1987	SD N	62	68	9	13	1	1	0	6	11-0	0	14	.191	.300	.235	47	-5	3-2	.960	-0	95	129	O28(17/6/7)	0	-0.6
1988	Tex A	36	53	4	10	1	0	0	5	0-0	0	15	.189	.185	.208	11	-6	2-0	1.000	-1	79	0	O17(9/1/7),1b7,D7	0	-0.7
1989	SF N	13	12	0	1	0	0	0	0	2-1	0	4	.083	.214	.083	-12	-2	0-0	1.000	1	177	0	1b3/rf	0	-0.1
Total	3	111	133	13	24	2	1	0	11	13-1	0	33	.180	.250	.211	28	-13	5-2	.973	-0	91	82	O46(26/7/15),1b10,D7	0	-1.4
STEERE, GENE Frederick Eugene; B8.16.1872 S.Scituate RI; D3.13.1942 San Francisco CA; d8.29; Col Brown																									
1894	Pit N	10	39	3	8	0	0	0	4	2	0	1	.205	.244	.205	9	-6	2	.896	-2	93	105	S10	—	-0.6
STEFERO, JOHN John Robert; B9.22.1959 Sumter SC; BL/TR/5´8˝/(184–185); d6.24																									
1983	Bal A	9	11	2	5	1	0	0	4	3-0	0	2	.455	.571	.545	212	2	0-0	.920	0	84	164	C9	0	0.3
1986	Bal A	52	120	14	28	2	0	2	13	16-0	0	25	.233	.321	.300	72	-4	0-1	.984	-4	65	145	C50/2	0	-0.7
1987	Mon N	18	56	4	11	0	0	1	3	3-1	0	17	.196	.237	.250	28	-6	0-0	.981	1	76	57	C17	0	-0.4
Total	3	79	187	20	44	3	0	3	20	22-1	0	44	.235	.314	.299	67	-8	0-1	.979	-2	69	124	C76/2	0	-0.8
STEGMAN, DAVE David William; B1.30.1954 Inglewood CA; BR/TR/5´11˝/(185–190); [DetA76 S1/2]; d9.4; Col Arizona																									
1978	Det A	8	14	3	4	2	0	1	3	1-0	0	2	.286	.313	.643	163	1	0-0	1.000	-1	91	0	O7(0/5/3)	0	0.0
1979	Det A	12	31	6	6	0	0	3	5	2-0	0	3	.194	.242	.484	88	-1	1-1	1.000	1	131	0	O12(0/11/1)	0	0.0
1980	Det A	65	130	12	23	5	0	2	9	14-0	0	23	.177	.255	.262	41	-11	1-1	.988	-4	85	34	O57(14/27/23),D2	0	-1.6
1982	NY A	2	0	0	0	0	0	0	0	0-0	0	0	ø	ø	ø	ø	0	0-0	ø	0	—	—	/D	0	0.0
1983	Chi A	30	53	5	9	2	0	0	4	10-0	0	9	.170	.292	.208	41	-4	0-1	1.000	-2	74	93	O29(5/19/5)	0	-0.7
1984	Chi A	55	92	13	24	1	2	2	11	4-0	2	18	.261	.306	.380	84	-2	3-0	.985	-2	89	54	O46(11/27/8),D3	0	-0.4
Total	6	172	320	39	66	10	2	8	32	31-0	2	55	.206	.277	.325	64	-17	5-3	.991	-8	89	44	O151(30/89/40),D6	0	-2.7
STEIN, JUSTIN Justin Marion "Ott"; B8.9.1911 St.Louis MO; D5.1.1992 Creve Coeur MO; BR/TR/5´11˝/180; d5.28; Col St. Louis																									
1938	Phi N	11	39	6	10	0	1	0	2	2	0	4	.256	.293	.308	67	-2	0	.880	-1	104	199	3b7,2b3	—	-0.2
	Cin N	11	18	3	6	1	0	0	1	0	0	1	.333	.333	.389	101	0	0	.857	-0	117	97	S7,2b2	—	0.0
	Year	22	57	9	16	1	1	0	3	2	0	5	.281	.305	.333	78	-2	0	.857	-1	104	199	3b7,S7,2b5	—	-0.2
STEIN, BILL William Allen; B1.21.1947 Battle Creek MI; BR/TR/5´10˝/(170–175); [StLN69 4/90]; d9.6; Col Southern Illinois; OF(15/0/14)																									
1972	StL N	14	35	2	11	0	1	2	3	0-0	0	7	.314	.314	.543	140	1	1-0	1.000	-3	48	0	3b4,O4(4/0/1)	0	-0.1
1973	StL N	32	55	4	12	2	0	0	2	7-0	0	18	.218	.306	.255	57	-3	0-0	1.000	-1	105	0	O10(2/0/8),1b2/3	0	-0.5
1974	Chi A	13	43	5	12	1	0	0	5	7-2	0	8	.279	.380	.302	96	0	0-0	.871	-3	80	0	3b11,D2	0	-0.3
1975	Chi A	76	226	23	61	7	1	3	21	18-0	1	32	.270	.327	.350	90	-3	2-2	.974	-1	115	82	2b28,3b24,D18/lf	0	-0.4
1976	Chi A	117	392	32	105	15	2	4	36	22-3	2	67	.268	.310	.347	92	-5	4-2	.960	-5	96	95	2b58,3b58/1SrfD	0	-0.7
1977	Sea A	151	556	53	144	26	5	13	67	29-2	5	79	.259	.299	.394	88	-10	3-4	.964	-9	89	70	3b147,S2,D3	0	-2.2
1978	Sea A	114	403	41	105	24	4	4	37	37-3	0	56	.261	.318	.370	94	-3	1-0	.929	-1	108	91	3b111/D	0	-0.6
1979	Sea A	88	250	28	62	9	2	7	27	17-1	2	28	.248	.297	.384	82	-7	1-2	.959	-1	99	113	3b67,2b17,S3	21	-0.8
1980	Sea A	67	198	16	53	5	1	5	27	16-4	1	25	.268	.321	.379	91	-3	1-1	.972	6	112	60	3b34,2b14,1b8,D5	50	0.3

YEAR	TM LG	G	AB	R	H	2B	3B	HR	RBI	BB-IB	HP	SO	AVG	OBP	SLG	AOPS	ABR	SB-CS	FA	FR	RNG	THR	GAMES AT POSITION	DL	BFW
1981	Tex A	53	115	21	38	6	0	2	22	7-3	0	15	.330	.360	.435	137	5	1-2	1.000	0	109	82	1b20,O8(7/0/1),3b7,2b3/S	0	0.4
1982	Tex A	85	184	14	44	8	0	1	16	12-0	2	23	.239	.293	.299	66	-9	0-0	.957	7	117	149	2b34,3b28,S6,1b2/lfD	0	-0.1
1983	Tex A	78	232	21	72	15	1	2	33	8-0	0	31	.310	.331	.409	104	1	2-3	.975	1	84	122	2b32,1b23,3b10,D6	0	0.1
1984	Tex A	27	43	3	12	1	0	0	3	5-2	0	9	.279	.354	.302	81	-1	0-0	.967	-2	91	74	2b11,1b3,3b3,D4	64	-0.3
1985	Tex A	44	79	5	20	3	1	1	12	1-1	1	15	.253	.272	.354	68	-4	0-0	.952	2	109	73	3b11,1b8,2b3,O3R,D6	15	-0.3
Total	14	959	2811	268	751	122	18	44	311	186-21	14	413	.267	.313	.370	90	-41	16-16	.950	-9	98	80	3b516,2b200,1b67,D49,O28L,S13	150	-5.5
STEINBACH, TERRY	Terry Lee; B3.2.1962 New Ulm MN; BR/TR/6´1˝/(195–212); [OakA83 9/215]; d9.12; Col Minnesota																								
1986	Oak A	6	15	3	5	0	0	2	4	1-0	0	0	.333	.375	.733	207	2	0-0	.962	0	35	357	C5	0	0.2
1987	Oak A	122	391	66	111	16	3	16	56	32-2	9	66	.284	.349	.463	121	12	1-2	.986	-3	115	**118**	C107,3b10/1D	0	1.2
1988	†Oak A★	104	351	42	93	19	1	9	51	33-2	6	47	.265	.334	.402	110	5	3-0	.983	7	104	**161**	C84,3b9,1b8/lfD	26	1.7
1989	†Oak A★	130	454	37	124	13	1	7	42	30-2	2	66	.273	.319	.352	93	-5	1-2	.985	2	**166**	88	C103,O14(6/0/8),1b10,3b3,D4	0	0.1
1990	†Oak A	114	379	32	95	15	2	9	57	19-1	4	66	.251	.291	.372	88	-8	0-1	.988	-2	115	75	C83,D25,1b3	25	-0.6
1991	Oak A	129	456	50	125	31	1	6	67	22-4	7	70	.274	.312	.386	99	-1	2-2	.980	-16	87	101	C117,1b9,D2	0	-1.1
1992	†Oak A	128	438	48	122	20	1	12	53	45-3	1	58	.279	.345	.411	117	10	2-3	.985	1	122	125	C124,1b5,D2	15	1.7
1993	Oak A★	104	389	47	111	19	1	10	43	25-1	3	65	.285	.333	.416	106	2	3-3	.989	-15	86	111	C86,1b15,D6	49	-0.9
1994	Oak A	103	369	51	105	21	2	11	57	26-4	0	62	.285	.327	.442	105	2	2-1	**.998**	9	119	144	C93,1b6,D6	0	1.5
1995	Oak A	114	406	43	113	26	1	15	65	25-4	3	74	.278	.322	.458	106	2	1-3	.993	8	112	**132**	C111,1b2	16	1.5
1996	Oak A	145	514	79	140	25	1	35	100	49-5	6	115	.272	.342	.529	117	12	0-1	.991	-6	102	94	C137/1D	0	1.3
1997	Min A	122	447	60	111	27	1	12	54	35-2	1	106	.248	.302	.394	79	-14	6-1	.993	-0	124	80	C116,1b2/D	0	-0.6
1998	Min A	124	422	45	102	25	2	14	54	38-0	4	89	.242	.310	.410	83	-11	0-1	.990	-1	131	91	C119,D3	0	-0.4
1999	Min A	101	338	35	96	16	4	4	42	38-1	2	54	.284	.358	.391	87	-6	2-2	.991	-4	124	53	C96/D	34	-0.4
Total	14	1546	5369	638	1453	273	21	162	745	418-31	48	938	.271	.326	.420	101	2	23-22	.989	-20	116	105	C1381,D69,1b62,3b22,O15(7/0/8)	165	5.2
STEINBACHER, HANK	Henry John; B3.22.1913 Sacramento CA; D4.3.1977 Sacramento CA; BL/TR/5´11˝/180; d4.21																								
1937	Chi A	26	73	13	19	4	1	1	9	4	0	7	.260	.299	.384	71	-4	2-0	.960	-1	90	0	O15L	—	-0.5
1938	Chi A	106	399	59	132	23	8	4	61	41	0	19	.331	.393	.459	110	6	1-3	.963	-4	96	74	O101(0/8/93)	—	-0.4
1939	Chi A	71	111	16	19	2	1	1	15	21	0	8	.171	.303	.234	38	-10	0-0	1.000	-1	95	64	O22(1/0/21)	—	-1.1
Total	3	203	583	88	170	29	10	6	85	66	0	34	.292	.364	.407	92	-8	3-3	.968	-6	95	65	O138(16/8/114)	—	-2.0
STEINBRENNER, GENE	Eugene Gass; B11.17.1892 Pittsburgh PA; D4.25.1970 Pittsburgh PA; BR/TR/5´8.5˝/155; d4.25																								
1912	Phi N	3	9	0	2	1	0	0	1	0	0	3	.222	.222	.333	48	-1	0	.900	-0	87	122	2b3	—	-0.1
STEINECKE, BILL	William Robert; B2.7.1907 Cincinnati OH; D7.20.1986 St.Augustine FL; BR/TR/5´8.5˝/175; d9.16; Col DePaul																								
1931	Pit N	4	4	0	0	0	0	0	0	0	0	1	.000	.000	.000	-99	-1	0	ø	0	*0*	*0*	/C	—	-0.1
STEINER, BEN	Benjamin Saunders; B7.28.1921 Alexandria VA; D10.27.1988 Venice FL; BL/TR/5´11˝/165; d4.17																								
1945	Bos A	78	304	39	78	8	3	3	20	31	1	29	.257	.327	.332	89	-4	10-6	.967	-2	96	118	2b77	0	-0.2
1946	Bos A	3	4	1	1	0	0	0	0	0	0	0	.250	.250	.250	38	0	0-0	.750	-0	54	0	/3	0	-0.1
1947	Det A	1	0	1	0	0	0	0	0	0	0	0	ø	ø	ø	ø	0	0-0	ø	0	—	—	/R	0	0.0
Total	3	82	308	41	79	8	3	3	20	31	1	29	.256	.326	.331	89	-4	10-6	.967	-2	96	118	2b77/3	0	-0.3
STEINER, RED	James Harry; B1.7.1915 Los Angeles CA; D11.16.2001 Gardena CA; BL/TR/6´0˝/185; d5.11																								
1945	Cle A	12	20	0	3	0	0	0	2	1	0	4	.150	.190	.150	-1	-3	0-0	1.000	1	*68*	*95*	C4	0	-0.2
	Bos A	26	59	6	12	1	0	0	4	14	0	2	.203	.356	.220	67	-2	0-0	.986	-3	*90*	*94*	C24	0	-0.3
	Year	38	79	6	15	1	0	0	6	15	0	6	.190	.319	.203	52	-4	0-0	.989	-2	*86*	*94*	C28	0	-0.5
STEINFELDT, HARRY	Harry M.; B9.29.1877 St.Louis MO; D8.17.1914 Bellevue KY; BR/TR/5´9.5˝/180; d4.22; OF(15/16/4)																								
1898	Cin N	88	308	47	91	18	6	0	43	27	1	—	.295	.354	.393	107	2	9	.917	-7	96	97	2b31,O29(14/15/0),3b22,S5,1b4	—	-0.5
1899	Cin N	108	390	63	96	16	8	0	43	40	6	—	.246	.326	.328	78	-11	19	.888	-8	94	67	3b60,2b40,S8,O2(0/1/1)	—	-1.5
1900	Cin N	134	510	57	125	29	7	2	66	27	7	—	.245	.292	.341	76	-17	14	.922	16	100	110	3b67,2b64,O2R,S2	—	0.3
1901	Cin N	105	382	40	95	18	7	6	47	28	2	—	.249	.303	.380	104	1	10	.886	7	116	76	3b55,2b50	—	1.0
1902	Cin N	129	479	53	133	20	7	1	49	24	3	—	.278	.316	.355	98	-2	12	.912	22	**118**	**174**	3b129/rf	—	2.4
1903	Cin N	118	439	71	137	**32**	12	6	83	47	6	—	.312	.386	.481	132	18	13	.937	6	101	104	3b104,S14	—	2.6
1904	Cin N	99	349	35	85	11	6	1	52	29	6	—	.244	.313	.318	87	-5	17	.887	-10	85	128	3b98	—	-1.3
1905	Cin N	114	384	49	104	16	9	1	39	30	3	—	.271	.329	.367	97	-2	15	.919	12	**111**	**122**	3b103/12lf	—	1.3
1906	†Chi N	151	539	81	**176**	27	10	3	**83**	47	14	—	.327	.395	.430	149	32	29	**.954**	-20	84	88	3b150/2	—	1.7
1907	†Chi N	152	542	52	144	25	5	1	70	37	9	—	.266	.323	.336	100	0	19	**.967**	-7	96	104	3b151	—	-0.3
1908	†Chi N	150	539	63	130	20	6	1	62	36	4	—	.241	.294	.306	88	-8	12	.940	-13	91	89	3b150	—	-1.9
1909	Chi N	151	528	73	133	27	6	2	59	57	5	—	.252	.331	.337	105	4	22	.940	1	99	101	3b151	—	1.0
1910	†Chi N	129	448	70	113	21	1	2	58	36	11	29	.252	.323	.317	88	-6	10	**.946**	1	102	97	3b128	—	-0.3
1911	Bos N	19	63	5	16	4	0	1	8	6	2	3	.254	.338	.365	89	-1	1	.810	-5	77	70	3b19	—	-0.5
Total	14	1647	5900	759	1578	284	90	27	762	471	79	32	.267	.330	.360	101	5	202	.926	-5	98	106	3b1387,2b187,O35C,S29,1b5	—	4.0
STELLBAUER, BILL	William Jennings; B3.20.1894 Bremond TX; D2.16.1974 New Braunfels TX; BR/TR/5´10˝/175; d4.12; Col Baylor																								
1916	Phi A	25	48	2	13	2	1	0	5	6	0	7	.271	.352	.354	118	1	2	.857	-3	79	0	O14L	—	-0.2
STELMASZEK, RICK	Richard Francis; B10.8.1948 Chicago IL; BL/TR/6´1˝/(190–195); [TexA67 11/205]; d6.25; C26																								
1971	Was A	6	9	0	0	0	0	0	0	0-0	0	3	.000	.000	.000	-99	-2	0-0	1.000	-1	0	243	C3	0	-0.3
1973	Tex A	7	9	0	1	0	0	0	0	1-0	0	2	.111	.200	.111	-11	-1	0-0	1.000	-1	157	0	C7	0	-0.2
	Cal A	22	26	2	4	1	0	0	3	6-0	0	7	.154	.313	.192	48	-1	0-0	1.000	-4	124	105	C22	0	-0.5
	Year	29	35	2	5	1	0	0	3	7-0	0	9	.143	.286	.171	33	-3	0-0	1.000	-4	131	83	C29	0	-0.7
1974	Chi N	25	44	2	10	2	0	1	7	10-0	0	6	.227	.364	.341	96	0	0-0	.983	-5	70	61	C16	0	-0.4
Total	3	60	88	4	15	3	0	1	10	17-0	0	18	.170	.302	.239	54	-4	0-0	.993	-10	99	83	C48	0	-1.4
STEM, FRED	Frederick Boothe; B9.22.1885 Oxford NC; D9.5.1964 Darlington SC; BL/TR/6´2˝/160; d9.15; Col North Carolina																								
1908	Bos N	20	72	9	20	0	1	0	3	2	0	—	.278	.297	.306	94	-1	1	.995	-1	80	111	1b19	—	-0.2
1909	Bos N	73	245	13	51	2	3	0	11	12	3	—	.208	.254	.241	51	-15	5	.989	11	172	86	1b68	—	-0.6
Total	2	93	317	22	71	2	4	0	14	14	3	—	.224	.263	.256	60	-16	6	.990	10	152	91	1b87	—	-0.8
STENGEL, CASEY	Charles Dillon "The Old Professor"; B7.30.1890 Kansas City MO; D9.29.1975 Glendale CA; BL/TL/5´11˝/175; d9.17; Mil 1918; M25/C2; HF1966																								
1912	Bro N	17	57	9	18	1	0	1	13	15	1	9	.316	.466	.386	140	5	5	.902	-2	94	40	O17C	—	0.1
1913	Bro N	124	438	60	119	16	8	7	43	56	1	58	.272	.356	.393	110	7	19-17	.960	-4	95	95	O119(0/117/2)	—	-0.8
1914	Bro N	126	412	55	130	13	10	4	60	56	5	55	.316	**.404**	.425	143	24	19	.964	-7	89	81	O121(0/2/119)	—	1.2
1915	Bro N	132	459	52	109	20	12	3	50	34	3	46	.237	.294	.353	94	-5	5-10	.959	-1	102	86	O129(1/0/128)	—	-1.7
1916	†Bro N	127	462	66	129	27	8	8	53	33	1	51	.279	.329	.424	127	14	11	.965	5	112	101	O121R	—	1.5
1917	Bro N	150	549	69	141	23	12	6	73	60	5	62	.257	.336	.375	115	11	18	.969	11	102	**157**	O150(0/1/149)	—	1.6
1918	Pit N	39	122	18	30	4	1	1	12	16	2	14	.246	.343	.320	99	1	11	.973	3	112	133	O37R	—	0.2
1919	Pit N	89	321	38	94	10	10	4	43	35	1	35	.293	.364	.424	131	12	12	.957	1	118	53	O87R	—	0.9
1920	Phi N	129	445	53	130	25	6	9	50	38	6	35	.292	.356	.436	121	13	7-13	.954	-2	97	110	O118(1/5/113)	—	0.2
1921	Phi N	24	59	7	18	3	1	0	4	6	0	7	.305	.369	.390	94	0	1-1	.969	2	93	251	O15R	—	0.1
	NY N	18	22	4	5	1	0	0	2	1	0	5	.227	.261	.273	41	-2	0-1	.875	-0	107	0	O8(0/2/6)	—	-0.3
	Year	42	81	11	23	4	1	0	6	7	0	12	.284	.341	.358	81	-2	1-2	.950	2	95	207	O23(0/2/21)	—	-0.2
1922	†NY N	84	250	48	92	8	10	7	48	21	**9**	17	.368	.436	.564	155	20	4-2	.969	-4	94	79	O77(0/75/2)	—	1.3
1923	†NY N	75	218	39	74	11	5	5	43	20	2	18	.339	.400	.505	139	12	6-2	.983	-6	83	59	O57(6/51/0)	—	0.4
1924	Bos N	131	461	57	129	20	6	5	39	45	3	39	.280	.348	.382	100	0	13-13	.978	-6	89	84	O126(0/5/121)	—	-1.7
1925	Bos N	12	13	0	1	0	0	0	2	1	0	2	.077	.143	.077	-46	-3	0-1	1.000	-0	68	0	/rf	—	-0.3
Total	14	1277	4288	575	1219	182	89	60	535	437	39	453	.284	.356	.410	119	109	131-60	.964	-10	99	98	O1183(8/275/901)	—	2.7
STENHOUSE, MIKE	Michael Steven; B5.29.1958 Pueblo CO; BL/TR/6´1˝/195; [MonN80*S1/4]; d10.3; f–Dave; Col Harvard																								
1982	Mon N	1	1	0	0	0	0	0	0	0-0	0	1	.000	.000	.000	-97	0	0-0	ø	0	—	—	/H	0	0.0
1983	Mon N	24	40	2	5	1	0	0	2	4-0	0	10	.125	.205	.150	-0	-5	0-0	1.000	-1	99	0	O9(3/0/7),1b5	0	-0.7
1984	Mon N	80	175	14	32	8	0	4	16	26-4	1	32	.183	.289	.297	69	-7	0-0	.986	-1	90	139	O48(30/0/19),1b14	0	-1.1
1985	Min A	81	179	23	40	5	0	5	21	29-1	0	18	.223	.330	.335	78	-5	1-0	.929	2	95	248	D27,O16(8/0/9),1b8	0	-0.5
1986	Bos A	21	21	1	2	1	0	0	1	12-0	0	5	.095	.424	.143	62	0	0-0	1.000	1	105	0	O4(2/0/2),1b3	0	0.0
Total	5	207	416	40	79	15	0	9	40	71-5	1	66	.190	.308	.291	67	-17	1-0	.973	0	92	146	O77(43/0/37),1b30,D27	0	-2.3

YEAR	TM LG	G	AB	R	H	2B	3B	HR	RBI	BB-IB	HP	SO	AVG	OBP	SLG	AOPS	ABR	SB-CS	FA	FR	RNG	THR	GAMES AT POSITION	DL	BFW
Stennett, Rennie	Renaldo Antonio (Porte); B4.5.1951 Colon, Pan; BR/TR/5´11˝/(154–188); d7.10																								
1971	Pit N	50	153	24	54	5	4	1	15	7-0	0	9	.353	.377	.458	136	6	1-1	.954	6	114	106	2b36	0	1.5
1972	†Pit N	109	370	43	106	14	5	3	30	9-1	2	43	.286	.307	.376	94	-5	4-3	.977	11	110	145	2b49,O41(31/5/10),S6	0	0.9
1973	Pit N	128	466	45	113	18	3	10	55	16-3	0	63	.242	.265	.358	73	-19	2-3	.981	17	107	119	2b84,S43,O5(3/0/2)	0	0.6
1974	†Pit N	157	673	84	196	29	3	7	56	32-8	2	51	.291	.322	.374	98	-4	8-9	.980	21	**112**	113	2b154,O2R	0	2.6
1975	†Pit N	148	616	89	176	25	7	7	62	33-1	4	42	.286	.324	.383	96	-6	5-4	.979	26	**114**	107	2b144	0	3.0
1976	Pit N	157	654	59	168	31	9	2	60	19-2	1	32	.257	.277	.341	74	-25	18-6	.981	24	**111**	111	2b157,S4	0	1.2
1977	Pit N	116	453	53	152	20	4	5	51	29-4	2	24	.336	.376	.430	112	8	28-18	.982	1	103	109	2b113	42	1.6
1978	Pit N	106	333	30	81	9	2	3	35	13-6	2	22	.243	.274	.309	60	-19	2-1	.971	-4	99	91	2b80,3b6	0	-2.0
1979	†Pit N	108	319	31	76	13	2	0	24	24-6	0	25	.238	.289	.292	56	-19	1-4	.974	0	107	115	2b102	0	-1.6
1980	SF N	120	397	34	97	13	2	2	37	22-10	2	31	.244	.286	.302	67	-18	4-4	.973	-7	98	80	2b111	0	-2.1
1981	SF N	38	87	8	20	0	0	1	7	3-0	1	6	.230	.264	.264	52	-6	2-1	1.000	-3	81	77	2b19	0	-0.9
Total	11	1237	4521	500	1239	177	41	41	432	207-41	16	348	.274	.306	.359	85	-107	75-54	.978	91	107	108	2b1049,S53,O48(34/5/14),3b6	42	4.8
Stenson, Dernell	Dernell Renauld; B6.17.1978 LaGrange GA; D11.4.2003 Chandler AZ; BL/TL/6´1˝/230; [BosA96 3/91]; d8.13																								
2003	Cin N	37	81	14	20	5	0	3	13	11-0	0	24	.247	.333	.420	101	0	0-0	.979	2	114	156	O22(18/0/7)/1	0	0.1
Stenzel, Jake	Jacob Charles (b Jacob Charles Stelzle); B6.24.1867 Cincinnati OH; D1.6.1919 Cincinnati OH; BR/TR/5´10˝/168; d6.16																								
1890	Chi N	11	41	3	11	1	0	0	3	1	0	0	.268	.286	.293	66	-2	0	.857	-1	0	0	O6R,C6	—	-0.2
1892	Pit N	3	9	0	0	0	0	0	0	1	0	3	.000	.100	.000	-69	-2	1	1.000	0	273	0	O2(1/1/0)/C	—	-0.2
1893	Pit N	60	224	57	81	13	4	4	37	24	0	17	.362	.423	.509	150	16	16	.905	-7	55	138	O45(4/18/23),C12/S2	—	0.6
1894	Pit N	132	525	150	185	39	20	13	121	76	6	13	.352	.440	.577	145	40	61	.926	-3	104	112	O132(5/127/0)	—	2.2
1895	Pit N	130	518	114	192	38	13	7	97	57	11	25	.371	.444	.535	160	50	53	.909	-10	116	137	O130C	—	2.6
1896	Pit N	114	479	104	173	26	14	2	82	32	8	13	.361	.410	.486	142	29	57	.922	-8	79	121	O114C/1	—	1.2
1897	†Bal N	131	536	113	189	**43**	7	4	116	36	10	—	.353	.404	.481	133	26	69	.932	-15	63	58	O131C	—	0.3
1898	Bal N	35	138	33	35	5	2	0	22	12	6	—	.254	.340	.319	87	-2	4	.926	-1	139	111	O35C	—	-0.4
	StL N	108	404	64	114	15	11	1	33	41	13	—	.282	.367	.381	112	7	21	.943	-3	53	54	O108C	—	-0.2
	Year	143	542	97	149	20	13	1	55	53	19	—	.275	.360	.365	106	5	25	.940	-3	72	67	O143C	—	-0.6
1899	StL N	35	128	21	35	9	0	1	19	16	3	—	.273	.367	.367	99	1	8	.949	-2	57	74	O33(8/21/4)	—	-0.3
	Cin N	9	29	5	9	1	0	0	3	4	1	—	.310	.412	.345	106	1	2	1.000	-1	0	0	O7C	—	0.0
	Year	44	157	26	44	10	0	1	22	20	4	—	.280	.376	.363	101	1	10	.957	-3	48	63	O40(8/28/4)	—	-0.3
Total	9	768	3031	664	1024	190	71	32	533	300	58	71	.338	.408	.479	135	164	292	.927	-49	83	98	O743(18/692/33),C19/12S	—	5.6
Stephens, Ray	Carl Ray; B9.22.1962 Houston TX; BR/TR/6´0˝/190; [StLN85 6/150]; d9.20; Col Troy St.																								
1990	StL N	5	15	2	2	1	0	1	1	0-0	0	3	.133	.133	.400	40	-1	0-0	1.000	-1	35	0	C5	0	-0.2
1991	StL N	6	7	0	2	0	0	0	0	1-0	0	3	.286	.375	.286	87	0	0-0	1.000	-1	51	81	C6	0	0.0
1992	Tex A	8	13	0	2	0	0	0	0	0-0	0	5	.154	.154	.154	-14	-2	0-0	1.000	-2	120	248	C6/D	0	-0.4
Total	3	19	35	2	6	1	0	1	1	1-0	0	11	.171	.194	.286	32	-3	0-0	1.000	-3	65	97	C17/D	0	-0.6
Stephens, Gene	Glen Eugene; B1.20.1933 Gravette AR; BL/TR/6´3.5˝/(175–185); d4.16																								
1952	Bos A	21	53	10	12	5	0	0	5	3	0	8	.226	.268	.321	59	-3	4-2	.962	0	107	104	O13(2/0/11)	0	-0.3
1953	Bos A	78	221	30	45	6	2	3	18	29	2	56	.204	.302	.290	57	-13	3-3	.966	-3	95	46	O72(71/0/3)	0	-2.0
1955	Bos A	109	157	25	46	9	4	3	18	20-0	2	34	.293	.374	.459	114	3	0-0	.947	3	100	220	O75(71/4/0)	0	0.4
1956	Bos A	104	63	22	17	2	0	1	7	12-0	0	12	.270	.387	.349	85	-1	0-1	.983	4	137	130	O71(69/2/2)	0	0.1
1957	Bos A	120	173	25	46	6	4	3	26	26-1	0	20	.266	.353	.399	102	1	0-2	.987	-3	72	148	O90(75/6/11)	0	-0.6
1958	Bos A	134	270	38	59	10	1	9	25	22-1	1	46	.219	.279	.363	71	-11	1-2	.975	0	97	112	O110(92/26/3)	0	-1.6
1959	Bos A	92	270	34	75	13	1	3	39	29-0	4	33	.278	.353	.367	95	-1	5-2	.981	4	94	240	O85(62/17/7)	42	0.0
1960	Bos A	35	109	9	25	4	0	2	11	14-0	0	22	.229	.312	.321	71	-4	5-1	.951	-1	93	103	O31(21/4/8)	0	-0.6
	Bal A	84	193	38	46	11	0	5	11	25-0	1	25	.238	.327	.373	91	-2	4-2	.992	5	118	149	O77(36/19/42)	0	0.1
	Year	119	302	47	71	15	0	7	22	39-0	1	47	.235	.322	.354	83	-6	9-3	.979	5	109	132	O108(57/23/50)	0	-0.5
1961	Bal A	32	58	4	11	2	0	0	2	14-0	0	7	.190	.347	.224	58	-3	1-1	1.000	-0	86	141	O30(27/5/5)	0	-0.4
	KC A	62	183	22	38	6	1	4	26	16-0	2	27	.208	.279	.317	58	-11	3-2	.968	4	110	194	O54(6/28/25)	0	-0.9
	Year	94	241	26	49	8	1	4	28	30-0	2	34	.203	.297	.295	59	-14	4-3	.975	4	103	178	O84(33/33/30)	0	-1.3
1962	KC A	5	4	0	0	0	0	0	0	1-0	0	1	.000	.200	.000	-39	-1	0-0	ø	0	—	—	/H	127	-0.1
1963	Chi A	6	18	5	7	0	0	1	2	1-0	0	3	.389	.421	.556	174	2	0-0	.909	1	88	614	O5(2/0/3)	0	0.2
1964	Chi A	82	141	21	33	4	2	3	17	21-3	2	28	.234	.335	.355	97	0	1-2	.969	3	122	89	O59(32/25/6)	0	0.1
Total	12	964	1913	283	460	78	15	37	207	233-5	14	322	.240	.325	.355	82	-44	27-20	.973	17	100	149	O772(566/136/126)	169	-5.6
Stephens, Jim	James Walter "Little Nemo"; B12.10.1883 Salineville OH; D1.2.1965 Oxford AL; BR/TR/5´6.5˝/157; d4.11; Col Villanova																								
1907	StL A	58	173	15	35	6	3	0	11	15	1	—	.202	.270	.272	73	-5	3	.967	-5	*91*	*96*	C56	—	-0.5
1908	StL A	47	150	14	30	4	1	0	6	9	2	—	.200	.255	.240	61	-6	0	.960	2	*121*	*107*	C45	—	0.0
1909	StL A	79	223	18	49	5	0	3	18	13	5	—	.220	.278	.283	83	-5	5	.980	2	*96*	*109*	C72	—	0.4
1910	StL A	99	289	24	62	3	7	0	23	16	2	—	.215	.261	.273	72	-11	2	.971	-1	*82*	***113***	C96	—	-0.3
1911	StL A	70	212	11	49	5	5	0	17	17	4	—	.231	.300	.302	71	-9	1	.949	-8	*75*	*102*	C66	—	-1.1
1912	StL A	75	205	13	51	7	5	0	22	7	0	—	.249	.274	.332	76	-8	3	.954	-1	*88*	*119*	C66	—	-0.4
Total	6	428	1252	95	276	30	21	3	97	77	14	—	.220	.273	.285	73	-44	14	.965	-11	*90*	*108*	C401	—	-1.9
Stephens, Vern	Vernon Decatur "Junior","Buster"; B10.23.1920 McAlister NM; D11.4.1968 Long Beach CA; BR/TR/5´10˝/(178–185); d9.13; Col Long Beach (CA) City																								
1941	StL A	3	2	0	1	0	0	0	0	0	0	0	.500	.500	.500	160	0	0-0	.500	-0	103	0	/S	0	0.0
1942	StL A	145	575	84	169	26	6	14	92	41	0	53	.294	.341	.433	115	9	1-3	.944	-13	98	92	S144	0	0.6
1943	StL A★	137	512	75	148	27	3	22	91	54	0	73	.289	.357	.482	142	25	3-2	.943	-22	91	62	S123,O11(9/0/3)	0	1.3
1944	†StL A★	145	559	91	164	32	1	20	**109**	62	1	54	.293	.365	.462	128	21	2-2	.954	-5	102	76	S143	0	2.8
1945	StL A✳	149	571	90	165	27	3	**24**	89	55	1	70	.289	.352	.473	132	21	2-1	**.961**	-18	94	80	S144,3b4	0	1.6
1946	StL A★	115	450	67	138	19	4	14	64	35	0	49	.307	.357	.460	121	11	0-1	.950	-1	103	93	S112	0	1.7
1947	StL A	150	562	74	157	18	4	15	83	70	0	61	.279	.359	.406	110	8	8-4	.970	13	**108**	103	S149	0	3.1
1948	Bos A★	**155**	635	114	171	25	8	29	137	77	2	56	.269	.350	.471	112	7	1-0	.971	9	**110**	99	S155	0	2.5
1949	Bos A★	**155**	610	113	177	31	2	39	**159**	101	0	73	.290	.391	.539	135	30	2-2	.966	2	**105**	108	S155	0	3.9
1950	Bos A☆	149	628	125	185	34	6	30	**144**	65	0	43	.295	.361	.511	110	7	1-0	.981	1	97	102	S146	0	1.6
1951	Bos A★	109	377	62	113	21	2	17	78	38	0	33	.300	.364	.501	120	10	1-2	.978	12	111	102	3b89,S2	0	2.0
1952	Bos A	92	295	35	75	13	2	7	44	39	1	31	.254	.343	.383	95	-2	2-2	.957	4	104	119	S53,3b29	0	0.5
1953	Chi A	44	129	14	24	6	0	1	14	13	0	18	.186	.261	.256	39	-11	2-0	.990	-0	99	97	3b38,S3	0	-1.1
	StL A	46	165	16	53	8	0	4	17	18	0	24	.321	.388	.442	121	5	0-0	.954	-2	95	77	3b46	0	0.3
	Year	90	294	30	77	14	0	5	31	31	0	42	.262	.332	.361	85	-6	2-0	.968	-2	97	85	3b84,S3	0	-0.8
1954	Bal A	101	365	31	104	17	1	8	46	17	0	36	.285	.311	.403	104	0	0-3	.966	-2	98	101	3b96	0	-0.3
1955	Bal A	3	6	0	1	0	0	0	0	0-0	1	0	.167	.286	.167	26	-1	0-0	1.000	-0	96	0	3b2	0	-0.1
	Chi A	22	56	10	14	3	0	3	7	7-0	0	11	.250	.328	.464	110	1	0-0	1.000	2	113	137	3b18	0	0.3
	Year	25	62	10	15	3	0	3	7	7-0	1	11	.242	.324	.435	102	0	0-0	1.000	2	112	129	3b20	0	0.2
Total	15	1720	6497	1001	1859	307	42	247	1174	692-0	6	685	.286	.355	.460	118	141	25-22	.960	-20	101	92	S1330,3b322,O11(9/0/3)	0	20.7
Stephenson, Riggs	Jackson Riggs "Old Hoss"; B1.5.1898 Akron AL; D11.15.1985 Tuscaloosa AL; BR/TR/5´10˝/185; d4.13; Col Alabama																								
1921	Cle A	65	206	45	68	17	2	2	34	23	4	15	.330	.408	.461	119	7	4-1	.942	-4	95	115	2b54,3b2	—	0.5
1922	Cle A	86	233	47	79	24	5	2	32	27	6	18	.339	.421	.511	141	16	3-0	.952	-4	96	75	3b34,2b25,O3(2/0/1)	—	1.4
1923	Cle A	91	301	48	96	20	6	5	65	15	3	25	.319	.357	.475	118	6	5-5	.970	11	106	124	2b66,O3R,3b2	—	1.8
1924	Cle A	71	240	33	89	20	0	4	44	27	2	10	.371	.439	.504	141	16	1-2	.961	-11	102	58	2b58,O7R	—	0.6
1925	Cle A	19	54	8	16	3	1	1	9	7	1	3	.296	.387	.444	110	1	1-1	.946	1	112	124	O16R	—	0.0
1926	Chi N	82	281	40	95	18	3	3	44	31	0	16	.338	.404	.456	129	13	2	.950	-4	90	105	O74(73/0/1)	—	0.4
1927	Chi N	152	579	101	199	**46**	9	7	82	65	6	28	.344	.415	.491	142	37	8	.975	0	96	129	O146L,3b6	—	2.5
1928	Chi N	137	512	75	166	36	9	8	90	68	3	29	.324	.407	.477	132	26	8	.982	-2	97	98	O135L	—	1.4
1929	†Chi N	136	495	91	179	36	6	17	110	67	7	21	.362	.445	.562	147	40	10	.984	-2	93	105	O130L	—	2.5
1930	Chi N	109	341	56	125	21	1	5	68	32	0	20	.367	.421	.478	116	11	2	.958	-3	91	99	O80L	—	0.2
1931	Chi N	80	263	34	84	14	4	1	52	37	1	14	.319	.405	.414	119	9	1	.985	-2	98	29	O66L	—	0.3
1932	†Chi N	147	583	86	189	49	4	4	85	54	2	27	.324	.383	.443	123	21	3	.984	-7	92	77	O147L	—	0.7
1933	Chi N	97	346	45	114	17	4	4	51	34	5	16	.329	.397	.436	138	19	5	.985	-1	99	73	O91L	—	1.3
1934	Chi N	38	74	5	16	0	0	0	7	7	1	5	.216	.293	.216	39	-6	0	1.000	2	93	327	O15L	—	-0.5
Total	14	1310	4508	714	1515	321	54	63	773	494	41	247	.336	.407	.473	130	216	53-9	.978	-25	95	98	O913(885/0/28),2b203,3b44	—	13.1

YEAR	TM LG	G	AB	R	H	2B	3B	HR	RBI	BB-IB	HP	SO	AVG	OBP	SLG	AOPS	ABR	SB-CS	FA	FR	RNG	THR	GAMES AT POSITION	DL	BFW
Stephenson, John	John Herman; B4.13.1941 S.Portsmouth KY; BL/TR/5´11˝/(180–185); d4.14; Col William Carey																								
1964	NY N	37	57	2	9	0	0	1	2	4-0	1	18	.158	.226	.211	24	-6	0-0	.800	-0	130	80	3b14,O8(5/3/0)	0	-0.7
1965	NY N	62	121	9	26	5	0	4	15	8-2	0	19	.215	.264	.355	75	-4	0-1	.981	-3	78	98	C47,O2R	0	-0.7
1966	NY N	63	143	17	28	1	1	1	11	8-0	2	28	.196	.248	.238	37	-13	0-0	.973	2	75	116	C52/lf	0	-0.9
1967	Chi N	18	49	3	11	3	1	0	5	1-1	1	6	.224	.255	.327	62	-2	0-0	1.000	-1	58	172	C13	0	-0.3
1968	Chi N	2	2	0	0	0	0	0	0	0-0	0	0	.000	.000	.000	-94	0	0-0	ø	0	—	—	/H	0	-0.1
1969	SF N	22	27	2	6	2	0	0	3	0-0	0	4	.222	.214	.296	45	-2	0-0	.941	-3	35	0	C9/3	0	-0.5
1970	SF N	23	43	3	3	1	0	0	6	2-0	0	7	.070	.109	.093	-45	-9	0-0	1.000	1	74	90	C9/lf	0	-0.7
1971	Cal A	98	279	24	61	17	0	3	25	22-6	3	21	.219	.281	.312	73	-10	0-0	.992	-2	106	61	C88	0	-0.9
1972	Cal A	66	146	14	40	3	1	2	17	11-5	4	8	.274	.342	.349	112	2	0-0	.993	-4	67	79	C56	0	0.0
1973	Cal A	60	122	9	30	5	0	1	9	7-1	1	7	.246	.292	.311	75	-4	0-0	.980	-4	94	58	C56	0	-0.7
Total	10	451	989	83	214	37	3	12	93	63-15	12	118	.216	.271	.296	64	-48	0-1	.986	-13	85	82	C330,3b15,O12(7/3/2)	0	-5.5
Stephenson, Joe	Joseph Chester; B6.30.1921 Detroit MI; D9.20.2001 Fullerton CA; BR/TR/6´2˝/185; d9.19; Mil 1944–45; s–Jerry; Col Western Michigan																								
1943	NY N	9	24	4	6	1	0	0	1	0	0	5	.250	.250	.292	56	-1	0	.973	1	*98*	*194*	C6	0	0.0
1944	Chi N	4	8	1	1	0	0	0	0	1	0	3	.125	.222	.125	-1	-1	1	1.000	1	*77*	*174*	C3	0	0.0
1947	Chi A	16	35	3	5	0	0	0	3	1	2	7	.143	.211	.143	-1	-5	0-0	.959	-1	*94*	*118*	C13	0	-0.5
Total	3	29	67	8	12	1	0	0	4	2	2	15	.179	.225	.194	19	-7	1-0	.970	1	*93*	*151*	C22	0	-0.5
Stephenson, Phil	Phillip Raymond; B9.19.1960 Guthrie OK; BL/TL/6´1˝/(195–201); [OakA82 3/80]; d4.5; Col Wichita St.																								
1989	Chi N	17	21	0	3	0	0	0	0	2-0	0	3	.143	.217	.143	5	-3	1-0	1.000	-1	57	0	O3L	15	-0.3
	SD N	10	17	4	6	0	0	2	2	3-0	0	2	.353	.450	.706	225	3	0-0	.977	0	121	90	1b8	0	0.3
	Year	27	38	4	9	0	0	2	2	5-0	0	5	.237	.326	.395	100	0	1-0	.977	-0	121	90	1b8,O3L	0	0.0
1990	SD N	103	182	26	38	9	1	4	19	30-1	0	43	.209	.319	.335	80	-4	2-1	.997	2	116	111	1b60	0	-0.5
1991	SD N	11	7	0	2	0	0	0	0	2-0	0	3	.286	.444	.286	106	0	0-0	ø	0	—	—	/H	153	0.0
1992	SD N	53	71	5	11	2	1	0	8	10-0	0	11	.155	.259	.211	34	-6	0-0	1.000	-1	79	0	O15(10/0/6),1b7	0	-0.9
Total	4	194	298	35	60	11	2	6	29	47-1	0	62	.201	.309	.312	73	-10	3-1	.993	1	117	107	1b75,O18(13/0/6)	168	-1.4
Stephenson, Dummy	Reuben Crandol; B9.22.1869 Petersburg NJ; D12.1.1924 Trenton NJ; BR/TR/5´11.5˝/180; d9.9																								
1892	Phi N	8	37	4	10	3	0	0	5	0	1	2	.270	.289	.351	94	0	0	.800	-1	84	0	O8C	—	-0.2
Stephenson, Bob	Robert Lloyd; B8.11.1928 Blair OK; BR/TR/6´0˝/165; d4.14; Col Oklahoma																								
1955	StL N	67	111	19	27	3	0	0	6	5-0	0	18	.243	.274	.270	46	-9	2-1	.938	-2	89	122	S48,2b7/3	0	-0.8
Stephenson, Walter	Walter McQueen "Tarzan"; B3.27.1911 Saluda NC; D7.4.1993 Shreveport LA; BR/TR/6´0˝/180; d4.29																								
1935	†Chi N	16	26	2	10	1	1	0	2	1	0	5	.385	.407	.500	142	1	0	1.000	1	*126*	*299*	C6	—	0.3
1936	Chi N	6	12	0	1	0	0	0	1	0	0	5	.083	.083	.083	-54	-3	0	1.000	0	*65*	*0*	C4	—	-0.2
1937	Phi N	10	23	1	6	0	0	0	2	2	0	3	.261	.320	.261	55	-1	0	.967	0	*102*	*112*	C7	—	-0.1
Total	3	32	61	3	17	1	1	0	5	3	0	13	.279	.313	.328	70	-3	0	.984	2	*104*	*156*	C17	—	0.0
Stern, Adam	Adam James; B2.12.1980 London ON, Can.; BL/TR/5´11˝/180; [AtlN01 3/105]; d7.7; Col Nebraska																								
2005	Bos A	36	15	4	2	0	0	1	2	0-0	1	4	.133	.188	.333	33	-2	1-1	1.000	-1	81	0	O21(2/6/13)	110	-0.2
2006	Bos A	10	20	3	3	1	0	0	4	0-0	1	4	.150	.190	.200	1	-3	1-0	1.000	1	125	335	O10(2/8/0)	35	-0.1
Total	2	46	35	7	5	1	0	1	6	0-0	2	8	.143	.189	.257	15	-5	2-1	1.000	1	103	171	O31(4/14/13)	145	-0.3
Sterrett, Dutch	Charles Hurlbut; B10.1.1889 Milroy PA; D12.9.1965 Baltimore MD; BR/TR/5´11.5˝/165; d6.20; Col Princeton																								
1912	NY A	66	230	30	61	4	7	1	32	11	4	—	.265	.310	.357	85	-6	8	.972	-5	96	63	O37(0/31/6),1b17,C10/2	—	-1.3
1913	NY A	21	35	0	6	0	0	0	3	1	1	5	.171	.216	.171	14	-4	1	1.000	-1	68	38	1b6/C	—	-0.5
Total	2	87	265	30	67	4	7	1	35	12	5	5	.253	.298	.332	77	-10	9	.972	-5	96	63	O37(0/31/6),1b23,C11/2	—	-1.8
Stevens, Chuck	Charles Augustus; B7.10.1918 Van Houten NM; BB/TL/6´1˝/180; d9.16; Mil 1943–45																								
1941	StL A	4	13	2	2	0	0	0	2	0	0	1	.154	.154	.154	-18	-2	0-0	.966	-1	0	121	1b4	0	-0.4
1946	StL A	122	432	53	107	17	4	3	27	47	2	62	.248	.324	.326	78	-12	4-6	**.995**	4	110	90	1b120	0	-1.4
1948	StL A	85	287	34	75	12	4	1	26	41	0	26	.261	.354	.341	83	-6	2-2	.991	1	103	101	1b85	0	-0.9
Total	3	211	732	89	184	29	8	4	55	88	2	89	.251	.333	.329	79	-20	6-8	.993	3	106	95	1b209	0	-2.7
Stevens, Lee	De Wain Lee; B7.10.1967 Kansas City MO; BL/TL/6´4˝/(205–235); [CalA86 1/22]; d7.16																								
1990	Cal A	67	248	28	53	10	0	7	32	22-3	0	75	.214	.275	.339	73	-10	1-1	.994	-2	85	105	1b67	0	-1.7
1991	Cal A	18	58	8	17	7	0	0	9	6-2	0	12	.293	.354	.414	113	1	1-2	.989	-0	113	72	1b11,O9(1/0/8)	0	0.0
1992	Cal A	106	312	25	69	19	0	7	37	29-6	1	64	.221	.288	.349	77	-10	1-4	.995	-1	92	121	1b91,D2	0	-1.9
1996	Tex A	27	78	6	18	2	3	3	12	6-0	1	22	.231	.291	.449	79	-3	0-0	.994	0	122	143	1b18,O5L	28	-0.4
1997	Tex A	137	426	58	128	24	2	21	74	23-2	1	83	.300	.336	.514	111	5	1-3	.994	-4	89	93	1b62,D38,O22(3/0/19)	0	-0.7
1998	†Tex A	120	344	52	91	17	4	20	59	31-4	0	93	.265	.324	.512	107	2	0-2	.996	0	94	56	D72,1b37,O7R	24	-0.4
1999	†Tex A	146	517	76	146	31	1	24	81	52-10	0	132	.282	.344	.485	103	2	2-3	.994	-9	73	**109**	1b133,D8	0	-1.8
2000	Mon N	123	449	60	119	27	2	22	75	48-6	2	105	.265	.337	.481	103	1	0-0	.991	0	102	97	1b123	0	-0.9
2001	Mon N	152	542	77	133	35	1	25	95	74-12	5	157	.245	.338	.452	103	4	2-1	.986	-4	94	94	1b152	0	-1.3
2002	Mon N	63	205	28	39	6	1	10	31	39-5	0	57	.190	.318	.376	78	-7	1-0	.993	4	125	101	1b58	0	-0.8
	Cle A	53	153	22	34	7	1	5	26	15-0	0	32	.222	.285	.379	75	-6	0-0	.987	-1	58	96	1b25,O16(11/0/5),D3	0	-0.9
Total	10	1012	3332	440	847	185	15	144	531	345-50	10	832	.254	.323	.448	97	-21	9-16	.992	-17	92	102	1b777,D123,O59(20/0/39)	52	-10.8
Stevens, Ed	Edward Lee "Big Ed"; B1.12.1925 Galveston TX; BL/TL/6´1˝/190; d8.9; C1																								
1945	Bro N	55	201	29	55	14	3	4	29	32	1	20	.274	.376	.433	125	8	0	.987	0	103	97	1b55	0	0.5
1946	Bro N	103	310	34	75	13	7	10	60	27	0	44	.242	.303	.426	104	0	2	.986	-4	84	90	1b99	0	-0.8
1947	Bro N	5	13	0	2	1	0	0	0	1	0	5	.154	.214	.231	18	-2	0	.971	1	193	79	1b4	0	-0.1
1948	Pit N	128	429	47	109	19	6	10	69	35	2	53	.254	.313	.396	89	-8	4	**.996**	4	112	**114**	1b117	0	-0.7
1949	Pit N	67	221	22	58	10	1	4	32	22	1	24	.262	.332	.371	86	-4	1	.995	10	167	131	1b58	62	0.4
1950	Pit N	17	46	2	9	2	0	0	3	4	0	5	.196	.260	.239	31	-5	0	1.000	1	115	109	1b12	0	-0.4
Total	6	375	1220	134	308	59	17	28	193	121	4	151	.252	.322	.398	95	-11	7	.992	12	114	107	1b345	62	-1.1
Stevens, R C	R C; B7.22.1934 Moultrie GA; BR/TL/6´5˝/(200–219); d4.15																								
1958	Pit N	59	90	16	24	3	1	7	18	5-0	2	25	.267	.320	.556	129	3	0-0	.991	1	112	121	1b52	0	0.2
1959	Pit N	3	7	2	2	0	0	1	1	0-0	0	0	.286	.286	.714	157	0	0-0	1.000	0	138	122	/1	0	0.1
1960	Pit N	9	3	1	0	0	0	0	0	0-0	0	1	.000	.000	.000	-99	-1	0-0	1.000	1	229	216	1b7	0	0.0
1961	Was A	33	62	2	8	1	0	0	2	7-0	0	15	.129	.217	.145	-1	-9	1-0	1.000	3	166	128	1b25	0	-0.7
Total	4	104	162	21	34	4	1	8	21	12-0	2	41	.210	.273	.395	77	-7	1-0	.995	5	135	126	1b85	0	-0.4
Stevens, Robert	Robert; d5.4																								
1875	Was NA	1	4	0	1	0	0	0	0	0	—	0	.250	.250	.250	77	0	0-0	.000	-0	0	0	/rf	—	0.0
Stevens, Bobby	Robert Jordan; B4.17.1907 Chevy Chase MD; D12.30.2005 Frederick MD; BL/TR/5´8˝/149; d7.3																								
1931	Phi N	12	35	3	12	0	0	0	4	2	2	2	.343	.410	.343	97	0	0	.870	-4	73	77	S10	—	-0.3
Steverson, Todd	Todd Anthony; B11.15.1971 Los Angeles CA; BR/TR/6´2˝/(194–200); [TorA92 1/25]; d4.28; Col Arizona St.																								
1995	Det A	30	42	11	11	0	0	2	6	6-0	0	10	.262	.340	.405	97	0	2-0	1.000	-2	73	100	O27(17/1/10)/D	77	-0.2
1996	SD N	1	1	0	0	0	0	0	0	0-0	0	1	.000	.000	.000	-99	0	0-0	ø	0	—	—	/H	0	0.0
Total	2	31	43	11	11	0	0	2	6	6-0	0	11	.256	.333	.395	93	0	2-0	1.000	-2	73	100	O27(17/1/10)/D	77	-0.2
Stewart, Andy	Andrew David; B12.5.1970 Oshawa ON, Can.; BR/TR/5´11˝/205; d9.6																								
1997	KC A	5	8	1	2	1	0	0	0	0-0	0	0	.250	.250	.375	58	0	0-0	1.000	0	113	185	C4/D	0	0.0
Stewart, Ace	Asa; B2.14.1869 Terre Haute IN; D4.17.1912 Terre Haute IN; BR/TR/5´10˝/176; d4.18																								
1895	Chi N	97	365	52	88	8	10	8	76	39	0	40	.241	.314	.384	75	-17	14	.911	-9	94	124	2b97	—	-1.7

THE BATTER REGISTER

YEAR	TM LG	G	AB	R	H	2B	3B	HR	RBI	BB-IB	HP	SO	AVG	OBP	SLG	AOPS	ABR	SB-CS	FA	FR	RNG	THR	GAMES AT POSITION	DL	BFW
Stewart, Tuffy	Charles Eugene; B7.31.1883 Chicago IL; D11.18.1934 Chicago IL; BL/TL/5´10˝/167; d8.8																								
1913	Chi N	9	8	1	1	1	0	0	2	2	0	5	.125	.300	.250	58	0	1	1.000	0	152	0	/rf	—	0.0
1914	Chi N	2	1	0	0	0	0	0	0	0	0	0	.000	.000	.000	-99	0	0	ø	0	—	—	/H	—	0.0
Total	2	11	9	1	1	1	0	0	2	2	0	5	.111	.273	.222	43	0	1	1.000	0	152	0	/rf	—	0.0
Stewart, Chris	Christopher David; B2.19.1982 Fontana CA; BR/TR/6´4˝/205; [ChiA01 12/373]; d9.6; Col Riverside (CA) JC																								
2006	Chi A	6	8	0	0	0	0	0	0	0-0	0	2	.000	.000	.000	-98	-2	0-0	1.000	2	91	526	C5/D	0	0.0
Stewart, Bud	Edward Perry; B6.15.1916 Sacramento CA; D6.21.2000 Palo Alto CA; BL/TR/5´11˝/170; d4.19; Def 1943; Mil 1944–45; Col UCLA																								
1941	Pit N	73	172	27	46	7	0	0	10	12	0	17	.267	.315	.308	76	-5	3	.962	1	97	176	O41(15/4/24)	0	-0.6
1942	Pit N	82	183	21	40	8	4	0	20	22	0	16	.219	.302	.306	76	-5	2	1.000	-1	110	42	O34(19/0/16),3b10,2b6	0	-0.9
1948	NY A	6	5	1	1	1	0	0	0	0	0	0	.200	.200	.400	58	0	0-0	ø	0	—	—	/H	0	0.0
	Was A	118	401	56	112	17	13	7	69	49	2	27	.279	.361	.439	115	7	8-9	.975	-1	104	60	O114(10/37/72)	0	0.1
	Year	124	406	57	113	18	13	7	69	49	2	27	.278	.359	.438	115	7	8-9	.975	-1	104	60	O114(10/37/72)	0	0.1
1949	Was A	118	388	58	110	23	4	8	43	49	3	33	.284	.368	.425	112	7	6-4	.982	-4	91	103	O105(75/16/20)	0	-0.3
1950	Was A	118	378	46	101	15	6	4	35	46	1	33	.267	.348	.370	88	-7	5-4	.991	2	99	126	O100(42/0/66)	0	-0.9
1951	Chi A	95	217	40	60	13	5	6	40	29	2	9	.276	.367	.465	127	8	1-6	.983	-1	93	97	O63(52/1/14)	0	0.1
1952	Chi A	92	225	23	60	10	0	5	30	28	1	17	.267	.350	.378	102	1	3-0	.982	-1	102	31	O60(57/0/3)	0	-0.3
1953	Chi A	53	59	16	16	2	0	2	13	14	0	3	.271	.411	.407	118	2	1-0	1.000	-1	83	0	O16(11/0/5)	51	0.1
1954	Chi A	18	13	0	1	0	0	0	0	3	0	2	.077	.250	.077	-7	-2	0-0	1.000	0	175	0	O2R	0	-0.2
Total	9	773	2041	288	547	96	32	32	260	252	9	157	.268	.351	.393	102	6	29-23	.982	-6	99	89	O535(281/58/222),3b10,2b6	51	-2.9
Stewart, Glen	Glen Weldon "Gabby"; B9.29.1912 Tullahoma TN; D2.11.1997 Memphis TN; BR/TR/6´0˝/175; d6.26; Col Ohio St.																								
1940	NY N	15	29	1	4	1	0	0	0	1	0	2	.138	.167	.172	-6	-4	0	.875	0	133	0	3b6,S5	—	-0.4
1943	Phi N	110	336	23	71	10	1	2	24	32	2	41	.211	.284	.265	61	-17	1	.947	-12	94	90	S77,2b18,1b8/C	0	-2.4
1944	Phi N	118	377	32	83	11	5	0	29	28	0	40	.220	.274	.276	57	-23	0	.963	1	105	88	3b83,S32/2	0	-1.9
Total	3	243	742	56	158	22	6	2	53	61	2	83	.213	.275	.267	56	-44	1	.953	-11	97	90	S114,3b89,2b19,1b8/C	0	-4.7
Stewart, Jimmy	James Franklin; B6.11.1939 Opelika AL; BB/TR/6´0˝/(160–175); d9.3; Col Austin Peay; OF(176/43/11)																								
1963	Chi N	13	37	1	11	2	0	0	1	1-0	0	7	.297	.316	.351	87	-1	1-1	.973	2	112	165	S9/2	0	0.2
1964	Chi N	132	415	59	105	17	0	3	33	49-0	2	61	.253	.331	.316	81	-8	10-8	.981	6	109	114	2b61,S45,O4C/3	0	0.6
1965	Chi N	116	282	26	63	9	4	0	19	30-1	2	53	.223	.301	.284	65	-13	13-3	.955	-2	97	156	O55(47/8/0),S48	0	-1.4
1966	Chi N	57	90	4	16	4	1	0	4	7-0	2	12	.178	.253	.244	38	-7	1-1	1.000	-2	118	116	O15(4/11/1),2b4,S2,3b2	0	-1.0
1967	Chi N	6	6	1	1	0	0	0	1	0-0	0	0	.167	.167	.167	-4	-1	0-0	ø	0	—	—	/H	0	-0.1
	Chi A	24	18	5	3	0	0	0	1	1-0	0	6	.167	.211	.167	13	-2	1-0	1.000	1	0	1192	O6L,2b5,S2	0	-0.1
1969	Cin N	119	221	26	56	3	4	4	24	19-3	0	33	.253	.311	.357	83	-6	4-2	.973	1	93	176	O66(55/10/1),2b18,3b6/S	0	-0.6
1970	†Cin N	101	105	15	28	3	1	1	8	8-1	1	13	.267	.322	.343	78	-3	5-3	1.000	2	73	120	O48(41/2/5),2b18,3b9/C1	0	-0.1
1971	Cin N	80	82	7	19	2	2	0	9	9-1	0	12	.232	.308	.305	75	-3	3-1	1.000	-2	45	0	O19(11/6/3),3b9,2b6	0	-0.4
1972	Hou N	68	96	14	21	5	2	0	9	6-2	0	9	.219	.257	.313	65	-5	0-1	1.000	-2	80	0	O11(9/2/1),1b9,2b8,3b2	0	-0.8
1973	Hou N	61	68	6	13	0	0	0	3	9-1	1	12	.191	.295	.191	38	-6	0-0	1.000	1	118	151	3b8,O3L/2	15	-0.5
Total	10	777	1420	164	336	45	14	8	112	139-9	8	218	.237	.306	.305	71	-55	38-20	.969	6	91	150	O227L,2b122,S107,3b37,1b10/C	15	-4.2
Stewart, Stuffy	John Franklin; B1.31.1894 Jasper FL; D12.30.1980 Lake City FL; BR/TR/5´9.5˝/160; d9.3																								
1916	StL N	9	17	0	3	0	0	0	1	0	0	3	.176	.176	.176	9	-2	0	.833	-1	75	112	2b8	—	-0.4
1917	StL N	13	9	4	0	0	0	0	0	0	0	4	.000	.000	.000	-99	-2	0	1.000	0	64	511	O7(2/3/2),2b2	—	-0.2
1922	Pit N	3	13	3	2	0	0	0	0	0	0	1	.154	.154	.154	-20	-2	0-0	.875	-1	84	122	2b3	—	-0.4
1923	Bro N	4	11	3	4	1	0	1	1	1	0	1	.364	.417	.727	202	2	0-0	.786	-1	86	68	2b3	—	0.0
1925	Was A	7	17	3	6	1	0	0	3	1	0	2	.353	.389	.412	105	0	1-0	.929	0	112	133	3b5/2	—	0.1
1926	Was A	62	63	27	17	6	1	0	9	6	0	6	.270	.333	.397	92	-1	8-4	.975	4	112	111	2b25/3	—	0.3
1927	Was A	56	129	24	31	6	2	0	4	8	0	15	.240	.285	.318	57	-9	12-2	.939	-0	102	96	2b37,3b2	—	-0.6
1929	Was A	22	6	10	0	0	0	0	0	1	0	0	.000	.143	.000	-60	-1	0-1	1.000	1	176	0	2b3	—	-0.1
Total	8	176	265	74	63	14	3	1	18	17	0	32	.238	.284	.325	61	-15	21-7	.932	1	101	99	2b82,3b8,O7(2/3/2)	—	-1.3
Stewart, Mark	Mark "Big Slick"; B10.14.1889 Whitlock TN; D1.17.1932 Memphis TN; BL/TR/6´1˝/180; d10.4; Col Washington and Lee																								
1913	Cin N	1	1	0	0	0	0	0	0	0	0	0	.000	.000	.000	-99	0	0	ø	-0	0	0	/C	—	0.0
Stewart, Shannon	Shannon Harold; B2.25.1974 Cincinnati OH; BR/TR/6´1˝/(190–210); [TorA92 1/19]; d9.2																								
1995	Tor A	12	38	2	8	0	0	0	1	5-0	1	5	.211	.318	.211	41	-3	2-0	.955	-1	76	196	O12C	0	-0.4
1996	Tor A	7	17	2	3	1	0	0	2	1-0	0	4	.176	.222	.235	16	-2	1-0	.800	-2	43	0	O6C	0	-0.3
1997	Tor A	44	168	25	48	13	7	0	22	19-1	4	24	.286	.368	.446	112	3	10-3	.980	-2	99	50	O41(2/39/0)/D	0	0.3
1998	Tor A	144	516	90	144	29	3	12	55	67-1	15	77	.279	.377	.417	106	7	51-18	.980	0	104	51	O144(110/44/0)	0	0.9
1999	Tor A	145	608	102	185	28	2	11	67	59-0	8	83	.304	.371	.411	98	0	37-14	.981	-10	91	44	O142(140/7/0),D2	0	-1.1
2000	Tor A	136	583	107	186	43	5	21	69	37-1	6	79	.319	.363	.518	116	14	20-5	.993	2	106	61	O136(136/1/0)	14	1.2
2001	Tor A	155	640	103	202	44	7	12	60	46-1	11	72	.316	.371	.463	115	15	27-10	.981	-7	88	79	O142L,D13	0	0.5
2002	Tor A	141	577	103	175	38	6	10	45	54-2	9	60	.303	.371	.442	111	11	14-2	.990	-4	92	51	O99L,D38	15	0.3
2003	Tor A	71	303	47	89	22	2	7	35	27-2	2	30	.294	.347	.449	106	3	1-2	.974	0	103	72	O69L,D2	25	0.0
	†Min A	65	270	43	87	22	0	6	38	25-1	4	36	.322	.384	.470	121	9	3-4	.993	4	115	113	O58(46/0/14),D6	0	1.0
	Year	136	573	90	176	44	2	13	73	52-3	6	66	.307	.364	.459	113	13	4-6	.983	5	108	91	O127(115/0/14),D8	0	1.0
2004	†Min A	92	378	46	115	17	2	11	47	47-4	1	44	.304	.380	.447	112	8	6-3	.972	-10	73	50	O71L,D21	58	-0.5
2005	Min A	132	551	69	151	27	3	10	56	34-2	8	73	.274	.323	.388	87	-10	7-5	.985	-2	96	99	O125L,D5	0	-1.6
2006	Min A	44	174	21	51	5	1	2	21	14-0	1	19	.293	.347	.368	86	-4	3-1	.984	0	94	132	O34L,D10	119	-0.5
Total	12	1188	4823	760	1444	289	38	102	518	435-15	70	606	.299	.364	.439	106	51	182-67	.983	-29	96	69	O1079(974/109/14),D98	231	-0.2
Stewart, Neb	Walter Nesbitt; B5.21.1918 S.Charleston OH; D6.8.1990 London OH; BR/TR/6´1˝/195; d9.8																								
1940	Phi N	10	31	3	4	0	0	0	0	1	0	5	.129	.156	.129	-21	-5	0	.944	1	86	342	O9(8/1/0)	—	-0.5
Stewart, Bill	William Wayne; B4.15.1928 Bay City MI; BR/TR/5´11˝/200; d4.17; Col Michigan St.																								
1955	KC A	11	18	2	2	1	0	0	0	1-0	0	6	.111	.158	.167	-13	-3	0-0	1.000	1	103	361	O6(4/0/2)	0	-0.2
Stillman, Royle	Royle Eldon; B1.2.1951 Santa Monica CA; BL/TL/5´11˝/(165–180); [LAN69 22/510]; d6.22																								
1975	Bal A	13	14	1	6	0	0	0	1	1-0	0	3	.429	.467	.429	163	1	0-0	1.000	0	141	0	O2(0/1/1)	0	0.1
1976	Bal A	20	22	0	2	0	0	0	1	3-1	0	4	.091	.200	.091	-14	-3	0-0	1.000	-0	0	0	1b2,D5	0	-0.3
1977	Chi A	56	119	18	25	7	1	3	13	17-1	0	21	.210	.307	.361	82	-3	2-1	.977	0	122	0	O26(19/0/8),D13/1	0	-0.4
Total	3	89	155	19	33	7	1	3	15	21-2	0	28	.213	.305	.329	77	-5	2-1	.978	0	123	0	O28(19/1/9),D18,1b3	0	-0.6
Stillwell, Kurt	Kurt Andrew; B6.4.1965 Glendale CA; BB/TR/5´11˝/(165–190); [CinN83 1/2]; d4.13; f–Ron																								
1986	Cin N	104	279	31	64	6	1	0	26	30-1	2	47	.229	.309	.258	56	-16	6-2	.951	-5	99	100	S80	0	-1.4
1987	Cin N	131	395	54	102	20	7	4	33	32-2	2	50	.258	.316	.375	79	-12	4-6	.914	-19	80	80	S51,2b37,3b20	0	-2.6
1988	KC A★	128	459	63	115	28	5	10	53	47-0	3	76	.251	.322	.399	100	0	6-5	.976	-10	97	78	S124	0	-0.1
1989	KC A	130	463	52	121	20	7	7	54	42-2	3	64	.261	.325	.380	99	-1	9-6	.970	-19	89	84	S130	28	-1.1
1990	KC A	144	506	60	126	35	4	3	51	39-1	4	60	.249	.304	.352	85	-10	0-2	.957	-12	94	88	S141	0	-1.3
1991	KC A	122	385	44	102	17	1	6	51	33-5	1	56	.265	.322	.361	89	-6	3-4	.959	-14	87	99	S118	16	-1.3
1992	SD N	114	379	35	86	15	3	2	24	26-9	1	58	.227	.274	.298	62	-19	4-1	.970	-12	87	105	2b111	15	-3.0
1993	SD N	57	121	9	26	4	0	1	11	11-2	1	22	.215	.286	.273	50	-9	4-3	.921	-5	82	77	S30,3b3	22	-1.2
	Cal A	22	61	2	16	2	2	0	3	4-0	0	11	.262	.299	.361	76	-2	2-0	.952	1	106	62	2b18,S7	0	0.0
1996	Tex A	46	77	12	21	4	0	1	4	10-0	1	11	.273	.364	.364	80	-2	0-0	.964	-9	68	40	2b21,S9,3b6/1D	28	-1.0
Total	9	998	3125	362	779	151	30	34	310	274-22	18	455	.249	.311	.349	82	-77	38-29	.958	-104	92	87	S690,2b187,3b29/D1	109	-13.0
Stillwell, Ron	Ronald Roy; B12.3.1939 Los Angeles CA; BR/TR/5´11˝/170; d7.3; s–Kurt; Col USC																								
1961	Was A	8	16	3	2	1	0	0	1	1-0	0	4	.125	.176	.188	-3	-2	0-0	.929	-3	66	131	S5	0	-0.5
1962	Was A	6	22	5	6	0	0	0	2	2-0	0	2	.273	.333	.273	66	-1	0-0	1.000	-1	79	80	2b6/S	0	-0.2
Total	2	14	38	8	8	1	0	0	3	3-0	0	6	.211	.268	.237	37	-3	0-0	1.000	-4	79	80	2b6,S6	0	-0.7

YEAR	TM LG	G	AB	R	H	2B	3B	HR	RBI	BB-IB	HP	SO	AVG	OBP	SLG	AOPS	ABR	SB-CS	FA	FR	RNG	THR	GAMES AT POSITION	DL	BFW
Stimac, Craig	Craig Steven; B11.18.1954 Oak Park IL; BR/TR/6´2˝/185; [SDN76 9/197]; d8.12; Col Denver																								
1980	SD N	20	50	5	11	2	0	0	7	1-0	0	6	.220	.222	.260	41	-4	0-0	.982	1	52	151	C11,3b2	0	-0.3
1981	SD N	9	9	0	1	0	0	0	0	0-0	0	3	.111	.111	.111	-40	-2	0-0	ø	0	—	—	/H	0	-0.2
Total	2	29	59	5	12	2	0	0	7	1-0	0	9	.203	.206	.237	29	-6	0-0	.982	1	52	151	C11,3b2	0	-0.5
Stinnett, Kelly	Kelly Lee; B2.14.1970 Lawton OK; BR/TR/5´11˝/(195–235); [CleA89 11/281]; d4.5; Col Seminole St. (OK) JC																								
1994	NY N	47	150	20	38	6	2	2	14	11-1	5	28	.253	.323	.360	79	-5	2-0	.979	-6	122	87	C44	0	-0.8
1995	NY N	77	196	23	43	8	1	4	18	29-3	6	65	.219	.338	.332	80	-5	2-0	.983	-10	67	86	C67	0	-1.1
1996	Mil A	14	26	1	2	0	0	0	0	2-0	1	11	.077	.172	.077	-33	-5	0-0	.960	-1	75	44	C14/D	0	-0.6
1997	Mil A	30	36	2	9	4	0	0	3	3-0	0	9	.250	.308	.361	73	-1	0-0	.989	3	250	84	C25/D	37	0.3
1998	Ari N	92	274	35	71	14	1	11	34	35-3	6	74	.259	.353	.438	107	3	0-1	.984	-5	104	124	C86/D	0	0.3
1999	†Ari N	88	284	36	66	13	0	14	38	24-2	5	83	.232	.302	.426	81	-9	2-1	.990	-7	86	120	C86	0	-1.0
2000	Ari N	76	240	22	52	7	0	8	33	19-4	6	56	.217	.291	.346	58	-16	0-1	.990	5	81	117	C74	0	-0.6
2001	Cin N	63	187	27	48	11	0	9	25	17-3	5	61	.257	.333	.460	97	-1	2-2	.966	-7	72	84	C59/D	33	-0.4
2002	Cin N	34	93	10	21	5	0	3	13	15-1	0	25	.226	.333	.376	83	-2	2-0	.990	2	83	95	C30	100	0.2
2003	Cin N	60	179	14	41	13	0	3	19	13-3	4	51	.229	.294	.352	72	-8	0-0	.993	-6	116	86	C50	0	-1.1
	Phi N	7	7	0	3	0	0	0	0	1-0	0	1	.429	.500	.429	157	1	0-0	1.000	1	0	0	/C	0	0.1
	Year	67	186	14	44	13	0	3	19	14-3	4	52	.237	.302	.355	75	-7	0-0	.993	-6	115	85	C51	0	-1.0
2004	KC A	20	59	10	18	0	0	3	7	5-0	2	16	.305	.379	.458	117	1	0-0	.971	-4	84	120	C20	106	-0.1
2005	Ari N	59	129	15	32	4	0	6	12	12-3	1	32	.248	.317	.419	86	-3	0-0	.977	-5	98	87	C56	21	-0.6
2006	NY A	34	79	6	18	3	0	1	9	5-1	1	29	.228	.282	.304	52	-6	0-0	.989	-0	65	87	C34	0	-0.4
	NY N	7	12	0	1	0	0	0	0	0-0	0	4	.083	.083	.083	-58	-3	0-0	.976	2	86	293	C7	0	-0.1
Total	13	708	1951	221	463	88	4	64	225	191-24	42	545	.237	.318	.385	80	-59	10-5	.984	-39	92	103	C653,D4	297	-5.9
Stinson, Bob	Gorrell Robert; B10.11.1945 Elkin NC; BB/TR (BR 1969 BL 1980p)/5´11.5˝/(180–185); [LAN66 S1/15]; d9.23; Col Miami–Dade North (FL) CC																								
1969	LA N	4	8	1	3	0	0	0	2	0-0	0	2	.375	.375	.375	118	0	0-1	.952	-1	65	115	C4	0	-0.1
1970	LA N	4	3	1	0	0	0	0	0	0-0	0	1	.000	.000	.000	-99	-1	0-0	1.000	-1	0	0	C3	0	-0.1
1971	StL N	17	19	3	4	1	0	0	1	1-0	0	7	.211	.250	.263	43	-1	0-0	.971	0	63	189	C6,O3(1/0/2)	0	-0.1
1972	Hou N	27	35	3	6	1	0	0	2	1-0	1	6	.171	.211	.200	19	-4	0-0	.964	-2	40	0	C12,O3(2/0/1)	0	-0.6
1973	Mon N	48	111	12	29	6	1	3	12	17-2	3	15	.261	.374	.414	114	3	0-1	.979	-4	98	71	C35/3	0	0.0
1974	Mon N	38	87	4	15	2	0	1	6	15-3	0	16	.172	.294	.230	45	-6	1-1	1.000	3	140	98	C29	39	-0.2
1975	KC A	63	147	18	39	9	1	1	9	18-1	1	29	.265	.345	.361	98	0	1-0	.993	7	110	105	C59/12rfD	0	1.0
1976	†KC A	79	209	26	55	7	1	2	25	25-2	1	29	.263	.342	.335	99	0	3-1	.979	-3	98	80	C79	0	0.1
1977	Sea A	105	297	27	80	11	1	8	32	37-4	6	50	.269	.360	.394	106	4	0-3	.984	-8	68	73	C99/D	0	-0.1
1978	Sea A	124	364	46	94	14	3	11	55	45-1	6	42	.258	.346	.404	111	6	2-1	.987	-17	71	117	C123/D	17	-0.6
1979	Sea A	95	247	19	60	8	0	6	28	33-3	4	38	.243	.338	.348	85	-4	1-2	.978	-10	71	71	C91	0	-1.1
1980	Sea A	48	107	6	23	2	0	1	8	9-0	1	19	.215	.277	.262	49	-7	0-0	.979	-8	55	78	C45	0	-1.5
Total	12	652	1634	166	408	61	7	33	180	201-16	23	254	.250	.337	.356	93	-10	8-10	.984	-45	81	89	C585,O7(3/0/4),D3/213	56	-3.3
Stires, Gat	Garrett; B10.13.1849 Hunterdon Co. NJ; D6.13.1933 Byron IL; BL/TR/5´8˝/180; d5.6																								
1871	Rok NA	**25**	110	23	30	4	6	2	24	7	—	5	.273	.316	.473	129	4	3-0	.837	-0	101	0	O25R	—	0.4
Stirnweiss, Snuffy	George Henry; B10.26.1918 New York NY; D9.15.1958 Newark Bay NJ; BR/TR/5´8.5˝/175; d4.22; Col North Carolina																								
1943	†NY A	83	274	34	60	8	4	1	25	47	0	37	.219	.333	.288	82	-5	11-9	.938	-2	99	129	S68,2b4	0	-0.2
1944	NY A	**154**	643	**125**	**205**	35	**16**	8	43	73	1	87	.319	.389	.460	137	32	**55**-11	**.982**	18	105	104	2b154	0	6.8
1945	NY A✳	**152**	632	**107**	**195**	32	**22**	10	64	78	1	62	**.309**	.385	**.476**	**143**	**34**	**33**-17	.970	**25**	110	**126**	2b152	0	**7.2**
1946	NY A★	129	487	75	122	19	7	0	37	66	0	58	.251	.340	.318	83	-9	18-6	.991	6	103	118	3b79,2b46,S4	0	0.1
1947	†NY A	148	571	102	146	18	8	5	41	89	2	47	.256	.358	.342	96	-1	5-3	.983	-9	92	107	2b148	0	-0.1
1948	NY A	141	515	90	130	20	7	3	32	86	1	62	.252	.360	.336	87	-8	5-4	**.993**	-8	88	107	2b141	0	-0.8
1949	†NY A	70	157	29	41	8	2	0	11	29	1	20	.261	.380	.338	90	-1	3-2	.974	2	91	105	2b51,3b4	0	0.3
1950	NY A	7	2	0	0	0	0	0	0	0	0	0	.000	.000	.000	-99	-1	0-0	1.000	0	203	0	2b4	0	0.0
	StL A	93	326	32	71	16	2	1	24	51	0	49	.218	.324	.288	56	-21	3-3	.975	-17	90	83	2b62,3b31,S5	0	-3.3
	Year	100	328	32	71	16	2	1	24	51	0	49	.216	.322	.287	55	-22	3-3	.975	-16	91	82	2b66,3b31,S5	0	-3.3
1951	Cle A	50	88	10	19	1	0	1	4	22	0	25	.216	.373	.261	78	-1	1-0	.992	5	116	116	2b25,3b2	0	0.5
1952	Cle A	1	0	0	0	0	0	0	0	0	0	0	ø	ø	ø	ø	0	0-0	ø	-0	0	0	/3	0	0.0
Total	10	1028	3695	604	989	157	68	29	281	541	6	447	.268	.362	.371	102	19	134-55	.980	21	99	109	2b787,3b117,S77	0	10.5
Stivetts, Jack	John Elmer "Happy Jack"; B3.31.1868 Ashland PA; D4.18.1930 Ashland PA; BR/TR/6´2˝/185; d6.26; OF(41/33/69); ▲																								
1889	StL AA	27	79	12	18	2	2	0	7	3	1	13	.228	.265	.304	55	-5	0	.896	-1	81	0	P26/rf	—	-0.1
1890	StL AA	67	226	36	65	15	6	7	43	16	1	—	.288	.337	.500	128	5	2	.894	3	102	119	P54,O10C,1b3	—	0.2
1891	StL AA	85	302	45	92	10	2	7	54	10	2	32	.305	.331	.421	100	-3	4	.898	4	104	63	P64,O24(1/0/23)	—	0.1
1892	†Bos N	71	240	40	71	14	2	3	36	27	1	28	.296	.369	.408	124	7	8	.904	1	103	177	P54,O18(16/2/0)/1	—	0.1
1893	Bos N	50	172	32	51	5	6	3	25	12	0	14	.297	.342	.448	101	-2	6	.955	-4	79	105	P38,O8(3/0/5),3b3	—	-0.3
1894	Bos N	68	244	55	80	12	7	8	64	16	0	21	.328	.369	.533	107	0	3	.943	-4	74	46	P45,O16(8/2/6),1b4	—	-0.2
1895	Bos N	46	158	20	30	6	4	0	24	6	0	18	.190	.220	.278	26	-19	1	.961	-2	76	49	P38,1b5,O2(0/1/1)	—	-0.4
1896	Bos N	67	222	43	77	9	6	3	49	12	1	10	.347	.383	.482	120	5	4	.946	-7	70	113	P42,O12(3/2/7),1b5/3	—	-0.3
1897	†Bos N	61	199	41	73	9	9	2	37	15	2	—	.367	.417	.533	141	11	2	.926	-3	75	144	O29(6/10/14),P18,2b2,1b2	—	0.2
1898	Bos N	41	111	16	28	1	1	2	16	10	0	—	.252	.314	.333	81	-3	1	.909	-4	59	0	O14(2/5/8),1b10,S4,2b2,P2	—	-0.7
1899	Cle N	18	39	8	8	1	1	0	2	6	1	—	.205	.326	.282	73	-1	0	1.000	1	112	0	O7(2/1/4),P7/S3	—	0.0
Total	11	601	1992	348	593	84	46	35	357	133	9	136	.298	.344	.439	104	-5	31	.924	-15	91	86	P388,O141R,1b30,S5,3b5,2b4	—	-1.4
Stock, Milt	Milton Joseph; B7.11.1893 Chicago IL; D7.16.1977 Fairhope AL; BR/TR/5´8˝/154; d9.29; C9																								
1913	NY N	7	17	2	3	1	0	0	1	2	0	1	.176	.263	.235	43	-1	2	.838	0	108	223	S7	—	0.0
1914	NY N	115	365	52	96	17	1	3	41	34	4	21	.263	.333	.340	103	2	11	.939	13	**122**	122	3b113/S	—	1.9
1915	†Phi N	69	227	37	59	7	3	1	15	22	0	26	.260	.325	.330	98	0	6-2	.971	-0	96	102	3b55,S4	—	0.2
1916	Phi N	132	509	61	143	25	6	1	43	27	2	33	.281	.320	.360	105	3	21-26	.955	-2	93	142	3b117,S15	—	0.1
1917	Phi N	150	564	76	149	27	6	3	53	51	1	34	.264	.326	.349	103	3	25	.942	-8	92	76	3b133,S19	—	0.0
1918	Phi N	123	481	62	132	14	1	1	42	35	1	22	.274	.325	.314	89	-5	20	.946	-5	102	74	3b123	—	-0.8
1919	StL N	135	492	56	151	16	4	0	52	49	1	21	.307	.371	.356	127	18	17	.966	19	109	98	2b77,3b58	—	4.4
1920	StL N	**155**	639	85	204	28	6	0	76	40	1	27	.319	.360	.382	117	15	15-17	.939	-10	97	78	3b155	—	0.7
1921	StL N	149	587	96	180	27	6	3	84	48	1	26	.307	.360	.388	100	2	11-3	.940	-20	83	77	3b149	—	-0.8
1922	StL N	151	581	85	177	33	9	5	79	42	0	29	.305	.352	.418	103	2	7-12	.950	-8	89	90	3b149/S	—	0.1
1923	StL N	151	603	63	174	33	3	2	96	40	1	21	.289	.334	.363	86	-12	9-6	.955	-15	91	90	3b150/2	—	-1.7
1924	Bro N	142	561	66	136	14	4	2	52	26	1	32	.242	.277	.292	54	-37	3-8	.931	-21	78	61	3b142	—	-5.2
1925	Bro N	146	615	98	202	28	9	1	62	38	0	28	.328	.368	.408	101	1	8-1	.978	-1	98	85	2b141,3b5	—	0.5
1926	Bro N	3	8	0	0	0	0	0	0	1	0	0	.000	.111	.000	-69	-2	0	.923	-0	98	70	2b3	—	-0.2
Total	14	1628	6249	839	1806	270	58	22	696	455	13	321	.289	.339	.361	98	-11	155-75	.945	-57	94	92	3b1349,2b222,S47	—	-0.8
Stocker, Kevin	Kevin Douglas; B2.13.1970 Spokane WA; BB/TR/6´1˝/(175–181); [PhiN91 2/54]; d7.7; Col Washington																								
1993	†Phi N	70	259	46	84	12	3	2	31	30-11	8	43	.324	.409	.417	124	11	5-0	.958	-4	91	101	S70	0	1.3
1994	Phi N	82	271	38	74	11	2	2	28	44-8	7	41	.273	.383	.351	93	0	2-2	.959	-1	102	90	S82	34	0.5
1995	Phi N	125	412	42	90	14	3	1	32	43-9	9	75	.218	.304	.274	54	-27	6-1	.969	5	106	100	S125	0	-1.2
1996	Phi N	119	394	46	100	22	6	5	41	43-9	8	89	.254	.336	.378	88	-6	6-4	.975	7	102	112	S119	0	0.9
1997	Phi N	149	504	51	134	23	5	4	40	51-7	2	91	.266	.335	.355	82	-13	11-6	.981	-12	90	83	S147	0	-1.4
1998	TB A	112	336	37	70	11	3	6	25	27-1	8	80	.208	.282	.313	53	-24	5-3	.979	11	106	**117**	S110	29	-0.4
1999	TB A	79	254	39	76	11	2	1	27	24-0	4	41	.299	.369	.370	88	-4	9-7	.957	4	100	97	S76	74	0.5
2000	TB A	40	114	20	30	7	1	2	8	19-0	2	27	.263	.378	.395	97	0	1-2	.933	-5	102	99	S40	0	-0.2
	Ana A	70	229	21	45	13	3	0	16	32-0	2	54	.197	.299	.279	47	-19	0-3	.978	3	110	112	S69	14	-1.1
	Year	110	343	41	75	20	4	2	24	51-0	4	81	.219	.326	.318	63	-18	1-5	.962	-2	107	107	S109	0	-1.3
Total	8	846	2773	340	703	124	28	23	248	313-45	50	541	.254	.338	.343	78	-82	45-28	.969	9	100	101	S838	151	-1.1

YEAR	TM LG	G	AB	R	H	2B	3B	HR	RBI	BB-IB	HP	SO	AVG	OBP	SLG	AOPS	ABR	SB-CS	FA	FR	RNG	THR	GAMES AT POSITION	DL	BFW
STOCKWELL, LEN	Leonard Clark; B8.25.1859 Cordova IL; D1.28.1905 Niles CA; BR/TR/5´11˝/165; d5.17																								
1879	Cle N	2	6	0	0	0	0	0	0	0	—	2	.000	.000	.000	-99	-1	—	1.000	1	471	1934	O2(0/1/1)	—	0.0
1884	Lou AA	2	9	0	1	0	0	0	—	0	0	—	.111	.111	.111	-29	-1	—	.667	-1	0	0	O2(1/1/0)/C	—	-0.2
1890	Cle N	2	7	2	2	1	0	0	0	0	0	3	.286	.286	.429	110	0	0	1.000	0	518	0	/lf1	—	0.0
Total	3	6	22	2	3	1	0	0	0	0	0	5	.136	.136	.182	-1	-2	0	.900	1	307	765	O5(2/2/1)/1C	—	-0.2
STODDARD	; d9.25																								
1875	Atl NA	2	9	1	1	1	0	0	0	0	—	1	.111	.111	.222	15	-1	0-0	.800	-1	0	0	O2(1/1/0)	—	-0.1
STOKES, AL	Albert John (b Albert John Stocek); B1.1.1900 Chicago IL; D12.19.1986 Grantham NH; BR/TR/5´9˝/175; d5.10																								
1925	Bos A	17	52	7	11	0	1	0	1	4	0	8	.212	.268	.250	32	-6	0-0	.969	1	*76*	*153*	C17	—	-0.3
1926	Bos A	30	86	7	14	3	3	0	6	8	0	28	.163	.234	.267	32	-9	0-0	.931	-5	*61*	*106*	C29	—	-1.3
Total	2	47	138	14	25	3	4	0	7	12	0	36	.181	.247	.261	32	-15	0-0	.946	-4	*67*	*124*	C46	—	-1.6
STONE, GENE	Eugene Daniel; B1.16.1944 Burbank CA; BL/TL/5´11˝/190; d5.13																								
1969	Phi N	18	28	4	6	0	1	0	0	4-1	0	9	.214	.313	.286	70	-1	0-0	1.000	-1	33	69	1b5	0	-0.2
STONE, GEORGE	George Robert; B9.3.1876 Lost Nation IA; D1.3.1945 Clinton IA; BL/TL/5´9˝/175; d4.20																								
1903	Bos A	2	2	0	0	0	0	0	0	0	0	—	.000	.000	.000	-95	0	0	ø	0	—	—	/H	—	0.0
1905	StL A	154	632	76	**187**	25	13	7	52	44	5	—	.296	.347	.410	147	32	26	.954	2	88	127	O154L	—	2.8
1906	StL A	**154**	581	91	208	25	20	6	71	52	7	—	**.358**	**.417**	**.501**	**195**	**63**	35	.968	0	52	79	O154L	—	5.9
1907	StL A	**155**	596	77	191	13	11	4	59	59	6	—	.320	.387	.399	151	36	23	.970	-3	60	112	O155L	—	2.6
1908	StL A	148	588	89	165	21	8	5	31	55	3	—	.281	.345	.369	131	21	20	.947	0	64	67	O148L	—	1.4
1909	StL A	83	310	33	89	5	4	1	15	24	1	—	.287	.340	.339	123	8	8	.928	-1	70	149	O81(63/0/18)	—	0.2
1910	StL A	152	562	60	144	17	12	0	40	48	0	—	.256	.315	.329	108	4	20	.972	-1	92	107	O145(139/1/5)	—	-0.5
Total	7	848	3271	426	984	106	68	23	268	282	22	—	.301	.360	.396	145	164	132	.958	-2	71	104	O837(813/1/23)	—	12.4
STONE, RON	Harry Ronald; B9.9.1942 Corning CA; BL/TL/6´2˝/(185–200); d4.13; Col Cal St.–Sacramento																								
1966	KC A	26	22	2	6	1	0	0	0	0-0	0	2	.273	.273	.318	71	-1	1-1	1.000	0	84	0	O4(2/2/1),1b3	0	-0.1
1969	Phi N	103	222	22	53	7	1	1	24	29-8	3	28	.239	.332	.293	79	-5	3-1	.978	-1	86	164	O69(37/2/32)	0	-0.9
1970	Phi N	123	321	30	84	12	5	3	39	38-1	1	45	.262	.338	.358	90	-4	5-6	.968	-1	102	87	O99(51/0/48),1b6	0	-1.1
1971	Phi N	95	185	16	42	8	1	2	23	25-3	0	36	.227	.315	.314	79	-4	2-2	.964	1	100	179	O51(22/1/33),1b3	0	-0.6
1972	Phi N	41	54	3	9	0	1	0	3	9-1	0	11	.167	.286	.204	40	-4	0-0	1.000	3	143	464	O15(6/1/9)	0	-0.1
Total	5	388	804	73	194	28	8	6	89	101-13	4	122	.241	.326	.318	81	-18	11-10	.973	3	99	147	O238(118/6/123),1b12	0	-2.8
STONE, JEFF	Jeffrey Glen; B12.26.1960 Kennett MO; BL/TR/6´0˝/(175–180); d9.9																								
1983	Phi N	9	4	2	3	0	2	0	3	0-0	0	1	.750	.750	1.750	578	2	4-0	ø	-0	0	0	/cf	0	0.3
1984	Phi N	51	185	27	67	4	6	1	15	9-0	2	26	.362	.394	.465	139	9	27-5	.916	-4	94	29	O46L	30	0.8
1985	Phi N	88	264	36	70	4	3	3	11	15-0	1	50	.265	.307	.337	78	-9	15-5	.966	-4	78	98	O69L	0	-1.5
1986	Phi N	82	249	32	69	6	4	6	19	20-0	4	52	.277	.341	.406	101	0	19-6	.982	1	89	224	O58(37/25/0)	0	0.1
1987	Phi N	66	125	19	32	7	1	1	16	8-0	3	38	.256	.316	.352	74	-5	3-1	1.000	0	80	221	O25(20/5/1)	34	-0.5
1988	Bal A	26	61	4	10	1	0	0	1	4-0	0	11	.164	.215	.180	12	-7	4-1	.963	0	70	331	O21(18/0/3)/D	44	-0.7
1989	Tex A	22	36	5	6	1	2	0	5	3-0	1	5	.167	.250	.306	55	-2	2-1	ø	-1	0	0	D15,O3(1/1/1)	0	-0.4
	Bos A	18	15	3	3	0	0	0	1	1-1	0	2	.200	.235	.200	27	-1	1-0	1.000	-0	106	0	O11(0/4/7),D3	0	-0.1
	Year	40	51	8	9	1	2	0	6	4-1	1	7	.176	.246	.275	46	-4	3-1	1.000	-1	75	0	D18,O14(1/5/8)	0	-0.5
1990	Bos A	10	2	1	1	0	0	0	1	0-0	0	1	.500	.500	.500	172	0	0-1	ø	0	—	—	D2	0	0.0
Total	8	372	941	129	261	23	18	11	72	60-1	11	186	.277	.327	.375	92	-13	75-20	.963	-8	84	146	O234(191/36/12),D21	108	-2.0
STONE, JOHN	John Thomas "Rocky"; B10.10.1905 Mulberry TN; D11.30.1955 Shelbyville TN; BL/TR/6´1˝/178; d8.31; Col Maryville																								
1928	Det A	26	113	20	40	10	3	2	21	5	1	8	.354	.387	.549	141	6	1-0	.962	-1	90	83	O26L	—	0.3
1929	Det A	51	150	23	39	11	2	2	15	11	0	13	.260	.311	.400	81	-5	1-1	.986	2	104	132	O36(35/0/2)	—	-0.5
1930	Det A	127	425	60	132	29	11	3	56	32	1	49	.311	.360	.452	102	1	6-9	.966	-1	102	63	O109(93/11/6)	—	-0.9
1931	Det A	147	584	86	191	28	11	10	76	56	2	48	.327	.388	.464	119	16	13-13	.959	5	108	107	O147(143/5/0)	—	1.1
1932	Det A	145	582	106	173	35	12	17	108	58	0	64	.297	.361	.486	113	10	2-1	.961	-1	99	99	O142(90/53/0)	—	0.2
1933	Det A	148	574	86	161	33	11	11	80	54	2	37	.280	.344	.434	103	1	1-4	.970	-2	100	84	O141(18/0/124)	—	-1.0
1934	Was A	113	419	77	132	28	7	7	67	52	3	26	.315	.395	.465	126	17	1-2	.966	5	103	144	O112(0/16/98)	—	1.4
1935	Was A	125	455	78	143	27	18	1	78	39	3	29	.314	.372	.459	118	10	4-5	.955	2	100	130	O114(19/7/90)	—	0.5
1936	Was A	123	437	95	149	22	11	15	90	60	0	26	.341	.421	.545	145	31	8-0	.967	6	108	121	O114(109/0/6)	—	2.8
1937	Was A	139	542	84	179	33	15	6	88	66	0	36	.330	.403	.480	127	23	6-4	.984	7	107	121	O137(37/7/95)	—	2.1
1938	Was A	56	213	24	52	12	4	3	28	30	0	16	.244	.337	.380	85	-5	2-1	.974	-1	95	110	O53(29/1/26)	—	-0.8
Total	11	1200	4494	739	1391	268	105	77	707	463	12	352	.310	.376	.467	116	105	45-40	.967	20	103	108	O1131(599/100/447)	—	5.2
STONE, TIGE	William Arthur; B9.18.1901 Macon GA; D1.1.1960 Jacksonville FL; BR/TR/5´8˝/145; d8.23; Col Mercer																								
1923	StL N	5	1	0	1	0	0	0	0	2	0	0	1.000	1.000	1.000	438	1	0-0	ø	0	0	0	O4(2/2/0)/P	—	0.0
STONEHAM, JOHN	John Andrew; B11.8.1908 Wood River IL; D1.1.2004 Owasso OK; BL/TR/5´9.5˝/168; d9.18; Col Washington–St. Louis																								
1933	Chi A	10	25	4	3	0	0	1	3	2	0	2	.120	.185	.240	12	-3	0-0	1.000	-0	100	0	O9(1/1/7)	—	-0.4
STORIE, HOWIE	Howard Edward "Sponge"; B5.15.1911 Pittsfield MA; D7.27.1968 Pittsfield MA; BR/TR/5´10˝/175; d9.7																								
1931	Bos A	6	17	2	2	0	0	0	0	3	0	2	.118	.250	.118	-1	-2	0-0	1.000	0	*145*	*49*	C6	—	-0.2
1932	Bos A	6	8	0	3	0	0	0	0	0	0	0	.375	.375	.375	98	0	0-0	1.000	0	*97*	*0*	C5	—	0.0
Total	2	12	25	2	5	0	0	0	0	3	0	2	.200	.286	.200	31	-2	0-0	1.000	0	*131*	*35*	C11	—	-0.2
STORKE, ALAN	Alan Marshall; B9.27.1884 Auburn NY; D3.18.1910 Newton MA; BR/TR/6´1˝/?; d9.24; Col Amherst																								
1906	Pit N	5	12	1	3	1	0	0	1	1	0	—	.250	.308	.333	96	0	1	1.000	0	121	770	3b2/S	—	0.0
1907	Pit N	112	357	24	92	6	6	1	39	16	3	—	.258	.295	.317	90	-6	6	.925	-9	94	128	3b67,1b23,2b7,S5	—	-1.4
1908	Pit N	64	202	20	51	5	3	1	12	9	0	—	.252	.284	.322	93	-2	4	.988	-6	56	96	1b49,3b6/2	—	-1.1
1909	Pit N	37	118	12	30	5	2	0	12	7	1	—	.254	.302	.331	89	-2	1	.994	-1	75	137	1b18,3b14	—	-0.3
	StL N	48	174	11	49	5	0	0	10	12	0	—	.282	.328	.310	105	1	5	.958	-1	99	81	S44,2b4/1	—	0.2
	Year	85	292	23	79	10	2	0	22	19	1	—	.271	.317	.318	97	-1	6	.958	-1	99	81	S44,1b19,3b14,2b4	—	-0.1
Total	4	266	863	68	225	22	11	2	74	45	4	—	.261	.300	.319	94	-9	17	.990	-15	68	99	1b91,3b89,S50,2b12	—	-2.6
STORTI, LIN	Lindo Ivan; B12.5.1906 Santa Monica CA; D7.24.1982 Ontario CA; BB/TR/5´11˝/165; d9.18																								
1930	StL A	7	28	6	9	1	1	0	2	2	0	6	.321	.367	.429	98	0	0-0	.975	1	96	201	2b6	—	0.1
1931	StL A	86	273	32	60	15	4	3	26	15	1	50	.220	.263	.337	55	-19	0-2	.926	5	105	168	3b67,2b7	—	-1.2
1932	StL A	53	193	19	50	11	2	3	26	5	0	20	.259	.278	.383	66	-11	1-0	.956	-0	96	104	3b51	—	-0.8
1933	StL A	70	210	26	41	7	4	3	21	25	0	31	.195	.281	.310	53	-15	2-2	.934	1	102	198	3b32,2b24	—	-1.1
Total	4	216	704	83	160	34	11	9	75	47	1	107	.227	.277	.345	59	-45	3-4	.936	7	102	154	3b150,2b37	—	-3.0
STOUCH, TOM	Thomas Carl; B12.2.1869 Perrysville OH; D10.7.1956 Lancaster PA; BR/TR/6´2˝/165; d7.7																								
1898	Lou N	4	16	4	5	1	0	0	6	1	0	—	.313	.353	.375	110	0	0	.850	-2	78	66	2b4	—	-0.1
STOVALL, DA ROND	Da Rond Tyrone; B1.3.1973 St.Louis MO; BB/TL/6´1˝/185; [StLN91 5/129]; d4.1																								
1998	Mon N	62	78	11	16	2	1	2	6	6-0	0	29	.205	.262	.333	57	-5	1-0	.925	-1	91	157	O47(27/14/7)	0	-0.6
STOVALL, GEORGE	George Thomas "Firebrand"; B11.23.1877 Leeds MO; D11.5.1951 Burlington IA; BR/TR/6´2˝/180; d7.4; M5; b–Jesse																								
1904	Cle A	52	181	18	54	10	1	1	31	2	3	—	.298	.317	.381	121	4	3	.978	-1	93	115	1b38,2b9,O3(2/1/0)/3	—	0.3
1905	Cle A	112	423	41	115	31	1	1	47	13	1	—	.272	.295	.357	105	2	13	.973	-3	133	115	1b60,2b46,O4C	—	-0.2
1906	Cle A	116	443	54	121	19	5	0	37	8	1	—	.273	.288	.339	97	-3	15	.985	-1	111	214	1b55,3b30,2b19	—	-0.6
1907	Cle A	124	466	38	110	17	6	1	36	18	2	—	.236	.267	.305	82	-11	13	.983	-3	89	**168**	1b122,3b2	—	-1.8
1908	Cle A	138	534	71	156	29	6	2	45	17	2	—	.292	.316	.380	126	13	14	**.990**	2	104	**146**	1b132,O5C/S	—	1.4
1909	Cle A	145	565	60	139	17	10	2	49	6	4	—	.246	.259	.322	80	-16	25	**.988**	10	**126**	**119**	1b145	—	-1.0
1910	Cle A	142	521	49	136	19	4	0	52	14	3	—	.261	.284	.313	86	-11	16	**.988**	7	**121**	94	1b132,2b2	—	-0.7
1911	Cle A	126	458	48	124	17	7	0	79	21	2	—	.271	.306	.338	79	-15	11	**.986**	7	**118**	103	1b118,2b2,M	—	-1.1
1912	StL A	116	398	35	101	17	5	0	45	14	4	—	.254	.286	.322	76	-14	11	.983	5	125	139	1b94,M	—	-1.1
1913	StL A	89	303	34	87	14	3	1	24	7	1	23	.287	.305	.363	98	-3	7	.988	8	143	91	1b76,M	—	0.3

YEAR	TM LG	G	AB	R	H	2B	3B	HR	RBI	BB-IB	HP	SO	AVG	OBP	SLG	AOPS	ABR	SB-CS	FA	FR	RNG	THR	GAMES AT POSITION	DL	BFW
1914	KC F	124	450	51	128	20	5	7	75	23	4	35	.284	.325	.398	100	-9	6	.989	5	117	**131**	1b116/3M	—	-0.8
1915	KC F	130	480	48	111	21	3	0	44	31	6	36	.231	.286	.287	64	-31	8	.987	5	**121**	91	1b129,M	—	-3.2
Total	12	1414	5222	547	1382	231	56	15	564	174	33	94	.265	.293	.339	91	-94	142	.986	40	117	125	1b1217,2b78,3b34,O12(2/9/0)/S	—	-8.5
STOVEY, HARRY	Harry Duffield (b Harry Duffield Stowe); B12.20.1856 Philadelphia PA; D9.20.1937 New Bedford MA; BR/TR/5´11.5˝/175; d5.1; M2; ▲																								
1880	Wor N	83	355	76	94	21	**14**	**6**	28	12	—	46	.265	.289	.454	136	12	—	.860	-6	54	54	O46(5/42/0),1b37,P2	—	0.2
1881	Wor N	75	341	57	92	25	7	2	30	12	—	23	.270	.295	.402	111	4	—	.955	-5	79	75	1b57,O18(1/0/17),M	—	-0.4
1882	Wor N	**84**	360	90	104	13	10	5	26	22	—	34	.289	.330	.422	136	14	—	.956	3	111	91	1b43,O41L	—	1.1
1883	Phi AA	94	421	**110**	128	**31**	6	**14**	66	27	—	—	.304	.346	**.506**	156	25	—	**.965**	1	81	74	1b93,O3C/P	—	1.5
1884	Phi AA	104	448	**124**	146	22	**23**	10	83	26	4	—	.326	.368	.545	182	38	—	.960	-1	90	99	1b104	—	2.5
1885	Phi AA	112	486	**130**	153	27	9	**13**	75	39	4	—	.315	.371	.488	160	32	—	.967	4	**128**	**106**	1b82,O30C,M	—	2.5
1886	Phi AA	123	489	115	144	28	11	7	59	64	1	—	.294	.377	.440	154	32	**68**	.870	-1	106	178	O63(0/46/17),1b62/P	—	2.0
1887	Phi AA	124	497	125	142	31	12	4	77	56	7	—	.286	.366	.421	119	14	74	.902	7	109	32	O80(49/29/2),1b46	—	1.1
1888	Phi AA	130	530	127	152	25	**20**	9	65	62	3	—	.287	.365	.460	165	**39**	87	.943	4	61	102	O118L,1b13	—	**3.5**
1889	Phi AA	137	556	**152**	171	38	13	**19**	**119**	77	1	68	.308	.393	**.525**	162	46	63	.897	18	146	153	O137L/1	—	**5.0**
1890	Bos P	118	481	142	144	25	11	12	84	81	5	38	.299	.406	.472	126	18	**97**	.921	0	109	69	O117(1/0/116)/1	—	1.3
1891	Bos N	134	544	118	152	31	**20**	**16**	95	79	2	69	.279	.373	**.498**	137	23	57	.910	7	101	123	O134(39/0/96)/1	—	2.4
1892	Bos N	38	146	21	24	8	1	0	12	14	3	19	.164	.252	.233	43	-10	20	.901	0	49	85	O38L	—	-1.3
	Bal N	74	283	58	77	14	11	4	55	40	1	32	.272	.364	.442	140	13	20	.913	-2	61	81	O64L,1b10	—	0.5
	Year	112	429	79	101	22	12	4	67	54	4	51	.235	.326	.371	105	2	40	.908	-2	56	83	O102L,1b10	—	-0.8
1893	Bal N	8	26	4	4	2	0	0	5	8	0	3	.154	.353	.231	55	-1	1	.864	-0	71	0	O7L	—	-0.2
	Bro N	48	175	43	44	6	6	1	29	44	0	11	.251	.402	.371	111	5	22	.901	-4	35	0	O48(19/26/3)	—	-0.2
	Year	56	201	47	48	8	6	1	34	52	0	14	.239	.395	.353	103	4	23	.895	-4	40	0	O55(26/26/3)	—	-0.4
Total	14	1486	6138	1492	1771	347	174	122	908	663	31	343	.289	.361	.461	141	304	509	.896	23	96	97	O944(519/176/251),1b550,P4	—	21.5
STOVIAK, RAY	Raymond Thomas; B6.6.1915 Scottdale PA; D2.23.1998 Nicoya, Costa Rica; BL/TL/6´1˝/195; d6.5; Col Villanova																								
1938	Phi N	10	10	1	0	0	0	0	0	0	0	3	.000	.000	.000	-99	-3	0	1.000	1	57	1233	O4R	—	-0.2
STOWERS, CHRIS	Christopher James; B8.18.1974 St.Louis MO; BL/TL/6´3˝/195; [MonN96 17/490]; d7.10; Col Georgia																								
1999	Mon N	4	2	0	0	0	0	0	0	0-0	0	0	.000	.000	.000	-99	-1	0-0	1.000	0	127	0	O2(0/1/1)	0	-0.1
STRAIN, JOE	Joseph Allan; B4.30.1954 Denver CO; BR/TR/5´10˝/(165–169); d6.28; Col Northern Colorado																								
1979	SF N	67	257	27	62	8	1	1	12	13-0	3	21	.241	.285	.292	62	-14	8-4	.982	7	110	75	2b67/3	0	-0.4
1980	SF N	77	189	26	54	6	0	0	16	10-0	0	10	.286	.320	.317	82	-5	1-2	.989	-5	95	63	2b42,3b6/S	31	-0.9
1981	Chi N	25	74	7	14	1	0	0	1	5-0	1	7	.189	.250	.203	28	-7	0-0	.975	9	142	83	2b20	15	0.3
Total	3	169	520	60	130	15	1	1	29	28-0	4	38	.250	.292	.288	64	-26	9-6	.983	11	110	72	2b129,3b7/S	46	-1.0
STRAND, PAUL	Paul Edward; B12.19.1893 Carbonado WA; D7.2.1974 Salt Lake City UT; BL/TL/6´0.5˝/190; d5.15; ▲																								
1913	Bos N	7	6	0	1	0	0	0	0	0	0	0	.167	.167	.167	-5	0	0	.875	0	137	0	P7	—	0.0
1914	Bos N	18	24	2	8	2	0	0	3	0	0	2	.333	.333	.417	123	2	0	.813	-0	89	237	P16	—	0.0
1915	Bos N	24	22	3	2	0	0	0	2	0	0	4	.091	.091	.091	-47	-4	0	.750	-1	32	0	P6,O5(2/1/0)	—	-0.2
1924	Phi A	47	167	15	38	9	4	0	13	4	2	9	.228	.254	.329	49	-14	3-3	.988	-3	83	81	O44(0/39/5)	—	-1.9
Total	4	96	219	20	49	11	4	0	18	4	2	15	.224	.244	.311	47	-16	3-3	.989	-4	82	98	O49(2/40/5),P29	—	-2.1
STRANDS, LARRY	John Lawrence; B12.5.1885 Chicago IL; D1.19.1957 Forest Park IL; BR/TR/5´10.5˝/165; d4.25																								
1915	New F	35	75	7	14	3	1	1	11	6	0	11	.187	.247	.293	55	-6	1	.852	-4	83	161	3b12,2b9,O2R	—	-1.1
STRANG, SAMMY	Samuel Nicklin "The Dixie Thrush" (b Samuel Strang Nicklin); B12.16.1876 Chattanooga TN; D3.13.1932 Chattanooga TN; BB/TR/5´8˝/160; d7.10; OF(11/63/92)																								
1896	Lou N	14	46	6	12	0	0	0	7	6	0	6	.261	.346	.261	64	-2	4	.803	-6	78	90	S14	—	-0.6
1900	Chi N	27	102	15	29	3	0	0	9	8	2	—	.284	.348	.314	86	-1	1	.887	-7	93	160	3b16,S9,2b2	—	-0.7
1901	NY N	135	493	55	139	14	6	1	34	59	5	—	.282	.364	.341	109	9	40	.877	8	113	155	3b91,2b37,O5R,S4	—	1.9
1902	Chi A	137	536	108	158	18	5	3	46	76	5	—	.295	.387	.364	114	15	38	.890	5	**109**	109	3b137	—	2.2
	Chi N	3	11	1	4	0	0	0	0	0	0	—	.364	.364	.364	128	0	1	1.000	-1	59	996	2b2,3b2	—	0.0
1903	Bro N	135	508	101	138	21	5	0	38	75	10	—	.272	.376	.333	106	9	46	.914	-5	100	105	3b124,O8C,2b3	—	0.7
1904	Bro N	77	271	28	52	11	0	1	9	45	4	—	.192	.316	.244	75	-5	16	.910	-29	84	65	2b63,3b12/S	—	-3.6
1905	†NY N	111	294	51	76	9	4	3	29	58	5	—	.259	.389	.347	117	10	23	.915	-7	97	81	2b47,O38(4/7/27),S9/13	—	0.3
1906	NY N	113	313	50	100	16	4	4	49	54	2	—	.319	.423	.435	164	27	21	.944	6	111	78	2b57,O39(5/17/17),S4,3b3/1	—	3.4
1907	NY N	123	306	56	77	20	4	4	30	60	8	—	.252	.388	.382	137	18	21	.947	-0	138	229	O70(1/28/41),2b13,3b7,1b5/S	—	1.6
1908	NY N	28	53	8	5	0	0	0	2	23	2	—	.094	.385	.094	52	0	5	.863	-3	98	138	2b14,O5(1/3/2),S3	—	-0.4
Total	10	903	2933	479	790	112	28	16	253	464	43	6	.269	.377	.343	113	80	216	.891	-38	106	119	3b393,2b238,O165R,S45,1b7	—	4.8
STRANGE, ALAN	Alan Cochrane "Inky"; B11.7.1906 Philadelphia PA; D6.27.1994 Seattle WA; BR/TR/5´9˝/162; d4.17; Col Penn St.																								
1934	StL A	127	430	39	100	17	2	1	45	48	0	28	.233	.310	.288	51	-31	3-1	.955	5	100	104	S125	—	-1.6
1935	StL A	49	147	8	34	6	1	0	17	17	0	7	.231	.311	.286	53	-10	0-0	.960	3	101	96	S49	—	-0.4
	Was A	20	54	3	10	2	1	0	5	4	0	1	.185	.241	.259	30	-6	0-0	.974	2	113	119	S16	—	-0.3
	Year	69	201	11	44	8	2	0	22	21	0	8	.219	.293	.279	47	-16	0-0	.963	5	104	102	S65	—	-0.7
1940	StL A	54	167	26	31	8	3	0	6	22	1	12	.186	.284	.269	43	-14	2-1	.962	5	115	105	S35,2b4	—	-0.6
1941	StL A	45	112	14	26	4	0	0	11	15	0	5	.232	.323	.268	56	-7	1-0	.973	0	98	91	S32,1b2/3	0	-0.4
1942	StL A	19	37	3	10	2	0	0	5	3	0	1	.270	.325	.324	82	-1	0-1	.935	2	142	218	3b10,S3/2	0	0.1
Total	5	314	947	93	211	39	7	1	89	109	1	54	.223	.304	.282	50	-69	6-3	.959	17	103	101	S260,3b11,2b5,1b2	0	-3.2
STRANGE, DOUG	Joseph Douglas; B4.13.1964 Greenville SC; BB/TR/6´1˝/(170–185); [DetA85 7/184]; d7.13; Col North Carolina St.; OF(18/0/2); [DL 1999 Pit N 182]																								
1989	Det A	64	196	16	42	4	1	1	14	17-0	1	36	.214	.280	.260	54	-12	3-3	.878	-1	100	118	3b54,2b9,S9/D	0	-1.4
1991	Chi N	3	9	0	4	1	0	0	1	0-0	1	1	.444	.455	.556	188	1	1-0	.800	-2	53	0	3b3	0	0.0
1992	Chi N	52	94	7	15	1	0	1	5	10-2	0	15	.160	.240	.202	26	-9	1-0	.900	-2	93	57	3b33,2b12	0	-1.2
1993	Tex A	145	484	58	124	29	0	7	60	43-3	3	69	.256	.318	.360	85	-10	6-4	.980	4	102	95	2b135,3b9/S	0	0.0
1994	Tex A	73	226	26	48	12	1	5	26	15-0	3	38	.212	.268	.341	56	-16	1-3	.970	3	107	114	2b53,3b13,O3(2/0/1)	15	-1.0
1995	†Sea A	74	155	19	42	9	2	2	21	10-0	2	25	.271	.323	.394	84	-4	0-3	.948	6	120	39	3b41,2b5,O4L/D	0	0.2
1996	Sea A	88	183	19	43	7	1	3	23	14-0	1	31	.235	.290	.333	58	-12	1-0	.961	-6	80	65	3b39,O11(10/0/1),D10,1b3,2b3	0	-1.7
1997	Mon N	118	327	40	84	16	2	12	47	36-9	2	76	.257	.332	.428	99	-1	0-2	.947	0	99	85	3b105,2b3,O2L/1	15	-0.1
1998	Pit N	90	185	9	32	8	0	0	14	10-1	1	39	.173	.217	.216	15	-23	1-0	.940	-4	83	51	3b42,2b9,1b3	29	-2.6
Total	9	707	1859	194	434	87	7	31	211	155-15	14	330	.233	.295	.338	69	-86	14-15	.927	-1	98	82	3b339,2b229,O20L,D12,S10,1b7	241	-7.8
STRATTON, ASA	Asa Evans; B2.10.1853 Grafton MA; D8.14.1925 Fitchburg MA; d6.17; Col Boston College																								
1881	Wor N	1	4	0	1	0	0	0	0	0	—	2	.250	.250	.250	55	0	—	.333	-1	38	0	/S	—	-0.1
STRATTON, SCOTT	Chilton Scott; B10.2.1869 Campbellsburg KY; D3.8.1939 Louisville KY; BL/TR/6´0˝/180; d4.21; ▲																								
1888	Lou AA	67	249	35	64	8	1	1	29	12	7	—	.257	.310	.309	101	1	10	.825	-1	146	0	O38(28/7/3),P33	—	-0.1
1889	Lou AA	62	229	30	66	7	5	4	34	13	2	36	.288	.332	.415	114	3	10	.915	6	173	75	O29(10/4/15),P19,1b17	—	0.4
1890	†Lou AA	55	189	29	61	3	5	0	24	16	3	—	.323	.385	.392	132	7	8	**.977**	5	128	88	P50,O5C	—	0.2
1891	Pit N	2	8	1	1	0	0	0	0	0	0	3	.125	.125	.125	-28	-1	0	.900	1	242	0	P2	—	0.0
	Lou AA	34	115	9	27	2	0	0	8	11	1	13	.235	.307	.252	61	-6	8	.939	3	133	**378**	P20,1b8,O6(2/3/1)	—	-0.1
1892	Lou N	63	219	22	56	2	9	0	23	17	3	21	.256	.318	.347	110	2	9	.915	2	109	152	P42,O17(1/0/16),1b6	—	0.1
1893	Lou N	61	221	34	50	8	5	0	16	25	1	15	.226	.308	.308	69	-10	6	.975	6	**131**	79	P37,O24R/1	—	-0.1
1894	Lou N	13	37	9	12	1	2	0	4	4	0	2	.324	.390	.459	112	1	1	.929	2	123	0	P7,O5R	—	0.1
	Chi N	24	99	30	37	5	4	3	23	7	1	1	.374	.421	.596	135	5	3	.938	-0	98	230	P16,O5R,1b2	—	0.1
	Year	37	136	39	49	6	6	3	27	11	1	3	.360	.412	.559	131	6	4	.935	1	105	169	P23,O10R,1b2	—	0.2
1895	Chi N	10	24	3	7	1	1	0	2	4	0	2	.292	.393	.417	102	0	1	.833	-0	147	0	P5,O4C	—	-0.1
Total	8	391	1390	202	381	37	32	8	163	109	18	93	.274	.335	.364	103	2	56	.938	22	120	143	P231,O133(41/23/68),1b34	—	0.5
STRAUB, JOE	Joseph; B1.19.1858 , Germany; D2.13.1929 Pueblo CO; BR/TR/5´10˝/160; d6.24																								
1880	Tro N	3	12	1	3	0	0	0	3	1	—	3	.250	.308	.250	87	0	—	.815	0	—	—	C3	—	0.0
1882	Phi AA	8	32	2	6	2	0	0	1	1	—	—	.188	.212	.250	52	-2	—	.830	-1	—	—	C7/rf	—	-0.2
1883	Col AA	27	100	4	13	0	0	0	—	4	—	—	.130	.163	.130	-5	-11	—	.860	-2	—	—	C14,1b12/cf	—	-1.1
Total	3	38	144	7	22	2	0	0	4	6	—	3	.153	.187	.167	17	-13	—	.843	-3	—	—	C24,1b12,O2(0/1/1)	—	-1.3

YEAR	TM LG	G	AB	R	H	2B	3B	HR	RBI	BB-IB	HP	SO	AVG	OBP	SLG	AOPS	ABR	SB-CS	FA	FR	RNG	THR	GAMES AT POSITION	DL	BFW
Strauss, Joe	Joseph “Dutch”,“The Socker” (b Joseph Strasser); B11.16.1858 Cincinnati OH; D6.24.1906 Cincinnati OH; BR/TR/5´9˝/175; d7.27																								
1884	KC U	16	60	4	12	3	0	0	—	1	—	—	.200	.213	.250	46	-6	—	.833	-2	81	0	O10(8/2/0),C3,2b2/3	—	-0.7
1885	Lou AA	2	6	0	1	0	0	0	0	0	0	—	.167	.167	.167	6	-1	—	ø	-1	0	0	/lfC	—	-0.2
1886	Lou AA	74	297	36	64	5	6	1	31	8	1	—	.215	.239	.283	60	-16	25	.857	3	158	0	O73(67/6/1),P2/C	—	-1.3
	Bro AA	9	36	6	9	1	1	0	5	1	0	—	.250	.270	.333	88	-1	4	1.000	1	108	0	O7L,C2	—	0.0
	Year	83	333	42	73	6	7	1	36	9	1	—	.219	.242	.288	63	-17	29	.866	4	154	0	O80(74/6/1),C3,P2	—	-1.3
Total	3	101	399	46	86	9	7	1	36	10	1	—	.216	.237	.281	59	-24	29	.861	1	146	0	O91(83/8/1),C7,P2,2b2/3	—	-2.2
Strawberry, Darryl	Darryl Eugene; B3.12.1962 Los Angeles CA; BL/TL/6´6˝/(190–215); [NYN80 1/1]; d5.6; [DL 1994 LA N 52]																								
1983	NY N	122	420	63	108	15	7	26	74	47-9	4	128	.257	.336	.512	133	17	19-6	.984	0	104	94	O117R	0	1.3
1984	NY N★	147	522	75	131	27	4	26	97	75-15	0	131	.251	.343	.467	128	20	27-8	.980	0	101	120	O146(0/21/134)	0	1.7
1985	NY N★	111	393	78	109	15	4	29	79	73-13	1	96	.277	.389	.557	166	36	26-11	.991	-4	95	68	O110(0/27/100)	47	3.0
1986	†NY N★	136	475	76	123	27	5	27	93	72-9	6	141	.259	.358	.507	140	27	28-12	.975	-3	93	95	O131(1/0/130)	0	1.9
1987	NY N★	154	532	108	151	32	5	39	104	97-13	7	122	.284	.398	.583	163	51	36-12	.972	-4	99	60	O151R	0	4.2
1988	†NY N★	153	543	101	146	27	3	**39**	101	85-21	3	127	.269	.366	**.545**	**166**	48	29-14	.971	3	109	58	O150R	0	**4.9**
1989	NY N✳	134	476	69	107	26	1	29	77	61-13	1	105	.225	.312	.466	126	15	11-4	.972	5	**114**	61	O131R	0	1.8
1990	NY N★	152	542	92	150	18	1	37	108	70-15	4	110	.277	.361	.518	140	29	15-8	.989	1	97	106	O149R	0	2.7
1991	LA N✳	139	505	86	134	22	4	28	99	75-4	3	125	.265	.361	.491	140	28	10-8	.978	-9	81	109	O136R	15	1.5
1992	LA N	43	156	20	37	8	0	5	25	19-4	1	34	.237	.322	.385	101	0	3-1	.986	-2	88	77	O42(2/0/40)	95	-0.3
1993	LA N	32	100	12	14	2	0	5	12	16-1	2	19	.140	.267	.310	58	-6	1-0	.905	-5	69	48	O29(4/0/25)	132	-1.2
1994	SF N	29	92	13	22	3	1	4	17	19-4	0	22	.239	.363	.424	110	2	0-3	.969	2	126	54	O27R	0	0.1
1995	†NY A	32	87	15	24	4	1	3	13	10-1	2	22	.276	.364	.448	111	1	0-0	.909	1	110	358	D15,O11(1/0/10)	0	0.1
1996	†NY A	63	202	35	53	13	0	11	36	31-5	1	55	.262	.359	.490	113	4	6-5	1.000	-2	82	53	O34(26/0/8),D26	0	-0.1
1997	NY A	11	29	1	3	1	0	0	2	3-0	0	9	.103	.188	.138	-13	-5	0-0	1.000	-1	78	0	O4L,D4	130	-0.5
1998	NY A	101	295	44	73	11	2	24	57	46-4	3	90	.247	.354	.542	134	14	8-7	.905	-2	88	0	D81,O16L	0	0.7
1999	†NY A	24	49	10	16	5	0	3	6	17-0	0	16	.327	.500	.612	185	8	2-0	ø	0	0	0	D17	0	0.7
Total	17	1583	5418	898	1401	256	38	335	1000	816-131	38	1352	.259	.357	.505	138	289	221-99	.977	-18	98	84	O1384(54/48/1308),D143	471	22.5
Street, Gabby	Charles Evard “Old Sarge”; B9.30.1882 Huntsville AL; D2.6.1951 Joplin MO; BR/TR/5´11˝/180; d9.13; M6/C2																								
1904	Cin N	11	33	1	4	1	0	0	0	1	0	—	.121	.147	.152	-7	-4	2	.973	3	127	109	C11	—	0.0
1905	Cin N	2	2	0	0	0	0	0	0	2	0	—	.000	.500	.000	48	0	0	1.000	0	118	207	/C	—	0.1
	Bos N	3	12	0	2	0	0	0	0	0	0	—	.167	.167	.167	-1	-2	1	.778	-2	69	89	C3	—	-0.4
	Cin N	29	91	8	23	5	1	0	8	6	1	—	.253	.306	.330	81	-2	1	.975	2	118	207	C26	—	0.3
	Year	34	105	8	25	5	1	0	8	8	1	—	.238	.298	.305	73	-3	2	.957	1	96	120	C30	—	0.0
1908	Was A	131	394	31	81	12	7	1	32	40	6	—	.206	.289	.279	92	-2	5	.973	4	109	103	C128	—	1.5
1909	Was A	137	407	25	86	12	1	0	29	26	2	—	.211	.262	.246	63	-17	2	.981	1	88	100	C137	—	-0.3
1910	Was A	89	257	13	52	6	0	1	16	23	2	—	.202	.273	.237	63	-11	1	**.978**	8	103	111	C86	—	0.6
1911	Was A	72	216	16	48	7	1	0	14	14	3	—	.222	.279	.264	53	-14	4	.973	9	105	92	C71	—	0.1
1912	NY A	29	88	4	16	1	1	0	6	7	2	—	.182	.258	.216	34	-8	1	.958	-1	89	109	C29	—	-0.7
1931	StL N	1	1	0	0	0	0	0	0	0	0	0	.000	.000	.000	-96	0	0	1.000	0	0	0	/CM	—	0.0
Total	8	504	1501	98	312	44	11	2	105	119	16	0	.208	.273	.256	66	-60	17	.974	25	100	103	C493	—	1.2
Streuli, Walt	Walter Herbert; B9.26.1935 Memphis TN; BR/TR/6´2˝/195; d9.25; Col Rhodes																								
1954	Det A	1	0	0	0	0	0	0	0	1	0	0	ø	1.000	ø	195	0	0-0	1.000	-0	0	0	/C	0	0.0
1955	Det A	2	4	1	1	1	0	0	1	0-0	0	0	.250	.200	.500	100	0	0-0	1.000	0	0	0	C2	0	0.0
1956	Det A	3	8	0	2	1	0	0	1	1-0	0	2	.250	.333	.375	87	0	0-0	.933	-0	0	204	C3	0	0.0
Total	3	6	12	1	3	2	0	0	2	2-0	0	2	.250	.333	.417	106	0	0-0	.957	-0	0	122	C6	0	0.0
Strick, Charles	Charles E. (b Charles E. Streck); B9.15.1858 Erie PA; D11.18.1933 Erie PA; d5.18																								
1882	Lou AA	32	110	17	18	6	1	0	—	9	—	—	.164	.227	.236	60	-4	—	.898	1	—	—	C21,O6C,2b6/S1	—	-0.1
Stricker, Cub	John A. (b John A. Streaker); B2.15.1860 Philadelphia PA; D11.19.1937 Philadelphia PA; BR/TR/5´3˝/138; d5.2; M1; OF(0/1/19); ▲																								
1882	Phi AA	72	272	34	59	6	1	0	18	15	—	—	.217	.258	.246	66	-10	—	.904	**23**	**123**	101	2b72,P2/rf	—	1.4
1883	Phi AA	89	330	67	90	8	0	1	40	19	—	—	.273	.312	.306	91	-4	—	.837	-22	86	68	2b88,C2	—	-2.0
1884	Phi AA	107	399	59	92	16	11	1	—	19	1	—	.231	.267	.333	89	-6	—	.870	-36	77	92	2b107/cfCP	—	-3.5
1885	Phi AA	106	398	71	93	9	3	1	41	21	7	—	.234	.284	.279	74	-12	—	.879	-14	92	86	2b106	—	-2.0
1887	Cle AA	131	534	122	141	19	4	2	53	53	3	—	.264	.334	.326	87	-7	86	.912	11	97	97	2b126,S6,P3	—	0.7
1888	Cle AA	127	493	80	115	13	6	1	33	50	6	—	.233	.311	.290	96	0	60	.929	24	102	121	2b122,O6R,P2	—	2.6
1889	Cle N	**136**	566	83	142	10	4	1	47	58	2	18	.251	.323	.288	72	-21	32	.932	8	96	108	2b135/S	—	-0.7
1890	Cle P	127	544	93	133	19	8	2	65	54	5	16	.244	.318	.320	77	-16	24	.905	3	104	98	2b109,S20	—	-0.7
1891	Bos AA	**139**	514	96	111	15	4	0	46	63	6	34	.216	.309	.261	64	-22	54	.942	24	101	**148**	2b139	—	0.5
1892	StL N	28	98	12	20	1	0	0	11	10	3	7	.204	.297	.214	58	-4	5	.939	-2	92	70	2b27/SM	—	-0.5
	Bal N	75	269	45	71	5	5	3	37	32	1	18	.264	.344	.353	108	3	13	.918	2	98	85	2b75	—	0.7
	Year	103	367	57	91	6	5	3	48	42	4	25	.248	.332	.316	95	-2	18	.923	-1	96	81	2b102/S	—	0.2
1893	Was N	59	218	28	39	7	1	0	20	20	0	12	.179	.248	.220	25	-24	4	.903	6	104	105	2b39,O12R,S4,3b4	—	-1.4
Total	11	1196	4635	790	1106	128	47	12	411	414	34	105	.239	.306	.294	78	-123	278	.907	26	97	103	2b1145,S32,O20R,P8,3b4,C3	—	-4.9
Strickland, George	George Bevan “Bo”; B1.10.1926 New Orleans LA; BR/TR/6´1˝/(175–180); d5.7; M2/C11																								
1950	Pit N	23	27	0	3	0	0	0	2	3	1	8	.111	.226	.111	-8	-4	0	.978	1	93	126	S19/3	0	-0.3
1951	Pit N	138	454	59	98	12	7	9	47	65	3	83	.216	.318	.333	73	-17	4-2	.943	9	105	104	S125,2b13	0	0.0
1952	Pit N	76	232	17	41	6	2	5	22	21	1	45	.177	.248	.284	46	-18	4-2	.953	11	112	103	2b45,S28/13	0	-0.3
	Cle A	31	88	8	19	4	0	1	8	14	0	15	.216	.324	.295	78	-2	0-0	.964	6	115	103	S30/2	0	0.6
1953	Cle A	123	419	43	119	17	4	5	47	51	0	52	.284	.362	.379	103	3	0-0	.974	**21**	**109**	**135**	S122/1	0	3.3
1954	†Cle A	112	361	42	77	12	3	6	37	55	1	62	.213	.314	.313	72	-13	2-1	.961	-13	95	95	S112	0	-1.7
1955	Cle A	130	388	34	81	9	5	2	34	49-0	3	60	.209	.302	.273	54	-25	1-0	**.976**	7	95	**115**	S128	0	-0.7
1956	Cle A	85	171	22	36	1	2	3	17	22-0	0	27	.211	.299	.292	56	-11	0-1	.986	8	106	128	2b28,S28,3b26	0	-0.1
1957	Cle A	89	201	21	47	8	2	1	19	26-1	1	29	.234	.323	.308	75	-7	0-3	.980	4	95	75	2b48,S23,3b19	0	0.0
1959	Cle A	132	441	55	105	15	2	3	48	51-2	0	64	.238	.313	.302	74	-15	1-1	.971	-12	84	83	3b80,S50,2b4	0	-2.3
1960	Cle A	32	42	4	7	0	0	1	3	4-1	1	8	.167	.255	.238	35	-4	0-0	.962	-2	98	120	S14,3b12,2b2	0	-0.6
Total	10	971	2824	305	633	84	27	36	284	361-4	11	453	.224	.313	.311	70	-113	12-10	.963	39	102	115	S679,2b141,3b139,1b2	0	-2.1
Strief, George	George Andrew; B10.16.1856 Cincinnati OH; D4.1.1946 Cleveland OH; BR/TR/5´7˝/172; d5.1; U1																								
1879	Cle N	71	264	24	46	7	1	0	15	10	—	23	.174	.204	.208	37	-17	—	.918	-8	64	0	O55(1/54/1),2b16	—	-2.5
1882	Pit AA	**79**	297	45	58	9	6	2	—	13	—	—	.195	.229	.286	76	-7	—	.917	0	91	93	2b78/S	—	-0.3
1883	StL AA	82	302	22	68	9	0	1	22	12	—	—	.225	.255	.265	64	-12	—	.899	5	104	127	2b67,O15(11/1/3)	—	-0.5
1884	StL AA	48	184	22	37	5	2	2	—	13	0	—	.201	.254	.283	72	-6	—	.848	-4	57	0	O44(43/1/0),2b3/1	—	-1.0
	KC U	15	56	5	6	5	0	0	—	4	—	—	.107	.167	.196	11	-8	—	.900	5	119	153	2b15	—	-0.2
	CP U	15	53	6	11	5	0	0	—	3	—	—	.208	.250	.302	67	-4	—	.905	-1	88	25	2b15	—	-0.3
	Year	30	109	11	17	10	0	0	—	7	—	—	.156	.207	.248	40	-11	—	.902	4	105	94	2b30	—	-0.5
	Cle N	8	29	2	7	2	0	0	0	0	—	5	.241	.241	.310	70	-1	—	1.000	1	240	0	O6L,3b2	—	0.0
1885	Phi AA	44	175	19	48	8	5	0	27	9	0	—	.274	.310	.377	110	1	—	.828	0	98	0	3b19,S10,O8(0/4/4),2b7	—	0.2
Total	5	362	1360	145	281	50	14	5	64	64	0	28	.207	.242	.275	67	-54	—	.899	-2	96	108	2b201,O128(61/60/8),3b21,S11/1	—	-4.6
Stringer, Lou	Louis Bernard; B5.13.1917 Grand Rapids MI; BR/TR/5´11˝/173; d4.15; Mil 1943–45																								
1941	Chi N	145	512	59	126	31	4	5	53	59	0	86	.246	.324	.352	94	-4	3	.960	24	**114**	101	2b137,S7	0	2.9
1942	Chi N	121	406	45	96	10	5	9	41	31	1	55	.236	.292	.352	92	-7	3	.955	-1	**106**	85	2b113/3	0	0.0
1946	Chi N	80	209	26	51	3	1	3	19	26	0	34	.244	.328	.311	83	-5	0	.956	-9	95	54	2b62/S3	0	-1.1
1948	Bos A	4	11	1	1	0	0	1	1	0	0	3	.091	.091	.364	17	-2	0-0	.947	2	146	231	2b2	0	0.0
1949	Bos A	35	41	10	11	4	0	1	6	5	0	10	.268	.348	.439	100	0	0-0	.978	2	96	208	2b9	0	0.3
1950	Bos A	24	17	7	5	1	0	0	2	0	0	4	.294	.294	.353	59	-1	1-0	.778	1	141	334	3b3/2S	0	0.0
Total	6	409	1196	148	290	49	10	19	122	121	1	192	.242	.313	.348	90	-19	7-0	.958	20	108	91	2b324,S9,3b5	0	2.1

YEAR	TM LG	G	AB	R	H	2B	3B	HR	RBI	BB-IB	HP	SO	AVG	OBP	SLG	AOPS	ABR	SB-CS	FA	FR	RNG	THR	GAMES AT POSITION	DL	BFW
Stripp, Joe	Joseph Valentine "Jersey Joe"; B2.3.1903 Harrison NJ; D6.10.1989 Orlando FL; BR/TR/5´11.5˝/175; d7.2; OF(10/0/12)																								
1928	Cin N	42	139	18	40	7	3	1	17	8	3	8	.288	.340	.403	95	-1	0	.931	-4	92	0	O21(10/0/11),3b17/S	—	-0.5
1929	Cin N	64	187	24	40	3	2	3	20	24	3	15	.214	.313	.299	55	-13	2	.960	3	115	52	3b55,2b2	—	-0.6
1930	Cin N	130	464	74	142	37	6	3	64	51	2	37	.306	.377	.431	100	2	15	.996	-0	83	113	1b75,3b48	—	0.0
1931	Cin N	105	426	71	138	26	2	3	42	21	2	31	.324	.359	.415	114	8	5	.957	6	108	126	3b96,1b9	—	1.7
1932	Bro N	138	534	94	162	36	9	6	64	36	2	30	.303	.350	.438	113	9	14	.954	16	115	133	3b93,1b43	—	2.4
1933	Bro N	141	537	69	149	20	7	1	51	26	1	23	.277	.312	.346	92	-7	5	.967	7	99	86	3b140	—	0.5
1934	Bro N	104	384	50	121	19	6	1	40	22	1	20	.315	.354	.404	108	4	2	.941	-4	90	159	3b96,1b7/S	—	0.2
1935	Bro N	109	373	44	114	13	5	3	43	22	0	15	.306	.344	.391	99	-1	2	.962	7	116	142	3b88,1b15/rf	—	0.7
1936	Bro N	110	439	51	139	31	1	1	60	22	1	12	.317	.351	.399	100	1	2	**.968**	7	97	99	3b106	—	1.1
1937	Bro N	90	300	37	73	10	2	1	26	20	0	18	.243	.291	.300	60	-17	1	.971	-4	89	52	3b66,1b14,S3	—	-2.0
1938	StL N	54	199	24	57	7	0	0	18	18	1	10	.286	.349	.322	81	-5	0	.977	-4	82	113	3b51	—	-0.7
	Bos N	59	229	19	63	10	0	1	19	10	0	7	.275	.305	.332	84	-6	2	.966	-1	100	126	3b58	—	-0.4
	Year	113	428	43	120	17	0	1	37	28	1	17	.280	.326	.327	82	-10	2	**.971**	-4	92	**120**	3b109	—	-1.1
Total	11	1146	4211	575	1238	219	43	24	464	280	16	226	.294	.340	.384	96	-26	50	.961	30	102	108	3b914,1b163,O22R,S5,2b2	—	2.4
Strittmatter, Mark	Mark Arthur; B4.4.1969 Huntington NY; BR/TR/6´1˝/210; [ColN92 28/795]; d9.3; Col Virginia Commonwealth																								
1998	Col N	4	4	0	0	0	0	0	0	0-0	0	3	.000	.000	.000	-83	-1	0-0	1.000	1	72	0	C3	0	0.0
Strobel, Allie	Albert Irving; B6.11.1884 Boston MA; D2.10.1955 Hollywood FL; BR/TR/6´0˝/160; d8.29; Col Boston College																								
1905	Bos N	5	19	1	2	0	0	0	2	0	0	—	.105	.105	.105	-38	-3	0	1.000	0	101	228	3b4/lf	—	-0.3
1906	Bos N	100	317	28	64	10	3	1	24	29	2	—	.202	.273	.262	69	-12	2	.946	-6	95	98	2b93,S6/cf	—	-1.8
Total	2	105	336	29	66	10	3	1	26	29	2	—	.196	.264	.253	63	-15	2	.946	-6	95	98	2b93,S6,3b4,O2(1/1/0)	—	-2.1
Stroner, Jim	James Melvin; B5.29.1901 Chicago IL; D12.6.1975 Tarboro NC; BR/TR/5´10˝/175; d5.1																								
1929	Pit N	6	8	0	3	1	0	0	0	1	0	0	.375	.444	.500	130	0	0	.571	-1	88	0	3b2	—	0.0
Strong, Jamal	Jamal Najar; B8.5.1978 Pasadena CA; BR/TR/5´10˝/(180–185); [SeaA00 6/176]; d9.2; Col Nebraska																								
2003	Sea A	12	2	2	0	0	0	0	0	0-0	0	0	.000	.000	.000	-99	-1	0-0	ø	-0	0	0	O2C,D7	0	-0.1
2005	Sea A	16	20	6	5	0	1	0	2	2-0	1	6	.250	.333	.350	93	0	0-0	1.000	0	87	327	O11(7/4/1),D3	21	0.0
Total	2	28	22	8	5	0	1	0	2	2-0	1	6	.227	.308	.318	76	-1	0-0	1.000	0	82	309	O13(7/6/1),D10	21	-0.1
Stroud, Ed	Edwin Marvin; B10.31.1939 Lapine AL; BL/TR/5´11˝/(175–180); d9.11																								
1966	Chi A	12	36	3	6	2	0	0	1	2-0	1	8	.167	.231	.222	33	-3	3-0	1.000	0	120	0	O11(4/0/7)	0	-0.3
1967	Chi A	20	27	6	8	0	1	0	3	1-0	1	5	.296	.345	.370	116	0	7-2	1.000	2	106	395	O12(11/0/5)	0	0.3
	Was A	87	204	36	41	5	3	1	10	25-0	1	29	.201	.289	.270	69	-8	8-6	.983	-7	88	28	O79(1/79/0)	0	-1.8
	Year	107	231	42	49	5	4	1	13	26-0	2	34	.212	.295	.281	75	-7	15-8	.985	-5	90	69	O91(12/79/5)	0	-1.5
1968	Was A	105	306	41	73	10	10	4	23	20-1	0	50	.239	.284	.376	102	-1	9-3	.979	-1	105	45	O84(25/7/58)	0	-0.6
1969	Was A	123	206	35	52	5	6	4	29	30-1	2	33	.252	.353	.393	114	4	12-2	.982	1	117	25	O85(28/1/58)	0	0.4
1970	Was A	129	433	69	115	11	5	5	32	40-2	3	79	.266	.331	.349	92	-5	29-8	.993	3	105	113	O118(9/106/9)	21	-0.2
1971	Chi A	53	141	19	25	4	3	0	2	11-0	0	20	.177	.237	.248	37	-12	4-5	1.000	-6	72	0	O44(8/22/20)	0	-2.2
Total	6	529	1353	209	320	37	28	14	100	129-4	8	224	.237	.306	.336	87	-25	72-26	.988	-7	101	62	O433(86/215/157)	21	-4.4
Stroughter, Steve	Stephen Lewis; B3.15.1952 Visalia CA; BL/TR/6´2˝/190; [SFN71 A1/6]; d4.7; Col Sequoias (CA) [JC]																								
1982	Sea A	26	47	4	8	1	0	1	3	3-1	1	9	.170	.235	.255	33	-4	0-0	1.000	1	194	975	O3L,D9	0	-0.3
Strueve, Al	Albert Frederick; B6.26.1860 Cincinnati OH; D1.28.1929 Buckskin Twp. OH; d6.22																								
1884	StL AA	2	7	2	2	0	0	0	—	0	0	—	.286	.286	.286	84	0	—	ø	1	0	0	/cfC	—	0.1
Strunk, Amos	Amos Aaron; B1.22.1889 Philadelphia PA; D7.22.1979 Llanerch PA; BL/TL/5´11.5˝/175; d9.24																								
1908	Phi A	12	34	4	8	1	0	0	0	4	0	—	.235	.316	.265	83	0	0	.903	0	74	271	O11(1/10/0)	—	-0.1
1909	Phi A	11	35	1	4	0	0	0	2	1	0	—	.114	.139	.114	-20	-5	2	1.000	0	245	0	O9(1/8/0)	—	-0.6
1910	†Phi A	16	48	9	16	0	1	0	2	3	0	—	.333	.373	.375	135	2	4	1.000	1	121	51	O14C	—	0.2
1911	†Phi A	74	215	42	55	7	2	1	21	35	1	—	.256	.363	.321	93	0	13	.958	2	104	116	O62(19/43/0),1b2	—	-0.2
1912	Phi A	122	412	58	119	13	12	3	63	47	3	—	.289	.366	.400	123	13	29	**.990**	8	112	98	O116(65/51/0)	—	1.4
1913	†Phi A	94	292	30	89	11	12	0	46	29	0	23	.305	.368	.425	135	12	14	.962	-2	100	74	O81C	—	0.4
1914	†Phi A	122	404	58	111	15	3	2	45	57	0	38	.275	.364	.342	117	11	25-22	**.987**	6	111	93	O120(12/108/0)	—	0.8
1915	Phi A	132	485	76	144	28	16	1	45	56	1	45	.297	.371	.427	144	25	17-19	.980	10	106	**165**	O111(0/59/52),1b19	—	2.6
1916	Phi A	150	544	71	172	30	9	3	49	66	3	59	.316	.393	.421	152	36	21-23	.978	0	98	108	O143(6/119/18),1b7	—	2.5
1917	Phi A	148	540	83	152	26	7	1	45	68	1	37	.281	.363	.361	123	17	16	**.986**	-5	100	63	O146C	—	0.1
1918	†Bos A	114	413	50	106	18	9	0	35	36	0	13	.257	.316	.344	101	-1	20	**.988**	-6	90	85	O113(1/112/0)	—	-1.6
1919	Bos A	48	184	27	50	11	3	0	17	13	1	13	.272	.323	.364	98	-1	3	.968	-4	94	55	O48C	—	-0.9
	Phi A	60	194	15	41	6	4	0	13	23	1	15	.211	.298	.284	63	-10	3	.981	-1	97	95	O52(0/10/42)	—	-1.4
	Year	108	378	42	91	17	7	0	30	36	2	28	.241	.310	.323	79	-11	6	.974	-5	96	75	O100(0/58/42)	—	-2.3
1920	Phi A	58	202	23	60	9	3	0	20	21	0	9	.297	.363	.371	94	-1	0-6	.990	-4	97	29	O54(6/10/38)	—	-1.0
	Chi A	53	188	33	45	8	1	1	16	28	0	15	.239	.338	.309	72	-7	1-0	.981	-1	109	47	O49(3/7/38)	—	-1.0
	Year	111	390	56	105	17	4	1	36	49	0	24	.269	.351	.341	83	-8	1-6	**.985**	-5	103	38	O103(9/17/76)	—	-2.0
1921	Chi A	121	401	68	133	19	10	3	69	38	1	27	.332	.391	.451	116	10	7-10	.970	-6	93	76	O111(9/69/33)	—	-0.4
1922	Chi A	92	311	36	90	11	4	0	33	33	0	28	.289	.358	.350	85	-6	9-6	.989	1	99	117	O74(14/56/4),1b7	—	-0.9
1923	Chi A	54	54	7	17	0	0	0	8	8	0	5	.315	.403	.315	92	0	1-0	1.000	0	136	0	O5(2/3/0),1b2	—	0.0
1924	Chi A	1	1	0	0	0	0	0	0	0	0	0	.000	.000	.000	-99	0	0-0	ø	0	—	—	/H	—	0.0
	Phi A	30	42	5	6	0	0	0	1	7	0	4	.143	.265	.143	7	-6	0-0	1.000	-1	62	0	O8(4/1/3)	—	-0.7
	Year	31	43	5	6	0	0	0	1	7	0	4	.140	.260	.140	5	-6	0-0	1.000	-1	62	0	O8(4/1/3)	—	-0.7
Total	17	1512	4999	696	1418	213	96	15	530	573	12	331	.284	.359	.374	112	89	185-86	.980	-2	102	91	O1327(143/955/228),1b37	—	-0.8
Stuart, Luke	Luther Lane; B5.23.1892 Alamance Co. NC; D6.15.1947 Winston–Salem NC; BR/TR/5´8˝/165; d7.28; Col Guilford																								
1921	StL A	3	3	2	1	0	0	1	2	0	0	1	.333	.333	1.333	291	1	0-0	1.000	-0	58	0	2b3	—	0.0
Stuart, Dick	Richard Lee "Dr. Strangeglove"; B11.7.1932 San Francisco CA; D12.15.2002 Redwood City CA; BR/TR/6´4˝/(200–215); d7.10																								
1958	Pit N	67	254	38	68	12	5	16	48	11-1	5	75	.268	.310	.543	124	7	0-0	.973	-0	113	128	1b64	0	0.3
1959	Pit N	118	397	64	118	15	2	27	78	42-7	2	86	.297	.362	.549	141	23	1-1	.976	1	**115**	110	1b105/lf	0	1.7
1960	†Pit N	122	438	48	114	17	5	23	83	39-5	0	107	.260	.317	.479	115	7	0-0	.986	0	106	117	1b108	0	0.2
1961	Pit N★	138	532	83	160	28	8	35	117	34-1	4	121	.301	.344	.581	140	28	0-3	.983	1	107	**123**	1b132/lf	0	1.9
1962	Pit N	114	394	52	90	11	4	16	64	32-1	2	94	.228	.286	.398	83	-11	0-1	.982	2	112	119	1b101	0	-1.6
1963	Bos A	157	612	81	160	25	4	42	**118**	44-2	1	144	.261	.312	.521	125	17	0-0	.979	7	**118**	81	1b155	0	1.5
1964	Bos A	156	603	73	168	27	1	33	114	37-7	3	130	.279	.320	.491	117	12	0-0	.981	-0	100	80	1b155	0	0.3
1965	Phi N	149	538	53	126	19	1	28	95	39-8	3	136	.234	.287	.429	101	-1	1-0	.986	3	109	92	1b143/3	0	-0.6
1966	NY N	31	87	7	19	0	0	4	13	9-2	0	26	.218	.292	.356	81	-2	0-1	.974	-1	96	109	1b23	17	-0.6
	†LA N	38	91	4	24	1	0	3	9	11-0	2	17	.264	.356	.374	112	2	0-1	.991	4	166	104	1b25	0	0.4
	Year	69	178	11	43	1	0	7	22	20-2	2	43	.242	.325	.365	97	-1	0-2	.982	3	131	106	1b48	0	-0.2
1969	Cal A	22	51	3	8	2	0	1	4	3-0	0	21	.157	.204	.255	29	-5	0-0	.991	-1	54	128	1b13	0	-0.8
Total	10	1112	3997	506	1055	157	30	228	743	301-34	22	957	.264	.316	.489	117	77	2-7	.982	14	110	103	1b1024,O2L/3	17	2.7
Stuart, Bill	William Alexander "Chauncey"; B8.28.1873 Boalsburg PA; D10.14.1928 Fort Worth TX; 5´11˝/170; d8.15; Col Penn St.																								
1895	Pit N	19	77	5	19	3	0	0	10	2	1	6	.247	.275	.286	47	-6	2	.913	-1	99	72	S17,2b2	—	-0.5
1899	NY N	1	3	0	0	0	0	0	0	0	0	—	.000	.000	.000	-99	-1	0	1.000	0	93	0	/2	—	-0.1
Total	2	20	80	5	19	3	0	0	10	2	1	6	.237	.265	.275	42	-7	2	.913	-1	99	72	S17,2b3	—	-0.6
Stubbs, Franklin	Franklin Lee; B10.21.1960 Richlands NC; BL/TL/6´2˝/(209–215); [LAN82 1/19]; d4.28; Col VPI																								
1984	LA N	87	217	22	42	2	3	8	17	24-3	0	63	.194	.273	.341	72	-9	2-2	.993	2	138	94	1b51,O20(6/3/13)	0	-1.2
1985	LA N	10	9	0	2	0	0	0	2	0-0	0	3	.222	.222	.222	25	-1	0-0	1.000	-0	0	117	1b4	0	-0.1
1986	LA N	132	420	55	95	11	1	23	58	37-11	2	107	.226	.291	.421	101	-2	7-1	.969	3	101	140	O124(108/23/15),1b13	0	-0.3
1987	LA N	129	386	48	90	16	3	16	52	31-9	1	85	.233	.290	.415	87	-9	8-1	**.994**	6	117	90	1b111,O18(13/0/6)	21	-0.8
1988	†LA N	115	242	30	54	13	0	8	34	23-3	1	61	.223	.288	.376	93	-2	11-3	.978	4	126	99	1b84,O13(7/1/6)	0	-0.2
1989	LA N	69	103	11	30	6	0	4	15	16-2	0	27	.291	.387	.466	145	7	3-2	.948	4	117	262	O28(22/5/3),1b7	43	1.0

YEAR	TM LG	G	AB	R	H	2B	3B	HR	RBI	BB-IB	HP	SO	AVG	OBP	SLG	AOPS	ABR	SB-CS	FA	FR	RNG	THR	GAMES AT POSITION	DL	BFW
1990	Hou N	146	448	59	117	23	2	23	71	48-3	2	114	.261	.334	.475	124	14	19-6	.991	-7	89	100	1b72,O71(67/0/5)	0	0.2
1991	Mil A	103	362	48	77	16	2	11	38	35-3	2	71	.213	.282	.359	79	-11	13-4	.991	4	124	100	1b92,O4L,D4	0	-1.2
1992	Mil A	92	288	37	66	11	1	9	42	27-3	1	68	.229	.297	.368	87	-6	11-8	.987	5	134	92	1b68,D16/rf	0	-0.7
1995	Det A	62	116	13	29	11	0	2	19	19-1	1	27	.250	.358	.397	97	0	0-1	.972	-4	56	111	1b20,O20L,D3	26	-0.5
Total	10	945	2591	323	602	109	12	104	348	260-38	10	626	.232	.303	.404	96	-19	74-28	.989	16	118	96	1b522,O299(247/32/49),D23	90	-3.8

STUBING, MOOSE Lawrence George; B3.31.1938 Bronx NY; BL/TL/6´3˝/220; d8.14; M1/C6

YEAR	TM LG	G	AB	R	H	2B	3B	HR	RBI	BB-IB	HP	SO	AVG	OBP	SLG	AOPS	ABR	SB-CS	FA	FR	RNG	THR	GAMES AT POSITION	DL	BFW
1967	Cal A	5	5	0	0	0	0	0	0	0-0	0	4	.000	.000	.000	-99	-1	0-0	ø	0	—	—	/H	0	-0.1

STUDLEY, SEEM Seymour L. "Warhorse"; B5.1841 Byron NY; D7.19.1901 Grand Island NE; 5´7.5˝/180; d4.20

YEAR	TM LG	G	AB	R	H	2B	3B	HR	RBI	BB-IB	HP	SO	AVG	OBP	SLG	AOPS	ABR	SB-CS	FA	FR	RNG	THR	GAMES AT POSITION	DL	BFW
1872	Nat NA	5	21	3	2	0	0	0	2	0	—	1	.095	.095	.095	-35	-4	0-0	.571	-2	0	0	O5C	—	-0.4

STUMPF, GEORGE George Frederick; B12.15.1910 New Orleans LA; D3.6.1993 Metairie LA; BL/TL/5´8˝/155; d9.19

YEAR	TM LG	G	AB	R	H	2B	3B	HR	RBI	BB-IB	HP	SO	AVG	OBP	SLG	AOPS	ABR	SB-CS	FA	FR	RNG	THR	GAMES AT POSITION	DL	BFW
1931	Bos A	7	28	2	7	1	1	0	4	1	0	2	.250	.276	.357	69	-2	0-0	1.000	-0	96	0	O7(6/2/0)	—	-0.2
1932	Bos A	79	169	18	34	2	2	1	18	18	0	21	.201	.278	.254	40	-16	1-1	.952	-2	95	65	O51(17/2/32)	—	-1.9
1933	Bos A	22	41	8	14	3	0	0	5	4	0	2	.341	.400	.415	117	1	4-0	1.000	-0	110	0	O15(3/8/4)	—	0.2
1936	Chi A	10	22	3	6	1	0	0	5	2	0	1	.273	.333	.318	59	-1	0-0	1.000	0	93	243	O4L	—	-0.1
Total	4	118	260	31	61	7	3	1	32	25	0	26	.235	.302	.296	57	-18	5-1	.969	-2	97	63	O77(30/12/36)	—	-2.0

STUMPF, BILL William Frederick; B3.21.1892 Baltimore MD; D2.14.1966 Crownsville MD; BR/TR/6´0.5˝/175; d5.11

YEAR	TM LG	G	AB	R	H	2B	3B	HR	RBI	BB-IB	HP	SO	AVG	OBP	SLG	AOPS	ABR	SB-CS	FA	FR	RNG	THR	GAMES AT POSITION	DL	BFW
1912	NY A	42	129	8	31	0	0	0	10	6	1	—	.240	.279	.240	46	-9	5	.892	-6	95	109	S26,2b8,3b5/1cf	—	-1.3
1913	NY A	12	29	5	6	1	0	0	1	3	0	3	.207	.281	.241	53	-2	0	.818	-3	96	0	S6,2b4/rf	—	-0.4
Total	2	54	158	13	37	1	0	0	11	9	1	3	.234	.280	.241	47	-11	5	.877	-8	95	87	S32,2b12,3b5,O2(0/1/1)/1	—	-1.7

STURDY, GUY Guy; B8.7.1899 Sherman TX; D5.4.1965 Marshall TX; BL/TL/6´0.5˝/180; d9.30

YEAR	TM LG	G	AB	R	H	2B	3B	HR	RBI	BB-IB	HP	SO	AVG	OBP	SLG	AOPS	ABR	SB-CS	FA	FR	RNG	THR	GAMES AT POSITION	DL	BFW
1927	StL A	5	21	5	9	1	0	0	5	1	0	0	.429	.455	.476	137	1	2-0	.974	-0	69	54	1b5	—	0.1
1928	StL A	54	45	3	10	1	0	1	8	8	0	4	.222	.340	.311	70	-2	1-0	1.000	-0	0	0	/1	—	-0.2
Total	2	59	66	8	19	2	0	1	13	9	0	4	.288	.373	.364	91	-1	3-0	.975	-1	66	51	1b6	—	-0.1

STURGEON, BOBBY Robert Howard; B8.6.1919 Clinton IN; BR/TR/6´0˝/175; d4.16; Mil 1943–45

YEAR	TM LG	G	AB	R	H	2B	3B	HR	RBI	BB-IB	HP	SO	AVG	OBP	SLG	AOPS	ABR	SB-CS	FA	FR	RNG	THR	GAMES AT POSITION	DL	BFW
1940	Chi N	7	21	1	4	1	0	0	2	0	0	1	.190	.190	.238	18	-2	0	.848	-1	91	123	S7	—	-0.3
1941	Chi N	129	433	45	106	15	3	0	25	9	0	30	.245	.260	.293	58	-26	5	.956	-0	101	98	S126/23	0	-1.9
1942	Chi N	63	162	8	40	7	1	0	7	4	1	13	.247	.269	.302	70	-7	2	.988	13	125	106	2b32,S29,3b2	0	1.0
1946	Chi N	100	294	26	87	12	2	1	21	10	0	18	.296	.319	.361	94	-4	0	.934	-10	90	92	S72,2b21	0	-1.0
1947	Chi N	87	232	16	59	10	5	0	21	7	0	12	.254	.276	.341	66	-13	0	.975	11	108	104	S45,2b30,3b5	0	0.1
1948	Bos N	34	78	10	17	3	1	0	4	4	0	5	.218	.256	.282	46	-6	0	.938	-4	97	113	2b18,S4,3b4	0	-0.9
Total	6	420	1220	106	313	48	12	1	80	34	1	79	.257	.277	.318	68	-58	7	.951	9	100	100	S283,2b102,3b12	0	-3.0

STURGIS, DEAN Dean Donnell; B12.1.1892 Beloit KS; D6.4.1950 Uniontown PA; BR/TR/6´1˝/180; d5.1; Col Bucknell

YEAR	TM LG	G	AB	R	H	2B	3B	HR	RBI	BB-IB	HP	SO	AVG	OBP	SLG	AOPS	ABR	SB-CS	FA	FR	RNG	THR	GAMES AT POSITION	DL	BFW
1914	Phi A	4	4	1	1	0	0	0	0	1	0	2	.250	.400	.250	100	0	0	1.000	0	*87*	*138*	/C	—	0.0

STURM, JOHNNY John Peter Joseph; B1.23.1916 St.Louis MO; D10.8.2004 St.Louis MO; BL/TL/6´1˝/185; d4.14; Mil 1942–45

YEAR	TM LG	G	AB	R	H	2B	3B	HR	RBI	BB-IB	HP	SO	AVG	OBP	SLG	AOPS	ABR	SB-CS	FA	FR	RNG	THR	GAMES AT POSITION	DL	BFW
1941	†NY A	124	524	58	125	17	3	3	36	37	3	50	.239	.293	.300	58	-33	3-5	.990	-2	94	**117**	1b124	0	-4.7

STUTZ, GEORGE George "Kid","Satan"; B2.12.1893 Philadelphia PA; D12.29.1930 Philadelphia PA; BR/TR/5´5˝/150; d8.17

YEAR	TM LG	G	AB	R	H	2B	3B	HR	RBI	BB-IB	HP	SO	AVG	OBP	SLG	AOPS	ABR	SB-CS	FA	FR	RNG	THR	GAMES AT POSITION	DL	BFW
1926	Phi N	6	9	0	0	0	0	0	0	0	0	2	.000	.000	.000	-95	-2	0	.938	0	95	127	S5	—	-0.2

STYLES, LENA William Graves; B11.27.1899 Gurley AL; D3.14.1956 Hunstville AL; BR/TR/6´1˝/185; d9.10; Col Alabama

YEAR	TM LG	G	AB	R	H	2B	3B	HR	RBI	BB-IB	HP	SO	AVG	OBP	SLG	AOPS	ABR	SB-CS	FA	FR	RNG	THR	GAMES AT POSITION	DL	BFW
1919	Phi A	8	22	0	6	1	0	0	5	1	0	6	.273	.304	.318	74	-1	0	.974	-0	*76*	*93*	C8	—	-0.1
1920	Phi A	24	50	5	13	3	1	0	5	6	0	7	.260	.339	.360	84	-1	1-0	.966	1	*111*	*195*	C9,1b7	—	0.0
1921	Phi A	4	5	0	1	0	0	0	0	0	0	2	.200	.200	.200	2	-1	0-0	.333	-1	*0*	*237*	C2	—	-0.2
1930	Cin N	7	12	2	3	0	1	0	1	1	1	2	.250	.357	.417	91	0	0	.875	-0	*70*	*184*	C5/1	—	0.0
1931	Cin N	34	87	7	21	3	0	0	5	8	1	7	.241	.313	.276	63	-4	0	.949	-5	*84*	*51*	C31	—	-0.8
Total	5	77	176	14	44	7	2	0	16	16	2	24	.250	.320	.313	71	-7	1-0	.929	-6	*83*	*93*	C55,1b8	—	-1.1

STYNES, CHRIS Christopher Desmond; B1.19.1973 Queens NY; BR/TR/5´10˝/(175–205); [TorA91 3/94]; d5.19; OF(134/2/22)

YEAR	TM LG	G	AB	R	H	2B	3B	HR	RBI	BB-IB	HP	SO	AVG	OBP	SLG	AOPS	ABR	SB-CS	FA	FR	RNG	THR	GAMES AT POSITION	DL	BFW
1995	KC A	22	35	7	6	1	0	0	2	4-0	0	3	.171	.256	.200	20	-4	0-0	.982	2	111	204	2b17,D2	0	-0.1
1996	KC A	36	92	8	27	6	0	0	6	2-0	0	5	.293	.309	.359	68	-5	5-2	.939	-3	93	91	O19L,2b5,3b2,D3	0	-0.7
1997	Cin N	49	198	31	69	7	1	6	28	11-1	4	13	.348	.394	.485	126	7	11-2	.976	3	112	204	O38L,2b8,3b3	0	1.1
1998	Cin N	123	347	52	88	10	1	6	27	32-1	4	36	.254	.323	.340	74	-13	15-1	1.000	5	108	100	O80(64/2/20),3b22,2b11,S2	0	-0.8
1999	Cin N	73	113	18	27	1	0	2	14	12-1	0	13	.239	.310	.301	54	-8	5-2	.956	-9	82	70	2b43,3b8,O4L	0	-1.4
2000	Cin N	119	380	71	127	24	1	12	40	32-2	2	54	.334	.386	.497	118	11	5-2	.966	-4	88	106	3b77,2b15,O8(6/0/2)	0	0.7
2001	Bos A	96	361	52	101	19	2	8	33	20-0	3	56	.280	.322	.410	91	-5	4-5	.949	-4	81	68	3b46,2b43,O3L	46	-0.8
2002	Chi N	98	195	25	47	9	1	5	26	21-1	1	29	.241	.314	.374	82	-5	1-1	.921	-3	74	48	3b40,2b20	0	-0.7
2003	Col N	138	443	71	113	31	3	11	73	48-1	6	76	.255	.335	.413	83	-10	3-1	.972	3	104	99	3b119,2b5	0	-0.6
2004	Pit N	74	162	16	35	10	0	1	16	9-2	2	23	.216	.266	.296	45	-13	0-0	.992	1	100	106	3b71	0	-1.2
Total	10	828	2326	351	640	118	9	51	265	191-9	22	308	.275	.335	.399	87	-45	49-16	.965	-10	95	93	3b388,2b167,O152L,D5,S2	46	-4.5

STYNES, NEIL Cornelius William; B12.10.1868 Arlington MA; D3.26.1944 Somerville MA; BR/TR/6´0˝/165; d9.8

YEAR	TM LG	G	AB	R	H	2B	3B	HR	RBI	BB-IB	HP	SO	AVG	OBP	SLG	AOPS	ABR	SB-CS	FA	FR	RNG	THR	GAMES AT POSITION	DL	BFW
1890	Cle P	2	8	0	0	0	0	0	0	0	0	0	.000	.000	.000	-99	-2	0	.786	-1	*70*	*0*	C2	—	-0.3

SUAREZ, KEN Kenneth Raymond; B4.12.1943 Tampa FL; BR/TR/5´9˝/175; d4.14; Col Florida St.

YEAR	TM LG	G	AB	R	H	2B	3B	HR	RBI	BB-IB	HP	SO	AVG	OBP	SLG	AOPS	ABR	SB-CS	FA	FR	RNG	THR	GAMES AT POSITION	DL	BFW
1966	KC A	35	69	5	10	0	1	0	2	15-0	0	26	.145	.298	.174	41	-5	2-0	.954	-1	58	175	C34	0	-0.4
1967	KC A	39	63	7	15	5	0	2	9	16-1	0	21	.238	.387	.413	143	5	1-0	.979	5	93	175	C36	0	1.2
1968	Cle A	17	10	1	1	0	0	0	0	1-0	0	3	.100	.182	.100	-13	-1	0-0	1.000	0	0	0	C12/23lf	0	-0.1
1969	Cle A	36	85	7	25	5	0	1	9	15-5	0	12	.294	.400	.388	118	3	1-0	.991	1	176	123	C36	0	0.6
1971	Cle A	50	123	10	25	7	0	1	9	18-3	2	15	.203	.310	.285	65	-5	0-1	.993	1	121	113	C48	0	-0.3
1972	Tex A	25	33	2	5	1	0	0	4	1-0	0	4	.152	.167	.182	7	-4	0-0	.965	1	318	147	C17	0	-0.3
1973	Tex A	93	278	25	69	11	0	1	27	33-0	5	16	.248	.334	.299	84	-4	1-2	.989	-1	91	111	C90	0	-0.2
Total	7	295	661	57	150	29	1	5	60	99-9	7	97	.227	.330	.297	81	-11	5-3	.984	6	111	127	C273/lf32	0	0.5

SUAREZ, LUIS Luis Abelardo; B8.24.1916 Alto Songo, Cuba; D6.5.1991 Havana, Cuba; BR/TR/5´11˝/170; d5.28

YEAR	TM LG	G	AB	R	H	2B	3B	HR	RBI	BB-IB	HP	SO	AVG	OBP	SLG	AOPS	ABR	SB-CS	FA	FR	RNG	THR	GAMES AT POSITION	DL	BFW
1944	Was A	1	2	0	0	0	0	0	0	0	0	0	.000	.000	.000	-99	-1	0-0	1.000	0	159	0	/3	0	0.0

SUCK, TONY Anthony (b Charles Anthony Zuck); B6.11.1858 Chicago IL; D1.29.1895 Chicago IL; 5´9˝/164; d8.9

YEAR	TM LG	G	AB	R	H	2B	3B	HR	RBI	BB-IB	HP	SO	AVG	OBP	SLG	AOPS	ABR	SB-CS	FA	FR	RNG	THR	GAMES AT POSITION	DL	BFW
1883	Buf N	2	7	1	0	0	0	0	0	1	—	4	.000	.125	.000	-56	-1	—	ø	-2	0	0	/lfC	—	-0.3
1884	CP U	53	188	18	28	2	0	0	—	13	—	—	.149	.204	.160	12	-26	—	.904	-4	—	—	C28,S15,O12(1/10/1)/3	—	-2.5
	Bal U	3	10	2	3	0	0	0	—	0	—	—	.300	.300	.300	75	-1	—	.882	1	—	—	C3	—	0.0
	Year	56	198	20	31	2	0	0	—	13	—	—	.157	.209	.167	15	-27	—	.901	-4	—	—	C31,S15,O12(1/10/1)/3	—	-2.5
Total	2	58	205	21	31	2	0	0	0	14	—	4	.151	.205	.161	13	-28	—	.894	-5	—	—	C32,S15,O13(2/10/1)/3	—	-2.8

SUDAKIS, BILL William Paul "Suds"; B3.27.1946 Joliet IL; BB/TR/6´1˝/(190–195); d9.3

YEAR	TM LG	G	AB	R	H	2B	3B	HR	RBI	BB-IB	HP	SO	AVG	OBP	SLG	AOPS	ABR	SB-CS	FA	FR	RNG	THR	GAMES AT POSITION	DL	BFW
1968	LA N	24	87	11	24	4	2	3	12	15-1	0	14	.276	.382	.471	167	8	1-0	.953	4	116	69	3b24	0	1.3
1969	LA N	132	462	50	108	17	5	14	53	40-5	1	94	.234	.294	.383	95	-5	3-2	.946	10	**110**	136	3b121	0	0.4
1970	LA N	94	269	37	71	11	0	14	44	35-4	3	46	.264	.352	.461	121	8	4-0	.983	-4	54	24	C38,3b37,O3R/1	0	0.6
1971	LA N	41	83	10	16	3	0	3	7	12-2	1	22	.193	.302	.337	85	-2	0-1	1.000	2	143	128	C19,3b/1O(1/0/1)	49	0.1
1972	NY N	18	49	3	7	0	0	1	7	6-0	0	14	.143	.236	.204	27	-5	0-0	.967	1	186	59	1b7,C5	86	-0.5
1973	Tex A	82	235	32	60	11	0	15	43	23-1	0	53	.255	.320	.494	131	9	0-1	.962	-2	89	19	3b29,1b24,C9,O2R,D8	0	0.5
1974	NY A	89	259	26	60	8	0	7	39	25-1	1	48	.232	.296	.344	86	-5	0-0	.990	1	126	120	D39,1b33,3b3/C	0	-0.8
1975	Cal A	30	58	4	7	2	0	1	6	12-3	1	15	.121	.274	.207	43	-4	1-1	.941	-0	14	186	D13,C5,1b2	0	-0.5
	Cle A	20	46	4	9	0	0	1	3	4-1	0	7	.196	.260	.261	47	-3	0-1	1.000	-0	58	118	1b12,C6	0	-0.5
	Year	50	104	8	16	2	0	2	9	16-4	1	22	.154	.268	.231	45	-7	1-2	1.000	-1	50	102	1b14,D13,C11	0	-1.0
Total	8	530	1548	177	362	56	7	59	214	172-18	7	313	.234	.311	.393	102	1	9-6	.942	11	112	116	3b217,C83,1b80,D60,O6(1/0/6)	135	0.6

Suder, Pete Peter "Pecky"; B4.16.1916 Aliquippa PA; D11.14.2006 Aliquippa PA; BR/TR/6´0˝/175; d4.15; Mil 1944–45

YEAR	TM LG	G	AB	R	H	2B	3B	HR	RBI	BB-IB	HP	SO	AVG	OBP	SLG	AOPS	ABR	SB-CS	FA	FR	RNG	THR	GAMES AT POSITION	DL	BFW
1941	Phi A	139	531	45	130	20	9	4	52	19	0	47	.245	.271	.339	62	-33	1-3	.957	-6	97	95	3b136,S3	0	-3.3
1942	Phi A	128	476	46	122	20	4	4	54	24	1	39	.256	.293	.340	78	-16	4-4	.954	-1	97	69	S69,3b34,2b31	0	-0.9
1943	Phi A	131	475	30	105	14	5	3	41	14	0	40	.221	.243	.291	56	-29	1-1	.971	-9	95	84	2b95,3b32,S5	0	-3.6
1946	Phi A	128	455	38	128	20	3	2	50	18	0	37	.281	.309	.352	85	-11	1-1	.959	2	102	85	S67,3b33,2b12,1b3,O2R	0	-0.4
1947	Phi A	145	528	45	127	28	4	5	60	35	2	44	.241	.290	.337	73	-21	0-3	**.986**	-21	97	96	2b140,S3,3b2	0	-3.7
1948	Phi A	148	519	64	125	23	5	7	60	60	1	60	.241	.321	.345	77	-18	1-3	.988	-4	101	103	2b148	0	-1.4
1949	Phi A	118	445	44	119	24	6	10	75	23	2	35	.267	.306	.416	93	-9	0-1	.975	5	107	122	2b89,3b36,S2	0	0.0
1950	Phi A	77	248	34	61	10	0	8	35	23	0	31	.246	.310	.383	78	-9	2-2	.979	2	106	120	2b47,3b11,S10,1b4	0	-0.4
1951	Phi A	123	440	46	108	18	1	1	42	30	1	42	.245	.295	.298	59	-26	5-5	**.987**	11	**107**	**119**	2b103,S18,3b3	0	-0.9
1952	Phi A	74	228	22	55	7	2	1	20	16	0	17	.241	.291	.303	61	-12	1-1	.991	1	98	109	2b43,S17,3b16	0	-0.9
1953	Phi A	115	454	44	130	11	3	4	35	17	0	35	.286	.312	.350	76	-17	3-3	.974	3	109	103	3b72,2b38,S7	0	-1.2
1954	Phi A	69	205	8	41	11	1	0	16	7	0	16	.200	.225	.263	34	-19	0-0	.961	4	105	102	2b35,3b20,S2	0	-1.4
1955	KC A	26	81	3	17	4	1	0	1	2-0	0	13	.210	.229	.284	37	-8	0-1	.990	-2	88	106	2b24	0	-0.9
Total	13	1421	5085	469	1268	210	44	49	541	288-0	7	456	.249	.290	.337	71	-228	19-28	.982	-15	101	103	2b805,3b395,S203,1b7,O2R	0	-19.0

Suero, William Williams (Urban); B11.7.1966 Santo Domingo, D.R.; D11.30.1995 Santo Domingo, D.R.; BR/TR/5´9˝/175; d4.9

YEAR	TM LG	G	AB	R	H	2B	3B	HR	RBI	BB-IB	HP	SO	AVG	OBP	SLG	AOPS	ABR	SB-CS	FA	FR	RNG	THR	GAMES AT POSITION	DL	BFW
1992	Mil A	18	16	4	3	1	0	0	0	2-0	1	1	.188	.316	.250	61	-1	1-1	.971	2	134	154	2b15/SD	0	0.1
1993	Mil A	15	14	0	4	0	0	0	0	1-0	0	3	.286	.333	.286	69	-1	0-1	.944	1	137	50	2b8/3	0	0.0
Total	2	33	30	4	7	1	0	0	0	3-0	1	4	.233	.324	.267	65	-2	1-2	.962	3	135	117	2b23,D2/3S	0	0.1

Sugden, Joe Joseph; B7.31.1870 Philadelphia PA; D6.28.1959 Philadelphia PA; BB/TR/5´10˝/180; d7.20; C7

YEAR	TM LG	G	AB	R	H	2B	3B	HR	RBI	BB-IB	HP	SO	AVG	OBP	SLG	AOPS	ABR	SB-CS	FA	FR	RNG	THR	GAMES AT POSITION	DL	BFW
1893	Pit N	27	92	20	24	4	3	0	12	10	1	11	.261	.340	.370	90	-1	1	.956	1	*99*	*103*	C27	—	0.1
1894	Pit N	39	139	23	46	13	2	2	23	14	3	2	.331	.404	.496	117	4	3	.910	-5	*103*	*89*	C31,3b4,S3/cf	—	0.2
1895	Pit N	50	158	28	48	4	1	1	17	16	3	12	.304	.379	.361	97	0	4	.901	-3	*88*	*122*	C50	—	0.1
1896	Pit N	80	301	42	89	5	7	0	36	19	5	9	.296	.348	.359	90	-5	5	.952	-5	*84*	*100*	C70,1b7,O4C	—	-0.3
1897	Pit N	84	288	31	64	6	4	0	38	18	3	—	.222	.275	.271	46	-23	9	.941	-12	*83*	*94*	C81,1b3	—	-2.4
1898	StL N	89	289	29	73	7	1	0	34	23	3	—	.253	.314	.284	70	-11	5	.937	-6	*74*	*137*	C60,O15(0/1/14),1b8	—	-1.2
1899	Cle N	76	250	19	69	5	1	0	14	11	0	—	.276	.307	.304	73	-10	2	.935	-18	*59*	*129*	C66,O4R,1b3/3	—	-2.0
1901	Chi A	48	153	21	42	7	1	0	19	13	2	—	.275	.339	.333	89	-2	4	.970	5	*115*	*103*	C42,1b5	—	0.7
1902	StL A	68	200	25	50	7	2	0	15	20	4	—	.250	.330	.305	78	-5	2	.956	-0	*110*	*100*	C61,1b4/P	—	0.0
1903	StL A	79	241	18	51	4	0	0	22	25	1	—	.212	.288	.228	58	-11	4	.983	7	*121*	*102*	C66,1b8	—	0.3
1904	StL A	105	348	25	93	6	3	0	30	28	5	—	.267	.331	.302	107	4	6	**.989**	-3	*94*	*100*	C79,1b28	—	0.9
1905	StL A	90	266	21	46	4	0	0	23	23	3	—	.173	.247	.188	41	-17	3	.983	7	*81*	*118*	C76,1b9	—	-0.3
1912	Det A	1	4	1	1	0	0	0	0	0	0	—	.250	.250	.250	44	0	0	.941	1	410	0	/1	—	0.0
Total	13	836	2729	303	696	72	25	3	283	220	33	34	.255	.318	.303	78	-77	48	.957	-32	*91*	*109*	C709,1b76,O24(0/6/18),3b5,S3/P	—	-3.9

Suhr, Gus August Richard; B1.3.1906 San Francisco CA; D1.15.2004 Scottsdale AZ; BL/TR/6´0˝/180; d4.15

YEAR	TM LG	G	AB	R	H	2B	3B	HR	RBI	BB-IB	HP	SO	AVG	OBP	SLG	AOPS	ABR	SB-CS	FA	FR	RNG	THR	GAMES AT POSITION	DL	BFW
1930	Pit N	151	542	93	155	26	14	17	107	80	2	56	.286	.380	.480	106	5	11	.992	-7	83	97	1b151	—	-1.0
1931	Pit N	87	270	26	57	13	4	4	32	38	0	25	.211	.308	.333	73	-10	4	.993	-0	100	118	1b76	—	-1.7
1932	Pit N	**154**	581	78	153	31	16	5	81	63	2	39	.263	.337	.398	99	-1	7	.988	-10	79	92	1b154	—	-2.6
1933	Pit N	**154**	566	72	151	31	11	10	75	72	0	52	.267	.350	.413	117	14	2	.991	-3	91	97	1b154	—	-0.4
1934	Pit N	**151**	573	67	162	36	13	13	103	66	3	52	.283	.360	.459	115	13	4	.994	-4	85	94	1b151	—	-0.5
1935	Pit N	**153**	529	68	144	33	12	10	81	70	0	54	.272	.357	.437	109	8	6	.989	-7	80	86	1b149,O2R	—	-1.2
1936	Pit N☆	**156**	583	111	182	33	12	11	118	95	2	34	.312	.410	.467	133	31	8	**.993**	-5	86	86	1b156	—	1.1
1937	Pit N	151	575	69	160	28	14	5	97	83	0	42	.278	.369	.402	109	10	2	.993	-4	85	94	1b151	—	-0.9
1938	Pit N	145	530	82	156	35	14	3	64	87	0	37	.294	.394	.430	126	22	4	.993	-10	77	**124**	1b145	—	-0.2
1939	Pit N	63	204	23	59	10	2	1	31	25	0	23	.289	.367	.373	101	1	4	.993	-5	66	88	1b52	—	-0.9
	Phi N	60	198	21	63	12	2	3	24	34	1	14	.318	.421	.444	137	12	1	.995	0	98	90	1b60	—	0.7
	Year	123	402	44	122	22	4	4	55	59	1	37	.303	.394	.408	118	13	5	.994	-4	83	89	1b112	—	-0.2
1940	Phi N	10	25	4	4	0	0	2	5	5	0	5	.160	.300	.400	95	0	0	.967	-2	25	96	1b7	—	-0.2
Total	11	1435	5176	714	1446	288	114	84	818	718	10	433	.279	.368	.428	112	105	53	.992	-56	84	97	1b1406,O2R	—	-7.8

Sukeforth, Clyde Clyde Leroy "Sukey"; B11.30.1901 Washington ME; D9.3.2000 Waldoboro ME; BL/TR/5´10˝/155; d5.23; M1/C15; Col Georgetown

YEAR	TM LG	G	AB	R	H	2B	3B	HR	RBI	BB-IB	HP	SO	AVG	OBP	SLG	AOPS	ABR	SB-CS	FA	FR	RNG	THR	GAMES AT POSITION	DL	BFW
1926	Cin N	1	1	0	0	0	0	0	0	0	0	1	.000	.000	.000	-99	0	0	ø	0	—	—	/H	—	0.0
1927	Cin N	38	58	12	11	2	0	0	2	7	0	2	.190	.277	.224	37	-5	2	.970	-0	*81*	*77*	C24	—	-0.4
1928	Cin N	33	53	5	7	2	1	0	3	3	0	5	.132	.179	.208	1	-8	0	.966	0	*99*	*83*	C26	—	-0.7
1929	Cin N	84	237	31	84	16	2	1	33	17	0	6	.354	.398	.451	115	6	8	.981	-2	*109*	*100*	C76	—	0.8
1930	Cin N	94	296	30	84	9	3	1	19	17	1	12	.284	.325	.345	65	-17	1	.976	-2	*92*	*109*	C82	—	-1.2
1931	Cin N	112	351	22	90	15	4	0	25	38	3	13	.256	.334	.322	82	-8	0	.965	-9	*84*	*97*	C106	—	-1.1
1932	Bro N	59	111	14	26	4	4	0	12	6	1	10	.234	.280	.342	68	-6	1	.991	-2	*93*	*89*	C36	—	-0.6
1933	Bro N	20	36	1	2	0	0	0	0	2	0	1	.056	.105	.056	-55	-7	0	.983	2	*85*	*103*	C18	—	-0.5
1934	Bro N	27	43	5	7	1	0	0	1	1	0	6	.163	.182	.186	-1	-6	0	1.000	-0	*83*	*101*	C18	—	-0.6
1945	Bro N	18	51	2	15	1	0	0	1	4	0	1	.294	.345	.314	85	-1	0	.947	-2	*98*	*0*	C13	0	-0.3
Total	10	486	1237	122	326	50	14	2	96	95	5	57	.264	.319	.331	71	-52	12	.974	-16	*92*	*95*	C399	0	-4.6

Sularz, Guy Guy Patrick; B11.7.1955 Minneapolis MN; BR/TR/5´11˝/(165–175); [SFN74 10/235]; d9.2

YEAR	TM LG	G	AB	R	H	2B	3B	HR	RBI	BB-IB	HP	SO	AVG	OBP	SLG	AOPS	ABR	SB-CS	FA	FR	RNG	THR	GAMES AT POSITION	DL	BFW
1980	SF N	25	65	3	16	1	1	0	3	9-1	0	6	.246	.333	.292	80	-2	1-0	.975	7	125	114	2b21,3b5	0	0.7
1981	SF N	10	20	0	4	0	0	0	2	2-0	1	4	.200	.292	.200	47	-1	0-1	1.000	2	118	95	2b6/3	0	0.1
1982	SF N	63	101	15	23	3	0	1	7	9-0	0	11	.228	.291	.287	63	-5	3-0	.961	6	111	166	S37,3b14,2b9	0	0.4
1983	SF N	10	20	3	2	0	0	0	0	3-0	0	2	.100	.217	.100	-10	-3	0-0	.917	1	98	83	S6,3b4	0	-0.1
Total	4	108	206	21	45	4	1	1	12	23-1	1	23	.218	.297	.262	60	-11	4-1	.954	16	109	153	S43,2b36,3b24	0	1.1

Sulik, Ernie Ernest Richard "Dave"; B7.7.1910 San Francisco CA; D5.31.1963 Oakland CA; BL/TL/5´10˝/178; d4.15; Col San Francisco

YEAR	TM LG	G	AB	R	H	2B	3B	HR	RBI	BB-IB	HP	SO	AVG	OBP	SLG	AOPS	ABR	SB-CS	FA	FR	RNG	THR	GAMES AT POSITION	DL	BFW
1936	Phi N	122	404	69	116	14	4	6	36	40	1	22	.287	.353	.386	90	-5	4	.971	-3	97	85	O105(41/65/1)	—	-1.1

Sullivan B Bristol RI; d5.15

YEAR	TM LG	G	AB	R	H	2B	3B	HR	RBI	BB-IB	HP	SO	AVG	OBP	SLG	AOPS	ABR	SB-CS	FA	FR	RNG	THR	GAMES AT POSITION	DL	BFW
1875	NH NA	2	8	3	3	0	0	0	2	0	—	1	.375	.375	.375	185	1	1-0	1.000	-0	0	0	O2R	—	0.1

Sullivan, Andy Andrew Raymond; B8.30.1884 Southborough MA; D2.14.1920 Framingham MA; TR; d9.13

YEAR	TM LG	G	AB	R	H	2B	3B	HR	RBI	BB-IB	HP	SO	AVG	OBP	SLG	AOPS	ABR	SB-CS	FA	FR	RNG	THR	GAMES AT POSITION	DL	BFW
1904	Bos N	1	1	0	0	0	0	0	0	1	0	—	.000	.500	.000	61	0	0	1.000	-0	0	0	/S	—	0.0

Sullivan, Jackie Carl Mancel; B2.22.1918 Princeton TX; D10.15.1992 Dallas TX; BR/TR/5´11˝/172; d7.6

YEAR	TM LG	G	AB	R	H	2B	3B	HR	RBI	BB-IB	HP	SO	AVG	OBP	SLG	AOPS	ABR	SB-CS	FA	FR	RNG	THR	GAMES AT POSITION	DL	BFW
1944	Det A	1	1	0	0	0	0	0	0	0	0	0	.000	.000	.000	-95	0	0-0	1.000	-0	0	0	/2	0	0.0

Sullivan, Cory Cory; B8.20.1979 Tulsa OK; BL/TL/6´0˝/(180–190); [ColN01 7/214]; d4.4; Col Wake Forest; [DL 2004 Col N 140]

YEAR	TM LG	G	AB	R	H	2B	3B	HR	RBI	BB-IB	HP	SO	AVG	OBP	SLG	AOPS	ABR	SB-CS	FA	FR	RNG	THR	GAMES AT POSITION	DL	BFW
2005	Col N	139	378	64	111	15	4	4	30	28-0	3	83	.294	.343	.386	82	-9	12-3	.986	3	103	148	O114(24/83/8)	0	-0.5
2006	Col N	126	386	47	103	26	10	2	30	32-3	1	100	.267	.321	.402	78	-13	10-6	.996	-6	93	83	O114C	0	-1.7
Total	2	265	764	111	214	41	14	6	60	60-3	4	183	.280	.332	.394	80	-22	22-9	.991	-2	98	114	O228(24/197/8)	140	-2.2

Sullivan, Dan Daniel C. "Link"; B5.9.1857 Providence RI; D10.26.1893 Providence RI; TR/5´11˝/194; d5.2

YEAR	TM LG	G	AB	R	H	2B	3B	HR	RBI	BB-IB	HP	SO	AVG	OBP	SLG	AOPS	ABR	SB-CS	FA	FR	RNG	THR	GAMES AT POSITION	DL	BFW
1882	Lou AA	67	286	44	78	8	2	0	—	9	—	—	.273	.295	.315	112	4	—	.878	5	—	—	C54,3b10,O4(0/3/1)/S	—	1.3
1883	Lou AA	36	145	8	31	5	2	0	—	3	—	—	.214	.230	.276	67	-5	—	.900	-6	—	—	C31,O2C,3b2/S	—	-0.7
1884	Lou AA	63	247	27	59	8	6	0	26	9	1	—	.239	.268	.320	95	-1	—	.930	-14	—	—	C63/lf	—	-0.9
1885	Lou AA	13	44	3	8	1	0	0	4	2	1	—	.182	.234	.205	40	-3	—	.948	-2	—	—	C13	—	-0.4
	StL AA	17	60	4	7	2	0	0	3	6	0	—	.117	.197	.150	10	-6	—	.956	2	—	—	C13,1b4	—	-0.3
	Year	30	104	7	15	3	0	0	7	8	1	—	.144	.212	.173	22	-9	—	.952	-0	—	—	C26,1b4	—	-0.7
1886	Pit AA	1	4	0	0	0	0	0	0	0	0	—	.000	.000	.000	-99	-1	0	.600	-1	—	—	/C	—	-0.2
Total	5	197	786	86	183	24	10	0	33	29	2	—	.233	.262	.289	84	-12	0	.909	-16	—	—	C175,3b12,O7(1/5/1),1b4,S2	—	-1.2

Sullivan, Denny Dennis J.; B6.26.1858 Boston MA; D12.31.1925 Boston MA; TR/5´9˝/170; d8.25; Col Holy Cross

YEAR	TM LG	G	AB	R	H	2B	3B	HR	RBI	BB-IB	HP	SO	AVG	OBP	SLG	AOPS	ABR	SB-CS	FA	FR	RNG	THR	GAMES AT POSITION	DL	BFW
1879	Pro N	5	19	5	5	2	0	0	2	1	—	1	.263	.300	.368	121	1	—	.429	-3	63	0	3b4/rf	—	-0.2
1880	Bos N	1	4	1	1	0	0	0	2	0	—	1	.250	.250	.250	72	0	—	.857	-0	—	—	/C	—	-0.1
Total	2	6	23	6	6	2	0	0	4	1	—	2	.261	.292	.348	113	1	—	.429	-4	—	—	3b4/Crf	—	-0.3

YEAR	TM LG	G	AB	R	H	2B	3B	HR	RBI	BB-IB	HP	SO	AVG	OBP	SLG	AOPS	ABR	SB-CS	FA	FR	RNG	THR	GAMES AT POSITION	DL	BFW
SULLIVAN, DENNY	Dennis William; B9.28.1882 Hillsboro WI; D6.2.1956 W.Los Angeles CA; BL/TR/5´10˝/?; d4.22																								
1905	Was A	3	11	0	0	0	0	0	0	1	0	—	.000	.083	.000	-76	-2	0	1.000	-0	0	0	O3R	—	-0.3
1907	Bos A	144	551	73	135	18	0	1	26	44	12	—	.245	.315	.283	92	-3	16	.975	-1	89	79	O143C	—	-1.2
1908	Bos A	101	355	33	85	7	8	0	25	14	4	—	.239	.276	.304	86	-7	4	.981	5	152	132	O97(0/92/5)	—	-0.8
	Cle A	4	6	0	0	0	0	0	0	0	0	—	.000	.000	.000	-99	-1	0	1.000	-0	0	0	O2(1/0/1)	—	-0.2
	Year	105	361	33	85	7	8	0	25	14	4	—	.235	.272	.299	83	-8	4	.982	4	150	130	O99(1/92/6)	—	-1.0
1909	Cle A	3	2	0	1	0	0	0	0	0	0	—	.500	.500	.500	207	0	0	ø	0	0	0	O2R	—	0.0
Total	4	255	925	106	221	25	8	1	51	59	16	—	.239	.296	.286	87	-13	20	.978	3	113	99	O247(1/235/11)	—	-2.5
SULLIVAN, HAYWOOD	Haywood Cooper; B12.15.1930 Donalsonville GA; D2.12.2003 Fort Myers FL; BR/TR/6´4˝/(210–215); d9.20; M1; s–Marc; Col Florida; [DL 1958 Bos A 168]																								
1955	Bos A	2	6	1	0	0	0	0	0	0-0	0	1	.000	.000	.000	-92	-2	0-0	1.000	1	*0*	*0*	C2	0	-0.1
1957	Bos A	2	1	0	0	0	0	0	0	0-0	0	0	.000	.000	.000	-95	0	0-0	1.000	0	0	0	/C	0	0.0
1959	Bos A	4	2	0	0	0	0	0	0	1-0	0	1	.000	.333	.000	-0	0	0-0	1.000	0	0	0	C2	0	0.0
1960	Bos A	52	124	9	20	1	0	3	10	16-2	0	24	.161	.255	.242	35	-12	0-0	.992	3	104	78	C50	0	-0.7
1961	KC A	117	331	42	80	16	2	6	40	46-0	0	45	.242	.333	.356	83	-7	1-0	.984	-3	106	106	C88,1b16,O5(2/0/3)	0	-0.7
1962	KC A	95	274	33	68	7	2	4	29	31-5	1	54	.248	.325	.332	74	-10	1-0	.980	-8	82	80	C94/1	0	-1.4
1963	KC A	40	113	9	24	6	1	0	8	15-2	0	15	.212	.300	.283	62	-5	0-0	.992	2	41	126	C37	0	-0.1
Total	7	312	851	94	192	30	5	13	87	109-9	1	140	.226	.312	.318	69	-36	2-0	.985	-5	*87*	*94*	C274,1b17,O5(2/0/3)	168	-3.0
SULLIVAN, JOHN	John Eugene; B2.16.1873 IL; D6.5.1924 St.Paul MN; BR/TR/5´10˝/170; d4.19																								
1905	Det A	13	32	4	5	0	0	0	4	4	0	—	.156	.250	.156	29	-2	0	.964	1	*80*	*165*	C12	—	-0.1
1908	Pit N	1	1	0	0	0	0	0	0	0	0	—	.000	.000	.000	-99	0	0	1.000	0	*0*	*321*	/C	—	0.0
Total	2	14	33	4	5	0	0	0	4	4	0	—	.152	.243	.152	26	-2	0	.965	1	*78*	*169*	C13	—	-0.1
SULLIVAN, CHUB	John Frank; B1.12.1856 Boston MA; D9.12.1881 Boston MA; BR/TR/6´0˝/164; d9.24																								
1877	Cin N	8	32	4	8	0	0	0	4	1	—	0	.250	.273	.250	74	-1	—	.944	-1	44	24	1b8	—	-0.1
1878	Cin N	**61**	244	29	63	4	2	0	20	2	—	9	.258	.264	.291	91	-2	—	**.975**	5	133	125	1b61	—	0.0
1880	Wor N	43	166	22	43	6	3	0	0	4	—	6	.259	.276	.331	97	-1	—	.983	3	108	104	1b43	—	0.0
Total	3	112	442	55	114	10	5	0	24	7	—	15	.258	.269	.303	92	-4	—	.976	7	118	110	1b112	—	-0.1
SULLIVAN, JOHN	John Lawrence; B3.21.1890 Williamsport PA; D4.1.1966 Milton PA; BR/TR/5´11˝/180; d4.18																								
1920	Bos N	81	250	36	74	14	4	1	28	29	2	29	.296	.374	.396	126	10	3-2	.977	-2	89	123	O66(16/5/45),1b6	—	0.5
1921	Bos N	5	5	0	0	0	0	0	0	0	0	0	.000	.000	.000	-99	-1	0-0	ø	0	—	—	/H	—	-0.1
	Chi N	76	240	28	79	14	4	4	41	19	1	26	.329	.381	.471	124	9	3-5	.962	-5	94	40	O66(63/1/1)	—	-0.2
	Year	81	245	28	79	14	4	4	41	19	1	26	.322	.374	.461	120	7	3-5	.962	-5	94	40	O66(63/1/1)	—	-0.3
Total	2	162	495	64	153	28	8	5	69	48	3	55	.309	.374	.428	123	18	6-7	.969	-7	91	83	O132(79/6/46),1b6	—	0.2
SULLIVAN, JOHN	John Paul; B11.2.1920 Chicago IL; BR/TR/5´10˝/170; d6.7; Mil 1945–46; C15; Col Wisconsin–Madison																								
1942	Was A	94	357	38	84	16	1	0	42	25	0	30	.235	.285	.286	61	-19	2-0	.936	-10	90	81	S92	0	-2.3
1943	Was A	134	456	49	95	12	2	1	55	57	1	59	.208	.298	.250	63	-20	6-2	.946	9	**109**	99	S133	0	0.0
1944	Was A	138	471	49	118	12	1	0	30	52	0	43	.251	.325	.280	77	-13	3-3	.934	-13	94	94	S138	0	-1.5
1947	Was A	49	133	13	34	0	1	0	5	22	0	14	.256	.361	.271	79	-3	0-2	.963	2	104	91	S40/2	0	0.1
1948	Was A	85	173	25	36	4	1	0	12	22	0	25	.208	.297	.243	46	-13	2-2	.951	-3	98	91	S57,2b4	0	-1.3
1949	StL A	105	243	29	55	8	3	0	18	38	0	35	.226	.331	.284	61	-13	5-2	.942	-7	91	78	S71,3b23,2b6	0	-1.6
Total	6	605	1833	203	422	52	9	1	162	216	1	206	.230	.312	.270	66	-81	18-11	.942	-22	98	91	S531,3b23,2b11	0	-6.6
SULLIVAN, JOHN	John Peter; B1.3.1941 Somerville NJ; BL/TR/6´0˝/(190–195); d9.20																								
1963	Det A	3	5	0	0	0	0	0	0	2-0	0	1	.000	.286	.000	-11	-1	0-0	1.000	-0	51	0	C2	0	-0.1
1964	Det A	2	3	0	0	0	0	0	0	0-0	0	1	.000	.000	.000	-99	-1	0-0	1.000	-1	0	905	C2	0	-0.1
1965	Det A	34	86	5	23	0	0	2	11	9-0	1	13	.267	.340	.337	93	-1	0-0	.994	-0	221	111	C29	0	0.1
1967	NY N	65	147	4	32	5	0	0	6	6-3	0	26	.218	.248	.252	44	-11	0-2	.991	-6	60	119	C57	0	-1.7
1968	Phi N	12	18	0	4	0	0	0	1	2-0	0	4	.222	.300	.222	59	-1	0-0	.967	1	0	191	C8	0	0.0
Total	5	116	259	9	59	5	0	2	18	19-3	1	45	.228	.282	.270	59	-15	0-2	.991	-5	116	131	C98	0	-1.8
SULLIVAN, JOE	Joseph Daniel; B1.6.1870 Charlestown MA; D11.2.1897 Charlestown MA; 5´10˝/178; d4.27																								
1893	Was N	128	508	72	134	16	13	2	64	36	8	24	.264	.322	.358	83	-14	7	.860	-29	91	56	S128	—	-3.0
1894	Was N	17	60	7	15	3	0	0	5	6	4	2	.250	.357	.300	62	-3	3	.900	-2	106	24	2b8,S6/3rf	—	-0.4
	Phi N	77	312	65	110	10	8	3	63	24	5	10	.353	.408	.465	112	6	12	.886	-18	85	99	S77	—	-0.6
	Year	94	372	72	125	13	8	3	68	30	9	12	.336	.399	.438	104	3	15	.883	-20	84	96	S83,2b8/3rf	—	-1.0
1895	Phi N	94	373	75	126	7	3	2	50	24	11	20	.338	.395	.389	102	2	15	.879	-19	89	83	S89,O6(3/2/1)	—	-1.1
1896	Phi N	48	191	45	48	5	3	2	24	18	10	12	.251	.347	.340	82	-4	9	.962	-3	52	0	O45(8/37/0),S2/3	—	-0.8
	StL N	51	212	25	62	4	2	2	21	9	10	12	.292	.351	.358	91	-3	5	.955	-4	66	60	O45L,2b7/3	—	-0.8
	Year	99	403	70	110	9	5	4	45	27	20	24	.273	.349	.350	87	-7	14	.959	-6	59	31	O90(53/37/0),2b7,S2,3b2	—	-1.6
Total	4	415	1656	289	495	45	29	11	227	117	48	80	.299	.362	.381	93	-16	51	.871	-74	88	75	S302,O97(56/39/2),2b15,3b3	—	-6.7
SULLIVAN, MARC	Marc Cooper; B7.25.1958 Quincy MA; BR/TR/6´4˝/(198–213); [BosA79 2/52]; d10.1; f–Haywood; Col Florida																								
1982	Bos A	2	6	0	2	0	0	0	0	0-0	0	2	.333	.333	.333	79	0	0-0	1.000	1	0	166	C2	0	0.1
1984	Bos A	2	6	1	3	0	0	0	1	1-0	0	0	.500	.571	.500	190	1	0-0	.950	1	114	0	C2	0	0.2
1985	Bos A	32	69	10	12	2	0	2	3	6-0	0	15	.174	.240	.290	42	-6	0-0	.993	-2	140	105	C32	46	-0.6
1986	Bos A	41	119	15	23	4	0	1	14	7-0	4	32	.193	.260	.252	40	-10	0-0	.986	-7	102	59	C41	0	-1.5
1987	Bos A	60	160	11	27	5	0	2	10	4-0	2	43	.169	.198	.237	15	-20	0-0	.994	-3	109	140	C60	0	-2.0
Total	5	137	360	37	67	11	0	5	28	18-0	6	92	.186	.236	.258	33	-35	0-0	.990	-10	112	105	C137	46	-3.8
SULLIVAN, MARTY	Martin C.; B10.20.1862 Lowell MA; D1.6.1894 Lowell MA; BR/TR; d4.30																								
1887	Chi N	115	472	98	134	13	16	7	77	36	4	53	.284	.340	.424	98	-4	35	.847	-9	47	0	O115(111/3/1)/P	—	-1.4
1888	Chi N	75	314	40	74	12	6	7	39	15	1	32	.236	.273	.379	99	-2	9	.927	3	102	272	O75(74/1/0)	—	-0.1
1889	Ind N	69	256	45	73	11	3	4	35	50	1	31	.285	.404	.398	121	10	15	.910	-6	74	176	O64(0/63/1),1b5	—	0.1
1890	Bos N	121	505	82	144	19	7	6	61	56	0	48	.285	.357	.386	108	4	33	.951	4	64	26	O120L/3	—	0.4
1891	Bos N	17	67	15	15	1	0	2	7	5	1	3	.224	.288	.328	71	-3	7	.926	-1	43	0	O17L	—	-0.4
	Cle N	1	4	0	1	0	0	0	1	0	0	1	.250	.250	.250	44	0	0	ø	0	0	0	/rf	—	0.0
	Year	18	71	15	16	1	0	2	8	5	1	4	.225	.286	.324	69	-3	7	.926	-1	43	0	O18(17/0/1)	—	-0.4
Total	5	398	1618	280	441	56	32	26	220	162	7	168	.273	.341	.395	104	5	99	.909	-9	67	89	O392(322/67/3),1b5/3P	—	-1.4
SULLIVAN, MIKE	Michael Joseph; B6.10.1860 Webster MA; D6.16.1929 Webster MA; BR/TR/5´8.5˝/165; d4.26																								
1888	Phi AA	28	112	20	31	5	6	1	19	3	0	—	.277	.296	.455	140	4	10	.742	-7	36	0	O18(16/0/2),3b10	—	-0.3
SULLIVAN, PAT	Patrick B.; B5.1861 Milwaukee WI; D4.14.1901 Milwaukee WI; TR/5´11˝/165; d7.17																								
1884	KC U	31	114	15	22	3	1	0	—	4	—	—	.193	.220	.237	44	-11	—	.767	1	108	231	3b21,O9(1/8/0)/CP	—	-0.8
SULLIVAN, RUSS	Russell Guy; B2.19.1923 Fredericksburg VA; BL/TR/6´0˝/(195–196); d9.8																								
1951	Det A	7	26	2	5	1	0	1	1	2	0	1	.192	.250	.346	60	-2	0-0	.938	0	91	187	O7(6/0/1)	0	-0.2
1952	Det A	15	52	7	17	2	1	3	5	3	1	5	.327	.375	.577	161	4	1-0	.826	-1	75	227	O14(6/0/9)	0	0.2
1953	Det A	23	72	7	18	5	1	1	6	13	2	5	.250	.379	.389	109	2	0-0	.958	2	98	261	O20L	0	0.2
Total	3	45	150	16	40	8	2	5	12	18	3	11	.267	.357	.447	118	4	1-0	.920	1	90	238	O41(32/0/10)	0	0.2
SULLIVAN, SUTER	Suter Grant; B10.14.1872 Baltimore MD; D4.19.1925 Baltimore MD; 6´0˝/170; d7.24																								
1898	StL N	42	144	10	32	3	0	0	12	13	3	—	.222	.300	.243	55	-8	1	.875	-10	78	59	S23,O10R,2b6/1P	—	-1.6
1899	Cle N	127	473	37	116	16	3	0	55	25	10	—	.245	.297	.292	67	-21	16	.938	12	115	118	3b101,O20(1/0/20),S3,1b3,2b2	—	-0.8
Total	2	169	617	47	148	19	3	0	67	38	13	—	.240	.298	.280	64	-29	17	.938	2	115	118	3b101,O30(1/0/30),S26,2b8,1b4/P	—	-2.4
SULLIVAN, TOM	Thomas Brandon; B12.19.1906 Nome AK; D8.16.1944 Seattle WA; BR/TR/6´0˝/190; d6.14																								
1925	Cin N	1	1	0	0	0	0	0	0	0	0	0	.000	.000	.000	-99	0	0-0	1.000	-0	*0*	*0*	/C	—	0.0

YEAR	TM LG	G	AB	R	H	2B	3B	HR	RBI	BB-IB	HP	SO	AVG	OBP	SLG	AOPS	ABR	SB-CS	FA	FR	RNG	THR	GAMES AT POSITION	DL	BFW
SULLIVAN, SLEEPER	Thomas Jefferson "Old Iron Hands"; B1859 , Ireland; D10.13.1909 St.Louis MO; BR/TR/?/175; d5.3																								
1881	Buf N	35	121	13	23	4	0	0	15	1	—	21	.190	.197	.223	32	-9	—	.853	-11	—	—	C31,O5(0/2/4)	—	-1.9
1882	StL AA	51	188	24	34	3	3	0	—	3	—	—	.181	.194	.229	40	-12	—	.840	-18	—	—	C51	—	-2.4
1883	StL AA	8	27	2	6	0	1	0	—	0	—	—	.222	.222	.296	62	-1	—	.939	3	—	—	C6,O2(0/1/1)	—	0.2
	Lou AA	1	2	0	0	0	0	0	—	0	—	—	.000	.000	.000	-99	0	—	.667	-0	—	—	/C	—	-0.1
	Year	9	29	2	6	0	1	0	—	0	—	—	.207	.207	.276	52	-2	—	.923	3	—	—	C7,O2(0/1/1)	—	0.1
1884	StL U	2	9	0	1	0	0	0	—	0	—	—	.111	.111	.111	-31	-2	—	ø	-1	0	0	/rfCP	—	-0.1
Total	4	97	347	39	64	7	4	0	15	4	—	21	.184	.194	.228	36	-24	—	.851	-27	—	—	C90,O8(0/3/6)/P	—	-4.3
SULLIVAN, TED	Timothy Paul; B1851 Co. Clare, Ireland; D7.5.1929 Washington DC; d9.9; M3/U2																								
1884	KC U	3	9	0	3	0	0	0	—	1	—	—	.333	.400	.333	143	0	—	1.000	-1	0	0	O2R/SM	—	-0.1
SULLIVAN, BILL	William; B7.4.1853 , Ireland; D11.13.1884 Holyoke MA; d8.9																								
1878	Chi N	2	6	1	1	0	0	0	0	0	—	0	.167	.167	.167	9	-1	—	1.000	-0	0	0	O2L	—	-0.1
SULLIVAN, BILLY	William Joseph Jr.; B10.23.1910 Chicago IL; D1.4.1994 Sarasota FL; BL/TR/6´0˝/170; d6.9; Mil 1944–46; f–Billy; Col Notre Dame/Portland; OF(33/0/33)																								
1931	Chi A	92	363	48	100	16	5	2	33	20	1	14	.275	.315	.364	83	-10	4-4	.912	-6	97	58	3b83,O2R/1	—	-1.3
1932	Chi A	93	307	31	97	16	1	1	45	20	0	9	.316	.358	.384	99	-1	1-3	.990	-2	114	95	1b52,3b17,C5,O3(1/0/2)	—	-0.7
1933	Chi A	54	125	9	24	0	1	0	13	10	0	5	.192	.252	.208	24	-14	0-0	.982	-3	108	138	1b22,C8	—	-1.8
1935	Cin N	85	241	29	64	9	4	2	36	19	2	16	.266	.324	.361	87	-5	4	.992	3	135	125	1b40,3b15,2b6	—	-0.4
1936	Cle A	93	319	39	112	32	6	2	48	16	0	9	.351	.382	.508	117	8	5-2	.968	-1	96	117	C72,3b5,1b3/O(1/0/1)	—	1.1
1937	Cle A	72	168	26	48	12	3	3	22	17	1	7	.286	.355	.446	100	0	1-4	.949	-5	81	116	C38,1b5/3	—	-0.4
1938	StL A	111	375	35	104	16	1	7	49	20	1	10	.277	.316	.381	74	-17	8-5	**.990**	0	77	**123**	C99,1b6	—	-1.0
1939	StL A	118	332	53	96	17	5	5	50	34	4	18	.289	.362	.416	96	-2	3-3	.954	1	104	152	O59(31/0/28),C19,1b4	—	-0.4
1940	†Det A	78	220	36	68	14	4	3	41	31	2	11	.309	.399	.450	109	4	2-0	.976	3	104	99	C57,3b6	—	1.0
1941	Det A	85	234	29	66	15	1	3	29	35	0	11	.282	.375	.393	94	-1	0-3	.976	3	90	77	C63	0	0.5
1942	Bro N	43	101	11	27	2	1	1	14	12	0	6	.267	.345	.337	98	0	1	.962	0	153	77	C41	0	0.2
1947	Pit N	38	55	1	14	3	0	0	8	6	0	3	.255	.328	.309	68	-2	1	1.000	0	93	90	C12	0	-0.1
Total	12	962	2840	347	820	152	32	29	388	240	11	119	.289	.346	.395	91	-40	30-24	.972	-7	94	102	C414,1b133,3b127,O65L,2b6	0	-3.3
SULLIVAN, BILLY	William Joseph Sr.; B2.1.1875 Oakland WI; D1.28.1965 Newberg OR; BR/TR/5´9˝/155; d9.13; M1; s–Billy																								
1899	Bos N	22	74	10	20	2	0	2	12	1	3	—	.270	.308	.378	80	-2	2	.952	4	120	87	C22	—	0.3
1900	Bos N	72	238	36	65	6	0	8	41	9	1	—	.273	.302	.399	83	-7	4	.974	4	101	85	C66/S2	—	0.2
1901	Chi A	98	367	54	90	15	6	4	56	10	3	—	.245	.271	.351	74	-15	12	**.967**	5	**110**	98	C97/3	—	0.0
1902	Chi A	76	263	36	64	12	3	1	26	6	3	—	.243	.268	.323	66	-13	11	.967	4	121	106	C70,1b2,O2(1/0/1)	—	-0.2
1903	Chi A	32	111	10	21	4	0	1	7	5	0	—	.189	.224	.252	45	-7	3	.988	-1	108	104	C31	—	-0.5
1904	Chi A	108	371	29	85	18	4	1	44	12	1	—	.229	.255	.307	81	-9	11	.964	6	128	107	C107	—	0.9
1905	Chi A	98	323	25	65	10	3	2	26	13	3	—	.201	.239	.269	64	-14	14	.974	3	**127**	94	C92,1b2/3	—	-0.3
1906	†Chi A	118	387	37	83	18	4	2	33	22	3	—	.214	.262	.297	77	-11	10	**.974**	6	**145**	92	C118	—	0.7
1907	Chi A	112	329	30	59	8	4	0	36	21	3	—	.179	.235	.228	49	-19	6	.983	2	**118**	92	C108/2	—	-0.8
1908	Chi A	137	430	40	82	8	4	0	29	22	3	—	.191	.235	.228	51	-24	15	**.985**	-12	109	97	C137	—	-2.7
1909	Chi A	97	265	11	43	3	0	0	16	17	5	—	.162	.226	.174	28	-22	9	.983	1	96	98	C97,M	—	-1.3
1910	Chi A	45	142	10	26	4	1	0	6	7	1	—	.183	.227	.225	43	-10	0	.976	9	130	92	C45	—	0.4
1911	Chi A	89	256	26	55	9	3	0	31	16	2	—	.215	.266	.273	52	-17	1	**.986**	7	**147**	91	C89	—	-0.3
1912	Chi A	41	91	9	19	2	1	0	15	9	1	—	.209	.287	.253	57	-5	0	.975	1	97	105	C41	—	-0.1
1914	Chi A	1	0	0	0	0	0	0	0	0	0	0	ø	ø	ø	ø	0	0	1.000	-0	0	0	/C	—	0.0
1916	Det A	1	0	0	0	0	0	0	0	0	0	0	ø	ø	ø	ø	0	0	ø	-0	0	0	/C	—	0.0
Total	16	1147	3647	363	777	119	33	21	378	170	32	0	.213	.254	.281	63	-175	98	.976	39	120	96	C1122,1b4,O2(1/0/1),3b2,2b2/S	—	-3.7
SUMMA, HOMER	Homer Wayne; B11.3.1898 Gentry MO; D1.29.1966 Los Angeles CA; BL/TR/5´10.5˝/170; d9.13; Col Missouri																								
1920	Pit N	10	22	1	7	1	1	0	1	3	0	1	.318	.400	.455	141	1	1-0	.950	0	112	110	O6(1/5/0)	—	0.2
1922	Cle A	12	46	9	16	3	3	1	6	1	3	1	.348	.400	.609	159	4	1-2	1.000	1	78	271	O12R	—	0.3
1923	Cle A	137	525	92	172	27	6	3	69	33	6	20	.328	.374	.419	109	6	9-13	.951	-12	81	84	O136(0/3/133)	—	-1.9
1924	Cle A	111	390	55	113	21	6	2	38	11	1	16	.290	.311	.390	79	-15	4-2	.941	-3	101	81	O95(0/3/92)	—	-2.3
1925	Cle A	75	224	28	74	10	1	0	25	13	3	6	.330	.375	.384	92	-2	3-2	.966	-5	94	42	O54(18/1/35),3b2	—	-1.0
1926	Cle A	**154**	581	74	179	31	6	4	76	47	8	9	.308	.368	.403	100	0	15-8	.975	6	109	102	O154R	—	-0.6
1927	Cle A	145	574	72	164	41	7	4	74	32	7	18	.286	.331	.402	89	-11	6-5	.955	-9	89	78	O145(0/1/144)	—	-3.0
1928	Cle A	134	504	60	143	26	3	3	57	20	6	15	.284	.319	.365	78	-17	4-2	.971	-6	90	88	O132R	—	-3.3
1929	†Phi A	37	81	12	22	4	0	0	10	2	1	1	.272	.298	.321	57	-5	1-1	.980	1	126	53	O24(18/0/16)	—	-0.5
1930	Phi A	25	54	10	15	2	1	1	5	4	1	1	.278	.339	.407	85	-1	0-0	.938	0	117	87	O15(3/0/12)	—	-0.2
Total	10	840	3001	413	905	166	34	18	361	166	36	88	.302	.346	.398	92	-40	44-35	.961	-27	95	87	O773(40/13/730),3b2	—	-12.3
SUMMERS, CHAMP	John Junior; B6.15.1946 Bremerton WA; BL/TR/6´2˝/(200–210); d5.4; C2; Col Southern Illinois Edwardsville																								
1974	Oak A	20	24	2	3	1	0	0	3	1-0	0	5	.125	.160	.167	-6	-3	0-0	1.000	-1	78	0	O12(8/0/4),D2	0	-0.4
1975	Chi N	76	91	14	21	5	1	1	16	10-0	1	13	.231	.311	.341	78	-3	0-0	.889	-2	80	0	O18(15/0/3)	0	-0.5
1976	Chi N	83	126	11	26	2	0	3	13	13-1	1	31	.206	.284	.294	59	-7	1-0	.964	-1	87	90	O26(19/0/7),1b10/C	0	-1.0
1977	Cin N	59	76	11	13	4	0	3	6	6-1	1	16	.171	.238	.342	53	-5	0-0	1.000	1	113	127	O16(3/0/13)/3	0	-0.5
1978	Cin N	13	35	4	9	2	0	1	3	7-1	0	4	.257	.381	.400	118	1	2-1	.933	-2	67	0	O12R	0	-0.2
1979	Cin N	27	60	10	12	2	1	1	11	13-0	1	15	.200	.351	.317	84	-1	0-1	.941	-1	74	119	O13(4/0/9),1b6	0	-0.3
	Det A	90	246	47	77	12	1	20	51	40-4	3	33	.313	.414	.614	168	24	7-6	.989	-8	75	70	O69(2/0/67),D10,1b4	0	1.2
1980	Det A	120	347	61	103	19	1	17	60	52-6	5	52	.297	.393	.504	141	22	4-3	.953	-5	81	37	D64,O47(21/0/26)/1	0	1.3
1981	Det A	64	165	16	42	8	0	3	21	19-3	3	35	.255	.339	.358	98	0	1-1	.964	-1	92	99	D37,O18R	15	-0.2
1982	SF N	70	125	15	31	5	0	4	19	16-0	3	17	.248	.342	.384	105	1	0-1	.913	-3	74	89	O31(30/0/1),1b3	0	-0.4
1983	SF N	29	22	3	3	0	0	0	3	7-0	0	8	.136	.333	.136	39	-1	0-0	1.000	0	179	0	/lf	66	-0.1
1984	†SD N	47	54	5	10	3	0	1	12	4-1	1	15	.185	.254	.296	54	-3	0-0	1.000	-1	30	196	1b8	0	-0.5
Total	11	698	1371	199	350	63	4	54	218	188-17	19	244	.255	.350	.425	111	25	15-13	.959	-22	80	67	O263(103/0/160),D113,1b32/3C	81	-1.6
SUMMERS, KID	William; B1868 Toronto ON, Can.; D10.16.1895 Toronto ON, Can.; BR/TR/5´10˝/169; d8.5																								
1893	StL N	2	1	1	0	0	0	0	0	0	1	0	.000	.500	.000	37	0	0	.500	-1	0	0	/lfC	—	0.0
SUMNER, CARL	Carl Ringdahl "Lefty"; B9.28.1908 Cambridge MA; D2.8.1999 Chatham MA; BL/TL/5´8˝/170; d7.28																								
1928	Bos A	16	29	6	8	1	1	0	3	5	0	6	.276	.382	.379	103	0	0-0	.923	-1	86	0	O10(5/4/1)	—	-0.1
SUNDAY, ART	Arthur (b August Hawker); B1.21.1862 Springfield IL; D10.2.1926 Reno NV; BL/TL/5´9˝/193; d5.5																								
1890	Bro P	24	83	26	22	5	1	0	13	15	7	9	.265	.419	.349	100	1	0	.909	-3	57	0	O24(0/5/20)	—	-0.1
SUNDAY, BILLY	William Ashley "Parson","The Evangelist"; B11.19.1862 Ames IA; D11.6.1935 Chicago IL; BL/TR/5´10˝/160; d5.22																								
1883	Chi N	14	54	6	13	4	0	0	5	1	—	18	.241	.255	.315	66	-2	—	.647	-3	43	0	O14(1/0/13)	—	-0.5
1884	Chi N	43	176	25	39	4	1	4	28	4	—	36	.222	.239	.324	70	-7	—	.663	-9	94	72	O43(0/9/34)	—	-1.5
1885	†Chi N	46	172	36	44	3	3	2	20	12	—	33	.256	.304	.343	96	-2	—	.825	-5	81	222	O46(1/4/43)	—	-0.7
1886	Chi N	28	103	16	25	2	2	0	6	7	—	26	.243	.291	.301	70	-4	10	.914	-1	49	0	O28(1/0/27)	—	-0.5
1887	Chi N	50	199	41	58	6	6	3	32	21	1	20	.291	.362	.427	105	0	34	.766	-10	42	119	O50(2/23/25)	—	-0.9
1888	Pit N	120	505	69	119	14	3	0	15	12	2	36	.236	.256	.275	76	-13	71	.939	15	133	125	O120(1/117/3)	—	-0.2
1889	Pit N	81	321	62	77	10	6	2	25	27	4	33	.240	.307	.327	84	-7	47	.946	8	110	73	O81(1/0/80)	—	0.0
1890	Pit N	86	358	58	92	9	2	1	33	32	5	20	.257	.327	.302	94	-1	56	.883	8	150	217	O86(0/51/35)/P	—	0.5
	Phi N	31	119	26	31	3	1	0	6	18	2	7	.261	.367	.303	93	0	28	.950	2	129	174	O31C	—	0.1
	Year	117	477	84	123	12	3	1	39	50	7	27	.258	.337	.302	94	-1	84	.900	10	145	**206**	O117(0/82/35)/P	—	0.6
Total	8	499	2007	339	498	55	24	12	170	134	14	229	.248	.300	.317	86	-36	246	.883	4	108	129	O499(7/235/260)/P	—	-3.7
SUNDBERG, JIM	James Howard; B5.18.1951 Galesburg IL; BR/TR/6´0˝/(190–196); [TexA73*S1/2]; d4.4; Col Iowa																								
1974	Tex A☆	132	368	45	91	13	3	3	36	62-0	0	61	.247	.354	.323	99	2	2-4	.990	6	114	93	C132	0	1.3
1975	Tex A	155	472	45	94	9	0	6	36	51-0	4	77	.199	.283	.256	54	-29	3-1	.981	10	135	103	C155	0	-1.2
1976	Tex A	140	448	33	102	24	2	3	34	37-0	0	61	.228	.285	.310	73	-15	0-0	**.991**	**20**	127	112	C140	0	1.2
1977	Tex A	149	453	61	132	20	3	6	65	53-0	2	77	.291	.365	.389	105	5	2-3	**.994**	**32**	**197**	100	C149	0	4.2
1978	Tex A★	149	518	54	144	23	6	6	58	64-6	3	70	.278	.358	.380	108	7	2-5	**.997**	17	118	126	C148/D	0	3.0

YEAR	TM LG	G	AB	R	H	2B	3B	HR	RBI	BB-IB	HP	SO	AVG	OBP	SLG	AOPS	ABR	SB-CS	FA	FR	RNG	THR	GAMES AT POSITION	DL	BFW
1979	Tex A	150	495	50	136	23	4	5	64	51-5	5	51	.275	.345	.368	94	-3	3-3	**.995**	15	127	100	C150	0	1.8
1980	Tex A	151	505	59	138	24	1	10	63	64-3	1	67	.273	.353	.384	106	6	2-2	.993	-1	92	104	C151	0	1.1
1981	Tex A	102	339	42	94	17	2	3	28	50-6	1	48	.277	.369	.366	119	11	2-5	.996	3	146	107	C98,O2L	0	1.7
1982	Tex A	139	470	37	118	22	5	10	47	49-2	1	57	.251	.322	.383	97	-2	2-6	.991	4	104	113	C132/lf	0	0.6
1983	Tex A	131	378	30	76	14	0	2	28	35-0	2	64	.201	.272	.254	46	-27	0-4	.993	4	101	**132**	C131	0	-1.9
1984	Mil A★	110	348	43	91	19	4	7	43	38-2	0	63	.261	.332	.399	106	3	1-1	**.995**	12	142	129	C109	26	1.9
1985	†KC A	115	367	38	90	12	4	10	35	33-3	1	67	.245	.308	.381	87	-7	0-2	.992	2	114	73	C112	0	-0.1
1986	KC A	140	429	41	91	9	1	12	42	57-1	0	91	.212	.303	.322	69	-18	1-1	**.995**	-1	118	102	C134	0	-1.4
1987	Chi N	61	139	9	28	2	0	4	15	19-3	2	40	.201	.306	.302	60	-8	0-0	.994	4	90	108	C57	0	-0.2
1988	Chi N	24	54	8	13	1	0	2	9	8-0	0	15	.241	.333	.370	99	0	0-0	1.000	-2	99	116	C20	0	-0.1
	Tex A	38	91	13	26	4	0	4	13	5-0	0	17	.286	.323	.462	114	1	0-0	1.000	-4	95	76	C36	0	-0.1
1989	Tex A	76	147	13	29	7	1	2	8	23-0	0	37	.197	.304	.299	70	-5	0-0	.992	-1	107	127	C73/D	0	-0.3
Total	16	1962	6021	621	1493	243	36	95	624	699-31	22	963	.248	.327	.348	89	-79	20-37	.993	121	123	107	C1927,O3L,D2	26	11.5

SURHOFF, B.J. William James; B8.4.1964 Bronx NY; BL/TR/6´1˝/(190–215); [MilA85 1/1]; d4.8; b–Rich; Col North Carolina; OF(904/5/94)

YEAR	TM LG	G	AB	R	H	2B	3B	HR	RBI	BB-IB	HP	SO	AVG	OBP	SLG	AOPS	ABR	SB-CS	FA	FR	RNG	THR	GAMES AT POSITION	DL	BFW
1987	Mil A	115	395	50	118	22	3	7	68	36-1	0	30	.299	.350	.423	103	2	11-10	.984	8	105	116	C98,3b10/1D	0	1.3
1988	Mil A	139	493	47	121	21	0	5	38	31-9	3	49	.245	.292	.318	71	-20	21-6	.990	0	113	89	C106,3b31,1b2/Slf	0	-1.1
1989	Mil A	126	436	42	108	17	4	5	55	25-1	3	29	.248	.287	.339	78	-14	14-12	.985	-3	84	88	C106,D12,3b6	0	-1.3
1990	Mil A	135	474	55	131	21	4	6	59	41-5	1	37	.276	.331	.376	99	-1	18-7	.985	-5	84	78	C125,3b11	0	0.3
1991	Mil A	143	505	57	146	19	4	5	68	26-2	0	33	.289	.319	.372	94	-6	5-8	.995	1	88	91	C127,3b5,O2(0/1/1)/2D	0	0.0
1992	Mil A	139	480	63	121	19	1	4	62	46-8	2	41	.252	.314	.321	81	-12	14-8	.990	13	122	107	C109,1b17,O7(5/1/1),3b3,D9	0	0.7
1993	Mil A	148	552	66	151	38	3	7	79	36-5	2	47	.274	.318	.391	91	-7	12-9	.949	-2	100	92	3b121,O24(12/0/14),1b8,C3/D	0	-1.0
1994	Mil A	40	134	20	35	11	2	5	22	16-0	0	14	.261	.336	.485	104	1	0-1	.923	-9	53	0	3b18,C12,1b8,O3R/D	82	-0.8
1995	Mil A	117	415	72	133	26	3	13	73	37-4	4	43	.320	.378	.492	118	11	7-3	.993	6	107	232	O60(54/3/9),1b55,C18,D3	0	1.2
1996	†Bal A	143	537	74	157	27	6	21	82	47-8	3	79	.292	.352	.482	109	6	0-1	.948	-7	90	118	3b106,O27L,D10,1b2	15	-0.2
1997	†Bal A	147	528	80	150	30	4	18	88	49-14	5	60	.284	.345	.458	112	9	1-1	.992	4	99	136	O133L,1b3,3b3,D9	0	0.7
1998	Bal A	**162**	573	79	160	34	1	22	92	49-9	1	81	.279	.332	.457	106	4	9-7	.989	-4	87	137	O157L/1	0	-0.5
1999	Bal A★	**162**	673	104	207	38	1	28	107	43-1	2	78	.308	.347	.492	116	14	5-1	**1.000**	7	96	171	O148L,D13,3b2	0	1.4
2000	Bal A	103	411	56	120	27	0	13	57	29-3	2	46	.292	.341	.453	104	2	7-2	.987	4	107	83	O102L/D	0	0.2
	†Atl N	44	128	13	37	9	2	1	11	12-0	1	12	.289	.352	.414	94	-1	3-0	1.000	-2	87	52	O32L	0	-0.3
2001	†Atl N	141	484	68	131	33	1	10	58	38-5	1	48	.271	.321	.405	86	-10	9-3	.986	-3	91	99	O129L,D3	0	-1.6
2002	Atl N	25	75	5	22	5	0	0	9	9-0	0	5	.293	.369	.360	93	0	1-3	1.000	3	105	140	1b11,O9R	155	0.1
2003	Bal A	93	319	32	94	20	0	5	41	29-3	1	29	.295	.353	.404	101	1	2-2	.978	-4	80	0	D39,O27(24/0/3),1b22	42	-0.8
2004	Bal A	100	343	49	106	12	1	8	50	30-2	1	46	.309	.365	.420	105	3	2-0	.986	1	103	75	O70(34/0/38),D18,1b10	38	0.0
2005	Bal A	91	303	30	78	11	2	5	34	11-1	1	32	.257	.282	.356	70	-14	0-0	.991	1	103	101	O60(46/0/16),1b18,D7	33	-1.6
Total	19	2313	8258	1062	2326	440	42	188	1153	640-81	33	839	.282	.332	.413	98	-32	141-84	.989	7	96	124	O991L,C704,3b316,1b158,D139/2S	365	-3.3

SUSCE, GEORGE George Cyril Methodius "Good Kid"; B8.13.1907 Pittsburgh PA; D2.25.1986 Sarasota FL; BR/TR/5´11.5˝/200; d4.23; C29; s–George; Col St. Bonaventure

YEAR	TM LG	G	AB	R	H	2B	3B	HR	RBI	BB-IB	HP	SO	AVG	OBP	SLG	AOPS	ABR	SB-CS	FA	FR	RNG	THR	GAMES AT POSITION	DL	BFW
1929	Phi N	17	17	5	5	3	0	1	1	1	1	2	.294	.368	.647	137	1	0	.900	-2	*82*	*0*	C11	—	0.0
1932	Det A	2	0	0	0	0	0	0	0	0	0	0	ø	ø	ø	ø	0	0-0	1.000	-0	*0*	*0*	C2	—	0.0
1939	Pit N	31	75	8	17	3	1	1	4	12	0	5	.227	.333	.333	81	-2	0	.984	1	*111*	*92*	C31	—	0.1
1940	StL A	61	113	6	24	4	0	0	13	9	2	9	.212	.282	.248	38	-10	1-0	.984	1	*111*	*84*	C61	—	-0.6
1941	Cle A	1	0	0	0	0	0	0	0	0	0	0	ø	ø	ø	ø	0	0-0	1.000	-0	*0*	*0*	/C	0	0.0
1942	Cle A	2	1	1	1	0	0	0	0	1	0	0	1.000	1.000	1.000	492	1	0-0	1.000	-0	*0*	*0*	C2	0	0.1
1943	Cle A	3	1	0	0	0	0	0	0	0	0	0	.000	.000	.000	-99	0	0-0	1.000	0	*0*	*838*	C3	0	0.0
1944	Cle A	29	61	3	14	1	0	0	4	2	0	5	.230	.254	.246	45	-5	0-0	.948	-0	*103*	*121*	C29	0	-0.4
Total	8	146	268	23	61	11	1	2	22	25	3	21	.228	.301	.299	60	-15	1-0	.974	0	*107*	*93*	C140	0	-0.8

SUSKO, PETE Peter Jonathan; B7.2.1904 Laura OH; D5.22.1978 Jacksonville FL; BL/TL/5´11˝/172; d8.1

YEAR	TM LG	G	AB	R	H	2B	3B	HR	RBI	BB-IB	HP	SO	AVG	OBP	SLG	AOPS	ABR	SB-CS	FA	FR	RNG	THR	GAMES AT POSITION	DL	BFW
1934	Was A	58	224	25	64	5	3	2	25	18	1	10	.286	.342	.362	85	-6	3-4	.988	3	129	112	1b58	—	-0.9

SUTCLIFFE, BUTCH Charles Inigo; B7.22.1915 Fall River MA; D3.2.1994 Fall River MA; BR/TR/5´8.5˝/165; d8.28

YEAR	TM LG	G	AB	R	H	2B	3B	HR	RBI	BB-IB	HP	SO	AVG	OBP	SLG	AOPS	ABR	SB-CS	FA	FR	RNG	THR	GAMES AT POSITION	DL	BFW
1938	Bos N	4	4	1	1	0	0	0	2	2	0	1	.250	.500	.250	124	0	0	.800	-0	*0*	*0*	C3	—	0.0

SUTCLIFFE, SY Elmer Ellsworth; B4.15.1862 Wheaton IL; D2.13.1893 Wheaton IL; BL/TL/6´2˝/170; d10.2; OF(10/5/43)

YEAR	TM LG	G	AB	R	H	2B	3B	HR	RBI	BB-IB	HP	SO	AVG	OBP	SLG	AOPS	ABR	SB-CS	FA	FR	RNG	THR	GAMES AT POSITION	DL	BFW
1884	Chi N	4	15	4	3	1	0	0	2	2	—	4	.200	.294	.267	72	0	—	.976	1	—	—	C4	—	0.1
1885	Chi N	11	43	5	8	1	1	0	4	2	—	5	.186	.222	.256	48	-3	—	.838	-4	—	—	C11/rf	—	-0.5
	StL N	16	49	2	6	1	0	0	4	5	—	10	.122	.204	.143	15	-4	—	.881	-3	—	—	C14,O2R	—	-0.6
	Year	27	92	7	14	2	1	0	8	7	—	15	.152	.212	.196	32	-7	—	.862	-7	—	—	C25,O3R	—	-1.1
1887	†Det N	0	0	0	0	0	0	0	0	0	0	0	ø	ø	ø	ø	0	0	.000	0	—	—	/H	—	0.0
1888	Det N	49	191	17	49	5	3	0	23	5	0	14	.257	.276	.314	87	-3	6	.901	3	111	85	S24,C14,1b5,O4R,2b2	—	0.1
1889	Cle N	46	161	17	40	3	2	1	21	14	0	6	.248	.309	.311	74	-6	5	.892	6	—	—	C37,1b8/rf	—	0.3
1890	Cle P	99	386	62	127	14	8	2	60	33	0	16	.329	.382	.422	125	14	10	.883	-19	*70*	*124*	C84,O15(1/0/14),S4,3b2	—	0.2
1891	Was AA	53	201	29	71	8	3	2	33	17	2	17	.353	.409	.453	154	14	8	.918	-4	107	71	O35(9/5/21),C22,S3/3	—	1.0
1892	Bal N	66	276	41	77	10	7	1	27	14	1	15	.279	.316	.377	106	0	12	.958	-7	71	92	1b66	—	-0.6
Total	8	344	1322	177	381	43	24	6	174	92	3	87	.288	.336	.371	107	12	41	.887	-25	*73*	*129*	C186,1b79,O58R,S31,3b3,2b2	—	0.0

SUTHERLAND, GARY Gary Lynn; B9.27.1944 Glendale CA; BR/TR/6´0˝/(175–185); d9.17; b–Darrell; Col USC; OF(31/0/6)

YEAR	TM LG	G	AB	R	H	2B	3B	HR	RBI	BB-IB	HP	SO	AVG	OBP	SLG	AOPS	ABR	SB-CS	FA	FR	RNG	THR	GAMES AT POSITION	DL	BFW
1966	Phi N	3	3	0	0	0	0	0	0	0-0	0	0	.000	.000	.000	-99	-1	0-0	1.000	1	282	745	/S	0	0.0
1967	Phi N	103	231	23	57	12	1	1	19	17-5	0	22	.247	.298	.320	76	-7	0-3	.928	-2	91	144	S66,O25L	0	-0.9
1968	Phi N	67	138	16	38	7	0	0	15	8-0	0	15	.275	.313	.326	93	-1	0-0	.968	-1	103	76	2b17,S10,3b10,O7(2/0/5)	0	-0.1
1969	Mon N	141	544	63	130	26	1	3	35	37-5	2	31	.239	.289	.307	67	-24	5-7	.971	11	101	**114**	2b139,S15/rf	21	-0.6
1970	Mon N	116	359	37	74	10	0	3	26	31-1	2	22	.206	.271	.259	43	-29	2-2	.975	3	105	123	2b97,S15/3	0	-2.1
1971	Mon N	111	304	25	78	7	2	4	26	18-3	2	12	.257	.302	.332	79	-9	3-4	.963	-1	108	121	2b56,S46,O4L,3b2	0	-0.4
1972	Hou N	5	8	0	1	0	0	0	1	0-0	0	0	.125	.125	.125	-30	-1	0-0	ø	0	0	0	/23	0	-0.1
1973	Hou N	16	54	8	14	5	0	0	3	3-0	0	5	.259	.298	.352	80	-1	0-0	.971	-2	81	123	2b14/S	0	-0.3
1974	Det A	149	619	60	157	20	1	5	49	26-1	0	37	.254	.282	.313	69	-26	1-3	.976	-11	94	90	2b147,S10,3b4	0	-2.9
1975	Det A	129	503	51	130	12	3	6	39	45-3	3	41	.258	.321	.330	81	-12	0-2	.968	-3	98	91	2b128	0	-0.8
1976	Det A	42	117	10	24	5	2	0	6	7-0	0	12	.205	.248	.282	53	-7	0-1	.984	5	112	125	2b42	0	0.0
	Mil A	59	115	9	25	2	0	1	9	8-2	1	7	.217	.268	.261	58	-6	0-2	.955	-0	96	101	2b45,1b2,D8	17	-0.6
	Year	101	232	19	49	7	2	1	15	15-2	1	19	.211	.258	.272	56	-13	0-3	.970	4	105	114	2b87,D8,1b2	0	-0.6
1977	SD N	80	103	5	25	3	0	1	11	7-0	0	15	.243	.291	.301	65	-5	0-0	.943	-3	98	100	2b30,3b21,1b4	0	-0.8
1978	StL N	10	6	1	1	0	0	0	0	0-0	0	0	.167	.167	.167	-7	-1	0-0	1.000	1	437	0	/2	0	0.0
Total	13	1031	3104	308	754	109	10	24	239	207-20	10	219	.243	.291	.308	69	-130	11-24	.971	-3	100	105	2b717,S164,3b39,O37L,D8,1b6	38	-9.6

SUTHERLAND, LEO Leonardo (Cantin); B4.6.1958 Santiago de Cuba, Cuba; BL/TL/5´10˝/(165–171); [ChiA76*S1/3]; d8.11; Col Golden West (CA) JC

YEAR	TM LG	G	AB	R	H	2B	3B	HR	RBI	BB-IB	HP	SO	AVG	OBP	SLG	AOPS	ABR	SB-CS	FA	FR	RNG	THR	GAMES AT POSITION	DL	BFW
1980	Chi A	34	89	9	23	3	0	0	5	1-1	0	11	.258	.264	.292	53	-6	4-1	.943	-1	110	0	O23(16/7/0)	0	-0.7
1981	Chi A	11	12	6	2	0	0	0	0	3-0	0	1	.167	.333	.167	49	-1	2-1	1.000	-1	66	0	O7(4/4/0)	0	-0.2
Total	2	45	101	15	25	3	0	0	5	4-1	0	12	.248	.274	.277	53	-7	6-2	.949	-2	103	0	O30(20/11/0)	0	-0.9

SUTKO, GLENN Glenn Edward; B5.9.1968 Atlanta GA; BR/TR/6´3˝/225; [CinN87 45/1103]; d10.3; Col Spartanburg Methodist (SC) JC

YEAR	TM LG	G	AB	R	H	2B	3B	HR	RBI	BB-IB	HP	SO	AVG	OBP	SLG	AOPS	ABR	SB-CS	FA	FR	RNG	THR	GAMES AT POSITION	DL	BFW
1990	Cin N	1	1	0	0	0	0	0	0	0-0	0	1	.000	.000	.000	-96	0	0-0	1.000	0	0	0	/C	0	0.0
1991	Cin N	10	10	0	1	0	0	0	1	2-0	0	6	.100	.250	.100	2	-1	0-0	.875	-1	61	265	C9	0	-0.2
Total	2	11	11	0	1	0	0	0	1	2-0	0	7	.091	.231	.091	-6	-1	0-0	.889	-1	54	236	C10	0	-0.2

SUTTON, EZRA Ezra Ballou; B9.17.1850 Palmyra NY; D6.20.1907 Braintree MA; BR/TR/5´8.5˝/153; d5.4; OF NA(0/1/2); OF(29/7/30)

YEAR	TM LG	G	AB	R	H	2B	3B	HR	RBI	BB-IB	HP	SO	AVG	OBP	SLG	AOPS	ABR	SB-CS	FA	FR	RNG	THR	GAMES AT POSITION	DL	BFW
1871	Cle NA	**29**	128	35	45	3	7	3	23	1	—	0	.352	.357	.555	166	11	3-1	**.795**	-0	89	89	3b29,O2(0/1/1)/C	—	0.6
1872	Cle NA	**22**	107	30	30	6	1	0	10	1	—	1	.280	.287	.355	102	1	1-0	.718	-6	77	67	3b22	—	-0.4
1873	Ath NA	51	243	51	81	7	6	0	34	2	—	2	.333	.339	.412	112	2	2-3	.803	-1	103	53	3b43,S8,2b2	—	-0.1
1874	Ath NA	**55**	243	54	71	10	3	0	28	0	—	2	.292	.292	.358	99	-2	6-4	.827	0	87	97	3b36,S20	—	-0.2
1875	Ath NA	75	358	83	116	11	7	1	59	1	—	3	.324	.326	.402	136	10	13-10	.803	13	**115**	**147**	3b73,P2,1b2/Srf	—	1.7
1876	Phi N	54	236	45	70	12	7	1	31	3	—	2	.297	.305	.419	141	10	—	.915	-5	201	47	1b29,2b15,3b8,O4R	—	0.3
1877	Bos N	58	253	43	74	10	6	0	39	4	—	10	.292	.304	.379	110	2	—	.882	-11	78	106	S36,3b22	—	-0.6
1878	Bos N	**60**	239	31	54	9	3	1	29	2	—	14	.226	.232	.301	69	-9	—	.888	-2	93	121	3b59/S	—	-0.8
1879	Bos N	**84**	339	54	84	13	4	0	34	2	—	18	.248	.252	.310	82	-7	—	.884	-9	99	147	S51,3b33	—	-1.1
1880	Bos N	76	288	41	72	9	2	0	25	7	—	7	.250	.268	.295	94	-2	—	.896	2	101	132	S39,3b37	—	0.3

YEAR	TM LG	G	AB	R	H	2B	3B	HR	RBI	BB-IB	HP	SO	AVG	OBP	SLG	AOPS	ABR	SB-CS	FA	FR	RNG	THR	GAMES AT POSITION	DL	BFW
1881	Bos N	**83**	333	42	97	12	4	0	31	13	—	9	.291	.318	.351	116	6	—	.877	-1	99	82	3b81,S2	—	0.7
1882	Bos N	81	319	44	80	8	1	2	38	24	—	25	.251	.303	.301	94	-1	—	.856	-5	89	67	3b77,S4	—	-0.4
1883	Bos N	94	414	101	134	28	15	3	73	17	—	12	.324	.350	.486	147	22	—	.866	-0	83	131	3b93/rfS	—	2.0
1884	Bos N	110	468	102	**162**	28	7	3	61	29	—	22	.346	.384	.455	164	35	—	**.908**	-5	86	63	3b110	—	2.8
1885	Bos N	110	457	78	143	23	8	4	47	17	—	25	.313	.338	.425	151	25	—	.875	3	93	150	3b91,S16,2b2/1	—	2.8
1886	Bos N	116	499	83	138	21	6	3	48	26	—	21	.277	.312	.361	107	4	18	.859	-9	55	71	O43(20/7/16),S28,3b28,2b18	—	-0.3
1887	Bos N	77	326	61	99	14	9	3	46	13	6	6	.304	.342	.429	112	4	17	.875	10	124	71	S37,O18(9/0/9),2b13,3b11	—	1.4
1888	Bos N	28	110	16	24	3	1	1	16	7	2	3	.218	.277	.291	79	-2	10	.859	-3	92	116	3b27/S	—	-0.5
Total	5NA	232	1079	253	343	37	24	4	154	5	—	8	.318	.321	.408	122	22	25-18	.795	5	100	101	3b203,S29,O3R,1b2,P2,2b2/C	—	1.6
Total	13	1031	4281	741	1231	190	73	21	518	164	8	174	.288	.315	.381	118	87	45	.871	-34	88	102	3b677,S216,O66R,2b48,1b30	—	6.6

SUTTON, LARRY Larry James; B5.14.1970 West Covina CA; BL/TL/6´0˝/(185–195); [KCA92 21/582]; d8.17; Col Illinois

YEAR	TM LG	G	AB	R	H	2B	3B	HR	RBI	BB-IB	HP	SO	AVG	OBP	SLG	AOPS	ABR	SB-CS	FA	FR	RNG	THR	GAMES AT POSITION	DL	BFW
1997	KC A	27	69	9	20	2	0	2	8	5-0	0	12	.290	.338	.406	90	-1	0-0	1.000	0	99	105	1b12/lfD	0	-0.2
1998	KC A	111	310	29	76	14	2	5	42	29-3	3	46	.245	.311	.352	70	-14	3-3	.987	-0	100	80	O79(39/0/47),1b6,D3	0	-1.7
1999	KC A	43	102	14	23	6	0	2	15	13-0	0	17	.225	.308	.343	65	-5	1-0	.987	-1	97	88	1b30/rfD	51	-0.8
2000	StL N	23	25	5	8	0	0	1	6	5-0	0	7	.320	.406	.440	119	1	0-0	1.000	0	101	89	1b6,O4(3/0/1)	0	0.1
2001	StL N	33	42	3	5	1	0	1	3	1-0	0	10	.119	.140	.214	-10	-7	0-0	1.000	1	214	108	1b11,O3R	0	-0.7
2002	Oak A	7	19	3	2	0	0	1	3	1-0	0	8	.105	.150	.263	7	-3	0-0	1.000	0	0	0	1b6,O3(2/0/1)	0	-0.3
2004	Fla N	8	5	0	1	0	0	0	1	1-0	0	2	.200	.333	.200	45	0	0-0	1.000	-0	0	0	/1	0	0.0
Total	7	252	572	63	135	23	2	12	78	55-3	3	102	.236	.302	.346	66	-29	4-3	.988	-0	99	94	O91(45/0/53),1b72,D11	51	-3.6

SUZUKI, ICHIRO Ichiro; B10.22.1973 Kasugai, Japan; BL/TR/5´9˝/(160–170); d4.2

YEAR	TM LG	G	AB	R	H	2B	3B	HR	RBI	BB-IB	HP	SO	AVG	OBP	SLG	AOPS	ABR	SB-CS	FA	FR	RNG	THR	GAMES AT POSITION	DL	BFW
2001	†Sea A★	157	692	127	**242**	34	8	8	69	30-10	8	53	**.350**	.381	.457	127	26	**56**-14	.997	7	113	80	O152R,D4	0	3.1
2002	Sea A★	157	647	111	208	27	8	8	51	68-**27**	5	62	.321	.388	.425	121	21	31-15	.991	7	113	87	O152(0/3/150),D4	0	2.1
2003	Sea A★	159	679	111	212	29	8	13	62	36-7	6	69	.312	.352	.436	112	10	34-8	.994	9	109	135	O159R	0	1.6
2004	Sea A★	161	704	101	**262**	24	5	8	60	49-**19**	4	63	**.372**	.414	.455	133	35	36-11	.992	9	110	109	O158R,D3	0	3.8
2005	Sea A★	**162**	679	111	206	21	12	15	68	48-23	4	66	.303	.350	.436	117	14	33-8	.995	13	117	105	O158R,D3	0	2.3
2006	Sea A★	161	695	110	**224**	20	9	9	49	49-16	5	71	.322	.370	.416	110	10	45-2	.992	4	106	95	O159(0/39/121),D2	0	1.6
Total	6	957	4096	671	1354	155	50	61	359	280-102	32	384	.331	.376	.438	120	116	235-58	.994	49	111	102	O938(0/42/898),D16	0	14.5

SVEUM, DALE Dale Curtis; B11.23.1963 Richmond CA; BB/TR/6´3˝/(185–212); [MilA82 1/25]; d5.12; C3; [DL 1989 Mil A 182]

YEAR	TM LG	G	AB	R	H	2B	3B	HR	RBI	BB-IB	HP	SO	AVG	OBP	SLG	AOPS	ABR	SB-CS	FA	FR	RNG	THR	GAMES AT POSITION	DL	BFW
1986	Mil A	91	317	35	78	13	2	7	35	32-0	1	63	.246	.316	.366	83	-8	4-3	.865	-12	95	70	3b65,2b13,S13	17	-1.8
1987	Mil A	153	535	86	135	27	3	25	95	40-4	1	133	.252	.303	.454	95	-6	2-6	.965	-20	88	96	S142,2b13	0	-1.2
1988	Mil A	129	467	41	113	14	4	9	51	21-0	1	122	.242	.274	.347	72	-19	1-0	.955	-2	99	**125**	S127/2D	0	-1.2
1990	Mil A	48	117	15	23	7	0	1	12	12-0	2	30	.197	.278	.282	59	-6	0-1	.918	-7	77	57	3b22,2b16,1b5,S5	0	-1.4
1991	Mil A	90	266	33	64	19	1	4	43	32-0	1	78	.241	.320	.365	92	-2	2-4	.968	-5	104	92	S51,3b38,2b2,D3	0	-0.5
1992	Phi N	54	135	13	24	4	0	2	16	16-4	0	39	.178	.261	.252	47	-9	0-0	.948	5	109	105	S34,3b5,1b4	15	-0.2
	Chi A	40	114	15	25	9	0	2	12	12-0	0	29	.219	.287	.351	80	-3	1-1	.944	-6	97	90	S37,1b2,3b2	0	-0.7
1993	Oak A	30	79	12	14	2	1	2	6	16-1	0	21	.177	.316	.304	71	-3	0-0	.976	-5	53	95	1b14,3b7,2b4/SlfD	0	-0.9
1994	Sea A	10	27	3	5	0	0	1	2	2-0	0	10	.185	.241	.296	37	-3	0-0	.909	2	181	0	3b3,D4	0	-0.1
1996	Pit N	12	34	9	12	5	0	1	5	6-0	0	6	.353	.450	.588	165	4	0-0	.913	-1	100	73	3b10	0	0.3
1997	Pit N	126	306	30	80	20	1	12	47	27-2	0	81	.261	.319	.451	98	-2	0-3	.941	1	107	58	3b47,S28,1b21,2b2	0	-0.1
1998	NY A	30	58	6	9	0	0	0	3	4-0	0	16	.155	.203	.155	-3	-9	0-0	.975	-1	125	110	1b21,3b6,D3	0	-1.1
1999	Pit N	49	71	7	15	5	1	3	13	7-1	0	28	.211	.278	.437	78	-3	0-0	.944	0	109	0	3b12,1b4,S4,2b2/lf	0	-0.3
Total	12	862	2526	305	597	125	13	69	340	227-12	6	656	.236	.298	.378	82	-69	10-18	.960	-51	97	105	S442,3b217,1b71,2b53,D13,O2L	214	-9.2

SWACINA, HARRY Harry Joseph "Swats"; B8.22.1881 St.Louis MO; D6.21.1944 Birmingham AL; BR/TR/6´2˝/190; d9.13

YEAR	TM LG	G	AB	R	H	2B	3B	HR	RBI	BB-IB	HP	SO	AVG	OBP	SLG	AOPS	ABR	SB-CS	FA	FR	RNG	THR	GAMES AT POSITION	DL	BFW
1907	Pit N	26	95	9	19	1	1	0	10	4	1	—	.200	.240	.232	47	-6	1	.996	-1	76	73	1b26	—	-0.9
1908	Pit N	53	176	7	38	6	1	0	13	5	0	—	.216	.238	.261	59	-9	4	.983	-5	63	95	1b50	—	-1.7
1914	Bal F	158	617	70	173	26	8	0	90	14	1	23	.280	.297	.348	73	-34	15	.985	10	**128**	93	1b158	—	-2.9
1915	Bal F	85	301	24	74	13	1	1	38	9	0	11	.246	.268	.306	59	-21	9	.986	6	137	111	1b75/2	—	-1.9
Total	4	322	1189	110	304	46	11	1	151	32	2	34	.256	.276	.315	66	-70	29	.986	10	115	96	1b309/2	—	-7.4

SWAN, ANDY Andrew J.; B8.1858 Falls PA; d7.23

YEAR	TM LG	G	AB	R	H	2B	3B	HR	RBI	BB-IB	HP	SO	AVG	OBP	SLG	AOPS	ABR	SB-CS	FA	FR	RNG	THR	GAMES AT POSITION	DL	BFW
1884	Was AA	5	21	3	3	1	0	0	—	0	0	—	.143	.143	.190	9	-2	—	.824	-2	0	0	1b3,3b2	—	-0.4
	Ric AA	3	10	2	5	0	0	0	—	0	0	—	.500	.500	.500	230	1	—	1.000	-0	0	0	1b3	—	0.1
	Year	8	31	5	8	1	0	0	—	0	0	—	.258	.258	.290	85	0	—	.902	-2	0	0	1b6,3b2	—	-0.3

SWANDELL, MARTY John Martin (b Martin Schwendel); B1841 Baden, Germany; D10.25.1906 Brooklyn NY; BL/TL/5´10.5˝/146; d5.7; U1

YEAR	TM LG	G	AB	R	H	2B	3B	HR	RBI	BB-IB	HP	SO	AVG	OBP	SLG	AOPS	ABR	SB-CS	FA	FR	RNG	THR	GAMES AT POSITION	DL	BFW
1872	Eck NA	14	52	8	12	1	0	0	4	4	—	1	.231	.286	.250	78	0	0-1	.564	-5	69	100	3b6,O5(0/4/1),2b2/1	—	-0.4
1873	Res NA	2	9	1	1	0	0	0	1	0	—	0	.111	.111	.111	-37	-1	0-0	.909	-0	0	0	1b2	—	-0.1
Total	2NA	16	61	9	13	1	0	0	5	4	—	1	.213	.262	.230	60	-1	0-1	.564	-5	69	100	3b6,O5(0/4/1),1b3,2b2	—	-0.5

SWANDER, PINKY Edward Ottis; B7.4.1880 Portsmouth OH; D10.24.1944 Springfield MA; BL/TL/5´9˝/180; d9.18

YEAR	TM LG	G	AB	R	H	2B	3B	HR	RBI	BB-IB	HP	SO	AVG	OBP	SLG	AOPS	ABR	SB-CS	FA	FR	RNG	THR	GAMES AT POSITION	DL	BFW
1903	StL A	14	51	9	14	2	2	0	6	10	2	—	.275	.413	.392	146	4	0	.833	-1	142	0	O14R	—	0.2
1904	StL A	1	1	0	0	0	0	0	0	0	0	—	.000	.000	.000	-99	0	0	ø	0	—	—	/H	—	0.0
Total	2	15	52	9	14	2	2	0	6	10	2	—	.269	.406	.385	142	4	0	.833	-1	142	0	O14R	—	0.2

SWANN, PEDRO Pedro Maurice; B10.27.1970 Wilmington DE; BL/TR/6´0˝/(195–200); [AtlN91 26/673]; d9.9; Col Delaware St.

YEAR	TM LG	G	AB	R	H	2B	3B	HR	RBI	BB-IB	HP	SO	AVG	OBP	SLG	AOPS	ABR	SB-CS	FA	FR	RNG	THR	GAMES AT POSITION	DL	BFW
2000	Atl N	4	2	0	0	0	0	0	0	0-0	0	2	.000	.000	.000	-99	-1	0-0	ø	-0	0	0	O3(1/1/2)	0	-0.1
2002	Tor A	13	12	3	1	0	0	0	1	1-0	0	6	.083	.154	.083	-33	-2	0-0	ø	-0	0	0	/rfD	0	-0.2
2003	Bal A	8	14	3	3	1	0	1	2	1-0	0	4	.214	.267	.500	96	0	0-0	1.000	-0	94	0	O6L/D	0	0.0
Total	3	25	28	6	4	1	0	1	3	2-0	0	12	.143	.200	.286	26	-3	0-0	1.000	-1	75	0	O10(7/1/3),D4	0	-0.3

SWANSON, EVAR Ernest Evar; B10.15.1902 DeKalb IL; D7.17.1973 Galesburg IL; BR/TR/5´9˝/170; d4.18; Col Knox

YEAR	TM LG	G	AB	R	H	2B	3B	HR	RBI	BB-IB	HP	SO	AVG	OBP	SLG	AOPS	ABR	SB-CS	FA	FR	RNG	THR	GAMES AT POSITION	DL	BFW
1929	Cin N	148	574	100	172	35	12	4	43	41	6	47	.300	.353	.423	96	-5	33	.970	-4	97	82	O142(91/51/0)	—	-1.6
1930	Cin N	95	301	43	93	15	3	2	22	11	1	17	.309	.335	.399	81	-10	4	.963	-1	101	92	O71(3/68/0)	—	-1.2
1932	Chi A	14	52	9	16	3	1	0	8	8	0	3	.308	.400	.404	116	2	3-1	.960	-2	87	0	O14L	—	0.0
1933	Chi A	144	539	102	165	25	7	1	63	93	3	35	.306	.411	.384	117	19	19-11	.973	-10	93	51	O139(6/8/129)	—	0.1
1934	Chi A	117	426	71	127	9	5	0	34	59	1	31	.298	.385	.343	86	-7	10-3	.980	-3	98	51	O105(4/1/100)	—	-1.4
Total	5	518	1892	325	573	87	28	7	170	212	11	133	.303	.376	.390	98	-1	69-15	.971	-19	96	65	O471(118/128/229)	—	-4.1

SWANSON, KARL Karl Edward; B12.17.1900 N.Henderson IL; D4.3.2002 Rock Island IL; BL/TR/5´10˝/155; d8.12

YEAR	TM LG	G	AB	R	H	2B	3B	HR	RBI	BB-IB	HP	SO	AVG	OBP	SLG	AOPS	ABR	SB-CS	FA	FR	RNG	THR	GAMES AT POSITION	DL	BFW
1928	Chi A	22	64	2	9	1	0	0	6	4	0	7	.141	.191	.156	-8	-10	3-0	.943	-1	110	81	2b21	—	-1.0
1929	Chi A	2	1	0	0	0	0	0	0	0	0	0	.000	.000	.000	-99	0	0-0	ø	0	—	—	/H	—	0.0
Total	2	24	65	2	9	1	0	0	6	4	0	7	.138	.188	.154	-9	-10	3-0	.943	-1	110	81	2b21	—	-1.0

SWANSON, STAN Stanley Lawrence; B5.19.1944 Yuba City CA; BR/TR/5´11˝/178; d6.23

YEAR	TM LG	G	AB	R	H	2B	3B	HR	RBI	BB-IB	HP	SO	AVG	OBP	SLG	AOPS	ABR	SB-CS	FA	FR	RNG	THR	GAMES AT POSITION	DL	BFW
1971	Mon N	49	106	14	26	3	0	2	11	10-1	0	13	.245	.310	.330	80	-3	1-3	1.000	-1	95	0	O38(24/16/2)	0	-0.6

SWANSON, BILL William Andrew; B10.12.1888 New York NY; D10.14.1954 New York NY; BB/TR/5´6˝/156; d9.2

YEAR	TM LG	G	AB	R	H	2B	3B	HR	RBI	BB-IB	HP	SO	AVG	OBP	SLG	AOPS	ABR	SB-CS	FA	FR	RNG	THR	GAMES AT POSITION	DL	BFW
1914	Bos A	11	20	0	4	2	0	0	0	3	0	4	.200	.304	.300	82	0	0-1	.875	-3	81	0	2b6,3b3/S	—	-0.4

SWARTWOOD, ED Cyrus Edward; B1.12.1859 Rockford IL; D5.15.1924 Pittsburgh PA; BL/TR/5´11˝/198; d8.11; U4

YEAR	TM LG	G	AB	R	H	2B	3B	HR	RBI	BB-IB	HP	SO	AVG	OBP	SLG	AOPS	ABR	SB-CS	FA	FR	RNG	THR	GAMES AT POSITION	DL	BFW
1881	Buf N	1	3	0	1	0	0	0	0	1	—	0	.333	.500	.333	170	0	—	.500	-1	0	0	/rf	—	0.0
1882	Pit AA	76	325	**86**	107	**18**	11	4	—	21	—	—	.329	.370	.489	197	33	—	.788	-12	49	112	O73(0/29/44),1b4	—	1.8
1883	Pit AA	94	412	86	**147**	24	8	3	—	25	—	—	**.357**	**.394**	.476	**186**	**41**	—	.936	-1	131	87	1b60,O37(0/31/6),C3	—	2.8
1884	Pit AA	102	399	74	115	19	6	0	—	33	**15**	—	.288	.365	.366	141	21	—	.804	-5	141	71	O79(0/2/77),1b22/3P	—	1.2
1885	Bro AA	99	399	80	106	8	9	0	49	36	5	—	.266	.334	.331	110	5	—	.851	-12	47	0	O95(47/0/48),1b4/SC	—	-0.8
1886	Bro AA	122	471	95	132	13	10	3	58	**70**	3	—	.280	.377	.369	133	21	37	.884	5	154	101	O122(0/20/103)/C	—	2.1
1887	Bro AA	91	363	72	92	14	8	1	54	46	3	—	.253	.342	.344	91	-4	29	.835	1	155	149	O91R	—	-0.3
1890	Tol AA	126	462	106	151	23	11	3	64	80	17	—	.327	.444	.444	157	38	53	.925	6	105	43	O126(0/7/119)/P	—	3.8
1892	Pit N	13	42	8	10	1	0	0	4	13	0	11	.238	.418	.262	106	2	1	.933	3	262	405	O13R	—	0.4
Total	9	724	2876	607	861	120	63	14	229	325	43	11	.299	.379	.400	142	157	120	.856	-15	114	78	O637(47/89/502),1b90,C5,P2/S3	—	11.0

YEAR	TM LG	G	AB	R	H	2B	3B	HR	RBI	BB-IB	HP	SO	AVG	OBP	SLG	AOPS	ABR	SB-CS	FA	FR	RNG	THR	GAMES AT POSITION	DL	BFW
Sweasy, Charlie	Charles James (b Charles James Swasey); B11.2.1847 Newark NJ; D3.30.1908 Newark NJ; BR/TR/5´9˝/172; d5.19; M1																								
1871	Oly NA	5	19	5	4	1	0	0	4	1	—	0	.211	.250	.263	50	-1	0-0	.788	-1	95	0	2b5	—	-0.2
1872	Cle NA	12	57	8	16	0	0	0	6	2	—	1	.281	.305	.281	86	-1	1-0	.833	2	116	74	2b11/rf	—	0.1
1873	Bos NA	1	4	0	1	0	0	0	0	0	—	0	.250	.250	.250	45	0	0-0	.714	0	140	244	/2	—	0.0
1874	Bal NA	8	33	2	8	0	0	0	4	2	—	0	.242	.286	.242	72	-1	0-0	.646	-6	53	96	2b8/rf	—	-0.6
	Atl NA	10	44	4	5	1	0	0	3	0	—	0	.114	.114	.136	-23	-5	0-0	.879	6	174	106	2b10	—	0.0
	Year	18	77	6	13	1	0	0	7	2	—	0	.169	.190	.182	21	-6	0-0	.781	-0	117	101	2b18/rf	—	-0.6
1875	RS NA	**19**	76	7	13	1	0	0	4	3	—	1	.171	.203	.184	39	-4	2-4	.828	-5	78	76	2b19,M	—	-1.0
1876	Cin N	56	225	18	46	5	2	0	10	2	—	5	.204	.211	.244	60	-8	—	.864	1	98	**130**	2b55/rf	—	-0.3
1878	Pro N	55	212	23	37	3	0	0	8	7	—	23	.175	.201	.189	29	-16	—	.846	-8	97	87	2b55	—	-2.1
Total	5NA	55	233	26	47	3	0	0	21	8	—	2	.202	.228	.215	47	-12	3-4	.808	-4	101	80	2b54,O2R	—	-1.7
Total	2	111	437	41	83	8	2	0	18	9	—	28	.190	.206	.217	44	-24	—	.855	-7	98	109	2b110/rf	—	-2.4
Sweeney, Buck	Charles Francis; B4.15.1890 Pittsburgh PA; D3.13.1955 Pittsburgh PA; 5´8˝/165; d9.28																								
1914	Phi A	1	1	0	0	0	0	0	0	0	0	1	.000	.000	.000	-99	0	0	1.000	0	161	0	/lf	—	0.0
Sweeney, Charlie	Charles J.; B4.13.1863 San Francisco CA; D4.4.1902 San Francisco CA; BR/TR/5´10.5˝/181; d5.11; ▲																								
1882	Pro N	1	4	0	0	0	0	0	0	0	—	1	.000	.000	.000	-99	-1	—	.500	0	443	0	/rf	—	-0.1
1883	Pro N	22	87	9	19	3	0	0	15	2	—	10	.218	.236	.253	47	-5	—	.863	1	128	144	P20,O7(2/3/2)	—	-0.2
1884	Pro N	41	168	24	50	9	0	1	19	11	—	17	.298	.341	.369	126	6	—	.940	0	104	89	P27,O17(0/5/13)/1	—	0.1
	StL U	45	171	31	54	14	2	1	—	10	—	—	.316	.354	.439	134	3	—	**.943**	5	124	**267**	P33,O13L/1	—	0.3
1885	StL N	71	267	27	55	7	1	0	24	12	—	33	.206	.240	.240	59	-11	—	.827	-4	70	100	O39(14/19/6),P35	—	-1.0
1886	StL N	17	64	4	16	2	0	0	7	3	—	10	.250	.284	.281	77	-2	0	.929	-0	104	159	P11,O4C,S2	—	-0.1
1887	Cle AA	36	133	22	30	4	4	0	19	21	0	—	.226	.331	.316	83	-2	11	.936	-4	79	35	1b20,O10(1/0/9),P3,S2,3b2	—	-0.6
Total	6	233	894	117	224	39	7	2	84	59	0	71	.251	.297	.317	90	-12	11	.909	-1	111	155	P129,O91(30/31/31),1b22,S4,3b2	—	-1.6
Sweeney, Dan	Daniel J.; B1.28.1868 Philadelphia PA; D7.13.1913 Louisville KY; 5´5˝/160; d4.18																								
1895	Lou N	22	90	18	24	5	0	1	16	17	1	2	.267	.389	.356	99	1	2	.800	-3	65	0	O22(0/1/21)	—	-0.2
Sweeney, Ed	Edward Francis "Jeff"; B7.19.1888 Chicago IL; D7.4.1947 Chicago IL; BR/TR/6´1˝/200; d5.16; Col Loyola–Chicago																								
1908	NY A	32	82	4	12	2	0	0	2	5	0	—	.146	.195	.171	19	-7	0	.955	-3	*84*	*92*	C25/1rf	—	-0.9
1909	NY A	67	176	18	47	3	0	0	21	16	0	—	.267	.328	.284	93	-1	3	.947	-1	*94*	*114*	C62,1b3	—	0.4
1910	NY A	78	215	25	43	4	4	0	13	17	4	—	.200	.271	.256	62	-10	12	.974	2	*105*	*104*	C77	—	0.0
1911	NY A	83	229	17	53	6	5	0	18	14	8	—	.231	.299	.301	63	-12	8	.964	-3	*94*	*95*	C83	—	-0.8
1912	NY A	110	351	37	94	12	1	0	30	27	3	—	.268	.325	.308	77	-10	6	.955	-5	*89*	***109***	C108	—	-0.6
1913	NY A	117	351	35	93	10	2	2	40	37	8	41	.265	.348	.322	96	0	11	.964	-7	*72*	***114***	C112/1cf	—	0.3
1914	NY A	87	258	25	55	8	1	1	22	35	4	30	.213	.316	.264	75	-7	19-6	.980	2	*92*	*98*	C78	—	0.5
1915	NY A	53	137	12	26	2	0	0	5	25	1	12	.190	.319	.204	57	-6	3-3	.975	-4	*91*	*92*	C53	—	-0.6
1919	Pit N	17	42	0	4	1	0	0	0	5	0	6	.095	.191	.119	-5	-5	1	.944	-1	*113*	*111*	C15	—	-0.6
Total	9	644	1841	173	427	48	13	3	151	181	28	89	.232	.310	.277	73	-58	63-9	.964	-19	*90*	*104*	C613,1b5,O2(0/1/1)	—	-2.3
Sweeney, Hank	Henry Leon; B12.28.1915 Franklin TN; D5.6.1980 Columbia TN; BL/TL/6´0˝/185; d10.1																								
1944	Pit N	1	2	0	0	0	0	0	0	0	0	1	.000	.000	.000	-96	-1	0	1.000	0	197	0	/1	0	0.0
Sweeney, Jerry	Jeremiah H.; B1860 Boston MA; D8.25.1891 Boston MA; 5´9.5˝/157; d8.22																								
1884	KC U	31	129	16	34	3	0	0	—	4	—	—	.264	.286	.287	85	-6	—	.958	3	156	119	1b31	—	-0.5
Sweeney, Rooney	John J.; B11.1.1858 New York NY; 5´8˝/155; d7.25																								
1883	Bal AA	25	101	13	21	5	2	0	—	4	—	—	.208	.238	.297	69	-3	—	.878	-0	—	—	C23,O3R	—	-0.2
1884	Bal U	48	186	37	42	7	1	0	—	15	—	—	.226	.284	.274	63	-14	—	.917	-5	—	—	C33,O16(0/6/10)/3	—	-1.5
1885	StL N	3	11	1	1	0	0	0	0	0	—	4	.091	.091	.091	-44	-2	—	.750	-0	0	0	O2(1/1/0)/C	—	-0.2
Total	3	76	298	51	64	12	3	0	0	19	—	4	.215	.262	.275	62	-19	—	.905	-6	—	—	C57,O21(1/7/13)/3	—	-1.9
Sweeney, Mark	Mark Patrick; B10.26.1969 Framingham MA; BL/TL/6´1˝/(195–215); [CalA91 9/246]; d8.4; Col Maine																								
1995	StL N	37	77	5	21	2	0	2	13	10-0	0	15	.273	.348	.377	92	-1	1-1	.994	-1	90	145	1b19/lf	0	-0.3
1996	†StL N	98	170	32	45	9	0	3	22	33-2	1	29	.265	.387	.371	101	2	3-0	.984	-1	106	55	O43(36/0/7),1b15	0	-0.1
1997	StL N	44	61	5	13	3	0	0	4	9-1	1	14	.213	.319	.262	56	-4	0-1	1.000	-1	100	0	O25(10/0/15),1b4	0	-0.5
	SD N	71	103	11	33	4	0	2	19	11-0	0	18	.320	.383	.417	118	3	2-2	.944	-2	74	0	O20(6/1/13),1b7	0	0.0
	Year	115	164	16	46	7	0	2	23	20-1	1	32	.280	.358	.360	93	-1	2-3	.976	-3	87	0	O45(16/1/28),1b11	0	-0.5
1998	†SD N	122	192	17	45	8	3	2	15	26-0	1	37	.234	.324	.339	82	-5	1-2	1.000	-3	99	0	O34(5/0/29),1b21/D	0	-1.1
1999	Cin N	37	31	6	11	3	0	2	7	4-1	0	9	.355	.429	.645	162	3	0-0	1.000	0	0	601	/1lf	0	0.3
2000	Mil N	71	73	9	16	6	0	1	6	12-1	1	18	.219	.337	.342	73	-3	0-0	1.000	1	315	0	O3L,1b2,D4	60	-0.2
2001	Mil N	48	89	9	23	3	1	3	11	12-0	0	23	.258	.347	.416	98	0	2-1	.968	-2	86	0	O20(20/0/3),1b2	0	-0.3
2002	SD N	48	65	3	11	3	0	1	4	4-0	0	19	.169	.217	.262	28	-7	0-0	.946	0	95	116	1b11,O5R/D	20	-0.8
2003	Col N	67	97	13	25	9	0	2	14	9-1	0	27	.258	.321	.412	79	-3	0-1	1.000	-2	77	0	O17(7/0/11),1b8/D	0	-0.6
2004	Col N	122	177	25	47	12	2	9	40	32-2	2	51	.266	.377	.508	114	5	1-0	1.000	3	111	248	O28(9/0/20),1b15,D4	0	0.6
2005	†SD N	135	221	31	65	12	1	8	40	40-3	0	58	.294	.395	.466	133	12	4-0	.988	-2	82	80	1b53,O6(1/1/4),D5	0	0.7
2006	SF N	114	259	32	65	15	2	5	37	28-3	3	50	.251	.330	.382	82	-7	0-1	.995	2	127	92	1b53,O21L	0	-0.9
Total	12	1014	1615	198	420	89	9	40	232	230-14	9	368	.260	.352	.401	96	-5	14-9	.979	-8	99	45	O224(120/2/107),1b211,D16	80	-3.2
Sweeney, Mike	Michael John; B7.22.1973 Orange CA; BR/TR/6´2˝/(195–235); [KCA91 10/262]; d9.4																								
1995	KC A	4	4	1	1	0	0	0	0	0-0	0	0	.250	.250	.250	30	0	0-0	.875	0	0	0	C4	0	0.0
1996	KC A	50	165	23	46	10	0	4	24	18-0	4	21	.279	.358	.412	95	-1	1-2	.994	2	139	120	C26,D22	0	0.1
1997	KC A	84	240	30	58	8	0	7	31	17-0	6	33	.242	.306	.363	72	-10	3-2	.993	9	136	110	C76,D3	0	0.3
1998	KC A	92	282	32	73	18	0	8	35	24-1	2	38	.259	.320	.408	85	-6	2-3	.984	-3	114	80	C91	0	-0.4
1999	KC A	150	575	101	185	44	2	22	102	54-0	10	48	.322	.387	.520	124	23	6-1	.981	-4	95	110	D71,1b74,C4	0	0.8
2000	KC A★	159	618	105	206	30	0	29	144	71-5	**15**	67	.333	.407	.523	128	29	8-3	.991	3	112	103	1b114,D45	0	1.8
2001	KC A★	147	559	97	170	46	0	29	99	64-13	2	64	.304	.374	.542	125	22	10-3	.989	3	115	**136**	1b108,D38	0	1.4
2002	KC A★	126	471	81	160	31	1	24	86	61-10	6	46	.340	.417	.563	141	30	9-7	.991	14	159	107	1b102,D24	30	3.2
2003	KC A✳	108	392	62	115	18	1	16	83	64-5	2	56	.293	.391	.467	118	13	3-2	.990	2	126	78	D62,1b45	48	0.7
2004	KC A	106	411	56	118	23	0	22	79	33-9	6	44	.287	.347	.504	119	11	3-2	.992	2	116	92	1b55,D48	43	0.5
2005	KC A★	122	470	63	141	39	0	21	83	33-7	4	61	.300	.347	.517	131	21	3-0	.998	-1	93	61	D73,1b49	15	1.3
2006	KC A	60	217	23	56	15	0	8	33	28-5	4	48	.258	.349	.438	105	2	2-0	ø	0	0	0	D59	98	0.0
Total	12	1208	4404	674	1329	282	4	190	799	467-55	61	526	.302	.373	.497	119	134	50-25	.990	27	119	104	1b547,D445,C201	234	9.7
Sweeney, Pete	Peter Jay; B12.31.1863 CA; D8.22.1901 San Francisco CA; BR/TR/5´9˝/170; d9.28																								
1888	Was N	11	44	3	8	0	1	0	5	0	0	4	.182	.182	.227	32	-4	0	.784	-1	68	77	3b8,O3L	—	-0.5
1889	Was N	49	193	13	44	7	3	1	23	11	4	26	.228	.284	.311	69	-8	8	.802	-10	87	65	3b47/2rf	—	-1.5
	StL AA	9	38	8	14	2	0	0	8	1	2	5	.368	.415	.421	122	1	2	.780	-2	81	71	3b8/cf	—	0.0
1890	StL AA	49	190	23	34	3	2	0	10	17	7	—	.179	.271	.216	38	-16	8	.880	-6	94	71	2b23,3b21,1b3,O2R	—	-1.9
	Lou AA	2	7	1	1	1	0	0	1	1	0	—	.143	.250	.286	59	0	1	.889	-1	33	0	S2	—	-0.1
	Phi AA	14	49	5	8	1	1	0	0	7	1	—	.163	.281	.224	49	-3	0	.915	-4	79	23	2b9,O4C,3b2	—	-0.6
	Year	65	246	29	43	5	3	0	11	25	8	—	.175	.272	.220	41	-19	9	.889	-11	90	58	2b32,3b23,O6(0/4/2),1b3,S2	—	-2.6
Total	3	134	521	53	109	14	7	1	47	37	14	35	.209	.280	.269	57	-30	19	.799	-24	77	79	3b86,2b33,O11(3/5/3),1b3,S2	—	-4.6
Sweeney, Ryan	Ryan Joseph; B2.20.1985 Cedar Rapids IA; BL/TL/6´4˝/200; [ChiA03 2/52]; d9.1																								
2006	Chi A	18	35	1	8	0	0	0	5	0-0	0	7	.229	.229	.229	18	-4	0-0	1.000	0	117	0	O15(6/7/6)	0	-0.4
Sweeney, Bill	William John; B3.6.1886 Covington KY; D5.26.1948 Cambridge MA; BR/TR/5´11˝/175; d6.14; OF(9/1/1)																								
1907	Chi N	3	10	1	1	0	0	0	1	1	0	—	.100	.182	.100	-11	-1	1	.571	-3	66	0	S3	—	-0.6
	Bos N	58	191	24	50	2	0	0	18	15	0	—	.262	.316	.272	85	-3	8	.871	-0	108	153	3b23,S15,O11(9/1/1),2b5/1	—	-0.4
	Year	61	201	25	51	2	0	0	19	16	0	—	.254	.309	.264	79	-5	9	.871	-4	108	153	3b23,S18,O11(9/1/1),2b5/1	—	-1.0
1908	Bos N	127	418	44	102	15	3	0	40	45	0	—	.244	.317	.294	97	0	17	.930	12	**114**	92	3b123,S3/2	—	1.8
1909	Bos N	138	493	44	120	19	3	1	36	37	0	—	.243	.296	.300	81	-11	25	.903	7	109	90	3b112,S26	—	0.0
1910	Bos N	150	499	43	133	22	4	5	46	61	2	28	.267	.349	.357	101	2	25	.903	-4	91	113	S110,3b21,1b17	—	0.2
1911	Bos N	137	523	92	164	33	6	3	63	77	2	26	.314	.404	.417	120	17	33	.944	11	104	87	2b136	—	3.1

YEAR	TM LG	G	AB	R	H	2B	3B	HR	RBI	BB-IB	HP	SO	AVG	OBP	SLG	AOPS	ABR	SB-CS	FA	FR	RNG	THR	GAMES AT POSITION	DL	BFW
1912	Bos N	153	593	84	204	31	13	1	100	68	5	34	.344	.416	.445	133	30	27	.959	26	**104**	108	2b153	—	5.6
1913	Bos N	139	502	65	129	17	6	0	47	66	3	50	.257	.347	.315	88	-5	18-18	.939	1	101	79	2b137	—	-0.5
1914	Chi N	134	463	45	101	14	5	1	38	53	0	15	.218	.298	.276	71	-16	18	.954	16	**107**	79	2b134	—	0.3
Total	8	1039	3692	442	1004	153	40	11	389	423	12	153	.272	.349	.344	100	13	172-18	.949	66	104	88	2b566,3b279,S157,1b18,O11L	—	9.5
Sweeney, Bill	William Joseph; B12.29.1904 Cleveland OH; D4.18.1957 San Diego CA; BR/TR/5´11˝/180; d4.13; C2																								
1928	Det A	89	309	47	78	15	5	0	19	15	0	28	.252	.287	.333	62	-18	12-8	.993	4	120	88	1b75,O3L	—	-1.9
1930	Bos A	88	243	32	75	13	0	4	30	9	0	15	.309	.333	.412	91	-4	5-3	.997	-1	93	113	1b56/3	—	-0.7
1931	Bos A	131	498	48	147	30	3	1	58	20	0	30	.295	.322	.373	87	-10	5-12	**.993**	8	132	92	1b124	—	-1.6
Total	3	308	1050	127	300	58	8	5	107	44	0	73	.286	.314	.370	80	-32	22-23	.994	12	120	95	1b255,O3L/3	—	-4.2
Sweet, Rick	Ricky Joe; B9.7.1952 Longview WA; BB/TR (BL 1978p)/6´1˝/(187–190); [SDN75*S3/65]; d4.8; C2; Col Gonzaga																								
1978	SD N	88	226	15	50	8	0	1	11	27-7	1	22	.221	.306	.270	67	-9	1-4	.984	6	164	111	C76	0	-0.2
1982	NY N	3	3	0	1	0	0	0	0	0-0	0	1	.333	.333	.333	87	0	0-0	ø	0	—	—	/H	0	0.0
	Sea A	88	258	29	66	6	1	4	24	20-0	2	24	.256	.311	.333	75	-9	3-0	.993	1	116	92	C83	0	-0.4
1983	Sea A	93	249	18	55	9	0	1	22	13-1	0	26	.221	.259	.269	44	-19	2-2	.987	5	81	131	C85	11	-1.2
Total	3	272	736	62	172	23	1	6	57	60-8	3	73	.234	.292	.292	62	-37	6-6	.988	12	119	111	C244	11	-1.8
Sweigert, Ham	Hampton; d10.12																								
1890	Phi AA	1	1	0	0	0	0	0	0	1	0	—	.000	.500	.000	48	0	1	1.000	1	722	0	/lf	—	0.1
Swentor, Augie	August William; B11.21.1899 Seymour CT; D11.10.1969 Waterbury CT; BR/TR/6´0˝/185; d9.12; Col Colgate																								
1922	Chi A	1	1	0	0	0	0	0	0	0	0	1	.000	.000	.000	-99	0	0-0	ø	0	—	—	/H	—	0.0
Swett, Pop	William E.; B4.16.1870 San Francisco CA; D11.22.1934 San Francisco CA; 6´0˝/175; d5.3																								
1890	Bos P	37	94	16	18	4	3	1	12	16	2	26	.191	.321	.330	69	-4	4	.820	-2	151	44	C34,O3R	—	-0.4
Swift, Bob	Robert Virgil; B3.6.1915 Salina KS; D10.17.1966 Detroit MI; BR/TR/5´11.5˝/180; d4.16; M2/C10																								
1940	StL A	130	398	37	97	20	1	0	39	28	1	39	.244	.295	.299	53	-27	1-0	.980	-15	93	79	C128	—	-3.4
1941	StL A	63	170	13	44	7	0	0	21	22	0	11	.259	.344	.300	69	-7	2-0	.985	-4	96	81	C58	0	-0.7
1942	StL A	29	76	3	15	4	0	1	8	3	0	5	.197	.228	.289	44	-6	0-2	1.000	-1	78	76	C28	0	-0.7
	Phi A	60	192	9	44	3	0	0	15	13	0	17	.229	.278	.245	48	-14	1-2	.970	-2	76	132	C60	0	-1.3
	Year	89	268	12	59	7	0	1	23	16	0	22	.220	.264	.257	47	-20	1-4	.977	-4	77	117	C88	0	-2.0
1943	Phi A	77	224	16	43	5	1	1	11	35	0	16	.192	.301	.237	58	-11	0-0	.976	-5	76	98	C77	0	-1.3
1944	Det A	80	247	15	63	11	1	1	19	27	1	27	.255	.331	.320	82	-5	2-0	.982	7	172	151	C76	0	0.7
1945	†Det A	95	279	19	65	5	0	0	24	26	0	22	.233	.298	.251	56	-15	1-0	.988	5	115	**120**	C94	0	-0.6
1946	Det A	42	107	13	25	2	0	2	10	14	0	7	.234	.322	.308	72	-4	0-0	.980	-3	98	59	C42	0	-0.5
1947	Det A	97	279	23	70	11	0	1	21	33	0	16	.251	.330	.301	74	-9	2-2	.989	3	120	95	C97	0	-0.2
1948	Det A	113	292	23	65	6	0	4	33	51	0	29	.223	.338	.284	65	-14	1-0	.991	3	100	89	C112	0	-0.5
1949	Det A	74	189	16	45	6	0	2	18	26	0	20	.238	.330	.302	68	-9	0-0	.989	-1	105	110	C69	0	-0.6
1950	Det A	67	132	14	30	4	0	2	9	25	0	6	.227	.350	.303	66	-6	0-0	.995	5	149	90	C66	0	0.1
1951	Det A	44	104	8	20	0	0	0	5	12	0	10	.192	.276	.192	28	-11	0-0	.982	-0	76	89	C43	50	-0.9
1952	Det A	28	58	3	8	1	0	0	4	7	1	7	.138	.242	.155	12	-7	0-0	.977	3	124	120	C28	0	-0.3
1953	Det A	2	3	0	1	1	0	0	1	2	0	1	.333	.600	.667	245	1	0-0	1.000	0	0	0	C2	0	0.1
Total	14	1001	2750	212	635	86	3	14	238	324	3	233	.231	.313	.280	61	-144	10-6	.985	-5	107	100	C980	50	-10.1
Swindells, Charlie	Charles Jay "Swin"; B10.26.1878 Rockford IL; D7.22.1940 Portland OR; BR/TR/5´11.5˝/180; d9.7; Col Stanford																								
1904	StL N	3	8	0	1	0	0	0	0	0	0	—	.125	.125	.125	-24	-1	0	1.000	0	101	39	C3	—	-0.1
Swisher, Nick	Nicholas Thompson; B11.25.1980 Columbus OH; BB/TL/6´0˝/(195–215); [OakA02 1/16]; d9.3; f–Steve; Col Ohio St.																								
2004	Oak A	20	60	11	15	4	0	2	8	8-0	2	11	.250	.352	.417	102	0	0-0	.889	-3	84	0	O16(12/1/4),1b3,D2	0	-0.3
2005	Oak A	131	462	66	109	32	1	21	74	55-3	4	110	.236	.322	.446	102	2	0-1	.990	-6	85	88	O121R,1b21	23	-1.1
2006	†Oak A	157	556	106	141	24	2	35	95	97-7	11	152	.254	.372	.493	125	23	1-2	.993	2	89	78	1b90,O80(79/1/1),D2	0	1.4
Total	3	308	1078	183	265	60	3	58	177	160-10	17	273	.246	.350	.468	114	25	1-3	.981	-7	96	83	O217(91/2/126),1b114,D4	23	-0.0
Swisher, Steve	Steven Eugene; B8.9.1951 Parkersburg WV; BR/TR/6´2˝/205; [ChiA73 1/21]; d6.14; C4; s–Nick; Col Ohio U.																								
1974	Chi N	90	280	21	60	5	0	5	27	37-1	2	63	.214	.307	.286	65	-13	0-3	.987	-3	113	96	C90	0	-1.3
1975	Chi N	93	254	20	54	16	2	1	22	30-7	4	57	.213	.301	.303	66	-11	1-0	.979	-11	104	95	C93	0	-1.9
1976	Chi N☆	109	377	25	89	13	3	5	42	20-3	2	82	.236	.275	.326	65	-18	2-1	.983	-4	119	104	C107	0	-1.8
1977	Chi N	74	205	21	39	7	0	5	15	9-5	2	47	.190	.229	.298	37	-19	0-0	.976	-4	100	103	C72	0	-2.0
1978	StL N	45	115	11	32	5	1	1	10	8-0	1	14	.278	.331	.365	95	-1	1-0	.991	-2	84	86	C42	0	-0.1
1979	StL N	38	73	4	11	1	1	1	3	6-0	0	17	.151	.213	.233	22	-8	0-0	.974	-4	140	58	C33	0	-1.1
1980	StL N	18	24	2	6	1	0	0	2	1-0	0	7	.250	.280	.292	57	-1	0-0	.957	-1	86	103	C8	0	-0.2
1981	SD N	16	28	2	4	0	0	0	0	2-0	0	11	.143	.200	.143	-2	-4	0-0	.971	-1	110	39	C10	26	-0.5
1982	SD N	26	58	2	10	1	0	2	3	5-0	0	24	.172	.238	.293	51	-4	0-0	.981	-3	89	64	C26	43	-0.6
Total	9	509	1414	108	305	49	7	20	124	118-16	11	322	.216	.279	.303	59	-79	4-4	.982	-31	109	94	C481	69	-9.5
Swoboda, Ron	Ronald Alan "Rocky"; B6.30.1944 Baltimore MD; BR/TR/6´2˝/(195–215); d4.12; Col Maryland																								
1965	NY N	135	399	52	91	15	3	19	50	33-3	3	102	.228	.291	.424	102	0	2-3	.947	2	101	153	O112(73/26/15)	0	-0.4
1966	NY N	112	342	34	76	9	4	8	50	31-4	5	76	.222	.296	.342	79	-10	4-2	.987	-1	89	109	O97(88/0/10)	0	-1.7
1967	NY N	134	449	47	126	17	3	13	53	41-4	1	96	.281	.340	.419	119	11	3-1	.957	1	101	105	O108R,1b20	0	0.4
1968	NY N	132	450	46	109	14	6	11	59	52-1	4	113	.242	.325	.373	109	5	8-1	.975	1	97	136	O125R	0	0.0
1969	†NY N	109	327	38	77	10	2	9	52	43-4	2	90	.235	.326	.361	90	-4	1-1	.988	-1	100	76	O97(22/0/77)	0	-1.0
1970	NY N	115	245	29	57	8	2	9	40	40-0	1	72	.233	.340	.392	95	-1	2-4	.984	-2	93	66	O100(1/0/100)	0	-0.8
1971	Mon N	39	75	7	19	4	3	0	6	11-0	2	16	.253	.364	.387	111	1	0-1	.977	2	98	286	O26(10/17/3)	0	0.2
	NY A	54	138	17	36	2	1	2	20	27-1	3	35	.261	.391	.333	113	4	0-0	.965	-1	97	71	O47(7/1/39)	0	0.1
1972	NY A	63	113	9	28	8	0	1	12	17-1	0	29	.248	.341	.345	108	2	0-1	.983	-0	96	98	O35(0/5/35),1b2	0	0.0
1973	NY A	35	43	6	5	0	0	1	2	4-0	0	18	.116	.191	.186	7	-6	0-0	1.000	-1	98	0	O20(0/8/12),D4	0	-0.7
Total	9	928	2581	285	624	87	24	73	344	299-18	21	647	.242	.324	.379	100	2	20-14	.972	0	97	111	O767(201/57/524),1b22,D4	0	-3.9
Sylvester, Lou	Louis J.; B2.14.1855 Springfield IL; D5.5.1936 Brooklyn NY; BR/TR/5´6˝/165; d4.18; ▲																								
1884	Cin U	82	333	67	89	13	8	2	—	18	—	—	.267	.305	.372	97	-12	—	.792	-3	110	71	O81(54/6/22),P6,S2	—	-1.3
1886	Lou AA	45	154	41	35	5	3	0	17	29	0	—	.227	.350	.299	98	1	3	.913	1	140	258	O45C	—	0.0
	Cin AA	17	55	10	10	0	0	3	8	7	1	—	.182	.286	.345	94	0	2	.909	1	144	367	O17(7/7/3)	—	0.0
	Year	62	209	51	45	5	3	3	25	36	1	—	.215	.333	.311	97	0	5	.912	2	141	291	O62(7/52/3)	—	0.0
1887	StL AA	29	112	20	25	4	3	1	18	13	1	—	.223	.310	.339	73	-5	13	.923	2	148	323	O29(12/4/13)/2	—	-0.3
Total	3	173	654	138	159	22	14	6	43	67	2	—	.243	.315	.347	93	-16	18	.854	2	127	186	O172(73/62/38),P6,S2/2	—	-1.6
Szekely, Joe	Joseph; B2.2.1925 Cleveland OH; D10.16.1995 Paris TX; BR/TR/5´11˝/180; d9.13; Col Baylor																								
1953	Cin N	5	13	0	1	0	0	0	0	0	0	3	.077	.077	.077	-59	-3	0-0	1.000	1	72	942	O3R	0	-0.2
Szotkiewicz, Ken	Kenneth John; B2.25.1947 Wilmington DE; BL/TR/6´0˝/165; [DetA68*S1/3]; d4.7; Col Georgia Southern																								
1970	Det A	47	84	9	9	1	0	3	9	12-2	0	29	.107	.216	.226	23	-9	0-0	.971	3	111	106	S44	50	-0.3
Tabb, Jerry	Jerry Lynn; B3.17.1952 Altus OK; BL/TR/6´2˝/(188–195); [ChiN73 1/16]; d9.8; Col Tulsa; [DL 1979 Oak A 47]																								
1976	Chi N	11	24	2	7	0	0	0	0	3-0	0	2	.292	.370	.292	82	0	0-0	1.000	-0	64	112	1b6	0	-0.1
1977	Oak A	51	144	8	32	3	0	6	19	10-2	0	26	.222	.269	.368	74	-6	0-1	.993	-2	77	98	1b36,D5	0	-1.0
1978	Oak A	12	9	0	1	0	0	0	1	2-1	0	5	.111	.273	.111	12	-1	0-0	1.000	-0	0	0	1b2,D2	0	-0.1
Total	3	74	177	10	40	3	0	6	20	15-3	0	33	.226	.284	.345	72	-7	0-1	.994	-2	74	98	1b44,D7	47	-1.2
Tabler, Pat	Patrick Sean; B2.2.1958 Hamilton OH; BR/TR/6´2˝/(195–200); [NYA76 1/16]; d8.21; OF(204/0/80)																								
1981	Chi N	35	101	11	19	3	1	1	5	13-0	0	26	.188	.281	.267	53	-6	0-1	.982	-2	94	82	2b35	0	-0.7
1982	Chi N	25	85	9	20	4	2	1	7	6-0	1	20	.235	.287	.365	80	-2	0-0	.949	-5	72	75	3b25	0	-0.8
1983	Cle A	124	430	56	125	23	5	6	65	56-1	1	63	.291	.370	.409	111	8	2-4	.948	-5	95	59	O88(87/0/1),3b25,2b2,D6	0	-0.2
1984	Cle A	144	473	66	137	21	3	10	68	47-2	3	62	.290	.354	.410	110	7	3-1	.998	-6	93	95	1b67,O43L,3b36/2D	0	-0.4
1985	Cle A	117	404	47	111	18	3	5	59	27-2	2	55	.275	.321	.371	90	-6	0-6	.983	3	119	99	1b92,D18,3b4/2	0	-1.1

THE BATTER REGISTER

YEAR	TM LG	G	AB	R	H	2B	3B	HR	RBI	BB-IB	HP	SO	AVG	OBP	SLG	AOPS	ABR	SB-CS	FA	FR	RNG	THR	GAMES AT POSITION	DL	BFW
1986	Cle A	130	473	61	154	29	2	6	48	29-3	3	75	.326	.368	.433	119	13	3-1	.990	-1	103	93	1b107,D18	19	0.5
1987	Cle A★	151	553	66	170	34	3	11	86	51-6	6	84	.307	.369	.439	113	12	5-2	.984	6	134	72	1b82,D66	0	1.1
1988	Cle A	41	143	16	32	5	1	1	17	23-1	1	27	.224	.333	.294	75	-4	1-0	1.000	-0	80	66	D29,1b10	0	-0.6
	KC A	89	301	37	93	17	2	1	49	23-0	2	41	.309	.358	.389	109	4	2-3	.986	-1	101	52	D40,O37(28/0/9),1b7/3	0	0.0
	Year	130	444	53	125	22	3	2	66	46-1	3	68	.282	.349	.358	98	0	3-3	.986	-2	101	52	D69,O37(28/0/9),1b17/3	0	-0.6
1989	KC A	123	390	36	101	11	1	2	42	37-0	2	42	.259	.325	.308	80	-10	0-0	.970	5	94	258	O55(26/0/28),D39,1b20,2b3/3	0	-0.8
1990	KC A	75	195	12	53	14	0	1	19	20-2	1	21	.272	.338	.359	98	0	0-2	.986	1	105	179	O42(11/0/31),D15,3b6,1b5	0	-0.1
	NY N	17	43	6	12	1	1	1	10	3-0	1	8	.279	.340	.419	107	0	0-0	1.000	1	116	168	O10(3/0/8)	0	0.1
1991	†Tor A	82	185	20	40	5	1	1	21	29-5	1	21	.216	.318	.270	64	-8	0-0	.985	0	103	70	D57,1b20/lf	0	-1.2
1992	†Tor A	49	135	11	34	5	0	0	16	11-0	0	14	.252	.306	.289	65	-6	0-0	1.000	0	98	81	1b34,O8(5/0/3)/3D	0	-0.8
Total	12	1202	3911	454	1101	190	25	47	512	375-22	24	559	.282	.345	.379	99	2	16-20	.988	-3	111	90	1b444,D291,O284L,3b99,2b42	19	-5.0

TABOR, GREG Gregory Steven; B5.21.1961 Castro Valley CA; BR/TR/6´0˝/165; [TexA81*1/10]; d9.10; Col Chabot (CA) JC

1987	Tex A	9	9	4	1	1	0	0	1	0-0	0	4	.111	.111	.222	-15	-1	0-0	.938	1	146	113	2b4/D	0	0.0

TABOR, JIM James Reubin "Rawhide"; B11.5.1916 New Hope AL; D8.22.1953 Sacramento CA; BR/TR/6´2˝/175; d8.2; Mil 1944–45; Col Alabama

1938	Bos A	19	57	8	18	3	2	1	8	1	0	6	.316	.328	.491	98	-1	0-1	.889	-1	100	91	3b11,S2	—	-0.1
1939	Bos A	149	577	76	167	33	8	14	95	40	1	54	.289	.337	.447	95	-7	16-10	.923	4	108	107	3b148	—	0.3
1940	Bos A	120	459	73	131	28	6	21	81	42	0	58	.285	.345	.510	114	8	14-10	.926	3	103	99	3b120	—	1.4
1941	Bos A	126	498	65	139	29	3	16	101	36	0	48	.279	.328	.446	100	-2	17-9	.930	0	104	99	3b125	0	0.4
1942	Bos A	139	508	56	128	18	2	12	75	37	0	47	.252	.303	.366	85	-12	6-13	.924	-8	90	103	3b138	0	-1.9
1943	Bos A	137	537	57	130	26	3	13	85	43	1	54	.242	.299	.374	95	-5	7-7	.938	-7	100	**125**	3b133,O2L	0	-1.3
1944	Bos A	116	438	58	125	25	3	13	72	31	1	38	.285	.334	.445	123	11	4-4	.950	4	105	63	3b114	0	1.7
1946	Phi N	124	463	53	124	15	2	10	50	36	1	51	.268	.322	.374	100	-2	3	.954	-2	**94**	89	3b124	0	-0.5
1947	Phi N	75	251	27	59	14	0	4	31	20	2	21	.235	.297	.339	71	-11	2	.916	-12	79	73	3b67	0	-2.3
Total	9	1005	3788	473	1021	191	29	104	598	286	6	377	.270	.322	.418	99	-21	69-54	.933	-18	99	97	3b980,O2L,S2	0	-2.3

TACKETT, JEFF Jeffrey Wilson; B12.1.1965 Fresno CA; BR/TR/6´2˝/(200–206); [BalA84 2/53]; d9.11

1991	Bal A	6	8	1	1	0	0	0	0	2-0	0	2	.125	.300	.125	23	-1	0-0	1.000	-1	75	0	C6	0	-0.1
1992	Bal A	65	179	21	43	8	1	5	24	17-1	2	28	.240	.307	.380	90	-3	0-0	.997	3	134	81	C64/3	0	0.4
1993	Bal A	39	87	8	15	3	0	0	9	13-0	0	28	.172	.277	.207	32	-8	0-0	.989	-1	93	150	C38/P	0	-0.7
1994	Bal A	26	53	5	12	3	1	2	9	5-0	2	13	.226	.317	.434	86	-1	0-0	.980	-3	114	68	C26	0	-0.2
Total	4	136	327	35	71	14	2	7	42	37-1	4	71	.217	.300	.336	72	-13	0-0	.992	-1	118	95	C134/P3	0	-0.6

TAGUCHI, SO So; B7.22.1969 Hyogo, Japan; BR/TR/5´10˝/(163–165); d6.10

2002	StL N	19	15	4	6	0	0	0	2	2-0	0	1	.400	.471	.400	131	1	1-0	.929	2	115	803	O14(8/6/0)	0	0.3
2003	StL N	43	54	9	14	3	1	3	13	4-1	0	11	.259	.310	.519	112	1	0-0	1.000	1	102	246	O38(11/16/13)/2	0	0.1
2004	†StL N	109	179	26	52	10	2	3	25	12-1	2	23	.291	.337	.419	94	-2	6-3	.980	-3	92	35	O103(53/31/28)	0	-0.5
2005	†StL N	143	396	45	114	21	2	8	53	20-2	2	62	.288	.322	.412	90	-7	11-2	.989	-6	86	88	O131(50/52/57)	0	-1.4
2006	†StL N	134	316	46	84	19	1	2	31	32-1	2	48	.266	.335	.351	76	-10	11-3	.969	-2	97	69	O123(70/59/7)/2D	0	-1.2
Total	5	448	960	130	270	53	6	16	124	70-5	6	145	.281	.331	.399	88	-17	29-8	.979	-8	92	91	O409(192/164/105),2b2/D	0	-2.7

TAITT, DOUG Douglas John "Poco"; B8.3.1902 Bay City MI; D12.12.1970 Portland OR; BL/TR/6´0˝/176; d4.10

1928	Bos A	143	482	51	144	28	14	3	61	36	2	32	.299	.350	.434	107	3	13-6	.975	6	102	140	O139(9/0/130)/P	—	-0.1
1929	Bos A	26	65	6	18	4	0	0	6	8	1	5	.277	.365	.338	84	-1	0-1	.955	1	106	163	O21(11/0/11)	—	-0.1
	Chi A	47	124	11	21	7	0	0	12	8	0	13	.169	.220	.226	15	-16	0-0	.966	1	101	141	O30R	—	-1.6
	Year	73	189	17	39	11	0	0	18	16	1	18	.206	.272	.265	39	-17	0-1	.961	2	103	150	O51(11/0/41)	—	-1.7
1931	Phi N	38	151	13	34	4	2	1	15	4	0	14	.225	.245	.298	42	-13	0	.990	4	113	190	O38L	—	-1.1
1932	Phi N	4	2	0	0	0	0	0	1	2	0	0	.000	.500	.000	43	0	0	ø	0	—	—	/H	—	0.0
Total	4	258	824	81	217	43	16	4	95	58	3	64	.263	.314	.369	79	-27	13-7	.975	12	104	151	O228(58/0/171)/P	—	-2.9

TALBOT, BOB Robert Dale; B6.6.1927 Visalia CA; BR/TR/6´0˝/170; d9.16

1953	Chi N	8	30	5	10	0	1	0	0	0	0	4	.333	.333	.400	88	-1	1-0	1.000	2	98	442	O7C	0	0.1
1954	Chi N	114	403	45	97	15	4	1	19	16	3	25	.241	.274	.305	50	-30	3-6	.985	-3	91	132	O111C	0	-4.0
Total	2	122	433	50	107	15	5	1	19	16	3	29	.247	.278	.312	53	-31	4-6	.986	-1	91	153	O118C	0	-3.9

TALTON, TIM Marion Lee; B1.14.1939 Pikeville NC; BL/TR/6´3˝/200; d7.8; Col East Carolina

1966	KC A	37	53	8	18	3	1	2	6	1-0	1	5	.340	.364	.547	163	4	0-1	1.000	-1	46	166	C14,1b9	0	0.3
1967	KC A	46	59	7	15	3	1	0	5	7-1	0	13	.254	.328	.339	102	0	0-0	.971	-1	37	79	C22/1	41	-0.1
Total	2	83	112	15	33	6	2	2	11	8-1	1	18	.295	.344	.438	131	4	0-1	.980	-2	40	108	C36,1b10	41	0.2

TAMARGO, JOHN John Felix; B11.7.1951 Tampa FL; BB/TR/5´10˝/(168–180); [StLN73 6/132]; d9.3; C6; Col Georgia Southern

1976	StL N	10	10	2	3	0	0	0	1	3-0	0	0	.300	.429	.300	117	1	0-0	1.000	-1	70	0	/C	0	0.0
1977	StL N	4	4	0	0	0	0	0	0	0-0	0	2	.000	.000	.000	-99	-1	0-0	1.000	0	0	0	/C	0	-0.1
1978	StL N	6	6	0	0	0	0	0	0	0-0	0	2	.000	.000	.000	-99	-2	0-0	ø	-0	0	0	/C	0	-0.2
	SF N	36	92	6	22	4	1	1	8	18-5	0	7	.239	.360	.337	100	1	1-1	.965	-5	63	29	C31	0	-0.3
	Year	42	98	6	22	4	1	1	8	18-5	0	9	.224	.342	.316	88	-1	1-1	.965	-5	63	29	C32	0	-0.5
1979	SF N	30	60	7	12	3	0	2	6	4-0	0	8	.200	.239	.350	67	-3	0-0	.985	-3	101	128	C17	0	-0.5
	Mon N	12	21	0	8	2	0	0	5	3-0	0	3	.381	.440	.476	155	2	0-0	1.000	-2	45	61	C4	0	0.0
	Year	42	81	7	20	5	0	2	11	7-0	0	11	.247	.293	.383	91	-1	0-0	.989	-5	87	111	C21	0	-0.5
1980	Mon N	37	51	4	14	3	0	1	13	6-0	0	5	.275	.345	.392	105	1	0-0	.975	-2	45	72	C12	25	-0.1
Total	5	135	244	19	59	12	1	4	33	34-5	0	27	.242	.326	.348	92	-1	1-1	.974	-12	68	60	C67	25	-1.2

TANKERSLEY, LEO Lawrence William; B6.8.1901 Terrell TX; D9.18.1980 Dallas TX; BR/TR/6´0˝/176; d7.2; Col TCU

1925	Chi A	1	3	0	0	0	0	0	0	0	0	0	.000	.000	.000	-99	-1	0-0	1.000	-0	*0*	*0*	/C	—	-0.1

TANNEHILL, JESSE Jesse Niles "Powder"; B7.14.1874 Dayton KY; D9.22.1956 Dayton KY; BB/TL (BL 1903)/5´8˝/150; d6.17; C1; b–Lee; ▲

1894	Cin N	5	11	0	0	0	0	0	1	1	0	2	.000	.083	.000	-76	-2	0	.600	-1	37	0	P5	—	0.0
1897	Pit N	56	184	22	49	8	2	0	22	18	2	—	.266	.338	.332	80	-5	4	.900	4	151	0	O33(4/27/2),P21	—	-0.2
1898	Pit N	60	152	25	44	9	3	1	17	7	0	—	.289	.321	.408	110	1	4	.956	3	116	81	P43,O7(3/4/0)	—	0.1
1899	Pit N	48	136	18	34	5	3	0	11	8	2	—	.250	.301	.331	74	-5	2	.955	3	124	311	P41/lf	—	0.1
1900	Pit N	34	110	19	37	7	0	0	17	5	0	—	.336	.365	.400	110	2	2	.924	1	109	0	P29,O4R	—	0.1
1901	Pit N	42	135	19	33	3	3	1	12	6	0	—	.244	.277	.333	74	-5	0	.917	-2	78	0	P32,O10(9/0/1)	—	-0.2
1902	Pit N	44	148	27	43	6	1	1	17	12	1	—	.291	.348	.365	116	3	3	.969	-1	96	197	P26,O16(5/0/11)	—	-0.1
1903	NY A	40	111	18	26	6	2	1	13	8	1	—	.234	.292	.351	87	-2	1	.969	2	115	124	P32,O5(4/1/0)	—	0.1
1904	Bos A	45	122	14	24	2	6	0	6	9	0	—	.197	.252	.311	73	-4	1	.991	2	117	173	P33,O2L	—	0.1
1905	Bos A	37	93	11	21	2	0	1	12	16	0	—	.226	.339	.280	96	6	1	.946	2	117	141	P37	—	0.0
1906	Bos A	31	79	12	22	2	2	0	4	6	0	—	.278	.329	.354	114	6	1	.948	0	98	63	P27	—	0.0
1907	Bos A	21	51	2	10	3	1	0	6	2	1	—	.196	.241	.294	71	1	0	.981	0	103	285	P18	—	0.0
1908	Bos A	1	2	0	1	0	0	0	0	0	0	—	.500	.500	.500	219	0	0	1.000	0	196	0	/P	—	0.0
	Was A	26	43	1	11	1	0	0	3	2	0	—	.256	.289	.279	92	2	0	.897	1	141	339	P10	—	0.0
	Year	27	45	1	12	1	0	0	3	2	0	—	.267	.298	.289	99	3	0	.907	2	145	317	P11	—	0.0
1909	Was A	16	36	2	6	1	0	0	1	5	1	—	.167	.286	.194	55	-2	0	1.000	0	0	0	O9R,P3	—	-0.2
1911	Cin N	1	1	0	0	0	0	0	0	0	0	1	.000	.000	.000	-99	0	0	1.000	-0	93	0	/P	—	0.0
Total	15	507	1414	190	361	55	23	5	142	105	8	3	.255	.310	.337	89	-4	19	.953	15	111	140	P359,O87(28/32/27)	—	-0.2

TANNEHILL, LEE Lee Ford; B10.26.1880 Dayton KY; D2.16.1938 Live Oak FL; BR/TR/5´11˝/170; d4.22; b–Jesse

1903	Chi A	**138**	503	48	113	14	3	2	50	25	1	—	.225	.263	.276	65	-22	10	.908	-9	103	118	S138	—	-2.7
1904	Chi A	153	547	50	125	31	5	0	61	20	3	—	.229	.260	.303	81	-12	14	.947	**27**	**123**	**172**	3b153	—	2.1
1905	Chi A	142	480	38	96	17	2	0	39	45	4	—	.200	.274	.244	67	-16	8	.931	25	**124**	**156**	3b142	—	1.4
1906	†Chi A	116	378	26	69	8	3	0	33	31	5	—	.183	.254	.220	50	-21	7	.951	**32**	136	139	3b99,S17	—	1.6
1907	Chi A	33	108	9	26	2	0	0	11	8	0	—	.241	.293	.259	79	-2	3	.912	4	125	97	3b31,S2	—	0.3
1908	Chi A	141	482	44	104	15	3	0	35	25	2	—	.216	.257	.259	69	-17	6	.935	17	**122**	112	3b136,S5	—	0.4
1909	Chi A	155	531	39	118	21	5	0	47	31	3	—	.222	.269	.281	77	-15	12	.941	7	92	112	3b91,S64	—	-0.4
1910	Chi A	67	230	17	51	10	0	1	21	11	2	—	.222	.263	.278	73	-8	3	.947	7	114	134	S38,1b23,3b6	—	0.1
1911	Chi A	141	516	60	131	17	6	0	49	32	2	—	.254	.300	.310	73	-20	0	.957	**36**	114	109	S102,2b27,3b7,1b5	—	2.3

YEAR	TM LG	G	AB	R	H	2B	3B	HR	RBI	BB-IB	HP	SO	AVG	OBP	SLG	AOPS	ABR	SB-CS	FA	FR	RNG	THR	GAMES AT POSITION	DL	BFW
1912	Chi A	4	3	0	0	0	0	0	0	1	1	—	.000	.400	.000	18	0	0	.667	-1	66	504	3b3/S	—	-0.1
Total	10	1090	3778	331	833	135	27	3	346	229	23	—	.220	.269	.273	70	-133	63	.938	147	120	141	3b668,S367,1b28,2b27	—	5.0
TANNER, CHUCK	Charles William; B7.4.1929 New Castle PA; BL/TL/6´0˝/(185–190); d4.12; M19; s–Bruce																								
1955	Mil N	97	243	27	60	9	3	6	27	27-3	0	32	.247	.319	.383	91	-4	0-0	.981	-2	91	94	O62(52/0/11)	0	-0.9
1956	Mil N	60	63	6	15	2	0	1	4	10-2	0	10	.238	.342	.317	84	-1	0-0	.800	-1	53	0	O8(7/0/1)	0	-0.2
1957	Mil N	22	69	5	17	3	0	2	6	5-0	0	4	.246	.297	.377	86	-2	0-0	1.000	-0	107	0	O18L	0	-0.3
	Chi N	95	318	42	91	16	2	7	42	23-2	2	20	.286	.336	.415	103	1	0-2	.988	-2	92	94	O82(59/25/0)	0	-0.6
	Year	117	387	47	108	19	2	9	48	28-2	2	24	.279	.329	.408	100	0	0-2	.990	-2	95	78	O100(77/25/0)	0	-0.9
1958	Chi N	73	103	10	27	6	0	4	17	9-2	0	10	.262	.321	.437	100	0	1-0	.955	-2	79	0	O15(2/3/10)	0	-0.3
1959	Cle A	14	48	6	12	2	0	1	5	2-0	0	9	.250	.280	.354	76	-2	0-0	1.000	-2	78	0	O10(3/7/0)	0	-0.4
1960	Cle A	21	25	2	7	1	0	0	4	4-0	0	6	.280	.367	.320	94	0	1-0	1.000	-0	84	0	O4L	49	0.0
1961	LA A	7	8	0	1	0	0	0	0	2-0	0	2	.125	.300	.125	16	-1	0-0	ø	-0	0	0	/rf	0	-0.1
1962	LA A	7	8	0	1	0	0	0	0	0-0	0	0	.125	.125	.125	-34	-2	0-0	ø	-0	0	0	O2(1/0/1)	0	-0.2
Total	8	396	885	98	231	39	5	21	105	82-9	2	93	.261	.323	.388	93	-11	2-2	.983	-10	90	69	O202(146/35/24)	49	-3.0
TAPPAN, WALTER	Walter Van Dorn "Tap"; B10.8.1890 Carlinville IL; D12.19.1967 Lynwood CA; BR/TR/5´8˝/158; d4.16																								
1914	KC F	18	39	1	8	1	0	1	3	1	0	0	.205	.225	.308	46	-4	1	.875	-2	126	80	S8,3b6/2	—	-0.5
TAPPE, EL	Elvin Walter; B5.21.1927 Quincy IL; D10.10.1998 Quincy IL; BR/TR/5´11˝/(180–190); d4.24; M2/C8																								
1954	Chi N	46	119	5	22	3	0	0	4	10	0	9	.185	.246	.210	21	-14	0-0	.986	1	*62*	*113*	C46	0	-1.1
1955	Chi N	2	0	0	0	0	0	0	0	0-0	0	0	ø	ø	ø	ø	0	0-0	1.000	1	*0*	*0*	C2	0	0.1
1956	Chi N	3	1	0	0	0	0	0	0	1-0	0	0	.000	.500	.000	51	0	0-0	1.000	0	*0*	*0*	C3	167	0.0
1958	Chi N	17	28	2	6	0	0	0	4	3-2	0	1	.214	.290	.214	37	-3	0-0	.962	-2	155	51	C16	0	-0.4
1960	Chi N	51	103	11	24	7	0	0	3	11-1	1	12	.233	.313	.301	70	-4	0-1	.992	1	65	219	C49	0	-0.1
1962	Chi N	26	53	3	11	0	0	0	6	4-0	2	3	.208	.288	.208	34	-5	0-0	1.000	1	92	107	C26,M	0	-0.3
Total	6	145	304	21	63	10	0	0	17	29-3	3	25	.207	.282	.240	41	-26	0-1	.989	1	77	*142*	C142	167	-1.8
TAPPE, TED	Theodore Nash; B2.2.1931 Seattle WA; D2.13.2004 Wenatchee WA; BL/TR/6´3˝/185; d9.14; Col Washington St.																								
1950	Cin N	7	5	1	1	0	0	1	1	1	0	1	.200	.333	.800	187	1	0	ø	0	—	—	/H	0	0.1
1951	Cin N	4	3	0	1	0	0	0	0	0	0	0	.333	.333	.333	79	0	0-0	ø	0	—	—	/H	0	0.0
1955	Chi N	23	50	12	13	2	0	4	10	11-3	2	11	.260	.413	.540	151	4	0-0	1.000	-1	81	101	O15R	120	0.3
Total	3	34	58	13	15	2	0	5	11	12-3	2	12	.259	.403	.552	151	5	0-0	1.000	-1	81	101	O15R	120	0.4
TARASCO, TONY	Anthony Giacinto; B12.9.1970 New York NY; BL/TR/6´1˝/205; [AtlN88 15/372]; d4.30																								
1993	†Atl N	24	35	6	8	2	0	0	2	0-0	1	5	.229	.243	.286	42	-3	0-1	1.000	-1	82	0	O12(4/0/8)	0	-0.4
1994	Atl N	87	132	16	36	6	0	5	19	9-1	0	17	.273	.313	.432	90	-2	5-0	1.000	-1	94	63	O45(26/0/22)	0	-0.3
1995	Mon N	126	438	64	109	18	4	14	40	51-12	2	78	.249	.329	.404	89	-7	24-3	.979	2	103	86	O116(11/0/105)	0	-0.6
1996	†Bal A	31	84	14	20	3	0	1	9	7-0	0	15	.238	.297	.310	54	-6	5-3	1.000	2	126	75	O23(0/1/22),D6	19	-0.4
1997	Bal A	100	166	26	34	8	1	7	26	25-1	1	33	.205	.313	.392	85	-4	2-2	.991	2	105	132	O81(7/8/68),D2	0	-0.4
1998	Cin N	15	24	5	5	2	0	1	4	3-0	0	5	.208	.296	.417	84	-1	0-0	1.000	0	114	0	O7(4/1/2)	0	-0.1
1999	NY A	14	31	5	5	2	0	0	3	3-0	0	5	.161	.229	.226	19	-4	1-0	1.000	-2	66	0	O12(9/0/5)	0	-0.5
2002	NY N	60	96	15	24	5	0	6	15	8-0	0	13	.250	.305	.490	112	1	2-1	.977	3	128	286	O29(18/2/13),1b7,D2	0	0.4
Total	8	457	1006	151	241	46	5	34	118	106-14	4	171	.240	.313	.397	84	-26	39-10	.987	7	104	98	O325(79/12/245),D10,1b7	19	-2.3
TARBERT, ARLIE	Wilbur Arlington; B9.10.1904 Cleveland OH; D11.27.1946 Cleveland OH; BR/TR/6´0˝/160; d6.18; Col Ohio St.																								
1927	Bos A	33	69	5	13	1	0	0	5	3	3	12	.188	.253	.203	20	-8	0-0	.944	1	85	222	O27(10/3/14)	—	-0.9
1928	Bos A	6	17	1	3	1	0	0	2	1	0	1	.176	.222	.235	21	-2	1-0	.900	0	91	202	O6R	—	-0.2
Total	2	39	86	6	16	2	0	0	7	4	3	13	.186	.247	.209	20	-10	1-0	.935	1	86	218	O33(10/3/20)	—	-1.1
TARTABULL, DANNY	Danilo (Mora); B10.30.1962 San Juan, PR; BR/TR/6´1˝/(185–210); [CinN80 3/71]; d9.7; f–Jose; OF(15/0/904)																								
1984	Sea A	10	20	3	6	1	0	2	7	2-0	1	3	.300	.375	.650	183	2	0-0	.931	2	120	109	S8/2	0	0.5
1985	Sea A	19	61	8	20	7	1	1	7	8-0	0	14	.328	.406	.525	151	5	1-0	.940	2	100	127	S16,3b4	0	0.8
1986	Sea A	137	511	76	138	25	6	25	96	61-2	1	157	.270	.347	.489	124	16	4-8	.953	-3	77	100	O101(14/0/87),2b31/3D	15	0.7
1987	KC A	158	582	95	180	27	3	34	101	79-2	1	136	.309	.390	.541	140	35	9-4	.976	-13	78	105	O149R,D6	0	1.4
1988	KC A	146	507	80	139	38	3	26	102	76-4	4	119	.274	.369	.515	144	32	8-5	.963	-8	84	103	O130R,D13	0	2.0
1989	KC A	133	441	54	118	22	0	18	62	69-2	3	123	.268	.369	.440	128	18	4-2	.982	-9	75	57	O71R,D55	15	0.6
1990	KC A	88	313	41	84	19	0	15	60	36-0	0	93	.268	.341	.473	128	12	1-1	.965	-5	88	30	O52R,D32	54	0.4
1991	KC A★	132	484	78	153	35	3	31	100	65-6	3	121	.316	.397	**.593**	170	47	6-3	.965	-14	80	46	O124R,D6	0	2.9
1992	NY A	123	421	72	112	19	0	25	85	103-14	0	115	.266	.409	.489	151	34	2-2	.980	-3	97	62	O69(1/0/68),D53	35	2.8
1993	NY A	138	513	87	128	33	2	31	102	92-9	2	156	.250	.363	.503	135	27	0-0	.978	-4	83	80	D88,O50R	21	1.6
1994	NY A	104	399	68	102	24	1	19	67	66-3	1	111	.256	.360	.464	115	10	1-1	1.000	-3	79	51	D78,O26R	0	0.2
1995	NY A	59	192	25	43	12	0	6	28	33-1	1	54	.224	.335	.380	88	-3	0-0	1.000	-0	90	98	D39,O18R	0	-0.5
	Oak A	24	88	9	23	4	0	2	7	10-0	0	28	.261	.337	.375	89	-1	0-2	1.000	0	115	0	D22/rf	29	-0.3
	Year	83	280	34	66	16	0	8	35	43-1	1	82	.236	.335	.379	88	-4	0-2	.911	-0	91	95	D61,O19R	0	-0.8
1996	Chi A	132	472	58	120	23	3	27	101	64-4	0	128	.254	.340	.487	111	7	1-2	.973	1	109	49	O122R,D10	0	0.1
1997	Phi N	3	7	2	0	0	0	0	0	4-0	0	4	.000	.364	.000	5	-1	0-0	1.000	-1	47	0	O3R	174	-0.1
Total	14	1406	5011	756	1366	289	22	262	925	768-47	17	1362	.273	.368	.496	133	240	37-30	.971	-58	85	75	O916R,D405,2b32,S24,3b5	343	13.1
TARTABULL, JOSE	Jose Milages (Guzman); B11.27.1938 Cienfuegos, Cuba; BL/TL/5´11˝/(160–165); d4.10; s–Danny																								
1962	KC A	107	310	49	86	6	5	0	22	20-0	1	19	.277	.321	.329	73	-12	19-5	.974	4	111	176	O85(1/85/0)	0	-0.9
1963	KC A	79	242	27	58	8	5	1	19	17-0	0	17	.240	.290	.326	68	-11	16-1	.986	-4	95	78	O71(1/70/0)	0	-1.4
1964	KC A	104	100	9	20	2	0	0	3	5-0	0	12	.200	.238	.220	28	-10	4-0	.978	2	104	252	O59(44/13/5)	0	-0.9
1965	KC A	68	218	28	68	11	4	1	19	18-0	0	20	.312	.361	.413	122	6	11-5	.986	8	128	182	O54(26/27/8)	0	1.3
1966	KC A	37	127	13	30	2	3	0	4	11-0	0	13	.236	.297	.299	74	-5	8-1	1.000	-2	92	50	O32(1/32/0)	0	-0.7
	Bos A	68	195	28	54	7	4	0	11	6-0	0	11	.277	.297	.354	79	-6	11-3	.989	-4	89	38	O47C	0	-1.1
	Year	105	322	41	84	9	7	0	15	17-0	0	24	.261	.297	.332	77	-10	19-4	.994	-7	90	43	O79(1/79/0)	0	-1.8
1967	†Bos A	115	247	36	55	1	2	0	10	23-0	0	26	.223	.287	.243	54	-14	6-6	.989	-3	87	83	O83(12/19/55)	0	-2.4
1968	Bos A	72	139	24	39	6	0	0	6	6-0	0	5	.281	.306	.324	87	-2	2-3	.984	1	111	58	O43(12/11/20)	25	-0.4
1969	Oak A	75	266	28	71	11	1	0	11	9-0	0	11	.267	.290	.316	72	-11	3-4	.993	-1	101	47	O63(28/36/0)	0	-1.6
1970	Oak A	24	13	5	3	2	0	0	2	0-0	0	2	.231	.231	.385	69	-1	1-0	1.000	-0	66	0	O6(4/2/0)	0	-0.1
Total	9	749	1857	247	484	56	24	2	107	115-0	1	136	.261	.303	.320	74	-66	81-28	.986	-1	102	104	O543(129/342/88)	25	-8.2
TARVER, LA SCHELLE	La Schelle; B1.30.1959 Modesto CA; BL/TL/5´11˝/165; d7.12; Col Cal St.–Sacramento																								
1986	Bos A	13	25	3	3	0	0	0	1	1-0	0	4	.120	.154	.120	-24	-4	0-1	1.000	-0	98	0	O9(3/7/0)	0	-0.5
TASBY, WILLIE	Willie; B1.8.1933 Shreveport LA; BR/TR/5´11˝/(175–183); d9.9																								
1958	Bal A	18	50	6	10	3	0	1	1	7-0	1	15	.200	.310	.320	78	-1	1-1	1.000	-1	99	0	O16(6/12/5)	0	-0.3
1959	Bal A	142	505	69	126	16	5	13	48	34-0	6	80	.250	.303	.378	88	-10	3-5	.968	0	98	146	O137(5/132/1)	0	-1.7
1960	Bal A	39	85	9	18	2	1	0	3	9-1	1	12	.212	.295	.259	52	-6	1-0	.980	-1	94	63	O36(17/9/18)	0	-0.8
	Bos A	105	385	68	108	17	1	7	37	51-0	5	54	.281	.371	.384	101	3	3-1	.979	-3	98	102	O102C	0	-0.5
	Year	144	470	77	126	19	2	7	40	60-1	6	66	.268	.358	.362	93	-2	4-1	.979	-5	97	94	O138(17/111/18)	0	-1.3
1961	Was A	141	494	54	124	13	2	17	63	58-2	2	94	.251	.330	.389	93	-5	4-10	.985	-7	97	67	O139(0/138/1)	0	-1.9
1962	Was A	11	34	4	7	0	0	0	0	2-0	0	6	.206	.250	.206	24	-4	0-0	.933	-1	80	0	O10(7/3/0)	0	-0.5
	Cle A	75	199	25	48	7	0	4	17	25-0	0	41	.241	.326	.337	81	-5	0-2	1.000	-4	91	38	O66(12/57/10)/3	0	-1.1
	Year	86	233	29	55	7	0	4	17	27-0	0	47	.236	.315	.318	73	-9	0-2	.992	-5	89	33	O76(19/60/10)/3	0	-1.6
1963	Cle A	52	116	11	26	3	1	4	5	15-4	1	25	.224	.318	.371	93	-1	0-1	.981	-3	87	0	O37(18/7/13)/2	0	-0.7
Total	6	583	1868	246	467	61	10	46	174	201-7	16	327	.250	.327	.367	89	-29	12-20	.980	-20	96	84	O543(65/460/48)/23	0	-7.5
TATE, POP	Edward Christopher "Dimples"; B12.22.1860 Richmond VA; D6.25.1932 Richmond VA; BR/TL/5´10˝/178; d9.26																								
1885	Bos N	4	13	1	2	0	0	0	2	1	—	3	.154	.214	.154	21	-1	—	.865	1	—	—	C4	—	0.0
1886	Bos N	31	106	13	24	3	1	0	3	7	—	17	.226	.274	.274	69	-4	0	.885	-5	—	—	C31	—	-0.6
1887	Bos N	60	231	34	60	5	3	0	27	8	4	9	.260	.296	.307	67	-11	7	.924	13	—	—	C53,O8R	—	0.6
1888	Bos N	41	148	18	34	7	1	1	6	8	2	7	.230	.278	.311	85	-2	3	.854	-4	—	—	C41/rf	—	-0.2
1889	Bal AA	72	253	28	46	6	3	1	27	13	5	37	.182	.236	.241	35	-22	4	.938	0	—	—	C62,1b10	—	-1.5

YEAR	TM LG	G	AB	R	H	2B	3B	HR	RBI	BB-IB	HP	SO	AVG	OBP	SLG	AOPS	ABR	SB-CS	FA	FR	RNG	THR	GAMES AT POSITION	DL	BFW
1890	Bal AA	19	71	7	13	1	1	0	6	4	6	—	.183	.284	.225	48	-5	3	.923	0	*118*	*124*	C11,1b8	—	-0.4
Total	6	227	822	101	179	22	9	2	71	41	17	73	.218	.269	.274	58	-45	17	.905	5	*118*	*124*	C202,1b18,O9R	—	-2.1

TATE, BENNIE Henry Bennett; B12.3.1901 Whitwell TN; D10.27.1973 W.Frankfort IL; BL/TR/5´8˝/165; d4.29

YEAR	TM LG	G	AB	R	H	2B	3B	HR	RBI	BB-IB	HP	SO	AVG	OBP	SLG	AOPS	ABR	SB-CS	FA	FR	RNG	THR	GAMES AT POSITION	DL	BFW
1924	†Was A	21	43	2	13	2	0	0	7	1	0	2	.302	.318	.349	74	-2	0-0	.841	-2	*129*	*48*	C14	—	-0.3
1925	Was A	16	27	0	13	3	0	0	7	2	0	2	.481	.517	.593	185	4	0-0	.955	2	*137*	*85*	C14	—	0.5
1926	Was A	59	142	17	38	5	2	1	13	15	0	1	.268	.338	.352	82	-4	0-0	.960	-3	*89*	*134*	C45	—	-0.5
1927	Was A	61	131	12	41	5	1	1	24	8	1	4	.313	.357	.389	95	-1	0-3	.977	3	*123*	*81*	C39	—	0.2
1928	Was A	57	122	10	30	6	0	0	15	10	0	4	.246	.303	.295	58	-7	0-4	.985	2	*123*	*100*	C30	—	-0.4
1929	Was A	81	265	26	78	12	3	0	30	16	0	8	.294	.335	.362	79	-9	2-6	.971	1	*116*	*107*	C74	—	-0.5
1930	Was A	14	20	1	5	0	0	0	2	0	0	1	.250	.250	.250	27	-2	0-0	.933	-1	*157*	*89*	C9	—	-0.2
	Chi A	72	230	26	73	11	2	0	27	18	0	10	.317	.367	.383	94	-2	2-1	.981	-6	*90*	*92*	C70	—	-0.3
	Year	86	250	27	78	11	2	0	29	18	0	11	.312	.358	.372	88	-4	2-1	.978	-6	*94*	*92*	C79	—	-0.5
1931	Chi A	89	273	27	73	12	3	0	22	26	0	10	.267	.331	.333	80	-8	1-1	.987	-0	*71*	*105*	C85	—	-0.3
1932	Chi A	4	10	1	1	0	0	0	0	1	0	0	.100	.182	.100	-27	-2	0-0	1.000	0	*117*	*223*	C4	—	-0.2
	Bos A	81	273	21	67	12	5	2	26	20	0	6	.245	.297	.348	68	-14	0-1	.974	-6	*63*	*110*	C76	—	-1.5
	Year	85	283	22	68	12	5	2	26	21	0	6	.240	.293	.339	65	-16	0-1	.975	-6	*65*	*114*	C80	—	-1.7
1934	Chi N	11	24	1	3	0	0	0	0	1	0	3	.125	.160	.125	-23	-4	0	1.000	-1	*116*	*108*	C8	—	-0.5
Total	10	566	1560	144	435	68	16	4	173	118	1	51	.279	.330	.351	78	-51	5-16	.974	-12	*93*	*103*	C468	—	-4.0

TATE, HUGHIE Hugh Henry; B5.19.1880 Everett PA; D8.7.1956 Greenville PA; BR/TR/5´11˝/190; d9.21; Col Penn

YEAR	TM LG	G	AB	R	H	2B	3B	HR	RBI	BB-IB	HP	SO	AVG	OBP	SLG	AOPS	ABR	SB-CS	FA	FR	RNG	THR	GAMES AT POSITION	DL	BFW
1905	Was A	4	13	1	4	0	1	0	2	0	0	—	.308	.308	.462	149	0	1	1.000	0	0	0	O3L	—	0.0

TATE, LEE Lee Willie "Skeeter"; B3.18.1932 Black Rock AR; BR/TR/5´10˝/165; d9.12

YEAR	TM LG	G	AB	R	H	2B	3B	HR	RBI	BB-IB	HP	SO	AVG	OBP	SLG	AOPS	ABR	SB-CS	FA	FR	RNG	THR	GAMES AT POSITION	DL	BFW
1958	StL N	10	35	4	7	2	0	0	1	4-0	0	3	.200	.282	.257	42	-3	0-0	.950	-1	90	86	S9	0	-0.3
1959	StL N	41	50	5	7	1	1	1	4	5-1	1	7	.140	.232	.260	29	-5	0-0	.927	-5	80	76	S39,2b2,3b2	0	-0.9
Total	2	51	85	9	14	3	1	1	5	9-1	1	10	.165	.253	.259	34	-8	0-0	.934	-6	83	79	S48,3b2,2b2	0	-1.2

TATIS, FERNANDO Fernando; B1.1.1975 San Pedro de Macoris, D.R.; BR/TR/5´10˝/(170–195); d7.26

YEAR	TM LG	G	AB	R	H	2B	3B	HR	RBI	BB-IB	HP	SO	AVG	OBP	SLG	AOPS	ABR	SB-CS	FA	FR	RNG	THR	GAMES AT POSITION	DL	BFW
1997	Tex A	60	223	29	57	9	0	8	29	14-0	0	42	.256	.297	.404	76	-8	3-0	.951	-10	81	46	3b60	0	-1.7
1998	Tex A	95	330	41	89	17	2	3	32	12-2	4	66	.270	.303	.361	68	-16	6-2	.945	11	116	102	3b94	0	-0.3
	StL N	55	202	28	58	16	2	8	26	24-1	2	57	.287	.367	.505	127	8	7-3	.928	1	114	71	3b55,S3	0	1.0
1999	StL N	149	537	104	160	31	2	34	107	82-4	16	128	.298	.404	.553	137	33	21-9	.958	-9	94	115	3b147	0	2.5
2000	†StL N	96	324	59	82	21	1	18	64	57-1	10	94	.253	.379	.491	116	9	2-3	.953	-12	85	102	3b91/1D	60	-0.3
2001	Mon N	41	145	20	37	9	0	2	11	16-0	4	43	.255	.339	.359	83	-3	0-0	.889	-9	78	29	3b41	142	-1.2
2002	Mon N	114	381	43	87	18	1	15	55	35-1	8	90	.228	.303	.399	80	-12	2-2	.948	-2	102	91	3b99,D4	29	-1.3
2003	Mon N	53	175	15	34	6	0	2	15	18-0	3	40	.194	.281	.263	42	-15	2-1	.968	1	102	110	3b49	105	-1.4
2006	Bal A	28	56	7	14	6	1	2	8	6-1	0	17	.250	.313	.500	112	1	0-0	1.000	0	111	0	3b5,1b4,O4(3/0/1)/2D	0	0.1
Total	8	691	2373	346	618	133	9	92	347	264-10	47	577	.260	.344	.440	98	-3	43-20	.948	-29	97	91	3b641,D15,1b5,O4(3/0/1),S3/2	336	-2.6

TATUM, JIM James Ray; B10.9.1967 Grossmont CA; BR/TR/6´2˝/200; [SDN85 3/76]; d9.18

YEAR	TM LG	G	AB	R	H	2B	3B	HR	RBI	BB-IB	HP	SO	AVG	OBP	SLG	AOPS	ABR	SB-CS	FA	FR	RNG	THR	GAMES AT POSITION	DL	BFW
1992	Mil A	5	8	0	1	0	0	0	0	1-0	0	2	.125	.222	.125	-0	-1	0-0	1.000	-1	39	0	3b5	0	-0.2
1993	Col N	92	98	7	20	5	0	1	12	5-0	1	27	.204	.245	.286	37	-9	0-0	.978	-2	111	136	1b12,3b6,O3(2/0/1)	0	-1.1
1995	Col N	34	34	4	8	1	1	0	4	1-0	0	7	.235	.257	.324	40	-3	0-0	1.000	-1	95	0	O2L/C	0	-0.3
1996	Bos A	2	8	1	1	0	0	0	0	0-0	0	2	.125	.125	.125	-36	-2	0-0	1.000	-0	53	0	3b2	0	-0.2
	SD N	5	3	0	0	0	0	0	0	0-0	0	1	.000	.000	.000	-99	-1	0-0	ø	-0	0	0	/3	0	-0.1
1998	NY N	35	50	4	9	1	2	2	13	3-0	0	19	.180	.211	.400	62	-3	0-0	1.000	0	35	33	1b9,C4,O4L,3b3/D	0	-0.4
Total	5	173	201	16	39	7	3	3	29	10-0	1	58	.194	.229	.303	37	-19	0-0	.987	-4	77	91	1b21,3b17,O9(8/0/1),C5/D	0	-2.3

TATUM, JARVIS Jarvis; B10.11.1946 Fresno CA; D1.6.2003 Los Angeles CA; BR/TR/6´0˝/185; [AnaA65 12/405]; d9.7

YEAR	TM LG	G	AB	R	H	2B	3B	HR	RBI	BB-IB	HP	SO	AVG	OBP	SLG	AOPS	ABR	SB-CS	FA	FR	RNG	THR	GAMES AT POSITION	DL	BFW
1968	Cal A	17	51	7	9	1	0	0	2	0-0	0	9	.176	.176	.196	13	-6	0-0	1.000	-1	94	0	O11C	0	-0.8
1969	Cal A	10	22	2	7	0	0	0	0	0-0	0	6	.318	.318	.318	82	-1	0-1	.857	-1	86	0	O5R	0	-0.2
1970	Cal A	75	181	28	43	7	0	0	6	17-1	0	35	.238	.302	.276	63	-9	1-0	.982	0	105	68	O58(8/43/12)	0	-1.1
Total	3	102	254	37	59	8	0	0	8	17-1	0	50	.232	.279	.264	55	-16	1-1	.979	-2	102	51	O74(8/54/17)	0	-2.1

TATUM, TOMMY V T; B7.16.1919 Decatur TX; D11.7.1989 Oklahoma City OK; BR/TR/6´0˝/185; d8.1; Mil 1942–45

YEAR	TM LG	G	AB	R	H	2B	3B	HR	RBI	BB-IB	HP	SO	AVG	OBP	SLG	AOPS	ABR	SB-CS	FA	FR	RNG	THR	GAMES AT POSITION	DL	BFW
1941	Bro N	8	12	1	2	1	0	0	1	1	0	3	.167	.231	.250	34	-1	0	1.000	-0	90	0	O4(1/3/0)	0	-0.1
1947	Bro N	4	6	0	0	0	0	0	0	0	0	1	.000	.000	.000	-96	-2	0	1.000	-0	90	0	O3(2/0/1)	0	-0.2
	Cin N	69	176	19	48	5	2	1	16	16	0	16	.273	.333	.341	80	-5	7	1.000	6	112	198	O49(9/37/4)/2	0	-0.1
	Year	73	182	19	48	5	2	1	16	16	0	17	.264	.323	.330	74	-7	7	1.000	5	111	193	O52(11/37/5)/2	0	-0.3
Total	2	81	194	20	50	6	2	1	17	17	0	20	.258	.318	.325	72	-8	7	1.000	5	111	185	O56(12/40/5)/2	0	-0.4

TAUBENSEE, EDDIE Edward Kenneth; B10.31.1968 Beeville TX; BL/TR/6´4˝/(205–230); [CinN86 6/150]; d5.18; [DL 2002 Cle A 183]

YEAR	TM LG	G	AB	R	H	2B	3B	HR	RBI	BB-IB	HP	SO	AVG	OBP	SLG	AOPS	ABR	SB-CS	FA	FR	RNG	THR	GAMES AT POSITION	DL	BFW
1991	Cle A	26	66	5	16	2	1	0	8	5-1	0	16	.242	.288	.303	65	-3	0-0	.979	-8	70	45	C25	0	-1.1
1992	Hou N	104	297	23	66	15	0	5	28	31-3	2	78	.222	.299	.323	80	-8	2-1	.992	3	106	102	C103	0	0.1
1993	Hou N	94	288	26	72	11	1	9	42	21-5	0	44	.250	.299	.389	86	-7	1-0	.992	5	122	78	C90	0	0.4
1994	Hou N	5	10	0	1	0	0	0	0	0-0	0	3	.100	.100	.100	-50	-2	0-0	1.000	1	183	114	C5	0	-0.1
	Cin N	61	177	29	52	8	2	8	21	15-2	0	28	.294	.345	.497	117	4	2-0	.990	-3	82	99	C61	0	0.4
	Year	66	187	29	53	8	2	8	21	15-2	0	31	.283	.333	.476	109	2	2-0	.990	-3	87	100	C66	0	0.3
1995	†Cin N	80	218	32	62	14	2	9	44	22-2	2	52	.284	.354	.491	119	6	2-2	.983	-8	95	64	C65,1b3	0	0.1
1996	Cin N	108	327	46	95	20	0	12	48	26-5	0	64	.291	.338	.462	108	4	3-4	.981	-4	68	109	C94	0	0.4
1997	Cin N	108	254	26	68	18	0	10	34	22-2	1	66	.268	.323	.457	101	0	0-1	.987	-1	76	67	C64,O11(6/0/5),1b7,D3	0	0.2
1998	Cin N	130	431	61	120	27	0	11	72	52-6	0	93	.278	.352	.418	102	2	1-0	.988	-9	89	71	C126	0	0.2
1999	Cin N	126	424	58	132	22	2	21	87	30-1	1	67	.311	.354	.521	115	9	0-2	.989	-3	83	50	C124	0	1.2
2000	Cin N	81	266	29	71	12	0	6	24	21-1	2	44	.267	.324	.380	75	-10	0-0	.989	-3	81	73	C76	61	-0.8
2001	Cle A	52	116	16	29	2	1	3	11	10-1	1	19	.250	.315	.362	75	-4	0-0	.986	-8	72	82	C38,D5	40	-1.0
Total	11	975	2874	351	784	151	9	94	419	255-29	9	574	.273	.331	.430	98	-9	11-10	.988	-38	89	78	C871,O11(6/0/5),1b10,D8	284	-0.0

TAUBY, FRED Frederick Joseph (b Frederick Joseph Taubensee); B3.27.1906 Canton OH; D11.23.1955 Concord CA; BR/TR/5´9.5˝/168; d9.1

YEAR	TM LG	G	AB	R	H	2B	3B	HR	RBI	BB-IB	HP	SO	AVG	OBP	SLG	AOPS	ABR	SB-CS	FA	FR	RNG	THR	GAMES AT POSITION	DL	BFW
1935	Chi A	13	32	5	4	1	0	0	2	2	0	3	.125	.176	.156	-13	-6	0-0	1.000	1	97	323	O7(1/1/5)	—	-0.4
1937	Phi N	11	20	2	0	0	0	0	3	0	0	5	.000	.000	.000	-93	-5	1	1.000	-0	105	0	O7(3/3/1)	—	-0.6
Total	2	24	52	7	4	1	0	0	5	2	0	8	.077	.111	.096	-43	-11	1-0	1.000	1	100	221	O14(4/4/6)	—	-1.0

TAUSSIG, DON Donald Franklin; B2.19.1932 New York NY; BR/TR/6´0˝/(180–190); d4.23; Col Hofstra

YEAR	TM LG	G	AB	R	H	2B	3B	HR	RBI	BB-IB	HP	SO	AVG	OBP	SLG	AOPS	ABR	SB-CS	FA	FR	RNG	THR	GAMES AT POSITION	DL	BFW
1958	SF N	39	50	10	10	0	0	1	4	3-1	0	8	.200	.245	.260	35	-5	0-0	1.000	-1	89	0	O36(27/0/11)	0	-0.7
1961	StL N	98	188	27	54	14	5	2	25	16-0	0	34	.287	.338	.447	98	0	2-2	.992	5	116	133	O87(48/20/30)	0	0.2
1962	Hou N	16	25	1	5	0	0	1	1	2-0	0	11	.200	.259	.320	59	-2	0-0	1.000	1	146	0	O4L	0	-0.1
Total	3	153	263	38	69	14	5	4	30	21-1	0	53	.262	.314	.399	84	-7	2-2	.994	4	112	97	O127(79/20/41)	0	-0.6

TAVAREZ, JESUS Jesus Rafael (Alcantaras); B3.26.1971 Santo Domingo, D.R.; BB/TR/6´0˝/170; d5.23

YEAR	TM LG	G	AB	R	H	2B	3B	HR	RBI	BB-IB	HP	SO	AVG	OBP	SLG	AOPS	ABR	SB-CS	FA	FR	RNG	THR	GAMES AT POSITION	DL	BFW
1994	Fla N	17	39	4	7	0	0	0	4	1-0	0	5	.179	.200	.179	-0	-6	1-1	1.000	3	168	177	O11(1/2/8)	0	-0.4
1995	Fla N	63	190	31	55	6	2	2	13	16-1	1	27	.289	.346	.374	89	-3	7-5	1.000	0	102	34	O61(4/47/32)	16	-0.4
1996	Fla N	98	114	14	25	3	0	0	6	7-0	0	18	.219	.264	.246	37	-11	5-1	1.000	0	105	0	O65(25/30/12)	0	-1.0
1997	Bos A	42	69	12	12	3	1	0	9	4-0	0	9	.174	.216	.246	21	-8	0-0	.980	-0	99	89	O35(4/29/4),D2	0	-0.8
1998	Bal A	8	11	2	2	0	0	1	1	2-0	0	3	.182	.308	.455	96	0	0-1	1.000	-1	77	0	O8(0/5/4)	0	-0.1
Total	5	228	423	63	101	12	3	3	33	30-1	1	62	.239	.289	.303	56	-28	13-8	.996	2	106	45	O180(34/113/60),D2	16	-2.7

TAVENER, JACKIE John Adam "Rabbit"; B12.27.1897 Celina OH; D9.14.1969 Fort Worth TX; BL/TR/5´5˝/138; d9.24

YEAR	TM LG	G	AB	R	H	2B	3B	HR	RBI	BB-IB	HP	SO	AVG	OBP	SLG	AOPS	ABR	SB-CS	FA	FR	RNG	THR	GAMES AT POSITION	DL	BFW
1921	Det A	2	4	0	0	0	0	0	0	0	0	1	.000	.000	.000	-99	-1	0-0	1.000	0	113	0	S2	—	-0.1
1925	Det A	134	453	45	111	11	11	0	47	39	3	60	.245	.309	.318	60	-30	5-4	.963	3	104	96	S134	—	-1.2
1926	Det A	156	532	65	141	22	14	1	58	52	1	53	.265	.332	.365	80	-17	8-7	.952	7	103	106	S156	—	0.6
1927	Det A	116	419	60	115	22	9	5	59	36	1	38	.274	.333	.406	90	-8	19-8	.948	2	100	116	S114	—	0.8
1928	Det A	132	473	59	123	24	15	5	52	33	4	51	.260	.314	.406	86	-12	13-8	.944	12	106	101	S131	—	1.4
1929	Cle A	92	250	25	53	9	4	2	27	26	1	28	.212	.289	.304	51	-19	1-4	.945	22	123	125	S89	—	0.9
Total	6	632	2131	254	543	88	53	13	243	186	10	231	.255	.318	.364	75	-87	46-31	.951	46	106	107	S626	—	2.4

YEAR	TM LG	G	AB	R	H	2B	3B	HR	RBI	BB-IB	HP	SO	AVG	OBP	SLG	AOPS	ABR	SB-CS	FA	FR	RNG	THR	GAMES AT POSITION	DL	BFW
TAVERAS, ALEX	Alejandro Antonio (Betances); B10.9.1955 Santiago, D.R.; BR/TR/5´10˝/(145–170); d9.9																								
1976	Hou N	14	46	3	10	0	0	0	2	2-0	0	1	.217	.250	.217	36	-4	1-2	.923	3	116	50	2b7,S7	0	-0.1
1982	LA N	11	3	1	1	1	0	0	2	0-0	0	1	.333	.333	.667	179	0	0-0	1.000	2	102	0	2b4,3b4,S2	0	0.2
1983	LA N	10	4	0	0	0	0	0	0	0-0	0	1	.000	.000	.000	-99	-1	0-0	ø	0	0	0	S3,2b2/3	0	-0.1
Total	3	35	53	4	11	1	0	0	4	2-0	0	3	.208	.236	.226	34	-5	1-2	.938	4	109	38	2b13,S12,3b5	0	0.0
TAVERAS, FRANK	Franklin Crisostomo (Fabian); B12.24.1949 Las Matas de Santa Cruz, D.R.; BR/TR/6´0˝/(150–170); d9.25																								
1971	Pit N	1	0	0	0	0	0	0	0	0-0	0	0	ø	ø	ø	ø	0	0-0	ø	0	—	—	/R	0	0.0
1972	Pit N	4	3	0	0	0	0	0	0	1-0	0	1	.000	.250	.000	-24	0	0-0	1.000	-1	56	155	S4	0	-0.1
1974	†Pit N	126	333	33	82	4	2	0	26	25-2	2	41	.246	.300	.270	63	-17	13-4	.941	-18	93	97	S124	0	-2.3
1975	†Pit N	134	378	44	80	9	4	0	23	37-0	2	42	.212	.284	.257	51	-25	17-6	.953	-6	95	110	S132	0	-1.6
1976	Pit N	144	519	76	134	8	6	0	24	44-1	4	79	.258	.321	.297	75	-17	58-11	.952	4	**108**	94	S141	0	1.2
1977	Pit N	147	544	72	137	20	10	1	29	38-2	6	71	.252	.306	.331	69	-24	**70**-18	.962	-22	97	84	S146	0	-2.3
1978	Pit N	157	654	81	182	31	9	0	38	29-3	5	60	.278	.313	.353	82	-17	46-25	.946	-26	91	92	S157	0	-2.7
1979	Pit N	11	45	4	11	3	0	0	1	0-0	0	2	.244	.244	.311	48	-3	2-1	.935	-3	80	70	S11	0	-0.6
	NY N	153	635	89	167	26	9	1	33	33-1	2	72	.263	.301	.337	76	-23	42-19	.966	-20	91	95	S153	0	-2.6
	Year	164	680	93	178	29	9	1	34	33-1	2	74	.262	.298	.335	74	-26	44-20	.964	-24	90	93	S164	0	-3.2
1980	NY N	141	562	65	157	27	0	0	25	23-0	1	64	.279	.308	.327	79	-16	32-18	.959	-25	82	79	S140	0	-2.9
1981	NY N	84	283	30	65	11	3	0	11	12-0	2	36	.230	.263	.290	58	-16	16-4	.931	-12	89	99	S79	0	-2.0
1982	Mon N	48	87	9	14	5	1	0	4	7-0	0	6	.161	.221	.241	29	-8	4-0	.947	-2	56	103	S26,2b19	0	-0.8
Total	11	1150	4043	503	1029	144	44	2	214	249-9	24	474	.255	.301	.313	70	-166	300-106	.953	-131	93	93	S1113,2b19	0	-16.7
TAVERAS, WILLY	Willy; B12.25.1981 Tenares, D.R.; BR/TR/6´0˝/160; d9.6																								
2004	Hou N	10	1	2	0	0	0	0	0	0-0	0	1	.000	.000	.000	-97	0	1-0	1.000	-0	40	0	O7(2/4/1)	0	0.0
2005	†Hou N	152	592	82	172	13	4	3	29	25-1	7	103	.291	.325	.341	74	-23	34-11	.991	2	101	140	O148C	0	-1.6
2006	Hou N	149	529	83	147	19	5	1	30	34-0	11	88	.278	.333	.338	71	-23	33-9	.986	6	109	146	O138C	0	-1.1
Total	3	311	1122	167	319	32	9	4	59	59-1	18	192	.284	.329	.340	73	-46	68-20	.988	8	104	142	O293(2/290/1)	0	-2.7
TAYLOR, TONY	Antonio Nemesio (Sanchez); B12.19.1935 Central Alara, Cuba; BR/TR/5´9˝/(170–185); d4.15; C9																								
1958	Chi N	140	497	63	117	15	3	6	27	40-0	7	93	.235	.299	.314	64	-26	21-6	.968	15	105	107	2b137/3	0	0.1
1959	Chi N	150	624	96	175	30	8	8	38	45-0	6	86	.280	.331	.393	94	-6	23-9	.970	10	**108**	114	2b149,S2	0	1.7
1960	Chi N	19	76	14	20	3	3	1	9	8-0	1	12	.263	.337	.421	108	1	2-0	.977	-3	92	158	2b19	0	0.0
	Phi N★	127	505	66	145	22	4	4	35	33-2	2	86	.287	.330	.370	92	-5	24-11	.968	-6	102	87	2b123,3b4	0	-0.1
	Year	146	581	80	165	25	7	5	44	41-2	3	98	.284	.331	.377	94	-5	26-11	.969	-8	101	97	2b142,3b4	0	-0.1
1961	Phi N	106	400	47	100	17	3	2	26	29-4	2	59	.250	.304	.322	67	-19	11-5	.980	-1	97	105	2b91,3b3	30	-1.2
1962	Phi N	152	625	87	162	21	5	7	43	68-4	5	82	.259	.336	.342	85	-12	20-9	.972	-14	90	99	2b150,S2	0	-1.2
1963	Phi N	157	640	102	180	20	10	5	49	42-1	7	99	.281	.330	.367	102	1	23-9	**.986**	-2	95	99	2b149,3b13	0	1.5
1964	Phi N	154	570	62	143	13	6	4	46	46-8	**13**	74	.251	.320	.316	81	-14	13-7	.977	-23	84	106	2b150	0	-2.5
1965	Phi N	106	323	41	74	14	3	3	27	22-0	12	58	.229	.302	.319	77	-10	5-4	.958	-8	92	97	2b86,3b5	0	-1.2
1966	Phi N	125	434	47	105	14	8	5	40	31-0	1	56	.242	.294	.346	77	-14	8-4	.988	1	100	89	2b68,3b52	0	-0.8
1967	Phi N	132	462	55	110	16	6	2	34	42-8	5	74	.238	.308	.312	77	-13	10-9	.991	-9	87	126	1b58,3b44,2b42,S3	0	-2.5
1968	Phi N	145	547	59	137	20	2	3	38	39-7	3	60	.250	.302	.311	85	-10	22-5	.966	13	111	95	3b138,2b5/1	0	0.7
1969	Phi N	138	557	68	146	24	5	3	30	42-1	4	62	.262	.317	.339	86	-10	19-10	.967	-1	112	66	3b71,2b57,1b10	0	-0.9
1970	Phi N	124	439	74	132	26	9	9	55	50-9	3	67	.301	.374	.462	126	17	9-11	.996	6	88	114	2b59,3b38,O18L/S	0	2.3
1971	Phi N	36	107	9	25	2	1	1	5	9-2	0	10	.234	.291	.299	68	-5	2-2	1.000	3	106	146	2b14,3b11,1b2	0	-0.1
	Det A	55	181	27	52	10	2	3	19	12-1	1	11	.287	.335	.414	107	1	5-1	.995	0	95	97	2b51,3b3	0	0.5
1972	†Det A	78	228	33	69	12	4	1	20	14-0	2	34	.303	.346	.404	119	5	5-1	.966	-2	87	84	2b67,3b8/1	0	0.8
1973	Det A	84	275	35	63	9	3	5	24	17-0	1	29	.229	.276	.338	68	-13	9-5	.987	-6	95	85	2b72,1b6,3b4/lfD	0	-1.5
1974	Phi N	62	64	5	21	4	0	2	13	6-0	1	6	.328	.389	.484	138	3	0-0	1.000	-1	63	0	1b7,3b5,2b4	0	0.2
1975	Phi N	79	103	13	25	5	1	1	17	17-2	1	18	.243	.350	.340	89	-1	3-3	.913	2	125	52	3b16,1b4,2b3	0	0.0
1976	Phi N	26	23	2	6	1	0	0	3	1-0	1	7	.261	.320	.304	75	-1	0-0	ø	-0	0	0	2b2/3	98	-0.1
Total	19	2195	7680	1005	2007	298	86	75	598	613-49	78	1083	.261	.321	.352	88	-131	234-111	.976	-27	95	102	2b1498,3b417,1b89,O19L,S8,D2	128	-4.3
TAYLOR, BEN	Benjamin Eugene; B9.30.1924 Metropolis IL; D5.11.1999 Alma OK; BL/TL/6´0˝/(185–186); d7.29																								
1951	StL A	33	93	14	24	2	1	3	6	9	2	22	.258	.337	.398	95	-1	1-1	.972	-2	82	78	1b25	0	-0.4
1952	Det A	7	18	0	3	0	0	0	0	0	0	5	.167	.167	.167	-7	-3	0-0	1.000	-0	78	112	1b4	0	-0.3
1955	Mil N	12	10	2	1	0	0	0	0	2-0	0	4	.100	.250	.100	-3	-1	0-0	1.000	-0	0	0	/1	0	-0.2
Total	3	52	121	16	28	2	1	3	6	11-0	2	31	.231	.306	.339	73	-5	1-1	.976	-2	81	82	1b30	0	-0.9
TAYLOR, CHINK	C L; B2.9.1898 Burnet TX; D7.7.1980 Temple TX; BR/TR/5´9˝/160; d4.18																								
1925	Chi N	8	6	2	0	0	0	0	0	0	0	0	.000	.000	.000	-99	-2	0-0	1.000	0	138	0	O2(1/0/1)	—	-0.2
TAYLOR, CARL	Carl Means; B1.20.1944 Sarasota FL; BR/TR/6´2˝/(200–207); d4.11																								
1968	Pit N	44	71	5	15	1	0	0	7	10-3	0	10	.211	.309	.225	63	-3	1-0	.979	-8	51	120	C29,O2(1/0/1)	0	-1.1
1969	Pit N	104	221	30	77	10	1	4	33	31-0	3	36	.348	.432	.457	154	18	0-1	.914	1	107	171	O36(19/0/19),1b24	0	1.6
1970	StL N	104	245	39	61	12	2	6	45	41-0	1	30	.249	.358	.388	97	0	5-2	.986	-3	85	106	O46R,1b15/3	0	-0.5
1971	Pit N	7	12	1	2	0	1	0	0	0-0	0	5	.167	.167	.333	38	-1	0-0	1.000	0	121	0	/rf	0	-0.1
	KC A	20	39	3	7	0	0	0	3	5-0	0	13	.179	.261	.179	30	-4	0-1	.964	1	145	0	O12(6/0/6)	0	-0.4
1972	KC A	63	113	17	30	2	1	0	11	17-1	1	16	.265	.361	.301	101	1	4-1	.982	-2	78	60	C21,O7(1/0/6),1b6,3b5	0	-0.1
1973	KC A	69	145	18	33	6	1	0	16	32-0	0	20	.228	.363	.283	79	-2	2-2	.980	-2	84	56	C63,1b2/D	0	-0.2
Total	6	411	846	113	225	31	6	10	115	136-4	5	130	.266	.367	.352	102	9	12-7	.980	-12	76	71	C113,O104(27/0/79),1b47,3b6/D	0	-0.8
TAYLOR, DANNY	Daniel Turney; B12.23.1900 Lash PA; D10.11.1972 Latrobe PA; BR/TR/5´10˝/190; d6.30																								
1926	Was A	21	50	10	15	0	1	1	5	5	0	7	.300	.364	.400	102	0	1-2	1.000	-0	95	98	O12(0/1/11)	—	-0.1
1929	Chi N	2	3	0	0	0	0	0	0	1	0	1	.000	.250	.000	-32	-1	0	1.000	-0	82	0	/rf	—	-0.1
1930	Chi N	74	219	43	62	14	3	2	37	27	1	34	.283	.364	.402	84	-5	6	.971	-1	97	86	O52L	—	-0.9
1931	Chi N	88	270	48	81	13	6	5	41	31	0	46	.300	.372	.448	117	7	4	.989	0	105	64	O67(39/22/4)	—	0.4
1932	Chi N	6	22	3	5	2	0	0	3	3	0	1	.227	.320	.318	73	-1	1	.900	-1	96	0	O6(0/4/2)	—	-0.2
	Bro N	105	395	84	128	22	7	11	48	33	1	41	.324	.378	.499	136	20	13	.989	-1	100	91	O96C	—	1.7
	Year	111	417	87	133	24	7	11	51	36	1	42	.319	.374	.489	133	19	14	.983	-2	100	85	O102(0/100/2)	—	1.5
1933	Bro N	103	358	75	102	21	9	9	40	47	0	45	.285	.368	.469	144	21	11	.977	-2	101	62	O91C	—	1.7
1934	Bro N	120	405	62	121	24	6	7	57	63	2	47	.299	.396	.440	130	20	12	.975	-2	90	121	O108(89/21/0)	—	1.3
1935	Bro N	112	352	51	102	19	5	7	59	46	0	32	.290	.372	.432	118	10	6	.970	-3	96	60	O99L	—	0.2
1936	Bro N	43	116	12	34	6	0	2	15	11	1	14	.293	.359	.397	102	1	2	.981	-0	94	107	O31L	—	-0.1
Total	9	674	2190	388	650	121	37	44	305	267	5	268	.297	.374	.446	121	72	56-2	.979	-11	98	82	O563(310/235/18)	—	3.9
TAYLOR, DWIGHT	Dwight Bernard; B3.24.1960 Los Angeles CA; BL/TL/5´9˝/166; [CleA81 7/168]; d4.14; Col Arizona																								
1986	KC A	4	2	1	0	0	0	0	0	0-0	0	0	.000	.000	.000	-98	-1	0-0	ø	-0	0	0	/cfD	0	-0.1
TAYLOR, ED	Edward James; B11.17.1901 Chicago IL; D1.30.1992 Chula Vista CA; BR/TR/5´6.5˝/160; d4.14																								
1926	Bos N	92	272	37	73	8	2	0	33	38	5	26	.268	.368	.313	93	0	4	.945	-1	98	102	3b62,S33	—	0.4
TAYLOR, LIVE OAK	Edward S.; B2.3.1851 Belfast ME; 5´9˝/170; d8.21																								
1877	Har N	2	8	0	3	0	0	0	0	0	—	2	.375	.375	.375	153	0	—	1.000	-0	0	0	O2L	—	0.0
1884	Pit AA	41	152	22	32	4	1	0	—	6	3	—	.211	.255	.250	66	-5	—	.798	-2	87	0	O41C	—	-0.8
Total	2	43	160	22	35	4	1	0	0	6	3	2	.219	.260	.256	70	-5	—	.802	-3	83	0	O43(2/41/0)	—	-0.8
TAYLOR, FRED	Frederick Rankin; B12.3.1924 Zanesville OH; D1.6.2002 Columbus OH; BL/TR/6´3˝/201; d9.12; Col Ohio St.																								
1950	Was A	6	16	1	2	0	0	0	0	1	0	2	.125	.176	.125	-23	-3	0-0	.968	0	144	147	1b3	0	-0.3
1951	Was A	6	12	1	2	1	0	0	0	0	0	4	.167	.167	.250	12	-2	0-0	.962	-1	57	165	1b2	0	-0.2
1952	Was A	10	19	3	5	1	0	0	4	3	0	2	.263	.364	.316	93	0	0-0	1.000	1	177	99	1b5	0	0.1
Total	3	22	47	5	9	2	0	0	4	4	0	8	.191	.255	.234	33	-5	0-0	.979	1	137	130	1b10	0	-0.4

YEAR	TM LG	G	AB	R	H	2B	3B	HR	RBI	BB-IB	HP	SO	AVG	OBP	SLG	AOPS	ABR	SB-CS	FA	FR	RNG	THR	GAMES AT POSITION	DL	BFW
Taylor, Harry	Harry Leonard; B4.4.1866 Halsey Valley NY; D7.12.1955 Buffalo NY; BL/6´2˝/160; d4.18; Col Cornell; OF(23/0/50)																								
1890	†Lou AA	**134**	553	115	169	7	7	0	53	68	1	—	.306	.383	.344	117	14	45	.982	3	104	100	1b118,S12,2b4/C	—	0.6
1891	Lou AA	91	348	80	103	7	3	2	35	55	4	30	.296	.398	.351	116	10	15	.978	2	118	106	1b90/32C	—	0.4
1892	Lou N	125	493	66	128	7	1	0	34	58	4	23	.260	.342	.278	96	1	24	.923	-6	81	116	O73(23/0/50),1b34,2b14,3b5,S2	—	-0.8
1893	Bal N	88	360	50	102	9	1	1	54	32	3	11	.283	.347	.322	77	-12	24	.976	-3	88	100	1b88	—	-1.2
Total	4	438	1754	311	502	30	12	3	176	213	12	64	.286	.367	.322	102	13	108	.979	-3	104	104	1b330,O73R,2b19,S14,3b6,C2	—	-1.0
Taylor, Harry	Harry Warren; B12.26.1907 McKeesport PA; D4.27.1969 Toledo OH; BL/TL/6´1.5˝/185; d4.14																								
1932	Chi N	10	8	1	1	0	0	0	0	1	0	1	.125	.222	.125	-4	-1	0	1.000	-0	0	0	/1	—	-0.1
Taylor, Sandy	James B.; 5´10.5˝/175; d8.11																								
1879	Tro N	24	97	10	21	4	0	0	8	1	—	8	.216	.224	.258	63	-3	—	.765	-3	37	0	O24L	—	-0.8
Taylor, Zack	James Wren; B7.27.1898 Yulee FL; D9.19.1974 Orlando FL; BR/TR/5´11.5˝/180; d6.15; M5/C8; Col Rollins																								
1920	Bro N	9	13	3	5	2	0	0	5	0	0	2	.385	.385	.538	158	1	0-1	.882	-1	*86*	*89*	C9	—	0.0
1921	Bro N	30	102	6	20	0	2	0	8	1	1	8	.196	.212	.235	17	-12	2-0	.965	-0	*86*	*96*	C30	—	-1.0
1922	Bro N	7	14	0	3	0	0	0	2	1	0	1	.214	.267	.214	26	-2	0-0	.950	-1	*79*	*99*	C6	—	-0.2
1923	Bro N	96	337	29	97	11	6	0	46	9	3	13	.288	.312	.356	78	-12	2-5	.967	7	*84*	*136*	C84	—	-0.1
1924	Bro N	99	345	36	100	9	4	1	39	14	1	14	.290	.319	.348	81	-10	0-1	**.988**	-4	*88*	*121*	C93	—	-0.9
1925	Bro N	109	352	33	109	16	4	3	44	17	1	19	.310	.343	.403	92	-5	0-0	.959	-10	*68*	***173***	C96	—	-0.8
1926	Bos N	125	432	36	110	22	3	0	42	28	2	27	.255	.303	.319	74	-16	1	.985	-0	*81*	***134***	C123	—	-0.8
1927	Bos N	30	96	8	23	2	1	1	14	8	0	5	.240	.298	.313	69	-5	0	.988	6	*100*	*127*	C27	—	0.3
	NY N	83	258	18	60	7	3	0	21	17	1	20	.233	.283	.283	52	-18	2	.972	-3	*119*	*92*	C81	—	-1.6
	Year	113	354	26	83	9	4	1	35	25	1	25	.234	.287	.291	56	-23	2	.978	3	*113*	***102***	C108	—	-1.3
1928	Bos N	125	399	36	100	15	1	2	30	33	3	29	.251	.313	.308	66	-20	2	.985	-12	*90*	*99*	C124	—	-2.4
1929	Bos N	34	101	8	25	7	0	0	10	7	1	9	.248	.303	.317	56	-7	0	.965	4	*104*	*164*	C31	—	-0.1
	†Chi N	64	215	29	59	16	3	1	31	19	1	18	.274	.336	.391	79	-7	0	.979	2	*129*	*89*	C64	—	-0.1
	Year	98	316	37	84	23	3	1	41	26	2	27	.266	.326	.367	72	-14	0	.974	6	*120*	*115*	C95	—	-0.2
1930	Chi N	32	95	12	22	2	1	1	11	2	1	12	.232	.255	.305	34	-11	0	1.000	0	*121*	*137*	C28	—	-0.8
1931	Chi N	8	4	0	1	0	0	0	0	2	0	1	.250	.500	.250	106	0	0	1.000	0	*0*	*229*	C5	—	0.1
1932	Chi N	21	30	2	6	1	0	0	3	1	0	4	.200	.226	.233	24	-3	0	1.000	2	*269*	*92*	C14	—	-0.1
1933	Chi N	16	11	0	0	0	0	0	0	0	0	1	.000	.000	.000	-99	-3	0	1.000	0	*0*	*0*	C12	—	-0.3
1934	NY A	4	7	0	1	0	0	0	0	0	0	1	.143	.143	.143	-28	-1	0-0	1.000	-0	*55*	*321*	C3	—	-0.1
1935	Bro N	26	54	2	7	3	0	0	5	2	1	8	.130	.175	.185	-3	-8	0	.970	1	*111*	*170*	C26	—	-0.6
Total	16	918	2865	258	748	113	28	9	311	161	16	192	.261	.304	.329	68	-139	9-7	.977	-10	*95*	*124*	C856	—	-9.5
Taylor, Joe	Joe Cephus; B3.2.1926 Chapman AL; D3.18.1993 Pittsburgh PA; BR/TR/6´1˝/(180–185); d8.26; Negro Lg 1949–50																								
1954	Phi A	18	58	5	13	1	1	1	8	2	0	9	.224	.250	.328	57	-4	0-1	.943	0	110	99	O16(9/0/8)	0	-0.5
1957	Cin N	33	107	14	28	7	0	4	9	6-0	0	24	.262	.301	.439	89	-2	0-1	.971	4	130	171	O27(19/0/8)	0	0.1
1958	StL N	18	23	2	7	3	0	1	3	2-0	0	4	.304	.346	.565	135	1	0-0	1.000	0	135	0	O5(2/2/1)	0	0.1
	Bal A	36	77	11	21	4	0	2	9	7-1	0	19	.273	.333	.403	107	1	0-0	.972	1	110	85	O21(3/4/15)	0	0.1
1959	Bal A	14	32	2	5	1	0	1	2	11-0	0	5	.156	.372	.281	84	0	0-0	1.000	-2	54	0	O12(2/0/10)	0	-0.3
Total	4	119	297	34	74	16	1	9	31	28-1	0	61	.249	.313	.401	92	-4	0-2	.969	3	110	103	O81(35/6/42)	0	-0.5
Taylor, Leo	Leo Thomas "Chink"; B5.13.1901 Walla Walla WA; D5.20.1982 Seattle WA; BR/TR/5´10.5˝/150; d5.3																								
1923	Chi A	1	0	0	0	0	0	0	0	0	0	0	ø	ø	ø	ø	0	0-0	ø	0	—	—	/R	—	0.0
Taylor, Reggie	Reginald Tremain; B1.12.1977 Newberry SC; BL/TR/6´1˝/(178–180); [PhiN95 1/14]; d9.17																								
2000	Phi N	9	11	1	1	0	0	0	0	0-0	0	8	.091	.091	.091	-54	-3	1-0	.800	-1	76	0	O3C	0	-0.3
2001	Phi N	5	7	1	0	0	0	0	0	1-0	0	1	.000	.125	.000	-67	-2	0-0	1.000	-0	96	0	O2C	0	-0.2
2002	Cin N	135	287	41	73	15	4	9	38	14-3	2	79	.254	.291	.429	84	-8	11-8	.973	1	109	49	O103(34/68/5)	0	-0.8
2003	Cin N	100	180	17	39	5	2	5	19	11-0	1	68	.217	.266	.350	62	-11	7-0	.990	1	107	89	O60(13/49/3)	34	-0.9
2005	TB A	11	22	2	4	2	0	0	1	2-0	0	7	.182	.250	.273	40	-2	2-0	1.000	0	116	0	O10(0/9/1)	0	-0.1
Total	5	260	507	62	117	22	6	14	58	28-3	3	163	.231	.274	.381	70	-26	21-8	.977	2	108	58	O178(47/131/9)	34	-2.3
Taylor, Hawk	Robert Dale; B4.3.1939 Metropolis IL; BR/TR/6´2˝/(190–195); d6.9																								
1957	Mil N	7	1	2	0	0	0	0	0	0-0	0	0	.000	.000	.000	-99	0	0-0	ø	0	0	0	/C	0	0.0
1958	Mil N	4	8	1	1	1	0	0	0	0-0	0	3	.125	.125	.250	-4	-1	0-0	1.000	0	107	0	O4L	0	-0.1
1961	Mil N	20	26	1	5	0	0	1	1	3-0	0	11	.192	.276	.308	58	-2	0-1	1.000	0	87	239	O5(4/0/1)/C	0	-0.2
1962	Mil N	20	47	3	12	0	0	0	2	2-0	0	10	.255	.286	.255	48	-4	0-1	.960	1	127	128	O11(7/0/4)	0	-0.3
1963	Mil N	16	29	1	2	0	0	0	0	1-0	0	12	.069	.100	.069	-51	-6	0-0	1.000	0	113	0	O8(4/3/1)	69	-0.7
1964	NY N	92	225	20	54	8	0	4	23	8-1	2	33	.240	.272	.329	70	-9	0-0	.981	-1	59	179	C45,O16L	0	-1.0
1965	NY N	25	46	5	7	0	0	4	10	1-0	0	8	.152	.167	.413	61	-3	0-0	.962	-2	29	93	C15/1	0	-0.5
1966	NY N	53	109	5	19	2	0	3	12	3-0	1	19	.174	.204	.275	32	-10	0-1	1.000	-3	61	172	C29,1b13	0	-1.4
1967	NY N	13	37	3	9	3	0	0	4	2-1	0	8	.243	.282	.324	74	-1	0-0	.955	-2	63	237	C12	0	-0.3
	Cal A	23	52	5	16	3	0	1	3	4-0	0	8	.308	.357	.423	135	2	0-0	1.000	3	291	177	C19	0	0.6
1969	KC A	64	89	7	24	5	0	3	21	6-0	0	18	.270	.313	.427	105	0	0-0	.909	1	122	148	O18(2/0/16),C6	0	0.1
1970	KC A	57	55	3	9	3	0	0	6	6-2	1	16	.164	.258	.218	33	-5	0-0	1.000	-1	67	0	C3/1	0	-0.6
Total	11	394	724	56	158	25	0	16	82	36-4	4	146	.218	.258	.319	62	-39	0-3	.984	-4	91	171	C131,O62(37/3/22),1b15	69	-4.4
Taylor, Bob	Robert Lee; B3.20.1944 Leland MS; BL/TR/5´9˝/170; d4.9																								
1970	SF N	63	84	12	16	0	0	2	10	12-0	4	13	.190	.320	.262	58	-5	0-0	1.000	-1	85	80	O26(22/0/5)/C	0	-0.6
Taylor, Sammy	Samuel Douglas; B2.27.1933 Woodruff SC; BL/TR/6´2˝/(185–189); d4.20																								
1958	Chi N	96	301	30	78	12	2	6	36	27-4	0	46	.259	.319	.372	84	-7	2-1	.988	-5	93	56	C87	0	-0.8
1959	Chi N	110	353	41	95	13	2	13	43	35-13	1	47	.269	.336	.428	103	1	1-0	.982	-24	54	91	C109	0	-1.8
1960	Chi N	74	150	14	31	9	0	3	17	6-0	1	18	.207	.241	.327	55	-10	0-1	.978	-3	97	130	C43	30	-1.2
1961	Chi N	89	235	26	56	8	2	8	23	23-7	4	39	.238	.316	.391	86	-5	0-0	.989	-7	76	74	C75	0	-0.9
1962	Chi N	7	15	0	2	1	0	0	1	3-1	0	3	.133	.278	.200	30	-1	0-0	1.000	-1	207	0	C6	0	-0.2
	NY N	68	158	12	35	4	2	3	20	23-1	2	17	.222	.323	.329	76	-5	0-0	.991	-7	81	130	C50	41	-1.0
	Year	75	173	12	37	5	2	3	21	26-2	2	20	.214	.319	.318	72	-6	0-0	.992	-7	93	118	C56	0	-1.2
1963	NY N	22	35	3	9	0	1	0	6	5-1	0	7	.257	.341	.314	91	0	0-0	1.000	2	78	93	C13	0	0.3
	Cin N	3	6	0	0	0	0	0	0	0-0	0	2	.000	.000	.000	-97	-2	0-0	.833	-1	0	0	C2	0	-0.3
	Year	25	41	3	9	0	1	0	6	5-1	0	9	.220	.298	.268	65	-2	0-0	.984	1	0	376	C15	0	0.0
	Cle A	4	10	1	3	0	0	0	1	0-0	0	2	.300	.300	.300	69	0	0-0	1.000	0	0	376	C2	0	0.0
Total	6	473	1263	127	309	47	9	33	147	122-27	8	181	.245	.313	.375	84	-29	3-2	.986	-45	77	88	C387	71	-5.9
Taylor, Tommy	Thomas Livingstone Carlton; B9.17.1892 Mexia TX; D4.5.1956 Greenville MS; BR/TR/5´8.5˝/160; d7.9																								
1924	†Was A	26	73	11	19	3	1	0	10	2	1	8	.260	.289	.329	61	-5	2-0	.923	-4	60	191	3b16,2b2/cf	—	-0.8
Taylor, Billy	William H.; B12.1870 Butler KY; D9.12.1905 Cincinnati OH; TR/5´10˝/160; d9.19																								
1898	Lou N	9	24	2	6	1	0	0	2	1	1	—	.250	.308	.292	73	-1	1	.909	-1	115	0	3b7/2	—	-0.2
Taylor, Billy	William Henry "Bollicky Bill"; B1855 Washington DC; D5.14.1900 Jacksonville FL; BR/TR/5´11.5˝/204; d5.21; OF(24/15/38); ▲																								
1881	Wor N	6	28	3	3	1	0	0	2	0	—	2	.107	.107	.143	-21	-4	—	.882	0	59	0	O5R/P	—	-0.3
	Det N	1	4	0	2	2	0	0	1	0	—	0	.500	.500	1.000	346	1	—	.750	-0	99	0	/3	—	0.1
	Cle N	24	103	6	25	1	0	0	12	0	—	8	.243	.243	.252	59	-5	—	.859	-2	61	108	O23L/P3	—	-0.8
	Year	31	135	9	30	4	0	0	15	0	—	10	.222	.222	.252	50	-8	—	.864	-2	61	86	O28(23/0/5),P2,3b2	—	-1.0
1882	Pit AA	70	299	40	84	16	13	3	—	7	—	—	.281	.297	.452	157	17	—	.862	-8	—	—	C27,1b23,3b14,O8(0/6/2)/P	—	0.8
1883	Pit AA	83	369	43	96	13	7	2	—	9	—	—	.260	.278	.350	105	2	—	.747	-16	135	0	O37(0/8/29),C33,P19,1b9	—	-1.0
1884	StL U	43	186	44	68	23	1	3	—	7	—	—	.366	.389	.548	174	12	—	.872	-2	86	138	P33,1b10,O4(1/1/2)	—	0.2
	Phi AA	30	111	8	28	6	2	0	—	2	1	—	.252	.272	.342	93	3	—	.788	2	126	95	P30	—	0.0
1885	Phi AA	6	21	0	4	0	0	0	2	0	0	—	.190	.190	.190	19	-1	—	.556	-1	58	0	P6	—	0.0
1886	Bal AA	10	39	4	12	0	1	0	8	1	0	—	.308	.325	.359	117	0	1	.800	-1	97	0	P8/1C	—	-0.1
1887	Phi AA	1	4	0	1	0	0	0	1	0	0	—	.250	.250	.250	40	0	0	1.000	-0	55	0	/P	—	0.0
Total	7	274	1164	148	323	62	24	8	26	26	1	10	.277	.294	.393	121	25	1	.822	-28	—	—	P100,O77R,C61,1b43,3b16	—	-1.1

YEAR	TM LG	G	AB	R	H	2B	3B	HR	RBI	BB-IB	HP	SO	AVG	OBP	SLG	AOPS	ABR	SB-CS	FA	FR	RNG	THR	GAMES AT POSITION	DL	BFW
TAYLOR, BILL	William Michael; B12.30.1929 Alhambra CA; BL/TR/6´3˝/(210–215); d4.14																								
1954	NY N	55	65	4	12	1	0	2	10	3	2	15	.185	.239	.292	38	-6	0-0	1.000	-1	66	0	O9(7/0/2)	0	-0.7
1955	NY N	65	64	9	17	4	0	4	12	1-0	0	16	.266	.273	.516	104	0	0-0	ø	-0	0	0	O2R	0	0.0
1956	NY N	1	4	0	1	1	0	0	0	0-0	0	1	.250	.250	.500	96	0	0-0	1.000	-0	67	0	/rf	0	0.0
1957	NY N	11	9	0	0	0	0	0	0	1-0	0	2	.000	.100	.000	-70	-2	0-0	ø	0	—	—	/H	0	-0.2
	Det A	9	23	4	8	2	0	1	3	0-0	0	3	.348	.348	.565	142	1	0-0	1.000	-1	60	0	O5L	0	0.0
1958	Det A	8	8	0	3	0	0	0	1	0-0	0	2	.375	.375	.375	100	0	0-0	1.000	0	116	0	/rf	0	0.0
Total	5	149	173	17	41	8	0	7	26	5-0	2	39	.237	.264	.405	74	-7	0-0	1.000	-2	65	0	O18(12/0/6)	0	-0.9
TAYLOR, ZACHARY	Zachary H.; d9.10																								
1874	Bal NA	13	48	3	12	0	0	0	3	0	—	1	.250	.250	.250	61	-2	0-0	.914	-1	112	17	1b13	—	-0.2
TEAHEN, MARK	Mark Thomas; B9.6.1981 Redlands CA; BL/TR/6´3˝/(210–220); [OakA02 1/39]; d4.4; Col St. Marys (CA)																								
2005	KC A	130	447	60	110	29	4	7	55	40-2	1	107	.246	.309	.376	84	-10	7-2	.947	9	105	95	3b128	21	0.0
2006	KC A	109	393	70	114	21	7	18	69	40-2	2	85	.290	.357	.517	125	14	10-0	.958	6	107	137	3b109	0	2.1
Total	2	239	840	130	224	50	11	25	124	80-4	3	192	.267	.332	.442	104	4	17-2	.952	14	106	114	3b237	21	2.1
TEBBETTS, BIRDIE	George Robert; B11.10.1912 Burlington VT; D3.24.1999 Manatee FL; BR/TR/5´11.5˝/(170–190); d9.16; Mil 1943–45; M11; Col Providence																								
1936	Det A	10	33	7	10	1	2	1	4	5	0	3	.303	.395	.545	129	1	0-0	.982	1	*158*	*76*	C10	—	0.2
1937	Det A	50	162	15	31	4	3	2	16	10	0	13	.191	.238	.290	32	-18	0-0	.963	-4	*89*	*91*	C48	—	-1.9
1938	Det A	53	143	16	42	6	2	1	25	12	0	13	.294	.348	.385	79	-5	1-2	.985	-1	*131*	*89*	C53	—	-0.4
1939	Det A	106	341	37	89	22	2	4	53	25	2	20	.261	.315	.372	70	-16	2-1	.970	11	*114*	*126*	C100	—	0.1
1940	†Det A	111	379	46	112	24	4	4	46	35	1	14	.296	.357	.412	90	-5	4-5	.975	15	*112*	***149***	C107	—	1.5
1941	Det A☆	110	359	28	102	19	4	2	47	38	1	29	.284	.354	.376	85	-7	1-2	.977	6	*88*	***130***	C98	0	0.4
1942	Det A★	99	308	24	76	11	0	1	27	39	2	17	.247	.335	.292	71	-10	4-0	.977	7	*102*	*107*	C97	0	0.3
1946	Det A	87	280	20	68	11	2	1	34	28	0	23	.243	.312	.307	69	-11	1-3	.982	-0	*105*	*86*	C87	0	-0.8
1947	Det A	20	53	1	5	1	0	0	2	3	0	3	.094	.143	.113	-27	-9	0-1	1.000	5	*139*	*158*	C20	0	-0.4
	Bos A	90	291	22	87	10	0	1	28	21	0	30	.299	.346	.344	86	-5	2-4	.974	-1	*88*	*75*	C89	0	-0.3
	Year	110	344	23	92	11	0	1	30	24	0	33	.267	.315	.308	69	-14	2-5	.980	4	*97*	*90*	C109	0	-0.7
1948	Bos A★	128	446	54	125	26	2	5	68	62	2	32	.280	.371	.381	95	-1	5-2	.981	-8	*116*	*68*	C126	0	-0.1
1949	Bos A★	122	403	42	109	14	0	5	48	62	1	22	.270	.369	.342	83	-8	8-1	.980	-2	*130*	*67*	C118	0	-0.2
1950	Bos A	79	268	33	83	10	1	8	45	29	0	26	.310	.377	.444	100	0	1-1	.988	-3	*110*	*90*	C74	0	0.0
1951	Cle A	55	137	8	36	6	0	2	18	8	1	7	.263	.308	.350	82	-4	0-0	.977	1	*93*	*118*	C44	0	-0.1
1952	Cle A	42	101	4	25	4	0	1	8	12	2	9	.248	.339	.317	89	-1	0-1	.986	-2	*93*	*98*	C37	0	-0.2
Total	14	1162	3704	357	1000	169	22	38	469	389	12	261	.270	.341	.358	81	-99	29-23	.978	23	*108*	*100*	C1108	0	-1.9
TEBEAU, PUSSY	Charles Alston; B2.22.1870 Worcester MA; D3.25.1950 Pittsfield MA; BR/TR/5´10˝/175; d7.22																								
1895	Cle N	2	6	3	3	0	0	0	1	2	0	1	.500	.625	.500	182	1	1	1.000	1	303	0	O2R	—	0.1
TEBEAU, GEORGE	George E. "White Wings"; B12.26.1861 St.Louis MO; D2.4.1923 Denver CO; BR/TR/5´9˝/175; d4.16; b–Patsy; ▲																								
1887	Cin AA	85	318	57	94	12	5	4	33	31	3	—	.296	.364	.403	111	5	37	.887	1	95	68	O84(80/1/3)/P	—	0.3
1888	Cin AA	121	411	72	94	12	12	3	51	61	7	—	.229	.338	.338	111	6	37	.911	2	99	72	O121L	—	0.5
1889	Cin AA	135	496	110	125	21	11	7	70	69	6	62	.252	.350	.381	105	3	61	.887	-7	69	53	O134L/1	—	-0.6
1890	Tol AA	94	381	71	102	16	10	1	36	51	3	—	.268	.359	.370	112	6	55	.951	1	87	30	O94(1/93/0)/P	—	0.3
1894	Was N	61	222	41	50	10	6	0	28	37	2	20	.225	.341	.324	63	-13	17	.857	-5	90	43	O61(8/53/0)	—	-1.7
	Cle N	40	150	32	47	9	4	0	25	25	0	18	.313	.411	.427	98	0	9	.928	-5	24	213	O27(4/23/0),1b12/3	—	-0.5
	Year	101	372	73	97	19	10	0	53	62	2	38	.261	.369	.366	78	-12	26	.880	-10	69	97	O88(12/76/0),1b12/3	—	-2.2
1895	Cle N	92	341	58	111	16	6	0	68	50	1	29	.326	.413	.408	106	5	12	.873	-7	48	0	O49(1/0/48),1b43	—	-0.4
Total	6	628	2319	441	623	96	54	15	311	324	22	129	.269	.364	.376	103	12	228	.900	-20	81	58	O570(349/170/51),1b56,P2/3	—	-2.1
TEBEAU, PATSY	Oliver Wendell; B12.5.1864 St.Louis MO; D5.15.1918 St.Louis MO; BR/TR/5´8˝/163; d9.20; M11; b–George																								
1887	Chi N	20	68	8	11	3	0	0	10	4	0	4	.162	.208	.206	14	-8	8	.855	-1	96	147	3b20	—	-0.8
1889	Cle N	**136**	521	72	147	20	6	8	76	37	2	41	.282	.332	.390	102	0	26	.897	1	100	110	3b136	—	0.3
1890	Cle P	110	450	86	134	26	6	5	74	34	3	20	.298	.351	.416	114	9	14	**.872**	13	103	120	3b110,M	—	1.9
1891	Cle N	61	249	38	65	8	3	1	41	16	3	13	.261	.313	.329	84	-6	12	.884	6	107	137	3b61/lfM	—	0.1
1892	†Cle N	86	340	47	83	13	3	2	49	23	8	34	.244	.307	.318	86	-6	6	.911	-3	94	172	3b74,2b5,1b4,S3,M	—	-0.7
1893	Cle N	116	486	90	160	32	8	2	102	32	4	11	.329	.375	.440	110	5	19	.980	5	128	82	1b57,3b56,2b3,M	—	0.8
1894	Cle N	125	523	82	158	23	7	3	89	35	1	35	.302	.347	.390	74	-24	30	.977	-5	75	100	1b115,2b10,3b2/SM	—	-2.2
1895	†Cle N	63	264	50	84	13	2	2	52	16	2	18	.318	.362	.405	92	-4	8	.992	3	76	113	1b49,2b9,3b6,M	—	0.0
1896	†Cle N	132	543	56	146	22	6	2	94	21	3	22	.269	.300	.343	65	-30	20	.985	3	112	**130**	1b122,3b7,2b5/SPM	—	-2.3
1897	Cle N	109	412	62	110	15	9	0	59	30	4	—	.267	.323	.347	73	-17	11	**.994**	1	89	107	1b92,2b18,3b2/SM	—	-1.4
1898	Cle N	131	477	53	123	11	4	1	63	53	7	—	.258	.341	.304	86	-7	5	.984	3	97	85	1b91,2b34,S7,3b3,M	—	-0.2
1899	StL N	77	281	27	69	10	3	1	26	18	5	—	.246	.303	.313	67	-13	5	.980	-3	73	96	1b65,S11/32M	—	-1.4
1900	StL N	1	4	0	0	0	0	0	0	0	0	—	.000	.000	.000	-99	-1	0	.700	-1	65	0	/SM	—	-0.2
Total	13	1167	4618	671	1290	196	57	27	735	319	42	198	.279	.332	.364	86	-102	164	.984	23	94	104	1b595,3b478,2b85,S25/Plf	—	-6.1
TEED, DICK	Richard Leroy; B3.8.1926 Springfield MA; BB/TR/5´11˝/180; d7.24																								
1953	Bro N	1	1	0	0	0	0	0	0	0	0	1	.000	.000	.000	-98	0	0-0	ø	0	—	—	/H	0	0.0
TEIXEIRA, MARK	Mark Charles; B4.11.1980 Annapolis MD; BB/TR/6´3˝/220; [TexA01 1/5]; d4.1; Col Georgia Tech																								
2003	Tex A	146	529	66	137	29	5	26	84	44-5	14	120	.259	.331	.480	104	2	1-2	.996	-3	96	96	1b116,O25(14/0/11),3b15,D5	0	-1.1
2004	Tex A	145	545	101	153	34	2	38	112	68-12	10	117	.281	.370	.560	133	27	4-1	.992	2	109	95	1b142,O7R,D2	16	1.6
2005	Tex A★	**162**	644	112	194	41	3	43	144	72-5	11	124	.301	.379	.575	145	43	4-0	**.998**	1	101	87	1b155,D8	0	3.0
2006	Tex A	**162**	628	99	177	45	1	33	110	89-12	4	128	.282	.371	.514	127	27	2-0	.997	-3	91	**108**	1b159,D3	0	1.0
Total	4	615	2346	378	661	149	11	140	450	273-34	39	489	.282	.364	.534	128	99	11-3	.996	-3	99	97	1b572,O32(14/0/18),D18,3b15	16	4.5
TEJADA, MIGUEL	Miguel Odalis (Martinez); B5.25.1976 Bani, D.R.; BR/TR/5´9˝/(170–215); d8.27																								
1997	Oak A	26	99	10	20	3	2	2	10	2-0	3	22	.202	.240	.333	48	-8	2-0	.968	-1	93	94	S26	0	-0.7
1998	Oak A	105	365	53	85	20	1	11	45	28-0	7	86	.233	.298	.384	77	-13	5-6	.951	3	106	110	S104	50	-0.3
1999	Oak A	159	593	93	149	33	4	21	84	57-3	10	94	.251	.325	.427	93	-7	8-7	.973	9	103	100	S159	0	1.2
2000	†Oak A	160	607	105	167	32	1	30	115	66-6	4	102	.275	.349	.479	109	7	6-0	.972	2	105	101	S160	0	2.0
2001	†Oak A	**162**	622	107	166	31	3	31	113	43-5	13	89	.267	.326	.476	108	5	11-5	.973	7	102	102	S162	0	2.4
2002	†Oak A★	**162**	662	108	204	30	0	34	131	38-3	11	84	.308	.354	.508	127	24	7-2	.975	8	107	107	S162	0	4.3
2003	†Oak A	**162**	636	98	177	42	0	27	106	53-7	6	65	.278	.336	.472	110	10	10-0	.972	7	104	97	S162	0	3.0
2004	Bal A★	**162**	653	107	203	40	2	34	**150**	48-6	10	73	.311	.360	.534	132	30	4-1	.970	28	**113**	106	S162	0	**6.6**
2005	Bal A★	**162**	654	89	199	**50**	5	26	98	40-9	7	83	.304	.349	.515	127	25	5-1	.971	14	**104**	99	S160,D2	0	4.9
2006	Bal A★	**162**	648	99	214	37	0	24	100	46-10	9	79	.330	.379	.498	129	29	6-2	.972	4	98	105	S150,D12	0	4.1
Total	10	1422	5539	869	1584	318	18	240	952	421-49	80	777	.286	.342	.480	113	102	64-24	.971	81	104	103	S1407,D14	50	27.5
TEJADA, WILFREDO	Wilfredo Aristides (Andujar); B11.12.1962 Santo Domingo, D.R.; BR/TR/6´0˝/(175–185); d9.9																								
1986	Mon N	10	25	1	6	1	0	0	2	2-1	0	8	.240	.296	.280	60	-1	0-0	1.000	-2	93	117	C10	0	-0.3
1988	Mon N	8	15	1	4	2	0	0	2	0-0	0	4	.267	.250	.400	85	0	0-0	1.000	0	94	0	C7	0	0.0
Total	2	18	40	2	10	3	0	0	4	2-1	0	12	.250	.279	.325	69	-1	0-0	1.000	-1	93	71	C17	0	-0.3
TEMPLE, JOHNNY	John Ellis; B8.8.1927 Lexington NC; D1.9.1994 Anderson SC; BR/TR/5´11˝/(154–175); d4.15; C1; Col Catawba																								
1952	Cin N	30	97	8	19	3	0	1	5	5	0	1	.196	.235	.258	37	-9	2-1	.984	-0	92	117	2b22	0	-0.8
1953	Cin N	63	110	14	29	4	0	1	9	7	1	12	.264	.314	.327	67	-5	1-0	.964	7	127	110	2b44	0	0.4
1954	Cin N	146	505	60	155	14	8	0	44	62	2	24	.307	.384	.366	94	-2	21-7	.973	-4	93	107	2b144	0	0.6
1955	Cin N	150	588	94	165	20	3	0	50	80-0	1	32	.281	.365	.325	81	-12	19-4	.971	2	99	**118**	2b149/S	0	0.3
1956	Cin N★	154	632	88	180	18	3	2	41	58-0	1	40	.285	.344	.332	78	-17	14-4	.981	-7	99	87	2b154/rf	0	-1.1
1957	Cin N★	145	557	85	158	24	4	0	37	**94**-0	4	34	.284	.387	.341	92	0	19-5	.974	-13	91	87	2b145	0	-0.1
1958	Cin N	141	542	82	166	31	6	3	47	91-0	4	41	.306	.405	.402	109	13	15-8	.979	-10	91	93	2b141/1	0	1.4
1959	Cin N★	149	598	102	186	35	6	8	67	72-2	2	40	.311	.380	.430	114	15	14-3	.974	-22	93	99	2b149	0	0.6
1960	Cle A	98	381	50	102	13	1	2	19	32-0	1	20	.268	.326	.323	79	-11	11-5	.974	-28	75	93	2b77,3b17	0	-3.4
1961	Cle A★	129	518	73	143	22	3	3	30	61-1	0	36	.276	.351	.347	90	-6	9-5	.969	-31	91	90	2b129	0	-2.5

YEAR	TM LG	G	AB	R	H	2B	3B	HR	RBI	BB-IB	HP	SO	AVG	OBP	SLG	AOPS	ABR	SB-CS	FA	FR	RNG	THR	GAMES AT POSITION	DL	BFW
1962	Bal A	78	270	28	71	8	1	1	17	36-0	1	22	.263	.352	.311	85	-4	7-4	.981	-11	90	96	2b71	0	-0.9
	Hou N	31	95	14	25	4	0	0	12	7-0	0	11	.263	.311	.305	72	-4	1-0	.941	-5	95	43	2b26/3	0	-0.7
1963	Hou N	100	322	22	85	12	1	1	17	41-1	0	24	.264	.347	.317	99	1	7-2	.970	-11	92	59	2b61,3b29	0	-0.5
1964	Cin N	6	3	0	0	0	0	0	0	2-1	0	1	.000	.400	.000	23	0	0-0	ø	0	—	—	/H	0	0.0
Total	13	1420	5218	720	1484	208	36	22	395	648-5	13	338	.284	.363	.351	91	-41	140-48	.974	-132	93	95	2b1312,3b47/1rfS	0	-6.7

TEMPLETON, GARRY Garry Lewis; B3.24.1956 Lockney TX; BB/TR/5´11˝/(170–209); [StLN74 1/13]; d8.9

YEAR	TM LG	G	AB	R	H	2B	3B	HR	RBI	BB-IB	HP	SO	AVG	OBP	SLG	AOPS	ABR	SB-CS	FA	FR	RNG	THR	GAMES AT POSITION	DL	BFW
1976	StL N	53	213	32	62	8	2	1	17	7-0	1	33	.291	.314	.362	90	-3	11-7	.922	5	104	127	S53	0	0.8
1977	StL N★	153	621	94	200	19	**18**	8	79	15-3	1	70	.322	.336	.449	110	5	28-24	.958	3	99	121	S151	0	2.1
1978	StL N	155	647	82	181	31	**13**	2	47	22-3	1	87	.280	.303	.377	90	-12	34-11	.953	**33**	111	124	S155	0	4.2
1979	StL N✱	154	672	105	**211**	32	**19**	9	62	18-4	1	91	.314	.331	.458	111	7	26-10	.960	24	**113**	121	S150	0	4.9
1980	StL N	118	504	83	161	19	9	4	43	18-6	0	43	.319	.342	.417	106	2	31-15	.959	36	**122**	**125**	S115	36	5.3
1981	StL N	80	333	47	96	16	8	1	33	14-3	0	55	.288	.315	.393	96	-3	8-12	.960	11	113	**123**	S76	17	1.4
1982	SD N	141	563	76	139	25	8	6	64	26-7	1	82	.247	.279	.352	81	-17	27-16	.961	-23	94	95	S136	0	-2.7
1983	SD N	126	460	39	121	20	2	3	40	21-7	0	57	.263	.294	.335	76	-16	16-6	.960	-7	95	98	S123	19	-1.0
1984	†SD N	148	493	40	127	19	3	2	35	39-**23**	1	81	.258	.312	.320	78	-14	8-3	.960	-24	92	99	S146	0	-2.4
1985	SD N★	148	546	63	154	30	2	6	55	41-**24**	1	88	.282	.332	.377	99	-1	16-6	.968	-4	101	115	S148	0	1.3
1986	SD N	147	510	42	126	21	2	2	44	35-21	1	86	.247	.296	.308	68	-23	10-5	.966	-25	88	74	S144	0	-3.5
1987	SD N	148	510	42	113	13	5	5	48	42-11	1	92	.222	.281	.296	55	-34	14-3	.972	13	106	92	S146	0	-0.4
1988	SD N	110	362	35	90	15	7	3	36	20-10	0	50	.249	.286	.354	85	-9	8-2	.968	9	106	118	S105,3b2	0	1.0
1989	SD N	142	506	43	129	26	3	6	40	23-12	0	80	.255	.286	.354	82	-13	1-3	.970	13	105	112	S140	0	1.0
1990	SD N	144	505	45	125	25	3	9	59	24-7	0	59	.248	.280	.362	75	-19	1-4	.957	-9	96	107	S135	0	-1.9
1991	SD N	32	57	5	11	1	1	1	6	1-0	0	9	.193	.203	.298	39	-5	0-1	.950	-3	86	131	3b15/S	0	-0.8
	NY N	80	219	20	50	9	1	2	20	9-3	0	29	.228	.257	.306	58	-13	3-1	.963	8	112	117	S40,1b25,3b2,O2R	0	-0.4
	Year	112	276	25	61	10	2	3	26	10-3	0	38	.221	.246	.304	54	-18	3-2	.963	5	110	115	S41,1b25,3b17,O2R	0	-1.2
Total	16	2079	7721	893	2096	329	106	70	728	375-144	9	1092	.271	.304	.369	87	-168	242-129	.961	61	103	109	S1964,1b25,3b19,O2R	72	8.9

TENACE, GENE Fury Gene (b Fiore Gino Tennaci); B10.10.1946 Russellton PA; BR/TR/6´0˝/(180–190); [OakA65 11/340]; d5.29; M1/C10; OF(1/0/10)

YEAR	TM LG	G	AB	R	H	2B	3B	HR	RBI	BB-IB	HP	SO	AVG	OBP	SLG	AOPS	ABR	SB-CS	FA	FR	RNG	THR	GAMES AT POSITION	DL	BFW
1969	Oak A	16	38	1	6	0	0	1	2	1-0	1	15	.158	.200	.237	23	-4	0-0	1.000	1	99	70	C13	0	-0.3
1970	Oak A	38	105	19	32	6	0	7	20	23-2	0	30	.305	.430	.562	177	12	0-2	.990	4	51	127	C30	0	1.7
1971	†Oak A	65	179	26	49	7	0	7	25	29-0	2	34	.274	.381	.430	132	9	2-1	.994	-2	132	67	C52/lf	0	0.9
1972	†Oak A	82	227	22	51	5	3	5	32	24-2	3	42	.225	.307	.339	97	-1	0-0	.979	-5	102	69	C49,O9R,1b7,2b2,3b2	0	-0.5
1973	†Oak A	160	510	83	132	18	2	24	84	101-8	10	94	.259	.387	.443	141	33	2-2	.989	-6	86	107	1b134,C33/2D	0	1.8
1974	†Oak A	158	484	71	102	17	1	26	73	**110**-6	12	105	.211	.367	.411	132	26	2-9	.995	5	80	107	1b106,C79,2b3	0	2.4
1975	†Oak A★	158	498	83	127	17	0	29	87	106-2	12	127	.255	.395	.464	146	36	7-4	.984	2	104	79	C125,1b68/D	0	4.0
1976	Oak A	128	417	64	104	19	1	22	66	81-2	4	91	.249	.373	.458	149	29	5-4	.995	-12	69	95	1b70,C65,D2	27	1.6
1977	SD N	147	437	66	102	24	4	15	61	**125**-10	**13**	119	.233	.415	.410	136	33	5-3	.980	2	96	129	C99,1b36,3b14	0	3.7
1978	SD N	142	401	60	90	18	4	16	61	101-8	11	98	.224	.392	.409	134	25	6-5	.993	5	95	118	1b80,C71/3	0	2.9
1979	SD N	151	463	61	122	16	4	20	67	105-4	7	106	.263	.403	.445	141	32	2-6	**.998**	8	140	**126**	C94,1b72	0	3.9
1980	SD N	133	316	46	70	11	1	17	50	92-11	4	63	.222	.399	.424	140	23	4-4	.979	-4	94	109	C104,1b19	0	2.3
1981	StL N	58	129	26	30	7	0	5	22	38-2	4	26	.233	.416	.403	129	8	0-0	.980	-6	94	82	C38,1b7	0	0.4
1982	†StL N	66	124	18	32	9	0	7	18	36-1	4	31	.258	.436	.500	158	13	1-1	.994	2	92	118	C37,1b7	32	1.6
1983	Pit N	53	62	7	11	5	0	0	6	12-0	4	17	.177	.346	.258	68	-2	0-1	.989	-0	76	83	1b19,C3/rf	24	-0.3
Total	15	1555	4390	653	1060	179	20	201	674	984-58	91	998	.241	.388	.429	137	272	36-42	.986	-8	105	100	C892,1b625,3b17,O11R,D6,2b6	83	26.1

TENNANT, TOM Thomas Francis; B7.3.1882 Monroe WI; D2.15.1955 San Carlos CA; BL/TL/5´11˝/165; d4.18; Col Northern Illinois

YEAR	TM LG	G	AB	R	H	2B	3B	HR	RBI	BB-IB	HP	SO	AVG	OBP	SLG	AOPS	ABR	SB-CS	FA	FR	RNG	THR	GAMES AT POSITION	DL	BFW
1912	StL A	2	2	1	0	0	0	0	0	0	0	—	.000	.000	.000	-99	-1	0	ø	0	—	—	/H	—	-0.1

TENNEY, FRED Fred Clay; B7.9.1859 Marlborough NH; D6.15.1919 Fall River MA; d4.28; Col Brown; ▲

YEAR	TM LG	G	AB	R	H	2B	3B	HR	RBI	BB-IB	HP	SO	AVG	OBP	SLG	AOPS	ABR	SB-CS	FA	FR	RNG	THR	GAMES AT POSITION	DL	BFW
1884	Was U	32	119	17	28	3	1	0	—	6	—	—	.235	.272	.277	69	-8	—	.867	0	85	209	O27(0/1/26),1b6	—	-0.8
	Bos U	4	17	1	2	0	0	0	—	0	—	—	.118	.118	.118	-29	-3	—	.750	-1	51	0	P4	—	0.0
	Wil U	1	3	0	0	0	0	0	—	0	—	—	.000	.000	.000	-97	-1	—	1.000	0	55	1698	/P	—	0.0
	Year	37	139	18	30	3	1	0	—	6	—	—	.216	.248	.252	54	-12	—	.867	-1	85	209	O27(0/1/26),1b6,P5	—	-0.8

TENNEY, FRED Frederick; B11.26.1871 Georgetown MA; D7.3.1952 Boston MA; BL/TL/5´9˝/155; d6.16; M4; Col Brown

YEAR	TM LG	G	AB	R	H	2B	3B	HR	RBI	BB-IB	HP	SO	AVG	OBP	SLG	AOPS	ABR	SB-CS	FA	FR	RNG	THR	GAMES AT POSITION	DL	BFW
1894	Bos N	27	86	23	34	7	1	2	21	12	0	9	.395	.469	.570	139	6	6	.893	2	*120*	*108*	C20,O6(3/2/1)/1	—	0.7
1895	Bos N	49	173	35	47	9	1	1	21	24	0	5	.272	.360	.353	78	-5	6	.885	2	160	129	O28(25/3/0),C21	—	-0.3
1896	Bos N	88	348	64	117	14	3	2	49	36	1	12	.336	.400	.411	108	4	18	.957	4	121	57	O60(7/0/53),C27	—	0.7
1897	†Bos N	132	566	125	180	24	3	1	85	49	4	—	.318	.376	.376	93	-5	34	.988	5	111	109	1b128,O4R	—	0.0
1898	Bos N	117	488	106	160	25	5	0	62	33	0	—	.328	.370	.400	114	9	23	.980	5	115	115	1b117/C	—	1.2
1899	Bos N	150	603	115	209	19	17	1	67	63	3	—	.347	.411	.439	122	18	28	.978	10	131	**134**	1b150	—	2.4
1900	Bos N	112	437	77	122	13	5	1	56	39	6	—	.279	.346	.339	80	-12	17	.981	9	**131**	85	1b111	—	-0.4
1901	Bos N	115	451	66	127	13	1	1	22	37	3	—	.282	.340	.322	85	-8	15	.976	7	**132**	112	1b113,C2	—	-0.2
1902	Bos N	134	489	88	154	18	3	2	30	73	5	—	.315	.409	.376	141	29	21	**.985**	12	**135**	104	1b134	—	**4.0**
1903	Bos N	122	447	79	140	22	3	3	41	70	8	—	.313	.415	.396	137	28	21	.974	9	**131**	93	1b122	—	3.2
1904	Bos N	147	533	76	144	17	9	1	37	57	9	—	.270	.351	.341	118	14	17	.986	8	120	95	1b144,O4(0/1/3)	—	2.0
1905	Bos N	149	549	84	158	18	3	0	28	67	3	—	.288	.368	.332	111	12	17	.982	22	**160**	87	1b148/PM	—	3.2
1906	Bos N	143	544	61	154	12	8	1	28	58	5	—	.283	.357	.340	121	14	17	.983	11	**130**	107	1b143,M	—	2.4
1907	Bos N	150	554	83	151	18	8	0	26	82	5	—	.273	.371	.334	121	18	15	.989	9	**122**	104	1b149,M	—	2.7
1908	NY N	156	583	**101**	149	20	1	2	49	72	7	—	.256	.344	.304	102	6	17	.990	10	121	111	1b156	—	1.5
1909	NY N	101	375	43	88	8	2	3	30	52	3	—	.235	.333	.291	92	-2	8	.986	8	131	115	1b98	—	0.5
1911	Bos N	102	369	52	97	13	4	1	36	50	1	17	.263	.352	.328	84	-7	5	.985	4	120	74	1b96,O2(0/1/1),M	—	-0.6
Total	17	1994	7595	1278	2231	270	77	22	688	874	63	43	.294	.371	.358	109	119	285	.983	135	128	104	1b1810,O104(35/7/62),C71/P	—	23.0

TEPEDINO, FRANK Frank Ronald; B11.23.1947 Brooklyn NY; BL/TL/5´11˝/(185–192); [BalA65 3/55]; d5.12

YEAR	TM LG	G	AB	R	H	2B	3B	HR	RBI	BB-IB	HP	SO	AVG	OBP	SLG	AOPS	ABR	SB-CS	FA	FR	RNG	THR	GAMES AT POSITION	DL	BFW
1967	NY A	9	5	0	2	0	0	0	0	1-0	0	1	.400	.500	.400	175	1	0-0	1.000	-0	0	0	/1	0	0.1
1969	NY A	13	39	6	9	0	0	0	4	4-0	0	4	.231	.302	.231	53	-2	1-0	.950	-1	99	0	O13R	0	-0.4
1970	NY A	16	19	2	6	2	0	0	2	1-0	0	2	.316	.350	.421	117	-0	0-1	1.000	-1	0	0	/1lf	0	-0.1
1971	NY A	6	6	0	0	0	0	0	0	0-0	0	0	.000	.000	.000	-99	-2	0-0	1.000	0	224	0	/lf	0	-0.2
	Mil A	53	106	11	21	1	0	2	7	4-0	1	17	.198	.234	.264	41	-9	2-2	.986	2	144	96	1b28	0	-0.9
	Year	59	112	11	21	1	0	2	7	4-0	1	17	.188	.222	.250	34	-10	2-2	.986	3	144	96	1b28/lf	0	-1.1
1972	NY A	8	8	0	0	0	0	0	0	0-0	0	1	.000	.000	.000	-99	-2	0-0	ø	0	—	—	/H	0	-0.2
1973	Atl N	74	148	20	45	5	0	4	29	13-3	0	21	.304	.354	.419	107	2	0-0	.992	1	108	91	1b58	0	-0.1
1974	Atl N	78	169	11	39	5	1	0	16	9-2	1	13	.231	.272	.272	51	-11	1-2	.988	-0	103	128	1b46	0	-1.6
1975	Atl N	8	7	0	0	0	0	0	0	1-0	0	2	.000	.125	.000	-61	-2	0-0	ø	0	—	—	/H	0	-0.2
Total	8	265	507	50	122	13	1	6	58	33-5	2	61	.241	.288	.306	65	-25	4-5	.989	2	113	105	1b134,O15(2/0/13)	0	-3.6

TEPSIC, JOE Joseph John; B9.18.1923 Slovan PA; BR/TR/5´9˝/170; d7.12; Col Penn St.

YEAR	TM LG	G	AB	R	H	2B	3B	HR	RBI	BB-IB	HP	SO	AVG	OBP	SLG	AOPS	ABR	SB-CS	FA	FR	RNG	THR	GAMES AT POSITION	DL	BFW
1946	Bro N	15	5	2	0	0	0	0	0	1	0	1	.000	.167	.000	-50	-1	0	1.000	0	138	0	/lf	0	-0.1

TERRELL, JERRY Jerry Wayne; B7.13.1946 Waseca MN; BR/TR (BB 1974p)/6´0˝/(165–170); [MinA68 18/412]; d4.14; Col Mankato St.; OF(12/1/11)

YEAR	TM LG	G	AB	R	H	2B	3B	HR	RBI	BB-IB	HP	SO	AVG	OBP	SLG	AOPS	ABR	SB-CS	FA	FR	RNG	THR	GAMES AT POSITION	DL	BFW
1973	Min A	124	438	43	116	15	2	1	32	21-0	1	56	.265	.297	.315	70	-18	13-7	.962	-12	87	74	S81,3b30,2b14/rfD	0	-2.0
1974	Min A	116	229	43	56	4	6	0	19	11-1	0	27	.245	.279	.314	68	-10	3-2	.960	12	109	105	S34,2b26,3b21,D12,O3L,1b2	0	0.5
1975	Min A	108	385	48	110	16	2	1	36	19-0	3	27	.286	.324	.345	88	-6	4-4	.947	2	98	131	S41,2b39,1b15,3b12,O6R,D2	0	0.0
1976	Min A	89	171	29	42	3	1	0	8	9-0	1	15	.246	.286	.275	64	-8	11-2	.988	2	88	101	2b31,3b26,S16,D12,O6(3/1/2)	0	-0.3
1977	Min A	93	214	32	48	6	0	1	20	11-1	1	21	.224	.263	.266	46	-16	10-4	.953	1	101	115	3b59,2b14,S7/1rfD	0	-1.5
1978	KC A	73	133	14	27	1	0	0	8	4-0	0	13	.203	.225	.211	23	-14	8-4	1.000	-2	95	68	2b31,3b25,S11,1b5	0	-1.5
1979	KC A	31	40	5	12	3	0	1	2	1-0	0	1	.300	.317	.450	102	0	1-0	.963	-1	97	54	3b19,2b7/PSD	50	0.0
1980	KC A	23	16	4	1	0	0	0	0	0-0	0	0	.063	.063	.063	-65	-4	0-0	1.000	1	112	0	O7(6/0/1),1b3,2b3/PD	0	-0.2
Total	8	657	1626	218	412	48	11	4	125	76-2	6	160	.253	.288	.304	66	-76	50-23	.961	3	102	132	3b192,S191,2b165,D39,1b26,O24L,P2	50	-5.0

TERRELL, TOM John Thomas; B6.19.1867 Louisville KY; D7.9.1893 Louisville KY; d10.5

YEAR	TM LG	G	AB	R	H	2B	3B	HR	RBI	BB-IB	HP	SO	AVG	OBP	SLG	AOPS	ABR	SB-CS	FA	FR	RNG	THR	GAMES AT POSITION	DL	BFW
1886	Lou AA	1	4	0	1	0	0	0	0	0	0	—	.250	.250	.250	54	0	0	ø	-1	0	0	/lfC	—	-0.1

YEAR	TM LG	G	AB	R	H	2B	3B	HR	RBI	BB-IB	HP	SO	AVG	OBP	SLG	AOPS	ABR	SB-CS	FA	FR	RNG	THR	GAMES AT POSITION	DL	BFW
TERRERO, LUIS	Luis Enrique; B5.18.1980 Santa Cruz de Barahona, D.R.; BR/TR/6´2˝/(205–225); d7.10																								
2003	Ari N	5	4	0	1	0	0	0	0	0-0	1	1	.250	.400	.250	69	0	0-0	1.000	-0	68	0	O3(0/2/1)	0	0.0
2004	Ari N	62	229	21	56	14	0	4	14	20-2	5	78	.245	.319	.358	70	-10	10-2	.938	-3	86	170	O61(1/57/4)	0	-1.1
2005	Ari N	88	161	23	37	6	1	4	20	14-0	6	40	.230	.313	.354	71	-7	3-2	.984	-1	104	38	O77(1/74/2)	22	-0.7
2006	Bal A	27	40	4	8	1	0	1	6	1-0	1	7	.200	.238	.300	39	-4	0-3	.973	3	125	412	O23(16/6/4)/D	0	-0.2
Total	4	182	434	48	102	21	1	9	40	35-2	13	126	.235	.311	.350	68	-21	13-7	.963	-1	97	140	O164(18/139/11)/D	22	-2.0
TERRY, WALLACE	Wallace W.; B10.1850 Attleborough (now Langhorne) PA; D1.21.1916 Philadelphia PA; d4.26																								
1875	Was NA	6	22	0	4	0	1	0	2	0	—	1	.182	.182	.273	58	-1	0-0	.810	-3	0	0	1b4,O3(0/1/2)	—	-0.3
TERRY, ADONIS	William H; B8.7.1864 Westfield MA; D2.24.1915 Milwaukee WI; BR/TR/5´11.5˝/168; d5.1; U1; ▲																								
1884	Bro AA	67	236	15	55	10	3	0	—	8	0	—	.233	.258	.301	81	-5	—	.764	-2	83	0	P56,O13(2/7/4)	—	-0.1
1885	Bro AA	71	264	23	45	1	3	1	20	10	0	—	.170	.201	.208	29	-22	—	.883	1	120	133	O47(26/11/10),P25/3	—	-1.4
1886	Bro AA	75	299	34	71	8	9	2	39	10	1	—	.237	.265	.344	89	-6	17	.934	1	**128**	127	P34,O32(10/11/11),S13	—	-0.4
1887	Bro AA	86	352	56	103	6	10	3	65	16	0	—	.293	.323	.392	98	-4	27	.895	2	62	55	O49(12/4/33),P40,S2	—	-0.3
1888	Bro AA	30	115	13	29	6	0	0	8	5	0	—	.252	.283	.304	89	-1	7	.909	2	93	203	P23,O7(2/4/1),1b2	—	0.1
1889	†Bro AA	49	160	29	48	6	6	2	26	14	0	14	.300	.356	.450	129	5	8	.963	5	125	113	P41,1b10	—	0.2
1890	†Bro N	99	363	63	101	17	9	4	59	40	4	34	.278	.356	.408	122	10	32	.930	-3	40	103	O54(42/5/7),P46/1	—	0.1
1891	Bro N	30	91	10	19	7	1	0	6	9	3	26	.209	.301	.308	78	-2	4	.957	-1	85	70	P25,O5R	—	-0.1
1892	Bal N	1	4	0	0	0	0	0	0	0	0	1	.000	.000	.000	-97	-1	0	1.000	0	149	0	/P	—	0.0
	Pit N	31	100	10	16	0	4	2	11	10	0	11	.160	.236	.300	62	-6	2	.938	-1	90	0	P30/cf	—	-0.1
	Year	32	104	10	16	0	4	2	11	10	0	12	.154	.228	.288	56	-7	2	.940	-1	92	0	P31/cf	—	-0.1
1893	Pit N	26	71	9	18	4	3	0	11	3	1	12	.254	.293	.394	84	2	1	.920	0	98	170	P26	—	0.0
1894	Pit N	1	0	0	0	0	0	0	0	0	0	0	ø	ø	ø	ø	0	0	ø	-0	0	0	/P	—	0.0
	Chi N	30	95	19	33	4	2	0	17	11	0	12	.347	.415	.432	99	0	3	.875	-1	85	0	P23,O7R,1b2	—	0.0
	Year	31	95	19	33	4	2	0	17	11	0	12	.347	.415	.432	99	0	3	.875	-1	84	0	P24,O7R,1b2	—	0.0
1895	Chi N	40	137	18	30	3	2	1	10	2	1	17	.219	.236	.292	33	-15	1	.895	1	115	123	P38/rfS	—	0.0
1896	Chi N	30	99	14	26	4	2	0	15	8	1	12	.263	.324	.343	73	2	4	.968	-2	74	0	P30	—	0.0
1897	Chi N	1	3	1	0	0	0	0	0	0	0	—	.000	.000	.000	-96	-1	0	.750	0	164	0	/P	—	0.0
Total	14	667	2389	314	594	76	54	15	287	146	11	139	.249	.295	.344	85	-44	106	.903	1	101	69	P440,O216(94/43/79),S16,1b15/3	—	-2.0
TERRY, BILL	William Harold "Memphis Bill"; B10.30.1898 Atlanta GA; D1.9.1989 Jacksonville FL; BL/TL/6´1˝/200; d9.24; M10; HF1954																								
1923	NY N	3	7	1	1	0	0	0	0	2	0	2	.143	.333	.143	30	-1	0-0	1.000	0	94	67	1b2	—	-0.1
1924	†NY N	77	163	26	39	7	2	5	24	17	0	18	.239	.311	.399	91	-2	1-1	.988	-1	82	120	1b35	—	-0.6
1925	NY N	133	489	75	156	31	6	11	70	42	1	52	.319	.374	.474	120	15	4-5	.990	4	**113**	84	1b126	—	0.9
1926	NY N	98	225	26	65	12	5	5	43	22	0	17	.289	.352	.453	117	5	3	.979	4	140	124	1b38,O14(1/0/13)	—	0.5
1927	NY N	150	580	101	189	32	13	20	121	46	2	53	.326	.377	.529	141	31	1	.993	5	**111**	111	1b150	—	2.6
1928	NY N	149	568	100	185	36	11	17	101	64	0	36	.326	.394	.518	136	30	7	.993	-2	93	**123**	1b149	—	1.8
1929	NY N	150	607	103	226	39	5	14	117	48	0	35	.372	.418	.522	132	31	10	.994	7	**118**	**129**	1b149/lf	—	2.5
1930	NY N	**154**	633	139	**254**	39	15	23	129	57	1	33	**.401**	.452	.619	159	61	8	.990	14	**137**	94	1b154	—	5.6
1931	NY N	**153**	611	**121**	213	43	**20**	9	112	47	2	36	.349	.397	.529	150	**42**	8	.990	10	129	89	1b153	—	**3.7**
1932	NY N	**154**	643	124	225	42	11	28	117	32	1	23	.350	.382	.580	158	49	4	.991	15	**135**	99	1b154,M	—	4.8
1933	†NY N★	123	475	68	153	20	5	6	58	40	0	23	.322	.375	.423	129	19	3	.992	1	101	**120**	1b117,M	—	0.9
1934	NY N★	**153**	602	109	213	30	6	8	83	60	2	47	.354	.414	.463	138	35	0	**.994**	6	115	**123**	1b153,M	—	2.5
1935	NY N★	145	596	91	203	32	8	6	64	41	0	55	.341	.383	.451	126	22	7	**.996**	6	**113**	109	1b143,M	—	1.4
1936	†NY N	79	229	36	71	10	5	2	39	19	0	19	.310	.363	.424	112	4	0	.996	3	120	142	1b56,M	—	0.2
Total	14	1721	6428	1120	2193	373	112	154	1078	537	9	449	.341	.393	.506	137	341	56-6	.992	72	117	110	1b1579,O15(2/0/13)	—	26.7
TERRY, ZEB	Zebulon Alexander; B6.17.1891 Denison TX; D3.14.1988 Los Angeles CA; BR/TR/5´8˝/129; d4.12; Mil 1918; Col Stanford																								
1916	Chi A	94	269	20	51	8	4	0	17	33	6	36	.190	.292	.249	62	-12	4	.935	-9	93	130	S93	—	-1.7
1917	Chi A	2	1	0	0	0	0	0	0	2	0	0	.000	.667	.000	102	0	0	1.000	-0	74	0	/S	—	0.0
1918	Bos N	28	105	17	32	2	2	0	8	8	1	14	.305	.360	.362	125	3	1	.977	7	115	116	S27	—	1.3
1919	Pit N	129	472	46	107	12	6	0	27	31	4	26	.227	.280	.278	65	-20	12	**.960**	-31	90	84	S127	—	-4.7
1920	Chi N	133	496	56	139	26	9	0	52	44	2	22	.280	.341	.369	102	2	12-16	.962	17	107	99	S70,2b63	—	2.4
1921	Chi N	123	488	59	134	18	1	2	45	27	4	19	.275	.318	.328	71	-20	1-13	.972	8	103	94	2b122	—	-1.2
1922	Chi N	131	496	56	142	24	2	0	67	34	2	16	.286	.335	.343	74	-19	2-11	.964	5	102	**111**	2b125,S4,3b3	—	-1.2
Total	7	640	2327	254	605	90	24	2	216	179	19	133	.260	.318	.322	78	-66	32-40	.956	-3	97	103	S322,2b310,3b3	—	-5.1
TERWILLIGER, WAYNE	Willard Wayne "Twig"; B6.27.1925 Clare MI; BR/TR/5´11˝/(170–175); d8.6; C18; Col Western Michigan																								
1949	Chi N	36	112	11	25	2	1	2	10	16	1	22	.223	.326	.313	74	-4	0	.978	4	119	48	2b34	0	0.2
1950	Chi N	133	480	63	116	22	3	10	32	43	5	63	.242	.311	.363	77	-16	13	.967	-7	**106**	78	2b126/13cf	0	-1.6
1951	Chi N	50	192	26	41	6	0	0	10	29	0	21	.214	.317	.245	52	-12	3-1	.969	-2	99	93	2b49	0	-1.1
	Bro N	37	50	11	14	1	0	0	4	8	1	7	.280	.390	.300	87	0	1-0	.949	4	126	102	2b24/3	0	0.4
	Year	87	242	37	55	7	0	0	14	37	1	28	.227	.332	.256	59	-12	4-1	.964	1	104	95	2b73/3	0	-0.7
1953	Was A	134	464	62	117	24	4	4	46	64	0	65	.252	.343	.347	89	-6	7-4	.982	7	**107**	112	2b133	0	1.1
1954	Was A	106	337	42	70	10	1	3	24	32	3	40	.208	.282	.270	55	-22	3-3	.972	10	117	115	2b90,3b10,S3	0	-0.6
1955	NY N	80	257	29	66	16	1	1	18	36-1	1	42	.257	.348	.339	84	-4	2-4	.985	17	112	128	2b78/S3	0	1.7
1956	NY N	14	18	0	4	1	0	0	0	0-0	0	5	.222	.222	.278	34	-2	0-0	.958	1	88	121	2b6	0	-0.1
1959	KC A	74	180	27	48	11	0	2	18	19-0	0	31	.267	.335	.361	90	-2	2-2	.972	11	115	109	2b63,S2/3	0	1.3
1960	KC A	2	1	0	0	0	0	0	0	0-0	0	0	.000	.000	.000	-99	0	0-0	1.000	0	78	282	2b2	0	0.0
Total	9	666	2091	271	501	93	10	22	162	247-1	11	296	.240	.323	.325	76	-68	31-14	.974	45	110	102	2b605,3b14,S6/cf1	0	1.3
TESCH, AL	Albert John "Tiny"; B1.27.1891 Jersey City NJ; D8.3.1947 Jersey City NJ; BB/TR/5´10˝/155; d8.21																								
1915	Bro F	8	7	2	2	1	0	0	2	0	0	0	.286	.286	.429	100	0	0	.867	1	176	151	2b3	—	0.1
TESTA, NICK	Nicholas; B6.29.1928 New York NY; BR/TR/5´8˝/170; d4.23; C1; Col Florida																								
1958	SF N	1	0	0	0	0	0	0	0	0-0	0	0	ø	ø	ø	ø	0	0-0	.000	-1	3	0	/C	0	-0.1
TETTELBACH, DICK	Richard Morley "Tut"; B6.26.1929 New Haven CT; D1.26.1995 E.Harwich MA; BR/TR/6´0˝/195; d9.25; Col Yale																								
1955	NY A	2	5	0	0	0	0	0	0	0-0	0	0	.000	.000	.000	-99	-1	0-0	1.000	0	0	1288	O2L	0	-0.1
1956	Was A	18	64	10	10	1	2	1	9	14-0	0	15	.156	.304	.281	56	-4	0-1	1.000	1	98	137	O18L	0	-0.5
1957	Was A	9	11	2	2	0	0	0	1	4-0	0	2	.182	.375	.182	65	0	0-0	.900	0	139	0	O3(2/2/0)	0	0.0
Total	3	29	80	12	12	1	2	1	10	18-0	0	17	.150	.300	.250	49	-5	0-1	.980	1	99	166	O23(22/2/0)	0	-0.6
TETTLETON, MICKEY	Mickey Lee; B9.16.1960 Oklahoma City OK; BB/TR/6´2˝/(195–214); [OakA81 5/118]; d6.30; Col Oklahoma St.																								
1984	Oak A	33	76	10	20	2	1	1	5	11-0	0	21	.263	.352	.355	104	1	0-0	.992	1	155	97	C32	0	0.2
1985	Oak A	78	211	23	53	12	0	3	15	28-0	2	59	.251	.344	.351	98	1	2-2	.989	-9	72	107	C76/D	21	-0.5
1986	Oak A	90	211	26	43	9	0	10	35	39-0	1	51	.204	.325	.389	102	2	7-1	.984	-8	80	111	C89	38	-0.2
1987	Oak A	82	211	19	41	3	0	8	26	30-0	0	65	.194	.292	.322	68	-10	1-1	.987	-6	94	72	C80/1D	15	-1.2
1988	Bal A	86	283	31	74	11	1	11	37	28-2	2	70	.261	.330	.424	113	5	0-1	.992	-7	80	101	C80	0	0.2
1989	Bal A★	117	411	72	106	21	2	26	65	73-4	1	117	.258	.369	.509	149	29	3-2	.994	-6	91	95	C75,D43	28	2.6
1990	Bal A	135	444	68	99	21	2	15	51	106-3	5	160	.223	.376	.381	116	15	2-4	.991	-6	103	71	C90,D40,1b5/rf	0	1.2
1991	Det A	154	501	85	132	17	2	31	89	101-9	2	131	.263	.387	.491	139	30	3-3	.990	-2	114	100	C125,D24,O3(2/0/1)/1	0	3.3
1992	Det A	157	525	82	125	25	0	32	83	**122**-18	1	137	.238	.379	.469	135	30	0-6	**.996**	-9	111	96	C113,D40,1b3,O2(1/0/1)	0	2.4
1993	Det A	152	522	79	128	25	4	32	110	109-12	0	139	.245	.372	.492	131	25	3-7	.992	-8	84	113	1b59,C56,O55(18/0/39),D4	0	1.2
1994	Det A★	107	339	57	84	18	2	17	51	97-10	5	98	.248	.419	.463	126	19	0-1	.992	-13	66	72	C53,1b24,D22,O18(1/0/17)	0	0.5
1995	Tex A	134	429	76	102	19	1	32	78	107-5	7	110	.238	.396	.510	130	22	0-0	.972	-3	92	81	O63(2/0/61),D58,1b9,C3	0	1.2
1996	†Tex A	143	491	78	121	26	1	24	83	95-8	3	137	.246	.366	.450	100	2	2-1	.977	-2	77	76	D115,1b23	0	-0.7
1997	Tex A	17	44	5	4	1	0	3	4	3-1	1	12	.091	.167	.318	21	-6	0-0	ø	0	0	0	D13	68	-0.6
Total	14	1485	4698	711	1132	210	16	245	732	949-72	30	1307	.241	.369	.449	121	165	23-29	.991	-78	95	90	C872,D361,O142(24/0/120),1b125	170	9.6
TEUFEL, TIM	Timothy Shawn; B7.7.1958 Greenwich CT; BR/TR/6´0˝/(170–175); [MinA80 2/38]; d9.3; Col Clemson																								
1983	Min A	21	78	11	24	7	1	3	6	2-0	0	8	.308	.325	.538	127	3	0-0	.990	2	105	102	2b18/SD	0	0.6
1984	Min A	157	568	76	149	30	3	14	61	76-8	2	73	.262	.349	.400	102	4	1-3	.984	-6	103	82	2b157	0	0.6
1985	Min A	138	434	58	113	24	3	10	50	48-2	3	70	.260	.335	.399	95	-2	4-2	.980	-24	91	78	2b137/D	0	-1.9

YEAR	TM LG	G	AB	R	H	2B	3B	HR	RBI	BB-IB	HP	SO	AVG	OBP	SLG	AOPS	ABR	SB-CS	FA	FR	RNG	THR	GAMES AT POSITION	DL	BFW
1986	†NY N	93	279	35	69	20	1	4	31	32-1	1	42	.247	.324	.369	93	-2	1-2	.971	-22	80	69	2b84,1b3/3	0	-2.2
1987	NY N	97	299	55	92	29	0	14	61	44-2	2	53	.308	.398	.545	154	25	3-2	.972	-7	96	93	2b92/1	15	2.2
1988	†NY N	90	273	35	64	20	0	4	31	29-1	1	41	.234	.306	.352	93	-2	0-1	.981	16	107	133	2b84,1b3	25	1.7
1989	NY N	83	219	27	56	7	2	2	15	32-1	1	50	.256	.350	.333	101	1	1-3	.960	-0	95	80	2b40,1b33	18	-0.1
1990	NY N	80	175	28	43	11	0	10	24	15-1	0	33	.246	.304	.480	112	2	0-0	.991	-6	93	125	1b24,2b24,3b10	0	-0.5
1991	NY N	20	34	2	4	0	0	1	2	2-0	0	8	.118	.167	.206	4	-5	1-1	1.000	0	59	32	1b6,3b5/2	0	-0.5
	SD N	97	307	39	70	16	0	11	42	49-4	1	69	.228	.334	.388	100	1	8-2	.987	-15	81	84	2b65,3b48	0	-1.2
	Year	117	341	41	74	16	0	12	44	51-4	1	77	.217	.319	.370	91	-3	9-3	.987	-15	82	83	2b66,3b53,1b6	0	-1.7
1992	SD N	101	246	23	55	10	0	6	25	31-3	1	45	.224	.312	.337	83	-5	2-1	.987	-3	98	77	2b52,3b26,1b5	0	-0.7
1993	SD N	96	200	26	50	11	2	7	31	27-0	0	39	.250	.338	.430	103	1	2-2	.990	-4	94	86	2b52,3b9,1b8	0	-0.1
Total	11	1073	3112	415	789	185	12	86	379	387-23	12	531	.254	.336	.404	103	21	23-19	.980	-69	94	86	2b806,3b99,1b83,D2/S	58	-2.1
TEXTOR, GEORGE	George Bernhardt; B12.27.1886 Newport KY; D3.10.1954 Massillon OH; BB/TR/5´10.5˝/174; d4.19																								
1914	Ind F	22	57	2	10	0	0	0	4	2	2	9	.175	.230	.175	10	-8	0	.955	1	*87*	*141*	C21	—	-0.6
1915	New F	3	6	1	2	0	0	0	0	0	0	0	.333	.333	.333	93	0	0	1.000	-1	*73*	*85*	C3	—	-0.1
Total	2	25	63	3	12	0	0	0	4	2	2	9	.190	.239	.190	17	-8	0	.957	1	*86*	*137*	C24	—	-0.7
THACKER, MOE	Morris Benton; B5.21.1934 Louisville KY; D11.13.1997 Louisville KY; BR/TR/6´3˝/(195–210); d8.3																								
1958	Chi N	11	24	4	6	1	0	2	3	1-1	0	7	.250	.269	.542	113	0	0-0	.952	-2	40	197	C9	0	-0.1
1960	Chi N	54	90	5	14	1	0	0	6	14-5	0	20	.156	.269	.167	23	-9	1-1	.980	0	127	151	C50	0	-0.8
1961	Chi N	25	35	3	6	0	0	0	2	11-1	1	11	.171	.383	.171	53	-2	0-0	.973	-2	176	62	C25	0	-0.3
1962	Chi N	65	107	8	20	5	0	0	9	14-1	1	40	.187	.287	.234	40	-9	0-1	.996	7	69	231	C65	0	0.0
1963	StL N	3	4	0	0	0	0	0	0	0-0	0	3	.000	.000	.000	-91	-1	0-0	1.000	-0	65	208	C3	0	-0.1
Total	5	158	260	20	46	7	0	2	20	40-8	2	81	.177	.290	.227	41	-21	1-2	.984	4	102	176	C152	0	-1.3
THAKE, AL	Albert; B9.21.1849 Wymondham, England; D9.1.1872 Brooklyn NY; 6´0˝/?; d6.13																								
1872	Atl NA	18	78	14	23	2	2	0	15	0	—	2	.295	.295	.372	89	-2	2-0	.808	-1	50	0	O18L/2	—	-0.2
THAMES, MARCUS	Marcus Markley; B3.6.1977 Louisville MS; BR/TR/6´2˝/(205–220); [NYA96 30/899]; d6.10; Col East Central (MO) JC																								
2002	NY A	7	13	2	3	1	0	1	2	0-0	0	4	.231	.231	.538	97	0	0-0	1.000	-0	104	0	O7(3/0/4)	0	0.0
2003	Tex A	30	73	12	15	2	0	1	4	8-0	2	18	.205	.298	.274	50	-5	0-1	1.000	-1	91	85	O24(4/0/20),D4	0	-0.7
2004	Det A	61	165	24	42	12	0	10	33	16-0	2	42	.255	.326	.509	118	4	0-1	1.000	3	114	123	O52(40/0/12),D5	0	0.5
2005	Det A	38	107	11	21	2	0	7	16	9-1	1	38	.196	.263	.411	78	-4	0-0	.978	-3	83	0	O31(21/0/10),D4	0	-0.8
2006	†Det A	110	348	61	89	20	2	26	60	37-0	4	92	.256	.333	.549	125	12	1-1	.977	-6	84	27	O59(54/0/5),D46	0	0.2
Total	5	246	706	110	170	37	2	45	115	70-1	9	194	.241	.316	.490	108	7	1-3	.989	-7	94	58	O173(122/0/51),D59	0	-0.8
THEOBALD, RON	Ronald Merrill; B7.28.1943 Oakland CA; BR/TR/5´8˝/165; d4.12; Col Arizona																								
1971	Mil A	126	388	50	107	12	2	1	23	38-0	3	39	.276	.342	.325	91	-3	11-8	.973	7	105	117	2b111/S3	0	1.0
1972	Mil A	125	391	45	86	11	0	1	19	68-2	5	38	.220	.342	.256	81	-5	0-7	.988	-9	104	99	2b113	0	-1.1
Total	2	251	779	95	193	23	2	2	42	106-2	8	77	.248	.342	.290	87	-8	11-15	.980	-2	104	108	2b224/3S	0	-0.1
THEODORE, GEORGE	George Basil; B11.13.1946 Salt Lake City UT; BR/TR/6´4˝/(185–190); d4.14; Col Utah																								
1973	†NY N	45	116	14	30	4	0	1	15	10-0	1	13	.259	.320	.319	79	-3	1-0	.984	3	118	169	O33(28/4/1),1b4	59	-0.2
1974	NY N	60	76	7	12	1	0	1	1	8-0	1	14	.158	.247	.211	29	-7	0-0	.990	-2	35	87	1b14,O12(8/0/4)	0	-1.1
Total	2	105	192	21	42	5	0	2	16	18-0	2	27	.219	.291	.276	59	-10	1-0	.958	1	107	188	O45(36/4/5),1b18	59	-1.3
THERIOT, RYAN	Ryan Stewart; B12.7.1979 Baton Rouge LA; BR/TR/5´11˝/175; [ChiN01 3/78]; d9.13; Col Louisiana St.																								
2005	Chi N	9	13	3	2	1	0	0	0	1-0	0	2	.154	.214	.231	16	-2	0-0	1.000	1	143	0	2b3	0	-0.1
2006	Chi N	53	134	34	44	11	3	3	16	17-0	2	18	.328	.412	.522	135	8	13-2	.984	-13	67	50	2b39,S2/3	0	-0.1
Total	2	62	147	37	46	12	3	3	16	18-0	2	20	.313	.395	.497	124	6	13-2	.985	-12	72	47	2b42,S2/3	0	-0.2
THEVENOW, TOMMY	Thomas Joseph; B9.6.1903 Madison IN; D7.29.1957 Madison IN; BR/TR/5´10˝/155; d9.4																								
1924	StL N	23	89	4	18	4	1	0	7	1	0	6	.202	.211	.270	28	-9	1-3	.951	4	110	87	S23	—	-0.3
1925	StL N	50	175	17	47	7	2	0	17	7	1	12	.269	.301	.331	60	-11	3-0	.950	1	104	60	S50	—	-0.4
1926	†StL N	**156**	563	64	144	15	5	2	63	27	1	26	.256	.291	.311	60	-33	8	.956	16	**111**	106	S156	—	0.0
1927	StL N	59	191	23	37	6	1	0	4	14	0	8	.194	.249	.236	29	-19	2	.945	5	111	124	S59	—	-0.8
1928	†StL N	69	171	11	35	8	3	0	13	20	0	12	.205	.288	.287	50	-13	0	.931	-8	96	99	S64,3b3/1	—	-1.5
1929	Phi N	90	317	30	72	11	0	0	35	25	2	25	.227	.288	.262	35	-32	3	.953	-1	101	87	S90	—	-2.2
1930	Phi N	**156**	573	57	164	21	1	0	78	23	2	26	.286	.316	.326	52	-44	1	.941	-6	104	84	S156	—	-3.0
1931	Pit N	120	404	35	86	12	1	0	38	28	1	22	.213	.266	.248	39	-35	0	.964	5	**109**	114	S120	—	-2.2
1932	Pit N	59	194	12	46	3	3	0	26	7	0	12	.237	.264	.284	48	-15	0	.918	-1	91	111	S29,3b22	—	-1.4
1933	Pit N	73	253	20	79	5	1	0	34	3	0	5	.312	.320	.340	89	-5	2	.975	-8	94	94	2b61,S3/3	—	-1.0
1934	Pit N	122	446	37	121	16	2	0	54	20	2	20	.271	.306	.316	65	-22	0	.969	-14	89	82	2b75,3b44/S	—	-3.0
1935	Pit N	110	408	38	97	9	9	0	47	12	1	23	.238	.261	.304	50	-30	1	.951	4	107	93	3b82,S13,2b8	—	-2.2
1936	Cin N	106	321	25	75	7	2	0	36	15	0	23	.234	.268	.268	48	-25	2	.945	-3	96	87	S68,2b33,3b12	—	-2.1
1937	Bos N	21	34	5	4	0	1	0	2	4	0	2	.118	.211	.176	7	-5	0	.969	0	120	69	S12,3b6,2b2	—	-0.4
1938	Pit N	15	25	2	5	0	0	0	2	4	1	0	.200	.333	.200	49	-2	0	1.000	2	129	44	2b9,S4/3	—	0.1
Total	15	1229	4164	380	1030	124	32	2	456	210	11	222	.247	.285	.294	52	-300	23-3	.950	-4	105	98	S848,2b188,3b171/1	—	-20.4
THOMAS, ANDRES	Andres Perez (b Andres Perez (Thomas)); B11.10.1963 Boca Chica, D.R.; BR/TR/6´1˝/(170–185); d9.3																								
1985	Atl N	15	18	6	5	0	0	0	2	0-0	0	2	.278	.278	.278	53	-1	0-0	.920	1	128	69	S10	0	0.0
1986	Atl N	102	323	26	81	17	2	6	32	8-2	0	49	.251	.267	.372	71	-14	4-6	.958	25	121	124	S97	0	1.9
1987	Atl N	82	324	29	75	11	0	5	39	14-0	2	50	.231	.268	.312	51	-23	6-5	.953	11	115	111	S81	79	-0.5
1988	Atl N	153	606	54	153	22	2	13	68	14-6	1	95	.252	.268	.360	76	-21	7-3	.959	-8	101	98	S150	0	-1.8
1989	Atl N	141	554	41	118	18	0	13	57	12-3	0	62	.213	.228	.316	53	-36	3-3	.956	9	102	119	S138	0	-1.9
1990	Atl N	84	278	26	61	8	0	5	30	11-2	0	43	.219	.248	.302	48	-20	2-1	.967	-1	97	101	S72,3b5	17	-1.7
Total	6	577	2103	182	493	76	4	42	228	59-13	3	301	.234	.255	.334	62	-115	22-18	.958	36	106	110	S548,3b5	96	-4.0
THOMAS, CHARLES	Charles Wesley; B12.26.1978 Fairfield CA; BL/TL/6´0˝/190; [AtlN00 19/580]; d6.23; Col Western Carolina																								
2004	†Atl N	83	236	35	68	8	4	7	31	21-9	9	45	.288	.368	.445	108	3	3-1	.993	7	114	189	O71(70/1/2)	0	0.7
2005	Oak A	30	46	4	5	0	0	0	1	5-0	4	8	.109	.255	.109	2	-6	0-1	.951	1	117	120	O27(13/9/8)	0	-0.6
Total	2	113	282	39	73	8	4	7	32	26-9	13	53	.259	.349	.390	91	-3	3-2	.984	8	115	176	O98(83/10/10)	0	0.1
THOMAS, PINCH	Chester David; B1.24.1888 Camp Point IL; D12.24.1953 Modesto CA; BL/TR/5´9.5˝/173; d4.24																								
1912	Bos A	13	30	0	6	0	0	0	5	2	0	—	.200	.250	.200	28	-3	1	.966	1	*129*	*118*	C8	—	-0.1
1913	Bos A	38	91	6	26	1	2	1	15	2	1	11	.286	.309	.374	97	-1	1	.983	0	*92*	*108*	C31	—	0.1
1914	Bos A	66	130	9	25	1	0	0	5	18	0	17	.192	.291	.200	48	-8	1	.966	2	*127*	*72*	C64/1	—	-0.2
1915	†Bos A	86	203	21	48	4	4	0	21	13	1	20	.236	.286	.296	76	-7	3-2	.969	7	*122*	*89*	C82	—	0.5
1916	†Bos A	99	216	21	57	10	1	1	21	33	1	13	.264	.364	.333	109	4	4	.981	0	135	75	C90	—	1.1
1917	Bos A	83	202	24	48	7	0	0	24	27	2	9	.238	.333	.272	86	-2	2	**.986**	4	*127*	*80*	C77	—	0.9
1918	Cle A	32	73	2	18	0	1	0	5	6	0	6	.247	.304	.274	68	-3	0	.948	1	*130*	*83*	C24	—	0.0
1919	Cle A	34	46	2	5	0	0	0	2	4	0	3	.109	.180	.109	-17	-7	0	.980	-1	*131*	*79*	C21	—	-0.7
1920	†Cle A	9	9	2	3	1	0	0	0	3	0	1	.333	.500	.444	147	1	0-0	1.000	1	*183*	*60*	C7	—	0.2
1921	Cle A	21	35	1	9	3	0	0	4	10	0	2	.257	.422	.343	96	1	0-0	.882	-4	*72*	*24*	C19	—	-0.3
Total	10	481	1035	88	245	27	8	2	102	118	5	82	.237	.318	.284	78	-25	12-2	.973	11	*124*	*81*	C423/1	—	1.5
THOMAS, DAN	Danny Lee; B5.9.1951 Birmingham AL; D6.12.1980 Mobile AL; BR/TR/6´2˝/190; [MilA72 1/6]; d9.2; Col Southern Illinois																								
1976	Mil A	32	105	13	29	5	1	4	15	14-1	2	28	.276	.372	.457	144	6	1-2	.955	-1	92	132	O32L	0	0.3
1977	Mil A	22	70	11	19	3	2	2	11	8-2	1	11	.271	.350	.457	119	2	0-2	1.000	1	126	0	O9L,D9	0	0.1
Total	2	54	175	24	48	8	3	6	26	22-3	3	39	.274	.363	.457	134	8	1-4	.966	-0	100	103	O41L,D9	0	0.4
THOMAS, DERREL	Derrel Osbon; B1.14.1951 Los Angeles CA; BB/TR/6´0˝/160; [HouN69*1/1]; d9.14; OF(93/394/65)																								
1971	Hou N	5	5	0	0	0	0	0	0	0-0	0	2	.000	.000	.000	-99	-1	0-1	1.000	-0	64	148	/2	0	-0.2
1972	SD N	130	500	48	115	15	5	5	36	41-1	2	73	.230	.290	.310	76	-17	9-9	.967	-6	99	91	2b83,S49,O3(0/2/1)	0	-1.4
1973	SD N	113	404	41	96	7	1	0	22	34-3	2	52	.238	.299	.260	61	-21	15-5	.914	4	106	91	S74,2b47	0	-0.6
1974	SD N	141	523	48	129	24	6	3	41	51-7	1	58	.247	.313	.333	85	-11	7-8	.976	2	103	62	2b104,3b22,O20(1/19/0),S5	0	-0.4

YEAR	TM LG	G	AB	R	H	2B	3B	HR	RBI	BB-IB	HP	SO	AVG	OBP	SLG	AOPS	ABR	SB-CS	FA	FR	RNG	THR	GAMES AT POSITION	DL	BFW
1975	SF N	144	540	99	149	21	9	6	48	57-0	3	56	.276	.347	.381	99	-1	28-13	.974	0	92	108	2b141/rf	0	1.0
1976	SF N	81	272	38	63	5	4	2	19	29-0	4	26	.232	.313	.301	73	-9	10-11	.964	6	108	118	2b69,O2(0/1/1)/S3	65	-0.1
1977	SF N	148	506	75	135	13	10	8	44	46-1	2	70	.267	.328	.379	90	-9	15-13	.991	8	111	208	O78(4/74/0),2b27,S26,3b6,1b3	0	0.1
1978	SD N	128	352	36	80	10	2	3	26	35-3	3	37	.227	.301	.293	72	-13	11-6	.991	19	119	246	O77(12/67/0),2b40,3b26,1b14	19	0.6
1979	LA N	141	406	47	104	15	4	5	44	41-7	5	49	.256	.330	.350	88	-6	18-5	.996	2	106	139	O119C,3b18,2b5,S3/1	0	-0.3
1980	LA N	117	297	32	79	18	3	1	22	26-3	1	48	.266	.326	.357	93	-2	7-9	.987	-1	119	114	O52(4/40/8),S49,2b18,C5,3b4	0	-0.1
1981	†LA N	80	218	25	54	4	0	4	24	25-2	0	23	.248	.322	.321	88	-3	7-2	.986	-6	86	102	2b30,S26,O18(3/10/6),3b10	0	-0.6
1982	LA N	66	98	13	26	2	1	0	2	10-1	0	12	.265	.333	.306	82	-2	2-3	1.000	-4	134	0	O28(6/16/8),2b18,3b14,S6	68	-0.6
1983	†LA N	118	192	38	48	6	6	2	8	27-2	2	36	.250	.345	.375	100	0	9-3	.990	0	108	142	O82(15/42/29),S13,2b9,3b7	32	0.2
1984	Mon N	108	243	26	62	12	2	0	20	20-1	0	33	.255	.308	.321	81	-6	0-4	.963	-11	83	111	S62,O48(41/0/7),2b15,3b4/1	0	-1.5
	Cal A	14	29	3	4	0	1	0	2	3-0	0	4	.138	.219	.207	19	-3	0-0	.889	-3	75	0	O7(2/2/4),S4,3b3	0	-0.6
1985	Phi N	63	92	16	19	2	0	4	12	11-1	0	14	.207	.291	.359	79	-3	2-0	.906	-2	92	50	S21,O7(5/2/0)/C23	0	-0.3
Total	15	1597	4677	585	1163	154	54	43	370	456-32	25	593	.249	.317	.332	83	-107	140-92	.970	8	99	98	2b608,O542C,S339,3b116,1b19,C6	184	-4.8
Thomas, Frank	Frank Edward "The Big Hurt"; B5.27.1968 Columbus GA; BR/TR/6´5˝/(240–275); [ChiA89 1/7]; d8.2; Col Auburn																								
1990	Chi A	60	191	39	63	11	3	7	31	44-0	2	54	.330	.454	.529	179	24	0-1	.989	-4	77	133	1b51,D8	0	1.6
1991	Chi A	158	559	104	178	31	2	32	109	**138**-13	1	112	.318	**.453**	.553	**181**	**71**	1-2	.996	-4	70	100	D101,1b56	0	5.8
1992	Chi A	160	573	108	185	**46**	2	24	115	**122**-6	5	88	.323	**.439**	.536	175	**66**	6-3	.992	-11	80	82	1b158,D2	0	4.4
1993	†Chi A★	153	549	106	174	36	0	41	128	112-23	2	54	.317	.426	.607	179	67	4-2	.989	-11	77	104	1b150,D4	0	4.1
1994	Chi A★	**113**	399	**106**	141	34	1	38	101	**109**-12	2	61	.353	**.487**	**.729**	**212**	**75**	2-3	.991	-8	68	99	1b99,D13	0	**5.2**
1995	Chi A★	**145**	493	102	152	27	0	40	111	**136-29**	6	74	.308	.454	.606	183	70	3-2	.991	-11	56	82	1b90,D54	0	4.5
1996	Chi A✱	141	527	110	184	26	0	40	134	109-**26**	5	70	.349	.459	.626	180	**72**	1-1	.992	-4	89	90	1b139	22	4.9
1997	Chi A✱	146	530	110	184	35	0	35	125	109-9	3	69	**.347**	**.456**	.611	**183**	**72**	1-1	.986	-6	79	87	1b97,D49	15	5.1
1998	Chi A	160	585	109	155	35	2	29	109	110-2	6	93	.265	.381	.480	126	26	7-0	.984	-1	72	107	D146,1b14	0	1.7
1999	Chi A	135	486	74	148	36	0	15	77	87-13	9	66	.305	.414	.471	125	24	3-3	.990	-4	65	90	D82,1b49	0	1.0
2000	†Chi A	159	582	115	191	44	0	43	143	112-18	5	94	.328	.436	.625	160	58	1-3	.996	-1	83	145	D127,1b30	0	4.3
2001	Chi A	20	68	8	15	3	0	4	10	10-2	0	12	.221	.316	.441	92	-1	0-0	.955	-0	66	106	D16,1b3	161	-0.2
2002	Chi A	148	523	77	132	29	1	28	92	88-2	7	115	.252	.361	.472	117	15	3-0	.955	0	176	175	D140,1b4	0	0.8
2003	Chi A	153	546	87	146	35	0	42	105	100-4	12	115	.267	.390	.562	142	37	0-0	.995	-3	56	101	D124,1b27	0	2.4
2004	Chi A	74	240	53	65	16	0	18	49	64-3	6	57	.271	.434	.563	152	23	0-2	1.000	0	132	68	D65,1b4	89	1.7
2005	Chi A	34	105	19	23	3	0	12	26	16-0	0	31	.219	.315	.590	131	4	0-0	ø	0	0	0	D28	131	0.2
2006	†Oak A	137	466	77	126	11	0	39	114	81-3	6	81	.270	.381	.545	140	29	0-0	ø	0	0	0	D135	15	2.0
Total	17	2096	7422	1404	2262	458	11	487	1579	1547-165	77	1246	.305	.424	.566	160	732	32-23	.991	-67	76	96	D1094,1b971	433	49.5
Thomas, Frank	Frank Joseph; B6.11.1929 Pittsburgh PA; BR/TR/6´3˝/(200–207); d8.17; OF(709/308/48)																								
1951	Pit N	39	148	21	39	9	2	2	16	9	0	15	.264	.306	.392	84	-4	0-2	1.000	0	92	163	O37C	0	-0.5
1952	Pit N	6	21	1	2	0	0	0	0	1	0	1	.095	.136	.095	-34	-4	0-0	1.000	0	77	254	O5C	0	-0.4
1953	Pit N	128	455	68	116	22	1	30	102	50	2	93	.255	.331	.505	115	9	1-2	.976	6	102	**166**	O118(6/96/16)	0	0.9
1954	Pit N★	153	577	81	172	32	7	23	94	51	**10**	74	.298	.359	.497	124	20	3-2	.989	7	106	122	O153(48/109/0)	0	1.8
1955	Pit N★	142	510	72	125	16	2	25	72	60-10	2	76	.245	.324	.431	101	0	2-0	.984	-2	99	77	O139(86/59/0)	0	-0.9
1956	Pit N	**157**	588	69	166	24	3	25	80	36-5	5	61	.282	.326	.461	112	8	0-5	.942	-4	91	117	3b111,O56L,2b4	0	0.0
1957	Pit N	151	594	72	172	30	1	23	89	44-9	3	66	.290	.335	.460	116	13	3-1	.977	4	97	91	1b71,O59(46/2/19),3b31	0	1.0
1958	Pit N★	149	562	89	158	26	4	35	109	42-2	7	79	.281	.334	.528	129	21	0-1	.926	-24	86	78	3b139,O8(5/0/3),1b2	0	-0.5
1959	Cin N	108	374	41	84	18	2	12	47	27-6	3	56	.225	.278	.380	72	-16	0-2	.927	-3	98	84	3b64,O33L,1b14	0	-2.2
1960	Chi N	135	479	54	114	12	1	21	64	28-4	0	74	.238	.280	.399	84	-13	1-0	.983	-5	100	93	1b50,O49(44/0/6),3b33	0	-2.4
1961	Chi N	15	50	7	13	2	0	2	6	2-0	0	8	.260	.288	.420	84	-1	0-0	1.000	-1	57	288	O10L,1b6	0	-0.3
	Mil N	124	423	58	120	13	3	25	67	29-7	6	70	.284	.335	.506	128	15	2-4	.954	-5	97	44	O109L,1b11	0	0.3
	Year	139	473	65	133	15	3	27	73	31-7	6	78	.281	.331	.497	123	13	2-4	.956	-5	94	62	O119L,1b17	0	0.0
1962	NY N	156	571	69	152	23	3	34	94	48-4	8	95	.266	.329	.496	117	12	2-1	.962	2	97	159	O126L,1b11,3b10	0	0.6
1963	NY N	126	420	34	109	9	1	15	60	33-5	3	48	.260	.317	.393	102	0	0-0	.988	3	101	138	O96L,1b15/3	0	-0.3
1964	NY N	60	197	19	50	6	1	3	19	10-1	2	29	.254	.295	.340	81	-5	1-1	1.000	4	106	99	O31L,1b19,3b2	0	-0.5
	Phi N	39	143	20	42	11	0	7	26	5-2	0	12	.294	.311	.517	132	6	0-1	.976	1	117	134	1b36	0	0.4
	Year	99	340	39	92	17	1	10	45	15-3	2	41	.271	.302	.415	103	0	1-2	.982	4	120	118	1b55,O31L,3b2	0	-0.1
1965	Phi N	35	77	7	20	4	0	1	7	4-0	0	10	.260	.289	.351	83	-2	0-0	1.000	-0	103	300	O12(9/0/4),1b11/3	0	-0.3
	Hou N	23	58	7	10	2	0	3	9	3-0	0	15	.172	.210	.362	63	-3	0-0	.984	-2	68	114	1b16,3b2/lf	0	-0.6
	Mil N	15	33	3	7	3	0	0	1	2-0	0	11	.212	.250	.303	57	-2	0-0	.979	-1	81	66	1b6,O3L	0	-0.3
	Year	73	168	17	37	9	0	4	17	9-0	0	36	.220	.254	.345	71	-7	0-0	.985	-3	70	111	1b33,O16(13/0/4),3b3	0	-1.2
1966	Chi N	5	5	0	0	0	0	0	0	0-0	0	1	.000	.000	.000	-99	-1	0-0	ø	0	—	—	/H	0	-0.1
Total	16	1766	6285	792	1671	262	31	286	962	484-55	51	894	.266	.320	.454	108	53	15-22	.978	-19	99	129	O1045L,3b394,1b268,2b4	0	-4.3
Thomas, Fred	Frederick Harvey "Tommy"; B12.19.1892 Milwaukee WI; D1.15.1986 Rice Lake WI; BR/TR/5´10˝/160; d4.22; Mil 1918																								
1918	†Bos A	44	144	19	37	2	1	1	11	15	1	20	.257	.331	.306	94	-1	4	.968	2	105	52	3b41/S	—	0.3
1919	Phi A	124	453	42	96	11	10	2	23	43	2	52	.212	.283	.294	61	-25	12	.945	-3	94	63	3b124	—	-2.6
1920	Phi A	76	255	27	59	6	3	1	11	26	2	17	.231	.307	.290	58	-15	8-4	.960	2	101	86	3b61,S12	—	-1.0
	Was A	3	7	0	1	0	0	0	0	0	0	1	.143	.143	.143	-25	-1	0-1	1.000	1	189	0	3b2	—	0.0
	Year	79	262	27	60	6	3	1	11	26	2	18	.229	.303	.286	56	-17	8-5	.962	4	104	83	3b63,S12	—	-1.0
Total	3	247	859	88	193	19	14	4	45	84	5	90	.225	.297	.293	65	-42	24-5	.954	3	99	66	3b228,S13	—	-3.3
Thomas, George	George Edward; B11.29.1937 Minneapolis MN; BR/TR/6´3.5˝/190; d9.11; C1; Col Minnesota; OF(136/170/186)																								
1957	Det A	1	1	0	0	0	0	0	0	0-0	0	1	.000	.000	.000	-97	0	0-0	.000	-0	0	0	/3	0	-0.1
1958	Det A	1	0	0	0	0	0	0	0	0-0	0	0	ø	ø	ø	ø	0	0-0	ø	-0	0	0	/rf	0	0.0
1961	Det A	17	6	2	0	0	0	0	0	0-0	0	4	.000	.000	.000	-97	-2	0-0	ø	-0	0	0	O2R/S	0	-0.2
	LA A	79	282	39	79	12	1	13	59	21-1	3	66	.280	.334	.468	101	0	3-6	.986	-9	90	0	O45(24/17/4),3b38	0	-1.2
	Year	96	288	41	79	12	1	13	59	21-1	3	70	.274	.328	.458	99	-1	3-6	.986	-9	89	0	O47(24/17/6),3b38/S	0	-1.4
1962	LA A	56	181	13	43	10	2	4	12	21-0	1	37	.238	.320	.381	91	-2	0-0	.957	2	109	141	O51(3/8/45)	0	-0.4
1963	LA A	53	167	14	35	7	1	4	15	9-1	1	32	.210	.254	.335	68	-8	0-0	.941	-1	101	45	O39(3/1/35),3b10,1b4	0	-1.2
	Det A	49	109	13	26	4	1	1	11	11-0	1	22	.239	.306	.321	76	-3	2-1	1.000	1	122	0	O40(2/30/9)/2	0	-0.4
	Year	102	276	27	61	11	2	5	26	20-1	2	54	.221	.276	.330	71	-11	2-1	.974	-0	111	23	O79(5/31/44),3b10,1b4/2	0	-1.6
1964	Det A	105	308	39	88	15	2	12	44	18-0	3	53	.286	.329	.464	117	6	4-1	.988	-0	101	80	O90(17/57/19)/3	0	0.3
1965	Det A	79	169	19	36	5	1	3	10	12-1	3	39	.213	.269	.308	64	-8	2-3	.948	0	103	173	O59(5/26/28)/2	0	-1.2
1966	Bos A	69	173	25	41	4	0	5	20	23-1	2	33	.237	.332	.347	87	-2	1-0	1.000	3	99	163	O48(10/25/15),3b6,C2,1b2	0	-0.2
1967	†Bos A	65	89	10	19	2	0	1	6	3-0	2	23	.213	.255	.270	51	-5	0-1	.973	-1	93	0	O43(20/3/20),1b3/C	23	-0.9
1968	Bos A	12	10	3	2	0	0	1	1	1-0	0	3	.200	.273	.500	123	0	1-0	1.000	0	144	0	O9(5/2/2)	0	0.1
1969	Bos A	29	51	9	18	3	1	0	8	3-0	1	11	.353	.400	.451	131	2	0-0	1.000	0	154	0	O12(8/1/3),1b10/C3	69	0.1
1970	Bos A	38	99	13	34	8	0	2	13	11-0	2	12	.343	.420	.485	139	6	0-0	.972	-4	109	0	O26(25/0/1),3b6	0	0.1
1971	Bos A	9	13	0	1	0	0	0	0	1-0	0	4	.077	.143	.077	-34	-2	0-0	1.000	-1	37	0	O5(3/0/2)	0	-0.4
	Min A	23	30	4	8	1	0	0	2	4-0	0	3	.267	.353	.300	84	0	0-0	1.000	-2	51	0	O11L/13	0	-0.3
	Year	32	43	4	9	1	0	0	3	5-0	0	7	.209	.292	.233	48	-3	0-0	1.000	-2	45	0	O16(14/0/2)/13	0	-0.7
Total	13	685	1688	203	430	71	9	46	202	138-4	18	343	.255	.316	.389	92	-18	13-12	.976	-12	102	79	O481R,3b64,1b20,C4,2b2/S	92	-5.9
Thomas, Herb	Herbert Mark; B5.26.1902 Sampson City FL; D12.4.1991 Starke FL; BR/TR/5´4.5˝/157; d8.28																								
1924	Bos N	32	127	12	28	4	1	1	8	9	3	8	.220	.288	.291	58	-8	5-2	.983	6	119	165	O32C	—	-0.3
1925	Bos N	5	17	2	4	0	1	0	0	2	1	0	.235	.350	.353	88	0	0-1	.963	-1	97	35	2b5	—	-0.2
1927	Bos N	24	74	11	17	6	1	0	6	3	1	9	.230	.269	.338	67	-4	2	.972	-7	80	75	2b17,S2	—	-1.0
	NY N	13	17	2	3	1	1	0	1	1	1	1	.176	.263	.353	64	-1	0	.900	-0	125	0	O3(1/0/2)/S	—	-0.1
	Year	37	91	13	20	7	2	0	7	4	2	10	.220	.268	.341	65	-5	2	.972	-7	80	75	2b17,S3,O3(1/0/2)	—	-1.1
Total	3	74	235	27	52	11	4	1	15	15	6	18	.221	.285	.315	63	-13	7-3	.976	-2	120	150	O35(1/32/2),2b22,S3	—	-1.6
Thomas, Ira	Ira Felix; B1.22.1881 Ballston Spa NY; D10.11.1958 Philadelphia PA; BR/TR/6´2˝/200; d5.18; C6																								
1906	NY A	44	115	12	23	1	2	0	15	8	1	—	.200	.258	.243	52	-6	2	.938	-3	*103*	*97*	C42	—	-0.7
1907	NY A	80	208	20	40	5	4	1	24	10	3	—	.192	.240	.269	58	-10	5	.953	5	*95*	*127*	C61,1b2	—	0.0
1908	†Det A	40	101	6	31	1	0	0	8	5	1	—	.307	.346	.317	111	1	0	.972	-3	*90*	*51*	C29	—	0.1
1909	Phi A	84	256	22	57	9	3	0	31	18	7	—	.223	.292	.281	79	-6	4	**.985**	14	***127***	*91*	C84	—	1.9
1910	†Phi A	60	180	14	50	8	2	1	19	6	0	—	.278	.301	.361	108	1	2	.967	7	*114*	*96*	C60	—	1.4
1911	†Phi A	103	297	33	81	14	3	0	39	23	8	—	.273	.341	.340	92	-3	4	.974	6	*116*	***110***	C103	—	1.1

YEAR	TM LG	G	AB	R	H	2B	3B	HR	RBI	BB-IB	HP	SO	AVG	OBP	SLG	AOPS	ABR	SB-CS	FA	FR	RNG	THR	GAMES AT POSITION	DL	BFW
1912	Phi A	48	139	14	30	4	2	1	13	8	2	—	.216	.268	.295	63	-7	3	.971	2	*131*	*89*	C48	—	-0.1
1913	Phi A	22	53	3	15	4	1	0	6	4	0	8	.283	.333	.396	116	1	0	.983	2	*120*	*97*	C21	—	0.4
1914	Phi A	2	3	0	0	0	0	0	0	0	0	0	.000	.000	.000	-99	-1	0	1.000	0	*101*	*118*	/C	—	-0.1
1915	Phi A	1	0	0	0	0	0	0	0	0	0	0	ø	ø	ø	ø	0	0	1.000	0	*0*	*.498*	/C	—	0.0
Total	10	484	1352	124	327	46	17	3	155	82	22	8	.242	.296	.308	82	-30	20	.970	29	*114*	99	C450,1b2	—	4.0
THOMAS, GORMAN	James Gorman; B12.12.1950 Charleston SC; BR/TR/6´2˝/(190–215); [MilA69 1/21]; d4.6																								
1973	Mil A	59	155	16	29	7	1	2	11	14-1	0	61	.187	.254	.284	52	-10	5-5	.957	-3	99	32	O50(4/1/46)/3D	0	-1.6
1974	Mil A	17	46	10	12	4	0	2	11	8-0	0	15	.261	.357	.478	143	3	4-0	1.000	-1	101	0	O13(4/1/8),D2	0	0.3
1975	Mil A	121	240	34	43	12	2	10	28	31-0	0	84	.179	.268	.371	80	-7	4-2	.961	-1	102	86	O113(23/92/1),D6	0	-1.0
1976	Mil A	99	227	27	45	9	2	8	36	31-1	1	67	.198	.294	.361	94	-2	2-3	.986	5	114	76	O94(1/66/29)/3D	0	0.0
1978	Mil A	137	452	70	111	24	1	32	86	73-4	2	133	.246	.351	.515	140	25	3-4	.983	-13	90	55	O137C	0	1.1
1979	Mil A	156	557	97	136	29	0	**45**	123	98-6	2	175	.244	.356	.539	138	31	1-5	.991	-7	98	37	O152C,D4	0	2.0
1980	Mil A	**162**	628	78	150	26	3	38	105	58-4	2	170	.239	.303	.471	112	7	8-5	.985	-9	97	51	O160C,D2	0	-0.3
1981	†Mil A★	103	363	54	94	22	0	21	65	50-8	2	85	.259	.348	.493	147	23	4-5	.979	-1	95	122	O97(0/49/49),D6	0	1.8
1982	†Mil A	158	567	96	139	29	1	**39**	112	84-5	4	143	.245	.343	.506	138	30	3-7	.991	-2	97	101	O157C	0	2.4
1983	Mil A	46	164	21	30	6	1	5	18	23-0	1	50	.183	.284	.323	73	-6	2-1	.992	-4	94	0	O46C	0	-1.1
	Cle A	106	371	51	82	17	0	17	51	57-2	1	98	.221	.322	.404	96	-1	8-3	.982	4	108	107	O106C	0	0.3
	Year	152	535	72	112	23	1	22	69	80-2	2	148	.209	.310	.379	89	-7	10-4	.985	0	104	74	O152C	0	-0.8
1984	Sea A	35	108	6	17	3	0	1	13	28-0	1	27	.157	.322	.213	56	-5	0-3	1.000	-3	73	99	O34L/D	138	-1.1
1985	Sea A	135	484	76	104	16	1	32	87	84-6	1	126	.215	.330	.450	111	8	3-2	ø	0	0	0	D133	20	0.4
1986	Sea A	57	170	24	33	4	0	10	26	27-3	1	55	.194	.308	.394	88	-3	1-2	ø	0	0	0	D52	0	-0.5
	Mil A	44	145	21	26	4	1	6	10	31-1	0	50	.179	.324	.345	79	-4	2-2	.980	-1	71	63	D36,1b6	0	-0.6
	Year	101	315	45	59	8	1	16	36	58-4	1	105	.187	.316	.371	84	-7	3-4	.980	-1	71	63	D88,1b6	0	-1.1
Total	13	1435	4677	681	1051	212	13	268	782	697-41	18	1339	.225	.324	.448	113	89	50-49	.984	-35	98	70	O1159(66/967/133),D246,1b6,3b2	158	2.1
THOMAS, LEE	James Leroy; B2.5.1936 Peoria IL; BL/TR/6´2˝/(187–198); d4.22; C2																								
1961	NY A	2	2	0	1	0	0	0	0	0-0	0	0	.500	.500	.500	177	0	0-0	ø	0	—	—	/H	0	0.0
	LA A	130	450	77	128	11	5	24	70	47-2	2	74	.284	.353	.491	111	6	0-5	.966	-1	104	152	O86(26/0/65),1b34	0	-0.4
	Year	132	452	77	129	11	5	24	70	47-2	2	74	.285	.353	.491	111	6	0-5	.966	-1	104	152	O86(26/0/65),1b34	0	-0.4
1962	LA A★	160	583	88	169	21	2	26	104	55-3	6	74	.290	.355	.467	124	19	6-1	.982	-10	71	92	1b90,O74(17/18/42)	0	0.0
1963	LA A	149	528	52	116	12	6	9	55	53-6	9	82	.220	.301	.316	78	-16	6-0	.996	2	113	107	1b104,O43(2/0/41)	0	-2.3
1964	LA A	47	172	14	47	8	1	2	24	18-1	0	22	.273	.340	.366	108	2	1-0	.949	-1	89	144	O47(1/0/46)/1	0	-0.3
	Bos A	107	401	44	103	19	2	13	42	34-4	4	29	.257	.319	.411	97	-1	2-1	.995	1	102	100	O107R/1	0	-0.8
	Year	154	573	58	150	27	3	15	66	52-5	4	51	.262	.325	.398	100	0	3-1	.981	-1	98	113	O154(1/0/153),1b2	0	-1.1
1965	Bos A	151	521	74	141	27	4	22	75	72-8	3	42	.271	.361	.464	126	19	6-2	.984	4	**115**	83	1b127,O20(14/0/6)	0	1.5
1966	Atl N	39	126	11	25	1	1	6	15	10-1	1	15	.198	.261	.365	71	-5	1-1	.987	2	122	81	1b36	0	-0.6
	Chi N	75	149	15	36	4	0	1	9	14-1	3	15	.242	.319	.289	70	-6	0-0	.992	-1	107	121	1b20,O17(16/1/0)	0	-0.8
	Year	114	275	26	61	5	1	7	24	24-2	4	30	.222	.293	.324	71	-11	1-1	.989	1	118	92	1b56,O17(16/1/0)	0	-1.4
1967	Chi N	77	191	16	42	4	1	2	23	15-5	3	22	.220	.284	.283	61	-10	1-0	.969	-3	83	70	O43(0/1/43),1b10	0	-1.7
1968	Hou N	90	201	14	39	4	0	1	11	14-4	1	22	.194	.249	.229	45	-13	2-1	.973	0	88	147	O48(7/0/42),1b2	0	-1.9
Total	8	1027	3324	405	847	111	22	106	428	332-35	32	397	.255	.327	.397	99	-5	25-11	.975	-8	95	113	O485(83/20/392),1b425	0	-7.3
THOMAS, BUD	John Tillman; B3.10.1929 Sedalia MO; BR/TR/6´0˝/180; d9.2																								
1951	StL A	14	20	3	7	0	0	1	1	0	0	3	.350	.350	.500	124	0	2-0	1.000	1	108	82	S14	0	0.2
THOMAS, KITE	Keith Marshall; B4.27.1923 Kansas City KS; D1.7.1995 Rocky Mount NC; BR/TR/6´1.5˝/195; d4.19; Col Kansas St.																								
1952	Phi A	75	116	24	29	6	1	6	18	20	1	27	.250	.365	.474	124	4	0-1	.957	-1	101	60	O29(12/0/17)	0	0.2
1953	Phi A	24	49	1	6	0	0	0	2	3	0	6	.122	.173	.122	-18	-8	0-0	1.000	0	121	0	O15(6/0/9)	0	-0.9
	Was A	38	58	10	17	3	2	1	12	11	1	7	.293	.414	.466	141	4	0-0	1.000	-1	84	0	O8(3/0/5)/C	0	0.2
	Year	62	107	11	23	3	2	1	14	14	1	13	.215	.311	.308	68	-5	0-0	1.000	-1	108	0	O23(9/0/14)/C	0	-0.7
Total	2	137	223	35	52	9	3	7	32	34	2	40	.233	.340	.395	98	0	0-1	.978	-2	104	32	O52(21/0/31)/C	0	-0.5
THOMAS, LEO	Leo Raymond "Tommy"; B7.26.1923 Turlock CA; D3.5.2001 Concord CA; BR/TR/5´11.5˝/178; d4.29																								
1950	StL A	35	121	19	24	6	0	1	9	20	0	14	.198	.312	.273	49	-9	0-1	.964	-2	102	83	3b35	0	-1.1
1952	StL A	41	124	12	29	5	1	0	12	17	2	7	.234	.336	.290	73	-4	2-0	.934	2	106	106	3b37,S3/2	0	-0.2
	Chi A	19	24	1	4	0	0	0	6	6	0	4	.167	.333	.167	42	-2	0-0	.952	1	116	75	3b9	0	-0.1
	Year	60	148	13	33	5	1	0	18	23	2	11	.223	.335	.270	68	-5	2-0	.936	2	107	101	3b46,S3/2	0	-0.3
Total	2	95	269	32	57	11	1	1	27	43	2	25	.212	.325	.271	59	-15	2-1	.948	-0	105	93	3b81,S3/2	0	-1.4
THOMAS, RAY	Raymond Joseph; B7.9.1910 Dover NH; D12.6.1993 Wilson NC; BR/TR/5´10.5˝/175; d7.22; Col Western Michigan																								
1938	Bro N	1	3	1	1	0	0	0	0	0	0	0	.333	.333	.333	82	0	0	1.000	0	*0*	*0*	/C	—	0.0
THOMAS, RED	Robert William; B4.25.1898 Hargrove AL; D3.22.1962 Fremont OH; BR/TR/5´11˝/165; d9.13																								
1921	Chi N	8	30	5	8	3	0	1	5	4	1	5	.267	.371	.467	120	1	0-1	.962	-0	103	76	O8C	—	0.0
THOMAS, ROY	Roy Allen; B3.24.1874 Norristown PA; D11.20.1959 Norristown PA; BL/TL/5´11˝/150; d4.14; C1; b–Bill; Col Penn																								
1899	Phi N	150	547	137	178	12	4	0	47	115	17	—	.325	.457	.362	130	37	42	.952	1	107	150	O135C,1b14	—	2.6
1900	Phi N	140	531	**132**	168	4	3	0	33	**115**	15	—	.316	.451	.335	119	27	37	.958	-6	98	110	O139C/P	—	1.1
1901	Phi N	129	479	102	148	5	2	1	28	**100**	9	—	.309	.437	.334	123	23	27	.967	-3	56	55	O129C	—	1.4
1902	Phi N	**138**	500	89	143	4	7	0	24	**107**	2	—	.286	**.414**	.322	127	25	17	.974	5	126	60	O138C	—	2.4
1903	Phi N	130	477	88	156	11	2	1	27	**107**	3	—	.327	**.453**	.365	139	35	17	.963	12	106	65	O130C	—	3.9
1904	Phi N	139	496	92	144	6	6	3	29	**102**	5	—	.290	.416	.345	141	33	28	.974	13	123	70	O139C	—	4.1
1905	Phi N	147	562	118	178	11	6	0	31	93	4	—	.317	.417	.358	137	33	23	.983	15	137	128	O147C	—	4.1
1906	Phi N	142	493	81	125	10	7	0	16	**107**	6	—	.254	.393	.302	117	18	22	**.986**	8	69	167	O142C	—	2.2
1907	Phi N	121	419	70	102	15	3	1	23	**83**	4	—	.243	.374	.301	113	13	11	.980	2	89	100	O121C	—	1.0
1908	Phi N	6	24	2	4	0	0	0	0	2	0	—	.167	.231	.167	26	-2	0	1.000	-1	0	0	O6C	—	-0.3
	Pit N	102	386	52	99	11	10	1	24	49	5	—	.256	.348	.345	121	11	11	.975	1	54	136	O101C	—	0.8
	Year	108	410	54	103	11	10	1	24	51	5	—	.251	.341	.334	116	9	11	.976	0	51	129	O107C	—	0.5
1909	Bos N	82	281	36	74	9	1	0	11	47	0	—	.263	.369	.302	104	4	5	.976	1	88	39	O76(75/2/0)	—	0.1
1910	Phi N	23	71	7	13	0	2	0	4	7	1	5	.183	.266	.239	46	-5	4	.952	-1	98	87	O20C	—	-0.7
1911	Phi N	21	30	5	5	2	0	0	2	8	0	6	.167	.342	.233	61	-1	0	1.000	1	96	249	O11R	—	0.0
Total	13	1470	5296	1011	1537	100	53	7	299	1042	71	11	.290	.413	.333	124	251	244	.972	49	97	101	O1434(75/1349/11),1b14/P	—	22.7
THOMAS, VALMY	Valmy; B10.21.1928 Santurce, PR; BR/TR/5´9˝/(165–175); d4.16																								
1957	NY N	88	241	30	60	10	3	6	31	16-1	1	29	.249	.296	.390	83	-6	0-0	.991	8	137	82	C88	0	0.5
1958	SF N	63	143	14	37	5	0	3	16	13-0	1	24	.259	.321	.357	82	-4	1-0	.992	-4	174	119	C61	0	-0.5
1959	Phi N	66	140	5	28	2	0	1	7	9-2	1	19	.200	.253	.236	31	-14	1-0	.980	11	85	181	C65/3	0	-0.1
1960	Bal A	8	16	0	1	0	0	0	0	1-0	0	0	.063	.118	.063	-51	-3	0-1	1.000	0	178	167	C8	0	-0.4
1961	Cle A	27	86	7	18	3	0	2	6	6-0	0	7	.209	.261	.314	54	-6	0-0	.988	7	177	157	C27	0	0.3
Total	5	252	626	56	144	20	3	12	60	45-3	3	79	.230	.283	.329	64	-33	2-1	.988	22	140	126	C249/3	0	-0.2
THOMAS, BILL	William Miskey; B12.8.1877 Norristown PA; D1.14.1950 Evansburg PA; BR/TR/5´10˝/190; d5.1; b–Roy; Col Ursinus																								
1902	Phi N	6	17	1	2	0	0	0	0	1	0	—	.118	.167	.118	-12	-2	0	.500	-1	0	1195	O3(2/0/1)/12	—	-0.3
THOMAS, WALT	William Walter "Tommy"; B4.28.1884 Foot Of Ten PA; D6.6.1950 Altoona PA; BR/TR/5´8˝/156; d9.18																								
1908	Bos N	5	13	2	2	0	0	0	1	3	0	—	.154	.313	.154	51	-1	2	.864	-1	96	83	S5	—	-0.1
THOMASON, ART	Arthur Wilson; B2.12.1889 Liberty MO; D5.2.1944 Kansas City MO; BL/TL/5´8˝/150; d8.10																								
1910	Cle A	20	70	4	12	0	1	0	2	5	0	—	.171	.227	.200	33	-6	3	.944	2	98	174	O20(0/1/19)	—	-0.6
THOMASSON, GARY	Gary Leah; B7.29.1951 San Diego CA; BL/TL/6´1˝/(170–195); [SFN69 7/160]; d9.5																								
1972	SF N	10	27	5	9	1	1	0	1	1-0	0	7	.333	.357	.444	124	1	0-0	1.000	-1	28	146	1b7,O2L	0	-0.1
1973	SF N	112	235	35	67	10	4	4	30	22-2	0	43	.285	.345	.413	105	1	2-0	.992	-3	76	64	1b47,O43(23/11/9)	0	-0.5
1974	SF N	120	315	41	77	14	3	2	29	38-2	0	56	.244	.325	.327	80	-8	7-1	.981	2	102	89	O76(20/32/26),1b15	0	-0.9
1975	SF N	114	326	44	74	12	3	7	32	37-1	1	48	.227	.304	.347	79	-10	9-3	.978	8	115	194	O74(27/34/18),1b17	0	-0.5

YEAR	TM LG	G	AB	R	H	2B	3B	HR	RBI	BB-IB	HP	SO	AVG	OBP	SLG	AOPS	ABR	SB-CS	FA	FR	RNG	THR	GAMES AT POSITION	DL	BFW
1976	SF N	103	328	45	85	20	5	8	38	30-7	1	45	.259	.321	.424	107	3	8-3	.959	-4	106	64	O54(5/35/19),1b39	34	-0.5
1977	SF N	145	446	63	114	24	6	17	71	75-8	1	102	.256	.358	.451	117	12	16-4	.959	-1	108	27	O113(62/49/20),1b31	0	0.8
1978	Oak A	47	154	17	31	4	1	5	16	15-2	0	44	.201	.272	.338	74	-6	4-1	.969	1	101	126	O44R,1b5	0	-0.7
	†NY A	55	116	20	32	4	1	3	20	13-0	0	22	.276	.346	.405	113	2	0-2	.972	6	126	173	O50(24/16/12)/D	0	0.6
	Year	102	270	37	63	8	2	8	36	28-2	0	66	.233	.304	.367	91	-4	4-3	.971	7	112	147	O94(24/16/56),1b5/D	0	-0.1
1979	LA N	115	315	39	78	11	1	14	45	43-4	1	70	.248	.339	.422	109	4	4-2	.980	-3	99	62	O100(10/61/43)/1	0	-0.1
1980	LA N	80	111	6	24	3	0	1	12	17-3	1	26	.216	.326	.270	70	-4	0-0	.974	-1	90	71	O31(9/9/15)/1	0	-0.6
Total	9	901	2373	315	591	103	25	61	294	291-29	5	463	.249	.330	.391	98	-5	50-16	.970	3	106	90	O587(182/247/206),1b163/D	34	-2.5

THOME, JIM James Howard; B8.27.1970 Peoria IL; BL/TR/6´4˝/(200–245); [CleA89 13/333]; d9.4; Col Illinois Central JC

YEAR	TM LG	G	AB	R	H	2B	3B	HR	RBI	BB-IB	HP	SO	AVG	OBP	SLG	AOPS	ABR	SB-CS	FA	FR	RNG	THR	GAMES AT POSITION	DL	BFW
1991	Cle A	27	98	7	25	4	2	1	9	5-1	1	16	.255	.298	.367	82	-3	1-1	.900	-1	108	109	3b27	0	-0.4
1992	Cle A	40	117	8	24	3	1	2	12	10-2	2	34	.205	.275	.299	63	-6	2-0	.882	-7	86	48	3b40	68	-1.3
1993	Cle A	47	154	28	41	11	0	7	22	29-1	4	36	.266	.385	.474	132	9	2-1	.950	1	105	122	3b47	0	1.0
1994	Cle A	98	321	58	86	20	1	20	52	46-5	0	84	.268	.359	.523	123	11	3-3	.940	7	115	83	3b94	0	1.6
1995	†Cle A	137	452	92	142	29	3	25	73	97-3	5	113	.314	.438	.558	154	42	4-3	.948	-9	94	106	3b134/D	0	3.1
1996	†Cle A	151	505	122	157	28	5	38	116	123-8	6	141	.311	.450	.612	166	57	2-2	.953	2	106	98	3b150/D	0	5.3
1997	†Cle A★	147	496	104	142	25	0	40	102	**120**-9	3	146	.286	.423	.579	154	44	1-1	.993	-0	98	101	1b145	0	3.0
1998	†Cle A★	123	440	89	129	34	2	30	85	89-8	4	141	.293	.413	.584	151	37	1-0	.991	-0	101	98	1b117,D6	39	2.4
1999	†Cle A★	146	494	101	137	27	2	33	108	**127**-13	4	171	.277	.426	.540	138	34	0-0	.994	7	**123**	96	1b111,D34	0	2.7
2000	Cle A	158	557	106	150	33	1	37	106	118-4	4	171	.269	.398	.531	129	28	1-0	.995	10	130	105	1b107,D48	0	2.4
2001	†Cle A	156	526	101	153	26	1	49	124	111-14	4	185	.291	.416	.624	163	52	0-1	.992	-5	81	83	1b148,D6	0	3.1
2002	Cle A	147	480	101	146	19	2	52	118	**122**-18	5	139	.304	.445	**.677**	**190**	**68**	1-2	.991	-1	94	104	1b128,D18	0	5.1
2003	Phi N	159	578	111	154	30	3	**47**	131	111-11	4	182	.266	.385	.573	158	51	0-3	.997	-6	83	103	1b156,D2	0	3.0
2004	Phi N★	143	508	97	139	28	1	42	105	104-26	2	144	.274	.396	.581	144	36	0-2	.994	-2	97	97	1b134,D6	0	2.1
2005	Phi N	59	193	26	40	7	0	7	30	45-4	2	59	.207	.360	.352	86	-2	0-0	1.000	0	94	91	1b52,D5	114	-0.7
2006	Chi A★	143	490	108	141	26	0	42	109	107-12	6	147	.288	.416	.598	156	45	0-0	1.000	-1	0	52	D136,1b3	0	3.5
Total	16	1881	6409	1259	1806	350	24	472	1302	1364-139	56	1909	.282	.409	.565	148	503	18-19	.994	-5	99	98	1b1101,3b492,D263	221	35.9

THOMPSON, ANDREW Andrew; d4.26

YEAR	TM LG	G	AB	R	H	2B	3B	HR	RBI	BB-IB	HP	SO	AVG	OBP	SLG	AOPS	ABR	SB-CS	FA	FR	RNG	THR	GAMES AT POSITION	DL	BFW
1875	Was NA	11	41	3	4	0	1	0	3	0	—	1	.098	.098	.146	-17	-5	0-0	.624	-8	—	—	C11/rf	—	-1.1

THOMPSON, ANDY Andrew John; B10.8.1975 Oconomowoc WI; BR/TR/6´3˝/215; [TorA94 23/651]; d5.2; [DL 2001 Tor A 45]

YEAR	TM LG	G	AB	R	H	2B	3B	HR	RBI	BB-IB	HP	SO	AVG	OBP	SLG	AOPS	ABR	SB-CS	FA	FR	RNG	THR	GAMES AT POSITION	DL	BFW
2000	Tor A	2	6	2	1	0	0	0	1	3-0	0	2	.167	.444	.167	62	0	0-0	1.000	-1	47	0	O2L	0	-0.1

THOMPSON, BOBBY Bobby La Rue; B11.3.1953 Charlotte NC; BB/TR/5´11˝/175; [TexA72 19/436]; d4.16

YEAR	TM LG	G	AB	R	H	2B	3B	HR	RBI	BB-IB	HP	SO	AVG	OBP	SLG	AOPS	ABR	SB-CS	FA	FR	RNG	THR	GAMES AT POSITION	DL	BFW
1978	Tex A	64	120	23	27	3	3	2	12	9-1	2	26	.225	.284	.350	79	-4	7-2	.982	1	109	40	O52(8/37/10),D3	37	-0.3

THOMPSON, TIM Charles Lemoine; B3.1.1924 Coalport PA; BL/TR/5´11˝/(180–190); d4.28; C1

YEAR	TM LG	G	AB	R	H	2B	3B	HR	RBI	BB-IB	HP	SO	AVG	OBP	SLG	AOPS	ABR	SB-CS	FA	FR	RNG	THR	GAMES AT POSITION	DL	BFW
1954	Bro N	10	13	2	2	1	0	0	1	1	0	1	.154	.214	.231	15	-2	0-0	.909	-1	*0*	*0*	C2/lf	0	-0.2
1956	KC A	92	268	21	73	13	2	1	27	17-1	2	23	.272	.319	.347	76	-6	2-4	.981	1	*88*	*120*	C68	0	-0.6
1957	KC A	81	230	25	47	10	0	7	19	18-6	0	26	.204	.262	.339	62	-13	0-0	.983	-2	84	76	C62	0	-1.2
1958	Det A	4	6	1	1	0	0	0	0	3-0	0	2	.167	.444	.167	70	0	0-0	1.000	-1	63	175	C4	0	-0.1
Total	4	187	517	49	123	24	2	8	47	39-7	2	52	.238	.293	.338	68	-25	2-4	.986	-3	*84*	*99*	C136/lf	0	-2.1

THOMPSON, DANNY Danny Leon; B2.1.1947 Wichita KS; D12.10.1976 Rochester MN; BR/TR/6´0˝/(180–183); [MinA68 S1/18]; d6.25; Col Oklahoma St.

YEAR	TM LG	G	AB	R	H	2B	3B	HR	RBI	BB-IB	HP	SO	AVG	OBP	SLG	AOPS	ABR	SB-CS	FA	FR	RNG	THR	GAMES AT POSITION	DL	BFW
1970	†Min A	96	302	25	66	9	0	0	22	7-0	0	39	.219	.234	.248	33	-28	0-0	.986	-0	105	83	2b81,3b37,S6	0	-2.4
1971	Min A	48	57	10	15	2	0	0	7	7-0	0	12	.263	.338	.298	81	-1	0-0	.897	-2	95	113	3b17,2b3/S	0	-0.3
1972	Min A	144	573	54	158	22	6	4	48	34-1	2	57	.276	.318	.356	96	-4	3-4	.957	-5	102	90	S144	0	0.9
1973	Min A	99	347	29	78	13	2	1	36	16-3	2	41	.225	.259	.282	51	-23	1-0	.950	8	111	85	S95/3D	0	-0.4
1974	Min A	97	264	25	66	6	1	4	25	22-0	2	29	.250	.311	.326	81	-6	1-1	.963	-9	83	91	S88,3b5/D	24	-0.7
1975	Min A	112	355	25	96	11	2	5	37	18-2	0	30	.270	.302	.355	85	-8	0-3	.941	-7	95	76	S100,3b7/2D	0	-0.6
1976	Min A	34	124	9	29	4	0	0	6	3-0	1	8	.234	.256	.266	53	-8	1-1	.988	-0	97	106	S34	0	-0.4
	Tex A	64	196	12	42	3	0	1	13	13-0	1	19	.214	.264	.245	49	-13	2-2	.976	-8	84	56	3b39,2b14,S10/D	0	-2.1
	Year	98	320	21	71	7	0	1	19	16-0	2	27	.222	.261	.253	51	-20	3-3	.981	-9	95	102	S44,3b39,2b14/D	0	-2.5
Total	7	694	2218	189	550	70	11	15	194	120-6	8	235	.248	.287	.310	70	-91	8-11	.956	-24	99	87	S478,3b106,2b99,D6	24	-6.0

THOMPSON, DON Donald Newlin; B12.28.1923 Swepsonville NC; BL/TL/6´0˝/185; d4.24

YEAR	TM LG	G	AB	R	H	2B	3B	HR	RBI	BB-IB	HP	SO	AVG	OBP	SLG	AOPS	ABR	SB-CS	FA	FR	RNG	THR	GAMES AT POSITION	DL	BFW
1949	Bos N	7	11	0	2	0	0	0	0	0	0	2	.182	.182	.182	-2	-2	0	.800	-0	116	0	O2R	0	-0.2
1951	Bro N	80	118	25	27	3	0	0	6	12	1	12	.229	.305	.254	51	-8	2-8	.987	2	110	110	O61(56/6/0)	0	-1.0
1953	†Bro N	96	153	25	37	5	0	1	12	14	1	13	.242	.310	.294	57	-9	2-3	.989	2	105	155	O81(51/8/25)	0	-0.9
1954	Bro N	34	25	2	1	0	0	0	1	5	1	5	.040	.226	.040	-25	-5	0-0	1.000	1	99	230	O29(27/2/0)	0	-0.5
Total	4	217	307	52	67	8	0	1	19	31	3	32	.218	.296	.254	46	-24	4-11	.984	5	107	140	O173(134/16/27)	0	-2.6

THOMPSON, FRANK Frank; d9.11

YEAR	TM LG	G	AB	R	H	2B	3B	HR	RBI	BB-IB	HP	SO	AVG	OBP	SLG	AOPS	ABR	SB-CS	FA	FR	RNG	THR	GAMES AT POSITION	DL	BFW
1875	Atl NA	1	5	1	2	0	0	0	1	0	—	0	.400	.400	.400	205	1	0-0	.000	-1	0	0	/rf	—	0.0

THOMPSON, FRANK Frank E; B7.2.1895 Springfield MO; D6.27.1940 Jasper Co. MO; BR/TR/5´8˝/155; d5.6

YEAR	TM LG	G	AB	R	H	2B	3B	HR	RBI	BB-IB	HP	SO	AVG	OBP	SLG	AOPS	ABR	SB-CS	FA	FR	RNG	THR	GAMES AT POSITION	DL	BFW
1920	StL A	22	53	7	9	0	0	0	5	13	1	10	.170	.343	.170	38	-4	1-1	.878	-4	88	44	3b14,2b2	—	-0.7

THOMPSON, HANK Henry Curtis; B12.8.1925 Oklahoma City OK; D9.30.1969 Fresno CA; BL/TR/5´9˝/(170–175); d7.17; Negro Lg 1943–48 Mil 1944–45

YEAR	TM LG	G	AB	R	H	2B	3B	HR	RBI	BB-IB	HP	SO	AVG	OBP	SLG	AOPS	ABR	SB-CS	FA	FR	RNG	THR	GAMES AT POSITION	DL	BFW
1947	StL A	27	78	10	20	1	1	0	5	10	0	7	.256	.341	.295	76	-2	2-1	.957	0	97	104	2b19	0	-0.1
1949	NY N	75	275	51	77	10	4	9	34	42	1	30	.280	.377	.444	120	8	5	.961	-6	91	97	2b69/3	0	0.6
1950	NY N	148	512	82	148	17	6	20	91	83	3	60	.289	.391	.463	123	19	8	.944	10	**108**	**165**	3b138,O10(0/2/9)	0	2.7
1951	†NY N	87	264	37	62	8	4	8	33	43	0	23	.235	.342	.386	95	-2	1-2	.925	-9	88	111	3b71	0	-1.2
1952	NY N	128	423	67	110	13	9	17	67	50	4	38	.260	.344	.454	119	10	4-4	.979	1	102	74	O72(20/51/1),3b46,2b4	0	0.7
1953	NY N	114	388	80	117	15	8	24	74	60	4	39	.302	.400	.567	146	27	6-5	.956	3	108	83	3b101,O9(1/0/8)/2	0	2.8
1954	†NY N	136	448	76	118	18	1	26	86	90	5	58	.263	.389	.482	126	20	3-0	.945	-2	98	114	3b130,2b2/lf	0	1.8
1955	NY N	135	432	65	106	13	1	17	63	84-4	4	56	.245	.367	.398	105	6	2-2	.943	1	**106**	99	3b124,2b7/S	0	0.7
1956	NY N	83	183	24	43	9	0	8	29	31-2	1	26	.235	.346	.415	105	2	2-1	.908	1	117	104	3b44,O10(8/0/3)/S	0	0.3
Total	9	933	3003	492	801	104	34	129	482	493-6	22	337	.267	.372	.453	118	88	33-15	.941	-2	104	116	3b655,O102(30/53/21),2b102,S2	0	8.3

THOMPSON, HOMER Homer Thomas; B6.1.1891 Spring City TN; D9.12.1957 Atlanta GA; BR/TR/5´9˝/160; d10.5; b–Tommy; Col Georgia

YEAR	TM LG	G	AB	R	H	2B	3B	HR	RBI	BB-IB	HP	SO	AVG	OBP	SLG	AOPS	ABR	SB-CS	FA	FR	RNG	THR	GAMES AT POSITION	DL	BFW
1912	NY A	1	0	0	0	0	0	0	0	0	0	—	ø	ø	ø	ø	0	0	.500	-0	*0*	*0*	/C	—	0.0

THOMPSON, SHAG James Alfred; B4.29.1893 Haw River NC; D1.7.1990 Black Mountain NC; BL/TR/5´8.5˝/165; d6.8; Col North Carolina

YEAR	TM LG	G	AB	R	H	2B	3B	HR	RBI	BB-IB	HP	SO	AVG	OBP	SLG	AOPS	ABR	SB-CS	FA	FR	RNG	THR	GAMES AT POSITION	DL	BFW
1914	Phi A	16	29	3	5	0	1	0	2	7	1	8	.172	.351	.241	82	0	1	.941	2	90	335	O8(2/6/0)	—	0.1
1915	Phi A	17	33	5	11	2	0	0	2	4	0	6	.333	.405	.394	144	2	0-1	1.000	1	87	257	O7C	—	0.2
1916	Phi A	15	17	4	0	0	0	0	0	7	0	6	.000	.292	.000	-12	-2	1	1.000	0	136	0	O8(1/6/1)	—	-0.2
Total	3	48	79	12	16	2	1	0	4	18	1	20	.203	.357	.253	87	0	2-1	.978	3	103	206	O23(3/19/1)	—	0.1

THOMPSON, JASON Jason Dolph; B7.6.1954 Hollywood CA; BL/TL/6´3˝/(200–220); [DetA75 4/75]; d4.23; Col Cal St.–Northridge

YEAR	TM LG	G	AB	R	H	2B	3B	HR	RBI	BB-IB	HP	SO	AVG	OBP	SLG	AOPS	ABR	SB-CS	FA	FR	RNG	THR	GAMES AT POSITION	DL	BFW
1976	Det A	123	412	45	90	12	1	17	54	68-6	1	72	.218	.328	.376	102	3	2-4	.994	4	112	103	1b117	0	-0.4
1977	Det A☆	158	585	87	158	24	5	31	105	73-2	1	91	.270	.347	.487	120	16	0-1	.991	-6	88	101	1b158	0	-0.1
1978	Det A★	153	589	79	169	25	3	26	96	74-3	0	96	.287	.364	.472	130	24	0-0	.993	-9	82	**123**	1b151	0	0.6
1979	Det A	145	492	58	121	16	1	20	79	70-8	1	90	.246	.338	.404	97	-1	2-0	.994	-1	94	115	1b140,D2	0	-1.0
1980	Det A	36	126	10	27	5	0	4	20	13-1	1	26	.214	.289	.349	73	-5	0-1	1.000	3	128	103	1b36	0	-0.4
	Cal A	102	312	59	99	14	0	17	70	70-9	0	60	.317	.439	.526	167	33	2-0	1.000	-3	71	76	1b47,D45	0	2.6
	Year	138	438	69	126	19	0	21	90	83-10	1	86	.288	.398	.475	140	28	2-1	1.000	0	96	88	1b83,D45	0	2.2
1981	Pit N	86	223	36	54	13	0	15	42	59-1	0	49	.242	.396	.502	147	17	0-0	.989	-2	93	115	1b78	0	1.1
1982	Pit N★	156	550	87	156	32	0	31	101	101-7	2	107	.284	.391	.511	145	38	1-0	.993	-0	97	98	1b155	0	2.9
1983	Pit N	152	517	70	134	20	1	18	76	99-7	1	128	.259	.376	.406	114	14	1-0	.993	-5	84	113	1b151	0	0.1
1984	Pit N	154	543	61	138	22	0	17	74	87-14	2	73	.254	.357	.389	110	10	0-0	.990	-8	79	99	1b152	0	-0.8
1985	Pit N	123	402	42	97	17	1	12	61	84-10	0	58	.241	.369	.378	111	10	0-0	.992	1	101	69	1b114	0	0.4
1986	Mon N	30	51	6	10	4	0	0	4	18-2	1	12	.196	.406	.275	92	1	0-1	.962	-3	45	81	1b15	0	-0.3
Total	11	1418	4802	640	1253	204	12	208	782	816-70	9	862	.261	.366	.438	121	160	8-7	.992	-28	91	103	1b1314,D47	0	4.7

YEAR	TM LG	G	AB	R	H	2B	3B	HR	RBI	BB-IB	HP	SO	AVG	OBP	SLG	AOPS	ABR	SB-CS	FA	FR	RNG	THR	GAMES AT POSITION	DL	BFW
Thompson, Jason	Jason Michael; B6.13.1971 Orlando FL; BL/TL/6´4˝/205; [SDN93 9/254]; d6.9; Col Arizona																								
1996	SD N	13	49	4	11	4	0	2	6	1-0	0	14	.224	.235	.429	75	-2	0-0	.964	1	136	63	1b13	0	-0.2
Thompson, Tug	John Parkinson; B9.5.1856 London ON, Can.; D8.1.1938 Guelph ON, Can.; BR/TR/5´8˝/160; d8.31																								
1882	Cin AA	1	5	0	1	0	0	0	—	0	—	—	.200	.200	.200	33	0	—	.000	-1	0	0	/cf	—	-0.1
1884	Ind AA	24	97	10	20	3	0	0	—	2	0	—	.206	.222	.237	51	-5	—	.429	-9	95	0	O12(0/7/5),C12	—	-1.2
Total	2	25	102	10	21	3	0	0	—	2	0	—	.206	.221	.235	50	-5	—	.409	-9	88	0	O13(0/8/5),C12	—	-1.3
Thompson, Kevin	Kevin Deshawn; B9.18.1979 Fort Worth TX; BR/TR/5´10˝/185; [NYA99 31/951]; d6.3; Col Grayson Co. (TX) JC																								
2006	NY A	19	30	5	9	3	0	1	6	6-0	0	9	.300	.417	.500	136	2	2-0	1.000	0	115	0	O15(3/2/10),D3	0	0.2
Thompson, Fresco	Lafayette Fresco "Tommy"; B6.6.1902 Centreville AL; D11.20.1968 Fullerton CA; BR/TR/5´8˝/150; d9.5; Col Columbia																								
1925	Pit N	14	37	4	9	2	1	0	8	4	0	1	.243	.317	.351	66	-2	2-1	.977	-1	88	135	2b12	—	-0.2
1926	NY N	2	8	1	5	0	0	0	1	2	0	0	.625	.700	.625	262	2	1	1.000	-0	113	0	2b2	—	0.2
1927	Phi N	153	597	78	181	32	14	1	70	34	2	36	.303	.343	.409	99	-2	19	.963	1	94	98	2b153	—	0.3
1928	Phi N	**152**	634	99	182	34	11	3	50	42	1	27	.287	.332	.390	85	-15	19	.966	8	101	91	2b152	—	-0.3
1929	Phi N	148	623	115	202	41	3	4	53	75	1	34	.324	.398	.419	96	0	16	.965	11	103	98	2b148	—	1.4
1930	Phi N	122	478	77	135	34	4	4	46	35	0	29	.282	.331	.395	70	-23	7	.955	-3	100	101	2b112	—	-2.1
1931	Bro N	74	181	26	48	6	1	1	21	23	1	16	.265	.351	.326	84	-3	5	.946	-2	94	138	2b43,S10,3b5	—	-0.2
1932	Bro N	3	1	0	0	0	0	0	0	0	0	0	.000	.000	.000	-99	0	0	ø	0	—	—	/H	—	0.0
1934	NY N	1	1	0	0	0	0	0	0	0	0	0	.000	.000	.000	-99	0	0	ø	0	—	—	/H	—	0.0
Total	9	669	2560	400	762	149	34	13	249	215	5	143	.298	.353	.398	88	-43	69-1	.962	13	99	100	2b622,S10,3b5	—	-0.9
Thompson, Milt	Milton Bernard; B1.5.1959 Washington DC; BL/TR/5´11˝/(160–203); [AtlN79*2/29]; d9.4; C3; Col Howard																								
1984	Atl N	25	99	16	30	1	0	2	4	11-1	0	11	.303	.373	.374	103	1	14-2	.956	1	75	302	O25L	0	0.3
1985	Atl N	73	182	17	55	7	2	0	6	7-0	3	36	.302	.339	.363	91	-2	9-4	.964	1	112	78	O49(23/5/27)	0	-0.3
1986	Phi N	96	299	38	75	7	1	6	23	26-1	1	62	.251	.311	.341	77	-10	19-4	.991	2	117	22	O89C	0	-0.6
1987	Phi N	150	527	86	159	26	9	7	43	42-2	0	87	.302	.351	.425	101	1	46-10	.989	4	114	54	O146(1/145/1)	0	1.0
1988	Phi N	122	378	53	109	16	2	2	33	39-6	1	59	.288	.354	.357	103	3	17-9	.983	7	**114**	116	O112(0/112/5)	0	1.0
1989	StL N	155	545	60	158	28	8	4	68	39-5	4	91	.290	.340	.393	106	4	27-8	.978	-4	99	66	O147(23/123/3)	0	0.1
1990	StL N	135	418	42	91	14	7	6	30	39-5	5	60	.218	.292	.328	70	-18	25-5	.971	-4	100	52	O116(12/14/96)	0	-2.2
1991	StL N	115	326	55	100	16	5	6	34	32-7	0	53	.307	.368	.442	125	11	16-9	.991	9	116	160	O91(72/12/12)	0	1.9
1992	StL N	109	208	31	61	9	1	4	17	16-3	2	39	.293	.350	.404	116	4	18-6	.974	-3	89	47	O45(35/1/11)	0	0.2
1993	†Phi N	129	340	42	89	14	2	4	44	40-9	2	57	.262	.341	.350	87	-5	9-4	.994	-1	97	93	O106(102/4/0)	0	-0.9
1994	Phi N	87	220	29	60	7	0	3	30	23-4	3	28	.273	.348	.345	81	-6	7-2	1.000	-1	100	27	O79(72/12/0)	0	-0.8
	Hou N	9	21	5	6	0	0	1	3	1-0	0	2	.286	.318	.429	97	0	2-0	1.000	0	82	306	O6R	0	0.0
	Year	96	241	34	66	7	0	4	33	24-4	3	30	.274	.346	.353	82	-6	9-2	**1.000**	-1	99	46	O85(72/12/6)	0	-0.8
1995	Hou N	92	132	14	29	9	0	2	19	14-3	1	37	.220	.297	.333	71	-5	4-2	.979	2	109	137	O34(15/1/21)	0	-0.5
1996	LA N	48	51	2	6	1	0	0	1	6-0	0	10	.118	.211	.137	-6	-8	1-1	1.000	-1	87	0	O17L	0	-0.9
	Col N	14	15	1	1	1	0	0	2	1-0	0	3	.067	.125	.133	-26	-3	0-0	1.000	0	135	0	/lf	0	-0.3
	Year	62	66	3	7	2	0	0	3	7-0	0	13	.106	.192	.136	-12	-11	1-1	1.000	-1	91	0	O18L	0	-1.2
Total	13	1359	3761	491	1029	156	37	47	357	336-46	22	635	.274	.335	.372	93	-33	214-66	.984	13	105	81	O1063(398/518/182)	0	-2.0
Thompson, Rich	Richard Charles; B4.23.1979 Reading PA; BL/TR/6´3˝/180; [TorA00 6/178]; d4.7; Col James Madison																								
2004	KC A	6	1	1	0	0	0	0	0	0-0	0	0	.000	.000	.000	-99	0	1-0	1.000	0	166	0	O3(1/0/2)	0	0.0
Thompson, Robby	Robert Randall; B5.10.1962 W.Palm Beach FL; BR/TR/5´11˝/(170–173); [SFN83 S1/2]; d4.8; C4; Col Florida																								
1986	SF N	149	549	73	149	27	3	7	47	42-0	5	112	.271	.328	.370	97	-3	12-15	.976	-3	101	116	2b149/S	0	0.0
1987	†SF N	132	420	62	110	26	5	10	44	40-3	8	91	.262	.338	.419	104	2	16-11	.972	4	99	**138**	2b126	15	1.2
1988	SF N*	138	477	66	126	24	6	7	48	40-0	4	111	.264	.323	.384	108	4	14-5	.978	-3	99	**128**	2b134	0	0.7
1989	†SF N	148	547	91	132	26	**11**	13	50	51-0	**13**	133	.241	.321	.400	108	5	12-2	.989	-2	100	116	2b148	0	0.9
1990	SF N	144	498	67	122	22	3	15	56	34-1	6	96	.245	.299	.392	92	-7	14-4	.989	20	112	127	2b142	0	1.9
1991	SF N	144	492	74	129	24	5	19	48	63-2	6	95	.262	.352	.447	127	18	14-7	.985	12	102	**133**	2b144	0	3.6
1992	SF N	128	443	54	115	25	1	14	49	43-1	8	75	.260	.333	.415	118	10	5-9	.978	**26**	109	**144**	2b120	23	3.9
1993	SF N*	128	494	85	154	30	2	19	65	45-0	7	97	.312	.375	.496	136	26	10-4	.988	17	106	**138**	2b128	17	4.8
1994	SF N	35	129	13	27	8	2	2	7	15-0	0	32	.209	.290	.349	69	-6	3-1	.989	5	114	114	2b35	86	0.0
1995	SF N	95	336	51	75	15	0	8	23	42-1	4	76	.223	.317	.339	75	-12	1-2	.993	-19	93	87	2b91	15	-2.7
1996	SF N	63	227	35	48	11	1	5	21	24-0	5	69	.211	.301	.335	69	-10	2-2	.976	-6	94	99	2b62	85	-1.4
Total	11	1304	4612	671	1187	238	39	119	458	439-8	66	987	.257	.329	.403	105	27	103-62	.983	50	103	124	2b1279/S	241	12.9
Thompson, Tommy	Rupert Lockhart; B5.19.1910 Elkhart IL; D5.24.1971 Auburn CA; BL/TR/5´9.5˝/155; d9.3																								
1933	Bos N	24	97	6	18	1	0	0	6	4	0	6	.186	.218	.196	21	-10	0	1.000	2	105	146	O24(1/13/10)	—	-1.1
1934	Bos N	105	343	40	91	12	3	0	37	13	4	19	.265	.300	.318	71	-15	2	.964	8	113	152	O82(6/1/75)	—	-1.2
1935	Bos N	112	297	34	81	7	1	4	30	36	1	17	.273	.353	.343	96	-1	2	.965	5	111	120	O85(12/12/62)	—	0.0
1936	Bos N	106	266	37	76	9	0	4	36	31	1	12	.286	.362	.365	103	2	3	1.000	-1	99	96	O39(10/22/7),1b25	—	-0.3
1938	Chi A	19	18	2	2	0	0	0	2	1	0	2	.111	.158	.111	-31	-4	0-0	1.000	-0	0	483	/1	—	-0.4
1939	Chi A	1	0	0	0	0	0	0	1	0	0	0	ø	ø	ø	ø	0	0-0	ø	0	—	—	/H	—	0.0
	StL A	30	86	23	26	5	0	1	7	23	1	7	.302	.455	.395	117	4	0-0	.977	0	90	172	O23R	—	0.3
	Year	31	86	23	26	5	0	1	8	23	1	7	.302	.455	.395	117	4	0-0	.977	0	90	172	O23R	—	0.3
Total	6	397	1107	142	294	34	4	9	119	108	7	63	.266	.335	.328	84	-24	7-0	.975	13	107	135	O253(29/48/177),1b26	—	-2.7
Thompson, Ryan	Ryan Orlando; B11.4.1967 Chestertown MD; BR/TR/6´3˝/(200–215); [TorA87 13/335]; d9.1																								
1992	NY N	30	108	15	24	7	1	3	10	8-0	0	24	.222	.274	.389	87	-2	2-2	.988	2	117	126	O29(0/26/10)	0	0.0
1993	NY N	80	288	34	72	19	2	11	26	19-4	3	81	.250	.302	.444	98	-2	2-7	.987	5	114	100	O76C	0	0.2
1994	NY N	98	334	39	75	14	1	18	59	28-7	10	94	.225	.301	.434	91	-6	1-1	.989	3	108	90	O98C	0	-0.2
1995	NY N	75	267	39	67	13	0	7	31	19-1	4	77	.251	.306	.378	83	-7	3-1	.985	7	123	86	O74(11/38/31)	66	-0.1
1996	Cle A	8	22	2	7	0	0	1	5	1-0	0	6	.318	.348	.455	101	0	0-0	1.000	-2	37	0	O8C	0	-0.2
1999	Hou N	12	20	2	4	1	0	1	5	2-0	0	7	.200	.273	.400	68	-1	0-0	.800	-1	32	394	O10(2/5/3)	0	-0.2
2000	NY A	33	50	12	13	3	0	3	14	5-0	1	12	.260	.339	.500	110	1	0-1	1.000	-0	104	0	O31(20/9/6)	0	0.0
2001	Fla N	18	31	6	9	5	0	0	2	1-0	0	8	.290	.313	.452	97	0	0-0	.923	-1	62	193	O16(1/4/12)	0	-0.1
2002	Mil N	62	137	16	34	9	2	8	24	7-0	2	38	.248	.295	.518	109	1	1-0	.985	0	101	99	O51(34/5/14)	0	0.0
Total	9	416	1257	165	305	71	6	52	176	90-12	20	347	.243	.301	.433	93	-16	9-12	.986	13	109	96	O393(68/269/76)	66	-0.6
Thompson, Sam	Samuel Luther "Big Sam"; B3.5.1860 Danville IN; D11.7.1922 Detroit MI; BL/TL/6´2˝/207; d7.2; HF1974																								
1885	Det N	63	254	58	77	11	9	7	44	16	—	22	.303	.344	.500	170	19	—	.885	6	203	0	O63R	—	2.3
1886	Det N	122	503	101	156	18	13	8	89	35	—	31	.310	.355	.445	137	21	13	.945	8	117	**329**	O122R	—	2.5
1887	†Det N	**127**	545	118	**203**	29	**23**	10	**166**	32	9	19	.372	.416	**.565**	164	45	22	.909	6	107	179	O127R	—	4.2
1888	Det N	56	238	51	67	10	8	6	40	23	3	10	.282	.352	.466	157	16	5	.882	-8	41	0	O56R	—	0.7
1889	Phi N	128	533	103	158	36	4	**20**	111	36	6	22	.296	.348	.492	122	12	24	.901	-8	78	150	O128R	—	0.2
1890	Phi N	132	549	116	**172**	**41**	9	4	102	42	8	29	.313	.371	.443	133	22	25	.939	0	126	103	O132R	—	1.9
1891	Phi N	133	554	108	163	23	10	7	90	52	8	20	.294	.363	.410	122	15	29	.937	18	153	164	O133(0/2/131)	—	2.8
1892	Phi N	153	609	109	186	28	11	9	104	59	11	19	.305	.377	.432	145	33	28	.937	1	112	138	O153(3/0/150)	—	2.5
1893	Phi N	131	600	130	**222**	**37**	13	11	126	50	6	17	.370	.424	.530	153	44	18	.931	-12	78	65	O131R/1	—	2.1
1894	Phi N	102	451	114	187	32	28	13	**147**	41	1	13	.415	.465	**.696**	**181**	57	27	**.972**	-4	73	50	O102R	—	3.6
1895	Phi N	119	538	131	211	45	21	**18**	**165**	31	5	11	.392	.430	**.654**	177	57	27	.943	12	**179**	49	O118R	—	5.0
1896	Phi N	119	517	103	154	28	7	12	100	28	6	13	.298	.341	.449	108	4	12	**.974**	18	**169**	**242**	O119R	—	1.3
1897	Phi N	3	13	2	3	0	1	0	3	1	0	—	.231	.286	.385	78	-1	0	.833	0	224	0	O3R	—	-0.1
1898	Phi N	14	63	14	22	5	3	1	15	4	0	—	.349	.388	.571	182	6	2	1.000	3	281	0	O14R	—	0.7
1906	Det A	8	31	4	7	0	1	0	3	1	0	—	.226	.250	.290	67	-1	0	1.000	-0	0	0	O8R	—	-0.2
Total	15	1410	5998	1262	1988	343	161	126	1305	451	63	226	.331	.384	.505	146	349	232	.934	41	121	133	O1409(3/2/1404)/1	—	29.5
Thompson, Scot	Vernon Scot; B12.7.1955 Grove City PA; BL/TL/6´3˝/(175–195); [ChiN74 1/7]; d9.3																								
1978	Chi N	19	36	7	15	3	0	0	2	2-0	0	4	.417	.447	.500	147	2	0-0	1.000	-1	50	0	O5(0/5/1),1b2	0	0.1
1979	Chi N	128	346	36	100	13	5	2	29	17-1	1	37	.289	.322	.373	82	-9	4-3	.971	-1	98	112	O100(12/26/72)	0	-1.4
1980	Chi N	102	226	26	48	10	1	2	13	28-3	1	31	.212	.301	.292	61	-11	6-6	.963	-3	89	90	O66(1/14/52),1b12	31	-1.9

YEAR	TM LG	G	AB	R	H	2B	3B	HR	RBI	BB-IB	HP	SO	AVG	OBP	SLG	AOPS	ABR	SB-CS	FA	FR	RNG	THR	GAMES AT POSITION	DL	BFW
1981	Chi N	57	115	8	19	5	0	0	8	7-1	0	8	.165	.208	.209	19	-12	2-0	.980	-4	78	54	O30(3/20/8),1b3	0	-1.7
1982	Chi N	49	74	11	27	5	1	0	7	5-0	0	4	.365	.405	.459	136	4	0-1	1.000	3	130	186	O23(20/1/4),1b4	34	0.6
1983	Chi N	53	88	4	17	3	1	0	10	3-0	0	14	.193	.220	.250	28	-9	0-0	1.000	-2	88	0	O29(23/0/6)/1	0	-1.2
1984	SF N	120	245	30	75	7	1	1	31	30-5	0	26	.306	.376	.355	111	5	5-3	.998	-2	92	93	1b87,O6(2/0/4)	0	-0.1
1985	SF N	64	111	8	23	5	0	0	6	2-0	0	10	.207	.221	.252	34	-10	0-0	.995	2	146	94	1b24	0	-1.0
	Mon N	34	32	2	9	1	0	0	4	3-0	0	7	.281	.333	.313	89	0	0-0	1.000	1	114	100	1b3,O3R	0	0.0
	Year	98	143	10	32	6	0	0	10	5-0	0	17	.224	.248	.266	46	-11	0-0	.995	3	144	94	1b27,O3R	0	-1.0
Total	8	626	1273	132	333	52	9	5	110	97-10	2	141	.262	.312	.328	76	-40	17-13	.973	-6	92	96	O262(61/66/150),1b136	65	-6.6

THOMSON, BOBBY Robert Brown "The Staten Island Scot"; B10.25.1923 Glasgow, Scotland; BR/TR/6´2˝/(185–190); d9.9

YEAR	TM LG	G	AB	R	H	2B	3B	HR	RBI	BB-IB	HP	SO	AVG	OBP	SLG	AOPS	ABR	SB-CS	FA	FR	RNG	THR	GAMES AT POSITION	DL	BFW
1946	NY N	18	54	8	17	4	1	2	9	4	0	5	.315	.362	.537	152	3	0	.935	-0	94	0	3b16	0	0.3
1947	NY N	138	545	105	154	26	5	29	85	40	4	78	.283	.336	.508	121	13	1	.980	-3	96	132	O127C,2b9	0	0.7
1948	NY N★	138	471	75	117	20	2	16	63	30	2	77	.248	.296	.401	87	-11	2	.970	3	105	105	O125(64/57/4)	0	-1.4
1949	NY N★	**156**	641	99	198	35	9	27	109	44	2	45	.309	.355	.518	132	25	10	.982	8	111	87	O156C	0	2.8
1950	NY N	149	563	79	142	22	7	25	85	55	5	45	.252	.324	.449	101	-2	3	.978	3	101	121	O149C	0	-0.3
1951	†NY N	148	518	89	152	27	8	32	101	73	4	57	.293	.385	.562	150	37	5-5	.966	-10	97	48	O77(33/43/3),3b69	0	2.2
1952	NY N★	153	608	89	164	29	**14**	24	108	52	4	74	.270	.331	.482	122	15	5-2	.940	-5	104	87	3b91,O63C	0	0.9
1953	NY N	154	608	80	175	22	6	26	106	43	3	57	.288	.338	.472	106	4	4-2	.983	-4	92	114	O154(0/153/1)	0	-0.7
1954	Mil N	43	99	7	23	3	0	2	15	12	0	29	.232	.315	.323	71	-4	0-0	.980	1	93	198	O26L	91	-0.5
1955	Mil N	101	343	40	88	12	3	12	56	34-4	0	52	.257	.319	.414	99	-1	2-1	.969	-3	97	72	O91(88/3/0)	0	-0.9
1956	Mil N	142	451	59	106	10	4	20	74	43-4	2	75	.235	.302	.408	95	-5	2-4	.974	-1	100	84	O136(128/18/0),3b3	0	-1.5
1957	Mil N	41	148	15	35	5	3	4	23	8-0	2	27	.236	.285	.392	86	-4	2-1	.988	-0	99	75	O38(36/5/1)	0	-0.7
	NY N	81	215	24	52	7	4	8	38	19-2	0	39	.242	.302	.423	93	-3	1-2	.992	1	111	50	O71(54/3/17)/3	0	-0.5
	Year	122	363	39	87	12	7	12	61	27-2	2	66	.240	.295	.410	90	-7	3-3	.990	1	106	60	O109(90/8/18)/3	0	-1.2
1958	Chi N	152	547	67	155	27	5	21	82	56-7	4	76	.283	.351	.466	117	13	0-2	.989	-2	97	114	O148(7/143/1),3b4	0	0.3
1959	Chi N	122	374	55	97	15	2	11	52	35-6	2	50	.259	.322	.398	93	-4	1-0	.987	3	101	119	O116(62/49/29)	0	-0.7
1960	Bos A	40	114	12	30	3	1	5	20	11-0	0	15	.263	.323	.439	102	0	0-1	.971	1	116	62	O27(12/13/2)/1	0	-0.1
	Bal A	3	6	0	0	0	0	0	0	0-0	0	3	.000	.000	.000	-99	-2	0-0	ø	-1	0	0	O2(1/0/1)	0	-0.2
	Year	43	120	12	30	3	1	5	20	11-0	0	18	.250	.308	.417	93	-2	0-1	.971	0	111	59	O29(13/13/3)/1	0	-0.3
Total	15	1779	6305	903	1705	267	74	264	1026	559-23	34	804	.270	.332	.462	111	74	38-20	.980	-10	100	99	O1506(511/982/59),3b184,2b9/1	91	-0.3

THON, DICKIE Richard William; B6.20.1958 South Bend IN; BR/TR/5´11˝/(150–178); d5.22

YEAR	TM LG	G	AB	R	H	2B	3B	HR	RBI	BB-IB	HP	SO	AVG	OBP	SLG	AOPS	ABR	SB-CS	FA	FR	RNG	THR	GAMES AT POSITION	DL	BFW
1979	†Cal A	35	56	6	19	3	0	0	8	5-0	0	10	.339	.393	.393	116	2	0-0	.923	-3	84	114	2b24,S8/3D	0	0.0
1980	Cal A	80	267	32	68	12	2	0	15	10-0	1	28	.255	.282	.315	65	-13	7-5	.928	-11	99	80	S22,2b21,D15,3b10/1	0	-2.2
1981	†Hou N	49	95	13	26	6	0	0	3	9-1	0	13	.274	.337	.337	97	0	6-1	.950	-10	63	93	2b28,S13,3b5	0	-0.8
1982	Hou N	136	496	73	137	31	**10**	3	36	37-2	1	48	.276	.327	.397	110	6	37-8	.975	18	109	125	S119,3b8/2	0	4.3
1983	Hou N★	154	619	81	177	28	9	20	79	54-10	2	73	.286	.341	.457	128	21	34-16	.966	22	111	**128**	S154	0	6.2
1984	Hou N	5	17	3	6	0	1	0	1	0-0	1	4	.353	.389	.471	150	1	0-1	1.000	-0	94	40	S5	175	0.1
1985	Hou N	84	251	26	63	6	1	6	29	18-4	0	50	.251	.299	.355	85	-6	8-3	.967	2	101	115	S79	20	0.4
1986	†Hou N	106	278	24	69	13	1	3	21	29-5	0	49	.248	.318	.335	83	-6	6-5	.972	-2	87	95	S104	17	0.0
1987	Hou N	32	66	6	14	1	0	1	3	16-3	0	13	.212	.366	.273	75	-2	3-0	.925	-5	87	62	S31	21	-0.4
1988	SD N	95	258	36	68	12	2	1	18	33-0	1	49	.264	.347	.337	100	1	19-4	.954	-11	92	87	S70,2b2/3	0	-0.3
1989	Phi N	136	435	45	118	18	4	15	60	33-6	0	81	.271	.321	.434	115	7	6-3	.972	20	**113**	102	S129	0	3.7
1990	Phi N	149	552	54	141	20	4	8	48	37-10	3	77	.255	.305	.350	80	-16	12-5	.964	2	105	108	S148	0	-0.3
1991	Phi N	146	539	44	136	18	4	9	44	25-6	0	84	.252	.283	.351	79	-17	11-5	.969	-9	96	85	S146	0	-1.6
1992	Tex A	95	275	30	68	15	3	4	37	20-1	0	40	.247	.293	.367	88	-5	12-2	.958	-2	98	72	S87	37	0.1
1993	Mil A	85	245	23	66	10	1	1	33	22-3	0	39	.269	.324	.331	79	-7	6-5	.966	-9	96	62	S28,3b25,2b22,D14	16	-1.5
Total	15	1387	4449	496	1176	193	42	71	435	348-51	9	658	.264	.317	.374	95	-34	167-63	.965	1	102	101	S1143,2b98,3b50,D30/1	286	7.7

THONEY, JACK John "Bullet Jack" (b John Thoeny); B12.8.1879 Ft.Thomas KY; D10.24.1948 Covington KY; BR/TR/5´10˝/175; d4.26

YEAR	TM LG	G	AB	R	H	2B	3B	HR	RBI	BB-IB	HP	SO	AVG	OBP	SLG	AOPS	ABR	SB-CS	FA	FR	RNG	THR	GAMES AT POSITION	DL	BFW
1902	Cle A	28	105	14	30	7	1	0	11	9	0	—	.286	.342	.371	102	1	4	.891	-11	102	21	2b14,S11,O2R	—	-1.0
	Bal A	3	11	1	0	0	0	0	0	1	0	—	.000	.083	.000	-72	-3	1	.778	-1	68	0	3b3	—	-0.4
	Year	31	116	15	30	7	1	0	11	10	0	—	.259	.317	.336	84	-2	5	.891	-12	102	21	2b14,S11,3b3,O2R	—	-1.4
1903	Cle A	32	122	10	25	3	0	1	9	2	0	—	.205	.218	.254	42	-9	7	.889	-1	217	148	O24(0/23/1),2b5,3b2	—	-1.1
1904	Was A	17	70	6	21	3	0	0	6	1	0	—	.300	.310	.343	108	0	2	.860	0	180	299	O17(0/8/9)	—	0.0
	NY A	36	128	17	24	4	2	0	12	8	1	—	.188	.241	.250	53	-7	9	.826	-2	82	100	3b26,O10C	—	-1.0
	Year	53	198	23	45	7	2	0	18	9	1	—	.227	.264	.283	71	-7	11	.886	-2	234	194	O27(0/18/9),3b26	—	-1.0
1908	Bos A	109	416	58	106	5	9	2	30	13	3	—	.255	.282	.325	94	-5	16	.948	4	94	58	O101(87/11/3)	—	-0.8
1909	Bos A	13	40	1	5	1	0	0	3	2	0	—	.125	.167	.150	0	-5	2	.960	1	67	297	O10L	—	-0.6
1911	Bos A	26	20	5	5	0	0	0	2	0	0	—	.250	.250	.250	40	-2	1	ø	0	—	—	/H	—	-0.2
Total	6	264	912	112	216	23	12	3	73	36	4	—	.237	.269	.298	75	-30	42	.929	-10	132	108	O164(97/52/15),3b31,2b19,S11	—	-5.1

THORMAN, SCOTT Scott Robert; B1.6.1982 Cambridge ON, Can.; BL/TR/6´3˝/235; [AtlN00 1/30]; d6.18

YEAR	TM LG	G	AB	R	H	2B	3B	HR	RBI	BB-IB	HP	SO	AVG	OBP	SLG	AOPS	ABR	SB-CS	FA	FR	RNG	THR	GAMES AT POSITION	DL	BFW
2006	Atl N	55	128	13	30	11	0	5	14	5-0	0	21	.234	.263	.438	74	-5	1-0	1.000	-1	65	125	O21L,1b18	0	-0.8

THORNTON, ANDY Andre; B8.13.1949 Tuskegee AL; BR/TR/6´2˝/205; d7.28; [DL 1980 Cle A 109]

YEAR	TM LG	G	AB	R	H	2B	3B	HR	RBI	BB-IB	HP	SO	AVG	OBP	SLG	AOPS	ABR	SB-CS	FA	FR	RNG	THR	GAMES AT POSITION	DL	BFW
1973	Chi N	17	35	3	7	3	0	0	2	7-0	0	9	.200	.333	.286	68	-1	0-0	.989	2	177	44	1b9	0	0.0
1974	Chi N	107	303	41	79	16	4	10	46	48-4	4	50	.261	.368	.439	120	9	2-1	.992	7	131	84	1b90/3	0	1.0
1975	Chi N	120	372	70	109	21	4	18	60	88-12	4	63	.293	.428	.516	155	33	3-2	.988	0	102	90	1b113,3b2	27	2.5
1976	Chi N	27	85	8	17	6	0	2	14	20-1	2	14	.200	.361	.341	93	0	2-0	.987	1	114	89	1b25	0	0.0
	Mon N	69	183	20	35	5	2	9	24	28-0	3	32	.191	.304	.388	92	-2	2-1	.994	-0	103	126	1b43,O11R	21	-0.6
	Year	96	268	28	52	11	2	11	38	48-1	5	46	.194	.323	.373	93	-2	4-1	.991	1	107	112	1b68,O11R	0	-0.6
1977	Cle A	131	433	77	114	20	5	28	70	70-1	11	82	.263	.378	.527	148	31	3-4	.995	-4	84	100	1b117,D9	0	1.8
1978	Cle A	145	508	97	133	22	4	33	105	93-4	6	72	.262	.377	.516	152	37	4-7	.995	7	116	87	1b145	0	3.5
1979	Cle A	143	515	89	120	31	1	26	93	90-2	4	93	.233	.347	.449	114	12	5-4	.994	-3	88	82	1b130,D13	0	0.0
1981	Cle A	69	226	22	54	12	0	6	30	23-1	0	37	.239	.303	.372	96	-1	3-1	.986	-1	74	78	D53,1b11	24	-0.4
1982	Cle A★	161	589	90	161	26	1	32	116	109-**18**	2	81	.273	.386	.484	137	34	6-7	1.000	-0	78	63	D152,1b8	0	2.7
1983	Cle A	141	508	78	143	27	1	17	77	87-14	2	72	.281	.383	.439	122	19	4-2	.991	1	114	83	D114,1b27	0	1.6
1984	Cle A★	155	587	91	159	26	0	33	99	91-11	2	79	.271	.366	.484	132	27	6-5	.979	0	108	113	D144,1b11	0	2.2
1985	Cle A	124	461	49	109	13	0	22	88	47-1	0	75	.236	.304	.408	94	-5	3-2	ø	0	0	0	D122	17	-0.8
1986	Cle A	120	401	49	92	14	0	17	66	65-0	1	67	.229	.333	.392	99	1	4-1	ø	0	0	0	D110	0	-0.2
1987	Cle A	36	85	8	10	2	0	0	5	10-0	0	25	.118	.206	.141	-4	-13	1-0	ø	0	0	0	D21	0	-1.3
Total	14	1565	5291	792	1342	244	22	253	895	876-69	41	851	.254	.360	.452	122	181	48-37	.992	9	104	90	D738,1b729,O11R,3b3	198	12.0

THORNTON, LOU Louis; B4.26.1963 Montgomery AL; BL/TR/6´2˝/(175–185); [NYN81 19/471]; d4.8

YEAR	TM LG	G	AB	R	H	2B	3B	HR	RBI	BB-IB	HP	SO	AVG	OBP	SLG	AOPS	ABR	SB-CS	FA	FR	RNG	THR	GAMES AT POSITION	DL	BFW
1985	†Tor A	56	72	18	17	1	1	1	8	2-0	1	24	.236	.267	.319	58	-4	1-0	.957	-2	99	0	O35(16/0/20),D16	0	-0.7
1987	Tor A	12	2	5	1	0	0	0	0	1-1	0	0	.500	.667	.500	211	0	0-1	ø	-0	0	0	O4L,D6	0	0.0
1988	Tor A	11	2	1	0	0	0	0	0	0-0	0	1	.000	.000	.000	-99	-1	0-0	1.000	-1	30	0	O10(9/0/1)/D	0	-0.1
1989	NY N	13	13	5	4	1	0	0	1	0-0	0	1	.308	.308	.385	101	0	2-0	1.000	1	149	0	O6(3/1/2)	0	0.1
1990	NY N	3	0	0	0	0	0	0	0	0-0	0	0	ø	ø	ø	ø	0	0-0	1.000	0	134	0	O2(0/1/1)	0	0.0
Total	5	95	89	29	22	2	1	1	9	3-1	1	25	.247	.280	.326	65	-5	3-1	.965	-2	98	0	O57(32/2/24),D23	0	-0.7

THORNTON, OTIS Otis Benjamin; B6.30.1945 Docena AL; BR/TR/6´1˝/186; d7.6

YEAR	TM LG	G	AB	R	H	2B	3B	HR	RBI	BB-IB	HP	SO	AVG	OBP	SLG	AOPS	ABR	SB-CS	FA	FR	RNG	THR	GAMES AT POSITION	DL	BFW
1973	Hou N	2	3	0	0	0	0	0	1	0-0	0	2	.000	.000	.000	-99	-1	0-0	1.000	0	27	0	C2	0	-0.1

THORNTON, WALTER Walter Miller; B2.18.1875 Lewiston ME; D7.14.1960 Los Angeles CA; BL/TL/6´1˝/180; d7.1; Col Cornell; ▲

YEAR	TM LG	G	AB	R	H	2B	3B	HR	RBI	BB-IB	HP	SO	AVG	OBP	SLG	AOPS	ABR	SB-CS	FA	FR	RNG	THR	GAMES AT POSITION	DL	BFW
1895	Chi N	8	22	4	7	1	0	1	7	3	0	1	.318	.400	.500	123	1	0	.900	-1	55	0	P7/1	—	0.0
1896	Chi N	9	22	6	8	0	1	0	1	5	0	2	.364	.481	.455	142	2	2	.800	-1	50	0	P5,O3(0/2/1)	—	0.0
1897	Chi N	75	265	39	85	9	6	0	55	30	6	—	.321	.402	.400	108	4	13	.781	-9	102	0	O59(48/8/3),P16	—	-0.9
1898	Chi N	62	210	34	62	5	2	0	14	22	0	—	.295	.362	.338	101	1	8	.877	-3	111	199	O34(2/26/6),P28	—	-0.3
Total	4	154	519	83	162	15	9	1	77	60	6	3	.312	.390	.382	108	8	23	.821	-14	101	71	O96(50/36/10),P56/1	—	-1.2

YEAR	TM LG	G	AB	R	H	2B	3B	HR	RBI	BB-IB	HP	SO	AVG	OBP	SLG	AOPS	ABR	SB-CS	FA	FR	RNG	THR	GAMES AT POSITION	DL	BFW
THORPE, BOB	Benjamin Robert; B11.19.1926 Caryville FL; D10.30.1996 Waveland MS; BR/TR/6´1.5˝/190; d4.19																								
1951	Bos N	2	2	1	1	0	1	0	1	0	0	0	.500	.500	1.500	448	1	0-0	ø	0	—	—	/H	0	0.1
1952	Bos N	81	292	20	76	8	2	3	26	5	1	42	.260	.275	.332	70	-13	3-1	.972	2	98	140	O72(8/0/70)	0	-1.5
1953	Mil N	27	37	1	6	1	0	0	5	1	0	6	.162	.184	.189	-3	-6	0-1	1.000	-1	96	0	O18(10/0/8)	0	-0.7
Total	3	110	331	22	83	9	3	3	32	6	1	48	.251	.266	.323	64	-18	3-2	.975	1	98	128	O90(18/0/78)	0	-2.1
THORPE, JIM	James Francis; B5.28.1887 Prague OK; D3.28.1953 Long Beach CA; BR/TR (BB 1915)/6´1˝/185; d4.14																								
1913	NY N	19	35	6	5	0	0	1	2	1	0	9	.143	.167	.229	12	-4	2-1	.944	1	92	202	O9(3/7/0)	—	-0.4
1914	NY N	30	31	5	6	1	0	0	2	0	0	4	.194	.194	.226	25	-3	1	.750	-0	101	0	O4(0/2/2)	—	-0.4
1915	NY N	17	52	8	12	3	1	0	1	2	0	16	.231	.259	.327	82	-1	4-2	.933	-2	99	0	O15(0/13/2)	—	-0.4
1917	Cin N	77	251	29	62	2	8	4	36	6	1	35	.247	.267	.367	98	-3	11	.962	2	111	80	O69(38/0/33)	—	-0.6
	†NY N	26	57	12	11	3	2	0	4	8	1	10	.193	.303	.316	93	0	1	.939	-1	111	0	O18(6/1/13)	—	-0.2
	Year	103	308	41	73	5	10	4	40	14	2	45	.237	.275	.357	97	-3	12	.958	1	111	66	O87(44/1/46)	—	-0.8
1918	NY N	58	113	15	28	4	4	1	11	4	2	18	.248	.286	.381	105	0	3	.983	-2	92	53	O44(2/33/12)	—	-0.5
1919	NY N	2	3	0	1	0	0	0	1	0	0	0	.333	.333	.333	102	0	0	1.000	-0	98	0	O2(1/1/0)	—	0.0
	Bos N	60	156	16	51	7	3	1	25	6	2	30	.327	.360	.429	143	7	7	.926	-4	98	43	O38(22/12/7),1b2	—	0.2
	Year	62	159	16	52	7	3	1	26	6	2	30	.327	.359	.428	142	7	7	.928	-4	98	42	O40(23/13/7),1b2	—	0.2
Total	6	289	698	91	176	20	18	7	82	27	6	122	.252	.286	.362	99	-4	29-3	.951	-7	103	59	O199(72/69/69),1b2	—	-2.3
THRASHER, BUCK	Frank Edward; B8.6.1889 Watkinsville GA; D6.12.1938 Cleveland OH; BL/TR/5´11˝/182; d9.27																								
1916	Phi A	7	29	4	9	2	1	0	4	2	0	1	.310	.355	.448	148	1	0	1.000	-1	98	0	O7R	—	0.1
1917	Phi A	23	77	5	18	2	1	0	2	3	1	12	.234	.272	.286	71	-3	0	.938	-3	85	36	O22R	—	-0.8
Total	2	30	106	9	27	4	2	0	6	5	1	13	.255	.295	.330	92	-2	0	.951	-3	88	28	O29R	—	-0.7
THRONEBERRY, MARV	Marvin Eugene "Marvelous Marv"; B9.2.1933 Collierville TN; D6.23.1994 Fisherville TN; BL/TL/6´0˝/(185–197); d9.25; b–Maynard																								
1955	NY A	1	2	1	2	1	0	0	3	0-0	0	0	1.000	.667	1.500	574	1	1-0	1.000	0	281	0	/1	0	0.2
1958	†NY A	60	150	30	34	5	2	7	19	19-0	1	40	.227	.316	.427	107	1	1-1	.991	-1	95	129	1b40,O5R	0	-0.2
1959	NY A	80	192	27	46	5	0	8	22	18-1	0	51	.240	.302	.391	93	-3	0-0	.989	0	106	118	1b54,O13(1/0/12)	0	-0.5
1960	KC A	104	236	29	59	9	2	11	41	23-1	0	60	.250	.315	.445	103	0	0-0	.991	0	104	103	1b71	0	-0.3
1961	KC A	40	130	17	31	2	1	6	24	19-1	0	30	.238	.336	.408	96	-1	0-0	.996	2	130	119	1b30,O10R	0	-0.2
	Bal A	56	96	9	20	3	0	5	11	12-0	0	20	.208	.296	.396	86	-2	0-0	.923	-1	53	0	O15R,1b11	0	-0.5
	Year	96	226	26	51	5	1	11	35	31-1	0	50	.226	.319	.403	93	-3	0-0	.991	0	144	117	1b41,O25R	0	-0.7
1962	Bal A	9	9	1	0	0	0	0	0	4-0	0	6	.000	.308	.000	-9	-1	0-0	1.000	0	120	0	O2R	0	-0.1
	NY N	116	357	29	87	11	3	16	49	34-4	0	83	.244	.306	.426	94	-4	1-3	.981	4	125	104	1b97	0	-0.7
1963	NY N	14	14	0	2	1	0	0	1	1-0	0	5	.143	.200	.214	19	-1	0-0	1.000	-0	0	93	1b3	0	-0.2
Total	7	480	1186	143	281	37	8	53	170	130-7	1	295	.237	.311	.416	96	-10	3-4	.987	4	115	111	1b307,O45(1/0/44)	0	-2.5
THRONEBERRY, FAYE	Maynard Faye; B6.22.1931 Fisherville TN; D4.26.1999 Memphis TN; BL/TR/6´0˝/(185–199); d4.15; Mil 1953–54; b–Marv																								
1952	Bos A	98	310	38	80	11	3	5	23	33	1	67	.258	.331	.361	86	-6	16-7	.955	1	98	148	O86(11/4/71)	0	-0.7
1955	Bos A	60	144	20	37	7	3	6	27	14-1	1	31	.257	.323	.472	104	0	0-0	.960	0	101	110	O34(32/0/3)	0	-0.2
1956	Bos A	24	50	6	11	2	0	1	3	3-0	0	16	.220	.264	.320	48	-4	0-0	.909	-2	86	0	O13(8/2/3)	56	-0.6
1957	Bos A	1	1	0	0	0	0	0	0	0-0	0	1	.000	.000	.000	-95	0	0-0	ø	0	—	—	/H	0	0.0
	Was A	68	195	21	36	8	2	2	12	17-0	1	37	.185	.252	.277	45	-15	0-1	.983	-3	93	58	O58(14/48/2)	0	-2.2
	Year	69	196	21	36	8	2	2	12	17-0	1	38	.184	.251	.276	45	-15	0-1	.983	-3	93	58	O58(14/48/2)	0	-2.2
1958	Was A	44	87	12	16	1	1	4	7	4-0	3	28	.184	.245	.356	64	-5	0-1	1.000	-2	81	76	O26(5/13/8)	0	-0.8
1959	Was A	117	327	36	82	11	2	10	42	33-3	3	61	.251	.322	.388	95	-2	6-4	.953	-3	90	147	O86(16/1/71)	0	-0.8
1960	Was A	85	157	18	39	7	1	1	23	18-3	1	33	.248	.326	.325	78	-4	1-1	.947	-2	87	104	O34(12/7/17)	0	-0.8
1961	LA A	24	31	1	6	1	0	0	0	5-0	0	10	.194	.306	.226	40	-3	0-0	1.000	0	91	294	O5(3/0/2)	0	-0.2
Total	8	521	1302	152	307	48	12	29	137	127-7	10	284	.236	.307	.358	79	-39	23-14	.962	-9	93	117	O342(101/75/177)	56	-6.3
THURMAN, GARY	Gary Montez; B11.12.1964 Indianapolis IN; BR/TR/5´10˝/(165–180); [KCA83 1/21]; d8.30																								
1987	KC A	27	81	12	24	2	0	0	5	8-0	0	20	.296	.360	.321	80	-2	7-2	.971	5	120	320	O27(22/6/0)	0	0.2
1988	KC A	35	66	6	11	1	0	0	2	4-0	0	20	.167	.214	.182	12	-8	5-1	.949	-2	77	93	O32(22/11/0)/D	0	-1.0
1989	KC A	72	87	24	17	2	1	0	5	15-0	0	26	.195	.311	.241	58	-4	16-0	.949	-4	73	104	O60(12/28/24),D4	56	-0.6
1990	KC A	23	60	5	14	3	0	0	3	2-0	0	12	.233	.258	.283	52	-4	1-1	1.000	-1	98	0	O21(5/2/15)	0	-0.6
1991	KC A	80	184	24	51	9	0	2	13	11-0	1	42	.277	.320	.359	87	-3	15-5	.970	4	122	67	O72(39/9/29)	34	0.1
1992	KC A	88	200	25	49	6	3	0	20	9-0	1	34	.245	.281	.305	62	-11	9-6	.986	5	117	132	O67(7/2/59),D9	0	-0.8
1993	Det A	75	89	22	19	2	2	0	13	11-0	0	30	.213	.297	.281	57	-6	7-0	.950	-3	77	161	O53(17/21/15),D9	0	-0.7
1995	Sea A	13	25	3	8	2	0	0	3	1-0	0	3	.320	.333	.400	92	0	5-2	1.000	0	113	0	O9(5/1/4)	0	0.0
1997	NY N	11	6	0	1	0	0	0	0	0-0	0	0	.167	.167	.167	-13	-1	0-1	1.000	0	157	0	O7(3/4/1)	0	-0.1
Total	9	424	798	121	194	27	6	2	64	61-0	2	187	.243	.297	.299	65	-39	65-18	.971	3	103	121	O348(132/84/147),D23	90	-3.5
THURMAN, BOB	Robert Burns; B5.14.1917 Kellyville OK; D10.31.1998 Wichita KS; BL/TL/6´1˝/(201–205); d4.14; Negro Lg 1946–49 Mil 1942–45																								
1955	Cin N	82	152	19	33	2	3	7	22	17-2	0	26	.217	.296	.408	80	-5	0-2	.949	-0	99	98	O36L	0	-0.8
1956	Cin N	80	139	25	41	5	2	8	22	10-2	0	14	.295	.340	.532	123	4	0-0	.953	-1	92	109	O29(9/0/20)	0	0.2
1957	Cin N	74	190	38	47	4	2	16	40	15-0	1	33	.247	.306	.542	114	3	0-0	.987	2	105	116	O44(29/0/15)	0	0.2
1958	Cin N	94	178	23	41	7	4	4	20	20-1	4	38	.230	.320	.382	81	-5	1-2	.976	3	120	75	O41(33/0/8)	0	-0.5
1959	Cin N	4	4	1	1	0	0	0	2	0-0	0	1	.250	.250	.250	33	0	0-0	ø	0	—	—	/H	0	0.0
Total	5	334	663	106	163	18	11	35	106	62-5	5	112	.246	.314	.465	99	-3	1-4	.970	3	106	99	O150(107/0/43)	0	-0.9
THURSTON, JOE	Joseph William; B9.29.1979 Fairfield CA; BL/TR/5´11˝/(175–190); [LAN99 4/134]; d9.2; Col Sacramento (CA) City																								
2002	LA N	8	13	1	6	1	0	0	1	0-0	0	1	.462	.429	.538	172	1	0-0	1.000	0	104	229	2b4	0	0.2
2003	LA N	12	10	2	2	0	0	0	0	1-0	0	1	.200	.273	.200	27	-1	0-0	.857	1	206	478	2b3	0	0.0
2004	LA N	17	17	1	3	1	1	0	1	0-0	0	5	.176	.167	.353	33	-2	0-0	1.000	-0	88	135	2b4	0	-0.2
2006	Phi N	18	18	3	4	1	0	0	0	1-0	1	2	.222	.300	.278	47	-1	0-0	1.000	1	63	132	2b4,O3(2/0/1)	0	0.0
Total	4	55	58	7	15	3	1	0	2	2-0	1	9	.259	.286	.345	65	-3	0-0	.967	3	105	218	2b15,O3(2/0/1)	0	0.0
TIEMEYER, EDDIE	Edward Carl; B5.9.1885 Cincinnati OH; D9.27.1946 Cincinnati OH; BR/TR/5´11.5˝/185; d8.19																								
1906	Cin N	5	11	3	2	0	0	0	0	1	0	—	.182	.250	.182	33	-1	0	1.000	0	133	377	3b3/P	—	0.0
1907	Cin N	1	0	1	0	0	0	0	0	1	0	—	ø	1.000	ø	206	0	0	ø	0	—	—	/H	—	0.0
1909	NY A	3	8	1	3	1	0	0	0	1	0	—	.375	.444	.500	197	1	0	.962	-1	0	0	1b3	—	0.0
Total	3	9	19	5	5	1	0	0	0	3	0	—	.263	.364	.316	110	0	0	.962	-0	0	0	1b3,3b3/P	—	0.0
TIERNAN, MIKE	Michael Joseph "Silent Mike"; B1.21.1867 Trenton NJ; D11.7.1918 New York NY; BL/TL/5´11˝/165; d4.30; ▲																								
1887	NY N	103	407	82	117	13	12	10	62	32	3	31	.287	.344	.452	125	13	28	.865	-7	58	101	O103(34/11/58),P5	—	0.4
1888	†NY N	113	443	75	130	16	8	9	52	42	7	42	.293	.364	.427	153	28	52	**.960**	-1	83	60	O113(0/1/112)	—	2.5
1889	†NY N	122	499	**147**	167	23	14	10	73	**96**	5	32	.335	.447	.497	162	47	33	.896	-3	82	48	O122(0/1/122)	—	3.7
1890	NY N	133	553	132	168	25	21	**13**	59	68	5	53	.304	.385	**.495**	**156**	**37**	56	.896	-15	59	105	O133(2/131/1)	—	1.6
1891	NY N	134	542	111	166	30	12	**16**	73	69	3	32	.306	.388	.494	**163**	**44**	53	.901	-8	78	116	O134(0/4/130)	—	3.0
1892	NY N	116	450	79	130	16	10	5	66	57	2	46	.289	.371	.402	136	21	20	.899	-4	81	49	O116R	—	1.0
1893	NY N	125	511	114	158	19	12	14	102	72	4	24	.309	.399	.476	131	23	26	.927	-11	56	45	O125R	—	0.4
1894	†NY N	113	429	87	120	20	13	5	79	55	1	21	.280	.363	.422	89	-8	28	.923	-12	48	24	O112R	—	-2.0
1895	NY N	120	476	127	165	23	21	7	70	66	1	19	.347	.427	.527	149	35	36	.946	-5	46	51	O119R	—	1.9
1896	NY N	**133**	521	132	192	24	16	7	89	77	2	18	.369	.452	.516	159	48	35	.970	-2	82	86	O133R	—	3.4
1897	NY N	128	532	123	174	29	10	5	72	61	1	—	.327	.397	.447	126	22	40	.931	-13	59	57	O128(38/0/90)	—	0.1
1898	NY N	103	415	90	116	15	11	5	49	43	7	—	.280	.357	.405	122	12	19	.973	-10	85	57	O103(96/0/7)	—	-0.6
1899	NY N	35	137	17	35	4	2	0	7	10	0	—	.255	.306	.314	73	-5	2	.938	-4	58	61	O35R	—	-1.0
Total	13	1478	5915	1316	1838	257	162	106	853	748	41	318	.311	.392	.463	138	317	428	.924	-96	68	67	O1476(170/148/1160),P5	—	14.4
TIERNEY, COTTON	James Arthur; B2.10.1894 Kansas City KS; D4.18.1953 Kansas City MO; BR/TR/5´8˝/175; d9.23																								
1920	Pit N	12	46	4	11	5	0	0	8	3	0	4	.239	.286	.348	79	-1	1-1	.964	-1	104	91	2b10,S2	—	-0.2
1921	Pit N	117	442	49	132	22	8	3	52	24	2	31	.299	.338	.405	93	-5	4-6	.965	-28	78	108	2b72,3b32,O4R,S3	—	-3.0
1922	Pit N	122	441	58	152	26	14	7	86	22	2	40	.345	.378	.515	127	16	7-8	.964	-30	86	97	2b105,O2R/S3	—	-1.2
1923	Pit N	29	120	22	35	5	2	2	23	2	1	10	.292	.309	.417	88	-3	2-1	.941	-2	95	130	2b29	—	-0.4
	Phi N	121	480	68	152	31	1	11	65	24	2	42	.317	.352	.454	100	0	3-4	.975	19	112	106	2b115,O7(3/0/4),3b2	—	2.0

YEAR	TM LG	G	AB	R	H	2B	3B	HR	RBI	BB-IB	HP	SO	AVG	OBP	SLG	AOPS	ABR	SB-CS	FA	FR	RNG	THR	GAMES AT POSITION	DL	BFW
	Year	150	600	90	187	36	3	13	88	26	3	52	.312	.343	.447	97	-3	5-5	.968	**17**	**108**	**111**	2b144,O7(3/0/4),3b2	—	1.6
1924	Bos N	136	505	38	131	16	1	6	58	22	4	37	.259	.296	.331	71	-22	11-8	.964	-8	99	112	2b115,3b22	—	-2.6
1925	Bro N	93	265	27	68	14	4	2	39	12	2	23	.257	.294	.362	68	-13	0-3	.963	-3	94	54	3b61/12	—	-1.3
Total	6	630	2299	266	681	119	30	31	331	109	13	187	.296	.332	.415	93	-28	28-31	.966	-52	96	107	2b447,3b118,O13(3/0/10),S6/1	—	-6.7
TIERNEY, BILL	William J.; B5.14.1858 Boston MA; D9.21.1898 Boston MA; d5.2																								
1882	Cin AA	1	5	1	0	0	0	0	—	0	—	—	.000	.000	.000	-95	-1	—	.917	0	317	0	/1	—	-0.1
1884	Bal U	1	3	0	1	0	0	0	—	1	—	—	.333	.500	.333	143	0	—	1.000	-0	0	0	/rf	—	0.0
Total	2	2	8	1	1	0	0	0	—	1	—	—	.125	.222	.125	13	-1	—	1.000	0	0	0	/rf1	—	-0.1
TIFFEE, TERRY	Terry R.; B4.21.1979 North Little Rock AR; BB/TR/6´3˝/(210–215); [MinA99 26/779]; d9.1; Col Pratt (KS) CC																								
2004	Min A	17	44	7	12	4	0	2	8	3-0	1	3	.273	.333	.500	110	1	0-0	.966	-1	86	0	3b12/1D	0	0.0
2005	Min A	54	150	9	31	8	1	1	15	8-1	0	15	.207	.245	.293	42	-13	1-0	.912	-2	87	188	3b24,1b13,D10	0	-1.5
2006	Min A	20	45	4	11	1	0	2	6	4-1	0	8	.244	.306	.400	81	-1	0-1	.941	0	108	184	3b6,1b3,D5	0	-0.2
Total	3	91	239	20	54	13	1	5	29	15-2	1	26	.226	.273	.351	62	-13	1-1	.932	-2	90	132	3b42,1b17,D16	0	-1.7
TILLEY, JOHN	John C.; B New York NY; BR/5´7˝/154; d8.23																								
1882	Cle N	15	56	2	5	1	1	0	4	2	—	11	.089	.121	.143	-16	-7	—	.857	1	110	135	O15(14/1/0)	—	-0.6
1884	Tol AA	17	56	5	10	2	0	0	—	4	1	—	.179	.246	.214	50	-3	—	.632	-3	0	0	O17L	—	-0.6
	StP U	**9**	26	2	4	1	0	0	—	3	—	—	.154	.241	.192	61	-2	—	.938	1	51	0	O9L	—	-0.1
Total	2	41	138	9	19	4	1	0	4	9	—	11	.138	.196	.181	23	-12	—	.818	-1	58	58	O41(40/1/0)	—	-1.3
TILLMAN, BOB	John Robert; B3.24.1937 Nashville TN; D6.23.2000 Gallatin TN; BR/TR/6´4˝/(200–210); d4.15; Col Middle Tennessee																								
1962	Bos A	81	249	28	57	6	4	14	38	19-0	1	65	.229	.283	.454	93	-4	0-0	.983	-7	79	98	C66	0	-0.8
1963	Bos A	96	307	24	69	10	2	8	32	34-8	1	64	.225	.304	.349	80	-8	0-0	.992	-7	75	52	C95	0	-1.1
1964	Bos A	131	425	43	118	18	1	17	61	49-11	0	74	.278	.352	.445	114	9	0-0	.989	-7	70	93	C131	0	0.8
1965	Bos A	111	368	20	79	10	3	6	35	40-3	0	69	.215	.288	.307	66	-16	0-0	.988	-6	90	83	C106	0	-1.9
1966	Bos A	78	204	12	47	8	0	3	24	22-3	0	35	.230	.303	.314	71	-7	0-0	.990	-8	53	98	C72	0	-1.3
1967	Bos A	30	64	4	12	1	0	1	4	3-0	0	18	.188	.224	.250	37	-5	0-0	.977	-3	42	78	C26	0	-0.7
	NY A	22	63	5	16	1	0	2	9	7-1	0	17	.254	.324	.365	109	1	0-0	.970	-2	62	124	C15	0	-0.1
	Year	52	127	9	28	2	0	3	13	10-1	0	35	.220	.275	.307	70	-5	0-0	.974	-5	51	100	C41	0	-0.8
1968	Atl N	86	236	16	52	4	0	5	20	16-2	3	55	.220	.278	.301	74	-8	1-0	.990	-7	76	88	C75	0	-1.4
1969	†Atl N	69	190	18	37	5	0	12	29	18-1	0	47	.195	.263	.411	86	-5	0-0	.988	-9	90	26	C69	0	-1.1
1970	Atl N	71	223	19	53	5	0	11	30	20-4	0	66	.238	.299	.408	83	-6	0-0	.988	-5	72	54	C70	0	-0.8
Total	9	775	2329	189	540	68	10	79	282	228-33	5	510	.232	.300	.371	85	-49	1-0	.988	-60	75	77	C725	0	-8.4
TILLMAN, RUSTY	Kerry Jerome; B8.29.1960 Jacksonville FL; BR/TR/6´0˝/(175–190); [NYN79*10/201]; d6.6; Col Florida JC																								
1982	NY N	12	13	4	2	1	0	0	0	0-0	0	4	.154	.154	.231	6	-2	1-0	1.000	-1	51	0	O3R	0	-0.2
1986	Oak A	22	39	6	10	1	0	1	6	3-0	0	11	.256	.310	.359	87	-1	2-0	.952	-1	97	0	O17(8/0/10)	15	-0.2
1988	SF N	4	4	1	1	0	0	1	3	2-0	0	1	.250	.500	1.000	335	1	0-0	1.000	0	143	0	/lf	0	0.1
Total	3	38	56	11	13	2	0	2	9	5-0	0	16	.232	.295	.375	87	-2	3-0	.958	-1	91	0	O21(9/0/13)	15	-0.3
TIMMONS, OZZIE	Osborne Llewellyn; B9.18.1970 Tampa FL; BR/TR/6´2˝/(220–225); [ChiN91 5/137]; d4.26; Col Tampa																								
1995	Chi N	77	171	30	45	10	1	8	28	13-2	0	32	.263	.314	.474	105	0	3-0	.970	-3	88	41	O55(49/0/6)	0	-0.3
1996	Chi N	65	140	18	28	4	0	7	16	15-0	1	30	.200	.282	.379	70	-7	1-0	1.000	1	111	50	O47(25/0/22)	0	-0.7
1997	Cin N	6	9	1	3	1	0	0	0	0-0	0	1	.333	.333	.444	100	0	0-0	.000	-1	0	0	/lf	0	-0.1
1999	Sea A	26	44	4	5	2	0	1	3	4-0	0	12	.114	.188	.227	5	-7	0-1	1.000	-2	69	0	O17(12/0/5)/1D	0	-0.8
2000	TB A	12	41	9	14	3	0	4	13	1-0	0	7	.341	.357	.707	163	4	0-0	1.000	-2	45	0	O9(2/0/7)/D	0	0.1
Total	5	186	405	62	95	20	1	20	60	33-2	1	82	.235	.293	.437	87	-10	4-1	.980	-6	89	35	O129(89/0/40),D6/1	0	-1.8
TINGLEY, RON	Ronald Irvin; B5.27.1959 Presque Isle ME; BR/TR/6´2˝/(160–195); [SDN77 10/242]; d9.25																								
1982	SD N	8	20	0	2	0	0	0	0	0-0	0	7	.100	.100	.100	-47	-4	0-0	.957	-1	40	72	C8	0	-0.5
1988	Cle A	9	24	1	4	0	0	1	2	2-0	0	8	.167	.231	.292	44	-2	0-0	1.000	2	55	133	C9	0	0.1
1989	Cal A	4	3	0	1	0	0	0	0	1-0	0	0	.333	.500	.333	141	0	0-0	.889	-1	32	0	C4	0	0.0
1990	Cal A	5	3	0	0	0	0	0	0	1-0	0	1	.000	.250	.000	-25	0	0-0	1.000	-0	0	0	C5	28	0.0
1991	Cal A	45	115	11	23	7	0	1	13	8-0	1	34	.200	.258	.287	50	-8	1-1	.988	6	117	184	C45	0	0.1
1992	Cal A	71	127	15	25	2	1	3	8	13-0	2	35	.197	.282	.299	62	-7	0-1	.987	8	121	139	C69	0	0.3
1993	Cal A	58	90	7	18	7	0	0	12	9-0	1	22	.200	.277	.278	49	-6	1-2	.995	4	155	84	C58	0	0.0
1994	Fla N	19	52	4	9	3	1	1	2	5-0	0	18	.173	.246	.327	46	-4	0-0	.990	2	173	144	C18	0	-0.1
	Chi A	5	5	0	0	0	0	0	0	0-0	0	2	.000	.000	.000	-99	-2	0-0	1.000	-0	50	0	C5	19	-0.2
1995	Det A	54	124	14	28	8	1	4	18	15-0	0	38	.226	.307	.403	84	-3	0-1	.991	-5	113	118	C53/1	0	-0.5
Total	9	278	563	52	110	27	3	10	55	54-0	4	165	.195	.270	.307	56	-36	2-5	.989	16	121	127	C274/1	47	-0.8
TINKER, JOE	Joseph Bert; B7.27.1880 Muscotah KS; D7.27.1948 Orlando FL; BR/TR/5´9˝/175; d4.17; M4; HF1946																								
1902	Chi N	133	501	55	132	19	5	2	55	26	0	—	.263	.300	.333	98	-3	27	.908	1	108	113	S126,3b8	—	0.3
1903	Chi N	124	460	67	134	21	7	2	70	37	1	—	.291	.345	.380	110	5	27	.906	0	105	106	S107,3b19	—	0.9
1904	Chi N	141	488	55	108	12	13	3	41	29	2	—	.221	.268	.318	80	-13	41	.925	16	105	120	S140/rf	—	0.7
1905	Chi N	149	547	70	135	18	8	2	66	34	1	—	.247	.292	.320	79	-15	31	.940	12	105	**130**	S149	—	0.2
1906	†Chi N	148	523	75	122	18	4	1	64	43	1	—	.233	.293	.289	77	-14	30	**.944**	-0	100	131	S147/3	—	-1.1
1907	†Chi N	117	402	36	89	11	3	1	36	25	1	—	.221	.269	.271	65	-17	20	.939	13	**111**	**135**	S113	—	0.1
1908	†Chi N	157	548	67	146	22	14	6	68	32	0	—	.266	.307	.391	117	8	30	**.958**	26	109	106	S157	—	4.5
1909	Chi N	143	516	56	132	26	11	4	57	17	0	—	.256	.280	.372	100	-4	23	**.940**	18	**105**	112	S143	—	2.1
1910	†Chi N	134	473	48	136	25	9	3	69	24	0	35	.288	.322	.397	110	3	20	.942	14	104	113	S132	—	2.3
1911	Chi N	144	536	61	149	24	12	4	69	39	0	31	.278	.327	.390	100	-2	30	**.937**	**22**	**109**	103	S143	—	2.9
1912	Chi N	142	550	80	155	24	7	0	75	38	2	21	.282	.331	.351	87	-11	25	.943	**26**	106	132	S142	—	2.5
1913	Cin N	110	382	47	121	20	13	1	57	20	1	26	.317	.352	.445	127	12	10-12	.968	21	111	95	S101,3b9,M	—	**3.8**
1914	Chi F	126	438	50	112	21	7	2	46	38	1	30	.256	.317	.349	86	-17	19	.947	12	109	**123**	S125,M	—	0.5
1915	Chi F	31	67	7	18	2	1	0	9	13	0	5	.269	.387	.328	109	1	3	.914	-2	109	50	S16,2b5,3b4,M	—	0.0
1916	Chi N	7	10	0	1	0	0	0	1	1	0	1	.100	.182	.100	-11	-1	0	.909	-0	106	0	S4,3b2,M	—	-0.2
Total	15	1806	6441	774	1690	263	114	31	783	416	10	149	.262	.308	.353	95	-68	336-12	.938	180	107	117	S1745,3b43,2b5/rf	—	19.5
TINSLEY, LEE	Lee Owen; B3.4.1969 Shelbyville KY; BB/TR/5´10˝/(185–198); [OakA87 1/11]; d4.6; C1																								
1993	Sea A	11	19	2	3	1	0	1	2	2-0	0	9	.158	.238	.368	59	-1	0-0	.900	0	147	0	O6(5/1/1),D2	0	-0.1
1994	Bos A	78	144	27	32	4	0	2	14	19-1	1	36	.222	.315	.292	56	-9	13-0	.991	1	111	35	O60(27/26/11),D10	0	-0.6
1995	†Bos A	100	341	61	97	17	1	7	41	39-1	1	74	.284	.359	.402	95	-2	18-8	.979	-0	103	93	O97C	36	0.0
1996	Phi N	31	52	1	7	0	0	0	2	4-0	0	22	.135	.196	.135	-11	-9	2-4	.960	0	107	0	O22(18/7/0)	16	-1.0
	Bos A	92	192	28	47	6	1	3	14	13-0	2	56	.245	.298	.333	59	-13	6-8	.993	1	94	237	O83(4/79/0)	0	-1.1
1997	Sea A	49	122	12	24	6	2	0	6	11-0	0	34	.197	.263	.279	42	-11	2-0	1.000	1	105	98	O41(34/6/2),D5	107	-1.0
Total	5	361	870	131	210	34	4	13	79	88-2	4	231	.241	.313	.334	66	-45	41-20	.985	3	103	112	O309(88/216/14),D17	159	-3.8
TIPPER, JIM	James; B6.18.1849 Middletown CT; D4.21.1895 New Haven CT; 5´5.5˝/148; d4.26																								
1872	Man NA	**24**	110	24	29	4	0	0	18	0	—	1	.264	.264	.300	77	-2	0-0	.773	-2	141	0	O20L,3b5	—	-0.3
1874	Har NA	45	197	36	60	8	0	0	19	1	—	7	.305	.308	.345	104	0	0-1	.812	-1	78	77	O45L	—	0.1
1875	NH NA	41	159	10	25	1	0	0	4	1	—	6	.157	.162	.164	16	-12	1-0	.790	-3	94	73	O41(8/32/3)	—	-1.2
Total	3NA	110	466	70	114	13	0	0	41	2	—	14	.245	.248	.273	72	-14	1-1	.798	-6	96	61	O106(73/32/3),3b5	—	-1.4
TIPTON, ERIC	Eric Gordon "Dukie","Blue Devil"; B4.20.1915 Petersburg VA; D8.29.2001 Newport News VA; BR/TR/5´11˝/190; d6.9; Col Duke																								
1939	Phi A	47	104	12	24	4	2	1	14	13	0	7	.231	.316	.337	68	-5	2-0	.942	-0	114	0	O34(33/0/2)	—	-0.6
1940	Phi A	2	8	2	1	0	1	0	0	1	0	1	.125	.222	.375	53	-1	0-0	1.000	-0	85	0	O2L	—	-0.1
1941	Phi A	1	4	0	2	0	0	0	0	0	0	0	.500	.500	.500	169	0	0-0	1.000	-0	96	0	/lf	0	0.0
1942	Cin N	63	207	22	46	5	5	4	18	25	1	14	.222	.309	.353	94	-2	1	.977	-2	97	67	O58(38/20/1)	0	-0.8
1943	Cin N	140	493	82	142	26	7	9	49	85	2	36	.288	.395	.424	138	28	1	.984	-5	99	57	O139L	0	1.6
1944	Cin N	140	479	62	144	28	3	3	36	59	2	32	.301	.380	.390	121	16	5	.983	2	107	73	O139L	0	1.0
1945	Cin N	108	331	32	80	17	1	5	34	40	2	37	.242	.327	.344	89	-4	11	.970	-2	102	32	O83L	0	-1.2
Total	7	501	1626	212	439	80	19	22	151	223	7	127	.270	.360	.383	112	32	20-0	.977	-8	103	55	O456(435/20/3)	0	-0.1

YEAR	TM LG	G	AB	R	H	2B	3B	HR	RBI	BB-IB	HP	SO	AVG	OBP	SLG	AOPS	ABR	SB-CS	FA	FR	RNG	THR	GAMES AT POSITION	DL	BFW
TIPTON, JOE	Joe Hicks; B2.18.1922 McCaysville GA; D3.1.1994 Birmingham AL; BR/TR/5´11˝/185; d5.2																								
1948	†Cle A	47	90	11	26	3	0	1	13	4	2	10	.289	.333	.356	85	-2	0-0	.971	2	125	123	C40	0	0.1
1949	Chi A	67	191	20	39	5	3	3	19	27	1	17	.204	.306	.309	65	-10	1-1	.992	1	85	113	C53	0	-0.6
1950	Phi A	64	184	15	49	5	1	6	20	19	0	16	.266	.335	.402	90	-4	0-0	.987	-4	88	71	C59	0	-0.5
1951	Phi A	72	213	23	51	9	0	3	20	51	1	25	.239	.389	.324	92	1	1-1	.969	5	149	149	C72	0	0.9
1952	Phi A	23	68	6	13	4	0	3	8	15	0	10	.191	.337	.382	94	0	0-0	.990	-1	121	174	C23	0	0.0
	Cle A	43	105	15	26	2	0	6	22	21	2	21	.248	.383	.438	137	6	1-0	.971	-5	85	110	C35	0	0.3
	Year	66	173	21	39	6	0	9	30	36	2	31	.225	.365	.416	119	6	1-0	.979	-6	100	137	C58	0	0.3
1953	Cle A	47	109	17	25	2	0	6	13	19	3	13	.229	.359	.413	111	2	0-0	1.000	-3	82	91	C46	0	0.0
1954	Was A	54	157	9	35	6	1	1	10	30	2	30	.223	.353	.293	83	-2	0-1	.992	0	93	98	C52	0	0.1
Total	7	417	1117	116	264	36	5	29	125	186	11	142	.236	.351	.355	91	-9	3-3	.984	-5	105	114	C380	0	0.3
TISCHINSKI, TOM	Thomas Arthur; B7.12.1944 Kansas City MO; BR/TR/5´10˝/(180–200); d4.11																								
1969	Min A	37	47	2	9	0	0	0	2	8-0	0	8	.191	.309	.191	42	-3	0-0	1.000	-3	198	69	C32	0	-0.6
1970	Min A	24	46	6	9	0	0	1	2	9-1	0	6	.196	.327	.261	63	-2	0-0	.990	-2	120	110	C22	0	-0.3
1971	Min A	21	23	0	3	2	0	0	2	1-0	1	4	.130	.200	.217	18	-2	0-0	.982	-0	55	124	C21	0	-0.3
Total	3	82	116	8	21	2	0	1	6	18-1	1	18	.181	.296	.224	46	-7	0-0	.992	-5	136	97	C75	0	-1.2
TITUS, JOHN	John Franklin "Silent John"; B2.21.1876 St.Clair PA; D1.8.1943 St.Clair PA; BL/TL/5´9˝/156; d6.8																								
1903	Phi N	72	280	38	80	15	6	2	34	19	4	—	.286	.340	.404	115	5	5	.952	3	129	77	O72(34/2/36)	—	0.4
1904	Phi N	146	504	60	148	25	5	4	55	46	8	—	.294	.362	.387	136	23	15	.952	10	122	122	O140(105/2/33)	—	2.7
1905	Phi N	147	548	99	169	36	14	2	89	69	12	—	.308	.397	.436	154	40	11	.962	7	122	86	O147R	—	4.1
1906	Phi N	145	484	67	129	22	5	1	57	78	9	—	.267	.378	.339	124	19	12	.974	7	131	118	O142(0/8/134)	—	2.1
1907	Phi N	145	523	72	144	23	12	3	63	47	9	—	.275	.345	.382	130	18	9	.928	-5	107	64	O142R	—	0.7
1908	Phi N	149	539	75	154	24	5	2	48	53	14	—	.286	.365	.360	127	19	27	.963	-4	116	69	O149R	—	1.0
1909	Phi N	151	540	69	146	22	6	3	46	66	**16**	—	.270	.367	.350	121	17	23	.971	4	108	130	O149R	—	1.5
1910	Phi N	143	535	91	129	26	5	3	35	93	4	44	.241	.358	.325	96	2	20	.976	-1	94	107	O142(1/0/142)	—	-0.6
1911	Phi N	76	236	35	67	14	1	8	26	32	1	16	.284	.372	.453	129	9	3	.979	-1	87	125	O60(1/0/59)	—	0.6
1912	Phi N	45	157	43	43	9	5	3	22	33	1	14	.274	.403	.452	125	7	6	.917	-5	85	36	O42R	—	-0.1
	Bos N	96	345	56	112	23	6	2	48	49	9	20	.325	.422	.443	134	20	5	.965	-3	96	86	O96(1/0/96)	—	1.1
	Year	141	502	99	155	32	11	5	70	82	10	34	.309	.416	.446	131	26	11	.952	-9	93	72	O138(1/0/138)	—	1.0
1913	Bos N	87	269	33	80	14	2	5	38	35	7	22	.297	.392	.420	129	12	4-7	.919	-5	85	93	O75R	—	0.2
Total	11	1402	4960	738	1401	253	72	38	561	620	94	116	.282	.373	.385	127	191	140-7	.959	5	110	96	O1356(142/12/1204)	—	13.7
TOBIN, JOHNNY	John Martin "Tip"; B9.15.1906 Jamaica Plain MA; D8.6.1983 Rhinebeck NY; BR/TR/6´3˝/187; d9.22; Col Fordham																								
1932	NY N	1	1	0	0	0	0	0	0	0	0	0	.000	.000	.000	-99	0	0	ø	0	—	—	/H	—	0.0
TOBIN, JOHNNY	John Patrick "Jackie"; B1.8.1921 Oakland CA; D1.18.1982 Oakland CA; BL/TR/6´0˝/165; d4.20; b–Jim; Col St. Marys (CA)																								
1945	Bos A	84	278	25	70	6	2	0	21	26	2	24	.252	.320	.288	75	-9	2-6	.951	7	112	121	3b72,2b5/cf	0	-0.2
TOBIN, JACK	John Thomas; B5.4.1892 St.Louis MO; D12.10.1969 St.Louis MO; BL/TL/5´8˝/142; d4.16; C3																								
1914	StL F	139	529	81	143	24	10	7	35	51	5	53	.270	.340	.393	94	-12	20	.952	6	94	151	O132(12/7/113)	—	-1.4
1915	StL F	158	625	92	**184**	26	13	6	51	68	3	42	.294	.366	.406	111	2	31	.965	-1	100	99	O158(0/31/128)	—	-0.9
1916	StL A	77	150	16	32	4	1	0	10	12	0	13	.213	.272	.253	61	-8	7	.842	-5	86	51	O41(0/6/35)	—	-1.6
1918	StL A	122	480	59	133	19	5	0	36	48	5	26	.277	.349	.338	111	7	13	.971	-4	86	114	O122(43/78/1)	—	-0.6
1919	StL A	127	486	54	159	22	7	6	57	36	2	24	.327	.376	.438	125	15	8	.953	1	97	124	O123L	—	1.1
1920	StL A	147	593	94	202	34	10	4	62	39	2	23	.341	.383	.452	117	14	21-13	.960	3	109	91	O147(34/0/113)	—	1.0
1921	StL A	150	671	132	236	31	**18**	8	59	45	3	22	.352	.395	.487	117	16	7-12	.956	5	98	134	O150(0/8/143)	—	0.5
1922	StL A	146	625	122	207	34	8	13	66	56	2	22	.331	.388	.474	119	18	7-9	.940	-9	85	94	O145(0/1/144)	—	-0.5
1923	StL A	151	637	91	202	32	15	13	73	42	4	13	.317	.363	.476	113	9	8-7	.969	-10	90	69	O151R	—	-1.4
1924	StL A	136	569	87	170	30	8	2	48	50	2	12	.299	.357	.390	87	-11	6-10	.957	-1	101	101	O132(1/1/130)	—	-2.3
1925	StL A	77	193	25	58	11	0	2	27	9	1	5	.301	.335	.389	79	-6	8-2	1.000	-3	98	29	O39(1/1/38),1b3	—	-1.0
1926	Was A	27	33	5	7	0	1	0	3	0	0	0	.212	.212	.273	26	-4	0-0	1.000	0	118	0	O7(0/4/3)	—	-0.4
	Bos A	51	209	26	57	9	0	1	14	16	0	3	.273	.324	.330	73	-8	6-5	.966	-4	79	118	O51(1/0/51)	—	-1.6
	Year	78	242	31	64	9	1	1	17	16	0	3	.264	.310	.322	67	-12	6-5	.970	-4	82	110	O58(1/4/54)	—	-2.0
1927	Bos A	111	374	52	116	18	3	2	40	36	0	9	.310	.371	.390	100	0	5-4	.947	-3	89	103	O93(5/0/89)	—	-1.0
Total	13	1619	6174	936	1906	294	99	64	581	508	29	267	.309	.364	.420	106	32	147-62	.957	-26	95	104	O1491(220/137/1139),1b3	—	-10.1
TOBIN, BILL	William F.; B10.10.1854 Hartford CT; D10.10.1912 Hartford CT; BL; d7.21																								
1880	Wor N	5	16	1	2	0	0	0	3	0	—	5	.125	.125	.125	-14	-2	—	1.000	-0	0	99	1b5	—	-0.2
	Tro N	33	136	14	22	1	1	0	8	4	—	20	.162	.186	.184	24	-11	—	.950	-1	94	160	1b33	—	-1.3
	Year	38	152	15	24	1	1	0	11	4	—	25	.158	.179	.178	20	-13	—	.958	-1	82	152	1b38	—	-1.5
TOCA, JORGE	Jorge Luis; B1.7.1975 Remedios, Cuba; BR/TR/6´3˝/220; d9.12; [DL 2002 NY N 61]																								
1999	NY N	4	3	0	1	0	0	0	0	0-0	0	2	.333	.333	.333	73	0	0-0	1.000	0	0	0	/1	0	0.0
2000	NY N	8	7	1	3	1	0	0	4	0-0	0	1	.429	.429	.571	158	1	0-0	1.000	-0	0	0	1b5/lf	0	0.0
2001	NY N	13	17	3	3	0	0	0	1	0-0	0	8	.176	.176	.176	-9	-3	0-0	1.000	0	113	93	1b3,O2L	0	-0.3
Total	3	25	27	4	7	1	0	0	5	0-0	0	11	.259	.259	.296	45	-2	0-0	1.000	-0	64	53	1b9,O3L	61	-0.3
TODD, AL	Alfred Chester; B1.7.1902 Troy NY; D3.8.1985 Elmira NY; BR/TR/6´1˝/198; d4.25; Col Mansfield																								
1932	Phi N	33	70	8	16	5	0	0	9	1	2	9	.229	.260	.300	45	-5	1	.899	-4	90	46	C25	—	-0.8
1933	Phi N	73	136	13	28	4	0	0	10	4	2	18	.206	.239	.235	32	-12	1	.983	1	72	150	C34,O2L	—	-0.9
1934	Phi N	91	302	33	96	22	2	4	41	10	2	39	.318	.344	.444	96	-1	3	.976	1	119	76	C82	—	0.5
1935	Phi N	107	328	40	95	18	3	3	42	19	3	35	.290	.334	.390	85	-6	3	.968	-7	99	82	C87	—	-0.8
1936	Pit N	76	267	28	73	10	5	2	28	11	2	24	.273	.307	.371	80	-9	4	.976	-1	76	88	C70	—	-0.5
1937	Pit N	133	514	51	158	18	10	8	86	16	1	36	.307	.330	.428	104	0	2	.972	-7	61	104	C128	—	0.1
1938	Pit N	133	491	52	130	19	7	7	75	18	4	31	.265	.296	.375	83	-14	2	.985	8	101	121	C132	—	0.3
1939	Bro N	86	245	28	68	10	0	5	32	13	1	16	.278	.317	.380	83	-6	1	.985	6	107	104	C73	—	0.4
1940	Chi N	104	381	31	97	13	2	6	42	11	4	29	.255	.283	.346	74	-15	1	.984	-4	101	95	C104	—	-1.3
1941	Chi N	6	6	1	1	0	0	0	0	0	0	1	.167	.167	.167	-6	-1	0	ø	0	—	—	/H	0	-0.1
1943	Chi N	21	45	1	6	0	0	0	1	1	0	5	.133	.152	.133	-17	-7	0	.986	1	133	64	C17	0	-0.5
Total	11	863	2785	286	768	119	29	35	366	104	21	243	.276	.307	.377	82	-76	18	.977	-4	93	98	C752,O2L	0	-3.6
TODT, PHIL	Philip Julius "Hook"; B8.9.1901 St.Louis MO; D11.15.1973 St.Louis MO; BL/TL/6´0˝/175; d4.25																								
1924	Bos A	52	103	17	27	8	2	1	14	6	1	9	.262	.309	.408	84	-3	0-1	.983	-1	91	63	1b18,O4(0/2/2)	—	-0.5
1925	Bos A	141	544	62	151	29	13	11	75	44	10	29	.278	.343	.439	97	-5	3-2	.991	3	105	103	1b140	—	-1.1
1926	Bos A	**154**	599	56	153	19	12	7	69	40	4	38	.255	.306	.362	76	-25	3-2	.988	10	**130**	97	1b154	—	-2.4
1927	Bos A	140	516	55	122	22	6	6	52	28	3	23	.236	.280	.337	61	-33	6-2	.991	8	121	106	1b139	—	-3.1
1928	Bos A	144	539	61	136	31	8	12	73	26	3	47	.252	.290	.406	83	-17	6-5	**.997**	3	102	87	1b144	—	-2.3
1929	Bos A	153	534	49	140	38	10	4	64	31	2	28	.262	.305	.393	80	-18	6-7	.991	3	108	101	1b153	—	-2.5
1930	Bos A	111	383	49	103	22	5	11	62	24	0	33	.269	.312	.439	92	-7	4-1	.993	2	**109**	105	1b104	—	-1.0
1931	†Phi A	62	197	23	48	14	2	5	44	8	0	22	.244	.273	.411	73	-9	1-1	.995	-4	53	117	1b52	—	-1.6
Total	8	957	3415	372	880	183	58	57	453	207	23	229	.258	.305	.395	81	-117	29-21	.992	23	109	100	1b904,O4(0/2/2)	—	-14.5
TOLAN, BOBBY	Robert; B11.19.1945 Los Angeles CA; BL/TL/5´11˝/(170–180); d9.3; C5; [DL 1971 Cin N 179]																								
1965	StL N	17	69	8	13	2	0	0	6	0-0	1	4	.188	.197	.217	16	-8	2-1	.970	-1	99	0	O17R	0	-1.1
1966	StL N	43	93	10	16	5	1	1	6	6-2	2	15	.172	.233	.280	43	-7	1-2	.952	-1	95	61	O26(10/0/16)/1	0	-1.1
1967	†StL N	110	265	35	67	7	3	6	32	19-0	4	43	.253	.309	.370	96	-2	12-7	.992	1	103	119	O80(6/54/25),1b13	0	-0.4
1968	†StL N	92	278	28	64	12	1	5	17	13-3	3	42	.230	.272	.335	82	-7	9-5	.967	-0	101	61	O67(2/9/57),1b9	0	-1.3
1969	Cin N	152	637	104	194	25	10	21	93	27-2	15	92	.305	.347	.474	122	16	26-12	.974	2	112	55	O150(0/88/62)	0	1.4
1970	†Cin N	152	589	112	186	34	6	16	80	62-3	8	94	.316	.384	.475	129	26	**57**-20	.978	-2	103	82	O150C	0	2.6
1972	†Cin N	149	604	88	171	28	5	8	82	44-5	6	88	.283	.334	.386	110	8	42-15	.990	3	103	94	O149C	0	1.1
1973	Cin N	129	457	42	94	14	2	9	51	27-2	3	68	.206	.251	.304	57	-29	15-10	.966	1	103	99	O120(0/76/65)	0	-3.5
1974	SD N	95	357	45	95	16	1	8	40	20-4	9	41	.266	.320	.384	101	0	7-9	.971	-3	98	86	O88(1/9/81)	58	-0.9
1975	SD N	147	506	58	129	19	4	5	43	28-3	10	45	.255	.306	.338	84	-12	11-13	.971	-3	96	56	O120(90/16/19),1b27	0	-2.6

YEAR	TM LG	G	AB	R	H	2B	3B	HR	RBI	BB-IB	HP	SO	AVG	OBP	SLG	AOPS	ABR	SB-CS	FA	FR	RNG	THR	GAMES AT POSITION	DL	BFW
1976	†Phi N	110	272	32	71	7	0	5	35	7-3	4	39	.261	.285	.342	76	-10	10-5	.992	-6	50	114	1b50,O35(20/10/5)	0	-2.1
1977	Phi N	15	16	1	2	0	0	0	1	1-0	0	4	.125	.176	.125	-17	-3	0-0	.944	-0	104	79	1b5	0	-0.3
	Pit N	49	74	7	15	4	0	2	9	4-0	0	10	.203	.241	.338	52	-5	1-1	1.000	0	93	109	1b20,O2L	0	-0.6
	Year	64	90	8	17	4	0	2	10	5-0	0	14	.189	.229	.300	40	-8	1-1	.992	0	94	105	1b25,O2L	0	-0.9
1979	SD N	22	21	2	4	0	1	0	2	0-0	0	2	.190	.190	.286	30	-2	0-0	1.000	0	232	172	1b5/rf	0	-0.2
Total	13	1282	4238	572	1121	173	34	86	497	258-27	65	587	.265	.314	.382	96	-35	193-100	.976	-10	102	77	O1005(131/561/348),1b130	237	-9.0
TOLENTINO, JOSE	Jose (Franco); B6.3.1961 Mexico City, Distrito Federal, Mexico; BL/TL/6´1˝/195; [OakA83 7/163]; d7.28; Col Texas																								
1991	Hou N	44	54	6	14	4	0	1	6	4-0	0	9	.259	.305	.389	101	0	0-0	.982	1	112	74	1b10/lf	0	0.0
TOLLESON, WAYNE	Jimmy Wayne; B11.22.1955 Spartanburg SC; BB/TR/5´9˝/(160–163); [TexA78 8/202]; d9.1; Col Western Carolina																								
1981	Tex A	14	24	6	4	0	0	0	1	1-0	0	5	.167	.200	.167	7	-3	2-0	1.000	-2	71	0	3b6,S2	0	-0.5
1982	Tex A	38	70	6	8	1	0	0	2	5-0	0	14	.114	.173	.129	-16	-11	1-1	.958	1	96	140	S26,3b4/2	0	-0.8
1983	Tex A	134	470	64	122	13	2	3	20	40-0	2	68	.260	.319	.315	76	-15	33-10	.972	-6	97	95	2b112,S26/D	0	-0.9
1984	Tex A	118	338	35	72	9	2	0	9	27-0	3	47	.213	.276	.251	46	-25	22-4	.979	-9	94	96	2b109,S7,3b5/cfD	0	-2.5
1985	Tex A	123	323	45	101	9	5	1	18	21-0	0	46	.313	.353	.381	99	-1	21-12	.972	-3	95	86	S81,2b29,3b12,D6	0	0.5
1986	Chi A	81	260	39	65	7	3	3	29	38-0	0	43	.250	.342	.335	83	-5	13-6	.955	-6	99	85	3b65,S18,O2(1/1/0),D2	0	-1.1
	NY A	60	215	22	61	9	2	0	14	14-0	2	33	.284	.332	.344	85	-4	4-4	.981	9	115	108	S56,3b7,2b3	0	1.0
	Year	141	475	61	126	16	5	3	43	52-0	2	76	.265	.338	.339	84	-10	17-10	.981	3	110	98	S74,3b72,2b3,O2(1/1/0),D2	0	-0.1
1987	NY A	121	349	48	77	4	0	1	22	43-0	0	72	.221	.306	.241	48	-26	5-3	.970	-3	100	100	S119,3b3	15	-1.7
1988	NY A	21	59	8	15	2	0	0	5	8-0	0	12	.254	.338	.288	79	-1	1-0	.981	6	136	120	2b12,3b10/S	144	0.5
1989	NY A	80	140	16	23	5	2	1	9	16-0	1	23	.164	.255	.250	43	-11	5-1	.912	2	89	130	3b28,S28,2b13,D10	13	-0.8
1990	NY A	73	74	12	11	1	1	0	4	6-0	0	21	.149	.210	.189	13	-9	1-0	.983	7	129	176	S45,2b13,3b3,D5	0	0.0
Total	10	863	2322	301	559	60	17	9	133	219-0	8	384	.241	.307	.293	65	-111	108-41	.974	-3	103	104	S409,2b292,3b143,D25,O3(1/2/0)	172	-6.3
TOLMAN, TIM	Timothy Lee; B4.20.1956 Santa Monica CA; BR/TR/6´0˝/(190–195); [HouN78 12/297]; d9.9; Col USC																								
1981	Hou N	4	8	0	1	0	0	0	0	0-0	0	0	.125	.125	.125	-31	-1	0-0	1.000	-0	65	0	O3(3/0/1)	0	-0.2
1982	Hou N	15	26	4	5	2	0	1	3	4-0	0	3	.192	.300	.385	98	0	0-0	1.000	-1	77	0	O5(4/0/1)/1	0	-0.1
1983	Hou N	43	56	4	11	4	0	2	10	6-0	0	9	.196	.270	.375	83	-1	0-1	1.000	-1	48	141	1b7,O3L	0	-0.4
1984	Hou N	14	17	2	3	1	0	0	0	0-0	0	3	.176	.176	.235	16	-2	0-0	1.000	0	123	0	O3(1/0/2)/1	0	-0.2
1985	Hou N	31	43	4	6	1	0	2	8	1-0	1	10	.140	.178	.302	33	-4	0-1	1.000	1	122	0	O9(6/0/3),1b6	0	-0.5
1986	Det A	16	34	4	6	1	0	0	2	6-0	0	4	.176	.293	.206	41	-3	1-1	1.000	-0	138	0	O4R,1b3,D9	0	-0.3
1987	Det A	9	12	3	1	1	0	0	1	7-1	1	2	.083	.429	.167	76	0	0-0	1.000	-1	80	0	O7(2/0/5),D2	0	0.0
Total	7	132	196	21	33	10	0	5	24	24-1	2	31	.168	.262	.296	58	-11	1-3	1.000	-2	97	0	O34(19/0/16),1b18,D11	0	-1.7
TOLSON, CHICK	Charles Julius "Toby"; B11.6.1898 Washington DC; D4.16.1965 Washington DC; BR/TR/6´0˝/185; d7.3																								
1925	Cle A	3	12	0	3	0	0	0	0	2	0	1	.250	.357	.250	56	-1	0-0	1.000	0	93	36	1b3	—	-0.1
1926	Chi N	57	80	4	25	6	1	1	8	5	0	8	.313	.353	.450	113	1	0	.991	0	112	128	1b13	—	0.1
1927	Chi N	39	54	6	16	4	0	2	17	4	0	9	.296	.345	.481	119	1	0	1.000	0	106	49	1b8	—	0.1
1929	†Chi N	32	109	13	28	5	0	1	19	9	2	16	.257	.325	.330	63	-6	0	.978	-2	83	88	1b31	—	-0.9
1930	Chi N	13	20	0	6	1	0	0	1	6	0	5	.300	.462	.350	99	1	1	.979	0	141	145	1b5	—	0.1
Total	5	144	275	23	78	16	1	4	45	26	2	39	.284	.350	.393	90	-4	1-0	.985	-1	97	92	1b60	—	-0.7
TOMBERLIN, ANDY	Andy Lee; B11.7.1966 Monroe NC; BL/TL/5´11˝/(180–185); d8.12																								
1993	Pit N	27	42	4	12	0	1	1	5	2-0	1	14	.286	.333	.405	97	0	0-0	1.000	-0	68	194	O7(6/0/1)	0	-0.1
1994	Bos A	18	36	1	7	0	1	1	1	6-0	0	12	.194	.310	.333	63	-2	1-0	1.000	1	75	345	O11(5/0/6)/PD	47	-0.2
1995	Oak A	46	85	15	18	0	0	4	10	5-0	0	22	.212	.256	.353	59	-6	4-1	.979	-2	80	74	O42(5/18/20),D2	0	-0.8
1996	NY N	63	66	12	17	4	0	3	10	9-0	1	27	.258	.355	.455	118	2	0-0	1.000	-1	58	214	O17(9/0/8)/1	0	0.1
1997	NY N	6	7	0	2	0	0	0	0	1-0	0	3	.286	.375	.286	80	0	0-0	1.000	0	111	0	O2(1/0/1)	173	0.0
1998	Det A	32	69	8	15	2	0	2	12	3-1	3	25	.217	.280	.333	58	-4	1-0	1.000	1	237	0	D22,O5(4/0/1)	0	-0.5
Total	6	192	305	40	71	6	2	11	38	26-1	5	103	.233	.304	.374	77	-10	6-1	.989	-2	78	154	O84(30/18/37),D29/1P	220	-1.5
TOMER, GEORGE	George Clarence; B11.26.1895 Perry IA; D12.15.1984 Perry IA; BL/TR/6´0˝/180; d9.17																								
1913	StL A	1	1	0	0	0	0	0	0	0	0	1	.000	.000	.000	-99	0	0	ø	0	—	—	/H	—	0.0
TOMNEY, PHIL	Philip Howard "Buster"; B7.17.1863 Reading PA; D3.18.1892 Reading PA; BR/TR/5´7˝/155; d9.7																								
1888	Lou AA	34	120	15	18	3	0	0	4	7	0	—	.150	.197	.175	20	-11	11	.882	6	114	87	S34	—	-0.3
1889	Lou AA	112	376	61	80	8	5	4	38	46	3	47	.213	.304	.293	71	-14	26	.857	22	**115**	121	S112	—	0.9
1890	†Lou AA	108	386	72	107	21	7	1	58	43	5	—	.277	.357	.376	119	10	27	**.902**	15	**112**	**111**	S108	—	2.4
Total	3	254	882	148	205	32	12	5	100	96	8	47	.232	.313	.313	86	-15	64	.878	43	114	112	S254	—	3.0
TONIS, MIKE	Michael Timothy; B2.9.1979 Sacramento CA; BR/TR/6´3˝/220; [KCA00 2/44]; d6.20; Col California																								
2004	KC A	2	6	0	0	0	0	0	0	1-0	0	0	.000	.143	.000	-58	-1	0-0	1.000	0	101	0	C2	0	-0.1
TONNEMAN, TONY	Charles Richard; B9.10.1881 Chicago IL; D8.4.1951 Prescott AZ; BR/TR/5´10.5˝/175; d9.19																								
1911	Bos A	2	5	0	1	1	0	0	3	1	0	—	.200	.333	.400	105	0	0	.900	0	*106*	77	C2	—	0.0
TOOLEY, BERT	Albert R.; B8.30.1886 Howell MI; D8.17.1976 Marshall MI; BR/TR/5´10˝/155; d4.12																								
1911	Bro N	119	433	55	89	11	3	1	29	53	2	63	.206	.295	.252	56	-25	18	.925	-6	98	94	S114	—	-2.4
1912	Bro N	77	265	34	62	6	5	2	37	19	0	21	.234	.285	.317	67	-13	12	.885	-17	90	74	S76	—	-2.5
Total	2	196	698	89	151	17	8	3	66	72	2	84	.216	.291	.277	60	-38	30	.909	-23	95	86	S190	—	-4.9
TOPORCER, SPECS	George (b George Toporczer); B2.9.1899 New York NY; D5.17.1989 Huntington Station NY; BL/TR/5´10.5˝/165; d4.13																								
1921	StL N	22	53	4	14	1	0	0	2	3	0	4	.264	.304	.283	57	-3	1-0	.938	-0	98	111	2b12,S2	—	-0.3
1922	StL N	116	352	56	114	25	6	3	36	24	2	18	.324	.370	.455	117	9	2-1	.939	-14	91	71	S91,3b6/2rf	—	0.3
1923	StL N	97	303	45	77	11	3	3	35	41	3	14	.254	.349	.340	84	-6	4-3	.945	-14	88	120	2b52,S33/13	—	-1.5
1924	StL N	70	198	30	62	10	3	1	24	11	4	14	.313	.362	.409	108	2	2-3	.974	-8	96	36	3b33,S25,2b3	—	-0.3
1925	StL N	83	268	38	76	13	4	2	26	36	2	15	.284	.373	.384	92	-2	7-2	.960	-1	97	97	S66,2b7	—	0.5
1926	†StL N	64	88	13	22	3	2	0	9	8	2	9	.250	.327	.330	74	-3	1	.983	-6	81	44	2b27,S5/3	—	-0.9
1927	StL N	86	290	37	72	13	4	0	19	27	1	16	.248	.314	.321	68	-13	5	.980	-8	92	101	3b54,S27,2b2/1	—	-1.5
1928	StL N	8	14	0	0	0	0	0	0	0	0	3	.000	.000	.000	-98	-4	0	1.000	0	536	0	/12	—	-0.4
Total	8	546	1566	223	437	76	22	9	151	150	14	93	.279	.347	.373	90	-20	22-9	.946	-51	93	87	S249,2b105,3b95,1b3/rf	—	-4.1
TORBORG, JEFF	Jeffrey Allen; B11.26.1941 Plainfield NJ; BR/TR/6´0.5˝/(190–200); d5.10; M11/C13; Col Rutgers																								
1964	LA N	28	43	4	10	1	1	0	4	3-1	1	8	.233	.292	.302	75	-2	0-0	.977	-6	48	86	C27	0	-0.7
1965	LA N	56	150	8	36	5	1	3	13	10-4	1	26	.240	.290	.347	85	-3	0-0	.991	3	101	71	C53	0	0.1
1966	LA N	46	120	4	27	3	0	1	13	10-3	0	23	.225	.278	.275	61	-6	0-0	.986	4	133	103	C45	0	0.0
1967	LA N	76	196	11	42	4	1	2	12	13-3	1	31	.214	.265	.276	60	-11	1-3	.989	4	147	108	C75	0	-0.5
1968	LA N	37	93	2	15	2	0	0	4	6-2	0	10	.161	.212	.183	21	-9	0-0	.991	4	109	143	C37	0	-0.5
1969	LA N	51	124	7	23	4	0	0	7	9-5	0	17	.185	.241	.218	31	-12	1-0	.996	3	102	100	C50	0	-0.7
1970	LA N	64	134	11	31	8	0	1	17	14-6	0	15	.231	.300	.313	68	-6	1-1	.983	4	128	91	C63	0	0.0
1971	Cal A	55	123	6	25	5	0	0	5	3-1	0	6	.203	.220	.244	34	-11	0-0	.987	-4	76	92	C49	32	-1.4
1972	Cal A	59	153	5	32	3	0	0	8	14-4	1	21	.209	.280	.229	55	-8	0-0	.998	6	67	115	C58	23	0.0
1973	Cal A	102	255	20	56	7	0	1	18	21-0	0	32	.220	.278	.259	56	-15	0-2	.991	2	80	77	C102	28	-0.9
Total	10	574	1391	78	297	42	3	8	101	103-29	4	189	.214	.268	.265	56	-83	3-6	.990	19	101	97	C559	83	-4.6
TORCATO, TONY	Anthony Dale; B10.25.1979 Woodland CA; BL/TR/6´1˝/(195–220); [SFN98 1/19]; d7.26																								
2002	SF N	5	11	0	3	1	0	0	0	0-0	0	2	.273	.273	.364	68	-1	0-0	1.000	-1	40	0	O3R	0	-0.1
2003	SF N	14	16	0	3	1	0	0	1	0-0	1	4	.188	.235	.250	26	-2	0-0	.833	-0	106	0	O6(4/0/2)	0	-0.2
2004	SF N	13	9	1	5	0	0	0	2	1-0	1	0	.556	.583	.556	205	2	0-0	ø	0	—	—	/H	0	0.1
2005	SF N	11	11	1	3	0	0	0	0	1-0	0	2	.273	.333	.273	60	-1	0-0	1.000	0	145	0	/rf	0	-0.1
Total	4	43	47	2	14	2	0	0	3	2-0	2	8	.298	.346	.340	81	-2	0-0	.889	-1	78	0	O10(4/0/6)	0	-0.3

Torgeson, Earl Clifford Earl "The Earl of Snohomish"; B1.1.1924 Snohomish WA; D11.8.1990 Everett WA; BL/TL/6´3˝/(180–190); d4.15; C1

YEAR	TM LG	G	AB	R	H	2B	3B	HR	RBI	BB-IB	HP	SO	AVG	OBP	SLG	AOPS	ABR	SB-CS	FA	FR	RNG	THR	GAMES AT POSITION	DL	BFW
1947	Bos N	128	399	73	112	20	6	16	78	82	0	59	.281	.403	.481	137	24	11	.984	-1	106	100	1b117	0	1.9
1948	†Bos N	134	438	70	111	23	5	10	67	81	2	54	.253	.372	.397	110	9	19	.993	0	101	103	1b129	0	0.5
1949	Bos N	25	100	17	26	5	1	4	19	13	0	4	.260	.345	.450	118	2	4	.988	-3	50	94	1b25	122	-0.2
1950	Bos N	**156**	576	**120**	167	30	3	23	87	119	1	69	.290	.412	.472	141	41	15	.986	0	**104**	87	1b156	0	3.5
1951	Bos N	**155**	581	99	153	21	4	24	92	102	2	70	.263	.375	.437	127	25	20-11	.988	0	100	90	1b155	0	2.0
1952	Bos N	122	382	49	88	17	0	5	34	81	1	38	.230	.366	.314	94	1	11-7	.989	-1	99	90	1b105,O5(2/0/3)	0	-0.3
1953	Phi N	111	379	58	104	25	8	11	64	53	2	57	.274	.366	.470	117	10	7-1	.987	-4	89	98	1b105	0	0.2
1954	Phi N	135	490	63	133	22	6	5	54	75	0	52	.271	.364	.371	93	-2	7-1	.990	-11	74	93	1b133	0	-2.0
1955	Phi N	47	150	29	40	5	3	1	17	32-1	0	20	.267	.393	.360	104	3	2-3	.995	-2	84	78	1b43	0	-0.2
	Det A	89	300	58	85	10	1	9	50	61-2	0	29	.283	.397	.413	123	13	9-0	.992	-1	98	111	1b83	0	0.9
1956	Det A	117	318	61	84	9	3	12	42	78-0	0	47	.264	.406	.425	120	13	6-4	.992	-6	65	84	1b83	0	0.2
1957	Det A	30	50	5	12	2	1	1	5	12-0	0	10	.240	.387	.380	108	1	0-0	1.000	0	94	106	1b17	0	0.0
	Chi A	86	251	53	74	11	2	7	46	49-0	0	44	.295	.406	.438	131	13	7-3	.998	-4	75	131	1b70/rf	0	0.7
	Year	116	301	58	86	13	3	8	51	61-0	0	54	.286	.403	.429	127	14	7-3	.999	-4	78	127	1b87/rf	0	0.7
1958	Chi A	96	188	37	50	8	0	10	30	48-1	0	29	.266	.415	.468	146	15	7-2	.978	-3	90	115	1b73	0	1.0
1959	†Chi A	127	277	40	61	5	3	9	45	62-1	0	55	.220	.359	.357	100	2	7-6	.983	-7	72	90	1b103	0	-1.1
1960	Chi A	68	57	12	15	2	0	2	9	21-2	0	8	.263	.462	.404	137	5	1-0	.983	0	126	66	1b10	0	0.5
1961	Chi A	20	15	1	1	0	0	0	1	3-0	0	5	.067	.211	.067	-19	-3	0-0	1.000	0	0	0	/1	0	-0.3
	NY A	22	18	3	2	0	0	0	0	8-0	0	3	.111	.385	.111	42	-1	0-1	.969	-0	70	217	1b8	0	-0.2
	Year	42	33	4	3	0	0	0	1	11-0	0	8	.091	.311	.091	16	-3	0-1	.970	-0	68	211	1b9	0	-0.5
Total	15	1668	4969	848	1318	215	46	149	740	980-7	8	653	.265	.385	.417	118	171	133-39	.989	-41	91	97	1b1416,O6(2/0/4)	122	7.1

Torphy, Red Walter Anthony; B11.6.1891 Fall River MA; D2.11.1980 Fall River MA; BR/TR/5´11˝/169; d9.25

YEAR	TM LG	G	AB	R	H	2B	3B	HR	RBI	BB-IB	HP	SO	AVG	OBP	SLG	AOPS	ABR	SB-CS	FA	FR	RNG	THR	GAMES AT POSITION	DL	BFW
1920	Bos N	3	15	1	3	2	0	0	2	0	0	1	.200	.200	.333	54	-1	0-0	.969	-1	0	95	1b3	—	-0.2

Torre, Frank Frank Joseph; B12.30.1931 Brooklyn NY; BL/TL/6´3˝/(200–205); d4.20; b–Joe

YEAR	TM LG	G	AB	R	H	2B	3B	HR	RBI	BB-IB	HP	SO	AVG	OBP	SLG	AOPS	ABR	SB-CS	FA	FR	RNG	THR	GAMES AT POSITION	DL	BFW
1956	Mil N	111	159	17	41	6	0	0	16	11-2	0	4	.258	.304	.296	67	-7	1-0	.993	5	142	108	1b89	0	-0.5
1957	†Mil N	129	364	46	99	19	5	5	40	29-1	9	19	.272	.339	.393	104	2	0-0	**.996**	1	103	113	1b117	0	-0.2
1958	†Mil N	138	372	41	115	22	5	6	55	42-7	7	14	.309	.386	.444	131	18	2-0	**.994**	5	117	103	1b122	0	1.8
1959	Mil N	115	263	23	60	15	1	1	33	35-6	3	12	.228	.321	.304	75	-8	0-0	.994	0	98	81	1b87	0	-1.2
1960	Mil N	21	44	2	9	1	0	0	5	3-1	0	2	.205	.245	.227	36	-4	0-0	1.000	-2	48	128	1b17	0	-0.6
1962	Phi N	108	168	13	52	8	2	0	20	24-1	4	6	.310	.404	.381	117	6	1-1	.980	2	119	102	1b76	0	0.5
1963	Phi N	92	112	8	28	7	2	1	10	11-2	3	7	.250	.333	.375	105	1	0-0	.989	3	141	118	1b56	0	0.3
Total	7	714	1482	150	404	78	15	13	179	155-20	26	64	.273	.349	.372	101	8	4-1	.993	15	113	104	1b564	0	0.1

Torre, Joe Joseph Paul; B7.18.1940 Brooklyn NY; BR/TR/6´2˝/(205–215); d9.25; M25; b–Frank

YEAR	TM LG	G	AB	R	H	2B	3B	HR	RBI	BB-IB	HP	SO	AVG	OBP	SLG	AOPS	ABR	SB-CS	FA	FR	RNG	THR	GAMES AT POSITION	DL	BFW
1960	Mil N	2	2	0	1	0	0	0	0	0-0	0	1	.500	.500	.500	189	0	0-0	ø	0	—	—	/H	0	0.0
1961	Mil N	113	406	40	113	21	4	10	42	28-4	4	60	.278	.330	.424	105	2	3-5	.982	-5	138	113	C112	0	0.1
1962	Mil N	80	220	23	62	8	1	5	26	24-2	2	24	.282	.355	.395	105	2	1-0	.986	8	128	122	C63	0	1.3
1963	Mil N☆	142	501	57	147	19	4	14	71	42-4	5	79	.293	.350	.431	126	17	1-5	.994	3	134	79	C105,1b37,O2L	0	2.2
1964	Mil N★	154	601	87	193	36	5	20	109	36-4	7	67	.321	.365	.498	140	31	2-4	**.995**	0	142	77	C96,1b70	0	3.2
1965	Mil N★	148	523	68	152	21	1	27	80	61-7	8	79	.291	.372	.489	140	29	0-1	.991	-9	84	96	C100,1b49	0	2.3
1966	Atl N★	148	546	83	172	20	3	36	101	60-8	2	61	.315	.382	.560	157	42	0-4	.984	0	129	112	C114,1b36	0	4.5
1967	Atl N★	135	477	67	132	18	1	20	68	49-7	3	75	.277	.345	.444	127	17	2-2	.991	0	92	**143**	C114,1b23	0	2.2
1968	Atl N	115	424	45	115	11	2	10	55	34-7	5	72	.271	.332	.377	112	6	1-0	**.996**	-5	78	68	C92,1b29	21	0.5
1969	StL N	159	602	72	174	29	6	18	101	66-13	5	85	.289	.361	.447	125	21	0-0	.996	-5	91	**108**	1b144,C17	0	0.5
1970	StL N★	161	624	89	203	27	9	21	100	70-10	7	91	.325	.398	.498	135	32	2-2	.987	-9	93	96	C90,3b73/1	0	2.7
1971	StL N★	161	634	97	**230**	34	8	24	**137**	63-20	4	70	**.363**	.421	.555	167	57	4-1	.951	-22	82	73	3b161	0	3.7
1972	StL N★	149	544	71	157	26	6	11	81	54-13	8	64	.289	.357	.419	122	16	3-0	.963	-9	86	88	3b117,1b27	0	0.5
1973	StL N★	141	519	67	149	17	2	13	69	65-14	10	78	.287	.376	.403	116	13	2-0	.993	-10	96	108	1b114,3b58	0	-0.4
1974	StL N	147	529	59	149	28	1	11	70	69-9	8	88	.282	.371	.401	116	14	1-2	.992	2	**119**	**130**	1b139,3b18	0	0.5
1975	NY N	114	361	33	89	16	3	6	35	35-3	2	55	.247	.317	.357	89	-6	0-0	.950	1	95	115	3b83,1b24	0	-0.7
1976	NY N	114	310	36	95	10	3	5	31	21-1	5	35	.306	.358	.406	123	9	1-3	.989	3	116	82	1b78,3b4	0	0.5
1977	NY N	26	51	2	9	3	0	1	9	2-1	0	10	.176	.204	.294	34	-5	0-0	.988	-2	35	128	1b16/3M	0	-0.8
Total	18	2209	7874	996	2342	344	59	252	1185	779-127	85	1094	.297	.365	.452	128	297	23-29	.990	-60	115	102	C903,1b787,3b515,O2L	21	22.8

Torrealba, Steve Steven Alexander; B2.24.1978 Barquisimeto, Lara, Venez.; BR/TR/6´0˝/175; d10.6; f–Pablo; [DL 2003 StL N 65]

YEAR	TM LG	G	AB	R	H	2B	3B	HR	RBI	BB-IB	HP	SO	AVG	OBP	SLG	AOPS	ABR	SB-CS	FA	FR	RNG	THR	GAMES AT POSITION	DL	BFW
2001	†Atl N	2	2	0	1	0	0	0	0	0-0	0	0	.500	.500	.500	158	0	0-0	1.000	0	0	0	C2	0	0.0
2002	Atl N	13	17	1	1	0	0	0	1	3-0	0	4	.059	.200	.059	-28	-3	0-0	1.000	-1	75	57	C12	0	-0.4
Total	2	15	19	1	2	0	0	0	1	3-0	0	4	.105	.227	.105	-9	-3	0-0	1.000	-1	71	54	C14	65	-0.4

Torrealba, Yorvit Yorvit Adolfo; B7.19.1978 Caracas, Distrito Capital, Venez.; BR/TR/5´11˝/(180–200); d9.5

YEAR	TM LG	G	AB	R	H	2B	3B	HR	RBI	BB-IB	HP	SO	AVG	OBP	SLG	AOPS	ABR	SB-CS	FA	FR	RNG	THR	GAMES AT POSITION	DL	BFW
2001	SF N	3	4	0	2	0	1	0	2	0-0	0	0	.500	.500	1.000	291	1	0-0	1.000	-0	0	0	C3	0	0.1
2002	SF N	53	136	17	38	10	0	2	14	14-2	2	20	.279	.355	.397	101	1	0-0	.993	2	86	96	C53	0	0.6
2003	†SF N	66	200	22	52	10	2	4	29	14-1	2	39	.260	.312	.390	81	-6	1-0	.997	8	130	151	C66/lf	0	0.6
2004	SF N	64	172	19	39	7	3	6	23	17-3	2	31	.227	.302	.407	79	-6	2-0	.995	6	129	86	C59	0	0.3
2005	SF N	34	93	18	21	8	0	1	7	9-1	1	25	.226	.301	.344	67	-4	1-0	1.000	2	129	192	C27/D	0	0.0
	Sea A	42	108	14	26	4	0	2	8	7-0	1	25	.241	.293	.333	71	-5	0-0	1.000	3	72	125	C41	0	0.1
2006	Col N	65	223	23	55	16	3	7	43	11-1	4	49	.247	.293	.439	77	-8	4-3	.987	1	115	159	C63	82	-0.3
Total	6	327	936	113	233	55	9	22	126	72-8	12	189	.249	.310	.397	81	-27	8-3	.995	21	111	132	C312/Dlf	82	1.4

Torres, Andres Andres Vungo (Feliciano); B1.26.1978 Aguadilla, PR; BB/TR/5´10˝/(175–190); [DetA98 4/117]; d4.7; Col Miami–Dade Wolfson (FL) CC

YEAR	TM LG	G	AB	R	H	2B	3B	HR	RBI	BB-IB	HP	SO	AVG	OBP	SLG	AOPS	ABR	SB-CS	FA	FR	RNG	THR	GAMES AT POSITION	DL	BFW
2002	Det A	19	70	7	14	1	1	0	3	6-0	1	16	.200	.266	.243	40	-6	2-2	.981	-1	104	0	O19C	0	-0.7
2003	Det A	59	168	23	37	4	3	1	9	10-0	0	35	.220	.263	.298	50	-13	5-5	.991	-0	91	179	O50(1/36/16),D3	0	-1.4
2004	Det A	3	0	1	0	0	0	0	0	0-0	0	0	ø	ø	ø	ø	0	1-0	ø	-0	0	0	/cfD	0	0.0
2005	Tex A	8	19	2	3	1	0	0	1	1-0	0	6	.158	.190	.211	9	-2	1-0	1.000	0	125	0	O5(0/4/2)	0	-0.2
Total	4	89	257	33	54	6	4	1	13	17-0	1	57	.210	.258	.276	44	-21	9-7	.988	-1	96	118	O75(1/60/18),D5	0	-2.3

Torres, Gil Don Gilberto (Nunez); B8.23.1915 Regla, Cuba; D1.10.1983 Regla, Cuba; BR/TR/6´0˝/155; d4.25; f–Ricardo; ▲

YEAR	TM LG	G	AB	R	H	2B	3B	HR	RBI	BB-IB	HP	SO	AVG	OBP	SLG	AOPS	ABR	SB-CS	FA	FR	RNG	THR	GAMES AT POSITION	DL	BFW
1940	Was A	2	0	0	0	0	0	0	0	0	0	0	ø	ø	ø	ø	0	0-0	1.000	0	184	0	P2	—	0.0
1944	Was A	134	524	42	140	20	6	0	58	21	1	24	.267	.297	.328	82	-15	10-7	.952	8	**110**	107	3b123,2b10,1b4	0	-0.5
1945	Was A	147	562	39	133	12	5	0	48	21	0	29	.237	.264	.276	62	-31	7-4	.953	-24	93	76	S145,3b2	0	-4.7
1946	Was A	63	185	18	47	8	0	0	13	11	0	12	.254	.296	.297	70	-8	3-2	.939	-2	97	88	S31,3b18,2b7,P3	0	-0.9
Total	4	346	1271	99	320	40	11	0	119	53	1	65	.252	.282	.301	72	-54	20-13	.951	-18	94	78	S176,3b143,2b17,P5,1b4	0	-6.1

Torres, Felix Felix (Sanchez); B5.1.1932 Ponce, PR; BR/TR/5´11˝/(165–180); d4.10

YEAR	TM LG	G	AB	R	H	2B	3B	HR	RBI	BB-IB	HP	SO	AVG	OBP	SLG	AOPS	ABR	SB-CS	FA	FR	RNG	THR	GAMES AT POSITION	DL	BFW
1962	LA A	127	451	44	117	19	4	11	74	28-5	4	73	.259	.306	.392	90	-8	0-0	.938	-0	105	88	3b123	0	-0.9
1963	LA A	138	463	40	121	32	1	4	51	30-0	3	73	.261	.307	.361	93	-4	1-0	.939	1	107	129	3b122,1b2	0	-0.3
1964	LA A	100	277	25	64	10	0	12	28	13-0	1	56	.231	.266	.397	91	-5	1-3	.970	-0	96	85	3b72,1b3	0	-0.7
Total	3	365	1191	109	302	61	5	27	153	71-5	8	202	.254	.297	.381	91	-17	2-3	.945	1	104	103	3b317,1b5	0	-1.9

Torres, Hector Hector Epitacio (Marroquin); B9.16.1945 Monterrey, Nuevo Leon, Mexico; BR/TR/6´0˝/175; d4.10; C2

YEAR	TM LG	G	AB	R	H	2B	3B	HR	RBI	BB-IB	HP	SO	AVG	OBP	SLG	AOPS	ABR	SB-CS	FA	FR	RNG	THR	GAMES AT POSITION	DL	BFW
1968	Hou N	128	466	44	104	11	1	1	24	18-2	0	64	.223	.252	.258	54	-27	2-3	.958	-3	100	77	S127/2	0	-2.4
1969	Hou N	34	69	5	11	1	0	1	8	2-0	0	12	.159	.183	.217	12	-8	0-0	.944	-3	74	71	S22	21	-1.1
1970	Hou N	31	65	6	16	1	2	0	5	6-0	0	8	.246	.310	.323	73	-3	0-0	.947	-4	92	71	S22,2b6	0	-0.4
1971	Chi N	31	58	4	13	3	0	0	2	4-0	0	10	.224	.274	.276	49	-4	0-0	.962	-4	97	76	S18,2b4	0	-0.7
1972	Mon N	83	181	14	28	4	1	2	7	13-1	1	26	.155	.215	.221	24	-19	0-2	.965	-7	95	94	2b60,S16,O2(1/0/1)/P3	0	-2.4
1973	Hou N	38	66	3	6	1	0	0	2	7-0	1	13	.091	.189	.106	-16	-11	0-1	.952	1	124	73	S22,2b13	0	-0.8
1975	SD N	112	352	31	91	12	0	5	26	22-3	0	32	.259	.297	.335	82	-10	2-3	.971	8	124	109	S75,3b42,2b16	0	0.6
1976	SD N	74	215	8	42	6	0	4	15	16-3	1	31	.195	.254	.279	56	-13	2-1	.949	-20	86	84	S63,3b4,2b3	0	-2.8
1977	Tor A	91	266	33	64	7	3	5	26	16-1	1	33	.241	.282	.346	70	-12	1-1	.980	-0	99	79	S68,2b23,3b2	0	-0.5
Total	9	622	1738	148	375	46	7	18	115	104-10	4	229	.216	.260	.281	55	-107	7-11	.962	-32	101	83	S433,2b126,3b49,O2(1/0/1)/P	21	-10.5

YEAR	TM LG	G	AB	R	H	2B	3B	HR	RBI	BB-IB	HP	SO	AVG	OBP	SLG	AOPS	ABR	SB-CS	FA	FR	RNG	THR	GAMES AT POSITION	DL	BFW
TORRES, RICARDO	Ricardo J. (Martinez); B4.16.1891 Regla, Cuba; D4.17.1960 Regla, Cuba; BR/TR/5´11˝/160; d5.18; s–Gil																								
1920	Was A	16	30	8	10	1	0	0	3	1	0	4	.333	.355	.367	94	0	0-0	1.000	-1	42	45	1b7,C5	—	-0.1
1921	Was A	2	3	1	1	0	0	0	0	1	0	1	.333	.500	.333	122	0	0-0	.750	-1	*0*	*0*	C2	—	0.0
1922	Was A	4	4	0	0	0	0	0	0	0	0	1	.000	.000	.000	-99	-1	0-0	1.000	1	*0*	*256*	C3	—	0.0
Total	3	22	37	9	11	1	0	0	3	2	0	6	.297	.333	.324	76	-1	0-0	.955	-1	*44*	*91*	C10,1b7	—	-0.1
TORRES, RUSTY	Rosendo (Hernandez); B9.30.1948 Aguadilla, PR; BB/TR/5´10˝/(175–180); [NYA66 54/811]; d9.20																								
1971	NY A	9	26	5	10	3	0	2	3	0-0	0	8	.385	.385	.731	220	4	0-1	1.000	0	122	0	O5(0/1/4)	0	0.4
1972	NY A	80	199	15	42	7	0	3	13	18-3	1	44	.211	.280	.291	72	-7	0-4	.978	-3	83	105	O62(1/1/60)	0	-1.6
1973	Cle A	122	312	31	64	8	1	7	28	50-5	3	62	.205	.317	.304	75	-9	6-5	.976	-2	92	136	O114(1/37/77)	0	-1.6
1974	Cle A	108	150	19	28	2	0	3	12	13-1	0	24	.187	.248	.260	48	-10	2-1	.959	2	92	220	O94(35/38/24)/D	0	-1.1
1976	Cal A	120	264	37	54	16	3	6	27	36-3	0	39	.205	.299	.356	97	0	4-4	.990	-4	92	88	O105(0/104/1)/3D	0	-0.8
1977	Cal A	58	77	9	12	1	1	3	10	10-0	0	18	.156	.250	.312	55	-5	0-1	.984	-1	92	55	O54(4/40/10)	41	-0.8
1978	Chi A	16	44	7	14	3	0	3	6	6-0	0	7	.318	.400	.591	173	4	0-1	.964	-1	98	0	O14(4/5/8)	0	0.3
1979	Chi A	90	170	26	43	5	0	8	24	23-1	2	37	.253	.349	.424	107	2	0-0	.976	-0	98	103	O85(36/17/35)	15	-0.1
1980	KC A	51	72	10	12	0	0	0	3	8-0	0	7	.167	.250	.167	16	-8	1-3	.973	5	130	221	O40(15/8/21)/D	0	-0.6
Total	9	654	1314	159	279	45	5	35	126	164-13	6	246	.212	.301	.334	82	-29	13-20	.977	-5	94	122	O573(96/251/240),D8/3	56	-5.9
TORVE, KELVIN	Kelvin Curtis; B1.10.1960 Rapid City SD; BL/TR/6´3˝/(190–205); [SFN81 2/36]; d6.25; Col Oral Roberts																								
1988	Min A	12	16	1	3	0	0	1	2	1-0	0	2	.188	.235	.375	66	-1	0-1	1.000	-0	58	50	1b4/D	0	-0.2
1990	NY N	20	38	0	11	4	0	0	2	4-0	2	9	.289	.386	.395	115	1	0-0	1.000	-2	0	118	1b9/lf	0	-0.1
1991	NY N	10	8	0	0	0	0	0	0	0-0	0	1	.000	.000	.000	-99	-2	0-0	1.000	1	2399	0	/1	0	-0.1
Total	3	42	62	1	14	4	0	1	4	5-0	2	12	.226	.304	.339	77	-2	0-1	1.000	-1	40	101	1b14/lfD	0	-0.4
TOVAR, CESAR	Cesar Leonardo "Pepito" (b Cesar Leonard Perez (Tovar)); B7.3.1940 Caracas, Distrito Capital, Venez.; D7.14.1994 Caracas, Distrito Capital, Venez.; BR/TR/5´9˝/(150–155); d4.12; OF(378/471/205)																								
1965	Min A	18	25	3	5	1	0	0	2	2-0	0	3	.200	.259	.240	41	-2	2-0	.800	1	136	197	2b4,3b2,O2C/S	0	-0.1
1966	Min A	134	465	57	121	19	5	2	41	44-1	4	50	.260	.325	.335	86	-7	16-6	.978	-4	104	79	2b76,S31,O24(4/20/0)	0	-0.1
1967	Min A	**164**	649	98	173	32	7	6	47	46-0	13	51	.267	.325	.365	97	-2	19-11	.994	-8	118	124	O74(10/64/5),3b70,2b36,S9	0	-1.0
1968	Min A	157	613	89	167	31	6	6	47	34-0	17	41	.272	.326	.372	106	5	35-13	.966	6	123	110	O78(39/34/10),3b75,S35,2b18/PC1	0	1.6
1969	†Min A	158	535	99	154	25	5	11	52	37-3	9	37	.288	.342	.415	109	6	45-12	.983	3	**117**	152	O113(39/70/8),2b41,3b20	0	1.3
1970	†Min A	161	650	120	195	**36**	**13**	10	54	52-5	8	47	.300	.356	.442	118	15	30-15	.977	1	111	127	O151(39/134/2),2b8,3b4	0	1.4
1971	Min A	157	657	94	**204**	29	3	1	45	45-5	3	39	.311	.356	.368	103	3	18-14	.986	13	**118**	150	O154(98/44/47),3b7,2b2	0	0.8
1972	Min A	141	548	86	145	20	6	2	31	39-6	**14**	39	.265	.329	.334	93	-4	21-10	.983	4	108	97	O139(38/5/101)	0	-0.7
1973	Phi N	97	328	49	88	18	4	1	21	29-2	5	35	.268	.335	.357	90	-4	6-4	.928	1	71	90	3b46,O24(6/3/16),2b22	18	-0.3
1974	Tex A	138	562	78	164	24	6	4	58	47-0	9	33	.292	.354	.377	114	11	13-9	.980	6	103	137	O135(66/87/11),D3	0	1.1
1975	Tex A	102	427	53	110	16	0	3	28	27-0	3	25	.258	.306	.316	77	-13	16-11	.919	-4	84	46	D66,O31(25/6/1)/2	15	-2.2
	†Oak A	19	26	5	6	1	0	0	3	3-0	0	3	.231	.310	.269	66	-1	4-0	1.000	-1	29	0	2b4,3b3/SD	0	-0.2
	Year	121	453	58	116	17	0	3	31	30-0	3	28	.256	.306	.313	76	-14	20-11	.938	-6	84	46	D73,O31(25/6/1),2b5,3b3/S	0	-2.4
1976	Oak A	29	45	1	8	0	0	0	4	4-0	2	4	.178	.275	.178	36	-4	1-2	.958	-1	88	0	O20(14/2/4),D4	73	-0.7
	NY A	13	39	2	6	1	0	0	2	4-1	1	3	.154	.250	.179	27	-3	0-1	1.000	1	149	189	D10,2b3	0	-0.3
	Year	42	84	3	14	1	0	0	6	8-1	3	7	.167	.263	.179	32	-7	1-3	.958	-0	88	0	O20(14/2/4),D14,2b3	0	-1.0
Total	12	1488	5569	834	1546	253	55	46	435	413-23	88	410	.278	.335	.368	99	0	226-108	.980	17	111	124	O945C,3b227,2b215,D90,S77/1CP	106	0.6
TOWNE, BABE	Jay King; B3.12.1880 Coon Rapids IA; D10.29.1938 Des Moines IA; BR/TR/5´10˝/180; d8.1																								
1906	†Chi A	14	36	3	10	0	0	0	6	7	0	—	.278	.395	.278	115	1	0	.923	-2	*141*	*69*	C13	—	0.0
TOWNSEND, GEORGE	George Hodgson "Sleepy"; B6.4.1867 Hartsdale NY; D3.15.1930 New Haven CT; BR/TR/5´7.5˝/180; d6.25; Col NYU																								
1887	Phi AA	31	109	12	21	3	0	0	14	3	0	—	.193	.214	.220	21	-12	8	.865	-5	—	—	C28,O3(1/0/2)	—	-1.2
1888	Phi AA	42	161	13	25	6	0	0	12	4	1	—	.155	.181	.193	20	-14	2	.912	1	—	—	C42	—	-0.9
1890	Bal AA	18	67	6	16	4	1	0	9	4	0	—	.239	.282	.328	76	-2	3	.930	4	*116*	*139*	C18	—	0.3
1891	Bal AA	61	204	29	39	5	4	0	18	20	5	21	.191	.279	.255	53	-13	3	.909	2	*141*	*94*	C58,O3(0/1/2)	—	-0.6
Total	4	152	541	60	101	18	5	0	53	31	6	21	.187	.239	.238	40	-41	16	.905	3	*135*	*105*	C146,O6(1/1/4)	—	-2.4
TOY, JIM	James Madison; B2.20.1858 Beaver Falls PA; D3.13.1919 Cresson PA; BR/TR/5´6˝/160; d4.20																								
1887	Cle AA	109	423	56	94	20	5	1	56	17	2	—	.222	.256	.300	56	-26	8	.975	4	113	111	1b82,O11(2/2/7),C10,3b8,S3	—	-2.4
1890	Bro AA	44	160	11	29	3	0	0	7	11	1	—	.181	.238	.200	30	-14	2	.867	-7	*82*	*121*	C44	—	-1.6
Total	2	153	583	67	123	23	5	1	63	28	3	—	.211	.251	.273	50	-40	10	.975	-4	113	111	1b82,C54,O11(2/2/7),3b8,S3	—	-4.0
TRABER, JIM	James Joseph; B12.26.1961 Columbus OH; BL/TL/6´0˝/(194–215); [BalA82 21/544]; d9.21; Col Oklahoma St.																								
1984	Bal A	10	21	3	5	0	0	0	2	2-0	0	4	.238	.292	.238	53	-1	0-0	ø	0	—	—	D9	0	-0.2
1986	Bal A	65	212	28	54	7	0	13	44	18-2	5	31	.255	.321	.472	116	4	0-0	.988	2	98	121	1b29,D21,O8(7/0/1)	0	0.3
1988	Bal A	103	352	25	78	6	0	10	45	19-3	1	42	.222	.261	.324	65	-18	1-2	.990	7	141	105	1b57,D30,O11(2/0/8)	0	-1.7
1989	Bal A	86	234	14	49	8	0	4	26	19-1	0	41	.209	.266	.295	60	-13	4-3	.998	5	132	119	1b69,D5	0	-1.3
Total	4	264	819	70	186	21	0	27	117	58-6	6	118	.227	.279	.352	77	-28	5-5	.993	13	129	114	1b155,D65,O19(9/0/9)	0	-2.9
TRACEWSKI, DICK	Richard Joseph; B2.3.1935 Eynon PA; BR/TR/5´11˝/(165–170); d4.12; M1/C24																								
1962	LA N	15	2	3	0	0	0	0	0	2-0	0	0	.000	.500	.000	50	0	0-0	1.000	1	186	0	S4	0	0.1
1963	†LA N	104	217	23	49	2	1	1	10	19-1	0	39	.226	.287	.258	63	-11	2-3	.957	-0	101	91	S81,2b23	0	-0.6
1964	LA N	106	304	31	75	13	4	1	26	31-4	0	61	.247	.315	.326	88	-5	3-3	.970	-8	89	81	2b56,3b30,S19	0	-0.8
1965	†LA N	78	186	17	40	6	0	1	20	25-4	2	30	.215	.313	.263	69	-7	2-6	.950	-2	110	96	3b53,2b14,S7	0	-1.0
1966	Det A	81	124	15	24	1	1	0	7	10-0	0	32	.194	.252	.218	36	-10	1-1	.947	1	100	118	2b70,S3	0	-0.7
1967	Det A	74	107	19	30	4	2	1	9	8-0	0	20	.280	.325	.383	107	1	1-1	.965	6	105	136	S44,2b12,3b10	0	0.9
1968	†Det A	90	212	30	33	3	1	4	15	24-0	0	51	.156	.239	.236	44	-14	3-0	.982	-8	94	102	S51,3b16,2b14	0	-2.0
1969	Det A	66	79	10	11	2	0	0	4	15-1	0	20	.139	.277	.165	25	-8	3-0	.957	5	97	153	S41,2b13,3b6	0	0.0
Total	8	614	1231	148	262	31	9	8	91	134-10	2	253	.213	.289	.272	65	-54	15-14	.958	-6	101	106	S250,2b202,3b115	0	-4.1
TRACY, ANDY	Andrew Michael; B12.11.1973 Bowling Green OH; BL/TR/6´3˝/(220–225); [MonN96 16/460]; d4.25; Col Bowling Green																								
2000	Mon N	83	192	29	50	8	1	11	32	22-1	2	61	.260	.339	.484	105	1	1-0	.882	-5	86	46	3b34,1b27	0	-0.5
2001	Mon N	38	55	4	6	1	0	2	8	6-0	0	26	.109	.190	.236	11	-8	0-0	1.000	-1	88	0	3b11,1b3,D2	0	-0.9
2004	Col N	15	16	1	3	1	0	0	1	1-0	0	8	.188	.235	.250	23	-2	0-0	1.000	-0	71	0	/3	0	-0.2
Total	3	136	263	34	59	10	1	13	41	29-1	2	95	.224	.302	.418	81	-9	1-0	.913	-7	86	34	3b46,1b30,D2	0	-1.6
TRACY, CHAD	Chad Austin; B5.22.1980 Charlotte NC; BL/TR/6´2˝/200; [AriN01 7/218]; d4.21; Col East Carolina																								
2004	Ari N	143	481	45	137	29	3	8	53	45-3	0	60	.285	.343	.407	88	-8	2-3	.935	11	104	116	3b135,1b11/lf	0	0.3
2005	Ari N	145	503	73	155	34	4	27	72	35-4	8	78	.308	.359	.553	129	20	3-1	.996	-1	100	113	1b80,O51(6/0/47)/D	0	1.1
2006	Ari N	154	597	91	168	41	0	20	80	54-5	5	129	.281	.343	.451	96	-2	5-1	.935	-3	101	98	3b147,1b6,D2	0	-0.3
Total	3	442	1581	209	460	104	7	55	205	134-12	13	267	.291	.348	.470	104	10	10-5	.935	7	102	106	3b282,1b97,O52(7/0/47),D3	0	1.1
TRACY, JIM	James Edwin; B12.31.1955 Hamilton OH; BL/TR/6´3˝/(185–193); [ChiN77*4/88]; d7.20; M6/C6; Col Marietta																								
1980	Chi N	42	122	12	31	3	3	3	9	13-1	0	37	.254	.326	.402	94	-1	2-2	.950	-6	66	0	O31(22/0/14)/1	0	-1.0
1981	Chi N	45	63	6	15	2	1	0	5	12-0	0	14	.238	.355	.302	84	-1	1-0	1.000	-2	76	0	O11(10/0/1)	0	-0.3
Total	2	87	185	18	46	5	4	3	14	25-1	0	51	.249	.336	.368	91	-2	3-2	.964	-8	69	0	O42(32/0/15)/1	0	-1.3
TRAFFLEY, JOHN	John M.; B1862 Chicago IL; D5.15.1900 Baltimore MD; 5´9˝/180; d6.15; b–Bill																								
1889	Lou AA	1	2	0	1	0	0	0	0	0	0	0	.500	.500	.500	189	0	0	.000	-0	0	0	/rf	—	0.0
TRAFFLEY, BILL	William Franklin; B12.21.1859 Staten Island NY; D6.23.1908 Des Moines IA; BR/TR/5´11.5˝/185; d7.27; b–John																								
1878	Chi N	2	9	1	1	0	0	0	1	0	—	1	.111	.111	.111	-25	-1	—	1.000	-1	—	—	C2	—	-0.2
1883	Cin AA	30	105	17	21	5	0	0	8	4	—	—	.200	.229	.248	51	-6	—	.851	0	—	—	C29,S2	—	-0.3
1884	Bal AA	53	210	25	37	4	6	0	—	3	1	—	.176	.192	.252	42	-14	—	.926	-4	—	—	C47,O6R/1	—	-1.3
1885	Bal AA	69	254	27	39	4	5	1	20	17	3	—	.154	.215	.220	38	-18	—	**.943**	4	—	—	C61,O10(0/5/5),2b3	—	-0.8
1886	Bal AA	25	85	15	18	0	1	0	7	10	0	—	.212	.295	.235	68	-3	8	.952	-3	—	—	C25	—	-0.3
Total	5	179	663	85	116	13	12	1	36	34	4	1	.175	.220	.235	45	-42	8	.927	-3	—	—	C164,O16(0/5/11),2b3,S2/1	—	-2.9

TRAGESSER, WALT Walter Joseph; B6.14.1887 Lafayette IN; D12.14.1970 Lafayette IN; BR/TR/6´0˝/175; d7.30; Mil 1918; Col Purdue

YEAR	TM LG	G	AB	R	H	2B	3B	HR	RBI	BB-IB	HP	SO	AVG	OBP	SLG	AOPS	ABR	SB-CS	FA	FR	RNG	THR	GAMES AT POSITION	DL	BFW
1913	Bos N	2	0	0	0	0	0	0	0	0	0	0	ø	ø	ø	ø	0	0	1.000	-0	0	0	C2	—	0.0
1915	Bos N	7	7	1	0	0	0	0	0	0	0	2	.000	.000	.000	-99	-2	0	.944	1	*231*	*51*	C7	—	-0.1
1916	Bos N	41	54	3	11	1	0	0	4	5	1	10	.204	.283	.222	59	-2	0	.971	4	178	113	C29	—	0.3
1917	Bos N	98	297	23	66	10	2	0	25	15	2	36	.222	.264	.269	68	-12	5	.971	0	*113*	*91*	C94	—	-0.4
1918	Bos N	7	1	0	0	0	0	0	0	0	0	0	.000	.000	.000	-99	0	0	.833	0	*0*	*156*	C7	—	0.0
1919	Bos N	20	40	3	7	2	0	0	3	2	1	10	.175	.233	.225	39	-3	1	.959	-1	*92*	*150*	C14	—	-0.3
	Phi N	35	114	7	27	7	0	0	8	9	1	31	.237	.298	.298	74	-3	4	.953	-2	*90*	*106*	C34	—	-0.2
	Year	55	154	10	34	9	0	0	11	11	2	41	.221	.281	.279	67	-6	5	.954	-3	*90*	*115*	C48	—	-0.5
1920	Phi N	62	176	17	37	11	1	6	26	4	2	36	.210	.236	.386	73	-7	4-0	.944	-10	*76*	*77*	C52	—	-1.2
Total	7	272	689	54	148	31	3	6	66	35	7	125	.215	.260	.295	67	-29	14-0	.961	-7	*105*	95	C239	—	-1.9

TRAMBACK, RED Stephen Joseph; B11.1.1915 Iselin PA; D12.28.1979 Buffalo NY; BL/TL/6´0˝/175; d9.15

YEAR	TM LG	G	AB	R	H	2B	3B	HR	RBI	BB-IB	HP	SO	AVG	OBP	SLG	AOPS	ABR	SB-CS	FA	FR	RNG	THR	GAMES AT POSITION	DL	BFW
1940	NY N	2	4	0	1	0	0	0	0	1	0	1	.250	.400	.250	82	0	1	.667	-0	79	0	/rf	—	-0.1

TRAMMELL, ALAN Alan Stuart; B2.21.1958 Garden Grove CA; BR/TR/6´0˝/(160–185); [DetA76 2/26]; d9.9; M3/C4

YEAR	TM LG	G	AB	R	H	2B	3B	HR	RBI	BB-IB	HP	SO	AVG	OBP	SLG	AOPS	ABR	SB-CS	FA	FR	RNG	THR	GAMES AT POSITION	DL	BFW
1977	Det A	19	43	6	8	0	0	0	0	4-0	0	12	.186	.255	.186	21	-5	0-0	.961	-8	74	57	S19	0	-1.1
1978	Det A	139	448	49	120	14	6	2	34	45-0	2	56	.268	.335	.339	88	-7	3-1	.979	5	103	118	S139	0	1.3
1979	Det A	142	460	68	127	11	4	6	50	43-0	0	55	.276	.335	.357	85	-10	17-14	.961	-4	92	109	S142	0	-0.1
1980	Det A★	146	560	107	168	21	5	9	65	69-2	3	63	.300	.376	.404	112	11	12-12	.980	-18	92	92	S144	0	0.7
1981	Det A	105	392	52	101	15	3	2	31	49-2	3	31	.258	.342	.327	91	-3	10-3	.983	13	107	102	S105	0	2.2
1982	Det A	157	489	66	126	34	3	9	57	52-0	0	47	.258	.325	.395	97	-1	19-8	.978	1	99	111	S157	0	1.7
1983	Det A	142	505	83	161	31	2	14	66	57-2	0	64	.319	.385	.471	138	28	30-10	.979	-8	90	92	S140	0	3.7
1984	†Det A✳	139	555	85	174	34	5	14	69	60-2	3	63	.314	.382	.468	134	28	19-13	.980	-3	95	110	S114,D22	22	3.5
1985	Det A★	149	605	79	156	21	7	13	57	50-4	2	71	.258	.312	.380	90	-9	14-5	.977	-13	93	98	S149	0	-0.5
1986	Det A	151	574	107	159	33	7	21	75	59-4	5	57	.277	.347	.469	120	16	25-12	.969	14	110	113	S149,D2	0	4.5
1987	†Det A★	151	597	109	205	34	3	28	105	60-8	3	47	.343	.402	.551	157	50	21-2	.971	-4	99	109	S149	0	6.1
1988	Det A✳	128	466	73	145	24	1	15	69	46-8	4	46	.311	.373	.464	139	25	7-4	.980	-1	100	91	S125	18	3.4
1989	Det A	121	449	54	109	20	3	5	43	45-1	4	45	.243	.314	.334	85	-8	10-2	.985	16	**112**	85	S117,D2	19	1.8
1990	Det A★	146	559	71	170	37	1	14	89	68-7	1	55	.304	.377	.449	130	24	12-10	.979	1	99	107	S142,D3	0	3.5
1991	Det A	101	375	57	93	20	0	9	55	37-1	3	39	.248	.320	.373	90	-5	11-2	.979	4	111	101	S92,D6	27	0.7
1992	Det A	29	102	11	28	7	1	1	11	15-0	1	4	.275	.370	.392	113	2	2-2	.977	-0	101	90	S27/D	142	0.4
1993	Det A	112	401	72	132	25	3	12	60	38-2	2	38	.329	.388	.496	136	21	12-8	.989	-6	104	64	S63,3b35,O8(4/4/0),D6	12	1.9
1994	Det A	76	292	38	78	17	1	8	28	16-1	1	35	.267	.307	.414	83	-8	3-0	.968	0	101	108	S63,D11	0	-0.3
1995	Det A	74	223	28	60	12	0	2	23	27-4	0	19	.269	.345	.350	82	-5	3-1	.980	-4	100	87	S60,D6	11	-0.5
1996	Det A	66	193	16	45	2	0	1	16	10-0	0	27	.233	.267	.259	35	-20	6-0	.976	-4	101	51	S43,2b11,3b8/lf	55	-1.8
Total	20	2293	8288	1231	2365	412	55	185	1003	850-48	37	874	.285	.352	.415	110	124	236-109	.977	-19	100	100	S2139,D59,3b43,2b11,O9(5/4/0)	306	31.1

TRAMMELL, BUBBA Thomas Bubba; B11.6.1971 Knoxville TN; BR/TR/6´2˝/(205–220); [DetA94 11/305]; d4.1; Col Tennessee

YEAR	TM LG	G	AB	R	H	2B	3B	HR	RBI	BB-IB	HP	SO	AVG	OBP	SLG	AOPS	ABR	SB-CS	FA	FR	RNG	THR	GAMES AT POSITION	DL	BFW
1997	Det A	44	123	14	28	5	0	4	13	15-0	0	35	.228	.307	.366	76	-4	3-1	1.000	0	104	63	O28(13/0/16),D15	0	-0.6
1998	TB A	59	199	28	57	18	1	12	35	16-0	0	45	.286	.338	.568	127	7	0-2	1.000	-2	77	140	O37(23/0/16),D19	0	0.2
1999	TB A	82	283	49	82	19	0	14	39	43-1	1	37	.290	.384	.505	123	11	0-2	.993	-1	103	44	O74(61/0/20),D6	0	0.6
2000	TB A	66	189	19	52	11	2	7	33	21-0	2	30	.275	.352	.466	107	2	3-0	1.000	-4	78	75	O48(26/0/24),D9	0	-0.3
	†NY N	36	56	9	13	2	0	3	12	8-0	0	19	.232	.323	.429	94	-1	1-0	.963	0	96	121	O25(11/0/16)	0	-0.1
2001	SD N	142	490	66	128	20	3	25	92	48-2	4	78	.261	.330	.467	112	7	2-2	.985	2	108	61	O132(34/0/102),D3	0	0.3
2002	SD N	133	403	54	98	16	1	17	56	53-2	3	71	.243	.333	.414	105	2	1-3	.973	-6	90	60	O122(23/0/104),D2	0	-0.9
2003	NY A	22	55	4	11	5	0	0	5	6-0	0	10	.200	.279	.291	51	-4	0-0	1.000	1	184	0	D15,O3L	0	-0.4
Total	7	584	1798	243	469	96	7	82	285	210-5	10	325	.261	.339	.459	109	20	10-10	.986	-10	97	67	O469(194/0/298),D69	0	-1.2

TRAVIS, CECIL Cecil Howell; B8.8.1913 Riverdale GA; BL/TR/6´1.5˝/185; d5.16; Mil 1942–45

YEAR	TM LG	G	AB	R	H	2B	3B	HR	RBI	BB-IB	HP	SO	AVG	OBP	SLG	AOPS	ABR	SB-CS	FA	FR	RNG	THR	GAMES AT POSITION	DL	BFW
1933	Was A	18	43	7	13	1	0	0	2	2	1	5	.302	.348	.326	80	-1	0-0	.974	2	132	52	3b15	—	0.1
1934	Was A	109	392	48	125	22	4	1	53	24	2	37	.319	.361	.403	101	0	1-5	.937	4	113	128	3b99	—	0.5
1935	Was A	138	534	85	170	27	8	0	61	41	**9**	28	.318	.377	.399	104	4	4-2	.963	21	**118**	**173**	3b114,O16L	—	2.6
1936	Was A	138	517	77	164	34	10	2	92	39	1	21	.317	.366	.433	102	1	4-4	.938	-5	98	119	S71,O53(1/0/52),2b4,3b2	—	-0.1
1937	Was A	135	526	72	181	27	7	3	66	39	5	34	.344	.395	.439	115	12	3-2	.965	-8	98	**122**	S129	—	1.3
1938	Was A☆	146	567	96	190	30	5	5	67	58	4	22	.335	.401	.432	117	16	6-5	.950	-4	102	110	S143	—	2.1
1939	Was A	130	476	55	139	20	9	5	63	34	2	25	.292	.342	.403	97	-4	0-3	.958	-5	101	106	S118	—	-0.1
1940	Was A★	136	528	60	170	37	11	2	76	48	2	23	.322	.381	.445	121	17	0-1	.934	11	108	**127**	3b113,S23	—	3.1
1941	Was A★	152	608	106	**218**	39	19	7	101	52	1	25	.359	.410	.520	152	44	2-2	.964	-0	98	104	S136,3b16	0	5.1
1945	Was A	15	54	4	13	2	1	0	10	4	0	5	.241	.293	.315	83	-1	0-1	.920	-1	94	154	3b14	0	-0.2
1946	Was A	137	465	45	117	22	3	1	56	45	4	47	.252	.323	.318	85	-9	2-4	.959	-18	95	95	S75,3b56	0	-2.5
1947	Was A	74	204	10	44	4	1	1	10	16	0	19	.216	.273	.260	50	-14	1-3	.932	-2	104	95	3b39,S15	0	-1.7
Total	12	1328	4914	665	1544	265	78	27	657	402	31	291	.314	.370	.416	109	65	23-32	.955	-4	99	110	S710,3b468,O69(17/0/52),2b4	0	10.2

TRAXLER, BRIAN Brian Lee; B9.26.1967 Waukegan IL; D11.19.2004 San Antonio TX; BL/TL/5´10˝/200; [LAN88 16/400]; d4.24; Col New Orleans

YEAR	TM LG	G	AB	R	H	2B	3B	HR	RBI	BB-IB	HP	SO	AVG	OBP	SLG	AOPS	ABR	SB-CS	FA	FR	RNG	THR	GAMES AT POSITION	DL	BFW
1990	LA N	9	11	0	1	1	0	0	0	0-0	0	4	.091	.091	.182	-28	-2	0-0	1.000	1	226	0	1b3	0	-0.2

TRAY, JIM James (b James Trahey); B2.14.1860 Jackson MI; D7.28.1905 Jackson MI; 5´11˝/180; d9.6

YEAR	TM LG	G	AB	R	H	2B	3B	HR	RBI	BB-IB	HP	SO	AVG	OBP	SLG	AOPS	ABR	SB-CS	FA	FR	RNG	THR	GAMES AT POSITION	DL	BFW
1884	Ind AA	6	21	2	6	0	0	0	—	2	0	—	.286	.348	.286	112	0	—	.857	-2	—	—	C4,1b2	—	-0.1

TRAYNOR, PIE Harold Joseph; B11.11.1898 Framingham MA; D3.16.1972 Pittsburgh PA; BR/TR/6´0˝/170; d9.15; M6; HF1948

YEAR	TM LG	G	AB	R	H	2B	3B	HR	RBI	BB-IB	HP	SO	AVG	OBP	SLG	AOPS	ABR	SB-CS	FA	FR	RNG	THR	GAMES AT POSITION	DL	BFW
1920	Pit N	17	52	6	11	3	1	0	2	3	1	6	.212	.268	.308	63	-2	1-3	.860	-7	74	61	S17	—	-1.1
1921	Pit N	7	19	0	5	0	0	0	2	1	0	2	.263	.300	.263	49	-1	0-0	.917	-0	104	0	3b3/S	—	-0.1
1922	Pit N	142	571	89	161	17	12	4	81	27	4	28	.282	.319	.375	77	-21	17-3	.945	-8	89	105	3b124,S18	—	-1.6
1923	Pit N	153	616	108	208	19	**19**	12	101	34	5	19	.338	.377	.489	124	19	28-13	.950	9	103	115	3b152/S	—	3.6
1924	Pit N	142	545	86	160	26	13	5	82	37	1	26	.294	.340	.417	100	-1	24-18	.968	6	102	**144**	3b141	—	1.3
1925	†Pit N	150	591	114	189	39	14	6	106	52	2	19	.320	.377	.464	106	6	15-9	**.957**	23	107	**154**	3b150/S	—	3.6
1926	Pit N	152	574	83	182	25	17	3	92	38	1	14	.317	.361	.436	108	5	8	.952	6	99	**128**	3b148,S3	—	2.0
1927	†Pit N	149	573	93	196	32	9	5	106	22	3	11	.342	.370	.455	112	9	11	.962	14	100	109	3b143,S9	—	3.2
1928	Pit N	144	569	91	192	38	12	3	124	28	1	10	.337	.370	.462	112	9	12	.946	6	103	57	3b144	—	2.3
1929	Pit N	130	540	94	192	27	12	4	108	30	3	7	.356	.393	.472	111	8	13	.951	-3	95	127	3b130	—	1.3
1930	Pit N	130	497	90	182	22	11	9	119	48	1	19	.366	.423	.509	124	20	7	.941	5	109	74	3b130	—	2.9
1931	Pit N	**155**	615	81	183	37	15	2	103	54	0	28	.298	.354	.416	107	6	6	.925	-10	97	76	3b155	—	0.2
1932	Pit N	135	513	74	169	27	10	2	68	32	4	20	.329	.373	.433	118	13	6	.936	-2	94	66	3b127	—	1.6
1933	Pit N★	**154**	624	85	190	27	6	1	82	35	1	24	.304	.342	.372	104	3	5	.946	-2	98	77	3b154	—	0.7
1934	Pit N★	119	444	62	137	22	10	1	61	21	1	27	.309	.341	.410	98	-2	3	.954	-10	84	**108**	3b110,M	—	-0.8
1935	Pit N	57	204	24	57	10	3	1	36	10	3	17	.279	.323	.373	84	-5	2	.888	-3	94	28	3b49/1M	—	-0.6
1937	Pit N	5	12	3	2	0	0	0	0	0	0	1	.167	.167	.167	-9	-2	0	1.000	1	152	0	3b3,M	—	-0.1
Total	17	1941	7559	1183	2416	371	164	58	1273	472	31	278	.320	.362	.435	107	64	158-46	.947	25	99	101	3b1863,S50/1	—	18.4

TREACEY, FRED Frederick S.; B1847 Brooklyn NY; TR/5´9.5˝/145; d5.16; b–Pete

YEAR	TM LG	G	AB	R	H	2B	3B	HR	RBI	BB-IB	HP	SO	AVG	OBP	SLG	AOPS	ABR	SB-CS	FA	FR	RNG	THR	GAMES AT POSITION	DL	BFW
1871	Chi NA	25	124	39	42	7	5	**4**	33	2	—	5	.339	.349	.573	144	5	13-5	**.918**	7	**229**	201	O25L	—	0.9
1872	Ath NA	**47**	236	53	65	7	3	2	31	5	—	10	.275	.290	.356	97	-1	7-5	.814	-2	59	108	O47C	—	-0.2
1873	Phi NA	51	243	49	62	7	2	1	31	5	—	7	.255	.270	.313	69	-10	4-3	.761	2	140	**316**	O51(2/50/0)	—	-0.6
1874	Chi NA	35	148	18	28	5	0	0	12	2	—	6	.189	.200	.223	35	-10	4-4	.790	7	302	350	O35(2/11/24)	—	-0.2
1875	Cen NA	11	46	9	12	3	0	0	2	2	—	0	.261	.292	.326	124	2	1-0	.848	1	108	214	O11L	—	0.3
	Phi NA	43	179	23	38	3	3	0	15	1	—	3	.212	.217	.263	63	-7	6-3	.858	1	40	75	O43(42/1/0)	—	-0.3
	Year	54	225	32	50	6	3	0	17	3	—	3	.222	.232	.276	75	-6	7-3	.856	3	54	103	O54(53/1/0)	—	0.0
1876	NY N	**57**	256	47	54	5	1	0	18	1	—	5	.211	.214	.238	58	-9	—	.844	9	84	36	O57(52/0/5)	—	-0.4
Total	5NA	212	976	191	247	32	13	7	124	17	—	31	.253	.266	.334	83	-21	35-20	.823	16	135	205	O212(82/109/24)	—	-0.1

TREACEY, PETE Peter; B1852 Brooklyn NY; d8.5; b–Fred; Col Fordham

YEAR	TM LG	G	AB	R	H	2B	3B	HR	RBI	BB-IB	HP	SO	AVG	OBP	SLG	AOPS	ABR	SB-CS	FA	FR	RNG	THR	GAMES AT POSITION	DL	BFW
1876	NY N	2	5	1	0	0	0	0	0	1	—	0	.000	.167	.000	-46	-1	—	.750	-1	84	0	S2	—	-0.1

YEAR	TM LG	G	AB	R	H	2B	3B	HR	RBI	BB-IB	HP	SO	AVG	OBP	SLG	AOPS	ABR	SB-CS	FA	FR	RNG	THR	GAMES AT POSITION	DL	BFW
Treadaway, Ray	Edgar Raymond; B10.31.1907 Ragland AL; D10.12.1935 Chattanooga TN; BL/TR/5´7˝/150; d9.17																								
1930	Was A	6	19	1	4	2	0	0	1	0	0	3	.211	.211	.316	31	-2	0-0	.833	-1	63	147	3b4	—	-0.3
Treadaway, George	George B.; B11.11.1866 Greenup Co. KY; BL/TL/6´0˝/185; d4.27																								
1893	Bal N	115	458	78	119	16	17	1	67	58	4	50	.260	.348	.376	91	-7	24	.901	8	141	94	O115(1/0/114)	—	-0.4
1894	Bro N	124	482	125	159	28	26	4	102	73	2	43	.330	.420	.521	135	29	27	.893	-1	75	39	O123(121/0/2)/1	—	1.4
1895	Bro N	87	343	56	89	14	3	8	57	33	2	22	.259	.328	.388	91	-4	9	.886	-8	58	157	O87R	—	-1.3
1896	Lou N	2	7	0	1	0	0	0	1	1	0	0	.143	.250	.143	5	-1	0	.500	-1	0	0	/rf1	—	-0.2
Total	4	328	1290	259	368	58	46	13	227	165	8	115	.285	.370	.432	108	17	60	.891	-2	94	87	O326(122/0/204),1b2	—	-0.5
Treadaway, Jeff	Hugh Jeffery; B1.22.1963 Columbus GA; BL/TR/5´11˝/(165–175); d9.4; Col Georgia																								
1987	Cin N	23	84	9	28	4	0	2	4	2-0	1	6	.333	.356	.452	108	1	1-0	.958	-4	85	113	2b21	0	-0.2
1988	Cin N	103	301	30	76	19	4	2	23	27-7	3	30	.252	.315	.362	92	-3	2-0	.984	7	109	104	2b97,3b2	27	0.8
1989	Atl N	134	473	58	131	18	3	8	40	30-3	0	38	.277	.317	.378	97	-3	3-2	.981	6	98	121	2b123,3b6	0	0.7
1990	Atl N	128	474	56	134	20	2	11	59	25-1	3	42	.283	.320	.403	93	-5	3-4	.976	24	**116**	107	2b122	0	2.1
1991	†Atl N	106	306	41	98	17	2	3	32	23-1	2	19	.320	.368	.418	115	7	2-2	.960	1	105	92	2b93	0	1.0
1992	†Atl N	61	126	5	28	6	1	0	5	9-4	0	16	.222	.274	.286	55	-7	1-2	.993	1	103	145	2b45/3	81	-0.6
1993	Cle A	97	221	25	67	14	1	2	27	14-2	2	21	.303	.347	.403	101	1	1-1	.933	-1	109	83	3b42,2b19,D4	0	0.0
1994	LA N	52	67	14	20	3	0	0	5	5-0	1	8	.299	.351	.343	88	-1	1-1	.950	1	106	104	2b24,3b3	23	0.0
1995	LA N	17	17	2	2	0	1	0	3	0-0	0	2	.118	.118	.235	-11	-3	0-0	ø	0	0	0	3b2/2	0	-0.3
	Mon N	41	50	4	12	2	0	0	10	5-1	0	2	.240	.309	.280	55	-3	0-1	1.000	-0	97	57	2b11/3	18	-0.4
	Year	58	67	6	14	2	1	0	13	5-1	0	4	.209	.264	.269	41	-6	0-1	1.000	-0	99	83	2b12,3b3	0	-0.7
Total	9	762	2119	244	596	103	14	28	208	140-19	12	184	.281	.326	.383	94	-16	14-13	.975	36	106	109	2b556,3b57,D4	149	3.1
Treadaway, Red	Thadford Leon; B4.28.1920 Athlone (now Bowlens Creek) NC; D5.26.1994 Atlanta GA; BL/TR/5´10˝/175; d7.25; Col Barton																								
1944	NY N	50	170	23	51	5	2	0	5	13	0	11	.300	.350	.353	98	0	2	.957	-0	106	77	O38(10/2/27)	0	-0.3
1945	NY N	88	224	31	54	4	2	4	23	20	0	13	.241	.303	.330	75	-8	3	.940	-4	91	72	O60(27/18/18)	0	-1.5
Total	2	138	394	54	105	9	4	4	28	33	0	24	.266	.323	.340	85	-8	5	.948	-4	98	74	O98(37/20/45)	0	-1.8
Treanor, Matt	Matthew Aaron; B3.3.1976 Garden Grove CA; BR/TR/6´2˝/(205–220); d6.2																								
2004	Fla N	29	55	7	13	2	0	0	1	4-0	2	13	.236	.311	.273	56	-4	0-0	.976	-2	81	87	C27	0	-0.4
2005	Fla N	58	134	10	27	8	0	0	13	16-1	3	28	.201	.301	.261	52	-9	0-0	.985	-1	89	103	C55	0	-0.7
2006	Fla N	67	157	12	36	6	1	2	14	19-4	5	34	.229	.328	.318	71	-6	0-1	.993	11	161	149	C61	14	0.7
Total	3	154	346	29	76	16	1	2	28	39-5	10	75	.220	.315	.289	61	-19	0-1	.987	8	121	122	C143	14	-0.4
Trechock, Frank	Frank Adam; B12.24.1915 Windber PA; D1.16.1989 Minneapolis MN; BR/TR/5´10˝/175; d9.19																								
1937	Was A	1	4	0	2	0	0	0	0	0	0	1	.500	.500	.500	160	0	0-0	.750	-0	100	249	/S	—	0.0
Tremark, Nick	Nicholas Joseph; B10.15.1912 Yonkers NY; D9.7.2000 Tomball TX; BL/TL/5´5˝/150; d8.9; Col Manhattan																								
1934	Bro N	17	28	3	7	1	0	0	6	2	0	2	.250	.300	.286	61	-2	0	1.000	0	123	0	O9(8/1/0)	—	-0.1
1935	Bro N	10	13	1	3	1	0	0	3	1	0	1	.231	.286	.308	61	-1	0	1.000	0	129	0	O4R	—	-0.1
1936	Bro N	8	32	6	8	2	0	0	1	3	1	2	.250	.333	.313	74	-1	0	1.000	1	97	261	O8(0/2/6)	—	0.0
Total	3	35	73	10	18	4	0	0	10	6	1	5	.247	.313	.301	67	-4	0	1.000	1	111	128	O21(8/3/10)	—	-0.2
Tremie, Chris	Christopher James; B10.17.1969 Houston TX; BR/TR/6´0˝/(200–215); [ChiA92 39/1100]; d7.1; Col Houston																								
1995	Chi A	10	24	0	4	0	0	0	0	1-0	0	2	.167	.200	.167	-3	-4	0-0	.976	-4	48	94	C9/D	0	-0.7
1998	Tex A	2	3	2	1	1	0	0	0	1-0	0	1	.333	.500	.667	189	1	0-0	ø	0	—	—	D2	0	0.0
1999	Pit N	9	14	1	1	0	0	0	1	2-0	0	4	.071	.188	.071	-31	-3	0-0	1.000	0	61	159	C8	0	-0.3
2004	Hou N	1	0	0	0	0	0	0	0	0-0	0	0	ø	ø	ø	ø	0	0-0	ø	-0	0	0	/C	0	0.0
Total	4	22	41	3	6	1	0	0	1	4-0	0	7	.146	.222	.171	3	-6	0-0	.986	-4	52	116	C18,D3	0	-1.0
Tremper, Overton	Carlton Overton; B3.22.1906 Brooklyn NY; D1.9.1996 Clearwater FL; BR/TR/5´10˝/163; d6.16; Col Penn																								
1927	Bro N	26	60	4	14	0	0	0	4	0	1	2	.233	.246	.233	29	-6	0	1.000	-1	62	210	O18L	—	-0.8
1928	Bro N	10	31	1	6	2	1	0	1	0	0	1	.194	.194	.323	33	-3	0	1.000	1	79	378	O9(7/1/1)	—	-0.3
Total	2	36	91	5	20	2	1	0	5	0	1	3	.220	.228	.264	30	-9	0	1.000	-0	69	275	O27(25/1/1)	—	-1.1
Trenwith, George	George W.; B1851 Philadelphia PA; D2.1.1890 Philadelphia PA; d4.21																								
1875	Cen NA	10	45	5	8	2	0	0	4	1	—	2	.178	.196	.222	49	-2	0-0	.583	-6	58	0	3b10	—	-0.7
	NH NA	6	25	1	6	2	0	0	3	0	—	1	.240	.240	.320	106	0	0-0	.692	-2	78	0	3b6	—	-0.1
	Year	16	70	6	14	4	0	0	7	1	—	3	.200	.211	.257	69	-1	0-0	.629	-7	66	0	3b16	—	-0.8
Tresh, Mike	Michael; B2.23.1914 Hazleton PA; D10.4.1966 Detroit MI; BR/TR/5´11˝/170; d9.4; s–Tom																								
1938	Chi A	10	29	3	7	2	0	0	2	8	0	4	.241	.405	.310	80	0	0-0	.978	1	*114*	*110*	C10	—	0.1
1939	Chi A	119	352	49	91	5	2	0	38	64	3	30	.259	.377	.284	70	-13	3-2	.985	2	*94*	*100*	C119	—	-0.3
1940	Chi A	135	480	62	135	15	5	1	64	49	1	40	.281	.349	.340	78	-15	3-10	.983	9	*111*	*80*	C135	—	0.0
1941	Chi A	115	390	38	98	10	1	0	33	38	1	27	.251	.319	.282	61	-22	1-0	.981	10	*103*	*125*	C115	0	-0.4
1942	Chi A	72	233	21	54	8	1	0	15	28	0	24	.232	.314	.275	68	-9	2-0	.977	-3	*100*	*69*	C72	0	-0.8
1943	Chi A	86	279	20	60	3	0	0	20	37	0	20	.215	.307	.226	57	-14	2-1	.982	1	*99*	*90*	C85	0	-0.8
1944	Chi A	93	312	22	81	8	1	0	25	37	2	15	.260	.342	.292	83	-6	0-3	.981	-1	*119*	*92*	C93	0	-0.2
1945	Chi A✳	**150**	458	50	114	12	0	0	47	65	0	37	.249	.342	.275	82	-8	6-3	.984	2	***148***	*114*	C150	0	0.3
1946	Chi A	80	217	28	47	5	2	0	21	36	3	24	.217	.336	.258	70	-7	0-2	.995	10	*91*	*109*	C79	0	0.7
1947	Chi A	90	274	19	66	6	2	0	20	26	2	26	.241	.311	.277	67	-12	2-0	.975	-6	*74*	*94*	C89	0	-1.4
1948	Chi A	39	108	10	27	1	0	1	11	9	0	9	.250	.308	.287	61	-6	0-0	.983	-2	*83*	*112*	C34	0	-0.6
1949	Cle A	38	37	4	8	0	0	0	1	5	0	7	.216	.310	.216	41	-3	0-0	1.000	4	*203*	*123*	C38	0	0.2
Total	12	1027	3169	326	788	75	14	2	297	402	12	263	.249	.335	.283	71	-115	19-21	.983	28	*108*	*99*	C1019	0	-3.2
Tresh, Tom	Thomas Michael; B9.20.1937 Detroit MI; BB/TR/6´0˝/(175–192); d9.3; f–Mike; Col Central Michigan																								
1961	NY A	9	8	1	2	0	0	0	0	0-0	0	1	.250	.250	.250	36	-1	0-0	1.000	1	160	119	S3	0	0.1
1962	†NY A★	157	622	94	178	26	5	20	93	67-3	8	74	.286	.359	.441	119	17	4-8	.970	-15	94	77	S111,O43L	0	0.8
1963	†NY A★	145	520	91	140	28	5	25	71	83-5	4	79	.269	.371	.487	140	31	3-3	.981	-5	99	65	O144(46/101/0)	0	2.0
1964	†NY A	153	533	75	131	25	5	16	73	73-3	7	110	.246	.342	.402	105	5	13-0	**.996**	-7	88	80	O146(106/69/6)	0	-0.6
1965	NY A	156	602	94	168	29	6	26	74	59-4	5	92	.279	.348	.477	133	25	5-2	.970	-4	91	135	O154(100/105/18)	0	1.5
1966	NY A	151	537	76	125	12	4	27	68	86-5	6	89	.233	.341	.421	123	18	5-4	.985	**27**	115	230	O84(69/18/0),3b64	0	4.2
1967	NY A	130	448	45	98	23	3	14	53	50-0	4	86	.219	.301	.377	104	2	1-0	.972	-1	91	107	O118L	0	-0.6
1968	NY A	152	507	60	99	18	3	11	52	76-8	4	97	.195	.304	.308	89	-5	10-5	.951	14	**117**	**114**	S119,O27L	0	2.1
1969	NY A	45	143	13	26	5	2	1	9	17-2	0	23	.182	.269	.266	52	-9	2-1	.980	1	100	94	S41	0	-0.4
	Det A	94	331	46	74	13	1	13	37	39-0	2	47	.224	.305	.387	90	-5	2-2	.965	-11	84	95	S77,O11(7/0/4)/3	0	-0.8
	Year	139	474	59	100	18	3	14	46	56-2	2	70	.211	.294	.350	79	-14	4-3	.971	-10	90	95	S118,O11(7/0/4)/3	0	-1.2
Total	9	1192	4251	595	1041	179	34	153	530	550-30	40	698	.245	.335	.411	113	78	45-25	.979	-0	95	112	O727(516/293/28),S351,3b65	0	8.3
Trevino, Alex	Alejandro (Castro); B8.26.1957 Monterrey, Nuevo Leon, Mexico; BR/TR/5´11˝/(165–179); d9.11; b–Bobby																								
1978	NY N	6	12	3	3	0	0	0	0	1-0	0	2	.250	.308	.250	59	-1	0-0	1.000	1	0	368	C5/3	0	0.0
1979	NY N	79	207	24	56	11	1	0	20	20-2	1	27	.271	.338	.333	86	-3	2-2	.976	8	111	162	C36,3b27,2b8	0	0.6
1980	NY N	106	355	26	91	11	2	0	37	13-1	1	41	.256	.281	.299	64	-18	0-3	.977	-1	128	143	C86,3b14/2	0	-1.8
1981	NY N	56	149	17	39	2	0	0	10	13-0	1	19	.262	.323	.275	72	-5	3-0	.963	5	164	83	C45,2b4,O2(2/0/1)/3	0	0.2
1982	Cin N	120	355	24	89	10	3	1	33	34-11	3	34	.251	.318	.304	76	-11	3-1	.979	9	110	80	C116,3b2	0	0.3
1983	Cin N	74	167	14	36	8	1	1	13	17-6	0	20	.216	.285	.293	59	-9	0-0	.987	12	143	93	C63,3b4/2	0	0.6
1984	Cin N	6	6	0	1	0	0	0	0	0-0	0	2	.167	.167	.167	-6	-1	0-0	1.000	-0	29	0	C4	0	-0.1
	Atl N	79	266	36	65	16	0	3	28	16-1	1	27	.244	.289	.338	71	-10	5-2	.989	13	92	143	C79	0	0.6
	Year	85	272	36	66	16	0	3	28	16-1	1	29	.243	.286	.335	69	-11	5-2	.989	13	91	**142**	C83	0	0.5
1985	SF N	57	157	17	34	10	1	6	19	20-0	0	24	.217	.303	.408	102	0	0-0	.978	-6	105	74	C55/3	0	-0.4
1986	LA N	89	202	31	53	13	0	4	26	27-2	1	35	.262	.351	.386	111	4	0-0	.969	-3	123	138	C63/1	0	0.4
1987	LA N	72	144	16	32	7	1	3	16	6-2	4	28	.222	.271	.347	64	-8	1-0	.987	-2	125	103	C45,O2(1/0/1)/3	0	-0.8
1988	Hou N	78	193	19	48	17	0	2	13	24-4	3	29	.249	.341	.368	108	3	5-2	.977	-16	73	60	C74/lf	0	-0.9
1989	Hou N	59	131	15	38	7	1	2	16	7-0	1	18	.290	.329	.405	113	2	0-0	.989	-2	148	72	C32,1b2,3b2	0	0.2

YEAR	TM LG	G	AB	R	H	2B	3B	HR	RBI	BB-IB	HP	SO	AVG	OBP	SLG	AOPS	ABR	SB-CS	FA	FR	RNG	THR	GAMES AT POSITION	DL	BFW
1990	Hou N	42	69	3	13	3	0	1	10	6-1	2	11	.188	.266	.275	53	-4	0-1	.992	5	106	94	C30/1	0	0.1
	NY N	9	10	0	3	1	0	0	2	1-0	0	0	.300	.333	.400	110	0	0-0	.929	-0	88	92	C7	0	0.0
	Cin N	7	7	0	3	1	0	0	1	0-0	1	0	.429	.500	.571	186	1	0-0	1.000	0	0	0	C2	0	0.1
	Year	58	86	3	19	5	0	1	13	7-1	3	11	.221	.293	.314	71	-3	0-1	.982	5	98	89	C39/1	0	0.2
Total	13	939	2430	245	604	117	10	23	244	205-30	19	317	.249	.310	.333	81	-60	19-11	.979	24	115	106	C742,3b53,2b14,O5(4/0/2),1b4	0	-0.9
TREVINO, BOBBY	Carlos (Castro); B8.15.1943 Monterrey, Nuevo Leon, Mexico; BR/TR/6´2˝/185; d5.22; b–Alex																								
1968	Cal A	17	40	1	9	1	0	0	1	2-0	0	9	.225	.262	.250	57	-2	0-1	.962	1	123	169	O11(1/7/5)	0	-0.2
TRIANDOS, GUS	Gus; B7.30.1930 San Francisco CA; BR/TR/6´3˝/(205–220); d8.13; Col St. Marys (CA)																								
1953	NY A	18	51	5	8	2	0	1	6	3	0	9	.157	.204	.255	24	-6	0-0	.991	-0	90	85	1b12,C5	0	-0.6
1954	NY A	2	1	0	0	0	0	0	0	0	0	1	.000	.000	.000	-99	0	0-0	ø	0	*0*	*0*	/C	0	0.0
1955	Bal A	140	481	47	133	17	3	12	65	40-4	2	55	.277	.333	.399	104	1	0-0	.989	-1	109	102	1b103,C36/3	0	-0.4
1956	Bal A	131	452	47	126	18	1	21	88	48-4	2	73	.279	.348	.462	122	13	0-0	.989	9	*76*	*120*	C89,1b52	0	2.2
1957	Bal A☆	129	418	44	106	21	1	19	72	38-7	3	73	.254	.317	.445	114	6	0-0	.992	3	145	**148**	C120	0	1.5
1958	Bal A★	137	474	59	116	10	0	30	79	60-4	1	65	.245	.327	.456	120	12	1-0	.987	9	**155**	79	C132	0	2.8
1959	Bal A★	126	393	43	85	7	1	25	73	65-6	3	56	.216	.330	.430	110	5	0-0	.981	8	115	106	C125	0	1.9
1960	Bal A	109	364	36	98	18	0	12	54	41-5	1	62	.269	.343	.418	107	4	0-0	.989	1	141	75	C105	34	1.0
1961	Bal A	115	397	35	97	21	0	17	63	44-7	1	60	.244	.320	.426	101	0	0-0	.989	11	177	94	C114	0	1.6
1962	Bal A	66	207	20	33	7	0	6	23	29-2	0	43	.159	.262	.280	49	-15	0-0	.985	0	98	131	C63	34	-1.2
1963	Det A	106	327	28	78	13	0	14	41	32-4	6	67	.239	.315	.407	98	-1	0-0	**.998**	-4	143	85	C90	0	0.0
1964	Phi N	73	188	17	47	9	0	8	33	26-5	1	41	.250	.339	.426	117	5	0-0	.985	1	84	102	C64/1	0	0.9
1965	Phi N	30	82	3	14	2	0	0	4	9-1	0	17	.171	.253	.195	29	-8	0-0	.975	-4	87	152	C28	0	-1.2
	Hou N	24	72	5	13	2	0	2	7	5-0	1	14	.181	.244	.292	54	-5	0-0	.970	-3	94	99	C20	0	-0.7
	Year	54	154	8	27	4	0	2	11	14-1	1	31	.175	.249	.240	40	-12	0-0	.973	-7	90	127	C48	0	-1.9
Total	13	1206	3907	389	954	147	6	167	608	440-49	21	636	.244	.322	.413	103	11	1-0	.987	28	*128*	*104*	C992,1b168/3	68	7.8
TRILLO, MANNY	Jesus Manuel Marcano (b Jesus Manuel Marcano (Trillo)); B12.25.1950 Caripito, Monagas, Venez.; BR/TR/6´1˝/(150–165); d6.28																								
1973	Oak A	17	12	0	3	2	0	0	3	0-0	0	4	.250	.250	.417	89	0	0-0	.941	1	111	137	2b16	0	0.1
1974	†Oak A	21	33	3	5	0	0	0	2	2-0	1	8	.152	.222	.152	10	-4	0-0	.949	4	133	118	2b21	34	0.1
1975	Chi N	154	545	55	135	12	2	7	70	45-3	3	78	.248	.306	.316	70	-22	1-7	.967	18	108	95	2b153/S	0	0.3
1976	Chi N	158	582	42	139	24	3	4	59	53-4	3	70	.239	.304	.311	69	-23	17-6	.981	9	105	97	2b156/S	0	-0.2
1977	Chi N★	152	504	51	141	18	5	7	57	44-6	5	58	.280	.339	.377	84	-11	3-5	.970	30	114	98	2b149	0	2.6
1978	Chi N	152	552	53	144	17	5	4	55	50-3	2	67	.261	.320	.332	75	-18	0-7	.978	29	**117**	109	2b149	0	1.8
1979	Phi N	118	431	40	112	22	1	6	42	20-3	4	59	.260	.296	.357	75	-15	4-7	.985	18	**112**	**116**	2b118	43	0.8
1980	†Phi N	141	531	68	155	25	9	7	43	32-8	3	46	.292	.334	.412	101	0	8-3	.987	24	111	101	2b140	17	3.4
1981	†Phi N★	94	349	37	100	14	3	6	36	26-3	3	37	.287	.338	.395	103	1	10-4	.987	18	104	107	2b94	0	2.6
1982	Phi N★	149	549	52	149	24	1	0	39	33-3	3	53	.271	.316	.319	76	-17	8-10	**.994**	14	97	114	2b149	0	0.3
1983	Cle A★	88	320	33	87	13	1	1	29	21-2	0	46	.272	.315	.328	75	-11	1-3	.989	8	107	95	2b87	15	0.0
	Mon N	31	121	16	32	8	0	2	16	10-0	2	18	.264	.331	.380	96	0	0-0	.979	-4	92	126	2b31	0	-0.2
1984	SF N	98	401	45	102	21	1	4	36	25-0	3	55	.254	.300	.342	83	-9	0-0	.988	-0	101	101	2b96,3b4	55	-0.5
1985	SF N	125	451	36	101	16	2	3	25	40-0	1	44	.224	.287	.288	65	-22	2-0	.981	12	106	94	2b120/3	0	-0.3
1986	Chi N	81	152	22	45	10	0	1	19	16-0	0	21	.296	.359	.382	98	0	0-2	.949	-3	89	59	3b53,1b11,2b6	38	-0.4
1987	Chi N	108	214	27	63	8	0	8	26	25-0	0	37	.294	.367	.444	110	3	0-3	.994	-5	89	106	1b47,3b35,2b10,S6	0	-0.5
1988	Chi N	76	164	15	41	5	0	1	14	8-0	0	32	.250	.283	.299	65	-8	2-0	.994	-1	54	61	1b24,3b17,2b13,S7	0	-0.9
1989	Cin N	17	39	3	8	0	0	0	0	2-0	1	9	.205	.262	.205	34	-3	0-0	1.000	-4	72	39	2b10,1b3/S	0	-0.8
Total	17	1780	5950	598	1562	239	33	61	571	452-35	34	742	.263	.316	.345	80	-159	56-57	.981	167	107	103	2b1518,3b110,1b85,S16	202	8.2
TRIPLETT, COAKER	Herman Coaker; B12.18.1911 Boone NC; D1.30.1992 Boone NC; BR/TR/5´11˝/185; d4.19; Col Appalachian St.																								
1938	Chi N	12	36	4	9	2	1	0	2	0	0	1	.250	.250	.361	65	-2	0	1.000	0	94	169	O9(6/2/1)	—	-0.2
1941	StL N	76	185	29	53	6	3	3	21	18	0	27	.286	.350	.400	104	1	0	.965	-0	93	140	O46(38/0/8)	0	-0.2
1942	StL N	64	154	18	42	7	4	1	23	17	0	15	.273	.345	.390	107	1	1	.966	2	114	86	O46(45/0/1)	0	0.1
1943	StL N	9	25	1	2	0	0	1	4	1	0	6	.080	.115	.200	-9	-4	0	1.000	-0	116	0	O6(2/0/4)	0	-0.5
	Phi N	105	360	45	98	16	4	14	52	28	0	28	.272	.325	.456	129	11	2	.970	3	103	133	O90L	0	0.9
	Year	114	385	46	100	16	4	15	56	29	0	34	.260	.312	.439	120	7	2	.972	3	104	125	O96(92/0/4)	0	0.4
1944	Phi N	84	184	15	43	5	1	1	25	19	0	10	.234	.305	.288	70	-7	1	.989	0	100	92	O44(41/1/2)	0	-1.0
1945	Phi N	120	363	36	87	11	1	7	46	40	0	27	.240	.315	.333	83	-9	6	.945	-3	103	46	O92(92/0/2)	0	-1.7
Total	6	470	1307	148	334	47	14	27	173	123	0	114	.256	.320	.375	97	-9	10	.965	2	103	95	O333(314/3/18)	0	-2.6
TROSKY, HAL	Harold Arthur Sr. (b Harold Arthur Trojovsky); B11.11.1912 Norway IA; D6.18.1979 Cedar Rapids IA; BL/TR (BB 1935p)/6´2˝/207; d9.11; s–Hal																								
1933	Cle A	11	44	6	13	1	2	1	8	2	1	12	.295	.340	.477	110	0	0-0	.990	-1	73	82	1b11	—	-0.1
1934	Cle A	**154**	625	117	206	45	9	35	142	58	2	49	.330	.388	.598	149	42	2-2	.986	0	104	**110**	1b154	—	2.5
1935	Cle A	154	632	84	171	33	7	26	113	46	1	60	.271	.321	.468	100	-4	1-2	.993	1	102	106	1b153	—	-1.7
1936	Cle A	151	629	124	216	45	9	42	**162**	36	3	58	.343	.382	.644	148	41	6-5	.985	1	107	96	1b151/2	—	2.4
1937	Cle A	153	601	104	179	36	9	32	128	65	1	60	.298	.367	.547	127	22	3-1	.993	-2	89	99	1b152	—	0.5
1938	Cle A	150	554	106	185	40	9	19	110	67	1	40	.334	.407	.542	138	33	5-1	.993	4	103	88	1b148	—	2.1
1939	Cle A	122	448	89	150	31	4	25	104	52	1	28	.335	.405	.589	157	38	2-3	.992	12	**137**	100	1b118	—	3.4
1940	Cle A	140	522	85	154	39	4	25	93	79	4	45	.295	.392	.529	140	33	1-2	.991	-6	79	**117**	1b139	—	1.3
1941	Cle A	89	310	43	91	17	0	11	51	44	1	21	.294	.383	.455	127	13	1-2	.989	-1	93	108	1b85	0	0.3
1944	Chi A	135	497	55	120	32	2	10	70	62	1	30	.241	.327	.374	101	2	3-2	.993	-9	71	107	1b130	0	-1.5
1946	Chi A	88	299	22	76	12	3	2	31	34	0	37	.254	.330	.334	89	-4	4-3	.991	-7	68	97	1b80	0	-1.5
Total	11	1347	5161	835	1561	331	58	228	1012	545	16	440	.302	.371	.522	130	216	28-23	.991	-8	96	103	1b1321/2	0	7.7
TROST, MIKE	Michael J.; B1866 Philadelphia PA; D3.24.1901 Philadelphia PA; TR/6´0.5˝/180; d8.21																								
1890	StL AA	17	51	10	13	2	0	1	7	6	1	—	.255	.345	.353	93	-1	4	.890	-1	*99*	*84*	C13,O4(0/3/1)	—	-0.1
1895	Lou N	3	12	1	1	0	0	0	1	0	0	1	.083	.083	.083	-61	-3	1	1.000	-0	0	63	1b3	—	-0.3
Total	2	20	63	11	14	2	0	1	8	6	1	1	.222	.300	.302	66	-4	5	.890	-2	*99*	*84*	C13,O4(0/3/1),1b3	—	-0.4
TROTT, SAM	Samuel W.; B3.1859 MD; D6.5.1925 Catonsville MD; BL/TL/5´9˝/190; d5.29; M1																								
1880	Bos N	39	125	14	26	4	1	0	9	3	—	5	.208	.227	.256	65	-4	—	.893	5	—	—	C36,O4(1/3/0)	—	0.1
1881	Det N	6	25	3	5	2	1	0	2	1	—	3	.200	.231	.360	80	-1	—	.868	-1	—	—	C6	—	-0.2
1882	Det N	32	129	11	31	7	1	0	12	0	—	13	.240	.240	.310	75	-4	—	.890	2	—	—	C23,S3,2b3,1b3,O2L/3	—	0.1
1883	Det N	75	295	27	72	14	1	0	29	10	—	23	.244	.269	.298	76	-8	—	.882	-15	82	97	2b42,C34,O6(0/1/5)/1	—	-1.6
1884	Bal AA	71	284	36	73	17	9	3	—	4	2	—	.257	.272	.412	116	4	—	.931	11	—	—	C60,2b6,O5(1/1/3)	—	1.8
1885	Bal AA	21	88	12	24	2	2	0	12	5	0	—	.273	.312	.341	108	1	—	.882	-3	—	—	C17,O4R,2b2/S	—	-0.1
1887	Bal AA	85	300	44	77	16	3	0	37	27	2	—	.257	.322	.330	87	-4	8	.915	2	—	—	C69,2b11,O3L,1b2/S	—	0.3
1888	Bal AA	31	108	19	30	11	4	0	22	4	0	—	.278	.304	.454	145	5	1	.908	-5	—	—	C27,O3(1/0/2)/21	—	0.2
Total	8	360	1354	166	338	73	22	3	123	54	4	44	.250	.280	.343	93	-11	9	.906	-4	—	—	C272,2b65,O27(8/5/14),1b7,S5/3	—	0.6
TROUPPE, QUINCY	Quincy Thomas; B12.25.1912 Dublin GA; D8.12.1993 Creve Coeur MO; BB/TR/6´2.5˝/225; d4.30; Negro Lg 1930–51																								
1952	Cle A	6	10	1	1	0	0	0	0	1	0	3	.100	.182	.100	-22	-2	0-0	1.000	1	*110*	*106*	C6	0	0.0
TROY, DASHER	John Joseph; B5.8.1856 New York NY; D3.30.1938 Ozone Park NY; BR/TR/5´5˝/154; d8.23																								
1881	Det N	11	44	2	15	3	0	0	4	3	—	8	.341	.383	.409	143	2	—	.792	-1	103	0	3b7,2b4	—	0.1
1882	Det N	40	152	22	37	7	2	0	14	5	—	10	.243	.268	.316	86	-2	—	.847	-17	80	65	2b31,S11	—	-1.7
	Pro N	4	17	1	4	0	0	0	1	0	—	1	.235	.235	.235	52	-1	—	.750	-1	96	93	S4	—	-0.2
	Year	44	169	23	41	7	2	0	15	5	—	11	.243	.264	.308	83	-3	—	.847	-19	80	65	2b31,S15	—	-1.9
1883	NY N	85	316	37	68	7	5	0	20	9	—	33	.215	.237	.269	54	-18	—	.879	-12	97	71	2b73,S12	—	-2.4
1884	†NY AA	107	421	80	111	22	10	2	—	19	3	—	.264	.300	.378	123	11	—	.879	-20	93	66	2b107	—	-0.5
1885	NY AA	45	177	24	39	3	3	2	12	5	4	—	.220	.258	.305	81	-4	—	.866	-12	80	90	2b42,O2R/S	—	-1.3
Total	5	292	1127	166	274	42	20	4	51	41	7	52	.243	.274	.327	91	-12	—	.873	-64	90	73	2b257,S28,3b7,O2R	—	-6.0
TRUAX, FRED	Frederick W.; B1868; D12.18.1899 Omaha NE; d8.18																								
1890	Pit N	1	3	0	1	0	0	0	1	1	0	1	.333	.500	.333	163	0	0	1.000	0	0	3185	/lf	—	0.0

YEAR	TM LG	G	AB	R	H	2B	3B	HR	RBI	BB-IB	HP	SO	AVG	OBP	SLG	AOPS	ABR	SB-CS	FA	FR	RNG	THR	GAMES AT POSITION	DL	BFW
TRUBY, CHRIS	Christopher John; B12.9.1973 Palm Springs CA; BR/TR/6´2˝/190; d6.16; [DL 2005 KC A 38]																								
2000	Hou N	78	258	28	67	15	4	11	59	10-1	5	56	.260	.295	.477	85	-7	2-1	.926	3	105	116	3b74	0	-0.4
2001	†Hou N	48	136	11	28	6	1	8	23	13-2	1	38	.206	.276	.441	77	-5	1-2	.923	-4	91	72	3b35/1	0	-0.9
2002	Mon N	35	105	12	27	5	2	2	7	5-1	1	27	.257	.297	.400	77	-4	1-1	.924	-3	95	75	3b31,1b2/lf	0	-0.7
	Det A	89	277	23	55	13	2	2	15	5-0	2	71	.199	.215	.282	33	-28	1-1	.958	10	116	147	3b89	25	-1.7
2003	TB A	13	43	4	12	3	0	0	3	5-0	0	13	.279	.354	.349	88	0	0-0	.976	4	138	170	3b13	0	0.3
Total	4	263	819	78	189	42	9	23	107	38-4	9	205	.231	.269	.388	67	-44	5-5	.942	9	108	119	3b242,1b3/lf	63	-3.4
TRUBY, HARRY	Harry Garvin "Bird Eye"; B5.12.1870 Ironton OH; D3.21.1953 Ironton OH; TR/5´11˝/185; d8.21; U1																								
1895	Chi N	33	119	17	40	3	0	0	16	10	3	7	.336	.402	.361	92	-1	7	.950	-0	90	143	2b33	—	0.0
1896	Chi N	29	109	13	28	2	2	2	31	6	3	5	.257	.314	.367	76	-4	4	.935	0	93	141	2b28	—	-0.3
	Pit N	8	32	1	5	0	0	0	3	2	0	4	.156	.206	.156	-4	-5	1	.949	-2	69	215	2b8	—	-0.6
	Year	37	141	14	33	2	2	2	34	8	3	9	.234	.289	.319	59	-9	5	.938	-2	88	157	2b36	—	-0.9
Total	2	70	260	31	73	5	2	2	50	18	6	16	.281	.342	.338	75	-10	12	.944	-2	89	150	2b69	—	-0.9
TRUESDALE, FRANK	Frank Day; B3.31.1884 St.Louis MO; D8.27.1943 Albuquerque NM; BB/TR/5´8˝/145; d4.27																								
1910	StL A	123	415	39	91	7	2	1	25	48	2	—	.219	.303	.253	79	-8	29	.914	-2	100	91	2b122	—	-1.1
1911	StL A	1	0	1	0	0	0	0	0	0	0	—	ø	ø	ø	ø	0	0	ø	0	—	—	/R	—	0.0
1914	NY A	77	217	22	46	4	0	0	13	39	3	35	.212	.340	.230	72	-5	11-11	.947	3	109	106	2b67,3b4	—	-0.2
1918	Bos A	15	36	6	10	1	0	0	2	4	0	5	.278	.350	.306	99	0	1	.913	-1	106	59	2b10	—	-0.1
Total	4	216	668	68	147	12	2	1	40	91	5	40	.220	.318	.249	78	-13	41-11	.924	0	103	94	2b199,3b4	—	-1.4
TRUMBULL, ED	Edward J. (b Edward J. Trembly); B11.3.1860 Chicopee MA; D1.14.1937 Kingston PA; d5.10; ▲																								
1884	Was AA	25	86	5	10	2	0	0	—	2	0	—	.116	.136	.140	-11	-10	—	.828	0	154	202	O15(2/8/5),P10	—	-0.5
TUBBS, GREG	Gregory Alan; B8.31.1962 Smithville TN; BR/TR/5´9˝/185; [AtlN84 22/565]; d8.1; Col Austin Peay																								
1993	Cin N	35	59	10	11	0	0	1	2	14-0	1	10	.186	.351	.237	61	-3	3-1	.975	1	105	109	O21(11/14/2)	0	-0.2
TUCKER, EDDIE	Eddie Jack "Scooter"; B11.18.1966 Greenville MS; BR/TR/6´2˝/205; [SFN88 5/126]; d6.14; Col Delta St.																								
1992	Hou N	20	50	5	6	1	0	0	3	3-0	2	13	.120	.200	.140	-2	-7	1-1	.976	-6	83	71	C19	0	-1.3
1993	Hou N	9	26	1	5	1	0	0	3	2-0	0	3	.192	.250	.231	31	-3	0-0	1.000	3	171	86	C8	0	0.0
1995	Hou N	5	7	1	2	0	0	1	1	0-0	0	0	.286	.286	.714	164	0	0-0	1.000	0	85	274	C3	0	0.1
	Cle A	17	20	2	0	0	0	0	0	5-0	1	4	.000	.231	.000	-33	-4	0-0	.982	-0	108	125	C17	0	-0.3
Total	3	51	103	9	13	2	0	1	7	10-0	3	20	.126	.224	.175	11	-14	1-1	.986	-3	109	96	C47	0	-1.5
TUCKER, MICHAEL	Michael Anthony; B6.25.1971 S.Boston VA; BL/TR/6´2˝/(185–210); [KCA92 1/10]; d4.26; Col Longwood; OF(301/195/783)																								
1995	KC A	62	177	23	46	10	0	4	17	18-2	1	51	.260	.332	.384	84	-4	2-3	.986	1	98	133	O36(30/1/5),D22	0	-0.6
1996	KC A	108	339	55	88	18	4	12	53	40-1	7	69	.260	.346	.442	98	-1	10-4	.989	-2	97	77	O98(28/0/73),1b9,D5	50	-0.6
1997	†Atl N	138	499	80	141	25	7	14	56	44-0	6	116	.283	.347	.445	104	3	12-7	.980	1	104	68	O129(53/0/102)	0	-0.2
1998	†Atl N	130	414	54	101	27	3	13	46	49-10	3	112	.244	.327	.418	95	-3	8-3	.995	-1	97	72	O118R	0	-0.9
1999	Cin N	133	296	55	75	8	5	11	44	37-3	3	81	.253	.338	.426	90	-5	11-4	.990	7	115	158	O114(0/13/107)	0	0.0
2000	Cin N	148	270	55	72	13	4	15	36	44-1	7	64	.267	.381	.511	120	9	13-6	.969	-0	99	109	O120(41/28/67)/2	0	0.6
2001	Cin N	86	231	31	56	10	1	7	30	23-1	1	55	.242	.308	.385	75	-9	12-5	.978	3	100	188	O70(37/32/19)	0	-0.6
	Chi N	63	205	31	54	9	7	5	31	23-3	1	47	.263	.339	.449	105	1	4-3	.991	2	103	72	O57(38/44/6),1b4	0	0.2
	Year	149	436	62	110	19	8	12	61	46-4	2	102	.252	.322	.415	88	-9	16-8	.984	5	101	133	O127(75/76/25),1b4	0	-0.4
2002	KC A	144	475	65	118	27	6	12	56	56-1	3	105	.248	.330	.406	84	-11	23-9	.991	4	102	142	O108(33/14/67),D23,1b5,2b2	0	-1.0
2003	KC A	104	389	61	102	20	5	13	55	39-3	2	88	.262	.331	.440	95	-3	8-10	.989	-3	88	145	O85(21/30/47),D15	50	-1.0
2004	SF N	140	464	77	119	21	6	13	62	70-3	2	106	.256	.353	.412	95	-3	5-2	.978	0	109	28	O124(0/25/106)	0	-0.6
2005	SF N	104	250	32	60	16	1	5	33	28-3	2	48	.240	.317	.372	79	-7	4-0	.983	0	92	178	O72(4/7/64)	0	-0.9
	Phi N	22	18	3	4	0	0	0	3	3-0	0	4	.222	.333	.222	48	-1	0-0	ø	-0	0	0	/cfD	0	-0.1
	Year	126	268	35	64	16	1	5	36	31-3	2	52	.239	.318	.362	77	-9	4-0	.983	0	92	178	O73(4/8/64),D4	0	-1.0
2006	†NY N	35	56	3	11	4	0	1	6	16-0	1	14	.196	.378	.321	85	0	2-0	1.000	1	100	267	O18(16/0/2)/1	0	0.0
Total	12	1417	4083	625	1047	208	49	125	528	490-31	39	960	.256	.339	.423	94	-34	114-56	.985	12	101	108	O1150R,D69,1b19,2b3	100	-5.7
TUCKER, OLLIE	Oliver Dinwiddie; B1.27.1902 Radiant VA; D7.13.1940 Radiant VA; BL/TR/5´11˝/180; d4.17																								
1927	Was A	20	24	1	5	2	0	0	8	4	0	2	.208	.321	.292	61	-1	0-0	1.000	0	122	0	O5R	—	-0.1
1928	Cle A	14	47	5	6	0	0	1	2	7	1	3	.128	.255	.191	19	-6	0-2	1.000	0	77	231	O14R	—	-0.7
Total	2	34	71	6	11	2	0	1	10	11	1	5	.155	.277	.225	33	-7	0-2	1.000	0	88	175	O19R	—	-0.8
TUCKER, TOMMY	Thomas Joseph "Foghorn"; B10.28.1863 Holyoke MA; D10.22.1935 Montague MA; BB/TR/5´11˝/165; d4.16																								
1887	Bal AA	136	524	114	144	15	9	6	84	29	**29**	—	.275	.347	.372	107	7	85	.976	4	113	75	1b136	—	-0.1
1888	Bal AA	136	520	74	149	17	12	6	61	16	18	—	.287	.330	.400	137	20	43	.975	3	**126**	105	1b129,O7(2/0/5)/P	—	1.1
1889	Bal AA	134	527	103	**196**	22	11	5	99	42	**33**	26	**.372**	**.450**	.484	**163**	**46**	63	.964	-1	103	93	1b123,O12(0/11/1)	—	2.8
1890	Bos N	132	539	104	159	17	8	1	62	56	**25**	22	.295	.387	.362	110	8	43	**.979**	-2	85	85	1b132	—	-0.5
1891	Bos N	**140**	548	103	148	16	5	2	69	37	**29**	30	.270	.349	.328	87	-9	26	.976	-3	87	100	1b140/P	—	-2.3
1892	†Bos N	149	542	85	153	15	7	1	62	45	**26**	35	.282	.365	.341	104	4	22	.972	-12	65	129	1b149	—	-0.8
1893	Bos N	121	486	83	138	13	2	7	91	27	20	31	.284	.347	.362	82	-14	8	.980	-11	58	**128**	1b121	—	-2.1
1894	Bos N	123	500	112	165	24	6	3	100	53	17	21	.330	.412	.420	94	-4	18	**.985**	2	99	108	1b123/cf	—	-0.2
1895	Bos N	126	465	87	115	19	6	3	73	63	19	29	.247	.360	.333	74	-17	15	.978	5	118	111	1b126	—	-1.0
1896	Bos N	122	474	74	144	27	5	2	72	30	14	29	.304	.363	.395	94	-4	6	.985	3	108	102	1b122	—	-0.1
1897	Bos N	4	14	0	3	2	0	0	4	2	0	—	.214	.313	.357	72	-1	0	.957	0	172	0	1b4	—	0.0
	Was N	93	352	52	119	18	5	5	61	27	11	—	.338	.403	.460	128	15	18	.984	-3	81	110	1b93	—	1.0
	Year	97	366	52	122	20	5	5	65	29	11	—	.333	.399	.456	126	14	18	.982	-2	85	105	1b97	—	1.0
1898	Bro N	73	283	35	79	9	4	1	34	12	7	—	.279	.325	.350	94	-3	1	.991	7	138	97	1b73	—	0.4
	StL N	72	252	18	60	7	2	0	20	18	12	—	.238	.319	.282	71	-9	1	.973	-0	105	89	1b72	—	-0.9
	Year	145	535	53	139	16	6	1	54	30	19	—	.260	.322	.318	83	-12	2	.982	7	122	93	1b145	—	-0.5
1899	Cle N	127	456	40	110	19	3	0	40	24	12	—	.241	.297	.296	68	-20	3	.977	0	99	77	1b127	—	-1.8
Total	13	1688	6482	1084	1882	240	85	42	932	481	272	223	.290	.364	.373	101	19	352	.978	-8	98	101	1b1670,O20(2/12/6),P2	—	-4.5
TUCKER, THURMAN	Thurman Lowell "Joe E."; B9.26.1917 Gordon TX; D5.7.1993 Oklahoma City OK; BL/TR/5´11˝/170; d4.14; Mil 1945																								
1942	Chi A	7	24	2	3	0	1	0	1	0	0	4	.125	.125	.208	-7	-4	0-0	.900	-0	71	326	O5C	0	-0.4
1943	Chi A	139	528	81	124	15	6	3	39	79	1	72	.235	.336	.303	87	-6	29-17	.988	9	109	133	O132C	0	-0.1
1944	Chi A★	124	446	59	128	15	6	2	46	57	0	40	.287	.368	.361	110	7	13-12	**.991**	11	**115**	96	O120C	0	1.4
1946	Chi A	121	438	62	126	20	3	1	36	54	1	45	.288	.367	.354	106	5	9-10	.990	-2	93	145	O110C	0	-0.1
1947	Chi A	89	254	28	60	9	4	1	17	38	0	25	.236	.336	.315	85	-5	10-4	.978	-1	96	119	O65C	0	-0.7
1948	†Cle A	83	242	52	63	13	2	1	19	31	1	17	.260	.347	.343	86	-4	11-2	1.000	-0	97	98	O66C	0	-0.4
1949	Cle A	80	197	28	48	5	2	0	14	18	0	19	.244	.307	.289	59	-12	4-2	.984	-2	98	64	O42(4/38/0)	0	-1.5
1950	Cle A	57	101	13	18	2	0	1	7	14	1	14	.178	.284	.228	34	-10	1-0	.968	1	103	107	O34(15/16/4)	0	-1.0
1951	Cle A	1	1	0	0	0	0	0	0	0	0	1	.000	.000	.000	-99	0	0-0	ø	0	—	—	/H	0	0.0
Total	9	701	2231	325	570	79	24	9	179	291	4	237	.255	.342	.325	89	-29	77-47	.988	16	103	117	O574(19/552/4)	0	-2.8
TULOWITZKI, TROY	Troy Trever; B10.10.1984 Santa Clara CA; BR/TR/6´3˝/205; [AriN05 1/7]; d8.30; Col Long Beach St.																								
2006	Col N	25	96	15	23	2	0	1	6	10-3	1	25	.240	.318	.292	53	-7	3-0	.983	1	95	153	S25	0	-0.3
TURANG, BRIAN	Brian Craig; B6.14.1967 Long Beach CA; BR/TR/5´10˝/170; [SeaA89 52/1299]; d8.13; Col Loyola Marymount																								
1993	Sea A	40	140	22	35	11	1	0	7	17-0	2	20	.250	.340	.343	82	-3	6-2	.986	-2	91	98	O38(26/14/1),3b2/2D	0	-0.5
1994	Sea A	38	112	9	21	5	1	1	8	7-0	1	25	.188	.242	.277	32	-12	3-1	.978	-2	98	77	O30(20/12/0),2b5,D4	16	-1.2
Total	2	78	252	31	56	16	2	1	15	24-0	3	45	.222	.297	.313	60	-15	9-3	.983	-4	94	90	O68(46/26/1),2b6,D5,3b2	16	-1.7
TURBIDY, JERRY	Jeremiah; B7.4.1852 Dudley MA; D9.5.1920 Webster MA; BR/TR/5´8˝/165; d7.27																								
1884	KC U	13	49	5	11	4	0	0	—	3	—	—	.224	.269	.306	85	-2	—	.830	4	125	141	S13	—	0.2
TURCHIN, EDDIE	Edward Lawrence "Smiley"; B2.10.1917 New York NY; D2.8.1982 Brookhaven NY; BR/TR/5´10˝/165; d5.9; Col Brooklyn																								
1943	Cle A	11	13	4	3	0	0	0	1	3	0	1	.231	.375	.231	84	0	0-0	1.000	1	118	257	3b4,S2	0	0.1

TURGEON, PETE Eugene Joseph; B1.3.1897 Minneapolis MN; D1.24.1977 Wichita Falls TX; BR/TR/5´6˝/145; d9.20

YEAR	TM LG	G	AB	R	H	2B	3B	HR	RBI	BB-IB	HP	SO	AVG	OBP	SLG	AOPS	ABR	SB-CS	FA	FR	RNG	THR	GAMES AT POSITION	DL	BFW
1923	Chi N	3	6	1	1	0	0	0	0	0	0	0	.167	.167	.167	-12	-1	0-0	.875	-0	.64	258	S2	—	-0.1

TURNER, CHRIS Christopher Wan; B3.23.1969 Bowling Green KY; BR/TR/6´3˝/(190–200); [CalA91 7/194]; d8.27; Col Western Kentucky

YEAR	TM LG	G	AB	R	H	2B	3B	HR	RBI	BB-IB	HP	SO	AVG	OBP	SLG	AOPS	ABR	SB-CS	FA	FR	RNG	THR	GAMES AT POSITION	DL	BFW
1993	Cal A	25	75	9	21	5	0	1	13	9-0	1	16	.280	.360	.387	99	0	1-1	.992	-1	62	63	C25	0	0.0
1994	Cal A	58	149	23	36	7	1	1	12	10-0	1	29	.242	.290	.322	58	-10	3-0	.997	1	91	91	C57	0	-0.4
1995	Cal A	5	10	0	1	0	0	0	1	0-0	0	3	.100	.100	.100	-48	-2	0-0	1.000	1	0	0	C4/D	0	-0.1
1996	Cal A	4	3	1	1	0	0	0	1	1-0	0	0	.333	.400	.333	115	0	0-0	1.000	1	0	791	C3/lf	0	0.1
1997	Ana A	13	23	4	6	1	1	1	2	5-0	0	8	.261	.393	.522	136	1	0-0	1.000	-4	53	0	C8,1b2/rfD	100	-0.2
1998	KC A	4	9	0	0	0	0	0	0	0-0	1	4	.000	.100	.000	-68	-2	0-0	1.000	-0	177	0	C4	0	-0.2
1999	Cle A	12	21	3	4	0	0	0	0	1-0	0	8	.190	.227	.190	8	-3	1-0	.964	-1	87	90	C12	0	-0.3
2000	NY A	37	89	9	21	3	0	1	7	10-0	1	21	.236	.320	.303	60	-5	0-1	1.000	-3	78	47	C36/1	0	-0.7
Total	8	158	379	49	90	16	2	4	36	36-0	4	89	.237	.307	.322	63	-21	5-2	.994	-7	79	69	C149,1b3,O2(1/0/1),D2	100	-1.8

TURNER, EARL Earl Edwin; B5.6.1923 Pittsfield MA; D10.20.1999 Lee MA; BR/TR/5´9˝/170; d9.25

YEAR	TM LG	G	AB	R	H	2B	3B	HR	RBI	BB-IB	HP	SO	AVG	OBP	SLG	AOPS	ABR	SB-CS	FA	FR	RNG	THR	GAMES AT POSITION	DL	BFW
1948	Pit N	2	1	0	0	0	0	0	0	0	0	0	.000	.000	.000	-98	0	0	ø	0	*0*	*0*	/C	0	0.0
1950	Pit N	40	74	10	18	0	0	3	5	4	0	13	.243	.282	.365	66	-4	1	.974	1	*127*	*99*	C34	0	-0.2
Total	2	42	75	10	18	0	0	3	5	4	0	13	.240	.278	.360	64	-4	1	.974	1	*126*	*98*	C35	0	-0.2

TURNER, TUCK George A.; B2.13.1873 W.New Brighton NY; D7.16.1945 Staten Island NY; BB/TL/5´6.5˝/155; d8.18

YEAR	TM LG	G	AB	R	H	2B	3B	HR	RBI	BB-IB	HP	SO	AVG	OBP	SLG	AOPS	ABR	SB-CS	FA	FR	RNG	THR	GAMES AT POSITION	DL	BFW
1893	Phi N	36	155	32	50	4	3	1	13	9	1	19	.323	.364	.406	105	0	7	.933	1	94	178	O36(1/35/0)	—	-0.1
1894	Phi N	82	347	95	145	21	9	1	84	24	2	13	.418	.458	.539	143	25	11	.902	-5	58	34	O80(56/3/22)/P	—	1.1
1895	Phi N	59	210	51	81	8	6	2	43	25	1	11	.386	.453	.510	147	16	14	.847	-4	70	0	O55(31/9/15)	—	0.6
1896	Phi N	13	32	12	7	2	0	0	0	8	0	5	.219	.375	.281	75	-1	6	.905	2	387	0	O8(1/7/0)	—	0.1
	StL N	51	203	30	50	7	8	1	27	14	1	21	.246	.298	.374	80	-7	6	.961	-3	64	57	O51R	—	-1.1
	Year	64	235	42	57	9	8	1	27	22	1	26	.243	.310	.362	79	-8	12	.948	-1	110	49	O59(1/7/51)	—	-1.0
1897	StL N	103	416	58	121	17	12	2	41	35	3	—	.291	.350	.404	101	-1	8	.945	-4	75	98	O102R	—	-0.8
1898	StL N	35	141	20	28	8	0	0	7	14	2	—	.199	.280	.255	53	-8	1	.929	-3	42	85	O34R	—	-1.3
Total	6	379	1504	298	482	67	38	7	215	129	10	69	.320	.378	.430	111	24	53	.916	-18	75	69	O366(89/54/224)/P	—	-1.5

TURNER, JERRY John Webber; B1.17.1954 Texarkana AR; BL/TL/5´9˝/180; [SDN72 10/217]; d9.2

YEAR	TM LG	G	AB	R	H	2B	3B	HR	RBI	BB-IB	HP	SO	AVG	OBP	SLG	AOPS	ABR	SB-CS	FA	FR	RNG	THR	GAMES AT POSITION	DL	BFW
1974	SD N	17	48	4	14	1	0	0	2	3-0	0	5	.292	.333	.313	85	-1	2-1	1.000	-1	68	135	O13L	0	-0.2
1975	SD N	11	22	1	6	0	0	0	0	2-1	0	1	.273	.333	.273	74	-1	0-0	.909	0	131	0	O4L	0	-0.1
1976	SD N	105	281	41	75	16	5	5	37	32-3	0	38	.267	.339	.413	123	8	12-6	.960	-2	89	128	O74L	0	0.3
1977	SD N	118	289	43	71	16	1	10	48	31-1	0	43	.246	.316	.412	105	1	12-4	.947	4	97	246	O69(65/4/2)	0	0.4
1978	SD N	106	225	28	63	9	1	8	37	21-5	3	32	.280	.348	.436	127	8	6-4	.970	-1	90	137	O58(28/17/24)	0	0.5
1979	SD N	138	448	55	111	23	2	9	61	34-0	2	58	.248	.301	.368	88	-9	4-2	.958	-2	97	85	O115(114/0/2)	0	-1.6
1980	SD N	85	153	22	44	5	0	3	18	10-4	2	18	.288	.335	.379	107	1	8-3	1.000	-1	91	93	O34(5/0/30)	52	0.0
1981	SD N	33	31	5	7	0	0	2	6	4-1	0	3	.226	.314	.419	116	0	0-1	.833	-0	107	0	O4R	0	0.0
	Chi A	10	12	1	2	0	0	0	2	1-0	0	2	.167	.231	.167	16	-1	0-0	1.000	0	106	0	/rf	0	-0.1
1982	Det A	85	210	21	52	3	0	8	27	20-1	0	37	.248	.310	.376	88	-4	1-3	.909	-2	58	0	D50,O13(2/0/12)	0	-0.9
1983	SD N	25	23	1	3	0	0	0	0	1-1	0	8	.130	.167	.130	-17	-4	0-0	ø	-0	0	0	/rf	0	-0.4
Total	10	733	1742	222	448	73	9	45	238	159-17	7	245	.257	.319	.387	101	-2	45-24	.959	-5	93	129	O386(305/21/76),D50	52	-2.1

TURNER, SHANE Shane Lee; B1.8.1963 Los Angeles CA; BL/TR/5´10˝/(180–190); [NYA85 6/155]; d8.19; Col Cal St.–Fullerton

YEAR	TM LG	G	AB	R	H	2B	3B	HR	RBI	BB-IB	HP	SO	AVG	OBP	SLG	AOPS	ABR	SB-CS	FA	FR	RNG	THR	GAMES AT POSITION	DL	BFW
1988	Phi N	18	35	1	6	0	0	0	1	5-0	0	9	.171	.275	.171	30	-3	0-0	.941	-3	83	76	3b8,S5	0	-0.6
1991	Bal A	4	1	0	0	0	0	0	0	0-0	0	0	.000	.000	.000	-99	0	0-0	1.000	0	290	0	/2D	0	0.0
1992	Sea A	34	74	8	20	5	0	0	5	9-0	0	15	.270	.341	.338	92	0	2-1	.881	-1	99	193	3b18,O15(15/0/1)	0	-0.1
Total	3	56	110	9	26	5	0	0	6	14-0	0	24	.236	.317	.282	71	-3	2-1	.898	-3	94	153	3b26,O15(15/0/1),S5/D2	0	-0.7

TURNER, TERRY Terrence Lamont "Cotton Top"; B2.28.1881 Sandy Lake PA; D7.18.1960 Cleveland OH; BR/TR/5´8˝/149; d8.25; C1

YEAR	TM LG	G	AB	R	H	2B	3B	HR	RBI	BB-IB	HP	SO	AVG	OBP	SLG	AOPS	ABR	SB-CS	FA	FR	RNG	THR	GAMES AT POSITION	DL	BFW
1901	Pit N	2	7	0	3	0	0	0	1	0	0	—	.429	.429	.429	145	0	0	.833	1	151	0	3b2	—	0.1
1904	Cle A	111	404	41	95	9	6	1	45	11	0	—	.235	.255	.295	74	-13	5	.940	3	106	85	S111	—	-0.8
1905	Cle A	**155**	586	49	155	16	14	4	72	14	6	—	.265	.289	.360	104	-1	17	.946	-25	94	106	S155	—	-2.4
1906	Cle A	147	584	85	170	27	7	2	62	35	6	—	.291	.338	.372	124	16	27	.960	19	**114**	**141**	S147	—	4.2
1907	Cle A	140	524	57	127	20	7	0	46	19	2	—	.242	.272	.307	84	-11	27	**.950**	-2	100	**155**	S139	—	-1.0
1908	Cle A	60	201	21	48	11	1	0	19	15	2	—	.239	.298	.303	95	-1	18	.952	-3	57	0	O36(0/2/34),S17	—	-0.5
1909	Cle A	53	208	25	52	7	4	0	16	14	2	—	.250	.304	.322	94	-2	14	.969	10	125	78	2b26,S26	—	1.0
1910	Cle A	150	574	71	132	14	6	0	33	53	5	—	.230	.301	.275	79	-13	31	.973	-1	102	113	S94,3b46,2b9	—	-1.1
1911	Cle A	117	417	59	105	16	9	0	28	34	1	—	.252	.310	.333	78	-13	29	.970	1	108	72	3b94,2b14,S10	—	-0.9
1912	Cle A	103	370	54	114	14	4	0	33	31	1	—	.308	.363	.368	106	3	19	**.951**	3	97	**144**	3b103	—	0.8
1913	Cle A	120	388	60	96	13	4	0	44	55	5	35	.247	.348	.302	88	-4	13	.954	13	99	272	3b71,2b25,S21	—	1.4
1914	Cle A	121	428	43	105	14	9	1	33	44	2	36	.245	.319	.327	91	-5	17-13	**.963**	22	113	**140**	3b104,2b17	—	2.1
1915	Cle A	75	262	35	66	14	1	0	14	29	1	13	.252	.329	.313	90	-2	12-11	.965	-4	94	58	2b51,3b20	—	-0.7
1916	Cle A	124	428	52	112	15	3	0	38	40	0	29	.262	.325	.311	86	-7	15	.963	9	112	70	3b77,2b42	—	0.5
1917	Cle A	69	180	16	37	7	0	0	15	14	0	19	.206	.263	.244	51	-10	4	.980	-0	91	68	3b40,2b23/S	—	-1.1
1918	Cle A	74	233	24	58	7	2	0	23	22	1	15	.249	.316	.296	77	-6	6	.969	2	110	39	3b46,2b26/S	—	-0.4
1919	Phi A	38	127	7	24	3	0	0	6	5	0	9	.189	.220	.213	21	-14	2	.946	3	117	155	S19,2b17/3	—	-0.9
Total	17	1659	5921	699	1499	207	77	8	528	435	34	156	.253	.308	.318	89	-83	256-24	.952	49	103	123	S741,3b604,2b250,O36(0/2/34)	—	0.3

TURNER, TOM Thomas Richard; B9.8.1916 Custer Co. OK; D5.14.1986 Kennewick WA; BR/TR/6´2˝/195; d4.25; Mil 1945

YEAR	TM LG	G	AB	R	H	2B	3B	HR	RBI	BB-IB	HP	SO	AVG	OBP	SLG	AOPS	ABR	SB-CS	FA	FR	RNG	THR	GAMES AT POSITION	DL	BFW
1940	Chi A	37	96	11	20	1	2	0	6	3	1	12	.208	.240	.260	29	-11	1-0	.969	2	*116*	*83*	C29	—	-0.7
1941	Chi A	38	126	7	30	5	0	0	8	9	0	15	.238	.289	.278	51	-9	2-0	.979	3	*104*	*101*	C35	0	-0.3
1942	Chi A	56	182	18	44	9	1	3	21	19	0	15	.242	.313	.352	89	-3	0-1	.971	-0	*101*	*81*	C54	0	0.0
1943	Chi A	51	154	16	37	7	1	2	11	13	0	21	.240	.299	.338	86	-3	1-0	.978	3	*105*	*92*	C49	0	0.3
1944	Chi A	36	113	9	26	6	0	2	13	5	0	16	.230	.263	.336	71	-5	0-1	.958	-2	*119*	*87*	C36	0	-0.5
	†StL A	15	25	2	8	1	0	0	4	2	0	5	.320	.370	.360	103	0	0-0	.969	-1	*97*	*56*	C11	0	0.0
	Year	51	138	11	34	7	0	2	17	7	0	21	.246	.283	.341	77	-5	0-1	.960	-2	*115*	*82*	C47	0	-0.5
Total	5	233	696	63	165	29	4	7	63	51	1	84	.237	.290	.320	70	-31	4-2	.972	5	*107*	*88*	C214	0	-1.2

TUTTLE, BILL William Robert; B7.4.1929 Elwood IL; D7.27.1998 Anoka MN; BR/TR/6´0˝/(185–190); d9.10; Col Bradley

YEAR	TM LG	G	AB	R	H	2B	3B	HR	RBI	BB-IB	HP	SO	AVG	OBP	SLG	AOPS	ABR	SB-CS	FA	FR	RNG	THR	GAMES AT POSITION	DL	BFW
1952	Det A	7	25	2	6	0	0	0	2	0	0	1	.240	.240	.240	34	-2	0-0	1.000	0	115	0	O6(3/3/0)	0	-0.3
1954	Det A	147	530	64	141	20	11	7	58	62	2	60	.266	.343	.385	102	1	5-8	.985	-2	93	133	O145(1/144/0)	0	-1.0
1955	Det A	**154**	603	102	168	23	4	14	78	76-2	1	54	.279	.358	.400	107	6	6-3	.985	5	104	127	O154C	0	0.4
1956	Det A	140	546	61	138	22	4	9	65	38-1	1	48	.253	.301	.357	73	-23	5-4	.976	3	102	149	O137C	0	-2.6
1957	Det A	133	451	49	113	12	4	5	47	44-4	1	41	.251	.316	.328	75	-16	2-6	.982	0	108	59	O128C	0	-2.4
1958	KC A	148	511	77	118	14	9	11	51	74-1	1	58	.231	.327	.358	88	-8	7-9	.988	-2	97	130	O145(0/107/46)	0	-1.8
1959	KC A	126	463	74	139	19	6	7	43	48-2	4	38	.300	.369	.413	113	9	10-6	.984	8	102	**218**	O121C	0	1.1
1960	KC A	151	559	75	143	21	3	8	40	66-2	2	52	.256	.336	.347	85	-11	1-5	.988	8	108	**183**	O148C	0	-1.1
1961	KC A	25	84	15	22	2	2	0	8	9-0	0	9	.262	.333	.333	77	-3	0-0	.951	-2	104	0	O25C	0	-0.5
	Min A	113	370	38	91	12	3	5	38	43-4	0	41	.246	.321	.335	73	-14	1-3	.943	-1	98	95	3b85,O64(0/63/6),2b2	0	-1.7
	Year	138	454	53	113	14	5	5	46	52-4	0	50	.249	.323	.335	73	-17	1-3	.970	-2	105	36	O89(0/88/6),3b85,2b2	0	-2.2
1962	Min A	110	123	21	26	4	1	1	13	19-1	1	14	.211	.317	.285	62	-6	1-0	.973	-6	75	98	O104(0/95/15)	0	-1.3
1963	Min A	16	3	0	0	0	0	0	0	1-1	0	0	.000	.250	.000	-22	0	0-0	1.000	1	156	823	O14C	0	0.1
Total	11	1270	4268	578	1105	149	47	67	443	480-18	13	416	.259	.334	.363	88	-67	38-44	.983	14	101	136	O1191(4/1139/67),3b85,2b2	0	-11.1

TUTWILER, GUY Guy Isbel "King Tut"; B7.17.1888 Coalburg AL; D8.15.1930 Birmingham AL; BL/TR/6´0˝/175; d8.29

YEAR	TM LG	G	AB	R	H	2B	3B	HR	RBI	BB-IB	HP	SO	AVG	OBP	SLG	AOPS	ABR	SB-CS	FA	FR	RNG	THR	GAMES AT POSITION	DL	BFW
1911	Det A	13	32	3	6	2	0	0	3	2	0	—	.188	.235	.250	34	-3	0	.778	-4	75	0	2b6,O3L	—	-0.6
1913	Det A	14	47	4	10	0	1	0	7	4	0	12	.213	.275	.255	56	-3	2	.987	1	127	135	1b14	—	-0.3
Total	2	27	79	7	16	2	1	0	10	6	0	12	.203	.259	.253	47	-6	2	.987	-3	127	135	1b14,2b6,O3L	—	-0.9

TWINEHAM, ART Arthur S. "Old Hoss"; B11.26.1866 Galesburg IL; BL/TL/6´1.5˝/190; d9.11

YEAR	TM LG	G	AB	R	H	2B	3B	HR	RBI	BB-IB	HP	SO	AVG	OBP	SLG	AOPS	ABR	SB-CS	FA	FR	RNG	THR	GAMES AT POSITION	DL	BFW
1893	StL N	14	48	8	15	2	0	0	11	1	1	2	.313	.340	.354	84	-1	0	.928	1	*85*	*120*	C14	—	0.0
1894	StL N	38	127	22	40	4	1	1	16	9	6	11	.315	.387	.386	87	-2	2	.939	3	*106*	*103*	C38	—	0.3
Total	2	52	175	30	55	6	1	1	27	10	7	13	.314	.375	.377	86	-3	2	.936	3	*100*	*107*	C52	—	0.3

YEAR	TM LG	G	AB	R	H	2B	3B	HR	RBI	BB-IB	HP	SO	AVG	OBP	SLG	AOPS	ABR	SB-CS	FA	FR	RNG	THR	GAMES AT POSITION	DL	BFW
TWITCHELL, LARRY	Lawrence Grant; B2.18.1864 Cleveland OH; D8.23.1930 Cleveland OH; BR/TR/6´0˝/185; d4.30; ▲																								
1886	Det N	4	16	0	1	0	0	0	0	0	—	2	.063	.063	.063	-60	-3	0	1.000	0	155	693	P4,O2(1/1/0)	—	-0.1
1887	†Det N	65	264	44	88	14	6	0	51	8	2	19	.333	.358	.432	114	4	12	.871	-5	45	64	O53(44/9/0),P15	—	-0.2
1888	Det N	131	524	71	128	19	4	5	67	28	3	45	.244	.286	.324	93	-4	14	.885	-9	59	98	O131L,P2	—	-1.6
1889	Cle N	134	549	73	151	16	11	4	95	29	3	37	.275	.315	.366	91	-10	17	.916	-10	39	0	O134L/P	—	-1.9
1890	Cle P	56	233	33	52	6	3	2	36	17	1	17	.223	.279	.300	60	-14	4	.821	-7	86	49	O56(1/0/56)	—	-1.7
	Buf P	44	172	24	38	3	1	2	17	23	1	12	.221	.316	.285	67	-7	4	.918	1	64	90	O32(4/0/28),P13,1b3	—	-0.4
	Year	100	405	57	90	9	4	4	53	40	2	29	.222	.295	.294	63	-21	8	.857	-5	79	63	O88(5/0/84),P13,1b3	—	-2.1
1891	Col AA	57	224	32	62	9	4	2	35	20	2	28	.277	.341	.379	113	3	10	.887	-7	46	0	O56L,P6	—	-0.4
1892	Was N	51	192	20	42	9	5	0	20	11	4	31	.219	.275	.318	82	-5	8	.897	-3	73	65	O48(46/0/2),S3/3	—	-1.0
1893	Lou N	45	187	37	58	11	3	2	31	17	3	20	.310	.377	.433	125	7	7	.874	-2	77	0	O45(43/0/2)	—	0.1
1894	Lou N	52	210	28	56	16	3	2	32	15	0	20	.267	.316	.400	77	-8	8	.908	7	179	189	O51L/P	—	-0.4
Total	9	639	2571	.362	676	103	40	19	384	168	19	231	.263	.313	.356	91	-37	84	.890	-34	67	57	O608(511/10/88),P42,S3,1b3/3	—	-7.6
TWOMBLY, BABE	Clarence Edward; B1.18.1896 Jamaica Plain MA; D11.23.1974 San Clemente CA; BL/TR/5´10˝/165; d4.14; b–George; Col Lehigh																								
1920	Chi N	78	183	25	43	1	1	2	14	17	1	20	.235	.303	.284	68	-7	5-9	.970	0	101	107	O45(5/15/25),2b2	—	-1.3
1921	Chi N	87	175	22	66	8	1	1	18	11	0	10	.377	.414	.451	129	8	4-6	.968	4	94	220	O45(10/29/6)	—	0.8
Total	2	165	358	47	109	9	2	3	32	28	1	30	.304	.357	.366	98	1	9-15	.969	4	98	158	O90(15/44/31),2b2	—	-0.5
TWOMBLY, GEORGE	George Frederick "Silent George"; B6.4.1892 Boston MA; D2.17.1975 Lexington MA; BR/TR/5´9˝/165; d7.9; b–Babe																								
1914	Cin N	68	240	22	56	0	5	0	19	14	3	27	.233	.284	.275	64	-11	12	.968	1	91	138	O68(68/0/1)	—	-1.5
1915	Cin N	46	66	5	13	0	1	0	5	8	1	8	.197	.293	.227	57	-3	5-3	1.000	1	106	129	O24(10/13/1)	—	-0.3
1916	Cin N	3	5	0	0	0	0	0	0	1	0	1	.000	.167	.000	-48	-1	0	1.000	-0	101	0	/lf	—	-0.1
1917	Bos N	32	102	8	19	1	1	0	9	18	1	5	.186	.314	.216	68	-3	4	.943	-4	87	30	O29(1/21/7)/1	—	-1.0
1919	Was A	1	4	0	0	0	0	0	0	0	0	0	.000	.000	.000	-99	-1	0	ø	-0	0	0	/lf	—	-0.1
Total	5	150	417	35	88	1	7	0	33	41	5	41	.211	.289	.247	62	-19	21-3	.967	-2	92	109	O123(81/34/9)/1	—	-3.0
TYACK, JIM	James Frederick; B1.9.1911 Florence MT; D1.3.1995 Bakersfield CA; BL/TR/6´2˝/195; d4.20																								
1943	Phi A	54	155	11	40	8	1	0	23	14	0	9	.258	.320	.323	88	-2	1-1	.977	1	103	144	O38(9/2/27)	0	-0.4
TYLER, FRED	Frederick Franklin "Clancy"; B12.16.1891 Derry NH; D10.14.1945 E.Derry NH; BR/TR/5´10.5˝/180; d10.3; b–Lefty																								
1914	Bos N	6	19	2	2	0	0	0	2	1	0	5	.105	.150	.105	-24	-3	0	1.000	-0	*117*	*107*	C6	—	-0.3
TYLER, JOHNNIE	John Anthony "Ty Ty","Katz" (b John Tylka); B7.30.1906 Mt.Pleasant PA; D7.11.1972 Mt.Pleasant PA; BB/TR/6´0˝/175; d9.16																								
1934	Bos N	3	6	0	1	0	0	0	1	0	0	3	.167	.167	.167	-11	-1	0	1.000	1	82	989	/cf	—	0.0
1935	Bos N	13	47	7	16	2	1	2	11	4	1	3	.340	.404	.553	168	4	0	.893	-0	100	127	O11L	—	0.3
Total	2	16	53	7	17	2	1	2	12	4	1	6	.321	.379	.509	148	3	0	.906	0	98	225	O12(11/1/0)	—	0.3
TYNER, JASON	Jason Renyt; B4.23.1977 Bedford TX; BL/TL/6´1˝/(170–185); [NYN98 1/21]; d6.5; Col Texas A&M																								
2000	NY N	13	41	3	8	2	0	0	5	1-0	1	4	.195	.222	.244	22	-5	1-1	.920	1	124	167	O12(12/2/0)	0	-0.4
	TB A	37	83	6	20	2	0	0	8	4-0	1	12	.241	.281	.265	41	-8	6-1	1.000	2	97	286	O31(27/4/0)/D	0	-0.5
2001	TB A	105	396	51	111	8	5	0	21	15-0	3	42	.280	.311	.326	70	-19	31-6	.978	4	106	147	O100(57/47/3)	0	-1.1
2002	TB A	44	168	17	36	2	1	0	9	7-0	1	19	.214	.249	.238	31	-17	7-1	.990	2	113	80	O42(41/1/0)/D	0	-1.5
2003	TB A	46	90	12	25	7	0	0	6	10-0	0	12	.278	.350	.356	89	-1	2-1	.962	-0	101	72	O32(9/2/23),D4	0	-0.2
2005	Min A	18	56	8	18	1	1	0	5	4-0	0	4	.321	.367	.375	97	0	2-0	1.000	0	112	0	O15(12/2/2),D3	0	0.0
2006	†Min A	62	218	29	68	5	2	0	18	11-2	1	18	.312	.345	.353	82	-6	4-2	.993	6	126	131	O50(33/18/1),D12	0	-0.1
Total	6	325	1052	126	286	27	9	0	72	52-2	7	111	.272	.309	.315	65	-56	53-12	.983	16	111	132	O282(191/76/29),D21	0	-3.8
TYREE, EARL	Earl Carlton "Ty"; B3.4.1890 Huntsville IL; D5.17.1954 Rushville IL; BR/TR/5´8˝/160; d10.5																								
1914	Chi N	1	4	1	0	0	0	0	0	0	0	0	.000	.000	.000	-99	-1	0	1.000	-1	*91*	*137*	/C	—	-0.2
TYRONE, JIM	James Vernon; B1.29.1949 Alice TX; BR/TR/6´1˝/185; [ChiN71 7/162]; d8.27; b–Wayne; Col Texas–Pan American																								
1972	Chi N	13	8	1	0	0	0	0	0	0-0	0	3	.000	.000	.000	-90	-2	1-0	1.000	1	180	839	O4(3/0/1)	0	-0.1
1974	Chi N	57	81	19	15	0	1	3	3	6-0	0	8	.185	.241	.321	54	-6	1-1	.962	-1	85	98	O32(21/1/12)/3	0	-0.8
1975	Chi N	11	22	0	5	0	1	0	3	1-0	0	4	.227	.250	.318	57	-1	1-1	1.000	0	73	271	O8L	0	-0.2
1977	Oak A	96	294	32	72	11	1	5	26	25-2	0	62	.245	.300	.340	76	-10	3-1	.950	1	107	90	O81(10/4/70)/1SD	0	-1.3
Total	4	177	405	52	92	11	3	8	32	32-2	0	77	.227	.281	.328	67	-19	6-3	.955	1	103	113	O125(42/5/83),D4/S13	0	-2.4
TYRONE, WAYNE	Oscar Wayne; B8.1.1950 Alice TX; BR/TR/6´1˝/185; [ChiN72 20/470]; d7.15; b–Jim; Col Texas–Pan American																								
1976	Chi N	30	57	3	13	1	0	1	8	3-2	0	21	.228	.262	.298	55	-3	0-0	1.000	-1	35	0	O7(6/0/1),1b5,3b5	0	-0.5
TYSON, TY	Albert Thomas; B6.1.1892 Wilkes–Barre PA; D8.16.1953 Buffalo NY; BR/TR/5´11˝/169; d4.13																								
1926	NY N	97	335	40	98	16	1	3	35	15	3	28	.293	.329	.373	90	-5	6	.980	1	99	105	O92(12/83/0)	—	-0.9
1927	NY N	43	159	24	42	7	2	1	17	10	0	19	.264	.308	.352	76	-6	5	.929	-2	87	132	O41(40/1/2)	—	-1.1
1928	Bro N	59	210	25	57	11	1	1	21	10	4	14	.271	.317	.348	75	-8	3	.965	-0	97	123	O55(1/41/14)	—	-1.1
Total	3	199	704	89	197	34	4	5	73	35	7	61	.280	.320	.361	82	-19	14	.966	-1	96	116	O188(53/125/16)	—	-3.1
TYSON, TURKEY	Cecil Washington "Slim"; B12.6.1914 Elm City NC; D2.17.2000 Elm City NC; BL/TR/6´5.5˝/225; d4.23																								
1944	Phi N	1	1	0	0	0	0	0	0	0	0	0	.000	.000	.000	-99	0	0	ø	0	—	—	/H	0	0.0
TYSON, MIKE	Michael Ray; B1.13.1950 Rocky Mount NC; BR/TR (BB 1972p, 76p, 79p, 80p)/5´9˝/(170–175); [StLN70*3/60]; d9.5; Col Indian River (FL) CC																								
1972	StL N	13	37	1	7	1	0	0	0	1-0	0	9	.189	.211	.216	22	-4	0-1	.981	2	121	56	2b11,S2	0	-0.2
1973	StL N	144	469	48	114	15	4	1	33	23-10	2	66	.243	.279	.299	60	-26	2-5	.944	-10	94	94	S128,2b16	0	-2.3
1974	StL N	151	422	35	94	14	5	1	37	22-9	3	70	.223	.264	.287	55	-27	4-2	.955	7	103	**145**	S143,2b12	0	-0.4
1975	StL N	122	368	45	98	16	3	2	37	24-4	3	39	.266	.316	.342	79	-11	5-2	.971	-8	91	83	S95,2b24,3b5	0	-0.8
1976	StL N	76	245	26	70	12	9	3	28	16-5	0	34	.286	.326	.445	116	4	3-1	.971	10	116	113	2b74	68	1.9
1977	StL N	138	418	42	103	15	2	7	57	30-11	2	48	.246	.299	.342	72	-17	3-4	.979	24	**118**	**134**	2b135	0	1.3
1978	StL N	125	377	26	88	16	0	3	26	24-7	0	41	.233	.277	.300	62	-20	2-0	.977	-8	90	**116**	2b124	0	-2.2
1979	StL N	75	190	18	42	8	2	5	20	13-6	1	28	.221	.272	.363	71	-8	2-1	.975	2	106	120	2b71	33	-0.3
1980	Chi N	123	341	34	81	19	3	3	23	15-3	2	61	.238	.273	.337	64	-16	1-2	.968	10	106	103	2b117	0	-0.2
1981	Chi N	50	92	6	17	2	0	2	8	7-1	1	15	.185	.248	.272	45	-7	1-0	.940	-3	97	85	2b36/S	0	-0.9
Total	10	1017	2959	281	714	118	28	27	269	175-56	14	411	.241	.285	.327	69	-132	23-18	.973	25	107	115	2b620,S369,3b5	101	-4.1
UECKER, BOB	Robert George; B1.26.1935 Milwaukee WI; BR/TR/6´1˝/(180–190); d4.13																								
1962	Mil N	33	64	5	16	2	0	1	8	7-0	0	15	.250	.324	.328	78	-2	0-0	.982	3	428	112	C24	0	0.2
1963	Mil N	13	16	3	4	2	0	0	0	2-0	0	5	.250	.333	.375	105	0	0-0	.958	1	116	119	C6	0	0.1
1964	StL N	40	106	8	21	1	0	1	6	17-0	1	24	.198	.315	.236	53	-6	0-1	.987	1	102	93	C40	0	-0.4
1965	StL N	53	145	17	33	7	0	2	10	24-1	2	27	.228	.345	.317	80	-3	0-1	.985	-7	60	107	C49	0	-0.8
1966	Phi N	78	207	15	43	6	0	7	30	22-6	0	36	.208	.279	.338	72	-8	0-0	.985	-2	91	112	C76	0	-0.8
1967	Phi N	18	35	3	6	2	0	0	7	5-1	0	9	.171	.275	.229	45	-2	0-0	.973	-1	48	105	C17	0	-0.3
	Atl N	62	158	14	23	2	0	3	13	19-4	0	51	.146	.236	.215	31	-14	0-1	.972	-5	77	55	C59	0	-1.9
	Year	80	193	17	29	4	0	3	20	24-5	0	60	.150	.243	.218	33	-17	0-1	.972	-6	72	64	C76	0	-2.2
Total	6	297	731	65	146	22	0	14	74	96-12	3	167	.200	.293	.287	63	-35	0-3	.981	-10	108	95	C271	0	-3.9
UGGLA, DAN	Daniel Cooley; B3.11.1980 Louisville KY; BR/TR/5´10˝/200; [AriN01 11/338]; d4.3; Col Memphis																								
2006	Fla N☆	154	611	105	172	26	7	27	90	48-1	9	123	.282	.339	.480	113	9	6-6	.980	10	104	107	2b151/D	0	2.5
UGUETO, LUIS	Luis Enrique; B2.15.1979 Caracas, Distrito Capital, Venezuela; BB/TR/5´11˝/170; d4.3																								
2002	Sea A	62	23	19	5	0	0	1	1	2-0	0	8	.217	.280	.348	68	-1	8-4	.960	2	118	119	D16,2b11,S8/3	24	0.0
2003	Sea A	12	5	4	1	0	0	0	1	1-0	0	0	.200	.333	.200	48	0	2-0	1.000	-0	98	334	2b4/3SD	0	0.0
Total	2	74	28	23	6	0	0	1	2	3-0	0	8	.214	.290	.321	65	-1	10-4	.967	1	114	161	D19,2b15,S9,3b2	24	0.0
UHALT, FRENCHY	Bernard Bartholomew; B4.27.1910 Bakersfield CA; D9.3.2004 Walnut Creek CA; BL/TR/5´10˝/180; d4.17																								
1934	Chi A	57	165	28	40	5	1	0	16	29	1	12	.242	.359	.285	66	-7	6-5	.935	-2	96	62	O40(4/14/22)	—	-1.1

UHLAENDER, TED Theodore Otto; B10.21.1940 Chicago Heights IL; BL/TR/6´2˝/(187–190); d9.4; C2; Col Baylor

YEAR	TM LG	G	AB	R	H	2B	3B	HR	RBI	BB-IB	HP	SO	AVG	OBP	SLG	AOPS	ABR	SB-CS	FA	FR	RNG	THR	GAMES AT POSITION	DL	BFW
1965	Min A	13	22	1	4	0	0	0	1	0-0	0	2	.182	.182	.182	3	-3	1-0	1.000	1	118	496	O4L	0	-0.2
1966	Min A	105	367	39	83	12	2	2	22	27-1	1	33	.226	.280	.286	60	-19	10-2	.985	3	113	66	O100(4/96/0)	0	-1.9
1967	Min A	133	415	41	107	19	7	6	49	13-1	3	45	.258	.285	.381	88	-7	4-4	**.996**	2	107	95	O118C	0	-1.1
1968	Min A	140	488	52	138	21	5	7	52	28-3	3	46	.283	.324	.389	110	5	16-7	.986	-7	96	36	O129C	0	-0.5
1969	†Min A	152	554	93	151	18	2	8	62	44-4	4	52	.273	.328	.356	89	-8	15-9	.997	-8	89	85	O150(44/108/1)	0	-2.2
1970	Cle A	141	473	56	127	21	2	11	46	39-3	1	44	.268	.321	.391	92	-5	3-6	.991	-11	83	66	O134(24/116/8)	0	-2.3
1971	Cle A	141	500	52	144	20	3	2	47	38-5	0	44	.288	.336	.352	87	-7	3-6	.992	-1	99	79	O131(87/33/13)	0	-1.7
1972	†Cin N	73	113	9	18	3	0	0	6	13-3	0	11	.159	.246	.186	25	-11	0-1	.976	-0	86	185	O27(3/2/23)	0	-1.4
Total	8	898	2932	343	772	114	21	36	285	202-20	12	277	.263	.311	.353	86	-55	52-35	.991	-21	97	76	O793(166/602/45)	0	-11.3

UHLE, GEORGE George Ernest "The Bull"; B9.18.1898 Cleveland OH; D2.26.1985 Lakewood OH; BR/TR/6´0˝/190; d4.30; C4; ▲

YEAR	TM LG	G	AB	R	H	2B	3B	HR	RBI	BB-IB	HP	SO	AVG	OBP	SLG	AOPS	ABR	SB-CS	FA	FR	RNG	THR	GAMES AT POSITION	DL	BFW
1919	Cle A	26	43	7	13	2	1	0	6	1	0	5	.302	.318	.395	94	3	0	.915	0	97	67	P26	—	0.0
1920	†Cle A	27	32	4	11	0	0	0	2	2	0	2	.344	.382	.344	91	2	1-0	1.000	0	96	0	P27	—	0.0
1921	Cle A	48	94	21	23	2	3	1	18	6	0	9	.245	.290	.362	64	3	0-0	.938	-3	75	102	P41	—	0.0
1922	Cle A	56	109	21	29	8	2	0	14	13	1	6	.266	.350	.376	88	9	1-2	.932	-3	75	153	P50	—	0.0
1923	Cle A	58	144	23	52	10	3	0	22	7	0	10	.361	.391	.472	127	17	2-1	.982	-0	96	184	P54	—	0.0
1924	Cle A	59	107	10	33	6	1	1	19	4	1	8	.308	.339	.411	92	7	0-1	**1.000**	1	92	220	P28	—	0.0
1925	Cle A	55	101	10	29	3	3	0	13	7	1	7	.287	.339	.376	81	6	0-0	.943	-3	72	80	P29	—	0.0
1926	Cle A	50	132	16	30	3	0	1	11	10	1	12	.227	.287	.273	46	4	2-2	.933	-0	84	77	P39	—	0.0
1927	Cle A	43	79	4	21	7	1	0	14	5	0	12	.266	.310	.380	78	5	0-1	.974	-1	82	159	P25	—	0.0
1928	Cle A	55	98	9	28	3	2	1	17	8	0	4	.286	.340	.388	90	7	0-0	.972	2	122	127	P31	—	0.0
1929	Det A	40	108	18	37	1	1	0	13	6	0	6	.343	.377	.370	93	8	0-0	.929	-3	73	64	P32	—	0.0
1930	Det A	59	117	15	36	4	2	2	21	8	0	13	.308	.352	.427	95	8	0-0	.975	-3	60	75	P33	—	0.0
1931	Det A	53	90	8	22	6	0	2	7	8	0	8	.244	.306	.378	76	5	0-1	**1.000**	-1	97	47	P29	—	0.0
1932	Det A	38	55	2	10	3	1	0	4	6	0	5	.182	.262	.273	37	1	0-0	1.000	-1	84	111	P33	—	0.0
1933	Det A	1	0	0	0	0	0	0	0	0	0	0	ø	ø	ø	ø	0	0-0	ø	0	0	0	/P	—	0.0
	NY N	8	5	1	0	0	0	0	0	1	0	3	.000	.167	.000	-50	0	0	1.000	0	130	0	P6	—	0.0
	NY A	12	20	1	8	1	0	0	1	4	0	2	.400	.500	.450	163	4	0-0	1.000	-1	69	137	P12	—	0.0
1934	NY A	10	5	1	3	0	1	0	1	0	0	0	.600	.600	1.000	329	2	0-0	1.000	-0	32	0	P10	—	0.0
1936	Cle A	24	21	1	8	1	0	1	4	2	0	0	.381	.435	.571	145	4	0-0	ø	-1	0	0	P7	—	0.0
Total	17	722	1360	172	393	60	21	9	187	98	4	112	.289	.339	.384	86	95	6-8	.960	-16	84	111	P513	—	0.0

UHLER, MAURY Maurice William; B12.14.1886 Pikesville MD; D5.4.1918 Baltimore MD; BR/TR/5´11˝/165; d4.14

YEAR	TM LG	G	AB	R	H	2B	3B	HR	RBI	BB-IB	HP	SO	AVG	OBP	SLG	AOPS	ABR	SB-CS	FA	FR	RNG	THR	GAMES AT POSITION	DL	BFW
1914	Cin N	46	56	12	12	2	0	0	3	5	0	11	.214	.279	.250	56	-3	4	.932	0	118	47	O36(22/11/3)	—	-0.4

UHLIR, CHARLIE Charles Karel; B7.30.1912 Chicago IL; D7.9.1984 Spirit Lake IA; BL/TL/5´7.5˝/150; d8.3

YEAR	TM LG	G	AB	R	H	2B	3B	HR	RBI	BB-IB	HP	SO	AVG	OBP	SLG	AOPS	ABR	SB-CS	FA	FR	RNG	THR	GAMES AT POSITION	DL	BFW
1934	Chi A	14	27	3	4	0	0	0	3	2	0	6	.148	.207	.148	-7	-4	0-0	1.000	-0	96	0	O6L	—	-0.5

ULICNY, MIKE Michael Edward "Slugs"; B9.28.1917 Greenwald PA; D9.22.2005 New Smyrna FL; BR/TR/5´9˝/165; d5.5

YEAR	TM LG	G	AB	R	H	2B	3B	HR	RBI	BB-IB	HP	SO	AVG	OBP	SLG	AOPS	ABR	SB-CS	FA	FR	RNG	THR	GAMES AT POSITION	DL	BFW
1945	Bos N	11	18	4	7	1	0	1	4	1	0	0	.389	.421	.611	184	2	0	.714	-1	*92*	*165*	C4	0	0.1

ULLGER, SCOTT Scott Matthew; B6.10.1955 New York NY; BR/TR/6´2˝/200; [MinA77 18/456]; d4.17; C12; Col St. Johns

YEAR	TM LG	G	AB	R	H	2B	3B	HR	RBI	BB-IB	HP	SO	AVG	OBP	SLG	AOPS	ABR	SB-CS	FA	FR	RNG	THR	GAMES AT POSITION	DL	BFW
1983	Min A	35	79	8	15	4	0	0	5	5-0	1	21	.190	.247	.241	33	-7	0-2	.990	-2	57	69	1b30,3b3/D	0	-1.1

ULRICH, GEORGE George T.; B6.5.1869 Philadelphia PA; d5.1

YEAR	TM LG	G	AB	R	H	2B	3B	HR	RBI	BB-IB	HP	SO	AVG	OBP	SLG	AOPS	ABR	SB-CS	FA	FR	RNG	THR	GAMES AT POSITION	DL	BFW
1892	Was N	6	24	1	7	1	0	0	0	0	0	4	.292	.292	.333	91	0	2	.889	0	71	0	3b3,S2,C2	—	0.0
1893	Cin N	1	3	0	0	0	0	0	0	0	1	0	.000	.250	.000	-31	-1	1	1.000	-0	0	0	/cf	—	-0.1
1896	NY N	14	45	4	8	1	0	0	1	1	2	1	.178	.229	.200	14	-6	0	.920	0	194	253	O11L,3b3	—	-0.6
Total	3	21	72	5	15	2	0	0	1	1	3	5	.208	.250	.236	35	-7	3	.923	0	183	238	O12(11/1/0),3b6,C2,S2	—	-0.7

UMPHLETT, TOM Thomas Mullen; B5.12.1930 Scotland Neck NC; BR/TR/6´2˝/(180–185); d4.16

YEAR	TM LG	G	AB	R	H	2B	3B	HR	RBI	BB-IB	HP	SO	AVG	OBP	SLG	AOPS	ABR	SB-CS	FA	FR	RNG	THR	GAMES AT POSITION	DL	BFW
1953	Bos A	137	495	53	140	27	5	3	59	34	2	30	.283	.331	.376	86	-10	4-2	.983	-1	100	100	O136C	0	-1.7
1954	Was A	114	342	21	75	8	3	1	33	17	0	42	.219	.255	.269	46	-27	1-2	.989	3	92	190	O101(12/4/86)	0	-3.0
1955	Was A	110	323	34	70	10	0	2	19	24-0	0	35	.217	.271	.266	47	-25	2-1	.988	5	108	128	O103(18/62/23)	0	-2.5
Total	3	361	1160	108	285	45	8	6	111	75-0	2	107	.246	.292	.314	65	-62	7-5	.986	7	100	133	O340(30/202/109)	0	-7.2

UNGLAUB, BOB Robert Alexander; B7.31.1881 Baltimore MD; D11.29.1916 Baltimore MD; BR/TR/5´11˝/178; d4.15; M1; Col Maryland

YEAR	TM LG	G	AB	R	H	2B	3B	HR	RBI	BB-IB	HP	SO	AVG	OBP	SLG	AOPS	ABR	SB-CS	FA	FR	RNG	THR	GAMES AT POSITION	DL	BFW
1904	NY A	6	19	2	4	0	0	0	2	0	0	—	.211	.211	.211	32	-2	0	.786	-1	88	290	3b4/S	—	-0.3
	Bos A	9	13	1	2	1	0	0	2	1	0	—	.154	.214	.231	39	-1	0	.625	-2	21	0	2b3,3b2/S	—	-0.4
	Year	15	32	3	6	1	0	0	4	1	0	—	.188	.212	.219	35	-2	0	.842	-3	85	218	3b6,2b3,S2	—	-0.7
1905	Bos A	43	121	18	27	5	1	0	11	6	0	—	.223	.260	.281	71	-4	2	.928	-1	102	131	3b21,2b7,1b2	—	-0.5
1907	Bos A	139	544	49	138	17	13	1	62	23	0	—	.254	.284	.338	89	-3	14	.986	-1	96	117	1b139,M	—	-0.8
1908	Bos A	72	266	23	70	11	3	1	25	7	2	—	.263	.287	.338	100	-1	6	.980	2	112	69	1b72	—	-0.1
	Was A	72	276	23	85	10	5	0	29	8	0	—	.308	.327	.380	142	11	8	.928	6	115	43	3b39,2b27,1b4	—	2.0
	Year	144	542	46	155	21	8	1	54	15	2	—	.286	.308	.360	120	9	14	.981	7	115	78	1b76,3b39,2b27	—	1.9
1909	Was A	130	480	43	127	14	9	3	41	22	3	—	.265	.301	.350	111	3	15	.992	2	109	111	1b57,O42(8/0/34),2b25,3b4	—	0.3
1910	Was A	124	431	29	101	9	4	0	44	21	0	—	.234	.270	.274	74	-15	21	.985	6	119	99	1b124	—	-1.2
Total	6	595	2150	188	554	67	35	5	216	88	5	—	.258	.288	.328	99	-12	66	.986	10	108	103	1b398,3b70,2b62,O42(8/0/34),S2	—	-1.0

UNROE, TIM Timothy Brian; B10.7.1970 Round Lake Beach IL; BR/TR/6´3˝/200; [MilA92 28/780]; d5.30; Col Lewis

YEAR	TM LG	G	AB	R	H	2B	3B	HR	RBI	BB-IB	HP	SO	AVG	OBP	SLG	AOPS	ABR	SB-CS	FA	FR	RNG	THR	GAMES AT POSITION	DL	BFW
1995	Mil A	2	4	0	1	0	0	0	0	0-0	0	0	.250	.250	.250	29	0	0-0	1.000	-0	0	233	1b2	0	-0.1
1996	Mil A	14	16	5	3	0	0	0	0	4-0	0	5	.188	.350	.188	40	-1	0-1	.976	2	0	117	1b11,3b3/lfD	0	0.0
1997	Mil A	32	16	3	4	1	0	2	5	2-0	0	9	.250	.333	.688	155	1	2-0	.969	1	129	88	1b23,3b2,O2(1/0/1)/2	0	0.2
1999	Ana A	27	54	5	13	2	0	1	6	4-0	1	16	.241	.305	.333	63	-3	0-0	1.000	-2	67	150	O12(4/0/8),3b3/2D	0	-0.5
2000	Atl N	4	5	0	0	0	0	0	0	1-0	0	2	.000	.167	.000	-54	-1	0-0	1.000	1	278	0	1b2/lf	0	-0.1
Total	5	79	95	13	21	3	0	3	11	11-0	1	32	.221	.308	.347	67	-4	2-1	.977	1	92	104	1b38,O16(7/0/9),D9,3b8,2b2	0	-0.5

UNSER, AL Albert Bernard; B10.12.1912 Morrisonville IL; D7.7.1995 Decatur IL; BR/TR/6´1˝/175; d9.14; s–Del

YEAR	TM LG	G	AB	R	H	2B	3B	HR	RBI	BB-IB	HP	SO	AVG	OBP	SLG	AOPS	ABR	SB-CS	FA	FR	RNG	THR	GAMES AT POSITION	DL	BFW
1942	Det A	4	8	2	3	0	0	0	0	0	0	2	.375	.375	.375	103	0	0-0	1.000	1	*110*	*130*	C4	0	0.1
1943	Det A	38	101	14	25	5	0	0	4	15	1	15	.248	.350	.297	84	-1	0-1	.982	-1	*90*	*113*	C37	0	0.0
1944	Det A	11	25	2	3	0	1	1	5	3	0	2	.120	.214	.320	49	-2	0-0	.864	-3	57	66	2b5/C	0	-0.5
1945	Cin N	67	204	23	54	10	3	3	21	14	2	24	.265	.318	.387	98	-1	0	.956	-2	*86*	*85*	C61	0	0.0
Total	4	120	338	41	85	15	4	4	30	32	3	43	.251	.322	.355	90	-4	0-1	.967	-5	*88*	*95*	C103,2b5	0	-0.4

UNSER, DEL Delbert Bernard; B12.9.1944 Decatur IL; BL/TL/6´1˝/(180–185); [TexA66 S1/18]; d4.10; C4; f–Al; Col Mississippi St.

YEAR	TM LG	G	AB	R	H	2B	3B	HR	RBI	BB-IB	HP	SO	AVG	OBP	SLG	AOPS	ABR	SB-CS	FA	FR	RNG	THR	GAMES AT POSITION	DL	BFW
1968	Was A	156	635	66	146	13	7	1	30	46-1	2	66	.230	.282	.277	73	-22	11-6	.988	10	100	**200**	O156C/1	0	-1.9
1969	Was A	153	581	69	166	19	**8**	7	57	58-3	0	54	.286	.349	.382	110	7	8-10	.972	-3	102	89	O149C	0	-0.1
1970	Was A	119	322	37	83	5	1	5	30	30-3	0	29	.258	.319	.326	82	-8	1-1	.984	3	102	151	O103(11/43/50)	0	-0.9
1971	Was A	153	581	63	148	19	6	9	41	59-10	2	68	.255	.325	.355	97	-3	11-6	.981	10	113	103	O151(8/105/68)	0	0.1
1972	Cle A	132	383	29	91	12	0	1	17	28-4	1	46	.238	.288	.277	67	-15	5-9	.989	4	104	146	O119(14/85/23)	0	-1.9
1973	Phi N	136	440	64	127	20	4	11	52	47-7	1	55	.289	.354	.427	114	9	5-8	.988	14	**119**	**194**	O132C	0	1.9
1974	Phi N	142	454	72	120	18	5	11	61	50-9	1	62	.264	.337	.399	101	0	6-4	.981	1	98	173	O135C	0	-0.3
1975	NY N	147	531	65	156	18	2	10	53	37-6	0	76	.294	.337	.392	106	2	4-3	.987	9	109	158	O144C	0	0.8
1976	NY N	77	276	28	63	13	2	5	25	18-1	1	40	.228	.275	.344	79	-9	4-4	.995	-1	98	112	O77(2/75/0)	0	-1.3
	Mon N	69	220	29	50	6	2	7	15	11-1	0	44	.227	.261	.368	74	-9	3-3	.983	-2	89	116	O65(29/13/34)	0	-1.5
	Year	146	496	57	113	19	4	12	40	29-2	1	84	.228	.269	.355	77	-17	7-7	.990	-3	94	114	O142(31/88/34)	0	-2.8
1977	Mon N	113	289	33	79	14	1	12	40	33-7	0	41	.273	.346	.453	115	6	2-5	.976	-6	86	45	O72(11/34/27),1b27	0	-0.4
1978	Mon N	130	179	16	35	5	0	2	15	24-5	1	29	.196	.293	.257	55	-10	2-0	.994	2	93	111	1b64,O33(7/12/14)	0	-1.1
1979	Phi N	95	141	26	42	8	0	6	29	14-2	0	33	.298	.354	.482	123	4	2-0	.978	-1	102	0	O30(16/11/3),1b22	0	0.3
1980	†Phi N	96	110	15	29	6	4	0	10	10-1	0	21	.264	.320	.391	93	-1	0-1	1.000	5	268	114	1b31,O23(13/12/1)	0	0.3
1981	Phi N	62	59	5	9	3	0	0	6	13-1	0	9	.153	.301	.203	44	-4	0-0	1.000	1	146	96	1b18,O16(7/6/4)	0	-0.4
1982	Phi N	19	14	0	0	0	0	0	0	3-1	0	2	.000	.176	.000	-45	-3	0-0	1.000	0	177	171	1b5,O2R	0	-0.3
Total	15	1799	5215	617	1344	179	42	87	481	481-62	9	675	.258	.319	.358	93	-56	64-60	.984	46	104	136	O1407(118/1112/226),1b168	0	-6.7

YEAR TM LG	G	AB	R	H	2B	3B	HR	RBI	BB-IB	HP	SO	AVG	OBP	SLG	AOPS	ABR	SB-CS	FA	FR	RNG	THR	GAMES AT POSITION	DL	BFW
UPHAM, JOHN	John Leslie; B12.29.1941 Windsor ON, Can.; BL/TL/6´0˝/180; d4.16																							
1967 Chi N	8	3	1	2	0	0	0	0	0-0	0	0	.667	.667	.667	270	1	0-0	ø	0	0	0	P5	0	0.0
1968 Chi N	13	10	0	2	0	0	0	0	0-0	0	3	.200	.200	.200	19	-1	0-0	1.000	-0	262	0	P2,O2(1/1/0)	0	-0.1
Total 2	21	13	1	4	0	0	0	0	0-0	0	3	.308	.308	.308	78	0	0-0	1.000	-0	229	0	P7,O2(1/1/0)	0	-0.1
UPRIGHT, DIXIE	Roy T.; B5.30.1926 Kannapolis NC; D11.13.1986 Concord NC; BL/TL/6´0˝/175; d4.18																							
1953 StL A	9	8	3	2	0	0	1	1	1	0	3	.250	.333	.625	151	0	0-0	ø	0	—	—	/H	0	0.0
UPSHAW, WILLIE	Willie Clay; B4.27.1957 Blanco TX; BL/TL/6´0˝/(185–195); [NYA75 5/115]; d4.9; C4																							
1978 Tor A	95	224	26	53	8	2	1	17	21-0	0	35	.237	.298	.304	69	-9	4-6	.943	-5	86	68	O52(46/6/1),D18,1b10	0	-1.9
1980 Tor A	34	61	10	13	3	1	1	5	6-1	0	14	.213	.284	.344	68	-3	1-0	.983	1	160	178	1b14,D12/lf	0	-0.3
1981 Tor A	61	111	15	19	3	1	4	10	11-0	1	16	.171	.252	.324	61	-6	2-1	1.000	-1	105	119	D15,1b14,O14(6/0/8)	0	-0.8
1982 Tor A	160	580	77	155	25	7	21	75	52-8	1	91	.267	.327	.443	101	0	8-8	.989	-6	89	95	1b155,D5	0	-1.7
1983 Tor A	160	579	99	177	26	7	27	104	61-8	5	98	.306	.373	.515	134	27	10-7	.985	-2	98	95	1b159/D	0	1.5
1984 Tor A	152	569	79	158	31	9	19	84	55-14	5	86	.278	.345	.464	117	13	10-4	.990	-8	84	105	1b151/D	0	-0.3
1985 †Tor A	148	501	79	138	31	5	15	65	48-7	4	71	.275	.342	.447	111	8	8-8	.992	-0	100	106	1b147/D	0	-0.2
1986 Tor A	155	573	85	144	28	6	9	60	78-4	2	87	.251	.341	.368	91	-5	23-5	.992	4	107	95	1b154/D	0	-0.8
1987 Tor A	150	512	68	125	22	4	15	58	58-4	3	78	.244	.324	.391	86	-10	10-11	.993	13	**129**	107	1b146	0	-0.8
1988 Cle A	149	493	58	121	22	3	11	50	62-4	2	66	.245	.330	.369	93	-3	12-9	.991	2	108	81	1b144	0	-1.1
Total 10	1264	4203	596	1103	199	45	123	528	452-50	23	642	.262	.335	.419	102	12	88-59	.990	-2	102	98	1b1094,O67(53/6/9),D54	0	-6.4
UPTON, B.J.	Melvin Emanuel; B8.21.1984 Norfolk VA; BR/TR/6´3˝/180; [TBA02 1/2]; d8.2																							
2004 TB A	45	159	19	41	8	2	4	12	15-0	1	46	.258	.324	.409	92	-2	4-1	.901	-9	89	76	S16,D14,3b13/lf	0	-0.9
2006 TB A	50	175	20	43	5	0	1	10	13-0	1	40	.246	.302	.291	55	-12	11-3	.906	-6	90	55	3b50	0	-1.5
Total 2	95	334	39	84	13	2	5	22	28-0	2	86	.251	.312	.347	73	-14	15-4	.908	-14	83	44	3b63,S16,D14/lf	0	-2.4
UPTON, TOM	Thomas Herbert "Muscles"; B12.29.1926 Esther MO; BR/TR/6´0˝/160; d4.19; b–Bill; Col Penn																							
1950 StL A	124	389	50	92	5	6	2	30	52	1	45	.237	.328	.296	58	-25	7-2	.946	-9	103	73	S115,2b2/3	0	-2.5
1951 StL A	52	131	9	26	4	3	0	12	12	1	22	.198	.271	.275	46	-10	1-1	.949	-4	93	100	S47	0	-1.2
1952 Was A	5	5	1	0	0	0	0	0	1	0	0	.000	.167	.000	-53	-1	0-0	1.000	1	156	85	S3	0	0.0
Total 3	181	525	60	118	9	9	2	42	65	2	67	.225	.313	.288	55	-36	8-3	.948	-12	101	80	S165,2b2/3	0	-3.7
URBAN, LUKE	Louis John; B3.22.1898 Fall River MA; D12.7.1980 Somerset MA; BR/TR/5´8˝/168; d7.19; Col Boston College																							
1927 Bos N	35	111	11	32	5	0	0	10	3	1	6	.288	.313	.333	79	-3	1	.947	-4	*98*	*172*	C34	—	-0.5
1928 Bos N	15	17	0	3	0	0	0	2	0	1	1	.176	.222	.176	6	-2	0	1.000	0	*92*	*202*	C10	—	-0.2
Total 2	50	128	11	35	5	0	0	12	3	2	7	.273	.301	.313	69	-5	1	.955	-4	*97*	*176*	C44	—	-0.7
URBANSKI, BILLY	William Michael; B6.5.1903 Linoleumville (now Travis) NY; D7.12.1973 Perth Amboy NJ; BR/TR/5´8˝/165; d7.4																							
1931 Bos N	82	303	22	72	13	4	0	17	10	5	32	.238	.274	.307	58	-19	3	.961	6	111	131	3b68,S19	—	-0.9
1932 Bos N	136	563	80	153	25	8	8	46	28	1	60	.272	.307	.387	89	-11	8	.946	-6	98	107	S136	—	-0.6
1933 Bos N	144	566	65	142	21	4	0	35	33	5	48	.251	.298	.302	78	-17	4	.953	-5	101	108	S143	—	-1.2
1934 Bos N	146	605	104	177	30	6	7	53	56	5	37	.293	.357	.397	110	9	4	**.961**	-10	98	101	S146	—	1.0
1935 Bos N	132	514	53	118	17	0	4	30	40	1	32	.230	.286	.286	59	-30	3	.939	-22	94	69	S129	—	-4.2
1936 Bos N	122	494	55	129	17	5	0	26	31	4	42	.261	.310	.316	74	-19	2	.937	-12	87	114	S80,3b38	—	-2.4
1937 Bos N	1	1	0	0	0	0	0	0	0	0	1	.000	.000	.000	-99	0	0	ø	0	—	—	/H	—	0.0
Total 7	763	3046	379	791	123	27	19	207	198	21	252	.260	.309	.337	81	-87	24	.949	-49	96	99	S653,3b106	—	-8.3
URIBE, JOSE	Jose Altagracia (Played Under Real Name of Jose Altagracia Gonzalez (Uribe) in 1984); B1.21.1959 San Cristobal, D.R.; D12.8.2006 Santo Domingo, D.R.; BB/TR (BR 1984, 89p)/5´10˝/(160–184); d9.13																							
1984 StL N	8	19	4	4	0	0	0	3	0-0	0	2	.211	.211	.211	19	-2	1-0	.955	-0	99	149	S5/2	0	-0.2
1985 SF N	147	476	46	113	20	4	3	26	30-8	2	57	.237	.285	.315	71	-20	8-2	.961	-1	98	91	S145/2	0	-0.5
1986 SF N	157	453	46	101	15	1	3	43	61-19	0	76	.223	.315	.280	69	-18	22-11	.977	13	103	118	S156	0	1.2
1987 †SF N	95	309	44	90	16	5	5	30	24-9	1	35	.291	.343	.424	107	3	12-2	.971	9	105	121	S95	71	2.2
1988 SF N	141	493	47	124	10	7	3	35	36-10	0	69	.252	.301	.318	82	-13	14-10	.970	-6	98	108	S140	16	-1.0
1989 †SF N	151	453	34	100	12	6	1	30	34-12	0	74	.221	.273	.280	61	-24	6-6	.973	17	**113**	**130**	S150	0	0.3
1990 SF N	138	415	35	103	8	6	1	24	29-13	0	49	.248	.297	.304	68	-20	5-9	.965	9	**113**	**113**	S134	0	-0.4
1991 SF N	90	231	23	51	8	4	1	12	20-6	0	33	.221	.283	.303	67	-11	3-4	.966	-0	105	98	S87	46	-0.7
1992 SF N	66	162	24	39	9	1	2	13	14-3	0	25	.241	.299	.346	87	-3	2-2	.971	4	107	138	S62	17	0.5
1993 Hou N	45	53	4	13	1	0	0	3	8-4	1	5	.245	.355	.264	71	-2	1-0	.944	2	92	187	S41	0	0.1
Total 10	1038	3064	307	738	99	34	19	219	256-84	4	425	.241	.300	.314	74	-110	74-46	.969	47	105	115	S1015,2b2	150	1.5
URIBE, JUAN	Juan C. (Tena); B7.22.1979 Bani, D.R.; BR/TR/5´11˝/(173–220); d4.8																							
2001 Col N	72	273	32	82	15	11	8	53	8-1	2	55	.300	.325	.524	95	-3	3-0	.983	-5	92	103	S69	0	-0.1
2002 Col N	155	566	69	136	25	7	6	49	34-1	5	120	.240	.286	.341	57	-35	9-2	.966	27	114	115	S155	0	0.4
2003 Col N	87	316	45	80	19	3	10	33	17-0	3	60	.253	.297	.427	76	-12	7-2	.972	27	121	118	S74,2b11/cf	65	2.1
2004 Chi A	134	502	82	142	31	6	23	74	32-1	3	96	.283	.327	.506	110	5	9-11	.984	20	103	109	2b77,S38,3b27,D2	0	2.7
2005 †Chi A	146	481	58	121	23	3	16	71	34-0	4	77	.252	.301	.412	85	-11	4-6	.977	2	100	113	S146	0	0.1
2006 Chi A	132	463	53	109	28	2	21	71	13-1	3	82	.235	.257	.441	75	-19	1-1	.977	5	101	106	S132	0	-0.4
Total 6	726	2601	339	670	141	32	84	351	138-4	20	490	.258	.297	.433	82	-75	33-22	.974	76	106	114	S614,2b88,3b27,D2/cf	65	4.8
URY, LON	Louis Newton "Old Sleep"; B1877 Ft.Scott KS; D3.4.1918 Kansas City MO; TR/6´0˝/?; d9.9																							
1903 StL N	2	7	0	1	0	0	0	0	0	0	—	.143	.143	.143	-19	-1	0	1.000	0	88	95	1b2	—	-0.1
USHER, BOB	Robert Royce; B3.1.1925 San Diego CA; BR/TR/6´1.5˝/(180–185); d4.16																							
1946 Cin N	92	152	16	31	5	1	1	14	13	1	27	.204	.271	.270	56	-9	2	.982	3	100	190	O80(23/32/25)/3	0	-0.8
1947 Cin N	9	22	2	4	0	0	1	1	2	0	2	.182	.250	.318	50	-2	0	1.000	1	116	249	O8(3/5/0)	0	-0.1
1950 Cin N	106	321	51	83	17	0	6	35	27	0	38	.259	.316	.368	79	-10	3	.985	-1	96	108	O93(4/80/12)	0	-1.3
1951 Cin N	114	303	27	63	12	2	5	25	19	1	36	.208	.257	.310	51	-22	4-5	.974	2	102	125	O98(14/82/2)	0	-2.4
1952 Chi N	1	0	0	0	0	0	0	0	1	0	0	ø	1.000	ø	197	0	0-0	ø	0	—	—	/H	0	0.0
1957 Cle A	10	8	1	1	0	0	0	0	1-0	0	3	.125	.222	.125	-3	-1	0-0	1.000	-0	102	0	O4(1/3/0)/3	0	-0.2
Was A	96	295	36	77	7	1	5	27	27-2	2	30	.261	.324	.342	84	-7	0-0	.979	2	106	117	O95(1/93/2)	0	-0.9
Year	106	303	37	78	7	1	5	27	28-2	2	33	.257	.321	.337	82	-8	0-0	.979	2	106	115	O99(2/96/2)/3	0	-1.1
Total 6	428	1101	133	259	41	4	18	102	90-2	4	136	.235	.295	.329	69	-51	9-5	.980	7	101	129	O378(46/295/41),3b2	0	-5.7
USSAT, DUTCH	William August; B4.11.1904 Dayton OH; D5.29.1959 Dayton OH; BR/TR/6´1˝/170; d9.13																							
1925 Cle A	1	1	0	0	0	0	0	0	0	0	0	.000	.000	.000	-99	0	0-0	1.000	0	142	0	/2	—	0.0
1927 Cle A	4	16	4	3	0	1	0	2	2	0	1	.188	.278	.313	53	-1	0-0	1.000	-0	82	134	3b4	—	-0.1
Total 2	5	17	4	3	0	1	0	2	2	0	1	.176	.263	.294	44	-1	0-0	1.000	-0	82	134	3b4/2	—	-0.1
UTLEY, CHASE	Chase Cameron; B12.17.1978 Pasadena CA; BL/TR/6´1˝/(170–185); [PhiN00 1/15]; d4.4; Col UCLA																							
2003 Phi N	43	134	13	32	10	1	2	21	11-0	6	22	.239	.322	.373	88	-2	2-0	.983	3	106	134	2b37	0	0.3
2004 Phi N	94	267	36	71	11	2	13	57	15-1	2	40	.266	.308	.468	94	-4	4-1	.982	-2	95	102	2b50,1b13	0	-0.3
2005 Phi N	147	543	93	158	39	6	28	105	69-5	9	109	.291	.376	.540	133	27	16-3	.978	6	95	86	2b135,1b8	0	4.1
2006 Phi N★	160	658	**131**	203	40	4	32	102	63-1	14	132	.309	.379	.527	123	24	15-4	.977	4	98	111	2b156,1b2/D	0	3.6
Total 4	444	1602	273	464	100	13	75	285	158-7	31	303	.290	.362	.509	119	45	37-8	.979	10	97	103	2b378,1b23/D	0	7.7
VACHE, TEX	Ernest Lewis; B11.17.1888 Santa Monica CA; D6.11.1953 Los Angeles CA; BR/TR/6´1˝/200; d4.16																							
1925 Bos A	110	252	41	79	15	7	3	48	21	7	33	.313	.382	.464	114	5	2-2	.908	-7	84	37	O53(52/0/1)	—	-0.6
VADEBONCOEUR, GENE	Onesime Eugene; B7.15.1858 Louiseville QC, Can.; BR/TR/5´6˝/150; d7.11																							
1884 Phi N	4	14	1	3	0	0	0	3	1	—	2	.214	.267	.214	56	-1	—	.846	-1	—	—	C4	—	-0.1
VAHRENHORST, HARRY	Harry Henry "Van"; B2.13.1885 St.Louis MO; D10.10.1943 St.Louis MO; BR/TR/6´1˝/175; d9.21																							
1904 StL A	1	1	0	0	0	0	0	0	0	0	—	.000	.000	.000	-99	0	0	ø	0	—	—	/H	—	0.0

YEAR	TM LG	G	AB	R	H	2B	3B	HR	RBI	BB-IB	HP	SO	AVG	OBP	SLG	AOPS	ABR	SB-CS	FA	FR	RNG	THR	GAMES AT POSITION	DL	BFW
VAIL, MIKE	Michael Lewis; B11.10.1951 San Francisco CA; BR/TR/6´0˝/(180–190); [StLN71*A4/86]; d8.18																								
1975	NY N	38	162	17	49	8	1	3	17	9-1	0	37	.302	.339	.420	113	2	0-0	.971	9	127	315	O36(35/1/0)	0	0.9
1976	NY N	53	143	8	31	5	1	0	9	6-0	0	19	.217	.243	.266	48	-10	0-1	.941	-1	103	40	O35(2/0/33)	68	-1.5
1977	NY N	108	279	29	73	12	1	8	35	19-0	2	58	.262	.310	.398	93	-4	0-7	.965	5	123	98	O85(2/0/83)	0	-0.4
1978	Cle A	14	34	2	8	2	1	0	2	1-1	0	9	.235	.250	.353	71	-2	1-1	1.000	1	142	0	O9(2/0/7)/D	0	-0.1
	Chi N	74	180	15	60	6	2	4	33	3-0	0	24	.333	.341	.456	109	1	0-1	.981	-5	74	34	O45(7/0/39)/3	0	-0.6
1979	Chi N	87	179	28	60	8	2	7	35	14-1	0	27	.335	.379	.520	131	8	0-2	.964	-3	81	112	O39(1/0/38),3b2	0	0.3
1980	Chi N	114	312	30	93	17	2	6	47	14-1	1	77	.298	.330	.423	100	0	2-5	.963	-1	101	91	O77(19/0/61)	0	-0.6
1981	Cin N	31	31	1	5	0	0	0	3	0-0	0	9	.161	.161	.161	-8	-5	0-0	1.000	0	130	0	O3R	0	-0.5
1982	Cin N	78	189	9	48	10	1	4	29	6-1	0	33	.254	.274	.381	82	-5	0-0	.988	3	95	227	O52(50/0/2)	0	-0.4
1983	SF N	18	26	1	4	1	0	0	3	0-0	1	7	.154	.185	.192	5	-3	0-0	1.000	-1	0	0	1b4,O2L	0	-0.5
	Mon N	34	53	5	15	2	0	2	4	8-0	1	10	.283	.387	.434	127	2	0-0	.958	2	91	501	O15(3/0/12)/13	0	0.4
	Year	52	79	6	19	3	0	2	7	8-0	2	17	.241	.326	.354	89	-1	0-0	.960	1	88	463	O17(5/0/12),1b5/3	0	-0.1
1984	LA N	16	16	1	1	0	0	0	2	1-0	0	7	.063	.118	.063	-48	-3	0-0	ø	-0	0	0	/lf	0	-0.4
Total	10	665	1604	146	447	71	11	34	219	81-5	5	317	.279	.313	.400	94	-19	3-17	.968	10	103	137	O399(124/1/278),1b5,3b4/D	68	-3.4
VALDERRAMA, CARLOS	Carlos Alberto; B11.30.1977 Bachaquero, Venezuela; BR/TR/6´0˝/180; d6.21																								
2003	SF N	7	7	0	1	0	0	0	0	0-0	0	3	.143	.143	.143	-25	-1	1-0	1.000	0	147	0	O5(4/2/0)/D	0	-0.1
VALDES, PEDRO	Pedro Jose (Manzo); B6.29.1973 Fajardo, PR; BL/TL/6´1˝/(180–190); [ChiN90 12/340]; d5.15																								
1996	Chi N	9	8	2	1	1	0	0	1	1-0	0	5	.125	.222	.250	23	-1	0-0	1.000	0	150	0	O2R	0	-0.1
1998	Chi N	14	23	1	5	1	1	0	2	1-0	0	3	.217	.250	.348	53	-2	0-1	1.000	0	134	0	O7(6/0/1)	57	-0.2
2000	Tex A	30	54	4	15	5	0	1	5	6-0	0	7	.278	.350	.426	94	0	0-0	1.000	-1	92	0	O14(1/0/13),D5	0	-0.1
Total	3	53	85	7	21	7	1	1	8	8-0	0	15	.247	.312	.388	77	-3	0-1	1.000	-0	106	0	O23(7/0/16),D5	57	-0.4
VALDES, ROY	Rogelio Lazaro (Rojas); B2.20.1920 Havana, Cuba; BR/TR/5´11˝/185; d5.3																								
1944	Was A	1	1	0	0	0	0	0	0	0	0	0	.000	.000	.000	-99	0	0-0	ø	0	—	—	/H	0	0.0
VALDESPINO, SANDY	Hilario (Borroto); B1.14.1939 San Jose de las Lajas, Cuba; BL/TL/5´8˝/(160–170); d4.12																								
1965	†Min A	108	245	38	64	8	2	1	22	20-3	2	28	.261	.319	.322	80	-6	7-4	.990	2	103	127	O57(43/0/17)	0	-0.7
1966	Min A	52	108	11	19	1	1	2	9	4-0	1	24	.176	.211	.259	33	-10	2-2	1.000	-1	99	0	O23(22/1/0)	0	-1.3
1967	Min A	99	97	9	16	2	0	1	3	5-1	0	22	.165	.204	.216	23	-9	3-1	.977	1	96	186	O65(64/0/1)	0	-1.0
1968	Atl N	36	86	8	20	1	0	1	4	10-5	1	20	.233	.320	.279	81	-2	0-0	.976	0	119	0	O20L	0	-0.3
1969	Hou N	41	119	17	29	4	0	0	12	15-0	0	19	.244	.326	.277	72	-4	2-2	.976	1	91	228	O29L	0	-0.5
	Sea A	20	38	3	8	1	0	0	2	1-0	1	7	.211	.250	.237	37	-3	0-1	.889	2	166	177	O7L	0	-0.2
1970	Mil A	8	9	0	0	0	0	0	0	0-0	0	4	.000	.000	.000	-99	-2	0-0	ø	-0	0	0	/lf	0	-0.3
1971	KC A	18	63	10	20	6	0	2	15	2-0	0	5	.317	.338	.508	138	3	0-0	.950	-2	65	109	O15(13/0/2)	0	0.0
Total	7	382	765	96	176	23	3	7	67	57-9	5	129	.230	.286	.295	65	-33	14-10	.974	4	101	121	O217(199/1/20)	0	-4.3
VALDEZ, JULIO	Julio Julian (b Julio Julian Castillo (Valdez); B6.3.1956 San Cristobal, D.R.; BB/TR (BR 1980)/6´2˝/160; d9.2																								
1980	Bos A	8	19	4	5	1	0	1	4	0-0	1	5	.263	.300	.474	103	0	2-0	.935	4	132	225	S8	0	0.5
1981	Bos A	17	23	1	5	0	0	0	3	0-0	0	2	.217	.208	.217	24	-2	0-1	.955	0	114	54	S17	0	-0.1
1982	Bos A	28	20	3	5	1	0	0	1	0-0	0	7	.250	.250	.300	47	-1	1-0	.976	1	102	108	S22,D3	0	0.1
1983	Bos A	12	25	3	3	0	0	0	0	1-0	1	4	.120	.185	.120	-13	-4	0-0	.939	-3	74	57	2b9,S2/D	0	-0.7
Total	4	65	87	11	18	2	0	1	8	1-0	2	18	.207	.231	.264	36	-7	3-1	.955	3	115	120	S49,2b9,D4	0	-0.2
VALDEZ, MARIO	Mario A.; B11.19.1974 Ciudad Obregon, Sonora, Mexico; BL/TL/6´2˝/(190–210); [ChiA93 48/1333]; d6.15; Col Miami–Dade North (FL) CC; [DL 2002 Oak A 36]																								
1997	Chi A	54	115	11	28	7	0	1	13	17-0	3	39	.243	.350	.330	83	-2	1-0	1.000	-4	51	62	1b47/3D	0	-0.9
2000	Oak A	5	12	0	0	0	0	0	0	0-0	0	3	.000	.000	.000	-99	-4	0-0	1.000	0	96	68	1b4	25	-0.4
2001	Oak A	32	54	7	15	1	0	1	8	12-1	1	18	.278	.418	.352	106	1	0-0	1.000	0	98	312	D12,O7L,1b6	132	0.1
Total	3	91	181	18	43	8	0	2	21	29-1	4	60	.238	.352	.315	79	-5	1-0	1.000	-4	53	67	1b57,D14,O7L/3	193	-1.2
VALDEZ, WILSON	Wilson Antonio; B5.20.1978 Nizao, D.R.; BR/TR/5´11˝/(160–170); d9.7																								
2004	Chi A	19	43	8	10	1	0	1	4	2-0	0	5	.233	.267	.326	52	-3	1-2	.973	-4	87	53	S12,2b5	0	-0.6
2005	Sea A	42	126	9	25	5	1	0	8	6-0	0	25	.198	.235	.254	32	-13	2-2	.973	-1	99	87	S42	0	-1.1
	SD N	9	13	0	3	2	0	0	1	2-0	0	1	.231	.333	.385	92	0	0-0	.944	-2	60	68	S8	0	-0.2
Total	2	70	182	17	38	8	1	1	13	10-0	0	31	.209	.250	.280	42	-16	3-4	.970	-7	93	79	S62,2b5	0	-1.9
VALDIVIELSO, JOSE	Jose (Lopez) (b Jose Martinez De Valdivielso (Lopez)); B5.22.1934 Matanzas, Cuba; BR/TR/6´1˝/175; d6.21																								
1955	Was A	94	294	32	65	12	5	2	28	21-1	3	38	.221	.277	.316	63	-17	1-2	.956	11	110	106	S94	0	0.1
1956	Was A	90	246	18	58	8	2	4	29	29-1	1	36	.236	.318	.333	72	-10	3-1	.947	9	110	97	S90	0	0.5
1959	Was A	24	14	1	4	0	0	0	0	1-1	0	3	.286	.333	.286	72	-1	0-0	1.000	0	89	142	S21	0	0.0
1960	Was A	117	268	23	57	1	1	2	19	20-0	4	36	.213	.276	.246	43	-22	1-2	.954	5	104	112	S115/3	0	-1.0
1961	Min A	76	149	15	29	5	0	1	9	8-0	0	19	.195	.234	.248	28	-15	1-1	.971	-12	80	78	S43,2b15,3b14	0	-2.5
Total	5	401	971	89	213	26	8	9	85	79-3	8	132	.219	.282	.290	55	-65	6-6	.955	12	104	103	S363,2b15,3b15	0	-2.9
VALENT, ERIC	Eric Christian; B4.4.1977 LaMirada CA; BL/TL/6´0˝/(191–195); [PhiN98 1/42]; d6.8; Col UCLA																								
2001	Phi N	22	41	3	4	2	0	0	1	4-0	1	11	.098	.196	.146	-10	-7	0-0	1.000	3	191	517	O8(7/0/1),D4	0	-0.4
2002	Phi N	7	10	1	2	0	0	0	0	0-0	0	3	.200	.200	.200	6	-1	0-0	ø	-1	0	0	O2R/1	0	-0.2
2003	Cin N	18	42	3	9	0	0	0	1	2-0	0	9	.214	.250	.214	24	-5	0-0	1.000	1	122	181	O8R	0	-0.4
2004	NY N	130	270	39	72	15	2	13	34	28-4	1	61	.267	.337	.481	111	4	0-1	1.000	1	90	48	O46(32/0/14),1b27	0	0.1
2005	NY N	28	43	4	8	3	0	0	1	7-3	0	17	.186	.300	.256	49	-3	0-0	.955	0	118	0	O12(2/2/8)	0	-0.3
Total	5	205	406	50	95	20	2	13	37	41-7	2	101	.234	.307	.389	81	-12	0-1	.992	4	107	104	O76(41/2/33),1b28,D4	0	-1.2
VALENTIN, JOHN	John William; B2.18.1967 Mineola NY; BR/TR/6´0˝/(170–185); [BosA88 5/121]; d7.27; Col Seton Hall																								
1992	Bos A	58	185	21	51	13	0	5	25	20-0	2	17	.276	.351	.427	109	3	1-0	.963	6	106	125	S58	0	1.3
1993	Bos A	144	468	50	130	40	3	11	66	49-2	2	77	.278	.346	.447	105	4	3-4	.971	16	**105**	**113**	S144	15	2.9
1994	Bos A	84	301	53	95	26	2	9	49	42-1	3	38	.316	.400	.505	127	14	3-1	.979	4	100	104	S83/D	33	2.2
1995	†Bos A	135	520	108	155	37	2	27	102	81-2	10	67	.298	.399	.533	137	31	20-5	.973	6	103	107	S135	0	4.6
1996	Bos A	131	527	84	156	29	3	13	59	63-0	7	59	.296	.374	.436	103	4	9-10	.971	6	102	100	S118,3b12/D	15	1.7
1997	Bos A	143	575	95	176	**47**	5	18	77	58-5	5	66	.306	.372	.499	123	20	7-4	.976	18	111	120	2b79,3b64	0	4.0
1998	†Bos A	153	588	113	145	44	1	23	73	77-3	9	82	.247	.340	.442	100	1	4-5	.965	18	**112**	132	3b153/2	0	1.8
1999	†Bos A	113	450	58	114	27	1	12	70	40-2	4	68	.253	.315	.398	79	-15	0-1	.954	12	109	100	3b111,D2	38	-0.2
2000	Bos A	10	35	6	9	1	0	2	2	2-0	0	5	.257	.297	.457	85	-1	0-1	1.000	-3	52	0	3b10	161	-0.4
2001	Bos A	20	60	8	12	2	0	1	5	9-0	1	8	.200	.314	.283	59	-3	0-0	.970	-1	98	92	S18,3b3	161	-0.3
2002	NY N	114	208	18	50	15	0	3	30	22-0	10	37	.240	.339	.356	89	-2	0-0	.971	-1	108	93	S24,1b22,3b18,2b3,D2	17	-0.4
Total	11	1105	3917	614	1093	281	17	124	558	463-15	53	524	.279	.360	.454	108	56	47-31	.972	82	103	108	S580,3b371,2b83,1b22,D6	440	17.2
VALENTIN, JOSE	Jose Antonio; B10.12.1969 Manati, PR; BB/TR (BL 2004)/5´10˝/(166–195); d9.17; b–Javier; OF(28/24/3)																								
1992	Mil A	4	3	1	0	0	0	0	1	0-0	0	0	.000	.000	.000	-99	-1	0-0	.667	-2	36	0	/2S	0	-0.3
1993	Mil A	19	53	10	13	1	2	1	7	7-1	1	16	.245	.344	.396	99	0	1-0	.922	-5	97	79	S19	0	-0.3
1994	Mil A	97	285	47	68	19	0	11	46	38-1	2	75	.239	.330	.421	88	-5	12-3	.954	**21**	**123**	**119**	S83,2b18/3	0	2.2
1995	Mil A	112	338	62	74	23	3	11	49	37-0	0	83	.219	.293	.402	75	-13	16-8	.971	6	111	**119**	S104/3D	0	0.1
1996	Mil A	154	552	90	143	33	7	24	95	66-9	0	145	.259	.336	.475	98	-3	17-4	.950	1	107	112	S151	0	1.0
1997	Mil A	136	494	58	125	23	1	17	58	39-4	4	109	.253	.310	.407	85	-12	19-8	.967	5	102	106	S134/D	21	0.4
1998	Mil N	151	428	65	96	24	0	16	49	63-8	1	105	.224	.323	.393	86	-8	10-7	.963	0	103	91	S139/D	0	0.1
1999	Mil N	89	256	45	58	9	5	10	38	48-7	2	52	.227	.347	.418	94	-2	3-2	.937	-8	100	78	S85	66	-0.4
2000	†Chi A	144	568	107	155	37	6	25	92	59-1	4	106	.273	.343	.491	105	3	19-2	.950	17	108	124	S141/rf	0	3.1
2001	Chi A	124	438	74	113	22	2	28	68	50-2	3	114	.258	.336	.509	112	7	9-6	.926	12	106	97	3b66,S43,O24C	15	2.1
2002	Chi A	135	474	70	118	26	4	25	75	43-2	2	99	.249	.311	.479	103	0	3-3	.952	5	107	112	3b83,S50/D	0	0.8
2003	Chi A	144	503	79	119	26	2	28	74	54-4	3	114	.237	.313	.463	97	-3	8-3	.969	14	102	**114**	S143	0	2.1
2004	Chi A	125	450	73	97	20	3	30	70	43-4	3	139	.216	.287	.473	91	-9	8-6	.965	17	110	**117**	S122,D2	18	1.6
2005	LA N	56	147	17	25	4	2	2	14	31-2	4	38	.170	.326	.265	58	-8	3-1	.913	2	117	90	3b29,O22L/S	88	-0.6
2006	†NY N	137	384	56	104	24	3	18	62	37-5	0	71	.271	.330	.490	110	5	6-2	.988	19	116	93	2b94,O7(6/0/2)/13	0	2.7
Total	15	1627	5373	854	1308	291	40	246	798	615-50	29	1266	.243	.322	.450	95	-49	134-55	.959	106	107	112	S1216,3b181,2b113,O54L,D9/1	208	14.6

YEAR	TM LG	G	AB	R	H	2B	3B	HR	RBI	BB-IB	HP	SO	AVG	OBP	SLG	AOPS	ABR	SB-CS	FA	FR	RNG	THR	GAMES AT POSITION	DL	BFW
VALENTIN, JAVIER	Jose Javier (Rosario); B9.19.1975 Manati, PR; BB/TR/5´10˝/(185–210); [MinA93 3/93]; d9.13; b–Jose																								
1997	Min A	4	7	1	2	0	0	0	0	0-0	0	3	.286	.286	.286	49	-1	0-0	1.000	1	111	363	C4	0	0.0
1998	Min A	55	162	11	32	7	1	3	18	11-1	0	30	.198	.247	.309	43	-14	0-0	.983	-3	97	67	C53/D	0	-1.3
1999	Min A	78	218	22	54	12	1	5	28	22-0	1	39	.248	.313	.381	74	-9	0-0	.998	6	159	108	C76	0	0.2
2002	Min A	4	4	0	2	0	0	0	0	0-0	0	0	.500	.500	.500	162	0	0-0	1.000	2	0	0	C4	0	0.2
2003	TB A	49	135	13	30	7	1	3	15	5-0	1	31	.222	.254	.356	60	-8	0-0	1.000	2	115	85	C42,D6	0	-0.3
2004	Cin N	82	202	18	47	10	1	6	20	17-3	1	36	.233	.293	.381	75	-8	0-0	.988	1	93	122	C55,1b7	0	-0.5
2005	Cin N	76	221	36	62	11	0	14	50	30-3	0	37	.281	.362	.520	128	9	0-0	.992	-6	121	80	C62,1b2	0	0.7
2006	Cin N	92	186	24	50	6	1	8	27	13-3	0	29	.269	.313	.441	86	-4	0-0	.974	5	204	100	C46,1b2/D	0	0.3
Total	8	440	1135	125	279	53	5	39	158	98-10	3	205	.246	.304	.404	81	-35	0-0	.990	8	130	95	C342,1b11,D8	0	-0.7
VALENTINE, ELLIS	Ellis Clarence; B7.30.1954 Helena AR; BR/TR/6´4˝/(207–218); [MonN72 2/29]; d9.3; [DL 1984 Cal A 182]																								
1975	Mon N	12	33	2	12	4	0	1	3	2-0	0	4	.364	.400	.576	160	3	0-0	.867	-1	67	158	O11R	0	0.1
1976	Mon N	94	305	36	85	15	2	7	39	30-0	0	51	.279	.339	.410	108	3	14-1	.972	-2	82	210	O88(2/55/31)	0	0.1
1977	Mon N★	127	508	63	149	28	2	25	76	30-3	0	58	.293	.331	.504	123	14	13-5	.972	-5	95	91	O126R	0	0.4
1978	Mon N	151	570	75	165	35	2	25	76	35-3	2	88	.289	.330	.489	127	19	13-8	.970	11	103	**198**	O146(0/3/145)	0	2.3
1979	Mon N	146	548	73	151	29	3	21	82	22-3	1	74	.276	.303	.454	104	0	11-9	.983	-4	96	82	O144R	0	-1.2
1980	Mon N	86	311	40	98	22	2	13	67	25-0	3	44	.315	.367	.524	144	18	5-5	.970	-1	102	86	O83R	36	1.3
1981	Mon N	22	76	8	16	3	0	3	15	6-0	0	11	.211	.259	.368	77	-3	0-1	1.000	-1	87	125	O21R	16	-0.5
	NY N	48	169	15	35	8	1	5	21	5-0	0	38	.207	.227	.355	64	-9	0-3	.957	1	97	163	O47R	0	-1.3
	Year	70	245	23	51	11	1	8	36	11-0	0	49	.208	.238	.359	68	-12	0-4	.969	0	94	152	O68R	0	-1.8
1982	NY N	111	337	33	97	14	1	8	48	5-0	1	38	.288	.294	.407	96	-4	1-3	.983	4	101	167	O98(14/4/82)	0	-0.5
1983	Cal A	86	271	30	65	10	2	13	43	18-0	0	48	.240	.283	.435	96	-3	2-1	.963	-4	92	82	O85(11/0/80)	32	-1.1
1985	Tex A	11	38	5	8	1	0	2	4	2-0	0	8	.211	.250	.395	72	-2	0-1	1.000	-1	64	0	O7R,D4	0	-0.3
Total	10	894	3166	380	881	169	15	123	474	180-9	7	462	.278	.315	.458	112	36	59-37	.972	-3	96	132	O856(27/62/777),D4	266	-0.7
VALENTINE, FRED	Fred Lee "Squeaky"; B1.19.1935 Clarksdale MS; BB/TR/6´1˝/190; d9.7; Col Tennessee St.																								
1959	Bal A	12	19	0	6	0	0	0	1	3-0	0	4	.316	.409	.316	104	0	0-1	.889	-1	59	267	O8(3/0/6)	0	-0.1
1963	Bal A	26	41	5	11	1	0	0	1	8-0	0	5	.268	.388	.293	98	0	0-0	1.000	-0	98	0	O10(1/0/10)	0	-0.1
1964	Was A	102	212	20	48	5	0	4	20	21-0	3	44	.226	.304	.307	71	-8	4-2	.978	-2	91	68	O57(22/14/22)	0	-1.4
1965	Was A	12	29	6	7	0	0	0	1	4-0	1	5	.241	.353	.241	73	-1	3-0	1.000	2	160	0	O11(5/6/1)	0	0.1
1966	Was A	146	508	77	140	29	7	16	59	51-1	10	63	.276	.351	.455	132	22	22-10	.980	3	109	76	O138(32/63/70),1b2	0	2.0
1967	Was A	151	457	52	107	16	1	11	44	56-1	10	76	.234	.330	.346	104	4	17-3	.989	-2	100	85	O136(26/70/55)	0	-0.1
1968	Was A	37	101	11	24	2	0	3	7	6-0	2	11	.238	.291	.347	97	-1	1-0	1.000	-1	81	145	O27(0/1/26)	0	-0.4
	Bal A	47	91	9	17	3	2	2	5	7-0	1	20	.187	.253	.330	75	-3	0-0	.972	1	97	183	O26(6/6/14)	0	-0.4
	Year	84	192	20	41	5	2	5	12	13-0	3	31	.214	.273	.339	86	-4	1-0	.986	-0	88	162	O53(6/7/40)	0	-0.8
Total	7	533	1458	180	360	56	10	36	138	156-2	27	228	.247	.330	.373	106	13	47-16	.983	-2	101	88	O413(95/160/204),1b2	0	-0.4
VALENTINE, BOB	Robert; d5.20																								
1876	NY N	1	3	0	0	0	0	0	0	0	—	0	.000	.000	.000	-99	-1	—	.333	-1	—	—	/C	—	-0.2
VALENTINE, BOBBY	Robert John; B5.13.1950 Stamford CT; BR/TR/5´10˝/(185–189); [LAN68 1/5]; d9.2; M15/C4; OF(87/18/26)																								
1969	LA N	5	0	3	0	0	0	0	0	0-0	0	0	ø	ø	ø	ø	0	0-0	ø	0	—	—	/R	0	0.0
1971	LA N	101	281	32	70	10	2	1	25	15-0	2	20	.249	.287	.310	74	-10	5-3	.961	-6	99	119	S37,3b23,2b21,O11(0/3/8)	0	-1.4
1972	LA N	119	391	42	107	11	2	3	32	27-2	2	33	.274	.319	.335	89	-6	5-5	.976	1	110	107	2b49,3b39,O16(5/8/4),S10	0	-0.2
1973	Cal A	32	126	12	38	5	2	1	13	5-0	0	9	.302	.323	.397	111	1	6-1	.948	-2	84	65	S25,O8(1/7/0)	138	0.3
1974	Cal A	117	371	39	97	10	3	3	39	25-0	3	25	.261	.308	.329	89	-6	8-5	.950	2	116	59	O62L,S36,3b15/2D	15	-0.4
1975	Cal A	26	57	5	16	2	0	0	5	4-0	1	3	.281	.323	.316	92	0	0-2	.958	-1	0	108	D13,1b3,3b2,O2(1/0/1)	0	-0.3
	SD N	7	15	1	2	0	0	1	1	4-0	0	0	.133	.316	.333	86	0	1-0	1.000	-1	54	0	O4L	0	-0.1
1976	SD N	15	49	3	18	4	0	0	4	6-0	0	2	.367	.436	.449	164	5	0-1	1.000	2	104	297	O10(7/0/5),1b4	0	0.6
1977	SD N	44	67	5	12	3	0	1	10	7-1	0	10	.179	.253	.269	46	-5	0-0	.962	-1	94	34	S10,3b10/1	0	-0.6
	NY N	42	83	8	11	1	0	1	3	6-0	0	9	.133	.191	.181	0	-12	0-0	1.000	-1	72	73	1b15,S14,3b4	0	-1.3
	Year	86	150	13	23	4	0	2	13	13-1	0	19	.153	.220	.220	20	-18	0-0	.969	-2	98	92	S24,1b16,3b14	0	-1.9
1978	NY N	69	160	17	43	7	0	1	18	19-1	1	18	.269	.346	.331	94	-1	1-1	.977	-2	100	67	2b45,3b9	0	-0.1
1979	Sea A	62	98	9	27	6	0	0	7	22-1	0	5	.276	.405	.337	101	2	1-2	.971	-4	73	42	S29,O15(7/0/8),2b4,3b4,C2/D	0	-0.2
Total	10	639	1698	176	441	59	9	12	157	140-5	9	134	.260	.315	.326	86	-32	27-20	.957	-12	93	76	S161,O128L,2b120,3b106,1b23,D18,C2	153	-3.7
VALENZUELA, BENNY	Benjamin Beltran "Papelero"; B6.2.1933 Los Mochis, Sinaloa, Mexico; BR/TR/5´10˝/175; d4.27																								
1958	StL N	10	14	0	3	1	0	0	0	1-0	0	0	.214	.267	.286	45	-1	0-0	.875	-1	67	0	3b3	0	-0.2
VALERA, YOHANNY	Yohanny; B8.17.1976 Santo Domingo, D.R.; BR/TR/6´1˝/196; d9.13																								
2000	Mon N	7	10	1	0	0	0	0	1	1-0	1	5	.000	.167	.000	-53	-2	0-0	1.000	1	99	112	C7	0	-0.1
VALLE, DAVE	David; B10.30.1960 Bayside NY; BR/TR/6´2˝/(200–220); [SeaA78 2/32]; d9.7																								
1984	Sea A	13	27	4	8	1	0	1	4	1-0	0	5	.296	.321	.444	110	0	0-0	1.000	1	113	116	C13	0	0.2
1985	Sea A	31	70	2	11	1	0	0	4	1-0	1	17	.157	.181	.171	-3	-10	0-0	.976	-2	93	31	C31	84	-1.1
1986	Sea A	22	53	10	18	3	0	5	15	7-0	0	7	.340	.417	.679	190	7	0-0	.982	-4	104	32	C12,1b4	0	0.3
1987	Sea A	95	324	40	83	16	3	12	53	15-2	3	46	.256	.292	.435	86	-8	2-0	.989	6	134	98	C75,D14,1b2/rf	15	0.2
1988	Sea A	93	290	29	67	15	2	10	50	18-0	9	38	.231	.295	.400	89	-5	0-1	.989	9	106	120	C84/1D	41	0.9
1989	Sea A	94	316	32	75	10	3	7	34	29-2	6	32	.237	.311	.354	85	-6	0-0	.993	7	131	**125**	C93	37	0.6
1990	Sea A	107	308	37	66	15	0	7	33	45-0	7	48	.214	.328	.331	84	-5	1-2	**.997**	1	97	85	C104/1	30	0.1
1991	Sea A	132	324	38	63	8	1	8	32	34-0	9	49	.194	.286	.299	63	-17	0-2	.992	10	**149**	89	C129,1b2	0	-0.1
1992	Sea A	124	367	39	88	16	1	9	30	27-1	8	58	.240	.305	.362	85	-8	0-0	.990	-7	98	96	C122	17	-0.8
1993	Sea A	135	423	48	109	19	0	13	63	48-4	**17**	56	.258	.354	.395	100	1	1-0	.995	13	129	118	C135	0	2.2
1994	Bos A	30	76	6	12	2	1	1	5	9-1	1	18	.158	.256	.250	30	-8	0-1	.982	-3	98	67	C28,1b2	0	-1.0
	Mil A	16	36	8	14	6	0	1	5	9-1	1	4	.389	.522	.639	188	6	0-1	1.000	-2	84	67	C12,D2	15	0.4
	Year	46	112	14	26	8	1	2	10	18-2	2	22	.232	.348	.375	83	-2	0-2	.986	-5	94	67	C40,1b2,D2	0	-0.6
1995	Tex A	36	75	7	18	3	0	0	5	6-0	1	18	.240	.305	.280	52	-5	1-0	.993	2	122	94	C29,1b7	0	-0.2
1996	Tex A	42	86	14	26	6	1	3	17	9-0	0	17	.302	.368	.500	110	1	0-0	.994	2	96	102	C35,1b5/D	0	0.4
Total	13	970	2775	314	658	121	12	77	350	258-11	63	413	.237	.314	.373	85	-57	5-7	.992	34	118	100	C902,1b24,D20/rf	239	2.1
VALLE, HECTOR	Hector Jose; B10.27.1940 Vega Baja, PR; BR/TR/5´9˝/180; d6.6																								
1965	LA N	9	13	1	4	0	0	0	2	2-0	0	3	.308	.400	.308	110	0	0-0	1.000	-2	36	114	C6	0	-0.1
VALO, ELMER	Elmer William; B3.5.1921 Ribnik, Czechoslovakia; D7.19.1998 Palmerton PA; BL/TR/5´11˝/(190–200); d9.22; Mil 1943–45; C2																								
1940	Phi A	6	23	6	8	0	0	0	0	3	0	0	.348	.423	.348	104	0	2-0	1.000	0	123	0	O6L	—	0.1
1941	Phi A	15	50	13	21	0	1	2	6	4	0	2	.420	.463	.580	179	5	0-0	1.000	-0	103	0	O10L	0	0.4
1942	Phi A	133	459	64	115	13	10	2	40	70	4	21	.251	.355	.336	95	-1	13-8	.964	-1	**108**	55	O122(1/1/120)	0	-1.0
1943	Phi A	77	249	31	55	6	2	3	18	35	1	13	.221	.319	.297	81	-5	2-6	.986	-0	101	85	O63(9/0/54)	0	-1.3
1946	Phi A	108	348	59	107	21	6	1	31	60	1	18	.307	.411	.411	131	18	9-8	.974	2	108	92	O90(5/0/85)	0	1.6
1947	Phi A	112	370	60	111	12	6	5	36	64	2	21	.300	.406	.405	123	14	11-3	.973	0	101	120	O104R	0	1.3
1948	Phi A	113	383	72	117	17	4	3	46	81	4	13	.305	.432	.394	120	17	10-6	.983	-4	99	48	O109R	0	0.9
1949	Phi A	150	547	86	155	27	12	5	85	119	2	32	.283	.413	.404	121	22	14-11	.981	9	**118**	71	O150L	0	1.9
1950	Phi A	129	446	62	125	16	5	10	46	82	7	22	.280	.400	.406	109	9	12-7	.982	2	106	91	O117(33/0/85)	0	0.6
1951	Phi A	123	444	75	134	27	8	7	55	75	8	20	.302	.412	.446	129	22	11-6	.981	-3	101	57	O116(1/22/95)	0	1.5
1952	Phi A	129	388	69	109	26	4	5	47	101	2	16	.281	.432	.407	126	21	12-11	.962	-4	100	73	O121(2/11/108)	0	1.3
1953	Phi A	50	85	15	19	3	0	0	9	22	0	7	.224	.383	.259	73	-2	0-1	1.000	0	107	55	O25(10/0/15)	0	-0.3
1954	Phi A	95	224	28	48	11	6	1	33	51	0	18	.214	.356	.330	90	-1	2-1	.965	1	111	72	O62(34/0/30)	0	-0.3
1955	KC A	112	283	50	103	17	4	3	37	52-2	0	18	.364	.460	.484	153	25	5-3	.987	1	104	90	O72(46/4/23)	0	2.3
1956	KC A	9	9	1	2	0	0	0	2	1-0	0	1	.222	.273	.222	40	-1	0-0	ø	-0	0	0	/lf	0	-0.1
	Phi N	98	291	40	84	13	3	5	37	48-6	3	21	.289	.392	.405	118	10	7-6	.966	-1	107	54	O87R	0	0.5
1957	Bro N	81	161	14	44	10	1	4	26	25-2	1	16	.273	.370	.422	104	2	0-1	1.000	-2	96	0	O36(26/0/14)	0	-0.2
1958	LA N	65	101	9	25	2	1	1	14	12-0	0	11	.248	.322	.317	69	-4	0-1	1.000	-2	77	0	O26(16/0/13)	0	-0.8
1959	Cle A	34	24	3	7	0	0	0	5	7-1	0	0	.292	.424	.292	113	1	0-0	1.000	0	247	0	O2R	0	0.1
1960	NY A	8	5	1	0	0	0	0	0	2-0	0	1	.000	.286	.000	-17	-1	0-0	ø	-0	0	0	O2R	0	-0.1

YEAR	TM LG	G	AB	R	H	2B	3B	HR	RBI	BB-IB	HP	SO	AVG	OBP	SLG	AOPS	ABR	SB-CS	FA	FR	RNG	THR	GAMES AT POSITION	DL	BFW
	Was A	76	64	6	18	3	0	0	16	17-0	1	4	.281	.424	.328	112	3	0-0	1.000	1	116	671	O6(1/0/5)	0	0.3
	Year	84	69	7	18	3	0	0	16	19-0	1	5	.261	.413	.304	103	2	0-0	1.000	1	93	537	O8(1/0/7)	0	0.2
1961	Min A	33	32	0	5	2	0	0	4	3-1	1	3	.156	.250	.219	25	-3	0-0	1.000	0	189	0	/lf	0	-0.3
	Phi N	50	43	4	8	2	0	1	8	8-0	1	6	.186	.327	.302	69	-2	0-0	ø	-0	0	0	/rf	0	-0.2
Total	20	1806	5029	768	1420	228	73	58	601	942-12	38	284	.282	.398	.391	114	149	110-79	.977	-0	105	71	O1329(352/38/952)	0	8.2
Van Buren, Deacon	Edward Eugene; B12.14.1870 LaSalle Co. IL; D6.29.1957 Portland OR; BL/TR/5´10˝/175; d4.21																								
1904	Bro N	1	1	0	1	0	0	0	0	0	0	—	1.000	1.000	1.000	531	0	0	ø	0	—	—	/H	—	0.0
	Phi N	12	43	2	10	2	0	0	3	3	0	—	.233	.283	.279	76	-1	2	.962	1	131	197	O12L	—	-0.1
	Year	13	44	2	11	2	0	0	3	3	0	—	.250	.298	.295	86	-1	2	.962	1	131	197	O12L	—	-0.1
Van Burkleo, Ty	Tyler Lee; B10.7.1963 Oakland CA; BL/TL/6´5˝/225; d7.28																								
1993	Cal A	12	33	2	5	3	0	1	1	6-0	0	9	.152	.282	.333	63	-2	1-0	1.000	-1	46	90	1b12	0	-0.4
1994	Col N	2	5	0	0	0	0	0	0	0-0	0	1	.000	.000	.000	-86	-1	0-0	1.000	0	127	104	1b2	0	-0.1
Total	2	14	38	2	5	3	0	1	1	6-0	0	10	.132	.250	.289	42	-3	1-0	1.000	-1	53	91	1b14	0	-0.5
Van Camp, Al	Albert Joseph; B9.7.1903 Moline IL; D2.2.1981 Davenport IA; BR/TR/5´11.5˝/175; d9.11																								
1928	Cle A	5	17	0	4	1	0	0	2	0	0	1	.235	.235	.294	38	-2	1-0	.980	-1	37	27	1b5	—	-0.2
1931	Bos A	101	324	34	89	15	4	0	33	20	1	24	.275	.319	.346	79	-11	3-2	.973	-2	89	73	O59(58/3/2),1b25	—	-1.6
1932	Bos A	34	103	10	23	4	2	0	6	4	0	17	.223	.252	.301	44	-9	0-0	.985	1	118	88	1b25	—	-1.0
Total	3	140	444	44	116	20	6	0	41	24	1	42	.261	.301	.333	69	-22	4-2	.973	-2	89	73	O59(58/3/2),1b55	—	-2.8
Vandagrift, Carl	Carl William; B4.22.1883 Cantrall IL; D10.9.1920 Fort Wayne IN; BR/TR/5´8˝/155; d5.19; Col Illinois																								
1914	Ind F	43	136	25	34	4	0	0	9	9	1	15	.250	.301	.279	53	-11	7	.925	-5	83	72	2b28,3b12,S5	—	-1.6
Vander Wal, John	John Henry; B4.29.1966 Grand Rapids MI; BL/TL/6´2˝/(190–205); [MonN87 3/70]; d9.6; Col Western Michigan																								
1991	Mon N	21	61	4	13	4	1	1	8	1-0	0	18	.213	.222	.361	63	-3	0-0	1.000	-1	99	0	O17L	0	-0.5
1992	Mon N	105	213	21	51	8	2	4	20	24-2	0	36	.239	.316	.352	90	-3	3-0	.981	3	112	96	O57(55/0/4),1b7	0	-0.1
1993	Mon N	106	215	34	50	7	4	5	30	27-2	1	30	.233	.320	.372	81	-6	6-3	.988	-6	74	90	1b42,O38(27/2/10)	0	-1.4
1994	Col N	91	110	12	27	3	1	5	15	16-0	0	31	.245	.339	.427	85	-2	2-1	1.000	-2	37	111	1b14,O7(5/0/2)	0	-0.5
1995	†Col N	105	101	15	35	8	1	5	21	16-5	0	23	.347	.432	.594	131	5	1-1	.957	1	95	85	1b10,O10(7/0/3)	0	0.5
1996	Col N	104	151	20	38	6	2	5	31	19-2	1	38	.252	.335	.417	79	-4	2-2	1.000	-2	91	0	O26(25/0/1),1b10	0	-0.8
1997	Col N	76	92	7	16	2	0	1	11	10-0	0	33	.174	.255	.228	23	-10	1-1	.923	-1	104	0	O9(2/0/7),1b5,D2	0	-1.2
1998	Col N	89	104	18	30	10	1	5	20	16-0	0	29	.288	.380	.548	117	3	0-0	1.000	1	88	237	O25(3/0/22),1b2	0	0.3
	†SD N	20	25	3	6	3	0	0	0	6-0	0	5	.240	.387	.360	105	1	0-0	1.000	1	169	0	O5(2/0/3),1b3,D3	0	0.1
	Year	109	129	21	36	13	1	5	20	22-0	0	34	.279	.382	.512	115	4	0-0	1.000	1	101	200	O30(5/0/25),1b5,D3	0	0.4
1999	SD N	132	246	26	67	18	0	6	41	37-1	2	59	.272	.368	.419	108	4	2-1	1.000	0	109	96	O48(45/0/3),1b28/D	0	0.2
2000	Pit N	134	384	74	115	29	0	24	94	72-5	2	92	.299	.410	.563	143	28	11-2	.965	-6	96	45	O78(13/0/65),1b33,D3	0	1.7
2001	Pit N	97	313	39	87	22	3	11	50	42-6	1	84	.278	.361	.473	111	6	7-4	.973	-8	78	44	O73(20/0/56),1b13,D7	0	-0.6
	SF N	49	139	19	35	6	1	3	20	26-3	0	38	.252	.370	.374	99	1	1-2	1.000	2	115	43	O41(3/0/38)/1	0	0.0
	Year	146	452	58	122	28	4	14	70	68-9	1	122	.270	.364	.442	108	7	8-6	.985	-7	91	44	O114(23/0/94),1b14,D7	0	-0.6
2002	†NY A	84	219	30	57	17	1	6	20	23-3	0	58	.260	.327	.429	101	1	1-1	.978	-4	99	0	O57(8/0/49),D16,1b6	0	-0.6
2003	Mil N	117	327	50	84	25	1	14	45	46-3	1	104	.257	.350	.468	112	6	1-2	.984	2	110	75	O89(6/0/83)	0	0.4
2004	Cin N	42	51	2	6	2	0	2	4	4-0	0	20	.118	.182	.275	16	-7	0-0	1.000	1	123	315	O7R,1b4	0	-0.6
Total	14	1372	2751	374	717	170	18	97	430	385-32	8	698	.261	.351	.441	102	20	38-20	.982	-19	100	61	O587(238/2/353),1b178,D32	0	-3.1
Van Dusen, Fred	Frederick William; B7.31.1937 Jackson Heights NY; BL/TL/6´3˝/180; d9.11																								
1955	Phi N	1	0	0	0	0	0	0	0	0-0	1	0	ø	1.000	ø	199	0	0-0	ø	0	—	—	/H	0	0.0
Van Dyke, Bill	William Jennings; B12.15.1863 Paris IL; D5.5.1933 El Paso TX; BR/TR/5´8˝/170; d4.17																								
1890	Tol AA	129	502	74	129	14	11	2	54	25	3	—	.257	.296	.341	85	-13	73	.924	-6	80	0	O110(109/1/0),3b18,2b2/C	—	-1.9
1892	StL N	4	16	2	2	0	0	0	1	0	0	1	.125	.125	.125	-26	-2	0	.875	-1	0	0	O4C	—	-0.3
1893	Bos N	3	12	2	3	1	0	0	1	0	0	1	.250	.250	.333	50	-1	1	1.000	-0	0	0	O3L	—	-0.1
Total	3	136	530	78	134	15	11	2	56	25	3	2	.253	.290	.334	81	-16	74	.924	-7	76	0	O117(112/5/0),3b18,2b2/C	—	-2.3
Van Gorder, Dave	David Thomas; B3.27.1957 Los Angeles CA; BR/TR/6´2˝/205; [CinN78 2/43]; d6.15; Col USC																								
1982	Cin N	51	137	4	25	3	1	0	7	14-2	1	19	.182	.263	.219	36	-12	1-0	.986	-8	78	49	C51	0	-1.9
1984	Cin N	38	101	10	23	2	0	0	6	12-2	0	17	.228	.310	.248	56	-6	0-0	1.000	-1	97	67	C36/1	0	-0.6
1985	Cin N	73	151	12	36	7	0	2	24	9-2	1	19	.238	.280	.325	67	-7	0-0	.989	-8	111	61	C70	15	-1.3
1986	Cin N	9	10	0	0	0	0	0	0	1-0	0	2	.000	.091	.000	-70	-2	0-0	1.000	0	135	0	C7	42	-0.2
1987	Bal A	12	21	4	5	0	0	1	1	3-0	0	6	.238	.333	.381	91	0	0-0	.978	-3	55	0	C12	0	-0.3
Total	5	183	420	30	89	12	1	3	38	39-6	2	63	.212	.280	.267	52	-27	1-0	.990	-20	94	53	C176/1	57	-4.3
Van Haltren, George	George Edward Martin "Rip"; B3.30.1866 St.Louis MO; D9.29.1945 Oakland CA; BL/TL/5´11˝/170; d6.27; M1; OF(313/1376/149); ▲																								
1887	Chi N	45	172	30	35	4	0	3	17	15	1	15	.203	.271	.279	47	-13	12	.927	-3	23	131	O27(4/0/23),P20	—	-0.9
1888	Chi N	81	318	46	90	9	14	4	34	22	0	34	.283	.329	.437	133	10	21	.872	0	102	0	O57(47/4/7),P30	—	0.4
1889	Chi N	134	543	126	175	20	10	9	81	82	5	41	.322	.416	.446	133	26	28	.898	-5	98	68	O130(115/15/0),S3/2	—	1.5
1890	Bro P	92	376	84	126	8	9	5	54	41	3	23	.335	.405	.444	119	9	35	.896	4	130	39	O67(6/12/49),P28,S3	—	0.7
1891	Bal AA	**139**	566	136	180	14	15	9	83	71	4	46	.318	.398	.443	139	28	75	.882	-15	146	234	O81(79/0/2),S59,P6,2b2	—	1.1
1892	Bal N	135	556	105	168	20	12	7	57	70	2	34	.302	.382	.419	138	26	49	.850	-2	128	94	O129(16/62/53),P4,3b3,1b2,S2,M	—	1.4
	Pit N	13	55	10	11	2	2	0	5	6	0	0	.200	.279	.309	77	-2	6	.905	-2	56	261	O13C	—	-0.4
	Year	148	611	115	179	22	14	7	62	76	2	34	.293	.373	.409	133	25	55	.854	-4	122	107	O142(16/75/53),P4,3b3,1b2,S2	—	1.0
1893	Pit N	124	529	129	179	14	11	3	79	75	2	25	.338	.422	.423	128	24	37	.869	-11	126	78	O111C,S12,2b2	—	0.5
1894	†NY N	**139**	528	109	175	22	4	7	105	55	4	23	.331	.399	.428	100	1	43	.915	-6	125	96	O139C	—	-1.0
1895	NY N	131	521	113	177	23	19	8	103	57	3	29	.340	.408	.503	137	28	32	.914	-5	134	69	O131C/P	—	1.2
1896	NY N	**133**	562	136	197	18	**21**	5	74	55	2	36	.351	.410	.484	139	31	39	.952	4	139	87	O133C,P2	—	2.3
1897	NY N	130	566	119	186	22	9	3	64	42	1	—	.329	.376	.415	112	9	50	.938	7	**166**	114	O130C	—	0.7
1898	NY N	**156**	654	129	204	28	16	2	68	59	4	—	.312	.372	.413	129	24	36	.917	-8	97	88	O156(17/138/3)	—	0.5
1899	NY N	**152**	607	118	183	22	3	2	58	75	1	—	.301	.379	.357	106	9	31	.932	-0	135	110	O152(23/129/0)	—	-0.1
1900	NY N	**141**	571	114	180	30	7	1	51	50	1	—	.315	.371	.398	118	15	**45**	.939	8	**148**	123	O141C/P	—	1.3
1901	NY N	135	543	82	182	23	6	1	47	51	4	—	.335	.396	.405	138	29	24	.941	5	139	109	O135C/P	—	2.6
1902	NY N	26	96	14	24	1	2	0	7	17	0	—	.250	.363	.302	107	2	6	.929	1	164	108	O26(3/13/10)	—	0.1
1903	NY N	84	280	42	72	6	1	0	28	28	1	—	.257	.327	.286	72	-9	14	.959	-5	31	46	O75(3/70/2)	—	-1.7
Total	17	1990	8043	1642	2544	286	161	69	1015	871	38	306	.316	.386	.418	122	247	583	.915	-33	125	96	O1833C,P93,S79,2b5,3b3,1b2	—	10.2
Vann, John	John Silas; B6.7.1890 Fairland OK; D6.10.1958 Shreveport LA; BR/TR/?/186; d6.11																								
1913	StL N	1	1	0	0	0	0	0	0	0	0	1	.000	.000	.000	-99	0	0	ø	0	—	—	/H	—	0.0
Van Noy, Jay	Jay Lowell; B11.4.1928 Garland UT; BL/TR/6´1˝/200; d6.18; Col Utah St.																								
1951	StL N	6	7	1	0	0	0	0	0	1	0	6	.000	.125	.000	-63	-2	0-0	1.000	0	126	0	/rf	0	-0.2
Van Robays, Maurice	Maurice Rene "Bomber"; B11.15.1914 Detroit MI; D3.1.1965 Detroit MI; BR/TR/6´0.5˝/190; d9.7; Mil 1944–45																								
1939	Pit N	27	105	13	33	9	0	2	16	6	0	10	.314	.351	.457	118	3	0	.919	-2	76	78	O25L/3	—	-0.1
1940	Pit N	145	572	82	156	27	7	11	116	33	3	58	.273	.316	.402	98	-4	2	.963	-5	90	96	O143(137/0/6)/1	—	-1.7
1941	Pit N	129	457	62	129	23	5	4	78	41	1	29	.282	.343	.381	104	2	0	.974	6	108	105	O121L	0	0.2
1942	Pit N	100	328	29	76	13	5	1	46	30	1	24	.232	.298	.311	76	-10	0	.986	4	108	103	O84L	0	-1.1
1943	Pit N	69	236	32	68	17	7	1	35	18	2	19	.288	.344	.432	119	5	0	.940	-3	97	80	O60(15/0/45)	0	-0.1
1946	Pit N	59	146	14	31	5	3	1	12	11	1	15	.212	.272	.308	63	-8	0	.955	-2	95	34	O37(21/3/13),1b2	0	-1.3
Total	6	529	1844	232	493	94	27	20	303	139	8	155	.267	.321	.380	97	-12	2	.966	-2	99	93	O470(403/3/64),1b3/3	0	-4.1
Van Slyke, Andy	Andrew James; B12.21.1960 Utica NY; BL/TR/6´2˝/(190–198); [StLN79 1/6]; d6.17; C1																								
1983	StL N	101	309	51	81	15	5	8	38	46-5	1	64	.262	.357	.421	115	7	21-7	.974	-1	97	99	O69(50/7/23),3b30,1b9	0	0.5
1984	StL N	137	361	45	88	16	4	7	50	63-9	0	71	.244	.354	.368	106	5	28-5	1.000	2	79	133	O81(34/15/35),3b32,1b30	0	0.8
1985	†StL N	146	424	61	110	25	6	13	55	47-6	2	54	.259	.335	.439	116	9	34-6	.996	6	101	160	O142(4/10/133),1b2	0	1.5
1986	StL N	137	418	48	113	23	7	13	61	47-5	1	85	.270	.343	.452	118	10	21-8	.969	8	108	148	O110(1/27/87),1b38	0	1.5
1987	Pit N	157	564	93	165	36	11	21	82	56-4	4	122	.293	.359	.507	125	20	34-8	.988	1	101	118	O150(0/114/37)/1	0	2.3

YEAR	TM LG	G	AB	R	H	2B	3B	HR	RBI	BB-IB	HP	SO	AVG	OBP	SLG	AOPS	ABR	SB-CS	FA	FR	RNG	THR	GAMES AT POSITION	DL	BFW
1988	Pit N★	154	587	101	169	23	**15**	25	100	57-2	1	126	.288	.345	.506	145	31	30-9	.991	5	102	170	O152C	0	4.1
1989	Pit N	130	476	64	113	18	9	9	53	47-3	3	100	.237	.308	.370	97	-3	16-4	.989	4	104	135	O123C,1b2	25	0.2
1990	†Pit N	136	493	67	140	26	6	17	77	66-2	1	89	.284	.367	.465	132	23	14-4	.976	-8	96	82	O133C	0	1.6
1991	†Pit N	138	491	87	130	24	7	17	83	71-1	4	85	.265	.355	.446	127	19	10-3	.996	-11	86	110	O135C	0	0.9
1992	†Pit N★	154	614	103	**199**	**45**	12	14	89	58-4	4	99	.324	.381	.505	151	41	12-3	.989	-3	98	117	O154C	0	4.1
1993	Pit N✳	83	323	42	100	13	4	8	50	24-5	2	40	.310	.357	.449	116	7	11-2	.995	-3	98	48	O78C	73	0.7
1994	Pit N	105	374	41	92	18	3	6	30	52-7	2	72	.246	.340	.358	81	-9	7-0	.992	2	99	170	O99C	0	-0.5
1995	Bal A	17	63	6	10	1	0	3	8	5-1	0	15	.159	.221	.317	37	-6	0-0	.978	1	104	247	O17(0/16/1)	31	-0.5
	Phi N	63	214	26	52	10	2	3	16	28-1	2	41	.243	.333	.350	81	-5	7-0	.984	-1	91	171	O56C	26	-0.4
Total	13	1658	5711	835	1562	293	91	164	792	667-55	27	1063	.274	.349	.443	119	149	245-59	.988	3	98	130	O1499(89/1119/316),1b82,3b62	155	16.8

VAN ZANDT, IKE Charles Isaac; B2.1876 Brooklyn NY; D9.14.1908 Nashua NH; BL/TL; d8.5; ▲

YEAR	TM LG	G	AB	R	H	2B	3B	HR	RBI	BB-IB	HP	SO	AVG	OBP	SLG	AOPS	ABR	SB-CS	FA	FR	RNG	THR	GAMES AT POSITION	DL	BFW
1901	NY N	3	6	1	1	0	0	0	0	0	0	—	.167	.167	.167	-3	-1	0	.333	-1	0	0	P2/lf	—	-0.1
1904	Chi N	3	11	0	0	0	0	0	0	0	0	—	.000	.000	.000	-99	-3	0	1.000	-0	0	0	O3R	—	-0.3
1905	StL A	94	322	31	75	15	1	1	20	7	1	—	.233	.252	.295	77	-9	7	.874	-11	93	0	O75(0/29/45)/P1	—	-2.6
Total	3	100	339	32	76	15	1	1	20	7	1	—	.224	.242	.283	69	-13	7	.868	-13	89	0	O79(1/29/46),P3/1	—	-3.0

VAN ZANT, DICK Richard "Foghorn Dick"; B11.1864 IN; D8.6.1912 Wayne Co. IN; 6´0˝/?; d10.4

YEAR	TM LG	G	AB	R	H	2B	3B	HR	RBI	BB-IB	HP	SO	AVG	OBP	SLG	AOPS	ABR	SB-CS	FA	FR	RNG	THR	GAMES AT POSITION	DL	BFW
1888	Cle AA	10	31	1	8	1	0	0	1	1	1	—	.258	.303	.290	93	0	1	.784	0	122	150	3b10	—	0.0

VARGAS, EDDIE Hediberto (Rodriguez); B2.23.1959 Guanica, PR; BR/TR/6´4˝/205; d9.8; [DL 1983 Pit N 81]

YEAR	TM LG	G	AB	R	H	2B	3B	HR	RBI	BB-IB	HP	SO	AVG	OBP	SLG	AOPS	ABR	SB-CS	FA	FR	RNG	THR	GAMES AT POSITION	DL	BFW
1982	Pit N	8	8	1	3	1	0	0	3	0-0	0	2	.375	.333	.500	136	0	0-0	1.000	-0	69	65	1b5	0	0.0
1984	Pit N	18	31	3	7	2	0	0	2	3-0	0	5	.226	.294	.290	65	-1	0-0	.982	-0	91	115	1b13	0	-0.2
Total	2	26	39	4	10	3	0	0	5	3-0	0	7	.256	.302	.333	80	-1	0-0	.986	-0	86	104	1b18	81	-0.2

VARITEK, JASON Jason Andrew; B4.11.1972 Rochester MN; BB/TR/6´2˝/(210–230); [SeaA94 1/14]; d9.24; Col Georgia Tech

YEAR	TM LG	G	AB	R	H	2B	3B	HR	RBI	BB-IB	HP	SO	AVG	OBP	SLG	AOPS	ABR	SB-CS	FA	FR	RNG	THR	GAMES AT POSITION	DL	BFW
1997	Bos A	1	1	0	1	0	0	0	0	0-0	0	0	1.000	1.000	1.000	415	0	0-0	1.000	0	0	0	/C	0	0.0
1998	†Bos A	86	221	31	56	13	0	7	33	17-1	2	45	.253	.309	.407	83	-6	2-2	.988	-1	88	97	C75,D3	0	-0.3
1999	†Bos A	144	483	70	130	39	2	20	76	46-2	2	85	.269	.330	.482	102	1	1-2	.990	9	69	110	C140,D2	0	1.7
2000	Bos A	139	448	55	111	31	1	10	65	60-3	6	84	.248	.342	.388	83	-10	1-1	.992	-0	71	107	C128/D	0	-0.2
2001	Bos A	51	174	19	51	11	1	7	25	21-3	1	35	.293	.371	.489	124	7	0-0	.996	10	72	122	C50	122	1.9
2002	Bos A	132	467	58	124	27	1	10	61	41-3	7	95	.266	.332	.392	91	-6	4-3	.996	12	82	99	C127/D	0	1.3
2003	†Bos A☆	142	451	63	123	31	1	25	85	51-8	7	106	.273	.351	.512	120	14	3-2	.990	-6	111	79	C137,D4	0	1.5
2004	†Bos A	137	463	67	137	30	1	18	73	62-9	10	126	.296	.390	.482	118	15	10-3	.998	10	82	78	C130/D	0	3.2
2005	†Bos A★	133	470	70	132	30	1	22	70	62-3	3	117	.281	.366	.489	120	15	2-0	.990	-6	104	72	C130	0	1.8
2006	Bos A	103	365	46	87	19	2	12	55	46-7	2	87	.238	.325	.400	85	-8	1-2	.994	-4	113	59	C99	33	-0.5
Total	10	1068	3543	479	952	231	10	131	543	406-39	40	780	.269	.348	.450	103	22	24-15	.993	24	88	90	C1017,D12	155	10.4

VARNER, BUCK Glen Gann; B8.17.1930 Hixson TN; D4.29.2000 Chattanooga TN; BL/TR/5´10˝/170; d9.19

YEAR	TM LG	G	AB	R	H	2B	3B	HR	RBI	BB-IB	HP	SO	AVG	OBP	SLG	AOPS	ABR	SB-CS	FA	FR	RNG	THR	GAMES AT POSITION	DL	BFW
1952	Was A	2	4	0	0	0	0	0	0	1	0	1	.000	.200	.000	-43	-1	0-0	1.000	-0	78	0	/rf	0	-0.1

VARNEY, PETE Richard Fred; B4.10.1949 Roxbury MA; BR/TR/6´3˝/(230–235); [ChiA71 A1/1]; d8.26; Col Harvard

YEAR	TM LG	G	AB	R	H	2B	3B	HR	RBI	BB-IB	HP	SO	AVG	OBP	SLG	AOPS	ABR	SB-CS	FA	FR	RNG	THR	GAMES AT POSITION	DL	BFW
1973	Chi A	5	4	0	0	0	0	0	0	1-0	0	0	.000	.200	.000	-38	-1	0-0	1.000	0	0	0	C5	0	0.0
1974	Chi A	9	28	1	7	0	0	0	2	1-0	0	8	.250	.267	.250	51	-2	0-0	.981	2	245	169	C9	0	0.0
1975	Chi A	36	107	12	29	5	1	2	8	6-1	1	28	.271	.316	.393	98	-1	2-0	.988	-2	101	114	C34,D2	0	0.0
1976	Chi A	14	41	5	10	2	0	3	5	2-0	0	9	.244	.279	.512	128	1	0-0	.988	-1	57	57	C14	0	0.0
	Atl N	5	10	0	1	0	0	0	0	0-0	0	2	.100	.100	.100	-41	-2	0-0	1.000	-1	27	153	C5	0	-0.2
Total	4	69	190	18	47	7	1	5	15	10-1	1	47	.247	.287	.374	87	-5	2-0	.988	-1	106	107	C67,D2	0	-0.2

VARSHO, GARY Gary Andrew; B6.20.1961 Marshfield WI; BL/TR/5´11˝/(185–190); [ChiN82 5/107]; d7.6; C5; Col Wisconsin–Oshkosh

YEAR	TM LG	G	AB	R	H	2B	3B	HR	RBI	BB-IB	HP	SO	AVG	OBP	SLG	AOPS	ABR	SB-CS	FA	FR	RNG	THR	GAMES AT POSITION	DL	BFW
1988	Chi N	46	73	6	20	3	0	0	5	1-0	0	6	.274	.280	.315	68	-3	5-0	.906	-0	116	0	O18(10/0/8)	0	-0.3
1989	Chi N	61	87	10	16	4	2	0	6	4-1	0	13	.184	.220	.276	38	-7	3-0	.929	-1	86	125	O21(17/0/4)	0	-0.8
1990	Chi N	46	48	10	12	4	0	0	1	1-1	0	6	.250	.265	.333	59	-3	2-0	1.000	-0	83	0	O3(2/0/1)	0	-0.2
1991	†Pit N	99	187	23	51	11	2	4	23	19-2	2	34	.273	.344	.417	115	4	9-2	.989	-0	100	67	O54(5/5/45),1b3	0	0.4
1992	†Pit N	103	162	22	36	6	3	4	22	10-1	0	32	.222	.266	.370	79	-5	5-2	.984	-1	101	54	O44(14/2/28)	0	-0.7
1993	Cin N	77	95	8	22	6	0	2	11	9-0	1	19	.232	.302	.358	76	-3	1-0	1.000	0	99	96	O22(13/0/9)	0	-0.3
1994	Pit N	67	82	15	21	6	3	0	5	4-1	2	19	.256	.307	.402	81	-2	0-1	.926	-2	85	0	O36(18/2/18)/1	0	-0.6
1995	Phi N	72	103	7	26	1	1	0	11	7-1	2	17	.252	.310	.282	58	-6	2-0	.939	-0	113	0	O25(9/0/16)	23	-0.7
Total	8	571	837	101	204	41	11	10	84	55-7	7	146	.244	.294	.355	78	-25	27-5	.963	-4	100	52	O223(88/9/129),1b4	23	-3.2

VATCHER, JIM James Ernest; B5.27.1965 Santa Monica CA; BR/TR/5´9˝/(165–175); [PhiN87 20/520]; d5.30; Col Cal St.–Northridge

YEAR	TM LG	G	AB	R	H	2B	3B	HR	RBI	BB-IB	HP	SO	AVG	OBP	SLG	AOPS	ABR	SB-CS	FA	FR	RNG	THR	GAMES AT POSITION	DL	BFW
1990	Phi N	36	46	5	12	1	0	1	4	4-0	0	6	.261	.320	.348	84	-1	0-0	1.000	-1	96	0	O24(12/0/12)	0	-0.2
	Atl N	21	27	2	7	1	1	0	3	1-0	0	9	.259	.286	.370	75	-1	0-0	1.000	-0	129	0	O6(2/0/4)	0	-0.1
	Year	57	73	7	19	2	1	1	7	5-0	0	15	.260	.308	.356	80	-2	0-0	1.000	-0	103	0	O30(14/0/16)	0	-0.3
1991	SD N	17	20	3	4	0	0	0	2	4-0	0	6	.200	.333	.200	52	-1	1-0	.900	-0	76	253	O11(2/0/9)	0	-0.1
1992	SD N	13	16	1	4	1	0	0	2	3-0	0	6	.250	.368	.313	93	0	0-0	1.000	1	95	229	O13(0/1/12)	0	0.0
Total	3	87	109	11	27	3	1	1	11	12-0	0	27	.248	.322	.321	77	-3	1-0	.980	-0	95	117	O54(16/1/37)	0	-0.4

VAUGHAN, GLENN Glenn Edward "Sparky"; B2.16.1944 Compton CA; D12.18.2004 Houston TX; BB/TR/5´11˝/170; d9.20; Col Houston

YEAR	TM LG	G	AB	R	H	2B	3B	HR	RBI	BB-IB	HP	SO	AVG	OBP	SLG	AOPS	ABR	SB-CS	FA	FR	RNG	THR	GAMES AT POSITION	DL	BFW
1963	Hou N	9	30	1	5	0	0	0	0	2-0	0	5	.167	.219	.167	14	-3	1-0	.914	-2	91	25	S9/3	0	-0.5

VAUGHAN, ARKY Joseph Floyd; B3.9.1912 Clifty AR; D8.30.1952 Eagleville CA; BL/TR/5´10.5˝/175; d4.17; HF1985

YEAR	TM LG	G	AB	R	H	2B	3B	HR	RBI	BB-IB	HP	SO	AVG	OBP	SLG	AOPS	ABR	SB-CS	FA	FR	RNG	THR	GAMES AT POSITION	DL	BFW
1932	Pit N	129	497	71	158	15	10	4	61	39	6	26	.318	.375	.412	113	10	10	.934	-16	96	101	S128	—	0.3
1933	Pit N	152	573	85	180	29	**19**	9	97	64	5	23	.314	.388	.478	146	35	3	.945	-10	98	104	S152	—	3.8
1934	Pit N★	149	558	115	186	41	11	12	94	**94**	2	38	.333	**.431**	.511	148	43	10	.952	3	101	91	S149	—	**5.5**
1935	Pit N★	137	499	108	192	34	10	19	99	**97**	7	18	**.385**	**.491**	**.607**	**187**	**69**	4	.950	-9	101	79	S137	—	**6.6**
1936	Pit N☆	**156**	568	**122**	190	30	11	9	78	**118**	5	21	.335	**.453**	.474	146	46	6	.945	-9	97	93	S156	—	4.7
1937	Pit N★	126	469	71	151	17	**17**	5	72	54	2	22	.322	.394	.463	132	21	7	.956	5	100	93	S108,O12L	—	3.2
1938	Pit N☆	148	541	88	174	35	5	7	68	104	2	21	.322	.433	.444	140	38	14	.961	17	108	**118**	S147	—	6.4
1939	Pit N★	152	595	94	182	30	11	6	62	70	6	20	.306	.385	.424	119	18	12	.962	11	**107**	96	S152	—	4.0
1940	Pit N★	**156**	594	**113**	178	40	**15**	7	95	88	3	25	.300	.393	.453	134	31	12	.942	9	**109**	89	S155,3b2	—	**5.1**
1941	Pit N★	106	374	69	118	20	7	6	38	50	2	13	.316	.399	.455	141	21	8	.958	-8	100	77	S97,3b3	0	2.1
1942	Bro N★	128	495	82	137	18	4	2	49	51	3	17	.277	.348	.341	100	1	8	.959	-10	88	89	3b119,S5/2	0	-0.5
1943	Bro N	149	610	**112**	186	39	6	5	66	60	3	13	.305	.370	.413	126	21	**20**	.965	-15	93	89	S99,3b55	0	1.6
1947	†Bro N	64	126	24	41	5	2	2	25	27	0	11	.325	.444	.444	132	7	4	1.000	1	112	0	O22L,3b10	0	0.7
1948	Bro N	65	123	19	30	3	0	3	22	21	0	8	.244	.354	.341	86	-2	0	1.000	2	93	210	O26L,3b8	0	-0.2
Total	14	1817	6622	1173	2103	356	128	96	926	937	46	276	.318	.406	.453	136	359	118	.951	-29	101	95	S1485,3b197,O60L/2	0	43.3

VAUGHN, FRED Frederick Thomas "Muscles"; B10.18.1918 Coalinga CA; D3.2.1964 Near Lake Wales FL; BR/TR/5´10˝/185; d8.20

YEAR	TM LG	G	AB	R	H	2B	3B	HR	RBI	BB-IB	HP	SO	AVG	OBP	SLG	AOPS	ABR	SB-CS	FA	FR	RNG	THR	GAMES AT POSITION	DL	BFW
1944	Was A	30	109	10	28	2	1	1	21	9	1	24	.257	.319	.321	87	-2	2-2	.942	-2	100	90	2b26,3b3	0	-0.3
1945	Was A	80	268	28	63	7	4	1	25	23	1	48	.235	.298	.302	81	-7	0-3	.946	-11	94	84	2b76/S	0	-1.8
Total	2	110	377	38	91	9	5	2	46	32	2	72	.241	.304	.308	83	-9	2-5	.945	-13	96	86	2b102,3b3/S	0	-2.1

VAUGHN, GREG Gregory Lamont; B7.3.1965 Sacramento CA; BR/TR/6´0˝/(193–205); [MilA86 S1/4]; d8.10; Col Miami

YEAR	TM LG	G	AB	R	H	2B	3B	HR	RBI	BB-IB	HP	SO	AVG	OBP	SLG	AOPS	ABR	SB-CS	FA	FR	RNG	THR	GAMES AT POSITION	DL	BFW
1989	Mil A	38	113	18	30	3	0	5	23	13-0	0	23	.265	.336	.425	115	2	4-1	.943	-2	83	90	O24L,D13	0	0.0
1990	Mil A	120	382	51	84	26	2	17	61	33-1	1	91	.220	.280	.432	98	-3	7-4	.967	-1	95	124	O106L,D8	15	-0.7
1991	Mil A	145	542	81	132	24	5	27	98	62-2	1	125	.244	.319	.456	115	9	2-2	.994	6	110	65	O135(134/0/1),D10	0	1.1
1992	Mil A	141	501	77	114	18	2	23	78	60-1	5	123	.228	.313	.409	103	1	15-15	.990	-2	99	65	O131(131/0/1),D7	0	-0.7
1993	Mil A★	154	569	97	152	28	2	30	97	89-14	5	118	.267	.369	.482	128	24	10-7	.986	-1	106	17	O94L,D58	0	1.6
1994	Mil A	95	370	59	94	24	1	19	55	51-6	1	93	.254	.345	.478	104	2	9-5	.982	-3	92	82	O81(81/1/0),D14	19	-0.4
1995	Mil A	108	392	67	88	19	1	17	59	55-3	0	89	.224	.317	.408	83	-10	10-4	ø	0	0	0	D104	0	-1.4
1996	Mil A☆	102	375	78	105	16	0	31	95	58-4	4	99	.280	.378	.571	131	18	5-2	.980	-4	94	72	O100(98/3/0)/D	0	1.0
	†SD N	43	141	20	29	3	1	10	22	24-2	2	31	.206	.329	.454	109	1	4-1	.974	1	109	92	O39L	0	0.2
1997	SD N	120	361	60	78	10	0	18	57	56-1	2	110	.216	.322	.393	92	-4	7-4	.994	0	92	120	O94L,D3	0	-0.7
1998	†SD N★	158	573	112	156	28	4	50	119	79-6	5	121	.272	.363	.597	159	47	11-4	.993	1	100	53	O151L,D4	0	4.2
1999	Cin N	153	550	104	135	20	2	45	118	85-3	3	137	.245	.347	.535	116	11	15-2	.986	1	100	93	O144L,D6	0	0.9

YEAR	TM LG	G	AB	R	H	2B	3B	HR	RBI	BB-IB	HP	SO	AVG	OBP	SLG	AOPS	ABR	SB-CS	FA	FR	RNG	THR	GAMES AT POSITION	DL	BFW
2000	TB A	127	461	83	117	27	1	28	74	80-3	2	128	.254	.365	.499	118	13	8-1	.993	1	95	138	O72L,D52	21	1.0
2001	TB A*	136	485	74	113	25	0	24	82	71-7	3	130	.233	.333	.433	102	2	11-5	.978	6	120	124	D76,O57L	0	0.2
2002	TB A	69	251	28	41	10	2	8	29	41-1	3	82	.163	.286	.315	61	-14	3-2	.987	3	119	110	D38,O31L	70	-1.4
2003	Col N	22	37	8	7	3	0	3	5	8-0	0	13	.189	.326	.514	102	0	0-0	1.000	1	144	0	O7(6/0/1),D3	0	0.1
Total	15	1731	6103	1017	1475	284	23	355	1072	865-54	37	1513	.242	.337	.470	112	99	121-59	.986	7	101	82	O1266(1261/4/3),D397	125	5.0

VAUGHN, FARMER Harry Francis; B3.1.1864 Ruraldale OH; D2.21.1914 Cincinnati OH; BR/TR/6´3˝/177; d10.7; OF(59/14/35)

YEAR	TM LG	G	AB	R	H	2B	3B	HR	RBI	BB-IB	HP	SO	AVG	OBP	SLG	AOPS	ABR	SB-CS	FA	FR	RNG	THR	GAMES AT POSITION	DL	BFW
1886	Cin AA	1	3	0	0	0	0	0	0	0	1	—	.000	.250	.000	-19	0	0	.917	0	—	—	/C	—	0.0
1888	Lou AA	51	189	15	37	4	2	1	21	4	1	—	.196	.216	.254	52	-11	4	.863	-1	95	207	O28(22/1/5),C25	—	-1.0
1889	Lou AA	90	360	39	86	11	5	3	45	7	0	41	.239	.253	.322	65	-19	13	.900	-2	—	—	C54,O20(5/9/4),1b18,3b3	—	-1.6
1890	NY P	44	166	27	44	7	0	1	22	10	0	9	.265	.307	.325	63	-9	6	.877	-8	*99*	*66*	C30,O12(8/1/3)/32	—	-1.2
1891	Cin AA	51	175	21	45	7	1	1	14	14	1	15	.257	.316	.326	77	-6	7	.923	4	*89*	*129*	C44,O6(3/1/2),1b2,3b2/P	—	0.1
	Mil AA	25	99	13	33	7	0	0	9	4	0	5	.333	.359	.404	98	-1	1	.924	5	*120*	*67*	C20,1b4/lf	—	0.4
	Year	76	274	34	78	14	1	1	23	18	1	20	.285	.331	.354	86	-7	8	.923	9	*100*	*107*	C64,O7(4/1/2),1b6,3b2/P	—	0.5
1892	Cin N	91	346	45	88	10	5	2	50	16	4	13	.254	.295	.329	90	-6	10	.929	-6	*118*	*73*	C67,1b14,O11(4/0/7),3b6	—	-0.6
1893	Cin N	121	483	68	135	17	12	1	108	35	3	17	.280	.332	.371	85	-13	16	**.969**	1	*110*	*84*	C80,O23(12/1/10),1b21	—	-0.5
1894	Cin N	72	284	50	88	15	5	8	64	12	0	11	.310	.338	.482	93	-6	5	.918	-3	*98*	*87*	C43,1b27,O8(4/1/3),S3	—	-0.4
1895	Cin N	92	334	60	102	23	5	1	48	17	0	10	.305	.339	.413	90	-6	15	.934	10	*102*	*107*	C77,1b15/32	—	0.9
1896	Cin N	114	433	71	127	20	9	2	66	16	1	7	.293	.320	.395	82	-14	7	.984	12	98	114	1b57,C57	—	0.3
1897	Cin N	54	199	21	58	13	5	0	30	2	0	—	.291	.299	.407	80	-7	2	.986	1	85	101	1b35,C15	—	-0.4
1898	Cin N	78	275	35	84	12	4	1	46	11	3	—	.305	.339	.389	101	-1	4	.979	0	51	111	1b39,C33	—	0.3
1899	Cin N	31	108	9	19	1	0	0	2	3	0	—	.176	.198	.185	5	-14	2	.982	3	124	82	1b21,C7/rf	—	-1.0
Total	13	915	3454	474	946	147	53	21	525	151	14	128	.274	.307	.365	80	-113	92	.926	17	*117*	*91*	C553,1b253,O110L,3b13,S3,2b2/P	—	-4.7

VAUGHN, MO Maurice Samuel; B12.15.1967 Norwalk CT; BL/TR/6´1˝/(225–268); [BosA89 1/23]; d6.27; Col Seton Hall; [DL 2001 Ana A 190, 2004 NY N 183]

YEAR	TM LG	G	AB	R	H	2B	3B	HR	RBI	BB-IB	HP	SO	AVG	OBP	SLG	AOPS	ABR	SB-CS	FA	FR	RNG	THR	GAMES AT POSITION	DL	BFW
1991	Bos A	74	219	21	57	12	0	4	32	26-2	2	43	.260	.339	.370	92	-1	2-1	.985	-1	93	127	1b49,D16	0	-0.6
1992	Bos A	113	355	42	83	16	2	13	57	47-7	3	67	.234	.326	.400	96	-2	3-3	.982	-1	102	108	1b85,D20	0	-1.0
1993	Bos A	152	539	86	160	34	1	29	101	79-23	8	130	.297	.390	.525	136	30	4-3	.987	-11	75	98	1b131,D19	0	0.6
1994	Bos A	111	394	65	122	25	1	26	82	57-**20**	10	112	.310	.408	.576	144	27	4-4	.989	-5	82	112	1b106/D	0	1.1
1995	†Bos A★	140	550	98	165	28	3	39	**126**	68-17	14	150	.300	.388	.575	143	35	11-4	.992	-3	94	106	1b138,D2	0	1.9
1996	Bos A★	161	635	118	207	29	1	44	143	95-19	14	154	.326	.420	.583	149	50	2-0	.988	-12	71	86	1b146,D15	0	2.3
1997	Bos A	141	527	91	166	24	0	35	96	86-17	12	154	.315	.420	.560	150	42	2-2	.988	-7	85	99	1b131,D9	23	2.3
1998	†Bos A*	154	609	107	205	31	2	40	115	61-13	8	144	.337	.402	.591	151	46	0-0	.991	-4	90	83	1b142,D12	0	2.7
1999	Ana A	139	524	63	147	20	0	33	108	54-7	11	127	.281	.358	.508	118	13	0-0	.995	-2	88	102	1b72,D67	15	0.2
2000	Ana A	161	614	93	167	31	0	36	117	79-11	14	181	.272	.365	.498	113	13	2-0	.990	-12	74	**120**	1b147,D14	0	-1.2
2002	NY N	139	487	67	126	18	0	26	72	59-6	10	145	.259	.349	.456	117	11	0-1	.984	-15	59	89	1b134	15	-1.5
2003	NY N	27	79	10	15	2	0	3	15	14-2	2	22	.190	.323	.329	75	-3	0-0	.974	-3	64	117	1b24	149	-0.7
Total	12	1512	5532	861	1620	270	10	328	1064	725-144	108	1429	.293	.383	.523	131	261	30-18	.988	-74	81	101	1b1305,D175	575	6.1

VAUGHN, BOBBY Robert; B6.4.1885 Stamford NY; D4.11.1965 Seattle WA; BR/TR/5´9˝/150; d6.12; Col Princeton

YEAR	TM LG	G	AB	R	H	2B	3B	HR	RBI	BB-IB	HP	SO	AVG	OBP	SLG	AOPS	ABR	SB-CS	FA	FR	RNG	THR	GAMES AT POSITION	DL	BFW
1909	NY A	5	14	1	2	0	0	0	0	1	0	—	.143	.200	.143	8	-1	1	.882	-3	46	0	2b4/S	—	-0.5
1915	StL F	144	521	69	146	19	9	0	32	58	3	38	.280	.356	.351	94	-10	24	.953	-7	97	94	2b127,S12,3b8	—	-1.5
Total	2	149	535	70	148	19	9	0	32	59	3	38	.277	.352	.346	92	-11	25	.951	-10	96	91	2b131,S13,3b8	—	-2.0

VAZQUEZ, RAMON Ramon Luis; B8.21.1976 Aibonito, PR; BL/TR/5´11˝/170; [SeaA95 27/734]; d9.7; Col Indian Hills (IA) CC

YEAR	TM LG	G	AB	R	H	2B	3B	HR	RBI	BB-IB	HP	SO	AVG	OBP	SLG	AOPS	ABR	SB-CS	FA	FR	RNG	THR	GAMES AT POSITION	DL	BFW
2001	†Sea A	17	35	5	8	0	0	0	4	0-0	0	3	.229	.222	.229	22	-4	0-0	1.000	-5	56	99	S10,2b6,3b2	0	-0.8
2002	SD N	128	423	50	116	21	5	2	32	45-3	1	79	.274	.344	.362	95	-3	7-2	.985	9	102	99	2b81,S41,3b20	0	1.2
2003	SD N	116	422	56	110	17	4	3	30	52-2	2	88	.261	.342	.341	88	-7	10-3	.969	-13	92	85	S108,3b4,2b3	36	-1.0
2004	SD N	52	115	12	27	3	2	1	13	11-2	0	24	.235	.297	.322	65	-6	1-1	.983	-6	79	56	S22,2b10,3b9,1b3	31	-1.1
2005	Bos A	27	61	6	12	2	0	0	4	3-0	0	14	.197	.234	.230	23	-7	0-0	.969	-5	66	56	S12,3b8,2b4/D	0	-1.0
	Cle A	12	24	1	6	3	0	0	1	2-0	0	3	.250	.308	.375	83	0	0-0	1.000	-0	68	163	2b8,S2	0	0.0
	Year	39	85	7	18	5	0	0	5	5-0	0	17	.212	.256	.271	40	-7	0-0	.974	-5	70	63	S14,2b12,3b8/D	0	-1.0
2006	Cle A	34	67	11	14	2	0	1	8	6-0	0	18	.209	.267	.284	47	-5	0-0	.960	0	89	44	3b14,2b7,S7	0	-0.4
Total	6	386	1147	141	293	48	11	7	92	119-7	3	229	.255	.324	.335	80	-32	18-6	.971	-18	93	81	S202,2b119,3b57,1b3/D	67	-3.1

VEACH, BOBBY Robert Hayes; B6.29.1888 St.Charles KY; D8.7.1945 Detroit MI; BL/TR/5´11˝/160; d9.6

YEAR	TM LG	G	AB	R	H	2B	3B	HR	RBI	BB-IB	HP	SO	AVG	OBP	SLG	AOPS	ABR	SB-CS	FA	FR	RNG	THR	GAMES AT POSITION	DL	BFW
1912	Det A	23	79	8	27	5	1	0	15	5	1	—	.342	.388	.430	138	4	2	.927	1	97	161	O22L	—	0.4
1913	Det A	137	491	54	132	22	10	0	64	53	5	31	.269	.346	.354	107	5	22	.917	-5	98	86	O135L	—	-0.7
1914	Det A	149	531	56	146	19	14	1	72	50	3	29	.275	.341	.369	110	5	20-20	.965	3	100	103	O145L	—	-0.1
1915	Det A	152	569	81	178	**40**	10	3	**112**	68	4	43	.313	.390	.434	140	29	16-19	.975	2	100	97	O152L	—	2.2
1916	Det A	150	566	92	173	33	15	3	91	52	3	41	.306	.367	.433	135	23	24-15	.967	3	109	70	O150L	—	2.1
1917	Det A	**154**	571	79	182	31	12	8	**103**	61	**9**	44	.319	.393	.457	160	41	21	.956	2	111	77	O154L	—	4.0
1918	Det A	127	499	59	139	21	13	3	**78**	35	4	23	.279	.331	.391	123	11	21	.977	2	107	83	O127(124/1/2)/P	—	0.8
1919	Det A	139	538	87	**191**	**45**	**17**	3	101	33	5	33	.355	.398	.519	160	41	19	.967	9	**117**	95	O138L	—	4.5
1920	Det A	154	612	92	188	39	15	11	113	36	7	22	.307	.353	.474	121	15	11-7	.967	14	112	129	O154L	—	2.1
1921	Det A	150	612	110	207	43	13	16	128	48	1	31	.338	.387	.529	133	29	14-10	.974	13	**115**	108	O149L	—	2.7
1922	Det A	**155**	618	96	202	34	13	9	126	42	8	27	.327	.377	.468	123	20	9-1	.982	10	**116**	84	O154L	—	1.8
1923	Det A	114	293	45	94	13	3	2	39	29	3	21	.321	.388	.406	111	5	10-3	.943	-6	88	72	O85(46/13/26)	—	-0.4
1924	Bos A	142	519	77	153	35	9	5	99	47	5	18	.295	.359	.426	102	1	5-5	.956	-4	97	82	O130L	—	-1.3
1925	Bos A	1	5	0	1	0	0	0	2	1	0	1	.200	.333	.200	38	0	0-0	1.000	-0	101	0	/lf	—	-0.1
	NY A	56	116	13	41	10	2	0	15	8	1	0	.353	.400	.474	123	4	1-4	.957	2	87	253	O33(13/0/30)	—	0.3
	†Was A	18	37	4	9	3	0	0	8	3	0	3	.243	.300	.324	60	-2	0-0	.923	-1	90	0	O11(4/0/7)	—	-0.4
	Year	75	158	17	51	13	2	0	25	12	1	4	.323	.374	.430	106	1	1-4	.952	1	88	186	O45(18/0/37)	—	-0.2
Total	14	1821	6656	953	2063	393	147	64	1166	571	59	367	.310	.370	.442	127	231	195-84	.964	43	106	94	O1740(1671/14/65)/P	—	17.9

VEACH, PEEK-A-BOO William Walter; B6.15.1862 Indianapolis IN; D11.12.1937 Indianapolis IN; 6´0˝/175; d8.24; ▲

YEAR	TM LG	G	AB	R	H	2B	3B	HR	RBI	BB-IB	HP	SO	AVG	OBP	SLG	AOPS	ABR	SB-CS	FA	FR	RNG	THR	GAMES AT POSITION	DL	BFW
1884	KC U	27	82	9	11	1	0	1	—	9	—	—	.134	.220	.183	27	-10	—	.833	2	150	268	O14(11/2/1),P12/21	—	-0.3
1887	Lou AA	1	3	0	0	0	0	0	0	1	0	—	.000	.250	.000	-26	0	0	.750	-0	55	0	/P	—	0.0
1890	Cle N	64	238	24	56	10	5	0	32	33	3	28	.235	.336	.319	93	-1	9	.971	6	184	105	1b64	—	0.0
	Pit N	8	30	6	9	1	1	2	5	8	0	3	.300	.447	.600	231	6	0	.968	0	136	17	1b8	—	0.4
	Year	72	268	30	65	11	6	2	37	41	3	31	.243	.349	.351	107	4	9	.971	7	178	95	1b72	—	0.4
Total	3	100	353	39	76	12	6	3	37	51	3	31	.215	.319	.309	90	-5	9	.971	8	175	93	1b73,O14(11/2/1),P13/2	—	0.1

VEAL, COOT Orville Inman; B7.9.1932 Sandersville GA; BR/TR/6´1˝/(160–165); d7.30; Col Auburn

YEAR	TM LG	G	AB	R	H	2B	3B	HR	RBI	BB-IB	HP	SO	AVG	OBP	SLG	AOPS	ABR	SB-CS	FA	FR	RNG	THR	GAMES AT POSITION	DL	BFW
1958	Det A	58	207	29	53	10	2	0	16	14-0	1	21	.256	.304	.324	69	-9	1-1	.981	-5	93	82	S58	0	-0.9
1959	Det A	77	89	12	18	1	0	1	15	8-1	1	7	.202	.273	.247	42	-7	0-0	.962	-1	95	83	S72	0	-0.5
1960	Det A	27	64	8	19	5	1	0	8	11-0	0	7	.297	.400	.406	115	2	0-0	.988	-3	97	92	S22,3b3/2	0	0.0
1961	Was A	69	218	21	44	10	0	0	8	19-0	3	29	.202	.273	.248	41	-18	1-8	.974	5	103	116	S63	0	-1.0
1962	Pit N	1	1	0	0	0	0	0	0	0-0	0	1	.000	.000	.000	-99	0	0-0	ø	0	—	—	/H	0	0.0
1963	Det A	15	32	5	7	0	0	0	4	4-0	0	4	.219	.297	.219	48	-2	0-0	.980	2	126	19	S12	0	0.0
Total	6	247	611	75	141	26	3	1	51	56-1	5	69	.231	.298	.288	59	-34	2-9	.976	-1	99	91	S227,3b3/2	0	-2.4

VEGA, JESUS Jesus Anthony (Morales); B10.14.1955 Bayamon, PR; BR/TR/6´1˝/(176–190); d9.5

YEAR	TM LG	G	AB	R	H	2B	3B	HR	RBI	BB-IB	HP	SO	AVG	OBP	SLG	AOPS	ABR	SB-CS	FA	FR	RNG	THR	GAMES AT POSITION	DL	BFW
1979	Min A	4	7	0	0	0	0	0	0	0-0	0	2	.000	.000	.000	-96	-2	0-0	ø	0	—	—	D3	0	-0.2
1980	Min A	12	30	3	5	0	0	0	4	3-0	0	7	.167	.242	.167	13	-4	1-0	1.000	0	697	0	1b2,D9	0	-0.3
1982	Min A	71	199	23	53	6	0	5	29	8-1	0	19	.266	.289	.372	79	-6	6-1	.974	-2	78	63	D39,1b18/lf	0	-0.9
Total	3	87	236	26	58	6	0	5	33	11-1	0	28	.246	.275	.335	65	-12	7-1	.975	-1	87	62	D51,1b20/lf	0	-1.4

VELANDIA, JORGE Jorge Luis (Macias); B1.12.1975 Caracas, Distrito Capital, Venez.; BR/TR/5´9˝/(160–185); d6.20

YEAR	TM LG	G	AB	R	H	2B	3B	HR	RBI	BB-IB	HP	SO	AVG	OBP	SLG	AOPS	ABR	SB-CS	FA	FR	RNG	THR	GAMES AT POSITION	DL	BFW
1997	SD N	14	29	0	3	2	0	0	0	1-0	0	7	.103	.133	.172	-22	-5	0-0	.941	-2	92	139	S6,2b5,3b3	0	-0.6
1998	Oak A	8	4	0	1	0	0	0	0	0-0	0	1	.250	.250	.250	31	0	0-0	.909	1	173	112	S7/2	0	0.1
1999	Oak A	63	48	4	9	1	0	0	2	2-0	1	13	.188	.235	.208	15	-6	2-0	.989	8	118	119	2b52,S8,3b2/D	58	0.3
2000	Oak A	18	24	1	3	1	0	0	2	0-0	1	6	.125	.160	.167	-17	-4	0-0	1.000	1	111	124	2b14,S4	0	-0.2
	NY N	15	7	1	0	0	0	0	0	2-0	0	2	.000	.222	.000	-39	-2	0-0	1.000	-2	35	0	2b7,S7,3b3	0	-0.3
2001	NY N	9	9	1	0	0	0	0	0	2-0	0	1	.000	.182	.000	-50	-2	0-0	1.000	-2	77	100	S8/3	71	-0.3

YEAR	TM LG	G	AB	R	H	2B	3B	HR	RBI	BB-IB	HP	SO	AVG	OBP	SLG	AOPS	ABR	SB-CS	FA	FR	RNG	THR	GAMES AT POSITION	DL	BFW
2003	NY N	23	58	6	11	3	1	0	8	10-1	0	15	.190	.304	.276	56	-4	0-0	.972	3	110	96	S23	0	0.1
Total	6	150	179	13	27	7	1	0	12	17-1	2	45	.151	.231	.201	14	-23	2-0	.987	8	108	104	2b79,S63,3b9/D	129	-0.9
VELARDE, RANDY	Randy Lee; B11.24.1962 Midland TX; BR/TR/6´0˝/(183–200); [ChiA85 19/475]; d8.20; Col Lubbock Christian; OF(97/4/12)																								
1987	NY A	8	22	1	4	0	0	0	1	0-0	0	6	.182	.182	.182	-3	-3	0-0	.933	-1	100	76	S8	0	-0.4
1988	NY A	48	115	18	20	6	0	5	12	8-0	2	24	.174	.240	.357	65	-6	1-1	.967	3	109	168	2b24,S14,3b11	0	-0.2
1989	NY A	33	100	12	34	4	2	2	11	7-0	1	14	.340	.389	.480	145	6	0-3	.954	-0	87	154	3b27,S9	20	0.5
1990	NY A	95	229	21	48	6	2	5	19	20-0	1	53	.210	.275	.319	65	-11	0-3	.945	8	113	105	3b74,S15,O5L,2b3,D3	0	-0.3
1991	NY A	80	184	19	45	11	1	1	15	18-0	3	43	.245	.322	.332	81	-4	3-1	.935	10	118	114	3b50,S31,O2L	0	0.8
1992	NY A	121	412	57	112	24	1	7	46	38-1	2	78	.272	.333	.386	102	1	7-2	.974	-1	103	91	S75,3b26,O23(14/2/7),2b3	0	0.6
1993	NY A	85	226	28	68	13	2	7	24	18-2	4	39	.301	.360	.469	125	8	2-2	.932	1	101	103	O50(48/2/0),S26,3b16/D	54	0.9
1994	NY A	77	280	47	78	16	1	9	34	22-0	4	61	.279	.338	.439	103	1	4-2	.944	2	107	116	S49,3b27,O7(6/0/1),2b5	0	0.5
1995	†NY A	111	367	60	102	19	1	7	46	55-0	4	64	.278	.375	.392	102	3	5-1	.976	-2	89	72	2b62,S28,O20(20/0/1),3b19	0	0.6
1996	Cal A	136	530	82	151	27	3	14	54	70-0	5	118	.285	.372	.426	100	2	7-7	.982	-17	81	99	2b114,3b28,S7	0	-1.0
1997	Ana A	1	0	0	0	0	0	0	0	0-0	0	0	ø	ø	ø	ø	0	0-0	ø	0	—	—	/R	175	0.0
1998	Ana A	51	188	29	49	13	1	4	26	34-0	1	42	.261	.375	.404	101	2	7-2	.982	-4	95	79	2b51	123	0.1
1999	Ana A	95	376	57	115	15	4	9	48	43-1	4	56	.306	.383	.439	109	6	13-4	.986	6	110	94	2b95	0	1.6
	Oak A	61	255	48	85	10	3	7	28	27-1	2	42	.333	.401	.478	127	11	11-4	.977	-3	100	102	2b61	0	1.0
	Year	156	631	105	200	25	7	16	76	70-2	6	98	.317	.390	.455	116	17	24-8	.983	2	106	97	2b156	0	2.6
2000	†Oak A	122	485	82	135	23	0	12	41	54-0	3	95	.278	.354	.400	92	-5	9-3	.982	**22**	**115**	111	2b122	34	2.1
2001	Tex A	78	296	46	88	16	2	9	31	29-0	5	73	.297	.369	.456	113	6	4-2	.988	0	100	109	2b52,1b9,3b7,O2R,D6	48	0.8
	†NY A	15	46	4	7	3	0	0	1	5-0	3	13	.152	.278	.217	33	-4	2-0	.952	2	135	106	3b7,O3(2/0/1)/1D	0	-0.2
	Year	93	342	50	95	19	2	9	32	34-0	8	86	.278	.356	.424	102	2	6-2	.988	3	100	109	2b52,3b14,D11,1b10,O5(2/0/3)	0	0.6
2002	†Oak A	56	133	22	30	8	0	2	8	15-1	5	32	.226	.325	.331	76	-4	3-0	.981	4	108	121	2b38,1b5/3D	29	0.2
Total	16	1273	4244	633	1171	214	23	100	445	463-6	49	853	.276	.352	.408	100	9	78-37	.980	31	101	102	2b630,3b293,S262,O112L,D20,1b15	483	7.6
VELASQUEZ, GUILLERMO	Guillermo (Burgara); B4.23.1968 Mexicali, Baja California, Mexico; BL/TR/6´3˝/(220–225); d9.14																								
1992	SD N	15	23	1	7	0	0	1	5	1-0	0	7	.304	.333	.435	114	0	0-0	.933	-0	82	83	1b3,O2L	0	0.0
1993	SD N	79	143	7	30	2	0	3	20	13-2	0	35	.210	.274	.287	50	-10	0-0	.984	-1	99	91	1b38,O6(4/0/2)	0	-1.4
Total	2	94	166	8	37	2	0	4	25	14-2	0	42	.223	.282	.307	59	-10	0-0	.981	-1	98	91	1b41,O8(6/0/2)	0	-1.4
VELAZQUEZ, FREDDIE	Federico Antonio (Velasquez); B12.6.1937 Santo Domingo, D.R.; BR/TR/6´1˝/185; d4.20																								
1969	Sea A	6	16	1	2	2	0	0	2	1-0	0	3	.125	.176	.250	18	-2	0-0	1.000	-2	40	0	C5	0	-0.3
1973	Atl N	15	23	2	8	1	0	0	3	1-0	0	3	.348	.375	.391	105	0	0-0	.975	1	146	60	C11	0	0.1
Total	2	21	39	3	10	3	0	0	5	2-0	0	6	.256	.293	.333	71	-2	0-0	.985	-1	102	35	C16	0	-0.2
VELEZ, OTTO	Otoniel (Franceschi); B11.29.1950 Ponce, PR; BR/TR/6´0˝/(170–195); d9.4																								
1973	NY A	23	77	9	15	4	0	2	7	15-0	0	24	.195	.326	.325	86	-1	0-1	.959	-0	99	128	O23R	0	-0.3
1974	NY A	27	67	9	14	1	1	2	10	15-1	0	24	.209	.345	.343	102	1	0-0	.986	-3	48	54	1b21,O3R,3b2	0	-0.4
1975	NY A	6	8	0	2	0	0	0	1	2-0	0	0	.250	.400	.250	88	0	0-0	1.000	-0	0	124	/1D	0	0.0
1976	†NY A	49	94	11	25	6	0	2	10	23-1	0	26	.266	.410	.394	137	6	0-0	.979	-1	107	66	O24(6/0/19),1b8/3D	0	0.4
1977	Tor A	120	360	50	92	19	3	16	62	65-1	1	87	.256	.366	.458	123	14	4-2	.973	0	100	98	O79R,D28	0	0.9
1978	Tor A	91	248	29	66	14	2	9	38	45-1	2	41	.266	.380	.448	130	12	1-3	.982	9	112	220	O74(39/0/39)/1D	0	1.7
1979	Tor A	99	274	45	79	21	0	15	48	46-2	3	45	.288	.396	.529	145	19	0-1	.971	-1	102	65	O73(43/0/34),1b6,D9	0	1.5
1980	Tor A	104	357	54	96	12	3	20	62	54-8	2	86	.269	.365	.487	127	14	0-0	.975	0	118	55	D97,1b3	38	1.1
1981	Tor A	80	240	32	51	9	2	11	28	55-3	3	60	.213	.363	.404	115	7	0-3	1.000	-0	0	0	D74/1	0	0.3
1982	Tor A	28	52	4	10	1	0	1	5	13-0	0	15	.192	.354	.269	68	-2	1-0	ø	0	0	0	D24	31	-0.2
1983	Cle A	10	25	1	2	0	0	0	1	3-0	0	6	.080	.179	.080	-25	-4	0-0	ø	0	—	—	D8	0	-0.5
Total	11	637	1802	244	452	87	11	78	272	336-17	11	414	.251	.369	.441	122	66	6-10	.973	3	104	122	O276(88/0/197),D255,1b41,3b3	69	4.5
VELTMAN, PAT	Arthur Patrick; B3.24.1906 Mobile AL; D10.1.1980 San Antonio TX; BR/TR/6´0˝/175; d4.17																								
1926	Chi A	5	4	1	1	0	0	0	0	1	0	1	.250	.400	.250	75	0	0-0	1.000	0	151	0	/S	—	0.0
1928	NY N	1	3	1	1	0	1	0	0	1	0	0	.333	.500	1.000	282	1	0	1.000	-0	95	0	/cf	—	0.1
1929	NY N	2	1	1	0	0	0	0	0	2	0	0	.000	.667	.000	81	0	0	1.000	-0	*0*	*0*	/C	—	0.0
1931	Bos N	1	1	0	0	0	0	0	0	0	0	0	.000	.000	.000	-99	0	0	ø	0	—	—	/H	—	0.0
1932	NY N	2	1	0	0	0	0	0	0	0	0	1	.000	.000	.000	-99	0	0	ø	0	—	—	/H	—	0.0
1934	Pit N	12	28	1	3	0	0	0	2	0	0	1	.107	.107	.107	-41	-6	0	1.000	-1	*65*	*0*	C11	—	-0.6
Total	6	23	38	4	5	0	1	0	2	4	0	3	.132	.214	.184	7	-5	0-0	1.000	-1	*62*	*0*	C12/cfS	—	-0.5
VENABLE, MAX	William McKinley; B6.6.1957 Phoenix AZ; BL/TR/5´10˝/(180–193); [LAN76 3/67]; d4.8																								
1979	SF N	55	85	12	14	1	1	0	3	10-1	1	18	.165	.260	.200	29	-8	3-3	.914	-2	78	127	O25(6/2/21)	0	-1.2
1980	SF N	64	138	13	37	5	0	0	10	15-0	0	22	.268	.333	.304	84	-2	8-2	1.000	-3	94	0	O40(16/14/11)	0	-0.5
1981	SF N	18	32	2	6	0	2	0	1	4-0	0	3	.188	.278	.313	69	-2	3-1	1.000	-0	102	0	O5(0/2/3)	0	-0.2
1982	SF N	71	125	17	28	2	1	1	7	7-0	0	16	.224	.265	.280	53	-8	9-3	.986	4	102	258	O53(33/12/8)	41	-0.5
1983	SF N	94	228	28	50	7	4	6	27	22-1	3	34	.219	.295	.364	84	-6	15-2	.993	6	117	139	O66(32/25/14)	0	0.1
1984	Mon N	38	71	7	17	2	0	2	7	3-1	1	7	.239	.276	.352	80	-2	1-0	1.000	-0	107	0	O27(23/3/3)	0	-0.3
1985	Cin N	77	135	21	39	12	3	0	10	6-0	0	17	.289	.315	.422	100	0	11-3	1.000	3	116	157	O39(31/7/3)	0	0.3
1986	Cin N	108	147	17	31	7	1	2	15	17-2	0	24	.211	.289	.313	65	-7	7-2	.969	-0	111	0	O57(49/8/3)	0	-0.8
1987	Cin N	7	7	2	1	0	0	0	2	0-0	0	0	.143	.143	.143	-23	-1	0-0	1.000	-0	72	0	O4C	0	-0.2
1989	Cal A	20	53	7	19	4	0	0	4	1-0	0	16	.358	.370	.434	128	2	0-0	1.000	-1	86	0	O13(4/4/7)	0	0.0
1990	Cal A	93	189	26	49	9	3	4	21	24-2	0	31	.259	.340	.402	109	3	5-1	.975	-1	96	101	O77(40/33/10)/D	0	0.1
1991	Cal A	82	187	24	46	8	2	3	21	11-2	2	30	.246	.292	.358	80	-6	2-1	.967	-5	76	101	O65(13/27/30),D3	0	-1.2
Total	12	727	1397	176	337	57	17	18	128	120-9	7	218	.241	.302	.345	81	-37	64-18	.982	-1	99	100	O471(247/141/113),D4	41	-4.4
VENTO, MIKE	Michael; B5.25.1978 Albuquerque NM; BR/TR/6´0˝/195; [NYA97 40/1219]; d9.13; Col San Ana (CA) JC																								
2005	NY A	2	2	0	0	0	0	0	0	0-0	0	1	.000	.000	.000	-99	-1	0-0	1.000	1	125	2139	O2R	0	0.0
2006	Was N	9	18	3	5	1	0	0	1	4-1	0	5	.278	.409	.333	98	0	0-0	1.000	0	115	0	O8R	0	0.0
Total	2	11	20	3	5	1	0	0	1	4-1	0	6	.250	.375	.300	80	-1	0-0	1.000	1	116	267	O10R	0	0.0
VENTURA, ROBIN	Robin Mark; B7.14.1967 Santa Maria CA; BL/TR/6´1˝/(185–200); [ChiA88 1/10]; d9.12; Col Oklahoma St.																								
1989	Chi A	16	45	5	8	3	0	0	7	8-0	1	6	.178	.298	.244	61	-2	0-0	.962	2	110	73	3b16	0	0.0
1990	Chi A	150	493	48	123	17	1	5	54	55-2	1	53	.249	.324	.318	83	-11	1-4	.939	3	100	**133**	3b147/1	0	-0.8
1991	Chi A	157	606	92	172	25	1	23	100	80-3	4	67	.284	.367	.442	126	24	2-4	.959	1	99	111	3b151,1b31	0	2.3
1992	Chi A★	157	592	85	167	38	1	16	93	93-9	0	71	.282	.375	.431	127	25	2-4	.957	26	**119**	106	3b157,1b2	0	**5.1**
1993	†Chi A	157	554	85	145	27	1	22	94	105-16	3	82	.262	.379	.433	121	20	1-6	.965	-2	97	97	3b155,1b4	0	1.7
1994	Chi A	109	401	57	113	15	1	18	78	61-15	2	69	.282	.373	.459	116	11	3-1	.935	-3	90	**143**	3b108,1b3/S	0	0.8
1995	Chi A	135	492	79	145	22	0	26	93	75-11	1	98	.295	.384	.498	134	26	4-3	.948	-0	94	70	3b121,1b18/D	0	2.4
1996	Chi A	158	586	96	168	31	2	34	105	78-10	2	81	.287	.368	.520	128	25	1-3	.974	3	93	**132**	3b150,1b14	0	2.5
1997	Chi A	54	183	27	48	10	1	6	26	34-5	0	21	.262	.373	.426	113	5	0-0	.956	3	101	120	3b54	114	0.8
1998	Chi A	161	590	84	155	31	4	21	91	79-**15**	1	111	.263	.349	.436	105	5	1-1	.966	14	**112**	**154**	3b161	0	1.8
1999	†NY N	161	588	88	177	38	0	32	120	74-10	3	109	.301	.379	.529	133	31	1-1	**.980**	19	107	**137**	3b160/1	0	4.6
2000	†NY N	141	469	61	109	23	1	24	84	75-12	2	91	.232	.338	.439	100	0	3-5	.954	5	99	122	3b137/1	14	0.4
2001	NY N	142	456	70	108	20	0	21	61	88-10	1	101	.237	.359	.419	108	8	2-5	.957	9	105	117	3b139	0	1.6
2002	†NY A★	141	465	68	115	17	0	27	93	90-9	2	101	.247	.368	.458	120	16	3-1	.941	11	105	109	3b137,1b5	0	2.6
2003	NY A	89	283	31	71	13	0	9	42	40-2	0	62	.251	.344	.392	95	-1	0-0	.974	-0	100	74	3b80/2D	0	-0.1
	LA N	49	109	11	24	5	1	5	13	18-2	0	25	.220	.331	.422	97	-1	0-0	.993	-2	92	118	1b42,3b3	0	-0.5
2004	†LA N	102	152	19	37	3	0	5	28	22-1	0	31	.243	.337	.362	83	-4	0-0	1.000	1	92	82	1b40,3b11/P	0	-0.5
Total	16	2079	7064	1006	1885	338	14	294	1182	1075-132	23	1179	.267	.362	.444	115	177	24-38	.958	89	102	119	3b1887,1b162,D5/P2S	128	24.7
VENTURA, VINCE	Vincent; B4.18.1917 New York NY; D9.11.2001 Lake Worth FL; BR/TR/6´1.5˝/190; d5.8																								
1945	Was A	18	58	4	12	0	0	0	2	4	0	4	.207	.258	.207	39	-5	0-0	.886	-1	99	78	O15L	0	-0.7
VERAS, QUILVIO	Quilvio Alberto (Perez); B4.3.1971 Santo Domingo, D.R.; BB/TR/5´9˝/(166–183); d4.25																								
1995	Fla N	124	440	86	115	20	7	5	32	80-0	9	68	.261	.384	.373	99	4	**56**-21	.986	5	93	110	2b122,O2(0/1/1)	0	1.8
1996	Fla N	73	253	40	64	8	1	4	14	51-1	2	42	.253	.381	.340	95	1	8-8	.986	10	102	126	2b67	42	1.3
1997	SD N	145	539	74	143	23	1	3	45	72-0	7	84	.265	.357	.328	87	-7	33-12	.984	-5	103	71	2b142	0	-0.2

YEAR	TM LG	G	AB	R	H	2B	3B	HR	RBI	BB-IB	HP	SO	AVG	OBP	SLG	AOPS	ABR	SB-CS	FA	FR	RNG	THR	GAMES AT POSITION	DL	BFW
1998	†SD N	138	517	79	138	24	2	6	45	84-2	6	78	.267	.373	.356	101	5	24-9	.987	20	**108**	113	2b131	0	3.2
1999	SD N	132	475	95	133	25	2	6	41	65-0	2	88	.280	.368	.379	97	0	30-17	.981	16	103	110	2b118	15	2.0
2000	Atl N	84	298	56	92	15	0	5	37	51-0	5	50	.309	.413	.409	111	9	25-12	.984	4	109	91	2b82	78	1.6
2001	Atl N	71	258	39	65	14	2	3	25	24-1	7	52	.252	.330	.357	77	-8	7-4	.991	5	106	102	2b67	17	0.0
Total	7	767	2780	469	750	129	15	32	239	427-4	38	462	.270	.372	.362	96	4	183-83	.985	55	103	102	2b729,O2(0/1/1)	152	9.7

VERAS, WILTON Wilton Andres; B1.19.1978 Monte Cristi, D.R.; BR/TR/6´2˝/198; d7.1

YEAR	TM LG	G	AB	R	H	2B	3B	HR	RBI	BB-IB	HP	SO	AVG	OBP	SLG	AOPS	ABR	SB-CS	FA	FR	RNG	THR	GAMES AT POSITION	DL	BFW
1999	Bos A	36	118	14	34	5	1	2	13	5-0	2	14	.288	.323	.398	81	-4	0-2	.929	0	95	141	3b35	0	-0.4
2000	Bos A	49	164	21	40	7	1	0	14	7-0	2	20	.244	.278	.299	46	-14	0-0	.907	4	109	145	3b49	0	-0.9
Total	2	85	282	35	74	12	2	2	27	12-0	4	34	.262	.297	.340	61	-18	0-2	.916	4	103	143	3b84	0	-1.3

VERBAN, EMIL Emil Matthew "Dutch","Antelope"; B8.27.1915 Lincoln IL; D6.8.1989 Quincy IL; BR/TR/5´11˝/165; d4.18

YEAR	TM LG	G	AB	R	H	2B	3B	HR	RBI	BB-IB	HP	SO	AVG	OBP	SLG	AOPS	ABR	SB-CS	FA	FR	RNG	THR	GAMES AT POSITION	DL	BFW
1944	†StL N	146	498	51	128	14	2	0	43	19	2	14	.257	.287	.293	62	-26	0	.968	-5	94	**150**	2b146	0	-2.4
1945	StL N✳	**155**	597	59	166	22	8	0	72	19	3	15	.278	.304	.342	77	-21	4	**.978**	-21	88	118	2b155	0	-3.4
1946	StL N	1	1	0	0	0	0	0	0	0	0	0	.000	.000	.000	-96	0	0	ø	0	—	—	/H	0	0.0
	Phi N★	138	473	44	130	17	5	0	34	21	0	18	.275	.306	.332	83	-13	5	.963	-2	100	100	2b138	0	-0.8
	Year	139	474	44	130	17	5	0	34	21	0	18	.274	.305	.331	83	-13	5	.963	-2	100	100	2b138	0	-0.8
1947	Phi N★	**155**	540	50	154	14	8	0	42	23	1	8	.285	.316	.341	77	-20	5	.982	**18**	**104**	111	2b155	0	0.6
1948	Phi N	55	169	14	39	5	1	0	11	11	1	5	.231	.282	.272	51	-12	0	.975	-2	100	91	2b54	0	-1.2
	Chi N	56	248	37	73	15	1	1	16	4	1	7	.294	.308	.375	88	-5	4	.964	5	106	134	2b56	0	0.3
	Year	111	417	51	112	20	2	1	27	15	2	12	.269	.297	.333	72	-17	4	.969	3	**103**	**115**	2b110	0	-0.9
1949	Chi N	98	343	38	99	11	1	0	22	8	2	2	.289	.309	.327	72	-14	3	.965	6	107	98	2b88	0	-0.4
1950	Chi N	45	37	7	4	1	0	0	1	3	0	5	.108	.175	.135	-17	-6	0	.966	3	165	202	2b8,S3/3cf	0	-0.3
	Bos N	4	5	1	0	0	0	0	0	0	0	0	.000	.000	.000	-99	-2	0	.833	-0	72	175	2b2	0	-0.2
	Year	49	42	8	4	1	0	0	1	3	0	5	.095	.156	.119	-27	-8	0	.927	3	138	194	2b10,S3/3cf	0	-0.5
Total	7	853	2911	301	793	99	26	1	241	108	10	74	.272	.301	.325	73	-119	21	.971	1	99	117	2b802,S3/cf3	0	-7.8

VERBLE, GENE Gene Kermit "Satchel"; B6.29.1928 Concord NC; BR/TR/5´10˝/(163–165); d4.17

YEAR	TM LG	G	AB	R	H	2B	3B	HR	RBI	BB-IB	HP	SO	AVG	OBP	SLG	AOPS	ABR	SB-CS	FA	FR	RNG	THR	GAMES AT POSITION	DL	BFW
1951	Was A	68	177	16	36	3	2	0	15	18	0	10	.203	.277	.243	42	-15	1-1	.978	-3	99	99	S28,2b19/3	0	-1.5
1953	Was A	13	21	4	4	0	0	0	2	2	0	1	.190	.261	.190	24	-2	0-0	1.000	1	113	126	S8	0	-0.1
Total	2	81	198	20	40	3	2	0	17	20	0	11	.202	.275	.237	40	-17	1-1	.981	-2	101	104	S36,2b19/3	0	-1.6

VERDI, FRANK Frank Michael; B6.2.1926 Brooklyn NY; BR/TR/5´10.5˝/170; d5.10

YEAR	TM LG	G	AB	R	H	2B	3B	HR	RBI	BB-IB	HP	SO	AVG	OBP	SLG	AOPS	ABR	SB-CS	FA	FR	RNG	THR	GAMES AT POSITION	DL	BFW
1953	NY A	1	0	0	0	0	0	0	0	0	0	0	ø	ø	ø	ø	0	0-0	ø	-0	0	0	/S	0	0.0

VERGEZ, JOHNNY Jean Louis; B7.9.1906 Oakland CA; D7.15.1991 Davis CA; BR/TR/5´8˝/165; d4.14

YEAR	TM LG	G	AB	R	H	2B	3B	HR	RBI	BB-IB	HP	SO	AVG	OBP	SLG	AOPS	ABR	SB-CS	FA	FR	RNG	THR	GAMES AT POSITION	DL	BFW
1931	NY N	152	565	67	157	24	2	13	81	29	6	65	.278	.320	.396	94	-7	11	.932	-6	92	95	3b152	—	-0.7
1932	NY N	118	376	42	98	21	3	6	43	25	2	36	.261	.310	.380	86	-8	1	.935	5	**107**	**123**	3b111/S	—	0.1
1933	NY N	123	458	57	124	21	6	16	72	39	3	66	.271	.332	.448	123	13	1	.928	-13	91	108	3b123	—	0.4
1934	NY N	108	320	31	64	18	1	7	27	28	2	55	.200	.269	.328	60	-18	1	.943	9	**116**	102	3b104	—	-0.6
1935	Phi N	148	546	56	136	27	4	9	63	46	4	67	.249	.312	.363	73	-20	8	**.953**	-4	88	102	3b148,S2	—	-1.9
1936	Phi N	15	40	4	11	2	0	1	5	3	0	11	.275	.326	.400	86	-1	0	.964	1	98	154	3b12	—	0.0
	StL N	8	18	1	3	1	0	0	1	1	0	3	.167	.211	.222	17	-2	0	.929	-0	76	166	3b8	—	-0.2
	Year	23	58	5	14	3	0	1	6	4	0	14	.241	.290	.345	66	-3	0	.952	0	91	158	3b20	—	-0.2
Total	6	672	2323	258	593	114	16	52	292	171	17	303	.255	.311	.385	87	-43	22	.939	-8	97	106	3b658,S3	—	-2.9

VERNON, MICKEY James Barton; B4.22.1918 Marcus Hook PA; BL/TL/6´2˝/(175–184); d7.8; Mil 1944–45; M3/C6; Col Villanova

YEAR	TM LG	G	AB	R	H	2B	3B	HR	RBI	BB-IB	HP	SO	AVG	OBP	SLG	AOPS	ABR	SB-CS	FA	FR	RNG	THR	GAMES AT POSITION	DL	BFW
1939	Was A	76	276	23	71	15	4	1	30	24	0	28	.257	.317	.351	76	-10	1-1	.985	-3	91	119	1b75	—	-1.9
1940	Was A	5	19	0	3	0	0	0	0	0	0	3	.158	.158	.158	-19	-3	0-0	1.000	-0	72	122	1b4	—	-0.4
1941	Was A	138	531	73	159	27	11	9	93	43	0	51	.299	.352	.443	114	9	9-3	.992	-7	81	101	1b132	0	-1.0
1942	Was A	**151**	621	76	168	34	6	9	86	59	3	63	.271	.337	.388	104	3	25-6	.982	-9	84	76	1b151	0	-1.8
1943	Was A	145	553	89	148	29	8	7	70	67	**10**	55	.268	.357	.387	122	17	24-8	.990	-11	75	99	1b143	0	0.1
1946	Was A★	148	587	88	207	**51**	8	8	85	49	0	64	**.353**	.403	.508	163	49	14-10	.990	-2	100	96	1b147	0	4.3
1947	Was A	**154**	600	77	159	29	12	7	85	49	0	42	.265	.320	.388	99	-4	12-12	.987	-3	94	83	1b154	0	-1.4
1948	Was A★	150	558	78	135	27	7	3	48	54	1	43	.242	.310	.332	73	-23	15-11	.989	5	114	83	1b150	0	-2.4
1949	Cle A	153	584	72	170	27	4	18	83	58	2	51	.291	.357	.443	113	8	9-7	.991	16	**134**	116	1b153	0	1.8
1950	Cle A	28	90	8	17	0	0	0	10	12	0	10	.189	.284	.189	24	-10	2-0	.996	1	102	126	1b25	0	-1.0
	Was A	90	327	47	100	17	3	9	65	50	4	29	.306	.404	.459	127	15	6-1	.990	2	111	104	1b85	0	1.4
	Year	118	417	55	117	17	3	9	75	62	4	39	.281	.379	.400	104	4	8-1	**.991**	3	109	109	1b110	0	0.4
1951	Was A	141	546	69	160	30	7	9	87	53	2	45	.293	.358	.423	112	9	7-6	**.994**	-5	86	87	1b137	0	-0.1
1952	Was A	154	569	71	143	33	9	10	80	89	0	66	.251	.353	.394	111	10	7-7	**.993**	-4	93	94	1b153	0	0.0
1953	Was A★	**152**	608	101	205	**43**	11	15	115	63	4	57	**.337**	.403	.518	151	43	4-6	.992	-3	93	116	1b152	0	3.0
1954	Was A★	151	597	90	173	**33**	14	20	97	61	5	61	.290	.357	.492	140	30	1-4	**.992**	-6	84	105	1b148	0	1.4
1955	Was A★	150	538	74	162	23	8	14	85	74-9	3	50	.301	.384	.452	133	26	0-4	.994	-6	81	97	1b144	0	1.0
1956	Bos A★	119	403	67	125	28	4	15	84	57-6	7	40	.310	.403	.511	125	16	1-0	.989	-5	85	99	1b108	0	0.6
1957	Bos A	102	270	36	65	18	1	7	38	41-2	5	35	.241	.350	.393	97	1	0-0	.992	3	117	75	1b70	0	0.0
1958	Cle A★	119	355	49	104	22	3	8	55	44-3	2	56	.293	.372	.439	126	14	0-4	.987	-2	92	104	1b96	0	0.5
1959	Mil N	74	91	8	20	4	0	3	14	7-1	1	20	.220	.283	.363	77	-3	0-0	.983	1	89	59	1b10,O4(2/0/2)	0	-0.3
1960	Pit N	9	8	0	1	0	0	0	1	1-1	0	0	.125	.222	.125	-2	-1	0-0	ø	0	—	—	/H	0	-0.1
Total	20	2409	8731	1196	2495	490	120	172	1311	955-22	49	869	.286	.359	.428	116	196	137-90	.990	-38	94	97	1b2237,O4(2/0/2)	0	3.7

VERSALLES, ZOILO Zoilo Casanova (Rodriguez) "Zorro"; B12.18.1939 Veldado, Cuba; D6.9.1995 Bloomington MN; BR/TR/5´10˝/(150–165); d8.1

YEAR	TM LG	G	AB	R	H	2B	3B	HR	RBI	BB-IB	HP	SO	AVG	OBP	SLG	AOPS	ABR	SB-CS	FA	FR	RNG	THR	GAMES AT POSITION	DL	BFW
1959	Was A	29	59	4	9	0	0	1	1	4-0	1	15	.153	.219	.203	17	-7	1-0	.943	3	107	113	S29	0	-0.2
1960	Was A	15	45	2	6	2	2	0	4	2-0	0	5	.133	.170	.267	16	-6	0-0	.935	-0	100	67	S15	0	-0.5
1961	Min A	129	510	65	143	25	5	7	53	25-2	1	61	.280	.314	.390	83	-13	16-9	.952	6	100	95	S129	0	0.4
1962	Min A	160	568	69	137	18	3	17	67	37-8	2	71	.241	.287	.373	74	-22	5-5	.970	**35**	106	**137**	S160	0	2.6
1963	Min A★	159	621	74	162	31	**13**	10	54	33-2	5	66	.261	.303	.401	94	-7	7-4	.961	-4	95	101	S159	0	0.4
1964	Min A	160	659	94	171	33	**10**	20	64	42-1	**8**	88	.259	.311	.431	103	1	14-4	.957	-22	89	95	S160	0	-0.5
1965	†Min A★	160	666	**126**	182	**45**	**12**	19	77	41-3	7	122	.273	.319	.462	115	12	27-5	.950	2	105	**123**	S160	0	3.3
1966	Min A	137	543	73	135	20	6	7	36	40-2	7	85	.249	.307	.346	82	-12	10-12	.942	-10	95	97	S135	0	-1.3
1967	Min A	160	581	63	116	16	7	6	50	33-2	6	113	.200	.249	.282	53	-35	5-3	.958	8	101	101	S159	0	-1.6
1968	LA N	122	403	29	79	16	3	2	24	26-4	0	84	.196	.244	.266	57	-22	6-4	.954	9	102	98	S119	0	-0.3
1969	Cle A	72	217	21	49	11	1	1	13	21-1	2	47	.226	.298	.300	66	-9	3-1	.975	-7	89	66	2b46,3b30,S3	0	-1.4
	Was A	31	75	9	20	2	1	0	6	3-0	1	13	.267	.304	.320	79	-2	1-0	.935	-1	110	34	S13,2b6,3b5	0	-0.2
	Year	103	292	30	69	13	2	1	19	24-1	3	60	.236	.299	.305	69	-12	4-1	.978	-8	91	64	2b52,3b35,S16	0	-1.6
1971	Atl N	66	194	21	37	11	0	5	22	11-1	0	40	.191	.233	.325	53	-12	2-1	.902	-14	84	41	3b30,S24/2	0	-2.6
Total	12	1400	5141	650	1246	230	63	95	471	318-26	40	810	.242	.290	.367	82	-134	97-48	.956	5	99	105	S1265,3b65,2b53	0	-1.9

VERYZER, TOM Thomas Martin; B2.11.1953 Port Jefferson NY; BR/TR/6´1˝/(170–185); [DetA71 1/11]; d8.14

YEAR	TM LG	G	AB	R	H	2B	3B	HR	RBI	BB-IB	HP	SO	AVG	OBP	SLG	AOPS	ABR	SB-CS	FA	FR	RNG	THR	GAMES AT POSITION	DL	BFW
1973	Det A	18	20	1	6	0	1	0	2	2-0	0	4	.300	.364	.400	108	0	0-0	.857	-4	63	28	S18	0	-0.3
1974	Det A	22	55	4	13	2	0	2	9	5-0	0	8	.236	.300	.382	92	-1	1-0	.927	-8	69	43	S20	0	-0.7
1975	Det A	128	404	37	102	13	1	5	48	23-1	5	76	.252	.297	.327	74	-14	2-6	.960	-3	96	79	S128	0	-0.5
1976	Det A	97	354	31	83	8	2	1	25	21-1	6	44	.234	.286	.277	63	-16	1-4	.966	4	102	89	S97	46	-0.3
1977	Det A	125	350	31	69	12	1	2	28	16-0	0	44	.197	.230	.254	31	-34	0-1	.969	12	112	95	S124	0	-1.0
1978	Cle A	130	421	48	114	18	4	1	32	13-0	5	36	.271	.298	.340	80	-12	1-2	.963	-11	98	75	S129	0	-1.1
1979	Cle A	149	449	41	99	9	3	0	34	34-0	4	54	.220	.279	.254	45	-35	2-5	.974	2	100	90	S148	0	-1.8
1980	Cle A	109	358	28	97	12	0	2	28	10-1	8	25	.271	.303	.321	71	-14	0-5	.971	4	100	81	S108	0	-0.1
1981	Cle A	75	221	13	54	4	0	0	14	10-1	1	10	.244	.278	.262	57	-12	1-0	.970	-1	94	98	S75	0	-0.6
1982	NY N	40	54	6	18	2	0	0	4	3-2	0	4	.333	.362	.370	107	1	1-0	.962	-11	107	66	2b26,S16	90	-0.9
1983	Chi N	59	88	5	18	3	0	1	3	3-1	0	13	.205	.231	.273	37	-8	0-0	.978	1	115	140	S28,3b17	0	-0.5
1984	†Chi N	44	74	5	14	1	0	0	4	3-1	4	11	.189	.259	.203	29	-7	0-0	.966	-3	82	89	S36,3b5,2b4	82	-0.8
Total	12	996	2848	250	687	84	12	14	231	143-8	33	329	.241	.283	.294	61	-152	9-23	.966	-17	99	85	S927,2b30,3b22	218	-8.6

YEAR	TM LG	G	AB	R	H	2B	3B	HR	RBI	BB-IB	HP	SO	AVG	OBP	SLG	AOPS	ABR	SB-CS	FA	FR	RNG	THR	GAMES AT POSITION	DL	BFW
Vick, Ernie	Henry Arthur; B7.2.1900 Toledo OH; D7.16.1980 Ann Arbor MI; BR/TR/5´9.5˝/185; d6.29; Col Michigan																								
1922	StL N	3	6	1	2	2	0	0	0	0	0	0	.333	.333	.667	159	1	0-0	.875	-0	*92*	*0*	C3	—	0.0
1924	StL N	16	23	2	8	1	0	0	0	3	0	3	.348	.423	.391	122	1	0-0	.974	2	*115*	*153*	C16	—	0.3
1925	StL N	14	32	3	6	2	1	0	3	3	0	1	.188	.257	.313	44	-3	0-0	.929	-0	*115*	*56*	C9	—	-0.2
1926	StL N	24	51	6	10	2	0	0	4	3	0	4	.196	.241	.235	27	-5	0	.944	0	*128*	*101*	C23	—	-0.4
Total	4	57	112	12	26	7	1	0	7	9	0	8	.232	.289	.313	58	-6	0-0	.944	1	*120*	*97*	C51	—	-0.3
Vick, Sammy	Samuel Bruce; B4.12.1895 Batesville MS; D8.17.1986 Memphis TN; BR/TR/5´10.5˝/163; d9.20; Mil 1918; Col Millsaps																								
1917	NY A	10	36	4	10	3	0	0	2	1	0	6	.278	.297	.361	100	0	2	.882	-1	95	83	O10R	—	-0.1
1918	NY A	2	3	1	2	0	0	0	1	0	0	0	.667	.667	.667	296	1	0	ø	-0	0	0	/rf	—	0.1
1919	NY A	106	407	59	101	15	9	2	27	35	0	55	.248	.308	.344	82	-11	9	.952	-6	92	78	O100R	—	-2.3
1920	NY A	51	118	21	26	7	1	0	11	14	2	20	.220	.313	.297	60	-6	1-1	.949	-2	113	0	O33(4/1/28)	—	-1.0
1921	Bos A	44	77	5	20	3	1	0	9	1	0	10	.260	.269	.325	52	-6	0-1	1.000	-0	104	65	O14R	—	-0.7
Total	5	213	641	90	159	28	11	2	50	51	2	91	.248	.305	.335	76	-22	12-2	.951	-8	97	63	O158(4/1/153)	—	-4.0
Vico, George	George Steve "Sam"; B8.9.1923 San Fernando CA; D1.14.1994 Redondo Beach CA; BL/TR/6´4˝/200; d4.20																								
1948	Det A	144	521	50	139	23	9	8	58	39	7	39	.267	.326	.392	88	-11	2-2	.988	-2	94	88	1b142	0	-1.7
1949	Det A	67	142	15	27	5	2	4	18	21	4	17	.190	.311	.338	72	-6	0-0	.985	1	112	93	1b53	0	-0.6
Total	2	211	663	65	166	28	11	12	76	60	11	56	.250	.323	.380	85	-17	2-2	.987	-0	98	89	1b195	0	-2.3
Victorino, Shane	Shane Patrick; B11.30.1980 Wailuku HI; BB/TR/5´9˝/160; [LAN99 6/194]; d4.2																								
2003	SD N	36	73	8	11	2	0	0	4	7-0	1	17	.151	.232	.178	11	-10	7-2	1.000	1	91	241	O32(15/16/3)	0	-0.8
2005	Phi N	21	17	5	5	0	0	2	8	0-0	0	3	.294	.263	.647	133	1	0-0	ø	-1	0	0	O12(4/5/3)	0	0.0
2006	Phi N	153	415	70	119	19	8	6	46	24-0	14	54	.287	.346	.414	89	-7	4-3	**1.000**	9	105	242	O122(44/67/21)	0	0.1
Total	3	210	505	83	135	21	8	8	58	31-0	15	74	.267	.326	.388	81	-16	11-5	1.000	9	101	238	O166(63/88/27)	0	-0.7
Vidal, Jose	Jose (Nicolas) "Papito"; B4.3.1940 Batey Lechuga, D.R.; BR/TR/6´0˝/(185–190); d9.5																								
1966	Cle A	17	32	4	6	1	1	0	3	5-0	0	11	.188	.297	.281	67	-1	0-1	1.000	-1	91	0	O11(0/3/8)	0	-0.3
1967	Cle A	16	34	4	4	0	0	0	0	7-0	0	12	.118	.268	.118	17	-3	0-1	1.000	1	106	162	O10(8/6/1)	0	-0.4
1968	Cle A	37	54	5	9	0	0	2	5	2-0	0	15	.167	.196	.278	43	-4	3-0	1.000	-1	75	0	O26(11/0/15)/1	0	-0.6
1969	Sea A	18	26	7	5	0	1	1	2	4-0	1	8	.192	.323	.385	98	0	1-1	.917	-0	107	0	O6(1/0/5)	0	-0.1
Total	4	88	146	20	24	1	2	3	10	18-0	1	46	.164	.261	.260	53	-8	4-3	.985	-1	92	42	O53(20/9/29)/1	0	-1.4
Vidro, Jose	Jose Angel (Cetty); B8.27.1974 Mayaguez, PR; BB/TR/5´11˝/(185–195); [MonN92 6/155]; d6.8																								
1997	Mon N	67	169	19	42	12	1	2	17	11-0	2	20	.249	.297	.367	75	-6	1-0	.958	-2	90	123	3b36,2b5,D5	0	-0.8
1998	Mon N	83	205	24	45	12	0	0	18	27-0	4	33	.220	.318	.278	61	-10	2-2	.975	-11	91	82	2b56,3b7	0	-1.9
1999	Mon N	140	494	67	150	45	2	12	59	29-2	4	51	.304	.346	.476	110	7	0-4	.982	-16	91	84	2b121,1b14,O3L,3b2	0	-0.6
2000	Mon N★	153	606	101	200	51	2	24	97	49-4	2	69	.330	.379	.540	129	27	5-4	.986	-1	105	101	2b153	0	3.1
2001	Mon N	124	486	82	155	34	1	15	59	31-2	10	49	.319	.371	.486	120	15	4-1	.983	-13	95	85	2b121,D2	23	0.8
2002	Mon N★	152	604	103	190	43	3	19	96	60-1	3	70	.315	.378	.490	120	19	2-1	.986	6	103	94	2b152	0	3.3
2003	Mon N★	144	509	77	158	36	0	15	65	69-6	7	50	.310	.397	.470	123	21	3-2	.983	-18	98	87	2b137	0	0.9
2004	Mon N	110	412	51	121	24	0	14	60	49-7	0	43	.294	.367	.454	107	5	3-1	.987	-15	92	109	2b105,D4	39	-0.4
2005	Was N	87	309	38	85	21	2	7	32	31-3	1	30	.275	.339	.424	104	2	0-0	.985	-23	84	77	2b79	61	-1.7
2006	Was N	126	463	52	134	26	1	7	47	41-3	3	48	.289	.348	.395	95	-3	1-0	.990	-25	84	72	2b107,1b8,D2	31	-2.2
Total	10	1186	4257	614	1280	304	12	115	550	397-28	36	463	.301	.363	.459	111	77	21-15	.985	-116	95	89	2b1036,3b45,1b22,D13,O3L	154	0.5
Villanueva, Hector	Hector (Balasquide); B10.2.1964 Rio Piedras, PR; BR/TR/6´1˝/220; d6.1; Col Alabama–Birmingham																								
1990	Chi N	52	114	14	31	4	1	7	18	4-2	2	27	.272	.308	.509	113	1	1-0	.991	3	729	50	C23,1b14	0	0.5
1991	Chi N	71	192	23	53	10	1	13	32	21-1	0	30	.276	.346	.542	140	10	0-0	.979	-5	91	86	C55,1b6	13	0.7
1992	Chi N	51	112	9	17	6	0	2	13	11-2	0	24	.152	.228	.259	36	-9	0-0	.978	5	97	116	C28,1b6	0	-0.4
1993	StL N	17	55	7	8	1	0	3	9	4-1	0	17	.145	.203	.327	40	-5	0-0	1.000	-3	70	92	C17	0	-0.7
Total	4	191	473	53	109	21	2	25	72	40-6	2	98	.230	.293	.442	98	-3	1-0	.984	0	189	89	C123,1b26	13	0.1
Vina, Fernando	Fernando; B4.16.1969 Sacramento CA; BL/TR/5´9˝/(160–180); [NYN90 9/253]; d4.10; Col Arizona St.; [DL 2005 Det A 183]																								
1993	Sea A	24	45	5	10	2	0	0	2	4-0	3	3	.222	.327	.267	60	-2	6-0	1.000	1	108	144	2b16,S4,D2	0	0.1
1994	NY N	79	124	20	31	6	0	0	6	12-0	**12**	11	.250	.372	.298	78	-3	3-1	.979	1	118	105	2b13,3b12,S9,O6L	15	-0.1
1995	Mil A	113	288	46	74	7	7	3	29	22-0	9	28	.257	.327	.361	75	-11	6-3	.983	12	107	**136**	2b99,S6,3b2	0	0.5
1996	Mil A	140	554	94	157	19	10	7	46	38-3	13	35	.283	.342	.392	82	-16	16-7	.979	18	108	**121**	2b137	0	0.9
1997	Mil A	79	324	37	89	12	2	4	28	12-1	7	23	.275	.312	.361	75	-13	8-7	.982	8	106	114	2b77/D	89	-0.2
1998	Mil N★	159	637	101	198	39	7	7	45	54-2	25	46	.311	.386	.427	112	14	22-16	.986	28	107	**128**	2b158	0	4.8
1999	Mil N	37	154	17	41	7	0	1	16	14-0	4	6	.266	.339	.331	71	-6	5-2	.995	2	103	122	2b37	137	-0.2
2000	†StL N	123	487	81	146	24	6	4	31	36-0	**28**	36	.300	.380	.398	95	-2	10-8	**.988**	11	100	118	2b122	16	1.4
2001	†StL N	154	631	95	191	30	8	9	56	32-3	22	35	.303	.357	.418	98	-2	17-7	**.987**	-4	94	114	2b151	0	0.2
2002	†StL N	150	622	75	168	29	5	1	54	44-2	18	36	.270	.333	.338	78	-19	17-11	.981	-16	94	109	2b150	0	-2.9
2003	StL N	61	259	35	65	14	4	4	23	11-0	11	24	.251	.309	.382	80	-8	4-4	.974	-9	87	108	2b60	96	-1.5
2004	Det A	29	115	21	26	5	0	0	7	9-0	5	9	.226	.308	.270	55	-7	2-1	.970	6	109	123	2b29	145	0.0
Total	12	1148	4240	627	1196	194	49	40	343	288-11	157	292	.282	.348	.379	87	-75	116-67	.984	57	101	119	2b1049,S19,3b14,O6L,D3	681	3.0
Vinson, Charlie	Charles Anthony "Chuck"; B1.5.1944 Washington DC; BL/TL/6´3˝/204; d9.19																								
1966	Cal A	13	22	3	4	2	0	1	6	5-0	1	9	.182	.357	.409	123	1	0-0	1.000	-1	40	130	1b11	0	-0.1
Vinson, Rube	Ernest Augustus; B3.20.1879 Dover DE; D10.12.1951 Chester PA; BL/TR/5´9˝/168; d9.27																								
1904	Cle A	15	49	12	15	1	0	0	2	10	1	—	.306	.433	.327	143	3	2	1.000	-1	0	0	O15L	—	0.2
1905	Cle A	39	134	12	26	3	1	0	9	7	2	—	.194	.245	.231	51	-8	4	.930	-2	27	0	O36(27/9/0)	—	-1.3
1906	Chi A	10	24	2	6	0	0	0	3	2	0	—	.250	.308	.250	77	-1	1	.600	-2	0	0	O7L	—	-0.4
Total	3	64	207	26	47	4	1	0	14	19	3	—	.227	.301	.256	77	-6	7	.914	-6	17	0	O58(49/9/0)	—	-1.5
Viox, Jim	James Harry; B12.30.1890 Lockland OH; D1.6.1969 Erlanger KY; BR/TR/5´7˝/150; d5.9																								
1912	Pit N	33	70	8	13	2	3	1	7	3	0	9	.186	.219	.343	53	-5	2	.957	-3	114	0	3b10,S8,O3R/2	—	-0.8
1913	Pit N	137	492	86	156	32	8	2	65	64	3	28	.317	.399	.427	142	30	14-14	.959	-40	85	59	2b124,S10	—	-0.9
1914	Pit N	143	506	52	134	18	5	1	57	63	4	33	.265	.351	.326	106	6	9	.939	-22	99	88	2b138,S2,O2R	—	-1.4
1915	Pit N	150	503	56	129	17	8	2	45	75	4	31	.256	.357	.334	111	10	12-8	.954	-20	95	69	2b134,3b13,O2C	—	-0.9
1916	Pit N	43	132	12	33	7	0	1	17	17	1	11	.250	.340	.326	104	2	2	.937	-11	82	64	2b25,3b11	—	-1.0
Total	5	506	1703	214	465	76	24	7	191	222	12	112	.273	.361	.358	116	43	39-22	.949	-96	93	72	2b422,3b34,S20,O7(0/2/5)	—	-5.0
Virdon, Bill	William Charles; B6.9.1931 Hazel Park MI; BL/TR/6´0˝/(175–185); d4.12; M13/C8																								
1955	StL N	144	534	58	150	18	6	17	68	36-3	1	64	.281	.322	.433	100	-2	2-4	.966	-5	99	63	O142(1/109/34)	0	-1.5
1956	StL N	24	71	10	15	2	0	2	9	5-2	1	8	.211	.269	.324	60	-4	0-1	.982	-1	90	121	O24C	0	-0.7
	Pit N	133	509	67	170	21	10	8	37	33-7	1	63	.334	.374	.462	126	18	6-6	.989	2	102	110	O130C	0	1.4
	Year	157	580	77	185	23	10	10	46	38-9	2	71	.319	.361	.445	118	14	6-7	.988	1	100	112	O154C	0	0.7
1957	Pit N	144	561	59	141	28	11	8	50	33-5	0	69	.251	.291	.383	82	-16	3-3	.986	5	105	123	O141C	0	-1.9
1958	Pit N	144	604	75	161	24	11	9	46	52-5	1	70	.267	.324	.387	90	-10	5-3	.993	2	106	94	O143C	0	-1.5
1959	Pit N	144	519	67	132	24	2	8	41	55-11	2	65	.254	.327	.355	83	-12	7-4	.979	12	114	**190**	O144C	0	-0.7
1960	†Pit N	120	409	60	108	16	9	8	40	40-2	0	44	.264	.326	.406	99	-1	8-2	.983	5	107	132	O109C	0	0.0
1961	Pit N	146	599	81	156	22	8	9	58	49-1	0	45	.260	.313	.369	81	-17	5-8	.985	-1	108	55	O145C	0	-2.4
1962	Pit N	156	663	82	164	27	**10**	6	47	36-0	1	65	.247	.286	.345	69	-31	5-13	.976	-3	98	107	O156C	0	-4.3
1963	Pit N	142	554	58	149	22	6	8	53	43-4	0	55	.269	.321	.374	99	-1	1-2	.988	-4	99	65	O142C	0	-1.0
1964	Pit N	145	473	59	115	11	3	3	27	30-1	0	48	.243	.287	.298	66	-22	1-5	.976	-7	95	67	O134C	0	-3.7
1965	Pit N	135	481	58	134	22	5	4	24	30-0	1	49	.279	.322	.370	94	-4	4-3	.970	-5	99	44	O128(1/127/0)	0	-1.4
1968	Pit N	6	3	1	1	0	0	1	2	0-0	0	2	.333	.333	1.333	388	1	0-0	1.000	-0	80	0	O4(1/0/3)	0	0.1
Total	12	1583	5980	735	1596	237	81	91	502	442-41	8	647	.267	.316	.379	89	-101	47-54	.982	0	103	96	O1542(3/1504/37)	0	-17.6

THE BATTER REGISTER

YEAR	TM LG	G	AB	R	H	2B	3B	HR	RBI	BB-IB	HP	SO	AVG	OBP	SLG	AOPS	ABR	SB-CS	FA	FR	RNG	THR	GAMES AT POSITION	DL	BFW
VIRGIL, OZZIE	Osvaldo Jose Jr.; B12.7.1956 Mayaguez, PR; BR/TR/6´1˝/(195–205); [PhiN76 6/137]; d10.5; f–Ozzie																								
1980	Phi N	1	5	1	1	1	0	0	0	0-0	0	1	.200	.200	.400	60	0	0-0	1.000	-2	21	0	/C	0	-0.2
1981	Phi N	6	6	0	0	0	0	0	0	0-0	0	2	.000	.000	.000	-95	-2	0-0	1.000	0	0	0	/C	0	-0.1
1982	Phi N	49	101	11	24	6	0	3	8	10-0	0	26	.238	.306	.386	90	-1	0-1	.964	1	80	59	C35	0	0.0
1983	†Phi N	55	140	11	30	7	0	6	23	8-0	3	34	.214	.272	.393	83	-4	0-2	.966	-11	63	97	C51	0	-1.5
1984	Phi N	141	456	61	119	21	2	18	68	45-5	5	91	.261	.331	.434	113	7	1-1	.992	-2	107	77	C137	0	1.1
1985	Phi N★	131	426	47	105	16	3	19	55	49-6	5	85	.246	.330	.432	109	5	0-0	**.994**	-9	81	84	C120	0	0.1
1986	Atl N	114	359	45	80	9	0	15	48	63-5	4	73	.223	.343	.373	94	-2	1-0	.984	13	75	132	C111	0	1.7
1987	Atl N★	123	429	57	106	13	1	27	72	47-4	7	81	.247	.331	.471	105	2	0-1	.989	-4	85	93	C122	0	0.3
1988	Atl N	107	320	23	82	10	0	9	31	22-1	5	54	.256	.313	.372	92	-3	2-0	.990	-6	102	93	C96	0	-0.4
1989	Tor A	9	11	2	2	1	0	1	2	4-0	0	3	.182	.400	.545	166	1	0-0	1.000	0	0	0	/CD	0	0.1
1990	Tor A	3	5	0	0	0	0	0	0	0-0	0	3	.000	.000	.000	-98	-1	0-0	1.000	-1	0	0	C2/D	0	-0.2
Total	11	739	2258	258	549	84	6	98	307	248-21	29	453	.243	.324	.416	101	2	4-5	.987	-21	88	93	C677,D7	0	0.9
VIRGIL, OZZIE	Osvaldo Jose Sr. (Pichardo); B5.17.1932 Monte Cristi, D.R.; BR/TR/6´0˝/175; d9.23; C19; s–Ozzie; OF(8/0/18)																								
1956	NY N	3	12	2	5	1	1	0	2	0-0	0	0	.417	.417	.667	186	1	1-0	.800	-1	22	259	3b3	0	0.0
1957	NY N	96	226	26	53	0	2	4	24	14-1	0	27	.235	.278	.305	57	-15	2-3	.926	4	127	120	3b62,O24(8/0/16)/S	0	-1.2
1958	Det A	49	193	19	47	10	2	3	19	8-0	0	20	.244	.272	.363	69	-9	1-0	.981	5	104	74	3b49	0	-0.4
1960	Det A	62	132	16	30	4	2	3	13	4-1	0	14	.227	.248	.356	60	-8	1-1	.974	3	102	159	3b42,2b8,S5/C	0	-0.5
1961	Det A	20	30	1	4	0	0	1	1	1-0	0	5	.133	.161	.233	4	-4	0-0	.938	-3	48	179	3b9,C3/2S	0	-0.7
	KC A	11	21	1	3	0	0	0	0	0-0	0	3	.143	.143	.143	-23	-4	0-0	.818	0	137	180	3b4,C3	0	-0.4
	Year	31	51	2	7	0	0	1	1	1-0	0	8	.137	.154	.196	-7	-8	0-0	.889	-3	74	179	3b13,C6/2S	0	-1.1
1962	Bal A	1	0	0	0	0	0	0	0	1-1	0	0	ø	1.000	ø	209	0	0-0	ø	0	—	—	/H	0	0.0
1965	Pit N	39	49	3	13	2	0	1	5	2-0	0	10	.265	.294	.367	85	-1	0-0	1.000	-0	137	65	C15,3b7,2b5	0	-0.1
1966	SF N	42	89	7	19	2	0	2	9	4-1	0	12	.213	.245	.303	51	-6	1-1	.984	-1	91	34	C13,3b13,1b5,2b2,O2R	0	-0.7
1969	SF N	1	1	0	0	0	0	0	0	0-0	0	0	.000	.000	.000	-99	0	0-0	ø	0	—	—	/H	0	0.0
Total	9	324	753	75	174	19	7	14	73	34-4	0	91	.231	.263	.331	59	-46	6-5	.951	7	111	111	3b189,C35,O26R,2b16,S7,1b5	0	-4.0
VIRTUE, JAKE	Jacob Kitchline "Guesses"; B3.2.1865 Philadelphia PA; D2.3.1943 Camden NJ; BB/TL/5´9.5˝/165; d7.21																								
1890	Cle N	62	223	39	68	6	5	2	25	49	1	15	.305	.432	.404	147	17	9	.982	0	99	96	1b62	—	1.0
1891	Cle N	139	517	82	135	19	14	2	72	75	8	40	.261	.363	.364	107	6	15	.972	-10	71	89	1b139	—	-1.5
1892	†Cle N	147	557	98	157	15	20	2	89	84	4	68	.282	.380	.391	128	20	14	.984	-4	78	85	1b147	—	1.4
1893	Cle N	97	378	87	100	16	10	1	60	54	1	14	.265	.358	.368	88	-7	11	.975	1	115	108	1b73,O13(0/9/4),S5,3b5/P	—	-0.6
1894	Cle N	29	89	15	23	4	1	0	10	13	1	3	.258	.359	.326	64	-5	1	.885	-2	93	0	O21(0/16/5),2b3,1b2/P	—	-0.6
Total	5	474	1764	321	483	60	50	7	256	275	15	140	.274	.376	.376	111	31	50	.978	-15	85	92	1b423,O34(0/25/9),3b5,S5,2b3,P2	—	-0.3
VISNER, JOE	Joseph Paul (b Joseph Paul Vezina); B9.27.1859 Minneapolis MN; D6.17.1945 Fosston MN; BL/TR/5´11˝/180; d7.4																								
1885	Bal AA	4	13	2	3	0	0	0	2	2	0	—	.231	.333	.231	82	0	—	.750	-1	0	0	O4(0/2/2)	—	-0.1
1889	†Bro AA	80	295	56	76	12	10	8	68	36	4	36	.258	.346	.447	125	9	13	.871	-11	—	—	C53,O29(2/0/27)	—	0.1
1890	Pit P	127	521	110	139	15	**22**	3	71	76	8	44	.267	.369	.397	114	13	18	.893	-7	78	91	O127R	—	0.4
1891	Was AA	18	68	13	19	2	3	1	7	8	0	7	.279	.355	.441	134	3	2	.806	-3	67	0	O17R/C3	—	0.0
	StL AA	6	27	2	4	0	1	0	1	0	0	3	.148	.148	.222	5	-4	0	1.000	0	112	0	O6R	—	-0.3
	Year	24	95	15	23	2	4	1	8	8	0	10	.242	.301	.379	94	-2	2	.846	-2	77	0	O23R/C3	—	-0.3
Total	4	235	924	183	241	29	36	12	149	122	12	90	.261	.354	.409	115	21	33	.892	-20	—	—	O183(2/2/179),C54/3	—	0.1
VITIELLO, JOE	Joseph David; B4.11.1970 Cambridge MA; BR/TR/6´3˝/(215–230); [KCA91 1/7]; d4.29; Col Alabama																								
1995	KC A	53	130	13	33	4	0	7	21	8-0	4	25	.254	.317	.446	94	-2	0-0	.982	-1	80	69	D38,1b8	0	-0.4
1996	KC A	85	257	29	62	15	1	8	40	38-2	3	69	.241	.342	.401	88	-4	2-0	1.000	0	120	76	D70,1b9/rf	0	-0.7
1997	KC A	51	130	11	31	6	0	5	18	14-1	2	37	.238	.322	.400	84	-3	0-0	.980	-0	111	0	O28(12/0/16),D12/1	92	-0.5
1998	KC A	3	7	0	1	0	0	0	0	1-0	0	2	.143	.250	.143	6	-1	0-0	ø	0	—	—	D2	40	-0.1
1999	KC A	13	41	4	6	1	0	1	4	2-0	2	9	.146	.222	.244	18	-5	0-0	1.000	1	132	128	1b10,D2	0	-0.5
2000	SD N	39	52	7	13	3	0	2	8	10-0	0	9	.250	.365	.423	107	1	0-0	.966	-1	95	128	1b17/rf	0	-0.1
2003	Mon N	38	76	12	26	6	0	3	13	7-0	2	14	.342	.407	.539	142	5	0-0	1.000	-1	76	0	O15L,1b12/D	0	0.3
Total	7	282	693	76	172	35	1	26	104	80-3	13	165	.248	.335	.414	90	-9	2-0	.983	-1	112	108	D125,1b57,O45(27/0/18)	132	-2.0
VITT, OSSIE	Oscar Joseph; B1.4.1890 San Francisco CA; D1.31.1963 Oakland CA; BR/TR/5´10˝/150; d4.11; M3																								
1912	Det A	76	273	39	67	4	4	0	19	18	2	—	.245	.297	.289	70	-11	17	.929	0	87	52	O28(26/1/1),3b24,2b15	—	-1.2
1913	Det A	99	359	45	86	11	3	2	33	31	2	18	.240	.304	.304	79	-10	5	.960	2	107	84	2b78,3b17,O2C	—	-0.7
1914	Det A	66	195	35	49	7	0	0	8	31	0	8	.251	.354	.287	90	-1	10-8	.964	3	117	90	2b36,3b16,O2L/S	—	0.3
1915	Det A	152	560	116	140	18	13	1	48	80	4	22	.250	.348	.334	99	1	26-18	**.964**	13	**112**	81	3b151,2b2	—	1.8
1916	Det A	153	597	88	135	17	12	0	42	75	1	28	.226	.314	.295	80	-14	18	**.964**	26	**118**	**107**	3b151,S2	—	1.8
1917	Det A	140	512	65	130	13	6	0	47	56	1	15	.254	.329	.303	93	-4	18	.940	-17	88	86	3b140	—	-1.8
1918	Det A	81	267	29	64	5	2	0	17	32	0	6	.240	.321	.273	83	-5	5	.953	3	97	108	3b66,2b9,O3C	—	-0.1
1919	Bos A	133	469	64	114	10	3	0	40	44	1	11	.243	.309	.277	69	-19	9	**.970**	18	**113**	115	3b133	—	0.3
1920	Bos A	87	296	50	65	10	4	1	28	43	1	10	.220	.321	.291	65	-14	5-4	.986	-1	104	51	3b64,2b21	—	-1.3
1921	Bos A	78	232	29	44	11	1	0	13	45	0	13	.190	.321	.246	48	-17	1-2	.962	-3	99	122	3b71,O3L,1b2	—	-1.5
Total	10	1065	3760	560	894	106	48	4	295	455	12	131	.238	.322	.295	80	-94	114-32	.960	45	107	96	3b833,2b161,O38(31/6/1),S3,1b2	—	-2.4
VIZCAINO, JOSE	Jose Luis (Pimental); B3.26.1968 San Cristobal, D.R.; BB/TR/6´1˝/(150–190); d9.10																								
1989	LA N	7	10	2	2	0	0	0	0	0-0	0	1	.200	.200	.200	15	-1	0-0	.882	1	114	148	S5	0	0.0
1990	LA N	37	51	3	14	1	1	0	2	4-1	0	8	.275	.327	.333	84	-1	1-1	.956	1	104	120	S11,2b6	0	0.0
1991	Chi N	93	145	7	38	5	0	0	10	5-0	0	18	.262	.283	.297	61	-8	2-1	.947	1	86	37	3b57,S33,2b9	0	-0.5
1992	Chi N	86	285	25	64	10	4	1	17	14-2	0	35	.225	.260	.298	56	-17	3-0	.969	7	115	117	S50,3b29,2b5	37	-0.6
1993	Chi N	151	551	74	158	19	4	4	54	46-2	3	71	.287	.340	.358	89	-8	12-9	.968	15	114	93	S81,3b44,2b34	0	1.4
1994	NY N	103	410	47	105	13	3	3	33	33-3	2	62	.256	.310	.324	68	-20	1-11	.970	-10	100	92	S102	0	-2.6
1995	NY N	135	509	66	146	21	5	3	56	35-4	1	76	.287	.332	.365	87	-10	8-3	**.984**	15	**109**	112	S134/2	0	1.5
1996	NY N	96	363	47	110	12	6	1	32	28-0	3	58	.303	.356	.377	99	-1	9-5	.986	1	100	123	2b93	0	0.5
	†Cle A	48	179	23	51	5	2	0	13	7-0	0	24	.285	.310	.335	64	-10	6-2	.981	-4	92	92	2b45,S4/D	0	-1.1
1997	†SF N	151	568	77	151	19	7	5	50	48-1	0	87	.266	.323	.350	78	-20	8-8	.976	6	106	110	S147,2b5	0	-0.4
1998	LA N	67	237	30	62	9	0	3	29	17-0	1	35	.262	.311	.338	75	-9	7-3	.985	-3	93	88	S66	79	-0.7
1999	LA N	94	266	27	67	9	0	1	29	20-0	1	23	.252	.304	.297	56	-18	2-1	.966	4	100	85	S44,2b30,3b9/lf	18	-1.0
2000	LA N	40	93	9	19	2	1	0	4	10-3	1	15	.204	.288	.247	39	-9	1-0	1.000	1	105	68	S19,3b12,2b3/1D	0	-0.6
	†NY A	73	174	23	48	8	1	0	10	12-0	0	28	.276	.319	.333	68	-9	5-7	.990	-2	94	94	2b62,3b6,S2,D4	0	-0.9
2001	†Hou N	107	256	38	71	8	3	1	14	15-0	2	33	.277	.322	.344	67	-13	3-2	.937	-3	102	90	S53,2b18,3b7	0	-1.2
2002	Hou N	125	406	53	123	19	2	5	37	24-2	1	40	.303	.342	.397	87	-7	3-5	.980	2	96	112	S58,3b30,2b25,1b5	0	-0.2
2003	Hou N	91	189	14	47	7	3	3	26	8-3	1	22	.249	.281	.365	64	-11	0-1	.963	-1	86	103	S32,2b20,3b2/1	53	-1.0
2004	†Hou N	138	358	34	98	21	3	3	33	20-5	0	39	.274	.311	.374	74	-14	1-1	.969	5	104	86	S64,2b37,3b21,1b8	0	-0.4
2005	†Hou N	98	187	15	46	10	2	1	23	15-4	0	40	.246	.299	.337	66	-9	2-0	1.000	2	109	190	2b23,S17,1b13,3b8	0	-0.6
2006	SF N	64	119	16	25	3	0	1	5	16-3	0	10	.210	.304	.261	47	-9	0-2	.961	2	119	47	S19,2b16,1b10,3b2	0	-0.7
	StL N	16	23	3	8	3	0	1	3	1-0	0	4	.348	.375	.609	145	2	0-0	.905	-0	94	130	S7,2b2/1	0	0.2
	Year	80	142	19	33	6	0	2	8	17-3	0	14	.232	.314	.317	62	-8	0-2	.944	2	0	0	S26,2b18,1b11,3b2	0	-0.5
Total	18	1820	5379	633	1453	204	47	36	480	378-33	16	729	.270	.318	.346	75	-202	74-62	.973	40	105	100	S948,2b434,3b227,1b39,D6/lf	187	-8.9
VIZQUEL, OMAR	Omar Enrique (Gonzalez); B4.24.1967 Caracas, Distrito Capital, Venez.; BB/TR/5´9˝/(155–185); d4.3																								
1989	Sea A	143	387	45	85	7	3	1	20	28-0	1	40	.220	.273	.261	50	-26	1-4	.971	5	100	**119**	S143	0	-1.3
1990	Sea A	81	255	19	63	3	2	2	18	18-0	0	22	.247	.295	.298	66	-12	4-1	.980	4	103	95	S81	34	-0.2
1991	Sea A	142	426	42	98	16	4	1	41	45-0	0	37	.230	.302	.293	66	-20	7-2	.980	26	108	128	S138/2	0	1.7
1992	Sea A	136	483	49	142	20	4	0	21	32-0	2	38	.294	.340	.352	93	-5	15-13	**.989**	8	99	100	S136	28	1.2
1993	Sea A	158	560	68	143	14	2	2	31	50-2	4	71	.255	.319	.298	66	-27	12-14	.980	20	103	112	S155,D2	0	0.2
1994	Cle A	69	286	39	78	10	1	1	33	23-0	0	23	.273	.325	.325	68	-14	13-4	.981	2	102	117	S69	51	-0.5
1995	†Cle A	136	542	87	144	28	0	6	56	59-0	1	59	.266	.333	.351	78	-16	29-11	.986	5	104	103	S136	0	0.1
1996	†Cle A	151	542	98	161	36	1	9	64	56-0	4	42	.297	.362	.417	98	0	35-9	.971	4	105	97	S150	0	1.7
1997	†Cle A	153	565	89	158	23	6	5	49	57-1	2	58	.280	.347	.368	84	-13	43-12	.985	10	102	100	S152	0	1.3
1998	†Cle A★	151	576	86	166	30	6	2	50	62-1	4	64	.288	.358	.372	88	-9	37-12	**.993**	8	102	96	S151	0	1.3
1999	†Cle A★	144	574	112	191	36	4	5	66	65-0	1	50	.333	.397	.436	108	10	42-9	.976	-0	98	92	S143/rf	0	2.4

YEAR	TM LG	G	AB	R	H	2B	3B	HR	RBI	BB-IB	HP	SO	AVG	OBP	SLG	AOPS	ABR	SB-CS	FA	FR	RNG	THR	GAMES AT POSITION	DL	BFW
2000	Cle A	156	613	101	176	27	3	7	66	87-0	5	72	.287	.377	.375	89	-7	22-10	**.995**	-0	92	94	S156	0	0.5
2001	†Cle A	155	611	84	156	26	8	2	50	61-0	2	72	.255	.323	.334	71	-25	13-9	**.989**	6	98	90	S154	0	-0.8
2002	Cle A★	151	582	85	160	31	5	14	72	56-3	8	64	.275	.341	.418	100	1	18-10	.990	13	102	95	S150	0	2.4
2003	Cle A	64	250	43	61	13	2	2	19	29-0	0	20	.244	.321	.336	74	-9	8-3	.978	13	111	146	S64	98	0.9
2004	Cle A	148	567	82	165	28	3	7	59	57-0	1	62	.291	.353	.388	98	-1	19-6	.982	-7	97	98	S147	0	0.5
2005	SF N	152	568	66	154	28	4	3	45	56-0	5	58	.271	.341	.350	80	-15	24-10	**.988**	-8	98	83	S150	0	-1.1
2006	SF N	153	579	88	171	22	10	4	58	56-3	6	51	.295	.361	.389	93	-6	24-7	**.993**	-14	93	95	S152	0	-0.6
Total	18	2443	8966	1283	2472	398	68	73	818	897-10	46	903	.276	.342	.360	84	-194	366-146	.984	93	100	101	S2427,D2/rf2	211	9.7
VOGEL, OTTO	Otto Henry; B10.26.1899 Mendota IL; D7.19.1969 Iowa City IA; BR/TR/6´0˝/195; d6.5; Col Illinois																								
1923	Chi N	41	81	10	17	0	1	1	6	7	3	11	.210	.297	.272	51	-6	2-3	.929	0	96	143	O24(3/0/21)/3	—	-0.7
1924	Chi N	70	172	28	46	11	2	1	24	10	3	26	.267	.319	.372	84	-4	4-4	.956	3	107	128	O53(12/1/40),3b2	—	-0.5
Total	2	111	253	38	63	11	3	2	30	17	6	37	.249	.312	.340	73	-10	6-7	.948	3	104	132	O77(15/1/61),3b3	—	-1.2
VOIGT, JACK	John David; B5.17.1966 Sarasota FL; BR/TR/6´1˝/(175–178); [BalA87 9/221]; d8.3; Col Louisiana St.																								
1992	Bal A	1	0	0	0	0	0	0	0	0-0	0	0	ø	ø	ø	ø	0	0-0	ø	0	—	—	/R	0	0.0
1993	Bal A	64	152	32	45	11	1	6	23	25-0	0	33	.296	.395	.500	133	8	1-0	.987	-0	99	121	O43(22/0/23),1b5,3b3,D9	0	0.6
1994	Bal A	59	141	15	34	5	0	3	20	18-1	1	25	.241	.327	.340	70	-6	0-0	.989	1	107	68	O54(17/1/37),1b6,D2	0	-0.7
1995	Bal A	3	1	1	1	0	0	0	0	0-0	0	0	1.000	1.000	1.000	415	0	0-0	1.000	0	409	0	/1D	0	0.1
	Tex A	33	62	8	10	3	0	2	8	10-0	0	14	.161	.274	.306	50	-5	0-0	1.000	-0	103	84	O25(8/0/17),1b5,D2	0	-0.6
	Year	36	63	9	11	3	0	2	8	10-0	0	14	.175	.284	.317	55	-4	0-0	1.000	-0	103	84	O25(8/0/17),1b6,D3	0	-0.5
1996	Tex A	5	9	1	1	0	0	0	0	0-0	0	2	.111	.111	.111	-41	-2	0-0	1.000	0	151	0	O3(2/0/1)/3	0	-0.2
1997	Mil A	72	151	20	37	9	2	8	22	19-2	1	36	.245	.331	.490	110	2	1-2	.985	-0	103	266	O40(35/2/5),1b19,3b6/D	0	-0.1
1998	Oak A	57	72	7	10	4	0	1	10	6-0	0	19	.139	.205	.236	15	-9	5-1	.987	-0	40	128	1b27,O20(9/10/2),3b2,D3	0	-0.9
Total	7	294	588	84	138	32	3	20	83	78-3	2	129	.235	.324	.401	86	-12	7-3	.990	1	103	143	O185(93/13/85),1b63,D18,3b12	0	-1.8
VOLLMER, CLYDE	Clyde Frederick "Dutch the Clutch"; B9.24.1921 Cincinnati OH; D10.2.2006 Florence KY; BR/TR/6´1˝/190; d5.31; Mil 1943–45																								
1942	Cin N	12	43	2	4	0	0	1	4	1	0	5	.093	.114	.163	-20	-7	0	1.000	0	113	0	O11(10/1/0)	0	-0.8
1946	Cin N	9	22	1	4	0	0	0	1	1	0	3	.182	.217	.182	14	-3	2	1.000	-1	75	0	O7(5/3/1)	0	-0.4
1947	Cin N	78	155	19	34	10	0	1	13	9	1	18	.219	.267	.303	51	-11	0	.984	4	123	72	O66(8/58/0)	0	-0.8
1948	Cin N	7	9	0	1	0	0	0	0	1	0	1	.111	.200	.111	-14	-1	0	ø	-0	0	0	O2(0/1/1)	0	-0.2
	Was A	1	5	1	2	0	0	0	0	0	0	1	.400	.400	.400	116	0	0-0	1.000	-0	74	0	/cf	0	0.0
1949	Was A	129	443	58	112	17	1	14	59	53	2	62	.253	.335	.391	94	-6	1-2	.982	1	109	37	O114(0/99/15)	0	-0.8
1950	Was A	6	14	4	4	0	0	0	1	2	0	3	.286	.375	.286	75	0	1-0	1.000	0	79	458	O3L	0	0.0
	Bos A	57	169	35	48	10	0	7	37	21	0	35	.284	.363	.467	102	0	1-0	.954	-2	93	98	O39(17/11/11)	0	-0.3
	Year	63	183	39	52	10	0	7	38	23	0	38	.284	.364	.454	100	0	2-0	.957	-1	92	123	O42(20/11/11)	0	-0.3
1951	Bos A	115	386	66	97	9	2	22	85	55	1	66	.251	.346	.456	105	2	0-0	.986	-4	97	66	O106(2/8/97)	0	-0.5
1952	Bos A	90	250	35	66	12	4	11	50	39	3	47	.264	.370	.476	124	9	2-2	1.000	1	104	66	O70(43/9/21)	0	0.5
1953	Bos A	1	0	0	0	0	0	0	0	1	0	0	ø	1.000	ø	180	0	0-0	ø	0	—	—	/H	0	0.0
	Was A	118	408	54	106	15	3	11	74	48	3	59	.260	.342	.392	100	0	0-2	.979	3	103	102	O106(104/0/2)	0	-0.5
	Year	119	408	54	106	15	3	11	74	49	3	59	.260	.343	.392	101	0	0-2	.979	3	103	102	O106(104/0/2)	0	-0.5
1954	Was A	62	117	8	30	4	0	2	15	12	1	28	.256	.331	.342	89	-2	0-0	1.000	-1	80	131	O26(5/0/21)	0	-0.4
Total	10	685	2021	283	508	77	10	69	339	243	11	328	.251	.335	.402	95	-19	7-6	.984	0	103	72	O551(197/191/169)	0	-4.2
VON KOLNITZ, FRITZ	Alfred Holmes; B5.20.1893 Charleston SC; D3.18.1948 Mount Pleasant SC; BR/TR/5´10.5˝/175; d4.18; Col South Carolina																								
1914	Cin N	41	104	8	23	2	0	0	6	6	1	16	.221	.270	.240	51	-6	4	.914	-1	112	72	3b20,O11(2/7/2),C2/1	—	-0.8
1915	Cin N	50	78	6	15	4	1	0	6	7	0	11	.192	.259	.269	59	-4	1-3	.933	-3	85	191	3b18,S6,1b3,C2/rf	—	-0.8
1916	Chi A	24	44	1	10	3	0	0	7	2	0	6	.227	.261	.295	66	-2	0	.909	-3	64	74	3b13	—	-0.5
Total	3	115	226	15	48	9	1	0	19	15	1	33	.212	.264	.261	56	-12	5-3	.918	-7	94	107	3b51,O12(2/7/3),S6,1b4,C4	—	-2.1
VOSMIK, JOE	Joseph Franklin; B4.4.1910 Cleveland OH; D1.27.1962 Cleveland OH; BR/TR/6´0˝/185; d9.13																								
1930	Cle A	9	26	1	6	2	0	0	4	1	0	1	.231	.259	.308	42	-2	0-0	.933	0	88	237	O5(1/4/0)	—	-0.2
1931	Cle A	149	591	80	189	36	14	7	117	38	2	30	.320	.363	.464	110	7	7-7	.970	4	104	116	O147(147/1/0)	—	0.1
1932	Cle A	**153**	621	106	194	39	12	10	97	58	5	42	.312	.376	.462	109	8	2-3	**.989**	19	**124**	99	O153L	—	1.6
1933	Cle A	119	438	53	115	20	10	4	56	42	3	13	.263	.331	.381	84	-11	0-2	.985	3	97	130	O113L	—	-1.4
1934	Cle A	104	405	71	138	33	2	6	78	35	0	10	.341	.393	.477	122	14	1-1	.976	-4	93	80	O104L	—	0.4
1935	Cle A★	152	620	93	**216**	**47**	**20**	10	110	59	4	30	.348	.408	.537	140	36	2-1	.986	3	110	41	O150L	—	2.8
1936	Cle A	138	506	76	145	29	7	7	94	79	0	21	.287	.383	.413	96	-2	5-1	.978	-3	95	95	O136(136/0/1)	—	-1.0
1937	StL A	144	594	81	193	47	9	4	93	49	1	38	.325	.377	.455	108	8	2-3	.972	7	109	107	O143L	—	0.6
1938	Bos A	146	621	121	**201**	37	6	9	86	59	2	26	.324	.384	.446	103	3	0-3	.978	4	100	131	O146(146/1/0)	—	-0.2
1939	Bos A	145	554	89	153	29	6	7	84	66	3	33	.276	.356	.388	87	-10	4-3	.974	-6	92	90	O144L	—	-2.2
1940	Bro N	116	404	45	114	14	6	1	42	22	1	21	.282	.321	.354	81	-11	0	.976	1	98	123	O99(39/9/51)	—	-1.6
1941	Bro N	25	56	0	11	0	0	0	4	4	0	4	.196	.250	.196	26	-6	0	1.000	-2	71	0	O18(2/0/16)	0	-0.8
1944	Was A	14	36	2	7	2	0	0	9	2	0	3	.194	.237	.250	41	-3	0-0	1.000	-0	102	0	O12(5/0/7)	0	-0.4
Total	13	1414	5472	818	1682	335	92	65	874	514	21	272	.307	.369	.438	104	31	23-24	.979	26	103	100	O1370(1283/15/75)	0	-2.3
VOSS, ALEX	Alexander; B5.16.1858 Roswell GA; D8.31.1906 Cincinnati OH; BR/TR/6´1˝/180; d4.17; ▲																								
1884	Was U	63	245	33	47	9	0	0	—	5	—	—	.192	.208	.229	33	-27	—	.848	6	126	156	P27,3b16,1b15,O13(0/7/6)/S	—	-1.3
	KC U	14	45	1	4	0	0	0	—	0	—	—	.089	.089	.089	-53	-10	—	.867	2	134	359	O8(5/3/0),P7	—	-0.3
	Year	77	290	34	51	9	0	0	—	5	—	—	.176	.190	.207	21	-37	—	.859	7	126	174	P34,O21(5/10/6),3b16,1b15/S	—	-1.6
VOSS, BILL	William Edward; B10.31.1943 Glendale CA; BL/TL/6´2˝/(160–170); d9.14																								
1965	Chi A	11	33	4	6	0	1	1	3	3-1	0	5	.182	.250	.333	68	-2	0-0	1.000	-1	76	0	O10R	0	-0.4
1966	Chi A	2	2	0	0	0	0	0	0	0-0	0	2	.000	.000	.000	-99	-1	0-0	1.000	0	95	0	/lf	0	-0.1
1967	Chi A	13	22	4	2	0	0	0	0	0-0	0	1	.091	.091	.091	-48	-4	1-1	1.000	0	113	0	O11(1/2/9)	0	-0.5
1968	Chi A	61	167	14	26	2	1	2	15	16-1	2	34	.156	.238	.216	38	-13	5-3	.963	-1	86	179	O55(5/2/53)	52	-1.9
1969	Cal A	133	349	33	91	11	4	2	40	35-6	0	40	.261	.327	.332	89	-5	5-3	.995	7	110	**161**	O111(6/4/104),1b2	0	-0.3
1970	Cal A	80	181	21	44	4	3	3	30	23-2	2	18	.243	.327	.348	91	-2	2-1	.979	3	99	224	O55R	32	-0.1
1971	Mil A	97	275	31	69	4	0	10	30	24-1	1	45	.251	.312	.375	95	-3	2-2	.987	-1	109	22	O79(4/13/67)	0	-0.7
1972	Mil A	27	36	1	3	1	0	0	1	5-0	0	4	.083	.195	.111	-7	-5	0-1	.929	-1	97	0	O11(3/0/9)	0	-0.7
	Oak A	40	97	10	22	5	1	1	5	9-3	1	16	.227	.296	.330	91	-1	0-0	1.000	1	102	157	O34(1/13/21)	0	-0.1
	Year	67	133	11	25	6	1	1	6	14-3	1	20	.188	.268	.271	63	-6	0-1	.987	0	92	0	O45(4/13/30)	0	-0.8
	StL N	11	15	1	4	2	0	0	3	2-0	0	2	.267	.333	.400	114	0	0-0	1.000	-0	92	0	O2C	0	0.0
Total	8	475	1177	119	267	29	10	19	127	117-14	6	167	.227	.298	.317	78	-36	15-11	.986	7	102	128	O369(21/36/328),1b2	84	-4.8
VOYLES, PHIL	Philip Vance; B5.12.1900 Murphy NC; D11.3.1972 Marlborough MA; BL/TR/5´11.5˝/175; d9.4																								
1929	Bos N	20	68	9	16	0	2	0	14	6	0	8	.235	.297	.294	49	-6	0	.922	-1	92	116	O20(1/19/0)	—	-0.7
VUKOVICH, GEORGE	George Stephen; B6.24.1956 Chicago IL; BL/TR/6´0˝/198; [PhiN77 4/100]; d4.13; Col Southern Illinois																								
1980	†Phi N	78	58	6	13	1	1	0	8	6-0	0	9	.224	.297	.276	57	-3	0-0	.933	-0	112	0	O28(13/0/15)	0	-0.4
1981	†Phi N	20	26	5	10	0	0	1	4	1-0	0	0	.385	.407	.500	148	1	1-0	1.000	0	118	0	O9(3/1/5)	0	0.2
1982	Phi N	123	335	41	91	18	2	6	42	32-14	0	47	.272	.334	.391	99	0	2-9	.977	1	108	67	O102(15/0/100)	0	-0.7
1983	Cle A	124	312	31	77	13	2	3	44	24-4	2	37	.247	.301	.330	72	-12	3-4	.986	0	111	44	O122(20/3/107)	0	-1.7
1984	Cle A	134	437	38	133	22	5	9	60	34-3	1	61	.304	.354	.439	116	10	1-4	.994	19	**128**	172	O130(16/0/124)	0	2.1
1985	Cle A	149	434	43	106	22	0	8	45	30-6	1	75	.244	.292	.350	76	-15	2-2	.988	-0	105	51	O137(10/0/131)	0	-2.1
Total	6	628	1602	164	430	76	10	27	203	127-27	4	229	.268	.322	.379	91	-19	9-19	.987	20	114	86	O528(77/4/482)	0	-2.6
VUKOVICH, JOHN	John Christopher; B7.31.1947 Sacramento CA; BR/TR/6´1˝/(187–190); [PhiN66*1/10]; d9.11; M2/C23; Col American River (CA) CC																								
1970	Phi N	3	8	1	1	0	0	0	0	1-0	0	0	.125	.222	.125	-4	-1	0-0	.778	0	72	95	S2/3	0	-0.1
1971	Phi N	74	217	11	36	5	0	0	14	12-1	1	34	.166	.211	.189	15	-25	2-1	.956	4	107	75	3b74	0	-2.3
1973	Mil A	55	128	10	16	3	0	2	9	9-0	0	40	.125	.182	.195	6	-16	0-2	.948	-4	94	42	3b40,1b13/S	0	-2.3
1974	Mil A	38	80	5	15	1	0	3	11	1-0	0	16	.188	.193	.313	45	-6	2-1	.945	-5	102	92	S12,3b12,2b11,1b4	0	-1.0
1975	Cin N	31	38	4	8	3	0	0	2	4-1	0	5	.211	.286	.289	59	-2	0-0	.925	0	109	148	3b31	0	-0.2
1976	Phi N	4	8	2	1	0	0	1	2	0-0	0	2	.125	.125	.500	69	0	0-0	1.000	-1	48	0	3b4/1	0	-0.2
1977	Phi N	2	2	0	0	0	0	0	0	0-0	0	1	.000	.000	.000	-95	-1	0-0	ø	0	—	—	/H	0	-0.1
1979	Phi N	10	15	0	3	1	0	0	1	0-0	0	3	.200	.200	.267	25	-2	0-0	1.000	-0	164	218	3b7,2b3	0	-0.2

YEAR	TM LG	G	AB	R	H	2B	3B	HR	RBI	BB-IB	HP	SO	AVG	OBP	SLG	AOPS	ABR	SB-CS	FA	FR	RNG	THR	GAMES AT POSITION	DL	BFW
1980	Phi N	49	62	4	10	1	1	0	5	2-1	1	7	.161	.197	.210	14	-7	0-1	.958	-4	84	0	3b34,2b9,S5/1	0	-1.3
1981	Phi N	11	1	0	0	0	0	0	0	0-0	0	1	.000	.000	.000	-95	0	0-0	.800	-1	105	0	3b9/12	0	-0.1
Total	10	277	559	37	90	14	1	6	44	29-3	2	109	.161	.203	.222	20	-60	4-5	.951	-12	103	62	3b212,2b24,1b20,S20	0	-7.8
WADDEY, FRANK	Frank Orum; B8.21.1905 Memphis TN; D10.21.1990 Knoxville TN; BL/TL/5´10.5˝/185; d4.16; Col Georgia Tech																								
1931	StL A	14	22	3	6	1	0	0	2	2	0	3	.273	.333	.318	70	-1	0-0	1.000	-1	71	0	O7(1/5/1)	—	-0.2
WADE, HAM	Abraham Lincoln; B12.20.1879 Spring City PA; D7.21.1968 Riverside NJ; BR/TR/5´8˝/155; d9.9																								
1907	NY N	1	0	0	0	0	0	0	0	0	1	—	ø	1.000	ø	208	0	0	1.000	0	0	0	/lf	—	0.0
WADE, GALE	Galeard Lee; B1.20.1929 Hollister MO; BL/TR/6´1.5˝/185; d4.11																								
1955	Chi N	9	33	5	6	1	0	1	1	4-0	0	3	.182	.270	.303	52	-2	0-0	.867	-2	62	175	O9C	0	-0.4
1956	Chi N	10	12	0	0	0	0	0	0	1-0	0	0	.000	.077	.000	-78	-3	0-0	.875	-0	119	0	O3C	0	-0.3
Total	2	19	45	5	6	1	0	1	1	5-0	0	3	.133	.220	.222	18	-5	0-0	.870	-2	75	134	O12C	0	-0.7
WADE, RIP	Richard Frank; B1.12.1898 Duluth MN; D7.15.1957 Duluth MN; BL/TR/5´11˝/174; d4.19																								
1923	Was A	33	69	8	16	2	2	2	14	5	0	10	.232	.284	.406	84	-2	0-0	.967	0	82	190	O19(5/12/2)	—	-0.3
WAGENHORST, WOODY	Ellwood Otto; B6.3.1863 Kutztown PA; D2.12.1946 Washington DC; 5´11˝/165; d6.25; Col Princeton																								
1888	Phi N	2	8	2	1	0	0	0	0	0	0	1	.125	.125	.125	-19	-1	0	.800	-1	53	414	3b2	—	-0.2
WAGNER, BUTTS	Albert; B9.17.1871 Chartiers (now Carnegie) PA; D11.26.1928 Pittsburgh PA; BR/TR/5´10˝/170; d4.27; b–Honus																								
1898	Was N	63	223	20	50	11	2	1	31	14	3	—	.224	.279	.305	67	-10	4	.833	-9	84	79	3b39,O10(1/9/0),S8,2b5	—	-1.7
	Bro N	11	38	2	9	1	1	0	3	2	0	—	.237	.275	.316	69	-2	0	.813	-3	88	53	3b11	—	-0.4
	Year	74	261	22	59	12	3	1	34	16	3	—	.226	.279	.307	68	-11	4	.828	-12	85	73	3b50,O10(1/9/0),S8,2b5	—	-2.1
WAGNER, HEINIE	Charles F.; B9.23.1880 New York NY; D3.20.1943 New Rochelle NY; BR/TR/5´9˝/183; d7.1; M1/C7																								
1902	NY N	17	56	4	12	1	0	0	2	0	0	—	.214	.214	.232	38	-4	3	.862	-4	86	91	S17	—	-0.8
1906	Bos A	9	32	1	9	0	0	0	4	1	0	—	.281	.303	.281	83	-1	2	.943	1	129	65	2b9	—	0.1
1907	Bos A	111	385	29	82	10	4	2	21	31	2	—	.213	.275	.275	76	-10	20	.931	-6	99	92	S109/23	—	-1.4
1908	Bos A	153	526	62	130	11	5	1	46	27	3	—	.247	.288	.293	86	-9	20	.939	32	**108**	108	S153	—	3.2
1909	Bos A	124	430	53	110	16	7	1	49	35	3	—	.256	.316	.333	103	1	18	.933	10	105	97	S123/2	—	1.7
1910	Bos A	142	491	61	134	26	7	1	52	44	2	—	.273	.335	.360	115	9	26	.927	-13	94	83	S140	—	0.0
1911	Bos A	80	261	34	67	13	8	1	38	29	4	—	.257	.340	.379	101	0	15	.946	-6	92	81	2b40,S32	—	-0.3
1912	†Bos A	144	504	75	138	25	6	2	68	62	4	—	.274	.358	.359	100	2	21	.922	-13	87	102	S144	—	-0.1
1913	Bos A	110	365	43	83	14	8	2	34	40	7	29	.227	.316	.326	86	-7	9	.937	-0	91	85	S103,2b5/3	—	0.0
1915	Bos A	84	267	38	64	11	2	0	29	37	3	34	.240	.339	.296	93	-1	8-4	.927	-15	87	70	2b79/3lf	—	-1.6
1916	Bos A	6	8	2	4	1	0	0	0	3	0	0	.500	.636	.625	278	2	2	1.000	1	149	0	3b4/2S	—	0.4
1918	Bos A	3	8	0	1	0	0	0	0	1	0	0	.125	.222	.125	5	-1	0	.900	-0	113	254	2b2/3	—	-0.1
Total	12	983	3333	402	834	128	47	10	343	310	28	63	.250	.319	.326	95	-19	144-4	.928	-14	97	96	S822,2b138,3b8/lf	—	1.1
WAGNER, HAL	Harold Edward; B7.2.1915 E.Riverton NJ; D8.7.1979 Riverside NJ; BL/TR/6´0˝/165; d10.3; Mil 1944–45; Col Duke																								
1937	Phi A	1	0	0	0	0	0	0	0	0	0	0	ø	ø	ø	ø	0	0-0	1.000	0	*0*	*0*	/C	—	0.0
1938	Phi A	33	88	10	20	2	1	0	8	8	1	9	.227	.299	.273	45	-8	0-0	.972	-2	*78*	*136*	C30	—	-0.7
1939	Phi A	5	8	0	1	0	0	0	0	0	0	3	.125	.125	.125	-37	-2	0-0	1.000	1	*127*	*264*	C5	—	-0.1
1940	Phi A	34	75	9	19	5	1	0	10	11	1	6	.253	.356	.347	85	-1	0-0	.964	1	*69*	*121*	C28	—	0.1
1941	Phi A	46	131	18	29	8	2	1	15	19	0	9	.221	.320	.336	75	-4	1-0	.976	-1	*89*	*91*	C42	0	-0.2
1942	Phi A☆	104	288	26	68	17	1	1	30	24	4	29	.236	.304	.313	74	-10	1-0	.986	-6	*74*	*110*	C94	0	-1.0
1943	Phi A	111	289	22	69	17	1	1	26	36	2	17	.239	.327	.315	89	-3	3-3	.980	-10	*75*	*88*	C99	0	-0.9
1944	Phi A	5	4	0	1	0	0	0	0	0	0	0	.250	.250	.250	44	0	0-0	1.000	0	*0*	*1076*	/C	0	0.0
	Bos A	66	223	21	74	13	4	1	38	29	4	14	.332	.418	.439	147	15	1-1	.970	-2	*101*	*80*	C64	0	1.8
	Year	71	227	21	75	13	4	1	38	29	4	14	.330	.415	.436	145	15	1-1	.971	-2	*100*	*85*	C65	0	1.8
1946	†Bos A★	117	370	39	85	12	2	6	52	69	2	32	.230	.354	.322	85	-5	3-1	.983	-5	***133***	*61*	C116	0	-0.4
1947	Bos A	21	65	5	15	3	0	0	6	9	0	5	.231	.324	.277	63	-3	0-0	.978	-1	*87*	*59*	C21	0	-0.3
	Det A	71	191	19	55	10	0	5	33	28	1	16	.288	.382	.419	119	6	0-1	.990	-0	*119*	*70*	C71	0	0.9
	Year	92	256	24	70	13	0	5	39	37	1	21	.273	.367	.383	105	3	0-1	.987	-1	*111*	*67*	C92	0	0.6
1948	Det A	54	109	10	22	3	0	0	10	20	0	11	.202	.326	.229	48	-8	1-0	.989	-2	*95*	*51*	C52	0	-0.7
	Phi N	3	4	0	0	0	0	0	0	0	0	0	.000	.000	.000	-99	-1	0	1.000	1	*0*	*540*	/C	0	-0.1
1949	Phi N	1	4	0	0	0	0	0	0	0	0	1	.000	.000	.000	-99	-1	0	.750	-0	*0*	*0*	/C	0	-0.2
Total	12	672	1849	179	458	90	12	15	228	253	15	152	.248	.343	.334	87	-25	10-6	.981	-26	*97*	*85*	C626	0	-1.8
WAGNER, HONUS	John Peter "The Flying Dutchman"; B2.24.1874 Chartiers (now Carnegie) PA; D12.6.1955 Carnegie PA; BR/TR/5´11˝/200; d7.19; M1/C19; HF1936; b–Butts; OF(35/67/272)																								
1897	Lou N	62	242	38	81	18	4	2	39	15	1	—	.335	.376	.467	126	9	20	.912	4	233	330	O53(1/53/0),2b9	—	0.8
1898	Lou N	151	588	80	176	29	3	10	105	31	6	—	.299	.341	.410	117	11	27	.972	-1	113	95	1b75,3b65,2b10	—	1.1
1899	Lou N	148	575	100	196	45	13	7	114	40	11	—	.341	.395	.501	145	35	37	.920	4	104	97	3b76,O61(3/0/58),2b7,1b4	—	3.4
1900	†Pit N	135	527	107	201	**45**	**22**	4	100	41	8	—	**.381**	.434	**.573**	**175**	53	38	.965	-3	71	109	O118R,3b9,2b7,1b3/P	—	4.1
1901	Pit N	**140**	549	101	194	37	11	6	**126**	53	7	—	.353	.417	.494	159	43	**49**	.918	3	99	139	S61,O54(1/0/53),3b24/2	—	4.4
1902	Pit N	136	534	**105**	176	**30**	16	3	**91**	43	**14**	—	.330	.394	**.463**	**159**	**37**	**42**	1.000	3	119	97	O61(20/11/30),S44,1b32/P2	—	3.9
1903	†Pit N	129	512	97	182	30	**19**	5	101	44	7	—	**.355**	.414	.518	160	39	46	.933	18	106	**132**	S111,O12(1/0/11),1b6	—	5.6
1904	Pit N	132	490	97	171	**44**	14	4	75	59	4	—	**.349**	**.423**	**.520**	**186**	**52**	**53**	.929	-4	97	110	S121,O8(6/2/0),1b3,2b2	—	**5.3**
1905	Pit N	147	548	114	199	32	14	6	101	54	7	—	.363	.427	.505	173	50	57	.935	19	**108**	117	S145,O2L	—	**7.5**
1906	Pit N	142	516	**103**	175	**38**	9	2	71	58	10	—	**.339**	.416	.459	166	42	53	.941	20	**109**	**137**	S137,O2R/3	—	**7.2**
1907	Pit N	142	515	98	180	**38**	14	6	82	46	5	—	**.350**	**.408**	**.513**	**186**	**50**	**61**	.938	6	102	73	S138,1b4	—	**6.7**
1908	Pit N	151	568	100	**201**	**39**	**19**	10	**109**	54	5	—	**.354**	**.415**	**.542**	**205**	**66**	**53**	.943	-11	93	106	S151	—	**6.9**
1909	†Pit N	137	495	92	168	**39**	10	5	**100**	66	3	—	**.339**	**.420**	**.489**	**168**	**42**	35	.940	5	99	**134**	S136/lf	—	**5.6**
1910	Pit N	150	556	90	**178**	34	8	4	81	59	5	47	.320	.390	.432	132	24	24	.935	5	97	**119**	S138,1b11,2b2	—	3.5
1911	Pit N	130	473	87	158	23	16	9	89	67	6	34	**.334**	.423	.507	154	35	20	.932	-0	97	153	S101,1b28/cf	—	4.1
1912	Pit N	145	558	91	181	35	20	7	**102**	59	6	38	.324	.395	.496	145	34	26	**.962**	17	100	**137**	S143	—	**5.9**
1913	Pit N	114	413	51	124	18	4	3	56	26	5	40	.300	.349	.385	114	7	21-11	**.962**	9	96	120	S105	—	2.5
1914	Pit N	150	552	60	139	15	9	1	50	51	2	51	.252	.317	.317	93	-5	23	**.950**	8	102	102	S132,3b17/1	—	1.2
1915	Pit N	**156**	566	68	155	32	17	6	78	39	4	64	.274	.325	.422	127	16	22-15	**.948**	1	97	105	S131,2b12,1b10	—	2.8
1916	Pit N	123	432	45	124	15	9	1	39	34	8	36	.287	.350	.370	120	11	11	.942	-14	86	79	S92,1b24,2b4	—	0.3
1917	Pit N	74	230	15	61	7	1	0	24	24	1	17	.265	.337	.304	94	0	5	.985	-4	89	93	1b47,3b18,2b2/SM	—	-0.6
Total	21	2794	10439	1739	3420	643	252	101	1733	963	125	327	.328	.391	.467	150	651	723-26	.940	84	100	116	S1887,O373R,1b248,3b210,2b57,P2	—	82.2
WAGNER, JOE	Joseph Bernard; B4.24.1889 New York NY; D11.15.1948 Bronx NY; BR/TR/5´11˝/165; d4.25																								
1915	Cin N	75	197	17	35	5	2	0	13	8	0	35	.178	.210	.223	31	-17	4-6	.961	6	101	162	2b46,S12,3b2	—	-1.3
WAGNER, LEON	Leon Lamar "Daddy Wags"; B5.13.1934 Chattanooga TN; D1.3.2004 Los Angeles CA; BL/TR/6´1˝/(192–205); d6.22; Col Tuskegee																								
1958	SF N	74	221	31	70	9	0	13	35	18-3	1	34	.317	.371	.534	139	12	1-0	.949	-0	92	134	O57L	0	0.9
1959	SF N	87	129	20	29	4	3	5	22	25-6	3	24	.225	.361	.419	110	2	0-0	.941	-0	116	0	O28L	0	0.1
1960	StL N	39	98	12	21	2	0	4	11	17-3	1	17	.214	.333	.357	83	-2	0-1	.963	1	98	182	O32(29/0/4)	0	-0.3
1961	LA A	133	453	74	127	19	2	28	79	48-2	3	65	.280	.348	.517	116	10	5-1	.971	0	89	148	O116(104/0/14)	0	0.4
1962	LA A★	160	612	96	164	21	5	37	107	50-4	5	87	.268	.326	.500	123	16	7-5	.972	-8	88	76	O156(102/0/62)	0	-0.1
1963	LA A★	149	550	73	160	11	1	26	90	49-8	7	73	.291	.352	.456	134	24	5-7	.960	-4	92	71	O141(136/0/7)	0	1.0
1964	Cle A	163	641	94	162	19	2	31	100	56-12	6	121	.253	.316	.434	108	5	14-2	.959	-6	92	63	O163L	0	-0.8
1965	Cle A	144	517	91	152	18	1	28	79	60-8	3	52	.294	.369	.495	143	29	12-2	.957	-12	78	40	O134L	0	1.2
1966	Cle A	150	549	70	153	20	0	23	66	46-9	1	69	.279	.334	.441	121	14	5-2	.990	-10	82	51	O139L	0	-0.2
1967	Cle A	135	433	56	105	15	1	15	54	37-6	12	76	.242	.317	.386	107	4	3-3	.980	-7	79	58	O117L	0	-1.1
1968	Cle A	38	49	5	9	4	0	0	6	6-0	0	6	.184	.273	.265	65	-2	0-0	.500	-3	27	0	O10(7/0/3)	0	-0.5
	Chi A	69	162	14	46	8	0	1	18	21-2	0	31	.284	.366	.352	117	4	2-1	.941	-6	72	0	O46(9/1/36)	0	-0.5
	Year	107	211	19	55	12	0	1	24	27-2	0	37	.261	.345	.332	105	3	2-1	.895	-9	65	0	O56(16/1/39)	0	-1.0
1969	SF N	11	12	0	4	0	0	0	2	2-1	1	1	.333	.467	.333	129	1	0-0	1.000	0	164	0	/lf	0	0.1
Total	12	1352	4426	636	1202	150	15	211	669	435-64	43	656	.272	.340	.455	121	117	54-24	.964	-54	87	72	O1140(1026/1/126)	0	0.2

WAGNER, MARK Mark Duane; B3.4.1954 Conneaut OH; BR/TR/6´1˝/(165–175); [DetA72 19/452]; d8.20

YEAR	TM LG	G	AB	R	H	2B	3B	HR	RBI	BB-IB	HP	SO	AVG	OBP	SLG	AOPS	ABR	SB-CS	FA	FR	RNG	THR	GAMES AT POSITION	DL	BFW
1976	Det A	39	115	9	30	2	3	0	12	6-0	0	18	.261	.298	.330	80	-3	0-2	.947	7	116	110	S39	0	0.8
1977	Det A	22	48	4	7	0	1	1	3	4-0	1	12	.146	.222	.250	28	-5	0-1	.923	-1	118	107	S21/2	0	-0.4
1978	Det A	39	109	10	26	1	2	0	6	3-0	2	11	.239	.272	.284	55	-7	1-0	.964	-3	92	107	S35,2b4	0	-0.7
1979	Det A	75	146	16	40	3	0	1	13	16-0	0	25	.274	.341	.315	77	-4	3-2	.974	-6	96	98	S41,2b29,3b2/D	0	-0.6
1980	Det A	45	72	5	17	1	0	0	3	7-0	0	11	.236	.304	.250	52	-5	0-1	.935	-10	71	49	S28,3b9,2b6	21	-1.3
1981	Tex A	50	85	15	22	4	1	1	14	8-0	0	13	.259	.323	.365	102	0	1-1	.964	0	92	89	S43,2b4,3b2	0	0.3
1982	Tex A	60	179	14	43	4	1	0	8	10-0	0	28	.240	.280	.274	55	-11	1-0	.955	2	110	88	S60	73	-0.3
1983	Tex A	2	2	0	0	0	0	0	0	0-0	0	1	.000	.000	.000	-99	-1	0-0	1.000	1	193	0	S2	18	0.0
1984	Oak A	82	87	8	20	5	1	0	12	7-0	0	11	.230	.284	.310	69	-4	2-0	.951	-4	86	84	S57,3b15,2b8/PD	0	-0.4
Total	9	414	843	81	205	20	9	3	71	61-0	3	130	.243	.295	.299	66	-40	8-7	.953	-13	100	92	S326,2b52,3b28,D4/P	112	-2.6

WAGNER, BILL William Joseph; B1.2.1894 Jesup IA; D1.11.1951 Waterloo IA; BR/TR/6´0˝/187; d7.16

YEAR	TM LG	G	AB	R	H	2B	3B	HR	RBI	BB-IB	HP	SO	AVG	OBP	SLG	AOPS	ABR	SB-CS	FA	FR	RNG	THR	GAMES AT POSITION	DL	BFW
1914	Pit N	3	1	0	0	0	0	0	0	0	0	0	.000	.000	.000	-99	0	0	1.000	0	*0*	*316*	C3	—	0.0
1915	Pit N	5	5	0	0	0	0	0	0	1	0	2	.000	.167	.000	-48	-1	0	1.000	1	*135*	*252*	C3	—	0.0
1916	Pit N	19	38	2	9	0	2	0	2	5	0	8	.237	.326	.342	104	0	0	.936	0	93	139	C15	—	0.1
1917	Pit N	53	151	15	31	7	2	0	9	11	1	22	.205	.264	.278	64	-6	1	.958	-6	*72*	*117*	C37,1b12	—	-1.1
1918	Bos N	13	47	2	10	0	0	1	7	4	0	5	.213	.275	.277	71	-2	0	.917	-4	*88*	*78*	C13	—	-0.5
Total	5	93	242	19	50	7	4	1	18	21	1	37	.207	.273	.281	69	-9	1	.947	-9	*81*	*117*	C71,1b12	—	-1.5

WAHL, KERMIT Kermit Emerson; B11.18.1922 Columbia SD; D9.16.1987 Tucson AZ; BR/TR/5´11˝/170; d6.23; Col Indiana

YEAR	TM LG	G	AB	R	H	2B	3B	HR	RBI	BB-IB	HP	SO	AVG	OBP	SLG	AOPS	ABR	SB-CS	FA	FR	RNG	THR	GAMES AT POSITION	DL	BFW
1944	Cin N	4	1	0	0	0	0	0	0	0	0	0	.000	.000	.000	-99	0	0	ø	-0	0	0	/3	0	0.0
1945	Cin N	71	194	18	39	8	2	0	10	23	0	22	.201	.286	.263	54	-12	2	.948	-1	101	82	2b32,S31,3b7	0	-0.9
1947	Cin N	39	81	8	14	0	0	1	4	6	1	12	.173	.239	.210	20	-10	0	.964	3	97	70	3b20,S9,2b2	0	-0.7
1950	Phi A	89	280	26	72	12	3	2	27	30	1	30	.257	.331	.343	74	-11	1-1	.946	4	108	77	3b61,S18,2b2	0	-0.6
1951	Phi A	20	59	4	11	2	0	0	6	9	0	5	.186	.294	.220	40	-5	0-0	.967	2	110	117	3b18	0	-0.3
	StL A	8	27	2	9	1	1	0	3	0	0	3	.333	.333	.444	106	0	0-0	.950	1	103	205	3b6	0	0.0
	Year	28	86	6	20	3	1	0	9	9	0	8	.233	.305	.291	60	-5	0-0	.962	2	108	141	3b24	0	-0.3
Total	5	231	642	58	145	23	6	3	50	68	2	72	.226	.302	.294	60	-38	3-1	.949	8	107	86	3b113,S58,2b36	0	-2.5

WAITKUS, EDDIE Edward Stephen; B9.4.1919 Cambridge MA; D9.16.1972 Jamaica Plain MA; BL/TL/6´1˝/175; d4.15; Mil 1942–45; Col Boston College

YEAR	TM LG	G	AB	R	H	2B	3B	HR	RBI	BB-IB	HP	SO	AVG	OBP	SLG	AOPS	ABR	SB-CS	FA	FR	RNG	THR	GAMES AT POSITION	DL	BFW
1941	Chi N	12	28	1	5	0	0	0	0	0	1	3	.179	.207	.179	10	-3	0	.949	-1	71	141	1b9	0	-0.6
1946	Chi N	113	441	50	134	24	5	4	55	23	1	14	.304	.340	.408	114	6	3	.996	3	105	89	1b106	0	0.6
1947	Chi N	130	514	60	150	28	6	2	35	32	2	17	.292	.336	.381	94	-6	3	.994	8	**124**	101	1b126	0	-0.1
1948	Chi N★	139	562	87	166	27	10	7	44	43	2	19	.295	.348	.416	110	7	11	.992	7	**123**	84	1b116,O20L	0	0.8
1949	Phi N✳	54	209	41	64	16	3	1	28	33	1	12	.306	.403	.426	126	10	3	.994	1	106	114	1b54	93	0.8
1950	†Phi N	154	641	102	182	32	5	2	44	55	1	29	.284	.341	.359	86	-13	3	.993	-3	91	107	1b154	0	-2.1
1951	Phi N	145	610	65	157	27	4	1	46	53	0	22	.257	.317	.320	73	-23	0-3	.992	-2	92	91	1b144	0	-3.2
1952	Phi N	146	499	51	144	29	4	2	49	64	1	23	.289	.371	.375	108	8	2-2	.991	-3	94	104	1b146	0	0.0
1953	Phi N	81	247	24	72	9	2	1	16	13	1	23	.291	.330	.356	79	-8	1-1	.989	-1	94	141	1b59	0	-1.2
1954	Bal A	95	311	35	88	17	4	2	33	28	1	25	.283	.341	.383	107	2	0-1	1.000	-0	91	104	1b78	0	-0.3
1955	Bal A	38	85	2	22	1	1	0	9	11-3	0	10	.259	.344	.294	78	-2	2-0	.974	-3	68	80	1b26	36	-0.6
	Phi N	33	107	10	30	5	0	2	14	17-1	0	7	.280	.379	.383	105	2	0-1	.996	0	96	126	1b31	0	-0.1
Total	11	1140	4254	528	1214	215	44	24	373	372-4	11	204	.285	.344	.374	96	-20	28-8	.993	5	101	101	1b1049,O20L	129	-6.0

WAITT, CHARLIE Charles C.; B10.14.1853 Hallowell ME; D10.21.1912 San Francisco CA; TR/5´11˝/165; d5.25

YEAR	TM LG	G	AB	R	H	2B	3B	HR	RBI	BB-IB	HP	SO	AVG	OBP	SLG	AOPS	ABR	SB-CS	FA	FR	RNG	THR	GAMES AT POSITION	DL	BFW
1875	StL NA	30	113	14	23	10	0	0	12	2	—	7	.204	.217	.292	83	0	3-2	.787	-2	72	284	O28(2/7/23),1b4	—	-0.1
1877	Chi N	10	41	2	4	0	0	0	2	0	—	3	.098	.098	.098	-34	-6	—	.793	1	135	264	O10R	—	-0.5
1882	Bal AA	72	250	19	39	4	0	0	—	13	—	—	.156	.198	.172	28	-17	—	.874	0	65	100	O72(60/0/12)	—	-1.7
1883	Phi N	1	3	0	1	0	0	0	0	0	—	1	.333	.333	.333	114	0	—	.333	-1	0	0	/cf	—	-0.1
Total	3	83	294	21	44	4	0	0	2	13	—	4	.150	.186	.163	18	-23	—	.855	0	74	122	O83(60/1/22)	—	-2.3

WAKAMATSU, DON Wilbur Donald; B2.22.1963 Hood River OR; BR/TR/6´2˝/200; [CinN85 11/266]; d5.22; C4; Col Arizona St.

YEAR	TM LG	G	AB	R	H	2B	3B	HR	RBI	BB-IB	HP	SO	AVG	OBP	SLG	AOPS	ABR	SB-CS	FA	FR	RNG	THR	GAMES AT POSITION	DL	BFW
1991	Chi A	18	31	2	7	0	0	0	0	1-0	0	6	.226	.250	.226	33	-3	0-0	1.000	-3	325	60	C18	0	-0.5

WAKEFIELD, HOWARD Howard John; B4.2.1884 Bucyrus OH; D4.16.1941 Chicago IL; BR/TR/6´1˝/185; d9.18; s–Dick

YEAR	TM LG	G	AB	R	H	2B	3B	HR	RBI	BB-IB	HP	SO	AVG	OBP	SLG	AOPS	ABR	SB-CS	FA	FR	RNG	THR	GAMES AT POSITION	DL	BFW
1905	Cle A	10	26	3	4	0	0	0	1	0	1	—	.154	.185	.154	8	-3	0	.926	-2	*96*	*108*	C8	—	-0.4
1906	Was A	77	211	17	59	9	2	1	21	7	0	—	.280	.303	.355	111	2	6	.946	-13	*74*	*92*	C60	—	-0.7
1907	Cle A	26	37	4	5	2	0	0	3	3	0	—	.135	.200	.189	24	-3	0	.930	-1	*111*	*32*	C11	—	-0.3
Total	3	113	274	24	68	11	2	1	25	10	1	—	.248	.277	.314	89	-4	6	.943	-15	*80*	*87*	C79	—	-1.4

WAKEFIELD, DICK Richard Cummings; B5.6.1921 Chicago IL; D8.26.1985 Redford MI; BL/TR/6´4˝/210; d6.26; Mil 1944–45; f–Howard; Col Michigan

YEAR	TM LG	G	AB	R	H	2B	3B	HR	RBI	BB-IB	HP	SO	AVG	OBP	SLG	AOPS	ABR	SB-CS	FA	FR	RNG	THR	GAMES AT POSITION	DL	BFW
1941	Det A	7	7	0	1	0	0	0	0	0	0	1	.143	.143	.143	-22	-1	0-0	1.000	0	114	0	/rf	0	-0.1
1943	Det A★	**155**	633	91	**200**	**38**	8	7	79	62	0	60	.316	.377	.434	127	22	4-5	.959	-7	92	90	O155(140/0/15)	0	0.5
1944	Det A	78	276	53	98	15	5	12	53	55	1	29	.355	.464	.576	186	34	2-2	.963	-5	93	46	O78L	0	2.4
1946	Det A	111	396	64	106	11	5	12	59	59	1	55	.268	.364	.412	110	6	3-5	.964	-2	96	87	O104L	0	-0.6
1947	Det A	112	368	59	104	15	5	8	51	80	1	44	.283	.412	.416	127	17	1-4	.950	-2	90	148	O101L	0	0.7
1948	Det A	110	322	50	89	20	5	11	53	70	0	55	.276	.406	.472	129	16	0-1	.948	-2	105	47	O86L	0	0.7
1949	Det A	59	126	17	26	3	1	6	19	32	0	24	.206	.367	.389	100	1	0-0	1.000	2	103	131	O32L	0	0.0
1950	NY A	3	2	0	1	0	0	0	1	1	0	1	.500	.667	.500	208	1	0-0	ø	0	—	—	/H	0	0.0
1952	NY N	3	2	0	0	0	0	0	0	1	0	1	.000	.333	.000	-0	0	0-0	ø	0	—	—	/H	0	0.0
Total	9	638	2132	334	625	102	29	56	315	360	3	270	.293	.396	.447	130	96	10-17	.959	-16	95	89	O557(541/0/16)	0	3.6

WAKELAND, CHRIS Christopher Robert; B6.15.1974 Huntington Beach CA; BL/TL/6´0˝/185; [DetA96 15/431]; d9.4; Col Oregon St.

YEAR	TM LG	G	AB	R	H	2B	3B	HR	RBI	BB-IB	HP	SO	AVG	OBP	SLG	AOPS	ABR	SB-CS	FA	FR	RNG	THR	GAMES AT POSITION	DL	BFW
2001	Det A	10	36	5	9	2	0	2	6	0-0	0	13	.250	.250	.472	86	-1	0-0	.941	2	164	0	O10R	0	0.0

WALBECK, MATT Matthew Lovick; B10.2.1969 Sacramento CA; BB/TR/5´11˝/(188–206); [ChiN87 8/192]; d4.7

YEAR	TM LG	G	AB	R	H	2B	3B	HR	RBI	BB-IB	HP	SO	AVG	OBP	SLG	AOPS	ABR	SB-CS	FA	FR	RNG	THR	GAMES AT POSITION	DL	BFW
1993	Chi N	11	30	2	6	2	0	1	6	1-0	0	6	.200	.226	.367	56	-2	0-0	1.000	-1	74	37	C11	0	-0.2
1994	Min A	97	338	31	69	12	0	5	35	17-1	2	37	.204	.246	.284	36	-33	1-1	.993	-3	94	**149**	C95/D	0	-2.8
1995	Min A	115	393	40	101	18	1	1	44	25-2	1	71	.257	.302	.316	61	-23	3-1	.991	-13	107	68	C113	0	-2.7
1996	Min A	63	215	25	48	10	0	2	24	9-0	0	34	.223	.252	.298	38	-21	3-1	.994	-3	106	93	C61	77	-1.9
1997	Det A	47	137	18	38	3	0	3	10	12-0	0	19	.277	.331	.365	83	-4	3-3	.988	-2	94	98	C44	81	-0.4
1998	Ana A	108	338	41	87	15	2	6	46	30-0	2	68	.257	.317	.367	77	-12	1-1	.990	3	72	131	C104,D2	0	-0.3
1999	Ana A	107	288	26	69	8	1	3	22	26-1	3	46	.240	.308	.306	58	-19	2-3	.989	-9	91	116	C97/D	0	-2.1
2000	Ana A	47	146	17	29	5	0	6	12	7-0	1	22	.199	.240	.356	47	-13	0-1	.991	-3	73	165	C44,1b2/D	14	-1.3
2001	Phi N	1	1	0	1	0	0	0	0	0-0	0	0	1.000	1.000	1.000	441	0	0-0	ø	0	—	—	/H	0	0.0
2002	Det A	27	85	4	20	2	0	0	3	3-0	0	14	.235	.258	.259	41	-7	0-0	.993	-1	229	32	C27	0	-0.7
2003	Det A	59	138	11	24	4	1	1	6	3-0	1	26	.174	.197	.239	15	-18	0-1	.979	-10	66	115	C55/D	0	-2.5
Total	11	682	2109	215	492	79	5	28	208	133-4	10	343	.233	.280	.315	54	-152	13-12	.991	-43	96	110	C651,D6,1b2	172	-14.9

WALCZAK, ED Edwin Joseph "Husky"; B9.21.1915 Arctic RI; D3.10.1998 Norwich CT; BR/TR/5´11˝/180; d9.3

YEAR	TM LG	G	AB	R	H	2B	3B	HR	RBI	BB-IB	HP	SO	AVG	OBP	SLG	AOPS	ABR	SB-CS	FA	FR	RNG	THR	GAMES AT POSITION	DL	BFW
1945	Phi N	20	57	6	12	3	0	0	2	6	0	9	.211	.286	.263	55	-3	0	.966	0	91	134	2b17,S2	0	-0.2

WALDEN, FRED Thomas Fred; B6.25.1890 Fayette MO; D9.27.1955 Jefferson Barracks MO; BR/TR; d6.3

YEAR	TM LG	G	AB	R	H	2B	3B	HR	RBI	BB-IB	HP	SO	AVG	OBP	SLG	AOPS	ABR	SB-CS	FA	FR	RNG	THR	GAMES AT POSITION	DL	BFW
1912	StL A	1	0	0	0	0	0	0	0	0	0	—	ø	ø	ø	ø	0	0	.000	-1	*34*	*0*	/C	—	-0.1

WALDRON, IRV Irving J.; B1.21.1872 Hillside NY; D7.22.1944 Worcester MA; BL/TR/5´5.5˝/155; d4.25

YEAR	TM LG	G	AB	R	H	2B	3B	HR	RBI	BB-IB	HP	SO	AVG	OBP	SLG	AOPS	ABR	SB-CS	FA	FR	RNG	THR	GAMES AT POSITION	DL	BFW
1901	Mil A	62	266	48	79	8	6	0	29	16	2	—	.297	.342	.372	103	1	12	.883	-2	112	0	O62R	—	-0.4
	Was A	79	332	54	107	14	3	0	23	22	2	—	.322	.368	.383	110	5	8	.955	-3	76	0	O78(0/69/9)	—	-0.1
	Year	141	598	102	186	22	9	0	52	38	4	—	.311	.356	.378	107	6	20	.923	-6	93	0	O140(0/69/71)	—	-0.5

WALEWANDER, JIM James; B5.2.1962 Chicago IL; BB/TR/5´10˝/(158–160); [DetA83 9/225]; d5.31; Col Iowa St.

YEAR	TM LG	G	AB	R	H	2B	3B	HR	RBI	BB-IB	HP	SO	AVG	OBP	SLG	AOPS	ABR	SB-CS	FA	FR	RNG	THR	GAMES AT POSITION	DL	BFW
1987	Det A	53	54	24	13	3	1	1	4	7-0	0	6	.241	.328	.389	93	-1	2-1	1.000	2	112	136	2b24,3b17,S3,D8	0	0.2
1988	Det A	88	175	23	37	5	0	0	6	12-0	0	26	.211	.261	.240	43	-13	11-4	.977	-5	93	109	2b61,S8,3b3,D9	0	-1.6
1990	NY A	9	5	1	1	1	0	0	1	0-0	0	0	.200	.200	.400	63	0	1-1	1.000	-0	50	0	2b2,3b2/SD	0	0.0

YEAR	TM LG	G	AB	R	H	2B	3B	HR	RBI	BB-IB	HP	SO	AVG	OBP	SLG	AOPS	ABR	SB-CS	FA	FR	RNG	THR	GAMES AT POSITION	DL	BFW
1993	Cal A	12	8	2	1	0	0	0	3	5-0	0	1	.125	.429	.125	64	0	1-1	1.000	1	114	163	S6,2b2,D3	0	0.1
Total	4	162	242	50	52	9	1	1	14	24-0	0	33	.215	.284	.273	57	-14	15-7	.982	-2	95	112	2b89,D22,3b22,S18	0	-1.3

WALKER, RUBE Albert Bluford; B5.16.1926 Lenoir NC; D12.12.1992 Morganton NC; BL/TR/6´1˝/(185–208); d4.20; C21

YEAR	TM LG	G	AB	R	H	2B	3B	HR	RBI	BB-IB	HP	SO	AVG	OBP	SLG	AOPS	ABR	SB-CS	FA	FR	RNG	THR	GAMES AT POSITION	DL	BFW
1948	Chi N	79	171	17	47	8	0	5	26	24	2	17	.275	.371	.409	115	4	0	.980	-2	*97*	*123*	C44	0	0.4
1949	Chi N	56	172	11	42	4	1	3	22	9	0	18	.244	.282	.331	66	-9	0	.964	-5	*64*	*124*	C43	70	-1.2
1950	Chi N	74	213	19	49	7	1	6	16	18	0	34	.230	.290	.357	70	-10	0	.975	-2	*66*	*129*	C62	0	-0.8
1951	Chi N	37	107	9	25	4	0	2	5	12	0	13	.234	.311	.327	71	-4	0-0	.969	-4	*57*	*107*	C31	0	-0.7
	Bro N	36	74	6	18	4	0	2	9	6	0	14	.243	.300	.378	80	-2	0-0	.972	-2	*242*	*102*	C23	0	-0.3
	Year	73	181	15	43	8	0	4	14	18	0	27	.238	.307	.348	74	-7	0-0	.970	-6	*121*	*105*	C54	0	-1.0
1952	Bro N	46	139	9	36	8	0	1	19	8	1	17	.259	.304	.338	77	-4	0-0	.987	2	*169*	*105*	C40	0	0.0
1953	Bro N	43	95	5	23	6	0	3	9	7	1	11	.242	.301	.400	79	-3	0-0	.978	1	*161*	*123*	C28	0	-0.1
1954	Bro N	50	155	12	28	7	0	5	23	24	1	17	.181	.291	.323	59	-9	0-0	.996	1	*152*	*84*	C47	0	-0.6
1955	Bro N	48	103	6	26	5	0	2	13	15-4	0	11	.252	.342	.359	86	-2	1-0	.987	2	*116*	*73*	C35	0	0.1
1956	†Bro N	54	146	5	31	6	1	3	20	7-2	0	18	.212	.245	.329	50	-11	0-1	.986	1	*139*	*123*	C43	0	-0.8
1957	Bro N	60	166	12	30	8	0	2	23	15-4	0	33	.181	.243	.265	35	-15	2-0	.992	-4	135	165	C50	0	-1.7
1958	LA N	25	44	3	5	2	0	1	7	5-2	0	10	.114	.200	.227	14	-6	0-0	.985	-4	189	127	C20	0	-0.9
Total	11	608	1585	114	360	69	3	35	192	150-12	5	213	.227	.294	.341	68	-71	3-1	.982	-15	*120*	*118*	C466	70	-6.6

WALKER, TONY Anthony Bruce; B7.1.1959 San Diego CA; BR/TR/6´2˝/204; d4.8

YEAR	TM LG	G	AB	R	H	2B	3B	HR	RBI	BB-IB	HP	SO	AVG	OBP	SLG	AOPS	ABR	SB-CS	FA	FR	RNG	THR	GAMES AT POSITION	DL	BFW
1986	Hou N	84	90	19	20	7	0	2	10	11-2	0	15	.222	.307	.367	87	-1	11-3	.986	0	119	0	O68C	0	0.0

WALKER, FRANK Charles Franklin; B9.22.1894 Enoree SC; D9.16.1974 Bristol TN; BR/TR/5´11˝/165; d9.6; Col Randolph–Macon

YEAR	TM LG	G	AB	R	H	2B	3B	HR	RBI	BB-IB	HP	SO	AVG	OBP	SLG	AOPS	ABR	SB-CS	FA	FR	RNG	THR	GAMES AT POSITION	DL	BFW
1917	Det A	2	2	0	0	0	0	0	0	0	0	1	.000	.000	.000	-99	0	0	ø	0	—	—	/H	—	-0.1
1918	Det A	55	167	10	33	10	3	1	20	7	1	29	.198	.234	.311	67	-8	3	.922	-2	103	80	O45(3/34/9)	—	-1.4
1920	Phi A	24	91	10	21	2	2	0	10	5	2	14	.231	.286	.297	54	-6	0-2	.983	-2	98	33	O24C	—	-1.1
1921	Phi A	19	66	6	15	3	0	1	6	8	0	11	.227	.311	.318	60	-4	1-0	.961	0	97	122	O19(3/16/0)	—	-0.4
1925	NY N	39	81	12	18	1	0	1	5	9	1	11	.222	.308	.272	51	-6	1-1	.960	-1	86	162	O21(0/21/1)	—	-0.7
Total	5	139	407	38	87	16	5	3	41	29	4	66	.214	.273	.300	58	-24	5-3	.949	-4	98	91	O109(6/95/10)	—	-3.7

WALKER, TILLY Clarence William; B9.4.1887 Telford TN; D9.20.1959 Unicoi TN; BR/TR/5´11˝/165; d6.10; Col Washington College

YEAR	TM LG	G	AB	R	H	2B	3B	HR	RBI	BB-IB	HP	SO	AVG	OBP	SLG	AOPS	ABR	SB-CS	FA	FR	RNG	THR	GAMES AT POSITION	DL	BFW
1911	Was A	95	356	44	99	6	4	2	39	15	2	—	.278	.311	.334	82	-10	12	.917	-2	98	98	O94L	—	-1.6
1912	Was A	39	110	22	30	2	1	0	9	8	2	—	.273	.333	.309	83	-2	11	.837	-1	80	164	O34(4/7/23)/2	—	-0.5
1913	StL A	23	85	7	25	4	1	0	11	2	0	9	.294	.310	.365	100	-1	5	.911	0	86	165	O23L	—	-0.2
1914	StL A	151	517	67	154	24	16	6	78	51	4	72	.298	.365	.441	148	28	29-17	.972	17	112	144	O145L	—	4.2
1915	StL A	144	510	53	137	20	7	5	49	36	5	77	.269	.323	.365	110	4	20-17	.940	9	106	135	O139(1/119/19)	—	0.1
1916	†Bos A	128	467	68	124	29	11	3	46	23	2	45	.266	.303	.394	109	2	14	.959	-5	101	69	O128(3/125/0)	—	-1.3
1917	Bos A	106	337	41	83	18	7	2	37	25	1	38	.246	.300	.359	102	-1	6	.972	4	96	144	O96C	—	-0.4
1918	Phi A	114	414	56	122	20	0	**11**	48	41	1	44	.295	.360	.423	135	17	8	.953	3	94	155	O109C	—	1.3
1919	Phi A	125	456	47	133	30	6	10	64	26	0	41	.292	.330	.450	116	8	8	.933	-4	98	89	O115(28/85/2)	—	-0.3
1920	Phi A	149	585	79	157	23	7	17	82	41	4	59	.268	.321	.419	94	-8	8-3	.940	-0	94	127	O149(123/26/0)	—	-1.5
1921	Phi A	142	556	89	169	32	5	23	101	73	4	41	.304	.389	.504	125	22	3-5	.955	5	102	125	O142L	—	1.3
1922	Phi A	153	565	111	160	31	4	37	99	61	4	67	.283	.357	.549	130	22	4-3	.956	-2	95	103	O148(137/11/0)	—	0.8
1923	Phi A	52	109	12	30	5	2	2	16	14	2	11	.275	.368	.413	104	1	1-2	1.000	-1	102	34	O26L	—	-0.2
Total	13	1421	5067	696	1423	244	71	118	679	416	31	504	.281	.339	.427	115	82	129-47	.949	23	99	119	O1348(726/578/44)/2	—	1.7

WALKER, CHICO Cleotha; B11.25.1958 Jackson MS; BB/TR/5´9˝/(160–185); [BosA76 22/525]; d9.2

YEAR	TM LG	G	AB	R	H	2B	3B	HR	RBI	BB-IB	HP	SO	AVG	OBP	SLG	AOPS	ABR	SB-CS	FA	FR	RNG	THR	GAMES AT POSITION	DL	BFW
1980	Bos A	19	57	3	12	0	0	1	5	6-1	1	10	.211	.292	.263	52	-4	3-2	.958	-2	101	98	2b11,D7	0	-0.5
1981	Bos A	6	17	3	6	0	0	0	2	1-0	0	2	.353	.389	.353	108	0	0-2	1.000	-2	81	35	2b5	0	-0.3
1983	Bos A	4	5	2	2	0	2	0	1	0-0	0	0	.400	.400	1.200	298	1	0-0	1.000	1	146	977	O3L	0	0.2
1984	Bos A	3	2	0	0	0	0	0	1	0-0	0	1	.000	.000	.000	-95	-1	0-0	1.000	0	146	0	/2	0	-0.1
1985	Chi N	21	12	3	1	0	0	0	0	0-0	0	5	.083	.083	.083	-48	-2	1-0	1.000	-0	92	0	O6(3/0/3),2b2	0	-0.3
1986	Chi N	28	101	21	28	3	2	1	7	10-0	0	20	.277	.339	.376	91	-1	15-4	.956	-3	83	56	O26(1/11/22)	0	-0.3
1987	Chi N	47	105	15	21	4	0	0	7	12-1	0	23	.200	.277	.238	38	-9	11-4	.974	-4	74	0	O33(25/3/5),3b2	0	-1.4
1988	Cal A	33	78	8	12	1	0	0	2	6-0	0	15	.154	.214	.167	8	-10	2-1	.933	-2	76	149	O17(5/12/0),2b7,3b2	0	-1.2
1991	Chi N	124	374	51	96	10	1	6	34	33-2	0	57	.257	.315	.337	80	-10	13-5	.929	-7	87	99	3b57,O53(20/36/8),2b6	0	-1.7
1992	Chi N	19	26	2	3	0	0	0	2	3-0	0	4	.115	.200	.115	-6	-4	1-0	1.000	1	206	0	O6(6/0/1),2b2,3b2	0	-0.3
	NY N	107	227	24	70	12	1	4	36	24-3	0	46	.308	.369	.423	127	8	14-1	.971	-0	102	44	3b36,2b16,O15(9/4/2)	0	1.2
	Year	126	253	26	73	12	1	4	38	27-3	0	50	.289	.351	.391	112	5	15-1	.960	1	105	42	3b38,O21(15/4/3),2b18	0	0.9
1993	NY N	115	213	18	48	7	1	5	19	14-0	0	29	.225	.271	.338	63	-12	7-0	.976	4	113	98	2b24,3b23,O15(15/0/1)	0	-0.6
Total	11	526	1217	150	299	37	7	17	116	109-7	1	212	.246	.305	.329	75	-44	67-19	.968	-14	84	127	O174(87/66/42),3b122,2b74,D7	0	-5.3

WALKER, DUANE Duane Allen; B3.13.1957 Pasadena TX; BL/TL/6´0˝/185; [CinN76*S1/22]; d5.25; Col San Jacinto North (TX) JC

YEAR	TM LG	G	AB	R	H	2B	3B	HR	RBI	BB-IB	HP	SO	AVG	OBP	SLG	AOPS	ABR	SB-CS	FA	FR	RNG	THR	GAMES AT POSITION	DL	BFW
1982	Cin N	86	239	26	52	10	0	5	22	27-0	2	58	.218	.298	.322	74	-8	9-3	.992	1	94	150	O69(40/2/31)	0	-0.9
1983	Cin N	109	225	14	53	12	1	2	29	20-4	0	43	.236	.296	.324	70	-9	6-3	.956	3	113	114	O60(35/0/26)	0	-0.9
1984	Cin N	83	195	35	57	10	3	10	28	33-2	0	35	.292	.391	.528	150	14	7-3	.950	-0	105	77	O68(51/13/9)	43	1.2
1985	Cin N	37	48	5	8	2	1	2	6	6-1	0	18	.167	.259	.375	72	-2	1-0	.882	-0	120	0	O10(8/0/2)	0	-0.2
	Tex A	53	132	14	23	2	0	5	11	15-0	1	29	.174	.264	.303	54	-9	2-1	1.000	3	94	340	O32(12/0/23),D10	0	-0.7
1988	StL N	24	22	1	4	1	0	0	3	2-0	0	7	.182	.250	.227	37	-2	0-0	ø	-1	0	0	O4(2/0/2)/1	0	-0.3
Total	5	392	861	95	197	37	5	24	99	103-7	3	190	.229	.311	.367	87	-16	25-10	.967	6	102	142	O243(148/15/93),D10/1	43	-1.8

WALKER, ERNIE Ernest Robert; B9.17.1890 Blossburg AL; D4.1.1965 Pell City AL; BL/TR/6´0˝/165; d4.13; b–Dixie

YEAR	TM LG	G	AB	R	H	2B	3B	HR	RBI	BB-IB	HP	SO	AVG	OBP	SLG	AOPS	ABR	SB-CS	FA	FR	RNG	THR	GAMES AT POSITION	DL	BFW
1913	StL A	7	14	0	3	0	0	0	2	0	0	5	.214	.214	.214	26	-1	0	1.000	-0	113	0	O2C	—	-0.2
1914	StL A	74	131	19	39	5	3	1	14	13	1	26	.298	.366	.405	137	6	6-4	.960	-1	96	87	O38(21/9/10)	—	0.4
1915	StL A	50	109	15	23	4	2	0	9	23	0	32	.211	.348	.284	93	0	5-8	.881	-3	89	32	O33(3/3/27)	—	-0.6
Total	3	131	254	34	65	9	5	1	25	36	1	63	.256	.351	.343	112	5	11-12	.928	-4	93	57	O73(24/14/37)	—	-0.4

WALKER, DIXIE Fred "The People's Cherce"; B9.24.1910 Villa Rica GA; D5.17.1982 Birmingham AL; BL/TR/6´1˝/175; d4.28; C5; b–Harry f–Dixie

YEAR	TM LG	G	AB	R	H	2B	3B	HR	RBI	BB-IB	HP	SO	AVG	OBP	SLG	AOPS	ABR	SB-CS	FA	FR	RNG	THR	GAMES AT POSITION	DL	BFW
1931	NY A	2	10	1	3	2	0	0	1	0	0	4	.300	.300	.500	113	0	0-0	1.000	-0	74	0	O2(1/0/1)	—	0.0
1933	NY A	98	328	68	90	15	7	15	51	26	1	28	.274	.330	.500	125	9	2-2	.962	1	102	117	O77(15/60/3)	—	0.6
1934	NY A	17	17	2	2	0	0	0	0	1	0	3	.118	.167	.118	-27	-3	0-0	1.000	-0	87	0	/lf	—	-0.3
1935	NY A	8	13	1	2	1	0	0	1	0	0	1	.154	.154	.231	-2	-2	0-0	.750	-0	85	0	O2L	—	-0.2
1936	NY A	6	20	3	7	0	2	1	5	1	0	3	.350	.381	.700	167	2	1-1	1.000	-0	90	0	O5C	—	0.1
	Chi A	26	70	12	19	2	0	0	11	14	1	6	.271	.400	.300	73	-2	1-0	1.000	1	101	134	O17(0/16/1)	—	-0.2
	Year	32	90	15	26	2	2	1	16	15	1	9	.289	.396	.389	92	-1	2-1	1.000	0	99	109	O22(0/21/1)	—	-0.1
1937	Chi A	**154**	593	105	179	28	**16**	9	95	78	0	26	.302	.383	.449	109	8	1-2	.952	-10	92	70	O154R	—	-1.0
1938	Det A	127	454	84	140	27	6	6	43	65	1	32	.308	.396	.434	102	3	5-4	.979	-3	94	96	O114(94/26/0)	—	-0.5
1939	Det A	43	154	30	47	4	5	4	19	15	0	8	.305	.367	.474	106	0	4-1	.970	2	105	138	O37(23/4/11)	—	0.1
	Bro N	61	225	27	63	6	4	2	38	20	0	10	.280	.339	.369	87	-4	1	.968	-1	97	104	O59C	—	-0.7
1940	Bro N	143	556	75	171	37	8	6	66	42	1	21	.308	.357	.435	111	8	3	.973	-5	102	50	O136(14/112/20)	—	-0.1
1941	†Bro N	148	531	88	165	32	8	9	71	70	0	18	.311	.391	.452	131	24	4	.976	10	106	**160**	O146(22/22/105)	0	2.6
1942	Bro N	118	393	57	114	28	1	6	54	47	1	15	.290	.367	.412	126	14	1	.986	0	103	87	O110(0/7/104)	0	0.9
1943	Bro N★	138	540	83	163	32	6	5	71	49	3	24	.302	.363	.411	123	16	3	.969	4	99	**152**	O136(57/0/82)	0	1.3
1944	Bro N★	147	535	77	191	37	8	13	91	72	1	27	**.357**	.434	.529	173	55	6	.962	2	100	127	O140(19/0/125)	0	4.9
1945	Bro N✳	154	607	102	182	42	9	8	**124**	75	5	16	.300	.381	.438	128	25	6	.992	10	109	124	O153R	0	2.4
1946	Bro N★	150	576	80	184	29	9	9	116	67	1	28	.319	.391	.448	136	28	14	.969	-9	85	103	O149R	0	1.6
1947	†Bro N★	148	529	77	162	31	3	9	94	97	1	26	.306	.415	.427	119	20	6	.964	-8	92	74	O147R	0	0.7
1948	Pit N	129	408	39	129	19	3	2	54	52	0	18	.316	.393	.392	111	9	1	.977	-6	91	57	O112(1/1/110)	0	0.0
1949	Pit N	88	181	26	51	4	1	1	18	26	0	11	.282	.372	.331	88	-2	0	.984	-2	93	69	O39R,1b3	0	-0.5
Total	18	1905	6740	1037	2064	376	96	105	1023	817	16	325	.306	.383	.437	121	208	59-10	.972	-14	98	102	O1736(249/312/1204),1b3	0	11.7

WALKER, GEE Gerald Holmes; B3.19.1908 Gulfport MS; D3.20.1981 Whitfield MS; BR/TR/5´11˝/188; d4.14; C1; b–Hub; Col U. of Mississippi

YEAR	TM LG	G	AB	R	H	2B	3B	HR	RBI	BB-IB	HP	SO	AVG	OBP	SLG	AOPS	ABR	SB-CS	FA	FR	RNG	THR	GAMES AT POSITION	DL	BFW
1931	Det A	59	189	20	56	17	2	1	28	14	0	21	.296	.345	.423	98	-1	10-7	.953	-5	86	59	O44(1/41/1)	—	-0.6
1932	Det A	127	480	71	155	32	6	8	78	13	3	38	.323	.345	.465	104	1	30-6	.949	1	105	96	O116(39/79/0)	—	0.2
1933	Det A	127	483	68	135	29	7	9	64	15	2	49	.280	.304	.424	89	-10	26-9	.942	-4	94	89	O113(92/8/13)	—	-1.7
1934	†Det A	98	347	54	104	19	2	6	39	19	2	20	.300	.340	.418	94	-4	20-9	.947	-0	104	80	O80(9/48/23)	—	-0.6

YEAR	TM LG	G	AB	R	H	2B	3B	HR	RBI	BB-IB	HP	SO	AVG	OBP	SLG	AOPS	ABR	SB-CS	FA	FR	RNG	THR	GAMES AT POSITION	DL	BFW
1935	†Det A	98	362	52	109	22	6	7	53	15	0	21	.301	.329	.453	104	0	6-4	.954	-3	103	31	O85(29/45/11)	—	-0.6
1936	Det A	134	550	105	194	55	5	12	93	23	8	30	.353	.387	.536	125	21	17-8	.948	1	101	117	O125(2/21/103)	—	1.4
1937	Det A★	151	635	105	213	42	4	18	113	41	5	74	.335	.380	.499	117	16	23-7	.956	-5	98	69	O151(88/11/54)	—	0.4
1938	Chi A	120	442	69	135	23	6	16	87	38	0	32	.305	.360	.493	109	4	9-4	.958	-5	91	102	O107(50/0/57)	—	-0.5
1939	Chi A	149	598	95	174	30	11	13	111	28	7	43	.291	.330	.443	94	-9	17-6	.967	8	110	108	O147L	—	-0.8
1940	Was A	140	595	87	175	29	7	13	96	24	3	58	.294	.325	.432	101	-3	21-4	.967	-2	96	100	O140L	—	-0.8
1941	Cle A	121	445	56	126	26	11	6	48	18	1	46	.283	.313	.431	100	-4	12-6	.982	5	111	98	O105(103/2/0)	0	-0.4
1942	Cin N	119	422	40	97	20	2	5	50	31	5	44	.230	.290	.322	79	-12	11	.973	-2	103	68	O110(20/74/19)	0	-1.9
1943	Cin N	114	429	48	105	23	2	3	54	12	3	38	.245	.270	.329	74	-16	6	.980	-6	91	79	O106(15/75/17)	0	-2.9
1944	Cin N	121	478	56	133	21	3	5	62	23	5	48	.278	.318	.366	96	-4	7	.967	-9	100	24	O117(1/59/61)	0	-1.9
1945	Cin N	106	316	28	80	11	2	2	21	16	0	38	.253	.289	.320	71	-14	8	.962	-5	93	67	O67(6/0/61),3b3	0	-2.3
Total	15	1784	6771	954	1991	399	76	124	997	330	44	600	.294	.331	.430	99	-35	223-70	.961	-31	100	82	O1613(742/463/420),3b3	0	-13.0

WALKER, GREG Gregory Lee; B10.6.1959 Douglas GA; BL/TR/6´3˝/(198–212); [PhiN77 20/511]; d9.18; C4

YEAR	TM LG	G	AB	R	H	2B	3B	HR	RBI	BB-IB	HP	SO	AVG	OBP	SLG	AOPS	ABR	SB-CS	FA	FR	RNG	THR	GAMES AT POSITION	DL	BFW
1982	Chi A	11	17	3	7	2	1	2	7	2-0	0	3	.412	.474	1.000	291	4	0-0	ø	0	—	—	D4	0	0.4
1983	†Chi A	118	307	32	83	16	3	10	55	28-3	2	57	.270	.332	.440	107	3	2-1	.985	-5	62	105	1b59,D21	0	-0.6
1984	Chi A	136	442	62	130	29	2	24	75	35-3	2	66	.294	.346	.532	133	19	8-5	.995	-5	78	93	1b101,D21	0	0.8
1985	Chi A	**163**	601	77	155	38	4	24	92	44-6	2	100	.258	.309	.454	102	0	5-2	.994	-1	91	91	1b151,D7	0	-0.9
1986	Chi A	78	282	37	78	10	6	13	51	29-4	2	44	.277	.345	.493	121	8	1-2	.993	-1	94	93	1b77/D	93	0.1
1987	Chi A	157	566	85	145	33	2	27	94	75-7	5	112	.256	.346	.465	110	9	2-1	.994	-15	71	112	1b154,D3	0	-1.5
1988	Chi A	99	377	45	93	22	1	8	42	29-3	3	77	.247	.304	.374	89	-5	0-1	.993	-13	58	106	1b98	65	-2.7
1989	Chi A	77	233	25	49	14	0	5	26	23-2	3	50	.210	.286	.335	77	-7	0-0	.987	-5	59	101	1b48,D23	16	-1.7
1990	Chi A	2	5	0	1	0	0	0	0	0-0	0	2	.200	.200	.200	12	-1	0-0	1.000	0	155	264	/1D	0	-0.1
	Bal A	14	34	2	5	0	0	0	2	3-0	1	9	.147	.237	.147	10	-4	1-0	ø	0	0	0	D11	0	-0.4
	Year	16	39	2	6	0	0	0	2	3-0	1	11	.154	.233	.154	10	-5	1-0	1.000	0	155	264	D12/1	0	-0.5
Total	9	855	2864	368	746	164	19	113	444	268-28	20	520	.260	.326	.449	107	26	19-12	.993	-45	76	101	1b689,D92	174	-6.6

WALKER, HARRY Harry William "Harry the Hat"; B10.22.1916 Pascagoula MS; D8.8.1999 Birmingham AL; BL/TR/6´2˝/190; d9.25; Mil 1944–45; M9/C4; b–Dixie f–Dixie

YEAR	TM LG	G	AB	R	H	2B	3B	HR	RBI	BB-IB	HP	SO	AVG	OBP	SLG	AOPS	ABR	SB-CS	FA	FR	RNG	THR	GAMES AT POSITION	DL	BFW
1940	StL N	7	27	2	5	2	0	0	6	0	0	2	.185	.185	.259	20	-3	0	1.000	2	125	350	O7(2/5/1)	—	-0.1
1941	StL N	7	15	3	4	1	0	0	1	2	0	1	.267	.353	.333	88	0	0	.875	-0	94	0	O5L	0	-0.1
1942	†StL N	74	191	38	60	12	2	0	16	11	1	14	.314	.355	.398	112	3	2	.968	2	104	145	O56(12/43/3),2b2	0	0.3
1943	†StL N★	148	564	76	166	28	6	2	53	40	0	24	.294	.341	.376	102	1	5	.965	-6	92	111	O144(0/143/1)/2	0	-0.9
1946	†StL N	112	346	53	82	14	6	3	27	30	1	29	.237	.300	.338	77	-11	12	.974	3	102	146	O92(13/79/0),1b8	0	-1.2
1947	StL N	10	25	2	5	1	0	0	0	4	0	2	.200	.310	.240	46	-2	0	.938	-1	87	0	O10(2/7/0)	0	-0.3
	Phi N★	130	488	79	181	28	16	1	41	59	4	37	.371	.443	.500	156	41	13	.966	5	103	167	O127C,1b4	0	4.1
	Year	140	513	81	186	29	**16**	1	41	63	4	39	**.363**	.436	.487	150	39	13	.964	4	102	**159**	O137(2/134/0),1b4	0	3.8
1948	Phi N	112	332	34	97	11	2	2	23	33	1	30	.292	.358	.355	95	-2	4	.981	2	106	108	O81(21/58/3),1b4/3	0	-0.2
1949	Chi N	42	159	20	42	6	3	1	14	11	0	6	.264	.312	.358	81	-5	2	.947	-3	85	92	O39(27/0/13)	0	-1.0
	Cin N	86	314	53	100	15	2	1	23	34	0	17	.318	.385	.389	107	4	4	.963	-2	97	106	O77(22/26/29)/1	0	0.0
	Year	128	473	73	142	21	5	2	37	45	0	23	.300	.361	.378	99	0	6	.959	-4	93	101	O116(49/26/42)/1	0	-1.0
1950	StL N	60	150	17	31	5	0	0	7	18	0	12	.207	.292	.240	40	-13	0	.969	-0	101	101	O46(9/30/3),1b2	0	-1.4
1951	StL N	8	26	6	8	1	0	0	2	2	0	1	.308	.357	.346	90	0	0-0	1.000	-1	84	0	O6(2/4/0)/1	0	-0.1
1955	StL N	11	14	2	5	2	0	0	1	1-0	0	0	.357	.400	.500	137	1	0-0	1.000	1	79	1064	/lfM	0	0.2
Total	11	807	2651	385	786	126	37	10	214	245-0	7	175	.296	.358	.383	103	14	42-0	.968	2	99	128	O691(116/522/53),1b20,2b3/3	0	-0.7

WALKER, HUB Harvey Willos; B8.17.1906 Gulfport MS; D11.26.1982 San Jose CA; BL/TR/5´10.5˝/175; d4.15; Mil 1942–44; b–Gee; Col U. of Mississippi

YEAR	TM LG	G	AB	R	H	2B	3B	HR	RBI	BB-IB	HP	SO	AVG	OBP	SLG	AOPS	ABR	SB-CS	FA	FR	RNG	THR	GAMES AT POSITION	DL	BFW
1931	Det A	90	252	27	72	13	1	0	16	23	4	25	.286	.355	.345	82	-6	10-1	.961	-2	98	78	O66(4/60/2)	—	-0.7
1935	Det A	9	25	4	4	3	0	0	1	3	0	4	.160	.250	.280	38	-2	0-0	1.000	0	112	0	O7C	—	-0.2
1936	Cin N	92	258	49	71	18	1	4	23	35	2	32	.275	.366	.399	113	6	8	.970	-0	101	85	O73(25/47/2)/C1	—	0.4
1937	Cin N	78	221	33	55	9	4	1	19	34	0	24	.249	.349	.339	92	-1	7	.993	1	101	110	O58(17/40/1),2b3	—	-0.2
1945	†Det A	28	23	4	3	0	0	0	1	9	0	4	.130	.375	.130	46	-1	1-0	1.000	-0	89	0	O7(5/0/2)	0	-0.1
Total	5	297	779	117	205	43	6	5	60	104	6	89	.263	.354	.353	92	-4	26-1	.975	-1	100	86	O211(51/154/7),2b3/1C	0	-0.8

WALKER, JOHNNY John Miles; B12.11.1896 Toulon IL; D8.19.1976 Hollywood FL; BR/TR/6´0˝/175; d9.19

YEAR	TM LG	G	AB	R	H	2B	3B	HR	RBI	BB-IB	HP	SO	AVG	OBP	SLG	AOPS	ABR	SB-CS	FA	FR	RNG	THR	GAMES AT POSITION	DL	BFW
1919	Phi A	3	9	0	0	0	0	0	0	0	0	2	.000	.000	.000	-99	-2	0	.941	-1	*73*	*56*	C3	—	-0.3
1920	Phi A	9	22	0	5	1	0	0	5	0	0	1	.227	.227	.273	32	-2	0-0	.960	-0	*106*	*102*	C6	—	-0.2
1921	Phi A	113	423	41	109	14	5	2	46	9	3	29	.258	.278	.329	54	-31	5-0	.989	-7	75	99	1b99,C7	—	-4.2
Total	3	125	454	41	114	15	5	2	51	9	3	32	.251	.270	.319	50	-35	5-0	.989	-8	75	99	1b99,C16	—	-4.7

WALKER, SPEED Joseph Richard; B1.23.1898 Munhall PA; D6.20.1959 W.Mifflin PA; BR/TR/6´0˝/170; d9.15

YEAR	TM LG	G	AB	R	H	2B	3B	HR	RBI	BB-IB	HP	SO	AVG	OBP	SLG	AOPS	ABR	SB-CS	FA	FR	RNG	THR	GAMES AT POSITION	DL	BFW
1923	StL N	2	7	1	2	0	0	0	0	0	0	1	.286	.286	.286	52	-1	0-0	1.000	-0	0	69	1b2	—	-0.1

WALKER, LARRY Larry Kenneth Robert; B12.1.1966 Maple Ridge BC, Can.; BL/TR/6´3˝/(205–237); d8.16; [DL 1988 Mon N 182]

YEAR	TM LG	G	AB	R	H	2B	3B	HR	RBI	BB-IB	HP	SO	AVG	OBP	SLG	AOPS	ABR	SB-CS	FA	FR	RNG	THR	GAMES AT POSITION	DL	BFW
1989	Mon N	20	47	4	8	0	0	0	4	5-0	1	13	.170	.264	.170	26	-4	1-1	1.000	0	78	292	O15(2/0/13)	0	-0.5
1990	Mon N	133	419	59	101	18	3	19	51	49-5	5	112	.241	.326	.434	112	6	21-7	.985	6	105	145	O124R	0	1.1
1991	Mon N	137	487	59	141	30	2	16	64	42-2	5	102	.290	.349	.458	127	18	14-9	.991	8	119	86	O102(0/5/99),1b39	15	2.1
1992	Mon N★	143	528	85	159	31	4	23	93	41-10	6	97	.301	.353	.506	143	29	18-6	.993	6	98	169	O139R	0	3.4
1993	Mon N	138	490	85	130	24	5	22	86	80-20	6	76	.265	.371	.469	119	15	29-7	.979	4	102	128	O132R,1b4	15	1.6
1994	Mon N	103	395	76	127	**44**	2	19	86	47-5	4	74	.322	.394	.587	151	32	15-5	.973	0	102	97	O68R,1b35	0	2.6
1995	†Col N	131	494	96	151	31	5	36	101	49-13	14	72	.306	.381	.607	122	16	16-3	.988	-1	91	140	O129(0/4/129)	0	1.1
1996	Col N	83	272	58	75	18	4	18	58	20-2	9	58	.276	.342	.570	110	4	18-2	.994	-1	97	101	O83(0/54/33)	66	0.5
1997	Col N★	153	568	143	208	46	4	**49**	130	78-14	14	90	.366	**.452**	**.720**	164	56	33-8	.992	-9	83	107	O151(0/2/150),1b3/D	0	4.4
1998	Col N★	130	454	113	165	46	3	23	67	64-2	4	61	**.363**	.445	.630	148	35	14-4	.984	2	104	100	O123(0/3/123)/23D	15	3.2
1999	Col N★	127	438	108	166	26	4	37	115	57-8	12	52	**.379**	**.458**	**.710**	152	37	11-4	.982	3	95	182	O114R/D	9	3.3
2000	Col N	87	314	64	97	21	7	9	51	46-4	9	40	.309	.409	.506	106	4	5-5	.994	7	104	202	O83(31/0/52),D3	70	0.7
2001	Col N★	142	497	107	174	35	3	38	123	82-6	14	103	**.350**	.449	.662	153	43	14-5	.984	-1	94	95	O129R,D5	0	3.6
2002	Col N	136	477	95	161	40	4	26	104	65-6	7	73	.338	.421	.602	146	35	6-5	.984	4	95	172	O123R,D7	0	3.2
2003	Col N	143	454	86	129	25	7	16	79	98-14	11	87	.284	.422	.476	118	17	7-4	.983	-5	90	93	O131R,D2	0	0.5
2004	Col N	38	108	22	35	9	3	6	20	25-2	4	23	.324	.464	.630	160	11	2-0	1.000	3	103	202	O34R	78	1.2
	†StL N	44	150	29	42	7	1	11	27	24-1	4	34	.280	.393	.560	141	10	4-0	.983	-5	77	40	O41(0/1/41)/D	0	0.4
	Year	82	258	51	77	16	4	17	47	49-3	8	57	.298	.424	.589	149	21	6-0	.992	-2	88	111	O75(0/1/75)/D	0	1.6
2005	†StL N	100	315	66	91	20	1	15	52	41-3	9	64	.289	.384	.502	128	14	2-1	.983	-8	73	114	O83(0/1/83),D6	28	0.3
Total	17	1988	6907	1355	2160	471	62	383	1311	913-117	138	1231	.313	.400	.565	136	378	230-76	.986	14	96	130	O1804(33/70/1716),1b81,D27/32	478	32.7

WALKER, FLEET Moses Fleetwood; B10.7.1856 Mt.Pleasant OH; D5.11.1924 Cleveland OH; BR/TR/?/159; d5.1; b–Welday; Col Michigan

YEAR	TM LG	G	AB	R	H	2B	3B	HR	RBI	BB-IB	HP	SO	AVG	OBP	SLG	AOPS	ABR	SB-CS	FA	FR	RNG	THR	GAMES AT POSITION	DL	BFW
1884	Tol AA	42	152	23	40	2	3	0	—	8	6	—	.263	.325	.316	106	1	—	.887	-5	—	—	C41/lf	—	0.0

WALKER, OSCAR Oscar; B3.18.1854 Brooklyn NY; D5.20.1889 Brooklyn NY; BL/TL/5´10˝/166; d9.17

YEAR	TM LG	G	AB	R	H	2B	3B	HR	RBI	BB-IB	HP	SO	AVG	OBP	SLG	AOPS	ABR	SB-CS	FA	FR	RNG	THR	GAMES AT POSITION	DL	BFW
1875	Atl NA	1	2	0	0	0	0	0	0	1	—	0	.000	.333	.000	30	0	0-0	.400	-0	0	366	/1rf	—	0.0
1879	Buf N	72	287	35	79	15	6	1	35	8	—	38	.275	.295	.380	118	5	—	.946	3	**165**	**181**	1b72	—	0.4
1880	Buf N	34	126	12	29	4	2	1	15	6	—	18	.230	.265	.317	95	-1	—	.917	-1	115	130	1b24,O11(3/7/1)	—	-0.4
1882	StL AA	76	318	48	76	15	7	**7**	—	10	—	—	.239	.262	.396	115	4	—	.846	6	101	212	O75(1/74/0)/21	—	0.6
1884	Bro AA	95	382	59	103	12	8	2	—	9	3	—	.270	.292	.359	110	3	—	.868	1	114	0	O59(16/43/0),1b36	—	-0.1
1885	Bal AA	4	13	1	0	0	0	0	1	0	0	—	.000	.000	.000	-99	-3	—	.667	-1	0	0	O4R	—	-0.4
Total	5	281	1126	155	287	46	23	11	51	33	3	56	.255	.278	.366	109	8	—	.850	7	105	126	O149(20/124/5),1b133/2	—	0.1

WALKER, TODD Todd Arthur; B5.25.1973 Bakersfield CA; BL/TR/6´0˝/(170–185); [MinA94 1/8]; d8.30; Col Louisiana St.

YEAR	TM LG	G	AB	R	H	2B	3B	HR	RBI	BB-IB	HP	SO	AVG	OBP	SLG	AOPS	ABR	SB-CS	FA	FR	RNG	THR	GAMES AT POSITION	DL	BFW
1996	Min A	25	82	8	21	6	0	0	6	4-0	0	13	.256	.281	.329	55	-6	2-0	.956	-0	103	100	3b20,2b4/D	0	-0.5
1997	Min A	52	156	15	37	7	1	3	16	11-1	1	30	.237	.288	.353	66	-8	7-0	.969	-1	106	67	3b40,2b8,D2	0	-0.7
1998	Min A	143	528	85	167	41	3	12	62	47-9	2	65	.316	.372	.473	116	13	19-7	.978	-20	96	86	2b140/D	0	0.1
1999	Min A	143	531	62	148	37	4	6	46	52-5	1	83	.279	.343	.397	84	-12	18-10	.984	-12	97	86	2b103,D34	0	-1.9
2000	Min A	23	77	14	18	1	0	2	8	7-0	0	10	.234	.287	.325	54	-6	3-0	.946	-4	78	105	2b19,D2	0	-0.8
	Col N	57	171	28	54	10	4	7	36	20-0	1	19	.316	.385	.544	108	2	4-1	.975	-6	96	84	2b52	0	-0.2
2001	Col N	85	290	52	86	18	2	12	43	25-1	0	40	.297	.349	.497	96	-1	1-3	.981	7	108	108	2b77	0	0.8
	Cin N	66	261	41	77	17	0	5	32	26-0	1	42	.295	.361	.418	95	-1	0-5	.987	-6	97	83	2b65/S	0	-0.5
	Year	151	551	93	163	35	2	17	75	51-1	1	82	.296	.355	.459	96	-2	1-8	.984	1	103	96	2b142/S	0	0.3

YEAR	TM LG	G	AB	R	H	2B	3B	HR	RBI	BB-IB	HP	SO	AVG	OBP	SLG	AOPS	ABR	SB-CS	FA	FR	RNG	THR	GAMES AT POSITION	DL	BFW
2002	Cin N	155	612	79	183	42	3	11	64	50-7	3	81	.299	.353	.431	102	3	8-5	**.989**	-7	100	91	2b154	0	0.3
2003	†Bos A	144	587	92	166	38	4	13	85	48-0	1	54	.283	.333	.428	96	-3	1-1	.975	-7	95	88	2b139,D2	0	-0.4
2004	Chi N	129	372	60	102	19	4	15	50	43-8	4	52	.274	.352	.468	107	4	0-3	.981	-12	86	63	2b89,1b5/lf	0	-0.5
2005	Chi N	110	397	50	121	25	3	12	40	31-1	1	40	.305	.355	.474	111	6	1-1	.985	-4	92	77	2b97,1b4,D2	44	0.7
2006	Chi N	94	318	38	88	16	1	6	40	38-1	1	27	.277	.352	.390	89	-4	0-1	.977	-3	89	94	2b46,1b37	0	-0.8
	†SD N	44	124	18	35	6	1	3	13	17-1	0	11	.282	.366	.419	107	2	2-0	.896	-4	101	69	3b23,2b14,1b3,D5	0	-0.1
	Year	138	442	56	123	22	2	9	53	55-2	1	38	.278	.356	.398	94	-3	2-1	.978	-6	89	98	2b60,1b40,3b23,D5	0	-0.9
Total	11	1270	4506	642	1303	283	30	107	541	419-34	16	567	.289	.349	.437	98	-11	66-37	.981	-78	96	87	2b1007,3b83,1b49,D49/lfS	44	-4.5
Walker, Wallie	Walter S.; B3.12.1860 Berlin (now Marne) MI; D2.28.1922 Pontiac MI; TR/5´10.5˝/162; d5.8																								
1884	Det N	1	4	1	1	0	0	0	0	0	—	0	.250	.250	.250	61	0	—	.750	-1	—	—	/C	—	-0.1
Walker, Welday	Welday Wilberforce; B6.1859 Steubenville OH; D11.23.1937 Steubenville OH; d7.15; b–Fleet; Col Michigan																								
1884	Tol AA	5	18	1	4	1	0	0	2	0	0	—	.222	.222	.278	60	-1	—	.667	-1	0	0	O5(4/1/0)	—	-0.2
Walker, Curt	William Curtis; B7.3.1896 Beeville TX; D12.9.1955 Beeville TX; BL/TR/5´9.5˝/170; d9.17; Col Southwestern (TX)																								
1919	NY A	1	1	0	0	0	0	0	0	0	0	0	.000	.000	.000	-99	0	0	ø	0	—	—	/H	—	0.0
1920	NY N	8	14	0	1	0	0	0	0	1	0	3	.071	.133	.071	-41	-3	0-0	1.000	-1	80	0	O4(1/2/1)	—	-0.4
1921	NY N	64	192	30	55	13	5	3	35	15	0	8	.286	.338	.453	107	2	4-3	.978	3	98	150	O58(0/46/13)	—	0.2
	Phi N	21	77	11	26	2	1	0	8	5	0	5	.338	.378	.390	96	0	0-2	.970	-2	79	85	O21(7/7/10)	—	-0.4
	Year	85	269	41	81	15	6	3	43	20	0	13	.301	.349	.435	104	1	4-5	.976	1	93	133	O79(7/53/23)	—	-0.2
1922	Phi N	148	581	102	196	36	11	12	89	56	4	46	.337	.399	.499	119	17	11-4	.955	5	100	125	O147R	—	1.1
1923	Phi N	140	527	66	148	26	5	5	66	45	0	31	.281	.337	.378	79	-15	12-12	.947	3	102	121	O137(12/0/125)/1	—	-2.4
1924	Phi N	24	71	11	21	6	1	1	8	7	0	4	.296	.359	.451	103	1	0-1	.900	-2	84	53	O20R	—	-0.3
	Cin N	109	397	55	119	21	10	4	46	44	1	15	.300	.371	.433	117	10	7-5	.978	1	97	116	O109(3/23/86)	—	0.3
	Year	133	468	66	140	27	11	5	54	51	1	19	.299	.369	.436	114	10	7-6	.969	-1	95	108	O129(3/23/106)	—	0.0
1925	Cin N	145	509	86	162	22	16	6	71	57	0	31	.318	.387	.460	118	14	14-11	**.983**	0	109	61	O141(4/15/124)	—	0.3
1926	Cin N	155	571	83	175	24	20	6	78	60	0	31	.306	.372	.450	124	18	3	.961	-0	99	97	O152(1/0/151)	—	0.6
1927	Cin N	146	527	60	154	16	10	6	80	47	0	19	.292	.350	.395	102	1	5	.957	2	107	87	O141R	—	-0.8
1928	Cin N	123	427	64	119	15	12	6	73	49	1	14	.279	.354	.412	101	0	19	.955	1	107	70	O122R	—	-0.9
1929	Cin N	141	492	76	154	28	15	7	83	85	2	17	.313	.416	.474	126	23	17	.969	-4	98	75	O138R	—	0.8
1930	Cin N	134	472	74	145	26	11	8	51	64	1	30	.307	.391	.460	110	9	4	.965	-3	102	49	O120(77/2/42)	—	-0.2
Total	12	1359	4858	718	1475	235	117	64	688	535	9	254	.304	.374	.440	110	77	96-38	.963	3	102	91	O1310(105/95/1120)/1	—	-2.1
Wall, Howard	Howard Cornelius; B12.1854 Washington DC; D3.15.1909 Washington DC; d9.13																								
1873	Was NA	1	3	1	1	0	0	0	0	1	—	0	.333	.500	.333	156	0	0-0	.000	-1	0	0	/S	—	-0.1
Wall, Joe	Joseph Francis "Gummy"; B7.24.1873 Brooklyn NY; D7.17.1936 Brooklyn NY; BL/TL; d9.22																								
1901	NY N	4	8	0	4	0	0	0	1	0	0	—	.500	.500	.500	198	1	0	1.000	-1	*48*	*0*	C2/rf	—	0.0
1902	NY N	6	14	2	5	2	0	0	0	2	0	—	.357	.438	.500	191	2	0	1.000	0	327	0	O3R	—	0.2
	Bro N	5	18	0	3	0	0	0	0	3	1	—	.167	.318	.167	50	-1	0	.893	-3	*75*	*41*	C5	—	-0.3
	Year	11	32	2	8	2	0	0	0	5	1	—	.250	.368	.313	111	1	0	.893	-3	*75*	*41*	C5,O3R	—	-0.1
Total	2	15	40	2	12	2	0	0	1	5	1	—	.300	.391	.350	127	2	0	.903	-4	*70*	*33*	C7,O4R	—	-0.1
Wallace, Jack	Clarence Eugene; B8.6.1890 Winnfield LA; D10.15.1960 Winnfield LA; BR/TR/5´10.5˝/175; d9.27; Col Louisiana St.																								
1915	Chi N	2	7	1	2	0	0	0	1	0	1	2	.286	.375	.286	101	0	0	1.000	1	*116*	*151*	C2	—	0.1
Wallace, Don	Donald Allen; B8.25.1940 Sapulpa OK; BL/TR/5´8˝/165; d4.12; Col Oklahoma St.																								
1967	Cal A	23	6	2	0	0	0	0	0	3-0	0	2	.000	.333	.000	6	0	0-1	1.000	-0	81	122	2b4/13	0	-0.1
Wallace, Doc	Frederick Renshaw "Jesse"; B9.30.1893 Church Hill MD; D12.31.1964 Haverford PA; BR/TR/5´6.5˝/135; d5.2; Col Washington College																								
1919	Phi N	2	4	0	1	0	0	0	0	0	0	1	.250	.250	.250	47	0	0	.875	-0	104	0	S2	—	0.0
Wallace, Jim	James Leo; B11.14.1881 Boston MA; D5.16.1953 Revere MA; BL/TL/5´9˝/150; d8.24																								
1905	Pit N	7	29	3	6	1	0	0	3	3	0	—	.207	.281	.241	55	-2	2	.929	1	291	0	O7R	—	-0.1
Wallace, Bobby	Rhoderick John; B11.4.1873 Pittsburgh PA; D11.3.1960 Torrance CA; BR/TR/5´8˝/170; d9.15; M3/C1/U1; HF1953; OF(4/6/16); ▲																								
1894	Cle N	4	13	0	2	1	0	0	1	0	0	1	.154	.154	.231	-8	-1	0	1.000	1	184	0	P4	—	0.0
1895	Cle N	30	98	16	21	2	3	0	10	6	2	17	.214	.274	.296	44	-3	0	.910	3	127	129	P30	—	0.0
1896	†Cle N	45	149	19	35	6	3	1	17	11	0	21	.235	.287	.336	60	-9	2	.950	-2	102	0	O23(3/6/15),P22/1	—	-0.7
1897	Cle N	**130**	516	99	173	33	21	4	112	48	2	—	.335	.394	.504	129	20	14	.928	4	99	68	3b130/lf	—	2.2
1898	Cle N	154	593	81	160	25	13	3	99	63	4	—	.270	.344	.371	106	5	7	.936	18	109	103	3b141,2b13	—	2.4
1899	StL N	151	577	91	170	28	14	12	108	54	2	—	.295	.357	.454	119	13	17	.919	30	109	107	S100,3b52	—	4.4
1900	StL N	126	485	70	130	25	9	4	70	40	3	—	.268	.328	.381	96	-3	7	.934	6	98	64	S126/3	—	0.8
1901	StL N	134	550	69	178	34	15	2	91	20	3	—	.324	.351	.451	138	24	15	.929	**27**	**116**	**131**	S134	—	5.4
1902	StL A	133	494	71	141	32	9	1	63	45	4	—	.285	.350	.393	107	6	18	.948	7	104	118	S131/Prf	—	1.6
1903	StL A	135	511	63	136	21	7	1	54	28	4	—	.266	.309	.341	97	-2	10	.924	18	**109**	117	S135	—	2.2
1904	StL A	139	541	57	149	29	4	2	69	42	2	—	.275	.330	.355	124	16	20	**.947**	3	105	84	S139	—	2.6
1905	StL A	**156**	587	67	159	25	9	1	59	45	1	—	.271	.324	.349	120	13	13	.935	21	108	82	S156	—	4.2
1906	StL A	139	476	64	123	21	7	2	67	58	4	—	.258	.344	.345	121	14	24	.949	2	99	115	S138	—	2.3
1907	StL A	147	538	56	138	20	7	0	70	54	3	—	.257	.328	.320	107	6	16	.941	8	105	116	S147	—	2.0
1908	StL A	137	487	59	123	24	4	1	60	52	2	—	.253	.327	.324	111	8	5	**.951**	15	107	108	S137	—	3.1
1909	StL A	116	403	36	96	12	2	0	35	38	4	—	.238	.310	.278	92	-2	7	.946	11	100	113	S87,3b29	—	1.4
1910	StL A	138	508	47	131	19	7	0	37	49	1	—	.258	.324	.323	110	6	12	.948	23	108	91	S99,3b39	—	3.6
1911	StL A	125	410	35	95	12	2	0	31	46	2	—	.232	.312	.271	66	-18	8	.943	4	107	101	S124/2M	—	-0.5
1912	StL A	100	323	39	78	14	5	0	31	43	1	—	.241	.332	.316	89	-3	3	.942	8	104	102	S87,3b10,2b2,M	—	1.1
1913	StL A	55	147	11	31	5	0	0	21	14	3	16	.211	.293	.245	59	-7	1	.931	-4	93	59	S39,3b7	—	-0.9
1914	StL A	26	73	3	16	2	1	0	5	5	0	13	.219	.269	.274	66	-3	1-1	.889	-7	89	30	S19,3b2	—	-1.0
1915	StL A	9	13	1	3	0	1	0	4	5	0	0	.231	.444	.385	154	1	0-1	.848	0	108	198	S9	—	0.2
1916	StL A	14	18	0	5	0	0	0	1	2	0	1	.278	.350	.278	93	0	0	.958	3	167	97	3b9,S5	—	0.3
1917	StL N	8	10	0	1	0	0	0	2	0	0	1	.100	.100	.100	-40	-2	0	1.000	-1	0	0	3b5,S2	—	-0.3
1918	StL N	32	98	3	15	1	0	0	4	6	0	9	.153	.202	.163	12	-10	1	.959	1	110	113	2b17,S12/3	—	-1.0
Total	25	2383	8618	1057	2309	391	143	34	1121	774	47	79	.268	.332	.358	106	69	201-2	.938	201	105	102	S1826,3b426,P57,2b33,O25R/1	—	35.4
Wallach, Tim	Timothy Charles; B9.14.1957 Huntington Park CA; BR/TR/6´3˝/(200–220); [MonN79 1/10]; d9.6; C2; Col Cal St.–Fullerton; OF(4/0/36)																								
1980	Mon N	5	11	1	2	0	0	1	2	1-0	0	5	.182	.250	.455	91	0	0-0	1.000	-1	57	0	O3(2/0/1)/1	0	-0.1
1981	†Mon N	71	212	19	50	9	1	4	13	15-2	4	37	.236	.299	.344	79	-6	0-1	1.000	-2	92	116	O35(1/0/34),1b16,3b15	0	-1.1
1982	Mon N	158	596	89	160	31	3	28	97	36-4	4	81	.268	.313	.471	113	8	6-4	.948	2	96	97	3b156,O2(1/0/1)/1	0	0.7
1983	Mon N	156	581	54	156	33	3	19	70	55-8	6	97	.269	.335	.434	112	10	0-3	.956	-3	93	103	3b156	0	0.4
1984	Mon N★	160	582	55	143	25	4	18	72	50-6	7	101	.246	.311	.395	102	0	3-7	.959	22	110	**118**	3b160/S	0	1.9
1985	Mon N★	155	569	70	148	36	3	22	81	38-8	5	79	.260	.310	.450	117	10	9-9	.967	36	**123**	**132**	3b154	0	4.4
1986	Mon N	134	480	50	112	22	1	18	71	44-8	**10**	72	.233	.308	.396	94	-5	8-4	.958	18	117	126	3b132	0	1.2
1987	Mon N★	153	593	89	177	**42**	4	26	123	37-5	7	98	.298	.343	.514	120	16	9-5	.952	7	102	88	3b150/P	0	2.0
1988	Mon N	159	592	52	152	32	5	12	69	38-7	3	88	.257	.302	.389	93	-6	2-6	.962	19	**114**	131	3b153/2	0	1.3
1989	Mon N★	154	573	76	159	**42**	0	13	77	58-10	1	81	.277	.341	.419	115	13	3-7	.958	9	104	82	3b153/P	0	2.2
1990	Mon N★	161	626	69	185	37	5	21	98	42-11	3	80	.296	.339	.471	126	20	6-9	.954	5	103	102	3b161	0	2.4
1991	Mon N	151	577	60	130	22	1	13	73	50-8	6	100	.225	.292	.334	77	-18	2-4	**.968**	6	105	110	3b149	0	-1.4
1992	Mon N	150	537	53	120	29	1	9	59	50-2	8	90	.223	.296	.331	79	-14	2-2	.964	19	122	133	3b85,1b71	0	-0.1
1993	LA N	133	477	42	106	19	1	12	62	32-2	3	70	.222	.271	.342	68	-24	0-2	.958	9	106	70	3b130/1	22	-1.4
1994	LA N	113	414	68	116	21	1	23	78	46-2	4	80	.280	.356	.502	128	17	0-2	.959	-4	94	63	3b113	0	1.2
1995	†LA N	97	327	24	87	22	2	9	38	27-4	4	69	.266	.326	.428	105	2	0-0	**.976**	-6	90	72	3b96/1	40	-0.3
1996	Cal A	57	190	23	45	7	0	8	20	18-2	1	47	.237	.306	.400	76	-8	1-0	.941	3	110	52	3b46,1b3,D8	0	-0.4
	†LA N	45	162	14	37	3	1	4	22	12-0	1	32	.228	.286	.333	67	-9	0-1	.971	-6	74	44	3b45	0	-1.5
Total	17	2212	8099	908	2085	432	36	260	1125	649-89	77	1307	.257	.316	.416	102	6	51-66	.959	133	105	100	3b2054,1b94,O40R,D8,P2/2S	62	11.4

YEAR	TM LG	G	AB	R	H	2B	3B	HR	RBI	BB-IB	HP	SO	AVG	OBP	SLG	AOPS	ABR	SB-CS	FA	FR	RNG	THR	GAMES AT POSITION	DL	BFW
WALLAESA, JACK	John; B8.31.1919 Easton PA; D12.27.1986 Easton PA; BB/TR (BR 1940)/6´3˝/191; d9.22; Mil 1943–45																								
1940	Phi A	6	20	0	3	0	0	0	2	0	0	2	.150	.150	.150	-22	-4	0-0	.903	-0	113	81	S6	—	-0.3
1942	Phi A	36	117	13	30	4	1	2	13	8	2	26	.256	.315	.359	90	-2	0-1	.920	-6	86	80	S36	0	-0.7
1946	Phi A	63	194	16	38	4	2	5	11	14	0	47	.196	.250	.314	57	-12	1-0	.916	-10	85	87	S59	0	-2.1
1947	Chi A	81	205	25	40	9	1	7	32	23	1	51	.195	.279	.351	78	-7	2-2	.968	6	113	114	S27,O22L/3	0	-0.2
1948	Chi A	33	48	2	9	0	0	1	3	1	0	12	.188	.204	.250	21	-6	0-0	1.000	1	107	124	S5/lf	0	-0.5
Total	5	219	584	56	120	17	4	15	61	46	3	138	.205	.267	.325	65	-31	3-3	.933	-10	94	92	S133,O23L/3	0	-3.8
WALLEN, NORM	Norman Edward (b Norman Edward Walentoski); B2.13.1917 Milwaukee WI; D6.20.1994 Milwaukee WI; BR/TR/5´11.5˝/175; d4.20																								
1945	Bos N	4	15	1	2	0	1	0	1	1	0	1	.133	.188	.267	25	-2	0	.800	-1	73	0	3b4	0	-0.3
WALLER, TY	Elliott Tyrone; B3.14.1957 Fresno CA; BR/TR/6´0˝/(180–188); [StLN77*4/82]; d9.6; C2; Col San Diego (CA) City																								
1980	StL N	5	12	3	1	0	0	0	0	1-0	0	5	.083	.154	.083	-31	-2	0-0	1.000	-3	27	0	3b5	0	-0.5
1981	Chi N	30	71	10	19	2	1	3	13	4-1	0	18	.268	.303	.451	106	0	2-0	.978	0	100	68	3b22,2b3,O3C	0	0.1
1982	Chi N	17	21	4	5	0	0	0	1	2-0	0	5	.238	.304	.238	52	-1	0-0	1.000	-0	84	0	O7(1/5/1)/3	0	-0.2
1987	Hou N	11	6	1	1	1	0	0	0	0-0	0	3	.167	.167	.333	29	-1	0-0	1.000	0	205	0	O3(1/2/0)	0	0.0
Total	4	63	110	18	26	3	1	3	14	7-1	0	31	.236	.280	.364	77	-4	2-0	.961	-2	89	55	3b28,O13(2/10/1),2b3	0	-0.6
WALLING, DENNY	Dennis Martin; B4.17.1954 Neptune NJ; BL/TR/6´1˝/(183–185); [OakA75 S1/1]; d9.7; C5; Col Clemson																								
1975	Oak A	6	8	0	1	1	0	0	2	0-0	0	4	.125	.125	.250	4	-1	0-0	1.000	-0	88	0	O3(1/2/0)	0	-0.1
1976	Oak A	3	11	1	3	0	0	0	0	0-0	0	3	.273	.273	.273	62	-1	0-0	.889	-0	108	0	O3(2/2/0)	0	-0.1
1977	Hou N	6	21	1	6	0	1	0	6	2-0	0	4	.286	.348	.381	103	0	0-1	1.000	0	125	0	O5(2/1/2)	0	0.0
1978	Hou N	120	247	30	62	11	3	3	36	30-3	1	24	.251	.332	.356	100	0	9-2	.980	4	116	81	O78(66/7/4)	0	0.3
1979	Hou N	82	147	21	48	8	4	3	31	17-2	0	21	.327	.394	.497	151	10	3-2	.985	-0	103	75	O42(7/0/35)	0	0.8
1980	†Hou N	100	284	30	85	6	5	3	29	35-4	0	26	.299	.374	.387	124	9	4-3	.989	-5	81	114	1b63,O19(1/0/18)	0	0.0
1981	†Hou N	65	158	23	37	6	0	5	23	28-1	0	17	.234	.346	.367	110	3	2-1	.990	-4	56	118	1b27,O27(5/1/21)	0	-0.3
1982	Hou N	85	146	22	30	4	1	1	14	23-3	0	19	.205	.312	.267	69	-5	4-2	1.000	-0	89	218	O32(4/11/18),1b20	0	-0.7
1983	Hou N	100	135	24	40	5	3	3	19	15-1	0	16	.296	.364	.444	131	5	2-2	.992	-1	76	112	1b42,3b13,O13(2/0/12)	0	0.3
1984	Hou N	87	249	37	70	11	5	3	31	16-2	1	28	.281	.325	.402	111	2	7-1	.956	6	116	202	3b52,1b16,O6(3/3/0)	22	0.8
1985	Hou N	119	345	44	93	20	1	7	45	25-2	0	26	.270	.316	.394	101	0	5-2	.938	2	111	112	3b51,1b46,O13(6/0/7)	0	-0.1
1986	†Hou N	130	382	54	119	23	1	13	58	36-5	0	31	.312	.367	.479	136	19	1-1	.960	3	95	49	3b102,O11(6/0/5),1b4	0	2.0
1987	Hou N	110	325	45	92	21	4	5	33	39-1	0	37	.283	.356	.418	109	5	5-1	.948	0	83	122	3b79,1b16,O7(6/0/2)	11	0.4
1988	Hou N	65	176	19	43	10	2	1	20	15-3	0	18	.244	.304	.341	88	-3	1-0	.950	8	115	207	3b51,1b3/lf	47	0.5
	StL N	19	58	3	13	3	0	0	1	2-0	0	7	.224	.250	.276	50	-4	1-0	1.000	-1	65	0	O11(10/0/1),3b5/1	0	-0.5
	Year	84	234	22	56	13	2	1	21	17-3	0	25	.239	.291	.325	79	-7	2-0	.941	7	118	218	3b56,O12(11/0/1),1b4	0	0.0
1989	StL N	69	79	9	24	7	0	1	11	14-2	0	12	.304	.409	.430	135	5	0-0	.969	-4	87	89	1b20,3b9,O6(3/0/3)	15	0.0
1990	StL N	78	127	7	28	5	0	1	19	8-0	0	15	.220	.265	.283	51	-9	0-0	1.000	1	92	63	1b15,3b11,O8(3/0/5)	0	-0.9
1991	Tex A	24	44	1	4	1	0	0	2	3-0	2	8	.091	.184	.114	-16	-7	0-0	.950	-1	97	0	3b14,O5(3/0/2)	21	-0.8
1992	Hou N	3	3	1	1	0	0	0	0	0-0	0	0	.333	.333	.333	93	0	0-0	ø	0	—	—	/H	177	0.0
Total	18	1271	2945	372	799	142	30	49	380	308-29	4	316	.271	.339	.390	107	28	44-18	.947	8	101	119	3b387,O290(131/27/135),1b273	293	1.6
WALLIS, JOE	Harold Joseph; B1.9.1952 E.St.Louis IL; BB/TR/5´10˝/(180–195); [ChiN73 6/136]; d9.2; Col Southern Illinois																								
1975	Chi N	16	56	9	16	2	2	1	4	5-0	0	14	.286	.344	.446	113	1	2-0	1.000	-0	98	123	O15(0/14/1)	0	0.1
1976	Chi N	121	338	51	86	11	5	5	21	33-3	1	62	.254	.322	.361	86	-6	3-9	.976	2	94	198	O90(10/68/16)	0	-1.1
1977	Chi N	56	80	14	20	3	0	2	8	16-1	0	25	.250	.375	.363	89	-1	0-1	.974	-3	69	146	O35C	29	-0.4
1978	Chi N	28	55	7	17	2	1	1	6	5-1	0	13	.309	.367	.436	110	1	0-2	1.000	-1	86	110	O25C	0	-0.1
	Oak A	85	279	28	66	16	1	6	26	26-1	0	42	.237	.300	.366	91	-3	1-4	.980	-3	102	146	O80(5/55/23)/D	0	-0.3
1979	Oak A	23	78	6	11	2	0	1	3	10-1	1	18	.141	.247	.205	25	-8	1-0	1.000	-1	93	62	O23(0/1/23)	109	-1.0
Total	5	329	886	115	216	36	9	16	68	95-7	2	174	.244	.317	.359	86	-16	7-16	.982	-1	94	153	O268(15/198/63)/D	138	-2.8
WALLS, LEE	Ray Lee; B1.6.1933 San Diego CA; D10.11.1993 Los Angeles CA; BR/TR/6´3˝/(190–205); d4.21; C5; Col Pasadena (CA) City																								
1952	Pit N	32	80	6	15	0	1	2	5	8	0	22	.188	.261	.287	51	-6	0-0	1.000	0	96	116	O19(1/18/0)	0	-0.6
1956	Pit N	143	474	72	130	20	11	11	54	50-0	2	83	.274	.345	.432	110	6	3-5	.967	4	109	101	O133(74/10/56)/3	0	0.3
1957	Pit N	8	22	3	4	1	0	0	0	2-0	0	5	.182	.250	.227	30	-2	1-0	1.000	1	120	271	O7L	0	-0.1
	Chi N	117	366	42	88	10	5	6	33	27-1	1	67	.240	.292	.344	72	-15	5-3	.984	-3	92	99	O94(67/29/6)/3	0	-2.4
	Year	125	388	45	92	11	5	6	33	29-1	1	72	.237	.290	.338	70	-18	6-3	.985	-2	94	109	O101(74/29/6)/3	0	-2.5
1958	Chi N★	136	513	80	156	19	3	24	72	47-0	**8**	62	.304	.370	.493	128	21	4-4	.992	1	104	96	O132R	0	1.6
1959	Chi N	120	354	43	91	18	3	8	33	42-1	5	73	.257	.342	.393	97	-1	0-2	.967	-4	104	12	O119R	0	-1.0
1960	Cin N	29	84	12	23	3	2	1	7	17-1	0	20	.274	.392	.393	115	3	2-0	.960	0	106	97	O24(12/0/12),1b2	0	0.2
	Phi N	65	181	19	36	6	1	3	19	14-1	0	32	.199	.253	.293	50	-13	3-2	.947	-4	97	86	3b34,O13(8/0/5),1b7	0	-1.8
	Year	94	265	31	59	9	3	4	26	31-2	0	52	.223	.300	.325	72	-10	5-2	.958	-4	102	65	O37(20/0/17),3b34,1b9	0	-1.6
1961	Phi N	91	261	32	73	6	4	8	30	19-1	0	48	.280	.329	.425	99	-1	2-2	.987	-3	100	126	1b28,3b26,O17(11/1/8)	0	-0.7
1962	LA N	60	109	9	29	3	1	0	17	10-0	0	21	.266	.325	.312	77	-3	1-0	.929	-1	64	127	O17(15/0/3),1b11,3b4	0	-0.6
1963	LA N	64	86	12	20	1	0	3	11	7-1	0	25	.233	.290	.349	89	-2	0-0	1.000	2	137	0	O18(10/0/8),1b5,3b2	0	0.0
1964	LA N	37	28	1	5	1	0	0	3	2-0	0	12	.179	.233	.214	29	-3	0-0	1.000	-0	88	0	O6(3/0/3)/C	0	-0.3
Total	10	902	2558	331	670	88	31	66	284	245-6	16	470	.262	.329	.398	96	-16	21-18	.977	-8	102	82	O599(208/58/352),3b68,1b53/C	0	-5.4
WALSH, AUSTIN	Austin Edward; B9.1.1891 Cambridge MA; D1.26.1955 Glendale CA; BL/TL/5´11˝/175; d4.19																								
1914	Chi F	57	121	14	29	6	1	1	10	4	0	25	.240	.264	.331	65	-9	0	1.000	-0	98	83	O30(21/1/8)	—	-1.0
WALSH, JIMMY	James Charles; B9.22.1885 Kallila, Ireland; D7.3.1962 Syracuse NY; BL/TR/5´10.5˝/170; d8.26; Mil 1918																								
1912	Phi A	31	107	11	27	8	2	0	15	12	0	—	.252	.328	.364	101	0	7	.947	-0	115	25	O30L	—	-0.1
1913	Phi A	97	303	56	77	16	5	0	27	38	2	40	.254	.341	.340	102	2	15	.961	2	109	87	O90(39/44/13)	—	-0.1
1914	NY A	43	136	13	26	1	3	1	11	29	0	21	.191	.333	.265	80	-2	6-9	.977	-1	103	69	O41(37/4/0)	—	-0.7
	†Phi A	68	216	35	51	11	6	3	36	30	4	27	.236	.340	.384	123	6	6-12	.966	-0	101	97	O56(25/26/6),1b3,3b3/S	—	0.0
	Year	111	352	48	77	12	9	4	47	59	4	48	.219	.337	.338	106	4	12-21	.971	-1	102	85	O97(62/30/6),1b3,3b3/S	—	-0.7
1915	Phi A	117	417	48	86	15	6	1	20	57	3	64	.206	.306	.278	78	-11	22-12	.976	5	110	105	O109(29/44/36),3b2/1	—	-1.2
1916	Phi A	114	390	42	91	13	6	1	27	54	2	36	.233	.330	.305	95	-1	27-14	.939	-1	101	100	O113(0/6/107)/1	—	-0.8
	†Bos A	14	17	5	3	1	0	0	2	4	0	2	.176	.333	.235	71	0	3-2	1.000	-1	104	0	O6(1/3/2),3b2	—	-0.1
	Year	128	407	47	94	14	6	1	29	58	2	38	.231	.330	.302	94	-2	30-16	.940	-2	101	98	O119(1/9/109),3b2/1	—	-0.9
1917	Bos A	57	185	25	49	6	3	0	12	25	0	14	.265	.352	.330	109	3	6	.982	-1	91	117	O47(2/43/2)	—	-0.2
Total	6	541	1771	235	410	71	31	6	150	249	11	204	.232	.330	.317	96	-3	92-49	.964	3	105	92	O492(163/170/166),3b7,1b5/S	—	-3.2
WALSH, JOHN	John Gabriel; B3.25.1879 Wilkes–Barre PA; D4.25.1947 Jamaica NY; BR/TR/5´8.5˝/162; d6.22; Col Notre Dame																								
1903	Phi N	1	3	0	0	0	0	0	0	0	0	—	.000	.000	.000	-99	-1	0	1.000	-0	123	0	/3	—	-0.1
WALSH, JOE	Joseph Francis; B10.14.1886 Minersville PA; D1.6.1967 Buffalo NY; BR/TR/6´2˝/170; d10.8; Col Villanova																								
1910	NY A	1	4	0	2	1	0	0	2	0	0	—	.500	.500	.750	275	1	0	.900	-0	*167*	*74*	/C	—	0.1
1911	NY A	4	9	2	2	1	0	0	0	0	0	—	.222	.222	.333	51	-1	0	1.000	-2	*71*	*58*	C4	—	-0.2
Total	2	5	13	2	4	2	0	0	2	0	0	—	.308	.308	.462	114	0	0	.933	-2	*115*	*65*	C5	—	-0.1
WALSH, JOE	Joseph Patrick "Tweet"; B3.13.1917 Boston MA; D10.5.1996 Boston MA; BR/TR/5´10˝/155; d7.1																								
1938	Bos N	4	8	0	0	0	0	0	0	0	0	2	.000	.000	.000	-99	-2	0	.900	-1	50	86	S4	—	-0.3
WALSH, JOE	Joseph R. "Reddy"; B11.5.1864 Chicago IL; D8.8.1911 Omaha NE; BL/TR; d9.3																								
1891	Bal AA	26	100	14	21	0	1	1	10	6	0	18	.210	.255	.260	47	-8	4	.865	1	85	215	S13,2b13	—	-0.5
WALSH, DEE	Leo Thomas; B3.28.1890 St.Louis MO; D7.14.1971 St.Louis MO; BB/TR/5´9.5˝/165; d4.10																								
1913	StL A	23	53	8	9	0	1	0	5	6	4	11	.170	.302	.208	51	-3	3	.933	0	112	81	S22/3	—	-0.2
1914	StL A	7	23	1	2	0	0	0	1	2	0	4	.087	.160	.087	-27	-4	1-1	.919	-0	97	188	S7	—	-0.4
1915	StL A	59	150	13	33	5	0	0	6	14	5	25	.220	.308	.253	71	-5	6-6	.951	4	95	227	O45(0/21/24),3b2/P2S	—	-0.4
Total	3	89	226	22	44	5	1	0	12	22	9	40	.195	.292	.226	56	-12	10-7	.951	4	95	227	O45(0/21/24),S30,3b3/2P	—	-1.0

YEAR	TM LG	G	AB	R	H	2B	3B	HR	RBI	BB-IB	HP	SO	AVG	OBP	SLG	AOPS	ABR	SB-CS	FA	FR	RNG	THR	GAMES AT POSITION	DL	BFW
WALSH, JIMMY	Michael Timothy "Runt"; B3.25.1886 Lima OH; D1.21.1947 Baltimore MD; BR/TR/5´9˝/174; d4.25; OF(29/16/33)																								
1910	Phi N	88	242	28	60	8	3	3	31	25	2	38	.248	.323	.343	91	-3	5	.947	-4	113	82	2b26,O26(7/14/6),S9,3b5	—	-0.8
1911	Phi N	94	289	29	78	20	3	1	31	21	2	30	.270	.324	.370	93	-3	5	.962	-3	92	50	O48(22/2/25),2b14,S9,3b7,C4/P1	—	-0.7
1912	Phi N	51	150	16	40	6	3	2	19	8	0	20	.267	.304	.387	83	-4	3	.944	1	108	81	2b31,3b12,C5	—	-0.3
1913	Phi N	26	30	3	10	4	0	0	5	1	0	5	.333	.355	.467	128	1	1	1.000	-0	90	219	2b6,S3/3rf	—	0.1
1914	Bal F	120	428	54	132	25	4	10	65	22	2	56	.308	.345	.456	113	0	18	.932	3	102	107	3b113/2Srf	—	0.7
1915	Bal F	106	401	43	121	20	1	9	60	21	2	44	.302	.340	.424	111	-1	12	.936	-5	94	91	3b106	—	-0.4
	StL F	17	31	5	6	1	0	0	1	3	2	4	.194	.306	.226	48	-2	1	.913	-0	106	0	3b9	—	-0.3
	Year	123	432	48	127	21	1	9	61	24	4	48	.294	.337	.410	106	-3	13	.934	-6	95	85	3b115	—	-0.7
Total	6	502	1571	178	447	84	14	25	212	101	10	197	.285	.332	.404	102	-12	45	.925	-8	97	95	3b253,2b78,O76R,S22,C9/1P	—	-1.7
WALSH, TOM	Thomas Joseph; B2.28.1886 Davenport IA; D3.16.1963 Naples FL; BR/TR/5´11˝/170; d8.15																								
1906	Chi N	2	1	0	0	0	0	0	0	0	0	—	.000	.000	.000	-95	0	0	1.000	-0	*0*	*323*	C2	—	0.0
WALSH, WALT	Walter William; B4.30.1897 Newark NJ; D1.15.1966 Avon By The Sea NJ; BR/TR/5´11˝/170; d5.4																								
1920	Phi N	2	0	0	0	0	0	0	0	0	0	0	ø	ø	ø	ø	0	0-0	ø	0	—	—	/R	—	0.0
WALTERS, ROXY	Alfred John; B11.5.1892 San Francisco CA; D6.3.1956 Alameda CA; BR/TR/5´8.5˝/160; d9.16																								
1915	NY A	2	3	0	1	0	0	0	0	0	0	0	.333	.333	.333	100	0	0	1.000	1	*141*	*189*	C2	—	0.1
1916	NY A	66	203	13	54	9	3	0	23	14	2	42	.266	.320	.340	96	-1	2	.974	12	143	139	C65	—	1.8
1917	NY A	61	171	16	45	2	0	0	14	9	1	22	.263	.304	.275	76	-5	2	.968	8	*139*	*105*	C57	—	0.9
1918	NY A	64	191	18	38	5	1	0	12	9	1	18	.199	.239	.236	42	-14	3	.953	-2	*120*	*76*	C50,O9R	—	-1.4
1919	Bos A	48	135	7	26	2	0	0	9	7	5	15	.193	.259	.207	33	-12	1	.982	3	*105*	*109*	C47	—	-0.6
1920	Bos A	88	258	25	51	11	1	0	28	30	9	21	.198	.303	.248	49	-18	2-2	.980	3	*77*	*100*	C85,1b2	—	-0.8
1921	Bos A	54	169	17	34	4	1	0	14	10	2	11	.201	.254	.237	27	-19	3-0	.990	11	*128*	*111*	C54	—	-0.4
1922	Bos A	38	98	4	19	2	0	0	6	6	0	8	.194	.240	.214	19	-12	0-0	.967	3	*99*	*90*	C36	—	-0.7
1923	Bos A	40	104	9	26	4	0	0	5	2	0	6	.250	.264	.288	45	-9	0-2	.974	3	*90*	*135*	C36/2	—	-0.4
1924	Cle A	32	74	10	19	2	0	0	5	10	0	6	.257	.345	.284	63	-4	0-1	.979	3	*104*	*129*	C25,2b7	—	0.0
1925	Cle A	5	20	0	4	0	0	0	0	0	0	2	.200	.200	.200	2	-3	0-0	1.000	0	*124*	*197*	C5	—	-0.2
Total	11	498	1426	119	317	41	6	0	116	97	20	151	.222	.281	.259	51	-97	13-5	.975	46	*113*	*111*	C462,O9R,2b8,1b2	—	-1.7
WALTERS, DAN	Daniel Gene; B8.15.1966 Brunswick ME; BR/TR/6´4˝/(225–230); [HouN84 5/123]; d6.1																								
1992	SD N	57	179	14	45	11	1	4	22	10-0	2	28	.251	.295	.391	92	-2	1-0	.992	3	85	97	C55	0	0.5
1993	SD N	27	94	6	19	3	0	1	10	7-2	0	13	.202	.255	.266	40	-8	0-0	.970	-5	75	140	C26	0	-1.2
Total	2	84	273	20	64	14	1	5	32	17-2	2	41	.234	.281	.348	73	-10	1-0	.985	-2	81	112	C81	0	-0.7
WALTERS, FRED	Fred James "Whale"; B9.4.1912 Laurel MS; D2.1.1980 Laurel MS; BR/TR/6´1˝/210; d4.17; Col Mississippi St.																								
1945	Bos A	40	93	2	16	2	0	0	5	10	0	9	.172	.252	.194	29	-8	1-1	.993	3	*115*	*196*	C38	0	-0.4
WALTERS, KEN	Kenneth Rogers; B11.11.1933 Fresno CA; BR/TR/6´1˝/180; d4.12																								
1960	Phi N	124	426	42	102	10	0	8	37	16-3	1	50	.239	.266	.319	60	-25	4-3	.988	9	**108**	**166**	O119(5/2/116)	0	-2.1
1961	Phi N	86	180	23	41	8	2	2	14	5-0	1	25	.228	.251	.328	53	-13	2-2	.975	0	100	112	O56(0/4/53),1b5/3	0	-1.6
1963	Cin N	49	75	6	14	2	0	1	7	4-1	1	14	.187	.237	.253	40	-6	0-2	.889	-2	73	0	O21(11/0/10)/1	0	-1.1
Total	3	259	681	71	157	20	2	11	58	25-4	3	89	.231	.259	.314	56	-44	6-7	.979	7	103	139	O196(16/6/179),1b6/3	0	-4.8
WALTERS, BUCKY	William Henry; B4.19.1909 Philadelphia PA; D4.20.1991 Abington PA; BR/TR/6´1˝/180; d9.18; M2/C8; ▲																								
1931	Bos N	9	38	2	8	2	0	0	0	0	0	3	.211	.211	.263	28	-4	0	.947	1	113	0	3b6,2b3	—	-0.3
1932	Bos N	22	75	8	14	3	1	0	4	2	0	18	.187	.208	.253	24	-8	0	.910	0	106	213	3b22	—	-0.8
1933	Bos A	52	195	27	50	8	3	4	28	19	1	24	.256	.326	.390	90	-3	1-1	.940	1	106	143	3b43,2b7	—	-0.1
1934	Bos A	23	88	10	19	4	4	4	18	3	0	12	.216	.242	.489	79	-4	0-0	.906	3	112	129	3b23	—	0.0
	Phi N	83	300	36	78	20	3	4	38	19	2	54	.260	.308	.387	75	-10	1	.950	-6	91	106	3b80,2b3,P2	—	-1.4
1935	Phi N	49	96	14	24	2	1	0	6	9	0	12	.250	.314	.292	58	-6	0	1.000	2	126	211	P24,O5L,2b2/3	—	0.0
1936	Phi N	64	121	12	29	10	1	1	16	7	0	15	.240	.281	.364	66	-6	0	.974	8	**176**	149	P40/23	—	0.4
1937	Phi N★	56	137	15	38	6	0	1	16	5	0	16	.277	.303	.343	69	-6	1	.988	5	143	**237**	P37,3b8	—	0.2
1938	Phi N	15	35	6	10	2	0	1	3	1	0	5	.286	.306	.429	103	3	1	.955	0	107	250	P12	—	0.0
	Cin N	36	64	10	9	1	0	0	5	7	1	18	.141	.236	.156	10	0	0	.981	2	141	100	P27	—	0.0
	Year	51	99	16	19	3	0	1	8	8	1	23	.192	.259	.253	42	3	1	.973	3	130	150	P39	—	0.0
1939	†Cin N☆	40	120	16	39	8	1	1	16	5	1	12	.325	.357	.433	111	13	1	.979	4	118	291	P39	—	0.0
1940	†Cin N★	37	117	11	24	3	0	1	18	4	0	14	.205	.231	.256	34	2	2	.945	-1	91	233	P36	—	0.0
1941	Cin N★	39	106	6	20	6	0	0	9	7	0	13	.189	.239	.245	36	2	0	.977	2	109	153	P37	0	0.0
1942	Cin N★	40	99	13	24	6	1	2	13	3	0	13	.242	.265	.384	89	-2	0	.961	1	110	198	P34/lf	0	0.1
1943	Cin N	37	90	11	24	7	1	1	12	6	0	15	.267	.313	.400	107	8	1	.971	1	97	**206**	P34	0	0.0
1944	Cin N★	37	107	9	30	4	0	0	13	8	0	18	.280	.330	.318	86	8	0	**1.000**	0	101	241	P34	0	0.0
1945	Cin N	24	61	11	14	3	0	3	8	3	0	14	.230	.266	.426	93	5	2	.975	-0	100	165	P22	0	0.0
1946	Cin N	24	55	6	7	2	0	0	5	4	0	12	.127	.186	.164	-0	-1	2	.940	2	123	371	P22	0	0.0
1947	Cin N	20	45	3	12	2	0	0	4	2	0	13	.267	.298	.311	62	3	0	.962	-1	83	0	P20	0	0.0
1948	Cin N	7	15	1	4	0	0	0	2	0	0	2	.267	.267	.267	46	1	0	1.000	1	169	0	P7,M	60	0.0
1950	Bos N	1	2	0	0	0	0	0	0	0	0	0	.000	.000	.000	-99	0	0	1.000	-0	0	0	/P	0	0.0
Total	19	715	1966	227	477	99	16	23	234	114	5	303	.243	.286	.344	69	-5	12-1	.974	24	117	205	P428,3b184,2b16,O6L	60	-1.9
WALTON, DANNY	Daniel James "Mickey"; B7.14.1947 Los Angeles CA; BR/TR (BB 1975–80)/6´0˝/(185–200); [HouN65 8/192]; d4.20																								
1968	Hou N	2	2	0	0	0	0	0	0	0-0	0	1	.000	.000	.000	-99	0	0-0	ø	0	—	—	/H	0	-0.1
1969	Sea A	23	92	12	20	1	2	3	10	5-0	3	26	.217	.275	.370	81	-3	2-0	.976	-2	87	0	O23L	0	-0.7
1970	Mil A	117	397	32	102	20	1	17	66	51-4	6	126	.257	.349	.441	117	10	2-3	.965	-5	86	62	O114L	0	-0.2
1971	Mil A	30	69	5	14	3	0	2	9	7-0	1	22	.203	.286	.333	76	-2	0-0	.923	-3	75	0	O19(19/1/0)/3	0	-0.7
	NY A	5	14	1	2	0	0	1	2	0-0	0	7	.143	.143	.357	40	-1	0-0	1.000	-1	62	0	O4(1/0/3)	0	-0.2
	Year	35	83	6	16	3	0	3	11	7-0	1	29	.193	.264	.337	70	-4	0-0	.933	-3	73	0	O23(20/1/3)/3	0	-0.9
1973	Min A	37	96	13	17	1	1	4	8	17-0	0	28	.177	.301	.333	75	-3	0-0	1.000	-2	61	0	O18(15/0/3),D11/3	0	-0.7
1975	Min A	42	63	4	11	2	0	1	8	4-2	0	18	.175	.224	.254	34	-6	0-0	.962	-0	52	169	1b7,C2,D6	0	-0.6
1976	LA N	18	15	0	2	0	0	0	2	1-0	0	2	.133	.176	.133	-8	-2	0-0	ø	0	—	—	/H	0	-0.3
1977	Hou N	13	21	0	4	0	0	0	1	0-0	0	5	.190	.190	.190	3	-3	0-0	.956	-1	85	37	1b5	0	-0.4
1980	Tex A	10	10	2	2	0	0	0	1	3-0	0	5	.200	.385	.200	67	0	0-0	ø	0	—	—	/D	0	0.0
Total	9	297	779	69	174	27	4	28	107	88-6	10	240	.223	.309	.376	90	-10	4-3	.966	-14	82	39	O178(172/1/6),D18,1b12,C2,3b2	0	-3.9
WALTON, JEROME	Jerome O'Terrell; B7.8.1965 Newnan GA; BR/TR/6´1˝/(175–200); [ChiN86*2/36]; d4.4; Col Enterprise St. (AL) JC																								
1989	†Chi N	116	475	64	139	23	3	5	46	27-1	6	77	.293	.335	.385	100	0	24-7	.990	-5	99	34	O115C	31	-0.3
1990	Chi N	101	392	63	103	16	2	2	21	50-1	4	70	.263	.350	.329	83	-7	14-7	.977	-5	99	56	O98C	45	-1.3
1991	Chi N	123	270	42	59	13	1	5	17	19-0	3	55	.219	.275	.330	67	-12	7-3	.983	-2	104	53	O101(0/100/1)	0	-1.4
1992	Chi N	30	55	7	7	0	1	0	1	9-0	2	13	.127	.273	.164	26	-5	1-2	.944	-1	94	0	O24(22/1/1)	18	-0.8
1993	Cal A	5	2	2	0	0	0	0	0	1-0	0	2	.000	.333	.000	-2	0	1-0	1.000	0	174	0	/lfD	0	0.0
1994	Cin N	46	68	10	21	4	0	1	9	4-0	0	12	.309	.347	.412	97	0	1-3	1.000	-0	107	166	O26(16/5/6),1b7	38	-0.2
1995	†Cin N	102	162	32	47	12	1	8	22	17-0	4	25	.290	.368	.525	132	8	10-7	.982	3	116	82	O89(36/50/8),1b3	0	0.9
1996	Atl N	37	47	9	16	5	0	1	4	5-0	0	10	.340	.389	.511	131	2	0-0	1.000	2	157	0	O28(23/1/5)	123	0.4
1997	†Bal A	26	68	8	20	1	0	3	9	4-0	0	10	.294	.333	.441	103	0	0-0	1.000	-0	111	0	O19(9/2/11),1b5,D2	129	-0.1
1998	TB A	12	34	4	11	3	0	0	3	2-0	0	6	.324	.361	.412	98	0	0-0	1.000	2	124	581	O8(4/0/4),D3	19	0.2
Total	10	598	1573	241	423	77	8	25	132	138-2	19	280	.269	.333	.376	91	-14	58-29	.984	-6	105	56	O509(111/373/36),1b15,D9	403	-2.6
WALTON, REGGIE	Reginald Sherard; B10.24.1952 Kansas City MO; BR/TR/6´3˝/(200–205); [SFN72*2/44]; d6.13; Col Compton (CA) CC																								
1980	Sea A	31	83	8	23	6	0	2	9	3-0	1	10	.277	.307	.422	97	0	2-2	.929	-0	118	0	O17(6/0/11),D11	0	-0.2
1981	Sea A	12	6	1	0	0	0	0	0	1-0	0	2	.000	.143	.000	-53	-1	0-0	ø	-0	0	0	O4(3/0/1)/D	23	-0.2
1982	Pit N	13	15	1	3	1	0	0	0	1-0	1	1	.200	.294	.267	55	-1	0-0	ø	-1	0	0	O2L	0	-0.1
Total	3	56	104	10	26	7	0	2	9	5-0	2	13	.250	.295	.375	82	-2	2-2	.929	-1	101	0	O23(11/0/12),D12	23	-0.5

YEAR	TM LG	G	AB	R	H	2B	3B	HR	RBI	BB-IB	HP	SO	AVG	OBP	SLG	AOPS	ABR	SB-CS	FA	FR	RNG	THR	GAMES AT POSITION	DL	BFW
WAMBSGANSS, BILL	William Adolph; B3.19.1894 Cleveland OH; D12.8.1985 Lakewood OH; BR/TR/5´11˝/175; d8.4; Mil 1918																								
1914	Cle A	43	143	12	31	6	2	0	12	8	4	24	.217	.277	.287	67	-6	2-7	.921	-2	103	105	S36,2b4	—	-0.8
1915	Cle A	121	375	30	73	4	4	0	21	36	4	50	.195	.272	.227	48	-24	8-9	.938	-2	104	81	2b78,3b35	—	-2.7
1916	Cle A	136	475	57	117	14	4	0	45	41	5	40	.246	.313	.293	77	-13	13	.925	-5	100	95	S106,2b24,3b5	—	-1.1
1917	Cle A	141	499	52	127	17	6	0	43	37	7	42	.255	.315	.313	85	-9	16	.951	15	**111**	**126**	2b137,1b3	—	0.9
1918	Cle A	87	315	34	93	15	2	0	40	21	3	21	.295	.345	.356	102	1	16	.952	-1	97	98	2b87	—	0.1
1919	Cle A	**139**	526	60	146	17	6	2	60	32	3	24	.278	.323	.344	82	-13	18	.963	11	103	109	2b139	—	0.0
1920	†Cle A	153	565	83	138	16	11	1	55	54	5	26	.244	.316	.317	66	-28	9-18	.960	8	101	114	2b153	—	-2.2
1921	Cle A	107	410	80	117	28	5	2	47	44	3	27	.285	.359	.393	90	-5	13-7	.963	-16	82	101	2b103,3b2	—	-1.7
1922	Cle A	142	538	89	141	22	6	0	47	60	4	26	.262	.341	.325	74	-19	17-10	.961	-7	98	101	2b125,S16	—	-2.1
1923	Cle A	101	345	59	100	20	4	1	59	43	3	15	.290	.373	.380	99	1	10-9	.963	7	105	92	2b88,3b4	—	0.9
1924	Bos A	156	636	93	174	41	5	0	49	54	4	33	.274	.334	.354	77	-21	14-8	.963	13	100	110	2b156	—	-0.3
1925	Bos A	111	360	50	83	12	4	1	41	52	1	21	.231	.329	.294	59	-22	3-5	.957	8	106	98	2b103,1b6	—	-1.1
1926	Phi A	54	54	11	19	3	0	0	1	8	1	8	.352	.444	.407	117	2	1-1	.923	0	107	122	S17,2b8	—	0.3
Total	13	1491	5241	710	1359	215	59	7	520	490	47	357	.259	.328	.327	78	-156	140-74	.958	29	101	105	2b1205,S175,3b46,1b9	—	-9.8
WANER, LLOYD	Lloyd James "Little Poison"; B3.16.1906 Harrah OK; D7.22.1982 Oklahoma City OK; BL/TR/5´9˝/150; d4.12; Def 1943; HF1967; b–Paul; Col East Central																								
1927	†Pit N	150	629	**133**	223	17	6	2	27	37	6	23	.355	.396	.410	108	9	14	.976	-4	103	58	O150(42/109/0)/2	—	-0.3
1928	Pit N	**152**	659	121	221	22	14	5	61	40	4	13	.335	.377	.434	107	6	8	.980	-1	99	107	O152(10/143/0)	—	-0.2
1929	Pit N	151	662	134	234	28	**20**	5	74	37	9	20	.353	.395	.479	113	12	6	.987	7	101	140	O151C	—	1.1
1930	Pit N	68	260	32	94	8	3	1	36	5	1	5	.362	.376	.427	93	-3	3	.983	3	105	125	O65C	—	-0.3
1931	Pit N	154	681	90	**214**	25	13	4	57	39	1	16	.314	.352	.407	104	2	7	.979	10	105	143	O153C/2	—	0.9
1932	Pit N	134	565	90	188	27	11	2	38	31	0	11	.333	.367	.430	116	12	6	.986	9	116	76	O131C	—	1.7
1933	Pit N	121	500	59	138	14	5	0	26	22	0	8	.276	.307	.324	80	-14	3	.982	1	101	107	O114(65/49/0)	—	-1.9
1934	Pit N	140	611	95	173	27	6	1	48	38	1	12	.283	.326	.352	80	-17	6	.979	7	113	81	O139C	—	-1.3
1935	Pit N	122	537	83	166	22	14	0	46	22	0	10	.309	.336	.402	95	-6	1	.989	2	108	50	O121C	—	-0.7
1936	Pit N	106	414	67	133	13	8	1	31	31	0	5	.321	.369	.399	104	2	1	.984	-3	100	30	O92C	—	-0.3
1937	Pit N	129	537	80	177	23	4	1	45	34	0	12	.330	.370	.393	107	6	3	.988	0	102	80	O123C	—	0.3
1938	Pit N☆	147	619	79	194	25	7	5	57	28	0	11	.313	.343	.401	103	1	5	.986	-5	92	121	O144C	—	-0.7
1939	Pit N	112	379	49	108	15	3	0	24	17	3	13	.285	.321	.340	79	-12	0	.992	5	105	130	O92C/3	—	-0.9
1940	Pit N	72	166	30	43	3	0	0	3	5	1	5	.259	.285	.277	56	-10	2	.989	0	101	102	O42(1/41/0)	—	-1.1
1941	Pit N	3	4	2	1	0	0	0	1	2	0	0	.250	.500	.250	116	0	0	1.000	0	114	0	/cf	0	0.0
	Bos N	19	51	7	21	1	0	0	4	2	0	0	.412	.434	.431	151	3	1	.969	0	104	106	O15(3/11/1)	0	0.3
	Cin N	55	164	17	42	4	1	0	6	8	0	0	.256	.291	.293	64	-8	0	.986	-1	93	101	O44(0/13/31)	0	-1.1
	Year	77	219	26	64	5	1	0	11	12	0	0	.292	.329	.324	85	-5	1	.981	-1	96	99	O60(3/25/32)	0	-0.8
1942	Phi N	101	287	23	75	7	3	0	10	16	0	6	.261	.300	.307	82	-8	1	.967	-2	100	92	O75C	0	-1.2
1944	Bro N	15	14	3	4	0	0	0	1	3	0	0	.286	.412	.286	101	0	0	1.000	-0	97	0	O4C	0	0.0
	Pit N	19	14	2	5	0	0	0	2	2	0	0	.357	.438	.357	120	1	0	1.000	1	162	0	O7(1/6/0)	0	0.1
	Year	34	28	5	9	0	0	0	3	5	0	0	.321	.424	.321	110	1	0	1.000	1	139	0	O11(1/10/0)	0	0.1
1945	Pit N	23	19	5	5	0	0	0	1	1	0	3	.263	.300	.263	55	-1	0	1.000	1	104	1380	O3(2/0/1)	0	0.0
Total	18	1993	7772	1201	2459	281	118	27	598	420	26	173	.316	.353	.393	99	-25	67	.983	31	103	97	O1818(124/1663/33),2b2/3	0	-5.6
WANER, PAUL	Paul Glee "Big Poison"; B4.16.1903 Harrah OK; D8.29.1965 Sarasota FL; BL/TL/5´8.5˝/153; d4.13; Mil 1945; C1; HF1952; b–Lloyd; Col East Central																								
1926	Pit N	144	536	101	180	35	**22**	8	79	66	4	19	.336	**.413**	.528	144	34	11	.976	4	103	108	O139(6/0/133)	—	2.6
1927	†Pit N	155	623	114	**237**	42	**18**	9	**131**	60	3	14	**.380**	.437	.549	152	47	5	.980	5	107	112	O143R,1b14	—	3.9
1928	Pit N	**152**	602	**142**	223	**50**	19	6	86	77	5	16	.370	.446	.547	152	49	6	.975	3	107	105	O131R,1b24	—	3.9
1929	Pit N	151	596	131	200	43	15	15	100	89	3	24	.336	.424	.534	133	33	15	.986	1	101	95	O143R,1b7	—	2.0
1930	Pit N	145	589	117	217	32	18	8	77	57	4	18	.368	.428	.525	128	28	18	.959	-4	106	50	O143(0/5/138)	—	1.2
1931	Pit N	150	559	88	180	35	10	6	70	73	4	21	.322	.404	.453	131	28	6	.976	**13**	**107**	**153**	O138R,1b10	—	3.1
1932	Pit N	**154**	630	107	215	**62**	10	8	82	56	2	24	.341	.397	.510	144	42	13	.974	1	105	81	O154(0/9/145)	—	3.3
1933	Pit N★	**154**	618	101	191	38	16	7	70	60	2	20	.309	.372	.456	136	29	3	.981	3	103	105	O154R	—	2.4
1934	Pit N★	146	599	**122**	**217**	32	16	14	90	68	2	24	**.362**	.429	.539	154	47	8	.985	7	108	113	O145R	—	4.3
1935	Pit N★	139	549	98	176	29	12	11	78	61	3	22	.321	.392	.477	128	23	2	.983	1	103	91	O136R	—	1.5
1936	Pit N	148	585	107	218	53	9	5	94	74	3	29	**.373**	.446	.520	156	51	7	.960	7	**114**	95	O145R	—	4.7
1937	Pit N★	**154**	619	94	219	30	9	2	74	63	0	34	.354	.413	.441	132	30	4	.970	-0	99	107	O150R,1b3	—	2.0
1938	Pit N	148	625	77	175	31	6	6	69	47	1	28	.280	.331	.378	94	-6	2	.977	-6	95	79	O147(0/1/148)	—	-2.1
1939	Pit N	125	461	62	151	30	6	3	45	35	0	18	.328	.375	.438	120	13	0	.978	1	97	122	O106R	—	0.7
1940	Pit N	89	238	32	69	16	1	1	32	23	0	14	.290	.352	.378	102	2	0	.985	-1	92	109	O45R,1b8	—	-0.2
1941	Bro N	11	35	5	6	0	0	0	4	8	0	0	.171	.326	.171	41	-2	0	.923	-1	83	0	O9R	0	-0.4
	Bos N	95	294	40	82	10	2	2	46	47	0	14	.279	.378	.347	110	6	1	.965	-1	95	120	O77(10/3/66),1b7	0	0.1
	Year	106	329	45	88	10	2	2	50	55	0	14	.267	.372	.328	102	3	1	.961	-2	94	108	O86(10/3/75),1b7	0	-0.3
1942	Bos N	114	333	43	86	17	1	1	39	62	1	20	.258	.376	.324	108	7	2	.969	-5	90	78	O94R	0	-0.3
1943	Bro N	82	225	29	70	16	0	1	26	35	1	9	.311	.406	.396	132	12	0	.960	-1	106	70	O57(1/0/56)	0	0.8
1944	Bro N	83	136	16	39	4	1	0	16	27	0	7	.287	.405	.331	111	4	0	.983	1	108	112	O32(1/0/31)	0	0.3
	NY A	9	7	1	1	0	0	0	1	2	0	1	.143	.333	.143	37	0	1-0	ø	0	—	—	/H	0	0.0
1945	NY A	1	0	0	0	0	0	0	0	1	0	0	ø	1.000	ø	191	0	0-0	ø	0	—	—	/H	0	0.0
Total	20	2549	9459	1627	3152	605	191	113	1309	1091	38	376	.333	.404	.473	133	477	104-0	.975	29	103	99	O2288(18/18/2256),1b73	0	33.8
WANNER, JACK	Clarence Curtis "Johnny"; B11.29.1885 Geneseo IL; D5.28.1919 Geneseo IL; BR/TR/5´11.5˝/190; d9.28																								
1909	NY A	3	8	0	1	0	0	0	0	2	0	—	.125	.300	.125	35	0	1	.600	-2	80	143	S2	—	-0.2
WANNINGER, PEE-WEE	Paul Louis; B12.12.1902 Birmingham AL; D3.7.1981 N.Augusta SC; BL/TR/5´7˝/150; d4.22																								
1925	NY A	117	403	35	95	13	6	1	22	11	0	34	.236	.256	.305	43	-38	3-5	.944	-5	93	98	S111,3b3/2	—	-3.1
1927	Bos A	18	60	4	12	0	0	0	1	6	1	2	.200	.284	.200	28	-6	2-4	.890	-1	104	125	S15	—	-0.6
	Cin N	28	93	14	23	2	2	0	8	6	0	7	.247	.293	.312	64	-5	0	.953	3	107	131	S28	—	0.1
Total	2	163	556	53	130	15	8	1	31	23	1	43	.234	.266	.295	45	-49	5-9	.941	-3	97	107	S154,3b3/2	—	-3.6
WARD, AARON	Aaron Lee; B8.28.1896 Booneville AR; D1.30.1961 New Orleans LA; BR/TR/5´10.5˝/160; d8.14; Mil 1918; Col Ouachita Baptist																								
1917	NY A	8	26	0	3	0	0	0	1	1	0	5	.115	.148	.115	-19	-4	0	.926	-1	75	126	S7	—	-0.6
1918	NY A	20	32	2	4	1	0	0	1	2	0	7	.125	.176	.156	0	-4	1	.941	3	121	186	S12,O4C,2b3	—	-0.1
1919	NY A	27	34	5	7	2	0	0	2	5	0	6	.206	.308	.265	61	-2	0	1.000	1	94	261	1b5,3b3,S2/2	—	0.0
1920	NY A	127	496	62	127	18	7	11	54	33	1	84	.256	.304	.387	79	-17	7-5	.965	17	**110**	127	3b114,S12	—	0.3
1921	†NY A	**153**	556	77	170	30	10	5	75	42	8	68	.306	.363	.423	98	-2	6-8	.961	19	110	58	2b124,3b33	—	1.9
1922	†NY A	**154**	558	69	149	19	5	7	68	45	6	64	.267	.328	.357	77	-20	6-4	.974	1	103	99	2b152,3b2	—	-1.4
1923	†NY A	**152**	567	79	161	26	11	10	82	56	3	65	.284	.351	.422	101	-1	8-8	**.980**	10	**105**	107	2b152	—	1.2
1924	NY A	120	400	42	101	13	10	8	66	40	2	45	.253	.324	.395	85	-12	1-4	.973	8	**104**	92	2b120/S	—	-0.2
1925	NY A	125	439	41	108	22	3	4	38	49	3	49	.246	.326	.337	70	-20	1-4	.966	-14	91	92	2b113,3b10	—	-2.9
1926	NY A	22	31	5	10	2	0	0	3	2	0	6	.323	.364	.387	97	0	0-0	1.000	-3	50	0	2b4/3	—	-0.3
1927	Chi A	145	463	75	125	25	8	5	56	63	2	56	.270	.360	.391	97	-1	6-5	.963	-24	95	85	2b139,3b6	—	-2.0
1928	Cle A	6	9	0	1	0	0	0	0	1	0	2	.111	.200	.111	-16	-2	0-0	.818	1	160	414	3b3,S2/2	—	-0.1
Total	12	1059	3611	457	966	158	54	50	446	339	25	457	.268	.335	.383	85	-85	36-38	.970	17	101	89	2b809,3b172,S36,1b5,O4C	—	-4.2
WARD, CHUCK	Charles William; B7.30.1894 St.Louis MO; D4.4.1969 Indian Rocks FL; BR/TR/5´11.5˝/170; d4.11; Mil 1918																								
1917	Pit N	125	423	25	100	12	3	0	43	32	8	43	.236	.302	.279	76	-11	5	.912	-26	87	98	S112,2b8,3b5	—	-3.3
1918	Bro N	2	6	0	2	0	0	0	3	0	0	0	.333	.333	.333	104	0	0	1.000	-0	103	0	3b2	—	0.0
1919	Bro N	45	150	7	35	1	2	0	8	7	2	11	.233	.277	.267	62	-7	0	.920	-7	88	0	3b45	—	-1.4
1920	Bro N	19	71	7	11	1	0	0	4	3	1	3	.155	.200	.169	6	-9	1-0	.928	-7	71	63	S19	—	-1.5
1921	Bro N	12	28	1	2	1	0	0	0	4	0	2	.071	.188	.107	-19	-5	0-0	.937	2	110	143	S12	—	-0.1
1922	Bro N	33	91	12	25	5	1	0	14	5	1	8	.275	.320	.352	74	-4	1-1	.934	-4	94	81	S31,3b2	—	-0.4
Total	6	236	769	52	175	20	6	0	72	51	12	67	.228	.286	.269	63	-36	7-1	.919	-40	88	94	S174,3b54,2b8	—	-6.7
WARD, CHRIS	Chris Gilbert; B5.18.1949 Oakland CA; BL/TL/6´0˝/180; d9.10; Col Chabot (CA) JC																								
1972	Chi N	1	1	0	0	0	0	0	0	0-0	0	0	.000	.000	.000	-90	0	0-0	ø	0	—	—	/H	0	0.0
1974	Chi N	92	137	8	28	4	0	1	15	18-3	0	13	.204	.293	.255	53	-8	0-2	.977	2	122	84	O22(21/0/1),1b6	0	-0.9
Total	2	93	138	8	28	4	0	1	15	18-3	0	13	.203	.291	.254	52	-8	0-2	.977	2	122	84	O22(21/0/1),1b6	0	-0.9

Ward, Daryle Daryle Lamar; B6.27.1975 Lynwood CA; BL/TL/6´2˝/(230–245); [DetA94 15/417]; d5.14; f–Gary; Col Santa Ana (CA) JC

YEAR	TM LG	G	AB	R	H	2B	3B	HR	RBI	BB-IB	HP	SO	AVG	OBP	SLG	AOPS	ABR	SB-CS	FA	FR	RNG	THR	GAMES AT POSITION	DL	BFW
1998	Hou N	4	3	1	1	0	0	0	0	1-0	0	2	.333	.500	.333	128	0	0-0	ø	0	—	—	/H	0	0.0
1999	†Hou N	64	150	11	41	6	0	8	30	9-0	0	31	.273	.311	.473	97	-2	0-0	.944	-3	74	70	O31L,1b10,D3	0	-0.5
2000	Hou N	119	264	36	68	10	2	20	47	15-2	0	61	.258	.295	.538	97	-3	0-0	.986	-3	88	40	O47(43/0/4),1b19,D4	0	-0.8
2001	†Hou N	95	213	21	56	15	0	9	39	19-4	1	48	.263	.323	.460	93	-2	0-0	.985	-2	89	82	O42(27/0/15),1b9,D3	0	-0.6
2002	Hou N	136	453	41	125	31	0	12	72	33-5	1	82	.276	.324	.424	89	-7	1-3	.981	-5	76	141	O122L/D	0	-1.7
2003	LA N	52	109	6	20	1	0	0	9	3-0	1	19	.183	.211	.193	7	-15	0-0	.992	-0	146	171	1b13,O11L	19	-1.7
2004	Pit N	79	293	39	73	17	2	15	57	22-3	3	45	.249	.305	.474	98	-2	0-0	.991	-5	82	134	1b71,O12R	50	-1.3
2005	Pit N	133	407	46	106	21	1	12	63	37-10	1	60	.260	.318	.405	89	-7	0-2	.994	7	131	124	1b109	0	-1.0
2006	Was N	78	104	15	32	9	0	6	19	14-1	2	21	.308	.390	.567	151	8	0-1	1.000	-1	97	0	O12(2/0/10),1b6	0	0.6
	Atl N	20	26	2	8	1	0	1	7	1-0	0	6	.308	.333	.462	99	0	0-0	1.000	0	103	75	1b4,O2L,D4	0	0.0
	Year	98	130	17	40	10	0	7	26	15-1	2	27	.308	.380	.546	140	8	0-1	1.000	-1	99	0	O14(4/0/10),1b10,D4	0	0.6
Total	9	780	2022	218	530	111	5	83	343	154-25	9	375	.262	.314	.445	92	-30	1-6	.981	-12	80	91	O279(238/0/41),1b241,D15	69	-7.0

Ward, Piggy Frank Gray; B4.16.1867 Chambersburg PA; D10.24.1912 Altoona PA; BB/TR/5´9.5˝/196; d6.12

YEAR	TM LG	G	AB	R	H	2B	3B	HR	RBI	BB-IB	HP	SO	AVG	OBP	SLG	AOPS	ABR	SB-CS	FA	FR	RNG	THR	GAMES AT POSITION	DL	BFW
1883	Phi N	1	5	0	0	0	0	0	0	0	—	2	.000	.000	.000	-99	-1	—	1.000	-0	111	0	/3	—	-0.1
1889	Phi N	7	25	0	4	1	0	0	4	0	0	7	.160	.160	.200	-0	-3	1	.848	-2	98	0	2b6/cf	—	-0.5
1891	Pit N	6	18	3	6	0	0	0	2	3	1	3	.333	.455	.333	134	1	3	.833	-1	0	0	O5L	—	0.0
1892	Bal N	56	186	28	54	6	5	1	33	31	4	18	.290	.403	.392	137	10	10	.892	3	205	251	O43R,2b7,S5/C	—	1.1
1893	Bal N	11	49	11	12	1	3	0	5	5	1	2	.245	.327	.388	88	-1	4	.862	-1	55	0	O9L,1b2	—	-0.3
	Cin N	42	150	44	42	4	1	0	10	37	6	10	.280	.440	.320	101	4	27	.827	-2	125	295	O40(1/0/39)/1	—	0.0
	Year	53	199	55	54	5	4	0	15	42	7	12	.271	.415	.337	99	2	31	.837	-3	110	230	O49(10/0/39),1b3	—	-0.3
1894	Was N	98	347	86	105	11	7	0	36	80	11	31	.303	.447	.375	103	9	41	.900	-14	99	54	2b79,O12(6/3/3),S3/3	—	-0.2
Total	6	221	780	172	223	23	16	1	90	156	23	73	.286	.419	.360	105	19	86	.854	-17	134	224	O110(21/4/85),2b92,S8,1b3,3b2/C	—	-0.0

Ward, Gary Gary Lamell; B12.6.1953 Los Angeles CA; BR/TR/6´2˝/(202–210); d9.3; C3; s–Daryle; OF(848/181/111)

YEAR	TM LG	G	AB	R	H	2B	3B	HR	RBI	BB-IB	HP	SO	AVG	OBP	SLG	AOPS	ABR	SB-CS	FA	FR	RNG	THR	GAMES AT POSITION	DL	BFW
1979	Min A	10	14	2	4	0	0	0	1	3-0	0	3	.286	.412	.286	88	0	0-1	1.000	0	138	0	O5(1/0/4),D3	0	0.0
1980	Min A	13	41	11	19	6	2	1	10	3-1	0	6	.463	.489	.780	229	7	0-0	1.000	-2	68	0	O12L	0	0.5
1981	Min A	85	295	42	78	7	6	3	29	28-4	0	48	.264	.325	.359	92	-3	5-2	.975	4	103	151	O80(61/19/1),D2	0	-0.2
1982	Min A	152	570	85	165	33	7	28	91	37-4	1	105	.289	.330	.519	126	18	13-1	.989	11	111	142	O150(127/4/25),D2	0	2.5
1983	Min A★	157	623	76	173	34	5	19	88	44-2	3	98	.278	.326	.440	105	3	8-1	.978	19	112	194	O152L,D2	0	1.6
1984	Tex A	155	602	97	171	21	7	21	79	55-3	0	95	.284	.343	.447	113	9	7-5	.987	5	105	110	O148(58/59/36),D5	0	0.9
1985	Tex A★	154	593	77	170	28	7	15	70	39-3	1	97	.287	.329	.433	105	3	26-7	.969	-2	94	116	O153(139/21/1)/D	0	-0.2
1986	Tex A	105	380	54	120	15	2	5	51	31-3	4	72	.316	.372	.405	109	5	12-8	.996	10	116	128	O104(102/4/0)/D	0	1.1
1987	NY A	146	529	65	131	22	1	16	78	33-2	1	101	.248	.291	.384	78	-18	9-1	.985	0	109	38	O94(69/30/5),D36,1b15	0	-2.0
1988	NY A	91	231	26	52	8	0	4	24	24-4	2	41	.225	.302	.312	73	-8	0-1	.992	-1	109	0	O54(17/39/3),1b11,3b2,D9	0	-1.1
1989	NY A	8	17	3	5	1	0	0	1	3-1	0	5	.294	.400	.353	115	1	0-0	1.000	-1	64	0	O6R/D	0	-0.1
	Det A	105	275	24	69	10	2	9	29	21-1	0	54	.251	.300	.400	99	-2	1-3	.990	4	119	78	O51(35/5/14),1b26,D26	0	-0.1
	Year	113	292	27	74	11	2	9	30	24-2	0	59	.253	.306	.397	100	-1	1-3	.991	3	113	69	O57(35/5/20),D27,1b26	0	-0.2
1990	Det A	106	309	32	79	11	2	9	46	30-0	1	50	.256	.322	.392	98	-1	2-0	.988	-1	102	41	O85(75/0/16),D13,1b2	15	-0.5
Total	12	1287	4479	594	1236	196	41	130	597	351-28	13	775	.276	.328	.425	104	14	83-30	.984	45	107	114	O1094L,D101,1b54,3b2	15	2.4

Ward, Jim James H. H.; B3.2.1855 Boston MA; D6.4.1886 Boston MA; d8.3

YEAR	TM LG	G	AB	R	H	2B	3B	HR	RBI	BB-IB	HP	SO	AVG	OBP	SLG	AOPS	ABR	SB-CS	FA	FR	RNG	THR	GAMES AT POSITION	DL	BFW
1876	Phi N	1	4	1	2	0	0	0	1	0	—	1	.500	.500	.500	236	1	—	.750	-1	—	—	/C	—	0.0

Ward, Rube John Andrew; B2.6.1879 New Lexington OH; D1.17.1945 Akron OH; 5´7˝/152; d4.28; Col Holy Cross

YEAR	TM LG	G	AB	R	H	2B	3B	HR	RBI	BB-IB	HP	SO	AVG	OBP	SLG	AOPS	ABR	SB-CS	FA	FR	RNG	THR	GAMES AT POSITION	DL	BFW
1902	Bro N	13	31	4	9	1	0	0	2	2	0	—	.290	.333	.323	102	0	0	.850	-0	88	0	O11(6/1/4)	—	-0.1

Ward, John John E.; B Washington DC; d5.23

YEAR	TM LG	G	AB	R	H	2B	3B	HR	RBI	BB-IB	HP	SO	AVG	OBP	SLG	AOPS	ABR	SB-CS	FA	FR	RNG	THR	GAMES AT POSITION	DL	BFW
1884	Was U	1	4	0	1	0	0	0	—	0	—	—	.250	.250	.250	54	0	—	.000	-1	0	0	/cf	—	-0.1

Ward, Jay John Francis; B9.9.1938 Brookfield MO; BR/TR/6´1˝/185; d5.6; C3

YEAR	TM LG	G	AB	R	H	2B	3B	HR	RBI	BB-IB	HP	SO	AVG	OBP	SLG	AOPS	ABR	SB-CS	FA	FR	RNG	THR	GAMES AT POSITION	DL	BFW
1963	Min A	9	15	0	1	1	0	0	2	1-0	0	5	.067	.125	.133	-27	-3	0-0	1.000	-2	61	0	3b4/lf	0	-0.4
1964	Min A	12	31	4	7	2	0	0	2	6-1	0	13	.226	.351	.290	80	0	0-0	.977	0	93	73	2b9,O3L	0	0.0
1970	Cin N	6	3	0	0	0	0	0	0	2-0	0	1	.000	.400	.000	17	0	0-0	1.000	0	114	0	3b2/12	0	0.0
Total	3	27	49	4	8	3	0	0	4	9-1	0	19	.163	.293	.224	46	-3	0-0	.977	-1	92	72	2b10,3b6,O4L/1	0	-0.4

Ward, John John Montgomery; B3.3.1860 Bellefonte PA; D3.4.1925 Augusta GA; BL/TR (TL 1884p, BB 1888)/5´9˝/165; d7.15; M7; HF1964; Col Penn St.; OF(4/110/100); ▲

YEAR	TM LG	G	AB	R	H	2B	3B	HR	RBI	BB-IB	HP	SO	AVG	OBP	SLG	AOPS	ABR	SB-CS	FA	FR	RNG	THR	GAMES AT POSITION	DL	BFW
1878	Pro N	37	138	14	27	5	4	1	15	2	—	13	.196	.207	.312	69	1	—	.866	2	107	179	P37	—	0.0
1879	Pro N	83	364	71	104	9	4	2	41	7	—	14	.286	.299	.349	115	5	—	.938	4	109	86	P70,3b16,O8(4/0/4)	—	0.3
1880	Pro N	86	356	53	81	12	2	0	27	6	—	16	.228	.240	.272	76	-9	—	.983	14	112	55	P70,3b25,O2R,M	—	0.9
1881	Pro N	**85**	357	56	87	18	6	0	53	5	—	10	.244	.254	.328	83	-7	—	.887	3	126	0	O40(0/4/36),P39,S13	—	-0.3
1882	Pro N	83	355	58	87	10	3	1	39	13	—	22	.245	.272	.299	83	-7	—	.824	5	174	142	O49(0/2/47),P34,S4	—	-0.1
1883	NY N	88	380	76	97	18	7	7	54	8	—	25	.255	.271	.395	100	-1	—	.859	14	198	88	O56(0/45/11),P34,3b5,S2/2	—	0.9
1884	NY N	113	482	98	122	11	8	2	51	28	—	47	.253	.294	.322	91	-6	—	.847	10	105	93	O59C,2b47,P9,M	—	0.4
1885	NY N	111	446	72	101	8	9	0	37	17	—	39	.226	.255	.285	75	-13	—	.904	4	95	**127**	S111	—	-0.6
1886	NY N	122	491	82	134	17	5	2	81	19	—	46	.273	.300	.340	93	-5	36	.890	11	99	113	S122	—	0.9
1887	NY N	**129**	545	114	184	16	5	1	53	29	4	12	.338	.375	.391	119	15	**111**	**.919**	32	109	**136**	S129	—	**4.3**
1888	†NY N	122	510	70	128	14	5	2	49	9	1	13	.251	.265	.310	84	-10	38	.857	-4	90	**129**	S122	—	-1.1
1889	†NY N	114	479	87	143	13	4	1	67	27	2	7	.299	.339	.349	91	-7	62	.890	9	95	104	S108,2b7	—	0.4
1890	Bro P	128	561	134	188	15	12	4	60	51	2	22	.335	.393	.426	112	7	63	.878	17	104	105	S128,M	—	2.2
1891	Bro N	105	441	85	122	13	5	0	39	36	3	10	.277	.335	.329	94	-3	57	.878	3	104	93	S87,2b18,M	—	0.2
1892	Bro N	148	614	109	163	13	3	1	47	82	3	19	.265	.355	.301	103	6	**88**	.920	-2	101	79	2b148,M	—	1.0
1893	NY N	135	588	129	193	27	9	2	77	47	1	5	.328	.379	.415	110	8	46	.918	4	105	65	2b134,M	—	1.4
1894	†NY N	138	549	102	146	12	5	0	79	35	1	6	.266	.311	.306	49	-46	39	.923	1	104	90	2b138,M	—	-3.1
Total	17	1827	7656	1410	2107	231	96	26	869	421	17	326	.275	.314	.341	93	-72	540	.887	123	99	115	S826,2b493,P293,O214C,3b46	—	7.7

Ward, Joe Joseph Aloysius; B9.2.1884 Philadelphia PA; D8.11.1934 Philadelphia PA; TR; d4.24

YEAR	TM LG	G	AB	R	H	2B	3B	HR	RBI	BB-IB	HP	SO	AVG	OBP	SLG	AOPS	ABR	SB-CS	FA	FR	RNG	THR	GAMES AT POSITION	DL	BFW
1906	Phi N	35	129	12	38	8	6	0	11	5	0	—	.295	.321	.450	140	5	2	.929	-5	80	66	3b27,2b3/S	—	0.0
1909	NY A	9	28	3	5	0	0	0	0	1	1	—	.179	.233	.179	30	-2	2	.846	-4	75	41	2b7/1	—	-0.7
	Phi N	74	184	21	49	8	2	0	23	9	1	—	.266	.304	.332	96	-1	7	.944	-6	95	126	2b48,S8,1b5,O2(1/1/0)	—	-0.8
1910	Phi N	48	124	11	18	2	1	0	13	3	2	11	.145	.178	.177	4	-16	1	.975	2	133	62	1b32/S3	—	-1.6
Total	3	166	465	47	110	18	9	0	47	18	4	11	.237	.271	.314	78	-14	12	.929	-13	91	102	2b58,1b38,3b28,S10,O2(1/1/0)	—	-3.1

Ward, Hap Joseph Nichols; B11.15.1885 Leesburg NJ; D9.13.1979 Elmer NJ; BR/5´5.5˝/166; d5.18

YEAR	TM LG	G	AB	R	H	2B	3B	HR	RBI	BB-IB	HP	SO	AVG	OBP	SLG	AOPS	ABR	SB-CS	FA	FR	RNG	THR	GAMES AT POSITION	DL	BFW
1912	Det A	1	2	0	0	0	0	0	0	0	0	—	.000	.000	.000	-99	-1	0	1.000	0	1107	0	/rf	—	0.0

Ward, Kevin Kevin Michael; B9.28.1961 Lansdale PA; BR/TR/6´1˝/195; [PhiN83 6/154]; d5.10; Col Arizona

YEAR	TM LG	G	AB	R	H	2B	3B	HR	RBI	BB-IB	HP	SO	AVG	OBP	SLG	AOPS	ABR	SB-CS	FA	FR	RNG	THR	GAMES AT POSITION	DL	BFW
1991	SD N	44	107	13	26	7	2	2	8	9-0	1	27	.243	.308	.402	95	-1	1-4	.982	-1	102	0	O33(31/0/2)	0	-0.4
1992	SD N	81	147	12	29	5	0	3	12	14-0	2	38	.197	.274	.293	60	-8	2-3	.946	-1	96	116	O51(36/9/8)	0	-1.1
Total	2	125	254	25	55	12	2	5	20	23-0	3	65	.217	.288	.339	75	-9	3-7	.961	-2	99	66	O84(67/9/10)	0	-1.5

Ward, Pete Peter Thomas; B7.26.1939 Montreal QC, Can.; BL/TR/6´1˝/(185–205); d9.21; C1; Col Lewis & Clark; OF(139/0/54)

YEAR	TM LG	G	AB	R	H	2B	3B	HR	RBI	BB-IB	HP	SO	AVG	OBP	SLG	AOPS	ABR	SB-CS	FA	FR	RNG	THR	GAMES AT POSITION	DL	BFW
1962	Bal A	8	21	1	3	2	0	0	2	4-0	0	5	.143	.280	.238	44	-2	0-0	1.000	-0	91	0	O6(2/0/4)	0	-0.2
1963	Chi A	157	600	80	177	34	6	22	84	52-1	5	77	.295	.353	.482	135	27	7-6	.923	-8	95	99	3b154/2S	0	1.9
1964	Chi A	144	539	61	152	28	3	23	94	56-11	2	76	.282	.348	.473	131	22	1-1	.958	4	106	113	3b138	0	2.7
1965	Chi A	138	507	62	125	25	3	10	57	56-11	6	83	.247	.327	.367	104	3	2-4	.952	4	**114**	91	3b134/2	0	0.6
1966	Chi A	84	251	22	55	7	1	3	28	24-0	3	49	.219	.290	.291	74	-8	3-1	.989	4	94	99	O59(44/0/18),3b16,1b5	47	-0.8
1967	Chi A	146	467	49	109	16	2	18	62	61-9	11	109	.233	.334	.392	119	12	3-2	.991	-10	72	52	O89(74/0/19),1b39,3b22	0	-0.5
1968	Chi A	125	399	43	86	15	0	15	50	76-8	10	85	.216	.354	.366	117	12	4-3	.946	-2	105	57	3b77,1b31,O22(16/0/7)	0	0.9
1969	Chi A	105	199	22	49	7	0	6	32	33-1	3	38	.246	.359	.372	101	1	0-0	.994	0	107	76	1b25,3b21,O9(3/0/6)	0	0.0
1970	NY A	66	77	5	20	2	2	1	18	9-0	0	17	.260	.333	.377	101	0	0-0	1.000	-1	48	97	1b13	0	-0.2
Total	9	973	3060	345	776	136	17	98	427	371-41	40	539	.254	.339	.405	116	67	20-17	.945	-9	106	96	3b562,O185L,1b113,2b2/S	47	4.4

Ward, Preston Preston Meyer; B7.24.1927 Columbia MO; BL/TR/6´3˝/(195–198); d4.20; Mil 1951–52

YEAR	TM LG	G	AB	R	H	2B	3B	HR	RBI	BB-IB	HP	SO	AVG	OBP	SLG	AOPS	ABR	SB-CS	FA	FR	RNG	THR	GAMES AT POSITION	DL	BFW
1948	Bro N	42	146	9	38	9	2	1	21	15	0	23	.260	.329	.370	86	-3	0	.990	-1	86	79	1b38	0	-0.5
1950	Chi N	80	285	31	72	11	2	6	33	27	0	42	.253	.317	.368	81	-8	3	.995	9	142	106	1b76	61	-0.2
1953	Chi N	33	100	10	23	5	0	4	12	18	0	21	.230	.347	.400	92	-1	3-1	.961	-4	89	0	O27C,1b7	0	-0.5
	Pit N	88	281	35	59	7	1	8	27	44	1	39	.210	.319	.327	69	-12	1-3	.991	3	117	88	1b78	0	-1.4
	Year	121	381	45	82	12	1	12	39	62	1	60	.215	.327	.346	76	-13	4-4	.991	-1	110	93	1b85,O27C	0	-1.9
1954	Pit N	117	360	37	97	16	2	7	48	39	0	61	.269	.337	.383	90	-5	0-0	.984	6	141	80	1b48,O42R,3b11	0	-0.3
1955	Pit N	84	179	16	38	7	4	5	25	22-4	0	28	.212	.296	.380	80	-6	0-0	.998	2	113	100	1b48/rf	0	-0.6
1956	Pit N	16	30	3	10	0	1	1	11	6-0	0	4	.333	.432	.500	157	3	0-0	1.000	-2	47	0	3b5,O5R	0	0.1
	Cle A	87	150	18	38	10	0	6	21	16-0	0	20	.253	.325	.440	98	-1	0-0	.988	3	127	91	1b60,O17(14/0/3)	0	0.0
1957	Cle A	10	11	2	2	1	0	0	0	0-0	0	2	.182	.182	.273	23	-1	0-0	1.000	-0	0	0	/1	0	-0.1
1958	Cle A	48	148	22	50	3	1	4	21	10-1	1	27	.338	.379	.453	133	6	0-1	.957	-2	79	55	3b24,1b21	0	0.3
	KC A	81	268	28	68	10	1	6	24	27-2	0	36	.254	.319	.366	87	-5	0-1	.989	-8	94	79	1b39,3b34,O2L	0	-1.7
	Year	129	416	50	118	13	2	10	45	37-3	1	63	.284	.340	.397	103	1	0-2	.992	-11	101	77	1b60,3b58,O2L	0	-1.4
1959	KC A	58	109	8	27	4	1	2	19	7-1	0	12	.248	.286	.358	76	-4	0-0	.982	-3	63	87	1b22/lf	0	-0.8
Total	9	744	2067	219	522	83	15	50	262	231-8	2	315	.253	.326	.380	88	-37	7-6	.992	3	115	91	1b438,O95(17/27/51),3b74	61	-5.7

Ward, Turner Turner Max; B4.11.1965 Orlando FL; BB/TR/6´2˝/(182–204); [NYA86 18/470]; d9.10; Col South Alabama

YEAR	TM LG	G	AB	R	H	2B	3B	HR	RBI	BB-IB	HP	SO	AVG	OBP	SLG	AOPS	ABR	SB-CS	FA	FR	RNG	THR	GAMES AT POSITION	DL	BFW
1990	Cle A	14	46	10	16	2	1	1	10	3-0	0	8	.348	.388	.500	147	3	3-0	.957	0	88	251	O13R/D	0	0.3
1991	Cle A	40	100	11	23	7	0	0	5	10-0	0	16	.230	.300	.300	66	-4	0-0	1.000	-1	101	45	O38(0/2/36)	0	-0.6
	Tor A	8	13	1	4	0	0	0	2	1-0	0	2	.308	.357	.308	82	0	0-0	1.000	-1	64	0	O6(1/0/5)	0	-0.1
	Year	48	113	12	27	7	0	0	7	11-0	0	18	.239	.306	.301	68	-5	0-0	1.000	-1	97	40	O44(1/2/41)	0	-0.7
1992	Tor A	18	29	7	10	3	0	1	3	4-0	0	4	.345	.424	.552	163	3	0-1	1.000	1	104	208	O12(2/4/6)	0	0.3
1993	Tor A	72	167	20	32	4	2	4	28	23-2	1	26	.192	.287	.311	61	-9	3-3	.990	-2	93	65	O65(33/10/22)/1	30	-1.4
1994	Mil A	102	367	55	85	15	2	9	45	52-4	3	68	.232	.328	.357	74	-14	6-2	.985	6	109	125	O99(35/52/25)/3	0	-0.8
1995	Mil A	44	129	19	34	3	1	4	16	14-1	1	21	.264	.338	.395	86	-3	6-1	.989	3	106	202	O40(26/7/19)/D	102	0.0
1996	Mil A	43	67	7	12	2	1	2	10	13-0	0	17	.179	.309	.328	60	-4	3-0	1.000	3	135	76	O32(15/3/18)/D	99	-0.1
1997	Pit N	71	167	33	59	16	1	7	33	18-2	2	17	.353	.420	.587	158	15	4-1	1.000	-2	85	94	O54(11/31/23)	0	1.2
1998	Pit N	123	282	33	74	13	3	9	46	27-1	4	40	.262	.328	.426	98	-1	5-4	.983	7	115	165	O97(41/48/22)/D	15	0.4
1999	Pit N	49	91	2	19	2	0	0	8	13-0	1	9	.209	.311	.231	41	-8	2-2	.955	-2	82	78	O34(5/22/13)	63	-1.0
	†Ari N	10	23	6	8	1	0	2	7	2-0	0	6	.348	.385	.652	159	2	0-0	1.000	0	113	0	O5(0/2/4)	15	0.2
	Year	59	114	8	27	3	0	2	15	15-0	1	15	.237	.326	.316	64	-6	2-2	.964	-2	87	65	O39(5/24/17)	0	-0.8
2000	Ari N	15	52	5	9	4	0	0	4	5-0	0	7	.173	.241	.250	25	-6	1-1	1.000	1	121	0	O15(0/1/14)	0	-0.6
2001	Phi N	17	15	1	4	1	0	0	2	1-1	1	6	.267	.353	.333	83	0	0-0	ø	0	—	—	/H	0	-0.1
Total	12	626	1548	210	389	73	11	39	219	186-11	13	247	.251	.332	.388	87	-26	33-15	.988	13	104	115	O510(169/182/220),D4/31	324	-2.3

Wares, Buzzy Clyde Ellsworth; B3.23.1886 Vandalia MI; D5.26.1964 South Bend IN; BR/TR/5´10˝/150; d9.15; C22

YEAR	TM LG	G	AB	R	H	2B	3B	HR	RBI	BB-IB	HP	SO	AVG	OBP	SLG	AOPS	ABR	SB-CS	FA	FR	RNG	THR	GAMES AT POSITION	DL	BFW
1913	StL A	11	35	5	10	2	0	0	1	1	0	3	.286	.306	.343	92	0	2	.973	-2	71	139	2b9	—	-0.3
1914	StL A	81	215	20	45	10	1	0	23	28	0	35	.209	.300	.265	73	-6	10-10	.903	-6	103	93	S68,2b8	—	-1.0
Total	2	92	250	25	55	12	1	0	24	29	0	38	.220	.301	.276	76	-6	12-10	.903	-8	103	93	S68,2b17	—	-1.3

Warner, Fred Frederick John Rodney; B1855 Philadelphia PA; D2.13.1886 Philadelphia PA; 5´7˝/155; d4.21

YEAR	TM LG	G	AB	R	H	2B	3B	HR	RBI	BB-IB	HP	SO	AVG	OBP	SLG	AOPS	ABR	SB-CS	FA	FR	RNG	THR	GAMES AT POSITION	DL	BFW
1875	Cen NA	**14**	57	11	14	4	0	0	2	1	—	2	.246	.259	.316	107	1	0-0	.784	-1	86	0	O14C	—	0.0
1876	Phi N	1	3	0	0	0	0	0	0	0	—	0	.000	.000	.000	-99	-1	—	.600	-1	0	0	/cf	—	-0.1
1878	Ind N	43	165	19	41	4	0	0	10	2	—	15	.248	.257	.273	86	-2	—	.907	-5	92	92	S41,O2L	—	-0.5
1879	Cle N	76	316	32	77	11	4	0	22	2	—	20	.244	.248	.304	82	-6	—	.827	1	99	72	3b54,O21(13/7/1)/1	—	-0.5
1883	Phi N	39	141	13	32	6	1	0	13	5	—	21	.227	.253	.284	69	-5	—	.775	-6	82	70	3b38/rf	—	-0.9
1884	Bro AA	84	352	40	78	4	0	1	—	17	1	—	.222	.259	.241	64	-14	—	.824	-6	97	133	3b84	—	-1.7
Total	5	243	977	104	228	25	5	1	45	26	1	56	.233	.254	.272	73	-28	—	.815	-17	95	102	3b176,S41,O25(15/8/2)/1	—	-3.7

Warner, Hooks Hoke Hayden; B5.22.1894 Del Rio TX; D2.19.1947 San Francisco CA; BL/TR/5´10.5˝/170; d8.21; Mil 1918

YEAR	TM LG	G	AB	R	H	2B	3B	HR	RBI	BB-IB	HP	SO	AVG	OBP	SLG	AOPS	ABR	SB-CS	FA	FR	RNG	THR	GAMES AT POSITION	DL	BFW
1916	Pit N	44	168	12	40	1	1	2	14	6	0	19	.238	.264	.292	70	-7	6	.899	-10	67	82	3b42/2	—	-1.8
1917	Pit N	3	5	0	1	0	0	0	0	0	0	1	.200	.200	.200	22	0	0	1.000	0	65	0	/3	—	0.0
1919	Pit N	6	8	0	1	0	0	0	2	3	0	1	.125	.364	.125	48	0	0	.818	-0	104	0	3b3	—	-0.1
1921	Chi N	14	38	4	8	1	0	0	3	2	1	1	.211	.268	.237	35	-4	1-1	.957	0	114	65	3b10	—	-0.3
Total	4	67	219	16	50	2	1	2	19	11	1	22	.228	.268	.274	61	-11	7-1	.906	-10	76	73	3b56/2	—	-2.2

Warner, John John Joseph; B8.15.1872 New York NY; D12.21.1943 Far Rockaway NY; BL/TR/5´11˝/165; d4.23

YEAR	TM LG	G	AB	R	H	2B	3B	HR	RBI	BB-IB	HP	SO	AVG	OBP	SLG	AOPS	ABR	SB-CS	FA	FR	RNG	THR	GAMES AT POSITION	DL	BFW
1895	Bos N	3	7	2	1	0	0	0	1	1	1	0	.143	.333	.143	24	-1	0	.917	1	135	168	C3	—	0.0
	Lou N	67	232	20	62	4	2	1	20	11	7	16	.267	.320	.315	68	-11	10	.931	-11	91	80	C64,1b3/2	—	-1.4
	Year	70	239	22	63	4	2	1	21	12	8	16	.264	.320	.310	67	-12	10	.930	-11	93	83	C67,1b3/2	—	-1.4
1896	Lou N	33	110	9	25	1	1	0	10	10	2	10	.227	.303	.255	50	-8	3	.939	2	78	120	C32/1	—	-0.3
	NY N	19	54	9	14	1	0	0	3	3	1	7	.259	.310	.278	57	-3	1	.922	-2	95	89	C19	—	-0.3
	Year	52	164	18	39	2	1	0	13	13	3	17	.238	.306	.262	52	-11	4	.934	-0	84	109	C51/1	—	-0.6
1897	NY N	111	400	50	109	6	3	2	51	26	16	—	.273	.342	.318	77	-13	8	.953	**32**	**169**	111	C111	—	2.5
1898	NY N	110	373	40	96	14	5	0	42	22	10	—	.257	.316	.322	86	-7	9	.968	9	91	**111**	C109/rf	—	1.0
1899	NY N	88	293	38	78	8	1	0	19	15	6	—	.266	.315	.300	72	-11	15	.952	0	86	**122**	C82,1b3	—	-0.3
1900	NY N	34	108	15	27	4	0	0	13	8	3	—	.250	.319	.287	71	-4	1	.948	4	111	109	C31	—	0.3
1901	NY N	87	291	19	70	6	1	0	20	3	8	—	.241	.268	.268	58	-16	3	.967	-4	84	112	C84	—	-1.2
1902	Bos A	65	222	19	52	5	7	0	12	13	3	—	.234	.286	.320	66	-11	0	.979	8	128	92	C64	—	0.3
1903	NY N	89	285	38	81	8	5	0	34	7	9	—	.284	.322	.347	88	-6	5	**.986**	12	119	108	C85	—	1.3
1904	NY N	86	287	29	57	5	1	1	15	14	7	—	.199	.253	.233	48	-17	7	**.982**	8	140	108	C86	—	-0.1
1905	StL N	41	137	9	35	2	2	1	12	6	3	—	.255	.301	.321	88	-2	2	.958	-2	90	116	C41	—	0.0
	Det A	36	119	12	24	2	3	0	7	8	0	—	.202	.252	.269	65	-5	2	.974	-2	75	98	C36	—	-0.4
1906	Det A	50	153	15	37	4	2	0	10	12	7	—	.242	.326	.294	92	-1	4	.978	9	110	120	C49	—	1.3
	Was A	32	103	5	21	4	1	1	9	2	1	—	.204	.226	.291	65	-5	3	.968	3	86	149	C32	—	0.2
	Year	82	256	20	58	8	3	1	19	14	8	—	.227	.288	.293	82	-5	7	.974	11	100	**132**	C81	—	1.5
1907	Was A	72	207	11	53	5	0	0	17	12	3	—	.256	.306	.280	95	-1	3	.971	-8	84	100	C64	—	-0.4
1908	Was A	51	116	8	28	2	1	0	8	8	4	—	.241	.313	.276	100	0	7	.982	2	112	83	C41/1	—	0.6
Total	14	1074	3497	348	870	81	35	6	303	181	91	33	.249	.303	.297	73	-122	83	.966	60	108	108	C1033,1b8/rf2	—	3.1

Warner, Jackie John Joseph; B8.1.1943 Monrovia CA; BR/TR/6´0˝/180; d4.12

YEAR	TM LG	G	AB	R	H	2B	3B	HR	RBI	BB-IB	HP	SO	AVG	OBP	SLG	AOPS	ABR	SB-CS	FA	FR	RNG	THR	GAMES AT POSITION	DL	BFW
1966	Cal A	45	123	22	26	4	1	7	16	9-0	0	55	.211	.263	.431	99	-1	0-0	.984	-2	94	51	O37R	0	-0.5

Warner, Jack John Ralph; B8.29.1903 Evansville IN; D3.13.1986 Mt.Vernon IL; BR/TR/5´9.5˝/165; d9.24

YEAR	TM LG	G	AB	R	H	2B	3B	HR	RBI	BB-IB	HP	SO	AVG	OBP	SLG	AOPS	ABR	SB-CS	FA	FR	RNG	THR	GAMES AT POSITION	DL	BFW
1925	Det A	10	39	7	13	0	0	0	2	3	0	6	.333	.381	.333	84	-1	0-0	1.000	-1	101	204	3b10	—	-0.1
1926	Det A	100	311	41	78	8	6	0	34	38	5	24	.251	.342	.315	71	-13	8-4	.956	-1	97	62	3b95,S3	—	-0.8
1927	Det A	139	559	78	149	22	9	1	45	47	6	45	.267	.330	.343	74	-22	14-4	.947	-4	99	116	3b138	—	-1.6
1928	Det A	75	206	33	44	4	4	0	13	16	1	15	.214	.274	.272	43	-18	4-5	.944	4	109	64	3b52,S7	—	-1.1
1929	Bro N	17	62	3	17	2	0	0	4	7	0	6	.274	.348	.306	65	-3	3	.945	-2	93	72	S17	—	-0.3
1930	Bro N	21	25	4	8	1	0	0	0	2	0	7	.320	.370	.360	79	-1	1	1.000	1	137	0	3b8	—	0.1
1931	Bro N	9	4	2	2	0	0	0	0	1	0	1	.500	.600	.500	200	1	0	1.000	1	211	0	S2/3	—	0.2
1933	Phi N	107	340	31	76	15	1	0	22	28	1	33	.224	.285	.274	53	-20	1	.973	4	102	98	2b71,3b30/S	—	-1.1
Total	8	478	1546	199	387	52	20	1	120	142	13	137	.250	.319	.312	65	-77	31-13	.950	2	103	100	3b334,2b71,S30	—	-4.7

Warnock, Hal Harold Charles; B1.6.1912 New York NY; D2.8.1997 Tucson AZ; BL/TR/6´2˝/180; d9.2; Col Arizona

YEAR	TM LG	G	AB	R	H	2B	3B	HR	RBI	BB-IB	HP	SO	AVG	OBP	SLG	AOPS	ABR	SB-CS	FA	FR	RNG	THR	GAMES AT POSITION	DL	BFW
1935	StL A	6	7	1	2	2	0	0	0	0	0	3	.286	.286	.571	112	0	0-0	1.000	-0	59	0	O2(1/1/0)		0.0

Warren, Bennie Bennie Louis; B3.2.1912 Elk City OK; D5.11.1994 Oklahoma City OK; BR/TR/6´1˝/184; d9.13; Mil 1943–45

YEAR	TM LG	G	AB	R	H	2B	3B	HR	RBI	BB-IB	HP	SO	AVG	OBP	SLG	AOPS	ABR	SB-CS	FA	FR	RNG	THR	GAMES AT POSITION	DL	BFW
1939	Phi N	18	56	4	13	0	0	1	7	7	0	7	.232	.317	.286	65	-3	0	.958	-3	53	100	C17	—	-0.5
1940	Phi N	106	289	33	71	6	1	12	34	40	1	46	.246	.339	.398	107	3	1	.975	-3	92	110	C97/1	—	0.5
1941	Phi N	121	345	34	74	13	2	9	35	44	3	66	.214	.309	.342	86	-6	0	.973	-5	73	**140**	C110	0	-0.5
1942	Phi N	90	225	19	47	6	3	7	20	24	1	36	.209	.288	.356	92	-3	0	.972	-6	67	**132**	C78/1	0	-0.5
1946	NY N	39	69	7	11	1	1	4	8	14	0	21	.159	.301	.377	91	-1	0	.965	-0	86	67	C30	0	0.0

YEAR	TM LG	G	AB	R	H	2B	3B	HR	RBI	BB-IB	HP	SO	AVG	OBP	SLG	AOPS	ABR	SB-CS	FA	FR	RNG	THR	GAMES AT POSITION	DL	BFW
1947	NY N	3	5	0	1	0	0	0	0	0	0	1	.200	.200	.200	6	-1	0	1.000	-0	*0*	*0*	C3	0	-0.1
Total	6	377	989	97	217	26	7	33	104	129	5	177	.219	.313	.360	92	-11	1	.972	-17	*77*	*122*	C335,1b2	0	-1.1
WARREN, BILL William Hackney "Hack"; B2.11.1884 MO; D1.28.1960 Whiteville TN; BL/TR/5´8˝/165; d4.30																									
1914	Ind F	26	50	5	12	2	0	0	5	5	0	7	.240	.309	.280	55	-4	2	.931	-3	*81*	*84*	C23	—	-0.6
1915	New F	5	3	0	1	0	0	0	1	0	0	0	.333	.333	.333	93	0	0	1.000	-0	*0*	*0*	/C1	—	0.0
Total	2	31	53	5	13	2	0	0	6	5	0	7	.245	.310	.283	57	-4	2	.932	-3	*80*	*83*	C24/1	—	-0.6
WARSTLER, RABBIT Harold Burton; B9.13.1903 N.Canton OH; D5.31.1964 N.Canton OH; BR/TR/5´7.5˝/150; d7.24																									
1930	Bos A	54	162	16	30	2	3	1	13	20	0	21	.185	.275	.253	36	-16	0-2	.947	-1	103	103	S54	—	-1.2
1931	Bos A	66	181	20	44	5	3	0	10	15	2	27	.243	.308	.304	65	-10	2-3	.933	-0	115	89	2b42,S19/3	—	-0.7
1932	Bos A	115	388	26	82	15	5	0	34	22	3	43	.211	.259	.276	40	-36	9-6	.939	**23**	**115**	**114**	S107	—	-0.5
1933	Bos A	92	322	44	70	13	1	1	17	42	0	36	.217	.308	.273	55	-20	2-4	.951	-1	103	82	S87	—	-1.5
1934	Phi A	117	419	56	99	19	3	1	36	51	1	30	.236	.321	.303	64	-22	9-3	.969	16	**117**	**116**	2b107,S2	—	0.1
1935	Phi A	138	496	62	124	20	7	3	59	56	0	53	.250	.326	.337	72	-21	8-4	.959	1	105	92	2b136,3b2	—	-1.1
1936	Phi A	66	236	27	59	8	6	1	24	36	2	16	.250	.354	.347	75	-9	0-0	.973	10	121	94	2b66	—	0.5
	Bos N	74	304	27	64	6	0	0	17	22	1	33	.211	.266	.230	37	-27	2	.948	7	114	120	S74	—	-1.4
1937	Bos N	149	555	57	124	20	0	3	36	51	2	62	.223	.291	.276	60	-30	4	.942	-9	106	104	S149	—	-2.8
1938	Bos N	142	467	37	108	10	4	0	40	48	0	38	.231	.303	.270	65	-22	3	.937	-7	103	94	S135,2b7	—	-2.0
1939	Bos N	114	342	34	83	11	3	0	24	24	0	31	.243	.292	.292	62	-19	2	.953	2	100	116	S49,2b43,3b21	—	-1.1
1940	Bos N	33	57	6	12	0	0	0	4	10	0	5	.211	.328	.211	54	-3	0	.974	0	100	161	2b24,3b2/S	—	-0.2
	Chi N	45	159	19	36	4	1	1	18	8	0	19	.226	.263	.283	52	-11	1	.939	-0	104	81	S28,2b17	—	-0.8
	Year	78	216	25	48	4	1	1	22	18	0	24	.222	.282	.264	53	-14	1	.960	-0	103	113	2b41,S29,3b2	—	-1.0
Total	11	1205	4088	431	935	133	36	11	332	405	11	414	.229	.300	.287	59	-246	42-22	.942	41	106	102	S705,2b442,3b26	—	-12.7
WARWICK, CARL Carl Wayne; B2.27.1937 Dallas TX; BR/TL/5´10˝/(168–170); d4.11; Col TCU																									
1961	LA N	19	11	2	1	0	0	0	1	2-0	0	3	.091	.231	.091	-9	-2	0-0	1.000	-1	38	0	O12(6/5/1)	0	-0.3
	StL N	55	152	27	38	6	2	4	16	18-0	0	33	.250	.324	.395	83	-4	3-0	.970	0	110	64	O48(15/34/10)	0	-0.4
	Year	74	163	29	39	6	2	4	17	20-0	0	36	.239	.317	.374	77	-5	3-0	.970	-1	105	60	O60(21/39/11)	0	-0.7
1962	StL N	13	23	4	8	0	0	1	4	2-0	0	2	.348	.385	.478	123	1	2-0	1.000	0	92	217	O10(1/0/9)	0	0.1
	Hou N	130	477	63	124	17	1	16	60	38-1	0	77	.260	.312	.400	98	-3	2-3	.986	2	98	150	O128(15/116/9)	0	-0.6
	Year	143	500	67	132	17	1	17	64	40-1	0	79	.264	.315	.404	98	-3	4-3	.986	2	98	153	O138(16/116/18)	0	-0.5
1963	Hou N	150	528	49	134	19	5	7	47	49-4	2	70	.254	.319	.348	98	-1	3-3	.988	-2	101	70	O141(23/11/114),1b2	0	-1.4
1964	†StL N	88	158	14	41	7	1	3	15	11-1	0	30	.259	.306	.373	83	-3	2-0	.933	-0	94	130	O49(11/0/41)	0	-0.6
1965	StL N	50	77	3	12	2	1	0	6	4-0	0	18	.156	.198	.208	13	-9	1-0	.960	-0	105	129	O21(4/2/15),1b4	0	-1.1
	Bal A	9	14	3	0	0	0	0	0	3-0	0	2	.000	.176	.000	-44	-3	0-0	1.000	-0	69	0	O3(1/0/2)	0	-0.3
1966	Chi N	16	22	3	5	0	0	0	0	0-0	0	6	.227	.227	.227	27	-2	0-0	1.000	0	88	335	O10(3/7/0)	0	-0.2
Total	6	530	1462	168	363	51	10	31	149	127-6	2	241	.248	.307	.360	87	-26	13-6	.980	-1	99	108	O422(79/175/201),1b6	0	-4.8
WARWICK, BILL Firmin Newton; B11.26.1897 Philadelphia PA; D12.19.1984 San Antonio TX; BR/TR/6´0.5˝/180; d7.18; Col Penn																									
1921	Pit N	1	1	0	0	0	0	0	0	0	0	0	.000	.000	.000	-97	0	0-0	.500	-0	*0*	*470*	/C	—	-0.1
1925	StL N	13	41	8	12	1	2	1	6	5	0	5	.293	.370	.488	114	1	0-1	1.000	-2	*91*	*47*	C13	—	-0.1
1926	StL N	9	14	0	5	0	0	0	2	0	0	2	.357	.357	.357	89	0	0	.923	1	*120*	*107*	C9	—	0.1
Total	3	23	56	8	17	1	2	1	8	5	0	7	.304	.361	.446	105	1	0-1	.954	-1	*99*	*76*	C23	—	-0.1
WASDELL, JIMMY James Charles; B5.15.1914 Cleveland OH; D8.6.1983 New Port Richey FL; BL/TL/5´11˝/185; d9.3																									
1937	Was A	32	110	13	28	4	4	2	12	7	0	13	.255	.299	.418	82	-4	0-1	.995	0	85	99	1b21,O7(3/0/4)	—	-0.6
1938	Was A	53	140	19	33	2	1	2	16	12	0	12	.236	.296	.307	55	-10	5-2	.996	-2	79	119	1b26,O6R	—	-1.3
1939	Was A	29	109	12	33	5	1	0	13	9	1	16	.303	.361	.367	94	-1	3-1	.964	-2	90	100	1b28	—	-0.5
1940	Was A	10	35	3	3	1	0	0	0	2	0	7	.086	.135	.114	-37	-7	0-0	1.000	-1	38	103	1b8	—	-0.9
	Bro N	77	230	35	64	14	4	3	37	18	1	24	.278	.333	.413	99	-1	4	.947	-5	93	33	O42(1/1/40),1b17	—	-1.0
1941	†Bro N	94	265	39	79	14	3	4	48	16	3	15	.298	.345	.419	110	3	2	.956	-3	97	54	O54(8/0/46),1b15	0	-0.4
1942	Pit N	122	409	44	106	11	2	3	38	47	1	22	.259	.337	.318	90	-4	1	.957	-2	99	102	O97(36/2/61),1b7	0	-1.3
1943	Pit N	4	2	0	1	0	0	0	1	2	0	0	.500	.750	.500	256	1	0	ø	0	—	—	/H	0	0.1
	Phi N	141	522	54	136	19	6	4	67	46	2	22	.261	.323	.343	96	-4	6	.988	1	110	91	1b82,O56(39/22/5)	0	-0.9
	Year	145	524	54	137	19	6	4	68	48	2	22	.261	.326	.344	97	-3	6	.988	1	110	91	1b82,O56(39/22/5)	0	-0.8
1944	Phi N	133	451	47	125	20	3	3	40	45	1	17	.277	.344	.355	100	1	0	.980	-6	96	66	O121(118/5/3),1b4	0	-1.2
1945	Phi N	134	500	65	150	19	8	7	60	32	3	11	.300	.346	.412	113	7	7	.967	-1	103	74	O65(17/13/37),1b63	0	-0.1
1946	Phi N	26	51	7	13	0	2	1	5	3	1	2	.255	.309	.392	101	0	0	.923	-1	79	0	O11(4/0/6),1b2	0	-0.2
	Cle A	32	41	1	11	0	0	0	4	4	0	4	.268	.333	.268	74	-1	1-0	.939	-1	105	223	1b4,O3(1/0/2)	0	-0.2
1947	Cle A	1	1	0	0	0	0	0	0	0	0	0	.000	.000	.000	-99	0	0-0	ø	0	—	—	/H	0	0.0
Total	11	888	2866	339	782	109	34	29	341	243	13	165	.273	.332	.365	96	-20	29-4	.966	-22	98	75	O462(227/43/210),1b277	0	-8.5
WASEM, LINK Lincoln William; B1.30.1911 Birmingham OH; D3.6.1979 S.Laguna CA; BR/TR/5´9.5˝/180; d5.5																									
1937	Bos N	2	1	0	0	0	0	0	0	0	0	0	.000	.000	.000	-99	0	0	1.000	0	*0*	*0*	C2	—	0.0
WASHBURN, LIBE Libeus; B6.16.1874 Lyme NH; D3.22.1940 Malone NY; BB/TL/5´10˝/180; d5.30; Col Brown; ▲																									
1902	NY N	6	9	1	4	0	0	0	0	2	2	—	.444	.615	.444	230	2	1	1.000	-0	0	0	O3(0/2/1)	—	0.2
1903	Phi N	8	18	1	3	0	0	0	1	1	0	—	.167	.211	.167	8	-2	0	1.000	-1	73	0	P4,O2L	—	-0.1
Total	2	14	27	2	7	0	0	0	1	3	2	—	.259	.375	.259	89	0	1	1.000	-1	0	0	O5(1/2/1),P4	—	0.1
WASHINGTON, CLAUDELL Claudell; B8.31.1954 Los Angeles CA; BL/TL/6´0˝/(190–195); d7.5																									
1974	†Oak A	73	221	16	63	10	5	0	19	13-1	1	44	.285	.326	.376	108	2	6-8	.985	1	110	107	D38,O32(14/10/10)	0	-0.1
1975	†Oak A★	148	590	86	182	24	7	10	77	32-9	5	80	.308	.345	.424	120	13	40-15	.978	-5	96	73	O148(112/35/11)	0	0.4
1976	Oak A	134	490	65	126	20	6	5	53	30-1	3	90	.257	.302	.353	96	-4	37-20	.963	-3	97	105	O126(0/30/105),D6	16	-1.3
1977	Tex A	129	521	63	148	31	2	12	68	25-9	3	112	.284	.318	.420	99	-2	21-8	.978	-2	92	120	O127(93/41/4)/D	15	-0.6
1978	Tex A	12	42	1	7	0	0	0	2	1-0	0	12	.167	.186	.167	-0	-6	0-1	.917	-2	71	0	O7(1/0/6),D4	0	-0.8
	Chi A	86	314	33	83	16	5	6	31	12-2	1	57	.264	.290	.404	93	-4	5-5	.959	-2	94	106	O82(15/8/63)/D	25	-1.1
	Year	98	356	34	90	16	5	6	33	13-2	1	69	.253	.278	.376	82	-10	5-6	.957	-4	92	97	O89(16/8/69),D5	0	-1.9
1979	Chi A	131	471	79	132	33	5	13	66	28-7	3	93	.280	.322	.454	107	4	19-11	.974	1	104	80	O122(0/1/121),D3	0	-0.1
1980	Chi A	32	90	15	26	4	2	1	12	5-0	1	19	.289	.333	.411	103	0	4-2	.933	-1	101	67	O23(21/0/3),D2	0	-0.1
	NY N	79	284	38	78	16	4	10	42	20-5	1	63	.275	.324	.465	120	6	17-5	.978	4	97	214	O70(23/1/58)	0	0.9
1981	Atl N	85	320	37	93	22	3	5	37	15-1	4	47	.291	.328	.425	113	5	12-6	.993	-3	94	74	O79R	65	-0.3
1982	†Atl N	150	563	94	150	24	6	16	80	50-9	6	107	.266	.330	.416	106	4	33-10	.950	-11	84	88	O139R	0	-1.2
1983	Atl N	134	496	75	138	24	8	9	44	35-6	0	103	.278	.322	.413	97	-3	31-9	.974	-3	97	94	O128R	0	-0.9
1984	Atl N★	120	416	62	119	21	2	17	61	59-8	1	77	.286	.374	.469	127	16	21-9	.967	-10	86	57	O107R	15	0.3
1985	Atl N	122	398	62	110	14	6	15	43	40-11	1	66	.276	.342	.455	115	7	14-4	.962	-15	67	45	O99R	0	-1.2
1986	Atl N	40	137	17	37	11	0	5	14	14-0	0	26	.270	.336	.460	113	2	4-7	.957	-5	75	39	O38R	29	-0.6
	NY A	54	135	19	32	5	0	6	16	7-0	2	33	.237	.285	.407	86	-3	6-1	.985	-2	100	0	O39(11/20/9)	0	-0.5
1987	NY A	102	312	42	87	17	0	9	44	27-2	0	54	.279	.336	.420	99	0	10-1	.988	0	101	102	O72(2/69/1),D13	15	0.1
1988	NY A	126	455	62	140	22	3	11	64	24-2	2	74	.308	.342	.442	119	10	15-6	.984	2	103	93	O117(13/103/8)	0	1.2
1989	Cal A	110	418	53	114	18	4	13	42	27-3	2	84	.273	.319	.428	111	4	13-5	.975	-5	90	80	O100(0/2/99),D7	17	-0.3
1990	Cal A	12	34	3	6	1	0	1	3	2-0	0	8	.176	.222	.294	44	-3	1-0	1.000	1	111	168	O9R	0	-0.2
	NY A	33	80	4	13	1	1	0	6	2-1	0	17	.162	.181	.200	7	-10	3-1	1.000	1	103	152	O21(19/0/4),D2	107	-1.0
	Year	45	114	7	19	2	1	1	9	4-1	0	25	.167	.193	.228	18	-13	4-1	1.000	2	105	157	O30(19/0/13),D2	0	-1.2
Total	17	1912	6787	926	1884	334	69	164	824	468-77	36	1266	.278	.325	.420	106	38	312-134	.973	-57	93	90	O1685(324/320/1101),D77	304	-7.4
WASHINGTON, HERB Herbert Lee; B11.16.1951 Belzoni MS; BR/TR/6´0˝/170; d4.4																									
1974	†Oak A	92	0	29	0	0	0	0	0	0-0	0	0	ø	ø	ø	ø	0	29-16	ø	0	—	—	/R	0	-0.2
1975	Oak A	13	0	4	0	0	0	0	0	0-0	0	0	ø	ø	ø	ø	0	2-1	ø	0	—	—	/R	0	0.0
Total	2	105	0	33	0	0	0	0	0	0-0	0	0	ø	ø	ø	ø	0	31-17	ø	0	—	—	0	—	-0.2
WASHINGTON, LA RUE La Rue; B9.7.1953 Long Beach CA; BR/TR/6´0˝/170; [TexA75 23/540]; d9.7; Col Cal St.–Dominguez Hills																									
1978	Tex A	3	3	0	0	0	0	0	0	0-0	0	1	.000	.000	.000	-99	-1	0-0	1.000	1	202	399	2b2/D	0	0.0
1979	Tex A	25	18	5	5	0	0	0	2	4-0	0	0	.278	.409	.278	90	0	2-1	1.000	-0	93	0	O13(0/12/1)/3D	0	0.0
Total	2	28	21	5	5	0	0	0	2	4-0	0	1	.238	.360	.238	66	-1	2-1	1.000	1	93	0	O13(0/12/1),D2,2b2/3	0	0.0

YEAR	TM LG	G	AB	R	H	2B	3B	HR	RBI	BB-IB	HP	SO	AVG	OBP	SLG	AOPS	ABR	SB-CS	FA	FR	RNG	THR	GAMES AT POSITION	DL	BFW
WASHINGTON, RON	Ronald; B4.29.1952 New Orleans LA; BR/TR/5´11˝/(155–170); d9.10; C11																								
1977	LA N	10	19	4	7	0	0	0	1	0-0	1	2	.368	.400	.368	107	0	1-1	.857	-3	83	73	S10	0	-0.2
1981	Min A	28	84	8	19	3	1	0	5	4-0	1	14	.226	.270	.286	57	-5	4-1	.951	4	100	107	S26,O2C	0	0.2
1982	Min A	119	451	48	122	17	6	5	39	14-0	0	79	.271	.291	.368	77	-15	3-3	.972	-22	77	79	S91,2b37/3	0	-2.8
1983	Min A	99	317	28	78	7	3	4	26	22-1	1	50	.246	.296	.325	68	-14	10-5	.962	-11	89	100	S81,2b14/3D	0	-1.6
1984	Min A	88	197	25	58	11	5	3	23	4-0	1	31	.294	.307	.447	102	0	1-1	.978	-8	91	78	S71,2b9,3b2,D4	0	-0.4
1985	Min A	70	135	24	37	6	4	1	14	8-0	0	15	.274	.308	.400	89	-3	5-1	.951	-2	102	62	S31,2b24,3b7/1D	0	-0.2
1986	Min A	48	74	15	19	3	0	4	11	3-0	0	21	.257	.278	.459	96	-1	1-2	.917	-2	68	71	2b16,D15,S7,3b3	0	-0.3
1987	Bal A	26	79	7	16	3	1	1	6	1-0	0	15	.203	.213	.304	36	-8	0-1	1.000	2	123	93	3b20,2b3,O2L/SD	0	-0.6
1988	Cle A	69	223	30	57	14	2	2	21	9-0	5	35	.256	.298	.363	82	-5	3-3	.933	-6	96	81	S54,3b8,2b7/D	0	-0.8
1989	Hou N	7	7	1	1	1	0	0	0	0-0	0	4	.143	.143	.286	20	-1	0-0	ø	-0	0	0	/23	0	-0.1
Total	10	564	1586	190	414	65	22	20	146	65-1	9	266	.261	.292	.368	78	-52	28-18	.958	-47	89	87	S372,2b111,3b43,D30,O4(2/2/0)/1	0	-6.8
WASHINGTON, GEORGE	Sloan Vernon "Vern"; B6.4.1907 Linden TX; D2.17.1985 Linden TX; BL/TR/5´11.5˝/190; d4.17																								
1935	Chi A	108	339	40	96	22	3	8	47	10	3	18	.283	.310	.437	89	-7	1-0	.974	2	96	162	O79R	—	-0.9
1936	Chi A	20	49	6	8	2	0	1	5	1	0	4	.163	.180	.265	8	-7	0-0	.938	0	75	248	O12R	—	-0.7
Total	2	128	388	46	104	24	3	9	52	11	3	22	.268	.294	.415	78	-14	1-0	.970	2	94	171	O91R	—	-1.6
WASHINGTON, U L	U L; B10.27.1953 Stringtown OK; BB/TR/5´11˝/(170–185); d9.6; Col Murray St. (OK) JC																								
1977	KC A	10	20	0	4	1	1	0	1	5-0	0	4	.200	.360	.350	93	0	1-0	.872	-1	98	101	S9	0	0.0
1978	KC A	69	129	10	34	2	1	0	9	10-0	0	20	.264	.314	.295	71	-5	12-6	.927	-14	69	55	S49,2b19/D	0	-1.5
1979	KC A	101	268	32	68	12	5	2	25	20-1	0	44	.254	.299	.358	77	-9	10-7	.970	-2	101	114	S50,2b46/3D	0	-0.5
1980	†KC A	153	549	79	150	16	11	6	53	53-0	0	78	.273	.336	.375	94	-5	20-7	.957	-20	98	88	S152	0	-0.8
1981	†KC A	98	339	40	77	19	1	2	29	41-1	0	43	.227	.310	.307	78	-8	10-10	.973	-20	93	92	S98	0	-2.0
1982	KC A	119	437	64	125	19	3	10	60	38-0	0	48	.286	.338	.412	105	3	23-7	.961	-4	102	96	S117/D	23	1.4
1983	KC A	144	547	76	129	19	6	5	41	48-0	1	78	.236	.298	.320	70	-23	40-7	.947	-8	103	104	S140/D	0	-1.0
1984	†KC A	63	170	18	38	6	0	1	10	14-0	0	31	.224	.281	.276	55	-10	4-6	.961	-2	99	127	S61	63	-0.8
1985	Mon N	68	193	24	48	9	4	1	17	15-1	0	33	.249	.301	.352	87	-4	6-3	.978	-5	96	96	2b43,S9,3b3	36	-0.7
1986	Pit N	72	135	14	27	0	4	0	10	15-2	0	27	.200	.278	.259	48	-10	6-0	.947	-1	98	135	S51,2b3	0	-0.6
1987	Pit N	10	10	1	3	0	0	0	0	2-1	0	3	.300	.417	.300	93	0	0-0	.833	-0	133	0	/S3	0	0.0
Total	11	907	2797	358	703	103	36	27	255	261-6	1	409	.251	.313	.343	81	-71	132-53	.956	-77	98	100	S737,2b111,D6,3b5	122	-6.5
WASINGER, MARK	Mark Thomas; B8.4.1961 Monterey CA; BR/TR/6´0˝/165; [SDN82 3/57]; d5.27; Col Old Dominion																								
1986	SD N	3	8	0	0	0	0	0	1	0-0	0	2	.000	.000	.000	-99	-2	0-0	.500	-2	57	325	3b3/2	0	-0.4
1987	SF N	44	80	16	22	3	0	1	3	8-0	0	14	.275	.341	.350	88	-1	2-0	.973	1	99	161	3b21,2b10,S2	0	0.0
1988	SF N	3	2	1	0	0	0	0	0	0-0	0	0	.000	.000	.000	-99	-1	0-0	ø	0	0	0	/3	0	-0.1
Total	3	50	90	17	22	3	0	1	4	8-0	0	16	.244	.306	.311	68	-4	2-0	.907	-0	94	179	3b25,2b11,S2	0	-0.5
WASZGIS, B.J.	Robert Michael; B8.24.1970 Omaha NE; BR/TR/6´2˝/215; [BalA91 10/264]; d7.29; Col McNeese St.																								
2000	Tex A	24	45	6	10	1	0	0	4	4-0	1	10	.222	.294	.244	40	-4	0-0	1.000	-4	265	30	C23,1b3	0	-0.7
WATERMAN, FRED	Frederick A.; B12.1845 New York NY; D12.16.1899 Cincinnati OH; 5´7.5˝/148; d5.5; M1																								
1871	Oly NA	**32**	158	46	50	7	4	0	17	10	—	0	.316	.357	.411	127	7	11-3	.695	2	117	**200**	3b28,C6	—	0.6
1872	Oly NA	**9**	45	13	17	1	2	0	6	0	—	0	.378	.378	.489	173	4	0-0	.843	4	170	260	3b7,C2,M	—	0.5
1873	Was NA	15	80	20	28	1	1	0	12	1	—	1	.350	.358	.387	124	2	0-0	.649	-6	70	0	S9,O4(0/3/1),3b2	—	-0.3
1875	Chi NA	5	20	2	6	0	0	0	3	0	—	2	.300	.300	.300	108	0	0-1	.545	-3	72	221	3b5	—	-0.3
Total	4NA	61	303	81	101	9	7	0	38	11	—	3	.333	.357	.409	131	13	11-4	.707	-3	118	204	3b42,S9,C8,O4(0/3/1)	—	0.5
WATHAN, DUSTY	Dustin James; B8.22.1973 Jacksonville FL; BR/TR/6´4˝/215; d9.24; f–John; Col Cerritos (CA) JC																								
2002	KC A	3	5	1	3	1	0	0	1	0-0	1	1	.600	.667	.800	256	1	0-0	1.000	1	82	0	C3	0	0.2
WATHAN, JOHN	John David; B10.4.1949 Cedar Rapids IA; BR/TR/6´2˝/205; [KCA71*1/4]; d5.26; M6/C4; s–Dusty; Col San Diego																								
1976	†KC A	27	42	5	12	1	0	0	5	2-0	1	5	.286	.333	.310	88	-1	0-2	.984	-1	103	63	C23,1b3	34	-0.1
1977	†KC A	55	119	18	39	5	3	2	21	5-1	0	8	.328	.346	.471	121	3	2-0	.993	-1	94	32	C35,1b5,D2	0	0.3
1978	†KC A	67	190	19	57	10	1	2	28	3-1	4	12	.300	.320	.395	98	-1	2-1	1.000	1	102	76	1b47,C21	21	-0.2
1979	KC A	90	199	26	41	7	3	2	28	7-1	0	24	.206	.227	.302	42	-17	2-1	.993	-3	98	118	1b49,C23,D11,O3(2/0/1)	0	-2.1
1980	†KC A	126	453	57	138	14	7	6	58	50-6	3	42	.305	.377	.406	113	9	17-3	.982	-9	76	83	C77,O35(19/0/17),1b12	0	0.4
1981	†KC A	89	301	24	76	9	3	1	19	19-1	2	23	.252	.298	.312	77	-9	11-6	.979	-5	89	73	C73,O16(3/0/13)/1	0	-1.2
1982	KC A	121	448	79	121	11	3	3	51	48-0	2	46	.270	.343	.328	85	-8	36-9	.980	-9	108	102	C120,1b3	35	-0.8
1983	KC A	128	437	49	107	18	3	2	32	27-0	1	56	.245	.289	.314	66	-21	28-7	.985	1	99	102	C92,1b37,O9(3/0/6)	0	-1.4
1984	†KC A	97	171	17	31	7	1	2	10	21-0	0	34	.181	.271	.269	49	-12	6-6	.975	-2	92	86	C59,1b33/lfD	0	-1.3
1985	†KC A	60	145	11	34	8	1	1	9	17-0	1	15	.234	.319	.324	76	-4	1-1	.986	12	126	121	C49,1b6,D2	0	0.9
Total	10	860	2505	305	656	90	25	21	261	199-10	14	265	.262	.318	.343	82	-61	105-36	.982	-17	100	88	C572,1b196,O64(28/0/37),D19	90	-5.5
WATKINS, DAVE	David Roger; B3.15.1944 Owensboro KY; BR/TR/5´10˝/185; d4.9																								
1969	Phi N	69	148	17	26	2	1	4	12	22-0	2	53	.176	.291	.284	63	-7	2-3	.981	-4	79	124	C54,O5(5/0/1)/3	0	-1.1
WATKINS, GEORGE	George Archibald; B6.4.1900 Freestone Co. TX; D6.1.1970 Houston TX; BL/TR/6´0˝/175; d4.15																								
1930	†StL N	119	391	85	146	32	7	17	87	24	4	49	.373	.415	.621	141	26	5	.956	-3	91	100	O89(3/1/85),1b13/2	—	1.3
1931	†StL N	131	503	93	145	30	13	13	51	31	5	66	.288	.336	.477	112	6	15	.958	-3	99	83	O129(0/9/121)	—	-0.4
1932	StL N	127	458	67	143	35	3	9	63	45	**8**	46	.312	.384	.461	122	17	18	.949	-2	99	106	O120(38/19/62)	—	0.8
1933	StL N	138	525	66	146	24	5	5	62	39	**12**	62	.278	.342	.371	98	0	11	.953	1	109	74	O135R	—	-0.7
1934	NY N	105	296	38	73	18	3	6	33	24	6	34	.247	.316	.389	90	-4	2	.944	-8	86	54	O81(8/68/5)	—	-1.5
1935	Phi N	150	600	80	162	25	5	17	76	40	4	78	.270	.320	.413	87	-12	3	.958	3	96	163	O148(128/20/1)	—	-1.6
1936	Phi N	19	70	7	17	4	0	2	5	5	0	13	.243	.293	.386	74	-3	2	.889	-2	75	93	O17L	—	-0.5
	Bro N	105	364	54	93	24	6	4	43	38	5	34	.255	.334	.387	93	-3	5	.969	-3	99	67	O98(72/1/25)	—	-1.1
	Year	124	434	61	110	28	6	6	48	43	5	47	.253	.328	.387	90	-6	7	.959	-4	96	70	O115(89/1/25)	—	-1.6
Total	7	894	3207	490	925	192	42	73	420	246	44	382	.288	.347	.443	105	27	61	.954	-16	98	97	O817(266/118/434),1b13/2	—	-3.7
WATKINS, ED	James Edward; B6.21.1877 Philadelphia PA; D3.29.1933 Kelvin AZ; d9.6																								
1902	Phi N	1	3	0	0	0	0	0	0	1	0	—	.000	.250	.000	-22	0	0	1.000	-0	0	0	/lf	—	-0.1
WATKINS, BILL	William Henry; B5.5.1858 Brantford ON, Can.; D6.9.1937 Port Huron MI; BR/5´10˝/156; d8.1; M9																								
1884	Ind AA	34	127	16	26	4	0	0	—	5	1	—	.205	.241	.236	58	-5	—	.845	-4	74	40	3b23,2b9,S2,M	—	-0.8
WATKINS, PAT	William Patrick; B9.2.1972 Raleigh NC; BR/TR/6´2˝/195; [CinN93 S1/32]; d9.9; Col East Carolina																								
1997	Cin N	17	29	2	6	2	0	0	0	0-0	0	5	.207	.207	.276	25	-3	1-0	1.000	-1	69	299	O15C	0	-0.3
1998	Cin N	83	147	11	39	8	1	2	15	8-0	1	26	.265	.300	.374	77	-5	1-3	.971	0	111	38	O77(13/39/28)	0	-0.6
1999	Col N	16	19	2	1	0	0	0	0	2-0	0	5	.053	.143	.053	-38	-4	0-0	1.000	0	113	0	O10(4/1/5)	0	-0.4
Total	3	116	195	15	46	10	1	2	15	10-0	1	36	.236	.271	.328	56	-12	2-3	.976	0	106	70	O102(17/55/33)	0	-1.3
WATLINGTON, NEAL	Julius Neal; B12.25.1922 Yanceyville NC; BL/TR/6´0˝/195; d7.10																								
1953	Phi A	21	44	4	7	1	0	0	3	3	0	8	.159	.213	.182	7	-6	0-1	.978	0	*117*	*174*	C9	0	-0.5
WATSON, ART	Arthur Stanhope "Watty"; B1.11.1884 Jeffersonville IN; D5.9.1950 Buffalo NY; BL/TR/5´10˝/175; d5.19																								
1914	Bro F	22	46	7	13	4	1	1	3	1	0	6	.283	.298	.478	110	0	0	.977	-0	*89*	*113*	C18	—	0.1
1915	Bro F	9	19	4	5	0	3	0	1	3	0	4	.263	.364	.579	164	1	0	.957	-2	*74*	72	C7	—	0.0
	Buf F	22	30	6	14	1	0	1	13	0	0	4	.467	.467	.600	195	3	0	.778	-3	*59*	*91*	C6/lf	—	0.0
	Year	31	49	10	19	1	3	1	14	3	0	8	.388	.423	.592	182	4	0	.878	-5	*68*	*80*	C13/lf	—	0.0
Total	2	53	95	17	32	5	4	2	17	4	0	14	.337	.364	.537	147	4	0	.946	-5	*80*	*100*	C31/lf	—	0.1
WATSON, BRANDON	Brandon Eric; B9.30.1981 Los Angeles CA; BL/TR/6´1˝/170; [MonN99 9/270]; d8.9																								
2005	Was N	25	40	8	7	1	1	1	5	4-0	0	8	.175	.250	.325	52	-3	0-2	.933	-0	78	205	O13(12/1/0)	0	-0.5
2006	Was N	9	28	0	5	0	0	0	0	1-0	0	3	.179	.207	.179	0	-4	0-2	1.000	-0	105	0	O8C	0	-0.5
	Cin N	1	0	0	0	0	0	0	0	0-0	0	0	ø	ø	ø	ø	0	1-0	ø	0	—	—	/R	0	0.0

YEAR	TM LG	G	AB	R	H	2B	3B	HR	RBI	BB-IB	HP	SO	AVG	OBP	SLG	AOPS	ABR	SB-CS	FA	FR	RNG	THR	GAMES AT POSITION	DL	BFW
	Year	10	28	0	5	0	0	0	0	1-0	0	3	.179	.207	.179	0	-4	1-2	1.000	-0	105	0	O8C	0	-0.5
Total	2	35	68	8	12	1	1	1	5	5-0	0	11	.176	.233	.265	30	-7	1-4	.969	-1	90	114	O21(12/9/0)	0	-1.0
WATSON, JOHNNY John Thomas; B1.16.1908 Tazewell VA; D4.29.1965 Huntington WV; BL/TR/6´0˝/175; d9.26; Col Marshall																									
1930	Det A	4	12	1	3	2	0	0	3	1	0	2	.250	.308	.417	80	0	0-0	.933	-1	73	151	S4	—	-0.1
WATSON, MATT Matthew Kyle; B9.5.1978 Lancaster PA; BL/TR/5´11˝/(190–200); [MonN99 16/480]; d9.12; Col Xavier																									
2003	NY N	15	23	0	4	2	0	0	2	1-0	0	5	.174	.208	.261	22	-3	0-0	.846	0	181	0	O5L	0	-0.2
2005	Oak A	19	48	4	9	3	0	0	5	2-0	0	4	.188	.220	.250	25	-5	0-0	1.000	1	127	0	O17(14/0/3)	0	-0.5
Total	2	34	71	4	13	5	0	0	7	3-0	0	9	.183	.216	.254	24	-8	0-0	.953	1	139	0	O22(19/0/3)	0	-0.7
WATSON, BOB Robert Jose "Bull"; B4.10.1946 Los Angeles CA; BR/TR/6´2˝/(200–218); d9.9; C3																									
1966	Hou N	1	1	0	0	0	0	0	0	0-0	0	0	.000	.000	.000	-99	0	0-0	ø	0	—	—	/H	0	0.0
1967	Hou N	6	14	1	3	0	0	1	2	0-0	0	3	.214	.214	.429	82	0	0-0	.958	0	117	0	1b3	0	-0.1
1968	Hou N	45	140	13	32	7	0	2	8	13-1	1	32	.229	.297	.321	88	-2	1-0	.885	-5	77	0	O40(40/0/1)	58	-1.1
1969	Hou N	20	40	3	11	3	0	0	3	6-0	2	5	.275	.396	.350	112	1	0-0	1.000	1	90	0	O6L,1b5/C	0	0.1
1970	Hou N	97	327	48	89	19	2	11	61	24-1	4	59	.272	.324	.443	109	3	1-1	.992	-6	70	81	1b83,C6/lf	0	-0.9
1971	Hou N	129	468	49	135	17	3	9	67	41-5	2	56	.288	.347	.395	114	8	0-3	.985	-10	79	35	O87L,1b45	0	-1.1
1972	Hou N	147	548	74	171	27	4	16	86	53-5	8	83	.312	.378	.464	143	31	1-1	.978	-10	80	61	O143L,1b2	0	1.4
1973	Hou N★	158	573	97	179	24	3	16	94	85-8	4	73	.312	.403	.449	137	33	1-4	.969	-4	99	84	O142L,1b26,C3	0	1.9
1974	Hou N	150	524	69	156	19	4	11	67	60-9	3	61	.298	.370	.412	125	18	3-4	.981	-7	83	79	O140L,1b35	0	0.2
1975	Hou N★	132	485	67	157	27	1	18	85	40-10	3	50	.324	.375	.495	152	32	3-5	.993	-2	92	107	1b118,O9L	0	2.1
1976	Hou N	157	585	76	183	31	3	16	102	62-10	4	64	.313	.377	.458	150	39	3-3	.990	-6	88	95	1b155	0	2.2
1977	Hou N	151	554	77	160	38	6	22	110	57-11	7	69	.289	.360	.498	139	30	5-0	.994	10	**126**	92	1b146	0	3.2
1978	Hou N	139	461	51	133	25	4	14	79	51-16	4	57	.289	.357	.451	135	22	3-1	.992	8	**122**	68	1b128	0	2.4
1979	Hou N	49	163	15	39	4	0	3	18	16-1	0	23	.239	.304	.319	75	-6	0-0	.993	3	121	77	1b44	0	-0.6
	Bos A	84	312	48	105	19	4	13	53	29-7	5	33	.337	.401	.548	145	20	3-2	.988	1	111	119	1b58,D26	0	1.7
1980	†NY A	130	469	62	144	25	3	13	68	48-5	1	56	.307	.368	.456	128	19	2-1	.990	3	113	105	1b104,D21	0	1.5
1981	†NY A	59	156	15	33	3	3	6	12	24-2	0	17	.212	.317	.385	102	0	0-0	.997	1	101	130	1b50,D6	23	-0.1
1982	NY A	7	17	3	4	3	0	0	3	3-0	0	0	.235	.350	.412	110	0	0-0	1.000	-1	0	144	1b6/D	0	-0.1
	Atl N	57	114	16	28	3	1	5	22	14-2	0	20	.246	.323	.421	106	1	1-1	1.000	-4	49	110	1b27,O2L	0	-0.5
1983	Atl N	65	149	14	46	9	0	6	37	18-3	0	23	.309	.376	.490	131	7	0-2	.984	-2	81	93	1b34	0	0.2
1984	Atl N	49	85	4	18	4	0	2	12	9-2	0	12	.212	.287	.329	68	-4	0-0	.983	0	114	147	1b19	18	-0.5
Total	19	1832	6185	802	1826	307	41	184	989	653-98	48	796	.295	.364	.447	130	252	27-28	.991	-29	99	95	1b1088,O570(570/0/1),D54,C10	99	11.9
WATT, ALLIE Albert Bailey; B12.12.1899 Philadelphia PA; D3.15.1968 Norfolk VA; BR/TR/5´8˝/154; d10.3; b–Frank																									
1920	Was A	1	1	0	1	1	0	0	1	0	0	0	1.000	1.000	2.000	700	1	0-0	1.000	0	143	0	/2	—	0.1
WATWOOD, JOHNNY John Clifford "Lefty"; B8.17.1905 Alexander City AL; D3.1.1980 Goodwater AL; BL/TL/6´1˝/186; d4.16; Col Auburn																									
1929	Chi A	85	278	33	84	12	6	2	28	22	1	21	.302	.355	.410	98	-1	6-3	.942	-1	102	90	O77(1/53/23)	—	-0.5
1930	Chi A	133	427	75	129	25	4	2	51	52	3	35	.302	.382	.393	100	3	5-7	.989	3	117	116	1b62,O52(1/36/14)	—	-0.2
1931	Chi A	128	367	51	104	16	6	1	47	56	1	30	.283	.380	.368	103	4	9-3	.944	5	105	161	O102(4/76/24),1b4	—	0.6
1932	Chi A	13	49	5	15	2	0	0	0	1	1	3	.306	.333	.347	82	-1	0-0	.960	-0	91	107	O13(4/1/11)	—	-0.2
	Bos A	95	266	26	66	11	0	0	30	20	0	11	.248	.301	.289	55	-18	7-4	.945	-2	92	83	O46(7/25/14),1b18	—	-2.1
	Year	108	315	31	81	13	0	0	30	21	1	14	.257	.306	.298	59	-19	7-4	.948	-2	92	88	O59(11/26/25),1b18	—	-2.3
1933	Bos A	13	30	2	4	0	0	0	2	3	0	3	.133	.212	.133	-7	-5	0-0	.950	-0	119	0	O9(5/0/4)	—	-0.5
1939	Phi N	2	6	0	1	0	0	0	0	0	0	0	.167	.167	.167	-11	-1	0	.933	-1	0	0	1b2	—	-0.2
Total	6	469	1423	192	403	66	16	5	158	154	6	103	.283	.356	.363	89	-19	27-17	.948	5	101	119	O299(22/191/90),1b86	—	-3.1
WAUXHAM ; d6.22																									
1872	Eck NA	1	2	0	0	0	0	0	0	0	—	1	.000	.000	.000	-99	0	0-0	.500	-1	122	0	/2	—	-0.1
WAY, BOB Robert Clinton; B4.2.1906 Emlenton PA; D6.20.1974 Pittsburgh PA; BR/TR/5´10.5˝/168; d4.12																									
1927	Chi A	5	3	3	1	0	0	0	1	0	0	0	.333	.333	.333	75	0	0-0	1.000	-0	0	0	/2	—	0.0
WEATHERLY, ROY Cyril Roy "Stormy"; B2.25.1915 Warren TX; D1.19.1991 Woodville TX; BL/TR/5´6.5˝/170; d6.27; Mil 1944–45																									
1936	Cle A	84	349	64	117	28	6	8	53	16	0	29	.335	.364	.519	115	6	3-8	.973	5	97	197	O84(3/5/80)	—	0.4
1937	Cle A	53	134	19	27	4	0	5	13	6	2	14	.201	.246	.343	47	-12	1-1	.964	1	84	227	O38(7/0/32)/3	—	-1.2
1938	Cle A	83	210	32	55	14	3	2	18	14	0	14	.262	.308	.386	74	-9	8-5	.975	2	97	170	O55(6/41/8)	—	-0.8
1939	Cle A	95	323	43	100	16	6	1	32	19	0	23	.310	.348	.406	95	-3	7-2	.961	-5	91	58	O76(36/27/14)	—	-0.9
1940	Cle A	135	578	90	175	35	11	12	59	27	1	26	.303	.335	.464	108	4	9-8	.969	2	103	101	O135(1/134/0)	—	0.1
1941	Cle A	102	363	59	105	21	5	3	37	32	2	20	.289	.350	.399	103	1	2-5	.968	-8	94	15	O88(0/87/1)	0	-0.9
1942	Cle A	128	473	61	122	23	7	5	39	35	1	25	.258	.310	.368	96	-5	8-13	.991	2	104	82	O117C	0	-0.8
1943	†NY A	77	280	37	74	8	3	7	28	18	1	9	.264	.311	.389	104	0	4-7	.983	-4	97	39	O68C	0	-0.8
1946	NY A	2	2	0	1	0	0	0	0	0	0	0	.500	.500	.500	178	0	0-0	ø	0	—	—	/H	0	0.0
1950	NY N	52	69	10	18	3	3	0	11	13	0	10	.261	.378	.391	102	1	0	1.000	1	95	261	O15(12/1/2)	0	0.1
Total	10	811	2781	415	794	152	44	43	290	180	7	170	.286	.331	.418	99	-17	42-49	.975	-3	98	101	O676(65/480/137)/3	0	-4.8
WEAVER, ART Arthur Coggshall "Six O'Clock"; B4.7.1879 Wichita KS; D3.23.1917 Denver CO; TR/6´1˝/160; d9.14																									
1902	StL N	11	33	2	6	2	0	0	3	1	0	—	.182	.206	.242	40	-2	0	.983	0	*99*	*136*	C11	—	-0.1
1903	StL N	16	49	4	12	0	0	0	5	4	0	—	.245	.302	.245	58	-3	1	.969	1	*94*	*124*	C16	—	0.0
	Pit N	16	48	8	11	0	1	0	3	2	0	—	.229	.260	.271	50	-3	0	.978	0	*142*	*85*	C11,1b5	—	-0.3
	Year	32	97	12	23	0	1	0	8	6	0	—	.237	.282	.258	54	-6	1	.972	1	*111*	*111*	C27,1b5	—	-0.3
1905	StL A	28	92	5	11	2	1	0	3	1	0	—	.120	.129	.163	-8	-12	0	.962	1	*79*	*113*	C28	—	-0.8
1908	Chi A	15	35	1	7	1	0	0	1	1	0	—	.200	.222	.229	47	-2	0	.953	-3	*92*	*78*	C15	—	-0.5
Total	4	86	257	20	47	5	2	0	15	9	0	—	.183	.211	.218	31	-22	1	.967	0	*94*	*111*	C81,1b5	—	-1.7
WEAVER, BUCK George Daniel; B8.18.1890 Pottstown PA; D1.31.1956 Chicago IL; BB/TR (BR 1912)/5´11˝/170; d4.11																									
1912	Chi A	147	523	55	117	21	8	1	43	9	6	—	.224	.245	.300	58	-32	13	.915	-7	93	115	S147	—	-2.9
1913	Chi A	151	533	51	145	17	8	4	52	15	8	60	.272	.302	.356	94	-8	20	.929	**36**	**111**	**132**	S151	—	4.0
1914	Chi A	136	541	64	133	20	9	2	28	20	5	40	.246	.279	.327	83	-14	14-20	.928	6	96	108	S134	—	-0.3
1915	Chi A	148	563	83	151	18	11	3	49	32	7	58	.268	.316	.355	98	-5	24-20	.939	-1	103	112	S148	—	0.4
1916	Chi A	151	582	78	132	27	6	3	38	30	13	48	.227	.280	.309	76	-19	22-13	.941	-0	100	145	3b85,S66	—	-1.3
1917	†Chi A	118	447	64	127	16	5	3	32	27	5	29	.284	.332	.362	110	4	19	**.949**	2	95	**120**	3b107,S10	—	1.0
1918	Chi A	112	420	37	126	12	5	0	29	11	3	24	.300	.323	.352	103	-1	20	.941	1	103	134	S98,3b11/2	—	0.7
1919	†Chi A	**140**	571	89	169	33	9	3	75	11	5	21	.296	.315	.401	100	-3	22	.963	-3	97	96	3b97,S43	—	0.0
1920	Chi A	151	629	102	208	34	8	2	74	28	6	23	.331	.365	.420	107	6	19-17	.933	-15	91	75	3b127,S25	—	-0.5
Total	9	1254	4809	623	1308	198	69	21	420	183	58	303	.272	.307	.355	92	-72	173-70	.935	19	100	121	S822,3b427/2	—	1.1
WEAVER, JIM James Francis; B10.10.1959 Kingston NY; BL/TL/6´3˝/200; [MinA80 2/35]; d4.10; Col Florida St.																									
1985	Det A	12	7	2	1	1	0	0	0	1-0	0	4	.143	.250	.286	46	0	0-1	1.000	-0	43	0	O4(0/3/1),D4	0	-0.1
1987	Sea A	7	4	2	0	0	0	0	0	2-0	0	3	.000	.333	.000	-1	-1	1-1	1.000	1	83	751	O4(1/2/2)	0	0.0
1989	SF N	12	20	2	4	3	0	0	2	0-0	0	7	.200	.200	.350	56	-1	1-0	1.000	-1	73	0	O8(1/0/7)	0	-0.2
Total	3	31	31	6	5	4	0	0	2	3-0	0	14	.161	.235	.290	47	-2	2-2	1.000	-1	72	210	O16(2/5/10),D4	0	-0.3
WEAVER, FARMER William B.; B3.23.1865 Parkersburg WV; D1.23.1943 Akron OH; BL/5´10˝/170; d9.16; OF(132/406/111)																									
1888	Lou AA	26	112	12	28	1	1	0	8	3	1	—	.250	.276	.277	79	-3	12	.878	-1	158	0	O26C	—	-0.4
1889	Lou AA	124	499	62	145	17	6	0	60	40	7	22	.291	.352	.349	102	2	21	.918	1	136	71	O123C,C2/32	—	-0.1
1890	†Lou AA	130	557	101	161	27	9	3	67	29	8	—	.289	.333	.386	114	8	45	.933	-6	101	96	O127(0/126/1),S2/3	—	-0.2
1891	Lou AA	133	556	74	157	25	7	1	53	33	11	23	.282	.335	.358	99	-2	30	**.958**	13	**139**	141	O130C,C4	—	0.6
1892	Lou N	138	551	58	140	15	4	0	57	40	9	17	.254	.315	.296	92	-4	30	.902	-10	94	75	O122(109/1/12),C15/1	—	-2.1
1893	Lou N	106	439	79	128	17	7	2	49	27	11	12	.292	.348	.376	100	0	17	.913	2	119	60	O85(20/0/65),C21	—	0.0
1894	Lou N	64	244	19	54	5	2	3	24	7	2	11	.221	.249	.295	33	-28	3	.958	1	133	0	O35(2/0/33),C17,1b10/2	—	-2.1
	Pit N	30	115	16	40	7	2	0	24	6	5	1	.348	.405	.443	105	1	4	.943	-8	*100*	*96*	C14,S12,3b5/lf	—	-0.4
	Year	94	359	35	94	12	4	3	48	13	7	12	.262	.301	.343	58	-26	7	.947	-7	128	0	O36(3/0/33),C31,S12,1b10,3b5/2	—	-2.5
Total	7	751	3073	421	853	114	38	9	342	185	54	86	.278	.330	.348	95	-26	162	.927	-8	120	83	O649C,C73,S14,1b11,3b7,2b2	—	-4.7

YEAR	TM LG	G	AB	R	H	2B	3B	HR	RBI	BB-IB	HP	SO	AVG	OBP	SLG	AOPS	ABR	SB-CS	FA	FR	RNG	THR	GAMES AT POSITION	DL	BFW
WEBB, SKEETER	James Laverne; B11.4.1909 Meridian MS; D7.8.1986 Meridian MS; BR/TR/5´9.5˝/150; d7.20; Col U. of Mississippi																								
1932	StL N	1	0	0	0	0	0	0	0	0	0	0	ø	ø	ø	ø	0	0	ø	-0	0	0	/S	—	0.0
1938	Cle A	20	58	11	16	2	0	0	2	8	0	7	.276	.364	.310	72	-2	1-0	.964	-2	85	94	S13,3b3,2b2	—	-0.3
1939	Cle A	81	269	28	71	14	1	2	26	15	1	24	.264	.305	.346	68	-13	1-1	.932	-8	89	91	S81	—	-1.4
1940	Chi A	84	334	33	79	11	2	1	29	30	0	33	.237	.299	.290	53	-23	3-6	.969	-9	100	95	2b74,S7/3	—	-2.8
1941	Chi A	29	84	7	16	2	0	0	6	3	1	9	.190	.227	.214	18	-10	1-0	.940	-0	103	121	2b18,S5,3b3	0	-0.9
1942	Chi A	32	94	5	16	2	1	0	4	4	0	13	.170	.204	.213	18	-11	1-2	.961	1	111	85	2b29	0	-0.9
1943	Chi A	58	213	15	50	5	2	0	22	6	0	19	.235	.256	.277	56	-13	5-4	.953	0	111	95	2b54	0	-1.1
1944	Chi A	139	513	44	108	19	6	0	30	20	1	39	.211	.242	.271	47	-38	7-3	.944	-3	**106**	95	S135,2b5	0	-3.2
1945	†Det A	118	407	43	81	12	2	0	21	30	0	35	.199	.254	.238	41	-31	8-7	.957	16	106	115	S104,2b11	0	-0.8
1946	Det A	64	169	12	37	1	1	0	17	9	0	18	.219	.258	.237	37	-15	3-3	.972	8	112	100	2b50,S8	0	-0.5
1947	Det A	50	79	13	16	3	0	0	6	7	0	9	.203	.267	.241	41	-6	3-0	.992	6	125	62	2b30,S6	0	0.1
1948	Phi A	23	54	5	8	2	0	0	3	0	0	9	.148	.148	.185	-12	-9	0-0	1.000	2	97	199	2b9,S8	0	-0.6
Total	12	699	2274	216	498	73	15	3	166	132	3	215	.219	.263	.268	46	-171	33-26	.946	11	102	99	S368,2b282,3b7	0	-12.4
WEBB, EARL	William Earl; B9.17.1897 Bon Air TN; D5.23.1965 Jamestown TN; BL/TR/6´1˝/185; d8.13																								
1925	NY N	4	3	0	0	0	0	0	0	1	0	1	.000	.250	.000	-31	-1	0-0	ø	0	—	—	/H	—	-0.1
1927	Chi N	102	332	58	100	18	4	14	52	48	1	31	.301	.391	.506	138	19	3	.959	0	93	133	O86(8/0/78)	—	1.2
1928	Chi N	62	140	22	35	7	3	3	23	14	0	17	.250	.318	.407	90	-3	0	.986	1	99	127	O31R	—	-0.4
1930	Bos A	127	449	61	145	30	6	16	66	44	1	56	.323	.385	.523	133	22	2-1	.959	-6	92	75	O116R	—	0.7
1931	Bos A	151	589	96	196	**67**	3	14	103	70	0	51	.333	.404	.528	151	47	2-2	.948	-5	86	136	O151R	—	3.0
1932	Bos A	52	192	23	54	9	1	5	27	25	0	15	.281	.364	.417	105	2	0-0	.964	-1	78	190	O50R,1b2	—	-0.2
	Det A	88	338	49	97	19	8	3	51	39	0	18	.287	.361	.417	97	-1	1-1	.955	0	98	125	O85R	—	-0.6
	Year	140	530	72	151	28	9	8	78	64	0	33	.285	.362	.417	100	0	1-1	.958	-1	91	148	O135R,1b2	—	-0.8
1933	Det A	6	11	1	3	0	0	0	3	3	0	0	.273	.429	.273	87	0	0-0	1.000	-0	38	0	O2R	—	0.0
	Chi A	58	107	16	31	5	0	1	8	16	0	13	.290	.382	.364	103	1	0-0	1.000	-2	92	197	O16(5/0/11),1b10	—	-0.2
	Year	64	118	17	34	5	0	1	11	19	0	13	.288	.387	.356	101	1	0-0	1.000	-2	86	174	O18(5/0/13),1b10	—	-0.2
Total	7	650	2161	326	661	155	25	56	333	260	2	202	.306	.381	.478	125	86	8-4	.958	-13	90	126	O537(13/0/524),1b12	—	3.4
WEBB, BILL	William Joseph; B6.25.1895 Chicago IL; D1.12.1943 Chicago IL; BR/TR/5´10˝/161; d9.17; Mil 1918; C5																								
1917	Pit N	5	15	1	3	0	0	0	0	2	0	3	.200	.294	.200	51	-1	0	1.000	0	104	82	2b4/S	—	-0.1
WEBER, HARRY	Henry J.; B3.1862 NY; D12.22.1926 Indianapolis IN; d7.22																								
1884	Ind AA	3	8	0	0	0	0	0	—	0	1	—	.000	.111	.000	-62	-1	—	.794	-1	—	—	C3	—	-0.2
WEBER, JOE	Joseph Edward; B2.15.1862 Hamilton ON, Can.; D12.15.1921 Hamilton ON, Can.; BR/5´9˝/167; d5.30																								
1884	Det N	2	8	0	0	0	0	0	0	0	—	2	.000	.000	.000	-99	-2	—	.750	0	227	0	O2(1/0/1)	—	-0.2
WEBSTER, LENNY	Leonard Irell; B2.10.1965 New Orleans LA; BR/TR/5´9˝/(185–202); [MinA85 21/535]; d9.1; Col Grambling St.																								
1989	Min A	14	20	3	6	2	0	0	1	3-0	0	2	.300	.391	.400	116	1	0-0	1.000	-3	50	0	C14	0	-0.2
1990	Min A	2	6	1	2	1	0	0	0	1-0	0	1	.333	.429	.500	149	0	0-0	1.000	-1	68	0	C2	0	0.0
1991	Min A	18	34	7	10	1	0	3	8	6-0	0	10	.294	.390	.588	162	3	0-0	.986	4	128	62	C17	0	0.7
1992	Min A	53	118	10	33	10	1	1	13	9-0	0	11	.280	.331	.407	102	0	0-2	.995	-5	91	69	C49/D	0	-0.4
1993	Min A	49	106	14	21	2	0	1	8	11-1	0	8	.198	.274	.245	40	-9	1-0	1.000	-1	111	94	C45/D	0	-0.8
1994	Mon N	57	143	13	39	10	0	5	23	16-1	6	24	.273	.370	.448	111	3	0-0	.996	-3	73	110	C46	0	0.2
1995	Phi N	49	150	18	40	9	0	4	14	16-0	0	27	.267	.337	.407	95	-1	0-0	.990	-8	68	51	C43	0	-0.6
1996	Mon N	78	174	18	40	10	0	2	17	25-2	2	21	.230	.332	.322	72	-6	0-0	.998	10	124	123	C63	0	0.7
1997	†Bal A	98	259	29	66	8	1	7	37	22-0	2	46	.255	.317	.375	82	-7	0-1	.995	-3	78	112	C97/D	0	-0.5
1998	Bal A	108	309	37	88	16	0	10	46	15-0	0	38	.285	.317	.434	95	-3	0-0	.993	-13	73	92	C102,D4	0	-1.0
1999	Bal A	16	36	1	6	1	0	0	3	8-0	1	5	.167	.333	.194	41	-3	0-0	.986	2	88	131	C12,D2	64	0.0
	Bos A	6	14	0	0	0	0	0	1	2-0	1	2	.000	.176	.000	-48	-3	0-0	1.000	-1	71	73	C6	0	-0.3
	Year	22	50	1	6	1	0	0	4	10-0	2	7	.120	.290	.140	15	-6	0-0	.990	1	83	113	C18,D2	0	-0.3
2000	Mon N	39	81	6	17	3	0	0	5	6-1	0	14	.210	.264	.247	30	-9	0-0	1.000	-5	74	50	C32	31	-1.2
Total	12	587	1450	157	368	73	2	33	176	140-5	12	209	.254	.324	.375	84	-34	1-3	.995	-26	85	91	C528,D9	95	-3.4
WEBSTER, MITCH	Mitchell Dean; B5.16.1959 Larned KS; BB/TL/6´1˝/(180–191); [LAN77 23/581]; d9.2																								
1983	Tor A	11	11	2	2	0	0	0	0	1-0	0	1	.182	.250	.182	20	-1	0-0	1.000	-1	52	0	O7C,D2	0	-0.2
1984	Tor A	26	22	9	5	2	1	0	4	1-0	0	7	.227	.261	.409	79	-1	0-0	.875	-0	119	0	O10(3/7/0)/1D	0	-0.1
1985	Tor A	4	1	0	0	0	0	0	0	0-0	0	0	.000	.000	.000	-97	0	0-1	ø	-0	0	0	O2L,D2	0	-0.1
	Mon N	74	212	32	58	8	2	11	30	20-3	0	33	.274	.335	.486	134	9	15-9	.993	0	101	86	O64(4/52/20)	0	0.8
1986	Mon N	151	576	89	167	31	**13**	8	49	57-4	4	78	.290	.355	.431	117	13	36-15	.977	0	100	130	O146(8/118/44)	0	1.3
1987	Mon N	156	588	101	165	30	8	15	63	70-5	6	95	.281	.361	.435	106	7	33-10	.982	-4	96	78	O153R	0	-0.2
1988	Mon N	81	259	33	66	5	2	2	13	36-2	5	37	.255	.354	.313	89	-2	12-10	.994	-4	91	59	O71(12/53/12)	0	-0.8
	Chi N	70	264	36	70	11	6	4	26	19-0	3	50	.265	.319	.398	101	0	10-4	.971	1	109	33	O65(8/52/10)	0	0.0
	Year	151	523	69	136	16	8	6	39	55-2	8	87	.260	.337	.356	95	-2	22-14	.982	-3	100	47	O136(20/105/22)	0	-0.8
1989	†Chi N	98	272	40	70	12	4	3	19	30-5	1	55	.257	.331	.364	93	-2	14-2	.965	3	116	82	O74(52/13/21)	15	0.2
1990	Cle A	128	437	58	110	20	6	12	55	20-1	3	61	.252	.285	.407	93	-7	22-6	.991	8	122	17	O118(25/95/0),1b3,D3	0	0.2
1991	Cle A	13	32	2	4	0	0	0	0	3-0	0	9	.125	.200	.125	-8	-5	2-2	1.000	0	115	0	O10(6/1/6)	0	-0.5
	Pit N	36	97	9	17	3	4	1	9	9-1	0	31	.175	.245	.320	58	-6	0-0	.963	-1	94	116	O29(2/9/20)	0	-0.8
	LA N	58	74	12	21	5	1	1	10	9-0	0	21	.284	.361	.419	121	2	0-1	1.000	1	120	0	O36(29/4/7)/1	0	0.2
	Year	94	171	21	38	8	5	2	19	18-1	0	52	.222	.296	.363	85	-4	0-1	.978	0	103	74	O65(31/13/27)/1	0	-0.6
1992	LA N	135	262	33	70	12	5	6	35	27-3	2	49	.267	.334	.420	115	5	11-5	.977	-2	103	0	O90(36/8/56)	0	0.2
1993	LA N	88	172	26	42	6	2	2	14	11-2	2	24	.244	.293	.337	73	-7	4-6	.950	-2	97	35	O56(32/2/27)	0	-1.2
1994	LA N	82	84	16	23	4	0	4	12	8-1	1	13	.274	.344	.464	114	2	1-2	1.000	-1	95	0	O48(45/0/6)	0	0.0
1995	†LA N	54	56	6	10	1	1	1	3	4-1	1	14	.179	.246	.286	43	-5	0-0	1.000	-1	72	0	O25(11/4/11)	21	-0.6
Total	13	1265	3419	504	900	150	55	70	342	325-28	28	578	.263	.330	.401	101	2	160-73	.980	-3	103	63	O1004(275/425/393),D16,1b5	36	-1.6
WEBSTER, RAY	Ramon Alberto; B8.31.1942 Colon, Pan; BL/TL/6´0˝/185; d4.11																								
1967	KC A	122	360	41	92	15	4	11	51	32-1	2	44	.256	.320	.411	118	7	5-3	.989	-3	76	75	1b83,O15(14/0/2)	0	-0.1
1968	Oak A	66	196	17	42	11	1	3	23	12-6	0	24	.214	.258	.327	80	-5	3-0	.988	-3	79	91	1b55	0	-1.2
1969	Oak A	64	77	5	20	0	1	1	13	12-5	1	8	.260	.359	.325	98	0	0-0	1.000	0	104	69	1b13	0	-0.1
1970	SD N	95	116	12	30	3	0	2	11	11-0	0	12	.259	.323	.336	80	-3	1-1	.981	-1	83	134	1b15/lf	0	-0.6
1971	SD N	10	8	0	1	0	0	0	0	2-0	0	1	.125	.300	.125	26	-1	0-0	ø	0	—	—	/H	0	-0.1
	Oak A	7	5	0	0	0	0	0	0	0-0	0	2	.000	.000	.000	-99	-1	0-0	1.000	-0	0	0	/1	0	-0.2
	Chi N	16	16	1	5	2	0	0	0	1-0	0	3	.313	.353	.438	107	0	0-0	1.000	0	316	266	/1	0	0.1
Total	5	380	778	76	190	31	6	17	98	70-12	3	94	.244	.308	.365	98	-3	9-4	.989	-7	80	85	1b168,O16(15/0/2)	0	-2.2
WEBSTER, RAY	Raymond George; B11.15.1937 Grass Valley CA; BR/TR/6´0˝/(160–175); d4.17																								
1959	Cle A	40	74	10	15	2	1	2	10	5-0	0	7	.203	.253	.338	63	-4	1-0	.929	-3	88	96	2b24,3b4	0	-0.6
1960	Bos A	7	3	1	0	0	0	0	1	1-0	0	0	.000	.200	.000	-25	-1	0-0	1.000	0	76	265	/2	0	0.0
Total	2	47	77	11	15	2	1	2	11	6-0	0	7	.195	.250	.325	59	-5	1-0	.931	-3	88	101	2b25,3b4	0	-0.6
WECKBECKER, PETE	Peter; B8.30.1864 Butler PA; D5.16.1935 Hampton VA; 5´7˝/150; d10.5																								
1889	Ind N	1	1	0	0	0	0	0	0	0	0	0	.000	.000	.000	-98	0	0	1.000	-0	—	—	/C	—	0.0
1890	†Lou AA	32	101	17	24	1	0	0	11	8	1	—	.238	.300	.248	63	-5	7	.941	4	*135*	*73*	C32	—	0.2
Total	2	33	102	17	24	1	0	0	11	8	1	0	.235	.297	.245	61	-5	7	.941	4	*135*	*73*	C33	—	0.2
WEDGE, ERIC	Eric Michael; B1.27.1968 Fort Wayne IN; BR/TR/6´3˝/(215–224); [BosA89 3/83]; d10.5; M4; Col Wichita St.																								
1991	Bos A	1	1	0	1	0	0	0	0	0-0	0	0	1.000	1.000	1.000	431	0	0-0	ø	0	—	—	/D	0	0.0
1992	Bos A	27	68	11	17	2	0	5	11	13-0	0	18	.250	.370	.500	132	3	0-0	1.000	-1	77	0	D20,C5	0	0.2
1993	Col N	9	11	2	2	0	0	0	1	0-0	0	4	.182	.182	.182	-2	-2	0-0	1.000	0	75	300	/C	111	-0.1
1994	Bos A	2	6	0	0	0	0	0	0	1-0	0	3	.000	.143	.000	-56	-1	0-0	ø	0	—	—	D2	0	-0.2
Total	4	39	86	13	20	2	0	5	12	14-0	0	25	.233	.340	.430	103	0	0-0	1.000	-1	77	61	D23,C6	111	-0.1

YEAR	TM LG	G	AB	R	H	2B	3B	HR	RBI	BB-IB	HP	SO	AVG	OBP	SLG	AOPS	ABR	SB-CS	FA	FR	RNG	THR	GAMES AT POSITION	DL	BFW
WEEDEN, BERT	Charles Albert; B12.21.1882 Northwood NH; D1.7.1939 Northwood NH; BL/TR/6´0˝/200; d6.4																								
1911	Bos N	1	1	0	0	0	0	0	0	0	0	0	.000	.000	.000	-93	0	0	ø	0	—	—	/H	—	0.0
WEEKLY, JOHNNY	Johnny; B6.14.1937 Waterproof LA; D11.24.1974 Walnut Creek CA; BR/TR/6´0˝/(180–200); d4.13; Col Diablo Valley (CA) JC; [DL 1960 SF N 102]																								
1962	Hou N	13	26	3	5	1	0	2	2	7-0	0	4	.192	.364	.462	129	1	0-0	1.000	-1	73	0	O7(4/0/4)	0	0.0
1963	Hou N	34	80	4	18	3	0	3	14	7-0	1	14	.225	.292	.375	98	0	0-0	1.000	2	113	160	O23(15/0/8)	33	0.0
1964	Hou N	6	15	0	2	0	0	0	3	1-0	0	3	.133	.167	.133	-8	-2	0-0	1.000	1	124	321	O5R	0	-0.2
Total	3	53	121	7	25	4	0	5	19	15-0	1	21	.207	.293	.364	92	-1	0-0	1.000	2	106	148	O35(19/0/17)	135	-0.2
WEEKS, RICKIE	Rickie Darnell; B9.13.1982 Altamonte Springs FL; BR/TR/6´0˝/(195–205); d9.15; Col Southern																								
2003	Mil N	7	12	1	2	1	0	0	0	1-0	1	6	.167	.286	.250	42	-1	0-0	.667	-4	15	0	2b4	0	-0.5
2005	Mil N	96	360	56	86	13	2	13	42	40-2	11	96	.239	.333	.394	89	-6	15-2	.951	-13	88	97	2b95	0	-1.1
2006	Mil N	95	359	73	100	15	3	8	34	30-1	**19**	92	.279	.363	.404	96	-1	19-5	.952	7	106	114	2b92/D	65	1.2
Total	3	198	731	130	188	29	5	21	76	71-3	31	194	.257	.346	.397	92	-8	34-7	.951	-10	96	104	2b191/D	65	-0.4
WEHNER, JOHN	John Paul; B6.29.1967 Pittsburgh PA; BR/TR/6´3˝/(204–206); [PitN88 7/174]; d7.17; Col Indiana; OF(69/29/54)																								
1991	Pit N	37	106	15	36	7	0	0	7	7-0	0	17	.340	.381	.406	122	3	3-0	.936	5	118	223	3b36	39	0.9
1992	†Pit N	55	123	11	22	6	0	0	4	12-2	0	22	.179	.252	.228	37	-10	3-0	.961	2	130	223	3b34,1b13,2b5	0	-0.9
1993	Pit N	29	35	3	5	0	0	0	0	6-1	0	10	.143	.268	.143	14	-4	0-0	1.000	2	121	294	O13(4/8/2),2b3,3b3	0	-0.2
1994	Pit N	2	4	1	1	1	0	0	3	0-0	0	1	.250	.250	.500	88	0	0-0	1.000	0	122	0	/3	23	0.0
1995	Pit N	52	107	13	33	0	3	0	5	10-1	0	17	.308	.361	.364	92	-1	3-1	1.000	0	104	137	O23(18/2/3),3b19/CS	0	-0.1
1996	Pit N	86	139	19	36	9	1	2	13	8-1	0	22	.259	.299	.381	75	-5	1-5	.971	-1	100	113	O29(9/13/8),3b24,2b12/C	0	-0.7
1997	†Fla N	44	36	8	10	2	0	0	2	2-0	1	5	.278	.333	.333	79	-1	1-0	1.000	-1	78	0	O27(10/1/19),3b6	65	-0.2
1998	Fla N	53	88	10	20	2	0	0	5	7-0	0	12	.227	.281	.250	45	-7	1-0	1.000	1	93	214	O23(12/2/11),3b8	0	-0.7
1999	Pit N	39	65	6	12	2	0	1	4	7-0	0	12	.185	.264	.262	33	-7	1-0	.958	-1	100	0	O17(12/2/6),3b2,S2/2	0	-0.7
2000	Pit N	21	50	10	15	3	0	1	9	4-0	0	6	.300	.352	.420	94	0	0-0	.973	1	100	0	3b16/lf	0	0.0
2001	Pit N	43	51	3	10	1	0	0	2	10-0	0	12	.196	.328	.216	44	-4	2-1	1.000	-0	37	52	1b11,O8(3/1/5),3b6/C2	28	-0.4
Total	11	461	804	99	200	33	4	4	54	73-5	1	136	.249	.311	.315	68	-36	15-7	.964	8	112	154	3b155,O141L,1b24,2b22,S3,C3	155	-3.0
WEIGEL, RALPH	Ralph Richard "Wig"; B10.2.1921 Coldwater OH; D4.15.1992 Memphis TN; BR/TR/6´1˝/180; d9.18																								
1946	Cle A	6	12	0	2	0	0	0	0	0	0	2	.167	.167	.167	-7	-2	1-0	1.000	-1	*90*	*0*	C6	0	-0.2
1948	Chi A	66	163	8	38	7	3	0	26	13	1	18	.233	.294	.313	64	-9	1-2	.969	-4	*78*	*105*	C39,O2L	0	-1.2
1949	Was A	34	60	4	14	2	0	0	4	8	0	6	.233	.324	.267	58	-3	0-1	.985	-1	*89*	*137*	C21	0	-0.3
Total	3	106	235	12	54	9	3	0	30	21	1	26	.230	.296	.294	59	-14	2-3	.976	-6	*82*	*108*	C66,O2L	0	-1.7
WEIHE, PODGE	John Garibaldi; B11.13.1862 Cincinnati OH; D4.15.1914 Cincinnati OH; BR/TR/5´11˝/175; d8.6																								
1883	Cin AA	1	4	1	1	0	0	0	—	0	—	—	.250	.250	.250	58	0	—	1.000	0	0	0	/cf	—	0.0
1884	Ind AA	63	256	29	65	13	2	4	—	9	0	—	.254	.279	.367	112	4	—	.860	-0	124	105	O58(1/23/35),2b4,1b3	—	0.2
Total	2	64	260	30	66	13	2	4	—	9	0	—	.254	.279	.365	111	4	—	.864	-0	121	102	O59(1/24/35),2b4,1b3	—	0.2
WEINGARTNER, ELMER	Elmer William "Dutch"; B8.13.1918 Cleveland OH; BR/TR/5´11˝/178; d4.19																								
1945	Cle A	20	39	5	9	1	0	0	1	4	0	11	.231	.302	.256	66	-2	0-0	.871	-3	81	90	S20	0	-0.4
WEINTRAUB, PHIL	Philip "Mickey"; B10.12.1907 Chicago IL; D6.21.1987 Palm Springs CA; BL/TL/6´1˝/195; d9.5; Col Loyola–Chicago																								
1933	NY N	8	15	3	3	0	0	1	1	3	0	2	.200	.333	.400	110	0	0	.667	-1	58	0	O6R	—	-0.1
1934	NY N	31	74	13	26	2	0	0	15	15	0	10	.351	.461	.378	130	5	0	.944	-3	82	0	O20(12/9/0)	—	0.1
1935	NY N	64	112	18	27	3	3	1	6	17	0	13	.241	.341	.348	87	-2	0	.975	-0	107	79	1b19,O7(1/0/6)	—	-0.4
1937	Cin N	49	177	27	48	10	4	3	20	19	1	25	.271	.345	.424	113	3	1	.976	-2	90	89	O47(41/0/6)	—	-0.1
	NY N	6	9	3	3	2	0	0	1	1	0	1	.333	.400	.556	155	1	0	1.000	-0	51	0	/lf	—	0.0
	Year	55	186	30	51	12	4	3	21	20	1	26	.274	.348	.430	115	4	1	.976	-2	89	87	O48(42/0/6)	—	-0.1
1938	Phi N	100	351	51	109	23	2	4	45	64	4	43	.311	.422	.422	137	23	1	.988	3	112	73	1b98	—	1.6
1944	NY N	104	361	55	114	18	9	13	77	59	0	59	.316	.412	.524	162	31	0	.992	3	109	88	1b99	0	3.0
1945	NY N	82	283	45	77	9	1	10	42	54	0	29	.272	.389	.417	122	10	2	.993	2	107	84	1b77	0	0.8
Total	7	444	1382	215	407	67	19	32	207	232	5	182	.295	.398	.440	133	71	4	.990	2	109	81	1b293,O81(55/9/18)	0	4.9
WEIS, AL	Albert John; B4.2.1938 Franklin Square NY; BB/TR (BR 1969–71)/6´0˝/(160–170); d9.15																								
1962	Chi A	7	12	2	1	0	0	0	0	2-0	1	3	.083	.267	.083	-1	-2	1-0	.882	-1	122	0	S4/23	0	-0.2
1963	Chi A	99	210	41	57	9	0	0	18	18-1	2	37	.271	.333	.314	85	-4	15-1	.990	6	110	139	2b48,S27/3	0	1.1
1964	Chi A	133	328	36	81	4	4	2	23	22-0	3	41	.247	.299	.302	70	-14	22-7	.966	3	111	**134**	2b116,S9,O2C	0	-0.1
1965	Chi A	103	135	29	40	4	3	1	12	12-1	2	22	.296	.360	.393	122	4	4-1	.975	5	109	111	2b74,S7,3b2,O2C	0	1.4
1966	Chi A	129	187	20	29	4	1	0	9	17-3	2	50	.155	.233	.187	24	-19	3-5	.987	13	120	142	2b96,S18	0	-0.1
1967	Chi A	50	53	9	13	2	0	0	4	1-0	1	7	.245	.273	.283	67	-2	3-3	.986	-2	115	24	2b32,S13	88	-0.3
1968	NY N	90	274	15	47	6	0	1	14	21-3	2	63	.172	.234	.204	33	-22	3-1	.958	-3	96	92	S59,2b29,3b2	0	-2.1
1969	†NY N	103	247	20	53	9	2	2	23	15-1	0	51	.215	.259	.291	53	-16	3-3	.960	-2	93	117	S52,2b43/3	0	-1.2
1970	NY N	75	121	20	25	7	1	1	11	7-1	1	21	.207	.254	.306	49	-9	1-1	.952	-12	73	58	2b44,S15	0	-1.8
1971	NY N	11	11	3	0	0	0	0	1	2-1	0	4	.000	.143	.000	-53	-2	0-0	1.000	-0	53	81	2b5,3b2	0	-0.2
Total	10	800	1578	195	346	45	11	7	115	117-11	14	299	.219	.278	.275	59	-86	55-22	.975	7	107	119	2b488,S204,3b9,O4C	88	-3.5
WEIS, BUTCH	Arthur John; B3.2.1901 St.Louis MO; D5.4.1997 St.Louis MO; BL/TL/5´11˝/180; d4.15																								
1922	Chi N	2	2	2	1	0	0	0	0	0	0	0	.500	.500	.500	156	0	0-0	ø	0	—	—	/H	—	0.0
1923	Chi N	22	26	2	6	1	0	0	2	5	0	8	.231	.355	.269	67	-1	0-1	1.000	-0	110	0	O6(4/0/2)	—	-0.2
1924	Chi N	37	133	19	37	8	1	0	23	15	1	14	.278	.356	.353	90	-1	4-5	.978	4	102	178	O36(14/0/22)	—	-0.2
1925	Chi N	67	180	16	48	5	3	2	25	23	0	22	.267	.350	.361	81	-5	2-4	.964	-3	88	76	O47(45/0/2)	—	-1.1
Total	4	128	341	39	92	14	4	2	50	43	1	44	.270	.353	.352	84	-7	6-10	.973	0	96	120	O89(63/0/26)	—	-1.5
WEISER, BUD	Harry Budson; B1.8.1891 Shamokin PA; D7.31.1961 Shamokin PA; BR/TR/5´11˝/165; d4.29																								
1915	Phi N	37	64	6	9	2	0	0	8	7	1	12	.141	.236	.172	24	-6	2-2	.897	-3	83	0	O20(4/16/0)	—	-1.1
1916	Phi N	4	10	1	3	1	0	0	1	0	0	3	.300	.300	.400	110	0	0	1.000	-0	110	0	O4L	—	0.0
Total	2	41	74	7	12	3	0	0	9	7	1	15	.162	.244	.203	36	-6	2-2	.912	-3	87	0	O24(8/16/0)	—	-1.1
WEISS, GARY	Gary Lee; B12.27.1955 Brenham TX; BB/TR (BR 1980)/5´10˝/170; [LAN78 19/486]; d9.13; Col Houston																								
1980	LA N	8	0	2	0	0	0	0	0	0-0	0	0	ø	ø	ø	ø	0	0-0	ø	0	—	—	/R	0	0.0
1981	LA N	14	19	2	2	0	0	0	1	1-0	0	4	.105	.143	.105	-28	-3	0-0	.920	-4	49	209	S13	0	-0.7
Total	2	22	19	4	2	0	0	0	1	1-0	0	4	.105	.143	.105	-28	-3	0-0	.920	-4	49	209	S13	0	-0.7
WEISS, JOE	Joseph Harold; B1.27.1894 Chicago IL; D7.7.1967 Cedar Rapids IA; BR/TR/6´0˝/165; d8.29																								
1915	Chi F	29	85	6	19	1	2	0	11	3	0	24	.224	.250	.282	53	-7	0	.992	-1	75	58	1b29	—	-1.0
WEISS, WALT	Walter William; B11.28.1963 Tuxedo NY; BB/TR/6´0˝/(175–188); [OakA85 1/11]; d7.12; Col North Carolina																								
1987	Oak A	16	26	3	12	4	0	0	1	2-0	0	2	.462	.500	.615	207	4	1-2	.974	1	125	81	S11,D2	0	0.6
1988	†Oak A	147	452	44	113	17	3	3	39	35-1	9	56	.250	.312	.321	81	-11	4-4	.979	10	104	95	S147	0	0.9
1989	†Oak A	84	236	30	55	11	0	3	21	21-0	1	39	.233	.298	.318	76	-7	6-1	.953	-14	87	99	S84	74	-1.5
1990	†Oak A	138	445	50	118	17	1	2	35	46-5	4	53	.265	.337	.321	89	-5	9-3	.979	-15	98	101	S137	15	-0.9
1991	Oak A	40	133	15	30	6	1	0	13	12-0	0	14	.226	.286	.286	63	-7	6-0	.970	-3	92	86	S40	137	-0.6
1992	†Oak A	103	316	36	67	5	2	0	21	43-1	1	39	.212	.305	.241	58	-17	6-3	.956	-13	94	89	S103	58	-2.2
1993	Fla N	158	500	50	133	14	2	1	39	79-13	3	73	.266	.367	.308	79	-11	7-3	.977	-18	91	86	S153	0	-1.7
1994	Col N	110	423	58	106	11	4	1	32	56-0	0	58	.251	.336	.303	59	-24	12-7	.973	7	105	94	S110	0	-0.9
1995	†Col N	137	427	65	111	17	3	1	25	98-8	5	57	.260	.403	.321	73	-12	15-3	.974	14	107	**119**	S136	0	1.4
1996	Col N	155	517	89	146	20	2	8	48	80-5	6	78	.282	.381	.375	82	-10	10-2	.957	-2	104	87	S155	0	0.0
1997	Col N	121	393	52	106	23	5	4	38	66-3	2	56	.270	.377	.384	82	-8	5-2	.983	19	**117**	**118**	S119	17	1.9
1998	†Atl N★	96	347	64	97	18	2	0	27	59-0	3	53	.280	.386	.343	95	1	7-1	.967	-1	96	130	S96	0	0.8
1999	†Atl N	110	279	38	63	13	4	2	29	35-1	3	48	.226	.315	.323	63	-16	7-3	.963	-10	90	95	S102	24	-1.8
2000	†Atl N	80	192	29	50	6	2	0	18	26-1	3	32	.260	.353	.313	72	-8	1-1	.949	7	113	110	S69	16	0.4
Total	14	1495	4686	623	1207	182	31	25	386	658-38	40	658	.258	.351	.326	77	-131	96-35	.970	-16	101	100	S1462,D2	341	-3.6

YEAR	TM LG	G	AB	R	H	2B	3B	HR	RBI	BB-IB	HP	SO	AVG	OBP	SLG	AOPS	ABR	SB-CS	FA	FR	RNG	THR	GAMES AT POSITION	DL	BFW
WELAJ, JOHNNY	John Ludwig; B5.27.1914 Moss Creek PA; D9.13.2003 Arlington TX; BR/TR/6´0″/164; d5.2; Mil 1943–45																								
1939	Was A	63	201	23	55	11	2	1	33	13	0	20	.274	.318	.363	80	-7	13-2	.975	0	106	55	O55(13/17/26)	—	-0.6
1940	Was A	88	215	31	55	9	0	3	21	19	2	20	.256	.322	.340	77	-7	8-7	.978	1	111	28	O53(15/35/3)	—	-0.9
1941	Was A	49	96	16	20	4	0	0	5	6	0	16	.208	.255	.250	36	-9	3-1	.979	0	120	0	O19(13/3/3)	0	-0.9
1943	Phi A	93	281	45	68	16	1	0	15	15	0	17	.242	.280	.306	72	-11	12-5	.960	0	110	54	O72(15/27/32)	0	-1.4
Total	4	293	793	115	198	40	3	4	74	53	2	73	.250	.298	.323	71	-34	36-15	.970	1	110	42	O199(56/82/64)	0	-3.8
WELCH, CURT	Curtis Benton; B2.10.1862 Williamsport OH; D8.29.1896 E.Liverpool OH; BR/TR/5´10″/175; d5.1; OF(17/1059/0)																								
1884	Tol AA	**109**	425	61	95	24	5	0	—	10	4	—	.224	.248	.304	76	-11	—	.888	14	119	97	O107(1/106/0),2b2,C2/1	—	0.0
1885	†StL AA	**112**	432	84	117	18	8	3	69	23	7	—	.271	.318	.370	112	5	—	**.946**	12	130	159	O112C	—	1.2
1886	†StL AA	138	563	114	158	31	13	2	95	29	14	—	.281	.332	.393	121	12	59	**.952**	10	83	109	O138C,2b2	—	1.5
1887	†StL AA	131	544	98	151	32	7	3	108	25	11	—	.278	.322	.379	86	-13	89	.941	12	140	172	O123C,2b8/1	—	-0.4
1888	Phi AA	**136**	549	125	155	22	8	1	61	33	**29**	—	.282	.355	.357	129	20	95	.952	1	104	135	O135C,2b3	—	1.5
1889	Phi AA	125	516	134	140	**39**	6	0	39	67	19	30	.271	.375	.370	114	15	66	.923	5	124	183	O125C	—	1.3
1890	Phi AA	103	396	100	106	21	4	2	40	49	32	—	.268	.392	.356	121	16	64	.919	11	134	149	O103C/P	—	2.0
	Bal AA	19	68	16	9	4	0	0	5	9	2	—	.132	.253	.191	30	-6	8	.974	1	97	149	O17C,1b2	—	-0.5
	Year	122	464	116	115	25	4	2	45	58	**34**	—	.248	.372	.332	107	9	72	.926	12	129	149	O120C,1b2/P	—	1.5
1891	Bal AA	132	514	122	138	22	10	3	55	77	**36**	42	.268	.400	.368	119	18	50	.946	13	111	97	O113(1/112/0),2b21,S2	—	2.4
1892	Bal N	63	237	42	56	1	3	1	22	36	11	9	.236	.363	.278	92	0	14	.905	-4	41	41	O63C	—	-0.7
	Cin N	25	94	14	19	0	2	1	7	7	6	8	.202	.299	.277	75	-3	7	.925	-1	47	114	O25(1/25/0)	—	-0.5
	Year	88	331	56	75	1	5	2	29	43	17	17	.227	.345	.278	88	-3	21	.911	-5	43	63	O88(1/88/0)	—	-1.2
1893	Lou N	14	47	5	8	1	0	0	2	16	2	4	.170	.400	.191	64	0	1	.912	0	84	0	O14L	—	-0.1
Total	10	1107	4385	915	1152	215	66	16	503	381	173	93	.263	.345	.353	107	53	453	.933	74	110	130	O1075C,2b36,1b4,S2,C2/P	—	7.7
WELCH, FRANK	Frank Tiguer "Bugger"; B8.10.1897 Birmingham AL; D7.25.1957 Birmingham AL; BR/TR/5´9″/175; d9.9																								
1919	Phi A	15	54	5	9	1	1	2	7	7	0	10	.167	.262	.333	66	-3	0	.909	-0	103	95	O15C	—	-0.5
1920	Phi A	100	360	43	93	17	5	4	40	26	2	41	.258	.312	.367	78	-12	2-9	.937	-5	89	117	O97(0/84/16)	—	-2.6
1921	Phi A	115	403	48	115	18	6	7	45	34	4	43	.285	.347	.412	92	-5	6-0	.943	-2	95	116	O104(3/93/8)	—	-1.1
1922	Phi A	114	375	43	97	17	3	11	49	40	3	40	.259	.335	.408	90	-6	3-4	.949	1	104	109	O104(4/6/94)	—	-1.3
1923	Phi A	125	421	56	125	19	9	4	55	48	4	40	.297	.374	.413	106	4	1-4	.967	6	**116**	88	O117R	—	-0.1
1924	Phi A	94	293	47	85	13	2	5	31	35	3	27	.290	.372	.399	98	0	2-3	.985	1	88	147	O74(0/2/72)	—	-0.6
1925	Phi A	85	202	40	56	5	4	4	41	29	2	14	.277	.373	.401	90	-3	2-1	.968	-2	86	110	O57R	—	-0.8
1926	Phi A	75	174	26	49	8	1	4	23	26	2	9	.282	.381	.408	100	1	2-5	.975	-1	92	96	O49(28/3/20)	—	-0.5
1927	Bos A	15	28	2	5	2	0	0	4	5	0	1	.179	.303	.250	46	-2	0-2	1.000	2	80	466	O6R	—	-0.1
Total	9	738	2310	310	634	100	31	41	295	250	20	225	.274	.350	.398	92	-26	18-28	.955	-2	98	115	O623(35/203/390)	—	-7.6
WELCH, HERB	Herbert M. "Dutch"; B10.19.1898 RoEllen TN; D4.13.1967 Memphis TN; BL/TR/5´6″/154; d9.15																								
1925	Bos A	13	38	2	11	0	1	0	2	0	0	6	.289	.289	.342	60	-3	0-0	.893	3	124	125	S13	—	0.1
WELCH, TUB	James T.; B7.3.1866 St.Louis MO; TR/5´11″/230; d6.12																								
1890	Tol AA	35	108	15	31	3	1	1	14	8	4	—	.287	.358	.361	109	1	7	.930	1	*114*	*116*	C25,1b10	—	0.3
1895	Lou N	47	153	18	37	4	1	1	8	13	2	7	.242	.310	.301	62	-9	2	.888	-3	*91*	*106*	C28,1b20	—	-0.8
Total	2	82	261	33	68	7	2	2	22	21	6	7	.261	.330	.326	81	-8	9	.911	-2	*102*	*111*	C53,1b30	—	-0.5
WELCH, MILT	Milton Edward; B7.26.1924 Farmersville IL; BR/TR/5´10″/175; d6.5																								
1945	Det A	1	2	0	0	0	0	0	0	0	0	1	.000	.000	.000	-94	0	0-0	1.000	0	*0*	*0*	/C	0	0.0
WELCHONCE, HARRY	Harry Monroe "Welch"; B11.20.1883 North Point PA; D2.26.1977 Arcadia CA; BL/TR/6´0″/170; d4.17																								
1911	Phi N	26	66	9	14	4	0	0	6	7	0	8	.212	.288	.273	56	-4	0	.929	-2	91	49	O17(1/6/11)	—	-0.6
WELDAY, MIKE	Lyndon Earl; B12.13.1878 Conway IA; D5.28.1942 Leavenworth KS; BL/TL/5´8″/165; d4.21																								
1907	Chi A	24	35	2	8	1	1	0	0	6	0	—	.229	.341	.314	113	1	0	.938	0	177	0	O15(4/8/3)	—	0.0
1909	Chi A	29	74	3	14	0	0	0	5	4	0	—	.189	.231	.189	34	-6	2	.886	-0	148	182	O20(7/10/3)	—	-0.8
Total	2	53	109	5	22	1	1	0	5	10	0	—	.202	.269	.229	60	-5	2	.900	-0	157	128	O35(11/18/6)	—	-0.8
WELF, OLLIE	Oliver Henry; B1.17.1889 Cleveland OH; D6.15.1967 Cleveland OH; BR/TL/5´9″/160; d8.30; Col Ohio St.																								
1916	Cle A	1	0	0	0	0	0	0	0	0	0	0	ø	ø	ø	ø	0	0	ø	0	—	—	/R	—	0.0
WELLMAN, BRAD	Brad Eugene; B8.17.1959 Lodi CA; BR/TR/6´0″/(165–170); d9.4																								
1982	SF N	6	4	1	1	0	0	0	0	0-0	0	1	.250	.250	.250	41	0	0-0	1.000	-1	48	0	2b2	0	-0.1
1983	SF N	82	182	15	39	3	0	1	16	22-1	0	39	.214	.296	.247	54	-11	5-3	.965	-8	99	74	2b74,S2	0	-1.6
1984	SF N	93	265	23	60	9	1	2	25	19-0	0	41	.226	.274	.291	62	-14	10-5	.977	6	109	71	2b54,S34,3b9	0	-0.3
1985	SF N	71	174	16	41	11	1	0	16	4-1	4	33	.236	.268	.310	64	-9	5-2	.983	-7	79	63	2b36,3b25,S3	29	-1.5
1986	SF N	12	13	0	2	0	0	0	1	1-0	0	2	.154	.214	.154	3	-2	0-0	1.000	-0	87	0	S8/23	0	-0.2
1987	LA N	3	4	1	1	0	0	0	1	0-0	0	1	.250	.250	.250	34	0	0-0	1.000	1	296	0	/2S3	30	0.0
1988	KC A	71	107	11	29	3	0	1	6	6-0	2	23	.271	.322	.327	81	-3	1-2	.972	2	111	118	2b46,S15,3b4,D3	0	0.0
1989	KC A	103	178	30	41	4	0	2	12	7-0	1	36	.230	.263	.287	55	-11	5-3	.995	1	107	109	2b64,S34,3b3/D	15	-0.8
Total	8	441	927	97	214	30	2	6	77	59-2	7	176	.231	.280	.287	61	-50	26-15	.978	-6	102	85	2b278,S97,3b43,D4	74	-4.5
WELLMAN, BOB	Robert Joseph; B7.15.1925 Norwood OH; D12.20.1994 Villa Hills KY; BR/TR/6´4″/210; d9.23																								
1948	Phi A	4	10	1	2	0	1	0	0	3	0	2	.200	.385	.400	109	0	0-0	1.000	-0	77	106	1b2/rf	0	0.0
1950	Phi A	11	15	1	5	0	0	1	1	0	0	3	.333	.333	.533	121	0	0-0	1.000	0	119	0	O2R	0	0.0
Total	2	15	25	2	7	0	1	1	1	3	0	5	.280	.357	.480	117	0	0-0	.889	-0	110	0	O3R,1b2	0	0.0
WELLS, GREG	Gregory De Wayne; B4.25.1954 McIntosh AL; BR/TR/6´5″/(218–225); d8.10																								
1981	Tor A	32	73	7	18	5	0	0	5	5-0	0	12	.247	.295	.315	71	-3	0-2	.994	-1	81	65	1b22,D3	0	-0.6
1982	Min A	15	54	5	11	1	2	0	3	1-0	0	8	.204	.211	.296	38	-5	0-0	.962	-2	33	72	1b10,D5	0	-0.8
Total	2	47	127	12	29	6	2	0	8	6-0	0	20	.228	.259	.307	58	-8	0-2	.983	-3	64	68	1b32,D8	0	-1.4
WELLS, JAKE	Jacob; B8.9.1863 Memphis TN; D3.16.1927 Hendersonville NC; BR/TR/5´11″/167; d8.10																								
1888	Det N	16	57	5	9	1	0	0	2	0	0	5	.158	.158	.175	6	-6	0	.917	2	—	—	C16	—	-0.3
1890	StL AA	30	105	17	25	3	0	0	12	10	5	—	.238	.333	.267	67	-4	1	.941	2	*99*	*102*	C28,O3L	—	0.0
Total	2	46	162	22	34	4	0	0	14	10	5	5	.210	.277	.235	50	-10	1	.932	3	*99*	*102*	C44,O3L	—	-0.3
WELLS, LEO	Leo Donald; B7.18.1917 Kansas City KS; D6.23.2006 St.Paul MN; BR/TR/5´9″/170; d4.16; Mil 1943–45																								
1942	Chi A	35	62	8	12	2	0	1	4	4	0	5	.194	.242	.274	46	-5	1-0	1.000	7	149	157	S12,3b6	0	0.3
1946	Chi A	45	127	11	24	4	1	1	11	12	0	34	.189	.259	.260	47	-9	3-4	.942	4	117	91	3b38,S2	0	-0.7
Total	2	80	189	19	36	6	1	2	15	16	0	39	.190	.254	.265	47	-14	4-4	.938	11	119	104	3b44,S14	0	-0.4
WELLS, VERNON	Vernon M.; B12.8.1978 Shreveport LA; BR/TR/6´1″/(210–225); [TorA97 1/5]; d8.30																								
1999	Tor A	24	88	8	23	5	0	1	8	4-0	0	18	.261	.293	.352	63	-5	1-1	1.000	0	84	272	O24C	0	-0.4
2000	Tor A	3	2	0	0	0	0	0	0	0-0	0	0	.000	.000	.000	-97	-1	0-0	1.000	-0	96	0	O3C	0	-0.1
2001	Tor A	30	96	14	30	8	0	1	6	5-0	1	15	.313	.350	.427	102	0	5-0	.969	-1	96	135	O30(0/27/3)	0	0.1
2002	Tor A	159	608	87	167	34	4	23	100	27-0	3	85	.275	.305	.457	96	-5	9-4	.992	-3	96	120	O159(0/146/13)	0	-0.6
2003	Tor A★	161	678	118	**215**	**49**	5	33	117	42-2	7	80	.317	.359	.550	131	30	4-1	.990	-13	90	41	O161C	0	1.8
2004	Tor A	134	536	82	146	34	2	23	67	51-2	2	83	.272	.337	.472	102	1	9-2	.997	-2	99	77	O131C,D3	30	0.2
2005	Tor A	156	620	78	167	30	3	28	97	47-3	3	86	.269	.320	.463	101	0	8-3	**1.000**	-6	87	154	O155C,D2	0	-0.4
2006	Tor A★	154	611	91	185	40	5	32	106	54-0	3	90	.303	.357	.542	124	21	17-4	.988	-10	91	56	O150C,D4	0	1.5
Total	8	821	3239	478	933	200	19	141	501	230-7	19	457	.288	.336	.492	110	41	53-15	.993	-35	92	97	O813(0/797/16),D9	30	2.1
WELSH, JIMMY	James Daniel; B10.9.1902 Denver CO; D10.30.1970 Oakland CA; BL/TR/6´1″/174; d4.14																								
1925	Bos N	122	484	69	151	25	8	7	63	20	8	24	.312	.350	.440	110	6	7-4	.960	5	93	157	O116(7/1/109),2b3	—	0.1
1926	Bos N	134	490	69	136	18	11	3	57	33	8	28	.278	.333	.378	100	-1	6	.965	8	105	129	O129R	—	-0.3
1927	Bos N	131	497	72	143	26	7	9	54	23	8	27	.288	.330	.423	109	4	11	.969	8	101	161	O129(1/121/11)/1	—	0.6
1928	NY N	124	476	77	146	22	5	9	54	29	8	30	.307	.357	.431	104	2	4	.981	-3	98	76	O117(6/110/1)	—	-0.6
1929	NY N	38	129	25	32	7	0	2	8	9	7	3	.248	.331	.349	69	-6	3	.940	-3	65	181	O35(30/7/0)	—	-1.1

YEAR	TM LG	G	AB	R	H	2B	3B	HR	RBI	BB-IB	HP	SO	AVG	OBP	SLG	AOPS	ABR	SB-CS	FA	FR	RNG	THR	GAMES AT POSITION	DL	BFW
	Bos N	53	186	24	54	8	7	2	16	13	4	9	.290	.350	.441	98	-1	1	.979	5	116	110	O51(1/49/2)	—	0.1
	Year	91	315	49	86	15	7	4	24	22	**11**	12	.273	.342	.403	86	-8	4	.970	2	98	135	O86(31/56/2)	—	-1.0
1930	Bos N	113	422	51	116	21	9	3	36	29	4	23	.275	.327	.389	75	-18	5	.980	7	113	90	O110C	—	-1.4
Total	6	715	2684	387	778	127	47	35	288	156	47	144	.290	.340	.411	98	-14	37-4	.971	26	101	126	O687(45/398/252),2b3/1	—	-2.6
Wendell, Lew	Lewis Charles; B3.22.1892 New York NY; D7.11.1953 Brooklyn NY; BR/TR/5´11˝/178; d6.10																								
1915	NY N	20	36	0	8	1	1	0	5	2	0	7	.222	.263	.306	76	-1	0	.920	-4	*76*	*115*	C18	—	-0.5
1916	NY N	2	2	0	0	0	0	0	0	0	0	2	.000	.000	.000	-99	0	0	ø	0	—	—	/H	—	-0.1
1924	Phi N	21	32	3	8	1	0	0	2	3	0	5	.250	.314	.281	54	-2	0-0	1.000	-1	*93*	*77*	C17	—	-0.2
1925	Phi N	18	26	0	2	0	0	0	3	1	0	3	.077	.111	.077	-47	-6	0-0	.909	-1	*99*	*92*	C9	—	-0.6
1926	Phi N	1	4	0	0	0	0	0	0	0	0	0	.000	.000	.000	-95	-1	0	.333	-1	*0*	*319*	/C	—	-0.2
Total	5	62	100	3	18	2	1	0	10	6	0	17	.180	.226	.220	23	-10	0-0	.925	-6	*84*	*104*	C45	—	-1.6
Wentz, Jack	John George (b John George Wernz); B3.4.1863 Louisville KY; D9.14.1907 Louisville KY; BR/TR/5´10.5˝/175; d4.15																								
1891	Lou AA	1	4	0	1	0	0	0	0	0	0	0	.250	.250	.250	44	0	0	.667	-1	59	0	/2	—	-0.1
Wentzel, Stan	Stanley Aaron; B1.13.1917 Lorane PA; D11.28.1991 St.Lawrence PA; BR/TR/6´1˝/200; d9.23																								
1945	Bos N	4	19	3	4	0	1	0	6	0	0	3	.211	.211	.316	45	-2	1	1.000	-1	80	0	O4C	0	-0.2
Wera, Julie	Julian Valentine; B2.9.1902 Winona MN; D12.12.1975 Rochester MN; BR/TR/5´8˝/164; d4.14																								
1927	NY A	38	42	7	10	3	0	1	8	1	1	5	.238	.273	.381	70	-2	0-0	1.000	0	86	0	3b19	—	-0.1
1929	NY A	5	12	1	5	0	0	0	2	1	0	1	.417	.462	.417	137	1	0-0	1.000	-0	114	0	3b4	—	0.1
Total	2	43	54	8	15	3	0	1	10	2	1	6	.278	.316	.389	85	-1	0-0	1.000	-0	92	0	3b23	—	0.0
Werber, Billy	William Murray; B6.20.1908 Berwyn MD; BR/TR/5´10˝/170; d6.25; Col Duke																								
1930	NY A	4	14	5	4	0	0	0	2	3	0	1	.286	.412	.286	84	0	0-0	.955	0	82	133	S3/3	—	0.0
1933	NY A	3	2	0	0	0	0	0	0	0	0	0	.000	.000	.000	-99	-1	0-0	ø	-0	0	0	/3	—	-0.1
	Bos A	108	425	64	110	30	6	3	39	33	0	39	.259	.312	.379	83	-11	15-5	.910	-14	90	90	S71,3b38,2b2	—	-1.7
	Year	111	427	64	110	30	6	3	39	33	0	39	.258	.311	.377	82	-12	15-5	.910	-14	90	90	S71,3b39,2b2	—	-1.8
1934	Bos A	152	623	129	200	41	10	11	67	77	1	37	.321	.397	.472	115	15	**40**-15	.941	17	**122**	97	3b130,S22	—	3.9
1935	Bos A	124	462	84	118	30	3	14	61	69	4	41	.255	.357	.424	95	-3	**29**-7	.942	14	109	118	3b123	—	1.8
1936	Bos A	145	535	89	147	29	6	10	67	89	4	37	.275	.382	.407	90	-7	23-13	.935	-11	81	104	3b101,O45(38/0/7)/2	—	-1.5
1937	Phi A	128	493	85	144	31	4	7	70	74	1	39	.292	.386	.414	103	5	**35**-13	.958	4	104	99	3b125,O3(1/2/0)	—	1.5
1938	Phi A	134	499	92	129	22	7	11	69	93	2	37	.259	.377	.397	96	0	19-15	.935	4	100	82	3b134	—	0.6
1939	†Cin N	147	599	**115**	173	35	5	5	57	91	6	46	.289	.388	.389	109	12	15	.933	9	104	**128**	3b147	—	2.7
1940	†Cin N	143	584	105	162	35	5	12	48	68	8	40	.277	.361	.416	113	12	16	**.962**	6	107	**126**	3b143	—	2.3
1941	Cin N	109	418	56	100	9	2	4	46	53	2	24	.239	.328	.299	77	-12	14	.959	10	108	**150**	3b107	0	0.2
1942	NY N	98	370	51	76	9	2	1	13	51	4	22	.205	.308	.249	64	-15	9	.927	13	126	88	3b93	0	0.0
Total	11	1295	5024	875	1363	271	50	78	539	701	32	363	.271	.364	.392	97	-5	215-68	.944	50	106	111	3b1143,S96,O48(39/2/7),2b3	0	9.7
Werden, Perry	Percival Wheritt; B7.21.1865 St.Louis MO; D1.9.1934 Minneapolis MN; BR/TR/6´2˝/220; d4.24; ▲																								
1884	StL U	18	76	7	18	2	0	0	—	2	—	—	.237	.256	.263	56	-6	—	.893	0	113	128	P16,O6(4/1/1)	—	-0.1
1888	Was N	3	10	0	3	0	0	0	2	1	0	4	.300	.364	.300	121	0	0	.857	-0	0	0	O3L	—	0.0
1890	Tol AA	128	498	113	147	22	**20**	6	72	78	13	—	.295	.404	.456	149	32	59	.972	5	121	93	1b124,O5(0/4/1)	—	2.3
1891	Bal AA	**139**	552	102	160	20	18	6	104	52	11	59	.290	.363	.424	124	15	46	.980	1	101	102	1b139	—	0.2
1892	StL N	149	598	73	154	22	6	8	84	59	4	52	.258	.328	.355	112	9	20	.982	12	131	91	1b149	—	1.9
1893	StL N	125	500	73	138	22	**29**	1	94	49	7	25	.276	.349	.442	109	3	11	.968	2	118	99	1b124/rf	—	0.4
1897	Lou N	133	512	76	154	21	14	5	83	41	12	—	.301	.366	.426	112	9	15	.984	19	**163**	94	1b133	—	2.3
Total	7	695	2746	444	774	109	87	26	439	282	47	140	.282	.359	.413	119	62	151	.978	40	127	96	1b669,P16,O15(7/5/3)	—	7.0
Werhas, Johnny	John Charles "Peaches"; B2.7.1938 Highland Park MI; BR/TR/6´2˝/200; d4.14; Col USC																								
1964	LA N	29	83	6	16	2	1	0	8	13-0	0	12	.193	.296	.241	59	-4	0-0	.952	-0	91	100	3b28	0	-0.5
1965	LA N	4	3	1	0	0	0	0	0	1-0	0	2	.000	.250	.000	-24	0	0-0	1.000	-0	0	0	/1	0	-0.1
1967	LA N	7	7	0	1	0	0	0	0	0-0	0	3	.143	.143	.143	-20	-1	0-0	ø	0	—	—	/H	0	-0.1
	Cal A	49	75	8	12	1	1	2	6	10-0	1	22	.160	.264	.280	64	-3	0-0	.963	-0	98	0	3b30,1b4/lf	0	-0.4
Total	3	89	168	15	29	3	2	2	14	24-0	1	39	.173	.276	.250	57	-8	0-0	.956	-0	94	62	3b58,1b5/lf	0	-1.1
Werner, Don	Donald Paul; B3.8.1953 Appleton WI; BR/TR/6´1˝/(170–185); [CinN71 5/120]; d9.2																								
1975	Cin N	7	8	0	1	0	0	0	0	0-0	1	0	.125	.222	.125	-2	-1	0-0	.923	-2	31	0	C7	0	-0.3
1976	Cin N	3	4	0	2	1	0	0	1	1-0	0	1	.500	.600	.750	274	1	0-0	1.000	-0	54	0	C3	0	0.1
1977	Cin N	10	23	3	4	0	0	2	4	2-1	0	3	.174	.231	.435	75	-1	0-1	1.000	0	88	68	C10	0	-0.1
1978	Cin N	50	113	7	17	2	1	0	11	14-2	1	30	.150	.242	.186	23	-12	1-0	.987	-4	81	87	C49	0	-1.5
1980	Cin N	24	64	2	11	2	0	0	5	7-0	1	10	.172	.260	.203	33	-6	1-0	.962	-5	64	46	C24	0	-1.0
1981	Tex A	2	8	1	2	0	0	0	0	0-0	0	2	.250	.250	.250	47	-1	0-1	ø	0	—	—	D2	0	-0.1
1982	Tex A	22	59	4	12	2	0	0	3	3-0	0	7	.203	.242	.237	34	-5	0-0	.980	-1	120	30	C22	0	-0.6
Total	7	118	279	17	49	7	1	2	24	27-3	3	53	.176	.251	.229	36	-25	2-2	.979	-12	84	59	C115,D2	0	-3.5
Werrick, Joe	Joseph Abraham; B10.25.1861 St.Paul MN; D5.10.1943 St.Peter MN; BR/TR/5´9˝/151; d9.27																								
1884	StP U	**9**	27	3	2	0	0	0	—	1	—	—	.074	.107	.074	-81	-7	—	.756	1	112	0	S9	—	-0.5
1886	Lou AA	136	561	75	140	20	14	3	62	33	2	—	.250	.294	.351	96	-6	19	.853	-2	94	47	3b136	—	-0.5
1887	Lou AA	136	533	90	152	21	13	7	99	38	3	—	.285	.336	.413	106	2	49	.831	-2	103	61	3b136	—	0.2
1888	Lou AA	111	413	49	89	12	7	0	51	30	3	—	.215	.274	.278	79	-10	15	.811	-15	92	69	3b89,S11,2b8,O3L	—	-2.1
Total	4	392	1534	217	383	53	34	10	212	102	8	—	.250	.300	.348	94	-21	83	.834	-18	97	58	3b361,S20,2b8,O3L	—	-2.9
Wert, Don	Donald Ralph; B7.29.1938 Strasburg PA; BR/TR/5´9˝/(160–165); d5.11; Col Franklin & Marshall																								
1963	Det A	78	251	31	65	6	2	7	25	24-2	2	51	.259	.326	.382	95	-2	3-3	.957	5	111	75	3b47,2b21,S8	0	0.5
1964	Det A	148	525	63	135	18	5	9	55	50-5	6	74	.257	.325	.362	91	-6	3-4	.965	2	101	121	3b142,S4	0	-0.6
1965	Det A	**162**	609	81	159	22	2	12	54	73-4	3	71	.261	.341	.363	100	1	5-6	**.976**	3	96	105	3b161,S3/2	0	0.3
1966	Det A	150	559	56	150	20	2	11	70	64-3	2	69	.268	.342	.370	103	4	6-3	.972	-19	83	74	3b150	0	-1.7
1967	Det A	142	534	60	137	23	2	6	40	44-2	7	59	.257	.320	.341	93	-4	1-1	.978	2	98	100	3b140/S	0	-0.2
1968	†Det A★	150	536	44	107	15	1	12	37	37-7	5	79	.200	.258	.299	66	-23	0-3	.966	-6	92	90	3b150,S2	0	-3.5
1969	Det A	132	423	46	95	11	1	14	50	49-6	1	60	.225	.303	.355	81	-11	3-1	.966	1	97	81	3b129	0	-1.1
1970	Det A	128	363	34	79	13	0	6	33	44-7	4	56	.218	.307	.303	69	-15	1-3	.953	-11	83	88	3b117,2b2	0	-2.8
1971	Was A	20	40	2	2	1	0	0	2	4-1	1	10	.050	.156	.075	-35	-7	0-0	1.000	-4	92	30	S7,3b7/2	15	-1.1
Total	9	1110	3840	417	929	129	15	77	366	389-37	31	529	.242	.314	.343	87	-63	22-24	.968	-27	94	94	3b1043,S25,2b25	15	-10.2
Werth, Dennis	Dennis Dean; B12.29.1952 Lincoln IL; BR/TR/6´1˝/(200–201); [NYA74 19/437]; d9.17; s–Jayson; Col Southern Illinois Edwardsville																								
1979	NY A	3	4	1	1	0	0	0	0	0-0	0	0	.250	.250	.250	36	0	0-0	1.000	0	329	0	/1	0	0.0
1980	NY A	39	65	15	20	3	0	3	12	12-0	0	19	.308	.416	.492	150	5	0-1	1.000	-1	63	126	1b12,O8(3/0/5)/C3D	0	0.3
1981	NY A	34	55	7	6	1	0	0	1	12-2	0	12	.109	.269	.127	17	-5	1-0	1.000	2	145	86	1b19,O8(4/0/4),C3,D4	77	-0.5
1982	KC A	41	15	5	2	0	0	0	2	4-0	0	2	.133	.316	.133	29	-1	0-0	.990	1	169	135	1b35,C2	0	-0.1
Total	4	117	139	28	29	4	0	3	15	28-2	0	33	.209	.341	.302	82	-1	1-1	.996	2	132	112	1b67,O16(7/0/9),D12,C6/3	77	-0.3
Werth, Jayson	Jayson Richard Gowan; B5.20.1979 Springfield IL; BR/TR/6´5˝/(210–215); [BalA97 1/22]; d9.1; f–Dennis gf–John Schofield; [DL 2006 LA N 182]																								
2002	Tor A	15	46	4	12	2	1	0	6	6-0	0	11	.261	.340	.348	82	-1	1-0	1.000	1	117	118	O15(4/1/10)	0	0.0
2003	Tor A	26	48	7	10	4	0	2	10	3-0	0	22	.208	.255	.417	70	-2	1-0	1.000	1	108	144	O20(0/1/19),D3	12	-0.2
2004	†LA N	89	290	56	76	11	3	16	47	30-0	4	85	.262	.338	.486	111	4	4-1	.974	3	108	145	O79(65/6/14)/D	59	0.5
2005	LA N	102	337	46	79	22	2	7	43	48-2	6	114	.234	.338	.374	86	-5	11-2	.987	6	113	112	O101(64/30/43)/D	67	0.0
Total	4	232	721	113	177	39	6	25	106	87-2	10	232	.245	.333	.420	95	-4	17-3	.984	11	111	127	O215(133/38/86),D5	320	0.3
Wertz, Del	Dwight Lyman Moody; B10.11.1888 Canton OH; D5.16.1958 Sarasota FL; BR/TR/5´10˝/160; d5.23; Col Case Western Reserve																								
1914	Buf F	3	0	1	0	0	0	0	0	0	0	0	ø	ø	ø	ø	0	0	1.000	-0	0	0	/S	—	0.0

YEAR	TM LG	G	AB	R	H	2B	3B	HR	RBI	BB-IB	HP	SO	AVG	OBP	SLG	AOPS	ABR	SB-CS	FA	FR	RNG	THR	GAMES AT POSITION	DL	BFW
Wertz, Vic	Victor Woodrow; B2.9.1925 York PA; D7.7.1983 Detroit MI; BL/TR/6´0˝/(186–203); d4.15																								
1947	Det A	102	333	60	96	22	4	6	44	47	0	66	.288	.376	.432	121	11	2-0	.965	-2	95	106	O83(38/2/43)	0	0.5
1948	Det A	119	391	49	97	19	9	7	67	48	3	70	.248	.335	.396	92	-6	0-0	.954	1	96	158	O98(64/1/36)	0	-1.0
1949	Det A★	**155**	608	96	185	26	6	20	133	80	0	61	.304	.385	.465	124	20	2-3	.981	-2	98	95	O155R	0	1.3
1950	Det A	149	559	99	172	37	4	27	123	91	4	55	.308	.408	.533	135	31	0-1	.967	-11	95	39	O145R	0	1.4
1951	Det A★	138	501	86	143	24	4	27	94	78	1	61	.285	.383	.511	139	28	0-3	.989	0	103	79	O131R	0	2.2
1952	Det A☆	85	285	46	70	15	3	17	51	46	1	44	.246	.352	.498	134	13	1-0	.986	2	103	136	O79R	0	1.3
	StL A	37	130	22	45	5	0	6	19	23	0	20	.346	.444	.523	164	12	0-0	.955	-3	103	0	O36R	0	0.9
	Year	122	415	68	115	20	3	23	70	69	1	64	.277	.381	.506	143	25	1-0	.976	-0	103	93	O115R	0	2.2
1953	StL A	128	440	61	118	18	6	19	70	72	4	44	.268	.376	.466	124	16	1-4	.974	4	103	134	O121(0/1/120)	0	1.4
1954	Bal A	29	94	5	19	1	0	1	13	11	0	17	.202	.283	.245	50	-7	0-0	.963	3	103	277	O27R	0	-0.5
	†Cle A	94	295	33	81	14	2	14	48	34	0	40	.275	.344	.478	123	8	0-2	.989	1	109	108	1b83,O5(2/0/3)	0	0.5
	Year	123	389	38	100	15	2	15	61	45	0	57	.257	.330	.422	106	2	0-2	.989	4	109	108	1b83,O32(2/0/30)	0	0.0
1955	Cle A	74	257	30	65	11	2	14	55	32-3	1	33	.253	.332	.475	112	4	1-1	.984	-2	86	100	1b63,O9(1/0/8)	0	-0.2
1956	Cle A	136	481	65	127	22	0	32	106	75-10	5	87	.264	.364	.509	127	19	0-0	.991	1	98	95	1b133	0	1.2
1957	Cle A★	144	515	84	145	21	0	28	105	78-6	2	88	.282	.371	.485	136	27	2-3	.988	0	101	92	1b139	0	1.9
1958	Cle A	25	43	5	12	1	0	3	12	5-0	0	7	.279	.354	.512	139	2	0-0	.980	0	131	82	1b8	98	0.2
1959	Bos A	94	247	38	68	13	0	7	49	22-5	2	32	.275	.337	.413	101	1	0-0	.992	2	115	94	1b64	0	0.0
1960	Bos A	131	443	45	125	22	0	19	103	37-4	1	54	.282	.335	.460	110	6	0-2	.987	3	110	86	1b117	0	0.2
1961	Bos A	99	317	33	83	16	2	11	60	38-3	2	43	.262	.339	.429	103	2	0-0	.991	4	117	95	1b86	0	0.1
	Det A	8	6	0	1	0	0	0	1	0-0	0	1	.167	.167	.167	-10	-1	0-0	ø	0	—	—	/H	0	-0.1
	Year	107	323	33	84	16	2	11	61	38-3	2	44	.260	.336	.424	101	1	0-0	.991	4	117	95	1b86	0	0.0
1962	Det A	74	105	7	34	2	0	5	18	5-0	1	13	.324	.357	.486	121	3	0-0	.988	0	100	48	1b16	0	0.2
1963	Det A	6	5	0	0	0	0	0	0	0-0	0	1	.000	.000	.000	-97	-1	0-0	ø	0	—	—	/H	0	-0.1
	Min A	35	44	3	6	0	0	3	7	6-2	0	5	.136	.240	.341	59	-3	0-0	1.000	1	149	53	1b6	0	-0.2
	Year	41	49	3	6	0	0	3	7	6-2	0	6	.122	.218	.306	44	-4	0-0	1.000	1	149	53	1b6	0	-0.3
Total	17	1862	6099	867	1692	289	42	266	1178	828-33	27	842	.277	.364	.469	121	185	9-19	.973	4	99	102	O889(105/4/783),1b715	98	11.2
Wessinger, Jim	James Michael; B9.25.1955 Utica NY; BR/TR/5´10˝/165; [AtlN76 6/123]; d8.4; Col LeMoyne (NY)																								
1979	Atl N	10	7	2	0	0	0	0	0	1-0	0	4	.000	.125	.000	-59	-2	0-0	.833	-1	66	0	2b2	0	-0.3
Wesson, Barry	Barry Jarvis; B4.6.1977 Tupelo MS; BR/TR/6´2˝/195; [HouN95 14/389]; d7.15																								
2002	Hou N	15	20	1	4	0	1	0	1	1-0	0	5	.200	.238	.300	38	-2	0-0	1.000	-1	81	0	O15(3/9/3)	0	-0.3
2003	Ana A	10	11	2	2	0	0	1	3	0-0	0	4	.182	.182	.455	62	-1	1-0	1.000	0	130	0	O9(5/0/4)/D	0	0.0
Total	2	25	31	3	6	0	1	1	4	1-0	0	9	.194	.219	.355	46	-3	1-0	1.000	-1	98	0	O24(8/9/7)/D	0	-0.3
West, Max	Max Edward; B11.28.1916 Dexter MO; D12.31.2003 Sierra Madre CA; BL/TR/6´1.5˝/182; d4.19; Mil 1943–45																								
1938	Bos N	123	418	47	98	16	5	10	63	38	1	38	.234	.300	.368	92	-6	5	.986	-4	94	70	O109(75/0/36),1b7	—	-1.7
1939	Bos N	130	449	67	128	26	6	19	82	51	5	55	.285	.364	.497	139	24	1	.974	1	104	80	O124(44/46/54)	—	1.9
1940	Bos N★	139	524	72	137	27	5	7	72	65	1	54	.261	.344	.372	103	4	2	.975	5	98	199	O102(4/59/49),1b36	—	0.1
1941	Bos N	138	484	63	134	28	4	12	68	72	2	68	.277	.373	.426	130	21	5	.981	5	101	135	O132(126/5/5)	0	2.0
1942	Bos N	134	452	54	115	22	0	16	56	68	2	59	.254	.354	.409	126	16	4	.991	-1	97	108	1b85,O50(36/2/13)	0	0.6
1946	Bos N	1	1	0	0	0	0	0	0	0	0	1	.000	.000	.000	-99	0	0	1.000	-0	0	0	/1	0	0.0
	Cin N	72	202	16	43	13	0	5	18	32	1	36	.213	.323	.351	95	-1	1	.952	-3	86	112	O58(54/3/1)	0	-0.8
	Year	73	203	16	43	13	0	5	18	32	1	37	.212	.322	.350	94	-1	1	.952	-3	86	112	O58(54/3/1)/1	0	-0.8
1948	Pit N	87	146	19	26	4	0	8	21	27	1	29	.178	.310	.370	82	-4	1	.991	1	123	78	1b32,O16(3/0/13)	0	-0.4
Total	7	824	2676	338	681	136	20	77	380	353	13	340	.254	.344	.407	114	54	19	.975	4	98	117	O591(342/115/171),1b161	0	1.7
West, Buck	Milton Douglas; B8.29.1860 Spring Mill OH; D1.13.1929 Mansfield OH; BL/TR/5´10˝/200; d8.24																								
1884	Cin AA	33	131	20	32	2	8	1	15	2	0	—	.244	.256	.405	107	0	—	.825	-4	19	0	O33C	—	-0.5
1890	Cle N	37	151	20	37	6	1	2	29	7	1	11	.245	.283	.338	82	-4	4	.831	-1	147	73	O37(0/4/33)	—	-0.5
Total	2	70	282	40	69	8	9	3	44	9	1	11	.245	.271	.369	94	-4	4	.828	-5	92	42	O70(0/37/33)	—	-1.0
West, Dick	Richard Thomas; B11.24.1915 Louisville KY; D3.13.1996 Fort Wayne IN; BR/TR/6´2˝/180; d9.28; Mil 1944–45; Col Georgia Southwestern																								
1938	Cin N	1	1	0	0	0	0	0	0	0	0	0	.000	.000	.000	-99	0	0	ø	0	—	—	/H	—	0.0
1939	Cin N	8	19	1	4	0	0	0	4	1	0	4	.211	.250	.211	25	-2	0	1.000	-0	90	0	O5L/C	—	-0.3
1940	Cin N	7	28	4	11	2	0	1	6	0	0	2	.393	.393	.571	161	2	1	1.000	-1	*102*	*60*	C7	—	0.1
1941	Cin N	67	172	15	37	5	2	1	17	6	1	23	.215	.246	.285	49	-12	4	.970	-4	*77*	*84*	C64	0	-1.4
1942	Cin N	33	79	9	14	3	0	1	8	5	0	13	.177	.226	.253	40	-6	1	.989	1	*92*	*150*	C17,O6L	0	-0.4
1943	Cin N	3	0	1	0	0	0	0	0	0	0	0	ø	ø	ø	ø	0	0	ø	0	—	—	/R	0	0.0
Total	6	119	299	30	66	10	2	3	35	12	1	42	.221	.253	.298	55	-18	6	.977	-4	*82*	*97*	C89,O11L	0	-2.0
West, Sam	Samuel Filmore; B10.5.1904 Longview TX; D11.23.1985 Lubbock TX; BL/TL/5´11˝/165; d4.17; Mil 1943–45; C3																								
1927	Was A	38	67	9	16	4	1	0	6	8	0	8	.239	.320	.328	69	-3	1-0	.939	1	95	223	O18(5/8/5)	—	-0.3
1928	Was A	125	378	59	114	30	7	3	40	20	1	23	.302	.338	.442	104	1	5-6	**.996**	2	97	138	O116(53/60/6)	—	-0.3
1929	Was A	142	510	60	136	16	8	3	75	45	0	41	.267	.326	.347	73	-22	10-8	.978	13	103	**178**	O139(4/136/0)	—	-1.4
1930	Was A	120	411	75	135	22	10	6	67	37	1	34	.328	.385	.474	116	10	5-5	.972	3	103	99	O118(1/117/0)	—	0.7
1931	Was A	132	526	77	175	43	13	3	91	30	0	37	.333	.369	.481	121	15	6-8	.990	14	**115**	128	O127C	—	2.2
1932	Was A	146	554	88	159	27	12	6	83	48	1	57	.287	.345	.412	96	-4	4-5	.979	15	115	126	O143C	—	0.6
1933	StL A★	133	517	93	155	25	12	11	48	59	1	49	.300	.373	.458	112	8	10-8	.988	5	102	157	O127C	—	0.9
1934	StL A★	122	482	90	157	22	10	9	55	62	0	55	.326	.403	.469	115	11	3-5	.972	5	101	**151**	O120C	—	1.1
1935	StL A☆	138	527	93	158	37	4	10	70	75	1	46	.300	.388	.442	109	9	1-6	**.989**	11	**118**	65	O135C	—	1.4
1936	StL A	152	533	78	148	26	4	7	70	94	0	70	.278	.386	.381	87	-8	2-0	.983	6	110	77	O148C	—	-0.4
1937	StL A★	122	457	68	150	37	4	7	58	46	0	28	.328	.390	.473	115	12	1-1	.987	9	103	169	O105C	—	1.7
1938	StL A	44	165	17	51	8	2	1	27	14	0	9	.309	.363	.400	91	-2	1-0	.971	-3	102	0	O41C	—	-0.5
	Was A	92	344	51	104	19	5	5	47	33	0	21	.302	.363	.430	105	2	1-1	.983	-3	98	50	O85(1/84/0)	—	-0.3
	Year	136	509	68	155	27	7	6	74	47	0	30	.305	.363	.420	100	0	2-1	.979	-6	99	34	O126(1/125/0)	—	-0.8
1939	Was A	115	390	52	110	20	8	3	52	67	0	29	.282	.387	.397	109	8	1-1	.992	1	104	98	O89(23/55/11),1b17	—	0.4
1940	Was A	57	99	7	25	6	1	1	18	16	0	13	.253	.357	.364	93	0	0-2	.990	0	100	127	1b12,O9(0/3/6)	—	-0.2
1941	Was A	26	37	3	10	0	0	0	6	11	0	2	.270	.438	.270	95	1	1-0	1.000	0	116	0	O8(4/1/3)	0	0.1
1942	Chi A	49	151	14	35	5	0	0	25	31	0	18	.232	.363	.265	80	-2	2-0	.983	-1	101	33	O45(1/44/0)	0	-0.4
Total	16	1753	6148	934	1838	347	101	75	838	696	5	540	.299	.371	.425	103	36	54-56	.983	79	106	115	O1573(92/1454/31),1b29	0	5.3
West, Max	Walter Maxwell; B7.14.1904 Sunset TX; D4.25.1971 Houston TX; BR/TR/5´11˝/165; d9.18; Col North Texas																								
1928	Bro N	7	21	4	6	1	1	0	1	4	0	1	.286	.400	.429	118	1	0	.882	1	78	544	O6(1/4/1)	—	0.1
1929	Bro N	5	8	1	2	1	0	0	1	1	0	0	.250	.333	.375	77	0	0	1.000	-0	68	0	O2(1/1/0)	—	-0.1
Total	2	12	29	5	8	2	1	0	2	5	0	1	.276	.382	.414	107	1	0	.895	1	76	453	O8(2/5/1)	—	0.0
West, Billy	William O.; B8.15.1853 Williamsburg NY; D10.27.1928 Richmond Hill NY; d5.22																								
1874	Atl NA	9	35	4	8	1	0	0	2	1	—	2	.229	.250	.257	71	-1	0-0	.707	-2	139	75	2b9/CS	—	-0.2
1876	NY N	1	4	0	0	0	0	0	0	0	—	0	.000	.000	.000	-99	-1	—	1.000	0	118	281	/2	—	-0.1
Westerberg, Oscar	Oscar William; B7.8.1882 Alameda CA; D4.17.1909 Alameda CA; BB/TR/6´0˝/186; d9.5; Col St. Marys (CA)																								
1907	Bos N	2	6	0	2	0	0	0	1	1	0	—	.333	.429	.333	139	0	0	1.000	-0	72	199	S2	—	0.0
Westlake, Jim	James Patrick; B7.3.1930 Sacramento CA; D1.3.2003 Sacramento CA; BL/TL/6´1˝/190; d4.16; b–Wally																								
1955	Phi N	1	1	0	0	0	0	0	0	0-0	0	1	.000	.000	.000	-99	0	0-0	ø	0	—	—	/H	0	0.0
Westlake, Wally	Waldon Thomas; B11.8.1920 Gridley CA; BR/TR/6´0˝/(186–196); d4.15; b–Jim																								
1947	Pit N	112	407	59	111	17	4	17	69	27	4	63	.273	.324	.459	103	0	5	.988	3	109	89	O109(0/12/97)	0	0.0
1948	Pit N	132	428	78	122	10	6	17	65	46	4	40	.285	.360	.456	117	9	2	.976	-2	98	91	O125(1/67/57)	0	0.4
1949	Pit N	147	525	77	148	24	8	23	104	45	6	69	.282	.345	.490	118	12	6	.982	3	104	103	O143(0/51/92)	0	1.0
1950	Pit N	139	477	69	136	15	6	24	95	48	7	78	.285	.359	.493	118	11	1	**.991**	1	108	40	O123(5/97/26)	0	0.8
1951	Pit N	50	181	28	51	4	0	16	45	9	2	26	.282	.323	.569	131	6	0-1	.908	5	120	136	3b34,O11(10/1/0)	0	1.0
	StL N★	73	267	36	68	8	5	6	39	24	4	42	.255	.325	.390	91	-4	1-2	.982	-1	96	113	O68(11/29/28)	0	-0.8

YEAR	TM LG	G	AB	R	H	2B	3B	HR	RBI	BB-IB	HP	SO	AVG	OBP	SLG	AOPS	ABR	SB-CS	FA	FR	RNG	THR	GAMES AT POSITION	DL	BFW
	Year	123	448	64	119	12	5	22	84	33	6	68	.266	.324	.462	107	2	1-3	.984	4	95	129	O79(21/30/28),3b34	0	0.2
1952	StL N	21	74	7	16	3	0	0	10	8	0	11	.216	.293	.257	53	-4	1-1	1.000	3	122	161	O15C	0	-0.2
	Cin N	59	183	29	37	4	0	3	14	31	2	29	.202	.324	.273	67	-7	0-2	.992	-1	98	98	O56(5/43/10)	0	-1.1
	Year	80	257	36	53	7	0	3	24	39	2	40	.206	.315	.268	63	-12	1-3	.995	2	100	245	O71(5/58/10)	0	-1.3
	Cle A	29	69	11	16	4	1	1	9	8	0	16	.232	.312	.362	93	-1	1-0	1.000	2	100	245	O28(12/4/20)	0	0.1
1953	Cle A	82	218	42	72	7	1	9	46	35	2	29	.330	.427	.495	153	18	2-0	.963	-2	99	59	O72(38/12/36)	0	1.3
1954	†Cle A	85	240	36	63	9	2	11	42	26	2	37	.262	.337	.454	114	4	0-1	.964	-4	97	23	O70(49/10/14)	0	-0.4
1955	Cle A	16	20	2	5	1	0	0	1	3-1	0	5	.250	.348	.300	73	-1	0-0	1.000	1	107	339	O7(4/3/0)	0	0.0
	Bal A	8	24	0	3	1	0	0	0	6-0	0	5	.125	.300	.167	30	-2	0-0	1.000	-1	76	0	O7(2/0/5)	0	-0.3
	Year	24	44	2	8	2	0	0	1	9-1	0	10	.182	.321	.227	49	-3	0-0	1.000	-0	90	151	O14(6/3/5)	0	-0.3
1956	Phi N	5	4	0	0	0	0	0	0	1-0	0	3	.000	.200	.000	-41	-1	0-0	ø	0	—	—	/H	0	-0.1
Total	10	958	3117	474	848	107	33	127	539	317-1	33	453	.272	.345	.450	111	40	19-7	.983	8	102	88	O834(137/344/385),3b34	0	1.7
Weston, Al	Alfred John; B12.11.1905 Lynn MA; D11.13.1997 San Diego CA; BR/TR/6´0˝/195; d7.7; Col Boston College																								
1929	Bos N	3	3	0	0	0	0	0	0	0	0	2	.000	.000	.000	-99	-1	0	ø	0	—	—	/H	—	-0.1
Westrum, Wes	Wesley Noreen; B11.28.1922 Clearbrook MN; D5.28.2002 Clearbrook MN; BR/TR/5´11˝/(185–190); d9.17; M5/C12																								
1947	NY N	6	12	1	5	1	0	0	2	0	0	2	.417	.417	.500	142	1	0	1.000	0	*0*	*202*	C2	0	0.1
1948	NY N	66	125	14	20	3	1	4	16	20	0	36	.160	.276	.296	54	-8	3	.981	5	*120*	*104*	C63	0	-0.1
1949	NY N	64	169	23	41	4	1	7	28	37	2	39	.243	.385	.402	111	4	1	.980	-0	*90*	*59*	C62	0	0.7
1950	NY N	140	437	68	103	13	3	23	71	92	2	73	.236	.371	.437	111	9	2	**.999**	14	***153***	*98*	C139	0	2.9
1951	†NY N	124	361	59	79	12	0	20	70	104	5	93	.219	.400	.418	119	16	1-0	.987	8	*142*	*123*	C122	0	3.0
1952	NY N☆	114	322	47	71	11	0	14	43	76	3	68	.220	.374	.385	110	8	1-2	.978	2	***182***	*88*	C112	0	1.5
1953	NY N☆	107	290	40	65	5	0	12	30	56	1	73	.224	.352	.366	86	-5	2-0	.982	5	*138*	*109*	C106/3	0	0.5
1954	†NY N	98	246	25	46	3	1	8	27	45	3	60	.187	.315	.305	63	-13	0-1	.985	10	*157*	*116*	C98	0	0.1
1955	NY N	69	137	11	29	1	0	4	18	24-3	1	18	.212	.327	.307	71	-5	0-1	.987	5	*130*	*105*	C68	0	0.2
1956	NY N	68	132	10	29	5	2	3	8	25-5	1	28	.220	.346	.356	91	-1	0-0	.982	8	*132*	*111*	C67	0	0.9
1957	NY N	63	91	4	15	1	0	1	2	10-1	1	24	.165	.255	.209	27	-9	0-1	.966	-8	88	131	C63	0	-1.6
Total	11	919	2322	302	503	59	8	96	315	489-9	19	514	.217	.356	.373	95	-3	10-5	.985	48	*141*	*105*	C902/3	0	8.2
Wetherby, Jeff	Jeffrey Barrett; B10.18.1963 Granada Hills CA; BL/TL/6´2˝/195; [AtlN85 21/536]; d6.7; Col USC																								
1989	Atl N	52	48	5	10	2	1	1	7	4-0	0	6	.208	.264	.354	75	-2	1-0	1.000	-0	100	0	O9(7/0/2)	0	-0.2
Wetzel, Dutch	Franklin Burton; B7.7.1893 Columbus IN; D3.5.1942 Hollywood CA; BR/TR/5´9.5˝/177; d9.15																								
1920	StL A	7	21	5	9	1	1	0	5	4	0	1	.429	.520	.571	183	3	0-1	.875	-0	96	121	O6(5/1/0)	—	0.2
1921	StL A	61	119	16	25	2	0	2	10	9	1	20	.210	.271	.277	38	-11	0-0	.981	0	115	35	O27(12/4/11)	—	-1.2
Total	2	68	140	21	34	3	1	2	15	13	1	21	.243	.312	.321	59	-8	0-1	.957	-0	111	54	O33(17/5/11)	—	-1.0
Whaley, Bill	William Carl; B2.10.1899 Indianapolis IN; D3.3.1943 Indianapolis IN; BR/TR/5´11˝/178; d4.18																								
1923	StL A	23	50	5	12	2	1	0	1	4	1	2	.240	.309	.320	62	-3	0-0	1.000	1	96	160	O13(4/9/0)	—	-0.3
Whaling, Bert	Albert James; B6.22.1888 Los Angeles CA; D1.21.1965 Los Angeles CA; BR/TR/6´0˝/185; d4.22																								
1913	Bos N	79	211	22	51	8	2	0	25	10	2	32	.242	.283	.299	65	-10	3-3	**.990**	1	101	101	C77	—	-0.4
1914	Bos N	60	172	18	36	7	0	0	12	21	2	28	.209	.303	.250	65	-6	2	.981	10	*142*	*106*	C59	—	0.9
1915	Bos N	72	190	10	42	6	2	0	13	8	3	38	.221	.264	.274	66	-8	0-1	.986	5	*144*	*82*	C69	—	0.1
Total	3	211	573	50	129	21	4	0	50	39	7	98	.225	.283	.276	65	-24	5-4	.986	15	*128*	*96*	C205	—	0.6
Wheat, Mack	McKinley Davis; B6.9.1893 Polo MO; D8.14.1979 Los Banos CA; BR/TR/5´11.5˝/167; d4.14; b–Zack																								
1915	Bro N	8	14	0	1	0	0	0	0	0	0	5	.071	.071	.071	-56	-3	0	.957	-1	*95*	*63*	C8	—	-0.3
1916	Bro N	2	2	0	0	0	0	0	0	0	0	1	.000	.000	.000	-97	0	0	1.000	-0	70	0	C2	—	-0.1
1917	Bro N	29	60	2	8	1	0	0	0	1	1	12	.133	.161	.150	-4	-7	1	.968	2	*108*	*130*	C18,O9(9/1/0)	—	-0.5
1918	Bro N	57	157	11	34	7	1	1	3	8	0	24	.217	.255	.293	67	-6	2	.966	-1	*87*	*109*	C38,O7(1/1/4)	—	-0.6
1919	Bro N	41	112	5	23	3	0	0	8	2	4	22	.205	.246	.232	43	-8	1	.944	-3	*86*	*100*	C38	—	-0.9
1920	Phi N	78	230	15	52	10	3	3	20	8	3	35	.226	.261	.335	67	-10	3-1	.961	2	*87*	*114*	C74	—	-0.2
1921	Phi N	10	27	1	5	2	1	0	4	0	2	3	.185	.241	.333	47	-2	0-0	.980	2	*90*	*119*	C9	—	0.0
Total	7	225	602	34	123	23	5	4	35	19	10	102	.204	.241	.279	52	-36	7-1	.961	0	*89*	*110*	C187,O16(10/2/4)	—	-2.6
Wheat, Zack	Zachary Davis "Buck"; B5.23.1888 Hamilton MO; D3.11.1972 Sedalia MO; BL/TR/5´10˝/170; d9.11; HF1959; b–Mack																								
1909	Bro N	26	102	15	31	7	3	0	4	6	0	—	.304	.343	.431	145	5	1	.952	1	126	105	O26(25/1/0)	—	0.4
1910	Bro N	**156**	606	78	172	36	15	2	55	47	6	80	.284	.341	.403	120	14	16	.962	5	105	99	O156L	—	0.9
1911	Bro N	140	534	55	153	26	13	5	76	29	7	58	.287	.332	.412	112	5	21	.955	-3	105	62	O136(135/1/0)	—	-0.4
1912	Bro N	123	453	70	138	28	7	8	65	39	6	40	.305	.367	.450	128	17	16	.968	1	108	70	O120L	—	1.2
1913	Bro N	138	535	64	161	28	10	7	58	25	2	45	.301	.335	.430	114	8	19-20	.978	8	**117**	69	O135L	—	0.7
1914	Bro N	145	533	66	170	26	9	9	89	47	3	50	.319	.377	.452	143	28	20	.962	15	**121**	118	O144L	—	3.8
1915	Bro N	146	528	64	136	15	12	5	66	52	5	42	.258	.330	.360	107	4	21-14	.953	9	**115**	101	O144L	—	0.7
1916	†Bro N	149	568	76	177	32	13	9	73	43	6	49	.312	.366	**.461**	149	**33**	19	.975	6	**114**	88	O149(149/1/0)	—	3.6
1917	Bro N	109	362	38	113	15	11	1	41	20	2	18	.312	.352	.423	133	13	5	.979	6	111	100	O98L	—	1.7
1918	Bro N	105	409	39	137	15	3	0	51	16	6	17	**.335**	.369	.386	131	15	9	.979	3	105	98	O105L	—	1.4
1919	Bro N	137	536	70	159	23	11	5	62	33	6	27	.297	.344	.409	123	14	15	.971	-3	108	51	O137L	—	0.6
1920	†Bro N	148	583	89	191	26	13	9	73	48	6	21	.328	.385	.463	138	29	8-10	.971	-4	100	63	O148L	—	1.8
1921	Bro N	148	568	91	182	31	10	14	85	44	3	19	.320	.372	.484	121	17	11-8	.965	-3	92	103	O148L	—	0.2
1922	Bro N	152	600	92	201	29	12	16	112	45	7	22	.335	.388	.503	129	25	9-6	**.991**	1	104	76	O152L	—	1.3
1923	Bro N	98	349	63	131	13	5	8	65	23	2	12	.375	.417	.510	148	23	3-3	.908	-8	86	57	O87(85/0/2)	—	0.8
1924	Bro N	141	566	92	212	41	8	14	97	49	4	18	.375	.428	.549	165	54	3-4	.965	4	106	97	O139L	—	4.5
1925	Bro N	150	616	125	221	42	14	14	103	45	1	22	.359	.403	.541	143	39	3-1	.962	-2	106	54	O149L	—	2.4
1926	Bro N	111	411	68	119	31	2	5	35	21	1	14	.290	.326	.411	99	-1	4	.955	1	105	99	O102L	—	-0.8
1927	Phi A	88	247	34	80	12	1	1	38	18	4	5	.324	.379	.393	95	-1	2-3	.983	-1	86	137	O62(57/2/3)	—	-0.7
Total	19	2410	9106	1289	2884	476	172	132	1248	650	77	559	.317	.367	.450	129	341	205-69	.966	34	107	84	O2337(2328/5/5)	—	24.1
Wheaton, Woody	Elwood Pierce; B10.3.1914 Philadelphia PA; D12.11.1995 Lancaster PA; BL/TL/5´8.5˝/160; d9.28; ▲																								
1943	Phi A	7	30	2	6	2	0	0	2	3	1	2	.200	.294	.267	65	-1	0-0	1.000	1	103	178	O7C	0	-0.1
1944	Phi A	30	59	1	11	2	0	0	5	5	0	3	.186	.250	.220	35	-5	1-2	1.000	0	56	0	P11,O8C	0	-0.4
Total	2	37	89	3	17	4	0	0	7	8	1	5	.191	.265	.236	45	-6	1-2	.981	1	103	192	O15C,P11	0	-0.5
Wheeler, Don	Donald Wesley "Scott"; B9.29.1922 Minneapolis MN; D12.10.2003 Bloomington MN; BR/TR/5´10˝/175; d4.23																								
1949	Chi A	67	192	17	46	9	2	1	22	27	0	19	.240	.333	.323	76	-6	2-0	.976	1	*88*	*125*	C58	0	-0.2
Wheeler, Ed	Edward Leroy; B6.15.1878 Sherman MI; D8.15.1960 Ft.Worth TX; BB/TR/5´10˝/160; d5.10																								
1902	Bro N	30	96	4	12	0	0	0	5	3	0	—	.125	.152	.125	-14	-13	1	.863	-6	74	0	3b11,2b10,S5	—	-2.0
Wheeler, Ed	Edward Raymond; B5.24.1915 Los Angeles CA; D8.4.1983 Centralia WA; BR/TR/5´9˝/160; d4.19; Col Loyola Marymount																								
1945	Cle A	46	72	12	14	2	0	0	2	8	0	13	.194	.275	.222	47	-5	1-1	.912	-6	56	0	3b14,S11,2b3	0	-1.1
Wheeler, George	George Harrison "Heavy"; B11.10.1881 Shelburn IN; D6.13.1918 Clinton IN; BL/TR/5´9.5˝/180; d7.27																								
1910	Cin N	3	3	0	0	0	0	0	0	0	0	2	.000	.000	.000	-99	-1	0	ø	0	—	—	/H	—	-0.1
Wheeler, Harry	Harry Eugene; B3.3.1858 Versailles IN; D10.9.1900 Cincinnati OH; BR/TR/5´11˝/165; d6.19; M1; ▲																								
1878	Pro N	7	27	7	4	0	0	0	1	2	—	15	.148	.207	.148	18	-1	—	.875	-2	39	0	P7	—	0.0
1879	Cin N	1	3	0	0	0	0	0	0	0	—	2	.000	.000	.000	-99	-1	—	1.000	-0	0	0	/rfP	—	-0.1
1880	Cle N	1	4	0	1	0	0	0	0	0	—	0	.250	.250	.250	72	0	—	1.000	-0	0	0	/lf	—	0.0
	Cin N	17	65	1	6	2	0	0	2	0	—	15	.092	.092	.123	-28	-8	—	.750	1	116	116	O17(16/1/0)	—	-0.9
	Year	18	69	1	7	2	0	0	2	0	—	15	.101	.101	.130	-22	-8	—	.759	0	107	107	O18(17/1/0)	—	-0.9
1882	Cin AA	76	344	59	86	11	11	1	29	7	—	—	.250	.265	.355	102	-1	—	.808	-7	72	76	O64R,1b12,P4	—	-0.9
1883	Col AA	82	371	42	84	6	7	0	—	6	—	—	.226	.239	.280	72	-11	—	.803	-2	83	48	O82L/2P	—	-1.3
1884	StL AA	5	19	0	5	2	0	0	—	1	0	—	.263	.300	.368	113	0	—	.600	-2	0	0	O5(4/1/0)	—	-0.1
	KC U	14	62	11	16	1	0	0	—	3	—	—	.258	.292	.274	84	-3	—	.769	-1	27	0	O13(12/0/1)/PM	—	-0.4

YEAR	TM LG	G	AB	R	H	2B	3B	HR	RBI	BB-IB	HP	SO	AVG	OBP	SLG	AOPS	ABR	SB-CS	FA	FR	RNG	THR	GAMES AT POSITION	DL	BFW
	CP U	37	158	29	36	5	3	1	—	4	—	—	.228	.247	.316	70	-11	—	.774	-5	35	0	O37C	—	-1.6
	Bal U	17	69	3	18	2	0	0	—	0	—	—	.261	.261	.290	61	-5	—	.815	-1	99	0	O17(0/1/16)	—	-0.6
	Year	68	289	43	70	8	3	1	—	7	—	—	.242	.260	.301	70	-20	—	.781	-7	49	0	O67(12/38/17)/P	—	-2.6
Total	6	257	1122	152	256	29	21	2	32	23	—	32	.228	.244	.297	74	-41	—	.791	-19	70	46	O237(115/40/82),P14,1b12/2	—	-5.9
WHEELER, DICK	Richard (b Richard Wheeler Maynard); B1.14.1898 Keene NH; D2.12.1962 Lexington MA; BR/TR/5´11˝/185; d6.17; Col Amherst																								
1918	StL N	3	6	0	0	0	0	0	0	0	0	3	.000	.000	.000	-99	-1	0	ø	-0	0	0	O2R	—	-0.2
WHEELOCK, BOBBY	Warren H.; B8.6.1864 Charlestown MA; D3.13.1928 Boston MA; BR/TR/5´8˝/160; d5.19																								
1887	Bos N	48	166	32	42	4	2	2	15	15	0	15	.253	.315	.337	80	-4	20	.878	-2	25	0	O28(9/1/18),S20,2b4	—	-0.5
1890	Col AA	52	190	24	45	6	1	1	16	25	0	—	.237	.326	.295	89	-2	34	.885	-0	95	89	S52	—	0.0
1891	Col AA	136	498	82	114	15	1	0	39	78	2	55	.229	.336	.263	76	-11	52	.899	16	110	**144**	S136	—	0.8
Total	3	236	854	138	201	25	4	3	70	118	2	70	.235	.330	.285	80	-17	106	.894	14	107	125	S208,O28(9/1/18),2b4	—	0.3
WHELAN, JIMMY	James Francis; B5.11.1890 Kansas City KS; D11.29.1929 Dayton OH; BR/TR/5´8.5˝/165; d4.24																								
1913	StL N	1	1	0	0	0	0	0	0	0	0	0	.000	.000	.000	-99	0	0	ø	0	—	—	/H	—	0.0
WHELAN, TOM	Thomas Joseph; B1.3.1894 Lynn MA; D6.26.1957 Boston MA; BR/TR/5´11˝/175; d8.13; Col Georgetown																								
1920	Bos N	1	1	0	0	0	0	0	0	1	0	1	.000	.500	.000	54	0	0-0	1.000	-0	0	0	/1	—	0.0
WHISENANT, PETE	Thomas Peter; B12.14.1929 Asheville NC; D3.22.1996 Port Charlotte FL; BR/TR/6´2˝/(190–200); d4.16; C2																								
1952	Bos N	24	52	3	10	2	0	0	7	4	0	13	.192	.250	.231	35	-5	1-1	.973	2	118	184	O14(9/5/0)	0	-0.4
1955	StL N	58	115	10	22	5	1	2	9	5-0	0	29	.191	.223	.304	39	-11	2-0	.964	3	116	162	O40(12/11/19)	0	-0.8
1956	Chi N	103	314	37	75	16	3	11	46	24-1	1	53	.239	.292	.414	89	-5	8-2	.992	2	105	93	O93(6/84/0)	0	-0.7
1957	Cin N	67	90	18	19	3	2	5	11	5-0	0	24	.211	.250	.456	80	-3	0-1	.982	1	122	0	O43(24/9/12)	0	-0.4
1958	Cin N	85	203	33	48	9	2	11	40	18-0	0	37	.236	.292	.463	93	-3	3-0	1.000	5	129	76	O66(26/2/42)/2	0	0.1
1959	Cin N	36	71	13	17	2	0	5	11	8-0	0	18	.239	.316	.479	105	0	0-0	.966	-0	97	86	O21(5/0/16)	0	0.0
1960	Cin N	1	1	0	0	0	0	0	0	0-0	0	0	.000	.000	.000	-98	0	0-0	ø	0	—	—	/H	0	0.0
	Cle A	7	6	0	1	0	0	0	0	0-0	0	2	.167	.167	.167	-10	-1	0-0	1.000	0	139	0	O2L	0	-0.1
	Was A	58	115	19	26	9	0	3	9	19-0	0	14	.226	.336	.383	95	0	2-1	1.000	-1	93	96	O47(23/31/1)	0	-0.3
	Year	65	121	19	27	9	0	3	9	19-0	0	16	.223	.329	.372	90	-1	2-1	1.000	-1	93	95	O49(25/31/1)	0	-0.4
1961	Min A	10	6	1	0	0	0	0	0	1-0	0	2	.000	.143	.000	-55	-1	0-0	1.000	0	105	0	O5L	0	-0.1
	Cin N	26	15	6	3	0	0	0	1	2-0	0	4	.200	.294	.200	34	-1	1-0	1.000	0	96	0	O12(10/0/2)/C3	0	-0.1
Total	8	475	988	140	221	46	8	37	134	86-1	1	196	.224	.284	.399	80	-30	17-5	.988	12	111	94	O343(122/142/92)/3C2	0	-2.8
WHISENTON, LARRY	Larry; B7.3.1956 St.Louis MO; BL/TL/6´1˝/190; [AtlN75 2/42]; d9.17																								
1977	Atl N	4	4	1	1	0	0	0	1	0-0	0	3	.250	.250	.250	31	0	0-0	ø	0	—	—	/H	0	-0.1
1978	Atl N	6	16	1	3	1	0	0	2	1-0	0	2	.188	.235	.250	32	-1	0-0	1.000	-1	67	0	O4R	0	-0.3
1979	Atl N	13	37	3	9	2	1	0	1	3-0	0	3	.243	.300	.351	73	-1	1-0	1.000	4	138	371	O13(9/0/4)	0	0.2
1981	Atl N	9	5	1	1	0	0	0	0	2-0	0	1	.200	.429	.200	83	0	0-0	.000	-0	0	0	O2(1/0/1)	0	0.0
1982	†Atl N	84	143	21	34	7	2	4	17	23-3	0	33	.238	.339	.399	105	1	2-2	.964	-2	88	42	O34(29/0/5)	0	-0.2
Total	5	116	205	27	48	10	3	4	21	29-3	0	42	.234	.326	.371	91	-1	3-2	.968	0	97	115	O53(39/0/14)	0	-0.4
WHISTLER, LEW	Lewis W. (b Lewis Wissler); B3.10.1868 St.Louis MO; D12.30.1959 St.Louis MO; TR/5´10.5˝/178; d8.7; OF(15/5/12)																								
1890	NY N	45	170	27	49	9	7	2	29	20	1	37	.288	.366	.459	140	8	8	.982	-2	62	111	1b45	—	0.2
1891	NY N	72	265	39	65	8	7	3	38	24	3	45	.245	.315	.362	101	0	4	.852	-14	91	60	S33,O22(14/5/3),1b7,2b6,3b5	—	-1.2
1892	Bal N	52	209	32	47	6	6	2	21	18	3	22	.225	.296	.340	90	-4	12	.973	-1	97	62	1b51/lf	—	-0.4
	Lou N	80	285	42	67	4	7	5	34	30	2	45	.235	.312	.351	109	3	14	.978	-2	84	131	1b72,2b10	—	0.1
	Year	132	494	74	114	10	13	7	55	48	5	67	.231	.305	.346	101	-1	26	.976	-3	89	102	1b123,2b10/lf	—	-0.3
1893	Lou N	13	47	5	10	1	1	0	9	5	1	5	.213	.302	.277	59	-3	1	.946	-1	116	93	1b13	—	-0.3
	StL N	10	38	5	9	1	0	0	2	3	0	2	.237	.293	.263	48	-3	0	.923	-1	82	0	O9R/1	—	-0.3
	Year	23	85	10	19	2	1	0	11	8	1	7	.224	.298	.271	54	-6	1	.949	-1	107	98	1b14,O9R	—	-0.6
Total	4	272	1014	150	247	29	28	12	133	100	10	156	.244	.318	.363	103	1	39	.976	-19	82	104	1b189,S33,O32L,2b16,3b5	—	-1.9
WHITAKER, LOU	Louis Rodman; B5.12.1957 Brooklyn NY; BL/TR/5´11˝/(155–180); [DetA75 5/99]; d9.9																								
1977	Det A	11	32	5	8	1	0	0	2	4-0	0	6	.250	.333	.281	66	-1	2-2	1.000	-4	71	37	2b9	0	-0.5
1978	Det A	139	484	71	138	12	7	3	58	61-0	1	65	.285	.361	.357	101	2	7-7	.978	20	111	115	2b136,D2	0	2.9
1979	Det A	127	423	75	121	14	8	3	42	78-2	1	66	.286	.395	.378	107	8	20-10	.986	17	102	**125**	2b126	15	3.1
1980	Det A	145	477	68	111	19	1	1	45	73-0	0	79	.233	.331	.283	69	-17	8-4	.985	-1	97	92	2b143	0	-1.0
1981	Det A	**109**	335	48	88	14	4	5	36	40-3	1	42	.263	.340	.373	102	2	5-3	.985	7	105	111	2b108	0	1.6
1982	Det A	152	560	76	160	22	8	15	65	48-4	1	58	.286	.341	.434	111	8	11-3	**.988**	13	104	**125**	2b149/D	0	3.0
1983	Det A★	161	643	94	206	40	6	12	72	67-8	0	70	.320	.380	.457	133	31	17-10	.983	-19	90	92	2b160	0	2.1
1984	†Det A★	143	558	90	161	25	1	13	56	62-5	0	63	.289	.357	.407	112	10	6-5	.979	-5	94	100	2b142	0	1.3
1985	Det A★	152	609	102	170	29	8	21	73	80-9	2	56	.279	.362	.456	123	21	6-4	.985	-14	89	103	2b150	0	1.5
1986	Det A★	144	584	95	157	26	6	20	73	63-5	0	70	.269	.338	.437	109	7	13-8	.984	6	106	113	2b141	0	2.1
1987	†Det A✳	149	604	110	160	38	6	16	59	71-2	1	108	.265	.341	.427	107	7	13-5	.976	-11	97	106	2b148	0	0.5
1988	Det A	115	403	54	111	18	2	12	55	66-5	0	61	.275	.376	.419	127	17	2-0	.984	-9	93	82	2b110	0	1.2
1989	Det A	148	509	77	128	21	1	28	85	89-6	3	59	.251	.361	.462	134	26	6-3	.985	6	98	99	2b146,D2	0	3.5
1990	Det A	132	472	75	112	22	2	18	60	74-7	0	71	.237	.338	.407	107	6	8-2	.991	18	**106**	114	2b130/D	0	2.8
1991	Det A	138	470	94	131	26	2	23	78	90-6	2	45	.279	.391	.489	141	30	4-2	**.994**	-5	103	103	2b135,D3	0	2.8
1992	Det A	130	453	77	126	26	0	19	71	81-5	1	46	.278	.386	.461	135	25	6-4	.984	-13	94	90	2b119,D10	0	1.4
1993	Det A	119	383	72	111	32	1	9	67	78-4	4	46	.290	.412	.449	132	23	3-3	.981	18	**114**	112	2b110	0	4.3
1994	Det A	92	322	67	97	21	2	12	43	41-4	1	47	.301	.377	.491	121	11	2-0	.970	-1	**110**	88	2b83,D5	0	1.3
1995	Det A	84	249	36	73	14	0	14	44	31-4	2	41	.293	.372	.518	130	11	4-0	.985	-1	105	83	2b63,D8	17	1.3
Total	19	2390	8570	1386	2369	420	65	244	1084	1197-79	20	1099	.276	.363	.426	116	227	143-75	.984	24	100	104	2b2308,D32	32	35.2
WHITAKER, STEVE	Stephen Edward; B5.7.1943 Tacoma WA; BL/TR/6´1˝/(182–187); d8.23																								
1966	NY A	31	114	15	28	3	2	7	15	9-0	1	24	.246	.306	.491	130	4	0-0	.955	-1	91	159	O31(4/20/10)	0	0.1
1967	NY A	122	441	37	107	12	3	11	50	23-2	3	89	.243	.283	.358	92	-6	2-5	.982	2	94	153	O114(26/12/78)	0	-1.5
1968	NY A	28	60	3	7	2	0	0	3	8-0	0	18	.117	.221	.150	14	-6	0-1	.917	-2	66	209	O14(6/7/2)	0	-1.0
1969	Sea A	69	116	15	29	2	1	6	13	12-1	1	29	.250	.323	.440	113	1	2-0	.962	1	87	227	O39(22/0/18)	0	0.1
1970	SF N	16	27	3	3	1	0	0	4	2-0	0	14	.111	.167	.148	-13	-4	0-0	.857	-1	58	0	O9L	0	-0.6
Total	5	266	758	73	174	20	6	24	85	54-3	5	174	.230	.283	.367	91	-11	4-6	.967	-1	89	164	O207(67/39/108)	0	-2.9
WHITE, FUZZ	Albert Eugene; B6.27.1916 Springfield MO; D4.24.2003 Springfield MO; BL/TR/6´0˝/175; d9.17																								
1940	StL A	2	2	0	0	0	0	0	0	0	0	0	.000	.000	.000	-98	-1	0-0	ø	0	—	—	/H	—	-0.1
1947	NY N	7	13	3	3	0	0	0	0	0	0	0	.231	.231	.231	23	-1	0	1.000	1	153	0	O5R	—	-0.1
Total	2	9	15	3	3	0	0	0	0	0	0	0	.200	.200	.200	6	-2	0-0	1.000	1	153	0	O5R	0	-0.2
WHITE, C. B.	C. B.; B Wakeman OH; d6.1																								
1883	Phi N	1	1	0	0	0	0	0	0	0	—	0	.000	.000	.000	-99	0	—	.667	-0	0	0	/S3	—	0.0
WHITE, CHARLIE	Charles; B8.12.1928 Kinston NC; D5.26.1998 Seatac WA; BL/TR/5´11˝/192; d4.18; Negro Lg 1950																								
1954	Mil N	50	93	14	22	4	0	1	8	9	0	8	.237	.304	.312	65	-5	0-0	.981	-1	*101*	*27*	C28	0	-0.5
1955	Mil N	12	30	3	7	1	0	0	4	5-0	1	7	.233	.361	.267	74	-1	0-0	1.000	-1	*127*	*50*	C10	0	-0.2
Total	2	62	123	17	29	5	0	1	12	14-0	1	15	.236	.319	.301	67	-6	0-0	.986	-2	*109*	*34*	C38	0	-0.7
WHITE, DERRICK	Derrick Ramon; B10.12.1969 San Rafael CA; BR/TR/6´1˝/(215–225); [MonN91 6/165]; d7.22; Col Oklahoma																								
1993	Mon N	17	49	6	11	3	0	2	4	2-1	1	12	.224	.269	.408	75	-2	2-0	.993	-1	87	162	1b17	0	-0.3
1995	Det A	39	48	3	9	2	0	0	2	0-0	0	7	.188	.188	.229	8	-7	1-0	.981	1	137	83	1b16,D11,O9(4/0/5)	0	-0.9
1998	Chi N	11	10	1	1	0	0	1	2	0-0	0	5	.100	.100	.400	23	-1	0-0	ø	0	0	0	/lf	0	-0.1
	Col N	9	9	0	0	0	0	0	0	0-0	0	4	.000	.000	.000	-83	-2	0-0	1.000	0	113	0	O2L/D	0	-0.2
	Year	20	19	1	1	0	0	1	2	0-0	0	9	.053	.053	.211	-31	-4	0-0	1.000	0	90	0	O3L/D	0	-0.3
Total	3	76	116	10	21	5	0	3	8	2-1	1	28	.181	.202	.302	29	-12	3-0	.990	-2	101	140	1b33,O12(8/0/5),D12	0	-1.5

YEAR	TM LG	G	AB	R	H	2B	3B	HR	RBI	BB-IB	HP	SO	AVG	OBP	SLG	AOPS	ABR	SB-CS	FA	FR	RNG	THR	GAMES AT POSITION	DL	BFW
White, Devon	Devon Markes; B12.29.1962 Kingston, Jamaica; BB/TR/6´2˝/(170–195); [CalA81 6/132]; d9.2																								
1985	Cal A	21	7	7	1	0	0	0	0	1-0	1	3	.143	.333	.143	36	-1	3-1	1.000	1	100	350	O16(14/1/3)	0	0.0
1986	†Cal A	29	51	8	12	1	1	1	3	6-0	0	8	.235	.316	.353	82	-1	6-0	.961	1	125	0	O28(17/7/5)	0	0.1
1987	Cal A	159	639	103	168	33	5	24	87	39-2	2	135	.263	.306	.443	99	-3	32-11	.980	18	120	156	O159(6/64/120)	0	1.1
1988	Cal A	122	455	76	118	22	2	11	51	23-1	2	84	.259	.297	.389	93	-6	17-8	.976	9	113	128	O116C	34	0.3
1989	Cal A★	156	636	86	156	18	13	12	56	31-3	2	129	.245	.282	.371	84	-17	44-16	.989	3	103	118	O154C/D	0	-1.2
1990	Cal A	125	443	57	96	17	3	11	44	44-5	3	116	.217	.290	.343	78	-14	21-6	.972	3	100	**186**	O122C	0	-1.0
1991	†Tor A	156	642	110	181	40	10	17	60	55-1	7	135	.282	.342	.455	115	12	33-10	**.998**	5	107	98	O156C	0	1.9
1992	†Tor A	153	641	98	159	26	7	17	60	47-0	5	133	.248	.303	.390	89	-11	37-4	.985	7	111	98	O152C/D	0	0.1
1993	†Tor A★	146	598	116	163	42	6	15	52	57-1	7	127	.273	.341	.438	106	5	34-4	.993	4	107	77	O145C	0	1.7
1994	Tor A	100	403	67	109	24	6	13	49	21-3	5	80	.270	.313	.457	95	-5	11-3	.978	5	115	64	O98C	0	0.2
1995	Tor A	101	427	61	121	23	5	10	53	29-1	5	97	.283	.334	.431	98	-2	11-2	.989	2	102	142	O99C	0	0.2
1996	Fla N	146	552	77	151	37	6	17	84	38-6	8	99	.274	.325	.455	107	4	22-6	.987	-8	91	71	O139C	0	0.1
1997	†Fla N	74	265	37	65	13	1	6	34	32-2	7	65	.245	.338	.370	90	-3	13-5	.987	0	102	128	O71C	85	-0.1
1998	Ari N★	146	563	84	157	32	1	22	85	42-4	9	102	.279	.335	.456	106	5	22-8	.987	-2	109	33	O144C	0	0.6
1999	LA N	134	474	60	127	20	2	14	68	39-2	11	88	.268	.337	.407	92	-7	19-5	.986	-11	90	45	O128C/D	0	-1.3
2000	LA N	47	158	26	42	5	1	4	13	9-0	1	30	.266	.310	.386	78	-6	3-6	.972	-4	84	99	O40C	80	-1.0
2001	Mil N	126	390	52	108	25	2	14	47	28-1	12	95	.277	.343	.459	107	4	18-3	1.000	-7	90	58	O100(13/86/2)	0	0.1
Total	17	1941	7344	1125	1934	378	71	208	846	541-32	87	1526	.263	.319	.419	97	-46	346-98	.986	25	105	100	O1867(50/1722/130),D3	199	1.8
White, Don	Donald William; B1.8.1919 Everett WA; D6.15.1987 Carlsbad CA; BR/TR/6´1˝/195; d4.19																								
1948	Phi A	86	253	29	62	14	2	1	28	19	2	16	.245	.303	.328	68	-12	0-1	.957	0	100	84	O54(33/7/17),3b17	0	-1.5
1949	Phi A	57	169	12	36	6	0	0	10	14	0	12	.213	.273	.249	40	-15	2-0	.989	1	106	103	O48(6/0/43),3b4	0	-1.5
Total	2	143	422	41	98	20	2	1	38	33	2	28	.232	.291	.296	57	-27	2-1	.971	1	103	93	O102(39/7/60),3b21	0	-3.0
White, Ed	Edward Perry; B4.6.1926 Anniston AL; D9.28.1982 Lakeland FL; BR/TR/6´2˝/200; d9.16; Col Alabama																								
1955	Chi A	3	4	0	2	0	0	0	0	1-0	0	1	.500	.600	.500	193	1	0-0	1.000	0	115	0	O2R	0	0.1
White, Elder	Elder Lafayette; B12.23.1934 Colerain NC; BR/TR/5´11˝/165; d4.10																								
1962	Chi N	23	53	4	8	2	0	0	1	8-0	1	11	.151	.274	.189	26	-5	3-0	.986	-1	102	63	S15/3	0	-0.4
White, Frank	Frank; B9.4.1950 Greenville MS; BR/TR/5´11˝/(170–190); d6.12; C8																								
1973	KC A	51	139	20	31	6	1	0	5	8-0	0	23	.223	.262	.281	50	-9	3-1	.937	5	103	139	S37,2b11	0	0.0
1974	KC A	99	204	19	45	6	3	1	18	5-0	0	33	.221	.239	.294	50	-14	3-4	.962	7	102	106	2b50,S29,3b16,D3	0	-0.3
1975	KC A	111	304	43	76	10	2	7	36	20-0	1	39	.250	.297	.365	85	-7	11-3	.984	5	106	92	2b68,S42,3b4/D	0	0.6
1976	†KC A	152	446	39	102	17	6	2	46	19-0	3	42	.229	.263	.307	67	-20	20-11	.973	18	**114**	105	2b130,S37	0	1.0
1977	†KC A	152	474	59	116	21	5	5	50	25-0	2	67	.245	.284	.342	69	-21	23-5	**.989**	-1	101	95	2b152,S4	0	-1.1
1978	†KC A★	143	461	66	127	24	6	7	50	26-1	3	59	.275	.317	.399	98	-2	13-10	.978	-8	96	112	2b140	0	-0.3
1979	KC A★	127	467	73	124	26	4	10	48	25-3	1	54	.266	.300	.403	87	-10	28-8	.982	-15	92	90	2b125	33	-1.4
1980	†KC A	154	560	70	148	23	4	7	60	19-0	2	69	.264	.289	.357	75	-20	19-6	.988	-2	98	98	2b153	0	-1.2
1981	†KC A★	94	364	35	91	17	1	9	38	19-0	0	50	.250	.285	.376	90	-6	4-2	.988	-10	93	109	2b93	0	-1.1
1982	KC A★	145	524	71	156	45	6	11	56	16-1	2	65	.298	.318	.469	113	8	10-7	.978	4	102	107	2b144	0	2.0
1983	KC A	146	549	52	143	35	6	11	77	20-4	0	51	.260	.283	.406	87	-11	13-5	**.990**	22	109	**118**	2b145	0	2.0
1984	†KC A	129	479	58	130	22	5	17	56	27-3	2	72	.271	.311	.445	106	2	5-5	.985	29	**118**	**124**	2b129	15	3.7
1985	†KC A	149	563	62	140	25	1	22	69	28-2	1	86	.249	.284	.414	88	-11	10-4	.980	23	**114**	101	2b149	0	2.0
1986	KC A★	151	566	76	154	37	3	22	84	43-5	2	88	.272	.322	.465	110	7	4-4	.987	13	107	98	2b151/S3	0	2.6
1987	KC A	154	563	67	138	32	2	17	78	51-5	2	86	.245	.308	.400	84	-13	1-3	.987	22	**112**	91	2b152/D	0	1.5
1988	KC A	150	537	48	126	25	1	8	58	21-3	4	67	.235	.266	.330	66	-26	7-3	**.994**	21	**110**	98	2b148,D3	0	-0.1
1989	KC A	135	418	34	107	22	1	2	36	30-0	2	52	.256	.307	.328	80	-11	3-2	.985	14	109	83	2b132/cf	0	0.6
1990	KC A	82	241	20	52	14	1	2	21	10-0	3	32	.216	.253	.307	57	-14	1-0	.978	1	96	98	2b79/rf	17	-1.2
Total	18	2324	7859	912	2006	407	58	160	886	412-27	30	1035	.255	.293	.383	85	-178	178-83	.984	149	105	102	2b2151,S150,3b21,D8,O2(0/1/1)	65	9.3
White, Doc	Guy Harris; B4.9.1879 Washington DC; D2.19.1969 Silver Spring MD; BL/TL/6´1˝/150; d4.22; Col Georgetown; ▲																								
1901	Phi N	31	98	15	27	3	1	1	10	2	1	—	.276	.297	.357	87	-2	1	.951	2	119	0	P31/lf	—	0.1
1902	Phi N	61	179	17	47	3	1	1	15	11	0	—	.263	.305	.307	89	-3	5	.931	0	107	0	P36,O19(17/0/2)	—	-0.3
1903	Chi A	38	99	10	20	3	0	0	5	19	0	—	.202	.331	.232	74	-2	1	.969	2	108	236	P37/cf	—	0.1
1904	Chi A	33	76	7	12	2	0	0	2	10	0	—	.158	.256	.184	42	-5	3	.951	1	92	101	P30,O2C	—	0.0
1905	Chi A	37	90	7	15	4	1	0	7	4	0	—	.167	.202	.233	40	-6	3	.953	2	101	104	P36/lf	—	0.1
1906	†Chi A	29	65	11	12	1	1	0	3	13	0	—	.185	.321	.231	75	-1	3	.922	2	117	64	P28/cf	—	0.1
1907	Chi A	48	90	12	20	1	0	0	2	12	0	—	.222	.314	.233	77	-2	2	**.986**	5	113	43	P46,O2R/2	—	0.2
1908	Chi A	51	109	12	25	1	0	0	10	12	0	—	.229	.306	.239	79	-2	4	**.986**	7	128	**326**	P41,O3(0/2/1)	—	0.4
1909	Chi A	72	192	24	45	1	5	0	7	33	0	—	.234	.347	.292	106	3	7	.926	-3	158	0	O40(1/35/4),P24	—	-0.2
1910	Chi A	56	126	14	25	1	2	0	8	14	0	—	.198	.279	.238	65	-5	2	.972	3	100	222	P33,O14(0/10/4)	—	0.0
1911	Chi A	39	78	12	20	1	1	0	6	7	0	—	.256	.318	.295	74	-3	1	.919	-1	97	133	P34,1b2/rf	—	-0.1
1912	Chi A	32	56	5	7	1	1	0	0	7	0	—	.125	.222	.179	15	-2	0	**1.000**	-1	92	74	P32	—	0.0
1913	Chi A	21	25	1	3	0	0	0	0	3	0	1	.120	.214	.120	-2	-3	0	.959	2	142	0	P19/1	—	0.1
Total	13	548	1283	147	278	22	13	2	75	147	1	1	.217	.298	.259	74	-33	32	.959	20	108	111	P427,O85(20/51/14),1b3/2	—	0.5
White, Deacon	James Laurie; B12.7.1847 Caton NY; D7.7.1939 Aurora IL; BL/TR/5´11˝/175; d5.4; M2; b–Will; OF(8/5/101); ▲																								
1871	Cle NA	**29**	146	40	47	6	5	1	21	4	—	1	.322	.340	.452	132	7	2-2	.821	-4	—	—	C29,S2/23rf	—	0.2
1872	Cle NA	**22**	109	21	37	2	2	0	22	4	—	1	.339	.363	.394	140	6	0-0	.882	1	—	—	C14,2b7,O5(2/1/3),M	—	0.4
1873	Bos NA	**60**	311	79	122	17	8	1	**77**	0	—	2	.392	.392	.508	152	17	19-3	.842	-0	—	—	C56,O12(2/2/8)	—	1.4
1874	Bos NA	70	352	75	106	5	7	3	52	5	—	0	.301	.311	.381	114	3	1-1	.839	1	—	—	C58,O21R/1	—	0.4
1875	Bos NA	80	371	76	136	23	3	1	60	3	—	2	**.367**	.372	.453	178	28	2-3	.880	19	—	—	C75,O14R/1	—	3.9
1876	Chi N	**66**	303	66	104	18	1	1	**60**	7	—	3	.343	.358	.419	141	12	—	.844	8	—	—	C63,O3L,1b3/3P	—	1.9
1877	Bos N	59	266	51	**103**	14	**11**	2	**49**	8	—	3	**.387**	.405	**.545**	**190**	**26**	—	.963	1	119	117	1b35,O19R,C7	—	2.2
1878	Cin N	**61**	258	41	81	4	1	0	29	10	—	5	.314	.340	.337	136	11	—	.909	0	—	—	C48,O16R/3	—	1.1
1879	Cin N	78	333	55	110	16	6	1	52	6	—	9	.330	.342	.423	159	21	—	.901	6	—	—	C59,O21(0/4/18),1b2,M	—	2.5
1880	Cin N	35	141	21	42	4	2	0	7	9	—	7	.298	.340	.355	137	6	—	.738	-4	115	64	O33(0/1/33),1b3/2	—	0.2
1881	Buf N	78	319	58	99	24	4	0	53	9	—	8	.310	.329	.411	133	12	—	.943	-9	91	67	1b26,2b25,O17(2/0/15),3b7,C4	—	0.4
1882	Buf N	83	337	51	95	17	0	1	33	15	—	16	.282	.313	.341	108	3	—	.837	-11	85	77	3b63,C20	—	-0.4
1883	Buf N	94	391	62	114	14	5	0	47	23	—	18	.292	.331	.353	106	3	—	.797	-14	85	82	3b77,C22	—	-0.7
1884	Buf N	110	452	82	147	16	11	5	74	32	—	13	.325	.370	.442	149	25	—	.825	-5	98	88	3b108,C3	—	1.9
1885	Buf N	98	404	54	118	6	6	0	57	12	—	11	.292	.313	.337	106	1	—	.888	2	103	83	3b98	—	0.4
1886	Det N	124	491	65	142	19	5	1	76	31	—	35	.289	.331	.354	105	3	9	.847	-9	97	141	3b124	—	-0.4
1887	†Det N	111	449	71	136	20	11	3	75	26	9	15	.303	.353	.416	109	5	20	.848	1	105	110	3b106,O3L,1b2	—	0.6
1888	Det N	125	527	75	157	22	5	4	71	21	9	24	.298	.336	.381	127	16	12	.857	-3	100	122	3b125	—	1.4
1889	Pit N	55	225	35	57	10	1	0	26	16	4	18	.253	.314	.307	81	-5	2	.872	-8	88	79	3b52,1b3	—	-1.1
1890	Buf P	122	439	62	114	13	4	0	47	67	19	30	.260	.381	.308	93	3	3	.905	18	117	140	3b64,1b57/SP	—	1.3
Total	5NA	261	1289	291	448	53	25	6	232	16	—	6	.348	.356	.441	145	61	24-9	.854	16	—	—	C232,O53(4/3/47),2b8,1b2,S2/3	—	6.3
Total	15	1299	5335	849	1619	217	73	18	756	292	41	215	.303	.344	.382	122	142	46	.853	-27	—	—	3b826,C226,1b131,O112R,2b26,P2/S	—	11.3
White, Jerry	Jerome Cardell; B8.23.1952 Shirley MA; BB/TR/5´11˝/(160–175); [MonN70 14/322]; d9.16; C11																								
1974	Mon N	9	10	0	4	1	1	0	2	0-0	0	0	.400	.400	.700	193	1	3-0	1.000	-1	76	0	O7(5/2/0)	0	0.1
1975	Mon N	39	97	14	29	4	1	2	7	10-1	0	7	.299	.364	.423	112	2	5-2	.976	2	120	58	O30(7/24/0)	0	0.4
1976	Mon N	114	278	32	68	11	1	2	21	27-2	2	31	.245	.316	.313	75	-8	15-7	.982	-3	94	90	O92(27/67/0)	0	-1.4
1977	Mon N	16	21	4	4	0	0	0	1	1-0	0	3	.190	.227	.190	14	-3	1-0	1.000	-0	73	0	O8(7/0/1)	0	-0.3
1978	Mon N	18	10	2	2	0	0	0	0	1-0	0	3	.200	.273	.200	34	-1	1-0	ø	-0	0	0	O3(1/0/2)	0	-0.1
	Chi N	59	136	22	37	6	0	1	10	23-1	0	16	.272	.373	.338	90	0	4-3	.981	1	99	178	O54C	23	0.0
	Year	77	146	24	39	6	0	1	10	24-1	0	19	.267	.366	.329	89	-1	5-3	.981	1	98	176	O57(1/54/2)	0	-0.1
1979	Mon N	88	138	30	41	7	1	3	18	21-2	1	23	.297	.391	.428	124	5	8-4	.983	-3	82	81	O43(6/13/26)	0	0.2
1980	Mon N	110	214	22	56	9	3	7	23	30-0	1	37	.262	.351	.430	116	5	8-7	.946	-1	96	122	O84(62/7/18)	0	0.1
1981	†Mon N	59	119	11	26	5	1	3	11	13-0	0	17	.218	.293	.353	81	-3	5-2	.952	-1	97	86	O39(7/13/20)	0	-0.6
1982	Mon N	69	115	13	28	6	1	2	13	8-1	2	26	.243	.304	.365	83	-3	3-3	1.000	0	100	72	O30(21/9/2)	15	-0.4
1983	Mon N	40	34	4	5	1	0	0	0	12-0	1	8	.147	.383	.176	60	-1	4-0	1.000	0	104	0	O13(2/5/6)	0	0.0

YEAR	TM LG	G	AB	R	H	2B	3B	HR	RBI	BB-IB	HP	SO	AVG	OBP	SLG	AOPS	ABR	SB-CS	FA	FR	RNG	THR	GAMES AT POSITION	DL	BFW
1986	StL N	25	24	1	3	0	0	1	3	2-0	0	3	.125	.179	.250	21	-3	0-0	1.000	0	154	0	O6(3/0/3)	0	-0.3
Total	11	646	1196	155	303	50	9	21	109	148-7	7	174	.253	.337	.363	93	-9	57-28	.974	-5	97	98	O409(148/194/78)	38	-2.3
WHITE, JACK	John Peter; B8.31.1905 New York NY; D6.19.1971 Flushing NY; BB/TR/5´7.5˝/150; d6.22; Col Fordham																								
1927	Cin N	5	4	1	0	0	0	0	0	0	0	0	.000	.000	.000	-99	-1	0	1.000	0	117	146	2b3,S2	—	-0.1
1928	Cin N	1	3	0	0	0	0	0	0	0	0	1	.000	.000	.000	-99	-1	0	.833	-1	0	0	/2	—	-0.2
Total	2	6	7	1	0	0	0	0	0	0	0	1	.000	.000	.000	-99	-2	0	.929	-1	68	85	2b4,S2	—	-0.3
WHITE, JACK	John Wallace; B1.19.1878 Traders Point IN; D9.30.1963 Indianapolis IN; BR/TR/5´6˝/?; d6.26																								
1904	Bos N	1	5	1	0	0	0	0	0	0	0	—	.000	.000	.000	-99	-1	0	1.000	1	497	0	/lf	—	-0.1
WHITE, JO-JO	Joyner Clifford; B6.1.1909 Red Oak GA; D10.9.1986 Tacoma WA; BL/TR/5´11˝/165; d4.15; M1/C10; s–Mike																								
1932	Det A	80	208	25	54	6	3	2	21	22	0	19	.260	.330	.346	73	-9	6-8	.962	2	96	176	O48(16/17/16)	—	-1.0
1933	Det A	91	234	43	59	9	5	2	34	27	3	26	.252	.337	.359	83	-6	5-5	.977	-1	98	93	O54(16/32/6)	—	-0.9
1934	†Det A	115	384	97	120	18	5	0	44	69	1	39	.313	.419	.385	108	9	28-6	.959	-0	98	123	O100(1/93/6)	—	0.9
1935	†Det A	114	412	82	99	13	12	2	32	68	0	42	.240	.348	.345	83	-10	19-10	.962	-4	94	94	O98C	—	-1.5
1936	Det A	58	51	11	14	3	0	0	6	9	0	10	.275	.383	.333	78	-1	2-0	.938	0	96	211	O18(0/18/1)	—	-0.1
1937	Det A	94	305	50	75	5	7	0	21	50	1	40	.246	.354	.308	67	-15	12-7	.973	-5	96	51	O82(3/79/0)	—	-2.0
1938	Det A	78	206	40	54	6	1	0	15	30	1	15	.262	.359	.301	63	-11	3-4	.967	1	106	85	O55(21/34/1)	—	-1.2
1943	Phi A	139	500	69	124	17	7	1	30	61	4	51	.248	.335	.316	91	-5	12-4	.966	-5	97	80	O133(2/131/0)	0	-1.3
1944	Phi A	85	267	30	59	4	2	1	21	40	3	27	.221	.329	.262	71	-9	5-4	.949	0	106	93	O74(10/9/57)/S	0	-1.4
	Cin N	24	85	9	20	2	0	0	5	10	0	7	.235	.316	.259	65	-4	0	1.000	1	99	177	O23(4/11/10)	0	-0.3
Total	9	878	2652	456	678	83	42	8	229	386	13	276	.256	.353	.328	82	-61	92-48	.965	-11	98	98	O685(73/522/97)/S	0	-8.8
WHITE, MIKE	Joyner Michael; B12.18.1938 Detroit MI; BR/TR/5´8˝/160; d9.21; f–Jo–Jo; Col American River (CA) CC																								
1963	Hou N	3	7	0	2	0	0	0	0	0-0	0	0	.286	.286	.286	69	0	0-0	1.000	-0	53	0	2b2	0	0.0
1964	Hou N	89	280	30	76	11	3	0	27	20-0	0	47	.271	.319	.332	89	-4	1-1	.978	7	99	100	O72(9/55/8),2b10,3b3	0	0.1
1965	Hou N	8	9	0	0	0	0	0	0	1-0	0	2	.000	.100	.000	-74	-2	0-0	1.000	-0	81	0	/3	0	-0.3
Total	3	100	296	30	78	11	3	0	27	21-0	0	49	.264	.311	.321	84	-6	1-1	.978	6	99	100	O72(9/55/8),2b12,3b4	0	-0.2
WHITE, MYRON	Myron Alan; B8.1.1957 Long Beach CA; BL/TL/5´11˝/180; [LAN75 2/48]; d9.4																								
1978	LA N	7	4	1	2	0	0	0	1	0-0	0	1	.500	.500	.500	180	0	0-1	1.000	-0	75	0	O4(1/0/3)	0	0.0
WHITE, RONDELL	Rondell Bernard; B2.23.1972 Milledgeville GA; BR/TR/6´1˝/(205–225); [MonN90 1/24]; d9.1																								
1993	Mon N	23	73	9	19	3	1	2	15	7-0	0	16	.260	.321	.411	91	-1	1-2	1.000	-2	88	0	O21(19/5/0)	0	-0.4
1994	Mon N	40	97	16	27	10	1	2	13	9-0	3	18	.278	.358	.464	111	2	1-1	.946	-2	80	75	O29(25/4/0)	0	-0.1
1995	Mon N	130	474	87	140	33	4	13	57	41-1	6	87	.295	.356	.464	111	8	25-5	.986	-3	99	78	O119(8/111/0)	0	1.0
1996	Mon N	88	334	35	98	19	4	6	41	22-0	2	53	.293	.340	.428	99	-1	14-6	.990	-0	98	121	O86C	79	0.1
1997	Mon N	151	592	84	160	29	5	28	82	31-3	10	111	.270	.316	.478	106	2	16-8	**.992**	3	109	83	O151C	0	0.7
1998	Mon N	97	357	54	107	21	2	17	58	30-2	7	57	.300	.363	.513	131	16	16-7	.996	9	120	117	O96(15/83/0)/D	69	2.6
1999	Mon N	138	539	83	168	26	6	22	64	32-2	11	85	.312	.359	.505	121	15	10-6	.964	-0	100	91	O135(102/73/0)	30	1.2
2000	Mon N	75	290	52	89	24	0	11	54	28-0	2	67	.307	.370	.503	118	8	5-1	.994	6	117	92	O74L	23	1.2
	Chi N	19	67	7	22	2	0	2	7	5-0	2	12	.328	.392	.448	113	1	0-2	1.000	2	133	0	O18L	40	0.2
	Year	94	357	59	111	26	0	13	61	33-0	4	79	.311	.374	.493	117	10	5-3	.995	8	120	75	O92L	0	1.4
2001	Chi N	95	323	43	99	19	1	17	50	26-4	7	56	.307	.371	.529	133	16	1-0	.979	-0	97	82	O90L	65	1.2
2002	†NY A	126	455	59	109	21	0	14	62	25-1	8	86	.240	.288	.378	77	-16	1-2	**1.000**	4	114	47	O113(113/1/0),D11	0	-1.7
2003	SD N★	115	413	49	115	17	3	18	66	25-2	8	71	.278	.330	.465	115	7	1-4	.978	1	99	104	O104L,D3	0	0.3
	KC A	22	75	13	26	6	1	4	21	6-0	2	8	.347	.400	.613	154	6	0-0	.978	2	144	0	O17L,D4	0	0.7
2004	Det A	121	448	76	121	21	2	19	67	39-4	8	77	.270	.337	.453	108	5	1-2	.977	-4	94	51	O74L,D43	0	-0.4
2005	Det A	97	374	49	117	24	3	12	53	17-0	5	48	.313	.348	.489	123	11	1-0	1.000	-3	98	0	O65L,D30	49	0.4
2006	†Min A	99	337	32	83	17	1	7	38	11-2	4	54	.246	.276	.365	65	-19	1-1	1.000	-2	92	0	D54,O38L	41	-2.4
Total	14	1436	5248	748	1500	292	34	194	748	354-21	85	906	.286	.339	.465	109	60	94-47	.987	10	104	75	O1230(762/514/0),D146	396	4.6
WHITE, ROY	Roy Hilton; B12.27.1943 Los Angeles CA; BB/TR/5´10˝/(165–172); d9.7; C5; OF(1520/63/56)																								
1965	NY A	14	42	7	14	2	0	0	3	4-0	1	7	.333	.404	.381	125	2	2-1	1.000	-0	84	0	O10(0/1/9)/2	0	0.1
1966	NY A	115	316	39	71	13	2	7	20	37-1	1	43	.225	.308	.345	91	-3	14-7	.957	-1	105	61	O82(72/12/0),2b2	0	-0.8
1967	NY A	70	214	22	48	8	0	2	18	19-0	1	25	.224	.287	.290	75	-7	10-4	.968	-7	96	43	O36(5/0/31),3b17	0	-1.7
1968	NY A	159	577	89	154	20	7	17	62	73-6	3	50	.267	.350	.414	136	26	20-11	.997	2	93	134	O154(119/25/12)	0	2.2
1969	NY A★	130	448	55	130	30	5	7	74	81-4	1	51	.290	.392	.426	136	26	18-10	.989	6	110	88	O126L	0	2.6
1970	NY A☆	162	609	109	180	30	6	22	94	95-11	0	66	.296	.387	.473	143	39	24-10	.994	0	101	55	O161(161/0/1)	0	3.1
1971	NY A	147	524	86	153	22	7	19	84	86-7	7	66	.292	.388	.469	152	39	14-7	**1.000**	5	107	84	O145L	0	3.8
1972	NY A	**155**	556	76	150	29	0	10	54	**99**-10	5	59	.270	.384	.376	130	27	23-7	.994	2	109	63	O155L	0	2.5
1973	NY A	**162**	639	88	157	22	3	18	60	78-3	2	81	.246	.329	.374	100	0	16-9	.977	-1	104	35	O162L	0	-1.0
1974	NY A	136	473	68	130	19	8	7	43	67-5	4	44	.275	.367	.393	121	15	15-6	.993	1	106	43	O67L,D53	0	1.2
1975	NY A	148	556	81	161	32	5	12	59	72-1	2	50	.290	.372	.430	128	22	16-15	.984	7	110	112	O135L,1b7,D2	0	1.9
1976	†NY A	156	626	**104**	179	29	3	14	65	83-1	0	52	.286	.365	.409	128	25	31-13	.987	-0	103	73	O156(140/21/1)	0	1.9
1977	†NY A	143	519	72	139	25	2	14	52	75-9	0	58	.268	.358	.405	109	9	18-11	.981	4	111	69	O135(133/1/2),D4	0	0.7
1978	†NY A	103	346	44	93	13	3	8	43	42-7	2	35	.269	.349	.393	111	6	10-4	.992	-6	89	22	O74(73/3/0),D23	15	-0.3
1979	NY A	81	205	24	44	6	0	3	27	23-1	0	21	.215	.290	.288	59	-12	2-2	1.000	-1	86	154	D29,O27L	0	-1.4
Total	15	1881	6650	964	1803	300	51	160	758	934-66	29	708	.271	.360	.404	121	214	233-117	.988	11	104	74	O1625L,D111,3b17,1b7,2b3	15	14.8
WHITE, SAMMY	Samuel Charles; B7.7.1927 Wenatchee WA; D9.4.1991 Princeville HI; BR/TR/6´3˝/195; d9.26; Col Washington																								
1951	Bos A	4	11	0	2	0	0	0	0	0	0	3	.182	.182	.182	-1	-2	0-0	1.000	1	*105*	*0*	C4	0	-0.1
1952	Bos A	115	381	35	107	20	2	10	49	16	0	43	.281	.310	.423	95	-4	2-3	.983	3	***124***	*93*	C110	0	0.4
1953	Bos A☆	136	476	59	130	34	2	13	64	29	2	48	.273	.318	.435	96	-4	3-2	.986	10	*106*	*93*	C131	0	1.3
1954	Bos A	137	493	46	139	25	2	14	75	21	0	50	.282	.307	.426	90	-8	1-3	.979	4	*81*	*99*	C133	0	0.2
1955	Bos A	143	544	65	142	30	4	11	64	44-4	7	58	.261	.323	.392	84	-12	1-2	.984	-2	*82*	*106*	C143	0	-0.7
1956	Bos A	114	392	28	96	15	2	5	44	35-7	0	40	.245	.304	.332	61	-22	2-1	.984	3	*124*	*102*	C114	0	-1.3
1957	Bos A	111	340	24	73	10	1	3	31	25-6	0	38	.215	.267	.276	46	-25	0-1	.985	-2	134	76	C111	0	-2.3
1958	Bos A	102	328	25	85	15	3	6	35	21-4	1	37	.259	.305	.378	81	-9	1-1	.988	-2	142	105	C102	0	-0.6
1959	Bos A	119	377	34	107	13	4	1	42	23-6	1	39	.284	.324	.347	81	-10	4-2	.990	2	112	98	C119	0	-0.2
1961	Mil N	21	63	1	14	1	0	1	5	2-0	0	9	.222	.242	.286	43	-5	0-0	.974	3	225	48	C20	0	-0.2
1962	Phi N	41	97	7	21	4	0	2	12	2-0	1	16	.216	.238	.320	50	-7	0-0	.975	0	82	152	C40	0	-0.6
Total	11	1043	3502	324	916	167	20	66	421	218-27	12	381	.262	.305	.377	79	-108	14-15	.984	20	*112*	*97*	C1027	0	-4.1
WHITE, SAM	Samuel Lambeth; B8.23.1892 Kinsley, England; D11.11.1929 Philadelphia PA; BL/TR/6´0˝/185; d9.8																								
1919	Bos N	1	1	0	0	0	0	0	0	0	0	0	.000	.000	.000	-99	0	0	1.000	1	*0*	*650*	/C	—	0.1
WHITE, ELMER	Willard Elmer; B12.7.1849 Caton NY; D3.17.1872 Caton NY; d5.4																								
1871	Cle NA	15	70	13	18	2	0	0	9	1	—	6	.257	.268	.286	63	-3	0-1	.783	-1	62	0	O15R,C3	—	-0.2
WHITE, BARNEY	William Barney "Bear"; B6.25.1923 Paris TX; D7.24.2002 Tyler TX; BR/TR/5´11˝/186; d6.5																								
1945	Bro N	4	1	2	0	0	0	0	0	1	0	1	.000	.500	.000	46	0	0	1.000	-0	93	0	/S3	0	0.0
WHITE, BILL	William De Kova; B1.28.1934 Lakewood FL; BL/TL/6´0˝/(185–200); d5.7; Mil 1957–58; Col Hiram																								
1956	NY N	138	508	63	130	23	7	22	59	47-3	4	72	.256	.321	.459	108	5	15-8	.989	5	113	91	1b138,O2(1/0/1)	0	0.2
1958	SF N	26	29	5	7	1	0	1	4	7-1	0	5	.241	.389	.379	107	1	1-0	1.000	-0	72	106	1b3,O2(1/0/1)	0	0.0
1959	StL N☆	138	517	77	156	33	9	12	72	34-1	2	61	.302	.344	.470	108	6	15-10	.962	-3	108	31	O92(86/9/0),1b71	0	-0.5
1960	StL N★	144	554	81	157	27	10	16	79	42-1	2	83	.283	.334	.455	105	3	12-6	.990	-5	79	**121**	1b123,O29(3/28/0)	0	-1.0
1961	StL N★	153	591	89	169	28	11	20	90	64-4	1	84	.286	.354	.472	107	6	8-11	.989	-2	95	93	1b151	0	-0.7
1962	StL N	159	614	93	199	31	3	20	102	58-6	6	69	.324	.386	.482	120	19	9-7	.993	2	98	104	1b146,O27(8/0/19)	0	1.1
1963	StL N★	**162**	658	106	200	26	8	27	109	59-9	0	100	.304	.360	.491	131	26	10-9	.991	-1	96	100	1b162	0	1.5
1964	†StL N★	160	631	92	191	37	4	21	102	52-7	1	103	.303	.355	.474	121	19	7-6	**.996**	1	98	103	1b160	0	1.0
1965	StL N	148	543	82	157	26	3	24	73	63-11	4	86	.289	.364	.481	125	19	3-3	.992	5	**113**	101	1b144	0	1.6
1966	Phi N	159	577	85	159	23	6	22	103	68-12	3	109	.276	.352	.451	122	18	16-6	**.994**	5	109	95	1b158	0	1.6
1967	Phi N	110	308	29	77	6	2	8	33	52-9	3	61	.250	.359	.360	107	5	6-1	.993	-0	96	127	1b95	0	0.0

YEAR	TM LG	G	AB	R	H	2B	3B	HR	RBI	BB-IB	HP	SO	AVG	OBP	SLG	AOPS	ABR	SB-CS	FA	FR	RNG	THR	GAMES AT POSITION	DL	BFW
1968	Phi N	127	385	34	92	16	2	9	40	39-6	2	79	.239	.309	.361	102	1	0-1	.994	6	118	114	1b111	0	0.0
1969	StL N	49	57	7	12	1	0	0	4	11-0	0	15	.211	.338	.228	61	-2	1-0	1.000	1	126	106	1b15	0	-0.2
Total	13	1673	5972	843	1706	278	65	202	870	596-70	28	927	.286	.351	.455	115	126	103-68	.992	12	101	102	1b1477,O152(99/37/21)	0	4.6
WHITE, BILL	William Dighton; B5.1.1860 Bridgeport OH; D12.29.1924 Bellaire OH; TR; d5.3																								
1884	Pit AA	74	291	25	66	7	10	0	—	13	1	—	.227	.262	.320	90	-4	—	.807	-9	102	72	S60,3b10,O4R	—	-1.0
1886	Lou AA	135	557	96	143	17	10	1	66	37	1	—	.257	.304	.329	93	-7	14	.871	17	99	123	S135/P	—	1.2
1887	Lou AA	132	512	85	129	7	9	2	79	47	0	—	.252	.315	.313	74	-19	41	.869	18	103	**137**	S132	—	0.2
1888	Lou AA	49	198	35	55	6	5	1	30	7	3	—	.278	.313	.374	122	4	15	.816	1	105	51	S38,3b11	—	0.5
	†StL AA	76	275	31	48	2	3	2	30	21	2	—	.175	.238	.225	44	-18	6	.892	-5	86	69	S74,2b2	—	-2.0
	Year	125	473	66	103	8	8	3	60	28	5	—	.218	.269	.288	74	-16	21	.864	-5	93	63	S112,3b11,2b2	—	-1.5
Total	4	466	1833	272	441	39	37	6	205	125	7	—	.241	.292	.312	82	-44	76	.860	20	99	105	S439,3b21,O4R,2b2/P	—	-1.1
WHITE, BILL	William Edward; B Milner GA; d6.21; Col Brown																								
1879	Pro N	1	4	1	1	0	0	0	0	0	—	1	.250	.250	.250	67	0	—	1.000	0	0	242	/1	—	0.0
WHITE, WARREN	William Warren (aka William Warren); B1844 Milrotn NY; D6.12.1890 Little Rock AR; 5´10.5˝/170; d6.17; M2																								
1871	Oly NA	1	4	0	0	0	0	0	0	0	—	0	.000	.000	.000	-99	-1	0-0	1.000	-0	54	0	/2	—	-0.1
1872	Nat NA	10	45	7	12	0	0	0	4	0	—	0	.267	.267	.267	55	-3	0-0	.861	7	148	120	3b9/SM	—	0.2
1873	Was NA	**39**	158	29	43	3	4	0	20	0	—	1	.272	.272	.342	83	-3	2-1	.728	3	116	124	3b37,S3	—	-0.1
1874	Bal NA	45	211	21	57	1	0	0	17	2	—	2	.270	.277	.275	78	-5	1-0	.782	**25**	**175**	82	3b45,C3,M	—	1.4
1875	Chi NA	**69**	287	37	71	9	0	0	23	0	—	3	.247	.247	.279	82	-5	5-10	.813	5	111	70	3b59,S5,O5C,2b2	—	-0.4
1884	Was U	4	18	2	1	0	0	0	—	0	—	—	.056	.056	.056	-69	-4	—	.692	-2	59	0	3b2/S2	—	-0.5
Total	5NA	164	705	94	183	13	4	0	64	2	—	6	.260	.262	.289	78	-17	8-11	.783	40	133	90	3b150,S9,O5C,C3,2b3	—	1.0
WHITED, ED	Edward Morris; B2.9.1964 Bristol PA; BR/TR/6´3˝/195; [HouN86 18/458]; d7.5; Col Rider																								
1989	Atl N	36	74	5	12	3	0	1	4	6-2	0	15	.162	.222	.243	33	-7	1-0	.914	-3	78	59	3b29,1b3	0	-1.0
WHITEHEAD, BURGESS	Burgess Urquhart "Whitey"; B6.29.1910 Tarboro NC; D11.25.1993 Windsor NC; BR/TR/5´10.5˝/160; d4.30; Mil 1942–45; Col North Carolina																								
1933	StL N	12	7	2	2	0	0	0	1	0	0	1	.286	.286	.286	60	0	0	1.000	0	74	128	S9,2b3	—	0.0
1934	†StL N	100	332	55	92	13	5	1	24	12	4	19	.277	.310	.355	73	-13	5	.962	-1	106	119	2b48,S29,3b28	—	-1.0
1935	StL N★	107	338	45	89	10	2	0	33	11	1	14	.263	.289	.305	57	-21	5	.980	1	97	119	2b80,3b8,S6	—	-1.5
1936	†NY N	**154**	632	99	176	31	3	4	47	29	7	32	.278	.317	.356	82	-17	14	.969	32	111	125	2b153	—	2.4
1937	†NY N★	**152**	574	64	164	15	6	5	52	28	4	20	.286	.323	.359	84	-14	7	**.974**	28	107	**126**	2b152	—	2.4
1939	NY N	95	335	31	80	6	3	2	24	24	5	19	.239	.299	.293	59	-20	1	.970	23	116	100	2b91,S4/3	—	0.9
1940	NY N	133	568	68	160	9	6	4	36	26	5	17	.282	.319	.340	81	-16	9	.947	11	91	46	3b74,2b57,S4	—	0.1
1941	NY N	116	403	41	92	15	4	1	23	14	2	10	.228	.258	.293	54	-26	7	.970	3	97	97	2b104/3	0	-1.7
1946	Pit N	55	127	10	28	1	2	0	5	6	1	6	.220	.261	.260	47	-9	3	.963	-3	92	92	2b30,3b4/S	0	-1.2
Total	9	924	3316	415	883	100	31	17	245	150	29	138	.266	.304	.331	72	-136	51	.972	94	106	116	2b718,3b116,S53	0	0.4
WHITEHEAD, MILT	Milton P.; B1862 Toronto ON, Can.; D8.15.1901 Highland CA; BB/TR; d4.20																								
1884	StL U	99	393	61	83	15	1	1	—	8	—	—	.211	.227	.262	46	-38	—	.803	-12	98	151	S94,O2C/P23	—	-4.1
	KC U	5	22	2	3	0	0	0	—	0	—	—	.136	.136	.136	-20	-4	—	.857	0	141	0	2b3/CS3	—	-0.3
	Year	104	415	63	86	15	1	1	—	8	—	—	.207	.222	.255	43	-41	—	.804	-12	98	**150**	S95,2b4,O2C,3b2/PC	—	-4.4
WHITEHOUSE, GIL	Gilbert Arthur; B10.15.1893 Somerville MA; D2.14.1926 Brewer ME; BB/TR/5´10˝/170; d6.20																								
1912	Bos N	2	3	0	0	0	0	0	0	0	0	3	.000	.000	.000	-98	-1	0	.667	-1	*120*	*0*	C2	—	-0.2
1915	New F	35	120	16	27	6	2	0	9	6	1	16	.225	.268	.308	66	-8	3	.949	-0	70	206	O28(0/2/26)/PC	—	-1.0
Total	2	37	123	16	27	6	2	0	9	6	1	19	.220	.262	.301	61	-9	3	.949	-1	70	206	O28(0/2/26),C3/P	—	-1.2
WHITELEY, GUERDON	Guerdon W.; B10.5.1859 Hopkinton RI; D11.23.1925 Cranston RI; 5´11˝/190; d8.7																								
1884	Cle N	8	34	4	5	0	0	0	0	1	—	8	.147	.171	.147	1	-4	—	.800	1	196	764	O8(4/3/1)	—	-0.3
1885	Bos N	33	135	14	25	2	2	1	7	1	—	25	.185	.191	.252	44	-9	—	.781	-3	123	218	O32(8/0/24)/C	—	-1.2
Total	2	41	169	18	30	2	2	1	7	2	—	33	.178	.187	.231	34	-13	—	.785	-2	136	316	O40(12/3/25)/C	—	-1.5
WHITEMAN, GEORGE	George "Lucky"; B12.23.1882 Peoria IL; D2.10.1947 Houston TX; BR/TR/5´7˝/160; d9.13																								
1907	Bos A	4	12	0	2	0	0	0	1	0	0	—	.167	.167	.167	6	-1	0	1.000	-0	0	0	O2L	—	-0.2
1913	NY A	11	32	8	11	3	1	0	2	7	0	2	.344	.462	.500	181	4	2	.938	-0	114	50	O11(4/4/3)	—	0.3
1918	†Bos A	71	214	24	57	14	0	1	28	20	2	9	.266	.335	.346	107	2	9	.935	-5	86	68	O69(65/0/4)	—	-0.6
Total	3	86	258	32	70	17	1	1	31	27	2	11	.271	.345	.357	113	5	11	.936	-6	89	63	O82(71/4/7)	—	-0.5
WHITEN, MARK	Mark Anthony; B11.25.1966 Pensacola FL; BB/TR/6´3˝/(210–235); [TorA86*5/130]; d7.12; Col Pensacola (FL) JC																								
1990	Tor A	33	88	12	24	1	1	2	7	7-0	0	14	.273	.323	.375	94	-1	2-0	1.000	3	115	165	O30(3/0/27),D2	0	0.1
1991	Tor A	46	149	12	33	4	3	2	19	11-1	1	35	.221	.274	.329	65	-8	0-1	1.000	1	107	67	O42R	0	-0.9
	Cle A	70	258	34	66	14	4	7	26	19-1	2	50	.256	.310	.422	100	-1	4-2	.962	10	119	230	O67(0/8/63),D3	0	0.7
	Year	116	407	46	99	18	7	9	45	30-2	3	85	.243	.297	.388	87	-9	4-3	.975	11	**114**	168	O109(0/8/105),D3	0	-0.2
1992	Cle A	148	508	73	129	19	4	9	43	72-10	2	102	.254	.347	.360	100	2	16-12	.980	5	103	137	O144R,D2	0	0.1
1993	StL N	152	562	81	142	13	4	25	99	58-9	2	110	.253	.323	.423	99	-3	15-8	.971	-3	99	77	O148(0/22/138)	0	-1.1
1994	StL N	92	334	57	98	18	2	14	53	37-9	1	75	.293	.364	.485	119	10	10-5	.964	11	**128**	130	O90R	17	1.6
1995	Bos A	32	108	13	20	3	0	1	10	8-0	0	23	.185	.239	.241	25	-12	1-0	1.000	2	95	213	O31R/D	18	-1.1
	Phi N	60	212	38	57	10	1	11	37	31-1	1	63	.269	.365	.481	120	7	7-0	.965	-1	98	100	O55R	0	0.5
1996	Phi N	60	182	33	43	8	0	7	21	33-2	1	62	.236	.356	.396	98	0	13-3	.945	3	107	199	O51(0/8/44)	0	0.3
	Atl N	36	90	12	23	5	1	3	17	16-0	0	25	.256	.364	.433	104	1	2-5	.933	-2	90	63	O29R	0	-0.3
	Year	96	272	45	66	13	1	10	38	49-2	1	87	.243	.359	.408	100	1	15-8	.942	1	116	149	O80(0/8/73)	0	0.0
	Sea A	40	140	31	42	7	0	12	33	21-4	2	40	.300	.399	.607	149	11	2-1	.969	3	116	149	O39(36/0/4)	0	1.1
1997	NY A	69	215	34	57	11	0	5	24	30-5	2	47	.265	.360	.386	96	0	4-2	.954	-2	100	60	O57(44/0/16),D6	0	-0.4
1998	†Cle A	88	226	31	64	14	0	6	29	29-0	3	60	.283	.372	.425	103	2	2-1	.970	2	99	194	O72(43/22/13)/PD	0	0.3
1999	Cle A	8	25	2	4	1	0	1	4	3-0	0	4	.160	.250	.320	42	-2	0-0	1.000	-0	77	238	O7(5/2/0)	79	-0.2
2000	Cle A	6	7	2	2	1	0	0	1	3-0	0	2	.286	.500	.429	134	1	0-0	1.000	-0	64	0	O5C	0	0.0
Total	11	940	3104	465	804	129	20	105	423	378-42	17	712	.259	.341	.415	101	7	78-40	.970	32	106	132	O867(131/67/696),D19/P	114	0.7
WHITESIDE, ELI	Dustin Eli; B10.22.1979 New Albany MS; BR/TR/6´2˝/210; [BalA01 6/173]; d7.5; Col Delta St.																								
2005	Bal A	9	12	1	3	0	0	0	1	0-0	0	2	.250	.250	.250	34	-1	0-0	.926	-0	66	119	C9	0	-0.1
WHITFIELD, FRED	Fred Dwight; B1.7.1938 Vandiver AL; BL/TL/6´1˝/(185–190); d5.27																								
1962	StL N	73	158	20	42	7	1	8	34	7-1	1	30	.266	.299	.475	95	-2	1-0	.987	1	119	133	1b38	0	-0.2
1963	Cle A	109	346	44	87	17	3	21	54	24-5	4	61	.251	.302	.500	123	9	0-1	.987	-4	83	97	1b92	0	-0.1
1964	Cle A	101	293	29	79	13	1	10	29	12-3	2	58	.270	.301	.423	100	-1	0-5	.992	-3	81	111	1b79	0	-1.0
1965	Cle A	132	468	49	137	23	1	26	90	16-7	2	42	.293	.316	.513	131	16	2-2	.993	4	107	94	1b122	0	1.4
1966	Cle A	137	502	59	121	15	2	27	78	27-9	4	76	.241	.283	.440	105	1	1-2	.991	-4	85	98	1b132	0	-1.3
1967	Cle A	100	257	24	56	10	0	9	31	25-8	1	45	.218	.290	.362	91	-3	3-3	.993	4	120	119	1b66	0	-0.3
1968	Cin N	87	171	15	44	8	0	6	32	9-1	2	29	.257	.302	.409	105	1	0-3	.981	-1	102	111	1b41	0	-0.3
1969	Cin N	74	74	2	11	0	0	1	8	18-0	0	27	.149	.315	.189	42	-5	0-0	.985	1	181	82	1b14	0	-0.5
1970	Mon N	4	15	0	1	0	0	0	0	1-0	0	3	.067	.125	.067	-47	-3	0-0	.976	2	253	89	1b4	0	-0.2
Total	9	817	2284	242	578	93	8	108	356	139-34	16	371	.253	.298	.443	107	13	7-16	.990	1	98	103	1b588	0	-2.5
WHITFIELD, TERRY	Terry Bertland; B1.12.1953 Blythe CA; BL/TR/6´1˝/(195–200); [NYA71 1/19]; d9.29																								
1974	NY A	2	5	0	1	0	0	0	0	0-0	0	1	.200	.200	.200	15	-1	0-0	ø	-1	0	0	/cf	0	-0.1
1975	NY A	28	81	9	22	1	1	0	7	1-0	0	17	.272	.274	.309	67	-4	1-0	.978	1	101	173	O25(2/0/23)/D	0	-0.4
1976	NY A	1	0	0	0	0	0	0	0	0-0	0	0	ø	ø	ø	ø	0	0-0	ø	-0	0	0	/lf	0	0.0
1977	SF N	114	326	41	93	21	3	7	36	20-1	2	46	.285	.329	.433	103	1	2-3	.972	0	107	72	O84(22/22/49)	0	-0.3
1978	SF N	149	488	70	141	20	2	10	32	33-5	2	69	.289	.335	.400	108	4	5-11	.988	-1	103	66	O140(138/5/0)	0	-0.5
1979	SF N	133	394	52	113	20	4	5	44	36-6	4	47	.287	.349	.396	112	7	5-4	.957	0	95	138	O106(105/1/0)	0	0.2
1980	SF N	118	321	38	95	16	2	4	26	20-3	1	44	.296	.337	.396	108	3	4-2	.987	2	94	188	O95L	0	0.2
1984	LA N	87	180	15	44	8	0	4	18	17-2	1	35	.244	.313	.356	88	-3	1-4	.988	-1	91	130	O58(23/2/37)	15	-0.7
1985	†LA N	79	104	8	27	7	0	3	16	6-1	0	27	.260	.300	.413	100	0	0-0	.926	-1	83	188	O28(21/1/7)	0	-0.2

YEAR	TM LG	G	AB	R	H	2B	3B	HR	RBI	BB-IB	HP	SO	AVG	OBP	SLG	AOPS	ABR	SB-CS	FA	FR	RNG	THR	GAMES AT POSITION	DL	BFW
1986	LA N	19	14	0	1	0	0	0	0	5-2	0	2	.071	.316	.071	14	-1	0-0	1.000	0	159	0	/lf	0	-0.1
Total	10	730	1913	233	537	93	12	33	179	138-20	10	288	.281	.330	.394	103	6	18-24	.976	1	98	118	O539(408/32/116)/D	15	-1.9
WHITING, ED	Edward C. (aka Harry Zieber); B1860 Philadelphia PA; BL/TR/?/188; d5.2																								
1882	Bal AA	**74**	308	43	80	14	5	0	—	7	—	—	.260	.276	.338	115	6	—	.834	-6	—	—	C72,1b3,O2(1/0/1)	—	0.4
1883	Lou AA	58	240	35	70	16	4	2	—	9	—	—	.292	.317	.417	145	13	—	.884	-9	—	—	C50,O6(3/3/0),2b2/31	—	0.7
1884	Lou AA	42	157	16	35	7	3	0	18	9	2	—	.223	.274	.306	93	-1	—	.891	-6	—	—	C40,O2(1/0/1),1b2	—	-0.3
1886	Was N	6	21	0	0	0	0	0	0	1	—	12	.000	.045	.000	-92	-5	0	.919	-2	—	—	C6	—	-0.6
Total	4	180	726	94	185	37	12	2	<u>18</u>	26	—	<u>12</u>	.255	.282	.347	114	13	0	.866	-24	—	—	C168,O10(5/3/2),1b6,2b2/3	—	0.2
WHITMAN, DICK	Dick Corwin; B11.9.1920 Woodburn OR; D2.12.2003 Peoria AZ; BL/TR/5´11˝/170; d4.16; Col Oregon																								
1946	Bro N	104	265	39	69	15	3	2	31	22	0	19	.260	.317	.362	92	-3	5	1.000	3	110	83	O85(30/54/1)	0	-0.4
1947	Bro N	4	10	1	4	0	0	0	2	1	0	0	.400	.455	.400	124	0	0	1.000	0	114	0	O3(2/0/1)	0	0.0
1948	Bro N	60	165	24	48	13	0	0	20	14	0	12	.291	.346	.370	91	-2	4	.990	1	108	95	O48(12/4/34)	0	-0.2
1949	†Bro N	23	49	8	9	2	0	0	2	4	0	4	.184	.245	.224	26	-5	0	.952	-1	98	0	O11(10/0/1)	0	-0.7
1950	†Phi N	75	132	21	33	7	0	0	12	10	3	10	.250	.317	.303	65	-6	1	.983	0	101	101	O32(7/13/15)	0	-0.7
1951	Phi N	19	17	0	2	0	0	0	0	0	0	1	.118	.118	.118	-37	-3	0-0	ø	-0	0	0	O6(5/1/0)	0	-0.3
Total	6	285	638	93	165	37	3	2	67	51	3	46	.259	.316	.335	78	-19	10-<u>0</u>	.992	3	107	82	O185(66/72/52)	0	-2.3
WHITMAN, FRANK	Walter Franklin "Hooker"; B8.15.1924 Marengo IN; D2.6.1994 Maryville IL; BR/TR/6´2˝/175; d6.30																								
1946	Chi A	17	16	7	1	0	0	0	1	2	1	6	.063	.211	.063	-22	-3	0-1	1.000	1	153	0	S6/12	0	-0.2
1948	Chi A	3	6	0	0	0	0	0	0	0	0	3	.000	.000	.000	-99	-2	0-0	.500	-1	63	124	/S	0	-0.3
Total	2	20	22	7	1	0	0	0	1	2	1	9	.045	.160	.045	-43	-5	0-1	.885	-0	128	35	S7/21	0	-0.5
WHITMER, DAN	Daniel Charles; B11.23.1955 Redlands CA; BR/TR/6´3˝/195; [AnaA78 14/352]; d7.20; C3; Col Cal St.–Fullerton																								
1980	Cal A	48	87	8	21	3	0	0	7	4-0	0	21	.241	.269	.276	52	-6	1-0	1.000	3	106	72	C48	0	-0.1
1981	Tor A	7	9	0	1	1	0	0	0	1-0	0	2	.111	.200	.222	20	-1	0-0	1.000	1	95	0	C7	0	0.0
Total	2	55	96	8	22	4	0	0	7	5-0	0	23	.229	.262	.271	49	-7	1-0	1.000	3	105	66	C55	0	-0.1
WHITMORE, DARRELL	Darrell Lamont; B11.18.1968 Front Royal VA; BL/TR/6´1˝/210; [CleA90 2/46]; d6.25; Col West Virginia																								
1993	Fla N	76	250	24	51	8	2	4	19	10-0	5	72	.204	.249	.300	44	-21	4-2	.979	0	108	60	O69(1/0/69)	0	-2.4
1994	Fla N	9	22	1	5	1	0	0	0	3-0	0	5	.227	.320	.273	54	-1	0-1	1.000	0	125	0	O6(5/0/1)	0	-0.2
1995	Fla N	27	58	6	11	2	0	1	2	5-0	0	15	.190	.250	.276	39	-5	0-0	.960	-2	85	0	O16(0/14/3)	120	-0.7
Total	3	112	330	31	67	11	2	5	21	18-0	5	92	.203	.254	.294	44	-27	4-3	.978	-1	106	47	O91(6/14/73)	120	-3.3
WHITNEY, PINKY	Arthur Carter; B1.2.1905 San Antonio TX; D9.1.1987 Center TX; BR/TR/5´10˝/165; d4.11																								
1928	Phi N	151	585	73	176	35	4	10	103	36	1	30	.301	.342	.426	96	-4	3	.955	5	99	83	3b149	—	1.0
1929	Phi N	**154**	612	89	200	43	14	8	115	61	2	35	.327	.390	.482	108	8	7	.967	**23**	**116**	113	3b154	—	3.7
1930	Phi N	149	606	87	207	41	5	8	117	40	1	41	.342	.383	.465	97	-2	3	.965	21	**113**	91	3b148	—	2.5
1931	Phi N	130	501	64	144	36	5	9	74	30	3	38	.287	.331	.433	96	-3	6	.948	-6	91	84	3b128	—	-0.4
1932	Phi N	**154**	624	93	186	33	11	13	124	35	0	66	.298	.335	.449	97	-3	6	**.960**	3	97	110	3b151,2b5	—	0.6
1933	Phi N	31	121	12	32	4	0	3	19	8	0	8	.264	.310	.372	83	-3	1	.963	-1	91	144	3b30	—	-0.3
	Bos N	100	382	42	94	17	2	8	49	25	2	23	.246	.296	.364	95	-3	2	.971	2	110	134	3b85,2b18	—	0.3
	Year	131	503	54	126	21	2	11	68	33	2	31	.250	.299	.366	92	-6	3	.969	1	105	**136**	3b115,2b18	—	0.0
1934	Bos N	146	563	58	146	26	2	12	79	25	3	54	.259	.294	.377	85	-14	7	**.968**	2	107	72	3b111,2b36,S2	—	-0.6
1935	Bos N	126	458	41	125	23	4	4	60	24	2	36	.273	.312	.367	89	-8	2	.958	3	110	65	3b74,2b49	—	0.1
1936	Bos N	10	40	1	7	0	0	0	5	2	1	4	.175	.233	.175	12	-5	0	.971	1	98	144	3b10	—	-0.4
	Phi N★	114	411	44	121	17	3	6	59	37	1	33	.294	.354	.394	92	-4	2	.955	12	120	100	3b111/2	—	1.2
	Year	124	451	45	128	17	3	6	64	39	2	37	.284	.343	.375	86	-9	2	.956	13	**118**	104	3b121/2	—	0.8
1937	Phi N	138	487	56	166	19	4	8	79	43	1	44	.341	.395	.446	118	13	6	**.982**	3	103	93	3b130	—	2.1
1938	Phi N	102	300	27	83	9	1	3	38	27	0	22	.277	.336	.343	90	-4	0	.934	-4	95	60	3b75,1b4,2b2	—	-0.6
1939	Phi N	34	75	9	14	0	1	1	6	7	0	4	.187	.256	.253	38	-7	0	.991	1	131	98	1b12,2b8,3b2	—	-0.6
Total	12	1539	5765	696	1701	303	56	93	927	400	17	438	.295	.343	.415	96	-39	45	.961	67	105	95	3b1358,2b119,1b16,S2	—	8.6
WHITNEY, ART	Arthur Wilson; B1.16.1858 Brockton MA; D8.15.1943 Lowell MA; BR/TR/5´8˝/155; d5.1; b–Frank; ▲																								
1880	Wor N	76	302	38	67	13	5	1	36	9	—	15	.222	.244	.308	79	-7	—	.860	-2	103	78	3b76	—	-0.6
1881	Det N	58	214	23	39	7	5	0	9	7	—	15	.182	.208	.262	45	-14	—	.849	7	121	111	3b58	—	-0.4
1882	Pro N	11	40	2	3	0	0	0	1	2	—	11	.075	.119	.075	-36	-6	—	.784	-3	97	75	S11	—	-0.8
	Det N	31	115	10	21	0	0	0	4	1	—	12	.183	.190	.183	20	-10	—	.854	-2	82	97	3b22,S8,P3	—	-1.0
	Year	42	155	12	24	0	0	0	5	3	—	23	.155	.171	.155	5	-16	—	.854	-5	82	97	3b22,S19,P3	—	-1.8
1884	Pit AA	23	94	10	28	4	0	0	—	1	0	—	.298	.305	.340	112	1	—	.916	3	121	37	3b21/cfS	—	0.4
1885	Pit AA	90	373	53	87	10	4	0	28	16	1	—	.233	.267	.282	74	-11	—	**.918**	-15	85	101	S75,3b8,2b4,O3L	—	-2.1
1886	Pit AA	136	511	70	122	13	4	0	55	51	6	—	.239	.315	.280	87	-5	15	**.906**	12	108	**139**	3b95,S42/P	—	0.8
1887	Pit N	119	431	57	112	11	4	0	51	55	2	18	.260	.346	.304	89	-2	10	**.924**	-8	96	68	3b119	—	-0.7
1888	†NY N	90	328	28	72	1	4	1	28	8	1	22	.220	.240	.256	59	-16	7	.887	5	103	104	3b90	—	-1.0
1889	†NY N	129	473	71	103	12	2	1	59	56	2	39	.218	.303	.258	57	-27	19	.882	2	98	120	3b129/P	—	-2.0
1890	NY P	119	442	71	97	12	3	0	45	64	3	19	.219	.322	.260	52	-31	8	.865	-12	89	74	3b88,S31	—	-3.2
1891	Cin AA	93	347	42	69	6	1	3	33	31	3	20	.199	.270	.248	45	-27	8	.903	-6	95	74	3b93	—	-2.7
	StL AA	3	11	0	0	0	0	0	0	1	0	2	.000	.083	.000	-66	-2	0	.867	1	170	0	3b3	—	-0.1
	Year	96	358	42	69	6	1	3	33	32	3	22	.193	.265	.240	41	-29	8	**.902**	-5	98	71	3b96	—	-2.8
Total	11	978	3681	475	820	89	32	6	<u>349</u>	302	18	<u>173</u>	.223	.285	.269	64	-157	67	.888	-18	101	94	3b802,S168,P5,2b4,O4(3/1/0)	—	-13.4
WHITNEY, FRANK	Frank Thomas "Jumbo"; B2.18.1856 Brockton MA; D10.30.1943 Baltimore MD; BR/TR/5´7.5˝/152; d5.17; b–Art																								
1876	Bos N	34	139	27	33	7	1	0	15	1	—	3	.237	.243	.302	79	-3	—	.818	1	129	278	O34(24/0/10)/2	—	-0.3
WHITT, ERNIE	Leo Ernest; B6.13.1952 Detroit MI; BL/TR/6´2˝/(200–205); [BosA72 15/352]; d9.12; C2; Col Macomb (MI) CC																								
1976	Bos A	8	18	4	4	2	0	1	3	2-0	0	2	.222	.300	.500	118	0	0-0	1.000	-1	264	38	C8	0	0.0
1977	Tor A	23	41	4	7	3	0	0	6	2-0	0	12	.171	.200	.244	23	-4	0-0	1.000	1	94	96	C14	41	-0.3
1978	Tor A	2	4	0	0	0	0	0	0	1-0	0	1	.000	.200	.000	-38	-1	0-0	1.000	1	0	279	/C	0	0.0
1980	Tor A	106	295	23	70	12	2	6	34	22-0	0	30	.237	.287	.353	72	-12	1-3	.986	6	87	107	C105	0	-0.2
1981	Tor A	74	195	16	46	9	0	1	16	20-3	0	30	.236	.307	.297	71	-7	5-2	.991	13	129	105	C72	0	0.9
1982	Tor A	105	284	28	74	14	2	11	42	26-5	0	34	.261	.317	.440	98	-1	3-1	.982	4	105	81	C98/D	0	0.7
1983	Tor A	123	344	53	88	15	2	17	56	50-5	0	55	.256	.346	.459	113	7	1-1	.992	14	118	108	C119	0	2.5
1984	Tor A	124	315	35	75	12	1	15	46	43-7	1	49	.238	.327	.425	104	2	0-3	.994	13	108	83	C118	15	1.8
1985	†Tor A★	139	412	55	101	21	2	19	64	47-9	1	59	.245	.323	.444	105	3	3-6	.988	13	121	80	C134	0	1.9
1986	Tor A	131	395	48	106	19	2	16	56	35-3	0	39	.268	.326	.448	106	3	0-1	.991	-1	114	89	C129	15	0.6
1987	Tor A	135	446	57	120	24	1	19	75	44-4	1	50	.269	.334	.455	105	3	0-1	.994	17	107	116	C131	0	2.3
1988	Tor A	127	398	63	100	11	2	16	70	61-4	1	38	.251	.348	.410	112	7	4-2	.994	-2	82	99	C123	0	1.2
1989	†Tor A	129	385	42	101	24	1	11	53	52-2	0	53	.262	.349	.416	117	10	5-4	.992	1	112	87	C115,D8	0	1.7
1990	Atl N	67	180	14	31	8	0	2	10	23-1	0	27	.172	.265	.250	41	-14	0-2	.991	-3	67	166	C59	57	-1.5
1991	Bal A	35	62	5	15	2	0	0	3	8-0	0	12	.242	.329	.274	71	-2	0-0	1.000	-1	80	133	C20,D2	0	-0.3
Total	15	1328	3774	447	938	176	15	134	534	436-43	4	491	.249	.324	.410	98	-6	22-26	.991	74	106	99	C1246,D11	128	11.3
WHITTED, POSSUM	George Bostic; B2.4.1890 Durham NC; D10.16.1962 Wilmington NC; BR/TR/5´8.5˝/168; d9.16; OF(442/94/117)																								
1912	StL N	12	46	7	12	3	0	0	7	3	0	5	.261	.306	.326	75	-2	1	.857	-3	71	56	3b12	—	-0.4
1913	StL N	123	404	44	89	10	5	0	38	31	4	44	.220	.282	.270	59	-22	9-16	.989	3	106	90	O41(20/3/18),S38,3b22,2b7,1b2	—	-2.3
1914	StL N	20	31	3	4	1	0	0	1	0	0	3	.129	.129	.161	-14	-4	1	.889	-2	97	148	3b5,O3(2/0/2)/2	—	-0.6
	†Bos N	66	218	36	57	11	4	2	31	18	3	18	.261	.326	.376	109	2	10	.967	-2	100	76	O38(4/25/10),2b15,1b4,3b4,S3	—	-0.2
	Year	86	249	39	61	12	4	2	32	18	3	21	.245	.304	.349	95	-2	11	.957	-3	97	74	O41(6/25/12),2b16,3b9,1b4,S3	—	-0.8
1915	†Phi N	128	448	46	126	17	3	1	43	29	2	47	.281	.328	.339	101	0	24-15	.978	-1	100	48	O119(53/66/0),1b7	—	-0.9
1916	Phi N	147	526	68	148	20	12	6	68	19	2	46	.281	.309	.399	113	5	29-17	.964	3	110	92	O136L,1b16	—	0.3
1917	Phi N	149	553	69	155	24	9	3	70	30	0	56	.280	.317	.373	107	3	10	.977	4	102	114	O141L,1b10,3b7/2	—	0.1
1918	Phi N	24	86	7	21	4	0	0	3	4	0	10	.244	.278	.291	69	-3	4	.982	1	112	112	O22L/1	—	-0.4
1919	Phi N	78	289	32	72	14	1	3	32	14	0	20	.249	.284	.336	80	-7	5	.955	-1	96	138	O47L,2b26,1b2	—	-1.1
	Pit N	35	131	15	51	7	7	0	21	6	1	4	.389	.420	.550	183	12	7	.988	3	140	131	1b33,3b2/lf	—	1.6
	Year	113	420	47	123	21	8	3	53	20	1	24	.293	.327	.402	112	5	12	.955	2	96	137	O48L,1b35,2b26,3b2	—	0.5

YEAR	TM LG	G	AB	R	H	2B	3B	HR	RBI	BB-IB	HP	SO	AVG	OBP	SLG	AOPS	ABR	SB-CS	FA	FR	RNG	THR	GAMES AT POSITION	DL	BFW
1920	Pit N	134	494	53	129	11	12	1	74	35	3	36	.261	.314	.338	85	-10	11-11	.961	-4	92	81	3b125,1b10/lf	—	-1.4
1921	Pit N	108	403	60	114	23	7	7	63	26	1	21	.283	.328	.427	96	-3	5-10	.988	6	118	62	O102(15/0/87),1b7	—	-0.9
1922	Bro N	1	1	0	0	0	0	0	0	0	0	0	.000	.000	.000	-99	0	0-0	ø	0	—	—	/H	—	0.0
Total	11	1025	3630	440	978	145	60	23	451	215	16	310	.269	.313	.361	95	-29	116-69	.975	5	105	87	O651L,3b177,1b92,2b50,S41	—	-6.2
Wicker, Floyd	Floyd Euliss; B9.12.1943 Burlington NC; BL/TR/6´2˝/(175–185); d6.23; Col East Carolina																								
1968	StL N	5	4	2	2	0	0	0	0	0-0	0	0	.500	.500	.500	204	0	0-0	ø	0	—	—	/H	0	0.1
1969	Mon N	41	39	2	4	0	0	0	2	2-0	0	20	.103	.146	.103	-29	-7	0-0	1.000	1	149	0	O11(2/7/2)	0	-0.7
1970	Mil A	15	41	3	8	1	0	1	3	1-0	0	8	.195	.214	.293	38	-4	0-0	1.000	-0	103	0	O12(8/0/4)	0	-0.5
1971	Mil A	11	8	0	1	0	0	0	0	2-0	0	0	.125	.300	.125	24	-1	0-0	ø	0	—	—	/H	24	-0.1
	SF N	9	21	3	3	0	0	0	1	2-0	1	5	.143	.250	.143	14	-2	0-0	1.000	1	108	253	O7L	0	-0.2
Total	4	81	113	10	18	1	0	1	6	7-0	1	33	.159	.215	.195	15	-14	0-0	1.000	1	114	83	O30(17/7/6)	24	-1.4
Wickland, Al	Albert; B1.27.1888 Chicago IL; D3.14.1980 Port Washington WI; BL/TL/5´7˝/155; d8.21																								
1913	Cin N	26	79	7	17	5	5	0	8	6	1	19	.215	.279	.405	94	-1	3-4	.983	1	111	66	O24C	—	-0.3
1914	Chi F	**157**	536	74	148	31	10	6	68	**81**	4	58	.276	.375	.405	119	9	17	.962	-2	101	88	O157(30/1/129)	—	-0.2
1915	Chi F	30	86	11	21	2	2	1	5	13	0	11	.244	.343	.349	101	-1	3	.946	-0	92	111	O24(5/0/20)	—	-0.3
	Pit F	110	389	63	117	12	8	1	30	52	2	47	.301	.386	.380	117	5	23	.968	4	116	77	O109(109/0/1)	—	0.5
	Year	140	475	74	138	14	10	2	35	65	2	58	.291	.378	.375	114	4	26	.966	4	112	82	O133(114/0/21)	—	0.2
1918	Bos N	95	332	55	87	7	13	4	32	53	2	39	.262	.367	.398	139	17	12	.975	-0	109	71	O95(1/0/94)	—	1.3
1919	NY A	26	46	2	7	1	0	0	1	2	0	10	.152	.188	.174	2	-6	0	1.000	-1	95	0	O15R	—	-0.8
Total	5	444	1468	212	397	58	38	12	144	207	9	184	.270	.364	.386	117	23	58-4	.968	1	107	79	O424(145/25/259)	—	0.2
Widger, Chris	Christopher Jon; B5.21.1971 Wilmington DE; BR/TR/6´3˝/(195–220); [SeaA92 3/82]; d6.23; Col George Mason; [DL 2001 Sea A 190]																								
1995	†Sea A	23	45	2	9	0	0	1	2	3-0	0	11	.200	.245	.267	34	-5	0-0	1.000	-6	88	0	C19,O3(2/0/1)/D	0	-1.0
1996	Sea A	8	11	1	2	0	0	0	0	0-0	1	5	.182	.250	.182	12	-2	0-0	.905	-2	224	0	C7	0	-0.3
1997	Mon N	91	278	30	65	20	3	7	37	22-1	1	59	.234	.290	.403	81	-9	2-0	.981	-25	54	80	C85	0	-2.8
1998	Mon N	125	417	36	97	18	1	15	53	29-2	0	85	.233	.281	.388	76	-16	6-1	.983	4	88	**143**	C123	0	-0.3
1999	Mon N	124	383	42	101	24	1	14	56	28-0	7	86	.264	.325	.441	95	-4	1-4	.992	-5	77	94	C118	0	-0.3
2000	Mon N	86	281	31	67	17	2	12	34	29-3	1	61	.238	.311	.441	87	-7	1-2	.985	-1	90	93	C85	14	-0.2
	Sea A	10	11	1	1	0	0	1	1	1-0	0	2	.091	.167	.364	30	-1	0-0	1.000	-1	0	0	C6,1b2/rf	0	-0.2
2002	NY A	21	64	4	19	5	0	0	5	2-0	2	9	.297	.338	.375	90	-1	0-0	.983	-3	120	66	C21	0	-0.3
2003	StL N	44	102	9	24	9	0	0	14	6-1	1	20	.235	.279	.324	59	-6	0-0	.995	-3	131	84	C41/1rf	23	-0.6
2005	†Chi A	45	141	18	34	8	0	4	11	10-0	1	22	.241	.296	.383	76	-5	0-2	.981	-2	82	24	C42/13D	0	-0.5
2006	Chi A	27	76	6	14	3	0	1	7	9-0	0	20	.184	.264	.263	38	-7	0-0	.973	-10	65	65	C22,D4	0	-1.5
	Bal A	9	17	0	2	0	0	0	2	2-0	0	4	.118	.211	.118	-12	-3	0-0	1.000	0	64	89	C6/D	24	-0.2
	Year	36	93	6	16	3	0	1	9	11-0	0	24	.172	.255	.237	29	-10	0-0	.979	-10	65	70	C28,D5	0	-1.7
Total	10	613	1826	180	435	104	7	55	222	141-7	14	384	.238	.296	.393	78	-66	10-9	.985	-52	84	92	C575,D7,O5(2/0/3),1b4/3	251	-8.2
Wiedenbauer, Tom	Thomas John; B11.5.1958 Menomonie WI; BR/TR/6´1˝/175; [HouN76 7/145]; d9.14																								
1979	Hou N	4	6	0	4	1	0	0	2	0-0	0	2	.667	.667	.833	326	2	0-0	1.000	-0	97	0	O3(1/1/1)	0	0.2
Wiedman, Stump	George Edward; B2.17.1861 Rochester NY; D3.2.1905 New York NY; BR/TR/5´7.5˝/165; d8.26; U1; ▲																								
1880	Buf N	23	78	8	8	1	0	0	3	2	—	11	.103	.125	.115	-18	-9	—	.893	-1	79	0	P17,O13(1/11/1)	—	-0.4
1881	Det N	13	47	9	12	1	0	0	5	2	—	2	.255	.286	.277	75	0	—	**1.000**	-2	68	0	P13	—	0.0
1882	Det N	50	193	20	42	7	1	0	20	2	—	19	.218	.226	.264	57	-9	—	.906	0	91	84	P46,O6(1/2/2)/S	—	0.0
1883	Det N	79	313	34	58	6	1	1	24	4	—	38	.185	.196	.220	27	-27	—	.909	-4	91	43	P52,O35(1/5/29),2b4	—	-1.4
1884	Det N	81	300	24	49	6	0	0	26	13	—	41	.163	.198	.183	22	-26	—	.846	-5	101	95	O53R,P26/S2	—	-2.1
1885	Det N	44	153	7	24	2	1	1	14	8	—	32	.157	.199	.203	30	-12	—	.867	-6	78	0	P38,O7(6/1/0)/2	—	-0.5
1886	KC N	51	179	13	30	2	0	0	7	5	—	46	.168	.190	.179	12	-19	3	.936	3	120	155	P51,O3(1/2/0)	—	0.1
1887	Det N	21	82	12	17	2	0	1	11	3	0	3	.207	.235	.268	38	-7	6	.837	-1	102	0	P21,O2L	—	0.0
	NY AA	14	46	5	7	1	1	0	1	4	0	—	.152	.220	.217	23	-5	2	.882	2	106	0	P12,O3(1/0/2)	—	0.1
	NY N	1	3	0	1	0	0	0	0	0	0	0	.333	.333	.333	90	0	0	.500	-0	67	0	/P	—	0.0
1888	NY N	2	7	1	0	0	0	0	1	2	0	1	.000	.222	.000	-24	0	0	.714	-0	51	0	P2	—	0.0
Total	9	379	1401	133	248	28	4	3	112	45	0	193	.177	.203	.209	28	-114	11	.885	-12	95	57	P279,O122(13/21/87),2b6,S2	—	-4.2
Wieghaus, Tom	Thomas Robert; B2.1.1957 Chicago Heights IL; BR/TR/6´0˝/195; [MonN78 10/243]; d10.4; Col Illinois St.																								
1981	Mon N	1	1	0	0	0	0	0	0	0-0	0	0	.000	.000	.000	-97	0	0-0	1.000	-0	9	0	/C	0	0.0
1983	Mon N	1	0	0	0	0	0	0	0	0-0	0	0	ø	ø	ø	ø	0	0-0	1.000	0	0	0	/C	0	0.0
1984	Hou N	6	10	0	0	0	0	0	1	1-0	0	3	.000	.083	.000	-77	-2	0-0	1.000	0	55	118	C6	0	-0.2
Total	3	8	11	0	0	0	0	0	1	1-0	0	3	.000	.077	.000	-79	-2	0-0	1.000	0	50	107	C8	0	-0.2
Wietelmann, Whitey	William Frederick; B3.15.1919 Zanesville OH; D3.26.2002 San Diego CA; BB/TR (BR 1939–41)/6´0˝/170; d9.6; C13																								
1939	Bos N	23	69	2	14	1	0	0	5	2	0	9	.203	.225	.217	21	-8	1	.953	1	111	81	S22/2	—	-0.6
1940	Bos N	35	41	3	8	1	0	0	1	5	0	5	.195	.283	.220	43	-3	0	.962	2	84	175	2b15,3b9,S3	—	-0.1
1941	Bos N	16	33	1	3	0	0	0	0	1	0	2	.091	.118	.091	-43	-6	0	1.000	1	110	0	2b10,S5,3b2	0	-0.5
1942	Bos N	13	34	4	7	2	0	0	0	4	0	5	.206	.289	.265	64	-1	0	.941	-1	101	107	S11/2	0	-0.2
1943	Bos N	**153**	534	33	115	14	1	0	39	46	3	40	.215	.281	.245	53	-32	9	.957	18	**115**	101	S153	0	-0.1
1944	Bos N	125	417	46	100	18	1	2	32	33	3	25	.240	.300	.302	67	-18	0	.954	-2	96	108	S103,2b23/3	0	-1.2
1945	Bos N	123	428	53	116	15	3	4	33	39	2	27	.271	.335	.348	89	-6	4	.972	-5	94	124	2b87,S39,3b2/P	0	-0.4
1946	Bos N	44	78	7	16	0	0	0	5	14	0	8	.205	.326	.205	52	-4	0	.915	-4	74	77	S16,3b8,2b4,P3	0	-0.8
1947	Pit N	48	128	21	30	4	1	1	7	12	0	10	.234	.300	.305	59	-8	0	.885	-12	77	59	S22,2b14,3b6/1	0	-1.8
Total	9	580	1762	170	409	55	6	7	122	156	8	131	.232	.298	.282	63	-86	14	.952	-2	104	100	S374,2b155,3b28,P4/1	0	-5.7
Wiggins, Alan	Alan Anthony; B2.17.1958 Los Angeles CA; D1.6.1991 Los Angeles CA; BB/TR/6´2˝/(164–165); [AnaA77*1/7]; d9.4; Col Pasadena (CA) City																								
1981	SD N	15	14	4	5	0	0	0	0	1-0	0	0	.357	.400	.357	127	0	2-0	.750	-0	115	0	O4L	0	0.0
1982	SD N	72	254	40	65	3	3	1	15	13-0	1	19	.256	.295	.303	72	-11	33-6	.967	4	104	167	O68(51/19/6)/2	60	-0.4
1983	SD N	144	503	83	139	20	2	0	22	65-3	1	43	.276	.360	.324	94	-2	66-13	.992	7	115	100	O105(63/48/14),1b45	0	1.0
1984	†SD N	158	596	106	154	19	7	3	34	75-1	3	57	.258	.342	.329	89	-6	70-21	.962	-20	92	100	2b157	0	-1.0
1985	SD N	10	37	3	2	1	0	0	0	2-0	0	4	.054	.103	.081	-48	-7	0-1	1.000	-4	74	67	2b9	0	-1.2
	Bal A	76	298	43	85	11	4	0	21	29-0	2	16	.285	.353	.349	95	-1	30-13	.960	-19	82	109	2b76	0	-1.4
1986	Bal A	71	239	30	60	3	1	0	11	22-0	0	20	.251	.309	.272	62	-13	21-7	.978	-5	90	105	2b66/D	0	-1.2
1987	Bal A	85	306	37	71	4	2	1	15	28-0	1	34	.232	.298	.268	53	-21	20-7	.983	1	102	95	D44,2b33,O5L	0	-1.7
Total	7	631	2247	346	581	61	19	5	118	235-4	8	193	.259	.330	.309	79	-61	242-68	.967	-37	90	101	2b342,O182(123/67/20),D45,1b45	60	-5.9
Wigginton, Ty	Ty Allen; B10.11.1977 San Diego CA; BR/TR/6´0˝/(200–225); [NYN98 17/514]; d5.16; Col North Carolina–Asheville																								
2002	NY N	46	116	18	35	8	0	6	18	8-0	2	19	.302	.354	.526	136	6	2-1	.900	2	87	133	3b14,1b13,2b12,O2(1/0/1)	0	0.7
2003	NY N	156	573	73	146	36	6	11	71	46-2	9	124	.255	.318	.396	89	-10	12-2	.962	-10	93	91	3b155	0	-1.7
2004	NY N	86	312	46	89	23	2	12	42	23-4	1	48	.285	.334	.487	112	5	6-1	.924	-3	102	76	3b66,2b25,1b5	16	0.3
	Pit N	58	182	17	40	7	0	5	24	22-2	1	34	.220	.306	.341	67	-9	1-0	.955	-4	91	83	3b56	0	-1.2
	Year	144	494	63	129	30	2	17	66	45-6	2	82	.261	.324	.433	95	-4	7-1	.938	-7	97	79	3b122,2b25,1b5	0	-0.9
2005	Pit N	57	155	20	40	9	1	7	25	14-0	1	30	.258	.324	.465	103	0	0-1	.894	-10	78	72	3b40,1b3/2	0	-1.0
2006	TB A	122	444	55	122	25	1	24	79	32-3	6	97	.275	.330	.498	112	7	4-3	.997	4	127	70	1b45,2b43,3b34,O12(5/0/7)/D	32	0.8
Total	5	525	1782	229	472	108	10	65	259	145-11	20	352	.265	.325	.446	101	-1	25-8	.944	-21	93	87	3b365,2b81,1b66,O14(6/0/8)/D	48	-2.1
Wilber, Del	Delbert Quentin "Babe"; B2.24.1919 Lincoln Park MI; D7.18.2002 St.Petersburg FL; BR/TR/6´3˝/200; d4.21; M1/C4																								
1946	StL N	4	4	0	0	0	0	0	0	1	0	0	.000	.200	.000	-39	-1	0	1.000	1	*0*	*0*	C4	0	0.0
1947	StL N	51	99	7	23	8	1	0	12	5	0	13	.232	.269	.333	57	-6	0	.983	0	*115*	*73*	C34	0	-0.5
1948	StL N	27	58	5	11	2	0	0	10	4	0	9	.190	.242	.224	25	-6	0	.949	-1	*301*	*75*	C26	0	-0.7
1949	StL N	2	4	0	1	0	0	0	0	0	0	0	.250	.250	.250	33	0	0	1.000	0	*0*	*0*	C2	0	0.0
1951	Phi N	84	245	30	68	7	3	8	34	17	0	26	.278	.324	.429	102	0	0-1	.978	2	*119*	*68*	C73	0	0.5
1952	Phi N	2	2	0	0	0	0	0	0	0	0	1	.000	.000	.000	-99	-1	0-0	ø	0	—	—	/H	0	-0.1
	Bos A	47	135	7	36	10	1	3	23	7	1	20	.267	.308	.422	94	-1	1-0	.995	2	*122*	*106*	C39	0	0.3
1953	Bos A	58	112	16	27	6	1	7	29	6	1	21	.241	.286	.500	103	0	0-0	.980	-1	*103*	*66*	C28,1b2	0	-0.1
1954	Bos A	24	61	2	8	2	1	1	7	4	0	6	.131	.179	.246	15	-7	0-0	.950	-3	*70*	*102*	C18	0	-1.0
Total	8	299	720	67	174	35	7	19	115	44	2	96	.242	.286	.389	79	-22	1-1	.978	-0	*128*	*78*	C224,1b2	0	-1.6

YEAR	TM LG	G	AB	R	H	2B	3B	HR	RBI	BB-IB	HP	SO	AVG	OBP	SLG	AOPS	ABR	SB-CS	FA	FR	RNG	THR	GAMES AT POSITION	DL	BFW
Wilborn, Claude	Claude Edward; B9.1.1912 Woodsdale NC; D11.13.1992 Roxboro NC; BL/TR/6´1˝/180; d9.8																								
1940	Bos N	5	7	0	0	0	0	0	0	0	0	1	.000	.000	.000	-99	-2	0	.500	-1	46	0	O3R	—	-0.3
Wilborn, Ted	Thaddeaus Iglehart; B12.16.1958 Waco TX; BB/TR/6´0˝/(165–170); [NYA76 4/88]; d4.5																								
1979	Tor A	22	12	3	0	0	0	0	0	1-0	0	7	.000	.077	.000	-76	-3	0-1	.875	-1	73	0	O7(4/1/2),D4	0	-0.4
1980	NY A	8	8	2	2	0	0	0	1	0-0	0	1	.250	.250	.250	38	-1	0-0	1.000	1	129	720	O3(1/1/1)	0	0.0
Total	2	30	20	5	2	0	0	0	1	1-0	0	8	.100	.143	.100	-33	-4	0-1	.933	0	91	227	O10(5/2/3),D4	0	-0.4
Wiley, John	John; d6.23																								
1884	Was U	1	4	0	0	0	0	0	—	0	—	—	.000	.000	.000	-99	-1	—	.333	-1	61	0	/3	—	-0.2
Wilfong, Rob	Robert Donald; B9.1.1953 Pasadena CA; BL/TR/6´1˝/(160–185); [MinA71 13/314]; d4.10																								
1977	Min A	73	171	22	42	1	1	1	13	17-0	2	26	.246	.321	.281	66	-8	10-4	.959	-1	102	112	2b66/D	0	-0.5
1978	Min A	92	199	23	53	8	0	1	11	19-1	2	27	.266	.336	.322	84	-4	8-4	.986	-8	94	82	2b80,D5	15	-0.7
1979	Min A	140	419	71	131	22	6	9	59	29-3	2	54	.313	.352	.458	114	8	11-4	.979	19	111	111	2b133,O3(1/1/1)	0	3.3
1980	Min A	131	416	55	103	16	5	8	45	34-3	3	61	.248	.308	.368	79	-13	10-6	**.995**	4	104	110	2b120,O6C	0	-0.2
1981	Min A	93	305	32	75	11	3	3	19	29-1	0	43	.246	.311	.331	80	-8	2-4	.980	0	102	82	2b93	0	-0.4
1982	Min A	25	81	7	13	1	0	0	5	7-0	1	13	.160	.236	.173	14	-10	0-2	.980	1	110	125	2b22	0	-0.9
	†Cal A	55	102	17	25	4	2	1	11	7-1	0	17	.245	.294	.353	76	-4	4-0	.982	6	133	106	2b28,3b5,O3(1/2/0),S2/D	0	0.4
	Year	80	183	24	38	5	2	1	16	14-1	1	30	.208	.268	.273	48	-13	4-2	.981	6	121	116	2b50,3b5,O3(1/2/0),S2/D	0	-0.5
1983	Cal A	65	177	17	45	7	1	2	17	10-1	0	25	.254	.293	.339	74	-7	0-2	.995	8	111	100	2b39,3b13,S6/D	0	0.3
1984	Cal A	108	307	31	76	13	2	6	33	20-0	2	53	.248	.296	.362	82	-8	3-2	.975	6	112	94	2b97,S4/D	0	0.2
1985	Cal A	83	217	16	41	3	0	4	13	16-1	0	32	.189	.243	.258	38	-19	4-1	.986	13	119	116	2b69,D2	0	-0.2
1986	†Cal A	92	288	25	63	11	3	3	33	16-2	2	34	.219	.263	.309	56	-18	1-4	.982	4	109	102	2b90	0	-1.1
1987	SF N	2	8	2	1	0	0	1	2	1-0	0	2	.125	.222	.500	89	0	1-0	.833	-1	55	177	2b2	0	-0.1
Total	11	959	2690	318	668	97	23	39	261	205-13	14	387	.248	.303	.345	77	-91	54-33	.982	51	108	102	2b839,3b18,S12,O12(2/9/1),D11	15	0.1
Wilhelm, Spider	Charles Ernest; B5.23.1929 Baltimore MD; D10.20.1992 Venice FL; BR/TR/5´9˝/170; d9.6																								
1953	Phi A	7	7	1	2	1	0	0	0	0	0	3	.286	.286	.429	87	0	0-0	.875	-0	108	0	S6	0	0.0
Wilhelm, Jim	James Webster; B9.20.1952 San Rafael CA; BR/TR/6´3˝/190; [SDN74 7/145]; d9.4; Col Santa Clara																								
1978	SD N	10	19	2	7	2	0	0	4	0-0	1	2	.368	.381	.474	154	1	1-0	1.000	-1	59	0	O10(3/7/0)	0	0.0
1979	SD N	39	103	8	25	4	3	0	8	2-0	0	12	.243	.255	.340	65	-6	1-1	.985	0	90	200	O30(4/25/1)	0	-0.6
Total	2	49	122	10	32	6	3	0	12	2-0	1	14	.262	.276	.361	79	-5	2-1	.987	-1	84	164	O40(7/32/1)	0	-0.6
Wilhoit, Joe	Joseph William; B12.20.1885 Hiawatha KS; D9.25.1930 Santa Barbara CA; BL/TR/6´2˝/175; d4.12; Col DePaul																								
1916	Bos N	116	383	44	88	13	4	2	38	27	1	45	.230	.282	.300	82	-8	18	.979	3	109	98	O108(1/1/106)	—	-1.2
1917	Bos N	54	186	20	51	5	0	1	10	17	0	15	.274	.335	.317	107	2	5	.928	-2	86	112	O52R	—	-0.3
	Pit N	9	10	0	2	0	0	0	0	1	0	1	.200	.273	.200	45	-1	0	1.000	1	49	686	O3(1/0/2)/1	—	0.0
	†NY N	34	50	9	17	2	2	0	8	8	0	5	.340	.431	.460	179	5	0	1.000	0	104	97	O11(0/2/10)	—	0.5
	Year	97	246	29	70	7	2	1	18	26	0	21	.285	.353	.341	118	6	5	.941	-2	88	121	O66(1/2/64)/1	—	0.2
1918	NY N	64	135	13	37	3	3	0	15	17	0	14	.274	.355	.341	115	3	4	.975	-1	85	137	O55(3/34/15)	—	0.0
1919	Bos A	6	18	7	6	0	0	0	2	5	0	2	.333	.478	.333	138	1	1	1.000	-1	81	0	O5R	—	0.0
Total	4	283	782	93	201	23	9	3	73	75	1	82	.257	.323	.321	101	2	28	.969	1	98	109	O234(5/37/190)/1	—	-1.0
Wilie, Denney	Dennis Ernest; B9.22.1890 Mt.Calm TX; D6.20.1966 Hayward CA; BL/TL/5´8˝/155; d7.27; Col Baylor																								
1911	StL N	28	51	10	12	3	1	0	3	8	2	11	.235	.361	.333	97	0	3	1.000	0	90	140	O15(11/3/2)	—	0.0
1912	StL N	30	48	2	11	0	1	0	6	7	2	9	.229	.351	.271	73	-1	0	.917	-1	101	58	O16(3/1/12)	—	-0.3
1915	Cle A	45	131	14	33	4	1	2	10	26	2	18	.252	.384	.344	115	4	2-6	.910	-3	104	21	O35(11/24/0)	—	-0.3
Total	3	103	230	26	56	7	3	2	19	41	6	38	.243	.372	.326	102	3	5-6	.925	-4	101	49	O66(25/28/14)	—	-0.6
Wilke, Harry	Henry Joseph; B12.14.1900 Cincinnati OH; D6.21.1991 Hamilton OH; BR/TR/5´10.5˝/171; d5.12																								
1927	Chi N	3	9	0	0	0	0	0	0	0	0	1	.000	.000	.000	-99	-3	0	1.000	0	124	0	3b3	—	-0.2
Wilkerson, Curtis	Curtis Vernon; B4.26.1961 Petersburg VA; BB/TR/5´9˝/(158–175); [TexA80 4/92]; d9.10																								
1983	Tex A	16	35	7	6	0	1	0	1	2-0	0	5	.171	.216	.229	23	-4	3-0	1.000	1	111	70	S9,2b2,3b2	0	-0.1
1984	Tex A	153	484	47	120	12	0	1	26	22-0	2	72	.248	.282	.279	54	-30	12-10	.944	-25	92	79	S116,2b47	0	-4.4
1985	Tex A	129	360	35	88	11	6	0	22	22-0	4	63	.244	.293	.308	64	-18	14-7	.957	0	103	84	S110,2b19,D2	0	-0.6
1986	Tex A	110	236	27	56	10	3	0	15	11-0	1	42	.237	.273	.305	56	-15	9-7	.968	-1	99	110	2b60,S56,D2	0	-1.1
1987	Tex A	85	138	28	37	5	3	2	14	6-0	2	16	.268	.308	.391	83	-4	6-3	.946	-2	89	67	S33,2b28,3b18,D4	0	-0.3
1988	Tex A	117	338	41	99	12	5	0	28	26-3	2	43	.293	.345	.358	95	-2	9-4	.970	5	106	98	2b87,S24,3b11/D	0	0.7
1989	†Chi N	77	160	18	39	4	2	1	10	8-0	0	33	.244	.278	.313	65	-8	4-2	.881	4	103	63	3b26,2b15,S7/lf	0	-0.3
1990	Chi N	77	186	21	41	5	1	0	16	7-2	0	36	.220	.249	.258	37	-16	2-2	.888	-3	95	71	3b52,2b14/Slf	0	-2.0
1991	†Pit N	85	191	20	36	9	1	2	18	15-0	0	40	.188	.243	.277	48	-14	2-1	.992	7	121	124	2b30,S15,3b14	0	-0.5
1992	KC A	111	296	27	74	10	1	2	29	18-3	1	47	.250	.292	.311	68	-13	18-7	.968	-4	92	83	S69,2b39,3b5/D	0	-1.1
1993	KC A	12	28	1	4	0	0	0	0	1-0	0	6	.143	.172	.143	-13	-5	2-0	1.000	-1	120	104	2b10,S4	140	-0.4
Total	11	972	2452	272	600	78	23	8	179	138-8	12	403	.245	.286	.305	62	-129	81-43	.957	-19	95	84	S444,2b351,3b128,D10,O2L	140	-10.1
Wilkerson, Brad	Stephen Bradley; B6.1.1977 Owensboro KY; BL/TL/6´0˝/(200–205); [MonN98 1/33]; d7.12; Col Florida																								
2001	Mon N	47	117	11	24	7	2	1	5	17-1	0	41	.205	.304	.325	64	-6	2-1	.970	-0	97	88	O38L	0	-0.8
2002	Mon N	153	507	92	135	27	8	20	59	81-7	5	161	.266	.370	.469	114	12	7-8	.972	-0	88	**188**	O129(72/73/3),1b23	0	0.7
2003	Mon N	146	504	78	135	34	4	19	77	89-0	4	155	.268	.380	.464	117	15	13-10	.982	3	101	145	O135(95/42/16),1b27	0	1.3
2004	Mon N	160	572	112	146	39	2	32	67	106-8	4	152	.255	.374	.498	118	18	13-6	.995	10	119	101	1b86,O80(59/18/10)	0	1.9
2005	Was N	148	565	76	140	42	7	11	57	84-9	7	147	.248	.351	.405	102	4	8-10	.985	3	107	87	O129(38/92/6),1b25	0	0.3
2006	Tex A	95	320	56	71	15	2	15	44	37-1	3	116	.222	.306	.422	86	-7	3-2	.993	-0	91	123	O82(80/1/3),D12	53	-1.1
Total	6	749	2585	425	651	164	25	98	309	414-26	23	772	.252	.358	.448	108	36	46-37	.981	16	99	141	O593(382/226/38),1b161,D12	53	2.3
Wilkins, Rick	Richard David; B6.4.1967 Jacksonville FL; BL/TR/6´2˝/(210–215); [ChiN86 23/582]; d6.6; Col Furman																								
1991	Chi N	86	203	21	45	9	0	6	22	19-2	6	56	.222	.307	.355	82	-5	3-3	.993	5	112	119	C82	0	0.4
1992	Chi N	83	244	20	66	9	1	8	22	28-7	0	53	.270	.344	.414	111	4	0-2	.993	12	111	114	C73	0	2.0
1993	Chi N	136	446	78	135	23	1	30	73	50-13	3	99	.303	.376	.561	148	30	2-1	.996	17	140	**131**	C133	0	5.4
1994	Chi N	100	313	44	71	25	2	7	39	40-5	2	86	.227	.317	.387	83	-7	4-3	.993	1	119	111	C95,1b2	0	-0.1
1995	Chi N	50	162	24	31	2	0	6	14	36-1	1	51	.191	.340	.315	75	-5	0-0	.988	-0	101	130	C49,1b2	0	-0.2
	Hou N	15	40	6	10	1	0	1	5	10-1	0	10	.250	.392	.350	107	1	0-0	1.000	-1	112	78	C13	65	0.1
	Year	65	202	30	41	3	0	7	19	46-2	1	61	.203	.351	.322	81	-4	0-0	.990	-2	103	119	C62,1b2	0	-0.1
1996	Hou N	84	254	34	54	8	2	6	23	46-10	1	81	.213	.330	.331	83	-5	0-1	.990	-1	101	98	C82	0	-0.2
	SF N	52	157	19	46	10	0	8	36	21-3	0	40	.293	.366	.510	134	8	0-2	.991	-5	85	164	C42,1b7	0	0.4
	Year	136	411	53	100	18	2	14	59	67-13	1	121	.243	.344	.399	103	3	0-3	.990	-6	96	119	C124,1b7	0	0.2
1997	SF N	66	190	18	37	5	0	6	23	17-0	0	65	.195	.257	.316	51	-15	0-0	.986	3	126	153	C57	0	-0.8
	†Sea A	5	12	2	3	1	0	1	4	1-0	0	2	.250	.286	.583	126	0	0-0	1.000	-1	31	167	C3,D2	19	-0.1
1998	Sea A	19	41	5	8	1	1	1	4	4-0	0	14	.195	.261	.341	56	-3	0-0	1.000	-1	171	63	C6,1b6,D2	0	-0.4
	NY N	5	15	3	2	0	0	0	1	2-0	0	2	.133	.235	.133	0	-2	0-0	.957	-2	82	90	C4	0	-0.4
1999	LA N	3	4	0	0	0	0	0	0	0-0	0	2	.000	.000	.000	-99	-1	0-0	1.000	0	0	0	/C	0	-0.1
2000	†StL N	4	11	3	3	0	0	0	1	2-0	0	2	.273	.385	.273	69	0	0-0	1.000	3	0	125	C3	0	0.2
2001	SD N	12	22	3	4	1	0	1	8	2-0	0	8	.182	.250	.364	60	-1	0-0	1.000	1	104	0	C7/1	0	0.0
Total	11	720	2114	280	515	95	7	81	275	278-42	13	571	.244	.332	.410	99	-1	9-12	.992	29	116	122	C650,1b18,D4	84	6.2
Wilkins, Bobby	Robert Linwood; B8.11.1922 Denton NC; BR/TR/5´9˝/165; d4.18; Col Catawba																								
1944	Phi A	24	25	7	6	0	0	0	3	1	1	4	.240	.296	.240	55	-1	0-0	.943	2	128	96	S9	0	0.1
1945	Phi A	62	154	22	40	6	0	0	4	10	0	17	.260	.305	.299	76	-5	2-4	.923	-1	102	96	S40,O4L	0	-0.5
Total	2	86	179	29	46	6	0	0	7	11	1	21	.257	.304	.291	73	-6	2-4	.926	1	105	96	S49,O4L	0	-0.4
Wilkinson, Ed	Edward Henry; B6.20.1890 Jacksonville OR; D4.9.1918 Tucson AZ; BR/TR/6´0˝/170; d7.4; Col St. Marys (CA)																								
1911	NY A	10	13	2	3	0	0	0	1	0	0	—	.231	.231	.231	27	-1	0	.800	-0	104	0	O3L/2	—	-0.2

YEAR	TM LG	G	AB	R	H	2B	3B	HR	RBI	BB-IB	HP	SO	AVG	OBP	SLG	AOPS	ABR	SB-CS	FA	FR	RNG	THR	GAMES AT POSITION	DL	BFW
WILL, BOB Robert Lee "Butch"; B7.15.1931 Berwyn IL; BL/TL/5´10.5˝/175; d4.16; Col Mankato St.																									
1957	Chi N	70	112	13	25	3	0	1	10	5-0	0	21	.223	.254	.277	44	-9	1-0	.963	-1	101	73	O30C	0	-1.1
1958	Chi N	6	4	1	1	0	0	0	0	2-0	0	0	.250	.500	.250	108	0	0-0	ø	-0	0	0	/rf	0	0.0
1960	Chi N	138	475	58	121	20	9	6	53	47-3	1	54	.255	.321	.373	91	-6	1-5	.992	1	103	91	O121(4/0/117)	0	-1.2
1961	Chi N	86	113	9	29	9	0	0	8	15-0	0	19	.257	.341	.336	80	-2	0-1	1.000	-1	109	0	O30(9/0/22)/1	0	-0.5
1962	Chi N	87	92	6	22	3	0	2	15	13-2	0	22	.239	.327	.337	78	-3	0-0	1.000	-0	107	0	O9R	0	-0.3
1963	Chi N	23	23	0	4	0	0	0	1	1-0	0	3	.174	.208	.174	11	-3	0-0	1.000	-0	0	170	/1	0	-0.3
Total	6	410	819	87	202	35	9	9	87	83-5	1	119	.247	.314	.344	80	-23	2-6	.988	-1	103	75	O191(13/30/149),1b2	0	-3.4
WILLARD, JERRY Gerald Duane; B3.14.1960 Oxnard CA; BL/TR/6´2˝/195; d4.11; Col Oxnard (CA) JC																									
1984	Cle A	87	246	21	55	8	1	10	37	26-0	0	55	.224	.295	.386	86	-5	1-0	.981	-5	85	109	C76/D	0	-0.7
1985	Cle A	104	300	39	81	13	0	7	36	28-1	1	59	.270	.333	.383	96	-1	0-0	.990	4	76	109	C96/D	0	0.6
1986	Oak A	75	161	17	43	7	0	4	26	22-0	2	28	.267	.354	.385	111	4	0-1	.994	-9	76	67	C71/D	0	-0.3
1987	Oak A	7	6	1	1	0	0	0	0	2-0	0	1	.167	.375	.167	54	0	0-0	1.000	-0	0	0	/13D	49	-0.1
1990	Chi A	3	3	0	0	0	0	0	0	0-0	0	2	.000	.000	.000	-99	-1	0-0	ø	-0	0	0	/C	0	-0.1
1991	†Atl N	17	14	1	3	0	0	1	4	2-0	0	5	.214	.313	.429	100	0	0-0	1.000	0	0	0	/C	0	0.0
1992	Atl N	26	23	2	8	1	0	2	7	1-1	0	3	.348	.375	.652	175	2	0-0	1.000	0	0	0	/C	0	0.2
	Mon N	21	25	0	3	0	0	0	1	1-0	0	7	.120	.154	.120	-22	-4	0-0	.952	0	139	0	1b5	0	-0.4
	Year	47	48	2	11	1	0	2	8	2-1	0	10	.229	.260	.375	75	-2	0-0	.952	0	139	0	1b5/C	0	-0.2
1994	Sea A	6	5	1	1	0	0	1	3	1-0	0	1	.200	.333	.800	176	0	0-0	ø	-0	0	0	/CD	0	0.0
Total	8	346	783	82	195	29	1	25	114	83-2	3	161	.249	.320	.384	94	-5	1-1	.988	-11	79	98	C247,D7,1b6/3	49	-0.8
WILLIAMS, RIP Alva Mitchel "Buff"; B1.31.1882 Carthage IL; D7.23.1933 Keokuk IA; BR/TR/6´0.5˝/187; d4.12																									
1911	Bos A	95	284	36	68	8	5	0	31	24	7	—	.239	.314	.303	73	-10	9	.975	-0	86	111	1b57,C38	—	-0.9
1912	Was A	60	157	14	50	11	4	0	22	7	1	—	.318	.352	.439	125	4	2	.978	8	*131*	*106*	C48	—	1.6
1913	Was A	66	106	9	30	6	2	1	12	9	0	16	.283	.339	.406	115	2	3	.985	-0	*100*	*95*	C18,1b9,O5(0/1/4)	—	0.2
1914	Was A	81	169	17	47	6	4	1	22	13	3	19	.278	.341	.379	112	2	2-2	.975	-3	*99*	*108*	C44,1b8/rf	—	0.2
1915	Was A	91	197	14	48	8	4	0	31	18	4	20	.244	.320	.325	91	-2	4-3	.967	7	*117*	*90*	C40,1b15/3	—	0.8
1916	Was A	76	202	16	54	10	2	0	20	15	2	19	.267	.324	.337	100	0	5	.982	-6	60	108	1b34,C23/3	—	-0.5
1918	Cle A	28	71	5	17	2	2	0	7	9	0	6	.239	.325	.324	87	-1	2	.980	-1	81	99	1b21/C	—	-0.3
Total	7	497	1186	111	314	51	23	2	145	95	17	<u>80</u>	.265	.328	.352	97	-5	27-<u>5</u>	.977	5	*110*	*94*	C212,1b144,O6(0/1/5),3b2	—	1.1
WILLIAMS, ART Arthur Franklin; B8.26.1877 Somerville MA; D5.16.1941 Arlington VA; BL/TR; d5.7; Col Tufts																									
1902	Chi N	49	167	20	38	3	0	0	14	17	3	—	.228	.310	.246	74	-4	9	.921	-2	33	0	O26(4/0/22),1b19	—	-0.8
WILLIAMS, GUS August Joseph "Gloomy Gus"; B5.7.1888 Omaha NE; D4.16.1964 Sterling IL; BL/TL/6´0˝/185; d4.12; b–Harry																									
1911	StL A	9	26	1	7	3	0	0	4	0	1	—	.269	.296	.385	93	0	0	.867	-1	106	0	O7L	—	-0.1
1912	StL A	64	216	32	63	13	7	2	32	27	0	—	.292	.370	.444	138	11	18	.930	2	101	136	O62R	—	0.9
1913	StL A	148	538	72	147	21	16	5	53	57	3	87	.273	.346	.400	121	13	31	.951	4	102	118	O143R	—	1.0
1914	StL A	144	499	51	126	19	6	4	47	36	4	120	.253	.308	.339	98	-3	35-20	.933	1	97	131	O142(1/0/141)	—	-0.9
1915	StL A	45	119	15	24	2	2	1	11	6	1	16	.202	.246	.277	59	-7	11-1	.949	-2	92	66	O35R	—	-0.8
Total	5	410	1398	171	367	58	31	12	147	126	9	<u>223</u>	.263	.327	.374	110	14	95-<u>21</u>	.939	5	99	120	O389(8/0/381)	—	0.1
WILLIAMS, BERNIE Bernabe (Figueroa); B9.13.1968 San Juan, PR; BB/TR/6´2˝/(180–205); d7.7																									
1991	NY A	85	320	43	76	19	4	3	34	48-0	1	57	.237	.336	.350	90	-3	10-5	.979	-1	104	68	O85C	0	-0.4
1992	NY A	62	261	39	73	14	2	5	26	29-1	1	36	.280	.354	.406	113	5	7-6	.995	5	109	135	O62(4/55/4)	0	0.8
1993	NY A	139	567	67	152	31	4	12	68	53-4	4	106	.268	.333	.400	99	-1	9-9	.989	-4	98	64	O139C	25	-0.4
1994	NY A	108	408	80	118	29	1	12	57	61-2	3	54	.289	.384	.453	120	14	16-9	.990	-2	95	119	O107C	0	1.3
1995	†NY A	144	563	93	173	29	9	18	82	75-1	5	98	.307	.392	.487	129	25	8-6	.982	5	117	14	O144C	0	3.0
1996	†NY A	143	551	108	168	26	7	29	102	82-8	0	72	.305	.391	.535	132	28	17-4	.986	-4	96	121	O140C,D2	15	2.6
1997	†NY A★	129	509	107	167	35	6	21	100	73-7	1	80	.328	.408	.544	149	39	15-8	.993	-15	85	31	O128C	35	2.5
1998	†NY A✳	128	499	101	169	30	5	26	97	74-9	1	81	**.339**	.422	.575	164	49	15-9	.990	-8	93	51	O123C,D5	37	4.0
1999	†NY A★	158	591	116	202	28	6	25	115	100-**17**	1	95	.342	.435	.536	149	48	9-10	.987	-2	100	96	O155C,D2	0	4.3
2000	†NY A★	141	537	108	165	37	6	30	121	71-11	5	84	.307	.391	.566	141	34	13-5	**1.000**	-2	104	30	O137C,D4	0	3.2
2001	†NY A★	146	540	102	166	38	0	26	94	78-11	6	67	.307	.395	.522	139	34	11-5	.994	-5	101	39	O144C/D	0	3.0
2002	†NY A	154	612	102	204	37	2	19	102	83-7	3	97	.333	.415	.493	142	41	8-4	.986	-12	91	26	O147C,D7	0	2.9
2003	†NY A	119	445	77	117	19	1	15	64	71-8	3	61	.263	.367	.411	107	7	5-0	.997	-3	99	59	O115C,D4	47	0.6
2004	†NY A	148	561	105	147	29	1	22	70	85-5	2	96	.262	.360	.435	106	7	1-5	.995	-7	90	43	O97C,D50	0	-0.2
2005	†NY A	141	485	53	121	19	1	12	64	53-1	1	75	.249	.321	.367	84	-11	1-2	.991	-4	91	124	O112C,D23	0	-1.5
2006	†NY A	131	420	65	118	29	0	12	61	33-5	2	53	.281	.332	.436	98	-1	2-0	.994	-6	92	22	O89(5/28/58),D31	0	-1.0
Total	16	2076	7869	1366	2336	449	55	287	1257	1069-97	39	1212	.297	.381	.477	125	315	147-87	.990	-63	98	62	O1924(9/1856/62),D129	159	24.7
WILLIAMS, BERNIE Bernard; B10.8.1948 Alameda CA; BR/TR/6´1˝/175; [SFN66 11/217]; d9.7																									
1970	SF N	7	16	2	5	2	0	0	1	2-0	0	1	.313	.389	.438	122	1	1-1	1.000	1	122	326	O6L	0	0.1
1971	SF N	35	73	8	13	1	0	1	5	12-2	0	24	.178	.294	.233	52	-4	1-1	.933	-3	75	0	O27(22/0/5)	0	-1.0
1972	SF N	46	68	12	13	3	1	3	9	7-0	0	22	.191	.267	.397	85	-2	0-0	1.000	2	121	100	O15(14/1/0)	0	-0.1
1974	SD N	14	15	1	2	0	0	0	0	0-0	0	6	.133	.133	.133	-27	-3	0-0	1.000	-1	48	0	O3(1/2/0)	0	-0.3
Total	4	102	172	23	33	6	1	4	15	21-2	0	53	.192	.280	.308	66	-8	2-2	.974	-1	95	70	O51(43/3/5)	0	-1.3
WILLIAMS, BILLY Billy Leo; B6.15.1938 Whistler AL; BL/TR/6´1˝/(170–175); d8.6; C18; HF1987																									
1959	Chi N	18	33	0	5	0	1	0	2	1-0	0	7	.152	.176	.212	3	-5	0-0	1.000	0	120	0	O10L	0	-0.5
1960	Chi N	12	47	4	13	0	2	2	7	5-0	0	12	.277	.346	.489	127	1	0-0	.962	-1	103	0	O12L	0	0.0
1961	Chi N	146	529	75	147	20	7	25	86	45-11	5	70	.278	.338	.484	114	9	6-0	.954	-6	89	80	O135(110/0/27)	0	-0.4
1962	Chi N★	159	618	94	184	22	8	22	91	70-3	4	72	.298	.369	.466	119	17	9-9	.967	4	93	156	O159(158/0/1)	0	1.1
1963	Chi N	161	612	87	175	36	9	25	95	68-9	2	78	.286	.358	.497	136	30	7-6	.987	6	102	120	O160L	0	2.7
1964	Chi N★	**162**	645	100	201	39	2	33	98	59-8	2	84	.312	.370	.532	145	39	10-7	.950	-7	80	129	O162(162/2/0)	0	2.4
1965	Chi N★	**164**	645	115	203	39	6	34	108	65-7	3	76	.315	.377	.552	155	48	10-1	.968	-6	93	91	O164(34/28/106)	0	3.5
1966	Chi N	**162**	648	100	179	23	5	29	91	69-16	4	61	.276	.347	.461	122	19	6-3	.976	1	108	77	O162(11/0/152)	0	1.0
1967	Chi N	**162**	634	92	176	21	12	28	84	68-8	2	67	.278	.346	.481	129	23	6-3	.989	-6	97	29	O162(161/0/6)	0	0.9
1968	Chi N★	**163**	642	91	185	30	8	30	98	48-10	2	53	.288	.336	.500	140	30	4-1	.967	-9	94	35	O163(137/0/47)	0	1.3
1969	Chi N	**163**	642	103	188	33	10	21	95	59-15	4	70	.293	.355	.474	116	13	3-2	.957	1	92	163	O159(153/0/28)	0	0.6
1970	Chi N	161	636	**137**	**205**	34	4	42	129	72-9	2	65	.322	.391	.586	141	37	7-1	.989	2	98	118	O160(155/0/9)	0	3.1
1971	Chi N	157	594	86	179	27	5	28	93	77-18	3	44	.301	.383	.505	131	26	7-5	.977	1	101	81	O154(151/0/4)	0	1.9
1972	Chi N★	150	574	95	191	34	6	37	122	62-20	6	59	**.333**	.398	**.606**	165	50	3-1	.984	-6	83	91	O144L,1b5	0	3.8
1973	Chi N★	156	576	72	166	22	2	20	86	76-14	1	72	.288	.369	.438	115	13	4-3	.985	9	94	158	O138L,1b19	0	1.4
1974	Chi N	117	404	55	113	22	0	16	68	67-12	1	44	.280	.382	.453	128	17	4-5	.986	3	116	84	1b65,O43(41/0/4)	15	1.2
1975	†Oak A	155	520	68	127	20	1	23	81	76-7	2	68	.244	.341	.419	117	12	0-0	.971	0	115	158	D145,1b7	0	0.8
1976	Oak A	120	351	36	74	12	0	11	41	58-15	0	44	.211	.320	.339	98	1	4-2	ø	-0	0	0	D106/lf	0	-0.2
Total	18	2488	9350	1410	2711	434	88	426	1475	1045-182	43	1046	.290	.361	.492	130	380	90-49	.973	-13	94	101	O2088(1738/30/384),D251,1b96	15	24.6
WILLIAMS, DALLAS Dallas McKinley; B2.28.1958 Brooklyn NY; BL/TL/5´11˝/165; [BalA76 1/20]; d9.19; C4																									
1981	Bal A	2	2	0	1	0	0	0	0	0-0	0	0	.500	.500	.500	190	0	0-0	1.000	0	399	0	/lf	0	0.0
1983	Cin N	18	36	2	2	0	0	0	1	3-0	0	6	.056	.128	.056	-46	-7	0-0	1.000	0	111	0	O12(6/3/3)	0	-0.8
Total	2	20	38	2	3	0	0	0	1	3-0	0	6	.079	.146	.079	-35	-7	0-0	1.000	0	115	0	O13(7/3/3)	0	-0.8
WILLIAMS, DANA Dana Lamont; B3.20.1963 Weirton WV; BR/TR/5´10˝/170; d6.19; Col Enterprise St. (AL) JC																									
1989	Bos A	8	5	1	1	1	0	0	0	0-0	1	1	.200	.333	.400	99	0	0-0	1.000	1	0	7581	/lfD	0	0.1
WILLIAMS, DAVEY David Carlous; B11.2.1927 Dallas TX; BR/TR/5´10˝/(160–165); d9.16; C2																									
1949	NY N	13	50	7	12	1	1	1	5	7	0	4	.240	.333	.360	86	-1	0	.953	-5	76	73	2b13	0	-0.6
1951	†NY N	30	64	17	17	1	0	2	8	5	0	8	.266	.319	.375	85	-2	1-1	1.000	1	104	71	2b22	0	0.0
1952	NY N	138	540	70	137	26	3	13	55	48	8	63	.254	.324	.385	95	-4	2-3	.973	-10	98	114	2b138	0	-0.7
1953	NY N★	112	340	51	101	11	2	3	34	44	3	19	.297	.382	.368	95	0	2-5	.982	-2	100	87	2b95	0	0.2
1954	†NY N	142	544	65	121	18	3	9	46	43	5	33	.222	.284	.316	56	-36	1-1	**.982**	-4	97	109	2b142	0	-3.0

YEAR	TM LG	G	AB	R	H	2B	3B	HR	RBI	BB-IB	HP	SO	AVG	OBP	SLG	AOPS	ABR	SB-CS	FA	FR	RNG	THR	GAMES AT POSITION	DL	BFW
1955	NY N	82	247	25	62	4	1	4	15	17-2	2	17	.251	.303	.324	67	-12	0-2	.968	-3	99	94	2b71	0	-1.2
Total	6	517	1785	235	450	61	10	32	163	164-2	18	144	.252	.320	.351	79	-55	6-12	.978	-24	98	102	2b481	0	-5.3
Williams, Keith	David Keith; B4.21.1972 Bedford PA; BR/TR/6´0˝/190; [SFN93 7/190]; d6.7; Col Clemson																								
1996	SF N	9	20	0	5	0	0	0	0	0-0	0	6	.250	.250	.250	33	-2	0-0	1.000	-0	107	0	O4(1/0/3)	0	-0.2
Williams, Dewey	Dewey Edgar "Dee"; B2.5.1916 Durham NC; D3.19.2000 Williston ND; BR/TR/6´0˝/160; d6.28																								
1944	Chi N	79	262	23	63	7	2	0	27	23	0	18	.240	.302	.282	65	-12	2	.981	2	*95*	***136***	C77	0	-0.6
1945	†Chi N	59	100	16	28	2	2	2	5	13	0	13	.280	.363	.400	114	2	0	.978	3	*147*	*116*	C54	0	0.7
1946	Chi N	4	5	0	1	0	0	0	0	0	0	2	.200	.200	.200	14	-1	0	1.000	0	*0*	*0*	C2	0	0.0
1947	Chi N	3	2	0	0	0	0	0	0	0	0	1	.000	.000	.000	-99	-1	0	ø	0	*0*	*0*	/C	0	-0.1
1948	Cin N	48	95	9	16	2	0	1	5	10	0	18	.168	.248	.221	29	-10	0	.961	-4	*71*	*56*	C47	0	-1.2
Total	5	193	464	48	108	11	4	3	37	46	0	52	.233	.302	.293	67	-22	2	.976	1	*100*	*114*	C181	0	-1.2
Williams, Earl	Earl Baxter; B1.27.1903 Cumberland Gap TN; D3.10.1958 Knoxville TN; BR/TR/6´0.5˝/185; d5.27; Col Maryville																								
1928	Bos N	3	2	0	0	0	0	0	0	0	0	1	.000	.000	.000	-99	-1	0	1.000	0	*0*	*0*	/C	—	0.0
Williams, Earl	Earl Craig; B7.14.1948 Newark NJ; BR/TR/6´3˝/(195–220); d9.13; [DL 1978 Oak A 42]																								
1970	Atl N	10	19	4	7	4	0	0	5	3-0	0	4	.368	.417	.579	165	2	0-0	1.000	2	56	51	1b4,3b3	0	0.3
1971	Atl N	145	497	64	129	14	1	33	87	42-5	7	80	.260	.324	.491	121	12	0-1	.981	-10	68	107	C72,3b42,1b31	0	0.3
1972	Atl N	151	565	72	146	24	2	28	87	62-6	6	118	.258	.336	.457	114	11	0-0	.980	-19	74	77	C116,3b21,1b20	0	-0.5
1973	†Bal A	132	459	58	109	18	1	22	83	66-8	3	107	.237	.333	.425	113	8	0-2	.987	-1	116	115	C95,1b42,D2	0	0.8
1974	†Bal A	118	413	47	105	16	0	14	52	40-3	7	79	.254	.327	.395	110	6	0-2	.983	-8	96	104	C75,1b47/D	0	-0.4
1975	Atl N	111	383	42	92	13	0	11	50	34-2	3	63	.240	.305	.360	82	-10	0-0	.989	-5	83	98	1b90,C11	0	-2.3
1976	Atl N	61	184	18	39	3	0	9	26	19-2	1	33	.212	.286	.375	83	-5	0-0	.995	-7	95	25	C38,1b17	0	-1.3
	Mon N	61	190	17	45	10	2	8	29	14-2	0	32	.237	.285	.437	99	-1	0-0	.981	4	150	100	1b47,C13	0	0.0
	Year	122	374	35	84	13	2	17	55	33-4	1	65	.225	.286	.406	91	-6	0-0	.986	-4	133	94	1b64,C51	0	-1.3
1977	Oak A	100	348	39	84	13	0	13	38	18-3	5	58	.241	.288	.391	84	-9	2-0	.989	-2	71	165	D45,C36,1b29	30	-1.1
Total	8	889	3058	361	756	115	6	138	457	298-31	32	574	.247	.318	.424	105	14	2-5	.984	-47	86	98	C456,1b327,3b66,D48	72	-4.2
Williams, Eddie	Edward Laquan; B11.1.1964 Shreveport LA; BR/TR/6´0˝/(175–210); [NYN83 1/4]; d4.18																								
1986	Cle A	5	7	2	1	0	0	0	1	0-0	0	3	.143	.143	.143	-22	-1	0-0	ø	-0	0	0	O4L	0	-0.2
1987	Cle A	22	64	9	11	4	0	1	4	9-0	1	19	.172	.280	.281	50	-4	0-0	.982	2	103	155	3b22	0	-0.3
1988	Cle A	10	21	3	4	0	0	0	1	0-0	1	3	.190	.227	.190	18	-2	0-0	1.000	1	123	0	3b10	0	-0.2
1989	Chi A	66	201	25	55	8	0	3	10	18-3	4	31	.274	.341	.358	100	1	1-2	.909	-0	103	193	3b65	0	0.0
1990	SD N	14	42	5	12	3	0	3	4	5-2	0	6	.286	.362	.571	151	3	0-1	.897	-2	92	118	3b13	0	0.1
1994	SD N	49	175	32	58	11	1	11	42	15-1	3	26	.331	.392	.594	158	15	0-1	.988	-2	89	83	1b46/3	0	0.9
1995	SD N	97	296	35	77	11	1	12	47	23-0	4	47	.260	.320	.426	98	-2	0-0	.989	-1	94	97	1b81	0	-0.9
1996	Det A	77	215	22	43	5	0	6	26	18-0	2	50	.200	.267	.307	45	-19	0-2	1.000	-1	49	228	D52,1b7,3b3,O2R	0	-2.2
1997	LA N	8	7	0	1	0	0	0	1	1-1	0	1	.143	.250	.143	7	-1	0-0	ø	0	—	—	/H	0	-0.1
	Pit N	30	89	12	22	5	0	3	11	10-1	2	24	.247	.333	.404	91	-1	1-0	.991	-3	57	101	1b26	0	-0.5
	Year	38	96	12	23	5	0	3	12	11-2	2	25	.240	.327	.385	87	-2	1-0	.991	-3	57	101	1b26	0	-0.6
1998	SD N	17	28	1	4	0	0	0	3	2-0	0	6	.143	.194	.143	-8	-5	0-0	1.000	-0	81	80	1b7	0	-0.5
Total	10	395	1145	146	288	47	2	39	150	101-8	17	216	.252	.319	.398	90	-16	2-6	.989	-7	85	96	1b167,3b114,D52,O6(4/0/2)	0	-3.9
Williams, Dib	Edwin Dibrell; B1.19.1910 Greenbrier AR; D4.2.1992 Searcy AR; BR/TR/5´11.5˝/175; d4.27; Col Hendrix																								
1930	Phi A	67	191	24	50	10	3	3	22	15	2	19	.262	.322	.393	77	-7	2-1	.951	0	103	77	2b39,S19/3	—	-0.4
1931	†Phi A	86	294	41	79	12	2	6	40	19	0	21	.269	.313	.384	78	-11	2-0	.931	2	93	158	S72,2b10/lf	—	-0.2
1932	Phi A	62	215	30	54	10	1	4	24	22	3	23	.251	.329	.363	76	-8	0-1	.952	1	105	96	2b53,S3	—	-0.3
1933	Phi A	115	408	52	118	20	5	11	73	32	1	35	.289	.342	.444	106	2	1-0	.921	-11	90	64	S84,2b29,1b2	—	-0.2
1934	Phi A	66	205	25	56	10	1	2	17	21	0	18	.273	.341	.361	84	-5	0-1	.956	1	109	88	2b53,S2	—	-0.1
1935	Phi A	4	10	0	1	0	0	0	0	0	0	1	.100	.100	.100	-49	-2	0-0	1.000	-1	111	0	2b2	—	-0.3
	Bos A	75	251	26	63	12	0	3	25	24	1	23	.251	.319	.335	65	-13	2-0	.952	-3	115	126	3b30,2b29,S15/1	—	-1.1
	Year	79	261	26	64	12	0	3	25	24	1	24	.245	.311	.326	61	-15	2-0	.973	-3	91	62	2b31,3b30,S15/1	—	-1.4
Total	6	475	1574	198	421	74	12	29	201	133	7	140	.267	.327	.385	82	-44	7-3	.955	-11	105	89	2b215,S195,3b31,1b3/lf	—	-2.6
Williams, Denny	Evon Daniel; B12.13.1896 Portland OR; D3.23.1929 San Clemente CA; BL/TR/5´8.5˝/150; d4.15																								
1921	Cin N	10	7	0	0	0	0	0	0	0	0	2	.000	.000	.000	-99	-2	0-1	1.000	0	138	0	/lf	—	-0.2
1924	Bos A	25	85	17	31	3	0	0	4	10	1	5	.365	.438	.400	117	3	3-3	.972	-1	89	54	O19L	—	0.0
1925	Bos A	69	218	28	50	1	3	0	13	17	0	11	.229	.285	.261	39	-21	2-6	.953	-2	99	69	O52(42/11/0)	—	-2.7
1928	Bos A	16	18	1	4	0	0	0	1	1	0	1	.222	.263	.222	29	-2	0-0	1.000	-0	97	0	O6(0/5/1)	—	-0.2
Total	4	120	328	46	85	4	3	0	18	28	1	19	.259	.319	.290	56	-22	5-10	.959	-3	97	63	O78(62/16/1)	—	-3.1
Williams, Cy	Fred; B12.21.1887 Wadena IN; D4.23.1974 Eagle River WI; BL/TL/6´2˝/180; d7.18; Col Notre Dame																								
1912	Chi N	28	62	3	15	1	1	0	1	6	0	14	.242	.309	.290	65	-3	2	1.000	1	101	126	O22(5/17/0)	—	-0.3
1913	Chi N	49	156	17	35	3	3	4	32	5	3	26	.224	.262	.359	76	-6	5-10	.976	-2	95	77	O44(36/9/0)	—	-1.2
1914	Chi N	55	94	12	19	2	2	0	5	13	2	13	.202	.312	.266	73	-3	2	.941	-0	105	74	O27(22/7/0)	—	-0.5
1915	Chi N	151	518	59	133	22	6	13	64	26	10	49	.257	.305	.398	112	5	15-10	.968	2	106	83	O149C	—	-0.3
1916	Chi N	118	405	55	113	19	9	**12**	66	51	9	64	.279	.372	.459	140	21	6	.989	-8	95	49	O116(0/115/1)	—	0.5
1917	Chi N	138	468	53	113	22	4	5	42	38	7	78	.241	.308	.338	91	-4	8	.960	11	113	135	O136C	—	-0.3
1918	Phi N	94	351	49	97	14	1	6	39	27	5	30	.276	.337	.373	109	4	10	.968	2	106	88	O91C	—	0.1
1919	Phi N	109	435	54	121	21	1	9	39	30	7	43	.278	.335	.393	111	6	9	.970	-2	99	89	O108C	—	-0.4
1920	Phi N	148	590	88	192	36	10	**15**	72	32	4	45	.325	.364	.497	139	28	18-12	.972	10	110	110	O147C	—	3.0
1921	Phi N	146	562	67	180	28	6	18	75	30	2	32	.320	.357	.488	112	9	5-15	.979	9	102	137	O146C	—	0.8
1922	Phi N	151	584	98	180	30	6	26	92	74	6	49	.308	.392	.514	120	18	11-14	.973	-5	93	102	O150C	—	0.5
1923	Phi N	136	535	98	157	22	3	**41**	114	59	7	57	.293	.371	.576	131	22	11-10	.981	-5	100	53	O135C	—	1.0
1924	Phi N	148	558	101	183	31	11	24	93	67	3	49	.328	.403	.552	137	30	7-12	.962	-6	95	85	O145C	—	1.5
1925	Phi N	107	314	78	104	11	5	13	60	53	5	34	.331	.435	.522	132	17	4-9	.989	3	104	104	O96R	—	1.1
1926	Phi N	107	336	63	116	13	4	18	53	38	4	35	.345	.418	**.568**	155	26	2	.963	-2	85	125	O93R	—	1.7
1927	Phi N	131	492	86	135	18	2	**30**	98	61	**9**	57	.274	.365	.502	128	19	0	.970	1	90	141	O130R	—	1.0
1928	Phi N	99	238	31	61	9	0	12	37	54	3	34	.256	.400	.445	117	8	0	1.000	2	92	165	O69(20/9/40)	—	0.5
1929	Phi N	66	65	11	19	2	0	5	21	22	0	9	.292	.471	.554	144	6	0	.966	1	119	122	O11(1/9/1)	—	0.6
1930	Phi N	21	17	1	8	2	0	0	2	4	0	3	.471	.571	.588	169	2	0	1.000	0	376	0	O3(1/1/1)	—	0.2
Total	19	2002	6780	1024	1981	306	74	251	1005	690	86	721	.292	.365	.470	123	205	115-92	.973	11	100	102	O1818(85/1374/362)	—	9.5
Williams, Papa	Fred; B7.17.1913 Meridian MS; D11.2.1993 Meridian MS; BR/TR/6´1˝/200; d4.19																								
1945	Cle A	16	19	0	4	0	0	0	0	1	0	2	.211	.250	.211	36	-2	0-0	1.000	0	164	149	1b3	0	-0.1
Williams, George	George; B10.23.1939 Detroit MI; BR/TR/5´11˝/165; d7.16																								
1961	Phi N	17	36	4	9	0	0	0	1	4-0	0	4	.250	.325	.250	56	-2	0-0	.967	2	117	115	2b15	0	0.0
1962	Hou N	5	8	1	3	1	0	0	2	0-0	0	1	.375	.375	.500	143	0	0-0	1.000	-0	117	105	2b3	0	0.1
1964	KC A	37	91	10	19	6	0	0	2	6-2	1	12	.209	.265	.275	49	-6	0-0	.970	-0	114	138	2b20,S2,3b2,O2L	0	-0.5
Total	3	59	135	15	31	7	0	0	5	10-2	1	17	.230	.288	.281	56	-8	0-0	.970	1	115	128	2b38,O2L,3b2,S2	0	-0.4
Williams, George	George Erik; B4.22.1969 LaCrosse WI; BB/TR/5´10˝/(190–214); [OakA91 24/645]; d7.14; Col Texas–Pan American; [DL 1998 Oak A 181]																								
1995	Oak A	29	79	13	23	5	1	3	14	11-2	2	21	.291	.383	.494	135	4	0-0	.956	-2	59	139	C13,D10	0	0.2
1996	Oak A	56	132	17	20	5	0	3	10	28-1	3	32	.152	.311	.258	47	-10	0-0	.982	-6	78	84	C43,D11	0	-1.4
1997	Oak A	76	201	30	58	9	1	3	22	35-0	2	46	.289	.397	.388	107	4	0-1	.984	-7	95	80	C67/D	53	0.0
2000	SD N	11	16	2	3	0	0	1	2	0-0	1	4	.188	.235	.375	54	-1	0-0	1.000	-1	58	0	C6	0	-0.2
Total	4	172	428	62	104	19	2	10	48	74-3	8	103	.243	.362	.367	91	-3	0-1	.981	-16	85	85	C129,D22	234	-1.4
Williams, Gerald	Gerald Floyd; B8.10.1966 New Orleans LA; BR/TR/6´2˝/(185–190); [NYA87 14/367]; d9.15; Col Grambling St.																								
1992	NY A	15	27	7	8	2	0	3	6	0-0	0	3	.296	.296	.704	173	2	2-0	.913	1	125	190	O12R	0	0.3
1993	NY A	42	67	11	10	2	3	0	6	1-0	2	14	.149	.183	.269	21	-8	2-0	.956	-1	87	162	O37(10/17/12)/D	0	-0.9
1994	NY A	57	86	19	25	8	0	4	13	4-0	0	17	.291	.319	.523	117	2	1-3	.957	-2	82	112	O43(26/8/12),D2	0	-0.2
1995	†NY A	100	182	33	45	18	2	6	28	22-1	1	34	.247	.327	.467	106	2	4-2	.993	8	124	162	O92(70/2/26),D2	0	0.7

YEAR	TM LG	G	AB	R	H	2B	3B	HR	RBI	BB-IB	HP	SO	AVG	OBP	SLG	AOPS	ABR	SB-CS	FA	FR	RNG	THR	GAMES AT POSITION	DL	BFW
1996	NY A	99	233	37	63	15	4	5	30	15-2	4	39	.270	.319	.433	90	-4	7-8	.978	-3	99	23	O92(70/14/10),D2	0	-1.0
	Mil A	26	92	6	19	4	0	0	4	4-1	1	18	.207	.247	.250	25	-11	3-1	.987	2	111	184	O26(0/25/1)	0	-0.7
	Year	125	325	43	82	19	4	5	34	19-3	5	57	.252	.299	.382	71	-15	10-9	.981	-1	102	67	O118(70/39/11),D2	0	-1.7
1997	Mil A	155	566	73	143	32	2	10	41	19-1	6	90	.253	.282	.369	68	-28	23-9	.992	1	98	137	O154(39/129/0)/D	0	-2.4
1998	†Atl N	129	266	46	81	19	2	10	44	17-1	3	48	.305	.352	.504	123	8	11-5	.970	5	**125**	47	O120(56/11/61)	0	1.1
1999	†Atl N	143	422	76	116	24	1	17	68	33-1	6	67	.275	.335	.457	99	-2	19-11	.985	0	93	136	O139(120/1/32)	0	-0.5
2000	TB A	146	632	87	173	30	2	21	89	34-0	3	103	.274	.312	.427	86	-16	12-12	.983	-6	96	85	O138C,D7	0	-2.0
2001	TB A	62	232	30	48	17	0	4	17	13-0	4	42	.207	.261	.332	56	-15	10-4	.989	9	127	159	O59C	0	-0.5
	NY A	38	47	12	8	1	0	0	2	5-0	1	13	.170	.264	.191	23	-5	3-1	.967	0	116	0	O26(6/11/12),D7	0	-0.5
	Year	100	279	42	56	18	0	4	19	18-0	5	55	.201	.262	.308	50	-20	13-5	.986	9	125	131	O85(6/70/12),D7	0	-1.0
2002	NY A	33	17	6	0	0	0	0	0	2-0	0	4	.000	.105	.000	-69	-4	2-0	1.000	-0	66	211	O30(7/6/17)	0	-0.4
2003	Fla N	27	31	5	4	1	0	0	3	2-0	0	5	.129	.182	.161	-10	-5	3-0	.941	-0	110	0	O16(11/2/3)	0	-0.5
2004	NY N	57	129	17	30	8	2	4	11	8-1	0	26	.233	.277	.419	78	-5	2-1	.982	-2	74	176	O45(21/20/7)	0	-0.7
2005	NY N	39	30	9	7	2	0	1	3	1-0	0	7	.233	.258	.400	71	-1	2-0	1.000	-0	80	207	O27(10/10/7)	0	-0.1
Total	14	1168	3059	474	780	183	18	85	365	180-8	31	530	.255	.301	.410	82	-90	106-57	.983	11	102	115	O1056(446/453/212),D22	0	-8.3
Williams, Glenn	Glenn David; B7.18.1977 Gosford, New South Wales, Australia; BB/TR/6´2˝/195; d6.7																								
2005	Min A	13	40	3	17	1	0	0	3	2-0	0	7	.425	.452	.450	139	2	1-2	.929	0	105	136	3b12	96	0.2
Williams, Harry	Harry Peter; B6.23.1890 Omaha NE; D12.21.1963 Huntington Park CA; BR/TR/6´1.5˝/200; d8.7; b–Gus																								
1913	NY A	27	82	18	21	3	1	1	12	15	1	10	.256	.378	.354	114	2	6	.981	-2	79	51	1b27	—	0.0
1914	NY A	59	178	9	29	5	2	1	17	26	5	26	.163	.287	.230	56	-9	3-6	.976	-6	69	74	1b58	—	-2.0
Total	2	86	260	27	50	8	3	2	29	41	6	36	.192	.316	.269	75	-7	9-6	.977	-8	72	67	1b85	—	-2.0
Williams, Jim	James Alfred; B4.29.1947 Zachary LA; BR/TR/6´2˝/190; [ChiN65 12/391]; d9.8																								
1969	SD N	13	25	4	7	1	0	0	2	3-0	0	11	.280	.345	.320	94	0	0-0	.900	-1	91	0	O6L	0	-0.1
1970	SD N	11	14	4	4	0	0	0	0	1-0	0	3	.286	.333	.286	70	-1	1-0	1.000	-0	88	0	O6(1/0/5)	0	-0.1
Total	2	24	39	8	11	1	0	0	2	4-0	0	14	.282	.341	.308	85	-1	1-0	.938	-1	90	0	O12(7/0/5)	0	-0.2
Williams, Jimy	James Francis; B10.4.1943 Santa Maria CA; BR/TR/5´10˝/170; d4.26; Mil 1966; M12/C13; Col Cal St.–Fresno																								
1966	StL N	13	11	1	3	0	0	0	1	1-0	0	5	.273	.333	.273	71	0	0-0	1.000	-3	51	57	S7,2b3	0	-0.4
1967	StL N	1	2	0	0	0	0	0	0	0-0	0	1	.000	.000	.000	-99	-1	0-0	1.000	0	39	0	/S	0	0.0
Total	2	14	13	1	3	0	0	0	1	1-0	0	6	.231	.286	.231	46	-1	0-0	1.000	-3	49	45	S8,2b3	0	-0.4
Williams, Jimmy	James Thomas; B12.20.1876 St.Louis MO; D1.16.1965 St.Petersburg FL; BR/TR/5´9˝/175; d4.15																								
1899	Pit N	153	621	126	220	28	**27**	9	116	60	6	—	.354	.416	.530	159	49	26	.900	1	101	62	3b153	—	4.7
1900	†Pit N	106	416	73	110	15	11	5	68	32	4	—	.264	.323	.389	95	-4	18	.889	5	101	**164**	3b103,S4	—	0.2
1901	Bal A	130	501	113	159	26	**21**	7	96	56	2	—	.317	.388	.495	138	25	21	.935	-1	101	81	2b130	—	2.2
1902	Bal A	125	498	83	156	27	**21**	8	83	36	1	—	.313	.361	.500	131	18	14	.945	1	107	93	2b104,3b19/1	—	2.0
1903	NY A	132	502	60	134	30	12	3	82	39	5	—	.267	.326	.392	108	5	9	**.957**	16	**112**	130	2b132	—	2.3
1904	NY A	146	559	62	147	31	7	2	74	38	4	—	.263	.314	.354	106	5	14	.951	15	106	**131**	2b146	—	2.3
1905	NY A	129	470	54	107	20	8	6	62	50	3	—	.228	.306	.343	95	-3	14	**.964**	3	92	**149**	2b129	—	0.2
1906	NY A	139	501	61	139	25	7	3	77	44	5	—	.277	.342	.373	112	8	8	.958	14	107	78	2b139	—	2.5
1907	NY A	139	504	53	136	17	11	2	63	35	1	—	.270	.319	.359	107	3	14	.966	-3	94	90	2b139	—	0.2
1908	StL A	148	539	63	127	20	7	4	53	55	3	—	.236	.310	.321	104	4	7	.963	3	99	114	2b148	—	0.9
1909	StL A	110	374	32	73	3	6	0	22	29	2	—	.195	.257	.235	60	-18	6	.962	-1	94	112	2b109	—	-2.1
Total	11	1457	5485	780	1508	242	138	49	796	474	36	—	.275	.337	.396	114	92	151	.955	52	101	109	2b1176,3b275,S4/1	—	15.4
Williams, Ken	Kenneth Roy; B6.28.1890 Grants Pass OR; D1.22.1959 Grants Pass OR; BL/TR/6´0˝/170; d7.14; Mil 1918																								
1915	Cin N	71	219	22	53	10	4	0	16	15	2	20	.242	.297	.324	86	-4	4-3	.948	3	97	156	O62(54/8/0)	—	-0.4
1916	Cin N	10	27	1	3	0	0	0	1	2	0	5	.111	.172	.111	-12	-4	1	.955	1	108	210	O10(8/1/0)	—	-0.3
1918	StL A	2	1	0	0	0	0	0	1	1	0	0	.000	.500	.000	53	0	0	ø	0	—	—	/H	—	0.0
1919	StL A	65	227	32	68	10	5	6	35	26	2	25	.300	.376	.467	133	10	7	.937	2	106	110	O63C	—	0.7
1920	StL A	141	521	90	160	34	13	10	72	41	4	26	.307	.362	.480	118	12	18-8	.961	4	107	92	O138(104/34/0)	—	1.0
1921	StL A	146	547	115	190	31	7	24	117	74	4	42	.347	.429	.561	142	36	20-17	.932	4	103	129	O145L	—	2.5
1922	StL A	153	585	128	194	34	11	**39**	**155**	74	7	31	.332	.413	.627	162	52	37-20	.970	2	105	80	O153(137/17/0)	—	4.1
1923	StL A	147	555	106	198	37	12	29	91	79	2	32	.357	.439	.623	168	55	18-17	.967	8	106	128	O145L	—	4.7
1924	StL A	114	398	78	129	21	4	18	84	69	1	17	.324	.425	.533	138	24	20-11	.968	6	109	113	O109L	—	2.0
1925	StL A	102	411	83	136	31	5	25	105	37	3	14	.331	.390	**.613**	144	25	10-5	.955	2	105	92	O102L	—	1.8
1926	StL A	108	347	55	97	15	7	17	74	39	1	23	.280	.354	.510	118	7	5-4	.948	2	101	136	O92(91/1/0)/2	—	0.2
1927	StL A	131	423	70	136	23	6	17	74	57	1	30	.322	.403	.525	135	22	9-7	.965	6	105	128	O113(110/4/0)	—	1.7
1928	Bos A	133	462	59	140	25	1	8	67	37	1	15	.303	.356	.413	104	2	4-9	.971	-3	95	85	O127L	—	-1.2
1929	Bos A	74	139	21	48	14	2	3	21	15	0	7	.345	.409	.540	146	10	1-5	.963	0	103	99	O39(0/30/10),1b2	—	0.7
Total	14	1397	4862	860	1552	285	77	196	913	566	28	287	.319	.393	.530	136	247	154-106	.958	38	104	111	O1298(1132/158/10),1b2/2	—	17.5
Williams, Kenny	Kenneth Royal; B4.6.1964 Berkeley CA; BR/TR/6´2˝/(184–195); [ChiA82 3/68]; d9.2																								
1986	Chi A	15	31	2	4	0	0	1	1	1-0	1	11	.129	.182	.226	10	-4	1-1	1.000	0	93	189	O10(1/4/5)/D	0	-0.4
1987	Chi A	116	391	48	110	18	2	11	50	10-0	9	83	.281	.314	.422	90	-6	21-10	.981	1	102	95	O115(0/111/4)	0	-0.5
1988	Chi A	73	220	18	35	4	2	8	28	10-0	8	64	.159	.221	.305	46	-17	6-5	.959	0	92	108	O38(0/12/29),3b32,D3	36	-1.9
1989	Det A	94	258	29	53	5	1	6	23	18-0	5	63	.205	.269	.302	62	-14	9-4	.979	9	110	257	O87(28/35/27)/1D	36	-0.5
1990	Det A	57	83	10	11	2	0	0	5	3-0	1	24	.133	.170	.157	-7	-12	2-2	1.000	5	109	299	O47(17/13/19),D6	0	-0.9
	Tor A	49	72	13	14	6	1	0	8	7-0	1	18	.194	.272	.306	61	-4	7-2	1.000	-1	95	0	O30(15/9/8),D9	0	-0.5
	Year	106	155	23	25	8	1	0	13	10-0	2	42	.161	.219	.226	25	-16	9-4	1.000	4	104	183	O77(32/22/27),D15	0	-1.4
1991	Tor A	13	29	5	6	2	0	1	3	4-0	1	5	.207	.314	.379	90	0	1-0	1.000	0	95	175	O9(1/1/8),D2	0	0.0
	Mon N	34	70	11	19	5	2	0	1	3-0	1	22	.271	.311	.400	100	0	2-1	.957	2	116	257	O24(9/4/11)	15	0.2
Total	6	451	1154	136	252	42	8	27	119	56-0	27	290	.218	.269	.339	66	-57	49-25	.981	17	103	164	O360(71/189/111),3b32,D22/1	87	-4.5
Williams, Mark	Mark Westley; B7.28.1953 Elmira NY; BL/TL/6´0˝/175; d5.20; Col Manatee (FL) CC																								
1977	Oak A	3	2	0	0	0	0	0	1	1-0	0	1	.000	.333	.000	0	0	0-0	1.000	0	220	0	/rf	0	0.0
Williams, Matt	Matthew Derrick; B11.28.1965 Bishop CA; BR/TR/6´2˝/(205–219); [SFN86 1/3]; d4.11; gf–Bert Griffith; Col Nevada–Las Vegas																								
1987	SF N	84	245	28	46	9	2	8	21	16-4	1	68	.188	.240	.339	54	-18	4-3	.975	15	114	141	S70,3b17	0	0.3
1988	SF N	52	156	17	32	6	1	8	19	8-0	2	41	.205	.251	.410	91	-3	0-1	.967	4	121	94	3b43,S14	0	0.2
1989	†SF N	84	292	31	59	18	1	18	50	14-1	2	72	.202	.242	.455	98	-3	1-2	.961	4	114	112	3b73,S30	0	0.3
1990	SF N★	159	617	87	171	27	2	33	**122**	33-9	7	138	.277	.319	.488	123	16	7-4	.959	9	107	**139**	3b159	0	2.6
1991	SF N	157	589	72	158	24	5	34	98	33-6	6	128	.268	.310	.499	129	18	5-5	.964	3	99	122	3b155,S4	0	2.2
1992	SF N	146	529	58	120	13	5	20	66	39-11	6	109	.227	.286	.384	93	-8	7-7	.945	7	105	**144**	3b144	0	-0.2
1993	SF N	145	579	105	170	33	4	38	110	27-4	4	80	.294	.325	.561	138	27	1-3	.970	1	95	**160**	3b144	16	2.7
1994	SF N★	112	445	74	119	16	3	**43**	96	33-7	2	87	.267	.319	.607	140	22	1-0	.963	12	**115**	130	3b110	0	3.3
1995	SF N✳	76	283	53	95	17	1	23	65	30-8	2	58	.336	.399	.647	175	30	2-0	.958	7	119	80	3b74	76	3.7
1996	SF N✳	105	404	69	122	16	1	22	85	39-9	6	91	.302	.367	.510	133	19	1-2	.951	2	99	117	3b92,1b13/S	56	1.9
1997	†Cle A	151	596	86	157	32	3	32	105	34-4	4	108	.263	.307	.488	100	-3	12-4	.970	13	114	82	3b151	0	1.1
1998	Ari N	135	510	72	136	26	1	20	71	43-8	3	102	.267	.327	.439	99	-2	5-1	.972	7	110	82	3b134	16	0.7
1999	†Ari N★	154	627	98	190	37	2	35	142	41-9	2	93	.303	.344	.536	118	15	2-0	.977	3	95	128	3b153	0	1.8
2000	Ari N	96	371	43	102	18	2	12	47	20-1	3	51	.275	.315	.431	83	-11	1-2	.964	1	92	123	3b94/D	66	-0.9
2001	†Ari N	106	408	58	112	30	0	16	65	22-3	3	70	.275	.314	.466	92	-5	1-0	.963	-0	94	115	3b102,S2	55	-0.4
2002	†Ari N	60	215	29	56	7	2	12	40	21-1	0	41	.260	.324	.479	99	-1	3-1	.969	-4	87	75	3b56	102	-0.4
2003	Ari N	44	134	17	33	9	0	4	16	16-1	2	26	.246	.327	.403	84	-3	0-0	.959	1	100	76	3b42	0	-0.2
Total	17	1866	7000	997	1878	338	35	378	1218	469-86	55	1363	.268	.317	.489	112	90	53-35	.963	86	104	118	3b1743,S121,1b13/D	387	18.7
Williams, Otto	Otto George; B11.2.1877 Newark NJ; D3.19.1937 Omaha NE; BR/TR/5´8˝/165; d10.5; C4																								
1902	StL N	2	5	0	2	0	0	0	2	1	0	—	.400	.500	.400	186	1	1	.813	0	119	0	S2	—	0.1
1903	StL N	53	187	10	38	4	2	0	9	9	0	—	.203	.240	.246	40	-15	6	.885	-4	103	86	S52/2	—	-1.7
	Chi N	38	130	14	29	5	0	0	13	4	0	—	.223	.246	.262	46	-9	8	.937	3	111	111	S26,2b7,1b3/3	—	-0.6
	Year	91	317	24	67	9	2	0	22	13	0	—	.211	.242	.252	42	-25	14	.904	-1	106	94	S78,2b8,1b3/3	—	-2.3
1904	Chi N	57	185	21	37	4	1	0	8	13	1	—	.200	.256	.232	51	-11	9	.973	0	110	139	O21(0/8/13),1b11,S10,2b6,3b6	—	-1.2

YEAR	TM LG	G	AB	R	H	2B	3B	HR	RBI	BB-IB	HP	SO	AVG	OBP	SLG	AOPS	ABR	SB-CS	FA	FR	RNG	THR	GAMES AT POSITION	DL	BFW
1906	Was A	20	51	3	7	0	0	0	2	2	1	—	.137	.185	.137	1	-6	0	.897	-0	100	42	S8,2b6,1b2/3	—	-0.7
Total	4	170	558	48	113	13	3	0	34	29	2	—	.203	.244	.237	43	-40	24	.905	-1	106	80	S98,O21(0/8/13),2b20,1b16,3b8	—	-4.1
WILLIAMS, REGGIE	Reginald Bernard; B5.5.1966 Laurens SC; BB/TR/6´1˝/(180–189); [SFN88 25/646]; d9.8; Col South Carolina–Aiken																								
1992	Cal A	14	26	5	6	1	1	0	2	1-0	0	10	.231	.259	.346	67	-1	0-2	1.000	0	110	0	O12C,D2	0	-0.2
1995	LA N	15	11	2	1	0	0	0	1	2-0	0	3	.091	.231	.091	-12	-2	0-0	1.000	-1	79	0	O14(10/1/4)	0	-0.2
1998	Ana A	29	36	7	13	1	0	1	5	7-0	1	11	.361	.477	.472	146	3	3-3	1.000	-0	106	0	O24(19/5/2),D2	0	0.2
1999	Ana A	30	63	8	14	1	2	1	6	5-0	1	21	.222	.286	.349	62	-4	2-1	.974	2	94	251	O24(4/3/18),D3	17	-0.3
Total	4	88	136	22	34	3	3	2	14	15-0	2	45	.250	.331	.360	81	-4	5-6	.989	1	99	104	O74(33/21/24),D7	17	-0.5
WILLIAMS, REGGIE	Reginald Dewayne; B8.29.1960 Memphis TN; BR/TR/5´11˝/(180–193); [LAN82 13/333]; d9.2; Col Southern A&M																								
1985	LA N	22	9	4	3	0	0	0	0	0-0	0	4	.333	.333	.333	89	0	1-0	.900	1	115	383	O15(12/2/1)	0	0.1
1986	LA N	128	303	35	84	14	2	4	32	23-9	2	57	.277	.331	.376	102	0	9-3	.984	-4	90	87	O124(26/79/35)	0	-0.6
1987	LA N	39	36	6	4	0	0	0	4	5-0	0	9	.111	.214	.111	-9	-6	1-1	.913	-1	95	0	O30(16/6/9)	0	-0.7
1988	Cle A	11	31	7	7	2	0	1	3	0-0	0	6	.226	.226	.387	66	-2	0-0	1.000	-0	78	212	O11(10/0/3)	0	-0.2
Total	4	200	379	52	98	16	2	5	39	28-9	2	76	.259	.311	.351	87	-8	11-4	.974	-5	90	97	O180(64/87/48)	0	-1.4
WILLIAMS, DICK	Richard Hirschfeld; B5.7.1929 St.Louis MO; BR/TR/6´0˝/190; d6.10; M21/C1; OF(283/156/64)																								
1951	Bro N	23	60	5	12	3	1	1	5	4	0	10	.200	.250	.333	54	-4	0-0	1.000	-1	84	97	O15L	0	-0.6
1952	Bro N	36	68	13	21	4	1	0	11	2	0	10	.309	.329	.397	99	0	0-0	1.000	1	117	76	O25(19/6/0)/13	0	0.0
1953	†Bro N	30	55	4	12	2	0	2	5	3	1	10	.218	.271	.364	62	-3	0-0	.923	-1	96	0	O24(17/2/9)	0	-0.5
1954	Bro N	16	34	5	5	0	0	1	2	2	0	7	.147	.189	.235	11	-5	0-0	1.000	-1	80	0	O14(13/2/0)	0	-0.6
1956	Bro N	7	7	0	2	0	0	0	0	0-0	0	1	.286	.286	.286	50	0	0-0	ø	0	—	—	/H	0	-0.1
	Bal A	87	353	45	101	18	4	11	37	30-1	0	40	.286	.342	.453	117	7	5-5	.990	-1	104	35	O81(9/66/19),1b10,2b10,3b4	0	0.1
1957	Bal A	47	167	16	39	10	2	1	17	14-3	0	21	.234	.293	.335	76	-6	0-1	1.000	4	110	256	O26(15/14/2),3b15,1b12	0	-0.4
	Cle A	67	205	33	58	7	0	6	17	12-0	1	19	.283	.324	.405	99	-1	3-4	.973	-3	106	54	O37(18/20/0),3b19	0	-0.6
	Year	114	372	49	97	17	2	7	34	26-3	1	40	.261	.310	.374	89	-7	3-5	.984	1	108	131	O63(33/34/2),3b34,1b12	0	-1.0
1958	Bal A	128	409	36	113	17	0	4	32	37-4	2	47	.276	.336	.347	94	-2	0-6	1.000	-0	122	171	O70(34/41/15),3b45,1b26,2b7	0	-0.9
1959	KC A	130	488	72	130	33	1	16	75	28-1	5	60	.266	.309	.436	102	0	4-1	.957	1	104	69	3b80,1b32,O23(13/2/8),2b3	0	-0.1
1960	KC A	127	420	47	121	31	0	12	65	39-3	1	68	.288	.346	.448	113	8	0-0	.951	6	101	109	3b57,1b34,O25L	0	1.1
1961	Bal A	103	310	37	64	15	2	8	24	20-0	0	38	.206	.251	.345	61	-19	0-4	.968	-5	73	89	O75(73/2/2),1b20,3b2	0	-2.9
1962	Bal A	82	178	20	44	7	1	1	18	14-0	1	26	.247	.303	.315	72	-7	0-0	1.000	0	108	0	O29(21/0/9),1b21,3b4	0	-0.9
1963	Bos A	79	136	15	35	8	0	2	12	15-0	0	25	.257	.329	.360	91	-1	0-0	.976	-2	94	38	3b17,1b11,O7L	0	-0.4
1964	Bos A	61	69	10	11	2	0	5	11	7-0	1	10	.159	.247	.406	74	-3	0-0	1.000	3	137	54	1b21,3b13,O5(4/1/0)	0	0.0
Total	13	1023	2959	358	768	157	12	70	331	227-12	12	392	.260	.312	.392	92	-36	12-21	.989	1	102	84	O456L,3b257,1b188,2b20	0	-6.8
WILLIAMS, RINALDO	Rinaldo Louis; B12.18.1893 Santa Cruz CA; D4.24.1966 Cottonwood AZ; BL/TR; d10.8																								
1914	Bro F	4	15	1	4	2	0	0	0	0	0	0	.267	.267	.400	81	-1	0	.923	0	111	0	3b4	—	-0.1
WILLIAMS, BOB	Robert Elias; B4.27.1884 Monday OH; D8.6.1962 Nelsonville OH; BR/TR/6´0˝/190; d7.3																								
1911	NY A	20	47	3	9	2	0	0	8	5	0	—	.191	.269	.234	38	-4	1	.942	-1	*95*	*123*	C20	—	-0.4
1912	NY A	20	44	7	6	1	0	0	3	9	0	—	.136	.283	.159	26	-4	0	.930	-2	*90*	*69*	C20	—	-0.5
1913	NY A	6	19	0	3	0	0	0	0	1	0	3	.158	.200	.158	5	-2	0	.971	-1	*72*	*120*	C6	—	-0.3
Total	3	46	110	10	18	3	0	0	11	15	0	3	.164	.264	.191	28	-10	1	.941	-4	*89*	*99*	C46	—	-1.2
WILLIAMS, TED	Theodore Samuel "The Kid", "The Thumper","The Splendid Splinter"; B8.30.1918 San Diego CA; D7.5.2002 Inverness FL; BL/TR/6´3˝/(190–205); d4.20; Mil 1943–45, 1952–53; M4; HF1966																								
1939	Bos A	149	565	131	185	44	11	31	**145**	107	2	64	.327	.436	.609	158	53	2-1	.945	1	106	94	O149R	—	4.1
1940	Bos A★	144	561	**134**	193	43	14	23	113	96	3	54	.344	**.442**	.594	159	53	4-4	.960	-1	96	119	O143(128/0/16)/P	—	4.0
1941	Bos A★	143	456	**135**	185	33	3	**37**	120	**147**	3	27	**.406**	**.553**	**.735**	**232**	**102**	2-4	.961	-3	95	100	O133(130/0/4)	0	**8.5**
1942	Bos A★	150	522	**141**	186	34	5	**36**	**137**	**145**	4	51	**.356**	**.499**	**.648**	**214**	**90**	3-2	.988	4	100	130	O150L	0	**8.5**
1946	†Bos A★	150	514	**142**	176	37	8	38	123	**156**	2	44	.342	**.497**	**.667**	**211**	**88**	0-0	.971	2	106	73	O150L	0	**8.1**
1947	Bos A★	156	528	**125**	181	40	9	**32**	**114**	**162**	2	47	**.343**	**.499**	**.634**	**199**	**83**	0-1	.975	1	100	94	O156L	0	**7.2**
1948	Bos A★	137	509	124	188	**44**	3	25	127	**126**	3	41	**.369**	**.497**	**.615**	**185**	**71**	4-0	.983	-0	99	92	O134L	0	5.9
1949	Bos A★	**155**	566	**150**	194	**39**	3	**43**	**159**	**162**	2	48	.343	**.490**	**.650**	**187**	**80**	1-1	.983	-0	98	103	O155L	0	**6.4**
1950	Bos A★	89	334	82	106	24	1	28	97	82	0	21	.317	.452	.647	163	34	3-0	.956	-5	87	106	O86L	0	2.2
1951	Bos A★	148	531	109	169	28	4	30	126	**144**	0	45	.318	**.464**	**.556**	159	**52**	1-1	.988	2	97	105	O147L	0	4.1
1952	Bos A	6	10	2	4	0	1	1	3	2	0	2	.400	.500	.900	264	2	0-0	1.000	0	103	0	O2L	0	0.2
1953	Bos A✱	37	91	17	37	6	0	13	34	19	0	10	.407	.509	.901	261	21	0-1	.970	-2	77	69	O26L	0	1.7
1954	Bos A★	117	386	93	133	23	1	29	89	**136**	1	32	.345	**.513**	.635	**193**	**61**	0-0	.982	-4	93	71	O115L	0	**5.1**
1955	Bos A★	98	320	77	114	21	3	28	83	91-**17**	2	24	.356	.496	.703	203	52	2-0	.989	-4	92	68	O93L	0	4.3
1956	Bos A★	136	400	71	138	28	2	24	82	102-**11**	1	39	.345	**.479**	.605	164	44	0-0	.973	-7	82	89	O110L	0	2.9
1957	Bos A★	132	420	96	163	28	1	38	87	119-**33**	5	43	**.388**	**.526**	**.731**	**227**	84	0-1	.995	-4	93	33	O125L	0	7.3
1958	Bos A★	129	411	81	135	23	2	26	85	98-12	4	49	**.328**	**.458**	.584	174	48	1-0	.957	-15	71	45	O114L	0	2.8
1959	Bos A★	103	272	32	69	15	0	10	43	52-6	2	27	.254	.372	.419	113	7	0-0	.970	-5	75	99	O76L	0	-0.2
1960	Bos A★	113	310	56	98	15	0	29	72	75-7	3	41	.316	.451	.645	187	42	1-1	.993	-3	81	112	O87L	0	3.4
Total	19	2292	7706	1798	2654	525	71	521	1839	2021-86	39	709	.344	.482	.634	186	1067	24-17	.974	-42	94	91	O2151(1984/0/169)/P	0	86.5
WILLIAMS, WALT	Walter Allen "No-Neck"; B12.19.1943 Brownwood TX; BR/TR/5´6˝/(185–195); d4.21; C1; Col San Francisco (CA) City																								
1964	Hou N	10	9	1	0	0	0	0	0	0-0	0	2	.000	.000	.000	-99	-2	1-0	1.000	-0	84	0	O5L	0	-0.3
1967	Chi A	104	275	35	66	16	3	3	15	17-0	2	20	.240	.289	.353	92	-3	3-2	.983	2	97	136	O73(59/0/21)	24	-0.5
1968	Chi A	63	133	6	32	6	0	1	8	4-1	2	17	.241	.271	.308	75	-4	0-1	1.000	-0	94	119	O34(9/0/28)	0	-0.7
1969	Chi A	135	471	59	143	22	1	3	32	26-1	3	33	.304	.343	.374	96	-2	6-2	.985	3	94	156	O111(34/0/83)	0	-0.5
1970	Chi A	110	315	43	79	18	1	3	15	19-0	2	30	.251	.296	.343	73	-11	3-3	.949	3	92	260	O79(13/3/64)	0	-1.3
1971	Chi A	114	361	43	106	17	3	8	35	24-1	5	27	.294	.344	.424	114	6	5-5	1.000	1	102	76	O90(35/0/62)/3	16	0.2
1972	Chi A	77	221	22	55	7	1	2	11	13-1	0	20	.249	.289	.317	79	-6	6-1	.990	3	102	174	O57(5/0/53)/3	0	-0.6
1973	Cle A	104	350	43	101	15	1	8	38	14-2	1	29	.289	.316	.406	100	-1	9-4	.970	4	102	167	O61L,D26	0	-0.1
1974	NY A	43	53	5	6	0	0	0	3	1-0	0	10	.113	.127	.113	-30	-9	1-0	.955	-1	88	119	O24(13/0/13),D3	0	-1.1
1975	NY A	82	185	27	52	5	1	5	16	8-1	3	23	.281	.320	.400	104	0	0-1	.982	-2	102	53	O31(8/10/14),D17,2b6	0	-0.4
Total	10	842	2373	284	640	106	11	33	173	126-7	18	211	.270	.310	.365	91	-32	34-19	.981	13	97	149	O565(242/13/338),D46,2b6,3b2	40	-5.3
WILLIAMS, WASH	Washington J.; B Philadelphia PA; D1.1890 Philadelphia PA; 5´11˝/180; d8.5																								
1884	Ric AA	2	8	0	2	0	0	0	—	0	0	—	.250	.250	.250	64	0	—	.500	-1	0	0	O2R	—	-0.1
1885	Chi N	1	4	0	1	0	0	0	0	0	—	0	.250	.250	.250	54	0	—	.500	-0	0	0	/rfP	—	-0.1
Total	2	3	12	0	3	0	0	0	0	0	—	0	.250	.250	.250	61	0	—	.500	-1	0	0	O3R/P	—	-0.2
WILLIAMS, BILLY	William; B6.13.1933 Newberry SC; BL/TR/6´3˝/195; d8.15																								
1969	Sea A	4	10	1	0	0	0	0	0	1-0	1	3	.000	.167	.000	-50	-2	0-0	1.000	1	19	884	O3R	0	-0.2
WILLIAMS, WOODY	Woodrow Wilson; B8.21.1912 Pamplin VA; D2.24.1995 Appomattox VA; BR/TR/5´11˝/175; d9.5																								
1938	Bro N	20	51	6	17	1	1	0	6	4	0	1	.333	.382	.392	111	1	1	.931	-5	74	52	S18/3	—	-0.3
1943	Cin N	30	69	8	26	2	1	0	11	1	0	3	.377	.386	.435	139	3	0	.986	-0	110	71	2b12,3b7,S5	0	0.4
1944	Cin N	**155**	653	73	157	23	3	1	35	44	2	24	.240	.290	.289	66	-30	7	**.971**	16	**116**	119	2b155	0	-0.6
1945	Cin N	133	482	46	114	14	0	0	27	39	2	24	.237	.296	.266	58	-27	6	.969	-8	102	85	2b133	0	-2.8
Total	4	338	1255	133	314	40	5	1	79	88	4	52	.250	.301	.292	69	-53	14	.971	3	110	103	2b300,S23,3b8	0	-3.3
WILLIAMSON, ANTONE	Anthony Joseph; B7.18.1973 Harbor City CA; BL/TR/6´1˝/195; [MilA94 1/4]; d5.31; Col Arizona St.																								
1997	Mil A	24	54	2	11	3	0	0	6	4-0	0	8	.204	.254	.259	35	-5	0-1	.977	-2	56	69	1b14,D4	0	-0.8
WILLIAMSON, ED	Edward Nagle; B10.24.1857 Philadelphia PA; D3.3.1894 Mountain Valley Springs AR; BR/TR/5´11˝/210; d5.1; ▲																								
1878	Ind N	**63**	250	31	58	10	2	1	19	5	—	15	.232	.247	.300	91	-1	—	.867	-5	93	77	3b63	—	-0.4
1879	Chi N	80	320	66	94	20	13	1	36	24	—	31	.294	.343	.447	149	17	—	**.871**	18	**131**	**158**	3b70,1b6,C4	—	3.3
1880	Chi N	75	311	65	78	20	2	0	31	15	—	26	.251	.285	.328	101	1	—	**.893**	11	113	88	3b63,C11,2b3	—	1.3
1881	Chi N	82	343	56	92	12	6	1	48	19	—	19	.268	.307	.347	100	0	—	**.909**	21	**128**	94	3b76,2b4,P3,S2/C	—	2.1
1882	Chi N	83	348	66	98	27	4	3	60	27	—	21	.282	.333	.408	130	13	—	**.881**	15	**120**	**171**	3b83/P	—	2.6
1883	Chi N	**98**	402	83	111	**49**	5	2	59	22	—	48	.276	.314	.438	116	8	—	.807	18	**133**	**155**	3b97,C3/P	—	2.4

YEAR	TM LG	G	AB	R	H	2B	3B	HR	RBI	BB-IB	HP	SO	AVG	OBP	SLG	AOPS	ABR	SB-CS	FA	FR	RNG	THR	GAMES AT POSITION	DL	BFW
1884	Chi N	107	417	84	116	18	8	**27**	84	42	—	56	.278	.344	.554	164	29	—	.861	22	**131**	**202**	3b99,C10,P2	—	4.7
1885	†Chi N	**113**	407	87	97	16	5	3	65	**75**	—	60	.238	.357	.324	107	5	—	**.892**	9	**115**	140	3b113,P2/C	—	1.5
1886	†Chi N	121	430	69	93	17	8	6	58	80	—	71	.216	.339	.335	92	-3	13	.869	-5	94	117	S121,C4,P2	—	-0.4
1887	Chi N	**127**	439	77	117	20	14	9	78	73	5	57	.267	.377	.437	111	6	45	.890	-33	84	78	S127/P	—	-2.0
1888	Chi N	132	452	75	113	9	14	8	73	65	6	71	.250	.352	.385	126	14	25	.884	-13	96	126	S132	—	0.6
1889	Chi N	47	173	16	41	3	1	1	30	23	4	22	.237	.340	.283	71	-6	2	.844	-22	86	44	S47	—	-2.4
1890	Chi P	73	261	34	51	7	3	2	26	36	8	35	.195	.311	.268	53	-17	3	.809	-17	85	77	3b52,S21	—	-2.7
Total	13	1201	4553	809	1159	228	85	64	667	506	23	532	.255	.332	.384	112	66	88	.866	20	119	137	3b716,S450,C34,P12,2b7,1b6	—	10.6
WILLIAMSON, HOWIE	Nathaniel Howard; B12.23.1904 Little Rock AR; D8.15.1969 Texarkana AR; BL/TL/6´0˝/170; d7.7; Col Texas																								
1928	StL N	10	9	0	2	0	0	0	0	1	0	4	.222	.300	.222	38	-1	0	ø	0	—	—	/H	—	-0.1
WILLIGROD, JULIUS	Julius; B10.27,1857 Marshalltown IA; D11.27.1906 San Francisco CA; BL; d7.15																								
1882	Det N	1	3	0	1	0	0	0	0	0	—	1	.333	.333	.333	115	0	—	1.000	-0	80	0	/S	—	0.0
	Cle N	9	36	5	5	1	1	0	2	3	—	7	.139	.205	.222	38	-2	—	.813	-2	0	0	O9(0/9/1)	—	-0.4
	Year	10	39	5	6	1	1	0	2	3	—	8	.154	.214	.231	44	-2	—	.813	-2	0	0	O9(0/9/1)/S	—	-0.4
WILLINGHAM, JOSH	Joshua David; B2.17.1979 Florence AL; BR/TR/6´1˝/200; [FlaN00 17/491]; d7.6; Col North Alabama																								
2004	Fla N	12	25	2	5	0	0	1	1	4-0	0	8	.200	.310	.320	67	-1	0-0	.938	-2	35	187	C5,O3L	0	-0.3
2005	Fla N	16	23	3	7	1	0	0	4	2-0	2	5	.304	.407	.348	106	0	0-0	1.000	-2	62	0	C8/lfD	64	-0.1
2006	Fla N	142	502	62	139	28	2	26	74	54-2	11	109	.277	.356	.496	122	16	2-0	.968	-6	90	78	O132L,C2,1b2,D3	15	0.6
Total	3	170	550	67	151	29	2	27	79	60-2	13	122	.275	.356	.482	119	15	2-0	.969	-10	91	76	O136L,C15,D4,1b2	79	0.2
WILLINGHAM, HUGH	Thomas Hugh; B5.30.1906 Dalhart TX; D6.15.1988 El Reno OK; BR/TR/6´0˝/180; d9.13																								
1930	Chi A	3	4	2	1	0	0	0	0	2	0	1	.250	.500	.250	100	0	0-0	1.000	-0	112	0	/2	—	0.0
1931	Phi N	23	35	5	9	2	1	1	3	2	0	9	.257	.297	.457	93	-1	0	.875	-1	77	94	S8,3b2/lf	—	-0.1
1932	Phi N	4	2	0	0	0	0	0	0	0	0	0	.000	.000	.000	-89	-1	0	ø	0	—	—	/H	—	-0.1
1933	Phi N	1	1	0	0	0	0	0	0	0	0	0	.000	.000	.000	-89	0	0	ø	0	—	—	/H	—	0.0
Total	4	31	42	7	10	2	1	1	3	4	0	10	.238	.304	.405	82	-2	0-0	.875	-2	77	94	S8,3b2/lf2	—	-0.2
WILLITS, REGGIE	Reggie Gene; B5.30.1981 Chickasta OK; BB/TR/5´11˝/185; [AnaA03 7/210]; d4.26; Col Oklahoma																								
2006	LA A	28	45	12	12	1	0	0	2	11-0	0	10	.267	.411	.289	89	0	4-3	.974	1	110	153	O20(0/19/1),D2	0	0.1
WILLS	; d5.14																								
1884	Was AA	4	15	1	2	2	0	0	—	0	0	—	.133	.133	.267	31	-1	—	.889	2	401	0	O4(1/3/0)	—	0.1
	KC U	5	21	2	3	1	0	0	—	0	—	—	.143	.143	.190	0	-3	—	1.000	1	208	0	O5C	—	-0.2
Total	1	9	36	3	5	3	0	0	—	0	—	—	.139	.139	.222	13	-4	—	.938	3	305	0	O9(1/8/0)	—	-0.1
WILLS, DAVE	Davis Bowles; B1.26.1877 Charlottesville VA; D10.13.1959 Washington DC; BL/TL; d6.8; Col Virginia																								
1899	Lou N	24	94	15	21	3	1	0	12	2	0	—	.223	.240	.277	41	-8	1	.957	-3	67	65	1b24	—	-1.0
WILLS, BUMP	Elliott Taylor; B7.27.1952 Washington DC; BB/TR/5´9˝/(170–178); [TexA75*S1/6]; d4.7; f–Maury; Col Arizona St.																								
1977	Tex A	152	541	87	155	28	6	9	62	65-7	0	96	.287	.361	.410	109	8	28-12	.982	6	104	98	2b150,S2/1D	0	2.5
1978	Tex A	157	539	78	135	17	4	9	57	63-3	4	91	.250	.331	.347	91	-5	52-14	.981	22	111	88	2b156	0	3.2
1979	Tex A	146	543	90	148	21	3	5	46	53-4	4	58	.273	.340	.350	88	-8	35-11	.976	12	104	96	2b146	14	1.5
1980	Tex A	146	578	102	152	31	5	5	58	51-1	3	71	.263	.322	.360	90	-7	34-9	.984	20	102	100	2b144	16	2.5
1981	Tex A	102	410	51	103	13	2	2	41	32-2	1	49	.251	.304	.307	81	-10	12-9	.983	11	101	103	2b101/D	0	0.6
1982	Chi N	128	419	64	114	18	4	6	38	46-3	5	76	.272	.347	.377	100	1	35-10	.963	-11	97	77	2b103	0	0.0
Total	6	831	3030	472	807	128	24	36	302	310-20	17	441	.266	.335	.360	94	-21	196-65	.979	60	104	94	2b800,D2,S2/1	30	10.3
WILLS, MAURY	Maurice Morning; B10.2.1932 Washington DC; BB/TR/5´11˝/(160–170); d6.6; M2; s–Bump																								
1959	†LA N	83	242	27	63	5	2	0	7	13-5	0	27	.260	.298	.298	55	-15	7-3	.966	0	97	88	S82	0	-0.9
1960	LA N	148	516	75	152	15	2	0	27	35-8	3	47	.295	.342	.331	80	-13	**50**-12	.945	26	105	103	S145	0	3.2
1961	LA N★	148	613	105	173	12	10	1	31	59-2	1	50	.282	.346	.339	76	-20	**35**-15	.959	10	95	108	S148	0	0.5
1962	LA N★	**165**	695	130	208	13	**10**	6	48	51-1	2	57	.299	.347	.373	100	-2	**104**-13	.956	-4	95	83	S165	0	2.7
1963	†LA N☆	134	527	83	159	19	3	0	34	44-0	1	48	.302	.355	.349	112	9	**40**-19	.959	10	105	84	S109,3b33	0	3.1
1964	LA N	158	630	81	173	15	5	2	34	41-0	0	73	.275	.318	.324	88	-11	**53**-17	.963	-13	91	94	S149,3b6	0	-0.5
1965	†LA N★	158	650	92	186	14	7	0	33	40-2	4	64	.286	.330	.329	93	-7	**94**-31	.970	18	105	107	S155	0	3.5
1966	†LA N★	143	594	60	162	14	2	1	39	34-0	2	60	.273	.314	.308	80	-17	38-24	.967	14	102	107	S139,3b4	0	1.0
1967	Pit N	149	616	92	186	12	9	3	45	31-1	1	44	.302	.334	.365	100	-2	29-10	.948	9	**117**	122	3b144,S2	0	1.1
1968	Pit N	153	627	76	174	12	6	0	31	45-1	1	57	.278	.326	.316	95	-4	52-21	.957	-10	98	102	3b141,S10	0	-1.2
1969	Mon N	47	189	23	42	3	0	0	8	20-0	0	21	.222	.295	.238	51	-12	15-6	.950	-2	98	100	S46/2	0	-0.7
	LA N	104	434	57	129	7	8	4	39	39-2	1	40	.297	.356	.378	113	6	25-15	.969	11	109	109	S104	0	3.1
	Year	151	623	80	171	10	8	4	47	59-2	1	61	.274	.337	.335	93	-6	40-21	.963	9	106	106	S150/2	0	2.4
1970	LA N	132	522	77	141	19	3	0	34	50-2	0	34	.270	.333	.318	78	-15	28-13	.959	-17	101	83	S126,3b4	0	-1.6
1971	LA N	149	601	73	169	14	3	3	44	40-2	0	44	.281	.323	.329	91	-9	15-8	.978	6	104	105	S144,3b4	0	1.5
1972	LA N	71	132	16	17	3	1	0	4	10-0	0	18	.129	.190	.167	2	-17	1-1	.984	-6	94	115	S31,3b26	0	-2.2
Total	14	1942	7588	1067	2134	177	71	20	458	552-26	16	684	.281	.330	.331	88	-129	586-208	.963	52	100	98	S1555,3b362/2	0	12.6
WILLSON, KID	Frank Hoxie; B11.3.1895 Bloomington NE; D4.17.1964 Union Gap WA; BL/TL/6´1˝/190; d7.2																								
1918	Chi A	4	1	2	0	0	0	0	0	1	0	1	.000	.500	.000	50	0	0	ø	0	—	—	/H	—	0.0
1927	Chi A	7	10	1	1	0	0	0	1	0	0	2	.100	.100	.100	-49	-2	0-0	1.000	0	143	0	O2(1/1/0)	—	-0.2
Total	2	11	11	3	1	0	0	0	1	1	0	3	.091	.167	.091	-31	-2	0-0	1.000	0	143	0	O2(1/1/0)	—	-0.2
WILMOT, WALT	Walter Robert; B10.18.1863 Plover WI; D2.1.1929 Chicago IL; BB/TR/5´9˝/165; d4.20																								
1888	Was N	119	473	61	106	16	9	4	43	23	2	55	.224	.263	.321	92	-5	46	.872	12	96	96	O119L	—	0.4
1889	Was N	108	432	88	125	19	**19**	9	57	51	2	32	.289	.367	.484	144	25	40	.927	14	106	92	O108(107/1/0)	—	3.1
1890	Chi N	**139**	571	114	159	15	13	**13**	99	64	2	44	.278	.353	.419	120	12	76	.938	11	110	90	O139(27/112/0)	—	1.6
1891	Chi N	121	498	102	137	14	10	11	71	55	5	21	.275	.353	.410	122	13	42	.922	-4	83	0	O121(62/60/0)	—	0.6
1892	Chi N	92	380	47	82	7	7	2	35	40	4	20	.216	.297	.287	76	-11	31	.903	-1	50	0	O92L	—	-2.0
1893	Chi N	94	392	69	118	14	14	3	61	40	1	8	.301	.367	.431	114	6	39	.873	-1	97	27	O93(84/10/0)	—	-0.3
1894	Chi N	135	604	136	199	45	12	5	130	36	1	27	.329	.368	.469	95	-7	76	.870	-7	71	84	O135L	—	-2.0
1895	Chi N	108	466	86	132	16	6	8	72	30	0	19	.283	.327	.395	80	-17	28	.914	3	114	130	O108L	—	-1.9
1897	NY N	11	34	8	9	2	0	1	4	2	0	—	.265	.306	.412	91	-1	1	.938	0	159	0	O9(5/1/3)	—	-0.1
1898	NY N	35	138	16	33	4	2	2	22	9	0	—	.239	.286	.341	82	-4	4	.886	-4	89	0	O34(6/0/29)	—	-0.9
Total	10	962	3988	727	1100	152	92	58	594	350	17	226	.276	.337	.404	105	11	383	.903	23	92	64	O958(745/184/32)	—	-1.5
WILSON, ARCHIE	Archie Clifton; B11.25.1923 Los Angeles CA; BR/TR/6´0˝/175; d9.18; Col USC																								
1951	NY A	4	4	0	0	0	0	0	0	0	1	0	.000	.200	.000	-44	-1	0-0	1.000	0	139	0	O2R	0	-0.1
1952	NY A	3	2	0	1	0	0	0	1	0	0	0	.500	.500	.500	190	0	0-0	ø	0	—	—	/H	0	0.0
	Was A	26	96	8	20	2	3	0	14	5	1	11	.208	.255	.292	54	-7	0-0	.971	-0	110	0	O24(14/10/0)	0	-0.9
	Bos A	18	38	1	10	3	0	0	2	2	0	3	.263	.300	.342	73	-1	0-0	.944	0	95	152	O13(2/2/9)	0	-0.2
	Year	47	136	9	31	5	3	0	17	7	1	14	.228	.271	.309	61	-8	0-0	.966	-0	106	39	O37(16/12/9)	0	-1.1
Total	2	51	140	9	31	5	3	0	17	7	2	14	.221	.268	.300	58	-9	0-0	.967	0	107	38	O39(16/12/11)	0	-1.2
WILSON, ART	Arthur Earl "Dutch"; B12.11.1885 Macon IL; D6.12.1960 Chicago IL; BR/TR/5´8˝/170; d9.29																								
1908	NY N	1	0	0	0	0	0	0	0	0	0	—	ø	ø	ø	ø	0	0	ø	0	—	—	/R	—	0.0
1909	NY N	19	42	4	10	2	1	0	5	4	0	—	.238	.304	.333	96	0	0	.985	-2	*97*	*86*	C19	—	-0.1
1910	NY N	26	52	10	14	4	1	0	5	9	1	6	.269	.387	.385	125	2	2	.975	-0	*96*	*93*	C25/1	—	0.4
1911	†NY N	66	109	17	33	9	1	1	17	19	1	12	.303	.411	.431	132	6	6	.963	-1	*125*	*82*	C64	—	0.8
1912	†NY N	65	121	17	35	6	0	3	19	13	0	14	.289	.358	.413	107	1	2	.960	3	*132*	*68*	C61	—	0.8
1913	†NY N	54	79	5	15	0	1	0	8	11	0	11	.190	.289	.215	45	-5	1-5	.965	6	127	79	C49	—	0.1
1914	Chi F	137	440	78	128	31	8	10	64	70	5	80	.291	.394	.466	142	21	13	.974	21	***143***	*94*	C132	—	**5.4**
1915	Chi F	96	269	44	82	11	2	7	31	65	1	38	.305	.442	.439	157	22	8	.980	-5	*116*	*79*	C87	—	2.6
1916	Pit N	53	128	11	33	5	2	1	12	13	1	27	.258	.331	.352	109	2	4	.981	-7	81	92	C39	—	-0.2
	Chi N	36	114	5	22	3	1	0	5	6	0	14	.193	.233	.237	40	-8	1	.953	-4	96	107	C34	—	-1.1

YEAR	TM LG	G	AB	R	H	2B	3B	HR	RBI	BB-IB	HP	SO	AVG	OBP	SLG	AOPS	ABR	SB-CS	FA	FR	RNG	THR	GAMES AT POSITION	DL	BFW
	Year	89	242	16	55	8	3	1	17	19	1	41	.227	.286	.298	76	-7	5	.967	-11	88	99	C73	—	-1.3
1917	Chi N	81	211	17	45	9	2	2	25	32	2	36	.213	.322	.303	85	-2	6	.968	6	*101*	*105*	C75	—	1.1
1918	Bos N	89	280	15	69	8	2	0	19	24	2	31	.246	.310	.289	87	-4	5	.977	-11	*89*	*100*	C85	—	-0.9
1919	Bos N	71	191	14	49	8	1	0	16	25	1	19	.257	.346	.309	102	2	2	.977	-2	*99*	*98*	C64/1	—	0.6
1920	Bos N	16	19	0	1	0	0	0	0	1	1	1	.053	.143	.053	-44	-4	0-0	1.000	-1	81	0	3b6,C2	—	-0.5
1921	Cle A	2	1	0	0	0	0	0	0	0	0	0	.000	.000	.000	-99	0	0-0	1.000	0	*0*	*0*	C2	—	0.0
Total	14	812	2056	237	536	96	22	24	226	292	15	289	.261	.357	.364	110	33	50-5	.972	4	*113*	*92*	C738,3b6,1b2	—	9.0
Wilson, Artie	Arthur Lee; B10.28.1920 Springville AL; BL/TR/5´10˝/162; d4.18; Negro Lg 1944–48																								
1951	NY N	19	22	2	4	0	0	0	1	2	0	1	.182	.250	.182	18	-3	2-0	1.000	1	94	235	2b3,S3,1b2	0	-0.1
Wilson, Charlie	Charles Woodrow "Swamp Baby"; B1.13.1905 Clinton SC; D12.19.1970 Rochester NY; BB/TR/5´10.5˝/178; d4.14; Col Presbyterian																								
1931	Bos N	16	58	7	11	4	0	1	11	3	0	5	.190	.230	.310	45	-5	0	.917	-1	100	0	3b14	—	-0.6
1932	StL N	24	96	7	19	3	3	1	2	3	0	8	.198	.222	.323	43	-8	0	.935	-3	97	98	S24	—	-0.9
1933	StL N	1	1	0	0	0	0	0	0	0	0	1	.000	.000	.000	-95	0	0	ø	-0	0	0	/S	—	0.0
1935	StL N	16	31	1	10	0	0	0	1	2	0	2	.323	.364	.323	83	-1	0	.933	-1	81	129	3b8	—	-0.1
Total	4	57	186	15	40	7	3	2	14	8	0	16	.215	.247	.317	50	-14	0	.935	-5	97	98	S25,3b22	—	-1.6
Wilson, Craig	Craig; B11.28.1964 Annapolis MD; BR/TR/5´11˝/(175–210); [StLN84 20/503]; d9.6; Col Anne Arundel (MD) CC																								
1989	StL N	6	4	1	1	0	0	0	1	1-0	0	2	.250	.400	.250	87	0	0-0	.500	-0	0	0	3b2	0	0.0
1990	StL N	55	121	13	30	2	0	0	7	8-0	0	14	.248	.290	.264	55	-8	0-2	.971	0	92	61	3b13,O13(7/0/7),2b9/1	0	-0.8
1991	StL N	60	82	5	14	2	0	0	13	6-2	0	10	.171	.222	.195	20	-9	0-0	.905	-0	77	242	3b12,O5L,1b4,2b3	0	-1.0
1992	StL N	61	106	6	33	6	0	0	13	10-2	0	18	.311	.368	.368	112	2	1-2	.970	-3	75	82	3b18,2b11,O3R	0	-0.1
1993	KC A	21	49	6	13	1	0	1	3	7-0	0	6	.265	.357	.347	84	-1	1-1	1.000	-0	91	204	3b15/2lf	0	-0.1
Total	5	203	362	31	91	11	0	1	37	32-4	0	50	.251	.308	.290	68	-16	2-5	.957	-3	83	133	3b60,2b24,O22(13/0/10),1b5	0	-2.0
Wilson, Craig	Craig Alan; B11.30.1976 Fountain Valley CA; BR/TR/6´2˝/(217–220); [TorA95 2/47]; d4.22																								
2001	Pit N	88	158	27	49	3	1	13	32	15-1	7	53	.310	.390	.589	145	10	3-1	.994	-3	123	114	1b26,O14(1/0/13),C10,D2	0	0.7
2002	Pit N	131	368	48	97	16	1	16	57	32-0	**21**	116	.264	.355	.443	107	4	2-3	.982	-1	85	142	O75(1/0/74),1b42,C5,D3	0	-0.3
2003	Pit N	116	309	49	81	15	4	18	48	35-4	13	89	.262	.360	.511	123	10	3-1	.978	3	124	126	O46(7/0/40),1b36,C21,D3	0	1.1
2004	Pit N	155	561	97	148	35	5	29	82	50-3	**30**	169	.264	.354	.499	118	15	2-2	.977	-5	100	38	O100(19/0/89),1b65,C4,D2	0	0.1
2005	Pit N	59	197	23	52	14	1	5	22	30-2	10	69	.264	.387	.421	112	5	3-0	.988	0	92	159	O47(19/0/30),1b15	105	0.3
2006	Pit N	85	255	38	68	11	2	13	41	24-2	5	88	.267	.339	.478	105	1	1-0	.997	-2	84	112	1b43,O30R	0	-0.5
	NY A	40	104	15	22	4	0	4	8	4-0	1	34	.212	.248	.365	56	-7	0-0	.992	-3	58	98	1b35,O2R	0	-1.2
Total	6	674	1952	297	517	98	14	98	290	190-12	87	618	.265	.354	.480	113	38	14-7	.981	-9	97	111	O314(47/0/278),1b262,C40,D10	105	0.2
Wilson, Craig	Craig Franklin; B9.3.1970 Chicago IL; BR/TR/6´0˝/185; [ChiA92 13/372]; d9.5; Col Kansas St.																								
1998	Chi A	13	47	14	22	5	0	3	10	3-0	0	6	.468	.490	.766	227	9	1-0	1.000	-3	67	72	S8,2b4,3b2	0	0.6
1999	Chi A	98	252	28	60	8	1	4	26	23-0	0	22	.238	.301	.325	59	-16	1-1	.969	-0	110	112	3b72,S22,2b7/1D	0	-1.4
2000	Chi A	28	73	12	19	3	0	0	4	5-0	1	11	.260	.316	.301	56	-5	1-0	.938	6	137	124	3b15,S10,2b4	36	0.2
Total	3	139	372	54	101	16	1	7	40	31-0	1	39	.272	.328	.376	78	-12	3-1	.964	2	114	112	3b89,S40,2b15/D1	36	-0.6
Wilson, Dan	Daniel Allen; B3.25.1969 Arlington Heights IL; BR/TR/6´3˝/(190–215); [CinN90 1/7]; d9.7; Col Minnesota																								
1992	Cin N	12	25	2	9	1	0	0	3	3-0	0	8	.360	.429	.400	132	1	0-0	1.000	1	127	125	C9	0	0.2
1993	Cin N	36	76	6	17	3	0	0	8	9-4	0	16	.224	.302	.263	54	-5	0-0	.994	-4	68	38	C35	0	-0.8
1994	Sea A	91	282	24	61	14	2	3	27	10-0	1	57	.216	.244	.312	42	-26	1-2	.986	12	124	110	C91	0	-0.8
1995	†Sea A	119	399	40	111	22	3	9	51	33-1	2	63	.278	.336	.416	93	-4	2-1	.995	14	111	117	C119	0	1.6
1996	Sea A★	138	491	51	140	24	0	18	83	32-2	3	88	.285	.330	.444	94	-6	1-2	.996	10	134	109	C135	0	1.1
1997	†Sea A	146	508	66	137	31	1	15	74	39-1	5	72	.270	.326	.423	94	-5	7-2	.995	13	125	**125**	C144	0	1.7
1998	Sea A	96	325	39	82	17	1	9	44	24-0	5	56	.252	.308	.394	82	-9	2-1	.994	-3	90	93	C94	43	-0.5
1999	Sea A	123	414	46	110	23	2	7	38	29-4	2	83	.266	.315	.382	78	-14	5-0	.995	-2	91	70	C121,1b5	0	-0.7
2000	†Sea A	90	268	31	63	12	0	5	27	22-0	0	51	.235	.291	.336	60	-17	1-2	.990	3	142	105	C88/13	28	-0.9
2001	†Sea A	123	377	44	100	20	1	10	42	20-0	2	69	.265	.305	.403	90	-7	3-2	**.999**	5	161	56	C122,1b2	0	0.5
2002	Sea A	115	359	35	106	16	1	6	44	18-1	2	81	.295	.326	.396	96	-3	1-0	.997	-2	124	67	C113,1b4	0	0.2
2003	Sea A	96	316	32	76	15	2	4	43	15-0	0	52	.241	.272	.339	64	-17	0-0	**.998**	1	**180**	54	C96	7	-1.0
2004	Sea A	103	319	23	80	13	0	2	33	26-0	1	57	.251	.305	.310	65	-16	0-1	.997	-3	107	98	C103	0	-1.2
2005	Sea A	11	27	2	5	0	0	0	2	0-0	1	10	.185	.214	.185	8	-4	0-1	.975	-2	106	167	C11	147	-0.6
Total	14	1299	4186	441	1097	211	13	88	519	280-13	24	763	.262	.309	.382	80	-132	23-14	.995	42	125	92	C1281,1b12/3	225	-1.2
Wilson, Desi	Desi Bernard; B5.9.1969 Glen Cove NY; BL/TL/6´7˝/230; [TexA91 30/794]; d8.7; Col Fairleigh Dickinson; [DL 1997 SF N 5]																								
1996	SF N	41	118	10	32	2	0	2	12	12-2	0	27	.271	.338	.339	81	-3	0-2	.984	-2	89	84	1b33	0	-0.8
Wilson, Eddie	Edward Francis; B9.7.1909 Hamden CT; D4.11.1979 Hamden CT; BL/TL/5´11˝/165; d6.21; Col Holy Cross																								
1936	Bro N	52	173	28	60	8	1	3	25	14	2	25	.347	.402	.457	129	8	3	.926	-3	92	68	O47R	—	0.2
1937	Bro N	36	54	11	12	4	1	1	8	17	0	14	.222	.408	.389	116	2	1	.966	-0	102	71	O21(0/1/20)	—	0.1
Total	2	88	227	39	72	12	2	4	33	31	2	39	.317	.404	.441	126	10	4	.936	-4	95	69	O68(0/1/67)	—	0.3
Wilson, Enrique	Enrique (Martes); B7.27.1973 Santo Domingo, D.R.; BB/TR/5´11˝/(160–195); d9.24																								
1997	Cle A	5	15	2	5	0	0	0	1	0-0	0	2	.333	.333	.333	72	-1	0-0	.941	1	120	205	S4/2	0	0.0
1998	†Cle A	32	90	13	29	6	0	2	12	4-0	1	8	.322	.354	.456	106	1	2-4	.989	1	107	58	2b22,S10,3b2	72	0.2
1999	†Cle A	113	332	41	87	22	1	2	24	25-1	1	41	.262	.310	.352	67	-17	5-4	.965	-12	98	25	3b61,S35,2b21/D	0	-2.5
2000	Cle A	40	117	16	38	9	0	2	12	7-0	0	11	.325	.360	.453	101	0	2-1	.950	-3	107	0	3b12,2b7,S7,D8	14	-0.2
	Pit N	40	122	11	32	6	1	3	15	11-2	0	13	.262	.321	.402	81	-4	0-1	.925	-0	110	34	3b16,2b11,S8	3	-0.3
2001	Pit N	46	129	7	24	3	0	1	8	3-0	0	23	.186	.203	.233	12	-17	0-3	.974	4	110	102	S28,2b10,3b2	0	-1.2
	†NY A	48	99	10	24	5	1	1	12	6-0	0	14	.242	.283	.343	64	-5	0-2	.952	4	99	71	S20,3b19,2b7/D	0	-0.1
2002	†NY A	60	105	17	19	2	2	2	11	8-0	0	22	.181	.239	.295	41	-9	1-1	.932	1	99	47	3b26,S14,2b7/rfD	0	-0.8
2003	†NY A	63	135	18	31	9	0	3	15	7-0	2	14	.230	.276	.363	68	-6	3-1	.987	-4	78	65	S33,3b17,2b10/D	0	-0.8
2004	NY A	93	240	19	51	9	0	6	31	15-0	0	20	.213	.254	.325	51	-18	1-2	.977	-6	92	57	2b80,S16	0	-2.0
2005	Chi N	15	22	1	3	2	0	0	0	3-0	0	1	.136	.240	.227	23	-2	0-0	.929	2	143	365	2b5,1b3,S3/3	0	0.0
Total	9	555	1406	155	343	73	5	22	141	89-3	4	169	.244	.288	.350	63	-78	14-19	.983	-13	95	72	2b181,S178,3b156,D13,1b3/rf	89	-7.7
Wilson, Frank	Francis Edward "Squash"; B4.20.1901 Malden MA; D11.25.1974 Leicester MA; BL/TR/6´0˝/185; d6.20; Col Boston College																								
1924	Bos N	61	215	20	51	7	0	1	15	23	0	22	.237	.311	.284	63	-11	3-4	.973	2	108	86	O55(35/20/0)	—	-1.3
1925	Bos N	12	31	3	13	1	1	0	0	4	0	1	.419	.486	.516	171	4	2-1	1.000	1	121	114	O10(9/0/1)	—	0.4
1926	Bos N	87	236	22	56	11	3	0	23	20	1	21	.237	.300	.309	70	-10	3	.934	1	107	109	O56(50/1/6)	—	-1.3
1928	Cle A	2	1	0	0	0	0	0	0	1	0	0	.000	.500	.000	41	0	0-0	ø	0	—	—	/H	—	0.0
	StL A	6	5	1	0	0	0	0	0	0	0	0	.000	.000	.000	-97	-1	0-0	ø	-0	0	0	/rf	—	-0.1
	Year	8	6	1	0	0	0	0	0	1	0	0	.000	.143	.000	-58	-1	0-0	ø	-0	0	0	/rf	—	-0.1
Total	4	168	488	46	120	19	4	1	38	48	1	44	.246	.315	.307	72	-18	8-5	.958	4	108	99	O122(94/21/8)	—	-2.3
Wilson, Tug	George Archer; B1860 Brooklyn NY; D11.28.1914 New York NY; 5´8˝/175; d5.9																								
1884	Bro AA	24	82	13	19	4	0	0	—	5	0	—	.232	.276	.280	81	-1	—	.826	-3	93	284	O12(5/6/1),C10,1b3/2	—	-0.4
Wilson, Squanto	George Francis; B3.29.1889 Old Town ME; D3.26.1967 Winthrop ME; BB/TR/5´9.5˝/170; d10.2; Col Bowdoin																								
1911	Det A	5	16	2	3	0	0	0	0	2	0	—	.188	.278	.188	29	-1	0	.900	-1	*106*	*97*	C5	—	-0.2
1914	Bos A	1	0	0	0	0	0	0	0	0	0	0	ø	ø	ø	ø	0	0	ø	0	0	0	/1	—	0.0
Total	2	6	16	2	3	0	0	0	0	2	0	0	.188	.278	.188	29	-1	0	.900	-1	*106*	*97*	C5/1	—	-0.2
Wilson, Icehouse	George Peacock; B9.14.1912 Maricopa CA; D10.13.1973 Moraga CA; BR/TR/6´0˝/186; d5.31; Col St. Marys (CA)																								
1934	Det A	1	1	0	0	0	0	0	0	0	0	0	.000	.000	.000	-99	0	0-0	ø	0	—	—	/H	—	0.0
Wilson, George	George Washington "Teddy"; B8.30.1925 Cherryville NC; D10.29.1974 Gastonia NC; BL/TR/6´1.5˝/185; d4.15																								
1952	Chi A	8	9	0	1	0	0	0	1	1	0	2	.111	.200	.111	-12	-1	0-0	1.000	0	109	0	/rf	0	-0.2
	NY N	62	112	9	27	7	0	2	16	3	0	14	.241	.261	.357	69	-5	0-0	.923	-2	100	0	O21(16/1/4),1b2	0	-0.9
1953	NY N	11	8	0	1	0	0	0	0	2	1	2	.125	.364	.125	34	-1	0-0	ø	0	—	—	/H	0	-0.1
1956	NY N	53	68	5	9	1	0	1	2	5-1	0	14	.132	.192	.191	3	-9	0-0	1.000	0	91	159	O8(2/0/6)	0	-1.0

YEAR	TM LG	G	AB	R	H	2B	3B	HR	RBI	BB-IB	HP	SO	AVG	OBP	SLG	AOPS	ABR	SB-CS	FA	FR	RNG	THR	GAMES AT POSITION	DL	BFW
	†NY A	11	12	1	2	0	0	0	0	3-0	0	0	.167	.333	.167	37	-1	0-0	.750	-1	68	0	O6(1/0/5)	0	-0.2
Total	3	145	209	15	40	8	0	3	19	14-1	1	32	.191	.246	.273	41	-17	0-0	.932	-3	96	42	O36(19/1/16),1b2	0	-2.4
Wilson, Glenn	Glenn Dwight; B12.22.1958 Baytown TX; BR/TR/6´1˝/(185–190); [DetA80 1/18]; d4.15; Col Sam Houston St.; OF(118/90/941)																								
1982	Det A	84	322	39	94	15	1	12	34	15-0	0	51	.292	.322	.457	111	4	2-3	.987	3	102	150	O80(2/71/8),D4	0	0.5
1983	Det A	144	503	55	135	25	6	11	65	25-1	3	79	.268	.306	.408	97	-4	1-1	.988	-7	86	122	O143(0/8/140)	0	-1.8
1984	Phi N	132	341	28	82	21	3	6	31	17-1	1	56	.240	.276	.372	80	-10	7-1	.968	-5	91	60	O109(92/3/18),3b4	0	-1.9
1985	Phi N★	161	608	73	167	39	5	14	102	35-1	0	117	.275	.311	.424	102	0	7-4	.968	16	117	170	O158(2/0/157)	0	0.8
1986	Phi N	155	584	70	158	30	4	15	84	42-1	4	91	.271	.319	.413	98	-3	5-1	.989	15	112	156	O154(1/0/153)	0	0.5
1987	Phi N	154	569	55	150	21	2	14	54	38-2	1	82	.264	.308	.381	79	-18	3-6	.968	10	106	169	O154R/P	0	-1.7
1988	Sea A	78	284	28	71	10	1	3	17	15-0	0	52	.250	.286	.324	68	-13	1-1	.980	-2	93	92	O75R,D2	0	-1.7
	Pit N	37	126	11	34	8	0	2	15	3-1	1	18	.270	.288	.381	93	-2	0-0	.985	-1	96	59	O35(0/4/32)	15	-0.4
1989	Pit N	100	330	42	93	20	4	9	49	32-5	1	39	.282	.342	.448	130	13	1-4	.977	-2	97	86	O85(0/1/85),1b10	0	0.7
	Hou N	28	102	8	22	6	0	2	15	5-0	0	14	.216	.250	.333	68	-5	0-1	.966	4	99	426	O25R	0	-0.2
	Year	128	432	50	115	26	4	11	64	37-5	1	53	.266	.321	.421	116	8	1-5	.974	2	97	167	O110(0/1/110),1b10	0	0.5
1990	Hou N	118	368	42	90	14	0	10	55	26-1	1	64	.245	.293	.364	83	-10	0-3	.975	10	112	172	O108(21/0/92)/1	0	-0.4
1993	Pit N	10	14	0	2	0	0	0	0	0-0	0	9	.143	.143	.143	-23	-2	0-0	.875	1	76	1203	O5(0/3/2)	0	-0.2
Total	10	1201	4151	451	1098	209	26	98	521	253-13	12	672	.265	.306	.398	93	-50	27-25	.977	42	103	145	O1131R,1b11,D6,3b4/P	15	-5.8
Wilson, Grady	Grady Herbert; B11.23.1922 Columbus GA; D7.23.2003 Columbus GA; BR/TR/6´0.5˝/170; d5.15; Col Troy St.																								
1948	Pit N	12	10	1	1	1	0	0	1	0	0	3	.100	.100	.200	-20	-2	0	.846	-0	68	185	S7	0	-0.2
Wilson, Henry	Henry C.; B4.8.1877 Baltimore MD; d10.12																								
1898	Bal N	1	2	0	0	0	0	0	0	1	0	—	.000	.333	.000	-2	0	0	1.000	0	*87*	*287*	/C	—	0.0
Wilson, Jack	Jack Eugene; B12.29.1977 Westlake Village CA; BR/TR/6´0˝/(175–190); [StLN98 9/258]; d4.3; Col Oxnard (CA) JC																								
2001	Pit N	108	390	44	87	17	1	3	25	16-2	1	70	.223	.255	.295	41	-35	1-3	.968	9	115	101	S107	0	-1.9
2002	Pit N	147	527	77	133	22	4	4	47	37-2	4	74	.252	.306	.332	67	-26	5-2	.977	20	**118**	100	S143	0	0.4
2003	Pit N	150	558	58	143	21	3	9	62	36-3	4	74	.256	.303	.353	70	-25	5-5	.975	4	**108**	109	S149	0	-1.0
2004	Pit N★	157	652	82	201	41	**12**	11	59	26-0	3	71	.308	.335	.459	103	1	8-4	.977	**27**	109	**129**	S156	0	3.9
2005	Pit N	158	587	60	151	24	7	8	52	31-6	6	58	.257	.299	.363	73	-25	7-3	.982	27	113	120	S157	0	1.4
2006	Pit N	142	543	70	148	27	1	8	35	33-0	4	65	.273	.316	.370	74	-21	4-3	.972	22	111	100	S131	0	1.0
Total	6	862	3257	391	863	152	28	43	280	179-13	22	412	.265	.306	.368	74	-131	30-20	.976	109	112	111	S843	0	3.8
Wilson, Jimmie	James "Ace"; B7.23.1900 Philadelphia PA; D5.31.1947 Bradenton FL; BR/TR/6´1.5˝/200; d4.17; M9/C5																								
1923	Phi N	85	252	27	66	9	0	1	25	4	1	17	.262	.276	.310	49	-19	4-2	.960	-9	*83*	*91*	C69,O2(1/1/0)	—	-2.2
1924	Phi N	95	280	32	78	16	3	6	39	17	1	12	.279	.322	.421	87	-5	5-4	.968	1	*92*	***131***	C82,1b2/rf	—	0.1
1925	Phi N	108	335	42	110	19	3	3	54	32	2	25	.328	.390	.430	100	2	5-3	.982	-7	*97*	*71*	C89/O	—	0.0
1926	Phi N	90	279	40	85	10	2	4	32	25	0	20	.305	.362	.398	99	0	3	.950	-4	*83*	*132*	C79	—	0.1
1927	Phi N	128	443	50	122	15	2	2	45	34	2	15	.275	.330	.332	77	-14	13	.975	-21	*82*	*80*	C124	—	-2.7
1928	Phi N	21	70	11	21	4	1	0	13	9	0	8	.300	.380	.386	97	0	3	.990	-0	*74*	*142*	C20	—	0.1
	†StL N	120	411	45	106	26	2	2	50	45	1	24	.258	.333	.345	76	-13	9	.983	4	*130*	*102*	C120	—	-0.1
	Year	141	481	56	127	30	3	2	63	54	1	32	.264	.340	.351	79	-13	12	.985	4	*122*	*108*	C140	—	0.0
1929	StL N	120	394	59	128	27	8	4	71	43	2	19	.325	.394	.464	111	8	4	.972	6	*115*	*106*	C119	—	1.9
1930	†StL N	107	362	54	115	25	7	1	58	28	1	17	.318	.368	.434	90	-5	8	.987	10	*113*	***121***	C99	—	1.0
1931	†StL N	115	383	45	105	20	2	0	51	28	5	15	.274	.332	.337	77	-11	5	.985	10	*100*	***128***	C110	—	0.5
1932	StL N	92	274	36	68	16	2	2	28	15	1	18	.248	.290	.343	67	-13	9	.982	2	*76*	*164*	C75,1b3/2	—	-0.6
1933	StL N★	113	369	34	94	17	0	1	45	23	1	33	.255	.300	.309	71	-13	6	.982	0	*87*	*122*	C107	—	-0.7
1934	Phi N	91	277	25	81	11	0	3	35	14	0	10	.292	.326	.365	75	-10	1	.987	5	*118*	*106*	C77/12M	—	-0.1
1935	Phi N★	93	290	38	81	20	0	1	37	19	1	19	.279	.326	.359	76	-9	4	.982	4	*99*	*92*	C78/2M	—	0.0
1936	Phi N	85	230	25	64	12	0	1	27	12	0	21	.278	.314	.343	70	-9	5	.960	-5	*96*	*84*	C63/1M	—	-1.1
1937	Phi N	39	87	15	24	3	0	1	8	6	0	4	.276	.323	.345	75	-3	1	.978	-1	*127*	*91*	C22,1b2,M	—	-0.3
1938	Phi N	3	2	0	0	0	0	0	0	0	0	1	.000	.000	.000	-99	-1	0	1.000	0	*0*	*0*	/CM	—	0.0
1939	Cin N	4	3	0	1	0	0	0	0	0	0	1	.333	.333	.333	79	0	0	ø	-0	*0*	*0*	/C	—	0.0
1940	†Cin N	16	37	2	9	2	0	0	3	2	0	1	.243	.282	.297	59	-2	1	.982	1	*101*	*122*	C16	—	0.0
Total	18	1525	4778	580	1358	252	32	32	621	356	18	280	.284	.336	.370	82	-117	86-9	.977	-3	*99*	*109*	C1351,1b9,O4(1/1/1),2b3	—	-4.1
Wilson, Gary	James Garrett; B1.12.1879 Baltimore MD; D5.1.1969 Randallstown MD; BR/TR/5´7˝/168; d9.27																								
1902	Bos A	2	8	0	1	0	0	0	1	0	0	—	.125	.125	.125	-30	-1	0	.800	-0	88	233	2b2	—	-0.2
Wilson, Jim	James George; B12.29.1960 Corvallis OR; BR/TR/6´3˝/225; [CleA82 2/40]; d9.13; Col Oregon St.																								
1985	Cle A	4	14	2	5	0	0	0	4	1-0	0	3	.357	.400	.357	110	0	0-0	1.000	-0	0	67	1b2,D2	0	0.0
1989	Sea A	5	8	0	0	0	0	0	0	0-0	0	3	.000	.000	.000	-97	-2	0-0	ø	0	—	—	D5	0	-0.2
Total	2	9	22	2	5	0	0	0	4	1-0	0	6	.227	.261	.227	36	-2	0-0	1.000	-0	0	67	D7,1b2	0	-0.2
Wilson, Chief	John Owen; B8.21.1883 Austin TX; D2.22.1954 Bertram TX; BL/TR/6´2˝/185; d4.15																								
1908	Pit N	144	529	47	120	8	7	3	43	22	2	—	.227	.260	.285	74	-18	12	.955	-1	108	72	O144(1/34/109)	—	-3.0
1909	†Pit N	**154**	569	64	155	22	12	4	59	19	6	—	.272	.303	.374	102	-2	17	.957	4	86	161	O154R	—	-0.6
1910	Pit N	146	536	59	148	14	13	4	50	21	7	68	.276	.312	.373	94	-8	8	.972	4	103	112	O146(1/7/138)	—	-1.1
1911	Pit N	148	544	72	163	34	12	12	**107**	41	4	55	.300	.353	.472	125	16	10	.977	5	110	98	O146(0/2/145)	—	1.3
1912	Pit N	**152**	583	80	175	19	**36**	11	95	35	2	67	.300	.342	.513	134	20	16	.961	-0	104	87	O152(0/87/69)	—	1.0
1913	Pit N	**155**	580	71	154	12	14	10	73	32	3	62	.266	.307	.386	102	-3	9-10	.969	2	115	69	O155(0/3/153)	—	-1.1
1914	StL N	154	580	64	150	27	12	9	73	32	4	66	.259	.302	.393	107	2	14	**.983**	12	107	126	O154(0/9/148)	—	0.6
1915	StL N	107	348	33	96	13	6	3	39	19	4	43	.276	.321	.374	110	3	8-15	**.984**	11	107	164	O105(3/70/33)	—	0.4
1916	StL N	120	355	30	85	8	2	3	32	20	5	46	.239	.289	.299	81	-8	4	.955	-4	93	91	O113(0/58/61)	—	-2.1
Total	9	1280	4624	520	1246	157	114	59	571	241	37	407	.269	.311	.391	105	2	98-25	.968	32	104	108	O1269(5/270/1010)	—	-4.6
Wilson, Josh	Joshua Aaron; B3.26.1981 Pittsburgh PA; BR/TR/6´1˝/180; [FlaN99 3/86]; d9.7; [DL 2006 Col N 65]																								
2005	Fla N	11	10	2	1	1	0	0	0	0-0	1	4	.100	.182	.200	0	-1	0-0	1.000	-1	100	145	S6,2b4	0	-0.2
Wilson, Les	Lester Wilbur "Tug"; B7.17.1885 St.Louis MI; D4.4.1969 Edmonds WA; BL/TR/5´11˝/170; d7.15																								
1911	Bos A	5	7	0	0	0	0	0	0	2	0	—	.000	.222	.000	-36	-1	0	1.000	-0	122	0	O3(2/0/1)	—	-0.1
Wilson, Hack	Lewis Robert; B4.26.1900 Ellwood City PA; D11.23.1948 Baltimore MD; BR/TR/5´6˝/190; d9.29; HF1979																								
1923	NY N	3	10	0	2	0	0	0	0	0	0	1	.200	.200	.200	6	-1	0-0	.857	-1	88	0	O3(1/2/0)	—	-0.2
1924	†NY N	107	383	62	113	19	12	10	57	44	1	46	.295	.369	.486	131	16	4-3	.967	-6	92	78	O103(14/90/1)	—	0.6
1925	NY N	62	180	28	43	7	4	6	30	21	1	33	.239	.322	.422	92	-3	5-2	.975	-5	77	76	O50(27/23/4)	—	-0.9
1926	Chi N	142	529	97	170	36	8	**21**	109	**69**	6	61	.321	.406	.539	**150**	**39**	10	.973	-5	95	85	O140C	—	2.8
1927	Chi N	146	551	119	175	30	12	**30**	129	71	6	70	.318	.401	.579	160	46	13	.967	-7	95	80	O146C	—	3.2
1928	Chi N	145	520	89	163	32	9	**31**	120	77	2	94	.313	.404	.588	159	45	4	.960	-13	87	90	O143C	—	2.5
1929	†Chi N	150	574	135	198	30	5	39	**159**	78	2	83	.345	.425	.618	155	49	3	.970	-3	97	101	O150C	—	3.6
1930	Chi N	155	585	146	208	35	6	**56**	**191**	**105**	1	84	.356	.454	**.723**	**177**	**76**	3	.951	-15	87	72	O155C	—	4.7
1931	Chi N	112	395	66	103	22	4	13	61	63	0	69	.261	.362	.435	112	8	1	.978	-4	88	129	O103(40/60/3)	—	0.0
1932	Bro N	135	481	77	143	37	5	23	123	51	1	85	.297	.366	.538	142	29	2	.955	-6	86	120	O125(1/8/116)	—	1.6
1933	Bro N	117	360	41	96	13	2	9	54	52	0	50	.267	.359	.389	119	10	7	.963	-5	99	46	O90(75/8/7),2b5	—	0.2
1934	Bro N	67	172	24	45	5	0	6	27	40	0	33	.262	.401	.395	120	7	0	.974	-1	89	101	O43(27/0/16)	—	0.4
	Phi N	7	20	0	2	0	0	0	3	3	0	4	.100	.217	.100	-11	-3	0	1.000	0	109	0	O6(5/0/1)	—	-0.3
	Year	74	192	24	47	5	0	6	30	43	0	37	.245	.383	.365	105	4	0	.977	-1	91	90	O49(32/0/17)	—	0.1
Total	12	1348	4760	884	1461	266	67	244	1063	674	20	713	.307	.395	.545	145	318	52-5	.965	-70	91	88	O1257(190/925/148),2b5	—	18.2
Wilson, Tack	Michael; B5.16.1955 Shreveport LA; BR/TR/5´10˝/185; d4.9; Col Laney (CA) JC																								
1983	Min A	5	4	4	1	1	0	0	1	0-0	0	0	.250	.250	.500	96	0	0-0	1.000	-0	39	0	/cfD	0	0.0
1987	Cal A	7	2	5	1	0	0	0	0	1-0	0	0	.500	.667	.500	223	1	0-0	1.000	-0	47	0	O4L,D2	0	0.0
Total	2	12	6	9	2	1	0	0	1	1-0	0	0	.333	.429	.500	150	1	0-0	1.000	-1	43	0	O5(4/1/0),D4	0	0.0

YEAR	TM LG	G	AB	R	H	2B	3B	HR	RBI	BB-IB	HP	SO	AVG	OBP	SLG	AOPS	ABR	SB-CS	FA	FR	RNG	THR	GAMES AT POSITION	DL	BFW
Wilson, Nigel	Nigel Edward; B1.12.1970 Oshawa ON, Can.; BL/TL/6´1˝/185; d9.8																								
1993	Fla N	7	16	0	0	0	0	0	0	0-0	0	11	.000	.000	.000	-94	-4	0-0	1.000	-0	75	0	O3L	0	-0.5
1995	Cin N	5	7	0	0	0	0	0	0	0-0	0	4	.000	.000	.000	-99	-2	0-0	1.000	-0	91	0	O2L	0	-0.2
1996	†Cle A	10	12	2	3	0	0	2	5	1-0	0	6	.250	.308	.750	156	1	0-0	ø	-1	0	0	/lfD	0	0.0
Total	3	22	35	2	3	0	0	2	5	1-0	0	21	.086	.111	.257	-7	-5	0-0	1.000	-1	63	0	O6L,D3	0	-0.7
Wilson, Parke	Parke Asel; B10.26.1867 Keithsburg IL; D12.20.1934 Hermosa Beach CA; BR/TR/5´11˝/166; d7.19																								
1893	NY N	31	114	16	28	4	1	2	21	7	0	9	.246	.289	.351	69	-6	5	.969	-3	*99*	*74*	C31	—	-0.5
1894	NY N	51	181	35	59	5	5	1	34	15	2	6	.326	.384	.425	95	-2	9	.841	-5	*108*	*64*	C35,1b16	—	-0.3
1895	NY N	67	238	32	56	9	0	0	30	14	1	16	.235	.281	.273	44	-20	11	.938	-1	*96*	*117*	C53,1b11,3b3	—	-1.3
1896	NY N	75	253	33	60	2	0	0	23	13	1	14	.237	.277	.245	39	-22	9	.936	-6	*94*	*95*	C71,1b2	—	-1.9
1897	NY N	47	158	29	47	9	3	0	23	15	1	—	.297	.362	.392	102	1	6	.929	2	*171*	*75*	C30,1b11,O4C/2	—	0.4
1898	NY N	1	4	0	0	0	0	0	0	0	0	—	.000	.000	.000	-99	-1	0	ø	-0	0	*0*	/lf	—	-0.1
1899	NY N	98	332	49	89	8	6	0	42	43	4	—	.268	.359	.328	92	-2	16	.925	-6	*87*	*85*	C31,1b29,S19,3b15,O7(3/0/4)	—	-0.4
Total	7	370	1280	194	339	37	15	3	173	107	9	45	.265	.326	.324	72	-52	56	.925	-19	*105*	*90*	C251,1b69,S19,3b18,O12(4/4/4)/2	—	-4.1
Wilson, Preston	Preston James Richard; B7.19.1974 Bamberg SC; BR/TR/6´2˝/(193–215); [NYN92 1/9]; d5.7; f–Mookie																								
1998	NY N	8	20	3	6	2	0	0	2	2-0	0	8	.300	.364	.400	104	0	1-1	.909	-1	93	0	O7(4/2/1)	0	-0.1
	Fla N	14	31	4	2	0	0	1	1	4-0	1	13	.065	.194	.161	-5	-5	0-0	1.000	-1	79	0	O11(3/7/1)	0	-0.6
	Year	22	51	7	8	2	0	1	3	6-0	1	21	.157	.259	.255	38	-5	1-1	.958	-2	85	0	O18(7/9/2)	0	-0.7
1999	Fla N	149	482	67	135	21	4	26	71	46-3	9	156	.280	.350	.502	120	13	11-4	.973	3	103	136	O136(23/111/15)	0	1.5
2000	Fla N	**161**	605	94	160	35	3	31	121	55-1	8	187	.264	.331	.486	109	6	36-14	.988	-3	101	94	O158C	0	0.8
2001	Fla N	123	468	70	128	30	2	23	71	36-2	6	107	.274	.331	.494	113	8	20-8	.993	3	100	183	O121C	39	1.3
2002	Fla N	141	510	80	124	22	2	23	65	58-3	9	140	.243	.329	.429	102	1	20-11	.981	-6	93	107	O138C	0	-0.3
2003	Col N★	155	600	94	169	43	1	36	**141**	54-1	4	139	.282	.343	.537	110	9	14-7	.980	-10	90	94	O155C	0	0.2
2004	Col N	58	202	24	50	11	0	6	29	17-2	3	49	.248	.315	.391	72	-8	2-1	.953	-2	97	117	O52C	110	-0.9
2005	Col N	71	267	39	69	15	1	15	47	25-0	1	77	.258	.322	.491	98	-1	3-2	.979	-6	88	58	O69C	0	-0.6
	Was N	68	253	34	66	14	1	10	43	20-0	6	71	.261	.329	.443	105	1	3-4	1.000	-3	91	80	O68(11/55/2)	0	-0.3
	Year	139	520	73	135	29	2	25	90	45-0	7	148	.260	.325	.467	101	0	6-6	.990	-9	90	69	O137(11/124/2)	0	-0.9
2006	Hou N	102	390	40	105	22	2	9	55	22-2	2	94	.269	.309	.405	80	-13	6-2	1.000	-8	82	38	O100(94/2/5)	0	-2.3
	†StL N	33	111	18	27	3	0	8	17	7-1	2	27	.243	.300	.486	96	-1	6-0	.960	-3	89	0	O28(8/5/19)	0	-0.4
	Year	135	501	58	132	25	2	17	72	29-3	4	121	.263	.307	.423	83	-14	12-2	.990	-11	83	30	O128(102/7/24)	0	-2.7
Total	9	1083	3939	567	1041	218	16	188	663	346-15	51	1068	.264	.330	.471	103	10	122-54	.983	-37	94	100	O1043(143/875/43)	149	-1.7
Wilson, Bob	Robert; B2.22.1925 Dallas TX; D4.23.1985 Dallas TX; BR/TR/5´11˝/197; d5.17; Negro Lg 1947–50																								
1958	LA N	3	5	0	1	0	0	0	0	0-0	0	1	.200	.200	.200	6	-1	0-0	1.000	0	97	0	/rf	0	-0.1
Wilson, Red	Robert James; B3.7.1929 Milwaukee WI; BR/TR/6´0˝/(190–205); d9.22; Col Wisconsin–Madison																								
1951	Chi A	4	11	1	3	1	0	0	0	1	0	2	.273	.333	.364	90	0	0-0	1.000	-0	*78*	*167*	C4	0	0.0
1952	Chi A	2	3	0	0	0	0	0	0	0	0	1	.000	.000	.000	-99	-1	0-0	1.000	1	*0*	*0*	C2	0	0.0
1953	Chi A	71	164	21	41	6	1	0	10	26	0	12	.250	.353	.299	75	-5	2-3	.981	5	*98*	*95*	C63	0	0.3
1954	Chi A	8	20	2	4	0	0	1	1	1	0	2	.200	.238	.350	58	-1	0-0	1.000	3	*158*	*72*	C8	0	0.2
	Det A	54	170	22	48	11	1	2	22	27	0	12	.282	.379	.394	115	5	3-1	.996	3	*134*	*104*	C53	0	1.0
	Year	62	190	24	52	11	1	3	23	28	0	14	.274	.365	.389	108	3	3-1	.997	5	*137*	*100*	C61	0	1.2
1955	Det A	78	241	26	53	9	0	2	17	26-3	0	23	.220	.296	.282	57	-14	1-2	.984	-5	*94*	*113*	C72	0	-1.7
1956	Det A	78	228	32	66	12	2	7	38	42-7	0	18	.289	.393	.452	124	10	2-1	.991	2	*136*	***127***	C78	0	1.5
1957	Det A	60	180	21	43	8	1	3	13	25-2	3	19	.239	.341	.344	86	-3	2-3	1.000	0	206	108	C60	0	0.0
1958	Det A	103	298	31	89	13	1	3	29	35-5	2	30	.299	.373	.379	101	2	10-0	.992	12	100	79	C101	0	2.1
1959	Det A	67	228	28	60	17	2	4	35	10-1	2	23	.263	.295	.408	88	-4	2-2	.988	3	85	79	C64	0	0.2
1960	Det A	45	134	17	29	4	0	1	14	16-1	0	14	.216	.298	.269	54	-8	3-0	.980	1	90	56	C45	0	-0.5
	Cle A	32	88	5	19	3	0	1	10	6-1	1	7	.216	.268	.284	53	-6	0-0	.989	4	90	110	C30	0	-0.1
	Year	77	222	22	48	7	0	2	24	22-2	1	21	.216	.286	.275	53	-14	3-0	.984	4	90	78	C75	0	-0.6
Total	10	602	1765	206	455	84	8	24	189	215-20	8	163	.258	.338	.355	87	-25	25-12	.990	28	*116*	*97*	C580	0	3.0
Wilson, Mike	Samuel Marshall; B12.2.1896 Edge Hill PA; D5.16.1978 Boynton Beach FL; BR/TR/5´10.5˝/160; d6.4; Col Lehigh																								
1921	Pit N	5	4	0	0	0	0	0	0	0	0	0	.000	.000	.000	-97	-1	0-0	.833	-0	*0*	*141*	C5	—	-0.1
Wilson, Neil	Samuel O'Neil; B6.14.1935 Lexington TN; BL/TR/6´1˝/175; d4.17																								
1960	SF N	6	10	0	0	0	0	0	0	1-1	0	2	.000	.091	.000	-77	-3	0-0	.958	-1	64	0	C6	0	-0.3
Wilson, Tom	Thomas G. "Slats"; B6.3.1890 Fleming KS; D3.7.1953 San Pedro CA; BB/TR/6´1.5˝/160; d9.8																								
1914	Was A	1	1	0	0	0	0	0	0	0	0	0	.000	.000	.000	-96	0	0	ø	-0	*0*	*0*	/C	—	-0.1
Wilson, Tom	Thomas Leroy; B12.19.1970 Fullerton CA; BR/TR/6´3˝/220; [NYA90 23/620]; d5.19; Col Fullerton (CA) JC																								
2001	Oak A	9	21	4	4	0	0	2	4	1-0	1	5	.190	.250	.476	88	-1	0-0	.974	-3	74	0	C9	0	-0.3
2002	Tor A	96	265	33	68	10	0	8	37	28-0	5	79	.257	.334	.385	89	-4	0-0	.988	-10	66	93	C65,D12,1b11	0	-1.1
2003	Tor A	96	256	37	66	19	0	5	35	28-0	1	80	.258	.331	.391	87	-4	0-0	.991	-2	63	93	C76,1b14,O2(1/0/1)/D	0	-0.2
2004	†LA N	9	8	1	1	0	0	0	0	0-0	0	3	.125	.125	.125	-35	-2	0-0	1.000	-1	0	252	C7	0	-0.2
	NY N	4	4	0	1	0	0	0	0	1-0	0	2	.250	.400	.250	75	0	0-0	1.000	-0	24	0	C3	0	0.0
	Year	13	12	1	2	0	0	0	0	1-0	0	5	.167	.231	.167	5	-2	0-0	1.000	-1	10	148	C10	0	-0.2
Total	4	214	554	75	140	29	0	15	76	58-0	7	169	.253	.327	.386	86	-11	0-0	.989	-15	63	89	C160,1b25,D13,O2(1/0/1)	0	-1.8
Wilson, Vance	Vance Allen; B3.17.1973 Mesa AZ; BR/TR/5´11˝/(190–215); [NYN93 44/1226]; d4.24; Col Mesa (AZ) CC; [DL 1998 NY N 20]																								
1999	NY N	1	0	0	0	0	0	0	0	0-0	0	0	ø	ø	ø	ø	0	0-0	ø	-0	0	0	/C	38	0.0
2000	NY N	4	4	0	0	0	0	0	0	0-0	0	2	.000	.000	.000	-99	-1	0-0	1.000	0	85	0	C3	0	-0.1
2001	NY N	32	57	3	17	3	0	0	6	2-0	2	16	.298	.339	.351	86	-1	0-1	.993	2	187	132	C27	0	0.2
2002	NY N	74	163	19	40	7	0	5	26	5-0	8	32	.245	.301	.380	83	-5	0-1	.983	6	101	206	C66/1	0	0.4
2003	NY N	96	268	28	65	9	1	8	39	15-1	5	56	.243	.293	.373	76	-11	1-2	.990	7	119	150	C89	0	0.0
2004	NY N	79	157	18	43	10	1	4	21	11-2	5	24	.274	.335	.427	99	0	1-0	.993	-1	109	119	C69	41	0.2
2005	Det A	61	152	18	30	4	0	3	19	11-0	6	26	.197	.275	.283	51	-11	0-0	.989	-3	91	133	C60	0	-1.0
2006	Det A	56	152	18	43	9	0	5	18	2-0	3	33	.283	.304	.441	92	-2	0-4	.997	7	103	89	C55	0	0.5
Total	8	403	953	104	238	42	2	25	129	46-3	29	189	.250	.302	.377	79	-31	2-8	.990	18	111	140	C370/1	99	0.2
Wilson, Bill	William Donald; B11.6.1928 Central City NE; BR/TR/6´2˝/200; d9.24; Mil 1951–52																								
1950	Chi A	3	6	0	0	0	0	0	0	2	0	2	.000	.250	.000	-33	-1	0-0	1.000	-0	80	0	O2C	0	-0.1
1953	Chi A	9	17	1	1	0	0	0	1	0	1	7	.059	.111	.059	-51	-4	0-0	1.000	-0	103	0	O3C	0	-0.4
1954	Chi A	20	35	4	6	1	0	2	5	7	0	5	.171	.310	.371	83	-1	0-1	.943	1	127	0	O19(15/0/4)	0	-0.1
	Phi A	94	323	43	77	10	1	15	33	39	8	59	.238	.334	.415	104	1	1-2	.989	4	110	82	O91C	0	0.1
	Year	114	358	47	83	11	1	17	38	46	8	64	.232	.332	.411	102	1	1-3	.984	5	112	72	O110(15/91/4)	0	0.0
1955	KC A	98	273	39	61	12	0	15	38	24-0	1	63	.223	.288	.432	91	-5	1-1	.969	-1	101	80	O82(23/57/4)/P	0	-1.0
Total	4	224	654	87	145	23	1	32	77	72-0	10	136	.222	.308	.407	92	-10	2-4	.979	3	107	73	O197(38/153/8)/P	0	-1.5
Wilson, Bill	William G.; B10.28.1867 Hannibal MO; D5.9.1924 St.Paul MN; TR; d4.30																								
1890	Pit N	83	304	30	65	11	3	0	21	22	2	50	.214	.271	.270	65	-13	5	.875	-16	*65*	*137*	C38,O25(4/8/13),1b18/S	—	-2.5
1897	Lou N	107	389	44	83	12	4	1	41	18	5	—	.213	.257	.272	41	-34	9	.940	-4	*92*	*111*	C105/3	—	-2.5
1898	Lou N	29	102	5	17	1	2	1	13	5	1	—	.167	.213	.245	32	-10	3	.895	-7	*83*	*119*	C28/1	—	-1.3
Total	3	219	795	79	165	24	9	2	75	45	8	50	.208	.257	.268	48	-57	17	.913	-27	*84*	*119*	C171,O25(4/8/13),1b19/3S	—	-6.3
Wilson, Mookie	William Hayward; B2.9.1956 Bamberg SC; BB/TR/5´10˝/(168–175); [NYN77 2/42]; d9.2; C6; s–Preston; Col South Carolina																								
1980	NY N	27	105	16	26	5	3	0	4	12-0	0	19	.248	.325	.352	90	-1	7-7	.973	-0	106	57	O26(1/26/0)	0	-0.3
1981	NY N	92	328	49	89	8	8	3	14	20-3	2	59	.271	.317	.372	95	-4	24-12	.983	5	118	56	O80(6/68/10)	0	0.1
1982	NY N	159	639	90	178	25	9	5	55	32-4	2	102	.279	.314	.369	90	-10	58-16	.988	8	110	131	O156C	0	0.4
1983	NY N	152	638	91	176	25	6	7	51	18-3	4	103	.276	.300	.367	84	-16	54-16	.984	1	106	66	O148C	0	-1.1
1984	NY N	154	587	88	162	28	10	10	54	26-2	2	90	.276	.308	.409	101	-2	46-9	.990	10	114	104	O146C	0	1.4
1985	NY N	93	337	56	93	16	8	6	26	28-6	0	52	.276	.331	.424	112	4	24-9	.964	-1	112	0	O83(4/83/0)	61	0.4

YEAR	TM LG	G	AB	R	H	2B	3B	HR	RBI	BB-IB	HP	SO	AVG	OBP	SLG	AOPS	ABR	SB-CS	FA	FR	RNG	THR	GAMES AT POSITION	DL	BFW
1986	†NY N	123	381	61	110	17	5	9	45	32-5	1	72	.289	.345	.430	115	7	25-7	.979	9	**119**	126	O114(78/65/3)	32	1.7
1987	NY N	124	385	58	115	19	7	9	34	35-8	2	85	.299	.359	.455	119	10	21-6	.963	0	108	61	O109(20/88/14)	0	1.1
1988	†NY N	112	378	61	112	17	5	8	41	27-2	2	63	.296	.345	.431	127	12	15-4	.976	0	102	102	O104(16/83/18)	0	1.4
1989	NY N	80	249	22	51	10	1	3	18	10-3	1	47	.205	.237	.289	52	-16	7-4	.975	5	124	70	O71(13/44/25)	0	-1.4
	†Tor A	54	238	32	71	9	1	2	17	3-0	2	37	.298	.311	.370	93	-3	12-1	.991	-6	83	54	O54(16/22/20)	0	-0.8
1990	Tor A	147	588	81	156	36	4	3	51	31-0	0	102	.265	.300	.355	81	-15	23-4	.992	-2	100	67	O141(8/133/0),D6	0	-1.6
1991	†Tor A	86	241	26	58	12	4	2	28	8-0	5	35	.241	.277	.349	70	-11	11-3	.973	-2	88	95	O41(36/5/0),D34	0	-1.4
Total	12	1403	5094	731	1397	227	71	67	438	282-36	23	866	.274	.314	.386	96	-45	327-98	.982	25	108	81	O1273(198/1067/90),D40	93	-0.1
Wilson, Willie	Willie James; B7.9.1955 Montgomery AL; BB/TR (BR 1976)/6´3˝/(187–200); [KCA74 1/18]; d9.4																								
1976	KC A	12	6	0	1	0	0	0	0	0-0	0	2	.167	.167	.167	-2	-1	2-1	.875	1	103	637	O6C	0	0.0
1977	KC A	13	34	10	11	2	0	0	1	1-0	0	8	.324	.343	.382	96	0	6-3	.960	-0	109	0	O9C,D2	0	0.0
1978	†KC A	127	198	43	43	8	2	0	16	16-0	2	33	.217	.280	.278	56	-11	46-12	.978	7	**119**	143	O112(82/35/0),D6	0	-0.1
1979	KC A	154	588	113	185	18	13	6	49	28-3	7	92	.315	.351	.420	105	2	**83**-12	.985	13	**120**	109	O152(130/23/5),D2	0	2.3
1980	†KC A	161	705	**133**	**230**	28	**15**	3	49	28-3	6	81	.326	.357	.421	111	8	79-10	.988	14	**121**	73	O159(102/62/0)	0	3.1
1981	†KC A	102	439	54	133	10	7	1	32	18-3	4	42	.303	.335	.364	102	0	34-8	.987	18	127	190	O101(83/19/0)	0	1.9
1982	KC A★	136	585	87	194	19	**15**	3	46	26-2	6	81	**.332**	.365	.431	117	12	37-11	.987	11	**127**	47	O135(119/19/0)	0	2.2
1983	KC A★	137	576	90	159	22	8	2	33	33-2	1	75	.276	.316	.352	83	-14	59-8	.975	-4	104	31	O136(63/75/0)	16	-1.2
1984	†KC A	128	541	81	163	24	9	2	44	39-2	3	56	.301	.350	.390	104	3	47-5	.990	-2	102	67	O128C	0	0.8
1985	†KC A	141	605	87	168	25	**21**	4	43	29-3	5	94	.278	.316	.408	96	-6	43-11	.995	-9	96	43	O140C	0	-1.1
1986	KC A	156	631	77	170	20	7	9	44	31-1	9	97	.269	.313	.366	82	-17	34-8	.993	-3	101	49	O155C	0	-1.6
1987	KC A	146	610	97	170	18	**15**	4	30	32-2	6	88	.279	.320	.377	82	-18	59-11	**.997**	-5	95	48	O143C,D2	0	-1.5
1988	KC A	147	591	81	155	17	**11**	1	37	22-1	2	106	.262	.289	.333	73	-23	35-7	.989	-8	97	16	O142C	0	-2.7
1989	KC A	112	383	58	97	17	7	3	43	27-0	1	78	.253	.300	.358	86	-8	24-6	.977	-3	102	40	O108C/D	21	-0.9
1990	KC A	115	307	49	89	13	3	2	42	30-1	2	57	.290	.354	.371	105	3	24-6	1.000	-1	99	43	O106(54/48/4)/D	0	0.3
1991	Oak A	113	294	38	70	14	4	0	28	18-1	4	43	.238	.290	.313	71	-12	20-5	.983	3	114	50	O87(40/33/19),D9	17	-0.9
1992	†Oak A	132	396	38	107	15	5	0	37	35-2	1	65	.270	.329	.333	91	-5	28-8	.981	8	**121**	33	O120(0/118/3),D5	15	0.6
1993	Chi N	105	221	29	57	11	3	1	11	11-1	3	40	.258	.301	.348	74	-9	7-2	.991	-5	88	40	O82C	0	-1.2
1994	Chi N	17	21	4	5	0	2	0	0	1-0	0	6	.238	.273	.429	79	-1	1-0	1.000	-1	78	0	O10C	16	-0.1
Total	19	2154	7731	1169	2207	281	147	41	585	425-27	62	1144	.285	.326	.376	93	-97	668-134	.987	34	109	62	O2031(673/1356/31),D28	85	-0.1
Winceniak, Ed	Edward Joseph; B4.16.1929 Chicago IL; BR/TR/5´9˝/165; d4.25																								
1956	Chi N	15	17	1	2	0	0	0	0	1-0	0	3	.118	.167	.118	-22	-3	0-0	.889	-1	64	0	3b4/2	0	-0.4
1957	Chi N	17	50	5	12	3	0	1	8	2-0	0	9	.240	.269	.360	68	-2	0-0	1.000	-4	59	62	S5,3b4,2b3	0	-0.6
Total	2	32	67	6	14	3	0	1	8	3-0	0	12	.209	.243	.299	45	-5	0-0	.955	-4	99	236	3b8,S5,2b4	0	-1.0
Windhorn, Gordie	Gordon Ray; B12.19.1933 Watseka IL; BR/TR/6´1˝/185; d9.10																								
1959	NY A	7	11	0	0	0	0	0	0	0-0	0	3	.000	.000	.000	-99	-3	0-0	1.000	-0	77	0	O4L	0	-0.4
1961	LA N	34	33	10	8	2	1	2	6	4-1	0	3	.242	.324	.545	115	1	0-1	.944	1	113	160	O17(5/3/9)	0	0.0
1962	KC A	14	19	1	3	1	0	0	1	0-0	0	3	.158	.158	.211	-2	-3	0-0	1.000	-0	78	0	O7L	0	-0.3
	LA A	40	45	9	8	6	0	0	1	7-1	0	10	.178	.288	.311	63	-2	1-1	1.000	-1	90	0	O27(22/3/5)	0	-0.4
	Year	54	64	10	11	7	0	0	2	7-1	0	13	.172	.254	.281	44	-5	1-1	1.000	-1	87	0	O34(29/3/5)	0	-0.7
Total	3	95	108	20	19	9	1	2	8	11-2	0	19	.176	.252	.333	55	-7	1-2	.981	-1	94	46	O55(38/6/14)	0	-1.1
Windle, Bill	Willis Brewer; B12.13.1904 Galena KS; D12.8.1981 Corpus Christi TX; BL/TL/5´11.5˝/170; d9.27; Col Missouri																								
1928	Pit N	1	1	1	1	1	0	0	0	0	0	0	1.000	1.000	2.000	641	1	0	1.000	-0	0	0	/1	—	0.1
1929	Pit N	2	1	0	0	0	0	0	0	0	0	1	.000	.000	.000	-98	0	0	1.000	-0	0	383	1b2	—	0.0
Total	2	3	2	1	1	1	0	0	0	0	0	1	.500	.500	1.000	264	1	0	1.000	-0	0	230	1b3	—	0.1
Wine, Robbie	Robert Paul Jr.; B7.13.1962 Norristown PA; BR/TR/6´2˝/200; [HouN83 1/8]; d9.2; f–Bobby; Col Oklahoma St.																								
1986	Hou N	9	12	2	3	1	0	0	0	1-0	0	4	.250	.308	.333	79	0	0-0	1.000	1	69	62	C8	0	0.1
1987	Hou N	14	29	1	3	1	0	0	0	1-0	0	10	.103	.133	.138	-29	-5	0-0	.979	-4	64	92	C12	0	-0.9
Total	2	23	41	3	6	2	0	0	0	2-0	0	14	.146	.186	.195	2	-5	0-0	.988	-3	66	83	C20	0	-0.8
Wine, Bobby	Robert Paul Sr.; B9.17.1938 New York NY; BR/TR/6´1˝/(185–187); d9.20; M1/C20; s–Robbie																								
1960	Phi N	4	14	1	2	0	0	0	0	0-0	0	2	.143	.143	.143	-22	-2	0-0	1.000	1	93	181	S4	0	-0.2
1962	Phi N	112	311	30	76	15	0	4	25	11-3	0	49	.244	.268	.331	62	-17	2-0	.979	-0	101	101	S89,3b20	0	-1.1
1963	Phi N	142	418	29	90	14	3	6	44	14-5	1	83	.215	.241	.306	58	-24	1-3	.971	14	102	105	S132,3b8	0	-0.1
1964	Phi N	126	283	28	60	8	3	4	34	25-6	0	37	.212	.274	.304	64	-14	1-0	.965	1	97	110	S108,3b16	0	-0.5
1965	Phi N	139	394	31	90	8	1	5	33	31-9	0	69	.228	.284	.292	64	-19	0-0	.967	17	105	112	S135,1b4	0	0.8
1966	Phi N	46	89	8	21	5	0	0	5	6-3	1	13	.236	.292	.292	63	-4	0-1	.974	5	107	118	S40,O2L	44	0.3
1967	Phi N	135	363	27	69	12	5	2	28	29-10	0	77	.190	.249	.267	48	-25	3-2	**.980**	18	105	**134**	S134,1b2	0	0.3
1968	Phi N	27	71	5	12	3	0	2	7	6-1	0	17	.169	.234	.296	58	-4	0-0	.972	-3	90	82	S25/3	124	-0.5
1969	Mon N	121	370	23	74	8	1	3	25	28-6	0	49	.200	.256	.251	42	-29	0-0	.949	20	107	**128**	S118/13	0	0.4
1970	Mon N	159	501	40	116	21	3	3	51	39-5	1	94	.232	.287	.303	59	-30	0-1	.976	19	103	**138**	S159	0	0.6
1971	Mon N	119	340	25	68	9	0	1	16	25-5	0	46	.200	.253	.235	39	-27	0-0	.982	5	96	103	S119	22	-1.0
1972	Mon N	34	18	2	4	1	0	0	0	0-0	0	2	.222	.222	.278	41	-1	0-0	1.000	2	88	0	3b21,S4/2	0	0.1
Total	12	1164	3172	249	682	104	16	30	268	214-53	3	538	.215	.264	.286	54	-196	7-7	.971	98	102	118	S1067,3b67,1b7,O2L/2	190	-0.9
Winfield, Dave	David Mark; B10.3.1951 St.Paul MN; BR/TR/6´6˝/(220–249); [SDN73 1/4]; d6.19; HF2001; Col Minnesota; OF(466/219/1879); [DL 1989 NY A 182]																								
1973	SD N	56	141	9	39	4	1	3	12	12-1	0	19	.277	.331	.383	107	1	0-0	.956	-2	92	42	O36(34/2/1)/1	0	-0.3
1974	SD N	145	498	57	132	18	4	20	75	40-2	1	96	.265	.318	.438	116	8	9-7	.960	6	108	129	O131(81/25/34)	0	0.7
1975	SD N	143	509	74	136	20	2	15	76	69-14	3	82	.267	.354	.403	119	14	23-4	.972	3	106	90	O138R	0	1.3
1976	SD N	137	492	81	139	26	4	13	69	65-8	3	78	.283	.366	.431	137	25	26-7	.982	8	106	132	O134(0/10/127)	0	3.1
1977	SD N★	157	615	104	169	29	7	25	92	58-10	0	75	.275	.335	.467	125	19	16-7	.972	12	115	120	O156R	0	2.3
1978	SD N★	158	587	88	181	30	5	24	97	55-20	2	81	.308	.367	.499	152	39	21-9	.979	-9	92	64	O154(1/84/112),1b2	0	2.7
1979	SD N★	159	597	97	184	27	10	34	**118**	85-**24**	2	71	.308	.395	.558	**168**	**56**	15-9	.986	4	105	103	O157R	0	5.2
1980	SD N★	162	558	89	154	25	6	20	87	79-14	2	83	.276	.365	.450	136	28	23-7	.987	-1	89	153	O159(0/20/154)	0	2.4
1981	†NY A★	105	388	52	114	25	1	13	68	43-3	1	41	.294	.360	.464	139	20	11-1	.985	-10	92	15	O102(80/23/0)/D	0	1.0
1982	NY A★	140	539	84	151	24	8	37	106	45-7	0	64	.280	.331	.560	143	28	5-3	.974	6	102	**208**	O135L,D4	15	2.8
1983	NY A★	152	598	99	169	26	8	32	116	58-2	2	77	.283	.345	.513	138	29	15-6	.978	-10	94	44	O151(122/39/9)	0	1.4
1984	NY A★	141	567	106	193	34	4	19	100	53-9	0	71	.340	.393	.515	155	43	6-4	.994	-2	102	35	O140(1/16/127)	15	3.4
1985	NY A★	155	633	105	174	34	6	26	114	52-8	0	96	.275	.328	.471	118	14	19-7	.991	4	101	126	O152R,D2	0	1.2
1986	NY A★	154	565	90	148	31	5	24	104	77-9	2	106	.262	.349	.462	120	17	6-5	.984	-1	98	88	O145R,3b2,D6	0	0.8
1987	NY A★	156	575	83	158	22	1	27	97	76-5	0	96	.275	.358	.457	115	14	5-6	.989	-11	85	57	O145R,D8	0	-0.6
1988	NY A★	149	559	96	180	37	2	25	107	69-10	2	88	.322	.398	.530	158	45	9-4	.989	-11	87	33	O141R,D4	0	3.0
1990	NY A	20	61	7	13	3	0	2	6	4-0	1	13	.213	.269	.361	75	-2	0-0	1.000	-2	62	0	O12L,D7	0	-0.5
	Cal A	112	414	63	114	18	2	19	72	48-3	1	68	.275	.348	.466	129	16	0-1	.989	-11	74	91	O108R,D3	0	0.1
	Year	132	475	70	127	21	2	21	78	52-3	2	81	.267	.338	.453	122	13	0-1	.989	-13	73	84	O120(12/0/108),D10	0	-0.4
1991	Cal A	150	568	75	149	27	4	28	86	56-4	1	109	.262	.326	.472	119	13	7-2	.990	-6	86	87	O115R,D34	0	0.3
1992	†Tor A	156	583	92	169	33	3	26	108	82-10	1	89	.290	.377	.491	135	29	2-3	1.000	-0	103	60	D130,O26R	0	2.3
1993	Min A	143	547	72	148	27	2	21	76	45-2	0	106	.271	.325	.442	103	1	2-3	1.000	-0	102	91	D105,O31R,1b5	0	-0.7
1994	Min A	77	294	35	74	15	3	10	43	31-5	0	51	.252	.321	.425	90	-5	2-1	1.000	0	139	0	D76/rf	16	-0.8
1995	Cle A	46	115	11	22	5	0	2	4	14-2	1	26	.191	.285	.287	48	-9	1-0	ø	0	0	0	D39	56	-1.0
Total	22	2973	11003	1669	3110	540	88	465	1833	1216-172	25	1686	.283	.353	.475	130	443	223-96	.982	-33	97	92	O2469R,D419,1b8,3b2	284	30.1
Wingo, Al	Absalom Holbrook "Red"; B5.6.1898 Norcross GA; D10.9.1964 Detroit MI; BL/TR/5´11˝/180; d9.9; b–Ivey; Col Oglethorpe																								
1919	Phi A	15	59	9	18	1	3	0	2	4	0	12	.305	.349	.424	115	1	0	.815	-2	77	72	O15L	—	-0.2
1924	Det A	78	150	21	43	12	2	1	26	21	0	13	.287	.374	.413	105	2	2-5	.925	-2	87	90	O43(30/7/6)	—	-0.4
1925	Det A	130	440	104	163	34	10	5	68	69	0	31	.370	.456	.527	151	38	14-13	.971	9	110	120	O122(120/2/0)	—	3.3
1926	Det A	108	298	45	84	19	0	1	45	52	0	32	.282	.389	.356	94	0	4-2	.923	2	97	166	O74(61/0/14),3b2	—	-0.4
1927	Det A	75	137	15	32	8	2	0	20	25	0	14	.234	.352	.321	74	-4	1-0	.891	-1	75	201	O34(9/4/21)	—	-0.7
1928	Det A	87	242	30	69	13	2	2	30	40	1	17	.285	.389	.380	101	2	2-2	.968	-2	97	77	O71(35/28/6)	—	-0.4
Total	6	493	1326	224	409	87	19	9	191	211	1	119	.308	.404	.423	114	39	23-22	.944	3	98	125	O359(270/41/47),3b2	—	1.2

YEAR	TM LG	G	AB	R	H	2B	3B	HR	RBI	BB-IB	HP	SO	AVG	OBP	SLG	AOPS	ABR	SB-CS	FA	FR	RNG	THR	GAMES AT POSITION	DL	BFW
WINGO, ED	Edmond Armand (b Edmond Armand La Riviere); B10.8.1895 St.Anne de Bellevue QC, Can.; D12.5.1964 Lachine QC, Can.; BR/TR/5´6˝/145; d10.2																								
1920	Phi A	1	4	0	1	0	0	0	1	0	0	0	.250	.250	.250	32	0	0-0	1.000	0	87	125	/C	—	0.0
WINGO, IVEY	Ivey Brown; B7.8.1890 Gainesville GA; D3.1.1941 Waycross GA; BL/TR/5´10˝/160; d4.20; M1/C3; b–Al																								
1911	StL N	25	57	4	12	2	0	0	3	3	0	7	.211	.250	.246	40	-5	0	.916	-2	82	114	C18	—	-0.6
1912	StL N	100	310	38	82	18	8	2	44	23	1	45	.265	.317	.394	96	-3	8	.957	-7	74	**127**	C92	—	-0.2
1913	StL N	112	307	25	78	5	8	2	35	17	1	41	.254	.295	.342	83	-9	18-11	.945	-10	79	**117**	C98,1b5/O(1/1/0)	—	-1.1
1914	StL N	80	237	24	71	8	5	4	26	18	1	17	.300	.352	.426	132	8	15	.958	-2	102	99	C70,O4R	—	1.3
1915	Cin N	119	339	26	75	11	6	3	29	13	0	33	.221	.250	.316	69	-14	10-11	.966	-0	96	**110**	C98/lf	—	-0.9
1916	Cin N	119	347	30	85	8	11	2	40	25	1	27	.245	.298	.349	100	-1	4	.958	-7	82	**138**	C107,M	—	0.1
1917	Cin N	121	399	37	106	16	11	2	39	25	1	13	.266	.311	.376	115	5	9	.967	-7	88	109	C120	—	1.0
1918	Cin N	100	323	35	82	15	6	0	31	19	1	18	.254	.297	.337	95	-3	6	.973	0	106	101	C93,O5(3/0/1)	—	0.6
1919	†Cin N	76	245	30	67	12	6	0	27	23	0	19	.273	.336	.371	115	5	4	.969	5	110	113	C75	—	1.8
1920	Cin N	108	364	32	96	11	5	2	38	19	0	13	.264	.300	.338	84	-8	6-4	.958	-5	105	101	C107,2b2	—	-0.5
1921	Cin N	97	295	20	79	7	6	3	38	21	1	14	.268	.319	.363	84	-8	3-2	.959	7	114	100	C92/lf	—	0.5
1922	Cin N	80	260	24	74	13	3	3	45	23	0	11	.285	.343	.392	91	-4	1-4	.964	5	119	120	C78	—	0.5
1923	Cin N	61	171	10	45	9	2	1	24	9	1	11	.263	.304	.357	75	-6	1-1	.969	2	110	124	C57	—	-0.1
1924	Cin N	66	192	21	55	5	4	1	23	14	1	8	.286	.338	.370	91	-3	1-1	.989	3	99	100	C65/1	—	0.4
1925	Cin N	55	146	6	30	7	0	0	12	11	0	8	.205	.261	.253	33	-15	1-2	.965	1	79	116	C55	—	-1.1
1926	Cin N	7	10	0	2	0	0	0	1	1	1	0	.200	.333	.200	48	-1	0	1.000	0	156	0	C7	—	0.0
1929	Cin N	1	1	0	0	0	0	0	0	0	0	0	.000	.000	.000	-99	0	0	ø	0	0	0	/C	—	0.0
Total	17	1327	4003	362	1039	147	81	25	455	264	10	285	.260	.307	.355	91	-62	87-36	.962	-17	97	112	C1233,O12(7/1/5),1b6,2b2	—	1.7
WINKELMAN, GEORGE	George Edward; B2.18.1865 Washington DC; D5.19.1960 Washington DC; BL/TL/5´9˝/140; d8.2																								
1886	Was N	1	5	0	1	0	0	0	0	0	—	1	.200	.200	.200	24	0	0	ø	-0	0	0	/rfP	—	0.0
WINKLEMAN, GEORGE	George W.; B1859 OH; D1.1.1921 New York NY; d8.4																								
1883	Lou AA	4	13	2	0	0	0	0	—	1	—	—	.000	.071	.000	-81	-3	—	.625	-0	185	0	O4(3/1/0)	—	-0.3
WINN, RANDY	Dwight Randolph; B6.9.1974 Los Angeles CA; BB/TR (BR 2000p)/6´2˝/(175–195); [FlaN95 3/65]; d5.11; Col Santa Clara																								
1998	TB A	109	338	51	94	9	9	1	17	29-0	1	69	.278	.337	.367	81	-10	26-12	.980	-1	95	134	O96(16/70/12),D4	0	-0.9
1999	TB A	79	303	44	81	16	4	2	24	17-0	1	63	.267	.307	.366	70	-14	9-9	.995	-0	101	92	O77C	0	-1.4
2000	TB A	51	159	28	40	5	0	1	16	26-0	2	25	.252	.362	.302	72	-6	6-7	.990	0	93	166	O47(29/18/0)/D	0	-0.7
2001	TB A	128	429	54	117	25	6	6	50	38-0	6	81	.273	.339	.401	96	-2	12-10	.981	5	103	**180**	O117(9/48/62),D3	0	-0.1
2002	TB A★	152	607	87	181	39	9	14	75	55-3	6	109	.298	.360	.461	119	17	27-8	.993	5	102	162	O146(0/138/8),D4	0	2.6
2003	Sea A	157	600	103	177	37	4	11	75	41-0	8	108	.295	.346	.425	108	7	23-5	.992	3	110	33	O157(139/20/4)	0	0.9
2004	Sea A	157	626	84	179	34	6	14	81	53-1	8	98	.286	.346	.427	106	5	21-7	.991	6	111	63	O154(40/128/0),D2	0	1.3
2005	Sea A	102	386	46	106	25	1	6	37	37-3	4	53	.275	.342	.391	103	3	12-6	1.000	8	124	57	O96(92/6/0),D2	0	0.8
	SF N	58	231	39	83	22	5	14	26	11-1	1	38	.359	.391	.680	169	22	7-5	.994	4	121	34	O55C	0	2.6
2006	SF N	149	573	82	150	34	5	11	56	48-3	7	63	.262	.324	.396	84	-14	10-8	.992	11	117	117	O141(20/59/89)	0	-0.7
Total	9	1142	4252	618	1208	246	49	80	457	355-11	44	707	.284	.343	.421	101	8	153-77	.991	42	109	101	O1086(345/619/175),D16	0	4.4
WINNINGHAM, HERM	Herman Son; B12.1.1961 Orangeburg SC; BL/TR/5´11˝/(170–190); [NYN81*S1/9]; d9.1; Col Georgia Perimeter JC																								
1984	NY N	14	27	5	11	1	1	0	5	1-0	0	7	.407	.429	.519	167	2	2-1	1.000	-1	55	0	O10(1/9/1)	0	0.1
1985	Mon N	125	312	30	74	6	5	3	21	28-3	0	72	.237	.297	.317	77	-11	20-9	.983	0	102	108	O116(1/115/0)	19	-1.1
1986	Mon N	90	185	23	40	6	3	4	11	18-3	0	51	.216	.286	.346	74	-7	12-7	.980	-4	92	72	O66(3/56/7)/S	0	-1.2
1987	Mon N	137	347	34	83	20	3	4	41	34-7	0	68	.239	.304	.349	71	-14	29-10	.975	-3	98	92	O131C	0	-1.6
1988	Mon N	47	90	10	21	2	1	0	6	12-1	0	18	.233	.320	.278	70	-3	4-5	.982	-1	98	0	O30(0/29/1)	0	-0.6
	Cin N	53	113	6	26	1	3	0	15	5-0	0	27	.230	.261	.292	57	-7	8-3	1.000	1	110	68	O42(14/21/8)	0	-0.6
	Year	100	203	16	47	3	4	0	21	17-1	0	45	.232	.288	.286	63	-10	12-8	.992	-0	105	38	O72(14/50/9)	0	-1.2
1989	Cin N	115	251	40	63	11	3	3	13	24-1	0	50	.251	.316	.355	89	-4	14-5	.980	1	106	92	O85(34/41/13)	15	-0.3
1990	†Cin N	84	160	20	41	8	5	3	17	14-1	0	31	.256	.314	.425	98	-1	6-4	1.000	-2	90	139	O64(5/58/1)	0	-0.3
1991	Cin N	98	169	17	38	6	1	1	4	11-1	0	40	.225	.272	.290	56	-10	4-4	.953	0	109	94	O66(12/55/1)	0	-1.1
1992	Bos A	105	234	27	55	8	1	1	14	10-0	0	53	.235	.266	.291	52	-15	6-5	.975	1	91	220	O67(36/32/0),D6	0	-1.7
Total	9	868	1888	212	452	69	26	19	147	157-17	0	417	.239	.296	.334	73	-70	105-53	.980	-8	99	104	O677(106/547/32),D6/S	34	-8.4
WINSETT, TOM	John Thomas "Long Tom"; B11.24.1909 McKenzie TN; D7.20.1987 Memphis TN; BL/TR/6´2˝/190; d4.20; Col Bethel																								
1930	Bos A	1	1	0	0	0	0	0	0	0	0	1	.000	.000	.000	-99	0	0-0	ø	0	—	—	/H	—	0.0
1931	Bos A	64	76	6	15	1	0	1	7	4	1	21	.197	.247	.250	33	-8	0-0	1.000	0	96	214	O8L	—	-0.7
1933	Bos A	6	12	1	1	0	0	0	0	1	0	6	.083	.154	.083	-36	-2	0-0	1.000	-1	28	0	O4(2/0/2)	—	-0.3
1935	StL N	7	12	2	6	1	0	0	2	2	0	3	.500	.571	.583	203	2	0	ø	-0	0	0	O2R	—	0.2
1936	Bro N	22	85	13	20	7	0	1	18	11	1	14	.235	.330	.353	83	-2	0	1.000	1	97	193	O21L	—	-0.2
1937	Bro N	118	350	32	83	15	5	5	42	45	3	64	.237	.329	.351	84	-7	3	.960	2	109	88	O101(100/1/0)/P	—	-1.1
1938	Bro N	12	30	6	9	1	0	1	7	6	0	4	.300	.417	.433	131	2	0	.882	-1	96	0	O9(5/0/4)	—	0.0
Total	7	230	566	60	134	25	5	8	76	69	5	113	.237	.325	.341	79	-15	3-0	.963	2	105	104	O145(136/1/8)/P	—	-2.1
WINTERS, MATT	Matthew Littleton; B3.18.1960 Buffalo NY; BL/TR/6´3˝/215; [NYA78 1/24]; d5.30																								
1989	KC A	42	107	14	25	6	0	2	9	14-1	0	23	.234	.320	.346	88	-1	0-0	.939	-2	89	54	O31R,D3	0	-0.4
WIRTS, KETTLE	Elwood Vernon; B10.30.1897 Consumne CA; D7.12.1968 Sacramento CA; BR/TR/5´11˝/170; d7.20; Col St. Marys (CA)																								
1921	Chi N	7	11	0	2	0	0	0	1	0	0	3	.182	.182	.182	-3	-2	0-0	1.000	1	92	119	C5	—	-0.1
1922	Chi N	31	58	7	10	2	0	1	6	12	0	15	.172	.314	.259	48	-4	0-0	.968	-3	112	56	C27	—	-0.5
1923	Chi N	5	5	2	1	0	0	0	1	2	0	0	.200	.429	.200	71	0	0-0	1.000	0	100	0	C3	—	0.1
1924	Chi A	6	12	0	1	0	0	0	0	2	0	2	.083	.214	.083	-22	-2	1-0	1.000	0	96	255	C5	—	-0.1
Total	4	49	86	9	14	2	0	1	8	16	0	20	.163	.294	.221	35	-8	1-0	.981	-1	106	89	C40	—	-0.6
WISE, HUGHIE	Hugh Edward; B3.9.1906 Campbellsville KY; D7.21.1987 Plantation FL; BB/TR/6´0˝/178; d9.26; Col Purdue																								
1930	Det A	2	6	0	2	0	0	0	0	0	0	0	.333	.333	.333	68	0	0-0	1.000	0	89	159	C2	—	0.0
WISE, CASEY	Kendall Cole; B9.8.1932 Lafayette IN; BB/TR/6´0˝/170; d4.16; Col Florida																								
1957	Chi N	43	106	12	19	3	1	0	7	11-0	0	14	.179	.256	.226	32	-10	0-0	.940	5	111	107	2b31,S5	0	-0.4
1958	†Mil N	31	71	8	14	1	0	0	0	4-0	0	8	.197	.240	.211	23	-8	1-1	1.000	0	116	69	2b10,S7/3	0	-0.7
1959	Mil N	22	76	11	13	2	0	1	5	10-0	0	5	.171	.267	.237	39	-7	0-0	.989	-2	85	122	2b20,S5	0	-0.7
1960	Det A	30	68	6	10	0	2	2	5	4-0	0	9	.147	.194	.294	29	-7	1-0	.983	0	109	92	2b17,S10/3	0	-0.6
Total	4	126	321	37	56	6	3	3	17	29-0	0	36	.174	.243	.240	31	-32	2-1	.968	3	104	103	2b78,S27,3b2	0	-2.4
WISE, DEWAYNE	Larry Dewayne; B2.24.1978 Columbia SC; BL/TL/6´1˝/180; [CinN97 5/158]; d4.6																								
2000	Tor A	28	22	3	3	0	0	0	0	1-0	1	5	.136	.208	.136	-10	-4	1-0	1.000	1	144	0	O18(14/1/3)	86	-0.3
2002	Tor A	42	112	14	20	4	1	3	13	4-0	0	15	.179	.207	.313	34	-11	5-0	1.000	7	132	276	O33(6/3/26),D3	0	-0.4
2004	†Atl N	77	162	24	37	9	4	6	17	9-1	1	28	.228	.272	.444	81	-6	6-1	1.000	-2	86	96	O56(34/7/15)	22	-0.8
2006	Cin N	31	38	3	7	2	0	0	1	0-0	0	6	.184	.184	.237	7	-5	0-0	.950	0	91	220	O18(9/5/4)	0	-0.5
Total	4	178	334	44	67	15	5	9	31	14-1	2	54	.201	.236	.356	50	-26	12-1	.995	6	108	167	O125(63/16/48),D3	108	-2.0
WISE, NICK	Nicholas Joseph; B6.15.1866 Boston MA; D1.25.1923 Boston MA; BR/TR/5´11˝/194; d6.20																								
1888	Bos N	1	3	0	0	0	0	0	0	0	0	0	.000	.000	.000	-97	-1	0	ø	-0	0	0	/rfC	—	-0.1
WISE, SAM	Samuel Washington "Modoc"; B8.18.1857 Akron OH; D1.22.1910 Akron OH; BL/TR/5´10.5˝/170; d7.30; OF(12/0/36)																								
1881	Det N	1	4	0	2	0	0	0	0	0	—	2	.500	.500	.500	207	0	—	.571	-1	111	0	/3	—	0.0
1882	Bos N	78	298	44	66	11	4	4	34	5	—	45	.221	.234	.326	77	-8	—	.852	-13	86	70	S72,3b6	—	-1.7
1883	Bos N	96	406	73	110	25	7	4	58	13	—	74	.271	.294	.397	105	2	—	.823	-1	93	92	S96	—	0.3
1884	Bos N	114	426	60	91	15	9	4	41	25	—	104	.214	.257	.319	81	-10	—	.884	2	92	81	S107,2b7	—	-0.4
1885	Bos N	107	424	71	120	20	10	4	46	25	—	61	.283	.323	.406	139	18	—	.858	6	101	112	S79,2b22,O6(4/0/2)	—	2.5
1886	Bos N	96	387	71	112	19	12	4	72	33	—	61	.289	.345	.432	139	18	31	.956	-21	78	75	1b57,2b20,S18/rf	—	-0.6
1887	Bos N	113	467	103	156	27	17	9	92	36	7	44	.334	.390	.522	150	31	43	.869	-1	105	98	S72,O27(4/0/23),2b16	—	2.7
1888	Bos N	105	417	66	100	19	12	4	40	34	6	66	.240	.306	.372	112	6	33	.888	3	98	131	S89,3b6,1b5,O4L,2b2	—	1.1
1889	Was N	121	472	79	118	15	8	4	62	61	4	62	.250	.341	.341	96	-1	24	.916	-16	98	71	2b72,S26,3b13,O10R	—	-1.2

YEAR	TM LG	G	AB	R	H	2B	3B	HR	RBI	BB-IB	HP	SO	AVG	OBP	SLG	AOPS	ABR	SB-CS	FA	FR	RNG	THR	GAMES AT POSITION	DL	BFW
1890	Buf P	119	505	95	148	29	11	5	102	46	6	45	.293	.359	.424	119	14	19	.906	8	104	87	2b119	—	2.1
1891	Bal AA	103	388	70	96	14	5	1	48	62	9	52	.247	.364	.317	94	0	33	.888	-9	**103**	76	2b99,S4	—	-0.5
1893	Was N	122	521	102	162	27	17	5	77	49	4	27	.311	.375	.457	124	16	20	.924	16	104	91	2b91,3b31	—	2.9
Total	12	1175	4715	834	1281	221	112	48	672	389	36	643	.272	.332	.397	114	86	203	.859	-26	95	96	S563,2b448,1b62,3b57,O48R	—	7.2
Wisner, Phil	Philip N.; B7.1869 Washington DC; D7.5.1936 Washington DC; TR; d8.30																								
1895	Was N	1	0	0	0	0	0	0	0	0	0	0	ø	ø	ø	ø	0	0	.250	-1	63	0	/S	—	-0.1
Wissman, Dave	David Alvin; B2.17.1941 Greenfield MA; BL/TR/6´2˝/178; d9.15; Col Bridgeport																								
1964	Pit N	16	27	2	4	0	0	0	0	1-0	0	9	.148	.179	.148	-7	-4	0-0	1.000	-0	101	0	O10(7/3/0)	0	-0.5
Wisterzil, Tex	George John; B3.7.1888 Detroit MI; D6.27.1964 San Antonio TX; BR/TR/5´9.5˝/150; d4.14																								
1914	Bro F	149	534	54	137	18	10	0	66	34	**11**	47	.257	.314	.328	76	-27	17	**.956**	16	107	101	3b149	—	-0.8
1915	Bro F	36	106	13	33	3	3	0	21	21	3	7	.311	.438	.396	137	5	8	.949	4	112	148	3b31	—	1.1
	Chi F	7	20	3	4	1	0	0	0	3	0	2	.200	.304	.250	60	-1	0	.955	0	106	0	3b6	—	-0.1
	StL F	8	24	1	5	1	0	0	4	2	1	2	.208	.296	.250	52	-2	2	.939	2	116	0	3b8	—	0.0
	Chi F	42	144	12	36	3	1	0	14	5	1	10	.250	.280	.285	63	-10	2	.968	5	106	0	3b42	—	-0.4
	Year	93	294	29	78	8	4	0	39	31	5	21	.265	.345	.320	90	-7	12	.958	10	112	103	3b87	—	0.6
Total	2	242	828	83	215	26	14	0	105	65	16	68	.260	.326	.325	81	-35	29	.957	26	109	102	3b236	—	-0.2
Witek, Mickey	Nicholas Joseph; B12.19.1915 Luzerne PA; D8.24.1990 Kingston PA; BR/TR/5´10˝/170; d4.16; Mil 1944–45																								
1940	NY N	119	433	34	111	7	0	3	31	24	0	17	.256	.295	.293	62	-23	2	.958	16	105	86	S89,2b32	—	0.2
1941	NY N	26	94	11	34	5	0	1	16	4	0	2	.362	.388	.447	132	4	0	.933	0	98	113	2b23	0	0.6
1942	NY N	148	553	72	144	19	6	5	48	36	0	20	.260	.306	.344	89	-9	2	**.978**	8	105	86	2b147	0	0.8
1943	NY N	153	622	68	195	17	0	6	55	41	0	23	.314	.356	.370	109	6	1	.967	15	**106**	83	2b153	0	3.2
1946	NY N	82	284	32	75	13	2	4	29	28	0	10	.264	.330	.366	97	-1	1	.962	-8	91	81	2b42,3b35	0	-0.8
1947	NY N	51	160	22	35	4	1	3	17	15	0	12	.219	.286	.313	58	-10	1	.983	9	120	108	2b40,3b3	0	0.1
1949	NY A	2	1	0	1	0	0	0	0	0	0	0	1.000	1.000	1.000	430	0	0-0	ø	0	—	—	/H	0	0.0
Total	7	581	2147	239	595	65	9	22	196	148	0	84	.277	.324	.347	90	-33	7-0	.969	40	106	88	2b437,S89,3b38	0	4.1
Withrow, Frank	Frank Blaine "Kid"; B6.14.1891 Greenwood MO; D9.5.1966 Omaha NE; BR/TR/5´11.5˝/187; d4.15																								
1920	Phi N	48	132	8	24	4	1	0	12	8	2	26	.182	.239	.227	33	-11	0-0	.973	1	*85*	*94*	C48	—	-0.7
1922	Phi N	10	21	3	7	2	0	0	3	3	0	5	.333	.417	.429	108	0	0-0	.909	0	*102*	*90*	C8	—	0.1
Total	2	58	153	11	31	6	1	0	15	11	2	31	.203	.265	.255	45	-11	0-0	.965	1	*87*	*93*	C56	—	-0.6
Withrow, Corky	Raymond Wallace; B11.28.1937 High Coal WV; BR/TR/6´3.5˝/200; d9.6; Col Georgetown																								
1963	StL N	6	9	0	0	0	0	0	1	0-0	0	2	.000	.000	.000	-91	-2	0-0	1.000	0	128	0	O2(1/0/1)	0	-0.2
Witmeyer, Ron	Ronald Herman; B6.28.1967 West Islip NY; BL/TL/6´3˝/215; [OakA88 7/177]; d8.25; Col Stanford																								
1991	Oak A	11	19	0	1	0	0	0	0	0-0	0	5	.053	.053	.053	-75	-5	0-0	1.000	0	103	58	1b8	0	-0.5
Witt, Kevin	Kevin Joseph; B1.5.1976 High Point NC; BL/TR/6´4˝/(185–220); [TorA94 1/28]; d9.15																								
1998	Tor A	5	7	0	1	0	0	0	0	0-0	0	3	.143	.143	.143	-25	-1	0-0	1.000	0	150	0	/1	0	-0.1
1999	Tor A	15	34	3	7	1	0	1	5	2-0	0	9	.206	.250	.324	44	-3	0-0	ø	0	0	0	D11	0	-0.3
2001	SD N	14	27	5	5	0	0	2	5	2-0	0	7	.185	.233	.407	68	-2	0-0	1.000	-1	66	76	1b9	0	-0.3
2003	Det A	93	270	25	71	9	0	10	26	15-0	1	68	.263	.301	.407	89	-5	1-1	1.000	1	118	135	D36,1b27,O13L,3b5	0	-0.9
2006	TB A	19	61	5	9	2	0	2	5	0-0	0	21	.148	.148	.279	7	-9	0-0	.935	-1	41	24	D10,1b5	0	-1.0
Total	5	146	399	38	93	12	0	15	41	19-0	1	108	.233	.267	.376	69	-20	1-1	.994	-0	101	108	D57,1b42,O13L,3b5	0	-2.6
Witt, Whitey	Lawton Walter (b Ladislaw Waldemar Wittkowski); B9.28.1895 Orange MA; D7.14.1988 Salem Co. NJ; BL/TR/5´7˝/150; d4.12; Mil 1918; Col Bowdoin																								
1916	Phi A	143	563	64	138	16	15	2	36	55	2	71	.245	.315	.337	101	-2	19	.902	5	99	96	S142	—	1.4
1917	Phi A	128	452	62	114	13	4	0	28	65	0	45	.252	.346	.299	98	2	12	.935	8	108	80	S111,O7L,3b6	—	1.9
1919	Phi A	122	460	56	123	15	6	0	33	46	0	26	.267	.334	.326	85	-9	11	.972	-4	103	43	O59(40/19/0),2b56,3b2	—	-1.6
1920	Phi A	65	218	29	70	11	3	1	25	27	0	16	.321	.396	.413	113	5	2-3	.960	-5	88	34	O50(0/5/45),2b10,S2	—	-0.3
1921	Phi A	154	629	100	198	31	11	4	45	77	1	52	.315	.390	.418	106	8	16-15	.959	-3	105	72	O154R	—	-0.8
1922	†NY A	140	528	98	157	11	6	4	40	**89**	1	29	.297	.400	.364	98	3	5-8	.976	-7	96	62	O139(0/109/30)	—	-1.3
1923	†NY A	146	596	113	187	18	10	6	56	67	3	42	.314	.386	.408	107	7	2-7	**.979**	-4	96	85	O144C	—	-0.5
1924	NY A	147	600	88	178	26	5	1	36	45	0	20	.297	.346	.362	83	-16	9-7	.976	-4	97	83	O144C	—	-2.6
1925	NY A	31	40	9	8	2	1	0	0	6	0	2	.200	.304	.300	55	-3	1-1	1.000	1	111	144	O10(0/9/1)	—	-0.2
1926	Bro N	63	85	13	22	1	1	0	3	12	0	6	.259	.351	.294	76	-2	1	.920	1	108	126	O22(3/17/2)	—	-0.3
Total	10	1139	4171	632	1195	144	62	18	302	489	7	309	.287	.362	.364	97	-7	78-41	.971	-13	99	73	O729(50/447/232),S255,2b66,3b8	—	-4.3
Witte, Jerry	Jerome Charles; B7.30.1915 St.Louis MO; D4.27.2002 Houston TX; BR/TR/6´1˝/190; d9.10																								
1946	StL A	18	73	7	14	2	0	2	4	0	0	18	.192	.192	.301	35	-7	0-0	.967	-2	70	95	1b18	0	-1.0
1947	StL A	34	99	4	14	2	1	2	12	11	0	22	.141	.227	.242	30	-10	0-0	.983	-1	86	86	1b27	0	-1.3
Total	2	52	172	11	28	4	1	4	16	11	0	40	.163	.213	.267	32	-17	0-0	.977	-4	80	90	1b45	0	-2.3
Wockenfuss, John	Johnny Bilton; B2.27.1949 Welch WV; BR/TR/6´0˝/(170–190); [TexA67 42/761]; d8.11; OF(42/0/69)																								
1974	Det A	13	29	1	4	1	0	0	2	3-0	0	2	.138	.212	.172	13	-3	0-0	.932	-2	112	145	C13	0	-0.5
1975	Det A	35	118	15	27	6	3	4	13	10-0	0	15	.229	.287	.432	97	-1	0-0	.982	3	92	107	C34	0	0.4
1976	Det A	60	144	18	32	7	2	3	10	17-0	1	14	.222	.309	.361	92	-1	0-3	.941	-6	102	93	C59	0	-0.7
1977	Det A	53	164	26	45	8	1	9	25	14-0	0	18	.274	.331	.500	117	3	0-0	.985	-1	111	85	C37,O9(6/0/3),D3	0	0.4
1978	Det A	71	187	23	53	5	0	7	22	21-4	1	14	.283	.357	.422	115	4	0-1	.978	-6	82	52	O60(6/0/55),D2	0	-0.5
1979	Det A	87	231	27	61	9	1	15	46	18-0	2	40	.264	.320	.506	116	4	2-2	.996	1	111	112	1b31,C20,D18,O6(5/0/1)	0	0.4
1980	Det A	126	372	56	102	13	2	16	65	68-4	3	64	.274	.390	.449	126	16	1-4	.983	0	112	95	1b52,D28,C25,O23(21/0/2)	0	1.1
1981	Det A	70	172	20	37	4	0	9	25	28-1	0	22	.215	.322	.395	103	1	0-0	.984	-3	37	172	D39,1b25,C5/lf	0	-0.5
1982	Det A	70	193	28	58	9	0	8	32	29-2	0	21	.301	.388	.472	135	10	0-0	.981	-4	66	105	C24,1b17,D17,O10(2/0/8)/3	0	0.6
1983	Det A	92	245	32	66	8	1	9	44	31-1	0	37	.269	.349	.420	114	5	1-1	1.000	5	112	114	D39,C29,1b13/3lf	0	0.9
1984	Phi N	86	180	20	52	3	1	6	24	30-1	0	24	.289	.390	.417	125	7	1-0	.996	-7	79	98	1b39,C21,3b2	0	-0.1
1985	Phi N	32	37	1	6	0	0	0	2	8-1	0	7	.162	.311	.162	35	-3	0-0	1.000	-0	33	126	1b7,C2	0	-0.4
Total	12	795	2072	267	543	73	11	86	310	277-14	7	278	.262	.349	.432	114	42	5-11	.972	-20	90	93	C269,1b184,D146,O110R,3b4	0	1.1
Woehr, Andy	Andrew Emil; B2.4.1896 Fort Wayne IN; D7.24.1990 Fort Wayne IN; BR/TR/5´11˝/165; d9.15																								
1923	Phi N	13	41	3	14	2	0	0	3	1	0	1	.341	.357	.390	87	-1	0-0	.975	2	112	173	3b13	—	0.2
1924	Phi N	50	152	11	33	4	5	0	17	5	2	8	.217	.252	.309	44	-13	2-2	.920	-5	85	113	3b44/2	—	-1.6
Total	2	63	193	14	47	6	5	0	20	6	2	9	.244	.274	.326	53	-14	2-2	.935	-3	91	127	3b57/2	—	-1.4
Woerlin, Joe	Joseph; B10.9.1864 Trenheim, France; D6.22.1919 St.Louis MO; d7.21																								
1895	Was N	1	3	1	1	0	0	0	0	0	0	0	.333	.333	.333	73	0	0	1.000	0	125	0	/S	—	0.0
Wohlford, Jim	James Eugene; B2.28.1951 Visalia CA; BR/TR/5´11˝/(167–180); [KCA70*S3/61]; d9.1; Col Sequoias (CA) [JC]																								
1972	KC A	15	25	3	6	1	0	0	0	2-0	1	6	.240	.321	.280	80	0	0-0	.950	-3	79	28	2b8	0	-0.4
1973	KC A	45	109	21	29	1	3	2	10	11-0	0	12	.266	.333	.385	95	-1	1-1	1.000	3	132	241	D19,O13(12/0/1)	0	0.0
1974	KC A	143	501	55	136	16	7	2	44	39-3	3	74	.271	.327	.343	88	-8	16-13	.982	-1	97	71	O138(126/0/16)/D	0	-1.8
1975	KC A	116	353	45	90	10	5	0	30	34-2	1	37	.255	.317	.312	78	-10	12-7	.953	-1	96	123	O102(43/0/66),D4	0	-1.6
1976	†KC A	107	293	47	73	10	2	1	24	29-0	1	24	.249	.314	.307	83	-6	22-16	.975	6	118	107	O93(84/2/8)/2D	0	-0.5
1977	Mil A	129	391	41	97	16	3	2	36	21-1	1	49	.248	.285	.320	65	-19	17-16	.981	4	112	74	O125(97/4/33)/2D	0	-2.2
1978	Mil A	46	118	16	35	7	2	1	19	6-0	0	10	.297	.325	.415	108	1	3-2	.982	-2	85	101	O35(21/4/12),D4	0	-0.2
1979	Mil A	63	175	19	46	13	1	1	17	8-0	0	28	.263	.290	.366	77	-6	6-2	.969	-1	112	0	O55(35/14/8),D5	0	-0.8
1980	SF N	91	193	17	54	6	4	1	24	13-0	1	23	.280	.324	.368	97	-1	1-4	.989	2	119	69	O49(40/4/8)/3	0	-0.3
1981	SF N	50	68	4	11	3	0	1	7	4-0	0	9	.162	.205	.250	30	-6	0-0	1.000	-2	21	152	O10L	0	-0.9
1982	SF N	97	250	37	64	12	1	2	25	30-4	0	36	.256	.331	.336	89	-3	8-3	.992	1	103	82	O72(68/0/6)	0	-0.4
1983	Mon N	83	141	7	39	8	0	1	14	5-0	0	14	.277	.297	.355	81	-4	0-0	.988	2	125	85	O61(8/6/48)	0	-0.3
1984	Mon N	95	213	20	64	13	2	5	29	14-0	0	19	.300	.342	.451	127	7	3-0	.989	-0	94	84	O59(44/1/14),3b2	0	0.6
1985	Mon N	70	125	7	24	5	1	1	15	16-5	0	18	.192	.284	.272	59	-7	0-2	1.000	-1	98	46	O43(8/0/36)	0	-1.1

YEAR	TM LG	G	AB	R	H	2B	3B	HR	RBI	BB-IB	HP	SO	AVG	OBP	SLG	AOPS	ABR	SB-CS	FA	FR	RNG	THR	GAMES AT POSITION	DL	BFW
1986	Mon N	70	94	10	25	4	2	1	11	9-3	0	17	.266	.327	.383	96	-1	0-2	1.000	-1	98	121	O22(10/0/12),3b6	0	-0.3
Total	15	1220	3049	349	793	125	33	21	305	241-18	8	376	.260	.313	.343	85	-64	89-68	.980	6	105	84	O877(606/35/268),D37,2b10,3b9	0	-10.2
Wojcik, John	John Joseph; B4.6.1942 Olean NY; BL/TR/6´0˝/(175–180); d9.9																								
1962	KC A	16	43	8	13	4	0	0	9	13-0	1	4	.302	.474	.395	131	3	3-0	1.000	-0	85	138	O12(10/0/5)	0	0.3
1963	KC A	19	59	7	11	0	0	0	2	8-2	0	8	.186	.284	.186	33	-5	2-0	1.000	1	105	89	O17(10/2/6)	0	-0.6
1964	KC A	6	22	1	3	0	0	0	0	2-0	0	8	.136	.208	.136	-2	-3	0-0	1.000	-0	100	0	O6L	0	-0.4
Total	3	41	124	16	27	4	0	0	11	23-2	1	20	.218	.345	.250	64	-5	5-0	1.000	0	97	92	O35(26/2/11)	0	-0.7
Wolf, Ray	Raymond Bernard "Grandpa"; B7.15.1904 Chicago IL; D10.6.1979 Fort Worth TX; BR/TR/5´11˝/175; d7.27; Col TCU																								
1927	Cin N	1	1	0	0	0	0	0	0	0	0	0	.000	.000	.000	-99	0	0	1.000	-0	0	0	/1	—	0.0
Wolf, Jimmy	William Van Winkle "Chicken"; B5.12.1862 Louisville KY; D5.16.1903 Louisville KY; BR/TR/5´9˝/190; d5.2; M1; OF(17/3/1024); ▲																								
1882	Lou AA	78	318	46	95	11	8	0	—	9	—	—	.299	.318	.384	144	14	—	.902	-2	**132**	134	O70(3/0/67),S9/1P	—	1.1
1883	Lou AA	**98**	389	59	102	17	9	1	—	5	—	—	.262	.272	.360	110	5	—	.890	14	**186**	**325**	O78(0/1/77),C20,S5/2	—	1.7
1884	Lou AA	**110**	486	79	146	24	11	3	73	4	3	—	.300	.310	.414	140	20	—	.884	-2	131	157	O101(0/1/101),C11/S31	—	1.7
1885	Lou AA	**112**	483	79	141	23	17	1	52	11	1	—	.292	.309	.416	128	13	—	.917	-1	100	117	O111R,C2/3P	—	1.0
1886	Lou AA	130	545	93	148	17	12	3	61	27	3	—	.272	.310	.363	105	-1	23	.934	7	132	130	O122(5/0/119),1b8,C3/2P	—	0.4
1887	Lou AA	**137**	569	103	160	27	13	2	102	34	8	—	.281	.331	.385	97	-4	45	.940	8	128	116	O128(8/1/120),1b11	—	0.1
1888	Lou AA	128	538	80	154	28	11	0	67	25	2	—	.286	.320	.379	126	15	41	.886	3	135	124	O85(1/0/84),S39,3b4,C3/1	—	1.7
1889	Lou AA	130	546	72	159	20	9	3	57	29	5	34	.291	.333	.377	104	1	18	.946	1	94	46	O88R,1b16,2b13,S10,3b7,M	—	0.1
1890	†Lou AA	**134**	543	100	**197**	29	11	4	98	43	12	—	**.363**	.421	.479	169	47	46	.939	-4	72	123	O123R,3b12	—	3.6
1891	Lou AA	136	528	67	135	16	8	1	81	42	8	36	.256	.320	.322	85	-11	13	.922	3	117	101	O131R,1b5/3	—	-0.9
1892	StL N	3	14	1	2	0	0	0	1	0	0	1	.143	.143	.143	-14	-2	0	1.000	-1	0	0	O3R	—	-0.3
Total	11	1196	4959	779	1439	212	109	18	592	229	42	71	.290	.327	.388	118	97	186	.918	26	120	133	O1040R,S64,1b43,C39,3b26,2b15,P3	—	10.2
Wolfe, Harry	Harold "Whitey"; B11.24.1892 Cleveland OH; D7.28.1971 Fort Wayne IN; BR/TR/5´8˝/160; d4.15																								
1917	Chi N	9	5	1	2	0	0	0	1	1	0	1	.400	.500	.400	164	0	0	1.000	0	115	0	O2L/S	—	0.1
	Pit N	3	5	0	0	0	0	0	0	1	0	4	.000	.167	.000	-45	-1	0	.875	0	81	343	/2S	—	-0.1
	Year	12	10	1	2	0	0	0	1	2	0	5	.200	.333	.200	61	0	0	1.000	0	115	0	O2L,S2/2	—	0.0
Wolfe, Larry	Laurence Marcy; B3.2.1953 Melbourne FL; BR/TR/5´11˝/170; [MinA73 9/203]; d9.16; Col Sacramento (CA) City																								
1977	Min A	8	25	3	6	1	0	0	6	1-1	0	0	.240	.269	.280	51	-2	0-0	1.000	1	110	88	3b8	0	-0.1
1978	Min A	88	235	25	55	10	1	3	25	36-0	0	27	.234	.332	.323	84	-4	0-1	.953	1	104	69	3b81,S7	0	-0.4
1979	Bos A	47	78	12	19	4	0	3	15	17-0	1	21	.244	.378	.410	109	2	0-0	.963	3	104	104	2b27,3b9,S2/C1D	0	0.5
1980	Bos A	18	23	3	3	1	0	1	4	0-0	0	5	.130	.125	.304	15	-3	0-0	1.000	-2	69	161	3b14,D4	0	-0.4
Total	4	161	361	43	83	16	1	7	50	54-1	1	53	.230	.327	.338	84	-7	0-1	.957	3	105	90	3b112,2b27,S9,D5/1C	0	-0.4
Wolfe, Polly	Roy Chamberlain; B9.1.1888 Knoxville IL; D11.21.1938 Morris IL; BL/TR/5´10˝/170; d9.22																								
1912	Chi A	1	1	0	0	0	0	0	0	0	0	—	.000	.000	.000	-99	0	0	ø	0	—	—	/H	—	0.0
1914	Chi A	8	28	0	6	0	0	0	0	3	0	6	.214	.290	.214	53	-2	1-1	.875	-1	81	0	O7R	—	-0.4
Total	2	9	29	0	6	0	0	0	0	3	0	6	.207	.281	.207	47	-2	1-1	.875	-1	81	0	O7R	—	-0.4
Wolstenholme, Abe	Abraham Lincoln; B3.4.1861 Philadelphia PA; D3.4.1916 Philadelphia PA; d6.4																								
1883	Phi N	3	11	0	1	1	0	0	0	0	—	0	.091	.091	.182	-22	-1	—	.727	-2	—	—	C2/lf	—	-0.3
Wolter, Harry	Harry Meiggs; B7.11.1884 Monterey CA; D7.6.1970 Palo Alto CA; BL/TR/5´10˝/175; d5.14; Col Santa Clara; ▲																								
1907	Cin N	4	15	1	2	0	0	0	1	0	0	—	.133	.133	.133	-16	-2	0	1.000	-0	0	0	O4R	—	-0.3
	Pit N	1	1	0	0	0	0	0	0	0	0	—	.000	.000	.000	-99	0	0	ø	-0	0	0	/P	—	0.0
	StL N	16	47	4	16	0	0	0	6	3	0	—	.340	.380	.340	130	2	1	.962	1	304	236	O9(1/6/2),P3	—	0.3
	Year	21	63	5	18	0	0	0	7	3	0	—	.286	.318	.286	91	-1	1	.969	1	241	187	O13(1/6/6),P4	—	0.0
1909	Bos A	54	121	14	29	2	4	2	10	9	0	—	.240	.292	.372	107	0	2	.978	-2	120	63	1b17,P11,O9R	—	-0.2
1910	NY A	135	479	84	128	15	9	4	42	66	7	—	.267	.364	.361	120	14	39	.940	-2	112	65	O129(1/0/128),1b2	—	0.7
1911	NY A	122	434	78	132	17	15	4	36	62	4	—	.304	.396	.440	125	15	28	.951	5	114	100	O113(0/7/106),1b2	—	1.4
1912	NY A	12	32	8	11	2	1	0	1	10	1	—	.344	.512	.469	171	4	5	.923	-1	76	91	O9(0/5/4)	—	0.3
1913	NY A	127	425	53	108	18	6	2	43	80	4	50	.254	.377	.339	109	10	13	.946	-7	92	82	O121(0/106/15)	—	-0.6
1917	Chi N	117	353	44	88	15	7	0	28	38	1	40	.249	.324	.331	94	-2	7	.942	1	93	132	O97(3/2/94)/1	—	-0.6
Total	7	588	1907	286	514	69	42	12	167	268	17	90	.270	.365	.369	114	41	95	.941	-5	106	92	O491(5/126/362),1b22,P15	—	1.0
Wolverton, Harry	Harry Sterling "Fighting Harry"; B12.6.1873 Mt.Vernon OH; D2.4.1937 Oakland CA; BL/TR/5´11˝/205; d9.25; M1; Col Kenyon																								
1898	Chi N	13	49	4	16	1	0	0	2	1	1	—	.327	.353	.347	101	0	1	.848	0	113	51	3b13	—	0.0
1899	Chi N	99	389	50	111	14	11	1	49	30	9	—	.285	.350	.386	105	2	14	.860	-7	102	85	3b98/S	—	-0.3
1900	Chi N	3	11	2	2	0	0	0	0	2	0	—	.182	.308	.182	38	-1	1	.875	-1	82	0	3b3	—	-0.1
	Phi N	101	383	42	108	10	8	3	58	20	3	—	.282	.323	.373	92	-6	4	.881	-10	98	109	3b101	—	-1.3
	Year	104	394	44	110	10	8	3	58	22	3	—	.279	.322	.368	91	-6	5	.881	-11	98	106	3b104	—	-1.4
1901	Phi N	93	379	42	117	15	4	0	43	22	6	—	.309	.356	.369	108	4	13	**.921**	3	**104**	100	3b93	—	1.0
1902	Was A	59	249	35	62	8	3	1	23	13	2	—	.249	.292	.317	68	-11	8	.904	3	106	90	3b59	—	-0.6
	Phi N	34	136	12	40	3	2	0	16	9	2	—	.294	.347	.346	114	2	3	.931	7	118	214	3b34	—	1.0
1903	Phi N	123	494	72	152	13	12	0	53	18	8	—	.308	.342	.383	110	4	10	**.941**	1	99	59	3b123	—	0.8
1904	Phi N	102	398	43	106	15	5	0	49	26	6	—	.266	.321	.329	105	2	18	.925	-1	93	117	3b102	—	0.5
1905	Bos N	122	463	38	104	15	7	2	55	23	10	—	.225	.276	.300	73	-16	10	.934	4	109	81	3b122	—	-0.9
1912	NY A	34	50	6	15	1	1	0	4	2	1	—	.300	.340	.360	94	-1	1	.821	-2	69	95	3b8,M	—	-0.2
Total	9	783	3001	346	833	95	53	7	352	166	48	—	.278	.326	.352	96	-21	83	.909	-2	102	95	3b756/S	—	-0.1
Womack, Tony	Anthony Darrell; B9.25.1969 Chatham VA; BL/TR/5´9˝/(150–175); [PitN91 7/201]; d9.10; Col Guilford																								
1993	Pit N	15	24	5	2	0	0	0	0	3-0	0	3	.083	.185	.083	-25	-4	2-0	.971	3	134	183	S6	0	-0.1
1994	Pit N	5	12	4	4	0	0	0	1	2-0	0	3	.333	.429	.333	100	0	0-0	.750	-2	44	62	2b3,S2	0	-0.2
1996	Pit N	17	30	11	10	3	1	0	7	6-0	1	1	.333	.459	.500	148	3	2-0	1.000	-1	71	0	O6(0/5/1),2b4	0	0.2
1997	Pit N★	155	641	85	178	26	9	6	50	43-2	3	109	.278	.326	.374	81	-19	**60**-7	.974	4	101	86	2b152,S4	0	0.4
1998	Pit N	159	655	85	185	26	7	3	45	38-1	0	94	.282	.319	.357	78	-22	**58**-8	.978	9	105	109	2b152,O5C,S2	0	0.4
1999	†Ari N	144	614	111	170	25	10	4	41	52-0	2	68	.277	.332	.370	78	-22	**72**-13	.992	-3	109	123	O123(0/6/122),2b19,S19	7	-1.6
2000	Ari N	146	617	95	167	21	**14**	7	57	30-0	5	74	.271	.307	.384	71	-30	45-11	.970	-12	88	89	S143,O2R	0	-2.4
2001	†Ari N	125	481	66	128	19	5	3	30	23-2	6	54	.266	.307	.345	64	-26	28-7	.955	-7	92	**118**	S118/cf	15	-2.0
2002	†Ari N	153	590	90	160	23	5	5	57	46-2	4	80	.271	.325	.353	72	-23	29-12	.964	-22	85	80	S149/rf	0	-3.3
2003	Ari N	61	219	30	52	10	3	2	15	8-0	2	27	.237	.270	.338	53	-16	8-3	.966	-5	87	89	S58	19	-1.6
	Col N	21	79	9	15	2	0	0	5	0-0	1	9	.190	.200	.215	7	-11	3-1	.959	-4	90	60	S14,2b7/cf	0	-1.3
	Chi N	21	51	4	12	2	1	0	2	1-0	0	11	.235	.250	.314	45	-4	2-1	1.000	-1	81	58	2b14/S	0	-0.5
	Year	103	349	43	79	14	4	2	22	9-0	3	47	.226	.251	.307	41	-31	13-5	.965	-10	88	84	S73,2b21/cf	0	-3.4
2004	†StL N	145	553	91	170	22	3	5	38	36-1	3	60	.307	.349	.385	90	-8	26-5	.976	-1	105	111	2b133	0	0.1
2005	†NY A	108	329	46	82	8	1	0	15	12-0	1	49	.249	.276	.280	49	-24	27-5	.983	7	91	65	O66(40/22/4),2b24,D11	0	-1.3
2006	Chi N	19	50	6	14	1	0	1	2	4-0	0	4	.280	.333	.360	76	-2	1-1	1.000	4	118	112	2b16	0	0.3
	Cin N	9	18	1	4	2	0	0	3	4-1	0	3	.222	.364	.333	76	0	0-0	1.000	2	134	99	2b5	0	0.2
	Year	28	68	7	18	3	0	1	5	8-1	0	7	.265	.342	.353	76	-2	1-1	1.000	6	122	108	2b21	0	0.5
Total	13	1303	4963	739	1353	190	59	36	368	308-9	28	649	.273	.317	.356	72	-208	363-74	.977	-29	104	100	2b529,S516,O205(40/40/130),D11	41	-12.7
Womack, Sid	Sidney Kirk "Tex"; B10.2.1896 Greensburg LA; D8.28.1958 Jackson MS; BR/TR/5´10.5˝/185; d8.15; Col Mississippi St.																								
1926	Bos N	1	3	0	0	0	0	0	1	0	0	0	.000	.000	.000	-99	-1	0	1.000	-0	*44*	*0*	/C	—	-0.1
Wood	; d9.30																								
1874	Bal NA	1	5	0	0	0	0	0	0	0	—	1	.000	.000	.000	-99	-1	0-0	.000	-1	0	0	/2	—	-0.2
Wood, Doc	Charles Spencer; B2.28.1900 Batesville MS; D11.3.1974 New Orleans LA; BR/TR/5´10˝/150; d7.21; Col U. of Mississippi																								
1923	Phi A	3	3	0	1	0	0	0	0	0	0	0	.333	.333	.333	75	0	0-0	.833	0	161	191	S3	—	0.0

YEAR	TM LG	G	AB	R	H	2B	3B	HR	RBI	BB-IB	HP	SO	AVG	OBP	SLG	AOPS	ABR	SB-CS	FA	FR	RNG	THR	GAMES AT POSITION	DL	BFW
Wood, Ted	Edward Robert; B1.4.1967 Mansfield OH; BL/TL/6´2˝/(178–187); [SFN88 1/29]; d9.4; Col New Orleans																								
1991	SF N	10	25	0	3	0	0	0	1	2-0	0	11	.120	.185	.120	-13	-4	0-0	.909	-1	80	0	O8R	0	-0.5
1992	SF N	24	58	5	12	2	0	1	3	6-0	1	15	.207	.292	.293	70	-2	0-0	.972	1	126	0	O16(6/0/10)	23	-0.2
1993	Mon N	13	26	4	5	1	0	0	3	3-1	0	3	.192	.276	.231	36	-2	0-0	1.000	0	117	0	O8(8/0/1)	0	-0.3
Total	3	47	109	9	20	3	0	1	7	11-1	1	29	.183	.264	.239	42	-8	0-0	.968	-0	113	0	O32(14/0/19)	23	-1.0
Wood, Fred	Frederick Llewellyn; B7.21.1865 Dundas ON, Can.; BR/5´5˝/150; d5.14; b–Pete																								
1884	Det N	12	42	4	2	0	0	0	1	3	—	18	.048	.111	.048	-51	-7	—	.889	-2	—	—	C7,O6R/S	—	-0.8
1885	Buf N	1	4	0	1	0	0	0	0	0	—	0	.250	.250	.250	60	0	—	.833	-0	—	—	/C	—	0.0
Total	2	13	46	4	3	0	0	0	1	3	—	18	.065	.122	.065	-41	-7	—	.883	-2	—	—	C8,O6R/S	—	-0.8
Wood, George	George A. "Dandy"; B11.9.1858 Boston MA; D4.4.1924 Harrisburg PA; BL/TR/5´10.5˝/175; d5.1; M1/U1; OF(1192/5/36); ▲																								
1880	Wor N	81	327	37	80	16	5	0	28	10	—	37	.245	.267	.324	91	-4	—	.887	-7	53	0	O80L,3b2/1	—	-1.5
1881	Det N	80	337	54	100	18	9	2	32	19	—	32	.297	.334	.421	131	11	—	.862	-2	85	124	O80L	—	0.4
1882	Det N	84	375	69	101	12	12	**7**	29	14	—	30	.269	.296	.421	127	10	—	.884	2	73	199	O84L	—	0.9
1883	Det N	99	441	81	133	26	11	5	47	25	—	37	.302	.339	.444	142	23	—	.876	7	65	76	O99(96/3/0)/P	—	2.3
1884	Det N	**114**	473	79	119	16	10	8	29	39	—	75	.252	.309	.378	122	14	—	.896	4	75	25	O114(114/0/1)/3	—	1.3
1885	Det N	82	362	62	105	19	8	5	28	13	—	19	.290	.315	.428	138	14	—	.885	2	79	51	O70L,3b12/SP	—	1.3
1886	Phi N	106	450	81	123	18	15	4	50	23	—	75	.273	.309	.407	115	6	9	.904	-4	67	77	O97(96/1/0),S6,3b3	—	0.0
1887	Phi N	113	491	118	142	22	19	14	66	40	6	51	.289	.350	.497	125	14	19	.873	-10	54	63	O104L,S3,3b3,2b3	—	0.2
1888	Phi N	106	433	67	99	19	6	6	51	39	7	44	.229	.303	.342	100	1	20	.905	-1	84	90	O104L,3b2,P2	—	-0.3
1889	Phi N	97	422	77	106	21	4	5	53	53	1	33	.251	.336	.355	85	-9	17	.915	-2	52	31	O92L,S6/P	—	-1.1
	Bal AA	3	10	1	2	0	0	0	1	0	0	2	.200	.200	.200	14	-1	1	1.000	-0	0	0	O3R	—	-0.1
1890	Phi P	**132**	539	115	156	20	14	9	102	51	8	35	.289	.360	.429	108	3	20	.895	14	142	180	O132(128/0/4)/3	—	1.2
1891	Phi AA	132	528	105	163	18	14	3	61	72	7	52	.309	.399	.413	132	23	22	.939	7	115	**222**	O122L,3b6,S5,M	—	2.3
1892	Bal N	21	76	9	17	1	1	0	10	10	2	8	.224	.330	.263	78	-2	1	.911	2	174	116	O21L	—	-0.1
	Cin N	30	107	10	21	2	4	0	14	10	1	17	.196	.271	.290	71	-4	4	.863	-1	113	109	O30(1/1/28)	—	-0.6
	Year	51	183	19	38	3	5	0	24	20	3	25	.208	.296	.279	74	-6	5	.885	1	140	112	O51(22/1/28)	—	-0.7
Total	13	1280	5371	965	1467	228	132	68	601	418	32	547	.273	.329	.403	116	99	113	.895	11	84	100	O1232L,3b30,S21,P5,2b3/1	—	6.2
Wood, Harry	Harold Austin; B2.10.1881 Waterville ME; D5.18.1955 Bethesda MD; BL/TR/5´10˝/155; d4.19; Col Maryland																								
1903	Cin N	2	3	0	0	0	0	0	0	1	0	—	.000	.250	.000	-24	0	0	ø	-0	0	0	O2(1/0/1)	—	-0.1
Wood, Jake	Jacob; B6.22.1937 Elizabeth NJ; BR/TR/6´1˝/170; d4.11; Col Delaware St.																								
1961	Det A	162	663	96	171	17	**14**	11	69	58-2	4	141	.258	.320	.376	83	-18	30-9	.969	-26	91	81	2b162	0	-2.7
1962	Det A	111	367	68	83	10	5	8	30	33-0	1	59	.226	.291	.346	68	-17	24-3	.950	-24	85	59	2b90	0	-3.0
1963	Det A	85	351	50	95	11	2	11	27	24-0	7	61	.271	.330	.407	102	1	18-5	.958	-8	93	97	2b81/3	58	0.2
1964	Det A	64	125	11	29	2	2	1	7	4-0	0	24	.232	.254	.304	54	-8	0-0	.989	-3	114	80	1b11,2b10,3b6/lf	0	-1.2
1965	Det A	58	104	12	30	3	0	2	7	10-0	1	19	.288	.357	.375	107	1	3-3	.977	-2	83	104	2b20/1S3	0	0.1
1966	Det A	98	230	39	58	9	3	2	27	28-0	1	48	.252	.336	.343	94	-1	4-3	.968	-9	81	87	2b52,3b4,1b2	0	-0.7
1967	Det A	14	20	2	1	1	0	0	0	1-0	0	7	.050	.095	.100	-41	-4	0-0	1.000	0	0	261	1b2,2b2	0	-0.3
	Cin N	16	17	1	2	0	0	0	1	1-0	0	3	.118	.167	.118	-15	-3	0-0	1.000	-0	88	0	O2R	0	-0.3
Total	7	608	1877	279	469	53	26	35	168	159-2	14	362	.250	.312	.362	82	-49	79-23	.963	-70	88	82	2b417,1b16,3b12,O3(1/0/2)/S	58	-7.9
Wood, Jimmy	James Leon; B12.1.1842 Brooklyn NY; D11.30.1927 San Francisco CA; TR/5´8.5˝/150; d5.8; M4																								
1871	Chi NA	**28**	135	45	51	10	6	1	29	11	—	3	.378	.425	.563	163	10	18-2	**.887**	8	107	**131**	2b28,M	—	1.2
1872	Tro NA	**25**	113	40	38	11	4	2	26	2	—	1	.336	.348	.558	172	9	0-0	.886	-1	82	54	2b25,M	—	0.5
	Eck NA	7	31	10	6	1	1	0	0	4	—	1	.194	.286	.290	91	1	1-0	.840	-0	95	30	2b7,M	—	0.0
	Year	32	144	50	44	12	5	2	26	6	—	2	.306	.333	.500	156	10	1-0	.875	-1	85	49	2b32	—	0.5
1873	Phi NA	42	209	67	67	11	1	0	27	8	—	1	.321	.346	.383	111	3	9-3	.856	2	93	**151**	2b42	—	0.2
Total	3NA	102	488	162	162	33	12	3	82	25	—	6	.332	.365	.467	139	23	28-5	.871	9	94	114	2b102	—	1.9
Wood, Jason	Jason William; B12.16.1969 San Bernardino CA; BR/TR/6´1˝/(170–200); [OakA91 11/307]; d4.1; Col Cal St.–Fresno																								
1998	Oak A	3	1	1	0	0	0	0	0	0-0	0	1	.000	.000	.000	-99	0	0-0	1.000	1	198	446	S2/3	0	0.1
	Det A	10	23	5	8	2	0	1	1	3-0	0	4	.348	.423	.565	152	2	0-1	1.000	-1	74	120	1b6/SD	0	0.0
	Year	13	24	6	8	2	0	1	1	3-0	0	5	.333	.407	.542	143	2	0-1	1.000	-0	74	120	1b6,S3,D3/3	0	0.1
1999	Det A	27	44	5	7	1	0	1	8	2-0	0	18	.159	.196	.250	12	-6	0-0	.909	-4	59	0	3b9,S9,1b5/2D	36	-1.0
2006	Fla N	12	13	3	6	2	0	0	1	1-0	0	2	.462	.500	.615	193	2	1-0	1.000	-0	114	153	1b5/2	0	0.2
Total	3	52	81	14	21	5	0	2	10	6-0	0	20	.259	.310	.395	79	-2	1-1	.989	-5	52	117	1b16,S12,3b10,D4,2b2	36	-0.7
Wood, Joe	Joe "Smoky Joe" (b Howard Ellsworth Wood); B10.25.1889 Kansas City MO; D7.27.1985 West Haven CT; BR/TR/5´11˝/180; d8.24; s–Joe; ▲																								
1908	Bos A	6	7	1	0	0	0	0	0	0	0	—	.000	.000	.000	-97	-1	0	.889	-0	71	531	P6	—	0.0
1909	Bos A	24	55	4	9	0	1	0	3	2	1	—	.164	.207	.200	28	0	0	.971	-4	55	0	P24	—	0.0
1910	Bos A	35	69	9	18	2	1	1	5	5	0	—	.261	.311	.362	108	5	0	.975	2	98	188	P35	—	0.0
1911	Bos A	44	88	15	23	4	2	2	11	10	1	—	.261	.343	.420	114	8	1	.947	2	88	143	P44	—	0.0
1912	†Bos A	43	124	16	36	13	1	1	13	11	0	—	.290	.348	.435	118	11	0	.974	8	110	79	P43	—	0.0
1913	Bos A	25	56	10	15	5	0	0	10	4	0	7	.268	.317	.357	95	4	1	.955	4	128	73	P23	—	0.0
1914	Bos A	21	43	2	6	1	0	0	1	3	1	14	.140	.213	.163	13	0	1	1.000	0	86	0	P18	—	0.0
1915	Bos A	29	54	6	14	1	1	1	7	5	0	10	.259	.322	.370	111	4	1-1	.982	1	103	**411**	P25	—	0.0
1917	Cle A	10	6	1	0	0	0	0	0	0	0	3	.000	.000	.000	-93	-1	0	1.000	0	108	0	P5	—	0.0
1918	Cle A	119	422	41	125	22	4	5	66	36	3	38	.296	.356	.403	118	9	8	.962	-2	101	79	O95(84/1/10),2b19,1b4	—	0.3
1919	Cle A	72	192	30	49	10	6	0	27	32	2	21	.255	.367	.370	101	1	3	.932	-4	88	85	O64(15/6/43)/P	—	-0.6
1920	†Cle A	61	137	25	37	11	2	1	30	25	2	16	.270	.390	.401	107	3	1-1	.987	0	99	95	O55(5/2/48)/P	—	0.1
1921	Cle A	66	194	32	71	16	5	4	60	25	0	17	.366	.438	.562	151	16	2-0	.973	-3	102	43	O64(0/21/56)	—	0.9
1922	Cle A	142	505	74	150	33	8	8	92	50	6	63	.297	.367	.442	109	7	5-1	.960	3	102	119	O141(2/1/138)	—	0.0
Total	14	697	1952	266	553	118	31	23	325	208	16	189	.283	.357	.411	110	66	23-3	.962	8	99	91	O419(106/31/295),P225,2b19,1b4	—	0.7
Wood, Joe	Joseph Perry "J.P.","Little Joe"; B10.3.1919 Houston TX; D3.25.1985 Houston TX; BR/TR/5´9.5˝/160; d5.2; Mil 1944–45; Col Rice																								
1943	Det A	60	164	22	53	4	4	1	17	6	0	13	.323	.347	.415	114	2	2-2	.896	-11	70	45	2b22,3b18	0	-0.9
Wood, Ken	Kenneth Lanier; B7.1.1924 Lincolnton NC; BR/TR/6´0˝/(200–205); d4.28																								
1948	StL A	10	24	2	2	0	1	0	2	1	0	4	.083	.120	.167	-24	-5	0-0	1.000	1	97	275	O5R	0	-0.4
1949	StL A	7	6	0	0	0	0	0	0	1	0	2	.000	.143	.000	-58	-1	0-0	ø	-0	0	0	O3(2/0/1)	0	-0.1
1950	StL A	128	369	42	83	24	0	13	62	38	1	58	.225	.299	.396	74	-16	0-4	.952	4	95	223	O94(7/0/88)	0	-1.6
1951	StL A	109	333	40	79	19	0	15	44	27	1	49	.237	.296	.429	92	-6	1-2	.959	0	101	111	O100(29/4/69)	0	-1.0
1952	Bos A	15	20	0	2	0	0	0	0	3	0	4	.100	.217	.100	-9	-3	0-0	.889	-1	93	0	O13(1/0/12)	0	-0.4
	Was A	61	210	26	50	8	6	6	32	30	0	21	.238	.333	.419	112	3	0-1	.954	4	111	144	O56(54/3/1)	0	0.2
	Year	76	230	26	52	8	6	6	32	33	0	25	.226	.323	.391	99	-1	0-1	.951	4	110	134	O69(55/3/13)	0	-0.2
1953	Was A	12	33	0	7	1	0	0	3	2	0	3	.212	.257	.242	36	-3	0-0	1.000	1	94	204	O7L	0	-0.3
Total	6	342	995	110	223	52	7	34	143	102	2	141	.224	.298	.393	81	-31	1-7	.956	8	101	160	O278(100/7/176)	0	-3.6
Wood, Bob	Robert Lynn; B7.28.1865 Thorn Hill (now part of Youngstown) OH; D5.22.1943 Churchill OH; BR/TR/5´8.5˝/153; d5.2																								
1898	Cin N	39	109	14	30	6	0	0	16	9	0	—	.275	.331	.330	84	-2	1	.943	3	*168*	*78*	C29/lf1	—	0.4
1899	Cin N	63	195	34	61	11	7	0	24	25	5	—	.313	.404	.441	129	9	3	.937	-3	*129*	*83*	C53,O2(1/1/0),3b2/1	—	0.9
1900	Cin N	45	139	17	37	8	1	0	22	10	1	—	.266	.320	.338	84	-3	3	.967	-3	*118*	*106*	C18,3b15/cf	—	-0.4
1901	Cle A	98	346	45	101	23	3	1	49	12	6	—	.292	.327	.384	101	1	6	.952	-3	*93*	*97*	C84,3b4,O3(1/0/2)/12S	—	0.5
1902	Cle A	81	258	23	76	18	2	0	40	27	6	—	.295	.375	.380	114	7	1	.941	-6	*87*	*91*	C52,1b16,O2R/23	—	0.5
1904	Det A	49	175	15	43	6	2	1	17	5	1	—	.246	.271	.320	89	-3	1	.974	4	*90*	*119*	C47	—	0.7
1905	Det A	8	24	1	2	1	0	0	0	1	0	—	.083	.120	.125	-22	-3	0	.886	-2	*75*	*165*	C7	—	-0.5
Total	7	383	1246	149	350	73	15	2	168	89	19	—	.281	.338	.368	101	6	15	.951	-9	*107*	*98*	C290,3b22,1b19,O9(3/2/4),2b2/S	—	2.1

YEAR	TM LG	G	AB	R	H	2B	3B	HR	RBI	BB-IB	HP	SO	AVG	OBP	SLG	AOPS	ABR	SB-CS	FA	FR	RNG	THR	GAMES AT POSITION	DL	BFW
Wood, Roy	Roy Winton “Woody”; B8.29.1892 Monticello AR; D4.6.1974 Fayetteville AR; BR/TR/6´0˝/175; d6.16; Col Arkansas																								
1913	Pit N	14	35	4	10	4	0	0	2	1	0	8	.286	.306	.400	105	0	0	.895	2	85	401	O8L/1	—	0.2
1914	Cle A	72	220	24	52	6	3	1	15	13	7	26	.236	.300	.305	79	-6	6-9	.946	1	102	128	O40(5/13/23),1b20	—	-1.1
1915	Cle A	33	78	5	15	2	1	0	3	2	2	13	.192	.232	.244	41	-6	1-2	.990	-1	77	77	1b21,O2(1/0/1)	—	-0.9
Total	3	119	333	33	77	12	4	1	20	16	9	47	.231	.285	.300	73	-12	7-11	.936	1	98	169	O50(14/13/24),1b42	—	-1.8
Woodall, Larry	Charles Lawrence; B7.26.1894 Staunton VA; D5.16.1963 Cambridge MA; BR/TR/5´9˝/165; d5.20; C7; Col North Carolina																								
1920	Det A	18	49	4	12	1	0	0	5	2	0	6	.245	.275	.265	45	-4	0-0	.988	1	*99*	*130*	C15	—	-0.2
1921	Det A	46	80	10	29	4	1	0	14	6	0	7	.363	.407	.438	117	2	1-0	.966	-5	*72*	*63*	C25	—	-0.1
1922	Det A	50	125	19	43	2	2	0	18	8	1	11	.344	.388	.392	107	1	0-1	.977	-8	*75*	*39*	C40	—	-0.5
1923	Det A	71	148	20	41	12	2	1	19	22	0	9	.277	.371	.405	106	2	2-1	.983	-2	*103*	*106*	C60	—	0.3
1924	Det A	67	165	23	51	9	2	0	25	21	0	5	.309	.387	.388	102	1	0-0	.986	-1	*96*	*100*	C62	—	0.3
1925	Det A	75	171	20	35	4	1	0	13	24	0	8	.205	.303	.240	39	-16	1-0	.967	-7	*86*	*85*	C75	—	-1.8
1926	Det A	67	146	18	34	5	0	0	15	15	0	2	.233	.304	.267	49	-11	0-0	.979	-4	*83*	*112*	C59	—	-1.1
1927	Det A	88	246	28	69	8	6	0	39	37	0	9	.280	.375	.362	90	-3	9-1	**.997**	3	*93*	*106*	C86	—	0.7
1928	Det A	65	186	19	39	7	1	0	13	24	0	10	.210	.300	.258	47	-14	3-1	.992	2	*101*	*142*	C62	—	-0.8
1929	Det A	1	1	0	0	0	0	0	0	0	0	0	.000	.000	.000	-99	0	0-0	ø	0	—	—	/H	—	0.0
Total	10	548	1317	161	353	52	15	1	161	159	1	67	.268	.347	.333	77	-42	16-4	.984	-21	*91*	*102*	C484	—	-3.2
Woodard, Darrell	Darrell Lee; B12.10.1956 Wilmar AR; BR/TR/5´11˝/160; [OakA74 12/286]; d8.6																								
1978	Oak A	33	9	10	0	0	0	0	0	1-0	0	1	.000	.100	.000	-73	-2	3-4	.964	2	114	112	2b14/3D	0	-0.1
Woodard, Mike	Michael Cary; B3.2.1960 Melrose Park IL; BL/TR/5´9˝/(155–160); [OakA78 4/82]; d9.11																								
1985	SF N	24	82	12	20	1	0	0	9	5-0	0	3	.244	.287	.256	56	-5	6-1	.990	-2	81	107	2b23	0	-0.6
1986	SF N	48	79	14	20	2	1	1	5	10-0	0	9	.253	.337	.342	92	-1	7-2	.986	-3	89	147	2b23,S2,3b2	0	-0.2
1987	SF N	10	19	0	4	1	0	0	1	0-0	0	1	.211	.211	.263	26	-2	0-0	1.000	2	123	158	2b8	0	0.1
1988	Chi A	18	45	3	6	0	1	0	4	1-0	1	5	.133	.170	.178	-2	-6	1-1	.975	4	111	99	2b14,D2	0	-0.2
Total	4	100	225	29	50	4	2	1	19	16-0	1	18	.222	.277	.271	54	-14	14-4	.985	1	94	121	2b68,D2,3b2,S2	0	-0.9
Woodhead, Red	James; B7.9.1851 Chelsea MA; D9.7.1881 Boston MA; 5´6˝/160; d4.15																								
1873	Mar NA	1	5	1	0	0	0	0	0	0	—	0	.000	.000	.000	-99	-1	0-0	.900	1	179	0	/S	—	0.0
1879	Syr N	34	131	4	21	1	0	0	2	0	—	23	.160	.160	.168	9	-12	—	.792	-9	72	86	3b34	—	-1.9
Woodling, Gene	Eugene Richard; B8.16.1922 Akron OH; D6.2.2001 Barberton OH; BL/TR/5´9.5˝/(175–200); d9.23; Mil 1943–45; C4																								
1943	Cle A	8	25	5	8	2	1	1	5	1	0	3	.320	.346	.600	186	2	0-0	1.000	-0	72	267	O6(0/1/5)	0	0.2
1946	Cle A	61	133	8	25	1	4	0	9	16	1	13	.188	.280	.256	54	-9	1-2	1.000	-1	106	0	O37(6/31/0)	0	-1.2
1947	Pit N	22	79	7	21	2	2	0	10	7	0	5	.266	.326	.342	75	-3	0	.968	1	111	70	O21(1/20/0)	0	-0.3
1949	†NY A	112	296	60	80	13	7	5	44	52	1	21	.270	.381	.412	110	5	2-2	.982	-2	95	89	O98(82/12/5)	0	-0.3
1950	†NY A	122	449	81	127	20	10	6	60	70	1	31	.283	.381	.412	106	5	5-3	.993	12	109	**190**	O118(117/2/0)	0	0.8
1951	†NY A	120	420	65	118	15	8	15	71	62	0	37	.281	.373	.462	130	17	0-4	.993	0	104	56	O116(101/17/0)	0	0.7
1952	†NY A	122	408	58	126	19	6	12	63	59	1	31	.309	.397	.473	151	29	1-4	**.996**	6	99	**169**	O118(112/6/0)	0	2.6
1953	†NY A	125	395	64	121	26	4	10	58	82	3	29	.306	**.429**	.468	147	32	2-7	**.996**	1	102	71	O119L	0	2.4
1954	NY A	97	304	33	76	12	5	3	40	53	0	35	.250	.358	.352	99	1	3-4	.983	-1	95	94	O89L	0	-0.6
1955	Bal A	47	145	22	32	6	2	3	18	24-4	1	18	.221	.329	.352	91	-2	1-1	1.000	-2	96	33	O44(26/4/25)	0	-0.5
	Cle A	79	259	33	72	15	1	5	35	36-2	3	15	.278	.368	.402	104	3	2-4	.993	-2	97	74	O70(64/0/16)	0	-0.3
	Year	126	404	55	104	21	3	8	53	60-6	4	33	.257	.354	.384	100	2	3-5	**.995**	-3	97	59	O114(90/4/41)	0	-0.8
1956	Cle A	100	317	56	83	17	0	8	38	69-2	3	29	.262	.395	.391	107	7	2-6	.981	-3	97	50	O85(85/0/2)	32	-0.3
1957	Cle A	133	430	74	138	25	2	19	78	64-2	3	35	.321	.408	.521	155	35	0-5	.992	9	107	178	O113L	0	3.6
1958	Bal A	133	413	57	114	16	1	15	65	66-3	2	49	.276	.378	.429	128	18	4-2	.974	-4	90	91	O116(61/0/68)	0	1.0
1959	Bal A★	140	440	63	132	22	2	14	77	78-4	0	35	.300	.402	.455	139	27	1-1	.981	-5	96	29	O124(85/0/57)	0	1.7
1960	Bal A	140	435	68	123	18	3	11	62	84-7	4	40	.283	.401	.414	123	19	3-0	.995	-1	91	94	O124(124/0/1)	0	1.2
1961	Was A	110	342	39	107	16	4	10	57	50-3	2	24	.313	.403	.471	135	19	1-0	.988	-1	91	122	O90(15/0/77)	0	1.2
1962	Was A	44	107	19	30	4	0	5	16	24-4	2	5	.280	.421	.458	138	7	1-0	.953	-4	81	0	O30(3/0/27)	0	0.2
	NY N	81	190	18	52	8	1	5	24	24-3	1	22	.274	.353	.405	103	1	0-0	.986	-2	99	0	O48(27/0/21)	0	-0.3
Total	17	1796	5587	830	1585	257	63	147	830	921-34	28	477	.284	.386	.431	123	213	29-45	.989	2	98	94	O1566(1230/93/304)	32	11.8
Woodruff, Pete	Franklin; B6.1873 NY; BR/TR; d9.19																								
1899	NY N	20	61	11	15	1	1	2	7	9	0	—	.246	.343	.393	105	0	3	1.000	-1	112	0	O19R/1	—	-0.1
Woodruff, Sam	Orville Francis; B12.27.1876 Chilo OH; D7.22.1937 Cincinnati OH; BR/TR/5´9˝/160; d4.14																								
1904	Cin N	87	306	20	58	14	3	0	20	19	3	—	.190	.244	.255	50	-18	9	.932	-3	100	67	3b61,2b17,S8/rf	—	-2.1
1910	Cin N	21	61	6	9	1	0	0	2	7	0	8	.148	.235	.164	18	-6	2	.933	-1	92	127	3b17,2b4	—	-0.8
Total	2	108	367	26	67	15	3	0	22	26	3	8	.183	.242	.240	45	-24	11	.932	-5	98	80	3b78,2b21,S8/rf	—	-2.9
Woods, Al	Alvis; B8.8.1953 Oakland CA; BL/TL/6´3˝/(190–200); [MinA72 S2/35]; d4.7; Col Laney (CA) JC																								
1977	Tor A	122	440	58	125	17	4	6	35	36-3	0	38	.284	.336	.382	95	-3	8-7	.969	-1	100	75	O115(106/0/15),D4	0	-1.0
1978	Tor A	62	220	19	53	12	3	3	25	11-1	1	23	.241	.278	.364	78	-7	1-2	.978	0	107	50	O60L	0	-1.1
1979	Tor A	132	436	57	121	24	4	5	36	40-0	1	28	.278	.337	.385	94	-3	6-4	.967	-1	97	107	O127L,D2	0	-0.9
1980	Tor A	109	373	54	112	18	2	15	47	37-3	1	35	.300	.364	.480	124	13	4-4	.991	2	104	74	O88L,D13	0	1.0
1981	Tor A	85	288	20	71	15	0	1	21	19-5	0	31	.247	.291	.309	69	-11	3-4	.973	-0	101	71	O77L,D2	0	-1.6
1982	Tor A	85	201	20	47	11	1	3	24	21-4	0	20	.234	.302	.343	72	-7	1-3	.970	-2	90	68	O64L,D10	0	-1.3
1986	Min A	23	28	5	9	1	0	2	8	3-0	0	5	.321	.375	.571	152	2	0-0	ø	0	—	—	D7	16	0.2
Total	7	618	1986	233	538	98	14	35	196	167-16	3	180	.271	.326	.387	93	-16	23-24	.974	-2	100	78	O531(522/0/15),D38	16	-4.7
Woods, Gary	Gary Lee; B7.20.1954 Santa Barbara CA; BR/TR/6´2˝/(185–190); d9.14; Col Santa Barbara (CA) City																								
1976	Oak A	6	8	0	1	0	0	0	0	0-0	0	3	.125	.125	.125	-28	-1	0-0	1.000	0	162	0	O4(1/2/1)/D	0	-0.1
1977	Tor A	60	227	21	49	9	1	0	17	7-0	2	38	.216	.246	.264	39	-20	5-4	.994	0	102	97	O60C	0	-2.1
1978	Tor A	8	19	1	3	1	0	0	0	1-0	0	1	.158	.200	.211	15	-2	1-0	1.000	0	111	0	O6(0/1/5)	0	-0.2
1980	†Hou N	19	53	8	20	5	0	2	15	2-0	0	9	.377	.400	.585	187	6	1-0	1.000	-1	80	93	O14(4/0/12)	0	0.5
1981	†Hou N	54	110	10	23	4	1	0	12	11-4	0	22	.209	.276	.264	58	-6	2-1	.984	0	112	45	O40(2/3/35)	0	-0.8
1982	Chi N	117	245	28	66	15	1	4	30	21-2	0	48	.269	.327	.388	96	-1	3-3	1.000	4	104	141	O103(37/67/12)	0	0.1
1983	Chi N	93	190	25	46	9	0	4	22	15-2	0	27	.242	.296	.353	76	-6	5-3	.971	2	103	141	O73(40/27/13)/2	15	-0.6
1984	†Chi N	87	98	13	23	4	1	3	10	15-0	0	21	.235	.333	.388	95	0	2-1	1.000	1	110	124	O62(36/11/18),2b3	0	0.0
1985	Chi N	81	82	11	20	3	0	0	4	14-0	0	18	.244	.354	.280	72	-2	0-1	1.000	0	105	68	O56(44/4/11)	15	-0.3
Total	9	525	1032	117	251	50	4	13	110	86-8	2	187	.243	.302	.337	76	-32	19-13	.992	7	104	107	O418(164/175/107),2b4/D	30	-3.5
Woods, Jim	James Jerome “Woody”; B9.17.1939 Chicago IL; BR/TR/6´0˝/(175–185); d9.27																								
1957	Chi N	2	0	1	0	0	0	0	0	0-0	0	0	ø	ø	ø	ø	0	0-0	ø	0	—	—	/R	0	0.0
1960	Phi N	11	34	4	6	0	0	1	3	3-1	0	13	.176	.243	.265	39	-3	0-0	.939	0	116	55	3b11	0	-0.3
1961	Phi N	23	48	6	11	3	0	2	9	4-2	1	15	.229	.296	.417	89	-1	0-0	.968	-2	77	122	3b15	0	-0.3
Total	3	36	82	11	17	3	0	3	12	7-3	1	28	.207	.275	.354	69	-4	0-0	.953	-2	95	91	3b26	0	-0.6
Woods, Ron	Ronald Lawrence; B2.1.1943 Hamilton OH; BR/TR/5´10˝/(165–173); d4.22																								
1969	Det A	17	15	3	4	0	0	1	3	2-0	0	3	.267	.353	.467	123	0	0-0	1.000	-0	103	0	O7(7/1/0)	0	0.0
	NY A	72	171	18	30	5	2	1	7	22-1	1	29	.175	.273	.246	48	-12	2-0	1.000	0	108	62	O67(1/66/0)	0	-1.3
	Year	89	186	21	34	5	2	2	10	24-1	1	32	.183	.280	.263	54	-12	2-0	1.000	0	108	59	O74(8/67/0)	0	-1.3
1970	NY A	95	225	30	51	5	3	8	27	33-3	0	35	.227	.324	.382	99	-1	4-2	.974	-3	86	136	O78(2/9/70)	21	-0.6
1971	NY A	25	32	4	8	1	0	1	2	4-0	0	2	.250	.333	.375	105	0	0-0	.929	0	136	0	O9(3/0/6)	0	0.0
	Mon N	51	138	26	41	7	3	1	17	19-0	0	18	.297	.382	.413	124	5	0-2	.989	6	114	239	O45(32/23/0)	0	0.9
1972	Mon N	97	221	21	57	5	1	10	31	22-2	0	33	.258	.321	.425	110	2	3-3	.991	-4	84	57	O73(8/58/10)	0	-0.4
1973	Mon N	135	318	45	73	11	3	3	31	56-3	0	34	.230	.344	.311	80	-7	12-6	.977	3	101	126	O114(29/91/4)	0	-0.7
1974	Mon N	90	127	15	26	0	0	1	12	17-1	1	17	.205	.299	.228	48	-9	6-5	.987	0	108	0	O61(40/20/5)	0	-1.1
Total	6	582	1247	162	290	34	12	26	130	175-10	2	171	.233	.326	.342	87	-22	27-18	.984	3	99	103	O454(122/268/95)	21	-3.2

YEAR	TM LG	G	AB	R	H	2B	3B	HR	RBI	BB-IB	HP	SO	AVG	OBP	SLG	AOPS	ABR	SB-CS	FA	FR	RNG	THR	GAMES AT POSITION	DL	BFW
Woodson, Tracy	Tracy Michael; B10.5.1962 Richmond VA; BR/TR/6´3˝/(215–216); [LAN84 3/77]; d4.7; Col North Carolina St.																								
1987	LA N	53	136	14	31	8	1	1	11	9-2	2	21	.228	.284	.324	63	-7	1-1	.958	-3	79	67	3b45,1b7	0	-1.1
1988	†LA N	65	173	15	43	4	1	3	15	7-1	1	32	.249	.279	.335	79	-6	1-2	.938	-5	86	59	3b41,1b25	0	-1.3
1989	LA N	4	6	0	0	0	0	0	0	0-0	0	1	.000	.000	.000	-99	-2	0-0	1.000	-0	68	0	/3	15	-0.2
1992	StL N	31	114	9	35	8	0	1	22	3-0	1	10	.307	.331	.404	109	1	0-0	.945	-6	71	103	3b26,1b3	0	-0.6
1993	StL N	62	77	4	16	2	0	0	2	1-0	0	14	.208	.215	.234	21	-9	0-0	.909	-0	117	195	3b28,1b11	0	-0.9
Total	5	215	506	42	125	22	2	5	50	20-3	4	78	.247	.279	.328	70	-23	2-3	.943	-14	83	85	3b141,1b46	15	-4.1
Woodward, Chris	Christopher Michael; B6.27.1976 Covina CA; BR/TR/6´0˝/(165–190); [TorA94 54/1438]; d6.7; Col Mt. San Antonio (CA) JC; OF(20/5/8)																								
1999	Tor A	14	26	1	6	1	0	0	2	2-0	0	6	.231	.276	.269	42	-2	0-0	.939	0	111	41	S10,3b2	0	-0.1
2000	Tor A	37	104	16	19	7	0	3	14	10-3	0	28	.183	.254	.337	46	-9	1-0	.955	1	103	68	S22,3b9,1b3,2b3	0	-0.6
2001	Tor A	37	63	9	12	3	2	2	5	1-0	0	14	.190	.203	.397	52	-5	0-1	.959	10	153	142	2b17,3b10,S4,1b2/D	26	0.5
2002	Tor A	90	312	48	86	13	4	13	45	26-0	3	72	.276	.330	.468	107	2	3-0	.965	11	107	120	S79,2b6,1b3,3b2,D2	20	1.9
2003	Tor A	104	349	49	91	22	2	7	45	28-0	3	72	.261	.316	.395	84	-8	1-2	.964	10	108	104	S103	0	0.8
2004	Tor A	69	213	21	50	13	4	1	24	14-0	1	46	.235	.283	.347	60	-13	1-2	.981	1	103	107	S64,D2	27	-0.7
2005	NY N	81	173	16	49	10	0	3	18	13-0	2	46	.283	.337	.393	94	-1	0-0	.991	-2	70	85	1b34,O23(13/5/6),S7,3b6,2b5/D	0	-0.6
2006	†NY N	83	222	25	48	10	1	3	25	23-2	1	55	.216	.289	.311	56	-15	1-1	.976	2	101	96	2b39,S13,3b11,O9(7/0/2)/1	0	-1.0
Total	8	515	1462	185	361	79	13	32	178	117-5	10	339	.247	.303	.384	78	-51	7-6	.967	34	106	107	S302,2b70,1b43,3b40,032L,D6	73	0.2
Woodward, Woody	William Frederick; B9.23.1942 Miami FL; BR/TR/6´2˝/(185–195); d9.9; Col Florida St.																								
1963	Mil N	10	2	1	0	0	0	0	0	0-0	0	0	.000	.000	.000	-99	-1	0-0	1.000	1	219	0	S5	0	0.1
1964	Mil N	77	115	18	24	2	1	0	11	6-1	2	28	.209	.260	.243	43	-9	0-1	.958	2	93	139	2b40,S18,3b7/1	0	-0.5
1965	Mil N	112	265	17	55	7	4	0	11	10-3	0	50	.208	.235	.264	41	-22	2-2	.977	4	96	123	S107,2b8	0	-1.2
1966	Atl N	144	455	46	120	23	3	0	43	37-9	4	54	.264	.323	.327	81	-10	2-2	.973	-5	106	103	2b79,S73	0	-0.5
1967	Atl N	136	429	30	97	15	2	0	25	37-5	1	51	.226	.287	.270	62	-21	0-6	**.982**	10	107	115	2b120,S16	0	-0.2
1968	Atl N	12	24	2	4	1	0	0	1	1-0	0	6	.167	.200	.208	23	-2	1-0	.973	1	123	97	S6,3b2/2	0	-0.1
	Cin N	56	119	13	29	2	0	0	10	7-3	2	23	.244	.297	.261	64	-5	1-0	.968	-9	87	77	S41,2b9/1	0	-1.2
	Year	68	143	15	33	3	0	0	11	8-3	2	29	.231	.281	.252	58	-7	2-0	.969	-8	92	80	S47,2b10,3b2/1	0	-1.3
1969	Cin N	97	241	36	63	12	0	0	15	24-3	2	40	.261	.333	.311	77	-6	3-2	.966	-7	101	71	S93,2b2	0	-0.4
1970	†Cin N	100	264	23	59	8	3	1	14	20-6	2	21	.223	.280	.288	53	-18	1-2	.973	4	109	120	S77,3b20,2b10,1b2	0	-0.7
1971	Cin N	136	273	22	66	9	1	0	18	27-4	0	28	.242	.309	.282	69	-10	4-0	.987	-9	91	109	S85,3b63,2b9	0	-1.2
Total	9	880	2187	208	517	79	14	1	148	169-34	13	301	.236	.294	.287	64	-104	14-15	.974	-9	99	98	S521,2b278,3b92,1b4	0	-5.9
Wooten, Junior	Earl Hazwell; B1.16.1924 Pelzer SC; D8.12.2006 Williamston SC; BR/TL/5´11˝/160; d9.16																								
1947	Was A	6	24	0	2	0	0	0	1	0	0	4	.083	.083	.083	-55	-5	1-0	.905	-0	113	0	O6(1/6/0)	0	-0.6
1948	Was A	88	258	34	66	8	3	1	23	24	2	21	.256	.324	.322	74	-10	2-1	.979	6	102	168	O73(0/55/22),1b6/P	0	-0.6
Total	2	94	282	34	68	8	3	1	24	24	2	25	.241	.305	.301	64	-15	3-1	.972	5	103	154	O79(1/61/22),1b6/P	0	-1.2
Wooten, Shawn	William Shawn; B7.24.1972 Glendora CA; BR/TR/5´10˝/(205–230); [DetA93 18/501]; d8.19; Col Mt. San Antonio (CA) JC																								
2000	Ana A	7	9	2	5	1	0	0	1	0-0	0	0	.556	.556	.667	202	1	0-0	1.000	-1	93	0	C4,1b3	0	0.1
2001	Ana A	79	221	24	69	8	1	8	32	5-0	3	42	.312	.332	.466	106	1	2-0	1.000	-1	174	140	D27,C25,1b21/3	0	-0.1
2002	†Ana A	49	113	13	33	8	0	3	19	6-1	1	24	.292	.331	.442	105	1	2-0	1.000	-2	80	52	D26,1b16,C2/3	102	-0.2
2003	Ana A	98	272	25	66	8	0	7	32	24-5	1	45	.243	.303	.349	75	-10	0-4	.995	-3	82	107	1b32,D28,C19,3b17	0	-1.7
2004	Phi N	33	53	2	9	3	0	0	2	2-0	2	9	.170	.228	.226	18	-7	0-0	1.000	-2	66	108	1b11,3b4	0	-0.9
2005	Bos A	1	1	0	0	0	0	0	0	0-0	0	0	.000	.000	.000	-96	0	0-0	ø	-0	0	0	/C	0	0.0
Total	6	267	669	66	182	28	1	18	86	37-6	7	120	.272	.314	.398	88	-14	4-4	.994	-8	91	116	1b83,D81,C51,3b23	102	-2.8
Wordsworth, Favel	Favel Perry; B11.22.1850 New York NY; D8.12.1888 New York NY; d4.28																								
1873	Res NA	12	40	5	10	0	0	0	3	2	—	1	.250	.286	.250	65	-1	1-0	.662	-4	97	35	S11/rf	—	-0.4
Workman, Chuck	Charles Thomas; B1.6.1915 Leeton MO; D1.3.1953 Kansas City MO; BL/TR/6´0˝/175; d9.18																								
1938	Cle A	2	5	1	2	0	0	0	0	0	0	0	.400	.400	.400	103	0	0-0	.500	-0	57	0	/rf	—	0.0
1941	Cle A	9	4	2	0	0	0	0	0	1	0	1	.000	.200	.000	-45	-1	0-0	ø	0	—	—	/H	0	-0.1
1943	Bos N	**153**	615	71	153	17	1	10	67	53	3	72	.249	.311	.328	86	-12	12	.988	2	95	130	O149(16/0/133),1b3/3	0	-2.1
1944	Bos N	140	418	46	87	18	3	11	53	42	4	41	.208	.287	.344	74	-15	1	.983	4	91	167	O103R,3b19	0	-1.7
1945	Bos N	139	514	77	141	16	2	25	87	51	6	58	.274	.347	.459	122	13	9	.910	-15	97	91	3b107,O24(5/0/19)	0	-0.2
1946	Bos N	25	48	5	8	2	0	2	7	3	1	11	.167	.231	.333	58	-3	0	.920	-1	94	114	O12(3/8/1)	0	-0.4
	Pit N	58	145	11	32	4	1	2	16	11	1	19	.221	.280	.303	64	-7	2	1.000	5	131	94	O40(3/0/38)/3	0	-0.4
	Year	83	193	16	40	6	1	4	23	14	2	30	.207	.268	.311	63	-10	2	.986	5	124	98	O52(6/8/39)/3	0	-0.8
Total	6	526	1749	213	423	57	7	50	230	161	15	202	.242	.311	.368	91	-25	24-0	.985	-4	99	125	O329(27/8/295),3b128,1b3	0	-4.9
Workman, Hank	Henry Kilgariff; B2.5.1926 Los Angeles CA; BL/TR/6´1˝/185; d9.4; Col USC																								
1950	NY A	2	5	1	1	0	0	0	0	0	0	1	.200	.200	.200	3	-1	0-0	1.000	-0	0	126	/1	0	-0.1
Worth, Herb	Herbert; B5.2.1847 Brooklyn NY; D4.27.1914 Brooklyn NY; d7.29																								
1872	Atl NA	1	5	1	1	1	0	0	1	0	—	0	.200	.200	.400	68	0	0-0	1.000	0	0	0	/rf	—	0.0
Worthington, Craig	Craig Richard; B4.17.1965 Los Angeles CA; BR/TR/6´0˝/(190–202); [BalA85 S1/11]; d4.26; Col Cerritos (CA) JC																								
1988	Bal A	26	81	5	15	2	0	2	4	9-0	0	24	.185	.267	.284	56	-5	1-0	.961	2	116	89	3b26	0	-0.2
1989	Bal A	145	497	57	123	23	0	15	70	61-2	4	114	.247	.334	.384	105	4	1-2	.951	-6	101	89	3b145	0	-0.2
1990	Bal A	133	425	46	96	17	0	8	44	63-2	3	96	.226	.328	.322	85	-6	1-2	.945	-7	96	128	3b131,D2	0	-1.4
1991	Bal A	31	102	11	23	3	0	4	12	12-0	1	14	.225	.313	.373	92	-1	0-1	.975	-2	89	54	3b30	39	-0.4
1992	Cle A	9	24	0	4	0	0	0	2	2-0	0	4	.167	.231	.167	13	-3	0-1	.857	1	123	155	3b9	0	-0.2
1995	Cin N	10	18	1	5	1	0	1	2	2-0	0	1	.278	.350	.500	120	0	0-0	1.000	1	92	126	1b4,3b2	0	0.1
	Tex A	26	68	4	15	4	0	2	6	7-0	0	8	.221	.293	.368	68	-3	0-0	.980	-2	90	79	3b26	0	-0.5
1996	Tex A	13	19	2	3	0	0	1	4	6-0	0	3	.158	.333	.316	69	-1	0-0	.917	0	89	96	3b7,1b6	0	-0.1
Total	7	393	1234	126	284	50	0	33	144	162-4	8	264	.230	.322	.351	90	-15	3-6	.950	-13	99	100	3b376,1b10,D2	39	-2.9
Worthington, Red	Robert Lee; B4.24.1906 Alhambra CA; D12.8.1963 Sepulveda CA; BR/TR/5´11˝/170; d4.14																								
1931	Bos N	128	491	47	143	25	10	4	44	26	1	38	.291	.328	.407	100	-2	1	**.988**	-2	95	113	O124(114/0/10)	—	-1.0
1932	Bos N	105	435	62	132	35	8	8	61	15	2	24	.303	.330	.476	118	10	1	.987	-2	92	120	O104L	—	0.2
1933	Bos N	17	45	3	7	4	0	0	0	1	0	3	.156	.174	.244	20	-5	0	.900	-1	86	119	O10(3/0/7)	—	-0.6
1934	Bos N	41	65	6	16	5	0	0	6	6	1	5	.246	.319	.323	78	-2	0	.920	-1	110	0	O11R	—	-0.3
	StL N	1	1	0	0	0	0	0	0	0	0	1	.000	.000	.000	-94	0	0	ø	0	—	—	/H	—	0.0
	Year	42	66	6	16	5	0	0	6	6	1	6	.242	.315	.318	75	-2	0	.920	-1	110	0	O11R	—	-0.3
Total	4	292	1037	118	298	69	18	12	111	48	4	71	.287	.321	.423	103	1	2	.981	-5	94	112	O249(221/0/28)	—	-1.7
Wortman, Chuck	William Lewis; B1.5.1892 Baltimore MD; D8.19.1977 Las Vegas NV; BR/TR/5´7˝/150; d7.20																								
1916	Chi N	69	234	17	47	4	2	2	16	18	0	22	.201	.258	.261	54	-13	4	.908	-15	90	88	S69	—	-2.7
1917	Chi N	75	190	24	33	4	1	0	9	18	0	23	.174	.245	.205	36	-14	6	.918	-11	88	104	S65/23	—	-2.4
1918	†Chi N	17	17	4	2	0	0	1	3	1	0	2	.118	.167	.294	39	-1	3	.864	-0	107	76	2b8,S4	—	-0.2
Total	3	161	441	45	82	8	3	3	28	37	0	47	.186	.249	.238	46	-28	13	.913	-25	89	95	S138,2b9/3	—	-5.3
Wotus, Ron	Ronald Allan; B3.3.1961 Colchester CT; BR/TR/6´1˝/(164–180); [PitN79 16/406]; d9.3; C9; [DL 1985 Pit N 95]																								
1983	Pit N	5	3	0	0	0	0	0	0	0-0	0	1	.000	.000	.000	-97	-1	0-0	1.000	0	71	0	S2/2	0	0.0
1984	Pit N	27	55	4	12	6	0	0	2	6-2	0	8	.218	.290	.327	74	-2	0-0	.976	8	138	153	S17,2b7	0	0.8
Total	2	32	58	4	12	6	0	0	2	6-2	0	9	.207	.277	.310	66	-3	0-0	.976	8	136	148	S19,2b8	95	0.8
Woulfe, Jimmy	James Joseph; B11.25.1859 New Orleans LA; D12.20.1924 New Orleans LA; TR/5´11˝/?; d5.16																								
1884	Cin AA	8	34	3	5	0	1	0	2	1	0	—	.147	.171	.206	22	-3	—	.625	-3	0	0	O7(1/0/6)/3	—	-0.6
	Pit AA	15	53	7	6	1	0	0	1	0	0	—	.113	.113	.132	-20	-7	—	.893	1	119	439	O15(0/14/1)	—	-0.6
	Year	23	87	10	11	1	1	0	3	1	0	—	.126	.136	.161	-3	-10	—	.795	-2	76	279	O22(1/14/7)/3	—	-1.2
Wright, Al	Albert Edgar "A-1"; B11.11.1912 San Francisco CA; D11.13.1998 Oakland CA; BR/TR/6´1.5˝/170; d4.25																								
1933	Bos N	4	1	0	1	0	0	0	0	0	0	0	1.000	1.000	1.000	515	1	0	.500	-1	0	0	2b3	—	0.0

YEAR	TM LG	G	AB	R	H	2B	3B	HR	RBI	BB-IB	HP	SO	AVG	OBP	SLG	AOPS	ABR	SB-CS	FA	FR	RNG	THR	GAMES AT POSITION	DL	BFW
Wright, Ab	Albert Owen; B11.16.1906 Terlton OK; D5.23.1995 Muskogee OK; BR/TR/6´3˝/200; d4.20; Col Oklahoma St.																								
1935	Cle A	67	160	17	38	11	1	2	18	10	2	17	.237	.291	.356	65	-9	2-1	.984	-2	80	141	O47(5/5/38)	—	-1.2
1944	Bos N	71	195	20	50	9	0	7	35	18	2	31	.256	.326	.410	102	0	0	.968	-3	91	53	O47(35/0/12)	0	-0.6
Total	2	138	355	37	88	20	1	9	53	28	4	48	.248	.310	.386	85	-9	2-1	.974	-5	86	91	O94(40/5/50)	0	-1.8
Wright, Cy	Ceylon; B8.16.1893 Minneapolis MN; D11.7.1947 Hines IL; BL/TR/5´9˝/150; d6.30																								
1916	Chi A	8	18	0	0	0	0	0	0	1	0	7	.000	.053	.000	-83	-4	0	.844	-1	103	102	S8	—	-0.6
Wright, David	David Allen; B12.20.1982 Norfolk VA; BR/TR/6´0˝/200; [NYN01 1/38]; d7.21																								
2004	NY N	69	263	41	77	17	1	14	40	14-0	3	40	.293	.332	.525	120	7	6-0	.942	-6	100	77	3b69	0	0.3
2005	NY N	160	575	99	176	42	1	27	102	72-2	7	113	.306	.388	.523	140	35	17-7	.948	2	107	79	3b160	0	3.9
2006	†NY N★	154	582	96	181	40	5	26	116	66-13	5	113	.311	.381	.531	134	31	20-5	.954	-6	93	112	3b153/D	0	2.8
Total	3	383	1420	236	434	99	7	67	258	152-15	15	266	.306	.375	.527	134	73	43-12	.949	-9	100	92	3b382/D	0	7.0
Wright, Glenn	Forest Glenn "Buckshot"; B2.6.1901 Archie MO; D4.6.1984 Olathe KS; BR/TR/5´11˝/170; d4.15; Col Missouri																								
1924	Pit N	**153**	616	80	177	28	18	7	111	27	1	52	.287	.318	.425	96	-6	14-6	.946	9	**110**	**112**	S153	—	2.0
1925	†Pit N	**153**	614	97	189	32	10	18	121	31	0	32	.308	.341	.480	100	-2	3-7	.939	2	102	116	S153/3	—	1.4
1926	Pit N	119	458	73	141	15	15	8	77	19	0	26	.308	.335	.459	106	1	6	.927	-8	99	116	S116	—	0.6
1927	†Pit N	143	570	78	160	26	4	9	105	39	1	46	.281	.328	.388	85	-12	4	.942	-14	94	103	S143	—	-1.1
1928	Pit N	108	407	63	126	20	8	8	66	21	0	53	.310	.343	.457	103	0	3	.927	-20	92	93	S101/1rf	—	-0.9
1929	Bro N	24	25	4	5	0	0	1	6	3	0	6	.200	.286	.320	51	-2	0	.667	-2	37	0	S3	—	-0.4
1930	Bro N	135	532	83	171	28	12	22	126	32	0	70	.321	.360	.543	116	11	2	.964	5	99	113	S134	—	2.6
1931	Bro N	77	268	36	76	9	4	9	32	14	2	35	.284	.324	.448	106	1	1	.942	8	107	109	S75	—	1.4
1932	Bro N	127	446	50	122	31	5	11	60	12	0	57	.274	.293	.439	96	-4	4	.939	8	103	**119**	S122,1b2	—	1.1
1933	Bro N	71	192	19	49	13	0	1	18	11	1	24	.255	.299	.339	85	-3	1	.936	-4	92	107	S51,1b9,3b2	—	-0.5
1935	Chi A	9	25	1	3	1	0	0	1	0	0	6	.120	.120	.160	-27	-5	0-0	.943	-0	105	82	2b7	—	-0.5
Total	11	1119	4153	584	1219	203	76	94	723	209	5	407	.294	.328	.447	99	-21	38-13	.941	-17	100	110	S1051,1b12,2b7,3b3/rf	—	5.7
Wright, George	George; B1.28.1847 Yonkers NY; D8.21.1937 Boston MA; BR/TR/5´9.5˝/150; d5.5; M1; HF1937; b–Sam b–Harry																								
1871	Bos NA	16	80	33	33	7	5	0	11	6	—	1	.412	.453	.625	200	10	9-1	.816	6	111	243	S15/1	—	1.1
1872	Bos NA	**48**	255	87	86	16	6	2	35	3	—	1	.337	.345	.471	141	10	14-4	.836	22	**119**	**324**	S48	—	2.2
1873	Bos NA	59	323	99	125	17	7	3	43	9	—	2	.387	.404	.511	156	20	9-9	**.826**	20	116	133	S59	—	2.6
1874	Bos NA	60	313	76	103	10	**15**	2	44	5	—	6	.329	.340	.476	150	15	2-0	.821	6	97	**218**	S60/3	—	1.5
1875	Bos NA	79	408	106	136	20	7	2	61	2	—	6	.333	.337	.431	159	22	13-6	.861	4	96	153	S79,P2	—	2.1
1876	Bos N	**70**	335	72	100	18	6	1	34	8	—	9	.299	.315	.397	134	12	—	.888	14	114	109	S68,2b2/P	—	2.5
1877	Bos N	**61**	290	58	80	15	1	0	35	9	—	15	.276	.298	.334	95	-1	—	.878	10	105	147	2b58,S3	—	1.0
1878	Bos N	59	267	35	60	5	1	0	12	6	—	22	.225	.242	.251	58	-13	—	**.947**	10	103	**188**	S59	—	0.0
1879	Pro N	**85**	388	79	107	15	10	1	42	13	—	20	.276	.299	.374	122	9	—	.924	20	**112**	95	S85,M	—	2.9
1880	Bos N	1	4	2	1	0	0	0	0	0	—	0	.250	.250	.250	72	0	—	1.000	0	118	0	/S	—	0.0
1881	Bos N	7	25	4	5	0	0	0	0	3	—	1	.200	.286	.200	58	-1	—	.963	-1	88	144	S7	—	-0.1
1882	Pro N	46	185	14	30	1	2	0	9	4	—	36	.162	.180	.189	19	-17	—	.873	-6	92	140	S46	—	-2.0
Total	5NA	262	1379	401	483	70	40	9	194	25	—	16	.350	.362	.479	155	77	47-20	.835	57	106	200	S261,P2/31	—	9.5
Total	7	329	1494	264	383	54	20	2	132	43	—	103	.256	.277	.323	93	-11	—	.911	48	106	128	S269,2b60/P	—	4.3
Wright, George	George De Witt; B12.22.1958 Oklahoma City OK; BB/TR/5´11˝/180; [TexA77 4/87]; d4.10																								
1982	Tex A	150	557	69	147	20	5	11	50	30-4	3	78	.264	.305	.377	90	-9	3-7	.981	6	104	147	O149(0/147/3)	0	-0.7
1983	Tex A	162	634	79	175	28	6	18	80	41-9	2	82	.276	.321	.424	105	2	8-7	.985	-4	100	58	O161C	0	-0.4
1984	Tex A	101	383	40	93	19	4	9	48	15-2	2	54	.243	.273	.384	77	-13	0-2	.983	-8	86	58	O80(0/54/26),D18	30	-2.5
1985	Tex A	109	363	21	69	13	0	2	18	25-5	0	49	.190	.241	.242	33	-34	4-7	.991	0	98	131	O102(0/53/55),D4	0	-3.9
1986	Tex A	49	106	10	23	3	1	2	7	4-1	1	23	.217	.250	.321	53	-7	3-5	.969	1	104	113	O42(10/8/27)	0	-0.9
	Mon N	56	117	12	22	5	2	0	5	11-0	1	28	.188	.258	.265	46	-9	1-1	1.000	-2	84	124	O32(10/21/3)	0	-1.2
Total	5	627	2160	231	529	88	18	42	208	126-21	9	314	.245	.288	.361	78	-70	19-29	.984	-7	98	100	O566(20/444/114),D22	30	-9.6
Wright, Joe	Joel Sherman; B1869 Oshkosh WI; D9.20.1909 Omaha NE; BL/TL/5´8˝/175; d7.14																								
1895	Lou N	60	228	30	63	10	4	1	30	12	1	28	.276	.315	.368	81	-7	7	.963	-1	49	47	O60(0/43/17)	—	-0.9
1896	Lou N	2	7	0	2	0	0	0	0	0	0	1	.286	.286	.286	53	-1	0	1.000	-0	0	0	O2R	—	-0.1
	Pit N	15	52	5	16	2	1	0	6	1	0	2	.308	.321	.385	89	-1	1	.958	-2	0	0	O12C/3	—	-0.3
	Year	17	59	5	18	2	1	0	6	1	0	3	.305	.317	.373	85	-2	1	.962	-2	0	0	O14(0/12/2)/3	—	-0.4
Total	2	77	287	35	81	12	5	1	36	13	1	31	.282	.316	.369	82	-9	8	.963	-3	40	38	O74(0/55/19)/3	—	-1.3
Wright, Pat	Patrick Francis; B7.5.1865 Pottsville PA; D5.29.1943 Springfield IL; BB/TR/6´2˝/190; d7.11																								
1890	Chi N	1	2	0	0	0	0	0	0	1	0	0	.000	.333	.000	-1	0	0	1.000	0	122	0	/2	—	0.0
Wright, Ron	Ronald Wade; B1.21.1976 Delta UT; BR/TR/6´1˝/230; [AtlN94 7/202]; d4.14																								
2002	Sea A	1	3	0	0	0	0	0	0	0-0	0	1	.000	.000	.000	-99	-1	0-0	ø	0	—	—	/D	0	-0.1
Wright, Sam	Samuel; B11.25.1848 New York NY; D5.6.1928 Boston MA; BR/TR/5´7.5˝/146; d4.19; b–George b–Harry																								
1875	NH NA	33	127	10	24	4	0	0	5	1	—	1	.189	.195	.220	51	-5	1-0	.807	11	138	76	S33	—	0.5
1876	Bos N	2	8	0	1	0	0	0	0	0	—	0	.125	.125	.125	-16	-1	—	.778	-0	111	0	S2	—	-0.1
1880	Cin N	9	34	0	3	0	0	0	0	0	—	5	.088	.088	.088	-40	-5	—	.889	-1	105	0	S9	—	-0.5
1881	Bos N	1	4	0	1	0	0	0	0	0	—	0	.250	.250	.250	60	0	—	.667	-1	80	0	/S	—	-0.1
Total	3	12	46	0	5	0	0	0	0	0	—	5	.109	.109	.109	-27	-6	—	.843	-2	103	0	S12	—	-0.7
Wright, Taffy	Taft Shedron; B8.10.1911 Tabor City NC; D10.22.1981 Orlando FL; BL/TR/5´10˝/180; d4.18; Mil 1943–45																								
1938	Was A	100	263	37	92	18	10	2	36	13	4	17	.350	.389	.517	134	12	1-2	.982	-2	97	63	O60(14/1/45)	—	0.7
1939	Was A	129	499	77	154	29	11	4	93	38	1	19	.309	.359	.435	110	6	1-2	.950	-0	98	115	O123(39/0/84)	—	-0.1
1940	Chi A	147	581	79	196	31	9	5	88	43	2	25	.337	.385	.448	114	12	4-7	.963	-6	92	90	O144R	—	-0.4
1941	Chi A	136	513	71	165	35	5	10	97	60	6	27	.322	.399	.468	130	24	5-4	.973	-6	97	59	O134R	0	0.9
1942	Chi A	85	300	43	100	13	5	0	47	48	4	9	.333	.432	.410	141	19	1-8	.968	-2	98	89	O81(81/0/1)	0	1.1
1946	Chi A	115	422	46	116	19	4	7	52	42	1	17	.275	.342	.389	108	4	10-3	.991	-5	97	51	O107(8/0/99)	0	-0.4
1947	Chi A	124	401	48	130	13	0	4	54	48	1	17	.324	.398	.387	123	14	8-6	.971	-5	92	81	O100(35/0/66)	0	0.4
1948	Chi A	134	455	50	127	15	6	4	61	38	5	18	.279	.341	.365	91	-7	2-1	.987	-1	95	107	O114(6/0/108)	0	-1.2
1949	Phi A	59	149	14	35	2	5	2	25	16	3	6	.235	.321	.356	82	-5	0-0	.970	-0	90	157	O35R	0	-0.6
Total	9	1029	3583	465	1115	175	55	38	553	346	27	155	.311	.376	.423	116	79	32-33	.972	-27	95	86	O898(183/1/716)	0	0.4
Wright, Tom	Thomas Everette; B9.22.1923 Shelby NC; BL/TR/5´11.5˝/180; d9.15																								
1948	Bos A	3	2	1	1	0	1	0	0	0	0	0	.500	.500	1.500	400	1	0-0	ø	0	—	—	/H	0	0.1
1949	Bos A	5	4	1	1	1	0	0	1	1	0	1	.250	.400	.500	128	0	0-0	ø	0	—	—	/H	0	0.0
1950	Bos A	54	107	17	34	7	0	0	20	6	1	18	.318	.360	.383	82	-3	0-0	.953	-1	97	60	O24(5/0/19)	0	-0.4
1951	Bos A	28	63	8	14	1	1	1	9	11	1	8	.222	.347	.317	73	-2	0-0	.950	-2	74	0	O18(1/0/17)	0	-0.5
1952	StL A	29	66	6	16	0	0	1	6	12	0	20	.242	.359	.288	79	-1	1-1	.976	1	106	188	O18L	0	-0.2
	Chi A	60	132	15	34	10	2	1	21	16	1	16	.258	.342	.386	102	1	1-0	.969	-0	99	95	O34(22/0/13)	0	-0.1
	Year	89	198	21	50	10	2	2	27	28	1	36	.253	.348	.354	94	-1	2-1	.971	1	101	128	O52(40/0/13)	0	-0.3
1953	Chi A	77	132	14	33	5	3	2	25	12	2	21	.250	.322	.379	86	-3	0-0	.978	-2	90	46	O33(10/0/24)	0	-0.6
1954	Was A	76	171	13	42	4	4	1	17	18	2	38	.246	.323	.333	85	-4	0-0	1.000	-1	104	0	O43(15/0/28)	0	-0.7
1955	Was A	7	7	0	0	0	0	0	0	0-0	0	1	.000	.000	.000	-99	-2	0-0	ø	0	—	—	/H	0	-0.2
1956	Was A	2	1	0	0	0	0	0	0	0-0	0	0	.000	.000	.000	-99	0	0-0	ø	0	—	—	/H	0	0.0
Total	9	341	685	75	175	28	11	6	99	76-0	7	123	.255	.336	.355	85	-13	2-1	.977	-6	97	58	O170(71/0/101)	0	-2.6
Wright, Dick	Willard James; B5.5.1890 Worcester NY; D1.24.1952 Bethlehem PA; BR/TR/5´10˝/170; d6.30; Col Lafayette																								
1915	Bro F	4	5	0	0	0	0	0	0	0	0	0	.000	.000	.000	-99	-1	0	.833	-1	*113*	*0*	C3	—	-0.2
Wright, Harry	William Henry; B1.10.1835 Sheffield, England; D10.3.1895 Atlantic City NJ; BR/TR/5´9.5˝/157; d5.5; M23; HF1953; b–George b–Sam; ▲																								
1871	Bos NA	**31**	147	42	44	5	2	0	26	13	—	2	.299	.356	.361	103	1	7-1	.855	-1	146	166	O30C,P9/SM	—	0.0
1872	Bos NA	**48**	208	39	53	5	1	0	24	9	—	2	.255	.286	.288	73	-7	0-0	.866	-5	78	121	O48C,P7,M	—	-0.8
1873	Bos NA	58	263	57	68	7	3	2	36	11	—	4	.259	.288	.331	76	-9	3-2	.819	-6	104	71	O58C,P14,M	—	-1.1

YEAR	TM LG	G	AB	R	H	2B	3B	HR	RBI	BB-IB	HP	SO	AVG	OBP	SLG	AOPS	ABR	SB-CS	FA	FR	RNG	THR	GAMES AT POSITION	DL	BFW
1874	Bos NA	40	184	44	58	4	2	2	27	4	—	3	.315	.330	.391	123	4	1-0	.827	-1	103	**367**	O40C,P6,M	—	0.2
1875	Bos NA	1	4	1	1	0	0	0	0	0	—	1	.250	.250	.250	72	0	0-0	1.000	-0	0	0	/rfM	—	0.0
1876	Bos N	1	3	0	0	0	0	0	0	0	—	1	.000	.000	.000	-98	-1	—	ø	0	0	0	/rfM	—	-0.1
1877	Bos N	1	4	0	0	0	0	0	0	0	—	1	.000	.000	.000	-97	-1	—	.667	0	398	2718	/cfM	—	0.0
Total	5NA	178	806	183	224	21	8	4	113	37	—	12	.278	.310	.339	91	-11	11-3	.841	-13	103	162	O177(0/176/1),P36/S	—	-1.7
Total	2	2	7	0	0	0	0	0	0	0	—	2	.000	.000	.000	-97	-2	—	.667	0	367	2509	O2(0/1/1)	—	-0.1
Wright, Bill	William Hiram; d9.16																								
1887	Was N	1	3	0	2	0	0	0	0	0	0	0	.667	.667	.667	290	1	0	.778	-1	—	—	/C	—	0.0
Wright, Rasty	William Smith; B1.31.1863 Birmingham MI; D10.14.1922 Duluth MN; BL/6´1˝/185; d4.17																								
1890	Syr AA	88	348	82	106	10	6	0	27	69	6	—	.305	.428	.368	150	30	30	.907	2	102	187	O88(0/70/18)	—	2.5
	Cle N	13	45	7	5	1	0	0	2	12	0	4	.111	.298	.133	27	-3	3	.917	-1	46	0	O13R	—	-0.4
Total	1	101	393	89	111	11	6	0	29	81	6	4	.282	.412	.341	135	27	33	.908	1	95	164	O101(0/70/31)	—	2.1
Wrightstone, Russ	Russell Guy; B3.18.1893 Bowmansdale PA; D2.25.1969 Harrisburg PA; BL/TR/5´10.5˝/176; d4.19; OF(85/0/33)																								
1920	Phi N	76	206	23	54	6	1	3	17	10	2	25	.262	.303	.345	82	-5	3-2	.934	3	106	71	3b56,S2/2	—	0.0
1921	Phi N	109	372	59	110	13	4	9	51	18	2	20	.296	.332	.425	92	-5	4-4	.922	5	111	60	3b54,O37(34/0/3),2b4	—	0.0
1922	Phi N	99	331	56	101	18	6	5	33	28	3	17	.305	.365	.441	98	-1	4-5	.973	10	120	66	3b40,S35,1b2	—	1.3
1923	Phi N	119	392	59	107	21	7	7	57	21	3	19	.273	.315	.416	82	-11	5-2	.942	-0	96	81	3b72,S21,2b9	—	-0.4
1924	Phi N	118	388	55	119	24	4	7	58	27	7	15	.307	.363	.443	102	2	5-4	.944	-9	91	108	3b97,2b9,S5/rf	—	0.0
1925	Phi N	92	286	48	99	18	5	14	61	19	1	18	.346	.389	.591	135	14	0-3	.937	-10	94	53	O45(37/0/10),S12,3b11,2b10,1b6	—	0.1
1926	Phi N	112	368	55	113	23	1	7	57	27	1	11	.307	.356	.432	106	3	5	.977	2	104	103	1b53,3b37,2b13,O5L	—	0.4
1927	Phi N	141	533	62	163	24	5	6	75	48	2	20	.306	.365	.403	104	4	9	.989	2	107	94	1b136/23	—	-0.3
1928	Phi N	33	91	7	19	5	1	1	11	14	1	5	.209	.321	.319	65	-4	0	.936	-2	91	48	O26(9/0/19),1b4	—	-0.8
	NY N	30	25	3	4	0	0	1	5	3	0	2	.160	.250	.280	38	-2	0	1.000	-0	0	0	1b2	—	-0.2
	Year	63	116	10	23	5	1	2	16	17	1	7	.198	.306	.310	60	-7	0	.936	-2	91	48	O26(9/0/19),1b6	—	-1.0
Total	9	929	2992	427	889	152	34	60	425	215	22	152	.297	.349	.431	99	-5	35-20	.942	3	103	87	3b368,1b203,O114L,S75,2b47	—	0.1
Wrigley, Zeke	George Watson; B1.18.1874 Philadelphia PA; D9.28.1952 Philadelphia PA; 5´8.5˝/150; d8.31																								
1896	Was N	5	9	1	1	0	0	0	2	1	0	1	.111	.200	.111	-17	-2	0	.909	2	172	0	2b3/S	—	0.1
1897	Was N	104	388	65	110	14	8	3	64	21	0	—	.284	.320	.384	86	-10	5	.885	4	231	455	O36(4/13/19),S33,3b30,2b9	—	-0.5
1898	Was N	111	400	50	98	9	10	2	39	20	1	—	.245	.283	.333	76	-15	10	.895	11	102	94	S97,2b11,O3(0/2/1)/3	—	0.1
1899	NY N	4	15	1	3	0	0	0	1	1	0	—	.200	.250	.200	25	-2	1	.818	-1	103	0	3b4	—	-0.2
	Bro N	15	49	4	10	2	2	0	11	3	0	—	.204	.250	.327	56	-3	2	.870	-4	78	84	S14/3	—	-0.6
	Year	19	64	5	13	2	2	0	12	4	0	—	.203	.250	.297	49	-5	3	.870	-5	78	84	S14,3b5	—	-0.8
Total	4	239	861	121	222	25	20	5	117	46	1	1	.258	.296	.351	78	-32	18	.892	12	101	85	S145,O39(4/15/20),3b36,2b23	—	-1.1
Wrona, Rick	Richard James; B12.10.1963 Tulsa OK; BR/TR/6´1˝/(185–190); [ChiN85 5/130]; d9.3; Col Wichita St.																								
1988	Chi N	4	6	0	0	0	0	0	0	0-0	0	1	.000	.000	.000	-96	-2	0-0	1.000	1	135	181	C2	0	-0.1
1989	†Chi N	38	92	11	26	2	1	2	14	2-1	1	21	.283	.299	.391	91	-1	0-0	.983	1	163	60	C37	0	0.2
1990	Chi N	16	29	3	5	0	0	0	0	2-1	0	11	.172	.226	.172	10	-4	1-0	.970	2	221	109	C16	0	-0.1
1992	Cin N	11	23	0	4	0	0	0	0	0-0	0	3	.174	.174	.174	-1	-3	0-0	.965	2	259	82	C10/1	0	-0.1
1993	Chi A	4	8	0	1	0	0	0	1	0-0	0	4	.125	.125	.125	-33	-2	0-0	1.000	-2	48	0	C4	0	-0.3
1994	Mil A	6	10	2	5	4	0	1	3	1-0	0	1	.500	.545	1.200	317	3	0-0	.923	-1	216	0	C5/1	0	0.2
Total	6	79	168	16	41	6	1	3	18	5-2	1	41	.244	.267	.345	68	-9	1-0	.976	4	182	69	C74,1b2	0	-0.2
Wuestling, Yats	George; B10.18.1903 St.Louis MO; D4.26.1970 St.Louis MO; BR/TR/5´11˝/167; d6.15																								
1929	Det A	54	150	13	30	4	1	0	16	9	1	24	.200	.250	.240	27	-17	1-3	.943	-4	104	62	S52/23	—	-1.6
1930	Det A	4	9	0	0	0	0	0	0	2	0	3	.000	.182	.000	-48	-2	0-0	.842	-0	105	101	S4	—	-0.2
	NY A	25	58	5	11	0	1	0	3	4	0	14	.190	.242	.224	20	-7	0-1	.918	1	104	100	S21,3b3	—	-0.4
	Year	29	67	5	11	0	1	0	3	6	0	17	.164	.233	.194	10	-10	0-1	.904	1	104	100	S25,3b3	—	-0.6
Total	2	83	217	18	41	4	2	0	19	15	1	41	.189	.245	.226	21	-26	1-4	.931	-3	104	73	S77,3b4/2	—	-2.2
Wyatt, Joe	Loral John; B4.6.1900 Petersburg IN; D12.5.1970 Oblong IL; BR/TR/6´1˝/175; d9.11; Col Wabash																								
1924	Cle A	4	12	1	2	0	0	0	1	2	0	1	.167	.286	.167	18	-1	0-0	.833	-1	83	0	O4R	—	-0.2
Wylie, Ren	James Renwick; B12.14.1861 Elizabeth PA; D8.17.1951 Wilkinsburg PA; BR/TR/5´11˝/155; d8.11; Col Geneva																								
1882	Pit AA	1	3	0	0	0	0	0	—	0	—	—	.000	.000	.000	-99	-1	—	1.000	1	745	0	/cf	—	0.0
Wyman, Frank	Frank H.; B5.10.1862 Haverhill MA; D2.4.1916 Everett MA; d6.10; ▲																								
1884	KC U	30	124	16	27	4	0	0	—	3	—	—	.218	.236	.250	55	-10	—	.743	2	158	231	O25(13/11/0),P3,1b3,3b3	—	-0.7
	CP U	2	8	1	3	0	0	0	—	0	—	—	.375	.375	.375	129	0	—	.846	-0	155	0	1b2	—	-0.1
	Year	32	132	17	30	4	0	0	—	3	—	—	.227	.244	.258	60	-10	—	.743	2	158	231	O25(13/11/0),1b5,P3,3b3	—	-0.8
Wynegar, Butch	Harold Delano; B3.14.1956 York PA; BB/TR/6´0˝/(185–200); [MinA74 2/38]; d4.9; C4																								
1976	Min A★	149	534	58	139	21	2	10	69	79-7	2	63	.260	.356	.363	109	9	0-0	.978	-7	101	106	C137,D15	0	0.8
1977	Min A★	144	532	76	139	22	3	10	79	68-5	2	61	.261	.344	.370	97	-1	2-3	.993	-6	111	104	C142/3	0	-0.1
1978	Min A	135	454	36	104	22	1	4	45	47-2	6	42	.229	.307	.308	72	-15	1-0	.988	2	114	115	C131/3	0	-0.7
1979	Min A	149	504	74	136	20	0	7	57	74-5	2	36	.270	.363	.351	90	-4	2-2	.992	6	167	122	C146,D2	0	0.8
1980	Min A	146	486	61	124	18	3	5	57	63-6	2	36	.255	.339	.335	81	-11	3-1	.988	14	146	105	C142/D	0	0.9
1981	Min A	47	150	11	37	5	0	0	10	17-2	1	9	.247	.322	.280	72	-5	0-1	.995	-0	75	145	C37,D9	54	-0.4
1982	Min A	24	86	9	18	4	0	1	8	10-1	0	12	.209	.292	.291	59	-5	0-0	.986	-2	75	71	C24	0	-0.6
	NY A	63	191	27	56	8	1	3	20	40-1	1	21	.293	.413	.393	126	10	0-1	.993	2	105	89	C62	38	1.3
	Year	87	277	36	74	12	1	4	28	50-2	1	33	.267	.378	.361	105	5	0-1	.991	-1	97	84	C86	0	0.7
1983	NY A	94	301	40	89	18	2	6	42	52-1	1	29	.296	.399	.429	132	16	1-1	.985	-9	102	128	C93	15	1.1
1984	NY A	129	442	48	118	13	1	6	45	65-6	0	35	.267	.360	.342	99	2	1-4	.993	-1	101	103	C126	0	0.5
1985	NY A	102	309	27	69	15	0	5	32	64-2	0	43	.223	.356	.320	89	-2	0-0	.990	2	109	111	C96	15	0.5
1986	NY A	61	194	19	40	4	1	7	29	30-2	0	21	.206	.310	.345	79	-6	0-0	.994	2	98	84	C57	15	-0.1
1987	Cal A	31	92	4	19	2	0	0	5	9-0	0	13	.207	.277	.228	37	-8	0-0	.994	4	107	110	C28/D	114	-0.3
1988	Cal A	27	55	8	14	4	1	1	8	8-1	0	7	.255	.338	.418	117	1	0-0	.981	2	123	162	C26	130	0.4
Total	13	1301	4330	498	1102	176	15	65	506	626-41	17	428	.255	.348	.347	93	-19	10-13	.989	9	116	110	C1247,D28,3b2	381	4.1
Wynn, Jimmy	James Sherman "The Toy Cannon"; B3.12.1942 Hamilton OH; BR/TR/5´9˝/(159–170); d7.10; Col Central St.; OF(298/1181/355)																								
1963	Hou N	70	250	31	61	10	5	4	27	30-4	0	53	.244	.319	.372	107	2	4-2	.963	-7	104	153	O53(43/10/0),S21,3b2	0	-0.6
1964	Hou N	67	219	19	49	7	0	5	18	24-2	1	58	.224	.301	.324	81	-5	5-5	.958	2	97	200	O64(13/51/0)	0	-0.7
1965	Hou N	157	564	90	155	30	7	22	73	84-3	5	126	.275	.371	.470	146	37	43-4	.978	9	111	147	O155C	0	5.1
1966	Hou N	105	418	62	107	21	1	18	62	41-4	1	81	.256	.321	.440	118	10	13-10	.978	4	112	85	O104C	59	1.0
1967	Hou N★	158	594	102	148	29	3	37	107	74-7	2	137	.249	.331	.495	139	29	16-4	.968	1	109	48	O157C	0	3.0
1968	Hou N	156	542	85	146	23	5	26	67	90-9	5	131	.269	.376	.474	158	41	11-17	.988	11	100	**212**	O153(56/93/7)	0	4.7
1969	Hou N	149	495	113	133	17	1	33	87	**148**-14	3	142	.269	.436	.507	167	55	23-7	.985	3	106	109	O149C	0	5.8
1970	Hou N	157	554	82	156	32	2	27	88	106-12	1	96	.282	.394	.493	143	38	24-5	.987	3	98	149	O151(66/87/0)	0	3.8
1971	Hou N	123	404	38	82	16	0	7	45	56-6	2	63	.203	.302	.295	72	-14	10-5	.988	2	96	118	O116(1/48/72)	0	-1.7
1972	Hou N	145	542	117	148	29	3	24	90	103-6	2	99	.273	.389	.470	148	39	17-7	.983	-1	102	75	O144(0/12/132)	0	3.4
1973	Hou N	139	481	90	106	14	5	20	55	91-9	4	102	.220	.347	.395	107	6	14-11	.986	2	108	79	O133(2/10/125)	0	0.1
1974	†LA N★	150	535	104	145	17	4	32	108	108-4	0	104	.271	.387	.497	153	41	18-15	.992	0	101	113	O148C	0	3.7
1975	LA N★	130	412	80	102	16	0	18	58	110-2	1	77	.248	.403	.417	135	26	7-3	.983	-3	99	79	O120(21/107/0)	0	2.1
1976	Atl N	148	449	75	93	19	1	17	66	**127**-1	0	111	.207	.377	.367	107	11	16-6	.971	7	99	**196**	O138(90/50/0)	0	1.4
1977	NY A	30	77	7	11	2	1	1	3	15-1	0	16	.143	.283	.234	43	-6	1-0	1.000	1	121	157	D15,O8(5/0/3)	0	-0.5
	Mil A	36	117	10	23	3	1	0	10	17-0	0	31	.197	.294	.239	49	-8	3-0	.967	-2	91	0	O17(1/0/16),D15	0	-1.0
	Year	66	194	17	34	5	2	1	13	32-1	0	47	.175	.289	.237	46	-14	4-0	.981	-0	102	55	D30,O25(6/0/19)	0	-1.5
Total	15	1920	6653	1105	1665	285	39	291	964	1224-84	27	1427	.250	.366	.436	129	302	225-101	.981	33	103	122	O1810C,D30,S21,3b2	59	29.6

YEAR	TM LG	G	AB	R	H	2B	3B	HR	RBI	BB-IB	HP	SO	AVG	OBP	SLG	AOPS	ABR	SB-CS	FA	FR	RNG	THR	GAMES AT POSITION	DL	BFW
WYNNE, MARVELL	Marvell; B12.17.1959 Chicago IL; BL/TL/5´11˝/(169–185); d6.15																								
1983	Pit N	103	366	66	89	16	2	7	26	38-0	3	52	.243	.319	.355	84	-8	12-10	.983	-5	93	66	O102C	0	-1.5
1984	Pit N	154	653	77	174	24	11	0	39	42-0	0	81	.266	.310	.337	82	-17	24-19	.990	-7	93	91	O154C	0	-2.9
1985	Pit N	103	337	21	69	6	3	2	18	18-2	1	48	.205	.247	.258	42	-27	10-5	.987	3	107	132	O99C	30	-2.7
1986	SD N	137	288	34	76	19	2	7	37	15-2	1	45	.264	.300	.417	99	-2	11-11	.986	2	113	67	O125C	0	-0.2
1987	SD N	98	188	17	47	8	2	2	24	20-1	0	37	.250	.321	.346	80	-5	11-6	.981	-1	100	71	O71(33/40/5)	15	-0.7
1988	SD N	128	333	37	88	13	4	11	42	31-2	0	62	.264	.325	.426	117	6	3-4	.987	4	105	124	O113(37/84/10)	0	0.9
1989	SD N	105	294	19	74	11	1	6	35	12-1	1	41	.252	.282	.357	82	-8	4-1	.971	0	92	169	O96(39/41/25)	0	-1.0
	†Chi N	20	48	8	9	2	1	1	4	1-1	1	7	.188	.220	.333	52	-3	2-0	.944	-3	64	0	O13(4/6/3)	0	-0.6
	Year	125	342	27	83	13	2	7	39	13-2	2	48	.243	.274	.354	77	-11	6-1	.968	-3	88	147	O109(43/47/28)	0	-1.6
1990	Chi N	92	186	21	38	8	2	4	19	14-3	1	25	.204	.264	.333	59	-11	3-2	.991	-0	97	116	O66(13/54/4)	0	-1.2
Total	8	940	2693	300	664	107	28	40	244	191-12	8	398	.247	.297	.352	81	-75	80-58	.985	-7	99	102	O839(126/706/47)	45	-9.9
WYROSTEK, JOHNNY	John Barney; B7.12.1919 Fairmont City IL; D12.12.1986 St.Louis MO; BL/TR/6´2˝/(180–185); d9.10; Mil 1944–45																								
1942	Pit N	9	35	0	4	0	1	0	3	3	0	2	.114	.184	.171	4	-4	0	1.000	1	100	177	O8L	0	-0.5
1943	Pit N	51	79	7	12	3	0	0	1	3	0	15	.152	.183	.190	7	-10	0	.919	-2	112	0	O20(5/6/9),3b2/12	0	-1.3
1946	Phi N	145	545	73	153	30	4	6	45	70	3	42	.281	.366	.383	116	13	7	.981	5	102	135	O142(6/138/0)	0	1.5
1947	Phi N	128	454	68	124	24	7	5	51	61	4	45	.273	.364	.390	104	4	7	.971	0	100	109	O126(0/27/100)	0	0.0
1948	Cin N	136	512	74	140	24	9	17	76	52	3	63	.273	.344	.455	119	12	7	.977	-5	96	85	O130C	0	0.3
1949	Cin N	134	474	54	118	20	4	9	46	58	2	63	.249	.333	.365	86	-9	7	.971	-2	99	95	O129(2/60/67)	0	-1.5
1950	Cin N★	131	509	70	145	34	5	8	76	52	5	38	.285	.357	.418	103	3	1	.980	1	106	89	O129(11/9/115),1b4	0	0.0
1951	Cin N★	142	537	52	167	31	3	2	61	54	2	54	.311	.376	.391	105	6	2-1	.970	-9	93	62	O139(1/0/139)	0	-0.7
1952	Cin N	30	106	12	25	1	3	1	10	18	0	7	.236	.347	.330	89	-1	1-2	1.000	1	93	203	O29(0/25/6)/1	0	-0.2
	Phi N	98	321	45	88	16	3	1	37	44	1	26	.274	.363	.352	100	2	1-7	.972	5	115	116	O88(2/1/87)	0	0.2
	Year	128	427	57	113	17	6	2	47	62	1	33	.265	.359	.347	97	1	2-9	.980	7	**110**	138	O117(2/26/93)/1	0	0.0
1953	Phi N	125	409	42	111	14	2	6	47	38	4	43	.271	.339	.359	83	-10	0-3	.962	1	97	141	O110(8/0/102)	0	-1.3
1954	Phi N	92	259	28	62	12	4	3	28	29	1	39	.239	.314	.351	74	-10	0-0	.990	-1	105	129	O55(6/0/49),1b22	0	-1.4
Total	11	1221	4240	525	1149	209	45	58	481	482	25	437	.271	.349	.383	98	-4	33-13	.975	-5	101	106	O1105(49/396/674),1b28,3b2/2	0	-4.9
YAIK, HENRY	Henry; B3.1.1864 Detroit MI; D9.21.1935 Detroit MI; BL/5´11˝/185; d10.3																								
1888	Pit N	2	6	0	2	0	0	0	1	1	0	0	.333	.429	.333	159	1	0	.625	0	436	1104	/lfC	—	0.1
YALE, AD	William M.; B4.17.1870 Bristol CT; D4.27.1948 Bridgeport CT; BR; d9.18																								
1905	Bro N	4	13	1	1	0	0	0	1	1	0	—	.077	.143	.077	-37	-2	0	1.000	-0	43	190	1b4	—	-0.3
YANCY, HUGH	Hugh; B10.16.1949 Sarasota FL; BR/TR/5´11˝/170; [ChiA68 2/34]; d7.5																								
1972	Chi A	3	9	0	1	0	0	0	0	0-0	0	0	.111	.111	.111	-33	-1	0-1	1.000	1	122	0	3b3	0	-0.2
1974	Chi A	1	0	0	0	0	0	0	0	0-0	0	0	ø	ø	ø	ø	0	0-0	ø	0	—	—	/D	0	0.0
1976	Chi A	3	10	0	1	1	0	0	0	0-0	0	3	.100	.100	.200	-14	-1	0-0	1.000	-1	50	157	2b3	0	-0.2
Total	3	7	19	0	2	1	0	0	0	0-0	0	3	.105	.105	.158	-23	-2	0-1	1.000	-0	50	157	2b3,3b3/D	0	-0.4
YANKOWSKI, GEORGE	George Edward; B11.19.1922 Cambridge MA; BR/TR/6´0˝/180; d8.17; Mil 1943–46; Col Northeastern																								
1942	Phi A	6	13	0	2	1	0	0	2	0	0	2	.154	.154	.231	7	-2	0-0	1.000	0	*75*	*191*	C6	0	-0.1
1949	Chi A	12	18	0	3	1	0	0	2	0	0	2	.167	.167	.222	3	-3	0-0	1.000	1	*96*	*131*	C6	0	-0.2
Total	2	18	31	0	5	2	0	0	4	0	0	4	.161	.161	.226	5	-5	0-0	1.000	1	*86*	*160*	C12	0	-0.3
YANTZ, GEORGE	George Webb; B7.27.1886 Louisville KY; D2.26.1967 Louisville KY; BR/TR/5´6.5˝/168; d9.30																								
1912	Chi N	1	1	0	1	0	0	0	0	0	0	0	1.000	1.000	1.000	450	0	0	ø	0	*0*	*0*	/C	—	0.0
YARYAN, YAM	Clarence Everett; B11.5.1892 Knowlton IA; D11.16.1964 Birmingham AL; BR/TR/5´10.5˝/180; d4.23																								
1921	Chi A	45	102	11	31	8	2	0	15	9	1	16	.304	.366	.422	102	0	0-0	.933	-5	*77*	*125*	C34	—	-0.2
1922	Chi A	36	71	9	14	2	0	2	9	6	1	10	.197	.269	.310	51	-5	1-0	.966	0	*115*	*84*	C26	—	-0.4
Total	2	81	173	20	45	10	2	2	24	15	2	26	.260	.326	.376	81	-5	1-0	.948	-5	*93*	*108*	C60	—	-0.6
YASTRZEMSKI, CARL	Carl Michael "Yaz"; B8.22.1939 Southampton NY; BL/TR/5´11˝/(170–185); d4.11; HF1989; Col Notre Dame; OF(1917/159/7)																								
1961	Bos A	148	583	71	155	31	6	11	80	50-3	3	96	.266	.324	.396	90	-9	6-5	.963	-5	87	111	O147L	0	-2.2
1962	Bos A	**160**	646	99	191	43	6	19	94	66-7	3	82	.296	.363	.469	118	18	7-4	.969	8	100	161	O160L	0	1.7
1963	Bos A★	151	570	91	**183**	**40**	3	14	68	**95**-6	1	72	**.321**	**.418**	.475	145	**41**	8-5	.980	9	98	**173**	O151(151/1/0)	0	**4.2**
1964	Bos A	151	567	77	164	29	9	15	67	75-6	2	90	.289	.374	.451	122	19	6-5	.973	20	**122**	207	O148(18/131/0),3b2	0	3.5
1965	Bos A✳	133	494	78	154	**45**	3	20	72	70-8	1	58	.312	**.395**	**.536**	**154**	**38**	7-6	.987	3	95	147	O130(125/7/1)	0	3.5
1966	Bos A☆	160	594	81	165	**39**	2	16	80	84-10	1	60	.278	.368	.431	117	17	8-9	.985	10	106	151	O158(157/1/0)	0	1.7
1967	†Bos A★	161	579	**112**	**189**	31	4	**44**	**121**	91-11	4	69	**.326**	**.418**	**.622**	**189**	**67**	10-8	.978	6	102	120	O161(161/1/0)	0	**6.9**
1968	Bos A★	157	539	90	162	32	2	23	74	**119**-13	2	90	**.301**	**.426**	.495	169	**53**	13-6	.991	11	112	124	O155(154/1/0),1b3	0	**6.3**
1969	Bos A★	**162**	603	96	154	28	2	40	111	101-9	1	91	.255	.362	.507	135	29	15-7	.985	6	90	154	O143(140/3/0),1b22	0	2.7
1970	Bos A★	161	566	**125**	186	29	0	40	102	128-12	1	66	.329	**.452**	**.592**	**174**	**65**	23-13	.990	1	104	83	1b94,O69(67/3/0)	0	5.5
1971	Bos A★	148	508	75	129	21	2	15	70	106-12	1	60	.254	.381	.392	112	13	8-7	.993	11	106	**181**	O146L	0	1.6
1972	Bos A★	125	455	70	120	18	2	12	68	67-3	4	44	.264	.357	.391	117	12	5-4	.974	6	95	164	O83L,1b42	30	1.1
1973	Bos A✳	152	540	82	160	25	4	19	95	105-13	0	58	.296	.407	.463	137	32	9-7	.994	-4	94	100	1b107,3b31,O14L	0	1.8
1974	Bos A★	148	515	**93**	155	25	2	15	79	104-16	3	48	.301	.414	.445	139	33	12-7	.997	-8	90	96	1b84,O63L,D4	0	1.5
1975	†Bos A★	149	543	91	146	30	1	14	60	87-12	2	67	.269	.371	.405	110	11	8-4	.996	-1	94	93	1b140,O8L,D2	0	-0.1
1976	Bos A★	155	546	71	146	23	2	21	102	80-6	1	67	.267	.357	.432	118	14	5-6	.998	-9	76	105	1b94,O51L,D10	0	-0.7
1977	Bos A★	150	558	99	165	27	3	28	102	73-6	1	40	.296	.372	.505	124	20	11-1	**1.000**	11	103	**159**	O140(138/0/2),1b7,D6	0	2.6
1978	Bos A✳	144	523	70	145	21	2	17	81	76-8	3	44	.277	.367	.423	111	10	4-5	.986	2	86	166	O71(63/8/0),1b50,D27	0	0.5
1979	Bos A★	147	518	69	140	28	1	21	87	62-8	2	46	.270	.346	.450	108	7	3-3	.996	4	142	94	D56,1b51,O36L	0	0.3
1980	Bos A	105	364	49	100	21	1	15	50	44-5	0	38	.275	.350	.462	115	8	0-2	1.000	-2	83	111	D49,O39(34/1/4),1b16	0	0.1
1981	Bos A	91	338	36	83	14	1	7	53	49-4	0	28	.246	.338	.355	95	-1	0-1	.992	3	136	77	D48,1b39	0	-0.2
1982	Bos A★	131	459	53	126	22	1	16	72	59-1	2	50	.275	.358	.431	109	7	0-1	1.000	1	130	116	D102,1b14,O2C	0	0.4
1983	Bos A★	119	380	38	101	24	0	10	56	54-11	2	29	.266	.359	.408	103	4	0-0	1.000	-1	80	56	D107,1b2/lf	0	0.0
Total	23	3308	11988	1816	3419	646	59	452	1844	1845-190	40	1393	.285	.379	.462	128	508	168-116	.981	80	99	143	O2076L,1b765,D411,3b33	30	42.7
YATES, AL	Albert Arthur; B5.26.1945 Jersey City NJ; BR/TR/6´2˝/210; d5.13																								
1971	Mil A	24	47	5	13	2	0	1	4	3-0	0	7	.277	.308	.383	99	0	1-0	1.000	1	104	317	O12(3/0/9)	0	0.1
YEABSLEY, BERT	Robert Watkins; B12.17.1893 Philadelphia PA; D2.8.1961 Philadelphia PA; BR/TR/5´9.5˝/175; d5.28																								
1919	Phi N	3	0	0	0	0	0	0	0	1	0	0	ø	1.000	ø	200	0	0	ø	0	—	—	/H	—	0.0
YEAGER, GEORGE	George J. "Doc"; B6.5.1874 Cincinnati OH; D7.5.1940 Cincinnati OH; BR/TR/5´10˝/190; d9.25; OF(8/5/13)																								
1896	Bos N	2	5	1	1	0	0	0	0	0	0	1	.200	.200	.200	5	-1	0	1.000	-0	0	411	1b2	—	-0.1
1897	†Bos N	30	95	20	23	2	3	2	15	7	0	—	.242	.294	.389	75	-4	2	.970	1	*153*	*78*	C13,O10(2/1/7),2b4/3	—	-0.2
1898	Bos N	68	221	37	59	13	1	3	24	16	4	—	.267	.328	.376	96	-1	1	.951	-2	*117*	*86*	C37,1b17,O9(6/3/1),S2	—	-0.1
1899	Bos N	3	8	1	1	0	0	0	0	1	0	—	.125	.222	.125	-3	-1	0	1.000	0	0	0	O2(0/1/1)/C	—	-0.1
1901	Cle A	39	139	13	31	5	0	0	14	4	1	—	.223	.250	.259	43	-11	2	.964	0	*97*	*130*	C25,1b5,O3R,2b2	—	-0.7
	Pit N	26	91	9	24	2	1	0	10	4	1	—	.264	.302	.308	75	-3	1	.971	0	*128*	*92*	C20,3b4/1	—	-0.1
1902	NY N	39	108	6	22	2	1	0	9	11	0	—	.204	.277	.241	61	-5	1	.946	-1	*96*	*100*	C27,1b3/rf	—	-0.3
	Bal A	11	38	3	7	1	0	0	1	2	0	—	.184	.225	.211	20	-4	0	.930	-1	*94*	*124*	C11	—	-0.3
Total	6	218	705	90	168	25	6	5	73	45	6	1	.238	.290	.312	69	-30	7	.953	-2	*112*	*100*	C134,1b28,O25R,2b6,3b5,S2	—	-1.9
YEAGER, JOE	Joseph Francis "Little Joe"; B8.28.1875 Philadelphia PA; D7.2.1937 Detroit MI; BR/TR/5´10˝/160; d4.22; ▲																								
1898	Bro N	43	134	12	23	5	1	0	15	7	1	—	.172	.218	.224	27	-13	1	.908	5	137	125	P36,O4(2/1/1),S2/2	—	0.1
1899	Bro N	23	47	12	9	0	1	0	4	6	4	—	.191	.333	.234	55	-3	0	.914	3	117	232	S11,P10/lf3	—	0.1
1900	Bro N	3	9	0	3	0	0	0	0	0	0	—	.333	.333	.333	79	0	0	1.000	-1	70	0	P2/3	—	0.0
1901	Det A	41	125	18	37	7	1	2	17	4	5	—	.296	.343	.416	105	1	3	.919	5	115	**209**	P26,S12/2	—	0.4
1902	Det A	50	161	17	39	6	5	1	23	5	4	—	.242	.282	.360	76	-6	0	.957	1	127	67	P19,O13(7/0/6),2b12,S3/3	—	-0.4
1903	Det A	109	402	36	103	15	6	0	43	18	9	—	.256	.303	.323	91	-5	9	.921	-9	86	78	3b107/PS	—	-1.1
1905	NY A	115	401	54	107	16	7	0	42	25	13	—	.267	.330	.342	102	1	8	.923	1	99	78	3b91,S21	—	0.6

YEAR	TM LG	G	AB	R	H	2B	3B	HR	RBI	BB-IB	HP	SO	AVG	OBP	SLG	AOPS	ABR	SB-CS	FA	FR	RNG	THR	GAMES AT POSITION	DL	BFW
1906	NY A	57	123	20	37	6	1	0	12	13	9	—	.301	.407	.366	129	6	3	.905	0	93	133	S22,2b13,3b3	—	0.7
1907	StL A	123	436	32	104	21	7	1	44	31	3	—	.239	.294	.326	98	-1	11	.938	5	104	129	3b91,2b17,S10	—	0.7
1908	StL A	10	15	3	5	1	0	0	1	1	3	—	.333	.474	.400	183	2	2	1.000	0	114	0	2b4/S	—	0.2
Total	10	574	1853	204	467	77	29	4	201	110	51	—	.252	.312	.331	92	-18	37	.927	10	96	93	3b295,P94,S83,2b48,O18(10/1/7)	—	1.3
YEAGER, STEVE	Stephen Wayne; B11.24.1948 Huntington WV; BR/TR/6´0˝/(190–205); [LAN67 4/80]; d8.2																								
1972	LA N	35	106	18	29	0	1	4	15	16-2	1	26	.274	.374	.406	123	4	0-0	.984	5	86	77	C35	0	1.1
1973	LA N	54	134	18	34	5	0	2	10	15-1	3	33	.254	.340	.336	91	-1	1-0	.981	-2	97	71	C50	0	-0.1
1974	†LA N	94	316	41	84	16	1	12	41	32-5	2	77	.266	.334	.437	120	8	2-2	.992	9	139	87	C93	0	2.1
1975	LA N	135	452	34	103	16	1	12	54	40-7	8	75	.228	.298	.347	83	-11	2-5	.992	14	151	56	C135	0	0.7
1976	LA N	117	359	42	77	11	3	11	35	30-3	7	84	.214	.286	.354	82	-10	3-1	.985	13	**137**	98	C115	0	0.9
1977	†LA N	125	387	53	99	21	2	16	55	43-11	4	84	.256	.334	.444	107	4	1-3	.977	18	**163**	73	C123	0	2.6
1978	†LA N	94	228	19	44	7	0	4	23	36-11	0	41	.193	.301	.276	63	-11	0-0	.988	11	138	132	C91	17	0.4
1979	LA N	105	310	33	67	9	2	13	41	29-8	0	68	.216	.282	.384	82	-9	1-0	.984	7	126	105	C103	0	0.2
1980	LA N	96	227	20	48	8	0	2	20	20-6	0	54	.211	.274	.273	55	-14	2-3	.984	1	119	62	C95	0	-1.1
1981	†LA N	42	86	5	18	2	0	3	7	6-0	0	14	.209	.261	.337	72	-4	0-0	.994	-1	149	84	C40	0	-0.3
1982	LA N	82	196	13	48	5	2	2	18	13-3	1	28	.245	.294	.321	75	-7	0-0	.990	5	144	112	C76	28	0.0
1983	†LA N	113	335	31	68	8	3	15	41	23-4	1	57	.203	.256	.379	74	-14	1-1	.985	1	139	114	C112	22	-0.9
1984	LA N	74	197	16	45	4	0	4	29	20-1	0	38	.228	.295	.310	72	-8	1-2	.994	-5	106	87	C65	0	-1.1
1985	†LA N	53	121	4	25	4	1	0	9	7-2	0	24	.207	.246	.256	43	-10	0-1	.992	8	135	185	C48	0	-0.1
1986	Sea A	50	130	10	27	2	0	2	12	12-0	0	23	.208	.273	.269	48	-10	0-0	1.000	-3	113	104	C49	15	-1.0
Total	15	1269	3584	357	816	118	16	102	410	342-64	27	726	.228	.298	.355	82	-93	14-18	.987	80	135	92	C1230	82	3.4
YEATMAN, BILL	William Suter; B3.1839 Alexandria VA; D4.20.1901 York PA; d4.20																								
1872	Nat NA	1	4	0	0	0	0	0	0	0	—	1	.000	.000	.000	-86	-1	0-0	.000	-0	0	0	/rf	—	-0.1
YELDING, ERIC	Eric Girard; B2.22.1965 Montrose AL; BR/TR/5´11˝/165; [TorA84*1/19]; d4.9; Col Chipola (FL) JC																								
1989	Hou N	70	90	19	21	2	0	0	9	7-0	1	19	.233	.290	.256	61	-5	11-5	1.000	2	102	87	S15,2b13,O8(1/4/3)	0	-0.1
1990	Hou N	142	511	69	130	9	5	1	28	39-1	0	87	.254	.305	.297	69	-23	64-25	.971	-4	109	106	O94(11/83/6),S40,2b10,3b3	0	-2.0
1991	Hou N	78	276	19	67	11	1	1	20	13-3	0	46	.243	.276	.301	66	-13	11-9	.939	-10	87	88	S72,O4(0/3/1)	0	-2.0
1992	Hou N	9	8	1	2	0	0	0	0	0-0	0	3	.250	.250	.250	44	-1	0-0	ø	-1	0	0	S2,O2(2/1/0)	0	-0.1
1993	Chi N	69	108	14	22	5	1	1	10	11-2	0	22	.204	.277	.296	54	-7	3-2	.984	5	120	106	2b32,3b7/Scf	0	-0.1
Total	5	368	993	122	242	27	7	3	67	70-6	1	177	.244	.292	.294	66	-49	89-41	.948	-8	89	85	S130,O109(14/92/10),2b55,3b10	0	-4.3
YELLE, ARCHIE	Archie Joseph; B6.11.1892 Saginaw MI; D5.2.1983 Woodland CA; BR/TR/5´10.5˝/170; d5.12																								
1917	Det A	25	51	4	7	1	0	0	0	5	0	4	.137	.214	.157	13	-5	2	.975	-2	*85*	*94*	C24	—	-0.6
1918	Det A	56	144	7	25	3	0	0	7	9	1	15	.174	.227	.194	28	-13	0	.948	-1	*85*	*142*	C52	—	-1.2
1919	Det A	6	4	1	0	0	0	0	0	1	0	0	.000	.200	.000	-42	-1	0	.833	-1	*99*	*125*	C6	—	-0.1
Total	3	87	199	12	32	4	0	0	7	15	1	19	.161	.223	.181	23	-19	2	.952	-4	*85*	*130*	C82	—	-1.9
YERKES, STEVE	Stephen Douglas; B5.15.1888 Hatboro PA; D1.31.1971 Lansdale PA; BR/TR/5´9˝/165; d9.29; Col Penn																								
1909	Bos A	5	7	0	2	0	0	0	0	0	0	—	.286	.286	.286	79	0	0	1.000	-0	77	0	S2	—	-0.1
1911	Bos A	142	502	70	140	24	3	1	57	52	6	—	.279	.354	.345	96	-1	14	.927	-14	91	92	S116,2b14,3b11	—	-0.6
1912	†Bos A	131	523	73	132	22	6	0	42	41	4	—	.252	.312	.317	76	-17	4	.943	-15	92	101	2b131	—	-3.0
1913	Bos A	137	483	67	129	29	6	1	48	50	2	32	.267	.338	.358	101	1	11	.957	-21	91	67	2b129	—	-1.8
1914	Bos A	92	293	23	64	17	2	1	23	14	2	23	.218	.259	.300	68	-12	5-6	.972	-1	98	154	2b91	—	-1.4
	Pit F	39	142	18	48	9	5	1	25	11	0	13	.338	.386	.493	139	5	2	.974	7	115	86	S39	—	1.5
1915	Pit F	121	434	44	125	17	8	1	49	30	2	27	.288	.337	.371	100	-7	17	**.967**	-1	**101**	92	2b114,S8	—	-0.6
1916	Chi N	44	137	12	36	6	2	1	10	9	0	7	.263	.308	.358	94	-1	1	.919	-1	102	95	2b41	—	-0.2
Total	7	711	2521	307	676	124	32	6	254	207	16	102	.268	.328	.350	93	-32	54-6	.956	-46	95	97	2b520,S165,3b11	—	-6.2
YEWCIC, TOM	Thomas "Kibby"; B5.9.1932 Conemaugh PA; BR/TR/5´11˝/180; d6.27; Col Michigan St.																								
1957	Det A	1	1	0	0	0	0	0	0	0-0	0	0	.000	.000	.000	-97	0	0-0	.833	0	10	0	/C	0	0.0
YEWELL, ED	Edwin Leonard; B8.22.1862 Washington DC; D9.15.1940 Washington DC; d5.12																								
1884	Was AA	27	93	14	23	3	1	0	—	1	1	—	.247	.263	.301	95	0	—	.885	0	112	103	2b11,O8(1/2/5),3b7,S2	—	0.0
	Was U	1	4	0	0	0	0	0	—	0	—	—	.000	.000	.000	-99	-1	—	.571	-1	76	0	/3	—	-0.2
Total	1	28	97	14	23	3	1	0	—	1	—	—	.237	.253	.289	85	-1	—	.885	-1	112	103	2b11,3b8,O8(1/2/5),S2	—	-0.2
YINGLING, CHARLIE	Charles Christian; B12.7.1865 Baltimore MD; D4.13.1897 Baltimore MD; d6.22; b–Joe																								
1894	Phi N	1	4	0	1	0	0	0	0	0	0	1	.250	.250	.250	21	-1	0	1.000	-0	83	0	/S	—	-0.1
YOHE, BILL	William Clyde; B9.2.1878 Mt.Erie IL; D12.24.1938 Bremerton WA; BR/TR/5´8˝/180; d8.30																								
1909	Was A	21	72	6	15	2	0	0	4	3	0	—	.208	.240	.236	53	-4	2	.921	2	115	39	3b19	—	-0.2
YORK, RUDY	Preston Rudolph; B8.17.1913 Ragland AL; D2.5.1970 Rome GA; BR/TR/6´1˝/209; d8.22; M1/C4																								
1934	Det A	3	6	0	1	0	0	0	0	1	0	3	.167	.286	.167	19	-1	0-0	1.000	0	*0*	*332*	C2	—	-0.1
1937	Det A	104	375	72	115	18	3	35	103	41	0	52	.307	.375	.651	150	25	3-2	.960	-16	*86*	*79*	C54,3b41,1b2	—	1.3
1938	Det A★	135	463	85	138	27	2	33	127	92	2	74	.298	.417	.579	139	29	1-2	.990	4	***141***	*89*	C116,O14L/1	—	3.5
1939	Det A	102	329	66	101	16	1	20	68	41	2	50	.307	.387	.544	126	12	5-0	.985	-3	*104*	*111*	C67,1b19	—	1.2
1940	†Det A	**155**	588	105	186	46	6	33	134	89	4	88	.316	.410	.583	141	37	3-2	.990	4	105	76	1b155	—	2.5
1941	Det A★	**155**	590	91	153	29	3	27	111	92	1	88	.259	.360	.456	104	4	3-1	.986	-2	95	81	1b155	0	-1.2
1942	Det A★	153	577	81	150	26	4	21	90	73	0	71	.260	.343	.428	107	5	3-3	.988	15	**133**	90	1b152	0	0.6
1943	Det A★	**155**	571	90	155	22	11	**34**	**118**	84	1	88	.271	.366	**.527**	148	33	5-5	.990	19	**141**	81	1b155	0	4.6
1944	Det A☆	151	583	77	161	27	7	18	98	68	1	73	.276	.353	.439	119	14	5-3	.989	7	120	**124**	1b151	0	1.4
1945	†Det A	**155**	595	71	157	25	5	18	87	60	0	85	.264	.331	.413	109	5	6-6	.988	-1	98	109	1b155	0	-0.5
1946	†Bos A★	154	579	78	160	30	6	17	119	86	1	93	.276	.371	.437	118	16	3-2	.994	6	**111**	**118**	1b154	0	1.7
1947	Bos A	48	184	16	39	7	0	6	27	22	0	32	.212	.296	.348	73	-7	0-0	.995	2	108	106	1b48	0	-0.7
	Chi A☆	102	400	40	97	18	4	15	64	36	0	55	.243	.305	.420	104	-1	1-0	.995	1	103	111	1b102	0	-0.3
	Year	**150**	584	56	136	25	4	21	91	58	0	87	.233	.302	.397	94	-8	1-0	**.995**	3	105	109	1b150	0	-1.0
1948	Phi A	31	51	4	8	0	0	0	6	7	0	15	.157	.259	.157	12	-6	0-0	.988	-1	83	116	1b14	0	-0.7
Total	13	1603	5891	876	1621	291	52	277	1152	792	12	867	.275	.362	.483	121	165	38-26	.990	35	112	99	1b1263,C239,3b41,O14L	0	13.3
YORK, TOM	Thomas Jefferson; B7.13.1850 Brooklyn NY; D2.17.1936 New York NY; BL/5´9˝/165; d5.9; M2/U2																								
1871	Tro NA	**29**	145	36	37	5	7	2	23	9	—	1	.255	.299	.428	104	0	2-2	.855	3	152	278	O29C	—	0.2
1872	Bal NA	51	250	66	66	10	4	0	40	3	—	1	.264	.273	.336	82	-6	6-1	.916	10	120	185	O51(51/0/1)	—	0.4
1873	Bal NA	**57**	278	70	84	11	7	2	50	3	—	4	.302	.310	.414	113	4	4-1	**.872**	11	123	71	O57(56/1/0)	—	1.2
1874	Phi NA	50	224	36	56	4	7	0	37	5	—	4	.250	.266	.330	87	-4	1-0	.861	8	80	0	O50(49/1/0)	—	0.4
1875	Har NA	**86**	375	68	111	14	7	0	37	3	—	6	.296	.302	.371	126	8	7-3	.868	4	50	48	O86L	—	1.3
1876	Har N	67	263	47	68	12	7	1	39	10	—	4	.259	.286	.369	108	1	—	.899	3	71	52	O67(66/1/0)	—	0.0
1877	Har N	56	237	43	67	16	7	1	37	3	—	11	.283	.292	.422	137	11	—	.865	0	46	58	O56L	—	0.6
1878	Pro N	**62**	269	56	83	19	**10**	1	26	8	—	19	.309	.329	.465	159	16	—	.873	4	87	118	O62L,M	—	1.5
1879	Pro N	81	342	69	106	25	5	1	50	19	—	28	.310	.346	.421	154	21	—	.898	-4	49	106	O81L	—	1.1
1880	Pro N	53	203	21	43	9	2	0	18	8	—	29	.212	.242	.276	78	-4	—	.934	-2	41	55	O53(50/1/2)	—	-0.9
1881	Pro N	**85**	316	57	96	23	5	2	47	29	—	26	.304	.362	.427	150	20	—	.859	-2	75	29	O85L,M	—	1.2
1882	Pro N	81	321	48	86	23	7	1	40	19	—	14	.268	.309	.393	124	9	—	.876	-2	59	88	O81L	—	0.5
1883	Cle N	**100**	381	56	99	29	5	2	46	**37**	—	55	.260	.325	.378	114	9	—	.864	-1	66	89	O100L	—	0.5
1884	Bal AA	83	314	64	70	14	7	1	—	34	10	—	.223	.318	.322	105	3	—	.843	-5	44	42	O83(68/0/15)	—	-0.3
1885	Bal AA	22	87	6	23	4	2	0	12	8	0	—	.264	.326	.356	117	2	—	.938	1	103	128	O22(2/1/19)	—	0.2
Total	5NA	273	1272	276	354	44	32	4	187	23	—	16	.278	.291	.373	104	2	20-7	.875	35	95	93	O273(242/31/1)	—	3.5
Total	10	690	2733	467	741	174	57	10	315	175	10	186	.271	.317	.387	126	88	—	.879	-8	62	73	O690(651/3/36)	—	4.4
YORK, TONY	Tony Batton; B11.27.1912 Irene TX; D4.18.1970 Hillsboro TX; BR/TR/5´10˝/165; d4.18; Mil 1945																								
1944	Chi N	28	85	4	20	1	0	0	7	4	0	11	.235	.270	.247	46	-6	0	.940	7	121	64	S15,3b12	0	0.2

YOST, NED Edgar Frederick; B8.19.1954 Eureka CA; BR/TR/6´1˝/185; [NYN74 S1/7]; d4.12; M4/C12; Col Chabot (CA) JC

YEAR	TM LG	G	AB	R	H	2B	3B	HR	RBI	BB-IB	HP	SO	AVG	OBP	SLG	AOPS	ABR	SB-CS	FA	FR	RNG	THR	GAMES AT POSITION	DL	BFW
1980	Mil A	15	31	0	5	0	0	0	0	0-0	0	6	.161	.161	.161	-12	-5	0-0	1.000	1	108	86	C15	0	-0.4
1981	Mil A	18	27	4	6	0	0	3	3	3-0	0	6	.222	.300	.556	148	1	0-0	.956	-1	112	120	C16	0	0.1
1982	†Mil A	40	98	13	27	6	3	1	8	7-0	0	20	.276	.324	.429	110	1	3-1	.977	-8	96	19	C39/D	0	-0.5
1983	Mil A	61	196	21	44	5	1	6	28	5-0	0	36	.224	.243	.352	66	-10	1-0	.971	-13	68	43	C61	35	-2.1
1984	Tex A	80	242	15	44	4	0	6	25	6-0	0	47	.182	.201	.273	29	-24	1-2	.995	-12	61	59	C78	0	-3.5
1985	Mon N	5	11	1	2	0	0	0	0	0-0	0	2	.182	.182	.182	2	-1	0-0	.962	-2	27	0	C5	0	-0.4
Total	6	219	605	54	128	15	4	16	64	21-0	0	117	.212	.237	.329	56	-38	5-3	.982	-36	74	51	C214/D	35	-6.8

YOST, EDDIE Edward Frederick Joseph "The Walking Man"; B10.13.1926 Brooklyn NY; BR/TR/5´10˝/(170–185); d8.16; Mil 1945–46; M1/C23; Col NYU

YEAR	TM LG	G	AB	R	H	2B	3B	HR	RBI	BB-IB	HP	SO	AVG	OBP	SLG	AOPS	ABR	SB-CS	FA	FR	RNG	THR	GAMES AT POSITION	DL	BFW
1944	Was A	7	14	3	2	0	0	0	0	1	0	2	.143	.200	.143	-1	-2	0-0	.917	-1	74	0	3b3,S2	0	-0.3
1946	Was A	8	25	2	2	1	0	0	1	5	0	5	.080	.233	.120	1	-3	2-1	1.000	1	115	60	3b7	0	-0.3
1947	Was A	115	428	52	102	17	3	0	14	45	2	57	.238	.314	.292	71	-16	3-5	.958	-8	91	52	3b114	0	-2.7
1948	Was A	145	555	74	138	32	11	2	50	82	4	51	.249	.349	.357	91	-6	4-3	.966	-11	88	71	3b145	0	-1.7
1949	Was A	124	435	57	110	19	7	9	45	91	1	41	.253	.383	.391	107	7	3-3	.954	1	100	75	3b122	0	0.7
1950	Was A	**155**	573	114	169	26	2	11	58	**141**	8	63	.295	.440	.405	123	32	6-6	.945	-2	96	131	3b155	0	2.7
1951	Was A	**154**	568	109	161	**36**	4	12	65	126	11	55	.283	.423	.424	132	34	6-4	.954	-21	80	67	3b152,O3L	0	1.2
1952	Was A☆	**157**	587	92	137	32	3	12	49	**129**	8	73	.233	.378	.359	110	15	4-3	.962	-30	78	68	3b157	0	-1.6
1953	Was A	**152**	577	107	157	30	7	9	45	**123**	4	59	.272	.403	.395	119	23	7-4	.965	-11	91	90	3b152	0	1.2
1954	Was A	**155**	539	101	138	26	4	11	47	131	5	71	.256	.405	.380	123	26	7-3	.968	-4	98	95	3b155	0	2.2
1955	Was A	122	375	64	91	17	5	7	48	95-0	11	54	.243	.407	.371	117	16	4-3	.943	-4	96	95	3b107	0	1.1
1956	Was A	152	515	94	119	17	2	11	53	**151**-9	8	82	.231	.412	.336	100	10	8-5	.963	8	104	96	3b135,O8R	0	1.7
1957	Was A	110	414	47	104	13	5	9	38	73-2	5	49	.251	.370	.372	104	5	1-11	.952	-7	94	80	3b107	0	-0.6
1958	Was A	134	406	55	91	16	0	8	37	81-2	9	43	.224	.361	.323	93	1	3-6	**.964**	-9	87	85	3b114,O4L,1b2	0	-1.1
1959	Det A	148	521	**115**	145	19	0	21	61	**135**-1	12	77	.278	**.435**	.436	133	34	9-2	**.962**	-9	84	84	3b146/2	0	2.6
1960	Det A	143	497	78	129	23	2	14	47	**125**-1	8	69	.260	**.414**	.398	118	21	5-4	.933	-26	75	67	3b142	0	-0.6
1961	LA A	76	213	29	43	4	0	3	15	50-0	2	48	.202	.358	.263	62	-10	0-1	.964	-8	83	31	3b67	0	-1.8
1962	LA A	52	104	22	25	9	1	0	10	30-0	1	21	.240	.412	.346	111	4	0-2	.950	-3	91	40	3b28,1b7	0	0.0
Total	18	2109	7346	1215	1863	337	56	139	683	1614-15	99	920	.254	.394	.371	109	191	72-66	.957	-144	90	81	3b2008,O15(7/0/8),1b9,S2/2	0	2.7

YOTER, ELMER Elmer Elsworth; B6.26.1900 Plainfield PA; D7.26.1966 Camp Hill PA; BR/TR/5´7˝/155; d9.9

YEAR	TM LG	G	AB	R	H	2B	3B	HR	RBI	BB-IB	HP	SO	AVG	OBP	SLG	AOPS	ABR	SB-CS	FA	FR	RNG	THR	GAMES AT POSITION	DL	BFW
1921	Phi A	3	3	0	0	0	0	0	0	0	0	0	.000	.000	.000	-99	-1	0-0	ø	0	—	—	/H	—	-0.1
1924	Cle A	19	66	3	18	1	1	0	7	5	0	8	.273	.324	.318	65	-4	0-0	.905	-1	108	33	3b19	—	-0.3
1927	Chi N	13	27	2	6	1	1	0	5	4	0	4	.222	.323	.333	76	-1	0	.947	0	118	0	3b11	—	0.0
1928	Chi N	1	0	0	0	0	0	0	0	0	0	0	ø	ø	ø	ø	0	0	ø	-0	0	0	/3	—	0.0
Total	4	36	96	5	24	2	2	0	12	9	0	12	.250	.314	.313	63	-6	0-0	.915	-1	110	24	3b31	—	-0.4

YOUKILIS, KEVIN Kevin Edmund; B3.15.1979 Cincinnati OH; BR/TR/6´1˝/220; [BosA01 8/243]; d5.15; Col Cincinnati

YEAR	TM LG	G	AB	R	H	2B	3B	HR	RBI	BB-IB	HP	SO	AVG	OBP	SLG	AOPS	ABR	SB-CS	FA	FR	RNG	THR	GAMES AT POSITION	DL	BFW
2004	†Bos A	72	208	38	54	11	0	7	35	33-0	4	45	.260	.367	.413	98	1	0-1	.968	5	108	78	3b65,D2	16	0.5
2005	Bos A	44	79	11	22	7	0	1	9	14-0	2	19	.278	.400	.405	111	2	0-1	1.000	-2	95	102	3b24,1b9,2b2	0	-0.1
2006	Bos A	147	569	100	159	42	2	13	72	91-0	9	120	.279	.381	.429	109	12	5-2	.995	5	96	104	1b127,O18L,3b16	0	0.6
Total	3	263	856	149	235	60	2	21	116	138-0	15	184	.275	.379	.423	106	15	5-4	.996	8	92	103	1b136,3b105,O18L,2b2,D2	16	1.0

YOUNG, CHRIS Christopher Brandon; B9.5.1983 Houston TX; BR/TR/6´2˝/180; [ChiA01 16/493]; d8.18

YEAR	TM LG	G	AB	R	H	2B	3B	HR	RBI	BB-IB	HP	SO	AVG	OBP	SLG	AOPS	ABR	SB-CS	FA	FR	RNG	THR	GAMES AT POSITION	DL	BFW
2006	Ari N	30	70	10	17	4	0	2	10	6-0	1	12	.243	.308	.386	73	-3	2-1	1.000	2	121	121	O24C	0	-0.1

YOUNG, DEL Delmer Edward; B5.11.1912 Cleveland OH; D12.8.1979 San Francisco CA; BB/TR/5´11˝/168; d4.19; f–Del

YEAR	TM LG	G	AB	R	H	2B	3B	HR	RBI	BB-IB	HP	SO	AVG	OBP	SLG	AOPS	ABR	SB-CS	FA	FR	RNG	THR	GAMES AT POSITION	DL	BFW
1937	Phi N	109	360	36	70	9	2	0	24	18	1	55	.194	.235	.231	25	-38	6	.950	7	**111**	103	2b108	—	-2.5
1938	Phi N	108	340	27	78	13	2	0	31	20	2	35	.229	.276	.279	55	-21	0	.933	-1	104	78	S87,2b17	—	-1.6
1939	Phi N	77	217	22	57	9	2	3	20	8	0	24	.263	.289	.364	77	-8	1	.946	-12	88	59	S55,2b17	—	-1.7
1940	Phi N	15	33	2	8	0	1	0	1	2	0	1	.242	.286	.303	65	-2	0	.962	-1	84	107	S6,2b5	—	-0.2
Total	4	309	950	87	213	31	7	3	76	48	3	115	.224	.264	.281	48	-69	7	.938	-7	98	73	S148,2b147	—	-6.0

YOUNG, DEL Delmer John; B10.24.1885 Macon MO; D12.17.1959 Cleveland OH; BL/TR/5´11˝/195; d9.24; s–Del

YEAR	TM LG	G	AB	R	H	2B	3B	HR	RBI	BB-IB	HP	SO	AVG	OBP	SLG	AOPS	ABR	SB-CS	FA	FR	RNG	THR	GAMES AT POSITION	DL	BFW
1909	Cin N	2	7	0	2	0	0	0	1	1	0	—	.286	.375	.286	106	0	0	1.000	0	371	0	O2(1/0/1)	—	0.0
1914	Buf F	80	174	17	48	5	5	4	22	3	0	13	.276	.288	.431	92	-6	0	.944	-3	98	39	O41(7/2/32)	—	-1.1
1915	Buf F	12	15	0	2	0	0	0	0	1	0	0	.133	.188	.133	-9	-2	1	.667	-1	70	0	O3(0/1/2)	—	-0.3
Total	3	94	196	17	52	5	5	4	23	5	0	13	.265	.284	.403	85	-8	1	.933	-3	112	35	O46(8/3/35)	—	-1.4

YOUNG, DELMON Delmon Damarcus; B9.14.1985 Birmingham AL; BR/TR/6´3˝/205; [TBA03 1/1]; d8.29; f–Dmitri

YEAR	TM LG	G	AB	R	H	2B	3B	HR	RBI	BB-IB	HP	SO	AVG	OBP	SLG	AOPS	ABR	SB-CS	FA	FR	RNG	THR	GAMES AT POSITION	DL	BFW
2006	TB A	30	126	16	40	9	1	3	10	1-0	3	24	.317	.336	.476	109	1	2-2	.983	0	89	216	O30(0/1/30)	0	0.0

YOUNG, DELWYN Delwyn Rudy; B6.30.1982 Los Angeles CA; BB/TR/5´8˝/210; [LAN02 4/121]; d9.7; Col Santa Barbara (CA) CC

YEAR	TM LG	G	AB	R	H	2B	3B	HR	RBI	BB-IB	HP	SO	AVG	OBP	SLG	AOPS	ABR	SB-CS	FA	FR	RNG	THR	GAMES AT POSITION	DL	BFW
2006	LA N	8	5	0	0	0	0	0	0	0-0	0	1	.000	.000	.000	-99	-2	0-0	ø	-0	0	0	O2(1/0/1)	0	-0.2

YOUNG, DMITRI Dmitri Dell; B10.11.1973 Vicksburg MS; BB/TR/6´2˝/(220–245); [StLN91 1/4]; d8.29; s–Delmon; OF(403/0/102)

YEAR	TM LG	G	AB	R	H	2B	3B	HR	RBI	BB-IB	HP	SO	AVG	OBP	SLG	AOPS	ABR	SB-CS	FA	FR	RNG	THR	GAMES AT POSITION	DL	BFW
1996	†StL N	16	29	3	7	0	0	0	2	4-0	1	5	.241	.353	.241	60	-1	0-1	.976	-2	22	103	1b10	0	-0.4
1997	StL N	110	333	38	86	14	3	5	34	38-3	2	63	.258	.335	.363	83	-8	6-5	.985	-2	88	95	1b74,O17(9/0/10)/D	18	-1.6
1998	Cin N	144	536	81	166	48	1	14	83	47-4	2	94	.310	.364	.481	120	17	2-4	.940	-8	89	49	O105(91/0/14),1b44	0	0.0
1999	Cin N	127	373	63	112	30	2	14	56	30-1	2	71	.300	.352	.504	111	6	3-1	.976	0	107	81	O91(23/0/75),1b9/D	0	0.2
2000	Cin N	152	548	68	166	37	6	18	88	36-6	3	80	.303	.346	.491	106	4	0-3	.978	-5	91	65	O111(111/0/1),1b36,D4	0	-0.8
2001	Cin N	142	540	68	163	28	3	21	69	37-10	5	77	.302	.350	.481	107	5	8-5	.957	-0	96	147	O87(86/0/1),1b38,3b36	0	0.0
2002	Det A	54	201	25	57	14	0	7	27	12-5	2	39	.284	.329	.458	111	3	2-0	.971	2	179	40	D35,1b15/3lf	107	0.2
2003	Det A☆	155	562	78	167	34	7	29	85	58-16	11	130	.297	.372	.537	143	35	2-1	.985	3	99	131	D75,O61L,3b16/1	0	3.0
2004	Det A	104	389	72	106	23	2	18	60	33-4	6	71	.272	.336	.481	115	8	0-1	1.000	1	114	73	D74,1b25,O2L/3	54	0.2
2005	Det A	126	469	61	127	25	3	21	72	29-7	9	100	.271	.325	.471	110	6	1-0	.990	2	123	100	D71,1b30,O20(19/0/1)	0	0.1
2006	Det A	48	172	19	43	4	1	7	23	11-0	0	39	.250	.293	.407	81	-6	1-1	.889	1	392	157	D44,1b3	80	-0.7
Total	11	1178	4152	576	1200	257	28	154	599	335-56	43	769	.289	.346	.476	111	69	25-22	.966	-8	97	93	O495L,D305,1b285,3b54	259	0.2

YOUNG, DON Donald Wayne; B10.18.1945 Houston TX; BR/TR/6´2˝/185; d9.9

YEAR	TM LG	G	AB	R	H	2B	3B	HR	RBI	BB-IB	HP	SO	AVG	OBP	SLG	AOPS	ABR	SB-CS	FA	FR	RNG	THR	GAMES AT POSITION	DL	BFW
1965	Chi N	11	35	1	2	0	0	1	2	0-0	0	11	.057	.056	.143	-45	-7	0-0	.933	-1	80	0	O11C	0	-0.9
1969	Chi N	101	272	36	65	12	3	6	27	38-5	5	74	.239	.343	.371	89	-3	1-5	.975	-2	100	75	O100(3/94/8)	0	-1.0
Total	2	112	307	37	67	12	3	7	29	38-5	5	85	.218	.313	.345	76	-10	1-5	.972	-3	98	69	O111(3/105/8)	0	-1.9

YOUNG, ERIC Eric Orlando; B5.18.1967 New Brunswick NJ; BR/TR/5´9˝/(170–185); [LAN89 43/1123]; d7.30; Col Rutgers

YEAR	TM LG	G	AB	R	H	2B	3B	HR	RBI	BB-IB	HP	SO	AVG	OBP	SLG	AOPS	ABR	SB-CS	FA	FR	RNG	THR	GAMES AT POSITION	DL	BFW
1992	LA N	49	132	9	34	1	0	1	11	8-0	0	9	.258	.300	.288	68	-6	6-1	.957	4	104	84	2b43	0	0.1
1993	Col N	144	490	82	132	16	8	3	42	63-3	4	41	.269	.355	.353	78	-14	42-19	.962	-1	104	82	2b79,O52(46/10/0)	0	-1.0
1994	Col N	90	228	37	62	13	1	7	30	38-1	2	17	.272	.378	.430	95	0	18-7	.981	-0	95	123	O60L/2	0	-0.1
1995	†Col N	120	366	68	116	21	**9**	6	36	49-3	5	29	.317	.404	.473	102	3	35-12	.973	8	107	112	2b77,O19L	0	1.6
1996	Col N★	141	568	113	184	23	4	8	74	47-1	21	31	.324	.393	.421	94	-3	**53**-19	.985	27	111	**114**	2b139	21	3.5
1997	Col N	118	468	78	132	29	6	6	45	57-0	5	37	.282	.363	.408	83	-9	32-12	.978	**26**	120	117	2b117	0	2.4
	LA N	37	154	28	42	4	2	2	16	14-1	4	17	.273	.347	.364	93	-2	13-2	.979	-16	70	82	2b37	0	-1.4
	Year	155	622	106	174	33	8	8	61	71-1	9	54	.280	.359	.397	85	-11	45-14	.978	10	107	108	2b154	0	1.0
1998	LA N	117	452	78	129	24	1	8	43	45-0	5	32	.285	.355	.396	103	3	42-13	.976	-3	96	96	2b113/D	18	1.0
1999	LA N	119	456	73	128	24	2	2	41	63-0	5	26	.281	.371	.355	90	-4	51-22	.984	-5	101	88	2b116	20	0.0
2000	Chi N	153	607	98	180	40	2	6	47	63-1	8	39	.297	.367	.399	96	-2	54-7	.979	-1	98	90	2b150	0	1.3
2001	Chi N	149	603	98	168	43	4	6	42	42-1	9	45	.279	.333	.393	90	-8	31-14	.981	-3	91	80	2b147	0	-0.3
2002	Mil N	138	496	57	139	29	3	3	28	39-0	6	38	.280	.338	.369	87	-9	31-11	.979	-2	99	95	2b123,O2(1/0/1),D2	0	-0.2
2003	Mil N	109	404	71	105	18	1	15	31	48-2	4	34	.260	.344	.421	99	-1	25-7	.968	-14	94	81	2b99	0	-0.7
	SF N	26	71	9	14	2	0	0	3	9-0	1	10	.197	.293	.225	38	-6	3-5	.989	2	112	109	2b18,O2C/D	0	-0.4
	Year	135	475	80	119	20	1	15	34	57-2	5	44	.251	.336	.392	89	-7	28-12	.971	-12	97	85	2b117,O2C/D	0	-1.1
2004	Tex A	104	344	55	99	25	2	1	27	43-0	8	28	.288	.377	.381	95	0	14-9	.976	-5	80	158	O53(47/9/0),D23,2b20,S8/3	0	-0.6
2005	†SD N	56	142	22	39	9	0	2	12	18-0	0	12	.275	.356	.380	98	0	7-6	1.000	1	126	0	O25(21/4/0),2b14	85	0.0
2006	SD N	56	128	19	26	5	0	3	13	13-1	2	16	.203	.281	.313	57	-9	8-2	.980	-3	87	0	O39(36/2/1)/2	0	-1.1

YEAR	TM LG	G	AB	R	H	2B	3B	HR	RBI	BB-IB	HP	SO	AVG	OBP	SLG	AOPS	ABR	SB-CS	FA	FR	RNG	THR	GAMES AT POSITION	DL	BFW
	Tex A	4	10	1	2	1	1	0	2	1-0	0	1	.200	.273	.500	94	0	0-0	1.000	2	200	269	/2lfD	0	0.1
Total	15	1730	6119	996	1731	327	46	79	543	660-14	89	462	.283	.359	.390	90	-67	465-168	.976	18	101	95	2b1295,O253(231/27/2),D28,S8/3	144	4.2
YOUNG, ERNIE	Ernest Wesley; B7.8.1969 Chicago IL; BR/TR/6´1˝/(190–234); [OakA90 10/289]; d5.17; Col Lewis																								
1994	Oak A	11	30	2	2	1	0	0	3	1-0	0	8	.067	.097	.100	-53	-7	0-0	.958	1	123	179	O10(7/3/1)/D	0	-0.6
1995	Oak A	26	50	9	10	3	0	2	5	8-0	0	12	.200	.310	.380	82	-1	0-0	.946	-1	103	0	O24(7/7/10)	0	-0.2
1996	Oak A	141	462	72	112	19	4	19	64	52-1	7	118	.242	.326	.424	89	-9	7-5	.997	3	104	97	O140(8/133/17)	0	-0.5
1997	Oak A	71	175	22	39	7	0	5	15	19-0	2	57	.223	.303	.349	70	-8	1-3	.980	2	102	169	O66(2/59/12)/D	0	-0.7
1998	KC A	25	53	2	10	3	0	1	3	2-0	1	9	.189	.232	.302	36	-5	2-1	1.000	3	130	183	O24(1/5/19)	23	-0.3
1999	Ari N	6	11	1	2	0	0	0	0	3-0	1	2	.182	.400	.182	54	-1	0-0	1.000	2	158	480	O4(1/0/3)	0	0.1
2003	Det A	5	11	0	2	0	0	0	0	4-0	0	5	.182	.400	.182	64	0	0-2	ø	0	—	—	D4	0	-0.1
2004	Cle A	3	4	0	2	0	0	0	0	1-0	0	2	.500	.600	.500	199	1	0-0	ø	0	—	—	D2	0	0.1
Total	8	288	796	108	179	33	4	27	90	90-1	11	213	.225	.310	.378	76	-30	10-11	.989	9	107	122	O268(26/207/62),D8	23	-2.2
YOUNG, GEORGE	George Joseph; B4.1.1890 Brooklyn NY; D3.13.1950 Brightwaters NY; BL/TR/6´0˝/185; d8.10																								
1913	Cle A	2	2	0	0	0	0	0	0	0	0	0	.000	.000	.000	-97	-1	0	ø	0	—	—	/H	—	-0.1
YOUNG, GERALD	Gerald Anthony; B10.22.1964 Tela, Honduras; BB/TR/6´2˝/185; [NYN82 5/111]; d7.8																								
1987	Hou N	71	274	44	88	9	2	1	15	26-0	1	27	.321	.380	.380	107	3	26-9	.980	-1	98	144	O67C	0	0.5
1988	Hou N	149	576	79	148	21	9	0	37	66-1	3	66	.257	.334	.325	94	-3	65-27	.992	1	99	156	O145C	0	0.2
1989	Hou N	146	533	71	124	17	3	0	38	74-4	2	60	.233	.326	.276	77	-14	34-25	**.998**	14	111	**197**	O143C	0	-0.2
1990	Hou N	57	154	15	27	4	1	1	4	20-0	0	23	.175	.269	.234	41	-12	6-3	.990	-1	94	177	O50C	0	-1.4
1991	Hou N	108	142	26	31	3	1	1	11	24-0	0	17	.218	.327	.275	76	-4	16-5	1.000	2	107	188	O84(6/76/5)	0	0.0
1992	Hou N	74	76	14	14	1	1	0	4	10-0	0	11	.184	.279	.224	46	-5	6-2	.964	1	114	0	O57(6/14/43)	80	-0.5
1993	Col N	19	19	5	1	0	0	0	1	4-0	0	1	.053	.217	.053	-20	-3	0-1	.882	0	137	0	O11(4/3/5)	0	-0.4
1994	StL N	16	41	5	13	3	2	0	3	3-0	0	8	.317	.364	.488	119	1	2-1	1.000	-1	94	0	O11(3/6/2)	0	0.0
Total	8	640	1815	259	446	58	19	3	113	227-5	6	213	.246	.329	.304	82	-37	155-73	.990	17	104	160	O568(19/504/55)	80	-1.8
YOUNG, HERMAN	Herman John; B4.14.1886 Boston MA; D12.13.1966 Ipswich MA; BR/TR/5´8˝/155; d6.11																								
1911	Bos N	9	25	2	6	0	0	0	0	0	1	3	.240	.269	.240	40	-2	0	.905	2	122	111	3b5,S3	—	0.0
YOUNG, JOHN	John Thomas; B2.9.1949 Los Angeles CA; BL/TL/6´3˝/210; d9.9; Col Chapman																								
1971	Det A	2	4	1	2	1	0	0	1	0-0	0	0	.500	.500	.750	240	1	0-0	1.000	-0	0	0	/1	0	0.1
YOUNG, KEVIN	Kevin Stacey; B6.16.1969 Alpena MI; BR/TR/6´3˝/(210–225); [PitN90 7/187]; d7.12; Col Southern Mississippi																								
1992	Pit N	10	7	2	4	0	0	0	4	2-0	0	0	.571	.667	.571	255	2	1-0	.750	-2	22	0	3b7/1	0	0.0
1993	Pit N	141	449	38	106	24	3	6	47	36-3	9	82	.236	.300	.343	74	-17	2-2	**.998**	10	**124**	112	1b135,3b6	0	-1.8
1994	Pit N	59	122	15	25	7	2	1	11	8-2	1	34	.205	.258	.320	49	-9	0-2	1.000	-0	66	138	1b37,3b17/O(1/0/1)	0	-1.2
1995	Pit N	56	181	13	42	9	0	6	22	8-0	2	53	.232	.268	.381	68	-9	1-3	.919	5	120	89	3b48,1b6	15	-0.5
1996	KC A	55	132	20	32	6	0	8	23	11-0	0	32	.242	.301	.470	90	-3	3-3	1.000	-1	114	142	1b27,O17(2/0/15),3b7,D3	0	-0.6
1997	Pit N	97	333	59	100	18	3	18	74	16-1	4	89	.300	.332	.535	122	9	11-2	.997	3	106	86	1b77,3b12,O11(10/0/1)	40	0.7
1998	Pit N	159	592	88	160	40	2	27	108	44-1	11	127	.270	.328	.481	110	7	15-7	.994	-13	70	112	1b157	0	-1.9
1999	Pit N	156	584	103	174	41	6	26	106	75-5	12	124	.298	.387	.522	127	26	22-10	.985	-4	96	**116**	1b155	0	0.9
2000	Pit N	132	496	77	128	27	0	20	88	32-1	8	96	.258	.311	.433	86	-12	8-3	.986	-11	73	110	1b129/D	0	-3.2
2001	Pit N	142	449	53	104	33	0	14	65	42-3	11	119	.232	.310	.399	80	-13	15-11	.994	-2	96	113	1b137	0	-2.6
2002	Pit N	146	468	60	115	26	1	16	51	50-2	4	101	.246	.322	.408	89	-7	4-6	.991	2	110	106	1b144	0	-1.9
2003	Pit N	52	84	8	17	4	0	2	7	12-0	0	25	.202	.302	.321	62	-5	1-0	.995	0	113	128	1b44/rf	0	-0.6
Total	12	1205	3897	536	1007	235	17	144	606	336-18	62	882	.258	.324	.438	95	-31	83-49	.992	-13	95	111	1b1049,3b97,O30(13/0/18),D4	55	-12.7
YOUNG, PEP	Lemuel Floyd; B8.29.1907 Jamestown NC; D1.14.1962 Jamestown NC; BR/TR/5´9˝/162; d4.25																								
1933	Pit N	25	20	3	6	1	1	0	0	0	0	5	.300	.300	.450	112	0	0	1.000	-0	93	0	/2S	—	0.0
1934	Pit N	19	17	3	4	0	0	0	2	0	0	6	.235	.235	.235	26	-2	0	1.000	1	203	189	2b2,S2	—	0.0
1935	Pit N	128	494	60	131	25	10	7	82	21	2	59	.265	.298	.399	83	-14	2	.952	-16	89	86	2b107,3b6,O6(1/0/5),S4	—	-2.2
1936	Pit N	125	475	47	118	23	10	6	77	29	1	52	.248	.293	.377	77	-17	3	.966	-22	88	57	2b123	—	-3.1
1937	Pit N	113	408	43	106	20	3	9	54	26	1	63	.260	.306	.390	88	-8	4	.942	13	116	133	S45,3b39,2b30	—	1.1
1938	Pit N	149	562	58	156	36	5	4	79	40	3	64	.278	.329	.381	94	-4	7	.973	25	**110**	**130**	2b149	—	3.0
1939	Pit N	84	293	34	81	14	3	3	29	23	2	29	.276	.333	.375	92	-4	1	.967	3	103	108	2b84	—	0.4
1940	Pit N	54	136	19	34	8	2	2	20	12	2	23	.250	.320	.382	94	-1	1	.909	-4	100	51	2b33,S7,3b5	—	-0.4
1941	Cin N	4	12	2	2	0	0	0	0	0	1	1	.167	.231	.167	13	-1	0	.923	0	97	164	3b3	0	-0.1
	StL N	2	2	0	0	0	0	0	0	0	0	2	.000	.000	.000	-94	-1	0	ø	0	—	—	/H	0	-0.1
	Year	6	14	2	2	0	0	0	0	0	1	3	.143	.200	.143	-2	-2	0	.923	0	97	164	3b3	0	-0.2
1945	StL N	27	47	5	7	1	0	1	4	1	0	8	.149	.167	.234	10	-6	0	.978	-1	80	72	S11,3b9,2b3	0	-0.7
Total	10	730	2466	274	645	128	34	32	347	152	12	312	.262	.308	.380	85	-58	18	.964	-1	98	94	2b532,S70,3b62,O6(1/0/5)	0	-2.1
YOUNG, MICHAEL	Michael Brian; B10.19.1976 Covina CA; BR/TR/6´0˝/(185–200); [TorA97 5/149]; d9.29; Col California–Santa Barbara																								
2000	Tex A	2	2	0	0	0	0	0	0	0-0	0	1	.000	.000	.000	-99	-1	0-0	ø	-1	0	0	/2	0	-0.1
2001	Tex A	106	386	57	96	18	4	11	49	26-0	3	91	.249	.298	.402	81	-12	3-1	.984	-1	99	107	2b104	0	-0.7
2002	Tex A	156	573	77	150	26	8	9	62	41-1	0	112	.262	.308	.382	81	-17	6-7	.988	14	**104**	95	2b152,S11,3b4	0	0.3
2003	Tex A	160	666	106	204	33	9	14	72	36-1	1	103	.306	.339	.446	99	-2	13-2	.987	8	100	102	2b159,S7	0	1.5
2004	Tex A★	160	690	114	216	33	9	22	99	44-1	1	89	.313	.353	.483	111	10	12-3	.972	-21	93	93	S158,D2	0	0.2
2005	Tex A★	159	668	114	**221**	40	5	24	91	58-0	3	91	**.331**	.385	.513	133	32	5-2	.974	-15	96	88	S155,D4	0	2.9
2006	Tex A★	**162**	691	93	217	52	3	14	103	48-0	1	96	.314	.356	.459	110	11	7-3	.981	23	**112**	109	S155,D7	0	4.2
Total	7	905	3676	561	1104	202	38	94	476	253-3	9	583	.300	.344	.453	105	21	46-18	.976	8	100	97	S486,2b416,D13,3b4	0	8.3
YOUNG, MIKE	Michael Darren; B3.20.1960 Oakland CA; BB/TR/6´2˝/(194–206); [BalA80*S1/11]; d9.14; Col St. Marys (CA)																								
1982	Bal A	6	2	2	0	0	0	0	0	0-0	0	1	.000	.000	.000	-99	-1	0-0	1.000	0	399	0	/lfD	0	0.0
1983	Bal A	25	36	5	6	2	1	0	2	2-0	1	8	.167	.231	.278	40	-3	1-0	.929	-0	100	108	O22(14/0/8),D3	0	-0.4
1984	Bal A	123	401	59	101	17	2	17	52	58-2	7	110	.252	.355	.431	119	12	6-2	.982	-7	92	55	O115(40/1/85)/D	0	0.0
1985	Bal A	139	450	72	123	22	1	28	81	48-5	4	104	.273	.348	.513	135	21	1-5	.975	2	104	106	O90(83/0/20),D37	0	1.6
1986	Bal A	117	369	43	93	15	1	9	42	49-2	3	90	.252	.342	.371	96	-1	3-1	.962	0	113	24	O69L,D38	0	-0.4
1987	Bal A	110	363	46	87	10	1	16	39	46-2	2	91	.240	.328	.405	95	-3	10-7	.975	-3	102	0	O60(54/7/0),D47	37	-0.9
1988	Phi N	75	146	13	33	14	0	1	14	26-1	1	43	.226	.343	.342	96	1	0-0	.938	1	126	0	O42(3/0/39)	0	0.1
	Mil A	8	14	2	0	0	0	0	0	2-1	1	5	.000	.176	.000	-45	-3	0-0	ø	-0	0	0	O2(1/0/1),D5	0	-0.3
1989	Cle A	32	59	2	11	0	0	1	5	6-1	1	13	.186	.273	.237	44	-4	1-2	1.000	-0	61	0	D15/lf	0	-0.6
Total	8	635	1840	244	454	80	6	72	235	237-14	20	465	.247	.338	.414	106	19	22-17	.969	-6	103	50	O402(266/8/153),D148	37	-0.9
YOUNG, BABE	Norman Robert; B7.1.1915 Astoria NY; D12.25.1983 Everett MA; BL/TL/6´2.5˝/185; d9.26; Mil 1943–45; Col Fordham																								
1936	NY N	1	1	0	0	0	0	0	0	0	0	0	.000	.000	.000	-99	0	0	ø	0	—	—	/H	—	0.0
1939	NY N	22	75	8	23	4	0	3	14	5	3	6	.307	.373	.480	127	3	0	.982	-2	70	101	1b22	—	-0.1
1940	NY N	149	556	75	159	27	4	17	101	69	2	28	.286	.367	.441	121	17	4	.992	-1	93	96	1b147	—	0.2
1941	NY N	152	574	90	152	28	5	25	104	66	5	39	.265	.346	.462	124	17	1	.986	-3	94	98	1b150	0	0.0
1942	NY N	101	287	37	80	17	1	11	59	34	5	22	.279	.365	.460	140	15	1	.972	-2	90	93	O54C,1b18	0	1.0
1946	NY N	104	291	30	81	11	0	7	33	30	0	21	.278	.346	.388	107	3	3	.988	-5	74	64	1b49,O24(0/17/7)	0	-0.5
1947	NY N	14	14	0	1	1	0	0	0	0	0	1	.071	.071	.143	-44	-3	0	ø	0	—	—	/H	0	-0.3
	Cin N	95	364	55	103	21	3	14	79	35	2	26	.283	.349	.473	117	8	0	.990	-1	96	86	1b93	0	0.4
	Year	109	378	55	104	22	3	14	79	35	2	27	.275	.340	.460	111	5	0	.990	-1	96	86	1b93	0	0.1
1948	Cin N	49	130	11	30	7	2	1	12	19	0	12	.231	.329	.338	84	-3	0	.993	1	106	128	1b31/rf	0	-0.3
	StL N	41	111	14	27	5	2	1	13	16	0	6	.243	.339	.351	82	-2	0	.996	-4	43	110	1b35	0	-0.7
	Year	90	241	25	57	12	4	2	25	35	0	18	.237	.333	.344	83	-5	0	.995	-3	75	119	1b66/rf	0	-1.0
Total	8	728	2403	320	656	121	17	79	415	274	17	161	.273	.352	.436	117	55	9	.989	-18	90	94	1b545,O79(0/71/8)	0	-0.3
YOUNG, RALPH	Ralph Stuart; B9.19.1888 Philadelphia PA; D1.24.1965 Philadelphia PA; BB/TR/5´5˝/165; d4.10; Col Washington College																								
1913	NY A	7	15	2	1	0	0	0	0	3	0	3	.067	.222	.067	-15	-2	2	.857	0	110	134	S7	—	-0.2
1915	Det A	123	378	44	92	6	5	0	31	53	2	31	.243	.339	.286	83	-7	12-11	.950	-1	107	101	2b119	—	-0.8
1916	Det A	153	528	60	139	16	6	1	45	62	1	43	.263	.342	.322	96	-2	20-20	.966	-6	97	87	2b146,S6/3	—	-0.8
1917	Det A	141	503	64	116	18	2	1	35	61	3	35	.231	.317	.280	83	-8	8	.958	5	107	77	2b141	—	-0.1

YEAR	TM LG	G	AB	R	H	2B	3B	HR	RBI	BB-IB	HP	SO	AVG	OBP	SLG	AOPS	ABR	SB-CS	FA	FR	RNG	THR	GAMES AT POSITION	DL	BFW
1918	Det A	91	298	31	56	7	1	0	21	54	0	17	.188	.313	.218	63	-11	15	.939	-12	96	67	2b91	—	-2.4
1919	Det A	125	456	63	96	13	5	1	25	53	1	32	.211	.294	.268	60	-24	8	.970	11	108	78	2b120,S5	—	-1.1
1920	Det A	150	594	84	173	21	6	0	33	85	2	30	.291	.382	.347	96	1	8-13	.969	-11	93	64	2b150	—	-1.0
1921	Det A	107	401	70	120	8	3	0	29	69	3	23	.299	.406	.334	91	-1	11-9	.947	-21	84	78	2b106	—	-1.9
1922	Phi A	125	470	62	105	19	2	1	35	55	3	21	.223	.309	.279	53	-32	8-6	.960	-7	97	81	2b120	—	-3.6
Total	9	1022	3643	480	898	108	30	4	254	495	15	235	.247	.339	.296	79	-86	92-59	.959	-42	99	79	2b993,S18/3	—	-11.9
Young, Dick	Richard Ennis; B6.3.1928 Seattle WA; BL/TR (BB 1952)/5´11˝/175; d9.11																								
1951	Phi N	15	68	7	16	5	0	0	2	3	0	6	.235	.268	.309	55	-4	0-1	.922	-6	83	77	2b15	0	-1.1
1952	Phi N	5	9	3	2	1	0	0	0	1	0	3	.222	.300	.333	76	0	1-0	.900	-1	80	96	2b2	0	0.0
Total	2	20	77	10	18	6	0	0	2	4	0	9	.234	.272	.312	58	-4	1-1	.919	-7	83	79	2b17	0	-1.1
Young, Bobby	Robert George; B1.22.1925 Granite MD; D1.28.1985 Baltimore MD; BL/TR/6´1˝/175; d8.30																								
1948	StL N	3	1	0	0	0	0	0	0	0	0	1	.000	.000	.000	-95	0	0	1.000	-0	0	0	/3	0	0.0
1951	StL A	147	611	75	159	13	9	1	31	44	0	51	.260	.310	.316	67	-30	8-7	.980	-4	102	88	2b147	0	-2.6
1952	StL A	149	575	59	142	15	9	4	39	56	0	48	.247	.314	.325	76	-20	3-3	.984	-7	97	112	2b149	0	-2.0
1953	StL A	148	537	48	137	22	2	4	25	41	1	40	.255	.309	.326	70	-23	2-1	.977	-19	87	97	2b148	0	-3.2
1954	Bal A	130	432	43	106	13	6	4	24	54	1	42	.245	.329	.331	88	-7	4-4	.976	-14	92	82	2b127	0	-1.3
1955	Bal A	59	186	5	37	3	0	1	8	11-1	0	23	.199	.244	.231	30	-19	1-4	.985	-1	104	100	2b58	0	-1.8
	Cle A	18	45	7	14	1	1	0	6	1-0	0	2	.311	.326	.378	86	-1	0-0	.983	4	121	192	2b11/3	0	0.4
	Year	77	231	12	51	4	1	1	14	12-1	0	25	.221	.259	.260	42	-20	1-4	.985	3	107	115	2b69/3	0	-1.4
1956	Cle A	1	0	0	0	0	0	0	0	0-0	0	0	ø	ø	ø	ø	0	0-0	ø	0	—	—	/R	0	0.0
1958	Phi N	32	60	7	14	1	1	1	4	1-0	0	5	.233	.246	.333	52	-4	0-0	.968	-4	85	61	2b21	0	-0.8
Total	8	687	2447	244	609	68	28	15	137	208-1	2	212	.249	.308	.318	71	-104	18-19	.980	-46	96	96	2b661,3b2	0	-11.3
Young, Russ	Russell Charles; B9.15.1902 Bryan OH; D5.13.1984 Roseville CA; BB/TR/6´0˝/175; d4.16																								
1931	StL A	16	34	2	4	0	0	1	2	2	0	4	.118	.167	.206	-3	-5	0-0	1.000	2	*124*	*90*	C16	—	-0.3
Young, Walter	Walter Ernest; B2.18.1980 Hattiesburg MS; BL/TR/6´5˝/320; [PitN99 31/932]; d9.6																								
2005	Bal A	14	33	2	10	1	0	1	3	4-1	0	7	.303	.378	.424	114	1	0-0	1.000	1	156	163	1b10,D3	0	0.1
Youngblood, Joel	Joel Randolph; B8.28.1951 Houston TX; BR/TR/6´0˝/(160–180); [CinN70*2/40]; d4.13; C5; OF(233/107/454)																								
1976	Cin N	55	57	8	11	1	1	0	1	2-0	1	8	.193	.233	.246	35	-5	1-0	.938	-0	112	241	O9(3/3/3),3b6/C2	0	-0.6
1977	StL N	25	27	1	5	2	0	0	1	3-0	0	5	.185	.267	.259	42	-2	0-2	1.000	-0	76	0	O11(10/0/1),3b6	0	-0.4
	NY N	70	182	16	46	11	1	0	11	13-1	0	40	.253	.301	.324	71	-8	1-3	.954	7	107	140	2b33,O22(4/7/13),3b10	0	-0.1
	Year	95	209	17	51	13	1	0	12	16-1	0	45	.244	.296	.316	67	-10	1-5	1.000	7	110	224	O33(14/7/14),2b33,3b16	0	-0.5
1978	NY N	113	266	40	67	12	8	7	30	16-1	1	39	.252	.294	.436	105	0	4-0	.989	6	116	303	O50(7/14/33),2b39,3b9/S	0	0.7
1979	NY N	158	590	90	162	37	5	16	60	60-7	7	84	.275	.346	.436	115	13	18-13	.985	9	107	155	O147(70/5/87),2b13,3b12	0	1.6
1980	NY N	146	514	58	142	26	2	8	69	52-10	2	69	.276	.340	.381	104	4	14-11	.984	21	**126**	**200**	O121(0/39/96),3b21,2b6	0	2.0
1981	NY N★	43	143	16	50	10	2	4	25	12-1	2	19	.350	.398	.531	165	12	2-5	.962	2	101	202	O41(4/2/36)	86	1.2
1982	NY N	80	202	21	52	12	0	3	21	8-1	5	37	.257	.302	.361	85	-4	0-4	.969	-1	99	156	O63(15/8/43),2b8/S3	0	-0.9
	Mon N	40	90	16	18	2	0	0	8	9-1	3	21	.200	.291	.222	45	-6	2-1	1.000	-0	106	57	O35(0/2/33)	0	-0.8
	Year	120	292	37	70	14	0	3	29	17-2	8	58	.240	.299	.318	72	-11	2-5	.979	-1	102	120	O98(15/10/76),2b8/S3	0	-1.7
1983	SF N	124	373	59	109	20	3	17	53	33-4	5	59	.292	.356	.499	139	19	7-4	.948	-14	94	79	2b64,3b28,O22(14/0/8)	0	0.7
1984	SF N	134	469	50	119	17	1	10	51	48-1	4	86	.254	.328	.358	95	-3	5-6	.887	-22	85	52	3b117,O11(4/0/8),2b5	0	-2.9
1985	SF N	95	230	24	62	6	0	4	24	30-1	1	37	.270	.355	.348	102	1	3-2	.955	-0	100	121	O56(7/17/34)/3	0	-0.1
1986	SF N	97	184	20	47	12	0	5	28	18-0	1	34	.255	.320	.402	104	1	1-1	1.000	-0	87	94	O45(29/0/17),1b7,3b5,2b4/S	0	-0.1
1987	SF N	69	91	9	23	3	0	3	11	5-0	1	13	.253	.296	.385	83	-3	1-1	1.000	1	96	220	O22(9/1/14),3b2	0	-0.3
1988	SF N	83	123	12	31	4	0	0	16	10-0	1	17	.252	.307	.285	76	-4	1-1	.980	-1	101	0	O45(22/9/18)	0	-0.6
1989	Cin N	76	118	13	25	5	0	3	13	13-2	2	21	.212	.299	.331	78	-3	0-1	.970	-3	65	75	O45(35/0/10)	0	-0.8
Total	14	1408	3659	453	969	180	23	80	422	332-30	36	589	.265	.329	.392	103	12	60-55	.981	3	106	159	O745R,3b218,2b173,1b7,S3/C	86	-1.4
Youngman, Henry	Henry; B1865 Indiana PA; D1.24.1936 Pittsburgh PA; TR/5´9˝/175; d4.19																								
1890	Pit N	13	47	6	6	1	1	0	4	6	0	9	.128	.226	.191	25	-4	1	.750	-3	101	198	3b7,2b6	—	-0.6
Youngs, Ross	Ross Middlebrook "Pep" (b Royce Middlebrook Youngs); B4.10.1897 Shiner TX; D10.22.1927 San Antonio TX; BL/TR/5´8˝/162; d9.25; HF1972																								
1917	NY N	7	26	5	9	2	3	0	1	1	0	5	.346	.370	.654	218	3	1	1.000	1	93	202	O7(1/6/0)	—	-0.4
1918	NY N	121	474	70	143	16	8	1	25	44	6	49	.302	.368	.376	129	18	10	.950	-4	99	89	O120R,2b7	—	0.8
1919	NY N	130	489	73	152	**31**	7	2	43	51	7	47	.311	.384	.415	142	28	24	.942	1	96	117	O130R	—	2.3
1920	NY N	153	581	92	204	27	14	6	78	75	2	55	.351	.427	.477	161	49	18-18	.935	0	96	129	O153R	—	4.1
1921	†NY N	141	504	90	165	24	16	3	102	71	1	47	.327	.411	.456	129	24	21-17	.978	-3	96	87	O137R	—	0.9
1922	†NY N	149	559	105	185	34	10	7	86	55	7	50	.331	.398	.465	121	19	17-9	.942	3	94	144	O147R	—	1.0
1923	†NY N	152	596	**121**	200	33	12	3	87	73	5	36	.336	.412	.446	128	28	13-19	.959	-2	90	123	O152R	—	0.9
1924	†NY N	133	526	112	187	33	12	10	74	77	3	31	.356	.441	.521	161	50	11-9	.955	-3	93	110	O132R,2b2	—	3.5
1925	NY N	130	500	82	132	24	6	6	53	66	4	51	.264	.354	.372	89	-6	17-11	.952	-10	80	123	O127R,2b3	—	-2.5
1926	NY N	95	372	62	114	12	5	4	43	37	2	19	.306	.372	.398	109	5	21	.974	0	87	138	O94R	—	-0.2
Total	10	1211	4627	812	1491	236	93	42	592	550	37	390	.322	.399	.441	131	218	153-83	.953	-17	92	119	O1199(1/6/1192),2b12	—	11.2
Yount, Eddie	Floyd Edwin; B12.19.1915 Newton NC; D10.26.1973 Newton NC; BR/TR/6´1˝/185; d9.9; Col Wake Forest																								
1937	Phi A	4	7	1	2	0	0	0	1	0	0	1	.286	.286	.286	45	-1	0-0	1.000	-0	91	0	O2(1/1/0)	—	-0.1
1939	Pit N	2	2	0	0	0	0	0	0	0	0	2	.000	.000	.000	-99	-1	0	ø	0	—	—	/H	—	-0.1
Total	2	6	9	1	2	0	0	0	1	0	0	3	.222	.222	.222	14	-2	0-0	1.000	-0	91	0	O2(1/1/0)	—	-0.2
Yount, Robin	Robin R; B9.16.1955 Danville IL; BR/TR/6´0˝/(160–180); [MilA73 1/3]; d4.5; C4; HF1999; b–Larry; OF(69/1150/0)																								
1974	Mil A	107	344	48	86	14	5	3	26	12-0	1	46	.250	.276	.346	79	-11	7-7	.962	-9	103	91	S107	0	-0.9
1975	Mil A	147	558	67	149	28	2	8	52	33-3	1	69	.267	.307	.367	90	-8	12-4	.939	-13	96	86	S145	0	-0.3
1976	Mil A	**161**	638	59	161	19	3	2	54	38-3	0	69	.252	.292	.301	76	-21	16-11	.963	-3	99	102	S161/cf	0	-0.4
1977	Mil A	154	605	66	174	34	4	4	49	41-1	2	80	.288	.333	.377	93	-5	16-7	.964	-3	99	102	S153	0	0.8
1978	Mil A	127	502	66	147	23	9	9	71	24-1	1	43	.293	.323	.428	110	4	16-5	.959	21	114	106	S125	28	4.0
1979	Mil A	149	577	72	154	26	5	8	51	35-3	1	52	.267	.308	.371	83	-15	11-8	.969	4	107	100	S149	0	0.4
1980	Mil A★	143	611	121	179	**49**	10	23	87	26-1	1	67	.293	.321	.519	130	22	20-5	.961	3	106	101	S133,D9	0	4.0
1981	†Mil A	96	377	50	103	15	5	10	49	22-1	2	37	.273	.312	.419	115	6	4-1	**.985**	30	**124**	**132**	S93,D3	0	4.7
1982	†Mil A★	156	635	129	**210**	**46**	12	29	114	54-2	1	63	.331	.379	**.578**	**168**	**58**	14-3	.969	-4	101	102	S154/D	0	**7.1**
1983	Mil A★	149	578	102	178	42	**10**	17	80	72-6	3	58	.308	.383	.503	153	44	12-5	.973	-3	98	100	S139,D8	0	5.6
1984	Mil A	160	624	105	186	27	7	16	80	67-7	1	67	.298	.362	.441	127	23	14-4	.971	17	111	104	S120,D39	0	5.2
1985	Mil A	122	466	76	129	26	3	15	68	49-3	2	56	.277	.342	.442	115	10	10-4	.970	-3	100	56	O108(69/40/0),D12,1b2	0	0.4
1986	Mil A	140	522	82	163	31	7	9	46	62-7	4	73	.312	.388	.450	124	19	14-5	**.997**	3	103	130	O131C,1b3,D6	0	2.2
1987	Mil A	158	635	99	198	25	9	21	103	76-10	1	94	.312	.384	.479	124	23	19-9	.987	-2	99	75	O150C,D8	0	1.9
1988	Mil A	**162**	621	92	190	38	**11**	13	91	63-10	3	63	.306	.369	.465	132	27	22-4	.996	3	99	157	O158C,D4	0	3.2
1989	Mil A	160	614	101	195	38	9	21	103	63-9	6	71	.318	.384	.511	152	43	19-3	.981	-4	96	104	O143C,D17	0	4.0
1990	Mil A	158	587	98	145	17	5	17	77	78-6	6	89	.247	.337	.380	102	2	15-8	.991	-6	100	36	O157C/D	0	-0.4
1991	Mil A	130	503	66	131	20	4	10	77	54-8	4	79	.260	.332	.376	99	0	6-4	.994	-5	101	16	O117C,D13	24	-0.7
1992	Mil A	150	557	71	147	40	3	8	77	53-9	3	81	.264	.325	.390	103	3	15-6	.995	-6	95	75	O139C,D11	0	-0.4
1993	Mil A	127	454	62	117	25	3	8	51	44-5	5	93	.258	.326	.379	91	-6	9-2	.997	-1	100	96	O114C,1b7,D6	17	-0.4
Total	20	2856	11008	1632	3142	583	126	251	1406	966-95	48	1350	.285	.342	.430	115	218	271-105	.964	20	104	102	S1479,O1218C,D138,1b12	69	40.0
Yurak, Jeff	Jeffrey Lynn; B2.26.1954 Pasadena CA; BB/TR/6´3˝/195; [SFN74 24/536]; d9.15; Col Citrus (CA) JC																								
1978	Mil A	5	5	0	0	0	0	0	0	1-0	0	0	.000	.167	.000	-49	-1	0-0	1.000	1	332	0	/lf	0	-0.1
Yvars, Sal	Salvador Anthony; B2.20.1924 New York NY; BR/TR/5´10˝/187; d9.27																								
1947	NY N	1	5	0	1	0	0	0	0	0	0	2	.200	.200	.200	6	-1	0	1.000	-0	*0*	*0*	/C	0	-0.1
1948	NY N	15	38	4	8	1	0	1	6	3	1	1	.211	.286	.316	62	-2	0	1.000	2	*104*	*109*	C15	0	0.0
1949	NY N	3	8	0	0	0	0	0	0	1	0	1	.000	.111	.000	-68	-2	0	1.000	0	*69*	*0*	C2	0	-0.2
1950	NY N	9	14	0	2	0	0	0	0	1	0	2	.143	.200	.143	-8	-2	0	.963	1	*137*	*185*	C9	0	-0.1
1951	†NY N	25	41	9	13	2	0	2	3	5	2	7	.317	.417	.512	147	3	0-0	.942	-2	*131*	*78*	C23	0	0.2
1952	NY N	66	151	15	37	3	0	4	18	10	1	16	.245	.296	.344	77	-5	0-0	.988	6	*205*	*138*	C59	0	0.3

YEAR	TM LG	G	AB	R	H	2B	3B	HR	RBI	BB-IB	HP	SO	AVG	OBP	SLG	AOPS	ABR	SB-CS	FA	FR	RNG	THR	GAMES AT POSITION	DL	BFW
1953	NY N	23	47	1	13	0	0	0	1	7	0	1	.277	.370	.277	71	-2	0-0	1.000	1	*134*	*118*	C20	0	0.0
	StL N	30	57	4	14	2	0	1	6	4	1	6	.246	.306	.333	67	-3	0-1	.989	1	*91*	*146*	C26	0	-0.1
	Year	53	104	5	27	2	0	1	7	11	1	7	.260	.336	.308	69	-4	0-1	.994	3	*112*	*133*	C46	0	-0.1
1954	StL N	38	57	8	14	4	0	2	8	6	1	5	.246	.328	.421	93	-1	1-0	1.000	-1	*140*	*154*	C21	0	-0.1
Total	8	210	418	41	102	12	0	10	42	37	6	41	.244	.315	.344	76	-15	1-1	.987	9	*150*	*127*	C176	0	-0.1
ZACHER, ELMER	Elmer Henry "Silver"; B9.17.1880 Buffalo NY; D12.20.1944 Buffalo NY; BR/TR/5´9˝/190; d4.30																								
1910	NY N	1	0	0	0	0	0	0	0	0	0	0	ø	ø	ø	ø	0	0	1.000	0	132	0	/cf	—	0.0
	StL N	47	132	7	28	5	1	0	10	10	2	19	.212	.278	.265	61	-7	3	.966	2	107	143	O36(11/12/13)/2	—	-0.6
	Year	48	132	7	28	5	1	0	10	10	2	19	.212	.278	.265	61	-7	3	.966	2	107	142	O37(11/13/13)/2	—	-0.6
ZAHNER, FRED	Frederick Joseph; B6.5.1870 Louisville KY; D7.24.1900 Louisville KY; d7.23																								
1894	Lou N	14	49	7	10	0	1	0	4	3	0	6	.204	.250	.245	21	-7	2	.778	-3	*102*	*60*	C10,O2R/1S	—	-0.7
1895	Lou N	21	49	7	11	1	1	0	6	6	1	4	.224	.321	.286	61	-3	0	.824	-5	*90*	*114*	C21	—	-0.6
Total	2	35	98	14	21	1	2	0	10	9	1	10	.214	.287	.265	41	-10	2	.805	-8	*94*	*94*	C31,O2R/S1	—	-1.3
ZAK, FRANKIE	Frank Thomas; B2.22.1922 Passaic NJ; D2.6.1972 Passaic NJ; BR/TR/5´10˝/150; d4.21																								
1944	Pit N☆	87	160	33	48	3	1	0	11	22	0	18	.300	.385	.331	99	1	6	.948	-1	104	88	S67	0	0.3
1945	Pit N	15	28	2	4	2	0	0	3	3	0	5	.143	.226	.214	22	-3	0	.971	1	117	83	S10/2	0	-0.2
1946	Pit N	21	20	8	4	0	0	0	0	1	0	0	.200	.238	.200	24	-2	0	.929	4	159	148	S10	0	0.3
Total	3	123	208	43	56	5	1	0	14	26	0	23	.269	.350	.303	82	-4	6	.948	4	110	93	S87/2	0	0.4
ZALUSKY, JACK	John Francis; B6.22.1879 Minneapolis MN; D8.11.1935 Minneapolis MN; BR/TR/5´11.5˝/172; d9.4																								
1903	NY A	7	16	2	5	0	0	0	1	1	0	—	.313	.353	.313	95	0	0	1.000	-1	*100*	*63*	C6/1	—	-0.1
ZAMBRANO, EDDIE	Eduardo Jose (Guerra); B2.1.1966 Maracaibo, Zulia, Venez.; BR/TR/6´2˝/(175–200); d9.19																								
1993	Chi N	8	17	1	5	0	0	0	2	1-0	0	3	.294	.333	.294	70	-1	0-0	1.000	-1	24	0	O4(1/0/3),1b2	0	-0.2
1994	Chi N	67	116	17	30	7	0	6	18	16-0	1	29	.259	.353	.474	113	2	2-1	.944	-3	85	71	O27(9/0/18),1b9,3b4	0	-0.2
Total	2	75	133	18	35	7	0	6	20	17-0	1	32	.263	.351	.451	108	1	2-1	.946	-4	79	64	O31(10/0/21),1b11,3b4	0	-0.4
ZAPUSTAS, JOE	Joseph John; B7.25.1907 Boston MA; D1.14.2001 Brockton MA; BR/TR/6´1˝/185; d9.28; Col Fordham																								
1933	Phi A	2	5	0	1	0	0	0	0	0	0	0	.200	.200	.200	6	-1	0-0	1.000	-0	83	0	O2(1/1/0)	—	-0.1
ZARDON, JOSE	Jose Antonio (Sanchez) "Guineo"; B5.20.1923 Havana, Cuba; BR/TR/6´0˝/150; d4.18																								
1945	Was A	54	131	13	38	5	3	0	13	7	0	11	.290	.326	.374	112	1	3-1	.972	2	121	64	O43(16/25/3)	0	0.2
ZARILLA, AL	Allen Lee "Zeke"; B5.1.1919 Los Angeles CA; D8.28.1996 Honolulu HI; BL/TR/5´11˝/180; d6.30; Mil 1945; C1																								
1943	StL A	70	228	27	58	7	1	2	17	17	1	20	.254	.309	.320	82	-5	1-1	.962	1	104	123	O60(0/6/56)	0	-0.8
1944	†StL A	100	288	43	86	13	6	6	45	29	6	33	.299	.375	.448	127	10	1-1	.977	-0	104	65	O79(74/2/4)	0	0.6
1946	StL A	125	371	46	96	14	9	4	43	27	1	37	.259	.311	.377	87	-8	3-5	.973	10	**111**	169	O107(46/17/51)	0	-0.4
1947	StL A	127	380	34	85	15	6	3	38	40	3	45	.224	.303	.318	71	-15	3-6	.986	-2	97	86	O110(23/22/72)	0	-2.4
1948	StL A★	144	529	77	174	39	3	12	74	48	4	48	.329	.389	.482	128	21	11-6	.962	-9	96	47	O136(26/58/61)	0	0.7
1949	StL A	15	56	10	14	1	0	1	6	8	1	2	.250	.354	.321	76	-2	1-1	1.000	-2	74	0	O15(10/1/8)	0	-0.5
	Bos A	124	474	68	133	32	4	9	71	48	4	51	.281	.352	.422	97	-3	4-4	.984	-5	98	52	O122(2/2/119)	0	-1.2
	Year	139	530	78	147	33	4	10	77	56	5	53	.277	.352	.411	95	-4	5-5	.985	-7	96	47	O137(12/3/127)	0	-1.7
1950	Bos A	130	471	92	153	32	10	9	74	76	4	47	.325	.423	.493	122	18	2-3	.976	-4	92	114	O128R	0	0.9
1951	Chi A	120	382	56	98	21	2	10	60	60	4	57	.257	.363	.401	109	6	2-4	.983	-9	80	94	O117(7/0/112)	0	-0.7
1952	Chi A	39	99	14	23	4	1	2	7	14	1	6	.232	.333	.354	90	-1	1-0	.974	-2	80	123	O32(17/0/18)	0	-0.4
	StL A	48	130	20	31	6	0	1	9	27	1	15	.238	.373	.308	88	0	2-1	.976	2	101	205	O35(21/10/8)	0	0.0
	Bos A	21	60	9	11	0	1	2	8	7	0	8	.183	.269	.317	58	-4	2-0	.941	1	92	247	O19(0/6/14)	0	-0.3
	Year	108	289	43	65	10	2	5	24	48	2	29	.225	.339	.325	83	-5	5-1	.968	1	92	188	O86(38/16/40)	0	-0.7
1953	Bos A	57	67	11	13	2	0	0	4	14	0	13	.194	.333	.224	50	-4	0-1	.947	-1	85	130	O18(3/7/9)	0	-0.5
Total	10	1120	3535	507	975	186	43	61	456	415	30	382	.276	.357	.405	102	13	33-33	.974	-19	96	97	O978(229/131/660)	0	-5.0
ZAUCHIN, NORM	Norbert Henry; B11.17.1929 Royal Oak MI; D1.31.1999 Birmingham AL; BR/TR/6´4.5˝/(220–225); d9.23; Mil 1952–53																								
1951	Bos A	5	12	0	2	1	0	0	0	0	0	4	.167	.167	.250	11	-2	0-1	.957	0	121	327	1b4	0	-0.2
1955	Bos A	130	477	65	114	10	0	27	93	69-1	3	105	.239	.335	.430	97	-3	3-0	**.995**	0	98	95	1b126	0	-1.0
1956	Bos A	44	84	12	18	2	0	2	11	14-0	1	22	.214	.333	.310	63	-4	0-0	.990	-1	75	95	1b31	0	-0.7
1957	Bos A	52	91	11	24	3	0	3	14	9-0	2	13	.264	.343	.396	96	0	0-0	.972	-1	106	138	1b36	0	-0.2
1958	Was A	96	303	35	69	8	2	15	37	38-1	1	68	.228	.310	.416	101	0	0-0	.995	1	100	86	1b91	0	-0.4
1959	Was A	19	71	11	15	4	0	3	4	7-0	1	14	.211	.291	.394	87	-1	2-0	.995	-2	48	104	1b19	0	-0.5
Total	6	346	1038	134	242	28	2	50	159	137-2	8	226	.233	.324	.408	93	-10	5-1	.993	-3	94	98	1b307	0	-3.0
ZAUN, GREGG	Gregory Owen; B4.14.1971 Glendale CA; BB/TR/5´10˝/(170–190); [BalA89 17/427]; d6.24																								
1995	Bal A	40	104	18	27	5	0	3	14	16-0	0	14	.260	.358	.394	94	-1	1-1	.987	3	117	98	C39/D	0	0.4
1996	Bal A	50	108	16	25	8	1	1	13	11-2	2	15	.231	.309	.352	68	-5	0-0	.987	-5	72	65	C49	0	-0.8
	Fla N	10	31	4	9	1	0	1	2	3-1	0	5	.290	.353	.419	105	0	1-0	1.000	2	336	38	C10	0	0.3
1997	†Fla N	58	143	21	43	10	2	2	20	26-4	2	18	.301	.415	.441	130	8	1-0	.978	5	95	97	C50/1	0	1.5
1998	Fla N	106	298	19	56	12	2	5	29	35-2	1	52	.188	.274	.292	53	-21	5-2	.986	-3	96	114	C88/2	0	-1.8
1999	Tex A	43	93	12	23	2	1	1	12	10-0	0	7	.247	.314	.323	61	-6	1-0	.984	2	127	136	C37,D2	0	-0.1
2000	KC A	83	234	36	64	11	0	7	33	43-3	3	34	.274	.390	.410	98	1	7-3	.988	-9	66	76	C76/12	43	-0.3
2001	KC A	39	125	15	40	9	0	6	18	12-0	0	16	.320	.377	.536	125	5	1-2	.975	-2	104	84	C35,D2	113	0.4
2002	Hou N	76	185	18	41	7	1	3	24	12-1	2	36	.222	.275	.319	52	-13	1-0	.985	-4	60	46	C44	0	-1.4
2003	Hou N	59	120	9	26	7	0	1	13	14-0	1	14	.217	.299	.300	55	-8	1-0	.976	-6	76	145	C31	0	-1.1
	Col N	15	46	6	12	1	0	3	8	5-0	0	7	.261	.333	.478	95	0	0-1	.973	-2	87	112	C14	0	-0.2
	Year	74	166	15	38	8	0	4	21	19-0	1	21	.229	.309	.349	67	-8	1-1	.975	-7	80	134	C45	0	-1.3
2004	Tor A	107	338	46	91	24	0	6	36	47-3	6	61	.269	.367	.393	93	-1	0-2	.987	1	79	105	C97,D6	0	0.5
2005	Tor A	133	434	61	109	18	1	11	61	73-2	0	70	.251	.355	.373	91	-3	2-3	.990	6	92	75	C132	15	1.0
2006	Tor A	99	290	39	79	19	0	12	40	41-3	3	42	.272	.363	.462	109	5	0-2	.994	4	61	120	C72,D19	5	1.1
Total	12	918	2549	320	645	134	8	62	323	348-21	20	391	.253	.345	.385	88	-39	21-16	.986	-7	88	94	C774,D30,2b2,1b2	176	-0.5
ZDEB, JOE	Joseph Edmund; B6.27.1953 Compton IL; BR/TR/5´11˝/185; [KCA71 4/76]; d4.7																								
1977	†KC A	105	195	26	58	5	2	2	23	16-3	0	23	.297	.346	.374	97	-1	6-5	.970	-2	93	106	O93(88/1/8)/3D	0	-0.5
1978	KC A	60	127	18	32	2	3	0	11	7-0	0	18	.252	.287	.315	68	-6	3-0	.957	-1	95	88	O52(43/0/12)/23D	0	-0.8
1979	KC A	15	23	3	4	1	1	0	0	2-0	0	4	.174	.240	.304	45	-2	1-0	1.000	-0	108	0	O9(6/0/3)	0	-0.2
Total	3	180	345	47	94	8	6	2	34	25-3	0	45	.272	.317	.348	83	-9	10-5	.967	-3	95	93	O154(137/1/23),D5,3b2/2	0	-1.5
ZEARFOSS, DAVE	David William Tilden; B1.1.1868 Schenectady NY; D9.12.1945 Wilmington DE; TR/5´9˝/174; d4.17; Col Washington College																								
1896	NY N	19	60	5	13	1	1	0	6	5	1	5	.217	.288	.267	48	-5	2	.893	-3	*93*	*91*	C19	—	-0.6
1897	NY N	5	10	1	3	0	1	0	0	0	0	—	.300	.300	.500	112	0	0	.880	2	*173*	*198*	C5	—	0.2
1898	NY N	1	1	0	1	0	0	0	0	0	0	—	1.000	1.000	1.000	489	0	0	1.000	0	*0*	*327*	/C	—	0.1
1904	StL N	27	80	7	17	2	0	0	9	10	0	—	.213	.300	.237	70	-2	0	.966	-3	*85*	*86*	C25	—	-0.3
1905	StL N	20	51	2	8	0	1	0	2	4	0	—	.157	.218	.196	24	-5	0	.966	-1	*88*	*109*	C19	—	-0.5
Total	5	72	202	15	42	3	3	0	17	19	1	5	.208	.279	.252	56	-12	2	.943	-6	*92*	*101*	C69	—	-1.1
ZEBER, GEORGE	George William; B8.29.1950 Ellwood City PA; BB/TR/5´11˝/(180–181); [NYA68 5/88]; d5.7																								
1977	†NY A	25	65	8	21	3	0	3	10	9-1	0	11	.323	.405	.508	148	5	0-0	.961	-0	107	102	2b21,S2,3b2/D	0	0.5
1978	NY A	3	6	0	0	0	0	0	0	0-0	0	0	.000	.000	.000	-99	-2	0-0	.750	-1	57	0	/2	0	-0.3
Total	2	28	71	8	21	3	0	3	10	9-1	0	11	.296	.375	.465	129	3	0-0	.953	-1	104	96	2b22,3b2,S2/D	0	0.2
ZEIDER, ROLLIE	Rollie Hubert "Bunions"; B11.16.1883 Auburn IN; D9.12.1967 Garrett IN; BR/TR/5´10˝/162; d4.14; OF(6/1/1)																								
1910	Chi A	136	498	57	108	9	2	0	31	62	1	—	.217	.305	.243	75	-12	49	.931	-6	96	108	2b87,S45,3b4	—	-1.8
1911	Chi A	73	217	39	55	3	0	2	21	29	2	—	.253	.347	.295	82	-4	28	.997	-4	115	80	1b29,S17,3b10,2b9	—	-0.7
1912	Chi A	130	420	57	103	12	10	1	42	50	3	—	.245	.330	.329	91	-4	48	.979	4	136	91	1b66,3b56/S	—	-0.1
1913	Chi A	16	20	4	7	0	0	0	2	4	0	1	.350	.458	.350	139	1	3	1.000	1	95	0	3b6,1b3/2	—	0.3
	NY A	50	159	15	37	2	0	0	12	25	1	9	.233	.341	.245	72	-4	3	.901	-9	78	104	S24,2b19,1b4,3b2	—	-1.2

YEAR	TM LG	G	AB	R	H	2B	3B	HR	RBI	BB-IB	HP	SO	AVG	OBP	SLG	AOPS	ABR	SB-CS	FA	FR	RNG	THR	GAMES AT POSITION	DL	BFW
	Year	66	179	19	44	2	0	0	14	29	1	10	.246	.354	.257	79	-3	6	.901	-8	78	104	S24,2b20,3b8,1b7	—	-0.9
1914	Chi F	119	452	60	124	13	2	1	36	44	4	28	.274	.344	.319	86	-15	35	.936	-5	94	**170**	3b117/S	—	-1.7
1915	Chi F	129	494	65	112	22	2	0	34	43	6	24	.227	.297	.279	66	-30	16	.941	-3	97	125	2b83,3b30,S21	—	-3.1
1916	Chi N	98	345	29	81	11	2	1	22	26	3	26	.235	.294	.287	71	-11	9	.928	-2	105	138	3b55,2b33,O7(6/0/1),S5,1b2	—	-1.3
1917	Chi N	108	354	36	86	14	2	0	27	28	2	30	.243	.302	.294	77	-9	17	.901	-14	66	82	S48,3b26,2b24/1cf	—	-2.2
1918	†Chi N	82	251	31	56	3	2	0	26	23	0	20	.223	.288	.251	63	-11	16	.956	-7	95	80	2b79/13	—	-1.9
Total	9	941	3210	393	769	89	22	5	253	334	22	138	.240	.315	.286	77	-99	224	.945	-45	95	97	2b335,3b307,S162,1b106,O8L	—	-13.7
Zeile, Todd	Todd Edward; B9.9.1965 Van Nuys CA; BR/TR/6´1˝/(190–205); [StLN86 2/55]; d8.18; Col UCLA																								
1989	StL N	28	82	7	21	3	1	1	8	9-1	0	14	.256	.326	.354	92	-1	0-0	.971	1	94	26	C23	0	0.2
1990	StL N	144	495	62	121	25	3	15	57	67-3	2	77	.244	.333	.398	101	1	2-4	.988	-5	93	119	C105,3b24,1b11/lf	0	0.1
1991	StL N	155	565	76	158	36	3	11	81	62-3	5	94	.280	.353	.412	114	12	17-11	.943	3	106	76	3b154	0	1.6
1992	StL N	126	439	51	113	18	4	7	48	68-4	0	70	.257	.352	.364	107	6	7-10	.960	-5	100	102	3b124	0	-0.1
1993	StL N	157	571	82	158	36	1	17	103	70-5	0	76	.277	.352	.433	110	10	5-4	.923	-10	103	110	3b153	0	0.0
1994	StL N	113	415	62	111	25	1	19	75	52-3	3	56	.267	.348	.470	112	8	1-3	.960	1	104	141	3b112	0	0.9
1995	StL N	34	127	16	37	6	0	5	22	18-1	1	23	.291	.378	.457	118	4	1-0	.980	2	129	118	1b34	14	0.3
	Chi N	79	299	34	68	16	0	9	30	16-0	3	53	.227	.271	.371	68	-15	0-0	.939	-8	95	107	3b75,O2L/1	0	-2.3
	Year	113	426	50	105	22	0	14	52	34-1	4	76	.246	.305	.397	84	-11	1-0	.939	-7	95	107	3b75,1b35,O2L	0	-2.0
1996	Phi N	134	500	61	134	24	0	20	80	67-4	1	88	.268	.353	.436	107	6	1-1	.962	-14	84	77	3b106,1b28	0	-1.0
	†Bal A	29	117	17	28	8	0	5	19	15-0	0	16	.239	.326	.436	91	-2	0-0	.964	2	102	170	3b29	0	0.0
1997	LA N	160	575	89	154	17	0	31	90	85-7	6	112	.268	.365	.459	123	20	8-7	.931	-18	83	105	3b160	0	0.2
1998	LA N	40	158	22	40	6	1	7	27	10-0	1	24	.253	.300	.437	96	-2	1-1	.929	-11	68	28	3b40/1	0	-1.3
	Fla N	66	234	37	68	12	1	6	39	31-2	2	34	.291	.374	.427	119	7	2-3	.971	-4	96	83	3b65	0	0.3
	Year	106	392	59	108	18	2	13	66	41-2	3	58	.276	.345	.431	110	5	3-4	.957	-15	103	86	3b105/1	0	-1.0
	†Tex A	52	180	26	47	14	1	6	28	28-0	1	32	.261	.358	.450	104	2	1-0	.915	0	103	86	3b52	0	0.2
1999	†Tex A	156	588	80	172	41	1	24	98	56-3	4	94	.293	.354	.488	107	6	1-2	.941	6	108	90	3b155/1D	0	1.1
2000	†NY N	153	544	67	146	36	3	22	79	74-4	2	85	.268	.356	.467	112	11	3-4	.992	4	111	78	1b151	0	0.1
2001	NY N	151	531	66	141	25	1	10	62	73-3	6	102	.266	.359	.373	97	0	1-0	.992	10	129	100	1b149	0	-0.2
2002	Col N	144	506	61	138	23	0	18	87	66-3	1	92	.273	.353	.425	93	-4	1-1	.942	-11	96	82	3b139/P	0	-1.5
2003	NY A	66	186	29	39	8	0	6	23	24-0	0	36	.210	.294	.349	72	-8	0-0	.917	2	101	199	3b30,1b23,D8	0	-0.7
	Mon N	34	113	11	29	2	2	5	19	10-0	3	18	.257	.331	.442	98	-1	1-0	.947	3	115	72	3b34	0	0.2
2004	NY N	137	348	30	81	16	0	9	35	44-1	1	83	.233	.319	.356	77	-12	0-0	.995	-4	87	99	1b67,3b46,C2/P	0	-1.9
Total	16	2158	7573	986	2004	397	23	253	1110	945-47	42	1279	.265	.346	.423	103	48	53-51	.942	-57	97	97	3b1498,1b466,C130,D9,O3L,P2	14	-3.8
Zeller, Bart	Barton Wallace; B7.22.1941 Chicago Heights IL; BR/TR/6´1˝/185; d5.21; C1; Col Arizona																								
1970	StL N	1	0	0	0	0	0	0	0	0-0	0	0	ø	ø	ø	ø	0	0-0	1.000	0	0	0	/C	0	0.0
Zernial, Gus	Gus Edward "Ozark Ike"; B6.27.1923 Beaumont TX; BR/TR/6´2.5˝/(205–210); d4.19																								
1949	Chi A	73	198	29	63	17	2	5	38	15	0	26	.318	.366	.500	132	8	0-1	1.000	-1	88	142	O46L	60	0.4
1950	Chi A	143	543	75	152	16	4	29	93	38	3	110	.280	.330	.484	110	2	0-2	.969	1	103	86	O137L	0	-0.7
1951	Chi A	4	19	2	2	0	0	0	4	2	0	2	.105	.190	.105	-19	-3	0-0	.933	1	107	241	O4L	0	-0.3
	Phi A	139	552	90	151	30	5	33	125	61	4	99	.274	.350	.525	132	21	2-2	.974	8	103	155	O138L	0	1.8
	Year	143	571	92	153	30	5	**33**	**129**	63	4	101	.268	.345	.511	127	18	2-2	.972	8	103	158	O142L	0	1.5
1952	Phi A	145	549	76	144	15	1	29	100	70	1	87	.262	.347	.452	114	9	5-1	.972	-3	98	65	O141L	0	-0.4
1953	Phi A★	147	556	85	158	21	3	42	108	57	4	79	.284	.355	.559	138	27	4-0	.972	5	99	**156**	O141L	0	2.4
1954	Phi A	97	336	42	84	8	2	14	62	30	4	60	.250	.316	.411	98	-2	0-0	.953	-1	102	74	O90L,1b2	0	-0.9
1955	KC A	120	413	62	105	9	3	30	84	30-1	3	90	.254	.304	.508	116	5	1-0	.964	5	**110**	106	O103L	0	0.4
1956	KC A	109	272	36	61	12	0	16	44	33-2	4	66	.224	.315	.445	99	-2	2-0	.984	3	93	201	O69L	0	-0.2
1957	KC A	131	437	56	103	20	1	27	69	34-0	1	84	.236	.290	.471	104	0	1-1	.952	-2	97	69	O113L/1	0	-0.9
1958	Det A	66	124	8	40	7	1	5	23	6-0	0	25	.323	.351	.516	127	4	0-0	.939	-2	81	88	O24L	0	0.2
1959	Det A	60	132	11	30	4	0	7	26	7-0	0	27	.227	.262	.417	80	-4	0-0	.972	-3	65	103	1b32/rf	0	-0.8
Total	11	1234	4131	572	1093	159	22	237	776	383-3	24	755	.265	.329	.486	115	65	15-7	.968	12	100	112	O1007(1006/0/1),1b35	60	1.0
Ziegler, Charlie	Charles Wallace; B1.13.1875 Canton OH; D4.18.1904 Canton OH; TR; d9.23																								
1899	Cle N	2	8	2	2	0	0	0	0	0	0	—	.250	.250	.250	40	-1	0	.750	-1	72	0	/S2	—	-0.1
1900	Phi N	3	11	0	3	0	0	0	1	0	0	—	.273	.273	.273	51	-1	0	.889	-1	69	0	3b3	—	-0.1
Total	2	5	19	2	5	0	0	0	1	0	0	—	.263	.263	.263	47	-2	0	.889	-1	69	0	3b3/2S	—	-0.2
Zientara, Benny	Benedict Joseph; B2.14.1918 Chicago IL; D4.16.1985 Lake Elsinore CA; BR/TR/5´9˝/165; d9.11; Mil 1942–45																								
1941	Cin N	9	21	3	6	0	0	0	2	1	0	3	.286	.318	.286	71	-1	0	.914	-0	105	91	2b6	0	-0.1
1946	Cin N	78	280	26	81	10	2	0	16	14	0	11	.289	.323	.339	91	-4	3	.970	18	136	151	2b39,3b36	0	1.6
1947	Cin N	117	418	60	108	18	1	2	24	23	0	23	.258	.297	.321	64	-22	2	.976	-10	92	81	2b100,3b13	0	-2.7
1948	Cin N	74	187	17	35	1	2	0	7	12	0	11	.187	.236	.214	23	-21	0	.990	7	103	103	2b60,3b3,S2	0	-1.1
Total	4	278	906	106	230	29	5	2	49	50	0	48	.254	.293	.304	64	-48	5	.976	15	103	100	2b205,3b52,S2	0	-2.3
Zies, Bill	William; B6.16.1867 Rock Island IL; D4.16.1907 Beardstown IL; BL; d8.9																								
1891	StL AA	2	3	0	1	0	0	0	0	0	0	0	.333	.333	.333	79	0	0	1.000	0	*155*	*106*	C2	—	0.0
Zimmer, Chief	Charles Louis; B11.23.1860 Marietta OH; D8.22.1949 Cleveland OH; BR/TR/6´0˝/190; d7.18; M1/U1																								
1884	Det N	8	29	0	2	1	0	0	0	1	—	14	.069	.100	.103	-38	-4	—	.830	-1	—	—	C6,O2R	—	-0.5
1886	NY AA	6	19	1	3	0	0	0	1	1	1	—	.158	.238	.158	27	-1	0	.893	2	—	—	C6	—	0.1
1887	Cle AA	14	52	9	12	5	0	0	4	4	1	—	.231	.298	.327	77	-1	1	.923	-2	—	—	C12,1b2	—	-0.2
1888	Cle AA	65	212	27	51	11	4	0	22	18	4	—	.241	.312	.330	109	3	15	.917	9	—	—	C59,O3(0/1/2),1b3/S	—	1.5
1889	Cle N	84	259	47	67	9	9	1	21	44	1	35	.259	.368	.375	109	4	14	.931	11	—	—	C81,1b3	—	1.8
1890	Cle N	125	444	54	95	16	6	2	57	46	11	54	.214	.303	.291	75	-13	15	.937	21	*117*	***114***	C125	—	1.6
1891	Cle N	116	440	55	112	21	4	3	69	33	4	49	.255	.312	.341	87	-8	15	.936	14	*92*	***138***	C116/3	—	1.4
1892	†Cle N	111	413	63	109	29	13	1	64	32	7	47	.264	.327	.404	116	7	18	.938	21	*130*	*82*	C111	—	3.4
1893	Cle N	57	227	27	70	13	7	2	41	16	1	15	.308	.357	.454	108	1	4	.968	11	*113*	*129*	C56/3	—	1.3
1894	Cle N	90	341	55	97	20	5	4	65	17	5	31	.284	.328	.408	73	-17	14	**.963**	27	***161***	*110*	C89	—	1.4
1895	†Cle N	88	315	60	107	21	2	5	56	33	9	30	.340	.417	.467	121	11	14	.975	10	*120*	*88*	C84,1b3	—	2.3
1896	†Cle N	91	336	46	93	18	3	3	46	31	9	48	.277	.354	.375	87	-6	4	**.972**	17	***150***	*83*	C91/3	—	1.6
1897	Cle N	80	294	50	93	22	3	0	40	25	4	—	.316	.378	.412	103	2	8	.976	11	*113*	*96*	C80	—	1.7
1898	Cle N	20	63	5	15	2	0	0	4	5	1	—	.238	.304	.270	66	-3	2	.970	4	*113*	*87*	C19	—	0.3
1899	Cle N	20	73	9	25	2	1	2	14	5	3	—	.342	.407	.479	154	6	1	.957	-5	*59*	*120*	C20	—	0.2
	Lou N	75	262	43	78	11	3	2	29	22	8	—	.298	.370	.385	107	3	9	.985	5	*115*	*102*	C62,1b11	—	1.2
	Year	95	335	52	103	13	4	4	43	27	11	—	.307	.378	.406	117	9	10	**.978**	-0	*102*	*106*	C82,1b11	—	1.4
1900	†Pit N	82	271	27	80	7	10	0	35	17	11	—	.295	.361	.395	108	2	4	.961	6	***129***	*93*	C78,1b2	—	1.4
1901	Pit N	69	236	17	52	7	3	0	21	20	4	—	.220	.292	.275	63	-11	6	.975	-0	*126*	*91*	C68	—	-0.4
1902	Pit N	42	142	13	38	4	2	0	17	11	4	—	.268	.338	.324	101	0	4	.969	2	*144*	*91*	C41/1	—	0.7
1903	Phi N	37	118	9	26	3	1	1	19	9	3	—	.220	.292	.288	68	-5	3	.968	1	*90*	*94*	C35,M	—	-0.1
Total	19	1280	4546	617	1225	222	76	26	625	390	91	323	.269	.339	.369	95	-30	151	.952	161	*122*	*102*	C1239,1b25,O5(0/1/4),3b3/S	—	20.7
Zimmer, Don	Donald William; B1.17.1931 Cincinnati OH; BR/TR/5´9˝/(165–187); d7.2; M14/C22																								
1954	Bro N	24	33	3	6	0	1	0	0	3	1	8	.182	.270	.242	34	-3	2-0	.939	2	120	107	S13	0	-0.1
1955	†Bro N	88	280	38	67	10	1	15	50	19-5	2	66	.239	.289	.443	89	-6	5-3	.976	3	97	138	2b62,S21,3b8	0	0.3
1956	Bro N	17	20	4	6	1	0	0	2	0-0	1	7	.300	.333	.350	78	-1	0-1	.944	1	94	160	S8,3b3/2	68	0.0
1957	Bro N	84	269	23	59	9	1	6	19	16-5	0	63	.219	.262	.327	52	-18	1-3	.957	-0	99	51	3b39,S37,2b5	0	-1.7
1958	LA N	127	455	52	119	15	2	17	60	28-1	1	92	.262	.305	.415	86	-11	14-2	.965	**30**	108	123	S114,3b12/2lf	0	3.1
1959	†LA N	97	249	21	41	7	1	4	28	37-7	1	56	.165	.274	.249	38	-22	3-1	.972	5	99	97	S88,3b5/2	0	-1.1
1960	Chi N	132	368	37	95	16	7	6	35	27-4	0	56	.258	.307	.389	90	-6	8-6	.980	8	119	60	2b75,3b45,S5,O2L	0	0.7
1961	Chi N★	128	477	57	120	25	4	13	40	25-1	2	70	.252	.291	.403	81	-14	5-1	.973	6	102	121	2b116,3b5/rf	0	0.1
1962	NY N	14	52	3	4	1	0	0	1	3-0	0	10	.077	.127	.096	-38	-10	0-1	.961	4	144	111	3b14	0	-0.7
	Cin N	63	192	16	48	11	2	2	16	14-1	1	30	.250	.304	.359	75	-7	1-2	.949	-5	90	87	3b43,2b17/S	0	-1.2
	Year	77	244	19	52	12	2	2	17	17-1	1	40	.213	.267	.303	51	-17	1-3	.952	-1	104	93	3b57,2b17/S	0	-1.9
1963	LA N	22	23	4	5	1	0	1	2	3-0	0	10	.217	.308	.391	107	0	0-0	.933	1	125	0	3b10/2S	0	0.1

YEAR	TM LG	G	AB	R	H	2B	3B	HR	RBI	BB-IB	HP	SO	AVG	OBP	SLG	AOPS	ABR	SB-CS	FA	FR	RNG	THR	GAMES AT POSITION	DL	BFW
	Was A	83	298	37	74	12	1	13	44	18-2	2	57	.248	.296	.426	100	-1	3-2	.935	5	111	110	3b78,2b2	0	0.3
1964	Was A	121	341	38	84	16	2	12	38	27-0	0	94	.246	.302	.411	96	-2	1-3	.955	-7	99	46	3b87,O4(2/0/3),C2/2	0	-1.1
1965	Was A	95	226	20	45	6	0	2	17	26-1	2	59	.199	.284	.252	56	-13	2-0	.966	-5	125	158	C33,3b26,2b12	0	-1.6
Total	12	1095	3283	353	773	130	22	91	352	246-27	13	678	.235	.290	.372	76	-114	45-25	.941	46	102	76	3b375,2b294,S288,C35,O8(5/0/4)	68	-2.9
ZIMMERMAN, EDDIE	Edward Desmond; B1.1.1883 Oceanic NJ; D5.6.1945 Emmaus PA; BR/TR/5´9˝/160; d9.29; Col Manhattan																								
1906	StL N	5	14	0	3	0	0	0	1	0	0	—	.214	.214	.214	35	-1	0	.929	-0	78	0	3b5	—	-0.2
1911	Bro N	122	417	31	77	10	7	3	36	34	2	37	.185	.249	.264	46	-33	9	**.961**	3	99	136	3b122	—	-2.7
Total	2	127	431	31	80	10	7	3	37	34	2	37	.186	.248	.262	45	-34	9	.960	2	98	132	3b127	—	-2.9
ZIMMERMAN, JERRY	Gerald Robert; B9.21.1934 Omaha NE; D9.9.1998 Neskowin OR; BR/TR/6´2˝/185; d4.14; C13																								
1961	†Cin N	76	204	8	42	5	0	0	10	11-0	2	21	.206	.252	.230	29	-21	1-1	.975	1	94	82	C76	0	-1.7
1962	Min A	34	62	8	17	4	0	0	7	3-0	1	5	.274	.318	.339	74	-2	0-0	.992	-1	139	126	C34	0	-0.2
1963	Min A	39	56	3	13	1	0	0	3	2-0	0	8	.232	.259	.250	43	-4	0-0	1.000	1	165	62	C39	0	-0.3
1964	Min A	63	120	6	24	3	0	0	12	10-0	3	15	.200	.278	.225	42	-9	0-0	.993	1	105	159	C63	0	-0.7
1965	†Min A	83	154	8	33	1	1	1	11	12-3	1	23	.214	.275	.253	49	-10	0-0	**.997**	1	115	69	C82	0	-0.7
1966	Min A	60	119	11	30	4	1	1	15	15-4	1	23	.252	.338	.328	88	-1	0-0	.996	7	148	102	C59	0	0.8
1967	Min A	104	234	13	39	3	0	1	12	22-5	2	49	.167	.243	.192	28	-21	0-1	.992	9	113	114	C104	0	-0.9
1968	Min A	24	45	3	5	1	0	0	2	3-0	1	10	.111	.180	.133	-3	-6	0-0	.991	1	131	108	C24	0	-0.5
Total	8	483	994	60	203	22	2	3	72	78-12	11	154	.204	.269	.239	43	-74	1-2	.991	19	118	102	C481	0	-4.2
ZIMMERMAN, HEINIE	Henry; B2.9.1887 New York NY; D3.14.1969 New York NY; BR/TR/5´11.5˝/176; d9.8; OF(3/8/2)																								
1907	†Chi N	5	9	0	2	1	0	0	1	0	0	—	.222	.222	.333	70	0	0	.789	0	114	274	2b4/Slf	—	0.0
1908	Chi N	46	113	17	33	4	1	0	9	1	0	—	.292	.298	.345	101	0	2	.923	-7	76	40	2b20,O8(2/4/2)/S3	—	-0.8
1909	Chi N	65	183	23	50	9	2	0	21	3	0	—	.273	.285	.344	93	-3	7	.945	-7	77	94	2b31,S12,3b4	—	-0.9
1910	†Chi N	99	335	35	95	16	6	3	38	20	1	36	.284	.326	.394	111	3	7	.948	-8	89	128	2b32,S26,3b23,O4C/1	—	-0.4
1911	Chi N	143	535	80	164	22	17	9	85	25	5	50	.307	.343	.462	124	13	23	.946	-5	98	96	2b108,3b20,1b11	—	1.0
1912	Chi N	145	557	95	**207**	**41**	14	**14**	99	38	6	60	**.372**	.418	**.571**	**170**	**51**	23	.916	1	106	103	3b121,1b22	—	5.3
1913	Chi N	127	447	69	140	28	12	9	95	41	6	40	.313	.379	.490	147	27	18-19	.912	5	107	115	3b125	—	3.3
1914	Chi N	146	564	75	167	36	12	4	87	20	5	46	.296	.326	.424	123	13	17	.897	-19	85	83	3b118,S15,2b12	—	-0.2
1915	Chi N	139	520	65	138	28	11	3	62	21	5	33	.265	.300	.379	105	1	19-13	.943	-6	97	75	2b100,3b36,S4	—	-0.2
1916	Chi N	107	398	54	116	25	5	6	64	16	3	33	.291	.324	.425	116	7	15-12	.932	8	116	92	3b85,2b14,S4	—	2.0
	NY N	40	151	22	41	4	0	0	19	7	0	10	.272	.304	.298	90	-2	9-8	.943	-1	98	94	3b40/2	—	-0.3
	Year	147	549	76	157	29	5	6	**83**	23	3	43	.286	.318	.390	110	6	24-20	.935	7	**110**	93	3b125,2b15,S4	—	1.7
1917	†NY N	150	585	61	174	22	9	5	**102**	16	1	43	.297	.317	.391	121	11	13	.947	14	**115**	101	3b149,2b5	—	3.2
1918	NY N	121	463	43	126	19	10	1	56	13	1	23	.272	.294	.363	102	-2	14	.955	-4	95	53	3b100,1b19	—	-0.4
1919	NY N	123	444	56	113	20	6	4	58	21	5	30	.255	.296	.354	96	-3	8	.940	-0	107	93	3b123	—	0.0
Total	13	1456	5304	695	1566	275	105	58	796	242	38	404	.295	.331	.419	121	116	175-52	.928	-29	103	92	3b945,2b327,S63,1b53,O13C	—	11.6
ZIMMERMAN, ROY	Roy Franklin; B9.13.1916 Pine Grove PA; D11.22.1991 Pine Grove PA; BL/TL/6´2˝/187; d8.27																								
1945	NY N	27	98	14	27	1	0	5	15	5	3	16	.276	.330	.439	111	1	1	.988	-2	76	73	1b25/rf	0	-0.2
ZIMMERMAN, RYAN	Ryan Wallace; B9.28.1984 Washington NC; BR/TR/6´3˝/220; [WasN05 1/4]; d9.1; Col Virginia																								
2005	Was N	20	58	6	23	10	0	0	6	3-0	0	12	.397	.419	.569	165	6	0-0	1.000	1	112	208	3b14/S	0	0.7
2006	Was N	157	614	84	176	47	3	20	110	61-7	2	120	.287	.351	.471	114	13	11-8	.965	-8	89	95	3b157	0	0.5
Total	2	177	672	90	199	57	3	20	116	64-7	2	132	.296	.357	.479	118	19	11-8	.967	-7	91	103	3b171/S	0	1.2
ZIMMERMAN, BILL	William Frederick; B1.20.1887 Kengen, Germany; D10.4.1952 Newark NJ; BR/TR/5´8.5˝/172; d4.14																								
1915	Bro N	22	57	3	16	2	0	0	7	4	0	8	.281	.328	.316	93	0	1	.864	-2	86	0	O18R	—	-0.4
ZINN, FRANK	Frank Patrick; B12.21.1865 Phoenixville PA; D5.12.1936 Philadelphia PA; 5´8˝/150; d4.18																								
1888	Phi AA	2	7	0	0	0	0	0	0	1	0	—	.000	.125	.000	-59	-1	0	.938	-0	—	—	C2	—	-0.1
ZINN, GUY	Guy; B2.13.1887 Holbrook WV; D10.6.1949 Park WV; BL/TR/5´10.5˝/170; d9.11																								
1911	NY A	9	27	5	4	0	2	0	1	4	1	—	.148	.281	.296	57	-2	0	.923	0	77	180	O8(2/4/2)	—	-0.2
1912	NY A	106	401	56	105	15	10	6	55	50	1	—	.262	.345	.394	105	2	17	.893	-9	92	65	O106(13/31/61)	—	-1.3
1913	Bos N	36	138	15	41	8	2	1	15	4	1	23	.297	.322	.406	105	0	3-4	.948	2	99	161	O35(1/34/0)	—	-0.1
1914	Bal F	61	225	30	63	10	6	3	25	16	3	26	.280	.336	.418	101	-4	6	.935	-4	92	65	O57(31/12/14)	—	-1.1
1915	Bal F	102	312	30	84	18	3	5	43	35	0	28	.269	.343	.394	104	-2	2	.949	-1	94	107	O88(63/17/8)	—	-0.8
Total	5	314	1103	136	297	51	23	15	139	109	6	77	.269	.338	.398	103	-6	28-4	.927	-12	93	93	O294(110/98/85)	—	-3.5
ZINTER, ALAN	Alan Michael; B5.19.1968 El Paso TX; BB/TR/6´2˝/200; [NYN89 1/24]; d6.18; Col Arizona																								
2002	Hou N	39	44	5	6	2	0	2	3	0-0	0	19	.136	.136	.318	14	-6	0-0	1.000	0	98	117	1b8/C	0	-0.6
2004	Ari N	28	34	2	7	2	0	1	6	5-0	0	15	.206	.300	.353	66	-2	0-0	.978	0	107	25	1b8,D2	60	-0.2
Total	2	67	78	7	13	4	0	3	9	5-0	0	34	.167	.214	.333	38	-8	0-0	.986	0	103	63	1b16,D2/C	60	-0.8
ZIPFEL, BUD	Marion Sylvester; B11.18.1938 Belleville IL; BL/TR/6´3˝/200; d7.26																								
1961	Was A	50	170	17	34	7	5	4	18	15-0	0	49	.200	.262	.371	69	-9	1-1	.983	-5	75	102	1b44	0	-1.6
1962	Was A	68	184	21	44	4	1	6	21	17-1	1	43	.239	.307	.370	82	-5	1-2	.976	-2	109	69	1b26,O23L	0	-1.0
Total	2	118	354	38	78	11	6	10	39	32-1	1	92	.220	.285	.370	76	-14	2-3	.981	-6	87	91	1b70,O23L	0	-2.6
ZISK, RICHIE	Richard Walter; B2.6.1949 Brooklyn NY; BR/TR/6´1˝/(200–220); [PitN67 3/56]; d9.8; [DL 1984 Sea A 181]																								
1971	Pit N	7	15	2	3	1	0	1	2	4-0	0	7	.200	.368	.467	134	1	0-0	1.000	-0	91	0	O6(3/0/3)	0	0.0
1972	Pit N	17	37	4	7	3	0	0	4	7-0	0	10	.189	.318	.270	70	-1	0-0	.938	-1	73	148	O12(12/0/1)	0	-0.2
1973	Pit N	103	333	44	108	23	7	10	54	21-0	0	63	.324	.364	.526	147	19	0-0	.987	2	90	175	O84(22/0/65)	0	1.8
1974	†Pit N	149	536	75	168	30	3	17	100	65-7	0	91	.313	.386	.476	144	33	1-1	.985	7	113	90	O141(9/0/135)	0	3.3
1975	†Pit N	147	504	69	146	27	3	20	75	68-9	2	109	.290	.374	.474	134	24	0-1	.975	-5	99	64	O140L	0	1.1
1976	Pit N	155	581	91	168	35	2	21	89	52-3	0	96	.289	.343	.465	127	20	1-0	.987	2	100	102	O152L	0	1.3
1977	Chi A★	141	531	78	154	17	6	30	101	55-7	3	98	.290	.355	.514	135	25	0-4	.982	3	101	120	O109(10/0/100),D28	0	1.9
1978	Tex A★	140	511	68	134	19	1	22	85	58-7	3	76	.262	.338	.432	115	10	3-3	.988	-6	83	94	O90(48/0/42),D49	15	-0.2
1979	Tex A	144	503	69	132	21	1	18	64	57-4	0	75	.262	.336	.416	103	2	1-1	.972	-6	88	103	O134(15/0/126),D3	0	-1.1
1980	Tex A	135	448	48	130	17	1	19	77	39-5	0	72	.290	.344	.460	122	13	0-2	.980	-3	73	129	D86,O37(2/0/35)	0	0.5
1981	Sea A	94	357	42	111	12	1	16	43	28-3	3	63	.311	.366	.485	137	16	0-2	ø	0	0	0	D93	0	1.3
1982	Sea A	131	503	61	147	28	1	21	62	49-4	1	89	.292	.354	.477	122	16	2-1	ø	0	0	0	D130	0	1.2
1983	Sea A	90	285	30	69	12	0	12	36	30-3	0	61	.242	.311	.411	94	-3	0-0	ø	0	0	0	D84	20	-0.5
Total	13	1453	5144	681	1477	245	26	207	792	533-52	12	910	.287	.353	.466	125	175	8-15	.981	-7	96	103	O905(413/0/507),D473	216	10.4
ZITZMANN, BILLY	William Arthur; B11.19.1895 Long Island City NY; D5.29.1985 Passaic NJ; BR/TR/5´10.5˝/175; d4.17																								
1919	Pit N	11	26	5	5	1	0	0	2	0	0	6	.192	.192	.231	26	-2	2	.917	-1	103	0	O8L	—	-0.4
	Cin N	2	1	0	0	0	0	0	0	0	0	0	.000	.000	.000	-99	0	0	ø	-0	0	0	/lf	—	0.0
	Year	13	27	5	5	1	0	0	2	0	0	6	.185	.185	.222	22	-3	2	.917	-1	101	0	O9L	—	-0.4
1925	Cin N	104	301	53	76	13	3	0	21	35	6	22	.252	.342	.316	71	-12	11-11	.959	-6	88	72	O89(80/4/7)/S	—	-2.3
1926	Cin N	53	94	21	23	2	1	0	3	6	2	7	.245	.304	.287	61	-5	3	.965	-1	111	0	O31(22/5/2)	—	-0.8
1927	Cin N	88	232	47	66	10	4	0	24	20	4	18	.284	.352	.362	94	-1	9	.958	-7	98	35	O60(17/36/7),S8,3b3	—	-1.1
1928	Cin N	101	266	53	79	9	3	3	33	13	3	22	.297	.337	.387	90	-5	13	.958	-1	104	68	O78(46/12/23)/3	—	-1.0
1929	Cin N	47	84	18	19	3	0	0	6	9	1	10	.226	.309	.262	45	-7	4	.940	-1	119	0	O22(15/0/7),1b5	—	-0.9
Total	6	406	1004	197	268	38	11	3	89	83	16	85	.267	.333	.336	77	-32	42-11	.956	-16	100	48	O289(189/57/46),S9,1b5,3b4	—	-6.5
ZOBRIST, BEN	Benjamin T.; B5.26.1981 Eureka IL; BB/TR/6´3˝/200; [HouN04 6/184]; d8.1; Col Dallas Baptist																								
2006	TB A	52	183	10	41	6	2	2	18	10-1	0	26	.224	.260	.311	49	-15	2-3	.963	2	102	85	S52	0	-0.9
ZOCCOLILLO, PETE	Peter Jude; B2.6.1977 Bronx NY; BL/TR/6´2˝/200; [ChiN99 23/710]; d9.5; Col Rutgers																								
2003	Mil N	20	37	0	4	1	0	0	3	2-0	0	13	.108	.154	.135	-24	-7	0-0	1.000	0	128	0	O7(3/0/4)	0	-0.7

YEAR	TM LG	G	AB	R	H	2B	3B	HR	RBI	BB-IB	HP	SO	AVG	OBP	SLG	AOPS	ABR	SB-CS	FA	FR	RNG	THR	GAMES AT POSITION	DL	BFW
Zosky, Eddie	Edward James; B2.10.1968 Whittier CA; BR/TR/6´0˝/(175–180); [TorA89 1/19]; d9.2; Col Cal St.–Fresno; [DL 1993 Tor A 128]																								
1991	Tor A	18	27	2	4	1	1	0	2	0-0	0	8	.148	.148	.259	10	-3	0-0	1.000	-2	89	89	S18	0	-0.4
1992	Tor A	8	7	1	2	0	1	0	1	0-0	0	2	.286	.250	.571	128	0	0-0	.923	1	126	124	S8	0	0.1
1995	Fla N	6	5	0	1	0	0	0	0	0-0	0	0	.200	.200	.200	6	-1	0-0	.667	-2	23	0	S4/2	0	-0.2
1999	Mil N	8	7	1	1	0	0	0	0	1-0	0	2	.143	.250	.143	3	-1	0-0	1.000	0	90	0	3b4,2b2	0	-0.1
2000	Hou N	4	4	0	0	0	0	0	0	0-0	0	1	.000	.000	.000	-93	-1	0-0	ø	0	—	—	/H	0	-0.1
Total	5	44	50	4	8	1	2	0	3	1-0	0	13	.160	.173	.260	16	-6	0-0	.963	-3	89	86	S30,3b4,2b3	128	-0.7
Zuber, Jon	Jon Edward; B12.10.1969 Encino CA; BL/TL/6´0˝/190; [PhiN92 12/333]; d4.19; Col California																								
1996	Phi N	30	91	7	23	4	0	1	10	6-1	0	11	.253	.296	.330	65	-5	1-0	.987	-1	77	61	1b22	0	-0.8
1998	Phi N	38	45	6	11	3	1	2	6	6-0	1	9	.244	.346	.489	116	1	0-0	1.000	-0	84	0	O5L,1b4	0	0.0
Total	2	68	136	13	34	7	1	3	16	12-1	1	20	.250	.313	.382	82	-4	1-0	.989	-2	77	62	1b26,O5L	0	-0.8
Zuleta, Julio	Julio Ernesto (Tapia); B3.28.1975 Panama City, Pan; BR/TR/6´6˝/(230–235); d4.6																								
2000	Chi N	30	68	13	20	8	0	3	12	2-0	3	19	.294	.342	.544	121	2	0-1	.966	-0	113	106	1b14,O6L	0	0.0
2001	Chi N	49	106	11	23	3	0	6	24	8-1	3	32	.217	.288	.415	82	-3	0-1	.991	-4	42	58	1b35	0	-0.9
Total	2	79	174	24	43	11	0	9	36	10-1	6	51	.247	.309	.466	97	-1	0-2	.984	-4	63	72	1b49,O6L	0	-0.9
Zupcic, Bob	Robert; B8.18.1966 Pittsburgh PA; BR/TR/6´4˝/(220–225); [BosA87 1/32]; d9.7; Col Oral Roberts																								
1991	Bos A	18	25	3	4	0	0	1	3	1-0	0	6	.160	.192	.280	27	-3	0-0	.875	-2	76	0	O16(3/7/6)	0	-0.4
1992	Bos A	124	392	46	108	19	1	3	43	25-1	4	60	.276	.322	.352	84	-8	2-2	.977	1	94	176	O114(32/68/22),D5	0	-1.0
1993	Bos A	141	286	40	69	24	2	2	26	27-2	2	54	.241	.308	.360	75	-10	5-2	.979	-0	95	129	O122(48/37/54),D5	0	-1.2
1994	Bos A	4	4	0	0	0	0	0	0	0-0	0	1	.000	.000	.000	-96	-1	0-1	1.000	-0	72	0	O2L/D	0	-0.2
	Chi A	32	88	10	18	4	1	1	8	4-0	0	16	.205	.237	.307	40	-8	0-0	1.000	1	107	128	O28(15/0/14),3b2/1	0	-0.8
	Year	36	92	10	18	4	1	1	8	4-0	0	17	.196	.227	.293	34	-10	0-1	1.000	0	105	121	O30(17/0/14),3b2/D1	0	-1.0
Total	4	319	795	99	199	47	4	7	80	57-3	6	137	.250	.303	.346	78	-30	7-5	.977	-1	95	146	O282(100/112/96),D11,3b2/1	0	-3.6
Zupo, Frank	Frank Joseph "Noodles"; B8.29.1939 San Francisco CA; D3.25.2005 Burlingame CA; BL/TR/5´11˝/182; d7.1																								
1957	Bal A	10	12	2	1	0	0	0	0	1-0	0	4	.083	.154	.083	-36	-2	0-0	.913	-0	42	128	C8	0	-0.2
1958	Bal A	1	2	0	0	0	0	0	0	0-0	0	1	.000	.000	.000	-99	-1	0-0	1.000	0	0	0	/C	0	0.0
1961	Bal A	5	4	1	2	1	0	0	0	1-0	0	1	.500	.600	.750	268	1	0-0	1.000	0	0	0	C4	0	0.1
Total	3	16	18	3	3	1	0	0	0	2-0	0	6	.167	.250	.222	31	-2	0-0	.941	0	29	88	C13	0	-0.1
Zuvella, Paul	Paul; B10.31.1958 San Mateo CA; BR/TR/6´0˝/(172–178); [AtlN80 15/367]; d9.4; C1; Col Stanford																								
1982	Atl N	2	1	0	0	0	0	0	0	0-0	0	0	.000	.000	.000	-98	0	0-0	.800	0	225	0	/S	0	0.0
1983	Atl N	3	5	0	0	0	0	0	0	2-0	1	1	.000	.375	.000	11	0	0-0	.750	-2	39	0	S2	0	-0.2
1984	Atl N	11	25	2	5	1	0	0	1	2-0	0	3	.200	.259	.240	38	-2	0-0	1.000	-0	114	143	2b6,S6	0	-0.2
1985	Atl N	81	190	16	48	8	1	0	4	16-1	0	14	.253	.311	.305	69	-8	2-0	.986	1	110	79	2b42,S33,3b5	0	-0.2
1986	NY A	21	48	2	4	1	0	0	2	5-0	0	4	.083	.170	.104	-23	-8	0-0	.966	2	109	115	S21	0	-0.4
1987	NY A	14	34	2	6	0	0	0	0	0-0	0	4	.176	.176	.176	-6	-5	0-0	1.000	-0	102	120	2b7,S6/3	0	-0.5
1988	Cle A	51	130	9	30	5	1	0	7	8-0	0	13	.231	.275	.285	55	-8	0-0	.959	-8	87	74	S49	0	-1.3
1989	Cle A	24	58	10	16	2	0	2	6	1-0	1	11	.276	.300	.414	97	0	0-0	.963	-4	79	25	S15,3b5,D3	0	-0.4
1991	KC A	2	0	0	0	0	0	0	0	0-0	0	0	ø	ø	ø	ø	0	0-0	ø	-0	0	0	3b2	0	0.0
Total	9	209	491	41	109	17	2	2	20	34-1	2	50	.222	.275	.277	52	-31	2-0	.959	-11	93	91	S133,2b55,3b13,D3	0	-3.2
Zwilling, Dutch	Edward Harrison; B11.2.1888 St.Louis MO; D3.27.1978 LaCrescenta CA; BL/TL/5´6.5˝/160; d8.14; C1																								
1910	Chi A	27	87	7	16	5	0	0	5	11	1	—	.184	.283	.241	67	-3	1	.940	-2	90	56	O27C	—	-0.7
1914	Chi F	154	592	91	185	38	8	**16**	95	46	1	68	.313	.363	.485	138	19	21	.962	-6	99	66	O154(0/153/1)	—	0.2
1915	Chi F	150	548	65	157	32	7	13	**94**	67	2	65	.286	.366	.442	135	17	24	.979	3	105	91	O148C,1b3	—	1.0
1916	Chi N	35	53	4	6	1	0	1	8	4	0	6	.113	.175	.189	11	-6	0	1.000	-1	79	0	O10(0/5/4)	—	-0.8
Total	4	366	1280	167	364	76	15	30	202	128	4	139	.284	.351	.438	127	27	46	.969	-7	101	75	O339(0/333/5),1b3	—	-0.3

THE ART OF PITCHING: THE PITCHER REGISTER

Pitching has always been thought of as an *art,* in contrast to hitting, which has generally been considered a *science.* Perhaps this is because the pitcher starts the action and controls the tempo of the game. Perhaps this is because good pitching is seen as aggressive, while hitting seems reactive. "Going after a hitter" is a sign of strength, and giving in to a hitter is a sign of weakness.

Good pitchers are creative, adjusting to the situation while inventing new ways to confound enemy batters. Pitchers who simply rock back and hurl the ball as hard as they can are derided as "throwers" and not "pitchers" – most throwers don't last long unless they can master the art of pitching. Pitchers of modest talent can fashion successful careers if they learn the art. Pitchers blessed with *a lot* of talent can achieve greatness if they combine their physical gifts with the art.

Two of the greatest books ever written on the subject of pitching show how similar the approach of the great pitchers has been over time, even under very different playing conditions. Christy Mathewson's *Pitching in a Pinch* and Tom Seaver's *The Art of Pitching* are both classics of baseball literature. Matty's book (with ghostwriter John Wheeler) was first published in 1912; it was reprinted by the University of Nebraska Press in 1993. Tom Terrific's book, co-authored with Lee Lowenfish, was first published in 1984 and remains in-print today.

During Mathewson's day, each at bat was a game of cat-and-mouse between and the man on the mound and the man at the plate. It was mostly a contest of deception, especially from the pitcher's end. It was not a power game – pitchers didn't have to throw that hard, but they were expected to start 35–40 games and complete almost all of them. If he remained healthy, a star pitcher could expect to log 350 or more innings, and pitch in relief 5–10 times in key games since the failed starters in the bullpen were relegated to mop-up and emergency duty.

What is now called "little ball" was the way of the day in the early twentieth century. Mathewson knew that the secret to being a successful pitcher was letting hitters get themselves out. "All batters who are good waiters, and will not hit at bad balls, are hard to deceive, because it means a twirler has to lay the ball over, and then the hitter always has the better chance," he said. "A pitcher will try to get a man to hit at a bad ball before he will put it near the plate."

What the "Big Six" didn't say – but what he understood and what he presumed the reader would understand as well – was that a *good* pitcher tries to get the batter to swing at *bad* pitches.

Mathewson also understood the critical nature of pacing himself. In his day, a batted ball wouldn't travel nearly as far as it would today, and the fences were usually farther away. Therefore, he could save his very best stuff, especially his devastating screwball (then called a "fadeaway") for when he needed it most: The term *pinches* refers to what would be called *clutch* situations today.

"Many persons have asked me why I do not use my 'fade-away' oftener when it is so effective," he wrote, "and the only answer is that every time I throw the 'fade-away' it takes so much out of my arm. It is a very hard ball to deliver. Pitching it ten or twelve times a game kills my arm, so I save it for the pinches."

Decades later, another dominant NL right-hander named Tom Seaver also talked about a pitcher pacing himself. Seaver wrote about pacing himself *during the at bat* as well as during the game in order to get the job done. In the 1970s Seaver knew that batters could connect for a long ball at almost any time, so he had to be able to reach back and strike a hitter out if necessary.

"If he is thinking ahead," Seaver wrote, "[a pitcher] will select pitches in sequence – for instance, throwing a sinking fastball in spot A in order to get the batter out with a slider in Spot B."

Seaver was the archetype of the modern power pitcher. He made his big league debut immediately after Sandy Koufax retired, and within three years he had joined the corps of great power pitchers of the 1960s like Don Drysdale, Bob Gibson, Jim Maloney, Jim Bunning, Juan Marichal, Bob Veale, and Sam McDowell. Seaver had better control than all of them except Marichal, and he clearly thought about the art of pitching in a very rigorous way.

The game in which Mathewson and Seaver pitched was fundamentally different. Scoring was much higher in Seaver's era, and the bullpens of the 1970s and 1980s were certainly more important than before World War II, so Seaver might expect to finish only about half the games he started.

As Seaver said, "You always have to throw more pitches when you walk batters. Even if they don't score, you are making pitches that you could save for key situations late in the ballgame."

While the game of 1970 was very different than the game of 1910, there is very little difference between Mathewson's "pitching in a pinch" and the following quote from Seaver:

"A game may ride on just three or four pitches that the pitcher must choose carefully and throw with accuracy . . . [Y]ou can train yourself to identify the outs that you *must* get, and within the bounds of sportsmanship, go about getting them." Sage advice, indeed.

This Pitcher Register chronicles the changes in pitching throughout baseball history, as shown by the records of the practitioners of the art. It allows for meaningful comparisons between Mathewson and Seaver, between Walter Johnson and Roger Clemens – the kind of reflection and analysis that adds so much to our understanding of the National Pastime.

Biographical Information

There are 7,601 pitchers in this Pitcher Register, of which 312 are also in the Batter Register. In order for a pitcher to be included in the batter register, he must have one season of 10 or more games where pitcher was not his prime position, or he must have 150 more career games played than games pitched. In order for a batter to be shown in the pitcher register, he must have at least 9 career innings pitched (as well as more games at another position than pitcher).

More details on many of the statistics and formulas shown in this register can be found in the glossary at the end of the encylopedia.

Every pitcher has (at least) a last name and a debut date. If an Hispanic pitcher has a matronymic name, it is placed in parentheses – for example, Marichal, Juan Antonio (Sanchez). Commonly used nicknames are also included on the biographical line; if a player was primarily known by his nickname during his career, it will be part of his listed name – such as Waddell, Rube. Other features and abbreviations for biographical information follow.

B (mm.dd.yyyy) is the place and date of birth.

D (mm.dd.yyyy) is the date and place of death.

The arm a pitcher threw with is expressed *TR* (throws right) or *TL* (throws left). The side of the plate a pitcher bats from is expressed *BR* (bats right), *BL* (bats left), or *BB* (bats both sides). In rare cases when a pitcher throws with both hands during a season, *TB* (throws both) is used and the season is included in parentheses. (The only pitcher to do this since 1901 is Greg A. Harris, who threw with both hands in one game in 1995.)

Height is shown by feet followed by inches. Weight is expressed in pounds. Many pitchers after 1950 now have expanded information about their playing weights; see page 6 in the Batter Register introduction for details.

Pitchers selected in the annual amateur/first-year player drafts since 1965 now have their draft information shown in their biographical line. See page 6 in the Batter Register introduction for complete details.

Debuts are marked *d*, followed by the date the pitcher made his first major league appearance. The debut year is the first year listed in the register, so it is not included in the biographical line.

Besides these basic pieces of information available in the biographical line, there are several other designations for players whose career, family, or duty took them beyond the norm.

If a pitcher on a major league roster missed significant parts of any season serving the United States during wartime, the following abbreviations are used to identify how the player served:

Mil indicates military service in the army, navy, air force, or marines;

Mer indicates the merchant marine;

Def indicates defense plant work.

The seasons the pitcher missed at least a part of are listed after the abbreviation for duty. At least one major leaguer missed time during the seasons below as a result of the following wars (dates include post-war service by some veterans):

Spanish-American War, 1898;

World War I, 1917–19;

World War II, 1941–46;

Korean War 1951–59;
Vietnam War 1962–72.

Negro Lg indicates years spent playing in big-league caliber Negro Leagues prior to playing in the major leagues. If a former Negro League player also served in the military during wartime, his military service will be shown even if it predates his major league debut.

If the pitcher spent time as a coach, manager, or umpire, that is indicated by the following symbols, which are followed by the number of seasons during which he performed those jobs. Abbreviations are:

C: Coach;
M: Manager;
U: Umpire.

HF indicates that the player is a member of the Hall of Fame; the year of election follows *HF*.

If the player had a close family member in the major leagues, the relative's relationship is identified by the codes listed below followed by the relative's first name (and, if it is different, the last name):

b: brother;
twb: twin brother;
f: father;
s: son;
gf: grandfather;
gs: grandson;
ggf: great grandfather;
ggs: great grandson.

Col indicates that the player played collegiate baseball at the university, college, or junior college shown. (See Batter Register introduction for full explanation.)

▲ at the end of the biographical information indicates that the pitcher is also listed in the Batter Register.

Statistical information

Symbols for the first two columns:

† before the team name means the pitcher participated in postseason play that season;

★ after team name means that the pitcher participated in the All-Star Game;

☆ after team name means that the pitcher was selected to the All-Star team that season but did not play;

✳ after team name means that the pitcher was selected to the All-Star team but replaced due to injury.

Boldface statistics in any category indicates a league-leading total or average.

The columns that appear in the pitcher register after **Year**:

TM: Team. Each team is identified by a three-letter code that is usually the first three letters of the city, state, or area where the team is located.

LG: League. The leagues in this book include the National League (N), the American League (A), the Federal League (F), the Players League (P), the Union Association (U), the National Association (NA) and the American Association (AA).

W: Wins.

L: Losses.

PCT: Winning Percentage. This is calculated by dividing wins by (wins plus losses).

G: Games.

GS: Games Started.

CG: Complete Games.

SHO: Shutouts.

SV: Saves. This became an official statistic in 1969. Saves are calculated based on the official definition of saves at the time. Saves before 1969 are based on how many winning games a relief pitcher finished for his team without getting a win.

BS: Blown Saves. From 1969–present, the number of times a pitcher entered the game in a save situation and allowed the opposing team to tie the game or take the lead.

IP: Innings Pitched. Exact innings pitched, including thirds of an inning, are available for all of baseball history, but thirds were not included in official innings pitched totals until 1982.

H: Hits Allowed.

R: Runs Allowed. This includes unearned runs.

HR: Home Runs Allowed.

HB: Hit Batsmen. The rule awarding first base to batters hit by pitches was instituted in 1884 by the American Association. It was adopted in 1887 by the National League.

BB: Bases On Balls Allowed. Generally referred to today as walks.

IB: Intentional Walks Allowed. Walking an opponent on purpose was first counted as a distinct category in 1955.

SO: Strikeouts. Unlike batter strikeouts, these are available for all pitchers in all seasons.

ERA: Earned Run Average. ERA is calculated by dividing earned runs by innings pitched and multiplying by 9.

AERA: Adjusted Earned Run Average. AERA is calculated by normalizing ERA for the context of the offensive level of the league and the player's home park(s) and converting to a scale in which 100 is average.

OAV: Opponents Batting Average. Hits allowed divided by opponent at bats.

OOB: Opponents On-Base Percentage.

AB: At Bats. At Bats by the pitcher as a batter.

HR: Home Runs. Home runs hit by the pitcher while batting.

SH: Sacrifice Hits. Sacrifice hits by the pitcher. (Sacrifice flies were counted as sacrifice hits from 1908–30 and in 1939.)

AVG: Average. The pitcher's batting average. No average is listed if he did not have an official at bat for a season or a career.

PB: Pitcher Batting Runs. Pitcher batting runs are calculated exactly the same way as adjusted batting runs except that the pitcher's offense is compared to the average offensive level of a pitcher, not an everyday player. The symbol * appears after pitcher batting if the pitcher played in games in addition to the ones in which he pitched.

SUP: Run Support. This is calculated by dividing the total number of runs scored for the pitcher's team(s) in his starts by the pitcher's total Games Started, normalizing the product for the context of the offensive level of the league and the player's home park(s), and converting to a scale in which 100 is average.

APR: Adjusted Pitching Runs. How many runs the pitcher allowed compared to the average pitcher. APR leaders are bolded for both starters and relievers.

DL: Disabled List. Days spent on the DL during the regular season. Before 1941, when there was no DL, an em dash (—) is shown. (See the introduction to the Batter Register for full explanation.)

PW: Pitcher Wins. This adds the pitcher's adjusted pitching wins, batting wins, and fielding wins to calculate how many wins the pitcher added to or subtracted from his team compared to what the average pitcher would have done.

YEAR	TM LG	W	L	PCT	G	GS	CG-SHO	SV-BS	IP	H	R	HR	HB	BB-IB	SO	ERA	AERA	OAV	OOB	AB-HR-SH	AVG	PB	SUP	APR	DL	PW
AARDSMA, DAVID	David Allan; B12.27.1981 Denver CO; BR/TR/6´5˝/(200–205); [SFN03 1/22]; d4.6; Col Rice																									
2004	SF N	1	0	1.000	11	0	0	0-1	10.2	20	8	1	2	10-0	5	6.75	64	.417	.525	0	ø	0	—	-3	0	-0.2
2006	Chi N	3	0	1.000	45	0	0	0-0	53	41	25	9	1	28-0	49	4.08	113	.214	.313	2-0-1	.000	-0	—	4	0	0.1
Total	2	4	0	1.000	56	0	0	0-1	63.2	61	33	10	3	38-0	54	4.52	100	.254	.358	2-0-1	.000	-0	—	1	0	-0.1
AASE, DON	Donald William; B9.8.1954 Orange CA; BR/TR/6´3˝/(185–222); [BosA72 6/136]; d7.26; [DL 1983 Cal A 182]																									
1977	Bos A	6	2	.750	13	13	4-2	0-0	92.1	85	36	6	1	19-1	49	3.12	144	.244	.283	0	ø	0	80	12	0	1.0
1978	Cal A	11	8	.579	29	29	6-1	0-0	178.2	185	88	14	2	80-4	93	4.03	90	.270	.348	0	ø	0	125	-7	0	-0.7
1979	†Cal A	9	10	.474	37	28	7-1	2-1	185.1	200	104	19	1	77-7	96	4.81	85	.277	.344	0	ø	0	121	-13	0	-1.3
1980	Cal A	8	13	.381	40	21	5-1	2-2	175	193	83	13	1	66-3	74	4.06	97	.287	.347	0	ø	0	69	0	0	-0.1
1981	Cal A	4	4	.500	39	0	0	11-0	65.1	56	17	4	0	24-2	38	2.34	157	.234	.303	0	ø	0	—	11	0	1.7
1982	Cal A	3	3	.500	24	0	0	4-4	52	45	20	5	0	23-2	40	3.46	118	.243	.327	0	ø	0	—	4	73	0.5
1984	Cal A	4	1	.800	23	0	0	8-5	39	30	7	1	0	19-5	28	1.62	247	.221	.312	0	ø	0	—	11	72	1.7
1985	Bal A	10	6	.625	54	0	0	14-5	88	83	44	6	1	35-7	67	3.78	107	.258	.330	0	ø	0	—	1	0	0.2
1986	Bal A★	6	7	.462	66	0	0	34-9	81.2	71	29	6	0	28-2	67	2.98	140	.234	.296	0	ø	0	—	11	0	2.3
1987	Bal A	1	0	1.000	7	0	0	2-0	8	8	2	1	0	4-0	3	2.25	197	.276	.364	0	ø	0	—	2	159	0.3
1988	Bal A	0	0	ø	35	0	0	0-1	46.2	40	22	4	0	37-5	28	4.05	97	.240	.374	0	ø	0	—	0	36	0.0
1989	NY N	1	5	.167	49	0	0	2-1	59.1	56	27	5	1	26-3	34	3.94	84	.245	.320	5	.000	-1	—	-4	0	-0.4
1990	LA N	3	1	.750	32	0	0	3-1	38	33	24	5	0	19-4	24	4.97	74	.232	.323	0	ø	0	—	-6	47	-0.7
Total	13	66	60	.524	448	91	22-5	82-29	1109.1	1085	503	89	7	457-45	641	3.80	104	.259	.331	5	.000	-1	104	22	569	4.5
ABBEY, BERT	Bert Wood; B11.29.1869 Essex VT; D6.11.1962 Essex Junction VT; BR/TR/5´11˝/175; d6.14; Col Vermont																									
1892	Was N	5	18	.217	27	22	19	1	195.2	207	139	7	6	76	77	3.45	94	.261	.330	75	.120	-3	88	-7	—	-0.9
1893	Chi N	2	4	.333	7	7	5	0	56	74	52	1	4	20	6	5.46	85	.308	.371	26	.231	-0	97	-6	—	-0.5
1894	Chi N	2	7	.222	11	11	10	0	92	119	74	3	3	37	24	5.18	109	.310	.375	39-0-2	.128	-5	75	5	—	-0.1
1895	Chi N	0	1	.000	1	1	1	0	8	10	8	0	1	2	3	4.50	113	.303	.361	3	.333	-0	42	0	—	0.0
	Bro N	5	2	.714	8	6	5	0	52	66	34	0	3	9	14	4.33	102	.304	.341	19	.263	1	111	0	—	0.1
	Year	5	3	.625	9	7	6	0	60	76	42	0	4	11	17	4.35	103	.304	.343	22	.273	1	100	1	—	0.1
1896	Bro N	8	8	.500	25	18	12	0	164.1	210	135	7	9	48	37	5.15	80	.308	.361	63-0-4	.190	-1	109	-21	—	-1.6
Total	5	22	40	.355	79	65	52	1	568	686	442	18	26	192	161	4.52	92	.292	.352	225-0-6	.169	-8	94	-29	—	-3.0
ABBOTT, JIM	James Anthony; B9.19.1967 Flint MI; BL/TL/6´3˝/(200–210); [CalA88 1/8]; d4.8; Col Michigan																									
1989	Cal A	12	12	.500	29	29	4-2	0-0	181.1	190	95	13	4	74-3	115	3.92	98	.274	.345	0	ø	0	98	-6	0	-0.7
1990	Cal A	10	14	.417	33	33	4-1	0-0	211.2	246	116	16	5	72-6	105	4.51	85	.295	.353	0	ø	0	94	-13	0	-1.3
1991	Cal A	18	11	.621	34	34	5-1	0-0	243	222	85	14	5	73-6	158	2.89	143	.244	.302	0	ø	0	93	33	0	4.0
1992	Cal A	7	15	.318	29	29	7	0-0	211	208	73	12	4	68-3	130	2.77	145	.263	.323	0	ø	0	58	28	27	2.9
1993	NY A	11	14	.440	32	32	4-1	0-0	214	221	115	22	3	73-4	95	4.37	96	.271	.332	0	ø	0	103	-5	15	-0.5
1994	NY A	9	8	.529	24	24	2	0-0	160.1	167	88	24	2	64-1	90	4.55	101	.273	.341	0	ø	0	101	1	0	0.1
1995	Chi A	6	4	.600	17	17	3	0-0	112.1	116	50	10	1	35-1	45	3.36	133	.269	.324	0	ø	0	116	13	0	1.0
	Cal A	5	4	.556	13	13	1-1	0-0	84.2	93	43	4	1	29-0	41	4.15	114	.280	.337	0	ø	0	84	5	0	0.5
	Year	11	8	.579	30	30	4-1	0-0	197	209	93	14	2	64-1	86	3.70	124	.274	.330	0	ø	0	102	16	0	1.5
1996	Cal A	2	18	.100	27	23	1	0-0	142	171	128	23	4	78-3	58	7.48	68	.306	.389	0	ø	0	65	-36	0	-3.9
1998	Chi A	5	0	1.000	5	5	0	0-0	31.2	35	16	2	1	12-0	14	4.55	101	.292	.358	0	ø	0	166	1	0	0.2
1999	Mil N	2	8	.200	20	15	0	0-0	82	110	71	14	2	42-3	37	6.91	67	.317	.393	21-0-3	.095	-1	95	-22	0	-2.2
Total	10	87	108	.446	263	254	31-6	0-0	1674	1779	880	154	32	620-30	888	4.25	100	.276	.340	21-0-3	.095	-1	92	-1	42	0.1
ABBOTT, KYLE	Lawrence Kyle; B2.18.1968 Newburyport MA; BL/TL/6´4˝/(195–215); [CalA89 1/9]; d9.10; Col Cal St.–Long Beach																									
1991	Cal A	1	2	.333	5	3	0	0-0	19.2	22	11	2	1	13-0	12	4.58	90	.301	.414	0	ø	0	52	-1	0	-0.1
1992	Phi N	1	14	.067	31	19	0	0-0	133.1	147	80	20	1	45-0	88	5.13	68	.283	.338	29-0-6	.069	-1	83	-22	0	-2.5
1995	Phi N	2	0	1.000	18	0	0	0-0	28.1	28	12	3	0	16-0	21	3.81	111	.267	.361	2	.500	0	—	2	70	0.2
1996	Cal A	0	1	.000	3	0	0	0-1	4	10	9	1	0	5-0	3	20.25	25	.500	.600	0	ø	0	—	-6	0	-1.0
Total	4	4	17	.190	57	22	0	0-1	185.1	207	112	26	2	79-0	124	5.20	72	.288	.358	31-0-6	.097	-1	75	-27	70	-3.4
ABBOTT, DAN	Leander Franklin "Big Dan"; B3.16.1862 Portage OH; D2.13.1930 Ottawa Lake MI; BR/TR/5´11˝/190; d4.19																									
1890	Tol AA	0	2	.000	3	1	1	1	13	19	14	0	1	8	1	6.23	63	.328	.418	7	.143	0	102	-3	—	-0.4
ABBOTT, PAUL	Paul David; B9.15.1967 Van Nuys CA; BR/TR/6´3˝/(185–205); [MinA85 3/67]; d8.21																									
1990	Min A	0	5	.000	7	7	0	0-0	34.2	37	24	0	1	28-0	25	5.97	70	.282	.410	0	ø	0	75	-6	0	-0.8
1991	Min A	3	1	.750	15	3	0	0-0	47.1	38	27	5	0	36-1	43	4.75	90	.232	.365	0	ø	0	85	-2	0	-0.2
1992	Min A	0	0	ø	6	0	0	0-0	11	12	4	1	1	5-0	13	3.27	125	.279	.360	0	ø	0	—	1	78	0.1
1993	Cle A	0	1	.000	5	5	0	0-0	18.1	19	15	5	0	11-1	7	6.38	69	.260	.357	0	ø	0	92	-4	0	-0.2
1998	Sea A	3	1	.750	4	4	0	0-0	24.2	24	11	2	0	10-0	22	4.01	117	.255	.324	0	ø	0	164	2	0	0.3
1999	Sea A	6	2	.750	25	7	0	0-2	72.2	50	31	9	0	32-3	68	3.10	155	.193	.278	0	ø	0	100	12	0	1.1
2000	†Sea A	9	7	.563	35	27	0	0-0	179	164	89	23	5	80-4	100	4.22	114	.243	.325	5-0-1	.400	1	95	13	0	1.0
2001	†Sea A	17	4	.810	28	27	1	0-0	163	145	79	21	7	87-5	118	4.25	100	.238	.338	4-0-1	.250	0	155	2	27	0.2
2002	Sea A	1	3	.250	7	5	0	0-0	26.1	40	36	5	1	20-0	22	11.96	36	.351	.449	0	ø	0	116	-23	147	-2.4
2003	KC A	1	2	.333	10	8	0	0-0	47.2	47	29	8	2	26-2	32	5.29	91	.257	.354	0	ø	0	105	-2	0	-0.1
2004	TB A	2	5	.286	10	9	0	0-0	47	49	39	8	3	27-0	25	6.70	70	.257	.356	0	ø	0	66	-11	0	-1.3
	Phi N	1	6	.143	10	10	0	0-0	49	57	37	14	1	31-1	21	6.24	71	.291	.390	11-0-3	.182	-0	55	-10	0	-1.2
Total	11	43	37	.538	162	112	1	0-2	720.2	682	421	101	21	393-17	496	4.92	92	.250	.346	20-0-5	.250	1	106	-28	252	-3.5
ABBOTT, GLENN	William Glenn; B2.16.1951 Little Rock AR; BR/TR/6´6˝/(195–210); [OakA69 8/175]; d7.29; Col Central Arkansas; [DL 1982 Sea A 182]																									
1973	Oak A	1	0	1.000	5	3	1	0-0	18.2	16	8	3	0	7-0	6	3.86	92	.225	.291	0	ø	0	159	0	0	0.0
1974	Oak A	5	7	.417	19	17	3	0-0	96	89	38	4	3	34-3	38	3.00	111	.247	.316	0	ø	0	90	4	0	0.4
1975	†Oak A	5	5	.500	30	15	3-1	0-0	114.1	109	61	12	2	50-7	51	4.25	86	.253	.330	0	ø	0	129	-8	0	-0.6
1976	Oak A	2	4	.333	19	10	0	0-0	62.1	87	41	6	1	16-0	27	5.49	61	.333	.371	0	ø	0	112	-14	0	-1.3
1977	Sea A	12	13	.480	36	34	7	0-0	204.1	212	111	32	12	56-2	100	4.45	93	.270	.327	0	ø	0	93	-6	0	-0.7
1978	Sea A	7	15	.318	29	28	8-1	0-0	155.1	191	99	22	2	44-5	67	5.27	73	.303	.349	0	ø	0	83	-23	20	-2.8
1979	Sea A	4	10	.286	23	19	3	0-0	116.2	138	78	19	3	38-2	25	5.17	85	.301	.351	0	ø	0	90	-11	20	-1.2
1980	Sea A	12	12	.500	31	31	7-2	0-0	215	228	110	27	3	49-4	78	4.10	102	.272	.314	0	ø	0	96	1	0	0.2
1981	Sea A	4	9	.308	22	20	1	0-0	130.1	127	64	14	0	28-1	35	3.94	99	.258	.296	0	ø	0	88	-1	0	-0.1
1983	Sea A	5	3	.625	14	14	2	0-0	82.1	103	46	9	4	15-2	38	4.59	93	.311	.347	0	ø	0	103	-2	66	-0.2
	Det A	2	1	.667	7	7	1-1	0-0	46.2	43	12	5	0	7-1	11	1.93	205	.244	.272	0	ø	0	69	10	0	0.6
	Year	7	4	.636	21	21	3-1	0-0	129	146	58	14	4	22-3	49	3.63	115	.288	.321	0	ø	0	92	8	0	0.4
1984	Det A	3	4	.429	13	8	1	0-0	44	62	39	9	2	8-1	8	5.93	67	.326	.356	0	ø	0	111	-12	0	-1.7
Total	11	62	83	.428	248	206	37-5	0-0	1286	1405	707	162	32	352-28	484	4.39	90	.280	.328	0	ø	0	96	-62	288	-7.4
ABER, AL	Albert Julius "Lefty"; B7.31.1927 Cleveland OH; D5.20.1993 Garfield Heights OH; BL/TL/6´2˝/(195–205); d9.15; Mil 1951–52																									
1950	Cle A	1	0	1.000	1	1	1	0	9	5	2	0	0	4	4	2.00	217	.167	.265	2	.000	0	83	3	0	0.3
1953	Cle A	1	1	.500	6	0	0	0	6	6	6	0	0	9	4	7.50	50	.240	.441	0	ø	1	—	-3	0	-0.5
	Det A	4	3	.571	17	10	2	0	66.2	63	35	3	0	41	34	4.45	91	.260	.367	23-0-1	.130	-1	122	-2	0	-0.3
	Year	5	4	.556	23	10	2	0	72.2	69	41	3	0	50	38	4.71	86	.258	.375	23-0-1	.130	-1	123	-5	0	-0.8
1954	Det A	5	11	.313	32	18	4	3	124.2	121	63	8	3	40	54	3.97	93	.257	.318	39-0-3	.128	-1	86	-4	0	-0.6
1955	Det A	6	3	.667	39	1	0	3	80	86	32	9	0	28-1	37	3.37	114	.275	.334	17-0-2	.059	-2	116	5	0	0.4
1956	Det A	4	4	.500	42	0	0	7	63	65	30	1	2	25-6	21	3.43	120	.270	.341	10-0-2	.300	1	—	4	0	0.5
1957	Det A	3	3	.500	28	0	0	1	37	46	33	6	1	11-3	15	6.81	57	.315	.363	8	.125	-0	—	-13	0	-1.9
	KC A	0	0	ø	3	0	0	0	3	6	4	2	0	2-0	0	12.00	33	.400	.471	1	1.000	0	—	-2	0	-0.1
	Year	3	3	.500	31	0	0	1	40	52	37	8	1	13-3	15	7.20	54	.323	.373	9	.222	0	—	-16	0	-2.0
Total	6	24	25	.490	168	30	7	14	389.1	398	205	29	6	160-10	169	4.18	93	.269	.341	100-0-8	.140	-3	99	-12	0	-2.2
ABERNATHIE, BILL	William Edward; B1.30.1929 Torrance CA; D2.19.2006 Yucaipa CA; BR/TR/5´10˝/190; d9.27																									
1952	Cle A	0	0	ø	1	0	0	1	2	4	3	1	0	1	0	13.50	25	.444	.500	1	.000	-0	—	-2	0	-0.2

YEAR	TM LG	W	L	PCT	G	GS	CG-SHO	SV-BS	IP	H	R	HR	HB	BB-IB	SO	ERA	AERA	OAV	OOB	AB-HR-SH	AVG	PB	SUP	APR	DL	PW
Abernathy, Ted	Talmadge Lafayette; B10.30.1921 Mebane NC; D11.16.2001 Charlotte NC; BR/TL/6´2˝/210; d9.19; Col Elon																									
1942	Phi A	0	0	ø	1	0	0	0	2.2	2	3	0	0	3	1	10.13	37	.222	.417	0	ø	0	—	-2	0	0.0
1943	Phi A	0	3	.000	5	2	1	0	14.2	24	22	0	0	13	10	12.89	26	.353	.457	4	.250	0	62	-14	0	-2.2
1944	Phi A	0	0	ø	1	0	0	0	3	5	1	0	0	1	2	3.00	116	.417	.462	1	.000	-0	—	0	0	0.0
Total	3	0	3	.000	7	2	1	0	20.1	31	26	0	0	17	13	11.07	31	.348	.453	5	.200	0	62	-16	0	-2.2
Abernathy, Ted	Theodore Wade; B3.6.1933 Stanley NC; D12.16.2004 Gastonia NC; BR/TR/6´4˝/(205–215); d4.13																									
1955	Was A	5	9	.357	40	14	3-2	0	119.1	136	87	9	7	67-1	79	5.96	64	.294	.386	26-0-4	.154	-1	78	-28	0	-2.9
1956	Was A	1	3	.250	5	4	2	0	30.1	35	16	2	1	10-0	18	4.15	104	.292	.348	11	.182	-0	57	1	0	0.1
1957	Was A	2	10	.167	26	16	2	0	85	100	65	9	4	65-1	50	6.78	57	.314	.433	24-0-2	.167	0	69	-24	0	-2.9
1960	Was A	0	0	ø	2	0	0	0	3	4	4	0	0	4-0	1	12.00	32	.308	.471	1	1.000	0	—	-2	0	-0.1
1963	Cle A	7	2	.778	43	0	0	12	59.1	54	25	3	0	29-6	47	2.88	126	.251	.339	5-0-1	.400	1	—	3	0	0.9
1964	Cle A	2	6	.250	53	0	0	11	72.2	66	40	5	2	46-5	57	4.33	83	.247	.360	6-0-1	.000	-1	—	-6	0	-0.8
1965	Chi N	4	6	.400	**84**	0	0	**31**	136.1	113	49	7	5	56-13	104	2.57	143	.227	.309	18-0-3	.167	0	—	15	0	2.1
1966	Chi N	1	3	.250	20	0	0	4	27.2	26	19	4	2	17-1	18	6.18	60	.255	.372	4	.000	-0	—	-6	0	-1.0
	Atl N	4	4	.500	38	0	0	4	65.1	58	34	5	0	36-10	42	3.86	94	.247	.343	8	.250	1	—	-3	0	-0.2
	Year	5	7	.417	58	0	0	8	93	84	53	9	2	53-11	60	4.55	80	.249	.352	12	.167	0	—	-10	0	-1.2
1967	Cin N	6	3	.667	**70**	0	0	**28**	106.1	63	19	1	5	41-5	88	1.27	295	.170	.261	17	.059	-1	—	**26**	0	3.8
1968	Cin N	10	7	.588	**78**	0	0	13	135.1	111	43	9	4	55-15	64	2.46	128	.228	.307	17	.000	-1	—	10	0	1.6
1969	Chi N	4	3	.571	56	0	0	3-3	85.1	75	38	8	1	42-11	55	3.16	127	.234	.322	8	.250	0	—	6	0	0.6
1970	Chi N	0	0	ø	11	0	0	1-0	9	9	2	0	1	5-1	2	2.00	225	.281	.395	0	ø	0	—	2	0	0.1
	StL N	1	0	1.000	11	0	0	1-2	18.1	15	6	0	3	12-4	8	2.95	141	.246	.385	3	.000	-0	—	3	0	0.2
	Year	1	0	1.000	22	0	0	2-2	27.1	24	8	0	4	17-5	10	2.63	162	.258	.388	3	.000	-0	—	5	0	0.3
	KC A	9	3	.750	36	0	0	12-3	55.2	41	23	3	1	38-0	49	2.59	144	.209	.340	14-0-3	.214	0	—	5	0	1.1
1971	KC A	4	6	.400	63	0	0	23-4	81	60	28	3	6	50-4	55	2.56	135	.210	.336	13-0-1	.077	-1	—	7	0	1.3
1972	KC A	3	4	.429	45	0	0	5-5	58.1	44	15	2	3	19-3	28	1.70	179	.210	.282	6	.000	-1	—	7	0	1.1
Total	14	63	69	.477	681	34	7-2	148-17	1148.1	1010	513	70	45	592-80	765	3.46	106	.241	.338	181-0-15	.138	-4	75	16	0	5.0
Abernathy, Woody	Virgil Woodrow; B2.1.1915 Forest City NC; D12.5.1994 Louisville KY; BL/TL/6´0˝/170; d7.28																									
1946	NY N	1	1	.500	15	1	0	1	40	32	16	5	0	10	6	3.37	102	.232	.284	8	.000	-1	100	1	0	-0.1
1947	NY N	0	0	ø	1	0	0	0	2	4	3	0	0	1	0	9.00	45	.400	.455	0	ø	0	—	-1	0	-0.1
Total	2	1	1	.500	16	1	0	1	42	36	19	5	0	11	6	3.64	95	.243	.296	8	.000	-1	100	0	0	-0.2
Ables, Harry	Harry Terrell "Hans"; B10.4.1883 Terrell TX; D2.8.1951 San Antonio TX; BR/TL/6´2.5˝/200; d9.4; Col Southwestern (TX)																									
1905	StL A	0	3	.000	6	3	1	0	30.2	37	22	0	0	13	11	3.82	67	.301	.368	10	.000	-1	37	-6	—	-0.7
1909	Cle A	1	1	.500	5	3	3	0	29.2	26	14	1	1	10	24	2.12	120	.226	.294	12	.000	-1	119	0	—	-0.2
1911	NY A	0	1	.000	3	2	0	0	11	16	15	1	0	7	6	9.82	37	.333	.418	4	.000	-1	140	-7	—	-0.6
Total	3	1	5	.167	14	8	4	0	71.1	79	51	2	1	30	41	4.04	67	.276	.347	26	.000	-4	102	-13	—	-1.5
Abrams, George	George Allen; B11.9.1899 Seattle WA; D12.5.1986 Clearwater FL; BR/TR/5´9˝/170; d4.19																									
1923	Cin N	0	0	ø	3	0	0	0	4.2	10	5	0	1	3	1	9.64	40	.500	.583	1	1.000	0	—	-3	—	-0.1
Abrego, Johnny	Johnny Ray; B7.4.1962 Corpus Christi TX; BR/TR/6´0˝/185; [PhiN81 1/20]; d9.4																									
1985	Chi N	1	1	.500	6	5	0	0-0	24	32	18	3	0	12-1	13	6.38	63	.352	.423	9	.000	-1	133	-5	0	-0.5
Abreu, Winston	Winston (Leonardo); B4.5.1977 Cotui, D.R.; BR/TR/6´2˝/170; d8.6																									
2006	Bal A	0	0	ø	7	0	0	0-0	8	10	10	1	1	6-1	6	10.13	45	.294	.405	0	ø	0	—	-5	0	-0.2
Accardo, Jeremy	Jeremy Lee; B12.18.1981 Phoenix AZ; BR/TR/6´2˝/190; d5.4; Col Illinois St.																									
2005	SF N	1	5	.167	28	0	0	0-1	29.2	26	13	2	1	9-1	16	3.94	108	.232	.293	2	.500	0	—	1	0	0.3
2006	SF N	1	3	.250	38	0	0	3-3	40.1	38	23	2	1	11-3	40	4.91	90	.247	.294	5	.000	-1	—	-2	0	-0.2
	Tor A	1	1	.500	27	0	0	0-2	28.2	38	19	5	0	9-2	14	5.97	79	.325	.373	0	ø	0	—	-3	0	-0.2
Total	2	3	9	.250	93	0	0	3-6	98.2	102	55	9	2	29-6	70	4.93	91	.266	.317	7	.143	-0	—	-4	0	-0.1
Acevedo, Jose	Jose Omar; B12.18.1977 Santo Domingo, D.R.; BR/TR/6´0˝/185; d6.19																									
2001	Cin N	5	7	.417	18	18	0	0-0	96	101	61	17	3	34-2	68	5.44	84	.272	.336	34-0-2	.118	-1	113	-7	0	-0.9
2002	Cin N	4	2	.667	6	5	0	0-0	23.2	28	21	8	2	12-0	14	7.23	59	.292	.382	7-0-2	.143	0	82	-7	0	-1.3
2003	Cin N	2	0	1.000	5	4	1	0-0	27	17	8	3	1	6-1	23	2.67	156	.183	.235	9-0-2	.000	-1	141	5	53	0.2
2004	Cin N	5	12	.294	39	27	0	0-0	157.2	188	108	30	5	45-8	117	5.94	72	.292	.340	43-0-5	.047	-3	102	-27	0	-2.8
2005	Col N	2	4	.333	36	5	0	1-1	64	86	48	13	1	16-3	31	6.47	72	.321	.355	8-0-1	.125	0	73	-11	49	-1.0
Total	5	18	25	.419	104	59	1	1-1	368.1	420	246	71	12	113-14	253	5.74	77	.285	.338	101-0-12	.079	-4	104	-47	102	-5.8
Acevedo, Juan	Juan Carlos (Lara); B5.5.1970 Ciudad Juarez, Chihuahua, Mexico; BR/TR/6´2˝/(195–243); [ColN92 14/403]; d4.30; Col Parkland (IL) JC; [DL 1996 NY N 38]																									
1995	Col N	4	6	.400	17	11	0	0-0	65.2	82	53	15	6	20-2	40	6.44	83	.317	.376	18	.056	-2	84	-7	0	-1.0
1997	NY N	3	1	.750	25	2	0	0-4	47.2	52	24	6	4	22-2	33	3.59	112	.286	.366	6-0-1	.000	-1	184	1	0	0.0
1998	StL N	8	3	.727	50	9	0	15-1	98.1	83	30	7	4	29-2	56	2.56	164	.236	.301	17-0-2	.176	0	90	19	29	2.5
1999	StL N	6	8	.429	50	12	0	4-2	102.1	115	71	17	4	48-3	52	5.89	78	.291	.369	20-0-2	.050	-2	115	-13	0	-1.9
2000	Mil N	3	7	.300	62	0	0	0-2	82.2	77	38	11	1	31-9	51	3.81	121	.246	.315	1	.000	0	—	8	22	0.8
2001	Col N	0	2	.000	39	0	0	0-5	32	37	24	4	1	19-6	26	5.63	95	.285	.377	0	ø	0	—	-2	40	-0.1
	Fla N	2	3	.400	20	0	0	0-0	28.1	31	11	2	1	16-3	21	2.54	164	.284	.375	3-0-1	.333	1	—	4	0	0.7
	Year	2	5	.286	59	0	0	0-5	60.1	68	35	6	2	35-9	47	4.18	115	.285	.376	3-0-1	.333	1	—	2	0	0.6
2002	Det A	1	5	.167	65	0	0	28-7	74.2	68	33	4	5	23-3	43	2.65	165	.246	.311	0	ø	0	—	11	0	1.5
2003	NY A	0	3	.000	25	0	0	6-1	25.2	34	24	5	2	10-3	19	7.71	57	.315	.374	0	ø	0	—	-10	0	-1.4
	Tor A	1	2	.333	14	0	0	0-1	12.2	18	8	1	0	8-1	9	4.26	111	.327	.413	0	ø	0	—	0	0	0.0
	Year	1	5	.167	39	0	0	6-2	38.1	52	32	6	2	18-4	28	6.57	69	.319	.387	0	ø	0	—	-9	0	-1.4
Total	8	28	40	.412	367	34	0	53-23	570	597	316	72	28	226-34	350	4.33	106	.274	.346	65-0-6	.092	-3	105	11	129	1.1
Acker, Jim	James Justin; B9.24.1958 Freer TX; BR/TR/6´2˝/(210–215); [AtlN80 1/21]; d4.7; Col Texas																									
1983	Tor A	5	1	.833	38	5	0	1-1	97.2	103	52	7	8	38-1	44	4.33	101	.273	.351	0	ø	0	205	0	0	0.1
1984	Tor A	3	5	.375	32	3	0	1-2	72	79	39	3	6	25-3	33	4.38	95	.286	.357	0	ø	0	73	-2	16	-0.2
1985	†Tor A	7	2	.778	61	0	0	10-3	86.1	86	35	7	3	43-1	42	3.23	131	.268	.358	0	ø	0	—	9	0	1.1
1986	Tor A	2	4	.333	23	5	0	0-2	60	63	34	6	2	22-3	32	4.35	98	.281	.344	0	ø	0	68	-2	0	-0.1
	Atl N	3	8	.273	21	14	0	0-1	95	100	47	7	1	26-3	37	3.79	105	.274	.321	28	.107	-1	58	1	0	0.0
1987	Atl N	4	9	.308	68	0	0	14-2	114.2	109	57	11	4	51-4	68	4.16	104	.253	.336	14	.214	0	—	3	0	0.5
1988	Atl N	0	4	.000	21	1	0	0-0	42	45	26	6	1	14-3	25	4.71	78	.280	.335	5	.400	1	0	-5	102	-0.4
1989	Atl N	0	6	.000	59	0	0	2-3	97.2	84	29	5	1	20-8	68	2.67	137	.237	.278	7	.143	-0	—	12	0	0.8
	†Tor A	2	1	.667	14	0	0	0-0	28.1	24	7	1	1	12-3	24	1.59	239	.235	.322	0	ø	0	—	6	0	0.7
1990	Tor A	4	4	.500	59	0	0	1-1	91.2	103	49	9	3	30-5	54	3.83	103	.281	.340	0	ø	0	—	-2	0	-0.1
1991	†Tor A	3	5	.375	54	4	0	1-2	88.1	77	53	16	2	36-5	44	5.20	81	.238	.313	0	ø	0	114	-8	0	-0.7
1992	Sea A	0	0	ø	17	0	0	0-0	30.2	45	19	4	0	12-1	11	5.28	76	.338	.388	0	ø	0	—	-4	36	-0.2
Total	10	33	49	.402	467	32	0	30-17	904.1	918	447	82	32	329-40	482	3.97	103	.267	.334	54	.167	0	91	8	154	1.5
Acker, Tom	Thomas James; B3.7.1930 Paterson NJ; BR/TR/6´4˝/(215–223); d4.20																									
1956	Cin N	4	3	.571	29	7	1-1	1	83.2	60	23	7	2	29-1	54	2.37	168	.201	.272	19	.053	-1	139	15	0	1.1
1957	Cin N	10	5	.667	49	6	1	4	108.2	122	63	16	8	41-8	67	4.97	83	.293	.361	19-0-2	.053	-1	111	-9	0	-1.2
1958	Cin N	4	3	.571	38	10	3	1	124.2	126	64	10	3	43-6	90	4.55	91	.266	.328	30-0-2	.067	-1	139	-3	0	-0.4
1959	Cin N	1	2	.333	37	0	0	2	63.1	57	31	10	4	37-5	45	4.12	98	.246	.356	9-0-2	.111	-0	—	0	0	-0.1
Total	4	19	13	.594	153	23	5-1	8	380.1	365	181	43	17	150-20	256	4.12	99	.257	.331	77-0-6	.065	-3	132	3	0	-0.6
Ackley, Fritz	Florian Frederick; B4.10.1937 Hayward WI; D5.22.2002 Duluth MN; BL/TR/6´1.5˝/193; d9.21																									
1963	Chi A	1	0	1.000	2	2	0	0	13	7	4	2	0	7-0	11	2.08	169	.167	.280	5	.200	0	127	2	0	0.2
1964	Chi A	0	0	ø	3	2	0	0	6.1	10	6	2	0	4-0	6	8.53	41	.345	.424	1	1.000	1	154	-3	0	0.0
Total	2	1	0	1.000	5	4	0	0	19.1	17	10	4	0	11-0	17	4.19	83	.239	.337	6	.333	1	140	-1	0	0.2
Acosta, Cy	Cecilio (Miranda); B11.22.1946 ElSabino, Sinaloa, Mexico; BR/TR/5´10˝/165; d6.4																									
1972	Chi A	3	0	1.000	26	0	0	5-0	34.2	25	6	2	0	17-3	28	1.56	201	.210	.309	4	.000	-0	—	6	0	0.7

THE PITCHER REGISTER

YEAR	TM LG	W	L	PCT	G	GS	CG-SHO	SV-BS	IP	H	R	HR	HB	BB-IB	SO	ERA	AERA	OAV	OOB	AB-HR-SH	AVG	PB	SUP	APR	DL	PW
1973	Chi A	10	6	.625	48	0	0	18-4	97	66	30	8	7	39-3	60	2.23	178	.193	.287	1	.000	-0	—	17	0	3.3
1974	Chi A	0	3	.000	27	0	0	3-4	45.2	43	22	3	5	18-2	19	3.74	100	.256	.338	2	.000	-0	—	0	44	0.0
1975	Phi N	0	0	ø	6	0	0	1-0	8.2	9	7	2	0	3-0	2	6.23	60	.273	.333	0	ø	0	—	-2	0	-0.1
Total	4	13	9	.591	107	0	0	27-8	186	143	65	15	12	77-8	109	2.66	141	.216	.306	7	.000	-1	—	21	44	3.9

Acosta, Ed Eduardo Elixbet; B3.9.1944 Boquete, Pan; BB/TR (BR 1970)/6´5˝/(208–215); d9.7

YEAR	TM LG	W	L	PCT	G	GS	CG-SHO	SV-BS	IP	H	R	HR	HB	BB-IB	SO	ERA	AERA	OAV	OOB	AB-HR-SH	AVG	PB	SUP	APR	DL	PW
1970	Pit N	0	0	ø	3	0	0	1-0	2.2	5	4	1	1	2-0	1	13.50	29	.417	.500	0	ø	0	—	-3	0	-0.2
1971	SD N	3	3	.500	8	6	3-1	0-0	46	43	18	4	0	7-1	16	2.74	121	.246	.272	17	.000	-2	80	2	0	0.1
1972	SD N	3	6	.333	46	2	0	0-1	89	105	49	7	3	30-7	53	4.45	74	.302	.358	12	.083	-0	147	-11	0	-1.2
Total	3	6	9	.400	57	8	3-1	1-1	137.2	153	71	12	4	39-8	70	4.05	82	.286	.334	29	.034	-2	96	-12	0	-1.3

Acosta, Jose Jose "Acostica"; B3.4.1891 Havana, Cuba; D11.16.1977 Havana, Cuba; BR/TR/5´6˝/134; d7.28; b–Merito

YEAR	TM LG	W	L	PCT	G	GS	CG-SHO	SV-BS	IP	H	R	HR	HB	BB-IB	SO	ERA	AERA	OAV	OOB	AB-HR-SH	AVG	PB	SUP	APR	DL	PW
1920	Was A	5	4	.556	17	5	4-1	1	82.2	92	40	1	0	26	9	4.03	93	.290	.344	25-0-2	.240	1	89	0	—	0.0
1921	Was A	5	4	.556	33	7	2	3	115.2	148	65	4	0	36	30	4.36	94	.317	.366	30-0-1	.067	-2	96	-2	—	-0.4
1922	Chi A	0	2	.000	5	1	0	0	15	25	14	4	0	6	6	8.40	48	.417	.470	5	.200	0	146	-6	—	-0.7
Total	3	10	10	.500	55	13	6-1	4	213.1	265	119	9	0	68	45	4.51	88	.314	.365	60-0-3	.150	-1	97	-8	—	-1.1

Acre, Mark Mark Robert; B9.16.1968 Concord CA; BR/TR/6´8˝/(240–246); d5.13; Col New Mexico St.

YEAR	TM LG	W	L	PCT	G	GS	CG-SHO	SV-BS	IP	H	R	HR	HB	BB-IB	SO	ERA	AERA	OAV	OOB	AB-HR-SH	AVG	PB	SUP	APR	DL	PW
1994	Oak A	5	1	.833	34	0	0	0-1	34.1	24	13	4	1	23-3	21	3.41	132	.202	.333	0	ø	0	—	5	0	0.7
1995	Oak A	1	2	.333	43	0	0	0-4	52	52	35	7	2	28-2	47	5.71	79	.256	.349	0	ø	0	—	-7	22	-0.4
1996	Oak A	1	3	.250	22	0	0	2-1	25	38	17	4	2	9-4	18	6.12	81	.339	.398	0	ø	0	—	-3	0	-0.4
1997	Oak A	2	0	1.000	15	0	0	0-2	15.2	21	10	1	0	8-0	12	5.74	80	.318	.387	0	ø	0	—	-2	0	-0.2
Total	4	9	6	.600	114	0	0	2-8	127	135	75	16	5	68-9	98	5.17	89	.270	.360	0	ø	0	—	-7	22	-0.3

Adams, Ace Ace Townsend; B3.2.1910 Willows CA; D2.26.2006 Albany GA; BR/TR/5´10.5˝/182; d4.15

YEAR	TM LG	W	L	PCT	G	GS	CG-SHO	SV-BS	IP	H	R	HR	HB	BB-IB	SO	ERA	AERA	OAV	OOB	AB-HR-SH	AVG	PB	SUP	APR	DL	PW
1941	NY N	4	1	.800	38	0	0	1	71	84	43	3	1	35	18	4.82	77	.304	.385	12	.083	-1	—	-8	0	-0.7
1942	NY N	7	4	.636	**61**	0	0	11	88	69	23	1	0	31	33	1.84	183	.223	.293	10	.100	-1	—	**14**	0	2.1
1943	NY N☆	11	7	.611	**70**	3	1	9	140.1	121	50	5	1	55	46	2.82	122	.236	.311	32-0-2	.125	-1	189	9	0	1.1
1944	NY N	8	11	.421	**65**	4	1	**13**	137.2	149	71	8	4	58	32	4.25	86	.279	.354	29-0-4	.103	-2	63	-6	0	-1.2
1945	NY N	11	9	.550	65	0	0	**15**	113	109	55	7	2	44	39	3.42	114	.252	.324	16-0-2	.188	0	—	3	0	0.7
1946	NY N	0	1	.000	3	0	0	0	2.2	9	5	2	0	1	3	16.88	20	.500	.526	0	ø	0	—	-4	0	-0.7
Total	6	41	33	.554	302	7	2	49	552.2	541	247	26	8	224	171	3.47	104	.260	.334	99-0-8	.121	-4	114	8	0	1.3

Adams, Babe Charles Benjamin; B5.18.1882 Tipton IN; D7.27.1968 Silver Spring MD; BL/TR/5´11.5˝/185; d4.18

YEAR	TM LG	W	L	PCT	G	GS	CG-SHO	SV-BS	IP	H	R	HR	HB	BB-IB	SO	ERA	AERA	OAV	OOB	AB-HR-SH	AVG	PB	SUP	APR	DL	PW
1906	StL N	0	1	.000	1	1	0	0	4	9	8	0	0	2	0	13.50	19	.474	.524	1	.000	-0	28	-5	—	-0.7
1907	Pit N	0	2	.000	4	3	1	0	22	40	25	1	3	3	11	6.95	35	.408	.442	7	.286	0	68	-11	—	-0.9
1909	†Pit N	12	3	.800	25	12	7-3	2	130	88	25	0	3	23	65	1.11	246	.196	.240	39-0-5	.051	-3	88	21	—	2.3
1910	Pit N	18	9	.667	34	30	16-3	0	245	217	95	4	6	60	101	2.24	138	.240	.291	83-0-5	.193	1	126	18	—	1.7
1911	Pit N	22	12	.647	40	37	24-6	0	293.1	253	97	5	8	42	133	2.33	147	.237	**.271**	103-0-1	.252	4	103	35	—	3.9
1912	Pit N	11	8	.579	28	20	11-2	0	170.1	169	73	4	3	35	63	2.91	112	.262	.303	53-0-1	.226	4	104	6	—	0.9
1913	Pit N	21	10	.677	43	37	24-4	0	313.2	271	94	7	0	49	144	2.15	140	.235	.267	114-0-3	.289	9	113	33	—	4.1
1914	Pit N	13	16	.448	40	35	19-3	1	283	253	97	5	7	39	91	2.51	105	.244	**.276**	97-1-2	.165	1	96	6	—	0.5
1915	Pit N	14	14	.500	40	30	17-2	2	245	229	90	6	2	34	62	2.87	95	.252	.280	85-0-2	.141	-2	103	1	—	-0.2
1916	Pit N	2	9	.182	16	10	4-1	0	72.1	91	51	2	3	12	22	5.72	47	.320	.355	22-0-1	.273	2	64	-20	—	-2.6
1918	Pit N	1	1	.500	3	3	2	0	22.2	15	4	0	0	4	6	1.19	241	.197	.237	9	.333	1	61	4	—	0.5
1919	Pit N	17	10	.630	34	29	23-6	1	263.1	213	66	1	3	23	92	1.98	152	.220	**.241**	92-0-3	.185	-0	83	30	—	3.0
1920	Pit N	17	13	.567	35	33	19-**8**	2	263	240	83	6	1	18	84	2.16	149	.244	**.259**	89-1-2	.146	-5	74	28	—	2.5
1921	Pit N	14	5	.737	25	20	11-2	0	160	155	57	4	0	18	55	2.64	**145**	.251	**.272**	63-0-2	.254	3	122	20	—	2.5
1922	Pit N	8	11	.421	27	19	12-4	0	171.1	191	77	1	4	15	39	3.57	114	.287	.307	56-1-5	.286	4	102	12	—	1.5
1923	Pit N	13	7	.650	26	22	11	1	158.2	196	83	8	1	25	38	4.42	91	.309	.336	55-0-1	.273	5	112	-4	—	-0.1
1924	Pit N	3	1	.750	9	3	2	0	39.2	31	9	1	0	3	5	1.13	338	.209	.225	11-0-1	.182	-0	74	11	—	0.9
1925	†Pit N	6	5	.545	33	10	3	3	101.1	129	67	7	3	17	18	5.42	82	.306	.338	31-0-1	.226	0	104	-7	—	-0.8
1926	Pit N	2	3	.400	19	0	0	3	36.2	51	32	5	0	8	7	6.14	64	.347	.381	9	.222	-0	—	-9	—	-1.3
Total	19	194	140	.581	482	354	206-44	15	2995.1	2841	1133	67	47	430	1036	2.76	118	.253	.284	1019-3-35	.212	24	101	169	—	17.7

Adams, Red Charles Dwight; B10.7.1921 Parlier CA; BR/TR/6´0˝/185; d5.5; C12

YEAR	TM LG	W	L	PCT	G	GS	CG-SHO	SV-BS	IP	H	R	HR	HB	BB-IB	SO	ERA	AERA	OAV	OOB	AB-HR-SH	AVG	PB	SUP	APR	DL	PW
1946	Chi N	0	1	.000	8	0	0	0	12	18	12	1	0	7	8	8.25	40	.353	.431	1	.000	-0	—	-6	0	-0.5

Adams, Dan Daniel Leslie "Rube"; B6.19.1887 St.Louis MO; D10.6.1964 St.Louis MO; BR/TR/5´11.5˝/165; d5.22

YEAR	TM LG	W	L	PCT	G	GS	CG-SHO	SV-BS	IP	H	R	HR	HB	BB-IB	SO	ERA	AERA	OAV	OOB	AB-HR-SH	AVG	PB	SUP	APR	DL	PW
1914	KC F	4	9	.308	36	14	6	3	136	141	67	3	7	52	38	3.51	79	.273	.347	46-1-1	.152	-1	85	-10	—	-1.2
1915	KC F	0	2	.000	11	2	0	0	35	41	20	2	1	13	16	4.63	57	.301	.367	9	.111	-0	27	-7	—	-0.4
Total	2	4	11	.267	47	16	6	3	171	182	87	5	8	65	54	3.74	74	.279	.351	55-1-1	.145	-2	78	-17	—	-1.6

Adams, Willie James Irvin; B9.27.1890 Clearfield PA; D6.18.1937 Albany NY; BR/TR/6´4˝/180; d6.30; Col Albright

YEAR	TM LG	W	L	PCT	G	GS	CG-SHO	SV-BS	IP	H	R	HR	HB	BB-IB	SO	ERA	AERA	OAV	OOB	AB-HR-SH	AVG	PB	SUP	APR	DL	PW
1912	StL A	2	3	.400	13	5	0	0	46.1	50	32	0	2	19	16	3.88	85	.284	.360	13	.000	-2	67	-5	—	-0.7
1913	StL A	0	0	ø	4	0	0	0	9	12	14	1	3	4	5	10.00	29	.293	.396	1	.000	0	—	-7	—	-0.4
1914	Pit F	1	1	.500	15	2	1	2	55.1	70	29	4	1	22	14	3.74	77	.326	.391	15	.067	-1	120	-5	—	-0.5
1918	Phi A	5	12	.294	32	14	7	0	169	164	95	2	12	97	39	4.42	66	.272	.383	57-0-1	.140	-3	57	-22	—	-2.4
1919	Phi A	0	0	ø	1	0	0	0	4.2	7	2	1	1	2	0	3.86	89	.389	.476	2	.000	-0	—	0	—	0.0
Total	5	8	16	.333	65	21	8	2	284.1	303	172	8	19	144	74	4.37	69	.287	.383	88-0-1	.102	-6	66	-39	—	-4.0

Adams, Mike Jon Michael; B7.29.1978 Corpus Christi TX; BR/TR/6´5˝/190; d5.18; Col Texas A&M–Kingsville

YEAR	TM LG	W	L	PCT	G	GS	CG-SHO	SV-BS	IP	H	R	HR	HB	BB-IB	SO	ERA	AERA	OAV	OOB	AB-HR-SH	AVG	PB	SUP	APR	DL	PW
2004	Mil N	2	3	.400	46	0	0	0-5	53	50	21	5	2	14-2	39	3.40	129	.248	.300	0	ø	0	—	6	0	0.5
2005	Mil N	0	1	.000	13	0	0	1-1	13.1	12	4	2	0	10-1	14	2.70	157	.235	.361	0	ø	0	—	2	0	0.2
2006	Mil N	0	0	ø	2	0	0	0-0	2.1	4	3	1	0	2-0	1	11.57	39	.364	.462	0	ø	0	—	-2	0	-0.1
Total	3	2	4	.333	61	0	0	1-6	68.2	66	28	8	2	26-3	54	3.54	123	.250	.320	0	ø	0	—	6	0	0.6

Adams, Joe Joseph Edward; B10.28.1877 Cowden IL; D10.8.1952 Montgomery City MO; BR/TL/6´0˝/190; d4.26

YEAR	TM LG	W	L	PCT	G	GS	CG-SHO	SV-BS	IP	H	R	HR	HB	BB-IB	SO	ERA	AERA	OAV	OOB	AB-HR-SH	AVG	PB	SUP	APR	DL	PW
1902	StL N	0	0	ø	1	0	0	0	4	9	6	0	1	2	0	9.00	30	.450	.522	2	.000	-0	—	-3	—	-0.1

Adams, Karl Karl Tutwiler "Rebel"; B8.11.1891 Columbus GA; D9.17.1967 Everett WA; BR/TR/6´2˝/170; d4.19

YEAR	TM LG	W	L	PCT	G	GS	CG-SHO	SV-BS	IP	H	R	HR	HB	BB-IB	SO	ERA	AERA	OAV	OOB	AB-HR-SH	AVG	PB	SUP	APR	DL	PW
1914	Cin N	0	0	ø	4	0	0	0	8	14	10	1	0	5	5	9.00	33	.424	.500	2	.500	0	—	-5	—	-0.2
1915	Chi N	1	9	.100	26	12	3	0	107	105	62	5	2	43	57	4.71	59	.267	.342	30-0-1	.000	-4	65	-19	—	-2.1
Total	2	1	9	.100	30	12	3	0	115	119	72	6	2	48	62	5.01	56	.279	.355	32-0-1	.031	-4	65	-24	—	-2.3

Adams, Rick Reuben Alexander; B12.23.1878 Paris TX; D3.10.1955 Paris TX; BL/TL/6´0˝/165; d7.13

YEAR	TM LG	W	L	PCT	G	GS	CG-SHO	SV-BS	IP	H	R	HR	HB	BB-IB	SO	ERA	AERA	OAV	OOB	AB-HR-SH	AVG	PB	SUP	APR	DL	PW
1905	Was A	2	5	.286	11	6	3-1	0	62.2	63	30	1	8	24	25	3.59	74	.264	.351	23	.174	0	71	-5	—	-0.4

Adams, Bob Robert Andrew; B1.20.1907 Birmingham AL; D3.6.1970 Jacksonville FL; BR/TR/6´0.5˝/165; d9.27

YEAR	TM LG	W	L	PCT	G	GS	CG-SHO	SV-BS	IP	H	R	HR	HB	BB-IB	SO	ERA	AERA	OAV	OOB	AB-HR-SH	AVG	PB	SUP	APR	DL	PW
1931	Phi N	0	1	.000	1	1	0	0	6	14	10	0	0	1	3	9.00	47	.424	.441	3	.000	-0	40	-4	—	-0.5
1932	Phi N	0	0	ø	4	0	0	0	6	7	1	0	0	2	2	1.50	294	.318	.375	0	ø	-0	—	2	—	0.1
Total	2	0	1	.000	5	1	0	0	12	21	11	0	0	3	5	5.25	82	.382	.414	3	.000	-0	40	-2	—	-0.4

Adams, Bob Robert Burdette; B7.24.1901 Holyoke MA; D10.17.1996 Lemoyne PA; BR/TR/5´11˝/168; d9.22; Col Lehigh

YEAR	TM LG	W	L	PCT	G	GS	CG-SHO	SV-BS	IP	H	R	HR	HB	BB-IB	SO	ERA	AERA	OAV	OOB	AB-HR-SH	AVG	PB	SUP	APR	DL	PW
1925	Bos A	0	0	ø	2	0	0	0	5.2	10	5	1	0	3	1	7.94	57	.417	.481	3	.333	0	—	-2	—	0.0

Adams, Terry Terry Wayne; B3.6.1973 Mobile AL; BR/TR/6´3˝/(205–225); [ChiN91 4/111]; d8.10

YEAR	TM LG	W	L	PCT	G	GS	CG-SHO	SV-BS	IP	H	R	HR	HB	BB-IB	SO	ERA	AERA	OAV	OOB	AB-HR-SH	AVG	PB	SUP	APR	DL	PW
1995	Chi N	1	1	.500	18	0	0	1-0	18	22	15	0	0	10-1	15	6.50	64	.289	.372	0	ø	0	—	-5	0	-0.5
1996	Chi N	3	6	.333	69	0	0	4-4	101	84	36	6	1	49-6	78	2.94	149	.231	.322	6	.000	-0	—	16	0	1.3
1997	Chi N	2	9	.182	74	0	0	18-4	74	91	43	3	1	40-6	64	4.62	94	.306	.388	2	.000	-0	—	-3	0	-0.6
1998	Chi N	7	7	.500	63	0	0	1-6	72.2	72	39	7	1	41-3	73	4.33	102	.255	.349	1	.000	-0	—	0	0	0.0
1999	Chi N	6	3	.667	52	0	0	13-5	65	60	33	9	0	28-2	57	4.02	114	.245	.319	2	.000	-0	—	4	48	0.5
2000	LA N	6	9	.400	66	0	0	2-5	84.1	80	42	6	0	39-0	56	3.52	126	.245	.325	2-0-1	.000	-0	—	6	0	1.1
2001	LA N	12	8	.600	43	22	0	0-1	166.1	172	84	9	3	54-1	141	4.33	95	.267	.326	39-0-5	.051	-2	103	-3	0	-0.3
2002	Phi N	7	9	.438	46	19	0	0-1	136.2	132	76	9	3	58-5	96	4.35	88	.255	.333	25-0-6	.080	-1	112	-11	0	-1.1
2003	Phi N	1	4	.200	66	0	0	0-0	68	68	22	1	2	23-4	51	2.65	150	.268	.331	1	.000	-0	—	11	15	0.7
2004	Tor A	4	4	.500	42	0	0	3-3	43	49	20	4	1	22-2	35	3.98	123	.290	.371	0	ø	0	—	4	0	0.7

YEAR	TM LG	W	L	PCT	G	GS	CG-SHO	SV-BS	IP	H	R	HR	HB	BB-IB	SO	ERA	AERA	OAV	OOB	AB-HR-SH	AVG	PB	SUP	APR	DL	PW
	Bos A	2	0	1.000	19	0	0	0-0	27	35	19	6	1	6-1	21	6.00	81	.321	.353	0	ø	0	—	-3	0	-0.2
	Year	6	4	.600	61	0	0	3-3	70	84	39	10	2	28-3	56	4.76	103	.302	.364	0	ø	0	—	2	0	0.5
2005	Phi N	0	2	.000	16	0	0	0-1	13.1	25	19	3	4	10-2	4	12.83	34	.403	.513	0	ø	0	—	-12	0	-1.5
Total	11	51	62	.451	574	41	0	42-30	869.1	890	448	63	17	380-33	691	4.17	102	.266	.342	78-0-12	.051	-3	100	4	63	0.1
ADAMS, WILLIE	William Edward; B10.8.1972 Gallup NM; BR/TR/6´7˝/(211–215); [OakA93 1/36]; d6.11; Col Stanford; [DL 1998 Oak A 181]																									
1996	Oak A	3	4	.429	12	12	1-1	0-0	76.1	76	39	11	5	23-3	68	4.01	124	.257	.319	0	ø	0	85	7	0	0.5
1997	Oak A	3	5	.375	13	12	0	0-0	58.1	73	53	9	4	32-2	37	8.18	56	.307	.391	0	ø	0	98	-21	0	-2.3
Total	2	6	9	.400	25	24	1-1	0-0	134.2	149	92	20	9	55-5	105	5.81	83	.279	.352	0	ø	0	91	-14	181	-1.8
ADAMSON, JOEL	Joel Lee; B7.2.1971 Lakewood CA; BL/TL/6´4˝/185; [PhiN90 7/185]; d4.10; Col Cerritos (CA) JC																									
1996	Fla N	0	0	ø	9	0	0	0-0	11	18	9	1	1	7-0	7	7.36	56	.400	.481	0	ø	0	—	-4	0	-0.2
1997	Mil A	5	3	.625	30	6	0	0-0	76.1	78	36	13	5	19-0	56	3.54	131	.265	.319	3	.000	-0	86	8	0	0.7
1998	Ari N	0	3	.000	5	5	0	0-0	23	25	21	5	3	11-0	14	8.22	52	.284	.379	7-0-1	.429	1	120	-9	154	-0.8
Total	3	5	6	.455	44	11	0	0-0	110.1	121	66	19	9	37-0	77	4.89	92	.283	.350	10-0-1	.300	1	100	-5	154	-0.3
ADAMSON, MIKE	John Michael; B9.13.1947 San Diego CA; BR/TR/6´2˝/190; [BalA67 S1/1]; d7.1; Col USC																									
1967	Bal A	0	1	.000	3	2	0	0	9.2	9	9	1	0	12-0	8	8.38	38	.257	.438	2	.500	1	97	-5	0	-0.4
1968	Bal A	0	2	.000	2	2	0	0	7.2	9	9	2	0	4-0	4	9.39	31	.281	.361	3	.333	0	89	-5	0	-0.9
1969	Bal A	0	1	.000	6	0	0	0-0	8	10	4	0	0	6-2	2	4.50	80	.357	.444	1-0-1	.000	-0	—	-1	0	-0.1
Total	3	0	4	.000	11	4	0	0-0	25.1	28	22	3	0	22-2	14	7.46	43	.295	.417	6-0-1	.333	1	88	-11	0	-1.4
ADKINS, GRADY	Grady Emmett "Butcher Boy"; B6.29.1897 Jacksonville AR; D3.31.1966 Little Rock AR; BR/TR/5´11˝/175; d4.13																									
1928	Chi A	10	16	.385	36	27	14	1	224.2	235	113	12	6	89	54	3.73	109	.278	.351	70-0-9	.143	-3*	74	7	—	0.3
1929	Chi A	2	11	.154	31	15	5	0	138.1	168	98	12	1	67	24	5.33	80	.303	.379	46-0-1	.239	3*	64	-16	—	-0.9
Total	2	12	27	.308	67	42	19	1	363	403	211	24	7	156	78	4.34	95	.288	.363	116-0-10	.181	-1	70	-9	—	-0.6
ADKINS, DEWEY	John Dewey; B5.11.1918 Norcatur KS; D12.26.1998 Santa Monica CA; BR/TR/6´2˝/195; d9.19																									
1942	Was A	0	0	ø	1	1	0	0	6.1	7	8	0	0	6	3	9.95	37	.259	.394	2-0-1	.500	0	257	-4	0	-0.2
1943	Was A	0	0	ø	7	0	0	0	10.1	9	3	0	0	5	1	2.61	123	.250	.341	0	ø	0	—	1	0	0.0
1949	Chi N	2	4	.333	30	5	1	0	82.1	98	58	11	0	39	43	5.68	71	.298	.372	20-1-0	.200	1	96	-15	0	-0.8
Total	3	2	4	.333	38	6	1	0	99	114	69	11	0	50	47	5.64	70	.291	.371	22-1-1	.227	1	123	-18	0	-1.0
ADKINS, JON	Jonathan Scott; B8.30.1977 Huntington WV; BL/TR/6´0˝/(200–215); [OakA98 9/255]; d8.14; Col Oklahoma St.																									
2003	Chi A	0	0	ø	4	0	0	0-0	9.1	8	5	1	1	7-0	3	4.82	95	.250	.390	0	ø	0	—	0	0	0.0
2004	Chi A	2	3	.400	50	0	0	0-0	62	75	35	13	1	20-3	44	4.65	101	.305	.358	0	ø	0	—	0	0	0.0
2005	Chi A	0	1	.000	5	0	0	0-0	8.1	13	8	0	1	4-2	1	8.64	52	.351	.429	0	ø	0	—	-3	0	-0.3
2006	SD N	2	1	.667	55	0	0	0-0	54.1	55	26	3	2	20-4	30	3.98	104	.271	.339	1	.000	-0	—	1	0	0.1
Total	4	4	5	.444	114	0	0	0-0	134	151	74	17	5	51-9	78	4.63	96	.292	.358	1	.000	-0	—	-2	0	-0.2
ADKINS, DOC	Merle Theron; B8.5.1872 Troy WI; D2.21.1934 Durham NC; BR/TR/5´10.5˝/220; d6.24; Col Beloit																									
1902	Bos A	1	1	.500	4	2	1	0	20	30	20	2	0	7	3	4.05	88	.345	.394	9	.222	-0	70	-3	—	-0.3
1903	NY A	0	0	ø	2	1	0	1	7	10	8	0	1	5	0	7.71	40	.333	.444	3	.000	-0	183	-3	—	-0.2
Total	2	1	1	.500	6	3	1	1	27	40	28	2	1	12	3	5.00	69	.342	.408	12	.167	-1	104	-6	—	-0.5
ADKINS, STEVE	Steven Thomas; B10.26.1964 Chicago IL; BR/TL/6´6˝/200; [NYA86 15/392]; d9.12; Col Penn																									
1990	NY A	1	2	.333	5	5	0	0-0	24	19	18	4	0	29-0	14	6.38	63	.226	.421	0	ø	0	105	-6	0	-0.6
AFFELDT, JEREMY	Jeremy David; B6.6.1979 Phoenix AZ; BL/TL/6´4˝/(185–225); [KCA97 3/91]; d4.6																									
2002	KC A	3	4	.429	34	7	0	0-1	77.2	85	41	8	3	37-4	67	4.64	108	.274	.356	0	ø	0	40	3	53	0.3
2003	KC A	7	6	.538	36	18	0	4-0	126	126	58	12	5	38-1	98	3.93	123	.261	.318	6	.333	1	109	12	16	1.3
2004	KC A	3	4	.429	38	8	0	13-4	76.1	91	49	6	3	32-2	49	4.95	94	.302	.371	0	ø	0	87	-3	55	-0.4
2005	KC A	0	2	.000	49	0	0	0-0	49.2	56	35	3	0	29-2	39	5.26	83	.277	.366	0	ø	0	—	-7	67	-0.3
2006	KC A	4	6	.400	27	9	0	0-0	70	71	51	9	1	42-0	28	5.91	79	.262	.360	2	.000	-0	83	-10	0	-1.2
	Col N	4	2	.667	27	0	0	1-2	27.1	30	23	4	1	13-3	20	6.91	69	.270	.349	1	.000	-0	—	-6	0	-1.1
Total	5	21	24	.467	211	42	0	18-7	427	459	257	42	13	191-12	301	4.91	97	.274	.349	9	.222	0	88	-11	191	-1.4
AGOSTO, JUAN	Juan Róberto (Gonzalez); B2.23.1958 Rio Piedras, PR; BL/TL/6´2˝/(175–190); d9.7																									
1981	Chi A	0	0	ø	2	0	0	0-0	5.2	5	3	1	1	0-0	3	4.76	76	.238	.273	0	ø	0	—	-1	0	0.0
1982	Chi A	0	0	ø	1	0	0	0-0	2	7	4	0	0	0-0	1	18.00	23	.538	.538	0	ø	0	—	-3	0	-0.1
1983	†Chi A	2	2	.500	39	0	0	7-1	41.2	41	20	2	1	11-1	29	4.10	103	.283	.329	0	ø	0	—	1	0	0.1
1984	Chi A	2	1	.667	49	0	0	7-3	55.1	54	20	2	3	34-7	26	3.09	135	.270	.382	0	ø	0	—	7	0	0.6
1985	Chi A	4	3	.571	54	0	0	1-3	60.1	45	27	3	3	23-1	39	3.58	121	.210	.292	0	ø	0	—	5	0	0.6
1986	Chi A	0	2	.000	9	0	0	0-0	4.2	6	5	0	0	4-0	3	7.71	56	.300	.417	0	ø	0	—	-2	0	-0.4
	Min A	1	2	.333	17	1	0	1-1	20.1	43	25	1	2	14-0	9	8.85	49	.443	.522	0	ø	0	21	-11	0	-1.5
	Year	1	4	.200	26	1	0	1-1	25	49	30	1	2	18-0	12	8.64	50	.419	.504	0	ø	0	21	-13	0	-1.9
1987	Hou N	1	1	.500	27	0	0	2-2	27.1	26	12	1	0	10-1	6	2.63	149	.248	.313	1	.000	-0	—	3	0	0.3
1988	Hou N	10	2	.833	75	0	0	4-6	91.2	74	27	6	0	30-13	33	2.26	147	.226	.287	5-0-1	.000	-0	—	11	0	1.7
1989	Hou N	4	5	.444	71	0	0	1-4	83	81	32	3	2	32-10	46	2.93	116	.256	.323	5	.200	0	—	4	0	0.5
1990	Hou N	9	8	.529	**82**	0	0	4-4	92.1	91	46	4	7	39-8	50	4.29	87	.261	.345	2	.000	-0	—	-4	0	-0.7
1991	StL N	5	3	.625	72	0	0	2-5	86	92	52	4	8	39-4	34	4.81	78	.291	.380	3	.333	1	—	-11	0	-0.9
1992	StL N	2	4	.333	22	0	0	0-1	31.2	39	24	2	3	9-2	13	6.25	55	.312	.364	4	.000	-0	—	-10	0	-1.8
	Sea A	0	0	ø	17	1	0	0-1	18.1	27	12	0	0	3-0	12	5.89	68	.346	.366	0	ø	0	114	-3	0	-0.2
1993	Hou N	0	0	ø	6	0	0	0-0	6	8	4	1	0	0-0	3	6.00	65	.308	.308	0	ø	0	—	-1	0	-0.1
Total	13	40	33	.548	543	2	0	29-31	626.1	639	313	30	30	248-47	307	4.01	94	.272	.345	20-0-1	.100	-1	71	-15	0	-1.9
AGUILERA, RICK	Richard Warren; B12.31.1961 San Gabriel CA; BR/TR/6´5˝/(193–210); [NYN83 3/58]; d6.12; Col Brigham Young																									
1985	NY N	10	7	.588	21	19	2	0-0	122.1	118	49	8	2	37-2	74	3.24	108	.258	.314	36-0-7	.278	3*	88	3	0	0.8
1986	†NY N	10	7	.588	28	20	2	0-1	141.2	145	70	15	7	36-1	104	3.88	93	.263	.314	51-2-3	.157	2*	124	-5	0	-0.3
1987	NY N	11	3	.786	18	17	1	0-0	115	124	53	12	3	33-2	77	3.60	106	.276	.329	40-1-6	.225	3	131	3	93	0.7
1988	†NY N	0	4	.000	11	3	0	0-0	24.2	29	20	2	1	10-2	16	6.93	47	.296	.367	4	.250	0	136	-10	118	-1.4
1989	NY N	6	6	.500	36	0	0	7-4	69.1	59	19	3	2	21-3	80	2.34	141	.231	.294	7	.000	-0	—	8	0	1.5
	Min A	3	5	.375	11	11	3	0-0	75.2	71	32	5	1	17-1	57	3.21	129	.245	.289	0	ø	0	93	6	0	0.7
1990	Min A	5	3	.625	56	0	0	32-7	65.1	55	27	5	4	19-6	61	2.76	151	.224	.291	0	ø	0	—	8	0	1.4
1991	†Min A★	4	5	.444	63	0	0	42-9	69	44	20	3	1	30-6	61	2.35	182	.183	.274	0	ø	0	—	14	0	2.9
1992	Min A★	2	6	.250	64	0	0	41-7	66.2	60	28	7	1	17-4	52	2.84	144	.238	.287	0	ø	0	—	7	0	1.3
1993	Min A★	4	3	.571	65	0	0	34-6	72.1	60	25	9	1	14-3	59	3.11	142	.223	.263	0	ø	0	—	11	0	1.9
1994	Min A	1	4	.200	44	0	0	23-6	44.2	57	23	7	0	10-3	46	3.63	136	.306	.340	0	ø	0	—	5	0	0.9
1995	Min A	1	1	.500	22	0	0	12-3	25	20	7	2	1	6-1	29	2.52	191	.222	.273	0	ø	0	—	7	0	1.0
	†Bos A	2	2	.500	30	0	0	20-1	30.1	26	9	4	0	7-0	23	2.67	182	.228	.268	0	ø	0	—	8	0	1.5
	Year	3	3	.500	52	0	0	32-4	55.1	46	16	6	1	13-1	52	2.60	186	.225	.270	0	ø	0	—	14	0	2.5
1996	Min A	8	6	.571	19	19	2	0-0	111.1	124	69	20	3	27-1	83	5.42	95	.276	.319	0	ø	0	108	-2	71	-0.3
1997	Min A	5	4	.556	61	0	0	26-7	68.1	65	29	9	2	22-3	68	3.82	122	.257	.318	0	ø	0	—	7	0	1.4
1998	Min A	4	9	.308	68	0	0	38-11	74.1	75	35	8	1	15-1	57	4.24	113	.262	.299	0	ø	0	—	6	0	1.1
1999	Min A	3	1	.750	17	0	0	6-2	21.1	10	3	2	0	2-0	13	1.27	409	.135	.158	0	ø	0	—	9	0	1.7
	Chi N	6	3	.667	44	0	0	8-5	46.1	44	22	6	2	10-1	32	3.69	124	.254	.299	1	.000	-0	—	4	24	0.8
2000	Chi N	1	2	.333	54	0	0	29-8	47.2	47	28	11	4	18-2	38	4.91	93	.251	.330	0	ø	0	—	-2	13	-0.3
Total	16	86	81	.515	732	89	10	318-77	1291.1	1233	568	138	36	351-42	1030	3.57	118	.251	.303	139-3-16	.201	8	106	87	319	17.3
AGUIRRE, HANK	Henry John; B1.31.1931 Azusa CA; D9.5.1994 Bloomfield Hills MI; BR/TL (BB 1965–70)/6´4˝/(195–210); d9.10; C3																									
1955	Cle A	2	0	1.000	4	1	1-1	0	12.2	6	3	0	0	12-0	6	1.42	281	.143	.333	4	.000	-1	156	3	0	0.4
1956	Cle A	3	5	.375	16	9	2-1	1	65.1	63	35	7	1	27-1	31	3.72	113	.253	.326	18-0-3	.111	-2	73	2	0	0.0
1957	Cle A	1	1	.500	10	1	0	0	20.1	26	15	0	0	13-3	9	5.75	65	.317	.394	4	.000	-1	96	-5	0	-0.5
1958	Det A	3	4	.429	44	3	0	5	69.2	67	31	5	1	27-2	38	3.75	108	.255	.322	14	.214	0	67	3	0	0.4
1959	Det A	0	0	ø	3	0	0	0	2.2	4	1	0	0	3-0	3	3.38	120	.364	.500	0	ø	0	—	0	0	0.0
1960	Det A	5	3	.625	37	6	1	10	94.2	75	31	7	3	30-1	80	2.85	139	.217	.283	28-0-2	.036	-3	115	13	0	0.9

YEAR	TM LG	W	L	PCT	G	GS	CG-SHO	SV-BS	IP	H	R	HR	HB	BB-IB	SO	ERA	AERA	OAV	OOB	AB-HR-SH	AVG	PB	SUP	APR	DL	PW
1961	Det A	4	4	.500	45	0	0	8	55.1	44	22	5	2	38-3	32	3.25	126	.224	.354	9-0-3	.000	-1	—	6	0	0.8
1962	Det A★	16	8	.667	42	22	11-2	3	216	162	67	14	5	65-7	156	**2.21**	**184**	**.205**	**.267**	75-0-4	.027	-8	80	**41**	0	3.4
1963	Det A	14	15	.483	38	33	14-3	0	225.2	222	96	25	8	68-3	134	3.67	102	.256	.314	76-0-2	.132	-2	102	5	0	0.3
1964	Det A	5	10	.333	32	27	3	1	161.2	134	76	15	8	59-4	88	3.79	97	.223	.300	53-0-4	.057	-4	92	-3	0	-0.8
1965	Det A	14	10	.583	32	32	10-2	0	208.1	185	89	24	10	60-2	141	3.59	97	.236	.295	70-0-4	.086	-2	116	-1	0	-0.4
1966	Det A	3	9	.250	30	14	2	0	103.2	104	50	14	3	26-2	50	3.82	91	.260	.310	25-0-2	.120	0	89	-4	0	-0.5
1967	Det A	0	1	.000	31	1	0	0	41.1	34	15	2	0	17-2	33	2.40	136	.219	.295	2	.500	1	294	3	0	0.3
1968	LA N	1	2	.333	25	0	0	3	39	32	8	0	3	13-3	25	0.69	400	.227	.298	3	.000	-0	—	8	0	0.7
1969	Chi N	1	0	1.000	41	0	0	1-1	45	45	13	2	2	12-1	19	2.60	155	.269	.324	5	.400	0	—	7	0	0.5
1970	Chi N	3	0	1.000	17	0	0	1-1	14	13	10	3	1	9-1	11	4.50	100	.250	.371	2	.000	-0	—	-1	0	-0.2
Total	16	75	72	.510	447	149	44-9	33-2	1375.1	1216	562	123	47	479-35	856	3.25	116	.236	.305	388-0-24	.085	-21	97	77	0	5.3
Ahearne, Pat	Patrick Howard; B12.10.1969 San Francisco CA; BR/TR/6´3˝/195; [DetA92 7/196]; d6.14; Col Pepperdine																									
1995	Det A	0	2	.000	4	3	0	0-0	10	20	13	2	0	5-1	4	11.70	41	.400	.455	0	ø	0	90	-7	0	-1.0
Ainsworth, Kurt	Kurt Harold; B9.9.1978 Baton Rouge LA; BR/TR/6´3˝/(192–210); [SFN99 1/24]; d9.5; Col Louisiana St.; [DL 2005 Bal A 183]																									
2001	SF N	0	0	ø	2	0	0	0-0	2	3	3	1	1	2-0	3	13.50	30	.333	.500	0	ø	0	—	-2	0	-0.1
2002	SF N	1	2	.333	6	4	0	0-0	25.2	22	7	1	1	12-0	15	2.10	188	.237	.330	6-0-1	.167	0	76	5	0	0.7
2003	SF N	5	4	.556	11	11	0	0-0	66	66	31	7	1	26-0	48	3.82	111	.262	.331	22-0-4	.045	-2*	94	3	61	0.1
	Bal A	0	1	.000	3	0	0	0-0	2.1	6	3	1	0	1-0	4	11.57	40	.429	.467	0	ø	0	—	-2	50	-0.3
2004	Bal A	0	1	.000	7	7	0	0-0	30.2	39	34	6	5	20-0	20	9.68	48	.320	.430	0	ø	0	116	-16	0	-0.7
Total	4	6	8	.429	29	22	0	0-0	126.2	136	78	16	8	61-0	90	5.19	83	.278	.364	28-0-5	.071	-2	100	-12	294	-0.3
Aitchison, Raleigh	Raleigh Leonidas; B12.5.1887 Tyndall SD; D9.26.1958 Columbus KS; BR/TL/5´11.5˝/175; d4.19																									
1911	Bro N	0	1	.000	1	0	0	0	1.1	1	2	0	0	1	0	0.00	ø	.200	.333	0	ø	0	—	0	—	-0.1
1914	Bro N	12	7	.632	26	17	8-3	0	172.1	156	71	4	3	60	87	2.66	107	.244	.312	51-0-3	.196	1	112	4	—	0.5
1915	Bro N	0	4	.000	7	5	2	0	32.2	36	25	3	2	6	14	4.96	56	.267	.308	8	.000	-0	80	-8	—	-0.9
Total	3	12	12	.500	34	22	10-3	0	206.1	193	98	7	5	67	101	3.01	95	.247	.311	59-0-3	.169	1	104	-4	—	-0.5
Aker, Jack	Jackie Delane; B7.13.1940 Tulare CA; BR/TR/6´2˝/(190–202); d5.3; C3; Col Sequoias (CA) [JC]																									
1964	KC A	0	1	.000	9	0	0	0	16.1	17	18	6	6	10-1	7	8.82	43	.266	.412	3	.000	-0*	—	-9	0	-0.5
1965	KC A	4	3	.571	34	0	0	3	51.1	45	18	3	3	18-6	26	3.16	111	.242	.317	8-0-1	.000	-1	—	3	0	0.3
1966	KC A	8	4	.667	66	0	0	**32**	113	81	27	6	3	28-10	68	1.99	171	.201	.256	21-0-1	.095	-1	—	**19**	0	3.2
1967	KC A	3	8	.273	57	0	0	12	88	87	44	9	3	32-8	65	4.30	74	.264	.334	8-0-3	.125	-0	—	-9	0	-1.4
1968	Oak A	4	4	.500	54	0	0	11	74.2	72	39	6	6	33-6	44	4.10	69	.258	.344	7-0-1	.143	-0	—	-11	0	-1.6
1969	Sea A	0	2	.000	15	0	0	3-1	16.2	25	15	4	1	13-4	7	7.56	48	.357	.464	1	.000	0	—	-7	0	-1.0
	NY A	8	4	.667	38	0	0	11-4	65.2	51	17	4	4	22-5	40	2.06	171	.217	.294	9	.111	-0	—	11	0	2.4
	Year	8	6	.571	53	0	0	14-5	82.1	76	32	8	5	35-9	47	3.17	112	.249	.335	10	.100	-0	—	4	0	1.4
1970	NY A	4	2	.667	41	0	0	16-4	70	57	19	3	4	20-5	36	2.06	174	.226	.291	16-0-1	.063	-1	—	12	0	1.4
1971	NY A	4	4	.500	41	0	0	4-8	55.2	48	20	3	0	26-9	24	2.59	127	.238	.320	3-0-3	.000	-0	—	4	0	0.6
1972	NY A	0	0	ø	4	0	0	0-0	6	5	2	0	1	3-0	1	3.00	100	.238	.360	0	ø	0	—	0	0	0.0
	Chi N	6	6	.500	48	0	0	17-3	67	65	31	4	5	23-5	36	2.96	129	.259	.330	6	.000	-0	—	3	0	0.8
1973	Chi N	4	5	.444	47	0	0	12-3	63.2	76	33	8	2	23-6	25	4.10	96	.308	.370	7	.000	-1	—	-1	0	-0.2
1974	Atl N	0	1	.000	17	0	0	0-1	16.2	17	11	3	0	9-2	7	3.78	100	.298	.382	1	.000	-0	—	-1	0	-0.1
	NY N	2	1	.667	24	0	0	2-0	41.1	33	18	4	2	14-1	18	3.48	104	.213	.285	2	.500	1	—	1	21	0.1
	Year	2	2	.500	41	0	0	2-1	58	50	29	7	2	23-3	25	3.57	103	.236	.313	3	.333	1	—	-1	0	0.0
Total	11	47	45	.511	495	0	0	123-24	746	679	312	63	40	274-68	404	3.28	105	.247	.322	92-0-10	.076	-5	—	15	21	4.0
Akerfelds, Darrel	Darrel Wayne; B6.12.1962 Denver CO; BR/TR/6´2˝/(210–218); [SeaA83 1/7]; d8.1; C6; Col Mesa St.																									
1986	Oak A	0	0	ø	2	0	0	0-0	5.1	7	5	2	0	3-1	5	6.75	58	.304	.385	0	ø	0	—	-2	0	-0.1
1987	Cle A	2	6	.250	16	13	1	0-0	74.2	84	60	18	7	38-1	42	6.75	68	.284	.374	0	ø	0	91	-16	0	-1.4
1989	Tex A	0	1	.000	6	0	0	0-1	11	11	6	1	0	5-2	9	3.27	122	.250	.320	0	ø	0	—	0	0	0.0
1990	Phi N	5	2	.714	71	0	0	3-0	93	65	45	10	3	54-8	42	3.77	102	.201	.316	6	.167	-0	—	0	0	0.0
1991	Phi N	2	1	.667	30	0	0	0-0	49.2	49	30	5	3	27-4	31	5.26	70	.257	.354	3	.000	-0	—	-8	0	-0.4
Total	5	9	10	.474	125	13	1	3-1	233.2	216	146	36	13	127-16	129	5.08	80	.246	.346	9	.111	-0	91	-26	0	-1.9
Akers, Jerry	Albert Earl; B11.1.1887 Shelbyville IN; D5.15.1979 Bay Pines FL; BR/TR/5´11˝/175; d5.4																									
1912	Was A	1	1	.500	5	1	0	0	20.1	24	17	1	2	15	11	4.87	68	.300	.423	6	.333	0	22	-4	—	-0.4
Alba, Gibson	Gibson Alberto (Rosado); B1.18.1960 Santiago, D.R.; BL/TL/6´2˝/160; d5.3																									
1988	StL N	0	0	ø	3	0	0	0-0	3.1	1	2	0	0	2-0	3	2.70	130	.091	.214	0	ø	0	—	0	0	0.0
Albanese, Joe	Joseph Peter; B6.26.1933 New York NY; D6.17.2000 New York NY; BR/TR/6´3˝/215; d7.18																									
1958	Was A	0	0	ø	6	0	0	0	6	8	3	1	0	2-0	3	4.50	85	.348	.370	0	ø	0	—	0	0	0.0
Alberro, Jose	Jose Edgardo; B6.29.1969 San Juan, PR; BR/TR/6´2˝/190; d4.27																									
1995	Tex A	0	0	ø	12	0	0	0-0	20.2	26	18	2	1	12-1	10	7.40	65	.299	.386	0	ø	0	—	-6	0	-0.2
1996	Tex A	0	1	.000	5	1	0	0-0	9.1	14	6	1	0	7-1	2	5.79	91	.368	.457	0	ø	0	35	0	0	0.0
1997	Tex A	0	3	.000	10	4	0	0-0	28.1	37	33	4	1	17-1	11	7.94	61	.303	.390	0	ø	0	85	-11	0	-1.0
Total	3	0	4	.000	27	5	0	0-0	58.1	77	57	7	2	36-3	23	7.41	66	.312	.399	0	ø	0	75	-17	0	-1.2
Albers, Matt	Matthew James; B1.20.1983 Houston TX; BL/TR/6´0˝/205; [HouN01 23/686]; d7.25; Col San Jacinto (TX) CC																									
2006	Hou N	0	2	.000	4	2	0	0-0	15	17	10	1	0	7-0	11	6.00	75	.298	.375	4	.000	-0	61	-2	0	-0.2
Alberts, Cy	Frederick Joseph; B1.14.1882 Grand Rapids MI; D8.27.1917 Fort Wayne IN; BR/TR/6´0˝/230; d9.17																									
1910	StL N	1	2	.333	4	3	2	0	27.2	35	22	1	0	20	10	6.18	48	.330	.437	7-0-1	.000	-0	83	-9	—	-0.9
Albosta, Ed	Edward John "Rube"; B10.27.1918 Saginaw MI; D1.7.2003 Saginaw MI; BR/TR/6´1˝/175; d9.3; Mil 1943–45																									
1941	Bro N	0	2	.000	2	2	0	0	13	11	9	1	0	8	5	6.23	59	.239	.352	4	.000	-1	46	-3	0	-0.4
1946	Pit N	0	6	.000	17	6	0	0	39.2	41	34	3	1	35	19	6.13	58	.266	.405	8	.125	-0	40	-12	0	-1.7
Total	2	0	8	.000	19	8	0	0	52.2	52	43	4	1	43	24	6.15	58	.260	.393	12	.083	-1	42	-15	0	-2.1
Albrecht, Ed	Edward Arthur; B2.28.1929 Affton MO; D12.29.1979 Cahokia IL; BR/TR/5´10.5˝/165; d10.2																									
1949	StL A	1	0	1.000	1	1	1	0	5	1	3	0	0	4	1	5.40	84	.063	.250	2	.000	-0	99	0	0	0.0
1950	StL A	0	1	.000	2	1	0	0	6.2	6	7	0	0	7	1	5.40	92	.250	.419	1	.000	-0	109	-1	0	-0.2
Total	2	1	1	.500	3	2	1	0	11.2	7	10	0	0	11	2	5.40	88	.175	.353	3	.000	-0	104	-1	0	-0.2
Albury, Vic	Victor; B5.12.1947 Key West FL; BL/TL/6´0˝/183; [CleA65 8/173]; d8.7																									
1973	Min A	1	0	1.000	14	0	0	0-0	23.1	13	7	1	0	19-2	13	2.70	147	.169	.333	0	ø	0	—	4	0	0.1
1974	Min A	8	9	.471	32	22	4-1	0-0	164	159	83	19	6	80-1	85	4.12	91	.259	.348	0	ø	0	102	-6	0	-0.6
1975	Min A	6	7	.462	32	15	2	1-0	135	115	82	16	4	97-1	72	4.53	85	.237	.364	1	.000	-0*	98	-12	0	-1.1
1976	Min A	3	1	.750	23	0	0	0-0	50.1	51	22	0	2	24-3	23	3.58	100	.271	.352	0	ø	0	—	1	24	0.0
Total	4	18	17	.514	101	37	6-1	1-0	372.2	338	194	36	12	220-7	193	4.11	92	.247	.353	1	.000	-0	101	-13	24	-1.6
Alcala, Santo	Santo (b Santo Anibal (Alcala)); B12.23.1952 San Pedro de Macoris, D.R.; BR/TR/6´5˝/185; d4.10; [DL 1978 Sea A 24]																									
1976	Cin N	11	4	.733	30	21	3-1	0-1	132	131	72	12	3	67-3	67	4.70	74	.261	.348	43-0-5	.140	-0	155	-16	0	-1.8
1977	Cin N	1	1	.500	7	2	0	0-0	15.2	22	11	1	1	7-1	9	5.74	69	.349	.417	3	.000	-0	79	-3	0	-0.4
	Mon N	2	6	.250	31	10	0	2-1	101.2	104	55	12	2	47-5	64	4.69	82	.263	.343	25-1-2	.080	-1	65	-8	0	-0.7
	Year	3	7	.300	38	12	0	2-1	117.1	126	66	13	3	54-6	73	4.83	80	.275	.353	28-1-2	.071	-1	67	-11	0	-1.1
Total	2	14	11	.560	68	33	3-1	2-2	249.1	257	138	25	6	121-9	140	4.76	77	.268	.351	71-1-7	.113	-2	120	-27	24	-2.9
Alderson, Dale	Dale Leonard; B3.9.1918 Belden NE; D2.12.1982 Garden Grove CA; BR/TR/5´10˝/190; d9.18; Mil 1944–45; Col Upper Iowa																									
1943	Chi N	0	1	.000	4	2	0	0	14	21	12	2	0	3	4	6.43	52	.356	.387	3	.000	-0	127	-5	0	-0.4
1944	Chi N	0	0	ø	12	1	0	0	21.2	31	18	2	0	9	7	6.65	53	.344	.404	4	.000	-1	166	-7	0	-0.4
Total	2	0	1	.000	16	3	0	0	35.2	52	30	4	0	12	11	6.56	53	.349	.398	7	.000	-1	138	-12	0	-0.8

Aldred, Scott Scott Phillip; B6.12.1968 Flint MI; BL/TL/6´4˝/(215–228); [DetA86 16/411]; d9.9

YEAR	TM LG	W	L	PCT	G	GS	CG-SHO	SV-BS	IP	H	R	HR	HB	BB-IB	SO	ERA	AERA	OAV	OOB	AB-HR-SH	AVG	PB	SUP	APR	DL	PW
1990	Det A	1	2	.333	4	3	0	0-0	14.1	13	6	0	1	10-1	7	3.77	106	.265	.393	0	ø	0	53	1	0	0.1
1991	Det A	2	4	.333	11	11	1	0-0	57.1	58	37	9	0	30-2	35	5.18	81	.266	.352	0	ø	0	115	-7	0	-0.6
1992	Det A	3	8	.273	16	13	0	0-0	65	80	51	12	3	33-4	34	6.78	59	.307	.387	0	ø	0	97	-19	0	-2.7
1993	Col N	0	0	ø	5	0	0	0-0	6.2	10	10	1	1	9-1	5	10.80	44	.357	.526	0	ø	0	—	-4	0	-0.2
	Mon N	1	0	1.000	3	0	0	0-1	5.1	9	4	1	0	1-0	4	6.75	62	.375	.400	0	ø	0	—	-1	119	-0.2
	Year	1	0	1.000	8	0	0	0-1	12	19	14	2	1	10-1	9	9.00	50	.365	.476	0	ø	0	—	-6	0	-0.4
1996	Det A	0	4	.000	11	8	0	0-0	43.1	60	52	9	3	26-3	36	9.35	54	.328	.416	0	ø	0	89	-21	0	-1.5
	Min A	6	5	.545	25	17	0	0-0	122	134	73	20	3	42-1	75	5.09	101	.281	.340	0	ø	0	127	1	0	0.0
	Year	6	9	.400	36	25	0	0-0	165.1	194	125	29	6	68-4	111	6.21	83	.294	.362	0	ø	0	115	-21	0	-1.5
1997	Min A	2	10	.167	17	15	0	0-0	77.1	102	66	20	3	28-2	33	7.68	61	.323	.382	0	ø	0	102	-23	0	-2.8
1998	TB A	0	0	ø	48	0	0	0-0	31.1	33	13	1	2	12-3	21	3.73	128	.280	.356	0	ø	0	—	4	0	0.2
1999	TB A	3	2	.600	37	0	0	0-0	24.1	26	15	1	2	14-0	22	5.18	96	.274	.375	0	ø	0	—	0	0	0.0
	Phi N	1	1	.500	29	0	0	1-3	32.1	33	15	1	0	15-3	19	3.90	120	.277	.345	1	.000	-0	—	3	0	0.2
2000	Phi N	1	3	.250	23	0	0	0-1	20.1	23	14	3	1	10-0	21	5.75	80	.284	.362	0	ø	0	—	-3	124	-0.4
Total	9	20	39	.339	229	67	1	1-5	499.2	581	356	78	19	230-20	312	6.02	78	.295	.371	1	.000	-0	105	-69	243	-7.9

Aldrich, Jay Jay Robert; B4.14.1961 Alexandria LA; BR/TR/6´3˝/210; [MilA82 10/261]; d6.5; Col Montclair St.

YEAR	TM LG	W	L	PCT	G	GS	CG-SHO	SV-BS	IP	H	R	HR	HB	BB-IB	SO	ERA	AERA	OAV	OOB	AB-HR-SH	AVG	PB	SUP	APR	DL	PW
1987	Mil A	3	1	.750	31	0	0	0-0	58.1	71	33	8	2	13-3	22	4.94	93	.306	.344	0	ø	0	—	-1	0	-0.1
1989	Mil A	1	0	1.000	16	0	0	1-1	26	24	11	3	1	13-2	12	3.81	101	.253	.349	0	ø	0	—	1	0	0.1
	Atl N	1	2	.333	8	0	0	0-1	12.1	7	5	0	0	6-1	7	2.19	167	.167	.265	1	.000	-0	—	1	0	0.2
1990	Bal A	1	2	.333	7	0	0	1-2	12	17	13	1	0	7-3	5	8.25	46	.327	.407	0	ø	0	—	-7	0	-1.2
Total	3	6	5	.545	62	0	0	2-4	108.2	119	62	12	3	39-9	46	4.72	90	.283	.345	1	.000	-0	—	-6	0	-1.0

Aldridge, Vic Victor Eddington; B10.25.1893 Indian Springs IN; D4.17.1973 Terre Haute IN; BR/TR/5´9.5˝/175; d4.15; Mil 1918

YEAR	TM LG	W	L	PCT	G	GS	CG-SHO	SV-BS	IP	H	R	HR	HB	BB-IB	SO	ERA	AERA	OAV	OOB	AB-HR-SH	AVG	PB	SUP	APR	DL	PW
1917	Chi N	6	6	.500	30	6	1-1	2	106.2	100	52	1	2	37	44	3.12	93	.252	.319	29-0-1	.138	-2	69	-3	—	-0.4
1918	Chi N	0	1	.000	3	0	0	0	12.1	11	3	0	0	6	10	1.46	191	.275	.370	3-0-1	.333	0	—	2	—	0.2
1922	Chi N	16	15	.516	36	34	20-2	0	258.1	287	129	14	12	56	66	3.52	119	.286	.332	100-0-7	.260	3	96	16	—	2.0
1923	Chi N	16	9	.640	30	30	15-2	0	217	209	101	17	1	67	64	3.48	115	.251	.307	71-0-5	.268	3	101	13	—	1.6
1924	Chi N	15	12	.556	32	32	20	0	244.1	261	110	10	7	80	74	3.50	112	.279	.341	85-0-7	.176	-3	107	12	—	0.9
1925	†Pit N	15	7	.682	30	26	14-1	0	213.1	218	99	15	5	74	88	3.63	123	.269	.334	86-1-2	.233	-1	119	21	—	1.6
1926	Pit N	10	13	.435	30	26	12-1	1	190	204	100	7	4	73	61	4.07	97	.279	.348	71-0-4	.225	-1	98	-1	—	-0.3
1927	†Pit N	15	10	.600	35	34	17-1	1	239.1	248	123	16	5	74	86	4.25	97	.270	.328	96-0-3	.219	-0	112	0	—	-0.2
1928	NY N	4	7	.364	22	16	3	2	119.1	133	68	7	3	45	33	4.83	81	.285	.352	40-1-2	.275	2	112	-10	—	-0.7
Total	9	97	80	.548	248	204	102-8	6	1600.2	1671	785	87	39	512	526	3.76	107	.273	.333	581-2-32	.229	2	106	50	—	4.7

Alexander, Doyle Doyle Lafayette; B9.4.1950 Cordova AL; BR/TR/6´3˝/(190–205); [LAN68 9/185]; d6.26

YEAR	TM LG	W	L	PCT	G	GS	CG-SHO	SV-BS	IP	H	R	HR	HB	BB-IB	SO	ERA	AERA	OAV	OOB	AB-HR-SH	AVG	PB	SUP	APR	DL	PW
1971	LA N	6	6	.500	17	12	4	0-0	92.1	105	45	6	1	18-0	30	3.80	86	.282	.316	33-0-1	.273	3	107	-7	0	-0.6
1972	Bal A	6	8	.429	35	9	2-2	2-1	106.1	78	36	5	1	30-8	49	2.45	127	.203	.261	25-0-3	.080	-1	92	6	0	0.8
1973	†Bal A	12	8	.600	29	26	10	0-0	174.2	169	85	19	7	52-5	63	3.86	98	.258	.317	0	ø	0	147	-2	27	-0.2
1974	Bal A	6	9	.400	30	12	2	0-2	114.1	127	65	7	4	43-4	40	4.01	87	.290	.356	0	ø	0	97	-10	0	-1.1
1975	Bal A	8	8	.500	32	11	3-1	1-3	133.1	127	47	7	1	47-7	46	3.04	117	.251	.316	0	ø	0	111	9	0	1.1
1976	Bal A	3	4	.429	11	6	2-1	0-0	64.1	58	27	3	0	24-2	17	3.50	94	.247	.312	0	ø	0	98	-1	0	-0.1
	†NY A	10	5	.667	19	19	5-2	0-0	136.2	114	54	9	3	39-0	41	3.29	104	.229	.287	0	ø	0	110	3	0	0.2
	Year	13	9	.591	30	25	7-3	0-0	201	172	81	12	3	63-2	58	3.36	101	.235	.295	0	ø	0	107	2	0	0.1
1977	Tex A	17	11	.607	34	34	12-1	0-0	237	221	103	24	2	82-2	82	3.65	112	.246	.309	0	ø	0	99	14	0	1.5
1978	Tex A	9	10	.474	31	28	7-1	0-0	191	198	84	18	1	71-1	81	3.86	97	.270	.333	0	ø	0	97	2	0	0.2
1979	Tex A	5	7	.417	23	18	0	0-0	113.1	114	65	3	1	69-3	50	4.45	93	.268	.366	0	ø	0	89	-5	25	-0.3
1980	Atl N	14	11	.560	35	35	7-1	0-0	231.2	227	120	20	4	74-5	114	4.20	88	.256	.315	83-0-3	.181	1	118	-13	0	-1.1
1981	SF N	11	7	.611	24	24	1-1	0-0	152.1	156	51	11	2	44-2	77	2.89	118	.263	.315	51-0-4	.176	1	115	11	0	1.4
1982	NY A	1	7	.125	16	11	0	0-0	66.2	81	52	14	0	14-2	26	6.08	66	.298	.329	0	ø	0	70	-16	89	-1.7
1983	NY A	0	2	.000	8	5	0	0-0	28.1	31	21	6	0	7-0	17	6.35	62	.277	.317	0	ø	0	111	-7	0	-0.5
	Tor A	7	6	.538	17	15	5	0-0	116.2	126	55	14	1	26-1	46	3.93	111	.279	.317	0	ø	0	85	5	0	0.6
	Year	7	8	.467	25	20	5	0-0	145	157	76	20	1	33-1	63	4.41	97	.278	.317	0	ø	0	90	-1	0	0.1
1984	Tor A	17	6	**.739**	36	35	11-2	0-0	261.2	238	99	21	3	59-1	139	3.13	132	.242	.284	0	ø	0	102	29	0	2.4
1985	†Tor A	17	10	.630	36	36	6-1	0-0	260.2	268	105	28	6	67-0	142	3.45	123	.266	.315	0	ø	0	91	25	0	2.4
1986	Tor A	5	4	.556	17	17	3	0-0	111	120	56	18	4	20-1	65	4.46	95	.273	.308	0	ø	0	122	-1	0	-0.1
	Atl N	6	6	.500	17	17	2	0-0	117.1	135	58	9	0	17-1	74	3.84	103	.287	.311	38-0-6	.211	1*	95	1	0	0.1
1987	Atl N	5	10	.333	16	16	3	0-0	117.2	115	57	21	2	27-5	64	4.13	105	.257	.300	35-0-6	.029	-3	74	4	0	0.1
	†Det A	9	0	1.000	11	11	3-3	0-0	88.1	63	16	3	0	26-0	44	1.53	279	.201	.263	0	ø	0	125	29	0	2.9
1988	Det A☆	14	11	.560	34	34	5-1	0-0	229	260	122	30	5	46-7	126	4.32	89	.282	.317	0	ø	0	112	-13	0	-1.4
1989	Det A	6	18	.250	33	33	5-1	0-0	223	245	118	28	5	76-3	95	4.44	86	.280	.337	0	ø	0	77	-12	0	-1.2
Total	19	194	174	.527	561	464	98-18	3-6	3367.2	3376	1541	324	53	978-60	1528	3.76	103	.261	.314	265-0-23	.166	1	103	51	141	5.4

Alexander, Gerald Gerald Paul; B3.26.1968 Baton Rouge LA; BR/TR/5´11˝/(190–200); [TexA89 21/535]; d9.9; Col Tulane

YEAR	TM LG	W	L	PCT	G	GS	CG-SHO	SV-BS	IP	H	R	HR	HB	BB-IB	SO	ERA	AERA	OAV	OOB	AB-HR-SH	AVG	PB	SUP	APR	DL	PW
1990	Tex A	0	0	ø	3	2	0	0-0	7	14	6	0	1	5-0	8	7.71	51	.438	.513	0	ø	0	139	-3	0	-0.1
1991	Tex A	5	3	.625	30	9	0	0-0	89.1	93	56	11	3	48-7	50	5.24	77	.272	.364	0	ø	0	130	-11	28	-0.9
1992	Tex A	1	0	1.000	3	0	0	0-0	1.2	5	5	1	0	1-0	1	27.00	14	.500	.500	0	ø	0	—	-4	0	-0.7
Total	3	6	3	.667	36	11	0	0-0	98	112	67	12	4	54-7	59	5.79	70	.292	.380	0	ø	0	132	-18	28	-1.7

Alexander, Grover Grover Cleveland "Old Pete"; B2.26.1887 Elba NE; D11.4.1950 St.Paul NE; BR/TR/6´1˝/185; d4.15; Mil 1918; HF1938

YEAR	TM LG	W	L	PCT	G	GS	CG-SHO	SV-BS	IP	H	R	HR	HB	BB-IB	SO	ERA	AERA	OAV	OOB	AB-HR-SH	AVG	PB	SUP	APR	DL	PW
1911	Phi N	**28**	13	.683	48	37	**31-7**	3	**367**	285	133	5	8	129	227	2.57	134	**.219**	.293	138	.174	-2*	101	37	—	3.7
1912	Phi N	19	17	.528	46	34	25-3	3	**310.1**	289	133	11	6	105	**195**	2.81	129	.251	.317	102-2-9	.186	0	90	27	—	3.0
1913	Phi N	22	8	.733	47	36	23-**9**	2	306.1	288	106	9	3	75	159	2.79	120	.254	.302	103-0-3	.126	-4	95	22	—	1.8
1914	Phi N	**27**	15	.643	46	39	**32**-6	1	**355**	327	133	8	11	76	**214**	2.38	123	.244	.290	137-0-2	.234	2*	105	22	—	3.1
1915	†Phi N	**31**	10	**.756**	49	42	**36-12**	3	**376.1**	253	86	3	10	64	**241**	**1.22**	**225**	**.191**	**.234**	130-1-5	.169	0	116	**58**	—	**7.5**
1916	Phi N	**33**	12	.733	48	**45**	**38-16**	3	**389**	323	90	6	10	50	**167**	**1.55**	**171**	.230	.262	138-0-3	.239	8*	96	**47**	—	**7.2**
1917	Phi N	**30**	13	.698	45	**44**	**34-8**	0	**388**	336	107	4	6	56	**200**	**1.83**	153	.234	.266	139-1-7	.216	4*	101	**39**	—	**5.4**
1918	Chi N	2	1	.667	3	3	3	0	26	19	7	0	1	3	15	1.73	161	.207	.240	10	.100	-1	127	3	—	0.3
1919	Chi N	16	11	.593	30	27	20-**9**	1	235	180	51	3	0	38	121	**1.72**	**167**	**.211**	.245	70-0-4	.171	1	92	34	—	**4.6**
1920	Chi N	**27**	14	.659	46	**40**	**33**-7	5	**363.1**	335	96	8	1	69	**173**	**1.91**	**168**	.248	.285	118-1-6	.229	4	83	**52**	—	**6.9**
1921	Chi N	15	13	.536	31	30	21-**3**	1	252	286	110	10	1	33	77	3.39	113	.296	.320	95-1-5	.305	6	100	12	—	1.8
1922	Chi N	16	13	.552	33	31	20-1	1	245.2	283	111	8	3	34	48	3.63	116	.295	.321	85-0-4	.176	-2	84	18	—	1.9
1923	Chi N	22	12	.647	39	36	26-3	2	305	308	128	17	0	30	72	3.19	126	.259	**.277**	111-1-7	.216	0	112	29	—	3.1
1924	Chi N	12	5	.706	21	20	12	0	169.1	183	82	9	1	25	33	3.03	129	.272	.299	65-1-4	.231	1	115	10	—	1.1
1925	Chi N	15	11	.577	32	30	20-1	0	236	270	106	14	3	29	63	3.39	127	.288	.312	79-2-9	.241	3	94	23	—	2.3
1926	Chi N	3	3	.500	7	7	4	0	52	55	26	0	0	7	12	3.46	111	.270	.294	15-0-3	.467	3	87	1	—	0.5
	†StL N	9	7	.563	23	16	11-2	2	148.1	136	57	8	2	24	35	2.91	134	.242	.276	50-0-3	.120	-4	79	16	—	1.3
	Year	12	10	.545	30	23	15-2	2	200.1	191	83	8	2	31	47	3.05	127	.250	**.281**	65-0-6	.200	-1	81	18	—	1.8
1927	StL N	21	10	.677	37	30	22-2	3	268	261	94	11	1	38	48	2.52	157	.258	**.286**	94-0-3	.245	3	109	**41**	—	**5.0**
1928	†StL N	16	9	.640	34	31	18-1	2	243.2	262	107	15	2	37	59	3.36	119	.277	.306	86-1-8	.291	6	122	18	—	2.2
1929	StL N	9	8	.529	22	19	8	0	132	149	65	10	1	23	33	3.89	120	.285	.317	41-0-3	.049	-4	103	12	—	1.0
1930	Phi N	0	3	.000	9	3	0	0	21.2	40	24	5	0	6	6	9.14	60	.396	.430	4	.000	-0	64	-7	—	-0.8
Total	20	373	208	.642	696	600	437-90	32	5190	4868	1852	164	70	951	2198	2.56	135	.250	.288	1810-11-88	.209	24	100	514	—	62.9

Alexander, Bob Robert Somerville; B8.7.1922 Vancouver BC, Can.; D4.7.1993 Oceanside CA; BR/TR/6´2.5˝/205; d4.11; Col Bethany

YEAR	TM LG	W	L	PCT	G	GS	CG-SHO	SV-BS	IP	H	R	HR	HB	BB-IB	SO	ERA	AERA	OAV	OOB	AB-HR-SH	AVG	PB	SUP	APR	DL	PW
1955	Bal A	1	0	1.000	4	0	0	0	4	8	6	0	1	2-0	1	13.50	28	.444	.500	0	ø	0	—	-4	0	-0.7
1957	Cle A	0	1	.000	5	0	0	0	7	10	7	0	1	5-2	1	9.00	41	.357	.457	1	.000	-0	—	-4	0	-0.5
Total	2	1	1	.500	9	0	0	0	11	18	13	0	2	7-2	2	10.64	35	.391	.474	1	.000	-0	—	-8	0	-1.2

Alfonseca, Antonio Antonio; B4.16.1972 LaRomana, D.R.; BR/TR/6´5˝/(225–250); d6.17

YEAR	TM LG	W	L	PCT	G	GS	CG-SHO	SV-BS	IP	H	R	HR	HB	BB-IB	SO	ERA	AERA	OAV	OOB	AB-HR-SH	AVG	PB	SUP	APR	DL	PW
1997	†Fla N	1	3	.250	17	0	0	0-2	25.2	36	16	3	1	10-3	19	4.91	83	.324	.385	3	.000	-0	—	-3	0	-0.4
1998	Fla N	4	6	.400	58	0	0	8-6	70.2	75	36	10	3	33-9	46	4.08	100	.281	.359	4	.000	-0	—	0	17	-0.2
1999	Fla N	4	5	.444	73	0	0	21-4	77.2	79	28	4	4	29-6	46	3.24	135	.274	.348	2	.000	-0	—	11	0	1.7
2000	Fla N	5	6	.455	68	0	0	**45**-4	70	82	35	7	1	24-3	47	4.24	103	.291	.347	0	ø	0	—	2	0	0.3

THE PITCHER REGISTER

YEAR	TM LG	W	L	PCT	G	GS	CG-SHO	SV-BS	IP	H	R	HR	HB	BB-IB	SO	ERA	AERA	OAV	OOB	AB-HR-SH	AVG	PB	SUP	APR	DL	PW
2001	Fla N	4	4	.500	58	0	0	28-6	61.2	68	24	6	5	15-3	40	3.06	136	.281	.335	0	ø	0	—	7	0	1.4
2002	Chi N	2	5	.286	66	0	0	19-9	74.1	73	34	5	3	36-3	61	4.00	101	.257	.344	3	.667	1	—	2	0	0.3
2003	†Chi N	3	1	.750	60	0	0	0-4	66.1	76	43	7	2	27-3	51	5.83	74	.290	.360	0-0-1	ø	0	—	-9	36	-0.5
2004	†Atl N	6	4	.600	79	0	0	0-1	73.2	71	24	5	0	28-5	45	2.57	168	.255	.322	1	.000	-0	—	14	0	1.6
2005	Fla N	1	1	.500	33	0	0	0-2	27.1	29	15	2	2	14-4	16	4.94	81	.299	.391	0	ø	0	—	-2	95	-0.1
2006	Tex A	0	0	ø	19	0	0	0-0	16	23	10	3	0	7-0	5	5.63	83	.348	.405	0	ø	0	—	-1	18	-0.1
Total	10	30	35	.462	531	0	0	121-38	563.1	612	265	52	21	223-39	376	3.99	106	.281	.351	13-0-1	.154	-0	—	21	166	4.0

ALLARD, BRIAN Brian Marshall; B1.3.1958 Spring Valley IL; BR/TR/6´1˝/175; [TexA76 4/84]; d8.8; [DL 1982 Sea A 182]

YEAR	TM LG	W	L	PCT	G	GS	CG-SHO	SV-BS	IP	H	R	HR	HB	BB-IB	SO	ERA	AERA	OAV	OOB	AB-HR-SH	AVG	PB	SUP	APR	DL	PW
1979	Tex A	1	3	.250	7	4	2	0-0	33.1	36	17	4	0	13-2	14	4.32	96	.283	.348	0	ø	0	44	0	0	0.0
1980	Tex A	0	1	.000	5	2	0	0-0	14.1	13	13	0	1	10-1	10	5.65	69	.236	.358	0	ø	0	115	-4	0	-0.3
1981	Sea A	3	2	.600	7	7	1	0-0	48	48	22	5	0	8-0	20	3.75	104	.265	.296	0	ø	0	102	1	60	0.1
Total	3	4	6	.400	19	13	3	0-0	95.2	97	52	9	1	31-3	44	4.23	94	.267	.325	0	ø	0	85	-3	242	-0.2

ALLEN, FRANK Frank Leon; B8.26.1888 Newbern AL; D7.30.1933 Gainesville AL; BR/TL/5´9˝/175; d4.24; Col Rhodes

YEAR	TM LG	W	L	PCT	G	GS	CG-SHO	SV-BS	IP	H	R	HR	HB	BB-IB	SO	ERA	AERA	OAV	OOB	AB-HR-SH	AVG	PB	SUP	APR	DL	PW
1912	Bro N	3	9	.250	20	15	5-1	0	109	119	70	1	1	57	58	3.63	92	.285	.373	36-1-2	.167	2	83	-8	—	-0.5
1913	Bro N	4	18	.182	34	25	11	2	174.2	144	75	6	10	81	82	2.83	116	.231	.329	51-1-2	.137	-1	74	7	—	0.6
1914	Bro N	8	14	.364	36	21	10-1	0	171.1	165	79	6	3	57	68	3.10	92	.265	.330	47-0-3	.128	0*	85	-2	—	-0.3
	Pit F	1	0	1.000	1	1	1	0	7	9	4	0	0	0	3	5.14	56	.321	.321	2	.500	1	191	-1	—	-0.1
1915	Pit F	23	13	.639	41	37	24-6	0	283.1	230	90	9	11	100	127	2.51	108	.227	.304	89-0-4	.079	-5	87	9	—	0.4
1916	Bos N	8	2	.800	19	14	7-2	1	113	102	32	1	4	31	63	2.07	120	.244	.302	34-0-3	.206	3	122	6	—	0.9
1917	Bos N	3	10	.231	29	14	2	0	112	124	61	3	6	47	56	3.94	65	.297	.376	29	.172	2	89	-18	—	-2.0
Total	6	50	66	.431	180	127	60-10	3	970.1	893	411	26	35	373	457	2.93	98	.252	.330	288-2-14	.135	2	88	-7	—	-1.0

ALLEN, JOHN John Marshall; B10.27.1890 Berkeley Springs WV; D9.24.1967 Hagerstown MD; BR/TR/6´1˝/170; d6.2

YEAR	TM LG	W	L	PCT	G	GS	CG-SHO	SV-BS	IP	H	R	HR	HB	BB-IB	SO	ERA	AERA	OAV	OOB	AB-HR-SH	AVG	PB	SUP	APR	DL	PW
1914	Bal F	0	0	ø	1	0	0	0	2	2	4	0	1	2	2	18.00	17	.286	.500	0	ø	0	—	-3	—	-0.1

ALLEN, JOHNNY John Thomas; B9.30.1904 Lenoir NC; D3.29.1959 St.Petersburg FL; BR/TR/6´0˝/180; d4.19

YEAR	TM LG	W	L	PCT	G	GS	CG-SHO	SV-BS	IP	H	R	HR	HB	BB-IB	SO	ERA	AERA	OAV	OOB	AB-HR-SH	AVG	PB	SUP	APR	DL	PW
1932	†NY A	17	4	**.810**	33	21	13-3	4	192	162	86	10	5	76	109	3.70	110	.228	.306	73-1-3	.123	-2	119	11	—	0.9
1933	NY A	15	7	.682	25	24	10-1	1	184.2	171	96	9	4	87	119	4.39	89	.242	.328	72-0-2	.181	0	131	-7	—	-0.8
1934	NY A	5	2	.714	13	10	4	0	71.2	62	30	3	2	32	54	2.89	141	.227	.313	26-0-2	.192	1	120	9	—	0.8
1935	NY A	13	6	.684	23	23	12-2	0	167	149	76	11	4	58	113	3.61	112	**.238**	.307	67-1-3	.224	1	133	11	—	1.2
1936	Cle A	20	10	.667	36	31	19-4	1	243	234	108	5	1	97	165	3.44	146	.256	.328	87-0-8	.161	-3*	116	43	—	4.3
1937	Cle A	15	1	**.938**	24	20	14	0	173	157	55	4	5	60	87	2.55	181	.244	.313	67-0-4	.090	-7	139	40	—	2.7
1938	Cle A★	14	8	.636	30	27	13	0	200	189	107	15	3	81	112	4.18	111	.246	.321	79-1-3	.253	4	122	10	—	1.4
1939	Cle A	9	7	.563	28	26	9-2	0	175	199	96	9	3	56	79	4.58	96	.291	.347	71-0-2	.225	1*	118	-1	—	0.1
1940	Cle A	9	8	.529	32	17	5-3	5	138.2	126	61	3	3	48	62	3.44	123	.243	.311	48	.208	0	66	12	—	1.4
1941	StL A	2	5	.286	20	9	2	1	67	89	53	4	2	29	27	6.58	65	.319	.387	22-1-1	.136	0	119	-15	0	-1.4
	†Bro N	3	0	1.000	11	4	1	0	57.1	38	18	6	0	12	21	2.51	146	.188	.234	20-0-1	.050	-2	145	8	0	0.2
1942	Bro N	10	6	.625	27	15	5-1	3	118	106	53	11	2	39	50	3.20	102	.238	.302	39-0-4	.179	-0	105	-1	0	-0.2
1943	Bro N	5	1	.833	17	1	0	1	38	42	21	3	2	25	15	4.26	79	.280	.390	7-0-2	.429	2	227	-4	0	-0.4
	NY N	1	3	.250	15	0	0	2	41	37	16	4	0	14	24	3.07	112	.245	.309	14-0-1	.000	-2	—	2	0	0.0
	Year	6	4	.600	32	1	0	3	79	79	37	7	2	39	39	3.65	93	.262	.351	21-0-3	.143	-0	224	-2	0	-0.4
1944	NY N	4	7	.364	18	13	2-1	0	84	88	48	7	2	24	33	4.07	90	.260	.313	24	.083	-2*	86	-5	0	-0.9
Total	13	142	75	.654	352	241	109-17	18	1950.1	1849	924	104	38	738	1070	3.75	113	.249	.321	716-4-36	.173	-8	119	113	0	9.3

ALLEN, LLOYD Lloyd Cecil; B5.8.1950 Merced CA; BR/TR/6´1˝/(184–185); [AnaA68 1/12]; d9.1

YEAR	TM LG	W	L	PCT	G	GS	CG-SHO	SV-BS	IP	H	R	HR	HB	BB-IB	SO	ERA	AERA	OAV	OOB	AB-HR-SH	AVG	PB	SUP	APR	DL	PW
1969	Cal A	0	1	.000	4	1	0	0-0	10	5	7	1	0	10-0	5	5.40	65	.147	.341	2	.500	1	0	-2	0	-0.1
1970	Cal A	1	1	.500	8	2	0	0-0	24	23	7	0	1	11-2	12	2.63	138	.261	.347	4	.000	-0	74	3	0	0.2
1971	Cal A	4	6	.400	54	1	0	15-3	94	75	29	4	0	40-8	72	2.49	131	.221	.302	17-1-0	.294	2	55	9	0	1.5
1972	Cal A	3	7	.300	42	6	0	5-3	85.1	76	38	7	3	55-5	53	3.48	84	.240	.356	17-0-3	.118	-1	50	-6	0	-0.9
1973	Cal A	0	0	ø	5	0	0	1-0	8.2	15	10	0	0	5-0	4	10.38	34	.417	.465	0	ø	0	—	-6	0	-0.3
	Tex A	0	6	.000	23	5	0	1-0	41	58	59	3	5	39-2	25	9.22	41	.326	.453	0	ø	0	119	-30	0	-3.8
	Year	0	6	.000	28	5	0	2-0	49.2	73	69	3	5	44-2	29	9.42	40	.341	.455	0	ø	0	120	-38	0	-4.1
1974	Tex A	0	1	.000	14	0	0	0-0	22	24	17	2	1	18-0	18	6.55	55	.276	.398	0	ø	0	—	-7	0	-0.4
	Chi A	0	1	.000	6	2	0	0-0	7	7	9	0	1	12-1	3	10.29	36	.259	.500	0	ø	0	176	-5	0	-0.6
	Year	0	2	.000	20	2	0	0-0	29	31	26	2	2	30-1	21	7.45	49	.272	.426	0	ø	0	182	-12	0	-1.0
1975	Chi A	0	2	.000	3	2	0	0-0	5.1	8	7	2	0	6-0	2	11.81	33	.348	.467	0	ø	0	11	-4	0	-0.7
Total	7	8	25	.242	159	19	0	22-6	297.1	291	183	19	11	196-18	194	4.69	71	.258	.369	40-1-3	.200	2	83	-48	0	-5.1

ALLEN, MYRON Myron Smith "Zeke"; B3.22.1854 Kingston NY; D3.8.1924 Kingston NY; BR/TR/5´8˝/150; d7.19; ▲

YEAR	TM LG	W	L	PCT	G	GS	CG-SHO	SV-BS	IP	H	R	HR	HB	BB-IB	SO	ERA	AERA	OAV	OOB	AB-HR-SH	AVG	PB	SUP	APR	DL	PW
1883	NY N	0	1	.000	1	1	1	0	8	8	5	0	—	3	0	1.13	275	.276	.344	4	.000	-1	69	1	—	0.0
1887	Cle AA	1	0	1.000	2	0	0	0	9.2	9	4	0	1	3	1	0.93	466	.243	.317	463-4	.276	0*	—	3	—	0.2
1888	KC AA	0	2	.000	2	2	2	0	18	17	7	0	2	1	2	2.50	135	.239	.270	136	.213	0*	34	2	—	0.2
Total	3	1	3	.250	5	3	3	0	35.2	34	16	0	3	7	3	1.77	203	.248	.299	603-4	.260	-0	44	6	—	0.4

ALLEN, NEIL Neil Patrick; B1.24.1958 Kansas City KS; BR/TR/6´2˝/(185–190); [NYN76 11/253]; d4.15

YEAR	TM LG	W	L	PCT	G	GS	CG-SHO	SV-BS	IP	H	R	HR	HB	BB-IB	SO	ERA	AERA	OAV	OOB	AB-HR-SH	AVG	PB	SUP	APR	DL	PW
1979	NY N	6	10	.375	50	5	0	8-1	99	100	46	4	0	47-13	65	3.55	105	.268	.345	14	.000	-2	52	1	24	0.0
1980	NY N	7	10	.412	59	0	0	22-5	97.1	87	43	7	0	40-9	79	3.70	98	.244	.317	14-0-1	.143	-0	—	0	0	-0.1
1981	NY N	7	6	.538	43	0	0	18-9	66.2	64	26	4	0	26-8	50	2.97	119	.259	.326	5-0-2	.200	1	—	4	0	1.0
1982	NY N	3	7	.300	50	0	0	19-5	64.2	65	22	5	1	30-5	59	3.06	120	.266	.348	6-0-1	.167	0	—	6	0	1.2
1983	NY N	2	7	.222	21	4	1-1	2-2	54	57	29	6	0	36-5	32	4.50	82	.278	.384	10-0-1	.000	-1	96	-4	0	-0.8
	StL N	10	6	.625	25	18	4-2	0-1	121.2	122	55	6	1	48-4	74	3.70	99	.265	.335	39-0-6	.128	-1	105	0	0	-0.1
	Year	12	13	.480	46	22	5-3	2-3	175.2	179	84	12	1	84-9	106	3.94	93	.269	.351	49-0-7	.102	-2	103	-6	0	-0.9
1984	StL N	9	6	.600	57	1	0	3-1	119	105	54	6	0	49-9	66	3.55	99	.239	.314	25	.240	1	50	-1	0	0.0
1985	StL N	1	4	.200	23	1	0	2-1	29	32	22	3	1	17-6	10	5.59	64	.283	.373	2	.000	-0	49	-7	0	-1.3
	NY A	1	0	1.000	17	0	0	1-0	29.1	26	9	1	0	13-0	16	2.76	146	.234	.315	0	ø	0	—	5	0	0.2
1986	Chi A	7	2	.778	22	17	2-2	0-0	113	101	50	8	2	38-1	57	3.82	114	.244	.306	0	ø	0	114	8	35	0.5
1987	Chi A	0	7	.000	15	10	0	0-0	49.2	74	40	6	2	26-0	26	7.07	66	.365	.438	0	ø	0	55	-12	70	-1.4
	NY A	0	1	.000	8	1	0	0-0	24.2	23	12	2	0	10-1	16	3.65	122	.242	.314	0	ø	0	62	2	0	0.1
	Year	0	8	.000	23	11	0	0-0	74.1	97	52	8	2	36-1	42	5.93	77	.326	.399	0	ø	0	56	-11	0	-1.3
1988	NY A	5	3	.625	41	2	0-1	0-2	117.1	121	51	14	2	37-7	61	3.84	104	.268	.322	0	ø	0	57	3	36	0.1
1989	Cle A	0	1	.000	3	0	0	0-0	3	8	5	1	0	0-0	0	15.00	27	.500	.471	0	ø	0	—	-3	65	-0.6
Total	11	58	70	.453	434	59	7-6	75-27	988.1	985	464	73	9	417-68	611	3.88	99	.264	.336	115-0-11	.130	-1	94	2	230	-1.2

ALLEN, EARL Robert Earl "Thin Man"; B7.2.1914 Smithville TN; D10.30.2005 Chesapeake VA; BR/TR/6´1˝/165; d9.19

YEAR	TM LG	W	L	PCT	G	GS	CG-SHO	SV-BS	IP	H	R	HR	HB	BB-IB	SO	ERA	AERA	OAV	OOB	AB-HR-SH	AVG	PB	SUP	APR	DL	PW
1937	Phi N	0	1	.000	3	1	0	0	12	18	12	2	0	8	8	6.75	64	.321	.406	3	.333	0	20	-4	—	-0.3

ALLEN, BOB Robert Gray; B10.23.1937 Tatum TX; BL/TL/6´2˝/(190–198); d4.14

YEAR	TM LG	W	L	PCT	G	GS	CG-SHO	SV-BS	IP	H	R	HR	HB	BB-IB	SO	ERA	AERA	OAV	OOB	AB-HR-SH	AVG	PB	SUP	APR	DL	PW
1961	Cle A	3	2	.600	48	0	0	3	81.2	96	42	7	1	40-5	42	3.75	105	.294	.373	12-0-1	.167	0	—	0	0	0.0
1962	Cle A	1	1	.500	30	0	0	4	30.2	29	24	5	0	25-3	23	5.87	66	.250	.378	5	.000	-1	—	-8	0	-0.7
1963	Cle A	1	2	.333	43	0	0	2	56	58	37	5	1	29-6	51	4.66	78	.266	.352	5	.200	-0	—	-8	0	-0.5
1966	Cle A	2	2	.500	36	0	0	5	51.1	56	27	2	2	13-6	33	4.21	82	.273	.318	9-0-1	.111	-0	—	-4	0	-0.4
1967	Cle A	0	5	.000	47	0	0	5	54.1	49	22	4	1	25-7	50	2.98	110	.243	.329	0	ø	0	—	1	0	0.2
Total	5	7	12	.368	204	0	0	19	274	288	152	23	5	132-27	199	4.11	89	.270	.351	31-0-2	.129	-1	—	-19	0	-1.4

ALLISON, DANA Dana Eric; B8.14.1966 Front Royal VA; BR/TL/6´3˝/215; [OakA89 21/556]; d4.12; Col James Madison

YEAR	TM LG	W	L	PCT	G	GS	CG-SHO	SV-BS	IP	H	R	HR	HB	BB-IB	SO	ERA	AERA	OAV	OOB	AB-HR-SH	AVG	PB	SUP	APR	DL	PW
1991	Oak A	1	1	.500	11	0	0	0-0	11	16	9	0	0	5-1	4	7.36	52	.381	.438	0	ø	0	—	-4	0	-0.7

ALLISON, MACK Mack Pendleton; B1.23.1887 Owensboro KY; D3.13.1964 Mount Vernon MO; BR/TR/6´1˝/185; d9.13

YEAR	TM LG	W	L	PCT	G	GS	CG-SHO	SV-BS	IP	H	R	HR	HB	BB-IB	SO	ERA	AERA	OAV	OOB	AB-HR-SH	AVG	PB	SUP	APR	DL	PW
1911	StL A	2	1	.667	3	3	3	0	26.1	24	9	0	2	5	2	2.05	165	.253	.304	10	.200	-0	93	4	—	0.3
1912	StL A	6	17	.261	31	20	11-1	1	169	171	102	4	6	49	43	3.62	92	.269	.327	52-0-1	.135	-3	58	-9	—	-1.5
1913	StL A	1	3	.250	11	4	3	0	51.1	52	24	0	3	13	12	2.28	129	.291	.349	14	.000	-2	19	1	—	-0.2
Total	3	9	21	.300	45	27	17-1	1	246.2	247	135	4	11	67	57	3.17	102	.271	.329	76-0-1	.118	-6	57	-4	—	-1.4

ALMANZA, ARMANDO Armando; B10.26.1972 ElPaso TX; BL/TL/6´3˝/(205–240); [StLN93 21/592]; d7.29; Col New Mexico JC

YEAR	TM LG	W	L	PCT	G	GS	CG-SHO	SV-BS	IP	H	R	HR	HB	BB-IB	SO	ERA	AERA	OAV	OOB	AB-HR-SH	AVG	PB	SUP	APR	DL	PW
1999	Fla N	0	1	.000	14	0	0	0-0	15.2	8	4	1	1	9-1	20	1.72	254	.154	.286	3	.000	-0	—	4	0	0.2
2000	Fla N	4	2	.667	67	0	0	0-4	46.1	38	27	3	2	43-6	46	4.86	90	.228	.388	1-0-1	.000	-0	—	-2	0	-0.3
2001	Fla N	2	2	.500	52	0	0	0-2	41	34	24	8	0	26-1	45	4.83	86	.230	.339	0	ø	0	—	-3	0	-0.3
2002	Fla N	3	2	.600	51	0	0	2-2	45.2	36	22	8	0	23-1	57	4.34	91	.224	.316	0	ø	0	—	-1	51	-0.1
2003	Fla N	4	5	.444	51	0	0	0-2	50.1	59	37	10	2	25-2	49	6.08	67	.296	.376	0	ø	0	—	-12	40	-1.9
2004	Atl N	1	1	.500	13	0	0	0-0	11.2	9	8	3	1	7-2	13	6.17	70	.200	.315	0-0-1	ø	0	—	-2	37	-0.3
2005	Ari N	0	0	ø	6	0	0	0-1	4	5	1	1	0	3-0	2	2.25	197	.313	.421	0	ø	0	—	1	0	0.1
Total	7	14	13	.519	254	0	0	2-11	214.2	189	123	34	6	136-13	232	4.82	87	.240	.351	4-0-2	.000	-0	—	-15	128	-2.6

ALMANZAR, CARLOS Carlos Manuel (Giron); B11.6.1973 Santiago, D.R.; BR/TR/6´2˝/(166–200); d9.4

YEAR	TM LG	W	L	PCT	G	GS	CG-SHO	SV-BS	IP	H	R	HR	HB	BB-IB	SO	ERA	AERA	OAV	OOB	AB-HR-SH	AVG	PB	SUP	APR	DL	PW
1997	Tor A	0	1	.000	4	0	0	0-0	3.1	1	1	1	0	1-0	4	2.70	170	.091	.167	0	ø	0	—	1	0	0.1
1998	Tor A	2	2	.500	25	0	0	0-3	28.2	34	18	4	1	8-2	20	5.34	87	.286	.336	0	ø	0	—	-2	0	-0.2
1999	SD N	0	0	ø	28	0	0	0-0	37.1	48	32	6	3	15-2	30	7.47	57	.316	.386	1	.000	-0	—	-13	33	-0.6
2000	SD N	4	5	.444	62	0	0	0-3	69.2	73	35	12	4	25-2	56	4.39	101	.266	.333	3	.000	-0	—	2	0	0.2
2001	NY A	0	1	.000	10	0	0	0-2	10.2	14	4	2	0	2-1	6	3.38	132	.333	.356	0	ø	0	—	1	0	0.1
2002	Cin N	0	1	.000	8	1	0	0-0	11.2	6	4	0	0	5-1	7	2.31	184	.158	.244	0	ø	0	43	2	111	0.2
2004	Tex A	7	3	.700	67	0	0	0-2	72.2	66	32	8	4	19-4	44	3.72	133	.244	.301	0	ø	0	—	10	0	1.1
2005	Tex A	0	0	ø	6	0	0	0-0	5	10	8	2	1	7-0	3	14.40	32	.435	.545	0	ø	0	—	-5	155	-0.2
Total	8	13	13	.500	210	1	0	0-10	239	252	134	35	13	82-12	170	4.82	95	.271	.335	4	.000	-0	43	-4	299	0.7

ALMONTE, ED Edwin; B12.17.1976 Santiago, D.R.; BR/TR/6´3˝/200; [ChiA98 26/779]; d7.7; Col St. Francis (NY)

YEAR	TM LG	W	L	PCT	G	GS	CG-SHO	SV-BS	IP	H	R	HR	HB	BB-IB	SO	ERA	AERA	OAV	OOB	AB-HR-SH	AVG	PB	SUP	APR	DL	PW
2003	NY N	0	0	ø	12	0	0	0-0	11.1	21	15	3	0	5-1	7	11.12	38	.412	.464	1	.000	-0	—	-9	0	-0.4

ALMONTE, HECTOR Hector Radhames (Moreta); B10.17.1975 Santo Domingo, D.R.; BR/TR/6´2˝/190; d7.26

YEAR	TM LG	W	L	PCT	G	GS	CG-SHO	SV-BS	IP	H	R	HR	HB	BB-IB	SO	ERA	AERA	OAV	OOB	AB-HR-SH	AVG	PB	SUP	APR	DL	PW
1999	Fla N	0	2	.000	15	0	0	0-0	15	20	7	1	0	6-2	8	4.20	104	.339	.394	0	ø	0	—	1	0	0.1
2003	Bos A	0	1	.000	7	0	0	0-0	7.2	9	7	1	0	7-1	6	8.22	57	.310	.421	0	ø	0	—	-3	0	-0.3
	Mon N	1	1	.500	28	0	0	0-1	29	34	22	4	2	17-2	26	6.83	65	.291	.390	1	.000	-0	—	-6	0	-0.4
Total	2	1	4	.200	50	0	0	0-1	51.2	63	36	6	2	30-5	40	6.27	71	.307	.396	1	.000	-0	—	-8	0	-0.6

ALOMA, LUIS Luis (Barba) "Witto"; B6.19.1923 Havana, Cuba; D4.7.1997 Park Ridge IL; BR/TR/6´2˝/(180–195); d4.19

YEAR	TM LG	W	L	PCT	G	GS	CG-SHO	SV-BS	IP	H	R	HR	HB	BB-IB	SO	ERA	AERA	OAV	OOB	AB-HR-SH	AVG	PB	SUP	APR	DL	PW
1950	Chi A	7	2	.778	42	0	0	4	87.2	77	44	6	1	53	49	3.80	118	.234	.342	15-0-1	.067	-2	—	6	0	0.4
1951	Chi A	6	0	1.000	25	1	1-1	3	69.1	52	14	3	2	24	25	1.82	222	.215	.291	20-0-1	.350	2	198	18	35	1.8
1952	Chi A	3	1	.750	25	0	0	6	40	42	20	5	1	11	18	4.27	85	.278	.331	7	.000	-1	—	-2	40	-0.4
1953	Chi A	2	0	1.000	24	0	0	2	38.1	41	20	7	0	23	23	4.70	86	.283	.381	6	.000	-1	—	-2	0	-0.2
Total	4	18	3	.857	116	1	1-1	15	235.1	212	98	21	4	111	115	3.44	120	.245	.333	48-0-2	.167	-2	198	20	75	1.6

ALSTON, GARVIN Garvin James; B12.8.1971 Mt.Vernon NY; BR/TR/6´2˝/185; [ColN92 10/291]; d6.6; Col Florida International; [DL 1997 Col N 181]

YEAR	TM LG	W	L	PCT	G	GS	CG-SHO	SV-BS	IP	H	R	HR	HB	BB-IB	SO	ERA	AERA	OAV	OOB	AB-HR-SH	AVG	PB	SUP	APR	DL	PW
1996	Col N	1	0	1.000	6	0	0	0-0	6	9	6	1	1	3-0	5	9.00	58	.375	.433	1	.000	-0	—	-2	0	-0.3

ALTAMIRANO, PORFI Porfirio (Ramirez); B5.17.1952 Darillo, Nicaragua; BR/TR/6´0˝/175; d5.9

YEAR	TM LG	W	L	PCT	G	GS	CG-SHO	SV-BS	IP	H	R	HR	HB	BB-IB	SO	ERA	AERA	OAV	OOB	AB-HR-SH	AVG	PB	SUP	APR	DL	PW
1982	Phi N	5	1	.833	29	0	0	2-1	39	41	19	2	1	14-3	26	4.15	89	.281	.339	4	.250	0	—	-1	23	-0.2
1983	Phi N	2	3	.400	31	0	0	0-0	41.1	38	18	9	2	15-3	24	3.70	97	.255	.329	2	.000	-0	—	0	0	0.0
1984	Chi N	0	0	ø	5	0	0	0-0	11.1	8	6	2	0	1-0	7	4.76	82	.195	.209	2	.000	-0	—	-1	0	0.0
Total	3	7	4	.636	65	0	0	2-1	91.2	87	43	13	3	30-6	57	4.03	91	.259	.320	8	.125	-0	—	-2	23	-0.2

ALTEN, ERNIE Ernest Matthias "Lefty"; B12.1.1894 Avon OH; D9.9.1981 Napa CA; BR/TL/6´0˝/175; d4.17

YEAR	TM LG	W	L	PCT	G	GS	CG-SHO	SV-BS	IP	H	R	HR	HB	BB-IB	SO	ERA	AERA	OAV	OOB	AB-HR-SH	AVG	PB	SUP	APR	DL	PW
1920	Det A	0	1	.000	14	1	0	0	23	40	27	2	1	9	4	9.00	41	.392	.446	3	.000	-1	213	-12	—	-0.6

ALTROCK, NICK Nicholas; B9.15.1876 Cincinnati OH; D1.20.1965 Washington DC; BB/TL/5´10˝/197; d7.14; C42

YEAR	TM LG	W	L	PCT	G	GS	CG-SHO	SV-BS	IP	H	R	HR	HB	BB-IB	SO	ERA	AERA	OAV	OOB	AB-HR-SH	AVG	PB	SUP	APR	DL	PW
1898	Lou N	3	3	.500	11	7	6	0	70	89	54	2	3	21	13	4.50	80	.307	.360	29	.241	0	127	-10	—	-0.6
1902	Bos A	0	2	.000	3	2	1	1	18	19	13	0	1	7	5	2.00	179	.271	.346	8	.000	-1	70	1	—	0.0
1903	Bos A	0	1	.000	1	1	1	0	8	13	10	0	0	4	3	9.00	34	.361	.425	3	.667	1	71	-5	—	-0.3
	Chi A	4	3	.571	12	8	6-1	0	71	59	35	3	3	19	19	2.15	130	.226	.286	30	.300	2*	130	2	—	0.6
	Year	4	4	.500	13	9	7-1	0	79	72	45	3	3	23	22	2.85	99	.242	.303	33	.333	4	123	-4	—	0.3
1904	Chi A	19	14	.576	38	36	31-6	1	307	274	117	2	3	48	87	2.96	83	.240	.272	111-1-6	.198	1*	126	-10	—	-0.8
1905	Chi A	23	12	.657	38	34	31-3	0	315.2	274	89	3	2	63	97	1.88	131	.236	.276	112-0-5	.125	-3*	122	24	—	2.7
1906	†Chi A	20	13	.606	38	30	25-4	0	287.2	269	95	0	3	42	99	2.06	123	.250	.281	100-0-2	.160	-1	105	15	—	1.9
1907	Chi A	7	13	.350	30	21	15-1	2	213.2	210	76	3	2	31	61	2.57	93	.259	.288	72	.181	1	67	-2	—	0.2
1908	Chi A	5	7	.417	23	13	8-1	2	136	127	55	2	2	18	21	2.71	85	.248	.276	49-0-1	.204	1	111	-6	—	-0.2
1909	Chi A	0	1	.000	1	1	1	0	9	16	6	0	0	1	2	5.00	47	.485	.500	3	.000	-0	60	-2	—	-0.3
	Was A	1	3	.250	9	5	2	0	38	55	23	0	1	5	9	5.45	45	.333	.357	19	.053	-1*	70	-10	—	-1.0
	Year	1	4	.200	10	6	3	0	47	71	29	0	1	6	11	5.36	45	.359	.380	22	.045	-1	68	-12	—	-1.3
1912	Was A	0	1	.000	1	0	0	0	1	1	2	0	0	2	0	18.00	19	.200	.429	1	.000	-0	—	-1	—	-0.2
1913	Was A	0	0	ø	4	0	0	0	9	7	5	0	1	4	2	5.00	59	.194	.293	1	.000	-0	—	-1	—	-0.1
1914	Was A	0	0	ø	1	0	0	0	1	3	0	0	0	0	1	0.00	ø	.750	.750	0	ø	0	—	0	—	0.0
1915	Was A	0	0	ø	1	0	0	1	3	7	4	0	0	1	2	9.00	33	.438	.471	1	.000	-0	—	-2	—	-0.2
1918	Was A	1	2	.333	5	3	1	0	24	24	11	1	1	6	5	3.00	91	.279	.333	8-1-1	.125	0	55	-1	—	0.0
1919	Was A	0	0	ø	1	0	0	0	0	4	4	0	0	0	0	(4)	ø	1.000	1.000	0	ø	0	—	-4	—	-0.3
1924	Was A	0	0	ø	1	0	0	0	2	4	1	0	0	0	0	0.00	ø	.500	.500	1	1.000	1	—	1	—	0.1
Total	16	83	75	.525	218	161	128-16	7	1514	1455	600	16	22	272	425	2.67	95	.255	.291	548-2-15	.175	1	108	-11	—	1.5

ALVAREZ, ABE Abraham; B10.17.1982 Los Angeles CA; BL/TL/6´2˝/190; [BosA02 2/49]; d7.22; Col Cal St.–Long Beach

YEAR	TM LG	W	L	PCT	G	GS	CG-SHO	SV-BS	IP	H	R	HR	HB	BB-IB	SO	ERA	AERA	OAV	OOB	AB-HR-SH	AVG	PB	SUP	APR	DL	PW
2004	Bos A	0	1	.000	1	1	0	0-0	5	8	5	2	0	5-0	2	9.00	54	.400	.520	0	ø	0	57	-2	0	-0.3
2005	Bos A	0	0	ø	2	0	0	0-0	2.1	6	4	1	0	0-0	1	15.43	29	.462	.462	0	ø	0	—	-3	0	-0.1
2006	Bos A	0	0	ø	1	0	0	0-0	3	5	4	2	0	2-0	2	12.00	39	.385	.467	1	.000	-0	—	-2	13	-0.1
Total	3	0	1	.000	4	1	0	0-0	10.1	19	13	5	0	7-0	5	11.32	42	.413	.491	1	.000	-0	57	-7	13	-0.5

ALVAREZ, TAVO Cesar Octavio; B11.25.1971 Ciudad Obregon, Sonora, Mexico; BR/TR/6´3˝/(235–245); [MonN90 2/50]; d8.21

YEAR	TM LG	W	L	PCT	G	GS	CG-SHO	SV-BS	IP	H	R	HR	HB	BB-IB	SO	ERA	AERA	OAV	OOB	AB-HR-SH	AVG	PB	SUP	APR	DL	PW
1995	Mon N	1	5	.167	8	8	0	0-0	37.1	46	30	2	3	14-0	17	6.75	64	.297	.366	12-0-2	.000	-1	95	-10	0	-1.4
1996	Mon N	2	1	.667	11	5	0	0-0	21	19	10	0	1	12-1	9	3.00	144	.235	.340	4-0-1	.500	1	100	2	16	0.3
Total	2	3	6	.333	19	13	0	0-0	58.1	65	40	2	4	26-1	26	5.40	80	.275	.357	16-0-3	.125	-1	97	-8	16	-1.1

ALVAREZ, JOSE Jose Lino; B4.12.1956 Tampa FL; BR/TR/5´10˝/(170–175); [AtlN78 8/183]; d10.1; Col Louisiana–Lafayette; [DL 1990 SF N 178]

YEAR	TM LG	W	L	PCT	G	GS	CG-SHO	SV-BS	IP	H	R	HR	HB	BB-IB	SO	ERA	AERA	OAV	OOB	AB-HR-SH	AVG	PB	SUP	APR	DL	PW
1981	Atl N	0	0	ø	1	0	0	0-0	2	0	0	0	0	0-0	2	0.00	ø	.000	.000	0	ø	0	—	1	0	0.0
1982	Atl N	0	0	ø	7	0	0	0-0	7.2	8	4	1	0	2-1	6	4.70	79	.308	.357	0	ø	0	—	-1	0	0.0
1988	Atl N	5	6	.455	60	0	0	3-1	102.1	88	34	7	6	53-12	81	2.99	123	.240	.343	8-0-1	.375	1*	—	9	0	1.2
1989	Atl N	3	3	.500	30	0	0	2-3	50.1	44	18	4	1	24-2	45	2.86	128	.237	.325	3-0-2	.000	-0	—	4	99	0.5
Total	4	8	9	.471	98	0	0	5-4	162.1	140	56	12	7	79-15	134	2.99	122	.240	.335	11-0-3	.273	1	—	13	277	1.7

ALVAREZ, JUAN Juan M.; B8.9.1973 Coral Gables FL; BL/TL/6´1˝/175; d9.1; Col St. Thomas (FL)

YEAR	TM LG	W	L	PCT	G	GS	CG-SHO	SV-BS	IP	H	R	HR	HB	BB-IB	SO	ERA	AERA	OAV	OOB	AB-HR-SH	AVG	PB	SUP	APR	DL	PW
1999	Ana A	0	1	.000	8	0	0	0-0	3	1	1	0	0	4-0	4	3.00	163	.111	.385	0	ø	0	—	1	0	0.1
2000	Ana A	0	0	ø	11	0	0	0-0	6	14	9	3	0	7-1	2	13.50	38	.467	.553	0	ø	0	—	-5	0	-0.2
2002	Tex A	0	4	.000	52	0	0	0-3	39.2	35	22	7	3	21-0	30	4.76	101	.241	.345	0	ø	0	—	0	0	0.0
2003	Fla N	0	0	ø	9	0	0	0-0	11.2	8	4	2	1	8-1	6	3.09	133	.216	.370	0	ø	0	—	2	0	0.1
Total	4	0	5	.000	80	0	0	0-3	60.1	58	36	12	4	40-2	42	5.22	90	.262	.381	0	ø	0	—	-2	0	0.0

ALVAREZ, VICTOR Victor Aurelio; B11.8.1976 Culiacan, Sinaloa, Mexico; BL/TL/5´10˝/150; d7.30

YEAR	TM LG	W	L	PCT	G	GS	CG-SHO	SV-BS	IP	H	R	HR	HB	BB-IB	SO	ERA	AERA	OAV	OOB	AB-HR-SH	AVG	PB	SUP	APR	DL	PW
2002	LA N	0	1	.000	4	1	0	0-0	10.1	9	5	1	0	2-0	7	4.35	90	.237	.275	2	.000	-0	0	0	0	-0.1
2003	LA N	0	1	.000	5	0	0	0-0	5.2	9	8	1	1	6-0	3	12.71	32	.391	.533	0	ø	0	—	-5	0	-0.8
Total	2	0	2	.000	9	1	0	0-0	16	18	13	2	1	8-0	10	7.31	54	.295	.386	2	.000	-0	0	-5	0	-0.9

ALVAREZ, WILSON Wilson Eduardo (Fuenmayor); B3.24.1970 Maracaibo, Zulia, Venez.; BL/TL/6´1˝/(175–255); d7.24; [DL 2001 TB A 190]

YEAR	TM LG	W	L	PCT	G	GS	CG-SHO	SV-BS	IP	H	R	HR	HB	BB-IB	SO	ERA	AERA	OAV	OOB	AB-HR-SH	AVG	PB	SUP	APR	DL	PW
1989	Tex A	0	1	.000	1	1	0	0-0	0	3	3	2	0	2-0	0	(3)	ø	1.000	1.000	0	ø	0	68	-3	0	-0.2
1991	Chi A	3	2	.600	10	9	2-1	0-0	56.1	47	26	9	0	29-0	32	3.51	114	.230	.325	0	ø	0	127	2	0	0.2
1992	Chi A	5	3	.625	34	9	0	1-0	100.1	103	64	12	4	65-2	66	5.20	75	.272	.381	0	ø	0	149	-15	0	-1.1

YEAR	TM LG	W	L	PCT	G	GS	CG-SHO	SV-BS	IP	H	R	HR	HB	BB-IB	SO	ERA	AERA	OAV	OOB	AB-HR-SH	AVG	PB	SUP	APR	DL	PW
1993	†Chi A	15	8	.652	31	31	1-1	0-0	207.2	168	78	14	7	122-8	155	2.95	143	.230	.344	0	ø	0	100	29	0	2.9
1994	Chi A★	12	8	.600	24	24	2-1	0-0	161.2	147	72	16	0	62-1	108	3.45	136	.241	.309	0	ø	0	102	22	0	2.3
1995	Chi A	8	11	.421	29	29	3	0-0	175	171	96	21	2	93-4	118	4.32	104	.258	.349	0	ø	0	101	1	0	0.2
1996	Chi A	15	10	.600	35	35	0	0-0	217.1	216	106	21	4	97-3	181	4.22	113	.258	.337	0	ø	0	119	16	0	1.5
1997	Chi A	9	8	.529	22	22	2-1	0-0	145.2	126	61	9	3	55-1	110	3.03	146	.232	.303	3	.000	-0	80	20	0	2.1
	†SF N	4	3	.571	11	11	0	0-0	66.1	54	36	9	1	36-3	69	4.48	92	.224	.326	23-0-1	.130	-0	130	-2	0	-0.2
1998	TB A	6	14	.300	25	25	0	0-0	142.2	130	78	18	9	68-0	107	4.73	101	.239	.332	0	ø	0	65	2	46	0.1
1999	TB A	9	9	.500	28	28	1	0-0	160	159	92	22	6	79-1	128	4.22	118	.260	.349	3	.000	-0	100	10	38	0.9
2002	TB A	2	3	.400	23	10	0	1-0	75	80	47	13	4	36-3	56	5.28	86	.272	.356	4	.000	-0	111	-6	67	-0.4
2003	LA N	6	2	.750	21	12	1-1	1-0	95	80	27	5	5	23-1	82	2.37	174	.231	.288	29-0-1	.172	0	102	19	0	1.6
2004	†LA N	7	6	.538	40	15	0	1-1	120.2	109	56	12	5	31-2	102	4.03	103	.244	.297	31-0-2	.161	-0	100	2	0	0.2
2005	LA N	1	4	.200	21	2	0	0-0	24	31	15	7	0	7-0	16	5.63	74	.316	.355	2-0-1	.000	-0	57	-3	123	-0.7
Total	14	102	92	.526	355	263	12-5	4-1	1747.2	1624	857	190	50	805-29	1330	3.96	113	.248	.333	95-0-5	.137	-1	102	94	464	9.4
Ames, Red	Leon Kessling; B8.2.1882 Warren OH; D10.8.1936 Warren OH; BB/TR/5´10.5˝/185; d9.14																									
1903	NY N	2	0	1.000	2	2	2-1	0	14	5	2	0	0	8	14	1.29	260	.114	.250	6	.000	-1	121	3	—	0.3
1904	NY N	4	6	.400	16	13	11-1	3	115	94	44	2	3	38	93	2.27	120	.222	.291	40	.125	-1	76	5	—	0.2
1905	†NY N	22	8	.733	34	31	21-2	0	262.2	220	113	2	3	105	198	2.74	107	.230	.308	97-0-6	.144	-1	140	5	—	0.4
1906	NY N	12	10	.545	31	25	15-1	1	203.1	166	79	1	3	93	156	2.66	98	.223	.312	61-0-1	.066	-3	109	0	—	-0.2
1907	NY N	10	12	.455	39	26	17-2	1	233.1	184	93	4	10	108	146	2.16	115	.219	.315	69-1-4	.174	2	113	2	—	0.5
1908	NY N	7	4	.636	18	15	5	1	114.1	96	35	0	1	27	81	1.81	133	.232	.281	36-0-4	.194	-0	132	6	—	0.7
1909	NY N	15	10	.600	34	27	20-2	1	244	217	109	2	4	81	156	2.69	95	.241	.306	81-0-3	.074	-5	118	-4	—	-0.5
1910	NY N	12	11	.522	33	23	13-3	0	190.1	161	78	3	6	63	94	2.22	133	.237	.308	62-1-2	.177	-1	96	11	—	1.4
1911	†NY N	11	10	.524	34	23	13-1	2	205	170	80	0	4	54	118	2.68	126	.223	.277	64-0-3	.094	-3	87	16	—	1.3
1912	†NY N	11	5	.688	33	22	9-2	2	179	194	82	3	4	35	83	2.46	137	.281	.320	58-0-1	.224	1	109	14	—	1.4
1913	NY N	2	1	.667	8	5	2	1	41.2	35	11	0	1	8	30	2.16	144	.241	.286	13-0-1	.154	-1	121	5	—	0.5
	Cin N	11	13	.458	31	24	12-1	2	187.1	185	82	7	5	70	80	2.88	113	.265	.336	59-0-4	.102	-4	86	7	—	0.4
	Year	13	14	.481	39	29	14-1	3	229	220	93	7	6	78	110	2.75	117	.261	.328	72-0-5	.111	-5	92	14	—	0.9
1914	Cin N	15	23	.395	47	37	18-4	**6**	297	274	125	7	6	94	128	2.64	111	.248	.311	94-1-5	.128	-4	78	9	—	1.0
1915	Cin N	2	4	.333	17	7	4-1	1	68	82	39	2	0	24	26	4.50	64	.311	.368	20	.050	-1	82	-10	—	-1.0
	StL N	9	3	.750	15	14	8-2	1	113.1	93	35	1	0	32	48	2.46	113	.226	.282	35-0-3	.114	-2	116	6	—	0.6
	Year	11	7	.611	32	21	12-3	2	181.1	175	74	3	0	56	74	3.23	87	.259	.316	55-0-3	.091	-3	104	-3	—	-0.4
1916	StL N	11	16	.407	45	25	10-2	**8**	228	225	100	3	5	57	98	2.64	100	.263	.313	68-0-2	.176	-0	90	-4	—	-0.6
1917	StL N	15	10	.600	43	19	10-2	3	209	189	75	2	3	57	62	2.71	99	.249	.304	64-0-3	.188	2	93	0	—	0.5
1918	StL N	9	14	.391	27	25	17	1	206.2	192	75	1	5	52	68	2.31	117	.252	.304	64-0-4	.156	-1	81	8	—	0.8
1919	StL N	3	5	.375	23	6	1	1	70	88	44	1	1	25	19	4.89	57	.314	.373	18-0-1	.222	-0	123	-15	—	-1.8
	Phi N	0	2	.000	3	2	1	1	16	26	12	0	0	3	4	6.19	52	.400	.426	5	.400	1	37	-4	—	-0.4
	Year	3	7	.300	26	8	2	2	86	114	56	1	1	28	23	5.13	56	.330	.382	23-0-1	.261	1	100	-19	—	-2.2
Total	17	183	167	.523	533	371	209-27	36	3198	2896	1313	41	64	1034	1702	2.63	108	.245	.310	1014-3-47	.141	-21	101	60	—	5.5
Amole, Doc	Morris George; B7.5.1878 Coatesville PA; D3.7.1912 Wilmington DE; BR/TL/5´9˝/165; d8.19																									
1897	Bal N	4	4	.500	11	7	6	0	70	67	34	0	6	17	19	2.57	162	.250	.309	28	.107	-3	73	11	—	0.8
1898	Was N	0	6	.000	7	5	4	0	49.1	83	57	0	6	22	11	7.84	47	.369	.439	20	.100	-2	93	-21	—	-2.0
Total	2	4	10	.286	18	12	10	0	119.1	150	91	0	12	39	30	4.75	83	.304	.369	48	.104	-4	81	-10	—	-1.2
Amor, Vicente	Vicente (Alvarez); B8.8.1932 Havana, Cuba; BR/TR/6´3˝/182; d4.16																									
1955	Chi N	0	1	.000	4	0	0	0	6	11	3	0	0	3-1	3	4.50	91	.407	.467	0	ø	0	—	0	0	0.0
1957	Cin N	1	2	.333	9	4	1	0	27.1	39	19	2	2	10-1	9	5.93	69	.345	.402	6	.167	-0	112	-5	0	-0.5
Total	2	1	3	.250	13	4	1	0	33.1	50	22	2	2	13-2	12	5.67	72	.357	.414	6	.167	-0	112	-5	0	-0.5
Ancker, Walter	Walter; B4.10.1893 New York NY; D2.13.1954 Englewood NJ; BR/TR/6´1˝/190; d9.3																									
1915	Phi A	0	0	ø	4	1	0	0	17.2	19	10	1	3	17	4	3.57	82	.279	.443	6	.000	-1	150	-1	—	-0.2
Andersen, Larry	Larry Eugene; B5.6.1953 Portland OR; BR/TR/6´3˝/(180–205); [CleA71 7/155]; d9.5																									
1975	Cle A	0	0	ø	3	0	0	0-0	5.2	4	3	0	0	2-0	4	4.76	80	.200	.261	0	ø	0	—	0	0	0.0
1977	Cle A	0	1	.000	11	0	0	0-0	14.1	10	7	1	0	9-3	8	3.14	127	.200	.322	0	ø	0	—	1	0	0.1
1979	Cle A	0	0	ø	8	0	0	0-0	16.2	25	14	3	0	4-0	7	7.56	57	.357	.382	0	ø	0	—	-5	0	-0.2
1981	Sea A	3	3	.500	41	0	0	5-3	67.2	57	27	4	2	18-2	40	2.66	146	.228	.282	0	ø	0	—	7	0	0.7
1982	Sea A	0	0	ø	40	1	0	1-0	79.2	100	56	16	4	23-1	32	5.99	72	.311	.361	0	ø	0	106	-13	21	-0.6
1983	†Phi N	1	0	1.000	17	0	0	0-1	26.1	19	7	0	0	9-1	14	2.39	151	.200	.267	2	.000	-0	—	4	0	0.2
1984	Phi N	3	7	.300	64	0	0	4-6	90.2	85	32	5	0	25-6	54	2.38	154	.248	.296	4	.000	-0	—	11	0	1.2
1985	Phi N	3	3	.500	57	0	0	3-6	73	78	41	5	3	26-4	50	4.32	86	.274	.340	4-0-1	.000	-0	—	-5	0	-0.4
1986	Phi N	0	0	ø	10	0	0	0-0	12.2	19	8	0	0	3-0	9	4.26	92	.388	.415	0-0-1	ø	0	—	-1	0	0.0
	†Hou N	2	1	.667	38	0	0	1-3	64.2	64	22	2	1	23-10	33	2.78	130	.276	.338	6	.000	-1	—	6	0	0.3
	Year	2	1	.667	48	0	0	1-3	77.1	83	30	2	1	26-10	42	3.03	121	.295	.351	6-0-1	.000	-1	—	5	0	0.3
1987	Hou N	9	5	.643	67	0	0	5-4	101.2	95	46	7	2	41-10	94	3.45	114	.246	.319	6	.167	0	—	4	0	0.6
1988	Hou N	2	4	.333	53	0	0	5-4	82.2	82	29	3	1	20-8	66	2.94	113	.254	.297	6	.333	1	—	4	15	0.4
1989	Hou N	4	4	.500	60	0	0	3-3	87.2	63	19	2	0	24-4	85	1.54	221	.198	.251	3-0-1	.333	0	—	18	30	1.7
1990	Hou N	5	2	.714	50	0	0	6-1	73.2	61	19	2	1	24-5	68	1.95	191	.229	.291	3-0-1	.000	-0	—	14	0	1.5
	†Bos A	0	0	ø	15	0	0	1-3	22	18	3	0	1	3-0	25	1.23	334	.220	.256	0	ø	0	—	7	0	0.3
1991	SD N	3	4	.429	38	0	0	13-3	47	39	13	0	0	13-3	40	2.30	166	.231	.283	2	.000	-0	—	8	41	1.5
1992	SD N	1	1	.500	34	0	0	2-0	35	26	14	2	1	8-2	35	3.34	108	.202	.252	1	.000	0	—	1	63	0.1
1993	†Phi N	3	2	.600	64	0	0	0-4	61.2	54	22	4	1	21-2	67	2.92	136	.233	.299	1	1.000	0	—	8	19	0.6
1994	Phi N	1	2	.333	29	0	0	0-0	32.2	33	20	2	0	15-3	27	4.41	97	.256	.333	0	ø	0	—	-1	49	-0.1
Total	17	40	39	.506	699	1	0	49-41	995.1	932	402	58	17	311-64	758	3.15	120	.249	.306	38-0-4	.132	-0	106	68	238	7.9
Anderson, Allan	Allan Lee; B1.7.1964 Lancaster OH; BL/TL/6´0˝/(180–201); [MinA82 2/32]; d6.11																									
1986	Min A	3	6	.333	21	10	1	0-0	84.1	106	54	11	1	30-3	51	5.55	78	.316	.371	0	ø	0*	77	-9	0	-0.9
1987	Min A	1	0	1.000	4	2	0	0-0	12.1	20	15	3	0	10-2	3	10.95	42	.392	.492	0	ø	0	177	-8	0	-0.5
1988	Min A	16	9	.640	30	30	3-1	0-0	202.1	199	70	14	7	37-1	83	**2.45**	**167**	.261	.299	0	ø	0	87	31	0	3.8
1989	Min A	17	10	.630	33	33	4-1	0-0	196.2	214	97	15	7	53-1	69	3.80	109	.275	.325	1	.000	-0*	125	4	0	0.5
1990	Min A	7	18	.280	31	31	5-1	0-0	188.2	214	106	20	5	39-1	82	4.53	92	.289	.325	0	ø	0	70	-8	0	-0.8
1991	Min A	5	11	.313	29	22	2	0-0	134.1	148	82	24	5	42-4	51	4.96	86	.281	.336	0	ø	0	79	-10	0	-1.1
Total	6	49	54	.476	148	128	15-3	0-0	818.2	901	424	87	25	211-12	339	4.11	102	.282	.329	1	.000	-0	92	0	0	1.0
Anderson, Red	Arnold Revola; B6.19.1912 Lawton IA; D8.7.1972 Sioux City IA; BR/TR/6´3˝/210; d9.19; Mil 1942																									
1937	Was A	0	1	.000	2	1	0	0	10.2	11	9	0	1	11	3	6.75	66	.282	.451	3	.000	-0	20	-3	—	-0.2
1940	Was A	1	1	.500	2	2	2	0	14	12	6	0	0	5	3	3.86	108	.245	.315	5	.600	1	74	1	—	0.3
1941	Was A	4	6	.400	32	6	1	0	112	127	69	7	3	53	34	4.18	97	.296	.377	31-0-2	.258	2	100	-5	0	-0.2
Total	3	5	8	.385	36	9	3	0	136.2	150	84	7	4	69	40	4.35	94	.290	.378	39-0-2	.282	3	85	-7	0	-0.1
Anderson, Brian	Brian James; B4.26.1972 Portsmouth VA; BL/TL (BB 2000)/6´1˝/(183–190); [CalA93 1/3]; d9.10; Col Wright St.																									
1993	Cal A	0	0	ø	4	1	0	0-0	11.1	11	5	1	0	2-0	4	3.97	114	.256	.289	0	ø	0	61	1	0	0.0
1994	Cal A	7	5	.583	18	18	0	0-0	101.2	120	63	13	5	27-0	47	5.22	94	.300	.347	0	ø	0	115	-4	31	-0.4
1995	Cal A	6	8	.429	18	17	1	0-0	99.2	110	66	24	3	30-2	45	5.87	80	.282	.334	0	ø	0	108	-11	45	-1.2
1996	Cle A	3	1	.750	10	9	0	0-0	51.1	58	29	9	0	14-1	21	4.91	100	.296	.338	0	ø	0	137	1	0	0.1
1997	†Cle A	4	2	.667	8	8	0	0-0	48	55	28	7	0	11-0	22	4.69	100	.301	.332	0	ø	0	112	0	38	0.0
1998	Ari N	12	13	.480	32	32	2-1	0-0	208	221	109	39	4	24-2	95	4.33	99	.274	.297	66-0-6	.106	-3*	95	-1	0	-0.2
1999	†Ari N	8	2	.800	31	19	2-1	1-1	130	144	69	18	1	28-3	75	4.57	101	.279	.317	38-1-1	.132	1*	118	2	0	0.4
2000	Ari N	11	7	.611	33	32	2	0-0	213.1	226	101	38	3	39-7	104	4.05	118	.275	.308	69-0-9	.188	1*	97	18	0	1.6
2001	†Ari N	4	9	.308	29	22	1	0-1	133.1	156	93	25	1	30-2	55	5.20	89	.295	.332	37	.135	-0*	103	-12	48	-1.0
2002	Ari N	6	11	.353	35	24	0	0-0	156	174	86	23	1	32-3	81	4.79	94	.284	.317	43-0-5	.116	-1*	87	-4	0	-0.4
2003	Cle A	9	10	.474	25	24	0	0-0	148	162	88	21	4	32-3	72	3.71	119	.282	.319	1	.000	0*	101	4	0	0.5
	KC A	5	1	.833	7	7	2-1	0-0	49.2	50	22	6	0	11-0	15	3.99	121	.272	.310	0	ø	0	139	5	0	0.5
	Year	14	11	.560	32	31	2-1	0-0	197.2	212	110	27	4	43-3	87	3.78	120	.279	.317	1	.000	0	110	8	0	1.0

YEAR	TM LG	W	L	PCT	G	GS	CG-SHO	SV-BS	IP	H	R	HR	HB	BB-IB	SO	ERA	AERA	OAV	OOB	AB-HR-SH	AVG	PB	SUP	APR	DL	PW
2004	KC A	6	12	.333	35	26	2-1	0-0	166	217	123	33	1	53-4	70	5.64	83	.320	.366	1-0-1	.000	-0	111	-21	0	-1.9
2005	KC A	1	2	.333	6	6	0	0-0	30.2	39	24	7	0	4-1	17	6.75	65	.305	.323	0	ø	0	127	-8	147	-0.6
Total	13	82	83	.497	291	245	12-4	1-2	1547	1743	906	264	23	337-28	723	4.74	97	.287	.324	255-1-22	.137	-3	106	-30	309	-2.6
Anderson, Dave	David S.; B10.10.1868 Chester PA; D3.22.1897 Chester PA; TL; d8.24																									
1889	Phi N	0	1	.000	5	2	1	0	23	30	21	2	0	14	8	7.43	59	.306	.393	11	.182	-0	93	-5	—	-0.2
1890	Phi N	1	1	.500	3	2	1	0	19.1	31	25	0	1	11	7	7.45	49	.352	.430	9	.111	-1	112	-8	—	-0.6
	Pit N	2	11	.154	13	13	13	0	108	116	84	2	7	49	41	4.67	71	.265	.349	42	.071	-5	65	-16	—	-1.7
	Year	3	12	.200	16	15	14	0	127.1	147	109	2	8	60	48	5.09	66	.280	.363	51	.078	-6	72	-26	—	-2.3
Total	2	3	13	.188	21	17	15	0	150.1	177	130	4	8	74	56	5.45	64	.284	.367	62	.097	-6	74	-29	—	-2.5
Anderson, Jimmy	James Drew; B1.22.1976 Portsmouth VA; BL/TL/6´1˝/(190–215); [PitN94 9/242]; d7.4																									
1999	Pit N	2	1	.667	13	4	0	0-0	29.1	25	15	2	1	16-2	13	3.99	115	.234	.336	9	.333	1	120	2	0	0.3
2000	Pit N	5	11	.313	27	26	1	0-0	144	169	94	13	7	58-2	73	5.25	88	.294	.364	50-0-4	.140	-1	93	-10	0	-1.0
2001	Pit N	9	17	.346	34	34	1	0-0	206.1	232	123	15	11	83-14	89	5.10	88	.287	.358	59-0-6	.119	-1	78	-13	0	-1.4
2002	Pit N	8	13	.381	28	25	1	0-0	140.2	167	91	20	5	63-5	47	5.44	77	.299	.372	42-0-3	.119	-1	96	-18	0	-2.3
2003	Cin N	1	5	.167	8	7	0	0-0	38.2	60	39	8	0	14-1	13	8.84	47	.359	.402	9-0-2	.111	0	119	-20	0	-2.3
2004	Chi N	0	0	ø	7	0	0	1-0	9.2	9	5	0	2	3-0	3	4.66	95	.243	.333	1	.000	-0	—	0	0	0.0
	Bos A	0	0	ø	5	0	0	0-0	6	10	4	0	0	3-0	3	6.00	81	.400	.464	0	ø	0	—	0	0	0.0
Total	6	25	47	.347	122	96	3	1-0	574.2	672	371	58	26	240-24	241	5.42	82	.295	.366	170-0-15	.135	-2	91	-59	0	-6.7
Anderson, Jason	Jason Roger; B6.9.1979 Danville IL; BL/TR/6´0˝/(170–190); [NYA00 10/308]; d3.31; Col Illinois																									
2003	NY A	1	0	1.000	22	0	0	0-0	20.2	23	13	3	2	14-4	9	4.79	92	.280	.390	0	ø	0	—	-1	0	-0.1
	NY N	0	0	ø	6	0	0	0-0	10.2	10	6	2	1	5-1	7	5.06	83	.256	.340	0	ø	0	—	-1	0	0.0
2004	Cle A	0	0	ø	1	0	0	0-0	1	1	5	1	0	4-1	1	45.00	10	.250	.625	0	ø	0	—	-5	0	-0.2
2005	NY A	1	0	1.000	3	0	0	0-0	5.2	4	5	0	0	7-1	2	7.94	54	.200	.407	0	ø	0	—	-2	0	-0.3
Total	3	2	0	1.000	32	0	0	0-0	38	38	29	6	3	30-7	19	6.39	68	.262	.390	0	ø	0	—	-9	0	-0.6
Anderson, John	John Charles; B11.23.1929 St.Paul MN; D12.20.1998 Houston TX; BR/TR/6´1˝/190; d8.17																									
1958	Phi N	0	0	ø	5	1	0	0	16	26	17	5	1	4-0	9	7.88	50	.361	.403	3	.000	-0	113	-7	0	-0.4
1960	Bal A	0	0	ø	4	0	0	0	4.2	8	7	0	0	4-0	1	13.50	28	.444	.522	0	ø	0	—	-5	0	-0.2
1962	StL N	0	0	ø	5	0	0	1	6.1	4	1	0	0	3-2	3	1.42	300	.182	.269	0	ø	0	—	2	0	0.1
	Hou N	0	0	ø	10	0	0	0	17.2	26	12	1	0	3-1	6	5.09	73	.338	.363	2	.000	-0	—	-3	0	-0.1
	Year	0	0	ø	15	0	0	1	24	30	13	1	0	6-3	9	4.13	94	.303	.340	2	.000	-0	—	-1	0	0.0
Total	3	0	0	ø	24	1	0	1	44.2	64	37	6	1	14-3	19	6.45	60	.339	.383	5	.000	-0	113	-13	0	-0.6
Anderson, Fred	John Frederick; B12.11.1885 Calahaln NC; D11.8.1957 Winston–Salem NC; BR/TR/6´2˝/180; d9.25; Mil 1918; Col Maryland																									
1909	Bos A	0	0	ø	1	1	0	0	8	3	3	0	0	1	5	1.13	222	.115	.148	3	.000	-0	113	1	—	0.0
1913	Bos A	0	6	.000	10	8	4	0	57.1	84	51	0	1	21	32	5.97	49	.353	.408	20	.050	-2	104	-19	—	-1.9
1914	Buf F	13	15	.464	37	28	21-2	0	260.1	243	115	8	2	64	144	3.08	96	.249	.297	90	.189	-2*	79	-5	—	-0.9
1915	Buf F	19	13	.594	36	28	14-5	0	240	192	80	5	3	72	142	2.51	111	.222	.285	80-0-1	.150	-4	88	9	—	0.5
1916	NY N	9	13	.409	38	27	13-2	2	188	206	99	7	5	38	98	3.40	72	.277	.316	58-0-4	.138	-0	130	-26	—	-3.3
1917	†NY N	8	8	.500	38	18	8-1	3	162	122	40	1	2	34	69	1.44	**177**	.209	**.255**	42-0-5	.071	-3	100	18	—	1.6
1918	NY N	4	2	.667	18	4	2-1	**3**	70.2	62	27	1	2	17	24	2.67	98	.246	.299	19-0-3	.000	-3	151	0	—	-0.2
Total	7	53	57	.482	178	114	62-11	8	986.1	912	415	22	15	247	514	2.86	95	.248	.298	312-0-13	.131	-14	99	-22	—	-4.2
Anderson, Bud	Karl Adam; B5.27.1956 Westbury NY; BR/TR/6´3˝/210; [SeaA77 3/78]; d6.11; Col Rutgers																									
1982	Cle A	3	4	.429	25	5	1	0-1	80.2	84	37	4	1	30-2	44	3.35	124	.268	.330	0	ø	0	57	5	0	0.4
1983	Cle A	1	6	.143	39	1	0	7-3	68.1	64	34	8	0	32-6	32	4.08	105	.255	.337	0	ø	0	21	2	0	0.1
Total	2	4	10	.286	64	6	1	7-4	149	148	71	12	1	62-8	76	3.68	114	.262	.333	0	ø	0	50	7	0	0.5
Anderson, Larry	Lawrence Dennis; B12.3.1952 Maywood CA; BR/TR/6´3˝/190; [MilA71 2/27]; d9.25																									
1974	Mil A	0	0	ø	2	0	0	0-0	2.1	2	0	0	0	1-0	3	0.00	ø	.250	.333	0	ø	0	—	1	0	0.1
1975	Mil A	1	0	1.000	8	1	1-1	0-0	30.1	36	18	3	0	6-0	13	5.04	76	.298	.328	0	ø	0	160	-3	0	-0.2
1977	Chi A	1	3	.250	6	0	0	0-1	8.2	10	10	1	0	15-4	7	9.35	44	.286	.490	0	ø	0	—	-5	0	-0.9
Total	3	2	3	.400	16	1	1-1	0-1	41.1	48	28	4	0	22-4	23	5.66	69	.293	.372	0	ø	0	160	-7	0	-1.0
Anderson, Matt	Matthew Jason; B8.17.1976 Louisville KY; BR/TR/6´4˝/200; [DetA97 1/1]; d6.25; Col Rice																									
1998	Det A	5	1	.833	42	0	0	0-4	44	38	16	3	2	31-4	44	3.27	145	.250	.378	0	ø	0	—	8	0	0.9
1999	Det A	2	1	.667	37	0	0	0-2	38	33	27	8	1	35-1	32	5.68	88	.232	.383	0	ø	0	—	-3	0	-0.3
2000	Det A	3	2	.600	69	0	0	1-0	74.1	61	44	8	3	45-4	71	4.72	104	.228	.339	0	ø	0	—	1	0	0.0
2001	Det A	3	1	.750	62	0	0	22-2	56	56	33	2	0	18-4	52	4.82	92	.257	.311	0	ø	0	—	-2	0	-0.3
2002	Det A	2	1	.667	12	0	0	0-2	11	17	13	1	2	8-1	8	9.00	49	.378	.474	0	ø	0	—	-6	145	-1.1
2003	Det A	0	1	.000	23	0	0	3-1	23.1	25	17	5	1	9-1	13	5.40	81	.272	.340	0	ø	0	—	-4	0	-0.2
2005	Col N	0	0	ø	12	0	0	0-0	10	19	17	3	2	11-0	4	12.60	37	.404	.525	0	ø	0	—	-9	0	-0.4
Total	7	15	7	.682	257	0	0	26-11	256.2	249	167	30	11	157-15	224	5.19	91	.258	.363	0	ø	0	—	-15	145	-1.4
Anderson, Mike	Michael James; B7.30.1966 Austin TX; BR/TR/6´3˝/205; d9.7; Col Southwestern (TX)																									
1993	Cin N	0	0	ø	3	0	0	0-0	5.1	12	11	3	0	3-0	4	18.56	22	.444	.500	1	.000	-0	—	-8	0	-0.4
Anderson, Craig	Norman Craig; B7.1.1938 Washington DC; BR/TR/6´2˝/(200–210); d6.23; Col Lehigh																									
1961	StL N	4	3	.571	25	0	0	1	38.2	38	15	3	1	12-0	21	3.26	135	.255	.313	9	.333	1	—	5	0	0.9
1962	NY N	3	17	.150	50	14	2	4	131.1	150	108	18	5	63-2	62	5.35	78	.278	.357	32-0-3	.094	-2	79	-22	0	-3.1
1963	NY N	0	2	.000	3	2	0	0	9.1	17	15	0	0	3-0	6	8.68	40	.362	.400	3	.333	0	25	-7	0	-1.1
1964	NY N	0	1	.000	4	1	0	0	13	21	9	0	0	3-0	5	5.54	65	.382	.407	3	.000	-0	0	-3	0	-0.2
Total	4	7	23	.233	82	17	2	5	192.1	226	147	21	6	81-2	94	5.10	81	.286	.355	47-0-3	.149	-1	69	-27	0	-3.5
Anderson, Rick	Richard Arlen; B11.29.1956 Everett WA; BR/TR/6´0˝/(175–180); [NYN78 24/580]; d6.9; C5; Col Washington																									
1986	NY N	2	1	.667	15	5	0	1-0	49.2	45	17	3	0	11-3	21	2.72	132	.245	.281	11-0-1	.091	-1	80	5	0	0.2
1987	KC A	0	2	.000	6	2	0	0-0	13	26	22	3	2	9-1	12	13.85	33	.394	.481	0	ø	0	10	-13	0	-1.5
1988	KC A	2	1	.667	7	3	0	0-0	34	41	17	3	1	9-2	9	4.24	95	.308	.349	0	ø	0	61	0	16	-0.1
Total	3	4	4	.500	28	10	0	1-0	96.2	112	56	9	3	29-6	42	4.75	81	.292	.341	11-0-1	.091	-1	58	-8	16	-1.4
Anderson, Rick	Richard Lee; B12.25.1953 Inglewood CA; D6.23.1989 Wilmington CA; BR/TR/6´2˝/210; [NYA72*S1/5]; d9.18; Col Los Angeles Valley (CA) JC; [DL 1981 Sea A 49]																									
1979	NY A	0	0	ø	1	0	0	0-0	2.1	1	1	0	0	4-0	0	3.86	107	.167	.500	0	ø	0	—	0	0	0.0
1980	Sea A	0	0	ø	5	2	0	0-0	9.2	8	5	1	0	10-2	7	3.72	112	.229	.400	0	ø	0	150	0	0	0.0
Total	2	0	0	ø	6	2	0	0-0	12	9	6	1	0	14-2	7	3.75	111	.220	.418	0	ø	0	150	0	49	0.0
Anderson, Bob	Robert Carl; B9.29.1935 E.Chicago IN; BR/TR/6´4.5˝/(206–210); d7.31; Col Western Michigan																									
1957	Chi N	0	1	.000	8	0	0	0	16.1	20	16	2	1	8-1	7	7.71	50	.317	.397	4	.000	-1	—	-7	0	-0.4
1958	Chi N	3	3	.500	17	8	2	0	65.2	61	29	3	1	29-1	51	3.97	99	.255	.335	17	.118	-1	109	1	0	0.0
1959	Chi N	12	13	.480	37	36	7-1	0	235.1	245	117	21	5	77-3	113	4.13	96	.272	.329	80-0-6	.075	-4	96	-4	0	-0.7
1960	Chi N	9	11	.450	38	30	5	1	203.2	201	105	26	7	68-8	115	4.11	92	.255	.320	71-0-5	.169	0*	90	-7	0	-0.6
1961	Chi N	7	10	.412	57	12	1	8	152	162	85	14	2	56-11	96	4.26	98	.275	.338	42-2-2	.143	0	81	-2	0	-0.1
1962	Chi N	2	7	.222	57	4	0	4	107.2	111	70	9	5	60-5	82	5.02	83	.266	.361	23-0-2	.130	0	79	-11	0	-0.9
1963	Det A	3	1	.750	32	3	0	0	60	58	28	5	6	21-2	38	3.30	113	.258	.335	9	.444	2	87	1	0	0.2
Total	7	36	46	.439	246	93	15-1	13	840.2	858	450	80	27	319-31	502	4.26	93	.266	.335	246-2-15	.134	-4	91	-29	0	-2.5
Anderson, Scott	Scott Richard; B8.1.1962 Corvallis OR; BR/TR/6´6˝/(185–200); [TexA84 7/170]; d4.8; Col Oregon St.																									
1987	Tex A	0	1	.000	8	0	0	0-1	11.1	17	12	0	1	8-2	6	9.53	47	.347	.448	0	ø	0	—	-6	0	-0.4
1990	Mon N	0	1	.000	4	3	0	0-0	18	12	6	1	0	5-0	16	3.00	123	.188	.243	4-0-1	.000	-0	123	2	0	0.0
1995	KC A	1	0	1.000	6	4	0	0-0	25.1	29	15	3	1	8-0	6	5.33	90	.290	.349	0	ø	0	116	-1	0	-0.1
Total	3	1	2	.333	18	7	0	0-1	54.2	58	33	4	2	21-2	28	5.43	80	.272	.342	4-0-1	.000	-0	117	-5	0	-0.5

YEAR	TM LG	W	L	PCT	G	GS	CG-SHO	SV-BS	IP	H	R	HR	HB	BB-IB	SO	ERA	AERA	OAV	OOB	AB-HR-SH	AVG	PB	SUP	APR	DL	PW
Anderson, Varney	Varney Samuel "Varn"; B6.18.1866 Geneva IL; D11.5.1941 Rockford IL; BR/TR/5´10˝/165; d8.1																									
1889	Ind N	0	1	.000	2	1	1	0	12	13	10	0	3	9	3	4.50	93	.271	.417	5	.000	-1	161	-1	—	-0.1
1894	Was N	0	2	.000	2	2	2	0	14	15	12	0	1	6	3	7.07	75	.273	.355	7	.429	0	60	-1	—	-0.1
1895	Was N	9	16	.360	29	25	18	0	204.2	288	199	13	10	97	35	5.89	82	.327	.400	97-0-2	.289	3*	104	-19	—	-1.3
1896	Was N	0	1	.000	2	2	1	0	9	23	16	0	0	3	0	13.00	34	.469	.500	5	.600	1	129	-7	—	-0.5
Total	4	9	20	.310	35	30	22	0	239.2	339	237	13	14	115	41	6.16	78	.328	.403	114-0-2	.298	4	104	-28	—	-2.0
Anderson, Walter	Walter Carl "Lefty"; B9.25.1897 Grand Rapids MI; D1.6.1990 Battle Creek MI; BL/TL/6´2˝/160; d5.14; Mil 1918; Col Western Michigan																									
1917	Phi A	0	0	ø	14	2	0	0	38.2	32	16	0	1	21	10	3.03	91	.246	.355	7	.429	1	78	0	—	0.1
1919	Phi A	1	0	1.000	3	0	0	0	14	13	8	0	1	8	10	3.86	89	.245	.355	4-0-1	.000	-1	—	-1	—	-0.1
Total	2	1	0	1.000	17	2	0	0	52.2	45	24	0	2	29	20	3.25	90	.246	.355	11-0-1	.273	0	78	-1	—	0.0
Anderson, Bill	William; B1.19.1865 Spencer Co. KY; D5.5.1936 Taylorsville KY; d8.12																									
1889	Lou AA	0	1	.000	1	1	1	0	8	10	10	2	0	6	2	10.13	38	.294	.400	3	.333	0	80	-4	—	-0.3
Anderson, Bill	William Edward "Lefty"; B11.28.1895 Boston MA; D3.13.1983 Medford MA; BR/TL/6´1˝/165; d9.10																									
1925	Bos N	0	0	ø	2	0	0	0	2.2	5	3	0	0	2	1	10.13	40	.500	.583	1	.000	-0	—	-2	—	-0.1
Anderson, Wingo	Wingo Charlie; B8.13.1886 Lillian TX; D12.19.1950 Fort Worth TX; BL/TL/5´10.5˝/150; d4.16																									
1910	Cin N	0	0	ø	7	2	0	0	17.1	16	15	0	1	17	11	4.67	62	.258	.425	5	.200	-0	153	-4	—	-0.3
Andrade, Steve	Stephen Michael; B2.6.1978 Woodland CA; BR/TR/6´1˝/220; [AnaA01 32/959]; d5.1; Col Cal St.–Stanislaus																									
2006	KC A	0	0	ø	4	0	0	0-0	4.2	5	5	0	0	4-0	5	9.64	49	.278	.409	0	ø	0	—	-2	0	-0.1
Andre, John	John Edward; B1.3.1923 Brockton MA; D11.25.1976 Barnstable MA; BL/TR/6´4˝/200; d4.16																									
1955	Chi N	0	1	.000	22	3	0	1	45	45	34	7	1	28-4	19	5.80	70	.259	.361	9	.111	-1	153	-9	0	-0.5
Andrews, Clayton	Clayton John; B5.15.1978 Dunedin FL; BR/TL/6´0˝/180; [TorA96 3/74]; d4.16																									
2000	Tor A	1	2	.333	8	2	0	0-0	20.2	34	23	6	0	9-0	12	10.02	50	.374	.426	3	.000	-0	140	-10	0	-1.2
Andrews, Elbert	Elbert De Vore; B12.11.1901 Greenwood SC; D11.25.1979 Greenwood SC; BL/TR/6´0˝/175; d5.1; Col Furman																									
1925	Phi A	0	0	ø	6	0	0	0	8	12	12	0	0	11	0	10.13	46	.375	.535	0	ø	0	—	-5	—	-0.2
Andrews, Hub	Herbert Carl; B8.31.1922 Burbank OK; BR/TR/6´0˝/170; d4.20																									
1947	NY N	0	0	ø	7	0	0	0	8.2	14	7	1	0	4	2	6.23	65	.368	.429	0	ø	0	—	-2	0	-0.1
1948	NY N	0	0	ø	1	0	0	0	3	3	1	0	0	0	0	0.00	ø	.300	.300	0	ø	0	—	1	0	0.1
Total	2	0	0	ø	8	0	0	0	11.2	17	8	1	0	4	2	4.63	87	.354	.404	0	ø	0	—	-1	0	0.0
Andrews, Ivy	Ivy Paul "Poison"; B5.6.1907 Dora AL; D11.24.1970 Birmingham AL; BR/TR/6´1˝/200; d8.15																									
1931	NY A	2	0	1.000	7	3	1	0	34.1	36	17	3	0	8	10	4.19	95	.273	.314	11	.182	0	248	0	—	0.0
1932	NY A	2	1	.667	4	1	1	0	24.2	20	8	0	0	9	7	1.82	223	.215	.284	9-0-1	.222	1	167	6	—	0.8
	Bos A	8	6	.571	25	19	8	0	141.2	144	76	4	2	53	30	3.81	118	.262	.329	51-0-2	.137	-3*	96	9	—	0.4
	Year	10	7	.588	29	20	9	0	166.1	164	84	4	2	62	37	3.52	126	.255	.322	60-0-3	.150	-2	100	15	—	1.2
1933	Bos A	7	13	.350	34	17	5	1	140	157	96	8	1	61	37	4.95	88	.279	.350	42-0-4	.214	-0*	87	-11	—	-1.4
1934	StL A	4	11	.267	43	13	2	3	139	166	84	7	0	65	51	4.66	107	.301	.375	40-0-1	.350	3	102	5	—	0.7
1935	StL A	13	7	.650	50	20	10	1	213.1	231	95	10	1	53	43	3.54	135	.273	.317	68-0-4	.132	-5	81	28	—	1.7
1936	StL A	7	12	.368	36	25	11	1	191.1	221	109	19	0	50	33	4.84	111	.286	.330	59-0-2	.169	-1	74	14	—	1.0
1937	Cle A	3	4	.429	20	4	1-1	0	59.2	76	33	3	0	9	16	4.37	105	.311	.336	12-0-1	.250	1	66	2	—	0.2
	†NY A	3	2	.600	11	5	3-1	1	49	49	19	2	0	17	17	3.12	142	.259	.320	15-0-2	.067	-1	67	8	—	0.6
	Year	6	6	.500	31	9	4-2	1	108.2	125	52	5	0	26	33	3.81	119	.289	.329	27-0-3	.148	-1	66	10	—	0.8
1938	NY A	1	3	.250	19	1	1	1	48	51	25	3	0	17	13	3.00	151	.268	.329	12	.167	-0	19	6	—	0.4
Total	8	50	59	.459	249	108	43-2	8	1041	1151	562	59	4	342	257	4.14	115	.279	.335	319-0-17	.185	-6	89	67	—	4.4
Andrews, John	John Richard; B2.9.1949 Monterey Park CA; BL/TL/5´10˝/180; d4.8; Col San Diego St.																									
1973	StL N	1	1	.500	16	0	0	0-0	18.1	16	10	3	0	11-1	5	4.42	83	.235	.342	2	.500	0	—	-1	0	-0.1
Andrews, Nate	Nathan Hardy; B9.30.1913 Pembroke NC; D4.26.1991 Winston–Salem NC; BR/TR/6´0˝/195; d5.1; Col North Carolina																									
1937	StL N	0	0	ø	4	0	0	0	9	12	4	1	0	3	6	4.00	100	.324	.375	0	ø	0	—	0	—	0.1
1939	StL N	1	2	.333	11	1	0	0	16	24	14	0	0	12	6	6.75	61	.343	.439	2	.000	-0	106	-5	—	-0.8
1940	Cle A	0	1	.000	6	0	0	0	12	16	9	1	0	6	3	6.00	70	.327	.400	0	ø	0	—	-2	—	-0.1
1941	Cle A	0	0	ø	2	0	0	0	2.1	3	4	0	0	2	1	11.57	34	.300	.417	1	.000	-0	—	-2	0	-0.1
1943	Bos N	14	20	.412	36	34	23-3	0	283.2	253	100	11	6	75	80	2.57	133	.238	.291	90-0-6	.156	-0	72	26	0	3.2
1944	Bos N☆	16	15	.516	37	34	16-2	2	257.1	263	106	14	2	74	76	3.22	119	.261	.312	88-0-3	.114	-4	85	18	0	1.7
1945	Bos N	7	12	.368	21	19	8	0	137.2	160	75	9	0	52	26	4.58	84	.295	.356	43-0-7	.209	0*	78	-8	0	-1.0
1946	Cin N	2	4	.333	7	7	3	0	43.1	50	29	2	1	8	13	3.95	85	.281	.316	14-0-3	.071	-1	113	-6	0	-0.8
	NY N	1	0	1.000	3	2	0	0	12	17	9	2	0	4	5	6.00	57	.362	.412	2	.500	1	236	-3	0	-0.2
	Year	3	4	.429	10	9	3	0	55.1	67	38	4	1	12	18	4.39	77	.298	.336	16-0-3	.125	-0	141	-9	0	-1.0
Total	8	41	54	.432	127	97	50-5	2	773.1	798	350	40	9	236	216	3.46	106	.265	.321	240-0-19	.146	-4	84	18	0	2.0
Andrus, Fred	Frederick Hotham; B8.23.1850 Washington MI; D11.10.1937 Detroit MI; BR/TR/6´2˝/185; d7.25.1876; ▲																									
1884	Chi N	1	0	1.000	1	1	1	0	9	11	3	1	—	2	2	2.00	157	.297	.333	5	.200	0	372	1	—	0.1
Andujar, Joaquin	Joaquin; B12.21.1952 San Pedro de Macoris, D.R.; BB/TR/6´0˝/(170–190); d4.8																									
1976	Hou N	9	10	.474	28	25	9-4	0-0	172.1	163	74	8	1	75-2	59	3.60	90	.255	.332	57-0-2	.140	-0	84	-5	0	-0.6
1977	Hou N☆	11	8	.579	26	25	4-1	0-0	158.2	149	80	11	4	64-3	69	3.69	98	.251	.325	53-0-4	.189	2	108	-5	0	-0.2
1978	Hou N	5	7	.417	35	13	2	1-0	110.2	88	45	3	4	58-6	55	3.42	98	.224	.327	23-0-4	.130	-0*	89	-1	22	0.0
1979	Hou N★	12	12	.500	46	23	8	4-3	194	168	86	7	2	88-6	77	3.43	102	.233	.316	57-2-5	.088	-0	82	1	0	0.3
1980	†Hou N	3	8	.273	35	14	0	2-2	122	132	59	8	0	43-2	75	3.91	84	.277	.335	29-1-5	.172	2	95	-8	0	-0.4
1981	Hou N	2	3	.400	9	3	0	0-1	23.2	29	17	2	0	12-0	18	4.94	66	.296	.366	4-0-1	.000	-0	108	-6	0	-1.1
	StL N	6	1	.857	11	8	1	0-1	55.1	56	24	4	0	11-1	19	3.74	97	.265	.302	19-0-1	.000	-2*	110	0	0	-0.2
	Year	8	4	.667	20	11	1	0-2	79	85	41	6	0	23-1	37	4.10	86	.275	.323	23-0-2	.000	-2	110	-4	0	-1.3
1982	†StL N	15	10	.600	38	37	9-5	0-0	265.2	237	85	11	7	50-7	137	2.47	149	.240	.281	95-0-9	.158	-1	95	33	0	3.0
1983	StL N	6	16	.273	39	34	5-2	1-0	225	215	112	23	3	75-7	125	4.16	88	.253	.315	73-0-5	.082	-4	97	-10	0	-1.0
1984	StL N✳	**20**	14	.588	36	36	12-**4**	0-0	**261.1**	218	104	20	7	70-13	147	3.34	105	.229	.284	84-2-7	.131	3	111	7	0	1.3
1985	†StL N✳	21	12	.636	38	38	10-2	0-0	269.2	265	113	15	11	82-12	112	3.40	105	.260	.321	94-0-7	.106	-2	121	6	0	0.5
1986	Oak A	12	7	.632	28	26	7-1	1-0	155.1	139	70	23	4	56-1	72	3.82	102	.239	.308	0	ø	0	99	3	41	0.3
1987	Oak A	3	5	.375	13	13	1	0-0	60.2	63	43	11	3	26-0	32	6.08	68	.269	.348	0	ø	0	120	-13	125	-1.4
1988	Hou N	2	5	.286	23	10	0	0-1	78.2	94	43	9	5	21-5	35	4.00	83	.297	.346	19-0-1	.211	2	128	-8	36	-0.4
Total	13	127	118	.518	405	305	68-19	9-8	2153	2016	955	155	51	731-65	1032	3.58	99	.250	.314	607-5-51	.127	-2	103	-6	224	0.1
Andujar, Luis	Luis (Sanchez); B11.22.1972 Bani, D.R.; BR/TR/6´2˝/(175–215); d9.8																									
1995	Chi A	2	1	.667	5	5	0	0-0	30.1	26	12	4	1	14-2	9	3.26	137	.230	.320	0	ø	0	92	4	0	0.3
1996	Chi A	0	2	.000	5	5	0	0-0	23	32	22	4	0	15-0	6	8.22	58	.337	.420	0	ø	0	117	-9	0	-0.6
	Tor A	1	1	.500	3	2	0	0-0	14.1	14	8	4	1	1-0	5	5.02	100	.264	.281	0	ø	0	74	0	0	0.0
	Year	1	3	.250	8	7	0	0-0	37.1	46	30	8	1	16-0	11	6.99	69	.311	.373	0	ø	0	104	-9	0	-0.6
1997	Tor A	0	6	.000	17	8	0	0-0	50	76	45	9	0	21-1	28	6.48	71	.352	.402	0	ø	0	95	-13	25	-1.3
1998	Tor A	0	0	ø	5	0	0	0-0	5.2	12	6	0	0	2-0	1	9.53	49	.429	.467	0	ø	0	—	-3	0	-0.1
Total	4	3	10	.231	35	20	0	0-0	123.1	160	93	21	2	53-3	49	5.98	78	.317	.379	0	ø	0	98	-21	25	-1.7
Angelini, Norm	Norman Stanley; B9.24.1947 San Francisco CA; BL/TL/5´11˝/175; d7.22; Col Washington St.																									
1972	KC A	2	1	.667	21	0	0	2-1	16	13	4	1	1	12-1	16	2.25	135	.228	.371	2	.000	-0	—	2	0	0.3
1973	KC A	0	0	ø	7	0	0	1-0	3.2	2	2	0	0	7-0	3	4.91	84	.200	.500	0	ø	0	—	0	0	0.0
Total	2	2	1	.667	28	0	0	3-1	19.2	15	6	1	1	19-1	19	2.75	118	.224	.398	2	.000	-0	—	2	0	0.3

Ankiel, Rick Richard Alexander; B7.19.1979 Fort Pierce FL; BL/TL/6´1˝/(210–215); [StLN97 2/72]; d8.23; [DL 2006 StL N 182]

YEAR	TM LG	W	L	PCT	G	GS	CG-SHO	SV-BS	IP	H	R	HR	HB	BB-IB	SO	ERA	AERA	OAV	OOB	AB-HR-SH	AVG	PB	SUP	APR	DL	PW
1999	StL N	0	1	.000	9	5	0	1-0	33	26	12	2	1	14-0	39	3.27	141	.215	.301	10-0-1	.100	-1	76	5	0	0.2
2000	†StL N	11	7	.611	31	30	0	0-0	175	137	80	21	6	90-2	194	3.50	133	.219	.320	68-2-1	.250	6*	104	20	0	2.3
2001	StL N	1	2	.333	6	6	0	0-0	24	25	21	7	3	25-0	27	7.13	61	.275	.434	8-0-1	.000	-1	117	-8	0	-0.8
2004	StL N	1	0	1.000	5	0	0	0-0	10	10	6	2	2	1-0	9	5.40	79	.256	.310	1	.000	0	—	-1	150	-0.1
Total	4	13	10	.565	51	41	0	1-0	242	198	119	32	12	130-2	269	3.90	118	.226	.331	87-2-3	.207	5	103	16	332	1.6

Antonelli, Johnny John August; B4.12.1930 Rochester NY; BL/TL/6´0˝/190; d7.4; Mil 1951–52

YEAR	TM LG	W	L	PCT	G	GS	CG-SHO	SV-BS	IP	H	R	HR	HB	BB-IB	SO	ERA	AERA	OAV	OOB	AB-HR-SH	AVG	PB	SUP	APR	DL	PW
1948	Bos N	0	0	ø	4	0	0	1	4	2	1	0	0	3	0	2.25	170	.143	.294	0	ø	0	—	1	0	0.1
1949	Bos N	3	7	.300	22	10	3-1	0	96	99	49	6	2	42	48	3.56	106	.273	.351	25-0-5	.120	-1	51	0	0	-0.1
1950	Bos N	2	3	.400	20	6	2-1	0	57.2	81	46	3	4	22	33	5.93	65	.335	.399	16	.125	-1	84	-15	0	-1.2
1953	Mil N	12	12	.500	31	26	11-2	1	175.1	167	83	15	1	71	131	3.18	123	.242	.314	62-0-4	.177	0	118	11	0	1.4
1954	†NY N★	21	7	**.750**	39	37	18-**6**	2	258.2	209	78	22	5	94	152	**2.30**	**176**	**.219**	.292	98-2-4	.163	0	109	**50**	0	**5.3**
1955	NY N	14	16	.467	38	34	14-2	1	235.1	206	105	24	11	82-5	143	3.33	121	.234	.306	82-4-3	.207	3	94	16	0	2.3
1956	NY N★	20	13	.606	41	36	15-5	1	258.1	225	93	20	3	75-10	145	2.86	132	.234	.291	89-3-6	.157	1*	76	26	0	3.5
1957	NY N☆	12	18	.400	40	30	8-3	0	212.1	228	98	19	3	67-7	114	3.77	104	.276	.330	72-3-1	.153	3*	66	5	0	0.9
1958	SF N☆	16	13	.552	41	34	13	3	241.2	216	101	31	3	87-7	143	3.28	116	.239	.306	84-1-5	.226	4*	110	14	0	1.9
1959	SF N★	19	10	.655	40	38	17-**4**	1	282	247	107	29	3	76-6	165	3.10	123	.233	.285	101-2-5	.158	1*	110	25	0	2.6
1960	SF N	6	7	.462	41	10	1-1	11	112.1	106	51	7	2	47-10	57	3.77	92	.253	.326	34-0-1	.235	2*	71	-2	0	0.0
1961	Cle A	0	4	.000	11	7	0	0	48	68	39	8	1	18-0	23	6.56	60	.338	.390	15-0-1	.267	1*	83	-14	0	-0.9
	Mil N	1	0	1.000	9	0	0	0	10.2	16	9	2	0	3-0	8	7.59	49	.340	.373	1	.000	-0	—	-5	0	-0.4
Total	12	126	110	.534	377	268	102-25	21	1992.1	1870	860	186	38	687-45	1162	3.34	116	.247	.312	679-15-35	.178	15	95	112	0	15.4

Apodaca, Bob Robert John; B1.31.1950 Los Angeles CA; BR/TR/5´11˝/170; d9.18; C10; Col Cal St.–Los Angeles; [DL 1978 NY N 155, 1979 NY N 127]

YEAR	TM LG	W	L	PCT	G	GS	CG-SHO	SV-BS	IP	H	R	HR	HB	BB-IB	SO	ERA	AERA	OAV	OOB	AB-HR-SH	AVG	PB	SUP	APR	DL	PW
1973	NY N	0	0	ø	1	0	0	0-0	0	0	1	0	0	2-0	0	(1)	ø	ø	1.000	0	ø	0	—	-1	0	-0.1
1974	NY N	6	6	.500	35	8	1	3-2	103	92	47	7	2	42-9	54	3.50	103	.241	.318	25-0-1	.120	0	112	1	0	0.1
1975	NY N	3	4	.429	46	0	0	13-1	84.2	66	18	4	0	28-9	45	1.49	236	.222	.286	11	.364	1	—	19	39	2.5
1976	NY N	3	7	.300	43	3	0	5-2	89.2	71	34	4	3	29-12	45	2.81	119	.223	.291	16-0-1	.125	0	88	5	0	0.6
1977	NY N	4	8	.333	59	0	0	5-5	84	83	38	7	1	30-11	53	3.43	111	.255	.318	6-0-1	.167	-0	—	2	0	0.4
Total	5	16	25	.390	184	11	1	26-10	361.1	312	138	22	6	131-41	197	2.86	124	.236	.305	58-0-3	.172	2	106	26	321	3.5

Aponte, Luis Luis Eduardo (Yuripe); B6.14.1953 ElTigre, Anzoategui, Venez.; BR/TR/6´0˝/(165–185); d9.4

YEAR	TM LG	W	L	PCT	G	GS	CG-SHO	SV-BS	IP	H	R	HR	HB	BB-IB	SO	ERA	AERA	OAV	OOB	AB-HR-SH	AVG	PB	SUP	APR	DL	PW
1980	Bos A	0	0	ø	4	0	0	0-0	7	6	1	0	0	2-1	1	1.29	332	.250	.308	0	ø	0	—	2	0	0.1
1981	Bos A	1	0	1.000	7	0	0	1-0	15.2	11	1	0	0	3-0	11	0.57	682	.208	.250	0	ø	0	—	6	0	0.5
1982	Bos A	2	2	.500	40	0	0	3-0	85	78	31	5	0	25-3	44	3.18	137	.246	.299	0	ø	0	—	11	0	0.6
1983	Bos A	5	4	.556	34	0	0	3-1	62	74	28	7	2	23-3	32	3.63	121	.301	.364	0	ø	0	—	5	0	0.7
1984	Cle A	1	0	1.000	25	0	0	0-0	50.1	53	25	5	1	15-0	25	4.11	100	.269	.322	0	ø	0	—	0	0	0.0
Total	5	9	6	.600	110	0	0	7-1	220	222	86	17	3	68-7	113	3.27	131	.265	.321	0	ø	0	—	24	0	1.9

Appier, Kevin Robert Kevin; B12.6.1967 Lancaster CA; BR/TR/6´2˝/(180–215); [KCA87 1/9]; d6.4; Col Antelope Valley (CA) JC

YEAR	TM LG	W	L	PCT	G	GS	CG-SHO	SV-BS	IP	H	R	HR	HB	BB-IB	SO	ERA	AERA	OAV	OOB	AB-HR-SH	AVG	PB	SUP	APR	DL	PW
1989	KC A	1	4	.200	6	5	0	0-0	21.2	34	22	3	0	12-1	10	9.14	42	.374	.434	0	ø	0	70	-12	0	-2.0
1990	KC A	12	8	.600	32	24	3-3	0-0	185.2	179	67	13	6	54-2	127	2.76	140	.252	.307	0	ø	0	99	22	0	2.3
1991	KC A	13	10	.565	34	31	6-3	0-0	207.2	205	97	13	2	61-3	158	3.42	121	.255	.307	0	ø	0	104	13	0	1.4
1992	KC A	15	8	.652	30	30	3	0-0	208.1	167	59	10	2	68-5	150	2.46	166	.217	.281	0	ø	0	77	38	0	4.1
1993	KC A	18	8	.692	34	34	5-1	0-0	238.2	183	74	8	1	81-3	186	**2.56**	**180**	.212	.279	0	ø	0	89	**51**	0	**5.1**
1994	KC A	7	6	.538	23	23	1	0-0	155	137	68	11	4	63-7	145	3.83	131	.240	.317	0	ø	0	96	21	0	1.5
1995	KC A★	15	10	.600	31	31	4-1	0-0	201.1	163	90	14	8	80-1	185	3.89	123	.221	.303	0	ø	0	95	22	17	2.4
1996	KC A	14	11	.560	32	32	5-1	0-0	211.1	192	87	17	5	75-2	207	3.62	139	.245	.314	0	ø	0	87	35	0	3.5
1997	KC A	9	13	.409	34	34	4-1	0-0	235.2	215	96	24	4	74-2	196	3.40	140	.243	.303	6	.000	-1	76	34	0	2.7
1998	KC A	1	2	.333	3	3	0	0-0	15	21	13	3	1	5-1	9	7.80	62	.339	.391	0	ø	0	64	-4	154	-0.6
1999	KC A	9	9	.500	22	22	1	0-0	140.1	153	81	18	6	51-3	78	4.87	104	.279	.345	2	.000	-0	97	4	0	0.4
	Oak A	7	5	.583	12	12	0	0-0	68.2	77	50	9	1	33-1	53	5.77	82	.280	.357	0	ø	0	110	-9	0	-1.2
	Year	16	14	.533	34	34	1	0-0	209	230	131	27	7	84-4	131	5.17	96	.279	.349	2	.000	-0	101	-5	0	-0.8
2000	†Oak A	15	11	.577	31	31	1-1	0-0	195.1	200	109	23	9	102-10	129	4.52	108	.262	.354	6	.167	-0	120	7	17	0.7
2001	NY N	11	10	.524	33	33	1-1	0-0	206.2	181	89	22	15	64-4	172	3.57	113	.237	.306	62-0-3	.113	-2	91	12	0	0.8
2002	†Ana A	14	12	.538	32	32	0	0-0	188.1	191	89	23	7	64-2	132	3.92	114	.267	.330	2-0-2	.000	-0	92	12	0	1.3
2003	Ana A	7	7	.500	19	19	0	0-0	92.2	105	60	17	8	36-4	50	5.63	78	.279	.353	5	.000	-0	101	-12	17	-1.6
	KC A	1	2	.333	4	4	0	0-0	19	15	9	4	0	7-0	5	4.26	113	.217	.289	0	ø	0	72	1	35	0.2
	Year	8	9	.471	23	23	0	0-0	111.2	120	69	21	8	43-4	55	5.40	82	.269	.343	5	.000	-0	95	-10	0	-1.4
2004	KC A	0	1	.000	2	2	0	0-0	4	7	8	0	0	3-0	2	13.50	35	.368	.455	0	ø	0	89	-5	176	-0.7
Total	16	169	137	.552	414	402	34-12	0-0	2595.1	2425	1168	232	79	933-51	1994	3.74	122	.247	.316	83-0-5	.096	-3	93	230	416	20.3

Applegate, Fred Frederick Romaine; B5.9.1879 Williamsport PA; D4.21.1968 Williamsport PA; BR/TR/6´2˝/180; d9.30

YEAR	TM LG	W	L	PCT	G	GS	CG-SHO	SV-BS	IP	H	R	HR	HB	BB-IB	SO	ERA	AERA	OAV	OOB	AB-HR-SH	AVG	PB	SUP	APR	DL	PW
1904	Phi A	1	2	.333	3	3	3	0	21	29	18	0	1	8	12	6.43	42	.330	.392	7-0-1	.286	0	115	-7	—	-0.9

Appleton, Ed Edward Samuel "Whitey"; B2.29.1892 Arlington TX; D1.27.1932 Arlington TX; BR/TR/6´0.5˝/173; d4.16

YEAR	TM LG	W	L	PCT	G	GS	CG-SHO	SV-BS	IP	H	R	HR	HB	BB-IB	SO	ERA	AERA	OAV	OOB	AB-HR-SH	AVG	PB	SUP	APR	DL	PW
1915	Bro N	4	10	.286	34	10	5	0	138.1	133	71	3	8	66	50	3.32	84	.263	.357	44	.159	-0	86	-9	—	-1.0
1916	Bro N	1	2	.333	14	3	1	1	47	49	25	1	1	18	14	3.06	88	.278	.349	12	.167	-0	102	-3	—	-0.3
Total	2	5	12	.294	48	13	6	1	185.1	182	96	4	9	84	64	3.25	85	.267	.355	56	.161	-1	89	-12	—	-1.3

Appleton, Pete Peter William "Jake" (aka Jablonowski in 1927-33); B5.20.1904 Terryville CT; D1.18.1974 Trenton NJ; BR/TR/5´11˝/180; d9.14; Mil 1943–45; Col Michigan

YEAR	TM LG	W	L	PCT	G	GS	CG-SHO	SV-BS	IP	H	R	HR	HB	BB-IB	SO	ERA	AERA	OAV	OOB	AB-HR-SH	AVG	PB	SUP	APR	DL	PW
1927	Cin N	2	1	.667	6	2	2-1	0	29.2	29	7	0	0	17	3	1.82	208	.261	.359	11	.545	2	45	7	—	0.9
1928	Cin N	3	4	.429	31	3	0	0	82.2	101	50	7	2	22	20	4.68	85	.311	.358	31-0-2	.323	3*	128	-7	—	-0.1
1930	Cle A	8	7	.533	39	7	2	1	118.2	122	71	8	5	53	45	4.02	120	.274	.357	40-0-1	.200	-1	84	8	—	0.8
1931	Cle A	4	4	.500	29	4	3	0	79.2	100	51	2	1	29	25	4.63	100	.293	.350	24-0-1	.208	0*	87	-1	—	-0.1
1932	Cle A	0	0	ø	4	0	0	0	5	11	11	1	0	3	1	16.20	29	.407	.467	0	ø	0	—	-6	—	-0.3
	Bos A	0	3	.000	11	3	0	0	46	49	35	2	2	26	15	4.11	109	.265	.362	17	.176	-0	51	-2	—	0.0
	Year	0	3	.000	15	3	0	0	51	60	46	3	2	29	16	5.29	85	.283	.374	17	.176	-0	50	-8	—	-0.3
1933	NY A	0	0	ø	1	0	0	0	2	3	0	0	0	1	0	0.00	ø	.375	.444	0	ø	0	—	1	—	0.1
1936	Was A	14	9	.609	38	20	12-1	3	201.2	199	94	7	3	77	77	3.53	135	.254	.324	76-0-1	.250	2	88	29	—	3.0
1937	Was A	8	15	.348	35	18	7-4	2	168	167	103	16	5	72	62	4.39	101	.260	.339	59-0-1	.186	-2	66	-2	—	-0.3
1938	Was A	7	9	.438	43	10	5	5	164.1	175	99	12	1	61	62	4.60	98	.270	.333	59-0-2	.254	3	103	-2	—	0.1
1939	Was A	5	10	.333	40	4	2	6	102.2	104	62	7	4	48	50	4.56	95	.265	.351	25-0-3	.160	-1	71	-4	—	-0.5
1940	Chi A	4	0	1.000	25	0	0	5	57.2	54	39	8	1	28	21	5.62	79	.248	.336	17-0-1	.176	-0	—	-6	—	-0.5
1941	Chi A	0	3	.000	13	0	0	1	27.1	27	21	4	2	17	12	5.27	78	.257	.371	4	.250	0	—	-5	0	-0.5
1942	Chi A	0	0	ø	4	0	0	0	4.2	2	2	0	0	3	2	3.86	93	.133	.278	0	ø	0	—	0	0	0.0
	StL A	1	1	.500	14	0	0	2	27.1	25	9	1	0	11	12	2.96	125	.243	.316	6	.167	1	—	3	0	0.4
	Year	1	1	.500	18	0	0	2	32	27	11	1	0	14	14	3.09	119	.229	.311	6	.167	1	—	3	0	0.4
1945	StL A	0	0	ø	2	0	0	0	2.1	3	5	0	0	7	1	15.43	23	.273	.556	0	ø	0	—	-3	0	-0.1
	Was A	1	0	1.000	6	2	1	1	21.1	16	8	1	0	11	12	3.38	92	.211	.310	5	.200	-0	137	0	0	0.0
	Year	1	0	1.000	8	2	1	1	23.2	19	13	1	0	18	13	4.56	69	.218	.352	5	.200	-0	135	-4	0	-0.1
Total	14	57	66	.463	341	73	34-6	26	1141	1187	667	76	26	486	420	4.30	104	.268	.343	374-0-12	.233	7	84	10	0	2.9

Aquino, Greg Gregori Emilio; B1.11.1978 Palenque, D.R.; BR/TR/6´1˝/190; d7.2

YEAR	TM LG	W	L	PCT	G	GS	CG-SHO	SV-BS	IP	H	R	HR	HB	BB-IB	SO	ERA	AERA	OAV	OOB	AB-HR-SH	AVG	PB	SUP	APR	DL	PW
2004	Ari N	0	2	.000	34	0	0	16-3	35.1	24	15	4	2	17-2	26	3.06	149	.194	.297	1	.000	-0	—	5	0	0.6
2005	Ari N	0	1	.000	35	0	0	1-2	31.1	42	29	7	4	17-1	34	7.76	57	.318	.409	0	ø	0	—	-11	68	-0.5
2006	Ari N	2	0	1.000	42	0	0	0-0	48.1	54	27	8	4	24-2	51	4.47	105	.283	.374	1	.000	-0	—	1	24	0.0
Total	3	2	3	.400	111	0	0	17-5	115	120	71	19	10	58-5	111	4.93	93	.268	.363	2	.000	-0	—	-5	92	0.1

Aquino, Luis Luis Antonio (Colon); B5.19.1964 Santurce, PR; BR/TR/6´1˝/(155–195); d8.8

YEAR	TM LG	W	L	PCT	G	GS	CG-SHO	SV-BS	IP	H	R	HR	HB	BB-IB	SO	ERA	AERA	OAV	OOB	AB-HR-SH	AVG	PB	SUP	APR	DL	PW
1986	Tor A	1	1	.500	7	0	0	0-1	11.1	14	8	2	0	3-1	5	6.35	67	.304	.340	0	ø	0	—	-2	0	-0.3
1988	KC A	1	0	1.000	7	5	1-1	0-0	29	33	15	1	1	17-0	11	2.79	144	.282	.375	0	ø	0	168	2	0	0.1
1989	KC A	6	8	.429	34	16	2-1	0-0	141.1	148	62	6	4	35-4	68	3.50	111	.271	.317	0	ø	0	99	5	15	0.5
1990	KC A	4	1	.800	20	3	1	0-0	68.1	59	25	6	4	27-6	28	3.16	122	.237	.319	0	ø	0	141	6	65	0.4
1991	KC A	8	4	.667	38	18	1-1	3-1	157	152	67	10	4	47-5	80	3.44	121	.253	.308	0	ø	0	104	13	0	0.9

YEAR	TM LG	W	L	PCT	G	GS	CG-SHO	SV-BS	IP	H	R	HR	HB	BB-IB	SO	ERA	AERA	OAV	OOB	AB-HR-SH	AVG	PB	SUP	APR	DL	PW
1992	KC A	3	6	.333	15	13	0	0-1	67.2	81	35	5	1	20-1	11	4.52	90	.303	.351	0	ø	0	60	-2	99	-0.2
1993	Fla N	6	8	.429	38	13	0	0-1	110.2	115	43	6	5	40-1	67	3.42	128	.276	.345	25-0-4	.080	-2	68	12	30	1.4
1994	Fla N	2	1	.667	29	1	0	0-0	50.2	39	22	3	3	22-4	22	3.73	119	.210	.300	6-0-1	.167	-0	61	5	38	0.3
1995	Mon N	0	2	.000	29	0	0	2-2	37.1	47	24	4	3	11-1	22	3.86	112	.301	.357	3	.333	1	—	-1	0	0.0
	SF N	0	1	.000	5	0	0	0-0	5	10	10	2	0	2-1	4	14.40	29	.400	.444	1	.000	-0	—	-6	35	-1.0
	Year	0	3	.000	34	0	0	2-2	42.1	57	34	6	3	13-2	26	5.10	84	.315	.369	4	.250	0	—	-7	0	-1.0
Total	9	31	32	.492	222	69	5-3	5-6	678.1	698	311	45	25	224-24	318	3.68	112	.267	.329	35-0-5	.114	-1	92	32	282	2.1
ARCHER, FRED	Frederick Marvin "Lefty"; B3.7.1910 Johnson City TN; D10.31.1981 Charlotte NC; BL/TL/6´0˝/193; d9.5																									
1936	Phi A	2	3	.400	6	5	2	0	36.2	41	28	3	3	15	9	6.38	80	.289	.369	15	.267	0	86	-4	—	-0.4
1937	Phi A	0	0	ø	1	0	0	0	3	4	2	0	0	0	2	6.00	79	.333	.333	0	ø	0	—	0	—	0.0
Total	2	2	3	.400	7	5	2	0	39.2	45	30	3	3	15	11	6.35	80	.292	.366	15	.267	1	86	-4	—	-0.4
ARCHER, JIM	James William; B5.25.1932 Max Meadows VA; BR/TL/6´0˝/190; d4.30																									
1961	KC A	9	15	.375	39	27	9-2	5	205.1	204	99	11	5	60-6	110	3.20	131	.257	.309	63-0-6	.063	-5	80	16	0	1.3
1962	KC A	0	1	.000	18	1	0	0	27.2	40	30	8	0	10-0	12	9.43	45	.342	.394	1	1.000	0	106	-14	0	-0.7
Total	2	9	16	.360	57	28	9-2	5	233	244	129	19	5	70-6	122	3.94	106	.268	.320	64-0-6	.078	-4	81	2	0	0.6
ARDIZOIA, RUGGER	Rinaldo Joseph; B11.20.1919 Oleggio, Italy; BR/TR/5´11˝/180; d4.30																									
1947	NY A	0	0	ø	1	0	0	0	2	4	2	1	0	1	0	9.00	39	.500	.556	0	ø	0	—	-1	0	-0.1
ARELLANES, FRANK	Frank Julian; B1.28.1882 Santa Cruz CA; D12.13.1918 San Jose CA; BR/TR/6´0˝/180; d7.28; Col Santa Clara																									
1908	Bos A	4	3	.571	11	8	6-1	0	79	60	26	1	3	18	33	1.82	135	.205	.259	30	.167	0*	97	5	—	0.3
1909	Bos A	16	12	.571	45	28	17-1	**8**	230.2	192	80	3	5	43	82	2.18	114	.229	.270	78-0-6	.167	-1*	114	7	—	0.8
1910	Bos A	4	7	.364	18	13	2	0	100	106	41	1	3	24	33	2.88	89	.283	.332	34-1-1	.176	0	93	-2	—	-0.2
Total	3	24	22	.522	74	49	25-2	8	409.2	358	147	5	11	85	148	2.28	110	.238	.283	142-1-7	.169	-1	105	10	—	0.9
ARIAS, RUDY	Rodolfo (Martinez); B6.6.1931 Las Villas, Cuba; BL/TL/5´10˝/165; d4.10																									
1959	Chi A	2	0	1.000	34	0	0	2	44	49	23	7	1	20-7	28	4.09	92	.277	.354	4	.000	-1	—	-2	0	-0.1
ARLICH, DON	Donald Louis; B2.15.1943 Wayne MI; BL/TL/6´2˝/185; d10.2																									
1965	Hou N	0	0	ø	1	1	0	0	6	5	2	0	0	1-0	0	3.00	112	.227	.261	2	.000	-0	78	0	0	0.0
1966	Hou N	0	1	.000	7	0	0	0	4	11	9	0	1	4-0	1	15.75	22	.478	.571	1	.000	-0	—	-6	0	-1.2
Total	2	0	1	.000	8	1	0	0	10	16	11	0	1	5-0	1	8.10	42	.356	.431	3	.000	-0	78	-6	0	-1.2
ARLIN, STEVE	Stephen Ralph; B9.25.1945 Seattle WA; BR/TR/6´3.5˝/195; d6.17; Col Ohio St.																									
1969	SD N	0	1	.000	4	1	0	0-0	10.2	13	11	2	0	9-1	9	9.28	39	.289	.407	2	.000	-0	0	-6	0	-0.5
1970	SD N	1	0	1.000	2	2	1-1	0-0	12.2	11	4	0	0	8-0	3	2.84	141	.244	.352	5	.000	-1	101	2	0	0.1
1971	SD N	9	19	.321	36	34	10-4	0-0	227.2	211	114	8	6	103-10	156	3.48	96	.244	.327	73-0-6	.123	-1	92	-8	0	-1.2
1972	SD N	10	21	.323	38	37	12-3	0-0	250	217	115	19	9	122-15	159	3.60	92	.237	.329	72-0-4	.153	3	74	-9	0	-0.8
1973	SD N	11	14	.440	34	27	7-3	0-1	180	196	107	26	1	72-7	98	5.10	69	.278	.343	60-0-2	.167	1	80	-28	0	-3.3
1974	SD N	1	7	.125	16	12	1	1-0	64	85	46	5	2	37-4	18	5.91	61	.326	.408	18-0-1	.111	-1	81	-16	0	-1.9
	Cle A	2	5	.286	11	10	1	0-0	43.2	59	34	1	0	22-4	20	6.60	55	.333	.405	0	ø	0	94	-13	0	-1.9
Total	6	34	67	.337	141	123	32-11	1-1	788.2	792	431	61	18	373-41	463	4.33	79	.263	.345	230-0-13	.139	1	83	-78	0	-9.5
ARMAS, TONY	Antonio Jose; B4.29.1978 Puerto Piritu, Anzoategui, Venez.; BR/TR/6´4˝/(205–225); d8.16; f–Tony																									
1999	Mon N	0	1	.000	1	1	0	0-0	6	8	4	0	0	2-1	2	1.50	297	.320	.357	2	.000	-0	82	1	0	0.1
2000	Mon N	7	9	.438	17	17	0	0-0	95	74	49	10	3	50-2	59	4.36	108	.218	.321	26-0-3	.038	-2	88	5	71	0.4
2001	Mon N	9	14	.391	34	34	0	0-0	196.2	180	101	18	10	91-6	176	4.03	107	.247	.336	53-0-6	.151	-1	85	4	0	0.3
2002	Mon N	12	12	.500	29	29	0	0-0	164.1	149	87	22	7	78-12	131	4.44	99	.243	.335	50-0-5	.100	-2	90	1	23	-0.1
2003	Mon N	2	1	.667	5	5	0	0-0	31	25	9	4	1	8-0	23	2.61	170	.225	.279	10	.200	0	101	7	161	0.6
2004	Mon N	2	4	.333	16	16	0	0-0	72	66	41	13	4	45-6	54	4.88	94	.247	.362	16-0-5	.000	-2*	88	-1	57	-0.2
2005	Was N	7	7	.500	19	19	0	0-0	101.1	100	57	16	5	54-4	59	4.97	83	.258	.355	32-0-1	.125	-1	80	-9	52	-1.1
2006	Was N	9	12	.429	30	30	0	0-0	154	167	96	19	13	64-7	97	5.03	87	.279	.358	50-0-5	.060	-3	105	-13	27	-1.8
Total	8	48	60	.444	151	151	0	0-0	820.1	769	444	102	43	392-38	601	4.45	99	.250	.341	239-0-25	.096	-11	91	-5	391	-1.8
ARMBRUST, ORVILLE	Orville Martin; B3.2.1908 Beirne AR; D10.2.1967 Mobile AL; BR/TR/5´10˝/195; d9.18																									
1934	Was A	1	0	1.000	3	2	0	0	12.2	10	3	1	0	3	3	2.13	203	.208	.255	4	.000	-1	50	3	—	0.2
ARMSTRONG, HOWARD	Howard Elmer; B12.2.1889 E.Claridon OH; D3.8.1926 Canisteo NY; BR/TR/5´9˝/165; d9.30																									
1911	Phi A	0	1	.000	1	0	0	0	3	3	2	0	0	1	0	0.00	ø	.273	.333	1	.000	-0	—	0	—	0.1
ARMSTRONG, JACK	Jack William; B3.7.1965 Englewood NJ; BR/TR/6´5˝/(215–220); [CinN87 1/18]; d6.21; Col Oklahoma																									
1988	Cin N	4	7	.364	14	13	0	0-0	65.1	63	44	8	0	38-2	45	5.79	62	.256	.349	21-0-1	.095	-1	77	-15	0	-2.2
1989	Cin N	2	3	.400	9	8	0	0-0	42.2	40	24	5	0	21-4	23	4.64	78	.245	.330	8-0-3	.000	-1*	92	-4	0	-0.5
1990	†Cin N★	12	9	.571	29	27	2-1	0-0	166	151	72	9	6	59-7	110	3.42	116	.241	.310	47-0-13	.106	-2	97	8	15	0.8
1991	Cin N	7	13	.350	27	24	1	0-0	139.2	158	90	25	2	54-2	93	5.48	69	.293	.354	43-0-5	.093	-2	92	-23	0	-3.0
1992	Cle A	6	15	.286	35	23	1	0-0	166.2	176	100	23	3	67-0	114	4.64	85	.269	.337	0	ø	0	89	-15	0	-1.7
1993	Fla N	9	17	.346	36	33	0	0-0	196.1	210	105	29	7	78-6	118	4.49	97	.271	.339	66-0-4	.152	-2	65	-2	0	-0.4
1994	Tex A	0	1	.000	2	2	0	0-0	10	9	4	3	0	2-0	7	3.60	134	.231	.268	0	ø	0	114	2	116	0.1
Total	7	40	65	.381	152	130	4-1	0-0	786.2	807	439	102	18	319-21	510	4.58	87	.265	.335	185-0-26	.114	-6	84	-49	131	-6.9
ARMSTRONG, MIKE	Michael Dennis; B3.7.1954 Glen Cove NY; BR/TR/6´3˝/(193–206); [CinN74*1/24]; d8.12; Col Miami																									
1980	SD N	0	0	ø	11	0	0	0-0	14.1	16	10	3	0	13-5	14	5.65	61	.296	.433	3	.000	-0	—	-4	0	-0.3
1981	SD N	0	2	.000	10	0	0	0-0	12	14	9	1	0	11-3	9	6.00	54	.311	.446	0	ø	0	—	-4	0	-0.7
1982	KC A	5	5	.500	52	0	0	6-2	112.2	88	45	9	3	43-4	75	3.20	128	.215	.290	0	ø	0	—	11	0	0.9
1983	KC A	10	7	.588	58	0	0	3-3	102.2	86	53	11	3	45-3	52	3.86	107	.228	.312	0	ø	0*	—	1	0	0.2
1984	NY A	3	2	.600	36	0	0	1-3	54.1	47	21	6	0	26-4	43	3.48	110	.239	.322	0	ø	0	—	3	75	0.3
1985	NY A	0	0	ø	9	0	0	0-0	14.2	9	5	4	0	2-0	11	3.07	132	.173	.204	0	ø	0	—	2	0	0.1
1986	NY A	0	1	.000	7	1	0	0-0	8.2	13	9	4	0	5-1	8	9.35	44	.351	.429	0	ø	0	176	-5	0	-0.5
1987	Cle A	1	0	1.000	14	0	0	1-0	18.2	27	18	4	0	10-0	9	8.68	53	.333	.407	0	ø	0	—	-7	0	-0.4
Total	8	19	17	.528	197	1	0	11-8	338	300	170	42	6	155-20	221	4.10	98	.240	.323	3	.000	-0	176	-3	75	-0.4
ARNOLD, JAMIE	James Lee; B3.24.1974 Dearborn MI; BR/TR/6´2˝/188; [AtlN92 1/21]; d4.20																									
1999	LA N	2	4	.333	36	3	0	1-2	69	81	50	6	6	34-2	26	5.48	80	.300	.390	10-0-1	.200	0	183	-11	0	-0.7
2000	Chi N	0	3	.000	12	4	0	1-0	32.2	34	28	1	3	19-0	13	6.61	69	.274	.376	9	.111	0	70	-9	0	-0.7
	LA N	0	0	ø	2	0	0	0-0	6.2	4	3	0	1	5-0	3	4.05	110	.174	.333	0	ø	0	—	0	0	0.0
	Year	0	3	.000	14	4	0	1-0	39.1	38	31	1	4	24-0	16	6.18	74	.259	.369	9	.111	0	71	-8	0	-0.7
Total	2	2	7	.222	50	7	0	2-2	108.1	119	81	7	10	58-2	42	5.73	77	.285	.382	19-0-1	.158	0	119	-20	0	-1.4
ARNOLD, SCOTT	Scott Gentry; B8.18.1962 Lexington KY; BR/TR/6´2˝/210; [StLN84 5/113]; d4.7; Col Miami–Ohio																									
1988	StL N	0	0	ø	6	0	0	0-0	6.2	9	4	0	0	4-1	8	5.40	65	.321	.406	0	ø	0	—	-1	0	-0.1
ARNOLD, TONY	Tony Dale; B5.3.1959 ElPaso TX; BR/TR/5´11˝/(170–185); [BalA81 10/258]; d8.9; Col Texas																									
1986	Bal A	0	2	.000	11	0	0	0-0	25.1	25	15	0	0	11-3	7	3.55	117	.278	.356	0	ø	0	—	0	0	0.1
1987	Bal A	0	0	ø	27	0	0	0-0	53	71	35	8	2	17-5	18	5.77	77	.330	.383	0	ø	0	—	-7	54	-0.2
Total	2	0	2	.000	38	0	0	0-0	78.1	96	50	8	2	28-8	25	5.06	86	.315	.375	0	ø	0	—	-7	54	-0.1
ARNSBERG, BRAD	Bradley James; B8.20.1963 Seattle WA; BR/TR/6´4˝/(205–215); [NYA83 S1/9]; d9.6; C6; Col Merced (CA) JC; [DL 1988 Tex A 150]																									
1986	NY A	0	0	ø	2	1	0	0-0	8	13	3	1	0	1-0	3	3.38	123	.342	.359	0	ø	0	110	1	0	0.0
1987	NY A	1	3	.250	6	2	0	0-0	19.1	22	12	5	0	13-3	14	5.59	79	.289	.385	0	ø	0	62	-2	22	-0.3
1989	Tex A	2	1	.667	16	1	0	1-0	48	45	27	6	3	22-0	26	4.13	97	.247	.337	0	ø	0	68	-1	0	0.0
1990	Tex A	6	1	.857	53	0	0	5-1	62.2	56	20	4	2	33-1	44	2.15	183	.235	.331	0	ø	0	—	11	0	1.3
1991	Tex A	0	1	.000	9	0	0	0-0	9.2	10	9	5	0	5-0	8	8.38	48	.256	.341	0	ø	0	—	-4	148	-0.4
1992	Cle A	0	0	ø	8	0	0	0-0	10.2	13	14	6	2	11-0	5	11.81	33	.317	.481	0	ø	0	—	-9	0	-0.4
Total	6	9	6	.600	94	4	0	6-1	158.1	159	85	27	7	85-4	100	4.26	95	.259	.353	0	ø	0	79	-4	320	0.2

YEAR	TM LG	W	L	PCT	G	GS	CG-SHO	SV-BS	IP	H	R	HR	HB	BB-IB	SO	ERA	AERA	OAV	OOB	AB-HR-SH	AVG	PB	SUP	APR	DL	PW
ARNTZEN, ORIE	Orie Edgar "Old Folks"; B10.18.1909 Beverly IL; D1.28.1970 Cedar Rapids IA; BR/TR/6´1˝/200; d4.20																									
1943	Phi A	4	13	.235	32	20	9	0	164.1	172	85	5	5	69	66	4.22	81	.277	.354	50-0-2	.160	-1	66	-13	0	-1.6
AROCHA, RENE	Rene (Magaly); B2.24.1966 Havana, Cuba; BR/TR/6´0˝/(180–205); d4.9																									
1993	StL N	11	8	.579	32	29	1	0-0	188	197	89	20	3	31-2	96	3.78	107	.271	.302	58-0-7	.103	-2	102	5	22	0.2
1994	StL N	4	4	.500	45	7	1-1	11-1	83	94	42	9	4	21-4	62	4.01	106	.286	.335	9-0-3	.111	0	101	1	0	0.1
1995	StL N	3	5	.375	41	0	0	0-7	49.2	55	24	6	3	18-4	25	3.99	107	.297	.365	1	.000	-0	—	2	63	0.3
1997	SF N	0	0	ø	6	0	0	0-1	10.1	17	14	2	1	5-2	7	11.32	36	.370	.434	1	.000	-0	—	-8	0	-0.4
Total	4	18	17	.514	124	36	2-1	11-9	331	363	169	37	11	75-12	190	4.11	100	.282	.325	69-0-10	.101	-2	101	0	85	0.2
ARRIGO, GERRY	Gerald William; B6.12.1941 Chicago IL; BL/TL/6´1˝/(175–195); d6.12																									
1961	Min A	0	1	.000	7	2	0	0	9.2	9	12	0	2	10-0	6	10.24	41	.265	.429	2	.500	0	198	-6	0	-0.5
1962	Min A	0	0	ø	1	0	0	0	1	3	3	0	0	1-0	1	18.00	23	.600	.667	0	ø	0	—	-2	0	-0.1
1963	Min A	1	2	.333	5	1	0	0	15.2	12	5	2	0	4-0	13	2.87	127	.211	.262	4	.000	-0	24	2	0	0.3
1964	Min A	7	4	.636	41	12	2-1	1	105.1	97	48	11	2	45-3	96	3.84	93	.244	.323	29-0-1	.172	1	122	-1	0	-0.1
1965	Cin N	2	4	.333	27	5	0	2	54	75	38	4	2	30-5	43	6.17	61	.342	.420	12-1-0	.167	1*	103	-12	0	-1.4
1966	Cin N	0	0	ø	3	0	0	0	7.1	7	4	2	0	3-0	3	4.91	79	.250	.323	1	.000	-0	—	-1	0	-0.1
	NY N	3	3	.500	17	5	0	0	43.1	47	20	5	0	16-2	28	3.74	97	.276	.337	10	.500	3	73	0	18	0.4
	Year	3	3	.500	20	5	0	0	50.2	54	24	7	0	19-2	31	3.91	94	.273	.335	11	.455	3	72	-1	0	0.3
1967	Cin N	6	6	.500	32	5	1-1	1	74	61	31	6	4	35-5	56	3.16	119	.232	.326	19-0-2	.211	1	61	4	0	0.6
1968	Cin N	12	10	.545	36	31	5-1	0	205.1	181	84	13	4	77-7	140	3.33	95	.237	.309	67-0-3	.075	-2	107	-3	0	-0.4
1969	Cin N	4	7	.364	20	16	1	0-0	91	89	50	9	8	61-3	35	4.15	91	.256	.376	31-0-1	.161	-0	79	-5	0	-0.6
1970	Chi A	0	3	.000	5	3	0	0-0	13.1	24	20	4	0	9-1	12	12.83	30	.393	.465	4-0-1	.000	-0	38	-12	0	-2.0
Total	10	35	40	.467	194	80	9-3	4-0	620	605	315	56	22	291-26	433	4.14	85	.258	.342	179-1-8	.151	2	96	-36	18	-3.9
ARROJO, ROLANDO	Luis Rolando; B7.18.1968 Santa Clara, Cuba; BR/TR/6´4˝/(215–220); d4.1																									
1998	TB A★	14	12	.538	32	32	2-2	0-0	202	195	84	21	19	65-2	152	3.56	135	.256	.329	3	.000	-0	84	28	7	3.3
1999	TB A	7	12	.368	24	24	2	0-0	140.2	162	84	23	14	60-2	107	5.18	96	.296	.378	0	ø	0	84	0	51	0.1
2000	Col N	5	9	.357	19	19	0	0-0	101.1	120	77	14	12	46-6	80	6.04	96	.299	.381	28-0-3	.107	-2	86	-4	14	-0.5
	Bos A	5	2	.714	13	13	0	0-0	71.1	67	41	10	4	22-0	44	5.05	99	.245	.310	0	ø	0	108	1	0	0.1
2001	Bos A	5	4	.556	41	9	0	5-2	103.1	88	44	8	12	35-4	78	3.48	127	.230	.313	4	.000	-0	104	11	20	1.0
2002	Bos A	4	3	.571	29	8	0	1-3	81.1	83	47	7	6	27-1	51	4.98	90	.269	.337	2-0-1	.000	-0	78	-3	58	-0.3
Total	5	40	42	.488	158	105	4-2	6-5	700	715	377	83	67	255-15	512	4.55	108	.267	.344	37-0-4	.081	-3	90	33	150	3.7
ARROYO, BRONSON	Bronson Anthony; B2.24.1977 Key West FL; BR/TR/6´5˝/(180–190); [PitN95 3/69]; d6.12																									
2000	Pit N	2	6	.250	20	12	0	0-0	71.2	88	61	10	4	36-6	50	6.40	72	.302	.384	21-0-2	.143	-0*	109	-16	0	-1.5
2001	Pit N	5	7	.417	24	13	1	0-0	88.1	99	54	12	4	34-6	39	5.09	88	.289	.355	21	.048	-1	97	-6	0	-0.8
2002	Pit N	2	1	.667	9	4	0	0-0	27	30	14	1	0	15-3	22	4.00	105	.283	.369	6	.000	-1	94	0	0	0.0
2003	†Bos A	0	0	ø	6	0	0	1-0	17.1	10	5	0	1	4-2	14	2.08	224	.164	.227	0	ø	0	—	5	0	0.2
2004	†Bos A	10	9	.526	32	29	0	0-0	178.2	171	99	17	20	47-3	142	4.03	121	.249	.314	6-0-1	.000	-1	105	13	0	1.1
2005	†Bos A	14	10	.583	35	32	0	0-0	205.1	213	116	22	14	54-3	100	4.51	101	.266	.322	1	.000	-0	107	-2	0	-0.3
2006	Cin N★	14	11	.560	35	**35**	3-1	0-0	**240.2**	222	98	31	5	64-7	184	3.29	143	.243	.296	81-2-10	.111	0	88	36	0	3.5
Total	7	47	44	.516	161	125	4-1	1-0	829	833	447	93	48	254-30	551	4.21	111	.260	.322	136-2-13	.096	-3	100	30	0	2.2
ARROYO, FERNANDO	Fernando; B3.21.1952 Sacramento CA; BR/TR/6´3˝/(180–195); [DetA70 10/243]; d6.28																									
1975	Det A	2	1	.667	14	2	1	0-0	53.1	56	28	5	1	22-2	25	4.56	89	.272	.343	0	ø	0	76	-1	0	0.0
1977	Det A	8	18	.308	38	28	8-1	0-0	209.1	227	102	23	1	52-5	60	4.17	103	.278	.319	0	ø	0	74	6	0	1.0
1978	Det A	0	0	ø	2	0	0	0-0	4.1	8	4	1	1	0-0	1	8.31	47	.400	.429	0	ø	0	—	-2	28	-0.1
1979	Det A	1	1	.500	6	0	0	0-0	12	17	11	3	0	4-2	7	8.25	53	.340	.382	0	ø	0	—	-5	0	-0.6
1980	Min A	6	6	.500	21	11	1-1	0-0	92.1	97	55	7	2	32-2	27	4.68	93	.273	.332	0	ø	0	89	-3	0	-0.4
1981	Min A	7	10	.412	23	19	2	0-0	128.1	144	66	11	5	34-1	39	3.93	101	.290	.341	0	ø	0	86	-1	0	-0.1
1982	Min A	0	1	.000	6	0	0	0-0	13.2	17	8	2	0	6-1	4	5.27	81	.321	.383	0	ø	0*	—	-1	0	0.0
	Oak A	0	0	ø	10	0	0	0-1	22.1	23	14	4	1	7-0	9	5.24	76	.271	.330	0	ø	0	—	-3	0	-0.2
	Year	0	1	.000	16	0	0	0-1	36	40	22	6	1	13-1	13	5.25	78	.290	.351	0	ø	0	—	-4	0	-0.2
1986	Oak A	0	0	ø	1	0	0	0-0	0	0	0	0	0	3-0	0	(0)	ø	ø	1.000	0	ø	0	—	0	0	0.0
Total	8	24	37	.393	121	60	12-2	0-1	535.2	589	288	56	11	160-13	172	4.44	95	.283	.335	0	ø	0	81	-10	28	-0.4
ARROYO, LUIS	Luis Enrique; B2.18.1927 Penuelas, PR; BL/TL/5´8˝/(175–190); d4.20																									
1955	StL N☆	11	8	.579	35	24	9-1	0	159	162	80	22	2	63-6	68	4.19	97	.261	.329	56-1-4	.232	1	99	-2	0	-0.3
1956	Pit N	3	3	.500	18	2	1	0	28.2	36	17	5	0	12-1	17	4.71	80	.298	.361	4-0-2	.500	1	163	-3	0	-0.5
1957	Pit N	3	11	.214	54	10	0	1	130.2	151	76	19	7	31-9	101	4.68	81	.282	.329	32-0-1	.156	-1*	67	-12	0	-1.3
1959	Cin N	1	0	1.000	10	0	0	0	13.2	17	11	0	0	11-3	8	3.95	103	.321	.418	2	.000	-0	—	-2	0	-0.1
1960	†NY A	5	1	.833	29	0	0	7	40.2	30	14	2	0	22-3	29	2.88	125	.207	.311	5	.000	-0	—	4	0	0.7
1961	†NY A☆	15	5	.750	**65**	0	0	**29**	119	83	34	5	3	49-8	87	2.19	169	.199	.284	25-0-3	.280	2	—	**21**	0	**4.4**
1962	NY A	1	3	.250	27	0	0	7	33.2	33	20	5	1	17-2	21	4.81	78	.262	.352	4	.500	1	—	-4	34	-0.6
1963	NY A	1	1	.500	6	0	0	0	6	12	9	0	0	3-1	5	13.50	26	.444	.484	0-0-1	ø	0	—	-6	0	-1.2
Total	8	40	32	.556	244	36	10-1	44	531.1	524	261	58	13	208-33	336	3.93	98	.256	.326	128-1-11	.227	3	97	-4	34	1.1
ARROYO, RUDY	Rudolph; B6.19.1950 New York NY; BL/TL/6´2˝/190; [StLN70*S4/79]; d6.1; Col Foothill (CA) JC																									
1971	StL N	0	1	.000	9	0	0	0-0	11.2	18	8	2	0	5-1	5	5.40	67	.375	.426	1	.000	-0	—	-2	0	-0.2
ARUNDEL, HARRY	Harry; B2.1855 Philadelphia PA; D3.25.1904 Cleveland OH; TR/5´6˝/145; d7.19																									
1875	Atl NA	0	1	.000	1	1	0	0	2.1	6	6	0	—	0	0	7.71	27	.400	.400	4	.000	-1	51	-2	—	-0.3
1882	Pit AA	4	10	.286	14	14	13	0	120	155	112	3	—	23	47	4.65	56	.294	.323	53	.189	0	105	-26	—	-2.1
1884	Pro N	1	0	1.000	1	1	1	0	9	8	2	0	—	4	4	1.00	285	.250	.333	3	.333	0	205	2	—	0.2
Total	2	5	10	.333	15	15	14	0	129	163	114	3	—	27	51	4.40	60	.291	.324	56	.196	0	112	-24	—	-1.9
ASENCIO, MIGUEL	Miguel (Depaula); B9.29.1980 Villa Mella, D.R.; BR/TR/6´2˝/190; d4.6; [DL 2004 KC A 183, 2005 SD N 68]																									
2002	KC A	4	7	.364	31	21	0	0-0	123.1	136	73	17	3	64-2	58	5.11	98	.282	.366	2	.000	-0	91	-1	0	-0.1
2003	KC A	2	1	.667	8	8	1	0-0	48.1	54	29	4	3	21-0	27	5.21	92	.295	.368	0	ø	0	134	-2	0	-0.1
2006	Col N	1	0	1.000	3	1	0	0-0	7.2	9	8	1	1	4-0	7	4.70	102	.281	.378	3	.000	-0	135	-1	0	-0.2
Total	3	7	8	.467	42	30	1	0-0	179.1	199	110	22	7	89-2	92	5.12	96	.286	.367	5	.000	-1	104	-4	251	-0.4
ASH, KEN	Kenneth Lowther; B9.16.1901 Anmoore WV; D11.15.1979 Clarksburg WV; BR/TR/5´11˝/165; d4.17; Col West Virginia Wesleyan																									
1925	Chi A	0	0	ø	2	0	0	0	4	7	4	2	0	0	0	9.00	46	.389	.389	0	ø	0	—	-2	—	-0.1
1928	Cin N	3	3	.500	8	5	2	0	36	43	26	1	1	13	6	6.50	61	.314	.377	14-0-1	.071	-1*	98	-9	—	-1.3
1929	Cin N	1	5	.167	29	7	2	2	82	91	57	2	5	30	26	4.83	95	.292	.363	21	.143	-1*	79	-6	—	-0.5
1930	Cin N	2	0	1.000	16	1	1	0	39.1	37	22	1	0	16	15	3.43	141	.268	.344	11	.182	-1*	90	4	—	0.2
Total	4	6	8	.429	55	13	5	2	161.1	178	109	6	6	59	47	4.96	90	.294	.363	46-0-1	.130	-3	85	-13	—	-1.7
ASHBY, ANDY	Andrew Jason; B7.11.1967 Kansas City MO; BR/TR/6´1˝/(180–202); d6.10; Col Crowder (MO) CC																									
1991	Phi N	1	5	.167	8	8	0	0-0	42	41	28	5	3	19-0	26	6.00	62	.256	.341	12-0-1	.083	-1	73	-10	0	-1.2
1992	Phi N	1	3	.250	10	8	0	0-0	37	42	31	6	1	21-0	24	7.54	47	.290	.379	11-0-2	.091	-0	113	-15	106	-1.5
1993	Col N	0	4	.000	20	9	0	1-0	54	89	54	5	3	32-4	33	8.50	56	.377	.453	15	.267	0	117	-18	0	-1.1
	SD N	3	6	.333	12	12	0	0-0	69	79	46	14	1	24-1	44	5.48	75	.295	.350	21-0-2	.048	-1	105	-9	0	-1.1
	Year	3	10	.231	32	21	0	1-0	123	168	100	19	4	56-5	77	6.80	65	.333	.399	36-0-2	.139	-1	111	-28	0	-2.2
1994	SD N	6	11	.353	24	24	4	0-0	164.1	145	75	16	3	43-12	121	3.40	122	.233	.285	49-0-9	.163	-0	70	11	0	1.0
1995	SD N	12	10	.545	31	**31**	2-2	0-0	192.2	180	79	17	11	62-3	150	2.94	138	.252	.320	49-0-17	.163	-0	105	21	0	2.2
1996	†SD N	9	5	.643	24	24	1	0-0	150.2	147	60	17	3	34-1	85	3.23	125	.259	.304	45-0-9	.244	3*	104	14	68	1.6
1997	SD N	9	11	.450	30	30	2	0-0	200.2	207	108	17	5	49-2	144	4.13	95	.266	.311	60-0-7	.067	-3*	120	-8	26	-0.9
1998	†SD N★	17	9	.654	33	33	5-1	0-0	226.2	223	90	23	7	58-8	151	3.34	119	.259	.309	72-0-9	.111	-2	113	17	0	1.7
1999	SD N★	14	10	.583	31	31	4-**3**	0-0	206	204	95	26	7	54-4	132	3.80	112	.258	.311	62-0-7	.129	-0	92	12	17	1.3
2000	Phi N	4	7	.364	16	16	1	0-0	101.1	113	75	17	5	38-5	51	5.68	81	.288	.351	28-0-5	.179	0	90	-15	14	-1.3
	†Atl N	8	6	.571	15	15	2-1	0-0	98	103	49	12	1	23-4	55	4.13	109	.271	.314	33-0-4	.121	-1*	95	4	0	0.4
	Year	12	13	.480	31	31	3-1	0-0	199.1	216	124	29	6	61-9	106	4.92	92	.280	.333	61-0-9	.148	-1	92	-12	0	-0.9

YEAR	TM LG	W	L	PCT	G	GS	CG-SHO	SV-BS	IP	H	R	HR	HB	BB-IB	SO	ERA	AERA	OAV	OOB	AB-HR-SH	AVG	PB	SUP	APR	DL	PW
2001	LA N	2	0	1.000	2	2	0	0-0	11.2	14	5	2	0	1-0	7	3.86	107	.292	.306	2-0-2	.500	1*	134	1	175	0.2
2002	LA N	9	13	.409	30	30	0	0-0	181.2	179	85	20	8	65-3	107	3.91	100	.261	.330	48-1-6	.125	-0	92	0	0	-0.1
2003	LA N	3	10	.231	21	12	0	0-0	73	90	42	8	3	17-2	41	5.18	80	.311	.354	14-0-3	.000	-2	53	-7	0	-1.2
2004	SD N	0	0	ø	2	0	0	0-0	2	1	0	0	0	0-0	2	0.00	ø	.143	.143	0	ø	0	—	1	0	0.0
Total	14	98	110	.471	309	285	21-7	1-0	1810.2	1857	922	205	61	540-49	1173	4.12	100	.268	.324	521-1-83	.134	-6	98	-1	406	0.0
ASSENMACHER, PAUL	Paul Andre; B12.10.1960 Detroit MI; BL/TL/6´3˝/(200–210); d4.12; Col Aquinas																									
1986	Atl N	7	3	.700	61	0	0	7-4	68.1	61	23	5	0	26-4	56	2.50	158	.241	.311	6	.000	-0	—	10	0	1.6
1987	Atl N	1	1	.500	52	0	0	2-4	54.2	58	41	8	1	24-4	39	5.10	85	.260	.333	4-0-2	.000	-0	—	-7	10	-0.4
1988	Atl N	8	7	.533	64	0	0	5-6	79.1	72	28	4	1	32-11	71	3.06	120	.251	.327	3-0-1	.333	1	—	6	15	1.3
1989	Atl N	1	3	.250	49	0	0	0-2	57.2	55	26	2	1	16-7	64	3.59	102	.249	.300	2	.000	-0	—	1	0	0.0
	†Chi N	2	1	.667	14	0	0	0-1	19	19	11	1	0	12-1	15	5.21	72	.275	.378	3	.000	-0	—	-2	0	-0.4
	Year	3	4	.429	63	0	0	0-3	76.2	74	37	3	1	28-8	79	3.99	92	.255	.320	5	.000	-1	—	-2	0	-0.4
1990	Chi N	7	2	.778	74	1	0	10-10	103	90	33	10	1	36-8	95	2.80	146	.239	.305	8-0-2	.000	-1	111	15	0	1.4
1991	Chi N	7	8	.467	75	0	0	15-9	102.2	85	41	10	3	31-6	117	3.24	120	.223	.284	4	.250	0	—	7	0	1.2
1992	Chi N	4	4	.500	70	0	0	8-5	68	72	32	6	3	26-5	67	4.10	88	.271	.340	4-0-2	.000	-0	—	-2	16	-0.3
1993	Chi N	2	1	.667	46	0	0	0-4	38.2	44	15	5	0	13-3	34	3.49	116	.288	.343	2	.500	0	—	3	0	0.2
	NY A	2	2	.500	26	0	0	0-1	17.1	10	6	0	1	9-3	11	3.12	134	.175	.299	0	ø	0	—	2	0	0.5
1994	Chi A	1	2	.333	44	0	0	1-2	33	26	13	2	1	13-2	29	3.55	132	.224	.301	0	ø	0	—	5	0	0.4
1995	†Cle A	6	2	.750	47	0	0	0-1	38.1	32	13	3	3	12-3	40	2.82	168	.225	.296	0	ø	0	—	8	0	1.5
1996	†Cle A	4	2	.667	63	0	0	1-2	46.2	46	18	1	4	14-5	44	3.09	158	.260	.325	0	ø	0	—	9	0	1.0
1997	†Cle A	5	0	1.000	75	0	0	4-1	49	43	17	5	1	15-5	53	2.94	160	.231	.289	0	ø	0	—	10	0	1.0
1998	†Cle A	2	5	.286	69	0	0	3-5	47	54	22	5	1	19-6	43	3.26	147	.286	.351	0	ø	0	—	6	0	0.8
1999	†Cle A	2	1	.667	55	0	0	0-2	33	50	32	6	1	17-5	29	8.18	62	.347	.415	0	ø	0	—	-11	0	-0.8
Total	14	61	44	.581	884	1	0	56-59	855.2	817	371	73	22	315-78	807	3.53	118	.252	.320	36-0-7	.083	-0	111	60	41	9.0
ASTACIO, EZEQUIEL	Ezequiel F.; B11.4.1979 Hato Mayor, D.R.; BR/TR/6´3˝/150; d5.3																									
2005	†Hou N	3	6	.333	22	14	0	0-0	81	100	56	23	1	25-2	66	5.67	74	.301	.346	21-0-2	.143	-1	99	-13	0	-1.4
2006	Hou N	2	0	1.000	6	0	0	0-0	5.2	7	7	2	0	6-3	6	11.12	41	.292	.433	0	ø	0	—	-4	0	-0.7
Total	2	5	6	.455	28	14	0	0-0	86.2	107	63	25	1	31-5	72	6.02	70	.301	.353	21-0-2	.143	-1	99	-17	0	-2.1
ASTACIO, PEDRO	Pedro Julio (Pura); B11.28.1969 Hato Mayor, D.R.; BR/TR/6´2˝/(174–210); d7.3																									
1992	LA N	5	5	.500	11	11	4-4	0-0	82	80	23	1	2	20-4	43	1.98	176	.255	.302	24-0-5	.125	-1	88	13	0	1.6
1993	LA N	14	9	.609	31	31	3-2	0-0	186.1	165	80	14	5	68-5	122	3.57	108	.239	.309	62-0-7	.161	-1	99	9	0	0.8
1994	LA N	6	8	.429	23	23	3-1	0-0	149	142	77	18	4	47-4	108	4.29	93	.252	.312	47-0-4	.064	-3	102	-5	0	-0.8
1995	†LA N	7	8	.467	48	11	1-1	0-1	104	103	53	12	4	29-5	80	4.24	91	.261	.316	24-0-2	.125	-0	100	-3	0	-0.4
1996	†LA N	9	8	.529	35	32	0	0-0	211.2	207	86	18	9	67-9	130	3.44	114	.261	.324	68-0-8	.088	-4	93	15	0	0.7
1997	LA N	7	9	.438	26	24	2-1	0-0	153.2	151	75	15	4	47-0	115	4.10	95	.256	.313	41-0-10	.146	-0	93	-3	0	-0.2
	Col N	5	1	.833	7	7	0	0-0	48.2	49	23	9	5	14-0	51	4.25	121	.262	.327	13-0-1	.077	-1	112	5	0	0.5
	Year	12	10	.545	33	31	2-1	0-0	202.1	200	98	24	9	61-0	166	4.14	102	.258	.317	54-0-11	.130	-1	98	4	0	0.3
1998	Col N	13	14	.481	35	34	0	0-0	209.1	245	160	39	17	74-0	170	6.23	83	.294	.363	62-0-11	.129	-3	97	-22	0	-2.6
1999	Col N	17	11	.607	34	34	7	0-0	232	258	140	38	11	75-6	210	5.04	115	.285	.343	86-0-7	.233	-0*	96	15	0	1.6
2000	Col N	12	9	.571	32	32	3	0-0	196.1	217	119	32	15	77-5	193	5.27	110	.281	.356	82-0-1	.098	-6	96	11	0	0.4
2001	Col N	6	13	.316	22	22	4-1	0-0	141	151	91	21	10	50-3	125	5.49	97	.276	.345	42-0-10	.095	-3	94	-1	0	-0.5
	Hou N	2	1	.667	4	4	0	0-0	28.2	30	10	1	3	4-0	19	3.14	146	.280	.322	11-0-1	.091	-1	101	5	47	0.4
	Year	8	14	.364	26	26	4-1	0-0	169.2	181	101	22	13	54-3	144	5.09	102	.276	.341	53-0-11	.094	-4	95	3	0	-0.1
2002	NY N	12	11	.522	31	31	3-1	0-0	191.2	192	106	32	16	63-5	152	4.79	83	.262	.330	62-0-6	.161	0	107	-15	0	-1.5
2003	NY N	3	2	.600	7	7	0	0-0	36.2	47	30	8	3	18-1	20	7.36	57	.311	.393	11-0-3	.091	-1	99	-12	148	-1.4
2004	Bos A	0	0	ø	5	1	0	0-0	8.2	13	10	2	0	5-0	6	10.38	47	.342	.419	0	ø	0	133	-4	0	-0.2
2005	Tex A	2	8	.200	12	12	0	0-0	67	79	45	13	1	11-1	45	6.04	75	.292	.319	1	.000	-0	76	-9	6	-1.1
	†SD N	4	2	.667	12	10	0	0-0	59.2	54	21	4	1	26-3	33	3.17	124	.247	.327	16-0-5	.063	-1	99	6	15	0.5
2006	Was N	5	5	.500	17	17	1-1	0-0	90.1	109	64	14	1	31-3	42	5.98	73	.301	.353	25-0-7	.200	1	119	-16	89	-1.4
Total	15	129	124	.510	392	343	31-12	0-1	2196.2	2292	1213	291	111	726-54	1664	4.67	97	.271	.334	677-0-88	.133	-23	98	-11	305	-3.6
ATCHISON, SCOTT	Scott Barham; B3.29.1976 Denton TX; BR/TR/6´2˝/(180–195); [SeaA98 49/1423]; d7.31; Col TCU																									
2004	Sea A	2	3	.400	25	0	0	0-0	30.2	29	12	4	0	14-2	36	3.52	127	.250	.328	0	ø	0	—	4	0	0.6
2005	Sea A	0	0	ø	6	0	0	0-0	6.2	7	5	1	0	1-0	9	6.75	62	.269	.296	0	ø	0	—	-2	153	-0.1
Total	2	2	3	.400	31	0	0	0-0	37.1	36	17	5	0	15-2	45	4.10	108	.254	.323	0	ø	0	—	2	153	0.5
ATCHLEY, JUSTIN	Justin Scott; B9.5.1973 Sedro–Woolley WA; BL/TL/6´3˝/215; [CinN95 12/335]; d4.7; Col Texas A&M																									
2001	Cin N	0	0	ø	15	0	0	0-2	10.1	12	7	4	1	5-2	8	6.10	75	.286	.375	1	.000	-0	—	-1	87	-0.1
ATHERTON, KEITH	Keith Rowe; B2.19.1959 Newport News VA; BR/TR/6´4˝/200; [OakA78 2/30]; d7.14																									
1983	Oak A	2	5	.286	29	0	0	4-4	68.1	53	22	7	1	23-4	40	2.77	141	.215	.280	1	.000	-0	—	10	0	1.0
1984	Oak A	7	6	.538	57	0	0	2-3	104	110	51	13	2	39-8	58	4.33	87	.274	.336	0	ø	0	—	-4	0	-0.6
1985	Oak A	4	7	.364	56	0	0	3-2	104.2	89	51	17	0	42-8	77	4.30	90	.231	.303	0	ø	0	—	-3	15	-0.4
1986	Oak A	1	2	.333	13	0	0	0-0	15.1	18	10	2	0	11-1	8	5.87	66	.295	.392	0	ø	0	—	-3	0	-0.5
	Min A	5	8	.385	47	0	0	10-4	81.2	82	37	9	1	35-3	59	3.75	116	.264	.336	0	ø	0	—	5	0	0.9
	Year	6	10	.375	60	0	0	10-4	97	100	47	11	1	46-4	67	4.08	105	.269	.346	0	ø	0	—	3	0	0.4
1987	†Min A	7	5	.583	59	0	0	2-4	79.1	81	46	10	4	30-4	51	4.54	102	.262	.332	0	ø	0	—	0	0	0.0
1988	Min A	7	5	.583	49	0	0	3-4	74	65	29	10	2	22-4	43	3.41	120	.235	.293	0	ø	0	—	6	0	0.9
1989	Cle A	0	3	.000	32	0	0	2-0	39	48	22	7	0	13-4	13	4.15	96	.293	.345	0	ø	0	—	-2	0	-0.2
Total	7	33	41	.446	342	0	0	26-21	566.1	546	268	75	10	215-36	349	3.99	102	.253	.320	1	.000	-0	—	9	15	1.1
ATKINS, TOMMY	Francis Montgomery; B12.9.1887 Ponca NE; D5.7.1956 Cleveland OH; BL/TL/5´10.5˝/165; d10.2																									
1909	Phi A	0	0	ø	1	1	0	0	6	6	4	0	0	5	4	4.50	53	.261	.393	2	.000	-0	176	-1	—	-0.1
1910	Phi A	3	2	.600	15	3	2	2	57	53	33	0	1	23	29	2.68	88	.254	.330	17	.118	-1	113	-4	—	-0.5
Total	2	3	2	.600	16	4	2	2	63	59	37	0	1	28	33	2.86	83	.254	.337	19	.105	-1	128	-5	—	-0.6
ATKINS, JAMES	James Curtis; B3.10.1921 Birmingham AL; BL/TR/6´3˝/205; d9.29																									
1950	Bos A	0	0	ø	1	0	0	0	4.2	4	2	1	1	4	0	3.86	127	.235	.409	2	.000	-0	—	1	0	0.0
1952	Bos A	0	1	.000	3	1	0	0	10.1	11	6	0	0	7	2	3.48	113	.275	.383	3	.667	1	44	0	0	0.1
Total	2	0	1	.000	4	1	0	0	15	15	8	1	1	11	2	3.60	118	.263	.391	5	.400	0	44	1	0	0.1
ATKINSON, AL	Albert Wright; B3.9.1861 Clinton IL; D6.17.1952 Elkhorn Twp. MO; BR/TR/5´11.5˝/165; d5.1																									
1884	Phi AA	11	11	.500	22	22	20-1	0	184.1	186	130	3	10	21	93	4.20	81	.244	.274	83	.193	-1	104	-16	—	-1.6
	CP U	6	10	.375	16	16	16-1	0	140	127	83	1	—	21	104	2.76	88	.226	.253	68	.206	-4*	66	-5	—	-0.9
	Bal U	3	5	.375	8	8	8	0	69.1	60	34	4	—	12	50	2.34	114	.217	.250	29	.138	-3	66	3	—	-0.1
	Year	9	15	.375	24	24	24-1	0	209.1	187	117	5	—	33	154	2.62	96	.223	.252	97	.186	-7	66	-3	—	-1.0
1886	Phi AA	25	17	.595	45	45	44-1	0	396.2	414	288	11	22	101	154	3.95	89	.256	.308	148	.122	-6	114	-15	—	-1.9
1887	Phi AA	6	8	.429	15	15	11	0	124.2	156	121	2	6	54	34	5.92	72	.292	.364	59-1	.203	-1*	120	-23	—	-1.8
Total	3	51	51	.500	106	106	99-3	0	915	943	656	21	38	209	435	3.96	85	.251	.297	387-1	.165	-14	102	-56	—	-6.3
ATKINSON, BILL	William Cecil Glenn; B10.4.1954 Chatham ON, Can.; BL/TR/5´7˝/(155–165); d9.18																									
1976	Mon N	0	0	ø	4	0	0	0-0	5	3	0	0	0	1-1	4	0.00	ø	.176	.222	0	ø	0	—	2	0	0.1
1977	Mon N	7	2	.778	55	0	0	7-1	83.1	72	33	12	0	29-11	56	3.35	115	.234	.296	5-0-1	.200	-0*	—	6	0	0.7
1978	Mon N	2	2	.500	29	0	0	3-1	45.1	45	23	5	1	28-4	32	4.37	82	.268	.370	4	.500	1	—	-3	0	-0.2
1979	Mon N	2	0	1.000	10	0	0	1-0	13.2	9	4	0	0	4-1	7	1.98	188	.170	.228	1	.000	-0	—	2	0	0.3
Total	4	11	4	.733	98	0	0	11-2	147.1	129	60	17	1	62-17	99	3.42	110	.236	.312	10-0-1	.300	1	—	7	0	0.9
AUCOIN, DEREK	Derek Alfred; B3.27.1970 Lachine QC, Can.; BR/TR/6´7˝/245; d5.21																									
1996	Mon N	0	1	.000	2	0	0	0-0	2.2	3	1	0	0	1-0	1	3.38	128	.300	.364	0	ø	0	—	0	0	0.1

YEAR	TM LG	W	L	PCT	G	GS	CG-SHO	SV-BS	IP	H	R	HR	HB	BB-IB	SO	ERA	AERA	OAV	OOB	AB-HR-SH	AVG	PB	SUP	APR	DL	PW
AUGUST, DON	Donald Glenn; B7.3.1963 Inglewood CA; BR/TR/6´3˝/190; [HouN84 1/17]; d6.2; Col Chapman																									
1988	Mil A	13	7	.650	24	22	6-1	0-0	148.1	137	55	12	0	48-6	66	3.09	129	.245	.303	0	ø	0	98	16	0	2.1
1989	Mil A	12	12	.500	31	25	2-1	0-0	142.1	175	93	17	2	58-2	51	5.31	73	.302	.364	0	ø	0	91	-23	0	-3.2
1990	Mil A	0	3	.000	5	0	0	0-1	11	13	10	0	0	5-0	2	6.55	59	.295	.367	0	ø	0	—	-4	0	-0.7
1991	Mil A	9	8	.529	28	23	1-1	0-0	138.1	166	87	18	3	47-2	62	5.47	73	.301	.358	0	ø	0	121	-21	0	-2.2
Total	4	34	30	.531	88	70	9-3	0-1	440	491	245	47	5	158-10	181	4.64	85	.283	.343	0	ø	0	103	-32	0	-4.0
AUGUSTINE, JERRY	Gerald Lee; B7.24.1952 Kewaunee WI; BL/TL/6´0˝/(180–185); [MilA74 15/342]; d9.9; Col Wisconsin–La Crosse																									
1975	Mil A	2	0	1.000	5	3	1	0-0	26.2	26	9	2	1	12-1	8	3.04	127	.274	.355	0	ø	0	122	3	0	0.2
1976	Mil A	9	12	.429	39	24	5-3	0-3	171.2	167	69	9	4	56-4	59	3.30	106	.261	.321	0	ø	0	94	5	0	0.5
1977	Mil A	12	18	.400	33	33	10-1	0-0	209	222	119	23	3	72-3	68	4.48	92	.277	.334	0	ø	0	88	-10	0	-1.2
1978	Mil A	13	12	.520	35	30	9-2	0-0	188.1	204	100	14	4	61-2	59	4.54	84	.280	.335	0	ø	0	127	-13	0	-1.4
1979	Mil A	9	6	.600	43	2	0	5-2	85.2	95	38	6	1	30-4	41	3.47	121	.284	.341	0	ø	0	129	7	0	1.0
1980	Mil A	4	3	.571	39	1	0	2-1	69.2	83	37	5	2	36-5	22	4.52	87	.301	.382	0	ø	0	46	-4	0	-0.3
1981	Mil A	2	2	.500	27	2	0	2-1	61.1	75	30	4	1	18-3	26	4.26	82	.300	.348	0	ø	0	194	-5	0	-0.3
1982	Mil A	1	3	.250	20	2	1	0-0	62	63	43	13	2	26-2	22	5.08	76	.267	.340	0	ø	0	83	-11	0	-0.7
1983	Mil A	3	3	.500	34	7	1	2-0	64.1	89	45	11	1	25-4	40	5.74	66	.328	.383	0	ø	0	134	-15	22	-1.3
1984	Mil A	0	0	ø	4	0	0	0-0	5.1	4	1	0	1	4-0	3	0.00	ø	.211	.375	0	ø	0	—	2	0	0.1
Total	10	55	59	.482	279	104	27-6	11-7	944	1028	491	87	20	340-28	348	4.23	91	.281	.342	0	ø	0	106	-41	22	-3.4
AUKER, ELDEN	Elden Le Roy "Submarine"; B9.21.1910 Norcatur KS; D8.4.2006 Vero Beach FL; BR/TR/6´2˝/194; d8.10; Col Kansas St.																									
1933	Det A	3	3	.500	15	6	2-1	0	55	63	34	3	2	25	17	5.24	82	.285	.363	17-0-1	.118	-1	109	-4	—	-0.5
1934	†Det A	15	7	.682	43	18	10-2	1	205	234	103	9	3	56	86	3.42	128	.288	.336	74-0-7	.149	-2	113	16	—	1.4
1935	†Det A	18	7	**.720**	36	25	13-2	0	195	213	86	13	9	61	63	3.83	109	.279	.340	74-0-4	.216	1	122	12	—	1.5
1936	Det A	13	16	.448	35	31	14-2	0	215.1	263	140	11	3	83	66	4.89	101	.302	.365	78-0-7	.308	7	100	-1	—	0.7
1937	Det A	17	9	.654	39	32	19-1	1	252.2	250	127	13	6	97	73	3.88	120	.260	.331	91-3-6	.198	4*	107	20	—	2.4
1938	Det A	11	10	.524	27	24	12-1	0	160.2	184	97	14	5	56	46	5.27	95	.284	.346	57-0-3	.088	-4	114	-1	—	-0.4
1939	Bos A	9	10	.474	31	25	6-1	0	151	183	108	13	1	61	43	5.36	88	.294	.358	53-2-3	.226	2	114	-12	—	-1.0
1940	StL A	16	11	.593	38	35	20-2	0	263.2	299	129	17	3	96	78	3.96	116	.281	.342	89-1-1	.213	3	105	18	—	2.0
1941	StL A	14	15	.483	34	31	13	0	216	268	150	20	1	85	60	5.50	78	.303	.365	80-0-3	.125	-3*	110	-28	0	-3.3
1942	StL A	14	13	.519	35	34	17-2	0	249	273	132	16	3	86	62	4.08	91	.277	.337	87-0-6	.161	-1*	111	-10	0	-1.1
Total	10	130	101	.563	333	261	126-14	2	1963.1	2230	1106	129	36	706	594	4.42	101	.285	.347	700-6-41	.187	6	110	10	0	1.7
AUSANIO, JOE	Joseph John; B12.9.1965 Kingston NY; BR/TR/6´1˝/205; [PitN88 11/278]; d7.14; Col Jacksonville																									
1994	NY A	2	1	.667	13	0	0	0-0	15.2	16	9	3	0	6-0	15	5.17	89	.254	.319	0	ø	0	—	-1	0	-0.1
1995	NY A	2	0	1.000	28	0	0	1-2	37.2	42	24	9	0	23-0	36	5.73	81	.286	.378	0	ø	0	—	-4	0	-0.2
Total	2	4	1	.800	41	0	0	1-2	53.1	58	33	12	0	29-0	51	5.57	83	.276	.361	0	ø	0	—	-5	0	-0.3
AUST, DENNIS	Dennis Kay; B11.25.1940 Tecumseh NE; BR/TR/5´11˝/180; d9.6; Col Florida																									
1965	StL N	0	0	ø	6	0	0	1	7.1	6	4	0	0	2-1	7	4.91	78	.214	.267	1	.000	-0	—	-1	0	0.0
1966	StL N	0	1	.000	9	0	0	1	9.2	12	7	1	0	6-2	7	6.52	55	.308	.391	1	.000	-0	—	-3	0	-0.3
Total	2	0	1	.000	15	0	0	2	17	18	11	1	0	8-3	14	5.82	64	.269	.342	2	.000	-0	—	-4	0	-0.3
AUSTIN, JIM	James Parker; B12.7.1963 Farmville VA; BR/TR/6´2˝/200; [SDN86 6/144]; d7.4; Col Virginia Commonwealth																									
1991	Mil A	0	0	ø	5	0	0	0-0	8.2	8	8	1	3	11-1	3	8.31	48	.276	.500	0	ø	0	—	-4	41	-0.2
1992	Mil A	5	2	.714	47	0	0	0-1	58.1	38	13	2	2	32-6	30	1.85	209	.191	.308	0	ø	0	—	13	0	1.4
1993	Mil A	1	2	.333	31	0	0	0-2	33	28	15	3	1	13-1	15	3.82	113	.230	.309	0	ø	0	—	2	15	0.1
Total	3	6	4	.600	83	0	0	0-3	100	74	36	6	6	56-8	48	3.06	132	.211	.329	0	ø	0	—	11	56	1.3
AUSTIN, JEFF	Jeffrey Wellington; B10.19.1976 San Bernardino CA; BR/TR/6´0˝/185; [KCA98 1/4]; d6.26; Col Stanford																									
2001	KC A	0	0	ø	21	0	0	0-0	26	27	17	4	1	14-2	27	5.54	90	.273	.362	0	ø	0	—	-1	0	-0.1
2002	KC A	0	0	ø	10	0	0	0-0	11	14	6	0	0	6-1	6	4.91	102	.318	.385	0	ø	0	—	0	0	0.0
2003	Cin N	2	3	.400	7	7	0	0-0	28.1	28	27	9	0	21-0	22	8.58	49	.255	.374	8-0-2	.125	-0	116	-13	0	-1.8
Total	3	2	3	.400	38	7	0	0-0	65.1	69	50	13	1	41-3	55	6.75	68	.273	.371	8-0-2	.125	-0	116	-14	0	-1.9
AUSTIN, RICK	Rick Gerald; B10.27.1946 Seattle WA; BR/TL/6´4˝/(190–195); [CleA68 S1/6]; d6.21; Col Washington St.																									
1970	Cle A	2	5	.286	31	8	1-1	3-0	67.2	74	36	10	3	26-6	53	4.79	84	.281	.352	18	.111	0	83	-4	0	-0.4
1971	Cle A	0	0	ø	23	0	0	1-1	23	25	15	3	3	20-4	20	5.09	76	.291	.429	1	.000	-0	—	-3	0	-0.2
1975	Mil A	2	3	.400	32	0	0	2-2	40	32	19	3	1	32-5	30	4.05	95	.222	.367	0	ø	0	—	0	0	0.0
1976	Mil A	0	0	ø	3	0	0	0-0	5.1	10	3	1	1	0-0	3	5.06	69	.435	.423	0	ø	0	—	-1	0	0.0
Total	4	4	8	.333	89	8	1-1	6-3	136	141	73	17	8	78-15	106	4.63	85	.273	.373	19	.105	0	83	-8	0	-0.6
AUTRY, AL	Albert; B2.29.1952 Modesto CA; BR/TR/6´5˝/197; [KCA69 4/93]; d9.14																									
1976	Atl N	1	0	1.000	1	1	0	0-0	5	4	3	2	0	3-0	3	5.40	70	.222	.333	2	.000	-0	93	-1	0	-0.1
AVERY, STEVE	Steven Thomas; B4.14.1970 Trenton MI; BL/TL/6´4˝/(180–205); [AtlN88 1/3]; d6.13																									
1990	Atl N	3	11	.214	21	20	1-1	0-0	99	121	79	7	2	45-2	75	5.64	72	.302	.372	30-0-2	.133	-1	92	-20	0	-2.5
1991	†Atl N	18	8	.692	35	35	3-1	0-0	210.1	189	89	21	3	65-0	137	3.38	115	.240	.299	79-0-5	.215	3*	122	12	0	1.7
1992	†Atl N	11	11	.500	35	**35**	2-2	0-0	233.2	216	95	14	0	71-3	129	3.20	115	.246	.300	76-0-9	.171	2	98	11	0	1.1
1993	†Atl N★	18	6	.750	35	35	3-1	0-0	223.1	216	81	14	0	43-5	125	2.94	138	.261	.295	75-0-8	.160	1	105	27	0	2.9
1994	Atl N	8	3	.727	24	24	1	0-0	151.2	127	71	15	4	55-4	122	4.04	107	.227	.298	49-0-6	.102	-2	122	6	0	0.3
1995	†Atl N	7	13	.350	29	29	3-1	0-0	173.1	165	92	22	6	52-4	141	4.67	93	.252	.311	53-2-8	.208	3	89	-4	0	0.0
1996	†Atl N	7	10	.412	24	23	1	0-0	131	146	70	10	4	40-8	86	4.47	100	.285	.339	46-2-1	.239	5	102	1	51	0.7
1997	Bos A	6	7	.462	22	18	0	0-0	96.2	127	76	15	2	49-0	51	6.42	72	.320	.394	1	.000	-0*	124	-19	62	-2.0
1998	Bos A	10	7	.588	34	23	0	0-1	123.2	128	74	14	4	64-0	57	5.02	94	.269	.361	1	.000	-0*	115	-3	0	-0.2
1999	Cin N	6	7	.462	19	19	0	0-0	96	75	62	11	1	78-0	51	5.16	91	.222	.364	26-0-2	.077	-2	92	-6	71	-0.8
2003	Det A	2	0	1.000	19	0	0	0-1	16	19	11	5	0	7-1	6	5.63	78	.302	.371	1	1.000	0	—	-2	0	-0.2
Total	11	96	83	.536	297	261	14-6	0-2	1554.2	1529	800	148	26	569-27	980	4.19	100	.259	.325	437-4-41	.174	9	107	3	184	1.0
AVREA, JAY	James Epherium; B7.6.1920 Cleburne TX; D6.26.1987 Dallas TX; BR/TR/6´1.5˝/175; d4.22																									
1950	Cin N	0	0	ø	2	0	0	0	5.1	6	2	0	0	3	2	3.38	125	.273	.360	2	.000	-0	—	1	0	0.0
AYALA, LUIS	Luis Ignacio; B1.12.1978 Los Mochis, Sinaloa, Mexico; BR/TR/6´2˝/(170–185); d3.31; [DL 2006 Was N 182]																									
2003	Mon N	10	3	.769	65	0	0	5-3	71	65	27	8	5	13-3	46	2.92	152	.244	.291	1	.000	-0	—	11	29	2.0
2004	Mon N	6	12	.333	81	0	0	2-5	90.1	92	30	6	5	15-2	63	2.69	171	.268	.307	9-0-1	.333	1	—	18	0	3.5
2005	Was N	8	7	.533	68	0	0	1-2	71	75	23	7	6	14-4	40	2.66	154	.286	.333	3-0-1	.333	0	—	12	0	2.3
Total	3	24	22	.522	214	0	0	8-10	232.1	232	80	21	16	42-9	149	2.75	160	.266	.310	13-0-2	.308	1	—	41	211	7.8
AYALA, BOBBY	Robert Joseph; B7.8.1969 Ventura CA; BR/TR/6´3˝/(190–210); d9.5																									
1992	Cin N	2	1	.667	5	5	0	0-0	29	33	15	1	1	13-2	23	4.34	83	.297	.376	9-0-1	.000	-1	131	-2	0	-0.3
1993	Cin N	7	10	.412	43	9	0	3-2	98	106	72	16	7	45-4	65	5.60	72	.274	.358	21-0-2	.095	-1	82	-20	0	-3.2
1994	Sea A	4	3	.571	46	0	0	18-6	56.2	42	25	2	0	26-0	76	2.86	172	.203	.289	0	ø	0	—	11	0	1.7
1995	†Sea A	6	5	.545	63	0	0	19-8	71	73	42	9	6	30-4	77	4.44	108	.262	.343	0	ø	0	—	1	0	0.2
1996	Sea A	6	3	.667	50	0	0	3-3	67.1	65	45	10	2	25-3	61	5.88	85	.256	.325	0	ø	0	—	-6	58	-0.6
1997	†Sea A	10	5	.667	71	0	0	8-4	96.2	91	45	14	3	41-3	92	3.82	119	.260	.338	0	ø	0	—	7	0	1.1
1998	Sea A	1	10	.091	62	0	0	8-9	75.1	100	66	9	1	26-4	68	7.29	64	.323	.370	0	ø	0	—	-21	0	-3.0
1999	Mon N	1	6	.143	53	0	0	0-1	66	60	36	6	4	34-1	64	3.68	121	.235	.331	1	.000	-0	—	3	0	0.3
	Chi N	0	1	.000	13	0	0	0-0	16	11	7	4	2	5-1	15	2.81	163	.193	.281	0	ø	0	—	2	0	0.1
	Year	1	7	.125	66	0	0	0-1	82	71	43	10	6	39-2	79	3.51	128	.228	.322	1	.000	-0	—	5	0	0.4
Total	8	37	44	.457	406	14	0	59-33	576	581	353	71	26	245-22	541	4.78	95	.263	.340	31-0-3	.065	-2	85	-25	58	-3.7
AYBAR, MANNY	Manuel Antonio; B5.4.1972 Bani, D.R.; BR/TR/6´1˝/(165–177); d8.4																									
1997	StL N	2	4	.333	12	12	0	0-0	68	66	33	8	4	29-0	41	4.24	99	.263	.344	21	.143	-1	92	1	0	0.0
1998	StL N	6	6	.500	20	14	0	0-0	81.1	90	58	6	2	42-1	57	5.98	70	.281	.367	27-1-1	.222	1	118	-15	0	-1.8
1999	StL N	4	5	.444	65	1	0	3-2	97	104	67	13	4	36-3	74	5.47	84	.272	.338	12-0-1	.083	-1*	180	-10	0	-1.0
2000	Col N	0	1	.000	1	0	0	0-0	1.2	5	3	1	0	0-0	0	16.20	36	.500	.500	0	ø	0	—	-1	0	-0.2

YEAR	TM LG	W	L	PCT	G	GS	CG-SHO	SV-BS	IP	H	R	HR	HB	BB-IB	SO	ERA	AERA	OAV	OOB	AB-HR-SH	AVG	PB	SUP	APR	DL	PW
	Cin N	1	1	.500	32	0	0	0-0	50.1	51	31	7	2	22-2	31	4.83	99	.262	.338	6-0-1	.000	-0	—	-1	21	0.0
	Fla N	1	0	1.000	21	0	0	0-1	27.1	18	8	3	0	13-1	14	2.63	166	.184	.277	0	ø	0	—	6	0	0.3
	Year	2	2	.500	54	0	0	0-1	79.1	74	42	11	2	35-3	45	4.31	108	.244	.323	6-0-1	.000	-0	—	2	0	0.1
2001	Chi N	2	1	.667	17	1	0	0-0	22.2	28	19	5	2	17-0	16	6.35	66	.304	.420	3-0-1	1.000	1	243	-6	0	-0.6
2002	†SF N	1	0	1.000	15	0	0	0-0	14.1	16	6	1	1	3-2	11	2.51	157	.271	.317	1	.000	-0	—	2	17	0.1
2003	SF N	0	0	ø	3	0	0	0-0	3	4	2	1	0	3-0	2	6.00	71	.333	.438	0	ø	0	—	-1	0	0.0
2005	NY N	0	0	ø	22	0	0	0-1	25.1	31	17	4	1	7-1	27	6.04	68	.301	.345	0	ø	0	—	-5	0	-0.3
Total	8	17	18	.486	208	28	0	3-4	391	413	244	49	16	172-10	273	5.11	86	.271	.348	70-1-4	.186	1	109	-30	38	-3.5
AYDELOTT, JAKE	Jacob Stuart; B7.6.1861 N.Manchester IN; D10.22.1926 Detroit MI; BL/TR/6´0˝/180; d5.15																									
1884	Ind AA	5	7	.417	12	12	11	0	106	129	100	0	0	29	30	4.92	67	.282	.324	44	.114	-3	93	-19	—	-1.9
1886	Phi AA	0	2	.000	2	2	2	0	18	21	11	0	0	12	5	4.00	88	.304	.407	6	.000	-1	34	0	—	-0.1
Total	2	5	9	.357	14	14	13	0	124	150	111	0	0	41	35	4.79	69	.285	.336	50	.100	-4	84	-19	—	-2.0
AYERS, BILL	William Oscar; B9.27.1919 Newnan GA; D9.24.1980 Newnan GA; BR/TR/6´3˝/185; d4.17																									
1947	NY N	0	3	.000	13	4	0	1	35.1	46	35	7	1	14	22	8.15	50	.322	.386	8-0-2	.250	0	87	-15	0	-1.1
AYERS, DOC	Yancey Wyatt; B5.21.1891 Snake Creek VA; D5.26.1968 Pulaski VA; BR/TR/6´1˝/185; d9.9; Col Roanoke																									
1913	Was A	1	1	.500	4	2	1-1	1	17.2	12	7	0	1	4	17	1.53	193	.188	.246	7	.000	-1	100	2	—	0.1
1914	Was A	11	15	.423	49	32	8-3	3	265.1	221	106	5	8	54	148	2.54	111	.238	.286	83-0-2	.169	-0	91	4	—	0.3
1915	Was A	14	9	.609	40	16	8-2	3	211.1	178	66	1	7	38	96	2.21	134	.234	.276	63-0-1	.190	-1	95	19	—	1.7
1916	Was A	5	8	.385	43	17	7	2	157	173	89	4	4	52	69	3.78	74	.285	.346	43-0-2	.140	-2	86	-19	—	-2.0
1917	Was A	11	10	.524	40	15	12-3	1	207.2	192	67	3	8	59	78	2.17	121	.256	.317	63-0-3	.206	-0	89	10	—	1.0
1918	Was A	10	12	.455	40	24	11-4	3	219.2	215	91	2	7	63	67	2.83	96	.261	.319	66-0-5	.152	-2	102	0	—	-0.2
1919	Was A	0	6	.000	11	5	0	1	43.2	52	27	0	4	17	12	2.89	111	.317	.395	12	.417	2	49	-2	—	0.0
	Det A	5	3	.625	24	5	3-1	0	93.2	88	34	2	3	31	32	2.69	119	.254	.320	24-0-2	.125	-1	113	6	—	0.3
	Year	5	9	.357	35	10	3-1	1	137.1	140	61	2	7	48	44	2.75	116	.274	.345	36-0-2	.222	0	81	4	—	0.3
1920	Det A	7	14	.333	46	23	8-3	1	208.2	217	115	6	8	62	103	3.88	96	.280	.340	59-0-2	.153	-2	86	-2	—	-0.4
1921	Det A	0	0	ø	2	1	0	0	4	9	6	0	0	2	0	9.00	47	.450	.500	0	ø	0	117	-2	—	-0.1
Total	9	64	78	.451	299	140	58-17	15	1428.2	1357	608	23	50	382	622	2.84	105	.259	.315	420-0-17	.171	-8	91	16	—	0.7
AYRAULT, BOB	Robert Cunningham; B4.27.1966 South Lake Tahoe CA; BR/TR/6´4˝/(230–235); d6.7; Col Nevada–Las Vegas																									
1992	Phi N	2	2	.500	30	0	0	0-0	43.1	32	16	0	1	17-1	27	3.12	113	.209	.287	0	ø	0	—	2	0	0.2
1993	Phi N	2	0	1.000	10	0	0	0-1	10.1	18	11	1	1	10-1	8	9.58	41	.375	.492	2	.000	-0	—	-6	0	-1.0
	Sea A	1	1	.500	14	0	0	0-1	19.2	18	8	1	0	6-1	7	3.20	140	.254	.304	0	ø	0	—	2	0	0.2
Total	2	5	3	.625	54	0	0	0-2	73.1	68	35	2	2	33-3	42	4.05	95	.250	.330	2	.000	-0	—	-2	0	-0.6
BABCOCK, BOB	Robert Ernest; B8.25.1949 New Castle PA; BR/TR/6´5˝/(190–210); d7.22; [DL 1982 Tex A 110]																									
1979	Tex A	0	0	ø	4	0	0	0-0	5.1	7	7	1	0	7-0	6	10.13	41	.318	.452	0	ø	0	—	-4	0	-0.2
1980	Tex A	1	2	.333	19	0	0	0-1	23.1	20	13	3	2	8-1	15	4.63	84	.238	.309	0	ø	0	—	-2	0	-0.2
1981	Tex A	1	1	.500	16	0	0	0-2	28.2	21	7	2	1	16-1	18	2.20	158	.219	.333	0	ø	0	—	5	0	0.3
Total	3	2	3	.400	39	0	0	0-3	57.1	48	27	6	3	31-2	39	3.92	94	.238	.339	0	ø	0	—	-1	110	-0.1
BABICH, JOHNNY	John Charles; B5.14.1913 Albion CA; D1.19.2001 Richmond CA; BR/TR/6´1.5˝/185; d6.19																									
1934	Bro N	7	11	.389	25	18	7	1	135	148	76	5	2	51	62	4.20	93	.281	.347	50-0-1	.140	-3	98	-5	—	-0.8
1935	Bro N	7	14	.333	37	24	7-2	0	143.1	191	124	7	2	52	55	6.66	60	.317	.373	49-0-2	.184	-0	102	-42	—	-5.0
1936	Bos N	0	0	ø	3	0	0	0	6	11	8	1	1	6	1	10.50	37	.440	.563	1	.000	-0	—	-5	—	-0.2
1940	Phi A	14	13	.519	31	30	16-1	0	229.1	222	111	16	1	80	94	3.73	119	.248	.310	86-0-2	.116	-6	98	19	—	1.4
1941	Phi A	2	7	.222	16	14	4	0	78.1	85	57	9	3	31	19	6.09	69	.281	.353	25-0-2	.400	4	106	-15	0	-1.0
Total	5	30	45	.400	112	86	34-3	1	592	657	376	38	9	220	231	4.93	85	.279	.343	211-0-7	.171	-5	100	-48	0	-5.6
BACKE, BRANDON	Brandon Allen; B4.5.1978 Galveston TX; BR/TR/6´0˝/(180–195); [TBA98 18/552]; d7.19; Col Galveston (TX) CC																									
2002	TB A	0	0	ø	9	0	0	0-0	13	15	10	3	2	7-0	6	6.92	65	.288	.393	0	ø	0	—	-3	0	-0.2
2003	TB A	1	1	.500	28	0	0	0-0	44.2	40	28	6	2	25-1	36	5.44	84	.247	.353	0	ø	0*	—	-4	0	-0.2
2004	†Hou N	5	3	.625	33	9	0	0-0	67	75	33	10	1	27-4	54	4.30	102	.290	.358	16-1-3	.313	3*	118	1	0	0.4
2005	†Hou N	10	8	.556	26	25	1-1	0-0	149.1	151	82	19	4	67-1	97	4.76	89	.263	.344	45-0-5	.222	4*	105	-7	40	-0.5
2006	Hou N	3	2	.600	8	8	0	0-0	43	43	18	4	3	18-0	19	3.77	120	.261	.340	14	.143	0*	85	4	143	0.5
Total	5	19	14	.576	104	42	1-1	0-0	317	324	171	42	12	144-6	212	4.71	92	.267	.350	75-1-8	.227	6	103	-9	183	0.0
BACKMAN, LES	Lester John; B3.20.1888 Cleves OH; D11.8.1975 Cincinnati OH; BR/TR/6´0.5˝/195; d7.3; Col Rose–Hulman Tech																									
1909	StL N	3	11	.214	21	15	8	0	128.1	146	69	1	3	39	35	4.14	61	.302	.357	39-0-1	.103	-1	81	-19	—	-2.1
1910	StL N	6	7	.462	26	11	4	2	116	117	55	4	2	53	41	3.03	98	.265	.346	35	.114	0	89	-3	—	-0.3
Total	2	9	18	.333	47	26	12	2	244.1	263	124	5	5	92	76	3.61	76	.284	.352	74-0-1	.108	-1	84	-22	—	-2.4
BACSIK, MIKE	Michael James; B4.1.1952 Dallas TX; BR/TR/6´1˝/(180–195); d6.15; s–Mike; Col Trinity (TX)																									
1975	Tex A	1	2	.333	7	3	0	0-0	26.2	28	17	1	1	9-1	13	3.71	102	.275	.336	0	ø	0	86	-2	0	-0.2
1976	Tex A	3	2	.600	23	0	0	0-2	55	66	31	3	2	26-4	21	4.25	84	.308	.385	0	ø	0	—	-4	0	-0.4
1977	Tex A	0	0	ø	2	0	0	0-0	2.1	9	5	1	0	0-0	1	19.29	21	.563	.563	0	ø	0	—	-4	0	-0.2
1979	Min A	4	2	.667	31	0	0	0-1	65.2	61	39	6	0	29-4	33	4.39	100	.249	.325	0	ø	0	—	-2	0	-0.2
1980	Min A	0	0	ø	10	0	0	0-0	23	26	12	1	0	11-0	9	4.30	102	.286	.359	0	ø	0	—	0	0	0.0
Total	5	8	6	.571	73	3	0	0-3	172.2	190	104	12	3	75-9	77	4.43	91	.284	.356	0	ø	0	86	-12	0	-1.0
BACSIK, MIKE	Michael Joseph; B11.11.1977 Dallas TX; BL/TL/6´3˝/190; [CleA96 18/543]; d8.5; f–Mike																									
2001	Cle A	0	0	ø	3	0	0	0-0	9	13	10	0	1	3-1	4	9.00	51	.325	.378	0	ø	0	—	-4	0	-0.2
2002	NY N	3	2	.600	11	9	1	0-0	55.2	63	29	8	4	19-3	30	4.37	91	.289	.355	18-0-3	.111	-0	125	-2	0	-0.1
2003	NY N	1	2	.333	5	3	0	0-0	17.2	28	21	5	0	8-0	12	10.19	41	.368	.424	3	.000	-0	60	-12	0	-1.5
2004	Tex A	1	1	.500	3	3	0	0-0	15.2	16	8	2	2	1-0	6	4.60	107	.267	.302	0	ø	0	106	1	0	0.1
Total	4	5	5	.500	22	15	1	0-0	98	120	68	15	7	31-4	52	5.88	72	.305	.363	21-0-3	.095	-1	107	-17	0	-1.7
BACZEWSKI, FRED	Frederic John "Lefty"; B5.15.1926 St.Paul MN; D11.14.1976 Culver City CA; BL/TL/6´2.5˝/(185–208); d4.26																									
1953	Chi N	0	0	ø	9	0	0	0	10	20	9	1	1	6	3	6.30	71	.435	.509	2-0-1	.500	0	—	-2	0	-0.1
	Cin N	11	4	.733	24	18	10-1	1	138.1	125	56	13	1	52	58	3.45	126	.244	.315	45-1-3	.178	-0	96	15	0	1.3
	Year	11	4	.733	33	18	10-1	1	148.1	145	65	14	2	58	61	3.64	120	.260	.332	47-1-4	.191	0	96	12	0	1.2
1954	Cin N	6	6	.500	29	22	4-1	0	130	159	82	22	1	53	43	5.26	80	.305	.368	42-0-6	.071	-3	107	-14	0	-1.5
1955	Cin N	0	0	ø	1	0	0	0	1	2	2	2	0	0-0	0	18.00	24	.400	.400	0	ø	0	—	-1	0	-0.1
Total	3	17	10	.630	63	40	14-2	1	279.1	306	149	38	3	111-0	104	4.45	96	.282	.349	89-1-10	.135	-3	102	-2	0	-0.4
BADER, LORE	Lore Verne "King"; B4.27.1888 Bader IL; D6.2.1973 LeRoy KS; BL/TR/6´0˝/175; d9.30; C1																									
1912	NY N	2	0	1.000	2	1	1	0	10	9	2	0	1	6	3	0.90	376	.250	.372	3	.000	-0	87	3	—	0.5
1917	Bos A	2	0	1.000	15	1	0	1	38.1	48	15	1	1	18	14	2.35	110	.306	.381	10-0-1	.300	1	84	0	—	0.1
1918	Bos A	1	3	.250	5	4	2-1	0	27	26	13	1	3	12	10	3.33	81	.271	.369	9	.111	-1	42	-2	—	-0.4
Total	3	5	3	.625	22	6	3-1	1	75.1	83	30	2	5	36	27	2.51	109	.287	.376	22-0-1	.182	-0	58	1	—	0.2
BAECHT, ED	Edward Joseph; B5.15.1907 Paden OK; D8.15.1957 Grafton IL; BR/TR/6´3˝/195; d4.24																									
1926	Phi N	2	0	1.000	28	1	1	0	56	73	43	4	1	28	14	6.11	68	.324	.402	14	.143	-1	101	-10	—	-0.5
1927	Phi N	0	1	.000	1	1	0	0	6	12	8	0	0	2	0	12.00	34	.429	.467	2	.000	-0	185	-5	—	-0.5
1928	Phi N	1	1	.500	9	1	0	0	24	37	16	1	0	9	10	6.00	71	.385	.438	7	.143	-0	59	-3	—	-0.3
1931	Chi N	2	4	.333	22	6	2	0	67	64	34	1	8	32	34	3.76	103	.250	.351	18-0-3	.278	1	119	0	—	0.1
1932	Chi N	0	0	ø	1	0	0	0	1	1	0	0	0	1	0	0.00	ø	.333	.500	0	ø	0	—	0	—	0.0
1937	StL A	0	0	ø	3	0	0	0	6.1	13	15	3	2	6	3	12.79	38	.419	.538	1	.000	-0	—	-7	—	-0.3
Total	6	5	6	.455	64	9	3	0	160.1	200	116	9	11	78	61	5.56	73	.313	.397	42-0-3	.190	-1	113	-25	—	-1.5
BAEK, CHA SEUNG	Cha Seung; B5.29.1980 Pusan, South Korea; BR/TR/6´4˝/(190–220); d8.8																									
2004	Sea A	2	4	.333	7	5	0	0-0	31	35	23	5	2	11-1	20	5.52	81	.278	.345	0	ø	0	104	-5	0	-0.8
2006	Sea A	4	1	.800	6	6	0	0-0	34.1	26	15	6	2	13-0	23	3.67	120	.208	.293	0	ø	0	103	3	7	0.4
Total	2	6	5	.545	13	11	0	0-0	65.1	61	38	11	4	24-1	43	4.55	98	.243	.319	0	ø	0	103	-2	7	-0.4

YEAR	TM LG	W	L	PCT	G	GS	CG-SHO	SV-BS	IP	H	R	HR	HB	BB-IB	SO	ERA	AERA	OAV	OOB	AB-HR-SH	AVG	PB	SUP	APR	DL	PW
BAEZ, BENITO	Benito (Ceri); B5.6.1977 Bonao, D.R.; BL/TL/6´0˝/160; d8.25; [DL 2002 Fla N 111]																									
2001	Fla N	0	0	ø	8	0	0	0-0	9.1	22	14	3	0	6-0	14	13.50	31	.449	.509	1	.000	-0	—	-10	0	-0.5
BAEZ, DANYS	Danys; B9.10.1977 Pinar Del Rio, Cuba; BR/TR/6´3˝/(225–230); d5.13																									
2001	†Cle A	5	3	.625	43	0	0	0-1	50.1	34	22	5	3	20-4	52	2.50	183	.191	.282	0	ø	0	—	8	0	1.1
2002	Cle A	10	11	.476	39	26	1	6-2	165.1	160	84	14	9	82-5	130	4.41	101	.256	.347	2	.000	-0	89	2	0	0.2
2003	Cle A	2	9	.182	73	0	0	25-10	75.2	65	36	9	4	23-0	66	3.81	116	.229	.295	1	.000	-0	—	6	0	1.0
2004	TB A	4	4	.500	62	0	0	30-3	68	60	31	6	7	29-4	52	3.57	131	.237	.331	0	ø	0	—	8	0	1.4
2005	TB A☆	5	4	.556	67	0	0	41-8	72.1	66	27	7	2	30-0	51	2.86	154	.244	.322	0	ø	0	—	11	0	2.3
2006	LA N	5	5	.500	46	0	0	9-7	49.2	53	29	3	6	11-2	29	4.35	101	.283	.335	0	ø	0	—	-1	0	-0.2
	Atl N	0	1	.000	11	0	0	0-1	10	7	6	0	1	6-1	10	5.40	84	.189	.318	0	ø	0	—	-1	40	-0.1
	Year	5	6	.455	57	0	0	9-8	59.2	60	35	3	7	17-3	39	4.53	97	.268	.332	0	ø	0	—	-2	0	-0.3
Total	6	31	37	.456	341	26	1	111-32	491.1	445	235	44	32	201-16	390	3.79	118	.243	.325	3	.000	-0	89	33	40	5.7
BAGBY, JIM	James Charles Jacob Jr.; B9.8.1916 Cleveland OH; D9.2.1988 Marietta GA; BR/TR/6´2˝/170; d4.18; Def 1944; f–Jim																									
1938	Bos A	15	11	.577	43	25	10-1	2	198.2	218	110	9	3	90	73	4.21	117	.283	.360	68-0-8	.191	-1*	119	14	—	1.6
1939	Bos A	5	5	.500	21	11	3	0	80	119	66	7	2	36	35	7.09	67	.347	.412	34-1-2	.294	3	117	-17	—	-1.5
1940	Bos A	10	16	.385	36	21	6-1	2	182.2	217	104	15	1	83	57	4.73	95	.296	.368	74-0-6	.203	-0*	93	-4	—	-0.5
1941	Cle A	9	15	.375	33	27	12	2	200.2	214	104	10	6	76	53	4.04	98	.273	.341	74-0-4	.243	2*	90	-4	0	-0.1
1942	Cle A☆	17	9	.654	38	**35**	16-4	1	270.2	267	105	19	1	64	54	2.96	117	.258	.302	95-1-7	.189	1*	109	15	0	1.5
1943	Cle A☆	17	14	.548	36	**33**	16-3	1	**273**	248	112	15	3	80	70	3.10	100	.240	.296	112-0-1	.268	4*	102	-1	0	0.6
1944	Cle A	4	5	.444	13	10	2	0	79	101	48	2	4	34	12	4.33	76	.312	.384	31-1-0	.226	1*	104	-11	0	-1.0
1945	Cle A	8	11	.421	25	19	11-3	1	159.1	171	70	3	2	59	38	3.73	87	.279	.344	58-0-1	.293	3	101	-6	0	-0.2
1946	†Bos A	7	6	.538	21	11	6-1	0	106.2	117	55	4	1	49	16	3.71	99	.279	.356	42	.119	-2	87	-3	0	-0.5
1947	Pit N	5	4	.556	37	6	2	0	115.2	143	75	14	5	37	23	4.67	90	.304	.361	32-0-3	.219	1	136	-8	0	-0.4
Total	10	97	96	.503	303	198	84-13	9	1666.1	1815	849	98	28	608	431	3.96	97	.278	.342	620-3-32	.226	12	104	-25	0	-0.5
BAGBY, JIM	James Charles Jacob Sr. "Sarge"; B10.5.1889 Barnett GA; D7.28.1954 Marietta GA; BB/TR/6´0˝/170; d4.22; s–Jim																									
1912	Cin N	2	1	.667	5	1	0	0	17.1	17	6	2	0	9	10	3.12	108	.270	.361	5	.000	-1	87	1	—	0.1
1916	Cle A	16	17	.485	48	27	14-3	5	272.2	253	109	2	8	67	88	2.61	115	.251	.303	90-0-9	.167	-1*	116	10	—	1.0
1917	Cle A	23	13	.639	49	37	26-8	7	320.2	277	91	6	6	73	83	1.99	142	.235	.283	108-0-3	.231	2	102	30	—	3.9
1918	Cle A	17	16	.515	**45**	31	23-2	6	271.1	274	107	0	2	78	57	2.69	112	.276	.330	99-0-3	.212	-0*	92	8	—	1.0
1919	Cle A	17	11	.607	35	32	21	3	241.1	258	96	3	4	44	61	2.80	120	.275	.310	89-1-4	.258	5*	121	15	—	2.2
1920	†Cle A	**31**	12	**.721**	**48**	38	**30**-3	0	**339.2**	338	122	9	5	79	73	2.89	132	.266	.311	131-1-7	.252	6*	133	39	—	4.7
1921	Cle A	14	12	.538	40	26	13	4	191.2	238	112	14	4	44	37	4.70	91	.308	.348	76-0-2	.197	-1*	108	-6	—	-0.9
1922	Cle A	4	5	.444	25	10	4	1	98.1	134	77	5	3	39	25	6.32	63	.340	.404	42	.262	3	136	-24	—	-1.6
1923	Pit N	3	2	.600	21	6	2	3	68.2	95	49	6	1	25	16	5.24	76	.336	.392	20-0-2	.050	-2	126	-10	—	-0.9
Total	9	127	89	.588	316	208	133-16	29	1821.2	1884	769	47	33	458	450	3.11	110	.273	.321	660-2-30	.218	11	114	63	—	9.5
BAHNSEN, STAN	Stanley Raymond; B12.15.1944 Council Bluffs IA; BR/TR/6´2˝/(185–198); [NYA65 4/68]; d9.9; Col Nebraska																									
1966	NY A	1	1	.500	4	3	1	1	23	15	9	3	0	7-0	16	3.52	94	.181	.244	7	.143	-0	141	0	0	0.0
1968	NY A	17	12	.586	37	34	10-1	0	267.1	216	72	14	2	68-6	162	2.05	142	.221	.271	81-0-10	.049	-4	97	26	0	2.4
1969	NY A	9	16	.360	40	33	5-2	1-0	220.2	222	102	28	0	90-9	130	3.83	92	.260	.330	60-0-9	.083	-3	87	-6	0	-0.9
1970	NY A	14	11	.560	36	35	6-2	0-0	232.2	227	100	23	2	75-4	116	3.33	107	.256	.312	74-0-8	.149	-1	102	6	0	0.6
1971	NY A	14	12	.538	36	34	14-3	0-0	242	221	99	20	5	72-8	110	3.35	98	.248	.304	79-0-8	.152	0	121	0	0	0.2
1972	Chi A	21	16	.568	43	41	5-1	0-0	252.1	263	107	22	6	73-1	157	3.60	87	.268	.321	92-0-3	.152	-1*	103	-10	0	-1.5
1973	Chi A	18	21	.462	42	42	14-4	0-0	282.1	290	128	20	5	117-2	120	3.57	111	.269	.341	0	ø	0	93	11	0	1.5
1974	Chi A	12	15	.444	38	35	10-1	0-0	216.1	230	128	17	4	110-6	102	4.70	80	.277	.362	0	ø	0	96	-22	0	-2.5
1975	Chi A	4	6	.400	12	12	2	0-0	67.1	78	49	9	3	40-0	31	6.01	65	.291	.389	0	ø	0	106	-15	0	-1.9
	Oak A	6	7	.462	21	16	2	0-1	100	88	42	2	3	37-1	49	3.24	113	.238	.310	1	.000	-0	101	4	0	0.5
	Year	10	13	.435	33	28	4	0-1	167.1	166	91	11	6	77-1	80	4.36	86	.261	.344	1	.000	-0	103	-11	0	-1.4
1976	Oak A	8	7	.533	35	14	1-1	0-2	143	124	55	13	2	43-3	82	3.34	101	.232	.290	0	ø	0	110	3	0	0.3
1977	Oak A	1	2	.333	11	2	0	1-1	22	24	16	5	1	13-5	21	6.14	66	.286	.380	0	ø	0	89	-5	0	-0.6
	Mon N	8	9	.471	23	22	3-1	0-0	127.1	142	76	14	0	38-2	58	4.81	80	.283	.332	42-0-4	.119	-1	103	-14	0	-1.7
1978	Mon N	1	5	.167	44	1	0	7-2	75	74	35	9	0	31-2	44	3.84	93	.261	.333	11-0-1	.091	-1	151	-2	22	-0.3
1979	Mon N	3	1	.750	55	0	0	5-2	94.1	80	34	10	0	42-4	71	3.15	118	.236	.319	14-1-0	.071	-0	—	8	0	0.4
1980	Mon N	7	6	.538	57	0	0	4-3	91.1	80	40	7	0	33-4	48	3.05	119	.235	.300	9	.111	1	—	3	0	0.6
1981	†Mon N	2	1	.667	25	3	0	1-1	49	45	27	7	1	24-0	28	4.96	72	.247	.338	9	.111	-0	58	-6	0	-0.5
1982	Cal A	0	1	.000	7	0	0	0-0	9.2	13	6	0	0	8-1	5	4.66	88	.310	.420	0	ø	0	—	-1	0	-0.1
	Phi N	0	0	ø	8	0	0	0-0	13.1	8	2	0	0	3-1	9	1.35	274	.182	.229	0	ø	0	—	3	0	0.2
Total	16	146	149	.495	574	327	73-16	20-12	2529	2440	1127	223	34	924-59	1359	3.60	97	.255	.321	479-1-43	.117	-9	100	-17	22	-3.3
BAHR, ED	Edson Garfield; B10.16.1919 Rouleau SK, Can.; BR/TR/6´1.5˝/172; d5.1																									
1946	Pit N	8	6	.571	27	14	7	0	136.2	128	57	8	5	52	44	2.63	134	.254	.330	45-0-1	.178	-1*	116	9	0	0.8
1947	Pit N	3	5	.375	19	11	1	0	82.1	82	45	5	3	43	25	4.59	92	.263	.358	23-0-3	.087	-2*	74	-2	0	-0.4
Total	2	11	11	.500	46	25	8	0	219	210	102	13	8	95	69	3.37	112	.257	.341	68-0-4	.147	-3	97	7	0	0.4
BAICHLEY, GROVER	Grover Cleveland; B12.10.1889 Toledo IL; D6.28.1956 San Jose CA; BR/TR/5´8˝/165; d8.24; Col Valparaiso																									
1914	StL A	0	0	ø	4	0	0	0	7	9	5	0	0	3	3	5.14	53	.346	.414	1	.000	-0	—	-2	—	-0.1
BAILES, SCOTT	Scott Alan; B12.18.1961 Chillicothe OH; BL/TL/6´2˝/(171–184); [PitN82 S4/71]; d4.9; Col Missouri St.																									
1986	Cle A	10	10	.500	62	10	0	7-6	112.2	123	70	12	1	43-5	60	4.95	85	.276	.339	0	ø	0	115	-10	0	-1.6
1987	Cle A	7	8	.467	39	17	0	6-2	120.1	145	75	21	4	47-1	65	4.64	98	.296	.358	0	ø	0	100	-3	0	-0.3
1988	Cle A	9	14	.391	37	21	5-2	0-2	145	149	89	22	2	46-0	53	4.90	84	.266	.322	0	ø	0	90	-13	0	-1.8
1989	Cle A	5	9	.357	34	11	0	0-1	113.2	116	57	7	3	29-4	47	4.28	93	.269	.316	0	ø	0	66	-2	24	-0.3
1990	Cal A	2	0	1.000	27	0	0	0-0	35.1	46	30	8	1	20-0	16	6.37	60	.315	.390	0	ø	0	—	-11	0	-0.5
1991	Cal A	1	2	.333	42	0	0	0-1	51.2	41	26	5	4	22-5	41	4.18	99	.218	.310	0	ø	0	—	0	15	0.0
1992	Cal A	3	1	.750	32	0	0	0-0	38.2	59	34	7	1	28-4	25	7.45	54	.351	.442	0	ø	0	—	-14	15	-1.3
1997	Tex A	1	0	1.000	24	0	0	0-0	22	18	9	2	0	10-2	14	2.86	170	.231	.315	0	ø	0	—	4	0	0.2
1998	Tex A	1	0	1.000	46	0	0	0-0	40.1	61	33	5	0	11-0	30	6.47	76	.351	.385	0	ø	0	—	-7	31	-0.4
Total	9	39	44	.470	343	59	5-2	13-12	679.2	758	423	89	16	256-21	351	4.95	86	.283	.345	0	ø	0	93	-56	85	-6.0
BAILEY, SWEETBREADS	Abraham Lincoln; B2.12.1895 Joliet IL; D9.27.1939 Joliet IL; BR/TR/6´0˝/184; d5.23																									
1919	Chi N	3	5	.375	21	5	0	0	71.1	75	30	2	3	20	19	3.15	91	.288	.346	18	.389	3	77	-1	—	0.3
1920	Chi N	1	2	.333	21	1	0	0	36.2	55	38	1	2	11	8	7.12	45	.359	.410	7-0-1	.143	-0	25	-16	—	-1.3
1921	Chi N	0	0	ø	3	0	0	0	5	6	2	0	1	2	2	3.60	106	.300	.391	0	ø	0	—	0	—	0.0
	Bro N	0	0	ø	7	0	0	0	24.1	35	15	1	1	7	6	5.18	75	.368	.417	5	.000	-0	—	-3	—	-0.2
	Year	0	0	ø	10	0	0	0	29.1	41	17	1	2	9	8	4.91	79	.357	.413	5	.000	-0	—	-2	—	-0.2
Total	3	4	7	.364	52	6	0	0	137.1	171	85	4	7	40	35	4.59	69	.324	.379	30-0-1	.267	2	63	-20	—	-1.2
BAILEY, ROGER	Charles Roger; B10.3.1970 Chattahoochee FL; BR/TR/6´1˝/180; [ColN92 3/95]; d4.27; Col Florida St.; [DL 1998 Col N 181]																									
1995	Col N	7	6	.538	39	6	0	0-0	81.1	88	49	9	1	39-3	33	4.98	108	.283	.363	16-0-3	.125	-1	140	3	0	0.3
1996	Col N	2	3	.400	24	11	0	1-0	83.2	94	64	7	1	52-0	45	6.24	84	.288	.384	19-1-3	.263	2	91	-8	23	-0.1
1997	Col N	9	10	.474	29	29	5-2	0-0	191	210	103	27	13	70-2	84	4.29	120	.283	.354	62-0-5	.210	-0*	111	14	15	1.5
Total	3	18	19	.486	92	46	5-2	1-0	356	392	216	43	15	161-5	162	4.90	107	.284	.363	97-1-11	.206	1	110	9	219	1.7
BAILEY, HARVEY	Harvey Francis; B11.24.1876 Adrian MI; D7.10.1922 Toledo OH; TL/6´0˝/160; d6.30																									
1899	Bos N	6	4	.600	12	11	8	0	86.2	83	42	7	6	35	26	3.95	105	.252	.334	34	.235	0	85	5	—	0.4
1900	Bos N	0	0	ø	4	1	0	0	20	24	16	0	2	11	9	4.95	83	.296	.394	9	.222	0	167	-2	—	0.0
Total	2	6	4	.600	16	12	8	0	106.2	107	58	7	8	46	35	4.13	100	.260	.346	43	.233	0	92	3	—	0.4
BAILEY, HOWARD	Howard L; B7.31.1957 Grand Haven MI; BR/TL/6´0˝/(185–195); d4.12; Col Grand Valley St.																									
1981	Det A	1	4	.200	9	5	0	0-0	36.2	45	31	4	3	13-2	17	7.36	51	.308	.372	0	ø	0	66	-14	0	-1.5
1982	Det A	0	0	ø	8	0	0	1-0	10	6	0	0	0	2-1	3	0.00	ø	.182	.222	0	ø	0	—	5	0	0.2

YEAR	TM LG	W	L	PCT	G	GS	CG-SHO	SV-BS	IP	H	R	HR	HB	BB-IB	SO	ERA	AERA	OAV	OOB	AB-HR-SH	AVG	PB	SUP	APR	DL	PW
1983	Det A	5	5	.500	33	3	0	0-1	72	69	45	11	2	25-3	21	4.88	81	.255	.321	0	ø	0	100	-9	0	-1.0
Total	3	6	9	.400	50	8	0	1-1	118.2	120	76	15	5	40-6	41	5.23	75	.267	.331	0	ø	0	78	-18	0	-2.3
Bailey, Jim	James Hopkins; B12.16.1934 Strawberry Plains TN; BB/TL/6´2.5˝/210; d9.10; b–Ed; Col Lincoln Memorial																									
1959	Cin N	0	1	.000	3	1	0	0	11.2	17	8	1	1	6-1	7	6.17	66	.333	.414	3	.000	-0	66	-2	0	-0.2
Bailey, King	Linwood C.; B11.1870 VA; D11.19.1917 Macon GA; BL/TL/6´0˝/185; d9.21																									
1895	Cin N	1	0	1.000	1	1	1	0	8	13	8	0	1	0	0	5.63	88	.361	.378	4	.500	1	273	-1	—	0.0
Bailey, Cory	Phillip Cory; B1.24.1971 Marion IL; BR/TR/6´1˝/(195–210); [BosA91 15/408]; d9.1; Col Southeastern Illinois JC																									
1993	Bos A	0	1	.000	11	0	0	0-0	15.2	12	7	0	0	12-3	11	3.45	134	.231	.369	0	ø	0	—	2	0	0.1
1994	Bos A	0	1	.000	5	0	0	0-1	4.1	10	6	2	0	3-1	4	12.46	40	.476	.542	0	ø	0	—	-3	0	-0.6
1995	StL N	0	0	ø	3	0	0	0-0	3.2	2	3	0	0	2-1	5	7.36	58	.154	.267	0	ø	0	—	-1	0	0.0
1996	StL N	5	2	.714	51	0	0	0-1	57	57	21	1	1	30-3	38	3.00	141	.263	.353	1-0-1	.000	1	—	8	0	0.9
1997	SF N	0	1	.000	7	0	0	0-0	9.2	15	9	1	0	4-0	5	8.38	49	.375	.422	1	1.000	0	—	-4	0	-0.3
1998	SF N	0	0	ø	5	0	0	0-0	3.1	2	1	1	0	1-0	2	2.70	149	.167	.231	0	ø	0	—	1	0	0.0
2001	KC A	1	1	.500	53	0	0	0-1	67.1	57	28	3	0	33-2	61	3.48	143	.234	.321	0	ø	0	—	10	0	0.5
2002	KC A	3	4	.429	37	0	0	1-6	46	53	24	5	2	31-7	24	4.11	121	.306	.413	0	ø	0	—	3	0	0.5
Total	8	9	10	.474	172	0	0	1-9	207	208	99	13	3	116-17	150	3.96	118	.269	.364	2-0-1	.500	1	—	16	0	1.1
Bailey, Steve	Steven John; B2.12.1942 Bronx NY; BR/TR/6´1˝/194; d4.14																									
1967	Cle A	2	5	.286	32	1	0	2	64.2	62	31	5	3	42-4	46	3.90	84	.259	.372	10	.000	-1	53	-4	0	-0.5
1968	Cle A	0	1	.000	2	1	0	0	5	4	3	1	0	2-0	1	3.60	83	.235	.300	0	ø	0	88	-1	0	-0.1
Total	2	2	6	.250	34	2	0	2	69.2	66	34	6	3	44-4	47	3.88	84	.258	.367	10	.000	-1	67	-5	0	-0.6
Bailey, Bill	William F.; B4.12.1888 Ft.Smith AR; D11.2.1926 Houston TX; BL/TL/5´11˝/165; d9.17																									
1907	StL A	4	1	.800	6	5	3	0	48.1	39	16	0	4	15	17	2.42	104	.223	.299	20-0-1	.150	-1	102	1	—	0.0
1908	StL A	3	5	.375	22	12	7	0	106.2	85	53	2	3	50	42	3.04	79	.220	.314	34-0-2	.088	-2	109	-8	—	-1.0
1909	StL A	9	10	.474	32	20	17-1	0	199	174	71	2	6	75	114	2.44	99	.248	.325	77-0-2	.286	5*	79	0	—	0.6
1910	StL A	3	18	.143	34	20	13	0	192.1	186	133	2	10	97	90	3.32	74	.262	.359	63-0-1	.206	0	64	-26	—	-2.7
1911	StL A	0	3	.000	7	2	2	0	31.2	42	26	1	2	16	8	4.55	74	.339	.423	11	.000	-2	43	-5	—	-0.6
1912	StL A	0	1	.000	3	2	0	0	10.2	15	12	0	0	10	2	9.28	36	.341	.463	2	.500	1	78	-6	—	-0.4
1914	Bal F	7	9	.438	19	18	10-1	0	128.2	106	58	2	7	68	131	3.08	99	.230	.338	43-0-1	.163	-1	78	-1	—	-0.1
1915	Bal F	6	19	.240	36	23	11-2	0	190.1	179	118	8	9	115	98	4.63	62	.255	.366	65-0-7	.231	0	103	-33	—	-4.0
	Chi F	3	1	.750	5	5	3-3	0	33.1	23	9	1	0	10	24	2.16	116	.202	.266	9	.222	0	117	2	—	0.3
	Year	9	20	.310	41	28	14-5	0	223.2	202	127	9	9	125	122	4.27	66	.247	.353	74-0-7	.230	0	105	-30	—	-3.7
1918	Det A	1	2	.333	8	4	1	0	37.2	53	34	0	1	26	13	5.97	45	.368	.468	13	.077	-1	85	-15	—	-1.2
1921	StL N	2	5	.286	19	6	3-1	0	74	95	41	1	2	22	20	4.26	86	.330	.381	22	.091	-2	60	-4	—	-0.5
1922	StL N	0	2	.000	12	0	0	0	31.2	38	22	1	0	23	11	5.40	72	.325	.436	7	.286	0	—	-5	—	-0.2
Total	11	38	76	.333	203	117	70-8	0	1084.1	1035	593	20	44	527	570	3.57	77	.261	.354	366-0-14	.194	-2	84	-100	—	-9.8
Bain, Loren	Herbert Loren; B7.4.1922 Staples MN; D11.24.1996 Chetek WI; BR/TR/6´0˝/190; d6.23																									
1945	NY N	0	0	ø	3	0	0	0	8	10	7	1	1	4	1	7.88	50	.323	.417	3	.333	0	—	-3	0	-0.1
Bair, Doug	Charles Douglas; B8.22.1949 Defiance OH; BR/TR/6´0˝/(165–185); [PitN71 2/46]; d9.13; Col Bowling Green																									
1976	Pit N	0	0	ø	4	0	0	0-0	6.1	4	4	0	0	5-1	4	5.68	62	.174	.321	0	ø	0	—	-1	0	-0.1
1977	Oak A	4	6	.400	45	0	0	8-6	83.1	78	39	11	0	57-9	68	3.46	117	.253	.364	0	ø	0	—	5	0	0.6
1978	Cin N	7	6	.538	70	0	0	28-5	100.1	87	23	6	0	38-3	91	1.97	180	.236	.305	14-0-1	.143	-0	—	18	0	3.4
1979	†Cin N	11	7	.611	65	0	0	16-7	94.1	93	47	7	3	51-12	86	4.29	86	.256	.350	8	.000	-1	—	-5	0	-1.1
1980	Cin N	3	6	.333	61	0	0	6-0	85	91	42	7	1	39-10	62	4.24	83	.277	.351	2	.000	-0	—	-6	0	-0.7
1981	Cin N	2	2	.500	24	0	0	0-2	39	42	28	5	0	17-4	16	5.77	61	.271	.343	3-1-0	.333	1	—	-10	0	-0.9
	StL N	2	0	1.000	11	0	0	1-0	15.2	13	6	0	0	2-0	14	3.45	105	.224	.250	3	.000	-0	—	1	0	0.0
	Year	4	2	.667	35	0	0	1-2	54.2	55	34	5	0	19-4	30	5.10	69	.258	.319	6-1-0	.167	1	—	-8	0	-0.9
1982	†StL N	5	3	.625	63	0	0	8-1	91.2	69	27	7	1	36-13	68	2.55	144	.211	.288	13-0-2	.077	-1	—	12	0	1.1
1983	StL N	1	1	.500	26	0	0	1-2	29.2	24	11	4	0	13-3	21	3.03	121	.224	.306	2	.000	-0	—	2	0	0.1
	Det A	7	3	.700	27	1	0	4-4	55.2	51	27	8	1	19-4	39	3.88	102	.242	.307	0	ø	0	46	0	0	0.0
1984	†Det A	5	3	.625	47	1	0	4-3	93.2	82	42	10	0	36-2	57	3.75	106	.238	.306	0	ø	0	160	3	0	0.3
1985	Det A	2	0	1.000	21	3	0	0-0	49	54	38	3	1	25-5	30	6.24	66	.281	.360	0	ø	0	170	-12	0	-0.5
	StL N	0	0	ø	2	0	0	0-0	2	1	0	0	0	2-0	0	0.00	ø	.167	.375	0	ø	0	—	1	0	0.0
1986	Oak A	2	3	.400	31	0	0	4-4	45	37	15	5	0	18-0	40	3.00	130	.224	.296	0	ø	0	—	6	0	0.7
1987	Phi N	2	0	1.000	11	0	0	0-1	13.2	17	9	4	0	5-0	10	5.93	72	.309	.361	1-0-1	.000	-0	—	-2	0	-0.3
1988	Tor A	0	0	ø	10	0	0	0-0	13.1	14	6	2	0	3-0	8	4.05	98	.280	.321	0	ø	0	—	0	0	0.0
1989	Pit N	2	3	.400	44	0	0	1-1	67.1	52	19	4	0	28-10	56	2.27	149	.211	.291	5	.200	0	—	9	0	0.7
1990	Pit N	0	0	ø	22	0	0	0-0	24.1	30	15	3	0	11-1	19	4.81	76	.306	.376	1	.000	-0	—	-3	0	-0.2
Total	15	55	43	.561	584	5	0	81-36	909.1	839	398	86	7	405-77	689	3.63	103	.246	.325	52-1-4	.096	-2	153	18	0	3.1
Baird, Bob	Robert Allen; B1.16.1940 Knoxville TN; D4.11.1974 Chattanooga TN; BL/TL/6´4˝/195; d9.3; Col Carson–Newman																									
1962	Was A	0	1	.000	3	3	0	0	10.2	13	8	0	0	8-0	3	6.75	60	.310	.412	3	.000	-0	66	-3	0	-0.3
1963	Was A	0	3	.000	5	3	0	0	11.2	12	15	1	1	7-0	7	7.71	48	.261	.364	3	.333	0	112	-7	0	-1.2
Total	2	0	4	.000	8	6	0	0	22.1	25	23	1	1	15-0	10	7.25	53	.284	.387	6	.167	-0	88	-10	0	-1.5
Bajenaru, Jeff	Jeffrey Michael; B3.21.1978 Pomona CA; BR/TR/6´1˝/(190–200); [ChiA99 36/1089]; d9.4; Col Oklahoma																									
2004	Chi A	0	1	.000	9	0	0	0-0	8.1	15	10	0	0	6-1	8	10.80	44	.405	.488	0	ø	0	—	-5	0	-0.5
2005	Chi A	0	0	ø	4	0	0	0-0	4.1	4	3	2	0	0-0	3	6.23	73	.222	.222	0	ø	0	—	-1	0	0.0
2006	Ari N	0	1	.000	1	0	0	0-1	1	4	4	3	0	0-0	0	36.00	13	.571	.571	0	ø	0	—	-3	0	-0.5
Total	3	0	2	.000	14	0	0	0-1	13.2	23	17	5	0	6-1	11	11.20	41	.371	.426	0	ø	0	—	-9	0	-1.0
Bakely, Jersey	Edward Enoch (b Edward Enoch Bakley); B4.17.1864 Blackwood NJ; D2.17.1915 Philadelphia PA; BR/TR/5´8˝/170; d5.11																									
1883	Phi AA	5	3	.625	8	8	7	0	61.1	65	47	0	—	12	14	3.23	110	.255	.288	26	.192	1	112	1	—	0.2
1884	Phi U	14	25	.359	39	38	38-1	0	344.2	390	305	0	—	76	204	4.47	52	.267	.303	167	.132	-11*	99	-87	—	-8.4
	Wil U	0	2	.000	2	2	2	0	17	24	17	0	—	1	9	4.24	63	.312	.321	5	.000	-1	32	-2	—	-0.3
	KC U	2	3	.400	5	5	3	0	33	29	16	0	—	4	13	2.45	91	.220	.243	20	.150	-1*	76	0	—	-0.2
	Year	16	30	.348	46	45	43-1	0	394.2	443	338	0	—	81	226	4.29	54	.265	.299	192	.130	-13	93	-87	—	-8.9
1888	Cle AA	25	33	.431	61	61	60-4	0	532.2	518	321	14	15	128	212	2.97	104	.246	.294	194-1	.134	-6	86	2	—	-0.3
1889	Cle N	12	22	.353	36	34	33-2	0	304.1	296	169	9	8	106	105	2.96	136	.248	.313	111-1	.135	-1	65	29	—	2.6
1890	Cle P	12	25	.324	43	38	32	0	326.1	412	307	13	7	147	67	4.47	89	.295	.365	138	.203	-2	95	-18	—	-1.7
1891	Was AA	2	10	.167	13	12	11	0	104.1	127	107	6	6	60	32	5.35	70	.291	.384	45	.222	-0	76	-19	—	-1.7
	Bal AA	4	2	.667	8	6	5	0	59	48	32	1	1	30	13	2.29	163	.214	.310	21	.095	0	103	8	—	0.6
	Year	6	12	.333	21	18	16	0	163.1	175	139	7	7	90	45	4.24	88	.265	.359	66	.182	-0	85	-12	—	-1.1
Total	6	76	125	.378	215	204	191-7	0	1782.2	1909	1321	43	37	564	669	3.66	91	.262	.318	727-2	.153	-21	87	-86	—	-9.2
Bakenhaster, Dave	David Lee; B3.5.1945 Columbus OH; BR/TR/5´10˝/168; d6.20																									
1964	StL N	0	0	ø	2	0	0	0	3	9	6	1	0	1-0	0	6.00	63	.474	.500	0	ø	0	—	-2	0	-0.1
Baker, Al	Albert Jones; B2.28.1906 Batesville MS; D11.6.1982 Kenedy TX; BR/TR/5´11˝/170; d8.20																									
1938	Bos A	0	0	ø	3	0	0	0	7.2	13	8	2	1	2	2	9.39	53	.371	.421	4	.000	-1	—	-3	—	-0.2
Baker, Bock	Charles "Smiling Bock"; B7.17.1878 Troy NY; D8.17.1940 New York NY; TL/5´9˝/181; d4.28																									
1901	Cle A	0	1	.000	1	1	1	0	8	23	13	0	1	6	0	5.63	63	.500	.566	4	.000	-1	19	-4	—	-0.4
	Phi A	0	1	.000	1	1	0	0	6	6	11	0	0	6	1	10.50	36	.261	.414	3	.333	0	90	-5	—	-0.5
	Year	0	2	.000	2	2	1	0	14	29	24	0	1	12	1	7.71	47	.420	.512	7	.143	-1	56	-8	—	-0.9
Baker, Ernie	Earnest Gould; B8.8.1875 Concord MI; D10.25.1945 Homer MI; BR/TR/5´10˝/160; d8.18																									
1905	Cin N	0	0	ø	1	0	0	0	4	7	4	1	1	0	1	4.50	73	.412	.444	2	.000	-0	—	-1	—	-0.1

YEAR	TM LG	W	L	PCT	G	GS	CG-SHO	SV-BS	IP	H	R	HR	HB	BB-IB	SO	ERA	AERA	OAV	OOB	AB-HR-SH	AVG	PB	SUP	APR	DL	PW
Baker, Jesse	Jesse Ormond; B6.3.1888 Anderson Island WA; D9.26.1972 Tacoma WA; BL/TL/5´11˝/188; d4.23																									
1911	Chi A	2	7	.222	22	8	3	1	94	101	52	3	4	30	51	3.93	82	.288	.351	29	.103	-2	70	-6	—	-0.6
Baker, Kirtley	Kirtley "Whitey"; B6.24.1869 Aurora IN; D4.15.1927 Covington KY; BR/TR/5´9˝/160; d5.7																									
1890	Pit N	3	19	.136	25	21	19-2	0	178.1	209	176	11	20	86	76	5.60	59	.283	.373	68	.147	-1*	63	-50	—	-4.6
1893	Bal N	3	8	.273	15	12	8	0	91.2	138	111	5	5	58	26	8.44	56	.337	.426	57	.298	2*	114	-33	—	-2.4
1894	Bal N	0	1	.000	1	0	0	0	0	1	5	0	0	2	0	(5)	ø	1.000	1.000	4	.000	-0*	—	-4	—	-0.3
1898	Was N	2	3	.400	6	5	4	0	47	56	31	1	0	18	7	3.06	120	.293	.354	18	.278	2	101	0	—	0.1
1899	Was N	1	7	.125	11	6	3	0	54	79	65	3	6	22	6	6.83	57	.339	.410	19	.158	-1*	89	-20	—	-2.2
Total	5	9	38	.191	58	44	34-2	0	371	483	388	20	31	186	115	6.28	60	.307	.391	166	.211	1	88	-107	—	-9.4
Baker, Neal	Neal Vernon; B4.30.1904 Harlingen TX; D1.5.1982 Houston TX; BR/TR/6´1˝/175; d6.26; Col Texas																									
1927	Phi A	0	0	ø	5	2	0	0	17.1	27	17	2	0	7	3	5.71	75	.365	.420	6	.167	-0	98	-4	—	-0.2
Baker, Norm	Norman Leslie; B10.14.1863 Philadelphia PA; D2.20.1949 Hurffville NJ; d5.21																									
1883	Pit AA	0	2	.000	3	3	2	0	19	24	16	0	—	11	5	3.32	98	.289	.372	12	.000	-2*	106	-2	—	-0.3
1885	Lou AA	13	12	.520	25	24	24-1	0	217	210	142	3	10	69	79	3.40	95	.241	.304	87	.207	-1	88	1	—	0.0
1890	Bal AA	1	1	.500	2	2	2	0	17	16	9	0	0	6	10	3.71	109	.242	.306	7	.000	-1	83	1	—	0.0
Total	3	14	15	.483	30	29	28-1	0	253	250	167	3	10	86	94	3.42	96	.245	.309	106	.170	-3	90	0	—	-0.3
Baker, Scott	Scott; B5.18.1970 San Jose CA; BL/TL/6´2˝/175; [StLN90 7/195]; d7.17; Col Taft (CA) JC																									
1995	Oak A	0	0	ø	1	0	0	0-0	3.2	5	4	0	1	5-0	3	9.82	46	.333	.500	0	ø	0	—	-2	0	-0.1
Baker, Steve	Steven Byrne; B8.30.1956 Eugene OR; BR/TR/6´0˝/(185–200); d5.25; Col Oregon																									
1978	Det A	2	4	.333	15	10	0	0-1	63.1	66	37	6	0	42-0	39	4.55	86	.276	.379	0	ø	0	76	-5	0	-0.5
1979	Det A	1	7	.125	21	12	0	1-1	84	97	63	13	6	51-2	54	6.64	66	.296	.396	0	ø	0	106	-19	0	-1.6
1982	Oak A	1	1	.500	5	3	0	0-0	25.2	30	14	3	0	4-0	14	4.56	87	.288	.312	0	ø	0	84	-2	0	-0.1
1983	Oak A	3	3	.500	35	1	0	5-6	54	59	32	4	2	26-4	23	4.33	90	.282	.363	0	ø	0	140	-4	0	-0.5
	StL N	0	1	.000	8	0	0	0-0	10	10	4	0	1	4-1	1	1.80	203	.286	.366	0	ø	0	—	1	0	0.1
Total	4	7	16	.304	84	26	0	6-8	237	262	150	26	9	127-7	131	5.13	79	.286	.374	0	ø	0	95	-29	0	-2.6
Baker, Tom	Thomas Calvin "Rattlesnake"; B6.11.1913 Nursery TX; D1.3.1991 Fort Worth TX; BR/TR/6´1.5˝/180; d8.15																									
1935	Bro N	1	0	1.000	11	1	1	0	42	48	25	2	0	20	10	4.29	93	.277	.352	19	.474	4	85	-2	—	0.2
1936	Bro N	1	8	.111	35	8	2	2	87.2	98	56	3	2	48	35	4.72	88	.288	.379	30	.233	1*	85	-6	—	-0.4
1937	Bro N	0	1	.000	7	0	0	0	8.1	14	10	1	1	5	2	8.64	47	.378	.465	0	ø	0	—	-4	—	-0.4
	NY N	1	0	1.000	13	0	0	0	31	30	15	0	0	16	11	4.06	96	.268	.359	9	.222	-0	—	0	—	0.0
	Year	1	1	.500	20	0	0	0	39.1	44	25	1	1	21	13	5.03	78	.295	.386	9	.222	-0	—	-4	—	-0.4
1938	NY N	0	0	ø	2	0	0	0	4	5	3	0	0	3	0	6.75	56	.313	.421	0	ø	0	—	-1	—	0.0
Total	4	3	9	.250	68	9	3	2	173	195	109	6	3	92	58	4.73	85	.288	.375	58	.310	5	87	-13	—	-0.6
Baker, Tom	Thomas Henry; B5.6.1934 Port Townsend WA; D3.9.1980 Port Townsend WA; BL/TL/6´0˝/195; d8.2																									
1963	Chi N	0	1	.000	10	1	0	0	18	20	12	2	1	7-0	14	3.00	117	.282	.346	3	.000	-0	25	-1	0	-0.1
Baker, Scott	Timothy Scott; B9.19.1981 Shreveport LA; BR/TR/6´4˝/(210–215); [MinA03 2/58]; d5.7; Col Oklahoma St.																									
2005	Min A	3	3	.500	10	9	0	0-0	53.2	48	21	5	0	14-0	32	3.35	131	.241	.288	0	ø	0	82	6	0	0.6
2006	Min A	5	8	.385	16	16	0	0-0	83.1	114	63	17	3	16-1	62	6.37	72	.324	.355	3	.000	-0	89	-16	0	-2.1
Total	2	8	11	.421	26	25	0	0-0	137	162	84	22	3	30-1	94	5.19	87	.294	.331	3	.000	-0	87	-10	0	-1.5
Balas, Mike	Mitchell Francis (b Mitchell Francis Balaski); B5.9.1910 Lowell MA; D10.15.1996 Westford MA; BR/TR/6´0˝/195; d4.27																									
1938	Bos N	0	0	ø	1	0	0	0	1.1	3	3	0	0	0	0	6.75	51	.375	.375	0	ø	0	—	-1	—	-0.1
Baldschun, Jack	Jack Edward; B10.16.1936 Greenville OH; BR/TR/6´0˝/(175–195); d4.28; Col Miami–Ohio																									
1961	Phi N	5	3	.625	**65**	0	0	3	99.2	90	53	7	5	49-11	59	3.88	105	.243	.337	11-0-1	.000	-1	—	0	0	-0.1
1962	Phi N	12	7	.632	67	0	0	13	112.2	95	41	6	2	58-9	95	2.96	131	.231	.326	16-0-2	.063	-1	—	12	0	2.1
1963	Phi N	11	7	.611	65	0	0	16	113.2	99	37	7	3	42-10	89	2.30	141	.232	.304	20-0-1	.000	-2	—	10	0	1.9
1964	Phi N	6	9	.400	71	0	0	21	118.1	111	50	8	3	40-7	96	3.12	111	.246	.310	16-0-2	.250	1	—	4	0	0.8
1965	Phi N	5	8	.385	65	0	0	6	99	102	53	4	4	42-12	81	3.82	91	.273	.347	7-0-2	.000	-1	—	-6	0	-0.9
1966	Cin N	1	5	.167	42	0	0	0	57.1	71	35	4	4	25-8	44	5.49	71	.318	.395	3	.333	0	—	-8	0	-0.8
1967	Cin N	0	0	ø	9	0	0	0	13	15	6	0	0	9-3	12	4.15	90	.283	.387	1	.000	-0	—	0	0	0.0
1969	SD N	7	2	.778	61	0	0	1-1	77	80	45	7	2	29-6	67	4.79	75	.264	.331	4	.250	0	—	-10	0	-1.1
1970	SD N	1	0	1.000	12	0	0	0-1	13.1	24	15	2	0	4-1	12	10.13	40	.375	.406	0	ø	0	—	-8	0	-0.6
Total	9	48	41	.539	457	0	0	60-2	704	687	335	45	23	298-67	555	3.69	99	.257	.334	78-0-8	.090	-3	—	-6	0	1.3
Baldwin, Lady	Charles B.; B4.8.1859 Oramel NY; D3.7.1937 Hastings MI; BR/TL/5´11˝/160; d9.30																									
1884	Mil U	1	1	.500	2	2	2	0	17	7	5	0	—	1	21	2.65	50	.117	.131	27	.222	0*	128	-3	—	-0.3
1885	Det N	11	9	.550	21	20	19-1	1	179.1	137	84	2	—	28	135	1.86	153	**.197**	**.228**	124	.242	3*	112	16	—	1.9
1886	Det N	**42**	13	.764	56	56	55-**7**	0	487	371	194	11	—	100	**323**	2.24	149	**.202**	**.243**	204	.201	3*	124	55	—	5.7
1887	†Det N	13	10	.565	24	24	24-1	0	211	225	136	8	5	61	60	3.84	106	.269	.323	85	.271	3	102	3	—	0.5
1888	Det N	3	3	.500	6	6	5	0	53	76	50	5	1	15	26	5.43	51	.322	.365	23	.261	2	172	-14	—	-1.2
1890	Bro N	1	0	1.000	2	1	0	0	7.2	15	6	0	0	4	4	7.04	49	.395	.452	3	.000	-0	312	-2	—	-0.2
	Buf P	2	5	.286	7	7	7	0	62	90	72	5	3	24	13	4.50	91	.325	.385	28	.286	1	85	-11	—	-0.7
Total	6	73	41	.640	118	116	112-9	1	1017	921	547	31	9	233	582	2.85	119	.232	.276	494	.231	11	117	44	—	5.7
Baldwin, Dave	David George; B3.30.1938 Tucson AZ; BR/TR/6´2˝/(175–205); d9.6; Col Arizona																									
1966	Was A	0	0	ø	4	0	0	0	7	8	3	0	0	1-0	4	3.86	90	.267	.290	0	ø	0	—	0	0	0.0
1967	Was A	2	4	.333	58	0	0	12	68.2	53	19	2	4	20-4	52	1.70	186	.215	.282	4	.000	-0	—	10	0	1.2
1968	Was A	0	2	.000	40	0	0	5	42	40	19	7	0	12-0	30	4.07	72	.260	.310	2	.000	0	—	-4	0	-0.3
1969	Was A	2	4	.333	43	0	0	4-0	66.2	57	31	4	5	34-2	51	4.05	87	.236	.337	7	.000	-1	—	-3	0	-0.4
1970	Mil A	2	1	.667	28	0	0	1-2	35.1	25	11	4	0	18-6	26	2.55	148	.205	.307	2	.500	0	—	5	25	0.6
1973	Chi A	0	0	ø	3	0	0	0-0	5	7	2	0	0	4-1	1	3.60	110	.368	.478	0	ø	0	—	0	0	0.0
Total	6	6	11	.353	176	0	0	22-2	224.2	190	85	17	9	89-13	164	3.08	108	.234	.313	15	.067	-1	—	8	25	1.1
Baldwin, Harry	Howard Edward; B6.3.1900 Baltimore MD; D1.23.1958 Baltimore MD; BR/TR/5´11˝/160; d5.4																									
1924	†NY N	3	1	.750	10	2	1	0	33.2	42	18	5	0	11	5	4.28	86	.309	.361	11-0-1	.364	1*	104	-2	—	-0.2
1925	NY N	0	0	ø	1	0	0	0	1	3	2	0	0	1	0	9.00	45	.500	.571	0	ø	0	—	-1	—	0.0
Total	2	3	1	.750	11	2	1	0	34.2	45	20	5	0	12	5	4.41	83	.317	.370	11-0-1	.364	1	104	-3	—	-0.2
Baldwin, James	James; B7.15.1971 Pinehurst NC; BR/TR/6´3˝/(210–265); [ChiA90 4/105]; d4.30																									
1995	Chi A	0	1	.000	6	4	0	0-0	14.2	32	22	6	0	9-1	10	12.89	35	.444	.506	0	ø	0	213	-14	0	-0.8
1996	Chi A	11	6	.647	28	28	0	0-0	169	168	88	24	4	57-3	127	4.42	108	.257	.319	0	ø	0	100	7	0	0.6
1997	Chi A	12	15	.444	32	32	1	0-0	200	205	128	19	5	83-3	140	5.27	84	.262	.334	3-0-1	.000	-0	116	-19	0	-2.1
1998	Chi A	13	6	.684	37	24	1	0-1	159	176	103	18	10	60-2	108	5.32	86	.278	.347	2	.000	-0	102	-13	0	-1.4
1999	Chi A	12	13	.480	35	33	1	0-0	199.1	219	119	34	7	81-1	123	5.10	97	.278	.348	2	.500	1	89	-1	0	-0.1
2000	†Chi A★	14	7	.667	29	28	2-1	0-0	178	185	96	34	8	59-3	116	4.65	109	.272	.335	4-0-1	.000	-0	103	11	0	1.1
2001	Chi A	7	5	.583	17	16	2-1	0-0	95.2	109	56	15	4	38-0	42	4.61	101	.286	.353	2	.000	-0	97	0	20	0.0
	LA N	3	6	.333	12	12	0	0-0	79.1	82	39	10	3	25-1	53	4.20	98	.274	.334	26-0-1	.077	-1	77	0	0	-0.2
2002	Sea A	7	10	.412	30	23	0	0-0	150	179	95	26	7	49-2	88	5.28	82	.298	.357	2	.500	0	110	-17	0	-1.6
2003	Min A	0	1	.000	10	0	0	1-1	15	21	10	6	0	4-1	7	5.40	83	.333	.362	0	ø	0	—	-2	0	-0.1
2004	NY N	0	2	.000	2	2	0	0-0	6	13	10	3	1	5-1	1	15.00	29	.448	.543	2	.000	-0	130	-7	0	-1.0
2005	Bal A	0	0	ø	12	0	0	0-0	22.1	17	4	2	1	3-0	12	1.61	273	.218	.253	1	.000	-0	—	7	0	0.3
	Tex A	0	2	.000	8	0	0	1-0	17.1	18	10	3	1	7-1	9	5.19	88	.273	.342	0	ø	0	—	-1	0	-0.1
	Bal A	0	0	ø	8	0	0	0-0	17	19	14	3	1	6-0	8	5.29	83	.275	.333	0	ø	0	—	-3	0	-0.2
	Year	0	2	.000	28	0	0	1-0	56.2	54	28	8	3	16-1	29	3.81	117	.254	.308	1	.000	-0	—	3	0	0.0
Total	11	79	74	.516	266	202	7-2	2-2	1322.2	1443	794	203	52	486-19	844	5.01	92	.278	.343	44-0-3	.091	-1	104	-52	20	-5.6

YEAR	TM LG	W	L	PCT	G	GS	CG-SHO	SV-BS	IP	H	R	HR	HB	BB-IB	SO	ERA	AERA	OAV	OOB	AB-HR-SH	AVG	PB	SUP	APR	DL	PW
BALDWIN, MARK	Marcus Elmore "Fido"; B10.29.1863 Pittsburgh PA; D11.10.1929 Pittsburgh PA; BR/TR/6´0˝/190; d5.2; Col Penn St.																									
1887	Chi N	18	17	.514	40	39	35-1	**1**	334	329	218	22	17	122	164	3.40	132	.248	.319	139-4	.187	-4*	83	33	—	2.2
1888	Chi N	13	15	.464	30	30	27-2	0	251	241	137	13	13	99	157	2.76	110	.249	.327	106-1	.151	-1	100	5	—	0.4
1889	Col AA	27	34	.443	**63**	**59**	54-6	1	**513.2**	458	358	9	20	274	**368**	3.61	100	.231	.331	208-2	.188	1*	92	-10	—	-0.9
1890	Chi P	**33**	24	.579	**58**	**56**	**53**-1	0	**492**	494	321	10	16	249	**206**	3.35	130	.250	.339	212-1	.212	-1	95	49	—	4.1
1891	Pit N	21	28	.429	53	51	48-2	1	437.2	385	278	10	23	227	197	2.76	119	.227	.327	177-1	.153	-3	94	21	—	1.6
1892	Pit N	26	27	.491	56	53	45	0	440.1	447	272	11	22	194	157	3.47	95	.253	.334	178-1	.101	-12	91	-3	—	-1.5
1893	Pit N	0	0	ø	1	1	0	0	2.1	6	4	0	0	1	0	11.57	39	.462	.500	1	.000	-0	61	-2	—	-0.1
	NY N	16	20	.444	45	39	33-2	2	331.1	335	228	6	12	141	100	4.10	114	.255	.332	134	.127	-11	87	18	—	0.4
	Year	16	20	.444	46	40	33-2	**2**	333.2	341	232	6	12	142	100	4.15	112	.257	.334	135	.126	-11	87	22	—	0.3
Total	7	154	165	.483	346	328	295-14	5	2802.1	2695	1816	81	123	1307	1349	3.37	113	.244	.331	1155-10	.163	-31	91	111	—	6.2
BALDWIN, O. F.	Orson F.; B11.3.1881 Carson City MI; D2.16.1942 Los Angeles CA; TR/?/185; d9.6																									
1908	StL N	1	3	.250	4	4	0	0	14.2	16	10	0	3	11	5	6.14	38	.302	.448	6	.000	-1	52	-4	—	-1.0
BALDWIN, RICK	Rickey Alan; B6.1.1953 Fresno CA; BL/TR/6´3˝/175; [NYN71 9/210]; d4.10																									
1975	NY N	3	5	.375	54	0	0	6-5	97.1	97	39	4	4	34-4	54	3.33	106	.263	.329	15-0-2	.200	0	—	3	0	0.3
1976	NY N	0	0	ø	11	0	0	0-0	22.2	14	6	0	2	10-1	9	2.38	141	.189	.292	3	.333	0	—	3	0	0.2
1977	NY N	1	2	.333	40	0	0	1-1	62.2	62	32	6	5	31-9	23	4.45	85	.265	.360	4	.500	1	—	-4	0	-0.1
Total	3	4	7	.364	105	0	0	7-6	182.2	173	77	10	11	75-14	86	3.60	100	.256	.336	22-0-2	.273	1	—	2	0	0.4
BALE, JOHN	John Robert; B5.22.1974 Cheverly MD; BL/TL/6´4˝/(195–210); [TorA96 5/129]; d9.30; Col Southern Mississippi																									
1999	Tor A	0	0	ø	1	0	0	0-0	2	2	3	1	0	2-0	4	13.50	36	.250	.400	0	ø	0	—	-2	0	-0.1
2000	Tor A	0	0	ø	2	0	0	0-0	3.2	5	7	1	2	3-0	6	14.73	34	.313	.455	0	ø	0	—	-4	0	-0.2
2001	Bal A	1	0	1.000	14	0	0	0-0	26.2	18	14	2	1	17-0	21	3.04	142	.194	.319	0	ø	0	—	2	0	0.1
2003	Cin N	1	2	.333	10	9	0	0-0	46.1	50	24	7	2	12-2	37	4.47	93	.281	.330	17	.118	-1	65	-1	0	-0.1
Total	4	2	2	.500	27	9	0	0-0	78.2	75	48	11	5	34-2	68	4.69	91	.254	.336	17	.118	-1	65	-5	0	-0.3
BALFOUR, GRANT	Grant Robert; B12.30.1977 Sydney, New South Wales, Australia; BR/TR/6´2˝/(170–190); d7.22; [DL 2006 Cin N 182]																									
2001	Min A	0	0	ø	2	0	0	0-0	2.2	3	4	2	0	3-0	2	13.50	35	.333	.462	0	ø	0	—	-2	0	-0.1
2003	Min A	1	0	1.000	17	1	0	0-1	26	23	12	4	0	14-2	30	4.15	108	.235	.327	0	ø	0	123	1	0	0.1
2004	†Min A	4	1	.800	36	0	0	0-1	39.1	35	19	4	2	21-1	42	4.35	106	.238	.341	0	ø	0	—	2	55	0.2
Total	3	5	1	.833	55	1	0	0-2	68	61	35	10	2	38-3	74	4.63	99	.240	.341	0	ø	0	123	1	237	0.2
BALLARD, JEFF	Jeffrey Scott; B8.13.1963 Billings MT; BL/TL/6´2˝/(198–210); [BalA85 7/177]; d5.9; Col Stanford																									
1987	Bal A	2	8	.200	14	14	0	0-0	69.2	100	60	15	0	35-1	27	6.59	67	.344	.413	0	ø	0	117	-19	0	-2.1
1988	Bal A	8	12	.400	25	25	6-1	0-0	153.1	167	83	15	6	42-2	41	4.40	89	.278	.330	0	ø	0	95	-8	0	-1.0
1989	Bal A	18	8	.692	35	35	4-1	0-0	215.1	240	95	16	4	57-5	62	3.43	111	.287	.334	0	ø	0	134	6	0	0.9
1990	Bal A	2	11	.154	44	17	0	0-0	133.1	152	79	22	3	42-6	50	4.93	78	.289	.344	0	ø	0	94	-17	0	-1.5
1991	Bal A	6	12	.333	26	22	0	0-0	123.2	153	91	16	2	28-2	37	5.60	71	.302	.340	0	ø	0	88	-27	0	-3.4
1993	Pit N	4	1	.800	25	5	0	0-0	53.2	70	31	3	2	15-3	16	4.86	84	.332	.380	11-0-1	.364	1	128	-5	0	-0.2
1994	Pit N	1	1	.500	28	0	0	2-3	24.1	32	19	5	1	10-3	11	6.66	66	.323	.387	2	.500	0	—	-5	0	-0.4
Total	7	41	53	.436	197	118	10-2	2-3	773.1	914	458	92	18	229-22	244	4.71	84	.298	.348	13-0-1	.385	2	109	-75	0	-7.7
BALLER, JAY	Jay Scot; B10.6.1960 Stayton OR; BR/TR/6´7˝/(215–225); [PhiN79 4/98]; d9.19																									
1982	Phi N	0	0	ø	4	1	0	0-0	8	7	4	1	1	2-0	7	3.38	109	.226	.294	0	ø	0	119	0	0	0.0
1985	Chi N	2	3	.400	20	4	0	1-0	52	52	21	8	1	17-7	31	3.46	116	.260	.320	8-0-1	.000	-1	50	3	0	0.2
1986	Chi N	2	4	.333	36	0	0	5-5	53.2	58	37	7	2	28-4	42	5.37	76	.275	.361	5-0-1	.000	-1	—	-8	0	-1.1
1987	Chi N	0	1	.000	23	0	0	0-1	29.1	38	22	4	0	20-2	27	6.75	64	.325	.423	1	1.000	0	—	-7	0	-0.3
1990	KC A	0	1	.000	3	0	0	0-1	2.1	4	4	1	1	2-1	1	15.43	25	.364	.500	0	ø	0	—	-3	0	-0.5
1992	Phi N	0	0	ø	8	0	0	0-0	11	10	10	5	0	10-0	9	8.18	43	.250	.392	0	ø	0	—	-5	0	-0.3
Total	6	4	9	.308	94	5	0	6-7	156.1	169	98	26	5	79-14	117	5.24	77	.277	.362	14-0-2	.071	-1	62	-20	0	-2.0
BALLINGER, MARK	Mark Alan; B1.31.1949 Glendale CA; BR/TR/6´6˝/205; [CleA67 2/31]; d8.6																									
1971	Cle A	1	2	.333	18	0	0	0-0	34.2	30	21	3	1	13-1	25	4.67	83	.233	.303	5	.200	-0	—	-3	0	-0.3
BALLOU, WIN	Noble Winfred; B11.30.1897 Mount Morgan KY; D1.29.1963 San Francisco CA; BR/TR/5´10.5˝/170; d8.24; Col Eastern Kentucky																									
1925	†Was A	1	1	.500	10	1	1	0	27.2	38	17	1	0	13	13	4.55	93	.342	.411	7	.143	-0	80	-1	—	-0.1
1926	StL A	11	10	.524	43	14	5	2	154	186	99	12	4	71	59	4.79	90	.311	.387	42-1-4	.048	-3	83	-9	—	-1.2
1927	StL A	5	6	.455	21	11	4	0	90.1	105	56	4	1	46	17	4.78	91	.309	.393	28-0-1	.036	-4	66	-3	—	-0.7
1929	Bro N	2	3	.400	25	2	0	0	57.2	69	52	5	0	38	20	6.71	69	.304	.404	16	.063	-2	76	-14	—	-1.1
Total	4	19	20	.487	99	28	10	2	329.2	398	224	22	5	168	109	5.11	86	.312	.394	93-1-5	.054	-9	75	-27	—	-3.1
BALSAMO, TONY	Anthony Fred; B11.21.1937 Brooklyn NY; BR/TR/6´2˝/185; d4.14; Col Fordham																									
1962	Chi N	0	1	.000	18	0	0	0	29.1	34	22	1	1	20-2	27	6.44	64	.293	.396	5	.200	0	—	-6	0	-0.2
BAMBERGER, GEORGE	George Irvin; B8.1.1923 Staten Island NY; D4.4.2004 North Redington Beach FL; BR/TR/6´0˝/(175–180); d4.19; M7/C10																									
1951	NY N	0	0	ø	2	0	0	0	2	4	4	2	0	2	1	18.00	22	.444	.545	0	ø	0	—	-3	0	-0.1
1952	NY N	0	0	ø	5	0	0	0	4	6	4	1	0	6	0	9.00	41	.353	.522	0	ø	0*	—	-2	0	-0.1
1959	Bal A	0	0	ø	3	1	0	1	8.1	15	7	1	0	2-0	2	7.56	50	.405	.436	2	.000	-0	163	-3	0	-0.2
Total	3	0	0	ø	10	1	0	1	14.1	25	15	4	0	10-0	3	9.42	40	.397	.479	2	.000	-0	163	-8	0	-0.4
BANE, EDDIE	Edward Norman; B3.22.1952 Chicago IL; BR/TL/5´9˝/(160–165); [MinA73 1/11]; d7.4; Col Arizona St.																									
1973	Min A	0	5	.000	23	6	0	2-2	60.1	62	40	5	2	30-0	42	4.92	81	.270	.353	0	ø	0	79	-7	0	-0.5
1975	Min A	3	1	.750	4	4	0	0-0	28.1	28	11	2	1	15-0	14	2.86	134	.262	.355	0	ø	0	81	3	0	0.3
1976	Min A	4	7	.364	17	15	1	0-0	79.1	92	52	6	0	39-2	24	5.11	70	.290	.367	0	ø	0*	134	-13	0	-1.7
Total	3	7	13	.350	44	25	1	2-2	168	182	103	13	3	84-2	80	4.66	81	.278	.360	0	ø	0	110	-17	0	-1.9
BANEY, DICK	Richard Lee; B11.1.1946 Fullerton CA; BR/TR/6´0˝/(185–200); [BosA66*S1/9]; d7.11																									
1969	Sea A	1	0	1.000	9	1	0	0-0	18.2	21	8	2	0	7-1	9	3.86	94	.292	.346	2-0-1	.000	-0	97	0	0	0.0
1973	Cin N	2	1	.667	11	1	0	2-0	30.2	26	10	1	4	6-1	17	2.93	118	.234	.298	9-0-1	.222	1	51	2	0	0.3
1974	Cin N	1	0	1.000	22	1	0	1-0	41	51	27	4	0	17-2	12	5.49	64	.305	.366	5-0-1	.000	-1	175	-9	0	-0.6
Total	3	4	1	.800	42	3	0	3-0	90.1	98	45	7	4	30-4	38	4.28	82	.280	.340	16-0-3	.125	-0	108	-7	0	-0.3
BANKHEAD, DAN	Daniel Robert; B5.3.1920 Empire AL; D5.2.1976 Houston TX; BR/TR/6´1˝/184; d8.26; Negro Lg 1941–48 Mil 1943–45																									
1947	†Bro N	0	0	ø	4	0	0	1	10	15	8	1	1	8	6	7.20	57	.341	.453	4-1-0	.250	1*	—	-3	0	0.0
1950	Bro N	9	4	.692	41	12	2-1	3	129.1	119	84	16	2	88	96	5.50	75	.252	.371	39	.231	1	128	-19	0	-1.7
1951	Bro N	0	1	.000	7	1	0	0	14	27	24	5	0	14	9	15.43	25	.422	.526	2	.000	-0*	157	-17	0	-1.0
Total	3	9	5	.643	52	13	2-1	4	153.1	161	116	22	3	110	111	6.52	63	.277	.395	45-1-0	.222	2	130	-39	0	-2.7
BANKHEAD, SCOTT	Michael Scott; B7.31.1963 Raleigh NC; BR/TR/5´10˝/(175–185); [KCA84 1/16]; d5.25; Col North Carolina																									
1986	KC A	8	9	.471	24	17	0	0-0	121	121	66	14	3	37-7	94	4.61	93	.259	.314	0	ø	0	96	-3	0	-0.5
1987	Sea A	9	8	.529	27	25	2	0-0	149.1	168	96	35	3	37-0	95	5.42	87	.283	.326	0	ø	0	98	-9	19	-1.0
1988	Sea A	7	9	.438	21	21	2-1	0-0	135	115	53	8	1	38-5	102	3.07	136	.224	.278	0	ø	0	66	15	40	1.7
1989	Sea A	14	6	.700	33	33	3-2	0-0	210.1	187	84	19	3	63-1	140	3.34	121	.239	.295	0	ø	0	101	18	0	1.5
1990	Sea A	0	2	.000	4	4	0	0-0	13	18	16	2	0	7-0	10	11.08	36	.333	.397	0	ø	0	132	-9	155	-1.1
1991	Sea A	3	6	.333	17	9	0	0-0	60.2	73	35	8	2	21-2	28	4.90	85	.297	.354	0	ø	0	74	-5	101	-0.6
1992	Cin N	10	4	.714	54	0	0	1-4	70.2	57	26	4	3	29-5	53	2.93	123	.218	.301	9-0-2	.222	0	—	5	0	0.9
1993	Bos A	2	1	.667	40	0	0	0-2	64.1	59	28	7	0	29-3	47	3.50	133	.250	.327	0	ø	0	—	8	0	0.3
1994	Bos A	3	2	.600	27	0	0	0-0	37.2	34	21	5	0	12-3	25	4.54	111	.239	.295	0	ø	0	—	2	53	0.2
1995	NY A	1	1	.500	20	1	0	0-0	39	44	26	9	0	16-0	20	6.00	77	.278	.343	0	ø	0	141	-5	0	-0.3
Total	10	57	48	.543	267	110	7-3	1-6	901	876	451	111	15	289-26	614	4.18	103	.254	.311	9-0-2	.222	0	92	17	368	1.1

YEAR	TM LG	W	L	PCT	G	GS	CG-SHO	SV-BS	IP	H	R	HR	HB	BB-IB	SO	ERA	AERA	OAV	OOB	AB-HR-SH	AVG	PB	SUP	APR	DL	PW
Banks, Bill	William John (b William John Yerrick); B2.26.1874 Danville PA; D9.8.1936 Danville PA; BR/TR/5´11˝/150; d9.27																									
1895	Bos N	1	0	1.000	1	1	1	0	7	7	2	0	0	4	4	0.00	ø	.259	.355	3	.000	-1	196	3	—	0.3
1896	Bos N	0	3	.000	4	3	2	0	23	42	31	2	2	13	6	10.57	43	.389	.463	11	.273	0	73	-11	—	-1.0
Total	2	1	3	.250	5	4	3	0	30	49	33	2	2	17	10	8.10	58	.363	.442	14	.214	-1	107	-8	—	-0.7
Banks, Willie	Willie Anthony; B2.27.1969 Jersey City NJ; BR/TR/6´1˝/(190–202); [MinA87 1/3]; d7.31																									
1991	Min A	1	1	.500	5	3	0	0-0	17.1	21	15	1	0	12-0	16	5.71	75	.288	.388	0	ø	0	114	-4	0	-0.4
1992	Min A	4	4	.500	16	12	0	0-0	71	80	46	6	2	37-0	37	5.70	72	.288	.370	0	ø	0	86	-11	0	-1.1
1993	Min A	11	12	.478	31	30	0	0-0	171.1	186	91	17	3	78-2	138	4.04	109	.280	.356	0	ø	0	97	4	0	0.4
1994	Chi N	8	12	.400	23	23	1-1	0-0	138.1	139	88	16	2	56-3	91	5.40	78	.261	.332	41-0-7	.122	-1	79	-17	0	-2.3
1995	Chi N	0	1	.000	10	0	0	0-1	11.2	27	23	5	0	12-4	9	15.43	27	.458	.542	1	.000	-0	—	-15	0	-1.1
	LA N	0	2	.000	6	6	0	0-0	29	36	21	2	1	16-2	23	4.03	96	.303	.387	8-0-1	.125	0	136	-3	0	-0.2
	Fla N	2	3	.400	9	9	0	0-0	50	43	27	7	1	30-1	30	4.32	99	.235	.344	17	.353	2*	65	0	0	0.1
	Year	2	6	.250	25	15	0	0-1	90.2	106	71	14	2	58-7	62	5.66	73	.294	.392	26-0-1	.269	2	92	-19	0	-1.2
1997	NY A	3	0	1.000	5	1	0	0-1	14	9	3	0	1	6-0	8	1.93	231	.188	.291	0	ø	0	83	4	0	0.9
1998	NY A	1	1	.500	9	0	0	0-0	14.1	20	16	4	1	12-2	8	10.05	44	.323	.440	0	ø	0	—	-9	0	-1.0
	Ari N	1	2	.333	33	0	0	1-1	43.2	34	21	2	1	25-2	32	3.09	138	.217	.326	1	.000	-0	—	4	0	0.2
2001	Bos A	0	0	ø	5	0	0	0-0	10.2	5	4	0	0	4-0	10	0.84	526	.132	.214	0	ø	0	—	3	0	0.1
2002	Bos A	2	1	.667	29	0	0	1-0	39	32	15	5	3	14-0	26	3.23	139	.222	.302	0	ø	0	—	6	0	0.4
Total	9	33	39	.458	181	84	1-1	2-3	610.1	632	370	65	15	302-16	428	4.75	90	.268	.353	68-0-8	.176	1	90	-38	0	-4.0
Bannister, Brian	Brian P.; B2.28.1981 Scottsdale AZ; BR/TR/6´2˝/200; [NYN03 7/199]; d4.5; f–Floyd; Col USC																									
2006	NY N	2	1	.667	8	6	0	0-0	38	34	18	4	2	22-2	19	4.26	103	.239	.341	12-0-1	.333	2	119	1	120	0.3
Bannister, Floyd	Floyd Franklin; B6.10.1955 Pierre SD; BL/TL/6´1˝/(188–195); [HouN76 1/1]; d4.19; s–Brian; Col Arizona St.																									
1977	Hou N	8	9	.471	24	23	4-1	0-0	142.2	138	70	11	4	68-1	112	4.04	90	.254	.339	48-0-6	.188	0	143	-6	27	-0.7
1978	Hou N	3	9	.250	28	16	2-2	0-0	110.1	120	59	13	1	63-4	94	4.81	69	.280	.372	31-0-5	.161	0	79	-17	0	-1.7
1979	Sea A	10	15	.400	30	30	6-2	0-0	182.1	185	92	25	4	68-4	115	4.05	108	.260	.327	0	ø	0	81	6	0	0.7
1980	Sea A	9	13	.409	32	32	8	0-0	217.2	200	96	24	2	66-6	155	3.47	120	.239	.295	0	ø	0	72	15	0	1.4
1981	Sea A	9	9	.500	21	20	5-2	0-0	121.1	128	62	14	3	39-0	85	4.45	87	.268	.327	0	ø	0	80	-5	21	-0.7
1982	Sea A★	12	13	.480	35	35	5-3	0-0	247	225	112	32	3	77-0	**209**	3.43	125	.243	.301	0	ø	0	98	19	0	1.8
1983	†Chi A	16	10	.615	34	34	5-2	0-0	217.1	191	88	19	2	71-3	193	3.35	126	.233	.294	0	ø	0	102	21	0	2.3
1984	Chi A	14	11	.560	34	33	4	0-0	218	211	127	30	6	80-2	152	4.83	87	.252	.318	1	.000	-0	100	-14	0	-1.5
1985	Chi A	10	14	.417	34	34	4-1	0-0	210.2	211	121	30	4	100-5	198	4.87	89	.261	.343	0	ø	0	95	-10	0	-1.0
1986	Chi A	10	14	.417	28	27	6-1	0-0	165.1	162	81	17	2	48-0	92	3.54	123	.259	.311	0	ø	0	69	10	29	1.3
1987	Chi A	16	11	.593	34	34	11-2	0-0	228.2	216	100	38	0	49-0	124	3.58	129	.246	.285	0	ø	0	89	25	0	2.5
1988	KC A	12	13	.480	31	31	2	0-0	189.1	182	102	22	5	68-6	113	4.33	93	.248	.316	0	ø	0	92	-7	0	-0.8
1989	KC A	4	1	.800	14	14	0	0-0	75.1	87	40	8	1	18-1	35	4.66	83	.290	.330	0	ø	0	112	-5	112	-0.3
1991	Cal A	0	0	ø	16	0	0	0-0	25	25	12	5	0	10-1	16	3.96	104	.266	.337	0	ø	0	—	0	31	0.0
1992	Tex A	1	1	.500	36	0	0	0-1	37	39	27	3	3	21-6	30	6.32	60	.281	.371	0	ø	0	—	-9	0	-0.5
Total	15	134	143	.484	431	363	62-16	0-1	2388	2320	1189	291	40	846-39	1723	4.06	102	.253	.317	80-0-11	.175	0	92	23	220	2.8
Bannon, Jimmy	James Henry "Foxy Grandpa"; B5.5.1871 Amesbury MA; D3.24.1948 Glen Rock NJ; BR/TR/5´5˝/160; d6.15; b–Tom; Col Holy Cross; ▲																									
1893	StL N	0	1	.000	1	1	0	0	4	10	18	1	2	5	1	22.50	21	.455	.586	107	.336	0*	370	-9	—	-0.9
1894	Bos N	0	0	ø	1	0	0	0	2	4	3	1	0	1	0	0.00	ø	.400	.455	494-13-6	.336	0*	—	0	—	0.0
1895	Bos N	0	0	ø	1	0	0	0	3	4	2	0	0	2	1	6.00	85	.308	.400	493-6-12	.347	0*	—	0	—	0.0
Total	3	0	1	.000	3	1	0	0	9	18	23	2	2	8	2	12.00	42	.400	.509	1094-19-18	.341	1	370	-9	—	-0.9
Banta, Jack	Jackie Kay; B6.24.1925 Hutchinson KS; D9.17.2006 Hutchinson KS; BL/TR/6´2.5˝/175; d9.18																									
1947	Bro N	0	1	.000	3	1	0	0	7.2	7	6	1	1	4	3	7.04	59	.226	.333	2	.000	-0	149	-2	0	-0.2
1948	Bro N	0	1	.000	2	1	0	0	3.1	5	6	0	0	5	1	8.10	49	.385	.556	1	.000	-0	0	-3	0	-0.5
1949	†Bro N	10	6	.625	48	12	2-1	3	152.1	125	63	12	6	68	97	3.37	122	.223	.314	46-0-1	.109	-2	102	12	0	1.0
1950	Bro N	4	4	.500	16	5	1	2	41.1	39	22	2	3	36	15	4.35	94	.252	.402	12	.167	-0	134	-1	0	-0.3
Total	4	14	12	.538	69	19	3-1	5	204.2	176	97	15	10	113	116	3.78	108	.232	.339	61-0-1	.115	-2	108	6	0	0.0
Baptist, Travis	Travis Steven; B12.30.1971 Forest Grove OR; BL/TL/6´0˝/195; [TorA90 45/1175]; d8.1																									
1998	Min A	0	1	.000	13	0	0	0-0	27	34	18	5	0	11-1	11	5.67	85	.321	.366	0	ø	0	—	-2	0	-0.1
Barber, Brian	Brian Scott; B3.4.1973 Hamilton OH; BR/TR/6´1˝/(175–190); [StLN91 1/22]; d8.12; [DL 1997 StL N 63]																									
1995	StL N	2	1	.667	9	4	0	0-0	29.1	31	17	4	0	16-0	27	5.22	82	.279	.362	8	.125	-0	137	-2	0	-0.2
1996	StL N	0	0	ø	1	1	0	0-0	3	4	5	0	1	6-0	1	15.00	28	.364	.550	0	ø	0	128	-3	0	-0.2
1998	KC A	2	4	.333	8	8	0	0-0	42	45	28	5	1	13-1	24	6.00	81	.276	.328	0	ø	0	67	-4	0	-0.5
1999	KC A	1	3	.250	8	3	0	1-0	18.2	31	20	6	2	10-2	7	9.64	53	.383	.457	0-0-1	ø	0	122	-8	0	-1.4
Total	4	5	8	.385	26	16	0	1-0	93	111	70	15	4	45-3	59	6.77	69	.303	.377	8-0-1	.125	-0	98	-17	63	-2.3
Barber, Steve	Stephen David; B2.22.1938 Takoma Park MD; BL/TL/6´0˝/(190–200); d4.21																									
1960	Bal A	10	7	.588	36	27	6-1	2	181.2	148	78	10	3	113-1	112	3.22	118	.226	.340	54-0-4	.056	-4	90	10	0	0.5
1961	Bal A	18	12	.600	37	34	14-**8**	1	248.1	194	102	13	2	130-4	150	3.33	115	.218	.317	80-2-9	.162	2	95	15	0	2.2
1962	Bal A	9	6	.600	28	19	5-2	0	140.1	145	66	9	1	61-2	89	3.46	107	.262	.335	42-0-5	.071	-2	107	2	33	0.0
1963	Bal A✳	20	13	.606	39	36	11-2	0	258.2	253	99	12	4	92-10	180	2.75	126	.258	.323	87-1-5	.138	-0	92	17	0	2.2
1964	Bal A	9	13	.409	36	26	4	1	157	144	72	15	7	81-5	118	3.84	93	.248	.345	47-1-1	.149	1	80	-4	0	-0.3
1965	Bal A	15	10	.600	37	32	7-2	0	220.2	177	79	16	2	81-5	130	2.69	129	.224	.294	65-1-6	.077	-2	83	19	0	2.0
1966	Bal A☆	10	5	.667	25	22	5-3	0	133.1	104	38	6	3	49-1	91	2.30	145	.218	.294	44-0-7	.068	-3	124	16	19	1.5
1967	Bal A	4	9	.308	15	15	1-1	0	74.2	47	39	5	5	61-2	48	4.10	77	.185	.351	22-0-1	.091	-1	83	-9	0	-1.5
	NY A	6	9	.400	17	17	3-1	0	97.2	103	47	4	3	54-3	70	4.05	77	.278	.371	29-0-2	.172	1	75	-9	0	-1.2
	Year	10	18	.357	32	32	4-2	0	172.1	150	86	9	8	115-5	118	4.07	77	.240	.363	51-0-3	.137	1	79	-16	0	-2.7
1968	NY A	6	5	.545	20	19	3-1	0	128.1	127	63	7	3	64-4	87	3.23	90	.256	.342	39-0-2	.051	-1	116	-9	0	-0.8
1969	Sea A	4	7	.364	25	16	0	0-0	86.1	99	51	9	1	48-2	69	4.80	76	.292	.379	25-0-1	.200	1	100	-11	37	-1.1
1970	Chi N	0	1	.000	5	0	0	0-0	5.2	10	6	0	0	6-3	3	9.53	47	.417	.533	0	ø	0	—	-3	0	-0.4
	Atl N	0	1	.000	5	2	0	0-0	14.2	17	10	3	1	5-0	11	4.91	87	.288	.354	4	.250	0	115	-1	0	-0.1
	Year	0	2	.000	10	2	0	0-0	20.1	27	16	3	1	11-3	14	6.20	70	.325	.411	4	.250	0	113	-4	0	-0.5
1971	Atl N	3	1	.750	39	3	0	2-0	75	92	42	6	2	25-2	40	4.80	78	.301	.356	13	.154	-0	127	-7	0	-0.4
1972	Atl N	0	0	ø	5	0	0	0-0	15.2	18	10	1	1	6-0	6	5.74	66	.290	.357	5	.200	-0	—	-3	0	-0.1
	Cal A	4	4	.500	34	3	0	2-2	58	37	16	4	1	30-11	34	2.02	146	.188	.297	7-0-2	.143	1	60	6	0	0.9
1973	Cal A	3	2	.600	50	1	0	4-2	89.1	90	40	5	3	32-3	58	3.53	102	.265	.332	0	ø	0	75	1	0	0.0
1974	SF N	0	1	.000	13	0	0	1-0	13.2	13	12	0	0	12-1	13	5.27	72	.255	.391	0	ø	0	—	-3	0	-0.3
Total	15	121	106	.533	466	272	59-21	13-4	1999	1818	870	125	42	950-59	1309	3.36	105	.245	.332	563-5-45	.115	-6	94	27	89	3.1
Barber, Steve	Steven Lee; B3.13.1948 Grand Rapids MI; BR/TR/6´1˝/(190–198); d4.9; Col La Verne																									
1970	Min A	0	0	ø	18	0	0	2-0	27.1	26	14	1	2	18-2	14	4.61	80	.263	.377	2-0-1	.000	-0*	—	-2	0	-0.1
1971	Min A	1	0	1.000	4	2	0	0-0	11.2	8	9	2	0	13-1	4	6.17	57	.190	.382	5	.000	-1*	139	-3	0	-0.3
Total	2	1	0	1.000	22	2	0	2-0	39	34	23	3	2	31-3	18	5.08	72	.241	.379	7-0-1	.000	-1	139	-5	0	-0.4
Barberich, Frank	Frank Frederick; B2.3.1882 Newtown NY; D5.1.1965 Ocala FL; BB/TR/5´10.5˝/175; d9.17																									
1907	Bos N	1	1	.500	2	2	1	0	12.1	19	10	0	0	5	1	5.84	44	.358	.414	4-0-1	.000	-0	167	-4	—	-0.6
1910	Bos A	0	0	ø	2	0	0	0	5	7	6	0	0	2	0	7.20	35	.350	.409	1	.000	-0	—	-3	—	-0.1
Total	2	1	1	.500	4	2	1	0	17.1	26	16	0	0	7	1	6.23	41	.356	.412	5-0-1	.000	-1	167	-7	—	-0.7
Barcelo, Lorenzo	Lorenzo Antonio; B8.10.1977 San Pedro de Macoris, D.R.; BR/TR/6´4˝/(220–230); d7.22																									
2000	†Chi A	4	2	.667	22	1	0	0-1	39	34	17	5	0	9-1	26	3.69	137	.231	.274	0	ø	0	93	6	0	0.7
2001	Chi A	1	0	1.000	17	0	0	0-0	21	24	13	1	1	8-2	15	4.71	99	.282	.347	0	ø	0	—	-1	126	0.0
2002	Chi A	0	1	.000	4	0	0	0-0	6	9	6	1	0	1-0	1	9.00	50	.333	.357	0	ø	0	—	-3	0	-0.3
Total	3	5	3	.625	43	1	0	0-1	66	67	36	7	1	18-3	42	4.50	109	.259	.307	0	ø	0	93	2	126	0.4

YEAR	TM LG	W	L	PCT	G	GS	CG-SHO	SV-BS	IP	H	R	HR	HB	BB-IB	SO	ERA	AERA	OAV	OOB	AB-HR-SH	AVG	PB	SUP	APR	DL	PW
BARCLAY, CURT	Curtis Cordell; B8.22.1931 Chicago IL; D3.25.1985 Missoula MT; BR/TR/6´3˝/(205–210); d4.21; Col Oregon																									
1957	NY N	9	9	.500	37	28	5-2	0	183	196	85	21	2	48-4	67	3.44	114	.274	.319	58-0-1	.190	0	94	7	0	0.8
1958	SF N	1	0	1.000	6	1	0	0	16	16	5	3	3	5-3	6	2.81	136	.258	.343	6	.667	2	188	2	0	0.4
1959	SF N	0	0	ø	1	0	0	0	0.1	2	5	0	0	2-0	0	54.00	7	.500	.667	0	ø	0	—	-3	0	-0.1
Total	3	10	9	.526	44	29	5-2	0	199.1	214	95	24	5	55-7	73	3.48	113	.274	.323	64-0-1	.234	2	97	6	0	1.1
BARE, RAY	Raymond Douglas; B4.15.1949 Miami FL; D3.29.1994 Miami FL; BR/TR/6´2˝/(185–195); [StLN69*S3/49]; d7.30; Col Miami–Dade North (FL) CC																									
1972	StL N	0	1	.000	14	0	0	1-1	16.2	18	2	0	0	6-2	5	0.54	635	.281	.343	0	ø	0	—	5	0	0.3
1974	StL N	1	2	.333	10	3	0	0-0	24.1	25	17	2	0	9-0	6	5.92	61	.281	.343	5	.200	-0	81	-6	0	-0.6
1975	Det A	8	13	.381	29	21	6-1	0-0	150.2	174	81	10	1	47-5	71	4.48	90	.293	.343	0	ø	0	76	-4	0	-0.4
1976	Det A	7	8	.467	30	21	3-2	0-0	134	157	85	13	0	51-6	59	4.63	80	.293	.353	0	ø	0	106	-15	0	-1.5
1977	Det A	0	2	.000	5	4	0	0-0	14.1	24	21	3	0	7-1	4	12.56	34	.381	.443	0	ø	-0	94	-12	0	-1.2
Total	5	16	26	.381	88	49	9-3	1-1	340	398	206	28	1	120-14	145	4.79	81	.296	.351	5	.200	-0	91	-32	0	-3.4
BARFIELD, JOHN	John David; B10.15.1964 Pine Bluff AR; BL/TL/6´1˝/(185–195); [TexA86 11/267]; d9.7; Col Oklahoma City; [DL 1992 Tex A 28]																									
1989	Tex A	0	1	.000	4	2	0	0-0	11.2	15	10	0	0	4-0	9	6.17	65	.319	.373	0	ø	0	102	-3	0	-0.2
1990	Tex A	4	3	.571	33	0	0	1-0	44.1	42	25	2	1	13-3	17	4.67	84	.268	.320	0	ø	0	—	-3	0	-0.4
1991	Tex A	4	4	.500	28	9	0	1-0	83.1	96	51	11	0	22-3	27	4.54	89	.289	.330	0	ø	0	133	-7	66	-0.6
Total	3	8	8	.500	65	11	0	2-0	139.1	153	86	13	1	39-6	53	4.72	85	.285	.330	0	ø	0	128	-13	94	-1.2
BARFOOT, CLYDE	Clyde Raymond "Foots"; B7.8.1891 Richmond VA; D3.11.1971 Highland Park CA; BR/TR/6´0˝/170; d4.13																									
1922	StL N	4	5	.444	42	2	1	2	117.2	139	75	2	10	30	19	4.21	92	.307	.363	34	.353	5	148	-8	—	-0.1
1923	StL N	3	3	.500	33	2	1-1	1	101.1	112	49	7	1	27	23	3.73	105	.289	.337	37-0-1	.189	-1*	168	3	—	0.1
1926	Det A	1	2	.333	11	1	0	2	31.1	42	27	4	0	9	7	4.88	83	.318	.362	5	.200	0	104	-5	—	-0.5
Total	3	8	10	.444	86	5	2-1	5	250.1	293	151	13	11	66	49	4.10	95	.301	.353	76-0-1	.263	4	147	-10	—	-0.5
BARGAR, GREG	Greg Robert; B1.27.1959 Inglewood CA; BR/TR/6´2˝/185; [MonN80 3/73]; d7.17; Col Arizona																									
1983	Mon N	2	0	1.000	8	3	0	0-0	20	23	15	6	1	8-0	9	6.75	54	.271	.340	6	.167	-0	138	-6	0	-0.6
1984	Mon N	0	1	.000	3	1	0	0-0	8	8	7	1	0	7-1	2	7.88	44	.286	.417	1	.000	-0	26	-4	0	-0.4
1986	StL N	0	2	.000	22	0	0	0-0	27.1	36	19	3	3	10-1	12	5.60	66	.330	.395	2	.000	-0	—	-6	0	-0.4
Total	3	2	3	.400	33	4	0	0-0	55.1	67	41	10	4	25-2	23	6.34	57	.302	.378	9	.111	-0	110	-16	0	-1.4
BARGER, CY	Eros Bolivar; B5.18.1885 Jamestown KY; D9.23.1964 Columbia KY; BL/TR/6´0˝/160; d8.30; Col Transylvania																									
1906	NY A	0	0	ø	2	1	0	1	5.1	7	8	0	0	3	3	10.13	29	.318	.400	3	.333	0	218	-4	—	-0.2
1907	NY A	0	0	ø	1	0	0	0	6	10	2	0	1	1	0	3.00	93	.370	.414	2	.000	-0	—	0	—	-0.1
1910	Bro N	15	15	.500	35	30	25-2	1	271.2	267	105	2	6	107	87	2.88	105	.275	.351	104-0-3	.231	3*	78	7	—	1.2
1911	Bro N	11	15	.423	30	30	21-1	0	217.1	224	112	4	7	71	60	3.52	95	.279	.342	145-0-5	.228	1*	82	-6	—	-0.4
1912	Bro N	1	9	.100	16	11	6	0	94	120	78	4	4	42	30	5.46	61	.326	.401	37	.189	-0*	76	-23	—	-2.0
1914	Pit F	10	16	.385	33	26	18-1	1	228.1	252	125	7	6	63	70	4.34	66	.290	.342	83-0-1	.205	-0*	78	-31	—	-3.4
1915	Pit F	9	8	.529	34	13	8-1	6	153	130	49	1	4	47	47	2.29	118	.238	.303	54	.278	2*	83	7	—	0.9
Total	7	46	63	.422	151	111	78-5	9	975.2	1010	479	18	28	334	297	3.56	85	.280	.346	428-0-9	.227	6	81	-50	—	-4.0
BARK, BRIAN	Brian Stuart; B8.26.1968 Baltimore MD; BL/TL/5´9˝/170; [AtlN90 12/318]; d7.6; Col North Carolina St.																									
1995	Bos A	0	0	ø	3	0	0	0-0	2.1	2	0	0	0	1-0	0	0.00	ø	.286	.375	0	ø	0	—	1	0	0.1
BARKER, LEN	Leonard Harold; B7.7.1955 Fort Knox KY; BR/TR/6´5˝/(215–235); [TexA73 3/49]; d9.14																									
1976	Tex A	1	0	1.000	2	2	1-1	0-0	15	7	4	0	2	6-0	7	2.40	150	.149	.273	0	ø	0	86	2	0	0.1
1977	Tex A	4	1	.800	15	3	0	1-1	47.1	36	15	1	1	24-3	51	2.66	153	.217	.318	0	ø	0	169	8	0	0.8
1978	Tex A	1	5	.167	29	0	0	4-2	52.1	63	31	6	2	29-2	33	4.82	78	.304	.395	0	ø	0	—	-6	0	-0.7
1979	Cle A	6	6	.500	29	19	2	0-0	137.1	146	79	6	2	70-1	93	4.92	87	.277	.360	0	ø	0	95	-8	0	-0.6
1980	Cle A	19	12	.613	36	36	8-1	0-0	246.1	237	127	17	3	92-3	**187**	4.17	99	.252	.318	0	ø	0	99	-2	0	-0.4
1981	Cle A★	8	7	.533	22	22	9-3	0-0	154.1	150	72	7	1	46-0	**127**	3.91	94	.249	.301	0	ø	0	130	-3	0	-0.3
1982	Cle A	15	11	.577	33	33	10-1	0-0	244.2	211	117	17	3	88-2	187	3.90	106	.232	.299	0	ø	0	102	7	0	0.7
1983	Cle A	8	13	.381	24	24	4-1	0-0	149.2	150	92	16	2	52-3	105	5.11	84	.266	.327	0	ø	0	94	-12	0	-1.6
	Atl N	1	3	.250	6	6	0	0-0	33	31	17	0	0	14-2	21	3.82	101	.248	.321	8-0-2	.125	-0	80	-1	0	-0.1
1984	Atl N	7	8	.467	21	20	1	0-0	126.1	120	59	10	2	38-2	95	3.85	100	.254	.309	38-0-4	.053	-1	102	1	58	0.2
1985	Atl N	2	9	.182	20	18	0	0-0	73.2	84	55	10	1	37-1	47	6.35	61	.288	.369	17	.000	-2	66	-17	42	-2.5
1987	Mil A	2	1	.667	11	11	0	0-0	43.2	54	27	6	2	17-1	22	5.36	86	.303	.371	0	ø	0	97	-3	49	-0.2
Total	11	74	76	.493	248	194	35-7	5-3	1323.2	1289	695	96	21	513-20	975	4.34	94	.256	.325	63-0-6	.048	-3	100	-34	149	-4.6
BARKER, RICHIE	Richard Frank; B10.29.1972 Revere MA; BR/TR/6´2˝/220; [ChiN94 37/1030]; d4.25; Col Quinsigamond (MA) CC																									
1999	Chi N	0	0	ø	5	0	0	0-0	5	6	4	0	0	4-1	3	7.20	63	.300	.400	0	ø	0	—	-1	0	-0.1
BARKLEY, BRIAN	Brian Edward; B12.8.1975 Conroe TX; BL/TL/6´2˝/180; [BosA94 5/131]; d5.28; gf–Red; Col Okaloosa–Walton (FL) CC; [DL 1999 Bos A 73]																									
1998	Bos A	0	0	ø	6	0	0	0-0	11	16	13	2	1	9-1	2	9.82	48	.340	.441	0	ø	0	—	-6	0	-0.3
BARKLEY, JEFF	Jeffrey Carver; B11.21.1959 Hickory NC; BB/TR/6´3˝/178; [CleA82 13/326]; d9.16; Col The Citadel																									
1984	Cle A	0	0	ø	3	0	0	0-0	4	6	3	0	0	1-0	4	6.75	61	.353	.368	0	ø	0	—	-1	0	0.0
1985	Cle A	0	3	.000	21	0	0	1-3	41	37	26	5	0	15-3	30	5.27	79	.243	.308	0	ø	0	—	-5	0	-0.3
Total	2	0	3	.000	24	0	0	1-3	45	43	29	5	0	16-3	34	5.40	77	.254	.314	0	ø	0	—	-6	0	-0.3
BARLOW, MIKE	Michael Roswell; B4.30.1948 Stamford NY; BL/TR/6´6˝/(200–220); d6.18; Col Syracuse																									
1975	StL N	0	0	ø	9	0	0	0-0	7.2	11	6	0	1	3-1	2	4.70	81	.355	.405	0	ø	0	—	-1	0	-0.1
1976	Hou N	2	2	.500	16	0	0	0-1	22	27	13	0	0	17-1	11	4.50	72	.318	.431	3	.000	-0	—	-4	0	-0.6
1977	Cal A	4	2	.667	20	1	0	1-0	59	53	33	3	4	27-6	25	4.58	86	.249	.343	0	ø	0	92	-4	0	-0.3
1978	Cal A	0	0	ø	1	0	0	0-0	2	3	1	0	0	0-0	1	4.50	81	.375	.375	0	ø	0	—	0	0	0.0
1979	†Cal A	1	1	.500	35	0	0	0-0	86	106	54	8	4	30-2	33	5.13	80	.314	.373	0	ø	0	—	-10	24	-0.5
1980	Tor A	3	1	.750	40	1	0	5-2	55	57	29	4	2	21-4	19	4.09	106	.273	.343	0	ø	0	83	1	0	0.1
1981	Tor A	0	0	ø	12	0	0	0-1	15	22	11	1	4	6-1	5	4.20	94	.338	.416	0	ø	0	—	-2	0	-0.1
Total	7	10	6	.625	133	2	0	6-4	246.2	279	147	16	15	104-15	96	4.63	86	.294	.370	3	.000	-0	90	-20	24	-1.5
BARNABE, CHUCK	Charles Edward; B6.12.1900 Russell Gulch CO; D8.16.1977 Waco TX; BL/TL/5´11.5˝/164; d4.14																									
1927	Chi A	0	5	.000	17	4	1	0	61	86	46	2	5	20	5	5.31	76	.351	.411	19-0-1	.158	1*	72	-10	—	-0.6
1928	Chi A	0	2	.000	7	2	0	0	9.2	17	9	0	1	0	3	6.52	62	.395	.409	8-1-0	.500	2*	52	-3	—	-0.2
Total	2	0	7	.000	24	6	1	0	70.2	103	55	2	6	20	8	5.48	74	.358	.411	27-1-1	.259	3	65	-13	—	-0.8
BARNES, BRIAN	Brian Keith; B3.25.1967 Roanoke Rapids NC; BL/TL/5´9˝/170; [MonN89 4/97]; d9.14; Col Clemson																									
1990	Mon N	1	1	.500	4	4	1	0-0	28	25	10	2	0	7-0	23	2.89	127	.236	.283	9	.000	-1	92	2	0	0.1
1991	Mon N	5	8	.385	28	27	1	0-0	160	135	82	16	6	84-2	117	4.22	86	.233	.333	49-0-3	.082	-1	85	-9	27	-0.7
1992	Mon N	6	6	.500	21	17	0	0-0	100	77	34	9	3	46-1	65	2.97	117	.213	.306	29-0-6	.276	2	107	7	0	1.1
1993	Mon N	2	6	.250	52	8	0	3-2	100	105	53	9	0	48-2	60	4.41	95	.274	.353	20-0-2	.150	-0	84	0	0	-0.1
1994	Cle A	0	1	.000	6	0	0	0-0	13.1	12	10	2	0	15-2	5	5.40	88	.235	.403	0	ø	0	—	-1	0	-0.1
	LA N	0	0	ø	5	0	0	0-0	5	10	4	1	0	4-1	5	7.20	55	.400	.483	0	ø	0	—	-2	0	-0.1
Total	5	14	22	.389	116	56	2	3-2	406.1	364	193	39	9	204-8	275	3.94	96	.242	.334	107-0-11	.140	1	89	-3	27	0.2
BARNES, FRANK	Frank; B8.26.1926 Longwood MS; BR/TR/6´0˝/170; d9.22; Negro Lg 1949–50																									
1957	StL N	0	1	.000	3	1	0	0	10	13	5	0	0	9-1	5	4.50	88	.317	.440	2	.000	-0*	67	0	0	-0.1
1958	StL N	1	1	.500	8	1	0	0	19	19	16	3	2	16-0	17	7.58	54	.260	.402	6	.167	-0*	131	-6	0	-0.6
1960	StL N	0	1	.000	4	1	0	1	7.2	8	5	1	1	9-0	8	3.52	116	.267	.450	2	.000	-0	0	0	0	-0.1
Total	3	1	3	.250	15	3	0	1	36.2	40	26	4	3	34-1	30	5.89	69	.278	.423	10	.100	-1	65	-6	0	-0.8
BARNES, FRANK	Frank Samuel "Lefty"; B1.9.1900 Dallas TX; D9.27.1967 Houston TX; BL/TL/6´2.5˝/195; d4.18																									
1929	Det A	0	1	.000	4	1	0	0	5	10	8	0	1	3	0	7.20	60	.400	.483	1	.000	-0	59	-3	—	-0.5
1930	NY A	0	1	.000	2	2	0	0	12.1	13	11	0	1	13	2	8.03	54	.283	.450	6	.333	1*	130	-4	—	-0.1
Total	2	0	2	.000	6	3	0	0	17.1	23	19	0	2	16	2	7.79	55	.324	.461	7	.286	1	106	-7	—	-0.6

YEAR	TM LG	W	L	PCT	G	GS	CG-SHO	SV-BS	IP	H	R	HR	HB	BB-IB	SO	ERA	AERA	OAV	OOB	AB-HR-SH	AVG	PB	SUP	APR	DL	PW
Barnes, Jesse	Jesse Lawrence "Nubby"; B8.26.1892 Perkins OK; D9.9.1961 Santa Rosa NM; BL/TR/6´0˝/170; d7.30; Mil 1918; b–Virgil																									
1915	Bos N	3	0	1.000	9	3	2	0	45.1	41	14	1	4	10	16	1.39	186	.244	.302	17-0-1	.176	0	124	5	—	0.3
1916	Bos N	6	15	.286	33	18	9-3	1	163	154	63	3	5	37	55	2.37	105	.254	.302	48-0-2	.188	0	97	-1	—	0.2
1917	Bos N	13	21	.382	50	33	26-2	1	295	261	115	3	3	50	107	2.68	95	.241	.277	101-0-1	.238	4*	83	-7	—	-0.1
1918	NY N	6	1	.857	9	9	4-2	0	54.2	53	15	0	0	13	12	1.81	145	.255	.299	18-0-3	.222	-0	141	5	—	0.7
1919	NY N	**25**	9	.735	38	34	23-4	1	295.2	263	98	8	2	35	92	2.40	117	.236	.260	120-0-7	.267	5*	127	14	—	2.4
1920	NY N	20	15	.571	43	34	23-2	0	292.2	271	108	9	2	56	63	2.64	113	.250	.288	108-0-4	.204	-2*	109	11	—	1.2
1921	†NY N	15	9	.625	42	31	15-1	6	258.2	298	108	13	3	44	56	3.10	118	.299	.331	92-0-4	.207	-1	125	15	—	1.3
1922	†NY N	13	8	.619	37	29	14-2	0	212.2	236	108	10	3	38	52	3.51	114	.278	.311	77-0-4	.182	-1	127	9	—	0.8
1923	NY N	3	1	.750	12	4	1	1	36	48	25	1	0	13	12	6.25	61	.329	.384	11	.273	0	161	-9	—	-0.8
	Bos N	10	14	.417	31	23	12-5	2	195.1	204	86	8	0	43	41	2.76	144	.270	.310	68-0-1	.147	-4	81	21	—	2.2
	Year	13	15	.464	43	27	13-5	3	231.1	252	111	9	0	56	53	3.31	120	.280	.322	79-0-1	.165	-4	92	10	—	1.4
1924	Bos N	15	20	.429	37	32	21-**4**	0	267.2	292	115	7	0	53	49	3.23	118	.284	.319	90-0-9	.222	-1	76	16	—	1.9
1925	Bos N	11	16	.407	32	28	17	0	216.1	255	127	14	1	63	55	4.53	88	.297	.346	81-1-3	.198	-1	95	-12	—	-1.3
1926	Bro N	10	11	.476	31	24	10-1	1	158	204	104	6	2	35	29	5.24	73	.321	.358	59-0-1	.237	-0	108	-22	—	-2.5
1927	Bro N	2	10	.167	18	10	2	0	78.2	106	64	5	0	25	14	5.72	69	.331	.380	23-0-1	.217	-0	67	-17	—	-2.2
Total	13	152	150	.503	422	312	179-26	13	2569.2	2686	1150	88	25	515	653	3.22	104	.273	.310	913-1-41	.214	1	105	28	—	4.1
Barnes, Junie	Junie Shoaf "Lefty"; B12.1.1911 Linwood NC; D12.31.1963 Jacksonville NC; BL/TL/5´11.5˝/170; d9.12; Col Wake Forest																									
1934	Cin N	0	0	ø	2	0	0	0	0.1	0	0	0	0	1	0	0.00	ø	.000	.500	0	ø	0	—	0	—	0.0
Barnes, Rich	Richard Monroe; B7.21.1959 Palm Beach FL; BR/TL/6´4˝/186; [ChiA77 2/27]; d7.18																									
1982	Chi A	0	2	.000	6	2	0	1-0	17	21	15	1	2	4-0	6	4.76	86	.292	.342	0	ø	0	45	-3	0	-0.4
1983	Cle A	1	1	.500	4	2	0	0-0	11.2	18	10	0	0	10-2	2	6.94	62	.375	.475	0	ø	0	127	-3	0	-0.5
Total	2	1	3	.250	10	4	0	1-0	28.2	39	25	1	2	14-2	8	5.65	74	.325	.399	0	ø	0	88	-6	0	-0.9
Barnes, Bob	Robert Avery "Lefty"; B1.6.1902 Washburn IL; D12.8.1993 Peoria IL; BL/TL/5´11.5˝/150; d7.8; Col Illinois																									
1924	Chi A	0	0	ø	2	0	0	0	4.2	14	11	1	0	0	1	19.29	21	.519	.519	2	.000	-0	—	-8	—	-0.4
Barnes, Virgil	Virgil Jennings "Zeke"; B3.5.1897 Ontario KS; D7.24.1958 Wichita KS; BR/TR/6´0˝/165; d9.25; b–Jesse																									
1919	NY N	0	0	ø	1	0	0	0	2	6	4	0	0	1	1	18.00	16	.545	.583	0	ø	0	—	-3	—	-0.2
1920	NY N	0	1	.000	1	1	0	0	7	9	3	0	0	1	2	3.86	78	.310	.333	1-0-1	.000	-0	52	0	—	-0.1
1922	NY N	1	0	1.000	22	2	1	2	51.2	46	27	1	0	11	16	3.48	115	.243	.285	12-0-1	.167	-1	214	2	—	0.1
1923	†NY N	2	3	.400	22	2	0	1	53	59	31	2	0	19	6	3.91	98	.285	.345	14	.000	-2	86	-3	—	-0.4
1924	†NY N	16	10	.615	35	29	15-1	3	229.1	239	87	10	0	57	59	3.06	120	.270	.314	77-0-4	.182	-2	139	18	—	1.8
1925	NY N	15	11	.577	32	27	17-1	2	221.2	242	110	9	1	53	53	3.53	114	.281	.323	89-0-2	.101	-9	114	10	—	0.1
1926	NY N	8	13	.381	31	25	9-2	1	185	183	73	4	3	56	54	2.87	131	.261	.318	56-0-1	.054	-7	78	17	—	1.0
1927	NY N	14	11	.560	35	29	12-2	2	228.2	251	116	14	4	51	66	3.98	97	.283	.325	83-0-4	.108	-7	110	-2	—	-0.9
1928	NY N	3	3	.500	10	9	3-1	0	55.1	71	32	3	0	18	11	5.04	78	.330	.382	22	.091	-2	127	-5	—	-0.7
	Bos N	2	7	.222	16	10	1	0	60.1	86	42	3	0	26	7	5.82	67	.344	.406	17-0-2	.059	-2	87	-11	—	-1.5
	Year	5	10	.333	26	19	4-1	0	115.2	157	74	6	0	44	18	5.45	72	.338	.395	39-0-2	.077	-3	106	-17	—	-2.2
Total	9	61	59	.508	205	134	58-7	11	1094	1192	525	46	8	293	275	3.66	105	.282	.329	371-0-15	.108	-31	111	23	—	-0.8
Barney, Rex	Rex Edward; B12.19.1924 Omaha NE; D8.12.1997 Baltimore MD; BR/TR/6´3˝/185; d8.18; Mil 1944–45																									
1943	Bro N	2	2	.500	9	8	1	0	45.1	36	32	4	2	41	23	6.35	53	.217	.378	18	.056	-2	139	-13	0	-1.2
1946	Bro N	2	5	.286	16	9	1	0	53.2	46	42	2	0	51	36	5.87	58	.240	.399	17	.235	1	93	-15	0	-1.7
1947	†Bro N	5	2	.714	28	9	0	0	77.2	66	52	4	2	59	36	4.75	87	.240	.378	27	.111	-1	159	-7	0	-0.8
1948	Bro N	15	13	.536	44	34	12-4	0	246.2	193	101	17	6	122	138	3.10	129	.217	.315	84-0-4	.167	-2	102	23	0	1.9
1949	†Bro N	9	8	.529	38	20	6-2	1	140.2	108	75	15	3	89	80	4.41	93	.216	.338	47-0-3	.213	0	128	-5	0	-0.6
1950	Bro N	2	1	.667	20	1	0	0	33.2	25	26	6	2	48	23	6.42	64	.214	.449	8	.125	0	151	-9	0	-0.7
Total	6	35	31	.530	155	81	20-6	1	597.2	474	328	48	15	410	336	4.31	91	.221	.350	201-0-7	.164	-4	117	-26	0	-3.1
Barnhart, Edgar	Edgar Vernon; B9.16.1904 Providence MO; D9.14.1984 Columbia MO; BL/TR/5´10˝/160; d9.23																									
1924	StL A	0	0	ø	1	0	0	0	1	0	0	0	0	2	0	0.00	ø	.000	.400	0	ø	0	—	0	—	0.0
Barnhart, Les	Leslie Earl "Barney"; B2.23.1905 Hoxie KS; D10.7.1971 Scottsdale AZ; BR/TR/6´0˝/180; d9.22																									
1928	Cle A	0	1	.000	2	1	0	0	9	13	7	1	0	4	1	7.00	59	.325	.386	2	.500	0	41	-2	—	-0.2
1930	Cle A	1	0	1.000	1	1	0	0	8.1	12	7	0	0	4	1	6.48	74	.364	.432	3-0-1	.000	-1	160	-1	—	-0.2
Total	2	1	1	.500	3	2	0	0	17.1	25	14	1	0	8	2	6.75	66	.342	.407	5-0-1	.200	-0	105	-3	—	-0.4
Barnicle, George	George Bernard "Barney"; B8.26.1917 Fitchburg MA; D10.10.1990 Largo FL; BR/TR/6´2˝/175; d9.6																									
1939	Bos N	2	2	.500	6	1	0	0	18.1	16	11	1	0	8	15	4.91	75	.235	.316	5	.000	-1	0	-2	—	-0.5
1940	Bos N	1	0	1.000	13	2	1	0	32.2	28	28	1	6	31	11	7.44	50	.233	.414	11	.000	-1	152	-13	—	-0.7
1941	Bos N	0	1	.000	1	1	0	0	6.2	5	5	0	1	4	2	6.75	53	.238	.385	2	.000	-0	0	-2	0	-0.3
Total	3	3	3	.500	20	4	1	0	57.2	49	44	2	7	43	28	6.55	56	.234	.382	18	.000	-2	76	-17	0	-1.5
Barnowski, Ed	Edward Anthony; B8.23.1943 Scranton PA; BR/TR/6´2˝/195; d9.8; Col Syracuse																									
1965	Bal A	0	0	ø	4	0	0	0	4.1	3	1	0	0	7-0	6	2.08	167	.200	.455	0	ø	0	—	1	0	0.0
1966	Bal A	0	0	ø	2	0	0	0	3	4	1	0	0	1-0	2	3.00	111	.364	.417	0	ø	0	—	0	0	0.0
Total	2	0	0	ø	6	0	0	0	7.1	7	2	0	0	8-0	8	2.45	139	.269	.441	0	ø	0	—	1	0	0.0
Barojas, Salome	Salome (Romero); B6.16.1957 Cordoba, Veracruz, Mexico; BR/TR/5´9˝/(160–188); d4.11																									
1982	Chi A	6	6	.500	61	0	0	21-6	106.2	96	43	9	1	46-6	56	3.54	115	.244	.322	0	ø	0	—	9	0	1.4
1983	†Chi A	3	3	.500	52	0	0	12-4	87.1	70	24	2	5	32-2	38	2.47	171	.224	.304	0	ø	0	—	17	0	1.6
1984	Chi A	3	2	.600	24	0	0	1-4	39.1	48	24	3	0	19-1	18	4.58	91	.310	.385	0	ø	0	—	-3	0	-0.3
	Sea A	6	5	.545	19	14	0	1-0	95.1	88	46	12	3	41-1	37	3.97	101	.249	.331	0	ø	0	125	1	0	0.1
	Year	9	7	.563	43	14	0	2-4	134.2	136	70	15	3	60-2	55	4.14	98	.268	.347	0	ø	0	124	-2	0	-0.2
1985	Sea A	0	5	.000	17	4	0	0-0	52.2	65	40	6	0	33-5	27	5.98	71	.305	.395	0	ø	0	38	-11	24	-0.9
1988	Phi N	0	0	ø	6	0	0	0-0	8.2	7	9	1	0	8-0	1	8.31	43	.250	.395	0	ø	0	—	-4	0	-0.2
Total	5	18	21	.462	179	18	0	35-14	390	374	186	33	9	179-15	177	3.95	104	.257	.340	0	ø	0	104	9	24	1.7
Barr, Jim	James Leland; B2.10.1948 Lynwood CA; BR/TR/6´3˝/(205–215); [SFN70 S3/49]; d7.31; Col USC																									
1971	†SF N	1	1	.500	17	0	0	0-0	35.1	33	15	3	1	5-1	16	3.57	96	.254	.281	4-0-1	.000	-0	—	0	0	0.0
1972	SF N	8	10	.444	44	18	8-2	2-1	179	166	66	16	3	41-8	86	2.87	122	.246	.290	49-0-4	.184	1	88	12	0	1.3
1973	SF N	11	17	.393	41	33	8-3	2-0	231.1	240	105	24	5	49-7	88	3.81	101	.268	.307	66-0-12	.152	-1	95	4	0	0.4
1974	SF N	13	9	.591	44	27	11-5	2-1	239.2	223	81	17	2	47-10	84	2.74	139	.251	.288	71-1-6	.254	4*	82	30	0	3.2
1975	SF N	13	14	.481	35	33	12-2	0-0	244	244	94	17	3	58-10	77	3.06	124	.265	.309	76-0-12	.118	-3*	93	19	0	1.9
1976	SF N	15	12	.556	37	37	8-3	0-0	252.1	260	104	9	2	60-7	75	2.89	126	.266	.308	74-0-12	.162	2*	102	18	0	2.2
1977	SF N	12	16	.429	38	38	6-2	0-0	234.1	286	130	18	3	56-4	97	4.76	83	.306	.345	76-0-13	.132	-2*	91	-15	0	-1.6
1978	SF N	8	11	.421	32	25	5-2	1-0	163	180	69	7	0	35-6	44	3.53	98	.281	.315	50-0-5	.100	-3*	87	0	0	-0.3
1979	Cal A	10	12	.455	36	25	5	0-1	197	217	100	22	3	55-5	69	4.20	97	.287	.335	0	ø	0	100	-2	0	-0.1
1980	Cal A	1	4	.200	24	7	0	1-0	68	90	43	12	3	23-2	22	5.56	71	.323	.373	0	ø	0	103	-11	40	-0.8
1982	SF N	4	3	.571	53	9	1-1	2-2	128.2	125	54	9	4	20-5	36	3.29	109	.262	.291	32-0-2	.250	1	120	4	0	0.4
1983	SF N	5	3	.625	53	0	0	2-3	92.2	106	47	7	1	20-9	47	3.98	89	.294	.325	15-0-1	.133	-0	—	-4	0	-0.4
Total	12	101	112	.474	454	252	64-20	12-8	2065.1	2170	908	161	30	469-74	741	3.56	106	.273	.313	513-1-68	.162	-0	95	55	40	6.2
Barr, Bob	Robert Alexander; B3.12.1908 Newton MA; D7.25.2002 Dover NH; BR/TR/6´0˝/175; d9.11																									
1935	Bro N	0	0	ø	2	0	0	0	2.1	5	3	0	0	2	0	3.86	103	.385	.467	0	ø	0	—	-1	—	0.0
Barr, Bob	Robert McClelland; B12.1856 Washington DC; D3.11.1930 Washington DC; BR/TR/6´1˝/192; d6.23																									
1883	Pit AA	6	18	.250	26	23	19	**1**	203.1	263	166	5	—	28	81	4.38	74	.294	.316	142	.246	3*	86	-27	—	-2.2
1884	Was AA	9	23	.281	32	32	32-2	0	281.1	312	210	9	13	31	138	3.45	88	.259	.285	135-2	.148	-2*	67	-13	—	-1.4
	Ind AA	3	11	.214	16	16	15	0	131.2	159	117	2	5	19	69	4.99	66	.274	.302	65	.185	0*	92	-22	—	-1.8
	Year	12	34	.261	48	48	47-2	0	413	471	327	11	18	50	207	3.94	79	.264	.291	200-2	.160	-2	76	-41	—	-3.2
1886	Was N	3	18	.143	23	23	21-1	0	191.2	221	153	7	—	54	80	4.41	73	.280	.326	79	.165	-2	72	-27	—	-2.5
1890	Roc AA	28	24	.538	57	54	52-3	0	493.1	458	267	7	14	219	209	3.25	110	.239	.321	201-2	.179	-1	107	21	—	1.8

YEAR	TM LG	W	L	PCT	G	GS	CG-SHO	SV-BS	IP	H	R	HR	HB	BB-IB	SO	ERA	AERA	OAV	OOB	AB-HR-SH	AVG	PB	SUP	APR	DL	PW
1891	NY N	0	4	.000	5	4	2	0	27	47	25	1	3	12	11	5.33	60	.367	.434	11	.091	-0	103	-6	—	-0.7
Total	5	49	98	.333	159	152	141-6	1	1328.1	1460	938	31	35	363	588	3.85	86	.265	.314	633-4	.185	-3	88	-74	—	-6.8
Barr, Steve	Steven Charles; B9.8.1951 St.Louis MO; BL/TL/6´4˝/200; [BosA69 7/155]; d10.1																									
1974	Bos A	1	0	1.000	1	1	1	0-0	9	7	4	0	0	6-0	3	4.00	96	.212	.333	0	ø	0	160	0	0	0.0
1975	Bos A	0	1	.000	3	2	0	0-0	7	11	9	1	0	7-0	2	2.57	158	.367	.474	0	ø	0	108	-2	0	-0.2
1976	Tex A	2	6	.250	20	10	3	0-0	67.2	70	51	10	0	44-1	27	5.59	64	.269	.373	0	ø	0	113	-16	23	-1.7
Total	3	3	7	.300	24	13	4	0-0	83.2	88	64	11	0	57-1	32	5.16	71	.272	.379	0	ø	0	117	-18	23	-1.9
Barrett, Red	Charles Henry; B2.14.1915 Santa Barbara CA; D7.28.1990 Wilson NC; BR/TR/5´11˝/183; d9.15																									
1937	Cin N	0	0	ø	1	0	0	0	6.1	5	1	0	0	2	1	1.42	263	.227	.292	3	.000	-0	—	2	—	0.0
1938	Cin N	2	0	1.000	6	2	2	0	28.2	28	13	2	0	15	5	3.14	116	.257	.347	7-0-4	.143	-0	151	1	—	0.0
1939	Cin N	0	0	ø	2	0	0	0	5.1	5	1	0	0	1	1	1.69	227	.263	.300	1	.000	-0	—	1	—	0.1
1940	Cin N	1	0	1.000	3	0	0	0	2.2	5	2	0	0	1	0	6.75	56	.455	.500	0	ø	0	—	-1	—	-0.1
1943	Bos N	12	18	.400	38	31	14-3	0	255	240	107	11	2	63	64	3.18	107	.250	.298	81-0-8	.136	-4	71	8	0	0.5
1944	Bos N	9	16	.360	42	30	11-1	2	230.1	257	124	13	2	63	54	4.06	94	.279	.327	75-0-12	.173	-1	97	-6	0	-0.6
1945	Bos N	2	3	.400	9	5	2	2	38	43	22	6	1	16	13	4.74	81	.281	.353	9-0-4	.222	-0	137	-3	0	-0.4
	StL N∗	21	9	.700	36	29	22-3	0	246.2	244	84	12	1	38	63	2.74	137	.256	.285	89-0-11	.112	-5	129	29	0	2.7
	Year	**23**	12	.657	45	34	**24**-3	2	**284.2**	287	106	18	2	54	76	3.00	125	.259	.295	98-0-15	.122	-5	130	25	0	2.3
1946	StL N	3	2	.600	23	9	1-1	2	67	75	35	5	2	24	22	4.03	86	.282	.346	17-0-2	.059	-1	152	-4	0	-0.4
1947	Bos N	11	12	.478	36	30	12-3	1	210.2	200	102	16	2	53	53	3.55	110	.244	.292	72-0-7	.111	-2	94	5	0	0.3
1948	†Bos N	7	8	.467	34	13	3	0	128.1	132	56	9	0	26	40	3.65	105	.268	.305	39-0-4	.179	-1	84	4	0	0.3
1949	Bos N	1	1	.500	23	0	0	0	44.1	58	32	4	2	10	17	5.68	66	.326	.368	5	.200	-0	—	-10	0	-0.4
Total	11	69	69	.500	253	149	67-11	7	1263.1	1292	579	78	12	312	333	3.53	105	.264	.309	398-0-52	.136	-16	102	26	0	2.0
Barrett, Frank	Francis Joseph "Red"; B7.1.1913 Ft.Lauderdale FL; D3.6.1998 Leesburg FL; BR/TR/6´2˝/173; d10.1; Col St. Leo																									
1939	StL N	0	1	.000	1	0	0	0	1.2	1	1	0	0	1	3	5.40	76	.167	.286	0	ø	0	—	0	—	0.0
1944	Bos A	8	7	.533	38	2	0	8	90.1	93	45	5	1	42	40	3.69	92	.271	.352	28-0-1	.143	-1	160	-4	0	-0.8
1945	Bos A	4	3	.571	37	0	0	3	86	77	30	0	0	29	35	2.62	130	.249	.314	20	.250	1	—	7	0	0.6
1946	Bos N	2	4	.333	23	0	0	1	35.1	35	21	2	1	17	12	5.09	67	.252	.338	6	.000	-1	—	-6	0	-0.9
1950	Pit N	1	2	.333	5	0	0	0	4.1	5	3	1	0	1	0	4.15	106	.357	.400	0	ø	0	—	0	0	0.0
Total	5	15	17	.469	104	2	0	12	217.2	211	100	8	2	90	90	3.51	98	.260	.336	54-0-1	.167	-1	160	-3	0	-1.1
Barrett, Tim	Timothy Wayne; B1.24.1961 Huntingburg IN; BL/TR/6´1˝/185; d7.18; Col Indiana St.																									
1988	Mon N	0	0	ø	4	0	0	1-0	9.1	10	6	2	0	2-0	5	5.79	63	.270	.308	2	.000	-0	—	-2	0	-0.1
Barrett, Dick	Tracy Souter "Kewpie Dick" (aka Richard Oliver 1933 and Richard Oliver Barrett 1934-43); B9.28.1906 Montoursville PA; D10.30.1966 Seattle WA; BR/TR/5´9˝/175; d6.27; Col Illinois																									
1933	Phi A	4	4	.500	15	7	3	0	70.1	74	51	2	1	49	26	5.76	74	.272	.385	21-0-2	.286	2	113	-10	—	-0.8
1934	Bos N	1	3	.250	15	3	0	0	32.1	50	27	2	0	12	14	6.68	57	.365	.416	7	.143	-0	83	-11	—	-1.1
1943	Chi N	0	4	.000	15	4	0	0	45	52	28	2	1	28	20	4.80	70	.291	.389	9-0-1	.111	-1	51	-7	0	-0.7
	Phi N	10	9	.526	23	20	10-2	1	169.1	137	53	5	2	51	65	2.39	141	.221	.282	49-0-6	.143	-0	80	18	0	2.1
	Year	10	13	.435	38	24	10-2	1	214.1	189	81	7	3	79	85	2.90	116	.237	.308	58-0-7	.138	-1	76	11	0	1.4
1944	Phi N	12	18	.400	37	28	11-1	0	221.1	223	110	7	3	88	74	3.86	94	.262	.333	74-0-6	.216	2	89	-6	0	-0.4
1945	Phi N	8	20	.286	36	30	8	1	190.2	217	129	11	7	92	72	5,38	71	.281	.363	62-0-2	.145	-1	83	-28	0	-3.6
Total	5	35	58	.376	141	92	32-3	2	729	753	398	29	14	320	271	4.28	86	.266	.343	222-0-17	.180	1	86	-44	0	-4.5
Barrios, Francisco	Francisco Javier (Jimenez); B6.10.1953 Hermosillo, Sonora, Mexico; D4.9.1982 Hermosillo, Sonora, Mexico; BR/TR/6´3˝/(154–207); d8.18																									
1974	Chi A	0	0	ø	2	0	0	0-0	2	7	6	0	0	2-0	2	27.00	14	.538	.600	0	ø	0	—	-5	0	-0.2
1976	Chi A	5	9	.357	35	14	6	3-1	141.2	136	72	13	4	46-3	81	4.32	83	.255	.314	0	ø	0	127	-11	0	-1.1
1977	Chi A	14	7	.667	33	31	9	0-0	231.1	241	117	22	5	58-1	119	4.12	99	.267	.313	0	ø	0	123	0	0	0.0
1978	Chi A	9	15	.375	33	32	9-2	0-0	195.2	180	93	13	7	85-2	79	4.05	94	.246	.327	0	ø	0	83	-3	0	-0.3
1979	Chi A	8	3	.727	15	15	2	0-0	94.2	88	49	9	5	33-1	28	3.61	118	.242	.311	0	ø	0	114	5	50	0.4
1980	Chi A	1	1	.500	3	3	0	0-0	16.1	21	9	4	1	8-0	2	4.96	82	.323	.400	0	ø	0	110	-1	34	-0.1
1981	Chi A	1	3	.250	8	7	1	0-0	36.1	45	23	3	1	14-1	12	3.96	91	.292	.355	0	ø	0	99	-3	89	-0.4
Total	7	38	38	.500	129	102	27-2	3-1	718	718	369	64	23	246-8	323	4.15	94	.260	.323	0	ø	0	108	-18	173	-1.7
Barrios, Manuel	Manuel Antonio; B9.21.1974 Cabecera, Pan; BR/TR/6´0˝/(170–185); d9.16																									
1997	Hou N	0	0	ø	2	0	0	0-0	3	6	4	0	0	3-0	3	12.00	33	.400	.500	0	ø	0	—	-3	0	-0.1
1998	Fla N	0	0	ø	2	0	0	0-0	2.2	4	1	1	0	2-0	1	3.38	120	.364	.462	0	ø	0	—	0	0	0.0
	LA N	0	0	ø	1	0	0	0-0	1	0	0	0	0	2-0	0	0.00	ø	.000	.500	0	ø	0	—	0	0	0.0
	Year	0	0	ø	3	0	0	0-0	3.2	4	1	1	0	4-0	1	2.45	165	.308	.471	0	ø	0	—	1	0	0.0
Total	2	0	0	ø	5	0	0	0-0	6.2	10	5	1	0	7-0	4	6.75	60	.357	.486	0	ø	0	—	-3	0	-0.1
Barron, Frank	Frank John; B8.6.1890 St.Marys WV; D9.18.1964 St.Marys WV; BL/TL/6´1˝/175; d8.19; Col West Virginia																									
1914	Was A	0	0	ø	1	0	0	0	1	1	0	0	0	0	1	0.00	ø	.333	.333	0	ø	0	—	0	—	0.0
Barry, Ed	Edward "Jumbo"; B10.2.1882 Madison WI; D6.19.1920 Montague MA; BR/TL/6´3˝/185; d8.21																									
1905	Bos A	1	2	.333	7	5	2	0	40.2	38	19	2	4	15	18	2.88	94	.248	.331	11-0-1	.091	-0	131	-2	—	-0.2
1906	Bos A	0	3	.000	3	3	3	0	21	23	22	2	3	5	10	6.00	46	.280	.344	9	.111	-0	44	-9	—	-1.0
1907	Bos A	0	1	.000	2	2	1	0	17.1	13	6	1	1	5	6	2.08	124	.210	.279	3-0-1	.000	-0	52	1	—	0.0
Total	3	1	6	.143	12	10	6	0	79	74	47	5	8	25	34	3.53	76	.249	.324	23-0-2	.087	-1	89	-10	—	-1.2
Barry, Hardin	Hardin "Finn"; B3.26.1891 Susanville CA; D11.5.1969 Carson City NV; BR/TR/6´0˝/185; d6.21; Col Santa Clara																									
1912	Phi A	0	0	ø	3	0	0	0	13	18	11	0	1	4	3	7.62	40	.360	.418	4	.000	-0	—	-6	—	-0.3
Barry, Kevin	Kevin Thomas; B8.18.1978 Princeton Junction NJ; BR/TR/6´2˝/235; [AtlN01 14/435]; d6.26; Col Rider																									
2006	Atl N	1	1	.500	19	1	0	0-1	25.2	24	16	2	1	14-0	19	5.61	81	.253	.348	2	.000	-0	102	-2	0	-0.1
Barry, Tom	Thomas Arthur; B4.10.1879 St.Louis MO; D6.4.1946 St.Louis MO; TR/5´9˝/155; d4.15																									
1904	Phi N	0	1	.000	1	1	0	0	0.2	6	5	0	0	1	1	40.50	7	.667	.700	0	ø	0	0	-3	—	-0.5
Barthelson, Bob	Robert Edward; B7.15.1924 New Haven CT; D4.14.2000 Branford CT; BR/TR/6´0˝/185; d7.4																									
1944	NY N	1	1	.500	7	1	0	0	9.2	13	9	2	0	5	4	4.66	79	.310	.383	0	ø	0	0	-2	0	-0.4
Barthold, John	John Francis "Hans"; B4.14.1882 Philadelphia PA; D11.4.1946 Fairview Village PA; BB/TR/5´11˝/180; d5.17																									
1904	Phi A	0	0	ø	4	0	0	0	10.2	12	9	0	1	8	5	5.06	53	.286	.412	3	.333	1	—	-3	—	-0.1
Bartholomew, Les	Lester Justin; B4.4.1903 Madison WI; D9.19.1972 Barrington IL; BR/TL/5´11.5˝/195; d4.11																									
1928	Pit N	0	0	ø	6	0	0	0	22.2	31	18	2	0	9	6	7.15	57	.356	.417	7	.143	-0	—	-6	—	-0.3
1932	Chi A	0	0	ø	3	0	0	0	5.1	5	3	0	0	6	1	5.06	85	.250	.423	1	.000	-0	—	0	—	0.0
Total	2	0	0	ø	9	0	0	0	28	36	21	2	0	15	7	6.75	61	.336	.418	8	.125	-0	—	-6	—	-0.3
Bartley, Bill	William Jackson; B1.8.1885 Cincinnati OH; D5.17.1965 Cincinnati OH; BR/TR/5´11.5˝/190; d9.15																									
1903	NY N	0	0	ø	1	0	0	0	3	3	4	0	0	4	2	0.00	ø	.273	.467	1	.000	-0	—	0	—	0.0
1906	Phi A	0	0	ø	3	0	0	1	8.2	10	9	0	0	6	6	9.35	29	.294	.400	3	.333	1	—	-5	—	-0.2
1907	Phi A	0	1	.000	15	3	2	0	56.1	44	22	0	0	19	16	2.24	116	.218	.285	21	.095	-2	130	2	—	-0.1
Total	3	0	1	.000	19	3	2	1	68	57	35	0	0	29	24	3.04	87	.231	.312	25	.120	-1	130	-3	—	-0.3
Barton, Shawn	Shawn Edward; B5.14.1963 Los Angeles CA; BR/TL/6´3˝/195; [PhiN84 21/542]; d8.6; Col Nevada–Reno																									
1992	Sea A	0	1	.000	14	0	0	0-1	12.1	10	5	1	0	7-2	4	2.92	137	.238	.347	0	ø	0	—	1	0	0.1
1995	SF N	4	1	.800	52	0	0	1-3	44.1	37	22	3	2	19-1	22	4.26	97	.237	.322	0-0-1	ø	0	—	0	0	0.0
1996	SF N	0	0	ø	7	0	0	0-0	8.1	19	12	2	0	1-0	3	9.72	43	.442	.455	0	ø	0	—	-6	0	-0.3
Total	3	4	2	.667	73	0	0	1-4	65	66	39	6	2	27-3	29	4.71	87	.274	.348	0-0-1	ø	0	—	-5	0	-0.2

YEAR	TM LG	W	L	PCT	G	GS	CG-SHO	SV-BS	IP	H	R	HR	HB	BB-IB	SO	ERA	AERA	OAV	OOB	AB-HR-SH	AVG	PB	SUP	APR	DL	PW
Bartosh, Cliff	Clifford Paul; B9.5.1979 West TX; BL/TL/6´2˝/180; [SDN98 29/862]; d5.15																									
2004	Cle A	1	0	1.000	34	0	0	0-2	19.1	22	10	4	0	11-0	25	4.66	93	.275	.363	0	ø	0	—	0	0	0.0
2005	Chi N	0	2	.000	19	0	0	0-0	19.2	23	13	7	2	11-0	15	5.49	80	.307	.404	1	1.000	0	—	-2	0	-0.2
Total	2	1	2	.333	53	0	0	0-2	39	45	23	11	2	22-0	40	5.08	86	.290	.383	1	1.000	0	—	-2	0	-0.2
Bartson, Charlie	Charles Franklin; B3.13.1865 Peoria IL; D6.9.1936 Peoria IL; 6´0˝/170; d5.14																									
1890	Chi P	9	10	.474	26	20	17	1	197	226	145	8	13	66	52	4.11	106	.276	.339	78	.167	-3	92	7	—	0.5
Barzilla, Philip	Philip Joseph; B1.25.1979 Houston TX; BL/TL/6´0˝/180; [HouN01 4/116]; d6.11; Col Rice																									
2006	Hou N	0	0	ø	1	0	0	0-0	0.1	1	0	0	0	0-0	0	0.00	ø	.500	.500	0	ø	0	—	0	0	0.0
Baskette, Jim	James Blaine "Big Jim"; B12.10.1887 Athens TN; D7.30.1942 Athens TN; BR/TR/6´2˝/185; d9.22																									
1911	Cle A	1	2	.333	4	2	2	0	21.1	21	8	0	1	9	8	3.38	101	.273	.356	6	.333	1	74	1	—	0.2
1912	Cle A	8	4	.667	29	11	7-1	1	116	109	50	2	7	46	51	3.18	107	.252	.334	40-0-1	.125	-1	114	5	—	0.3
1913	Cle A	0	0	ø	2	1	0	0	4.2	8	3	1	0	2	0	5.79	52	.400	.455	1	1.000	1	268	-1	—	0.1
Total	3	9	6	.600	35	14	9-1	1	142	138	61	3	8	57	59	3.30	103	.261	.342	47-0-1	.170	1	118	5	—	0.6
Bass, Norm	Norman Delaney; B1.21.1939 Laurel MS; BR/TR/6´3˝/205; d4.23; Col Pacific (CA)																									
1961	KC A	11	11	.500	40	23	6-2	0	170.2	164	98	17	4	82-0	74	4.69	89	.255	.340	59-1-3	.119	-2*	116	-7	0	-1.2
1962	KC A	2	6	.250	22	10	0	0	75.1	96	55	7	0	46-2	33	6.09	69	.317	.402	22-0-1	.045	-2	97	-14	0	-1.4
1963	KC A	0	0	ø	3	1	0	0	7.2	11	11	2	0	9-0	4	11.74	33	.333	.465	1	.000	-0	137	-6	0	-0.3
Total	3	13	17	.433	65	34	6-2	0	253.2	271	164	26	4	137-2	111	5.32	79	.277	.364	82-1-4	.098	-4	111	-27	0	-2.9
Bass, Dick	Richard William; B7.7.1906 Rogersville TN; D2.3.1989 Graceville FL; BR/TR/6´2˝/175; d9.21; Col Miami–Ohio																									
1939	Was A	0	1	.000	1	1	0	0	8	7	6	0	1	6	1	6.75	64	.241	.389	2	.000	-0	61	-2	—	-0.2
Batchelder, Joe	Joseph Edmund "Win"; B7.11.1898 Wenham MA; D5.5.1989 Beverly MA; BR/TL/5´7˝/165; d9.29																									
1923	Bos N	1	0	1.000	4	1	1	0	9	12	7	2	1	1	2	7.00	57	.353	.389	1	.000	0	83	-2	—	-0.2
1924	Bos N	0	0	ø	3	0	0	0	4.2	4	2	0	0	2	2	3.86	99	.235	.316	1	.000	-0	—	0	—	0.0
1925	Bos N	0	0	ø	4	0	0	0	7	10	5	0	0	1	2	5.14	78	.357	.379	1	.000	-0	—	-1	—	0.0
Total	3	1	0	1.000	11	1	1	0	20.2	26	14	2	1	4	6	5.66	70	.329	.369	3	.000	-0	83	-3	—	-0.2
Batchelor, Richard	Richard Anthony; B4.8.1967 Florence SC; BR/TR/6´1˝/195; d9.3; Col South Carolina–Aiken																									
1993	StL N	0	0	ø	9	0	0	0-0	10	14	12	1	0	3-1	4	8.10	50	.359	.386	1	.000	-0	—	-5	0	-0.3
1996	StL N	2	0	1.000	11	0	0	0-0	15	9	2	0	0	1-0	11	1.20	353	.173	.189	1	.000	-0	—	5	0	0.6
1997	StL N	1	1	.500	10	0	0	0-1	16	21	12	0	2	7-1	8	4.50	93	.323	.405	0	ø	0	—	-2	0	-0.2
	SD N	2	0	1.000	13	0	0	0-1	12.2	19	11	2	1	7-1	10	7.82	50	.358	.443	0	ø	0	—	-5	0	-0.7
	Year	3	1	.750	23	0	0	0-2	28.2	40	23	2	3	14-2	18	5.97	68	.339	.422	0	ø	0	—	-7	0	-0.9
Total	3	5	1	.833	43	0	0	0-2	53.2	63	37	3	3	18-3	33	5.03	82	.301	.362	2	.000	-0	—	-7	0	-0.6
Bates, Dick	Charles Richard; B10.7.1945 McArthur OH; BL/TR/6´0˝/190; d4.27																									
1969	Sea A	0	0	ø	1	0	0	0-0	1.2	3	5	1	0	3-0	3	27.00	13	.375	.545	0	ø	0	—	-4	0	-0.2
Bates, Frank	Creed Napoleon; B9.28.1876 Cleveland TN; TR; d10.7																									
1898	Cle N	2	1	.667	4	4	4	0	29	30	15	0	1	11	5	3.10	117	.265	.336	9-0-1	.111	0	73	1	—	0.1
1899	StL N	0	0	ø	2	0	0	0	8.2	7	2	0	0	5	0	1.04	383	.219	.324	3	.333	1	—	3	—	0.2
	Cle N	1	18	.053	20	19	17	0	153	239	181	6	23	105	13	7.24	51	.355	.458	65	.215	1*	58	-67	—	-5.7
	Year	1	18	.053	22	19	17	0	161.2	246	183	6	23	110	13	6.90	54	.348	.452	68	.221	2	57	-59	—	-5.5
Total	2	3	19	.136	26	23	21	0	190.2	276	198	6	24	121	18	6.33	58	.337	.437	77-0-1	.208	2	60	-63	—	-5.4
Bates, John	John William; B5.28.1868 OH; D3.24.1919 Oakland CA; d8.25																									
1889	KC AA	0	1	.000	1	1	1	0	8	15	14	0	0	5	3	13.50	31	.385	.455	4	.000	-1	44	-6	—	-0.5
Batista, Miguel	Miguel Jerez (Decartes); B2.19.1971 Santo Domingo, D.R.; BR/TR/6´0˝/(160–195); d4.11																									
1992	Pit N	0	0	ø	1	0	0	0-0	2	4	2	1	0	3-0	1	9.00	39	.400	.538	0	ø	0	—	-1	0	-0.1
1996	Fla N	0	0	ø	9	0	0	0-0	11.1	9	8	0	0	7-2	6	5.56	74	.231	.348	0	ø	0	—	-2	0	-0.1
1997	Chi N	0	5	.000	11	6	0	0-0	36.1	36	24	4	1	24-2	27	5.70	76	.267	.372	8	.000	-1	82	-5	0	-0.7
1998	Mon N	3	5	.375	56	13	0	0-0	135	141	66	12	6	65-7	92	3.80	111	.274	.359	32-0-2	.000	-4	82	5	0	-0.1
1999	Mon N	8	7	.533	39	17	2-1	1-0	134.2	146	88	10	7	58-2	95	4.88	91	.280	.353	35-1-4	.200	2	120	-9	25	-0.6
2000	Mon N	0	1	.000	4	0	0	0-2	8.1	19	14	2	2	3-0	7	14.04	34	.452	.500	1	.000	0	—	-8	0	-0.8
	KC A	2	6	.250	14	9	0	0-0	57	66	54	17	0	34-2	30	7.74	68	.292	.383	3	.000	-0	84	-16	0	-1.8
2001	†Ari N	11	8	.579	48	18	0	0-0	139.1	113	57	13	10	60-2	90	3.36	138	.226	.320	32-0-2	.063	-2	83	18	0	2.0
2002	†Ari N	8	9	.471	36	29	1	0-0	184.2	172	99	12	6	70-3	112	4.29	105	.245	.316	51-1-2	.157	1	98	2	0	0.2
2003	Ari N	10	9	.526	36	29	2-1	0-0	193.1	197	85	13	8	60-3	142	3.54	131	.267	.326	57-0-4	.070	-4	99	21	0	1.5
2004	Tor A	10	13	.435	38	31	2-1	5-0	198.2	206	115	22	3	96-1	104	4.80	102	.273	.355	5	.000	-1	89	1	0	0.1
2005	Tor A	5	8	.385	71	0	0	31-8	74.2	80	39	9	2	27-5	54	4.10	112	.268	.331	0	ø	0	—	3	0	0.5
2006	Ari N	11	8	.579	34	33	3-1	0-0	206.1	231	116	18	6	84-5	110	4.58	102	.288	.357	60-0-9	.100	-2	108	1	0	-0.1
Total	12	68	79	.463	397	185	10-4	37-10	1381.2	1420	767	133	51	591-34	870	4.46	103	.269	.345	284-2-23	.095	-10	97	10	25	0.0
Batton, Chris	Christopher Sean; B8.24.1954 Los Angeles CA; BR/TR/6´4˝/195; [OakA72 12/286]; d9.19																									
1976	Oak A	0	0	ø	2	1	0	0-0	4	5	4	1	0	3-0	4	9.00	37	.313	.421	0	ø	0	235	-2	0	-0.1
Bauer, Albert	Albert; B8.7.1859 Columbus OH; D2.23.1944 Columbus OH; TL/5´9˝/190; d9.22; U1																									
1884	Col AA	1	2	.333	3	3	3	0	25	22	21	1	0	14	13	4.68	65	.224	.321	11	.273	0	47	-5	—	-0.4
1886	StL N	0	4	.000	4	4	3	0	28.2	31	27	1	—	27	13	5.97	54	.267	.406	12	.167	-1	86	-7	—	-0.8
Total	2	1	6	.143	7	7	6	0	53.2	53	48	2	—	41	26	5.37	58	.248	.369	23	.217	-0	69	-12	—	-1.2
Bauer, Lou	Louis Walter; B11.30.1898 Egg Harbor City NJ; D2.4.1979 Pomona NJ; BR/TR/6´0˝/175; d8.13																									
1918	Phi A	0	0	ø	1	0	0	0	0	0	2	0	0	2	0	(1)	ø	ø	1.000	0	ø	0	—	-1	—	-0.1
Bauer, Rick	Richard Edward; B1.10.1977 Garden Grove CA; BR/TR/6´6˝/(212–225); [BalA97 5/165]; d9.2; Col Treasure Valley (OR) CC																									
2001	Bal A	0	5	.000	6	6	0	0-0	33	35	22	7	1	9-0	16	4.64	93	.265	.315	0	ø	0	54	-3	0	-0.4
2002	Bal A	6	7	.462	56	1	0	1-4	83.2	84	41	12	4	36-4	45	3.98	109	.268	.348	0	ø	0	64	3	0	0.4
2003	Bal A	0	0	ø	35	0	0	0-1	61.1	58	36	5	4	24-3	43	4.55	101	.256	.333	0	ø	0	—	-1	0	0.0
2004	Bal A	2	1	.667	23	2	0	0-1	53.2	49	31	4	4	20-0	37	4.70	99	.238	.317	0	ø	0	69	0	15	0.0
2005	Bal A	0	0	ø	5	0	0	0-0	8.1	13	9	2	0	4-0	5	9.72	45	.361	.425	0	ø	0	—	-4	0	-0.2
2006	Tex A	3	1	.750	58	1	0	2-3	71	73	31	4	4	25-0	35	3.55	132	.272	.338	0	ø	0	80	8	0	0.4
Total	6	11	14	.440	183	10	0	3-9	311	312	170	34	17	118-7	181	4.34	104	.264	.336	0	ø	0	60	3	15	0.2
Bauers, Russ	Russell Lee; B5.10.1914 Townsend WI; D1.1.1995 Hines IL; BL/TR/6´3˝/195; d8.20; Mil 1944–45																									
1936	Pit N	0	0	ø	1	1	0	0	1.1	2	5	0	1	4	0	33.75	12	.500	.778	0	ø	0	167	-4	—	-0.2
1937	Pit N	13	6	.684	34	19	11-2	1	187.2	174	70	2	4	80	118	2.88	134	.245	.325	69-0-1	.217	1	115	21	—	2.2
1938	Pit N	13	14	.481	40	34	12-2	3	243	207	102	7	6	99	117	3.07	124	.233	.314	88-0-3	.239	4	89	18	—	2.1
1939	Pit N	2	4	.333	15	8	1	1	53.2	46	27	4	1	25	12	3.35	114	.240	.330	19-0-1	.211	-0	94	1	—	0.1
1940	Pit N	0	2	.000	15	2	0	0	30.2	42	29	2	2	18	11	7.63	50	.323	.413	7	.286	0	80	-13	—	-0.7
1941	Pit N	1	3	.250	8	5	1	0	37.1	40	28	1	0	25	20	5.54	65	.267	.371	14	.357	1	136	-8	0	-0.7
1946	Chi N	2	1	.667	15	2	2	1	43.1	45	17	1	1	19	22	3.53	94	.273	.351	10	.300	1	90	0	0	0.2
1950	StL A	0	0	ø	1	0	0	0	2	6	4	0	0	1	0	4.50	110	.600	.636	0	ø	0	—	-1	0	0.0
Total	8	31	30	.508	129	71	27-4	6	599	562	282	17	15	271	300	3.53	107	.250	.334	207-0-5	.242	7	101	14	0	3.0
Baumann, Frank	Frank Matt "The Beau"; B7.1.1933 St.Louis MO; BL/TL/6´1˝/(200–210); d7.31																									
1955	Bos A	2	1	.667	7	5	0	0	34	38	28	2	1	17-0	27	5.82	74	.281	.361	13	.231	-0	108	-7	0	-0.5
1956	Bos A	2	1	.667	7	1	0	0	24.2	22	11	3	0	14-0	18	3.28	141	.234	.333	9-0-1	.333	1	231	3	0	0.4
1957	Bos A	1	0	1.000	4	1	0	0	12	13	5	1	1	3-0	7	3.75	106	.277	.333	2-0-1	.500	0	67	1	0	0.1
1958	Bos A	2	2	.500	10	7	2	0	52.1	56	27	4	4	27-2	31	4.47	90	.276	.370	14-0-1	.214	1	77	-1	0	0.0
1959	Bos A	6	4	.600	26	10	2	1	95.2	96	47	11	1	55-3	48	4.05	100	.259	.356	29-0-1	.207	1	104	0	0	0.1

YEAR	TM LG	W	L	PCT	G	GS	CG-SHO	SV-BS	IP	H	R	HR	HB	BB-IB	SO	ERA	AERA	OAV	OOB	AB-HR-SH	AVG	PB	SUP	APR	DL	PW
1960	Chi A	13	6	.684	47	20	7-2	3	185.1	169	67	11	1	53-8	71	**2.67**	142	.247	.300	52	.154	1	122	21	0	2.1
1961	Chi A	10	13	.435	53	23	5-1	3	187.2	249	128	22	2	59-4	75	5.61	70	.318	.366	61-2-1	.262	6*	124	-35	0	-3.2
1962	Chi A	7	6	.538	40	10	3-1	4	119.2	117	46	10	2	36-5	55	3.38	115	.258	.314	30-0-1	.267	4	101	9	0	1.4
1963	Chi A	2	1	.667	24	1	0	1	50.1	52	22	2	0	17-2	31	3.04	115	.265	.322	11	.091	-0	25	1	31	0.1
1964	Chi A	0	3	.000	22	0	0	1	32	40	22	4	0	16-8	19	6.19	56	.320	.392	4-0-1	.000	-0	—	-9	0	-0.9
1965	Chi N	0	1	.000	4	0	0	0	3.2	4	3	0	0	3-0	2	7.36	50	.286	.412	0	ø	0	—	-1	0	-0.2
Total	11	45	38	.542	244	78	19-4	13	797.1	856	406	70	12	300-32	384	4.11	95	.276	.340	225-2-7	.218	14	113	-18	31	-0.6
Baumgardner, George	George Washington; B7.22.1891 Barboursville WV; D12.13.1970 Barboursville WV; BL/TR/5´11˝/178; d4.14																									
1912	StL A	11	13	.458	30	27	18-2	0	218.1	222	101	1	11	79	102	3.38	98	.274	.346	76-0-1	.145	-0	91	3	—	0.3
1913	StL A	10	20	.333	38	31	23-2	1	253.1	267	119	6	10	84	78	3.13	94	.286	.351	78	.167	2	86	-5	—	-0.4
1914	StL A	16	14	.533	45	18	9-3	1	183.2	152	72	3	8	84	93	2.79	97	.229	.323	53-0-4	.132	-1	109	0	—	-0.1
1915	StL A	0	2	.000	7	1	1	0	22.1	29	15	0	0	11	6	4.43	65	.358	.435	6	.000	-1	0	-4	—	-0.4
1916	StL A	1	0	1.000	4	2	0	0	8	12	8	0	0	5	4	7.88	35	.364	.447	2	.000	0	96	-4	—	-0.5
Total	5	38	49	.437	124	79	51-7	2	685.2	682	315	10	29	263	283	3.22	93	.270	.346	215-0-5	.144	-0	93	-10	—	-1.1
Baumgarten, Ross	Ross; B5.27.1955 Highland Park IL; BL/TL/6´1˝/(180–183); [ChiA77 20/491]; d8.16; Col Florida																									
1978	Chi A	2	2	.500	7	4	1-1	0-0	23	29	15	3	1	9-0	15	5.87	65	.315	.375	0	ø	0	106	-5	0	-0.7
1979	Chi A	13	8	.619	28	28	4-3	0-0	190.2	175	82	18	1	83-1	72	3.54	120	.243	.319	0	ø	0	104	17	0	1.7
1980	Chi A	2	12	.143	24	23	3-1	0-0	136	127	60	10	1	52-0	66	3.44	118	.256	.324	0	ø	0	45	9	31	1.0
1981	Chi A	5	9	.357	19	19	2-1	0-0	101.2	101	56	9	1	40-3	52	4.07	89	.260	.329	0	ø	0*	118	-6	0	-0.8
1982	Pit N	0	5	.000	12	10	0	0-0	44	60	33	3	0	27-1	17	6.55	57	.347	.429	12	.083	-1	99	-12	69	-1.3
Total	5	22	36	.379	90	84	10-6	0-0	495.1	492	246	43	4	211-5	222	4.00	100	.263	.336	12	.083	-1	89	3	100	-0.1
Baumgartner, Harry	Harry E.; B10.8.1892 S.Pittsburg TN; D12.3.1930 Augusta GA; BR/TR/5´11˝/175; d9.6																									
1920	Det A	0	1	.000	9	0	0	0	18	18	10	1	0	6	7	4.00	93	.273	.333	4	.250	0	—	0	—	0.0
Baumgartner, Stan	Stanwood Fulton; B12.14.1894 Houston TX; D10.4.1955 Philadelphia PA; BL/TL/6´0˝/175; d6.26; Col Chicago																									
1914	Phi N	2	2	.500	15	4	2-1	0	60.1	60	29	0	2	16	24	3.28	90	.270	.325	19	.053	-1	105	-1	—	-0.3
1915	Phi N	0	2	.000	16	1	0	0	48.1	38	22	2	1	23	27	2.42	113	.226	.323	12	.083	-1*	81	0	—	0.0
1916	Phi N	0	0	ø	1	0	0	0	4	5	2	0	0	1	0	2.25	118	.333	.375	1	.000	-0	—	0	—	0.0
1921	Phi N	3	6	.333	22	7	2	0	66.2	103	72	8	2	22	13	7.02	60	.355	.404	30	.200	0*	72	-19	—	-2.1
1922	Phi N	1	1	.500	6	1	0	0	9.2	18	9	1	0	5	2	6.52	72	.409	.469	3	.333	0	105	-2	—	-0.2
1924	Phi A	13	6	.684	36	16	12-1	4	181	181	72	6	4	73	45	2.88	**149**	.271	.347	60-0-5	.217	-0	91	26	—	2.4
1925	Phi A	6	3	.667	37	12	2-1	3	113.1	120	55	2	7	35	18	3.57	130	.275	.338	30-0-1	.233	-0	101	12	—	0.9
1926	Phi A	1	1	.500	10	1	0	0	22.1	28	10	0	0	10	0	4.03	103	.326	.396	3-0-1	.333	0	182	1	—	0.2
Total	8	26	21	.553	143	42	18-3	7	505.2	553	271	19	16	185	129	3.70	109	.287	.354	158-0-7	.190	-2	98	17	—	0.9
Bausewine, George	George W.; B3.22.1869 Philadelphia PA; D7.29.1947 Norristown PA; 6´2˝/207; d9.14; U1																									
1889	Phi AA	1	4	.200	7	6	6	0	55.1	64	46	1	9	33	18	3.90	97	.281	.393	21	.048	-2	85	-3	—	-0.3
Bauta, Ed	Eduardo (Galvez); B1.6.1935 Florida, Cuba; BR/TR/6´3˝/200; d7.6																									
1960	StL N	0	0	ø	9	0	0	1	15.2	14	11	4	1	11-1	6	6.32	65	.237	.366	1	.000	-0	—	-3	0	-0.2
1961	StL N	2	0	1.000	13	0	0	5	19.1	12	5	2	0	5-1	12	1.40	315	.171	.224	4	.500	1	—	5	0	0.9
1962	StL N	1	0	1.000	20	0	0	1	32.1	28	18	5	1	21-1	25	5.01	85	.239	.357	4	.250	0	—	-1	0	-0.1
1963	StL N	3	4	.429	38	0	0	3	52.2	55	26	2	2	21-4	30	3.93	90	.279	.351	5-0-1	.000	-1	—	-2	0	-0.4
	NY N	0	0	ø	9	0	0	0	19	22	11	0	0	9-0	13	5.21	67	.289	.360	3	.000	-0	—	-3	0	-0.2
	Year	3	4	.429	47	0	0	3	71.2	77	37	2	2	30-4	43	4.27	83	.282	.354	8-0-1	.000	-1	—	-4	0	-0.6
1964	NY N	0	2	.000	8	0	0	1	10	17	6	1	0	3-1	3	5.40	66	.395	.435	0	ø	0	—	-2	0	-0.3
Total	5	6	6	.500	97	0	0	11	149	148	77	14	4	70-8	89	4.35	89	.263	.346	17-0-1	.176	-0	—	-6	0	-0.3
Bautista, Denny	Denny M. (German); B8.23.1980 Sanchez Ramirez, D.R.; BR/TR/6´5˝/(170–190); d5.25																									
2004	Bal A	0	0	ø	2	0	0	0-0	2	6	8	1	1	2-0	1	36.00	13	.545	.600	0	ø	0	—	-7	0	-0.3
	KC A	0	4	.000	5	5	0	0-0	27.2	38	20	2	2	11-1	18	6.51	72	.333	.402	0	ø	0	44	-5	0	-0.6
	Year	0	4	.000	7	5	0	0-0	29.2	44	28	3	3	13-1	19	8.49	55	.352	.423	0	ø	0	44	-11	0	-0.9
2005	KC A	2	2	.500	7	7	0	0-0	35.2	36	23	2	2	17-0	23	5.80	75	.259	.346	0	ø	0	106	-5	144	-0.4
2006	KC A	0	2	.000	8	7	0	0-0	35	38	24	5	4	17-0	22	5.66	83	.277	.369	0	ø	0	103	-4	24	-0.1
	Col N	0	1	.000	4	1	0	0-0	6.2	9	10	0	0	4-0	5	5.40	89	.310	.394	1	.000	-0	115	-3	0	-0.4
Total	3	2	9	.182	26	20	0	0-0	107	127	85	10	9	51-1	69	6.48	71	.295	.379	1	.000	-0	89	-24	168	-1.8
Bautista, Jose	Jose Joaquin (Arias); B7.25.1964 Bani, D.R.; BR/TR/6´2˝/(195–210); d4.9																									
1988	Bal A	6	15	.286	33	25	3	0-0	171.2	171	86	21	7	45-3	76	4.30	92	.258	.310	0	ø	0	63	-5	0	-0.6
1989	Bal A	3	4	.429	15	10	0	0-0	78	84	46	17	1	15-0	30	5.31	72	.274	.309	0	ø	0	83	-12	22	-1.0
1990	Bal A	1	0	1.000	22	0	0	0-0	26.2	28	15	4	0	7-3	15	4.05	94	.272	.315	0	ø	0	—	-2	0	-0.1
1991	Bal A	0	1	.000	5	0	0	0-0	5.1	13	10	1	1	5-0	3	16.88	24	.464	.559	0	ø	0	—	-8	0	-1.1
1993	Chi N	10	3	.769	58	7	1	2-0	111.2	105	38	11	5	27-3	63	2.82	143	.250	.301	21-0-2	.190	0*	153	15	0	1.7
1994	Chi N	4	5	.444	58	0	0	1-3	69.1	75	30	10	3	17-7	45	3.89	108	.284	.330	2	.000	-0	—	4	6	0.4
1995	SF N	3	8	.273	52	6	0	0-0	100.2	120	77	24	5	26-3	45	6.44	64	.295	.341	18-0-1	.000	-2	77	-25	0	-2.6
1996	SF N	3	4	.429	37	1	0	0-1	69.2	66	32	10	2	15-5	28	3.36	123	.249	.291	9-0-1	.111	-0	44	5	17	0.4
1997	Det A	2	2	.500	21	0	0	0-0	40.1	55	32	6	2	12-3	19	6.69	69	.324	.375	0	ø	0	—	-9	0	-0.8
	StL N	0	0	ø	11	0	0	0-0	12.1	15	10	2	1	2-1	4	6.57	64	.300	.340	0	ø	0	—	-3	0	-0.2
Total	9	32	42	.432	312	49	4	3-4	685.2	732	376	106	27	171-28	328	4.62	88	.273	.321	50-0-4	.100	-2	79	-40	45	-3.9
Bayliss, Jonah	Jonah James; B8.13.1980 North Adams MA; BR/TR/6´2˝/(200–210); [KCA02 7/198]; d6.21; Col Trinity (CT)																									
2005	KC A	0	0	ø	11	0	0	0-0	11.2	7	6	2	2	4-0	10	4.63	95	.167	.271	0	ø	0	—	0	0	0.0
2006	Pit N	1	1	.500	11	0	0	0-0	14.2	13	7	1	1	11-2	15	4.30	107	.241	.373	0	ø	0	—	1	0	0.1
Total	2	1	1	.500	22	0	0	0-0	26.1	20	13	3	3	15-2	25	4.44	101	.208	.330	0	ø	0	—	1	0	0.1
Bayne, Bill	William Lear "Beverly"; B4.18.1899 Pittsburgh PA; D5.22.1981 St.Louis MO; BL/TL/5´9˝/160; d9.20																									
1919	StL A	1	1	.500	2	2	1	0	12	16	8	0	0	6	0	5.25	63	.320	.393	5	.400	0	118	-2	—	-0.3
1920	StL A	5	6	.455	18	13	6-1	0	99.2	102	51	3	7	41	38	3.70	106	.279	.363	35-0-1	.171	-2	89	2	—	-0.1
1921	StL A	11	5	.688	47	14	6-1	3	164	167	103	8	5	80	82	4.72	95	.270	.358	60-1-0	.300	5	121	-4	—	0.0
1922	StL A	4	5	.444	26	9	3	2	92.2	86	49	5	9	37	38	4.56	91	.249	.338	30	.233	-1	87	-1	—	-0.2
1923	StL A	2	2	.500	19	2	0	0	46	49	25	4	3	31	15	4.50	93	.287	.405	13-0-2	.231	-0	79	-1	—	-0.1
1924	StL A	1	3	.250	22	3	0	0	50.2	47	31	4	8	29	20	4.44	102	.250	.373	14	.429	2	118	0	—	0.2
1928	Cle A	2	5	.286	37	6	3	3	108.2	128	68	3	10	43	39	5.13	81	.309	.388	30	.367	3	119	-9	—	-0.2
1929	Bos A	5	5	.500	27	6	2	0	84.1	111	72	9	8	29	26	6.72	64	.326	.392	25-0-1	.320	2	63	-21	—	-1.8
1930	Bos A	0	0	ø	1	0	0	0	4	5	2	1	0	1	1	4.50	102	.294	.333	2	.500	0	—	0	—	0.0
Total	9	31	32	.492	199	55	21-2	8	662	711	409	37	50	297	259	4.84	87	.283	.370	214-1-4	.290	10	99	-36	—	-2.5
Bazardo, Yorman	Yorman Michael (Osorio); B7.11.1984 Maracay, Aragua, Venezuela; BR/TR/6´2˝/170; d5.26																									
2005	Fla N	0	0	ø	1	0	0	0-0	1.2	5	5	0	0	2-0	2	21.60	19	.500	.583	1	.000	-0	—	-4	0	-0.2
Beall, Walter	Walter Esau; B7.29.1899 Washington DC; D1.28.1959 Suitland MD; BR/TR/5´10˝/178; d9.3																									
1924	NY A	2	0	1.000	4	2	0	0	23	19	11	2	0	17	18	3.52	118	.237	.371	7	.143	-1	152	1	—	0.0
1925	NY A	0	1	.000	8	1	0	0	11.1	11	17	0	3	19	8	12.71	34	.282	.541	3	.000	-1	39	-10	—	-0.8
1926	NY A	2	4	.333	20	9	1	1	81.2	71	46	2	6	68	56	3.53	109	.240	.392	22-0-1	.136	0	124	0	—	0.0
1927	NY A	0	0	ø	1	0	0	0	1	1	1	0	0	0	0	9.00	43	.333	.333	0	ø	0	—	-1	—	0.0
1929	Was A	1	0	1.000	3	0	0	0	7	8	4	0	0	7	3	3.86	110	.348	.500	3	.000	-1	—	0	—	0.0
Total	5	5	5	.500	36	12	1	1	124	110	79	4	9	111	85	4.43	90	.249	.410	35-0-1	.114	-1	120	-10	—	-0.8
Beam, Alex	Alexander Rodger; B11.21.1869 Johnstown PA; D4.17.1938 Nogales AZ; d5.25																									
1889	Pit N	1	1	.500	2	2	2	0	18	11	16	0	0	15	1	6.50	58	.172	.329	6	.167	0	63	-5	—	-0.4
Beam, Ernie	Ernest Joseph; B3.17.1867 Mansfield OH; D9.12.1918 Mansfield OH; TR/6´0.5˝/185; d5.2																									
1895	Phi N	0	2	.000	9	1	1	**3**	24.2	33	33	1	1	25	3	11.31	42	.317	.454	11	.182	-1*	179	-15	—	-1.2

YEAR	TM LG	W	L	PCT	G	GS	CG-SHO	SV-BS	IP	H	R	HR	HB	BB-IB	SO	ERA	AERA	OAV	OOB	AB-HR-SH	AVG	PB	SUP	APR	DL	PW
Beam, T.J.	Theodore Lester; B8.28.1980 Scottsdale AZ; BR/TR/6´7˝/215; [NYA02 10/306]; d6.17; Col Mississippi																									
2006	NY A	2	0	1.000	20	0	0	0-1	18	26	17	5	2	6-2	12	8.50	53	.338	.400	1	.000	-0	—	-7	0	-0.7
Beamon, Charlie	Charles Alfonzo Sr.; B12.25.1934 Oakland CA; BR/TR/5´11˝/195; d9.26; s–Charlie																									
1956	Bal A	2	0	1.000	2	1	1-1	0	13	9	2	0	0	8-0	14	1.38	283	.191	.309	5	.000	-1	23	4	0	0.6
1957	Bal A	0	0	ø	4	1	0	0	8.2	8	6	1	1	7-0	5	5.19	69	.229	.372	2	.000	-0	273	-2	0	-0.1
1958	Bal A	1	3	.250	21	3	0	0	49.2	47	27	3	6	21-1	26	4.35	83	.266	.361	10-0-1	.000	-1*	108	-5	0	-0.3
Total	3	3	3	.500	27	5	1-1	0	71.1	64	35	4	7	36-1	45	3.91	93	.247	.353	17-0-1	.000	-2	123	-3	0	0.2
Bean, Belve	Beveric Benton "Bill"; B4.23.1905 Mullin TX; D6.1.1988 Comanche TX; BR/TR/6´1.5˝/197; d5.30																									
1930	Cle A	3	3	.500	23	3	1	2	74.1	99	58	7	0	32	19	5.45	89	.331	.396	26	.346	2	107	-6	—	-0.2
1931	Cle A	0	1	.000	4	0	0	0	7	11	5	0	1	4	3	6.43	72	.379	.471	1	.000	-0	—	-1	—	-0.1
1933	Cle A	1	2	.333	27	2	0	0	70.1	80	43	6	1	20	41	5.25	85	.300	.351	22	.182	-1	105	-4	—	-0.2
1934	Cle A	5	1	.833	21	1	0	0	51.1	53	25	2	3	21	20	3.86	118	.265	.344	15-0-1	.200	0	96	4	—	0.5
1935	Cle A	0	0	ø	1	0	0	0	1	2	1	1	0	0	0	9.00	50	.400	.400	0	ø	0	—	0	—	0.0
	Was A	2	0	1.000	10	2	0	0	31	43	28	5	0	19	6	7.26	60	.339	.425	8-1-0	.375	3	181	-10	—	-0.3
	Year	2	0	1.000	11	2	0	0	32	45	29	6	0	19	6	7.31	59	.341	.424	8-1-0	.375	3	181	-11	—	-0.3
Total	5	11	7	.611	86	8	1	2	235	288	160	21	5	96	89	5.32	86	.311	.378	72-1-1	.264	4	122	-17	—	-0.3
Bean, Colter	Randall Colter; B1.16.1977 Anniston AL; BL/TR/6´6˝/255; d4.26; Col Auburn																									
2005	NY A	0	0	ø	1	0	0	0-0	2	1	1	0	0	2-0	2	4.50	96	.143	.333	0	ø	0	—	0	0	0.0
2006	NY A	0	0	ø	2	0	0	0-0	2	2	2	0	1	2-0	1	9.00	50	.333	.500	0	ø	0	—	-1	0	0.0
Total	2	0	0	ø	3	0	0	0-0	4	3	3	0	1	4-0	3	6.75	65	.231	.421	0	ø	0	—	-1	0	0.0
Beard, Dave	Charles David; B10.2.1959 Atlanta GA; BL/TR/6´5˝/(190–215); [OakA77 6/147]; d7.16																									
1980	Oak A	0	1	.000	13	0	0	1-0	16	12	6	0	1	7-1	12	3.38	113	.218	.313	0	ø	0	—	1	0	0.1
1981	†Oak A	1	1	.500	8	0	0	3-1	13	9	5	1	1	4-1	15	2.77	127	.191	.264	0	ø	0	—	1	0	0.2
1982	Oak A	10	9	.526	54	2	0	11-8	91.2	85	41	9	1	35-6	73	3.44	115	.244	.308	0	ø	0	58	5	0	0.9
1983	Oak A	5	5	.500	43	0	0	10-3	61	55	39	8	2	36-4	40	5.61	69	.246	.351	0	ø	0	—	-11	22	-1.9
1984	Sea A	3	2	.600	43	0	0	5-3	76	88	56	15	4	33-5	40	5.80	69	.291	.362	0	ø	0	—	-16	34	-1.1
1985	Chi N	0	0	ø	9	0	0	0-0	12.2	16	9	2	0	7-2	4	6.39	63	.314	.397	0	ø	0	—	-3	0	-0.1
1989	Det A	0	2	.000	2	1	0	0-0	5.1	9	7	2	1	2-0	1	5.06	76	.375	.444	0	ø	0	47	-2	70	-0.4
Total	7	19	20	.487	172	3	0	30-15	275.2	274	163	37	10	124-19	185	4.70	84	.261	.339	0	ø	0	54	-25	126	-2.3
Beard, Mike	Michael Richard; B6.21.1950 Little Rock AR; BL/TL/6´1˝/185; [AtlN71 D1/18]; d9.7; Col Texas																									
1974	Atl N	0	0	ø	6	0	0	0-0	9.1	5	3	1	1	1-0	7	2.89	131	.156	.206	0	ø	0	—	1	0	0.1
1975	Atl N	4	0	1.000	34	2	0	0-3	70.1	71	31	4	2	28-5	27	3.20	118	.265	.333	9-0-1	.111	-0	105	4	0	0.2
1976	Atl N	0	2	.000	30	0	0	1-2	33.2	38	18	1	0	14-3	8	4.28	89	.299	.364	1	.000	-0	—	-2	0	-0.1
1977	Atl N	0	0	ø	4	0	0	0-0	4.2	14	11	3	0	2-0	1	9.64	46	.452	.485	0	ø	0	—	-4	0	-0.2
Total	4	4	2	.667	74	2	0	1-5	118	128	63	9	3	45-8	43	3.74	102	.279	.343	10-0-1	.100	-0	105	-1	0	0.0
Beard, Ralph	Ralph William; B2.11.1929 Cincinnati OH; D2.10.2003 West Palm Beach FL; BR/TR/6´5˝/200; d6.29; Col Cincinnati																									
1954	StL N	0	4	.000	13	10	0	0	58	62	32	2	2	28	17	3.72	110	.278	.357	17	.059	-1	69	0	0	-0.2
Bearden, Gene	Henry Eugene; B9.5.1920 Lexa AR; D3.18.2004 Alexander City AL; BL/TL/6´3˝/204; d5.10																									
1947	Cle A	0	0	ø	1	0	0	0	0.1	2	3	0	0	1	0	81.00	4	.667	.750	0	ø	0	—	-3	0	-0.1
1948	†Cle A	20	7	.741	37	29	15-6	1	229.2	187	72	9	3	106	80	**2.43**	**167**	.229	.320	90-2-2	.256	5	145	**43**	0	5.5
1949	Cle A	8	8	.500	32	19	5	0	127	140	77	6	2	92	41	5.10	78	.286	.401	45-0-2	.111	-3	99	-15	0	-1.7
1950	Cle A	1	3	.250	14	3	0	0	45.1	57	32	5	0	32	10	6.15	70	.328	.432	13	.154	1	111	-8	0	-0.6
	Was A	3	5	.375	12	9	4	0	68.1	81	35	1	2	33	20	4.21	107	.297	.377	22-0-1	.227	1*	74	3	0	0.4
	Year	4	8	.333	26	12	4	0	113.2	138	67	6	2	65	30	4.99	89	.309	.399	35-0-1	.200	2	83	-5	0	-0.2
1951	Was A	0	0	ø	1	1	0	0	2.2	6	5	0	0	2	1	16.88	24	.429	.500	0	ø	0	152	-4	0	-0.2
	Det A	3	4	.429	37	4	2-1	0	106	112	58	6	1	58	38	4.33	96	.275	.366	32-2-1	.188	1	101	-2	0	0.0
	Year	3	4	.429	38	5	2-1	0	108.2	118	63	6	1	60	39	4.64	90	.280	.371	32-2-1	.188	1	111	-5	0	-0.2
1952	StL A	7	8	.467	34	16	3	0	150.2	158	89	13	1	78	45	4.30	91	.270	.357	65-0-1	.354	6*	81	-9	0	-0.1
1953	Chi A	3	3	.500	25	3	0	0	58.1	48	27	8	0	33	24	2.93	137	.223	.327	21-0-2	.190	-1*	169	4	0	0.3
Total	7	45	38	.542	193	84	29-7	1	788.1	791	398	48	9	435	259	3.96	103	.266	.361	288-4-9	.236	10	111	9	0	3.5
Beare, Gary	Gary Ray; B8.22.1952 San Diego CA; BR/TR/6´4˝/200; [MilA74 5/102]; d9.7; Col Cal St.–Long Beach																									
1976	Mil A	2	3	.400	6	5	2	0-0	41	43	16	4	0	15-0	32	3.29	107	.274	.335	0	ø	0	125	1	0	0.2
1977	Mil A	3	3	.500	17	6	0	0-0	58.2	63	46	6	1	38-3	32	6.44	64	.276	.378	0	ø	0	124	-15	0	-1.2
Total	2	5	6	.455	23	11	2	0-0	99.2	106	62	10	1	53-3	64	5.15	75	.275	.361	0	ø	0	124	-14	0	-1.0
Bearnarth, Larry	Lawrence Donald; B9.11.1941 New York NY; D12.31.1999 Seminole FL; BR/TR/6´2˝/(202–205); d4.16; C11; Col St. Johns																									
1963	NY N	3	8	.273	58	2	0	4	126.1	127	61	7	5	47-9	48	3.42	102	.268	.338	30	.200	1	111	-1	0	0.2
1964	NY N	5	5	.500	44	1	0	3	78	79	38	6	2	38-1	31	4.15	86	.271	.358	14	.143	-0	123	-4	0	-0.4
1965	NY N	3	5	.375	40	3	0	1	60.2	75	43	6	4	28-2	16	4.60	77	.304	.381	9	.111	0	49	-11	0	-1.3
1966	NY N	2	3	.400	29	1	0	0	54.2	59	31	11	1	20-6	27	4.45	82	.281	.342	9	.111	-0	0	-5	0	-0.4
1971	Mil A	0	0	ø	2	0	0	0-0	3	10	6	1	0	2-0	2	18.00	19	.556	.600	0	ø	0	—	-4	0	-0.2
Total	5	13	21	.382	173	7	0	8-0	322.2	350	179	31	12	135-18	124	4.13	86	.282	.356	62	.161	1	70	-25	0	-2.1
Bearse, Kevin	Kevin Gerard; B11.7.1965 Jersey City NJ; BL/TL/6´2˝/195; [CleA87 22/567]; d4.15; Col Old Dominion																									
1990	Cle A	0	2	.000	3	3	0	0-0	7.2	16	11	2	2	5-0	2	12.91	31	.421	.511	0	ø	0	62	-7	0	-1.2
Beasley, Chris	Christopher Charles; B6.23.1962 Jackson TN; BR/TR/6´2˝/190; [CleA84 9/214]; d7.20; Col Arizona St.																									
1991	Cal A	0	1	.000	22	0	0	0-0	26.2	26	14	2	1	10-1	14	3.38	122	.257	.327	0	ø	0	—	1	0	0.1
Beatin, Ed	Ebenezer Ambrose; B8.10.1866 Baltimore MD; D5.9.1925 Baltimore MD; BR/TL/5´9˝/162; d8.2																									
1887	Det N	1	1	.500	2	2	2	0	18	13	11	2	1	8	6	4.00	102	.203	.301	7	.000	-1	103	0	—	-0.1
1888	Det N	5	7	.417	12	12	12-1	0	107	111	60	6	2	16	44	2.86	98	.251	.280	56-2	.250	5*	84	-1	—	0.3
1889	Cle N	20	15	.571	36	36	35-3	0	317.2	316	179	12	6	141	126	3.57	113	.252	.330	121-1	.116	-5*	86	19	—	1.1
1890	Cle N	22	30	.423	54	54	53-1	0	474.1	518	300	11	15	186	155	3.83	94	.269	.338	191-1	.141	-9	80	-11	—	-1.6
1891	Cle N	0	3	.000	5	4	2	0	29	39	44	1	6	21	4	5.28	66	.310	.431	13	.077	-1	86	-9	—	-0.8
Total	5	48	56	.462	109	108	104-5	0	946	997	594	32	30	372	335	3.68	99	.261	.332	388-4	.144	-13	83	-2	—	-1.1
Beattie, Jim	James Louis; B7.4.1954 Hampton VA; BR/TR/6´6˝/(205–225); [NYA75 4/91]; d4.25; Col Dartmouth																									
1978	†NY A	6	9	.400	25	22	0	0-0	128	123	60	8	8	51-2	65	3.73	98	.255	.335	0	ø	0	102	-1	0	-0.1
1979	NY A	3	6	.333	15	13	1-1	0-0	76	85	45	5	0	41-0	32	5.21	79	.294	.375	0	ø	0	90	-8	27	-0.7
1980	Sea A	5	15	.250	33	29	3	0-0	187.1	205	115	19	4	98-9	67	4.85	86	.286	.372	0	ø	0	93	-15	0	-1.4
1981	Sea A	3	2	.600	13	9	0	1-0	66.2	59	24	2	2	18-0	36	2.97	131	.232	.288	0	ø	0	80	7	0	0.5
1982	Sea A	8	12	.400	28	26	6-1	0-0	172.1	149	73	13	1	65-0	140	3.34	128	.233	.303	0	ø	0	81	16	0	1.8
1983	Sea A	10	15	.400	30	29	8-2	0-0	196.2	197	89	12	3	66-6	132	3.84	112	.259	.320	0	ø	0	72	11	23	1.5
1984	Sea A	12	16	.429	32	32	12-2	0-0	211	206	86	13	5	75-6	119	3.41	118	.260	.326	0	ø	0	91	16	0	2.0
1985	Sea A	5	6	.455	18	15	1-1	0-0	70.1	93	61	9	3	33-0	45	7.29	58	.316	.385	0	ø	0	131	-23	84	-2.9
1986	Sea A	0	6	.000	9	7	0	0-0	40.1	57	28	7	3	14-2	24	6.02	71	.341	.398	0	ø	0	73	-7	125	-0.8
Total	9	52	87	.374	203	182	31-7	1-0	1148.2	1174	581	88	29	461-25	660	4.17	99	.267	.338	0	ø	0	90	-4	259	-0.1
Beatty, Blaine	Gordon Blaine; B4.25.1964 Victoria TX; BL/TL/6´2˝/(185–190); [BalA86 9/227]; d9.16; Col Baylor; [DL 1990 NY N 178]																									
1989	NY N	0	0	ø	2	1	0	0-0	6	5	1	1	0	2-0	3	1.50	220	.217	.280	2	.500	0	188	1	0	0.1
1991	NY N	0	0	ø	5	0	0	0-0	9.2	9	3	0	0	4-1	7	2.79	131	.250	.317	0	ø	0	—	1	0	0.1
Total	2	0	0	ø	7	1	0	0-0	15.2	14	4	1	0	6-1	10	2.30	153	.237	.303	2	.500	0	188	2	178	0.2
Beazley, Johnny	John Andrew "Nig"; B5.25.1918 Nashville TN; D4.21.1990 Nashville TN; BR/TR/6´1.5˝/190; d9.28; Mil 1943–45																									
1941	StL N	1	0	1.000	1	1	1	0	9	10	1	0	0	3	4	1.00	376	.294	.351	3	.000	-0	68	3	0	0.3
1942	†StL N	21	6	.778	43	23	13-3	3	215.1	181	67	4	3	73	91	2.13	161	.226	.293	73-0-9	.137	-1	120	28	0	3.5
1946	†StL N	7	5	.583	19	18	5	0	103	109	55	6	4	55	36	4.46	77	.275	.368	33-0-3	.242	1	114	-9	0	-0.9

YEAR	TM LG	W	L	PCT	G	GS	CG-SHO	SV-BS	IP	H	R	HR	HB	BB-IB	SO	ERA	AERA	OAV	OOB	AB-HR-SH	AVG	PB	SUP	APR	DL	PW
1947	Bos N	2	0	1.000	9	2	2	0	28.2	30	15	1	0	19	12	4.40	89	.273	.380	7-0-2	.000	-1	193	-1	0	-0.2
1948	Bos N	0	1	.000	3	2	0	0	16	19	13	2	0	7	4	4.50	85	.284	.351	4-0-1	.000	-1	127	-3	94	-0.2
1949	Bos N	0	0	ø	1	0	0	0	2	0	0	0	0	0	0	0.00	ø	.000	.000	0	ø	0	—	1	0	0.0
Total	6	31	12	.721	76	46	21-3	3	374	349	151	13	7	157	147	3.01	116	.247	.325	120-0-15	.150	-1	120	19	94	2.5

Becannon, Buck James Melvin; B8.22.1859 New York NY; D11.5.1923 New York NY; 5´10˝/165; d10.15

YEAR	TM LG	W	L	PCT	G	GS	CG-SHO	SV-BS	IP	H	R	HR	HB	BB-IB	SO	ERA	AERA	OAV	OOB	AB-HR-SH	AVG	PB	SUP	APR	DL	PW
1884	†NY AA	1	0	1.000	1	1	1	0	6	2	2	0	0	2	2	1.50	208	.091	.167	3	.000	-0	251	1	—	0.1
1885	NY AA	2	8	.200	10	10	10	0	85	108	84	5	5	24	13	6.25	50	.296	.348	33	.303	2	108	-28	—	-2.2
Total	2	3	8	.273	11	11	11	0	91	110	86	5	5	26	15	5.93	53	.284	.337	36	.278	1	121	-27	—	-2.1

Bechler, Steve Steven Scott; B11.18.1979 Medford OR; D2.17.2003 Ft.Lauderdale FL; BR/TR/6´2˝/207; [BalA98 3/99]; d9.6

YEAR	TM LG	W	L	PCT	G	GS	CG-SHO	SV-BS	IP	H	R	HR	HB	BB-IB	SO	ERA	AERA	OAV	OOB	AB-HR-SH	AVG	PB	SUP	APR	DL	PW
2002	Bal A	0	0	ø	3	0	0	0-0	4.2	6	7	3	1	4-0	3	13.50	32	.300	.440	0	ø	0	—	-5	0	-0.2

Bechtel, George George A.; B1848 Philadelphia PA; 5´11˝/165; d5.20; ▲

YEAR	TM LG	W	L	PCT	G	GS	CG-SHO	SV-BS	IP	H	R	HR	HB	BB-IB	SO	ERA	AERA	OAV	OOB	AB-HR-SH	AVG	PB	SUP	APR	DL	PW
1871	Ath NA	1	2	.333	3	3	2	0	26	43	42	0	—	11	1	7.96	51	.319	.370	94-1	.351	1*	99	-11	—	-0.6
1873	Phi NA	0	2	.000	3	2	1	0	16	27	24	0	—	2	0	4.50	77	.318	.333	258-1	.244	0*	103	-3	—	-0.2
1874	Phi NA	1	3	.250	6	4	4	0	39	57	42	0	—	1	0	1.62	137	.297	.301	151-1	.278	1*	85	1	—	0.1
1875	Cen NA	2	12	.143	14	14	14	0	126	169	138	0	—	5	6	2.71	80	.274	.280	61	.279	3	81	-8	—	-0.3
	Ath NA	3	1	.750	4	4	4	0	36	41	19	0	—	3	3	2.50	96	.279	.293	164	.280	0*	158	0	—	0.0
	Year	5	13	.278	18	18	18	0	162	210	157	0	—	8	9	2.67	83	.275	.283	225	.280	4	99	-15	—	-0.3
Total	4NA	7	20	.259	30	27	25	0	243	337	265	0	—	22	10	3.19	79	.287	.300	728-3	.276	6	98	-21	—	-1.0

Beck, George Ernest George Bernard; B2.21.1890 South Bend IN; D10.29.1973 South Bend IN; BR/TR/5´11˝/165; d5.15

YEAR	TM LG	W	L	PCT	G	GS	CG-SHO	SV-BS	IP	H	R	HR	HB	BB-IB	SO	ERA	AERA	OAV	OOB	AB-HR-SH	AVG	PB	SUP	APR	DL	PW
1914	Cle A	0	0	ø	1	0	0	0	1	1	0	0	1	0	0	0.00	ø	.250	.400	0	ø	0	—	0	—	0.0

Beck, Frank Frank J. (b Frank J. Hengstebeck); B11.1858; TR/5´9˝/141; d5.2

YEAR	TM LG	W	L	PCT	G	GS	CG-SHO	SV-BS	IP	H	R	HR	HB	BB-IB	SO	ERA	AERA	OAV	OOB	AB-HR-SH	AVG	PB	SUP	APR	DL	PW
1884	Pit AA	0	3	.000	3	3	3	0	25	33	29	0	5	6	11	6.12	54	.306	.370	12	.333	1	79	-8	—	-0.7
	Bal U	0	2	.000	2	2	1	0	9	17	13	0	—	4	7	8.00	33	.378	.429	20	.100	-1*	112	-4	—	-0.7
Total	1	0	5	.000	5	5	4	0	34	50	42	0	5	10	18	6.62	48	.327	.387	32	.188	-0	95	-12	—	-1.4

Beck, Rich Richard Henry; B1.21.1941 Pasco WA; BB/TR/6´3˝/190; d9.14; Mil 1966–67; Col Gonzaga

YEAR	TM LG	W	L	PCT	G	GS	CG-SHO	SV-BS	IP	H	R	HR	HB	BB-IB	SO	ERA	AERA	OAV	OOB	AB-HR-SH	AVG	PB	SUP	APR	DL	PW
1965	NY A	2	1	.667	3	3	1-1	0	21	22	6	1	0	7-1	10	2.14	159	.275	.333	7	.000	-0	77	3	0	0.4

Beck, Rod Rodney Roy; B8.3.1968 Burbank CA; BR/TR/6´1˝/(215–236); [OakA86 13/327]; d5.6

YEAR	TM LG	W	L	PCT	G	GS	CG-SHO	SV-BS	IP	H	R	HR	HB	BB-IB	SO	ERA	AERA	OAV	OOB	AB-HR-SH	AVG	PB	SUP	APR	DL	PW
1991	SF N	1	1	.500	31	0	0	1-0	52.1	53	22	4	1	13-2	38	3.78	95	.273	.319	2	.500	0	—	0	0	0.0
1992	SF N	3	3	.500	65	0	0	17-6	92	62	20	4	2	15-2	87	1.76	189	.190	.228	2	.500	0	—	17	0	1.7
1993	SF N★	3	1	.750	76	0	0	48-4	79.1	57	20	11	3	13-4	86	2.16	182	.201	.241	4-0-1	.000	-0	—	16	0	2.4
1994	SF N★	2	4	.333	48	0	0	28-0	48.2	49	17	10	0	13-2	39	2.77	146	.261	.304	3	.000	-0	—	7	24	1.3
1995	SF N	5	6	.455	60	0	0	33-10	58.2	60	31	7	2	21-3	42	4.45	93	.267	.331	3	.333	0	—	-2	0	-0.3
1996	SF N	0	9	.000	63	0	0	35-7	62	56	23	9	1	10-2	48	3.34	124	.238	.270	3	.333	0	—	7	0	1.4
1997	†SF N☆	7	4	.636	73	0	0	37-8	70	67	31	7	2	8-2	53	3.47	119	.248	.275	0	ø	0	—	5	0	0.9
1998	†Chi N	3	4	.429	**81**	0	0	51-7	80.1	86	33	11	2	20-4	81	3.02	146	.269	.311	1	.000	-0	—	10	0	1.9
1999	Chi N	2	4	.333	31	0	0	7-4	30	41	26	5	0	13-3	13	7.80	59	.331	.388	0	ø	0	—	-10	65	-1.8
	†Bos A	0	1	.000	12	0	0	3-1	14	9	3	0	1	5-0	12	1.93	258	.184	.273	0	ø	0	—	5	0	0.5
2000	Bos A	3	0	1.000	34	0	0	0-3	40.2	34	15	2	2	12-1	35	3.10	162	.222	.287	0	ø	0	—	9	94	0.5
2001	Bos A	6	4	.600	68	0	0	6-5	80.2	77	42	15	3	28-6	63	3.90	114	.252	.319	1	.000	-0	—	3	0	0.4
2003	SD N	3	2	.600	36	0	0	20-0	35.1	25	7	4	1	11-2	32	1.78	225	.197	.266	0	ø	0	—	10	0	2.0
2004	SD N	0	2	.000	26	0	0	0-0	24	27	18	8	0	9-0	15	6.38	62	.278	.333	0	ø	0	—	-7	0	-0.5
Total	13	38	45	.458	704	0	0	286-55	768	703	308	97	20	191-33	644	3.30	124	.242	.291	19-0-1	.211	0	—	70	183	10.4

Beck, Boom-Boom Walter William; B10.16.1904 Decatur IL; D5.7.1987 Champaign IL; BR/TR/6´2˝/200; d9.22; C3

YEAR	TM LG	W	L	PCT	G	GS	CG-SHO	SV-BS	IP	H	R	HR	HB	BB-IB	SO	ERA	AERA	OAV	OOB	AB-HR-SH	AVG	PB	SUP	APR	DL	PW
1924	StL A	0	0	ø	1	0	0	0	1	2	0	0	0	1	0	0.00	ø	.667	.750	0	ø	0	—	0	—	0.0
1927	StL A	1	0	1.000	3	1	1	0	11.1	15	8	0	1	5	6	5.56	78	.333	.412	4	.250	-0	153	-1	—	-0.1
1928	StL A	2	3	.400	16	4	2	0	49	52	29	4	4	20	17	4.41	95	.289	.373	14	.429	1	96	-2	—	0.0
1933	Bro N	12	20	.375	43	**35**	15-3	1	257	270	128	9	11	69	89	3.54	91	.267	.321	95-0-2	.189	0	111	-12	—	-1.4
1934	Bro N	2	6	.250	22	9	2	0	57	72	50	6	5	32	24	7.42	53	.301	.395	17-0-1	.235	1	118	-21	—	-2.3
1939	Phi N	7	14	.333	34	16	12	3	182.2	203	104	11	3	64	77	4.73	85	.284	.345	68-0-4	.132	-3	68	-13	—	-1.6
1940	Phi N	4	9	.308	29	15	4	0	129.1	147	69	13	9	41	38	4.31	90	.286	.349	36-0-3	.056	-3	58	-5	—	-0.7
1941	Phi N	1	9	.100	34	7	2	0	95.1	104	52	8	2	35	34	4.63	80	.276	.341	25-0-1	.120	-2	62	-8	0	-1.0
1942	Phi N	0	1	.000	26	1	0	0	53	69	30	4	1	17	10	4.75	70	.325	.378	12	.333	1*	102	-8	0	-0.3
1943	Phi N	0	0	ø	4	0	0	0	13.2	24	15	1	2	5	3	9.88	34	.393	.456	4	.500	1	—	-9	0	-0.4
1944	Det A	1	2	.333	28	2	0	1	74	67	36	5	3	27	25	3.89	92	.243	.317	22-0-1	.318	2	105	-1	0	0.0
1945	Cin N	2	4	.333	11	6	2	1	47.2	42	21	0	1	12	9	3.40	111	.236	.288	14-0-2	.214	-0	68	2	0	0.2
	Pit N	6	1	.857	14	5	4	0	63	54	19	2	0	14	20	2.14	184	.234	.278	16-0-5	.125	-1	94	12	0	1.1
	Year	8	5	.615	25	11	6	1	110.2	96	40	2	1	26	29	2.68	144	.235	.282	30-0-7	.167	-1	81	13	0	1.3
Total	12	38	69	.355	265	101	44-3	6	1034	1121	561	63	42	342	352	4.30	86	.277	.340	327-0-19	.187	-2	89	-66	0	-6.5

Becker, Charlie Charles Schlagel "Buck"; B10.14.1890 Washington DC; D7.30.1928 Washington DC; BL/TL/6´2˝/180; d8.2

YEAR	TM LG	W	L	PCT	G	GS	CG-SHO	SV-BS	IP	H	R	HR	HB	BB-IB	SO	ERA	AERA	OAV	OOB	AB-HR-SH	AVG	PB	SUP	APR	DL	PW
1911	Was A	3	5	.375	11	5	5-1	0	71.1	80	44	2	7	23	31	4.04	81	.268	.335	22-0-1	.227	-0	48	-5	—	-0.5
1912	Was A	0	0	ø	4	0	0	0	9	8	6	0	0	6	5	3.00	111	.258	.378	2	.500	0	—	0	—	0.0
Total	2	3	5	.375	15	5	5-1	0	80.1	88	50	2	7	29	36	3.92	84	.267	.340	24-0-1	.250	0	48	-5	—	-0.5

Becker, Bob Robert Charles; B8.15.1875 Syracuse NY; D10.11.1951 Syracuse NY; TL; d9.6

YEAR	TM LG	W	L	PCT	G	GS	CG-SHO	SV-BS	IP	H	R	HR	HB	BB-IB	SO	ERA	AERA	OAV	OOB	AB-HR-SH	AVG	PB	SUP	APR	DL	PW
1897	Phi N	0	2	.000	5	2	2	0	24	32	18	0	1	7	10	5.63	75	.317	.367	9	.111	-0	85	-3	—	-0.3
1898	Phi N	0	0	ø	1	0	0	0	5	6	6	0	0	5	0	10.80	32	.300	.440	1	.000	0	—	-3	—	-0.1
Total	2	0	2	.000	6	2	2	0	29	38	24	0	1	12	10	6.52	62	.314	.381	10	.100	-0	85	-6	—	-0.4

Beckett, Josh Joshua Patrick; B5.15.1980 Spring TX; BR/TR/6´4˝/(190–220); [FlaN99 1/2]; d9.4

YEAR	TM LG	W	L	PCT	G	GS	CG-SHO	SV-BS	IP	H	R	HR	HB	BB-IB	SO	ERA	AERA	OAV	OOB	AB-HR-SH	AVG	PB	SUP	APR	DL	PW
2001	Fla N	2	2	.500	4	4	0	0-0	24	14	9	3	1	11-0	24	1.50	278	.161	.263	7-0-2	.286	1	116	5	0	1.0
2002	Fla N	6	7	.462	23	21	0	0-0	107.2	93	56	13	1	44-2	113	4.10	96	.232	.307	31-0-5	.032	-3	109	-4	75	-0.7
2003	†Fla N	9	8	.529	24	23	0	0-0	142	132	54	9	2	56-4	152	3.04	135	.246	.319	46-0-5	.152	0	120	16	54	1.8
2004	Fla N	9	9	.500	26	26	1-1	0-0	156.2	137	72	16	6	54-3	152	3.79	108	.235	.305	44-0-9	.159	0	89	5	58	0.5
2005	Fla N	15	8	.652	29	29	2-1	0-0	178.2	153	75	14	7	58-2	166	3.38	119	.234	.303	59-1-4	.153	3	121	12	32	1.9
2006	Bos A	16	11	.593	33	33	0	0-0	204.2	191	120	36	10	74-1	158	5.01	93	.245	.317	7-1-0	.429	2	102	-7	0	-0.6
Total	6	57	45	.559	139	136	3-2	0-0	813.2	720	386	91	27	297-12	765	3.85	109	.237	.309	194-2-25	.149	4	108	27	219	3.9

Beckett, Robbie Robert Joseph; B7.16.1972 Austin TX; BR/TL/6´5˝/(225–240); [SDN90 1/25]; d9.12

YEAR	TM LG	W	L	PCT	G	GS	CG-SHO	SV-BS	IP	H	R	HR	HB	BB-IB	SO	ERA	AERA	OAV	OOB	AB-HR-SH	AVG	PB	SUP	APR	DL	PW
1996	Col N	0	0	ø	5	0	0	0-1	5.1	6	8	3	0	9-0	6	13.50	39	.286	.484	0	ø	0	—	-4	0	-0.2
1997	Col N	0	0	ø	2	0	0	0-0	1.2	1	1	0	0	1-1	2	5.40	96	.167	.286	0	ø	0	—	0	0	0.0
Total	2	0	0	ø	7	0	0	0-1	7	7	9	3	0	10-1	8	11.57	45	.259	.447	0	ø	0	—	-4	0	-0.2

Beckman, Jim James Joseph (b Reinhardt Boeckman); B3.1.1905 Cincinnati OH; D12.5.1974 Montgomery OH; BR/TR/5´10˝/172; d7.27

YEAR	TM LG	W	L	PCT	G	GS	CG-SHO	SV-BS	IP	H	R	HR	HB	BB-IB	SO	ERA	AERA	OAV	OOB	AB-HR-SH	AVG	PB	SUP	APR	DL	PW
1927	Cin N	0	1	.000	4	1	0	0	12.1	18	10	2	1	6	0	5.84	65	.340	.417	1	.000	0	67	-3	—	-0.2
1928	Cin N	0	1	.000	6	0	0	0	15.1	19	12	1	0	9	4	5.87	67	.306	.394	3	.000	-0	—	-4	—	-0.3
Total	2	0	2	.000	10	1	0	0	27.2	37	22	3	1	15	4	5.86	66	.322	.405	4	.000	-0	67	-7	—	-0.5

Beckmann, Bill William Aloysius; B12.8.1907 Clayton MO; D1.2.1990 Florissant MO; BR/TR/6´0˝/175; d5.2; Col Washington–St. Louis

YEAR	TM LG	W	L	PCT	G	GS	CG-SHO	SV-BS	IP	H	R	HR	HB	BB-IB	SO	ERA	AERA	OAV	OOB	AB-HR-SH	AVG	PB	SUP	APR	DL	PW
1939	Phi A	7	11	.389	27	19	7-2	0	155.1	198	104	15	1	41	20	5.39	87	.312	.355	52-0-6	.250	0	98	-9	—	-0.9
1940	Phi A	8	4	.667	34	9	6-2	1	127.1	132	68	11	1	35	47	4.17	107	.265	.314	39-0-3	.205	-1	81	5	—	0.2
1941	Phi A	5	9	.357	22	15	4	1	130	141	76	11	2	33	28	4.57	92	.270	.315	47-0-4	.191	0	92	-6	0	-0.6
1942	Phi A	0	1	.000	5	1	0	0	20.1	24	17	1	0	9	10	7.08	53	.289	.359	4-0-1	.500	1	113	-6	0	-0.2
	StL N	1	0	1.000	2	0	0	0	7	4	0	0	0	1	3	0.00	ø	.200	.238	1	.000	-0	—	3	0	0.4
Total	4	21	25	.457	90	44	17-4	2	440	499	265	38	4	119	108	4.79	92	.284	.330	143-0-14	.224	1	94	-13	0	-1.1

YEAR	TM LG	W	L	PCT	G	GS	CG-SHO	SV-BS	IP	H	R	HR	HB	BB-IB	SO	ERA	AERA	OAV	OOB	AB-HR-SH	AVG	PB	SUP	APR	DL	PW
BECKWITH, JOE	Thomas Joseph; B1.28.1955 Opelika AL; BL/TR/6´3˝/(185–200); [LAN77 2/46]; d7.21; Col Auburn; [DL 1981 LA N 180]																									
1979	LA N	1	2	.333	17	0	0	2-0	37.1	42	18	4	0	15-1	28	4.34	83	.284	.350	5-0-1	.000	-1	—	-2	0	-0.2
1980	LA N	3	3	.500	38	0	0	0-0	59.2	60	17	1	1	23-4	40	1.96	177	.263	.331	2	.000	0	—	9	0	0.9
1982	LA N	2	1	.667	19	1	0	1-0	40	38	14	2	0	14-5	33	2.70	129	.252	.311	7-0-1	.000	-1	229	3	0	0.1
1983	†LA N	3	4	.429	42	3	0	1-0	71	73	40	5	1	35-11	50	3.55	102	.264	.347	5	.200	0	49	-2	0	-0.1
1984	KC A	8	4	.667	49	1	0	2-1	100.2	92	39	13	2	25-1	75	3.40	119	.247	.293	0	ø	0	0	8	0	1.0
1985	†KC A	1	5	.167	49	0	0	1-2	95	99	45	9	3	32-8	80	4.07	103	.269	.330	0	ø	0	—	3	0	0.2
1986	LA N	0	0	ø	15	0	0	0-1	18.1	28	16	5	0	6-0	13	6.87	50	.350	.395	0	ø	0	—	-8	0	-0.4
Total	7	18	19	.486	229	5	0	7-4	422	432	189	39	7	150-30	319	3.54	107	.266	.328	19-0-2	.053	-1	71	11	180	1.5
BEDARD, ERIK	Erik Joseph; B3.5.1979 Navan ON, Can.; BL/TL/6´1˝/(180–195); [BalA99 6/187]; d4.17; Col Norwalk (CT) CC; [DL 2003 Bal A 183]																									
2002	Bal A	0	0	ø	2	0	0	0-0	0.2	2	1	0	0	0-0	1	13.50	32	.500	.500	0	ø	0	—	-1	0	0.0
2004	Bal A	6	10	.375	27	26	0	0-0	137.1	149	83	13	7	71-1	121	4.59	102	.270	.359	4	.000	-0	105	-2	0	-0.2
2005	Bal A	6	8	.429	24	24	0	0-0	141.2	139	66	10	5	57-1	125	4.00	110	.260	.333	0	ø	0	83	8	57	0.8
2006	Bal A	15	11	.577	33	33	0	0-0	196.1	196	92	16	5	69-0	171	3.76	120	.258	.322	2	.000	-0	102	15	0	1.7
Total	4	27	29	.482	86	83	0	0-0	476	486	242	39	17	197-2	418	4.08	111	.263	.337	6	.000	-0	98	20	240	2.3
BEDGOOD, PHIL	Phillip Burlette; B3.8.1898 Harrison GA; D11.8.1927 Fort Pierce FL; BR/TR/6´3˝/218; d9.20																									
1922	Cle A	1	0	1.000	1	1	1	0	9	7	4	0	3	4	5	4.00	100	.233	.378	2-0-1	.000	-0	106	0	—	0.0
1923	Cle A	0	2	.000	9	2	0	0	18.2	16	13	0	2	14	7	5.30	75	.246	.395	4	.250	0	167	-3	—	-0.2
Total	2	1	2	.333	10	3	1	0	27.2	23	17	0	5	18	12	4.88	82	.242	.390	6-0-1	.167	0	147	-3	—	-0.2
BEDIENT, HUGH	Hugh Carpenter; B10.23.1889 Gerry NY; D7.21.1965 Jamestown NY; BR/TR/6´0˝/185; d4.26																									
1912	†Bos A	20	9	.690	41	28	19	2	231	206	93	6	3	55	122	2.92	116	.240	.288	73-0-6	.192	1	102	14	—	1.7
1913	Bos A	15	14	.517	43	28	15-1	5	259	255	104	0	6	67	122	2.78	106	.263	.314	80-0-5	.125	-3	80	7	—	0.2
1914	Bos A	8	12	.400	42	16	7-1	2	177.1	187	97	4	5	45	70	3.60	75	.281	.331	50-0-1	.100	-2	129	-19	—	-2.3
1915	Buf F	16	18	.471	53	30	16-2	**10**	269.1	284	131	5	3	69	106	3.17	88	.274	.321	83-0-5	.108	-5	92	-16	—	-2.7
Total	4	59	53	.527	179	102	57-4	19	936.2	932	425	15	17	236	420	3.08	96	.264	.313	286-0-17	.133	-9	98	-14	—	-3.1
BEDNAR, ANDY	Andrew Jackson; B8.16.1908 Streator IL; D11.26.1937 Graham TX; BR/TR/5´10.5˝/180; d9.6																									
1930	Pit N	0	0	ø	2	0	0	0	1.1	4	4	0	0	1	1	27.00	18	.500	.556	0	ø	0	—	-3	—	-0.1
1931	Pit N	0	0	ø	3	0	0	0	4	10	5	1	0	0	2	11.25	34	.476	.476	0	ø	0	—	-3	—	-0.1
Total	2	0	0	ø	5	0	0	0	5.1	14	9	1	0	1	3	15.19	27	.483	.500	0	ø	0	—	-6	—	-0.2
BEDROSIAN, STEVE	Stephen Wayne; B12.6.1957 Methuen MA; BR/TR/6´3˝/(195–205); [AtlN78 3/53]; d8.14; Col New Haven																									
1981	Atl N	1	2	.333	15	1	0	0-1	24.1	15	14	2	1	15-2	9	4.44	79	.169	.292	2	.000	-0	101	-3	0	-0.4
1982	†Atl N	8	6	.571	64	3	0	11-6	137.2	102	39	7	4	57-5	123	2.42	152	.206	.292	26-0-4	.038	-2	80	20	0	2.1
1983	Atl N	9	10	.474	70	1	0	19-7	120	100	50	11	4	51-8	114	3.60	107	.229	.313	19-0-1	.105	-1	69	4	0	0.7
1984	Atl N	9	6	.600	40	4	0	11-2	83.2	65	23	5	1	33-5	81	2.37	163	.210	.288	17-0-1	.118	-1	109	14	15	2.6
1985	Atl N	7	15	.318	37	37	0	0-0	206.2	198	101	17	5	111-6	134	3.83	101	.254	.349	64-0-6	.078	-4	86	0	0	-0.5
1986	Phi N	8	6	.571	68	0	0	29-9	90.1	79	39	12	0	34-10	82	3.39	115	.232	.299	5	.200	0	—	5	0	1.0
1987	Phi N★	5	3	.625	65	0	0	**40**-8	89	79	31	11	1	28-5	74	2.83	152	.237	.297	4	.000	-0	—	14	0	2.1
1988	Phi N	6	6	.500	57	0	0	28-6	74.1	75	34	6	0	27-5	61	3.75	96	.257	.317	2	.000	-0	—	-1	46	-0.2
1989	Phi N	2	3	.400	28	0	0	6-3	33.2	21	13	7	1	17-1	24	3.21	112	.183	.289	0	ø	0	—	2	0	0.3
	†SF N	1	4	.200	40	0	0	17-5	51	35	18	5	0	22-4	34	2.65	128	.192	.277	6	.167	-0	—	4	0	0.5
	Year	3	7	.300	68	0	0	23-8	84.2	56	31	12	1	39-5	58	2.87	121	.189	.282	6	.167	-0	—	5	0	0.8
1990	SF N	9	9	.500	68	0	0	17-5	79.1	72	40	6	2	44-9	43	4.20	87	.241	.341	4	.500	1	—	-5	0	-0.9
1991	†Min A	5	3	.625	56	0	0	6-1	77.1	70	42	11	3	35-6	44	4.42	97	.243	.327	0	ø	0	—	-1	0	-0.2
1993	Atl N	5	2	.714	49	0	0	0-0	49.2	34	11	4	2	14-2	33	1.63	248	.194	.256	2	.000	-0	—	13	0	1.6
1994	Atl N	0	2	.000	46	0	0	0-2	46	41	20	4	2	18-5	43	3.33	130	.243	.319	2	.500	0	—	4	0	0.2
1995	Atl N	1	2	.333	29	0	0	0-2	28	40	21	6	1	12-2	22	6.11	71	.354	.414	0	ø	0	—	-5	0	-0.5
Total	14	76	79	.490	732	46	0	184-57	1191	1026	496	114	27	518-75	921	3.38	115	.232	.314	153-0-12	.098	-7	87	65	61	8.4
BEEBE, FRED	Frederick Leonard; B12.31.1879 Lincoln NE; D10.30.1957 Elgin IL; BR/TR/6´1˝/190; d4.17; Col Illinois																									
1906	Chi N	6	1	.857	14	6	4	1	70	56	27	1	5	32	55	2.70	98	.210	.306	29	.103	-1	170	0	—	-0.2
	StL N	9	9	.500	20	19	16-1	0	160.2	115	65	1	9	68	116	3.02	87	.208	.305	58-0-3	.172	0	88	-5	—	-0.5
	Year	15	10	.600	34	25	20-1	1	230.2	171	92	2	14	100	**171**	2.93	90	.209	.305	87-0-3	.149	-1	107	-5	—	-0.7
1907	StL N	7	19	.269	31	29	24-4	0	238.1	192	95	1	10	109	141	2.72	92	.230	.326	86-0-3	.128	-3	62	-2	—	-0.5
1908	StL N	5	13	.278	29	19	12	0	174.1	134	88	3	4	66	72	2.63	90	**.193**	.267	56-0-3	.125	-2	83	-8	—	-1.0
1909	StL N	15	21	.417	44	34	18-1	1	287.2	256	142	5	7	104	105	2.82	90	.229	.299	108-0-3	.167	-2	114	-16	—	-2.1
1910	Cin N	12	14	.462	35	26	11-2	0	214.1	193	101	3	7	94	93	3.07	95	.246	.333	73-0-1	.164	-2	89	-2	—	-0.4
1911	Phi N	3	3	.500	9	8	3	0	48.1	52	26	2	3	24	20	4.47	77	.297	.391	19	.263	2*	104	-3	—	-0.1
1916	Cle A	5	3	.625	20	12	5-1	2	100.2	92	43	1	1	37	32	2.41	125	.251	.321	28-0-3	.214	1	88	4	—	0.3
Total	7	62	83	.428	202	153	93-9	4	1294.1	1090	587	17	46	534	634	2.86	93	.227	.311	457-0-16	.158	-8	93	-32	—	-4.5
BEECH, MATT	Lucas Matthew; B1.20.1972 Oakland CA; BL/TL/6´2˝/(190–205); [PhiN94 7/198]; d8.8; Col Houston; [DL 1999 Phi N 176]																									
1996	Phi N	1	4	.200	8	8	0	0-0	41.1	49	32	8	3	11-0	33	6.97	62	.306	.350	14	.071	-1	94	-10	0	-1.1
1997	Phi N	4	9	.308	24	24	0	0-0	136.2	147	81	25	5	57-9	120	5.07	83	.279	.351	30-0-11	.167	-0	94	-11	16	-0.9
1998	Phi N	3	9	.250	21	21	0	0-0	117	126	78	19	4	63-2	113	5.15	84	.275	.366	33-0-6	.152	-1	83	-13	49	-1.3
Total	3	8	22	.267	53	53	0	0-0	295	322	191	52	12	131-11	266	5.37	80	.281	.357	77-0-17	.143	-2	90	-34	241	-3.3
BEECHER, ROY	Leroy "Colonel"; B5.10.1884 Swanton OH; D10.11.1952 Toledo OH; BL/TR/6´2˝/180; d9.29																									
1907	NY N	0	2	.000	2	2	2	0	14	17	8	0	0	6	5	2.57	96	.293	.359	5	.000	-1	43	-1	—	-0.2
1908	NY N	0	0	ø	2	0	0	1	5.2	11	5	0	0	3	0	7.94	30	.440	.500	3	.333	1*	—	-3	—	-0.1
Total	2	0	2	.000	4	2	2	1	19.2	28	13	0	0	9	5	4.12	60	.337	.402	8	.125	-0	43	-4	—	-0.3
BEENE, FRED	Freddy Ray; B11.24.1942 Angleton TX; BB/TR (BR 1968)/5´9˝/(155–160); d9.18; Col Sam Houston St.																									
1968	Bal A	0	0	ø	1	0	0	0	1	2	1	0	0	1-0	1	9.00	33	.500	.500	0	ø	0	—	-1	0	0.0
1969	Bal A	0	0	ø	2	0	0	0-0	2.2	2	0	0	0	1-0	0	0.00	ø	.200	.273	0	ø	0	—	1	0	0.1
1970	Bal A	0	0	ø	4	0	0	0-0	6	8	5	1	0	5-4	4	6.00	61	.320	.433	0	ø	0	—	-2	0	-0.1
1972	NY A	1	3	.250	29	1	0	3-0	57.2	55	21	3	1	24-5	37	2.34	128	.256	.332	9	.000	-1*	533	2	0	0.1
1973	NY A	6	0	1.000	19	4	0	1-0	91	67	21	5	1	27-5	49	1.68	221	.209	.271	0	ø	0	108	21	0	1.4
1974	NY A	0	0	ø	6	0	0	1-0	10	9	4	1	1	2-0	10	2.70	131	.231	.286	0	ø	0	—	1	0	0.1
	Cle A	4	4	.500	32	0	0	2-3	73	68	44	7	1	26-2	35	4.93	74	.246	.310	0	ø	0*	—	-10	0	-1.0
	Year	4	4	.500	38	0	0	3-3	83	77	48	8	2	28-2	45	4.66	78	.244	.307	0	ø	0	—	-10	0	-0.9
1975	Cle A	1	0	1.000	19	1	0	1-1	46.2	63	42	4	3	25-3	20	6.94	55	.323	.406	0	ø	0*	254	-16	62	-0.8
Total	7	12	7	.632	112	6	0	8-4	288	274	138	21	7	111-19	156	3.63	98	.253	.324	9	.000	-1	195	-4	62	-0.2
BEENE, ANDY	Ramon Andrew; B10.13.1956 Freeport TX; BR/TR/6´3˝/205; [MilA79 5/127]; d9.22; Col Baylor																									
1983	Mil A	0	0	ø	1	0	0	0-0	2	3	3	0	0	1-1	0	4.50	84	.333	.400	0	ø	0	—	-1	0	-0.1
1984	Mil A	0	2	.000	5	3	0	0-0	18.2	28	23	1	2	9-0	11	11.09	35	.350	.424	0	ø	0	101	-14	0	-1.2
Total	2	0	2	.000	6	3	0	0-0	20.2	31	26	1	2	10-1	11	10.45	37	.348	.422	0	ø	0	101	-15	0	-1.3
BEERS, CLARENCE	Clarence Scott; B12.9.1918 ElDorado KS; D12.6.2002 Tucson AZ; BR/TR/6´0˝/175; d5.2																									
1948	StL N	0	0	ø	1	0	0	0	0.2	3	4	0	0	1	0	13.50	30	.500	.571	0	ø	0	—	-2	0	-0.1
BEGGS, JOE	Joseph Stanley "Fireman"; B11.4.1910 Rankin PA; D7.19.1983 Indianapolis IN; BR/TR/6´1˝/182; d4.19; Mil 1944–45; Col Geneva																									
1938	NY A	3	2	.600	14	9	4	0	58.1	69	41	7	0	20	8	5.40	84	.299	.355	20	.250	1	95	-6	—	-0.3
1940	†Cin N	12	3	.800	37	1	0	**7**	76.2	68	19	1	1	21	25	2.00	190	.243	.298	21-0-1	.190	-0	275	**15**	—	3.2
1941	Cin N	4	3	.571	37	0	0	5	57	57	29	2	0	27	19	3.79	95	.313	.402	10	.300	1	—	-2	0	-0.2
1942	Cin N	6	5	.545	38	0	0	8	88.2	65	28	4	1	33	24	2.13	154	.206	.283	21-0-1	.000	-3	—	11	0	1.4
1943	Cin N	7	6	.538	39	4	4-2	6	115.1	121	38	0	0	25	28	2.34	142	.276	.315	35-0-2	.143	-1	58	**11**	0	1.2
1944	Cin N	1	0	1.000	1	1	1	0	9	8	2	0	0	0	2	2.00	174	.222	.222	4	.000	-1	96	2	0	0.1
1946	Cin N	12	10	.545	28	22	14-2	1	190	175	63	15	1	39	38	2.32	144	.247	.287	63-0-7	.222	2	97	20	0	2.6
1947	Cin N	0	3	.000	11	4	0	0	32.1	42	26	4	0	6	11	5.29	78	.316	.345	11-0-1	.091	-1	118	-6	0	-0.6
	NY N	3	3	.500	32	0	0	2	66	81	38	6	1	18	23	4.23	96	.300	.346	13-0-2	.077	-1	—	-2	0	-0.3

YEAR	TM LG	W	L	PCT	G	GS	CG-SHO	SV-BS	IP	H	R	HR	HB	BB-IB	SO	ERA	AERA	OAV	OOB	AB-HR-SH	AVG	PB	SUP	APR	DL	PW
	Year	3	6	.333	43	4	0	2	98.1	123	64	10	1	24	34	4.58	89	.305	.346	24-0-3	.083	-2	119	-9	0	-0.9
1948	NY N	0	0	ø	1	0	0	0	0.1	2	0	0	0	0	0	0.00	ø	.667	.667	0	ø	0	—	0	0	0.0
Total	9	48	35	.578	238	41	23-4	29	693.2	688	284	39	4	189	178	2.96	122	.265	.316	198-0-14	.167	-3	101	43	0	7.1

BEGLEY, ED Edward N. (b Edward N. Bagley); B10.1863 New York NY; D7.24.1919 Waterbury CT; d5.3

YEAR	TM LG	W	L	PCT	G	GS	CG-SHO	SV-BS	IP	H	R	HR	HB	BB-IB	SO	ERA	AERA	OAV	OOB	AB-HR-SH	AVG	PB	SUP	APR	DL	PW
1884	NY N	12	18	.400	31	30	30	0	266	296	209	9	—	99	104	4.16	72	.263	.323	121	.182	-3*	93	-33	—	-3.2
1885	NY AA	4	9	.308	15	14	10	0	115	131	102	5	8	48	44	4.93	63	.278	.355	52-1	.173	-1	91	-25	—	-2.1
Total	2	16	27	.372	46	44	40	0	381	427	311	14	8	147	148	4.39	69	.268	.333	173-1	.179	-3	92	-58	—	-5.3

BEHAN, PETIE Charles Frederick; B12.11.1887 Dallas City PA; D1.22.1957 Bradford PA; BR/TR/5´10˝/160; d9.16

YEAR	TM LG	W	L	PCT	G	GS	CG-SHO	SV-BS	IP	H	R	HR	HB	BB-IB	SO	ERA	AERA	OAV	OOB	AB-HR-SH	AVG	PB	SUP	APR	DL	PW
1921	Phi N	0	1	.000	2	2	1	0	10.2	17	8	0	0	1	3	5.91	72	.354	.367	4	.000	-1	68	-1	—	-0.2
1922	Phi N	4	2	.667	7	5	3-1	0	47.1	49	27	3	1	14	13	2.47	189	.259	.314	20	.250	-0	112	7	—	0.7
1923	Phi N	3	12	.200	31	17	5	2	131	182	102	11	1	57	27	5.50	84	.336	.401	43-0-4	.186	-2*	88	-13	—	-1.5
Total	3	7	15	.318	40	24	9-1	2	189	248	137	14	2	72	43	4.76	97	.319	.378	67-0-4	.194	-3	91	-7	—	-1.0

BEHENNA, RICK Richard Kipp; B3.6.1960 Miami FL; BR/TR/6´2˝/170; [AtlN78 4/79]; d4.12

YEAR	TM LG	W	L	PCT	G	GS	CG-SHO	SV-BS	IP	H	R	HR	HB	BB-IB	SO	ERA	AERA	OAV	OOB	AB-HR-SH	AVG	PB	SUP	APR	DL	PW
1983	Atl N	3	3	.500	14	6	0	0-0	37.1	37	20	7	1	12-2	17	4.58	84	.255	.314	12-1-0	.333	2	91	-2	0	-0.2
	Cle A	0	2	.000	5	4	0	0-0	26	22	13	0	1	14-1	9	4.15	103	.232	.336	0	ø	0	69	0	0	0.0
1984	Cle A	0	3	.000	3	3	0	0-0	9.2	17	15	5	1	8-0	6	13.97	30	.386	.491	0	ø	0	37	-10	139	-1.5
1985	Cle A	0	2	.000	4	4	0	0-0	19.2	29	17	3	0	8-0	4	7.78	54	.354	.407	0	ø	0	93	-7	139	-0.6
Total	3	3	10	.231	26	17	0	0-0	92.2	105	65	15	3	42-3	36	6.12	67	.287	.363	12-1-0	.333	2	77	-19	278	-2.3

BEHNEY, MEL Melvin Brian; B9.2.1947 Newark NJ; BL/TL/6´2˝/175; [CinN68 S1/5]; d8.14; Mil 1970; Col Michigan St.

YEAR	TM LG	W	L	PCT	G	GS	CG-SHO	SV-BS	IP	H	R	HR	HB	BB-IB	SO	ERA	AERA	OAV	OOB	AB-HR-SH	AVG	PB	SUP	APR	DL	PW
1970	Cin N	0	2	.000	5	1	0	0-0	10	15	11	1	0	8-2	2	4.50	90	.341	.442	1	.000	-0	89	-3	0	-0.5

BEHRMAN, HANK Henry Bernard; B6.27.1921 Brooklyn NY; D1.20.1987 New York NY; BR/TR/5´11˝/174; d4.17

YEAR	TM LG	W	L	PCT	G	GS	CG-SHO	SV-BS	IP	H	R	HR	HB	BB-IB	SO	ERA	AERA	OAV	OOB	AB-HR-SH	AVG	PB	SUP	APR	DL	PW
1946	Bro N	11	5	.688	47	11	2	4	150.2	138	63	3	2	69	78	2.93	115	.241	.325	42-0-4	.095	-3	134	6	0	0.2
1947	†Bro N	0	0	ø	2	0	0	0	3.2	3	4	1	0	4	2	9.82	42	.231	.412	0	ø	0	—	-2	0	-0.1
	Pit N	0	2	.000	10	2	0	0	24.2	33	26	6	2	17	11	9.12	46	.347	.456	6-0-1	.000	-1	125	-12	0	-0.9
	†Bro N	5	3	.625	38	6	0	8	88.1	94	60	9	0	44	31	5.30	78	.274	.357	26-0-4	.231	1	164	-11	0	-1.1
	Year	5	5	.500	50	8	0	8	116.2	130	90	16	2	65	44	6.25	66	.288	.380	32-0-5	.188	-0	154	-26	0	-2.1
1948	Bro N	5	4	.556	34	4	2-1	7	91	95	51	7	3	42	42	4.05	99	.268	.350	28-0-4	.107	-2	128	-2	0	-0.4
1949	NY N	3	3	.500	43	4	1-1	0	71.1	64	46	5	0	52	25	4.92	81	.239	.363	13	.077	-1	100	-7	0	-0.6
Total	4	24	17	.585	174	27	5-2	19	429.2	427	250	31	7	228	189	4.40	87	.259	.352	115-0-13	.122	-5	133	-28	0	-2.9

BEIMEL, JOE Joseph Ronald; B4.19.1977 St.Marys PA; BL/TL/6´3˝/(205–215); [PitN98 18/538]; d4.8; Col Duquesne

YEAR	TM LG	W	L	PCT	G	GS	CG-SHO	SV-BS	IP	H	R	HR	HB	BB-IB	SO	ERA	AERA	OAV	OOB	AB-HR-SH	AVG	PB	SUP	APR	DL	PW
2001	Pit N	7	11	.389	42	15	0	0-0	115.1	131	72	12	6	49-4	58	5.23	86	.290	.366	26-0-4	.269	1	88	-9	0	-1.1
2002	Pit N	2	5	.286	53	8	0	0-1	85.1	88	49	9	4	45-12	53	4.64	90	.267	.359	10-0-2	.300	1	110	-4	0	-0.2
2003	Pit N	1	3	.250	69	0	0	0-5	62.1	69	35	7	4	33-6	42	5.05	86	.299	.388	5	.000	-1*	—	-4	0	-0.2
2004	Min A	0	0	ø	3	0	0	0-0	1.2	8	8	1	0	2-0	2	43.20	11	.615	.667	0	ø	0	—	-7	0	-0.3
2005	TB A	0	0	ø	7	0	0	0-0	11	15	4	1	0	4-1	3	3.27	134	.319	.373	0	ø	0	—	2	0	0.1
2006	LA N	2	1	.667	62	0	0	2-0	70	70	26	7	0	21-3	30	2.96	148	.262	.313	1	.000	-0	—	11	0	0.7
Total	6	12	20	.375	236	23	0	2-6	345.2	381	194	37	14	154-26	188	4.71	92	.284	.361	42-0-6	.238	2	96	-11	0	-1.0

BEIRNE, KEVIN Kevin Patrick; B1.1.1974 Houston TX; BL/TR/6´4˝/210; [ChiA95 11/308]; d5.17; Col Texas A&M

YEAR	TM LG	W	L	PCT	G	GS	CG-SHO	SV-BS	IP	H	R	HR	HB	BB-IB	SO	ERA	AERA	OAV	OOB	AB-HR-SH	AVG	PB	SUP	APR	DL	PW
2000	Chi A	1	3	.250	29	1	0	0-1	49.2	50	41	9	4	20-1	41	6.70	75	.263	.338	0	ø	0	56	-9	0	-0.6
2001	Tor A	0	0	ø	5	0	0	0-0	7	13	10	1	0	6-1	5	12.86	36	.394	.487	0	ø	0	—	-6	0	-0.3
2002	LA N	2	0	1.000	12	3	0	0-1	29	26	11	4	2	17-2	17	3.41	114	.245	.357	5-0-1	.400	1	174	2	0	0.2
Total	3	3	3	.500	46	4	0	0-2	85.2	89	62	14	6	43-4	63	6.09	76	.271	.359	5-0-1	.400	1	126	-13	0	-0.7

BELCHER, TIM Timothy Wayne; B10.19.1961 Mount Gilead OH; BR/TR/6´3˝/(210–235); [NYA84*S1/1]; d9.6; Col Mount Vernon Nazarene

YEAR	TM LG	W	L	PCT	G	GS	CG-SHO	SV-BS	IP	H	R	HR	HB	BB-IB	SO	ERA	AERA	OAV	OOB	AB-HR-SH	AVG	PB	SUP	APR	DL	PW
1987	LA N	4	2	.667	6	5	0	0-0	34	30	11	2	0	7-0	23	2.38	167	.240	.278	10	.200	0	64	6	0	1.0
1988	†LA N	12	6	.667	36	27	4-1	4-1	179.2	143	65	8	2	51-7	152	2.91	115	.217	.275	56-1-5	.071	-2	110	9	0	0.7
1989	LA N	15	12	.556	39	30	**10-8**	1-0	230	182	81	20	7	80-5	200	2.82	122	.217	.289	70-0-10	.100	-2	92	16	0	1.5
1990	LA N	9	9	.500	24	24	5-2	0-0	153	136	76	17	2	48-0	102	4.00	92	.240	.299	43-0-9	.163	1	93	-5	48	-0.5
1991	LA N	10	9	.526	33	33	2-1	0-0	209.1	189	76	10	2	75-3	156	2.62	138	.240	.306	67-0-7	.119	-2	93	20	0	1.5
1992	Cin N	15	14	.517	35	34	2-1	0-0	227.2	201	104	17	3	80-2	149	3.91	92	.238	.303	76-1-7	.105	-2	109	-6	0	-1.0
1993	Cin N	9	6	.600	22	22	4-2	0-0	137	134	72	11	7	47-4	101	4.47	90	.254	.322	50-0-3	.200	1	118	-6	0	-0.6
	†Chi A	3	5	.375	12	11	1-1	0-0	71.2	64	36	8	1	27-0	34	4.40	96	.242	.313	0	ø	0	77	0	0	-0.1
1994	Det A	7	15	.318	25	25	3	0-0	162	192	124	21	4	78-10	76	5.89	84	.290	.367	0	ø	0	103	-20	0	-2.1
1995	†Sea A	10	12	.455	28	28	1	0-0	179.1	188	101	19	5	88-5	96	4.52	106	.269	.352	0	ø	0	92	4	0	0.4
1996	KC A	15	11	.577	35	35	4-1	0-0	238.2	262	117	28	6	68-4	113	3.92	128	.281	.331	0	ø	0	92	27	0	2.4
1997	KC A	13	12	.520	32	32	3-1	0-0	213.1	242	128	31	5	70-2	113	5.02	95	.288	.345	6	.000	-1	109	-6	0	-0.7
1998	KC A	14	14	.500	34	34	2	0-0	234	247	127	37	7	73-0	130	4.27	114	.272	.328	5-0-1	.200	0	92	12	0	1.1
1999	Ana A	6	8	.429	24	24	0	0-0	132.1	168	104	27	5	46-0	52	6.73	73	.315	.369	5	.200	0	95	-25	41	-2.1
2000	Ana A	4	5	.444	9	9	1	0-0	40.2	45	31	8	2	22-1	22	6.86	75	.281	.373	0	ø	0	87	-6	139	-1.1
Total	14	146	140	.510	394	373	42-18	5-1	2442.2	2423	1253	264	58	860-43	1519	4.16	102	.259	.323	388-2-42	.124	-6	98	20	228	0.4

BELINDA, STAN Stanley Peter; B8.6.1966 Huntingdon PA; BR/TR/6´3˝/(187–215); [PitN86 10/238]; d9.8; Col Allegany (MD) CC

YEAR	TM LG	W	L	PCT	G	GS	CG-SHO	SV-BS	IP	H	R	HR	HB	BB-IB	SO	ERA	AERA	OAV	OOB	AB-HR-SH	AVG	PB	SUP	APR	DL	PW
1989	Pit N	0	1	.000	8	0	0	0-0	10.1	13	8	0	0	2-0	10	6.10	56	.295	.326	0	ø	0	—	-3	0	-0.3
1990	†Pit N	3	4	.429	55	0	0	8-5	58.1	48	23	4	1	29-3	55	3.55	103	.227	.321	5-0-1	.000	-1	—	2	0	0.2
1991	†Pit N	7	5	.583	60	0	0	16-4	78.1	50	30	10	4	35-4	71	3.45	104	.184	.283	7-0-2	.000	-0	—	3	0	0.5
1992	†Pit N	6	4	.600	59	0	0	18-6	71.1	58	26	8	0	29-5	57	3.15	110	.223	.295	3	.667	1	—	3	0	0.6
1993	Pit N	3	1	.750	40	0	0	19-3	42.1	35	18	4	1	11-4	30	3.61	113	.224	.276	1	.000	-0	—	2	0	0.3
	KC A	1	1	.500	23	0	0	0-1	27.1	30	13	2	1	6-0	25	4.28	108	.280	.325	0	ø	0	—	1	0	0.1
1994	KC A	2	2	.500	37	0	0	1-1	49	47	36	6	5	24-3	37	5.14	98	.250	.345	0	ø	0	—	-3	0	-0.2
1995	†Bos A	8	1	.889	63	0	0	10-4	69.2	51	25	5	4	28-3	57	3.10	157	.205	.291	0	ø	0	—	14	11	1.8
1996	Bos A	2	1	.667	31	0	0	2-2	28.2	31	22	3	4	20-1	18	6.59	77	.272	.399	0	ø	0	—	-4	113	-0.4
1997	Cin N	1	5	.167	84	0	0	1-4	99.1	84	42	11	9	33-6	114	3.71	115	.229	.304	3	.333	0	—	7	0	0.3
1998	Cin N	4	8	.333	40	0	0	1-1	61.1	46	23	7	1	28-6	57	3.23	133	.212	.304	1	.000	-0	—	7	85	1.3
1999	Cin N	3	1	.750	29	0	0	2-0	42.2	42	26	11	1	18-3	40	5.27	89	.258	.333	4	.250	0	—	-2	81	-0.2
2000	Col N	1	3	.250	46	0	0	1-6	35.2	39	32	10	2	17-4	40	7.07	82	.277	.358	1	.000	-0*	—	-5	0	-0.5
	Atl N	0	0	ø	10	0	0	0-0	11	16	12	4	1	5-1	11	9.82	46	.348	.407	0	ø	0	—	-6	0	-0.3
	Year	1	3	.250	56	0	0	1-6	46.2	55	44	14	3	22-5	51	7.71	71	.294	.370	1	.000	-0	—	-10	0	-0.8
Total	12	41	37	.526	585	0	0	79-37	685.1	590	336	85	34	285-43	622	4.15	103	.233	.315	25-0-3	.160	1	—	16	290	3.2

BELINSKY, BO Robert; B12.7.1936 New York NY; D11.23.2001 Las Vegas NV; BL/TL/6´2˝/(187–191); d4.18

YEAR	TM LG	W	L	PCT	G	GS	CG-SHO	SV-BS	IP	H	R	HR	HB	BB-IB	SO	ERA	AERA	OAV	OOB	AB-HR-SH	AVG	PB	SUP	APR	DL	PW
1962	LA A	10	11	.476	33	31	5-3	1	187.1	149	86	12	13	122-3	145	3.56	109	.216	.343	60-0-2	.167	1*	81	7	0	0.8
1963	LA A	2	9	.182	13	13	2	0	76.2	78	54	12	4	35-2	60	5.75	60	.262	.345	27	.074	-2	88	-20	0	-2.5
1964	LA A	9	8	.529	23	22	4-1	0	135.1	120	45	8	6	49-5	91	2.86	115	.240	.314	42-0-5	.095	-1	95	10	0	1.0
1965	Phi N	4	9	.308	30	14	3	1	109.2	103	72	13	6	48-5	71	4.84	71	.248	.331	32-0-1	.188	1*	105	-19	0	-2.1
1966	Phi N	0	2	.000	9	1	0	0	15.1	14	5	3	3	5-1	8	2.93	123	.250	.344	3	.333	0	147	1	0	0.2
1967	Hou N	3	9	.250	27	18	0	0	115.1	112	74	12	8	54-0	80	4.68	71	.255	.345	39-0-1	.077	-2	103	-20	0	-2.2
1969	Pit N	0	3	.000	8	3	0	0-0	17.2	17	10	1	2	14-2	15	4.58	76	.266	.412	2	.000	-0	42	-2	0	-0.4
1970	Cin N	0	0	ø	3	0	0	0-0	8	10	6	0	0	6-0	6	4.50	90	.294	.400	1	1.000	1	—	-1	0	0.0
Total	8	28	51	.354	146	102	14-4	2-0	665.1	603	352	61	42	333-18	476	4.10	86	.241	.339	206-0-9	.131	-2	91	-44	0	-5.2

BELISLE, MATT Matthew Thomas; B6.6.1980 Austin TX; BR/TR/6´3˝/(190–195); [AtlN98 2/52]; d9.7

YEAR	TM LG	W	L	PCT	G	GS	CG-SHO	SV-BS	IP	H	R	HR	HB	BB-IB	SO	ERA	AERA	OAV	OOB	AB-HR-SH	AVG	PB	SUP	APR	DL	PW
2003	Cin N	1	1	.500	6	0	0	0-1	8.2	10	5	1	1	2-0	6	5.19	80	.303	.351	1	.000	-0	—	-1	0	-0.2
2005	Cin N	4	8	.333	60	5	0	1-3	85.2	101	49	11	6	26-6	59	4.41	97	.294	.352	7-0-1	.143	-0*	133	-3	0	-0.4
2006	Cin N	2	0	1.000	30	2	0	0-1	40	43	18	5	3	19-1	26	3.60	131	.277	.363	5-0-2	.000	-1	49	5	71	0.2
Total	3	7	9	.438	96	7	0	1-5	134.1	154	72	17	10	47-7	91	4.22	104	.289	.355	13-0-3	.077	-1	107	1	71	-0.4

YEAR	TM LG	W	L	PCT	G	GS	CG-SHO	SV-BS	IP	H	R	HR	HB	BB-IB	SO	ERA	AERA	OAV	OOB	AB-HR-SH	AVG	PB	SUP	APR	DL	PW
Belitz, Todd	Todd Stephen; B10.23.1975 Des Moines IA; BL/TL/6´1˝/200; [TBA97 4/144]; d9.4; Col Washington St.																									
2000	Oak A	0	0	ø	5	0	0	0-0	3.1	4	2	0	0	4-0	3	2.70	180	.267	.421	0	ø	0	—	0	0	0.0
2001	Col N	1	1	.500	8	0	0	0-0	9.1	9	8	2	0	3-0	5	7.71	69	.250	.308	1	.000	-0	—	-2	0	-0.3
Total	2	1	1	.500	13	0	0	0-0	12.2	13	10	2	0	7-0	8	6.39	82	.255	.345	1	.000	-0	—	-2	0	-0.3
Bell, Charlie	Charles C.; B8.12.1868 Cincinnati OH; D2.7.1937 Cincinnati OH; TR; d10.13; b–Frank																									
1889	KC AA	1	0	1.000	1	1	1	0	9	4	5	0	1	3	3	1.00	425	.129	.229	6	.167	0*	87	2	—	0.3
1891	Lou AA	2	6	.250	10	9	8	0	77	93	65	4	8	20	16	4.68	78	.289	.346	28	.036	-2	64	-10	—	-1.0
	Cin AA	1	0	1.000	1	1	1	0	9	2	2	0	1	3	1	0.00	ø	.069	.182	4	.500	0	121	3	—	0.4
	Year	3	6	.333	11	10	9	0	86	95	67	4	9	23	17	4.19	88	.271	.332	32	.094	-2	70	-4	—	-0.6
Total	2	4	6	.400	12	11	10	0	95	99	72	4	10	26	20	3.88	97	.259	.323	38	.105	-2	72	-5	—	-0.3
Bell, Eric	Eric Alvin; B10.27.1963 Modesto CA; BL/TL/6´0˝/165; [BalA82 9/234]; d9.24																									
1985	Bal A	0	0	ø	4	0	0	0-0	5.2	4	3	1	0	4-0	4	4.76	85	.200	.333	0	ø	0	—	0	0	0.0
1986	Bal A	1	2	.333	4	4	0	0-0	23.1	23	14	4	0	14-0	18	5.01	83	.258	.356	0	ø	0	93	-2	0	-0.3
1987	Bal A	10	13	.435	33	29	2	0-0	165	174	113	32	2	78-0	111	5.45	81	.271	.350	0	ø	0	86	-20	0	-2.4
1991	Cle A	4	0	1.000	10	0	0	0-0	18	5	2	0	1	5-0	7	0.50	835	.091	.180	0	ø	0	—	7	0	1.5
1992	Cle A	0	2	.000	7	1	0	0-0	15.1	22	13	1	1	9-0	10	7.63	52	.349	.432	0	ø	0	23	-6	0	-0.6
1993	Hou N	0	1	.000	10	0	0	0-0	7.1	10	5	0	0	2-0	2	6.14	63	.313	.353	0	ø	0	—	-2	0	-0.2
Total	6	15	18	.455	68	34	2	0-0	234.2	238	150	38	4	112-0	152	5.18	84	.264	.346	0	ø	0	86	-23	0	-2.0
Bell, Gary	Gary; B11.17.1936 San Antonio TX; BR/TR/6´1˝/(195–198); d6.1; Col San Antonio (TX) JC																									
1958	Cle A	12	10	.545	33	23	10	1	182	141	70	18	5	73-0	110	3.31	110	.213	.294	56-0-5	.196	2	112	9	0	1.1
1959	Cle A	16	11	.593	44	28	12-1	5	234	208	107	28	5	105-4	136	4.04	91	.238	.321	75-0-8	.240	3	113	-5	0	-0.3
1960	Cle A★	9	10	.474	28	23	6-2	1	154.2	139	78	15	7	82-2	109	4.13	90	.242	.340	47-0-8	.149	-0*	94	-6	0	-0.6
1961	Cle A	12	16	.429	34	34	11-2	0	228.1	214	125	32	6	100-2	163	4.10	96	.245	.324	81-0-9	.198	1	116	-8	0	-0.8
1962	Cle A	10	9	.526	57	6	1	12	107.2	104	56	14	3	52-8	80	4.26	91	.264	.349	24	.208	1	100	-4	0	-0.7
1963	Cle A	8	5	.615	58	7	0	5	119	91	48	13	4	52-10	98	2.95	123	.208	.298	26-0-2	.115	-1	67	7	0	0.7
1964	Cle A	8	6	.571	56	2	0	4	106	106	56	15	4	53-5	89	4.33	83	.260	.349	16-0-3	.375	2	136	-8	0	-0.9
1965	Cle A	6	5	.545	60	0	0	17	103.2	86	43	7	2	50-10	86	3.04	115	.226	.318	16-1-1	.063	-0	—	4	0	0.4
1966	Cle A☆	14	15	.483	40	37	12	0	254.1	211	102	19	4	79-3	194	3.22	107	.228	.289	76-0-8	.132	-1	77	6	0	0.7
1967	Cle A	1	5	.167	9	9	1	0	60.2	50	28	7	1	24-1	39	3.71	88	.234	.311	15-0-5	.000	-2	89	-3	0	-0.4
	†Bos A	12	8	.600	29	24	8	3	165.1	143	70	16	4	47-3	115	3.16	110	.231	.288	59-0-2	.203	1	115	4	0	0.6
	Year	13	13	.500	38	33	9	3	226	193	98	23	5	71-4	154	3.31	104	.232	.294	74-0-7	.162	-1	108	2	0	0.2
1968	Bos A☆	11	11	.500	35	27	9-3	1	199.1	177	82	7	5	68-6	103	3.12	101	.239	.306	59-0-5	.220	2	101	-1	0	0.2
1969	Sea A	2	6	.250	13	11	1-1	2-0	61.1	76	40	8	2	34-8	30	4.70	78	.305	.389	14-0-5	.214	1	80	-9	0	-0.9
	Chi A	0	0	ø	23	2	0	0-0	38.2	48	27	8	2	23-2	26	6.28	61	.308	.403	5	.000	-0	161	-9	0	-0.5
	Year	2	6	.250	36	13	1-1	2-0	100	124	67	16	4	57-10	56	5.31	70	.306	.394	19-0-5	.158	1	91	-17	0	-1.4
Total	12	121	117	.508	519	233	71-9	51-0	2015	1794	932	207	54	842-64	1378	3.68	98	.239	.318	569-1-61	.185	9	101	-23	0	-1.4
Bell, George	George Glenn "Farmer"; B11.2.1874 Greenwood NY; D12.25.1941 New York NY; BR/TR/6´0˝/195; d4.17																									
1907	Bro N	8	16	.333	35	27	20-3	1	263.2	222	102	1	6	77	88	2.25	104	.238	.300	84-0-2	.095	-2	99	0	—	-0.1
1908	Bro N	4	15	.211	29	19	12-2	1	155.1	162	80	3	2	45	63	3.59	65	.270	.324	47-0-5	.170	1	70	-20	—	-2.3
1909	Bro N	16	15	.516	33	30	29-6	1	256	236	103	5	4	73	95	2.71	96	.251	.307	90-0-2	.167	1	85	-4	—	-0.3
1910	Bro N	10	27	.270	44	36	25-4	1	310	267	127	4	4	82	102	2.64	115	.241	.296	97-0-2	.134	-4	69	9	—	0.5
1911	Bro N	5	6	.455	19	12	6-2	0	101	123	59	2	2	28	28	4.28	78	.315	.364	33-0-1	.121	-1	88	-10	—	-1.0
Total	5	43	79	.352	160	124	92-17	4	1086	1010	471	15	18	305	376	2.85	94	.254	.310	351-0-12	.137	-6	81	-25	—	-3.2
Bell, Heath	Heath Justin; B9.29.1977 Oceanside CA; BR/TR/6´3˝/(225–230); d8.24; Col Santa Ana (CA) JC																									
2004	NY N	0	2	.000	17	0	0	0-1	24.1	22	9	5	0	6-0	27	3.33	129	.253	.301	1	.000	-0	—	3	0	0.2
2005	NY N	1	3	.250	42	0	0	0-0	46.2	56	30	3	1	13-3	43	5.59	74	.298	.347	3	.000	-0	—	-7	0	-0.6
2006	NY N	0	0	ø	22	0	0	0-0	37	51	25	6	0	11-2	35	5.11	86	.331	.376	1	.000	-0	—	-4	0	-0.2
Total	3	1	5	.167	81	0	0	0-1	108	129	64	14	1	30-5	105	4.92	87	.301	.348	5	.000	-1	—	-8	0	-0.6
Bell, Hi	Herman S; B7.16.1897 Mt.Sherman KY; D6.7.1949 Glendale CA; BR/TR/6´0˝/185; d4.16																									
1924	StL N	3	8	.273	28	10	5	1	113.1	124	68	5	5	29	29	4.92	77	.292	.344	31	.065	-2	83	-12	—	-1.3
1926	†StL N	6	6	.500	27	8	3	2	85	82	41	1	2	17	27	3.18	123	.255	.296	25-0-1	.120	-1	67	5	—	0.4
1927	StL N	1	3	.250	25	1	0	0	57.1	71	37	5	1	22	31	3.92	101	.317	.381	11	.091	-1	172	-2	—	-0.3
1929	StL N	0	2	.000	7	0	0	0	13	19	15	1	0	4	4	6.92	67	.339	.383	3	.000	-0	—	-5	—	-0.6
1930	†StL N	4	3	.571	39	9	2	**8**	115.1	143	65	4	2	23	42	3.90	129	.299	.334	26-0-3	.077	-3	108	**11**	—	0.5
1932	NY N	8	4	.667	35	10	3	2	120	132	58	12	2	16	25	3.68	101	.280	.307	34-0-1	.088	-2	129	1	—	-0.2
1933	†NY N	6	5	.545	38	7	1-1	5	105.1	100	31	4	2	20	24	2.05	157	.246	.285	29-0-1	.138	-1	104	**13**	—	1.4
1934	NY N	4	3	.571	22	2	0	6	54	72	25	2	2	12	9	3.67	105	.319	.358	19-0-1	.105	-1	268	2	—	0.1
Total	8	32	34	.485	221	47	14-1	24	663.1	743	340	34	16	143	191	3.69	107	.285	.326	178-0-7	.096	-12	108	13	—	-0.0
Bell, Jerry	Jerry Houston; B10.6.1947 Madison TN; BB/TR/6´4˝/(180–190); d9.6; Col Rhodes																									
1971	Mil A	2	1	.667	8	0	0	0-0	14.2	10	5	0	0	6-1	8	3.07	114	.200	.281	0	ø	0	—	1	0	0.2
1972	Mil A	5	1	.833	25	3	0	0-0	70.2	50	15	1	3	33-4	20	1.66	185	.209	.310	14-0-1	.071	-1	135	11	20	0.9
1973	Mil A	9	9	.500	31	25	8	1-3	183.2	185	95	14	5	70-5	57	3.97	96	.263	.332	0	ø	0	126	-5	0	-0.4
1974	Mil A	1	0	1.000	5	0	0	0-0	14	17	6	2	0	5-0	4	2.57	142	.315	.373	0	ø	0	—	1	0	0.1
Total	4	17	11	.607	69	28	8	1-3	283	262	121	17	8	114-10	89	3.28	110	.250	.327	14-0-1	.071	-1	131	8	20	0.8
Bell, Ralph	Ralph Albert "Lefty"; B11.6.1890 Kahoka MO; D10.18.1959 Burlington IA; BL/TL/5´11.5˝/170; d7.16																									
1912	Chi A	0	0	ø	3	0	0	0	6	8	7	1	0	8	5	9.00	36	.333	.500	2	.000	-0	—	-4	—	-0.2
Bell, Rob	Robert Allen; B1.17.1977 Newburgh NY; BR/TR/6´5˝/225; [AtlN95 3/85]; d4.8																									
2000	Cin N	7	8	.467	26	26	1	0-0	140.1	130	84	32	1	73-6	112	5.00	95	.243	.334	45-0-3	.067	-3	105	-3	0	-0.6
2001	Cin N	0	5	.000	9	9	0	0-0	44.1	46	28	9	3	17-1	33	5.48	84	.275	.351	7-0-2	.143	0	65	-3	0	-0.3
	Tex A	5	5	.500	18	18	0	0-0	105.1	130	87	23	4	47-0	64	7.18	67	.310	.378	0	ø	0	125	-25	0	-2.0
2002	Tex A	4	3	.571	17	15	0	0-0	94	113	69	16	1	35-0	70	6.22	77	.296	.351	1	.000	0	124	-14	0	-0.8
2003	TB A	5	4	.556	19	18	0	0-0	101	103	64	15	5	39-1	44	5.52	83	.263	.336	2	.000	-0	106	-9	0	-0.7
2004	TB A	8	8	.500	24	19	1	0-0	123	121	71	16	5	41-0	57	4.46	105	.253	.317	5	.200	0	103	1	0	0.2
2005	TB A	1	1	.500	8	3	0	0-0	25	41	25	7	2	12-0	13	8.28	53	.360	.426	0	ø	0	161	-11	56	-0.7
Total	6	30	34	.469	121	108	2	0-0	633	684	428	118	21	264-8	393	5.69	83	.275	.347	60-0-5	.083	-2	109	-64	56	-4.9
Bell, Bill	William Samuel "Ding Dong"; B10.24.1933 Goldsboro NC; D10.11.1962 Durham NC; BR/TR/6´3˝/(200–218); d9.5; Mil 1953–54																									
1952	Pit N	0	1	.000	4	1	0	0	15.2	16	11	3	0	13	4	4.60	87	.254	.382	4	.000	-0	0	-2	0	-0.1
1955	Pit N	0	0	ø	1	0	0	0	1	0	0	0	0	1-0	0	0.00	ø	.000	.250	0	ø	0	0	0	0	0.0
Total	2	0	1	.000	5	1	0	0	16.2	16	11	3	0	14-0	4	4.32	93	.242	.375	4	.000	-0	0	-2	0	-0.1
Beltran, Francis	Francis Lebron; B7.25.1979 Santo Domingo, D.R.; BR/TR/6´5˝/(220–230); d6.28; [DL 2005 Was N 183]																									
2002	Chi N	0	0	ø	11	0	0	0-0	12	14	11	2	0	16-1	11	7.50	54	.311	.484	1	.000	-0	—	-5	0	-0.2
2004	Chi N	2	2	.500	34	0	0	0-0	35	27	19	8	0	22-0	40	4.63	96	.214	.329	1	.000	-0	—	-1	0	-0.1
	Mon N	0	0	ø	11	0	0	1-0	14.1	20	12	3	2	5-1	8	7.53	61	.333	.397	2	.500	0	—	-4	15	-0.2
	Year	2	2	.500	45	0	0	1-0	49.1	47	31	11	2	27-1	48	5.47	82	.253	.350	3	.333	0	—	-4	0	-0.3
Total	2	2	2	.500	56	0	0	1-0	61.1	61	42	13	2	43-2	59	5.87	75	.264	.380	4	.250	0	—	-10	198	-0.5
Beltran, Rigo	Rigoberto; B11.13.1969 Tijuana, Baja California, Mexico; BL/TL/5´11˝/(185–215); [StLN91 26/675]; d6.2; Col Wyoming																									
1997	StL N	1	2	.333	35	4	0	1-0	54.1	47	25	3	0	17-0	50	3.48	120	.237	.294	7	.143	0	88	4	0	0.2
1998	NY N	0	0	ø	7	0	0	0-0	8	6	3	1	0	4-0	5	3.38	122	.214	.303	1	.000	-0	—	1	0	0.0
1999	NY N	1	1	.500	21	0	0	0-0	31	30	15	5	0	12-2	35	3.48	125	.250	.318	1	.000	-0	—	2	0	0.1
	Col N	0	0	ø	12	0	0	0-0	11	20	9	2	1	7-1	15	7.36	79	.385	.467	2	.500	0	—	-1	0	0.0
	Year	1	1	.500	33	0	0	0-0	42	50	24	7	1	19-3	50	4.50	105	.291	.365	3	.333	0	—	0	0	0.1
2000	Col N	0	0	ø	1	1	0	0-0	1.1	6	6	2	0	3-0	1	40.50	14	.600	.692	0	ø	0	158	-4	0	-0.2
2004	Mon N	0	0	ø	2	0	0	0-0	0.2	1	1	0	0	0-0	0	13.50	34	.333	.333	0	ø	0	—	-1	37	0.0
Total	5	2	3	.400	78	5	0	1-0	106.1	110	59	13	1	43-3	106	4.40	100	.268	.336	11	.182	0	108	1	37	0.1

YEAR	TM LG	W	L	PCT	G	GS	CG-SHO	SV-BS	IP	H	R	HR	HB	BB-IB	SO	ERA	AERA	OAV	OOB	AB-HR-SH	AVG	PB	SUP	APR	DL	PW
BENDER, CHIEF	Charles Albert; B5.5.1884 Crow Wing Co. MN; D5.22.1954 Philadelphia PA; BR/TR/6´2˝/185; d4.20; C6; HF1953; Col Dickinson																									
1903	Phi A	17	14	.548	36	33	29-2	0	270	239	115	6	25	65	127	3.07	100	.237	.299	120-0-4	.183	-1*	114	1	—	0.0
1904	Phi A	10	11	.476	29	20	18-4	0	203.2	167	90	1	4	59	149	2.87	93	.225	.285	79-0-2	.228	3*	78	-4	—	-0.2
1905	†Phi A	18	11	.621	35	23	18-4	0	229	193	103	5	11	90	142	2.83	94	.230	.313	92-0-2	.217	2*	111	-4	—	-0.2
1906	Phi A	15	10	.600	36	27	24	**3**	238.1	208	98	5	8	48	159	2.53	108	.238	.284	99-3-2	.253	7*	116	4	—	1.2
1907	Phi A	16	8	.667	33	24	20-4	3	219.1	185	67	1	3	34	112	2.05	127	.231	.265	100-0-4	.230	3*	112	15	—	2.0
1908	Phi A	8	9	.471	18	17	14-2	1	138.2	121	48	1	3	21	85	1.75	146	.236	.270	50-0-1	.220	2*	85	8	—	1.3
1909	Phi A	18	8	.692	34	29	24-5	1	250	196	68	1	5	45	161	1.66	145	.214	.254	93-0-5	.215	4*	130	20	—	2.7
1910	†Phi A	23	5	**.821**	30	28	25-3	0	250	182	63	1	10	47	155	1.58	150	.207	.255	93-0-4	.269	8*	130	25	—	4.1
1911	†Phi A	17	5	**.773**	31	24	16-2	3	216.1	198	66	2	4	58	114	2.16	146	.252	.307	79-0-5	.165	-3*	117	26	—	2.2
1912	Phi A	13	8	.619	27	19	12-1	2	171	169	63	1	1	33	90	2.74	113	.277	.315	60-0-3	.150	-1	115	10	—	0.9
1913	†Phi A	21	10	.677	48	21	14-2	**13**	236.2	208	78	2	3	59	135	2.21	125	.236	.287	78-0-5	.154	0	154	13	—	1.7
1914	†Phi A	17	3	**.850**	28	23	14-7	2	179	159	49	4	1	55	107	2.26	115	.240	.299	62-1-4	.145	0	152	10	—	1.2
1915	Bal F	4	16	.200	26	23	15	1	178.1	198	103	5	7	37	89	3.99	72	.298	.342	60-1-0	.267	4	81	-22	—	-2.0
1916	Phi N	7	7	.500	27	13	4	3	122.2	137	71	3	10	34	43	3.74	71	.287	.347	43-0-1	.279	4*	143	-16	—	-1.4
1917	Phi N	8	2	.800	20	10	8-4	2	113	84	24	1	7	26	43	1.67	168	.215	.277	39-1-0	.205	1	113	15	—	1.5
1925	Chi A	0	0	ø	1	0	0	0	1	1	2	1	0	1	0	18.00	23	.333	.500	0	ø	0	—	-1	—	-0.1
Total	16	212	127	.625	459	334	255-40	34	3017	2645	1108	40	102	712	1711	2.46	111	.239	.292	1147-6-42	.212	34	117	100	—	14.9
BENES, ALAN	Alan Paul; B1.21.1972 Evansville IN; BR/TR/6´5˝/(215–235); [StLN93 1/16]; d9.19; b–Andy; Col Creighton; [DL 1998 StL N 181]																									
1995	StL N	1	2	.333	3	3	0	0-0	16	24	15	2	1	4-0	20	8.44	51	.343	.387	6	.000	-1	42	-6	0	-1.0
1996	†StL N	13	10	.565	34	32	3-1	0-0	191	192	120	27	7	87-3	131	4.90	87	.266	.347	61-0-7	.148	-0	108	-17	0	-1.8
1997	StL N	9	9	.500	23	23	2	0-0	161.2	128	60	13	4	68-3	160	2.89	145	.219	.303	52-0-2	.173	0	74	23	60	2.3
1999	StL N	0	0	ø	2	0	0	0-0	2	2	0	0	0	0-0	2	0.00	ø	.286	.286	0	ø	0	—	1	153	0.1
2000	StL N	2	2	.500	30	0	0	0-1	46	54	33	7	2	23-2	26	5.67	82	.290	.373	4	.500	1	—	-6	0	-0.4
2001	StL N	2	0	1.000	9	1	0	0-0	14.2	14	12	5	0	12-0	10	7.36	59	.250	.382	2	.500	0	128	-5	0	-0.5
2002	Chi N	2	2	.500	7	7	0	0-0	39.1	42	22	3	0	12-1	32	4.35	93	.276	.325	13	.077	-1	95	-2	0	-0.2
2003	Chi N	0	0	ø	3	0	0	1-0	8.1	8	2	0	0	6-0	9	2.16	201	.267	.389	1	.000	-0	—	2	0	0.1
	Tex A	0	3	.000	4	4	0	0-0	15	29	20	2	0	8-0	11	11.40	44	.414	.468	0	ø	0	88	-10	0	-1.4
Total	8	29	28	.509	115	70	5-1	1-1	494	493	284	59	14	220-9	401	4.59	93	.263	.341	139-0-9	.158	0	92	-20	394	-2.8
BENES, ANDY	Andrew Charles; B8.20.1967 Evansville IN; BR/TR/6´6˝/(235–245); [SDN88 1/1]; d8.11; b–Alan; Col Evansville																									
1989	SD N	6	3	.667	10	10	0	0-0	66.2	51	28	7	1	31-0	66	3.51	100	.213	.303	24-1-1	.250	2	111	1	0	0.3
1990	SD N	10	11	.476	32	31	2	0-0	192.1	177	87	18	1	69-5	140	3.60	107	.242	.306	60-0-5	.100	-2	92	5	0	0.1
1991	SD N	15	11	.577	33	33	4-1	0-0	223	194	76	23	4	59-7	167	3.03	126	.232	.285	62-1-7	.032	-2	77	22	0	2.3
1992	SD N	13	14	.481	34	34	2-2	0-0	231.1	230	90	14	5	61-6	169	3.35	107	.264	.314	67-1-5	.149	2	71	8	0	1.1
1993	SD N★	15	15	.500	34	34	4-2	0-0	230.2	200	111	23	4	86-7	179	3.78	109	.232	.303	72-1-14	.125	-0	85	9	0	0.9
1994	SD N	6	14	.300	25	25	2-2	0-0	172.1	155	82	20	1	51-2	**189**	3.86	107	.237	.293	49-0-13	.163	-0	88	6	0	0.6
1995	SD N	4	7	.364	19	19	1-1	0-0	118.2	121	65	10	4	45-3	126	4.17	98	.262	.330	40-0-3	.150	-0	102	-3	0	-0.3
	†Sea A	7	2	.778	12	12	0	0-0	63	72	42	8	2	33-2	45	5.86	81	.287	.369	0	ø	0	138	-6	0	-0.7
1996	†StL N	18	10	.643	36	34	3-1	1-0	230.1	215	107	28	6	77-7	160	3.83	111	.247	.310	73-0-9	.151	-0	108	11	0	1.0
1997	StL N	10	7	.588	26	26	0	0-0	177	149	64	9	5	61-4	175	3.10	135	.230	.298	55-0-8	.218	2	96	24	27	2.2
1998	Ari N	14	13	.519	34	34	1	0-0	231.1	221	111	25	6	74-3	164	3.97	108	.251	.311	65-1-10	.169	3*	98	8	0	1.2
1999	Ari N	13	12	.520	33	32	0	0-0	198.1	216	117	34	4	82-3	141	4.81	96	.273	.343	58-1-10	.155	1	110	-4	0	-0.5
2000	†StL N	12	9	.571	30	27	1	0-0	166	174	95	30	1	68-0	137	4.88	95	.275	.342	50-1-6	.080	-1	114	-2	18	-0.5
2001	StL N	7	7	.500	27	19	0	0-1	107.1	122	92	30	6	61-0	78	7.38	59	.286	.380	32-0-2	.156	1	124	-35	0	-3.7
2002	†StL N	5	4	.556	18	17	1	0-0	97	80	39	10	5	51-3	64	2.78	145	.228	.330	34-1-2	.206	2*	116	11	91	1.1
Total	14	155	139	.527	403	387	21-9	1-1	2505.1	2377	1206	289	55	909-52	2000	3.97	104	.250	.317	741-8-95	.143	6	99	55	136	5.1
BENGE, RAY	Raymond Adelphia; B4.22.1902 Jacksonville TX; D6.27.1997 Centerville TX; BR/TR/5´9.5˝/160; d9.26; Col Sam Houston St.																									
1925	Cle A	1	0	1.000	2	2	1-1	0	11.2	9	2	0	0	3	3	1.54	286	.205	.255	5	.400	0	133	4	—	0.3
1926	Cle A	1	0	1.000	8	0	0	0	11.2	15	11	0	0	4	3	3.86	105	.313	.365	3	.333	0	—	-2	—	-0.1
1928	Phi N	8	18	.308	40	28	12-1	1	201.2	219	117	15	5	88	68	4.55	94	.286	.363	58-0-7	.207	-0*	80	-6	—	-0.8
1929	Phi N	11	15	.423	38	26	9-2	4	199	255	147	24	4	77	78	6.29	83	.322	.385	74-0-3	.203	-3*	91	-18	—	-2.3
1930	Phi N	11	15	.423	38	29	14	1	225.2	305	178	22	1	81	70	5.70	96	.328	.382	88-0-3	.205	-3	108	-10	—	-1.2
1931	Phi N	14	18	.438	38	31	16-2	2	247	251	107	12	5	61	117	3.17	134	.262	.310	88-0-6	.205	-2	81	26	—	2.9
1932	Phi N	13	12	.520	41	28	13-2	6	222.1	247	119	15	4	58	89	4.05	109	.281	.329	75-0-2	.173	-3	102	7	—	0.4
1933	Bro N	10	17	.370	37	30	16-2	1	228.2	238	104	11	6	55	74	3.42	94	.268	.315	76-0-6	.184	0	103	-5	—	-0.7
1934	Bro N	14	12	.538	36	32	14-1	0	227	252	124	11	3	61	64	4.32	90	.272	.319	89-0-2	.169	-2	117	-9	—	-1.1
1935	Bro N	9	9	.500	23	17	5-1	1	124.2	142	77	12	1	47	39	4.48	89	.289	.353	47-0-1	.191	-1	93	-8	—	-1.2
1936	Bos N	7	9	.438	21	19	2	0	115	161	79	6	1	38	32	5.79	66	.333	.382	43-0-4	.140	-3	91	-23	—	-3.0
	Phi N	1	4	.200	15	6	0	1	45.2	70	35	3	0	19	13	4.73	96	.350	.406	10	.000	-1	56	-3	—	-0.5
	Year	8	13	.381	36	25	2	1	160.2	231	114	9	1	57	45	5.49	73	.338	.389	53-0-4	.113	-4	81	-23	—	-3.5
1938	Cin N	1	1	.500	9	0	0	2	15.1	13	8	1	0	6	5	4.11	89	.228	.302	3	.333	0	—	-1	—	-0.1
Total	12	101	130	.437	346	248	102-12	19	1875.1	2177	1108	132	30	598	655	4.52	95	.292	.347	659-0-34	.188	-17	96	-48	—	-7.4
BENITEZ, ARMANDO	Armando German; B11.3.1972 Ramon Santana, D.R.; BR/TR/6´4˝/(180–245); d7.28																									
1994	Bal A	0	0	ø	3	0	0	0-0	10	8	1	0	1	4-0	14	0.90	562	.216	.310	0	ø	0	—	4	0	0.2
1995	Bal A	1	5	.167	44	0	0	2-3	47.2	37	33	8	5	37-2	56	5.66	84	.213	.361	0	ø	0	—	-5	0	-0.6
1996	†Bal A	1	0	1.000	18	0	0	4-1	14.1	7	6	2	0	6-0	20	3.77	131	.143	.232	0	ø	0	—	2	128	0.2
1997	†Bal A	4	5	.444	71	0	0	9-1	73.1	49	22	7	1	43-5	106	2.45	180	.191	.305	0	ø	0	—	16	0	2.0
1998	Bal A	5	6	.455	71	0	0	22-4	68.1	48	29	10	4	39-2	87	3.82	119	.199	.318	0	ø	0	—	6	0	1.2
1999	†NY N	4	3	.571	77	0	0	22-6	78	40	17	4	0	41-4	128	1.85	235	.148	.260	5	.000	-1	—	22	0	2.8
2000	†NY N	4	4	.500	76	0	0	41-5	76	39	24	10	0	38-2	106	2.61	168	.148	.255	0	ø	0	—	16	0	2.9
2001	NY N	6	4	.600	73	0	0	43-3	76.1	59	32	12	1	40-6	93	3.77	107	.214	.314	1	.000	-0	—	4	0	0.7
2002	NY N	1	0	1.000	62	0	0	33-4	67.1	46	20	8	3	25-0	79	2.27	174	.190	.272	0	ø	0	—	13	0	1.3
2003	NY N☆	3	3	.500	45	0	0	21-7	49.1	41	18	5	0	24-1	50	3.10	135	.223	.311	1	.000	-0	—	6	0	1.1
	NY A	1	1	.500	9	0	0	0-0	9.1	8	4	0	0	6-1	10	1.93	228	.235	.350	0	ø	0	—	2	0	0.3
	Sea A	0	0	ø	15	0	0	0-1	14.1	10	5	1	0	11-1	15	3.14	138	.189	.328	0	ø	0	—	2	0	0.1
	Year	1	1	.500	24	0	0	0-1	23.2	18	9	1	0	17-2	25	2.66	164	.207	.337	0	ø	0	—	4	0	0.4
2004	Fla N☆	2	2	.500	64	0	0	**47**-4	69.2	36	11	6	0	21-4	62	1.29	318	.152	.220	1	.000	-0	—	23	20	3.7
2005	SF N	2	3	.400	30	0	0	19-4	30	25	17	5	0	16-0	23	4.50	94	.229	.323	0	ø	0	—	-1	110	-0.3
2006	SF N	4	2	.667	41	0	0	17-8	38.1	39	15	6	0	21-2	31	3.52	126	.267	.353	0	ø	0	—	4	35	0.8
Total	13	38	38	.500	699	0	0	280-51	722.1	492	254	84	15	372-30	880	2.95	146	.191	.295	8	.000	-1	—	114	293	16.4
BENN, HENRY	Henry Omer; B1.25.1890 Viola WI; D6.4.1967 Madison WI; BR/TR/6´0˝/190; d9.24																									
1914	Cle A	0	0	ø	1	0	0	0	1	0	0	0	0	0	1	0.00	ø	.000	.000	0	ø	0	—	0	—	0.0
BENNETT, DAVE	David Hans; B11.7.1945 Berkeley CA; BR/TR/6´5˝/205; d6.12; b–Dennis																									
1964	Phi N	0	0	ø	1	0	0	0	1	2	1	0	0	0-0	1	9.00	39	.400	.400	0	ø	0	—	-1	0	0.0
BENNETT, JEFF	David Jeffrey; B6.10.1980 Donelson TN; BR/TR/6´3˝/206; [PitN98 19/568]; d4.6																									
2004	Mil N	1	5	.167	60	0	0	0-1	71.1	78	43	12	2	26-2	45	4.79	92	.278	.338	2	.000	-0	—	-4	0	-0.3
BENNETT, DENNIS	Dennis John; B10.5.1939 Oakland CA; BL/TL/6´5˝/(185–205); d5.12; b–Dave; Col Shasta (CA) JC																									
1962	Phi N	9	9	.500	31	24	7-2	3	174.2	144	78	17	6	68-3	149	3.81	102	.224	.302	63-1-3	.127	-1	98	3	0	0.2
1963	Phi N	9	5	.643	23	16	6-1	1	119.1	102	44	12	4	33-5	82	2.64	122	.231	.287	40-1-1	.225	3	123	6	74	1.1
1964	Phi N	12	14	.462	41	32	7-2	1	208	222	92	23	5	58-8	125	3.68	94	.280	.331	66-0-2	.197	3	84	-2	0	0.0
1965	Bos A	5	7	.417	34	18	3	0	141.2	152	76	15	6	53-6	85	4.38	85	.279	.346	39-0-2	.179	2	98	-8	0	-0.5
1966	Bos A	3	3	.500	16	13	0	0	75	75	30	9	1	23-2	47	3.24	117	.261	.316	23-1-2	.130	1	82	5	80	0.4
1967	Bos A	4	3	.571	13	11	4-1	0	69.2	72	32	12	2	22-2	34	3.88	90	.268	.327	25-1-1	.120	-0	141	-2	0	-0.2
	NY N	1	1	.500	8	6	0	0	26.1	37	15	4	1	7-1	14	5.13	66	.336	.378	8	.250	0	91	-4	0	-0.3
1968	Cal A	0	5	.000	16	7	1	1	48.1	46	22	6	4	17-0	36	3.54	82	.250	.324	13-0-2	.077	-1	47	-4	0	-0.5
Total	7	43	47	.478	182	127	28-6	6	863	850	389	98	29	281-27	572	3.69	96	.260	.322	277-4-13	.166	7	97	-6	154	0.2

BENNETT, ERIK Erik Hans; B9.13.1968 Yreka CA; BR/TR/6´2˝/205; [CalA89 4/96]; d5.15; Col Cal St.–Sacramento

YEAR	TM LG	W	L	PCT	G	GS	CG-SHO	SV-BS	IP	H	R	HR	HB	BB-IB	SO	ERA	AERA	OAV	OOB	AB-HR-SH	AVG	PB	SUP	APR	DL	PW
1995	Cal A	0	0	ø	1	0	0	0-0	0.1	0	0	0	0	0-0	0	0.00	ø	.000	.000	0	ø	0	—	0	0	0.0
1996	Min A	2	0	1.000	24	0	0	1-0	27.1	33	24	7	2	16-1	13	7.90	65	.306	.402	0	ø	0	—	-8	0	-0.5
Total	2	2	0	1.000	25	0	0	1-0	27.2	33	24	7	2	16-1	13	7.81	66	.303	.398	0	ø	0	—	-8	0	-0.5

BENNETT, FRANK Francis Allen "Chip"; B10.27.1904 Mardela Springs MD; D3.18.1966 Wilmington DE; BR/TR/5´10.5˝/163; d9.17

YEAR	TM LG	W	L	PCT	G	GS	CG-SHO	SV-BS	IP	H	R	HR	HB	BB-IB	SO	ERA	AERA	OAV	OOB	AB-HR-SH	AVG	PB	SUP	APR	DL	PW
1927	Bos A	0	1	.000	4	1	0	0	12.1	15	4	0	0	6	1	2.92	145	.333	.412	3	.000	-1	40	2	—	0.1
1928	Bos A	0	0	ø	1	0	0	0	1	1	0	0	0	0	0	0.00	ø	.250	.250	0	ø	0	—	0	—	0.0
Total	2	0	1	.000	5	1	0	0	13.1	16	4	0	0	6	1	2.70	156	.327	.400	3	.000	-1	40	2	—	0.1

BENNETT, JOEL Joel Todd; B1.31.1970 Binghamton NY; BR/TR/6´1˝/(160–171); [BosA91 21/564]; d7.15; Col East Stroudsburg

YEAR	TM LG	W	L	PCT	G	GS	CG-SHO	SV-BS	IP	H	R	HR	HB	BB-IB	SO	ERA	AERA	OAV	OOB	AB-HR-SH	AVG	PB	SUP	APR	DL	PW
1998	Bal A	0	0	ø	2	0	0	0-0	2	2	1	0	0	3-0	0	4.50	101	.250	.455	0	ø	0	—	0	0	0.0
1999	Phi N	2	1	.667	5	3	0	0-1	17	26	17	10	0	7-0	13	9.00	52	.351	.407	4-0-1	.000	-0	105	-7	0	-1.0
Total	2	2	1	.667	7	3	0	0-1	19	28	18	10	0	10-0	13	8.53	55	.341	.413	4-0-1	.000	-0	105	-7	0	-1.0

BENNETT, SHAYNE Shayne Anthony; B4.10.1972 Adelaide, South Australia, Australia; BR/TR/6´5˝/(200–220); [BosA93 25/695]; d8.22; Col Du Page (IL) [JC]

YEAR	TM LG	W	L	PCT	G	GS	CG-SHO	SV-BS	IP	H	R	HR	HB	BB-IB	SO	ERA	AERA	OAV	OOB	AB-HR-SH	AVG	PB	SUP	APR	DL	PW
1997	Mon N	0	1	.000	16	0	0	0-0	22.2	21	9	2	0	9-3	8	3.18	132	.247	.309	1	.000	0	—	3	0	0.1
1998	Mon N	5	5	.500	62	0	0	1-1	91.2	97	61	8	6	45-3	59	5.50	77	.276	.363	6-0-1	.000	-0	—	-12	0	-1.2
1999	Mon N	0	1	.000	5	1	0	0-0	11.1	24	18	4	1	3-0	4	14.29	31	.444	.475	2	.000	-0	82	-12	0	-0.8
Total	3	5	7	.417	83	1	0	1-1	125.2	142	88	14	7	57-6	71	5.87	72	.290	.365	9-0-1	.000	-0	82	-21	0	-1.9

BENOIT, JOAQUIN Joaquin Antonio (Pena); B7.26.1977 Santiago, D.R.; BR/TR/6´3˝/(205–220); d8.8

YEAR	TM LG	W	L	PCT	G	GS	CG-SHO	SV-BS	IP	H	R	HR	HB	BB-IB	SO	ERA	AERA	OAV	OOB	AB-HR-SH	AVG	PB	SUP	APR	DL	PW
2001	Tex A	0	0	ø	1	1	0	0-0	5	8	6	3	0	3-0	4	10.80	44	.364	.423	0	ø	0	116	-3	0	-0.1
2002	Tex A	4	5	.444	17	13	0	1-0	84.2	91	51	6	5	58-2	59	5.31	90	.272	.384	0	ø	0	89	-4	0	-0.4
2003	Tex A	8	5	.615	25	17	0	0-0	105	99	67	23	3	51-0	87	5.49	91	.246	.332	2	.000	-0	92	-5	21	-0.5
2004	Tex A	3	5	.375	28	15	0	0-0	103	113	67	19	8	31-0	95	5.68	87	.279	.335	6	.000	-1	111	-6	15	-0.5
2005	Tex A	4	4	.500	32	9	0	0-0	87	69	39	9	2	38-0	78	3.72	122	.212	.297	1	.000	-0*	104	8	48	0.6
2006	Tex A	1	1	.500	56	0	0	0-2	79.2	68	49	5	3	38-4	85	4.86	96	.224	.314	0	ø	0	—	-3	0	-0.2
Total	6	20	20	.500	159	55	0	1-2	464.1	448	279	65	21	219-6	408	5.12	94	.250	.335	9	.000	-1	100	-13	84	-1.1

BENSON, ALLEN Allen Wilbert "Bullet Ben"; B7.12.1908 Hurley SD; D11.16.1999 Viborg SD; BR/TR/6´1˝/185; d8.19

YEAR	TM LG	W	L	PCT	G	GS	CG-SHO	SV-BS	IP	H	R	HR	HB	BB-IB	SO	ERA	AERA	OAV	OOB	AB-HR-SH	AVG	PB	SUP	APR	DL	PW
1934	Was A	0	1	.000	2	2	0	0	9.2	19	14	0	2	5	4	12.10	36	.413	.491	3-0-2	.000	-0	131	-8	—	-0.7

BENSON, KRIS Kristen James; B11.7.1974 Kennesaw GA; BR/TR/6´4˝/(190–205); [PitN96 1/1]; d4.9; Col Clemson; [DL 2001 Pit N 190]

YEAR	TM LG	W	L	PCT	G	GS	CG-SHO	SV-BS	IP	H	R	HR	HB	BB-IB	SO	ERA	AERA	OAV	OOB	AB-HR-SH	AVG	PB	SUP	APR	DL	PW
1999	Pit N	11	14	.440	31	31	2	0-0	196.2	184	105	16	6	83-5	139	4.07	113	.249	.327	65-0-6	.154	0	90	9	0	1.1
2000	Pit N	10	12	.455	32	32	2-1	0-0	217.2	206	104	24	10	86-5	184	3.85	121	.249	.325	65-0-9	.092	-2	88	19	0	1.5
2002	Pit N	9	6	.600	25	25	0	0-0	130.1	152	76	18	3	50-8	79	4.70	89	.295	.359	40-0-4	.175	-0*	108	-8	43	-0.9
2003	Pit N	5	9	.357	18	18	0	0-0	105	127	67	14	1	36-4	68	4.97	87	.295	.347	30-0-6	.000	-3	89	-10	73	-1.4
2004	Pit N	8	8	.500	20	20	0	0-0	132.1	137	69	7	6	44-5	83	4.22	103	.272	.336	39-0-10	.179	-0	98	1	0	0.1
	NY N	4	4	.500	11	11	1-1	0-0	68	65	37	8	4	17-3	51	4.50	95	.244	.298	19-0-5	.053	-1	77	-1	0	-0.3
	Year	12	12	.500	31	31	1-1	0-0	200.1	202	106	15	10	61-8	134	4.31	100	.263	.323	58-0-15	.138	-1	90	1	0	-0.2
2005	NY N	10	8	.556	28	28	0	0-0	174.1	171	86	24	4	49-5	95	4.13	100	.253	.306	49-0-6	.184	2	117	0	32	0.2
2006	Bal A	11	12	.478	30	30	3	0-0	183	199	105	33	7	58-2	88	4.82	94	.287	.342	9-1-0	.111	1	99	-6	17	-0.6
Total	7	68	73	.482	195	195	8-2	0-0	1207.1	1241	649	144	41	423-37	787	4.34	102	.267	.331	316-1-46	.130	-3	97	4	355	-0.3

BENTLEY, CY Clytus George; B11.23.1850 East Haven CT; D2.26.1873 Middletown CT; d4.26

YEAR	TM LG	W	L	PCT	G	GS	CG-SHO	SV-BS	IP	H	R	HR	HB	BB-IB	SO	ERA	AERA	OAV	OOB	AB-HR-SH	AVG	PB	SUP	APR	DL	PW
1872	Man NA	2	15	.118	18	17	14	0	144	259	253	4	—	12	5	6.06	60	.331	.341	114-1	.219	-0*	74	-39	—	-2.6

BENTLEY, JACK John Needles; B3.8.1895 Sandy Spring MD; D10.24.1969 Olney MD; BL/TL/5´11.5˝/200; d9.6; ▲

YEAR	TM LG	W	L	PCT	G	GS	CG-SHO	SV-BS	IP	H	R	HR	HB	BB-IB	SO	ERA	AERA	OAV	OOB	AB-HR-SH	AVG	PB	SUP	APR	DL	PW
1913	Was A	1	0	1.000	3	1	0	1	11	5	0	0	0	2	5	0.00	ø	.152	.200	3	.000	-0	25	4	—	0.4
1914	Was A	5	7	.417	30	11	3-2	**4**	125.1	110	49	3	3	53	55	2.37	119	.249	.334	40	.275	2	89	4	—	0.6
1915	Was A	0	2	.000	4	2	0	0	11.1	8	4	0	0	3	0	0.79	374	.200	.256	2	.000	-0	12	2	—	0.3
1916	Was A	0	0	ø	2	0	0	0	1.1	0	0	0	0	1	1	0.00	ø	.000	.250	0	ø	0	—	0	—	0.0
1923	†NY N	13	8	.619	31	26	12-1	3	183	198	102	10	5	67	80	4.48	85	.277	.343	89-1-2	.427	16*	118	-13	—	0.1
1924	†NY N	16	5	.762	28	24	13-1	1	188	196	85	11	4	56	60	3.78	97	.273	.329	98-0-1	.265	4*	134	0	—	0.4
1925	NY N	11	9	.550	28	22	11	0	157	200	90	10	1	59	47	5.04	80	.323	.383	99-3-1	.303	6*	111	-12	—	-0.3
1926	Phi N	0	2	.000	7	3	0	0	25.1	37	28	2	0	10	7	8.17	51	.327	.382	240-2-7	.258	1*	107	-11	—	-0.7
	NY N	0	0	ø	1	0	0	0	2	0	0	0	0	2	1	0.00	ø	.000	.250	4	.250	-0*	—	1	—	0.0
	Year	0	2	.000	8	3	0	0	27.1	37	28	2	0	12	8	7.57	54	.311	.374	244-2-7	.258	1	108	-10	—	-0.7
1927	NY N	0	0	ø	4	0	0	0	9.2	7	7	1	1	10	3	2.79	138	.206	.400	9-1-0	.222	1*	—	0	—	0.0
Total	9	46	33	.582	138	89	39-4	9	714	761	365	37	14	263	259	4.01	91	.280	.346	584-7-11	.291	28	115	-25	—	0.8

BENTON, AL John Alton; B3.18.1911 Noble OK; D4.14.1968 Lynwood CA; BR/TR/6´4˝/215; d4.18; Mil 1943–44

YEAR	TM LG	W	L	PCT	G	GS	CG-SHO	SV-BS	IP	H	R	HR	HB	BB-IB	SO	ERA	AERA	OAV	OOB	AB-HR-SH	AVG	PB	SUP	APR	DL	PW
1934	Phi A	7	9	.438	32	21	7	1	155	145	98	7	2	88	58	4.88	90	.249	.349	55-0-2	.109	-4	109	-10	—	-1.3
1935	Phi A	3	4	.429	27	9	0	0	78.1	110	81	7	1	47	42	7.70	59	.328	.413	25-0-1	.040	-3	127	-29	—	-2.4
1938	Det A	5	3	.625	19	10	6	0	95.1	93	40	10	1	39	33	3.30	151	.259	.333	33-0-2	.121	-3	95	17	—	1.0
1939	Det A	6	8	.429	37	16	3	5	150	182	94	11	1	58	67	4.56	107	.294	.355	44-0-7	.091	-4	101	3	—	-0.1
1940	Det A	6	10	.375	42	0	0	**17**	79.1	93	44	5	0	36	50	4.42	107	.294	.366	17-0-4	.000	-3	—	3	—	0.4
1941	Det A☆	15	6	.714	38	14	7-1	7	157.2	130	63	11	3	65	63	2.97	153	**.221**	.302	50-0-9	.060	-5	103	24	0	2.6
1942	Det A★	7	13	.350	35	30	9-1	2	226.2	210	87	9	0	84	110	2.90	136	.246	.314	67-0-9	.075	-5	65	25	0	1.5
1945	†Det A	13	8	.619	31	27	12-5	3	191.2	175	68	7	2	63	76	2.02	174	.241	.303	63-0-8	.063	-6	91	24	0	2.2
1946	Det A	11	7	.611	28	15	6-1	1	140.2	132	69	9	1	58	60	3.65	100	.245	.319	49-0-5	.184	-1	116	-2	0	-0.3
1947	Det A	6	7	.462	36	14	4	7	133	147	77	11	1	61	33	4.40	86	.288	.365	39-0-3	.154	-2	101	-10	0	-1.2
1948	Det A	2	2	.500	30	0	0	3	44.1	45	34	4	1	36	18	5.68	77	.273	.406	11-0-2	.182	-0	—	-7	0	-0.7
1949	Cle A	9	6	.600	40	11	4-2	10	135.2	116	33	7	1	51	41	2.12	188	.238	.312	38-0-3	.132	-2	65	31	0	3.3
1950	Cle A	4	2	.667	36	0	0	4	63	57	32	7	1	30	26	3.57	121	.243	.331	12-0-2	.083	-1	—	4	0	0.3
1952	Bos A	4	3	.571	24	0	0	6	37.2	37	11	1	0	17	20	2.39	165	.268	.348	9-0-2	.000	-1	—	6	0	1.2
Total	14	98	88	.527	455	167	58-10	66	1688.1	1672	831	106	15	733	697	3.66	115	.259	.336	512-0-59	.098	-39	94	79	0	6.5

BENTON, RUBE John Cleave; B6.27.1890 Clinton NC; D12.12.1937 Dothan AL; BR/TL/6´1˝/190; d6.28; Mil 1918

YEAR	TM LG	W	L	PCT	G	GS	CG-SHO	SV-BS	IP	H	R	HR	HB	BB-IB	SO	ERA	AERA	OAV	OOB	AB-HR-SH	AVG	PB	SUP	APR	DL	PW
1910	Cin N	0	1	.000	12	2	0	0	38	44	34	1	1	23	15	4.74	62	.282	.378	11	.091	-1	64	-10	—	-0.6
1911	Cin N	3	3	.500	6	6	5	0	44.2	44	18	0	3	23	28	2.01	164	.270	.370	14-0-2	.143	-0	57	5	—	0.5
1912	Cin N	18	20	.474	**50**	**39**	22-2	2	302	316	143	2	18	118	162	3.10	108	.278	.356	104-0-3	.135	-6	88	9	—	0.5
1913	Cin N	11	7	.611	23	22	9-1	0	144.1	140	76	4	9	60	68	3.49	93	.265	.350	48-0-2	.208	1	108	-4	—	-0.4
1914	Cin N	16	18	.471	41	35	16-4	2	271	223	124	3	11	95	121	2.96	99	.228	.303	91-0-3	.143	-3	75	0	—	-0.3
1915	Cin N	6	13	.316	35	21	6-2	4	176.1	165	79	2	14	67	83	3.32	86	.257	.340	53-0-2	.208	-0	73	-7	—	-0.7
	NY N	3	5	.375	10	6	3	1	60.2	57	26	0	5	9	26	2.82	91	.253	.297	23-0-1	.217	1	131	-2	—	-0.2
	Year	9	18	.333	45	27	9-2	5	237	222	105	2	19	76	109	3.19	87	.256	.329	76-0-3	.211	1	85	-7	—	-0.9
1916	NY N	16	8	.667	38	29	15-3	2	238.2	210	84	5	10	58	115	2.87	85	.241	.296	78-0-4	.090	-4	109	-8	—	-1.4
1917	†NY N	15	9	.625	35	25	14-3	3	215	190	78	5	7	41	70	2.72	94	.238	.281	72-0-5	.167	-1	115	-3	—	-0.5
1918	NY N	1	2	.333	3	3	2	0	24	17	8	0	0	3	9	1.88	140	.202	.230	7	.143	1	86	1	—	0.3
1919	NY N	17	11	.607	35	28	11-1	2	209	181	71	5	4	52	53	2.63	107	.237	.289	67-1-3	.194	-1	120	6	—	0.7
1920	NY N	9	16	.360	33	25	12-4	2	193.1	222	82	8	3	31	52	3.03	99	.291	.321	65-0-4	.092	-7	96	-1	—	-0.6
1921	NY N	5	2	.714	18	9	3-1	0	72	72	28	2	0	17	11	2.88	128	.266	.309	21-0-2	.143	-1	139	6	—	0.4
1923	Cin N	14	10	.583	33	26	15	1	219	243	106	10	5	57	59	3.66	106	.284	.333	80-0-3	.287	4	123	8	—	1.2
1924	Cin N	7	9	.438	32	19	6-1	1	162.2	166	70	2	4	24	42	2.77	136	.266	.297	46	.261	2	85	15	—	1.6
1925	Cin N	9	10	.474	33	16	6-1	1	146.2	182	88	3	1	34	36	4.05	102	.301	.340	45-0-4	.200	1	94	-1	—	-0.2
Total	15	150	144	.510	437	311	145-23	21	2517.1	2472	1115	52	95	712	950	3.09	102	.261	.319	825-1-38	.172	-14	99	14	—	0.3

BENTON, LARRY Lawrence James; B11.20.1897 St.Louis MO; D4.3.1953 Amberley OH; BR/TR/5´11˝/165; d4.25

YEAR	TM LG	W	L	PCT	G	GS	CG-SHO	SV-BS	IP	H	R	HR	HB	BB-IB	SO	ERA	AERA	OAV	OOB	AB-HR-SH	AVG	PB	SUP	APR	DL	PW
1923	Bos N	5	9	.357	35	9	2	0	128	141	78	4	4	57	42	4.99	80	.293	.373	31-0-4	.161	-1	53	-11	—	-1.0
1924	Bos N	5	7	.417	30	13	4	1	128	129	63	4	3	64	41	4.15	92	.274	.365	33-0-2	.091	-3	77	-2	—	-0.5
1925	Bos N	14	7	.667	31	21	16-2	1	183.1	170	72	6	2	70	49	3.09	130	.249	.320	58-0-8	.241	2*	96	21	—	2.3
1926	Bos N	14	14	.500	43	27	12-1	1	231.2	244	113	10	7	81	103	3.85	92	.280	.346	78-0-6	.154	-4*	81	-7	—	-1.2
1927	Bos N	4	2	.667	11	10	3	0	60.1	72	33	3	2	27	25	4.48	83	.310	.387	18-0-3	.222	1	142	-4	—	-0.3

YEAR	TM LG	W	L	PCT	G	GS	CG-SHO	SV-BS	IP	H	R	HR	HB	BB-IB	SO	ERA	AERA	OAV	OOB	AB-HR-SH	AVG	PB	SUP	APR	DL	PW
	NY N	13	5	.722	29	23	8-1	2	173	183	83	9	2	54	65	3.95	98	.275	.331	50-0-8	.160	-2*	106	1	—	-0.1
	Year	17	7	**.708**	40	33	11-1	2	233.1	255	116	12	4	81	90	4.09	93	.284	.346	68-0-11	.176	-1	116	-2	—	-0.4
1928	NY N	**25**	9	**.735**	42	36	**28**-2	4	310.1	299	106	14	0	71	90	2.73	144	.258	.300	112-0-6	.143	-3	124	43	—	4.1
1929	NY N	11	17	.393	39	31	14-3	3	237	276	129	16	0	61	63	4.14	111	.297	.340	86-1-1	.105	-6*	82	11	—	0.6
1930	NY N	1	3	.250	8	4	1	1	30	42	31	8	0	14	16	7.80	61	.323	.389	10-1-1	.300	2	166	-11	—	-1.1
	Cin N	7	12	.368	35	22	9	1	177.2	246	124	7	0	45	47	5.12	94	.337	.375	62-0-2	.177	-2	78	-10	—	-1.1
	Year	8	15	.348	43	26	10	2	207.2	288	155	15	0	59	63	5.50	87	.334	.377	72-1-3	.194	-0	91	-22	—	-2.2
1931	Cin N	10	15	.400	38	23	12-2	2	204.1	240	98	6	1	53	35	3.35	112	.299	.343	66-0-2	.167	-1	80	5	—	0.6
1932	Cin N	6	13	.316	35	22	7	2	179.2	201	104	10	0	27	35	4.31	90	.285	.311	54-0-5	.204	0	89	-9	—	-0.8
1933	Cin N	10	11	.476	34	19	7-2	2	152.2	160	70	5	3	36	33	3.71	91	.271	.316	53-0-2	.170	-1	92	-2	—	-0.5
1934	Cin N	0	1	.000	16	1	0	2	29	53	25	1	0	7	5	6.52	63	.393	.423	7	.286	0	85	-8	—	-0.3
1935	Bos N	2	3	.400	29	0	0	0	72	103	61	6	1	24	21	6.88	55	.338	.388	20-0-2	.200	0	—	-25	—	-1.4
Total	13	127	128	.498	455	261	123-13	22	2297	2559	1190	109	25	691	670	4.03	98	.288	.341	738-2-52	.165	-17	94	-8	—	-0.7
Benton, Sid	Sidney Wright; B8.4.1894 Buckner AR; D3.8.1977 Fayetteville AR; BR/TR/6´1˝/170; d4.18; Col Arkansas																									
1922	StL N	0	0	ø	1	0	0	0	0	0	0	0	0	2	0	(0)	ø	ø	1.000	0	ø	0	—	0	—	0.0
Bentz, Chad	Chad Robert; B5.5.1980 Seward AK; BR/TL/6´2˝/(210–215); [MonN01 7/202]; d4.7; Col Cal St.–Long Beach																									
2004	Mon N	0	3	.000	36	0	0	0-0	27.2	23	19	5	2	23-3	18	5.86	78	.228	.381	2	.500	0	—	-3	0	-0.3
2005	Fla N	0	0	ø	4	0	0	0-0	2	8	7	2	0	0-0	0	31.50	13	.571	.571	0	ø	0	—	-6	0	-0.3
Total	2	0	3	.000	40	0	0	0-0	29.2	31	26	7	2	23-3	18	7.58	60	.270	.400	2	.500	0	—	-9	0	-0.6
Benz, Joe	Joseph Louis "Blitzen","Butcher Boy"; B1.21.1886 New Alsace IN; D4.22.1957 Chicago IL; BR/TR/6´1.5˝/196; d8.16																									
1911	Chi A	3	2	.600	12	6	1	0	55.2	52	23	0	2	13	28	2.26	142	.251	.302	17	.059	-2	101	5	—	0.2
1912	Chi A	13	17	.433	42	31	12-3	0	238.2	231	107	5	8	70	97	2.90	110	.259	.319	76-0-8	.132	-5	89	7	—	0.3
1913	Chi A	7	10	.412	33	17	6-1	1	151	146	64	1	2	59	79	2.74	107	.257	.329	50-0-2	.180	-1	106	3	—	0.5
1914	Chi A	15	19	.441	48	35	16-4	2	283.1	245	103	4	2	66	142	2.26	119	.236	.282	92-0-4	.130	-3	78	14	—	1.7
1915	Chi A	15	11	.577	39	28	17-2	0	238.1	209	78	4	3	43	81	2.11	141	.238	.276	79-0-4	.127	-5	113	21	—	1.9
1916	Chi A	9	5	.643	28	16	6-4	0	142	108	40	0	3	32	57	2.03	136	.214	.265	46-0-2	.065	-4	103	13	—	0.9
1917	Chi A	7	3	.700	19	13	7-2	0	94.2	76	36	1	2	23	25	2.47	108	.220	.272	30-0-3	.167	-1	150	2	—	0.1
1918	Chi A	8	8	.500	29	17	10-1	0	154	156	57	1	2	28	30	2.63	104	.269	.304	51-0-4	.216	-1	110	2	—	0.4
1919	Chi A	0	0	ø	1	0	0	0	2	2	1	0	0	0	0	0.00	ø	.250	.250	0	ø	0	—	0	—	0.0
Total	9	77	75	.507	251	163	75-17	3	1359.2	1225	509	16	24	334	539	2.43	119	.244	.294	441-0-27	.138	-21	101	67	—	6.0
Bere, Jason	Jason Phillip; B5.26.1971 Cambridge MA; BR/TR/6´3˝/(185–225); [ChiA90 36/952]; d5.27; Col Middlesex (MA) CC																									
1993	†Chi A	12	5	.706	24	24	1	0-0	142.2	109	60	12	5	81-0	129	3.47	122	.210	.322	0	ø	0	126	13	0	1.3
1994	Chi A★	12	2	**.857**	24	24	0	0-0	141.2	119	65	17	1	80-0	127	3.81	123	.229	.331	0	ø	0	120	15	0	1.2
1995	Chi A	8	15	.348	27	27	1	0-0	137.2	151	120	21	6	106-6	110	7.19	62	.277	.396	0	ø	0	99	-44	15	-5.5
1996	Chi A	0	1	.000	5	5	0	0-0	16.2	26	19	3	0	18-1	19	10.26	46	.356	.478	0	ø	0	117	-10	150	-0.5
1997	Chi A	4	2	.667	6	6	0	0-0	28.2	20	15	4	3	17-0	21	4.71	94	.198	.328	0	ø	0	83	0	140	-0.1
1998	Chi A	3	7	.300	18	15	0	0-0	83.2	98	71	14	2	58-0	53	6.45	71	.293	.395	0	ø	0	96	-20	0	-1.9
	Cin N	3	2	.600	9	7	0	0-0	43.2	39	20	3	1	20-0	31	4.12	104	.242	.326	14	.000	-1	122	1	0	0.0
1999	Cin N	3	0	1.000	12	10	0	0-0	43.1	56	37	6	2	40-3	28	6.85	68	.326	.456	14-0-2	.286	1	125	-10	48	-0.5
	Mil N	2	0	1.000	5	4	0	0-0	23.1	23	15	3	0	10-0	19	4.63	99	.256	.327	8	.375	1	175	-1	0	0.0
	Year	5	0	1.000	17	14	0	0-0	66.2	79	52	9	2	50-3	47	6.08	77	.302	.415	22-0-2	.318	2	139	-12	0	-0.5
2000	Mil N	6	7	.462	20	20	0	0-0	115	115	66	19	1	63-7	98	4.93	94	.264	.356	39-0-1	.205	1	94	-3	0	-0.1
	Cle A	6	3	.667	11	11	0	0-0	54.1	65	41	6	4	26-0	44	6.63	76	.297	.377	0	ø	0	126	-9	0	-1.2
2001	Chi N	11	11	.500	32	32	2	0-0	188	171	99	24	1	77-7	175	4.31	97	.241	.314	62-0-7	.194	2	103	-3	0	-0.2
2002	Chi N	1	10	.091	16	16	0	0-0	85.2	98	63	13	3	28-1	65	5.67	71	.290	.343	24-0-7	.125	-0	90	-17	89	-1.9
2003	Cle A	0	0	ø	2	2	0	0-0	6.2	5	3	0	0	2-0	1	4.05	109	.208	.259	0	ø	0	73	0	177	0.0
Total	11	71	65	.522	211	203	4	0-0	1111	1095	694	145	29	626-25	920	5.14	87	.258	.354	161-0-17	.186	3	109	-88	619	-9.4
Berenguer, Juan	Juan Bautista; B11.30.1954 Aguadulce, Pan; BR/TR/5´11˝/(186–225); d8.17																									
1978	NY N	0	2	.000	5	3	0	0-0	13	17	12	1	1	11-0	8	8.31	43	.327	.446	3	.000	-0	59	-6	0	-0.9
1979	NY N	1	1	.500	5	5	0	0-0	30.2	28	13	2	1	12-0	25	2.93	127	.252	.328	7-0-1	.143	0	81	2	0	0.1
1980	NY N	0	1	.000	6	0	0	0-0	9.1	9	9	1	0	10-2	7	5.79	62	.250	.413	0	ø	0	—	-3	0	-0.3
1981	KC A	0	4	.000	8	3	0	0-0	19.2	22	21	4	2	16-0	20	8.69	42	.289	.412	0	ø	0	83	-11	0	-1.9
	Tor A	2	9	.182	12	11	1	0-0	71	62	41	7	3	35-1	29	4.31	92	.235	.327	0	ø	0	56	-3	0	-0.5
	Year	2	13	.133	20	14	1	0-0	90.2	84	62	11	5	51-1	49	5.26	74	.247	.347	0	ø	0	61	-14	0	-2.4
1982	Det A	0	0	ø	2	1	0	0-0	6.2	5	5	0	0	9-1	8	6.75	61	.200	.412	0	ø	0	134	-2	0	-0.1
1983	Det A	9	5	.643	37	19	2-1	1-1	157.2	110	58	19	6	71-3	129	3.14	126	.193	.288	0	ø	0	119	16	0	1.2
1984	Det A	11	10	.524	31	27	2-1	0-0	168.1	146	75	14	5	79-2	118	3.48	114	.232	.320	0	ø	0	108	8	0	0.9
1985	Det A	5	6	.455	31	13	0	0-0	95	96	67	12	1	48-3	82	5.59	73	.259	.343	0	ø	0	111	-16	0	-1.6
1986	SF N	2	3	.400	46	4	0	4-4	73.1	64	23	4	2	44-3	72	2.70	131	.242	.353	7-0-3	.143	-0	114	8	21	0.5
1987	†Min A	8	1	.889	47	6	0	4-5	112	100	51	10	0	47-7	110	3.94	118	.238	.312	0	ø	0	124	10	19	0.7
1988	Min A	8	4	.667	57	1	0	2-3	100	74	44	7	1	61-7	99	3.96	103	.207	.322	0	ø	0	178	3	0	0.3
1989	Min A	9	3	.750	56	0	0	3-4	106	96	44	11	2	47-0	93	3.48	119	.246	.326	0	ø	0	—	8	0	0.8
1990	Min A	8	5	.615	51	0	0	0-2	100.1	85	43	9	2	58-4	77	3.41	122	.232	.338	0	ø	0	—	7	0	0.8
1991	Atl N	0	3	.000	49	0	0	17-1	64.1	43	18	5	3	20-2	53	2.24	173	.189	.261	5	.000	-1	—	11	19	1.0
1992	Atl N	3	1	.750	28	0	0	1-2	33.1	35	22	7	1	16-4	19	5.13	71	.269	.354	2	.000	-0	—	-6	0	-0.7
	KC A	1	4	.200	19	2	0	0-1	44.2	42	30	3	1	20-3	26	5.64	72	.247	.325	0	ø	0	22	-7	0	-0.7
Total	15	67	62	.519	490	95	5-2	32-23	1205.1	1034	576	116	31	604-42	975	3.90	103	.232	.325	24-0-4	.083	-1	100	19	59	-0.4
Berenyi, Bruce	Bruce Michael; B8.21.1954 Bryan OH; BR/TR/6´3˝/(205–215); [CinN76 S1/3]; d7.5; Col Truman St.																									
1980	Cin N	2	2	.500	6	6	0	0-0	27.2	34	26	1	0	23-0	19	7.81	45	.318	.438	7-0-4	.000	-1	135	-14	0	-1.7
1981	Cin N	9	6	.600	21	20	5-3	0-0	126	97	55	3	0	77-0	106	3.50	100	.211	.322	42-0-3	.190	1	111	0	0	0.1
1982	Cin N	9	18	.333	34	34	4-1	0-0	222.1	208	90	8	2	96-5	157	3.36	109	.255	.332	62-0-12	.242	3	62	9	0	1.4
1983	Cin N	9	14	.391	32	31	4-1	0-0	186.1	173	92	9	2	102-3	151	3.86	99	.247	.343	55-0-10	.218	2	99	-2	0	0.0
1984	Cin N	3	7	.300	13	11	0	0-0	51	63	35	0	0	42-2	53	6.00	63	.306	.422	16-0-2	.063	-1	78	-11	0	-1.9
	NY N	9	6	.600	19	19	0	0-0	115	100	58	6	1	53-2	81	3.76	95	.238	.324	37-0-5	.243	2	109	-3	0	-0.3
	Year	12	13	.480	32	30	0	0-0	166	163	93	6	1	95-4	134	4.45	82	.260	.357	53-0-7	.189	0	98	-14	0	-2.2
1985	NY N	1	0	1.000	3	3	0	0-0	13.2	8	6	0	1	10-0	10	2.63	133	.170	.328	4-0-2	.250	0	118	1	130	0.1
1986	NY N	2	2	.500	14	7	0	0-0	39.2	47	30	5	1	22-0	30	6.35	56	.299	.383	11-0-1	.000	-1	114	-12	0	-1.2
Total	7	44	55	.444	142	131	13-5	0-0	781.2	730	392	32	7	425-12	607	4.03	91	.251	.345	234-0-39	.197	5	94	-32	130	-3.5
Berger, Heinie	Charles Carl; B1.7.1882 LaSalle IL; D2.10.1954 Lakewood OH; TR/5´9˝/?; d5.6																									
1907	Cle A	3	3	.500	14	7	5-1	0	87.1	74	35	0	1	20	50	2.99	84	.232	.279	28-0-3	.179	0	81	-2	—	-0.2
1908	Cle A	13	8	.619	29	24	16	0	199.1	152	60	1	4	66	101	2.12	113	.219	.290	74-0-5	.108	-4	134	8	—	0.4
1909	Cle A	13	14	.481	34	29	19-4	1	247	221	95	2	12	58	162	2.73	94	.256	.312	83-0-2	.133	-1	78	0	—	-0.1
1910	Cle A	3	4	.429	13	8	2	0	65.1	57	25	0	3	32	24	3.03	85	.243	.341	21-0-3	.143	-1	88	-1	—	-0.3
Total	4	32	29	.525	90	68	42-5	1	599	504	215	3	20	176	337	2.60	96	.239	.303	206-0-13	.131	-6	98	5	—	-0.2
Bergman, Dusty	Dustin Michael; B2.1.1978 Carson City NV; BL/TL/6´5˝/200; [AnaA99 6/191]; d6.9; Col Hawaii																									
2004	Ana A	0	0	ø	1	0	0	0-0	2	4	3	0	0	1-0	1	13.50	33	.444	.455	0	ø	0	—	-2	0	-0.1
Bergman, Sean	Sean Frederick; B4.11.1970 Joliet IL; BR/TR/6´4˝/(205–225); [DetA91 4/114]; d7.7; Col Southern Illinois																									
1993	Det A	1	4	.200	9	6	1	0-0	39.2	47	29	6	1	23-3	19	5.67	77	.294	.382	0	ø	0	109	-6	0	-0.7
1994	Det A	2	1	.667	3	3	0	0-0	17.2	22	11	2	1	7-0	12	5.60	88	.301	.366	0	ø	0	149	-1	0	-0.1
1995	Det A	7	10	.412	28	28	1-1	0-0	135.1	169	95	19	4	67-8	86	5.12	94	.307	.384	0	ø	0	91	-10	21	-1.1
1996	SD N	6	8	.429	41	14	0	0-0	113.1	119	63	14	2	33-3	85	4.37	92	.274	.325	30-1-0	.100	-1*	115	-6	0	-0.6
1997	SD N	2	4	.333	44	9	0	0-2	99	126	72	11	3	38-4	74	6.09	64	.316	.376	13-0-3	.231	1	141	-24	0	-1.2
1998	Hou N	12	9	.571	31	27	1	0-0	172	183	81	20	5	42-3	100	3.72	109	.268	.315	60-0-8	.083	-3	134	5	0	0.1
1999	Hou N	4	6	.400	19	16	2-1	0-0	99	130	60	9	3	26-1	38	5.36	82	.332	.374	28-2-1	.107	1	90	-9	40	-0.8
	Atl N	1	0	1.000	6	0	0	0-1	6.1	5	2	0	0	3-0	6	2.84	157	.217	.308	0	ø	0	—	1	0	0.2
	Year	5	6	.455	25	16	2-1	0-1	105.1	135	62	9	3	29-1	44	5.21	85	.325	.370	28-2-1	.107	1	90	-7	0	-0.6

YEAR	TM LG	W	L	PCT	G	GS	CG-SHO	SV-BS	IP	H	R	HR	HB	BB-IB	SO	ERA	AERA	OAV	OOB	AB-HR-SH	AVG	PB	SUP	APR	DL	PW
2000	Min A	4	5	.444	15	14	0	0-0	68	111	76	18	2	33-1	35	9.66	55	.374	.436	2	.500	1	108	-30	0	-2.9
Total	8	39	47	.453	196	117	5-2	0-3	750.1	912	489	99	21	272-23	455	5.28	83	.303	.362	133-3-12	.113	-2	113	-80	61	-7.1
BERGMANN, JASON	Jason Chris; B9.25.1981 Neptune NJ; BR/TR/6´4˝/205; [MonN02 11/317]; d8.28; Col Rutgers																									
2005	Was N	2	0	1.000	15	1	0	0-0	19.2	14	6	1	2	11-1	21	2.75	150	.200	.321	3	.333	1	161	3	0	0.4
2006	Was N	0	2	.000	29	6	0	0-0	64.2	81	49	12	6	27-6	54	6.68	65	.312	.384	8-0-2	.000	-0	81	-16	0	-0.8
Total	2	2	2	.500	44	7	0	0-0	84.1	95	55	13	8	38-7	75	5.76	75	.288	.370	11-0-2	.091	0	92	-13	0	-0.4
BERLY, JACK	John Chambers; B5.24.1903 Natchitoches LA; D6.26.1977 Houston TX; BR/TR/5´11.5˝/190; d4.22																									
1924	StL N	0	0	ø	4	0	0	0	8	8	5	2	0	4	2	5.63	67	.267	.353	2	.000	-0	—	-1	—	-0.1
1931	NY N	7	8	.467	27	11	4-1	0	111.1	114	55	6	4	51	45	3.88	95	.270	.354	35	.171	-1	122	-1	—	-0.2
1932	Phi N	1	2	.333	21	1	1	2	46	61	42	4	1	21	15	7.63	58	.333	.405	10	.000	-1	76	-13	—	-1.0
1933	Phi N	2	3	.400	13	6	1-1	0	50	62	30	5	2	22	4	5.04	76	.307	.381	13-0-1	.308	0	87	-5	—	-0.4
Total	4	10	13	.435	65	18	6-2	2	215.1	245	132	17	7	98	66	5.02	78	.292	.371	60-0-1	.167	-2	104	-20	—	-1.7
BERNAL, VICTOR	Victor Hugo; B10.6.1953 Los Angeles CA; D9.2.2006 Arcadia CA; BR/TR/6´1˝/175; [SDN75 6/122]; d4.6; Col Cal Poly–Pomona																									
1977	SD N	1	1	.500	15	0	0	0-0	20.1	23	13	4	0	9-2	6	5.31	67	.287	.360	1	.000	-0	—	-4	0	-0.4
BERNARD, DWIGHT	Dwight Vern; B5.31.1952 Mt.Vernon IL; BR/TR/6´2˝/(170–180); [NYN74 2/41]; d6.29; Col Belmont																									
1978	NY N	1	4	.200	30	1	0	0-2	48	54	25	4	0	27-3	26	4.31	82	.297	.386	5	.200	0	127	-4	0	-0.4
1979	NY N	0	3	.000	32	1	0	0-0	44	59	26	2	0	26-4	20	4.70	79	.331	.411	0-0-2	ø	0	119	-5	0	-0.3
1981	†Mil A	0	0	ø	6	0	0	0-0	5	5	3	0	0	6-1	1	3.60	96	.263	.407	0	ø	0	—	0	0	0.0
1982	†Mil A	3	1	.750	47	0	0	6-3	79	78	39	4	1	27-0	45	3.76	102	.263	.321	0	ø	0	—	0	0	-0.1
Total	4	4	8	.333	115	2	0	6-5	176	196	93	10	1	86-8	92	4.14	90	.290	.366	5-0-2	.200	1	121	-9	0	-0.8
BERNARD, JOE	Joseph Carl "J.C."; B3.24.1882 Brighton IL; D9.22.1960 Springfield IL; BR/TR/6´1˝/175; d9.23																									
1909	StL N	0	0	ø	1	0	0	0	1	1	0	0	0	2	2	0.00	ø	.250	.500	0	ø	0	—	0	—	0.0
BERNERO, ADAM	Adam Gino; B11.28.1976 San Jose CA; BR/TR/6´4˝/(205–225); d8.1; Col Armstrong Atlantic																									
2000	Det A	0	1	.000	12	4	0	0-0	34.1	33	18	3	1	13-1	20	4.19	117	.270	.338	0	ø	0	96	2	0	0.1
2001	Det A	0	0	ø	5	0	0	0-0	12.1	13	13	4	1	4-0	8	7.30	61	.260	.321	0	ø	0	—	-5	0	-0.2
2002	Det A	4	7	.364	28	11	0	0-0	101.2	128	74	17	6	31-1	69	6.20	71	.309	.362	4-0-1	.000	-0	98	-19	0	-1.8
2003	Det A	1	12	.077	18	17	0	0-0	100.2	104	68	14	7	41-0	54	6.08	72	.267	.342	4	.000	-0*	56	-17	0	-1.8
	Col N	0	2	.000	31	0	0	0-2	32.2	33	22	5	1	13-1	26	5.23	94	.266	.336	2	.000	-0	—	-2	0	-0.1
2004	Col N	1	1	.500	16	2	0	0-1	32.1	36	20	7	0	17-2	21	5.57	85	.283	.361	5-0-1	.000	-1	137	-2	87	-0.2
2005	Atl N	4	3	.571	36	0	0	0-1	47	61	35	5	4	12-3	37	6.51	65	.313	.360	1-0-1	1.000	0	—	-12	0	-1.5
2006	KC A	1	0	1.000	3	2	0	0-0	13	15	2	0	0	0-0	12	1.38	338	.283	.283	0	ø	0	131	5	24	0.3
	Phi N	0	1	.000	1	1	0	0-0	2	7	8	3	0	2-0	0	36.00	13	.538	.600	0	ø	0	20	-6	0	-0.8
Total	7	11	27	.289	150	37	0	0-4	376	430	260	58	20	133-8	247	5.91	76	.289	.350	16-0-3	.063	-1	80	-56	111	-6.0
BERNHARD, BILL	William Henry "Strawberry Bill"; B3.16.1871 Clarence NY; D3.30.1949 San Diego CA; BB/TR/6´1˝/205; d4.24																									
1899	Phi N	6	6	.500	21	12	10-1	0	132.1	120	66	3	6	36	23	2.65	139	.242	.301	54	.241	0	109	12	—	0.9
1900	Phi N	15	10	.600	32	27	20	2	218.2	284	151	3	5	74	49	4.77	76	.313	.368	91	.154	-5	131	-25	—	-2.8
1901	Phi A	17	10	.630	31	27	26-1	0	257	328	169	6	2	50	58	4.52	84	.307	.339	107-0-3	.187	-1*	97	-16	—	-1.3
1902	Phi A	1	0	1.000	1	1	1	0	9	7	1	0	0	3	1	1.00	367	.212	.278	4	.000	-1	157	3	—	0.2
	Cle A	17	5	.773	27	24	22-3	1	217	169	78	4	5	34	57	2.20	157	.216	.253	90	.200	-1	120	32	—	2.9
	Year	18	5	**.783**	28	25	23-3	1	226	176	79	4	5	37	58	2.15	161	**.215**	**.254**	94	.191	-2	122	33	—	3.1
1903	Cle A	14	5	.737	20	19	18-3	0	165.2	151	62	1	0	21	60	2.12	135	.242	.267	65	.185	-1	121	13	—	1.5
1904	Cle A	23	13	.639	38	37	35-4	0	320.2	323	107	3	4	55	137	2.13	119	.263	.296	124-0-3	.177	-1	127	15	—	1.6
1905	Cle A	7	13	.350	22	19	17	0	174.1	185	93	5	1	34	56	3.36	78	.274	.309	69	.087	-6	72	-16	—	-2.3
1906	Cle A	16	15	.516	31	30	23-2	0	255.1	235	99	1	5	47	85	2.54	103	.248	.287	99-0-2	.212	2	123	5	—	0.9
1907	Cle A	0	4	.000	8	4	3	0	42	58	32	0	0	11	19	3.21	78	.330	.369	15	.200	0	74	-7	—	-0.6
Total	9	116	81	.589	231	200	175-14	3	1792	1860	858	26	28	365	545	3.04	102	.268	.307	718-0-8	.180	-13	114	16	—	1.0
BERNHARDT, WALTER	Walter Jacob; B5.20.1893 Pleasant Valley Twp. PA; D7.26.1958 Watertown NY; BR/TR/6´2˝/175; d7.16; Col Penn																									
1918	NY A	0	0	ø	1	0	0	0	0.2	0	0	0	0	0	1	0.00	ø	.000	.000	0	ø	0	—	0	—	0.0
BERRY, JOE	Jonas Arthur "Jittery Joe"; B12.16.1904 Huntsville AR; D9.27.1958 Anaheim CA; BL/TR/5´10.5˝/145; d9.6																									
1942	Chi N	0	0	ø	2	0	0	0	2	7	4	0	0	2	1	18.00	18	.538	.600	0	ø	0	—	-3	0	-0.2
1944	Phi A	10	8	.556	53	0	0	**12**	111.1	78	32	4	2	23	44	1.94	179	.192	.238	25-0-3	.120	-1	—	**17**	0	3.2
1945	Phi A	8	7	.533	**52**	0	0	5	130.1	114	40	5	0	38	51	2.35	146	.232	.287	35-0-2	.143	-1	—	**15**	0	1.8
1946	Phi A	0	1	.000	5	0	0	0	13	15	5	1	1	3	5	2.77	128	.288	.339	3-0-1	.333	0	—	1	0	0.1
	Cle A	3	6	.333	21	0	0	1	37.1	32	18	4	0	21	16	3.38	98	.235	.338	7-0-1	.286	0	—	-1	0	-0.3
	Year	3	7	.300	26	0	0	1	50.1	47	23	5	1	24	21	3.22	105	.250	.338	10-0-2	.300	1	—	0	0	-0.2
Total	4	21	22	.488	133	0	0	18	294	246	99	14	3	87	117	2.45	140	.224	.282	70-0-7	.157	-2	—	29	0	4.6
BERTAINA, FRANK	Frank Louis; B4.14.1944 San Francisco CA; BL/TL/5´11˝/(180–185); d8.1																									
1964	Bal A	1	0	1.000	6	4	1-1	0	26	18	8	3	0	13-1	18	2.77	129	.198	.298	5-0-2	.000	-1	93	3	0	0.1
1965	Bal A	0	0	ø	2	1	0	0	6	9	4	0	0	4-0	5	6.00	58	.360	.433	1	.000	-0	152	-1	0	-0.1
1966	Bal A	2	5	.286	16	9	0	0	63.1	52	29	3	4	36-2	46	3.13	107	.226	.338	19	.105	-1	120	-1	0	-0.2
1967	Bal A	1	1	.500	5	2	0	0	21.2	17	9	4	0	14-0	19	3.32	95	.224	.341	9	.111	-0	14	-1	0	-0.1
	Was A	6	5	.545	18	17	4-4	0	95.2	90	36	8	0	37-1	67	2.92	108	.251	.320	35-0-2	.057	-3*	102	3	0	0.0
	Year	7	6	.538	23	19	4-4	0	117.1	107	45	12	0	51-1	86	2.99	106	.247	.324	44-0-2	.068	-3	93	2	0	-0.1
1968	Was A	7	13	.350	27	23	1	0	127.1	133	76	15	6	69-1	81	4.66	63	.273	.366	38-0-1	.132	-0	101	-25	0	-3.8
1969	Was A	1	3	.250	14	5	0	0-0	35.2	43	30	8	0	23-0	25	6.56	53	.291	.384	11-1-1	.364	2	131	-13	0	-1.0
	Bal A	0	0	ø	3	0	0	0-0	6	1	0	0	0	3-0	5	0.00	ø	.063	.200	1	1.000	1	—	2	0	0.2
	Year	1	3	.250	17	5	0	0-0	41.2	44	30	8	0	26-0	30	5.62	63	.268	.365	12-1-1	.417	3	131	-10	0	-0.8
1970	StL N	1	2	.333	8	5	0	0-1	31.1	36	16	1	0	15-3	14	3.16	131	.293	.367	7	.143	0	87	2	0	0.2
Total	7	19	29	.396	99	66	6-5	0-1	413	399	208	42	10	214-8	280	3.84	85	.257	.347	126-1-6	.127	-1	102	-31	0	-4.7
BERTOTTI, MIKE	Michael David; B1.18.1970 Jersey City NJ; BL/TL/6´1˝/185; [ChiA91 31/826]; d7.29; Col Iona																									
1995	Chi A	1	1	.500	4	4	0	0-0	14.1	23	20	6	3	11-0	15	12.56	36	.365	.463	0	ø	0	135	-13	0	-1.3
1996	Chi A	2	0	1.000	15	2	0	0-1	28	28	18	5	0	20-3	19	5.14	93	.257	.369	0	ø	0	117	-2	0	-0.1
1997	Chi A	0	0	ø	9	0	0	0-0	3.2	9	3	0	0	2-0	4	7.36	60	.450	.478	0	ø	0	—	-1	0	-0.1
Total	3	3	1	.750	28	6	0	0-1	46	60	41	11	3	33-3	38	7.63	61	.313	.412	0	ø	0	127	-16	0	-1.5
BERTRAND, LEFTY	Roman Mathias; B2.28.1909 Cobden MN; D3.17.2002 The Dalles OR; BR/TL/6´0˝/180; d4.15; Col St. Marys (MN)																									
1936	Phi N	0	0	ø	1	0	0	0	2	3	2	1	0	2	1	9.00	50	.333	.455	0	ø	0	—	-1	—	0.0
BERUMEN, ANDRES	Andres; B4.5.1971 Tijuana, Baja California, Mexico; BR/TR/6´2˝/(205–210); [KCA89 27/699]; d4.27																									
1995	SD N	2	3	.400	37	0	0	1-3	44.1	37	29	3	3	36-3	42	5.68	72	.226	.369	1	.000	-0	—	-7	21	-0.8
1996	SD N	0	0	ø	3	0	0	0-0	3.1	3	2	1	1	2-1	4	5.40	75	.231	.375	0	ø	0	—	0	0	0.0
Total	2	2	3	.400	40	0	0	1-3	47.2	40	31	4	4	38-4	46	5.66	72	.226	.369	1	.000	-0	—	-7	21	-0.8
BESANA, FRED	Frederick Cyril; B4.5.1931 Lincoln CA; BR/TL/6´3.5˝/200; d4.18; Col Cal St.–Sacramento																									
1956	Bal A	1	0	1.000	7	2	0	0	17.2	22	12	0	2	14-0	7	5.60	70	.310	.427	4	.000	-0	136	-3	0	-0.2
BESSE, HERMAN	Herman A.; B8.16.1911 St.Louis MO; D8.13.1972 Los Angeles CA; BL/TL/6´2˝/190; d4.19; Mil 1944–45																									
1940	Phi A	0	3	.000	17	5	0	0	53	70	56	10	3	34	19	8.83	50	.315	.413	19	.263	2	130	-23	—	-0.9
1941	Phi A	2	0	1.000	6	2	1	0	19.2	28	22	4	0	12	8	10.07	42	.329	.412	5	.200	-0	103	-11	0	-0.9
1942	Phi A	2	9	.182	30	14	4	1	133	163	99	7	4	69	78	6.16	61	.300	.383	53	.226	2*	110	-31	0	-2.2
1943	Phi A	1	1	.500	5	1	0	0	16.1	18	6	2	1	4	3	3.31	103	.295	.348	8	.000	-1*	199	1	0	-0.1
1946	Phi A	0	2	.000	7	3	0	1	20.2	19	12	1	0	9	10	5.23	68	.247	.326	5	.000	-0	81	-3	0	-0.3
Total	5	5	15	.250	65	25	5	2	242.2	298	195	24	8	128	118	6.79	58	.302	.386	90	.200	2	114	-67	0	-4.4

YEAR	TM LG	W	L	PCT	G	GS	CG-SHO	SV-BS	IP	H	R	HR	HB	BB-IB	SO	ERA	AERA	OAV	OOB	AB-HR-SH	AVG	PB	SUP	APR	DL	PW
BESSENT, DON	Fred Donald; B3.13.1931 Jacksonville FL; D7.7.1990 Jacksonville FL; BR/TR/6´0˝/(173–180); d7.17																									
1955	†Bro N	8	1	.889	24	2	1	3	63.1	51	19	7	0	21-2	29	2.70	150	.220	.283	20-0-3	.100	-2	132	11	0	1.3
1956	†Bro N	4	3	.571	38	0	0	9	79.1	63	23	5	0	31-6	52	2.50	159	.221	.295	18-0-1	.111	-1	—	13	0	1.2
1957	Bro N	1	3	.250	27	0	0	0	44	58	28	5	0	19-3	24	5.73	73	.328	.387	4	.250	0	—	-6	0	-0.5
1958	LA N	1	0	1.000	19	0	0	0	24.1	24	14	3	1	17-0	13	3.33	123	.270	.393	2-0-1	.000	-0	—	0	77	0.0
Total	4	14	7	.667	108	2	1	12	211	196	84	20	1	88-11	118	3.33	122	.250	.324	44-0-5	.114	-3	132	18	77	2.0
BEST, KARL	Karl Jon; B3.6.1959 Aberdeen WA; BR/TR/6´4˝/(190–210); [SeaA77 12/312]; d8.19; [DL 1989 SF N 182]																									
1983	Sea A	0	1	.000	4	0	0	0-0	5.1	14	9	2	2	5-0	3	13.50	32	.483	.583	0	ø	0	—	-5	0	-0.8
1984	Sea A	1	1	.500	5	0	0	0-0	6	7	2	0	0	0-0	6	3.00	134	.292	.280	0	ø	0	—	1	0	0.2
1985	Sea A	2	1	.667	15	0	0	4-0	32.1	25	9	1	1	6-0	32	1.95	217	.207	.250	0	ø	0	—	7	105	0.8
1986	Sea A	2	3	.400	26	0	0	1-2	35.2	35	19	3	1	21-2	23	4.04	106	.255	.354	0	ø	0	—	0	11	0.0
1988	Min A	0	0	ø	11	0	0	0-0	12	15	9	1	0	7-1	9	6.00	68	.306	.379	0	ø	0	—	-3	0	-0.1
Total	5	5	6	.455	61	0	0	5-2	91.1	96	48	7	4	39-3	73	4.04	104	.267	.341	0	ø	0	—	0	298	0.1
BETANCOURT, RAFAEL	Rafael Jose; B4.29.1975 Cumana, Sucre, Venezuela; BR/TR/6´2˝/(170–200); d7.13																									
2003	Cle A	2	2	.500	33	0	0	1-2	38	27	11	5	1	13-2	36	2.13	208	.196	.268	0	ø	0	—	10	0	0.9
2004	Cle A	5	6	.455	68	0	0	4-7	66.2	71	32	7	0	18-6	76	3.92	111	.268	.312	0	ø	0	—	3	15	0.4
2005	Cle A	4	3	.571	54	0	0	1-2	67.2	57	23	5	0	17-2	73	2.79	149	.224	.273	0	ø	0	—	11	18	1.0
2006	Cle A	3	4	.429	50	0	0	3-3	56.2	52	25	7	0	11-5	48	3.81	113	.241	.275	0	ø	0	—	4	26	0.4
Total	4	14	15	.483	205	0	0	9-14	229	207	91	24	1	59-15	233	3.26	132	.237	.285	0	ø	0	—	28	59	2.7
BETHKE, JIM	James Charles; B11.5.1946 Falls City NE; BR/TR/6´3˝/185; d4.12																									
1965	NY N	2	0	1.000	25	0	0	0	40	41	24	3	6	22-2	19	4.27	83	.266	.377	4	.000	-0	—	-4	0	-0.2
BETTENDORF, JEFF	Jeffrey Allen; B12.10.1960 Lompoc CA; BR/TR/6´3˝/190; [NYN79 2/28]; d4.8																									
1984	Oak A	0	0	ø	3	0	0	1-0	9.2	9	5	3	0	5-0	5	4.66	81	.243	.333	0	ø	0	—	-1	0	-0.1
BETTS, HARRY	Harold Matthew "Chubby","Ginger"; B6.19.1881 Alliance OH; D5.22.1946 San Antonio TX; BR/TR/5´10˝/200; d9.22																									
1903	StL N	0	1	.000	1	1	1	0	9	11	10	0	2	5	2	10.00	33	.297	.409	3	.000	-0	21	-5	—	-0.4
1913	Cin N	0	0	ø	1	0	0	0	3.1	1	1	0	1	3	0	2.70	120	.143	.455	1	.000	-0	—	0	—	0.0
Total	2	0	1	.000	2	1	1	0	12.1	12	11	0	3	8	2	8.03	41	.273	.418	4	.000	-1	21	-5	—	-0.4
BETTS, HUCK	Walter McKinley; B2.18.1897 Millsboro DE; D6.13.1987 Millsboro DE; BR/TR/5´11˝/170; d4.26																									
1920	Phi N	1	1	.500	27	4	1	0	88.1	86	48	3	2	33	18	3.57	96	.261	.332	25	.080	-2	115	-2	—	-0.4
1921	Phi N	3	7	.300	32	2	1	4	100.2	141	65	8	4	14	28	4.47	95	.337	.365	30	.267	0	10	-1	—	-0.1
1922	Phi N	1	0	1.000	7	0	0	0	15	23	17	3	0	8	4	9.60	49	.348	.419	4	.000	-0	—	-6	—	-0.4
1923	Phi N	2	4	.333	19	4	3	1	84.1	100	38	7	4	14	18	3.09	149	.314	.351	31-0-1	.097	-3*	45	11	—	0.4
1924	Phi N	7	10	.412	37	9	2	2	144.1	160	76	8	5	42	46	4.30	104	.286	.341	45-0-6	.156	-2*	93	4	—	0.1
1925	Phi N	4	5	.444	35	7	1	1	97.1	146	86	10	3	38	28	5.55	86	.342	.400	34	.294	2*	121	-12	—	-0.7
1932	Bos N	13	11	.542	31	27	16-3	1	221.2	229	84	9	0	35	32	2.80	134	.267	.295	79-0-1	.241	2	94	23	—	2.4
1933	Bos N	11	11	.500	35	26	17-2	4	242	225	79	9	0	55	40	2.79	110	.248	.290	76-0-9	.224	2	93	11	—	1.5
1934	Bos N	17	10	.630	40	27	10-2	3	213	258	105	17	3	42	69	4.06	94	.296	.330	69-0-6	.188	1	107	-3	—	-0.4
1935	Bos N	2	9	.182	44	19	2-1	0	159.2	213	118	9	2	40	40	5.47	69	.321	.362	44-0-2	.159	-0	85	-34	—	-2.0
Total	10	61	68	.473	307	125	53-8	16	1366.1	1581	716	83	23	321	323	3.93	98	.292	.334	437-0-25	.197	-2	91	-9	—	0.4
BEVENS, BILL	Floyd Clifford; B10.21.1916 Hubbard OR; D10.26.1991 Salem OR; BR/TR/6´3.5˝/210; d5.12; [DL 1948 NY A 63]																									
1944	NY A	4	1	.800	8	5	3	0	43.2	44	18	4	1	13	16	2.68	130	.273	.331	16-0-1	.063	-2	163	3	0	0.1
1945	NY A	13	9	.591	29	25	14-2	0	184	174	83	12	1	68	76	3.67	94	.254	.322	63-1-4	.111	-4	118	-2	0	-0.7
1946	NY A	16	13	.552	31	31	18-3	0	249.2	213	73	11	1	78	120	2.23	154	.232	.293	84-2-8	.083	-4	88	34	0	3.2
1947	†NY A	7	13	.350	28	23	11-1	0	165	167	79	13	1	77	77	3.82	93	.264	.345	58-0-3	.121	-3	104	-7	0	-1.0
Total	4	40	36	.526	96	84	46-6	0	642.1	598	253	40	4	236	289	3.08	113	.250	.318	221-3-16	.100	-13	106	28	63	1.6
BEVERLIN, JASON	Jason Robert; B11.27.1973 Ashtabula OH; BL/TR/6´5˝/220; [OakA94 4/93]; d7.29; Col Western Carolina																									
2002	Cle A	0	0	ø	4	0	0	0-0	7.1	9	7	1	0	4-0	9	7.36	60	.290	.371	0	ø	0	—	-3	0	-0.1
	Det A	0	3	.000	3	3	0	0-0	12.1	18	15	2	0	5-0	7	9.49	46	.327	.383	0	ø	0	49	-7	0	-1.2
	Year	0	3	.000	7	3	0	0-0	19.2	27	22	3	0	9-0	16	8.69	51	.314	.379	0	ø	0	49	-10	0	-1.3
BEVIL, BRIAN	Brian Scott; B9.5.1971 Houston TX; BR/TR/6´3˝/(190–225); [KCA90 30/817]; d6.17; Col Angelina (TX) JC																									
1996	KC A	1	0	1.000	3	1	0	0-0	11	9	7	2	0	5-0	7	5.73	88	.237	.318	0	ø	0	111	-1	0	0.0
1997	KC A	1	2	.333	18	0	0	1-4	16.1	16	13	1	1	9-2	13	6.61	72	.267	.361	0	ø	0	—	-3	0	-0.6
1998	KC A	3	1	.750	39	0	0	0-2	40	47	29	4	3	22-1	47	6.30	77	.283	.373	0	ø	0	—	-5	67	-0.5
Total	3	5	3	.625	60	1	0	1-6	67.1	72	49	7	4	36-3	67	6.28	77	.273	.362	0	ø	0	111	-9	67	-1.1
BEVIL, LOU	Louis Eugene (b Louis Eugene Bevilacqua); B11.27.1922 Nelson IL; D2.1.1973 Dixon IL; BB/TR/5´11.5˝/190; d9.2; Mil 1943–45; Col Notre Dame																									
1942	Was A	0	1	.000	4	1	0	0	9.2	9	7	0	1	11	2	6.52	56	.265	.457	3	.000	-0	140	-3	0	-0.3
BEVILLE, BEN	Clarence Benjamin; B8.28.1877 Colusa CA; D1.5.1937 Yountville CA; BR/TR/5´9˝/190; d5.24																									
1901	Bos A	0	2	.000	2	2	1	0	9	8	7	0	1	9	1	4.00	88	.235	.409	7	.286	0*	29	-1	—	-0.1
BIBBY, JIM	James Blair; B10.29.1944 Franklinton NC; BR/TR/6´5˝/(230–250); d9.4; Col Fayetteville St.; [DL 1982 Pit N 182]																									
1972	StL N	1	3	.250	6	6	0	0-0	40.1	29	18	4	1	19-4	28	3.35	102	.206	.302	8-0-2	.125	0	103	0	0	0.0
1973	StL N	0	2	.000	6	3	0	0-0	16	19	17	2	2	17-2	12	9.56	38	.306	.463	2	.000	0	80	-9	0	-1.0
	Tex A	9	10	.474	26	23	11-2	1-0	180.1	121	73	14	6	106-4	155	3.24	116	**.192**	.312	0	ø	0*	81	11	0	1.0
1974	Tex A	19	19	.500	41	41	11-5	0-0	264	255	146	25	9	113-4	149	4.74	76	.255	.334	0	ø	0	119	-29	0	-3.7
1975	Tex A	2	6	.250	12	12	4-1	0-0	68.1	73	41	2	2	28-0	31	5.00	75	.274	.342	0	ø	0	115	-8	0	-0.9
	Cle A	5	9	.357	24	12	2	1-2	112.2	99	48	7	0	50-3	62	3.20	119	.235	.313	0	ø	0	85	7	0	0.8
	Year	7	15	.318	36	24	6-1	1-2	181	172	89	9	2	78-3	93	3.88	98	.250	.324	0	ø	0	100	-1	0	-0.1
1976	Cle A	13	7	.650	34	21	4-3	1-0	163.1	162	61	6	1	56-1	84	3.20	110	.266	.325	0	ø	0	96	7	0	0.8
1977	Cle A	12	13	.480	37	30	9-2	2-0	206.2	197	100	17	4	73-2	141	3.57	112	.250	.315	0	ø	0	96	6	0	0.6
1978	Pit N	8	7	.533	34	14	3-2	1-2	107	100	52	10	2	39-7	72	3.53	106	.246	.314	31-1-0	.129	1	95	1	0	0.2
1979	†Pit N	12	4	.750	34	17	4-1	0-1	137.2	110	51	9	4	47-6	103	2.81	139	.218	.289	45-2-6	.178	2	117	15	0	1.8
1980	Pit N★	19	6	**.760**	35	34	6-1	0-0	238.1	210	95	20	6	88-3	144	3.32	111	.238	.311	77-1-10	.156	2	126	11	0	1.2
1981	Pit N	6	3	.667	14	14	2-2	0-0	93.2	79	30	4	2	26-1	48	2.50	146	.225	.279	28-1-4	.143	1	103	11	0	1.2
1983	Pit N	5	12	.294	29	12	0	2-1	78	92	60	10	1	51-0	44	6.69	56	.297	.393	18-0-2	.111	-1	89	-23	0	-4.4
1984	Tex A	0	0	ø	8	0	0	0-0	16.1	19	8	1	0	10-1	6	4.41	95	.297	.392	0	ø	0	—	0	0	0.0
Total	12	111	101	.524	340	239	56-19	8-6	1722.2	1565	800	131	40	723-38	1079	3.76	99	.243	.321	209-5-24	.148	5	104	0	182	-2.4
BICKFORD, VERN	Vernon Edgell; B8.17.1920 Hellier KY; D5.6.1960 Concord VA; BR/TR/6´0˝/185; d4.24																									
1948	†Bos N	11	5	.688	33	22	10-1	1	146	125	59	9	3	63	60	3.27	117	.226	.309	49-0-6	.204	1	131	10	0	1.0
1949	Bos N★	16	11	.593	37	36	15-2	0	230.2	246	125	20	6	106	101	4.25	89	.273	.354	81-0-10	.185	-1	123	-12	0	-1.3
1950	Bos N	19	14	.576	40	**39**	**27**-2	0	**311.2**	293	135	25	6	122	126	3.47	111	.248	.321	116-0-9	.138	-4	122	16	0	1.0
1951	Bos N	11	9	.550	25	20	12-3	0	164.2	146	68	7	6	76	76	3.12	118	.240	.330	52-0-6	.115	-2	125	10	0	1.0
1952	Bos N	7	12	.368	26	22	7-1	0	161.1	165	73	7	2	64	62	3.74	97	.269	.340	51-0-5	.176	-0	58	-2	0	-0.2
1953	Mil N	2	5	.286	20	9	2	1	58	60	35	8	2	35	25	5.28	74	.279	.385	15-0-1	.067	-1	114	-7	0	-0.8
1954	Bal A	0	1	.000	1	1	0	0	4	5	5	0	0	1	0	9.00	40	.333	.316	1	.000	-0	98	-3	0	-0.4
Total	7	66	57	.537	182	149	73-9	2	1076.1	1040	500	76	25	467	450	3.71	102	.254	.334	365-0-37	.156	-7	114	12	0	0.3
BICKHAM, DAN	Daniel Denison; B10.31.1864 Dayton OH; D3.3.1951 Dayton OH; BR/TR/5´10˝/160; d8.13; Col Princeton																									
1886	Cin AA	1	0	1.000	1	1	1	0	9	13	11	0	0	3	6	3.00	117	.351	.400	3	.333	0	202	-2	—	-0.1
BICKNELL, CHARLIE	Charles Stephen "Bud"; B7.27.1928 Plainfield NJ; BR/TR/5´11˝/170; d4.22																									
1948	Phi N	0	1	.000	17	1	0	0	25.2	29	20	5	0	17	5	5.96	66	.287	.390	5	.000	-1	67	-6	0	-0.4
1949	Phi N	0	0	ø	13	0	0	0	28.1	32	24	3	2	17	4	7.62	52	.291	.395	1	.000	1	—	-11	0	-0.5
Total	2	0	1	.000	30	1	0	0	54	61	44	8	2	34	9	6.83	58	.289	.393	6	.000	-0	67	-17	0	-0.9

YEAR	TM LG	W	L	PCT	G	GS	CG-SHO	SV-BS	IP	H	R	HR	HB	BB-IB	SO	ERA	AERA	OAV	OOB	AB-HR-SH	AVG	PB	SUP	APR	DL	PW
Biddle, Rocky	Lee Francis; B5.21.1976 Las Vegas NV; BR/TR/6´3˝/(220–230); [ChiA97 1/51]; d8.10; Col Cal St.–Long Beach																									
2000	Chi A	1	2	.333	4	4	0	0-0	22.2	31	25	5	0	8-0	7	8.34	61	.326	.371	0	ø	0	153	-9	0	-0.9
2001	Chi A	7	8	.467	30	21	0	0-3	128.2	137	87	16	8	52-3	85	5.39	87	.272	.347	1-0-1	.000	-0	104	-11	17	-1.1
2002	Chi A	3	4	.429	44	7	0	1-2	77.2	72	42	13	5	39-4	64	4.06	111	.245	.342	0	ø	0	112	2	33	0.2
2003	Mon N	5	8	.385	73	0	0	34-7	71.2	71	43	10	6	40-5	54	4.65	95	.254	.359	1	.000	-0	—	-2	0	-0.6
2004	Mon N	4	8	.333	47	9	0	11-4	78	98	69	15	8	31-3	51	6.92	66	.307	.380	11-0-3	.000	-1	76	-20	0	-3.2
Total	5	20	30	.400	198	41	0	46-16	378.2	409	266	59	27	170-15	261	5.47	84	.274	.357	13-0-4	.000	-1	106	-40	50	-5.6
Bielecki, Mike	Michael Joseph; B7.31.1959 Baltimore MD; BR/TR/6´3˝/(195–200); [PitN79 S1/8]; d9.14; Col Valencia (FL) CC																									
1984	Pit N	0	0	ø	4	0	0	0-0	4.1	4	0	0	0	0-0	1	0.00	ø	.250	.250	0	ø	0	—	2	0	0.1
1985	Pit N	2	3	.400	12	7	0	0-0	45.2	45	26	5	1	31-1	22	4.53	80	.257	.372	10-0-1	.000	-1*	63	-5	0	-0.5
1986	Pit N	6	11	.353	31	27	0	0-0	148.2	149	87	10	2	83-3	83	4.66	83	.262	.355	48-0-4	.063	-3	102	-13	0	-1.7
1987	Pit N	2	3	.400	8	8	2	0-0	45.2	43	25	6	1	12-0	25	4.73	88	.250	.299	16-0-2	.063	-1	103	-2	0	-0.3
1988	Chi N	2	2	.500	19	5	0	0-0	48.1	55	22	4	0	16-1	33	3.35	109	.284	.332	10	.100	-0	97	1	0	0.0
1989	†Chi N	18	7	**.720**	33	33	4-3	0-0	212.1	187	82	16	0	81-8	147	3.14	120	.237	.307	70-0-9	.043	-5	105	14	0	1.0
1990	Chi N	8	11	.421	36	29	0	1-0	168	188	101	13	5	70-11	103	4.93	83	.287	.359	43-0-10	.163	-0	95	-14	0	-1.4
1991	Chi N	13	11	.542	39	25	0	0-1	172	169	91	18	2	54-6	72	4.50	87	.262	.318	46-0-4	.065	-2	110	-9	0	-1.3
	Atl N	0	0	ø	2	0	0	0-0	1.2	2	0	0	0	2-0	3	0.00	ø	.286	.444	0	ø	0	—	1	0	0.0
	Year	13	11	.542	41	25	0	0-1	173.2	171	91	18	2	56-6	75	4.46	88	.262	.319	46-0-4	.065	-2	110	-9	0	-1.3
1992	Atl N	2	4	.333	19	14	1-1	0-0	80.2	77	27	2	1	27-1	62	2.57	143	.254	.315	24-0-4	.125	-1	90	9	68	0.6
1993	Cle A	4	5	.444	13	13	0	0-0	68.2	90	47	8	2	23-3	38	5.90	74	.310	.363	0	ø	0	110	-10	0	-1.1
1994	Atl N	2	0	1.000	19	1	0	0-0	27	28	12	2	1	12-1	18	4.00	108	.277	.360	3-0-1	.000	-0	148	1	0	0.1
1995	Cal A	4	6	.400	22	11	0	0-0	75.1	80	56	15	3	31-1	45	5.97	79	.273	.343	0	ø	0	106	-11	46	-1.3
1996	†Atl N	4	3	.571	40	5	0	2-0	75.1	63	24	8	0	33-6	71	2.63	169	.224	.303	10	.100	-0	101	15	0	1.3
1997	Atl N	3	7	.300	50	0	0	2-4	57.1	56	33	9	1	21-3	60	4.08	103	.250	.316	2	.000	-0	—	-1	43	-0.1
Total	14	70	73	.490	347	178	7-4	5-5	1231	1236	633	116	19	496-45	783	4.18	96	.262	.332	282-0-35	.078	-14	101	-22	157	-4.6
Biemiller, Harry	Harry Lee; B10.9.1897 Baltimore MD; D5.25.1965 Orlando FL; BR/TR/6´1˝/171; d8.26																									
1920	Was A	1	0	1.000	5	2	1	0	17	21	13	1	0	13	10	4.76	78	.318	.430	4-0-1	.000	-1	128	-3	—	-0.2
1925	Cin N	0	1	.000	23	1	0	2	47	45	28	2	7	21	9	4.02	102	.280	.386	9	.000	-0	103	0	—	0.0
Total	2	1	1	.500	28	3	1	2	64	66	41	3	7	34	19	4.22	95	.291	.399	13-0-1	.000	-1	117	-3	—	-0.2
Bierbauer, Lou	Louis W.; B9.28.1865 Erie PA; D1.31.1926 Erie PA; BL/TR/5´8˝/140; d4.17; ▲																									
1886	Phi AA	0	0	ø	2	0	0	0	10.2	8	9	0	0	5	1	4.22	83	.178	.260	522-2	.226	-0*	—	-1	—	-0.1
1887	Phi AA	0	0	ø	1	0	0	1	1	0	0	0	0	0	1	0.00	ø	.000	.000	530-1	.272	0*	—	0	—	0.1
1888	Phi AA	0	0	ø	1	0	0	0	3	5	1	0	0	0	3	0.00	ø	.357	.357	535	.267	0*	—	1	—	0.0
Total	3	0	0	ø	4	0	0	1	14.2	13	10	0	0	5	5	3.07	112	.210	.269	1587-3	.255	0	—	0	—	0.0
Bierbrodt, Nick	Nicholas Raymond; B5.16.1978 Tarzana CA; BL/TL/6´5˝/(185–215); [AriN96 1/30]; d6.7																									
2001	Ari N	2	2	.500	5	5	0	0-0	23	29	21	6	0	12-0	17	8.22	56	.305	.380	6-0-2	.667	2*	195	-8	18	-0.8
	TB A	3	4	.429	11	11	0	0-0	61.1	71	38	11	4	27-1	56	4.55	99	.285	.363	0	ø	0	92	-2	0	-0.2
2003	TB A	0	2	.000	13	5	0	0-0	35.1	59	41	9	5	23-3	20	9.68	47	.376	.463	0	ø	0	117	-20	0	-0.9
	Cle A	0	0	ø	5	0	0	0-0	8	5	6	0	0	4-0	9	6.75	66	.185	.273	0	ø	0	—	-2	0	-0.1
	Year	0	2	.000	18	5	0	0-0	43.1	64	47	9	5	27-3	29	9.14	50	.348	.434	0	ø	0	117	-21	0	-1.0
2004	Tex A	1	1	.500	4	4	0	0-0	17	14	11	4	2	19-0	10	5.82	85	.246	.443	2-0-1	.000	-0	89	-1	0	-0.1
Total	3	6	9	.400	38	25	0	0-0	144.2	178	117	30	11	85-4	112	6.66	69	.304	.398	8-0-3	.500	2	118	-33	18	-2.1
Bigbee, Lyle	Lyle Randolph "Al"; B8.22.1893 Waterloo OR; D8.5.1942 Portland OR; BL/TR/6´0˝/180; d4.15; b–Carson; Col Oregon; ▲																									
1920	Phi A	0	3	.000	12	2	0	0	45	66	42	5	0	25	12	8.00	50	.369	.446	75-1-1	.187	0*	128	-14	—	-0.8
1921	Pit N	0	0	ø	5	0	0	0	8	4	1	0	0	4	1	1.13	341	.154	.267	2	.000	-0	—	2	—	0.1
Total	2	0	3	.000	17	2	0	0	53	70	43	5	0	29	13	6.96	57	.341	.423	77-1-1	.182	-0	128	-12	—	-0.7
Biggs, Charlie	Charles Orval; B9.15.1906 French Lick IN; D5.24.1954 French Lick IN; BR/TR/6´1˝/185; d9.3																									
1932	Chi A	1	1	.500	6	4	0	0	24.2	32	22	2	3	12	1	6.93	62	.314	.402	9	.111	-0	138	-7	—	-0.5
Bilbrey, Jim	James Melvin; B4.20.1924 Rickman TN; D12.26.1985 Toledo OH; BR/TR/6´2.5˝/205; d5.17																									
1949	StL A	0	0	ø	1	0	0	0	1	1	2	0	0	3	0	18.00	25	.250	.571	0	ø	0	—	-1	0	-0.1
Bildilli, Emil	Emil "Hill Billy"; B9.16.1912 Diamond IN; D9.16.1946 Hartford City IN; BR/TL/5´10˝/170; d8.24																									
1937	StL A	0	1	.000	4	1	0	0	8	12	9	1	0	3	2	10.13	48	.353	.405	2	.000	-0	108	-4	—	-0.4
1938	StL A	1	2	.333	5	3	2	0	21.2	33	18	3	0	11	11	7.06	70	.359	.427	8	.250	-0	53	-4	—	-0.5
1939	StL A	1	1	.500	2	2	2	0	19	21	8	0	0	6	8	3.32	147	.266	.318	5-0-1	.000	-0	72	3	—	0.2
1940	StL A	2	4	.333	28	11	3	1	97	113	68	12	2	52	32	5.57	82	.298	.386	30-0-1	.200	-1*	105	-10	—	-0.5
1941	StL A	0	0	ø	2	0	0	0	2.1	5	3	0	0	3	2	11.57	37	.417	.533	0	ø	0	—	-2	0	-0.1
Total	5	4	8	.333	41	17	7	1	148	184	106	16	2	75	55	5.84	80	.309	.388	45-0-2	.178	-2	92	-17	0	-1.3
Billiard, Harry	Harry Pree "Pree"; B11.11.1883 Monroe IN; D6.3.1923 Wooster OH; BR/TR/6´0˝/190; d7.31																									
1908	NY A	0	0	ø	6	0	0	0	17	15	15	1	5	14	10	2.65	94	.234	.410	6	.167	-0	—	-3	—	-0.2
1914	Ind F	8	7	.533	32	16	5	2	125.2	117	71	4	7	63	45	3.72	84	.257	.356	38	.184	-1	111	-9	—	-1.2
1915	New F	0	1	.000	14	2	0	1	28.1	32	23	0	3	28	7	5.72	45	.291	.447	6-0-1	.333	0	82	-10	—	-0.5
Total	3	8	8	.500	52	18	5	3	171	164	109	5	15	105	62	3.95	75	.260	.379	50-0-1	.200	-1	112	-22	—	-1.9
Billingham, Jack	John Eugene; B2.21.1943 Orlando FL; BR/TR/6´4˝/(185–215); d4.11																									
1968	LA N	3	0	1.000	50	1	0	8	71.1	54	18	0	2	30-9	46	2.14	129	.215	.304	3-0-2	.000	0	31	6	0	0.5
1969	Hou N	6	7	.462	52	4	1	2-3	82.2	92	45	12	5	29-11	71	4.25	84	.290	.357	14-0-1	.071	0	81	-6	0	-1.0
1970	Hou N	13	9	.591	46	24	8-2	0-2	187.2	190	102	10	10	63-2	134	3.98	98	.259	.325	58-0-7	.103	-2	104	-6	0	-0.8
1971	Hou N	10	16	.385	33	33	8-3	0-0	228.1	205	98	9	16	68-8	139	3.39	99	.243	.310	73-0-6	.123	-3	85	-2	0	-0.5
1972	†Cin N	12	12	.500	36	31	8-4	1-0	217.2	197	83	18	7	64-8	137	3.18	102	.241	.300	71-0-5	.070	-4	120	3	0	-0.2
1973	†Cin N☆	19	10	.655	40	**40**	16-**7**	0-0	**293.1**	257	112	20	10	95-10	155	3.04	114	.236	.303	93-0-13	.065	-5	115	13	0	0.8
1974	Cin N	19	11	.633	36	35	8-3	0-0	212.1	233	105	16	6	64-9	103	3.94	89	.288	.343	67-0-11	.075	-5	117	-11	0	-1.9
1975	†Cin N	15	10	.600	33	32	5	0-0	208	222	100	22	9	76-12	79	4.11	87	.279	.347	65-0-10	.108	-1	133	-11	0	-1.5
1976	†Cin N	12	10	.545	34	29	5-2	1-1	177	190	96	17	4	62-5	76	4.32	81	.279	.340	59-0-8	.237	3	147	-17	0	-1.7
1977	Cin N	10	10	.500	36	23	3-2	0-2	161.2	195	105	16	10	56-9	76	5.23	75	.306	.368	56-0-6	.161	-1	146	-25	0	-2.7
1978	Det A	15	8	.652	30	30	10-4	0-0	201.2	218	95	16	8	65-2	59	3.88	100	.284	.341	0	ø	0	114	1	0	0.0
1979	Det A	10	7	.588	35	19	2	3-0	158	163	74	13	7	60-11	59	3.30	132	.275	.347	0	ø	0	96	13	0	1.3
1980	Det A	0	0	ø	8	0	0	0-1	7.1	11	6	1	0	6-1	3	7.36	56	.355	.447	0	ø	0	—	-2	0	-0.1
	Bos A	1	3	.250	7	4	0	0-0	24.1	45	30	6	4	12-0	4	11.10	38	.413	.484	0	ø	0	73	-16	0	-2.1
	Year	1	3	.250	15	4	0	0-1	31.2	56	36	7	4	18-1	7	10.23	41	.400	.476	0	ø	0	74	-18	0	-2.2
Total	13	145	113	.562	476	305	74-27	15-9	2231.1	2272	1069	176	98	750-97	1141	3.83	94	.268	.333	559-0-69	.111	-17	117	-60	0	-9.9
Billings, Josh	Haskell Clark; B9.27.1907 New York NY; D12.26.1983 Greenbrae CA; BR/TR/5´11˝/180; d8.17; Col Brown																									
1927	Det A	5	4	.556	10	9	5	0	67	64	36	3	6	39	18	4.84	87	.259	.373	27	.259	0	123	-1	—	-0.1
1928	Det A	5	10	.333	21	16	3-1	0	110.2	118	83	4	5	59	48	5.12	80	.276	.371	35-0-4	.286	3	109	-15	—	-1.4
1929	Det A	0	1	.000	8	0	0	0	19.1	27	14	0	1	9	1	5.12	84	.365	.440	6	.000	-1	—	-2	—	-0.1
Total	3	10	15	.400	39	25	8-1	0	197	209	133	7	12	107	67	5.03	83	.279	.378	68-0-4	.250	2	114	-18	—	-1.6
Billingsley, Brent	Brent Aaron; B4.19.1975 Downey CA; BL/TL/6´2˝/200; [FlaN96 5/134]; d5.20; Col Cal St.–Fullerton																									
1999	Fla N	0	0	ø	8	0	0	0-0	7.2	11	14	3	2	10-0	3	16.43	27	.379	.548	0	ø	0	—	-10	0	-0.5
Billingsley, Chad	Chad Ryan; B7.29.1984 Defiance OH; BR/TR/6´0˝/245; [LAN03 1/24]; d6.15																									
2006	†LA N	7	4	.636	18	16	0	0-0	90	92	43	7	3	58-3	59	3.80	115	.272	.383	24-0-1	.083	-0	100	5	0	0.5
Bird, Doug	James Douglas; B3.5.1950 Corona CA; BR/TR/6´4˝/(180–195); [KCA69 S3/60]; d4.29; Col Mt. San Antonio (CA) JC																									
1973	KC A	4	4	.500	54	0	0	20-4	102.1	81	37	10	2	30-7	83	2.99	138	.217	.276	0	ø	0	—	12	0	1.3
1974	KC A	7	6	.538	55	1	1	10-7	92.1	100	31	6	1	27-9	62	2.73	140	.286	.333	0	ø	0	23	11	0	1.8
1975	KC A	9	6	.600	51	4	0	11-7	105.1	100	42	7	2	40-10	81	3.25	119	.258	.326	0	ø	0	80	8	0	1.2

YEAR	TM LG	W	L	PCT	G	GS	CG-SHO	SV-BS	IP	H	R	HR	HB	BB-IB	SO	ERA	AERA	OAV	OOB	AB-HR-SH	AVG	PB	SUP	APR	DL	PW
1976	†KC A	12	10	.545	39	27	2-1	2-1	197.2	191	90	17	3	31-3	107	3.37	104	.251	.279	0	ø	0	104	1	0	0.1
1977	†KC A	11	4	.733	53	5	0	14-4	118.1	120	52	14	3	29-4	83	3.88	104	.270	.314	0	ø	0	152	5	0	0.6
1978	†KC A	6	6	.500	40	6	0	1-4	98.2	110	63	8	2	31-5	48	5.29	72	.284	.336	0	ø	0	117	-14	0	-1.6
1979	Phi N	2	0	1.000	32	1	1	0-0	61	73	35	7	2	16-4	33	5.16	75	.305	.349	6	.167	0	137	-7	21	-0.4
1980	NY A	3	0	1.000	22	1	0	1-1	50.2	47	16	3	1	14-1	17	2.66	149	.257	.307	0	ø	0	294	8	0	0.5
1981	NY A	5	1	.833	17	4	0	0-1	53.1	58	19	5	0	16-3	28	2.70	134	.280	.326	0	ø	0	68	5	0	0.6
	Chi N	4	5	.444	12	12	2-1	0-0	75.1	72	34	5	1	16-3	34	3.58	105	.254	.293	20-0-2	.100	-1	75	1	0	0.0
1982	Chi N	9	14	.391	35	33	2-1	0-0	191	230	119	26	3	30-3	71	5.14	74	.297	.324	56-0-4	.143	-2	103	-26	0	-3.1
1983	Bos A	1	4	.200	22	6	0	1-0	67.2	91	52	14	2	16-4	33	6.65	66	.324	.360	0	ø	0	76	-14	0	-1.0
Total	11	73	60	.549	432	100	8-3	60-29	1213.2	1273	590	122	22	296-56	680	3.99	96	.272	.315	82-0-6	.134	-2	99	-10	21	0.0
Bird, Red	James Edward; B4.25.1890 Stephenville TX; D3.23.1972 Murfreesboro AR; BL/TL/5´11˝/170; d9.17																									
1921	Was A	0	0	ø	1	0	0	0	5	5	3	0	1	1	2	5.40	76	.294	.368	1	.000	-0	—	0	—	0.0
Birkbeck, Mike	Michael Lawrence; B3.10.1961 Orrville OH; BR/TR/6´1˝/(185–190); [MilA83 4/106]; d8.17; Col Akron; [DL 1990 Mil A 43]																									
1986	Mil A	1	1	.500	7	4	0	0-0	22	24	12	0	0	12-0	13	4.50	97	.282	.371	0	ø	0	99	0	0	0.0
1987	Mil A	1	4	.200	10	10	1	0-0	45	63	33	8	0	19-0	25	6.20	74	.335	.392	0	ø	0	103	-7	105	-0.6
1988	Mil A	10	8	.556	23	23	0	0-0	124	141	69	10	1	37-1	64	4.72	85	.285	.335	0	ø	0	110	-8	0	-1.0
1989	Mil A	0	4	.000	9	9	1	0-0	44.2	57	32	4	3	22-2	31	5.44	71	.310	.387	0	ø	0	94	-9	90	-0.7
1992	NY N	0	1	.000	1	1	0	0-0	7	12	7	3	0	1-1	2	9.00	39	.387	.406	2	.000	-0	129	-4	0	-0.4
1995	NY N	0	1	.000	4	4	0	0-0	27.2	22	5	2	0	2-0	14	1.63	248	.220	.235	6-0-1	.333	1	34	8	0	0.5
Total	6	12	19	.387	54	51	2	0-0	270.1	319	158	27	4	93-4	149	4.86	84	.295	.351	8-0-1	.250	1	100	-20	238	-2.2
Birkins, Kurt	Kurt Daniel; B8.11.1980 West Hills CA; BL/TL/6´2˝/190; [BalA00 33/984]; d5.4; Col Los Angeles Pierce (CA) JC																									
2006	Bal A	5	2	.714	35	0	0	0-1	31	25	19	4	3	16-0	27	4.94	92	.221	.328	0	ø	0	—	-2	64	-0.3
Birkofer, Ralph	Ralph Joseph "Lefty"; B11.5.1908 Cincinnati OH; D3.16.1971 Cincinnati OH; BL/TL/5´11˝/213; d4.25																									
1933	Pit N	4	2	.667	9	8	3-1	0	50.2	43	22	1	1	17	20	2.31	144	.229	.296	22	.318	1	135	3	—	0.5
1934	Pit N	11	12	.478	41	23	11	1	204	227	106	11	5	66	71	4.10	100	.277	.335	75-0-2	.227	1	90	1	—	0.0
1935	Pit N	9	7	.563	37	18	8-1	1	150.1	173	87	5	6	42	80	4.07	101	.283	.335	58	.241	2*	94	0	—	0.0
1936	Pit N	7	5	.583	34	13	2	0	109.1	130	73	4	5	41	44	4.69	86	.295	.362	41	.220	-0	166	-10	—	-1.1
1937	Bro N	0	2	.000	11	1	0	0	29.2	45	28	3	0	9	9	6.67	60	.341	.383	11	.273	1*	43	-9	—	-0.5
Total	5	31	28	.525	132	63	24-2	2	544	618	316	24	17	175	224	4.19	96	.282	.340	207-0-2	.242	5	111	-15	—	-1.1
Birrer, Babe	Werner Joseph; B7.4.1929 Buffalo NY; BR/TR/6´0˝/195; d6.5																									
1955	Det A	4	3	.571	36	3	1	3	80.1	77	39	9	0	29-4	28	4.15	93	.248	.311	19-2-0	.158	2	85	-1	0	0.1
1956	Bal A	0	0	ø	4	0	0	0	5.1	9	5	0	0	1-0	1	6.75	58	.360	.385	1	.000	-0	—	-2	0	-0.1
1958	LA N	0	0	ø	16	0	0	1	34	43	20	4	1	7-3	16	4.50	91	.309	.342	7	.571	2	—	-2	0	0.1
Total	3	4	3	.571	56	3	1	4	119.2	129	64	13	1	37-7	45	4.36	90	.272	.324	27-2-0	.259	4	85	-5	0	0.1
Birtsas, Tim	Timothy Dean; B9.5.1960 Pontiac MI; BL/TL/6´7˝/(225–245); [NYA82 2/36]; d5.3; Col Michigan St.																									
1985	Oak A	10	6	.625	29	25	2	0-0	141.1	124	72	18	3	91-0	94	4.01	97	.238	.352	0	ø	0	111	-3	0	-0.4
1986	Oak A	0	0	ø	2	0	0	0-0	2	2	5	1	0	4-1	1	22.50	17	.286	.545	0	ø	0	—	-4	0	-0.2
1988	Cin N	1	3	.250	36	4	0	0-0	64.1	61	34	6	3	24-5	38	4.20	85	.250	.321	10	.000	-1	56	-5	0	-0.4
1989	Cin N	2	2	.500	42	1	0	1-0	69.2	68	33	5	3	27-8	57	3.75	96	.261	.330	4-1-0	.250	1	74	-1	0	0.0
1990	Cin N	1	3	.250	29	0	0	0-0	51.1	69	24	7	1	24-6	41	3.86	102	.325	.395	4-0-3	.000	-0	—	0	0	0.0
Total	5	14	14	.500	138	30	2	1-0	328.2	324	168	37	10	170-20	231	4.08	93	.260	.350	18-1-3	.056	-0	103	-13	0	-1.0
Biscan, Frank	Frank Stephen "Porky"; B3.13.1920 Mt.Olive IL; D5.22.1959 St.Louis MO; BL/TL/5´11˝/190; d5.3; Mil 1942–45																									
1942	StL A	0	1	.000	11	0	0	1	27	13	8	1	0	11	10	2.33	159	.143	.235	6	.000	-0	—	4	0	0.2
1946	StL A	1	1	.500	16	0	0	1	22.2	28	13	0	0	22	9	5.16	72	.318	.455	3	.000	-0	—	-2	0	-0.3
1948	StL A	6	7	.462	47	4	1	2	98.2	129	78	3	9	71	45	6.11	75	.322	.435	26	.192	1	79	-18	0	-2.0
Total	3	7	9	.438	74	4	1	4	148.1	170	99	4	9	104	64	5.28	81	.294	.409	35	.143	-0	79	-16	0	-2.1
Bishop, Charlie	Charles Tuller; B1.1.1924 Atlanta GA; D7.5.1993 Lawrenceville GA; BR/TR/6´2˝/195; d8.22																									
1952	Phi A	2	2	.500	6	5	1	0	30.2	29	24	2	0	24	17	6.46	61	.238	.363	9-0-1	.111	-0	110	-8	0	-0.9
1953	Phi A	3	14	.176	39	20	1-1	2	160.2	174	106	15	5	86	66	5.66	76	.282	.375	56	.089	-4*	81	-21	0	-2.3
1954	Phi A	4	6	.400	20	12	4	1	96	98	49	10	5	50	34	4.41	89	.275	.369	33-0-1	.121	-2*	88	-4	0	-0.6
1955	KC A	1	0	1.000	4	0	0	0	6.2	6	7	1	3	8-2	4	5.40	77	.261	.486	2	.500	0	—	-2	0	-0.2
Total	4	10	22	.313	69	37	6-1	3	294	307	186	28	13	168-2	121	5.33	77	.275	.375	100-0-2	.110	-6	87	-35	0	-4.0
Bishop, Jim	James Morton; B1.28.1898 Montgomery City MO; D9.20.1973 Montgomery City MO; BR/TR/6´0˝/195; d4.26																									
1923	Phi N	0	3	.000	15	0	0	1	32.2	48	31	2	3	11	5	6.34	73	.353	.413	10	.000	-2	—	-6	—	-0.7
1924	Phi N	0	1	.000	7	1	0	0	16.2	24	14	3	0	7	3	6.48	69	.348	.408	5	.200	-0	76	-3	—	-0.2
Total	2	0	4	.000	22	1	0	1	49.1	72	45	5	3	18	8	6.39	71	.351	.412	15	.067	-2	76	-9	—	-0.9
Bishop, Lloyd	Lloyd Clifton; B4.25.1890 Conway Springs KS; D6.18.1968 Wichita KS; BR/TR/6´0˝/180; d9.5; Col Wichita St.																									
1914	Cle A	0	1	.000	3	1	0	0	8	14	5	0	0	3	1	5.63	51	.389	.436	2	.000	-0	101	-2	—	-0.2
Bishop, Bill	William Henry "Lefty"; B10.22.1900 Houtzdale PA; D2.14.1956 St.Joseph MO; BL/TL/5´8˝/170; d9.15																									
1921	Phi A	0	0	ø	2	0	0	0	7	8	9	0	0	10	4	9.00	50	.267	.450	3	.000	-1	—	-4	—	-0.2
Bishop, Bill	William Robinson; B12.27.1869 Adamsburg PA; D12.15.1932 Pittsburgh PA; BR/TR/5´8˝/187; d9.13																									
1886	Pit AA	0	1	.000	2	2	2	0	17	17	14	0	1	11	4	3.18	107	.221	.326	7	.143	-1	105	-1	—	-0.1
1887	Pit N	0	3	.000	3	3	3	0	27	45	46	2	2	22	4	13.33	29	.354	.457	9	.000	-1	34	-26	—	-1.8
1889	Chi N	0	0	ø	2	0	0	2	3	6	13	0	0	6	1	18.00	23	.400	.571	1	.000	0	—	-6	—	-0.6
Total	3	0	4	.000	7	5	5	2	47	68	73	2	3	39	9	9.96	37	.311	.421	17	.059	-2	61	-33	—	-2.5
Bithorn, Hi	Hiram Gabriel (Sosa); B3.18.1916 Santurce, PR; D12.30.1951 Ciudad Victoria, Tamaulipas, Mexico; BR/TR/6´1˝/200; d4.15; Mil 1944–45																									
1942	Chi N	9	14	.391	38	16	9	2	171.1	191	93	8	0	81	65	3.68	87	.296	.374	57-0-1	.123	-1	95	-14	0	-1.9
1943	Chi N	18	12	.600	39	30	19-**7**	2	249.2	227	79	8	2	65	86	2.60	129	.244	.294	92-0-5	.174	-0	110	23	0	2.9
1946	Chi N	6	5	.545	26	7	2-1	1	86.2	97	42	5	0	25	34	3.84	86	.283	.332	28-0-2	.179	-0	111	-5	0	-0.7
1947	Chi A	1	0	1.000	2	0	0	0	2	2	0	0	0	0	0	0.00	ø	.286	.286	0	ø	0	—	1	0	0.2
Total	4	34	31	.523	105	53	30-8	5	509.2	517	214	21	2	171	185	3.16	104	.268	.328	177-0-8	.158	-2	106	5	0	0.5
Bitker, Joe	Joseph Anthony; B2.12.1964 Glendale CA; BR/TR/6´1˝/175; [SDN84 S2/32]; d7.31; Col Sacramento (CA) City																									
1990	Oak A	0	0	ø	1	0	0	0-0	3	1	0	0	0	1-0	2	0.00	ø	.111	.200	0	ø	0	—	1	0	0.1
	Tex A	0	0	ø	5	0	0	0-0	9	7	3	0	1	3-0	6	3.00	131	.212	.289	0	ø	0	—	1	0	0.1
	Year	0	0	ø	6	0	0	0-0	12	8	3	0	1	4-0	8	2.25	173	.190	.271	0	ø	0	—	2	0	0.2
1991	Tex A	1	0	1.000	9	0	0	0-0	14.2	17	11	4	0	8-3	16	6.75	60	.274	.357	0	ø	0	—	-4	0	-0.2
Total	2	1	0	1.000	15	0	0	0-0	26.2	25	14	4	1	12-3	24	4.73	84	.240	.322	0	ø	0	—	-2	0	0.0
Bittiger, Jeff	Jeffrey Scott; B4.13.1962 Jersey City NJ; BR/TR/5´10˝/175; [NYN80 7/157]; d9.2																									
1986	Phi N	1	1	.500	3	3	0	0-0	14.2	16	10	2	1	7-1	8	5.52	71	.271	.358	3-1-1	.333	1	114	-2	0	-0.2
1987	Min A	1	0	1.000	3	1	0	0-0	8.1	11	5	2	1	0-0	5	5.40	86	.314	.333	0	ø	0	157	0	0	0.0
1988	Chi A	2	4	.333	25	7	0	0-0	61.2	59	31	11	0	29-2	33	4.23	95	.255	.333	0	ø	0	49	-1	20	-0.1
1989	Chi A	0	1	.000	2	1	0	0-0	9.2	9	7	2	0	6-0	7	6.52	59	.257	.366	0	ø	0	71	-3	44	-0.2
Total	4	4	6	.400	33	12	0	0-0	94.1	95	53	17	2	42-3	53	4.77	84	.264	.341	3-1-1	.333	1	77	-6	64	-0.5
Bivin, Jim	James Nathaniel; B12.11.1909 Jackson MS; D11.7.1982 Pueblo CO; BR/TR/6´0˝/155; d4.16																									
1935	Phi N	2	9	.182	47	14	0	1	161.2	220	129	20	3	65	54	5.79	78	.316	.377	48	.146	-1	72	-22	—	-1.4
Black, Dave	David; B4.19.1892 Chicago IL; D10.27.1936 Pittsburgh PA; BL/TR/6´2˝/175; d5.2																									
1914	Chi F	1	0	1.000	8	1	1	0	25	28	19	1	0	4	19	6.12	43	.311	.340	6	.333	1	207	-9	—	-0.4
1915	Chi F	6	7	.462	25	10	2	0	121.1	104	46	4	6	33	43	2.45	103	.241	.304	37-0-4	.108	-2	123	0	—	-0.3
	Bal F	1	3	.250	8	4	1	0	34	32	18	2	2	15	10	3.71	77	.260	.350	12-0-2	.250	0	110	-3	—	-0.3
	Year	7	10	.412	33	14	3	0	155.1	136	64	6	8	48	53	2.72	95	.245	.315	49-0-6	.143	-2	120	-3	—	-0.6

YEAR	TM LG	W	L	PCT	G	GS	CG-SHO	SV-BS	IP	H	R	HR	HB	BB-IB	SO	ERA	AERA	OAV	OOB	AB-HR-SH	AVG	PB	SUP	APR	DL	PW
1923	Bos A	0	0	ø	2	0	0	0	1	2	0	0	0	0	0	0.00	ø	.500	.500	0	ø	0	—	0	—	0.0
Total	3	8	10	.444	43	15	4	0	181.1	166	83	7	8	52	72	3.18	82	.256	.319	55-0-6	.164	-1	125	-12	—	-1.0

BLACK, DON Donald Paul; B7.20.1916 Salix IA; D4.21.1959 Cuyahoga Falls OH; BR/TR/6´0˝/185; d4.24

YEAR	TM LG	W	L	PCT	G	GS	CG-SHO	SV-BS	IP	H	R	HR	HB	BB-IB	SO	ERA	AERA	OAV	OOB	AB-HR-SH	AVG	PB	SUP	APR	DL	PW
1943	Phi A	6	16	.273	33	26	12-1	1	208	193	105	8	6	110	65	4.20	81	.247	.344	69-0-2	.188	-1	75	-15	0	-1.6
1944	Phi A	10	12	.455	29	27	8	0	177.1	177	94	6	4	75	78	4.06	86	.259	.336	59-0-3	.186	-1	100	-11	0	-1.3
1945	Phi A	5	11	.313	26	18	8	0	125.1	154	77	5	0	69	47	5.17	66	.307	.391	37-0-1	.162	-2	81	-21	0	-2.7
1946	Cle A	1	2	.333	18	4	0	0	43.2	45	26	5	1	21	15	4.53	73	.273	.358	10-0-1	.200	0	123	-7	0	-0.4
1947	Cle A	10	12	.455	30	28	8-3	0	190.2	177	90	17	1	85	72	3.92	89	.249	.330	66-0-3	.182	-1	110	-9	0	-1.1
1948	Cle A	2	2	.500	18	10	1	0	52	57	33	5	1	40	16	5.37	76	.282	.403	15-0-1	.200	-0	107	-7	0	-0.5
Total	6	34	55	.382	154	113	37-4	1	797	803	425	46	13	400	293	4.35	80	.264	.352	256-0-11	.184	-4	95	-70	0	-7.6

BLACK, BUD Harry Ralston; B6.30.1957 San Mateo CA; BL/TL/6´2˝/(180–188); [SeaA79 17/417]; d9.5; C7; Col San Diego St.

YEAR	TM LG	W	L	PCT	G	GS	CG-SHO	SV-BS	IP	H	R	HR	HB	BB-IB	SO	ERA	AERA	OAV	OOB	AB-HR-SH	AVG	PB	SUP	APR	DL	PW
1981	Sea A	0	0	ø	2	0	0	0-0	1	2	0	0	0	3-1	0	0.00	ø	.500	.714	0	ø	0	—	0	0	0.0
1982	KC A	4	6	.400	22	14	0	0-0	88.1	92	48	10	3	34-6	40	4.58	89	.269	.338	0	ø	0*	78	-4	0	-0.4
1983	KC A	10	7	.588	24	24	3	0-0	161.1	159	75	19	2	43-1	58	3.79	108	.257	.305	0	ø	0	120	6	0	0.7
1984	†KC A	17	12	.586	35	35	8-1	0-0	257	226	99	22	4	64-2	140	3.12	130	.233	**.283**	0	ø	0	85	25	0	2.9
1985	†KC A	10	15	.400	33	33	5-2	0-0	205.2	216	111	17	8	59-4	122	4.33	96	.268	.323	0	ø	0	84	-3	0	-0.4
1986	KC A	5	10	.333	56	4	0	9-2	121	100	49	14	7	43-5	68	3.20	134	.225	.301	0	ø	0	80	13	0	1.7
1987	KC A	8	6	.571	29	18	0	1-1	122.1	126	63	16	5	35-2	61	3.60	127	.265	.320	0	ø	0	108	10	26	1.0
1988	KC A	2	1	.667	17	0	0	0-1	22	23	12	2	0	11-2	19	4.91	82	.267	.351	0	ø	0	—	-2	0	-0.2
	Cle A	2	3	.400	16	7	0	1-0	59	59	35	6	4	23-1	44	5.03	82	.262	.337	0	ø	0	91	-5	33	-0.4
	Year	4	4	.500	33	7	0	1-1	81	82	47	8	4	34-3	63	5.00	82	.264	.341	0	ø	0	92	-7	0	-0.6
1989	Cle A	12	11	.522	33	32	6-3	0-0	222.1	213	95	14	1	52-0	88	3.36	118	.252	.295	0	ø	0	87	14	0	1.3
1990	Cle A	11	10	.524	29	29	5-2	0-0	191	171	79	17	4	58-1	103	3.53	112	.236	.294	0	ø	0	104	10	0	1.0
	Tor A	2	1	.667	3	2	0	0-1	15.2	10	7	2	1	3-0	3	4.02	99	.189	.237	0	ø	0	69	0	0	0.1
	Year	13	11	.542	32	31	5-2	0-1	206.2	181	86	19	5	61-1	106	3.57	110	.233	.290	0	ø	0	101	12	0	1.1
1991	SF N	12	16	.429	34	34	3-3	0-0	214.1	201	104	25	4	71-8	104	3.99	90	.251	.313	71-0-9	.183	1*	93	-10	0	-1.0
1992	SF N	10	12	.455	28	28	2-1	0-0	177	178	88	23	1	59-11	82	3.97	84	.263	.321	54-0-10	.056	-3	84	-14	31	-1.8
1993	SF N	8	2	.800	16	16	0	0-0	93.2	89	44	13	2	33-2	45	3.56	111	.256	.321	37-0-3	.243	2	139	2	99	0.5
1994	SF N	4	2	.667	10	10	0	0-0	54.1	50	31	9	3	16-1	28	4.47	91	.245	.307	17-0-5	.059	-1	119	-3	77	-0.4
1995	Cle A	4	2	.667	11	10	0	0-0	47.1	63	42	8	0	16-2	34	6.85	69	.317	.362	0	ø	0	122	-12	0	-1.2
Total	15	121	116	.511	398	296	32-12	11-5	2053.1	1978	982	217	49	623-49	1039	3.84	104	.253	.310	179-0-27	.145	-1	97	27	266	3.4

BLACK, JOE Joseph; B2.8.1924 Plainfield NJ; D5.17.2002 Scottsdale AZ; BR/TR/6´2˝/(215–229); d5.1; Negro Lg 1943–50 Mil 1943–45; Col Morgan St.

YEAR	TM LG	W	L	PCT	G	GS	CG-SHO	SV-BS	IP	H	R	HR	HB	BB-IB	SO	ERA	AERA	OAV	OOB	AB-HR-SH	AVG	PB	SUP	APR	DL	PW
1952	†Bro N	15	4	.789	56	2	1	15	142.1	102	40	9	1	41	85	2.15	169	.201	.262	36-0-6	.139	-1*	135	**23**	0	3.3
1953	†Bro N	6	3	.667	34	3	0	5	72.2	74	46	12	1	27	42	5.33	80	.259	.325	17	.235	0	56	-8	0	-1.0
1954	Bro N	0	0	ø	5	0	0	0	7	11	9	3	0	5	3	11.57	35	.355	.432	0	ø	0	—	-5	0	-0.3
1955	Bro N	1	0	1.000	6	0	0	0	15.1	15	5	1	0	5-1	9	2.93	138	.273	.328	3	.333	0	—	2	0	0.1
	Cin N	5	2	.714	32	11	1	3	102.1	106	58	13	0	25-3	54	4.22	100	.263	.303	30-0-3	.100	-2	134	-1	0	-0.3
	Year	6	2	.750	38	11	1	3	117.2	121	63	14	0	30-4	63	4.05	104	.264	.306	33-0-3	.121	-2	134	1	0	-0.2
1956	Cin N	3	2	.600	32	0	0	2	61.2	61	31	11	0	25-3	27	4.52	88	.256	.326	10	.000	-1*	—	-2	0	-0.3
1957	Was A	0	1	.000	7	0	0	0	12.2	22	11	4	0	1-0	2	7.11	55	.393	.397	0	ø	0	—	-4	0	-0.3
Total	6	30	12	.714	172	16	2	25	414	391	200	53	2	129-7	222	3.91	102	.248	.304	96-0-9	.135	-5	124	5	0	1.2

BLACK, BOB Robert Benjamin; B12.10.1862 Cincinnati OH; D3.21.1933 Sioux City IA; 5´5.5˝/155; d8.19; ▲

YEAR	TM LG	W	L	PCT	G	GS	CG-SHO	SV-BS	IP	H	R	HR	HB	BB-IB	SO	ERA	AERA	OAV	OOB	AB-HR-SH	AVG	PB	SUP	APR	DL	PW
1884	KC U	4	9	.308	16	15	13	0	123	127	79	1	—	17	93	3.22	69	.249	.273	146-1	.247	3*	64	-13	—	-0.8

BLACK, BUD William Carroll; B7.9.1932 St.Louis MO; D10.2.2005 St.Louis MO; BR/TR/6´3˝/197; d9.13; Mil 1953–54

YEAR	TM LG	W	L	PCT	G	GS	CG-SHO	SV-BS	IP	H	R	HR	HB	BB-IB	SO	ERA	AERA	OAV	OOB	AB-HR-SH	AVG	PB	SUP	APR	DL	PW
1952	Det A	0	1	.000	2	2	0	0	8	14	11	0	0	5	0	10.13	38	.389	.463	3	.000	-0	103	-6	0	-0.6
1955	Det A	1	1	.500	3	2	1-1	0	14	12	5	0	2	8-0	7	1.29	299	.231	.355	4-0-1	.250	0	81	3	0	0.4
1956	Det A	1	1	.500	5	1	0	0	10	10	4	2	0	5-0	7	3.60	114	.256	.333	2	.000	-0	86	1	0	0.1
Total	3	2	3	.400	10	5	1-1	0	32	36	20	2	2	18-0	14	4.22	93	.283	.378	9-0-1	.111	-1	90	-2	0	-0.1

BLACKBURN, CHARLIE Foster Edwin; B1.6.1895 Chicago IL; D3.9.1984 New Port Richey FL; BR/TR/6´1˝/165; d4.17; Col Chicago

YEAR	TM LG	W	L	PCT	G	GS	CG-SHO	SV-BS	IP	H	R	HR	HB	BB-IB	SO	ERA	AERA	OAV	OOB	AB-HR-SH	AVG	PB	SUP	APR	DL	PW
1915	KC F	0	1	.000	7	2	0	0	15.2	19	15	2	0	13	7	8.62	31	.306	.427	4	.000	-1	160	-9	—	-0.6
1921	Chi A	0	0	ø	1	0	0	0	1	0	0	0	0	1	0	0.00	ø	.000	.333	0	ø	0	—	0	—	0.0
Total	2	0	1	.000	8	2	0	0	16.2	19	15	2	0	14	7	8.10	34	.297	.423	4	.000	-1	160	-9	—	-0.6

BLACKBURN, GEORGE George W. "Smiling George"; B9.21.1871 Ozark MO; TR/5´11˝/184; d7.6

YEAR	TM LG	W	L	PCT	G	GS	CG-SHO	SV-BS	IP	H	R	HR	HB	BB-IB	SO	ERA	AERA	OAV	OOB	AB-HR-SH	AVG	PB	SUP	APR	DL	PW
1897	Bal N	2	2	.500	5	4	3	0	33	34	30	2	1	12	1	6.82	61	.264	.331	13	.077	-2	115	-8	—	-0.9

BLACKBURN, JIM James Ray "Bones"; B6.19.1924 Warsaw KY; D10.26.1969 Cincinnati OH; BR/TR/6´4˝/175; d7.24

YEAR	TM LG	W	L	PCT	G	GS	CG-SHO	SV-BS	IP	H	R	HR	HB	BB-IB	SO	ERA	AERA	OAV	OOB	AB-HR-SH	AVG	PB	SUP	APR	DL	PW
1948	Cin N	0	2	.000	16	0	0	0	32.1	38	18	1	0	14	10	4.18	94	.302	.371	6	.000	-0	—	-1	0	-0.1
1951	Cin N	0	0	ø	2	0	0	0	3.2	8	7	3	2	2	1	17.18	24	.444	.545	0	ø	0	—	-5	0	-0.2
Total	2	0	2	.000	18	0	0	0	36	46	25	4	2	16	11	5.50	71	.319	.395	6	.000	-0	—	-6	0	-0.3

BLACKBURN, RON Ronald Hamilton; B4.23.1935 Mt.Airy NC; D4.29.1998 Morganton NC; BR/TR/6´0.5˝/(160–170); d4.15; Mil 1959

YEAR	TM LG	W	L	PCT	G	GS	CG-SHO	SV-BS	IP	H	R	HR	HB	BB-IB	SO	ERA	AERA	OAV	OOB	AB-HR-SH	AVG	PB	SUP	APR	DL	PW
1958	Pit N	2	1	.667	38	2	0	3	63.2	61	33	7	3	27-5	31	3.39	114	.261	.338	7-0-1	.286	1	58	1	0	0.2
1959	Pit N	1	1	.500	26	0	0	1	44.1	50	21	5	2	15-4	19	3.65	106	.286	.345	5-1-0	.200	1	—	1	0	0.1
Total	2	3	2	.600	64	2	0	4	108	111	54	12	5	42-9	50	3.50	110	.271	.341	12-1-1	.250	2	58	2	0	0.3

BLACKLEY, TRAVIS Travis Jarrod; B11.4.1982 Melbourne, Victoria, Australia; BL/TL/6´3˝/190; d7.1; [DL 2005 Sea A 183]

YEAR	TM LG	W	L	PCT	G	GS	CG-SHO	SV-BS	IP	H	R	HR	HB	BB-IB	SO	ERA	AERA	OAV	OOB	AB-HR-SH	AVG	PB	SUP	APR	DL	PW
2004	Sea A	1	3	.250	6	6	0	0-0	26	35	31	9	1	22-0	16	10.04	45	.321	.436	0	ø	0	128	-17	0	-1.9

BLACKWELL, EWELL Ewell "The Whip"; B10.23.1922 Fresno CA; D10.29.1996 Hendersonville NC; BR/TR/6´6˝/(185–195); d4.21; Mil 1943–45; Col La Verne

YEAR	TM LG	W	L	PCT	G	GS	CG-SHO	SV-BS	IP	H	R	HR	HB	BB-IB	SO	ERA	AERA	OAV	OOB	AB-HR-SH	AVG	PB	SUP	APR	DL	PW
1942	Cin N	0	0	ø	2	0	0	0	3	3	4	0	0	3	1	6.00	55	.231	.375	1	.000	-0	—	-2	0	-0.1
1946	Cin N★	9	13	.409	33	25	10-**5**	0	194.1	160	62	1	4	79	100	2.45	136	.226	.307	56-0-6	.107	-3	69	20	0	2.1
1947	Cin N★	**22**	8	.733	33	33	**23**-6	0	273	227	91	10	4	95	**193**	2.47	166	.234	.304	106-0-7	.123	-5	94	46	0	4.5
1948	Cin N★	7	9	.438	22	20	4-1	0	138.2	134	73	12	4	52	114	4.54	86	.251	.323	48-0-3	.229	1	96	-7	0	-0.4
1949	Cin N★	5	5	.500	30	4	0	1	76.2	80	36	7	3	34	55	4.23	99	.271	.352	19-0-1	.211	-0	42	2	0	0.3
1950	Cin N★	17	15	.531	40	32	18-1	4	261	203	105	12	13	112	188	2.97	143	**.210**	.301	89-0-7	.146	-2	81	32	0	3.6
1951	Cin N★	16	15	.516	38	32	11-2	2	232.2	204	110	16	9	97	120	3.44	118	.233	.315	82-1-2	.293	7*	81	13	0	2.5
1952	Cin N	3	12	.200	23	17	3	0	102	107	66	6	5	60	48	5.38	70	.275	.379	32-0-1	.156	-0	71	-18	0	-2.4
	†NY A	1	0	1.000	5	2	0	1	16	12	2	0	0	12	7	0.56	591	.203	.338	5	.200	-0	105	5	0	0.4
1953	NY A	2	0	1.000	8	4	0	1	19.2	17	10	2	1	13	11	3.66	101	.233	.356	5	.000	-1	144	0	0	-0.1
1955	KC A	0	1	.000	2	0	0	1	4	3	3	1	1	5-0	2	6.75	62	.250	.500	0-0-1	ø	0	—	-1	0	-0.2
Total	10	82	78	.512	236	169	69-15	11	1321	1150	562	67	44	562-0	839	3.30	120	.235	.319	443-1-28	.174	-3	83	90	0	10.2

BLAEHOLDER, GEORGE George Franklin; B1.26.1904 Orange CA; D12.29.1947 Garden Grove CA; BR/TR/5´11˝/175; d4.20

YEAR	TM LG	W	L	PCT	G	GS	CG-SHO	SV-BS	IP	H	R	HR	HB	BB-IB	SO	ERA	AERA	OAV	OOB	AB-HR-SH	AVG	PB	SUP	APR	DL	PW
1925	StL A	0	0	ø	2	0	0	0	2	6	7	3	1	1	1	31.50	15	.600	.667	0	ø	0	—	-5	—	-0.2
1927	StL A	0	1	.000	1	1	1	0	9	8	5	1	1	4	2	5.00	87	.258	.361	3	.333	0	77	0	—	0.0
1928	StL A	10	15	.400	38	26	9-1	3	214.1	235	123	23	2	52	87	4.37	96	.280	.324	71-2-1	.211	2	95	-5	—	-0.1
1929	StL A	14	15	.483	42	24	13-**4**	2	222	237	113	18	0	61	72	4.18	106	.275	.323	74-1-2	.122	-4	74	8	—	0.8
1930	StL A	11	13	.458	37	23	10-1	4	191.1	235	119	20	2	46	70	4.61	106	.303	.343	65-0-4	.185	-1	99	3	—	0.1
1931	StL A	11	15	.423	35	32	13-1	0	226.1	280	137	15	1	56	79	4.53	102	.295	.335	77-0-3	.143	-3	84	3	—	0.2
1932	StL A	14	14	.500	42	36	16-1	0	258.1	304	163	19	3	76	80	4.70	103	.290	.340	88-0-2	.136	-4	91	2	—	-0.1
1933	StL A	15	19	.441	38	36	14-3	0	255.2	283	146	24	0	69	63	4.72	99	.280	.326	77-0-7	.182	-1	71	0	—	0.1
1934	StL A	14	18	.438	39	33	14-1	3	234.1	276	130	16	0	68	66	4.22	118	.296	.343	75-0-10	.093	-5	75	18	—	1.7
1935	StL A	1	1	.500	6	2	0	0	17.2	25	15	3	0	6	0	7.13	67	.342	.392	3-0-1	.000	-1	109	-4	—	-0.4
	Phi A	6	10	.375	23	22	10-1	0	149	173	78	10	0	49	22	3.99	114	.289	.343	47-0-6	.043	-6	88	8	—	0.2
	Year	7	11	.389	29	24	10-1	0	166.2	198	93	13	0	55	22	4.32	106	.295	.348	50-0-7	.040	-7	89	4	—	-0.2
1936	Cle A	8	4	.667	35	16	6-1	0	134.1	158	83	21	3	47	30	5.09	99	.295	.356	46-0-3	.130	-3	126	1	—	-0.1
Total	11	104	125	.454	338	251	106-14	12	1914.1	2220	1119	173	13	535	572	4.54	103	.290	.337	626-3-39	.142	-25	87	29	—	2.2

YEAR	TM LG	W	L	PCT	G	GS	CG-SHO	SV-BS	IP	H	R	HR	HB	BB-IB	SO	ERA	AERA	OAV	OOB	AB-HR-SH	AVG	PB	SUP	APR	DL	PW
BLAIR, DENNIS	Dennis Herman; B6.5.1954 Middletown OH; BR/TR/6´5˝/182; [MonN72 5/101]; d5.26																									
1974	Mon N	11	7	.611	22	22	4-1	0-0	146	113	61	7	5	72-4	76	3.27	118	.210	.307	51-0-6	.118	-2	127	9	0	1.0
1975	Mon N	8	15	.348	30	27	1	0-0	163.1	150	77	14	3	106-3	82	3.80	102	.251	.362	49-0-2	.143	-1	64	1	0	0.0
1976	Mon N	0	2	.000	5	4	1	0-0	15.2	21	11	1	2	11-0	9	4.02	93	.300	.405	4	.000	-0	76	-2	0	-0.2
1980	SD N	0	1	.000	5	1	0	0-0	14	18	10	3	0	3-0	11	6.43	53	.310	.344	5	.200	0	78	-4	0	-0.3
Total	4	19	25	.432	62	54	6-1	0-0	339	302	159	25	10	192-7	178	3.69	104	.239	.341	109-0-8	.128	-4	91	4	0	0.5
BLAIR, WILLIE	William Allen; B12.18.1965 Paintsville KY; BR/TR/6´1˝/(182–185); [TorA86 11/289]; d4.11; Col Morehead St.																									
1990	Tor A	3	5	.375	27	6	0	0-0	68.2	66	33	4	1	28-4	43	4.06	97	.250	.320	0	ø	0	80	-1	0	-0.1
1991	Cle A	2	3	.400	11	5	0	0-1	36	58	27	7	1	10-0	13	6.75	62	.377	.413	0	ø	0	74	-9	0	-1.0
1992	Hou N	5	7	.417	29	8	0	0-0	78.2	74	47	5	2	25-2	48	4.00	85	.249	.309	17-0-1	.059	-1	83	-9	0	-1.5
1993	Col N	6	10	.375	46	18	1	0-0	146	184	90	20	3	42-4	84	4.75	101	.306	.350	36-0-3	.111	-2	60	-1	0	-0.3
1994	Col N	0	5	.000	47	1	0	3-3	77.2	98	57	9	4	39-3	68	5.79	86	.308	.390	6	.000	-1	37	-7	0	-0.6
1995	SD N	7	5	.583	40	12	0	0-0	114	112	60	11	2	45-3	83	4.34	94	.262	.333	24-0-4	.000	-2	81	-2	0	-0.5
1996	†SD N	2	6	.250	60	0	0	1-4	88	80	52	13	7	29-5	67	4.60	87	.240	.311	3	.000	-0	—	-7	0	-0.7
1997	Det A	16	8	.667	29	27	2	0-0	175	186	85	18	3	46-2	90	4.17	111	.273	.319	4	.000	-0	101	10	29	1.0
1998	Ari N	4	15	.211	23	23	0	0-0	146.2	165	91	27	3	51-2	71	5.34	80	.292	.352	48-0-4	.083	-3	67	-15	0	-1.9
	NY N	1	1	.500	11	2	0	0-0	28.2	23	10	4	1	10-0	21	3.14	131	.228	.301	4	.250	1	11	3	0	0.3
	Year	5	16	.238	34	25	0	0-0	175.1	188	101	31	4	61-2	92	4.98	85	.282	.344	52-0-4	.096	-2	63	-13	0	-1.6
1999	Det A	3	11	.214	39	16	0	0-0	134	169	107	29	4	44-0	82	6.85	73	.308	.361	1	.000	-0	84	-26	0	-2.2
2000	Det A	10	6	.625	47	17	0	0-2	156.2	185	89	20	2	35-0	74	4.88	101	.296	.331	3	.333	0	124	2	0	0.1
2001	Det A	1	4	.200	9	4	0	0-0	24	38	30	3	3	11-3	15	10.50	42	.369	.437	2	.000	-0	79	-16	0	-2.5
Total	12	60	86	.411	418	139	3	4-10	1274	1438	778	170	36	415-28	759	5.04	89	.286	.342	148-0-12	.074	-8	85	-78	29	-9.9
BLAIR, BILL	William Ellsworth; B9.17.1863 Pittsburgh PA; D2.22.1890 Pittsburgh PA; BL/TL/5´8.5˝/172; d7.19																									
1888	Phi AA	1	3	.250	4	4	3	0	31	29	21	0	1	8	16	2.61	114	.238	.290	13	.308	1	44	0	—	0.2
BLAISDELL, DICK	Howard Carleton; B6.18.1862 Bradford MA; D8.20.1886 Malden MA; d7.9																									
1884	KC U	0	3	.000	3	3	3	0	26	49	39	0	—	4	8	8.65	26	.377	.396	16	.313	0*	70	-17	—	-1.3
BLAKE, ED	Edward James; B12.23.1925 E.St.Louis IL; BR/TR/5´11˝/175; d5.1																									
1951	Cin N	0	0	ø	3	0	0	0	4	10	5	3	0	1	1	11.25	36	.476	.500	0	ø	0	—	-3	0	-0.1
1952	Cin N	0	0	ø	2	0	0	0	3	3	0	0	0	0	0	0.00	ø	.250	.250	0	ø	0	—	1	0	0.1
1953	Cin N	0	0	ø	1	0	0	0	0	1	2	0	0	1	0	(2)	ø	1.000	1.000	0	ø	0	—	-2	0	-0.2
1957	KC A	0	0	ø	2	0	0	0	1.2	1	1	1	0	2-1	0	5.40	73	.167	.375	0	ø	0	—	0	0	0.0
Total	4	0	0	ø	8	0	0	0	8.2	15	8	4	0	4-1	1	8.31	48	.375	.432	0	ø	0	—	-4	0	-0.2
BLAKE, SHERIFF	John Frederick; B9.17.1899 Ansted WV; D10.31.1982 Beckley WV; BB/TR/6´0˝/180; d6.29; Col West Virginia Wesleyan																									
1920	Pit N	0	0	ø	6	0	0	0	13.1	21	14	0	1	6	7	8.10	40	.368	.438	4	.250	-0	—	-7	—	-0.3
1924	Chi N	6	6	.500	29	11	4	1	106.1	123	58	3	2	44	42	4.57	85	.299	.370	31-0-1	.290	1	99	-5	—	-0.4
1925	Chi N	10	18	.357	36	31	14	2	231.1	260	144	17	5	114	93	4.86	89	.287	.370	79-0-3	.152	-4	78	-14	—	-1.8
1926	Chi N	11	12	.478	39	27	11-4	1	197.2	204	91	7	6	92	95	3.60	107	.280	.366	65-0-3	.215	-1	80	7	—	0.7
1927	Chi N	13	14	.481	32	27	13-2	0	224.1	238	101	3	4	82	64	3.29	117	.282	.348	83-0-4	.193	-2	104	12	—	1.3
1928	Chi N	17	11	.607	34	29	16-4	1	240.2	209	80	4	3	101	78	2.47	156	.240	.321	88-0-7	.216	0*	98	37	—	4.0
1929	†Chi N	14	13	.519	35	29	13-1	1	218.1	244	122	8	2	103	70	4.29	108	.291	.370	81-0-5	.173	-2*	123	8	—	0.6
1930	Chi N	10	14	.417	34	24	7	0	186.2	213	127	14	3	99	80	4.82	101	.291	.378	66-0-3	.227	-1*	95	-3	—	-0.4
1931	Chi N	0	4	.000	16	5	0	0	50	64	34	4	1	26	29	5.22	74	.312	.392	16	.500	3	124	-8	—	-0.2
	Phi N	4	5	.444	14	9	1	1	71	90	49	2	3	35	31	5.58	76	.305	.384	25	.240	0	97	-8	—	-0.8
	Year	4	9	.308	30	14	1	1	121	154	83	6	4	61	60	5.43	75	.308	.388	41	.341	3	106	-17	—	-1.0
1937	StL A	2	2	.500	15	1	0	1	36.2	55	33	5	0	20	12	7.61	63	.350	.424	10-0-1	.100	-1	144	-10	—	-1.0
	StL N	0	3	.000	14	2	2	0	43.2	45	23	1	0	18	20	3.71	107	.271	.342	10-0-1	.300	0	65	1	—	0.1
Total	10	87	102	.460	304	195	81-11	8	1620	1766	876	68	30	740	621	4.13	101	.284	.363	558-0-28	.211	-6	97	10	—	1.8
BLANCHE, AL	Prosper Albert (b Prosper Bilangio); B9.21.1909 Somerville MA; D4.2.1997 Melrose MA; BR/TR/6´0˝/178; d8.23; Col Providence																									
1935	Bos N	0	0	ø	6	0	0	0	17.1	14	3	0	0	5	4	1.56	243	.230	.288	6	.167	-0	—	5	—	0.2
1936	Bos N	0	1	.000	11	0	0	1	16	20	15	1	1	8	4	6.19	62	.303	.387	4	.250	0	—	-5	—	-0.3
Total	2	0	1	.000	17	0	0	1	33.1	34	18	1	1	13	8	3.78	101	.268	.340	10	.200	-0	—	0	—	-0.1
BLANCO, GIL	Gilbert Henry; B12.15.1945 Phoenix AZ; BL/TL/6´5˝/(205–217); d4.24; Col Phoenix (AZ) JC																									
1965	NY A	1	1	.500	17	1	0	0	20.1	16	10	1	1	12-0	14	3.98	85	.232	.341	0	ø	0	26	-1	0	-0.1
1966	KC A	2	4	.333	11	8	0	0	38.1	31	26	3	4	36-1	21	4.70	72	.237	.415	12-0-1	.167	-0	84	-7	0	-1.0
Total	2	3	5	.375	28	9	0	0	58.2	47	36	4	5	48-1	35	4.45	76	.235	.391	12-0-1	.167	-0	78	-8	0	-1.1
BLAND, NATE	Nathan Garrett; B12.27.1974 Birmingham AL; BL/TL/6´5˝/190; [LAN93 4/102]; d5.5																									
2003	Hou N	1	2	.333	22	0	0	0-1	20.1	22	13	3	2	12-2	18	5.75	77	.286	.391	0	ø	0	—	-2	0	-0.3
BLANDING, FRED	Frederick James "Fritz"; B2.8.1886 Redlands CA; D7.16.1950 Salem VA; BR/TR/5´11˝/185; d9.15; Col Michigan																									
1910	Cle A	2	2	.500	6	5	4-1	0	45.1	43	19	0	4	12	25	2.78	93	.254	.319	18	.111	-1	99	-1	—	-0.2
1911	Cle A	7	11	.389	29	16	11	2	176	190	95	5	6	60	80	3.68	93	.283	.347	65-0-1	.262	2*	70	-4	—	-0.2
1912	Cle A	18	14	.563	39	31	23-1	1	262	259	117	4	3	79	75	2.92	117	.267	.324	93-1-9	.226	1	106	14	—	1.7
1913	Cle A	15	10	.600	41	22	14-3	0	215	234	79	6	3	72	63	2.55	119	.284	.344	86-0-2	.244	4	101	13	—	1.7
1914	Cle A	4	9	.308	29	12	5	0	116	133	82	0	1	54	35	3.96	73	.301	.378	39	.103	-2*	69	-16	—	-1.9
Total	5	46	46	.500	144	86	57-5	3	814.1	859	392	15	17	277	278	3.13	102	.279	.342	301-1-12	.216	4	92	6	—	1.1
BLANK, MATT	Clarence Matthew; B4.5.1976 Texarkana TX; BL/TL/6´2˝/195; [MonN97 11/346]; d4.3; Col Texas A&M																									
2000	Mon N	0	1	.000	13	0	0	0-1	14	12	8	1	1	5-1	4	5.14	92	.222	.295	1	.000	-0	—	0	135	0.0
2001	Mon N	2	2	.500	5	4	0	0-0	22.2	23	14	5	2	13-1	11	5.16	84	.267	.369	8	.500	2	112	-2	0	-0.1
Total	2	2	3	.400	18	4	0	0-1	36.2	35	22	6	3	18-2	15	5.15	87	.250	.341	9	.444	2	112	-2	135	-0.1
BLANK, FRED	Frederick August; B6.18.1874 DeSoto MO; D2.5.1936 St.Louis MO; BL/TL/6´0.5˝/175; d6.20																									
1894	Cin N	0	1	.000	1	1	1	0	8	5	4	0	0	9	1	4.50	123	.179	.378	3	.000	-1	26	1	—	0.1
BLANKENSHIP, HOMER	Homer "Si"; B8.4.1902 Bonham TX; D6.22.1974 Longview TX; BR/TR/6´0˝/185; d9.6; b–Ted																									
1922	Chi A	0	0	ø	4	0	0	0	13	21	7	1	0	5	3	4.85	84	.389	.441	4	.000	-1	—	-1	—	-0.1
1923	Chi A	1	1	.500	4	0	0	1	5	9	5	0	0	1	1	3.60	110	.429	.455	0	ø	0	—	-1	—	-0.2
1928	Pit N	0	2	.000	5	2	1	0	21.2	27	15	1	0	9	6	5.82	70	.321	.387	8	.375	1	31	-3	—	-0.2
Total	3	1	3	.250	13	2	1	1	39.2	57	27	2	0	15	10	5.22	78	.358	.414	12	.250	0	31	-5	—	-0.5
BLANKENSHIP, KEVIN	Kevin De Wayne; B1.26.1963 Anaheim CA; BR/TR/6´0˝/(180–185); d9.20; Col Arizona																									
1988	Atl N	0	1	.000	2	2	0	0-0	10.2	7	4	0	1	7-0	5	3.38	109	.194	.341	3	.000	-0	61	1	0	0.0
	Chi N	1	0	1.000	1	1	0	0-0	5	7	4	2	0	1-0	4	7.20	51	.318	.348	3	.000	-0	219	-2	0	-0.3
	Year	1	1	.500	3	3	0	0-0	15.2	14	8	2	1	8-0	9	4.60	80	.241	.343	6	.000	-1	113	-1	0	-0.3
1989	Chi N	0	0	ø	2	0	0	0-0	5.1	4	1	0	0	2-0	2	1.69	224	.200	.273	1	.000	-0	—	1	0	0.0
1990	Chi N	0	2	.000	3	2	0	0-0	12.1	13	10	1	0	6-0	5	5.84	70	.265	.333	4	.000	-0	66	-3	0	-0.4
Total	3	1	3	.250	8	5	0	0-0	33.1	31	19	3	1	16-0	16	4.59	84	.244	.329	11	.000	-1	93	-3	0	-0.7
BLANKENSHIP, TED	Theodore; B5.10.1901 Bonham TX; D1.14.1945 Atoka OK; BR/TR/6´1˝/170; d7.2; b–Homer																									
1922	Chi A	8	10	.444	24	15	7	1	127.2	124	58	4	2	47	42	3.81	107	.266	.335	41-0-3	.171	-1	78	5	—	0.5
1923	Chi A	9	14	.391	44	23	9-1	0	204.2	219	115	8	4	100	57	4.35	91	.287	.372	76-3-2	.211	2	88	-8	—	-0.7
1924	Chi A	7	6	.538	25	11	7	1	129.1	167	79	1	1	38	36	5.01	82	.317	.364	46-1-3	.326	6	140	-10	—	-0.5
1925	Chi A	17	8	.680	40	23	16-3	1	232	218	90	11	0	69	81	3.03	137	.253	.308	88-2-4	.205	2	110	31	—	2.9
1926	Chi A	13	10	.565	29	26	15-1	1	209.1	217	96	13	1	65	66	3.61	107	.273	.328	76-0-6	.132	-2	114	7	—	0.4
1927	Chi A	12	17	.414	37	34	11-3	0	236.2	280	156	14	2	74	51	5.06	80	.299	.352	80-3-1	.188	3*	93	-26	—	-2.5
1928	Chi A	9	11	.450	27	22	8	0	158	186	92	9	2	80	36	4.61	88	.306	.388	59-0-3	.169	-2	91	-8	—	-1.1
1929	Chi A	0	2	.000	8	1	0	0	18.1	28	18	3	0	9	7	8.84	48	.359	.425	4	.250	-0	20	-8	—	-0.7

YEAR	TM LG	W	L	PCT	G	GS	CG-SHO	SV-BS	IP	H	R	HR	HB	BB-iB	SO	ERA	AERA	OAV	OOB	AB-HR-SH	AVG	PB	SUP	APR	DL	PW
1930	Chi A	2	1	.667	7	1	0	0	14.2	23	15	0	1	7	2	9.20	50	.371	.443	5	.200	-0	74	-6	—	-1.0
Total	9	77	79	.494	241	156	73-8	4	1330.2	1462	719	63	13	489	378	4.29	94	.287	.351	475-9-22	.196	7	99	-23	—	-2.7
Blanton, Cy	Darrell Elijah; B7.6.1908 Waurika OK; D9.13.1945 Norman OK; BL/TR/5´11.5˝/180; d9.23																									
1934	Pit N	0	1	.000	1	1	0	0	8	5	3	1	1	4	5	3.38	122	.161	.278	1	.000	0	42	1	—	0.1
1935	Pit N	18	13	.581	35	30	23-**4**	1	254.1	220	93	3	2	55	142	**2.58**	**159**	**.229**	**.272**	97-0-3	.134	-4	91	**41**	—	4.4
1936	Pit N	13	15	.464	44	32	15-**4**	3	235.2	235	114	9	3	55	127	3.51	115	.257	.301	84-0-5	.155	-3	94	12	—	1.0
1937	Pit N★	14	12	.538	36	**34**	14-4	0	242.2	250	115	13	5	76	143	3.30	117	.266	.324	85-0-4	.165	-0	102	12	—	1.1
1938	Pit N	11	7	.611	29	26	10-1	0	172.2	190	84	13	2	46	80	3.70	103	.281	.329	64-0-4	.203	-1	132	2	—	0.2
1939	Pit N	2	3	.400	10	6	1	0	42	45	23	4	0	10	11	4.29	90	.266	.307	14	.286	1	102	-2	—	-0.1
1940	Phi N	4	3	.571	13	10	5	0	77	82	43	7	1	21	24	4.32	90	.272	.322	24-0-2	.083	-1	85	-4	—	-0.5
1941	Phi N☆	6	13	.316	28	25	7-1	0	163.2	186	98	11	3	57	64	4.51	82	.284	.344	51-0-4	.118	-2	82	-16	0	-2.0
1942	Phi N	0	4	.000	6	3	0	0	22.1	30	15	3	1	13	15	5.64	59	.345	.436	8	.125	-0	59	-5	0	-0.9
Total	9	68	71	.489	202	167	75-14	4	1218.1	1243	588	64	18	337	611	3.55	110	.262	.314	428-0-22	.154	-11	98	41	0	3.3
Blanton, Joe	Joseph Matthew; B12.11.1980 Bowling Green KY; BR/TR/6´3˝/(225–240); [OakA02 1/24]; d9.21; Col Kentucky																									
2004	Oak A	0	0	ø	3	0	0	0-0	8	6	5	1	0	2-0	6	5.63	82	.214	.267	0	ø	0	—	-1	0	0.0
2005	Oak A	12	12	.500	33	33	2	0-0	201.1	178	86	23	5	67-3	116	3.53	124	.236	.300	3-0-1	.333	0	91	19	0	2.0
2006	†Oak A	16	12	.571	32	31	1-1	0-0	194.1	241	111	17	5	58-4	107	4.82	94	.309	.356	2-0-1	.000	-0	99	-6	0	-0.9
Total	3	28	24	.538	68	64	3-1	0-0	403.2	425	202	41	10	127-7	229	4.19	106	.272	.328	5-0-2	.200	0	95	12	0	1.1
Blasingame, Wade	Wade Allen; B11.22.1943 Deming NM; BL/TL/6´1˝/(185–190); d9.17																									
1963	Mil N	0	0	ø	2	0	0	0	3	7	4	0	0	2-0	3	12.00	27	.467	.529	0	ø	0	—	-3	0	-0.1
1964	Mil N	9	5	.643	28	13	3-1	2	116.2	113	58	15	0	51-2	70	4.24	83	.257	.333	40-1-0	.175	3*	142	-7	0	-0.5
1965	Mil N	16	10	.615	38	36	10-1	1	224.2	200	103	17	5	116-10	117	3.77	94	.244	.339	81-1-3	.185	3	119	-5	0	-0.1
1966	Atl N	3	7	.300	16	12	0	0	67.2	71	42	5	2	25-2	34	5.32	68	.272	.340	23	.217	1*	75	-11	22	-1.4
1967	Atl N	1	0	1.000	10	4	0	0	25.1	27	13	1	1	21-1	20	4.62	72	.287	.422	7	.143	0	165	-3	0	-0.1
	Hou N	4	7	.364	15	14	0	0	77	91	57	9	2	27-2	46	5.96	56	.298	.357	22-0-2	.182	2*	133	-22	0	-2.6
	Year	5	7	.417	25	18	0	0	102.1	118	70	10	3	48-3	66	5.63	59	.296	.374	29-0-2	.172	2	140	-25	0	-2.7
1968	Hou N	1	2	.333	22	2	0	1	36	45	21	3	0	10-1	22	4.75	62	.308	.348	5	.000	0	147	-7	51	-0.5
1969	Hou N	0	5	.000	26	5	0	1-1	52	66	47	4	2	33-7	33	5.37	66	.306	.396	12	.000	-1*	50	-15	0	-1.5
1970	Hou N	3	3	.500	13	13	1	0-0	77.2	76	34	4	2	23-3	55	3.48	112	.261	.318	24	.083	-0	96	3	0	0.2
1971	Hou N	9	11	.450	30	28	2	0-0	158.1	177	90	11	13	45-3	93	4.60	73	.285	.344	49-1-2	.204	4	119	-23	0	-2.1
1972	Hou N	0	0	ø	10	0	0	0-0	8.1	4	9	1	2	8-0	9	8.64	39	.148	.368	0	ø	0	—	-5	0	-0.3
	NY A	0	1	.000	12	1	0	0-0	17	14	8	5	1	11-1	7	4.24	71	.250	.382	2-0-1	.000	0	59	-2	0	0.0
Total	10	46	51	.474	222	128	16-2	5-1	863.2	891	486	75	30	372-32	512	4.52	77	.271	.348	265-3-8	.166	14	115	-100	73	-9.0
Blass, Steve	Stephen Robert; B4.18.1942 Canaan CT; BR/TR/6´0˝/(160–170); d5.10																									
1964	Pit N	5	8	.385	24	13	3-1	0	104.2	107	52	9	1	45-5	67	4.04	87	.266	.339	30-0-2	.067	-1	91	-6	0	-0.8
1966	Pit N	11	7	.611	34	25	1	0	155.2	173	80	12	2	46-1	76	3.87	92	.284	.336	52-0-2	.231	1	109	-8	0	-0.8
1967	Pit N	6	8	.429	32	16	2	0	126.2	126	65	12	2	47-7	72	3.55	95	.261	.328	39-0-2	.128	-1	104	-6	0	-0.7
1968	Pit N	18	6	**.750**	33	31	12-7	0	220.1	191	64	13	4	57-5	132	2.12	138	.234	.287	80-0-4	.138	-1*	142	19	0	2.0
1969	Pit N	16	10	.615	38	32	9	2-0	210	207	119	21	6	86-3	147	4.46	78	.258	.333	84-1-2	.250	6*	146	-24	0	-2.1
1970	Pit N	10	12	.455	31	31	6-1	0-0	196.2	187	92	14	5	73-8	120	3.52	112	.254	.324	70-0-3	.114	-2*	106	7	29	0.4
1971	†Pit N	15	8	.652	33	33	12-**5**	0-0	240	226	81	16	2	68-8	136	2.85	119	.249	.302	83-0-8	.120	-3*	132	17	0	1.3
1972	†Pit N★	19	8	.704	33	32	11-2	0-0	249.2	227	80	18	4	84-8	117	2.49	134	.246	.311	82-0-12	.183	1*	115	24	0	2.9
1973	Pit N	3	9	.250	23	18	1	0-0	88.2	109	98	11	12	84-4	27	9.85	36	.313	.454	24-0-5	.417	4*	129	-59	0	-6.0
1974	Pit N	0	0	ø	1	0	0	0-0	5	5	8	2	0	7-0	2	9.00	39	.238	.429	2	.000	-0	—	-4	0	-0.2
Total	10	103	76	.575	282	231	57-16	2-0	1597.1	1558	739	128	38	597-49	896	3.63	95	.258	.327	546-1-40	.172	4	122	-40	29	-4.0
Blateric, Steve	Stephen Lawrence; B3.20.1944 Denver CO; BR/TR/6´3˝/200; d9.17; Col Denver																									
1971	Cin N	0	0	ø	2	0	0	0-0	2.2	5	4	2	1	0-0	4	13.50	25	.385	.429	0	ø	0	—	-3	0	-0.1
1972	NY A	0	0	ø	1	0	0	0-0	4	2	0	0	0	0-0	4	0.00	ø	.143	.143	1	.000	-0	—	1	0	0.1
1975	Cal A	0	0	ø	2	0	0	0-0	4.1	9	5	0	0	1-0	5	6.23	57	.429	.435	0	ø	0	—	-2	0	-0.1
Total	3	0	0	ø	5	0	0	0-0	11	16	9	2	1	1-0	13	5.73	58	.333	.353	1	.000	-0	—	-4	0	-0.1
Blauvelt, Henry	Henry Russell; B4.8.1873 Nyack NY; D12.28.1926 Portland OR; d6.22																									
1890	Roc AA	0	0	ø	2	0	0	0	12.1	19	23	0	0	8	5	10.22	35	.339	.422	6	.500	1	—	-10	—	-0.3
Blaylock, Gary	Gary Nelson; B10.11.1931 Clarkton MO; BR/TR/6´0˝/198; d4.10; C4																									
1959	StL N	4	5	.444	26	12	3	0	100	117	61	14	2	43-3	61	5.13	83	.298	.366	34-2-1	.118	0*	81	-8	0	-0.7
	NY A	0	1	.000	15	1	0	0	25.2	30	13	0	1	15-0	20	3.51	104	.306	.400	2	.500	1	48	0	0	0.0
Total	1	4	6	.400	41	13	3	0	125.2	147	74	14	3	58-3	81	4.80	86	.300	.373	36-2-1	.139	1	80	-8	0	-0.7
Blaylock, Bob	Robert Edward; B6.28.1935 Chattanooga OK; BR/TR/6´1˝/(185–198); d7.22																									
1956	StL N	1	6	.143	14	6	0	0	41	45	32	7	0	24-1	39	6.37	59	.276	.369	11	.091	-1	101	-11	0	-1.7
1959	StL N	0	1	.000	3	1	0	0	9	8	5	1	0	3-0	3	4.00	106	.229	.289	1	.000	-0	232	0	0	0.0
Total	2	1	7	.125	17	7	0	0	50	53	37	8	0	27-1	42	5.94	65	.268	.356	12	.083	-1	121	-11	0	-1.7
Blazier, Ron	Ronald Patrick; B7.30.1971 Altoona PA; BR/TR/6´6˝/(205–248); d5.31; [DL 1998 Phi N 181]																									
1996	Phi N	3	1	.750	27	0	0	0-0	38.1	49	30	6	0	10-3	25	5.87	73	.310	.347	1	1.000	0	—	-7	0	-0.7
1997	Phi N	1	1	.500	36	0	0	0-0	53.2	62	31	8	0	21-3	42	5.03	84	.290	.347	5-0-1	.400	1	—	-4	0	-0.2
Total	2	4	2	.667	63	0	0	0-0	92	111	61	14	0	31-6	67	5.38	79	.298	.347	6-0-1	.500	1	—	-11	181	-0.9
Blemker, Ray	Raymond; B8.9.1937 Huntingburg IN; D2.15.1994 Evansville IN; BR/TL/5´11˝/190; d7.3; Col Georgia Tech																									
1960	KC A	0	0	ø	1	0	0	0	1.2	3	5	1	1	2-0	0	27.00	15	.375	.545	0	ø	0	—	-4	0	-0.2
Blethen, Clarence	Clarence Waldo "Climax"; B7.11.1893 Dover-Foxcroft ME; D4.11.1973 Frederick MD; BL/TR/5´11˝/165; d9.17; Col Maine																									
1923	Bos A	0	0	ø	5	0	0	0	17.2	29	15	0	0	7	2	7.13	58	.382	.434	6	.000	-1	—	-5	—	-0.4
1929	Bro N	0	0	ø	2	0	0	0	2	4	2	0	0	3	0	9.00	51	.444	.583	0	ø	0	—	-1	—	0.0
Total	2	0	0	ø	7	0	0	0	19.2	33	17	0	0	10	2	7.32	57	.388	.453	6	.000	-1	—	-6	—	-0.4
Blewett, Bob	Robert Lawrence; B6.28.1877 Fond Du Lac WI; D3.17.1958 Sedro Woolley WA; BL/TL/5´11˝/170; d6.17; Col Beloit																									
1902	NY N	0	2	.000	5	3	2	0	28	39	26	0	1	7	8	4.82	58	.328	.370	10	.000	-1	81	-7	—	-0.6
Bliss, Elmer	Elmer Ward; B3.9.1875 Penfield PA; D3.18.1962 Bradford PA; BL/TR/6´0˝/180; d9.28																									
1903	NY A	1	0	1.000	1	0	0	0	7	4	1	0	0	0	3	0.00	ø	.167	.167	3	.000	-0	—	2	—	0.2
Blomdahl, Ben	Benjamin Earl; B12.30.1970 Long Beach CA; BR/TR/6´2˝/185; [DetA90 14/373]; d4.28; Col Riverside (CA) CC																									
1995	Det A	0	0	ø	14	0	0	1-0	24.1	36	21	5	0	13-0	15	7.77	62	.356	.430	0	ø	0	—	-7	0	-0.3
Blong, Joe	Joseph Myles; B9.17.1853 St.Louis MO; D9.17.1892 St.Louis MO; BR/TR; d5.4; ▲																									
1875	RS NA	3	12	.200	15	15	12-1	0	129	169	121	0	—	2	14	3.07	71	.284	.286	68	.147	-4*	47	-10	—	-0.9
1876	StL N	0	0	ø	1	0	0	0	4	2	0	0	—	1	0	0.00	ø	.154	.214	264	.235	-0*	—	1	—	0.1
1877	StL N	10	9	.526	25	21	17	0	187.1	203	121	0	—	38	51	2.74	95	.262	.296	218	.216	0*	106	-5	—	-0.5
Total	2	10	9	.526	26	21	17	0	191.1	205	121	0	—	39	51	2.68	97	.260	.295	482	.226	0	106	-4	—	-0.4
Blue, Vida	Vida Rochelle; B7.28.1949 Mansfield LA; BB/TL (BL 1969)/6´0˝/(182–200); [OakA67 2/27]; d7.20																									
1969	Oak A	1	1	.500	12	4	0	1-0	42	49	34	13	0	18-1	24	6.64	52	.290	.358	10	.000	-0	154	-16	0	-0.9
1970	Oak A	2	0	1.000	6	6	2-2	0-0	38.2	20	12	0	1	12-0	35	2.09	168	.152	.228	15-1-1	.200	2	131	6	0	0.5
1971	†Oak A★	24	8	.750	39	39	24-**8**	0-0	312	209	73	19	4	88-3	301	**1.82**	183	**.189**	**.251**	18-0-13	.118	-2	107	54	0	5.3
1972	†Oak A	6	10	.375	25	23	5-4	0-0	151	117	55	11	1	48-3	111	2.80	102	.215	.277	45-0-2	.044	-2*	92	0	0	-0.4
1973	†Oak A	20	9	.690	37	37	13-4	0-0	263.2	214	108	26	4	105-2	158	3.28	109	.224	.300	1	.000	-0*	125	10	0	1.0
1974	†Oak A	17	15	.531	40	40	12-1	0-0	282.1	246	118	17	1	98-7	174	3.25	103	.236	.299	0	ø	0	122	4	0	0.1
1975	†Oak A★	22	11	.667	39	38	13-2	1-0	278	243	103	21	5	99-4	189	3.01	121	.236	.305	0	ø	0	135	22	0	2.4
1976	Oak A	18	13	.581	37	37	20-6	0-0	298.1	268	90	9	1	63-3	166	2.35	143	.239	.279	0	ø	0	92	34	0	3.5
1977	Oak A✳	14	19	.424	38	38	16-1	0-0	279.2	284	138	23	1	86-5	157	3.83	105	.264	.317	1	.000	-0	70	6	0	0.6

YEAR	TM LG	W	L	PCT	G	GS	CG-SHO	SV-BS	IP	H	R	HR	HB	BB-IB	SO	ERA	AERA	OAV	OOB	AB-HR-SH	AVG	PB	SUP	APR	DL	PW
1978	SF N★	18	10	.643	35	35	9-4	0-0	258	233	87	12	0	70-4	171	2.79	124	.246	.295	79-1-5	.076	2	101	21	0	2.4
1979	SF N	14	14	.500	34	34	10	0-0	237	246	143	23	1	111-11	138	5.01	70	.272	.348	83-1-8	.120	0*	124	-40	0	-4.0
1980	SF N✳	14	10	.583	31	31	10-3	0-0	224	202	79	14	0	61-8	129	2.97	118	.242	.292	68-0-7	.074	-4	83	16	35	1.4
1981	SF N★	8	6	.571	18	18	1	0-0	124.2	97	40	7	1	54-3	63	2.45	139	.217	.302	35-0-5	.200	2	80	13	0	1.8
1982	KC A	13	12	.520	31	31	6-2	0-0	181	163	80	20	0	80-3	103	3.78	108	.238	.316	0	ø	0	97	8	0	1.0
1983	KC A	0	5	.000	19	14	1	0-0	85.1	96	62	12	2	35-0	53	6.01	68	.286	.352	0	ø	0	101	-17	0	-0.9
1985	SF N	8	8	.500	33	20	1	0-0	131	115	70	17	1	80-1	103	4.47	78	.240	.348	30-0-8	.133	0	122	-13	0	-1.3
1986	SF N	10	10	.500	28	28	0	0-0	156.2	137	65	19	0	77-3	100	3.27	108	.239	.326	43-1-4	.093	1	100	5	26	0.7
Total	17	209	161	.565	502	473	143-37	2-0	3343.1	2939	1357	263	23	1185-61	2175	3.27	108	.237	.303	512-4-53	.104	-2	106	113	61	13.2
BLUEJACKET, JIM	James (b James Smith); B7.8.1887 Adair OK; D3.26.1947 Pekin IL; BR/TR/6´2.5˝/200; d8.6; ggs–Bill Wilkinson																									
1914	Bro F	4	5	.444	17	7	3-1	1	67	77	34	2	0	19	29	3.76	76	.302	.350	22	.136	-1	89	-6	—	-0.7
1915	Bro F	10	11	.476	24	21	10-2	0	162.2	155	74	2	0	75	48	3.15	86	.258	.340	61-0-1	.131	-4	98	-7	—	-1.5
1916	Cin N	0	1	.000	3	2	0	0	7	12	6	0	0	3	1	7.71	34	.400	.455	2	.000	-0	144	-3	—	-0.5
Total	3	14	17	.452	44	30	13-3	1	236.2	244	114	4	0	97	78	3.46	80	.275	.347	85-0-1	.129	-5	98	-16	—	-2.7
BLUMA, JAIME	James Andrew; B5.18.1972 Beaufort SC; BR/TR/5´11˝/195; [KCA94 3/79]; d8.9; Col Wichita St.; [DL 1997 KC A 181]																									
1996	KC A	0	0	ø	17	0	0	5-0	20	18	9	2	2	4-1	14	3.60	140	.247	.300	0	ø	0	—	3	0	0.2
BLUME, CLINT	Clinton Willis; B10.17.1898 Brooklyn NY; D6.12.1973 Islip NY; BR/TR/5´11˝/175; d9.30; Col Colgate																									
1922	NY N	1	0	1.000	1	1	1	0	9	7	3	0	0	1	2	1.00	400	.212	.235	1	1.000	1	102	2	—	0.4
1923	NY N	2	0	1.000	12	1	0	0	24	22	11	0	2	20	2	3.75	102	.265	.419	5	.000	-0	129	0	—	0.0
Total	2	3	0	1.000	13	2	1	0	33	29	14	0	2	21	4	3.00	129	.250	.374	6	.167	1	117	2	—	0.4
BLYLEVEN, BERT	Rik Aalbert; B4.6.1951 Zeist, Netherlands; BR/TR/6´3˝/(190–220); [MinA69 3/55]; d6.5; [DL 1991 Cal A 182]																									
1970	†Min A	10	9	.526	27	25	5-1	0-0	164	143	66	17	2	47-6	135	3.18	116	.232	.288	50-0-7	.140	-1	94	10	0	0.9
1971	Min A	16	15	.516	38	38	17-5	0-0	278.1	267	95	21	5	59-1	224	2.81	126	.255	.297	91-0-7	.132	-3	87	23	0	2.2
1972	Min A	17	17	.500	39	38	11-3	0-0	287.1	247	93	22	10	69-7	228	2.73	118	.233	.285	94-0-11	.160	-1	105	20	0	2.4
1973	Min A★	20	17	.541	40	40	25-**9**	0-0	325	296	109	16	9	67-4	258	2.52	**158**	.242	.284	0	ø	0	93	**48**	0	5.3
1974	Min A	17	17	.500	37	37	19-3	0-0	281	244	99	14	9	77-3	249	2.66	141	.233	.290	0	ø	0	96	31	0	3.7
1975	Min A	15	10	.600	35	35	20-3	0-0	275.2	219	104	24	4	84-2	233	3.00	128	.219	.281	0	ø	0	110	26	0	2.3
1976	Min A	4	5	.444	12	12	4	0-0	95.1	101	39	3	4	35-5	75	3.12	115	.283	.351	0	ø	0	74	5	0	0.4
	Tex A	9	11	.450	24	24	14-6	0-0	202.1	182	67	11	8	46-1	144	2.76	130	.242	.292	0	ø	0	64	20	0	2.1
	Year	13	16	.448	36	36	18-6	0-0	297.2	283	106	14	12	81-6	219	2.87	125	.255	.312	0	ø	0	67	24	0	2.5
1977	Tex A	14	12	.538	30	30	15-5	0-0	234.2	181	81	20	7	69-1	182	2.72	150	.214	.278	0	ø	0	107	35	0	3.7
1978	Pit N	14	10	.583	34	34	11-4	0-0	243.2	217	94	17	6	66-5	182	3.03	123	.235	.290	85-0-7	.129	-2*	102	19	0	1.6
1979	†Pit N	12	5	.706	37	37	4	0-0	237.1	238	102	21	6	92-8	172	3.60	109	.265	.335	70-0-15	.129	-3*	105	10	0	0.3
1980	Pit N	8	13	.381	34	32	5-2	0-2	216.2	219	102	20	0	59-5	168	3.82	97	.262	.310	61-0-9	.082	-4*	82	-3	0	-0.7
1981	Cle A	11	7	.611	20	20	9-1	0-0	159.1	145	52	9	5	40-1	107	2.88	128	.245	.296	0	ø	0	99	16	0	1.7
1982	Cle A	2	2	.500	4	4	0	0-0	20.1	16	14	2	0	11-0	19	4.87	85	.211	.303	0	ø	0	121	-2	155	-0.4
1983	Cle A	7	10	.412	24	24	5	0-0	156.1	160	74	8	10	44-4	123	3.91	109	.267	.325	0	ø	0	81	6	0	0.7
1984	Cle A	19	7	.731	33	32	12-4	0-0	245	204	86	19	6	74-4	170	2.87	144	.224	.285	0	ø	0	116	33	18	3.4
1985	Cle A★	9	11	.450	23	23	15-4	0-0	179.2	163	76	14	7	49-1	129	3.26	128	.240	.296	0	ø	0	92	16	0	1.6
	Min A	8	5	.615	14	14	9-1	0-0	114	101	45	9	2	26-0	77	3.00	148	.237	.281	0	ø	0	78	16	0	1.7
	Year	17	16	.515	37	**37**	**24-5**	0-0	**293.2**	264	121	23	9	75-1	**206**	3.16	135	.239	.290	0	ø	0	86	32	0	3.3
1986	Min A	17	14	.548	36	36	16-3	0-0	**271.2**	262	134	50	10	58-4	215	4.01	108	.250	.294	0	ø	0	95	9	0	0.9
1987	†Min A	15	12	.556	37	37	8-1	0-0	267	249	132	46	9	101-4	196	4.01	116	.249	.321	0	ø	0	98	17	0	1.6
1988	Min A	10	17	.370	33	33	7	0-0	207.1	240	128	21	16	51-1	145	5.43	75	.294	.345	0	ø	0	93	-27	16	-3.1
1989	Cal A	17	5	.773	33	33	8-**5**	0-0	241	225	76	14	8	44-2	131	2.73	140	.248	.287	0	ø	0	114	32	0	2.8
1990	Cal A	8	7	.533	23	23	2	0-0	134	163	85	15	7	25-0	69	5.24	73	.303	.339	0	ø	0	109	-19	54	-1.9
1992	Cal A	8	12	.400	25	24	1	0-0	133	150	76	17	5	29-2	70	4.74	85	.285	.326	0	ø	0	72	-10	0	-1.4
Total	22	287	250	.534	692	685	242-60	0-2	4970	4632	2029	430	155	1322-71	3701	3.31	118	.247	.301	451-0-56	.131	-14	96	331	425	31.8
BLYZKA, MIKE	Michael John (b Michael John Bliska); B12.25.1928 Hamtramck MI; D10.13.2004 Cheyenne WY; BR/TR/5´11.5˝/190; d4.21																									
1953	StL A	2	6	.250	33	9	2	0	94.1	110	78	6	0	56	23	6.39	66	.292	.383	23-0-2	.000	-3	73	-23	0	-2.0
1954	Bal A	1	5	.167	37	0	0	1	86.1	83	48	2	0	51	35	4.69	76	.254	.351	15-0-1	.133	-1	—	-10	0	-0.7
Total	2	3	11	.214	70	9	2	1	180.2	193	126	8	0	107	58	5.58	70	.274	.368	38-0-3	.053	-4	73	-33	0	-2.7
BOARDMAN, CHARLIE	Charles Louis; B3.27.1893 Seneca Falls NY; D8.10.1968 Sacramento CA; BL/TR/6´2.5˝/194; d9.26																									
1913	Phi A	0	2	.000	2	2	1	0	9	10	5	0	0	6	4	2.00	138	.323	.432	3	.000	-0	54	0	—	-0.1
1914	Phi A	0	0	ø	2	0	0	0	7.1	10	5	0	0	4	2	4.91	53	.357	.438	2	.000	-0	—	-2	—	-0.1
1915	StL N	1	0	1.000	3	1	1	0	19	12	12	0	0	15	7	2.84	98	.188	.342	7	.286	0	160	-2	—	-0.1
Total	3	1	2	.333	7	3	2	0	35.1	32	22	0	0	25	13	3.06	90	.260	.385	12	.167	-0	90	-4	—	-0.3
BOCHTLER, DOUG	Douglas Eugene; B7.5.1970 W.Palm Beach FL; BR/TR/6´3˝/(200–205); [MonN89 9/228]; d5.5; Col Indian River (FL) CC																									
1995	SD N	4	4	.500	34	0	0	1-3	45.1	38	18	5	0	19-0	45	3.57	114	.239	.318	2	.000	-0	—	4	0	0.6
1996	†SD N	2	4	.333	63	0	0	3-4	65.2	45	25	6	1	39-8	68	3.02	134	.195	.311	0	ø	0	—	7	0	0.6
1997	SD N	3	6	.333	54	0	0	2-1	60.1	51	35	3	1	50-4	46	4.77	82	.229	.368	0	ø	0	—	-6	15	-0.8
1998	Det A	0	2	.000	51	0	0	0-2	67.1	73	48	17	3	42-6	45	6.15	77	.279	.381	0	ø	0	—	-9	0	-0.5
1999	LA N	0	0	ø	12	0	0	0-0	13	11	8	3	1	6-1	7	5.54	79	.224	.316	0	ø	0	—	-1	0	-0.1
2000	KC A	0	2	.000	6	0	0	0-0	8.1	13	6	2	0	10-4	4	6.48	81	.371	.511	0	ø	0	—	-1	0	-0.2
Total	6	9	18	.333	220	0	0	6-10	260	231	140	36	6	166-23	215	4.57	93	.241	.353	2	.000	-0	—	-6	15	-0.4
BOCKUS, RANDY	Randy Walter; B10.5.1960 Canton OH; BL/TR/6´2˝/(195–205); [SFN82 34/796]; d9.10; Col Kent St.																									
1986	SF N	0	0	ø	5	0	0	0-0	7	7	5	1	0	6-1	4	2.57	137	.241	.371	1	.000	-0*	—	0	0	0.0
1987	SF N	1	0	1.000	12	0	0	0-1	17.1	17	8	2	0	4-1	9	3.63	106	.266	.309	1	.000	-0	—	0	0	0.0
1988	SF N	1	1	.500	20	0	0	0-1	32	35	19	2	1	13-2	18	4.78	68	.297	.368	6	.167	0	—	-6	0	-0.3
1989	Det A	0	0	ø	2	0	0	0-0	5.1	7	3	0	0	2-1	2	5.06	76	.333	.391	0	ø	0	—	-1	0	0.0
Total	4	2	1	.667	39	0	0	0-2	61.2	66	35	5	1	25-5	33	4.23	83	.284	.355	8	.125	-0	—	-7	0	-0.3
BODDICKER, MIKE	Michael James; B8.23.1957 Cedar Rapids IA; BR/TR/5´11˝/(172–190); [BalA78 6/152]; d10.4; Col Iowa																									
1980	Bal A	0	1	.000	1	1	0	0-0	7.1	6	6	1	0	5-0	4	6.14	65	.207	.324	0	ø	0	90	-2	0	-0.2
1981	Bal A	0	0	ø	2	0	0	0-0	5.2	6	4	1	0	2-0	2	4.76	77	.261	.320	0	ø	0	—	-1	0	-0.1
1982	Bal A	1	0	1.000	7	0	0	0-0	25.2	25	10	2	0	12-2	20	3.51	116	.258	.339	0	ø	0	—	2	0	0.1
1983	†Bal A	16	8	.667	27	26	10-**5**	0-0	179	141	65	13	0	52-1	120	2.77	145	**.216**	.273	0	ø	0	104	23	0	3.1
1984	Bal A☆	**20**	11	.645	34	34	16-4	0-0	261.1	218	95	23	5	81-1	128	**2.79**	140	.228	.290	0	ø	0*	100	32	0	3.9
1985	Bal A	12	17	.414	32	32	9-2	0-0	203.1	227	104	13	5	89-7	135	4.07	100	.286	.361	0	ø	0*	99	-1	0	0.1
1986	Bal A	14	12	.538	33	33	7	0-0	218.1	214	125	30	11	74-4	175	4.70	89	.255	.321	0	ø	0	110	-12	20	-1.1
1987	Bal A	10	12	.455	33	33	7-2	0-0	226	212	114	29	7	78-4	152	4.18	106	.248	.315	0	ø	0*	87	7	0	0.8
1988	Bal A	6	12	.333	21	21	4	0-0	147	149	72	14	11	51-5	100	3.86	102	.265	.333	0	ø	0	71	0	0	0.0
	†Bos A	7	3	.700	15	14	1-1	0-0	89	85	30	3	3	26-1	56	2.63	157	.257	.313	0	ø	0	121	14	0	1.6
	Year	13	15	.464	36	35	5-1	0-0	236	234	102	17	14	77-6	156	3.39	118	.262	.326	0	ø	0	92	14	0	1.6
1989	Bos A	15	11	.577	34	34	3-2	0-0	211.2	217	101	19	10	71-4	145	4.00	103	.267	.330	0	ø	0	104	5	0	0.6
1990	†Bos A	17	8	.680	34	34	4	0-0	228	225	92	16	10	69-6	143	3.36	122	.258	.319	0	ø	0	111	19	0	2.0
1991	KC A	12	12	.500	30	29	1	0-0	180.2	188	89	13	13	59-0	79	4.08	101	.272	.340	0	ø	0	94	3	16	0.4
1992	KC A	1	4	.200	29	8	0	3-0	86.2	92	50	5	8	37-3	47	4.98	82	.269	.351	0	ø	0	61	-7	57	-0.4
1993	Mil A	3	5	.375	10	10	1	0-0	54	77	35	6	4	15-1	24	5.67	76	.338	.387	0	ø	0	96	-7	39	-0.9
Total	14	134	116	.536	342	309	63-16	3-0	2123.2	2082	992	188	87	721-39	1330	3.80	108	.257	.323	0	ø	0	99	75	132	9.9
BOEHLER, GEORGE	George Henry; B1.2.1892 Lawrenceburg IN; D6.23.1958 Lawrenceburg IN; BR/TR/6´2˝/180; d9.13																									
1912	Det A	0	2	.000	5	4	2	0	32	50	31	0	2	14	15	6.47	50	.365	.431	10	.100	-1	108	-11	—	-0.6
1913	Det A	0	1	.000	1	1	1	0	8	11	9	0	2	6	2	6.75	43	.367	.500	3	.333	1	0	-4	—	-0.3
1914	Det A	2	3	.400	18	6	2	0	63	54	39	1	8	48	37	3.57	79	.242	.394	17	.176	1	121	-7	—	-0.5
1915	Det A	1	1	.500	8	0	0	0	15	19	10	0	1	4	7	1.80	168	.328	.381	4	.750	2*	—	0	—	0.1
1916	Det A	1	1	.500	5	2	1	0	13.1	12	8	0	2	9	8	4.73	61	.261	.404	3	.000	0	158	-2	—	-0.3
1920	StL A	0	1	.000	3	1	0	0	7	10	10	1	0	4	2	7.71	51	.303	.378	1	.000	0	162	-4	—	-0.4

YEAR	TM LG	W	L	PCT	G	GS	CG-SHO	SV-BS	IP	H	R	HR	HB	BB-IB	SO	ERA	AERA	OAV	OOB	AB-HR-SH	AVG	PB	SUP	APR	DL	PW
1921	StL A	0	0	ø	1	0	0	0	1	1	0	0	0	0	0	0.00	ø	.500	.500	0	ø	0	—	0	—	0.0
1923	Pit N	1	3	.250	10	3	1	0	28.1	33	26	1	1	26	12	6.04	66	.314	.455	10	.300	1	103	-8	—	-0.9
1926	Bro N	1	0	1.000	10	1	0	0	34.2	42	23	1	3	23	10	4.41	87	.302	.412	12	.250	0*	65	-3	—	-0.2
Total	9	6	12	.333	61	18	7	0	202.1	232	156	4	19	134	93	4.71	70	.300	.416	60	.233	3	110	-39	—	-3.1

BOEHLING, JOE John Joseph; B3.20.1891 Richmond VA; D9.8.1941 Richmond VA; BL/TL/5´11˝/168; d6.20

YEAR	TM LG	W	L	PCT	G	GS	CG-SHO	SV-BS	IP	H	R	HR	HB	BB-IB	SO	ERA	AERA	OAV	OOB	AB-HR-SH	AVG	PB	SUP	APR	DL	PW
1912	Was A	0	0	ø	3	0	0	0	5	4	4	0	2	6	2	7.20	46	.235	.480	0	ø	0	—	-2	—	-0.1
1913	Was A	17	7	.708	38	25	18-3	4	235.1	197	82	3	9	82	110	2.14	138	.236	.312	86-0-1	.221	1	106	18	—	2.2
1914	Was A	13	8	.619	27	24	14-2	0	196	180	76	3	9	76	91	3.03	93	.258	.339	71-0-2	.239	4	107	-1	—	0.4
1915	Was A	14	13	.519	40	32	14-2	0	229.1	217	105	5	9	119	108	3.22	92	.255	.352	75-1-4	.173	0*	97	-4	—	-0.2
1916	Was A	9	11	.450	27	19	7-2	0	139.2	134	62	1	3	54	52	3.09	90	.260	.333	41-0-1	.171	1	66	-5	—	-0.5
	Cle A	2	4	.333	12	9	3	0	60.2	63	23	0	2	23	18	2.67	113	.281	.353	19	.263	1*	67	2	—	0.4
	Year	11	15	.423	39	28	10-2	0	200.1	197	85	1	5	77	70	2.97	96	.266	.339	60-0-1	.200	1	66	-3	—	-0.1
1917	Cle A	1	6	.143	12	7	1	0	46.1	50	27	1	3	16	11	4.66	61	.291	.361	16-0-1	.188	-0*	54	-7	—	-1.0
1920	Cle A	0	1	.000	3	2	0	0	13	16	10	0	0	10	4	4.85	78	.333	.448	4	.500	1	115	-2	—	0.0
Total	7	56	50	.528	162	118	57-9	4	925.1	861	389	13	37	386	396	2.97	98	.256	.340	312-1-9	.212	7	92	-1	—	1.2

BOEHRINGER, BRIAN Brian Edward; B1.8.1969 St.Louis MO; BB/TR/6´2˝/(190–195); [ChiA91 4/124]; d4.30; Col Nevada–Las Vegas

YEAR	TM LG	W	L	PCT	G	GS	CG-SHO	SV-BS	IP	H	R	HR	HB	BB-IB	SO	ERA	AERA	OAV	OOB	AB-HR-SH	AVG	PB	SUP	APR	DL	PW
1995	NY A	0	3	.000	7	3	0	0-1	17.2	24	27	5	1	22-1	10	13.75	34	.320	.475	0	ø	0	74	-18	0	-2.2
1996	†NY A	2	4	.333	15	3	0	0-1	46.1	46	28	6	1	21-2	37	5.44	91	.260	.337	0	ø	0	75	-2	0	-0.2
1997	†NY A	3	2	.600	34	0	0	0-3	48	39	16	4	0	32-6	53	2.63	170	.225	.343	0	ø	0	—	10	87	0.9
1998	†SD N	5	2	.714	56	1	0	0-1	76.1	75	38	10	4	45-4	67	4.36	91	.257	.363	7	.000	-0	23	-3	0	-0.3
1999	SD N	6	5	.545	33	11	0	0-2	94.1	97	38	10	1	35-4	64	3.24	132	.267	.330	16-0-2	.063	-1	92	11	50	1.1
2000	SD N	0	3	.000	7	3	0	0-1	15.2	18	15	4	0	10-0	9	5.74	78	.286	.378	4-0-1	.250	0	41	-4	152	-0.6
2001	NY A	0	1	.000	22	0	0	1-0	34.2	35	15	3	3	12-0	33	3.12	143	.255	.325	0	ø	0	—	4	0	0.2
	SF N	0	3	.000	29	0	0	1-0	34.1	32	20	4	2	17-5	27	4.19	98	.239	.329	3	.000	-0	—	-2	0	-0.2
2002	Pit N	4	4	.500	70	0	0	1-5	79.2	65	30	5	2	33-6	65	3.39	124	.229	.311	0	ø	0	—	8	0	0.7
2003	Pit N	5	4	.556	62	0	0	0-3	62.1	64	39	11	3	30-3	47	5.49	79	.267	.353	0	ø	0	—	-7	0	-1.0
2004	Pit N	1	1	.500	21	0	0	0-2	25.1	27	14	2	1	17-3	20	4.62	94	.293	.398	1	.000	-0	—	-1	124	-0.1
Total	10	26	32	.448	356	21	0	3-19	534.2	522	280	64	18	274-34	432	4.36	99	.257	.347	31-0-3	.065	-1	78	-4	413	-1.7

BOERNER, LARRY Lawrence Hyer; B1.21.1905 Staunton VA; D10.16.1969 Staunton VA; BR/TR/6´4.5˝/175; d6.30; Col McDaniel

YEAR	TM LG	W	L	PCT	G	GS	CG-SHO	SV-BS	IP	H	R	HR	HB	BB-IB	SO	ERA	AERA	OAV	OOB	AB-HR-SH	AVG	PB	SUP	APR	DL	PW
1932	Bos A	0	4	.000	21	5	0	0	61	71	41	2	3	37	19	5.02	90	.302	.404	17-0-1	.000	-3	61	-4	—	-0.4

BOEVER, JOE Joseph Martin; B10.4.1960 Kirkwood MO; BR/TR/6´1˝/(200–215); d7.19; Col Nevada–Las Vegas

YEAR	TM LG	W	L	PCT	G	GS	CG-SHO	SV-BS	IP	H	R	HR	HB	BB-IB	SO	ERA	AERA	OAV	OOB	AB-HR-SH	AVG	PB	SUP	APR	DL	PW
1985	StL N	0	0	ø	13	0	0	0-1	16.1	17	8	3	0	4-1	20	4.41	81	.270	.309	0	ø	0	—	-1	0	-0.1
1986	StL N	0	1	.000	11	0	0	0-0	21.2	19	5	2	0	11-0	8	1.66	222	.232	.323	2	.500	0	—	5	0	0.3
1987	Atl N	1	0	1.000	14	0	0	0-0	18.1	29	15	4	0	12-1	18	7.36	59	.367	.446	0	ø	0	—	-5	0	-0.3
1988	Atl N	0	2	.000	16	0	0	1-0	20.1	12	4	1	1	1-0	7	1.77	207	.182	.206	0	ø	0	—	4	0	0.5
1989	Atl N	4	11	.267	66	0	0	21-9	82.1	78	37	6	1	34-5	68	3.94	93	.252	.328	1	.000	-0	—	-1	0	-0.1
1990	Atl N	1	3	.250	33	0	0	8-4	42.1	40	23	6	0	35-10	35	4.68	86	.252	.383	2	.000	-0	—	-2	0	-0.3
	Phi N	2	3	.400	34	0	0	6-1	46	37	12	0	0	16-2	40	2.15	179	.215	.282	1	.000	-0	—	9	0	1.1
	Year	3	6	.333	67	0	0	14-5	88.1	77	35	6	0	51-12	75	3.36	117	.233	.333	3	.000	-0	—	6	0	0.8
1991	Phi N	3	5	.375	68	0	0	0-2	98.1	90	45	10	0	54-11	89	3.84	96	.245	.336	3	.333	0	—	-1	0	-0.1
1992	Hou N	3	6	.333	**81**	0	0	2-4	111.1	103	38	3	4	45-9	67	2.51	135	.248	.324	7	.000	-1	—	10	0	0.7
1993	Oak A	4	2	.667	42	0	0	0-1	79.1	87	40	8	4	33-4	49	3.86	107	.280	.353	0	ø	0	—	1	0	0.1
	Det A	2	1	.667	19	0	0	3-1	23	14	10	1	0	11-3	14	2.74	159	.179	.269	0	ø	0	—	3	0	0.4
	Year	6	3	.667	61	0	0	3-2	102.1	101	50	9	4	44-7	63	3.61	116	.260	.336	0	ø	0	—	5	0	0.5
1994	Det A	9	2	.818	46	0	0	3-3	81.1	80	40	12	2	37-12	49	3.98	124	.263	.345	0	ø	0	—	8	0	1.0
1995	Det A	5	7	.417	60	0	0	3-3	98.2	128	74	17	3	44-12	71	6.39	75	.319	.384	0	ø	0	—	-16	0	-1.8
1996	Pit N	0	2	.000	13	0	0	2-1	15	17	11	2	1	6-0	6	5.40	81	.288	.364	1	.000	-0	—	-2	0	-0.3
Total	12	34	45	.430	516	0	0	49-30	754.1	751	362	75	16	343-70	541	3.93	103	.262	.341	17	.118	-1	—	12	0	1.1

BOGART, JOHN John Renzie "Big John"; B9.21.1900 Bloomsburg PA; D12.7.1986 Clarence NY; BR/TR/6´2˝/195; d9.17

YEAR	TM LG	W	L	PCT	G	GS	CG-SHO	SV-BS	IP	H	R	HR	HB	BB-IB	SO	ERA	AERA	OAV	OOB	AB-HR-SH	AVG	PB	SUP	APR	DL	PW
1920	Det A	2	1	.667	4	2	0	0	23.2	16	12	0	0	18	5	3.04	122	.195	.340	8	.250	-0	149	1	—	0.1

BOGGS, RAY Raymond Joseph "Lefty"; B12.12.1904 Reamsville KS; D11.27.1989 Grand Junction CO; BL/TL/6´0.5˝/170; d9.1; Col Denver

YEAR	TM LG	W	L	PCT	G	GS	CG-SHO	SV-BS	IP	H	R	HR	HB	BB-IB	SO	ERA	AERA	OAV	OOB	AB-HR-SH	AVG	PB	SUP	APR	DL	PW
1928	Bos N	0	0	ø	4	0	0	0	5	2	3	0	3	7	0	5.40	72	.167	.545	0	ø	0	—	-1	—	0.0

BOGGS, TOMMY Thomas Winton; B10.25.1955 Poughkeepsie NY; BR/TR/6´2˝/(200–209); [TexA74 1/2]; d7.19

YEAR	TM LG	W	L	PCT	G	GS	CG-SHO	SV-BS	IP	H	R	HR	HB	BB-IB	SO	ERA	AERA	OAV	OOB	AB-HR-SH	AVG	PB	SUP	APR	DL	PW
1976	Tex A	1	7	.125	13	13	3	0-0	90.1	87	42	7	1	34-1	36	3.49	103	.257	.322	0	ø	0	64	0	0	0.0
1977	Tex A	0	3	.000	6	6	0	0-0	27.1	40	18	1	1	12-0	15	5.93	69	.351	.417	0	ø	0	107	-5	0	-0.5
1978	Atl N	2	8	.200	16	12	1-1	0-0	59	80	46	8	1	26-3	21	6.71	60	.323	.386	18-1-1	.167	0	48	-14	0	-2.1
1979	Atl N	0	2	.000	3	3	0	0-0	12.2	21	11	0	1	4-0	1	6.39	63	.362	.413	4	.250	0	81	-3	0	-0.4
1980	Atl N	12	9	.571	32	26	4-3	0-0	192.1	180	80	14	4	46-0	84	3.42	108	.249	.295	63-0-6	.159	-2	97	6	0	0.3
1981	Atl N	3	13	.188	25	24	2	0-0	142.2	140	72	11	3	54-4	81	4.10	86	.265	.332	46-0-1	.152	-1	77	-9	0	-1.0
1982	Atl N	2	2	.500	10	10	0	0-0	46.1	43	22	2	2	22-1	29	3.30	112	.253	.345	17-0-1	.235	0	110	1	129	0.1
1983	Atl N	0	0	ø	5	0	0	0-0	6.1	8	4	1	0	1-0	5	5.68	68	.320	.346	0	ø	0	—	-1	151	0.0
1985	Tex A	0	0	ø	4	0	0	0-1	7	13	9	3	0	2-0	6	11.57	37	.382	.417	0	ø	0	—	-5	0	-0.2
Total	9	20	44	.313	114	94	10-4	0-1	584	612	304	47	13	201-9	278	4.22	88	.273	.334	148-1-9	.169	-2	83	-30	280	-3.8

BOGLE, WARREN Warren Frederick; B10.19.1946 Passaic NJ; BL/TL/6´4˝/230; [OakA67 S4/73]; d7.31; Col Miami

YEAR	TM LG	W	L	PCT	G	GS	CG-SHO	SV-BS	IP	H	R	HR	HB	BB-IB	SO	ERA	AERA	OAV	OOB	AB-HR-SH	AVG	PB	SUP	APR	DL	PW
1968	Oak A	0	0	ø	16	1	0	0	23	26	12	3	0	8-1	26	4.30	66	.283	.337	5	.000	-1	185	-4	0	-0.2

BOHANON, BRIAN Brian Edward; B8.1.1968 Denton TX; BL/TL/6´2˝/(210–250); [TexA87 1/19]; d4.10

YEAR	TM LG	W	L	PCT	G	GS	CG-SHO	SV-BS	IP	H	R	HR	HB	BB-IB	SO	ERA	AERA	OAV	OOB	AB-HR-SH	AVG	PB	SUP	APR	DL	PW
1990	Tex A	0	3	.000	11	6	0	0-0	34	40	30	6	2	18-0	15	6.62	60	.296	.380	0	ø	0	77	-11	0	-0.8
1991	Tex A	4	3	.571	11	11	1	0-0	61.1	66	35	4	2	23-0	34	4.84	84	.274	.336	0	ø	0	152	-5	84	-0.5
1992	Tex A	1	1	.500	18	7	0	0-0	45.2	57	38	7	1	25-0	29	6.31	61	.297	.377	0	ø	0	130	-14	15	-0.7
1993	Tex A	4	4	.500	36	8	0	0-1	92.2	107	54	8	4	46-3	45	4.76	88	.296	.377	0	ø	0	104	-6	21	-0.4
1994	Tex A	2	2	.500	11	5	0	0-0	37.1	51	31	7	1	8-1	26	7.23	67	.321	.357	0	ø	0	91	-9	0	-0.7
1995	Det A	1	1	.500	52	10	0	1-0	105.2	121	68	10	4	41-5	63	5.54	87	.285	.350	0	ø	0	139	-7	0	-0.3
1996	Tor A	0	1	.000	20	0	0	1-0	22	27	19	4	2	19-4	17	7.77	64	.303	.429	0	ø	0	—	-6	0	-0.3
1997	NY N	6	4	.600	19	14	0	0-0	94.1	95	49	9	4	34-2	66	3.82	105	.258	.328	33-0-1	.182	0*	122	0	0	0.0
1998	NY N	2	4	.333	25	4	0	0-1	54.1	47	21	4	6	21-2	39	3.15	131	.234	.325	14	.429	2	84	6	0	0.9
	LA N	5	7	.417	14	14	2	0-0	97.1	74	35	9	5	36-0	72	2.40	168	.213	.294	29-0-4	.207	2	73	16	0	2.2
	Year	7	11	.389	39	18	2	0-1	151.2	121	56	13	11	57-2	111	2.67	152	.220	.305	43-0-4	.279	4	75	21	0	3.1
1999	Col N	12	12	.500	33	33	3-1	0-0	197.1	236	146	30	14	92-1	120	6.20	93	.304	.386	71-1-5	.197	-0*	92	-7	0	-0.7
2000	Col N	12	10	.545	34	26	2-1	0-0	177	181	101	24	6	79-4	98	4.68	124	.266	.346	53-2-11	.208	1*	104	17	0	1.9
2001	Col N	5	8	.385	20	19	0	0-0	97	127	79	20	7	47-3	47	7.14	75	.323	.404	31-0-1	.323	2*	104	-14	83	-1.4
Total	12	54	60	.474	304	157	8-2	2-2	1116	1229	706	142	58	489-25	671	5.19	93	.281	.359	231-3-22	.229	8	106	-40	203	-0.8

BOHEN, PAT Leo Ignatius; B9.30.1890 Oakland IA; D4.8.1942 Napa CA; BR/TR/5´10.5˝/155; d10.1

YEAR	TM LG	W	L	PCT	G	GS	CG-SHO	SV-BS	IP	H	R	HR	HB	BB-IB	SO	ERA	AERA	OAV	OOB	AB-HR-SH	AVG	PB	SUP	APR	DL	PW
1913	Phi A	0	1	.000	1	1	1	0	8	3	1	0	0	2	5	1.13	246	.120	.185	3	.000	-0	0	2	—	0.2
1914	Pit N	0	0	ø	1	0	0	0	1	2	2	0	1	2	0	18.00	15	.500	.714	1	.000	-0	—	-2	—	-0.1
Total	2	0	1	.000	2	1	1	0	9	5	3	0	1	4	5	3.00	92	.172	.294	4	.000	-1	0	0	—	0.1

BOHN, CHARLIE Charles; B5.1856 Cleveland OH; D8.1.1903 Cleveland OH; BR/TR/5´9˝/165; d6.20

YEAR	TM LG	W	L	PCT	G	GS	CG-SHO	SV-BS	IP	H	R	HR	HB	BB-IB	SO	ERA	AERA	OAV	OOB	AB-HR-SH	AVG	PB	SUP	APR	DL	PW
1882	Lou AA	1	1	.500	2	2	2	0	18	21	8	0	—	3	1	3.00	83	.273	.300	13	.154	-0*	52	0	—	0.0

BOHNET, JOHN John Kelly; B1.18.1961 Pasadena CA; BB/TL/6´0˝/180; [CleA79 1/7]; d5.10

YEAR	TM LG	W	L	PCT	G	GS	CG-SHO	SV-BS	IP	H	R	HR	HB	BB-IB	SO	ERA	AERA	OAV	OOB	AB-HR-SH	AVG	PB	SUP	APR	DL	PW
1982	Cle A	0	0	ø	3	3	0	0-0	11.2	11	9	4	1	7-0	4	6.94	60	.250	.365	0	ø	0	88	-3	0	-0.1

BOITANO, DAN Danny Jon; B3.22.1953 Sacramento CA; BR/TR/6´0˝/(185–190); [PhiN73 S1/11]; d10.1; Col Fresno (CA) City

YEAR	TM LG	W	L	PCT	G	GS	CG-SHO	SV-BS	IP	H	R	HR	HB	BB-IB	SO	ERA	AERA	OAV	OOB	AB-HR-SH	AVG	PB	SUP	APR	DL	PW
1978	Phi N	0	0	ø	1	0	0	0-0	1	0	0	0	0	1-0	0	0.00	ø	.000	.250	0	ø	0	—	0	0	0.0
1979	Mil A	0	0	ø	5	0	0	0-0	6	6	1	1	0	3-0	5	1.50	280	.273	.360	0	ø	0	—	2	0	0.1
1980	Mil A	0	1	.000	11	0	0	0-0	17.2	26	17	7	1	6-0	11	8.15	48	.342	.393	0	ø	0	—	-8	0	-0.4

YEAR	TM LG	W	L	PCT	G	GS	CG-SHO	SV-BS	IP	H	R	HR	HB	BB-IB	SO	ERA	AERA	OAV	OOB	AB-HR-SH	AVG	PB	SUP	APR	DL	PW
1981	NY N	2	1	.667	15	0	0	0-1	16.1	21	10	2	2	5-0	8	5.51	64	.309	.368	0	ø	0*	—	-3	0	-0.5
1982	Tex A	0	0	ø	19	0	0	0-1	30.1	33	19	5	2	13-2	28	5.34	73	.280	.356	0	ø	0	—	-5	0	-0.2
Total	5	2	2	.500	51	0	0	0-2	71.1	86	47	15	5	28-2	52	5.68	68	.300	.367	0	ø	0	—	-14	0	-1.0
Bokelmann, Dick	Richard Werner; B10.26.1926 Arlington Heights IL; BR/TR/6´0.5˝/180; d8.3; Col Northwestern																									
1951	StL N	3	3	.500	20	1	0	3	52.1	49	30	2	1	31	22	3.78	105	.245	.349	14-0-2	.000	-2	67	-2	0	-0.4
1952	StL N	0	1	.000	11	0	0	0	12.2	20	17	0	0	7	5	9.24	40	.357	.429	0	ø	0	—	-9	0	-0.6
1953	StL N	0	0	ø	3	0	0	0	3	4	2	0	0	0	0	6.00	71	.308	.308	0	ø	0	—	0	0	0.0
Total	3	3	4	.429	34	1	0	3	68	73	49	2	1	38	27	4.90	80	.271	.364	14-0-2	.000	-2	67	-11	0	-1.0
Bokina, Joe	Joseph; B4.4.1910 Northampton MA; D10.25.1991 Chattanooga TN; BR/TR/6´0˝/184; d4.16																									
1936	Was A	0	2	.000	5	1	0	0	8.1	15	8	0	0	6	5	8.64	55	.395	.477	1	.000	-0	18	-3	—	-0.5
Boland, Bernie	Bernard Anthony; B1.21.1892 Rochester NY; D9.12.1973 Detroit MI; BR/TR/5´8.5˝/168; d4.14																									
1915	Det A	13	7	.650	45	18	8-1	3	202.2	167	86	2	6	75	72	3.11	98	.230	.307	63-0-1	.175	-1*	124	1	—	0.0
1916	Det A	10	3	.769	46	9	5-1	3	130.1	111	69	1	4	73	59	3.94	73	.240	.349	32-0-2	.250	2*	173	-14	—	-1.4
1917	Det A	16	11	.593	43	28	13-3	6	238	192	89	0	6	95	89	2.68	99	.226	.308	72-0-5	.056	-5*	111	4	—	-0.2
1918	Det A	14	10	.583	29	25	14-4	0	204	176	69	1	6	67	63	2.65	101	.236	.304	69	.174	0	103	3	—	0.3
1919	Det A	14	16	.467	35	30	18-1	1	242.2	222	93	7	3	80	71	3.04	105	.253	.318	74-0-3	.108	-3	76	8	—	0.6
1920	Det A	0	2	.000	4	3	1	0	17.1	23	18	0	2	14	4	7.79	48	.348	.476	7	.143	-0	114	-7	—	-0.7
1921	StL A	1	4	.200	7	6	0	0	27	34	36	2	1	28	6	9.33	48	.309	.453	10	.100	-1	109	-15	—	-2.1
Total	7	68	53	.562	209	119	59-10	13	1062	925	460	13	28	432	364	3.25	91	.241	.322	327-0-11	.138	-8	108	-20	—	-3.5
Bolden, Bill	William Horace "Big Bill"; B5.9.1893 Dandridge TN; D12.8.1966 Jefferson City TN; BR/TR/6´4˝/200; d6.27																									
1919	StL N	0	1	.000	3	1	0	0	12	17	7	0	1	4	4	5.25	53	.340	.400	3	.333	0	57	-3	—	-0.2
Bolen, Stew	Stewart O'Neal; B10.12.1902 Jackson AL; D8.30.1969 Mobile AL; BL/TL/5´11˝/180; d4.15																									
1926	StL A	0	0	ø	5	0	0	0	14.2	21	10	2	0	6	7	6.14	70	.356	.415	4	.500	1	—	-2	—	-0.1
1927	StL A	0	1	.000	3	1	1	0	9.2	14	9	0	0	5	7	8.38	52	.368	.442	3	.333	0	96	-3	—	-0.2
1931	Phi N	3	12	.200	28	16	2	0	98.2	117	75	5	4	63	55	6.39	66	.297	.399	32	.156	-1	82	-18	—	-2.4
1932	Phi N	0	0	ø	5	0	0	0	16	18	8	0	2	10	3	2.81	157	.281	.395	7	.143	-0	—	2	—	0.0
Total	4	3	13	.188	41	17	3	0	139	170	102	7	6	84	72	6.09	70	.306	.403	46	.196	-0	82	-21	—	-2.7
Bolin, Bobby	Bobby Donald; B1.29.1939 Hickory Grove SC; BR/TR/6´4˝/(200–212); d4.18																									
1961	SF N	2	2	.500	37	1	0	5	48	37	20	6	3	37-8	48	3.19	120	.210	.352	7	.286	0	186	3	0	0.3
1962	†SF N	7	3	.700	41	5	2	5	92	84	41	10	5	35-5	74	3.62	105	.243	.320	23	.261	2	162	2	0	0.4
1963	SF N	10	6	.625	47	12	2	7	137.1	128	73	13	7	57-4	134	3.28	98	.242	.322	35-1-4	.143	2	110	-7	0	-0.9
1964	SF N	6	9	.400	38	23	5-3	1	174.2	143	71	16	10	77-3	146	3.25	110	.220	.312	50-0-4	.100	0*	102	6	0	0.5
1965	SF N	14	6	.700	45	13	2	2	163	125	51	17	4	56-4	135	2.76	130	.214	.285	54-1-1	.167	1	106	17	0	2.2
1966	SF N	11	10	.524	36	34	10-4	1	224.1	174	85	25	10	70-10	143	2.89	127	.211	.280	76-2-1	.171	3	82	19	15	2.0
1967	SF N	6	8	.429	37	15	0	0	120	120	71	16	3	50-9	69	4.88	67	.258	.331	33-0-2	.242	2	116	-20	0	-2.0
1968	SF N	10	5	.667	34	19	6-3	0	176.2	128	44	9	4	46-9	126	1.99	148	.200	.258	55-0-1	.091	-1	101	20	0	1.7
1969	SF N	7	7	.500	30	22	2	0-0	146.1	149	86	17	7	49-3	102	4.43	79	.260	.323	39-1-2	.154	3	126	-15	0	-1.0
1970	Mil A	5	11	.313	32	20	3	1-0	132	131	84	20	4	67-7	81	4.91	77	.256	.343	36-1-6	.194	2	86	-18	0	-1.9
	Bos A	2	0	1.000	6	0	0	2-0	8	2	0	0	1	5-2	8	0.00	ø	.080	.250	1	.000	-0	—	3	0	0.7
	Year	7	11	.389	38	20	3	3-0	140	133	84	20	5	72-9	89	4.63	82	.248	.338	37-1-6	.189	2	86	-13	0	-1.2
1971	Bos A	5	3	.625	52	0	0	6-3	69.2	74	34	7	0	24-4	51	4.26	87	.273	.329	12	.250	0	—	-3	0	-0.4
1972	Bos A	0	1	.000	21	0	0	5-1	30.2	24	11	3	1	11-1	27	2.93	110	.209	.283	2	.000	-0	—	1	0	0.1
1973	Bos A	3	4	.429	39	0	0	15-5	53.1	45	16	5	1	13-2	31	2.70	149	.232	.282	0	ø	0	—	8	0	1.6
Total	13	88	75	.540	495	164	32-10	50-9	1576	1364	687	164	60	597-71	1175	3.40	103	.231	.306	423-6-21	.163	15	103	16	15	3.3
Bollo, Greg	Gregory Gene; B11.16.1943 Detroit MI; BR/TR/6´4˝/(180–185); d5.9; Col Western Michigan																									
1965	Chi A	0	0	ø	15	0	0	0	22.2	12	11	5	2	9-1	16	3.57	89	.152	.256	0	ø	0	—	-1	0	-0.1
1966	Chi A	0	1	.000	3	1	0	0	7	7	2	0	1	3-0	4	2.57	123	.269	.367	1	.000	-0	0	1	0	0.1
Total	2	0	1	.000	18	1	0	0	29.2	19	13	5	3	12-1	20	3.34	96	.181	.283	1	.000	-0	0	0	0	0.0
Bolton, Rod	Rodney Earl; B9.23.1968 Chattanooga TN; BR/TR/6´2˝/190; [ChiA90 13/348]; d4.10; Col Kentucky																									
1993	Chi A	2	6	.250	9	8	0	0-0	42.1	55	40	4	1	16-0	17	7.44	57	.314	.367	0	ø	0	76	-16	0	-2.3
1995	Chi A	0	2	.000	8	3	0	0-0	22	33	23	4	0	14-1	10	8.18	55	.351	.431	0	ø	0	118	-10	0	-0.7
Total	2	2	8	.200	17	11	0	0-0	64.1	88	63	8	1	30-1	27	7.69	56	.327	.390	0	ø	0	88	-26	0	-3.0
Bolton, Tom	Thomas Edward; B5.6.1962 Nashville TN; BL/TL/6´3˝/(175–185); [BosA80 20/518]; d5.17																									
1987	Bos A	1	0	1.000	29	0	0	0-0	61.2	83	33	5	2	27-2	49	4.38	104	.329	.394	0	ø	0	—	1	0	0.1
1988	Bos A	1	3	.250	28	0	0	1-0	30.1	35	17	1	0	14-1	21	4.75	87	.285	.355	0	ø	0	—	-2	0	-0.2
1989	Bos A	0	4	.000	4	4	0	0-0	17.1	21	18	1	0	10-1	9	8.31	50	.292	.373	0	ø	0	33	-8	0	-1.3
1990	†Bos A	10	5	.667	21	16	3	0-0	119.2	111	46	6	3	47-3	65	3.38	121	.251	.323	0	ø	0	97	11	0	1.3
1991	Bos A	8	9	.471	25	19	0	0-0	110	136	72	16	1	51-2	64	5.24	83	.308	.378	0	ø	0	87	-11	22	-1,5
1992	Bos A	1	2	.333	21	1	0	0-0	29	34	11	0	2	14-1	23	3.41	125	.286	.370	0	ø	0	21	3	0	0.3
	Cin N	3	3	.500	16	8	0	0-0	46.1	52	28	9	2	23-2	27	5.24	69	.284	.368	14-0-1	.000	-1	113	-8	0	-1.0
1993	Det A	6	6	.500	43	8	0	0-0	102.2	113	57	5	7	45-10	66	4.47	97	.282	.363	0	ø	0	127	-1	0	-0.1
1994	Bal A	1	2	.333	22	0	0	0-0	23.1	29	15	3	0	13-1	12	5.40	94	.309	.389	0	ø	0	—	-1	0	-0.1
Total	8	31	34	.477	209	56	3	1-0	540.1	614	297	46	17	244-23	336	4.56	93	.289	.364	14-0-1	.000	-1	92	-16	22	-2.5
Bomback, Mark	Mark Vincent; B4.14.1953 Portsmouth VA; BR/TR/5´11˝/170; [BosA71 25/584]; d9.12																									
1978	Mil A	0	0	ø	2	1	0	0-0	1.2	5	3	1	0	1-0	1	16.20	23	.500	.545	0	ø	0	118	-2	0	-0.1
1980	NY N	10	8	.556	36	25	2-1	0-0	162.2	191	80	17	4	49-3	68	4.09	88	.297	.347	43-0-5	.233	3	84	-7	0	-0.3
1981	Tor A	5	5	.500	20	11	0	0-1	90.1	84	42	6	1	35-2	33	3.89	102	.251	.321	0	ø	0*	84	2	0	0.2
1982	Tor A	1	5	.167	16	8	0	0-0	59.2	87	44	10	3	25-0	22	6.03	75	.343	.405	0	ø	0	73	-9	0	-0.8
Total	4	16	18	.471	74	45	2-1	0-1	314.1	367	169	34	8	110-5	124	4.47	87	.295	.353	43-0-5	.233	3	82	-16	0	-1.0
Bond, Tommy	Thomas Henry; B4.2.1856 Granard, Ireland; D1.24.1941 Boston MA; BR/TR/5´7.5˝/160; d5.5; M1/U2																									
1874	Atl NA	22	32	.407	55	55	55-1	0	497	606	440	15	—	8	42	2.03	102	.266	.268	245	.220	-0	76	1	—	0.6
1875	Har NA	19	16	.543	40	39	37-6	0	352	302	152	3	—	7	70	1.41	167	.216	.219	289	.266	3*	81	33	—	3.1
1876	Har N	31	13	.705	45	45	45-6	0	408	355	164	2	—	13	88	1.68	141	.220	.227	182	.275	1	97	32	—	3.1
1877	Bos N	**40**	17	**.702**	58	58	58-**6**	0	521	530	248	5	—	36	**170**	**2.11**	133	.249	**.261**	259	.228	-4*	115	40	—	3.3
1878	Bos N	**40**	19	**.678**	**59**	**59**	**57-9**	0	**532.2**	571	222	5	—	33	**182**	2.06	115	.269	.280	236	.212	-4	91	14	—	0.9
1879	Bos N	43	19	.694	64	64	59-**11**	0	555.1	543	206	8	—	24	155	**1.96**	**126**	.251	.259	257	.241	2*	136	**39**	—	**4.1**
1880	Bos N	26	29	.473	63	57	49-3	0	493	559	298	1	—	45	118	2.67	85	.274	.290	282	.220	-2*	106	-33	—	-2.9
1881	Bos N	0	3	.000	3	3	2	0	25.1	40	17	3	—	2	2	4.26	62	.360	.372	10	.200	-0	27	-3	—	-0.3
1882	Wor N	0	1	.000	2	2	0	0	12.1	12	13	0	—	7	2	4.38	71	.218	.306	30	.133	-1*	60	-2	—	-0.2
1884	Bos U	13	9	.591	23	21	19	0	189	185	120	3	—	14	128	3.00	79	.239	.253	162	.296	2*	117	-13	—	-1.1
	Ind AA	0	5	.000	5	5	5	0	43	62	51	5	2	4	15	5.65	58	.310	.330	23	.130	-1*	48	-12	—	-1.2
Total	2NA	41	48	.461	95	94	92-7	0	849	908	592	18	—	15	112	1.77	123	.247	.250	534	.245	2	77	34	—	3.7
Total	8	193	115	.627	322	314	294-35	0	2779.2	2857	1339	32	2	178	860	2.25	110	.255	.267	1441	.236	-7	109	62	—	5.7
Bonderman, Jeremy	Jeremy Allen; B10.28.1982 Kennewick WA; BR/TR/6´2˝/(210–220); [OakA01 1/26]; d4.2																									
2003	Det A	6	19	.240	33	28	0	0-0	162	193	118	23	4	58-2	108	5.56	79	.294	.352	2	.000	-0	76	-26	0	-3.3
2004	Det A	11	13	.458	33	32	2-**2**	0-0	184	168	101	24	10	73-5	168	4.89	92	.242	.321	7	.000	-1	112	-6	0	-0.7
2005	Det A	14	13	.519	29	29	4	0-0	189	199	101	21	4	57-0	145	4.57	94	.271	.326	6	.000	-1	111	-5	0	-0.7
2006	†Det A	14	8	.636	34	**34**	0	0-0	214	214	104	18	3	64-7	202	4.08	110	.259	.312	4	.000	-0	102	11	0	0.8
Total	4	45	53	.459	129	123	6-2	0-0	749	774	424	86	21	252-14	623	4.72	93	.266	.327	19	.000	-2	101	-26	0	-3.9
Bones, Ricky	Ricardo Ricky; B4.7.1969 Salinas, PR; BR/TR/6´0˝/(175–219); d8.11																									
1991	SD N	4	6	.400	11	11	0	0-0	54	57	33	3	0	18-0	31	4.83	79	.269	.321	13-0-4	.077	-0	139	-6	0	-1.1
1992	Mil A	9	10	.474	31	28	0	0-0	163.1	169	90	27	9	48-0	65	4.57	85	.264	.321	0	ø	0	99	-13	0	-1.4
1993	Mil A	11	11	.500	32	31	3	0-0	203.2	222	122	28	8	63-3	63	4.86	89	.278	.334	0	ø	0*	113	-13	0	-1.2

YEAR	TM LG	W	L	PCT	G	GS	CG-SHO	SV-BS	IP	H	R	HR	HB	BB-IB	SO	ERA	AERA	OAV	OOB	AB-HR-SH	AVG	PB	SUP	APR	DL	PW
1994	Mil A☆	10	9	.526	24	24	4-1	0-0	170.2	166	76	17	3	45-1	57	3.43	148	.255	.304	0	ø	0	85	28	0	2.6
1995	Mil A	10	12	.455	32	31	3	0-0	200.1	218	108	26	4	83-2	77	4.63	108	.281	.349	0	ø	0	104	10	0	1.0
1996	Mil A	7	14	.333	32	23	0	0-0	145	170	104	28	9	62-2	59	5.83	89	.294	.369	0	ø	0	101	-11	0	-1.3
	NY A	0	0	ø	4	1	0	0-0	7	14	11	2	1	6-0	4	14.14	35	.438	.525	0	ø	0	94	-7	0	-0.3
	Year	7	14	.333	36	24	0	0-0	152	184	115	30	10	68-2	63	6.22	83	.301	.378	0	ø	0	101	-18	0	-1.6
1997	Cin N	0	1	.000	9	2	0	0-0	17.2	31	22	2	2	11-2	8	10.19	42	.378	.454	2	.000	-0	140	-12	0	-0.6
	KC A	4	7	.364	21	11	1	0-1	78.1	102	59	10	5	25-2	36	5.97	79	.325	.377	0	ø	0*	107	-11	0	-1.3
1998	KC A	2	2	.500	32	0	0	1-1	53.1	49	18	4	1	24-5	38	3.04	160	.244	.327	1	.000	-0	—	11	0	0.8
1999	Bal A	0	3	.000	30	2	0	0-3	43.2	59	29	7	2	19-0	26	5.98	79	.322	.390	0	ø	0*	40	-5	15	-0.3
2000	Fla N	2	3	.400	56	0	0	0-3	77.1	94	43	6	3	27-8	59	4.54	97	.303	.358	2	.000	0	—	-2	14	-0.1
2001	Fla N	4	4	.500	61	0	0	0-0	64	71	39	7	3	33-9	41	5.06	82	.286	.374	2	.500	0	—	-7	0	-0.6
Total	11	63	82	.434	375	164	11-1	1-8	1278.1	1422	754	167	50	464-34	564	4.85	95	.283	.346	20-0-4	.100	-0	103	-38	29	-3.8
Bonetti, Julio	Julio Giacomo; B7.14.1911 Genoa, Italy; D6.17.1952 Belmont CA; BR/TR/6´0˝/180; d4.22																									
1937	StL A	4	11	.267	28	16	7	1	143.1	190	103	13	2	60	43	5.84	83	.321	.385	47-0-2	.149	-2	77	-15	—	-1.3
1938	StL A	2	3	.400	17	0	0	0	28.1	41	21	1	0	13	7	6.35	78	.350	.415	8	.000	-1	—	-4	—	-0.6
1940	Chi N	0	0	ø	1	0	0	0	1.1	3	3	0	0	4	0	20.25	19	.429	.636	0	ø	0	—	-2	—	-0.1
Total	3	6	14	.300	46	16	7	1	173	234	127	14	2	77	50	6.03	80	.327	.394	55-0-2	.127	-3	77	-21	—	-2.0
Boney, Hank	Henry Tate "Haney"; B10.28.1903 Wallace NC; D6.12.2002 Lake Worth FL; BL/TR/5´11˝/176; d6.28; Col Florida																									
1927	NY N	0	0	ø	3	0	0	0	4	4	1	0	0	2	0	2.25	171	.267	.353	0	ø	0	—	1	—	0.0
Bong, Jung	Jung Keun; B7.15.1980 Seoul, South Korea; BL/TL/6´3˝/(175–215); d4.23; [DL 2005 Cin N 183]																									
2002	Atl N	0	1	.000	1	1	0	0-0	6	8	5	0	0	2-0	4	7.50	54	.320	.370	2	.000	-0*	46	-2	0	-0.3
2003	Atl N	6	2	.750	44	0	0	1-2	57	56	32	8	2	31-6	47	5.05	83	.267	.365	5-0-1	.000	-0	—	-4	0	-0.4
2004	Cin N	1	1	.500	3	3	0	0-0	15.1	17	13	3	0	10-0	11	4.70	92	.270	.370	4	.000	-0	122	-3	0	-0.3
Total	3	7	4	.636	48	4	0	1-2	78.1	81	50	11	2	43-6	62	5.17	81	.272	.366	11-0-1	.000	-1	106	-9	183	-1.0
Bonham, Tiny	Ernest Edward; B8.16.1913 Ione CA; D9.15.1949 Pittsburgh PA; BR/TR/6´2˝/215; d8.5																									
1940	NY A	9	3	.750	12	12	10-3	0	99.1	83	24	4	0	13	37	1.90	212	.224	.250	37	.189	0	76	25	—	2.8
1941	†NY A	9	6	.600	23	14	7-1	2	126.2	118	44	12	1	31	43	2.98	132	.246	.294	50-0-1	.160	-1	116	16	0	1.5
1942	†NY A☆	21	5	**.808**	28	27	**22-6**	0	226	199	65	11	1	24	71	2.27	152	.237	**.259**	74-0-10	.122	-2	112	31	0	3.0
1943	†NY A☆	15	8	.652	28	26	17-4	1	225.2	197	63	13	1	52	71	2.27	142	.236	.282	76-0-5	.197	0	102	26	0	2.5
1944	NY A	12	9	.571	26	25	17-1	0	213.2	228	84	14	0	41	54	2.99	116	.273	.307	75-0-5	.133	-3	98	11	0	0.6
1945	NY A	8	11	.421	23	23	12	0	180.2	186	72	11	1	22	42	3.29	105	.265	.288	63-0-3	.238	3	79	5	0	0.7
1946	NY A	5	8	.385	18	14	6-2	3	104.2	97	47	6	0	23	30	3.70	93	.243	.284	31-0-1	.129	-0	85	-2	0	-0.3
1947	Pit N	11	8	.579	33	18	7-3	3	149.2	167	67	17	2	35	63	3.85	110	.277	.319	45-0-6	.156	-0	116	9	0	0.8
1948	Pit N	6	10	.375	22	20	7	0	135.2	145	71	18	3	23	42	4.31	94	.276	.310	49-0-1	.163	-2	94	-3	0	-0.7
1949	Pit N	7	4	.636	18	14	5-1	0	89	81	43	11	0	23	25	4.25	99	.246	.295	22-0-5	.045	-1	90	1	0	-0.1
Total	10	103	72	.589	231	193	110-21	9	1551	1501	580	117	9	287	478	3.06	120	.254	.289	522-0-37	.161	-7	98	119	0	10.8
Bonham, Bill	William Gordon; B10.1.1948 Glendale CA; BR/TR/6´3˝/(190–210); d4.7; Col UCLA; [DL 1981 Cin N 104]																									
1971	Chi N	2	1	.667	33	2	0	0-1	60	63	38	6	5	36-5	41	4.65	85	.281	.390	12	.167	-0	56	-6	0	-0.3
1972	Chi N	1	1	.500	19	4	0	4-1	57.2	56	22	4	1	25-2	49	3.12	122	.260	.340	14-0-3	.286	1	116	4	0	0.4
1973	Chi N	7	5	.583	44	15	3	6-0	152	126	55	10	4	64-7	121	3.02	131	.230	.313	43-0-6	.093	-3	88	15	0	1.2
1974	Chi N	11	22	.333	44	36	10-2	1-0	242.2	246	133	13	6	109-8	191	3.86	99	.263	.342	84-0-5	.143	-3*	75	-5	0	-0.6
1975	Chi N	13	15	.464	38	36	7-2	0-0	229.1	254	133	15	5	109-6	165	4.71	82	.281	.359	82-0-8	.183	-0*	113	-19	0	-2.0
1976	Chi N	9	13	.409	32	31	3	0-0	196	215	102	11	2	96-2	110	4.27	91	.283	.361	65-0-7	.200	1	101	-6	0	-0.5
1977	Chi N	10	13	.435	34	34	1	0-0	214.2	207	111	15	3	82-16	134	4.36	101	.254	.324	65-0-11	.231	1*	91	3	0	0.6
1978	Cin N	11	5	.688	23	23	1	0-0	140.1	151	59	9	1	50-8	83	3.53	101	.276	.336	43-0-8	.186	2	132	2	0	0.6
1979	Cin N	9	7	.563	29	29	2	0-0	175.2	173	80	14	8	60-3	78	3.79	98	.261	.329	57-0-6	.140	-1	114	0	0	-0.1
1980	Cin N	2	1	.667	4	4	0	0-0	19	21	10	1	0	5-0	13	4.74	74	.276	.321	6	.000	-0	108	-2	91	-0.4
Total	10	75	83	.475	300	214	27-4	11-2	1487.1	1512	743	98	35	636-57	985	4.01	97	.266	.342	471-0-54	.172	-2	100	-14	195	-1.1
Bonikowski, Joe	Joseph Peter; B1.16.1941 Philadelphia PA; BR/TR/6´0˝/176; d4.12																									
1962	Min A	5	7	.417	30	13	3	2	99.2	95	47	6	1	38-2	45	3.88	105	.255	.323	27-0-2	.148	-1	106	3	0	0.3
Bonness, Bill	William John "Lefty"; B12.15.1923 Cleveland OH; D12.3.1977 Detroit MI; BR/TL/6´4˝/200; d9.26																									
1944	Cle A	0	1	.000	2	1	0	0	7	11	6	0	2	5	1	7.71	43	.367	.486	3	.000	-0	51	-3	0	-0.4
Bono, Gus	Adlai Wendell; B8.29.1894 Doe Run MO; D12.3.1948 Dearborn MI; BR/TR/5´11˝/175; d9.13																									
1920	Was A	0	2	.000	4	1	0	0	12.1	17	13	0	0	6	4	8.76	43	.315	.383	3	.000	-0	149	-6	—	-0.8
Bonser, Boof	Boof; B10.14.1981 St.Petersburg FL; BR/TR/6´4˝/260; [SFN00 1/21]; d5.21																									
2006	†Min A	7	6	.538	18	18	0	0-0	100.1	104	50	18	1	24-0	84	4.22	108	.267	.309	3-0-1	.000	-0	99	4	0	0.4
Booker, Chris	Christopher Scott; B12.9.1976 Monroeville AL; BR/TR/6´3˝/235; [ChiN95 20/539]; d9.5																									
2005	Cin N	0	0	ø	3	0	0	0-0	2	6	8	2	0	4-0	2	31.50	14	.545	.667	0	ø	0	—	-6	0	-0.3
2006	KC A	0	0	ø	1	0	0	0-0	1	5	6	3	0	3-0	0	54.00	9	.625	.727	0	ø	0	—	-5	56	-0.2
	Was N	0	0	ø	10	0	0	0-0	7.1	5	3	1	0	1-0	7	3.68	119	.192	.222	0	ø	0	—	1	0	0.0
Total	2	0	0	ø	14	0	0	0-0	10.1	16	17	6	0	8-0	9	13.94	31	.356	.453	0	ø	0	—	-10	56	-0.5
Booker, Greg	Gregory Scott; B6.22.1960 Lynchburg VA; BR/TR/6´6˝/(230–245); [SDN81 10/239]; d9.11; C7; Col Elon																									
1983	SD N	0	1	.000	6	1	0	0-0	11.2	18	10	2	0	9-0	5	7.71	45	.375	.474	1	.000	-0	76	-5	0	-0.4
1984	†SD N	1	1	.500	32	1	0	0-1	57.1	67	27	4	0	27-4	28	3.30	109	.295	.367	7	.286	1	74	0	0	0.1
1985	SD N	0	1	.000	17	0	0	0-0	22.1	20	17	3	1	17-2	7	6.85	52	.247	.376	1	.000	-0	—	-7	0	-0.4
1986	SD N	1	0	1.000	9	0	0	0-0	11	10	5	0	0	4-2	7	1.64	224	.233	.298	0	ø	0	—	1	0	0.1
1987	SD N	1	1	.500	44	0	0	1-0	68.1	62	29	5	3	30-1	17	3.16	126	.246	.332	6	.000	-1	—	5	9	0.2
1988	SD N	2	2	.500	34	2	0	0-0	63.2	68	31	5	1	19-2	43	3.39	100	.278	.327	8	.250	1	144	-2	0	0.0
1989	SD N	0	1	.000	11	0	0	0-0	19	15	10	2	0	10-1	8	4.26	82	.224	.325	0	ø	0	—	-1	0	-0.1
	Min A	0	0	ø	6	0	0	0-0	8.2	11	4	1	0	2-0	3	4.15	100	.306	.342	0	ø	0	—	0	0	0.0
1990	SF N	0	0	ø	2	0	0	0-0	2	7	3	0	0	0-0	1	13.50	27	.538	.538	0	ø	0	—	-2	0	-0.1
Total	8	5	7	.417	161	4	0	1-1	264	278	136	22	5	118-12	119	3.89	94	.275	.351	23	.174	1	104	-11	9	-0.6
Booles, Red	Seabron Jesse; B7.14.1880 Bernice LA; D3.16.1955 Monroe LA; BL/TR/5´10˝/150; d7.30																									
1909	Cle A	0	1	.000	4	1	0	0	22.2	20	12	0	1	8	6	1.99	129	.235	.309	6	.167	0	55	0	—	0.0
Boone, Danny	Daniel Hugh; B1.14.1954 Long Beach CA; BL/TL/5´8˝/(131–140); [CalA76 S2/33]; d4.11; Col Cal St.–Fullerton																									
1981	SD N	1	0	1.000	37	0	0	2-0	63.1	63	23	2	1	21-7	43	2.84	114	.267	.327	4-0-1	.500	1	—	3	0	0.3
1982	SD N	1	0	1.000	10	0	0	1-2	16	21	10	2	0	3-0	8	5.63	61	.323	.353	5	.200	0	—	-3	0	-0.2
	Hou N	0	1	.000	10	0	0	1-1	12.2	7	6	1	0	4-1	4	3.55	94	.171	.239	1	.000	-0	—	-1	0	-0.1
	Year	1	1	.500	20	0	0	2-3	28.2	28	16	3	0	7-1	12	4.71	72	.264	.307	6	.167	0	—	-4	0	-0.3
1990	Bal A	0	0	ø	4	1	0	0-0	9.2	12	3	1	1	3-0	2	2.79	137	.308	.372	0	ø	0	72	1	0	0.1
Total	3	2	1	.667	61	1	0	4-3	101.2	103	42	6	2	31-8	57	3.36	99	.270	.326	10-0-1	.300	1	72	0	0	0.1
Boone, George	George Morris; B3.1.1871 Louisville KY; D9.24.1910 Louisville KY; d4.23																									
1891	Lou AA	0	0	ø	4	1	0	1	15	15	15	0	0	9	4	7.80	47	.250	.348	6	.333	0	68	-5	—	-0.2
Boone, Dan	James Albert; B1.19.1895 Samantha AL; D5.11.1968 Tuscaloosa AL; BR/TR/6´2˝/190; d9.10; b–Ike; Col Alabama																									
1919	Phi A	0	1	.000	3	2	0	0	14.2	24	14	0	0	10	1	6.75	51	.375	.459	4	.000	-1	91	-5	—	-0.3
1921	Det A	0	0	ø	1	0	0	1	2	1	1	0	0	2	0	0.00	ø	.200	.429	1	.000	-0	—	1	—	0.0
1922	Cle A	4	6	.400	11	10	4-2	0	75.1	87	39	3	1	19	9	4.06	99	.298	.343	26-0-1	.192	-1	72	0	—	-0.1
1923	Cle A	4	6	.400	27	4	2	0	70.1	93	56	3	3	31	15	6.01	66	.322	.393	19	.211	0	78	-15	—	-1.6
Total	4	8	13	.381	42	16	6-2	1	162.1	205	110	6	4	62	25	5.10	77	.315	.378	50-0-1	.180	-1	75	-19	—	-2.0

YEAR	TM LG	W	L	PCT	G	GS	CG-SHO	SV-BS	IP	H	R	HR	HB	BB-IB	SO	ERA	AERA	OAV	OOB	AB-HR-SH	AVG	PB	SUP	APR	DL	PW
BOOTCHECK, CHRIS	Christopher Brandon; B10.24.1978 Laporte IN; BR/TR/6´5˝/200; [AnaA00 1/20]; d9.9; Col Auburn																									
2003	Ana A	0	1	.000	4	1	0	0-0	10.1	16	13	5	0	6-0	7	9.58	46	.340	.415	0	ø	0	21	-7	0	-0.5
2005	LA A	0	1	.000	5	2	0	1-0	18.2	19	7	1	0	4-1	8	3.38	127	.257	.291	0	ø	0	119	2	0	0.1
2006	LA A	0	1	.000	7	0	0	0-0	10.1	16	12	3	0	9-0	7	10.45	43	.364	.472	0	ø	0	—	-6	19	-0.5
Total	3	0	3	.000	16	3	0	1-0	39.1	51	32	9	0	19-1	22	6.86	63	.309	.378	0	ø	0	85	-11	19	-0.9
BOOTH, AMOS	Amos Smith "Darling"; B9.14.1848 Lebanon OH; D7.1.1921 Miamisburg OH; BR/TR/5´9˝/159; d4.25; ▲																									
1876	Cin N	0	1	.000	3	1	0	0	9.2	22	18	0	—	0	0	9.31	24	.431	.431	272	.261	0*	264	-7	—	-0.5
1877	Cin N	1	7	.125	12	8	6	0	86	114	75	1	—	13	18	3.56	74	.296	.319	157	.172	-1*	74	-11	—	-0.9
Total	2	1	8	.111	15	9	6	0	95.2	136	93	1	—	13	18	4.14	63	.312	.332	429	.228	-1	96	-18	—	-1.4
BOOZER, JOHN	John Morgan; B7.6.1938 Columbia SC; D1.24.1986 Lexington SC; BR/TR/6´3˝/(205–210); d7.22; Col Wofford																									
1962	Phi N	0	0	ø	9	0	0	0	20.1	22	13	3	0	10-1	13	5.75	67	.282	.364	1	.000	-0	—	-4	0	-0.2
1963	Phi N	3	4	.429	26	8	2	1	83	67	31	11	1	33-5	69	2.93	110	.227	.303	21	.143	-0	70	3	0	0.1
1964	Phi N	3	4	.429	22	3	0	2	60.1	64	37	6	2	18-2	51	5.07	68	.271	.327	13	.077	-1*	51	-10	0	-1.2
1966	Phi N	0	0	ø	2	2	0	0	5.1	8	5	1	0	3-0	5	6.75	53	.348	.423	2	.000	-0	135	-2	0	-0.1
1967	Phi N	5	4	.556	28	7	1	1	74.2	86	39	6	1	24-5	48	4.10	83	.292	.347	19	.211	1	129	-5	0	-0.6
1968	Phi N	2	2	.500	38	0	0	5	68.2	76	32	3	2	15-3	49	3.67	82	.279	.320	9-0-2	.111	-0	—	-5	0	-0.4
1969	Phi N	1	2	.333	46	2	0	6-3	82	91	46	12	0	36-5	47	4.28	83	.283	.354	9-0-2	.333	1	50	-8	0	-0.3
Total	7	14	16	.467	171	22	3	15-3	394.1	414	203	42	6	139-21	282	4.09	82	.272	.334	74-0-4	.162	-0	91	-31	0	-2.7
BORBON, PEDRO	Pedro (Rodriguez); B12.2.1946 Mao, D.R.; BR/TR/6´2˝/(185–200); d4.9; s–Pedro																									
1969	Cal A	2	3	.400	22	0	0	0-0	41	55	31	5	4	11-2	20	6.15	57	.324	.376	3	.000	-0	—	-12	29	-1.4
1970	Cin N	0	2	.000	12	1	0	0-0	17.1	21	15	2	3	6-1	6	6.75	60	.309	.390	3	.000	-0	22	-5	0	-0.5
1971	Cin N	0	0	ø	3	0	0	0-0	4.1	3	3	1	0	1-0	4	4.15	81	.200	.250	0	ø	0	—	-1	0	0.0
1972	†Cin N	8	3	.727	62	2	0	11-1	122	115	45	5	3	32-11	48	3.17	102	.254	.304	21	.048	-1	68	2	0	0.1
1973	†Cin N	11	4	.733	80	0	0	14-5	121	137	33	4	1	35-15	60	2.16	160	.298	.345	15	.333	1	—	18	0	2.7
1974	Cin N	10	7	.588	73	0	0	14-6	139	133	54	11	4	32-16	53	3.24	108	.255	.300	26-0-1	.192	-0	—	5	0	0.7
1975	†Cin N	9	5	.643	67	0	0	5-1	125	145	47	6	3	21-6	29	2.95	121	.301	.333	24-0-3	.292	2	—	7	0	1.0
1976	†Cin N	4	3	.571	69	1	0	8-3	121	135	49	4	4	31-11	53	3.35	105	.292	.338	18-0-2	.222	0	252	2	0	0.2
1977	Cin N	10	5	.667	73	0	0	18-5	127	131	48	7	3	24-4	48	3.19	124	.268	.304	22-0-2	.182	-0	—	11	0	1.4
1978	Cin N	8	2	.800	62	0	0	4-1	99.1	102	56	6	3	27-8	35	4.98	71	.274	.324	11-0-1	.182	-0	—	-13	0	-1.4
1979	Cin N	2	2	.500	30	0	0	2-2	44.2	48	17	2	0	8-4	23	3.43	108	.277	.303	6	.333	0	—	2	0	0.3
	SF N	4	3	.571	30	0	0	3-1	46	56	28	7	0	13-3	26	4.89	71	.303	.347	3	.333	0	—	-8	0	-1.2
	Year	6	5	.545	60	0	0	5-3	90.2	104	45	9	0	21-7	49	4.17	86	.291	.326	9	.333	1	—	-5	0	-0.9
1980	StL N	1	0	1.000	10	0	0	1-0	19	17	10	3	0	10-2	4	3.79	99	.250	.329	4	.250	0	—	-1	0	0.0
Total	12	69	39	.639	593	4	0	80-25	1026.2	1098	436	63	28	251-83	409	3.52	101	.280	.325	156-0-9	.205	2	100	7	29	1.9
BORBON, PEDRO	Pedro Felix (Marte); B11.15.1967 Mao, D.R.; BR/TL/6´1˝/(205–230); d10.2; f–Pedro; Col Ranger (TX) JC; [DL 1998 Atl N 181]																									
1992	Atl N	0	1	.000	2	0	0	0-0	1.1	2	1	0	0	1-1	1	6.75	54	.333	.429	0	ø	0	—	0	0	-0.1
1993	Atl N	0	0	ø	3	0	0	0-0	1.2	3	4	0	0	3-0	2	21.60	19	.429	.600	0	ø	0	—	-3	0	-0.2
1995	†Atl N	2	2	.500	41	0	0	2-2	32	29	12	2	1	17-4	33	3.09	140	.240	.336	1	.000	-0	—	4	0	0.5
1996	Atl N	3	0	1.000	43	0	0	1-0	36	26	12	1	1	7-0	31	2.75	162	.203	.250	1	1.000	0	—	7	56	0.6
1999	LA N	4	3	.571	70	0	0	1-1	50.2	39	23	5	1	29-1	33	4.09	107	.209	.314	2-0-1	.000	-0	—	3	0	0.3
2000	Tor A	1	1	.500	59	0	0	1-0	41.2	45	37	5	5	38-5	29	6.48	78	.280	.417	0	ø	0	—	-8	0	-0.3
2001	Tor A	2	4	.333	71	0	0	0-5	53.1	48	24	8	4	12-3	45	3.71	124	.244	.298	0	ø	0	—	5	0	0.5
2002	Tor A	1	2	.333	16	0	0	0-2	12.2	12	8	3	1	6-3	11	4.97	93	.231	.317	0	ø	0	—	-1	0	-0.1
	Hou N	3	2	.600	56	0	0	1-2	37.2	41	24	7	2	19-5	39	5.50	79	.287	.367	3	.000	-0	—	-4	0	-0.6
2003	StL N	0	1	.000	7	0	0	0-0	4	14	9	2	1	2-2	0	20.25	20	.560	.607	0	ø	0	—	-7	0	-1.3
Total	9	16	16	.500	368	0	0	6-12	271	259	154	33	16	134-24	224	4.68	96	.252	.342	7-0-1	.143	-0	—	-4	237	-0.7
BORCHERS, GEORGE	George Benard "Chief"; B4.18.1869 Sacramento CA; D10.24.1938 Sacramento CA; BB/TR/5´10˝/180; d5.18																									
1888	Chi N	4	4	.500	10	10	7-1	0	67	67	45	2	6	29	26	3.49	87	.251	.338	33	.061	-2	124	-4	—	-0.5
1895	Lou N	0	1	.000	1	1	0	0	0.2	1	2	0	0	3	0	27.00	17	.333	.667	0	ø	0	0	-1	—	-0.2
Total	2	4	5	.444	11	11	7-1	0	67.2	68	47	2	6	32	26	3.72	82	.252	.344	33	.061	-2	112	-5	—	-0.7
BORDEN, JOE	Joseph Emley (aka Joseph Emley Josephs in 1875); B5.9.1854 Jacobstown NJ; D10.14.1929 Yeadon PA; BR/TR/5´9˝/140; d7.24																									
1875	Phi NA	2	4	.333	7	7	7-2	0	66	47	30	0	—	7	9	1.50	152	**.181**	**.203**	28	.107	-3	80	5	—	0.1
1876	Bos N	11	12	.478	29	24	16-2	1	218.1	257	155	4	—	51	34	2.89	78	.276	.313	121	.207	-3*	105	-11	—	-1.3
BORDI, RICH	Richard Albert; B4.18.1959 San Francisco CA; BR/TR/6´7˝/(210–220); [OakA80 3/56]; d7.16; Col Cal St.–Fresno																									
1980	Oak A	0	0	ø	1	0	0	0-0	2	4	1	0	0	0-0	0	4.50	85	.400	.400	0	ø	0	—	0	0	0.0
1981	Oak A	0	0	ø	2	0	0	0-0	2	1	0	0	0	1-0	0	0.00	ø	.143	.250	0	ø	0	—	1	0	0.0
1982	Sea A	0	2	.000	7	2	0	0-0	13	18	12	4	1	1-0	10	8.31	52	.310	.333	0	ø	0	74	-5	0	-0.7
1983	Chi N	0	2	.000	11	1	0	1-0	25.1	34	15	2	0	12-1	20	4.97	77	.321	.390	4	.000	-0	23	-3	0	-0.3
1984	Chi N	5	2	.714	31	7	0	4-0	83.1	78	37	11	0	20-4	41	3.46	113	.242	.284	19	.053	-1	136	3	15	0.1
1985	NY A	6	8	.429	51	3	0	2-0	98	95	41	5	1	29-4	64	3.21	126	.253	.306	0	ø	0	112	8	15	1.1
1986	Bal A	6	4	.600	52	1	0	3-2	107	105	56	13	4	41-5	83	4.46	94	.254	.325	0	ø	0	0	-2	0	-0.2
1987	NY A	3	1	.750	16	1	0	0-1	33	42	28	7	0	12-0	23	7.64	58	.309	.365	0	ø	0	82	-11	0	-1.1
1988	Oak A	0	1	.000	2	2	0	0-0	7.2	6	6	0	0	5-0	6	4.70	81	.214	.324	0	ø	0	132	-2	0	-0.2
Total	9	20	20	.500	173	17	0	10-3	371.1	383	196	42	6	121-14	247	4.34	94	.263	.320	23	.043	-2	104	-11	30	-1.3
BORDLEY, BILL	William Clarke; B1.9.1958 Los Angeles CA; BR/TL/6´3˝/200; d6.30; Col USC; [DL 1982 SF N 49]																									
1980	SF N	2	3	.400	8	6	0	0-0	30.2	34	19	3	0	21-1	11	4.70	75	.288	.396	6-0-2	.167	0	119	-4	0	-0.6
BORIS, PAUL	Paul Stanley; B12.13.1955 Irvington NJ; BR/TR/6´2˝/200; d5.21; Col Rutgers																									
1982	Min A	1	2	.333	23	0	0	0-0	49.2	46	24	8	2	19-3	30	3.99	107	.246	.318	0	ø	0	—	1	0	0.0
BORK, FRANK	Frank Bernard; B7.13.1940 Buffalo NY; BR/TL/6´2˝/175; d4.15																									
1964	Pit N	2	2	.500	33	2	0	2	42	51	22	6	1	11-3	31	4.07	86	.295	.341	5-0-1	.200	0	138	-3	0	-0.2
BORKOWSKI, DAVE	David Richard; B2.7.1977 Detroit MI; BR/TR/6´1˝/(200–230); [DetA95 11/294]; d7.17																									
1999	Det A	2	6	.250	17	12	0	0-0	76.2	86	58	10	4	40-0	50	6.10	82	.283	.371	3	.000	-0	99	-10	0	-0.9
2000	Det A	0	1	.000	2	1	0	0-0	5.1	11	13	2	0	7-1	1	21.94	22	.423	.529	0	ø	0	76	-10	0	-1.1
2001	Det A	0	2	.000	15	0	0	0-0	29.2	30	21	5	3	15-3	30	6.37	69	.261	.356	0	ø	0	—	-6	93	-0.3
2004	Bal A	3	4	.429	17	8	0	0-1	56	65	37	6	3	15-1	45	5.14	91	.289	.339	0	ø	0	79	-4	0	-0.5
2006	Hou N	3	2	.600	40	0	0	0-0	71	70	38	8	0	23-7	52	4.69	96	.257	.313	5	.000	-1	—	-1	0	-0.1
Total	5	8	15	.348	91	21	0	0-1	238.2	262	167	31	10	100-12	178	5.84	80	.278	.351	8	.000	-1	94	-31	93	-2.9
BORLAND, TOM	Thomas Bruce "Spike"; B2.14.1933 ElDorado KS; BL/TL/6´3˝/175; d5.15; Col Oklahoma St.																									
1960	Bos A	0	4	.000	26	4	0	3	51	67	40	4	0	23-4	32	6.53	62	.322	.388	13	.000	-2	125	-13	0	-1.2
1961	Bos A	0	0	ø	1	0	0	0	1	3	2	0	0	0-0	0	18.00	23	.500	.500	0	ø	0	—	-1	0	-0.1
Total	2	0	4	.000	27	4	0	3	52	70	42	4	0	23-4	32	6.75	60	.327	.391	13	.000	-2	125	-14	0	-1.3
BORLAND, TOBY	Toby Shawn; B5.29.1969 Ruston LA; BR/TR/6´6˝/(186–215); [PhiN87 27/702]; d5.27																									
1994	Phi N	1	0	1.000	24	0	0	1-0	34.1	31	10	1	4	14-3	26	2.36	181	.248	.343	3	.000	-0	—	7	0	0.3
1995	Phi N	1	3	.250	50	0	0	6-3	74	81	37	3	5	37-7	59	3.77	112	.277	.366	5	.200	0	—	2	24	0.1
1996	Phi N	7	3	.700	69	0	0	0-2	90.2	83	51	9	3	43-3	76	4.07	106	.239	.327	4	.000	-0	—	0	0	-0.1
1997	NY N	0	1	.000	13	0	0	1-1	13.1	11	9	1	1	14-0	7	6.08	66	.220	.400	0-0-1	ø	0	—	-3	0	-0.2
	Bos A	0	0	ø	3	0	0	0-0	3.1	6	5	1	2	7-0	1	13.50	34	.400	.625	0	ø	0	—	-3	0	-0.1
1998	Phi N	0	0	ø	6	0	0	0-0	9	8	5	1	0	5-0	9	5.00	86	.242	.342	0	ø	0	—	-1	0	0.0
2001	Ana A	0	1	.000	2	0	0	0-1	3.1	8	5	1	0	1-0	0	10.80	43	.471	.500	0	ø	0	—	-2	0	-0.4
2002	Fla N	1	0	1.000	15	0	0	0-0	13.2	14	8	3	3	5-0	11	5.27	75	.269	.355	0	ø	0	—	-2	0	-0.1
2003	Fla N	0	0	ø	7	0	0	0-0	9.2	3	3	0	0	8-1	4	1.86	220	.097	.275	0	ø	0	—	2	137	0.1
2004	Fla N	1	1	.500	18	0	0	0-1	18.1	18	11	3	0	12-5	18	5.40	76	.254	.357	0	ø	0	—	-2	0	-0.2
Total	9	11	9	.550	207	0	0	8-8	269.2	263	144	23	18	146-19	211	4.17	102	.254	.354	12-0-1	.083	-1	—	-2	161	-0.6

YEAR	TM LG	W	L	PCT	G	GS	CG-SHO	SV-BS	IP	H	R	HR	HB	BB-IB	SO	ERA	AERA	OAV	OOB	AB-HR-SH	AVG	PB	SUP	APR	DL	PW
Borowski, Joe	Joseph Thomas; B5.4.1971 Bayonne NJ; BR/TR/6´2˝/225; [ChiA89 32/823]; d7.9																									
1995	Bal A	0	0	ø	6	0	0	0-0	7.1	5	1	0	0	4-0	3	1.23	390	.192	.300	0	ø	0	—	3	0	0.1
1996	Atl N	2	4	.333	22	0	0	0-0	26	33	15	4	1	13-4	15	4.85	92	.324	.405	2-0-1	.000	-0	—	-1	0	-0.1
1997	Atl N	2	2	.500	20	0	0	0-0	24	27	11	2	0	16-4	6	3.75	112	.287	.391	0	ø	0	—	1	0	0.2
	NY A	0	1	.000	1	0	0	0-0	2	2	2	0	0	4-1	2	9.00	49	.250	.500	0	ø	0	—	-1	0	-0.2
1998	NY A	1	0	1.000	8	0	0	0-0	9.2	11	7	0	0	4-0	7	6.52	67	.289	.357	0	ø	0	—	-2	15	-0.2
2001	Chi N	0	1	.000	1	1	0	0-0	1.2	6	6	1	0	3-0	1	32.40	13	.667	.750	0	ø	0	88	-5	0	-0.7
2002	Chi N	4	4	.500	73	0	0	2-4	95.2	84	31	10	1	29-6	97	2.73	149	.238	.295	7	.286	0	—	15	0	1.2
2003	†Chi N	2	2	.500	68	0	0	33-4	68.1	53	23	5	1	19-1	66	2.63	165	.207	.264	0	ø	0	—	12	0	1.7
2004	Chi N	2	4	.333	22	0	0	9-2	21.1	27	19	3	0	15-2	17	8.02	55	.303	.400	0	ø	0	—	-8	121	-1.5
2005	Chi N	0	0	ø	11	0	0	0-0	11	12	8	5	0	1-0	11	6.55	67	.261	.277	0	ø	0	—	-2	47	-0.1
	TB A	1	5	.167	32	0	0	0-4	35.1	26	15	3	0	11-1	16	3.82	115	.208	.272	0	ø	0	—	3	0	0.4
2006	Fla N	3	3	.500	72	0	0	36-7	69.2	63	31	7	2	33-7	64	3.75	114	.235	.323	0	ø	0	—	5	0	0.8
Total	10	17	26	.395	336	1	0	80-21	372	349	169	40	5	152-26	305	3.87	111	.247	.321	9-0-1	.222	0	88	20	183	1.6
Borowy, Hank	Henry Ludwig; B5.12.1916 Bloomfield NJ; D8.23.2004 Brick NJ; BR/TR/6´0˝/175; d4.18; Col Fordham																									
1942	†NY A	15	4	.789	25	21	13-4	1	178.1	157	56	6	0	66	85	2.52	136	.233	.301	70-0-4	.157	-1	132	20	0	2.0
1943	†NY A	14	9	.609	29	27	14-3	0	217.1	195	75	11	2	72	113	2.82	114	.241	.305	74-0-8	.203	3	106	12	0	1.6
1944	NY A★	17	12	.586	35	30	19-3	2	252.2	224	93	15	0	88	107	2.64	132	.236	.301	90-0-7	.133	-3	97	21	0	2.1
1945	NY A✳	10	5	.667	18	18	7-1	0	132.1	107	61	6	1	58	35	3.13	111	.221	.305	50-0-3	.220	1	134	2	0	0.3
	†Chi N	11	2	.846	15	14	11-1	1	122.1	105	33	2	0	47	47	**2.13**	171	.231	.303	41-0-7	.171	0	137	22	0	2.3
1946	Chi N	12	10	.545	32	28	8-1	0	201	220	96	9	1	61	95	3.76	88	.274	.326	72-0-7	.181	1*	123	-10	0	-0.9
1947	Chi N	8	12	.400	40	25	7-1	2	183	190	99	19	1	63	75	4.38	90	.267	.328	56	.125	-1*	90	-6	0	-0.7
1948	Chi N	5	10	.333	39	17	2-1	1	127	156	80	9	0	49	50	4.89	80	.308	.369	36	.222	2	75	-14	0	-1.2
1949	Phi N	12	12	.500	28	28	12-1	0	193.1	188	99	19	0	63	43	4.19	94	.259	.319	61-0-5	.213	3	101	-5	0	-0.3
1950	Phi N	0	0	ø	3	0	0	0	6.1	5	4	0	0	4	3	5.68	71	.250	.375	0-0-1	ø	0	—	-1	0	-0.1
	Pit N	1	3	.250	11	3	0	0	25.1	32	19	6	1	9	9	6.39	69	.311	.372	6-0-2	.167	-0	94	-5	0	-0.7
	Year	1	3	.250	14	3	0	0	31.2	37	23	6	1	13	12	6.25	69	.301	.372	6-0-3	.167	-0	95	-6	0	-0.8
	Det A	1	1	.500	13	2	1	0	32.2	23	15	3	0	16	12	3.31	142	.205	.305	7-0-2	.143	-0	106	4	0	0.2
1951	Det A	2	2	.500	26	1	0	0	45.1	58	39	3	1	27	16	6.95	60	.314	.404	8	.000	-1	85	-14	0	-1.1
Total	10	108	82	.568	314	214	94-16	7	1717	1660	769	108	7	623	690	3.50	104	.254	.320	571-0-46	.173	3	108	26	0	3.5
Bosio, Chris	Christopher Louis; B4.3.1963 Carmichael CA; BR/TR/6´3˝/(220–235); [MilA82*S2/44]; d8.3; C1; Col Sacramento (CA) City																									
1986	Mil A	0	4	.000	10	4	0	0-0	34.2	41	27	9	0	13-0	29	7.01	62	.293	.353	0	ø	0	78	-8	0	-0.8
1987	Mil A	11	8	.579	46	19	2-1	2-2	170	187	102	18	1	50-3	150	5.24	88	.276	.326	0	ø	0	103	-9	0	-0.8
1988	Mil A	7	15	.318	38	22	9-1	6-0	182	190	80	13	2	38-6	84	3.36	119	.268	.303	0	ø	0	69	11	0	1.4
1989	Mil A	15	10	.600	33	33	8-2	0-0	234.2	225	90	16	6	48-1	173	2.95	131	.249	.289	0	ø	0	123	22	0	2.3
1990	Mil A	4	9	.308	20	20	4-1	0-0	132.2	131	67	15	3	38-1	76	4.00	97	.258	.311	0	ø	0	89	-1	79	0.0
1991	Mil A	14	10	.583	32	32	5-1	0-0	204.2	187	80	15	8	58-0	117	3.25	123	.244	.302	0	ø	0	114	18	15	1.9
1992	Mil A	16	6	.727	33	33	4-2	0-0	231.1	223	100	21	4	44-1	120	3.62	107	.254	.291	0	ø	0	121	7	0	0.6
1993	Sea A	9	9	.500	29	24	3-1	1-1	164.1	138	75	14	6	59-3	119	3.45	130	.229	.303	0	ø	0*	79	15	48	1.5
1994	Sea A	4	10	.286	19	19	4	0-0	125	137	72	15	2	40-3	67	4.32	114	.277	.330	0	ø	0	81	6	33	0.7
1995	†Sea A	10	8	.556	31	31	0	0-0	170	211	98	18	5	69-3	85	4.92	97	.312	.375	0	ø	0	110	-1	0	-0.1
1996	Sea A	4	4	.500	18	9	0	0-0	60.2	72	44	8	4	24-1	39	5.93	84	.299	.364	0	ø	0	151	-7	80	-0.7
Total	11	94	93	.503	309	246	39-9	9-3	1710	1742	835	162	41	481-22	1059	3.96	107	.264	.315	0	ø	0	104	53	255	6.0
Boskie, Shawn	Shawn Kealoha; B3.28.1967 Hawthorne NV; BR/TR/6´3˝/(200–210); [ChiN86*1/10]; d5.20; Col Modesto (CA) JC																									
1990	Chi N	5	6	.455	15	15	1	0-0	97.2	99	42	8	1	31-3	49	3.69	111	.265	.322	36-0-2	.222	1	83	5	52	0.7
1991	Chi N	4	9	.308	28	20	0	0-0	129	150	78	14	5	52-4	62	5.23	75	.294	.361	41-1-3	.171	2*	94	-15	0	-1.2
1992	Chi N	5	11	.313	23	18	0	0-0	91.2	96	55	14	4	36-3	39	5.01	72	.284	.354	27-0-3	.185	1	76	-13	36	-1.8
1993	Chi N	5	3	.625	39	2	0	0-3	65.2	63	30	7	7	21-2	39	3.43	118	.258	.333	11	.273	1	134	3	0	0.4
1994	Chi N	0	0	ø	2	0	0	0-0	3.2	3	0	0	0	0-0	2	0.00	ø	.214	.214	0	ø	0	—	2	0	0.1
	Phi N	4	6	.400	18	14	1	0-1	84.1	85	56	14	3	29-2	59	5.23	82	.258	.321	26-0-1	.115	1*	93	-9	0	-0.8
	Year	4	6	.400	20	14	1	0-1	88	88	56	14	3	29-2	61	5.01	85	.256	.317	26-0-1	.115	1	93	-9	0	-0.7
	Sea A	0	1	.000	2	1	0	0-0	2.2	4	2	1	0	1-1	0	6.75	73	.333	.385	0	ø	0	37	0	12	-0.1
1995	Cal A	7	7	.500	20	20	1	0-0	111.2	127	73	16	7	25-0	51	5.64	84	.281	.324	0	ø	0	109	-10	57	-1.1
1996	Cal A	12	11	.522	37	28	1	0-0	189.1	226	126	40	13	67-7	133	5.32	95	.294	.358	0	ø	0	95	-6	0	-0.6
1997	Bal A	6	6	.500	28	9	0	1-0	77	95	57	14	2	26-1	50	6.43	69	.304	.354	0	ø	0*	97	-17	16	-2.2
1998	Mon N	1	3	.250	5	5	0	0-0	17.2	34	21	5	2	4-1	10	9.17	46	.415	.449	4	.000	-0	136	-10	0	-1.7
Total	9	49	63	.438	217	132	4	1-4	870.1	982	540	133	44	292-24	494	5.14	85	.286	.346	145-1-9	.179	5	95	-70	173	-8.3
Bosman, Dick	Richard Allen; B2.17.1944 Kenosha WI; BR/TR/6´3˝/(205–208); d6.1; C11																									
1966	Was A	2	6	.250	13	7	0	0	39	60	36	4	0	12-4	20	7.62	45	.361	.402	12-0-2	.250	0	98	-17	0	-3.0
1967	Was A	3	1	.750	7	7	2-1	0	51.1	38	12	3	0	10-2	25	1.75	180	.204	.242	15-0-2	.200	0*	98	8	0	0.7
1968	Was A	2	9	.182	46	10	0	1	139	139	63	9	4	35-5	63	3.69	79	.262	.310	30-0-1	.200	1	80	-11	0	-0.8
1969	Was A	14	5	.737	31	26	5-2	1-0	193	156	59	11	2	39-0	99	**2.19**	**160**	.220	.260	64-0-5	.094	-1*	119	27	0	2.6
1970	Was A	16	12	.571	36	34	7-3	0-0	230.2	212	81	16	2	71-8	134	3.00	120	.245	.302	80-0-6	.138	-2	84	18	0	1.9
1971	Was A	12	16	.429	35	35	7-1	0-0	236.2	245	110	29	5	71-9	113	3.73	91	.272	.327	75-0-5	.093	-1	102	-9	0	-1.2
1972	Tex A	8	10	.444	29	29	1-1	0-0	173.1	183	87	11	6	48-6	105	3.63	84	.273	.326	53-0-13	.094	-2	122	-14	21	-1.6
1973	Tex A	2	5	.286	7	7	1-1	0-0	40.1	42	24	6	1	17-1	14	4.24	89	.268	.341	0	ø	0	68	-3	0	-0.5
	Cle A	1	8	.111	22	17	2	0-0	97	130	74	19	6	29-5	41	6.22	64	.320	.373	0	ø	0	96	-23	0	-1.9
	Year	3	13	.188	29	24	3-1	0-0	137.1	172	98	25	7	46-6	55	5.64	69	.306	.364	0	ø	0	88	-27	0	-2.4
1974	Cle A	7	5	.583	25	18	2-1	0-0	127.1	126	69	13	1	29-3	56	4.10	89	.255	.297	0	ø	0	112	-8	0	-0.8
1975	Cle A	0	2	.000	6	3	0	0-0	28.2	33	17	3	3	8-1	11	4.08	93	.292	.349	0	ø	0	54	-2	0	-0.1
	†Oak A	11	4	.733	22	21	2	0-0	122.2	112	50	12	3	24-3	42	3.52	104	.240	.280	0	ø	0	115	4	0	0.4
	Year	11	6	.647	28	24	2	0-0	151.1	145	67	15	6	32-4	53	3.63	101	.250	.294	0	ø	0	107	2	0	0.3
1976	Oak A	4	2	.667	27	15	0	0-0	112	118	54	13	1	19-1	34	4.10	82	.274	.305	0	ø	0	136	-8	0	-0.4
Total	11	82	85	.491	306	229	29-10	2-0	1591	1594	736	149	34	412-48	757	3.67	94	.261	.310	329-0-34	.125	-5	105	-38	21	-4.7
Bosser, Mel	Melvin Edward; B2.8.1914 Johnstown PA; D3.26.1986 Crossville TN; BR/TR/6´0˝/173; d4.29																									
1945	Cin N	2	0	1.000	7	1	0	0	16	9	6	0	0	17	3	3.38	111	.158	.351	4	.000	-1	68	1	0	0.0
Boswell, Andy	Andrew Cottrell; B9.26.1873 New Gretna NJ; D2.3.1936 Ocean City NJ; TR/6´1˝/165; d5.10; Col Penn																									
1895	NY N	2	2	.500	5	4	3	0	34	41	35	1	3	22	18	5.82	80	.293	.400	16	.188	-1	115	-6	—	-0.6
	Was N	1	2	.333	6	3	3	0	30	44	32	1	2	19	12	6.00	80	.336	.428	14	.286	0*	114	-4	—	-0.3
	Year	3	4	.429	11	7	6	0	64	85	67	2	5	41	30	5.91	80	.314	.413	30	.233	-1	114	-11	—	-0.9
Boswell, Dave	David Wilson; B1.20.1945 Baltimore MD; BR/TR/6´3˝/(180–195); d9.18																									
1964	Min A	2	0	1.000	4	4	0	0	23.1	21	11	4	0	12-1	25	4.24	84	.236	.327	9-0-1	.222	0	118	-1	0	0.0
1965	†Min A	6	5	.545	27	12	1	0	106	77	43	20	5	46-0	85	3.40	105	.204	.298	38	.316	4*	117	4	30	0.7
1966	Min A	12	5	.706	28	21	8-1	0	169.1	120	66	19	5	65-2	173	3.14	115	.197	.279	63-0-2	.143	-1*	117	9	0	0.8
1967	Min A	14	12	.538	37	32	11-3	0	222.2	162	84	14	7	107-5	204	3.27	106	.202	.301	73-1-3	.219	4*	100	8	0	1.3
1968	Min A	10	13	.435	34	28	7-2	0	190	148	79	19	7	87-2	143	3.32	93	.213	.305	60-1-5	.233	5*	98	-3	0	0.0
1969	†Min A	20	12	.625	39	38	10	0-0	256.1	215	105	18	8	99-2	190	3.23	113	.226	.303	94-2-6	.170	3*	116	12	0	1.5
1970	Min A	3	7	.300	18	15	0	0-0	68.2	80	55	12	2	44-3	45	6.42	58	.292	.390	25	.160	-0*	128	-20	29	-2.6
1971	Det A	0	0	ø	3	0	0	0-0	4.1	3	3	0	0	6-0	3	6.23	58	.200	.409	0	ø	0	—	-1	0	0.0
	Bal A	1	2	.333	15	1	0	0-0	24.2	32	16	4	0	15-1	14	4.38	78	.305	.388	5	.200	0	53	-4	0	-0.4
	Year	1	2	.333	18	1	0	0-0	29	35	19	4	0	21-1	17	4.66	74	.292	.392	5	.200	0	52	-5	0	-0.4
Total	8	68	56	.548	205	151	37-6	0-0	1065.1	858	462	110	34	481-16	882	3.52	99	.219	.309	367-4-17	.202	13	111	4	59	1.3
Botelho, Derek	Derek Wayne; B8.2.1956 Long Beach CA; BR/TR/6´2˝/180; [PhiN76*2/42]; d7.18; Col Miami–Dade Kendall (FL) CC																									
1982	KC A	2	1	.667	8	4	0	0-0	24	25	11	4	0	8-0	12	4.13	99	.275	.330	0	ø	0	145	0	0	0.0
1985	Chi N	1	3	.250	11	7	1	0-0	44	52	27	8	2	23-1	23	5.32	75	.299	.387	14	.143	-0	117	-5	0	-0.5
Total	2	3	4	.429	19	11	1	0-0	68	77	38	12	2	31-1	35	4.90	83	.291	.368	14	.143	-0	127	-5	0	-0.5

YEAR	TM LG	W	L	PCT	G	GS	CG-SHO	SV-BS	IP	H	R	HR	HB	BB-IB	SO	ERA	AERA	OAV	OOB	AB-HR-SH	AVG	PB	SUP	APR	DL	PW
Bottalico, Ricky	Ricky Paul; B8.26.1969 New Britain CT; BL/TR/6´2˝/(200–217); d7.29; Col Central Connecticut																									
1994	Phi N	0	0	ø	3	0	0	0-0	3	3	0	0	0	1-0	3	0.00	ø	.250	.308	0	ø	0	—	1	0	0.1
1995	Phi N	5	3	.625	62	0	0	1-4	87.2	50	25	7	4	42-3	87	2.46	171	.167	.277	5-0-1	.000	-1	—	17	0	1.4
1996	Phi N★	4	5	.444	61	0	0	34-4	67.2	47	24	6	2	23-2	74	3.19	135	.197	.272	3	.333	1	—	9	0	1.9
1997	Phi N	2	5	.286	69	0	0	34-7	74	68	31	7	2	42-4	89	3.65	116	.245	.347	1	.000	-0	—	5	0	0.9
1998	Phi N	1	5	.167	39	0	0	6-1	43.1	54	31	7	1	25-5	27	6.44	67	.305	.390	0	ø	0	—	-9	68	-1.3
1999	StL N	3	7	.300	68	0	0	20-8	73.1	83	45	8	3	49-1	66	4.91	94	.284	.392	3	.000	-0	—	-3	0	-0.5
2000	KC A	9	6	.600	62	0	0	16-7	72.2	65	40	12	2	41-3	56	4.83	108	.239	.342	0	ø	0	—	4	0	0.7
2001	Phi N	3	4	.429	66	0	0	3-4	67	58	31	11	4	25-2	57	3.90	106	.241	.318	3	.333	1	—	2	21	0.2
2002	Phi N	0	3	.000	30	0	0	0-1	27.1	33	16	3	2	13-2	24	4.61	83	.300	.381	0	ø	0	—	-3	99	-0.3
2003	Ari N	1	0	1.000	2	0	0	0-0	1.2	3	1	0	0	2-1	2	5.40	86	.375	.500	0	ø	0	—	0	0	0.0
2004	NY N	3	2	.600	60	0	0	0-4	69.1	54	30	3	4	34-7	61	3.38	127	.215	.314	2	.000	-0	—	7	0	0.4
2005	Mil N	2	2	.500	40	0	0	2-4	41.2	43	24	7	3	19-0	29	4.54	94	.265	.349	0	ø	0	—	-2	0	-0.2
Total	12	33	42	.440	562	0	0	116-44	628.2	561	298	71	27	316-30	575	3.99	110	.240	.335	17-0-1	.118	-0	—	28	188	3.3
Bottenfield, Kent	Kent Dennis; B11.14.1968 Portland OR; BR/TR/6´3˝/(225–245); [MonN86 4/96]; d7.6																									
1992	Mon N	1	2	.333	10	4	0	1-0	32.1	26	9	1	1	11-1	14	2.23	157	.217	.284	8-0-1	.375	1	58	4	0	0.5
1993	Mon N	2	5	.286	23	11	0	0-0	83	93	49	11	5	33-2	33	4.12	101	.288	.362	24-0-1	.167	-0	76	-1	0	-0.1
	Col N	3	5	.375	14	14	1	0-0	76.2	86	53	13	1	38-1	30	6.10	78	.302	.382	26-0-2	.269	1	89	-8	0	-0.5
	Year	5	10	.333	37	25	1	0-0	159.2	179	102	24	6	71-3	63	5.07	88	.294	.372	50-0-3	.220	1	85	-10	0	-0.6
1994	Col N	3	1	.750	15	1	0	1-0	24.2	28	16	1	2	10-0	15	5.84	85	.283	.360	1	.000	-0	55	-1	36	-0.3
	SF N	0	0	ø	1	0	0	0-0	1.2	5	2	1	0	0-0	0	10.80	38	.556	.556	0	ø	0	—	-1	0	-0.1
	Year	3	1	.750	16	1	0	1-0	26.1	33	18	2	2	10-0	15	6.15	80	.306	.375	1	.000	-0	56	-3	0	-0.4
1996	Chi N	3	5	.375	48	0	0	1-2	61.2	59	25	3	3	19-4	33	2.63	166	.255	.320	2-0-1	.500	0	—	9	0	1.2
1997	Chi N	2	3	.400	64	0	0	2-2	84	82	39	13	2	35-7	74	3.86	112	.259	.333	4-0-4	.000	-0	—	4	0	0.1
1998	StL N	4	6	.400	44	17	0	4-1	133.2	128	72	13	4	57-3	98	4.44	95	.254	.333	34-0-5	.088	-2	122	-3	0	-0.4
1999	StL N★	18	7	.720	31	31	0	0-0	190.1	197	91	21	5	89-5	124	3.97	116	.270	.350	61-0-8	.148	-1	105	14	0	1.6
2000	Ana A	7	8	.467	21	21	0	0-0	127.2	144	82	25	3	56-4	75	5.71	90	.285	.357	3	.667	1	99	-5	15	-0.4
	Phi N	1	2	.333	8	8	1-1	0-0	44	41	24	5	0	21-0	31	4.50	102	.240	.320	14-0-3	.000	-2	75	0	0	-0.1
2001	Hou N	2	5	.286	13	9	0	1-0	52	61	44	16	2	16-0	39	6.40	72	.288	.338	14-0-1	.143	-0	83	-12	120	-1.4
Total	9	46	49	.484	292	116	2-1	10-5	911.2	950	506	123	28	385-27	566	4.54	100	.271	.345	191-0-26	.162	-3	97	0	171	0.1
Botting, Ralph	Ralph Wayne; B5.12.1955 Houlton ME; BL/TL/6´0˝/195; [AnaA74 7/154]; d6.28																									
1979	Cal A	2	0	1.000	12	1	0	0-0	29.2	46	30	6	1	15-1	22	8.80	46	.362	.428	0	ø	0	111	-15	0	-0.9
1980	Cal A	0	3	.000	6	6	0	0-0	26.1	40	20	1	0	13-0	12	5.81	68	.348	.411	0	ø	0	98	-6	0	-0.6
Total	2	2	3	.400	18	7	0	0-0	56	86	50	7	1	28-1	34	7.39	54	.355	.420	0	ø	0	99	-21	0	-1.5
Botz, Bob	Robert Allen; B4.28.1935 Milwaukee WI; BR/TR/5´11˝/170; d5.8																									
1962	LA A	2	1	.667	35	0	0	2	63	71	30	7	2	11-0	24	3.43	113	.285	.319	9-0-1	.000	-1	—	2	0	-0.1
Boucher, Denis	Denis; B3.7.1968 Montreal QC, Can.; BR/TL/6´1˝/195; d4.12																									
1991	Tor A	0	3	.000	7	7	0	0-0	35.1	39	20	6	2	16-1	16	4.58	92	.279	.358	0	ø	0	93	-2	0	-0.1
	Cle A	1	4	.200	5	5	0	0-0	22.2	35	21	6	0	8-0	13	8.34	50	.350	.398	0	ø	0	53	-9	0	-1.5
	Year	1	7	.125	12	12	0	0-0	58	74	41	12	2	24-1	29	6.05	69	.308	.375	0	ø	0	76	-10	0	-1.6
1992	Cle A	2	2	.500	8	7	0	0-0	41	48	29	9	1	20-0	17	6.37	62	.302	.377	0	ø	0	129	-10	0	-0.8
1993	Mon N	3	1	.750	5	5	0	0-0	28.1	24	7	1	0	3-1	14	1.91	219	.229	.243	6-0-2	.167	0	82	7	0	1.0
1994	Mon N	0	1	.000	10	2	0	0-1	18.2	24	16	6	0	7-0	17	6.75	63	.324	.378	3-0-1	.333	1	54	-5	0	-0.2
Total	4	6	11	.353	35	26	0	0-1	146	170	93	28	3	54-2	77	5.42	76	.294	.353	9-0-3	.222	1	89	-19	0	-1.6
Bouldin, Carl	Carl Edward; B9.17.1939 Germantown KY; BB/TR (BL 1961)/6´2˝/178; d9.2; Col Cincinnati																									
1961	Was A	0	1	.000	2	1	0	0	3.1	9	6	0	0	2-0	2	16.20	25	.500	.550	1	.000	-0	66	-4	0	-0.7
1962	Was A	1	2	.333	6	3	1	0	20	26	13	0	1	9-0	12	5.85	69	.321	.387	7	.000	-1*	81	-3	0	-0.5
1963	Was A	2	2	.500	10	3	0	0	23.1	31	18	3	0	8-1	10	5.79	64	.307	.355	7	.000	-1	88	-6	0	-0.9
1964	Was A	0	3	.000	9	3	0	0	25	30	20	2	2	11-2	12	5.40	69	.294	.368	6	.000	-0*	64	-6	0	-0.7
Total	4	3	8	.273	27	10	1	0	71.2	96	57	5	3	30-3	36	6.15	62	.318	.379	21	.000	-2	77	-19	0	-2.8
Boultes, Jake	Jacob John; B8.6.1884 St.Louis MO; D12.24.1955 St.Louis MO; BR/TR/6´3˝/?; d4.18																									
1907	Bos N	5	9	.357	24	12	11	0	139.2	140	75	1	8	50	49	2.71	94	.266	.338	68	.132	-2*	86	-10	—	-0.9
1908	Bos N	3	5	.375	17	5	1	0	74.2	80	40	7	1	8	28	3.01	80	.274	.296	21-0-4	.143	-0*	134	-7	—	-0.8
1909	Bos N	0	0	ø	1	0	0	0	8	9	7	2	1	0	1	6.75	42	.290	.313	3	.333	0	—	-3	—	-0.1
Total	3	8	14	.364	42	17	12	0	222.1	229	122	10	10	58	78	2.96	85	.269	.324	92-0-4	.141	-2	100	-20	—	-1.8
Bourgeois, Steve	Steven James; B8.4.1972 Lutcher LA; BR/TR/6´1˝/220; [SFN93 21/582]; d4.3; Col Louisiana–Monroe																									
1996	SF N	1	3	.250	15	5	0	0-0	40	60	35	4	4	21-4	17	6.30	66	.355	.434	11-0-1	.273	2	104	-11	0	-0.7
Bouton, Jim	James Alan; B3.8.1939 Newark NJ; BR/TR/6´0˝/(174–185); d4.22; Col Western Michigan																									
1962	NY A	7	7	.500	36	16	3-1	2	133	124	63	9	0	59-1	71	3.99	94	.254	.330	32-0-4	.063	-2*	122	-2	0	-0.4
1963	†NY A★	21	7	.750	40	30	12-6	1	249.1	191	79	18	3	87-2	148	2.53	139	.212	.282	83-0-11	.072	-6	111	27	0	2.3
1964	†NY A	18	13	.581	38	**37**	11-4	0	271.1	227	100	32	6	60-4	125	3.02	120	.225	.272	100-0-7	.130	-3	110	18	0	1.4
1965	NY A	4	15	.211	30	25	2	0	151.1	158	89	23	5	60-1	97	4.82	71	.269	.339	43-0-2	.093	-0*	97	-23	0	-2.7
1966	NY A	3	8	.273	24	19	3	1	120.1	117	49	13	1	38-5	65	2.69	123	.257	.313	38-0-3	.105	-2	91	5	0	0.3
1967	NY A	1	0	1.000	17	1	0	0	44.1	47	31	5	1	18-5	31	4.67	67	.275	.344	7-0-1	.000	-0	195	-10	0	-0.6
1968	NY A	1	1	.500	12	3	1	0	44	49	20	5	2	9-0	24	3.68	79	.287	.326	7	.000	-0	90	-3	0	-0.2
1969	Sea A	2	1	.667	57	1	0	1-0	92	77	48	12	2	38-4	68	3.91	93	.219	.298	9	.000	-1	170	-4	0	-0.3
	Hou N	0	2	.000	16	1	1	1-0	30.2	32	16	1	2	12-1	32	4.11	87	.267	.343	4	.000	-0	50	-2	0	-0.2
1970	Hou N	4	6	.400	29	6	1	0-0	73.1	84	53	5	1	33-3	49	5.40	72	.285	.358	17-0-1	.353	2	154	-15	0	-1.5
1978	Atl N	1	3	.250	5	5	0	0-0	29	25	18	4	0	21-1	10	4.97	81	.234	.357	7	.000	-1	67	-3	0	-0.4
Total	10	62	63	.496	304	144	34-11	6-0	1238.2	1131	566	127	23	435-27	720	3.57	99	.243	.309	347-0-29	.101	-13	108	-12	0	-2.3
Bovee, Mike	Michael Craig; B8.21.1973 San Diego CA; BR/TR/5´10˝/200; [KCA91 6/158]; d9.13																									
1997	Ana A	0	0	ø	3	0	0	0-0	3.1	3	2	1	0	1-0	5	5.40	85	.231	.286	0	ø	0	—	0	0	0.0
Bowen, Ryan	Ryan Eugene; B2.10.1968 Hanford CA; BR/TR/6´0˝/185; [HouN86 1/13]; d7.22																									
1991	Hou N	6	4	.600	14	13	0	0-0	71.2	73	43	4	3	36-1	49	5.15	69	.268	.353	22-0-1	.182	1*	114	-12	0	-1.4
1992	Hou N	0	7	.000	11	9	0	0-0	33.2	48	43	8	2	30-3	22	10.96	31	.333	.455	9	.111	-0*	80	-28	0	-4.5
1993	Fla N	8	12	.400	27	27	2-1	0-0	156.2	156	83	11	3	87-7	98	4.42	99	.263	.358	51-0-3	.118	-1	86	-1	0	-0.2
1994	Fla N	1	5	.167	8	8	1	0-0	47.1	50	28	9	2	19-0	32	4.94	90	.273	.345	14-0-1	.357	2	77	-2	89	0.0
1995	Fla N	2	0	1.000	4	3	0	0-0	16.2	23	11	3	0	12-2	15	3.78	114	.329	.417	6	.333	0	119	-1	131	0.0
Total	5	17	28	.378	64	60	3-1	0-0	326	350	208	35	10	184-13	216	5.30	77	.277	.370	102-0-5	.176	2	90	-44	220	-6.1
Bowen, Cy	Sutherland McCoy; B2.17.1871 Kingston IN; D1.25.1925 Greensburg IN; BR/TR/6´0˝/175; d4.28																									
1896	NY N	0	1	.000	2	1	1	0	12	12	13	0	3	9	3	6.00	70	.261	.414	3-0-2	.333	0	51	-3	—	-0.1
Bowers, Shane	Shane Patrick; B7.27.1971 Glendora CA; BR/TR/6´4˝/213; [MinA93 21/597]; d7.26; Col Loyola Marymount																									
1997	Min A	0	3	.000	5	5	0	0-0	19	27	20	2	1	8-0	7	8.05	58	.329	.391	0	ø	0	67	-8	0	-1.0
Bowers, Stew	Stewart Cole "Doc"; B2.26.1915 New Freedom PA; D12.14.2005 Havertown PA; BB/TR/6´0˝/170; d8.5; Col Gettysburg																									
1935	Bos A	2	1	.667	10	2	1	0	23.2	26	14	1	0	17	5	3.42	139	.283	.394	5	.200	0*	46	2	—	0.2
1936	Bos A	0	0	ø	5	0	0	0	5.2	10	7	1	0	2	0	9.53	56	.370	.414	0	ø	0*	—	-3	—	-0.1
Total	2	2	1	.667	15	2	1	0	29.1	36	21	2	0	19	5	4.60	106	.303	.399	5	.200	0	46	-1	—	0.1
Bowie, Micah	Micah Andrew; B11.10.1974 Humble TX; BL/TL/6´4˝/(185–210); [AtlN93 8/236]; d7.24																									
1999	Atl N	0	1	.000	3	0	0	0-0	4	8	6	1	0	4-0	2	13.50	33	.421	.522	0	ø	0	—	-4	0	-0.6
	Chi N	2	6	.250	11	11	0	0-0	47	73	54	8	2	30-2	39	9.96	46	.358	.439	14	.214	0	101	-27	0	-3.3
	Year	2	7	.222	14	11	0	0-0	51	81	60	9	2	34-2	41	10.24	45	.363	.447	14	.214	0	101	-31	0	-3.9
2002	†Oak A	2	0	1.000	13	0	0	0-0	12	12	2	1	1	8-1	8	1.50	299	.261	.382	0	ø	0	—	4	0	0.6

YEAR	TM LG	W	L	PCT	G	GS	CG-SHO	SV-BS	IP	H	R	HR	HB	BB-IB	SO	ERA	AERA	OAV	OOB	AB-HR-SH	AVG	PB	SUP	APR	DL	PW
2003	Oak A	0	1	.000	6	0	0	0-0	8.1	13	7	1	0	2-0	4	7.56	61	.361	.395	0	ø	0	—	-2	129	-0.2
2006	Was N	0	1	.000	15	0	0	0-0	19.2	11	3	1	0	7-0	11	1.37	318	.164	.243	1	.000	-0	—	7	53	0.3
Total	4	4	9	.308	48	11	0	0-0	91	117	72	12	3	51-3	64	6.92	65	.315	.399	15	.200	0	102	-22	182	-3.2
BOWLER, GRANT	Grant Tierney "Moose"; B10.24.1907 Denver CO; D6.25.1968 Denver CO; BR/TR/6´0˝/190; d8.21; Col DePaul																									
1931	Chi A	0	1	.000	13	3	1	0	35.1	40	26	1	0	24	15	5.35	80	.288	.393	10	.100	-0	106	-5	—	-0.3
1932	Chi A	0	0	ø	4	0	0	0	6.1	15	12	1	0	3	2	15.63	28	.484	.529	2	.000	-0	—	-8	—	-0.4
Total	2	0	1	.000	17	3	1	0	41.2	55	38	2	0	27	17	6.91	62	.324	.416	12	.083	-1	106	-13	—	-0.7
BOWLES, BRIAN	Brian Christopher; B8.18.1976 Harbor City CA; BR/TR/6´5˝/220; [TorA94 50/1361]; d6.27																									
2001	Tor A	0	0	ø	2	0	0	0-0	3.2	4	0	0	0	1-0	4	0.00	ø	.286	.333	0	ø	0	—	2	0	0.1
2002	Tor A	2	1	.667	17	0	0	0-1	20	13	11	0	3	14-1	19	4.05	114	.183	.337	0	ø	0	—	1	0	0.1
2003	Tor A	0	0	ø	5	0	0	0-0	7	8	4	1	2	2-0	2	2.57	185	.267	.353	0	ø	0	—	1	0	0.0
Total	3	2	1	.667	24	0	0	0-1	30.2	25	15	1	5	17-1	25	3.23	144	.217	.341	0	ø	0	—	4	0	0.2
BOWLES, CHARLIE	Charles James; B3.15.1917 Norwood MA; D12.23.2003 Newton NC; BR/TR/6´3˝/180; d9.25; Mil 1943–45																									
1943	Phi A	1	1	.500	2	2	2	0	18	17	10	0	0	4	6	3.00	113	.258	.300	8	.125	-1*	136	-1	0	-0.1
1945	Phi A	0	3	.000	8	4	1	0	33.1	35	19	3	0	23	11	5.13	67	.273	.384	21	.238	0*	93	-5	0	-0.4
Total	2	1	4	.200	10	6	3	0	51.1	52	29	3	0	27	17	4.38	78	.268	.357	29	.207	-0	108	-6	0	-0.5
BOWLES, EMMETT	Emmett Jerome "Chief"; B8.2.1898 Wanette OK; D9.3.1959 Flagstaff AZ; BR/TR/6´0˝/180; d9.12																									
1922	Chi A	0	0	ø	1	0	0	0	1	2	3	0	0	1	0	27.00	15	.500	.600	0	ø	0	—	-2	—	-0.1
BOWMAN, ABE	Alvah Edson; B1.25.1893 Greenup IL; D10.11.1979 Longview TX; BR/TR/6´1˝/190; d5.19																									
1914	Cle A	2	7	.222	22	10	2-1	0	72.2	74	45	0	4	45	27	4.46	65	.277	.389	21	.048	-2	78	-10	—	-1.4
1915	Cle A	0	1	.000	2	1	0	0	1.1	1	4	0	0	3	0	20.25	15	.250	.571	0	ø	0	72	-2	—	-0.4
Total	2	2	8	.200	24	11	2-1	0	74	75	49	0	4	48	27	4.74	61	.277	.393	21	.048	-2	78	-12	—	-1.8
BOWMAN, JOE	Joseph Emil; B6.17.1910 Kansas City KS; D11.22.1990 Kansas City MO; BL/TR/6´2˝/190; d4.18																									
1932	Phi A	0	1	.000	7	0	0	0	11	14	10	2	3	6	4	8.18	55	.318	.434	1	1.000	0	—	-4	—	-0.2
1934	NY N	5	4	.556	30	10	3	3	107.1	119	52	9	2	36	36	3.61	107	.279	.338	29-0-1	.172	0*	125	3	—	0.2
1935	Phi N	7	10	.412	33	17	6-1	1	148.1	157	86	13	4	56	58	4.25	107	.269	.337	67-1-1	.194	0*	85	3	—	0.4
1936	Phi N	9	20	.310	40	28	12	1	203.2	243	140	14	7	53	80	5.04	90	.289	.336	77-0-1	.195	-1*	90	-10	—	-1.4
1937	Pit N	8	8	.500	30	19	7	1	128	161	78	11	1	35	38	4.57	85	.306	.351	47-0-3	.213	2*	110	-10	—	-1.0
1938	Pit N	3	4	.429	17	1	0	1	60	68	33	2	0	20	25	4.65	82	.285	.340	21-0-2	.333	2*	134	-4	—	-0.3
1939	Pit N	10	14	.417	37	27	10-1	1	184.2	217	105	15	7	43	58	4.48	86	.292	.336	96-0-4	.344	12*	109	-13	—	-0.3
1940	Pit N	9	10	.474	32	24	10	2	187.2	209	113	10	7	66	57	4.46	85	.274	.337	90-1-0	.244	9*	132	-16	—	-0.5
1941	Pit N	3	2	.600	18	7	1-1	1	69.1	77	24	3	1	28	22	2.99	121	.278	.346	31	.258	1*	121	6	0	0.6
1944	Bos A	12	8	.600	26	24	10-1	0	168.1	175	95	14	2	64	53	4.81	71	.269	.336	100	.200	3*	138	-23	0	-2.3
1945	Bos A	0	2	.000	3	3	0	0	11.2	18	12	1	0	9	0	9.26	37	.360	.458	9	.222	0*	92	-7	0	-0.9
	Cin N	11	13	.458	25	24	15-1	0	185.2	198	89	8	7	68	71	3.59	105	.270	.338	71-0-2	.070	-5*	88	2	0	-0.4
Total	11	77	96	.445	298	184	74-5	11	1465.2	1656	837	102	41	484	502	4.40	89	.282	.341	639-2-14	.221	24	108	-73	0	-6.1
BOWMAN, BOB	Robert James; B10.3.1910 Keystone WV; D9.4.1972 Bluefield WV; BR/TR/5´10.5˝/160; d4.21																									
1939	StL N	13	5	.722	51	15	4-2	**9**	169.1	141	54	8	1	60	78	2.60	158	.232	.302	47-0-5	.085	-3	108	28	—	2.7
1940	StL N	7	5	.583	28	17	7	0	114.1	118	66	9	4	43	43	4.33	92	.267	.337	33-0-2	.061	-2	121	-5	—	-0.7
1941	NY N	6	7	.462	29	6	2	1	80.1	100	55	10	1	36	25	5.71	65	.302	.372	21-1-3	.048	-1	119	-16	0	-2.4
1942	Chi N	0	0	ø	1	0	0	0	1	1	0	0	0	0	0	0.00	ø	.250	.250	0	ø	0	—	0	0	0.0
Total	4	26	17	.605	109	38	13-2	10	365	360	175	27	6	139	146	3.82	104	.260	.330	101-1-10	.069	-5	115	7	0	-0.4
BOWMAN, ROGER	Roger Clinton; B8.18.1927 Amsterdam NY; D7.21.1997 Los Angeles CA; BR/TL/6´0˝/175; d9.22																									
1949	NY N	0	0	ø	2	2	0	0	6.1	6	3	1	0	7	4	4.26	93	.261	.433	2	.000	-0	100	0	0	0.0
1951	NY N	2	4	.333	9	5	0	0	26.1	35	18	2	1	22	24	6.15	64	.297	.411	6-0-1	.000	-0	86	-5	0	-1.1
1952	NY N	0	0	ø	2	1	0	0	3	6	4	0	1	3	3	12.00	31	.429	.556	1	.000	-0	216	-2	0	-0.1
1953	Pit N	0	4	.000	30	2	0	0	65.1	65	42	9	1	29	36	4.82	93	.261	.341	7	.286	0	20	-4	0	-0.1
1955	Pit N	0	3	.000	7	2	0	0	16.2	25	18	2	1	10-2	8	8.64	48	.347	.434	2-0-1	.500	0	54	-8	0	-1.1
Total	5	2	11	.154	50	12	0	0	117.2	137	85	14	4	71-2	75	5.81	73	.288	.385	18-0-2	.167	-0	77	-19	0	-2.4
BOWMAN, SUMNER	Sumner Sallade; B2.9.1867 Millersburg PA; D1.11.1954 Millersburg PA; BL/TL/6´0˝/160; d6.11; Col Penn																									
1890	Phi N	0	0	ø	1	1	0	0	8	11	7	0	1	2	2	7.88	46	.314	.368	4	.500	1	138	-2	—	-0.1
	Pit N	2	5	.286	9	7	6	0	70.2	100	90	1	11	50	22	6.62	50	.323	.434	36	.278	2*	134	-31	—	-2.0
	Year	2	5	.286	10	8	6	0	78.2	111	97	1	12	52	24	6.75	49	.322	.428	40	.300	2	135	-34	—	-2.1
1891	Phi AA	2	5	.286	8	8	8	0	68	73	54	0	5	37	22	3.44	110	.265	.363	54	.241	0*	82	-3	—	-0.2
Total	2	4	10	.286	18	16	14	0	146.2	184	151	1	17	89	46	5.22	68	.297	.399	94	.266	3	107	-36	—	-2.3
BOWSFIELD, TED	Edward Oliver; B1.10.1935 Vernon BC, Can.; BR/TL/6´1˝/190; d7.20																									
1958	Bos A	4	2	.667	16	10	2	0	65.2	58	32	3	1	36-1	38	3.84	104	.233	.331	26	.154	-1*	121	1	0	0.0
1959	Bos A	0	1	.000	5	2	0	0	9	16	15	2	0	9-0	4	15.00	27	.390	.500	1	.000	-0	152	-10	0	-0.9
1960	Bos A	1	2	.333	17	2	0	2	21	20	12	1	1	13-0	18	5.14	79	.260	.366	4-0-2	.250	0	163	-2	0	-0.2
	Cle A	3	4	.429	11	6	1-1	0	40.2	47	30	1	0	20-1	14	5.09	73	.296	.372	10-0-1	.100	-0	67	-8	0	-1.2
	Year	4	6	.400	28	8	1-1	2	61.2	67	42	2	1	33-1	32	5.11	75	.284	.370	14-0-3	.143	-0	92	-10	0	-1.4
1961	LA A	11	8	.579	41	21	4-1	0	157	154	75	18	1	63-3	88	3.73	121	.255	.323	51-0-2	.137	-1*	95	12	0	1.1
1962	LA A	9	8	.529	34	25	1	1	139	154	82	12	2	40-0	52	4.40	88	.277	.325	37-0-4	.162	1*	104	-10	0	-1.0
1963	KC A	5	7	.417	41	11	2-1	3	111.1	115	60	14	3	47-5	67	4.45	88	.269	.343	23-0-2	.043	-1*	83	-6	0	-0.6
1964	KC A	4	7	.364	50	9	2-1	0	118.2	135	63	12	4	31-4	45	4.10	93	.285	.331	21-0-2	.095	-1*	78	-5	0	-0.5
Total	7	37	39	.487	215	86	12-4	6	662.1	699	369	63	12	259-14	326	4.35	93	.270	.336	173-0-13	.127	-3	99	-28	0	-3.3
BOWYER, TRAVIS	Travis Charlton; B8.3.1981 Lynchburg VA; BR/TR/6´3˝/210; [MinA19 9/599]; d9.10																									
2005	Min A	0	1	.000	8	0	0	0-1	9.2	10	6	3	1	3-0	12	5.59	78	.270	.333	0	ø	0	—	-1	0	-0.1
BOYD, OIL CAN	Dennis Ray; B10.6.1959 Meridian MS; BR/TR/6´1˝/(144–160); [BosA80 16/414]; d9.13; Col Jackson St.																									
1982	Bos A	0	1	.000	3	1	0	0-1	8.1	11	5	2	0	2-0	2	5.40	81	.314	.351	0	ø	0	21	-1	0	-0.1
1983	Bos A	4	8	.333	15	13	5	0-0	98.2	103	46	9	1	23-0	43	3.28	134	.269	.308	0	ø	0	81	9	0	0.9
1984	Bos A	12	12	.500	29	26	10-3	0-0	197.2	207	109	18	1	53-5	134	4.37	96	.269	.314	0	ø	0	108	-3	0	-0.3
1985	Bos A	15	13	.536	35	35	13-3	0-0	272.1	273	117	26	4	67-3	154	3.70	117	.261	.306	0	ø	0	107	20	0	2.1
1986	†Bos A	16	10	.615	30	30	10	0-0	214.1	222	99	32	2	45-1	129	3.78	111	.265	.302	0	ø	0	119	11	0	1.2
1987	Bos A	1	3	.250	7	7	0	0-0	36.2	47	31	6	2	9-1	12	5.89	78	.315	.356	0	ø	0	108	-8	143	-0.6
1988	Bos A	9	7	.563	23	23	1	0-0	129.2	147	82	25	2	41-2	71	5.34	77	.289	.341	0	ø	0	112	-16	57	-1.7
1989	Bos A	3	2	.600	10	10	0	0-0	59	57	31	8	0	19-0	26	4.42	93	.253	.309	0	ø	0	128	-1	122	-0.1
1990	Mon N	10	6	.625	31	31	3-3	0-0	190.2	164	64	19	3	52-10	113	2.93	126	.233	.287	59-0-12	.051	-4	110	18	0	0.9
1991	Mon N	6	8	.429	19	19	1-1	0-0	120.1	115	49	9	0	40-2	82	3.52	104	.256	.314	36-0-3	.083	-1	94	3	0	0.2
	Tex A	2	7	.222	12	12	0	0-0	62	81	47	12	0	17-1	33	6.68	61	.314	.356	0	ø	0	68	-16	0	-2.0
Total	10	78	77	.503	214	207	43-10	0-1	1389.2	1427	680	166	15	368-25	799	4.04	102	.266	.313	95-0-15	.063	-5	105	16	322	0.5
BOYD, GARY	Gary Lee; B8.22.1946 Pasadena CA; BR/TR/6´4˝/200; d8.1; Col El Camino (CA) JC																									
1969	Cle A	0	2	.000	8	3	0	0-0	11	8	11	1	0	14-1	9	9.00	42	.205	.407	1	.000	-0	54	-5	0	-0.9
BOYD, JAKE	Jacob Henry; B1.19.1874 Martinsburg WV; D8.12.1932 Gettysburg PA; TL/?/160; d9.20; ▲																									
1894	Was N	0	3	.000	3	3	3	0	19	37	35	1	1	14	3	8.53	62	.402	.486	21	.143	-1*	76	-9	—	-0.9
1895	Was N	2	11	.154	15	13	8	0	92.2	132	95	1	11	40	18	6.80	71	.329	.405	159-1-0	.270	2*	73	-15	—	-1.3
1896	Was N	1	2	.333	4	2	2	0	32	45	34	0	6	15	6	6.75	65	.328	.418	13	.077	-1	56	-7	—	-0.6
Total	3	3	16	.158	22	18	13	0	143.2	214	164	2	18	69	27	7.02	68	.340	.420	193-1-0	.244	-1	73	-31	—	-2.8
BOYD, JASON	Jason Pernell; B2.23.1973 St.Clair IL; BR/TR/6´3˝/(170–175); [PhiN94 8/226]; d9.10; Col John A. Logan (IL) CC																									
1999	Pit N	0	0	ø	4	0	0	0-0	5.1	5	2	0	1	2-0	4	3.38	136	.250	.333	1	.000	-0	—	1	0	0.0
2000	Phi N	0	1	.000	30	0	0	0-1	34.1	39	28	2	1	24-4	32	6.55	70	.293	.405	0	ø	0	—	-8	90	-0.4
2002	SD N	1	0	1.000	23	0	0	0-3	28.1	33	29	6	0	15-1	18	7.94	49	.300	.375	0	ø	0	—	-14	0	-0.7

YEAR	TM LG	W	L	PCT	G	GS	CG-SHO	SV-BS	IP	H	R	HR	HB	BB-IB	SO	ERA	AERA	OAV	OOB	AB-HR-SH	AVG	PB	SUP	APR	DL	PW
2003	Cle A	3	1	.750	44	0	0	0-1	52.1	38	25	4	3	26-1	31	4.30	103	.200	.303	0	ø	0	—	2	19	0.2
2004	Pit N	1	0	1.000	12	0	0	0-0	13	13	9	4	3	8-1	12	5.54	78	.260	.393	0	ø	0	—	-2	0	-0.1
Total	5	5	2	.714	113	0	0	0-5	133.1	128	93	16	8	75-7	97	5.74	76	.254	.356	1	.000	-0	—	-21	109	-1.0
Boyd, Ray	Raymond C.; B2.11.1887 Hortonville IN; D2.11.1920 Hortonville IN; BR/TR/5´10˝/160; d9.24																									
1910	StL A	0	2	.000	3	2	1	0	14.1	16	10	0	1	5	6	4.40	56	.286	.355	5	.200	-0	41	-3	—	-0.4
1911	Cin N	2	2	.500	7	4	3	1	44	34	22	0	2	19	20	2.66	124	.206	.296	12-0-1	.083	-0	62	2	—	0.1
Total	2	2	4	.333	10	6	4	1	58.1	50	32	0	3	24	26	3.09	101	.226	.310	17-0-1	.118	-0	55	-1	—	-0.3
Boyer, Blaine	Blaine Thomas; B7.11.1981 Atlanta GA; BR/TR/6´3˝/215; [AtlN00 3/100]; d6.12																									
2005	Atl N	4	2	.667	43	0	0	0-2	37.2	32	13	1	2	17-0	33	3.11	136	.234	.325	0	ø	0	—	5	0	0.7
2006	Atl N	0	0	ø	2	0	0	0-0	0.2	4	3	0	0	1-0	0	40.50	11	.667	.714	0	ø	0	—	-3	100	-0.1
Total	2	4	2	.667	45	0	0	0-2	38.1	36	16	1	2	18-0	33	3.76	113	.252	.341	0	ø	0	—	2	100	0.6
Boyer, Cloyd	Cloyd Victor "Junior"; B9.1.1927 Alba MO; BR/TR/6´1˝/188; d4.23; C8; b–Clete b–Ken																									
1949	StL N	0	0	ø	3	1	0	0	3.1	5	4	0	0	7	0	10.80	39	.357	.571	0	ø	0*	85	-2	0	-0.1
1950	StL N	7	7	.500	36	14	6-1	1	120.1	105	52	15	3	49	82	3.52	122	.233	.312	33-0-3	.182	0	123	10	0	1.1
1951	StL N	2	5	.286	19	8	1	1	63.1	68	42	9	3	46	40	5.26	75	.286	.408	20-0-1	.200	0	123	-10	0	-1.0
1952	StL N	6	6	.500	23	14	4-2	0	110.1	108	56	11	4	47	44	4.24	88	.258	.338	38	.211	2*	101	-5	0	-0.4
1955	KC A	5	5	.500	30	11	2	0	98.1	107	81	21	7	69-3	32	6.22	67	.282	.398	29-0-1	.069	-2	97	-24	0	-2.3
Total	5	20	23	.465	111	48	13-3	2	395.2	393	235	56	17	218-3	198	4.73	86	.262	.361	120-0-5	.167	1	110	-31	0	-2.7
Boyle, Henry	Henry J. "Handsome Henry"; B9.20.1860 Philadelphia PA; D5.25.1932 Philadelphia PA; BR/TR; d7.9; ▲																									
1884	StL U	15	3	.833	19	16	16-2	1	150	118	63	3	—	10	88	1.74	137	.202	.215	262-4	.260	1*	127	10	—	0.7
1885	StL N	16	24	.400	42	39	39-1	0	366.2	346	207	2	—	100	133	2.75	100	.239	.288	258-1	.202	1*	80	-7	—	-0.6
1886	StL N	9	15	.375	25	24	23-2	0	210	183	106	5	—	46	101	**1.76**	**183**	.220	.261	108-1	.250	4*	85	26	—	3.0
1887	Ind N	13	24	.351	38	38	37	0	328	356	204	11	12	69	85	3.65	114	.265	.307	141-2	.191	-1*	73	17	—	1.3
1888	Ind N	15	22	.405	37	37	36-3	0	323	315	179	11	10	58	98	3.26	91	.245	.283	125-1	.144	-3	108	-14	—	-1.5
1889	Ind N	21	23	.477	46	45	38-2	0	378.2	422	224	14	14	95	97	3.92	106	.274	.322	155-1	.245	5	84	14	—	1.6
Total	6	89	111	.445	207	199	189-10	1	1756.1	1740	983	46	36	378	602	3.06	110	.247	.289	1049-10	.219	7	89	46	—	4.5
Boyles, Harry	Harry "Stretch"; B11.29.1913 Granite City IL; D1.7.2005 McAllen TX; BR/TR/6´5˝/185; d8.3																									
1938	Chi A	0	4	.000	9	2	1	1	29.1	31	27	2	2	25	18	5.22	94	.263	.400	8	.125	-1	36	-4	—	-0.5
1939	Chi A	0	0	ø	2	0	0	0	3.1	4	4	0	0	6	1	10.80	44	.308	.526	1	.000	-0	—	-2	—	-0.1
Total	2	0	4	.000	11	2	1	1	32.2	35	31	2	2	31	19	5.79	84	.267	.415	9	.111	-1	36	-6	—	-0.6
Boze, Marshall	Marshall Wayne; B5.23.1971 San Manuel AZ; BR/TR/6´1˝/214; [MilA90 12/331]; d4.28; Col Southwestern (CA) CC																									
1996	Mil A	0	2	.000	25	0	0	1-1	32.1	47	29	5	6	25-4	19	7.79	67	.362	.481	0	ø	0	—	-8	0	-0.4
Brabender, Gene	Eugene Mathew; B8.16.1941 Madison WI; D12.27.1996 Madison WI; BR/TR/6´5.5˝/220; d5.11; Col Wisconsin–Whitewater																									
1966	Bal A	4	3	.571	31	1	0	2	71	57	30	4	1	29-0	62	3.55	94	.229	.310	13	.077	-1	159	-1	0	-0.2
1967	Bal A	6	4	.600	14	14	3-1	0	94	77	38	6	1	23-1	71	3.35	94	.220	.269	28-0-1	.071	-1	109	-2	0	-0.3
1968	Bal A	6	7	.462	37	15	3-2	3	124.2	116	52	9	3	48-4	92	3.32	88	.248	.320	35-1-3	.086	-0	105	-5	0	-0.7
1969	Sea A	13	14	.481	40	29	7-1	0-1	202.1	193	111	26	13	103-7	139	4.36	84	.254	.350	70-1-2	.129	-1*	100	-16	0	-2.2
1970	Mil A	6	15	.286	29	21	2	1-0	128.2	127	94	9	2	79-7	76	6.02	63	.255	.357	41-0-3	.098	-2	82	-31	0	-4.5
Total	5	35	43	.449	151	80	15-4	6-1	620.2	570	325	54	20	282-19	440	4.25	80	.245	.330	187-2-9	.102	-5	99	-55	0	-7.9
Bracken, Jack	John James; B4.14.1881 Cleveland OH; D7.16.1954 Highland Park MI; BR/TR/5´11˝/175; d8.7																									
1901	Cle A	4	8	.333	12	12	12	0	100	137	94	4	10	31	18	6.21	57	.322	.381	44	.227	0	87	-26	—	-2.4
Brackenridge, John	John Givler; B12.24.1880 Harrisburg PA; D3.20.1953 Harrisburg PA; BR/TR/6´0˝/?; d4.15																									
1904	Phi N	0	1	.000	7	1	0	0	34	37	32	4	4	16	11	5.56	48	.298	.396	13	.154	-0	77	-11	—	-0.5
Bradey, Don	Donald Eugene; B10.4.1934 Charlotte NC; BR/TR/5´9˝/180; d9.25																									
1964	Hou N	0	2	.000	3	1	0	0	2.1	6	7	0	0	3-1	2	19.29	18	.429	.500	0	ø	0	26	-5	0	-0.9
Bradford, Chad	Chadwick Lee; B9.14.1974 Jackson MS; BR/TR/6´5˝/205; [ChiA96 13/377]; d8.1; Col Southern Mississippi; [DL 2005 Oak A 86]																									
1998	Chi A	2	1	.667	29	0	0	1-2	30.2	27	16	0	0	7-0	11	3.23	142	.229	.272	0	ø	0	—	3	0	0.3
1999	Chi A	0	0	ø	3	0	0	0-0	3.2	9	8	1	0	5-0	0	19.64	25	.474	.583	0	ø	0	—	-6	0	-0.2
2000	†Chi A	1	0	1.000	12	0	0	0-0	13.2	13	4	0	0	1-1	9	1.98	256	.255	.269	0	ø	0	—	4	0	0.3
2001	†Oak A	2	1	.667	35	0	0	1-3	36.2	41	12	6	1	6-0	34	2.70	169	.281	.314	0	ø	0	—	8	0	0.6
2002	†Oak A	4	2	.667	75	0	0	2-3	75.1	73	29	2	5	14-5	56	3.11	144	.253	.298	0	ø	0	—	11	0	0.9
2003	†Oak A	7	4	.636	72	0	0	2-3	77	67	28	7	7	30-9	62	3.04	151	.236	.324	0	ø	0	—	13	0	1.8
2004	Oak A	5	7	.417	68	-0	0	1-3	59	51	32	5	5	24-9	34	4.42	105	.234	.323	0	ø	0	—	1	15	0.2
2005	†Bos A	2	1	.667	31	0	0	0-1	23.1	29	10	1	3	4-1	10	3.86	118	.312	.356	0	ø	0	—	2	0	0.2
2006	†NY N	4	2	.667	70	0	0	2-1	62	59	22	1	0	13-4	45	2.90	151	.254	.290	0	ø	0	—	10	0	0.9
Total	9	27	18	.600	395	0	0	9-16	381.1	369	161	23	21	104-29	261	3.40	134	.255	.312	0	ø	0	—	46	101	5.0
Bradford, Larry	Larry; B12.21.1949 Chicago IL; D9.11.1998 Atlanta GA; BR/TL/6´1˝/(200–205); [AtlN73 19/442]; d9.24																									
1977	Atl N	0	0	ø	2	0	0	0-0	2.2	3	1	1	0	0-0	1	3.38	132	.273	.273	0	ø	0	—	0	0	0.0
1979	Atl N	1	0	1.000	21	0	0	2-1	19	11	5	0	1	10-1	11	0.95	424	.172	.286	1	.000	-0	—	5	0	0.4
1980	Atl N	3	4	.429	56	0	0	4-3	55.1	49	20	3	1	22-8	32	2.44	151	.243	.317	3	.000	-0	—	6	0	0.8
1981	Atl N	2	0	1.000	25	0	0	1-0	26.2	26	13	1	0	12-0	14	3.71	95	.268	.342	1	1.000	0	—	-1	0	0.0
Total	4	6	4	.600	104	0	0	7-4	103.2	89	39	5	2	44-9	58	2.52	148	.238	.317	5	.200	-0	—	10	0	1.2
Bradford, Bill	William D; B8.28.1921 Choctaw AR; D8.22.2000 Fairfield Bay AR; BR/TR/6´2˝/180; d4.24																									
1956	KC A	0	0	ø	1	0	0	0	2	2	2	2	0	1-0	0	9.00	48	.250	.333	0	ø	0	—	-1	0	0.0
Bradley, Fred	Fred Langdon; B7.31.1920 Parsons KS; BR/TR/6´1˝/180; d5.1																									
1948	Chi A	0	0	ø	8	0	0	0	15.2	11	12	2	1	4	2	4.60	93	.190	.254	1	.000	-0	—	-2	108	-0.1
1949	Chi A	0	0	ø	1	1	0	0	2	4	3	0	0	3	0	13.50	31	.444	.583	1	.000	-0	300	-2	0	-0.1
Total	2	0	0	ø	9	1	0	0	17.2	15	15	2	1	7	2	5.60	76	.224	.307	2	.000	-0	300	-4	108	-0.2
Bradley, Foghorn	George H.; B7.1.1855 Milford MA; D3.31.1900 Philadelphia PA; BR/TR/6´0˝/175; d8.23; U6																									
1876	Bos N	9	10	.474	22	21	16-1	1	173.1	201	116	1	—	16	16	2.49	91	.263	.279	82	.232	-1	103	-3	—	-0.4
Bradley, George	George Washington "Grin"; B7.13.1852 Reading PA; D10.2.1931 Philadelphia PA; BR/TR/5´10.5˝/175; d5.4; ▲																									
1875	StL NA	33	26	.559	60	60	57-5	0	535.2	540	304	3	—	17	60	2.13	94	.241	.247	254	.244	7	93	-5	—	0.3
1876	StL N	45	19	.703	64	64	63-**16**	0	573	470	229	3	—	38	103	**1.23**	**174**	**.211**	**.224**	265	.249	4	109	63	—	6.2
1877	Chi N	18	23	.439	50	44	35-2	0	394	452	266	4	—	39	59	3.31	90	.269	.286	214	.243	0*	100	-13	—	-1.1
1879	Tro N	13	40	.245	54	54	53-3	0	487	590	361	12	—	26	133	2.85	88	.275	.284	251	.247	4*	82	-14	—	-0.4
1880	Pro N	13	8	.619	28	20	16-4	2	196	158	66	2	—	6	54	1.38	160	.210	.217	309	.227	1*	106	18	—	1.9
1881	Cle N	2	4	.333	6	6	5	0	51	70	36	2	—	3	6	3.88	67	.320	.329	241-2	.249	0*	69	-6	—	-0.6
1882	Cle N	6	9	.400	18	16	15	0	147	164	102	5	—	22	32	3.73	75	.264	.289	115	.183	-3*	84	-14	—	-1.2
1883	Phi AA	16	7	.696	26	23	22	0	214.1	215	129	7	—	22	56	3.15	112	.244	.263	312-1	.234	-0*	114	13	—	1.0
1884	Cin U	25	15	.625	41	38	36-3	0	342	350	203	7	—	23	168	2.71	94	.248	.260	226	.190	-8*	98	-7	—	-1.6
Total	8	138	125	.525	287	265	245-28	2	2404.1	2469	1392	42	—	179	611	2.50	103	.248	.262	1933-3	.231	-1	99	40	—	4.2
Bradley, Herb	Herbert Theodore; B1.3.1903 Agenda KS; D10.16.1959 Clay Center KS; BR/TR/6´0˝/170; d5.9; Col Kansas																									
1927	Bos A	1	1	.500	6	2	2	0	23	16	9	0	2	7	6	3.13	135	.198	.278	7	.429	1	69	3	—	0.3
1928	Bos A	0	3	.000	15	5	1-1	0	47.1	64	41	2	2	16	14	7.23	57	.339	.396	13-0-2	.154	-1	74	-15	—	-0.8
1929	Bos A	0	0	ø	3	0	0	0	4	7	3	1	0	2	0	6.75	63	.438	.500	1	.000	-0	—	-1	—	0.0
Total	3	1	4	.200	24	7	3-1	0	74.1	87	53	3	4	25	20	5.93	70	.304	.368	21-0-2	.238	-0	72	-13	—	-0.5
Bradley, Ryan	Ryan J.; B10.26.1975 Covina CA; BR/TR/6´4˝/226; [NYA97 1/40]; d8.22; Col Arizona St.																									
1998	NY A	2	1	.667	5	1	0	0-0	12.2	12	9	2	1	9-0	13	5.68	77	.250	.373	0	ø	0	85	-2	0	-0.4

YEAR	TM LG	W	L	PCT	G	GS	CG-SHO	SV-BS	IP	H	R	HR	HB	BB-IB	SO	ERA	AERA	OAV	OOB	AB-HR-SH	AVG	PB	SUP	APR	DL	PW
Bradley, Bert	Steven Bert; B12.23.1956 Athens GA; BB/TR/6´1˝/190; [OakA79 27/670]; d9.3; Col Brigham Young																									
1983	Oak A	0	0	ø	6	0	0	0-0	8.1	14	7	1	0	4-1	3	6.48	60	.400	.450	0	ø	0	—	-3	0	-0.1
Bradley, Tom	Thomas William; B3.16.1947 Asheville NC; BR/TR/6´3˝/(173–195); [AnaA68 7/144]; d9.9; Col Maryland																									
1969	Cal A	0	1	.000	3	0	0	0-0	2	9	9	1	0	0-0	2	27.00	13	.600	.600	0	ø	0	—	-6	0	-1.1
1970	Cal A	2	5	.286	17	11	1-1	0-0	69.2	71	38	3	1	33-6	53	4.13	88	.270	.350	18-0-3	.167	0	94	-5	0	-0.4
1971	Chi A	15	15	.500	45	39	7-6	2-2	285.2	273	111	16	2	74-5	206	2.96	120	.248	.295	96-1-7	.156	-1*	88	19	0	1.7
1972	Chi A	15	14	.517	40	40	11-2	0-0	260	225	94	19	2	65-4	209	2.98	105	.231	.280	91-0-9	.132	-2*	110	5	0	0.3
1973	SF N	13	12	.520	35	34	6-1	0-0	224	212	109	26	3	69-10	136	3.90	99	.246	.302	77-0-6	.195	1	113	0	0	0.0
1974	SF N	8	11	.421	30	21	2	0-0	134.1	152	90	15	1	52-4	72	5.16	74	.282	.342	40-0-6	.075	-2	105	-18	0	-2.6
1975	SF N	2	3	.400	13	6	0	0-0	42	57	33	6	1	18-4	13	6.21	61	.326	.390	10-0-1	.000	-1	108	-11	0	-1.2
Total	7	55	61	.474	183	151	27-10	2-2	1017.2	999	484	86	10	311-33	691	3.72	96	.254	.309	332-1-32	.145	-5	103	-16	0	-3.3
Bradshaw, Joe	Joe Siah; B8.17.1897 RoEllen TN; D1.30.1985 Tavares FL; BR/TR/6´2.5˝/200; d5.9																									
1929	Bro N	0	0	ø	2	0	0	0	4	3	3	0	2	4	1	4.50	103	.231	.474	0	ø	0	—	0	—	0.0
Brady, Neal	Cornelius Joseph; B3.4.1897 Covington KY; D6.19.1947 Fort Mitchell KY; BR/TR/6´0.5˝/197; d9.25; Mil 1918																									
1915	NY A	0	0	ø	2	1	0	0	8.2	9	3	0	0	7	6	3.12	94	.281	.410	4	.000	-1	99	0	—	-0.1
1917	NY A	1	0	1.000	2	1	0	0	9	6	2	0	0	5	4	2.00	134	.188	.297	2	.500	0	80	1	—	0.2
1925	Cin N	1	3	.250	20	3	2	1	63.2	73	44	4	4	20	12	4.66	88	.289	.350	25	.240	1	103	-5	—	-0.2
Total	3	2	3	.400	24	5	2	1	81.1	88	49	4	4	32	22	4.20	91	.278	.351	31	.226	1	94	-4	—	-0.1
Brady, Jim	James Joseph "Diamond Jim"; B3.2.1936 Jersey City NJ; BL/TL/6´2˝/185; d5.12; Col Notre Dame																									
1956	Det A	0	0	ø	6	0	0	0	6.1	15	21	3	0	11-1	3	28.42	14	.484	.619	0	ø	0	—	-17	0	-0.7
Brady, King	James Ward; B5.28.1881 Elmer NJ; D8.21.1947 Albany NY; BR/TR/6´0˝/190; d9.21																									
1905	Phi N	1	1	.500	2	2	2	0	13	19	7	0	0	2	3	3.46	84	.333	.356	5	.200	-0	86	-1	—	-0.1
1906	Pit N	1	1	.500	3	2	1	0	23	30	7	0	0	4	14	2.35	114	.313	.340	10	.100	-1	123	1	—	0.0
1907	Pit N	0	0	ø	1	0	0	0	2	2	1	0	0	1	0	0.00	ø	.286	.375	0	ø	0	—	0	—	0.0
1908	Bos A	1	0	1.000	1	1	1-1	0	9	8	0	0	0	0	3	0.00	ø	.242	.242	2	.000	-0	111	2	—	0.3
1912	Bos N	0	0	ø	1	0	0	0	2.2	5	6	0	0	3	0	20.25	18	.313	.421	1	.000	-0	—	-4	—	-0.2
Total	5	3	2	.600	8	5	4-1	0	49.2	64	21	0	0	10	20	3.08	89	.306	.338	18	.111	-1	105	-2	—	0.0
Brady, Bill	William Aloysius "King"; B8.18.1889 New York NY; D4.10.1956 Brooklyn NY; TR/6´2˝/?; d7.9																									
1912	Bos N	0	0	ø	1	0	0	0	1	2	0	0	0	0	0	0.00	ø	.500	.500	0	ø	0	—	0	—	0.0
Braggins, Dick	Richard Realf; B12.25.1879 Mercer PA; D8.16.1963 Lake Wales FL; BR/TR/5´11˝/170; d5.16; Col Case Western Reserve																									
1901	Cle A	1	2	.333	4	3	2	0	32	44	28	1	1	15	1	4.78	74	.324	.395	13-0-1	.154	-1	82	-5	—	-0.5
Brainard, Asa	Asahel "Count"; B1841 Albany NY; D12.29.1888 Denver CO; TR/5´8.5˝/150; d5.5																									
1871	Oly NA	12	15	.444	30	30	30	0	264	361	292	4	—	37	13	4.50	93	.288	.308	134	.224	-6	89	-10	—	-0.9
1872	Oly NA	2	7	.222	9	9	9	0	79	148	140	0	—	5	1	6.38	57	.333	.341	43	.372	3	64	-25	—	-1.4
	Man NA	0	2	.000	2	2	1	0	8	13	17	1	—	0	0	5.63	64	.260	.260	25	.200	-0*	69	-2	—	-0.3
	Year	2	9	.182	11	11	10	0	87	161	157	1	—	5	1	6.31	57	.326	.333	68	.309	3	65	-26	—	-1.7
1873	Bal NA	5	7	.417	14	14	12	0	108.2	182	139	0	—	9	3	4.14	82	.326	.336	69	.261	0*	126	-11	—	-0.8
1874	Bal NA	5	22	.185	30	27	25	0	240	405	329	1	—	27	8	3.71	60	.327	.341	196	.240	-1*	73	-37	—	-3.0
Total	4NA	24	53	.312	85	82	77	0	699.2	1109	917	6	—	78	25	4.40	76	.313	.327	467	.248	-4	88	-85	—	-6.4
Braithwood, Al	Alfred; B2.15.1892 Braceville IL; D11.24.1960 Rowlesburg WV; BR/TL/6´1.5˝/145; d9.1																									
1915	Pit F	0	0	ø	2	0	0	0	3	0	0	0	0	0	2	0.00	ø	.000	.000	0	ø	0	—	1	—	0.0
Brame, Erv	Ervin Beckham; B10.12.1901 Big Rock TN; D11.22.1949 Hopkinsville KY; BL/TR/6´2˝/190; d4.14																									
1928	Pit N	7	4	.636	24	11	6	0	95.2	110	62	5	1	44	22	5.08	80	.291	.366	49-1-1	.265	4*	138	-10	—	-0.6
1929	Pit N	16	11	.593	37	28	19-1	0	229.2	250	123	17	0	71	68	4.55	105	.278	.331	116-4-2	.310	12*	106	11	—	2.0
1930	Pit N	17	8	.680	32	28	**22**	1	235.2	291	153	21	5	56	55	4.70	106	.305	.346	116-3-5	.353	11*	113	4	—	1.1
1931	Pit N	9	13	.409	26	21	15-2	0	179.2	211	102	14	0	45	33	4.21	91	.295	.336	95	.274	6*	103	-7	—	-0.3
1932	Pit N	3	1	.750	23	3	0	0	51	84	52	6	0	16	10	7.41	51	.365	.407	20	.250	1*	154	-21	—	-1.4
Total	5	52	37	.584	142	91	62-3	1	791.2	946	492	63	6	232	188	4.76	94	.298	.347	396-8-8	.306	33	113	-23	—	0.8
Branca, Ralph	Ralph Theodore Joseph "Hawk"; B1.6.1926 Mt.Vernon NY; BR/TR/6´3˝/220; d6.12																									
1944	Bro N	0	2	.000	21	1	0	1	44.2	46	36	2	5	32	16	7.05	50	.274	.405	6	.000	-1	94	-15	0	-0.9
1945	Bro N	5	6	.455	16	15	7	1	109.2	73	44	4	0	79	69	3.04	124	.189	.327	40-0-2	.100	-3	81	10	0	0.7
1946	Bro N	3	1	.750	24	10	2-2	3	67.1	62	34	4	0	41	42	3.88	87	.246	.352	18	.111	0	177	-4	0	-0.3
1947	†Bro N☆	21	12	.636	43	**36**	15-4	1	280	251	100	22	6	98	148	2.67	155	.240	.309	97-0-9	.124	-3	94	43	0	4.2
1948	Bro N★	14	9	.609	36	28	11-1	1	215.2	189	93	24	4	80	122	3.51	114	.232	.304	74-0-3	.203	1	101	13	0	1.2
1949	†Bro N☆	13	5	.722	34	27	9-2	1	186.2	181	100	21	2	91	109	4.39	93	.253	.339	62-0-8	.081	-2	147	-6	0	-0.9
1950	Bro N	7	9	.438	43	15	5	7	142	152	80	24	0	55	100	4.69	87	.271	.336	34-2-7	.118	1	132	-9	0	-0.9
1951	Bro N	13	12	.520	42	27	13-3	3	204	180	81	19	3	85	118	3.26	120	.237	.316	63-0-6	.175	-1	87	15	0	1.5
1952	Bro N	4	2	.667	16	7	2	0	61	52	29	8	4	21	26	3.84	95	.232	.309	19-0-1	.158	-0	136	-2	37	-0.2
1953	Bro N	0	0	ø	7	0	0	0	11	15	12	4	2	5	5	9.82	43	.341	.431	0	ø	0	—	-6	0	-0.3
	Det A	4	7	.364	17	14	7	1	102	98	55	7	2	31	50	4.15	98	.253	.311	34-0-1	.118	-1	108	-2	0	-0.4
1954	Det A	3	3	.500	17	5	0	0	45.1	63	33	10	2	30	15	5.76	64	.330	.424	13	.308	2	115	-11	0	-1.1
	NY A	1	0	1.000	5	3	0	0	12.2	9	5	0	1	13	7	2.84	121	.209	.390	4	.500	1	77	1	0	0.1
	Year	4	3	.571	22	8	0	0	58	72	38	10	3	43	22	5.12	71	.308	.417	17	.353	2	100	-10	0	-1.0
1956	Bro N	0	0	ø	1	0	0	0	2	1	0	0	0	2-0	2	0.00	ø	.143	.333	0	ø	0	—	1	0	0.1
Total	12	88	68	.564	322	188	71-12	19	1484	1372	702	149	31	663-0	829	3.79	104	.245	.328	464-2-37	.142	-6	111	28	37	-2.8
Branch, Harvey	Harvey Alfred; B2.8.1939 Memphis TN; BR/TL/6´0˝/175; d9.18; Col Alabama St.																									
1962	StL N	0	1	.000	1	1	0	0	5	5	3	1	0	5-0	2	5.40	79	.263	.417	1	.000	-0	62	0	0	-0.1
Branch, Norm	Norman Downs "Red"; B3.22.1915 Spokane WA; D11.21.1971 Navasota TX; BR/TR/6´3˝/200; d5.5; Mil 1942–45; Col Texas																									
1941	NY A	5	1	.833	27	0	0	2	47	37	16	2	0	26	28	2.87	137	.224	.330	10	.000	-1	—	6	0	0.7
1942	NY A	0	1	.000	10	0	0	2	15.2	18	15	3	0	16	13	6.32	54	.290	.436	3	.333	0	—	-6	0	-0.5
Total	2	5	2	.714	37	0	0	4	62.2	55	31	5	0	42	41	3.73	102	.242	.361	13	.077	-1	—	0	0	0.2
Branch, Roy	Roy; B7.12.1953 St.Louis MO; BR/TR/6´0˝/175; [KCA71 1/5]; d9.11																									
1979	Sea A	0	1	.000	2	2	0	0-0	11.1	12	11	2	0	7-1	6	7.94	55	.273	.365	0	ø	0	83	-4	0	-0.3
Brandenburg, Mark	Mark Clay; B7.14.1970 Houston TX; BR/TR/6´0˝/180; [TexA92 26/734]; d7.20; Col Texas Tech; [DL 1998 Tex A 181]																									
1995	Tex A	0	1	.000	11	0	0	0-0	27.1	36	18	5	1	7-1	21	5.93	82	.316	.358	0	ø	0	—	-3	0	-0.1
1996	Tex A	1	3	.250	26	0	0	0-1	47.2	48	22	3	2	25-1	37	3.21	164	.262	.354	0	ø	0	—	9	0	0.6
	Bos A	4	2	.667	29	0	0	0-1	28.1	28	13	5	1	8-1	29	3.81	134	.250	.301	0	ø	0	—	4	0	0.8
	Year	5	5	.500	55	0	0	0-2	76	76	35	8	3	33-2	66	3.43	151	.258	.334	0	ø	0	—	13	0	1.4
1997	Bos A	0	2	.000	31	0	0	0-0	41	49	25	3	2	16-3	34	5.49	85	.299	.364	0	ø	0	—	-3	62	-0.1
Total	3	5	8	.385	97	0	0	0-2	144.1	161	78	16	6	56-6	121	4.49	111	.281	.347	0	ø	0	—	7	243	1.2
Brandom, Chick	Chester Milton; B3.31.1887 Coldwater KS; D10.7.1958 Santa Ana CA; BR/TR/5´8˝/161; d9.3; Col Oklahoma																									
1908	Pit N	1	0	1.000	3	1	1	1	17	13	5	0	1	4	8	0.53	435	.228	.290	7	.143	-0	92	2	—	0.2
1909	Pit N	1	0	1.000	13	2	0	2	40.2	33	12	0	1	10	21	1.11	246	.239	.295	10	.100	-1	77	5	—	0.3
1915	New F	1	1	.500	16	1	1	0	50.1	55	36	0	1	15	15	3.40	75	.293	.348	10	.200	1	137	-9	—	-0.4
Total	3	3	1	.750	32	4	2	3	108	101	53	0	3	29	44	2.08	124	.264	.320	27	.148	-0	95	-2	—	0.1
Brandon, Bucky	Darrell G; B7.8.1940 Nacogdoches TX; BR/TR/6´2˝/200; d4.19																									
1966	Bos A	8	8	.500	40	17	5-2	2	157.2	129	70	13	4	70-3	101	3.31	115	.222	.309	44-0-6	.182	1*	98	6	0	0.8
1967	Bos A	5	11	.313	39	19	2	3	157.2	147	86	21	7	59-7	96	4.17	84	.245	.318	43-0-5	.186	1	96	-13	0	-1.2
1968	Bos A	0	0	ø	8	0	0	0	12.2	19	11	1	1	9-0	10	6.39	49	.333	.433	1	.000	-0	—	-5	0	-0.3

YEAR	TM LG	W	L	PCT	G	GS	CG-SHO	SV-BS	IP	H	R	HR	HB	BB-IB	SO	ERA	AERA	OAV	OOB	AB-HR-SH	AVG	PB	SUP	APR	DL	PW
1969	Sea A	0	1	.000	8	1	0	0-0	15	15	15	4	2	16-1	10	8.40	43	.250	.423	0	ø	0	170	-8	0	-0.5
	Min A	0	0	ø	3	0	0	0-0	3.1	5	3	1	0	3-2	1	2.70	135	.357	.471	1	.000	0	—	0	0	0.0
	Year	0	1	.000	11	1	0	0-0	18.1	20	18	5	2	19-3	11	7.36	49	.270	.432	1	.000	0	170	-8	0	-0.5
1971	Phi N	6	6	.500	52	0	0	4-4	83	81	42	5	0	47-9	44	3.90	91	.264	.357	13-0-2	.154	-0	—	-4	0	-0.6
1972	Phi N	7	7	.500	42	6	0	2-2	104.1	106	49	9	6	46-8	67	3.45	105	.268	.352	15-0-4	.067	-1	98	0	0	-0.2
1973	Phi N	2	4	.333	36	0	0	2-0	56.1	54	35	5	3	25-7	25	5.43	70	.261	.343	5	.200	0	—	-9	0	-0.9
Total	7	28	37	.431	228	43	7-2	13-6	590	556	311	59	23	275-37	354	4.04	90	.250	.337	122-0-17	.164	1	99	-33	0	-2.9
Brandt, Ed	Edward Arthur "Big Ed"; B2.17.1905 Spokane WA; D11.1.1944 Spokane WA; BL/TL/6´1˝/190; d4.26																									
1928	Bos N	9	21	.300	38	32	12-1	0	225.1	234	141	22	7	109	84	5.07	77	.273	.359	70-0-3	.243	5*	80	-25	—	-2.2
1929	Bos N	8	13	.381	26	21	13	0	167.2	196	111	12	5	83	50	5.53	85	.302	.385	64-0-3	.234	2*	82	-13	—	-1.0
1930	Bos N	4	11	.267	41	13	4-1	1	147.1	168	88	15	0	59	65	5.01	99	.291	.356	50-0-1	.240	1	68	1	—	0.2
1931	Bos N	18	11	.621	33	29	23-3	2	250	228	94	11	4	77	112	2.92	130	.244	.304	82-0-7	.256	5*	90	24	—	3.4
1932	Bos N	16	16	.500	35	31	19-2	1	254	271	122	11	5	57	79	3.97	95	.275	.318	92-0-5	.207	-0	87	-2	—	-0.1
1933	Bos N	18	14	.563	41	32	23-4	4	287.2	256	85	10	3	77	104	2.60	118	.245	.298	97-0-4	.309	9*	93	21	—	3.5
1934	Bos N	16	14	.533	40	29	20-3	5	255	249	111	13	4	83	106	3.53	108	.254	.315	96-0-2	.240	4*	114	11	—	1.5
1935	Bos N	5	19	.208	29	25	12	0	174.2	224	110	12	1	66	61	5.00	76	.319	.378	62	.210	-0*	81	-23	—	-2.6
1936	Bro N	11	13	.458	38	29	12-1	2	234	246	105	14	4	65	104	3.50	118	.268	.319	84-0-2	.190	0*	93	18	—	1.6
1937	Pit N	11	10	.524	33	25	7-2	2	176.1	177	73	11	2	67	74	3.11	124	.263	.332	59-0-1	.169	1	96	15	—	1.8
1938	Pit N	5	4	.556	24	13	5-1	0	96.1	93	44	3	0	35	38	3.46	110	.250	.314	37-0-2	.297	2	91	4	—	0.5
Total	11	121	146	.453	378	279	150-18	17	2268.1	2342	1084	134	35	778	877	3.86	101	.269	.332	793-0-30	.236	30	89	31	—	6.6
Brandt, Bill	William George; B3.21.1915 Aurora IN; D5.16.1968 Fort Wayne IN; BR/TR/5´8.5˝/170; d9.20; Mil 1944–45																									
1941	Pit N	0	1	.000	2	1	0	0	7	5	3	0	0	3	0	3.86	94	.200	.286	1	.000	-0	71	0	0	0.0
1942	Pit N	1	1	.500	3	3	1	0	16.1	23	10	1	0	5	4	4.96	68	.343	.389	7	.143	-0	108	-3	0	-0.3
1943	Pit N	4	1	.800	29	3	0	0	57.1	57	25	3	1	19	17	3.14	111	.248	.308	7-0-1	.143	-0	65	2	0	0.1
Total	3	5	3	.625	34	7	1	0	80.2	85	38	4	1	27	21	3.57	97	.264	.323	15-0-1	.133	-1	84	-1	0	-0.2
Brantley, Cliff	Clifford; B4.12.1968 Staten Island NY; BR/TR/6´1˝/190; [PhiN86 2/35]; d9.3																									
1991	Phi N	2	2	.500	6	5	0	0-0	31.2	26	12	0	2	19-0	25	3.41	108	.228	.341	8-0-2	.000	-1	102	1	0	0.1
1992	Phi N	2	6	.250	28	9	0	0-0	76.1	71	45	6	4	58-4	32	4.60	76	.251	.382	14-0-7	.214	1	137	-10	0	-0.9
Total	2	4	8	.333	34	14	0	0-0	108	97	57	6	6	77-4	57	4.25	84	.244	.370	22-0-9	.136	0	125	-9	0	-0.8
Brantley, Jeff	Jeffrey Hoke; B9.5.1963 Florence AL; BR/TR/5´11˝/(180–197); [SFN85 6/134]; d8.5; Col Mississippi St.																									
1988	SF N	0	1	.000	9	1	0	1-0	20.2	22	13	2	1	6-1	11	5.66	58	.275	.333	2	.500	0	27	-5	0	-0.2
1989	†SF N	7	1	.875	59	1	0	0-1	97.1	101	50	10	2	37-8	69	4.07	83	.271	.337	12-0-3	.083	-1	52	-8	0	-0.7
1990	SF N★	5	3	.625	55	0	0	19-5	86.2	77	18	3	3	33-6	61	1.56	235	.240	.315	7-0-4	.286	1	—	20	0	2.7
1991	SF N	5	2	.714	67	0	0	15-4	95.1	78	27	8	5	52-10	81	2.45	146	.225	.332	3-0-1	.000	-0	—	13	0	1.2
1992	SF N	7	7	.500	56	4	0	7-2	91.2	67	32	8	3	45-5	86	2.95	113	.207	.307	9	.111	0	102	5	0	0.7
1993	SF N	5	6	.455	53	12	0	0-3	113.2	112	60	19	7	46-2	76	4.28	92	.259	.336	28-0-1	.107	-1	114	-5	0	-0.7
1994	Cin N	6	6	.500	50	0	0	15-6	65.1	46	20	6	0	28-5	63	2.48	169	.202	.288	3	.000	-0	—	13	0	2.6
1995	†Cin N	3	2	.600	56	0	0	28-4	70.1	53	22	11	1	20-3	62	2.82	148	.206	.263	3	.000	-0	—	11	0	1.5
1996	Cin N	1	2	.333	66	0	0	**44**-5	71	54	21	7	0	28-6	76	2.41	178	.215	.289	1-0-1	.000	-0	—	15	5	2.1
1997	Cin N	1	1	.500	13	0	0	1-2	11.2	9	5	2	2	7-1	16	3.86	111	.205	.340	0	ø	0	—	1	146	0.1
1998	StL N	0	5	.000	48	0	0	14-8	50.2	40	26	12	1	18-3	48	4.44	95	.220	.289	0-0-1	ø	0	—	-1	9	-0.1
1999	Phi N	1	2	.333	10	0	0	5-1	8.2	5	6	0	0	8-0	11	5.19	90	.161	.325	0	ø	0	—	-1	150	-0.1
2000	Phi N	2	7	.222	55	0	0	23-5	55.1	64	36	12	2	29-0	57	5.86	78	.288	.373	0	ø	0	—	-6	30	-1.3
2001	Tex A	0	1	.000	18	0	0	0-0	21	26	12	5	0	9-1	11	5.14	93	.310	.372	0	ø	0	—	0	0	-0.1
Total	14	43	46	.483	615	18	0	172-46	859.1	754	348	105	27	366-51	728	3.39	114	.237	.319	68-0-11	.118	-2	101	52	340	7.7
Brashear, Kitty	Norman Cobb; B8.27.1877 Mansfield OH; D12.22.1934 Los Angeles CA; BR/TR; d6.25; b–Roy																									
1899	Lou N	1	0	1.000	3	0	0	0	8	8	7	0	1	2	5	4.50	86	.258	.324	2	.500	0	—	-1	—	-0.1
Braun, John	John Paul; B12.26.1939 Madison WI; BR/TR/6´5˝/205; d10.2																									
1964	Mil N	0	0	ø	1	0	0	0	2	2	0	0	0	1-0	1	0.00	ø	.286	.375	0	ø	0	—	1	0	0.0
Braun, Ryan	Ryan Zachary; B7.29.1980 Kitchener ON, Can.; BR/TR/6´1˝/215; [KCA03 6/162]; d9.2; Col Nevada–Las Vegas																									
2006	KC A	0	1	.000	9	0	0	0-2	10.2	13	8	2	0	3-0	6	6.75	69	.317	.356	0	ø	0	—	-2	0	-0.2
Braxton, Garland	Edgar Garland; B6.10.1900 Snow Camp NC; D2.25.1966 Norfolk VA; BB/TL/5´11˝/152; d5.27																									
1921	Bos N	1	3	.250	17	2	0	0	37.1	44	26	0	2	17	16	4.82	76	.310	.391	7	.000	-1	0	-6	—	-0.7
1922	Bos N	1	2	.333	25	5	2	0	66.2	75	37	3	4	24	15	3.38	118	.286	.355	16-0-3	.063	-2	102	2	—	-0.1
1925	NY A	1	1	.500	3	2	0	0	19.1	26	14	1	1	5	11	6.52	65	.338	.386	6	.333	0	69	-4	—	-0.3
1926	NY A	5	1	.833	37	1	0	2	67.1	71	28	1	0	19	30	2.67	144	.275	.325	20	.300	1	153	8	—	0.7
1927	Was A	10	9	.526	**58**	2	0	**13**	155.1	144	62	5	2	33	96	2.95	138	.246	.289	39-0-3	.231	0	41	**19**	—	2.3
1928	Was A	13	11	.542	38	24	15-2	6	218.1	177	78	7	5	44	94	**2.51**	**160**	**.222**	**.267**	72-0-5	.125	-4	88	34	—	3.2
1929	Was A	12	10	.545	37	20	9	4	182	219	116	6	2	51	59	4.85	88	.299	.346	54-0-5	.148	-1	97	-12	—	-1.4
1930	Was A	3	2	.600	15	0	0	5	27.1	22	11	3	0	9	7	3.29	140	.222	.287	5-0-1	.000	-1	—	4	—	0.7
	Chi A	4	10	.286	19	10	2	1	90.2	127	80	9	1	33	44	6.45	72	.333	.388	23-0-1	.087	-2	69	-18	—	-2.4
	Year	7	12	.368	34	10	2	6	118	149	91	12	1	42	51	5.72	81	.310	.367	28-0-2	.071	-2	69	-15	—	-1.7
1931	Chi A	0	3	.000	17	3	0	1	47.1	71	43	1	2	23	28	6.85	62	.338	.409	11	.091	-1	99	-14	—	-0.8
	StL A	0	0	ø	11	1	0	0	18	27	24	2	1	10	7	10.50	44	.370	.452	3	.667	1	109	-11	—	-0.4
	Year	0	3	.000	28	4	0	1	65.1	98	67	3	3	33	35	7.85	56	.346	.420	14	.214	0	102	-25	—	-1.2
1933	StL A	0	1	.000	5	1	0	0	8.1	11	10	0	1	8	5	9.72	48	.289	.426	1	.000	-0	146	-4	—	-0.4
Total	10	50	53	.485	282	71	28-2	32	938	1014	529	38	21	276	412	4.13	101	.278	.332	257-0-18	.156	-8	88	-2	—	0.4
Bray, Bill	Bill Alan; B6.5.1983 Virginia Beach VA; BL/TL/6´3˝/215; [MonN04 1/13]; d6.3; Col William & Mary																									
2006	Was N	1	1	.500	19	0	0	0-0	23	24	11	2	1	9-2	16	3.91	112	.273	.343	1	.000	-0	—	1	0	0.1
	Cin N	2	1	.667	29	0	0	2-1	27.2	33	16	3	0	9-1	23	4.23	112	.292	.344	0	ø	0	—	1	0	0.1
	Year	3	2	.600	48	0	0	2-1	50.2	57	27	5	1	18-3	39	4.09	112	.284	.344	1	.000	-0	—	2	0	0.2
Brazelton, Dewon	Dewon Cortez; B6.16.1980 Tullahoma TN; BR/TR/6´4˝/215; [TBA01 1/3]; d9.13; Col Middle Tennessee																									
2002	TB A	0	1	.000	2	2	0	0-0	13	12	7	3	2	6-0	5	4.85	93	.279	.392	0	ø	0	51	0	0	0.0
2003	TB A	1	6	.143	10	10	0	0-0	48.1	57	49	9	3	23-1	24	6.89	67	.292	.372	1	.000	-0	87	-16	0	-1.9
2004	TB A	6	8	.429	22	21	0	0-0	120.2	121	71	12	11	53-2	64	4.77	98	.260	.346	1	.000	-0	78	-1	0	-0.2
2005	TB A	1	8	.111	20	8	0	0-1	71	87	65	12	4	60-3	43	7.61	58	.307	.431	0	ø	0	53	-25	0	-2.5
2006	SD N	0	2	.000	9	2	0	0-0	18	28	25	6	0	9-1	9	12.00	35	.354	.411	4	.250	1	67	-17	0	-1.4
Total	5	8	25	.242	63	43	0	0-1	271	305	217	42	20	151-7	145	6.38	71	.286	.381	6	.167	0	74	-59	0	-6.0
Brazle, Al	Alpha Eugene "Cotton"; B10.19.1913 Loyal OK; D10.24.1973 Grand Junction CO; BL/TL/6´2˝/185; d7.25; Mil 1944–45																									
1943	†StL N	8	2	.800	13	9	8-1	0	88	74	18	0	0	29	26	1.53	219	.231	.295	32	.281	2	106	18	0	2.4
1946	†StL N	11	10	.524	37	15	6-2	0	153.1	152	69	1	2	55	58	3.29	105	.261	.327	52-0-2	.212	-0	119	1	0	0.1
1947	StL N	14	8	.636	44	19	7	4	168	186	65	7	2	48	85	2.84	146	.284	.335	64-0-3	.219	1	113	22	0	3.0
1948	StL N	10	6	.625	42	23	6-2	1	156.1	171	77	8	0	50	55	3.80	108	.281	.335	55	.145	-2*	96	3	0	0.2
1949	StL N	14	8	.636	39	25	9-1	0	206.1	208	85	18	6	61	75	3.18	131	.263	.321	82-0-1	.134	-4	119	21	0	1.6
1950	StL N	11	9	.550	46	12	3	6	164.2	188	81	12	4	80	47	4.10	105	.296	.378	61	.213	-1*	91	5	0	0.5
1951	StL N	6	5	.545	56	8	5	7	154.1	139	61	13	5	60	66	3.09	128	.245	.322	46	.109	-3	81	14	0	0.6
1952	StL N	12	5	.706	46	6	3-1	**16**	109.1	75	38	6	1	42	55	2.72	137	.198	.280	32-0-1	.125	-1	88	12	0	2.0
1953	StL N	6	7	.462	60	0	0	**18**	92	101	47	8	2	43	57	4.21	101	.280	.360	15-0-2	.333	1	—	1	0	0.3
1954	StL N	5	4	.556	58	0	0	8	84.1	93	48	10	3	24	30	4.16	99	.288	.339	14	.000	-2	—	-2	0	-0.4
Total	10	97	64	.602	441	117	47-7	60	1376.2	1387	589	83	25	492	554	3.31	120	.266	.332	453-0-9	.177	-9	105	95	0	10.3

Brazoban, Yhency Yhency Jose; B6.11.1980 Santo Domingo, D.R.; BR/TR/6´1˝/170; d8.5

YEAR	TM LG	W	L	PCT	G	GS	CG-SHO	SV-BS	IP	H	R	HR	HB	BB-IB	SO	ERA	AERA	OAV	OOB	AB-HR-SH	AVG	PB	SUP	APR	DL	PW
2004	†LA N	6	2	.750	31	0	0	0-0	32.2	25	9	2	0	15-2	27	2.48	167	.219	.310	1	.000	-0	—	7	0	1.3
2005	LA N	4	10	.286	74	0	0	21-6	72.2	70	46	11	5	32-4	61	5.33	78	.258	.345	2	.000	-0	—	-9	0	-1.9
2006	LA N	0	0	ø	5	0	0	0-1	5	7	3	0	0	2-0	4	5.40	81	.350	.391	0	ø	0	—	0	172	0.0
Total	3	10	12	.455	110	0	0	21-7	110.1	102	58	13	5	49-6	92	4.49	93	.252	.338	3	.000	-0	—	-2	172	-0.6

Brea, Lesli Lesli Guillermo; B10.12.1973 San Pedro de Macoris, D.R.; BR/TR/5´10˝/170; d8.13

YEAR	TM LG	W	L	PCT	G	GS	CG-SHO	SV-BS	IP	H	R	HR	HB	BB-IB	SO	ERA	AERA	OAV	OOB	AB-HR-SH	AVG	PB	SUP	APR	DL	PW
2000	Bal A	0	1	.000	6	1	0	0-0	9	12	11	1	1	10-0	5	11.00	43	.324	.469	0	ø	0	100	-6	0	-0.6
2001	Bal A	0	0	ø	2	0	0	0-0	2	6	4	2	0	3-0	0	18.00	24	.545	.643	0	ø	0	—	-3	0	-0.1
Total	2	0	1	.000	8	1	0	0-0	11	18	15	3	1	13-0	5	12.27	38	.375	.508	0	ø	0	100	-9	0	-0.7

Brecheen, Harry Harry David "Harry the Cat"; B10.14.1914 Broken Bow OK; D1.17.2004 Bethany OK; BL/TL/5´10˝/(160–165); d4.22; C14; Col East Central

YEAR	TM LG	W	L	PCT	G	GS	CG-SHO	SV-BS	IP	H	R	HR	HB	BB-IB	SO	ERA	AERA	OAV	OOB	AB-HR-SH	AVG	PB	SUP	APR	DL	PW
1940	StL N	0	0	ø	3	0	0	0	3.1	2	1	0	0	2	4	0.00	ø	.167	.286	0	ø	0	—	1	—	0.1
1943	†StL N	9	6	.600	29	13	8-1	4	135.1	98	41	4	3	39	68	2.26	149	.206	.270	42-0-4	.190	1	97	16	0	2.0
1944	†StL N	16	5	.762	30	22	13-3	0	189.1	174	67	8	3	46	88	2.85	124	.242	.290	68-0-4	.162	-1*	125	16	0	1.7
1945	StL N	15	4	**.789**	24	18	13-3	2	157.1	136	48	5	5	44	63	2.52	149	.238	.298	57-0-2	.123	-1	97	23	0	2.5
1946	†StL N	15	15	.500	36	30	14-**5**	3	231.1	212	73	8	4	67	117	2.49	139	.244	.301	83-0-1	.133	-3*	78	25	0	3.1
1947	StL N★	16	11	.593	29	28	18-1	1	223.1	220	92	20	3	66	89	3.30	125	.260	.316	83-0-4	.241	5	109	21	0	2.9
1948	StL N☆	20	7	**.741**	33	30	21-**7**	1	233.1	193	62	6	2	49	**149**	**2.24**	**183**	.222	**.265**	82-0-2	.146	-1	98	**47**	0	5.3
1949	StL N	14	11	.560	32	31	14-2	1	214.2	207	96	18	7	65	88	3.35	124	.252	.312	77-0-3	.273	5	94	17	0	2.3
1950	StL N	8	11	.421	27	23	12-2	1	163.1	151	77	18	3	45	80	3.80	113	.244	.298	58-1-0	.241	3	95	9	0	1.2
1951	StL N	8	4	.667	24	16	5	2	138.2	134	54	11	1	54	57	3.25	122	.256	.327	55-1-1	.218	2	97	12	0	1.1
1952	StL N	7	5	.583	25	13	4-1	2	100.1	82	39	12	3	28	54	3.32	112	.223	.283	29-0-1	.207	1	109	6	0	1.0
1953	StL A	5	13	.278	26	16	3	1	117.1	122	51	7	3	31	44	3.07	137	.269	.320	39-0-2	.179	-1*	41	12	0	1.7
Total	12	133	92	.591	318	240	125-25	18	1907.2	1731	701	117	37	536	901	2.92	133	.242	.298	673-2-24	.192	11	95	205	0	24.9

Breckinridge, Bill William Robertson; B10.16.1907 Tulsa OK; D8.23.1958 Tulsa OK; BR/TR/5´11˝/175; d6.30; Col Dartmouth

YEAR	TM LG	W	L	PCT	G	GS	CG-SHO	SV-BS	IP	H	R	HR	HB	BB-IB	SO	ERA	AERA	OAV	OOB	AB-HR-SH	AVG	PB	SUP	APR	DL	PW
1929	Phi A	0	0	ø	3	1	0	0	10	10	10	0	0	16	2	8.10	52	.270	.491	4	.000	-1	199	-4	—	-0.3

Breining, Fred Fred Lawrence; B11.15.1955 San Francisco CA; BR/TR/6´4˝/(180–185); [PitN74*3/57]; d9.4; Col San Mateo (CA) [JC]

YEAR	TM LG	W	L	PCT	G	GS	CG-SHO	SV-BS	IP	H	R	HR	HB	BB-IB	SO	ERA	AERA	OAV	OOB	AB-HR-SH	AVG	PB	SUP	APR	DL	PW
1980	SF N	0	0	ø	5	0	0	0-0	6.2	8	4	0	1	4-1	3	5.40	65	.333	.448	0	ø	0	—	-1	0	-0.1
1981	SF N	5	2	.714	45	1	0	1-0	77.2	66	28	4	2	38-8	37	2.55	134	.243	.334	11-0-1	.000	-1	104	6	0	0.4
1982	SF N	11	6	.647	54	9	2	0-1	143.1	146	61	6	1	52-10	98	3.08	116	.269	.333	29-0-5	.207	1	109	6	0	0.9
1983	SF N	11	12	.478	32	32	6	0-0	202.2	202	97	15	5	60-11	117	3.82	93	.259	.312	67-0-5	.149	1	108	-5	0	-0.5
1984	Mon N	0	0	ø	4	0	0	0-0	6.2	4	1	0	0	5-0	5	1.35	256	.190	.346	1	.000	-0	—	2	139	0.1
Total	5	27	20	.574	140	42	8	1-1	437	426	191	25	9	159-30	260	3.34	106	.260	.325	108-0-11	.148	1	109	8	139	0.8

Breitenstein, Alonzo Alonzo; B11.9.1857 Utica NY; D6.19.1932 Utica NY; d7.7

YEAR	TM LG	W	L	PCT	G	GS	CG-SHO	SV-BS	IP	H	R	HR	HB	BB-IB	SO	ERA	AERA	OAV	OOB	AB-HR-SH	AVG	PB	SUP	APR	DL	PW
1883	Phi N	0	1	.000	1	1	0	0	5	8	9	0	—	2	0	9.00	34	.320	.370	2	.000	-0	69	-3	—	-0.5

Breitenstein, Ted Theodore P. "Theo"; B6.1.1869 St.Louis MO; D5.3.1935 St.Louis MO; BL/TL/5´9˝/167; d4.28

YEAR	TM LG	W	L	PCT	G	GS	CG-SHO	SV-BS	IP	H	R	HR	HB	BB-IB	SO	ERA	AERA	OAV	OOB	AB-HR-SH	AVG	PB	SUP	APR	DL	PW
1891	StL AA	2	0	1.000	6	1	1-1	1	28.2	15	14	2	0	14	13	2.20	191	.150	.254	12	.000	-2	118	5	—	0.2
1892	StL N	9	19	.321	39	32	28-1	0	282.1	280	192	8	6	148	126	4.69	68	.248	.339	131	.122	-3*	88	-40	—	-3.3
1893	StL N	19	24	.442	48	42	38-1	1	382.2	359	197	8	8	156	102	**3.18**	**149**	.241	.316	160-1	.181	-5*	78	68	—	5.6
1894	StL N	27	23	.540	**56**	**50**	**46**-1	0	**447.1**	497	320	21	11	191	140	4.79	113	.278	.352	182-0-9	.220	-1*	82	35	—	2.8
1895	StL N	19	30	.388	55	**51**	**47**-1	1	438.2	468	299	16	14	182	131	4.37	111	.269	.343	221-0-2	.190	-7*	92	22	—	1.3
1896	StL N	18	26	.409	44	43	37-1	0	339.2	376	236	12	5	138	114	4.48	97	.278	.347	162-0-7	.259	3*	81	-6	—	-0.1
1897	Cin N	23	12	.657	40	39	32-2	0	320.1	345	172	3	9	91	98	3.62	126	.273	.326	124-0-4	.266	3*	96	31	—	2.9
1898	Cin N	20	14	.588	39	37	32-3	0	315.2	313	170	2	11	123	68	3.42	112	.257	.330	121-0-5	.215	1*	98	12	—	1.3
1899	Cin N	13	9	.591	26	24	21	0	210.2	219	111	2	9	71	59	3.59	109	.268	.333	105-1-4	.352	9*	98	9	—	1.6
1900	Cin N	10	10	.500	24	20	18-1	0	192.1	205	111	4	14	79	39	3.65	101	.272	.352	126-2-1	.190	-0*	106	-1	—	0.0
1901	StL N	0	3	.000	3	3	1	0	15	24	26	1	0	14	3	6.60	48	.358	.469	6	.333	0	149	-10	—	-1.4
Total	11	160	170	.485	380	342	301-12	3	2973.1	3101	1848	79	87	1207	893	4.03	109	.265	.338	1350-4-32	.216	-4	89	125	—	10.9

Brennan, Ad Addison Foster; B7.18.1887 LaHarpe KS; D1.7.1962 Kansas City MO; BL/TL/5´11˝/170; d5.19

YEAR	TM LG	W	L	PCT	G	GS	CG-SHO	SV-BS	IP	H	R	HR	HB	BB-IB	SO	ERA	AERA	OAV	OOB	AB-HR-SH	AVG	PB	SUP	APR	DL	PW
1910	Phi N	2	0	1.000	19	5	2	0	73.1	72	36	2	3	28	28	2.33	134	.264	.339	25	.280	1*	162	2	—	0.2
1911	Phi N	2	1	.667	5	3	1	0	22.2	22	12	0	1	12	12	3.57	96	.259	.357	9-0-1	.222	-0	124	0	—	0.0
1912	Phi N	11	9	.550	27	19	13-1	2	174	185	88	4	3	49	78	3.57	102	.274	.326	59-1-2	.254	4	106	4	—	0.9
1913	Phi N	14	12	.538	40	24	12-1	1	207	204	76	5	6	46	94	2.39	139	.268	.314	67-0-3	.164	-2	97	18	—	1.9
1914	Chi F	5	5	.500	16	11	5-1	0	85.2	84	44	7	2	21	31	3.57	74	.256	.305	32-0-2	.250	1	96	-9	—	-0.9
1915	Chi F	3	9	.250	19	13	7-2	0	106	117	55	4	7	30	40	3.74	67	.287	.346	27-0-3	.185	0*	86	-15	—	-1.6
1918	Was A	0	0	ø	2	1	0	0	5.1	7	4	0	1	5	0	5.06	54	.241	.371	1	.000	-0	110	-1	—	-0.1
	Cle A	0	0	ø	1	0	0	0	3	3	1	0	0	3	0	3.00	100	.333	.500	0	ø	0	—	0	—	0.0
	Year	0	0	ø	3	1	0	0	8.1	10	5	0	1	8	0	4.32	65	.263	.404	1	.000	-0	107	-1	—	-0.1
Total	7	37	36	.507	129	76	40-5	3	677	694	316	22	23	194	283	3.11	102	.270	.327	220-1-11	.218	4	103	-1	—	0.4

Brennan, Don James Donald; B12.2.1903 Augusta ME; D4.26.1953 Boston MA; BR/TR/6´0˝/210; d4.16; Col Georgetown

YEAR	TM LG	W	L	PCT	G	GS	CG-SHO	SV-BS	IP	H	R	HR	HB	BB-IB	SO	ERA	AERA	OAV	OOB	AB-HR-SH	AVG	PB	SUP	APR	DL	PW
1933	NY A	5	1	.833	18	10	3	3	85	92	56	4	0	47	46	4.98	78	.275	.365	27-0-3	.259	2	193	-12	—	-0.6
1934	Cin N	4	3	.571	28	7	2	2	78	89	51	3	1	35	31	3.81	107	.290	.364	22-0-1	.227	0	109	-2	—	-0.1
1935	Cin N	5	5	.500	38	5	2-1	5	114.1	101	43	4	4	44	48	3.15	126	.242	.320	30	.100	-1	115	13	—	0.9
1936	Cin N	5	2	.714	41	4	0	9	94.1	117	60	2	1	35	40	4.39	87	.305	.364	25-0-2	.080	-3	105	-9	—	-1.0
1937	Cin N	1	1	.500	10	0	0	0	16	25	14	1	0	10	6	6.75	55	.347	.427	5	.000	-1	—	-6	—	-0.7
	†NY N	1	0	1.000	6	0	0	0	9.1	12	8	0	1	9	1	6.75	58	.316	.458	1	.000	0	—	-3	—	-0.3
	Year	2	1	.667	16	0	0	0	25.1	37	22	1	1	19	7	6.75	56	.336	.438	6	.000	-1	—	-8	—	-1.0
Total	5	21	12	.636	141	26	7-1	19	397	436	232	14	7	180	172	4.19	94	.281	.358	110-0-6	.155	-2	142	-19	—	-1.8

Brennan, Tom Thomas Martin; B10.30.1952 Chicago IL; BR/TR/6´1˝/180; [CleA74 1/4]; d9.5; Col Lewis

YEAR	TM LG	W	L	PCT	G	GS	CG-SHO	SV-BS	IP	H	R	HR	HB	BB-IB	SO	ERA	AERA	OAV	OOB	AB-HR-SH	AVG	PB	SUP	APR	DL	PW
1981	Cle A	2	2	.500	7	6	1	0-0	48.1	49	20	5	0	14-1	15	3.17	116	.259	.310	0	ø	0	89	2	0	0.2
1982	Cle A	4	2	.667	30	4	0	2-2	92.2	112	51	9	2	10-1	46	4.27	97	.300	.317	0	ø	0	66	-2	0	-0.1
1983	Cle A	2	2	.500	11	5	1-1	0-0	39.2	45	22	3	1	8-1	21	3.86	111	.288	.323	0	ø	0	98	0	0	0.0
1984	Chi A	0	1	.000	4	1	0	0-0	6.2	8	5	1	0	3-0	3	4.05	103	.308	.379	0	ø	0	22	-1	0	-0.1
1985	LA N	1	3	.250	12	4	0	0-0	31.2	41	26	2	0	11-4	17	7.39	47	.333	.374	8-0-1	.125	-0	69	-12	0	-1.3
Total	5	9	10	.474	64	20	2-1	2-2	219	255	124	20	3	46-7	102	4.40	90	.294	.327	8-0-1	.125	-0	78	-13	0	-1.3

Brennan, William William Raymond; B1.15.1963 Tampa FL; BR/TR/6´3˝/185; d7.19; Col Mercer

YEAR	TM LG	W	L	PCT	G	GS	CG-SHO	SV-BS	IP	H	R	HR	HB	BB-IB	SO	ERA	AERA	OAV	OOB	AB-HR-SH	AVG	PB	SUP	APR	DL	PW
1988	LA N	0	1	.000	4	2	0	0-0	9.1	13	7	0	0	6-1	7	6.75	50	.342	.432	2	.000	-0	106	-3	0	-0.3
1993	Chi N	2	1	.667	8	1	0	0-0	15	16	8	2	1	8-1	11	4.20	96	.291	.385	1-0-1	.000	0	0	0	0	0.0
Total	2	2	2	.500	12	3	0	0-0	24.1	29	15	2	1	14-2	18	5.18	73	.312	.404	3-0-1	.000	0	63	-3	0	-0.3

Brenneman, Jim James Leroy; B2.13.1941 San Diego CA; D3.10.1994 Pearl MS; BR/TR/6´2˝/180; d7.9; Col Mesa St.

YEAR	TM LG	W	L	PCT	G	GS	CG-SHO	SV-BS	IP	H	R	HR	HB	BB-IB	SO	ERA	AERA	OAV	OOB	AB-HR-SH	AVG	PB	SUP	APR	DL	PW
1965	NY A	0	0	ø	3	0	0	0	2	5	5	1	0	3-0	2	18.00	19	.455	.571	0	ø	0	—	-4	0	-0.2

Brenner, Bert Delbert Henry "Dutch"; B7.18.1887 Minneapolis MN; D4.11.1971 St.Louis Park MN; BR/TR/6´0˝/175; d9.21

YEAR	TM LG	W	L	PCT	G	GS	CG-SHO	SV-BS	IP	H	R	HR	HB	BB-IB	SO	ERA	AERA	OAV	OOB	AB-HR-SH	AVG	PB	SUP	APR	DL	PW
1912	Cle A	1	0	1.000	2	1	1	0	13	14	8	0	0	4	3	2.77	123	.286	.340	5	.000	-1	108	0	—	-0.1

Brenton, Lynn Lynn Davis "Buck","Herb"; B10.7.1889 Peoria IL; D10.14.1968 Los Angeles CA; BR/TR/5´10˝/165; d8.10

YEAR	TM LG	W	L	PCT	G	GS	CG-SHO	SV-BS	IP	H	R	HR	HB	BB-IB	SO	ERA	AERA	OAV	OOB	AB-HR-SH	AVG	PB	SUP	APR	DL	PW
1913	Cle A	0	0	ø	1	0	0	0	2	4	2	0	0	0	2	9.00	34	.400	.400	0	ø	0	—	-1	—	-0.1
1915	Cle A	2	3	.400	11	5	1-1	0	51	60	31	1	2	20	18	3.35	91	.308	.378	17	.118	-1	62	-3	—	-0.5
1920	Cin N	2	1	.667	5	1	1	1	18.1	17	14	0	0	4	13	4.91	62	.236	.276	8	.250	0	181	-4	—	-0.6
1921	Cin N	1	8	.111	17	8	2	1	60	80	35	0	1	17	19	4.05	88	.342	.389	15-0-3	.133	-0	60	-4	—	-0.4
Total	4	5	12	.294	34	14	4-1	2	131.1	161	82	1	3	41	52	3.97	83	.315	.369	40-0-3	.150	-1	69	-12	—	-1.6

Breslow, Craig Craig Andrew; B8.8.1980 New Haven CT; BL/TL/6´1˝/180; [MilN02 26/769]; d7.23; Col Yale

YEAR	TM LG	W	L	PCT	G	GS	CG-SHO	SV-BS	IP	H	R	HR	HB	BB-IB	SO	ERA	AERA	OAV	OOB	AB-HR-SH	AVG	PB	SUP	APR	DL	PW
2005	SD N	0	0	ø	14	0	0	0-0	16.1	15	6	1	1	13-0	14	2.20	178	.238	.372	1	.000	-0	—	3	0	0.1
2006	Bos A	0	2	.000	13	0	0	0-0	12	12	5	0	1	6-1	12	3.75	125	.261	.345	0	ø	0	—	1	0	0.2
Total	2	0	2	.000	27	0	0	0-0	28.1	27	11	1	2	19-1	26	2.86	148	.248	.361	1	.000	-0	—	4	0	0.3

YEAR	TM LG	W	L	PCT	G	GS	CG-SHO	SV-BS	IP	H	R	HR	HB	BB-IB	SO	ERA	AERA	OAV	OOB	AB-HR-SH	AVG	PB	SUP	APR	DL	PW
Bresnahan, Roger	Roger Philip "The Duke of Tralee"; B6.11.1879 Toledo OH; D12.4.1944 Toledo OH; BR/TR/5´9˝/200; d8.27; M5/C6; HF1945; ▲																									
1897	Was N	4	0	1.000	6	5	3-1	0	41	52	21	1	3	10	12	3.95	110	.306	.355	16	.375	1	112	4	—	0.4
1901	Bal A	0	1	.000	2	1	0	0	6	10	8	0	0	4	3	6.00	64	.370	.452	295-1-4	.268	0*	105	-2	—	-0.2
1910	StL N	0	0	ø	1	0	0	0	3.1	6	1	0	0	1	0	0.00	ø	.400	.438	234-0-8	.278	0*	—	1	—	0.1
Total	3	4	1	.800	9	6	3-1	0	50.1	68	30	1	3	15	15	3.93	107	.321	.374	545-1-12	.275	2	113	3	—	0.3
Bressler, Rube	Raymond Bloom; B10.23.1894 Coder PA; D11.7.1966 Cincinnati OH; BR/TL/6´0˝/187; d4.24; Mil 1918; ▲																									
1914	Phi A	10	4	.714	29	10	8-1	2	147.2	112	37	1	4	56	96	1.77	148	.220	.302	51-0-2	.216	4	165	14	—	1.7
1915	Phi A	4	17	.190	32	20	7-1	0	178.1	183	133	3	7	118	69	5.20	56	.283	.399	55-1-3	.145	1*	87	-42	—	-4.2
1916	Phi A	0	2	.000	4	2	0	0	15	16	11	0	2	14	8	6.60	43	.296	.457	5-0-1	.200	1	79	-5	—	-0.6
1917	Cin N	0	0	ø	2	1	0	0	9	15	11	0	0	5	2	6.00	44	.429	.500	5	.200	-0*	259	-4	—	-0.2
1918	Cin N	8	5	.615	17	13	10	0	128	124	48	3	1	39	37	2.46	108	.261	.318	62-0-1	.274	4*	129	2	—	0.9
1919	Cin N	2	4	.333	13	4	1	0	41.2	37	19	1	0	8	13	3.46	80	.248	.287	165-2-7	.206	2*	65	-3	—	-0.3
1920	Cin N	2	0	1.000	10	2	1-1	0	20.1	24	8	0	0	2	4	1.77	172	.300	.317	30-0-1	.267	0*	142	2	—	0.2
Total	7	26	32	.448	107	52	27-3	2	540	511	267	8	14	242	229	3.40	81	.262	.348	373-3-15	.214	12	115	-36	—	-2.5
Brett, Herb	Herbert James "Duke"; B5.23.1900 Lawrenceville VA; D11.25.1974 St.Petersburg FL; BR/TR/6´0˝/175; d8.8																									
1924	Chi N	0	0	ø	1	1	0	0	5.1	6	4	0	0	7	1	5.06	77	.300	.481	2	.000	-0	217	-1	—	-0.1
1925	Chi N	1	1	.500	10	1	0	0	17.1	12	7	0	1	3	6	3.63	119	.194	.242	1	.000	-0	20	2	—	0.2
Total	2	1	1	.500	11	2	0	0	22.2	18	11	0	1	10	7	3.97	106	.220	.312	3	.000	-0	110	1	—	0.1
Brett, Ken	Kenneth Alven; B9.18.1948 Brooklyn NY; D11.18.2003 Spokane WA; BL/TL/5´11˝/(180–195); [BosA66 1/4]; d9.27; b–George																									
1967	†Bos A	0	0	ø	1	0	0	0	2	3	1	0	0	0-0	2	4.50	77	.375	.375	0	ø	0	—	0	0	0.0
1969	Bos A	2	3	.400	8	8	0	0-0	39.1	41	24	6	3	22-1	23	5.26	73	.275	.377	10-1-2	.300	2	101	-5	0	-0.4
1970	Bos A	8	9	.471	41	14	1	2-0	139.1	118	71	17	3	79-6	155	4.07	98	.223	.327	41-2-1	.317	6	101	-1	0	0.6
1971	Bos A	0	3	.000	29	2	0	1-0	59	57	38	7	1	35-6	57	5.34	70	.253	.356	10-0-1	.200	-0	36	-10	0	-0.5
1972	Mil A	7	12	.368	26	22	2-1	0-0	133	121	76	13	1	49-9	74	4.53	68	.242	.310	44-0-1	.227	2*	93	-22	24	-2.9
1973	Phi N	13	9	.591	31	25	10-1	0-0	211.2	206	91	19	0	74-12	111	3.44	111	.259	.320	80-4-0	.250	8*	120	8	0	1.9
1974	†Pit N★	13	9	.591	27	27	10-3	0-0	191	192	81	9	2	52-9	96	3.30	106	.257	.306	87-2-3	.310	11*	142	4	0	1.6
1975	†Pit N	9	5	.643	23	16	4-1	0-0	118	110	47	10	2	43-5	47	3.36	107	.250	.318	52-1-1	.231	4*	101	5	30	1.0
1976	NY A	0	0	ø	2	0	0	1-0	2.1	2	0	0	0	0-0	1	0.00	ø	.222	.222	0	ø	0	—	1	0	0.1
	Chi A	10	12	.455	27	26	16-1	1-0	200.2	171	82	5	3	76-3	91	3.32	107	.234	.305	12	.083	-1*	85	5	0	0.5
	Year	10	12	.455	29	26	16-1	2-0	203	173	82	5	3	76-3	92	3.28	109	.233	.304	12	.083	-1	85	7	0	0.6
1977	Chi A	6	4	.600	13	13	2	0-0	82.2	101	47	10	1	15-0	39	5.01	82	.305	.334	0	ø	0	151	-6	0	-0.7
	Cal A	7	10	.412	21	21	5	0-0	142	157	73	15	3	38-0	41	4.25	93	.287	.334	0	ø	0*	88	-3	0	-0.2
	Year	13	14	.481	34	34	7	0-0	224.2	258	120	25	4	53-0	80	4.53	88	.294	.334	0	ø	0	113	-10	0	-0.9
1978	Cal A	3	5	.375	31	10	1-1	1-1	100	100	60	12	1	42-5	43	4.95	73	.262	.335	0	ø	0	94	-14	0	-1.0
1979	Min A	0	0	ø	9	0	0	0-1	12.2	16	7	1	0	6-0	3	4.97	88	.320	.393	0	ø	0	—	-1	0	0.0
	LA N	4	3	.571	30	0	0	2-1	47	52	20	1	1	12-2	13	3.45	105	.277	.322	11	.273	1	—	1	0	0.3
1980	KC A	0	0	ø	8	0	0	1-0	13.1	8	0	0	1	5-0	4	0.00	ø	.174	.269	0	ø	0	—	6	0	0.3
1981	KC A	1	1	.500	22	0	0	2-0	32.1	35	16	2	1	14-4	7	4.18	87	.282	.355	0	ø	0	—	-2	0	-0.1
Total	14	83	85	.494	349	184	51-8	11-3	1526.1	1490	734	127	23	562-62	807	3.93	94	.257	.323	347-10-9	.262	32	107	-34	54	0.5
Breuer, Marv	Marvin Howard "Baby Face"; B4.29.1914 Rolla MO; D1.17.1991 Rolla MO; BR/TR/6´2˝/185; d5.4																									
1939	NY A	0	0	ø	1	0	0	0	1	2	1	0	0	1	0	9.00	48	.667	.750	0	ø	0	—	0	—	0.0
1940	NY A	8	9	.471	27	22	10	0	164	175	89	20	0	61	71	4.55	89	.267	.329	54-0-6	.037	-5	123	-8	—	-1.2
1941	†NY A	9	7	.563	26	18	7-1	2	141	131	73	10	2	49	77	4.09	96	.243	.308	46-0-4	.087	-3	99	-2	0	-0.6
1942	†NY A	8	9	.471	27	19	6	1	164.1	157	67	11	1	37	72	3.07	112	.252	.295	54-0-5	.056	-3	89	6	0	0.1
1943	NY A	0	1	.000	5	1	0	0	14	22	16	0	0	6	6	8.36	39	.349	.406	3	.333	0	79	-8	0	-0.5
Total	5	25	26	.490	86	60	23-1	3	484.1	487	246	41	3	154	226	4.03	94	.258	.315	157-0-15	.064	-11	105	-12	0	-2.2
Brewer, Jack	Jack Herndon "Buddy"; B7.21.1919 Los Angeles CA; D11.30.2003 Sun City CA; BR/TR/6´2˝/170; d7.15; Col USC																									
1944	NY N	1	4	.200	14	7	2	0	55	66	40	8	3	16	21	5.56	66	.288	.343	19	.211	0	85	-11	0	-0.9
1945	NY N	8	6	.571	28	21	8	0	159.2	162	77	14	3	58	49	3.83	102	.260	.326	56-0-7	.179	-1	97	1	0	-0.1
1946	NY N	0	0	ø	1	0	0	0	2	3	3	0	0	2	3	13.50	25	.333	.455	0	ø	0	—	-2	0	-0.1
Total	3	9	10	.474	43	28	10	0	216.2	231	120	22	6	76	73	4.36	88	.268	.332	75-0-7	.187	-1	94	-12	0	-1.1
Brewer, Jim	James Thomas; B11.17.1937 Merced CA; D11.16.1987 Tyler TX; BL/TL/6´2˝/(186–195); d7.17; C3																									
1960	Chi N	0	3	.000	5	4	0	0	21.2	25	14	2	1	6-2	7	5.82	65	.272	.323	6	.167	0*	47	-4	58	-0.5
1961	Chi N	1	7	.125	36	11	0	0	86.2	116	65	17	1	21-2	57	5.82	72	.321	.358	22-0-1	.182	0	114	-15	0	-1.3
1962	Chi N	0	1	.000	6	1	0	0	5.2	10	6	2	0	3-0	1	9.53	44	.435	.500	0	ø	0	169	-3	0	-0.4
1963	Chi N	3	2	.600	29	1	0	0	49.2	59	32	10	0	15-0	35	4.89	72	.294	.339	6-0-1	.000	0	49	-7	0	-0.8
1964	LA N	4	3	.571	34	5	1-1	1	93	79	33	5	0	25-5	63	3.00	108	.232	.282	22	.273	2	130	4	0	0.4
1965	†LA N	3	2	.600	19	2	0	2	49.1	33	13	1	0	28-4	31	1.82	179	.196	.311	10	.000	-1*	80	8	43	0.8
1966	†LA N	0	2	.000	13	0	0	2	22	17	9	0	0	11-0	8	3.68	90	.221	.315	0	ø	0	—	0	0	0.0
1967	LA N	5	4	.556	30	11	0	1	100.2	78	32	8	1	31-7	74	2.68	116	.218	.281	22-0-1	.045	-1	85	6	0	0.4
1968	LA N	8	3	.727	54	0	0	14	76	59	22	5	0	33-13	75	2.49	111	.219	.303	9-0-1	.222	0	—	4	0	0.8
1969	LA N	7	6	.538	59	0	0	20-10	88.1	71	30	5	4	41-6	92	2.55	132	.221	.316	11	.091	0	—	8	0	1.5
1970	LA N	7	6	.538	58	0	0	24-5	89	66	36	10	0	33-9	91	3.13	123	.207	.280	12-0-1	.083	-0	—	7	0	1.2
1971	LA N	6	5	.545	55	0	0	22-5	81.1	55	17	4	0	24-5	66	1.88	173	.194	.254	9	.333	1	—	14	0	3.0
1972	LA N	8	7	.533	51	0	0	17-7	78.1	41	16	6	2	25-11	69	1.26	266	.157	.233	1	.000	0	—	18	0	4.0
1973	LA N★	6	8	.429	56	0	0	20-8	71.2	58	26	8	0	25-9	56	3.01	116	.229	.293	5-0-2	.400	1	—	5	0	1.0
1974	†LA N	4	4	.500	24	0	0	0-2	39.1	29	14	5	0	10-1	26	2.52	136	.207	.258	2	.000	-0	—	4	49	0.7
1975	LA N	3	1	.750	21	0	0	2-2	33	44	20	2	1	12-2	21	5.18	66	.333	.380	3	.000	-0	—	-6	0	-0.8
	Cal A	1	0	1.000	21	0	0	5-1	34.2	38	9	2	0	11-1	22	1.82	197	.279	.325	0	ø	0	—	7	0	0.4
1976	Cal A	3	1	.750	13	0	0	2-3	20	20	7	0	0	6-0	16	2.70	124	.256	.306	0	ø	0	—	1	126	0.3
Total	17	69	65	.515	584	35	1-1	132-43	1040.1	898	401	92	10	360-77	810	3.07	111	.236	.300	140-0-7	.150	1	103	51	276	10.7
Brewer, Tom	Thomas Austin; B9.3.1931 Wadesboro NC; BR/TR/6´1˝/175; d4.18; Col Elon																									
1954	Bos A	10	9	.526	33	23	7	0	162.2	152	90	15	7	95	69	4.65	88	.249	.355	60-0-2	.267	3*	123	-6	0	-0.5
1955	Bos A	11	10	.524	31	28	9-2	0	192.2	198	101	21	8	87-3	91	4.20	102	.263	.344	73-0-3	.151	-2*	121	2	0	0.2
1956	Bos A★	19	9	.679	32	32	15-4	0	244.1	200	103	14	5	112-6	127	3.50	132	.220	.307	94-1-1	.298	4*	98	30	0	3.9
1957	Bos A	16	13	.552	32	32	15-2	0	238.1	225	113	24	7	93-9	128	3.85	103	.250	.324	94-0-4	.202	-1*	119	4	0	0.6
1958	Bos A	12	12	.500	33	32	10-1	0	227.1	227	122	21	8	93-2	124	3.72	108	.259	.333	82-0-3	.195	-0*	111	1	0	0.3
1959	Bos A	10	12	.455	36	32	11-3	2	215.1	219	96	14	2	88-5	121	3.76	108	.265	.336	72-1-7	.111	-4*	103	8	0	0.6
1960	Bos A	10	15	.400	34	29	8-1	1	186.2	220	115	13	6	72-5	60	4.82	84	.301	.364	62-1-3	.194	0*	92	-17	0	-1.9
1961	Bos A	3	2	.600	10	9	0	0	42	37	21	4	0	29-0	13	3.43	122	.242	.357	14	.286	1*	85	2	90	0.4
Total	8	91	82	.526	241	217	75-13	3	1509.1	1478	761	126	43	669-30	733	4.00	104	.257	.337	551-3-23	.207	1	108	24	90	3.6
Brewer, Billy	William Robert; B4.15.1968 Fort Worth TX; BL/TL/6´1˝/(175–200); [MonN90 28/751]; d4.8; Col Dallas Baptist																									
1993	KC A	2	2	.500	46	0	0	0-2	39	31	16	6	0	20-4	28	3.46	133	.230	.327	0	ø	0	—	5	0	0.4
1994	KC A	4	1	.800	50	0	0	3-4	38.2	28	11	4	2	16-1	25	2.56	196	.207	.297	0	ø	0	—	11	0	1.3
1995	KC A	2	4	.333	48	0	0	0-4	45.1	54	28	9	2	20-1	31	5.56	86	.290	.365	0	ø	0	—	-3	0	-0.3
1996	NY A	1	0	1.000	4	0	0	0-0	5.2	7	6	0	0	8-0	8	9.53	52	.292	.469	0	ø	0	—	-3	0	-0.4
1997	Oak A	0	0	ø	3	0	0	0-0	2	4	3	1	0	2-0	1	13.50	34	.444	.500	0	ø	0	—	-2	22	-0.1
	Phi N	1	2	.333	25	0	0	0-2	22	15	8	2	0	11-0	16	3.27	129	.188	.280	1	.000	-0	—	3	42	0.3
1998	Phi N	0	1	.000	2	0	0	0-0	0.1	3	4	0	0	2-0	0	108.00	4	.750	.833	0	ø	0	—	-4	172	-0.6
1999	Phi N	1	1	.500	25	0	0	2-0	25.2	30	20	4	0	14-1	28	7.01	67	.294	.376	0	ø	0	—	-6	0	-0.5
Total	7	11	11	.500	203	0	0	5-12	178.2	172	96	26	4	93-7	137	4.79	99	.255	.345	1	.000	-0	—	1	236	0.1
Brewington, Jamie	Jamie Chancellor; B9.28.1971 Greenville NC; BR/TR/6´4˝/(180–190); [SFN92 10/271]; d7.24; Col Virginia Commonwealth																									
1995	SF N	6	4	.600	13	13	0	0-0	75.1	68	38	8	4	45-6	45	4.54	91	.245	.355	23-0-4	.217	0*	101	-2	0	-0.2
2000	Cle A	3	0	1.000	26	0	0	0-0	45.1	56	28	3	2	19-0	34	5.36	93	.311	.379	1	.000	0	—	-2	0	-0.1
Total	2	9	4	.692	39	13	0	0-0	120.2	124	66	11	6	64-6	79	4.85	92	.271	.364	24-0-4	.208	1	101	-4	0	-0.3

YEAR	TM LG	W	L	PCT	G	GS	CG-SHO	SV-BS	IP	H	R	HR	HB	BB-IB	SO	ERA	AERA	OAV	OOB	AB-HR-SH	AVG	PB	SUP	APR	DL	PW
Brice, Alan	Alan Healey; B10.1.1937 New York NY; BR/TR/6´5˝/210; d9.22																									
1961	Chi A	0	1	.000	3	0	0	0	3.1	4	2	0	0	3-0	3	0.00	ø	.308	.438	0	ø	0	—	1	0	0.1
Brickner, Ralph	Ralph Harold "Brick"; B5.2.1925 Cincinnati OH; D5.9.1994 Port Jefferson NY; BR/TR/6´3.5˝/215; d5.4; Col Indiana																									
1952	Bos A	3	1	.750	14	1	0	1	33	32	8	1	0	11	9	2.18	181	.264	.326	8	.250	0	44	6	0	0.8
Bridges, Marshall	Marshall "Sheriff"; B6.2.1931 Jackson MS; D9.3.1990 Jackson MS; BB/TL (BR 1962–65)/6´1˝/(165–190); d6.17																									
1959	StL N	6	3	.667	27	4	1	1	76	67	38	10	0	37-8	76	4.26	99	.240	.324	23-1-2	.217	2	95	1	0	0.1
1960	StL N	2	2	.500	20	1	0	1	31.1	33	15	2	1	16-1	27	3.45	119	.266	.350	6	.000	-0	65	1	0	0.1
	Cin N	4	0	1.000	14	0	0	2	25.1	14	3	1	0	7-0	26	1.07	359	.161	.223	4-0-1	.250	0	—	8	0	1.4
	Year	6	2	.750	34	1	0	3	56.2	47	18	3	1	23-1	53	2.38	167	.223	.300	10-0-1	.100	-0	67	9	0	1.5
1961	Cin N	0	1	.000	13	0	0	0	20.2	26	19	4	1	11-0	17	7.84	52	.317	.400	2	.000	-0	—	-8	0	-0.4
1962	†NY A	8	4	.667	52	0	0	18	71.2	49	30	4	0	48-6	66	3.14	119	.194	.321	14-0-1	.000	-2	—	4	0	0.8
1963	NY A	2	0	1.000	23	0	0	1	33	27	18	2	1	30-2	35	3.82	92	.237	.392	0	ø	0	—	-2	0	-0.1
1964	Was A	0	3	.000	17	0	0	2	30	37	22	3	0	17-2	16	5.70	65	.303	.383	3	.000	-0	—	-7	0	-0.7
1965	Was A	1	2	.333	40	0	0	0	57.1	62	26	3	0	25-4	39	2.67	130	.268	.340	7-0-1	.143	0	—	2	0	0.2
Total	7	23	15	.605	206	5	1	25	345.1	315	171	29	3	191-23	302	3.75	102	.244	.339	59-1-5	.119	-0	97	-1	0	1.4
Bridges, Tommy	Thomas Jefferson Davis; B12.28.1906 Gordonsville TN; D4.19.1968 Nashville TN; BR/TR/5´10.5˝/155; d8.13; Mil 1944–45; C2; Col Tennessee																									
1930	Det A	3	2	.600	8	5	2	0	37.2	28	18	4	0	23	17	4.06	118	.215	.333	10-0-2	.300	1	104	4	—	0.5
1931	Det A	8	16	.333	35	23	8-2	0	173	182	120	13	0	108	105	4.99	92	.263	.363	54-0-5	.148	-2	67	-10	—	-1.4
1932	Det A	14	12	.538	34	26	10-**4**	1	201	174	95	14	1	119	108	3.36	140	.233	.339	67-0-5	.164	-1	93	27	—	2.9
1933	Det A	14	12	.538	33	28	17-2	2	233	192	102	8	6	110	120	3.09	140	**.226**	.319	78-0-7	.205	2	71	29	—	3.2
1934	†Det A☆	22	11	.667	36	**35**	23-3	1	275	249	117	16	3	104	151	3.67	120	.241	.312	98-0-8	.122	-4	117	28	—	2.4
1935	†Det A☆	21	10	.677	36	34	23-4	1	274.1	277	129	22	3	113	**163**	3.51	119	.259	.332	109-0-4	.239	3	126	19	—	2.1
1936	Det A✳	**23**	11	.676	39	**38**	26-5	0	294.2	289	141	21	5	115	**175**	3.60	137	.255	.326	118-0-6	.212	0	115	43	—	4.2
1937	Det A★	15	12	.556	34	31	18-3	0	245.1	267	129	15	3	91	138	4.07	115	.274	.338	96-0-3	.240	2	108	15	—	1.6
1938	Det A	13	9	.591	25	20	13	1	151	171	83	14	2	58	101	4.59	109	.287	.353	54-0-4	.130	-1	113	8	—	0.7
1939	Det A★	17	7	.708	29	26	16-2	2	198	186	87	11	6	61	129	3.50	140	.243	.304	71-0-8	.197	0	114	30	—	3.2
1940	†Det A☆	12	9	.571	29	28	12-2	0	197.2	171	89	11	0	88	133	3.37	141	.229	.311	68-0-4	.176	-2	104	27	—	2.3
1941	Det A	9	12	.429	25	22	10-1	0	147.2	128	66	10	1	70	90	3.41	133	.233	.320	47-0-4	.085	-3	65	17	0	1.9
1942	Det A	9	7	.563	23	22	11-2	1	174	164	66	6	4	61	97	2.74	144	.246	.313	63-0-1	.095	-2	84	21	0	1.6
1943	Det A	12	7	.632	25	22	11-3	0	191.2	159	57	9	0	61	124	2.39	147	.226	.287	64-0-4	.219	2	102	24	0	2.6
1945	†Det A	1	0	1.000	4	1	0	0	11	14	6	2	0	2	6	3.27	107	.311	.340	3	.000	-0	145	0	0	0.0
1946	Det A	1	1	.500	9	1	0	1	21.1	24	16	5	1	8	17	5.91	62	.279	.347	3	.000	0	117	-5	0	-0.5
Total	16	194	138	.584	424	362	200-33	10	2826.1	2675	1321	181	35	1192	1674	3.57	126	.248	.325	1003-0-65	.180	-5	101	277	0	27.3
Briggs, Buttons	Herbert Theodore; B7.8.1875 Poughkeepsie NY; D2.18.1911 Cleveland OH; BR/TR/6´1˝/180; d4.23																									
1896	Chi N	12	8	.600	26	21	19	1	194	202	129	6	15	108	84	4.31	105	.266	.368	78	.128	-6	97	5	—	-0.3
1897	Chi N	4	17	.190	22	22	21	0	186.2	246	166	6	9	85	60	5.26	85	.315	.388	81-0-2	.160	-6	90	-18	—	-2.0
1898	Chi N	1	3	.250	4	4	3	0	30	38	22	0	1	10	14	5.70	63	.306	.363	14	.429	2	119	-4	—	-0.3
1904	Chi N	19	11	.633	34	30	28-3	3	277	252	102	3	8	77	112	2.05	130	.246	.304	94-1-2	.170	-0	95	16	—	1.4
1905	Chi N	8	8	.500	20	20	13-5	0	168	141	58	1	6	52	68	2.14	139	.237	.304	57-0-3	.053	-4	91	15	—	0.7
Total	5	44	47	.484	106	97	84-8	4	855.2	879	477	16	39	332	338	3.41	104	.268	.342	324-1-7	.148	-15	95	14	—	-0.5
Briggs, John	Jonathan Tift; B1.24.1934 Natoma CA; BR/TR/5´10˝/(170–175); d4.17																									
1956	Chi N	0	0	ø	3	0	0	0	5.1	5	1	1	3	4-1	1	1.69	223	.238	.429	0	ø	0	—	1	0	0.1
1957	Chi N	0	1	.000	3	0	0	0	4.1	7	6	2	0	3-0	1	12.46	31	.368	.435	0	ø	0	—	-4	0	-0.7
1958	Chi N	5	5	.500	20	17	3-1	0	95.2	99	52	12	1	45-1	46	4.52	87	.270	.351	35-0-1	.257	2	107	-5	0	-0.4
1959	Cle A	0	1	.000	4	1	0	0	12.2	12	5	1	0	3-0	5	2.13	173	.245	.283	2	.000	-0	96	2	0	0.1
1960	Cle A	4	2	.667	21	2	0	1	36.1	32	20	4	1	15-0	19	4.46	84	.250	.329	8-0-1	.125	-0	165	-3	0	-0.5
	KC A	0	2	.000	8	1	0	0	11.1	19	17	3	0	12-0	8	12.71	31	.380	.500	3	.000	-0	66	-10	0	-1.5
	Year	4	4	.500	29	3	0	1	47.2	51	37	7	1	27-0	27	6.42	59	.287	.380	11-0-1	.091	-1	132	-13	0	-2.0
Total	5	9	11	.450	59	21	3-1	1	165.2	174	101	23	5	82-2	80	5.00	77	.275	.360	48-0-2	.208	1	110	-19	0	-2.9
Briles, Nelson	Nelson Kelley; B8.5.1943 Dorris CA; D2.13.2005 Orlando FL; BR/TR/5´11˝/(195–205); d4.19; Col Santa Clara																									
1965	StL N	3	3	.500	37	2	0	4	82.1	79	33	4	6	26-6	52	3.50	110	.258	.327	15	.133	-0	216	4	0	0.2
1966	StL N	4	15	.211	49	17	0	6	154	162	65	14	7	54-11	100	3.21	112	.279	.345	38-0-1	.079	-2	91	5	0	0.5
1967	†StL N	14	5	.737	49	14	4-2	6	155.1	139	45	8	5	40-8	94	2.43	135	.236	.289	40-0-5	.150	0	109	16	0	2.1
1968	†StL N	19	11	.633	33	33	13-4	0	243.2	251	90	18	7	55-12	141	2.81	103	.266	.310	80-0-9	.138	1	128	1	0	0.1
1969	StL N	15	13	.536	36	33	10-3	0-0	227.2	218	104	17	2	63-7	126	3.52	102	.251	.301	76-1-5	.105	-1	103	0	0	-0.2
1970	StL N	6	7	.462	30	19	1-1	0-0	106.2	129	84	14	3	36-7	59	6.24	66	.297	.349	39-0-3	.179	1	154	-25	23	-2.6
1971	†Pit N	8	4	.667	37	14	4-2	1-1	136	131	51	12	3	35-12	76	3.04	112	.250	.301	39-1-3	.256	4	151	6	0	0.9
1972	†Pit N	14	11	.560	28	27	9-2	0-0	195.2	185	83	14	1	43-8	120	3.08	108	.249	.288	70-0-5	.157	-0	119	3	0	0.3
1973	Pit N	14	13	.519	33	33	7-1	0-0	218.2	201	87	19	1	51-3	94	2.84	124	.244	.287	72-1-6	.194	3	106	14	0	1.9
1974	KC A	5	7	.417	18	17	3	0-0	103	118	48	9	2	21-1	41	4.02	95	.293	.329	0	ø	0	85	0	73	0.0
1975	KC A	6	6	.500	24	16	3	2-0	112	127	60	19	5	25-1	73	4.26	91	.285	.329	0	ø	0	94	-4	0	-0.4
1976	Tex A	11	9	.550	32	31	7-1	1-0	210	224	87	17	2	47-0	98	3.26	110	.273	.312	0	ø	0	103	8	0	0.6
1977	Tex A	6	4	.600	28	15	2-1	1-0	108.1	114	58	13	6	30-1	57	4.24	96	.275	.332	0	ø	0	109	-2	0	-0.2
	Bal A	0	0	ø	2	0	0	1-0	4	5	3	2	0	0-0	2	6.75	57	.294	.294	0	ø	0	—	-1	0	-0.1
	Year	6	4	.600	30	15	2-1	2-0	112.1	119	61	15	6	30-1	59	4.33	94	.276	.330	0	ø	0	109	-3	0	-0.3
1978	Bal A	4	4	.500	16	8	1	0-0	54.1	58	31	6	2	21-2	30	4.64	76	.279	.345	0	ø	0	124	-7	28	-1.0
Total	14	129	112	.535	452	279	64-17	22-1	2111.2	2141	929	186	51	547-79	1163	3.44	103	.264	.312	469-3-37	.154	5	113	18	124	2.1
Brill, Frank	Francis Hasbrouck (b Francis Hasbrouck Briell); B3.30.1864 Astoria NY; D11.19.1944 Flushing NY; BR/TR/5´8˝/155; d6.23																									
1884	Det N	2	10	.167	12	12	12-1	0	103	148	98	7	—	26	18	5.50	53	.312	.348	44	.136	-3*	79	-24	—	-2.3
Brillheart, Jim	James Benson; B9.28.1903 Dublin VA; D9.2.1972 Radford VA; BR/TL/5´11˝/170; d4.17; Col Roanoke																									
1922	Was A	4	6	.400	31	10	3	1	119.2	120	58	3	8	72	47	3.61	107	.275	.388	36-0-1	.083	-4	114	4	—	-0.2
1923	Was A	0	1	.000	12	0	0	0	18	27	15	1	1	12	8	7.00	54	.360	.455	2	.000	-0	—	-6	—	-0.3
1927	Chi N	4	2	.667	32	12	4	0	128.2	140	67	4	4	38	36	4.13	94	.286	.343	44-0-6	.023	-5	123	-3	—	-0.7
1931	Bos A	0	0	ø	11	1	0	0	19.2	27	16	2	0	15	7	5.49	78	.325	.429	4-1-0	.500	2	79	-4	—	0.0
Total	4	8	9	.471	86	23	7	1	286	314	156	10	13	137	98	4.19	93	.290	.376	86-1-7	.070	-8	117	-9	—	-1.2
Brink, Brad	Bradford Albert; B1.20.1965 Roseville CA; BR/TR/6´2˝/(195–208); [PhiN86 1/7]; d5.17; Col USC																									
1992	Phi N	0	4	.000	8	7	0	0-0	41.1	53	27	2	1	13-2	16	4.14	85	.308	.360	12-0-1	.083	-0	63	-6	0	-0.6
1993	Phi N	0	0	ø	2	0	0	0-0	6	3	2	1	0	3-0	8	3.00	132	.143	.250	1	.000	-0	—	1	0	0.0
1994	SF N	0	0	ø	4	0	0	0-0	8.1	4	1	1	0	4-1	3	1.08	376	.143	.250	1	.000	-0	—	3	0	0.1
Total	3	0	4	.000	14	7	0	0-0	55.2	60	30	4	1	20-3	27	3.56	103	.271	.335	14-0-1	.071	-1	63	-2	0	-0.5
Briscoe, John	John Eric; B9.22.1967 LaGrange IL; BR/TR/6´3˝/(185–190); [OakA88 3/73]; d4.18; Col TCU																									
1991	Oak A	0	0	ø	11	0	0	0-0	14	12	11	3	0	10-0	9	7.07	55	.235	.355	0	ø	0	—	-5	0	-0.3
1992	Oak A	0	1	.000	2	2	0	0-0	7	12	6	0	0	9-0	4	6.43	59	.400	.538	0	ø	0	109	-2	0	-0.3
1993	Oak A	1	0	1.000	17	0	0	0-0	24.2	26	25	2	0	26-3	24	8.03	52	.277	.426	0	ø	0	—	-12	0	-0.6
1994	Oak A	4	2	.667	37	0	0	1-1	49.1	31	24	7	1	39-2	45	4.01	112	.185	.340	0	ø	0*	—	3	26	0.3
1995	Oak A	0	1	.000	16	0	0	0-0	18.1	25	17	4	2	21-1	19	8.35	54	.347	.495	0	ø	0	—	-7	91	-0.3
1996	Oak A	0	1	.000	17	0	0	1-1	26.1	18	11	2	0	24-2	14	3.76	132	.205	.368	0	ø	0*	—	4	0	0.2
Total	6	5	5	.500	100	2	0	2-2	139.2	124	94	18	3	129-8	115	5.67	78	.247	.398	0	ø	0	109	-19	117	-1.0
Brissie, Lou	Leland Victor; B6.5.1924 Anderson SC; BL/TL/6´4˝/215; d9.28; Col Presbyterian																									
1947	Phi A	0	1	.000	1	1	0	0	7	9	5	1	0	5	4	6.43	59	.310	.412	2	.000	-0	70	-2	0	-0.2
1948	Phi A	14	10	.583	39	25	11	5	194	202	100	6	2	95	127	4.13	104	.269	.352	76-0-5	.237	0	101	2	0	0.2
1949	Phi A★	16	11	.593	34	29	18	3	229.1	220	113	20	5	118	118	4.28	96	.251	.344	90-0-6	.267	3	107	0	0	0.1
1950	Phi A	7	19	.269	46	31	15-2	8	246	237	127	22	4	117	101	4.02	113	.253	.338	87-0-1	.172	-3	81	12	0	0.9
1951	Phi A	0	2	.000	2	2	0	0	13.1	20	10	0	0	8	3	6.75	63	.357	.438	5-0-1	.200	-0	83	-3	0	-0.4

YEAR	TM LG	W	L	PCT	G	GS	CG-SHO	SV-BS	IP	H	R	HR	HB	BB-IB	SO	ERA	AERA	OAV	OOB	AB-HR-SH	AVG	PB	SUP	APR	DL	PW
	Cle A	4	3	.571	54	4	1	9	112.1	90	44	5	3	61	50	3.20	118	.223	.329	23-0-1	.261	0	135	9	0	0.6
	Year	4	5	.444	56	6	1	9	125.2	110	54	5	3	69	53	3.58	107	.239	.342	28-0-2	.250	0	120	5	0	0.2
1952	Cle A	3	2	.600	42	1	0	2	82.2	68	41	5	0	34	28	3.48	96	.221	.299	12-0-3	.250	1	52	-3	0	-0.1
1953	Cle A	0	0	ø	16	0	0	2	13	21	11	2	0	13	5	7.62	49	.389	.507	0	ø	0	—	-5	0	-0.3
Total	7	44	48	.478	234	93	45-2	29	897.2	867	451	61	14	451	436	4.07	102	.254	.343	295-0-17	.227	1	98	10	0	0.8
Brito, Eude	Eude Ezequiel; B8.19.1978 Saban de la Mar, D.R.; BL/TL/5´11˝/160; d8.21																									
2005	Phi N	1	2	.333	6	5	0	0-0	22	20	9	2	2	11-1	15	3.68	118	.250	.351	7	.143	-0	87	2	0	0.3
2006	Phi N	1	2	.333	5	2	0	0-0	18.1	21	15	2	1	12-2	9	7.36	64	.296	.400	6	.000	-0	39	-5	0	-0.7
Total	2	2	4	.333	11	7	0	0-0	40.1	41	24	4	3	23-3	24	5.36	84	.272	.374	13	.077	-1	71	-3	0	-0.4
Britt, Jim	James Edward; B2.25.1856 Brooklyn NY; D2.28.1923 San Francisco CA; d5.2																									
1872	Atl NA	9	28	.243	37	37	37	0	336	568	473	6	—	21	13	4.53	100	.326	.334	155	.265	-7	54	0	—	-0.3
1873	Atl NA	17	36	.321	54	**54**	**51**-1	0	480.2	696	519	6	—	41	16	4.08	78	.301	.313	240	.196	-3	79	-52	—	-3.7
Total	2NA	26	64	.289	91	91	88-1	0	816.2	1264	992	12	—	62	29	4.26	87	.312	.322	395	.223	-10	67	-52	—	-4.0
Brittin, Jack	John Albert; B3.4.1924 Athens IL; D1.5.1994 Springfield IL; BR/TR/5´11˝/175; d9.15; Col Illinois																									
1950	Phi N	0	0	ø	3	0	0	0	4	2	2	0	0	3	3	4.50	90	.143	.294	0	ø	0	—	0	0	0.0
1951	Phi N	0	0	ø	3	0	0	0	4	5	5	0	0	6	3	9.00	43	.294	.478	0	ø	0	—	-3	0	-0.1
Total	2	0	0	ø	6	0	0	0	8	7	7	0	0	9	6	6.75	58	.226	.400	0	ø	0	—	-3	0	-0.1
Britton, Chris	Christopher Daniel; B12.16.1982 Hollywood FL; BR/TR/6´3˝/280; [BalA01 8/233]; d4.12																									
2006	Bal A	0	2	.000	52	0	0	1-2	53.2	46	22	4	0	17-3	41	3.35	135	.228	.286	0	ø	0	—	7	0	0.3
Britton, Jim	James Allan; B3.25.1944 N.Tonawanda NY; BR/TR/6´5˝/(215–230); d9.20; [DL 1970 Mon N 156]																									
1967	Atl N	0	2	.000	2	2	0	0	13.1	15	9	2	0	2-0	4	6.08	55	.278	.304	4	.000	-0	66	-4	0	-0.5
1968	Atl N	4	6	.400	34	9	2-2	3	90.1	81	35	1	2	34-5	61	3.09	97	.245	.318	21-0-2	.143	-0	106	-1	0	-0.1
1969	†Atl N	7	5	.583	24	13	2-1	1-0	88	69	38	10	0	49-1	60	3.78	96	.218	.322	21-0-4	.190	0	87	0	0	0.0
1971	Mon N	2	3	.400	16	6	0	0-0	45.2	49	33	10	2	27-1	23	5.72	62	.274	.375	9-0-1	.000	-1	54	-11	78	-1.3
Total	4	13	16	.448	76	30	4-3	4-0	237.1	214	115	23	4	112-7	148	4.02	83	.243	.331	55-0-7	.127	-2	85	-16	234	-1.9
Brizzolara, Tony	Anthony John; B1.14.1957 Santa Monica CA; BR/TR/6´5˝/(210–217); [AtlN77 2/30]; d5.19; Col Texas																									
1979	Atl N	6	9	.400	20	19	2	0-0	107.1	133	70	6	3	33-1	64	5.28	76	.303	.352	35-0-1	.029	-3	88	-13	0	-1.8
1983	Atl N	1	0	1.000	14	0	0	1-0	20.1	22	8	2	0	6-0	17	3.54	109	.278	.329	0	ø	0	—	1	0	0.0
1984	Atl N	1	2	.333	10	4	0	0-0	29	33	22	4	0	13-1	17	5.28	73	.284	.351	7-0-2	.000	-1	115	-5	0	-0.6
Total	3	8	11	.421	44	23	2	1-0	156.2	188	100	12	3	52-2	98	5.06	79	.297	.349	42-0-3	.024	-4	93	-17	0	-2.4
Broaca, Johnny	John Joseph; B10.3.1909 Lawrence MA; D5.16.1985 Lawrence MA; BR/TR/5´11˝/190; d6.2; Col Yale																									
1934	NY A	12	9	.571	26	24	13-1	0	177.1	203	94	9	1	65	74	4.16	98	.284	.344	66-0-4	.030	-7	120	-2	—	-0.9
1935	NY A	15	7	.682	29	27	14-2	0	201	199	96	16	0	79	78	3.58	113	.254	.323	80-0-5	.150	-4	133	11	—	0.5
1936	NY A	12	7	.632	37	27	12-1	3	206	235	110	16	0	66	84	4.24	110	.284	.337	82-0-3	.110	-6	115	10	—	0.0
1937	NY A	1	4	.200	7	6	3	0	44	58	27	5	0	17	9	4.70	94	.324	.383	14-0-1	.000	-2	72	-1	—	-0.4
1939	Cle A	4	2	.667	22	2	0	0	46	53	39	5	0	28	13	4.70	94	.288	.382	12	.000	-2	100	-7	—	-0.9
Total	5	44	29	.603	121	86	42-4	3	674.1	748	366	51	1	255	258	4.08	105	.278	.341	254-0-13	.091	-21	118	11	—	-1.7
Broberg, Pete	Peter Sven; B3.2.1950 W.Palm Beach FL; BR/TR/6´3˝/205; [TexA71 D1/1]; d6.20; Col Dartmouth																									
1971	Was A	5	9	.357	18	18	7-1	0-0	124.2	104	57	10	10	53-2	89	3.47	97	.228	.319	44-1-3	.114	-0	100	-2	0	-0.3
1972	Tex A	5	12	.294	39	25	3-2	1-0	176.1	153	93	14	13	85-3	133	4.29	71	.237	.332	51-0-5	.078	-2	93	-22	0	-2.4
1973	Tex A	5	9	.357	22	20	6-1	0-0	118.2	130	77	8	5	66-3	57	5.61	67	.283	.375	0	ø	0*	80	-21	0	-2.2
1974	Tex A	0	4	.000	12	2	0	0-0	29	29	29	7	1	13-0	15	8.07	44	.264	.344	0	ø	0	74	-14	0	-1.7
1975	Mil A	14	16	.467	38	32	7-2	0-0	220.1	219	114	18	16	106-2	100	4.13	93	.263	.356	0	ø	0	106	-6	0	-0.7
1976	Mil A	1	7	.125	20	11	1	0-0	92.1	99	59	5	4	72-6	28	4.97	71	.281	.403	0	ø	0	86	-16	0	-1.3
1977	Chi N	1	2	.333	22	0	0	0-0	36	34	22	8	0	18-4	20	4.75	93	.256	.340	6	.000	-1	—	-1	0	-0.2
1978	Oak A	10	12	.455	35	26	2	0-0	165.2	174	101	16	3	65-5	94	4.62	79	.269	.336	0	ø	0	90	-18	0	-2.1
Total	8	41	71	.366	206	134	26-6	1-0	963	942	552	86	52	478-25	536	4.56	78	.259	.350	101-1-8	.089	-3	93	-100	0	-10.9
Brocail, Doug	Douglas Keith; B5.16.1967 Clearfield PA; BL/TR/6´5˝/(220–250); [SDN86*1/12]; d9.8; Col Lamar (CO) CC; [DL 2002 Hou N 183]																									
1992	SD N	0	0	ø	3	3	0	0-0	14	17	10	2	0	5-0	15	6.43	56	.298	.355	5	.200	0	118	-4	0	-0.2
1993	SD N	4	13	.235	24	24	0	0-0	128.1	143	75	16	4	42-4	70	4.56	91	.282	.337	33-0-11	.182	-0*	87	-6	0	-0.7
1994	SD N	0	0	ø	12	0	0	0-1	17	21	13	1	2	5-3	11	5.82	71	.304	.364	2	.000	-0*	—	-4	86	-0.2
1995	Hou N	6	4	.600	36	7	0	1-0	77.1	87	40	10	4	22-2	39	4.19	92	.280	.334	16-0-4	.250	1*	127	-3	0	-0.2
1996	Hou N	1	5	.167	23	4	0	0-0	53	58	31	7	2	23-1	34	4.58	85	.289	.364	11	.000	-1*	23	-5	96	-0.6
1997	Det A	3	4	.429	61	4	0	2-7	78	74	31	10	3	36-4	60	3.23	143	.256	.341	0	ø	0	104	12	0	1.0
1998	Det A	5	2	.714	60	0	0	0-1	62.2	47	23	2	1	18-3	55	2.73	174	.211	.269	0	ø	0	—	13	15	1.2
1999	Det A	4	4	.500	70	0	0	2-2	82	60	23	7	4	25-1	78	2.52	198	.206	.276	0	ø	0	—	23	0	2.0
2000	Det A	5	4	.556	49	0	0	0-5	50.2	57	25	5	1	14-2	41	4.09	120	.285	.330	0	ø	0	—	5	19	0.7
2004	Tex A	4	1	.800	43	0	0	1-0	52.1	54	29	2	5	20-1	43	4.13	119	.269	.346	0	ø	0	—	3	44	0.3
2005	Tex A	5	3	.625	61	0	0	1-3	73.1	90	48	2	4	34-3	61	5.52	82	.301	.375	0	ø	0	—	-7	0	-0.6
2006	SD N	2	2	.500	25	0	0	0-0	28.1	27	16	1	0	8-2	19	4.76	87	.252	.302	0	ø	0	—	-2	113	-0.2
Total	12	39	42	.481	467	42	0	7-19	717	735	364	65	30	252-26	526	4.09	108	.267	.332	67-0-15	.164	-0	85	25	556	2.5
Brock, Chris	Terrence Christopher; B2.5.1970 Orlando FL; BR/TR/6´0˝/(180–185); [AtlN92 12/341]; d6.11; Col Florida St.																									
1997	Atl N	0	0	ø	7	6	0	0-0	30.2	34	23	2	0	19-2	16	5.58	75	.288	.376	10	.100	-0	146	-5	0	-0.3
1998	SF N	0	0	ø	13	0	0	0-0	27.2	31	13	3	0	7-1	19	3.90	103	.279	.322	4	.250	0	—	0	0	0.0
1999	SF N	6	8	.429	19	19	0	0-0	106.2	124	69	18	4	41-2	76	5.48	78	.291	.357	35-0-4	.200	1	118	-14	72	-1.4
2000	Phi N	7	8	.467	63	5	0	1-2	93.1	85	48	21	3	41-0	69	4.34	106	.239	.321	9-1-2	.222	1	52	3	0	0.5
2001	Phi N	3	0	1.000	24	0	0	0-1	32.2	35	16	6	2	15-2	26	4.13	100	.276	.359	3	.333	0	—	0	0	0.0
2002	Bal A	2	1	.667	22	0	0	0-0	44	52	24	6	1	14-1	21	4.70	92	.297	.349	2	.000	-0	—	-1	48	-0.1
Total	6	18	17	.514	148	30	0	1-3	335	361	193	56	10	137-8	227	4.81	90	.275	.345	63-1-6	.190	3	111	-17	120	-1.3
Brockett, Lew	Lewis Albert "King"; B7.23.1880 Brownsville IL; D9.19.1960 Norris City IL; BR/TR/5´10.5˝/168; d4.25																									
1907	NY A	1	2	.333	8	4	1	0	46.1	58	36	1	2	26	13	6.22	45	.309	.398	22	.182	-0*	73	-13	—	-0.9
1909	NY A	10	8	.556	26	18	10-3	1	170	148	68	3	6	59	70	2.12	119	.245	.318	60-0-3	.283	3	94	5	—	1.1
1911	NY A	2	4	.333	16	8	2	0	75.1	73	45	2	5	39	25	4.66	77	.256	.356	39	.308	2*	93	-6	—	-0.2
Total	3	13	14	.481	50	30	13-3	1	291.2	279	149	6	13	124	108	3.43	83	.259	.343	121-0-3	.273	5	91	-14	—	0.0
Brodowski, Dick	Richard Stanley; B7.26.1932 Bayonne NJ; BR/TR/6´2˝/(190–195); d6.15; Mil 1953–54																									
1952	Bos A	5	5	.500	20	12	4	0	114.2	111	66	12	3	50	42	4.40	90	.252	.333	39-1-1	.205	1	124	-6	0	-0.4
1955	Bos A	1	0	1.000	16	0	0	0	32	36	25	5	1	25-2	10	5.63	76	.295	.416	10-1-0	.500	3	—	-5	0	0.0
1956	Was A	0	3	.000	7	3	1	0	17.2	31	18	5	0	12-0	8	9.17	47	.397	.473	5	.000	-1	48	-8	0	-1.2
1957	Was A	0	1	.000	6	0	0	0	11.1	12	15	2	1	10-0	4	11.12	35	.261	.404	1	.000	-0	—	-9	0	-0.7
1958	Cle A	1	0	1.000	5	0	0	0	10	3	0	0	0	6-0	12	0.00	ø	.100	.250	1	.000	-0	—	4	0	0.4
1959	Cle A	2	2	.500	18	0	0	5	30	19	13	3	3	21-1	9	1.80	205	.181	.328	6-0-2	.333	0	—	4	0	0.6
Total	6	9	11	.450	72	15	5	5	215.2	212	137	27	8	124-3	85	4.76	84	.258	.359	62-2-3	.242	3	109	-20	0	-1.3
Broglio, Ernie	Ernest Gilbert; B8.27.1935 Berkeley CA; BR/TR/6´2˝/(195–200); d4.11																									
1959	StL N	7	12	.368	35	25	6-3	0	181.1	174	104	20	0	89-10	133	4.72	90	.250	.334	61-0-3	.098	-3	80	-9	0	-1.0
1960	StL N	**21**	9	**.700**	52	24	9-3	0	226.1	172	76	18	2	100-5	188	2.74	**149**	.213	.299	68-0-4	.206	2	87	32	0	4.4
1961	StL N	9	12	.429	29	26	7-2	0	174.2	166	97	19	1	75-5	113	4.12	107	.248	.322	62-0-4	.145	-2	88	4	0	0.1
1962	StL N	12	9	.571	34	30	11-4	0	222.1	193	80	22	2	93-5	132	3.00	143	.237	.316	72-0-6	.139	-2	83	31	0	2.5
1963	StL N	18	8	.692	39	35	11-5	0	250	202	97	24	4	90-4	145	2.99	119	.216	.286	89-0-10	.112	-3	128	14	0	1.2
1964	StL N	3	5	.375	11	11	3-1	0	69.1	65	33	7	1	26-2	36	3.50	109	.247	.317	21-0-2	.095	-0	86	2	0	0.1
	Chi N	4	7	.364	18	16	3	1	100.1	111	51	12	0	30-4	46	4.04	92	.281	.331	35-0-2	.286	3	81	-4	0	-0.2
	Year	7	12	.368	29	27	6-1	1	169.2	176	84	19	1	56-6	82	3.82	98	.267	.325	56-0-4	.214	2	83	-1	0	-0.1
1965	Chi N	1	6	.143	26	6	0	0	50.2	63	44	7	0	46-8	22	6.93	53	.313	.440	4-0-1	.000	-0	111	-17	0	-2.2

YEAR	TM LG	W	L	PCT	G	GS	CG-SHO	SV-BS	IP	H	R	HR	HB	BB-IB	SO	ERA	AERA	OAV	OOB	AB-HR-SH	AVG	PB	SUP	APR	DL	PW
1966	Chi N	2	6	.250	15	11	2	1	62.1	70	46	14	0	38-6	34	6.35	58	.290	.384	19-0-1	.368	3	104	-16	0	-1.5
Total	8	77	74	.510	259	184	52-18	2	1337.1	1216	628	143	10	587-49	849	3.74	107	.242	.321	431-0-33	.158	-2	94	37	0	3.4

BROHAWN, TROY Michael Troy; B1.14.1973 Cambridge MD; BL/TL/6´1˝/190; [SFN94 4/116]; d4.14; Col Nebraska; [DL 1999 Ari N 34]

YEAR	TM LG	W	L	PCT	G	GS	CG-SHO	SV-BS	IP	H	R	HR	HB	BB-IB	SO	ERA	AERA	OAV	OOB	AB-HR-SH	AVG	PB	SUP	APR	DL	PW
2001	†Ari N	2	3	.400	59	0	0	1-2	49.1	55	27	5	1	23-2	30	4.93	94	.289	.362	1	.000	-0	—	-1	0	-0.1
2002	SF N	0	1	.000	11	0	0	0-0	5.2	5	4	1	2	1-0	3	6.35	62	.227	.320	0	ø	0	—	-1	0	-0.2
2003	LA N	2	0	1.000	12	0	0	0-0	11.2	10	6	2	0	4-0	13	3.86	107	.227	.292	1	1.000	0	—	0	139	0.1
Total	3	4	4	.500	82	0	0	1-2	66.2	70	37	8	3	28-2	46	4.86	92	.273	.347	2	.500	0	—	-2	173	-0.2

BRONDELL, KEN Kenneth Leroy; B10.17.1921 Bradshaw NE; D10.3.2004 Van Nuys CA; BR/TR/6´1˝/195; d5.3

YEAR	TM LG	W	L	PCT	G	GS	CG-SHO	SV-BS	IP	H	R	HR	HB	BB-IB	SO	ERA	AERA	OAV	OOB	AB-HR-SH	AVG	PB	SUP	APR	DL	PW
1944	NY N	0	1	.000	7	2	1	0	19.1	27	18	3	0	8	1	8.38	44	.329	.389	4	.000	-1*	114	-9	0	-0.5

BRONKEY, JEFF Jacob Jeffrey; B9.18.1965 Kabul, Afghanistan; BR/TR/6´3˝/(210–215); [MinA86 2/38]; d5.2; Col Oklahoma St.

YEAR	TM LG	W	L	PCT	G	GS	CG-SHO	SV-BS	IP	H	R	HR	HB	BB-IB	SO	ERA	AERA	OAV	OOB	AB-HR-SH	AVG	PB	SUP	APR	DL	PW
1993	Tex A	1	1	.500	21	0	0	1-2	36	39	20	4	1	11-4	18	4.00	105	.285	.338	1	.000	-0	—	0	0	0.0
1994	Mil A	1	1	.500	16	0	0	1-1	20.2	20	10	3	0	12-4	13	4.35	117	.247	.344	0	ø	0	—	2	79	0.2
1995	Mil A	0	0	ø	8	0	0	0-0	12.1	15	6	0	0	6-0	5	3.65	137	.313	.389	0	ø	0	—	2	115	0.1
Total	3	2	2	.500	45	0	0	2-3	69	74	36	7	1	29-8	36	4.04	114	.278	.349	1	.000	-0	—	4	194	0.3

BRONSTAD, JIM James Warren; B6.22.1936 Ft.Worth TX; BR/TR/6´3˝/(195–196); d6.7

YEAR	TM LG	W	L	PCT	G	GS	CG-SHO	SV-BS	IP	H	R	HR	HB	BB-IB	SO	ERA	AERA	OAV	OOB	AB-HR-SH	AVG	PB	SUP	APR	DL	PW
1959	NY A	0	3	.000	16	3	0	2	29.1	34	19	2	1	13-0	14	5.22	70	.288	.361	5	.000	-0	73	-5	0	-0.6
1963	Was A	1	3	.250	25	0	0	1	57.1	66	38	9	1	22-2	22	5.65	66	.297	.359	12	.000	-1*	—	-11	0	-0.8
1964	Was A	0	1	.000	4	0	0	0	7	10	4	0	0	2-0	9	5.14	72	.345	.387	0	ø	0	—	-1	0	-0.1
Total	3	1	7	.125	45	3	0	3	93.2	110	61	11	2	37-2	45	5.48	67	.298	.362	17	.000	-2	73	-17	0	-1.5

BROOKENS, IKE Edward Dwain; B1.3.1949 Chambersburg PA; BR/TR/6´5˝/170; [TexA67 5/85]; d6.17

YEAR	TM LG	W	L	PCT	G	GS	CG-SHO	SV-BS	IP	H	R	HR	HB	BB-IB	SO	ERA	AERA	OAV	OOB	AB-HR-SH	AVG	PB	SUP	APR	DL	PW
1975	Det A	0	0	ø	3	0	0	0-0	10.1	11	6	3	1	5-0	8	5.23	77	.282	.378	0	ø	0	—	-1	0	0.0

BROOKS, FRANK Frank J.; B9.6.1978 Brooklyn NY; BL/TL/6´1˝/200; [PhiN99 13/396]; d8.27; Col St. Peters

YEAR	TM LG	W	L	PCT	G	GS	CG-SHO	SV-BS	IP	H	R	HR	HB	BB-IB	SO	ERA	AERA	OAV	OOB	AB-HR-SH	AVG	PB	SUP	APR	DL	PW
2004	Pit N	0	1	.000	11	1	0	0-0	17.1	13	10	5	0	9-2	18	4.67	93	.203	.301	1	.000	-0	43	-1	0	-0.1
2005	Atl N	0	0	ø	1	0	0	0-0	0.1	1	0	0	0	0-0	0	0.00	ø	1.000	1.000	0	ø	0	—	0	0	0.0
Total	2	0	1	.000	12	1	0	0-0	17.2	14	10	5	0	9-2	18	4.58	94	.215	.311	1	.000	-0	43	-1	0	-0.1

BROOKS, HARRY Harry Frank; B11.30.1865 Philadelphia PA; D12.5.1945 Philadelphia PA; d7.24

YEAR	TM LG	W	L	PCT	G	GS	CG-SHO	SV-BS	IP	H	R	HR	HB	BB-IB	SO	ERA	AERA	OAV	OOB	AB-HR-SH	AVG	PB	SUP	APR	DL	PW
1886	NY AA	0	1	.000	1	1	0	0	2	9	13	0	0	2	0	36.00	9	.429	.478	1	.000	-0	55	-8	—	-0.9

BROSNAN, JIM James Patrick; B10.24.1929 Cincinnati OH; BR/TR/6´4˝/(197–250); d4.15

YEAR	TM LG	W	L	PCT	G	GS	CG-SHO	SV-BS	IP	H	R	HR	HB	BB-IB	SO	ERA	AERA	OAV	OOB	AB-HR-SH	AVG	PB	SUP	APR	DL	PW
1954	Chi N	1	0	1.000	18	0	0	0	33.1	44	35	9	1	18	17	9.45	44	.331	.409	8	.125	-0	—	-17	0	-0.8
1956	Chi N	5	9	.357	30	10	1-1	1	95	95	44	9	0	45-8	51	3.79	100	.270	.349	22-0-2	.182	-0	98	1	0	0.1
1957	Chi N	5	5	.500	41	5	1	0	98.2	79	38	11	1	46-4	73	3.38	115	.219	.308	20-0-2	.250	2	96	7	0	0.9
1958	Chi N	3	4	.429	8	8	2	0	51.2	41	20	3	0	29-3	24	3.14	125	.225	.327	19	.105	-1	83	5	0	0.6
	StL N	8	4	.667	33	12	2	7	115	107	46	10	1	50-3	65	3.44	120	.250	.328	31-0-3	.097	-1	111	10	0	1.0
	Year	11	8	.579	41	20	4	7	166.2	148	66	13	1	79-6	89	3.35	121	.243	.328	50-0-3	.100	-2	99	14	0	1.6
1959	StL N	1	3	.250	20	1	0	2	33	34	18	5	1	15-5	18	4.91	86	.276	.357	7	.286	1	190	-2	0	-0.1
	Cin N	8	3	.727	26	9	1-1	2	83.1	79	35	7	5	26-2	56	3.35	121	.248	.313	23-0-1	.043	-2	98	6	0	0.7
	Year	9	6	.600	46	10	1-1	4	116.1	113	53	12	6	41-7	74	3.79	108	.256	.325	30-0-1	.100	-1	107	5	0	0.6
1960	Cin N	7	2	.778	57	2	0	12	99	79	31	5	0	22-5	62	2.36	162	.225	.269	15-1-1	.200	2	219	15	0	1.9
1961	†Cin N	10	4	.714	53	0	0	16	80	77	34	7	0	18-3	40	3.04	134	.249	.288	13-0-1	.154	-0	—	8	0	1.5
1962	Cin N	4	4	.500	48	0	0	13	64.2	76	27	6	0	18-5	51	3.34	120	.292	.335	6-0-2	.000	-1	—	5	0	0.7
1963	Cin N	0	1	.000	6	0	0	0	4.2	8	4	2	0	3-1	4	7.71	43	.421	.500	0	ø	0	—	-2	0	-0.4
	Chi A	3	8	.273	45	0	0	14	73	71	24	7	0	22-5	46	2.84	124	.263	.315	13	.308	1	—	6	0	1.3
Total	9	55	47	.539	385	47	7-2	67	831.1	790	356	81	9	312-44	507	3.54	111	.254	.322	177-1-12	.153	1	106	42	0	7.4

BROSS, TERRY Terrence Paul; B3.30.1966 ElPaso TX; BR/TR/6´9˝/230; [NYN87 13/342]; d9.4; Col St. Johns

YEAR	TM LG	W	L	PCT	G	GS	CG-SHO	SV-BS	IP	H	R	HR	HB	BB-IB	SO	ERA	AERA	OAV	OOB	AB-HR-SH	AVG	PB	SUP	APR	DL	PW
1991	NY N	0	0	ø	8	0	0	0-0	10	7	2	1	0	3-0	5	1.80	204	.200	.263	0	ø	0	—	2	0	0.1
1993	SF N	0	0	ø	2	0	0	0-0	2	3	2	1	0	1-0	1	9.00	44	.333	.400	0	ø	0	—	-1	0	-0.1
Total	2	0	0	ø	10	0	0	0-0	12	10	4	2	0	4-0	6	3.00	124	.227	.292	0	ø	0	—	1	0	0.0

BROSSEAU, FRANK Franklin Lee; B7.31.1944 Drayton ND; BR/TR/6´1˝/180; [PitN66 S1/19]; d9.10; Col Minnesota

YEAR	TM LG	W	L	PCT	G	GS	CG-SHO	SV-BS	IP	H	R	HR	HB	BB-IB	SO	ERA	AERA	OAV	OOB	AB-HR-SH	AVG	PB	SUP	APR	DL	PW
1969	Pit N	0	0	ø	2	0	0	0-0	1.2	2	2	0	0	2-1	2	10.80	32	.286	.444	0	ø	0	—	-1	0	-0.1
1971	Pit N	0	0	ø	1	0	0	0-0	2	1	0	0	0	0-0	0	0.00	ø	.200	.200	0	ø	0	—	1	0	0.1
Total	2	0	0	ø	3	0	0	0-0	3.2	3	2	0	0	2-1	2	4.91	70	.250	.357	0	ø	0	—	0	0	0.0

BROUTHERS, DAN Dennis Joseph "Big Dan"; B5.8.1858 Sylvan Lake NY; D8.2.1932 E.Orange NJ; BL/TL/6´2˝/207; d6.23; HF1945; ▲

YEAR	TM LG	W	L	PCT	G	GS	CG-SHO	SV-BS	IP	H	R	HR	HB	BB-IB	SO	ERA	AERA	OAV	OOB	AB-HR-SH	AVG	PB	SUP	APR	DL	PW
1879	Tro N	0	2	.000	3	2	2	0	21	35	30	0	—	8	6	5.57	45	.343	.391	168-4	.274	1*	0	-7	—	-0.5
1883	Buf N	0	0	ø	1	0	0	0	2	9	7	0	—	3	2	31.50	10	.643	.706	425-3	.374	1*	—	-5	—	-0.2
Total	2	0	2	.000	4	2	2	0	23	44	37	0	—	11	8	7.83	33	.379	.433	593-7	.346	1	0	-12	—	-0.7

BROW, SCOTT Scott John; B3.17.1969 Butte MT; BR/TR/6´3˝/200; [TorA90 7/204]; d4.28; Col Washington

YEAR	TM LG	W	L	PCT	G	GS	CG-SHO	SV-BS	IP	H	R	HR	HB	BB-IB	SO	ERA	AERA	OAV	OOB	AB-HR-SH	AVG	PB	SUP	APR	DL	PW
1993	Tor A	1	1	.500	6	3	0	0-0	18	19	15	2	1	10-1	7	6.00	73	.275	.366	0	ø	0	168	-4	0	-0.3
1994	Tor A	0	3	.000	18	0	0	2-0	29	34	27	4	1	19-2	15	5.90	83	.288	.386	0	ø	0	—	-6	0	-0.6
1996	Tor A	1	0	1.000	18	1	0	0-1	38.2	45	25	5	0	25-1	23	5.59	90	.294	.391	0	ø	0	111	-2	0	-0.1
1998	Ari N	1	0	1.000	17	0	0	0-0	21.1	22	17	2	0	14-2	13	7.17	60	.272	.375	1	.000	-0	—	-6	0	-0.3
Total	4	3	4	.429	59	4	0	2-1	107	120	84	13	2	68-6	58	6.06	78	.285	.382	1	.000	-0	146	-18	0	-1.3

BROWER, FRANK Frank Willard "Turkeyfoot"; B3.26.1893 Gainesville VA; D11.20.1960 Baltimore MD; BL/TR/6´2˝/180; d8.14.1920; Col Washington and Lee; ▲

YEAR	TM LG	W	L	PCT	G	GS	CG-SHO	SV-BS	IP	H	R	HR	HB	BB-IB	SO	ERA	AERA	OAV	OOB	AB-HR-SH	AVG	PB	SUP	APR	DL	PW
1924	Cle A	0	0	ø	4	0	0	0	9.2	7	2	0	1	4	0	0.93	459	.212	.316	107-3-0	.280	1*	—	3	—	0.2

BROWER, JIM James Robert; B12.29.1972 Edina MN; BR/TR/6´2˝/(205–215); [TexA94 6/169]; d9.5; Col Minnesota

YEAR	TM LG	W	L	PCT	G	GS	CG-SHO	SV-BS	IP	H	R	HR	HB	BB-IB	SO	ERA	AERA	OAV	OOB	AB-HR-SH	AVG	PB	SUP	APR	DL	PW
1999	Cle A	3	1	.750	9	2	0	0-0	25.2	27	13	8	1	10-1	18	4.56	112	.270	.339	0	ø	0	229	2	0	0.2
2000	Cle A	2	3	.400	17	11	0	0-0	62	80	45	11	2	31-1	32	6.24	80	.309	.387	3	.000	-0	90	-8	0	-0.5
2001	Cin N	7	10	.412	46	10	0	1-1	129.1	119	65	17	5	60-5	94	3.97	116	.247	.335	26-0-2	.308	2*	125	8	0	1.2
2002	Cin N	2	0	1.000	22	0	0	0-0	39.1	38	18	2	0	10-1	24	3.89	110	.260	.306	4-0-1	.000	-0	—	2	0	0.1
	Mon N	1	2	.333	30	0	0	0-1	41	39	22	5	4	22-1	33	4.83	91	.245	.351	5	.000	-1	—	-1	0	-0.1
	Year	3	2	.600	52	0	0	0-1	80.1	77	40	7	4	32-2	57	4.37	99	.252	.330	9-0-1	.000	-1	—	1	0	0.0
2003	†SF N	8	5	.615	51	5	0	2-1	100	90	48	8	1	39-2	65	3.96	107	.249	.320	17-0-1	.176	0	119	3	0	0.3
2004	SF N	7	7	.500	**89**	0	0	1-4	93	90	42	6	4	36-2	63	3.29	132	.259	.333	2	.500	1	—	9	0	1.3
2005	SF N	2	1	.667	32	0	0	1-2	30.1	40	22	5	2	15-0	25	6.53	65	.320	.399	2	.000	-0	—	-7	0	-0.7
	†Atl N	1	2	.333	37	0	0	0-0	30	33	14	6	3	17-3	28	4.20	101	.282	.387	0	ø	0	—	0	0	0.0
	Year	3	3	.500	69	0	0	1-2	60.1	73	36	11	5	32-3	53	5.37	79	.302	.393	2	.000	-0	—	-6	0	-0.7
2006	Bal A	0	1	.000	12	0	0	0-1	12.1	21	19	1	3	13-1	9	13.86	33	.389	.521	0	ø	0	—	-12	0	-0.8
	SD N	0	0	ø	6	0	0	0-0	7.2	11	8	1	2	1-0	5	9.39	44	.344	.400	0	ø	0	—	-5	0	-0.2
Total	8	33	32	.508	351	28	0	5-10	570.2	588	316	70	27	254-17	396	4.62	97	.269	.351	59-0-4	.203	1	124	-9	0	0.8

BROWN, ALTON Alton Leo "Deacon"; B4.16.1925 Norfolk VA; BR/TR/6´2˝/195; d4.21

YEAR	TM LG	W	L	PCT	G	GS	CG-SHO	SV-BS	IP	H	R	HR	HB	BB-IB	SO	ERA	AERA	OAV	OOB	AB-HR-SH	AVG	PB	SUP	APR	DL	PW
1951	Was A	0	0	ø	7	0	0	0	11.2	14	12	1	1	12	7	9.26	44	.298	.450	1	.000	-0	—	-6	0	-0.3

BROWN, ANDREW Andrew Aaron; B2.17.1981 Chardon OH; BR/TR/6´6˝/230; [AtlN99 6/204]; d8.13

YEAR	TM LG	W	L	PCT	G	GS	CG-SHO	SV-BS	IP	H	R	HR	HB	BB-IB	SO	ERA	AERA	OAV	OOB	AB-HR-SH	AVG	PB	SUP	APR	DL	PW
2006	Cle A	0	0	ø	9	0	0	0-0	10	6	4	0	1	8-1	7	3.60	120	.171	.341	0	ø	0	—	1	0	0.1

BROWN, BOARDWALK Carroll William; B2.20.1889 Woodbury NJ; D2.8.1977 Burlington NJ; BR/TR/6´1.5˝/178; d9.27

YEAR	TM LG	W	L	PCT	G	GS	CG-SHO	SV-BS	IP	H	R	HR	HB	BB-IB	SO	ERA	AERA	OAV	OOB	AB-HR-SH	AVG	PB	SUP	APR	DL	PW
1911	Phi A	0	1	.000	2	1	1	0	12	12	7	0	0	2	6	4.50	70	.267	.298	4	.000	-1	91	-2	—	-0.2
1912	Phi A	13	11	.542	34	24	15-3	0	199	204	115	2	9	87	64	3.66	84	.283	.367	76-0-4	.145	-3	142	-17	—	-2.0
1913	Phi A	17	11	.607	43	35	11-3	1	235.1	200	94	6	10	87	70	2.94	94	.233	.310	82-1-2	.159	-1	145	-5	—	-0.8
1914	Phi A	1	5	.167	15	7	2	0	66	64	34	1	0	26	20	4.09	64	.268	.340	20-0-1	.000	-2	96	-10	—	-1.1
	NY A	6	5	.545	20	14	8	0	122.1	123	57	2	1	42	57	3.24	85	.271	.334	44-0-2	.182	1	123	-7	—	-0.3
	Year	7	10	.412	35	21	10	0	188.1	187	91	3	1	68	77	3.54	77	.270	.336	64-0-3	.125	-0	114	-14	—	-1.4

YEAR	TM LG	W	L	PCT	G	GS	CG-SHO	SV-BS	IP	H	R	HR	HB	BB-IB	SO	ERA	AERA	OAV	OOB	AB-HR-SH	AVG	PB	SUP	APR	DL	PW
1915	NY A	3	6	.333	19	11	5	0	96.2	95	49	4	5	47	34	4.10	72	.275	.370	32	.188	-1*	66	-10	—	-1.0
Total	5	40	39	.506	133	92	42-6	1	731.1	698	356	15	25	291	251	3.47	83	.262	.340	258-1-9	.147	-6	126	-51	—	-5.4
BROWN, CHARLIE	Charles Edward; B8.17.1871 Bluffton IN; D4.3.1938 Monclova OH; TL/6´0˝/180; d8.4																									
1897	Cle N	1	2	.333	4	4	2	0	24.1	30	25	2	5	17	8	7.77	58	.300	.426	11	.273	0	91	-7	—	-0.6
BROWN, BUSTER	Charles Edward "Yank"; B8.31.1881 Boone IA; D2.9.1914 Sioux City IA; BR/TR/6´0˝/180; d6.22; Col Iowa St.																									
1905	StL N	8	11	.421	23	21	17-3	0	178.2	172	80	5	10	62	57	2.97	100	.260	.332	65	.092	-3	73	0	—	-0.2
1906	StL N	8	16	.333	32	27	21	0	238.1	208	98	2	11	112	109	2.64	99	.234	.327	85-1-6	.165	0	88	-3	—	-0.1
1907	StL N	1	6	.143	9	8	6	0	63.2	57	38	2	5	45	17	3.39	74	.263	.401	26-0-1	.269	2	107	-7	—	-0.4
	Phi N	9	6	.600	21	16	13-4	0	130	118	47	3	6	56	38	2.42	100	.246	.333	53	.189	2	120	0	—	0.1
	Year	10	12	.455	30	24	19-4	0	193.2	175	85	5	11	101	55	2.74	89	.251	.355	79-0-1	.215	3	115	-6	—	-0.3
1908	Phi N	0	0	ø	3	0	0	0	7	9	6	0	1	5	3	2.57	94	.346	.469	5	.200	-0*	—	-1	—	0.0
1909	Phi N	0	0	ø	7	1	0	0	25	22	10	1	1	16	10	3.24	80	.259	.382	9	.000	-1	81	-1	—	-0.2
	Bos N	4	8	.333	18	17	8-2	0	123.1	108	45	1	7	56	32	3.14	90	.244	.339	48	.146	-2	64	1	—	-0.1
	Year	4	8	.333	25	18	8-2	0	148.1	130	55	2	8	72	42	3.16	88	.247	.346	57	.123	-3	66	0	—	-0.3
1910	Bos N	9	23	.281	46	29	16-1	2	263	251	113	4	4	94	88	2.67	125	.268	.337	81-1-5	.198	0	63	16	—	2.1
1911	Bos N	8	18	.308	42	25	13	2	241	258	161	11	10	116	76	4.29	89	.284	.371	84-1-3	.250	3	80	-15	—	-1.0
1912	Bos N	4	15	.211	31	21	12	0	168.1	146	107	7	2	66	68	4.01	89	.239	.315	61-0-1	.213	1	98	-10	—	-0.8
1913	Bos N	0	0	ø	2	0	0	0	13.1	19	10	0	2	3	3	4.73	70	.396	.453	5	.000	-0	—	-2	—	-0.1
Total	9	51	103	.331	234	165	106-10	4	1451.2	1368	715	36	59	631	501	3.21	96	.258	.343	522-3-16	.182	3	82	-22	—	-0.7
BROWN, CURLY	Charles Roy "Lefty"; B12.9.1888 Spring Hill KS; D6.10.1968 Spring Hill KS; BL/TL/5´10.5˝/165; d9.8																									
1911	StL A	1	2	.333	3	2	2	0	23	22	9	0	1	5	8	2.74	123	.247	.295	9	.000	-1	53	2	—	0.1
1912	StL A	1	3	.250	16	4	2-1	0	64.2	69	56	0	3	35	28	4.87	68	.277	.373	24	.208	-0*	78	-14	—	-0.9
1913	StL A	1	1	.500	2	2	2	0	14	12	5	0	0	4	3	2.57	114	.245	.302	5	.400	1	76	1	—	0.2
1915	Cin N	0	2	.000	7	3	0	0	27	26	20	2	2	6	13	4.67	61	.245	.298	11	.364	1*	147	-6	—	-0.4
Total	4	3	8	.273	28	11	6-1	0	128.2	129	90	2	6	50	52	4.20	76	.262	.337	49	.224	0	88	-17	—	-1.0
BROWN, CLINT	Clinton Harold; B7.8.1903 Blackash PA; D12.31.1955 Rocky River OH; BL/TR/6´1˝/190; d9.27																									
1928	Cle A	0	1	.000	2	1	1	0	11	14	6	0	0	2	2	4.91	84	.304	.333	5	.200	-0	102	0	—	0.0
1929	Cle A	0	2	.000	3	1	1	0	16.1	18	8	0	0	6	1	3.31	134	.286	.348	7	.000	-1	38	2	—	0.1
1930	Cle A	11	13	.458	35	31	16-**3**	1	213.2	271	138	14	4	51	54	4.97	97	.314	.356	73-0-3	.247	2	86	0	—	0.3
1931	Cle A	11	15	.423	39	33	12-2	0	233.1	284	143	10	1	55	50	4.71	98	.295	.333	87-0-3	.172	-2	104	-1	—	-0.1
1932	Cle A	15	12	.556	37	32	21-1	1	262.2	298	143	14	4	50	59	4.08	116	.279	.314	100-2-5	.250	6*	100	18	—	2.2
1933	Cle A	11	12	.478	33	23	10-2	1	185	202	83	10	2	34	47	3.41	130	.276	.310	62-0-3	.145	-3*	81	21	—	2.2
1934	Cle A	4	3	.571	17	2	0	1	50.1	83	42	3	0	14	15	5.90	77	.359	.396	17	.294	1	105	-9	—	-0.9
1935	Cle A	4	3	.571	23	5	1	2	49	61	34	3	1	14	20	5.14	88	.300	.349	10	.200	0	77	-4	—	-0.5
1936	Chi A	6	2	.750	38	2	0	5	83	106	50	5	3	24	19	4.99	104	.315	.366	25-0-2	.160	-0	127	**3**	—	0.2
1937	Chi A	7	7	.500	**53**	0	0	**18**	100	92	47	7	1	36	51	3.42	135	.242	.309	18-0-1	.222	1	—	**12**	—	2.1
1938	Chi A	1	3	.250	8	0	0	2	13.2	16	8	0	0	9	2	4.61	106	.333	.439	2	.500	1	—	1	—	0.2
1939	Chi A	11	10	.524	**61**	0	0	18	118.1	127	58	8	0	27	41	3.88	122	.281	.322	19-0-4	.211	1	—	**11**	—	2.1
1940	Chi A	4	6	.400	37	0	0	10	66	75	30	5	2	16	23	3.68	120	.284	.330	14-0-3	.071	-1	—	6	—	0.9
1941	Cle A	3	3	.500	41	0	0	5	74.1	77	30	3	1	28	22	3.27	120	.279	.348	17	.118	0	—	6	0	0.7
1942	Cle A	1	1	.500	7	0	0	0	9	16	10	2	1	2	4	6.00	57	.356	.396	1	.000	-0	—	-4	0	-0.8
Total	15	89	93	.489	434	130	62-8	64	1485.2	1740	830	84	20	368	410	4.26	109	.291	.335	457-2-24	.199	5	95	62	0	8.7
BROWN, CURT	Curtis Steven; B1.15.1960 Ft.Lauderdale FL; BR/TR/6´5˝/(165–175); d6.10; Col Broward (FL) CC																									
1983	Cal A	1	1	.500	10	0	0	0-0	16	25	13	1	0	4-1	7	7.31	55	.368	.397	0	ø	0	—	-5	0	-0.6
1984	NY A	1	1	.500	13	0	0	0-1	16.2	18	5	1	0	4-0	10	2.70	142	.281	.319	0	ø	0	—	2	0	0.3
1986	Mon N	0	1	.000	6	0	0	0-0	12	15	6	0	0	2-2	4	3.00	125	.319	.340	1	.000	-0	—	0	0	0.0
1987	Mon N	0	1	.000	5	0	0	0-0	7	10	7	2	0	4-1	6	7.71	55	.333	.412	0	ø	0	—	-3	0	-0.3
Total	4	2	4	.333	34	0	0	0-1	51.2	68	31	4	0	14-4	27	4.88	81	.325	.363	1	.000	-0	—	-6	0	-0.6
BROWN, ED	Edward P.; B Chicago IL; TR/?/178; d8.19; ▲																									
1882	StL AA	0	0	ø	1	0	0	0	2	2	1	0	—	0	1	0.00	ø	.250	.250	60	.183	-0*	—	0	—	0.0
1884	Tol AA	0	1	.000	1	1	1	0	9	19	16	0	1	4	1	9.00	38	.396	.453	153	.176	-0*	0	-5	—	-0.4
Total	2	0	1	.000	2	1	1	0	11	21	17	0	1	4	2	7.36	45	.375	.426	213	.178	-0	0	-5	—	-0.4
BROWN, ELMER	Elmer Young "Shook"; B8.25.1883 Southport IN; D1.23.1955 Indianapolis IN; BL/TR/5´11.5˝/172; d9.16																									
1911	StL A	1	1	.500	5	3	1-1	0	16.2	16	17	0	0	14	5	6.48	52	.242	.375	8	.125	-1	135	-6	—	-0.6
1912	StL A	5	8	.385	23	13	2-1	0	120.1	122	56	2	12	42	45	2.99	111	.280	.359	36-0-2	.167	-1	96	4	—	0.2
1913	Bro N	0	0	ø	3	1	0	0	13	6	3	0	1	10	6	2.08	159	.158	.347	4	.000	-1	91	2	—	0.0
1914	Bro N	1	2	.333	11	5	1	0	36.2	33	28	2	7	23	22	3.93	73	.402	.563	12-0-1	.083	-1	175	-6	—	-0.5
1915	Bro N	0	0	ø	1	0	0	0	2	4	4	0	0	3	1	9.00	31	.500	.636	0	ø	0	—	-2	—	-0.1
Total	5	7	11	.389	43	22	4-2	0	188.2	181	108	4	20	92	79	3.48	93	.287	.395	60-0-3	.133	-3	116	-8	—	-1.0
BROWN, HAL	Hector Harold "Skinny"; B12.11.1924 Greensboro NC; BR/TR/6´2˝/(181–185); d4.19; C1; Col North Carolina																									
1951	Chi A	0	0	ø	3	0	0	1	8.2	15	9	3	0	4	4	9.35	43	.385	.442	2	1.000	1*	—	-5	0	-0.1
1952	Chi A	2	3	.400	24	8	1	0	72.1	82	39	8	0	21	31	4.23	86	.284	.332	19-1-1	.158	1*	108	-5	0	-0.3
1953	Bos A	11	6	.647	30	25	6-1	0	166.1	177	94	16	0	57	62	4.65	90	.269	.327	58-1-4	.293	5	89	-6	0	-0.1
1954	Bos A	1	8	.111	40	5	1	0	118	126	64	6	3	41	66	4.12	100	.269	.329	24-0-1	.125	-0	82	-1	0	-0.1
1955	Bos A	1	0	1.000	2	0	0	0	4	2	1	0	0	2-0	2	2.25	191	.143	.250	1	1.000	0	—	1	0	0.2
	Bal A	0	4	.000	15	5	1	0	57	51	30	5	0	26-1	26	4.11	93	.241	.322	16	.000	-1*	84	-2	0	-0.3
	Year	1	4	.200	17	5	1	0	61	53	31	5	0	28-1	28	3.98	97	.235	.318	17	.059	-1	83	-1	0	-0.1
1956	Bal A	9	7	.563	35	14	4-1	2	151.2	142	72	18	1	37-3	57	4.04	97	.247	.292	42-0-3	.190	1*	101	0	0	0.1
1957	Bal A	7	8	.467	25	20	7-2	1	150	132	68	17	2	37-3	62	3.90	92	.236	.283	48-0-6	.208	2*	86	-4	0	-0.2
1958	Bal A	7	5	.583	19	17	4-2	1	96.2	96	35	9	0	20-0	44	3.07	117	.259	.296	27-0-1	.148	-0*	88	7	45	0.8
1959	Bal A	11	9	.550	31	21	2	3	164	158	73	16	1	32-5	81	3.79	100	.252	.289	42-0-9	.048	-3	77	2	0	-0.1
1960	Bal A	12	5	.706	30	20	6-1	0	159	155	61	14	1	22-3	66	3.06	125	.258	**.283**	44-0-5	.182	3	135	13	0	1.6
1961	Bal A	10	6	.625	27	23	6-3	1	166.2	153	62	14	1	33-0	61	3.19	121	.247	.284	50-0-3	.140	-0	91	15	0	1.3
1962	Bal A	6	4	.600	22	11	0	1	85.2	88	41	12	3	21-2	25	4.10	90	.268	.317	28-0-2	.286	2	112	-3	0	-0.2
	NY A	0	1	.000	2	1	0	0	6.2	9	10	3	0	2-0	2	6.75	56	.333	.367	1	.000	-0	71	-4	0	-0.5
	Year	6	5	.545	24	12	0	1	92.1	97	51	15	3	23-2	27	4.29	86	.273	.321	29-0-2	.276	1	109	-8	0	-0.7
1963	Hou N	5	11	.313	26	20	6-3	0	141.1	137	54	14	0	8-0	68	3.31	95	.255	.264	43-0-3	.093	-2	66	0	0	-0.3
1964	Hou N	3	15	.167	27	21	3	1	132	154	68	18	2	26-10	53	3.95	86	.292	.326	39-0-2	.128	-1	45	-8	0	-1.2
Total	14	85	92	.480	358	211	47-13	11	1680	1677	781	173	14	389-27	710	3.81	98	.260	.302	484-2-40	.169	8	88	0	45	0.6
BROWN, JACKIE	Jackie Gene; B5.31.1943 Holdenville OK; BR/TR/6´1˝/195; d7.2; C9; b–Paul																									
1970	Was A	2	2	.500	24	5	1	0-0	57	49	28	8	0	37-1	47	3.95	91	.231	.344	13	.154	-0	94	-2	0	-0.2
1971	Was A	3	4	.429	14	9	0	0-0	47	60	34	9	1	27-2	21	5.94	57	.316	.404	15	.133	-1	91	-13	0	-1.8
1973	Tex A	5	5	.500	25	3	2-1	2-4	66.2	82	31	7	2	25-0	45	3.92	96	.309	.372	0	ø	0	143	0	0	-0.1
1974	Tex A	13	12	.520	35	26	9-2	0-0	216.2	219	97	13	4	74-4	134	3.57	100	.265	.327	0	ø	0	108	1	0	0.1
1975	Tex A	5	5	.500	17	7	2-1	0-0	70.1	70	37	7	2	35-2	35	4.22	89	.266	.355	0	ø	0	97	-3	0	-0.5
	Cle A	1	2	.333	25	3	1	1-2	69.1	72	40	9	0	29-6	41	4.28	89	.276	.342	0	ø	0	177	-5	0	-0.3
	Year	6	7	.462	42	10	3-1	1-2	139.2	142	77	16	2	64-8	76	4.25	89	.271	.349	0	ø	0	121	-8	0	-0.8
1976	Cle A	9	11	.450	32	27	5-2	0-0	180	193	94	14	7	55-4	104	4.25	83	.276	.332	0	ø	0	107	-15	0	-1.5
1977	Mon N	9	12	.429	42	25	6-2	0-0	185.2	189	99	15	4	71-5	89	4.51	86	.264	.332	56-0-4	.125	-2	99	-11	0	-1.5
Total	7	47	53	.470	214	105	26-8	3-6	892.2	934	460	82	20	353-24	516	4.18	88	.272	.341	84-0-4	.131	-3	105	-48	0	-5.8
BROWN, KEVIN	James Kevin; B3.14.1965 Milledgeville GA; BR/TR/6´4˝/(188–220); [TexA86 1/4]; d9.30; Col Georgia Tech																									
1986	Tex A	1	0	1.000	1	1	0	0-0	5	6	2	0	0	0-0	4	3.60	120	.316	.316	0	ø	0	189	0	0	0.1
1988	Tex A	1	1	.500	4	4	1	0-0	23.1	33	15	2	1	8-0	12	4.24	97	.330	.385	0	ø	0	156	-1	0	-0.1
1989	Tex A	12	9	.571	28	28	7	0-0	191	167	81	10	4	70-2	104	3.35	119	.234	.303	0	ø	0	96	13	0	1.6
1990	Tex A	12	10	.545	26	26	6-2	0-0	180	175	84	13	3	60-3	88	3.60	109	.255	.315	1	.000	-0*	108	6	15	0.6
1991	Tex A	9	12	.429	33	33	0	0-0	210.2	233	116	17	13	90-5	96	4.40	92	.284	.362	0	ø	0	111	-9	0	-0.8

YEAR	TM LG	W	L	PCT	G	GS	CG-SHO	SV-BS	IP	H	R	HR	HB	BB-IB	SO	ERA	AERA	OAV	OOB	AB-HR-SH	AVG	PB	SUP	APR	DL	PW
1992	Tex A★	**21**	11	.656	35	35	11-1	0-0	**265.2**	262	117	11	10	76-2	173	3.32	115	.260	.316	0	ø	0	110	13	0	1.5
1993	Tex A	15	12	.556	34	34	12-3	0-0	233	228	105	14	15	74-5	142	3.59	117	.252	.318	0	ø	0*	107	15	6	1.7
1994	Tex A	7	9	.438	26	25	3	0-0	170	218	109	18	6	50-3	123	4.82	100	.314	.361	0	ø	0	93	-3	0	-0.1
1995	Bal A	10	9	.526	26	26	3-1	0-0	172.1	155	73	10	9	48-1	117	3.60	133	.241	.302	0	ø	0	85	22	0	2.5
1996	Fla N★	17	11	.607	32	32	5-**3**	0-0	233	187	60	8	16	33-2	159	**1.89**	**218**	.220	.262	75-0-4	.120	-1*	66	**57**	15	**6.9**
1997	†Fla N★	16	8	.667	33	33	6-2	0-0	237.1	214	77	10	14	66-7	205	2.69	151	.240	.303	72-0-6	.125	-0	95	37	0	3.8
1998	†SD N★	18	7	.720	36	**35**	7-3	0-0	257	225	77	8	10	49-4	257	2.38	167	.235	.279	82-0-7	.207	4	101	47	0	4.9
1999	LA N	18	9	.667	35	**35**	5-1	0-0	252.1	210	99	19	7	59-1	221	3.00	145	.222	.273	78-0-13	.064	-5	93	37	0	3.2
2000	LA N★	13	6	.684	33	33	5-1	0-0	230	181	76	21	9	47-1	216	**2.58**	172	**.213**	**.261**	66-0-14	.076	-3	95	48	15	3.4
2001	LA N	10	4	.714	20	19	1	0-0	115.2	94	41	8	2	38-2	104	2.65	156	.224	.291	36-1-2	.083	-0	99	18	77	2.1
2002	LA N	3	4	.429	17	10	0	0-0	63.2	68	36	9	5	23-1	58	4.81	81	.274	.348	20-1-2	.250	2	88	-7	96	-0.4
2003	LA N✳	14	9	.609	32	32	0	0-0	211	184	67	11	5	56-2	185	2.39	173	.236	.290	63-0-6	.159	0	85	39	15	4.2
2004	†NY A	10	6	.625	22	22	0	0-0	132	132	65	14	3	35-0	83	4.09	112	.262	.309	0	ø	0	103	7	50	0.7
2005	NY A	4	7	.364	13	13	0	0-0	73.1	107	57	5	7	19-1	50	6.50	66	.341	.388	2	.500	1	119	-18	117	-2.1
Total	19	211	144	.594	486	476	72-17	0-0	3256.1	3079	1357	208	139	901-42	2397	3.28	128	.249	.306	495-2-54	.129	-3	97	321	406	33.7
BROWN, JIM	James W. H.; B12.12.1860 Clinton Co. PA; D4.6.1908 Williamsport PA; d4.17; ▲																									
1884	Alt U	1	9	.100	11	11	7	0	74	99	80	0	—	36	39	5.35	50	.301	.370	88-1	.250	-1*	58	-20	—	-2.0
	NY N	0	1	.000	1	1	1	0	9	10	9	0	—	8	2	5.00	60	.263	.391	3	.000	-1	0	-2	—	-0.2
	StP U	1	4	.200	6	6	4-1	0	36	43	34	1	—	14	20	3.75	35	.277	.337	16	.313	4	96	-18	—	-1.4
1886	Phi AA	0	1	.000	1	1	1	0	8.1	9	5	0	0	3	4	3.24	108	.265	.324	3	.000	-1	68	0	—	0.0
Total	2	2	15	.118	19	19	13-1	0	127.1	161	128	1	0	61	65	4.74	50	.290	.360	110-1	.245	2	62	-40	—	-3.6
BROWN, JAMIE	Jamie Monroe; B3.31.1977 Meridian MS; BR/TR/6´2˝/200; [CleA96 21/633]; d5.20; Col Meridian (MS) CC; [DL 2000 Cle A 27]																									
2004	Bos A	0	0	ø	4	0	0	0-0	7.2	15	7	1	0	4-0	6	5.87	83	.417	.463	0	ø	0	—	-1	0	-0.1
BROWN, JOHN	John J. "Ad"; B8.24.1876 Philadelphia PA; D7.18.1908 Philadelphia PA; d8.11																									
1897	Bro N	0	1	.000	1	1	0	0	5	7	8	0	3	4	0	7.20	57	.333	.500	2	.500	0	52	-3	—	-0.3
BROWN, JOPHERY	Jophery Clifford; B1.22.1945 Grambling LA; BL/TR/6´2˝/190; [ChiN66 S2/23]; d9.21; Col Grambling St.																									
1968	Chi N	0	0	ø	1	0	0	0	2	2	1	0	0	1-1	0	4.50	70	.286	.375	0	ø	0	—	0	0	0.0
BROWN, JOE	Joseph E.; B4.4.1859 Warren PA; D6.28.1888 Warren PA; 5´10˝/162; d8.16; ▲																									
1884	Chi N	4	2	.667	7	6	5	0	50	56	36	4	—	7	27	4.68	67	.258	.281	61	.213	-1*	155	-5	—	-0.5
1885	Bal AA	0	4	.000	4	4	4	0	38	52	33	0	0	4	9	5.68	57	.306	.322	19	.158	-1*	113	-8	—	-0.7
Total	2	4	6	.400	11	10	9	0	88	108	69	4	0	11	36	5.11	62	.279	.299	80	.200	-2	139	-13	—	-1.2
BROWN, JOE	Joseph Henry; B7.3.1900 Little Rock AR; D3.7.1950 Los Angeles CA; BR/TR/6´0˝/176; d5.17																									
1927	Chi A	0	0	ø	1	1	0	0	0	2	3	0	0	1	0	(3)	ø	1.000	1.000	0	ø	0	62	-3	—	-0.2
BROWN, KEITH	Keith Edward; B2.14.1964 Flagstaff AZ; BB/TR/6´4˝/(205–215); [CinN86 21/540]; d8.25; Col Cal St.–Sacramento																									
1988	Cin N	2	1	.667	4	3	0	0-0	16.1	14	5	1	0	4-0	6	2.76	130	.237	.286	4-0-1	.000	-0	50	2	0	0.3
1990	Cin N	0	0	ø	8	0	0	0-0	11.1	12	6	2	0	3-0	8	4.76	83	.286	.333	0	ø	0	—	-1	0	0.0
1991	Cin N	0	0	ø	11	0	0	0-0	12	15	4	0	0	6-1	4	2.25	169	.306	.382	0	ø	0	—	2	0	0.1
1992	Cin N	0	1	.000	2	2	0	0-0	8	10	5	2	0	5-0	5	4.50	80	.313	.405	2-0-1	.000	-0	113	-1	0	-0.2
Total	4	2	2	.500	25	5	0	0-0	47.2	51	20	5	0	18-1	23	3.40	110	.280	.345	6-0-2	.000	-1	72	2	0	0.2
BROWN, KEVIN	Kevin Dewayne; B3.5.1966 Oroville CA; BL/TL/6´1˝/185; [AtlN86*S1/2]; d7.27; Col Sacramento (CA) City																									
1990	NY N	0	0	ø	2	0	0	0-0	2	2	0	0	0	1-0	0	0.00	ø	.250	.333	0	ø	0	—	1	0	0.1
	Mil A	1	1	.500	5	3	0	0-0	21	14	7	1	1	7-1	12	2.57	151	.182	.256	0	ø	0	55	3	0	0.3
1991	Mil A	2	4	.333	15	10	0	0-1	63.2	66	39	6	1	34-2	30	5.51	72	.270	.361	0	ø	0	119	-9	0	-0.7
1992	Sea A	0	0	ø	2	0	0	0-0	3	4	3	1	0	3-0	2	9.00	45	.333	.467	0	ø	0	—	-2	0	-0.1
Total	3	3	5	.375	24	13	0	0-1	89.2	86	49	8	2	45-3	44	4.82	82	.252	.341	0	ø	0	105	-7	0	-0.4
BROWN, LLOYD	Lloyd Andrew "Gimpy"; B12.25.1904 Beeville TX; D1.14.1974 Opa–Locka FL; BL/TL/5´9˝/170; d7.17																									
1925	Bro N	0	3	.000	17	5	1	0	63.1	79	39	1	2	25	23	4.12	101	.319	.385	23-0-1	.087	-2	113	-1	—	-0.3
1928	Was A	4	4	.500	27	10	2	1	107	112	62	7	2	40	38	4.04	99	.273	.341	31	.161	0	99	-3	—	0.0
1929	Was A	8	7	.533	40	15	7-1	0	168	186	92	7	1	69	48	4.18	101	.297	.368	50-0-2	.220	3	101	1	—	0.5
1930	Was A	16	12	.571	38	22	10-1	0	197	220	99	6	5	65	59	4.25	108	.293	.354	65-1-2	.215	2	79	11	—	1.7
1931	Was A	15	14	.517	42	32	15-1	0	258.2	256	120	13	0	79	79	3.20	134	.257	.311	96-0-3	.229	3	100	27	—	3.0
1932	Was A	15	12	.556	46	24	10-2	5	202.2	239	115	11	1	55	53	4.44	97	.296	.342	70-0-6	.100	-5	99	-4	—	-0.9
1933	StL A	1	6	.143	8	6	0	0	39	57	35	1	0	17	7	7.15	65	.350	.411	11	.273	1	82	-10	—	-1.3
	Bos A	8	11	.421	33	21	9-2	1	163.1	180	93	4	0	64	37	4.02	109	.281	.347	57-2-4	.281	6	85	4	—	1.2
	Year	9	17	.346	41	27	9-2	1	202.1	237	128	5	0	81	44	4.63	96	.295	.360	68-2-4	.279	7	85	-6	—	-0.1
1934	Cle A	5	10	.333	38	15	5	6	117	116	67	7	2	51	39	3.85	118	.263	.342	30-0-1	.233	1	61	6	—	0.7
1935	Cle A	8	7	.533	42	8	4-2	4	122	123	52	6	3	37	45	3.61	125	.265	.323	37-0-2	.108	-2	75	**14**	—	1.4
1936	Cle A	8	10	.444	24	16	12-1	1	140.1	166	78	13	3	45	34	4.17	121	.294	.349	45-1-4	.222	2	76	12	—	1.5
1937	Cle A	2	6	.250	31	5	2	0	77	107	59	4	3	27	32	6.55	70	.329	.386	24	.167	-1	49	-14	—	-1.3
1940	Phi N	1	3	.250	18	2	0	3	37.2	58	26	3	0	16	16	6.21	63	.354	.411	13-0-1	.077	-1	123	-8	—	-1.0
Total	12	91	105	.464	404	181	77-10	21	1693	1899	937	83	22	590	510	4.20	105	.288	.348	552-4-26	.192	6	88	35	—	5.2
BROWN, MACE	Mace Stanley; B5.21.1909 North English IA; D3.24.2002 Greensboro NC; BR/TR/6´1˝/190; d5.21; Mil 1944–45; C1; Col Iowa																									
1935	Pit N	4	1	.800	18	5	2	0	72.2	84	41	5	0	22	28	3.59	114	.287	.337	24-0-2	.167	-0	141	2	—	0.2
1936	Pit N	10	11	.476	47	10	3	3	165	178	89	8	1	55	56	3.87	105	.275	.332	60-0-3	.167	-2	98	1	—	0.0
1937	Pit N	7	2	.778	50	2	0	**7**	107.2	109	59	2	1	45	60	4.18	92	.261	.334	30	.300	2	134	-4	—	-0.2
1938	Pit N★	15	9	.625	**51**	2	0	5	132.2	155	68	5	0	44	55	3.80	100	.294	.349	38-0-5	.132	-2	123	-1	—	-0.3
1939	Pit N	9	13	.409	47	19	8-1	7	200.1	232	90	8	2	52	71	3.37	114	.293	.338	64-0-4	.109	-4	83	9	—	0.6
1940	Pit N	10	9	.526	48	17	5-1	**7**	173	181	78	5	2	49	73	3.49	109	.267	.318	52-0-5	.115	-1	129	6	—	0.6
1941	Pit N	0	0	ø	1	0	0	0	1.1	2	0	0	0	0	0	0.00	ø	.333	.333	0	ø	0	—	1	0	0.0
	Bro N	3	2	.600	24	0	0	3	42.2	31	17	3	1	26	22	3.16	116	.208	.330	8	.000	-1	—	3	0	0.3
	Year	3	2	.600	25	0	0	3	44	33	17	3	1	26	22	3.07	119	.213	.330	8	.000	-1	—	3	0	0.3
1942	Bos A	9	3	.750	34	0	0	6	60.1	56	27	4	0	28	20	3.43	109	.255	.339	15-0-3	.067	-1	—	2	0	0.3
1943	Bos A	6	6	.500	**49**	0	0	9	93.1	71	26	2	0	51	40	2.12	156	.222	.329	17-0-1	.059	-1	—	**12**	0	1.6
1946	†Bos A	3	1	.750	18	0	0	1	26.1	26	7	2	0	16	10	2.05	179	.268	.372	5-0-1	.000	-1	—	4	0	0.7
Total	10	76	57	.571	387	55	18-2	48	1075.1	1125	502	44	7	388	435	3.46	110	.271	.335	313-0-24	.137	-11	110	35	0	3.8
BROWN, MARK	Mark Anthony; B7.13.1959 Bellows Falls VT; BB/TR/6´2˝/(190–200); [BalA80 6/156]; d8.9; Col Massachusetts																									
1984	Bal A	1	2	.333	9	0	0	0-0	23	22	11	2	1	7-0	10	3.91	100	.256	.319	0	ø	0	—	0	0	0.0
1985	Min A	0	0	ø	6	0	0	0-0	15.2	21	13	1	0	7-0	5	6.89	64	.333	.384	0	ø	0	—	-4	0	-0.2
Total	2	1	2	.333	15	0	0	0-0	38.2	43	24	3	1	14-0	15	5.12	80	.289	.347	0	ø	0	—	-4	0	-0.2
BROWN, MIKE	Michael Gary; B3.4.1959 Camden Co. NJ; BR/TR/6´2˝/(195–205); [BosA80 2/48]; d9.16; C1; Col Clemson																									
1982	Bos A	1	0	1.000	3	0	0	0-0	6	7	0	0	0	1-0	4	0.00	ø	.304	.333	0	ø	0	—	3	0	0.4
1983	Bos A	6	6	.500	19	18	3-1	0-0	104	110	62	12	2	43-1	35	4.67	94	.276	.345	0	ø	0	134	-4	22	-0.4
1984	Bos A	1	8	.111	15	11	0	0-0	67	104	63	9	3	19-1	32	6.85	61	.347	.388	0	ø	0	76	-21	0	-2.3
1985	Bos A	0	0	ø	2	1	0	0-0	3.1	9	8	0	0	3-0	3	21.60	20	.500	.545	0	ø	0	126	-6	0	-0.3
1986	Bos A	4	4	.500	15	10	0	0-0	57.1	72	35	10	1	25-1	32	5.34	79	.316	.381	0	ø	0	84	-6	0	-0.7
	Sea A	0	2	.000	6	2	0	0-0	15.2	19	14	4	0	11-0	9	7.47	57	.302	.405	0	ø	0	0	-5	0	-0.6
	Year	4	6	.400	21	12	0	0-0	73	91	49	14	1	36-1	41	5.79	73	.313	.387	0	ø	0	70	-11	0	-1.3
1987	Sea A	0	0	ø	1	0	0	0-0	0.1	3	2	0	0	0-0	0	54.00	9	.750	.750	0	ø	0	—	-2	0	-0.1
Total	6	12	20	.375	61	42	3-1	0-0	253.2	324	184	35	6	102-3	115	5.75	75	.313	.374	0	ø	0	101	-41	22	-4.0
BROWN, MORDECAI	Mordecai Peter Centennial "Three Finger","Miner"; B10.19.1876 Nyesville IN; D2.14.1948 Terre Haute IN; BB/TR/5´10˝/175; d4.19; M1; HF1949																									
1903	StL N	9	13	.409	26	24	19-1	0	201	231	105	7	6	59	83	2.60	126	.293	.347	77-0-2	.195	-0	77	11	—	1.1
1904	Chi N	15	10	.600	26	23	21-4	1	212.1	155	74	1	6	50	81	1.86	143	**.199**	**.253**	89-0-1	.213	1*	100	16	—	1.9
1905	Chi N	18	12	.600	30	24	24-4	0	249	219	89	3	1	44	89	2.17	138	.235	.271	93-1-7	.140	-1*	111	20	—	2.2

YEAR	TM LG	W	L	PCT	G	GS	CG-SHO	SV-BS	IP	H	R	HR	HB	BB-IB	SO	ERA	AERA	OAV	OOB	AB-HR-SH	AVG	PB	SUP	APR	DL	PW
1906	†Chi N	26	6	.813	36	32	27-**9**	3	277.1	198	56	1	4	61	144	**1.04**	**254**	.202	**.252**	98-0-5	.204	1	141	**45**	—	**6.1**
1907	†Chi N	20	6	.769	34	27	20-6	3	233	180	51	2	6	40	107	1.39	179	.221	.262	85-1-5	.153	-0*	123	29	—	3.7
1908	†Chi N	29	9	.763	44	31	27-9	**5**	312.1	214	64	1	5	49	123	1.47	160	.195	.232	121-0-5	.207	1*	105	32	—	4.4
1909	Chi N	**27**	9	.750	**50**	34	**32**-8	**7**	**342.2**	246	78	1	7	53	172	1.31	193	.202	.239	125-0-5	.176	1	125	**45**	—	5.3
1910	†Chi N	25	14	.641	46	31	**27-6**	**7**	295.1	256	95	3	4	64	143	1.86	155	.232	**.277**	103-0-6	.175	-0	132	29	—	4.0
1911	Chi N	21	11	.656	**53**	27	21	**13**	270	267	110	5	6	55	129	2.80	118	.262	.303	91-0-3	.253	5	113	16	—	2.3
1912	Chi N	5	6	.455	15	8	5-2	0	88.2	92	35	2	1	20	34	2.64	126	.275	.317	31-0-1	.290	2*	113	6	—	0.8
1913	Cin N	11	12	.478	39	16	11-1	6	173.1	174	79	7	1	44	41	2.91	112	.277	.325	54-0-3	.204	-0	80	5	—	0.6
1914	StL F	12	6	.667	26	18	13-2	0	175	172	73	7	3	43	81	3.29	92	.254	.302	59-0-2	.254	2	101	-1	—	-0.1
	Bro F	2	5	.286	9	8	5	0	57.2	63	33	1	0	18	32	4.21	68	.276	.329	19	.211	-0	128	-8	—	-0.9
	Year	14	11	.560	35	26	18-2	0	232.2	235	106	8	3	61	113	3.52	85	.260	.309	78-0-2	.244	1	109	-7	—	-1.0
1915	Chi F	17	8	.680	35	25	17-3	4	236.1	189	75	2	7	64	95	2.09	120	.220	.279	82-0-4	.293	5*	125	11	—	1.8
1916	Chi N	2	3	.400	12	4	2	0	48.1	52	27	0	4	9	21	3.91	74	.289	.337	16	.250	0	167	-5	—	-0.5
Total	14	239	130	.648	481	332	271-55	49	3172.1	2708	1044	43	61	673	1375	2.06	137	.233	.278	1143-2-49	.206	16	114	251	—	32.7
Brown, Myrl	Myrl Lincoln; B10.10.1894 Waynesboro PA; D2.23.1981 Harrisburg PA; BR/TR/5´11˝/172; d8.19; Col Lebanon Valley																									
1922	Pit N	3	1	.750	7	5	2	0	34.2	42	25	2	0	13	9	5.97	68	.296	.355	11-0-2	.273	1	164	-6	—	-0.5
Brown, Norm	Norman Ladelle; B2.1.1919 Evergreen NC; D5.31.1995 Bennettsville SC; BB/TR/6´3˝/180; d10.3; Mil 1944–45																									
1943	Phi A	0	0	ø	1	1	0	0	7	5	4	0	0	0	1	0.00	ø	.185	.185	3	.000	-0	99	1	0	0.0
1946	Phi A	0	1	.000	4	0	0	0	7.1	8	8	2	0	6	3	6.14	58	.267	.389	0	ø	0	—	-3	0	-0.4
Total	2	0	1	.000	5	1	0	0	14.1	13	12	2	0	6	4	3.14	111	.228	.302	3	.000	-0	99	-2	0	-0.4
Brown, Paul	Paul Dwayne; B6.18.1941 Ft.Smith AR; BR/TR/6´1˝/(184–190); d7.23; b–Jackie																									
1961	Phi N	0	1	.000	5	1	0	0	10	13	9	3	1	8-0	1	8.10	50	.325	.440	2	.500	0	0	-4	0	-0.3
1962	Phi N	0	6	.000	23	9	0	1	63.2	74	45	9	3	33-0	29	5.94	65	.298	.385	13-0-1	.154	0	93	-14	72	-1.2
1963	Phi N	0	1	.000	6	2	0	0	15.1	15	10	2	2	5-0	11	4.11	79	.238	.314	2	.500	0	173	-2	0	-0.1
1968	Phi N	0	0	ø	2	0	0	0	4	6	4	0	0	1-0	4	9.00	33	.353	.389	0	ø	0	—	-2	0	-0.1
Total	4	0	8	.000	36	12	0	1	93	108	68	14	6	47-0	45	6.00	63	.293	.380	17-0-1	.235	1	97	-22	72	-1.7
Brown, Ray	Paul Percival; B1.31.1889 Chicago IL; D5.29.1955 Los Angeles CA; BR/TR/6´1˝/172; d9.29																									
1909	Chi N	1	0	1.000	1	1	1	0	9	5	3	0	0	4	2	2.00	127	.172	.273	3	.000	-0	165	0	—	0.0
Brown, Stub	Richard P.; B8.3.1870 Baltimore MD; D3.10.1948 Baltimore MD; TL/6´2˝/220; d8.15																									
1893	Bal N	0	0	ø	2	0	0	0	9	13	8	0	1	5	0	6.00	79	.325	.413	5	.200	-0	—	-1	—	-0.1
1894	Bal N	4	0	1.000	9	6	3	0	49.2	59	39	3	1	24	8	4.89	112	.292	.370	23-0-1	.087	-4	104	2	—	-0.2
1897	Cin N	0	1	.000	2	1	1	0	13	17	8	1	0	8	2	4.15	110	.315	.403	5	.000	-1	0	1	—	-0.1
Total	3	4	1	.800	13	7	4	0	71.2	89	55	4	2	37	10	4.90	106	.301	.382	33-0-1	.091	-5	93	2	—	-0.4
Brown, Bob	Robert Murray; B4.1.1911 Dorchester MA; D8.3.1990 Pembroke MA; BR/TR/6´0.5˝/190; d4.21																									
1930	Bos N	0	0	ø	3	0	0	0	6	10	7	0	0	8	1	10.50	47	.417	.563	2	.000	-0	—	-3	—	-0.2
1931	Bos N	0	1	.000	3	1	0	0	6.1	9	7	0	0	3	2	8.53	44	.375	.444	2	.500	0	45	-3	—	-0.4
1932	Bos N	14	7	.667	35	28	9	1	213	187	89	6	2	104	110	3.30	114	.238	.329	67-0-5	.194	-0	104	13	—	1.1
1933	Bos N	0	0	ø	5	0	0	0	6.2	6	4	0	0	3	3	2.70	114	.250	.333	2	.000	-0*	—	-1	—	-0.1
1934	Bos N	1	3	.250	16	8	2-1	0	58.1	59	40	2	3	36	21	5.71	67	.262	.371	21	.238	0	141	-12	—	-0.7
1935	Bos N	1	8	.111	15	10	2-1	0	65	79	55	2	0	36	17	6.37	59	.302	.386	19-0-1	.105	-1*	87	-20	—	-2.4
1936	Bos N	0	2	.000	2	2	0	0	8.1	10	6	1	0	3	5	5.40	71	.278	.333	2	.000	-0	55	-2	—	-0.3
Total	7	16	21	.432	79	49	13-2	1	363.2	360	208	11	5	193	159	4.48	84	.261	.354	115-0-6	.183	-2	103	-28	—	-3.0
Brown, Scott	Scott Edward; B8.30.1956 DeQuincy LA; BR/TR/6´2˝/220; [CinN75 4/94]; d8.11; [DL 1982 KC A 181]																									
1981	Cin N	1	0	1.000	10	0	0	0-2	13	16	4	0	0	1-1	7	2.77	127	.314	.321	1	.000	-0	—	1	0	0.1
Brown, Steve	Steven Elbert; B2.12.1957 San Francisco CA; BR/TR/6´5˝/200; d8.1; Col California–Davis																									
1983	Cal A	2	3	.400	12	4	2-1	0-0	46	45	19	4	0	16-1	23	3.52	115	.256	.314	0	ø	0	34	3	0	0.3
1984	Cal A	0	1	.000	3	3	0	0-0	11	16	13	0	0	9-1	5	9.00	44	.340	.439	0	ø	0	121	-7	0	-0.5
Total	2	2	4	.333	15	7	2-1	0-0	57	61	32	4	0	25-2	28	4.58	88	.274	.343	0	ø	0	71	-4	0	-0.2
Brown, Tom	Thomas Dale; B8.10.1949 Lafayette LA; BR/TR/6´1˝/170; d9.14; Col Louisiana–Monroe																									
1978	Sea A	0	0	ø	6	0	0	0-0	13	14	6	2	0	4-0	8	4.15	93	.286	.340	0	ø	0	—	0	0	0.0
Brown, Tom	Thomas Tarlton; B9.21.1860 Liverpool, England; D10.25.1927 Washington DC; BL/TR/5´10˝/168; d7.6; M2/U4; ▲																									
1882	Bal AA	0	0	ø	2	0	0	0	8.1	13	7	0	—	6	2	1.08	255	.333	.422	181-1	.304	1*	—	0	—	0.0
1883	Col AA	0	1	.000	3	1	1	0	14	14	17	0	—	10	6	5.79	53	.246	.358	420-5	.274	1*	93	-5	—	-0.2
1884	Col AA	2	1	.667	4	0	0	0	19	27	24	0	0	7	5	7.11	43	.281	.330	451-5	.273	1*	—	-9	—	-1.0
1885	Pit AA	0	0	ø	2	0	0	0	6	0	3	0	3	3	2	3.00	107	.000	.207	437-4	.307	1*	—	0	—	0.0
1886	Pit AA	0	0	ø	1	0	0	0	2	2	4	0	0	5	1	9.00	38	.125	.333	460-1	.285	0*	—	-1	—	0.0
Total	5	2	2	.500	12	1	1	0	49.1	56	55	0	3	31	16	5.29	57	.242	.340	1949-16	.286	4	93	-15	—	-1.2
Brown, Jumbo	Walter George; B4.30.1907 Greene RI; D10.2.1966 Freeport NY; BR/TR/6´4˝/295; d8.26																									
1925	Chi N	0	0	ø	2	0	0	0	6	5	5	0	0	4	0	3.00	144	.217	.333	1	.000	-0	—	0	—	0.0
1927	Cle A	0	2	.000	8	0	0	0	18.2	19	14	3	1	26	8	6.27	67	.284	.489	3	.667	1	—	-4	—	-0.2
1928	Cle A	0	1	.000	5	0	0	0	14.2	19	15	0	0	15	12	6.75	61	.365	.507	3	.667	1	—	-5	—	-0.2
1932	NY A	5	2	.714	19	3	3-1	1	55.2	58	30	1	2	30	31	4.53	90	.270	.364	23-0-1	.174	-1	70	-2	—	-0.2
1933	NY A	7	5	.583	21	8	1	0	74	78	48	3	0	52	55	5.23	74	.269	.380	28-0-1	.179	-1	145	-11	—	-1.5
1935	NY A	6	5	.545	20	8	3-1	0	87.1	94	41	2	0	37	41	3.61	112	.279	.350	32	.313	3	102	5	—	0.8
1936	NY A	1	4	.200	20	3	0	1	64	93	47	4	0	29	19	5.91	79	.352	.416	19	.000	-3	107	-9	—	-0.8
1937	Cin N	1	0	1.000	4	1	0	0	9.2	16	10	0	0	3	4	8.38	45	.390	.432	2	.000	0	139	-5	—	-0.4
	NY N	1	0	1.000	4	0	0	0	8.2	5	2	0	0	5	4	1.04	374	.172	.294	0	ø	0	—	2	—	0.3
	Year	2	0	1.000	8	1	0	0	18.1	21	12	0	0	8	8	4.91	78	.300	.372	2	.000	0	136	-2	—	-0.1
1938	NY N	5	3	.625	43	0	0	5	90	65	26	5	1	28	42	1.80	209	.204	.271	16	.188	1	—	**18**	—	1.7
1939	NY N	4	0	1.000	31	0	0	7	56.1	69	30	1	1	25	24	4.15	95	.304	.375	11	.364	1	—	-1	—	0.0
1940	NY N	2	4	.333	41	0	0	**7**	55.1	49	25	5	0	25	31	3.42	114	.232	.314	10	.100	-1	—	2	—	0.2
1941	NY N	1	5	.167	31	0	0	**8**	57	49	23	2	0	21	30	3.32	111	.238	.308	9	.111	-1	—	3	0	0.3
Total	12	33	31	.516	249	23	7-2	29	597.1	619	316	26	5	300	301	4.07	99	.271	.357	157-0-2	.204	2	116	-7	0	0.0
Brown, Walter	Walter Irving; B4.23.1915 Jamestown NY; D2.3.1991 Westfield NY; BR/TR/5´11˝/175; d5.16																									
1947	StL A	1	0	1.000	19	0	0	0	46	50	27	3	0	28	10	4.89	79	.294	.394	11	.000	-1	—	-4	0	-0.3
Browning, Cal	Calvin Duane; B3.16.1938 Burns Flat OK; BL/TL/5´11˝/190; d6.12; Col Oklahoma St.																									
1960	StL N	0	0	ø	1	0	0	0	0.2	5	3	1	0	1-0	0	40.50	10	.714	.750	0	ø	0	—	-2	0	-0.1
Browning, Frank	Frank "Dutch"; B10.29.1882 Falmouth KY; D5.20.1948 San Antonio TX; BR/TR/5´6˝/155; d4.16; Col Georgetown																									
1910	Det A	2	2	.500	11	6	2	3	49	51	22	0	0	10	16	2.57	102	.262	.298	14-0-2	.000	-2	119	-1	—	-0.2
Browning, Tom	Thomas Leo; B4.28.1960 Casper WY; BL/TL/6´1˝/(180–195); [CinN82 9/233]; d9.9; Col Tennessee Wesleyan																									
1984	Cin N	1	0	1.000	3	3	0	0-0	23.1	27	4	0	0	5-0	14	1.54	246	.303	.340	7	.143	-0	70	6	0	0.3
1985	Cin N	20	9	.690	38	38	6-4	0-0	261.1	242	111	29	3	73-8	155	3.55	107	.245	.297	88-0-9	.193	2*	112	8	0	1.1
1986	Cin N	14	13	.519	39	**39**	4-2	0-0	243.1	225	123	26	1	70-6	147	3.81	101	.245	.295	86-0-7	.163	-1*	109	-2	0	-0.4
1987	Cin N	10	13	.435	32	31	2	0-0	183	201	107	27	5	61-7	117	5.02	84	.284	.342	52-0-6	.154	0*	92	-13	0	-1.5
1988	Cin N	18	5	.783	36	**36**	5-2	0-0	250.2	205	98	36	7	64-3	124	3.41	105	.224	.277	83-0-9	.145	1*	123	7	0	0.6
1989	Cin N	15	12	.556	37	**37**	9-2	0-0	249.2	241	109	31	3	64-10	118	3.39	106	.255	.302	78-0-14	.090	-3*	106	5	0	0.1
1990	†Cin N	15	9	.625	35	**35**	2-1	0-0	227.2	235	98	24	5	52-13	99	3.80	104	.266	.309	75-0-9	.093	-3*	93	7	0	0.3
1991	Cin N☆	14	14	.500	36	36	1	0-0	230.1	241	124	32	4	56-4	115	4.18	91	.266	.309	70-1-10	.171	2	114	-11	0	-1.2
1992	Cin N	6	5	.545	16	16	0	0-0	87	108	49	6	2	28-7	33	5.07	71	.311	.362	31-0-2	.226	1	99	-12	95	-1.2
1993	Cin N	7	7	.500	21	20	0	0-0	114	159	61	15	1	20-2	53	4.74	85	.333	.359	37-1-4	.216	2	102	-7	58	-0.4
1994	Cin N	3	1	.750	7	7	2-1	0-0	40.2	34	20	8	1	13-1	22	4.20	99	.222	.284	14-0-2	.143	-0	131	0	94	0.0

YEAR	TM LG	W	L	PCT	G	GS	CG-SHO	SV-BS	IP	H	R	HR	HB	BB-IB	SO	ERA	AERA	OAV	OOB	AB-HR-SH	AVG	PB	SUP	APR	DL	PW
1995	KC A	0	2	.000	2	2	0	0-0	10	13	9	2	0	5-0	3	8.10	59	.302	.375	0	ø	0	39	-3	135	-0.5
Total	12	123	90	.577	302	300	31-12	0-0	1921	1931	913	236	32	511-61	1000	3.94	97	.262	.310	621-2-72	.153	2	106	-15	382	-2.8
Brownson, Mark	Mark Phillip; B6.17.1975 Lake Worth FL; BL/TR/6´2˝/185; [ColN93 30/856]; d7.21; Col Palm Beach (FL) CC																									
1998	Col N	1	0	1.000	2	2	1-1	0-0	13.1	16	7	2	1	2-0	8	4.73	110	.296	.333	5	.000	-1	115	1	0	0.0
1999	Col N	0	2	.000	7	7	0	0-0	29.2	42	26	8	1	8-0	21	7.89	73	.333	.378	9-0-2	.111	-1	77	-5	0	-0.3
2000	Phi N	1	0	1.000	2	0	0	0-1	5	7	4	1	0	3-0	3	7.20	64	.333	.417	0	ø	0	—	-1	0	-0.2
Total	3	2	2	.500	11	9	1-1	0-1	48	65	37	11	2	13-0	32	6.94	79	.323	.370	14-0-2	.071	-1	87	-5	0	-0.5
Broxton, Jonathan	Jonathan Roy; B6.16.1984 Augusta GA; BR/TR/6´4˝/(275–290); [LAN01 2/60]; d7.29																									
2005	LA N	1	0	1.000	14	0	0	0-1	13.2	13	11	0	1	12-2	22	5.93	70	.245	.382	0	ø	0	—	-3	0	-0.2
2006	†LA N	4	1	.800	68	0	0	3-4	76.1	61	25	7	1	33-6	97	2.59	169	.216	.300	2-0-1	.000	0	—	15	0	0.9
Total	2	5	1	.833	82	0	0	3-5	90	74	36	7	2	45-8	119	3.10	140	.221	.314	2-0-1	.000	0	—	12	0	0.7
Brubaker, Bruce	Bruce Ellsworth; B12.29.1941 Harrisburg PA; BR/TR/6´1˝/198; d4.15																									
1967	LA N	0	0	ø	1	0	0	0	1.1	3	3	1	0	0-0	2	20.25	15	.429	.429	0	ø	0	—	-3	0	-0.1
1970	Mil A	0	0	ø	1	0	0	0-0	2	2	2	1	0	1-0	0	9.00	42	.250	.333	0	ø	0	—	-1	0	-0.1
Total	2	0	0	ø	2	0	0	0-0	3.1	5	5	2	0	1-0	2	13.50	26	.333	.375	0	ø	0	—	-4	0	-0.2
Bruce, Lou	Louis R.; B1.16.1877 St.Regis NY; D2.9.1968 Ilion NY; BL/TR/5´5˝/145; d6.22; Col Syracuse; ▲																									
1904	Phi A	0	0	ø	2	0	0	0	11	11	7	1	0	2	2	4.91	55	.262	.295	101-0-6	.267	0*	—	-2	—	-0.1
Bruce, Bob	Robert James; B5.16.1933 Detroit MI; BR/TR/6´3˝/(200–210); d9.14; Col Alma																									
1959	Det A	0	1	.000	2	1	0	0	2	2	5	1	0	3-0	1	9.00	45	.250	.455	0	ø	0	87	-2	0	-0.4
1960	Det A	4	7	.364	34	15	1	0	130	127	68	16	5	56-1	76	3.74	106	.250	.331	39-0-2	.179	0	89	0	0	0.1
1961	Det A	1	2	.333	14	6	0	0	44.2	57	28	6	2	24-2	25	4.43	92	.320	.403	9-0-1	.111	0	129	-3	0	-0.2
1962	Hou N	10	9	.526	32	27	6	0	175	164	92	16	12	82-3	135	4.06	92	.248	.339	55-0-1	.200	5	112	-7	0	-0.1
1963	Hou N	5	9	.357	30	25	1-1	0	170.1	162	73	7	8	60-3	123	3.59	88	.250	.318	55-0-3	.127	2*	87	-6	0	-0.3
1964	Hou N	15	9	.625	35	29	9-4	0	202.1	191	70	8	3	33-4	135	2.76	124	.246	.277	63-0-5	.190	2*	82	16	0	2.2
1965	Hou N	9	18	.333	35	34	7-1	0	229.2	241	107	22	9	38-4	145	3.72	90	.270	.305	74-0-4	.122	-1	83	-9	0	-1.1
1966	Hou N	3	13	.188	25	23	1	0	129.2	160	83	16	8	29-4	71	5.34	64	.301	.344	39-0-7	.077	-2	91	-27	30	-3.1
1967	Atl N	2	3	.400	12	7	1	1	38.2	42	25	3	1	15-4	22	4.89	68	.269	.337	12	.167	0	132	-7	0	-0.9
Total	9	49	71	.408	219	167	26-6	1	1122.1	1146	551	95	48	340-25	733	3.85	91	.263	.321	346-0-23	.150	6	94	-45	30	-3.8
Bruckbauer, Fred	Frederick John; B5.27.1938 New Ulm MN; BR/TR/6´1˝/185; d4.25; Col Minnesota																									
1961	Min A	0	0	ø	1	0	0	0	0	3	3	0	0	1-0	0	(3)	ø	1.000	1.000	0	ø	0	—	-3	0	-0.2
Bruckmiller, Andy	Andrew; B1.1.1882 Pittsburgh PA; D1.12.1970 McKeesport PA; BR/TR/5´11˝/175; d6.26																									
1905	Det A	0	0	ø	1	0	0	0	1	4	3	0	0	1	1	27.00	10	.571	.625	1	.000	-0	—	-2	—	-0.1
Bruhert, Mike	Michael Edwin; B6.24.1951 Jamaica NY; BR/TR/6´6˝/220; d4.9																									
1978	NY N	4	11	.267	27	22	1-1	0-0	133.2	171	83	6	1	34-5	56	4.78	74	.317	.357	40-0-1	.075	-3	100	-21	0	-2.4
Brumley, Duff	Duff Lechaun; B8.25.1970 Cleveland TN; BR/TR/6´4˝/220; [StLN90 24/649]; d6.1; Col Cleveland St. (TN) CC																									
1994	Tex A	0	0	ø	2	0	0	0-0	3.1	6	6	1	0	5-0	4	16.20	30	.400	.500	0	ø	0	—	-4	0	-0.2
Brummett, Greg	Gregory Scott; B4.20.1967 Wichita KS; BR/TR/6´0˝/180; [SFN89 11/284]; d5.29; Col Wichita St.																									
1993	SF N	2	3	.400	8	8	0	0-0	46	53	25	9	0	13-1	20	4.70	84	.294	.338	15-0-2	.000	-1	126	-4	0	-0.5
	Min A	2	1	.667	5	5	0	0-0	26.2	29	17	3	0	15-1	10	5.74	77	.299	.383	0	ø	0	146	-3	0	-0.3
Total	1	4	4	.500	13	13	0	0-0	72.2	82	42	12	0	28-2	30	5.08	81	.296	.355	15-0-2	.000	-1	134	-7	0	-0.8
Bruner, Jack	Jack Raymond; B7.1.1924 Waterloo IA; D6.24.2003 Lincoln NE; BL/TL/6´1˝/185; d9.16; Col Iowa																									
1949	Chi A	1	2	.333	4	2	0	0	7.2	10	7	0	0	8	4	8.22	51	.357	.500	1	.000	-0	43	-3	0	-0.6
1950	Chi A	0	0	ø	9	0	0	0	12.1	7	6	0	1	14	8	3.65	123	.184	.415	0	ø	0	—	1	0	0.0
	StL A	1	2	.333	13	1	0	1	35	36	21	4	2	23	16	4.63	107	.267	.381	10	.000	-1	55	1	0	0.0
	Year	1	2	.333	22	1	0	1	47.1	43	27	4	3	37	24	4.37	110	.249	.390	10	.000	-1	56	2	0	0.0
Total	2	2	4	.333	26	3	0	1	55	53	34	4	3	45	28	4.91	96	.264	.406	11	.000	-1	44	-1	0	-0.6
Bruner, Roy	Walter Roy; B2.10.1917 Cecilia KY; D11.30.1986 St.Matthews KY; BR/TR/6´0˝/165; d9.14; Mil 1941–45																									
1939	Phi N	0	4	.000	4	4	2	0	27	38	22	3	0	13	11	6.67	60	.339	.408	9-0-1	.111	-1	65	-8	—	-1.0
1940	Phi N	0	0	ø	2	0	0	0	6.1	5	4	2	0	6	4	5.68	69	.227	.393	2	.500	0	—	-1	—	0.0
1941	Phi N	0	3	.000	13	1	0	0	29.1	37	17	1	0	25	13	4.91	75	.336	.459	6	.000	-0	23	-3	0	-0.4
Total	3	0	7	.000	19	5	2	0	62.2	80	43	6	0	44	28	5.74	67	.328	.431	17-0-1	.118	-1	58	-12	0	-1.4
Brunet, George	George Stuart "Lefty"; B6.8.1935 Houghton MI; D10.25.1991 Poza Rica, Veracruz, Mexico; BR/TL/6´1˝/(193–210); d9.14																									
1956	KC A	0	0	ø	6	1	0	0	9	10	8	1	0	11-0	5	7.00	62	.286	.457	2	.000	-0	144	-3	0	-0.1
1957	KC A	0	1	.000	4	2	0	0	11.1	13	7	2	0	4-0	3	5.56	71	.277	.333	2	.000	-0	68	-2	0	-0.2
1959	KC A	0	0	ø	2	0	0	0	4.2	10	9	2	1	7-1	7	11.57	35	.435	.581	0	ø	0	—	-5	0	-0.2
1960	KC A	0	2	.000	3	2	0	0	10.1	12	6	0	1	10-2	4	4.35	91	.308	.460	3	.000	-0	22	-1	0	-0.1
	Mil N	2	0	1.000	17	6	0	0	49.2	53	31	6	1	22-5	39	5.07	68	.275	.345	11	.091	-1	150	-10	0	-0.6
1961	Mil N	0	0	ø	5	0	0	0	5	7	3	1	0	2-0	0	5.40	69	.412	.450	0	ø	0	—	-1	30	0.0
1962	Hou N	2	4	.333	17	11	2	0	54	62	31	2	0	21-1	36	4.50	83	.291	.353	17-0-1	.059	-1	92	-5	0	-0.5
1963	Hou N	0	3	.000	5	2	0	0	12.2	24	11	2	0	6-1	11	7.11	44	.393	.448	3	.000	-0	55	-6	0	-1.1
	Bal A	0	1	.000	16	0	0	1	20	25	15	3	1	9-0	13	5.40	64	.301	.372	1	.000	-0	—	-5	0	-0.3
1964	LA A	2	2	.500	10	7	0	0	42.1	38	17	2	0	25-1	36	3.61	91	.237	.337	11-0-1	.182	0	77	0	0	0.0
1965	Cal A	9	11	.450	41	26	8-3	2	197	149	64	9	3	69-8	141	2.56	133	.209	.280	56-0-6	.054	-2	78	18	0	1.5
1966	Cal A	13	13	.500	41	32	8-2	0	212	183	88	21	5	106-8	148	3.31	101	.234	.327	68-1-1	.103	-2	98	1	0	-0.1
1967	Cal A	11	19	.367	40	37	7-2	1	250	203	99	19	4	90-9	165	3.31	95	.223	.293	78-0-4	.077	-4	91	-2	0	-0.7
1968	Cal A	13	17	.433	39	36	8-5	0	245.1	191	83	23	2	68-3	132	2.86	102	.215	.270	74-0-4	.081	-3	78	4	0	-0.1
1969	Cal A	6	7	.462	23	19	2-2	0-1	100.2	98	51	15	1	39-4	56	3.84	91	.255	.324	27-0-2	.037	-1	87	-5	0	-0.7
	Sea A	2	5	.286	12	11	2	0-0	63.2	70	41	11	0	28-5	37	5.37	68	.280	.353	20-1-0	.150	1	97	-11	0	-1.0
	Year	8	12	.400	35	30	4-2	0-1	164.1	168	92	26	1	67-9	93	4.44	80	.265	.335	47-1-2	.085	-0	90	-16	0	-1.7
1970	Was A	8	6	.571	24	20	2-1	0-0	118	124	64	10	1	48-4	67	4.42	82	.275	.345	38-1-4	.158	1	117	-11	0	-1.0
	Pit N	1	1	.500	12	1	0	0-0	16.2	19	5	1	1	9-1	17	2.70	147	.311	.408	4	.000	-0	45	3	0	0.2
1971	StL N	0	1	.000	7	0	0	0-1	9.1	12	6	3	0	7-0	4	5.79	63	.316	.422	3	.333	0	—	-2	0	-0.2
Total	15	69	93	.426	324	213	39-15	4-2	1431.2	1303	639	133	21	581-53	921	3.62	92	.244	.318	418-3-23	.089	-14	91	-43	30	-5.2
Brunette, Justin	Justin Thomas; B10.7.1975 Los Alamitos CA; BL/TL/6´1˝/200; [StLN97 20/614]; d4.13; Col San Diego St.																									
2000	StL N	0	0	ø	4	0	0	0-0	4.2	8	3	0	0	5-0	2	5.79	80	.364	.481	1	1.000	0	—	0	0	0.0
Bruney, Brian	Brian Anthony; B2.17.1982 Astoria OR; BR/TR/6´3˝/(225–245); [AriN00 12/369]; d5.8																									
2004	Ari N	3	4	.429	30	0	0	0-1	31.1	20	16	2	1	27-5	34	4.31	106	.189	.358	0	ø	0	—	1	40	0.2
2005	Ari N	1	3	.250	47	0	0	12-4	46	56	39	6	5	35-2	51	7.43	60	.299	.421	1	.000	-0	—	-14	0	-1.7
2006	†NY A	1	1	.500	19	0	0	0-0	20.2	14	2	1	1	15-0	25	0.87	521	.189	.333	0	ø	0	—	9	0	0.7
Total	3	5	8	.385	96	0	0	12-5	98	90	57	9	7	77-7	110	5.05	89	.245	.385	1	.000	-0	—	-4	40	-0.8
Bruno, Tom	Thomas Michael; B1.26.1953 Chicago IL; BR/TR/6´5˝/(205–210); d8.1																									
1976	KC A	1	0	1.000	12	0	0	0-0	17.1	20	13	3	0	9-1	11	6.75	52	.290	.367	0	ø	0	—	-5	0	-0.3
1977	Tor A	0	1	.000	12	0	0	0-0	18.1	30	18	4	1	13-1	9	7.85	54	.366	.444	0	ø	0	—	-7	0	-0.3
1978	StL N	4	3	.571	18	3	0	1-2	49.2	38	12	3	0	17-1	33	1.99	179	.209	.275	12-0-2	.083	-1	92	9	0	1.2
1979	StL N	2	3	.400	27	1	0	0-1	38.1	37	18	1	2	22-5	27	4.23	90	.253	.355	5-0-1	.200	0	46	-1	0	-0.1
Total	4	7	7	.500	69	4	0	1-3	123.2	125	61	11	3	61-8	80	4.22	88	.261	.344	17-0-3	.118	-1	78	-4	0	0.5

YEAR	TM LG	W	L	PCT	G	GS	CG-SHO	SV-BS	IP	H	R	HR	HB	BB-IB	SO	ERA	AERA	OAV	OOB	AB-HR-SH	AVG	PB	SUP	APR	DL	PW
Brunson, Will	William Donald; B3.20.1970 Irving TX; BL/TL/6´4˝/185; [CinN92 21/577]; d6.21; Col Southwest Texas																									
1998	LA N	0	1	.000	2	0	0	0-0	2.1	3	3	0	0	2-0	1	11.57	35	.333	.455	0	ø	0	—	-2	0	-0.3
	Det A	0	0	ø	8	0	0	0-0	3	2	0	0	0	1-0	1	0.00	ø	.200	.273	0	ø	0	—	2	0	0.1
1999	Det A	1	0	1.000	17	0	0	0-0	12	18	9	3	0	6-1	9	6.00	83	.367	.421	0	ø	0	—	-2	0	-0.1
Total	2	1	1	.500	27	0	0	0-0	17.1	23	12	3	0	9-1	11	5.71	84	.338	.405	0	ø	0	—	-2	0	-0.3
Bruske, Jim	James Scott; B10.7.1964 E.St.Louis IL; BR/TR/6´1˝/185; [CleA86 S1/6]; d8.25; Col Loyola Marymount																									
1995	LA N	0	0	ø	9	0	0	1-0	10	12	7	0	1	4-0	5	4.50	86	.300	.378	0	ø	0	—	-1	0	-0.1
1996	LA N	0	0	ø	11	0	0	0-0	12.2	17	8	2	1	3-1	12	5.68	69	.315	.362	0	ø	0	—	-2	0	-0.1
1997	SD N	4	1	.800	28	0	0	0-1	44.2	37	22	4	1	25-1	32	3.63	108	.228	.330	6	.167	0*	—	1	19	0.1
1998	LA N	3	0	1.000	35	0	0	1-1	44	47	18	2	3	19-1	31	3.48	116	.272	.354	3	.000	-0	—	3	0	0.1
	SD N	0	0	ø	4	0	0	0-0	7	10	4	1	0	4-2	4	3.86	103	.333	.412	0	ø	0	—	0	0	0.0
	Year	3	0	1.000	39	0	0	1-1	51	57	22	3	3	23-3	35	3.53	114	.281	.362	3	.000	-0	—	3	0	0.1
	NY A	1	0	1.000	3	1	0	0-0	9	9	3	2	0	1-0	3	3.00	146	.257	.278	0	ø	0	170	2	0	0.2
2000	Mil N	1	0	1.000	15	0	0	0-0	16.2	22	15	5	2	12-1	8	6.48	71	.314	.424	1	.000	-0	—	-4	73	-0.2
Total	5	9	1	.900	105	1	0	2-2	144	154	77	16	8	68-6	95	4.13	98	.273	.357	10	.100	-0	170	-1	92	0.0
Brusstar, Warren	Warren Scott; B2.2.1952 Oakland CA; BR/TR/6´3˝/(200–210); [PhiN74*S4/67]; d5.6; Col Cal St.–Fresno																									
1977	†Phi N	7	2	.778	46	0	0	3-1	71.1	64	26	7	1	24-3	46	2.65	152	.250	.316	6-0-1	.000	-1	—	9	0	1.2
1978	†Phi N	6	3	.667	58	0	0	0-3	88.2	74	25	0	3	30-7	60	2.33	155	.239	.310	7	.143	0	—	13	0	1.4
1979	Phi N	1	0	1.000	13	0	0	1-1	14.1	23	12	1	0	4-2	3	6.91	56	.383	.415	0	ø	0	—	-5	84	-0.4
1980	†Phi N	2	2	.500	26	0	0	0-1	38.2	42	16	3	0	13-2	21	3.72	103	.286	.344	1	.000	-0	—	1	94	0.1
1981	†Phi N	0	1	.000	14	0	0	0-1	12.1	12	6	0	1	10-4	8	4.38	84	.250	.383	0	ø	0	—	-1	0	-0.1
1982	Phi N	2	3	.400	22	0	0	2-1	22.2	31	12	2	1	5-3	11	4.76	78	.348	.381	2	.000	-0	—	-2	0	-0.4
	Chi A	2	0	1.000	10	0	0	0-0	18.1	19	7	2	1	3-0	8	3.44	119	.257	.295	0	ø	0	—	2	0	0.2
1983	Chi N	3	1	.750	59	0	0	1-3	80.1	67	21	1	2	37-10	46	2.35	162	.234	.321	4-0-1	.000	-0	—	13	0	0.7
1984	†Chi N	1	1	.500	41	0	0	3-2	63.2	57	23	4	1	21-7	36	3.11	126	.247	.307	5-0-1	.200	1	—	6	14	0.4
1985	Chi N	4	3	.571	51	0	0	4-1	74.1	87	55	8	3	36-11	34	6.05	66	.292	.368	7	.143	0	—	-15	0	-1.6
Total	9	28	16	.636	340	0	0	14-14	484.2	476	203	28	13	183-49	273	3.51	110	.265	.333	32-0-3	.094	-1	—	21	192	1.5
Bryant, Clay	Claiborne Henry; B11.16.1911 Madison Heights VA; D4.9.1999 Boca Raton FL; BR/TR/6´2.5˝/195; d4.19; C3																									
1935	Chi N	1	2	.333	9	1	0	2	22.2	34	15	1	0	7	13	5.16	76	.358	.402	6-1-1	.333	2*	173	-3	—	-0.2
1936	Chi N	1	2	.333	26	0	0	0	57.1	57	25	0	2	24	35	3.30	121	.259	.337	12-0-1	.417	1*	—	4	—	0.3
1937	Chi N	9	3	.750	38	9	4-1	3	135.1	117	69	1	1	78	75	4.26	94	.232	.336	45-1-2	.311	5*	99	-3	—	0.1
1938	†Chi N	19	11	.633	44	30	17-3	2	270.1	235	105	6	1	125	**135**	3.10	124	.235	.321	106-3-1	.226	4*	97	22	—	2.6
1939	Chi N	2	1	.667	4	4	2	0	31.1	42	23	3	1	14	9	5.74	69	.307	.375	14	.214	0*	116	-6	—	-0.5
1940	Chi N	0	1	.000	8	0	0	0	26.1	26	17	2	0	14	5	4.78	78	.265	.357	9	.333	1*	—	-3	—	-0.1
Total	6	32	20	.615	129	44	23-4	7	543.1	511	254	13	5	262	272	3.73	104	.249	.335	192-5-5	.266	13	101	11	—	2.2
Bryant, Ron	Ronald Raymond; B11.12.1947 Redlands CA; BB/TL/6´0˝/(180–190); [SFN65 12/422]; d9.29																									
1967	SF N	0	0	ø	1	0	0	0	4	3	2	0	1	0-0	2	4.50	73	.200	.250	1	.000	-0	—	0	0	0.0
1969	SF N	4	3	.571	16	8	0	1-0	57.2	60	29	8	2	25-1	30	4.37	80	.271	.349	16-0-3	.188	1	123	-4	0	-0.4
1970	SF N	5	8	.385	34	11	1	0-1	96	103	58	7	2	38-0	66	4.78	83	.274	.342	27-0-2	.111	-1	76	-9	0	-1.1
1971	†SF N	7	10	.412	27	22	3-2	0-0	140	146	69	9	3	49-3	79	3.79	90	.272	.333	50-0-1	.200	1	96	-5	0	-0.5
1972	SF N	14	7	.667	35	28	11-4	0-0	214	176	81	20	2	77-5	107	2.90	121	.224	.293	70-0-6	.171	1	125	13	0	1.1
1973	SF N	**24**	12	.667	41	39	8	0-0	270	240	125	23	9	115-12	143	3.53	109	.234	.315	95-0-3	.168	1*	103	8	0	1.1
1974	SF N	3	15	.167	41	23	0	0-1	126.2	142	92	11	4	68-4	75	5.61	68	.286	.372	31-0-4	.129	-1	76	-23	18	-3.1
1975	StL N	0	1	.000	10	1	0	0-0	8.2	20	17	2	0	7-1	7	16.62	23	.444	.519	1	.000	-0	93	-11	0	-1.1
Total	8	57	56	.504	205	132	23-6	1-2	917	890	473	80	23	379-26	509	4.02	92	.254	.329	291-0-19	.165	0	100	-31	18	-4.0
Bryden, T.R.	Thomas Ray; B1.17.1959 Moses Lake WA; BR/TR/6´4˝/190; d4.10; Col Gonzaga																									
1986	Cal A	2	1	.667	16	0	0	0-1	34.1	38	25	4	2	21-0	25	6.55	63	.290	.386	0	ø	0	—	-8	0	-0.6
Brynan, Tod	Charles Ruley; B7.1863 Philadelphia PA; D5.10.1925 Philadelphia PA; BR/TR/5´10˝/?; d6.22																									
1888	Chi N	2	1	.667	3	3	2	0	25	29	26	2	2	7	11	6.48	47	.271	.328	11	.182	0	128	-8	—	-0.7
1891	Bos N	0	1	.000	1	1	0	0	1	4	6	0	0	3	0	54.00	7	.571	.700	0	ø	0	163	-4	—	-0.5
Total	2	2	2	.500	4	4	2	0	26	33	32	2	2	10	11	8.31	37	.289	.357	11	.182	0	146	-12	—	-1.2
Buchanan, Jim	James Forrest; B7.1.1876 Chatham Hill VA; D6.15.1949 Norfolk NE; BL/TR/5´10˝/165; d4.16; Col Austin																									
1905	StL A	5	9	.357	22	15	12-1	**2**	141.1	149	76	2	2	27	54	3.50	73	.272	.309	46-0-1	.152	-0	96	-15	—	-1.4
Buchanan, Bob	Robert Gordon; B5.3.1961 Ridley Park PA; BL/TL/6´1˝/(180–185); [CinN79 2/41]; d7.13																									
1985	Cin N	1	0	1.000	14	0	0	0-0	16	25	15	4	0	9-1	3	8.44	45	.368	.442	1	.000	-0	—	-7	21	-0.4
1989	KC A	0	0	ø	2	0	0	0-0	3.1	5	6	1	0	3-2	3	16.20	24	.333	.444	0	ø	0	—	-4	0	-0.2
Total	2	1	0	1.000	16	0	0	0-0	19.1	30	21	5	0	12-3	6	9.78	39	.361	.442	1	.000	-0	—	-11	21	-0.6
Buchholz, Taylor	Taylor; B10.13.1981 Lower Merion Twsp. PA; BR/TR/6´4˝/220; [PhiN00 6/175]; d4.7																									
2006	Hou N	6	10	.375	22	19	1-1	0-0	113	107	80	21	3	34-4	77	5.89	76	.248	.304	30-0-4	.033	-2*	76	-18	0	-2.3
Buckels, Gary	Gary Scott; B7.22.1965 LaMirada CA; BR/TR/6´0˝/185; d7.23; Col Cal St.–Fullerton																									
1994	StL N	0	1	.000	10	0	0	0-0	12	8	5	2	0	7-1	9	2.25	189	.186	.300	1	.000	-0	—	2	0	0.1
Buckeye, Garland	Garland Maiers "Gob"; B10.16.1897 Heron Lake MN; D11.14.1975 Stone Lake WI; BB/TL/6´0˝/260; d6.19; Col Wabash																									
1918	Was A	0	0	ø	1	0	0	0	2	3	4	0	0	6	2	18.00	15	.333	.600	0	ø	0	—	-3	—	-0.1
1925	Cle A	13	8	.619	30	18	11-1	0	153	161	74	3	6	58	49	3.65	121	.267	.338	62-3-3	.226	2	104	13	—	1.7
1926	Cle A	6	9	.400	32	18	5-1	0	165.2	160	79	3	6	69	36	3.10	131	.264	.345	60-2-2	.200	2	103	12	—	1.1
1927	Cle A	10	17	.370	35	25	13-2	1	204.2	231	106	6	5	74	38	3.96	106	.296	.360	71-0-2	.268	3	69	6	—	0.9
1928	Cle A	1	5	.167	9	6	0	0	35	58	32	2	2	5	6	6.69	62	.389	.417	9	.111	-1	95	-10	—	-1.4
	NY N	0	0	ø	1	0	0	0	3.2	9	6	1	0	2	3	14.73	27	.409	.458	2	.500	1	—	-4	—	-0.1
Total	5	30	39	.435	108	67	29-4	1	564	622	301	15	19	214	134	3.91	108	.287	.356	204-5-7	.230	7	90	14	—	2.1
Buckingham, Fred	Frederick Bristol; B2.13.1876 Blenheim NY; D12.3.1958 Washington DC; d8.30; Col Yale																									
1895	Was N	0	0	ø	1	1	0	0	3	6	5	0	0	2	1	6.00	80	.400	.471	1	.000	-0	74	-1	—	-0.1
Buckles, Jess	Jesse Robert "Jim"; B5.20.1890 Lordsburg CA; D8.2.1975 Westminster CA; BL/TL/6´2.5˝/205; d9.17																									
1916	NY A	0	0	ø	2	0	0	0	4	3	2	0	0	1	2	2.25	128	.188	.235	1	.000	-0	—	0	—	0.0
Buckley, John	John Edward; B3.20.1869 Marlborough MA; D5.3.1942 Westborough MA; BL/TR/6´1˝/200; d7.15																									
1890	Buf P	1	3	.250	4	4	4	0	34	49	32	5	0	16	4	7.68	53	.325	.389	15	.000	-2	82	-10	—	-0.9
Buddie, Mike	Michael Joseph; B12.12.1970 Berea OH; BR/TR/6´3˝/(210–219); [NYA92 4/102]; d4.6; Col Wake Forest																									
1998	NY A	4	1	.800	24	2	0	0-0	41.2	46	29	5	3	13-1	20	5.62	78	.284	.346	0	ø	0	149	-7	0	-0.7
1999	NY A	0	0	ø	2	0	0	0-0	2	3	1	1	0	0-0	1	4.50	105	.333	.333	0	ø	0	—	0	0	0.0
2000	Mil N	0	0	ø	5	0	0	0-0	6	8	3	0	0	1-1	5	4.50	103	.320	.346	0	ø	0	—	0	0	0.0
2001	Mil N	0	1	.000	31	0	0	2-0	41.2	34	20	2	4	17-2	22	3.89	110	.225	.316	4	.250	0	—	2	20	0.2
2002	Mil N	1	2	.333	25	0	0	0-2	39.2	46	23	5	1	21-7	28	4.54	91	.293	.378	2	.000	-0	—	-2	0	-0.1
Total	5	5	4	.556	87	2	0	2-2	131	137	76	13	8	52-11	76	4.67	92	.272	.347	6	.167	-0	149	-7	20	-0.6
Budnick, Mike	Michael Joe; B9.15.1919 Astoria OR; D12.2.1999 Seattle WA; BR/TR/6´1˝/200; d4.18																									
1946	NY N	2	3	.400	35	7	1-1	3	88.1	75	40	13	0	48	36	3.16	109	.231	.330	20-1-0	.300	3	107	1	0	0.4
1947	NY N	0	0	ø	7	1	0	0	12	16	16	0	0	10	6	10.50	39	.314	.426	4	.250	0	217	-9	0	-0.4
Total	2	2	3	.400	42	8	1-1	3	100.1	91	56	13	0	58	42	4.04	87	.242	.343	24-1-0	.292	3	122	-8	0	0.0

YEAR	TM LG	W	L	PCT	G	GS	CG-SHO	SV-BS	IP	H	R	HR	HB	BB-IB	SO	ERA	AERA	OAV	OOB	AB-HR-SH	AVG	PB	SUP	APR	DL	PW
Buehrle, Mark	Mark Alan; B3.23.1979 St.Charles MO; BL/TL/6´2˝/(200–225); [ChiA98 38/1139]; d7.16; Col Jefferson (MO) CC																									
2000	†Chi A	4	1	.800	28	3	0	0-2	51.1	55	27	5	3	19-1	37	4.21	120	.272	.344	0	ø	0	93	5	0	0.4
2001	Chi A	16	8	.667	32	32	4-2	0-0	221.1	188	89	24	8	48-2	126	3.29	142	.230	.279	3	.000	-0	104	32	0	3.4
2002	Chi A★	19	12	.613	34	34	5-2	0-0	239	236	102	25	3	61-7	134	3.58	126	.260	.308	6	.167	-0	126	26	0	3.2
2003	Chi A	14	14	.500	35	35	2	0-0	230.1	250	124	22	5	61-2	119	4.14	111	.278	.325	6	.167	-0	96	7	0	0.8
2004	Chi A	16	10	.615	35	**35**	4-1	0-0	**245.1**	257	119	33	8	51-2	165	3.89	121	.271	.312	3-0-2	.000	-0	120	19	0	1.9
2005	†Chi A★	16	8	.667	33	33	3-1	0-0	**236.2**	240	99	20	4	40-4	149	3.12	145	.262	.295	3	.000	-0	86	31	0	3.0
2006	Chi A☆	12	13	.480	32	32	1	0-0	204	247	124	36	6	48-5	98	4.99	94	.305	.346	4-0-1	.000	-0	95	-8	0	-0.8
Total	7	97	66	.595	229	204	19-6	0-2	1428	1473	684	165	37	328-23	828	3.83	121	.268	.312	25-0-3	.080	-1	104	112	0	11.9
Buffinton, Charlie	Charles G.; B6.14.1861 Fall River MA; D9.23.1907 Fall River MA; BR/TR/6´1˝/180; d5.17; M1; ▲																									
1882	Bos N	2	3	.400	5	5	4-1	0	42	53	34	2	—	14	17	4.07	70	.296	.347	50	.260	0*	111	-6	—	-0.5
1883	Bos N	25	14	.641	43	41	34-4	1	333	346	187	4	—	51	188	3.03	102	.254	.281	341-1	.238	0*	135	9	—	0.7
1884	Bos N	48	16	.750	67	67	63-8	0	587	506	225	15	—	76	417	2.15	135	.219	.244	352-1	.267	12*	116	51	—	5.8
1885	Bos N	22	27	.449	51	50	49-6	0	434.1	425	238	10	—	112	242	2.88	93	.246	.292	338-1	.240	5*	99	-7	—	0.0
1886	Bos N	7	10	.412	18	17	16	0	151	203	129	4	—	39	47	4.59	70	.308	.346	176-1	.290	4*	106	-22	—	-1.6
1887	Phi N	21	17	.553	40	38	35-1	0	332.1	352	224	16	4	92	160	3.66	116	.264	.313	269-1	.268	2*	102	18	—	2.0
1888	Phi N	28	17	.622	46	46	43-6	0	400.1	324	139	6	4	59	199	1.91	156	.213	.244	160	.181	-1	76	45	—	**5.1**
1889	Phi N	28	16	.636	47	43	37-2	0	380	390	196	10	6	121	153	3.24	134	.258	.315	154	.208	-3	89	45	—	4.0
1890	Phi P	19	15	.559	36	33	28	1	283.1	312	211	8	7	126	89	3.81	112	.268	.343	150-1	.273	4*	102	10	—	1.2
1891	Bos AA	29	9	**.763**	48	43	33-2	1	363.2	303	153	8	7	120	158	2.55	137	.219	**.284**	181-1	.188	-0*	112	45	—	4.0
1892	Bal N	4	8	.333	13	13	9	0	97	130	88	4	3	46	30	4.92	70	.309	.381	43	.349	4	115	-16	—	-1.1
Total	11	233	152	.605	414	396	351-30	3	3404	3344	1824	87	31	856	1700	2.96	114	.246	.292	2214-7	.245	27	105	172	—	19.6
Buhl, Bob	Robert Ray; B8.12.1928 Saginaw MI; D2.16.2001 Titusville FL; BR/TR (BB 1958–60, 66)/6´2˝/(180–190); d4.17																									
1953	Mil N	13	8	.619	30	18	8-3	0	154.1	133	59	9	3	73	83	2.97	132	.235	.326	53-0-5	.113	-3	101	18	0	1.9
1954	Mil N	2	7	.222	31	14	2-1	3	110.1	117	54	5	2	65	57	4.00	93	.277	.374	31	.032	-3	97	-3	0	-0.5
1955	Mil N	13	11	.542	38	27	11-1	1	201.2	168	85	13	1	109-5	117	3.21	117	.227	.324	57-0-7	.105	-4	105	11	0	0.8
1956	Mil N	18	8	.692	38	33	13-2	0	216.2	190	96	18	2	105-7	86	3.32	104	.236	.325	73-0-6	.096	-4	116	3	0	-0.1
1957	†Mil N	18	7	**.720**	34	31	14-2	0	216.2	191	77	15	0	121-4	117	2.74	128	.241	.338	73-0-3	.082	-3	123	19	0	1.6
1958	Mil N	5	2	.714	11	10	3	1	73	74	33	5	1	30-0	27	3.45	102	.260	.330	25-0-1	.200	0	115	0	72	0.0
1959	Mil N	15	9	.625	31	25	12-**4**	0	198	181	76	19	2	74-3	105	2.86	124	.243	.312	70-0-2	.057	-5	124	15	0	1.3
1960	Mil N★	16	9	.640	36	33	11-2	0	238.2	202	89	23	3	103-7	121	3.09	111	.229	.310	89-0-3	.157	-2	115	12	0	1.1
1961	Mil N	9	10	.474	32	28	9-1	0	188.1	180	99	23	5	98-4	77	4.11	91	.256	.350	60-0-2	.067	-4	123	-11	0	-1.3
1962	Mil N	0	1	.000	1	1	0	0	2	6	5	0	0	4-1	1	22.50	17	.545	.625	1	.000	-0	92	-4	0	-0.6
	Chi N	12	13	.480	34	30	8-1	0	212	204	108	23	6	94-6	109	3.69	112	.255	.334	69-0-7	.000	-6	91	6	0	0.0
	Year	12	14	.462	35	31	8-1	0	214	210	113	23	6	98-7	110	3.87	107	.259	.339	70-0-7	.000	-6	91	2	0	-0.6
1963	Chi N	11	14	.440	37	34	6	0	226	219	96	24	3	62-1	108	3.38	104	.259	.310	74-0-7	.108	-3	94	4	0	0.1
1964	Chi N	15	14	.517	36	35	11-3	0	227.2	208	103	22	5	68-4	107	3.83	97	.244	.301	73-0-5	.096	-2	101	-1	0	-0.2
1965	Chi N	13	11	.542	32	31	2	0	184.1	207	100	26	0	57-4	92	4.39	84	.284	.333	67-0-2	.060	-4	101	-12	0	-1.8
1966	Chi N	0	0	ø	1	1	0	0	2.1	4	4	1	0	1-0	1	15.43	24	.400	.417	1	.000	-0	215	-3	0	-0.1
	Phi N	6	8	.429	32	18	1	1	132	156	74	10	4	39-6	59	4.77	75	.298	.349	41-0-3	.098	-2	111	-16	0	-1.7
	Year	6	8	.429	33	19	1	1	134.1	160	78	11	4	40-6	60	4.96	73	.300	.351	42-0-3	.095	-2	117	-20	0	-1.8
1967	Phi N	0	0	ø	3	0	0	0	3	6	4	2	0	2-0	1	12.00	28	.462	.533	0	ø	0	—	-3	0	-0.1
Total	15	166	132	.557	457	369	111-20	6	2587	2446	1162	238	37	1105-52	1268	3.55	103	.251	.328	857-0-53	.089	-43	108	35	72	0.4
Buice, De Wayne	De Wayne Allison; B8.20.1957 Lynwood CA; BR/TR/6´0˝/(170–185); d4.25; Col Cal St.–Dominguez Hills																									
1987	Cal A	6	7	.462	57	0	0	17-4	114	87	45	12	2	40-3	109	3.39	128	.213	.285	0	ø	0	—	14	0	1.8
1988	Cal A	2	4	.333	32	0	0	3-4	41.1	45	29	5	0	19-3	38	5.88	66	.287	.360	0	ø	0	—	-9	50	-1.3
1989	Tor A	1	0	1.000	7	0	0	0-0	17	13	12	2	0	13-1	10	5.82	65	.220	.351	0	ø	0	—	-4	15	-0.2
Total	3	9	11	.450	96	0	0	20-8	172.1	145	86	19	2	72-7	157	4.23	99	.232	.311	0	ø	0	—	1	65	0.3
Buker, Cy	Cyril Owen; B2.5.1919 Greenwood WI; BL/TR/5´11˝/190; d5.17; Col Wisconsin–Madison																									
1945	Bro N	7	2	.778	42	4	0	5	87.1	90	41	2	1	45	48	3.30	114	.268	.356	16-0-3	.188	-0	147	4	0	0.4
Bukvich, Ryan	Ryan Adrien; B5.13.1978 Naperville IL; BR/TR/6´3˝/250; [KCA00 11/314]; d7.12; Col U. of Mississippi																									
2002	KC A	1	0	1.000	26	0	0	0-1	25	26	19	2	1	19-3	20	6.12	82	.277	.393	0	ø	0	—	-3	0	-0.2
2003	KC A	1	0	1.000	9	0	0	0-0	10.1	12	11	2	0	9-0	8	9.58	50	.293	.412	0	ø	0	—	-5	0	-0.4
2004	KC A	0	0	ø	9	0	0	1-0	7.1	4	3	0	0	7-0	7	3.68	127	.182	.379	0	ø	0	—	1	0	0.0
2005	Tex A	0	0	ø	4	0	0	0-0	4	2	5	0	0	6-0	4	11.25	40	.167	.444	0	ø	0	—	-3	169	-0.1
Total	4	2	0	1.000	48	0	0	1-1	46.2	44	38	4	1	41-3	39	6.94	70	.260	.400	0	ø	0	—	-10	169	-0.7
Bulger, Jason	Jason Patrick; B12.6.1979 Atlanta GA; BR/TR/6´4˝/215; [AriN01 1/22]; d8.26; Col Valdosta St.																									
2005	Ari N	1	0	1.000	9	0	0	0-0	10	14	6	1	0	5-1	9	5.40	82	.333	.404	0	ø	0	—	-1	0	-0.1
2006	LA A	0	0	ø	2	0	0	0-0	1.2	1	3	0	0	3-0	1	16.20	27	.167	.444	0	ø	0	—	-2	0	-0.1
Total	2	1	0	1.000	11	0	0	0-0	11.2	15	9	1	0	8-1	10	6.94	64	.313	.411	0	ø	0	—	-3	0	-0.2
Bullinger, Jim	James Eric; B8.21.1965 New Orleans LA; BR/TR/6´2˝/(185–190); [ChiN86 9/220]; d5.27; b–Kirk; Col New Orleans																									
1992	Chi N	2	8	.200	39	9	1	7-0	85	72	49	9	4	54-6	36	4.66	78	.233	.350	20-1-1	.250	2	78	-9	0	-0.8
1993	Chi N	1	0	1.000	15	0	0	1-0	16.2	18	9	1	0	9-0	10	4.32	93	.277	.360	1	.000	-0	—	-1	0	-0.1
1994	Chi N	6	2	.750	33	10	1	2-0	100	87	43	6	1	34-2	72	3.60	117	.235	.298	22-0-5	.136	1	97	7	0	0.6
1995	Chi N	12	8	.600	24	24	1-1	0-0	150	152	80	14	9	65-7	93	4.14	101	.265	.346	47-0-8	.128	1*	118	-1	32	0.0
1996	Chi N	6	10	.375	37	20	1-1	1-0	129.1	144	101	15	8	68-5	90	6.54	67	.283	.373	32-2-3	.250	5*	105	-29	0	-2.5
1997	Mon N	7	12	.368	36	25	2-2	0-1	155.1	165	106	17	12	74-5	87	5.56	75	.276	.364	43-1-3	.209	2	91	-24	0	-2.2
1998	Sea A	0	1	.000	2	1	0	0-0	5.2	13	10	3	0	2-0	4	15.88	29	.433	.455	0	ø	0	139	-7	0	-0.8
Total	7	34	41	.453	186	89	6-4	11-1	642	651	398	65	34	306-25	392	5.06	82	.265	.351	165-4-20	.188	10	102	-64	32	-5.8
Bullinger, Kirk	Kirk Matthew; B10.28.1969 New Orleans LA; BR/TR/6´2˝/170; [StLN92 32/895]; d8.30; b–Jim; Col Southeastern Louisiana																									
1998	Mon N	1	0	1.000	8	0	0	0-1	7	14	8	1	0	0-0	2	9.00	47	.400	.400	1	.000	-0	—	-4	0	-0.5
1999	Bos A	0	0	ø	4	0	0	0-0	2	2	1	0	0	2-0	0	4.50	111	.286	.444	0	ø	0	—	0	0	0.0
2000	Phi N	0	0	ø	3	0	0	0-0	3.1	4	2	0	0	0-0	4	5.40	85	.308	.286	0	ø	0	—	0	69	0.0
2003	Hou N	0	0	ø	7	0	0	0-0	8	7	6	2	0	1-0	5	6.75	65	.219	.242	0	ø	0	—	-2	0	-0.1
2004	Hou N	1	0	1.000	27	0	0	1-1	30.2	36	22	5	1	10-2	11	6.16	71	.286	.341	3	.000	-0	—	-6	0	-0.2
Total	5	2	0	1.000	49	0	0	1-2	51	63	39	8	1	13-2	22	6.53	67	.296	.336	4	.000	-0	—	-12	69	-0.8
Bullington, Bryan	Bryan Paul; B9.30.1980 Indianapolis IN; BR/TR/6´4˝/220; [PhiN02 1/1]; d9.18; Col Ball St.; [DL 2006 Pit N 182]																									
2005	Pit N	0	0	ø	1	0	0	0-0	1.1	1	2	0	1	1-0	1	13.50	31	.250	.429	0	ø	0	—	-1	0	-0.1
Bullock, Red	Malton Joseph; B10.12.1911 Biloxi MS; D6.27.1988 Pascagoula MS; BL/TL/6´1˝/192; d5.19; Col Millsaps																									
1936	Phi A	0	2	.000	12	2	0	0	16.2	19	32	0	0	37	7	14.04	36	.271	.523	4	.000	-1	52	-17	—	-1.6
Bump, Nate	Nathan Louis; B1.24.1976 Towanda PA; BL/TR/6´2˝/(180–195); [SFN98 1/25]; d6.28; Col Penn St.																									
2003	†Fla N	4	0	1.000	32	0	0	0-0	36.1	34	21	3	7	20-0	17	4.71	87	.246	.367	0-0-1	ø	0	—	-3	0	-0.3
2004	Fla N	2	4	.333	50	2	0	1-3	73.2	86	46	7	3	32-8	44	5.01	82	.297	.370	5	.000	-1	147	-9	0	-0.7
2005	Fla N	0	3	.000	31	0	0	0-1	38	43	18	5	2	12-1	18	4.03	99	.289	.350	5-0-1	.200	0	—	0	78	0.0
Total	3	6	7	.462	113	2	0	1-4	148	163	85	15	12	64-9	79	4.68	87	.282	.364	10-0-2	.100	-1	147	-12	78	-1.0
Bunch, Melvin	Melvin Lynn; B11.4.1971 Texarkana TX; BR/TR/6´1˝/(165–170); [KCA92 15/414]; d5.6; Col Texarkana (TX) JC																									
1995	KC A	1	3	.250	13	5	0	0-0	40	42	25	11	0	14-1	19	5.62	85	.261	.320	0	ø	0	89	-3	0	-0.3
1999	Sea A	0	0	ø	5	1	0	0-0	10	20	13	3	0	7-0	4	11.70	41	.426	.491	0	ø	0	117	-7	0	-0.3
Total	2	1	3	.250	18	6	0	0-0	50	62	38	14	0	21-1	23	6.84	70	.298	.361	0	ø	0	94	-10	0	-0.6
Bunker, Wally	Wallace Edward; B1.25.1945 Seattle WA; BR/TR/6´2˝/(195–205); d9.29																									
1963	Bal A	0	1	.000	1	1	0	0	4	10	6	1	0	3-0	1	13.50	26	.476	.542	2	.500	0	77	-4	0	-0.6
1964	Bal A	19	5	**.792**	29	29	12-1	0	214	161	72	17	3	62-5	96	2.69	133	.207	.267	72-0-2	.069	-2	122	21	0	2.1
1965	Bal A	10	8	.556	34	27	4-1	2	189	170	79	16	4	58-2	84	3.38	103	.242	.301	55-0-3	.073	-1	133	4	0	0.1

YEAR	TM LG	W	L	PCT	G	GS	CG-SHO	SV-BS	IP	H	R	HR	HB	BB-IB	SO	ERA	AERA	OAV	OOB	AB-HR-SH	AVG	PB	SUP	APR	DL	PW
1966	†Bal A	10	6	.625	29	24	3	0	142.2	151	74	16	2	48-2	89	4.29	78	.269	.327	48-0-3	.104	-0*	143	-15	20	-1.6
1967	Bal A	3	7	.300	29	9	1	1	88	83	46	7	2	31-1	51	4.09	77	.254	.322	26-0-1	.077	-2	132	-10	0	-1.3
1968	Bal A	2	0	1.000	18	10	2-1	0	71	59	25	4	1	14-1	44	2.41	121	.225	.265	18-0-2	.111	-0	158	3	0	0.1
1969	KC A	12	11	.522	35	31	10-1	2-0	222.2	198	89	29	4	62-3	130	3.23	114	.238	.293	70-0-7	.143	0	90	12	0	1.4
1970	KC A	2	11	.154	24	15	2-1	0-0	121.2	109	63	16	0	50-2	59	4.22	89	.238	.312	31-0-1	.065	-0	59	-5	43	-0.6
1971	KC A	2	3	.400	7	6	0	0-0	32.1	35	19	7	0	6-0	15	5.01	69	.271	.301	9	.000	-1	87	-5	0	-0.8
Total	9	60	52	.536	206	152	34-5	5-0	1085.1	976	473	113	16	334-16	569	3.51	99	.240	.299	331-0-19	.094	-5	114	1	63	-1.2
Bunning, Jim	James Paul David; B10.23.1931 Southgate KY; BR/TR/6´3˝/(185–203); d7.20; HF1996; Col Xavier																									
1955	Det A	3	5	.375	15	8	0	1	51	59	38	8	3	32-2	37	6.35	60	.291	.395	15-0-2	.200	-0	84	-13	0	-1.8
1956	Det A	5	1	.833	15	3	0	1	53.1	55	24	6	0	28-4	34	3.71	111	.257	.339	18-0-2	.333	2	137	3	0	0.4
1957	Det A★	**20**	8	.714	45	30	14-1	1	**267.1**	214	91	33	11	72-5	182	2.69	143	.218	.277	94-1-5	.213	3	95	32	0	3.4
1958	Det A	14	12	.538	35	34	10-3	0	219.2	188	96	28	10	79-4	177	3.52	115	.228	.302	75-0-6	.187	-1*	105	12	0	1.1
1959	Det A★	17	13	.567	40	35	14-1	1	249.2	220	111	37	11	75-0	**201**	3.89	104	.234	.297	89-1-8	.191	1	106	10	0	0.9
1960	Det A	11	14	.440	36	34	10-3	0	252	217	92	20	11	64-7	**201**	2.79	**142**	.236	.292	81-0-8	.160	-2*	72	**31**	0	2.5
1961	Det A★	17	11	.607	38	37	12-4	1	268	232	113	25	9	71-3	194	3.19	128	.229	.284	100-0-2	.130	-4	103	26	0	2.0
1962	Det A★	19	10	.655	41	35	12-2	6	258	262	112	28	13	74-3	184	3.59	113	.261	.319	95-1-4	.242	4*	111	15	0	1.8
1963	Det A★	12	13	.480	39	35	6-2	1	248.1	245	119	38	5	69-3	196	3.88	97	.254	.306	84-0-6	.155	-1*	91	-4	0	-0.5
1964	Phi N★	19	8	.704	41	39	13-5	2	284.1	248	99	23	14	46-3	219	2.63	132	.233	.274	99-0-9	.121	-2	133	26	0	1.9
1965	Phi N	19	9	.679	39	39	15-7	0	291	253	92	23	12	62-10	268	2.60	133	.232	.279	103-1-4	.214	4	102	31	0	3.4
1966	Phi N★	19	14	.576	43	**41**	16-**5**	1	314	260	91	26	19	55-8	252	2.41	149	.223	.268	106-0-4	.179	1	97	42	0	4.4
1967	Phi N	17	15	.531	40	**40**	16-**6**	0	**302.1**	241	94	18	13	73-20	**253**	2.29	149	.217	.271	104-2-7	.163	2	100	**35**	0	**3.9**
1968	Pit N	4	14	.222	27	26	3-1	0	160	168	75	14	8	48-6	95	3.88	75	.272	.332	51-0-2	.098	-2	96	-15	0	-2.0
1969	Pit N	10	9	.526	25	25	4	0-0	156	147	74	10	6	49-4	124	3.81	91	.249	.311	47-0-7	.043	-3	103	-6	0	-1.1
	LA N	3	1	.750	9	9	1	0-0	56.1	65	23	5	1	10-0	33	3.36	100	.288	.321	18-0-3	.111	-1	106	0	0	-0.1
	Year	13	10	.565	34	34	5	0-0	212.1	212	97	15	7	59-4	157	3.69	93	.259	.314	65-0-10	.062	-4	104	-5	0	-1.2
1970	Phi N	10	15	.400	34	33	4	0-0	219	233	111	19	8	56-9	147	4.11	98	.274	.321	71-0-3	.127	-2*	85	-4	0	-0.7
1971	Phi N	5	12	.294	29	16	1	1-1	110	126	72	11	6	37-7	58	5.48	65	.297	.358	25-1-3	.120	0*	90	-21	0	-3.1
Total	17	224	184	.549	591	519	151-40	16-1	3760.1	3433	1527	372	160	1000-98	2855	3.27	114	.242	.297	1275-7-85	.167	-1	100	200	0	16.4
Burba, Dave	David Allen; B7.7.1966 Dayton OH; BR/TR/6´4˝/(220–255); [SeaA87 2/33]; d9.8; Col Ohio St.																									
1990	Sea A	0	0	ø	6	0	0	0-0	8	8	6	0	1	2-0	4	4.50	88	.267	.333	0	ø	0	—	-1	0	0.0
1991	Sea A	2	2	.500	22	2	0	1-0	36.2	34	16	6	0	14-3	16	3.68	112	.245	.314	0	ø	0	88	2	0	0.2
1992	SF N	2	7	.222	23	11	0	0-0	70.2	80	43	4	2	31-2	47	4.97	67	.287	.358	15-0-3	.067	-1	76	-13	0	-1.7
1993	SF N	10	3	.769	54	5	0	0-0	95.1	95	49	14	3	37-5	88	4.25	93	.265	.336	17-0-3	.294	2	128	-4	0	-0.2
1994	SF N	3	6	.333	57	0	0	0-3	74	59	39	5	6	45-3	84	4.38	93	.221	.345	3	.000	-0	—	-2	0	-0.3
1995	SF N	4	2	.667	37	0	0	0-1	43.1	38	26	5	0	25-2	46	4.98	83	.235	.335	0	ø	0	—	-4	0	-0.5
	†Cin N	6	2	.750	15	9	1-1	0-0	63.1	52	24	4	0	26-1	50	3.27	128	.223	.301	15-0-4	.067	-0	101	7	0	0.7
	Year	10	4	.714	52	9	1-1	0-1	106.2	90	50	9	0	51-3	96	3.97	105	.228	.315	15-0-4	.067	-0	101	3	0	0.2
1996	Cin N	11	13	.458	34	33	0	0-0	195	179	96	18	2	97-9	148	3.83	112	.244	.329	67-2-3	.104	-1	92	8	0	0.7
1997	Cin N	11	10	.524	30	27	2	0-0	160	157	88	22	9	73-10	131	4.72	91	.255	.341	46-0-4	.196	1	91	-7	20	-0.6
1998	†Cle A	15	10	.600	32	31	0	0-0	203.2	210	100	30	7	69-4	132	4.11	116	.269	.330	6-1-0	.167	1	104	15	0	1.7
1999	†Cle A	15	9	.625	34	34	1	0-0	220	211	113	30	8	96-3	174	4.25	120	.254	.336	3	.333	1	102	19	0	1.9
2000	Cle A	16	6	.727	32	32	0	0-0	191.1	199	99	19	2	91-2	180	4.47	112	.267	.346	1-0-2	.000	-0	109	12	0	1.2
2001	†Cle A	10	10	.500	32	27	1	0-0	150.2	188	112	16	3	54-2	118	6.21	74	.306	.361	2-0-2	.000	-0	129	-26	0	-2.8
2002	Tex A	4	5	.444	23	18	1	0-1	111.1	125	71	13	7	40-3	70	5.42	88	.279	.346	5	.200	0	107	-7	0	-0.5
	Cle A	1	0	1.000	12	3	0	0-1	34	30	20	3	2	17-0	25	4.50	99	.236	.333	0	ø	0	139	-1	0	-0.1
	Year	5	5	.500	35	21	1	0-2	145.1	155	91	16	9	57-3	95	5.20	90	.270	.343	5	.200	0	112	-7	0	-0.6
2003	Mil N	1	1	.500	17	2	0	0-0	43.1	42	19	5	4	19-2	35	3.53	122	.250	.340	10-0-1	.000	-1	87	3	0	0.1
2004	Mil N	3	1	.750	45	0	0	2-2	70.2	63	36	6	2	24-2	47	4.08	108	.237	.302	3	.000	-0	—	2	0	0.1
	SF N	1	0	1.000	6	0	0	0-1	6.1	7	4	1	0	2-0	3	5.68	76	.280	.333	1	.000	-0	—	-1	0	-0.1
	Year	4	1	.800	51	0	0	2-3	77	70	40	7	2	26-2	50	4.21	104	.241	.304	4	.000	-0	—	2	0	0.0
Total	15	115	87	.569	511	234	6-1	3-9	1777.2	1777	961	201	58	762-53	1398	4.49	100	.260	.337	194-3-22	.134	0	106	2	20	-0.2
Burbach, Bill	William David; B8.22.1947 Dickeyville WI; BR/TR/6´4˝/(215–222); [NYA65 1/19]; d4.11																									
1969	NY A	6	8	.429	31	24	2-1	0-0	140.2	112	68	15	2	102-1	82	3.65	97	.219	.349	40-0-6	.100	-1	97	-3	0	-0.5
1970	NY A	0	2	.000	4	4	0	0-0	16.2	23	19	2	1	9-0	10	10.26	35	.324	.402	5	.000	-1	150	-12	0	-1.2
1971	NY A	0	1	.000	2	0	0	0-0	3.1	6	6	0	0	5-2	3	10.80	30	.400	.524	2	.000	-0	—	-4	0	-0.7
Total	3	6	11	.353	37	28	2-1	0-0	160.2	141	93	17	3	116-3	95	4.48	79	.236	.360	47-0-6	.085	-2	105	-19	0	-2.4
Burchart, Larry	Larry Wayne; B2.8.1946 Tulsa OK; BR/TR/6´3˝/210; [LAN67 S3/54]; d4.10; Col Oklahoma St.																									
1969	Cle A	0	2	.000	29	0	0	0-0	42.1	42	28	2	1	24-2	26	4.25	89	.266	.358	0	ø	0	—	-4	62	-0.3
Burchell, Fred	Frederick Duff; B7.14.1879 Perth Amboy NJ; D11.20.1951 Jordan NY; BR/TL/5´11˝/175; d4.17																									
1903	Phi N	0	3	.000	6	3	2	0	44	48	28	0	2	14	12	2.86	114	.293	.356	16	.188	-1	7	-1	—	-0.1
1907	Bos A	0	1	.000	2	1	0	0	10	8	5	0	1	2	6	2.70	95	.222	.282	5	.200	-0	131	0	—	-0.1
1908	Bos A	10	8	.556	31	19	9	0	179.2	161	84	2	11	65	94	2.96	83	.247	.326	69-0-3	.246	1*	133	-9	—	-0.9
1909	Bos A	3	3	.500	10	5	1	0	52	51	22	1	2	11	12	2.94	85	.271	.318	19	.158	-0	102	-2	—	-0.2
Total	4	13	15	.464	49	28	12	0	285.2	268	139	3	16	92	124	2.93	89	.258	.328	109-0-3	.220	-0	108	-12	—	-1.3
Burdette, Freddie	Freddie Thomason; B9.15.1936 Moultrie GA; BR/TR/6´1˝/170; d9.5																									
1962	Chi N	0	0	ø	8	0	0	1	9.2	5	4	2	0	8-3	5	3.72	111	.161	.325	1	.000	-0	—	1	0	0.0
1963	Chi N	0	0	ø	4	0	0	0	4.2	5	2	1	0	2-0	1	3.86	91	.313	.389	0	ø	0	—	0	0	0.0
1964	Chi N	1	0	1.000	18	0	0	0	20	17	7	2	1	10-2	4	3.15	118	.243	.333	1	1.000	0	—	2	0	0.1
Total	3	1	0	1.000	30	0	0	1	34.1	27	13	5	1	20-5	10	3.41	112	.231	.338	2	.500	0	—	3	0	0.1
Burdette, Lew	Selva Lewis; B11.22.1926 Nitro WV; BR/TR/6´2˝/(180–195); d9.26; C2; Col Richmond																									
1950	NY A	0	0	ø	2	0	0	0	1.1	3	1	0	0	0	0	6.75	64	.500	.500	0	ø	0	—	0	0	0.0
1951	Bos N	0	0	ø	3	0	0	0	4.1	6	4	0	1	5	1	6.23	59	.375	.545	1	.000	-0	—	-2	0	-0.1
1952	Bos N	6	11	.353	45	9	5	7	137	138	58	8	2	47	47	3.61	100	.265	.328	35-0-6	.114	-0	77	1	0	0.2
1953	Mil N	15	5	.750	46	13	6-1	8	175	177	73	7	5	56	58	3.24	121	.264	.326	53-0-5	.170	-1	100	15	0	1.5
1954	Mil N	15	14	.517	38	32	13-4	0	238	224	87	17	4	62	79	2.76	135	.251	.300	79-0-5	.089	-5*	84	26	0	2.5
1955	Mil N	13	8	.619	42	33	11-2	0	230	253	114	25	6	73-9	70	4.03	93	.280	.336	86-0-3	.233	3*	124	-6	0	-0.2
1956	Mil N	19	10	.655	39	35	16-**6**	1	256.1	234	92	22	3	52-7	110	**2.70**	128	.241	.281	86-0-11	.186	1*	125	23	0	2.6
1957	†Mil N★	17	9	.654	37	33	14-1	0	256.2	260	117	25	2	59-8	78	3.72	94	.264	.304	88-2-4	.148	1*	137	-6	0	-0.3
1958	†Mil N	20	10	**.667**	40	36	19-3	0	275.1	279	102	18	5	50-7	113	2.91	121	.264	.300	99-3-5	.242	9*	123	19	0	2.9
1959	Mil N★	**21**	15	.583	41	**39**	20-**4**	1	289.2	312	144	38	1	38-3	105	4.07	87	.273	.295	104-0-5	.202	6*	126	-16	0	-1.2
1960	Mil N	19	13	.594	45	32	**18**-4	4	275.2	277	116	19	5	35-7	83	3.36	102	.260	.287	91-2-2	.176	5*	126	3	0	1.1
1961	Mil N	18	11	.621	40	36	14-3	0	**272.1**	295	131	31	3	33-3	92	4.00	94	.273	.295	103-3-3	.204	5*	114	-8	0	-0.2
1962	Mil N	10	9	.526	37	19	6-1	2	143.2	172	85	26	2	23-6	59	4.89	78	.298	.325	51-0-2	.176	0*	114	-16	0	-1.9
1963	Mil N	6	5	.545	15	13	4-1	0	84	71	40	15	1	24-4	28	3.64	88	.228	.284	26-0-4	.038	-0*	109	-5	0	-0.7
	StL N	3	8	.273	21	14	3	2	98	106	50	6	7	16-2	45	3.77	94	.278	.314	31-0-3	.097	-1	88	-3	0	-0.6
	Year	9	13	.409	36	27	7-1	2	182	177	90	21	8	40-6	73	3.71	92	.255	.300	57-0-7	.070	-2	98	-7	0	-1.3
1964	StL N	1	0	1.000	8	0	0	0	10	10	3	1	0	3-0	3	1.80	211	.256	.302	1	.000	-0	—	2	0	0.2
	Chi N	9	9	.500	28	17	8-2	0	131	152	74	15	1	19-2	40	4.88	76	.292	.317	43-2-3	.279	6	103	-14	0	-1.1
	Year	10	9	.526	36	17	8-2	0	141	162	77	16	1	22-2	43	4.66	80	.290	.316	44-2-3	.273	6	103	-11	0	-0.9
1965	Chi N	0	2	.000	7	3	0	0	20.1	26	17	3	1	4-1	5	5.31	69	.299	.337	6	.333	1*	95	-5	0	-0.3
	Phi N	3	3	.500	19	9	1-1	0	70.2	95	50	5	5	17-2	23	5.48	63	.329	.374	20-0-2	.300	1	107	-16	0	-1.1
	Year	3	5	.375	26	12	1-1	0	91	121	67	8	6	21-3	28	5.44	65	.322	.365	26-0-2	.308	2	104	-22	0	-1.4
1966	Cal A	7	2	.778	54	0	0	5	79.2	80	32	4	1	12-2	27	3.39	99	.268	.297	8	.125	-0	—	0	0	0.0
1967	Cal A	1	0	1.000	19	0	0	1	18.1	16	10	4	1	0-0	8	4.91	64	.232	.243	0	ø	0	—	-3	0	-0.2
Total	18	203	144	.585	626	373	158-33	31	3067.1	3186	1400	289	56	628-63	1074	3.66	99	.268	.306	1011-12-63	.183	30	115	-11	0	3.1

YEAR	TM LG	W	L	PCT	G	GS	CG-SHO	SV-BS	IP	H	R	HR	HB	BB-IB	SO	ERA	AERA	OAV	OOB	AB-HR-SH	AVG	PB	SUP	APR	DL	PW
Burdick, Bill	William Byron; B10.11.1859 Austin MN; D10.23.1949 Spokane WA; BR/TR; d7.23																									
1888	Ind N	10	10	.500	20	20	20	0	176	168	88	12	6	43	55	2.81	105	.242	.292	68	.147	-2*	82	0	—	-0.3
1889	Ind N	2	4	.333	10	4	2	1	45.2	58	42	7	0	13	16	4.53	92	.301	.345	17	.118	-0	141	-5	—	-0.5
Total	2	12	14	.462	30	24	22	1	221.2	226	130	19	6	56	71	3.17	101	.255	.304	85	.141	-3	93	-5	—	-0.8
Burgmeier, Tom	Thomas Henry; B8.2.1943 St.Paul MN; BL/TL/5´11˝/(180–187); d4.10; C4																									
1968	Cal A	1	4	.200	56	2	0	5	72.2	65	41	5	0	24-3	33	4.33	67	.250	.310	2	.000	0*	75	-12	0	-0.9
1969	KC A	3	1	.750	31	0	0	0-3	54	67	31	5	1	21-3	23	4.17	89	.316	.374	18	.167	-0*	—	-4	0	-0.2
1970	KC A	6	6	.500	41	0	0	1-1	68.1	59	31	6	0	23-1	43	3.16	118	.236	.297	14-0-1	.143	-0*	—	3	0	0.6
1971	KC A	9	7	.563	67	0	0	17-4	88.1	71	23	3	7	30-4	44	1.73	199	.223	.303	20	.250	2*	—	15	0	3.7
1972	KC A	6	2	.750	51	0	0	9-3	55.1	67	32	0	1	33-6	18	4.23	72	.313	.401	12	.333	1	—	-9	0	-1.5
1973	KC A	0	0	ø	6	0	0	1-0	10	13	6	2	1	4-0	4	5.40	76	.310	.383	0	ø	0	—	-1	0	-0.1
1974	Min A	5	3	.625	50	0	0	4-1	91.2	92	46	7	2	26-2	34	4.52	83	.270	.319	0	ø	0*	—	-5	0	-0.3
1975	Min A	5	8	.385	46	0	0	11-4	75.2	76	32	7	1	23-2	41	3.09	124	.264	.318	0	ø	0*	—	5	0	1.0
1976	Min A	8	1	.889	57	0	0	1-2	115.1	95	36	11	2	29-3	45	2.50	143	.226	.279	0	ø	0	—	14	0	1.2
1977	Min A	6	4	.600	61	0	0	7-4	97.1	113	56	15	2	33-0	35	5.09	78	.299	.354	0	ø	0	—	-10	0	-1.0
1978	Bos A	2	1	.667	35	1	0	4-2	61.1	74	33	7	3	23-1	24	4.40	94	.302	.368	0	ø	0	87	-1	0	0.0
1979	Bos A	3	2	.600	44	0	0	4-3	88.2	89	32	8	4	16-4	60	2.74	163	.263	.302	0	ø	0	—	15	0	0.9
1980	Bos A☆	5	4	.556	62	0	0	24-2	99	87	30	3	2	20-3	54	2.00	213	.241	.283	0	ø	0	—	21	0	3.1
1981	Bos A	4	5	.444	32	0	0	6-1	59.2	61	23	5	4	17-4	35	2.87	137	.268	.329	0	ø	0	—	6	0	1.1
1982	Bos A	7	0	1.000	40	0	0	2-2	102.1	98	30	6	2	22-7	44	2.29	191	.259	.300	0	ø	0	—	21	0	1.6
1983	Oak A	6	7	.462	49	0	0	4-2	96	89	33	2	0	32-8	39	2.81	138	.244	.303	0	ø	0*	—	12	0	1.7
1984	Oak A	3	0	1.000	17	0	0	2-0	23	15	6	2	0	8-4	8	2.35	161	.190	.261	0	ø	0	—	4	97	0.6
Total	17	79	55	.590	745	3	0	102-34	1258.2	1231	521	94	32	384-55	584	3.23	118	.261	.318	66-0-1	.212	2	70	74	97	11.5
Burgos, Ambiorix	Ambiorix; B4.19.1984 Nagua, D.R.; BR/TR/6´3˝/235; d4.23																									
2005	KC A	3	5	.375	59	0	0	2-4	63.1	60	29	6	5	31-1	65	3.98	110	.251	.348	0	ø	0	—	3	24	0.3
2006	KC A	4	5	.444	68	1	0	18-12	73.1	83	49	16	6	37-4	72	5.52	85	.288	.376	0	ø	0	181	-7	0	-1.0
Total	2	7	10	.412	127	1	0	20-16	136.2	143	78	22	11	68-5	137	4.81	94	.271	.363	0	ø	0	181	-4	24	-0.7
Burgos, Enrique	Enrique (Calles); B10.7.1965 Chorrera, Pan; BL/TL/6´4˝/(195–230); d7.15																									
1993	KC A	0	1	.000	5	0	0	0-0	5	5	5	0	1	6-1	6	9.00	51	.238	.429	0	ø	0	—	-2	0	-0.4
1995	SF N	0	0	ø	5	0	0	0-0	8.1	14	8	1	1	6-0	12	8.64	48	.378	.477	0	ø	0	—	-4	0	-0.2
Total	2	0	1	,000	10	0	0	0-0	13.1	19	13	1	2	12-1	18	8.78	49	.328	.458	0	ø	0	—	-6	0	-0.6
Burk, Sandy	Charles Sanford; B4.22.1887 Columbus OH; D10.11.1934 Brooklyn NY; BR/TR/5´8˝/155; d9.12																									
1910	Bro N	0	3	.000	4	3	1	0	19.1	17	16	0	2	27	14	6.05	50	.258	.484	5	.000	-1	49	-6	—	-0.9
1911	Bro N	1	3	.250	13	7	1	0	58	54	36	1	3	47	15	5.12	65	.261	.405	19-0-1	.105	-1	103	-9	—	-0.7
1912	Bro N	0	0	ø	2	0	0	0	8.1	9	3	0	0	3	2	3.24	103	.273	.333	4	.250	0	—	0	—	0.1
	StL N	1	3	.250	12	4	2	1	44.2	37	19	0	1	12	17	2.42	142	.236	.294	11	.000	-2	43	4	—	0.1
	Year	1	3	.250	14	4	2	1	53	46	22	0	1	15	19	2.55	134	.242	.301	15	.067	-1	43	4	—	0.2
1913	StL N	0	2	.000	19	7	0	1	70	81	45	1	6	33	29	5.14	63	.290	.377	22	.091	-2	113	-14	—	-0.9
1915	Pit F	2	0	1.000	2	2	1	0	18	8	3	0	0	11	9	1.00	271	.140	.279	6	.167	-0	77	3	—	0.3
Total	5	4	11	.267	52	23	5	2	218.1	206	122	2	12	133	86	4.25	76	.258	.372	67-0-1	.090	-5	86	-22	—	-2.0
Burkart, Elmer	Elmer Robert "Swede"; B2.1.1917 Philadelphia PA; D2.6.1995 Baltimore MD; BR/TR/6´2˝/190; d9.14; Col Temple																									
1936	Phi N	0	0	ø	2	2	0	0	7.2	4	3	0	0	12	2	3.52	129	.160	.432	2	.000	-0	65	1	—	0.0
1937	Phi N	0	0	ø	7	0	0	0	16	20	11	0	0	9	4	6.19	70	.323	.408	6	.000	-1	—	-2	—	-0.2
1938	Phi N	0	1	.000	2	1	1	0	10	12	5	0	1	3	1	4.50	86	.286	.348	3	.000	-0	22	0	—	-0.1
1939	Phi N	1	0	1.000	5	0	0	0	8.1	11	4	0	0	2	2	4.32	93	.344	.382	1	1.000	1	—	0	—	0.1
Total	4	1	1	.500	16	3	1	0	42	47	23	0	1	26	9	4.93	85	.292	.394	12	.083	-1	55	-1	—	-0.2
Burke, James	James; B Attleboro MA; d6.10																									
1882	Buf N	0	1	.000	1	1	0	0	4	10	9	0	—	0	0	11.25	26	.435	.435	4	.000	-1	72	-4	—	-0.5
1883	Buf N	0	0	ø	1	1	0	0	8	9	8	0	—	3	1	5.63	56	.243	.300	5	.200	-0	152	-2	—	-0.1
1884	Bos U	19	15	.559	38	36	34	0	322	326	201	10	—	31	255	2.85	83	.245	.263	184	.223	-3*	109	-18	—	-2.2
Total	3	19	16	.543	40	38	34	0	334	345	218	10	—	34	256	3.02	80	.249	.267	193	.218	-4	109	-24	—	-2.8
Burke, John	John C.; B2.9.1970 Durango CO; BB/TR/6´4˝/215; [ColN92 1/27]; d8.13; Col Florida; [DL 1998 Col N 181]																									
1996	Col N	2	1	.667	11	0	0	0-0	15.2	21	13	3	1	7-0	19	7.47	70	.318	.387	2	.500	0	—	-3	0	-0.4
1997	Col N	2	5	.286	17	9	0	0-0	59	83	46	13	6	26-0	39	6.56	79	.329	.401	19-0-2	.158	-1*	58	-7	0	-0.8
Total	2	4	6	.400	28	9	0	0-0	74.2	104	59	16	7	33-0	58	6.75	77	.327	.398	21-0-2	.190	-1	58	-10	181	-1.2
Burke, John	John Patrick; B1.27.1877 Hazleton PA; D8.4.1950 Jersey City NJ; BR/TR; d6.27; Col St. Bonaventure																									
1902	NY N	0	1	.000	2	1	1	0	14	21	11	0	0	3	3	5.79	49	.344	.375	13	.154	-0*	24	-4	—	-0.3
Burke, Bobby	Robert James "Lefty"; B1.23.1907 Joliet IL; D2.8.1971 Joliet IL; BL/TL/6´0.5˝/150; d4.16																									
1927	Was A	3	2	.600	36	6	1	0	100	91	48	6	7	32	20	3.96	103	.245	.316	24-0-3	.125	-2	109	3	—	-0.1
1928	Was A	2	4	.333	26	7	2-1	0	85.1	87	44	1	2	18	27	3.90	103	.277	.320	20-0-1	.250	1	69	1	—	0.1
1929	Was A	6	8	.429	37	17	4	0	141	154	91	6	4	55	51	4.79	89	.279	.349	43-0-7	.140	-3	81	-9	—	-1.1
1930	Was A	3	4	.429	24	4	2	3	74.1	62	41	2	3	29	35	3.63	127	.229	.310	23-0-1	.174	-1	168	5	—	0.3
1931	Was A	8	3	.727	30	13	3-1	2	128.2	124	67	6	2	50	38	4.27	101	.255	.327	47-0-2	.213	-0	148	3	—	0.2
1932	Was A	3	6	.333	22	10	2	0	91	98	55	4	1	44	32	5.14	84	.272	.353	25-0-1	.200	0*	97	-7	—	-0.6
1933	Was A	4	3	.571	25	6	4-1	0	64	64	29	1	2	31	28	3.23	129	.256	.343	17-0-2	.235	0	88	6	—	0.6
1934	Was A	8	8	.500	37	15	7-1	0	168	155	67	2	1	72	52	3.21	134	.245	.323	57-0-3	.228	2*	75	22	—	2.0
1935	Was A	1	8	.111	15	10	2	0	66.1	90	63	7	2	27	16	7.46	58	.327	.391	22-0-1	.182	-0*	72	-24	—	-2.6
1937	Phi N	0	0	ø	2	0	0	0	0	1	1	0	0	2	0	(1)	ø	.500	.750	0	ø	0	—	-1	—	-0.1
Total	10	38	46	.452	254	88	27-4	5	918.2	926	506	35	24	360	299	4.29	99	.263	.336	278-0-21	.194	-3	97	-1	—	-1.3
Burke, Steve	Steven Michael; B3.5.1955 Stockton CA; BB/TR/6´2˝/200; [BosA74*S2/31]; d9.10; Col Merritt (CA) JC																									
1977	Sea A	0	1	.000	6	0	0	0-0	15.2	12	6	0	0	7-1	6	2.87	144	.226	.311	0	ø	0	—	2	0	0.1
1978	Sea A	0	1	.000	18	0	0	0-0	49	46	22	2	1	24-0	16	3.49	110	.258	.346	0	ø	0	—	2	0	0.1
Total	2	0	2	.000	24	0	0	0-0	64.2	58	28	2	1	31-1	22	3.34	117	.251	.338	0	ø	0	—	4	0	0.2
Burke, Tim	Timothy Philip; B2.19.1959 Omaha NE; BR/TR/6´3˝/(200–205); [PitN80 2/49]; d4.8; Col Nebraska																									
1985	Mon N	9	4	.692	**78**	0	0	8-1	120.1	86	32	9	7	44-14	87	2.39	144	.204	.288	10	.100	-0	—	16	0	1.9
1986	Mon N	9	7	.563	68	2	0	4-6	101.1	103	37	7	4	46-13	82	2.93	128	.262	.344	7-0-1	.000	-0	83	9	0	1.4
1987	Mon N	7	0	1.000	55	0	0	18-4	91	64	18	3	0	17-6	58	1.19	359	.196	.234	10-0-2	.000	-1	—	**28**	16	2.9
1988	Mon N	3	5	.375	61	0	0	18-6	82	84	36	7	3	25-13	42	3.40	107	.272	.327	2	.000	-0	—	2	0	0.3
1989	Mon N★	9	3	.750	68	0	0	28-11	84.2	68	24	6	0	22-7	54	2.55	140	.225	.274	3	.000	-0	—	11	0	2.2
1990	Mon N	3	3	.500	58	0	0	20-5	75	71	29	6	2	21-6	47	2.52	146	.247	.300	6	.167	0	—	7	42	1.0
1991	Mon N	3	4	.429	37	0	0	5-7	46	41	24	3	4	14-6	25	4.11	89	.243	.314	1	.000	-0	—	-3	0	-0.4
	NY N	3	3	.500	35	0	0	1-3	55.2	55	22	5	0	12-2	34	2.75	133	.255	.291	5	.000	-1	—	5	0	0.5
	Year	6	7	.462	72	0	0	6-10	101.2	96	46	8	4	26-8	59	3.36	109	.249	.301	6	.000	-1	—	1	0	0.1
1992	NY N	1	2	.333	15	0	0	0-2	15.2	26	15	1	0	3-0	7	5.74	61	.366	.387	0	ø	0	—	-6	0	-1.0
	NY A	2	2	.500	23	0	0	0-0	27.2	26	14	2	1	15-4	8	3.25	121	.250	.350	0	ø	0	—	1	31	0.1
Total	8	49	33	.598	498	2	0	102-45	699.1	624	251	49	21	219-71	444	2,72	137	.240	.302	44-0-3	.045	-2	83	70	89	8.9
Burke, Billy	William Ignatius; B7.11.1889 Clinton MA; D2.9.1967 Worcester MA; BL/TL/5´10˝/165; d4.30; Col Notre Dame																									
1910	Bos N	1	0	1.000	19	1	1	0	64	68	32	1	2	29	22	4.08	82	.302	.387	21-0-1	.190	-1*	179	-2	—	-0.2
1911	Bos N	0	1	.000	2	1	0	0	3.1	6	7	0	0	5	1	18.90	20	.429	.579	1	1.000	0	39	-4	—	-0.7
Total	2	1	1	.500	21	2	1	0	67.1	74	39	1	2	34	23	4.81	70	.310	.400	22-0-1	.227	-0	111	-6	—	-0.9
Burke, Turk	William R.; B11.1865 Cincinnati OH; D3.17.1939 Atchison KS; TR/6´0˝/200; d7.20																									
1887	Det N	0	1	.000	2	2	1	0	15	21	14	0	2	5	3	6.00	68	.318	.384	8	.250	-0	151	-3	—	-0.2

YEAR	TM LG	W	L	PCT	G	GS	CG-SHO	SV-BS	IP	H	R	HR	HB	BB-IB	SO	ERA	AERA	OAV	OOB	AB-HR-SH	AVG	PB	SUP	APR	DL	PW
Burkett, Jesse	Jesse Cail "Crab"; B12.4.1868 Wheeling WV; D5.27.1953 Worcester MA; BL/TL/5´8˝/155; d4.22; C1; HF1946; ▲																									
1890	NY N	3	10	.231	21	14	6	0	118	134	123	3	14	92	82	5.57	63	.277	.407	401-4	.309	8*	80	-26	—	-1.7
1894	Cle N	0	0	ø	1	0	0	0	4	6	2	0	0	1	0	4.50	122	.333	.368	523-8-10	.358	0*	—	1	—	0.0
1902	StL A	0	1	.000	1	0	0	0	1	4	4	0	0	1	2	9.00	39	.571	.625	553-5-7	.306	0*	—	-2	—	-0.3
Total	3	3	11	.214	23	14	6	0	123	144	129	3	14	94	84	5.56	64	.283	.408	1477-17-17	.325	9	80	-27	—	-2.0
Burkett, John	John David; B11.28.1964 New Brighton PA; BR/TR/6´2˝/(175–215); [SFN83 6/148]; d9.15																									
1987	SF N	0	0	ø	3	0	0	0-0	6	7	4	2	1	3-0	5	4.50	86	.304	.407	1	.000	-0	—	-1	0	0.0
1990	SF N	14	7	.667	33	32	2	1-0	204	201	92	18	4	61-7	118	3.79	96	.257	.313	63-0-8	.048	-3	128	-3	0	-0.6
1991	SF N	12	11	.522	36	34	3-1	0-0	206.2	223	103	19	10	60-2	131	4.18	86	.277	.332	55-0-9	.091	-2	93	-14	0	-1.6
1992	SF N	13	9	.591	32	32	3-1	0-0	189.2	194	96	13	4	45-6	107	3.84	87	.264	.308	55-0-8	.018	-3	127	-14	0	-2.0
1993	SF N★	**22**	7	.759	34	34	2-1	0-0	231.2	224	100	18	11	40-4	145	3.65	108	.255	.294	76-0-12	.118	-1	125	8	0	0.9
1994	SF N	6	8	.429	25	25	0	0-0	159.1	176	72	14	7	36-7	85	3.62	112	.286	.330	51-0-3	.059	-4	87	7	0	0.2
1995	Fla N	14	14	.500	30	30	4	0-0	188.1	208	95	22	6	57-5	126	4.30	100	.282	.339	66-0-4	.106	-2*	89	2	0	0.0
1996	Fla N	6	10	.375	24	24	1	0-0	154	154	84	15	3	42-2	108	4.32	95	.263	.314	52-0-3	.173	0	88	-4	0	-0.4
	†Tex A	5	2	.714	10	10	1-1	0-0	68.2	75	33	4	2	16-2	47	4.06	130	.280	.323	0	ø	0	86	9	0	0.7
1997	Tex A	9	12	.429	30	30	2	0-0	189.1	240	106	20	4	30-1	139	4.56	107	.307	.333	5	.200	0	101	6	26	0.6
1998	Tex A	9	13	.409	32	32	0	0-0	195	230	131	19	8	46-1	131	5.68	86	.292	.335	3	.000	-0	82	-15	0	-1.5
1999	Tex A	9	8	.529	30	25	0	0-0	147.1	184	95	18	3	46-1	96	5.62	92	.307	.358	2	.000	-0	96	-6	18	-0.6
2000	†Atl N	10	6	.625	31	22	0	0-1	134.1	162	79	13	4	51-2	110	4.89	92	.303	.365	42-0-6	.143	0	118	-5	0	-0.5
2001	†Atl N★	12	12	.500	34	34	1-1	0-0	219.1	187	83	17	6	70-13	187	3.04	142	.230	.294	65-0-7	.092	-3	98	31	0	2.8
2002	Bos A	13	8	.619	29	29	1-1	0-0	173	199	93	25	8	50-5	124	4.53	99	.287	.340	3-0-1	.000	-0	121	0	20	-0.1
2003	†Bos A	12	9	.571	32	30	1	0-0	181.2	202	108	20	9	47-1	107	5.15	90	.281	.330	1-0-1	.000	-0	109	-7	0	-0.7
Total	15	166	136	.550	445	423	21-6	1-1	2648.1	2866	1374	257	90	700-59	1766	4.31	99	.277	.326	540-0-62	.093	-19	104	-6	64	-2.8
Burkhart, Ken	Kenneth William (b Kenneth William Burkhardt); B11.18.1916 Knoxville TN; D12.29.2004 Knoxville TN; BR/TR/6´1˝/190; d4.21; U17																									
1945	StL N	18	8	.692	42	22	12-4	2	217.1	206	76	9	3	66	67	2.90	129	.251	.309	72-0-4	.181	1	98	23	0	2.5
1946	StL N	6	3	.667	25	13	5-2	2	100	111	34	4	2	36	32	2.88	120	.282	.346	34	.147	-0	143	8	0	0.6
1947	StL N	3	6	.333	34	6	1	1	95	108	55	13	4	23	44	5.21	79	.292	.340	24-0-2	.125	-1	103	-8	0	-0.8
1948	StL N	0	0	ø	20	0	0	1	37.1	50	24	4	2	14	16	5.54	74	.331	.395	4	.250	0*	—	-5	0	-0.2
	Cin N	0	3	.000	16	0	0	0	41.2	42	34	3	1	16	14	6.91	57	.255	.324	9-1-0	.333	2	—	-13	0	-0.7
	Year	0	3	.000	36	0	0	1	79	92	58	7	3	30	30	6.27	64	.291	.358	13-1-0	.308	2	—	-18	0	-0.9
1949	Cin N	0	0	ø	11	0	0	1	28.1	29	10	2	0	10	8	3.18	132	.282	.345	7	.286	0	—	4	0	0.2
Total	5	27	20	.574	148	41	18-6	7	519.2	546	233	35	12	165	181	3.84	99	.273	.332	150-1-6	.180	2	110	9	0	1.6
Burnett, A.J.	Allan James; B1.3.1977 North Little Rock AR; BR/TR/6´5˝/(204–230); [NYN95 8/217]; d8.17																									
1999	Fla N	4	2	.667	7	7	0	0-0	41.1	37	23	3	0	25-2	33	3.48	126	.242	.343	17	.118	-1	102	2	0	0.1
2000	Fla N	3	7	.300	13	13	0	0-0	82.2	80	46	8	2	44-3	57	4.79	91	.259	.352	25-1-2	.280	4	85	-3	107	0.1
2001	Fla N	11	12	.478	27	27	2-1	0-0	173.1	145	82	20	7	83-3	128	4.05	103	.231	.323	50-0-7	.080	-2	80	3	36	0.2
2002	Fla N	12	9	.571	31	29	7-**5**	0-1	204.1	153	84	12	9	90-5	203	3.30	119	.209	.302	57-1-7	.105	1	91	13	26	1.3
2003	Fla N	0	2	.000	4	4	0	0-0	23	18	13	2	2	18-2	21	4.70	87	.217	.365	7	.143	0	74	-2	166	-0.1
2004	Fla N	7	6	.538	20	19	1	0-0	120	102	50	9	4	38-0	113	3.68	112	.231	.296	29-0-8	.138	-1	109	7	60	0.7
2005	Fla N	12	12	.500	32	32	4-2	0-0	209	184	97	12	7	79-1	198	3.44	116	.237	.312	68-1-9	.147	2	100	9	0	1.1
2006	Tor A	10	8	.556	21	21	2-1	0-0	135.2	138	67	14	8	39-3	118	3.98	119	.264	.323	3	.000	-0	100	10	73	1.2
Total	8	59	58	.504	155	152	16-9	0-1	989.1	857	462	80	39	416-19	871	3.77	111	.235	.318	256-3-33	.133	4	94	39	468	4.6
Burnett, Sean	Sean Richard; B9.17.1982 Dunedin FL; BL/TL/5´11˝/190; [PitN00 1/19]; d5.30; [DL 2005 Pit N 183]																									
2004	Pit N	5	5	.500	13	13	1-1	0-0	71.2	86	41	9	1	28-2	30	5.02	86	.301	.364	23-0-2	.000	-2	94	-4	43	-0.7
Burnette, Wally	Wallace Harper; B6.20.1929 Blairs VA; D2.12.2003 Danville VA; BR/TR/6´0.5˝/(178–195); d7.15																									
1956	KC A	6	8	.429	18	14	4-1	0	121.1	115	48	13	2	39-3	54	2.89	150	.252	.312	39-0-5	.051	-4	79	17	0	1.3
1957	KC A	7	12	.368	38	9	1	1	113	115	62	8	1	44-3	57	4.30	92	.268	.333	32-0-3	.250	1	78	-5	0	-0.6
1958	KC A	1	1	.500	12	4	0	0	28.1	29	14	2	0	14-0	11	3.49	112	.264	.344	6-0-1	.167	0	132	0	0	0.0
Total	3	14	21	.400	68	27	5-1	1	262.2	259	124	23	3	97-6	122	3.56	116	.260	.325	77-0-9	.143	-4	87	12	0	0.7
Burns, Dennis	Dennis; B5.24.1898 Tiff City MO; D5.21.1969 Tulsa OK; BR/TR/5´10˝/180; d9.22; Col Missouri																									
1923	Phi A	2	1	.667	4	3	2	0	27	21	9	1	0	7	8	2.00	205	.210	.262	9	.111	-1	81	5	—	0.5
1924	Phi A	6	8	.429	37	17	7	1	154	191	101	3	1	68	26	5.08	84	.314	.384	42-0-2	.143	-2	96	-13	—	-1.2
Total	2	8	9	.471	41	20	9	1	181	212	110	4	1	75	34	4.62	92	.299	.367	51-0-2	.137	-3	94	-8	—	-0.7
Burns, Farmer	James Joseph "Slab"; B6.2.1876 Ashtabula OH; TR/5´7˝/168; d7.6; Col Washington & Jefferson																									
1901	StL N	0	0	ø	1	0	0	0	1	2	1	0	1	1	0	9.00	35	.400	.571	0	ø	0	—	-1	—	0.0
Burns, Mike	Michael John; B7.14.1978 Westminster CA; BR/TR/6´0˝/(205–210); [HouN00 30/907]; d5.13; Col Cal St.–Los Angeles																									
2005	Hou N	0	0	ø	27	0	0	0-0	31	29	18	6	5	8-1	20	4.94	86	.238	.311	0	ø	0	—	-2	0	-0.1
2006	Cin N	0	0	ø	11	0	0	0-0	13.1	30	13	2	2	3-1	9	8.78	54	.469	.507	0	ø	0	—	-5	0	-0.2
	Bos A	0	0	ø	7	0	0	0-0	7.2	10	4	0	0	1-1	7	4.70	100	.323	.324	0	ø	0	—	0	0	0.0
Total	2	0	0	ø	45	0	0	0-0	52	69	35	8	7	12-3	36	5.88	75	.318	.370	0	ø	0	—	-7	0	-0.3
Burns, Dick	Richard Simon; B12.26.1863 Holyoke MA; D11.16.1937 Holyoke MA; BL/TL/5´7˝/140; d5.3; ▲																									
1883	Det N	2	12	.143	17	13	13	0	127.2	172	122	8	—	33	30	4.51	69	.301	.339	140	.186	-2*	78	-21	—	-1.9
1884	Cin U	23	15	.605	40	40	34-1	0	329.2	298	179	7	—	47	167	2.46	104	.225	.252	350-4	.306	7*	113	2	—	0.4
1885	StL N	0	0	ø	1	0	0	0	3	3	3	0	—	0	2	9.00	31	.250	.250	54	.222	0*	—	-2	—	0.0
Total	3	25	27	.481	58	53	47-1	0	460.1	473	304	15	—	80	199	3.07	89	.248	.278	544-4	.267	6	105	-21	—	-1.5
Burns, Britt	Robert Britt; B6.8.1959 Houston TX; BL/TL/6´5˝/(215–231); [ChiA78 3/70]; d8.5; [DL 1986 NY A 182]																									
1978	Chi A	0	2	.000	2	2	0	0-0	7.2	14	12	2	0	3-0	3	12.91	29	.378	.425	0	ø	0	35	-8	0	-1.1
1979	Chi A	0	0	ø	6	0	0	0-1	5	10	5	1	0	1-0	2	5.40	79	.435	.423	0	ø	0	—	-1	0	-0.1
1980	Chi A	15	13	.536	34	32	11-1	0-0	238	213	83	17	4	63-2	133	2.84	143	.241	.293	0	ø	0	67	34	0	3.8
1981	Chi A☆	10	6	.625	24	23	5-1	0-0	156.2	139	52	14	6	49-1	108	2.64	137	.238	.300	0	ø	0	102	18	0	1.6
1982	Chi A	13	5	.722	28	28	5-1	0-0	169.1	168	89	12	3	67-1	116	4.04	101	.257	.328	0	ø	0	115	0	0	-0.1
1983	†Chi A	10	11	.476	29	26	8-4	0-0	173.2	165	79	14	5	55-2	115	3.58	118	.249	.310	0	ø	0	77	11	35	1.1
1984	Chi A	4	12	.250	34	16	2	3-2	117	130	74	7	4	45-1	85	5.00	84	.280	.347	0	ø	0	78	-11	32	-1.4
1985	Chi A	18	11	.621	36	34	8-4	0-0	227	206	105	26	2	79-1	172	3.96	110	.242	.306	0	ø	0	108	11	0	1.3
Total	8	70	60	.538	193	161	39-11	3-3	1094.1	1045	499	93	24	362-8	734	3.66	112	.251	.313	0	ø	0	91	54	249	5.1
Burns, Tommy	Thomas P. "Oyster"; B9.6.1864 Philadelphia PA; D11.11.1928 Brooklyn NY; BL/TR/5´8˝/183; d8.18; ▲																									
1884	Bal AA	0	0	ø	2	0	0	**1**	9	12	5	0	0	2	6	3.00	116	.343	.378	131-6	.298	1*	—	1	—	0.1
1885	Bal AA	7	4	.636	15	11	10-1	**3**	105.2	112	76	2	13	21	30	3.58	91	.266	.321	321-5	.231	3*	101	-6	—	-0.4
1887	Bal AA	1	0	1.000	3	0	0	0	11.1	16	16	0	3	4	2	9.53	43	.291	.371	551-9	.341	2*	—	-6	—	-0.3
1888	Bal AA	0	1	.000	5	0	0	0	12.2	12	8	0	0	3	2	4.26	70	.240	.283	325-4	.298	2*	—	-1	—	0.0
Total	4	8	5	.615	25	11	10-1	4	138.2	152	105	2	16	30	40	4.09	81	.271	.326	1328-24	.300	7	101	-12	—	-0.6
Burns, Todd	Todd Edward; B7.6.1963 Maywood CA; BR/TR/6´2˝/(186–195); [OakA84 7/168]; d5.31; Col Oral Roberts																									
1988	†Oak A	8	2	.800	17	14	2	1-0	102.2	93	38	8	1	34-1	57	3.16	121	.241	.303	0	ø	0	125	8	0	0.7
1989	†Oak A	6	5	.545	50	2	0	8-3	96.1	66	27	3	1	28-5	49	2.24	165	.196	.259	0	ø	0	86	17	0	2.0
1990	†Oak A	3	3	.500	43	2	0	3-1	78.2	78	28	8	0	32-4	43	2.97	126	.263	.331	0	ø	0	97	7	0	0.5
1991	Oak A	1	0	1.000	9	0	0	0-0	13.1	10	5	2	0	8-1	3	3.38	114	.217	.321	0	ø	0	—	1	61	0.1
1992	Tex A	3	5	.375	35	10	0	1-1	103	97	54	8	4	32-1	55	3.84	100	.248	.309	0	ø	0	67	-2	0	-0.2
1993	Tex A	0	4	.000	25	5	0	0-3	65	63	36	6	2	32-3	35	4.57	92	.253	.339	0	ø	0	57	-3	0	-0.2
	StL N	0	4	.000	24	0	0	0-2	30.2	32	21	8	0	9-6	10	6.16	65	.274	.320	3-0-1	.000	-0	—	-6	0	-0.8
Total	6	21	23	.477	203	33	2	13-10	489.2	439	209	43	8	175-21	252	3.47	111	.241	.307	3-0-1	.000	-0	93	22	61	2.1

YEAR	TM LG	W	L	PCT	G	GS	CG-SHO	SV-BS	IP	H	R	HR	HB	BB-IB	SO	ERA	AERA	OAV	OOB	AB-HR-SH	AVG	PB	SUP	APR	DL	PW
BURNS, BILL	William Thomas "Sleepy Bill"; B1.27.1880 San Saba TX; D6.6.1953 Ramona CA; BB/TL/6´2˝/195; d4.18																									
1908	Was A	6	11	.353	23	19	11-2	0	164	135	58	3	4	18	55	1.70	134	.229	.257	54	.148	-1	71	7	—	0.8
1909	Was A	1	1	.500	6	4	1	0	29.1	25	7	0	3	7	13	1.23	198	.229	.294	11	.273	0	51	3	—	0.3
	Chi A	7	13	.350	23	19	10-3	0	168	161	64	2	8	34	50	2.04	115	.264	.312	59-0-1	.153	1	70	2	—	0.4
	Year	8	14	.364	29	23	11-3	0	197.1	186	71	2	11	41	63	1.92	123	.259	.309	70-0-1	.171	1	66	7	—	0.7
1910	Chi A	0	0	ø	1	0	0	0	0.1	0	0	0	0	1	0	0.00	ø	.000	.500	0	ø	0	—	0	—	0.0
	Cin N	8	13	.381	31	21	13-2	0	178.2	183	103	3	12	49	57	3.48	84	.273	.333	61-0-1	.262	2*	100	-13	—	-1.1
1911	Cin N	1	0	1.000	6	3	0	1	17.2	17	11	1	3	3	5	3.06	108	.254	.315	7	.429	2	151	-1	—	0.2
	Phi N	6	10	.375	21	14	8-3	1	121	132	59	5	6	26	47	3.42	101	.287	.333	40	.150	-1	59	1	—	0.0
	Year	7	10	.412	27	17	8-3	2	138.2	149	70	6	9	29	52	3.38	102	.283	.331	47	.191	0	75	0	—	0.2
1912	Det A	1	4	.200	6	5	2	0	38.2	52	29	0	2	9	6	5.35	61	.338	.382	13	.231	1	104	-8	—	-0.8
Total	5	30	52	.366	117	85	45-10	2	717.2	705	331	14	38	147	233	2.72	100	.265	.313	245-0-2	.196	4	81	-9	—	-0.2
BURNSIDE, PETE	Peter Willits; B7.2.1930 Evanston IL; BR/TL/6´2˝/(180–190); d9.20																									
1955	NY N	1	0	1.000	2	2	1	0	12.2	10	9	1	0	9-0	2	2.84	142	.204	.328	5	.200	0	210	0	0	0.0
1957	NY N	1	4	.200	10	9	1-1	0	30.2	47	30	5	1	13-0	18	8.80	45	.356	.415	9-0-2	.000	-1	114	-15	0	-2.1
1958	SF N	0	0	ø	6	1	0	0	10.2	20	10	3	0	5-0	4	6.75	56	.400	.455	0	ø	0	141	-4	0	-0.2
1959	Det A	1	3	.250	30	0	0	1	62	55	31	7	2	25-1	49	3.77	108	.237	.315	10-0-1	.000	-1	—	1	0	0.0
1960	Det A	7	7	.500	31	15	2	2	113.2	122	56	14	4	50-1	71	4.28	93	.277	.355	27-0-5	.148	-1	96	-2	0	-0.3
1961	Was A	4	9	.308	33	16	4-2	2	113.1	106	66	11	3	51-2	56	4.53	89	.251	.330	34-0-3	.059	-3	74	-6	0	-1.0
1962	Was A	5	11	.313	40	20	6	2	149.2	152	82	20	2	51-3	74	4.45	91	.263	.322	35-0-5	.057	-3	83	-7	0	-1.0
1963	Bal A	0	1	.000	6	0	0	0	7.1	11	4	0	1	2-0	6	4.91	71	.344	.400	1	.000	-0	—	-1	0	-0.2
	Was A	0	1	.000	38	1	0	0	67.1	84	49	12	0	24-1	23	6.15	60	.308	.359	11	.091	-0	48	-16	0	-0.9
	Year	0	2	.000	44	1	0	0	74.2	95	53	12	1	26-1	29	6.03	61	.311	.363	12	.083	-1	48	-17	0	-1.1
Total	8	19	36	.345	196	64	14-3	7	567.1	607	337	73	13	230-8	303	4.81	82	.275	.344	132-0-16	.076	-8	93	-50	0	-5.7
BURNSIDE, SHELDON	Sheldon John; B12.22.1954 South Bend IN; BR/TL/6´5˝/200; d9.4																									
1978	Det A	0	0	ø	2	0	0	0-0	4	4	4	0	0	2-0	3	9.00	43	.250	.333	0	ø	0	—	-2	0	-0.1
1979	Det A	1	1	.500	10	0	0	0-0	21.1	28	16	2	1	8-2	13	6.33	69	.333	.394	0	ø	0	—	-4	0	-0.3
1980	Cin N	1	0	1.000	7	0	0	0-0	4.2	6	1	1	0	1-0	2	1.93	183	.333	.368	1	.000	-0	—	1	0	0.2
Total	3	2	1	.667	19	0	0	0-0	30	38	21	3	1	11-2	18	6.00	69	.322	.382	1	.000	-0	—	-5	0	-0.2
BURPO, GEORGE	George Harvie; B6.19.1922 Jenkins KY; BR/TL/6´0˝/195; d6.9																									
1946	Cin N	0	0	ø	2	0	0	0	2.1	4	4	0	0	5	1	15.43	22	.400	.600	0	ø	0	—	-3	0	-0.2
BURRELL, HARRY	Harry J.; B5.26.1869 Bethel VT; D12.11.1914 Omaha NE; BR/TL; d9.13																									
1891	StL AA	4	2	.667	7	4	3	1	43	51	36	4	2	21	19	4.81	87	.285	.366	20	.200	-1*	52	-2	—	-0.3
BURRES, BRIAN	Brian James; B4.8.1981 Oregon City OR; BL/TL/6´1˝/180; [SFN00 31/931]; d9.8; Col Mt. Hood (OR) CC																									
2006	Bal A	0	0	ø	11	0	0	0-0	8	6	2	1	0	1-0	6	2.25	201	.200	.226	0	ø	0	—	2	0	0.1
BURRIS, AL	Alva Burton; B1.28.1874 Warwick MD; D3.25.1938 Salisbury MD; BR/TR; d6.22; Col Washington College																									
1894	Phi N	0	0	ø	1	0	0	0	5	14	10	0	0	2	0	18.00	29	.500	.533	4	.500	1	—	-6	—	-0.2
BURRIS, RAY	Bertram Ray; B8.22.1950 Idabel OK; BR/TR/6´5˝/(192–210); [ChiN72 17/399]; d4.8; C3; Col Southwestern Oklahoma																									
1973	Chi N	1	1	.500	31	1	0	0-0	64.2	65	22	2	0	27-7	57	2.92	135	.261	.331	7-0-1	.143	0	22	7	0	0.4
1974	Chi N	3	5	.375	40	5	0	1-1	75	91	61	8	4	26-6	40	6.60	58	.300	.359	13-0-1	.077	-1*	50	-20	0	-2.1
1975	Chi N	15	10	.600	36	35	8-2	0-0	238.1	259	121	25	4	73-6	108	4.12	94	.281	.334	82-0-7	.183	1*	111	-5	0	-0.6
1976	Chi N	15	13	.536	37	36	10-4	0-0	249	251	102	22	5	70-5	112	3.11	125	.263	.315	81-0-8	.111	-4*	81	17	0	1.5
1977	Chi N	14	16	.467	39	39	5-1	0-0	221	270	132	29	3	67-9	105	4.72	93	.305	.355	69-1-9	.174	1*	98	-7	0	-0.7
1978	Chi N	7	13	.350	40	32	4-1	1-1	199	210	112	15	10	79-11	94	4.75	85	.274	.346	61-0-7	.115	-1*	96	-12	0	-1.2
1979	Chi N	0	0	ø	14	0	0	0-0	21.2	23	17	0	1	15-1	14	6.23	67	.284	.398	1	.000	0	—	-5	0	-0.2
	NY A	1	3	.250	15	0	0	0-2	27.2	40	22	5	0	10-1	19	6.18	67	.342	.388	0	ø	0	—	-7	0	-0.9
	NY N	0	2	.000	4	4	0	0-0	21.2	21	10	2	1	6-3	10	3.32	112	.247	.304	6-0-1	.167	-0	66	0	15	0.0
1980	NY N	7	13	.350	29	29	1	0-0	170.1	181	86	20	4	54-5	83	4.02	90	.277	.333	51-0-3	.098	-2	85	-8	32	-1.2
1981	†Mon N	9	7	.563	22	21	4	0-0	135.2	117	56	9	3	41-3	52	3.05	117	.235	.294	37-0-7	.189	1	118	5	0	0.6
1982	Mon N	4	14	.222	37	15	2	2-3	123.2	143	77	14	2	53-7	55	4.73	78	.297	.365	28-0-4	.179	1	76	-15	0	-2.0
1983	Mon N	4	7	.364	40	17	2-1	0-0	154	139	68	13	2	56-4	100	3.68	98	.244	.312	39-0-2	.231	3	83	0	0	0.3
1984	Oak A	13	10	.565	34	28	5-1	0-0	211.2	193	84	15	8	90-1	93	3.15	120	.244	.325	0	ø	0*	106	15	0	1.3
1985	Mil A	9	13	.409	29	28	6	0-0	170.1	182	95	25	3	53-0	81	4.81	87	.272	.325	0	ø	0	98	-8	0	-0.9
1986	StL N	4	5	.444	23	10	0	0-0	82	92	52	13	4	32-4	34	5.60	66	.287	.359	27	.148	0	101	-15	0	-1.5
1987	Mil A	2	2	.500	10	2	0	0-0	23	33	16	4	0	12-3	8	5.87	79	.351	.417	0	ø	0	79	-3	0	-0.4
Total	15	108	134	.446	480	302	47-10	4-7	2188.2	2310	1133	221	54	764-76	1065	4.17	94	.274	.335	502-1-50	.151	-1	95	-61	47	-7.6
BURROWS, JOHN	John; B10.30.1913 Winnfield LA; D4.27.1987 Coal Run OH; BR/TL/5´10˝/200; d4.25																									
1943	Phi A	0	1	.000	4	1	0	0	7.2	8	7	0	1	9	3	8.22	41	.276	.462	1	.000	-0	0	-4	0	-0.4
	Chi N	0	2	.000	23	1	0	2	32.2	25	17	0	2	16	18	3.86	87	.205	.307	3	.667	1	51	-2	0	0.0
1944	Chi N	0	0	ø	3	0	0	0	3	7	7	0	0	3	1	18.00	20	.467	.556	0	ø	0	—	-5	0	-0.2
Total	2	0	3	.000	30	2	0	2	43.1	40	31	0	3	28	22	5.61	60	.241	.360	4	.500	1	25	-11	0	-0.6
BURROWS, TERRY	Terry Dale; B11.28.1968 Lake Charles LA; BL/TL/6´1˝/(185–195); [TexA90 7/198]; d6.12; Col McNeese St.																									
1994	Tex A	0	0	ø	1	0	0	0-0	1	1	1	1	0	1-0	0	9.00	54	.250	.400	0	ø	0	—	0	0	0.0
1995	Tex A	2	2	.500	28	3	0	1-2	44.2	60	37	11	2	19-0	22	6.45	75	.323	.391	0	ø	0	96	-9	0	-0.7
1996	Mil A	2	0	1.000	8	0	0	0-0	12.2	12	4	2	1	10-0	5	2.84	183	.261	.404	0	ø	0	—	3	0	0.4
1997	SD N	0	2	.000	13	0	0	0-0	10.1	12	13	1	1	8-1	8	10.45	38	.286	.412	0	ø	0	—	-8	0	-1.3
Total	4	4	4	.500	50	3	0	1-2	68.2	85	55	15	4	38-1	35	6.42	74	.306	.397	0	ø	0	96	-14	0	-1.6
BURTON, JIM	Jim Scott; B10.27.1949 Royal Oak MI; BR/TL/6´3˝/195; [BosA71 D1/5]; d6.10; Col Michigan																									
1975	†Bos A	1	2	.333	29	4	0	1-1	53	58	30	6	0	19-2	39	2.89	141	.276	.333	0	ø	0	87	2	0	0.1
1977	Bos A	0	0	ø	1	0	0	0-0	2.2	2	0	0	0	1-0	3	0.00	ø	.200	.273	0	ø	0	—	1	0	0.1
Total	2	1	2	.333	30	4	0	1-1	55.2	60	30	6	0	20-2	42	2.75	149	.273	.331	0	ø	0	87	3	0	0.2
BURTSCHY, MOE	Edward Frank; B4.18.1922 Cincinnati OH; D5.2.2004 Cincinnati OH; BR/TR/6´3˝/208; d6.17																									
1950	Phi A	0	1	.000	9	1	0	0	19	22	16	2	1	21	12	7.11	64	.289	.449	5	.000	-0	20	-5	0	-0.2
1951	Phi A	0	0	ø	7	0	0	0	17	18	11	0	1	12	4	5.29	81	.277	.397	3	.333	0	—	-2	64	-0.1
1954	Phi A	5	4	.556	46	0	0	4	94.2	80	45	7	8	53	54	3.80	103	.234	.346	17	.118	-1	—	1	0	0.0
1955	KC A	2	0	1.000	7	0	0	0	11.1	17	13	0	1	10-1	9	10.32	40	.354	.467	3	.333	0	—	-7	0	-1.0
1956	KC A	3	1	.750	21	0	0	0	43.1	41	22	6	3	30-4	18	3.95	110	.263	.389	8	.125	-1	—	1	0	0.1
Total	5	10	6	.625	90	1	0	4	185.1	178	107	15	14	126-5	97	4.71	88	.259	.381	36	.139	-1	20	-12	64	-1.2
BURTT, DENNIS	Dennis Allen; B11.29.1957 San Diego CA; BB/TR/6´0˝/187; [BosA76*2/45]; d9.4; Col Santa Ana (CA) JC																									
1985	Min A	2	2	.500	5	2	0	0-0	28.1	20	13	2	0	7-0	9	3.81	116	.200	.250	0	ø	0	103	2	0	0.3
1986	Min A	0	0	ø	3	0	0	0-0	2	7	7	1	0	3-1	1	31.50	14	.538	.625	0	ø	0	—	-6	0	-0.3
Total	2	2	2	.500	8	2	0	0-0	30.1	27	20	3	0	10-1	10	5.64	78	.239	.298	0	ø	0	103	-4	0	0.0
BURWELL, DICK	Richard Matthew; B1.23.1940 Alton IL; BR/TR/6´1˝/190; d9.13; Col Illinois Wesleyan																									
1960	Chi N	0	0	ø	3	1	0	0	9.2	11	6	2	1	7-0	1	5.59	68	.306	.432	3	.333	0	140	-2	0	-0.1
1961	Chi N	0	0	ø	2	0	0	0	4	6	4	0	0	4-0	0	9.00	46	.375	.476	1	.000	-0	—	-2	0	-0.1
Total	2	0	0	ø	5	1	0	0	13.2	17	10	2	1	11-0	1	6.59	59	.327	.446	4	.250	0	140	-4	0	-0.2
BURWELL, BILL	William Edwin; B3.27.1895 Jarbalo KS; D6.11.1973 Ormond Beach FL; BL/TR/5´11˝/175; d5.1; M1/C8																									
1920	StL A	6	4	.600	33	2	0	4	113.1	133	55	5	4	42	30	3.65	107	.303	.369	42-0-2	.167	-2*	91	4	—	0.1
1921	StL A	2	4	.333	33	3	1	2	84.1	102	62	2	2	29	17	5.12	87	.309	.368	25	.240	-0	130	-8	—	-0.5
1928	Pit N	1	0	1.000	4	1	0	0	20.2	18	12	2	0	8	2	5.23	78	.234	.306	9-0-1	.222	-0	125	-2	—	-0.1
Total	3	9	8	.529	70	6	1	6	218.1	253	129	9	6	79	49	4.37	95	.299	.363	76-0-3	.197	-2	118	-6	—	-0.5

YEAR	TM LG	W	L	PCT	G	GS	CG-SHO	SV-BS	IP	H	R	HR	HB	BB-IB	SO	ERA	AERA	OAV	OOB	AB-HR-SH	AVG	PB	SUP	APR	DL	PW
Busby, Mike	Michael James; B12.27.1972 Lomita CA; BR/TR/6´4˝/(210–225); [StLN91 14/363]; d4.7																									
1996	StL N	0	1	.000	1	1	0	0-0	4	9	13	4	1	4-0	4	18.00	24	.409	.519	2	.500	0	64	-8	0	-0.9
1997	StL N	0	2	.000	3	3	0	0-0	14.1	24	14	2	0	4-0	6	8.79	48	.393	.424	4	.500	1	73	-7	0	-0.7
1998	StL N	5	2	.714	26	2	0	0-2	46	45	23	3	5	15-0	33	4.50	93	.254	.327	3	.000	-0	98	0	101	-0.1
1999	StL N	0	1	.000	15	0	0	0-0	17.2	21	15	2	2	14-0	7	7.13	65	.300	.430	0	ø	0	—	-5	0	-0.2
Total	4	5	6	.455	45	6	0	0-2	82	99	65	11	8	37-0	50	6.48	66	.300	.381	9	.333	1	79	-20	101	-1.9
Busby, Steve	Steven Lee; B9.29.1949 Burbank CA; BR/TR/6´2˝/(190–195); [KCA71 D2/39]; d9.8; Col USC; [DL 1977 KC A 28]																									
1972	KC A	3	1	.750	5	5	3	0-0	40	28	9	1	0	8-0	31	1.57	193	.200	.238	15	.200	0	116	6	0	0.7
1973	KC A	16	15	.516	37	37	7-1	0-0	238.1	246	125	18	6	105-7	174	4.23	97	.271	.347	0	ø	0	94	-3	0	-0.3
1974	KC A☆	22	14	.611	38	38	20-3	0-0	292.1	284	118	14	9	92-6	198	3.39	113	.258	.319	0	ø	0	119	17	0	2.2
1975	KC A★	18	12	.600	34	34	18-3	0-0	260.1	233	96	18	3	81-4	160	3.08	125	.242	.302	0	ø	0	93	25	0	2.9
1976	KC A	3	3	.500	13	13	1	0-0	71.2	58	42	7	3	49-1	29	4.40	80	.218	.344	0	ø	0	154	-8	95	-0.6
1978	KC A	1	0	1.000	7	5	0	0-0	21.1	24	18	2	2	15-1	10	7.59	50	.282	.402	0	ø	0	127	-8	0	-0.4
1979	KC A	6	6	.500	22	12	4	0-0	94.1	71	45	10	0	64-3	45	3.63	118	.220	.343	0	ø	0	87	6	0	0.8
1980	KC A	1	3	.250	11	6	0	0-0	42.1	59	30	3	2	19-0	12	6.17	66	.335	.402	0	ø	0	77	-9	0	-0.7
Total	8	70	54	.565	167	150	53-7	0-0	1060.2	1003	483	73	25	433-22	659	3.72	105	.253	.328	15	.200	0	105	26	123	4.6
Buschhorn, Don	Donald Lee; B4.29.1946 Independence MO; BR/TR/6´0˝/168; d5.15																									
1965	KC A	0	1	.000	12	3	0	0	31	36	17	7	1	8-0	9	4.35	80	.295	.341	4	.500	1*	101	-3	32	-0.1
Bush, Dave	David T.; B11.9.1979 Pittsburgh PA; BR/TR/6´2˝/(210–212); [TorA02 2/55]; d7.2; Col Wake Forest																									
2004	Tor A	5	4	.556	16	16	1-1	0-0	97.2	95	47	11	6	25-2	64	3.69	133	.255	.309	2	.000	-0	85	10	0	0.8
2005	Tor A	5	11	.313	25	24	2	0-0	136.1	142	73	20	13	29-3	75	4.49	102	.269	.322	0	ø	0	96	2	0	0.2
2006	Mil N	12	11	.522	34	32	3-2	0-0	210	201	111	26	18	38-2	166	4.41	102	.252	.299	62-0-9	.177	1	101	2	0	0.4
Total	3	22	26	.458	75	72	6-3	0-0	444	438	231	57	37	92-7	305	4.28	108	.258	.308	64-0-9	.172	1	95	14	0	1.4
Bush, Guy	Guy Terrell "The Mississippi Mudcat"; B8.23.1901 Aberdeen MS; D7.2.1985 Shannon MS; BR/TR/6´0˝/175; d9.17; Col Tupelo Mil. Inst. [JC]																									
1923	Chi N	0	0	ø	1	0	0	0	1	1	0	0	0	0	2	0.00	ø	.250	.250	0	ø	0	—	0	—	0.0
1924	Chi N	2	5	.286	16	8	4	0	80.2	91	51	7	2	24	36	4.02	97	.285	.339	26	.154	-1	82	-4	—	-0.6
1925	Chi N	6	13	.316	42	15	5	**4**	182	213	102	15	3	52	76	4.30	101	.300	.350	57-0-3	.193	-2	83	0	—	0.0
1926	Chi N	13	9	.591	35	15	7-2	2	157.1	149	58	3	3	42	32	2.86	134	.258	.311	48-0-3	.167	-2	94	18	—	2.1
1927	Chi N	10	10	.500	36	22	9-1	2	193.1	177	76	3	6	79	62	3.03	128	.250	.330	65-0-5	.123	-4	86	18	—	1.3
1928	Chi N	15	6	.714	42	24	9-2	2	204.1	229	104	10	5	86	61	3.83	100	.293	.367	73-0-4	.082	-6	112	0	—	-0.7
1929	†Chi N	18	7	.720	**50**	30	18-2	**8**	270.2	277	135	16	4	107	82	3.66	126	.265	.335	91-0-10	.165	-4	115	27	—	1.8
1930	Chi N	15	10	.600	46	25	11	3	225	291	174	22	2	86	75	6.20	79	.316	.376	78-0-3	.282	3	121	-31	—	-2.4
1931	Chi N	16	8	.667	39	24	14-1	2	180.1	190	104	9	2	66	54	4.49	86	.268	.332	57-0-5	.123	-2	132	-13	—	-1.5
1932	†Chi N	19	11	.633	40	30	15-1	0	238.2	262	106	13	7	70	73	3.21	118	.278	.332	84-0-6	.179	0	108	13	—	1.5
1933	Chi N	20	12	.625	41	32	20-4	2	259	261	95	9	1	68	84	2.75	119	.257	.304	88-0-5	.125	-1	117	16	—	2.0
1934	Chi N	18	10	.643	40	27	15-1	2	209.1	213	96	15	1	54	75	3.83	101	.262	.309	70-0-6	.229	1*	110	3	—	0.5
1935	Pit N	11	11	.500	41	25	8-1	2	204.1	237	115	16	5	40	42	4.32	95	.285	.321	63-0-3	.127	-1	102	-2	—	-0.3
1936	Pit N	1	3	.250	16	0	0	2	34.2	49	28	3	0	11	10	5.97	68	.336	.382	9	.333	0	—	-8	—	-0.8
	Bos N	4	5	.444	15	11	5	0	90.1	98	38	2	0	20	28	3.39	113	.281	.320	25-0-6	.120	-1	86	5	—	0.4
	Year	5	8	.385	31	11	5	2	125	147	66	5	0	31	38	4.10	95	.297	.338	34-0-6	.176	-0	85	-1	—	-0.4
1937	Bos N	8	15	.348	32	20	11-1	1	180.2	201	77	8	0	48	56	3.54	101	.282	.328	54-0-2	.111	-2*	71	3	—	0.2
1938	StL N	0	1	.000	6	0	0	1	6	6	3	1	0	3	1	4.50	88	.286	.375	0	ø	0	—	0	—	0.0
1945	Cin N	0	0	ø	4	0	0	1	4.1	5	4	0	0	3	1	8.31	45	.278	.381	0	ø	0	—	-2	0	-0.1
Total	17	176	136	.564	542	308	151-16	34	2722	2950	1366	152	41	859	850	3.86	103	.277	.334	888-0-61	.161	-22	105	43	0	3.4
Bush, Joe	Leslie Ambrose "Bullet Joe"; B11.27.1892 Brainerd MN; D11.1.1974 Ft.Lauderdale FL; BR/TR/5´9˝/173; d9.30																									
1912	Phi A	0	0	ø	1	1	0	0	8	14	10	0	0	4	3	7.88	39	.368	.429	4	.500	1	264	-5	—	-0.1
1913	†Phi A	15	6	.714	39	16	6-1	3	200.1	199	95	3	5	66	81	3.82	72	.261	.324	70-0-2	.157	-0	126	-21	—	-1.9
1914	†Phi A	17	13	.567	38	23	14-2	2	206	184	84	2	8	81	109	3.06	85	.242	.322	74-1-4	.189	2	113	-10	—	-1.2
1915	Phi A	5	15	.250	25	18	8	0	145.2	137	86	3	4	89	89	4.14	71	.263	.375	49-0-2	.143	-3	78	-17	—	-2.4
1916	Phi A	15	24	.385	40	33	25-8	0	286.2	222	109	3	3	130	157	2.57	111	.219	.310	100-0-2	.140	-4*	69	9	—	1.1
1917	Phi A	11	17	.393	37	31	17-4	2	233.1	207	101	3	1	111	121	2.47	111	.241	.328	80	.200	1	75	3	—	0.5
1918	†Bos A	15	15	.500	36	31	26-7	2	272.2	241	88	3	3	91	125	2.11	127	.242	.307	98-0-1	.276	6	80	16	—	2.8
1919	Bos A	0	0	ø	3	2	0	0	9	11	5	0	0	4	3	5.00	60	.324	.395	5	.400	1*	195	-2	—	0.0
1920	Bos A	15	15	.500	35	32	18	1	243.2	287	138	3	10	94	88	4.25	86	.300	.369	102-0-3	.245	2*	95	-18	—	-1.6
1921	Bos A	16	9	.640	37	32	21-3	1	254.1	244	111	10	6	93	96	3.50	121	.260	.330	120-0-3	.325	6*	107	22	—	2.8
1922	†NY A	26	7	**.788**	39	30	20	3	255.1	240	109	16	1	85	92	3.31	121	.252	.314	95-0-5	.326	8	118	20	—	3.2
1923	†NY A	19	15	.559	37	30	22-3	0	275.2	263	115	7	5	117	125	3.43	115	.260	.340	113-2-0	.274	7*	103	17	—	2.6
1924	NY A	17	16	.515	39	31	19-3	1	252	262	117	9	7	109	80	3.57	116	.273	.352	124-1-1	.339	14*	102	16	—	3.2
1925	StL A	14	14	.500	33	30	15-2	0	208.2	230	129	18	2	91	63	5.09	92	.284	.357	102-2-1	.255	3*	103	-4	—	0.2
1926	Was A	1	8	.111	12	11	3	0	71.1	83	54	6	5	35	27	6.69	58	.292	.380	30	.233	1*	87	-20	—	-1.9
	Pit N	6	6	.500	19	12	9-2	3	110.2	97	45	7	2	35	38	3.01	131	.236	.299	49-1-0	.265	2*	85	11	—	1.4
1927	Pit N	1	2	.333	5	3	0	0	6.2	14	14	1	0	5	1	13.50	30	.412	.487	5	.600	1*	76	-8	—	-1.2
	NY N	1	1	.500	3	2	1	0	12	18	10	1	0	5	6	7.50	51	.340	.397	4	.500	1	99	-4	—	-0.5
	Year	2	3	.400	8	5	1	0	18.2	32	24	2	0	10	7	9.64	41	.368	.433	9	.556	2	86	-12	—	-1.7
1928	Phi A	2	1	.667	11	2	1	1	35.1	39	21	1	1	18	15	5.09	79	.300	.389	15	.067	-1*	106	-3	—	-0.3
Total	17	196	184	.516	489	370	225-35	19	3087.1	2992	1441	96	63	1263	1319	3.51	99	.260	.336	1239-7-24	.253	49	98	2	—	6.7
Bushelman, Jack	John Francis; B8.29.1885 Cincinnati OH; D10.26.1955 Roanoke VA; BR/TR/6´2˝/175; d10.5; Col Cincinnati																									
1909	Cin N	0	1	.000	1	1	1	0	7	7	7	1	0	4	3	2.57	101	.241	.333	1	.000	-0	108	-1	—	-0.2
1911	Bos A	0	1	.000	3	1	1	0	12	8	9	0	1	10	5	3.00	109	.186	.352	3	.000	-0	22	-1	—	-0.1
1912	Bos A	1	0	1.000	3	0	0	0	7.2	9	4	0	0	5	5	4.70	72	.310	.412	3	.000	-0	—	-1	—	-0.1
Total	3	1	2	.333	7	2	2	0	26.2	24	20	1	1	19	13	3.38	93	.238	.364	7	.000	-1	57	-3	—	-0.4
Bushey, Frank	Francis Clyde; B8.1.1906 Wheaton KS; D3.18.1972 Topeka KS; BR/TR/6´0˝/180; d9.17																									
1927	Bos A	0	0	ø	1	0	0	0	1.1	2	1	0	0	2	0	6.75	63	.500	.667	0	ø	0	—	0	—	0.0
1930	Bos A	0	1	.000	11	0	0	0	30	34	22	1	2	15	4	6.30	73	.306	.398	9	.111	-1	—	-5	—	-0.3
Total	2	0	1	.000	12	0	0	0	31.1	36	23	1	2	17	4	6.32	73	.313	.410	9	.111	-1	—	-5	—	-0.3
Bushing, Chris	Christopher Shaun; B11.4.1967 Rockville Centre NY; BR/TR/6´0˝/190; d9.3; Col Broward (FL) CC																									
1993	Cin N	0	0	ø	6	0	0	0-0	4.1	9	7	1	0	4-0	3	12.46	32	.450	.520	0	ø	0	—	-4	0	-0.2
Buskey, Tom	Thomas William; B2.20.1947 Harrisburg PA; D6.7.1998 Harrisburg PA; BR/TR/6´3˝/(200–228); d8.5; Col North Carolina																									
1973	NY A	0	1	.000	8	0	0	1-1	16.2	18	12	2	1	4-0	8	5.40	69	.286	.324	0	ø	0	—	-3	0	-0.2
1974	NY A	0	1	.000	4	0	0	1-0	5.2	10	4	1	1	3-1	3	6.35	56	.400	.483	0	ø	0	—	-2	0	-0.3
	Cle A	2	6	.250	51	0	0	17-7	93	93	36	10	1	33-8	40	3.19	114	.263	.322	0	ø	0	—	5	0	0.7
	Year	2	7	.222	55	0	0	18-7	98.2	103	40	11	2	36-9	43	3.38	108	.272	.333	0	ø	0	—	3	0	0.4
1975	Cle A	5	3	.625	50	0	0	7-3	77	69	27	7	1	29-10	29	2.57	148	.252	.324	0	ø	0	—	10	38	1.2
1976	Cle A	5	4	.556	39	0	0	1-2	94.1	88	42	9	3	34-8	32	3.63	97	.256	.326	0	ø	0	—	-1	0	-0.1
1977	Cle A	0	0	ø	21	0	0	0-0	34	45	24	6	1	8-1	15	5.29	75	.313	.348	0	ø	0	—	-6	0	-0.3
1978	Tor A	0	1	.000	8	0	0	0-0	13.1	14	5	1	0	5-4	7	3.38	117	.275	.339	0	ø	0	—	1	0	0.1
1979	Tor A	6	10	.375	44	0	0	7-4	78.2	74	33	10	1	25-7	44	3.43	128	.249	.310	0	ø	0	—	8	7	1.8
1980	Tor A	3	1	.750	33	0	0	0-1	66.2	68	35	11	0	26-6	34	4.45	97	.278	.341	0	ø	0	—	0	0	0.0
Total	8	21	27	.438	258	0	0	34-18	479.1	479	218	57	9	167-45	212	3.66	106	.267	.328	0	ø	0	—	12	45	2.9
Butcher, Max	Albert Maxwell; B9.21.1910 Holden WV; D9.15.1957 Man WV; BR/TR/6´2˝/220; d4.20																									
1936	Bro N	6	6	.500	38	15	5	2	147.2	154	85	11	1	59	55	3.96	104	.268	.337	48	.125	-3*	89	0	—	-0.3
1937	Bro N	11	15	.423	39	24	8-1	0	191.2	203	106	12	7	75	57	4.27	94	.280	.354	62-0-1	.161	-1*	69	-2	—	-0.3
1938	Bro N	5	4	.556	24	8	3	2	72.2	104	66	9	1	39	21	6.56	59	.334	.410	25-1-2	.160	0*	141	-22	—	-2.4
	Phi N	4	8	.333	12	12	11	0	98.1	94	40	6	2	31	29	2.93	133	.253	.314	35	.257	1	42	9	—	1.1
	Year	9	12	.429	36	20	14	2	171	198	106	15	3	70	50	4.47	87	.290	.359	60-1-2	.217	1	82	-13	—	-1.3

YEAR	TM LG	W	L	PCT	G	GS	CG-SHO	SV-BS	IP	H	R	HR	HB	BB-IB	SO	ERA	AERA	OAV	OOB	AB-HR-SH	AVG	PB	SUP	APR	DL	PW
1939	Phi N	2	13	.133	19	16	3	0	104.1	131	72	10	1	51	27	5.61	71	.308	.383	38-0-3	.184	-1	75	-18	—	-2.3
	Pit N	4	4	.500	14	12	5-2	0	86.2	104	37	2	0	23	21	3.43	112	.297	.340	31-0-3	.097	-2	70	5	—	0.3
	Year	6	17	.261	33	28	8-2	0	191	235	109	12	1	74	48	4.62	85	.303	.364	69-0-6	.145	-3	73	-13	—	-2.0
1940	Pit N	8	9	.471	35	24	6-2	2	136.1	161	99	13	1	46	40	6.01	63	.290	.346	50-0-1	.300	4*	120	-31	—	-3.0
1941	Pit N	17	12	.586	33	32	19	0	236	249	98	11	1	66	61	3.05	118	.265	.314	82-0-5	.183	-1	101	14	0	1.6
1942	Pit N	5	8	.385	24	18	9	1	150.2	144	59	7	2	44	49	2.93	116	.247	.303	49-0-2	.143	-2	90	7	0	0.4
1943	Pit N	10	8	.556	33	21	10-2	1	193.2	191	65	4	2	57	45	2.60	134	.262	.317	61-0-7	.164	-1	100	20	0	1.8
1944	Pit N	13	11	.542	35	27	13-5	1	199	216	83	8	1	46	43	3.12	119	.273	.314	63-0-5	.190	-0*	104	13	0	1.6
1945	Pit N	10	8	.556	28	20	12-2	0	169.1	184	76	7	4	46	37	3.03	130	.277	.328	54-0-6	.222	0	105	13	0	1.3
Total	10	95	106	.473	334	229	104-14	9	1786.1	1935	886	100	23	583	485	3.73	101	.276	.333	598-1-35	.184	-6	93	8	0	-0.2
Butcher, John	John Daniel; B3.8.1957 Glendale CA; BR/TR/6´4˝/(185–190); [TexA77 S1/18]; d9.8; Col Yavapai (AZ) JC																									
1980	Tex A	3	3	.500	6	6	1	0-0	35.1	34	19	2	0	13-0	27	4.08	95	.248	.313	0	ø	0	100	-1	0	-0.1
1981	Tex A	1	2	.333	5	3	1-1	0-0	27.2	18	6	0	0	8-1	19	1.63	214	.186	.248	0	ø	0	43	6	0	0.7
1982	Tex A	1	5	.167	18	13	2	1-0	94.1	102	53	10	2	34-4	39	4.87	80	.280	.342	0	ø	0	94	-9	0	-0.5
1983	Tex A	6	6	.500	38	6	1-1	5-3	123	128	50	8	1	41-4	58	3.51	115	.270	.328	0	ø	0	86	9	0	0.9
1984	Min A	13	11	.542	34	34	8-1	0-0	225	242	98	18	4	53-5	83	3.44	123	.276	.317	0	ø	0	92	17	0	1.6
1985	Min A	11	14	.440	34	33	8-2	0-0	207.2	239	125	24	6	43-4	92	4.98	89	.289	.325	0	ø	0	98	-11	0	-1.2
1986	Min A	0	3	.000	16	10	1	0-1	70	82	50	11	1	24-1	29	6.30	69	.294	.349	0	ø	0	105	-13	0	-0.6
	Cle A	1	5	.167	13	8	1-1	0-0	50.2	86	43	6	3	13-0	16	6.93	60	.381	.416	0	ø	0	103	-15	15	-1.5
	Year	1	8	.111	29	18	2-1	0-1	120.2	168	93	17	4	37-1	45	6.56	65	.333	.379	0	ø	0	104	-28	0	-2.1
Total	7	36	49	.424	164	113	23-6	6-4	833.2	931	444	79	17	229-19	363	4.42	95	.284	.331	0	ø	0	96	-17	15	-0.7
Butcher, Mike	Michael Dana; B5.10.1965 Davenport IA; BR/TR/6´1˝/200; [KCA86 S2/36]; d7.6; C1; Col NE Oklahoma A&M JC																									
1992	Cal A	2	2	.500	19	0	0	0-1	27.2	29	11	3	2	13-1	24	3.25	124	.264	.352	0	ø	0	—	2	0	0.3
1993	Cal A	1	0	1.000	23	0	0	8-2	28.1	21	12	2	2	15-1	24	2.86	159	.204	.309	0	ø	0	—	4	71	0.3
1994	Cal A	2	1	.667	33	0	0	1-2	29.2	31	24	2	2	23-5	19	6.67	74	.274	.406	0	ø	0	—	-6	0	-0.5
1995	Cal A	6	1	.857	40	0	0	0-2	51.1	49	28	7	1	31-2	29	4.73	100	.257	.358	0	ø	0	—	0	0	0.0
Total	4	11	4	.733	115	0	0	9-7	137	130	75	14	7	82-9	96	4.47	103	.251	.358	0	ø	0	—	0	71	0.1
Butland, Bill	Wilburn Rue; B3.22.1918 Terre Haute IN; D9.19.1997 Terre Haute IN; BR/TR/6´5˝/185; d5.29; Mil 1943–45																									
1940	Bos A	1	2	.333	3	3	1	0	21	27	13	0	0	10	5	5.57	81	.307	.378	7-0-1	.000	-1	59	-2	—	-0.3
1942	Bos A	7	1	.875	23	10	6-2	1	111.1	85	35	8	3	33	46	2.51	149	.206	.270	28-0-2	.036	-1	126	15	0	1.0
1946	Bos A	1	0	1.000	5	2	0	0	16.1	23	20	3	0	13	10	11.02	33	.343	.450	4	.250	0	164	-12	0	-0.6
1947	Bos A	0	0	ø	1	0	0	0	2	3	1	0	0	0	1	4.50	86	.333	.333	0	ø	0	—	0	0	0.0
Total	4	9	3	.750	32	15	7-2	1	150.2	138	69	11	3	56	62	3.88	99	.240	.310	39-0-3	.051	-2	117	1	0	0.1
Butler, Adam	Adam Christopher; B8.17.1973 Fairfax VA; BL/TL/6´2˝/225; d3.31; Col William and Mary																									
1998	Atl N	0	1	.000	8	0	0	0-0	5	5	7	1	1	6-1	7	10.80	39	.278	.462	0	ø	0	—	-4	0	-0.7
Butler, Cecil	Cecil Dean "Slewfoot"; B10.23.1937 Dallas GA; BR/TR/6´4˝/(195–200); d4.23																									
1962	Mil N	2	0	1.000	9	2	1	0	31	26	13	4	0	9-1	22	2.61	145	.217	.271	8	.000	-1	92	3	65	0.1
1964	Mil N	0	0	ø	2	0	0	0	4.1	7	4	2	0	0-0	2	8.31	42	.368	.368	0	ø	0	—	-2	0	-0.1
Total	2	2	0	1.000	11	2	1	0	35.1	33	17	6	0	9-1	24	3.31	114	.237	.284	8	.000	-1	92	1	65	0.0
Butler, Charlie	Charles Thomas; B5.12.1906 Green Cove Springs FL; D5.10.1964 Brunswick GA; BR/TL/6´1.5˝/210; d5.1																									
1933	Phi N	0	0	ø	1	0	0	0	1	1	1	0	0	2	0	9.00	42	.250	.500	0	ø	0	—	0	—	0.0
Butler, Ike	Isaac Burr; B8.22.1873 Langston MI; D3.17.1948 Oakland CA; TR/6´0˝/175; d8.5																									
1902	Bal A	1	10	.091	16	14	12	0	116.1	168	103	1	2	45	13	5.34	71	.337	.394	53-0-2	.113	-3*	90	-20	—	-1.8
Butler, Bill	William Franklin; B3.12.1947 Hyattsville MD; BL/TL/6´2˝/(185–210); [DetA65 16/610]; d4.9																									
1969	KC A	9	10	.474	34	29	5-4	0-0	193.2	174	91	15	3	91-5	156	3.90	95	.240	.326	60-0-5	.050	-4	97	-2	0	-0.7
1970	KC A	4	12	.250	25	25	2-1	0-0	140.2	117	66	17	1	87-1	75	3.77	99	.229	.340	44-0-1	.045	-3	77	0	0	-0.4
1971	KC A	1	2	.333	14	6	0	0-0	44.1	45	19	6	0	18-0	32	3.45	100	.268	.339	12	.083	-1	122	0	0	-0.1
1972	Cle A	0	0	ø	6	2	0	0-0	11.2	9	3	1	0	10-0	6	1.54	211	.220	.373	1	.000	-0	122	2	0	0.1
1974	Min A	4	6	.400	26	12	2	1-0	98.2	91	47	9	1	56-2	79	4.10	91	.251	.350	0	ø	0	90	-2	0	-0.3
1975	Min A	5	4	.556	23	8	1	0-0	81.2	100	61	12	0	35-0	55	5.95	64	.301	.363	0	ø	0	152	-19	0	-1.8
1977	Min A	0	1	.000	6	4	0	0-0	21	19	17	5	1	15-0	5	6.86	58	.244	.372	0	ø	0	203	-7	0	-0.3
Total	7	23	35	.397	134	86	10-5	1-0	591.2	555	304	65	6	312-8	408	4.21	88	.250	.342	117-0-6	.051	-7	103	-28	0	-3.5
Butters, Tom	Thomas Arden; B4.8.1938 Delaware OH; BR/TR/6´2˝/195; d9.8; Col Ohio Wesleyan																									
1962	Pit N	0	0	ø	4	0	0	0	6	5	1	0	1	6-1	10	1.50	262	.238	.429	0	ø	0	—	2	0	0.1
1963	Pit N	0	0	ø	6	1	0	0	16.1	15	8	1	2	8-0	11	4.41	75	.259	.352	3	.333	0	105	-1	0	-0.1
1964	Pit N	2	2	.500	28	4	0	0	64.1	52	21	3	0	37-1	58	2.38	148	.221	.324	11-0-2	.182	0	69	7	0	0.4
1965	Pit N	0	1	.000	5	0	0	0	9	9	8	2	0	5-0	6	7.00	50	.250	.341	1	.000	-0	—	-3	38	-0.4
Total	4	2	3	.400	43	5	0	0	95.2	81	38	6	3	56-2	85	3.10	113	.231	.337	15-0-2	.200	0	75	5	38	0.0
Buttery, Frank	Frank; B5.13.1851 Silvermine CT; D12.16.1902 Norwalk CT; d4.26; ▲																									
1872	Man NA	3	2	.600	8	5	5	0	59	94	78	1	—	3	5	4.27	85	.322	.329	93	.215	-2*	187	-5	—	-0.3
Buxton, Ralph	Ralph Stanley "Buck"; B6.7.1914 Rainton SK, Can.; D1.6.1988 San Leandro CA; BR/TR/5´11.5˝/163; d9.11																									
1938	Phi A	0	1	.000	5	0	0	0	9.1	12	7	1	0	5	9	4.82	100	.324	.405	1	.000	-0	—	0	—	-0.1
1949	NY A	0	1	.000	14	0	0	2	26.2	22	13	3	0	16	14	4.05	100	.229	.339	3	.000	-0	—	0	0	0.0
Total	2	0	2	.000	19	0	0	2	36	34	20	4	0	21	23	4.25	100	.256	.357	4	.000	-1	—	0	0	-0.1
Buzhardt, John	John William; B8.17.1936 Prosperity SC; BR/TR/6´2˝/(195–200); d9.10																									
1958	Chi N	3	0	1.000	6	2	1	0	24.1	16	5	2	0	7-1	9	1.85	212	.184	.245	8	.125	-0	57	6	0	0.7
1959	Chi N	4	5	.444	31	10	1-1	0	101.1	107	64	12	1	29-4	33	4.97	79	.271	.318	29-0-2	.069	-1	109	-12	0	-1.1
1960	Phi N	5	16	.238	30	29	5	0	200.1	198	101	14	2	68-12	73	3.86	100	.259	.319	62-0-2	.161	-1*	69	-1	0	-0.3
1961	Phi N	6	18	.250	41	27	6-1	0	202.1	200	107	28	6	65-6	92	4.49	91	.263	.324	57-0-7	.105	-2	92	-6	0	-0.9
1962	Chi A	8	12	.400	28	25	8-2	0	152.1	156	75	16	4	59-3	64	4.19	93	.264	.332	51-0-4	.118	-2	91	-4	0	-0.5
1963	Chi A	9	4	.692	19	18	6-3	0	126.1	100	35	8	5	31-5	59	2.42	145	.216	.272	48-0-1	.083	-3*	101	17	30	1.5
1964	Chi A	10	8	.556	31	25	8-3	0	160	150	60	13	4	35-4	97	2.98	116	.250	.291	54-0-4	.204	2	119	9	0	1.2
1965	Chi A	13	8	.619	32	30	4-1	1	188.2	167	69	12	7	56-9	108	3.01	106	.242	.304	56-0-9	.125	0*	114	5	0	0.5
1966	Chi A	6	11	.353	33	22	5-4	1	150.1	144	74	13	4	30-4	66	3.83	83	.248	.288	43-0-1	.116	-1*	104	-11	0	-1.2
1967	Chi A	3	9	.250	28	7	0	0	88.2	100	44	11	6	37-5	33	3.96	78	.294	.370	20-0-2	.200	0	104	-7	0	-0.9
	Bal A	0	1	.000	7	1	0	0	11.2	14	6	1	0	5-1	7	4.63	68	.298	.365	1	.000	-0	111	-2	0	-0.1
	Year	3	10	.231	35	8	0	0	100.1	114	50	12	6	42-6	40	4.04	77	.295	.370	21-0-2	.190	0	105	-10	0	-1.0
	Hou N	0	0	ø	1	0	0	0	0.2	0	0	0	0	0-0	0	0.00	ø	.000	.000	0	ø	0	—	0	0	0.0
1968	Hou N	4	4	.500	39	4	0	5	83.2	73	35	0	4	35-13	37	3.12	95	.239	.319	16-0-1	.250	1	198	-3	0	-0.1
Total	11	71	96	.425	326	200	44-15	7	1490.2	1425	675	130	43	457-67	678	3.66	97	.253	.312	445-0-33	.135	-7	100	-9	30	-1.2
Byerly, Bud	Eldred William; B10.26.1920 Webster Groves MO; BR/TR/6´2.5˝/185; d9.26																									
1943	StL N	1	0	1.000	2	2	0	0	13	14	6	0	0	5	6	3.46	97	.280	.345	3	.000	-0	88	0	0	-0.1
1944	†StL N	2	2	.500	9	4	2	0	42.1	37	18	2	0	20	13	3.40	104	.228	.313	12	.167	-0	107	1	0	0.0
1945	StL N	4	5	.444	33	8	2	0	95	111	61	3	1	41	39	4.74	79	.288	.358	23-0-5	.217	1	158	-12	0	-0.9
1950	Cin N	0	1	.000	4	1	0	0	14.2	12	4	1	0	4	5	2.45	173	.218	.271	3	.000	-0	21	3	0	0.1
1951	Cin N	2	1	.667	40	0	0	0	66	69	33	6	2	25	28	3.27	125	.267	.337	6	.000	-0*	—	4	0	0.2
1952	Cin N	0	1	.000	12	2	0	1	24.2	29	15	0	0	7	14	5.11	74	.309	.356	5	.200	0	24	-4	0	-0.2
1956	Was A	2	4	.333	25	0	0	4	51.2	45	19	6	2	14-3	19	2.96	146	.243	.303	11	.091	-1	—	8	0	0.8
1957	Was A	6	6	.500	47	0	0	6	95	94	38	6	1	22-5	39	3.13	125	.264	.305	15	.067	-1	—	7	0	0.9
1958	Was A	2	0	1.000	17	0	0	1	24	34	20	4	1	11-2	13	6.75	56	.347	.411	2	.000	-0	—	-8	0	-0.7
	Bos A	1	2	.333	18	0	0	0	30.1	31	12	1	1	7-3	16	1.78	225	.272	.312	4	.000	-1	—	5	0	0.4
	Year	3	2	.600	35	0	0	1	54.1	65	32	5	2	18-5	29	3.98	99	.307	.359	6	.000	-1	—	-3	0	-0.3
1959	SF N	1	0	1.000	11	0	0	0	13	11	2	2	0	5-1	4	1.38	275	.234	.308	0	ø	0	—	4	0	0.3

YEAR	TM LG	W	L	PCT	G	GS	CG-SHO	SV-BS	IP	H	R	HR	HB	BB-IB	SO	ERA	AERA	OAV	OOB	AB-HR-SH	AVG	PB	SUP	APR	DL	PW
1960	SF N	1	0	1.000	19	0	0	2	22	32	14	3	1	6-0	13	5.32	65	.340	.379	1-0-1	.000	-0	—	-4	0	-0.3
Total	11	22	22	.500	237	17	4	14	491.2	519	242	34	9	167-14	209	3.70	105	.273	.333	85-0-6	.118	-4	112	4	0	0.5
BYNUM, MIKE Michael Alan; B3.20.1978 Tampa FL; BL/TL/6´4˝/(195–200); [SDN99 1/49]; d8.17; Col North Carolina																										
2002	SD N	1	0	1.000	14	3	0	0-0	27.1	33	16	3	3	15-2	17	5.27	74	.308	.402	8	.000	-1	207	-4	0	-0.3
2003	SD N	1	4	.200	13	5	0	0-0	36	44	35	14	1	15-0	35	8.75	46	.297	.366	10-0-1	.300	1	103	-19	0	-2.1
2004	SD N	0	1	.000	2	0	0	0-0	0.2	1	4	0	0	3-0	0	54.00	7	.333	.667	0	ø	0	—	-4	0	-0.6
Total	3	2	5	.286	29	8	0	0-0	64	78	55	17	4	33-2	52	7.73	51	.302	.387	18-0-1	.167	-0	141	-27	0	-3.0
BYRD, HARRY Harry Gladwin; B2.3.1925 Darlington SC; D5.14.1985 Darlington SC; BR/TR (BB 1955)/6´1˝/188; d4.21																										
1950	Phi A	0	0	ø	6	0	0	0	10.2	25	20	3	2	9	2	16.88	27	.481	.571	2	.000	-0	—	-14	0	-0.6
1952	Phi A	15	15	.500	37	28	15-3	2	228.1	244	100	12	7	98	116	3.31	120	.274	.351	75-0-6	.133	-3	83	13	0	1.4
1953	Phi A	11	20	.355	40	**37**	11-2	0	236.2	279	155	23	14	115	122	5.51	78	.294	.379	81-0-3	.222	-1	82	-29	0	-3.4
1954	NY A	9	7	.563	25	21	5-1	0	132.1	131	56	10	7	43	52	2.99	115	.258	.321	46-0-3	.196	1	136	4	0	0.5
1955	Bal A	3	2	.600	14	8	1-1	1	65.1	64	33	7	7	28-1	25	4.55	84	.261	.350	19-0-3	.158	-0	125	-3	0	-0.3
	Chi A	4	6	.400	25	12	1-1	1	91	85	49	10	2	30-4	44	4.65	85	.251	.313	30-0-3	.067	-3	96	-6	0	-0.9
	Year	7	8	.467	39	20	2-2	2	156.1	149	82	17	9	58-5	69	4.61	85	.255	.329	49-0-6	.102	-3	107	-8	0	-1.2
1956	Chi A	0	1	.000	3	1	0	0	4.1	9	6	0	0	4-0	0	10.38	39	.474	.542	1	.000	-0	0	-3	0	-0.6
1957	Det A	4	3	.571	37	1	0	5	59	53	23	6	2	28-4	20	3.36	115	.249	.339	8-0-2	.000	-1	208	4	0	0.3
Total	7	46	54	.460	187	108	33-8	9	827.2	890	442	71	41	355-9	381	4.35	91	.277	.355	262-0-20	.160	-8	96	-34	0	-3.6
BYRD, JEFF Jeffrey Alan; B11.11.1956 LaMesa CA; BR/TR/6´3˝/185; [TexA74 2/26]; d6.20																										
1977	Tor A	2	13	.133	17	17	1	0-0	87.1	98	68	5	0	68-1	40	6.18	69	.286	.399	0	ø	0	76	-18	0	-2.5
BYRD, PAUL Paul Gregory; B12.3.1970 Louisville KY; BR/TR/6´1˝/(184–190); [CleA91 4/112]; d7.28; Col Louisiana St.; [DL 2003 Atl N 183]																										
1995	NY N	2	0	1.000	17	0	0	0-0	22	18	6	1	1	7-1	26	2.05	197	.222	.286	1	1.000	0	—	5	0	0.4
1996	NY N	1	2	.333	38	0	0	0-2	46.2	48	22	7	0	21-4	31	4.24	95	.265	.340	2	.000	-0	—	0	69	0.0
1997	Atl N	4	4	.500	31	4	0	0-0	53	47	34	6	4	28-4	37	5.26	80	.235	.338	7-0-2	.143	-0	88	-6	0	-0.8
1998	Atl N	0	0	ø	1	0	0	0-0	2	4	3	0	0	1-0	1	13.50	31	.400	.455	0	ø	0	—	-2	0	-0.1
	Phi N	5	2	.714	8	8	2-1	0-0	55	41	16	6	0	17-1	38	2.29	189	.203	.264	18	.167	0	104	12	0	1.5
	Year	5	2	.714	9	8	2-1	0-0	57	45	19	6	0	18-1	39	2.68	161	.212	.273	18	.167	0	104	10	0	1.4
1999	Phi N☆	15	11	.577	32	32	1	0-0	199.2	205	119	34	17	70-2	106	4.60	102	.265	.337	55-0-11	.127	-1	117	-3	0	-0.4
2000	Phi N	2	9	.182	17	15	0	0-0	83	89	67	17	3	35-2	53	6.51	71	.271	.345	20-0-2	.150	0	76	-19	66	-2.0
2001	Phi N	0	1	.000	3	1	0	0-0	10	10	9	1	1	4-0	3	8.10	51	.278	.349	2-0-1	.500	0*	67	-4	0	-0.3
	KC A	6	6	.500	16	15	1	0-0	93.1	110	45	11	1	22-1	49	4.05	123	.297	.335	4-0-1	.000	-0	86	9	16	1.0
2002	KC A	17	11	.607	33	33	**7**-2	0-0	228.1	224	111	36	7	38-1	129	3.90	128	.256	.288	2	.000	-0	92	22	0	2.3
2004	†Atl N	8	7	.533	19	19	0	0-0	114.1	123	57	18	2	19-0	79	3.94	109	.270	.301	30-0-8	.200	2	113	4	76	0.6
2005	†LA A	12	11	.522	31	31	2-1	0-0	204.1	216	95	22	7	28-1	102	3.74	114	.272	.301	4	.250	0	97	11	0	1.0
2006	Cle A	10	9	.526	31	31	1	0-0	179	232	120	26	6	38-3	88	4.88	89	.308	.343	4-0-2	.250	0	137	-17	0	-1.6
Total	11	82	73	.529	277	189	14-4	0-2	1290.2	1367	704	185	49	328-20	742	4.32	105	.270	.318	149-0-27	.161	1	105	12	410	1.6
BYRDAK, TIM Timothy Christopher; B10.31.1973 Oak Lawn IL; BL/TL/5´11˝/(160–195); [KCA94 5/135]; d8.7; Col Rice																										
1998	KC A	0	0	ø	3	0	0	0-0	1.2	5	1	1	0	0-0	1	5.40	90	.556	.556	0	ø	0	—	0	0	0.0
1999	KC A	0	3	.000	33	0	0	1-3	24.2	32	24	5	1	20-2	17	7.66	66	.308	.424	2	.500	1	—	-7	0	-0.7
2000	KC A	0	1	.000	12	0	0	0-2	6.1	11	8	3	0	4-0	8	11.37	46	.367	.441	0	ø	0	—	-4	0	-0.5
2005	Bal A	0	1	.000	41	0	0	1-0	26.2	27	14	1	1	21-1	31	4.05	109	.255	.380	0	ø	0	—	1	0	0.0
2006	Bal A	1	0	1.000	16	0	0	0-0	7	14	10	2	0	8-1	2	12.86	35	.438	.550	0	ø	0	—	-6	102	-0.7
Total	5	1	5	.167	105	0	0	2-5	66.1	89	57	12	2	53-4	59	7.06	67	.317	.427	2	.500	1	—	-16	102	-1.9
BYRNE, JERRY Gerald Wilfred; B2.2.1907 Parnell MI; D8.11.1955 Lansing MI; BR/TR/6´0˝/170; d8.31; Col Michigan St.																										
1929	Chi A	0	1	.000	3	1	0	0	7.1	11	6	0	0	6	1	7.36	58	.379	.486	2	.000	-0	59	-2	—	-0.3
BYRNE, TOMMY Thomas Joseph; B12.31.1919 Baltimore MD; BL/TL/6´1˝/(182–187); d4.27; Mil 1944–45; Col Wake Forest																										
1943	NY A	2	1	.667	11	2	0	0	31.2	28	26	1	3	35	22	6.54	49	.248	.437	11-0-1	.091	-0*	105	-11	0	-1.0
1946	NY A	0	1	.000	4	1	0	0	9.1	7	8	1	1	8	5	5.79	60	.194	.356	9	.222	0*	75	-3	0	-0.2
1947	NY A	0	0	ø	4	1	0	0	4.1	5	2	0	0	6	2	4.15	85	.294	.478	0	ø	0	225	0	0	0.0
1948	NY A	8	5	.615	31	11	5-1	2	133.2	79	55	8	9	101	93	3.30	124	.172	.332	46-1-4	.326	6	123	12	0	1.6
1949	†NY A	15	7	.682	32	30	12-3	0	196	125	84	11	13	179	129	3.72	109	**.183**	.362	83-0-1	.193	1*	140	11	0	1.0
1950	NY A☆	15	9	.625	31	31	10-2	0	203.1	188	115	23	17	160	118	4.74	91	.245	.387	81-2-0	.272	7*	140	-10	0	-0.4
1951	NY A	2	1	.667	9	3	0	0	21	16	17	0	3	36	14	6.86	56	.213	.482	9-1-0	.222	1	124	-7	0	-0.8
	StL A	4	10	.286	19	17	7-2	0	122.2	104	56	5	12	114	57	3.82	115	.235	.404	57-1-2	.281	3*	64	8	0	1.2
	Year	6	11	.353	28	20	7-2	0	143.2	120	73	5	15	150	71	4.26	101	.232	.417	66-2-2	.273	4	72	3	0	0.4
1952	StL A	7	14	.333	29	24	14	0	196	182	117	16	10	112	91	4.68	84	.247	.354	84-1-0	.250	5*	90	-16	0	-1.2
1953	Chi A	2	0	1.000	6	6	0	0	16	18	18	0	0	26	4	10.13	40	.295	.506	18-1-0	.167	1*	158	-10	0	-0.9
	Was A	0	5	.000	6	5	2	0	33.2	35	17	3	1	22	22	4.28	91	.276	.387	17	.059	-1*	55	-1	0	-0.2
	Year	2	5	.286	12	11	2	0	49.2	53	35	3	1	48	26	6.16	64	.282	.430	35-1-0	.114	-0	113	-11	0	-1.1
1954	NY A	3	2	.600	5	5	4-1	0	40	36	13	1	0	19	24	2.70	127	.240	.325	19	.368	4*	149	4	0	1.0
1955	†NY A	16	5	**.762**	27	22	9-3	2	160	137	69	12	7	87-3	76	3.15	119	.237	.340	78-1-1	.205	4*	117	9	0	1.5
1956	†NY A	7	3	.700	37	8	1	6	109.2	108	50	9	2	72-5	52	3.36	115	.262	.372	52-3-2	.269	6*	129	5	0	1.0
1957	†NY A	4	6	.400	30	4	1	2	84.2	70	41	8	7	60-2	57	4.36	82	.227	.363	37-3-0	.189	4*	87	-5	0	-0.2
Total	13	85	69	.552	281	170	65-12	12	1362	1138	688	98	85	1037-10	766	4.11	97	.229	.370	601-14-11	.238	41	118	-14	0	2.4
BYSTROM, MARTY Martin Eugene; B7.26.1958 Coral Gables FL; BR/TR/6´5˝/(200–210); d9.7; Col Miami–Dade Kendall (FL) CC																										
1980	†Phi N	5	0	1.000	6	5	1-1	0-0	36	26	6	1	0	9-0	21	1.50	255	.195	.246	14	.071	-1	168	9	0	1.3
1981	Phi N	4	3	.571	9	9	1	0-0	53.2	55	21	3	1	16-1	24	3.35	109	.264	.319	17-0-1	.118	-1	105	2	0	0.2
1982	Phi N	5	6	.455	19	16	1	0-0	89	93	53	2	5	35-4	50	4.85	76	.277	.350	24-0-3	.125	-0	99	-11	64	-1.3
1983	†Phi N	6	9	.400	24	23	1-1	0-0	119.1	136	75	6	7	44-2	87	4.60	78	.285	.348	38-0-1	.237	2	107	-15	50	-1.6
1984	Phi N	4	4	.500	11	11	0	0-0	56.2	66	36	5	0	22-1	36	5.08	72	.283	.341	19-0-3	.158	-0	110	-8	0	-1.1
	NY A	2	2	.500	7	7	0	0-0	39.1	34	16	3	1	13-1	24	2.97	129	.230	.296	0	ø	0	77	3	33	0.3
1985	NY A	3	2	.600	8	8	0	0-0	41	44	29	8	1	19-0	16	5.71	71	.280	.360	0	ø	0	107	-8	106	-0.8
Total	6	29	26	.527	84	79	4-2	0-0	435	454	236	28	15	158-9	258	4.26	87	.268	.333	112-0-8	.161	-0	107	-28	253	-3.0
CABRERA, DANIEL Daniel Alberto; B5.28.1981 San Pedro de Macoris, D.R.; BR/TR/6´7˝/(230–260); d5.13																										
2004	Bal A	12	8	.600	28	27	1-1	1-0	147.2	145	85	14	2	89-2	76	5.00	93	.259	.359	4	.000	-0	116	-3	0	-0.6
2005	Bal A	10	13	.435	29	29	0	0-0	161.1	144	92	14	11	87-2	157	4.52	97	.235	.339	1	.000	-0	80	-3	20	-0.4
2006	Bal A	9	10	.474	26	26	2-1	0-0	148	130	82	11	5	104-1	157	4.74	95	.241	.364	1-0-1	.000	-0	114	-3	21	-0.4
Total	3	31	31	.500	83	82	3-2	1-0	457	419	259	39	18	280-5	390	4.75	95	.245	.353	6-0-1	.000	-1	103	-9	41	-1.4
CABRERA, FERNANDO Fernando Jose; B11.16.1981 Toa Baja, PR; BR/TR/6´4˝/(170–225); [CleA99 10/317]; d8.20																										
2004	Cle A	0	0	ø	4	0	0	0-0	5.1	3	3	0	0	1-0	6	3.38	129	.167	.200	0	ø	0	—	0	0	0.0
2005	Cle A	2	1	.667	15	0	0	0-0	30.2	24	7	1	0	11-1	29	1.47	284	.212	.282	0	ø	0	—	9	0	0.8
2006	Cle A	3	3	.500	51	0	0	0-4	60.2	53	36	12	1	32-2	71	5.19	83	.243	.337	0	ø	0	—	-5	16	-0.4
Total	3	5	4	.556	70	0	0	0-4	96.2	80	46	13	1	44-3	106	3.91	109	.229	.313	0	ø	0	—	4	16	0.4
CABRERA, JOSE Jose Alberto; B3.24.1972 Santiago, D.R.; BR/TR/6´0˝/(160–180); d7.15																										
1997	Hou N	0	0	ø	12	0	0	0-1	15.1	6	2	1	0	6-0	18	1.17	341	.125	.211	2	.000	-0	—	5	0	0.2
1998	Hou N	0	0	ø	3	0	0	0-0	4.1	7	4	0	0	1-1	1	8.31	49	.389	.421	0	ø	0	—	-2	176	-0.1
1999	†Hou N	4	0	1.000	26	0	0	0-1	29.1	21	7	3	0	9-2	28	2.15	206	.196	.252	0	ø	0	—	8	0	0.9
2000	Hou N	2	3	.400	52	0	0	2-1	59.1	74	40	10	3	17-2	41	5.92	83	.308	.357	1	.000	-0	—	-5	0	-0.4
2001	Atl N	7	4	.636	55	0	0	2-6	59.1	52	24	5	2	25-4	43	2.88	150	.239	.315	1	.000	-0	—	8	0	1.4
2002	Mil N	6	10	.375	50	11	0	0-1	103.1	131	84	23	9	36-9	61	6.79	61	.314	.378	19-0-1	.105	-1	106	-30	0	-4.2
Total	6	19	17	.528	198	11	0	4-10	271	291	161	42	14	94-18	192	4.95	88	.278	.340	23-0-1	.087	-1	106	-16	176	-2.2
CADARET, GREG Gregory James; B2.27.1962 Detroit MI; BL/TL/6´3˝/(205–230); [OakA83 11/267]; d7.5; Col Grand Valley St.																										
1987	Oak A	6	2	.750	29	0	0	0-1	39.2	37	22	6	1	24-1	30	4.54	92	.252	.356	0	ø	0	—	-2	0	-0.2
1988	†Oak A	5	2	.714	58	0	0	3-1	71.2	60	26	2	1	36-1	64	2.89	132	.226	.317	0	ø	0	—	7	0	0.7
1989	Oak A	0	0	ø	26	0	0	0-1	27.2	21	9	0	0	19-3	14	2.28	163	.214	.336	0	ø	0	—	4	0	0.2

YEAR	TM LG	W	L	PCT	G	GS	CG-SHO	SV-BS	IP	H	R	HR	HB	BB-IB	SO	ERA	AERA	OAV	OOB	AB-HR-SH	AVG	PB	SUP	APR	DL	PW
	NY A	5	5	.500	20	13	3-1	0-1	92.1	109	53	7	2	38-1	66	4.58	85	.298	.364	0	ø	0	95	-7	0	-0.7
	Year	5	5	.500	46	13	3-1	0-2	120	130	62	7	2	57-4	80	4.05	95	.280	.358	0	ø	0	96	-4	0	-0.5
1990	NY A	5	4	.556	54	6	0	3-1	121.1	120	62	8	1	64-5	80	4.15	96	.268	.359	0	ø	0	84	-2	0	0.0
1991	NY A	8	6	.571	68	5	0	3-4	121.2	110	52	8	2	59-6	105	3.62	115	.246	.335	0	ø	0	167	8	0	0.9
1992	NY A	4	8	.333	46	11	1-1	1-2	103.2	104	53	12	2	74-7	73	4.25	93	.267	.385	0	ø	0	107	-3	0	-0.3
1993	Cin N	2	1	.667	34	0	0	1-0	32.2	40	19	3	1	23-5	23	4.96	81	.305	.413	2	.000	-0	—	-3	0	-0.3
	KC A	1	1	.500	13	0	0	0-0	15.1	14	5	0	1	7-0	2	2.93	157	.264	.361	0	ø	0	—	3	0	0.3
1994	Tor A	0	1	.000	21	0	0	0-0	20	24	15	4	0	17-2	15	5.85	83	.289	.410	0	ø	0	—	-3	0	-0.1
	Det A	1	0	1.000	17	0	0	2-0	20	17	9	0	0	16-3	14	3.60	137	.227	.363	0	ø	0	—	3	0	0.2
	Year	1	1	.500	38	0	0	2-0	40	41	24	4	0	33-5	29	4.72	104	.259	.387	0	ø	0	—	1	0	0.1
1997	Ana A	0	0	ø	15	0	0	0-0	13.2	11	5	1	2	8-2	11	3.29	140	.220	.350	0	ø	0	—	2	0	0.1
1998	Ana A	1	2	.333	39	0	0	1-1	37	38	17	6	3	15-0	37	4.14	115	.257	.337	0	ø	0	—	3	0	0.2
	Tex A	0	0	ø	11	0	0	0-0	7.2	11	4	1	0	3-0	5	4.70	104	.355	.400	0	ø	0	—	0	0	0.0
	Year	1	2	.333	50	0	0	1-1	44.2	49	21	7	3	18-0	42	4.23	113	.274	.348	0	ø	0	—	4	0	0.2
Total	10	38	32	.543	451	35	4-2	14-12	724.1	716	351	58	16	403-36	539	3.99	103	.262	.358	2	.000	-0	104	10	0	1.0
CADORE, LEON Leon Joseph "Caddy"; B11.20.1890 Chicago IL; D3.16.1958 Spokane WA; BR/TR/6´1˝/190; d4.28; Mil 1918; Col Gonzaga																										
1915	Bro N	0	2	.000	7	2	1	0	21	28	15	0	2	8	12	5.57	50	.337	.409	6	.000	-1	40	-5	—	-0.6
1916	Bro N	0	0	ø	1	0	0	0	6	10	4	0	0	0	2	4.50	60	.370	.370	3	.000	-0	—	-1	—	-0.1
1917	Bro N	13	13	.500	37	30	21-1	3	264	231	86	3	7	63	115	2.45	114	.241	.292	92-0-5	.261	5	92	12	—	1.7
1918	Bro N	1	0	1.000	2	2	1-1	0	17	6	1	0	1	2	5	0.53	526	.115	.164	4	.000	-0	54	4	—	0.2
1919	Bro N	14	12	.538	35	27	16-3	0	250.2	228	80	5	6	39	94	2.37	125	.245	.280	87	.161	-3	94	19	—	1.5
1920	†Bro N	15	14	.517	35	30	16-4	0	254.1	256	91	4	3	56	79	2.62	122	.270	.313	91-2-4	.220	2	106	17	—	2.3
1921	Bro N	13	14	.481	35	30	12-1	0	211.2	243	112	17	6	46	79	4.17	93	.292	.334	75-1-3	.187	-1	101	-4	—	-0.6
1922	Bro N	8	15	.348	29	21	13	0	190.1	224	115	13	1	57	49	4.35	94	.299	.349	71-2-3	.268	4	88	-8	—	-0.5
1923	Bro N	4	1	.800	8	4	3	0	36	39	14	2	0	13	5	3.25	119	.291	.354	13	.077	-1*	106	4	—	0.3
	Chi A	0	1	.000	1	1	0	0	2.1	6	7	0	0	2	3	23.14	17	.500	.571	0	ø	0	42	-5	—	-0.7
1924	NY N	0	0	ø	2	0	0	0	4	2	0	0	0	3	2	0.00	ø	.154	.313	0	ø	0	—	2	—	0.1
Total	10	68	72	.486	192	147	83-10	3	1257.1	1273	525	44	26	289	445	3.14	106	.269	.314	442-5-15	.208	5	96	35	—	3.6
CADY, CHARLIE Charles B.; B12.1865 Chicago IL; D6.7.1909 Kankakee IL; 5´11˝/180; d9.5; ▲																										
1883	Cle N	0	1	.000	1	1	1	0	8	13	13	0	—	4	5	7.88	40	.361	.425	11	.000	-1*	17	-4	—	-0.4
1884	CP U	3	1	.750	4	4	4	0	35	37	25	0	—	13	15	2.83	86	.253	.314	20	.100	-1*	158	-2	—	-0.3
Total	2	3	2	.600	5	5	5	0	43	50	38	0	—	17	20	3.77	68	.275	.337	31	.065	-2	129	-6	—	-0.7
CAHILL, JOHN John Patrick Parnell "Patsy"; B4.30.1865 San Francisco CA; D10.31.1901 Pleasanton CA; BR/TR/5´7.5˝/168; d5.31; ▲																										
1884	Col AA	1	0	1.000	2	1	1	0	16	15	15	0	3	4	1	5.06	60	.211	.282	210	.219	0*	299	-4	—	-0.2
1886	StL N	1	0	1.000	2	0	0	0	12	11	5	0	—	3	2	3.00	107	.268	.318	463-1	.199	-0*	—	1	—	0.1
1887	Ind N	0	2	.000	6	1	1	0	22	40	38	3	2	19	5	14.32	29	.430	.535	263	.205	-1*	47	-19	—	-1.3
Total	3	2	2	.500	10	2	2	0	50	66	58	3	5	26	8	8.64	41	.322	.411	936-1	.205	-1	159	-22	—	-1.4
CAIN, LES Leslie; B1.13.1948 San Luis Obispo CA; BL/TL/6´1˝/(190–200); [DetA66 4/74]; d4.28																										
1968	Det A	1	0	1.000	8	4	0	0	24	25	9	1	0	20-1	13	3.00	100	.269	.398	7	.143	0	137	0	0	0.0
1970	Det A	12	7	.632	29	29	5	0-0	180.2	167	92	15	7	98-1	156	3.84	98	.247	.346	68-1-3	.162	0	115	-4	0	-0.4
1971	Det A	10	9	.526	26	26	3-1	0-0	144.2	121	77	14	6	91-1	118	4.35	83	.228	.346	55-1-2	.145	-0*	116	-12	0	-1.5
1972	Det A	0	3	.000	5	5	0	0-0	23.2	18	12	2	0	16-0	16	3.80	83	.209	.330	7-0-1	.143	-0	73	-2	29	-0.3
Total	4	23	19	.548	68	64	8-1	0-0	373	331	190	32	13	225-3	303	3.98	91	.239	.349	137-2-6	.153	-0	113	-18	29	-2.2
CAIN, MATT Matthew Thomas; B10.1.1984 Dothan AL; BR/TR/6´3˝/230; [SFN02 1/15]; d8.29																										
2005	SF N	2	1	.667	7	7	1	0-0	46.1	24	12	4	0	19-1	30	2.33	182	.151	.240	15-0-1	.067	-1	73	10	0	0.5
2006	SF N	13	12	.520	32	31	1-1	0-0	190.2	157	93	18	6	87-1	179	4.15	107	.222	.310	57-0-8	.140	-0	94	7	0	0.7
Total	2	15	13	.536	39	38	2-1	0-0	237	181	105	22	6	106-2	209	3.80	116	.209	.297	72-0-9	.125	-1	90	17	0	1.2
CAIN, SUGAR Merritt Patrick; B4.5.1907 Macon GA; D4.3.1975 Atlanta GA; BL/TR (BB 1932–33)/5´11˝/190; d4.15																										
1932	Phi A	3	4	.429	10	6	3	0	45	42	27	1	0	28	24	5.00	90	.256	.365	12	.250	1	75	-2	—	-0.2
1933	Phi A	13	12	.520	38	32	16-1	1	218	244	132	18	3	137	43	4.25	101	.280	.379	80-0-4	.200	-1*	109	-3	—	-0.4
1934	Phi A	9	17	.346	36	32	15	0	230.2	235	128	15	3	128	66	4.41	99	.266	.360	82-0-5	.159	-3	97	-1	—	-0.4
1935	Phi A	0	5	.000	6	5	0	0	26	39	22	1	0	19	5	6.58	69	.382	.479	8	.000	-1	53	-6	—	-1.0
	StL A	9	8	.529	31	24	8	0	167.2	197	112	7	4	104	68	5.26	91	.290	.388	57-0-3	.193	-2	107	-8	—	-1.0
	Year	9	13	.409	37	29	8	0	193.2	236	134	8	4	123	73	5.44	88	.302	.400	65-0-3	.169	-4	98	-14	—	-2.0
1936	StL A	1	1	.500	4	3	1	0	16.1	20	13	0	0	9	8	6.61	81	.286	.367	7	.286	0	147	-2	—	-0.2
	Chi A	14	10	.583	30	26	14-1	0	195.1	228	112	18	5	75	42	4.75	110	.293	.359	68-0-4	.103	-4*	97	12	—	0.6
	Year	15	11	.577	34	29	15-1	0	211.2	248	125	18	5	84	50	4.89	107	.292	.360	75-0-4	.120	-4	102	11	—	0.4
1937	Chi A	4	2	.667	18	6	1	0	68.2	88	48	7	0	51	17	6.16	75	.325	.432	22-0-2	.182	-1	133	-9	—	-0.7
1938	Chi A	0	1	.000	5	3	0	0	19.2	26	17	0	0	18	6	4.58	107	.321	.444	8	.000	-1	78	-1	—	-0.2
Total	7	53	60	.469	178	137	58-2	1	987.1	1119	611	67	15	569	279	4.83	96	.287	.380	344-0-18	.163	-13	101	-20	—	-3.5
CAIN, BOB Robert Max "Sugar"; B10.16.1924 Longford KS; D4.8.1997 Cleveland OH; BL/TL/6´0˝/165; d9.18																										
1949	Chi A	0	0	ø	6	0	0	1	11	7	3	0	0	5	5	2.45	170	.179	.273	3	.000	-0	—	2	0	0.0
1950	Chi A	9	12	.429	34	23	11-1	2	171.2	153	80	12	5	109	77	3.93	114	.244	.361	61-0-3	.197	-0*	93	13	0	1.3
1951	Chi A	1	2	.333	4	4	1	0	26.1	25	14	3	3	13	3	3.76	107	.248	.350	9	.333	1	88	0	0	0.1
	Det A	11	10	.524	35	22	6-1	2	149.1	135	88	13	11	82	58	4.70	89	.239	.347	53-0-2	.245	2	120	-9	0	-0.9
	Year	12	12	.500	39	26	7-1	2	175.2	160	102	16	14	95	61	4.56	91	.241	.348	62-0-2	.258	3	115	-8	0	-0.8
1952	StL A	12	10	.545	29	27	8-1	2	170	169	79	15	2	62	70	4.13	95	.264	.331	58-0-5	.138	-1*	97	0	0	-0.2
1953	StL A	4	10	.286	32	13	1	1	99.2	129	74	8	1	45	36	6.23	67	.310	.379	30	.200	0*	106	-20	0	-2.5
Total	5	37	44	.457	140	89	27-3	8	628	618	338	51	22	316	249	4.50	93	.259	.351	214-0-10	.196	0	102	-14	0	-2.2
CAIRNCROSS, CAMERON Cameron; B5.11.1972 Cairns, Queensland, Australia; BL/TL/6´0˝/195; d7.20; [DL 2001 Cle A 190]																										
2000	Cle A	1	0	1.000	15	0	0	0-0	9.1	11	4	1	0	3-1	8	3.86	130	.306	.350	0	ø	0	—	1	0	0.1
CALDWELL, CHARLIE Charles William "Chuck"; B8.2.1901 Bristol VA; D11.1.1957 Princeton NJ; BR/TR/5´10˝/180; d7.7; Col Princeton																										
1925	NY A	0	0	ø	3	0	0	0	2.2	7	6	0	0	3	1	16.88	25	.467	.556	1	.000	-0	—	-4	—	-0.2
CALDWELL, EARL Earl Welton "Teach"; B4.9.1905 Sparks TX; D9.15.1981 Mission TX; BR/TR/6´1˝/178; d9.8																										
1928	Phi N	1	4	.200	5	5	1-1	0	34.2	46	23	5	0	17	6	5.71	75	.348	.423	9-0-1	.111	-0	44	-4	—	-0.5
1935	StL A	3	2	.600	6	5	2-1	0	36.2	34	16	2	0	17	5	3.68	130	.245	.327	11-0-1	.182	-0	65	5	—	0.6
1936	StL A	7	16	.304	41	25	10-2	2	189	252	146	15	15	83	59	6.00	90	.319	.394	58-1-4	.190	-1	79	-13	—	-1.4
1937	StL A	0	0	ø	9	2	0	0	29	39	22	3	2	13	8	6.83	71	.317	.391	9-0-1	.222	0	99	-5	—	-0.2
1945	Chi A	6	7	.462	27	11	5-1	4	105.1	108	50	8	3	37	45	3.59	92	.265	.331	37-0-3	.216	-0	110	-4	0	-0.3
1946	Chi A	13	4	.765	39	0	0	8	90.2	60	28	2	1	29	42	2.08	164	.186	.255	18-0-2	.167	1	—	**13**	0	2.8
1947	Chi A	1	4	.200	40	0	0	8	54.1	53	23	4	1	30	22	3.64	100	.261	.359	7-0-1	.000	-1	—	1	0	0.0
1948	Chi A	1	5	.167	25	1	0	3	39	53	25	3	2	22	10	5.31	80	.335	.423	5	.000	-0	42	-4	0	-0.7
	Bos A	1	1	.500	8	0	0	0	9	11	14	2	1	11	5	13.00	34	.333	.511	3	.333	0	—	-8	0	-1.5
	Year	2	6	.250	33	1	0	3	48	64	39	5	3	33	15	6.75	63	.335	.441	8	.125	-0	42	-12	0	-2.2
Total	8	33	43	.434	200	49	18-5	25	587.2	656	347	44	25	259	202	4.69	92	.284	.363	157-1-13	.178	-2	87	-19	0	-1.2
CALDWELL, RALPH Ralph Grant "Lefty"; B1.18.1884 Philadelphia PA; D8.5.1969 W.Trenton NJ; BL/TL/5´9˝/155; d9.10; Col Penn																										
1904	Phi N	2	2	.500	6	5	5	0	41	40	29	1	2	15	30	4.17	64	.242	.313	18	.444	3	154	-7	—	-0.3
1905	Phi N	1	3	.250	7	2	1	1	34	44	25	1	3	7	29	4.24	69	.321	.367	15	.000	-2	136	-6	—	-0.9
Total	2	3	5	.375	13	7	6	1	75	84	54	2	5	22	59	4.20	66	.278	.337	33	.242	1	148	-13	—	-1.2
CALDWELL, MIKE Ralph Michael; B1.22.1949 Tarboro NC; BR/TL/6´0˝/185; [SDN71 12/271]; d9.4; Col North Carolina St.																										
1971	SD N	1	0	1.000	6	0	0	0-0	6.2	4	0	0	0	3-3	5	0.00	ø	.174	.269	1	1.000	1	—	3	0	0.5
1972	SD N	7	11	.389	42	20	4-2	2-3	163.2	183	92	10	4	49-14	102	4.01	83	.282	.335	50-0-4	.140	-1	108	-18	0	-1.8
1973	SD N	5	14	.263	55	13	3-1	10-2	149	146	77	8	2	53-10	86	3.74	94	.260	.325	35-0-3	.143	-1*	75	-6	0	-0.8
1974	SF N	14	5	.737	31	27	6-2	0-1	189.1	176	80	17	4	63-1	83	2.95	129	.249	.312	63-0-7	.143	-2	120	15	0	1.4

YEAR	TM LG	W	L	PCT	G	GS	CG-SHO	SV-BS	IP	H	R	HR	HB	BB-IB	SO	ERA	AERA	OAV	OOB	AB-HR-SH	AVG	PB	SUP	APR	DL	PW
1975	SF N	7	13	.350	38	21	4	1-0	163.1	194	102	16	5	48-7	57	4.79	79	.296	.346	44-0-7	.159	-0	109	-19	0	-2.0
1976	SF N	1	7	.125	50	9	0	2-0	107.1	145	74	5	2	20-2	55	4.86	75	.324	.354	19-0-1	.158	-0	102	-16	0	-1.1
1977	Cin N	0	0	ø	14	0	0	1-0	24.2	25	11	1	0	8-1	11	4.01	98	.260	.317	4	.500	2	—	0	0	0.2
	Mil A	5	8	.385	21	12	2	0-0	94.1	101	58	6	2	36-7	38	4.58	90	.271	.337	0	ø	0	88	-7	0	-0.7
1978	Mil A	22	9	.710	37	34	**23**-6	1-0	293.1	258	90	14	7	54-3	131	2.36	161	.234	.273	0	ø	0	101	45	0	4.8
1979	Mil A	16	6	**.727**	30	30	16-4	0-0	235	252	96	18	4	39-2	89	3.29	128	.278	.309	0	ø	0	114	24	0	2.3
1980	Mil A	13	11	.542	34	33	11-2	1-0	225.1	248	112	29	2	56-2	74	4.03	97	.285	.328	0	ø	0	133	-2	0	-0.2
1981	†Mil A	11	9	.550	24	23	3	0-0	144.1	151	70	18	1	38-4	41	3.93	88	.272	.317	0	ø	0	120	-9	0	-1.1
1982	†Mil A	17	13	.567	35	34	12-3	0-1	258	269	119	30	0	58-3	75	3.91	98	.271	.310	0	ø	0	114	0	0	0.1
1983	Mil A	12	11	.522	32	32	10-2	0-0	228.1	269	125	35	1	51-1	58	4.53	84	.296	.332	0	ø	0	119	-20	0	-1.8
1984	Mil A	6	13	.316	26	19	4-1	0-0	126	160	76	11	1	21-2	34	4.64	84	.314	.338	0	ø	0	85	-12	27	-1.5
Total	14	137	130	.513	475	307	98-23	18-7	2408.2	2581	1182	218	35	597-62	939	3.81	100	.276	.320	216-0-22	.157	-2	111	-22	27	-1.7
Caldwell, Ray	Raymond Benjamin "Rube","Sum"; B4.26.1888 Corydon PA; D8.17.1967 Salamanca NY; BL/TR/6´2˝/190; d9.9; ▲																									
1910	NY A	1	0	1.000	6	2	1	1	19.1	19	8	1	0	9	17	3.72	71	.260	.341	6	.000	-1	126	-1	—	-0.2
1911	NY A	14	14	.500	41	26	19-1	1	255	240	115	7	13	79	145	3.35	107	.260	.327	147-0-1	.272	3*	83	11	—	1.3
1912	NY A	8	16	.333	30	26	13-3	0	183.1	196	111	1	6	67	95	4.47	80	.277	.344	76-0-1	.237	1*	92	-11	—	-1.1
1913	NY A	9	8	.529	27	16	15-2	1	164.1	131	59	5	9	60	87	2.41	124	.221	.303	97-0-2	.289	3*	113	11	—	1.7
1914	NY A	18	9	.667	31	23	22-5	0	213	153	53	5	4	51	92	1.94	142	.205	.260	113-0-5	.195	1*	99	21	—	3.0
1915	NY A	19	16	.543	36	35	31-3	0	305	266	115	6	5	107	130	2.89	101	.244	.315	144-4-2	.243	8*	108	4	—	1.2
1916	NY A	5	12	.294	21	18	14-1	0	165.2	142	62	6	8	65	76	2.99	97	.243	.327	93	.204	-0*	61	1	—	0.1
1917	NY A	13	16	.448	32	29	21-1	0	236	199	92	8	6	76	102	2.86	94	.234	.302	124-2-0	.258	6*	93	-2	—	0.8
1918	NY A	9	8	.529	24	21	14-1	1	176.2	173	69	2	1	62	59	3.06	93	.261	.325	151-1-4	.291	4*	114	-3	—	0.3
1919	Bos A	7	4	.636	18	12	6-1	0	86.1	92	49	1	3	31	23	3.96	76	.279	.346	48-0-3	.271	1*	115	-11	—	-1.1
	Cle A	5	1	.833	6	6	4-1	0	52.2	33	13	1	2	19	24	1.71	196	.181	.266	23	.348	2	105	9	—	1.4
	Year	12	5	.706	24	18	10-2	0	139	125	62	2	5	50	47	3.11	101	.244	.317	71-0-3	.296	4	111	0	—	0.3
1920	†Cle A	20	10	.667	34	33	20-1	0	237.2	286	135	9	4	63	80	3.86	98	.303	.350	89-0-5	.213	1*	137	-6	—	-0.7
1921	Cle A	6	6	.500	37	12	4-1	4	147	159	91	7	2	49	76	4.90	87	.275	.333	53-1-1	.208	0*	144	-9	—	-0.6
Total	12	134	120	.528	343	259	184-21	8	2242	2089	972	59	63	738	1006	3.22	99	.253	.319	1164-8-24	.248	31	105	14	—	6.1
Calero, Kiko	Enrique Nomar; B1.9.1975 Santurce, PR; BR/TR/6´1˝/(180–200); [KCA96 27/799]; d4.2; Col St. Thomas (FL)																									
2003	StL N	1	1	.500	26	1	0	1-3	38.1	29	12	5	1	20-2	51	2.82	146	.212	.311	4	.250	0	91	6	92	0.3
2004	†StL N	3	1	.750	41	0	0	2-1	45.1	27	14	5	1	10-1	47	2.78	153	.176	.232	1	.000	-0	—	8	28	0.7
2005	Oak A	4	1	.800	58	0	0	1-1	55.2	45	20	6	1	18-2	52	3.23	135	.216	.281	1	.000	-0	—	8	27	0.6
2006	†Oak A	3	2	.600	70	0	0	2-3	58	50	22	4	0	24-3	67	3.41	133	.231	.307	0	ø	0	—	8	0	0.6
Total	4	11	5	.688	195	1	0	6-8	197.1	151	68	20	3	72-8	217	3.10	140	.211	.285	6	.167	-0	91	30	147	2.2
Calhoun, Jeff	Jeffrey Wilton; B4.11.1958 LaGrange GA; BL/TL/6´2˝/190; [HouN80 3/69]; d9.2; Col U. of Mississippi																									
1984	Hou N	0	1	.000	9	0	0	0-0	15.1	5	3	0	0	2-2	11	1.17	285	.100	.135	0	ø	0	—	4	0	0.2
1985	Hou N	2	5	.286	44	0	0	4-3	63.2	56	21	2	0	24-4	47	2.54	137	.243	.313	5	.000	-0	—	7	15	0.8
1986	†Hou N	1	0	1.000	20	0	0	0-0	26.2	28	16	3	0	12-1	14	3.71	97	.264	.339	0	ø	0	—	-2	0	-0.1
1987	Phi N	3	1	.750	42	0	0	1-0	42.2	25	13	1	1	26-8	31	1.48	291	.168	.292	1	.000	-0	—	10	26	1.0
1988	Phi N	0	0	ø	3	0	0	0-1	2.1	6	4	2	0	1-0	1	15.43	23	.462	.500	0	ø	0	—	-3	62	-0.1
Total	5	6	7	.462	118	0	0	5-4	150.2	120	57	8	1	65-15	104	2.51	148	.219	.301	6	.000	-0	—	16	103	1.8
Cali, Carmen	Carmen S.; B11.4.1978 Cleveland OH; BL/TL/5´10˝/185; [StLN00 10/293]; d9.8; Col Florida Atlantic																									
2004	StL N	0	0	ø	10	0	0	0-0	7.1	13	7	1	0	6-1	8	8.59	50	.394	.475	0	ø	0	—	-3	0	-0.2
2005	StL N	0	0	ø	6	0	0	0-0	6	10	8	3	0	6-1	5	10.50	40	.385	.485	0	ø	0	—	-4	0	-0.2
Total	2	0	0	ø	16	0	0	0-0	13.1	23	15	4	0	12-2	13	9.45	45	.390	.479	0	ø	0	—	-7	0	-0.4
Caligiuri, Fred	Frederick John; B10.22.1918 W.Hickory PA; BR/TR/6´0˝/190; d9.3; Mil 1943–46																									
1941	Phi A	2	2	.500	5	5	4	0	43	45	22	2	0	14	7	2.93	143	.257	.312	20-0-1	.200	1	107	3	0	0.3
1942	Phi A	0	3	.000	13	2	0	1	36.2	45	27	2	2	18	20	6.38	59	.300	.382	12	.083	-0	79	-9	0	-0.7
Total	2	2	5	.286	18	7	4	1	79.2	90	49	4	2	32	27	4.52	89	.277	.345	32-0-1	.156	1	101	-6	0	-0.4
Calihan, Will	William T. (b William T. Callahan); B5.1868 Oswego NY; D12.20.1917 Rochester NY; 5´8˝/150; d4.17																									
1890	Roc AA	18	15	.545	37	36	31	0	296.1	276	170	4	16	125	127	3.28	109	.239	.322	159-1	.145	-3*	96	9	—	0.6
1891	Phi AA	6	6	.500	13	11	11	0	112	151	103	7	12	47	28	6.43	59	.312	.387	56	.196	-1*	97	-28	—	-2.2
Total	2	24	21	.533	50	47	42	0	408.1	427	273	11	28	172	155	4.14	88	.261	.341	215-1	.158	-4	96	-19	—	-1.6
Callahan, Ben	Benjamin Franklin; B5.19.1957 Mt.Airy NC; BR/TR/6´7˝/230; [NYA80 31/742]; d6.22; Col Catawba																									
1983	Oak A	1	2	.333	4	2	0	0-0	9.1	18	16	0	0	5-1	2	12.54	31	.400	.451	0	ø	0	140	-10	0	-1.6
Callahan, Nixey	James Joseph; B3.18.1874 Fitchburg MA; D10.4.1934 Boston MA; BR/TR/5´10.5˝/180; d5.12; M7; ▲																									
1894	Phi N	1	2	.333	9	2	1	2	33.2	64	52	3	5	17	9	9.89	52	.398	.470	21	.238	-1	76	-19	—	-1.3
1897	Chi N	12	9	.571	23	22	21-1	0	189.2	221	111	6	8	55	52	4.03	111	.289	.343	360-3-8	.292	3*	108	13	—	1.5
1898	Chi N	20	10	.667	31	31	30-2	0	274.1	267	137	2	10	71	73	2.46	146	.253	.307	164-0-4	.262	4*	119	29	—	3.3
1899	Chi N	21	12	.636	35	34	33-3	0	294.1	327	155	5	24	76	77	3.06	123	.281	.338	150-0-5	.260	4*	92	22	—	2.8
1900	Chi N	13	16	.448	32	32	32-2	0	285.1	347	195	5	22	74	77	3.82	94	.299	.353	115-0-5	.235	2	104	-6	—	0.0
1901	Chi A	15	8	.652	27	22	20-1	0	215.1	195	94	4	9	50	70	2.42	144	.239	.290	118-1-4	.331	8*	100	25	—	3.7
1902	Chi A	16	14	.533	35	31	29-2	0	282.1	287	150	8	11	89	75	3.60	94	.264	.326	218-0-13	.234	3*	114	-9	—	-0.2
1903	Chi A	1	2	.333	3	3	3	0	28	40	24	0	1	5	12	4.50	62	.333	.365	439-2-11	.292	1*	161	-7	—	-0.5
Total	8	99	73	.576	195	177	169-11	2	1603	1748	918	33	90	437	445	3.39	109	.276	.332	1585-6-50	.276	25	106	48	—	9.3
Callahan, John	John W.; B Moberly MO; d9.3																									
1898	StL N	0	2	.000	2	2	1	0	8.1	18	20	2	2	7	2	16.20	23	.429	.529	4	.000	-1	56	-11	—	-1.4
Callahan, Joe	Joseph Thomas; B10.8.1916 E.Boston MA; D5.24.1949 S.Boston MA; BR/TR/6´2˝/170; d9.13; Col Northeastern																									
1939	Bos N	1	0	1.000	4	1	1	0	17.1	17	6	0	1	3	8	3.12	119	.250	.292	4	.000	-0	71	2	—	0.1
1940	Bos N	0	2	.000	6	2	0	0	15	20	17	1	0	13	3	10.20	36	.351	.471	5	.000	-1	35	-10	—	-1.1
Total	2	1	2	.333	10	3	1	0	32.1	37	23	1	1	16	11	6.40	58	.296	.380	9	.000	-1	47	-8	—	-1.0
Callahan, Ray	Raymond James "Pat"; B8.29.1891 Ashland WI; D1.23.1973 Olympia WA; BL/TL/5´10.5˝/170; d9.12																									
1915	Cin N	0	0	ø	3	0	0	0	6.1	12	7	1	0	1	4	8.53	34	.364	.382	3	.333	0	—	-4	—	-0.2
Callaway, Mickey	Michael Christopher; B5.13.1975 Memphis TN; BR/TR/6´2˝/(190–215); [TBA96 7/214]; d6.12; Col U. of Mississippi																									
1999	TB A	1	2	.333	5	4	0	0-0	19.1	30	20	2	0	14-1	11	7.45	67	.357	.444	3	.667	1*	70	-6	17	-0.6
2001	TB A	0	0	ø	2	0	0	0-0	5	3	4	2	0	2-0	2	7.20	63	.167	.250	0	ø	0	—	-1	0	-0.1
2002	Ana A	2	1	.667	6	6	0	0-0	34.1	31	20	4	3	11-0	23	4.19	107	.235	.308	0	ø	0	127	0	0	0.0
2003	Ana A	1	4	.200	17	4	0	0-0	38.1	57	32	7	1	16-1	22	6.81	64	.345	.402	0	ø	0	148	-11	47	-1.2
	Tex A	0	3	.000	6	3	0	0-0	22.1	27	18	0	1	8-0	19	6.45	77	.314	.367	0	ø	0	56	-4	0	-0.4
	Year	1	7	.125	23	7	0	0-0	60.2	84	50	7	2	24-1	41	6.68	69	.335	.390	0	ø	0	106	-14	0	-1.6
2004	Tex A	0	1	.000	4	3	0	0-0	11.1	18	10	2	1	7-0	9	7.94	62	.367	.448	0	ø	0	119	-3	167	-0.2
Total	5	4	11	.267	40	20	0	0-0	130.2	166	104	17	6	58-2	86	6.27	74	.311	.380	3	.667	1	108	-25	231	-2.5
Calmus, Dick	Richard Lee; B1.7.1944 Los Angeles CA; BR/TR/6´4˝/(185–191); d4.22																									
1963	LA N	3	1	.750	21	1	0	0	44	32	14	3	0	16-1	25	2.66	114	.204	.277	6	.000	-1	29	3	0	0.1
1967	Chi N	0	0	ø	1	1	0	0	4.1	5	4	2	0	0-0	1	8.31	43	.278	.278	2	.500	0	99	-2	0	-0.1
Total	2	3	1	.750	22	2	0	0	48.1	37	18	5	0	16-1	26	3.17	97	.211	.277	8	.125	-0	70	1	0	0.0
Calvert, Mark	Mark; B9.29.1956 Tulsa OK; BR/TR/6´1˝/195; [SFN78 21/521]; d4.17; Col Tulsa																									
1983	SF N	1	4	.200	18	4	0	0-0	37.1	46	33	2	3	34-4	14	6.27	57	.307	.441	8-0-1	.000	-1	150	-13	0	-1.6
1984	SF N	2	4	.333	10	5	1	0-0	32	40	21	4	1	9-1	5	5.06	70	.303	.350	8	.000	-1	115	-6	15	-1.0
Total	2	3	8	.273	28	9	1	0-0	69.1	86	54	6	4	43-5	19	5.71	62	.305	.402	16-0-1	.000	-1	130	-19	15	-2.6

YEAR	TM LG	W	L	PCT	G	GS	CG-SHO	SV-BS	IP	H	R	HR	HB	BB-IB	SO	ERA	AERA	OAV	OOB	AB-HR-SH	AVG	PB	SUP	APR	DL	PW
Calvert, Paul	Paul Leo Emile; B10.6.1917 Montreal QC, Can.; D2.1.1999 Sherbrooke QC, Can.; BR/TR/6´0˝/185; d9.24																									
1942	Cle A	0	0	ø	1	0	0	0	2	0	0	0	0	2	2	0.00	ø	.000	.286	0	ø	0	—	1	0	0.0
1943	Cle A	0	0	ø	5	0	0	0	8.1	6	4	0	1	6	2	4.32	72	.200	.351	1	.000	-0	—	-1	0	-0.1
1944	Cle A	1	3	.250	35	4	0	0	77	89	48	4	0	38	31	4.56	72	.289	.367	15-0-1	.267	1	120	-12	0	-0.4
1945	Cle A	0	0	ø	1	0	0	0	1.1	3	2	0	0	1	1	13.50	24	.429	.500	0	ø	0	—	-1	0	-0.1
1949	Was A	6	17	.261	34	23	5	1	160.2	175	111	11	2	86	52	5.43	78	.279	.368	51-0-4	.137	-2*	91	-21	0	-2.6
1950	Det A	2	2	.500	32	0	0	4	51.1	71	42	7	2	25	14	6.31	74	.324	.398	7	.000	-1	—	-10	0	-0.8
1951	Det A	0	0	ø	1	0	0	0	1	1	0	0	0	0	0	0.00	ø	.250	.250	0	ø	0	—	0	0	0.0
Total	7	9	22	.290	109	27	5	5	301.2	345	207	22	5	158	102	5.31	76	.287	.373	74-0-5	.149	-2	95	-44	0	-4.0
Camacho, Ernie	Ernest Carlos; B2.1.1955 Salinas CA; BR/TR/6´1˝/180; [OakA76 S1/17]; d5.22; Col Hartnell (CA) CC																									
1980	Oak A	0	0	ø	5	0	0	0-0	11.2	20	9	2	1	5-0	9	6.94	55	.364	.426	0	ø	0	—	-4	0	-0.2
1981	Pit N	0	1	.000	7	3	0	0-0	21.2	23	13	0	0	15-1	11	4.98	73	.295	.400	4-0-1	.000	-0	89	-3	0	-0.2
1983	Cle A	0	1	.000	4	0	0	0-0	5.1	5	3	1	1	2-0	2	5.06	84	.250	.348	0	ø	0	—	0	0	-0.1
1984	Cle A	5	9	.357	69	0	0	23-10	100	83	31	6	1	37-5	48	2.43	170	.229	.300	0	ø	0	—	18	0	3.1
1985	Cle A	0	1	.000	2	0	0	0-2	3.1	4	3	0	0	1-0	2	8.10	51	.333	.333	0	ø	0	—	-1	177	-0.2
1986	Cle A	2	4	.333	51	0	0	20-10	57.1	60	26	1	2	31-6	36	4.08	103	.269	.355	0	ø	0	—	2	15	0.4
1987	Cle A	0	1	.000	15	0	0	1-3	13.2	21	14	1	3	5-1	9	9.22	50	.350	.426	0	ø	0	—	-6	0	-0.4
1988	Hou N	0	3	.000	13	0	0	1-0	17.2	25	15	1	0	12-2	13	7.64	44	.352	.446	1	.000	-0	—	-8	0	-1.3
1989	SF N	3	0	1.000	13	0	0	0-0	16.1	10	5	1	0	11-2	14	2.76	123	.175	.309	1	.000	-0	—	1	0	0.3
1990	SF N	0	0	ø	8	0	0	0-0	10	10	4	1	0	3-0	8	3.60	102	.256	.310	0	ø	0	—	0	0	0.0
	StL N	0	0	ø	6	0	0	0-1	5.2	7	6	2	0	6-1	7	7.94	48	.318	.433	0	ø	0	—	-3	0	-0.1
	Year	0	0	ø	14	0	0	0-1	15.2	17	10	3	0	9-1	15	5.17	72	.279	.361	0	ø	0	—	-3	0	-0.1
Total	10	10	20	.333	193	3	0	45-26	262.2	268	129	16	8	128-18	159	4.21	95	.268	.351	6-0-1	.000	-1	89	-4	192	1.3
Cambria, Fred	Frederick Dennis; B1.22.1948 Cambria Heights NY; BR/TR/6´2˝/195; [PitN69 3/58]; d8.26; Col St. Leo																									
1970	Pit N	1	2	.333	6	5	0	0-0	33.1	37	15	2	1	12-0	14	3.51	113	.272	.336	10-0-2	.200	1	95	1	0	0.2
Cammack, Eric	Eric Wade; B8.14.1975 Nederland TX; BR/TR/6´1˝/180; [NYN97 13/390]; d4.28; Col Lamar; [DL 2001 NY N 190]																									
2000	NY N	0	0	ø	8	0	0	0-0	10	7	7	1	1	10-1	9	6.30	69	.194	.375	1	1.000	1	—	-2	0	0.0
Camnitz, Harry	Henry Richardson; B10.26.1884 McKinney KY; D1.6.1951 Louisville KY; BR/TR/6´1˝/168; d9.29; b–Howie; Col Centre																									
1909	Pit N	0	0	ø	1	0	0	0	4	6	2	0	0	1	1	4.50	60	.353	.389	2	.000	-0	—	0	—	-0.1
1911	StL N	1	0	1.000	2	0	0	0	2	0	0	0	0	1	2	0.00	ø	.000	.143	0	ø	0	—	1	—	0.2
Total	2	1	0	1.000	3	0	0	0	6	6	2	0	0	2	3	3.00	98	.261	.320	2	.000	-0	—	1	—	0.1
Camnitz, Howie	Samuel Howard "Red"; B8.22.1881 Covington KY; D3.2.1960 Louisville KY; BR/TR/5´9˝/169; d4.22; b–Harry; Col Centre																									
1904	Pit N	1	4	.200	10	2	2	0	49	48	39	0	3	20	21	4.22	65	.259	.341	16	.063	-1	50	-11	—	-1.2
1906	Pit N	1	0	1.000	2	1	1-1	0	9	6	2	0	0	5	5	2.00	134	.188	.297	3	.000	-0	27	1	—	0.0
1907	Pit N	13	8	.619	31	19	15-4	1	180	135	65	0	3	59	85	2.15	113	.211	.281	60-0-3	.050	-5	103	5	—	0.0
1908	Pit N	16	9	.640	38	26	17-3	2	236.2	182	76	6	5	69	118	1.56	148	.210	.272	72-0-6	.083	-3	98	13	—	1.1
1909	†Pit N	25	6	**.806**	41	30	20-6	3	283	207	75	1	7	68	133	1.62	168	.211	.267	87-0-9	.138	-0	120	31	—	3.5
1910	Pit N	12	13	.480	38	31	16-1	2	260	246	110	1	12	61	120	3.22	96	.256	.308	88-1-7	.125	-3	97	1	—	-0.4
1911	Pit N	20	15	.571	40	33	18-1	1	267.2	245	112	8	4	84	139	3.13	110	.248	.309	84-0-12	.143	-3	107	12	—	0.9
1912	Pit N	22	12	.647	41	32	22-2	2	276.2	256	104	8	13	82	121	2.83	115	.251	.315	98-0-8	.235	1	119	17	—	1.8
1913	Pit N	6	17	.261	36	22	5-1	2	192.1	203	106	7	8	84	64	3.74	81	.282	.363	59	.153	-1	80	-18	—	-2.1
	Phi N	3	3	.500	9	5	1	1	49	49	25	1	2	23	21	3.67	91	.268	.356	16	.063	-1	81	-2	—	-0.4
	Year	9	20	.310	45	27	6-1	3	241.1	252	131	8	10	107	85	3.73	83	.279	.362	75	.133	-3	81	-14	—	-2.5
1914	Pit F	14	19	.424	36	34	20-1	1	262	256	132	8	8	90	82	3.23	89	.258	.324	87-0-8	.161	-4	101	-15	—	-2.4
1915	Pit F	0	0	ø	4	2	0	0	20	19	11	1	0	11	6	4.50	60	.257	.353	7	.000	-1	77	-4	—	-0.3
Total	11	133	106	.556	326	237	137-20	15	2085.1	1852	857	41	65	656	915	2.75	106	.242	.307	677-1-53	.136	-24	103	30	—	0.5
Camp, Rick	Rick Lamar; B6.10.1953 Trion GA; BR/TR/6´0˝/198; [AtlN74 7/149]; d9.15; Col West Georgia																									
1976	Atl N	0	1	.000	5	1	0	0-0	11.1	13	9	0	0	2-0	6	6.35	60	.302	.326	2	.000	-0	70	-3	0	-0.2
1977	Atl N	6	3	.667	54	0	0	10-4	78.2	89	47	6	1	47-13	51	4.00	111	.283	.373	6	.000	-1	—	1	35	0.0
1978	Atl N	2	4	.333	42	4	0	0-4	74.1	99	42	5	3	32-10	23	3.75	107	.329	.396	8-0-1	.000	-1	72	-1	0	-0.1
1980	Atl N	6	4	.600	77	0	0	22-2	108.1	92	26	3	4	29-8	33	1.91	193	.235	.291	9	.111	-0	—	21	0	2.9
1981	Atl N	9	3	.750	48	0	0	17-5	76	68	17	5	1	12-3	47	1.78	199	.239	.271	12-0-1	.000	-1	—	**15**	0	2.9
1982	†Atl N	11	13	.458	51	21	3	5-2	177.1	199	84	18	1	52-8	68	3.65	101	.291	.339	41-0-5	.024	-3	73	0	0	-0.4
1983	Atl N	10	9	.526	40	16	1	0-0	140	146	64	16	4	38-2	61	3.79	102	.270	.321	39-0-3	.077	-2	101	1	0	0.0
1984	Atl N	8	6	.571	31	21	1	0-0	148.2	134	59	11	2	63-3	69	3.27	118	.245	.324	45-0-3	.111	-2	86	10	15	0.7
1985	Atl N	4	6	.400	66	2	0	3-0	127.2	130	72	8	5	61-11	49	3.95	98	.263	.347	13-1-1	.231	1	92	-4	0	-0.3
Total	9	56	49	.533	414	65	5	57-17	942.1	970	420	72	21	336-58	407	3.37	114	.269	.333	175-1-14	.074	-8	85	40	50	5.5
Camp, Shawn	Shawn Anthony; B11.18.1975 Fairfax VA; BR/TR/6´1˝/200; [SDN97 16/500]; d4.5; Col George Mason/North Alabama																									
2004	KC A	2	2	.500	42	0	0	2-1	66.2	74	37	10	5	16-1	51	3.92	119	.285	.335	0	ø	0	—	3	0	0.2
2005	KC A	1	4	.200	29	0	0	0-2	49	69	40	4	4	13-3	28	6.43	68	.332	.377	0	ø	0	—	-12	0	-1.1
2006	TB A	7	4	.636	75	0	0	4-2	75	93	43	9	7	19-3	53	4.68	100	.313	.365	0	ø	0	—	0	0	0.0
Total	3	10	10	.500	146	0	0	6-5	190.2	236	120	23	16	48-7	132	4.86	94	.308	.358	0	ø	0	—	-9	0	-0.9
Camp, Kid	Winfield Scott; B12.8.1869 New Albany OH; D3.2.1895 Omaha NE; BB/TR/6´0˝/160; d5.3; b–Lew																									
1892	Pit N	0	1	.000	4	1	1	0	23	31	23	4	1	9	6	6.26	53	.310	.373	11	.091	-1	77	-6	—	-0.4
1894	Chi N	0	1	.000	3	2	2	0	22	34	24	0	1	12	6	6.55	86	.351	.427	11-0-1	.000	-3	57	-2	—	-0.3
Total	2	0	2	.000	7	3	3	0	45	65	47	4	2	21	12	6.40	69	.330	.400	22-0-1	.045	-4	66	-8	—	-0.7
Campbell, Archie	Archibald Stewart "Iron Man"; B10.20.1903 Maplewood NJ; D12.22.1989 Sparks NV; BR/TR/6´0˝/180; d4.21																									
1928	NY A	0	1	.000	13	1	0	2	24	30	22	0	0	11	9	5.25	72	.288	.357	4-0-2	.250	0	90	-7	—	-0.4
1929	Was A	0	1	.000	4	0	0	0	4	10	7	1	0	5	1	15.75	27	.500	.600	0	ø	0	—	-5	—	-0.8
1930	Cin N	2	4	.333	23	3	1	4	58	71	38	2	1	31	19	5.43	89	.311	.396	15	.267	0	42	-3	—	-0.2
Total	3	2	6	.250	40	4	1	6	86	111	67	3	1	47	29	5.86	77	.315	.398	19-0-2	.263	0	53	-15	—	-1.4
Campbell, Dave	David Alan; B9.3.1951 Princeton IN; BR/TR/6´3˝/210; d5.6; Col East Tennessee																									
1977	Atl N	0	6	.000	65	0	0	13-0	88.2	78	32	7	3	33-6	42	3.05	146	.239	.311	12-0-2	.083	-1	—	13	0	1.0
1978	Atl N	4	4	.500	53	0	0	1-1	69.1	67	39	10	5	49-12	45	4.80	84	.258	.383	0	ø	0	—	-4	0	-0.5
Total	2	4	10	.286	118	0	0	14-1	158	145	71	17	8	82-18	87	3.82	112	.247	.345	12-0-2	.083	-1	—	9	0	0.5
Campbell, Hugh	Hugh F.; B1846 , Ireland; D3.1.1881 Newark NJ; d4.28; b–Mat																									
1873	Res NA	2	16	.111	19	18	18	0	165	251	213	6	—	8	7	2.95	119	.297	.304	86	.151	-5*	42	10	—	0.5
Campbell, Jim	James Marcus; B5.19.1966 Santa Maria CA; BL/TL/5´11˝/175; [KCA87 32/821]; d8.21; Col San Diego St.																									
1990	KC A	1	0	1.000	2	2	0	0-0	9.2	15	9	1	0	1-0	2	8.38	46	.349	.364	0	ø	0	189	-4	0	-0.4
Campbell, John	John Millard; B9.13.1907 Washington DC; D4.24.1995 Daytona Beach FL; BR/TR/6´1.5˝/184; d7.23; Col Alabama																									
1933	Was A	0	0	ø	1	0	0	0	1	1	1	0	0	1	0	0.00	ø	.200	.333	0	ø	0	—	0	—	0.0
Campbell, Kevin	Kevin Wade; B12.6.1964 Marianna AR; BR/TR/6´2˝/(225–231); [LAN86 5/126]; d7.19; Col Arkansas																									
1991	Oak A	1	0	1.000	14	0	0	0-1	23	13	7	4	1	14-0	16	2.74	141	.167	.301	0	ø	0	—	3	0	0.2
1992	Oak A	2	3	.400	32	5	0	1-0	65	66	39	4	0	45-3	38	5.12	74	.267	.378	0	ø	0	87	-9	0	-0.7
1993	Oak A	0	0	ø	11	0	0	0-0	16	20	13	1	1	11-1	9	7.31	57	.313	.416	0	ø	0	—	-5	0	-0.3
1994	Min A	1	0	1.000	14	0	0	0-0	24.2	20	8	2	1	5-0	15	2.92	169	.233	.274	0	ø	0	—	6	0	0.3
1995	Min A	0	0	ø	6	0	0	0-0	9.2	8	5	0	0	5-0	5	4.66	103	.235	.333	0	ø	0	—	0	0	0.0
Total	5	4	3	.571	77	5	0	1-1	138.1	127	72	11	3	80-4	83	4.55	90	.250	.351	0	ø	0	87	-5	0	-0.5

YEAR	TM LG	W	L	PCT	G	GS	CG-SHO	SV-BS	IP	H	R	HR	HB	BB-IB	SO	ERA	AERA	OAV	OOB	AB-HR-SH	AVG	PB	SUP	APR	DL	PW
CAMPBELL, MIKE Michael Thomas; B2.17.1964 Seattle WA; BR/TR/6´3˝/(210–220); [SeaA85 1/7]; d7.4; Col Hawaii–Manoa; [DL 1990 KC A 18]																										
1987	Sea A	1	4	.200	9	9	1	0-0	49.1	41	29	9	2	25-2	35	4.74	100	.224	.319	0	ø	0	77	0	0	0.0
1988	Sea A	6	10	.375	20	20	2	0-0	114.2	128	81	18	0	43-1	63	5.89	71	.280	.339	0	ø	0	112	-19	0	-2.3
1989	Sea A	1	2	.333	5	5	0	0-0	21	28	22	4	0	10-0	6	7.29	55	.301	.369	0	ø	0	121	-8	0	-1.0
1992	Tex A	0	1	.000	1	0	0	0-0	3.2	3	4	1	0	2-0	2	9.82	39	.231	.333	0	ø	0	—	-2	0	-0.4
1994	SD N	1	1	.500	3	2	0	0-1	8.1	13	12	5	0	5-0	10	12.96	32	.351	.429	3	.333	0	110	-8	0	-1.2
1996	Chi N	3	1	.750	13	5	0	0-0	36.1	29	19	7	0	10-0	19	4.46	98	.216	.269	11-0-1	.364	2	165	0	63	0.1
Total	6	12	19	.387	51	41	3	0-1	233.1	242	167	44	2	95-3	135	5.86	74	.264	.331	14-0-1	.357	2	111	-37	81	-4.8
CAMPBELL, BRETT Richard Brett; B10.17.1981 Atlanta GA; BR/TR/6´0˝/170; [MonN04 34/1012]; d9.7; Col Kennesaw St.																										
2006	Was N	0	0	ø	4	0	0	0-0	4.1	4	5	1	1	2-0	4	10.38	42	.250	.368	0	ø	0	—	-3	0	-0.1
CAMPBELL, BILLY William James; B11.5.1873 Pittsburgh PA; D10.6.1957 Cincinnati OH; BL/TL/5´10˝/165; d4.17																										
1905	StL N	1	1	.500	2	2	2	0	17	27	17	0	0	7	2	7.41	40	.365	.420	7-0-1	.143	-0	133	-8	—	-0.7
1907	Cin N	3	0	1.000	3	3	3	0	21	19	5	0	0	3	4	2.14	121	.244	.272	8	.250	0	174	2	—	0.3
1908	Cin N	12	13	.480	35	24	19-2	2	221.1	203	99	3	10	44	73	2.60	89	.252	.299	72-0-6	.083	-3	93	-9	—	-1.2
1909	Cin N	7	11	.389	30	15	7	2	148.1	162	65	0	9	39	37	2.67	97	.288	.344	43-0-6	.140	-1	104	-1	—	0.0
Total	4	23	25	.479	70	44	31-2	4	407.2	411	186	3	19	93	116	2.80	88	.270	.320	130-0-13	.115	-4	105	-16	—	-1.6
CAMPBELL, BILL William Richard; B8.9.1948 Highland Park MI; BR/TR/6´3˝/(190–200); d7.14; C1; Col Mt. San Antonio (CA) JC																										
1973	Min A	3	3	.500	28	2	0	7-2	51.2	44	20	5	1	20-1	42	3.14	127	.226	.301	0	ø	0	45	5	0	0.7
1974	Min A	8	7	.533	63	0	0	19-8	120.1	109	37	4	2	55-4	89	2.62	143	.242	.326	0	ø	0	—	16	0	2.5
1975	Min A	4	6	.400	47	7	2-1	5-6	121	119	58	13	2	46-2	76	3.79	101	.262	.330	1	.000	-0	161	1	0	0.1
1976	Min A	17	5	**.773**	**78**	0	0	20-10	167.2	145	63	9	5	62-11	115	3.01	119	.234	.305	0	ø	0	—	11	0	1.8
1977	Bos A★	13	9	.591	69	0	0	**31**-11	140	112	48	13	5	60-10	114	2.96	152	.224	.311	0	ø	0	—	22	0	**4.5**
1978	Bos A	7	5	.583	29	0	0	4-11	50.2	62	25	3	0	17-3	47	3.91	105	.308	.362	0	ø	0	—	1	0	0.3
1979	Bos A	3	4	.429	41	0	0	9-8	54.2	55	28	5	1	23-6	25	4.28	104	.262	.338	0	ø	0	—	1	0	0.3
1980	Bos A	4	0	1.000	23	0	0	0-0	41.1	44	26	1	0	22-0	17	4.79	89	.284	.367	0	ø	0	—	-3	72	-0.3
1981	Bos A	1	1	.500	30	0	0	7-0	48.1	45	23	5	0	20-4	37	3.17	124	.245	.316	0	ø	0	—	2	0	0.2
1982	Chi N	3	6	.333	62	0	0	8-5	100	89	44	6	0	40-13	71	3.69	102	.245	.314	7	.143	-0	—	2	0	0.3
1983	Chi N	6	8	.429	**82**	0	0	8-5	122.1	128	65	4	1	49-18	97	4.49	85	.275	.342	10	.100	-1	—	-8	0	-0.9
1984	Phi N	6	5	.545	57	0	0	1-4	81.1	68	43	2	0	35-13	52	3.43	107	.222	.301	1	.000	-0	—	-1	0	-0.2
1985	†StL N	5	3	.625	50	0	0	4-1	64.1	55	32	5	2	21-9	41	3.50	102	.230	.294	6	.333	1	—	-1	0	-0.1
1986	Det A	3	6	.333	34	0	0	3-1	55.2	46	26	5	1	21-5	37	3.88	107	.230	.302	0	ø	0	—	2	32	0.3
1987	Mon N	0	0	ø	7	0	0	0-0	10	18	12	2	0	4-1	4	8.10	53	.360	.400	1	.000	0	—	-5	0	-0.2
Total	15	83	68	.550	700	9	2-1	126-72	1229.1	1139	550	82	20	495-100	864	3.54	110	.248	.321	26	.154	1	134	45	104	9.3
CAMPER, CARDELL Cardell; B7.6.1952 Boley OK; BR/TR/6´3˝/203; d9.11; Col Glendale (AZ) CC																										
1977	Cle A	1	0	1.000	3	1	0	0-0	9.1	7	4	0	0	4-1	9	3.86	104	.200	.282	0	ø	0	113	0	0	0.0
CAMPFIELD, SAL William Holton; B2.19.1868 Meadville PA; D5.16.1952 Meadville PA; BR/TR/6´0.5˝/?; d5.15																										
1896	NY N	1	1	.500	6	2	2	0	27	31	15	1	2	6	6	4.00	105	.284	.333	12	.167	-0	127	1	—	0.0
CAMPILLO, JORGE Jorge Hidalgo; B8.10.1978 Tijuana, Baja California, Mexico; BR/TR/6´1˝/190; d5.20																										
2005	Sea A	0	0	ø	2	1	0	0-0	2	1	0	0	0	1-0	1	0.00	ø	.125	.222	0	ø	0	89	1	61	0.0
2006	Sea A	0	0	ø	1	0	0	0-0	2.1	4	4	0	0	0-0	1	15.43	29	.364	.364	0	ø	0	—	-3	0	-0.1
Total	2	0	0	ø	3	1	0	0-0	4.1	5	4	0	0	1-0	2	8.31	52	.263	.300	0	ø	0	89	-2	61	-0.1
CAMPISI, SAL Salvatore John; B8.11.1942 Brooklyn NY; BR/TR/6´2˝/(210–212); d8.15; Col Long Island–Brooklyn																										
1969	StL N	1	0	1.000	7	0	0	0-0	9.2	4	1	0	0	6-2	7	0.93	385	.121	.256	0	ø	0	—	3	0	0.3
1970	StL N	2	2	.500	37	0	0	4-0	49.1	53	19	2	3	37-11	26	2.92	142	.282	.406	1	.000	-0	—	6	0	0.5
1971	Min A	0	0	ø	6	0	0	0-1	4.1	5	2	1	0	4-0	2	4.15	85	.294	.429	0	ø	0	—	0	0	0.0
Total	3	3	2	.600	50	0	0	4-1	63.1	62	22	3	3	47-13	35	2.70	149	.261	.388	1	.000	-0	—	9	0	0.8
CANAVAN, HUGH Hugh Edward "Hugo"; B5.13.1897 Worcester MA; D9.4.1967 Boston MA; BL/TL/5´8˝/160; d4.23; Mil 1918																										
1918	Bos N	0	4	.000	11	3	3	0	46.2	70	42	0	5	15	18	6.36	42	.366	.427	21	.095	-0*	94	-19	—	-1.5
CANDELARIA, JOHN John Robert "Candy Man"; B11.6.1953 New York NY; BL/TL (BB 1982p, 83–86 BR 1987–90)/6´7˝/(210–250); [PitN72 2/47]; d6.8																										
1975	†Pit N	8	6	.571	18	18	4-1	0-0	120.2	95	47	8	2	36-9	95	2.76	130	.212	.271	43	.140	-0	142	10	0	1.0
1976	Pit N	16	7	.696	32	31	11-4	1-0	220	173	87	22	2	60-5	138	3.15	112	.216	.271	76-0-5	.184	3	123	10	0	1.3
1977	Pit N☆	20	5	**.800**	33	33	6-1	0-0	230.2	197	64	29	2	50-2	133	**2.34**	**172**	.232	.274	80-0-4	.225	4	93	**43**	0	5.0
1978	Pit N	12	11	.522	30	29	3-1	1-0	189	191	73	15	5	49-6	94	3.24	115	.261	.311	52-0-7	.173	3*	92	12	0	1.8
1979	†Pit N	14	9	.609	33	30	8	0-0	207	201	83	25	3	41-6	101	3.22	122	.253	.290	68-0-8	.132	-1	104	16	0	1.6
1980	Pit N	11	14	.440	35	34	7	1-0	233.1	246	114	14	3	50-4	97	4.01	92	.276	.313	77-0-3	.195	2	100	-7	0	-0.6
1981	Pit N	2	2	.500	6	6	0	0-0	40.2	42	17	3	0	11-1	14	3.54	103	.271	.317	13-0-2	.231	0	126	1	147	0.1
1982	Pit N	12	7	.632	31	30	1-1	1-0	174.2	166	62	13	4	37-3	133	2.94	128	.255	.296	54-0-3	.222	3*	94	16	0	2.0
1983	Pit N	15	8	.652	33	32	2	0-0	197.2	191	73	15	2	45-3	157	3.23	116	.257	.300	65-0-5	.138	-0	94	14	0	1.4
1984	Pit N	12	11	.522	33	28	3-1	2-1	185.1	179	69	19	1	34-3	133	2.72	134	.256	.289	62-1-4	.129	1	104	16	0	1.9
1985	Pit N	2	4	.333	37	0	0	9-6	54.1	57	23	7	1	14-2	47	3.64	100	.275	.319	1-0-2	.000	-0	—	1	0	0.1
	Cal A	7	3	.700	13	13	1-1	0-0	71	70	33	7	3	24-1	53	3.80	108	.262	.327	0	ø	0	119	3	0	0.3
1986	†Cal A	10	2	.833	16	16	1-1	0-0	91.2	68	30	4	3	26-2	81	2.55	162	.206	.268	0	ø	0	132	16	84	1.9
1987	Cal A	8	6	.571	20	20	0	0-0	116.2	127	70	17	1	20-0	74	4.71	92	.279	.308	0	ø	0	111	-6	62	-0.5
	NY N	2	0	1.000	3	3	0	0-0	12.1	17	8	1	0	3-0	10	5.84	66	.333	.364	5	.200	0	110	-2	0	-0.3
1988	NY A	13	7	.650	25	24	6-2	1-0	157	150	69	18	2	23-2	121	3.38	117	.248	.275	0	ø	0	112	8	0	1.0
1989	NY A	3	3	.500	10	6	1	0-0	49	49	28	8	0	12-1	37	5.14	76	.258	.299	0	ø	0	101	-5	105	-0.6
	Mon N	0	2	.000	12	0	0	0-0	16.1	17	8	3	0	4-2	14	3.31	108	.283	.313	0	ø	0	—	0	0	0.0
1990	Min A	7	3	.700	34	1	0	4-3	58.1	55	23	9	0	9-2	44	3.39	123	.244	.270	0	ø	0	66	5	0	0.9
	Tor A	0	3	.000	13	2	0	1-0	21.1	32	13	2	2	11-3	19	5.48	72	.356	.425	0	ø	0	57	-3	0	-0.4
	Year	7	6	.538	47	3	0	5-3	79.2	87	36	11	2	20-5	63	3.95	104	.276	.318	0	ø	0	59	3	0	0.5
1991	LA N	1	1	.500	59	0	0	2-3	33.2	31	16	3	0	11-2	38	3.74	96	.252	.307	0	ø	0	—	-1	0	-0.1
1992	LA N	2	5	.286	50	0	0	5-2	25.1	20	9	1	0	13-3	23	2.84	122	.220	.311	0	ø	0	—	2	0	0.5
1993	Pit N	0	3	.000	24	0	0	1-2	19.2	25	19	2	1	9-1	17	8.24	50	.313	.385	0	ø	0	—	-9	17	-1.3
Total	19	177	122	.592	600	356	54-13	29-17	2525.2	2399	1038	245	37	592-63	1673	3.33	115	.251	.295	596-1-43	.174	14	106	140	415	17.0
CANDINI, MILO Mario Cain; B8.3.1917 Manteca CA; D3.17.1998 Manteca CA; BR/TR/6´0˝/187; d5.1; Mil 1945																										
1943	Was A	11	7	.611	28	21	8-3	1	166	144	55	3	1	65	67	2.49	128	.238	.313	56-1-6	.161	-1	109	14	0	1.5
1944	Was A	6	7	.462	28	10	4-2	1	103	110	53	3	1	49	31	4.11	79	.276	.357	32-0-6	.313	3	118	-8	0	-0.6
1946	Was A	2	0	1.000	9	0	0	1	21.2	15	5	1	0	4	6	2.08	161	.192	.232	6	.333	1	—	4	0	0.4
1947	Was A	3	4	.429	38	2	0	1	87	96	53	5	0	35	31	5.17	72	.273	.339	18-0-2	.167	-0	83	-13	0	-0.9
1948	Was A	2	3	.400	35	4	1	3	94.1	96	56	1	1	63	23	5.15	84	.267	.378	22	.364	3	73	-6	0	0.0
1949	Was A	0	0	ø	3	0	0	1	5.2	4	3	0	0	1	1	4.76	89	.200	.238	1	1.000	0	—	0	0	0.0
1950	Phi N	1	0	1.000	18	0	0	0	30	32	11	2	0	15	10	2.70	150	.281	.364	6	.167	-0	—	4	0	0.2
1951	Phi N	1	0	1.000	15	0	0	0	30	33	22	3	0	18	14	6.00	64	.275	.370	3	.333	1	—	-7	0	-0.3
Total	8	26	21	.553	174	37	13-5	8	537.2	530	258	18	3	250	183	3.92	92	.259	.341	144-1-14	.243	7	100	-12	0	0.3
CANDIOTTI, TOM Thomas Caesar; B8.31.1957 Walnut Creek CA; BR/TR/6´2˝/(200–230); d8.8; Col St. Marys (CA)																										
1983	Mil A	4	4	.500	10	8	2-1	0-0	55.2	62	21	4	2	16-0	21	3.23	117	.291	.343	0	ø	0	78	4	0	0.5
1984	Mil A	2	2	.500	8	6	0	0-0	32.1	38	21	5	0	10-0	23	5.29	74	.277	.327	0	ø	0	81	-5	30	-0.6
1986	Cle A	16	12	.571	36	34	**17**-3	0-0	252.1	234	112	18	8	106-0	167	3.57	117	.246	.324	0	ø	0	113	18	0	1.9
1987	Cle A	7	18	.280	32	32	7-2	0-0	201.2	193	132	28	4	93-2	111	4.78	96	.250	.330	0	ø	0	74	-9	0	-0.9
1988	Cle A	14	8	.636	31	31	11-1	0-0	216.2	225	86	15	6	53-3	137	3.28	126	.272	.319	0	ø	0	99	20	15	2.0
1989	Cle A	13	10	.565	31	31	4	0-0	206	188	80	10	4	55-5	124	3.10	128	.242	.294	0	ø	0	75	19	15	2.2
1990	Cle A	15	11	.577	31	29	3-1	0-0	202	207	92	23	6	55-1	128	3.65	108	.263	.315	0	ø	0	108	5	15	0.8
1991	Cle A	7	6	.538	15	15	3	0-0	108.1	88	35	6	2	28-0	86	2.24	186	.218	.268	0	ø	0	77	21	0	2.4
	†Tor A	6	7	.462	19	19	3	0-0	129.2	114	47	6	4	45-1	81	2.98	142	.236	.304	0	ø	0	79	17	0	1.7

YEAR	TM LG	W	L	PCT	G	GS	CG-SHO	SV-BS	IP	H	R	HR	HB	BB-IB	SO	ERA	AERA	OAV	OOB	AB-HR-SH	AVG	PB	SUP	APR	DL	PW
	Year	13	13	.500	34	34	6	0-0	238	202	82	12	6	73-1	167	2.65	159	.228	.288	0	ø	0	78	39	0	4.1
1992	LA N	11	15	.423	32	30	6-2	0-0	203.2	177	78	13	3	63-5	152	3.00	116	.237	.297	56-0-12	.107	-1	82	11	15	1.3
1993	LA N	8	10	.444	33	32	2	0-0	213.2	192	86	12	6	71-1	155	3.12	124	.241	.305	60-0-9	.133	-1	68	18	0	1.3
1994	LA N	7	7	.500	23	22	5	0-0	153	149	77	9	5	54-2	102	4.12	97	.259	.323	50-0-7	.140	-1	112	-3	0	-0.3
1995	LA N	7	14	.333	30	30	1-1	0-0	190.1	187	93	18	9	58-2	141	3.50	111	.255	.316	55-0-5	.109	-2	79	5	0	0.3
1996	†LA N	9	11	.450	28	27	1	0-0	152.1	172	91	18	3	43-3	79	4.49	87	.288	.336	45-0-9	.089	-2	96	-12	24	-1.4
1997	LA N	10	7	.588	41	18	0	0-0	135	128	60	21	11	40-4	89	3.60	109	.248	.314	32-0-9	.094	-1*	119	5	0	0.4
1998	Oak A	11	16	.407	33	33	3	0-0	201	222	124	30	9	63-2	98	4.84	96	.281	.338	1-0-1	1.000	1	92	-6	0	-0.5
1999	Oak A	3	5	.375	11	11	0	0-0	56.2	67	46	11	2	23-0	30	6.35	75	.298	.362	0	ø	0	98	-11	0	-1.3
	Cle A	1	1	.500	7	2	0	0-0	14.2	19	18	3	1	7-0	11	11.05	46	.306	.386	0	ø	0	174	-9	0	-0.9
	Year	4	6	.400	18	13	0	0-0	71.1	86	64	14	3	30-0	41	7.32	66	.300	.367	0	ø	0	110	-21	0	-2.2
Total	16	151	164	.479	451	410	68-11	0-0	2725	2662	1299	250	85	883-31	1735	3.73	109	.256	.317	299-0-52	.117	-7	91	88	114	8.9
CANEIRA, JOHN	John Cascaes; B10.7.1952 Waterbury CT; BR/TR/6´3˝/200; [AnaA74 S1/2]; d9.10; Col Eastern Connecticut																									
1977	Cal A	2	2	.500	6	4	0	0-0	28.2	27	15	5	0	16-2	17	4.08	96	.252	.347	0	ø	0	86	0	0	-0.1
1978	Cal A	0	0	ø	2	2	0	0-0	7.2	8	6	2	0	3-0	0	7.04	52	.286	.344	0	ø	0	74	-3	0	-0.2
Total	2	2	2	.500	8	6	0	0-0	36.1	35	21	7	0	19-2	17	4.71	82	.259	.346	0	ø	0	81	-3	0	-0.3
CANO, JOSE	Joselito (Soriano); B3.7.1962 Boca Del Soco, D.R.; BR/TR/6´3˝/175; d8.28; s–Robinson; [DL 1990 Hou N 63]																									
1989	Hou N	1	1	.500	6	3	1	0-0	23	24	13	2	0	7-2	8	5.09	67	.267	.316	6	.000	-1	113	-4	0	-0.4
CANTRELL, GUY	Guy Dewey "Gunner"; B4.9.1904 Clarita OK; D1.31.1961 McAlester OK; BR/TR/6´0˝/190; d8.18																									
1925	Bro N	1	0	1.000	14	3	1	0	36	42	27	0	1	14	13	3.00	139	.294	.361	9	.000	-1	121	0	—	-0.1
1927	Bro N	0	0	ø	6	0	0	0	10	10	3	0	0	6	5	2.70	147	.250	.348	3	.333	0	—	2	—	0.1
	Phi A	0	2	.000	2	2	2	0	18	25	10	0	0	7	7	5.00	85	.338	.395	6	.167	-0	39	-1	—	-0.1
1930	Det A	1	5	.167	16	2	1	0	35	38	30	5	1	20	20	5.66	85	.271	.366	9	.000	-2	81	-5	—	-0.8
Total	3	2	7	.222	38	7	4	0	99	115	70	5	2	47	45	4.27	103	.290	.368	27	.074	-3	86	-4	—	-0.9
CANTWELL, BEN	Benjamin Caldwell; B4.13.1902 Milan TN; D12.4.1962 Salem MO; BR/TR/6´1˝/168; d8.19; Col Tennessee																									
1927	NY N	1	1	.500	5	2	1	0	19.2	26	9	1	1	2	6	4.12	94	.313	.337	8	.250	0	99	0	—	0.0
1928	NY N	1	0	1.000	7	1	0	1	18.1	20	10	1	1	4	0	4.42	89	.282	.329	4	.500	1	173	-1	—	0.0
	Bos N	3	3	.500	22	10	3	0	90	112	63	7	2	36	18	5.10	77	.304	.369	29	.172	-1	115	-13	—	-0.8
	Year	4	3	.571	29	11	3	1	108.1	132	73	8	3	40	18	4.98	79	.301	.363	33	.212	-0	120	-15	—	-0.8
1929	Bos N	4	13	.235	27	20	8	2	157	171	98	11	2	52	25	4.47	105	.280	.338	50-0-3	.180	0	74	-1	—	0.2
1930	Bos N	9	15	.375	31	21	10	2	173.1	213	99	15	1	45	43	4.88	101	.312	.355	63-0-2	.302	2*	62	4	—	0.9
1931	Bos N	7	9	.438	33	16	9-2	2	156.1	160	73	4	0	34	32	3.63	104	.262	.301	57-0-2	.228	0*	83	2	—	0.4
1932	Bos N	13	11	.542	37	9	3-1	5	146	133	56	6	5	33	33	2.96	127	.247	.296	50	.280	2	99	14	—	2.6
1933	Bos N	20	10	**.667**	40	29	18-2	2	254.2	242	89	12	3	54	57	2.62	117	.249	.291	85-0-3	.141	-1*	97	12	—	1.5
1934	Bos N	5	11	.313	27	19	6-1	5	143.1	163	88	8	2	34	45	4.33	88	.285	.327	43-0-5	.279	1*	86	-13	—	-1.1
1935	Bos N	4	25	.138	39	24	13	0	210.2	235	117	15	2	44	34	4.61	82	.282	.320	67-0-5	.284	4*	54	-16	—	-1.5
1936	Bos N	9	9	.500	34	12	4	2	133.1	127	55	8	4	35	42	3.04	126	.252	.306	41-0-3	.195	-1*	82	11	—	1.4
1937	NY N	0	1	.000	1	1	0	0	4	6	4	1	0	1	1	9.00	43	.375	.412	0	ø	0	44	-2	—	-0.3
	Bro N	0	0	ø	13	0	0	0	27.1	32	17	1	0	8	12	4.61	88	.288	.336	6	.167	-0	—	-2	—	0.0
	Year	0	1	.000	14	1	0	0	31.1	38	21	2	0	9	13	5.17	78	.299	.346	6	.167	0	43	-4	—	-0.3
Total	11	76	108	.413	316	164	75-6	21	1534	1640	778	90	23	382	348	3.91	100	.275	.321	503-0-23	.231	8	81	-5	—	3.3
CANTWELL, MIKE	Michael Joseph; B6.15.1894 Washington DC; D1.5.1953 Oteen NC; BL/TL/5´10˝/155; d8.17; b–Tom; Col Georgetown																									
1916	NY A	0	0	ø	1	0	0	0	2	0	2	0	0	2	0	0.00	ø	.000	.333	0	ø	0	—	0	—	0.0
1919	Phi N	1	3	.250	5	3	2	0	27.1	36	19	1	2	9	6	5.60	58	.343	.405	9	.222	-0	107	-6	—	-0.8
1920	Phi N	0	3	.000	5	1	0	0	23.1	25	18	1	3	15	8	3.86	89	.284	.406	7-0-1	.143	-1	138	-3	—	-0.4
Total	3	1	6	.143	11	4	2	0	52.2	61	39	2	5	26	14	4.61	71	.310	.404	16-0-1	.188	-1	114	-9	—	-1.2
CANTWELL, TOM	Thomas Aloysius; B12.23.1888 Washington DC; D4.1.1968 Washington DC; BR/TR/6´0˝/170; d5.19; b–Mike; Col Georgetown																									
1909	Cin N	1	0	1.000	6	1	1	0	21.2	16	10	0	1	7	7	1.66	156	.205	.279	5	.600	1	81	1	—	0.2
1910	Cin N	0	0	ø	2	0	0	0	1.1	2	2	0	0	3	0	13.50	22	.400	.625	0	ø	0	—	-1	—	-0.1
Total	2	1	0	1.000	8	1	1	0	23	18	12	0	1	10	7	2.35	111	.217	.309	5	.600	1	81	0	—	0.1
CAPEL, MIKE	Michael Lee; B10.13.1961 Marshall TX; BR/TR/6´1˝/175; [ChiN83 13/320]; d5.7; Col Texas																									
1988	Chi N	2	1	.667	22	0	0	0-3	29.1	34	19	5	3	13-2	19	4.91	74	.293	.379	2	.000	-0	—	-5	0	-0.5
1990	Mil A	0	0	ø	2	0	0	0-0	0.1	6	6	0	1	1-0	1	135.00	3	.857	.889	0	ø	0	—	-5	0	-0.2
1991	Hou N	1	3	.250	25	0	0	3-1	32.2	33	14	3	0	15-1	23	3.03	117	.266	.343	0	ø	0	—	1	0	0.1
Total	3	3	4	.429	49	0	0	3-4	62.1	73	39	8	4	29-3	43	4.62	78	.296	.377	2	.000	-0	—	-9	0	-0.6
CAPELLAN, JOSE	Jose Francisco; B1.13.1981 Cotui, D.R.; BR/TR/6´4˝/235; d9.12																									
2004	Atl N	0	1	.000	3	2	0	0-0	8	14	10	2	0	5-0	4	11.25	38	.400	.463	2	.000	-0	140	-6	0	-0.6
2005	Mil N	1	1	.500	17	0	0	0-0	15.2	17	6	1	0	5-0	14	2.87	148	.293	.338	0	ø	0	—	2	0	0.2
2006	Mil N	4	2	.667	61	0	0	0-2	71.2	65	37	11	3	31-7	58	4.40	102	.244	.328	2	.000	-0	—	1	12	0.0
Total	3	5	4	.556	81	2	0	0-2	95.1	96	53	14	3	41-7	76	4.72	94	.267	.343	4	.000	-0	140	-3	12	-0.4
CAPILLA, DOUG	Douglas Edmund; B1.7.1952 Honolulu HI; BL/TL/5´8˝/(170–175); [SFN70 25/600]; d9.12																									
1976	StL N	1	0	1.000	7	0	0	0-1	8.1	8	5	0	0	4-0	5	5.40	66	.242	.324	0	ø	0	—	-1	0	-0.1
1977	StL N	0	0	ø	2	0	0	0-0	2.1	2	4	0	0	2-0	1	15.43	25	.222	.364	0	ø	0	—	-3	0	-0.1
	Cin N	7	8	.467	22	16	1	0-0	106.1	94	53	10	2	59-1	74	4.23	93	.237	.338	34-0-3	.059	-3	100	-3	0	-0.7
	Year	7	8	.467	24	16	1	0-0	108.2	96	57	10	2	61-1	75	4.47	88	.236	.339	34-0-3	.059	-3	100	-5	0	-0.8
1978	Cin N	0	1	.000	6	3	0	0-0	11	14	12	1	0	11-0	9	9.82	36	.318	.439	2	.000	-0*	169	-7	0	-0.6
1979	Cin N	1	0	1.000	5	0	0	0-0	6.1	7	6	1	1	5-0	0	8.53	43	.269	.406	1	1.000	0	—	-3	0	-0.4
	Chi N	0	1	.000	13	1	0	0-0	17.1	14	6	1	0	7-0	10	2.60	160	.206	.280	0	ø	0	64	3	0	0.2
	Year	1	1	.500	18	1	0	0-0	23.2	21	12	2	1	12-0	10	4.18	96	.223	.318	1	1.000	0	66	0	0	-0.2
1980	Chi N	2	8	.200	39	11	0	0-1	89.2	82	46	7	3	51-5	51	4.12	96	.253	.355	21-0-1	.190	0*	39	-1	0	0.0
1981	Chi N	1	0	1.000	42	0	0	0-3	51	52	20	1	2	34-3	28	3.18	118	.284	.396	3	.000	-0	—	3	0	0.1
Total	6	12	18	.400	136	31	1	0-5	292.1	273	152	21	8	173-9	178	4.34	90	.252	.356	61-0-4	.115	-3	83	-12	0	-1.6
CAPPS, MATT	Matthew Dicus; B9.3.1983 Douglasville GA; BR/TR/6´3˝/240; [PitN02 7/193]; d9.16																									
2005	Pit N	0	0	ø	4	0	0	0-0	4	5	2	0	1	0-0	3	4.50	94	.333	.375	0	ø	0	—	0	0	0.0
2006	Pit N	9	1	.900	85	0	0	1-9	80.2	81	37	12	3	12-5	56	3.79	121	.266	.299	2	.000	0	—	7	0	0.8
Total	2	9	1	.900	89	0	0	1-9	84.2	86	39	12	4	12-5	59	3.83	119	.270	.303	2	.000	0	—	7	0	0.8
CAPPUZZELLO, GEORGE	George Angelo; B1.15.1954 Youngstown OH; BR/TL/6´0˝/(175–195); [DetA72 27/623]; d5.31																									
1981	Det A	1	1	.500	18	3	0	1-0	33.2	28	14	2	2	18-2	19	3.48	109	.222	.329	0	ø	0	111	1	0	0.1
1982	Hou N	0	1	.000	17	0	0	0-2	19.1	16	6	2	3	7-1	13	2.79	119	.232	.321	1	.000	-0	—	2	59	0.1
Total	2	1	2	.333	35	3	0	1-2	53	44	20	4	5	25-3	32	3.23	112	.226	.326	1	.000	-0	111	3	59	0.2
CAPRA, BUZZ	Lee William; B10.1.1947 Chicago IL; BR/TR/5´10˝/(160–168); [NYN69 27/625]; d9.15; Col Illinois St.																									
1971	NY N	0	1	.000	3	0	0	0-0	5.1	3	6	0	0	5-1	6	8.44	41	.167	.348	1	.000	-0	—	-3	0	-0.5
1972	NY N	3	2	.600	14	6	0	0-0	53	50	27	7	0	27-1	45	4.58	74	.253	.341	12	.250	1	83	-6	0	-0.3
1973	NY N	2	7	.222	24	0	0	4-3	42	35	18	4	2	28-9	35	3.86	95	.233	.357	2-0-1	.000	0	—	0	0	0.0
1974	Atl N☆	16	8	.667	39	27	11-5	1-0	217	163	67	13	3	84-6	137	**2.28**	**166**	**.208**	.286	67-0-7	.164	0	95	33	0	3.5
1975	Atl N	4	7	.364	12	12	5	0-0	78.1	77	41	8	1	28-1	35	4.25	89	.257	.320	23-0-5	.043	-2	85	-3	111	-0.5
1976	Atl N	0	1	.000	5	0	0	0-0	9.1	9	9	0	0	6-2	4	8.68	44	.265	.366	0	ø	0	—	-4	82	-0.4
1977	Atl N	6	11	.353	45	16	0	0-0	139.1	142	88	28	4	80-12	100	5.36	83	.263	.360	36-0-3	.111	-2	66	-10	0	-1.3
Total	7	31	37	.456	142	61	16-5	5-3	544.1	479	256	60	10	258-32	362	3.87	101	.237	.324	141-0-16	.135	-2	84	7	193	0.5
CAPUANO, CHRIS	Christopher Frank; B8.19.1978 Springfield MA; BL/TL/6´3˝/(210–220); [AriN99 8/238]; d5.4; Col Duke																									
2003	Ari N	2	4	.333	9	5	0	0-0	33	27	19	3	6	11-1	23	4.64	100	.231	.326	8	.000	-1	81	0	0	-0.1
2004	Mil N	6	8	.429	17	17	0	0-0	88.1	91	55	18	5	37-1	80	4.99	88	.269	.349	30	.200	1	85	-6	93	-0.7
2005	Mil N	18	12	.600	35	**35**	0	0-0	219	212	105	31	12	91-6	176	3.99	107	.256	.337	71-0-5	.169	1	110	7	0	1.0

YEAR	TM LG	W	L	PCT	G	GS	CG-SHO	SV-BS	IP	H	R	HR	HB	BB-IB	SO	ERA	AERA	OAV	OOB	AB-HR-SH	AVG	PB	SUP	APR	DL	PW
2006	Mil N☆	11	12	.478	34	34	3-2	0-0	221.1	229	108	29	9	47-4	174	4.03	112	.265	.307	68-0-5	.118	-1*	80	11	0	0.9
Total	4	37	36	.507	95	91	3-2	0-0	561.2	559	287	81	32	186-12	453	4.20	105	.261	.327	177-0-10	.147	-1	92	12	93	1.1
Caraway, Pat	Cecil Bradford Patrick; B9.26.1905 Erath Co. TX; D6.9.1974 ElPaso TX; BL/TL/6´4˝/175; d4.19																									
1930	Chi A	10	10	.500	38	21	9-1	1	193.1	194	96	11	3	57	83	3.86	120	.267	.323	64-0-3	.172	-1	93	19	—	1.7
1931	Chi A	10	24	.294	51	32	11-1	2	220	268	177	17	7	101	55	6.22	68	.295	.370	72-0-8	.194	-1*	79	-47	—	-5.9
1932	Chi A	2	6	.250	19	9	1	0	64.2	80	55	6	3	37	13	6.82	63	.304	.396	21-0-1	.143	-1	68	-16	—	-1.7
Total	3	22	40	.355	108	62	21-2	3	478	542	328	34	13	195	151	5.35	83	.286	.356	157-0-12	.178	-3	82	-44	—	-5.9
Carden, John	John Bruton; B5.19.1921 Killeen TX; D2.8.1949 Mexia TX; BR/TR/6´5˝/210; d5.18; Col Texas A&M																									
1946	NY N	0	0	ø	1	0	0	0	2	4	7	0	1	4	1	22.50	15	.400	.600	0	ø	0	—	-5	0	-0.2
Cardinal, Conrad	Conrad Seth; B3.30.1942 Brooklyn NY; BR/TR/6´1˝/190; d4.11																									
1963	Hou N	0	1	.000	6	1	0	0	13.1	15	14	0	0	7-0	7	6.08	52	.283	.355	2	.000	-0	82	-6	0	-0.4
Cardoni, Ben	Armand Joseph "Big Ben"; B8.21.1920 Jessup PA; D4.2.1969 Jessup PA; BR/TR/6´3˝/195; d8.22																									
1943	Bos N	0	0	ø	11	0	0	1	28	38	20	1	1	14	5	6.43	53	.336	.414	7	.000	-1	—	-8	0	-0.5
1944	Bos N	0	6	.000	22	5	1	0	75.2	83	40	5	1	37	24	3.93	97	.284	.367	17-0-4	.235	-0*	48	-1	0	-0.1
1945	Bos N	0	0	ø	3	0	0	0	4	6	5	0	1	3	5	9.00	43	.300	.417	0	ø	0	—	-2	0	-0.1
Total	3	0	6	.000	36	5	1	1	107.2	127	65	6	3	54	34	4.76	78	.299	.382	24-0-4	.167	-1	48	-11	0	-0.7
Cardwell, Don	Donald Eugene; B12.7.1935 Winston–Salem NC; BR/TR/6´4˝/(210–220); d4.21; Col Appalachian St.																									
1957	Phi N	4	8	.333	30	19	5-1	1	128.1	122	71	17	4	42-1	92	4.91	78	.251	.313	35-1-3	.200	1	86	-13	0	-1.0
1958	Phi N	3	6	.333	16	14	3	0	107.2	99	55	16	2	37-4	77	4.51	88	.241	.306	38-0-1	.211	1	84	-4	0	-0.2
1959	Phi N	9	10	.474	25	22	5-1	0	153	135	77	22	4	65-5	106	4.06	101	.238	.317	55-1-1	.055	-3*	84	1	0	-0.3
1960	Phi N	1	2	.333	5	4	0	0	28.1	28	14	4	1	11-1	21	4.45	87	.262	.336	8-2-2	.250	2	119	-1	0	0.1
	Chi N	8	14	.364	31	26	6-1	0	177	166	101	19	5	68-10	129	4.37	86	.249	.320	69-3-0	.203	3*	97	-13	0	-1.2
	Year	9	16	.360	36	30	6-1	0	205.1	194	115	23	6	79-11	150	4.38	87	.251	.322	77-5-2	.208	5	100	-14	0	-1.1
1961	Chi N	15	14	.517	39	**38**	13-3	0	259.1	243	121	22	10	88-0	156	3.82	110	.246	.312	95-3-4	.105	-1*	97	13	0	1.3
1962	Chi N	7	16	.304	41	29	6-1	4	195.2	205	116	27	9	60-7	104	4.92	84	.267	.326	61-0-4	.148	-0	74	-14	0	-1.5
1963	Pit N	13	15	.464	33	32	7-2	0	213.2	195	92	21	16	52-10	112	3.07	107	.245	.303	71-0-3	.085	-2	91	3	0	0.2
1964	Pit N	1	2	.333	4	4	1-1	0	19.1	15	9	1	3	7-1	10	2.79	126	.217	.313	7	.143	-0	88	1	35	0.1
1965	Pit N	13	10	.565	37	34	12-2	0	240.1	214	101	21	12	59-1	107	3.18	110	.239	.294	74-2-10	.162	3	117	8	0	1.2
1966	Pit N	6	6	.500	32	14	1	1	101.2	112	58	15	6	27-8	60	4.60	78	.282	.335	29-0-1	.103	-1	106	-12	0	-1.3
1967	NY N	5	9	.357	26	16	3-3	0	118.1	112	55	8	7	39-8	71	3.57	95	.249	.319	38-1-0	.158	2*	84	-3	44	0.0
1968	NY N	7	13	.350	29	25	5-1	1	180	156	69	9	10	50-11	82	2.95	102	.233	.293	61-1-3	.049	-3*	75	0	0	-0.3
1969	†NY N	8	10	.444	30	21	4	0-0	152.1	145	63	15	5	47-10	60	3.01	122	.252	.313	47-1-2	.170	1	92	8	0	1.1
1970	NY N	0	2	.000	16	1	0	0-0	25	31	19	3	3	6-1	8	6.48	63	.316	.364	5	.000	-1	44	-6	0	-0.5
	Atl N	2	1	.667	16	2	1-1	0-1	23	31	23	5	1	13-2	16	9.00	48	.326	.409	5	.400	1	115	-10	0	-1.1
	Year	2	3	.400	32	3	1-1	0-1	48	62	42	8	4	19-3	24	7.69	54	.321	.386	10	.200	-0	93	-16	0	-1.6
Total	14	102	138	.425	410	301	72-17	7-1	2123	2009	1044	225	98	671-80	1211	3.92	95	.250	.313	698-15-34	.135	2	92	-42	79	-3.4
Carleton, Tex	James Otto; B8.19.1906 Comanche TX; D1.11.1977 Fort Worth TX; BB/TR/6´1.5˝/180; d4.17; Col TCU																									
1932	StL N	10	13	.435	44	22	9-3	0	196.1	198	94	12	3	70	113	4.08	96	.261	.326	60-1-0	.150	-2	88	1	—	0.0
1933	StL N	17	11	.607	44	33	15-4	3	277	263	117	15	4	97	147	3.38	103	.249	.315	91-1-8	.187	1*	130	5	—	0.5
1934	†StL N	16	11	.593	40	31	16	2	240.2	260	126	14	7	52	103	4.26	99	.271	.314	88-1-3	.193	1*	109	1	—	0.2
1935	†Chi N	11	8	.579	31	22	8	1	171	169	82	17	3	60	84	3.89	101	.257	.322	62-0-1	.129	-3	116	3	—	0.1
1936	Chi N	14	10	.583	35	26	12-**4**	1	197.1	204	85	14	6	67	88	3.65	109	.268	.332	60-3-4	.233	6	115	9	—	1.7
1937	Chi N	16	8	.667	32	27	18-4	0	208.1	183	80	10	4	94	105	3.15	126	.236	.321	71-0-6	.169	1*	117	19	—	2.2
1938	†Chi N	10	9	.526	33	24	9	0	167.2	213	118	11	8	74	80	5.42	71	.307	.381	65	.231	3	125	-31	—	-2.7
1940	Bro N	6	6	.500	34	17	4-1	2	149	140	68	12	3	47	88	3.81	105	.245	.305	43-0-5	.186	-0	100	4	—	0.2
Total	8	100	76	.568	293	202	91-16	9	1607.1	1630	770	105	38	561	808	3.91	100	.261	.326	540-6-27	.185	6	114	11	—	2.2
Carlos, Cisco	Francisco Manuel; B9.17.1940 Monrovia CA; BR/TR/6´3˝/205; d8.25; Col Northern Colorado																									
1967	Chi A	2	0	1.000	8	7	1-1	0	41.2	23	5	0	1	9-0	27	0.86	359	.161	.216	16	.063	-1	88	11	0	0.5
1968	Chi A	4	14	.222	29	21	0	0	122.1	121	64	13	10	37-5	57	3.90	78	.258	.324	31-0-4	.065	-1	67	-12	0	-1.9
1969	Chi A	4	3	.571	25	4	0	0-1	49.1	52	33	4	5	23-3	28	5.66	68	.274	.367	10-0-2	.000	-1	132	-9	0	-1.2
	Was A	1	1	.500	6	4	0	0-0	17.2	23	9	2	0	6-0	5	4.58	76	.348	.403	5	.200	1	114	-2	0	-0.1
	Year	5	4	.556	31	8	0	0-1	67	75	42	6	5	29-3	33	5.37	70	.293	.376	15-0-2	.067	-0	121	-10	0	-1.3
1970	Was A	0	0	ø	5	0	0	0-0	6	3	1	0	0	4-0	2	1.50	241	.150	.292	0	ø	0	—	2	0	0.1
Total	4	11	18	.379	73	36	1-1	0-1	237	222	112	19	16	79-8	119	3.72	88	.250	.322	62-0-6	.065	-3	84	-10	0	-2.6
Carlsen, Don	Donald Herbert; B10.15.1926 Chicago IL; D9.22.2002 Denver CO; BR/TR/6´1˝/(175–180); d4.28																									
1948	Chi N	0	0	ø	1	0	0	0	1	5	4	0	0	2	1	36.00	11	.625	.700	0	ø	0	—	-3	0	-0.2
1951	Pit N	2	3	.400	7	6	2	0	43	50	22	4	1	14	20	4.19	101	.292	.349	16	.250	0	66	1	0	0.1
1952	Pit N	0	1	.000	5	1	0	0	10	20	13	1	0	5	2	10.80	37	.417	.472	3	.333	0	0	-7	0	-0.5
Total	3	2	4	.333	13	7	2	0	54	75	39	5	1	21	23	6.00	70	.330	.390	19	.263	0	57	-9	0	-0.6
Carlson, Dan	Daniel Steven; B1.26.1970 Portland OR; BR/TR/6´1˝/(185–200); [SFN89 33/856]; d9.13; Col Mt. Hood (OR) CC																									
1996	SF N	1	0	1.000	5	0	0	0-0	10	13	6	2	0	2-0	4	2.70	153	.310	.326	1	.000	-0	—	0	0	0.0
1997	SF N	0	0	ø	6	0	0	0-0	15.1	20	14	5	0	8-1	14	7.63	54	.317	.389	3	.000	-0	—	-6	10	-0.3
1998	TB A	0	0	ø	10	0	0	0-0	17.2	25	15	3	3	8-0	16	7.64	63	.347	.429	0	ø	0	—	-5	0	-0.2
1999	Ari N	0	0	ø	2	0	0	0-0	4	5	4	0	0	0-0	3	9.00	51	.278	.278	0	ø	0	—	-2	0	-0.1
Total	4	1	0	1.000	23	0	0	0-0	47	63	39	10	3	18-1	37	6.70	66	.323	.382	4	.000	-0	—	-13	10	-0.6
Carlson, Hal	Harold Gust; B5.17.1892 Rockford IL; D5.28.1930 Chicago IL; BR/TR/6´0˝/180; d4.13; Mil 1918																									
1917	Pit N	7	11	.389	34	17	9-1	1	161.1	140	64	0	4	49	68	2.90	98	.241	.304	49-0-3	.122	-2	70	-1	—	-0.2
1918	Pit N	0	1	.000	3	2	0	0	12	12	5	1	0	5	5	3.75	77	.286	.362	5	.200	-0	53	-1	—	-0.1
1919	Pit N	8	10	.444	22	14	7-1	0	141	114	41	0	2	39	49	2.23	135	.243	.303	43-0-1	.163	-1	58	12	—	1.5
1920	Pit N	14	13	.519	39	31	16-3	3	246.2	262	102	4	8	63	62	3.36	96	.281	.331	85-0-2	.271	3	94	0	—	0.1
1921	Pit N	4	8	.333	31	10	3	4	109.2	121	59	6	2	23	37	4.27	90	.290	.330	34	.294	1	79	-4	—	-0.2
1922	Pit N	9	12	.429	39	18	6	2	145.1	193	106	10	4	58	64	5.70	72	.323	.386	56-1-4	.268	3	131	-25	—	-2.6
1923	Pit N	0	0	ø	4	0	0	0	13.1	19	9	2	1	2	4	4.73	85	.358	.393	5	.000	-0	—	-1	—	-0.1
1924	Phi N	8	17	.320	38	23	12-1	2	203.2	267	122	9	3	55	66	4.86	92	.329	.374	76-2-2	.276	2*	78	-6	—	-0.4
1925	Phi N	13	14	.481	35	32	18-**4**	0	234	281	131	19	6	52	80	4.23	113	.298	.338	93-2-2	.183	-2*	101	14	—	1.2
1926	Phi N	17	12	.586	35	34	20-3	0	267.1	293	116	9	2	47	55	3.23	128	.281	.313	96-0-3	.240	2*	85	25	—	2.6
1927	Phi N	4	5	.444	11	9	4	1	63.2	80	41	7	0	18	13	5.23	79	.316	.362	25-0-1	.240	0*	149	-7	—	-0.9
	Chi N	12	8	.600	27	22	15-2	0	184.1	201	73	9	2	27	27	3.17	122	.280	.307	67-0-3	.164	-3	104	16	—	1.2
	Year	16	13	.552	38	31	19-2	1	248	281	114	16	2	45	40	3.70	106	.289	.322	92-0-4	.185	-3	118	10	—	0.3
1928	Chi N	3	2	.600	20	4	2	4	56.1	74	42	4	0	15	11	5.91	65	.329	.371	19	.263	0	77	-13	—	-1.1
1929	†Chi N	11	5	.688	31	13	6-2	2	111.2	131	71	8	1	31	35	5.16	90	.292	.340	39-0-3	.231	1	144	-5	—	-0.5
1930	Chi N	4	2	.667	8	6	3	0	51.2	68	31	5	1	14	14	5.05	97	.313	.358	20	.250	0	119	0	—	0.1
Total	14	114	120	.487	377	235	121-17	19	2002	2256	1013	93	36	498	590	3.97	99	.291	.337	712-5-24	.223	4	98	4	—	0.6
Carlson, Leon	Leon Alton "Swede"; B2.17.1895 Jamestown NY; D9.15.1961 Jamestown NY; BR/TR/6´3˝/195; d5.31																									
1920	Was A	0	0	ø	3	0	0	0	12.1	14	7	1	0	2	3	3.65	102	.292	.320	6	.167	-0	—	0	—	-0.1
Carlton, Steve	Steven Norman "Lefty"; B12.22.1944 Miami FL; BL/TL/6´4˝/(178–220); d4.12; HF1994																									
1965	StL N	0	0	ø	15	2	0	0	25	27	7	3	1	8-1	21	2.52	153	.287	.350	2	.000	-0	148	4	0	0.2
1966	StL N	3	3	.500	9	9	2-1	0	52	56	22	2	0	18-1	25	3.12	115	.280	.335	15-0-2	.267	1	82	2	0	0.4
1967	†StL N	14	9	.609	30	28	11-2	1	193	173	71	10	2	62-1	168	2.98	110	.238	.299	72-0-1	.153	1	114	7	0	0.9
1968	†StL N★	13	11	.542	34	33	10-5	0	232	214	87	11	3	61-4	162	2.99	97	.246	.295	73-2-6	.164	2*	107	-2	0	0.0
1969	StL N★	17	11	.607	31	31	12-2	0-0	236.1	185	66	15	4	93-6	210	2.17	165	.216	.294	80-1-4	.213	5*	81	37	0	5.0
1970	StL N	10	19	.345	34	33	13-2	0-0	253.2	239	123	25	2	109-16	193	3.73	111	.251	.326	80-0-3	.200	2	75	9	0	1.1
1971	StL N☆	20	9	.690	37	36	18-4	0-0	273.1	275	120	23	5	98-11	172	3.56	102	.262	.326	96-0-7	.177	1	122	2	0	0.3
1972	Phi N★	**27**	10	.730	41	**41**	**30**-8	0-0	**346.1**	257	84	17	1	87-8	**310**	**1.97**	**183**	.206	.257	117-1-7	.197	4	92	**60**	0	**7.4**

YEAR	TM LG	W	L	PCT	G	GS	CG-SHO	SV-BS	IP	H	R	HR	HB	BB-IB	SO	ERA	AERA	OAV	OOB	AB-HR-SH	AVG	PB	SUP	APR	DL	PW
1973	Phi N	13	20	.394	40	**40**	**18**-3	0-0	**293.1**	293	146	29	3	113-12	223	3.90	98	.260	.329	100-2-4	.160	0	83	-5	0	-0.5
1974	Phi N☆	16	13	.552	39	39	17-1	0-0	291	249	118	21	5	136-8	**240**	3.22	118	.234	.321	102-0-7	.245	2	114	17	0	1.8
1975	Phi N	15	14	.517	37	37	14-3	0-0	255.1	217	116	24	2	104-5	192	3.56	106	.233	.308	90-0-7	.156	-0	106	5	0	0.4
1976	†Phi N	20	7	**.741**	35	35	13-2	0-0	252.2	224	94	19	1	72-4	195	3.13	114	.237	.290	92-0-7	.217	2	150	14	0	1.5
1977	†Phi N☆	**23**	10	.697	36	36	17-2	0-0	283	229	99	25	4	89-5	198	2.64	153	.223	.286	97-3-7	.268	8	107	40	0	5.5
1978	†Phi N	16	13	.552	34	34	12-3	0-0	247.1	228	91	30	3	63-7	161	2.84	127	.246	.295	86-0-3	.291	7	118	19	0	3.1
1979	Phi N★	18	11	.621	35	35	13-4	0-0	251	202	112	25	5	89-11	213	3.62	107	.219	.290	94-0-2	.223	3*	111	5	0	0.9
1980	†Phi N☆	**24**	9	.727	38	**38**	13-3	0-0	**304**	243	87	15	2	90-12	**286**	2.34	**163**	.218	.276	101-0-6	.188	-1	103	**48**	0	**5.2**
1981	†Phi N☆	13	4	.765	24	24	10-1	0-0	190	152	59	9	1	62-3	179	2.42	151	.222	.286	67-0-2	.134	-0	107	24	0	2.0
1982	Phi N★	**23**	11	.676	38	**38**	**19-6**	0-0	**295.2**	253	114	17	1	86-5	**286**	3.10	119	.232	.288	101-2-8	.218	4	104	19	0	2.5
1983	†Phi N	15	16	.484	37	37	8-3	0-0	**283.2**	277	117	20	3	84-10	**275**	3.11	116	.258	.313	97-0-6	.196	3	92	15	0	1.8
1984	Phi N	13	7	.650	33	33	1	0-0	229	214	104	14	0	79-7	163	3.58	102	.246	.306	84-1-3	.190	2*	127	3	0	0.4
1985	Phi N	1	8	.111	16	16	0	0-0	92	84	43	6	0	53-4	48	3.33	112	.249	.349	28-0-1	.179	0	58	2	73	0.3
1986	Phi N	4	8	.333	16	16	0	0-0	83	102	70	15	0	45-4	62	6.18	63	.297	.376	34-0-1	.206	1	111	-22	0	-2.7
	SF N	1	3	.250	6	6	0	0-0	30	36	20	4	1	16-0	18	5.10	69	.303	.390	11-1-0	.182	1	139	-6	0	-0.6
	Year	5	11	.313	22	22	0	0-0	113	138	90	19	1	61-4	80	5.89	65	.299	.380	45-1-1	.200	2	118	-28	0	-3.3
	Chi A	4	3	.571	10	10	0	0-0	63.1	58	30	6	0	25-0	40	3.69	118	.252	.323	0	ø	0	84	4	0	0.4
1987	Cle A	5	9	.357	23	14	3	1-3	109	111	76	17	2	63-3	71	5.37	85	.266	.361	0	ø	0	107	-10	0	-1.1
	Min A	1	5	.167	9	7	0	0-0	43	54	35	7	2	23-1	20	6.70	69	.310	.397	0	ø	0	65	-9	0	-1.1
	Year	6	14	.300	32	21	3	1-3	152	165	111	24	4	86-4	91	5.74	80	.279	.372	0	ø	0	93	-22	0	-2.2
1988	Min A	0	1	.000	4	1	0	0-0	9.2	20	19	5	0	5-1	5	16.76	24	.408	.463	0	ø	0	45	-13	0	-1.1
Total	24	329	244	.574	741	709	254-55	2-3	5217.2	4672	2130	414	53	1833-150	4136	3.22	116	.240	.306	1719-13-94	.201	48	104	269	73	34.0
Carlyle, Buddy	Earl L.; B12.21.1977 Omaha NE; BL/TR/6´3˝/(170–175); [CinN96 2/38]; d8.29																									
1999	SD N	1	3	.250	7	7	0	0-0	37.2	36	28	7	2	17-0	29	5.97	71	.257	.342	9	.222	1	111	-8	0	-0.6
2000	SD N	0	0	ø	4	0	0	0-0	3	6	7	0	0	3-0	2	21.00	21	.400	.500	0	ø	0	—	-5	0	-0.2
2005	LA N	0	0	ø	10	0	0	0-1	14	16	13	4	1	4-0	13	8.36	50	.291	.350	0	ø	0	—	-6	0	-0.3
Total	3	1	3	.250	21	7	0	0-1	54.2	58	48	11	3	24-0	44	7.41	57	.276	.356	9	.222	1	111	-19	0	-1.1
Carman, Don	Donald Wayne; B8.14.1959 Oklahoma City OK; BL/TL/6´3˝/(190–201); d10.1; Col Seminole St. (OK) JC																									
1983	Phi N	0	0	ø	1	0	0	1-0	1	0	0	0	0	0-0	0	0.00	ø	.000	.000	0	ø	0	—	0	0	0.1
1984	Phi N	0	1	.000	11	0	0	0-0	13.1	14	9	2	0	6-4	16	5.40	68	.255	.328	1	.000	-0	—	-2	0	-0.2
1985	Phi N	9	4	.692	71	0	0	7-5	86.1	52	25	6	2	38-3	87	2.08	178	.178	.273	3-0-1	.000	-0	—	14	0	2.3
1986	Phi N	10	5	.667	50	14	2-1	1-6	134.1	113	50	11	3	52-11	98	3.22	121	.234	.311	31-0-2	.000	-3	78	12	0	1.0
1987	Phi N	13	11	.542	35	35	3-2	0-0	211	194	110	34	5	69-7	125	4.22	102	.244	.306	61-0-10	.082	-3	96	2	0	-0.3
1988	Phi N	10	14	.417	36	32	2	0-0	201.1	211	101	20	4	70-6	116	4.29	84	.270	.330	63-0-8	.048	-5	95	-12	0	-2.0
1989	Phi N	5	15	.250	49	20	0	0-0	149.1	152	98	21	3	86-6	81	5.24	68	.260	.355	34-0-7	.029	-3	83	-26	0	-3.6
1990	Phi N	6	2	.750	59	1	0	1-1	86.2	69	43	13	4	38-7	58	4.15	93	.218	.307	11	.273	1	94	-2	0	-0.1
1991	Cin N	0	2	.000	28	0	0	1-0	36	40	23	8	1	19-1	15	5.25	72	.286	.373	5	.000	-1	—	-5	0	-0.3
1992	Tex A	0	0	ø	2	0	0	0-0	2.1	4	3	0	0	0-0	2	7.71	50	.364	.364	0	ø	0	—	-1	0	-0.1
Total	10	53	54	.495	342	102	7-3	11-12	921.2	849	462	115	22	378-45	598	4.11	94	.245	.321	209-0-28	.057	-14	91	-20	0	-3.2
Carmichael, Chet	Chester Keller; B1.9.1888 Muncie IN; D8.22.1960 Rochester NY; BR/TR/5´11.5˝/200; d9.5																									
1909	Cin N	0	0	ø	2	0	0	0	7	9	6	0	2	3	2	0.00	ø	.321	.424	2	.000	-0	—	0	—	0.0
Carmona, Fausto	Fausto C.; B12.7.1983 Santo Domingo, D.R.; BR/TR/6´4˝/220; d4.15																									
2006	Cle A	1	10	.091	38	7	0	0-3	74.2	88	46	9	7	31-3	58	5.42	80	.297	.373	0	ø	0	103	-8	0	-0.9
Carmona, Rafael	Rafael; B10.2.1972 Rio Piedras, PR; BL/TR/6´2˝/185; [SeaA93 13/353]; d5.18; Col Indian Hills (IA) CC; [DL 1998 Sea A 181]																									
1995	Sea A	2	4	.333	15	3	0	1-1	47.2	55	31	9	2	34-1	28	5.66	84	.293	.397	0	ø	0	124	-4	0	-0.4
1996	Sea A	8	3	.727	53	1	0	1-4	90.1	95	47	11	3	55-9	62	4.28	116	.273	.375	0	ø	0	75	7	0	0.7
1997	Sea A	0	0	ø	4	0	0	0-0	5.2	3	3	1	0	2-0	6	3.18	143	.150	.227	0	ø	0	—	0	0	0.0
1999	Sea A	1	0	1.000	9	0	0	0-0	11.1	18	11	3	0	9-1	0	7.94	60	.409	.491	0	ø	0	—	-4	59	-0.3
Total	4	11	7	.611	81	4	0	2-5	155	171	92	24	5	100-11	96	4.94	99	.285	.387	0	ø	0	109	-1	240	-0.0
Carney, Pat	Patrick Joseph "Doc"; B8.7.1876 Holyoke MA; D1.9.1953 Worcester MA; BL/TL/6´0˝/200; d9.20.1901; Col Holy Cross; ▲																									
1902	Bos N	0	1	.000	2	1	0	0	5	6	5	1	1	3	3	9.00	31	.300	.417	522-2-4	.270	0*	48	-3	—	-0.4
1903	Bos N	4	5	.444	10	9	9	0	78	93	52	2	2	31	29	4.04	79	.284	.349	392-1-5	.240	2*	105	-7	—	-0.5
1904	Bos N	0	4	.000	4	3	1	0	26.1	40	27	1	1	12	5	5.81	47	.364	.431	279-0-8	.204	0*	62	-10	—	-1.2
Total	3	4	10	.286	16	13	10	0	109.1	139	84	4	4	46	37	4.69	66	.303	.372	1193-3-17	.245	2	95	-20	—	-2.1
Carpenter, Chris	Christopher John; B4.27.1975 Exeter NH; BR/TR/6´6˝/(215–230); [TorA93 1/15]; d5.12; [DL 2003 StL N 183]																									
1997	Tor A	3	7	.300	14	13	1-1	0-0	81.1	108	55	7	2	37-0	55	5.09	90	.325	.394	0	ø	0	71	-6	0	-0.7
1998	Tor A	12	7	.632	33	24	1-1	0-0	175	177	97	18	5	61-1	136	4.37	107	.265	.329	1	.000	-0	114	4	0	0.3
1999	Tor A	9	8	.529	24	24	4-1	0-0	150	177	81	16	3	48-1	106	4.38	112	.294	.346	1	.000	0	104	8	25	0.8
2000	Tor A	10	12	.455	34	27	2	0-0	175.1	204	130	30	5	83-1	113	6.26	80	.290	.369	2	.000	-0	94	-22	0	-2.3
2001	Tor A	11	11	.500	34	34	3-2	0-0	215.2	229	112	29	16	75-5	157	4.09	112	.274	.345	6-0-1	.167	-0	107	9	0	0.8
2002	Tor A	4	5	.444	13	13	1	0-0	73.1	89	45	11	4	27-0	45	5.28	88	.306	.368	1-0-1	1.000	0	85	-5	125	-0.5
2004	StL N	15	5	.750	28	28	1	0-0	182	169	75	24	8	38-2	152	3.46	123	.245	.291	62-0-4	.081	-4	90	17	0	1.4
2005	†StL N★	21	5	**.808**	33	33	**7**-4	0-0	241.2	204	82	18	3	51-0	213	2.83	148	.231	.273	77-0-10	.065	-4	118	39	0	3.7
2006	†StL N☆	15	8	.652	32	32	5-**3**	0-0	221.2	194	81	21	10	43-3	184	3.09	141	.235	**.279**	71-0-9	.127	-2	100	32	15	2.7
Total	9	100	68	.595	245	228	25-12	0-0	1516	1551	758	174	56	463-13	1161	4.09	111	.266	.324	221-0-25	.095	-9	101	76	348	6.2
Carpenter, Cris	Cris Howell; B4.5.1965 St.Augustine FL; BR/TR/6´1˝/(185–190); [StLN87 1/14]; d5.14; Col Georgia																									
1988	StL N	2	3	.400	8	8	1	0-0	47.2	56	27	3	1	9-2	24	4.72	75	.298	.327	14-0-3	.143	-0	101	-6	0	-0.6
1989	StL N	4	4	.500	36	5	0	0-2	68	70	30	4	2	26-9	35	3.18	115	.262	.328	9-0-2	.444	1	101	2	0	0.4
1990	StL N	0	0	ø	4	0	0	0-0	8	5	4	2	0	2-1	6	4.50	86	.167	.219	1	.000	-0	—	0	0	0.0
1991	StL N	10	4	.714	59	0	0	0-0	66	53	31	6	0	20-9	47	4.23	89	.220	.278	3	.333	0	—	-2	0	-0.4
1992	StL N	5	4	.556	73	0	0	1-7	88	69	29	10	4	27-8	46	2.97	115	.220	.288	3-0-1	.333	0	—	6	0	0.6
1993	Fla N	0	1	.000	29	0	0	0-2	37.1	29	15	1	2	13-2	26	2.89	151	.212	.288	0-0-1	ø	0	—	5	0	0.3
	Tex A	4	1	.800	27	0	0	1-1	32	35	15	4	2	12-1	27	4.22	99	.289	.355	0	ø	0	—	1	0	0.1
1994	Tex A	2	5	.286	47	0	0	5-6	59	69	35	7	0	20-7	39	5.03	96	.291	.342	0	ø	0	—	0	0	0.0
1996	Mil A	0	0	ø	8	0	0	0-0	8.1	12	8	1	0	2-0	2	7.56	69	.333	.359	0	ø	0	—	-2	0	-0.1
Total	8	27	22	.551	291	13	1	7-18	414.1	398	194	38	11	131-39	252	3.91	100	.254	.312	30-0-7	.267	1	94	4	0	0.3
Carpenter, Lew	Lewis Emmett; B8.16.1913 Woodstock GA; D4.25.1979 Marietta GA; BR/TR/6´2˝/195; d5.1; Col Georgia Tech																									
1943	Was A	0	0	ø	4	0	0	0	3.1	1	0	0	1	4	1	0.00	ø	.125	.462	0	ø	0	—	1	0	0.1
Carpenter, Paul	Paul Calvin; B8.12.1894 Granville OH; D3.14.1968 Newark OH; BR/TR/5´11˝/165; d7.26																									
1916	Pit N	0	0	ø	5	0	0	0	7.2	8	3	0	0	4	5	1.17	229	.258	.343	2	.000	-0	—	1	—	0.0
Carpenter, Bob	Robert Louis; B12.12.1917 Chicago IL; D10.19.2005 Evergreen Park IL; BR/TR/6´3˝/195; d9.12; Mil 1943–45																									
1940	NY N	2	0	1.000	5	3	2	0	33	29	11	2	0	14	25	2.73	142	.238	.316	10	.100	-0	127	4	—	0.2
1941	NY N	11	6	.647	29	19	8-1	2	131.2	138	71	15	2	42	42	3.83	97	.265	.323	45-0-2	.156	-0	128	-5	0	-0.7
1942	NY N	11	10	.524	28	25	12-2	0	185.2	192	73	13	1	51	53	3.15	107	.263	.312	65-0-6	.185	-1	117	6	0	0.4
1946	NY N	1	3	.250	12	6	1-1	0	39	37	22	7	0	18	13	4.85	71	.245	.325	10-0-2	.100	-0	54	-5	0	-0.5
1947	NY N	0	0	ø	2	0	0	0	3	5	5	0	0	3	0	12.00	34	.385	.500	0	ø	0	—	-3	0	-0.1
	Chi N	0	1	.000	4	1	0	0	7.1	10	5	1	0	4	1	4.91	80	.323	.400	1	1.000	0	45	-1	0	-0.1
	Year	0	1	.000	6	1	0	0	10.1	15	10	1	0	7	1	6.97	57	.341	.431	1	1.000	0	44	-4	0	-0.2
Total	5	25	20	.556	80	54	23-4	2	399.2	411	187	38	3	132	134	3.60	98	.262	.321	131-0-10	.168	-1	113	-4	0	-0.8
Carpin, Frank	Frank Dominic; B9.14.1938 Brooklyn NY; BL/TL/5´10˝/172; d5.25; Col Notre Dame																									
1965	Pit N	3	1	.750	39	0	0	4	39.2	35	16	0	3	24-3	27	3.18	111	.243	.360	1	.000	-0	—	2	0	0.3
1966	Hou N	1	0	1.000	10	0	0	0	6	9	7	0	0	6-0	2	7.50	46	.346	.469	0	ø	0	—	-3	0	-0.5
Total	2	4	1	.800	49	0	0	4	45.2	44	23	0	3	30-3	29	3.74	93	.259	.377	1	.000	-0	—	-1	0	-0.2

YEAR	TM LG	W	L	PCT	G	GS	CG-SHO	SV-BS	IP	H	R	HR	HB	BB-IB	SO	ERA	AERA	OAV	OOB	AB-HR-SH	AVG	PB	SUP	APR	DL	PW
Carrara, Giovanni	Giovanni (Jimenez); B3.4.1968 Edo Anzoategui, Venezuela; BR/TR/6´2˝/(210–235); d7.29																									
1995	Tor A	2	4	.333	12	7	1	0-0	48.2	64	46	10	1	25-1	27	7.21	66	.320	.395	0	ø	0	115	-14	0	-1.5
1996	Tor A	0	1	.000	11	0	0	0-1	15	23	19	5	0	12-2	10	11.40	44	.359	.461	0	ø	0	—	-10	0	-0.5
	Cin N	1	0	1.000	8	5	0	0-0	23	31	17	6	2	13-1	13	5.87	73	.323	.414	7	.000	-1	160	-4	0	-0.3
1997	Cin N	0	1	.000	2	2	0	0-0	10.1	14	9	4	0	6-1	5	7.84	55	.333	.417	2-0-2	.000	-0	65	-4	0	-0.3
2000	Col N	0	1	.000	8	0	0	0-1	13.1	21	19	5	1	11-2	15	12.83	45	.356	.458	1	.000	-0	—	-8	32	-0.5
2001	LA N	6	1	.857	47	3	0	0-3	85.1	73	30	12	1	24-3	70	3.16	130	.231	.287	12	.250	1	134	11	0	0.8
2002	LA N	6	3	.667	63	1	0	1-5	90.2	83	34	14	6	32-4	56	3.28	119	.243	.318	6-0-1	.000	-0	71	7	20	0.7
2003	Sea A	2	0	1.000	23	0	0	0-0	29	40	22	6	2	14-0	13	6.83	63	.333	.412	0	ø	0	—	-8	0	-0.4
2004	†LA N	5	2	.714	42	0	0	2-1	53.2	46	15	1	1	20-3	48	2.18	190	.228	.300	2	.000	-0	—	12	0	1.5
2005	LA N	7	4	.636	72	0	0	0-2	75.2	65	35	6	6	38-5	56	3.93	106	.243	.344	1-0-1	.000	-0	—	2	0	0.4
2006	LA N	0	1	.000	25	0	0	1-1	27.2	27	14	5	1	7-0	25	4.55	96	.250	.302	0	ø	0	—	0	0	0.0
Total	10	29	18	.617	313	18	1	4-14	472.1	487	260	74	21	202-22	338	4.69	91	.268	.346	31-0-4	.097	-1	128	-16	52	-0.1
Carrasco, D.J.	Daniel; B4.12.1977 Safford AZ; BR/TR/6´1˝/(210–215); [BalA97 26/795]; d4.2; Col Pima (AZ) CC																									
2003	KC A	6	5	.545	50	2	0	2-3	80.1	82	44	8	7	40-4	57	4.82	100	.271	.364	2	.000	-0	124	1	0	0.1
2004	KC A	2	2	.500	30	0	0	0-3	35.1	41	22	5	3	15-3	22	4.84	96	.287	.364	0	ø	0	—	-1	0	-0.1
2005	KC A	6	8	.429	21	20	1	0-0	114.2	129	67	11	6	51-2	49	4.79	91	.289	.366	7-0-1	.000	-1	93	-6	0	-0.6
Total	3	14	15	.483	101	22	1	2-6	230.1	252	133	24	16	106-9	128	4.81	95	.283	.365	9-0-1	.000	-1	93	-6	0	-0.6
Carrasco, Hector	Hector (Pacheco); B10.22.1969 San Pedro de Macoris, D.R.; BR/TR/6´2˝/(175–220); d4.4																									
1994	Cin N	5	6	.455	45	0	0	6-2	56.1	42	17	3	2	30-1	41	2.24	187	.210	.319	6	.000	-1	—	12	20	2.2
1995	†Cin N	2	7	.222	64	0	0	5-4	87.1	86	45	1	2	46-5	64	4.12	101	.257	.344	7	.000	-1	—	0	0	-0.2
1996	Cin N	4	3	.571	56	0	0	0-2	74.1	58	37	6	1	45-5	59	3.75	114	.214	.324	5	.200	0	—	3	0	0.3
1997	Cin N	1	2	.333	38	0	0	0-0	51.1	51	25	3	4	25-2	46	3.68	116	.250	.342	0	ø	0	—	2	0	0.1
	KC A	1	6	.143	28	0	0	0-2	34.2	29	21	4	4	16-3	30	5.45	87	.227	.327	0	ø	0	—	-2	0	-0.3
1998	Min A	4	2	.667	63	0	0	1-1	61.2	75	30	4	1	31-1	46	4.38	110	.304	.373	0	ø	0	—	4	0	0.3
1999	Min A	2	3	.400	39	0	0	1-1	49	48	29	3	1	18-0	35	4.96	104	.261	.328	0	ø	0	—	1	81	0.0
2000	Min A	4	3	.571	61	0	0	1-4	72	75	38	6	3	33-0	57	4.25	124	.270	.349	0	ø	0	—	7	0	0.6
	Bos A	1	1	.500	8	1	0	0-1	6.2	15	8	2	1	5-1	7	9.45	53	.469	.553	0	ø	0	37	-3	0	-0.6
	Year	5	4	.556	69	1	0	1-5	78.2	90	46	8	4	38-1	64	4.69	112	.290	.371	0	ø	0	36	4	0	0.0
2001	Min A	4	3	.571	56	0	0	1-1	73.2	77	40	8	0	30-3	70	4.64	101	.277	.344	0	ø	0	—	0	0	0.0
2003	Bal A	2	6	.250	40	0	0	1-2	38.1	40	22	5	2	20-3	27	4.93	93	.270	.365	0	ø	0	—	-1	0	-0.2
2005	Was N	5	4	.556	64	5	0	2-2	88.1	59	23	6	6	38-7	75	2.04	202	.193	.291	8-0-2	.000	-1	83	20	0	1.8
2006	LA A	7	3	.700	56	3	0	1-1	100.1	93	42	10	5	27-1	72	3.41	131	.244	.301	0	ø	0	56	12	0	1.1
Total	11	42	49	.462	618	9	0	19-23	794	748	377	61	32	364-32	629	3.88	117	.250	.334	26-0-2	.038	-2	64	55	101	5.1
Carrasquel, Alex	Alejandro Eloy (Aparicio); B7.24.1912 Caracas, Distrito Capital, Venez.; D8.19.1969 Caracas, Distrito Capital, Venez.; BR/TR/6´1˝/182; d4.23																									
1939	Was A	5	9	.357	40	17	7	2	159.1	165	89	7	1	68	41	4.69	93	.266	.340	42-1-5	.167	1	91	-3	—	-0.2
1940	Was A	6	2	.750	28	0	0	0	48	42	26	4	0	29	19	4.88	86	.240	.348	7	.000	-1	—	-2	—	-0.4
1941	Was A	6	2	.750	35	5	4	2	96.2	103	44	7	1	49	30	3.44	117	.278	.364	21-0-2	.095	0	133	7	0	0.7
1942	Was A	7	7	.500	35	15	7-1	4	152.1	161	74	7	1	53	40	3.43	107	.267	.327	44-0-4	.136	-0	103	2	0	0.2
1943	Was A	11	7	.611	39	13	4-1	5	144.1	160	76	3	1	54	48	3.68	87	.279	.342	43-0-4	.186	1	144	-10	0	-1.1
1944	Was A	8	7	.533	43	7	3	2	134	143	68	8	2	50	35	3.43	95	.273	.339	36	.194	1	110	-5	0	-0.3
1945	Was A	7	5	.583	35	7	5-2	1	122.2	105	43	5	0	40	38	2.71	114	.228	.289	36-0-1	.083	-2	145	7	0	0.5
1949	Chi A	0	0	ø	3	0	0	0	3.2	8	6	1	0	4	1	14.73	28	.421	.522	0	ø	0	—	-4	0	-0.2
Total	8	50	39	.562	258	64	30-4	16	861	887	426	42	6	347	252	3.73	98	.265	.335	229-1-16	.144	0	115	-8	0	-0.8
Carreno, Amalio	Amalio Rafael (Adrian); B4.11.1964 Chacachacare, Nueva Esparta, Venez.; BR/TR/6´0˝/170; d7.7																									
1991	Phi N	0	0	ø	3	0	0	0-0	3.1	5	6	1	2	3-0	2	16.20	23	.333	.500	1	.000	-0	—	-4	0	-0.2
Carrick, Bill	William Martin "Doughnut Bill"; B9.5.1873 Erie PA; D3.7.1932 Philadelphia PA; BR/TR/5´10˝/150; d7.30																									
1898	NY N	3	1	.750	5	4	4	0	39.2	39	23	0	5	21	10	3.40	102	.255	.363	18	.167	-1	138	0	—	0.0
1899	NY N	16	27	.372	44	**43**	**40**-3	0	361.2	485	250	4	18	122	60	4.65	81	.320	.378	130-0-4	.138	-6	87	-32	—	-3.4
1900	NY N	19	22	.463	**45**	**41**	32-1	0	341.2	415	224	7	13	92	63	3.53	102	.299	.348	115-0-4	.174	-3	97	-2	—	-0.5
1901	Was A	14	22	.389	42	37	34	0	324	367	198	12	20	93	70	3.75	98	.282	.339	126-0-3	.159	-5	76	-5	—	-0.8
1902	Was A	11	17	.393	31	30	28	0	257.2	344	194	10	9	72	36	4.86	76	.320	.368	108-0-4	.185	-2*	100	-34	—	-3.3
Total	5	63	89	.414	167	155	138-4	0	1324.2	1650	889	33	65	400	239	4.14	89	.304	.359	497-0-15	.163	-16	91	-73	—	-8.0
Carrithers, Don	Donald George; B9.15.1949 Lynwood CA; BR/TR/6´2˝/180; [SFN67 3/58]; d8.1																									
1970	SF N	2	1	.667	11	2	0	0-0	22	31	19	5	0	14-1	14	7.36	54	.333	.417	6	.000	-0	56	-8	0	-1.0
1971	†SF N	5	3	.625	22	12	2-1	1-0	80.1	77	48	6	2	37-1	41	4.03	85	.254	.331	17-0-4	.176	0	136	-8	0	-0.7
1972	SF N	4	8	.333	25	14	2	1-0	90	108	66	10	5	42-4	42	5.80	60	.296	.375	29-0-1	.207	1*	128	-23	0	-2.7
1973	SF N	1	2	.333	25	3	0	0-1	58	64	40	2	4	35-2	36	4.81	80	.278	.381	16-0-1	.250	0*	84	-8	0	-0.3
1974	Mon N	5	2	.714	22	3	0	1-1	60	56	22	6	3	17-4	31	3.00	128	.249	.306	14-0-1	.286	0	121	6	0	0.8
1975	Mon N	5	3	.625	19	14	5-2	0-0	101	90	39	7	4	38-1	37	3.30	117	.240	.316	34-0-1	.176	0	104	7	35	0.7
1976	Mon N	6	12	.333	34	19	2	0-0	140.1	153	84	9	7	78-13	71	4.43	85	.286	.381	37-0-3	.108	-1*	55	-12	0	-1.5
1977	Min A	0	1	.000	7	0	0	0-0	14.1	16	13	2	1	6-1	3	6.91	58	.271	.348	0	ø	0	—	-5	88	-0.3
Total	8	28	32	.467	165	67	11-3	3-2	566	595	331	47	26	267-27	275	4.45	84	.272	.355	153-0-11	.176	0	97	-51	123	-5.0
Carroll, Clay	Clay Palmer "Hawk"; B5.2.1941 Clanton AL; BR/TR/6´1˝/(178–205); d9.2																									
1964	Mil N	2	0	1.000	11	1	0	1	20.1	15	4	1	0	3-1	17	1.77	199	.200	.231	2	.000	-0	200	4	0	0.5
1965	Mil N	0	1	.000	19	1	0	1	34.2	35	18	3	1	13-2	16	4.41	80	.269	.336	5-0-1	.000	-1	99	-3	0	-0.2
1966	Atl N	8	7	.533	**73**	3	0	11	144.1	127	45	8	4	29-4	67	2.37	154	.236	.277	30-0-8	.100	-2	201	19	0	2.1
1967	Atl N	6	12	.333	42	7	1	0	93	111	62	6	3	29-10	35	5.52	60	.304	.357	16-0-2	.063	-1	113	-22	0	-3.9
1968	Atl N	0	1	.000	10	0	0	0	22.1	26	15	1	0	6-2	10	4.84	62	.310	.348	5	.000	-0	—	-5	0	-0.3
	Cin N	7	7	.500	58	1	0	17	121.2	102	35	3	6	32-10	61	2.29	138	.230	.289	24-0-1	.250	1	27	11	0	2.0
	Year	7	8	.467	68	1	0	17	144	128	50	4	6	38-12	71	2.69	117	.242	.299	29-0-1	.207	1	28	6	0	1.7
1969	Cin N	12	6	.667	71	4	0	7-10	150.2	149	70	9	7	78-18	90	3.52	107	.262	.356	29-1-5	.207	2	183	3	0	0.7
1970	†Cin N	9	4	.692	65	0	0	16-2	104.1	104	38	4	2	27-9	63	2.59	156	.259	.309	14	.071	-1	—	15	0	2.2
1971	Cin N☆	10	4	.714	61	0	0	15-3	93.2	78	26	5	2	42-9	64	2.50	135	.234	.323	10-0-3	.100	-1	—	10	0	2.1
1972	†Cin N☆	6	4	.600	**65**	0	0	**37**-3	96	89	27	5	1	32-9	51	2.25	144	.256	.316	11-0-1	.182	0	—	11	0	2.2
1973	†Cin N	8	8	.500	53	5	0	14-4	92.2	111	47	5	5	34-11	41	3.69	93	.307	.372	14-0-4	.214	0	87	-5	0	-0.9
1974	Cin N	12	5	.706	57	3	0	6-3	100.2	96	27	3	0	30-9	46	2.15	163	.256	.308	18	.167	-0	100	16	0	2.8
1975	†Cin N	7	5	.583	56	2	0	7-6	96.1	93	30	2	3	32-8	44	2.62	137	.255	.315	19-0-2	.000	-2	147	11	0	1.2
1976	Chi A	4	4	.500	29	0	0	6-4	77.1	67	26	1	2	24-2	38	2.56	139	.242	.306	0	ø	0	—	8	30	0.9
1977	StL N	4	2	.667	51	1	0	4-4	90	77	28	8	1	24-8	34	2.50	156	.238	.290	11-0-3	.091	-1	68	14	0	1.0
	Chi A	1	3	.250	8	0	0	1-0	11.1	14	7	3	0	4-0	4	4.76	86	.311	.367	0	ø	0	—	-1	0	-0.2
1978	Pit N	0	0	ø	2	0	0	0-0	4	2	1	0	0	3-0	0	2.25	166	.143	.294	0	ø	0	—	1	0	0.0
Total	15	96	73	.568	731	28	1	143-39	1353.1	1296	506	67	37	442-112	681	2.94	121	.257	.319	208-1-30	.130	-5	127	87	30	12.2
Carroll, Ed	Edgar Fleischer; B7.27.1907 Baltimore MD; D10.13.1984 Rossville MD; BR/TR/6´3˝/185; d5.1																									
1929	Bos A	1	0	1.000	24	2	0	0	67.1	77	46	6	4	20	13	5.61	76	.291	.349	16-0-3	.063	-2	99	-8	—	-0.6
Carroll, Ownie	Owen Thomas; B11.11.1902 Kearny NJ; D6.8.1975 Orange NJ; BR/TR/5´10.5˝/165; d6.20; Col Holy Cross																									
1925	Det A	2	2	.500	10	4	1	0	40.2	46	30	1	2	28	12	3.76	114	.293	.406	16	.375	1*	112	-2	—	-0.1
1927	Det A	10	6	.625	31	15	8	0	172	186	99	5	6	73	41	3.98	106	.281	.358	69-0-1	.174	-2*	110	3	—	0.1
1928	Det A	16	12	.571	34	28	19-2	2	231	219	100	6	7	87	51	3.27	126	.262	.337	98-0-9	.194	-0*	95	22	—	2.5
1929	Det A	9	17	.346	34	26	12	1	202	249	133	10	8	86	54	4.63	93	.310	.383	74-0-2	.230	2*	94	-11	—	-0.9
1930	Det A	0	5	.000	6	3	0	0	20.1	30	24	3	0	9	4	10.62	45	.333	.394	7	.143	-1	66	-11	—	-1.8
	NY A	0	1	.000	10	1	0	0	32.2	49	32	2	4	18	8	6.61	65	.374	.464	10-0-1	.200	0*	140	-10	—	-0.4
	Year	0	6	.000	16	4	0	0	53	79	56	5	4	27	12	8.15	55	.357	.437	17-0-1	.176	-0	86	-21	—	-2.2
	Cin N	0	1	.000	3	2	1	0	14	17	9	3	0	3	0	4.50	107	.309	.345	5	.200	-0	45	0	—	0.0
1931	Cin N	3	9	.250	29	12	4	0	107.1	135	76	6	4	51	24	5.53	67	.314	.392	34-0-1	.206	0*	86	-21	—	-2.0
1932	Cin N	10	19	.345	32	26	15	1	210	245	124	7	9	44	55	4.50	86	.286	.328	77-0-2	.208	2*	76	-14	—	-1.5

YEAR	TM LG	W	L	PCT	G	GS	CG-SHO	SV-BS	IP	H	R	HR	HB	BB-IB	SO	ERA	AERA	OAV	OOB	AB-HR-SH	AVG	PB	SUP	APR	DL	PW
1933	Bro N	13	15	.464	33	31	11	0	226.1	248	117	9	7	54	45	3.78	85	.281	.327	74-0-4	.149	-1*	112	-16	—	-1.7
1934	Bro N	1	3	.250	26	5	0	1	74.1	108	64	9	1	33	17	6.42	61	.342	.406	25	.240	1*	115	-22	—	-0.8
Total	9	64	90	.416	248	153	71-2	5	1330.2	1532	808	61	48	486	311	4.43	89	.294	.359	489-0-20	.200	2	95	-82	—	-6.6
Carroll, Dick	Richard Thomas "Shadow"; B7.21.1884 Cleveland OH; D11.22.1945 Cleveland OH; BR/TR/6´2˝/?; d9.25
1909	NY A	0	0	ø	2	1	0	0	5	7	6	1	0	1	1	3.60	70	.292	.320	2	.500	0	307	-2	—	-0.1
Carroll, Tom	Thomas Michael; B11.5.1952 Utica NY; BL/TR/6´3˝/(183–190); [CinN70 6/138]; d7.7
1974	Cin N	4	3	.571	16	13	0	0-0	78.1	68	44	11	0	44-3	37	3.68	95	.231	.331	26-0-2	.154	-1	123	-5	0	-0.5
1975	Cin N	4	1	.800	12	7	0	0-0	47	52	28	1	2	26-0	14	4.98	72	.284	.379	14	.000	-2	116	-7	0	-0.9
Total	2	8	4	.667	28	20	0	0-0	125.1	120	72	12	2	70-3	51	4.16	85	.252	.350	40-0-2	.100	-2	120	-12	0	-1.4
Carsey, Kid	Wilfred; B10.22.1870 New York NY; D3.29.1960 Miami FL; BL/TR/5´7˝/168; d4.8
1891	Was AA	14	37	.275	54	53	46-1	0	415	513	358	17	28	161	174	4.99	75	.293	.362	187	.150	-5*	79	-49	—	-4.7
1892	Phi N	19	16	.543	43	36	30-1	1	317.2	317	160	6	12	104	76	3.12	104	.250	.312	131-1	.153	-3*	109	7	—	0.4
1893	Phi N	20	15	.571	39	35	30-1	0	318.1	375	229	7	19	124	50	4.81	95	.285	.355	145	.186	-7	110	-7	—	-1.2
1894	Phi N	18	12	.600	37	32	26	0	288.1	366	241	22	18	106	43	5.52	93	.306	.371	129-0-1	.279	4	136	-12	—	-0.5
1895	Phi N	24	16	.600	44	40	35	1	342.1	460	274	14	21	118	64	4.92	97	.317	.376	141-0-11	.291	3	124	-13	—	-0.9
1896	Phi N	11	11	.500	27	21	18-1	1	187.1	273	164	4	9	72	36	5.62	77	.337	.397	81-0-3	.222	1	130	-29	—	-2.3
1897	Phi N	2	1	.667	4	4	2	0	28	35	20	0	1	16	1	5.14	82	.304	.394	13-0-1	.231	-1	153	-2	—	-0.3
	StL N	3	8	.273	12	11	11	0	99	133	81	5	4	31	14	6.00	73	.319	.372	43	.302	2*	74	-13	—	-0.9
	Year	5	9	.357	16	15	13	0	127	168	101	5	5	47	15	5.81	75	.316	.377	56-0-1	.286	2	94	-16	—	-1.2
1898	StL N	2	12	.143	20	13	10	0	123.2	177	112	2	10	37	10	6.33	60	.333	.387	105-1-4	.200	-0*	72	-30	—	-2.7
1899	Cle N	1	8	.111	10	9	8	0	77.2	109	66	2	2	24	11	5.68	65	.330	.379	36	.278	1*	89	-17	—	-1.3
	Was N	1	2	.333	4	3	2	0	29	27	14	0	1	4	3	3.72	105	.248	.281	11-0-1	.000	-2	92	1	—	0.0
	Year	2	10	.167	14	12	10	0	106.2	136	80	2	3	28	14	5.15	73	.310	.355	47-0-1	.213	-1	90	-13	—	-1.3
1901	Bro N	1	0	1.000	2	0	0	0	7	9	9	1	1	3	4	10.29	33	.310	.394	2	.000	-0	—	-5	—	-0.5
Total	10	116	138	.457	296	257	218-4	3	2233.1	2794	1728	80	126	800	486	4.95	85	.300	.363	1024-2-21	.212	-8	108	-169	—	-14.9
Carson, Al	Albert James "Soldier"; B8.22.1882 Chicago IL; D11.26.1962 San Diego CA; BR/TR/5´10.5˝/162; d5.6; Col Santa Clara
1910	Chi N	0	0	ø	2	0	0	0	6.2	6	5	0	0	1	2	4.05	71	.240	.269	1	.000	0	—	-1	—	-0.1
Carter, Andy	Andrew Godfrey; B11.9.1968 Philadelphia PA; BL/TL/6´5˝/(200–220); [PhiN87 37/952]; d5.3
1994	Phi N	0	2	.000	20	0	0	0-0	34.1	34	18	5	6	12-2	18	4.46	96	.268	.351	6	.000	-1	—	0	0	-0.1
1995	Phi N	0	0	ø	4	0	0	0-0	7.1	4	5	3	1	2-1	6	6.14	69	.167	.250	1	1.000	0	—	-1	0	0.0
Total	2	0	2	.000	24	0	0	0-0	41.2	38	23	8	7	14-3	24	4.75	90	.252	.335	7	.143	-0	—	-1	0	-0.1
Carter, Arnold	Arnold Lee "Hook","Lefty"; B3.14.1918 Rainelle WV; D4.12.1989 Louisville KY; BL/TL/5´10˝/170; d4.29
1944	Cin N	11	7	.611	33	18	9-3	3	148.2	143	54	1	3	40	33	2.60	134	.256	.309	48-2-2	.250	5*	91	13	0	2.2
1945	Cin N	2	4	.333	13	6	2-1	0	46.2	54	21	2	2	13	4	3.09	122	.286	.338	17	.176	0*	38	2	0	0.3
Total	2	13	11	.542	46	24	11-4	3	195.1	197	75	3	5	53	37	2.72	131	.264	.317	65-2-2	.231	5	77	15	0	2.5
Carter, Nick	Conrad Powell; B5.19.1879 Oatlands VA; D11.23.1961 Grasonville MD; BR/TR/5´8˝/140; d4.14; Col Virginia
1908	Phi A	2	5	.286	14	4	2	0	60.2	58	26	1	2	17	17	2.97	86	.270	.329	20	.100	-2	40	-2	—	-0.3
Carter, Jeff	Jeffrey Allen; B12.3.1964 Tampa FL; BR/TR/6´3˝/195; [MonN87 19/486]; d7.31; Col Tampa
1991	Chi A	0	1	.000	5	2	0	0-0	12	8	8	1	0	5-0	2	5.25	76	.182	.265	0	ø	0	160	-2	0	-0.2
Carter, Lance	Lance David; B12.18.1974 Bradenton FL; BR/TR/6´1˝/190; [KCA94 21/583]; d9.15; Col Manatee (FL) CC
1999	KC A	0	1	.000	6	0	0	0-0	5.1	3	3	2	0	3-0	3	5.06	100	.167	.286	0	ø	0	—	0	0	0.0
2002	TB A	2	0	1.000	8	0	0	2-0	20.1	15	3	2	0	5-1	14	1.33	340	.203	.253	0	ø	0	—	7	0	0.8
2003	TB A☆	7	5	.583	62	0	0	26-7	79	72	39	12	4	19-6	47	4.33	106	.242	.291	0	ø	0	—	3	0	0.5
2004	TB A	3	3	.500	56	0	0	0-1	80.1	77	32	12	1	23-2	36	3.47	134	.252	.301	0	ø	0	—	12	0	0.7
2005	TB A	1	2	.333	39	0	0	1-3	57	61	31	9	1	15-1	13	4.89	90	.279	.324	0	ø	0	—	-2	0	-0.1
2006	LA N	0	1	.000	10	0	0	0-1	11.2	17	11	1	0	8-0	5	8.49	52	.347	.424	0	ø	0	—	-5	0	-0.3
Total	6	13	12	.520	181	0	0	29-12	253.2	245	119	38	6	73-10	127	4.15	110	.254	.306	0	ø	0	—	15	0	1.6
Carter, Larry	Larry Gene; B5.22.1965 Charleston WV; BR/TR/6´5˝/195; [StLN86 10/260]; d9.6; Col West Virginia St.
1992	SF N	1	5	.167	6	6	0	0-0	33	34	17	6	0	18-0	21	4.64	72	.270	.359	10-0-1	.200	1	68	-4	0	-0.7
Carter, Paul	Paul Warren "Nick"; B5.1.1894 Lake Park GA; D9.11.1984 Lake Park GA; BL/TR/6´3˝/175; d9.15; Col Rhodes
1914	Cle A	1	3	.250	5	4	1	0	24.2	35	15	0	0	5	9	2.92	99	.340	.370	7	.000	-1	69	-1	—	-0.3
1915	Cle A	1	1	.500	11	2	2	0	42	44	22	1	0	18	14	3.21	95	.272	.344	14-0-1	.214	1*	72	-1	—	0.0
1916	Chi N	2	2	.500	8	5	2	0	36	26	16	1	0	17	14	2.75	106	.203	.297	12-0-1	.167	-0	98	0	—	0.0
1917	Chi N	5	8	.385	23	13	6	2	113.1	115	47	2	3	19	34	3.26	89	.276	.313	35-0-1	.171	-0	76	-1	—	-0.2
1918	Chi N	3	2	.600	21	4	1	2	73	78	29	2	1	19	13	2.71	103	.290	.339	25	.240	0	129	1	—	0.2
1919	Chi N	5	4	.556	28	7	2	1	85	81	36	1	2	28	17	2.65	109	.252	.316	26	.269	1*	110	1	—	0.1
1920	Chi N	3	6	.333	31	8	2	2	106	131	68	3	5	36	14	4.67	69	.324	.387	35-0-1	.171	-1	144	-16	—	-1.5
Total	7	20	26	.435	127	43	16	7	480	510	233	10	11	142	115	3.32	89	.283	.339	154-0-4	.195	-1	101	-17	—	-1.7
Carter, Sol	Solomon Mobley "Buck"; B12.23.1908 Picayune MS; BR/TR/6´0˝/178; d4.15; Col Auburn
1931	Phi A	0	0	ø	2	0	0	0	2.1	1	5	0	0	4	1	19.29	23	.143	.455	0	ø	0	—	-3	—	-0.1
Caruthers, Bob	Robert Lee "Parisian Bob"; B1.5.1864 Memphis TN; D8.5.1911 Peoria IL; BL/TR/5´7˝/138; d9.7; M1/U2; ▲
1884	StL AA	7	2	.778	13	7	7	0	82.2	61	34	1	3	15	58	2.61	125	.189	.232	82-2	.268	2*	122	9	—	0.9
1885	†StL AA	**40**	13	**.755**	53	53	53-6	0	482.1	430	196	3	19	57	190	**2.07**	**158**	.230	.260	222-1	.225	6*	103	**61**	—	**6.3**
1886	†StL AA	30	14	.682	44	43	42-2	0	387.1	323	164	3	7	86	166	2.32	148	.217	.263	317-4	.334	26*	113	51	—	7.2
1887	†StL AA	29	9	**.763**	39	39	39-2	0	341	337	185	6	16	61	74	3.30	138	.247	.287	364-8	.357	20*	122	45	—	5.9
1888	Bro AA	29	15	.659	44	43	42-4	0	391.2	337	176	4	10	53	140	2.39	125	.224	.255	335-5	.230	10*	112	28	—	3.7
1889	†Bro AA	**40**	11	**.784**	56	50	46-**7**	1	445	444	215	16	13	104	118	3.13	119	.252	.298	172-2	.250	17*	123	33	—	4.6
1890	†Bro N	23	11	.676	37	33	30-1	0	300	292	163	9	12	87	64	3.09	112	.247	.305	238-1	.265	11*	100	12	—	2.2
1891	Bro N	18	14	.563	38	32	29-2	1	297	323	185	7	13	107	69	3.12	106	.267	.333	171-2	.281	11*	111	-1	—	1.0
1892	StL N	2	10	.167	16	10	10	1	101.2	131	75	10	6	27	21	5.84	55	.300	.350	513-3	.277	6*	55	-23	—	-1.8
Total	9	218	99	.688	340	310	298-24	3	2828.2	2678	1393	59	99	597	900	2.83	123	.240	.285	2414-28	.282	111	112	215	—	30.0
Carvajal, Marcos	Marcos Jose (Rendon); B8.19.1984 Ciudad Bolivar, Bolivar, Venezuela; BR/TR/6´4˝/175; d4.6
2005	Col N	0	2	.000	39	0	0	0-1	53	52	30	8	3	21-0	47	5.09	92	.259	.335	4	.250	0	—	-1	0	0.0
Cary, Chuck	Charles Douglas; B3.3.1960 Whittier CA; BL/TL/6´4˝/(210–216); [DetA81 7/172]; d8.22; Col California
1985	Det A	0	1	.000	16	0	0	2-1	23.2	16	9	2	2	8-1	22	3.42	120	.190	.274	0	ø	0	—	2	0	0.1
1986	Det A	1	2	.333	22	0	0	0-1	31.2	33	18	3	0	15-4	21	3.41	122	.273	.348	0	ø	0	—	1	0	0.0
1987	Atl N	1	1	.500	13	0	0	1-1	16.2	17	7	3	1	4-3	15	3.78	115	.266	.319	1	.000	-0	—	1	0	0.2
1988	Atl N	0	0	ø	7	0	0	0-0	8.1	8	6	1	1	4-0	7	6.48	57	.250	.351	0	ø	0	—	-2	129	-0.1
1989	NY A	4	4	.500	22	11	2	0-0	99.1	78	42	13	0	29-6	79	3.26	119	.209	.266	0	ø	0	99	6	26	0.3
1990	NY A	6	12	.333	28	27	2	0-0	156.2	155	77	21	1	55-1	134	4.19	95	.260	.321	0	ø	0	76	-2	36	-0.2
1991	NY A	1	6	.143	10	9	0	0-0	53.1	61	35	6	0	32-2	34	5.91	71	.285	.378	0	ø	0	76	-9	0	-1.0
1993	Chi A	1	0	1.000	16	0	0	0-0	20.2	22	12	1	3	11-0	10	5.23	81	.286	.379	0	ø	0	—	-2	127	-0.1
Total	8	14	26	.350	134	47	4	3-3	410.1	390	206	50	8	158-17	322	4.17	97	.250	.319	1	.000	-0	81	-5	318	-0.8
Cary, Scott	Scott Russell "Red"; B4.11.1923 Kendallville IN; BL/TL/5´11.5˝/168; d5.1
1947	Was A	3	1	.750	23	3	1	0	54.2	73	38	5	1	20	25	5.93	63	.312	.369	13-0-1	.077	-1	119	-12	0	-0.9
Casale, Jerry	Jerry Joseph; B9.27.1933 Brooklyn NY; BR/TR/6´2˝/(200–205); d9.14
1958	Bos A	0	0	ø	2	0	0	0	3	1	0	0	0	2-0	3	0.00	ø	.111	.273	0	ø	0	—	1	0	0.1
1959	Bos A	13	8	.619	31	26	9-3	0	179.2	162	89	20	5	89-3	93	4.31	94	.238	.329	59-3-4	.169	3	110	-2	0	-0.2
1960	Bos A	2	9	.182	29	14	1	0	96.1	113	78	14	1	67-5	54	6.17	66	.294	.394	33	.273	3	87	-24	0	-2.1
1961	LA A	1	5	.167	13	7	0	1	42.2	52	34	9	1	25-0	35	6.54	69	.297	.386	13-1-0	.462	3	56	-8	0	-0.7

YEAR	TM LG	W	L	PCT	G	GS	CG-SHO	SV-BS	IP	H	R	HR	HB	BB-IB	SO	ERA	AERA	OAV	OOB	AB-HR-SH	AVG	PB	SUP	APR	DL	PW
	Det A	0	0	ø	3	1	0	0	12	15	8	3	0	3-0	6	5.25	78	.313	.353	3	.000	-0	108	-1	0	-0.1
	Year	1	5	.167	16	8	0	1	54.2	67	42	12	1	28-0	41	6.26	71	.300	.379	16-1-0	.375	3	63	-10	0	-0.8
1962	Det A	1	2	.333	18	1	0	0	36.2	33	19	5	0	18-1	16	4.66	87	.236	.321	8	.000	-1	88	-1	0	-0.2
Total	5	17	24	.415	96	49	10-3	1	370.1	376	228	51	7	204-9	207	5.08	81	.262	.354	116-4-4	.216	7	95	-35	0	-3.2

CASCARELLA, JOE Joseph Thomas "Crooning Joe"; B6.28.1907 Philadelphia PA; D5.22.2002 Baltimore MD; BR/TR/6´10.5˝/175; d4.17

YEAR	TM LG	W	L	PCT	G	GS	CG-SHO	SV-BS	IP	H	R	HR	HB	BB-IB	SO	ERA	AERA	OAV	OOB	AB-HR-SH	AVG	PB	SUP	APR	DL	PW
1934	Phi A	12	15	.444	42	22	9-2	1	194.1	214	111	8	3	104	71	4.68	94	.288	.377	64-0-3	.094	-4	86	-5	—	-0.9
1935	Phi A	1	6	.143	9	3	1	0	32.1	29	21	1	0	22	15	5.29	86	.252	.372	8-0-2	.125	-1	32	-2	—	-0.4
	Bos A	0	3	.000	6	4	0	0	17	25	17	3	0	11	9	6.88	69	.329	.414	2-0-1	.000	-0	78	-4	—	-0.7
	Year	1	9	.100	15	7	1	0	49.1	54	38	4	0	33	24	5.84	79	.283	.388	10-0-3	.100	-1	59	-7	—	-1.1
1936	Bos A	0	2	.000	10	1	0	0	20.2	27	16	0	0	9	7	6.97	76	.329	.396	4	.000	-1	265	-3	—	-0.3
	Was A	9	8	.529	22	16	7-1	1	139.1	147	66	7	6	54	34	4.07	117	.276	.349	49-0-4	.143	-2	113	15	—	1.2
	Year	9	10	.474	32	17	7-1	1	160	174	82	7	6	63	41	4.44	109	.283	.355	53-0-4	.132	-3	122	12	—	0.9
1937	Was A	0	5	.000	10	4	1	1	32.1	50	41	3	1	23	10	8.07	55	.347	.440	9	.222	-0	59	-17	—	-2.0
	Cin N	1	2	.333	11	3	2	1	43.2	44	24	1	0	22	16	3.92	95	.263	.349	11	.091	-1	54	-2	—	-0.2
1938	Cin N	4	7	.364	33	1	0	4	61	66	33	2	0	22	30	4.57	80	.275	.336	18	.167	-1	116	-5	—	-1.0
Total	5	27	48	.360	143	54	20-3	8	540.2	602	329	25	10	267	192	4.84	91	.287	.370	165-0-10	.121	-9	93	-23	—	-4.3

CASE, CHARLIE Charles Emmett; B9.7.1879 Smith Landing OH; D4.16.1964 Batavia OH; BR/TR/6´0˝/170; d7.5

YEAR	TM LG	W	L	PCT	G	GS	CG-SHO	SV-BS	IP	H	R	HR	HB	BB-IB	SO	ERA	AERA	OAV	OOB	AB-HR-SH	AVG	PB	SUP	APR	DL	PW
1901	Cin N	1	2	.333	3	3	3	0	27	34	21	0	0	6	5	4.67	69	.306	.342	10	.100	-1	66	-5	—	-0.5
1904	Pit N	10	5	.667	18	17	14-3	0	141	129	56	0	4	31	49	2.94	93	.243	.290	53	.170	1	118	-1	—	0.0
1905	Pit N	11	11	.500	31	24	18-3	1	217	202	81	2	15	66	57	2.57	117	.251	.319	68-0-1	.103	-2	79	10	—	0.6
1906	Pit N	1	1	.500	2	2	1	0	11	8	9	0	1	5	3	5.73	47	.190	.292	2	.500	1	150	-3	—	-0.5
Total	4	23	19	.548	54	46	36-6	1	396	373	167	2	20	108	114	2.93	99	.251	.310	133-0-1	.135	-1	95	1	—	-0.4

CASEY, DAN Daniel Maurice; B11.20.1862 Binghamton NY; D2.8.1943 Washington DC; BR/TL/6´0˝/180; d8.18; b–Dennis

YEAR	TM LG	W	L	PCT	G	GS	CG-SHO	SV-BS	IP	H	R	HR	HB	BB-IB	SO	ERA	AERA	OAV	OOB	AB-HR-SH	AVG	PB	SUP	APR	DL	PW
1884	Wil U	1	1	.500	2	2	2	0	18	23	17	0	—	4	10	1.00	267	.291	.325	6	.167	-1	32	1	—	0.0
1885	Det N	4	8	.333	12	12	12-1	0	104	105	61	1	—	35	79	3.29	86	.256	.315	43	.116	-3	90	-2	—	-0.4
1886	Phi N	24	18	.571	44	44	39-4	0	369	326	169	9	—	104	193	2.41	136	.223	.275	151	.152	-5	95	37	—	3.0
1887	Phi N	28	13	.683	45	45	43-**4**	0	390.1	377	199	15	14	115	119	**2.86**	**148**	.246	.305	164-1	.165	-11	91	57	—	3.6
1888	Phi N	14	18	.438	33	33	31-2	0	285.2	298	156	6	5	48	108	3.15	94	.259	.291	118	.153	-4	76	-3	—	-0.7
1889	Phi N	6	10	.375	20	20	15-1	0	152.2	170	92	4	8	72	65	3.77	115	.274	.357	68	.221	-2	74	10	—	0.7
1890	Syr AA	19	22	.463	45	42	40-2	0	360.2	365	249	8	14	165	169	4.14	85	.255	.337	160	.162	-4*	97	-35	—	-3.3
Total	7	96	90	.516	201	198	182-14	0	1680.1	1664	943	43	41	543	743	3.18	113	.249	.309	710-1	.162	-27	88	65	—	2.9

CASEY, HUGH Hugh Thomas; B10.14.1913 Atlanta GA; D7.3.1951 Atlanta GA; BR/TR/6´1˝/207; d4.29; Mil 1943–45

YEAR	TM LG	W	L	PCT	G	GS	CG-SHO	SV-BS	IP	H	R	HR	HB	BB-IB	SO	ERA	AERA	OAV	OOB	AB-HR-SH	AVG	PB	SUP	APR	DL	PW
1935	Chi N	0	0	ø	13	0	0	0	25.2	29	13	2	0	14	10	3.86	102	.279	.364	6	.167	-0	—	0	—	0.0
1939	Bro N	15	10	.600	40	25	15	1	227.1	228	88	13	11	54	79	2.93	137	.260	.311	74-0-10	.203	0	101	25	—	2.7
1940	Bro N	11	8	.579	44	10	5-2	2	154	136	63	13	6	51	53	3.62	110	.237	.306	36-0-8	.250	2*	130	9	—	1.3
1941	†Bro N	14	11	.560	45	18	4-1	7	162	155	81	8	1	57	61	3.89	94	.251	.316	50-0-5	.120	-1	96	-4	0	-0.6
1942	Bro N	6	3	.667	50	2	0	**13**	112	91	32	3	2	44	54	2.25	145	.221	.300	27-0-4	.148	-0	51	13	0	1.3
1946	Bro N	11	5	.688	46	1	0	5	99.2	101	31	2	2	33	31	1.99	170	.267	.329	22-0-5	.136	-1	101	**14**	0	2.4
1947	†Bro N	10	4	.714	46	0	0	**18**	76.2	75	36	7	2	29	40	3.99	104	.260	.331	18-0-2	.056	-1	—	2	0	0.3
1948	Bro N	3	0	1.000	22	0	0	4	36	59	36	6	2	17	7	8.00	50	.391	.459	7-0-1	.000	-1	—	-16	60	-1.6
1949	Pit N	4	1	.800	33	0	0	5	38.2	50	24	4	1	14	9	4.66	90	.314	.374	3-0-1	.333	0	—	-3	0	-0.4
	NY A	1	0	1.000	4	0	0	0	7.2	11	10	0	0	8	5	8.22	49	.324	.452	1	.000	-0	—	-5	0	-0.5
Total	9	75	42	.641	343	56	24-3	55	939.2	935	414	58	27	321	349	3.45	110	.260	.325	244-0-36	.164	-2	105	35	60	4.9

CASEY, BILL William B.; B St.Louis MO; d8.17

YEAR	TM LG	W	L	PCT	G	GS	CG-SHO	SV-BS	IP	H	R	HR	HB	BB-IB	SO	ERA	AERA	OAV	OOB	AB-HR-SH	AVG	PB	SUP	APR	DL	PW
1887	Phi AA	0	0	ø	1	0	0	0	1	4	3	0	0	1	0	18.00	24	.667	.714	0	ø	0	—	-2	—	-0.1

CASHION, CARL Jay Carl; B6.6.1891 Mecklenburg Co. NC; D11.17.1935 Lake Millicent WI; BL/TR/6´2˝/200; d8.4; Col Erskine

YEAR	TM LG	W	L	PCT	G	GS	CG-SHO	SV-BS	IP	H	R	HR	HB	BB-IB	SO	ERA	AERA	OAV	OOB	AB-HR-SH	AVG	PB	SUP	APR	DL	PW
1911	Was A	1	5	.167	11	9	5	0	71.1	67	45	4	7	47	26	4.16	79	.220	.338	37-0-1	.324	2*	51	-6	—	-0.2
1912	Was A	10	6	.625	26	17	13-1	0	170.1	150	84	4	5	103	84	3.17	105	.250	.365	103-2-1	.214	2*	109	4	—	0.5
1913	Was A	1	1	.500	4	3	0	0	9	7	11	0	3	14	3	6.00	49	.333	.632	12	.250	0*	134	-4	—	-0.8
1914	Was A	0	1	.000	2	1	0	0	5	4	7	0	1	6	1	10.80	26	.250	.478	1	.000	-0	52	-4	—	-0.7
Total	4	12	13	.480	43	30	18-1	1	255.2	228	147	8	16	170	114	3.70	89	.243	.368	153-2-2	.242	5	91	-10	—	-1.2

CASIAN, LARRY Lawrence Paul; B10.28.1965 Lynwood CA; BR/TL/6´0˝/(170–175); [MinA87 6/139]; d9.9; Col Cal St.–Fullerton

YEAR	TM LG	W	L	PCT	G	GS	CG-SHO	SV-BS	IP	H	R	HR	HB	BB-IB	SO	ERA	AERA	OAV	OOB	AB-HR-SH	AVG	PB	SUP	APR	DL	PW
1990	Min A	2	1	.667	5	3	0	0-0	22.1	26	9	2	0	4-0	11	3.22	129	.306	.333	0	ø	0	95	2	0	0.3
1991	Min A	0	0	ø	15	0	0	0-0	18.1	28	16	4	1	7-2	6	7.36	58	.354	.414	0	ø	0	—	-6	0	-0.3
1992	Min A	1	0	1.000	6	0	0	0-0	6.2	7	2	0	0	1-0	2	2.70	151	.259	.286	0	ø	0	—	1	0	0.2
1993	Min A	5	3	.625	54	0	0	1-2	56.2	59	23	1	1	14-2	31	3.02	146	.268	.311	0	ø	0	—	8	44	0.9
1994	Min A	1	3	.250	33	0	0	1-0	40.2	57	34	11	2	12-2	18	7.08	70	.343	.390	0	ø	0	—	-9	0	-0.7
	Cle A	0	2	.000	7	0	0	0-0	8.1	16	9	1	0	4-1	2	8.64	55	.421	.476	0	ø	0	—	-4	0	-0.6
	Year	1	5	.167	40	0	0	1-0	49	73	43	12	2	16-3	20	7.35	67	.358	.406	0	ø	0	—	-12	0	-1.3
1995	Chi N	1	0	1.000	42	0	0	0-3	23.1	23	6	1	0	15-6	11	1.93	216	.258	.358	2	.000	-0	—	6	48	0.3
1996	Chi N	1	1	.500	35	0	0	0-1	24	14	5	2	1	11-3	15	1.88	233	.187	.295	0	ø	0	—	7	0	0.5
1997	Chi N	0	1	.000	12	0	0	0-0	9.2	16	9	3	1	2-1	7	7.45	58	.364	.388	1	.000	-0	—	-3	15	-0.3
	KC A	0	2	.000	32	0	0	0-2	26.2	32	15	5	0	6-1	16	5.06	94	.299	.333	0	ø	0	—	0	0	0.0
1998	Chi A	0	0	ø	4	0	0	0-0	4	8	5	0	2	1-0	6	11.25	41	.400	.478	0	ø	0	—	-3	0	-0.1
Total	9	11	13	.458	245	3	0	2-8	240.2	286	133	30	8	77-18	125	4.56	98	.301	.354	3	.000	-0	95	-1	107	0.2

CASILLA, SANTIAGO Santiago (aka Jairo Garcia in 2004-05); B6.25.1980 Don Gregorio, D.R.; BR/TR/6´0˝/165; d8.9

YEAR	TM LG	W	L	PCT	G	GS	CG-SHO	SV-BS	IP	H	R	HR	HB	BB-IB	SO	ERA	AERA	OAV	OOB	AB-HR-SH	AVG	PB	SUP	APR	DL	PW
2004	Oak A	0	0	ø	4	0	0	0-0	5.2	5	8	3	1	9-0	5	12.71	36	.227	.469	0	ø	0	—	-5	0	-0.2
2005	Oak A	0	0	ø	3	0	0	0-0	3	2	1	0	0	1-0	1	3.00	146	.182	.250	0	ø	0	—	1	0	0.0
2006	Oak A	0	0	ø	2	0	0	0-0	2.1	2	3	0	0	2-0	2	11.57	39	.250	.400	0	ø	0	—	-2	0	-0.1
Total	3	0	0	ø	9	0	0	0-0	11	9	12	3	1	12-0	8	9.82	46	.220	.407	0	ø	0	—	-6	0	-0.3

CASKEY, CRAIG Craig Douglas; B12.11.1949 Visalia CA; BB/TL/5´11˝/185; [MonN72 S1/12]; d7.19; Col Puget Sound

YEAR	TM LG	W	L	PCT	G	GS	CG-SHO	SV-BS	IP	H	R	HR	HB	BB-IB	SO	ERA	AERA	OAV	OOB	AB-HR-SH	AVG	PB	SUP	APR	DL	PW
1973	Mon N	0	0	ø	9	1	0	0-1	14.1	15	11	3	1	4-0	6	5.65	68	.278	.339	1-0-1	.000	-0	139	-3	0	-0.2

CASSIAN, ED Edward T.; B11.28.1867 Wilbraham MA; D9.10.1918 Meriden CT; TR/5´8˝/160; d6.26

YEAR	TM LG	W	L	PCT	G	GS	CG-SHO	SV-BS	IP	H	R	HR	HB	BB-IB	SO	ERA	AERA	OAV	OOB	AB-HR-SH	AVG	PB	SUP	APR	DL	PW
1891	Phi N	1	3	.250	6	4	3	0	38	40	20	0	3	16	10	2.84	120	.260	.341	17	.118	-1	57	2	—	0.0
	Was AA	2	4	.333	7	5	5	0	53	73	63	4	5	35	14	5.60	67	.316	.417	26	.346	2	133	-13	—	-0.9
Total	1	3	7	.300	13	9	8	0	91	113	83	4	8	51	24	4.45	81	.294	.387	43	.256	1	100	-11	—	-0.9

CASSIDY, JOHN John P.; B1857 Brooklyn NY; D7.2.1891 Brooklyn NY; BR/TL/5´8˝/168; d4.24; ▲

YEAR	TM LG	W	L	PCT	G	GS	CG-SHO	SV-BS	IP	H	R	HR	HB	BB-IB	SO	ERA	AERA	OAV	OOB	AB-HR-SH	AVG	PB	SUP	APR	DL	PW
1875	Atl NA	1	21	.045	30	22	18	0	213.2	284	242	3	—	11	9	3.03	69	.277	.285	166-1	.175	-3*	47	-27	—	-2.2
1877	Har N	1	1	.500	2	2	2	0	18	24	11	0	—	1	2	5.00	49	.320	.329	251	.378	1*	170	-3	—	-0.2

CASSIDY, SCOTT Scott Robert; B10.3.1975 Syracuse NY; BR/TR/6´2˝/(175–180); d4.1; Col LeMoyne (NY)

YEAR	TM LG	W	L	PCT	G	GS	CG-SHO	SV-BS	IP	H	R	HR	HB	BB-IB	SO	ERA	AERA	OAV	OOB	AB-HR-SH	AVG	PB	SUP	APR	DL	PW
2002	Tor A	1	4	.200	58	0	0	0-7	66	52	42	12	7	32-3	48	5.73	81	.222	.327	0	ø	0	—	-6	0	-0.4
2005	Bos A	0	0	ø	1	0	0	0-0	0.2	4	3	0	0	0-0	0	40.50	11	.667	.667	0	ø	0	—	-2	0	-0.1
	SD N	1	1	.500	10	0	0	0-0	12.1	15	10	3	0	3-0	12	6.57	60	.306	.346	1	.000	0	—	-4	0	-0.5
2006	SD N	6	4	.600	42	0	0	0-2	42.2	39	18	8	1	19-2	49	2.53	164	.248	.331	1	.000	-0	—	6	0	1.1
Total	3	8	9	.471	111	0	0	0-9	121.2	110	73	23	8	54-5	109	4.88	90	.247	.335	2	.000	0	—	-6	0	0.1

CASTER, GEORGE George Jasper "Ug"; B8.4.1907 Colton CA; D12.18.1955 Lakewood CA; BR/TR/6´1.5˝/180; d9.10; Col San Bernardino Valley (CA) JC

YEAR	TM LG	W	L	PCT	G	GS	CG-SHO	SV-BS	IP	H	R	HR	HB	BB-IB	SO	ERA	AERA	OAV	OOB	AB-HR-SH	AVG	PB	SUP	APR	DL	PW
1934	Phi A	3	2	.600	5	3	2	0	37	32	16	3	3	14	15	3.41	129	.235	.320	15	.267	0	106	4	—	0.5
1935	Phi A	1	4	.200	25	1	0	1	63.1	86	59	8	2	37	24	6.25	73	.322	.408	22	.227	0*	0	-15	—	-1.0
1937	Phi A	12	19	.387	34	33	19-3	0	231.2	227	141	23	2	107	100	4.43	106	.258	.339	90-0-1	.211	-1*	85	5	—	0.5
1938	Phi A	16	20	.444	42	**40**	20-2	1	281.1	310	156	25	3	117	112	4.35	111	.277	.347	101-0-2	.198	1	84	17	—	2.0
1939	Phi A	9	9	.500	28	17	7-1	0	136	144	82	16	3	45	59	4.90	96	.276	.337	43-0-2	.209	-1	78	-1	—	-0.1
1940	Phi A	4	19	.174	36	24	11	2	178.1	234	160	18	3	69	75	6.56	68	.312	.372	62-0-2	.129	-3	82	-43	—	-4.8
1941	StL A	3	7	.300	32	9	3	3	104.1	105	66	12	2	37	36	5.00	86	.259	.324	29-0-1	.103	-2	74	-8	0	-0.9

YEAR	TM LG	W	L	PCT	G	GS	CG-SHO	SV-BS	IP	H	R	HR	HB	BB-IB	SO	ERA	AERA	OAV	OOB	AB-HR-SH	AVG	PB	SUP	APR	DL	PW
1942	StL A	8	2	.800	39	0	0	5	80	62	30	3	3	39	34	2.81	132	.217	.317	15	.067	-1	—	8	0	0.9
1943	StL A	6	8	.429	35	0	0	8	76.1	69	22	4	1	41	43	2.12	157	.246	.345	22	.136	-1	—	10	0	2.0
1944	StL A	6	6	.500	42	0	0	**12**	81	91	37	5	0	33	46	2.44	147	.284	.351	20	.250	0	—	6	0	1.0
1945	StL A	1	2	.333	10	0	0	1	15.2	20	13	0	0	7	9	6.89	51	.308	.375	3	.333	0	—	-5	0	-1.0
	†Det A	5	1	.833	22	0	0	2	51.1	47	25	3	2	27	23	3.86	91	.250	.350	11-0-2	.182	0	—	-1	0	-0.1
	Year	6	3	.667	32	0	0	3	67	67	38	3	2	34	32	4.57	77	.265	.356	14-0-2	.214	0	—	-7	0	-1.1
1946	Det A	2	1	.667	26	0	0	4	41.1	42	26	1	1	24	19	5.66	65	.264	.364	7-0-1	.143	-0	—	-7	0	-0.7
Total	12	76	100	.432	376	127	62-6	39	1377.2	1469	833	121	25	597	595	4.54	96	.273	.349	440-0-11	.184	-7	87	-30	0	-1.7

Castillo, Tony Antonio Jose (Jimenez); B3.1.1963 Quibor, Lara, Venez.; BL/TL/5´10˝/(177–190); d8.14

YEAR	TM LG	W	L	PCT	G	GS	CG-SHO	SV-BS	IP	H	R	HR	HB	BB-IB	SO	ERA	AERA	OAV	OOB	AB-HR-SH	AVG	PB	SUP	APR	DL	PW
1988	Tor A	1	0	1.000	14	0	0	0-0	15	10	5	2	0	2-0	14	3.00	132	.200	.222	0	ø	0	—	2	0	0.1
1989	Tor A	1	1	.500	17	0	0	1-0	17.2	23	14	0	1	10-5	10	6.11	62	.333	.405	0	ø	0	—	-5	0	-0.6
	Atl N	0	1	.000	12	0	0	0-0	9.1	8	5	0	0	4-1	5	4.82	76	.222	.300	1	.000	-0	—	-1	0	-0.1
1990	Atl N	5	1	.833	52	3	0	1-1	76.2	93	41	5	1	20-3	64	4.23	95	.302	.342	7-0-2	.143	0	142	-2	0	-0.1
1991	Atl N	1	1	.500	7	0	0	0-0	8.2	13	9	3	0	5-0	8	7.27	53	.342	.419	0	ø	0	—	-4	0	-0.7
	NY N	1	0	1.000	10	3	0	0-0	23.2	27	7	1	0	6-1	10	1.90	193	.281	.320	4-0-2	.000	-0	74	4	0	0.2
	Year	2	1	.667	17	3	0	0-0	32.1	40	16	4	0	11-1	18	3.34	112	.299	.349	4-0-2	.000	-0	72	0	0	-0.5
1993	†Tor A	3	2	.600	51	0	0	0-1	50.2	44	19	4	0	22-5	28	3.38	130	.242	.320	0	ø	0	—	6	0	0.6
1994	Tor A	5	2	.714	41	0	0	1-3	68	66	22	7	3	28-1	43	2.51	194	.260	.337	0	ø	0	—	17	0	1.6
1995	Tor A	1	5	.167	55	0	0	13-8	72.2	64	27	7	3	24-1	38	3.22	148	.243	.308	0	ø	0	—	13	0	1.3
1996	Tor A	2	3	.400	40	0	0	1-1	72.1	72	38	9	2	20-1	48	4.23	118	.260	.312	0	ø	0	—	6	0	0.4
	Chi A	3	1	.750	15	0	0	1-3	22.2	23	7	1	1	4-1	9	1.59	300	.267	.298	0	ø	0	—	7	0	1.1
	Year	5	4	.556	55	0	0	2-4	95	95	45	10	3	24-2	57	3.60	138	.262	.309	0	ø	0	—	12	0	1.5
1997	Chi A	4	4	.500	64	0	0	4-5	62.1	74	48	6	1	23-7	42	4.91	90	.296	.358	1	.000	-0	—	-8	15	-0.9
1998	Chi A	1	2	.333	25	0	0	0-0	27	38	25	7	2	11-0	14	8.00	57	.328	.395	0	ø	0	—	-10	0	-0.8
Total	10	28	23	.549	403	6	0	22-22	526.2	555	267	52	14	179-26	333	3.93	114	.274	.333	13-0-4	.077	-1	96	25	15	2.1

Castillo, Carlos Carlos; B4.21.1975 Boston MA; BR/TR/6´2˝/(240–250); [ChiA94 3/89]; d4.2

YEAR	TM LG	W	L	PCT	G	GS	CG-SHO	SV-BS	IP	H	R	HR	HB	BB-IB	SO	ERA	AERA	OAV	OOB	AB-HR-SH	AVG	PB	SUP	APR	DL	PW
1997	Chi A	2	1	.667	37	2	0	1-0	66.1	68	35	9	1	33-3	43	4.48	99	.265	.346	1	1.000	0	135	0	0	0.0
1998	Chi A	6	4	.600	54	2	0	0-2	100.1	94	61	17	5	35-1	64	5.11	90	.246	.312	1	.000	-0	81	-5	0	-0.4
1999	Chi A	2	2	.500	18	2	0	0-0	41	45	26	10	0	14-1	23	5.71	87	.274	.331	0	ø	0	113	-2	0	-0.2
2001	Bos A	0	0	ø	2	0	0	0-0	3	3	2	1	0	0-0	0	6.00	74	.273	.250	0	ø	0	—	0	0	0.0
Total	4	10	7	.588	111	6	0	1-2	210.2	210	124	37	6	82-5	130	5.04	91	.258	.326	2	.500	0	111	-7	0	-0.6

Castillo, Frank Frank Anthony; B4.1.1969 ElPaso TX; BR/TR/6´1˝/(180–200); [ChiN87 6/140]; d6.27

YEAR	TM LG	W	L	PCT	G	GS	CG-SHO	SV-BS	IP	H	R	HR	HB	BB-IB	SO	ERA	AERA	OAV	OOB	AB-HR-SH	AVG	PB	SUP	APR	DL	PW
1991	Chi N	6	7	.462	18	18	4	0-0	111.2	107	56	5	0	33-2	73	4.35	90	.252	.304	35-0-6	.143	-0	88	-3	16	-0.5
1992	Chi N	10	11	.476	33	33	0	0-0	205.1	179	91	19	6	63-6	135	3.46	105	.232	.293	65-0-5	.092	-2	86	3	0	0.0
1993	Chi N	5	8	.385	29	25	2	0-0	141.1	162	83	20	9	39-4	84	4.84	83	.293	.348	43-0-8	.163	-0	96	-12	0	-0.9
1994	Chi N	2	1	.667	4	4	1	0-0	23	25	13	3	0	5-0	19	4.30	98	.278	.316	9	.000	-1	151	-1	39	-0.2
1995	Chi N	11	10	.524	29	29	2-2	0-0	188	179	75	22	6	52-4	135	3.21	130	.248	.302	59-0-7	.102	-2	83	20	0	1.8
1996	Chi N	7	16	.304	33	33	1-1	0-0	182.1	209	112	28	8	46-4	139	5.28	83	.288	.335	57-0-4	.088	-3	87	-16	0	-2.0
1997	Chi N	6	9	.400	20	19	0	0-0	98	113	64	9	4	44-1	67	5.42	80	.292	.370	33-0-4	.152	-1	92	-12	0	-1.6
	Col N	6	3	.667	14	14	0	0-0	86.1	107	57	16	4	25-3	59	5.42	95	.308	.360	25-0-6	.080	-2	121	-2	0	-0.4
	Year	12	12	.500	34	33	0	0-0	184.1	220	121	25	8	69-4	126	5.42	87	.300	.365	58-0-10	.121	-2	105	-13	0	-2.0
1998	Det A	3	9	.250	27	19	0	1-0	116	150	91	17	5	44-0	81	6.83	70	.316	.376	1	.000	-0	99	-24	28	-2.1
2000	Tor A	10	5	.667	25	24	0	0-0	138	112	58	18	5	56-0	104	3.59	140	.220	.303	7	.143	-0	106	23	32	2.2
2001	Bos A	10	9	.526	26	26	0	0-0	136.2	138	72	14	5	35-2	89	4.21	105	.260	.308	2-0-1	.000	-0	95	3	40	0.3
2002	Bos A	6	15	.286	36	23	0	1-1	163.1	174	101	19	7	58-6	112	5.07	88	.274	.337	1-0-1	.000	-0	82	-11	0	-1.2
2004	Bos A	0	0	ø	2	0	0	0-0	1	1	0	0	0	1-0	0	0.00	ø	.333	.500	0	ø	0	—	1	0	0.0
2005	Fla N	0	1	.000	1	1	0	0-0	4.1	4	5	0	0	5-0	4	10.38	39	.235	.409	1	.000	-0	94	-3	0	-0.5
Total	13	82	104	.441	297	268	10-3	2-1	1595.1	1660	878	190	59	506-32	1101	4.56	95	.268	.327	338-0-42	.109	-12	94	-34	155	-5.1

Castillo, Juan Juan Francisco (Azdura); B6.23.1970 Caracas, Distrito Capital, Venez.; BR/TR/6´5˝/205; d7.26

YEAR	TM LG	W	L	PCT	G	GS	CG-SHO	SV-BS	IP	H	R	HR	HB	BB-IB	SO	ERA	AERA	OAV	OOB	AB-HR-SH	AVG	PB	SUP	APR	DL	PW
1994	NY N	0	0	ø	2	2	0	0-0	11.2	17	9	2	0	5-0	1	6.94	60	.362	.423	5	.200	0	175	-3	0	-0.1

Castillo, Bobby Robert Ernie; B4.18.1955 Los Angeles CA; BR/TR/5´10˝/(170–180); d9.10; Col Los Angeles Valley (CA) JC

YEAR	TM LG	W	L	PCT	G	GS	CG-SHO	SV-BS	IP	H	R	HR	HB	BB-IB	SO	ERA	AERA	OAV	OOB	AB-HR-SH	AVG	PB	SUP	APR	DL	PW
1977	LA N	1	0	1.000	6	1	0	0-0	11.1	12	5	2	0	2-0	7	3.97	97	.279	.304	1	.000	-0	69	0	0	0.0
1978	LA N	0	4	.000	18	0	0	1-1	34	28	19	2	0	33-7	30	3.97	88	.239	.399	7	.000	-1	—	-3	0	-0.4
1979	LA N	2	0	1.000	19	0	0	7-1	24.1	26	5	0	1	13-1	25	1.11	326	.277	.364	3	.000	-0	—	6	0	0.9
1980	LA N	8	6	.571	61	0	0	5-1	98.1	70	31	4	1	45-5	60	2.75	127	.206	.297	9-0-1	.111	-0*	—	9	0	1.4
1981	†LA N	2	4	.333	34	1	0	5-2	50.2	50	31	5	0	24-4	35	5.33	62	.262	.341	9	.444	2	81	-12	0	-1.3
1982	Min A	13	11	.542	40	25	6-1	0-0	218.2	194	96	26	0	85-7	123	3.66	117	.241	.310	0	ø	0	89	14	0	1.3
1983	Min A	8	12	.400	27	25	3	0-0	158.1	170	91	17	1	65-4	90	4.77	90	.278	.347	0	ø	0	83	-8	0	-0.8
1984	Min A	2	1	.667	10	2	0	0-0	25.1	14	7	2	0	19-2	7	1.78	238	.177	.327	0	ø	0	32	6	94	0.6
1985	†LA N	2	2	.500	35	5	0	0-0	68	59	42	9	1	41-6	57	5.43	65	.230	.337	10-0-2	.100	-0*	131	-12	11	-0.7
Total	9	38	40	.487	250	59	9-1	18-5	689	623	327	67	4	327-36	434	3.94	100	.246	.329	39-0-3	.154	0	92	0	105	1.0

Castleman, Slick Clydell; B9.8.1913 Donelson TN; D3.2.1998 Nashville TN; BR/TR/6´0˝/185; d5.9

YEAR	TM LG	W	L	PCT	G	GS	CG-SHO	SV-BS	IP	H	R	HR	HB	BB-IB	SO	ERA	AERA	OAV	OOB	AB-HR-SH	AVG	PB	SUP	APR	DL	PW
1934	NY N	1	0	1.000	7	0	0	0	16.2	18	11	1	0	10	5	5.40	72	.277	.373	4	.250	1	—	-3	—	0.0
1935	NY N	15	6	.714	29	25	9-1	0	173.2	186	93	14	1	64	64	4.09	94	.268	.330	67-1-0	.179	-0	110	-6	—	-0.6
1936	†NY N	4	7	.364	29	12	2-1	1	111.2	148	80	6	5	56	54	5.64	69	.323	.403	39-1-0	.128	-1*	94	-22	—	-1.9
1937	NY N	11	6	.647	23	23	10-2	0	160.1	148	66	19	0	33	78	3.31	117	.247	.287	57-0-3	.070	-5	109	11	—	0.5
1938	NY N	4	5	.444	21	14	4	0	90.2	108	55	4	3	37	18	4.17	90	.296	.365	31-0-3	.097	-2*	130	-7	—	-0.8
1939	NY N	1	2	.333	12	4	0	0	33.2	36	18	1	0	23	6	4.54	86	.286	.396	9-0-1	.333	1	106	-2	—	-0.1
Total	6	36	26	.581	121	78	25-4	1	586.2	644	323	45	9	223	225	4.25	91	.279	.345	207-2-7	.135	-6	110	-29	—	-2.9

Castleton, Roy Royal Eugene; B7.26.1885 Salt Lake City UT; D6.24.1967 Los Angeles CA; BR/TL/5´11˝/167; d4.16

YEAR	TM LG	W	L	PCT	G	GS	CG-SHO	SV-BS	IP	H	R	HR	HB	BB-IB	SO	ERA	AERA	OAV	OOB	AB-HR-SH	AVG	PB	SUP	APR	DL	PW
1907	NY A	1	1	.500	3	2	1	0	16	11	6	1	0	3	3	2.81	99	.196	.237	5	.000	-1	60	0	—	0.0
1909	Cin N	1	1	.500	4	1	1	0	14	14	6	0	2	6	5	1.93	135	.275	.373	3	.667	1	350	1	—	0.2
1910	Cin N	1	2	.333	4	2	1	0	13.2	15	5	0	1	6	5	3.29	89	.288	.373	5	.000	-1	128	0	—	0.0
Total	3	3	4	.429	11	5	3	0	43.2	40	17	1	3	15	13	2.68	104	.252	.328	13	.154	-0	142	1	—	0.2

Castner, Paul Paul Henry "Lefty"; B2.16.1897 St.Paul MN; D3.3.1986 St.Paul MN; BL/TL/5´11˝/187; d8.6; Col Notre Dame

YEAR	TM LG	W	L	PCT	G	GS	CG-SHO	SV-BS	IP	H	R	HR	HB	BB-IB	SO	ERA	AERA	OAV	OOB	AB-HR-SH	AVG	PB	SUP	APR	DL	PW
1923	Chi A	0	0	ø	6	0	0	0	10	14	9	0	0	5	0	6.30	63	.326	.396	3-0-2	.000	-0	—	-3	—	-0.2

Castro, Fabio Fabio Enrique; B1.20.1985 Monte Cristi, D.R.; BL/TL/5´7˝/175; d4.6

YEAR	TM LG	W	L	PCT	G	GS	CG-SHO	SV-BS	IP	H	R	HR	HB	BB-IB	SO	ERA	AERA	OAV	OOB	AB-HR-SH	AVG	PB	SUP	APR	DL	PW
2006	Tex A	0	0	ø	4	0	0	0-0	8.1	6	5	0	0	7-0	5	4.32	108	.200	.351	0	ø	0	—	0	54	0.0
	Phi N	0	1	.000	16	0	0	1-1	23.1	12	4	1	2	6-0	13	1.54	304	.158	.233	2	.000	-0	—	8	0	0.4
Total	1	0	1	.000	20	0	0	1-1	31.2	18	9	1	2	13-0	18	2.27	206	.170	.268	2	.000	-0	—	8	54	0.4

Castro, Bill William Radhames (Checo); B12.13.1953 Santiago, D.R.; BR/TR/5´11˝/(170–180); d8.20; C15

YEAR	TM LG	W	L	PCT	G	GS	CG-SHO	SV-BS	IP	H	R	HR	HB	BB-IB	SO	ERA	AERA	OAV	OOB	AB-HR-SH	AVG	PB	SUP	APR	DL	PW
1974	Mil A	0	0	ø	8	0	0	0-0	18	19	10	2	0	5-0	10	4.50	81	.264	.308	0	ø	0	—	-2	0	-0.1
1975	Mil A	3	2	.600	18	5	0	1-0	75	78	28	3	2	17-5	25	2.52	153	.271	.313	0	ø	0	119	9	40	0.6
1976	Mil A	4	6	.400	39	0	0	8-2	70.1	70	29	4	3	19-5	23	3.45	102	.265	.322	0	ø	0	—	1	21	0.2
1977	Mil A	8	6	.571	51	0	0	13-6	69.1	76	34	7	2	23-10	28	4.15	99	.293	.347	0	ø	0	—	0	0	0.1
1978	Mil A	5	4	.556	42	0	0	8-5	49.2	43	14	2	6	14-5	17	1.81	209	.234	.306	0	ø	0	—	10	0	2.0
1979	Mil A	3	1	.750	39	0	0	6-6	44.1	40	14	2	0	13-5	10	2.03	207	.244	.296	0	ø	0	—	9	0	1.0
1980	Mil A	2	4	.333	56	0	0	8-4	84.1	89	35	2	2	17-6	32	2.77	141	.274	.311	0	ø	0	—	9	0	0.8
1981	NY A	1	1	.500	11	0	0	0-0	19	26	13	2	0	5-1	4	3.79	95	.329	.369	0	ø	0	—	-2	0	-0.2
1982	KC A	3	2	.600	21	4	0	1-0	75.2	72	34	8	2	20-4	37	3.45	118	.243	.292	0	ø	0	139	4	0	0.2
1983	KC A	2	0	1.000	18	0	0	0-0	40.2	51	34	4	5	12-1	17	6.64	62	.300	.358	0	ø	0	—	-11	0	-0.6
Total	10	31	26	.544	303	9	0	45-23	546.1	564	245	36	22	145-42	203	3.33	118	.268	.319	0	ø	0	130	27	61	4.0

Cates, Eli Eli Eldo; B1.26.1877 Greens Fork IN; D5.29.1964 Anderson IN; BR/TR/5´9.5˝/175; d4.20; ▲

YEAR	TM LG	W	L	PCT	G	GS	CG-SHO	SV-BS	IP	H	R	HR	HB	BB-IB	SO	ERA	AERA	OAV	OOB	AB-HR-SH	AVG	PB	SUP	APR	DL	PW
1908	Was A	4	8	.333	19	10	7	0	113.2	112	46	3	1	32	33	2.53	90	.261	.314	59-0-5	.186	1*	90	-3	—	0.0

YEAR	TM LG	W	L	PCT	G	GS	CG-SHO	SV-BS	IP	H	R	HR	HB	BB-IB	SO	ERA	AERA	OAV	OOB	AB-HR-SH	AVG	PB	SUP	APR	DL	PW
CATHER, MIKE	Michael Peter; B12.17.1970 San Diego CA; BR/TR/6´2˝/(195–205); [TexA93 41/1151]; d7.13; Col California																									
1997	†Atl N	2	4	.333	35	0	0	0-3	37.2	23	12	1	2	19-4	29	2.39	176	.174	.288	1	.000	-0	—	7	0	1.0
1998	Atl N	2	2	.500	36	0	0	0-3	41.1	39	21	7	2	12-1	33	3.92	106	.255	.314	0	ø	0	—	1	28	0.1
1999	Atl N	1	0	1.000	4	0	0	0-1	2.2	5	3	2	0	1-0	0	10.13	44	.417	.462	0	ø	0	—	-2	0	-0.3
Total	3	5	6	.455	75	0	0	0-7	81.2	67	36	10	4	32-5	62	3.42	123	.226	.307	1	.000	-0	—	6	28	0.8
CATHEY, HARDIN	Hardin Abner "Lil Abner"; B7.6.1919 Burns TN; D7.27.1997 Nashville TN; BR/TR/6´4˝/190; d4.16																									
1942	Was A	1	1	.500	12	2	0	0	30.1	44	26	1	0	16	8	7.42	49	.341	.414	8-0-1	.375	1	187	-11	0	-0.6
CATO, KEEFE	John Keefe; B5.6.1958 Yonkers NY; BR/TR/6´1˝/185; [CinN79 2/30]; d6.13; Col Fairfield																									
1983	Cin N	1	0	1.000	4	0	0	0-0	3.2	2	1	0	0	1-0	3	2.45	156	.154	.214	0-0-1	ø	0	—	1	0	0.1
1984	Cin N	0	1	.000	8	0	0	1-0	15.2	22	14	5	0	4-0	12	8.04	47	.344	.371	4	.500	1	—	-6	0	-0.4
Total	2	1	1	.500	12	0	0	1-0	19.1	24	15	5	0	5-0	15	6.98	54	.312	.345	4-0-1	.500	1	—	-5	0	-0.3
CATTANACH, JOHN	John Leckie; B5.10.1863 Providence RI; D11.10.1926 Providence RI; 5´10˝/190; d6.5																									
1884	Pro N	0	0	ø	1	1	0	0	5	2	7	0	—	4	2	9.00	32	.100	.250	4	.000	-1	149	-3	—	-0.2
	StL U	1	1	.500	2	2	2	0	17	12	10	0	—	4	13	2.12	113	.185	.232	7	.000	-1	80	0	—	-0.1
Total	1	1	1	.500	3	3	2	0	22	14	17	0	—	8	15	3.68	68	.165	.237	11	.000	-2	102	-3	—	-0.3
CAUDILL, BILL	William Holland; B7.13.1956 Santa Monica CA; BR/TR/6´1˝/(175–225); [StLN74 8/181]; d5.12																									
1979	Chi N	1	7	.125	29	12	0	0-0	90	89	57	16	4	41-5	104	4.80	87	.255	.337	17-0-4	.059	-1	76	-7	0	-0.7
1980	Chi N	4	6	.400	72	2	0	1-3	127.2	100	37	10	1	59-12	112	2.19	181	.223	.309	9-0-1	.222	0	68	22	0	1.7
1981	Chi N	1	5	.167	30	10	0	0-2	71	87	50	9	2	31-2	45	5.83	64	.301	.368	14-0-1	.143	0	97	-14	0	-1.2
1982	Sea A	12	9	.571	70	0	0	26-6	95.2	65	25	9	1	35-4	111	2.35	182	.192	.269	0	ø	0	—	21	0	**4.2**
1983	Sea A	2	8	.200	63	0	0	26-3	72.2	70	39	10	2	38-6	73	4.71	91	.257	.348	0	ø	0	—	-2	18	-0.4
1984	Oak A★	9	7	.563	68	0	0	36-8	96.1	77	30	9	0	31-4	89	2.71	139	.218	.278	1	.000	-0	—	13	0	2.6
1985	Tor A	4	6	.400	67	0	0	14-5	69.1	53	26	9	2	35-6	46	2.99	142	.209	.306	0	ø	0	—	9	0	1.5
1986	Tor A	2	4	.333	40	0	0	2-2	36.1	36	25	6	2	17-1	32	6.19	69	.254	.342	0	ø	0	—	-7	15	-1.1
1987	Oak A	0	0	ø	6	0	0	1-0	8	10	8	3	0	1-0	8	9.00	46	.294	.314	0	ø	0	—	-4	31	-0.2
Total	9	35	52	.402	445	24	0	106-29	667	587	297	81	14	288-40	620	3.68	111	.237	.316	41-0-6	.122	-1	83	31	64	6.4
CAUSEY, RED	Cecil Algernon; B8.11.1893 Georgetown FL; D11.11.1960 Avon Park FL; BR/TR/6´1˝/160; d4.26																									
1918	NY N	11	6	.647	29	18	10-2	2	158.1	143	58	2	7	42	48	2.79	94	.245	.304	48-0-1	.125	-3	126	-1	—	-0.5
1919	NY N	9	3	.750	19	16	6	0	105	99	52	5	2	38	25	3.69	76	.251	.320	38-0-1	.132	-1*	160	-10	—	-1.3
	Bos N	4	5	.444	10	10	3	0	69	81	38	1	1	20	14	4.57	63	.308	.359	21-0-2	.095	-2	86	-11	—	-1.5
	Year	13	8	.619	29	26	9	0	174	180	90	6	3	58	39	4.03	70	.274	.336	59-0-3	.119	-3	131	-21	—	-2.8
1920	Phi N	7	14	.333	35	26	11-1	3	181.1	203	109	4	5	79	30	4.32	79	.299	.376	59-0-2	.186	-2*	104	-16	—	-2.1
1921	Phi N	3	3	.500	7	7	4	0	50.2	58	22	4	1	11	8	2.84	149	.294	.335	20	.150	-1*	83	7	—	0.7
	NY N	1	1	.500	7	1	0	0	14.2	13	8	0	0	6	1	2.45	149	.228	.302	3	.333	0*	67	1	—	0.1
	Year	4	4	.500	14	8	4	0	65.1	71	30	4	1	17	9	2.76	149	.280	.327	23	.174	-1	83	7	—	0.8
1922	NY N	4	3	.571	24	2	1	1	70.2	69	34	2	0	34	13	3.18	126	.262	.347	21-0-1	.238	-0*	214	5	—	0.5
Total	5	39	35	.527	131	80	35-3	6	649.2	666	321	18	16	230	139	3.59	89	.273	.340	210-0-7	.157	-9	115	-25	—	-4.1
CAVET, PUG	Tillar H.; B12.26.1889 McGregor TX; D8.4.1966 San Luis Obispo CA; BL/TL/6´3˝/176; d4.25																									
1911	Det A	0	0	ø	1	1	0	0	4	6	5	0	0	1	1	4.50	77	.316	.350	1	.000	-0	229	-1	—	-0.1
1914	Det A	7	7	.500	31	14	6-1	2	151.1	129	61	2	9	44	51	2.44	115	.238	.306	47-0-2	.106	-2	102	4	—	0.3
1915	Det A	4	2	.667	17	7	2	1	71	83	39	2	2	22	26	4.06	75	.300	.355	24-0-1	.250	1	131	-7	—	-0.4
Total	3	11	9	.550	49	22	8-1	3	226.1	218	105	4	11	67	78	2.98	97	.260	.323	72-0-3	.153	-0	119	-4	—	-0.2
CECCARELLI, ART	Arthur Edward "Chic"; B4.2.1930 New Haven CT; BR/TL (BB 1957)/6´0˝/190; d5.3																									
1955	KC A	4	7	.364	31	16	3-1	0	123.2	123	81	20	0	71-2	68	5.31	79	.258	.351	38-0-3	.079	-3	84	-15	0	-1.5
1956	KC A	0	1	.000	3	2	0	0	10	13	13	3	1	4-1	2	7.20	60	.317	.391	3	.000	-0	123	-5	0	-0.4
1957	Bal A	0	5	.000	20	8	1	0	58	62	34	3	2	31-3	30	4.50	80	.278	.371	14	.000	-2	62	-7	0	-0.8
1959	Chi N	5	5	.500	18	15	4-2	0	102	95	58	19	1	37-6	56	4.76	83	.245	.309	33-0-2	.091	-1	110	-8	0	-0.9
1960	Chi N	0	0	ø	7	1	0	0	13	16	12	1	0	4-0	10	5.54	68	.296	.339	0-0-1	ø	0	210	-4	0	-0.2
Total	5	9	18	.333	79	42	8-3	0	306.2	309	198	46	4	147-12	166	5.05	79	.261	.342	88-0-6	.068	-6	94	-39	0	-3.8
CEÇENA, JOSE	Jose Isabel (Lugo); B8.20.1963 Ciudad Obregon, Sonora, Mexico; BR/TR/5´11˝/180; d4.6																									
1988	Tex A	0	0	ø	22	0	0	1-1	26.1	20	16	2	2	23-1	27	4.78	86	.213	.372	0	ø	0	—	-2	74	-0.1
CECIL, REX	Rex Rolston; B10.8.1916 Lindsay OK; D10.30.1966 Long Beach CA; BL/TR/6´3˝/195; d8.13																									
1944	Bos A	4	5	.444	11	9	4	0	61	72	44	5	1	33	33	5.16	66	.286	.371	18-0-2	.278	2	112	-14	0	-1.6
1945	Bos A	2	5	.286	7	7	1	0	45	46	37	4	0	27	30	5.20	66	.261	.360	20	.300	1	114	-12	0	-1.5
Total	2	6	10	.375	18	16	5	0	106	118	81	9	1	60	63	5.18	66	.276	.366	38-0-2	.289	2	113	-26	0	-3.1
CENTER, PETE	Marvin Earl; B4.22.1912 Hazel Green KY; D8.8.2004 Campton KY; BR/TR/6´4˝/190; d9.11; Mil 1943–44; Col Morehead St.																									
1942	Cle A	0	0	ø	1	0	0	0	3.1	7	6	0	1	4	0	16.20	21	.438	.571	1	.000	-0	—	-5	0	-0.2
1943	Cle A	1	2	.333	24	1	0	1	42.1	29	18	3	0	18	10	2.76	112	.201	.290	5	.000	-1	108	0	0	-0.1
1945	Cle A	6	3	.667	31	8	2	1	85.2	89	42	2	1	28	34	3.99	81	.270	.329	22	.091	-2	141	-7	0	-1.0
1946	Cle A	0	2	.000	21	0	0	1	29	29	16	2	1	20	6	4.97	67	.269	.388	3	.000	-0	—	-5	0	-0.4
Total	4	7	7	.500	77	9	2	3	160.1	154	82	7	3	70	50	4.10	79	.258	.338	31	.065	-3	138	-17	0	-1.7
CERDA, JAIME	Jaime Magana; B10.26.1978 Fresno CA; BL/TL/6´0˝/(175–200); [NYN98 23/694]; d6.28; Col Fresno (CA) City																									
2002	NY N	0	0	ø	32	0	0	0-0	25.2	22	7	0	1	14-0	21	2.45	161	.232	.327	1	.000	-0	—	5	0	0.2
2003	NY N	1	1	.500	27	0	0	0-1	32.1	32	21	4	0	20-1	19	5.85	72	.267	.366	1	.000	-0	—	-5	0	-0.3
2004	KC A	1	4	.200	53	0	0	2-1	45.2	41	21	1	3	30-3	33	3.15	148	.244	.363	0	ø	0	—	6	0	0.7
2005	KC A	1	4	.200	20	0	0	0-1	19	21	14	3	0	11-2	18	6.63	66	.284	.372	0	ø	0	—	-4	0	-0.8
Total	4	3	9	.250	132	0	0	2-3	122.2	116	63	8	4	75-6	91	4.26	102	.254	.358	2	.000	-0	—	2	0	-0.2
CERROS, JUAN	R.Juan; B9.25.1976 Monterrey, Nuevo Leon, Mexico; BR/TR/6´1˝/200; d9.8																									
2003	Cin N	0	0	ø	11	0	0	0-0	13	11	7	1	2	5-2	9	4.85	86	.224	.316	0	ø	0	—	-1	0	0.0
CERUTTI, JOHN	John Joseph; B4.28.1960 Albany NY; D10.3.2004 Toronto ON, Can.; BL/TL/6´2˝/(195–200); [TorA81 1/21]; d9.1; Col Amherst																									
1985	Tor A	0	2	.000	4	1	0	0-0	6.2	10	7	1	1	4-0	5	5.40	79	.323	.417	0	ø	0	0	-2	0	-0.4
1986	Tor A	9	4	.692	34	20	2-1	1-0	145.1	150	73	25	1	47-2	89	4.15	102	.268	.324	0	ø	0	122	2	0	0.2
1987	Tor A	11	4	.733	44	21	2	0-0	151.1	144	75	30	1	59-5	92	4.40	103	.251	.321	0	ø	0	119	5	0	0.3
1988	Tor A	6	7	.462	46	12	0	1-1	123.2	120	56	12	3	42-6	65	3.13	127	.256	.320	0	ø	0	104	8	0	0.9
1989	†Tor A	11	11	.500	33	31	3-1	0-0	205.1	214	90	19	6	53-2	69	3.07	124	.273	.322	0	ø	0	109	11	0	1.3
1990	Tor A	9	9	.500	30	23	0	0-0	140	162	77	23	4	49-3	49	4.76	83	.297	.356	0	ø	0	112	-11	0	-1.3
1991	Det A	3	6	.333	38	8	1	2-3	88.2	94	49	9	2	37-9	29	4.57	91	.276	.348	0	ø	0	93	-4	0	-0.3
Total	7	49	43	.533	229	116	8-2	4-4	861	894	427	119	18	291-27	398	3.94	104	.271	.331	0	ø	0	111	9	0	0.7
CHACIN, GUSTAVO	Gustavo G. (Adolfo); B12.4.1980 Maracaibo, Zulia, Venezuela; BL/TL/5´11˝/(193–195); d9.20																									
2004	Tor A	1	1	.500	2	2	0	0-0	14	8	4	0	1	3-0	6	2.57	190	.167	.231	0	ø	0	57	4	0	0.5
2005	Tor A	13	9	.591	34	34	0	0-0	203	213	93	20	8	70-3	121	3.72	123	.274	.337	7-0-1	.000	-1	102	18	0	1.6
2006	Tor A	9	4	.692	17	17	0	0-0	87.1	90	51	19	6	38-2	47	5.05	94	.266	.351	0	ø	0	125	-2	93	-0.3
Total	3	23	14	.622	53	53	0	0-0	304.1	311	148	39	15	111-5	174	4.05	115	.268	.337	7-0-1	.000	-1	108	20	93	1.8
CHACON, SHAWN	Shawn Anthony; B12.23.1977 Anchorage AK; BR/TR/6´3˝/(210–220); [ColN96 3/86]; d4.29																									
2001	Col N	6	10	.375	27	27	0	0-0	160	157	96	26	10	87-10	134	5.06	105	.260	.360	47-0-7	.043	-4	86	4	0	-0.1
2002	Col N	5	11	.313	21	21	0	0-0	119.1	122	84	25	7	60-3	67	5.73	83	.263	.355	35-0-2	.257	1	68	-12	28	-1.3
2003	Col N✷	11	8	.579	23	23	0	0-0	137	124	73	12	12	58-4	93	4.60	106	.243	.331	46-1-2	.196	1	98	5	62	0.7
2004	Col N	1	9	.100	66	0	0	35-9	63.1	71	52	12	5	52-7	52	7.11	67	.282	.414	0	ø	0	—	-15	0	-2.9
2005	Col N	1	7	.125	13	12	0	0-0	72.2	69	33	7	8	36-4	39	4.09	114	.260	.361	20-0-3	.150	-0	57	5	33	0.5
	†NY A	7	3	.700	14	12	0	0-0	79	66	26	7	6	30-0	40	2.85	151	.225	.309	0	ø	0	97	14	0	1.6
2006	NY A	5	3	.625	17	11	0	0-0	63	77	54	11	5	36-2	35	7.00	65	.300	.389	2	.000	0	115	-18	25	-1.8

YEAR	TM LG	W	L	PCT	G	GS	CG-SHO	SV-BS	IP	H	R	HR	HB	BB-IB	SO	ERA	AERA	OAV	OOB	AB-HR-SH	AVG	PB	SUP	APR	DL	PW
	Pit N	2	3	.400	9	9	0	0-0	46	47	32	12	4	27-1	27	5.48	84	.272	.379	13-0-2	.077	-0	69	-5	0	-0.5
Total	6	38	54	.413	190	115	0	35-9	740.1	733	450	112	57	386-31	487	5.12	94	.260	.358	163-1-16	.147	-3	85	-22	148	-3.8
CHADWICK, RAY	Ray Charles; B11.17.1962 Durham NC; BB/TR/6´2˝/180; [AnaA83 16/415]; d7.29; Col Winston–Salem St.																									
1986	Cal A	0	5	.000	7	7	0	0-0	27.1	39	26	5	1	15-0	9	7.24	57	.336	.417	0	ø	0	75	-10	0	-1.5
CHAGNON, LEON	Leon Wilbur "Shag"; B9.28.1902 Pittsfield NH; D7.30.1953 Amesbury MA; BR/TR/6´0˝/182; d10.5																									
1929	Pit N	0	0	ø	1	1	0	0	7	11	7	1	0	1	4	9.00	53	.333	.353	2	.000	-0	146	-3	—	-0.1
1930	Pit N	0	3	.000	18	4	3	0	62	92	52	9	5	23	27	6.82	73	.355	.418	20	.200	-1	118	-11	—	-0.5
1932	Pit N	9	6	.600	30	10	4-1	0	128	140	62	10	2	34	52	3.94	97	.276	.324	40-0-1	.225	2	88	1	—	0.2
1933	Pit N	6	4	.600	39	5	1	1	100	100	48	2	3	17	35	3.69	90	.259	.296	21-0-2	.048	-2	156	-3	—	-0.5
1934	Pit N	4	1	.800	33	0	0	1	58	68	32	5	1	24	19	4.81	86	.288	.356	13	.231	0	—	-3	—	-0.1
1935	NY N	0	2	.000	14	1	0	1	38.1	32	17	7	0	5	16	3.52	109	.232	.259	9	.000	-1	0	2	—	0.0
Total	6	19	16	.543	135	21	8-1	3	393.1	443	218	34	11	104	153	4.51	87	.284	.333	105-0-3	.162	-2	109	-17	—	-1.0
CHAKALES, BOB	Robert Edward "Chick"; B8.10.1927 Asheville NC; BR/TR/6´1˝/(180–185); d4.21																									
1951	Cle A	3	4	.429	17	10	2-1	0	68.1	80	40	3	0	43	32	4.74	80	.292	.388	20-1-1	.350	2	82	-7	0	-0.5
1952	Cle A	1	2	.333	5	1	0	0	12	19	13	2	0	8	7	9.75	34	.388	.474	4	.500	1	287	-8	0	-1.4
1953	Cle A	0	2	.000	7	3	1	0	27	28	13	2	1	10	6	2.67	141	.283	.355	7	.286	0	32	2	0	0.1
1954	Cle A	2	0	1.000	3	0	0	0	10.1	4	1	0	0	12	3	0.87	422	.114	.340	3-0-1	.333	1	—	3	0	0.7
	Bal A	3	7	.300	38	6	0	3	89.1	81	43	8	1	43	44	3.73	96	.245	.331	22-0-2	.364	2	131	-2	0	0.0
	Year	5	7	.417	41	6	0	3	99.2	85	44	8	1	55	47	3.43	105	.232	.332	25-0-3	.360	3	131	1	0	0.7
1955	Chi A	0	0	ø	7	0	0	0	12.1	11	2	2	0	6-1	6	1.46	271	.256	.347	2	.000	-0	—	3	0	0.2
	Was A	2	3	.400	29	0	0	0	54.2	55	38	4	1	25-3	28	5.27	73	.263	.342	8	.000	-1	—	-10	0	-0.9
	Year	2	3	.400	36	0	0	0	67	66	40	6	1	31-4	34	4.57	84	.262	.343	10	.000	-1	—	-6	0	-0.7
1956	Was A	4	4	.500	43	1	0	4	96	94	53	3	3	57-7	33	4.03	107	.268	.369	20-0-3	.150	-1	123	1	0	0.1
1957	Was A	0	1	.000	4	2	0	0	18.1	20	13	2	0	10-1	12	5.40	72	.274	.357	7	.143	0	172	-3	0	-0.1
	Bos A	0	2	.000	18	0	0	3	32	53	30	5	1	11-0	16	8.16	49	.379	.425	3-0-1	.667	1	—	-13	0	-1.0
	Year	0	3	.000	22	2	0	3	50.1	73	43	7	1	21-1	28	7.15	55	.343	.401	10-0-1	.300	1	169	-17	0	-1.1
Total	7	15	25	.375	171	23	3-1	10	420.1	445	246	31	7	225-12	187	4.54	85	.277	.366	96-1-8	.271	5	102	-34	0	-2.8
CHALMERS, GEORGE	George W. "Dut"; B6.7.1888 Aberdeen, Scotland; D8.5.1960 Bronx NY; BR/TR/6´1˝/189; d9.21; Col Manhattan																									
1910	Phi N	1	1	.500	4	3	2	0	22	21	17	0	1	11	12	5.32	59	.280	.379	7	.143	-0	151	-5	—	-0.4
1911	Phi N	13	10	.565	38	22	11-3	4	208.2	196	107	5	4	101	101	3.11	111	.256	.346	73-0-2	.178	-1	96	3	—	0.2
1912	Phi N	3	4	.429	12	8	3	0	57.2	64	34	4	2	37	22	3.28	111	.296	.404	16-0-1	.188	-0	111	1	—	0.0
1913	Phi N	3	10	.231	26	15	4	1	116	133	75	3	5	51	46	4.81	69	.296	.374	33-0-1	.212	-1	83	-17	—	-1.8
1914	Phi N	0	3	.000	3	2	1	0	18	23	17	0	1	15	6	5.50	53	.324	.448	6	.000	-1	73	-5	—	-0.8
1915	†Phi N	8	9	.471	26	20	13-1	1	170.1	159	58	3	0	45	82	2.48	110	.255	.305	59-0-2	.169	-0	89	8	—	0.7
1916	Phi N	1	4	.200	12	8	2	0	53.2	49	31	2	2	19	21	3.19	83	.244	.315	15-0-3	.000	-2	106	-5	—	-0.7
Total	7	29	41	.414	121	78	36-4	6	646.1	645	339	17	15	279	290	3.41	93	.269	.348	209-0-9	.163	-5	96	-20	—	-2.8
CHAMBERLAIN, CRAIG	Craig Philip; B2.2.1957 Hollywood CA; BR/TR/6´1˝/190; [KCA78 S1/2]; d8.12; Col Arizona																									
1979	KC A	4	4	.500	10	10	4	0-0	69.2	68	31	7	1	18-0	30	3.75	114	.261	.306	0	ø	0	102	5	0	0.4
1980	KC A	0	1	.000	5	0	0	0-1	9.1	10	8	3	0	5-2	3	6.75	60	.270	.349	0	ø	0	—	-3	0	-0.3
Total	2	4	5	.444	15	10	4	0-1	79	78	39	10	1	23-2	33	4.10	103	.262	.312	0	ø	0	102	2	0	0.1
CHAMBERLAIN, ELTON	Elton P. "Icebox"; B11.5.1867 Buffalo NY; D9.22.1929 Baltimore MD; BR/TR (TB 1888p)/5´9˝/168; d9.13																									
1886	Lou AA	0	3	.000	4	4	4	0	31.1	39	43	0	0	17	18	6.61	55	.287	.366	19	.158	-0*	57	-9	—	-0.7
1887	Lou AA	18	16	.529	36	36	35-1	0	309	340	226	8	14	117	118	3.79	116	.274	.343	131-1	.198	-3*	97	17	—	1.2
1888	Lou AA	14	9	.609	24	24	21-1	0	196	178	123	2	11	59	119	2.53	122	.233	.298	94	.191	0*	131	8	—	0.9
	†StL AA	11	2	.846	14	14	13-1	0	112	61	34	1	6	27	57	1.61	203	.154	.220	50-1	.100	-3	128	20	—	1.7
	Year	25	11	.694	38	38	34-2	0	308	239	157	3	17	86	176	2.19	143	.206	.271	144-1	.160	-3	130	26	—	2.6
1889	StL AA	32	15	.681	53	51	44-3	1	421.2	376	220	18	17	165	202	2.97	142	.231	.309	171-2	.199	-2	94	**56**	—	4.6
1890	StL AA	3	1	.750	5	5	3	0	35	47	37	1	0	26	14	5.91	73	.311	.412	15	.133	-1	125	-6	—	-0.7
	Col AA	12	6	.667	25	21	19-6	0	175	128	69	2	8	70	114	2.21	162	.198	.285	65	.231	3	87	28	—	2.6
	Year	15	7	.682	30	26	22-**6**	0	210	175	106	3	8	96	128	2.83	131	.220	.310	80	.213	1	95	16	—	1.9
1891	Phi AA	22	23	.489	49	46	44	0	405.2	397	263	10	12	206	204	4.22	90	.248	.338	176-2	.188	2*	86	-15	—	-1.1
1892	Cin N	19	23	.452	52	49	43-2	0	406.1	391	230	8	17	170	169	3.39	96	.243	.322	160-2	.225	2*	88	-5	—	-0.5
1893	Cin N	16	12	.571	34	27	19-1	0	241	248	148	3	15	112	59	3.73	128	.258	.345	97	.196	-3	95	24	—	1.7
1894	Cin N	10	9	.526	23	22	18-1	0	177.2	220	155	10	12	91	57	5.77	96	.301	.387	70-1-3	.314	4	91	-2	—	0.2
1896	Cle N	0	1	.000	2	2	1	0	11	21	12	0	1	5	2	7.36	62	.396	.458	3	.000	-0	180	-3	—	-0.2
Total	10	157	120	.567	321	301	264-16	1	2521.2	2446	1560	63	113	1065	1133	3.57	112	.247	.327	1051-9-3	.203	-2	97	113	—	9.7
CHAMBERLAIN, BILL	William Vincent; B4.21.1909 Stoughton MA; D2.6.1994 Brockton MA; BR/TL/5´10.5˝/173; d8.2; Col St. Anselm																									
1932	Chi A	0	5	.000	12	5	0	0	41.1	39	30	3	0	25	11	4.57	95	.250	.354	10	.100	-1	32	-3	—	-0.4
CHAMBERS, CLIFF	Clifford Day "Lefty"; B1.10.1922 Portland OR; BL/TL/6´3˝/(208–210); d4.24; Col Washington St.																									
1948	Chi N	2	9	.182	29	12	3-1	0	103.2	100	57	4	3	48	51	4.43	88	.254	.339	30-0-3	.133	-1	74	-5	0	-0.6
1949	Pit N	13	7	.650	34	21	10-1	0	177.1	186	89	15	5	58	93	3.96	106	.268	.329	55-0-6	.236	3	99	3	0	0.7
1950	Pit N	12	15	.444	37	33	11-2	0	249.1	262	138	18	6	92	93	4.30	102	.265	.332	90-2-2	.289	7	92	1	0	0.7
1951	Pit N	3	6	.333	10	10	2-1	0	59.2	64	38	5	4	31	19	5.58	76	.276	.371	21-1-1	.333	2	67	-7	0	-0.7
	StL N	11	6	.647	21	16	9-1	0	129.1	120	59	13	0	56	45	3.83	104	.251	.329	49-0-1	.163	0	129	3	0	0.3
	Year	14	12	.538	31	26	11-2	0	189	184	97	18	4	87	64	4.38	92	.259	.343	70-1-2	.214	2	105	-2	0	-0.4
1952	StL N	4	4	.500	26	13	2-1	1	98.1	110	51	8	2	33	47	4.12	90	.285	.344	32-0-1	.281	3	105	-4	30	0.1
1953	StL N	3	6	.333	32	8	0	0	79.2	82	50	7	1	43	26	4.86	88	.266	.358	17	.118	-1	76	-7	0	-0.7
Total	6	48	53	.475	189	113	37-7	1	897.1	924	482	70	21	361	374	4.29	96	.266	.338	294-3-14	.235	13	95	-16	30	-0.2
CHAMBERS, JOHNNIE	Johnnie Monroe; B9.10.1911 Copperhill TN; D5.11.1977 Palatka FL; BL/TR/6´0˝/185; d5.4																									
1937	StL N	0	0	ø	2	0	0	0	2	5	4	0	0	2	1	18.00	22	.455	.538	0	ø	0	—	-3	—	-0.1
CHAMBERS, ROME	Richard Jerome; B8.31.1875 Weaverville NC; D8.30.1902 Weaverville NC; BL/TL/6´2˝/173; d5.7																									
1900	Bos N	0	0	ø	1	0	0	1	4	5	6	0	0	5	2	11.25	37	.313	.476	1	.000	-0	—	-2	—	-0.1
CHAMBERS, BILL	William Christopher; B9.13.1888 Cameron WV; D3.27.1962 Fort Wayne IN; BR/TR/5´9˝/185; d7.11																									
1910	StL N	0	0	ø	1	0	0	0	1	1	1	0	0	0	0	0.00	ø	.250	.250	0	ø	0	—	0	—	0.0
CHAMPION, BILL	Buford Billy; B9.18.1947 Shelby NC; BR/TR/6´4˝/(178–200); [PhiN65 3/58]; d6.4																									
1969	Phi N	5	10	.333	23	20	4-2	1-0	116.2	130	68	7	3	63-4	70	5.01	71	.286	.373	35-0-3	.171	0	114	-17	0	-1.9
1970	Phi N	0	2	.000	7	1	0	0-0	14	21	14	3	1	10-2	12	9.00	45	.375	.471	3	.000	-0	67	-7	0	-0.9
1971	Phi N	3	5	.375	37	9	0	0-0	108.2	100	61	10	3	48-4	49	4.39	81	.249	.329	27	.111	-1	61	-10	0	-0.8
1972	Phi N	4	14	.222	30	22	2	0-0	132.2	155	80	11	1	54-8	54	5.09	71	.301	.366	34-1-5	.147	0*	73	-19	0	-2.4
1973	Mil A	5	8	.385	37	11	2	1-1	136.1	139	58	10	4	62-4	67	3.70	103	.267	.349	0	ø	0	90	4	0	0.5
1974	Mil A	11	4	.733	31	23	2	0-0	161.2	168	72	12	0	49-3	60	3.62	101	.270	.321	0	ø	0	99	0	0	-0.1
1975	Mil A	6	6	.500	27	13	3-1	0-0	110	125	77	11	0	55-8	40	5.89	65	.290	.367	0	ø	0	97	-22	56	-2.1
1976	Mil A	0	1	.000	10	3	0	0-0	24.1	35	20	0	1	13-2	8	7.03	50	.361	.430	0	ø	0	100	-9	0	-0.4
Total	8	34	50	.405	202	102	13-3	2-1	804.1	873	450	64	13	354-35	360	4.69	78	.282	.355	99-1-8	.141	-1	91	-80	56	-8.1
CHANCE, DEAN	Wilmer Dean; B6.1.1941 Plain Twp. OH; BR/TR/6´3˝/(200–210); d9.11																									
1961	LA A	0	2	.000	5	4	0	0	18.1	33	15	0	1	5-1	11	6.87	66	.412	.443	5	.000	-1	69	-4	0	-0.4
1962	LA A	14	10	.583	50	24	6-2	8	206.2	195	83	14	5	66-5	127	2.96	130	.250	.311	65-0-7	.062	-5	109	20	0	1.8
1963	LA A	13	18	.419	45	35	6-2	3	248	229	109	10	10	90-7	168	3.19	107	.243	.315	80-0-7	.150	-1	89	4	0	0.4
1964	LA A★	**20**	9	.690	46	35	**15-11**	4	**278.1**	194	56	7	2	86-9	207	**1.65**	**199**	.195	.260	89-0-8	.079	-5	80	**58**	0	**5.6**
1965	Cal A	15	10	.600	36	33	10-4	0	225.2	197	86	12	9	101-10	164	3.15	108	.238	.327	75-0-5	.093	-2	104	7	0	0.8
1966	Cal A	12	17	.414	41	37	11-2	1	259.2	206	113	18	7	114-9	180	3.08	109	.222	.310	76-0-8	.026	-6	103	2	0	-0.4
1967	Min A★	20	14	.588	41	**39**	**18**-5	1	**283.2**	244	109	17	7	68-7	220	2.73	127	.229	.278	92-0-7	.033	-6	107	18	0	1.6
1968	Min A	16	16	.500	43	39	15-6	1	292	224	96	15	10	63-8	234	2.53	122	.211	.260	93-0-9	.054	-6	94	18	0	1.6

YEAR	TM LG	W	L	PCT	G	GS	CG-SHO	SV-BS	IP	H	R	HR	HB	BB-IB	SO	ERA	AERA	OAV	OOB	AB-HR-SH	AVG	PB	SUP	APR	DL	PW
1969	†Min A	5	4	.556	20	15	1	0-0	88.1	76	39	6	4	35-3	50	2.95	123	.233	.314	24-0-5	.042	-1	118	4	54	0.2
1970	Cle A	9	8	.529	45	19	1-1	4-0	155	172	80	18	6	59-11	109	4.24	95	.287	.355	42-0-4	.071	-3	92	-4	0	-0.8
	NY N	0	1	.000	3	0	0	1-0	2	3	3	0	0	2-1	0	13.50	30	.500	.625	0	ø	0	—	-2	0	-0.4
1971	Det A	4	6	.400	31	14	0	0-0	89.2	91	43	5	4	50-4	64	3.51	103	.265	.363	21-0-1	.000	-2	76	-1	21	-0.4
Total	11	128	115	.527	406	294	83-33	23-0	2147.1	1864	832	122	65	739-75	1534	2.92	119	.234	.303	662-0-61	.066	-37	97	120	75	9.6
Chandler, Ed	Edward Oliver; B2.17.1922 Pinson AL; D7.6.2003 Las Vegas NV; BR/TR/6´2˝/190; d4.18																									
1947	Bro N	0	1	.000	15	1	0	1	29.2	31	23	7	0	12	8	6.37	65	.263	.331	2-0-1	.000	0	85	-7	0	-0.3
Chandler, Spud	Spurgeon Ferdinand; B9.12.1907 Commerce GA; D1.9.1990 S.Pasadena FL; BR/TR/6´0˝/181; d5.6; Mil 1944–45; C2; Col Georgia																									
1937	NY A	7	4	.636	12	10	6-2	0	82.1	79	31	8	1	20	31	2.84	156	.253	.300	30-0-5	.133	-2	129	15	—	1.7
1938	NY A	14	5	.737	23	23	14-2	0	172	183	86	7	2	47	36	4.03	113	.271	.320	69-3-3	.203	2	128	12	—	1.5
1939	NY A	3	0	1.000	11	0	0	0	19	26	7	0	0	9	4	2.84	153	.329	.398	5	.400	1	—	3	—	0.6
1940	NY A	8	7	.533	27	24	6-1	0	172	184	100	12	6	60	56	4.60	88	.275	.341	60-2-4	.150	1	141	-12	—	-0.7
1941	†NY A	10	4	.714	28	20	11-4	4	163.2	146	68	5	0	60	60	3.19	123	.239	.307	60-0-3	.183	-1	120	14	0	1.2
1942	†NY A★	16	5	.762	24	24	17-3	0	200.2	176	64	13	4	74	74	2.38	145	.237	.309	71-0-6	.211	4	138	24	0	3.0
1943	†NY A☆	**20**	4	**.833**	30	30	**20-5**	0	253	197	62	5	4	54	134	**1.64**	**197**	.215	**.261**	97-2-3	.258	7	110	**42**	0	**5.3**
1944	NY A	0	0	ø	1	1	0	0	6	6	3	1	1	1	1	4.50	77	.300	.364	1-0-1	.000	-0	144	0	0	0.0
1945	NY A	2	1	.667	4	4	2-1	0	31	30	16	2	0	7	12	4.65	75	.250	.291	12	.333	1	111	-3	0	-0.2
1946	NY A☆	20	8	.714	34	32	20-6	2	257.1	200	71	7	1	90	138	2.10	164	.218	.288	94-0-5	.149	-0	119	38	0	4.5
1947	†NY A☆	9	5	.643	17	16	13-2	0	128	100	41	4	0	41	68	2.46	144	.214	.277	49-2-3	.245	4	106	15	0	2.2
Total	11	109	43	.717	211	184	109-26	6	1485	1327	549	64	19	463	614	2.84	132	.240	.301	548-9-33	.201	17	124	148	0	19.1
Chaney, Esty	Esty Clyon; B1.29.1891 Hadley PA; D2.5.1952 Cleveland OH; BR/TR/5´11˝/170; d8.2																									
1913	Bos A	0	0	ø	1	0	0	0	1	1	1	0	0	2	0	9.00	33	.200	.429	0	ø	0	—	-1	—	0.0
1914	Bro F	0	0	ø	1	0	0	0	4	7	3	0	0	2	1	6.75	43	.389	.450	1	.000	-0	—	-1	—	-0.1
Total	2	0	0	ø	2	0	0	0	5	8	4	0	0	4	1	7.20	40	.348	.444	1	.000	-0	—	-2	—	-0.1
Chapin, Darrin	Darrin John; B2.1.1966 Warren OH; BR/TR/6´0˝/170; [NYA86*6/155]; d9.21; Col Cleveland St.																									
1991	NY A	0	1	.000	3	0	0	0-0	5.1	3	3	0	0	6-0	5	5.06	82	.158	.360	0	ø	0	—	0	0	-0.1
1992	Phi N	0	0	ø	1	0	0	0-0	2	2	2	1	0	0-0	1	9.00	39	.250	.250	0	ø	0	—	-1	0	-0.1
Total	2	0	1	.000	4	0	0	0-0	7.1	5	5	1	0	6-0	6	6.14	65	.185	.333	0	ø	0	—	-1	0	-0.2
Chaplin, Tiny	James Bailey; B7.13.1905 Los Angeles CA; D3.25.1939 National City CA; BR/TR/6´1˝/195; d4.13; Col Florida																									
1928	NY N	0	2	.000	12	1	0	0	24	27	15	0	0	8	5	4.50	87	.284	.340	5	.000	-1	152	-2	—	-0.2
1930	NY N	2	6	.250	19	8	3	1	73	89	45	8	4	16	20	5.18	91	.305	.349	19-1-1	.105	-0	62	-2	—	-0.2
1931	NY N	3	0	1.000	16	3	1	1	42.1	39	17	2	2	16	7	3.19	116	.242	.318	11-0-1	.182	0	155	3	—	0.2
1936	Bos N	10	15	.400	40	31	14	2	231.2	273	131	21	3	62	86	4.12	93	.294	.340	84-0-5	.202	-0	113	-12	—	-1.1
Total	4	15	23	.395	87	43	18	4	371	428	208	31	9	102	118	4.25	94	.290	.340	119-1-7	.176	-1	105	-13	—	-1.3
Chapman, Ed	Edwin Volney; B11.28.1905 Courtland MS; D5.3.2000 Clarksdale MS; BB/TR/6´1˝/185; d8.6; b–Calvin; Col Mississippi St.																									
1933	Was A	0	0	ø	6	1	0	0	9	10	9	2	0	2	4	8.00	52	.270	.308	3	.000	-0	163	-4	—	-0.2
Chapman, Fred	Frederick Joseph; B11.24.1872 Little Cooley PA; D12.14.1957 Union City PA; BR/TR/5´8˝/165; d7.22																									
1887	Phi AA	0	0	ø	1	1	1	0	5	8	6	0	0	2	4	7.20	60	.364	.417	2	.000	-0	59	-2	—	-0.1
Chapman, Ben	William Benjamin; B12.25.1908 Nashville TN; D7.7.1993 Hoover AL; BR/TR/6´0˝/190; d4.15.1930; M4/C1; ▲																									
1944	Bro N	5	3	.625	11	9	6	0	79.1	75	36	4	3	33	37	3.40	104	.242	.321	38-0-1	.368	6*	157	1	0	0.7
1945	Bro N	3	3	.500	10	7	2	0	53.2	64	33	3	3	32	23	5.53	68	.296	.394	22	.136	-1*	110	-7	0	-0.7
	Phi N	0	0	ø	3	0	0	0	7	7	8	0	0	6	4	7.71	50	.259	.394	51	.314	0*	—	-3	0	-0.1
	Year	3	3	.500	13	7	2	0	60.2	71	41	3	3	38	27	5.79	65	.292	.394	73	.260	-0	109	-12	0	-0.8
1946	Phi N	0	0	ø	1	0	0	0	1	1	0	0	0	0	1	0.00	ø	.200	.200	1	.000	-0	—	0	0	0.0
Total	3	8	6	.571	25	16	8	0	141	147	77	7	6	71	65	4.40	83	.263	.353	112-0-1	.295	6	136	-9	0	-0.1
Chappelle, Bill	William Hogan "Big Bill"; B3.22.1881 Waterloo NY; D12.31.1944 Mineola NY; BR/TR/6´2˝/206; d8.20																									
1908	Bos N	2	4	.333	13	6	3-1	0	70.1	60	28	0	4	17	23	1.79	135	.233	.290	21-0-2	.048	-1	54	2	—	0.1
1909	Bos N	1	1	.500	5	3	2	0	29	31	13	0	1	11	8	1.86	151	.279	.350	11-1-0	.364	2	107	1	—	0.4
	Cin N	0	0	ø	1	0	0	1	4	5	2	0	1	2	0	2.25	115	.278	.381	1	.000	-0	—	0	—	0.0
	Year	1	1	.500	6	3	2	1	33	36	15	0	2	13	8	1.91	146	.279	.354	12-1-0	.333	2	108	1	—	0.4
1914	Bro F	4	2	.667	16	6	4	0	74.1	71	43	1	3	29	31	3.15	91	.255	.332	23-0-1	.000	-4	119	-6	—	-0.9
Total	3	7	7	.500	35	15	9-1	1	177.2	167	86	1	9	59	62	2.38	113	.251	.321	56-1-3	.089	-3	91	-3	—	-0.4
Charlton, Norm	Norman Wood; B1.6.1963 Fort Polk LA; BB/TL/6´3˝/(195–210); [MonN84 1/28]; d8.19; Col Rice; [DL 1987 Cin N 81, 1994 Phi N 131, 2002 Sea A 138]																									
1988	Cin N	4	5	.444	10	10	0	0-0	61.1	60	27	6	2	20-2	39	3.96	90	.256	.318	15-0-4	.000	-1	72	-1	0	-0.3
1989	Cin N	8	3	.727	69	0	0	0-1	95.1	67	38	5	2	40-7	98	2.93	123	.197	.284	5	.000	-1	—	6	0	0.6
1990	†Cin N	12	9	.571	56	16	1-1	2-1	154.1	131	53	10	4	70-4	117	2.74	144	.231	.319	37	.135	0*	77	19	0	2.6
1991	Cin N	3	5	.375	39	11	0	1-3	108.1	92	37	6	6	34-4	77	2.91	131	.236	.306	23-0-4	.043	-2*	64	12	48	0.7
1992	Cin N★	4	2	.667	64	0	0	26-8	81.1	79	39	7	3	26-4	90	2.99	121	.262	.323	5-0-2	.200	0	—	1	0	0.1
1993	Sea A	1	3	.250	34	0	0	18-3	34.2	22	12	4	0	17-0	48	2.34	191	.179	.277	0	ø	0	—	7	72	1.3
1995	Phi N	2	5	.286	25	0	0	0-1	22	23	19	2	3	15-3	12	7.36	57	.280	.406	1	1.000	1	—	-7	0	-1.4
	†Sea A	2	1	.667	30	0	0	14-1	47.2	23	12	2	1	16-0	58	1.51	316	.143	.223	0	ø	0	—	16	0	1.7
1996	Sea A	4	7	.364	70	0	0	20-7	75.2	68	37	7	1	38-1	73	4.04	123	.244	.334	0	ø	0	—	8	0	1.3
1997	†Sea A	3	8	.273	71	0	0	14-11	69.1	89	59	7	4	47-2	55	7.27	62	.312	.417	0	ø	0	—	-21	0	-3.4
1998	Bal A	2	1	.667	36	0	0	0-1	35	46	27	5	0	25-0	41	6.94	66	.305	.401	0	ø	0	—	-9	0	-0.6
	Atl N	0	0	ø	13	0	0	1-0	13	7	2	0	1	8-0	6	1.38	301	.167	.308	1	.000	-0	—	4	0	0.2
1999	TB A	2	3	.400	42	0	0	0-1	50.2	49	29	4	1	36-0	45	4.44	112	.257	.372	0	ø	0	—	3	0	0.2
2000	Cin N	0	0	ø	2	0	0	0-0	3	6	9	1	0	6-0	1	27.00	18	.429	.600	0	ø	0	—	-7	0	-0.3
2001	†Sea A	4	2	.667	44	0	0	1-1	47.2	36	19	4	4	11-0	48	3.02	141	.212	.274	0	ø	0	—	6	48	0.7
Total	13	51	54	.486	605	37	1-1	97-39	899.1	798	419	70	32	409-27	808	3.71	112	.240	.327	87-0-10	.092	-2	67	37	518	3.4
Charton, Pete	Frank Lane; B12.21.1942 Jackson TN; BL/TR/6´2˝/190; d4.19; Col Baylor																									
1964	Bos A	0	2	.000	25	5	0	0	65	67	39	12	1	24-1	37	5.26	73	.275	.342	10	.100	-0	55	-8	0	-0.4
Chase, Ken	Kendall Fay "Lefty"; B10.6.1913 Oneonta NY; D1.16.1985 Oneonta NY; BL/TL/6´2˝/210; d4.23																									
1936	Was A	0	0	ø	1	0	0	0	2.1	2	3	0	0	4	1	11.57	41	.250	.500	1	1.000	1	—	-2	—	0.0
1937	Was A	4	3	.571	14	9	4	0	76.1	74	41	4	0	60	43	4.13	107	.257	.385	29-0-1	.034	-4	79	3	—	-0.2
1938	Was A	9	10	.474	32	21	7	1	150	151	99	4	4	113	64	5.58	81	.268	.394	48-0-4	.208	1	91	-14	—	-1.4
1939	Was A	10	19	.345	32	31	15-1	0	232	215	116	10	1	114	118	3.80	114	.243	.330	89	.169	-3	78	13	—	1.2
1940	Was A	15	17	.469	35	34	20-1	0	261.2	260	120	14	5	143	129	3.23	129	.261	.357	92-1-5	.163	-1	81	24	—	2.6
1941	Was A	6	18	.250	33	30	8-1	0	205.2	228	136	11	3	115	98	5.08	80	.280	.371	74-0-1	.149	-2	90	-23	0	-2.4
1942	Bos A	5	1	.833	13	10	4	0	80.1	82	37	5	0	41	34	3.81	98	.263	.348	33-0-3	.182	1	154	0	0	0.0
1943	Bos A	0	4	.000	7	5	0	0	27.1	36	25	0	0	30	9	6.91	48	.316	.458	11	.091	-1	66	-12	0	-1.5
	NY N	4	12	.250	21	20	4-1	0	129.1	140	70	7	2	74	86	4.11	84	.275	.369	42-0-3	.214	0*	76	-11	0	-1.3
Total	8	53	84	.387	188	160	62-4	1	1165	1188	647	55	15	694	582	4.27	97	.265	.365	419-1-17	.165	-8	86	-22	0	-3.0
Chavez, Anthony	Anthony Francisco; B10.22.1970 Turlock CA; BR/TR/5´11˝/180; [AnaA92 50/1392]; d9.2; Col San Jose St.																									
1997	Ana A	0	0	ø	7	0	0	0-0	9.2	7	1	1	0	5-1	10	0.93	495	.206	.300	0	ø	0	—	4	0	0.2
Chavez, Nestor	Nestor Isais (Silva); B7.6.1947 Chacao, Miranda, Venez.; D3.16.1969 Maracaibo, Zulia, Venez.; BR/TR/6´0˝/150; d9.9																									
1967	SF N	1	0	1.000	2	0	0	0	5	4	2	0	0	3-1	3	0.00	ø	.211	.318	1	.000	-0	—	1	0	0.2
Cheadle, Dave	David Baird; B2.19.1952 Greensboro NC; BL/TL/6´2˝/190; [NYA70 1/12]; d9.16																									
1973	Atl N	0	1	.000	2	0	0	0-0	2	2	4	1	0	3-2	2	18.00	22	.250	.455	0	ø	0	—	-3	0	-0.5

YEAR	TM LG	W	L	PCT	G	GS	CG-SHO	SV-BS	IP	H	R	HR	HB	BB-IB	SO	ERA	AERA	OAV	OOB	AB-HR-SH	AVG	PB	SUP	APR	DL	PW
CHECH, CHARLIE	Charles William; B4.27.1878 Madison WI; D1.31.1938 Los Angeles CA; BR/TR/5´11.5˝/190; d4.14; Col Wisconsin–Madison																									
1905	Cin N	14	14	.500	39	25	20-1	0	267.2	300	139	4	11	77	79	2.89	114	.288	.344	89-0-8	.191	1	113	9	—	0.9
1906	Cin N	1	4	.200	11	5	5	3	66	59	32	1	6	24	17	2.32	119	.243	.326	25	.200	1	74	0	—	0.1
1908	Cle A	11	7	.611	27	20	14-4	0	165.2	136	51	2	7	34	51	1.74	137	.229	.279	48-0-3	.104	-1	92	10	—	1.2
1909	Bos A	7	5	.583	17	13	6-1	0	106.2	107	51	3	5	27	40	2.95	85	.260	.314	36	.083	-2	115	-6	—	-1.0
Total	4	33	30	.524	94	63	45-6	3	606	602	273	10	29	162	187	2.52	113	.263	.320	198-0-11	.152	-1	103	13	—	1.2
CHECO, ROBINSON	Robinson (Perez); B9.9.1971 Santo Domingo, D.R.; BR/TR/6´1˝/185; d9.16																									
1997	Bos A	1	1	.500	5	2	0	0-0	13.1	12	5	0	0	3-0	14	3.38	138	.235	.278	0	ø	0	49	2	42	0.3
1998	Bos A	0	2	.000	2	2	0	0-0	7.2	11	8	3	0	5-0	5	9.39	50	.379	.471	0	ø	0	89	-4	0	-0.6
1999	LA N	2	2	.500	9	2	0	0-0	15.2	24	20	5	0	13-1	11	10.34	42	.333	.435	3-0-1	.333	0	137	-11	45	-1.9
Total	3	3	5	.375	16	6	0	0-0	36.2	47	33	8	0	21-1	30	7.61	60	.309	.393	3-0-1	.333	0	91	-13	87	-2.2
CHEEVES, VIRGIL	Virgil Earl "Chief"; B2.12.1901 Oklahoma City OK; D5.5.1979 Dallas TX; BR/TR/6´0˝/195; d9.7																									
1920	Chi N	0	0	ø	5	2	0	0	18	16	7	0	0	7	3	3.50	92	.250	.324	4	.000	-0	61	0	—	-0.1
1921	Chi N	11	12	.478	37	22	9-1	0	163	192	97	8	9	47	39	4.64	82	.309	.366	48-0-4	.167	-2	85	-14	—	-2.1
1922	Chi N	12	11	.522	39	22	9-1	2	182.2	195	99	9	10	76	40	4.09	103	.281	.360	62-1-2	.210	1	88	2	—	0.3
1923	Chi N	3	4	.429	19	8	0	0	71.1	89	54	8	3	37	13	6.18	65	.314	.399	23	.174	-1	121	-15	—	-1.3
1924	Cle A	0	0	ø	8	1	0	0	17.1	26	17	2	1	17	2	7.79	55	.388	.518	4	.250	0	138	-6	—	-0.3
1927	NY N	0	0	ø	3	0	0	0	6.1	8	3	1	0	4	1	4.26	90	.333	.429	0-0-1	ø	0	—	0	—	0.0
Total	6	26	27	.491	111	55	18-2	2	458.2	526	277	28	23	188	98	4.73	84	.300	.375	141-1-7	.184	-1	92	-33	—	-3.5
CHELINI, ITALO	Italo Vincent "Chilly","Lefty"; B10.10.1914 San Francisco CA; D8.25.1972 San Francisco CA; BL/TL/5´10.5˝/175; d9.12																									
1935	Chi A	0	0	ø	2	0	0	0	5	7	7	1	1	4	1	12.60	37	.350	.480	2	.500	0	—	-4	—	-0.2
1936	Chi A	4	3	.571	18	6	5	0	83.2	100	51	8	0	30	16	4.95	105	.291	.348	32	.156	-1	110	3	—	0.0
1937	Chi A	0	1	.000	4	0	0	0	8.2	15	10	2	1	0	3	10.38	44	.405	.421	1	.000	0	—	-5	—	-0.4
Total	3	4	4	.500	24	6	5	0	97.1	122	68	11	2	34	20	5.83	88	.304	.362	35	.171	-1	110	-6	—	-0.6
CHEN, BRUCE	Bruce Kastulo; B6.19.1977 Panama City, Pan; BL/TL/6´2˝/(150–215); d9.7																									
1998	Atl N	2	0	1.000	4	4	0	0-0	20.1	23	9	3	1	9-1	17	3.98	105	.287	.367	7-0-2	.143	-0	149	1	0	0.0
1999	Atl N	2	2	.500	16	7	0	0-0	51	38	32	11	2	27-3	45	5.47	82	.208	.315	11-0-1	.000	-1	73	-5	0	-0.5
2000	Atl N	4	0	1.000	22	0	0	0-0	39.2	35	15	4	1	19-2	32	2.50	181	.232	.318	5-0-2	.000	-1	—	8	0	0.6
	Phi N	3	4	.429	15	15	0	0-0	94.1	81	39	14	1	27-2	80	3.63	127	.232	.288	25-0-5	.040	-2	91	11	0	0.5
	Year	7	4	.636	37	15	0	0-0	134	116	54	18	2	46-4	112	3.29	139	.232	.298	30-0-7	.033	-3	91	18	0	1.1
2001	Phi N	4	5	.444	16	16	0	0-0	86.1	90	53	19	1	31-4	79	5.00	82	.262	.322	28-0-3	.107	-1	122	-10	0	-1.0
	NY N	3	2	.600	11	11	0	0-0	59.2	56	37	10	0	28-0	47	4.68	86	.255	.335	19-0-2	.158	-0	131	-6	0	-0.4
	Year	7	7	.500	27	27	0	0-0	146	146	90	29	1	59-4	126	4.87	84	.259	.327	47-0-5	.128	-1	126	-15	0	-1.4
2002	NY N	0	0	ø	1	0	0	0-0	0.2	1	0	0	0	0-0	0	0.00	ø	.333	.333	0	ø	0	—	0	0	0.0
	Mon N	2	3	.400	15	5	0	0-0	37.1	47	29	9	1	23-3	43	6.99	63	.303	.397	12-0-1	.417	2	59	-9	0	-0.9
	Cin N	0	2	.000	39	1	0	0-0	39.2	37	24	7	1	20-2	37	4.31	99	.243	.330	3-0-1	.000	-0	65	-1	0	-0.1
	Year	2	5	.286	55	6	0	0-0	77.2	85	53	16	2	43-5	80	5.56	78	.274	.363	15-0-2	.333	1	61	-11	0	-1.0
2003	Hou N	0	0	ø	11	0	0	0-0	12	14	8	2	2	8-1	8	6.00	74	.311	.421	1	.000	-0	—	-2	0	-0.1
	Bos A	0	1	.000	5	2	0	0-0	12.1	12	8	4	0	2-0	12	5.11	91	.255	.280	0	ø	0	129	-1	0	-0.1
2004	Bal A	2	1	.667	8	7	1	0-0	47.2	39	19	7	0	16-0	32	3.02	154	.220	.284	0	ø	0	105	8	0	0.5
2005	Bal A	13	10	.565	34	32	1	0-0	197.1	187	94	33	9	63-0	133	3.83	115	.248	.312	3	.333	1	108	12	0	1.3
2006	Bal A	0	7	.000	40	12	0	0-0	98.2	137	81	28	0	35-3	70	6.93	65	.334	.382	1	1.000	0	75	-27	0	-1.5
Total	9	35	37	.486	237	112	2	0-0	797	797	448	151	19	308-21	635	4.60	96	.260	.328	115-0-17	.130	-3	102	-21	0	-1.7
CHENEY, LARRY	Laurance Russell; B5.2.1886 Belleville KS; D1.6.1969 Daytona Beach FL; BR/TR/6´1.5˝/185; d9.9																									
1911	Chi N	1	0	1.000	3	1	0	0	10	8	0	0	0	3	11	0.00	ø	.229	.289	4	.250	0	113	4	—	0.4
1912	Chi N	**26**	10	.722	42	37	**28**-4	0	303.1	262	122	5	7	111	140	2.85	117	.234	.307	106-1-10	.226	5	119	17	—	2.2
1913	Chi N	21	14	.600	**54**	36	25-2	**11**	305	271	117	7	8	98	136	2.57	124	.241	.306	104-0-6	.192	2*	108	20	—	2.6
1914	Chi N	20	18	.526	**50**	40	21-6	5	311.1	239	136	9	10	140	157	2.54	109	.215	.308	100-0-5	.180	3	100	8	—	1.3
1915	Chi N	8	9	.471	25	18	6-2	0	131.1	120	69	1	4	55	68	3.56	78	.246	.327	40-0-2	.150	-1	107	-12	—	-1.6
	Bro N	0	2	.000	5	4	1	0	27	16	10	0	2	17	11	1.67	167	.174	.315	7	.143	0	94	2	—	0.2
	Year	8	11	.421	30	22	7-2	0	158.1	136	79	1	6	72	79	3.24	86	.234	.325	47-0-2	.149	-1	105	-9	—	-1.4
1916	†Bro N	18	12	.600	41	32	15-5	0	253	178	91	5	10	105	166	1.92	140	**.198**	.289	79-0-4	.114	-3	105	15	—	1.6
1917	Bro N	8	12	.400	35	24	14-1	2	210.1	185	80	4	5	73	102	2.35	119	.239	.309	68-0-1	.206	2	88	6	—	0.8
1918	Bro N	11	13	.458	32	21	15	1	200.2	177	84	2	10	74	83	3.00	93	.241	.319	66-0-3	.242	2*	71	-3	—	-0.1
1919	Bro N	1	3	.250	9	4	2	0	39	45	21	1	2	14	14	4.15	72	.300	.367	11	.182	-0	80	-4	—	-0.5
	Bos N	0	2	.000	8	2	0	0	33	35	20	0	0	15	13	3.55	81	.294	.373	11	.182	0	125	-4	—	-0.2
	Phi N	2	5	.286	9	6	5	0	57.1	69	34	2	1	28	25	4.55	71	.315	.395	21	.095	-2	82	-7	—	-1.1
	Year	3	10	.231	26	12	7	0	129.1	149	75	3	3	57	52	4.18	73	.305	.381	43	.140	-2	89	-15	—	-1.8
Total	9	116	100	.537	313	225	132-20	19	1881.1	1605	784	36	59	733	926	2.70	109	.234	.313	617-1-31	.186	9	102	42	—	5.6
CHENEY, TOM	Thomas Edgar; B10.14.1934 Morgan GA; D11.1.2001 Rome GA; BR/TR/6´0˝/(170–180); d4.21																									
1957	StL N	0	1	.000	4	3	0	0	9	6	6	0	0	15-0	10	5.00	79	.207	.477	2-0-1	.000	-0	126	-1	0	-0.1
1959	StL N	0	1	.000	11	2	0	0	11.2	17	9	2	2	11-2	8	6.94	61	.354	.484	0	ø	0	105	-3	0	-0.2
1960	†Pit N	2	2	.500	11	8	1-1	0	52	44	25	5	0	33-0	35	3.98	94	.238	.352	17-0-1	.176	0	103	-1	0	-0.1
1961	Pit N	0	0	ø	1	0	0	0	0	1	5	1	0	4-0	0	(4)	ø	.500	.833	0	ø	0	—	-4	0	-0.3
	Was A	1	3	.250	10	7	0	0	29.2	32	30	8	0	26-0	20	8.80	46	.283	.408	8-0-1	.500	2*	91	-14	38	-1.4
1962	Was A	7	9	.438	37	23	4-3	1	173.1	134	68	12	2	97-0	147	3.17	127	.213	.318	48-0-6	.063	-3	79	16	0	1.1
1963	Was A	8	9	.471	23	21	7-4	0	136.1	99	51	14	1	40-3	97	2.71	137	.202	.262	46-0-2	.109	-3*	75	13	0	1.2
1964	Was A	1	3	.250	15	6	1	1	48.2	45	26	10	0	13-1	25	3.70	100	.245	.293	12-0-4	.250	0	84	-1	101	-0.1
1966	Was A	0	1	.000	3	1	0	0	5.1	4	4	1	1	6-0	3	5.06	68	.222	.440	0	ø	0	178	-1	0	-0.2
Total	8	19	29	.396	115	71	13-8	2	466	382	224	53	6	245-6	345	3.77	103	.225	.322	133-0-15	.135	-3	86	4	139	-0.1
CHESBRO, JACK	John Dwight "Happy Jack"; B6.5.1874 N.Adams MA; D11.6.1931 Conway MA; BR/TR/5´9˝/180; d7.12; C1; HF1946																									
1899	Pit N	6	9	.400	19	17	15	0	149	165	99	3	11	59	28	4.11	93	.280	.357	58-0-2	.155	-3	88	-6	—	-0.9
1900	Pit N	15	13	.536	32	26	20-3	1	215.2	220	123	4	12	79	56	3.67	99	.264	.336	85	.176	-1	112	1	—	-0.1
1901	Pit N	21	10	**.677**	36	28	26-**6**	1	287.2	261	104	4	14	52	129	2.38	137	.240	.284	116-1-4	.216	3	108	32	—	3.3
1902	Pit N	**28**	6	**.824**	35	33	31-**8**	1	286.1	242	81	1	21	62	136	2.17	126	.229	.285	112-0-4	.179	-2	147	23	—	2.3
1903	NY A	21	15	.583	40	36	33-1	0	324.2	300	140	7	9	74	147	2.77	113	.245	.293	124-2-3	.185	-1	93	12	—	1.2
1904	NY A	**41**	12	**.774**	**55**	**51**	**48**-6	0	**454.2**	338	128	4	7	88	239	1.82	149	**.208**	.252	174-1-3	.236	6*	113	**41**	—	**6.1**
1905	NY A	19	15	.559	41	38	24-3	0	303.1	262	125	5	6	71	156	2.20	134	.235	.284	112-0-2	.188	0	98	16	—	1.8
1906	NY A	23	17	.575	**49**	**42**	24-4	1	325	314	138	2	10	75	152	2.96	100	.257	.305	125-1-0	.208	-1	103	0	—	-0.1
1907	NY A	10	10	.500	30	25	17-1	0	206	192	83	0	6	46	78	2.53	110	.249	.297	76	.197	-1	82	6	—	0.6
1908	NY A	14	20	.412	45	31	20-3	1	288.2	276	134	6	14	67	124	2.93	85	.256	.307	102-0-3	.176	-2	80	-12	—	-1.6
1909	NY A	0	4	.000	9	4	2	0	49.2	70	47	2	3	13	17	6.34	40	.347	.394	17	.176	-0	77	-19	—	-1.4
	Bos A	0	1	.000	1	1	0	0	6	7	4	1	0	4	3	4.50	56	.318	.423	2	.500	0	141	-1	—	-0.2
	Year	0	5	.000	10	5	2	0	55.2	77	51	3	3	17	20	6.14	41	.344	.398	19	.211	0	89	-20	—	-1.6
Total	11	198	132	.600	392	332	260-35	5	2896.2	2647	1206	39	113	690	1265	2.68	111	.244	.297	1103-5-21	.197	-2	104	93	—	11.0
CHESNES, BOB	Robert Vincent; B5.6.1921 Oakland CA; D5.23.1979 Everett WA; BB/TR/6´0˝/180; d5.6																									
1948	Pit N	14	6	.700	25	23	15	0	194.1	180	92	13	4	90	69	3.57	114	.247	.333	91-1-0	.275	7*	134	8	0	1.6
1949	Pit N	7	13	.350	27	25	8-1	1	145.1	153	104	16	5	82	49	5.88	71	.276	.374	68-1-0	.250	6*	98	-26	0	-2.3
1950	Pit N	3	3	.500	9	7	2	0	39	44	26	7	3	17	12	5.54	79	.293	.376	13	.154	-0	118	-4	0	-0.5
Total	3	24	22	.522	61	55	25-1	1	378.2	377	222	36	12	189	130	4.66	89	.263	.354	172-2-0	.256	12	116	-22	0	-1.2
CHETKOVICH, MITCH	Mitchell; B7.21.1917 Fairpoint OH; D8.24.1971 Grass Valley CA; BR/TR/6´3.5˝/208; d4.19																									
1945	Phi N	0	0	ø	4	0	0	0	3	2	2	0	0	3	0	0.00	ø	.182	.357	0	ø	0	—	0	0	0.0
CHEVEZ, TONY	Silvio Antonio (b Silvio Antonio Aguilera (Chevez)); B6.20.1954 Telica, Nicaragua; BR/TR/5´11˝/175; d5.31																									
1977	Bal A	0	0	ø	4	0	0	0-0	8	10	13	3	2	8-1	7	12.38	31	.294	.435	0	ø	0	—	-9	0	-0.4

YEAR	TM LG	W	L	PCT	G	GS	CG-SHO	SV-BS	IP	H	R	HR	HB	BB-IB	SO	ERA	AERA	OAV	OOB	AB-HR-SH	AVG	PB	SUP	APR	DL	PW
CHIAMPARINO, SCOTT	Scott Michael; B8.22.1966 San Mateo CA; BR/TR/6´2˝/(190–205); [OakA87 4/95]; d9.5; Col Santa Clara; [DL 1993 Fla N 182]																									
1990	Tex A	1	2	.333	6	6	0	0-0	37.2	36	14	1	2	12-0	19	2.63	150	.250	.314	0	ø	0	69	5	0	0.3
1991	Tex A	1	0	1.000	5	5	0	0-0	22.1	26	11	1	0	12-0	8	4.03	101	.295	.380	0	ø	0	122	0	134	0.0
1992	Tex A	0	4	.000	4	4	0	0-0	25.1	25	11	2	0	5-0	13	3.55	108	.260	.294	0	ø	0	48	1	112	0.1
Total	3	2	6	.250	15	15	0	0-0	85.1	87	36	4	2	29-0	40	3.27	120	.265	.327	0	ø	0	82	6	428	0.4
CHIASSON, SCOTT	Scott Christopher; B8.14.1977 Norwich CT; BR/TR/6´3˝/200; [KCA98 5/137]; d9.19; Col Eastern Connecticut; [DL 2003 Chi N 183]																									
2001	Chi N	1	1	.500	6	0	0	0-0	6.2	5	2	2	1	2-0	6	2.70	155	.200	.286	0	ø	0	—	1	0	0.3
2002	Chi N	0	0	ø	4	0	0	0-0	4.2	11	12	2	0	6-1	3	23.14	18	.440	.548	0	ø	0	—	-9	0	-0.4
Total	2	1	1	.500	10	0	0	0-0	11.1	16	14	4	1	8-1	9	11.12	37	.320	.424	0	ø	0	—	-8	183	-0.1
CHICK, TRAVIS	Travis Cole; B6.10.1984 Irving TX; BR/TR/6´3˝/215; [FlaN02 14/413]; d9.13																									
2006	Sea A	0	0	ø	3	0	0	0-0	5	7	7	0	0	10-0	2	12.60	35	.333	.548	0	ø	0	—	-4	0	-0.2
CHIFFER, FLOYD	Floyd John; B4.20.1956 Glen Cove NY; BR/TR/6´2˝/180; [SDN78 5/109]; d4.7; Col UCLA																									
1982	SD N	4	3	.571	51	0	0	4-7	79.1	73	33	9	4	34-1	48	2.95	116	.247	.330	8	.000	-1	—	3	0	0.1
1983	SD N	0	2	.000	15	0	0	1-0	22.2	17	10	0	0	10-1	15	3.18	110	.210	.297	1	.000	-0	—	0	0	0.0
1984	SD N	1	0	1.000	15	1	0	0-0	28	42	24	1	0	16-2	20	7.71	47	.347	.417	3	.000	-0	197	-12	0	-0.7
Total	3	5	5	.500	81	1	0	5-7	130	132	67	10	4	60-4	83	4.02	87	.266	.346	12	.000	-1	197	-9	0	-0.6
CHILD, HARRY	Harry Stephen Patrick (b Harry Stephen Patrick Chesley); B5.23.1905 Baltimore MD; D11.8.1972 Alexandria VA; BB/TR/5´11˝/187; d7.16; Col Loyola–Maryland																									
1930	Was A	0	0	ø	5	0	0	0	10	10	7	1	0	5	5	6.30	73	.263	.349	4	.250	-0	—	-1	—	-0.1
CHILDERS, JASON	Jason Lee; B1.13.1975 Statesboro GA; BR/TR/6´0˝/160; d4.3; b–Matt; Col Kennesaw St.																									
2006	TB A	0	1	.000	5	0	0	0-0	7.2	12	6	1	0	4-0	5	4.70	99	.343	.400	0	ø	0	—	-1	0	-0.1
CHILDERS, MATT	Matthew Wilkie; B12.3.1978 Douglas GA; BR/TR/6´5˝/215; [MilA97 9/277]; d8.3; b–Jason																									
2002	Mil N	0	0	ø	8	0	0	0-0	9	13	12	2	1	8-1	6	12.00	34	.342	.468	1	.000	-0	—	-7	0	-0.4
2005	Atl N	0	0	ø	3	0	0	0-0	4	5	2	1	1	3-0	2	4.50	94	.294	.429	0	ø	0	—	0	0	0.0
Total	2	0	0	ø	11	0	0	0-0	13	18	14	3	2	11-1	8	9.69	43	.327	.456	1	.000	-0	—	-7	0	-0.4
CHILDERS, BILL	William; B St.Louis MO; d7.27																									
1895	Lou N	0	0	ø	1	0	0	0	0	2	6	0	0	5	0	(6)	ø	1.000	1.000	0	ø	0	—	-5	—	-0.4
CHILDRESS, ROCKY	Rodney Osborne; B2.18.1962 Santa Rosa CA; BR/TR/6´2˝/195; [PhiN80 21/532]; d5.17																									
1985	Phi N	0	1	.000	16	1	0	0-0	33.1	45	23	3	0	9-3	14	6.21	60	.326	.362	6-0-2	.167	-0	0	-8	0	-0.4
1986	Phi N	0	0	ø	2	0	0	0-0	2.2	4	3	0	0	1-0	1	6.75	58	.364	.417	0	ø	0	—	-1	0	-0.1
1987	Hou N	1	2	.333	32	0	0	0-4	48.1	46	17	4	0	18-6	26	2.98	132	.260	.323	2	.000	-0	—	6	0	0.3
1988	Hou N	1	0	1.000	11	0	0	0-0	23.1	26	17	3	1	9-2	24	6.17	54	.280	.350	4	.250	0	—	-7	0	-0.4
Total	4	2	3	.400	61	1	0	0-4	107.2	121	60	10	1	37-11	65	4.76	78	.289	.344	12-0-2	.167	-0	0	-10	0	-0.6
CHIPMAN, BOB	Robert Howard "Mr. Chips"; B10.11.1918 Brooklyn NY; D11.8.1973 Huntington NY; BL/TL/6´2˝/(180–190); d9.28																									
1941	Bro N	1	0	1.000	1	0	0	0	5	3	0	0	0	1	3	0.00	ø	.150	.190	3	.000	-0	—	2	0	0.4
1942	Bro N	0	0	ø	2	0	0	0	1.1	1	0	0	0	2	1	0.00	ø	.250	.500	0	ø	0	—	0	0	0.0
1943	Bro N	0	0	ø	1	0	0	0	1.2	2	0	0	0	2	0	0.00	ø	.400	.571	0	ø	0	—	1	0	0.0
1944	Bro N	3	1	.750	11	3	1	0	36.1	38	19	1	0	24	20	4.21	84	.270	.376	11-0-2	.182	-0	197	-2	0	-0.2
	Chi N	9	9	.500	26	21	8-1	2	129	147	62	9	0	40	41	3.49	101	.288	.340	48	.104	-3	122	0	0	-0.3
	Year	12	10	.545	37	24	9-1	2	165.1	185	81	10	0	64	61	3.65	97	.284	.348	59-0-2	.119	-3	131	-2	0	-0.5
1945	†Chi N	4	5	.444	25	10	3-1	0	72	63	37	4	1	34	29	3.50	104	.230	.317	17-0-3	.176	1	100	-1	0	0.0
1946	Chi N	6	5	.545	34	10	5-3	2	109.1	103	44	8	1	54	42	3.13	106	.255	.344	33-0-1	.061	-3	80	2	0	-0.1
1947	Chi N	7	6	.538	32	17	5-1	0	134.2	135	58	6	0	66	51	3.68	107	.264	.348	44-0-3	.091	-3*	80	7	0	0.4
1948	Chi N	2	1	.667	34	3	0	4	60.1	73	34	5	0	24	16	3.58	109	.293	.355	16	.250	1	129	0	0	0.1
1949	Chi N	7	8	.467	38	11	3-1	1	113.1	110	65	8	2	63	46	3.97	102	.248	.344	24-0-3	.125	-0	83	-3	0	-0.4
1950	Bos N	7	7	.500	27	12	4	1	124	127	75	10	4	37	40	4.43	87	.262	.319	39-0-1	.154	-1	94	-11	0	-1.2
1951	Bos N	4	3	.571	33	0	0	4	52	59	29	5	2	19	17	4.85	76	.284	.349	10	.100	-1	—	-6	0	-0.9
1952	Bos N	1	1	.500	29	0	0	0	41.2	28	15	5	0	20	16	2.81	129	.188	.284	5	.400	1	—	4	0	0.3
Total	12	51	46	.526	293	87	29-7	14	880.2	889	438	61	10	386	322	3.72	100	.261	.338	250-0-13	.128	-8	101	-7	0	-1.9
CHITREN, STEVE	Stephen Vincent; B6.8.1967 Tokyo, Japan; BR/TR/6´0˝/180; [OakA89 6/166]; d9.5; Col Stanford																									
1990	Oak A	1	0	1.000	8	0	0	0-0	17.2	7	2	0	0	4-0	19	1.02	367	.117	.172	0	ø	0	—	6	0	0.3
1991	Oak A	1	4	.200	56	0	0	4-3	60.1	59	31	8	4	32-4	47	4.33	89	.258	.356	0	ø	0	—	-4	0	-0.3
Total	2	2	4	.333	64	0	0	4-3	78	66	33	8	4	36-4	66	3.58	107	.228	.320	0	ø	0	—	2	0	0.0
CHITTUM, NELSON	Nelson Boyd; B3.25.1933 Harrisonburg VA; BR/TR/6´1˝/180; d8.17; Col Elizabethtown																									
1958	StL N	0	1	.000	13	2	0	0	29.1	31	21	5	1	7-0	13	6.44	64	.265	.310	4	.250	0	141	-6	0	-0.3
1959	Bos A	3	0	1.000	21	0	0	0	30.1	29	9	0	0	11-2	12	1.19	342	.266	.333	5-0-1	.200	0	—	7	0	0.7
1960	Bos A	0	0	ø	6	0	0	0	8.1	8	4	0	0	6-1	5	4.32	94	.242	.359	1	.000	-0	—	0	0	0.0
Total	3	3	1	.750	40	2	0	0	68	68	34	5	1	24-3	30	3.84	106	.263	.326	10-0-1	.200	0	141	1	0	0.4
CHLUPSA, BOB	Robert Joseph; B9.16.1945 New York NY; BR/TR/6´7˝/(215–220); [StLN67 S5/90]; d7.16; Col Manhattan																									
1970	StL N	0	2	.000	14	0	0	0-0	16.1	26	16	2	0	9-3	10	8.82	47	.366	.432	0	ø	0	—	-7	0	-0.8
1971	StL N	0	0	ø	1	0	0	0-0	2	3	2	0	0	0-0	1	9.00	40	.333	.333	0	ø	0	—	-1	0	0.0
Total	2	0	2	.000	15	0	0	0-0	18.1	29	18	2	0	9-3	11	8.84	46	.363	.422	0	ø	0	—	-8	0	-0.8
CHO, JIN HO	Jin Ho; B8.16.1975 Jun Ju City, South Korea; BR/TR/6´0˝/(207–220); d7.4; [DL 2000 Bos A 24]																									
1998	Bos A	0	3	.000	4	4	0	0-0	18.2	28	17	4	1	3-0	15	8.20	58	.341	.368	0	ø	0	93	-6	0	-0.8
1999	Bos A	2	3	.400	9	7	0	0-0	39.1	45	26	7	2	8-0	16	5.72	87	.287	.324	1	.000	-0	72	-2	0	-0.3
Total	2	2	6	.250	13	11	0	0-0	58	73	43	11	3	11-0	31	6.52	75	.305	.339	1	.000	-0	80	-8	24	-1.1
CHOATE, DON	Donald Leon; B7.2.1938 Potosi MO; BR/TR/6´0˝/185; d9.12																									
1960	SF N	0	0	ø	4	0	0	0	8	7	4	0	0	4-0	7	2.25	155	.233	.324	0	ø	0	—	0	0	0.0
CHOATE, RANDY	Randol Doyle; B9.5.1975 San Antonio TX; BL/TL/6´3˝/(180–195); [NYA97 5/169]; d7.1; Col Florida St.																									
2000	†NY A	0	1	.000	22	0	0	0-0	17	14	10	3	1	8-0	12	4.76	100	.215	.307	0	ø	0	—	0	0	0.0
2001	†NY A	3	1	.750	37	0	0	0-0	48.1	34	21	0	9	27-2	35	3.35	133	.202	.341	3	.000	-0	—	5	0	0.4
2002	NY A	0	0	ø	18	0	0	0-0	22.1	18	18	1	3	15-0	17	6.04	72	.217	.356	1	.000	-0	—	-5	0	-0.3
2003	NY A	0	0	ø	5	0	0	0-0	3.2	7	3	0	0	1-0	0	7.36	60	.467	.500	0	ø	0	—	-1	0	-0.1
2004	Ari N	2	4	.333	74	0	0	0-2	50.2	52	26	1	5	28-11	49	4.62	99	.267	.366	1	.000	-0	—	1	0	0.1
2005	Ari N	0	0	ø	8	0	0	0-0	7	8	7	0	1	5-1	4	9.00	49	.276	.400	0	ø	0	—	-3	0	-0.1
2006	Ari N	0	1	.000	30	0	0	0-0	16	21	9	0	3	3-0	12	3.94	119	.304	.360	0	ø	0	—	1	0	0.1
Total	7	5	7	.417	194	0	0	0-2	165	154	94	5	22	87-14	129	4.64	98	.247	.356	5	.000	-1	—	-2	0	0.1
CHOUINARD, BOBBY	Robert William; B5.1.1972 Manila, Philippines; BR/TR/6´1˝/(170–190); [BalA90 5/148]; d5.26																									
1996	Oak A	4	2	.667	13	11	0	0-0	59	75	41	10	3	32-3	32	6.10	82	.316	.400	0	ø	0	127	-7	0	-0.5
1998	Mil N	0	0	ø	1	0	0	0-0	3	5	1	0	0	0-0	1	3.00	145	.455	.417	0	ø	0	—	0	0	0.0
	Ari N	0	2	.000	26	2	0	0-1	38.1	41	23	5	0	11-2	26	4.23	101	.268	.315	2	.000	-0	172	-1	17	-0.1
	Year	0	2	.000	27	2	0	0-1	41.1	46	24	5	0	11-2	27	4.14	104	.280	.322	2	.000	-0	172	-1	0	-0.1
1999	†Ari N	5	2	.714	32	0	0	1-1	40.1	31	16	3	0	12-2	23	2.68	172	.220	.274	3-0-1	.000	-0	—	7	0	1.1
2000	Col N	2	2	.500	31	0	0	0-2	32.2	35	17	4	1	9-2	23	3.86	150	.273	.324	3	.333	0	—	5	0	0.5
2001	Col N	0	0	ø	8	0	0	0-0	7.2	10	7	4	0	1-1	5	8.22	65	.303	.324	0	ø	0	—	-2	49	-0.1
Total	5	11	8	.579	111	13	0	1-4	181	197	105	26	4	65-10	110	4.57	107	.280	.340	8-0-1	.125	-0	132	2	66	0.9
CHOUNEAU, CHIEF	William (b William Cadreau); B9.2.1888 Cloquet MN; D9.17.1946 Cloquet MN; BR/TR/5´9˝/150; d10.9																									
1910	Chi A	0	1	.000	1	1	0	0	5.1	7	2	0	0	0	1	3.38	71	.292	.292	1	.000	1	28	0	—	0.0

YEAR	TM LG	W	L	PCT	G	GS	CG-SHO	SV-BS	IP	H	R	HR	HB	BB-IB	SO	ERA	AERA	OAV	OOB	AB-HR-SH	AVG	PB	SUP	APR	DL	PW
Chris, Mike	Michael; B10.8.1957 Santa Monica CA; BL/TL/6´3˝/(175–180); [DetA77*S1/10]; d7.31; Col Los Angeles Pierce (CA) JC																									
1979	Det A	3	3	.500	13	8	0	0-0	39	46	30	3	0	21-0	31	6.92	63	.297	.376	0	ø	0	68	-10	0	-1.2
1982	SF N	0	2	.000	9	6	0	0-0	26	23	16	2	1	26-2	10	4.85	74	.245	.410	7	.143	-0	107	-4	0	-0.2
1983	SF N	0	0	ø	7	0	0	0-0	13.1	16	14	1	2	16-2	5	8.10	44	.308	.479	2	.000	-0	—	-7	0	-0.4
Total	3	3	5	.375	29	14	0	0-0	78.1	85	60	6	3	63-4	46	6.43	61	.282	.407	9	.111	-0	84	-21	0	-1.8
Christenson, Gary	Gary Richard; B5.5.1953 Mineola NY; BL/TL/6´5˝/(200–212); [DetA71 13/304]; d9.1																									
1979	KC A	0	0	ø	6	0	0	0-1	10.2	10	5	1	0	2-0	4	3.38	126	.250	.279	0	ø	0	—	1	0	0.0
1980	KC A	3	0	1.000	24	0	0	1-2	31.1	35	23	4	2	18-1	16	5.17	78	.278	.372	0	ø	0	—	-5	0	-0.5
Total	2	3	0	1.000	30	0	0	1-3	42	45	28	5	2	20-1	20	4.71	87	.271	.351	0	ø	0	—	-4	0	-0.5
Christenson, Larry	Larry Richard; B11.10.1953 Everett WA; BR/TR/6´4˝/(210–215); [PhiN72 1/3]; d4.13																									
1973	Phi N	1	4	.200	10	9	1	0-0	34.1	53	25	3	1	20-1	11	6.55	58	.366	.443	10	.000	-1	72	-9	0	-1.2
1974	Phi N	1	1	.500	10	1	0	2-0	23	20	11	2	0	15-3	18	4.30	88	.241	.357	4-0-1	.000	-1	46	-1	0	-0.1
1975	Phi N	11	6	.647	29	26	5-2	1-0	171.2	149	73	12	1	45-2	88	3.67	103	.236	.286	57-2-8	.246	5	108	4	0	0.8
1976	Phi N	13	8	.619	32	29	2	0-0	168.2	199	77	8	1	42-4	54	3.68	97	.297	.338	51-2-6	.196	4	122	-2	0	0.0
1977	†Phi N	19	6	.760	34	34	5-1	0-0	219.1	229	113	21	7	69-1	118	4.06	99	.268	.324	74-3-10	.135	1	140	-2	0	-0.3
1978	†Phi N	13	14	.481	33	33	9-3	0-0	228	209	90	16	1	47-7	131	3.24	112	.244	.282	67-1-7	.075	-2	85	10	0	0.8
1979	Phi N	5	10	.333	19	17	2	0-0	106	118	56	9	2	30-3	53	4.50	86	.291	.339	31-1-3	.290	5	67	-7	67	-0.4
1980	†Phi N	5	1	.833	14	14	0	0-0	73.2	62	35	4	3	27-4	49	4.03	95	.227	.303	19-1-3	.368	3	117	-1	77	0.3
1981	†Phi N	4	7	.364	20	15	0	1-0	106.2	108	48	8	1	30-3	70	3.54	103	.267	.313	30-0-3	.100	-1	95	0	21	-0.2
1982	Phi N	9	10	.474	33	33	3	0-0	223	212	95	15	3	53-5	145	3.47	106	.253	.297	67-1-12	.075	-3	98	6	0	0.2
1983	Phi N	2	4	.333	9	9	0	0-0	48.1	42	25	2	1	17-1	44	3.91	92	.233	.297	17-0-1	.059	-1	87	-2	118	-0.3
Total	11	83	71	.539	243	220	27-6	4-0	1402.2	1401	648	100	21	395-34	781	3.79	99	.262	.313	427-11-54	.150	9	104	-4	283	-0.4
Christiansen, Clay	Clay C.; B6.28.1958 Wichita KS; BR/TR/6´5˝/205; [NYA80 15/386]; d5.10; Col Kansas																									
1984	NY A	2	4	.333	24	1	0	2-2	38.2	50	28	4	1	12-0	27	6.05	63	.309	.356	0	ø	0	0	-10	0	-1.4
Christiansen, Jason	Jason Samuel; B9.21.1969 Omaha NE; BR/TL/6´5˝/(230–246); d4.26; Col Cameron																									
1995	Pit N	1	3	.250	63	0	0	0-4	56.1	49	28	5	3	34-9	53	4.15	105	.234	.345	1	.000	-0	—	1	0	0.1
1996	Pit N	3	3	.500	33	0	0	0-2	44.1	56	34	7	1	19-2	38	6.70	66	.311	.374	4-0-1	.000	-0	—	-10	0	-1.2
1997	Pit N	3	0	1.000	39	0	0	0-2	33.2	37	11	2	2	17-3	37	2.94	146	.274	.364	0	ø	0	—	5	78	0.4
1998	Pit N	3	3	.500	60	0	0	6-4	64.2	51	22	2	0	27-7	71	2.51	171	.216	.295	4	.250	0	—	12	0	1.2
1999	Pit N	2	3	.400	39	0	0	3-2	37.2	26	17	2	2	22-4	35	4.06	113	.198	.321	1	.000	-0*	—	3	75	0.4
2000	Pit N	2	8	.200	44	0	0	1-2	38	28	22	2	0	25-4	41	4.97	93	.207	.329	0	ø	0	—	-1	0	-0.1
	†StL N	1	0	1.000	21	0	0	0-1	10	13	7	1	2	2-1	12	5.40	86	.317	.378	0	ø	0	—	-1	0	-0.1
	Year	3	8	.273	65	0	0	1-3	48	41	29	3	2	27-5	53	5.06	92	.233	.340	0	ø	0	—	-2	0	-0.2
2001	StL N	1	1	.500	30	0	0	3-0	19.1	15	10	4	1	10-1	19	4.66	93	.211	.313	0	ø	0	—	0	36	0.0
	SF N	1	0	1.000	25	0	0	0-1	17	14	3	1	0	5-0	12	1.59	258	.241	.292	0	ø	0	—	5	0	0.3
	Year	2	1	.667	55	0	0	3-1	36.1	29	13	5	1	15-1	31	3.22	131	.225	.304	0	ø	0	—	5	0	0.3
2002	SF N	0	1	.000	6	0	0	0-0	5	6	3	1	0	2-0	1	5.40	73	.316	.381	0	ø	0	—	-1	165	-0.1
2003	†SF N	0	0	ø	40	0	0	0-1	26	25	15	3	1	11-0	22	5.19	82	.243	.322	0	ø	0	—	-2	65	-0.1
2004	SF N	4	3	.571	60	0	0	3-3	36	34	20	3	3	26-1	22	4.50	96	.250	.377	0	ø	0	—	-1	17	-0.2
2005	SF N	6	1	.857	56	0	0	0-2	42	48	27	4	0	15-2	17	5.36	79	.286	.337	0	ø	0	—	-5	0	-0.8
	LA A	0	0	ø	12	0	0	0-0	3.2	7	1	0	0	2-0	4	2.45	174	.389	.450	0	ø	0	—	1	0	0.0
Total	11	27	26	.509	528	0	0	16-24	433.2	409	220	37	15	217-34	384	4.30	101	.249	.339	10-0-1	.100	-1	—	6	436	-0.2
Christman, Tim	Timothy Arthur; B3.31.1975 Oneonta NY; BL/TL/6´0˝/195; [ColN96 11/326]; d4.21; Col Siena																									
2001	Col N	0	0	ø	1	0	0	0-0	2	1	1	1	0	0-0	2	4.50	119	.143	.143	0	ø	0	—	0	0	0.0
Christopher, Mike	Michael Wayne; B11.3.1963 Petersburg VA; BR/TR/6´5˝/205; [NYA85 7/181]; d9.10; Col East Carolina																									
1991	LA N	0	0	ø	3	0	0	0-0	4	2	0	0	0	3-0	2	0.00	ø	.167	.333	0	ø	0	—	2	0	0.1
1992	Cle A	0	0	ø	10	0	0	0-0	18	17	8	2	0	10-1	13	3.00	131	.254	.346	0	ø	0	—	1	0	0.1
1993	Cle A	0	0	ø	9	0	0	0-0	11.2	14	6	3	0	2-1	8	3.86	114	.286	.314	0	ø	0	—	0	0	0.0
1995	Det A	4	0	1.000	36	0	0	1-1	61.1	71	28	8	2	14-2	34	3.82	126	.292	.333	0	ø	0	—	7	0	0.4
1996	Det A	1	1	.500	13	0	0	0-0	30	47	36	12	0	11-2	19	9.30	55	.351	.389	0	ø	0	—	-15	0	-0.8
Total	5	5	1	.833	71	0	0	1-1	125	151	78	25	2	40-6	76	4.90	95	.299	.348	0	ø	0	—	-5	0	-0.2
Christopher, Russ	Russell Ormand; B9.12.1917 Richmond CA; D12.5.1954 Richmond CA; BR/TR/6´3˝/180; d4.14; b–Loyd																									
1942	Phi A	4	13	.235	30	18	10	1	165	154	78	8	3	99	58	3.82	99	.254	.362	56-0-3	.089	-3	78	1	0	0.1
1943	Phi A	5	8	.385	24	15	5	2	133	120	58	3	3	58	56	3.45	98	.242	.325	45-0-1	.156	-1	93	-1	0	0.2
1944	Phi A	14	14	.500	35	24	13-1	1	215.1	200	91	6	9	63	84	2.97	117	.245	.306	81-1-1	.222	3	68	9	0	1.8
1945	Phi A✶	13	13	.500	33	27	17-2	2	227.1	213	92	9	9	75	100	3.17	108	.251	.319	76-1-6	.171	-1*	80	6	0	1.1
1946	Phi A	5	7	.417	30	13	1	0	119.1	119	71	5	3	44	79	4.30	82	.254	.322	36-0-1	.139	-0	112	-12	0	-0.9
1947	Phi A	10	7	.588	44	0	0	12	80.2	70	30	4	0	33	33	2.90	131	.236	.313	16-0-2	.125	-0	—	8	0	1.6
1948	†Cle A	3	2	.600	45	0	0	**17**	59	55	21	3	0	27	14	2.90	140	.247	.328	6-0-2	.000	-0	—	8	0	1.1
Total	7	54	64	.458	241	97	46-3	35	999.2	931	441	38	27	399	424	3.37	106	.248	.325	316-2-16	.158	-3	82	19	0	5.0
Chulk, Vinnie	Charles Vincent; B12.19.1978 Miami FL; BR/TR/6´2˝/(180–195); [TorA00 12/358]; d9.8; Col St. Thomas (FL)																									
2003	Tor A	0	0	ø	3	0	0	0-1	5.1	6	3	0	0	3-0	2	5.06	94	.273	.360	0	ø	0	—	0	0	0.0
2004	Tor A	1	3	.250	47	0	0	2-3	56	59	30	6	1	27-1	44	4.66	105	.271	.352	0	ø	0	—	2	0	0.1
2005	Tor A	0	1	.000	62	0	0	0-1	72	68	33	9	1	26-3	39	3.88	119	.255	.319	0	ø	0	—	6	0	0.3
2006	Tor A	1	0	1.000	20	0	0	0-1	24	29	16	4	2	5-0	18	5.25	90	.293	.336	0	ø	0	—	-2	0	-0.1
	SF N	0	3	.000	28	0	0	0-1	22.1	17	13	2	1	15-2	25	5.24	85	.210	.337	1	.000	-0	—	-2	0	-0.2
Total	4	2	7	.222	160	0	0	2-7	179.2	179	95	21	5	76-6	128	4.51	104	.261	.335	1	.000	-0	—	4	0	0.1
Church, Bubba	Emory Nicholas; B9.12.1924 Birmingham AL; D9.17.2001 Birmingham AL; BR/TR/6´0˝/180; d4.30																									
1950	Phi N	8	6	.571	31	18	8-2	1	142	113	50	12	0	56	50	2.73	149	.225	.303	44-0-3	.182	0*	84	21	0	1.9
1951	Phi N	15	11	.577	38	33	15-4	1	247	246	107	17	1	90	104	3.53	109	.261	.326	86-1-7	.256	5*	99	9	0	1.2
1952	Phi N	0	0	ø	2	1	0	0	5	11	6	0	1	1	3	10.80	34	.440	.481	1	.000	-0	195	-4	0	-0.2
	Cin N	5	9	.357	29	22	5-1	0	153.1	173	85	21	3	48	47	4.34	87	.301	.358	50-1-1	.240	3*	98	-12	0	-0.7
	Year	5	9	.357	31	23	5-1	0	158.1	184	91	21	4	49	50	4.55	83	.307	.363	51-1-1	.235	3	102	-13	0	-0.9
1953	Cin N	3	3	.500	11	7	2	0	42.2	55	32	9	2	19	12	5.98	73	.318	.392	15	.267	1*	129	-8	0	-0.8
	Chi N	4	5	.444	27	11	1	1	104.1	115	67	16	2	49	47	5.00	89	.276	.355	33-1-1	.212	1	97	-6	0	-0.4
	Year	7	8	.467	38	18	3	1	148	170	99	25	4	68	59	5.29	84	.289	.366	48-1-1	.229	2	108	-16	0	-1.2
1954	Chi N	1	3	.250	7	3	1	0	14.2	21	18	8	0	13	8	9.82	43	.350	.459	5	.000	-1*	156	-9	0	-1.6
1955	Chi N	0	0	ø	2	0	0	1	3.1	4	2	1	0	1-0	3	5.40	76	.286	.333	1	.000	-0*	—	0	0	0.0
Total	6	36	37	.493	147	95	32-7	4	713.1	738	367	84	9	277-0	274	4.10	97	.272	.342	235-3-12	.226	9	100	-9	0	-0.6
Church, Len	Leonard; B3.21.1942 Chicago IL; D4.22.1988 Richardson TX; BB/TR/6´0˝/190; d8.27; Col Wilbur Wright (IL) JC																									
1966	Chi N	0	1	.000	4	0	0	0	6	10	6	1	0	7-2	3	7.50	49	.400	.515	1	.000	-0	—	-3	0	-0.4
Churn, Chuck	Clarence Nottingham; B2.1.1930 Bridgetown VA; BR/TR/6´3˝/205; d4.18																									
1957	Pit N	0	0	ø	5	0	0	0	8.1	9	4	1	0	4-1	4	4.32	88	.333	.406	1	.000	-0	—	0	0	0.0
1958	Cle A	0	0	ø	6	0	0	0	8.2	12	7	1	0	5-0	4	6.23	59	.343	.425	0	ø	0	—	-3	0	-0.1
1959	†LA N	3	2	.600	14	0	0	1	30.2	28	17	2	1	10-4	24	4.99	85	.255	.315	6	.167	0	—	-2	0	-0.2
Total	3	3	2	.600	25	0	0	1	47.2	49	28	4	1	19-5	32	5.10	79	.285	.352	7	.143	0	—	-5	0	-0.3
Ciardi, Mark	Mark Thomas; B8.19.1961 New Brunswick NJ; BR/TR/6´0˝/180; [MilA83 15/392]; d4.9; Col Maryland																									
1987	Mil A	1	1	.500	4	3	0	0-0	16.1	26	17	5	0	9-0	8	9.37	49	.361	.432	0	ø	0	86	-8	0	-0.7
Cicotte, Al	Alva Warren "Bozo"; B12.23.1929 Melvindale MI; D11.29.1982 Westland MI; BR/TR/6´3˝/(185–190); d4.22																									
1957	NY A	2	2	.500	20	2	0	2	65.1	57	25	5	1	30-1	36	3.03	118	.237	.324	20	.150	-0	50	4	0	0.2
1958	Was A	0	3	.000	8	4	0	0	28	36	18	3	0	14-0	14	4.82	79	.316	.388	10	.200	-0*	59	-4	0	-0.4
	Det A	3	1	.750	14	2	0	0	43	50	19	1	0	15-1	21	3.56	113	.307	.359	17	.176	-1*	134	2	0	0.2
	Year	3	4	.429	22	6	0	0	71	86	37	4	0	29-1	35	4.06	97	.310	.371	27	.185	-1	83	-1	0	-0.2

YEAR	TM LG	W	L	PCT	G	GS	CG-SHO	SV-BS	IP	H	R	HR	HB	BB-IB	SO	ERA	AERA	OAV	OOB	AB-HR-SH	AVG	PB	SUP	APR	DL	PW
1959	Cle A	3	1	.750	26	1	0	1	44	46	29	4	2	25-3	23	5.32	69	.299	.395	3-0-1	.333	1	192	-8	0	-0.7
1961	StL N	2	6	.250	29	7	0	1	75	83	47	16	2	34-2	51	5.28	83	.283	.362	21	.286	1	72	-5	0	-0.4
1962	Hou N	0	0	ø	5	0	0	0	4.2	8	4	1	0	1-0	4	3.86	97	.381	.409	0	ø	0	—	-1	0	0.0
Total	5	10	13	.435	102	16	0	4	260	280	142	30	5	119-7	149	4.36	90	.284	.361	71-0-1	.211	0	83	-12	0	-1.1
CICOTTE, EDDIE	Edward Victor "Knuckles"; B6.19.1884 Springwells MI; D5.5.1969 Detroit MI; BB/TR/5´9˝/175; d9.3																									
1905	Det A	1	1	.500	3	1	1	0	18	25	8	0	0	5	6	3.50	78	.329	.370	7	.429	1	78	-1	—	0.0
1908	Bos A	11	12	.478	39	24	17-2	2	207.1	198	77	0	11	59	95	2.43	101	.256	.318	72	.236	2*	109	2	—	0.5
1909	Bos A	14	5	.737	27	17	10-1	1	162.1	117	63	3	1	56	82	1.94	129	.207	.280	51-0-3	.235	3	134	5	—	0.9
1910	Bos A	15	11	.577	36	30	20-3	0	250	213	94	4	13	86	104	2.74	93	.233	.308	85-0-4	.141	-1	116	0	—	0.1
1911	Bos A	11	15	.423	35	25	16-1	0	220	236	121	2	4	73	106	2.82	116	.282	.342	71-0-5	.141	-2	99	7	—	0.5
1912	Bos A	1	3	.250	9	6	2	0	46	58	34	0	1	15	20	5.67	60	.319	.374	13	.154	0	137	-10	—	-0.7
	Chi A	9	7	.563	20	18	13-1	0	152	159	63	3	0	37	70	2.84	113	.277	.320	53-0-3	.245	1	97	7	—	0.9
	Year	10	10	.500	29	24	15-1	0	198	217	97	3	1	52	90	3.50	93	.287	.333	66-0-3	.227	1	108	-2	—	0.2
1913	Chi A	18	11	.621	41	30	18-3	1	268	224	77	2	3	73	121	1.58	185	.227	.283	91-0-4	.143	-3	93	36	—	4.1
1914	Chi A	11	16	.407	45	30	15-4	3	269.1	220	96	0	3	72	122	2.04	132	.232	.288	86-0-6	.163	-1	79	17	—	2.1
1915	Chi A	13	12	.520	39	26	15-1	3	223.1	216	89	2	6	48	106	3.02	99	.261	.306	67-0-10	.209	1*	121	3	—	0.4
1916	Chi A	15	7	**.682**	44	19	11-2	5	187	138	56	1	1	70	91	1.78	155	.218	.296	57-0-8	.211	2	143	18	—	2.6
1917	†Chi A	**28**	12	.700	49	35	29-7	4	**346.2**	246	76	2	3	70	150	**1.53**	**174**	.203	**.248**	112-0-8	.179	1	105	**45**	—	**5.7**
1918	Chi A	12	19	.387	38	30	24-1	2	266	275	102	2	2	40	104	2.77	99	.271	.300	86-0-1	.163	2	84	1	—	0.2
1919	†Chi A	**29**	7	**.806**	40	35	**30**-5	1	**306.2**	256	77	5	2	49	110	1.82	175	.228	.261	99-0-11	.202	1	108	47	—	5.5
1920	Chi A	21	10	.677	37	35	28-4	2	303.1	316	128	6	2	74	87	3.26	115	.275	.320	112-0-4	.196	-3	121	19	—	1.5
Total	14	209	148	.585	502	361	249-35	24	3226	2897	1161	32	52	827	1374	2.38	123	.245	.297	1062-0-67	.186	4	108	196	—	24.3
CIMINO, PETE	Peter William; B10.17.1942 Philadelphia PA; BR/TR/6´2˝/(195–213); d9.22																									
1965	Min A	0	0	ø	1	0	0	0	1	0	0	0	0	0-0	0	0.00	ø	.000	.000	0	ø	0	—	0	0	0.0
1966	Min A	2	5	.286	35	0	0	4	64.2	53	27	4	1	30-3	57	2.92	123	.222	.310	6-0-1	.000	-0	—	4	0	0.3
1967	Cal A	3	3	.500	46	1	0	1	88.1	73	38	12	2	31-4	80	3.26	96	.229	.297	12	.417	2	111	-2	0	0.0
1968	Cal A	0	0	ø	4	0	0	0	7	7	5	0	0	4-0	2	2.57	113	.259	.355	0	ø	0	—	-1	0	-0.1
Total	4	5	8	.385	86	1	0	5	161	133	70	16	3	65-7	139	3.07	108	.226	.304	18-0-1	.278	1	111	1	0	0.2
CIMORELLI, FRANK	Frank Thomas; B8.2.1968 Poughkeepsie NY; BR/TR/6´0˝/175; [StLN89 37/952]; d4.30; Col Dominican																									
1994	StL N	0	0	ø	11	0	0	1-0	13.1	20	14	0	2	10-2	1	8.78	48	.345	.444	2	.000	-0	—	-7	0	-0.4
CIOLA, LOU	Louis Alexander; B9.6.1922 Norfolk VA; D10.18.1981 Austin MN; BR/TR/5´9˝/165; d7.25; Mil 1944–46; Col Richmond																									
1943	Phi A	1	3	.250	12	3	2	0	43.2	48	33	2	1	22	7	5.56	61	.273	.357	18	.167	-1	157	-11	0	-1.0
CISCO, GALEN	Galen Bernard; B3.7.1936 St.Marys OH; BR/TR/5´11˝/(200–215); d6.11; C28; Col Ohio St.																									
1961	Bos A	2	4	.333	17	8	0	0	52.1	67	40	5	0	28-0	26	6.71	62	.325	.397	10-0-3	.100	-0*	72	-12	0	-1.2
1962	Bos A	4	7	.364	23	9	1	0	83	95	66	11	3	50-1	43	6.72	61	.292	.387	25	.080	-1	77	-21	0	-2.4
	NY N	1	1	.500	4	2	1	0	19.1	15	7	0	3	11-2	13	3.26	128	.208	.337	7	.000	-1	63	2	0	0.1
1963	NY N	7	15	.318	51	17	1	0	155.2	165	88	15	7	64-1	81	4.34	80	.273	.348	38-0-2	.132	0	62	-14	0	-1.8
1964	NY N	6	19	.240	36	25	5-2	0	191.2	182	85	17	6	54-4	78	3.62	99	.256	.311	54-0-6	.111	-0	83	0	0	0.1
1965	NY N	4	8	.333	35	17	1-1	0	112.1	119	63	12	1	51-2	58	4.49	79	.272	.348	27-0-4	.259	2	102	-11	0	-1.0
1967	Bos A	0	1	.000	11	0	0	1	22.1	21	10	4	0	8-0	8	3.63	96	.266	.326	3	.000	-0	—	0	0	-0.1
1969	KC A	1	1	.500	15	0	0	1-0	22.1	17	11	4	0	15-0	18	3.63	102	.215	.340	0	ø	0	—	0	0	0.0
Total	7	25	56	.309	192	78	9-3	2-0	659	681	370	68	20	281-10	325	4.56	81	.271	.346	164-0-15	.128	0	80	-56	0	-6.3
CITARELLA, RALPH	Ralph Alexander; B2.7.1958 East Orange NJ; BR/TR/6´0˝/180; [StLN79 S1/12]; d9.13; Col Florida Southern																									
1983	StL N	0	0	ø	6	0	0	0-0	11	8	2	0	0	3-1	4	1.64	224	.205	.262	1	.000	-0	—	3	0	0.1
1984	StL N	0	1	.000	10	2	0	0-0	22.1	20	9	0	3	7-2	15	3.63	97	.238	.319	4	.250	0	164	0	15	0.0
1987	Chi A	0	0	ø	5	0	0	0-0	11	13	9	4	2	4-0	9	7.36	63	.302	.388	0	ø	0	—	-3	0	-0.1
Total	3	0	1	.000	21	2	0	0-0	44.1	41	20	4	5	14-3	28	4.06	94	.247	.324	5	.200	0	164	0	15	0.0
CLANCY, JIM	James; B12.18.1955 Chicago IL; BR/TR/6´4˝/(185–220); [TexA74 4/74]; d7.26																									
1977	Tor A	4	9	.308	13	13	4-1	0-0	76.2	80	47	7	0	47-1	44	5.05	84	.280	.374	0	ø	0	81	-6	0	-0.8
1978	Tor A	10	12	.455	31	30	7	0-0	193.2	199	96	10	1	91-1	106	4.09	97	.270	.347	0	ø	0	76	-3	0	-0.3
1979	Tor A	2	7	.222	12	11	2	0-0	63.2	65	44	8	0	31-0	33	5.51	80	.272	.349	0	ø	0	71	-8	110	-0.9
1980	Tor A	13	16	.448	34	34	15-2	0-0	250.2	217	108	19	2	128-4	152	3.30	131	.233	.326	0	ø	0	68	24	0	2.6
1981	Tor A	6	12	.333	22	22	2	0-0	125	126	77	12	5	64-0	56	4.90	81	.262	.352	0	ø	0	82	-11	0	-1.6
1982	Tor A★	16	14	.533	40	**40**	11-3	0-0	266.2	251	122	26	2	77-1	139	3.71	121	.248	.301	0	ø	0	87	21	0	2.1
1983	Tor A	15	11	.577	34	34	11-1	0-0	223	238	115	23	1	61-0	99	3.91	111	.271	.315	0	ø	0	101	6	0	0.6
1984	Tor A	13	15	.464	36	**36**	5	0-0	219.2	249	132	25	3	88-2	118	5.12	81	.287	.353	0	ø	0	92	-21	0	-2.3
1985	†Tor A	9	6	.600	23	23	1	0-0	128.2	117	54	15	0	37-0	66	3.78	112	.241	.292	0	ø	0	112	9	59	0.9
1986	Tor A	14	14	.500	34	34	6-3	0-0	219.1	202	100	24	4	63-0	126	3.94	108	.243	.296	0	ø	0	100	10	0	1.1
1987	Tor A	15	11	.577	37	37	5-1	0-0	241.1	234	103	24	1	80-5	180	3.54	128	.255	.314	0	ø	0	104	26	0	2.6
1988	Tor A	11	13	.458	36	31	4	1-0	196.1	207	106	26	9	47-3	118	4.49	88	.272	.321	0	ø	0	101	-10	0	-1.2
1989	Hou N	7	14	.333	33	26	1	0-0	147	155	100	13	0	66-15	91	5.08	67	.269	.342	41-0-7	.146	-0	84	-32	0	-4.2
1990	Hou N	2	8	.200	33	10	0	1-1	76	100	58	4	3	33-9	44	6.51	57	.322	.387	14-0-2	.214	0	63	-22	0	-2.6
1991	Hou N	0	3	.000	30	0	0	5-1	55	37	19	5	0	20-3	33	2.78	127	.193	.266	3-0-1	.000	-0	—	5	0	0.2
	†Atl N	3	2	.600	24	0	0	3-2	34.2	36	23	3	1	14-1	17	5.71	68	.267	.336	3	.000	-0	—	-6	0	-0.9
	Year	3	5	.375	54	0	0	8-3	89.2	73	42	8	1	34-4	50	3.91	94	.223	.295	6-0-1	.000	-1	—	-2	0	-0.7
Total	15	140	167	.456	472	381	74-11	10-4	2517.1	2513	1304	244	32	947-45	1422	4.23	99	.261	.326	61-0-10	.148	-1	90	-18	169	-4.7
CLARK, BRYAN	Bryan Donald; B7.12.1956 Madera CA; BL/TL/6´2˝/(185–200); [PitN74 10/227]; d4.11																									
1981	Sea A	2	5	.286	29	9	1	2-3	93.1	92	54	3	1	55-4	52	4.34	89	.261	.359	0	ø	0*	87	-6	0	-0.4
1982	Sea A	5	2	.714	37	5	1-1	0-0	114.2	104	44	6	0	58-2	70	2.75	156	.241	.330	0	ø	0	98	16	0	1.0
1983	Sea A	7	10	.412	41	17	2	0-0	162.1	160	82	14	3	72-6	76	3.94	109	.261	.340	0	ø	0	77	5	0	0.6
1984	Tor A	1	2	.333	20	3	0	0-0	45.2	66	33	6	1	22-2	21	5.91	70	.342	.410	0	ø	0	109	-9	0	-0.5
1985	Cle A	3	4	.429	31	3	0	2-2	62.2	78	47	8	0	34-2	24	6.32	66	.311	.390	0	ø	0	80	-14	0	-1.4
1986	Chi A	0	0	ø	5	0	0	0-0	8	8	4	0	0	2-0	5	4.50	97	.276	.323	0	ø	0	—	0	0	0.0
1987	Chi A	0	0	ø	11	0	0	0-0	18.2	19	5	1	0	8-0	8	2.41	192	.297	.365	0	ø	0	—	5	0	0.2
1990	Sea A	2	0	1.000	12	0	0	0-0	11	9	4	0	0	10-0	3	3.27	122	.237	.396	0	ø	0	—	1	0	0.2
Total	8	20	23	.465	186	37	4-1	4-5	516.1	536	273	38	5	261-16	259	4.15	101	.272	.356	0	ø	0	85	-2	0	-0.3
CLARK, ED	Edward C.; B Cincinnati OH; d7.4																									
1886	Phi AA	0	1	.000	1	1	1	0	8	10	8	2	2	2	2	6.75	52	.294	.368	2	.000	-0	0	-2	—	-0.2
1891	Col AA	0	0	ø	1	0	0	0	2	2	0	0	0	0	1	0.00	ø	.250	.250	1	.000	-0	—	1	—	0.0
Total	2	0	1	.000	2	1	1	0	10	12	8	2	2	2	3	5.40	65	.286	.348	3	.000	-0	0	-1	—	-0.2
CLARK, GEORGE	George Myron; B5.19.1891 Smithland IA; D11.14.1940 Sioux City IA; BR/TL/6´0˝/190; d5.16; Col Iowa St.																									
1913	NY A	0	1	.000	11	1	0	0	19	22	23	1	3	19	5	9.00	33	.278	.436	4	.500	1	50	-11	—	-0.5
CLARK, GINGER	Harvey Daniel; B3.7.1879 Wooster OH; D5.10.1943 Lake Charles LA; BR/TR/5´11˝/165; d8.11																									
1902	Cle A	1	0	1.000	1	0	0	0	6	10	6	0	1	3	1	6.00	57	.370	.452	4	.500	1	—	-2	—	-0.2
CLARK, MARK	Mark Willard; B5.12.1968 Bath IL; BR/TR/6´5˝/(225–235); [StLN88 9/236]; d9.6; Col MacMurray																									
1991	StL N	1	1	.500	7	2	0	0-0	22.1	17	10	3	0	11-0	13	4.03	93	.215	.301	7-0-1	.000	-1	84	0	0	-0.1
1992	StL N	3	10	.231	20	20	1-1	0-0	113.1	117	59	12	0	36-2	44	4.45	77	.265	.318	36-0-4	.139	-1	95	-12	0	-1.5
1993	Cle A	7	5	.583	26	15	1	0-0	109.1	119	55	18	1	25-1	57	4.28	102	.279	.320	0	ø	0	95	2	54	0.1
1994	Cle A	11	3	.786	20	20	4-1	0-0	127.1	133	61	14	4	40-0	60	3.82	125	.273	.329	0	ø	0	126	13	22	1.3
1995	Cle A	9	7	.563	22	21	2	0-0	124.2	143	77	13	4	42-0	68	5.27	90	.288	.344	0	ø	0	100	-6	0	-0.7
1996	NY N	14	11	.560	32	32	2	0-0	212.1	217	98	20	3	48-8	142	3.43	117	.265	.306	69-0-10	.043	-5	110	13	0	0.7
1997	NY N	8	7	.533	23	22	1	0-0	142	158	74	18	3	47-2	72	4.25	94	.289	.347	43-1-4	.047	-2	99	-4	0	-0.6
	Chi N	6	1	.857	9	9	2	0-0	63	55	22	6	1	12-1	51	2.86	151	.226	.264	23-0-2	.000	-2	111	10	0	0.8
	Year	14	8	.636	32	31	3	0-0	205	213	96	24	4	59-3	123	3.82	107	.270	.322	66-1-6	.030	-4	103	6	0	0.2

YEAR	TM LG	W	L	PCT	G	GS	CG-SHO	SV-BS	IP	H	R	HR	HB	BB-IB	SO	ERA	AERA	OAV	OOB	AB-HR-SH	AVG	PB	SUP	APR	DL	PW
1998	†Chi N	9	14	.391	33	33	2-1	0-0	213.2	236	116	23	4	48-4	161	4.84	91	.278	.318	62-0-8	.065	-3	87	-7	0	-1.0
1999	Tex A	3	7	.300	15	15	0	0-0	74.1	103	73	17	1	34-1	44	8.60	60	.329	.392	2	.000	-0	101	-26	106	-2.7
2000	Tex A	3	5	.375	12	8	0	0-0	44	66	42	10	3	24-2	16	7.98	64	.347	.425	0	ø	0	106	-13	0	-1.8
Total	10	74	71	.510	219	197	15-3	0-0	1246.1	1364	687	154	24	367-21	728	4.61	94	.279	.330	242-1-29	.058	-14	103	-30	182	-5.5
Clark, Mike	Michael John; B2.12.1922 Camden NJ; D1.25.1996 Camden NJ; BR/TR/6´4˝/(190–200); d7.27																									
1952	StL N	2	0	1.000	12	4	0	0	25.1	32	18	2	0	14	10	6.04	61	.311	.393	5	.000	-1	150	-6	0	-0.5
1953	StL N	1	0	1.000	23	2	0	1	35.2	46	21	2	2	21	17	4.79	89	.315	.408	6	.000	-1	115	-2	0	-0.2
Total	2	3	0	1.000	35	6	0	1	61	78	39	4	2	35	27	5.31	76	.313	.402	11	.000	-1	133	-8	0	-0.7
Clark, Phil	Philip James; B10.3.1932 Albany GA; BR/TR/6´3˝/(190–210); d4.15																									
1958	StL N	0	1	.000	7	0	0	1	7.2	11	5	2	0	3-0	1	3.52	117	.355	.412	1	.000	-0*	—	0	0	-0.1
1959	StL N	0	1	.000	7	0	0	0	7	8	11	0	0	8-1	5	12.86	33	.286	.444	0	ø	0	—	-6	0	-0.7
Total	2	0	2	.000	14	0	0	1	14.2	19	16	2	0	11-1	6	7.98	52	.322	.429	1	.000	-0	—	-6	0	-0.8
Clark, Rickey	Rickey Charles; B3.21.1946 Mt.Clemens MI; BR/TR/6´2˝/170; d4.22																									
1967	Cal A	12	11	.522	32	30	1-1	0	174	144	69	15	6	69-0	81	2.59	121	.224	.303	50-0-9	.040	-4	100	6	0	0.4
1968	Cal A	1	11	.083	21	17	0	0	94.1	74	51	4	1	54-1	60	3.53	83	.217	.323	28-0-3	.107	-1	91	-11	0	-1.5
1969	Cal A	0	0	ø	6	1	0	0-0	9.2	12	6	2	0	7-1	6	5.59	63	.300	.404	2	.500	0	25	-2	0	-0.1
1971	Cal A	2	1	.667	11	7	1-1	1-0	44	36	15	6	2	28-2	28	2.86	113	.220	.340	15-0-1	.267	1	122	2	0	0.2
1972	Cal A	4	9	.308	26	15	2	1-1	109.2	105	59	10	2	55-2	61	4.51	65	.261	.345	31-0-1	.097	-1*	72	-19	0	-2.3
Total	5	19	32	.373	96	70	4-2	2-1	431.2	371	200	37	11	213-6	236	3.38	91	.233	.325	126-0-14	.103	-5	93	-24	0	-3.3
Clark, Bob	Robert William; B8.22.1897 Newport PA; D5.18.1944 Carlsbad NM; BR/TR/6´3˝/188; d5.26; Col Susquehanna																									
1920	Cle A	1	2	.333	11	2	2-1	0	42	59	19	0	1	13	8	3.43	111	.383	.435	10	.200	-0	73	2	—	0.1
1921	Cle A	0	0	ø	5	0	0	0	9.1	23	17	2	1	6	2	14.46	29	.511	.577	3	.000	-1	—	-10	—	-0.5
Total	2	1	2	.333	16	2	2-1	0	51.1	82	36	2	2	19	10	5.44	71	.412	.468	13	.154	-1	73	-8	—	-0.4
Clark, Terry	Terry Lee; B10.18.1960 Los Angeles CA; BR/TR/6´2˝/(190–196); [StLN79 23/575]; d7.7; Col Mt. San Antonio (CA) JC																									
1988	Cal A	6	6	.500	15	15	2-1	0-0	94	120	54	8	0	31-6	39	5.07	77	.323	.370	0	ø	0	122	-11	0	-1.2
1989	Cal A	0	2	.000	4	2	0	0-0	11	13	8	0	0	3-0	7	4.91	78	.310	.348	0	ø	0	83	-2	30	-0.3
1990	Hou N	0	0	ø	1	1	0	0-0	4	9	7	0	0	3-0	2	13.50	28	.429	.500	2	.500	0	193	-5	0	-0.2
1995	Atl N	0	0	ø	3	0	0	0-0	3.2	3	2	0	0	5-0	2	4.91	88	.231	.444	0	ø	0	—	0	0	0.0
	Bal A	2	5	.286	38	0	0	1-0	39	40	15	3	1	15-5	18	3.46	138	.276	.346	0	ø	0	—	6	0	0.9
1996	KC A	1	1	.500	12	0	0	0-0	17.1	28	15	3	0	7-1	12	7.79	65	.350	.402	0	ø	0	—	-5	0	-0.5
	Hou N	0	2	.000	5	0	0	0-0	6.1	16	10	1	1	2-1	5	11.37	34	.471	.514	0	ø	0	—	-6	53	-1.1
1997	Cle A	0	3	.000	4	4	0	0-0	26.1	29	21	3	0	13-1	13	6.15	76	.284	.359	0	ø	0	44	-5	0	-0.4
	Tex A	1	4	.200	9	5	0	0-0	30.2	41	20	3	2	10-0	11	5.87	83	.325	.384	1	1.000	0	42	-2	0	-0.2
	Year	1	7	.125	13	9	0	0-0	57	70	41	6	2	23-1	24	6.00	80	.307	.373	1	1.000	0	43	-7	0	-0.6
Total	6	10	23	.303	91	27	2-1	1-0	232.1	299	152	21	4	89-14	109	5.54	78	.320	.378	3	.667	1	89	-30	83	-3.0
Clark, Otey	William Otis; B5.22.1915 Boscobel WI; BR/TR/6´1.5˝/190; d4.17																									
1945	Bos A	4	4	.500	12	9	4-1	0	82	86	33	6	1	19	20	3.07	111	.268	.311	24-0-3	.208	0	75	3	0	0.1
Clark, Watty	William Watson "Lefty"; B5.16.1902 St.Joseph LA; D3.4.1972 Clearwater FL; BL/TL/6´0.5˝/175; d5.28; Col Mississippi College																									
1924	Cle A	1	3	.250	12	1	0	0	25.2	38	27	0	2	14	6	7.01	61	.345	.429	9	.222	1	20	-9	—	-1.0
1927	Bro N	7	2	.778	27	3	1	2	73.2	74	23	2	0	19	32	2.32	171	.265	.312	21-0-1	.143	-1	86	**13**	—	1.5
1928	Bro N	12	9	.571	40	19	10-2	3	194.2	193	75	4	1	50	85	2.68	148	.259	.306	66-0-6	.152	-2	105	28	—	2.6
1929	Bro N	16	19	.457	41	**39**	19-3	1	**279**	295	136	14	3	71	140	3.74	123	.270	.316	97-0-4	.165	-3*	96	29	—	2.7
1930	Bro N	13	13	.500	44	24	9-1	6	200	209	110	20	0	38	81	4.18	117	.271	.306	68-1-1	.206	0	87	17	—	2.0
1931	Bro N	14	10	.583	34	28	16-3	1	233.1	243	86	4	1	52	96	3.20	119	.267	.308	84-0-3	.250	4	93	21	—	2.3
1932	Bro N	20	12	.625	40	**36**	19-2	0	273	282	122	10	4	49	99	3.49	109	.264	.299	97-0-4	.216	1	105	9	—	1.2
1933	Bro N	2	4	.333	11	8	4-1	1	50.2	61	29	2	3	6	14	4.80	67	.303	.333	13-0-2	.154	-0	68	-8	—	-0.9
	NY N	3	4	.429	16	5	0	0	44	58	25	3	1	11	11	4.70	68	.317	.359	11	.273	1	161	-6	—	-0.8
	Year	5	8	.385	27	13	4-1	1	94.2	119	54	5	4	17	25	4.75	68	.310	.346	24-0-2	.208	1	104	-15	—	-1.7
1934	NY N	1	2	.333	5	4	1	0	18.2	23	15	5	0	5	6	6.75	57	.295	.337	6-0-1	.167	0	78	-5	—	-0.7
	Bro N	2	0	1.000	17	1	0	0	25.1	40	19	0	1	9	10	5.33	73	.345	.397	8	.125	-1	111	-5	—	-0.4
	Year	3	2	.600	22	5	1	0	44	63	34	5	1	14	16	5.93	66	.325	.373	14-0-1	.143	-0	84	-10	—	-1.1
1935	Bro N	13	8	.619	33	25	11-1	0	207	215	93	11	1	28	35	3.30	120	.264	.289	79-0-3	.177	-0*	97	15	—	1.4
1936	Bro N	7	11	.389	33	16	1-1	2	120	162	73	11	0	28	28	4.43	93	.316	.351	39	.231	0	63	-4	—	-0.6
1937	Bro N	0	0	ø	2	0	0	0	2.1	4	3	0	0	3	0	7.71	52	.308	.438	0	ø	0	—	-1	—	0.0
Total	12	111	97	.534	355	209	91-14	16	1747.1	1897	836	86	17	383	643	3.66	112	.275	.315	598-1-25	.196	1	94	94	—	9.3
Clarke, Lefty	Alan Thomas; B3.8.1896 Clarksville MD; D3.11.1975 Cheverly MD; BB/TL/5´11˝/180; d10.2																									
1921	Cin N	0	1	.000	1	1	1	0	5	7	7	0	0	2	1	5.40	66	.304	.360	1	.000	-0	0	-2	—	-0.4
Clarke, Henry	Henry Tefft; B8.28.1875 Bellevue NE; D3.28.1950 Colorado Springs CO; BR/TR; d6.26; Col Chicago																									
1897	Cle N	0	4	.000	5	4	3	0	30.2	32	29	4	3	12	3	5.87	76	.267	.348	25	.280	0*	83	-5	—	-0.5
1898	Chi N	1	0	1.000	1	1	1	0	9	8	4	0	1	5	1	2.00	179	.235	.350	4	.250	0*	99	1	—	0.1
Total	2	1	4	.200	6	5	4	0	39.2	40	33	4	4	17	4	4.99	86	.260	.349	29	.276	0	86	-4	—	-0.4
Clarke, Rufe	Rufus Rivers; B4.13.1900 Estill SC; D2.8.1983 Columbia SC; BR/TR/6´1˝/203; d9.3; b–Sumpter; Col Davidson																									
1923	Det A	1	1	.500	5	0	0	0	6	6	3	0	1	6	2	4.50	86	.300	.481	0	ø	0	—	0	—	0.0
1924	Det A	0	0	ø	2	0	0	0	5.1	3	2	0	1	5	1	3.38	122	.158	.360	1	.000	-0	—	1	—	0.0
Total	2	1	1	.500	7	0	0	0	11.1	9	5	0	2	11	3	3.97	100	.231	.423	1	.000	-0	—	1	—	0.0
Clarke, Stan	Stanley Martin; B8.9.1960 Toledo OH; BL/TL/6´1˝/(180–190); [TorA81 6/134]; d6.7; Col Toledo																									
1983	Tor A	1	1	.500	10	0	0	0-1	11	10	4	2	0	5-0	7	3.27	133	.256	.333	0	ø	0	—	1	0	0.2
1985	Tor A	0	0	ø	4	0	0	0-1	4	3	2	1	0	2-0	2	4.50	94	.214	.313	0	ø	0	—	0	0	0.0
1986	Tor A	0	1	.000	10	0	0	0-0	12.2	18	13	4	0	10-1	9	9.24	46	.375	.475	0	ø	0	—	-6	0	-0.4
1987	Sea A	2	2	.500	22	0	0	0-0	23	31	14	7	0	10-1	13	5.48	87	.333	.387	0	ø	0	—	-1	0	-0.2
1989	KC A	0	2	.000	2	2	0	0-0	7	14	12	2	0	4-0	2	15.43	25	.438	.500	0	ø	0	35	-8	0	-1.2
1990	StL N	0	0	ø	2	0	0	0-0	3.1	2	1	0	0	0-0	3	2.70	143	.167	.167	0	ø	0	—	0	0	0.0
Total	6	3	6	.333	50	2	0	0-2	61	78	46	16	0	31-2	36	6.79	65	.328	.398	0	ø	0	35	-14	0	-1.6
Clarke, Webbo	Vibert Ernesto; B6.8.1928 Colon, Pan; D6.14.1970 Cristobal, Canal Zone; BL/TL/6´0˝/165; d9.4																									
1955	Was A	0	0	ø	7	2	0	0	21.1	17	11	2	0	14-0	9	4.64	83	.221	.341	6	.167	-0	151	-1	0	-0.1
Clarke, Dad	William H.; B1.7.1865 Oswego NY; D6.3.1911 Lorain OH; BB/TR/5´7˝/160; d4.23																									
1888	Chi N	1	0	1.000	2	2	1	0	16	23	17	2	2	6	6	5.06	60	.315	.383	7-1	.286	2	223	-4	—	0.0
1891	Col AA	1	2	.333	4	3	2	0	21	30	21	0	1	16	2	6.86	50	.326	.431	9	.111	0	150	-7	—	-0.7
1894	NY N	3	4	.429	15	6	5	1	84	114	76	3	3	26	15	4.93	107	.320	.371	37	.216	-0*	108	1	—	0.0
1895	NY N	18	15	.545	37	30	27-1	1	281.2	336	174	5	11	60	67	3.39	137	.292	.333	121	.240	-2	105	33	—	2.6
1896	NY N	17	24	.415	48	40	33-1	1	351	431	246	9	11	60	66	4.26	99	.300	.332	147-0-1	.204	-4*	89	-5	—	-1.0
1897	NY N	2	1	.667	6	4	2	0	31	43	34	1	2	11	10	6.10	68	.326	.386	18	.167	-1*	137	-8	—	-0.6
	Lou N	2	4	.333	7	6	6	0	54.2	74	33	3	2	10	7	3.95	108	.320	.354	22	.227	-1	56	3	—	0.2
	Year	4	5	.444	13	10	8	0	85.2	117	67	4	4	21	17	4.73	89	.322	.366	40	.200	-2	88	-7	—	-0.4
1898	Lou N	0	1	.000	1	1	1	0	9	10	7	1	2	2	1	5.00	72	.278	.350	3	.000	-1	139	-2	—	-0.2
Total	7	44	51	.463	120	92	77-2	3	848.1	1061	608	24	34	191	174	4.17	106	.302	.344	364-1-1	.214	-6	100	11	—	0.3
Clarkson, Dad	Arthur Hamilton; B8.31.1866 Cambridge MA; D2.5.1911 Somerville MA; BR/TR/5´10˝/165; d8.20; b–John b–Walter																									
1891	NY N	1	2	.333	5	2	1	0	28	24	23	0	3	18	11	2.89	111	.222	.349	9	.444	2	121	-1	—	0.1
1892	Bos N	1	0	1.000	1	1	1	0	7	5	1	0	0	3	0	1.29	273	.192	.276	3	.000	-0	54	2	—	0.2
1893	StL N	12	9	.571	24	21	17-1	0	186.1	194	116	4	14	79	37	3.48	136	.260	.342	75	.133	-5*	82	23	—	1.6
1894	StL N	8	17	.320	32	32	24-1	0	233.1	318	236	9	11	117	46	6.36	85	.321	.399	88	.182	-4*	74	-26	—	-2.1
1895	StL N	1	6	.143	7	7	7	0	61	91	66	7	2	26	9	7.38	65	.340	.402	23	.043	-3	53	-16	—	-1.5

YEAR	TM LG	W	L	PCT	G	GS	CG-SHO	SV-BS	IP	H	R	HR	HB	BB-IB	SO	ERA	AERA	OAV	OOB	AB-HR-SH	AVG	PB	SUP	APR	DL	PW
	Bal N	12	3	.800	20	14	10	0	142	169	84	5	4	64	23	3.87	123	.291	.365	57-1-3	.140	-4	119	13	—	0.8
	Year	13	9	.591	27	21	17	0	203	260	150	12	6	90	32	4.92	97	.306	.377	80-1-3	.112	-7	96	0	—	-0.7
1896	Bal N	4	2	.667	7	4	3	0	47	72	40	1	2	18	7	4.98	86	.348	.405	18-0-1	.278	0	116	-5	—	-0.5
Total	6	39	39	.500	96	81	63-2	0	704.2	873	566	26	36	325	133	4.90	99	.298	.376	273-1-4	.161	-14	85	-10	—	-1.4
CLARKSON, JOHN	John Gibson; B7.1.1861 Cambridge MA; D2.4.1909 Belmont MA; BR/TR/5´10˝/155; d5.2; HF1963; b–Dad b–Walter																									
1882	Wor N	1	2	.333	3	3	2	0	24	49	31	0	—	2	3	4.50	69	.392	.402	11	.364	1	74	-5	—	-0.4
1884	Chi N	10	3	.769	14	13	12	0	118	94	64	10	—	25	102	2.14	147	.208	.249	84-3	.262	4*	168	10	—	1.4
1885	†Chi N	**53**	16	.768	**70**	**70**	**68-10**	0	**623**	497	255	21	—	97	**308**	1.85	163	.208	.239	283-4	.216	2*	131	**71**	—	**7.3**
1886	†Chi N	36	17	.679	55	55	50-3	0	466.2	419	248	19	—	86	313	2.41	150	.229	.264	210-3	.233	1	110	50	—	5.0
1887	Chi N	**38**	21	.644	**60**	**59**	**56**-2	0	**523**	513	283	19	8	92	**237**	3.08	146	.246	.281	215-6	.242	2*	101	**76**	—	**7.5**
1888	Bos N	33	20	.623	54	54	53-3	0	**483.1**	448	247	17	10	119	223	2.76	104	.236	.284	205-1	.195	2*	129	9	—	1.2
1889	Bos N	**49**	19	**.721**	**73**	**72**	**68-8**	1	**620**	589	280	16	17	203	**284**	**2.73**	**153**	.243	**.306**	262-2	.206	0	85	**93**	—	**8.9**
1890	Bos N	26	18	.591	44	44	43-2	0	383	370	186	14	16	140	138	3.27	115	.246	.316	173-2	.249	3*	91	28	—	2.8
1891	Bos N	33	19	.635	55	51	47-3	**3**	460.2	435	244	18	15	154	141	2.79	131	.240	.305	187	.225	3	84	41	—	4.4
1892	Bos N	8	6	.571	16	16	15-4	0	145.2	115	65	4	5	60	48	2.35	150	.208	.292	57-1	.228	1	107	15	—	1.4
	†Cle N	17	10	.630	29	28	27-1	1	243.1	235	132	4	4	72	91	2.55	133	.244	.299	101	.139	-5	118	18	—	1.1
	Year	25	16	.610	45	44	42-5	1	389	350	197	8	9	132	139	2.48	139	.231	.296	158-1	.171	-4	114	36	—	2.5
1893	Cle N	16	17	.485	36	35	31	0	295	358	240	11	5	95	62	4.45	110	.291	.344	131-1	.206	-4*	110	10	—	0.7
1894	Cle N	8	10	.444	22	18	13-1	0	150.2	173	109	6	0	46	28	4.42	124	.285	.335	55-1-4	.200	-3	93	16	—	1.2
Total	12	328	178	.648	531	518	485-37	5	4536.1	4295	2384	159	80	1191	1978	2.81	134	.240	.291	1974-24-4	.219	9	106	432	—	42.5
CLARKSON, WALTER	Walter Hamilton; B11.3.1878 Cambridge MA; D10.10.1946 Cambridge MA; BR/TR/5´10˝/150; d7.2; b–Dad b–John; Col Harvard																									
1904	NY A	1	2	.333	13	4	2	1	66.1	63	42	3	10	25	43	5.02	54	.251	.343	26	.269	2	105	-14	—	-0.6
1905	NY A	3	3	.500	9	4	3	0	46	40	26	1	2	13	35	3.91	75	.235	.297	19	.053	-2	72	-4	—	-0.7
1906	NY A	9	4	.692	32	16	9-3	0	151	135	59	6	5	55	64	2.32	128	.242	.316	51-0-3	.157	-1	106	7	—	0.4
1907	NY A	1	1	.500	5	2	0	1	17.1	19	12	1	2	8	3	6.23	45	.279	.372	7	.286	0	145	-4	—	-0.5
	Cle A	4	6	.400	17	10	9-1	0	90.2	77	40	1	3	29	32	1.99	126	.232	.299	28-0-1	.036	-3	75	2	—	-0.2
	Year	5	7	.417	22	12	9-1	1	108	96	52	2	5	37	35	2.67	96	.240	.312	35-0-1	.086	-3	88	-3	—	-0.7
1908	Cle A	0	0	ø	2	1	0	0	3.1	6	4	0	2	2	1	10.80	22	.400	.526	1	1.000	0	315	-3	—	-0.1
Total	5	18	16	.529	78	37	23-4	2	374.2	340	183	12	24	132	178	3.17	88	.244	.320	132-0-4	.152	-4	102	-16	—	-1.7
CLARKSON, BILL	William Henry "Blackie"; B9.27.1898 Portsmouth VA; D8.27.1971 Raleigh NC; BR/TR/5´11˝/160; d5.2																									
1927	NY N	3	9	.250	26	7	2	2	86.2	92	50	3	1	52	28	4.36	88	.280	.380	20	.050	-1*	44	-5	—	-0.8
1928	NY N	0	0	ø	4	0	0	0	5.2	10	6	0	0	1	3	7.94	49	.455	.478	0	ø	0	—	-3	—	-0.1
	Bos N	0	2	.000	19	2	0	0	34.2	53	29	2	1	22	8	6.75	58	.349	.434	3	.000	-0	0	-10	—	-0.5
	Year	0	2	.000	23	2	0	0	40.1	63	35	2	1	23	11	6.92	57	.362	.439	3	.000	-0	0	-14	—	-0.6
1929	Bos N	0	1	.000	2	1	0	0	7	16	10	0	0	4	0	10.29	45	.485	.541	2	.500	0	112	-5	—	-0.5
Total	3	3	12	.200	51	10	2	2	134	171	95	5	2	79	39	5.44	72	.319	.408	25	.080	-1	48	-23	—	-1.9
CLARY, MARTY	Martin Keith; B4.3.1962 Detroit MI; BR/TR/6´4˝/(190–195); [AtlN83 3/74]; d9.5; Col Northwestern																									
1987	Atl N	0	1	.000	7	1	0	0-0	14.2	20	13	2	1	4-0	7	6.14	71	.328	.373	1	.000	-0	63	-3	0	-0.2
1989	Atl N	4	3	.571	18	17	2-1	0-0	108.2	103	47	6	1	31-3	30	3.15	116	.249	.301	31-0-5	.161	0	88	4	0	0.3
1990	Atl N	1	10	.091	33	14	0	0-0	101.2	128	72	9	1	39-4	44	5.67	71	.308	.364	28-0-2	.000	-3	82	-17	0	-1.9
Total	3	5	14	.263	58	32	2-1	0-0	225	251	132	17	3	74-7	81	4.48	86	.282	.336	60-0-7	.083	-2	84	-16	0	-1.8
CLASET, GOWELL	Gowell Sylvester "Lefty"; B11.26.1907 Battle Creek MI; D3.8.1981 St.Petersburg FL; BB/TL/6´3.5˝/210; d4.12																									
1933	Phi A	2	0	1.000	8	1	0	0	11.1	23	15	1	0	11	1	9.53	45	.426	.523	2	.500	1	258	-7	—	-0.9
CLAUSEN, FRITZ	Frederick William; B4.26.1869 New York NY; D2.11.1960 Memphis TN; BR/TL/5´11˝/190; d7.23																									
1892	Lou N	9	13	.409	24	24	24-2	0	200	181	120	3	3	87	94	3.06	100	.232	.311	84	.155	-3	87	-3	—	-0.6
1893	Lou N	1	4	.200	5	5	3	0	33	41	25	2	1	22	4	6.00	73	.295	.395	14	.214	-1	89	-5	—	-0.5
	Chi N	6	2	.750	10	9	8	1	76	71	46	1	5	39	31	3.08	150	.240	.338	33	.121	-3	96	10	—	0.6
	Year	7	6	.538	15	14	11	1	109	112	71	3	6	61	35	3.96	115	.257	.357	47	.149	-4	93	9	—	0.1
1894	Chi N	0	1	.000	2	2	0	0	4.1	5	7	0	0	5	1	14.54	39	.294	.455	1	.000	-0	75	-3	—	-0.4
1896	Lou N	0	2	.000	2	2	1	0	11	17	13	1	3	6	4	6.55	66	.347	.448	4	.000	-1	123	-3	—	-0.4
Total	4	16	22	.421	43	42	36-2	1	324.1	315	211	7	12	159	134	3.64	100	.246	.334	136	.147	-8	93	-4	—	-1.3
CLAUSS, AL	Albert Stanley "Lefty"; B6.24.1891 New Haven CT; D9.13.1952 New Haven CT; BR/TL/5´10.5˝/178; d4.22																									
1913	Det A	0	1	.000	5	1	0	0	13.1	11	9	0	2	12	1	4.73	62	.224	.397	4	.000	-1	0	-2	—	-0.2
CLAUSSEN, BRANDON	Brandon Allen Falker; B5.1.1979 Rapid City SD; BR/TL/6´2˝/200; [NYA98 34/1027]; d6.28; Col Howard (TX) JC																									
2003	NY A	1	0	1.000	1	1	0	0-0	6.1	8	2	1	0	1-0	5	1.42	309	.296	.321	4	.250	0	189	2	0	0.3
2004	Cin N	2	8	.200	14	14	0	0-0	66	80	50	9	2	35-2	45	6.14	70	.299	.380	19-0-2	.105	-1	76	-14	0	-1.9
2005	Cin N	10	11	.476	29	29	0	0-0	166.2	178	89	24	7	57-5	121	4.21	101	.273	.335	55-0-6	.091	-2	115	-1	0	-0.4
2006	Cin N	3	8	.273	14	14	0	0-0	77	93	56	14	6	28-1	57	6.19	76	.301	.368	21-0-3	.095	-1	71	-11	107	-1.3
Total	4	16	27	.372	58	58	0	0-0	316	359	197	48	15	121-8	228	5.04	87	.286	.353	99-0-11	.101	-4	96	-24	107	-3.3
CLAY, DANNY	Danny Bruce; B10.24.1961 Sun Valley CA; BR/TR/6´1˝/200; d5.1; Col Loyola Marymount																									
1988	Phi N	0	1	.000	17	0	0	0-0	24	27	17	5	0	21-2	12	6.00	60	.303	.432	2-0-1	.000	-0	—	-6	0	-0.4
CLAY, KEN	Kenneth Earl; B4.6.1954 Lynchburg VA; BR/TR/6´3˝/(190–195); [NYA72 2/38]; d6.7																									
1977	†NY A	2	3	.400	21	3	0	1-1	55.2	53	32	6	1	24-3	20	4.37	91	.251	.329	0	ø	0	128	-3	0	-0.3
1978	†NY A	3	4	.429	28	6	0	0-0	75.2	89	41	3	2	21-3	32	4.28	85	.291	.338	0	ø	0	131	-6	21	-0.5
1979	NY A	1	7	.125	32	5	0	2-2	78.1	88	49	12	2	25-1	28	5.40	76	.291	.346	0	ø	0	57	-10	0	-1.0
1980	Tex A	2	3	.400	8	8	0	0-0	43	43	24	4	3	29-2	17	4.60	84	.256	.373	0	ø	0	109	-3	0	-0.3
1981	Sea A	2	7	.222	22	14	0	0-0	101	116	62	10	3	42-3	32	4.63	84	.294	.363	0	ø	0	69	-10	66	-0.9
Total	5	10	24	.294	111	36	0	3-3	353.2	389	208	35	11	141-12	129	4.68	83	.281	.350	0	ø	0	91	-32	87	-3.0
CLEAR, MARK	Mark Alan; B5.27.1956 Los Angeles CA; BR/TR/6´4˝/(200–215); [PhiN74 8/171]; d4.4																									
1979	†Cal A★	11	5	.688	52	0	0	14-7	109	87	48	6	3	68-5	98	3.63	112	.219	.333	0	ø	0	—	6	0	0.9
1980	Cal A	11	11	.500	58	0	0	9-6	106.1	82	51	2	5	65-9	105	3.30	120	.216	.336	0	ø	0	—	4	0	0.8
1981	Bos A	8	3	.727	34	0	0	9-5	76.2	69	36	11	2	51-2	82	4.11	95	.239	.357	0	ø	0	—	0	0	0.0
1982	Bos A☆	14	9	.609	55	0	0	14-9	105	92	39	11	7	61-6	109	3.00	145	.238	.348	0	ø	0	—	15	0	3.0
1983	Bos A	4	5	.444	48	0	0	4-1	96	101	71	10	3	68-5	81	6.28	70	.273	.385	0	ø	0	—	-17	0	-1.6
1984	Bos A	8	3	.727	47	0	0	8-2	67	47	38	2	2	70-3	76	4.03	104	.198	.378	0	ø	0	—	0	0	-0.1
1985	Bos A	1	3	.250	41	0	0	3-3	55.2	45	26	1	5	50-10	55	3.72	116	.225	.389	0	ø	0	—	3	0	0.3
1986	Mil A	5	5	.500	59	0	0	16-3	73.2	53	23	4	1	36-2	85	2.20	198	.201	.295	0	ø	0	—	16	0	2.6
1987	Mil A	8	5	.615	58	1	0	6-3	78.1	70	46	9	5	55-3	81	4.48	103	.239	.363	0	ø	0	99	-1	0	0.0
1988	Mil A	1	0	1.000	25	0	0	0-0	29	23	12	4	0	21-0	26	2.79	143	.215	.338	0	ø	0	—	3	63	0.1
1990	Cal A	0	0	ø	4	0	0	0-0	7.2	5	7	0	2	9-0	6	5.87	65	.200	.421	0	ø	0	—	-2	0	-0.1
Total	11	71	49	.592	481	1	0	83-39	804.1	674	397	60	35	554-45	804	3.85	110	.228	.353	0	ø	0	99	27	63	5.9
CLEARY, JOE	Joseph Christopher "Fire"; B12.3.1918 Cork, Ireland; D6.3.2004 Yonkers NY; BR/TR/5´9˝/150; d8.4																									
1945	Was A	0	0	ø	1	0	0	0	0.1	5	7	0	0	3	1	189.00	2	.833	.889	0	ø	0	—	-7	0	-0.3
CLEMENS, ROGER	William Roger "Rocket"; B8.4.1962 Dayton OH; BR/TR/6´4˝/(205–235); [BosA83 1/19]; d5.15; Col Texas																									
1984	Bos A	9	4	.692	21	20	5-1	0-0	133.1	146	67	13	2	29-3	126	4.32	97	.271	.309	0	ø	0	132	1	0	0.1
1985	Bos A	7	5	.583	15	15	3-1	0-0	98.1	83	38	5	3	37-0	74	3.29	131	.228	.303	0	ø	0	86	11	73	1.3
1986	†Bos A★	**24**	4	**.857**	33	33	10-1	0-0	254	179	77	21	4	67-0	238	**2.48**	**169**	**.195**	**.252**	0	ø	0	132	**49**	0	5.1
1987	Bos A	**20**	9	**.690**	36	36	**18-7**	0-0	281.2	248	100	19	9	83-4	256	2.97	154	.235	.295	0	ø	0	111	**49**	0	**4.5**
1988	†Bos A★	18	12	.600	35	35	**14-8**	0-0	264	217	93	17	6	62-4	**291**	2.93	141	.220	.270	0	ø	0	97	34	0	3.7
1989	Bos A	17	11	.607	35	35	8-3	0-0	253.1	215	101	20	8	93-5	230	3.13	132	.231	.305	0	ø	0	100	26	0	2.7
1990	†Bos A☆	21	6	.778	31	31	7-**4**	0-0	228.1	193	59	7	7	54-3	209	**1.93**	**212**	.228	.278	0	ø	0	94	**51**	0	**6.2**
1991	Bos A★	18	10	.643	35	**35**	13-**4**	0-0	**271.1**	219	93	15	5	65-12	**241**	**2.62**	**165**	.221	.270	0	ø	0	95	**47**	0	**4.7**
1992	Bos A★	18	11	.621	32	32	11-**5**	0-0	246.2	203	80	11	9	62-5	208	**2.41**	**177**	.224	.278	0	ø	0	86	**45**	0	**5.3**

THE PITCHER REGISTER

YEAR	TM LG	W	L	PCT	G	GS	CG-SHO	SV-BS	IP	H	R	HR	HB	BB-IB	SO	ERA	AERA	OAV	OOB	AB-HR-SH	AVG	PB	SUP	APR	DL	PW
1993	Bos A	11	14	.440	29	29	2-1	0-0	191.2	175	99	17	11	67-4	160	4.46	104	.244	.315	0	ø	0	64	7	27	0.8
1994	Bos A	9	7	.563	24	24	3-1	0-0	170.2	124	62	15	4	71-1	168	2.85	**177**	**.203**	.288	0	ø	0	71	38	0	3.2
1995	†Bos A	10	5	.667	23	23	0	0-0	140	141	70	15	14	60-0	132	4.18	116	.259	.346	0	ø	0	108	11	38	1.1
1996	Bos A	10	13	.435	34	34	6-2	0-0	242.2	216	106	19	4	106-2	**257**	3.63	140	.237	.317	1	1.000	0	80	41	0	3.3
1997	Tor A★	**21**	7	.750	34	34	**9-3**	0-0	**264**	204	65	9	12	68-1	**292**	**2.05**	**224**	.213	**.273**	2	.500	1	91	**75**	0	**7.9**
1998	Tor A★	**20**	6	.769	33	33	5-3	0-0	234.2	169	78	11	7	88-0	**271**	**2.65**	**176**	**.197**	.277	4-0-1	.000	-0	91	**52**	0	**5.2**
1999	†NY A	14	10	.583	30	30	1-1	0-0	187.2	185	101	20	9	90-0	163	4.60	103	.261	.350	4-0-1	.000	-0	88	5	23	0.6
2000	†NY A	13	8	.619	32	32	1	0-0	204.1	184	96	26	10	84-0	188	3.70	129	.236	.317	3	.000	-0	95	23	16	2.1
2001	†NY A★	20	3	**.870**	33	33	0	0-0	220.1	205	94	19	5	72-1	213	3.51	126	.246	.309	2	.000	-0	123	23	0	2.2
2002	†NY A	13	6	.684	29	29	0	0-0	180	172	94	18	7	63-6	192	4.35	100	.250	.317	3	.667	1	116	1	25	0.2
2003	†NY A★	17	9	.654	33	33	1-1	0-0	211.2	199	99	24	5	58-1	190	3.91	112	.247	.299	1-0-1	.000	-0	107	12	0	1.4
2004	†Hou N★	18	4	**.818**	33	33	0	0-0	214.1	169	76	15	6	79-5	218	2.98	147	.217	.292	72-0-3	.167	0	100	33	0	3.1
2005	†Hou N★	13	8	.619	32	32	1	0-0	211.1	151	51	11	3	62-5	185	**1.87**	**225**	**.198**	.261	58-0-5	.207	3	76	**54**	0	5.7
2006	Hou N	7	6	.538	19	19	0	0-0	113.1	89	34	7	4	29-1	102	2.30	196	.216	.274	27-0-7	.074	-0	81	26	0	2.8
Total	23	348	178	.662	691	690	118-46	0-0	4817.2	4086	1833	354	154	1549-63	4604	3.10	144	.228	.294	177-0-18	.169	5	97	714	202	73.2
CLEMENSEN, BILL	William Melville; B6.20.1919 New Brunswick NJ; D2.18.1994 Alta CA; BR/TR/6´1˝/193; d5.22; Mil 1942–45; Col San Jose St.																									
1939	Pit N	0	1	.000	12	1	0	0	27	32	26	0	3	20	13	7.33	52	.311	.437	6	.333	1	23	-11	—	-0.4
1941	Pit N	1	0	1.000	2	1	1	0	13	7	5	0	0	7	4	2.77	130	.159	.275	4	.000	-1	71	1	0	0.0
1946	Pit N	0	0	ø	1	0	0	0	2	0	0	0	0	0	2	0.00	ø	.000	.000	0	ø	0	—	1	0	0.0
Total	3	1	1	.500	15	2	1	0	42	39	31	0	3	27	19	5.57	67	.255	.377	10	.200	0	46	-9	0	-0.4
CLEMENT, MATT	Matthew Paul; B8.12.1974 McCandless Twp. PA; BR/TR/6´3˝/(180–210); [SDN93 3/86]; d9.6																									
1998	SD N	2	0	1.000	4	2	0	0-0	13.2	15	8	0	0	7-1	13	4.61	86	.283	.367	2-0-2	.000	-0	93	-1	0	-0.2
1999	SD N	10	12	.455	31	31	0	0-0	180.2	190	106	18	9	86-2	135	4.48	95	.273	.358	52-0-6	.077	-2	101	-8	0	-1.1
2000	SD N	13	17	.433	34	34	0	0-0	205	194	131	22	16	125-4	170	5.14	87	.248	.361	60-0-5	.067	-3	94	-17	0	-2.2
2001	Fla N	9	10	.474	31	31	0	0-0	169.1	172	102	15	15	85-2	134	5.05	83	.267	.365	50-0-8	.080	-2*	114	-17	0	-1.9
2002	Chi N	12	11	.522	32	32	3-2	0-0	205	162	84	18	6	85-7	215	3.60	113	.215	.299	61-0-10	.049	-3	110	13	0	1.0
2003	†Chi N	14	12	.538	32	32	2-1	0-0	201.2	169	100	22	14	79-2	171	4.11	106	.227	.312	62-0-8	.145	-1	88	6	0	0.6
2004	Chi N	9	13	.409	30	30	0	0-0	181	155	79	23	12	77-4	190	3.68	121	.229	.317	55-0-4	.145	-1	83	15	0	1.5
2005	†Bos A★	13	6	.684	32	32	1	0-0	191	192	102	18	16	68-1	146	4.57	99	.260	.333	3	.000	-0	120	0	0	0.0
2006	Bos A	5	5	.500	12	12	0	0-0	65.1	77	50	8	6	38-0	43	6.61	71	.291	.392	3	.333	0	114	-13	109	-1.6
Total	9	87	86	.503	238	236	6-3	0-0	1412.2	1326	762	144	94	650-23	1217	4.47	97	.248	.338	348-0-43	.095	-12	102	-22	109	-3.9
CLEMENTS, PAT	Patrick Brian; B2.2.1962 McCloud CA; BR/TL/6´0˝/(175–185); [CalA83 4/103]; d4.9; Col UCLA																									
1985	Cal A	5	0	1.000	41	0	0	1-1	62	47	23	4	2	25-2	19	3.34	124	.218	.305	0	ø	0	—	7	0	0.6
	Pit N	0	2	.000	27	0	0	2-4	34.1	39	14	2	0	15-3	17	3.67	99	.289	.358	3-0-1	.333	0	—	1	0	0.0
1986	Pit N	0	4	.000	65	0	0	2-3	61	53	20	1	2	32-6	31	2.80	139	.251	.349	6	.000	-1	—	8	0	0.5
1987	NY A	3	3	.500	55	0	0	7-3	80	91	45	4	3	30-2	36	4.95	90	.299	.364	0	ø	0	—	-4	0	-0.2
1988	NY A	0	0	ø	6	1	0	0-1	8.1	12	8	1	0	4-0	3	6.48	61	.343	.390	0	ø	0	69	-3	0	-0.1
1989	SD N	4	1	.800	23	1	0	0-1	39	39	17	4	0	15-5	18	3.92	89	.267	.333	6	.000	-1	76	-1	0	-0.1
1990	SD N	0	0	ø	9	0	0	0-0	13	20	9	1	0	7-1	6	4.15	92	.357	.429	0	ø	0	—	-1	0	-0.1
1991	SD N	1	0	1.000	12	0	0	0-0	14.1	13	8	0	0	9-4	8	3.77	101	.255	.349	1	.000	-0	—	0	131	0.0
1992	SD N	2	1	.667	27	0	0	0-1	23.2	25	9	0	2	12-4	11	2.66	135	.281	.379	1	.000	-0	—	2	0	0.2
	Bal A	2	0	1.000	23	0	0	0-0	24.2	23	10	0	2	11-0	9	3.28	124	.258	.350	0	ø	0	—	2	0	0.2
Total	8	17	11	.607	288	2	0	12-14	360.1	362	163	17	11	160-27	158	3.77	106	.272	.351	17-0-1	.059	-1	68	11	131	1.0
CLEMONS, CHRIS	Christopher Hale; B10.31.1972 Baytown TX; BR/TR/6´4˝/225; [ChiA94 S1/33]; d7.23; Col Texas A&M																									
1997	Chi A	0	2	.000	5	2	0	0-0	12.2	19	13	4	1	11-0	8	8.53	52	.345	.463	0	ø	0	21	-6	0	-0.7
CLEMONS, LANCE	Lance Levis; B7.6.1947 Philadelphia PA; BL/TL/6´2˝/205; [KCA68 7/156]; d8.12; Col West Chester																									
1971	KC A	1	0	1.000	10	3	0	0-0	24	26	16	2	1	12-0	20	4.13	83	.263	.345	7-1-1	.286	2	122	-4	0	0.0
1972	StL N	0	1	.000	3	1	0	0-0	5.1	8	7	1	1	5-0	2	10.13	34	.364	.500	1	.000	-0	52	-4	0	-0.7
1974	Bos A	1	0	1.000	6	0	0	0-0	6.1	8	8	1	1	4-3	1	9.95	39	.296	.406	0	ø	0	—	-4	0	-0.6
Total	3	2	1	.667	19	4	0	0-0	35.2	42	31	4	3	21-3	23	6.06	58	.284	.382	8-1-1	.250	2	102	-12	0	-1.3
CLEVELAND, REGGIE	Reginald Leslie; B5.23.1948 Swift Current SK, Can.; BR/TR/6´1˝/(185–205); d10.1																									
1969	StL N	0	0	ø	1	1	0	0-0	4	7	4	0	0	1-0	3	9.00	40	.368	.400	1-0-1	.000	-0	148	-2	0	-0.1
1970	StL N	0	4	.000	16	1	0	0-0	26	31	27	3	0	18-6	22	7.62	54	.298	.392	4	.250	0	152	-11	0	-1.4
1971	StL N	12	12	.500	34	34	10-2	0-0	222	238	107	20	6	53-12	148	4.01	91	.271	.315	82-0-4	.171	-1	100	-8	0	-0.9
1972	StL N	14	15	.483	33	33	11-3	0-0	230.2	229	120	21	5	60-12	153	3.94	87	.258	.306	71-0-11	.239	3	102	-16	0	-1.7
1973	StL N	14	10	.583	32	32	6-3	0-0	224	211	88	13	4	61-12	122	3.01	122	.246	.298	74-0-9	.230	4	101	15	0	1.9
1974	Bos A	12	14	.462	41	27	10	0-0	221.1	234	121	25	9	69-5	103	4.31	89	.271	.329	0	ø	0	115	-13	0	-1.3
1975	†Bos A	13	9	.591	31	20	3-1	0-1	170.2	173	90	19	3	52-1	78	4.43	92	.263	.317	0	ø	0	104	-5	0	-0.6
1976	Bos A	10	9	.526	41	14	3	2-2	170	159	73	3	4	61-4	76	3.07	127	.246	.314	0	ø	0	82	12	0	1.3
1977	Bos A	11	8	.579	36	27	9-1	2-1	190.1	211	97	20	4	43-2	85	4.26	105	.281	.320	0	ø	0	108	5	0	0.3
1978	Bos A	0	1	.000	1	0	0	0-0	0.1	1	1	0	0	0-0	0	0.00	ø	.333	.333	0	ø	0	—	0	0	-0.1
	Tex A	5	7	.417	53	0	0	12-7	75.2	65	33	5	3	23-6	46	3.09	121	.236	.295	0	ø	0	—	4	0	0.8
	Year	5	8	.385	54	0	0	12-7	76	66	34	5	3	23-6	46	3.08	122	.237	.296	0	ø	0	—	4	0	0.7
1979	Mil A	1	5	.167	29	1	0	4-2	55	77	44	9	0	23-4	22	6.71	63	.344	.394	0	ø	0	129	-15	0	-1.6
1980	Mil A	11	9	.550	45	13	5-2	4-2	154.1	150	73	9	5	49-2	54	3.73	105	.254	.312	0	ø	0	109	3	0	0.3
1981	Mil A	2	3	.400	35	0	0	1-0	64.2	57	41	5	1	30-2	18	5.15	67	.239	.326	0	ø	0	—	-13	0	-1.1
Total	13	105	106	.498	428	203	57-12	25-15	1809	1843	919	152	44	543-68	930	4.01	96	.264	.318	232-0-25	.211	6	104	-44	0	-4.2
CLEVENGER, TEX	Truman Eugene; B7.9.1932 Visalia CA; BR/TR/6´1˝/(180–185); d4.18; Col Cal St.–Fresno																									
1954	Bos A	2	4	.333	23	8	1	0	67.2	67	42	9	2	29	43	4.79	86	.262	.337	14	.214	0*	70	-5	0	-0.4
1956	Was A	0	0	ø	20	1	0	0	31.2	33	22	4	0	21-0	17	5.40	80	.264	.365	2	.000	-0	144	-4	0	-0.2
1957	Was A	7	6	.538	52	9	2	8	139.2	139	69	11	4	47-4	75	4.19	93	.261	.322	33-0-4	.212	1	87	-4	0	-0.1
1958	Was A	9	9	.500	**55**	4	0	6	124	119	65	12	1	50-6	70	4.35	88	.251	.321	22-0-2	.136	0	59	-8	0	-1.0
1959	Was A	8	5	.615	50	7	2-2	8	117.1	114	56	8	2	51-3	71	3.91	100	.256	.332	23-0-4	.174	1	84	1	0	0.5
1960	Was A	5	11	.313	53	11	1	7	128.2	150	77	10	3	49-10	49	4.20	93	.298	.358	22-0-4	.091	-1	70	-7	0	-1.0
1961	LA A	2	1	.667	12	0	0	1	16	13	5	1	0	13-1	11	1.69	267	.220	.361	3	.000	-0	—	4	0	0.7
	NY A	1	1	.500	21	0	0	0	31.2	35	20	3	1	21-1	14	4.83	77	.287	.396	4	.250	0	—	-5	0	-0.2
	Year	3	2	.600	33	0	0	1	47.2	48	25	4	1	34-2	25	3.78	105	.265	.384	7	.143	0	—	0	0	0.5
1962	NY A	2	0	1.000	21	0	0	0	38	36	14	3	1	17-5	11	2.84	132	.248	.329	4	.000	-0*	—	4	0	0.1
Total	8	36	37	.493	307	40	6-2	30	694.2	706	370	61	14	298-30	361	4.18	94	.265	.339	127-0-14	.157	1	78	-24	0	-1.6
CLIBURN, STEW	Stewart Walker; B12.19.1956 Jackson MS; BR/TR/6´0˝/(187–195); [PitN77 4/96]; d9.17; twb–Stan; Col Delta St.																									
1984	Cal A	0	0	ø	1	0	0	0-0	2	3	3	0	0	1-1	1	13.50	30	.333	.400	0	ø	0	—	-2	0	-0.1
1985	Cal A	9	3	.750	44	0	0	6-1	99	87	25	5	1	26-6	48	2.09	197	.241	.292	0	ø	0	—	23	0	2.9
1988	Cal A	4	2	.667	40	1	0	0-4	84	83	45	11	6	32-6	42	4.07	95	.266	.342	0	ø	0*	47	-3	0	-0.2
Total	3	13	5	.722	85	1	0	6-5	185	173	73	16	7	59-13	91	3.11	129	.254	.317	0	ø	0	47	18	0	2.6
CLINTON, JIM	James Lawrence "Big Jim"; B8.10.1850 New York NY; D9.3.1921 Brooklyn NY; BR/TR/5´8.5˝/174; d5.18; U1; ▲																									
1872	Eck NA	0	1	.000	1	1	1	0	9	25	36	1	—	1	1	7.00	49	.373	.382	98	.245	0*	0	-8	—	-0.4
1875	Atl NA	1	13	.071	17	14	9	0	123	141	104	0	—	5	7	2.41	86	.262	.268	81	.123	-5*	40	-5	—	-0.7
1876	Lou N	0	1	.000	1	1	1	0	9	12	11	0	—	1	1	6.00	45	.279	.279	65	.338	0*	28	-2	—	-0.1
Total	2NA	1	14	.067	18	15	10	0	132	166	140	1	—	6	8	2.73	80	.274	.281	179	.190	-5	36	-13	—	-1.1
CLONINGER, TONY	Tony Lee; B8.13.1940 Lincoln Co. NC; BR/TR/6´0˝/(200–215); d6.15; C12																									
1961	Mil N	7	2	.778	19	10	3	0	84	84	49	16	1	33-1	51	5.25	71	.258	.326	30-0-2	.167	-0	154	-13	0	-1.2
1962	Mil N	8	3	.727	24	15	4-1	0	111	113	61	10	1	46-1	69	4.30	88	.264	.335	39-0-2	.103	-2	123	-7	0	-0.8
1963	Mil N	9	11	.450	41	18	4-2	1	145.1	131	68	17	2	63-12	100	3.78	85	.239	.318	37-0-5	.135	0	125	-9	0	-1.3
1964	Mil N	19	14	.576	38	34	15-3	2	242.2	206	112	20	3	82-9	163	3.56	99	.231	.294	87-0-11	.241	3	112	-2	0	0.0
1965	Mil N	24	11	.686	40	38	16-1	1	279	247	115	20	3	119-5	211	3.29	107	.236	.315	105-1-7	.162	2*	133	7	0	0.9
1966	Atl N	14	11	.560	39	38	11-1	1	257.2	253	134	29	6	116-9	178	4.12	88	.258	.336	111-5-2	.234	10*	129	-14	0	-0.3

YEAR	TM LG	W	L	PCT	G	GS	CG-SHO	SV-BS	IP	H	R	HR	HB	BB-IB	SO	ERA	AERA	OAV	OOB	AB-HR-SH	AVG	PB	SUP	APR	DL	PW
1967	Atl N	4	7	.364	16	16	1	0	76.2	85	50	13	0	31-4	55	5.17	64	.285	.348	25	.200	1	111	-16	51	-2.0
1968	Atl N	1	3	.250	8	1	0	0	19	15	9	0	0	11-2	7	4.26	70	.227	.329	4	.000	-0	58	-2	0	-0.5
	Cin N	4	3	.571	17	17	2-2	0	91.1	81	49	7	3	48-6	65	4.04	78	.233	.330	34-2-3	.206	3*	156	-9	0	-0.4
	Year	5	6	.455	25	18	2-2	0	110.1	96	58	7	3	59-8	72	4.08	77	.232	.330	38-2-3	.184	3	152	-12	0	-0.9
1969	Cin N	11	17	.393	35	34	6-2	0-0	189.2	184	123	24	5	103-4	103	5.03	75	.250	.344	72-1-3	.167	1*	118	-26	0	-3.5
1970	†Cin N	9	7	.563	30	18	0	1-1	148	136	69	10	4	78-6	56	3.83	106	.249	.346	47-2-2	.213	3	97	5	0	0.9
1971	Cin N	3	6	.333	28	8	1-1	0-0	97.1	79	42	12	4	49-3	51	3.88	87	.230	.328	27-0-2	.259	1	128	-4	0	-0.2
1972	StL N	0	2	.000	17	0	0	0-1	26	29	17	2	1	19-3	11	5.19	66	.293	.405	3	.000	-0	—	-5	0	-0.4
Total	12	113	97	.538	352	247	63-13	6-2	1767.2	1643	898	180	33	798-65	1120	4.07	88	.247	.328	621-11-39	.192	21	124	-95	51	-8.8

CLONTZ, BRAD John Bradley; B4.25.1971 Stuart VA; BR/TR/6´1˝/(180–203); [AtlN92 10/285]; d4.26; Col VPI

YEAR	TM LG	W	L	PCT	G	GS	CG-SHO	SV-BS	IP	H	R	HR	HB	BB-IB	SO	ERA	AERA	OAV	OOB	AB-HR-SH	AVG	PB	SUP	APR	DL	PW
1995	†Atl N	8	1	.889	59	0	0	4-2	69	71	29	5	4	22-4	55	3.65	118	.269	.332	2	.000	-0	—	6	0	0.7
1996	†Atl N	6	3	.667	**81**	0	0	1-5	80.2	78	53	11	2	33-8	49	5.69	78	.255	.328	2-0-1	.000	0	—	-9	0	-0.8
1997	Atl N	5	1	.833	51	0	0	1-1	48	52	24	3	1	18-3	42	3.75	112	.286	.350	1	.000	-0	—	2	0	0.1
1998	LA N	2	0	1.000	18	0	0	0-1	20.2	15	13	3	2	10-4	14	5.66	71	.200	.310	2	.000	-0	—	-3	0	-0.3
	NY N	0	0	ø	2	0	0	0-0	3	4	3	1	0	2-0	2	9.00	46	.333	.429	0	ø	0	—	-2	18	-0.1
	Year	2	0	1.000	20	0	0	0-1	23.2	19	16	4	2	12-4	16	6.08	66	.218	.327	2	.000	-0	—	-5	0	-0.4
1999	Pit N	1	3	.250	56	0	0	2-1	49.1	49	21	6	3	24-5	40	2.74	168	.254	.344	3	.000	-0	—	8	0	0.6
2000	Pit N	0	0	ø	5	0	0	0-0	7	7	4	1	0	11-2	8	5.14	90	.269	.486	0	ø	0	—	0	153	0.0
Total	6	22	8	.733	272	0	0	8-10	277.2	276	147	30	12	120-26	210	4.34	101	.261	.340	10-0-1	.000	-0	—	2	171	0.2

CLOSTER, AL Alan Edward; B6.15.1943 Creighton NE; BL/TL/6´2˝/(190–212); d4.19; Col Iowa St.

YEAR	TM LG	W	L	PCT	G	GS	CG-SHO	SV-BS	IP	H	R	HR	HB	BB-IB	SO	ERA	AERA	OAV	OOB	AB-HR-SH	AVG	PB	SUP	APR	DL	PW
1966	Was A	0	0	ø	1	0	0	0	0.1	1	0	0	0	2-0	0	0.00	ø	.500	.750	0	ø	0	—	0	0	0.0
1971	NY A	2	2	.500	14	1	0	0-0	28.1	33	22	4	2	13-7	22	5.08	65	.289	.364	6-0-1	.000	-1	27	-8	0	-1.0
1972	NY A	0	0	ø	2	0	0	0-0	2.1	2	3	1	0	4-0	2	11.57	26	.250	.500	1	.000	-0	—	-2	0	-0.1
1973	Atl N	0	0	ø	4	0	0	0-1	4.1	7	7	1	0	4-1	2	14.54	27	.389	.500	0	ø	0	—	-4	0	-0.2
Total	4	2	2	.500	21	1	0	0-1	35.1	43	32	6	2	23-8	26	6.62	51	.303	.400	7-0-1	.000	-1	27	-14	0	-1.3

CLOUDE, KEN Kenneth Brian; B1.9.1975 Baltimore MD; BR/TR/6´1˝/180; [SeaA93 6/157]; d8.9; [DL 2000 Sea A 31]

YEAR	TM LG	W	L	PCT	G	GS	CG-SHO	SV-BS	IP	H	R	HR	HB	BB-IB	SO	ERA	AERA	OAV	OOB	AB-HR-SH	AVG	PB	SUP	APR	DL	PW
1997	Sea A	4	2	.667	10	9	0	0-0	51	41	32	8	3	26-0	46	5.12	89	.218	.321	2	.000	-0	122	-4	0	-0.4
1998	Sea A	8	10	.444	30	30	0	0-0	155.1	187	116	29	3	80-4	114	6.37	73	.296	.376	3	.000	-0	109	-27	0	-2.6
1999	Sea A	4	4	.500	31	6	0	1-2	72.1	106	67	10	5	46-5	35	7.96	60	.346	.435	2	.000	-0	156	-25	0	-2.3
Total	3	16	16	.500	71	45	0	1-2	278.2	334	215	47	11	152-9	195	6.56	71	.297	.383	7	.000	-1	117	-56	31	-5.3

CLOUGH, ED Edgar George "Big Ed","Spec"; B10.28.1906 Wiconisco PA; D1.30.1944 Harrisburg PA; BL/TL/6´0˝/188; d8.28.1924; ▲

YEAR	TM LG	W	L	PCT	G	GS	CG-SHO	SV-BS	IP	H	R	HR	HB	BB-IB	SO	ERA	AERA	OAV	OOB	AB-HR-SH	AVG	PB	SUP	APR	DL	PW
1925	StL N	0	1	.000	3	1	0	0	10	11	9	1	1	5	3	8.10	53	.289	.386	4	.250	-0	59	-3	—	-0.3
1926	StL N	0	0	ø	1	0	0	0	2	5	6	0	1	3	0	22.50	17	.556	.692	1	.000	-0	—	-4	—	-0.2
Total	2	0	1	.000	4	1	0	0	12	16	15	1	2	8	3	10.50	40	.340	.456	5	.200	-0	59	-7	—	-0.5

CLOWERS, BILL William Perry; B8.14.1898 San Marcos TX; D1.13.1978 Sweeny TX; BL/TL/5´11˝/175; d7.20

YEAR	TM LG	W	L	PCT	G	GS	CG-SHO	SV-BS	IP	H	R	HR	HB	BB-IB	SO	ERA	AERA	OAV	OOB	AB-HR-SH	AVG	PB	SUP	APR	DL	PW
1926	Bos A	0	0	ø	2	0	0	0	1.2	2	1	0	0	0	0	0.00	ø	.333	.333	0	ø	0	—	0	—	0.0

CLUTTERBUCK, BRYAN Bryan Richard; B12.17.1959 Detroit MI; BR/TR/6´4˝/225; [MilA81 7/176]; d7.18; Col Eastern Michigan

YEAR	TM LG	W	L	PCT	G	GS	CG-SHO	SV-BS	IP	H	R	HR	HB	BB-IB	SO	ERA	AERA	OAV	OOB	AB-HR-SH	AVG	PB	SUP	APR	DL	PW
1986	Mil A	0	1	.000	20	0	0	0-0	56.2	68	32	8	2	16-2	38	4.29	102	.296	.345	0	ø	0	—	0	0	0.0
1989	Mil A	2	5	.286	14	11	1	0-0	67.1	73	39	11	0	16-1	29	4.14	93	.269	.306	0	ø	0	94	-4	86	-0.5
Total	2	2	6	.250	34	11	1	0-0	124	141	71	19	2	32-3	67	4.21	97	.281	.324	0	ø	0	94	-4	86	-0.5

CLYDE, DAVID David Eugene; B4.22.1955 Kansas City KS; BL/TL/6´1˝/(185–186); [TexA73 1/1]; d6.27

YEAR	TM LG	W	L	PCT	G	GS	CG-SHO	SV-BS	IP	H	R	HR	HB	BB-IB	SO	ERA	AERA	OAV	OOB	AB-HR-SH	AVG	PB	SUP	APR	DL	PW
1973	Tex A	4	8	.333	18	18	0	0-0	93.1	106	63	8	4	54-1	74	5.01	75	.293	.388	0	ø	0	102	-15	0	-1.7
1974	Tex A	3	9	.250	28	21	4	0-0	117	129	64	14	4	47-0	52	4.38	82	.286	.355	0	ø	0	96	-10	0	-1.0
1975	Tex A	0	1	.000	1	1	0	0-0	7	6	3	0	0	6-0	2	2.57	147	.273	.429	0	ø	0	47	1	0	0.1
1978	Cle A	8	11	.421	28	25	5	0-0	153.1	166	80	4	3	60-3	83	4.28	88	.280	.345	0	ø	0*	92	-8	0	-0.9
1979	Cle A	3	4	.429	9	8	1	0-0	45.2	50	33	7	1	13-0	17	5.91	73	.279	.330	0	ø	0	95	-8	82	-1.0
Total	5	18	33	.353	84	73	10	0-0	416.1	457	243	33	12	180-4	228	4.63	82	.285	.358	0	ø	0	95	-40	82	-4.5

CLYDE, TOM Thomas Knox; B8.17.1923 Wachapreague VA; D10.1.2005 Dallas TX; BR/TR/6´3˝/195; d5.31; Mil 1944–46; Col Presbyterian

YEAR	TM LG	W	L	PCT	G	GS	CG-SHO	SV-BS	IP	H	R	HR	HB	BB-IB	SO	ERA	AERA	OAV	OOB	AB-HR-SH	AVG	PB	SUP	APR	DL	PW
1943	Phi A	0	0	ø	4	0	0	0	6	7	8	1	1	4	0	9.00	38	.304	.429	2	.000	-0	—	-4	0	-0.3

COAKLEY, ANDY Andrew James (aka Jack McAllister in 1902); B11.20.1882 Providence RI; D9.27.1963 New York NY; BL/TR/6´0˝/165; d9.17; Col Holy Cross

YEAR	TM LG	W	L	PCT	G	GS	CG-SHO	SV-BS	IP	H	R	HR	HB	BB-IB	SO	ERA	AERA	OAV	OOB	AB-HR-SH	AVG	PB	SUP	APR	DL	PW
1902	Phi A	2	1	.667	3	3	3	0	27	25	15	0	2	9	9	2.67	138	.245	.319	8	.375	1	92	2	—	0.3
1903	Phi A	0	3	.000	6	3	2	0	37.2	48	31	2	2	11	20	5.50	56	.310	.363	15	.200	-0	70	-10	—	-0.8
1904	Phi A	4	3	.571	8	8	7-2	0	62	48	19	1	2	23	33	1.89	142	.215	.294	23-0-1	.087	-2	63	5	—	0.3
1905	†Phi A	18	8	.692	35	31	21-3	0	255	227	93	2	6	73	145	1.84	145	.240	.299	94-0-4	.138	-3	123	17	—	1.3
1906	Phi A	7	8	.467	22	16	10	0	149	144	78	0	3	44	59	3.14	87	.257	.314	49-0-2	.143	-2	115	-8	—	-1.1
1907	Cin N	17	16	.515	37	30	21-1	1	265.1	269	97	1	7	79	89	2.34	111	.274	.332	84-0-6	.071	-6	91	8	—	0.2
1908	Cin N	8	18	.308	32	28	20-4	2	242.1	219	79	3	4	64	61	1.86	124	.249	.303	76-0-5	.092	-4	66	10	—	0.4
	Chi N	2	0	1.000	4	3	2-1	0	20.1	14	4	0	0	6	7	0.89	266	.192	.253	6	.000	-1	140	3	—	0.2
	Year	10	18	.357	36	31	22-5	2	262.2	233	83	3	4	70	68	1.78	130	.245	.299	82-0-5	.085	-5	74	10	—	0.6
1909	Chi N	0	1	.000	1	1	0	0	2	7	7	0	0	3	1	18.00	14	.583	.667	0	ø	0	55	-4	—	-0.6
1911	NY A	0	1	.000	2	1	1	0	11.2	20	13	0	0	2	4	5.40	67	.377	.400	4	.250	0	60	-3	—	-0.2
Total	9	58	59	.496	150	124	87-11	3	1072.1	1021	436	9	26	314	428	2.35	111	.256	.315	359-0-18	.117	-16	95	20	—	-0.0

COATES, JIM James Alton; B8.4.1932 Farnham VA; BR/TR/6´4˝/(180–192); d9.21

YEAR	TM LG	W	L	PCT	G	GS	CG-SHO	SV-BS	IP	H	R	HR	HB	BB-IB	SO	ERA	AERA	OAV	OOB	AB-HR-SH	AVG	PB	SUP	APR	DL	PW
1956	NY A	0	0	ø	2	0	0	0	2	1	3	0	1	4-0	0	13.50	29	.167	.545	0	ø	0	—	-2	0	-0.1
1959	NY A	6	1	.857	37	4	2	3	100.1	89	39	10	3	36-4	64	2.87	127	.234	.305	21	.095	-1	133	8	0	0.4
1960	†NY A★	13	3	.813	35	18	6-2	1	149.1	139	78	16	2	66-4	73	4.28	84	.248	.327	48-0-8	.250	4	189	-11	0	-0.8
1961	†NY A	11	5	.688	43	11	4-1	5	141.1	128	60	15	7	53-0	80	3.44	108	.243	.318	35-0-8	.029	-3	104	4	0	0.1
1962	†NY A	7	6	.538	50	6	0	6	117.2	119	62	9	5	50-5	67	4.44	84	.263	.339	32-0-3	.125	-1	107	-8	0	-1.1
1963	Was A	2	4	.333	20	2	0	0	44.1	51	29	4	3	21-4	31	5.28	70	.297	.377	6	.000	-1	144	-7	0	-1.0
	Cin N	0	0	ø	9	0	0	0	16.1	21	10	2	0	7-1	11	5.51	61	.313	.378	3	.000	-0	—	-3	0	-0.2
1965	Cal A	2	0	1.000	17	0	0	3	28	23	13	1	0	16-2	15	3.54	96	.228	.325	1	.000	-0	—	-1	0	-0.1
1966	Cal A	1	1	.500	9	4	1-1	0	31.2	32	16	3	0	10-0	16	3.98	84	.258	.311	11	.091	-1	118	-2	0	-0.2
1967	Cal A	1	2	.333	25	1	0	0	52.1	47	26	5	4	23-5	39	4.30	73	.244	.336	3	.333	1	28	-6	0	-0.2
Total	9	43	22	.662	247	46	13-4	18	683.1	650	336	65	25	286-25	396	4.00	90	.252	.330	160-0-19	.131	-3	142	-28	0	-3.2

COBB, GEORGE George Woodworth; B9.25.1865 Independence IA; D8.19.1926 Pomona CA; 6´0˝/168; d4.15

YEAR	TM LG	W	L	PCT	G	GS	CG-SHO	SV-BS	IP	H	R	HR	HB	BB-IB	SO	ERA	AERA	OAV	OOB	AB-HR-SH	AVG	PB	SUP	APR	DL	PW
1892	Bal N	10	37	.213	53	47	42	0	394.1	495	333	21	19	140	159	4.86	71	.295	.356	172-1	.209	5*	93	-55	—	-4.6

COBB, HERB Herbert Edward; B8.6.1904 Pinetops NC; D1.8.1980 Tarboro NC; BR/TR/5´11˝/150; d4.21

YEAR	TM LG	W	L	PCT	G	GS	CG-SHO	SV-BS	IP	H	R	HR	HB	BB-IB	SO	ERA	AERA	OAV	OOB	AB-HR-SH	AVG	PB	SUP	APR	DL	PW
1929	StL A	0	0	ø	1	0	0	0	1	3	4	1	0	1	0	36.00	12	.600	.667	0	ø	0	—	-3	—	-0.1

COCANOWER, JAIME James Stanley; B2.14.1957 San Juan, PR; BR/TR/6´4˝/(190–200); d9.7; Col Baylor

YEAR	TM LG	W	L	PCT	G	GS	CG-SHO	SV-BS	IP	H	R	HR	HB	BB-IB	SO	ERA	AERA	OAV	OOB	AB-HR-SH	AVG	PB	SUP	APR	DL	PW
1983	Mil A	2	0	1.000	5	3	1	0-0	30	21	8	1	1	12-0	8	1.80	211	.200	.288	0	ø	0	192	6	0	0.4
1984	Mil A	8	16	.333	33	27	1	0-1	174.2	188	99	13	9	78-3	65	4.02	97	.279	.359	0	ø	0	83	-7	0	-0.8
1985	Mil A	6	8	.429	24	15	3-1	0-0	116.1	122	72	6	8	73-2	44	4.33	97	.274	.383	0	ø	0	97	-5	0	-0.6
1986	Mil A	0	1	.000	17	2	0	0-0	44.2	40	29	1	2	38-0	22	4.43	98	.248	.396	0	ø	0	94	-2	0	0.0
Total	4	16	25	.390	79	47	5-1	0-1	365.2	371	208	21	20	201-5	139	3.99	101	.268	.366	0	ø	0	94	-8	0	-1.0

COCHRAN, GOAT Alvah Jackson "Al","Goat"; B1.31.1891 Concord GA; D5.23.1947 Atlanta GA; BR/TR/5´10˝/175; d8.25

YEAR	TM LG	W	L	PCT	G	GS	CG-SHO	SV-BS	IP	H	R	HR	HB	BB-IB	SO	ERA	AERA	OAV	OOB	AB-HR-SH	AVG	PB	SUP	APR	DL	PW
1915	Cin N	0	0	ø	1	0	0	0	2	5	3	0	0	0	1	9.00	32	.455	.455	0	ø	0	—	-1	—	-0.1

COCO, PASQUAL Pasqual (Reynoso); B9.8.1977 Santo Domingo, D.R.; BR/TR/6´1˝/185; d7.17

YEAR	TM LG	W	L	PCT	G	GS	CG-SHO	SV-BS	IP	H	R	HR	HB	BB-IB	SO	ERA	AERA	OAV	OOB	AB-HR-SH	AVG	PB	SUP	APR	DL	PW
2000	Tor A	0	0	ø	1	1	0	0-0	4	5	4	1	1	5-0	2	9.00	56	.294	.478	0	ø	0	93	-2	0	-0.1
2001	Tor A	1	0	1.000	7	1	0	0-0	14.1	12	8	0	2	6-0	9	4.40	104	.226	.323	0	ø	0	141	0	0	0.0
2002	Tor A	0	1	.000	2	0	0	0-0	1	4	2	0	0	3-1	0	18.00	26	.571	.700	0	ø	0	—	-1	0	-0.2
Total	3	1	1	.500	10	2	0	0-0	19.1	21	14	1	3	14-1	11	6.05	77	.273	.400	0	ø	0	119	-3	0	-0.3

YEAR	TM LG	W	L	PCT	G	GS	CG-SHO	SV-BS	IP	H	R	HR	HB	BB-IB	SO	ERA	AERA	OAV	OOB	AB-HR-SH	AVG	PB	SUP	APR	DL	PW
Cocreham, Gene	Eugene; B11.14.1884 Luling TX; D12.27.1945 Luling TX; BR/TR/6´3.5˝/192; d9.25																									
1913	Bos N	0	1	.000	1	1	0	0	8.1	13	7	0	1	4	3	7.56	43	.371	.450	4	.000	-1	138	-3	—	-0.3
1914	Bos N	3	4	.429	15	3	1	0	44.2	48	30	2	0	27	15	4.84	57	.296	.397	10-0-1	.100	-0	112	-10	—	-1.6
1915	Bos N	0	0	ø	1	0	0	0	1.2	3	2	0	0	0	0	5.40	48	.429	.429	0	ø	0	—	-1	—	-0.1
Total	3	3	5	.375	17	4	1	0	54.2	64	39	2	1	31	18	5.27	54	.314	.407	14-0-1	.071	-1	121	-14	—	-2.0
Codiroli, Chris	Christopher Allen; B3.26.1958 Oxnard CA; BR/TR/6´1˝/(160–165); [DetA78*1/11]; d9.11; Col San Jose St.																									
1982	Oak A	1	2	.333	3	3	0	0-0	16.2	16	8	1	0	4-0	5	4.32	92	.246	.290	0	ø	0	46	0	0	0.0
1983	Oak A	12	12	.500	37	31	7-2	1-0	205.2	208	115	17	7	72-4	85	4.46	87	.264	.328	0	ø	0	109	-14	0	-1.6
1984	Oak A	6	4	.600	28	14	1	1-1	89.1	111	67	16	3	34-4	44	5.84	65	.304	.366	0	ø	0	113	-23	0	-2.3
1985	Oak A	14	14	.500	37	**37**	4	0-0	226	228	125	23	3	78-2	111	4.46	87	.259	.318	0	ø	0	112	-16	0	-1.8
1986	Oak A	5	8	.385	16	16	1	0-0	91.2	91	54	15	2	38-2	43	4.03	97	.250	.323	0	ø	0	112	-6	100	-0.7
1987	Oak A	0	2	.000	3	3	0	0-0	11.1	12	11	1	1	8-0	4	8.74	48	.273	.396	0	ø	0	95	-6	0	-0.7
1988	Cle A	0	4	.000	14	2	0	1-1	19.1	32	22	2	3	10-2	12	9.31	44	.372	.455	0	ø	0	55	-11	0	-2.0
1990	KC A	0	1	.000	6	2	0	0-0	10.1	13	11	1	4	17-1	8	9.58	40	.325	.557	0	ø	0	12	-6	0	-0.5
Total	8	38	47	.447	144	108	13-2	3-2	670.1	711	413	76	23	261-15	312	4.87	80	.270	.339	0	ø	0	106	-82	100	-9.6
Coffey, Todd	Justin Todd; B9.9.1980 Shelby NC; BR/TR/6´5˝/230; [CinN98 41/1220]; d4.19																									
2005	Cin N	4	1	.800	57	0	0	1-1	58	84	33	5	5	11-2	26	4.50	95	.344	.382	3	.000	-0	—	-2	0	-0.3
2006	Cin N	6	7	.462	81	0	0	8-4	78	85	34	7	2	27-5	60	3.58	132	.274	.335	0	ø	0	—	9	0	1.5
Total	2	10	8	.556	138	0	0	9-5	136	169	67	12	7	38-7	86	3.97	114	.305	.355	3	.000	-0	—	7	0	1.2
Coffman, Slick	George David; B12.11.1910 Veto AL; D5.8.2003 Birmingham AL; BR/TR/6´0˝/155; d5.21; b–Dick																									
1937	Det A	7	5	.583	28	5	1	0	101	121	61	8	3	39	22	4.37	107	.295	.361	29-0-4	.172	0	116	1	—	0.1
1938	Det A	4	4	.500	39	6	1	2	95.2	120	70	6	0	48	31	6.02	83	.310	.386	24-0-1	.167	-0	103	-10	—	-0.8
1939	Det A	2	1	.667	23	1	0	0	42.1	51	36	4	1	22	10	6.38	77	.295	.378	5	.000	-0	126	-7	—	-0.5
1940	StL A	2	2	.500	31	4	1	1	74.2	108	62	5	0	23	26	6.27	73	.334	.379	15-0-2	.200	-0*	101	-15	—	-0.7
Total	4	15	12	.556	121	16	3	3	313.2	400	229	23	4	132	89	5.60	85	.309	.375	73-0-7	.164	-0	108	-31	—	-1.9
Coffman, Kevin	Kevin Reese; B1.19.1965 Austin TX; BR/TR/6´2˝/(175–206); [AtlN83 11/282]; d9.5																									
1987	Atl N	2	3	.400	5	5	0	0-0	25.1	31	14	2	3	22-0	14	4.62	94	.313	.448	10	.100	-0	63	0	0	-0.1
1988	Atl N	2	6	.250	18	11	0	0-0	67	62	52	3	4	54-2	24	5.78	63	.251	.390	22-0-1	.227	2*	90	-16	0	-1.6
1990	Chi N	0	2	.000	8	2	0	0-0	18.1	26	24	0	0	19-0	9	11.29	36	.333	.459	5	.200	0	99	-13	0	-1.2
Total	3	4	11	.267	31	18	0	0-0	110.2	119	90	5	7	95-2	47	6.42	60	.281	.416	37-0-1	.189	1	83	-29	0	-2.9
Coffman, Dick	Samuel Richard; B12.18.1906 Veto AL; D3.24.1972 Athens AL; BR/TR/6´2˝/195; d4.28; b–Slick																									
1927	Was A	0	1	.000	5	2	0	0	16	20	9	0	2	2	5	3.38	120	.313	.353	3-0-1	.333	0	62	0	—	0.1
1928	StL A	4	5	.444	29	7	3	1	85.2	122	68	7	1	37	25	6.09	69	.359	.423	23-0-2	.043	-3	95	-18	—	-1.9
1929	StL A	1	1	.500	27	3	1-1	1	52.2	61	40	3	3	14	11	5.98	74	.295	.348	7	.000	-1	70	-9	—	-0.5
1930	StL A	8	18	.308	38	30	12-1	1	196	250	134	14	5	69	54	5.14	95	.311	.369	66-0-2	.136	-5	78	-8	—	-1.3
1931	StL A	9	13	.409	32	17	11-2	1	169.1	159	81	10	2	51	39	3.88	119	.241	.298	51-0-6	.078	-5	72	16	—	1.3
1932	StL A	5	3	.625	9	6	3-1	0	61	66	24	3	2	21	14	3.10	157	.277	.341	22	.045	-2	85	11	—	1.1
	Was A	1	6	.143	22	9	2	0	76.1	92	45	2	1	31	17	4.83	89	.307	.373	22	.091	-1	88	-4	—	-0.4
	Year	6	9	.400	31	15	5-1	0	137.1	158	69	5	3	52	31	4.06	112	.294	.359	44	.068	-3	86	10	—	0.7
1933	StL A	3	7	.300	21	13	3-1	1	81	114	57	9	2	39	19	5.89	79	.329	.399	27	.037	-3	86	-9	—	-1.2
1934	StL A	9	10	.474	40	21	6-1	3	173	212	112	11	1	59	55	4.53	110	.303	.358	51-0-5	.216	-1	71	5	—	0.4
1935	StL A	5	11	.313	41	18	5	2	143.2	206	116	14	2	46	34	6.14	78	.335	.383	41-0-4	.146	-1	87	-21	—	-2.1
1936	†NY N	7	5	.583	42	2	0	7	101.2	119	53	7	2	23	26	3.90	100	.296	.337	20-0-1	.200	-0	0	-1	—	-0.1
1937	†NY N	8	3	.727	42	1	0	3	80	93	36	4	4	31	30	3.04	128	.289	.359	19	.368	2	222	**6**	—	1.0
1938	NY N	8	4	.667	**51**	3	1-1	**12**	111.1	116	50	3	3	21	21	3.48	108	.268	.306	28	.071	-3	67	4	—	0.1
1939	NY N	1	2	.333	28	0	0	3	38	50	18	1	3	6	9	3.08	128	.316	.353	4	.000	-1	—	2	—	0.1
1940	Bos N	1	5	.167	31	0	0	3	48.1	63	33	4	2	11	11	5.40	69	.323	.365	12	.083	-1	—	-9	—	-1.3
1945	Phi N	2	1	.667	14	0	0	0	26.1	39	18	0	0	2	2	5.13	75	.351	.363	4	.250	0	—	-4	0	-0.3
Total	15	72	95	.431	472	132	47-8	38	1460.1	1782	894	92	35	463	372	4.65	96	.302	.357	400-0-21	.127	-22	83	-39	0	-5.0
Cogan, Tony	Anthony Michael; B12.21.1976 Chicago IL; BL/TL/6´2˝/205; [KCA99 12/361]; d4.2; Col Stanford																									
2001	KC A	0	4	.000	39	0	0	0-2	24.2	32	17	7	5	13-0	17	5.84	85	.320	.420	0	ø	0	—	-2	0	-0.3
Cogan, Dick	Richard Henry; B12.5.1871 Paterson NJ; D5.2.1948 Paterson NJ; BR/TR/5´7˝/150; d5.10																									
1897	Bal N	0	0	ø	1	0	0	0	2	4	3	0	1	2	0	13.50	31	.400	.538	1	.000	-0	—	-2	—	-0.1
1899	Chi N	2	3	.400	5	5	5	0	44	54	32	1	4	24	9	4.30	87	.302	.396	25-0-1	.200	1*	92	-3	—	-0.2
1900	NY N	0	0	ø	2	0	0	0	8	10	6	0	0	6	1	6.75	54	.303	.410	8	.125	-0*	—	-2	—	-0.1
Total	3	2	3	.400	8	5	5	0	54	68	41	1	5	32	10	5.00	75	.306	.405	34-0-1	.176	0	92	-7	—	-0.4
Coggin, David	David Raymond; B10.30.1976 Covina CA; BR/TR/6´4˝/205; [PhiN95 1/30]; d6.23; [DL 2003 Phi N 183]																									
2000	Phi N	2	0	1.000	5	5	0	0-0	27	35	20	2	1	12-0	17	5.33	86	.315	.387	7-0-1	.000	-1	160	-4	0	-0.3
2001	Phi N	6	7	.462	17	17	0	0-0	95	99	46	7	5	39-6	62	4.17	99	.272	.348	33-0-1	.061	-1	78	0	0	-0.1
2002	Phi N	2	5	.286	38	7	0	0-0	77	65	42	4	4	51-3	64	4.68	82	.231	.355	8-0-2	.000	-1	86	-7	0	-0.7
Total	3	10	12	.455	60	29	0	0-0	199	199	108	13	10	102-9	143	4.52	90	.263	.356	48-0-4	.042	-3	97	-11	183	-1.1
Cohen, Hy	Hyman; B1.29.1931 Brooklyn NY; BR/TR/6´5˝/215; d4.17																									
1955	Chi N	0	0	ø	7	1	0	0	17	28	17	2	1	10-0	4	7.94	51	.378	.459	3	.000	-0	174	-7	0	-0.4
Cohen, Syd	Sydney Harry; B5.7.1906 Baltimore MD; D4.9.1988 ElPaso TX; BB/TL/5´11˝/180; d9.18; b–Andy; Col SMU																									
1934	Was A	1	1	.500	3	2	2	0	18	25	15	2	0	6	6	7.50	58	.333	.383	11	.273	0*	91	-6	—	-0.4
1936	Was A	0	2	.000	19	1	0	1	36	44	27	4	3	14	21	5.25	91	.303	.377	8	.000	-1	111	-3	—	-0.2
1937	Was A	2	4	.333	33	0	0	4	55	64	30	1	0	17	22	3.11	142	.299	.351	14	.143	-1	—	5	—	0.6
Total	3	3	7	.300	55	3	2	5	109	133	72	7	3	37	49	4.54	100	.306	.365	33	.152	-2	97	-4	—	0.0
Colbert, Vince	Vincent Norman; B12.20.1945 Washington DC; BR/TR/6´4˝/200; [CleA68 11/234]; d5.19; Col East Carolina																									
1970	Cle A	1	1	.500	23	0	0	2-1	31	37	25	4	1	16-2	17	7.26	55	.298	.380	2	.000	-0	—	-10	0	-0.7
1971	Cle A	7	6	.538	50	10	2	2-1	142.2	140	71	11	6	71-9	74	3.97	97	.265	.355	29-0-2	.138	-0*	63	-2	0	-0.2
1972	Cle A	1	7	.125	22	11	1-1	0-0	74.2	74	42	8	7	38-5	36	4.58	71	.267	.365	20-0-1	.200	1*	77	-10	0	-1.0
Total	3	9	14	.391	95	21	3-1	4-2	248.1	251	138	23	14	125-16	127	4.57	81	.270	.361	51-0-3	.157	0	67	-22	0	-1.9
Colborn, Jim	James William; B5.22.1946 Santa Paula CA; BR/TR/6´0˝/(185–191); d7.13; C6; Col Whittier																									
1969	Chi N	1	0	1.000	6	2	0	0-0	14.2	15	6	2	1	9-1	4	3.07	131	.283	.397	3	.000	-0	88	1	0	0.1
1970	Chi N	3	1	.750	34	5	0	4-3	72.2	88	37	3	1	23-6	50	3.59	125	.298	.347	15-0-1	.067	-1	147	5	0	0.2
1971	Chi N	0	1	.000	14	0	0	0-0	10.1	18	8	1	0	3-0	2	6.97	56	.383	.420	0	ø	0	—	-3	0	-0.2
1972	Mil A	7	7	.500	39	12	4-1	0-0	147.2	135	53	14	2	43-7	97	3.11	99	.245	.300	37-0-2	.081	-1	99	1	0	-0.1
1973	Mil A☆	20	12	.625	43	36	22-4	1-0	314.1	297	133	21	3	87-5	135	3.18	120	.251	.302	0	ø	0	109	19	0	1.9
1974	Mil A	10	13	.435	33	31	10-1	0-0	224	230	104	27	6	60-4	83	4.06	90	.268	.319	0	ø	0	93	-8	0	-0.8
1975	Mil A	11	13	.458	36	29	8-1	2-0	206.1	215	111	18	5	65-5	79	4.27	90	.270	.327	0	ø	0	109	-9	0	-0.9
1976	Mil A	9	15	.375	32	32	7	0-0	225.2	232	97	20	2	54-9	101	3.71	95	.268	.310	0	ø	0	87	-1	0	-0.2
1977	KC A	18	14	.563	36	35	6-1	0-0	239	233	106	22	13	81-2	103	3.62	112	.255	.323	0	ø	0*	109	12	0	1.6
1978	KC A	1	2	.333	8	3	0	0-0	28.1	31	18	4	2	12-1	8	4.76	80	.282	.363	0	ø	0	86	-3	0	-0.3
	Sea A	3	10	.231	20	19	3	0-0	114.1	125	77	21	6	38-1	26	5.35	72	.279	.341	0	ø	0	85	-19	0	-1.8
	Year	4	12	.250	28	22	3	0-0	142.2	156	95	25	8	50-2	34	5.24	73	.280	.345	0	ø	0	85	-22	0	-2.1
Total	10	83	88	.485	301	204	60-8	7-3	1597.1	1619	750	153	41	475-41	688	3.80	99	.265	.320	55-0-3	.073	-3	102	-5	0	-0.5
Colcolough, Tom	Thomas Bernard; B10.8.1870 Charleston SC; D12.10.1919 Charleston SC; BR/TR/5´10.5˝/180; d8.1																									
1893	Pit N	1	0	1.000	8	3	1	**2**	43.2	45	30	1	0	32	7	4.12	110	.259	.374	14	.143	0	113	2	—	0.1
1894	Pit N	8	5	.615	23	14	11	0	150.2	213	147	5	5	72	29	7.23	73	.329	.401	70-0-1	.200	-3	129	-28	—	-1.8
1895	Pit N	1	1	.500	7	6	3	0	43.1	54	49	1	3	5	21	6.65	68	.300	.388	17-0-1	.294	3*	140	-11	—	-0.3
1899	NY N	4	5	.444	11	8	7	0	81.2	85	49	3	3	41	14	3.97	95	.268	.357	37	.270	1*	101	-1	—	0.0
Total	4	14	11	.560	49	31	22	2	319.1	397	275	10	13	166	66	5.89	79	.301	.385	138-0-2	.225	1	123	-38	—	-2.0

YEAR	TM LG	W	L	PCT	G	GS	CG-SHO	SV-BS	IP	H	R	HR	HB	BB-IB	SO	ERA	AERA	OAV	OOB	AB-HR-SH	AVG	PB	SUP	APR	DL	PW
COLE, BERT	Albert George; B7.1.1896 San Francisco CA; D5.30.1975 San Mateo CA; BL/TL/6´1˝/180; d4.19																									
1921	Det A	7	4	.636	20	11	7-1	1	109.2	134	66	3	4	36	22	4.27	100	.305	.363	46-0-3	.283	3*	115	0	—	0.2
1922	Det A	1	6	.143	23	5	2-1	0	79.1	105	60	4	1	39	21	4.88	80	.313	.387	25	.160	-1*	92	-13	—	-1.0
1923	Det A	13	5	.722	52	13	6-1	5	163	183	95	9	5	61	32	4.14	93	.284	.351	55-1-1	.255	2*	161	-8	—	-0.6
1924	Det A	3	9	.250	28	12	2-1	2	109.1	135	69	4	4	35	16	4.69	88	.314	.371	37-0-2	.270	1*	82	-7	—	-0.5
1925	Det A	2	3	.400	14	2	1	1	33.2	44	27	2	1	15	7	5.88	73	.336	.408	11	.273	0	146	-7	—	-0.8
	Cle A	1	1	.500	13	2	0	1	44	55	33	1	1	25	9	6.14	72	.322	.411	13	.154	-0	95	-7	—	-0.3
	Year	3	4	.429	27	4	1	2	77.2	99	60	3	2	40	16	6.03	73	.328	.410	24	.208	0	120	-12	—	-1.1
1927	Chi A	1	4	.200	27	2	0	0	66.2	79	43	3	3	19	12	4.72	86	.309	.363	18-0-2	.167	-1	93	-6	—	-0.4
Total	6	28	32	.467	177	47	18-4	10	605.2	735	393	26	19	230	119	4.67	87	.305	.370	205-1-8	.239	5	116	-48	—	-3.4
COLE, DAVE	David Bruce; B8.29.1930 Williamsport MD; BR/TR/6´2˝/175; d9.9																									
1950	Bos N	0	1	.000	4	0	0	0	8	7	2	0	1	3	8	1.13	342	.259	.355	1	.000	-0	—	2	0	0.2
1951	Bos N	2	4	.333	23	7	1	0	67.2	64	43	3	2	64	33	4.26	86	.254	.409	17-1-0	.353	4	117	-8	0	-0.2
1952	Bos N	1	1	.500	22	3	0	0	44.2	38	21	2	3	42	22	4.03	90	.241	.409	8	.000	-1	132	-2	0	-0.2
1953	Mil N	0	1	.000	10	0	0	0	14.2	17	14	1	0	14	13	8.59	46	.279	.413	2-1-0	.500	1	—	-7	0	-0.3
1954	Chi N	3	8	.273	18	14	2-1	0	84	74	56	7	1	62	37	5.36	78	.241	.365	28-1-1	.214	-1*	85	-11	49	-1.1
1955	Phi N	0	3	.000	7	3	0	0	18.1	21	15	3	0	14-0	6	6.38	62	.304	.412	5	.200	-0	82	-5	0	-0.7
Total	6	6	18	.250	84	27	3-1	0	237.1	221	151	16	7	199-0	119	4.93	79	.253	.393	61-3-1	.230	5	99	-31	49	-2.3
COLE, ED	Edward William (b Edward William Kisleauskas); B3.22.1909 Wilkes–Barre PA; D7.28.1999 Nashville TN; BR/TR/5´11˝/170; d4.22																									
1938	StL A	1	5	.167	36	6	1	3	88.2	116	69	8	5	48	26	5.18	96	.313	.399	21	.143	-1	97	-7	—	-0.6
1939	StL A	0	2	.000	6	0	0	0	6.1	8	7	1	0	6	5	7.11	68	.308	.438	1	.000	-0	—	-2	—	-0.4
Total	2	1	7	.125	42	6	1	3	95	124	76	9	5	54	31	5.31	94	.312	.401	22	.136	-2	97	-9	—	-1.0
COLE, KING	Leonard Leslie; B4.15.1886 Toledo IA; D1.6.1916 Bay City MI; BR/TR/6´1˝/170; d10.6																									
1909	Chi N	1	0	1.000	1	1	1-1	0	9	6	0	0	0	3	1	0.00	ø	.194	.265	4	.750	2	220	3	—	0.7
1910	†Chi N	20	4	**.833**	33	29	21-4	1	239.2	174	64	2	9	130	114	1.80	**160**	**.211**	.325	91-0-5	.231	2*	138	29	—	3.1
1911	Chi N	18	7	.720	32	27	13-2	0	221.1	188	87	3	9	99	101	3.13	106	.236	.328	79-0-3	.152	-2	120	10	—	0.8
1912	Chi N	1	2	.333	8	3	0	0	19	36	26	2	2	8	9	10.89	31	.409	.469	5	.400	1	147	-15	—	-1.8
	Pit N	2	2	.500	12	5	2	0	49	61	42	1	2	18	11	6.43	51	.330	.395	15-0-1	.133	-1	180	-17	—	-1.2
	Year	3	4	.429	20	8	2	0	68	97	68	3	4	26	20	7.68	43	.355	.419	20-0-1	.200	0	168	-32	—	-3.0
1914	NY A	10	9	.526	33	15	8-2	0	141.2	151	63	3	1	51	43	3.30	84	.288	.352	42-0-2	.048	-3	90	-8	—	-1.5
1915	NY A	2	3	.400	10	6	2	1	51	41	27	2	3	22	19	3.18	92	.224	.317	13-0-2	.077	-1	87	-3	—	-0.4
Total	6	54	27	.667	129	86	47-9	2	730.2	657	309	13	26	331	298	3.12	97	.250	.340	249-0-13	.173	-2	125	-1	—	-0.3
COLE, VICTOR	Victor Alexander; B1.23.1968 Leningrad, USSR; BB/TR/5´10˝/160; [KCA88 14/361]; d6.6; Col Santa Clara																									
1992	Pit N	0	2	.000	8	4	0	0-0	23	23	14	1	0	14-0	12	5.48	63	.261	.359	4-0-1	.000	-0	72	-5	0	-0.4
COLEMAN, JOHN	John Francis; B3.6.1863 Saratoga Springs NY; D5.31.1922 Detroit MI; BL/TR (BB 1887)/5´9.5˝/170; d5.1; Col Syracuse; ▲																									
1883	Phi N	12	48	.200	65	61	59-3	0	538.1	772	510	17	—	48	159	4.87	63	.309	.322	354	.234	4*	82	-110	—	-8.5
1884	Phi N	5	15	.250	21	19	14-1	0	154.1	216	147	9	—	22	37	4.90	61	.308	.329	171	.246	2*	78	-29	—	-2.6
	Phi AA	0	2	.000	3	2	2	0	21	28	14	0	4	2	5	3.43	99	.304	.347	107-2	.206	0*	36	-1	—	0.0
1885	Phi AA	2	2	.500	8	3	3	0	60.1	82	46	0	0	5	12	3.43	100	.366	.380	398-3	.299	2*	92	0	—	0.2
1886	Phi AA	1	1	.500	3	1	1	0	20.2	18	9	1	1	5	2	2.61	134	.225	.279	492	.246	0*	85	2	—	0.2
1889	Phi AA	3	2	.600	5	5	4	0	34	38	23	2	1	14	6	2.91	130	.273	.344	19	.053	-2*	144	2	—	0.0
1890	Pit N	0	2	.000	2	2	1	0	14	28	23	1	0	6	3	9.64	34	.400	.447	11	.182	0*	105	-10	—	-0.9
Total	6	23	72	.242	107	93	84-4	0	842.2	1182	772	30	6	102	224	4.68	67	.311	.330	1552-5	.251	7	84	-146	—	-11.6
COLEMAN, JOHN	John W.; B1.29.1860 Philadelphia PA; D1.27.1915 Bristol PA; TR; d6.23																									
1890	Phi N	0	1	.000	1	1	0	0	1.2	4	8	0	0	3	2	21.60	17	.444	.583	0	ø	0	207	-4	—	-0.5
COLEMAN, JOE	Joseph Howard; B2.3.1947 Boston MA; BR/TR/6´3˝/(170–195); [TexA65 1/3]; d9.28; C11; f–Joe																									
1965	Was A	2	0	1.000	2	2	2	0	18	9	3	0	0	8-0	7	1.50	232	.153	.254	6-0-1	.000	-1	114	4	0	0.5
1966	Was A	1	0	1.000	1	1	1	0	9	6	2	0	0	2-0	4	2.00	173	.188	.235	3	.000	-0	76	2	0	0.2
1967	Was A	8	9	.471	28	22	3	0	134	154	78	6	9	47-4	77	4.63	68	.291	.355	36-0-5	.056	-1	120	-22	0	-2.8
1968	Was A	12	16	.429	33	33	12-2	0	223	212	98	18	12	51-3	139	3.27	89	.250	.299	70-0-6	.129	-1*	92	-11	0	-1.6
1969	Was A	12	13	.480	40	36	12-4	1-2	247.2	222	102	26	6	100-7	182	3.27	107	.243	.320	84-0-4	.107	-3	100	7	0	0.5
1970	Was A	8	12	.400	39	29	6-1	0-1	218.2	190	98	25	4	89-6	152	3.58	101	.233	.309	67-0-4	.119	2	95	0	0	0.3
1971	Det A	20	9	.690	39	38	16-3	0-0	286	241	106	17	7	96-3	236	3.15	115	.229	.296	96-0-9	.094	-3	108	16	15	1.1
1972	†Det A✱	19	14	.576	40	39	9-3	0-0	280	216	99	23	9	110-7	222	2.80	113	.214	.296	82-0-15	.110	-3	106	11	0	0.9
1973	Det A	23	15	.605	40	40	13-2	0-0	288.1	283	125	32	10	93-2	202	3.53	116	.258	.321	0	ø	0	87	16	0	1.9
1974	Det A	14	12	.538	41	41	11-2	0-0	285.2	272	160	30	12	158-13	177	4.32	89	.254	.355	0	ø	0	100	-16	0	-1.3
1975	Det A	10	18	.357	31	31	6-1	0-0	201	234	137	27	9	85-6	125	5.55	73	.291	.363	0	ø	0	87	-28	0	-3.4
1976	Det A	2	5	.286	12	12	1	0-0	66.2	80	44	1	5	34-0	38	4.86	77	.308	.395	0	ø	0	100	-9	0	-0.8
	Chi N	2	8	.200	39	4	0	4-4	79	72	43	9	2	35-8	66	4.10	95	.246	.327	13	.154	-0	51	-3	0	-0.4
1977	Oak A	4	4	.500	43	12	2	2-2	127.2	114	51	11	2	49-2	55	2.96	136	.241	.313	0	ø	0	124	14	0	0.8
1978	Oak A	3	0	1.000	10	0	0	0-0	19.2	12	3	1	0	5-0	4	1.37	267	.185	.239	0	ø	0	—	5	0	0.8
	Tor A	2	0	1.000	31	0	0	0-1	60.2	67	34	6	1	30-3	28	4.60	86	.286	.364	0	ø	0	—	-4	0	-0.3
	Year	5	0	1.000	41	0	0	0-1	80.1	79	37	7	1	35-3	32	3.81	102	.264	.338	0	ø	0	—	1	0	0.5
1979	SF N	0	0	ø	5	0	0	0-0	3.2	3	2	0	1	2-0	0	0.00	ø	.231	.353	0	ø	0	—	1	0	0.0
	Pit N	0	0	ø	10	0	0	0-0	20.2	29	17	1	1	9-1	14	6.10	64	.326	.390	5	.200	0	—	-5	0	-0.3
	Year	0	0	ø	15	0	0	0-0	24.1	32	19	1	2	11-1	14	5.18	74	.314	.385	5	.200	0	—	-5	0	-0.3
Total	15	142	135	.513	484	340	94-18	7-10	2569.1	2416	1202	233	90	1003-65	1728	3.70	98	.250	.324	462-0-44	.106	-10	98	-22	15	-3.9
COLEMAN, JOE	Joseph Patrick; B7.30.1922 Medford MA; D4.9.1997 Ft.Myers FL; BR/TR/6´2.5˝/(193–200); d9.19; Mil 1943–45; s–Joe; Col Boston College																									
1942	Phi A	0	1	.000	1	0	0	0	6	8	5	0	0	1	0	3.00	126	.308	.333	4	.000	-1	—	-1	0	-0.1
1946	Phi A	0	2	.000	4	2	0	0	13	19	8	1	0	8	8	5.54	64	.345	.429	5	.400	1	97	-2	0	-0.3
1947	Phi A	6	12	.333	32	21	9-2	1	160.1	171	84	17	0	62	65	4.32	88	.275	.341	48-0-3	.146	-1	65	-8	0	-1.0
1948	Phi A★	14	13	.519	33	29	13-3	0	215.2	224	105	11	1	90	86	4.09	105	.269	.341	74-0-6	.122	-4	95	6	0	0.2
1949	Phi A	13	14	.481	33	30	18-1	1	240.1	249	119	12	3	127	109	3.86	107	.271	.361	79-1-7	.177	0	80	6	0	0.4
1950	Phi A	0	5	.000	15	6	2	0	54	74	54	9	0	50	12	8.50	54	.332	.454	17-1-0	.059	-1	83	-23	0	-1.8
1951	Phi A	1	6	.143	28	9	1	1	96.1	117	69	12	3	59	34	5.98	72	.305	.402	27-0-1	.259	1	108	-17	0	-1.0
1953	Phi A	3	4	.429	21	9	2-1	0	90	85	46	8	1	49	18	4.00	107	.254	.352	28	.286	1	78	2	0	0.2
1954	Bal A	13	17	.433	33	32	15-4	0	221.1	184	102	16	3	96	103	3.50	102	.232	.315	74-2-4	.176	2	75	0	0	0.3
1955	Bal A	0	1	.000	6	2	0	0	11.2	19	15	5	1	10-0	4	10.80	35	.373	.469	3	.667	1	116	-9	32	-0.5
	Det A	2	1	.667	17	0	0	3	25.1	22	9	1	1	14-0	5	3.20	120	.239	.346	4-0-1	.750	1	—	2	0	0.5
	Year	2	2	.500	23	2	0	3	37	41	24	6	2	24-0	9	5.59	69	.287	.392	7-0-1	.714	3	116	-6	0	0.0
Total	10	52	76	.406	223	140	60-11	6	1134	1172	616	92	13	566-0	444	4.38	92	.271	.356	363-4-22	.182	2	82	-44	32	-3.1
COLEMAN, PERCY	Pierce Devon; B10.15.1876 Mason OH; D2.16.1948 Van Nuys CA; TR; d7.2																									
1897	StL N	1	2	.333	13	5	3	0	66.1	108	76	0	8	33	10	7.19	61	.362	.440	31	.226	-1	133	-21	—	-0.9
1898	Cin N	0	1	.000	1	1	1	0	9	13	7	0	1	3	2	3.00	128	.333	.395	3	.000	-1	56	0	—	-0.1
Total	2	1	3	.250	14	6	4	0	75.1	121	83	0	9	36	12	6.69	65	.359	.435	34	.206	-1	120	-21	—	-1.0
COLEMAN, RIP	Walter Gary; B7.31.1931 Troy NY; D5.14.2004 Wolfeboro NH; BL/TL/6´2˝/185; d8.15; Col Syracuse																									
1955	†NY A	2	1	.667	10	6	0	1	29	40	19	2	1	16-0	15	5.28	71	.331	.413	10-0-1	.200	1	135	-5	0	-0.4
1956	NY A	3	5	.375	29	9	0	2	88.1	97	42	6	1	42-1	42	3.67	105	.285	.363	24-0-2	.042	-3	153	2	0	-0.1
1957	KC A	0	7	.000	19	6	1-1	0	41	53	32	5	0	25-0	15	5.93	67	.325	.408	9-0-1	.000	-1	64	-9	0	-1.5
1959	KC A	2	10	.167	29	11	2	2	81	85	46	8	1	34-0	54	4.56	88	.273	.345	25-0-1	.080	-2	78	-4	0	-0.8
	Bal A	0	0	ø	3	0	0	0	4	4	0	0	0	2-0	4	0.00	ø	.267	.353	0	ø	0	—	2	0	0.1
	Year	2	10	.167	32	11	2	2	85	89	46	8	1	36-0	58	4.34	92	.273	.345	25-0-1	.080	-2	78	-3	0	-0.7
1960	Bal A	0	2	.000	5	1	0	0	4	8	5	0	1	5-1	0	11.25	34	.444	.583	1	.000	-0	46	-3	0	-0.6
Total	5	7	25	.219	95	33	3-1	5	247.1	287	144	21	4	124-2	130	4.58	85	.296	.376	69-0-5	.072	-5	104	-17	0	-3.3

YEAR	TM LG	W	L	PCT	G	GS	CG-SHO	SV-BS	IP	H	R	HR	HB	BB-IB	SO	ERA	AERA	OAV	OOB	AB-HR-SH	AVG	PB	SUP	APR	DL	PW
COLEMAN, WALTER	Walter Lee; B6.13.1873 Lees Summit MO; D11.20.1925 Bunceton MO; TL/5´10˝/174; d9.25																									
1895	StL N	0	1	.000	1	1	1	0	8	12	15	1	1	8	5	13.50	36	.343	.477	5	.200	-0	118	-7	—	-0.5
COLLAMORE, ALLAN	Allan Edward; B6.5.1887 Worcester MA; D8.8.1980 Battle Creek MI; BR/TR/6´0˝/170; d4.15																									
1911	Phi A	0	1	.000	2	0	0	0	2	6	9	0	2	3	1	36.00	9	.600	.733	0	ø	0	—	-7	—	-1.1
1914	Cle A	3	7	.300	27	8	3	0	105.1	100	52	3	6	49	32	3.25	89	.264	.357	32-0-1	.094	-2	73	-3	—	-0.6
1915	Cle A	2	5	.286	11	6	5-2	0	64.1	52	22	1	0	22	15	2.38	128	.235	.305	23	.174	0*	72	5	—	0.6
Total	3	5	13	.278	40	14	8-2	0	171.2	158	83	4	8	74	48	3.30	89	.259	.347	55-0-1	.127	-2	72	-5	—	-1.1
COLLARD, HAP	Earl Clinton; B8.29.1898 Williams AZ; D7.9.1968 Jamestown CA; BR/TR/6´0˝/170; d4.23																									
1927	Cle A	0	0	ø	4	0	0	0	5.1	8	7	0	0	3	2	5.06	83	.333	.407	0	ø	0	—	-2	—	-0.1
1928	Cle A	0	0	ø	1	0	0	0	4	4	3	0	0	4	1	2.25	184	.250	.400	1	1.000	0	—	0	—	0.0
1930	Phi N	6	12	.333	30	15	4	0	127	188	106	15	3	39	25	6.80	80	.350	.397	44	.205	-2*	88	-15	—	-1.7
Total	3	6	12	.333	35	15	4	0	136.1	200	116	15	3	46	28	6.60	81	.347	.398	45	.222	-1	88	-17	—	-1.8
COLLIER, ORLIN	Orlin Edward; B2.17.1907 E.Prairie MO; D9.9.1944 Memphis TN; BR/TR/5´11.5˝/180; d9.11; Col U. of Mississippi																									
1931	Det A	0	1	.000	2	2	0	0	10.1	17	12	0	0	7	3	7.84	59	.362	.444	3	.000	-0	83	-4	—	-0.4
COLLIFLOWER, HARRY	James Harry "Collie"; B3.11.1869 Petersville MD; D8.12.1961 Washington DC; BL/TL/5´11.5˝/175; d7.21; U1																									
1899	Cle N	1	11	.083	14	12	11	0	98	152	122	6	11	41	8	8.17	45	.353	.422	76	.303	2*	85	-50	—	-4.1
COLLINS, DAN	Daniel Thomas; B7.12.1854 St.Louis MO; D9.21.1883 New Orleans LA; d6.8; ▲																									
1874	Chi NA	1	1	.500	2	2	1	0	11	22	17	0	—	2	0	4.91	45	.386	.407	12	.083	-1*	59	-3	—	-0.4
COLLINS, DON	Donald Edward; B9.15.1952 Lyons GA; BR/TL/6´2˝/195; [AtlN72 S2/30]; d5.4; Col South Georgia JC																									
1977	Atl N	3	9	.250	40	6	0	2-1	70.2	82	43	8	1	41-8	27	5.09	87	.299	.389	11-0-1	.000	-1	47	-3	0	-0.7
1980	Cle A	0	0	ø	4	0	0	0-0	6	9	5	0	0	7-1	0	7.50	55	.346	.485	0	ø	0	—	-2	0	-0.1
Total	2	3	9	.250	44	6	0	2-1	76.2	91	48	8	1	48-9	27	5.28	84	.303	.398	11-0-1	.000	-1	47	-5	0	-0.8
COLLINS, RIP	Harry Warren; B2.26.1896 Weatherford TX; D5.27.1968 Bryan TX; BR/TR (BB 1920–23)/6´1˝/205; d4.19; Col Texas A&M																									
1920	NY A	14	8	.636	36	18	10-2	1	187.1	171	83	6	14	79	66	3.22	119	.247	.337	62-0-8	.129	-4	109	12	—	0.9
1921	†NY A	11	5	.688	28	16	7-2	0	137.1	158	103	6	10	78	64	5.44	78	.293	.392	56-0-2	.196	-1	128	-19	—	-2.0
1922	Bos A	14	11	.560	32	29	15-3	0	210.2	219	101	4	10	103	69	3.76	109	.274	.364	76-0-1	.158	-3*	86	9	—	0.6
1923	Det A	3	7	.300	17	14	3-1	0	92.1	104	61	3	10	22	25	4.87	79	.284	.342	27-0-2	.111	-2	99	-11	—	-1.2
1924	Det A	14	7	.667	34	30	11-1	0	216	199	99	6	4	63	75	3.21	128	.249	.307	76-0-5	.145	-5*	117	20	—	1.2
1925	Det A	6	11	.353	26	20	5	0	140	149	86	7	6	52	33	4.56	94	.281	.352	42-0-2	.119	-4	88	-5	—	-0.7
1926	Det A	8	8	.500	30	13	5-3	1	122	128	53	4	7	44	44	2.73	149	.278	.350	39-0-1	.154	-1*	105	15	—	1.7
1927	Det A	13	7	.650	30	25	10-1	0	172.2	207	116	5	8	59	37	4.69	90	.312	.375	54-0-7	.204	0	126	-10	—	-0.8
1929	StL A	11	6	.647	26	20	10-1	1	155.1	162	79	16	6	73	47	4.00	111	.270	.355	62-1-1	.274	4	120	7	—	1.1
1930	StL A	9	7	.563	35	20	6-1	2	171.2	168	90	11	5	63	75	4.35	112	.259	.330	54-0-4	.130	-2	89	12	—	0.7
1931	StL A	5	5	.500	17	14	2	0	107	130	55	5	1	38	34	3.79	122	.307	.366	34-0-2	.147	-1	82	9	—	0.8
Total	11	108	82	.568	311	219	84-15	5	1712.1	1795	926	73	81	674	569	3.99	106	.275	.351	582-1-35	.165	-18	105	39	—	2.3
COLLINS, PHIL	Philip Eugene "Fidgety Phil"; B8.27.1901 Chicago IL; D8.14.1948 Chicago IL; BR/TR/5´11˝/175; d10.7																									
1923	Chi N	1	0	1.000	1	1	0	0	5	8	2	0	0	1	2	3.60	111	.400	.429	2	.000	-0	205	0	—	0.1
1929	Phi N	9	7	.563	43	11	3	5	153.1	172	106	18	4	83	61	5.75	90	.284	.374	58-1-0	.190	-0*	125	-7	—	-0.7
1930	Phi N	16	11	.593	47	25	17-1	3	239	287	148	22	10	86	87	4.78	114	.299	.363	87-3-2	.253	3*	101	17	—	1.8
1931	Phi N	12	16	.429	42	27	16-2	4	240.1	268	126	14	5	83	73	3.86	110	.283	.344	95	.168	-4*	92	8	—	0.6
1932	Phi N	14	12	.538	43	21	6	3	184.1	231	117	21	6	65	66	5.27	84	.314	.375	68	.265	2	123	-12	—	-1.4
1933	Phi N	8	13	.381	42	13	5-1	**6**	151	178	79	9	6	57	40	4.11	93	.293	.360	53-0-1	.132	-2*	57	-4	—	-0.8
1934	Phi N	13	18	.419	45	32	15	1	254	277	138	30	3	87	72	4.18	113	.273	.333	88-0-7	.170	-5*	83	13	—	0.8
1935	Phi N	0	2	.000	3	3	0	0	14.2	24	20	5	0	9	4	11.66	39	.348	.423	6	.000	-1	94	-9	—	-1.0
	StL N	7	6	.538	26	9	2	2	82.2	96	48	6	3	26	18	4.57	90	.290	.347	25-0-4	.160	-1	129	-4	—	-0.7
	Year	7	8	.467	29	12	2	2	97.1	120	68	11	3	35	22	5.64	74	.300	.361	31-0-4	.129	-2	120	-13	—	-1.7
Total	8	80	85	.485	292	142	64-4	24	1324.1	1541	784	125	37	497	423	4.66	100	.291	.356	482-4-14	.193	-8	99	2	—	-1.3
COLLINS, RAY	Ray Williston; B2.11.1887 Colchester VT; D1.9.1970 Burlington VT; BL/TL/6´1˝/185; d7.19; Col Vermont																									
1909	Bos A	4	3	.571	12	8	4-2	0	73.2	70	29	2	0	18	31	2.81	89	.269	.317	23-0-1	.130	-0	120	-1	—	-0.1
1910	Bos A	13	11	.542	35	26	18-4	1	244.2	205	73	1	1	41	109	1.62	158	.229	.264	84-0-4	.179	-1	90	22	—	1.9
1911	Bos A	11	12	.478	31	24	14	1	194.2	184	81	1	4	44	86	2.40	136	.256	.302	60-0-3	.150	0	76	19	—	2.0
1912	†Bos A	13	8	.619	27	24	17-4	0	199.1	192	65	4	2	42	82	2.53	135	.256	.297	65-0-3	.169	0	118	22	—	2.1
1913	Bos A	19	8	.704	30	30	19-3	0	246.2	242	88	3	2	37	88	2.63	112	.264	.294	80-1-7	.150	2	108	12	—	1.3
1914	Bos A	20	13	.606	39	30	16-6	0	272.1	252	95	3	0	56	72	2.51	107	.258	.298	79-0-9	.139	-0	91	8	—	0.7
1915	Bos A	4	7	.364	25	9	2	2	104.2	101	62	1	1	31	43	4.30	65	.261	.317	28-0-1	.286	5	122	-17	—	-1.4
Total	7	84	62	.575	199	151	90-19	4	1336	1246	493	15	10	269	511	2.51	115	.254	.294	419-1-28	.165	6	100	65	—	6.5
COLLUM, JACKIE	Jack Dean; B6.21.1927 Victor IA; BL/TL/5´7˝/(160–167); d9.21																									
1951	StL N	2	1	.667	3	2	1-1	0	17	11	3	0	0	10	5	1.59	250	.204	.328	7	.429	1	111	5	0	1.0
1952	StL N	0	0	ø	2	0	0	0	3	2	1	0	0	1	0	0.00	ø	.200	.273	0	ø	0	—	1	0	0.1
1953	StL N	0	0	ø	7	0	0	0	11.1	15	10	1	0	4	5	6.35	67	.326	.380	3	.000	-0	—	-3	0	-0.1
	Cin N	7	11	.389	30	12	4-1	3	124.2	123	57	8	6	39	51	3.75	116	.263	.328	36-0-3	.278	3	92	9	0	1.5
	Year	7	11	.389	37	12	4-1	3	136	138	67	9	6	43	56	3.97	109	.269	.333	39-0-3	.256	2	92	5	0	1.4
1954	Cin N	7	3	.700	36	2	1	0	79	86	43	8	5	32	28	3.76	112	.283	.359	13-1-2	.231	2	106	1	0	0.4
1955	Cin N	9	8	.529	32	17	5	1	134	128	65	17	2	37-4	49	3.63	117	.254	.306	40-0-5	.250	2	131	7	0	1.1
1956	StL N	6	2	.750	38	1	0	7	60	63	29	6	2	27-6	17	4.20	90	.281	.358	14	.214	1	140	-1	0	-0.1
1957	Chi N	1	1	.500	9	0	0	1	10.2	8	8	0	1	9-1	7	6.75	57	.211	.367	0	ø	0	—	-3	0	-0.6
	Bro N	0	0	ø	3	0	0	0	4.1	7	4	1	0	1-0	3	8.31	50	.368	.381	0	ø	0	—	-2	0	-0.1
	Year	1	1	.500	12	0	0	1	15	15	12	1	1	10-1	10	7.20	55	.263	.371	0	ø	0	—	-5	0	-0.7
1958	LA N	0	0	ø	2	0	0	0	3.1	4	3	2	0	2-0	0	8.10	51	.308	.400	1	.000	-0	—	-1	0	-0.1
1962	Min A	0	2	.000	8	3	0	0	15.1	29	22	1	0	11-0	5	11.15	37	.414	.482	4	.000	-0	95	-12	0	-1.3
	Cle A	0	0	ø	1	0	0	0	1.1	4	2	0	0	0-0	1	13.50	29	.571	.571	0	ø	0	—	-1	0	-0.1
	Year	0	2	.000	9	3	0	0	16.2	33	24	1	0	11-0	6	11.34	36	.429	.489	4	.000	-0	95	-13	0	-1.4
Total	9	32	28	.533	171	37	11-2	12	464	480	247	44	16	173-11	171	4.15	101	.273	.342	118-1-10	.246	8	115	0	0	1.7
COLOME, JESUS	Jesus (De La Cruz); B12.23.1977 San Pedro de Macoris, D.R.; BR/TR/6´2˝/(170–205); d6.21																									
2001	TB A	2	3	.400	30	0	0	0-0	48.2	37	22	8	2	25-4	31	3.33	135	.208	.309	0	ø	0	—	6	0	0.4
2002	TB A	2	7	.222	32	0	0	0-5	41.1	56	41	6	2	33-5	33	8.27	55	.341	.455	0	ø	0	—	-17	0	-3.0
2003	TB A	3	7	.300	54	0	0	2-6	74	69	37	9	3	46-5	69	4.50	102	.247	.355	0	ø	0	—	2	0	0.3
2004	TB A	2	2	.500	33	0	0	3-1	41.1	28	16	4	1	18-1	40	3.27	143	.193	.287	1-0-1	.000	-0	—	7	20	0.7
2005	TB A	2	3	.400	36	0	0	0-1	45.1	54	29	7	2	18-3	28	4.57	96	.283	.351	0	ø	0	—	-3	68	-0.2
2006	TB A	0	0	ø	1	0	0	0-0	0.1	0	1	0	0	1-0	0	27.00	17	.000	.500	0	ø	0	—	-1	0	0.0
Total	6	11	22	.333	186	0	0	5-13	251	244	146	34	10	141-18	201	4.73	96	.255	.354	1-0-1	.000	-0	—	-6	88	-1.8
COLON, BARTOLO	Bartolo; B5.24.1973 Altamira, D.R.; BR/TR/6´0˝/(185–250); d4.4																									
1997	Cle A	4	7	.364	19	17	1	0-0	94	107	66	12	3	45-1	66	5.65	83	.286	.366	1	.000	-0	103	-10	0	-1.0
1998	†Cle A★	14	9	.609	31	31	6-2	0-0	204	205	91	15	3	79-5	158	3.71	129	.260	.329	2	.500	0	101	24	0	2.4
1999	†Cle A	18	5	.783	32	32	1-1	0-0	205	185	97	24	7	76-5	161	3.95	129	.242	.314	7-0-1	.143	-0	120	25	0	2.5
2000	Cle A	15	8	.652	30	30	2-1	0-0	188	163	86	21	4	98-4	212	3.88	129	.233	.329	5	.000	-1	100	23	25	2.4
2001	†Cle A	14	12	.538	34	34	1	0-0	222.1	220	106	26	2	90-2	201	4.09	112	.261	.332	7	.143	-0	100	14	0	1.5
2002	Cle A	10	4	.714	16	16	4-2	0-0	116.1	104	37	11	2	31-1	75	2.55	174	.245	.297	6	.167	-0	81	24	0	2.7
	Mon N	10	4	.714	17	17	4-1	0-0	117	115	48	9	0	39-4	74	3.31	132	.259	.317	39-0-2	.128	-1	111	13	0	1.3
2003	Chi A	15	13	.536	34	34	**9**	0-0	242	223	107	30	5	67-3	173	3.87	119	.248	.301	6-0-1	.000	-1	103	22	0	2.0
2004	†Ana A	18	12	.600	34	34	0	0-0	208.1	215	122	38	3	71-1	158	5.01	89	.265	.324	3	.000	-0	118	-12	0	-1.5
2005	†LA A★	**21**	8	.724	33	33	2	0-0	222.2	215	93	26	3	43-0	157	3.48	123	.254	.291	3	.333	0	118	20	0	2.2
2006	LA A	1	5	.167	10	10	1-1	0-0	56.1	71	39	11	3	11-0	31	5.11	87	.306	.344	1-0-1	.000	-0	99	-6	127	-0.5
Total	10	140	87	.617	290	288	31-8	0-0	1876	1823	892	223	35	650-26	1466	3.98	117	.256	.319	80-0-5	.125	-3	107	137	152	14.0

YEAR	TM LG	W	L	PCT	G	GS	CG-SHO	SV-BS	IP	H	R	HR	HB	BB-IB	SO	ERA	AERA	OAV	OOB	AB-HR-SH	AVG	PB	SUP	APR	DL	PW
Colon, Roman	Roman Benedicto; B8.13.1979 Monte Cristi, D.R.; BR/TR/6´6˝/225; d8.21																									
2004	Atl N	2	1	.667	18	0	0	0-1	19	18	9	0	0	8-1	15	3.32	130	.254	.321	0	ø	0	—	2	0	0.2
2005	Atl N	1	5	.167	23	4	0	0-0	44.1	47	28	10	0	14-1	30	5.28	80	.272	.323	7-0-1	.000	-1	89	-5	0	-0.8
	Det A	1	1	.500	12	3	0	0-1	25	35	17	7	0	7-0	17	6.12	70	.327	.365	0	ø	0	22	-4	0	-0.3
2006	Det A	2	0	1.000	20	1	0	1-0	38.2	46	21	6	1	14-2	25	4.89	92	.303	.361	0	ø	0	126	-1	49	-0.1
Total	3	6	7	.462	73	8	0	1-2	127	146	75	23	1	43-4	87	5.03	86	.290	.343	7-0-1	.000	-1	68	-8	49	-1.0
Colpaert, Dick	Richard Charles; B1.3.1944 Fraser MI; BR/TR/5´10˝/182; d7.21																									
1970	Pit N	1	0	1.000	8	0	0	0-0	10.2	9	7	3	0	8-2	6	5.91	67	.237	.370	0	ø	0	—	-2	0	-0.2
Colson, Loyd	Loyd Albert; B11.4.1947 Wellington TX; BR/TR/6´1˝/195; [NYA67 28/530]; d9.25; Col Bacone																									
1970	NY A	0	0	ø	1	0	0	0-0	2	3	1	0	0	0-0	3	4.50	79	.333	.333	0	ø	0	—	0	0	0.0
Colton, Larry	Lawrence Robert; B6.8.1942 Los Angeles CA; BL/TR/6´3˝/200; d5.6; Col California																									
1968	Phi N	0	0	ø	1	0	0	0	2	3	1	0	0	0-0	2	4.50	67	.333	.333	0	ø	0	—	0	30	0.0
Colyer, Steve	Stephen Edward; B2.22.1979 St.Louis MO; BL/TL/6´4˝/(200–205); [LAN97 2/83]; d4.3; Col St. Louis–Meramec (MO) CC																									
2003	LA N	0	0	ø	13	0	0	0-0	19.2	22	6	0	0	9-0	16	2.75	150	.297	.373	0	ø	0	—	3	0	0.2
2004	Det A	1	0	1.000	41	0	0	0-0	32	33	24	8	1	24-1	31	6.47	69	.270	.395	0	ø	0	—	-7	0	-0.3
Total	2	1	0	1.000	54	0	0	0-0	51.2	55	30	8	1	33-1	47	5.05	86	.281	.387	0	ø	0	—	-4	0	-0.1
Combe, Geoff	Geoffrey Wade; B2.1.1956 Melrose MA; BR/TR/6´2˝/185; d9.2																									
1980	Cin N	0	0	ø	4	0	0	0-0	6.2	9	8	0	0	4-1	10	10.80	33	.346	.433	0	ø	0	—	-5	0	-0.3
1981	Cin N	1	0	1.000	14	0	0	0-0	17.2	27	15	3	0	10-1	9	7.64	46	.370	.440	0	ø	0	—	-7	0	-0.4
Total	2	1	0	1.000	18	0	0	0-0	24.1	36	23	3	0	14-2	19	8.51	41	.364	.439	0	ø	0	—	-12	0	-0.7
Combs, Pat	Patrick Dennis; B10.29.1966 Newport RI; BL/TL/6´3˝/(200–207); [PhiN88 1/11]; d9.5; Col Baylor																									
1989	Phi N	4	0	1.000	6	6	1-1	0-0	38.2	36	10	2	0	6-1	30	2.09	171	.248	.278	12-0-1	.167	0	103	6	0	0.7
1990	Phi N	10	10	.500	32	31	3-2	0-0	183.1	179	90	12	4	86-7	108	4.07	95	.257	.339	60-0-4	.150	0	91	-4	0	-0.3
1991	Phi N	2	6	.250	14	13	1	0-0	64.1	64	41	7	2	43-1	41	4.90	76	.254	.365	15-0-2	.133	1	101	-10	102	-1.1
1992	Phi N	1	1	.500	4	4	0	0-0	18.2	20	16	0	0	12-0	11	7.71	46	.278	.376	8-0-1	.125	0	135	-8	0	-0.7
Total	4	17	17	.500	56	54	5-3	0-0	305	299	157	21	6	147-9	190	4.22	89	.257	.340	95-0-8	.147	1	98	-16	102	-1.4
Comellas, Jorge	Jorge (Pous) "Pancho"; B12.7.1916 Havana, Cuba; D9.13.2001 Miami FL; BR/TR/6´0˝/190; d4.19																									
1945	Chi N	0	2	.000	7	1	0	0	12	11	7	1	0	6	6	4.50	81	.244	.333	3	.000	-0	93	-1	0	-0.1
Comer, Steve	Steven Michael; B1.13.1954 Minneapolis MN; BB/TR/6´3˝/(195–207); d4.15; C1; Col Minnesota																									
1978	Tex A	11	5	.688	30	11	3-2	1-2	117.1	107	36	5	1	37-3	65	2.30	163	.249	.309	0	ø	0	137	18	0	2.5
1979	Tex A	17	12	.586	36	36	6-1	0-0	242.1	230	114	24	8	84-4	86	3.68	113	.252	.319	0	ø	0	94	12	0	1.3
1980	Tex A	2	4	.333	12	11	0	0-0	41.2	65	41	5	2	22-0	9	7.99	49	.367	.441	0	ø	0	151	-19	61	-2.2
1981	Tex A	8	2	.800	36	1	0	6-3	77.1	70	25	1	1	31-8	22	2.56	136	.241	.313	0	ø	0	0	8	0	1.2
1982	Tex A	1	6	.143	37	3	1	6-2	97	133	64	11	2	36-9	23	5.10	76	.342	.395	0	ø	0	78	-16	27	-1.2
1983	Phi N	1	0	1.000	3	1	0	0-0	8.2	11	6	0	0	3-0	1	5.19	69	.314	.368	1-0-1	.000	-0	196	-2	0	-0.2
1984	Cle A	4	8	.333	22	20	1	0-0	117.1	146	80	11	4	39-2	39	5.68	73	.309	.360	0	ø	0	83	-19	0	-1.7
Total	7	44	37	.543	176	83	11-3	13-7	701.2	762	366	57	18	252-26	245	4.13	96	.281	.344	1-0-1	.000	-0	106	-18	88	-0.3
Comiskey, Charlie	Charles Albert "Commy","The Old Roman"; B8.15.1859 Chicago IL; D10.26.1931 Eagle River WI; BR/TR/6´0˝/180; d5.2; M12; HF1939; ▲																									
1882	StL AA	0	1	.000	2	1	1	0	8	12	8	0	—	3	2	0.00	ø	.324	.375	329-1	.243	0*	55	1	—	0.1
1884	StL AA	0	0	ø	1	0	0	0	4	1	1	0	0	0	4	2.25	145	.059	.059	460-2	.237	0*	—	1	—	0.0
1889	StL AA	0	0	ø	1	0	0	0	0.1	0	0	0	0	0	0	0.00	ø	.000	.000	587-3	.286	0*	—	0	—	0.0
Total	3	0	1	.000	4	1	1	0	12.1	13	9	0	0	3	6	0.73	410	.236	.276	1376-6	.259	0	55	2	—	0.1
Compton, Jack	Harry Leroy; B3.9.1882 Lancaster OH; D7.4.1974 Lancaster OH; BR/TR/5´9˝/157; d9.7																									
1911	Cin N	0	1	.000	8	3	0	1	25.1	19	11	0	1	15	6	3.91	85	.204	.321	6	.333	0	129	0	—	0.0
Compton, Clint	Robert Clinton; B11.1.1950 Montgomery AL; BL/TL/5´11˝/185; d10.3																									
1972	Chi N	0	0	ø	1	0	0	0-0	2	2	2	0	0	2-0	0	9.00	42	.286	.444	0	ø	0	—	-1	0	-0.1
Comstock, Keith	Keith Martin; B12.23.1955 San Francisco CA; BL/TL/6´0˝/(171–175); [CalA76*5/93]; d4.3; Col Canada (CA) JC																									
1984	Min A	0	0	ø	4	0	0	0-0	6.1	6	6	2	0	4-0	2	8.53	50	.261	.370	0	ø	0	—	-3	0	-0.1
1987	SF N	2	0	1.000	15	0	0	1-1	20.2	19	8	1	0	10-2	21	3.05	126	.253	.337	1	.000	-0	—	2	0	0.2
	SD N	0	1	.000	26	0	0	0-0	36	33	22	4	0	21-3	38	5.50	72	.252	.348	1	.000	-0	—	-5	0	-0.3
	Year	2	1	.667	41	0	0	1-1	56.2	52	30	5	0	31-5	59	4.61	85	.252	.344	2	.000	-0	—	-3	0	-0.1
1988	SD N	0	0	ø	7	0	0	0-1	8	8	6	1	0	3-1	9	6.75	50	.250	.314	0	ø	0	—	-3	0	-0.1
1989	Sea A	1	2	.333	31	0	0	0-1	25.2	26	8	2	0	10-2	22	2.81	144	.268	.330	0	ø	0	—	4	0	0.4
1990	Sea A	7	4	.636	60	0	0	2-5	56	40	22	4	0	26-5	50	2.89	138	.206	.296	0	ø	0	—	6	0	1.2
1991	Sea A	0	0	ø	1	0	0	0-0	0.1	2	2	0	0	1-0	0	54.00	8	.667	.750	0	ø	0	—	-2	62	-0.1
Total	6	10	7	.588	144	0	0	3-8	153	134	74	14	0	75-13	142	4.06	97	.241	.327	2	.000	-0	—	-1	62	1.2
Comstock, Ralph	Ralph Remick "Commy"; B11.24.1890 Sylvania OH; D9.13.1966 Toledo OH; BR/TR/5´10˝/168; d8.26																									
1913	Det A	2	5	.286	10	7	1	1	60.1	90	55	0	1	16	37	5.37	54	.346	.386	22	.227	1	112	-18	—	-1.8
1915	Bos A	1	0	1.000	3	0	0	0	9	10	3	2	0	2	1	2.00	139	.294	.333	2	.000	0	—	1	—	0.1
	Pit F	3	3	.500	12	7	3	2	52.2	44	25	2	1	7	18	3.25	83	.237	.268	16-0-1	.000	-2	103	-4	—	-0.7
1918	Pit N	5	6	.455	15	8	6	1	81	78	33	0	2	14	44	3.00	96	.259	.297	26	.192	-0	69	0	—	-0.1
Total	3	11	14	.440	40	22	10	4	203	222	116	4	4	39	100	3.72	76	.284	.322	66-0-1	.152	-1	94	-21	—	-2.5
Condrey, Clay	Clayton Lee; B11.19.1975 Beaumont TX; BR/TR/6´3˝/195; d8.28; Col McNeese St.																									
2002	SD N	1	2	.333	9	3	0	0-0	26.2	20	7	1	2	8-1	16	1.69	230	.217	.288	6	.000	-1	32	6	0	0.6
2003	SD N	1	2	.333	9	6	0	0-0	34	43	32	7	3	21-4	25	8.47	47	.305	.406	10	.200	0	133	-17	55	-1.2
2006	Phi N	2	2	.500	21	0	0	0-1	28.2	35	11	3	0	9-2	16	3.14	149	.318	.367	2	.000	-0	—	5	0	0.6
Total	3	4	6	.400	39	9	0	0-1	89.1	98	50	11	5	38-7	57	4.74	88	.286	.362	18	.111	-1	94	-6	55	0.0
Cone, David	David Brian; B1.2.1963 Kansas City MO; BL/TR/6´1˝/(180–200); [KCA81 3/74]; d6.8																									
1986	KC A	0	0	ø	11	0	0	0-0	22.2	29	14	2	1	13-1	21	5.56	77	.309	.398	0	ø	0	—	-3	0	-0.1
1987	NY N	5	6	.455	21	13	1	1-0	99.1	87	46	11	5	44-1	68	3.71	103	.239	.327	31-0-3	.065	-1	89	1	78	0.0
1988	†NY N★	20	3	**.870**	35	28	8-4	0-0	231.1	178	67	10	4	80-7	213	2.22	147	.213	.283	80-0-5	.150	1	126	28	0	2.8
1989	NY N	14	8	.636	34	33	7-2	0-0	219.2	183	92	20	4	74-6	190	3.52	94	.223	.289	77-0-6	.234	4	122	-4	0	-0.1
1990	NY N	14	10	.583	31	30	6-2	0-0	211.2	177	84	21	1	65-1	**233**	3.23	117	.226	.284	70-0-9	.200	3*	118	13	0	1.7
1991	NY N	14	14	.500	34	34	5-2	0-0	232.2	204	95	13	5	73-2	**241**	3.29	112	.235	.296	72-0-6	.125	-1	94	11	0	1.1
1992	NY N★	13	7	.650	27	27	7-**5**	0-0	196.2	162	75	12	9	82-5	214	2.88	122	.223	.307	65-0-7	.092	-2	111	11	0	0.9
	†Tor A	4	3	.571	8	7	0	0-0	53	39	16	3	3	29-2	47	2.55	161	.206	.317	0	ø	0	76	9	0	1.1
1993	KC A	11	14	.440	34	34	6-1	0-0	254	205	102	20	10	114-2	191	3.33	139	.223	.312	0	ø	0	59	33	0	3.0
1994	KC A★	16	5	.762	23	23	4-3	0-0	171.2	130	60	15	7	54-0	132	2.94	171	.209	.277	0	ø	0	90	**39**	0	**4.3**
1995	Tor A	9	6	.600	17	17	5-2	0-0	130.1	113	53	12	5	41-2	102	3.38	140	.232	.297	0	ø	0	103	20	0	2.1
	†NY A	9	2	.818	13	13	1	0-0	99	82	42	12	1	47-0	89	3.82	121	.223	.312	0	ø	0	128	10	0	1.0
	Year	18	8	.692	30	30	6-2	0-0	**229.1**	195	95	24	6	88-2	191	3.57	132	.228	.304	0	ø	0	114	29	0	3.1
1996	†NY A	7	2	.778	11	11	1	0-0	72	50	25	3	2	34-0	71	2.88	172	.198	.293	0	ø	0	126	16	122	1.8
1997	†NY A★	12	6	.667	29	29	1	0-0	195	155	67	17	4	86-2	222	2.82	158	.218	.305	3	.000	-0	97	36	33	2.9
1998	†NY A	**20**	7	.741	31	31	3	0-0	207.2	186	89	20	15	59-1	209	3.55	123	.237	.302	3-0-1	.000	-0	134	19	0	2.2
1999	†NY A★	12	9	.571	31	31	1-1	0-0	193.1	164	84	21	11	90-2	177	3.44	137	.229	.322	3	.333	1	109	27	0	2.5
2000	†NY A	4	14	.222	30	29	0	0-0	155	192	124	25	9	82-3	120	6.91	69	.306	.389	3	.333	0	93	-36	0	-3.2
2001	Bos A	9	7	.563	25	25	0	0-0	135.2	148	74	17	10	57-4	115	4.31	103	.275	.351	1-0-1	.000	-0	96	1	43	0.0
2003	NY N	1	3	.250	5	4	0	0-0	18	20	13	4	0	13-1	13	6.50	65	.282	.393	4	.250	0	50	-4	34	-0.8
Total	17	194	126	.606	450	419	56-22	1-0	2898.2	2504	1222	258	106	1137-42	2668	3.46	120	.232	.309	412-0-38	.155	5	103	227	310	23.2

YEAR	TM LG	W	L	PCT	G	GS	CG-SHO	SV-BS	IP	H	R	HR	HB	BB-IB	SO	ERA	AERA	OAV	OOB	AB-HR-SH	AVG	PB	SUP	APR	DL	PW
Cone, Bob	Robert Earl; B2.27.1894 Galveston TX; D5.24.1955 Galveston TX; BR/TR/6´2˝/172; d7.25; Col Texas																									
1915	Phi A	0	0	ø	1	1	0	0	0.2	5	3	0	0	0	0	40.50	7	.714	.714	0	ø	0	100	-2	—	-0.1
Conger, Dick	Richard; B4.3.1921 Los Angeles CA; D2.16.1970 Los Angeles CA; BR/TR/6´0˝/185; d4.22; Mil 1944–46; Col UCLA																									
1940	Det A	1	0	1.000	2	0	0	0	3	2	1	0	0	3	1	3.00	159	.200	.385	0	ø	0	—	1	—	0.1
1941	Pit N	0	0	ø	2	1	0	0	4	3	0	0	0	3	2	0.00	ø	.214	.353	0	ø	0	24	2	0	0.1
1942	Pit N	0	0	ø	2	1	0	0	8.1	9	3	0	0	5	3	2.16	157	.290	.389	3	.000	-0*	74	1	0	0.0
1943	Phi N	2	7	.222	13	10	2	0	54.2	72	46	3	5	24	18	6.09	55	.327	.406	16	.063	-1	91	-18	0	-2.6
Total	4	3	7	.300	19	12	2	0	70	86	50	3	5	35	24	5.14	67	.313	.400	19	.053	-1	82	-14	0	-2.4
Conkwright, Allen	Allen Howard "Red"; B12.4.1896 Sedalia MO; D7.30.1991 LaMesa CA; BR/TR/5´10˝/170; d9.16; Col Utah St.																									
1920	Det A	2	1	.667	5	3	0	1	19.1	29	16	0	0	16	4	6.98	53	.397	.506	5	.200	1	164	-6	—	-0.7
Conley, Gene	Donald Eugene; B11.10.1930 Muskogee OK; BR/TR/6´8˝/(220–227); d4.17; Col Washington St.																									
1952	Bos N	0	3	.000	4	3	0	0	12.2	23	16	4	2	9	6	7.82	46	.397	.493	5	.400	1	66	-8	0	-1.3
1954	Mil N★	14	9	.609	28	27	12-2	0	194.1	171	73	17	7	79	113	2.96	126	.240	.320	77-0-3	.156	-2	100	18	0	1.6
1955	Mil N★	11	7	.611	22	21	10	0	158	152	81	23	1	52-9	107	4.16	90	.254	.313	54-0-8	.204	-1	122	-7	0	-0.8
1956	Mil N	8	9	.471	31	19	5-1	3	158.1	169	74	13	2	52-10	68	3.13	111	.276	.333	45-0-8	.156	-1	106	2	30	0.1
1957	†Mil N	9	9	.500	35	18	6-1	1	148	133	63	9	2	64-5	61	3.16	111	.244	.323	46-0-2	.196	1	94	4	0	0.6
1958	Mil N	0	6	.000	26	7	0	2	72	89	44	8	4	17-1	53	4.88	72	.309	.353	16-1-0	.188	1	106	-13	0	-0.9
1959	Phi N★	12	7	.632	25	22	12-3	1	180	159	68	13	2	42-6	102	3.00	**137**	.235	.280	67-0-4	.239	2	119	21	39	2.4
1960	Phi N	8	14	.364	29	25	9-2	0	183.1	192	85	10	2	42-4	117	3.68	105	.272	.311	63-1-2	.127	-1	77	4	0	0.2
1961	Bos A	11	14	.440	33	30	6-2	1	199.2	229	116	33	3	65-2	113	4.91	85	.287	.343	73-2-2	.219	4	94	-12	0	-1.0
1962	Bos A	15	14	.517	34	33	9-2	1	241.2	238	116	28	5	68-5	134	3.95	105	.256	.308	87-1-1	.207	3	98	6	0	1.0
1963	Bos A	3	4	.429	9	9	0	0	40.2	51	31	4	1	21-0	14	6.64	57	.305	.386	15-0-1	.200	0	128	-11	66	-1.7
Total	11	91	96	.487	276	214	69-13	9	1588.2	1606	767	162	31	511-42	888	3.82	101	.264	.322	548-5-31	.192	8	101	4	135	0.2
Conley, Ed	Edward J.; B7.10.1864 Sandwich MA; D10.16.1894 Cumberland RI; 5´8˝/142; d7.20; Col Holy Cross																									
1884	Pro N	4	4	.500	8	8	8-1	0	71	63	47	4	—	22	33	2.15	132	.223	.280	28	.143	-2	88	3	—	0.0
Conley, Snipe	James Patrick; B4.25.1894 Cressona PA; D1.7.1978 DeSoto TX; BR/TR/5´11.5˝/179; d5.20																									
1914	Bal F	4	6	.400	35	11	4-2	1	125	112	49	2	6	47	86	2.52	120	.259	.340	35	.114	-3	84	5	—	0.0
1915	Bal F	1	4	.200	25	6	4	0	86	97	48	5	4	32	40	4.29	67	.314	.386	24	.250	1	69	-11	—	-0.5
1918	Cin N	2	0	1.000	5	0	0	1	13.2	17	10	2	0	5	2	5.27	51	.321	.379	4-0-1	.250	0	—	-4	—	-0.6
Total	3	7	10	.412	65	17	8-2	2	224.2	226	107	9	10	84	128	3.36	88	.284	.360	63-0-1	.175	-1	80	-10	—	-1.1
Conley, Bob	Robert Burns; B2.1.1934 Mousie KY; BR/TR/6´1˝/188; d9.11																									
1958	Phi N	0	0	ø	2	2	0	0	8.1	9	7	0	0	1-0	0	7.56	52	.273	.278	1-0-1	.000	-0	136	-3	0	-0.2
Conn, Bert	Albert Thomas; B9.22.1879 Philadelphia PA; D11.2.1944 Philadelphia PA; TR/6´0˝/178; d9.16; ▲																									
1898	Phi N	0	1	.000	1	1	0	0	7	13	9	1	0	2	3	6.43	53	.394	.429	3	.333	1	103	-3	—	-0.3
1900	Phi N	0	2	.000	4	1	1	0	17.1	29	29	0	6	16	2	8.31	44	.372	.510	9	.333	1*	76	-12	—	-1.0
Total	2	0	3	.000	5	2	1	0	24.1	42	38	1	6	18	5	7.77	46	.378	.489	12	.333	2	88	-15	—	-1.3
Connally, Sarge	George Walter; B8.31.1898 McGregor TX; D1.27.1978 Houston TX; BR/TR/5´11˝/170; d9.10; Col Meridian (TX) JC																									
1921	Chi A	0	1	.000	5	2	0	0	22.1	29	16	0	1	10	6	6.45	66	.330	.404	8	.500	2	59	-5	—	-0.1
1923	Chi A	0	0	ø	3	0	0	0	8.2	7	6	0	1	12	3	6.23	64	.241	.476	3-0-1	.333	0	—	-2	—	-0.1
1924	Chi A	7	13	.350	44	13	6	6	160	177	95	4	9	68	55	4.05	102	.290	.369	50-0-1	.220	-1	82	-3	—	-0.3
1925	Chi A	6	7	.462	40	2	0	8	104.2	122	66	2	2	58	45	4.64	89	.310	.402	28-0-4	.250	1	91	-7	—	-0.6
1926	Chi A	6	5	.545	31	8	5	3	108.1	128	51	0	2	35	47	3.16	122	.300	.356	32-0-4	.156	-1	117	6	—	0.5
1927	Chi A	10	15	.400	43	18	11-1	5	198.1	217	108	8	9	83	58	4.08	99	.292	.370	67-0-7	.328	4	77	-1	—	0.3
1928	Chi A	2	5	.286	28	5	1	2	74.1	89	52	1	4	29	28	4.84	84	.313	.385	19-0-1	.105	-1	67	-8	—	-0.9
1929	Chi A	0	0	ø	11	0	0	1	11.1	13	6	0	0	8	3	4.76	90	.317	.429	0	ø	0	—	0	—	0.0
1931	Cle A	5	5	.500	17	9	5	1	85.2	87	56	7	6	50	37	4.20	110	.256	.361	27-0-4	.185	0	73	1	—	0.1
1932	Cle A	8	6	.571	35	7	4-1	3	112.1	119	59	6	3	42	32	4.33	110	.266	.333	40-1-2	.175	-0	126	7	—	0.7
1933	Cle A	5	3	.625	41	3	1	1	103	112	60	4	3	49	30	4.89	91	.271	.353	26-0-3	.231	1	83	-2	—	-0.2
1934	Cle A	0	0	ø	5	0	0	1	5.1	4	3	0	0	5	1	5.06	90	.222	.391	1	.000	-0	—	0	—	0.0
Total	12	49	60	.450	303	67	33-2	31	994.1	1104	578	32	40	449	345	4.30	98	.288	.368	301-1-27	.233	5	87	-14	—	-0.6
Connelly, Steve	Steven Lee; B4.27.1974 Long Beach CA; BR/TR/6´4˝/210; [OakA95 24/652]; d6.28; Col Oklahoma																									
1998	Oak A	0	0	ø	3	0	0	0-0	4.2	10	1	0	1	4-0	1	1.93	240	.435	.536	0	ø	0	—	1	0	0.1
Connelly, Bill	William Wirt "Wild Bill"; B6.29.1925 Alberta VA; D11.27.1980 Richmond VA; BL/TR/6´0˝/(175–185); d8.22																									
1945	Phi A	1	1	.500	2	1	0	0	8	7	4	0	0	8	0	4.50	76	.259	.429	1	.000	0	25	-1	0	-0.1
1950	Chi A	0	0	ø	2	0	0	0	2.1	5	3	1	0	1	0	11.57	39	.455	.500	0	ø	0	—	-2	0	-0.1
	Det A	0	0	ø	2	0	0	0	4	4	3	1	0	2	1	6.75	69	.250	.333	1	.000	0	—	-1	0	0.0
	Year	0	0	ø	4	0	0	0	6.1	9	6	2	0	3	1	8.53	54	.333	.400	1	.000	0	—	-2	0	-0.1
1952	NY N	5	0	1.000	11	4	0	0	31.2	22	18	4	0	25	22	4.55	81	.208	.359	11	.364	3	150	-3	0	-0.1
1953	NY N	0	1	.000	8	2	0	0	20.1	33	26	4	0	17	11	11.07	39	.371	.472	6	.000	-1	73	-14	0	-0.7
Total	4	6	2	.750	25	7	0	0	66.1	71	54	10	0	53	34	6.92	57	.285	.411	19	.211	3	106	-21	0	-1.0
Connolly, Ed	Edward Joseph Jr.; B12.3.1939 Brooklyn NY; D7.1.1998 New Canaan CT; BL/TL/6´1˝/(188–190); d4.19; f–Ed; Col Massachusetts																									
1964	Bos A	4	11	.267	27	15	1-1	0	80.2	80	50	3	6	64-2	73	4.91	79	.261	.395	18-0-2	.167	0	57	-9	0	-1.6
1967	Cle A	2	1	.667	15	4	0	0	49.1	63	46	6	1	34-2	45	7.48	44	.315	.414	11-0-1	.182	0	133	-22	0	-1.3
Total	2	6	12	.333	42	19	1-1	0	130	143	96	9	7	98-4	118	5.88	62	.282	.402	29-0-3	.172	0	73	-31	0	-2.9
Connor, John	John; B7.1861 Nashua NH; D11.14.1905 Nashua NH; d7.26																									
1884	Bos N	1	4	.200	7	7	7	0	60	70	44	1	—	18	29	3.15	92	.275	.322	25	.080	-3	79	-5	—	-0.5
1885	Buf N	0	1	.000	1	1	1	0	9	14	9	0	—	2	0	4.00	75	.378	.410	3	.000	-0	76	-2	—	-0.2
	Lou AA	1	3	.250	4	4	4	0	35	43	27	0	2	12	19	4.89	66	.295	.356	14	.143	-1	69	-4	—	-0.5
Total	2	2	8	.200	12	12	12	0	104	127	80	1	2	32	48	3.81	79	.290	.341	42	.095	-4	75	-11	—	-1.2
Connors, Joe	Joseph C. (b Joseph C. O'Connor); B1862 Paterson NJ; D1.13.1891 Denver CO; d5.3																									
1884	Alt U	0	1	.000	1	1	1	0	9	18	14	0	—	5	0	7.00	38	.391	.451	11	.091	-1*	80	-4	—	-0.3
	KC U	0	1	.000	2	1	1	0	12	24	14	1	—	0	1	4.50	50	.393	.393	11	.091	-1*	57	-4	—	-0.3
	Year	0	2	.000	3	2	2	0	21	42	28	1	—	5	1	5.57	43	.393	.420	22	.091	-1	71	-8	—	-0.6
Connors, Bill	William Joseph; B11.2.1941 Schenectady NY; BR/TR/6´1˝/(180–185); d5.3; C17; Col Syracuse																									
1966	Chi N	0	1	.000	11	0	0	0	16	20	13	4	0	7-1	3	7.31	50	.308	.370	0	ø	0	—	-5	0	-0.3
1967	NY N	0	0	ø	6	1	0	0	13	8	9	3	1	5-0	13	6.23	54	.170	.264	1	.000	-0	130	-4	0	-0.2
1968	NY N	0	1	.000	9	0	0	0	14	21	14	0	1	7-1	8	9.00	34	.339	.414	1-0-1	1.000	1	—	-8	0	-0.5
Total	3	0	2	.000	26	1	0	0	43	49	36	7	2	19-2	24	7.53	45	.282	.357	2-0-1	.500	1	130	-17	0	-1.0
Conovar, Ted	Theodore "Huck"; B3.10.1868 Lexington KY; D7.27.1910 Paris KY; BR/TR/5´10.5˝/165; d5.26																									
1889	Cin AA	0	0	ø	1	0	0	1	2	4	4	0	0	2	1	13.50	29	.400	.500	0	ø	0	—	-2	—	-0.2
Conroy, Tim	Timothy James; B4.3.1960 McKeesport PA; BL/TL/5´11˝/185; [OakA78 1/20]; d6.23																									
1978	Oak A	0	0	ø	2	2	0	0-0	4.2	3	6	0	1	9-0	0	7.71	47	.188	.481	0	ø	0	160	-3	0	-0.1
1982	Oak A	2	2	.500	5	5	1	0-0	25.1	20	13	1	0	18-0	17	3.55	111	.222	.349	0	ø	0	111	0	0	0.0
1983	Oak A	7	10	.412	39	18	3-1	0-0	162.1	141	89	17	2	98-2	112	3.94	99	.232	.338	0	ø	0	83	-6	0	-0.6
1984	Oak A	1	6	.143	38	14	0	0-1	93	82	58	11	2	63-0	69	5.23	72	.236	.353	0	ø	0	84	-15	0	-1.0
1985	Oak A	0	1	.000	16	2	0	0-1	25.1	22	15	3	1	15-1	8	4.26	91	.237	.345	0	ø	0	70	-2	0	-0.1
1986	StL N	5	11	.313	25	21	1	0-0	115.1	122	72	15	3	56-7	79	5.23	71	.275	.353	29-0-8	.138	1*	90	-19	53	-2.3
1987	StL N	3	2	.600	10	9	0	0-0	40.2	48	26	0	1	25-3	22	5.53	76	.306	.400	15-0-2	.000	-2	148	-5	109	-0.7
Total	7	18	32	.360	135	71	5-1	0-2	466.2	438	279	47	10	284-13	307	4.69	82	.249	.353	44-0-10	.091	-1	98	-50	162	-4.8

YEAR	TM LG	W	L	PCT	G	GS	CG-SHO	SV-BS	IP	H	R	HR	HB	BB-IB	SO	ERA	AERA	OAV	OOB	AB-HR-SH	AVG	PB	SUP	APR	DL	PW
CONSTABLE, JIM	Jimmy Lee "Sheriff"; B6.14.1933 Jonesborough TN; D9.4.2002 Johnson City TN; BB/TL/6´1˝/(185–190); d6.24																									
1956	NY N	0	0	ø	3	0	0	0	4.1	9	7	0	1	7-0	1	14.54	26	.429	.586	0	ø	0	—	-5	0	-0.2
1957	NY N	1	1	.500	16	0	0	0	28.1	27	10	2	4	7-0	13	2.86	138	.262	.333	5	.000	-0	—	3	0	0.2
1958	SF N	1	0	1.000	9	0	0	1	8	10	6	1	0	3-0	4	5.63	68	.323	.382	1	1.000	1	—	-2	0	-0.1
	Cle A	0	1	.000	6	2	0	0	9.1	17	13	2	1	4-0	3	11.57	32	.415	.478	2	1.000	1	74	-8	0	-0.7
	Was A	0	1	.000	15	2	0	0	27.2	29	15	3	1	15-0	25	4.88	78	.271	.360	4	.250	0	71	-3	0	-0.1
	Year	0	2	.000	21	4	0	0	37	46	28	5	2	19-0	28	6.57	57	.311	.392	6	.500	1	71	-11	0	-0.8
1962	Mil N	1	1	.500	3	2	1-1	1	18	14	4	1	0	4-0	12	2.00	190	.222	.265	5-0-1	.000	-0	46	4	0	0.4
1963	SF N	0	0	ø	4	0	0	0	2.1	3	1	0	0	1-0	1	3.86	83	.333	.400	0	ø	0	—	0	0	0.0
Total	5	3	4	.429	56	6	1-1	2	98	109	56	9	7	41-0	59	4.87	78	.291	.369	17-0-1	.235	2	62	-11	0	-0.5
CONSUEGRA, SANDY	Sandalio Simeon (Castello); B9.3.1920 Potrerillos, Cuba; D11.16.2005 Miami FL; BR/TR/5´10˝/(150–165); d6.10																									
1950	Was A	7	8	.467	21	18	8-2	2	124.2	132	71	6	1	57	38	4.40	102	.270	.347	40-0-4	.175	-1*	102	1	0	0.0
1951	Was A	7	8	.467	40	12	5	3	146	140	71	10	0	63	31	4.01	102	.251	.327	43-0-3	.233	-0	112	2	0	0.2
1952	Was A	6	0	1.000	30	2	0	5	73.2	80	30	2	0	27	19	3.05	116	.276	.338	17-0-2	.176	-0	368	4	0	0.3
1953	Was A	0	0	ø	4	0	0	0	5	9	6	0	0	4	0	10.80	36	.391	.481	0	ø	0	—	-4	0	-0.2
	Chi A	7	5	.583	29	13	5-1	3	124	122	39	9	2	28	30	2.54	158	.258	.302	35-0-6	.057	-4	65	20	0	1.7
	Year	7	5	.583	33	13	5-1	3	129	131	45	9	2	32	30	2.86	141	.264	.311	35-0-6	.057	-4	65	16	0	1.5
1954	Chi A★	16	3	**.842**	39	17	3-2	3	154	142	52	9	0	35	31	2.69	139	.248	.289	48-0-4	.229	1	107	17	0	2.3
1955	Chi A	6	5	.545	44	7	3	7	126.1	120	42	4	2	18-7	35	2.64	150	.256	.283	29-0-3	.103	-2	125	**18**	0	1.4
1956	Chi A	1	2	.333	28	1	0	3	38.1	45	25	0	1	11-3	7	5.17	79	.296	.345	4	.000	-1	22	-5	0	-0.5
	Bal A	1	1	.500	4	1	0	0	8.2	10	4	2	0	2-0	1	4.15	94	.294	.324	2	.500	0	91	0	0	0.0
	Year	2	3	.400	32	2	0	3	47	55	29	2	1	13-3	8	4.98	82	.296	.342	6	.167	-0	55	-5	0	-0.5
1957	Bal A	0	0	ø	5	0	0	0	5	4	1	0	0	0-0	0	1.80	200	.211	.200	0	ø	0	—	1	0	0.1
	NY N	0	0	ø	4	0	0	0	3.2	7	5	1	0	1-1	1	2.45	160	.389	.400	0	ø	0	—	-1	0	0.0
Total	8	51	32	.614	248	71	24-5	26	809.1	811	346	43	6	246-11	193	3.37	119	.262	.316	218-0-22	.170	-5	107	53	0	5.3
CONTRERAS, NARDI	Arnaldo Juan; B9.19.1951 Tampa FL; BB/TR/6´2˝/193; [CinN69 12/276]; d5.23; C7																									
1980	Chi A	0	0	ø	8	0	0	0-0	13.2	18	10	1	2	7-2	8	5.93	69	.333	.422	0	ø	0	—	-3	0	-0.1
CONTRERAS, JOSE	Jose Ariel; B12.6.1971 Las Martinas, Cuba; BR/TR/6´4˝/(230–245); d3.31																									
2003	†NY A	7	2	.778	18	9	0	0-1	71	52	27	4	5	30-1	72	3.30	133	.202	.297	3	.000	-0	107	10	78	1.0
2004	NY A	8	5	.615	18	18	0	0-0	95.2	93	66	22	6	42-1	82	5.64	81	.250	.333	8	.000	-1	125	-12	0	-1.5
	Chi A	5	4	.556	13	13	0	0-0	74.2	73	48	9	2	42-0	68	5.30	89	.256	.353	0	ø	0	101	-6	0	-0.6
	Year	13	9	.591	31	31	0	0-0	170.1	166	114	31	8	84-1	150	5.50	84	.253	.342	8	.000	-1	115	-17	0	-2.1
2005	†Chi A	15	7	.682	32	32	1	0-0	204.2	177	91	23	9	75-2	154	3.61	125	.232	.307	3	.000	-0	83	19	0	1.8
2006	Chi A✳	13	9	.591	30	30	1-1	0-0	196	194	101	20	10	55-4	134	4.27	110	.256	.312	4	.000	0	106	8	16	0.7
Total	4	48	27	.640	111	102	2-1	0-1	642	589	333	78	32	244-8	510	4.28	107	.242	.317	18	.000	-1	102	19	94	1.4
CONVERSE, JIM	James Daniel; B8.17.1971 San Francisco CA; BL/TR/5´9˝/(180–185); [SeaA90 16/431]; d5.22; [DL 1996 KC A 182]																									
1993	Sea A	1	3	.250	4	4	0	0-0	20.1	23	12	0	0	14-2	10	5.31	84	.295	.398	0	ø	0	52	-1	0	-0.2
1994	Sea A	0	5	.000	13	8	0	0-0	48.2	73	49	5	1	40-4	39	8.69	57	.353	.454	0	ø	0	56	-18	0	-1.5
1995	Sea A	0	3	.000	6	1	0	1-0	11	16	9	2	0	8-0	9	7.36	65	.348	.444	0	ø	0	39	-3	0	-0.5
	KC A	1	0	1.000	9	0	0	0-0	12.1	12	8	0	0	8-2	5	5.84	82	.267	.377	0	ø	0	—	-1	0	-0.1
	Year	1	3	.250	15	1	0	1-0	23.1	28	17	2	0	16-2	14	6.56	73	.308	.411	0	ø	0	39	-4	0	-0.6
1997	KC A	0	0	ø	3	0	0	0-0	5	4	2	2	0	5-0	3	3.60	132	.222	.391	0	ø	0	—	1	0	0.0
Total	4	2	11	.154	35	13	0	1-0	97.1	128	80	9	1	75-8	66	7.21	66	.325	.430	0	ø	0	53	-22	182	-2.3
CONWAY, JIM	James P.; B10.8.1858 Clifton PA; TR; d5.5; b–Pete																									
1884	Bro AA	3	9	.250	13	13	10	0	105.1	132	84	4	3	15	25	4.44	75	.289	.316	47	.128	-4*	110	-13	—	-1.5
1885	Phi AA	0	1	.000	2	2	1	0	12.1	19	16	0	0	2	0	7.30	47	.358	.382	6	.000	-0	154	-4	—	-0.3
1889	KC AA	19	19	.500	41	37	33	0	335	334	232	12	14	90	115	3.25	131	.252	.306	149	.208	-6	91	29	—	2.1
Total	3	22	29	.431	56	52	44	0	452.2	485	332	16	17	107	140	3.64	110	.264	.311	202	.183	-10	97	12	—	0.3
CONWAY, JERRY	Jerome Patrick; B6.7.1901 Holyoke MA; D4.16.1980 Holyoke MA; BL/TL/6´2˝/190; d8.31; Col St. Anselm																									
1920	Was A	0	0	ø	1	0	0	0	2	1	0	0	0	1	0	0.00	ø	.167	.286	0	ø	0	—	1	—	0.0
CONWAY, PETE	Peter J.; B10.30.1866 Burmont PA; D1.13.1903 Clifton Heights PA; BR/TR/5´10.5˝/162; d8.10; b–Jim; ▲																									
1885	Buf N	10	17	.370	27	27	26-1	0	210	256	173	10	—	44	94	4.67	64	.287	.320	90-1	.111	-4*	71	-35	—	-3.8
1886	KC N	5	15	.250	23	20	19	0	180	236	185	6	—	61	81	5.75	65	.294	.343	194-1	.242	0*	76	-38	—	-3.2
	Det N	6	5	.545	11	11	11	0	91	93	55	1	—	25	35	3.36	99	.255	.303	43-2	.186	1*	127	-1	—	-0.1
	Year	11	20	.355	34	31	30	0	271	329	240	7	—	86	116	4.95	73	.282	.331	237-3	.232	1	93	-38	—	-3.3
1887	†Det N	8	9	.471	17	17	16	0	146	132	95	3	5	47	40	2.90	141	.235	.300	95-1	.232	0*	95	9	—	0.9
1888	Det N	30	14	.682	45	45	43-4	0	391	315	170	11	13	57	176	2.26	124	.208	**.243**	167-3	.275	14	131	23	—	3.9
1889	Pit N	2	1	.667	3	3	2	0	22	26	16	1	0	16	2	4.91	76	.286	.393	10-1	.100	0	113	-3	—	-0.2
Total	5	61	61	.500	126	123	117-5	0	1040	1058	694	32	18	250	428	3.59	90	.250	.295	599-9	.224	12	101	-45	—	-2.5
CONWAY, DICK	Richard Butler; B4.25.1865 Lowell MA; D9.9.1926 Lowell MA; BL/TR/5´7.5˝/140; d7.22; b–Bill																									
1886	Bal AA	2	7	.222	9	9	8	0	76.2	106	91	6	3	43	64	6.81	50	.312	.394	34	.206	0	121	-28	—	-2.3
1887	Bos N	9	15	.375	26	26	25	0	222.1	249	161	10	7	86	45	4.66	88	.276	.343	145	.248	2*	81	-12	—	-0.8
1888	Bos N	4	2	.667	6	6	6	0	53	49	31	2	4	8	12	2.38	121	.240	.282	25	.160	-1*	117	1	—	0.0
Total	3	15	24	.385	41	41	39	0	352	404	283	18	14	137	121	4.78	79	.279	.347	204	.230	1	94	-39	—	-3.1
CONZELMAN, JOE	Joseph Harrison; B7.14.1885 Bristol CT; D4.17.1979 Mountain Brook AL; BR/TR/6´0˝/170; d5.1; Col Brown																									
1913	Pit N	0	1	.000	3	2	1	0	15	13	4	0	1	5	9	1.20	252	.245	.322	4	.000	-1	37	3	—	0.1
1914	Pit N	5	6	.455	33	9	4-1	2	101	88	39	2	3	40	39	2.94	90	.254	.337	27	.111	-2	66	-2	—	-0.3
1915	Pit N	1	1	.500	18	1	0	0	47.1	41	18	0	3	20	22	3.42	80	.248	.340	11	.091	-1	82	-2	—	-0.2
Total	3	6	8	.429	54	12	5-1	2	163.1	142	61	2	7	65	70	2.92	93	.252	.336	42	.095	-3	63	-1	—	-0.4
COOK, AARON	Aaron Lane; B2.8.1979 Fort Campbell KY; BR/TR/6´3˝/(175–215); [ColN97 2/70]; d8.10																									
2002	Col N	2	1	.667	9	5	0	0-0	35.2	41	18	4	2	13-0	14	4.54	104	.295	.364	11-0-1	.091	-1	86	1	0	0.1
2003	Col N	4	6	.400	43	16	1	0-0	124	160	89	8	8	57-7	43	6.02	81	.317	.391	29-0-6	.172	-0	105	-13	0	-0.9
2004	Col N	6	4	.600	16	16	1	0-0	96.2	112	47	7	7	39-5	40	4.28	111	.294	.369	34-0-2	.118	-1	98	5	57	0.4
2005	Col N	7	2	.778	13	13	2	0-0	83.1	101	38	8	2	16-2	24	3.67	127	.301	.334	30-0-5	.167	0	121	8	118	0.7
2006	Col N	9	15	.375	32	32	0	0-0	212.2	242	107	17	7	55-11	92	4.23	113	.288	.335	58-0-13	.052	-3	76	13	0	1.1
Total	5	28	28	.500	113	82	4	0-0	552.1	656	299	44	26	180-25	213	4.58	105	.298	.356	162-0-27	.111	-6	94	14	175	1.4
COOK, ANDY	Andrew Bernard; B8.30.1967 Memphis TN; BR/TR/6´5˝/205; [NYA88 11/287]; d5.9; Col Memphis																									
1993	NY A	0	1	.000	4	0	0	0-0	5.1	4	3	1	0	7-0	4	5.06	83	.200	.407	0	ø	0	—	0	0	-0.1
COOK, DENNIS	Dennis Bryan; B10.4.1962 LaMarque TX; BL/TL/6´3˝/(185–190); [SFN85 18/446]; d9.12; Col Texas																									
1988	SF N	2	1	.667	4	4	1-1	0-0	22	9	8	1	0	11-1	13	2.86	114	.125	.233	4-0-1	.000	1	116	1	0	0.2
1989	SF N	1	0	1.000	2	2	1	0-0	15	13	3	1	0	5-0	9	1.80	188	.245	.310	6	.167	1	131	3	0	0.3
	Phi N	6	8	.429	21	16	1-1	0-0	106	97	56	17	2	33-6	58	3.99	90	.243	.303	36-0-2	.222	1*	97	-6	0	-0.7
	Year	7	8	.467	23	18	2-1	0-0	121	110	59	18	2	38-6	67	3.72	96	.243	.304	42-0-2	.214	2	101	-4	0	-0.4
1990	Phi N	8	3	.727	42	13	2-1	1-1	141.2	132	61	13	2	54-9	58	3.56	108	.250	.319	42-1-4	.310	4*	126	5	0	0.8
	LA N	1	1	.500	5	3	0	0-0	14.1	23	13	7	0	2-0	6	7.53	49	.365	.373	7	.286	1	123	-6	0	-0.6
	Year	9	4	.692	47	16	2-1	1-1	156	155	74	20	2	56-9	64	3.92	98	.262	.325	49-1-4	.306	5	125	0	0	0.2
1991	LA N	1	0	1.000	20	1	0	0-1	17.2	12	3	0	0	7-1	8	0.51	709	.203	.279	1-0-1	.000	-0	50	5	0	0.3
1992	Cle A	5	7	.417	32	25	1	0-0	158	156	79	29	2	50-2	96	3.82	103	.255	.312	0	ø	0	105	0	0	-0.1
1993	Cle A	5	5	.500	25	6	0	0-2	54	62	36	9	2	16-1	34	5.67	77	.295	.348	0	ø	0	88	-7	0	-1.1
1994	Chi A	3	1	.750	38	0	0	0-1	33	29	17	4	0	14-3	26	3.55	132	.230	.307	0	ø	0	—	3	0	0.3
1995	Cle A	0	0	ø	11	0	0	0-0	12.2	16	9	3	1	10-2	13	6.39	74	.320	.443	0	ø	0	—	-2	0	-0.1
	Tex A	0	2	.000	35	1	0	2-0	45	47	23	6	1	16-1	40	4.00	121	.280	.337	0	ø	0	115	3	0	0.1
	Year	0	2	.000	46	1	0	2-0	57.2	63	32	9	2	26-3	53	4.53	106	.289	.363	0	ø	0	116	1	0	0.0
1996	†Tex A	5	2	.714	60	0	0	0-2	70.1	53	34	2	7	35-7	64	4.09	129	.214	.322	0	ø	0	—	9	0	0.7

YEAR	TM LG	W	L	PCT	G	GS	CG-SHO	SV-BS	IP	H	R	HR	HB	BB-IB	SO	ERA	AERA	OAV	OOB	AB-HR-SH	AVG	PB	SUP	APR	DL	PW
1997	†Fla N	1	2	.333	59	0	0	0-2	62.1	64	28	4	2	28-4	63	3.90	104	.267	.347	9-1-0	.556	3*	—	2	0	0.4
1998	NY N	8	4	.667	73	0	0	1-4	68	60	21	5	3	27-4	79	2.38	173	.240	.318	3	.000	-0	—	13	0	2.0
1999	†NY N	10	5	.667	71	0	0	3-3	63	50	27	11	1	27-1	68	3.86	113	.216	.299	1	.000	-0	—	4	0	0.8
2000	†NY N	6	3	.667	68	0	0	2-6	59	63	35	8	5	31-4	53	5.34	82	.270	.368	0-0-1	ø	0	—	-5	0	-0.6
2001	NY N	1	1	.500	43	0	0	0-2	36	28	18	6	1	10-1	34	4.25	95	.207	.265	1	.000	-0	—	-1	0	-0.1
	Phi N	0	0	ø	19	0	0	0-1	9.2	15	6	2	1	4-2	4	5.59	74	.385	.455	0	ø	0	—	-1	16	-0.1
	Year	1	1	.500	62	0	0	0-3	45.2	43	24	8	2	14-3	38	4.53	90	.247	.309	1	.000	-0	—	-2	0	-0.2
2002	Ana A	1	1	.500	37	0	0	0-1	24	21	9	2	1	10-0	13	3.38	133	.241	.320	0	ø	0	—	3	68	0.2
Total	15	64	46	.582	665	71	6-3	9-26	1011.2	950	486	130	31	390-49	739	3.91	106	.250	.322	110-2-9	.264	9	100	23	84	2.7

COOK, EARL Earl Davis; B12.10.1908 Stouffville ON, Can.; D11.21.1996 Markham ON, Can.; BR/TR/6´0˝/195; d9.12

YEAR	TM LG	W	L	PCT	G	GS	CG-SHO	SV-BS	IP	H	R	HR	HB	BB-IB	SO	ERA	AERA	OAV	OOB	AB-HR-SH	AVG	PB	SUP	APR	DL	PW
1941	Det A	0	0	ø	1	0	0	0	2	4	1	0	0	0	1	4.50	101	.400	.400	0	ø	0	—	0	0	0.0

COOK, GLEN Glen Patrick; B9.8.1959 Buffalo NY; BR/TR/5´11˝/180; [TexA81 24/604]; d6.23; Col Ithaca

YEAR	TM LG	W	L	PCT	G	GS	CG-SHO	SV-BS	IP	H	R	HR	HB	BB-IB	SO	ERA	AERA	OAV	OOB	AB-HR-SH	AVG	PB	SUP	APR	DL	PW
1985	Tex A	2	3	.400	9	7	0	0-0	40	53	42	12	3	18-1	19	9.45	45	.327	.396	0	ø	0	107	-21	0	-2.1

COOK, MIKE Michael Horace; B8.14.1963 Charleston SC; BR/TR/6´3˝/(200–225); [CalA85 1/19]; d7.1; Col South Carolina

YEAR	TM LG	W	L	PCT	G	GS	CG-SHO	SV-BS	IP	H	R	HR	HB	BB-IB	SO	ERA	AERA	OAV	OOB	AB-HR-SH	AVG	PB	SUP	APR	DL	PW
1986	Cal A	0	2	.000	5	1	0	0-1	9	13	12	3	0	7-1	6	9.00	46	.333	.435	0	ø	0	66	-6	0	-1.0
1987	Cal A	1	2	.333	16	1	0	0-1	34.1	34	21	7	0	18-0	27	5.50	79	.264	.354	0	ø	0	0	-3	0	-0.2
1988	Cal A	0	1	.000	3	0	0	0-0	3.2	4	2	0	1	1-0	2	4.91	79	.308	.400	0	ø	0	—	0	0	-0.1
1989	Min A	0	1	.000	15	0	0	0-0	21.1	22	12	1	1	17-1	15	5.06	82	.268	.392	0	ø	0	—	-2	0	-0.1
1993	Bal A	0	0	ø	2	0	0	0-0	3	1	0	0	0	2-1	3	0.00	ø	.091	.231	0	ø	0	—	1	0	0.1
Total	5	1	6	.143	41	2	0	0-2	71.1	74	47	11	2	45-3	53	5.55	76	.270	.375	0	ø	0	32	-10	0	-1.3

COOK, ROLLIN Rollin Edward; B10.5.1890 Toledo OH; D8.11.1975 Toledo OH; BR/TR/5´9˝/152; d7.6; Col Ohio St.

YEAR	TM LG	W	L	PCT	G	GS	CG-SHO	SV-BS	IP	H	R	HR	HB	BB-IB	SO	ERA	AERA	OAV	OOB	AB-HR-SH	AVG	PB	SUP	APR	DL	PW
1915	StL A	0	0	ø	5	0	0	0	13.2	16	14	0	1	9	7	7.24	40	.276	.382	4	.250	0	—	-6	—	-0.3

COOK, RON Ronald Wayne; B7.11.1947 Jefferson TX; BL/TL/6´1˝/175; d4.10; Col Kilgore (TX) JC

YEAR	TM LG	W	L	PCT	G	GS	CG-SHO	SV-BS	IP	H	R	HR	HB	BB-IB	SO	ERA	AERA	OAV	OOB	AB-HR-SH	AVG	PB	SUP	APR	DL	PW
1970	Hou N	4	4	.500	41	7	0	2-0	82.1	80	37	4	3	42-4	50	3.72	105	.274	.367	17-0-1	.235	2*	102	2	0	0.4
1971	Hou N	0	4	.000	5	4	0	0-0	25.2	23	14	2	1	8-1	10	4.91	69	.237	.299	8	.250	0*	26	-4	9	-0.5
Total	2	4	8	.333	46	11	0	2-0	108	103	51	6	4	50-5	60	4.00	94	.265	.350	25-0-1	.240	2	76	-2	9	-0.1

COOKE, STEVE Steven Montague; B1.14.1970 Lihue HI; BR/TL/6´6˝/(220–240); [PitN89 35/912]; d7.28; Col Southern Idaho [JC]; [DL 1995 Pit N 160]

YEAR	TM LG	W	L	PCT	G	GS	CG-SHO	SV-BS	IP	H	R	HR	HB	BB-IB	SO	ERA	AERA	OAV	OOB	AB-HR-SH	AVG	PB	SUP	APR	DL	PW
1992	Pit N	2	0	1.000	11	0	0	1-0	23	22	9	2	0	4-1	10	3.52	99	.253	.286	3-0-2	.333	0	—	0	0	0.0
1993	Pit N	10	10	.500	32	32	3-1	0-0	210.2	207	101	22	3	59-4	132	3.89	105	.258	.310	71-0-6	.155	-1	103	2	0	0.0
1994	Pit N	4	11	.267	25	23	2	0-0	134.1	157	79	21	5	46-7	74	5.02	87	.298	.358	42-0-5	.190	0	83	-7	0	-0.8
1996	Pit N	0	0	ø	3	0	0	0-0	8.1	11	7	1	0	5-0	7	7.56	58	.314	.390	1	.000	-0	—	-2	79	-0.1
1997	Pit N	9	15	.375	32	32	0	0-0	167.1	184	95	15	9	77-11	109	4.30	100	.284	.366	52-0-7	.058	-4	76	-3	0	-0.7
1998	Cin N	1	0	1.000	1	1	0	0-0	6	4	1	0	1	0-0	3	1.50	286	.182	.217	2	.500	0	107	2	177	0.4
Total	6	26	36	.419	104	88	5-1	1-0	549.2	585	292	61	18	191-23	335	4.31	97	.276	.339	171-0-20	.140	-4	89	-8	416	-1.2

COOMBS, DANNY Daniel Bernard; B3.23.1942 Lincoln ME; BR/TL/6´5˝/(200–210); d9.27; Mil 1964; Col Seton Hall

YEAR	TM LG	W	L	PCT	G	GS	CG-SHO	SV-BS	IP	H	R	HR	HB	BB-IB	SO	ERA	AERA	OAV	OOB	AB-HR-SH	AVG	PB	SUP	APR	DL	PW
1963	Hou N	0	0	ø	1	0	0	0	0.1	3	1	0	0	0-0	0	27.00	12	.750	.750	0	ø	0	—	-1	0	0.0
1964	Hou N	1	1	.500	7	1	0	0	18	21	10	1	1	10-0	14	5.00	68	.300	.395	4	.000	-0	154	-3	0	-0.3
1965	Hou N	0	2	.000	26	3	0	0	47	54	26	3	3	23-1	35	4.79	70	.292	.374	9	.111	0	35	-7	0	-0.3
1966	Hou N	0	0	ø	2	0	0	0	2.2	4	1	0	0	0-0	3	3.38	101	.333	.333	1	.000	-0	—	0	0	0.0
1967	Hou N	3	0	1.000	6	2	0	0	24.1	21	9	0	0	9-4	23	3.33	99	.233	.300	8	.125	0	80	1	0	0.1
1968	Hou N	4	3	.571	40	2	0	2	46.2	52	21	0	1	17-4	29	3.28	90	.286	.345	10	.400	1	88	-3	0	-0.2
1969	Hou N	0	1	.000	8	0	0	0-0	8	12	6	0	1	2-1	3	6.75	53	.364	.417	2	.000	-0	—	-2	0	-0.3
1970	SD N	10	14	.417	35	27	5-1	0-0	188.1	185	83	12	2	76-14	105	3.30	122	.256	.326	52-0-7	.096	-2	80	13	0	1.3
1971	SD N	1	6	.143	19	7	0	0-1	57.2	81	52	10	0	25-5	37	6.24	53	.327	.387	14-0-2	.214	1	130	-22	0	-2.2
Total	9	19	27	.413	144	42	5-1	2-1	393	433	209	26	8	162-29	249	4.08	89	.280	.349	100-0-9	.140	-0	89	-24	0	-1.9

COOMBS, JACK John Wesley "Colby Jack"; B11.18.1882 LeGrand IA; D4.15.1957 Palestine TX; BB/TR/6´0˝/185; d7.5; M1/C1; Col Colby; ▲

YEAR	TM LG	W	L	PCT	G	GS	CG-SHO	SV-BS	IP	H	R	HR	HB	BB-IB	SO	ERA	AERA	OAV	OOB	AB-HR-SH	AVG	PB	SUP	APR	DL	PW
1906	Phi A	10	10	.500	23	18	13-1	0	173	144	65	0	7	68	90	2.50	109	.229	.312	67-0-1	.239	1*	81	5	—	0.7
1907	Phi A	6	9	.400	23	17	10-2	2	132.2	109	58	2	9	64	73	3.12	83	.227	.329	48-1-2	.167	-1*	93	-5	—	-0.7
1908	Phi A	7	5	.583	26	18	10-4	0	153	130	63	1	3	64	80	2.00	128	.233	.316	220-1-9	.255	4*	104	4	—	0.7
1909	Phi A	12	11	.522	30	24	18-6	1	205.2	156	63	1	6	73	97	2.32	104	.213	.289	83-0-2	.169	1*	104	6	—	0.8
1910	†Phi A	**31**	9	.775	**45**	38	35-**13**	1	353	248	74	0	7	115	224	1.30	183	.201	.273	132-0-1	.220	4*	110	**47**	—	5.8
1911	†Phi A	**28**	12	.700	47	**40**	26-1	2	336.2	360	166	8	16	119	185	3.53	89	.280	.348	141-2-3	.319	14*	150	-12	—	-0.2
1912	Phi A	21	10	.677	40	32	23-1	2	262.1	227	120	5	10	94	120	3.29	93	.241	.316	110-0-2	.255	6*	121	-4	—	0.2
1913	Phi A	0	0	ø	2	2	0	0	5.1	5	9	0	1	6	0	10.13	27	.313	.522	3	.333	1	201	-5	—	-0.2
1914	Phi A	0	1	.000	2	2	0	0	8	8	4	0	1	3	1	4.50	58	.267	.353	11	.273	0*	56	-1	—	-0.1
1915	Bro N	15	10	.600	29	24	17-2	0	195.2	166	71	1	16	91	56	2.58	108	.236	.337	75-0-1	.280	4	88	6	—	1.0
1916	†Bro N	13	8	.619	27	19	10-3	0	159	136	54	3	2	44	47	2.66	101	.239	.296	61	.180	-0	94	4	—	0.3
1917	Bro N	7	11	.389	31	14	9	0	141	147	76	7	8	49	34	3.96	71	.284	.355	44-0-1	.227	2*	79	-17	—	-2.1
1918	Bro N	8	14	.364	27	20	16-2	0	189	191	97	10	2	49	44	3.81	73	.266	.315	113-0-1	.168	-0*	74	-18	—	-2.2
1920	Det A	0	0	ø	2	0	0	0	5.2	7	5	0	0	2	1	3.18	117	.318	.375	2	.000	-0	—	-1	—	-0.1
Total	14	158	110	.590	354	268	187-35	8	2320	2034	925	38	88	841	1052	2.78	99	.241	.316	1110-4-23	.235	36	107	9	—	3.9

COOMBS, BOBBY Raymond Franklin; B2.2.1908 Goodwins Mills ME; D10.21.1991 Ogunquit ME; BR/TR/5´9.5˝/160; d6.8; Col Duke

YEAR	TM LG	W	L	PCT	G	GS	CG-SHO	SV-BS	IP	H	R	HR	HB	BB-IB	SO	ERA	AERA	OAV	OOB	AB-HR-SH	AVG	PB	SUP	APR	DL	PW
1933	Phi A	0	1	.000	21	0	0	2	31.1	47	30	4	0	20	8	7.47	57	.348	.432	5	.400	1	—	-11	—	-0.4
1943	NY N	0	1	.000	9	0	0	0	16	33	26	1	0	8	5	12.94	27	.423	.477	2	.000	0	—	-17	0	-0.9
Total	2	0	2	.000	30	0	0	2	47.1	80	56	5	0	28	13	9.32	43	.376	.448	7	.286	1	—	-28	0	-1.3

COONEY, JOHNNY John Walter; B3.18.1901 Cranston RI; D7.8.1986 Sarasota FL; BR/TL/5´10˝/165; d4.19; M1/C21; f–Jimmy b–Jimmy; ▲

YEAR	TM LG	W	L	PCT	G	GS	CG-SHO	SV-BS	IP	H	R	HR	HB	BB-IB	SO	ERA	AERA	OAV	OOB	AB-HR-SH	AVG	PB	SUP	APR	DL	PW
1921	Bos N	0	1	.000	8	1	0	0	20.2	19	12	3	0	10	9	3.92	93	.241	.326	5	.200	-0	113	-1	—	-0.1
1922	Bos N	1	2	.333	4	3	1	0	25	19	10	0	1	6	7	2.16	185	.224	.283	8	.000	-1	41	4	—	0.3
1923	Bos N	3	5	.375	23	8	5-2	0	98	92	43	3	3	22	23	3.31	121	.246	.293	66-0-3	.379	4*	64	8	—	0.9
1924	Bos N	8	9	.471	34	19	12-2	2	181	176	79	4	4	50	67	3.18	120	.260	.314	130-0-5	.254	2*	64	11	—	1.1
1925	Bos N	14	14	.500	31	29	20-2	0	245.2	267	123	18	3	50	65	3.48	115	.274	.312	103-0-5	.320	5*	95	11	—	2.1
1926	Bos N	3	3	.500	19	8	3-1	0	83.1	106	52	0	7	29	23	4.00	89	.320	.387	126-0-8	.302	3*	132	-8	—	-0.2
1928	Bos N	3	7	.300	24	5	2	1	89.2	106	47	7	0	31	18	4.32	91	.303	.360	41-0-1	.171	-0*	105	-2	—	-0.1
1929	Bos N	2	3	.400	14	2	1	3	45	57	29	4	0	22	11	5.00	94	.315	.389	72	.319	2*	56	-2	—	0.0
1930	Bos N	0	0	ø	2	0	0	0	7	16	14	2	1	3	1	18.00	27	.471	.526	3	.000	-1*	—	-9	—	-0.4
Total	9	34	44	.436	159	75	44-7	6	795.1	858	409	41	19	223	224	3.72	106	.278	.331	554-0-22	.289	15	85	12	—	3.6

COONEY, BOB Robert Daniel; B7.12.1907 Glens Falls NY; D5.4.1976 Glens Falls NY; BR/TR/5´11˝/160; d9.6; Col Fordham

YEAR	TM LG	W	L	PCT	G	GS	CG-SHO	SV-BS	IP	H	R	HR	HB	BB-IB	SO	ERA	AERA	OAV	OOB	AB-HR-SH	AVG	PB	SUP	APR	DL	PW
1931	StL A	0	3	.000	5	4	1	0	39.1	46	21	1	1	20	13	4.12	113	.291	.374	13	.385	1	64	2	—	0.3
1932	StL A	1	2	.333	23	3	1	1	71	94	61	8	2	36	23	6.97	70	.324	.402	22	.000	-3*	82	-14	—	-1.0
Total	2	1	5	.167	28	7	2	1	110.1	140	82	9	3	56	36	5.95	80	.313	.393	35	.143	-2	71	-12	—	-0.7

COOPER, WILBUR Arley Wilbur; B2.24.1892 Bearsville WV; D8.7.1973 Encino CA; BR/TL/5´11˝/175; d8.29

YEAR	TM LG	W	L	PCT	G	GS	CG-SHO	SV-BS	IP	H	R	HR	HB	BB-IB	SO	ERA	AERA	OAV	OOB	AB-HR-SH	AVG	PB	SUP	APR	DL	PW
1912	Pit N	3	0	1.000	6	4	3-2	0	38	32	7	1	0	15	30	1.66	197	.227	.301	13-0-2	.154	-0	129	8	—	0.5
1913	Pit N	5	3	.625	30	9	3-1	0	93	98	52	0	2	45	39	3.29	92	.276	.361	26-0-1	.077	-1	166	-6	—	-0.7
1914	Pit N	16	15	.516	40	34	19	0	266.2	246	99	4	5	79	102	2.13	125	.254	.313	92-0-3	.207	1	100	9	—	1.1
1915	Pit N	5	16	.238	38	20	11-1	4	185.2	180	92	4	9	52	71	3.30	83	.262	.323	60-0-2	.117	-3	101	-13	—	-1.8
1916	Pit N	12	11	.522	42	23	16-2	2	246	189	72	4	4	74	111	1.87	144	.215	.279	79-0-7	.215	0*	73	20	—	2.1
1917	Pit N	17	11	.607	40	34	23-7	1	297.2	276	96	4	4	54	99	2.36	120	.258	.297	103-0-2	.204	2*	100	16	—	1.7
1918	Pit N	19	14	.576	38	29	26-2	**3**	273.1	219	86	2	10	65	117	2.11	136	.223	.279	95-0-5	.242	3	84	22	—	3.0
1919	Pit N	19	13	.594	35	32	**27**-4	1	286.2	229	97	10	15	74	106	2.67	113	.225	.287	101-0-1	.287	6*	90	11	—	1.7
1920	Pit N	24	15	.615	44	37	28-3	2	327	307	113	4	11	52	114	2.39	134	.253	.290	113-0-2	.221	1	85	26	—	3.0
1921	Pit N	**22**	14	.611	38	**38**	29-2	0	**327**	341	145	9	10	80	134	3.25	118	.272	.320	122-0-4	.254	4	95	19	—	2.2
1922	Pit N	23	14	.622	41	36	**27**-4	0	294.2	330	130	13	7	61	129	3.18	128	.286	.326	108-4-3	.269	9	110	**27**	—	**3.9**
1923	Pit N	17	19	.472	39	**38**	26-1	0	294.2	331	136	11	11	71	77	3.57	112	.288	.335	107-0-3	.262	4	90	15	—	1.8
1924	Pit N	20	14	.588	38	35	25-**4**	1	268.2	296	116	13	5	40	62	3.28	117	.283	.313	104-0-1	.346	10	122	16	—	2.7

YEAR	TM LG	W	L	PCT	G	GS	CG-SHO	SV-BS	IP	H	R	HR	HB	BB-IB	SO	ERA	AERA	OAV	OOB	AB-HR-SH	AVG	PB	SUP	APR	DL	PW
1925	Chi N	12	14	.462	32	26	13	0	212.1	249	115	18	4	61	41	4.28	101	.291	.341	82-2-1	.207	1	100	2	—	0.1
1926	Chi N	2	1	.667	8	8	3-2	0	55	65	32	6	0	21	18	4.42	87	.311	.374	18	.389	3	168	-3	—	0.1
	Det A	0	4	.000	8	3	0	0	13.2	27	18	0	3	9	2	11.20	36	.443	.534	4-0-1	.000	-1	83	-10	—	-1.7
Total	15	216	178	.548	517	406	279-35	14	3480	3415	1406	103	100	853	1252	2.89	116	.262	.312	1227-6-38	.239	39	101	159	—	19.7

Cooper, Brian Brian John; B8.19.1974 Hollywood CA; BR/TR/6´1˝/(180–195); [AnaA95 4/88]; d9.7; Col USC

YEAR	TM LG	W	L	PCT	G	GS	CG-SHO	SV-BS	IP	H	R	HR	HB	BB-IB	SO	ERA	AERA	OAV	OOB	AB-HR-SH	AVG	PB	SUP	APR	DL	PW
1999	Ana A	1	1	.500	5	5	0	0-0	27.2	23	15	3	4	18-0	15	4.88	100	.228	.363	0	ø	0	126	1	0	0.1
2000	Ana A	4	8	.333	15	15	1-1	0-0	87	105	66	18	2	35-1	36	5.90	88	.299	.362	4	.000	-0	75	-9	0	-1.0
2001	Ana A	0	1	.000	7	1	0	0-0	13.2	10	5	2	0	4-0	7	2.63	177	.200	.255	0	ø	0	40	3	0	0.2
2002	Tor A	0	1	.000	2	2	0	0-0	8.1	14	13	5	0	4-0	3	14.04	33	.400	.450	0	ø	0	200	-8	0	-0.7
2004	SF N	0	2	.000	5	2	0	0-0	13.1	15	13	4	1	5-1	7	8.78	49	.288	.356	3	.000	-0	0	-6	0	-0.8
2005	SF N	0	1	.000	8	1	0	0-0	17.2	15	6	0	0	8-0	7	3.06	139	.234	.319	2	.500	0	22	3	0	0.1
Total	6	5	14	.263	42	26	1-1	0-0	167.2	182	118	32	7	74-2	75	5.80	84	.279	.354	9	.111	-0	87	-16	0	-2.1

Cooper, Cal Calvin Asa; B8.11.1922 Great Falls SC; D7.4.1994 Clinton SC; BR/TR/6´2.5˝/180; d9.14; Col Newberry

YEAR	TM LG	W	L	PCT	G	GS	CG-SHO	SV-BS	IP	H	R	HR	HB	BB-IB	SO	ERA	AERA	OAV	OOB	AB-HR-SH	AVG	PB	SUP	APR	DL	PW
1948	Was A	0	0	ø	1	0	0	0	1	5	5	1	0	1	0	45.00	10	.625	.667	0	ø	0	—	-4	0	-0.2

Cooper, Don Donald James; B1.15.1957 New York NY; BR/TR/6´1˝/(175–185); [NYA78 17/442]; d4.9; C5; Col New York Tech

YEAR	TM LG	W	L	PCT	G	GS	CG-SHO	SV-BS	IP	H	R	HR	HB	BB-IB	SO	ERA	AERA	OAV	OOB	AB-HR-SH	AVG	PB	SUP	APR	DL	PW
1981	Min A	1	5	.167	27	2	0	0-0	58.2	61	33	9	1	32-4	33	4.30	92	.274	.364	0	ø	0	91	-3	0	-0.3
1982	Min A	0	1	.000	6	1	0	0-0	11.1	14	12	0	0	11-2	5	9.53	45	.311	.439	0	ø	0	149	-6	0	-0.5
1983	Tor A	0	0	ø	4	0	0	0-0	5.1	8	4	3	0	0-0	5	6.75	65	.348	.348	0	ø	0	—	-1	0	-0.1
1985	NY A	0	0	ø	7	0	0	0-0	10	12	6	2	0	3-0	4	5.40	75	.300	.341	0	ø	0	—	-1	0	-0.1
Total	4	1	6	.143	44	3	0	0-0	85.1	95	55	14	1	46-6	47	5.27	77	.287	.372	0	ø	0	112	-11	0	-1.0

Cooper, Guy Guy Evans "Rebel"; B1.28.1893 Rome GA; D8.2.1951 Santa Monica CA; BB/TR/6´1˝/185; d5.2

YEAR	TM LG	W	L	PCT	G	GS	CG-SHO	SV-BS	IP	H	R	HR	HB	BB-IB	SO	ERA	AERA	OAV	OOB	AB-HR-SH	AVG	PB	SUP	APR	DL	PW
1914	NY A	0	0	ø	1	0	0	0	3	3	3	0	0	2	3	9.00	31	.273	.385	1	.000	-0	—	-2	—	-0.1
	Bos A	1	0	1.000	9	1	0	0	22	23	15	1	3	9	5	5.32	51	.299	.393	7	.000	-1*	244	-6	—	-0.4
	Year	1	0	1.000	10	1	0	0	25	26	18	1	3	11	8	5.76	47	.295	.392	8	.000	-1	243	-7	—	-0.5
1915	Bos A	0	0	ø	1	0	0	0	2	0	0	0	0	2	0	0.00	ø	.000	.286	0	ø	0	—	1	—	0.0
Total	2	1	0	1.000	11	1	0	0	27	26	18	1	3	13	8	5.33	51	.280	.385	8	.000	-1	242	-7	—	-0.5

Cooper, Mort Morton Cecil; B3.2.1913 Atherton MO; D11.17.1958 Little Rock AR; BR/TR/6´2˝/210; d9.14; b-Walker

YEAR	TM LG	W	L	PCT	G	GS	CG-SHO	SV-BS	IP	H	R	HR	HB	BB-IB	SO	ERA	AERA	OAV	OOB	AB-HR-SH	AVG	PB	SUP	APR	DL	PW
1938	StL N	2	1	.667	4	3	1	1	23.2	17	11	1	1	12	11	3.04	130	.195	.300	9-0-1	.222	0	86	2	—	0.3
1939	StL N	12	6	.667	45	26	7-2	4	210.2	208	94	6	2	97	130	3.25	127	.260	.342	69-2-6	.232	3*	96	16	—	1.5
1940	StL N	11	12	.478	38	29	16-3	3	230.2	225	103	12	3	86	95	3.63	110	.253	.321	83-0-7	.157	-2	97	11	—	0.7
1941	StL N	13	9	.591	29	25	12	0	186.2	175	88	15	3	69	118	3.91	106	.244	.313	70-0-1	.186	-0	92	0	0	-0.1
1942	†StL N★	**22**	7	.759	37	35	22-**10**	0	278.2	207	73	9	5	68	152	**1.78**	**193**	**.204**	**.258**	103-0-7	.184	-1	106	**47**	0	**4.7**
1943	†StL N★	**21**	8	**.724**	37	32	24-6	3	274	228	81	5	5	79	141	2.30	146	.226	.286	100-1-5	.170	-1	117	**33**	0	3.3
1944	†StL N	22	7	.759	34	33	22-**7**	1	252.1	227	74	6	5	60	97	2.46	143	.239	.288	94-0-4	.202	2	146	33	0	3.7
1945	StL N	2	0	1.000	4	3	1	0	23.2	20	7	1	1	7	14	1.52	246	.227	.292	6-0-1	.333	1	143	5	0	0.5
	Bos N✳	7	4	.636	20	11	4-1	1	78	77	35	4	1	27	45	3.35	115	.257	.320	26-1-0	.231	1	135	4	0	0.6
	Year	9	4	.692	24	14	5-1	1	101.2	97	42	5	2	34	59	2.92	130	.250	.314	32-1-1	.250	2	136	8	0	1.1
1946	Bos N☆	13	11	.542	28	27	15-4	1	199	181	76	16	0	39	83	3.12	110	.239	**.276**	67-1-8	.209	1	107	9	0	1.0
1947	Bos N	2	5	.286	10	7	2	0	46.2	48	26	2	2	13	15	4.05	96	.271	.328	13-0-1	.000	-1	71	-2	0	-0.4
	NY N	1	5	.167	8	8	2	0	36.2	51	32	7	0	13	12	7.12	57	.323	.374	14-1-2	.429	4	89	-12	0	-1.3
	Year	3	10	.231	18	15	4	0	83.1	99	58	9	2	26	27	5.40	74	.296	.350	27-1-3	.222	2	81	-14	0	-1.7
1949	Chi N	0	0	ø	1	0	0	0	0	2	3	1	0	1	0	(3)	ø	1.000	1.000	0	ø	0	—	-3	0	-0.2
Total	11	128	75	.631	295	239	128-33	14	1840.2	1666	703	85	28	571	913	2.97	123	.240	.300	654-6-43	.194	6	109	143	0	14.3

Copeland, Mays Mays; B8.31.1913 Mountain View AR; D11.29.1982 Indio CA; BR/TR/6´0˝/180; d4.27

YEAR	TM LG	W	L	PCT	G	GS	CG-SHO	SV-BS	IP	H	R	HR	HB	BB-IB	SO	ERA	AERA	OAV	OOB	AB-HR-SH	AVG	PB	SUP	APR	DL	PW
1935	StL N	0	0	ø	1	0	0	0	0.2	2	1	0	0	0	0	13.50	30	.667	.667	0	ø	0	—	-1	—	0.0

Coppinger, Rocky John Thomas; B3.19.1974 ElPaso TX; BR/TR/6´5˝/(225–250); [BalA93 19/539]; d6.11; Col Hill (TX) JC; [DL 2000 Mil N 181]

YEAR	TM LG	W	L	PCT	G	GS	CG-SHO	SV-BS	IP	H	R	HR	HB	BB-IB	SO	ERA	AERA	OAV	OOB	AB-HR-SH	AVG	PB	SUP	APR	DL	PW
1996	†Bal A✳	10	6	.625	23	22	0	0-0	125	126	76	25	2	60-1	104	5.18	95	.263	.344	0	ø	0	123	-3	0	-0.4
1997	Bal A	1	1	.500	5	4	0	0-0	20	21	14	2	1	16-1	22	6.30	70	.273	.400	0	ø	0	146	-4	156	-0.3
1998	Bal A	0	0	ø	6	1	0	0-0	15.2	16	9	3	0	7-1	13	5.17	88	.246	.319	0	ø	0	245	-1	0	-0.1
1999	Bal A	0	1	.000	11	2	0	0-0	21.2	25	21	8	0	19-0	17	8.31	57	.294	.419	1	1.000	0	119	-9	0	-0.4
	Mil N	5	3	.625	29	0	0	0-2	36.2	35	16	5	0	23-3	39	3.68	125	.250	.354	2	.000	-0	—	4	0	0.7
2001	Mil N	1	0	1.000	8	3	0	0-0	22.2	24	17	5	1	15-0	15	6.75	64	.282	.392	5-0-1	.000	-1	143	-6	0	-0.3
Total	5	17	11	.607	82	32	0	0-2	241.2	247	153	48	4	140-6	210	5.47	87	.265	.361	8-0-1	.125	-0	132	-19	337	-0.8

Coppola, Henry Henry Peter; B8.4.1912 E.Douglas MA; D7.10.1990 Norfolk MA; BR/TR/5´11˝/175; d4.19

YEAR	TM LG	W	L	PCT	G	GS	CG-SHO	SV-BS	IP	H	R	HR	HB	BB-IB	SO	ERA	AERA	OAV	OOB	AB-HR-SH	AVG	PB	SUP	APR	DL	PW
1935	Was A	3	4	.429	19	5	2-1	0	59.1	72	40	6	1	29	19	5.92	73	.300	.378	14	.071	-0	88	-9	—	-0.9
1936	Was A	0	0	ø	6	0	0	1	14	17	9	1	0	12	2	4.50	106	.315	.439	3	.333	1	—	0	—	0.1
Total	2	3	4	.429	25	5	2-1	1	73.1	89	49	7	1	41	21	5.65	78	.303	.390	17	.118	0	88	-9	—	-0.8

Corbett, Doug Douglas Mitchell; B11.4.1952 Sarasota FL; BR/TR/6´1˝/(185–192); d4.10; Col Florida

YEAR	TM LG	W	L	PCT	G	GS	CG-SHO	SV-BS	IP	H	R	HR	HB	BB-IB	SO	ERA	AERA	OAV	OOB	AB-HR-SH	AVG	PB	SUP	APR	DL	PW
1980	Min A	8	6	.571	73	0	0	23-7	136.1	102	31	7	1	42-8	89	1.98	221	.213	.277	0	ø	0	—	**35**	0	**4.8**
1981	Min A☆	2	6	.250	**54**	0	0	17-8	87.2	80	29	5	0	34-13	60	2.57	154	.239	.305	0	ø	0	—	12	0	1.7
1982	Min A	0	2	.000	10	0	0	3-3	22	27	13	3	0	10-1	15	5.32	80	.300	.370	0	ø	0	—	-2	0	-0.2
	Cal A	1	7	.125	33	0	0	8-4	57	46	32	8	0	25-5	37	5.05	81	.223	.307	0	ø	0	—	-5	0	-0.7
	Year	1	9	.100	43	0	0	11-7	79	73	45	11	0	35-6	52	5.13	81	.247	.326	0	ø	0	—	-6	0	-0.9
1983	Cal A	1	1	.500	11	0	0	0-1	17.1	26	10	1	1	4-2	18	3.63	111	.351	.392	0	ø	0	—	0	0	0.0
1984	Cal A	5	1	.833	45	1	0	4-3	85	76	22	2	2	30-12	48	2.12	189	.244	.310	0	ø	0	136	18	0	1.3
1985	Cal A	3	3	.500	30	0	0	0-1	46	49	33	7	1	20-3	24	4.89	84	.274	.348	0	ø	0	—	-6	35	-0.7
1986	†Cal A	4	2	.667	46	0	0	10-0	78.2	66	36	11	1	22-2	36	3.66	113	.231	.286	0	ø	0	—	4	0	0.4
1987	Bal A	0	2	.000	11	0	0	1-1	23	25	20	5	0	13-3	16	7.83	57	.281	.369	0	ø	0	—	-8	21	-0.6
Total	8	24	30	.444	313	1	0	66-28	553	497	226	49	6	200-49	343	3.32	125	.242	.310	0	ø	0	136	48	56	6.0

Corbett, Joe Joseph Aloysius; B12.4.1875 San Francisco CA; D5.2.1945 San Francisco CA; BR/TR/5´10˝/175; d8.23; Col St. Marys (CA)

YEAR	TM LG	W	L	PCT	G	GS	CG-SHO	SV-BS	IP	H	R	HR	HB	BB-IB	SO	ERA	AERA	OAV	OOB	AB-HR-SH	AVG	PB	SUP	APR	DL	PW
1895	Was N	0	2	.000	3	3	3	0	19	26	22	3	2	9	3	5.68	84	.321	.402	15	.133	-1*	69	-3	—	-0.3
1896	†Bal N	3	0	1.000	8	3	3	1	41	31	17	0	5	17	28	2.20	195	.208	.310	22	.273	1*	116	9	—	0.5
1897	†Bal N	24	8	.750	37	37	34-1	0	313	330	173	2	21	115	149	3.11	134	.269	.341	150-0-1	.247	-0*	147	31	—	2.5
1904	StL N	5	8	.385	14	14	12	0	108.2	110	75	2	8	51	68	4.39	61	.240	.327	43	.209	1	118	-20	—	-1.9
Total	4	32	18	.640	62	57	52-1	1	481.2	497	287	7	36	192	248	3.42	113	.259	.338	230-0-1	.235	1	134	17	—	0.8

Corbett, Sherman Sherman Stanley; B11.3.1962 New Braunfels TX; BL/TL/6´4˝/(203–210); [CalA84 3/60]; d5.29; Col Texas A&M

YEAR	TM LG	W	L	PCT	G	GS	CG-SHO	SV-BS	IP	H	R	HR	HB	BB-IB	SO	ERA	AERA	OAV	OOB	AB-HR-SH	AVG	PB	SUP	APR	DL	PW
1988	Cal A	2	1	.667	34	0	0	1-1	45.2	47	23	2	0	23-3	28	4.14	94	.273	.350	0	ø	0	—	-1	0	-0.1
1989	Cal A	0	0	ø	4	0	0	0-0	5.1	3	2	1	0	1-0	3	3.38	113	.158	.200	0	ø	0	—	0	0	0.0
1990	Cal A	0	0	ø	4	0	0	0-0	5	8	5	0	0	3-0	2	9.00	43	.364	.423	0	ø	0	—	-3	0	-0.1
Total	3	2	1	.667	42	0	0	1-1	56	58	30	3	0	27-3	33	4.50	86	.272	.346	0	ø	0	—	-4	0	-0.2

Corbin, Ray Alton Ray; B2.12.1949 Live Oak FL; BR/TR/6´2˝/190; d4.6; Col Lake City (FL) JC/North Florida CC

YEAR	TM LG	W	L	PCT	G	GS	CG-SHO	SV-BS	IP	H	R	HR	HB	BB-IB	SO	ERA	AERA	OAV	OOB	AB-HR-SH	AVG	PB	SUP	APR	DL	PW
1971	Min A	8	11	.421	52	11	2	3-1	140.1	141	74	19	3	70-11	83	4.10	86	.265	.351	34-0-4	.206	1	87	-10	0	-1.2
1972	Min A	8	9	.471	31	19	5-3	0-0	161.2	135	56	12	6	53-3	83	2.62	123	.230	.299	49-0-2	.082	-2*	97	10	0	0.8
1973	Min A	8	5	.615	51	7	1	14-2	148.1	124	58	7	5	60-4	83	3.03	131	.229	.308	0	ø	0	129	14	0	1.4
1974	Min A	7	6	.538	29	15	1	0-1	112.1	133	78	8	3	40-4	50	5.29	71	.294	.352	0	ø	0	110	-20	0	-2.0
1975	Min A	5	7	.417	18	11	3	0-0	89.2	105	59	13	2	38-5	49	5.12	75	.295	.363	0	ø	0	86	-13	49	-1.5
Total	5	36	38	.486	181	63	12-3	17-4	652.1	638	325	59	19	261-27	348	3.84	95	.258	.331	83-0-6	.133	-2	99	-19	49	-2.5

Corbin, Archie Archie Ray; B12.30.1967 Beaumont TX; BR/TR/6´4˝/(190–230); [NYN86 16/414]; d9.10

YEAR	TM LG	W	L	PCT	G	GS	CG-SHO	SV-BS	IP	H	R	HR	HB	BB-IB	SO	ERA	AERA	OAV	OOB	AB-HR-SH	AVG	PB	SUP	APR	DL	PW
1991	KC A	0	0	ø	2	0	0	0-0	2.1	3	1	0	0	2-0	1	3.86	107	.300	.417	0	ø	0	—	0	0	0.0
1996	Bal A	2	0	1.000	18	0	0	0-0	27.1	22	7	2	1	22-0	20	2.30	215	.222	.366	0	ø	0	—	8	0	0.5
1999	Fla N	0	1	.000	17	0	0	0-0	21	25	20	2	1	15-0	30	7.29	60	.291	.398	1	.000	-0	—	-8	36	-0.4
Total	3	2	1	.667	37	0	0	0-0	50.2	50	28	4	2	39-0	51	4.44	105	.256	.382	1	.000	-0	—	0	36	0.1

YEAR	TM LG	W	L	PCT	G	GS	CG-SHO	SV-BS	IP	H	R	HR	HB	BB-IB	SO	ERA	AERA	OAV	OOB	AB-HR-SH	AVG	PB	SUP	APR	DL	PW
CORCORAN, LARRY	Lawrence J.; B8.10.1859 Brooklyn NY; D10.14.1891 Newark NJ; BL/TR (TB 1884p)/5´3˝/127; d5.1; b–Mike; ▲																									
1880	Chi N	43	14	.754	63	60	57-4	2	536.1	404	218	6	—	99	**268**	1.95	124	.199	.236	286	.231	-0*	128	29	—	2.9
1881	Chi N	**31**	14	.689	45	44	43-4	0	396.2	380	205	10	—	78	150	2.31	118	.242	.278	189	.222	-1*	128	16	—	1.2
1882	Chi N	27	12	**.692**	39	39	38-3	0	355.2	281	153	5	—	63	170	**1.95**	**148**	**.200**	**.234**	169-1	.207	-2*	136	34	—	2.9
1883	Chi N	34	20	.630	56	53	51-3	0	473.2	483	281	7	—	82	216	2.49	132	.247	.277	263	.209	-2*	116	37	—	3.2
1884	Chi N	35	23	.603	60	59	57-7	0	516.2	473	286	35	—	116	272	2.40	130	.229	.270	251-1	.243	2*	118	35	—	3.5
1885	Chi N	5	2	.714	7	7	6-1	0	59.1	63	38	2	—	24	10	3.64	83	.259	.326	22	.273	2	156	-2	—	-0.1
	NY N	2	1	.667	3	3	2	0	25	24	12	1	—	11	10	2.88	93	.245	.321	14	.357	1	191	0	—	0.2
	Year	7	3	.700	10	10	8-1	0	84.1	87	50	3	—	35	20	3.42	85	.255	.324	36	.306	3	165	-4	—	0.1
1886	Was N	0	1	.000	2	1	1	0	14	16	11	0	—	4	3	5.79	56	.271	.317	81	.185	0*	76	-3	—	-0.2
1887	Ind N	0	2	.000	2	2	1	0	15	23	31	2	2	19	4	12.60	33	.338	.494	10	.200	-0*	94	-14	—	-1.1
Total	8	177	89	.665	277	268	256-22	2	2392.1	2147	1235	68	2	496	1103	2.36	123	.226	.264	1285-2	.223	-1	125	132	—	12.5
CORCORAN, MIKE	Michael; B Brooklyn NY; d7.15; b–Larry																									
1884	Chi N	0	1	.000	1	1	1	0	9	16	14	1	—	7	2	4.00	78	.372	.460	3	.000	-0	0	-2	—	-0.2
CORCORAN, ROY	Roy Elliot; B5.11.1980 Baton Rouge LA; BR/TR/5´10˝/170; d7.30; Col Louisiana St.																									
2003	Mon N	0	0	ø	5	0	0	0-0	7.1	7	2	0	0	3-0	2	1.23	362	.250	.323	1	.000	-0	—	2	0	0.1
2004	Mon N	0	0	ø	5	0	0	0-0	5.1	7	4	0	0	5-0	4	6.75	68	.304	.429	0	ø	0	—	-1	0	-0.1
2006	Was N	0	1	.000	6	0	0	0-1	5.2	12	8	1	0	4-0	6	11.12	39	.414	.471	1	.000	0	—	-5	0	-0.6
Total	3	0	1	.000	16	0	0	0-1	18.1	26	14	1	0	12-0	12	5.89	76	.325	.409	2	.000	0	—	-4	0	-0.6
CORCORAN, TIM	Timothy Hugh; B4.15.1978 Baton Rouge LA; BR/TR/6´2˝/205; [NYN96 44/1300]; d6.14; Col Gulf Coast (FL) CC																									
2005	TB A	0	0	ø	10	1	0	0-0	22.2	19	15	1	1	12-0	13	5.96	74	.226	.330	0	ø	0	42	-3	0	-0.2
2006	TB A	5	9	.357	21	16	0	0-0	90.1	92	48	10	4	48-3	59	4.38	106	.271	.365	4-0-1	.000	-0	88	3	0	0.3
Total	2	5	9	.357	31	17	0	0-0	113	111	63	11	5	60-3	72	4.70	98	.262	.358	4-0-1	.000	-0	86	0	0	0.1
CORDERO, CHAD	Chad Patrick; B4.18.1982 Upland CA; BR/TR/6´0˝/(190–200); d8.30; Col Cal St.–Fullerton																									
2003	Mon N	1	0	1.000	12	0	0	1-0	11	4	2	1	0	3-1	12	1.64	271	.111	.179	0-0-1	ø	0	—	3	0	0.3
2004	Mon N	7	3	.700	69	0	0	14-4	82.2	68	28	8	1	43-4	83	2.94	156	.221	.315	2-0-1	.000	-0	—	15	0	2.0
2005	Was N★	2	4	.333	74	0	0	**47**-7	74.1	55	24	9	2	17-2	61	1.82	226	.198	.248	0	ø	0	—	16	0	2.8
2006	Was N	7	4	.636	68	0	0	29-4	73.1	59	27	13	3	22-5	69	3.19	137	.215	.279	2	.000	-0	—	10	0	2.0
Total	4	17	11	.607	223	0	0	91-15	241.1	186	81	31	6	85-12	225	2.61	167	.208	.279	4-0-2	.000	-0	—	44	0	7.1
CORDERO, FRANCISCO	Francisco Javier; B5.11.1975 Santo Domingo, D.R.; BR/TR/6´2˝/(200–235); d8.2																									
1999	Det A	2	2	.500	20	0	0	0-0	19	19	7	2	0	18-2	19	3.32	151	.284	.416	0	ø	0	—	4	0	0.7
2000	Tex A	1	2	.333	56	0	0	0-3	77.1	87	51	11	4	48-3	49	5.35	95	.285	.383	0	ø	0	—	-2	0	-0.1
2001	Tex A	0	1	.000	3	0	0	0-0	2.1	3	1	0	0	2-1	1	3.86	124	.300	.417	0	ø	0	—	0	186	0.0
2002	Tex A	2	0	1.000	39	0	0	10-2	45.1	33	12	2	2	13-1	41	1.79	268	.204	.271	1	.000	-0	—	13	32	1.0
2003	Tex A	5	8	.385	73	0	0	15-10	82.2	70	33	4	2	38-6	90	2.94	169	.230	.315	0	ø	0	—	15	0	2.6
2004	Tex A☆	3	4	.429	67	0	0	49-5	71.2	60	19	1	1	32-2	79	2.13	231	.226	.311	0	ø	0	—	21	0	4.1
2005	Tex A	3	1	.750	69	0	0	37-8	69	61	28	5	4	30-2	79	3.39	134	.234	.319	0	ø	0	—	9	0	1.2
2006	Tex A	7	4	.636	49	0	0	6-9	48.2	49	27	5	3	16-1	54	4.81	97	.265	.325	0	ø	0	—	0	0	0.0
	Mil N	3	1	.750	28	0	0	16-2	26.2	20	5	2	0	16-1	30	1.69	266	.213	.327	0	ø	0	—	9	0	1.7
Total	8	26	23	.531	404	0	0	133-39	442.2	402	183	32	16	213-19	442	3.33	145	.243	.331	1	.000	-0	—	69	218	11.2
CORDOVA, FRANCISCO	Francisco; B4.26.1972 Cerro Azul, Veracruz, Mexico; BR/TR/6´1˝/(163–197); d4.2; [DL 2001 Pit N 190]																									
1996	Pit N	4	7	.364	59	6	0	12-6	99	103	49	11	2	20-6	95	4.09	107	.263	.303	16-0-2	.125	-1	127	4	0	0.4
1997	Pit N	11	8	.579	29	29	2-2	0-0	178.2	175	80	14	9	49-4	121	3.63	118	.259	.314	56-0-8	.089	-2	111	13	15	1.1
1998	Pit N	13	14	.481	33	33	3-2	0-0	220.1	204	91	22	3	69-5	157	3.31	129	.245	.303	75-0-2	.120	-2	87	24	0	2.5
1999	Pit N	8	10	.444	27	27	2	0-0	160.2	166	83	16	4	59-6	98	4.43	104	.273	.339	49-0-5	.163	-0	95	6	38	0.6
2000	Pit N	6	8	.429	18	17	0	0-0	95	107	63	12	2	38-4	66	5.21	89	.285	.352	35	.114	-1	95	-7	90	-0.9
Total	5	42	47	.472	166	112	7-4	12-6	753.2	755	366	75	20	235-25	537	3.96	111	.262	.320	231-0-17	.121	-6	98	40	333	3.7
COREY, BRYAN	Bryan Scott; B10.21.1973 Thousand Oaks CA; BR/TR/6´1˝/(170–180); [DetA93 12/333]; d5.13; Col Los Angeles Pierce (CA) JC																									
1998	Ari N	0	0	ø	3	0	0	0-0	4	6	4	1	1	2-0	1	9.00	48	.375	.474	0	ø	0	—	-2	0	-0.1
2002	LA N	0	0	ø	1	0	0	0-0	1	0	0	0	0	0-0	0	0.00	ø	.000	.000	0	ø	0	—	0	15	0.0
2006	Tex A	1	1	.500	16	0	0	0-0	17.1	15	5	0	0	8-0	13	2.60	180	.231	.311	0	ø	0	—	4	0	0.4
	Bos A	1	0	1.000	16	0	0	0-0	21.2	20	11	1	2	7-0	15	4.57	102	.250	.319	0	ø	0	—	1	0	0.0
	Year	2	1	.667	32	0	0	0-0	39	35	16	1	2	15-0	28	3.69	127	.241	.315	0	ø	0	—	5	0	0.4
Total	3	2	1	.667	36	0	0	0-0	44	41	20	2	3	17-0	29	4.09	113	.250	.326	0	ø	0	—	3	15	0.3
COREY, ED	Edward Norman "Ike" (b Abraham Simon Cohen); B7.13.1894 Chicago IL; D9.17.1970 Kenosha WI; BR/TR/6´0˝/170; d7.2																									
1918	Chi A	0	0	ø	1	0	0	0	2	2	1	0	0	1	0	4.50	61	.333	.429	1	.000	-0	—	0	—	0.0
COREY, FRED	Frederick Harrison; B1855 Coventry RI; D11.27.1912 Providence RI; BR/TR/5´7˝/160; d5.1; ▲																									
1878	Pro N	1	2	.333	5	5	2	0	23	22	10	0	—	7	7	2.35	94	.250	.305	21	.143	-1*	146	0	—	0.0
1880	Wor N	8	9	.471	25	17	9-2	2	148.1	131	72	6	—	16	47	2.43	107	.219	.239	138	.174	-3*	77	4	—	0.0
1881	Wor N	6	15	.286	23	21	20-1	0	188.2	231	127	3	—	31	33	3.72	81	.299	.326	203	.222	-1*	79	-12	—	-1.2
1882	Wor N	1	13	.071	21	14	12	0	139	180	132	5	—	19	36	3.56	87	.286	.307	255	.247	0*	83	-10	—	-0.7
1883	Phi AA	10	7	.588	18	16	15	0	148.1	182	106	3	—	24	42	3.40	104	.283	.309	298-1	.258	2*	123	3	—	0.4
1885	Phi AA	1	0	1.000	1	1	1	0	9	18	9	2	0	1	3	7.00	49	.419	.432	384-1	.245	0*	257	-2	—	-0.2
Total	6	27	46	.370	93	74	59-3	2	656.1	764	456	19	0	98	168	3.32	92	.276	.300	1299-2	.236	-3	96	-17	—	-1.7
COREY, MARK	Mark Franklin; B11.16.1974 Coudersport PA; BR/TR/6´2˝/(210–225); [CinN95 4/111]; d10.2; Col Edinboro																									
2001	NY N	0	0	ø	2	0	0	0-0	1.2	5	3	0	0	3-1	3	16.20	25	.500	.615	0	ø	0	—	-2	0	-0.1
2002	NY N	0	3	.000	12	0	0	0-0	10	10	7	2	1	8-1	9	4.50	88	.250	.388	1	.000	-0*	—	-1	15	-0.3
	Col N	0	0	ø	14	0	0	0-0	12	22	16	7	2	8-1	12	12.00	39	.400	.492	1	.000	-0	—	-8	0	-0.4
	Year	0	3	.000	26	0	0	0-0	22	32	23	9	3	16-2	21	8.59	51	.337	.447	2	.000	-0	—	-10	0	-0.7
2003	Pit N	1	2	.333	22	0	0	0-0	30.1	29	19	2	1	11-1	27	5.34	81	.252	.315	0	ø	0	—	-3	0	-0.3
2004	Pit N	1	2	.333	31	0	0	0-1	35.2	39	20	3	2	19-3	28	4.54	95	.275	.366	1	.000	-0	—	-1	0	-0.1
Total	4	2	7	.222	81	0	0	0-1	89.2	105	65	14	6	49-7	79	6.02	72	.290	.380	3	.000	-0	—	-15	15	-1.2
CORKHILL, POP	John Stewart; B4.11.1858 Parkesburg PA; D4.3.1921 Pennsauken NJ; BL/TR/5´10˝/180; d5.1.1883; ▲																									
1884	Cin AA	1	0	1.000	1	0	0	0	5	1	1	0	0	2	4	1.80	185	.063	.167	452-4	.274	0*	—	1	—	0.2
1885	Cin AA	1	4	.200	8	1	0	1	37	36	25	2	1	10	12	3.65	89	.243	.296	440-1	.252	1*	18	-2	—	-0.2
1886	Cin AA	0	0	ø	1	0	0	0	0.2	1	1	0	0	0	1	13.50	26	.333	.333	540-5	.265	0*	—	-1	—	0.0
1887	Cin AA	1	0	1.000	5	0	0	0	14.2	22	15	0	0	5	3	5.52	79	.324	.370	541-5	.311	1*	—	-2	—	-0.1
1888	Cin AA	0	0	ø	2	0	0	1	5	8	6	1	0	0	1	10.80	29	.348	.348	490-1	.271	0*	—	-3	—	-0.1
Total	5	3	4	.429	17	1	0	2	62.1	68	48	3	1	17	21	4.62	76	.264	.312	2463-16	.276	3	18	-7	—	-0.2
CORKINS, MIKE	Michael Patrick; B5.25.1946 Riverside CA; BR/TR/6´1˝/(190–200); d9.8																									
1969	SD N	1	3	.250	6	4	0	0-0	17	27	17	3	0	8-1	13	8.47	42	.370	.427	3	.000	0	74	-9	0	-1.6
1970	SD N	5	6	.455	24	18	1	0-1	111	109	62	11	4	79-10	75	4.62	87	.258	.377	37-1-5	.216	2*	113	-7	0	-0.4
1971	SD N	0	0	ø	8	0	0	0-0	13	14	6	1	0	6-0	16	3.46	96	.280	.357	0	ø	0	—	0	0	0.0
1972	SD N	6	9	.400	47	9	2-1	6-4	140	125	61	14	4	62-9	108	3.54	94	.240	.322	38-1-4	.237	2	65	-3	0	0.0
1973	SD N	5	8	.385	47	11	2	3-2	122	130	79	12	11	61-10	82	4.50	78	.274	.367	33-3-1	.212	4*	114	-17	0	-1.4
1974	SD N	2	2	.500	25	2	0	0-0	56.1	53	32	5	1	32-4	41	4.79	75	.255	.354	8-0-1	.000	-0*	122	-7	0	-0.5
Total	6	19	28	.404	157	44	5-1	9-7	459.1	458	257	46	20	248-34	335	4.39	82	.262	.357	119-5-11	.202	9	104	-43	0	-3.9
CORMIER, LANCE	Lance Robert; B8.19.1980 Lafayette LA; BR/TR/6´1˝/(190–200); [AriN02 4/129]; d6.19; Col Alabama																									
2004	Ari N	1	4	.200	17	5	0	0-0	45.1	62	42	13	2	25-2	24	8.14	56	.333	.412	8-0-1	.250	1	90	-15	0	-1.4
2005	Ari N	7	3	.700	67	0	0	0-1	79.1	86	50	7	5	43-5	63	5.11	87	.284	.381	6-0-1	.333	0	—	-6	0	-0.7
2006	Atl N	4	5	.444	29	9	0	0-0	73.2	90	44	8	2	39-7	43	4.89	93	.314	.395	12-0-2	.083	-1	63	-3	15	-0.4
Total	3	12	12	.500	113	14	0	0-1	198.1	238	136	28	9	107-14	130	5.72	79	.307	.393	26-0-4	.192	1	74	-24	15	-2.5

YEAR	TM LG	W	L	PCT	G	GS	CG-SHO	SV-BS	IP	H	R	HR	HB	BB-IB	SO	ERA	AERA	OAV	OOB	AB-HR-SH	AVG	PB	SUP	APR	DL	PW
CORMIER, RHEAL	Rheal Paul; B4.23.1967 Moncton NB, Can.; BL/TL/5´10˝/(185–200); [StLN88 6/158]; d8.15; Col CC of Rhode Island																									
1991	StL N	4	5	.444	11	10	2	0-0	67.2	74	35	5	2	8-1	38	4.12	91	.277	.300	21-0-1	.238	1	77	-3	0	-0.3
1992	StL N	10	10	.500	31	30	3	0-0	186	194	83	15	5	33-2	117	3.68	93	.269	.305	59-0-10	.102	-2	105	-6	0	-0.7
1993	StL N	7	6	.538	38	21	1	0-0	145.1	163	80	18	4	27-3	75	4.33	93	.284	.319	47-0-6	.234	2	113	-6	26	-0.2
1994	StL N	3	2	.600	7	7	0	0-0	39.2	40	24	6	3	7-0	26	5.45	78	.256	.298	14	.286	1*	104	-5	89	-0.4
1995	†Bos A	7	5	.583	48	12	0	0-2	115	131	60	12	3	31-2	69	4.07	119	.294	.342	0	ø	0	97	9	0	0.8
1996	Mon N	7	10	.412	33	27	1-1	0-0	159.2	165	80	16	9	41-3	100	4.17	104	.270	.321	43-0-11	.186	1	79	4	15	0.6
1997	Mon N	0	1	.000	1	1	0	0-0	1.1	4	5	1	0	1-0	0	33.75	12	.500	.556	0	ø	0	66	-4	176	-0.6
1999	†Bos A	2	0	1.000	60	0	0	0-3	63.1	61	34	4	5	18-2	39	3.69	135	.246	.307	0	ø	0	—	7	0	0.3
2000	Bos A	3	3	.500	64	0	0	0-2	68.1	74	40	7	0	17-2	43	4.61	109	.275	.316	0	ø	0	—	2	0	0.2
2001	Phi N	5	6	.455	60	0	0	1-5	51.1	49	26	5	4	17-4	37	4.21	98	.247	.320	1	.000	-0	—	-1	19	-0.1
2002	Phi N	5	6	.455	54	0	0	0-3	60	61	38	6	4	32-6	49	5.25	73	.265	.362	3	.333	1	—	-10	0	-1.5
2003	Phi N	8	0	1.000	65	0	0	1-3	84.2	54	18	4	1	25-2	67	1.70	234	.182	.248	2	.500	1	—	23	0	2.2
2004	Phi N	4	5	.444	84	0	0	0-7	81	70	32	7	5	26-6	46	3.56	125	.237	.309	1	.000	-0	—	9	0	0.9
2005	Phi N	4	2	.667	57	0	0	0-2	47.1	56	33	9	2	16-1	34	5.89	74	.296	.354	1-0-2	.000	-0	—	-8	0	-0.8
2006	Phi N	2	2	.500	43	0	0	0-4	34	27	6	2	3	13-3	13	1.59	295	.225	.316	0	ø	0	—	11	0	1.3
	Cin N	0	1	.000	21	0	0	0-0	14	21	7	3	0	4-0	6	4.50	105	.350	.391	0	ø	0	—	1	0	0.0
	Year	2	3	.400	64	0	0	0-4	48	48	13	5	3	17-3	19	2.44	193	.267	.340	0	ø	0	—	12	0	1.3
Total	15	71	64	.526	677	108	7-1	2-31	1218.2	1244	601	120	50	316-37	759	4.02	105	.265	.316	192-0-30	.188	4	92	23	325	1.7
CORNEJO, NATE	Nathan J.; B9.24.1979 Wellington KS; BR/TR/6´5˝/(200–245); [DetA98 1/34]; d8.8; f–Mardie																									
2001	Det A	4	4	.500	10	10	0	0-0	42.2	63	38	10	3	28-4	22	7.38	60	.342	.437	0	ø	0	124	-14	0	-2.0
2002	Det A	1	5	.167	9	9	1	0-0	50	63	33	6	2	18-0	23	5.04	87	.303	.362	0	ø	0	73	-5	0	-0.5
2003	Det A	6	17	.261	32	32	2	0-0	194.2	236	111	18	3	58-8	46	4.67	94	.307	.356	4-0-1	.000	-0	66	-7	0	-0.7
2004	Det A	1	3	.250	5	5	0	0-0	25.2	42	25	4	1	11-1	12	8.42	53	.375	.435	0	ø	0	124	-11	154	-1.3
Total	4	12	29	.293	56	56	3	0-0	313	404	207	38	9	115-13	103	5.41	81	.318	.376	4-0-1	.000	-0	83	-37	154	-4.5
CORNEJO, MARDIE	Nieves Mardie; B8.5.1951 Wellington KS; BR/TR/6´3˝/200; [NYN73 21/493]; d4.8; s–Nate; Col Tulsa																									
1978	NY N	4	2	.667	25	0	0	3-0	36.2	37	12	1	3	14-5	17	2.45	144	.285	.358	0	ø	0	—	4	0	0.7
CORNELIUS, REID	Jonathan Reid; B6.2.1970 Thomasville AL; BR/TR/6´0˝/(200–210); [MonN88 11/284]; d4.29																									
1995	Mon N	0	0	ø	8	0	0	0-0	9	11	8	3	2	5-0	4	8.00	54	.306	.419	0	ø	0	—	-3	0	-0.2
	NY N	3	7	.300	10	10	0	0-0	57.2	64	36	8	1	25-5	35	5.15	78	.284	.354	20	.100	-1	101	-7	0	-1.1
	Year	3	7	.300	18	10	0	0-0	66.2	75	44	11	3	30-5	39	5.54	74	.287	.364	20	.100	-1	100	-11	0	-1.3
1999	Fla N	1	0	1.000	5	2	0	0-0	19.1	16	7	0	0	5-1	12	3.26	134	.229	.280	5-0-1	.200	0	84	3	0	0.2
2000	Fla N	4	10	.286	22	21	0	0-0	125	135	74	19	4	50-4	50	4.82	91	.282	.351	37-0-4	.135	-1*	76	-7	0	-0.6
Total	3	8	17	.320	45	33	0	0-0	211	226	125	30	7	85-10	101	4.91	87	.279	.349	62-0-5	.129	-2	83	-14	0	-1.7
CORNELL, JEFF	Jeffery Ray; B2.10.1957 Kansas City MO; BB/TR/5´11˝/170; [KCA78 8/207]; d6.2; Col Missouri																									
1984	SF N	1	3	.250	23	0	0	0-1	38.1	51	30	4	1	22-6	19	6.10	58	.340	.423	4	.000	-0	—	-11	0	-1.2
CORNETT, BRAD	Brad Byron; B2.4.1969 Lamesa TX; BR/TR/6´3˝/(188–190); d6.8; Col Lubbock Christian																									
1994	Tor A	1	3	.250	9	4	0	0-0	31	40	25	1	3	11-2	22	6.68	73	.331	.394	0	ø	0	52	-6	0	-0.6
1995	Tor A	0	0	ø	5	0	0	0-0	5	9	6	1	1	3-0	4	9.00	53	.429	.520	0	ø	0	—	-3	30	-0.1
Total	2	1	3	.250	14	4	0	0-0	36	49	31	2	4	14-2	26	7.00	69	.345	.414	0	ø	0	52	-9	30	-0.7
CORNUTT, TERRY	Terry Stanton; B10.2.1952 Roseburg OR; BR/TR/6´2˝/(185–195); [SFN72 S4/49]; d4.9; Col Linn–Benton (OR) CC																									
1977	SF N	1	2	.333	28	1	0	0-0	44.1	38	24	4	0	22-5	23	3.86	102	.229	.316	1-0-1	.000	-0	0	0	0	-0.1
1978	SF N	0	0	ø	1	0	0	0-0	3	1	0	0	0	0-0	0	0.00	ø	.100	.100	0	ø	0	—	1	0	0.1
Total	2	1	2	.333	29	1	0	0-0	47.1	39	24	4	0	22-5	23	3.61	108	.222	.305	1-0-1	.000	-0	0	1	0	0.0
CORPAS, MANUEL	Manuel; B12.3.1982 Panama City, Pan; BR/TR/6´3˝/170; d7.18																									
2006	Col N	1	2	.333	35	0	0	0-2	32.1	36	13	3	2	8-1	27	3.62	133	.286	.338	0	ø	0	—	4	0	0.3
CORREA, ED	Edwin Josue (Andino); B4.29.1966 Hato Rey, PR; BR/TR/6´2˝/(192–205); d9.18; [DL 1988 Tex A 150, 1989 Tex A 151]																									
1985	Chi A	1	0	1.000	5	1	0	0-0	10.1	11	9	2	0	11-0	10	6.97	62	.275	.431	0	ø	0	63	-3	0	-0.3
1986	Tex A	12	14	.462	32	32	4-2	0-0	202.1	167	102	15	3	126-2	189	4.23	102	.223	.336	0	ø	0	82	4	0	0.6
1987	Tex A	3	5	.375	15	15	0	0-0	70	83	63	17	4	52-2	61	7.59	60	.296	.411	0	ø	0	110	-22	63	-2.0
Total	3	16	19	.457	52	48	4-2	0-0	282.2	261	174	34	7	189-4	260	5.16	85	.244	.360	0	ø	0	91	-21	364	-1.7
CORREIA, KEVIN	Kevin John; B8.24.1980 San Diego CA; BR/TR/6´3˝/(200–210); [SFN02 4/127]; d7.10; Col Cal Poly–San Luis Obispo																									
2003	SF N	3	1	.750	10	7	0	0-0	39.1	41	16	6	4	18-1	28	3.66	116	.275	.366	13-0-1	.154	-0	120	3	0	0.2
2004	SF N	0	1	.000	12	1	0	0-0	19	25	20	3	1	10-0	14	8.05	54	.333	.404	3	.333	1	257	-8	0	-0.3
2005	SF N	2	5	.286	16	11	0	0-0	58.1	61	31	12	4	31-2	44	4.63	92	.274	.371	14-0-1	.071	-0	81	-2	0	-0.3
2006	SF N	2	0	1.000	48	0	0	0-1	69.2	64	27	5	3	22-0	57	3.49	127	.242	.303	12	.083	-1	—	8	0	0.3
Total	4	7	7	.500	86	19	0	0-1	186.1	191	94	26	12	81-3	143	4.35	100	.268	.349	42-0-2	.119	-0	102	1	0	-0.1
CORRIDON, FRANK	Francis Joseph "Fiddler"; B11.25.1880 Newport RI; D2.21.1941 Syracuse NY; BB/TR/6´0˝/170; d4.15																									
1904	Chi N	5	5	.500	12	10	9	0	100.1	88	43	2	7	37	34	3.05	87	.240	.321	58-0-1	.224	0*	72	-2	—	0.0
	Phi N	6	5	.545	12	11	11-1	0	94.1	88	33	2	8	28	44	2.19	122	.250	.320	35	.171	-0	65	6	—	0.8
	Year	11	10	.524	24	21	20-1	0	194.2	176	76	4	15	65	78	2.64	101	.245	.320	93-0-1	.204	0	69	4	—	0.8
1905	Phi N	10	12	.455	35	26	18-1	1	212	203	109	2	16	57	79	3.48	84	.257	.319	72-1-2	.208	4	101	-12	—	-0.6
1907	Phi N	18	14	.563	37	32	23-3	2	274	228	107	0	9	89	131	2.46	98	.230	.299	97	.165	0*	112	-4	—	-0.2
1908	Phi N	14	10	.583	27	24	18-2	1	208.1	178	69	0	6	48	50	2.51	97	.239	.290	73-0-3	.123	-2	109	1	—	0.2
1909	Phi N	11	7	.611	27	19	11-3	0	171	147	61	0	6	61	69	2.11	123	.242	.318	59-0-3	.186	0	119	7	—	1.0
1910	StL N	6	14	.300	30	18	9	3	156	168	88	1	9	55	51	3.81	78	.283	.353	51-0-1	.196	-0	83	-16	—	-1.8
Total	6	70	67	.511	180	140	99-10	7	1216	1100	510	7	61	375	458	2.80	95	.247	.315	445-1-10	.180	3	99	-20	—	-0.6
CORSI, JIM	James Bernard; B9.9.1961 Newton MA; BR/TR/6´1˝/(210–230); [NYA82 25/642]; d6.28; Col St. Leo; [DL 1990 Oak A 178]																									
1988	Oak A	0	1	.000	11	1	0	0-0	21.1	20	10	1	0	6-1	10	3.80	100	.260	.302	0	ø	0	168	0	0	0.0
1989	Oak A	1	2	.333	22	0	0	0-0	38.1	26	8	2	1	10-0	21	1.88	197	.194	.252	0	ø	0	—	9	0	0.6
1991	Hou N	0	5	.000	47	0	0	0-3	77.2	76	37	6	0	23-5	53	3.71	95	.259	.310	1	.000	-0	—	-2	0	-0.1
1992	†Oak A	4	2	.667	32	0	0	0-0	44	44	12	2	0	18-2	19	1.43	264	.273	.343	0	ø	0	—	10	0	1.3
1993	Fla N	0	2	.000	15	0	0	0-0	20.1	28	15	1	0	10-3	7	6.64	66	.337	.404	0	ø	0	—	-4	115	-0.4
1995	Oak A	2	4	.333	38	0	0	2-2	45	31	14	2	2	26-1	26	2.20	206	.203	.324	0	ø	0	—	11	47	1.4
1996	Oak A	6	0	1.000	56	0	0	3-3	73.2	71	33	6	3	34-4	43	4.03	123	.269	.356	0	ø	0	—	9	21	0.7
1997	Bos A	5	3	.625	52	0	0	2-7	57.2	56	26	1	4	21-7	40	3.43	136	.255	.327	0	ø	0	—	7	29	0.9
1998	†Bos A	3	2	.600	59	0	0	0-3	66	58	23	6	1	23-2	49	2.59	182	.235	.301	1	.000	-0	—	14	19	1.0
1999	Bos A	1	2	.333	23	0	0	0-3	24	25	15	4	2	19-3	14	5.25	95	.284	.418	0	ø	0	—	0	0	0.0
	Bal A	0	1	.000	13	0	0	0-1	13.1	15	4	2	0	1-0	8	2.70	174	.294	.308	0	ø	0	—	3	15	0.2
	Year	1	3	.250	36	0	0	0-4	37.1	40	19	6	2	20-3	22	4.34	113	.288	.383	0	ø	0	—	2	0	0.2
Total	10	22	24	.478	368	1	0	7-22	481.1	450	197	33	13	191-28	290	3.25	133	.254	.328	2	.000	-0	168	57	424	5.6
CORT, BARRY	Barry Lee; B4.15.1956 Toronto ON, Can.; BR/TR/6´5˝/195; [MilA74 4/78]; d4.22																									
1977	Mil A	1	1	.500	7	3	1	0-0	24.1	25	9	1	1	9-1	17	3.33	123	.281	.350	0	ø	0	80	3	22	0.2
CORTES, DAVID	David C.; B10.15.1973 Mexicali, Baja California, Mexico; BR/TR/5´11˝/(195–225); d8.30; [DL 2000 Atl N 181]																									
1999	Atl N	0	0	ø	4	0	0	0-0	3.2	3	3	0	0	4-0	2	4.91	91	.214	.389	0	ø	0	—	-1	0	0.0
2003	Cle A	0	0	ø	2	0	0	0-0	3	8	5	1	0	0-0	1	12.00	37	.471	.444	0	ø	0	—	-3	0	-0.1
2005	Col N	2	0	1.000	50	0	0	2-1	52.2	50	24	9	1	10-2	36	4.10	114	.251	.288	2	.000	-0	—	4	0	0.2
2006	Col N	3	1	.750	30	0	0	0-1	29.1	35	14	3	1	6-1	14	4.30	112	.310	.344	0	ø	0	—	2	0	0.2
Total	4	5	1	.833	86	0	0	2-2	88.2	96	46	13	2	20-3	53	4.47	105	.280	.319	2	.000	-0	—	2	181	0.3

YEAR	TM LG	W	L	PCT	G	GS	CG-SHO	SV-BS	IP	H	R	HR	HB	BB-IB	SO	ERA	AERA	OAV	OOB	AB-HR-SH	AVG	PB	SUP	APR	DL	PW
Corwin, Al	Elmer Nathan; B12.3.1926 Newburgh NY; D10.23.2003 Geneva IL; BR/TR/6´1˝/170; d7.25																									
1951	†NY N	5	1	.833	15	8	3-1	1	59	49	27	7	0	21	30	3.66	107	.222	.289	20-0-2	.050	-2	110	2	0	-0.1
1952	NY N	6	1	.857	21	7	1	2	67.2	58	23	5	0	36	36	2.66	139	.237	.335	21-0-1	.095	-1*	117	8	0	0.7
1953	NY N	6	4	.600	48	7	2-1	2	106.2	122	65	17	3	68	49	4.98	86	.290	.393	32-2-2	.281	4*	110	-7	0	-0.3
1954	NY N	1	3	.250	20	0	0	0	31.1	35	19	4	0	14	14	4.02	100	.297	.363	3	.000	-0*	—	-1	0	-0.2
1955	NY N	0	1	.000	13	0	0	0	24.2	25	11	3	0	17-2	13	4.01	100	.263	.372	3	.000	-0	—	1	0	0.0
Total	5	18	10	.643	117	22	6-2	5	289.1	289	145	36	3	156-2	142	3.98	101	.263	.355	79-2-5	.152	0	111	3	0	0.1
Cosgrove, Mike	Michael John; B2.17.1951 Phoenix AZ; BL/TL/6´1˝/170; [HouN70*S2/38]; d9.10; Col Phoenix (AZ) JC																									
1972	Hou N	0	1	.000	7	1	0	1-0	13.2	16	8	2	0	3-0	7	4.61	73	.286	.317	2-0-1	.000	-0	53	-2	0	-0.2
1973	Hou N	1	1	.500	13	0	0	0-1	10	11	2	1	0	8-2	2	1.80	203	.282	.396	0	ø	0	—	2	0	0.4
1974	Hou N	7	3	.700	45	0	0	2-3	90	76	35	2	1	39-3	47	3.50	100	.232	.313	18-0-2	.056	-1	—	2	0	0.1
1975	Hou N	1	2	.333	32	3	1	5-3	71.1	62	24	2	0	37-1	32	3.03	112	.245	.338	13-0-2	.154	0	95	4	0	0.3
1976	Hou N	3	4	.429	22	16	1-1	0-0	89.2	106	63	6	2	58-2	34	5.52	58	.303	.399	23-0-5	.087	-1	126	-25	0	-1.8
Total	5	12	11	.522	119	20	2-1	8-7	274.2	271	132	13	3	145-8	122	4.03	84	.264	.353	56-0-10	.089	-2	113	-19	0	-1.2
Cosman, Jim	James Henry; B2.19.1943 Brockport NY; BR/TR/6´4.5˝/(205–211); d10.2; Col Middle Tennessee																									
1966	StL N	1	0	1.000	1	1	1-1	0	9	2	0	0	1	2-0	5	0.00	ø	.074	.167	3	.000	-0	49	4	0	0.4
1967	StL N	1	0	1.000	10	5	0	0	31.1	21	12	2	5	24-2	11	3.16	104	.198	.368	8-0-1	.125	-0	112	1	0	0.0
1970	Chi N	0	0	ø	1	0	0	0-0	1	3	3	1	0	1-1	0	27.00	17	.600	.667	0	ø	0	—	-2	0	-0.1
Total	3	2	0	1.000	12	6	1-1	0-0	41.1	26	15	3	6	27-3	16	3.05	111	.188	.343	11-0-1	.091	-1	100	3	0	0.3
Costello, John	John Reilly; B12.24.1960 Bronx NY; BR/TR/6´1˝/(180–190); [StLN83 24/612]; d6.2; Col Mercyhurst																									
1988	StL N	5	2	.714	36	0	0	1-1	49.2	44	15	3	0	25-4	38	1.81	194	.235	.324	5	.000	-0	—	8	0	1.0
1989	StL N	5	4	.556	48	0	0	3-3	62.1	48	24	5	2	20-7	40	3.32	110	.213	.278	6-0-2	.000	-1	—	3	21	0.3
1990	StL N	0	0	ø	4	0	0	0-0	4.1	7	3	1	1	1-1	1	6.23	62	.368	.429	0	ø	0	—	-1	6	-0.1
	Mon N	0	0	ø	4	0	0	0-1	6.1	5	5	2	0	1-0	1	5.68	65	.208	.231	0	ø	0	—	-2	46	-0.1
	Year	0	0	ø	8	0	0	0-1	10.2	12	8	3	1	2-1	2	5.91	63	.279	.319	0	ø	0	—	-3	0	-0.2
1991	SD N	1	0	1.000	27	0	0	0-1	35	37	15	2	0	17-3	24	3.09	123	.276	.353	1-0-1	.000	-0	—	2	0	0.1
Total	4	11	6	.647	119	0	0	4-6	157.2	141	62	13	3	64-15	104	2.97	123	.239	.313	12-0-3	.000	-1	—	10	73	1.2
Cotter, Dan	Daniel Joseph; B4.14.1867 Boston MA; D9.4.1935 Boston MA; BR/TR; d7.16																									
1890	Buf P	0	1	.000	1	1	1	0	9	18	19	1	0	7	0	14.00	29	.400	.481	4	.000	-1	0	-9	—	-0.6
Cottrell, Ensign	Ensign Stover; B8.29.1888 Hoosick Falls NY; D2.27.1947 Syracuse NY; BL/TL/5´9.5˝/173; d6.21; Col Syracuse																									
1911	Pit N	0	0	ø	1	0	0	0	1	4	4	0	0	1	0	9.00	38	.667	.714	0	ø	0	—	-2	—	-0.1
1912	Chi N	0	0	ø	1	0	0	0	4	8	4	0	0	1	1	9.00	37	.444	.474	1	.000	-0	—	-2	—	-0.1
1913	Phi A	1	0	1.000	2	1	1	0	10	15	7	0	0	2	3	5.40	51	.333	.362	4	.250	1	268	-3	—	-0.2
1914	Bos N	0	1	.000	1	1	0	0	1	2	2	0	0	3	1	9.00	31	.333	.556	0	ø	0	26	-1	—	-0.2
1915	NY A	0	1	.000	7	0	0	0	21.1	29	12	2	1	7	7	3.38	87	.330	.385	7	.000	-1	—	-2	—	-0.2
Total	5	1	2	.333	12	2	1	0	37.1	58	29	2	1	14	12	4.82	61	.356	.410	12	.083	-0	137	-10	—	-0.8
Cotts, Neal	Neal James; B3.25.1980 Belleville IL; BL/TL/6´2˝/(195–205); [OakA01 2/69]; d8.12; Col Illinois St.																									
2003	Chi A	1	1	.500	4	4	0	0-0	13.1	15	12	1	0	17-0	10	8.10	57	.294	.471	0	ø	0	131	-5	0	-0.6
2004	Chi A	4	4	.500	56	1	0	0-2	65.1	61	45	13	3	30-2	58	5.65	83	.247	.335	1	1.000	1	20	-7	0	-0.7
2005	†Chi A	4	0	1.000	69	0	0	0-2	60.1	38	15	1	4	29-5	58	1.94	233	.179	.286	0	ø	0	—	16	0	1.0
2006	Chi A	1	2	.333	70	0	0	1-3	54	64	33	12	3	24-6	43	5.17	91	.291	.367	0	ø	0	—	-3	0	-0.1
Total	4	10	7	.588	199	5	0	1-7	193	178	105	27	10	100-13	169	4.52	102	.244	.341	1	1.000	1	108	1	0	-0.4
Couch, Johnny	John Daniel; B3.31.1891 Vaughn MT; D12.8.1975 Palo Alto CA; BL/TR/6´0˝/180; d4.11; Mil 1918; Col Stanford																									
1917	Det A	0	0	ø	3	0	0	0	13.1	13	6	0	0	1	1	2.70	98	.255	.269	4	.000	-0	—	0	—	0.0
1922	Cin N	16	9	.640	43	33	18-2	1	264	301	132	13	5	56	45	3.89	103	.289	.328	91-0-3	.132	-3	105	7	—	0.3
1923	Cin N	2	7	.222	19	8	1	0	69.1	98	60	2	0	15	14	5.97	65	.344	.377	23-0-1	.174	-1	85	-18	—	-2.0
	Phi N	2	4	.333	11	7	2	0	65	91	45	4	3	21	18	5.26	87	.335	.389	24	.250	0*	105	-4	—	-0.3
	Year	4	11	.267	30	15	3	0	134.1	189	105	6	3	36	32	5.63	75	.339	.383	47-0-1	.213	-1	95	-24	—	-2.3
1924	Phi N	4	8	.333	37	7	3	3	137	170	97	13	1	39	23	4.73	94	.306	.352	49-2-2	.204	-1	65	-9	—	-0.7
1925	Phi N	5	6	.455	34	7	2-1	2	94.1	112	71	9	1	39	11	5.44	88	.298	.365	31-1-1	.161	-1	76	-7	—	-0.7
Total	5	29	34	.460	147	62	26-3	6	643	785	411	41	10	171	112	4.63	91	.304	.350	222-3-7	.167	-6	93	-31	—	-3.4
Couchee, Mike	Michael Eugene; B12.4.1957 San Jose CA; BR/TR/6´0˝/190; [SDN80 19/473]; d4.5; C1; Col USC																									
1983	SD N	0	1	.000	8	0	0	0-0	14	12	8	1	0	6-1	5	5.14	68	.214	.286	2	.500	0	—	-2	36	-0.1
Coughlin, Roscoe	William Edward; B3.15.1868 Walpole MA; D3.20.1951 Chelsea MA; TR/5´10˝/160; d4.22																									
1890	Chi N	4	6	.400	11	10	10	0	95	102	60	3	4	40	29	4.26	86	.266	.341	39	.256	1	84	-3	—	-0.2
1891	NY N	3	4	.429	8	7	6	0	61	74	50	5	3	23	22	3.84	83	.289	.355	23	.130	1	115	-6	—	-0.4
Total	2	7	10	.412	19	17	16	0	156	176	110	8	7	63	51	4.10	85	.275	.346	62	.210	2	96	-9	—	-0.6
Coumbe, Fritz	Frederick Nicholas; B12.13.1889 Antrim PA; D3.21.1978 Paradise CA; BL/TL/6´0˝/152; d4.22																									
1914	Bos A	1	2	.333	17	5	1	1	62.1	49	20	0	0	16	17	1.44	186	.222	.274	18	.111	-1	97	6	—	0.3
	Cle A	1	5	.167	14	5	2	0	55.1	59	31	0	4	16	22	3.25	89	.288	.351	23	.261	1	71	-3	—	-0.2
	Year	2	7	.222	31	10	3	1	117.2	108	51	0	4	32	39	2.29	121	.254	.312	41	.195	0	84	3	—	0.1
1915	Cle A	4	7	.364	30	12	4-1	2	114	123	63	1	3	37	37	3.47	88	.294	.355	37-0-3	.270	1*	74	-6	—	-0.3
1916	Cle A	7	5	.583	29	13	7-2	0	120.1	121	36	1	1	27	39	2.02	149	.279	.323	35-0-2	.057	-3*	87	12	—	1.2
1917	Cle A	8	6	.571	34	10	4-1	5	134.1	119	54	0	3	35	30	2.14	132	.251	.307	39-0-2	.154	-1*	109	6	—	0.7
1918	Cle A	13	7	.650	30	17	9	3	150	164	61	4	1	52	41	3.06	98	.286	.347	56-0-5	.214	-1*	131	1	—	0.3
1919	Cle A	1	1	.500	8	2	0	1	23.2	32	15	2	0	9	7	5.32	63	.348	.406	6-0-1	.500	1	129	-4	—	-0.2
1920	Cin N	0	1	.000	3	0	0	0	14.2	17	13	0	0	4	7	4.91	62	.304	.350	13-1-0	.231	1*	—	-4	—	-0.2
1921	Cin N	3	4	.429	28	6	3	1	86.2	89	42	2	1	21	12	3.22	111	.280	.326	25-0-1	.320	1*	80	2	—	0.4
Total	8	38	38	.500	193	70	30-4	13	761.1	773	335	10	13	217	212	2.80	108	.277	.332	252-1-14	.206	-1	98	10	—	2.0
Courtney, Harry	Henry Seymour; B11.19.1898 Asheville NC; D12.11.1954 Lyme CT; BL/TL/6´4˝/185; d9.13																									
1919	Was A	3	0	1.000	4	3	2-1	0	26.1	25	9	0	0	19	6	2.73	117	.269	.393	10-0-1	.200	-0	163	2	—	0.1
1920	Was A	8	11	.421	37	24	10-1	0	188	223	128	6	9	77	48	4.74	79	.298	.371	69-1-3	.232	4	99	-23	—	-1.7
1921	Was A	6	9	.400	30	15	3	1	132.2	159	103	7	8	71	26	5.63	73	.305	.397	47-0-1	.298	2*	95	-24	—	-2.1
1922	Was A	0	1	.000	5	0	0	0	10	11	4	0	0	9	4	3.60	107	.306	.444	4	.000	-1	—	1	—	0.0
	Chi A	5	6	.455	18	11	5	0	86.2	100	52	5	1	37	28	4.98	82	.299	.371	33	.273	3	82	-8	—	-0.6
	Year	5	7	.417	23	11	5	0	96.2	111	56	5	1	46	32	4.84	84	.300	.379	37	.243	2	82	-5	—	-0.6
Total	4	22	27	.449	94	53	20-2	1	443.2	518	296	18	18	213	112	4.91	79	.299	.382	163-1-5	.252	7	97	-52	—	-4.3
Courtright, John	John Charles; B5.30.1970 Marion OH; BL/TL/6´2˝/185; [CinN91 8/223]; d5.6; Col Duke																									
1995	Cin N	0	0	ø	1	0	0	0-0	1	2	1	0	0	0-0	0	9.00	46	.500	.500	0	ø	0	—	-1	0	0.0
Coveleski, Harry	Harry Frank "The Giant Killer" (b Harry Frank Kowalewski); B4.23.1886 Shamokin PA; D8.4.1950 Shamokin PA; BB/TL/6´0˝/180; d9.10; b–Stan																									
1907	Phi N	1	0	1.000	4	0	0	0	20	10	2	0	1	3	6	0.00	ø	.147	.194	8	.000	-0	—	5	—	0.2
1908	Phi N	4	1	.800	6	5	5-2	0	43.2	29	7	0	2	12	22	1.24	196	.196	.265	15-0-2	.133	-0	99	6	—	0.8
1909	Phi N	6	10	.375	24	17	8-2	1	121.2	109	51	0	5	49	56	2.74	95	.247	.329	37-0-3	.108	-2	63	-2	—	-0.5
1910	Cin N	1	1	.500	7	4	2	0	39.1	35	41	1	4	42	27	5.26	55	.246	.431	16-0-1	.063	-1	172	-14	—	-0.8
1914	Det A	22	12	.647	44	36	23-5	2	303.1	251	109	4	12	100	124	2.49	113	.227	.298	95-0-6	.242	5	97	13	—	2.3
1915	Det A	22	13	.629	**50**	38	20-1	4	312.2	271	123	2	20	87	150	2.45	124	.233	.298	103-0-8	.175	-2	114	16	—	1.7
1916	Det A	21	11	.656	44	39	22-3	2	324.1	278	105	6	11	63	108	1.97	145	.237	.282	118-0-1	.212	1	100	26	—	3.1
1917	Det A	4	6	.400	16	11	2	0	69	70	39	0	2	14	15	2.61	101	.265	.307	22-0-1	.227	-0	146	-3	—	-0.4
1918	Det A	0	1	.000	3	1	1	0	14	17	9	0	0	6	3	3.86	69	.315	.383	4	.250	0	57	-3	—	-0.1
Total	9	81	55	.596	198	151	83-13	9	1248	1070	486	13	57	376	511	2.39	118	.235	.301	418-0-22	.189	-0	104	44	—	6.3

YEAR	TM LG	W	L	PCT	G	GS	CG-SHO	SV-BS	IP	H	R	HR	HB	BB-IB	SO	ERA	AERA	OAV	OOB	AB-HR-SH	AVG	PB	SUP	APR	DL	PW
COVELESKI, STAN	Stanley Anthony (b Stanislaus Kowalewski); B7.13.1889 Shamokin PA; D3.20.1984 South Bend IN; BR/TR/5´11˝/166; d9.10; HF1969; b–Harry																									
1912	Phi A	2	1	.667	5	2	2-1	0	21	18	9	0	1	4	9	3.43	90	.231	.277	7	.143	-0	48	0	—	-0.1
1916	Cle A	15	13	.536	45	27	11-1	3	232	247	100	6	1	58	76	3.41	88	.278	.323	75-1-4	.173	-0	115	-4	—	-0.4
1917	Cle A	19	14	.576	45	36	24-**9**	4	298.1	202	78	3	1	94	133	1.81	157	**.194**	.261	97-0-7	.134	-4*	77	33	—	3.2
1918	Cle A	22	13	.629	38	33	25-2	1	311	261	90	2	4	76	87	1.82	165	.229	.279	110-0-5	.191	-3	87	35	—	3.9
1919	Cle A	24	12	.667	43	34	24-4	4	286	286	99	2	5	60	118	2.61	128	.267	.308	94-0-3	.213	4	98	26	—	3.9
1920	†Cle A	24	14	.632	41	38	26-3	2	315	284	110	6	4	65	**133**	2.49	153	**.243**	**.285**	111-0-9	.225	3	105	**44**	—	**5.5**
1921	Cle A	23	13	.639	43	**40**	28-2	2	315	341	137	6	4	84	99	3.37	126	.280	.329	116-0-11	.155	-6	116	33	—	3.0
1922	Cle A	17	14	.548	35	33	21-3	2	276.2	292	120	14	2	64	98	3.32	121	.274	.316	99-0-2	.101	-7	96	20	—	1.4
1923	Cle A	13	14	.481	33	31	17-**5**	2	228	251	98	8	2	42	54	**2.76**	**143**	.282	.316	79-0-9	.089	-8	98	26	—	2.2
1924	Cle A	15	16	.484	37	33	18-2	0	240.1	286	140	6	4	73	58	4.04	106	.294	.346	82-0-4	.134	-5	96	3	—	-0.1
1925	†Was A	20	5	**.800**	32	32	15-3	0	241	230	86	7	2	73	58	**2.84**	**149**	.255	.312	81-0-11	.111	-8	107	**41**	—	2.9
1926	Was A	14	11	.560	36	34	11-3	1	245.1	272	112	1	0	81	50	3.12	124	.286	.342	82-0-3	.207	1	108	16	—	1.6
1927	Was A	2	1	.667	5	4	0	0	14.1	13	7	0	0	8	3	3.14	129	.250	.350	6	.333	0	113	1	—	0.2
1928	NY A	5	1	.833	12	8	2	0	58	72	41	5	0	20	5	5.74	66	.323	.379	19-0-4	.053	-2	158	-12	—	-1.2
Total	14	215	142	.602	450	385	224-38	21	3082	3055	1227	66	30	802	981	2.89	128	.262	.311	1058-1-72	.159	-34	102	262	—	26.0
COVINGTON, CHET	Chester Rogers "Chesty"; B11.6.1910 Cairo IL; D6.11.1976 Pembroke Park FL; BB/TL/6´2˝/195; d4.23																									
1944	Phi N	1	1	.500	19	0	0	0	38.2	46	22	2	0	8	13	4.66	78	.297	.331	6	.000	-1	—	-4	0	-0.3
COVINGTON, TEX	William Wilkes; B3.19.1887 Henryville TN; D12.10.1931 Denison TX; BL/TR/6´1˝/175; d4.25; b–Sam																									
1911	Det A	7	1	.875	17	6	5	0	83.2	94	43	2	10	33	29	4.09	85	.297	.381	32	.188	-1	160	-3	—	-0.4
1912	Det A	3	4	.429	14	9	2-1	0	63.1	58	33	0	3	30	19	4.12	79	.253	.347	15	.133	0	75	-4	—	-0.4
Total	2	10	5	.667	31	15	7-1	0	147	152	76	2	13	63	48	4.10	82	.278	.367	47	.170	-1	109	-7	—	-0.8
COWLEY, JOE	Joseph Alan; B8.15.1958 Lexington KY; BR/TR/6´5˝/(207–220); d4.13																									
1982	Atl N	1	2	.333	17	8	0	0-0	52.1	53	27	6	1	16-2	27	4.47	82	.265	.321	15-0-1	.200	0	96	-3	33	-0.2
1984	NY A	9	2	.818	16	11	3-1	0-0	83.1	75	34	12	2	31-1	71	3.56	108	.234	.303	0	ø	0	163	4	0	0.5
1985	NY A	12	6	.667	30	26	1	0-0	159.2	132	75	29	6	85-2	97	3.95	103	.224	.327	0	ø	0	116	3	0	0.3
1986	Chi A	11	11	.500	27	27	4	0-0	162.1	133	81	20	3	83-1	132	3.88	112	.223	.319	0	ø	0*	97	7	0	0.8
1987	Phi N	0	4	.000	5	4	0	0-0	11.2	21	26	2	2	17-1	5	15.43	28	.389	.548	3	.333	1	42	-15	0	-2.3
Total	5	33	25	.569	95	76	8-1	0-0	469.1	414	243	69	14	232-7	332	4.20	97	.235	.327	18-0-1	.222	1	110	-4	33	-0.9
COX, DANNY	Danny Bradford; B9.21.1959 Northampton, England; BR/TR/6´4˝/(225–250); [StLN81 13/319]; d8.6; Col Troy St.; [DL 1990 StL N 178]																									
1983	StL N	3	6	.333	12	12	0	0-0	83	92	38	6	0	23-2	36	3.25	112	.286	.332	27-0-3	.074	-2	68	2	0	0.1
1984	StL N	9	11	.450	29	27	1-1	0-0	156.1	171	81	9	7	54-6	70	4.03	87	.289	.353	53-0-1	.132	0*	96	-11	0	-1.2
1985	†StL N	18	9	.667	35	35	10-4	0-0	241	226	91	19	3	64-5	131	2.88	124	.251	.300	79-0-8	.152	0	106	17	0	1.9
1986	StL N	12	13	.480	32	32	8	0-0	220	189	85	14	2	60-6	108	2.90	127	.234	.288	65-0-16	.077	-3	83	17	17	1.2
1987	†StL N	11	9	.550	31	31	2	0-0	199.1	224	99	17	3	71-6	101	3.88	108	.290	.351	69-0-4	.116	-2*	105	4	29	0.1
1988	StL N	3	8	.273	13	13	0	0-0	86	89	40	6	1	25-7	47	3.98	89	.272	.323	23-0-5	.043	-2	70	-3	115	-0.6
1991	Phi N	4	6	.400	23	17	0	0-0	102.1	98	57	14	1	39-2	46	4.57	81	.258	.323	29-0-4	.103	-1	119	-10	29	-1.0
1992	Phi N	2	2	.500	9	7	0	0-0	38.1	46	28	3	0	19-1	30	5.40	65	.299	.371	11	.091	-1	114	-9	0	-0.9
	†Pit N	3	1	.750	16	0	0	3-2	24.1	20	9	2	0	8-1	18	3.33	104	.225	.286	3	.000	-0	—	1	0	0.1
	Year	5	3	.625	25	7	0	3-2	62.2	66	37	5	0	27-2	48	4.60	76	.272	.341	14	.071	-1	115	-9	0	-0.8
1993	†Tor A	7	6	.538	44	0	0	2-4	83.2	73	31	8	0	29-5	84	3.12	140	.230	.293	0	ø	0	—	12	0	1.6
1994	Tor A	1	1	.500	10	0	0	3-0	18.2	7	3	0	1	7-1	14	1.45	337	.113	.211	0	ø	0	—	7	97	0.9
1995	Tor A	1	3	.250	24	0	0	0-2	45	57	40	4	1	33-4	38	7.40	64	.317	.419	0	ø	0	—	-13	39	-0.9
Total	11	74	75	.497	278	174	21-5	8-8	1298	1292	602	102	19	432-46	723	3.64	104	.263	.323	359-0-41	.109	-9	95	14	504	1.3
COX, ERNIE	Ernest Thompson; B2.19.1894 Birmingham AL; D4.29.1974 Birmingham AL; BL/TR/6´1˝/180; d5.5																									
1922	Chi A	0	0	ø	1	0	0	0	1	1	2	0	0	2	0	18.00	23	.250	.500	0	ø	0	—	-1	—	-0.1
COX, GEORGE	George Melvin; B11.15.1904 Sherman TX; D12.17.1995 Bedford TX; BR/TR/6´1˝/170; d4.12																									
1928	Chi A	1	2	.333	26	2	0	0	89	110	58	6	2	39	22	5.26	77	.313	.385	26-0-1	.077	-2	94	-10	—	-0.6
COX, GLENN	Glenn Melvin; B2.3.1931 Montebello CA; BR/TR/6´2˝/210; d9.20																									
1955	KC A	0	2	.000	2	2	0	0	2.1	11	8	0	0	1-0	2	30.86	14	.611	.632	1	.000	-0	32	-6	0	-1.0
1956	KC A	0	2	.000	3	3	1	0	23.1	15	11	2	0	22-0	6	4.24	102	.203	.381	7	.000	-1	34	1	0	-0.1
1957	KC A	1	0	1.000	10	0	0	0	14.1	18	9	1	0	9-1	8	5.02	79	.321	.415	2	.000	0	—	-2	0	-0.1
1958	KC A	0	0	ø	2	0	0	0	3.2	6	4	1	0	3-0	1	9.82	40	.400	.500	0	ø	0	—	-2	0	-0.1
Total	4	1	4	.200	17	5	1	0	43.2	50	32	4	0	35-1	17	6.39	65	.307	.427	10	.000	-1	34	-9	0	-1.3
COX, CASEY	Joseph Casey; B7.3.1941 Long Beach CA; BR/TR/6´5˝/(200–215); d4.15; Col Cal St.–Los Angeles																									
1966	Was A	4	5	.444	66	0	0	7	113	104	53	6	4	35-15	46	3.50	99	.250	.310	8-0-1	.000	-1	—	-2	0	-0.3
1967	Was A	7	4	.636	54	0	0	1	73	67	33	2	4	21-7	32	2.96	107	.250	.311	3	.000	-0	—	-1	0	-0.1
1968	Was A	0	1	.000	4	0	0	0	7.2	7	2	0	0	0-0	4	2.35	124	.250	.241	0	ø	0	—	1	0	0.1
1969	Was A	12	7	.632	52	13	4	0-2	171.2	161	62	15	1	64-7	73	2.78	126	.251	.318	47-0-6	.106	-2	120	14	0	1.2
1970	Was A	8	12	.400	37	30	1	1-1	192.1	211	108	27	4	44-4	68	4.45	81	.285	.324	58-0-7	.121	-2	97	-19	0	-2.1
1971	Was A	5	7	.417	54	11	0	7-3	124.1	131	69	9	7	40-8	43	3.98	85	.273	.335	26-0-1	.077	-1	99	-12	0	-1.4
1972	Tex A	3	5	.375	35	4	0	4-3	65.1	73	41	7	1	26-7	27	4.41	69	.277	.341	9	.111	1	36	-12	22	-1.5
	NY A	0	1	.000	5	1	0	0-0	11.2	13	6	0	2	3-1	4	4.63	65	.289	.353	0-0-1	ø	0	0	-2	0	-0.2
	Year	3	6	.333	40	5	0	4-3	77	86	47	7	3	29-8	31	4.44	68	.278	.343	9-0-1	.111	1	29	-14	0	-1.7
1973	NY A	0	0	ø	1	0	0	0-0	3	5	3	0	2	1-0	0	6.00	62	.357	.444	0	ø	0	—	-1	0	-0.1
Total	8	39	42	.481	308	59	5	20-9	762	772	377	66	25	234-49	297	3.70	93	.266	.323	151-0-16	.099	-6	99	-34	22	-4.4
COX, LES	Leslie Warren; B8.14.1904 Junction TX; D10.14.1934 San Angelo TX; BR/TR/6´0˝/164; d9.11; Col Texas																									
1926	Chi A	0	1	.000	2	0	0	0	5	6	10	2	0	5	3	5.40	72	.261	.393	2	.500	0	—	-4	—	-0.6
COX, RED	Plateau Preston; B2.16.1895 Laurel Springs NC; D10.15.1984 Roanoke VA; BL/TR/6´2˝/190; d4.17																									
1920	Det A	0	0	ø	3	0	0	0	5	9	4	0	0	3	1	5.40	69	.375	.444	1	.000	-0	—	-1	—	-0.1
COX, TERRY	Terry Lee; B3.30.1949 Odessa TX; BR/TR/6´5˝/215; d9.7																									
1970	Cal A	0	0	ø	3	0	0	0-0	2.1	4	1	0	0	0-0	3	3.86	94	.400	.400	0	ø	0	—	0	0	0.0
COX, BILL	William Donald; B6.23.1913 Ashmore IL; D2.16.1988 Charleston IL; BR/TR/6´1˝/185; d6.6																									
1936	StL N	0	0	ø	2	0	0	0	2.2	4	5	0	0	1	1	6.75	58	.333	.385	0	ø	0	—	-2	—	-0.1
1937	Chi A	1	0	1.000	3	2	1-1	0	12.2	9	1	0	0	5	8	0.71	648	.200	.280	4	.250	0	47	6	—	0.4
1938	Chi A	0	2	.000	7	1	0	0	11.2	11	14	0	0	13	5	6.94	70	.244	.414	2	.000	-0	18	-4	—	-0.6
	StL A	1	4	.200	22	7	1	0	63	81	53	8	0	35	16	7.00	71	.315	.397	17	.059	-1*	81	-13	—	-0.9
	Year	1	6	.143	29	8	1	0	74.2	92	67	8	0	48	21	6.99	71	.305	.400	19	.053	-2	73	-17	—	-1.5
1939	StL A	0	2	.000	4	2	1	0	9.1	10	10	0	0	8	8	9.64	50	.256	.383	1	.000	-0	63	-4	—	-0.7
1940	StL A	0	1	.000	12	0	0	0	17.1	23	17	3	0	12	7	7.27	63	.333	.432	1	.000	-0*	—	-5	—	-0.3
Total	5	2	9	.182	50	12	3-1	0	116.2	138	100	11	0	74	45	6.56	74	.296	.392	25	.080	-2	68	-22	—	-2.2
COYLE, BILL	William Claude; B9.20.1871 KY; D6.4.1941 San Francisco CA; TR; d7.7																									
1893	Bos N	0	1	.000	2	1	0	0	8	14	10	1	0	3	2	9.00	55	.368	.415	4	.000	-1	184	-3	—	-0.3
COZART, CHARLIE	Charles Rhubin; B10.17.1919 Lenoir NC; D12.31.2004 Lenoir NC; BR/TL/6´0˝/190; d4.17																									
1945	Bos N	1	0	1.000	5	0	0	0	8	10	11	2	0	15	4	10.13	38	.303	.521	2	.000	-0	—	-6	0	-0.6
CRABB, ROY	James Roy; B8.23.1890 Monticello IA; D3.30.1940 Lewistown MT; BR/TR/5´11˝/160; d8.10																									
1912	Chi A	0	1	.000	2	1	0	0	8.2	6	2	0	0	4	3	1.04	308	.214	.313	3	.000	-0	23	2	—	0.2
	Phi A	2	4	.333	7	7	3	0	43.1	48	22	0	4	17	12	3.74	82	.287	.367	16-0-1	.000	-3	103	-3	—	-0.6
	Year	2	5	.286	9	8	3	0	52	54	24	0	4	21	15	3.29	94	.277	.359	19-0-1	.000	-3	92	0	—	-0.4

YEAR	TM LG	W	L	PCT	G	GS	CG-SHO	SV-BS	IP	H	R	HR	HB	BB-IB	SO	ERA	AERA	OAV	OOB	AB-HR-SH	AVG	PB	SUP	APR	DL	PW
Crable, George	George Elmer; B1.9.1885 NE; BL/TL/6´1˝/190; d8.3																									
1910	Bro N	0	0	ø	2	1	1	0	7.1	5	4	0	2	5	3	4.91	62	.217	.400	2	.000	0	123	-1	—	-0.1
Crabtree, Tim	Timothy Lyle; B10.13.1969 Jackson MI; BR/TR/6´4˝/(195–225); [TorA92 2/63]; d6.23; Col Michigan St.																									
1995	Tor A	0	2	.000	31	0	0	0-2	32	30	16	1	2	13-0	21	3.09	154	.240	.319	0	ø	0	—	4	0	0.3
1996	Tor A	5	3	.625	53	0	0	1-4	67.1	59	26	4	3	22-4	57	2.54	197	.231	.298	0	ø	0	—	16	21	1.7
1997	Tor A	3	3	.500	37	0	0	2-3	40.2	65	32	7	2	17-3	26	7.08	65	.374	.431	0	ø	0	—	-10	61	-1.3
1998	†Tex A	6	1	.857	64	0	0	0-1	85.1	86	40	3	3	35-2	60	3.59	136	.264	.335	1	.000	-0	—	11	0	0.7
1999	†Tex A	5	1	.833	68	0	0	0-3	65	71	26	4	1	18-1	54	3.46	149	.280	.328	0	ø	0	—	12	0	0.9
2000	Tex A	2	7	.222	68	0	0	2-7	80.1	86	52	7	2	31-6	54	5.15	99	.274	.339	0	ø	0	—	-1	0	-0.1
2001	Tex A	0	5	.000	21	0	0	4-2	23.1	37	18	3	1	14-2	16	6.56	73	.385	.456	0	ø	0	—	-4	127	-0.8
Total	7	21	22	.488	342	0	0	9-22	394	434	210	29	14	150-18	288	4.20	118	.281	.346	1	.000	-0	—	28	209	1.4
Craddock, Walt	Walter Anderson; B3.25.1932 Pax WV; D7.6.1980 Parma Heights OH; BR/TL/5´11.5˝/176; d9.3; Col Syracuse																									
1955	KC A	0	2	.000	4	2	0	0	15	18	14	3	0	10-0	9	7.80	54	.300	.400	5	.000	-1	43	-6	0	-0.7
1956	KC A	0	2	.000	2	2	0	0	9.1	9	7	1	0	10-0	8	6.75	64	.265	.432	2	.000	-0	21	-2	0	-0.4
1958	KC A	0	3	.000	23	1	0	0	36.2	41	25	4	1	20-0	22	5.89	66	.289	.376	2	.000	-0	69	-7	0	-0.5
Total	3	0	7	.000	29	5	0	0	61	68	46	8	1	40-0	39	6.49	62	.288	.391	9	.000	-1	40	-15	0	-1.6
Craft, Molly	Maurice Montague; B11.28.1895 Portsmouth VA; D10.25.1978 Los Angeles CA; BR/TR/6´2˝/165; d8.8; Mil 1918																									
1916	Was A	0	1	.000	2	1	1	0	11	12	5	0	0	6	9	3.27	85	.316	.409	4	.000	-0*	27	-1	—	0.0
1917	Was A	0	0	ø	8	0	0	1	14	17	10	0	0	8	2	3.86	68	.315	.403	2	.500	0	—	-3	—	-0.1
1918	Was A	0	0	ø	3	0	0	0	7	5	1	0	0	1	5	1.29	212	.208	.240	2	.000	-0	—	1	—	0.0
1919	Was A	0	3	.000	16	2	0	1	48.2	59	28	2	2	18	17	3.88	83	.309	.374	18-0-1	.111	-2	98	-4	—	-0.4
Total	4	0	4	.000	29	3	1	2	80.2	93	44	2	2	33	33	3.57	84	.303	.374	26-0-1	.115	-2	77	-7	—	-0.5
Craghead, Howard	Howard Oliver "Judge"; B5.25.1908 Selma CA; D7.14.1962 San Diego CA; BR/TR/6´2˝/200; d4.30																									
1931	Cle A	0	0	ø	4	0	0	0	5.2	8	4	0	0	2	2	6.35	73	.320	.370	0	ø	0	—	-1	—	0.0
1933	Cle A	0	0	ø	11	0	0	0	17.1	19	13	1	1	10	2	6.23	71	.292	.395	3	.000	-0	—	-3	—	-0.2
Total	2	0	0	ø	15	0	0	0	23	27	17	1	1	12	4	6.26	72	.300	.388	3	.000	-0	—	-4	—	-0.2
Craig, George	George McCarthy "Lefty"; B11.15.1887 Philadelphia PA; D4.23.1911 Indianapolis IN; TL; d7.19																									
1907	Phi A	0	0	ø	2	0	0	0	1.2	2	3	0	2	3	0	10.80	24	.286	.583	1	.000	-0	—	-2	—	-0.1
Craig, Pete	Peter Joel; B7.10.1940 LaSalle ON, Can.; BL/TR/6´5˝/220; d9.6; Col Detroit Mercy																									
1964	Was A	0	0	ø	2	1	0	0	1.2	8	9	1	0	4-1	0	48.60	8	.667	.750	0	ø	0	192	-8	0	-0.4
1965	Was A	0	3	.000	3	3	0	0	14.1	18	15	1	0	8-1	2	8.16	43	.321	.394	3	.667	1	101	-7	0	-1.1
1966	Was A	0	0	ø	1	0	0	0	2	2	2	0	0	1-1	1	4.50	77	.250	.333	0	ø	0	—	-1	0	0.0
Total	3	0	3	.000	6	4	0	0	18	28	26	2	0	13-3	3	11.50	30	.368	.451	3	.667	1	126	-16	0	-1.5
Craig, Roger	Roger Lee; B2.17.1930 Durham NC; BR/TR/6´4˝/(180–200); d7.17; M10/C13; Col North Carolina St.																									
1955	†Bro N	5	3	.625	21	10	3	2	90.2	81	37	8	1	43-6	48	2.78	146	.238	.323	26-0-1	.077	-2	132	11	0	0.6
1956	†Bro N	12	11	.522	35	32	8-2	1	199	169	90	25	4	87-5	109	3.71	107	.231	.313	61-0-5	.016	-5	104	6	0	-0.1
1957	Bro N	6	9	.400	32	13	1	0	111.1	102	58	18	2	47-5	69	4.61	90	.249	.328	29-0-2	.138	-1	67	-2	0	-0.4
1958	LA N	2	1	.667	9	2	1	0	32	30	20	3	0	12-1	16	4.50	91	.242	.309	9	.000	-1	121	-2	0	-0.3
1959	†LA N	11	5	.688	29	17	7-**4**	0	152.2	122	49	13	1	45-3	76	2.06	205	.217	.275	52-0-4	.058	-4	88	30	0	2.6
1960	LA N	8	3	.727	21	15	6-1	0	115.2	99	48	8	3	43-4	69	3.27	121	.230	.304	36-0-3	.056	-2	117	8	44	0.5
1961	LA N	5	6	.455	40	14	2	2	112.2	130	87	22	4	52-7	63	6.15	71	.288	.365	27-0-3	.148	-0	104	-21	0	-2.0
1962	NY N	10	24	.294	42	33	13	3	233.1	261	133	35	7	70-3	118	4.51	93	.288	.341	76-0-4	.053	-5	79	-6	0	-1.1
1963	NY N	5	22	.185	46	31	14	2	236	249	117	28	6	58-2	108	3.78	92	.267	.312	69-0-3	.087	-2	57	-7	0	-0.9
1964	†StL N	7	9	.438	39	19	3	5	166	180	76	16	4	35-4	84	3.25	117	.276	.316	48-0-1	.208	2	80	7	0	1.1
1965	Cin N	1	4	.200	40	0	0	3	64.1	74	33	6	3	25-7	30	3.64	103	.289	.355	11-0-2	.182	-0	—	-1	0	-0.1
1966	Phi N	2	1	.667	14	0	0	1	22.2	31	15	4	0	5-1	13	5.56	65	.326	.353	4	.000	-0	—	-5	15	-0.6
Total	12	74	98	.430	368	186	58-7	19	1536.1	1528	763	186	35	522-48	803	3.83	104	.259	.321	448-0-28	.085	-22	89	18	59	-0.7
Crain, Jesse	Jesse Alan; B7.5.1981 Toronto ON, Can.; BR/TR/6´1˝/205; [MinA02 2/61]; d8.5; Col Houston																									
2004	†Min A	3	0	1.000	22	0	0	0-1	27	17	6	2	1	12-1	14	2.00	231	.179	.278	0	ø	0	—	8	0	0.8
2005	Min A	12	5	.706	75	0	0	1-3	79.2	61	28	6	5	29-7	25	2.71	162	.218	.300	0	ø	0	—	14	0	2.7
2006	†Min A	4	5	.444	68	0	0	1-3	76.2	79	31	6	2	18-2	60	3.52	130	.262	.306	0	ø	0	—	10	0	1.0
Total	3	19	10	.655	165	0	0	2-7	183.1	157	65	14	8	59-10	99	2.95	153	.232	.299	0	ø	0	—	32	0	4.5
Cram, Jerry	Gerald Allen; B12.9.1947 Los Angeles CA; BR/TR/6´0˝/(175–185); d9.3; Col Riverside (CA) CC																									
1969	KC A	0	1	.000	5	2	0	0-0	16.2	15	8	0	0	6-1	10	3.24	114	.231	.296	3	.000	-0	108	0	0	0.0
1974	NY N	0	1	.000	10	0	0	0-0	22.1	22	4	1	0	4-3	8	1.61	224	.275	.310	3	.333	0	—	5	0	0.3
1975	NY N	0	1	.000	4	0	0	0-0	5	7	3	2	0	2-0	2	5.40	65	.333	.391	0	ø	0	—	-1	0	-0.2
1976	KC A	0	0	ø	4	0	0	0-0	4.1	8	3	0	0	1-0	2	6.23	56	.421	.450	0	ø	0	—	-1	0	-0.1
Total	4	0	3	.000	23	2	0	0-0	48.1	52	18	3	0	13-4	22	2.98	121	.281	.328	6	.167	-0	108	3	0	0.0
Cramer, Bill	William Wendell; B5.22.1891 Bedford IN; D9.11.1966 Fort Wayne IN; BR/TR/6´0˝/175; d6.25																									
1912	Cin N	0	0	ø	1	0	0	0	2.1	6	6	0	0	0	2	0.00	ø	.500	.500	1	.000	-0	—	-1	—	-0.1
Crandall, Doc	James Otis; B10.8.1887 Wadena IN; D8.17.1951 Bell CA; BR/TR/5´10.5˝/180; d4.24; C4; ▲																									
1908	NY N	12	12	.500	32	24	13	0	214.2	198	83	3	9	59	77	2.93	82	.248	.307	72-2-6	.222	5*	125	-8	—	-0.5
1909	NY N	6	4	.600	30	8	4	6	122	117	58	5	3	33	55	2.88	89	.252	.305	41-1-2	.244	3	150	-4	—	0.0
1910	NY N	17	4	.810	42	18	13-2	5	207.2	194	86	10	4	43	73	2.56	116	.246	.289	73-1-3	.342	10*	157	8	—	1.8
1911	†NY N	15	5	.750	41	15	9-2	5	198.2	199	82	10	6	51	94	2.63	128	.256	.307	113-2-5	.239	5*	138	14	—	2.1
1912	†NY N	13	7	.650	37	10	7	2	162	181	85	7	2	35	60	3.61	94	.286	.326	80-0-3	.313	6*	167	-1	—	0.6
1913	†NY N	2	4	.333	24	1	1	5	55.1	61	28	2	1	13	28	3.09	101	.293	.338	25	.280	2*	0	-1	—	0.1
	†NY N	2	0	1.000	11	1	1	1	42.1	41	17	1	0	11	14	2.55	122	.248	.295	22	.364	3*	289	2	—	0.5
	Year	4	4	.500	35	2	2	6	97.2	102	45	3	1	24	42	2.86	109	.273	.319	47	.319	5	145	**2**	—	0.6
1914	StL F	13	9	.591	27	21	18-1	0	196	194	94	8	2	52	84	3.54	86	.256	.305	278-2-5	.309	8*	104	-9	—	0.0
1915	StL F	21	15	.583	51	33	22-4	1	312.2	307	116	5	10	77	117	2.59	111	.263	.314	141-1-0	.284	13*	102	7	—	2.2
1916	StL A	0	0	ø	2	0	0	0	1.1	7	9	0	1	1	0	27.00	10	.636	.692	12	.083	-0*	—	-5	—	-0.3
1918	Bos N	1	2	.333	5	3	3	0	34	39	11	1	1	4	4	2.38	113	.307	.333	28	.286	1*	56	1	—	0.3
Total	10	102	62	.622	302	134	91-9	25	1546.2	1538	669	52	39	379	606	2.92	101	.261	.310	885-9-24	.286	55	124	4	—	6.8
Crane, Ed	Edward Nicholas "Cannon-Ball"; B5.27.1862 Boston MA; D9.20.1896 Rochester NY; BR/TR/5´10.5˝/204; d4.17; ▲																									
1884	Bos U	0	2	.000	4	2	1	0	18	17	14	1	—	6	13	4.00	59	.233	.291	428-12	.285	1*	36	-3	—	-0.2
1886	Was N	1	7	.125	10	8	7-1	0	70	91	85	4	—	53	39	7.20	45	.313	.419	292	.171	-1*	38	-30	—	-2.5
1888	†NY N	5	6	.455	12	11	11-2	1	92.2	70	51	3	2	40	58	2.43	113	.193	.277	37-1	.162	1	75	2	—	0.3
1889	†NY N	14	11	.560	29	25	23	0	230.2	221	159	10	10	136	130	3.63	109	.245	.350	103-2	.204	3	112	5	—	0.5
1890	NY P	16	19	.457	43	35	28	0	330.1	323	280	12	10	208	116	4.63	98	.245	.352	146	.315	7	108	-5	—	0.0
1891	Cin AA	14	14	.500	32	31	25-1	0	250	216	151	3	14	139	122	**2.45**	**167**	.225	.332	110-1	.155	-6*	76	35	—	2.6
	Cin N	4	8	.333	15	13	11-1	0	116.2	134	91	3	3	64	51	4.09	83	.277	.365	46	.109	-3	90	-10	—	-1.1
1892	NY N	16	24	.400	47	42	35-2	1	364.1	350	276	10	12	189	174	3.80	85	.243	.335	163	.245	4*	112	-28	—	-2.3
1893	NY N	2	4	.333	10	7	4	0	68.1	84	62	2	6	41	11	5.93	79	.294	.393	26	.462	4*	144	-8	—	-0.1
	Bro N	0	2	.000	2	2	1	0	10	19	19	2	1	9	5	13.50	33	.388	.492	5	.400	0*	79	-10	—	-1.1
	Year	2	6	.250	12	9	5	0	78.1	103	81	4	7	50	16	6.89	67	.307	.408	31	.452	5	129	-16	—	-1.2
Total	8	72	97	.426	204	176	146-7	2	1551	1525	1188	50	58	885	719	3.99	95	.247	.347	1356-16	.237	12	98	-52	—	-3.9
Crawford, Carlos	Carlos Lamonte; B10.4.1971 Charlotte NC; BR/TR/6´1˝/190; [CleA90 51/1279]; d6.7; Col Montreat																									
1996	Phi N	0	1	.000	1	1	0	0-0	3.2	7	10	1	1	2-0	4	4.91	88	.389	.476	1	.000	-0	105	-4	0	-0.5
Crawford, Larry	Charles Lowrie; B4.27.1914 Swissvale PA; D12.20.1994 Hanover PA; BL/TL/6´1˝/165; d7.21																									
1937	Phi N	0	0	ø	6	0	0	0	6	12	10	2	0	1	2	15.00	29	.387	.406	0	ø	0	—	-6	—	-0.3

CRAWFORD, JIM James Frederick "Catfish"; B9.29.1950 Chicago IL; BL/TL/6´3˝/200; [HouN72 14/321]; d4.6; Col Arizona St.

YEAR	TM LG	W	L	PCT	G	GS	CG-SHO	SV-BS	IP	H	R	HR	HB	BB-IB	SO	ERA	AERA	OAV	OOB	AB-HR-SH	AVG	PB	SUP	APR	DL	PW
1973	Hou N	2	4	.333	48	0	0	6-4	70	69	41	7	2	33-8	56	4.50	81	.256	.338	13	.231	1	—	-8	0	-0.6
1975	Hou N	3	5	.375	44	2	0	4-3	86.2	92	40	0	2	37-4	37	3.63	93	.280	.354	17-0-1	.294	2	91	-3	0	-0.1
1976	Det A	1	8	.111	32	5	1	2-1	109.1	115	65	4	0	43-4	68	4.53	82	.275	.335	0	ø	0	57	-10	0	-0.6
1977	Det A	7	8	.467	37	7	0	1-2	126	156	82	13	1	50-5	91	4.79	90	.310	.369	0	ø	0	77	-9	0	-0.9
1978	Det A	2	3	.400	20	0	0	0-0	39.1	45	24	3	2	19-3	24	4.35	90	.292	.371	0	ø	0	—	-3	0	-0.4
Total	5	15	28	.349	181	14	1	13-10	431.1	477	252	27	7	182-24	276	4.40	87	.285	.353	30-0-1	.267	3	74	-33	0	-2.6

CRAWFORD, JOE Joseph Randal; B5.2.1970 Gainesville FL; BL/TL/6´3˝/225; [NYN91 17/459]; d4.7; Col Kent St.

YEAR	TM LG	W	L	PCT	G	GS	CG-SHO	SV-BS	IP	H	R	HR	HB	BB-IB	SO	ERA	AERA	OAV	OOB	AB-HR-SH	AVG	PB	SUP	APR	DL	PW
1997	NY N	4	3	.571	19	2	0	0-0	46.1	36	18	7	0	13-1	25	3.30	121	.216	.272	11	.000	-1	46	4	0	0.5

CRAWFORD, PAXTON Paxton Keith; B8.4.1977 Little Rock AR; BR/TR/6´3˝/205; [BosA95 9/242]; d7.1; [DL 2002 Bos A 82]

YEAR	TM LG	W	L	PCT	G	GS	CG-SHO	SV-BS	IP	H	R	HR	HB	BB-IB	SO	ERA	AERA	OAV	OOB	AB-HR-SH	AVG	PB	SUP	APR	DL	PW
2000	Bos A	2	1	.667	7	4	0	0-0	29	25	15	0	2	13-2	17	3.41	147	.240	.325	0	ø	0	75	4	0	0.3
2001	Bos A	3	0	1.000	8	7	0	0-0	36	40	19	3	2	13-0	25	4.75	93	.276	.342	0	ø	0	143	0	0	0.0
Total	2	5	1	.833	15	11	0	0-0	65	65	34	3	4	26-2	42	4.15	113	.261	.335	0	ø	0	115	4	82	0.3

CRAWFORD, STEVE Steven Ray; B4.29.1958 Pryor OK; BR/TR/6´5˝/(220–240); d9.2

YEAR	TM LG	W	L	PCT	G	GS	CG-SHO	SV-BS	IP	H	R	HR	HB	BB-IB	SO	ERA	AERA	OAV	OOB	AB-HR-SH	AVG	PB	SUP	APR	DL	PW
1980	Bos A	2	0	1.000	6	4	2	0-0	32.1	41	14	3	0	8-2	10	3.62	118	.306	.345	0	ø	0	142	2	0	0.1
1981	Bos A	0	5	.000	14	11	0	0-0	57.2	69	38	10	3	18-0	29	4.99	78	.301	.354	0	ø	0	106	-7	0	-0.6
1982	Bos A	1	0	1.000	5	0	0	0-0	9	14	3	0	0	0-0	2	2.00	218	.341	.341	0	ø	0	—	2	129	0.2
1984	Bos A	5	0	1.000	35	0	0	1-3	62	69	31	6	1	21-5	21	3.34	126	.286	.341	0	ø	0	—	4	0	0.3
1985	Bos A	6	5	.545	44	1	0	12-4	91	103	47	5	0	28-8	58	3.76	115	.289	.338	0	ø	0	105	3	30	0.4
1986	†Bos A	0	2	.000	40	0	0	4-4	57.1	69	29	5	0	19-7	32	3.92	107	.308	.359	0	ø	0	—	1	45	0.1
1987	Bos A	5	4	.556	29	0	0	0-0	72.2	91	48	13	2	32-2	43	5.33	86	.314	.386	0	ø	0	—	-7	15	-0.7
1989	KC A	3	1	.750	25	0	0	0-1	54	48	19	2	3	19-3	33	2.83	137	.242	.317	0	ø	0	—	6	0	0.5
1990	KC A	5	4	.556	46	0	0	1-1	80	79	38	7	3	23-3	54	4.16	93	.254	.310	0	ø	0	—	-1	29	0.0
1991	KC A	3	2	.600	33	0	0	1-0	46.2	60	31	3	1	18-5	38	5.98	69	.311	.367	0	ø	0	—	-8	72	-0.8
Total	10	30	23	.566	277	16	2	19-13	562.2	643	298	54	13	186-35	320	4.17	100	.290	.346	0	ø	0	113	-5	320	-0.5

CREEK, DOUG Paul Douglas; B3.1.1969 Winchester VA; BL/TL/6´0˝/(200–225); [StLN91 7/181]; d9.17; Col Georgia Tech

YEAR	TM LG	W	L	PCT	G	GS	CG-SHO	SV-BS	IP	H	R	HR	HB	BB-IB	SO	ERA	AERA	OAV	OOB	AB-HR-SH	AVG	PB	SUP	APR	DL	PW
1995	StL N	0	0	ø	6	0	0	0-0	6.2	2	0	0	0	3-0	10	0.00	ø	.095	.208	0	ø	0	—	3	0	0.1
1996	SF N	0	2	.000	63	0	0	0-1	48.1	45	41	11	2	32-2	38	6.52	64	.243	.361	1-0-1	.000	-0	—	-14	0	-0.7
1997	SF N	1	2	.333	3	3	0	0-0	13.1	12	12	1	0	14-0	14	6.75	61	.240	.406	3-0-2	.333	0	89	-4	0	-0.7
1999	Chi N	0	0	ø	3	0	0	0-0	6	6	7	1	0	8-1	6	10.50	44	.261	.438	0	ø	0	—	-4	0	-0.2
2000	TB A	1	3	.250	45	0	0	1-2	60.2	49	33	10	2	39-3	73	4.60	107	.224	.342	0	ø	0	—	2	0	0.2
2001	TB A	2	5	.286	66	0	0	0-3	62.2	51	34	7	4	49-5	66	4.31	105	.230	.374	0	ø	0	—	1	0	0.1
2002	TB A	2	1	.667	29	0	0	0-2	37.1	39	27	8	3	21-1	37	6.27	72	.264	.366	1	.000	-0	—	-7	0	-0.5
	Sea A	1	1	.500	23	0	0	0-0	18.1	18	10	2	4	14-1	19	4.91	88	.257	.404	0	ø	0	—	-1	0	-0.1
	Year	3	2	.600	52	0	0	0-2	55.2	57	37	10	7	35-2	56	5.82	76	.261	.379	1	.000	-0	—	-7	0	-0.6
2003	Tor A	0	0	ø	21	0	0	0-1	13.2	14	6	2	2	12-3	11	3.29	144	.264	.406	0	ø	0	—	2	135	0.1
2005	Det A	0	0	ø	20	0	0	0-0	22.1	27	18	7	0	7-0	18	6.85	62	.293	.340	0	ø	0	—	-6	0	-0.3
Total	9	7	14	.333	279	3	0	1-9	289.1	263	188	49	17	199-16	292	5.32	84	.243	.366	5-0-3	.200	0	89	-28	135	-2.0

CREEL, JACK Jack Dalton "Tex"; B4.23.1916 Kyle TX; D8.13.2002 Houston TX; BR/TR/6´0˝/165; d4.22

YEAR	TM LG	W	L	PCT	G	GS	CG-SHO	SV-BS	IP	H	R	HR	HB	BB-IB	SO	ERA	AERA	OAV	OOB	AB-HR-SH	AVG	PB	SUP	APR	DL	PW
1945	StL N	5	4	.556	26	8	2	2	87	78	41	5	6	45	34	4.14	90	.245	.349	26-0-4	.077	-2*	116	-2	0	-0.3

CREEL, KEITH Steven Keith; B2.4.1959 Dallas TX; BR/TR/6´2˝/180; [KCA80 S1/4]; d5.25; Col Texas

YEAR	TM LG	W	L	PCT	G	GS	CG-SHO	SV-BS	IP	H	R	HR	HB	BB-IB	SO	ERA	AERA	OAV	OOB	AB-HR-SH	AVG	PB	SUP	APR	DL	PW
1982	KC A	1	4	.200	9	6	0	0-0	41.2	43	28	8	0	25-0	13	5.40	76	.267	.362	0	ø	0	74	-6	0	-0.6
1983	KC A	2	5	.286	25	10	1	0-0	89.1	116	66	17	2	35-0	31	6.35	65	.320	.380	0	ø	0	86	-20	0	-1.4
1985	Cle A	2	5	.286	15	8	0	0-0	62	73	35	7	2	23-2	31	4.79	87	.296	.354	0	ø	0	109	-4	0	-0.4
1987	Tex A	0	0	ø	6	0	0	0-0	9.2	12	5	2	0	5-0	5	4.66	97	.293	.370	0	ø	0	—	0	0	0.0
Total	4	5	14	.263	55	24	1	0-0	202.2	244	134	34	4	88-2	80	5.60	74	.300	.368	0	ø	0	91	-30	0	-2.4

CREMINS, BOB Robert Anthony "Lefty","Crooked Arm"; B2.15.1906 Pelham Manor NY; D3.27.2004 Pelham NY; BL/TL/5´11˝/178; d8.17

YEAR	TM LG	W	L	PCT	G	GS	CG-SHO	SV-BS	IP	H	R	HR	HB	BB-IB	SO	ERA	AERA	OAV	OOB	AB-HR-SH	AVG	PB	SUP	APR	DL	PW
1927	Bos A	0	0	ø	4	0	0	0	5.1	5	4	0	0	3	0	5.06	83	.250	.348	0	ø	0	—	-1	—	0.0

CRESS, WALKER Walker James "Foots"; B3.6.1917 Ben Hur VA; D4.21.1996 Baton Rouge LA; BR/TR/6´5˝/205; d4.27; Col Louisiana St.

YEAR	TM LG	W	L	PCT	G	GS	CG-SHO	SV-BS	IP	H	R	HR	HB	BB-IB	SO	ERA	AERA	OAV	OOB	AB-HR-SH	AVG	PB	SUP	APR	DL	PW
1948	Cin N	0	1	.000	30	2	1	0	60	60	32	2	1	42	33	4.50	87	.271	.390	8-0-1	.500	2*	79	-3	0	0.0
1949	Cin N	0	0	ø	3	0	0	0	2	2	0	0	0	3	0	0.00	ø	.286	.500	0	ø	0	—	1	0	0.0
Total	2	0	1	.000	33	2	1	0	62	62	32	2	1	45	33	4.35	90	.272	.394	8-0-1	.500	2	79	-2	0	0.0

CRESSEND, JACK John Baptiste; B5.13.1975 New Orleans LA; BR/TR/6´1˝/(185–195); d8.26; Col Tulane

YEAR	TM LG	W	L	PCT	G	GS	CG-SHO	SV-BS	IP	H	R	HR	HB	BB-IB	SO	ERA	AERA	OAV	OOB	AB-HR-SH	AVG	PB	SUP	APR	DL	PW
2000	Min A	0	0	ø	11	0	0	0-0	13.2	20	8	0	0	6-0	6	5.27	100	.364	.426	0	ø	0	—	0	0	0.0
2001	Min A	3	2	.600	44	0	0	0-2	56.1	50	24	6	1	16-0	40	3.67	127	.237	.291	0	ø	0	—	6	0	0.5
2002	Min A	0	1	.000	23	0	0	0-0	32	40	25	6	1	19-4	22	5.91	76	.305	.392	0	ø	0	—	-6	114	-0.3
2003	Cle A	2	1	.667	33	0	0	0-1	43	40	12	1	2	9-1	28	2.51	176	.252	.300	0	ø	0	—	10	0	0.5
2004	Cle A	0	1	.000	11	0	0	0-0	15.2	22	11	4	0	10-2	8	6.32	69	.333	.416	0	ø	0	—	-3	0	-0.2
Total	5	5	5	.500	122	0	0	0-3	160.2	172	80	17	4	60-7	104	4.20	109	.277	.342	0	ø	0	—	7	114	0.5

CREWS, TIM Stanley Timothy; B4.3.1961 Tampa FL; D3.23.1993 Orlando FL; BR/TR/6´0˝/(180–195); [MilA81*2/48]; d7.27; Col Valencia (FL) CC

YEAR	TM LG	W	L	PCT	G	GS	CG-SHO	SV-BS	IP	H	R	HR	HB	BB-IB	SO	ERA	AERA	OAV	OOB	AB-HR-SH	AVG	PB	SUP	APR	DL	PW
1987	LA N	1	1	.500	20	0	0	3-3	29	30	9	2	2	8-1	20	2.48	160	.268	.325	2	.000	-0	—	5	0	0.4
1988	LA N	4	0	1.000	42	0	0	0-1	71.2	77	29	3	0	16-7	45	3.14	107	.278	.312	5-0-1	.200	0	—	1	0	0.0
1989	LA N	0	1	.000	44	0	0	1-2	61.2	69	27	7	2	23-9	56	3.21	107	.284	.351	0	ø	0	—	0	0	0.0
1990	LA N	4	5	.444	66	2	0	5-4	107.1	98	40	9	1	24-6	76	2.77	133	.238	.280	7	.000	-1	98	10	0	0.7
1991	LA N	2	3	.400	60	0	0	6-2	76	75	30	7	0	19-11	53	3.43	105	.256	.299	1	.000	0	—	3	0	0.2
1992	LA N	0	3	.000	49	2	0	0-1	78	95	46	6	2	20-9	43	5.19	67	.310	.351	7	.286	0	65	-12	0	-0.6
Total	6	11	13	.458	281	4	0	15-13	423.2	444	181	34	7	110-43	293	3.44	103	.270	.316	22-0-1	.136	-0	82	7	0	0.7

CRIDER, JERRY Jerry Stephen; B9.2.1941 Sioux Falls SD; BR/TR/6´2˝/200; d5.21

YEAR	TM LG	W	L	PCT	G	GS	CG-SHO	SV-BS	IP	H	R	HR	HB	BB-IB	SO	ERA	AERA	OAV	OOB	AB-HR-SH	AVG	PB	SUP	APR	DL	PW
1969	Min A	1	0	1.000	21	1	0	1-1	28.2	31	15	3	2	15-6	16	4.71	77	.284	.378	9	.444	2	267	-2	0	0.1
1970	Chi A	4	7	.364	32	8	0	4-0	91	101	49	13	2	34-2	40	4.45	87	.288	.350	24-0-2	.083	-1	83	-5	0	-0.8
Total	2	5	7	.417	53	9	0	5-1	119.2	132	64	16	4	49-8	56	4.51	85	.287	.357	33-0-2	.182	1	103	-7	0	-0.7

CRIM, CHUCK Charles Robert; B7.23.1961 Van Nuys CA; BR/TR/6´0˝/(170–190); [MilA82 17/443]; d4.8; Col Hawaii–Manoa

YEAR	TM LG	W	L	PCT	G	GS	CG-SHO	SV-BS	IP	H	R	HR	HB	BB-IB	SO	ERA	AERA	OAV	OOB	AB-HR-SH	AVG	PB	SUP	APR	DL	PW
1987	Mil A	6	8	.429	53	5	0	12-5	130	133	60	15	3	39-5	56	3.67	126	.266	.322	0	ø	0	115	12	0	1.3
1988	Mil A	7	6	.538	**70**	0	0	9-2	105	95	38	11	2	28-3	58	2.91	137	.247	.298	0	ø	0	—	13	0	1.6
1989	Mil A	9	7	.563	**76**	0	0	7-7	117.2	114	42	7	2	36-9	59	2.83	136	.259	.314	0	ø	0	—	13	0	1.8
1990	Mil A	3	5	.375	67	0	0	11-5	85.2	88	39	7	2	23-4	39	3.47	112	.261	.309	0	ø	0	—	4	19	0.4
1991	Mil A	8	5	.615	66	0	0	3-2	91.1	115	52	9	2	25-9	39	4.63	86	.305	.351	0	ø	0	—	-7	0	-0.9
1992	Cal A	7	6	.538	57	0	0	1-2	87	100	56	11	6	29-6	30	5.17	78	.293	.355	0	ø	0	—	-12	0	-1.6
1993	Cal A	2	2	.500	11	0	0	0-0	15.1	17	11	2	2	5-1	10	5.87	77	.298	.369	0	ø	0	—	-2	0	-0.4
1994	Chi N	5	4	.556	49	1	0	2-3	64.1	69	36	9	1	24-6	43	4.48	94	.271	.336	2	.000	-0	173	-2	0	-0.3
Total	8	47	43	.522	449	6	0	45-26	696.1	731	334	71	20	209-43	334	3.83	107	.272	.326	2	.000	-0	137	19	19	1.9

CRIMIAN, JACK John Melvin; B2.17.1926 Philadelphia PA; BR/TR/5´10˝/(175–180); d7.3

YEAR	TM LG	W	L	PCT	G	GS	CG-SHO	SV-BS	IP	H	R	HR	HB	BB-IB	SO	ERA	AERA	OAV	OOB	AB-HR-SH	AVG	PB	SUP	APR	DL	PW
1951	StL N	1	0	1.000	11	0	0	1	17	24	17	3	0	8	5	9.00	44	.338	.405	3	.333	0	—	-9	0	-0.6
1952	StL N	0	0	ø	5	0	0	0	8.1	15	9	4	0	4	4	9.72	38	.417	.475	1	.000	0	—	-5	0	-0.2
1956	KC A	4	8	.333	54	7	0	3	129	129	87	19	5	49-2	59	5.51	79	.265	.334	22-0-5	.227	1*	94	-16	0	-1.3
1957	Det A	0	1	.000	4	0	0	0	5.2	9	8	1	0	4-2	1	12.71	30	.375	.448	0	ø	0	—	-5	0	-0.8
Total	4	5	9	.357	74	7	0	4	160	177	121	27	5	65-4	69	6.36	67	.287	.355	26-0-5	.231	1	94	-35	0	-2.9

CRISS, DODE Dode; B3.12.1885 Sherman MS; D9.8.1955 Sherman MS; BL/TR/6´2˝/200; d4.20; ▲

YEAR	TM LG	W	L	PCT	G	GS	CG-SHO	SV-BS	IP	H	R	HR	HB	BB-IB	SO	ERA	AERA	OAV	OOB	AB-HR-SH	AVG	PB	SUP	APR	DL	PW
1908	StL A	0	1	.000	9	1	0	0	18	15	14	1	3	13	9	6.50	37	.250	.408	82	.341	1*	343	-7	—	-0.2
1909	StL A	1	5	.167	11	6	3	0	55.1	53	33	0	2	32	43	3.42	71	.262	.369	48	.292	5*	78	-8	—	-0.3
1910	StL A	2	1	.667	6	0	0	0	19.1	12	7	0	4	9	9	1.40	177	.176	.309	91-1-0	.231	1*	—	2	—	0.4

YEAR	TM LG	W	L	PCT	G	GS	CG-SHO	SV-BS	IP	H	R	HR	HB	BB-IB	SO	ERA	AERA	OAV	OOB	AB-HR-SH	AVG	PB	SUP	APR	DL	PW
1911	StL A	0	2	.000	4	2	0	0	18.1	24	21	0	2	10	9	8.35	40	.333	.429	83-2-1	.253	0*	43	-9	—	-0.7
Total	4	3	9	.250	30	9	3	0	111	104	75	1	11	64	70	4.38	59	.259	.375	304-3-1	.276	8	96	-22	—	-0.8

CRISTALL, BILL William Arthur "Lefty"; B9.12.1875 Odessa, Russia; D1.28.1939 Buffalo NY; BL/TL/5´7˝/145; d9.3

YEAR	TM LG	W	L	PCT	G	GS	CG-SHO	SV-BS	IP	H	R	HR	HB	BB-IB	SO	ERA	AERA	OAV	OOB	AB-HR-SH	AVG	PB	SUP	APR	DL	PW
1901	Cle A	1	5	.167	6	6	5-1	0	48.1	54	42	1	4	30	12	4.84	73	.280	.388	20-0-1	.350	2	111	-8	—	-0.5

CRISTANTE, LEO Dante Leo; B12.10.1926 Detroit MI; D8.24.1977 Dearborn MI; BR/TR/6´1˝/195; d4.21

YEAR	TM LG	W	L	PCT	G	GS	CG-SHO	SV-BS	IP	H	R	HR	HB	BB-IB	SO	ERA	AERA	OAV	OOB	AB-HR-SH	AVG	PB	SUP	APR	DL	PW
1951	Phi N	1	1	.500	10	1	0	0	22	28	13	3	1	9	6	4.91	78	.318	.388	6-0-1	.167	-0	206	-3	0	-0.2
1955	Det A	0	1	.000	20	1	0	0	36.2	37	15	1	0	14-2	9	3.19	120	.261	.325	7	.000	-1	162	3	0	0.0
Total	2	1	2	.333	30	2	0	0	58.2	65	28	4	1	23-2	15	3.84	100	.283	.349	13-0-1	.077	-1	184	0	0	-0.2

CRITCHLEY, MORRIE Morris Arthur; B3.26.1850 New London CT; D3.6.1910 Pittsburgh PA; 6´1˝/190; d5.8

YEAR	TM LG	W	L	PCT	G	GS	CG-SHO	SV-BS	IP	H	R	HR	HB	BB-IB	SO	ERA	AERA	OAV	OOB	AB-HR-SH	AVG	PB	SUP	APR	DL	PW
1882	Pit AA	1	0	1.000	1	1	1-1	0	9	7	0	0	—	1	3	0.00	ø	.200	.222	5	.000	-1	39	3	—	0.2
	StL AA	0	4	.000	4	4	4	0	34	43	31	3	—	7	2	4.24	66	.289	.321	14	.214	-0	87	-4	—	-0.5
	Year	1	4	.200	5	5	5-1	0	43	50	31	3	—	8	5	3.35	83	.272	.302	19	.158	-1	78	-3	—	-0.3

CROCKER, CLAUDE Claude Arthur; B7.20.1924 Caroleen NC; D12.19.2002 Clinton SC; BR/TR/6´2˝/185; d8.1; Col North Carolina

YEAR	TM LG	W	L	PCT	G	GS	CG-SHO	SV-BS	IP	H	R	HR	HB	BB-IB	SO	ERA	AERA	OAV	OOB	AB-HR-SH	AVG	PB	SUP	APR	DL	PW
1944	Bro N	0	0	ø	2	0	0	0	3.1	6	4	0	0	5	1	10.80	33	.400	.550	1	1.000	0	—	-2	0	-0.1
1945	Bro N	0	0	ø	1	0	0	1	2	2	0	0	0	1	1	0.00	ø	.286	.375	0	ø	0	—	1	0	0.1
Total	2	0	0	ø	3	0	0	1	5.1	8	4	0	0	6	2	6.75	54	.364	.500	1	1.000	0	—	-1	0	0.0

CRONE, RAY Raymond Hayes; B8.7.1931 Memphis TN; BR/TR/6´2˝/(165–190); d4.13

YEAR	TM LG	W	L	PCT	G	GS	CG-SHO	SV-BS	IP	H	R	HR	HB	BB-IB	SO	ERA	AERA	OAV	OOB	AB-HR-SH	AVG	PB	SUP	APR	DL	PW
1954	Mil N	1	0	1.000	19	2	1	1	49	44	11	6	1	19	33	2.02	184	.247	.322	10	.200	-0	48	11	0	0.5
1955	Mil N	10	9	.526	33	15	6-1	0	140.1	117	63	11	0	42-7	76	3.46	108	.227	.285	44-0-3	.159	-1	90	4	0	0.4
1956	Mil N	11	10	.524	35	21	6	2	169.2	173	92	19	1	44-3	73	3.87	89	.263	.307	49-0-5	.122	1	122	-11	0	-1.2
1957	Mil N	3	1	.750	11	5	2	0	42.1	54	23	8	0	15-2	15	4.46	78	.312	.365	11-0-1	.182	1	161	-5	0	-0.3
	NY N	4	8	.333	25	17	2	1	120.2	131	68	11	3	40-1	56	4.33	91	.272	.330	40-0-1	.025	-4	113	-6	0	-0.8
	Year	7	9	.438	36	22	4	1	163	185	91	19	3	55-3	71	4.36	88	.282	.339	51-0-2	.059	-3	124	-11	0	-1.1
1958	SF N	1	2	.333	14	1	0	0	24	35	18	5	0	13-0	7	6.75	56	.354	.421	2	.000	-0	94	-7	0	-0.8
Total	5	30	30	.500	137	61	17-1	4	546	554	275	60	5	173-13	260	3.87	95	.263	.319	156-0-10	.115	-3	112	-14	0	-2.2

CRONIN, JACK John J.; B5.26.1874 Staten Island NY; D7.12.1929 Middletown NY; BR/TR/6´0˝/200; d8.24

YEAR	TM LG	W	L	PCT	G	GS	CG-SHO	SV-BS	IP	H	R	HR	HB	BB-IB	SO	ERA	AERA	OAV	OOB	AB-HR-SH	AVG	PB	SUP	APR	DL	PW
1895	Bro N	0	0	ø	2	0	0	2	5	10	8	0	0	3	1	10.80	41	.417	.481	2	.500	1	—	-4	—	-0.2
1898	Pit N	2	2	.500	4	4	2-1	0	28	35	14	0	0	8	9	3.54	101	.304	.350	10	.100	-0	140	1	—	0.1
1899	Cin N	2	2	.500	5	5	5	0	41	56	35	2	5	16	9	5.49	71	.324	.397	17	.118	-1	136	-7	—	-0.7
1901	Det A	13	16	.448	30	28	21-1	0	219.2	261	145	6	11	42	62	3.89	99	.292	.331	85-0-4	.247	2*	83	1	—	0.1
1902	Det A	0	0	ø	4	0	0	0	17.1	26	23	1	3	8	5	9.35	39	.347	.430	7	.000	-1	—	-10	—	-0.5
	Bal A	3	5	.375	10	8	8	0	75.2	66	29	1	0	24	20	2.62	144	.236	.296	27-0-2	.148	-1	69	10	—	1.0
	Year	3	5	.375	14	8	8	0	93	92	52	2	3	32	25	3.87	97	.259	.326	34-0-2	.118	-2	70	1	—	0.5
	NY N	5	6	.455	13	12	11	0	114	105	49	3	0	18	52	2.45	115	.245	.275	65-0-2	.169	-1*	73	4	—	0.3
1903	NY N	6	4	.600	20	11	8	1	115.2	130	67	5	6	37	50	3.81	88	.284	.345	46-0-2	.196	0	114	-6	—	-0.5
1904	Bro N	12	23	.343	40	34	33-4	0	307	284	132	10	12	79	110	2.70	102	.245	.300	108-0-3	.157	-3	80	4	—	0.2
Total	7	43	58	.426	128	102	88-6	3	923.1	973	502	28	37	235	318	3.40	96	.270	.321	367-0-13	.180	-5	89	-7	—	-0.2

CROSBY, GEORGE George Washington; B1860 IA; D1.9.1913 San Francisco CA; d5.22

YEAR	TM LG	W	L	PCT	G	GS	CG-SHO	SV-BS	IP	H	R	HR	HB	BB-IB	SO	ERA	AERA	OAV	OOB	AB-HR-SH	AVG	PB	SUP	APR	DL	PW
1884	Chi N	1	2	.333	3	3	3	0	28	27	21	3	—	12	11	3.54	89	.227	.298	13-1	.308	1	85	-1	—	0.0

CROSBY, KEN Kenneth Stewart; B12.15.1947 New Denver BC, Can.; BR/TR/6´2˝/(179–186); [NYA69 10/225]; d8.5; Col Brigham Young

YEAR	TM LG	W	L	PCT	G	GS	CG-SHO	SV-BS	IP	H	R	HR	HB	BB-IB	SO	ERA	AERA	OAV	OOB	AB-HR-SH	AVG	PB	SUP	APR	DL	PW
1975	Chi N	1	0	1.000	9	0	0	0-0	8.1	10	3	0	0	7-0	6	3.24	120	.294	.415	0	ø	0	—	1	0	0.1
1976	Chi N	0	0	ø	7	1	0	0-0	12	20	16	3	0	8-0	5	12.00	32	.377	.459	2	.500	0	113	-9	0	-0.4
Total	2	1	0	1.000	16	1	0	0-0	20.1	30	19	3	0	15-0	11	8.41	46	.345	.441	2	.500	1	113	-8	0	-0.3

CROSS, LEM George Lewis; B1.9.1872 Sanbornton NH; D10.9.1930 Manchester NH; TR/5´9˝/155; d8.6

YEAR	TM LG	W	L	PCT	G	GS	CG-SHO	SV-BS	IP	H	R	HR	HB	BB-IB	SO	ERA	AERA	OAV	OOB	AB-HR-SH	AVG	PB	SUP	APR	DL	PW
1893	Cin N	0	2	.000	3	3	2	0	21	24	16	3	0	9	7	5.57	86	.279	.347	6	.333	1	54	-1	—	0.0
1894	Cin N	3	4	.429	8	7	3	0	53	94	73	9	5	21	11	8.49	65	.381	.440	26	.231	-1*	111	-17	—	-1.5
Total	2	3	6	.333	11	10	5	0	74	118	89	12	5	30	18	7.66	69	.354	.416	32	.250	-0	95	-18	—	-1.5

CROTHERS, DOUG Douglas; B11.16.1859 Natchez MS; D3.29.1907 St.Louis MO; BR/TR/5´9˝/140; d8.3

YEAR	TM LG	W	L	PCT	G	GS	CG-SHO	SV-BS	IP	H	R	HR	HB	BB-IB	SO	ERA	AERA	OAV	OOB	AB-HR-SH	AVG	PB	SUP	APR	DL	PW
1884	KC U	1	2	.333	3	3	3	0	25	26	15	0	—	6	11	1.80	124	.250	.291	15	.133	-1*	114	0	—	-0.2
1885	NY AA	7	11	.389	18	18	18-1	0	154	192	135	4	2	49	40	5.08	61	.293	.344	51	.157	0	117	-34	—	-2.9
Total	2	8	13	.381	21	21	21-1	0	179	218	150	4	2	55	51	4.63	65	.287	.337	66	.152	-1	116	-34	—	-3.1

CROUCH, BILL William Henry "Skip"; B12.3.1886 Kiamensi DE; D12.22.1945 Highland Park MI; BL/TL/6´1˝/210; d7.12; s–Bill

YEAR	TM LG	W	L	PCT	G	GS	CG-SHO	SV-BS	IP	H	R	HR	HB	BB-IB	SO	ERA	AERA	OAV	OOB	AB-HR-SH	AVG	PB	SUP	APR	DL	PW
1910	StL A	0	0	ø	1	1	1	0	8	6	4	0	0	7	2	3.38	73	.231	.394	3	.000	-0	108	-1	—	-0.1

CROUCH, BILL Wilmer Elmer; B8.20.1910 Wilmington DE; D12.26.1980 Howell MI; BB/TR/6´1˝/180; d5.9; f–Bill; Col Eastern Michigan

YEAR	TM LG	W	L	PCT	G	GS	CG-SHO	SV-BS	IP	H	R	HR	HB	BB-IB	SO	ERA	AERA	OAV	OOB	AB-HR-SH	AVG	PB	SUP	APR	DL	PW
1939	Bro N	4	0	1.000	6	3	3	0	38.1	37	14	3	0	14	10	2.58	156	.255	.321	15-0-1	.133	-1	224	5	—	0.4
1941	Phi N	2	3	.400	20	5	1	1	59	65	31	4	0	17	26	4.42	84	.286	.336	11-0-3	.091	-0	83	-4	0	-0.2
	StL N	1	2	.333	18	4	0	6	45	45	16	2	0	14	15	3.00	125	.271	.328	13-0-1	.000	-1	39	4	0	0.2
	Year	3	5	.375	38	9	1	7	104	110	47	6	0	31	41	3.81	98	.280	.333	24-0-4	.042	-2	63	1	0	0.0
1945	StL N	1	0	1.000	6	0	0	0	13.1	12	5	1	1	7	4	3.38	111	.255	.364	2	.000	-0	—	1	0	0.0
Total	3	8	5	.615	50	12	4	7	155.2	159	66	10	1	52	55	3.47	110	.272	.332	41-0-5	.073	-3	105	6	0	0.4

CROUCH, ZACH Zachary Quinn; B10.26.1965 Folsom CA; BL/TL/6´3˝/190; [BosA84 13/328]; d6.4

YEAR	TM LG	W	L	PCT	G	GS	CG-SHO	SV-BS	IP	H	R	HR	HB	BB-IB	SO	ERA	AERA	OAV	OOB	AB-HR-SH	AVG	PB	SUP	APR	DL	PW
1988	Bos A	0	0	ø	3	0	0	0-0	1.1	4	1	0	0	2-0	0	6.75	61	.571	.667	0	ø	0	—	0	0	0.0

CROUSHORE, RICH Richard Steven; B8.7.1970 Lakehurst NJ; BR/TR/6´4˝/210; d5.18; Col James Madison; [DL 2001 NY N 17]

YEAR	TM LG	W	L	PCT	G	GS	CG-SHO	SV-BS	IP	H	R	HR	HB	BB-IB	SO	ERA	AERA	OAV	OOB	AB-HR-SH	AVG	PB	SUP	APR	DL	PW
1998	StL N	0	3	.000	41	0	0	8-3	54.1	44	31	6	4	29-2	47	4.97	85	.213	.320	0-0-2	ø	0	—	-4	0	-0.2
1999	StL N	3	7	.300	59	0	0	3-7	71.2	68	42	9	3	43-4	88	4.14	111	.247	.354	3	.333	1	—	1	0	0.1
2000	Col N	2	0	1.000	6	0	0	0-0	11.1	15	11	1	1	6-1	11	8.74	66	.313	.393	1-0-1	1.000	0	—	-3	0	-0.4
	Bos A	0	1	.000	5	0	0	0-0	4.2	4	3	0	1	5-1	3	5.79	87	.250	.435	0	ø	0	—	0	0	0.0
Total	3	5	11	.313	111	0	0	11-10	142	131	87	16	9	83-8	149	4.88	93	.240	.347	4-0-3	.500	1	—	-6	17	-0.5

CROW, DEAN Paul Dean; B8.21.1972 Garland TX; BL/TR/6´4˝/215; [SeaA93 10/269]; d5.29; Col Baylor

YEAR	TM LG	W	L	PCT	G	GS	CG-SHO	SV-BS	IP	H	R	HR	HB	BB-IB	SO	ERA	AERA	OAV	OOB	AB-HR-SH	AVG	PB	SUP	APR	DL	PW
1998	Det A	2	2	.500	32	0	0	0-0	45.2	55	22	6	2	16-6	18	3.94	121	.313	.374	0	ø	0	—	4	0	0.3

CROWDER, ALVIN Alvin Floyd "General"; B1.11.1899 Winston–Salem NC; D4.3.1972 Winston–Salem NC; BL/TR/5´10˝/170; d7.24

YEAR	TM LG	W	L	PCT	G	GS	CG-SHO	SV-BS	IP	H	R	HR	HB	BB-IB	SO	ERA	AERA	OAV	OOB	AB-HR-SH	AVG	PB	SUP	APR	DL	PW
1926	Was A	7	4	.636	19	12	6	1	100	97	52	3	2	60	26	3.96	98	.261	.367	38-0-2	.237	1	122	-1	—	0.0
1927	Was A	4	7	.364	15	11	4-2	0	67.1	58	44	3	2	42	22	4.54	89	.232	.347	22-0-1	.136	-1	95	-5	—	-0.9
	StL A	3	5	.375	21	8	2-1	3	73.2	71	44	3	1	42	30	5.01	87	.260	.361	23-0-1	.261	0	103	-3	—	-0.3
	Year	7	12	.368	36	19	6-3	3	141	129	88	6	3	84	52	4.79	88	.247	.354	45-0-2	.200	-1	98	-9	—	-1.2
1928	StL A	21	5	**.808**	41	31	19-1	2	244	238	113	11	1	91	99	3.69	114	.258	.325	80-0-9	.188	-2	114	15	—	1.0
1929	StL A	17	15	.531	40	34	19-**4**	4	266.2	272	133	22	0	93	79	3.92	113	.271	.332	96-0-1	.188	-3	89	14	—	1.1
1930	StL A	3	7	.300	13	10	5-1	1	77.1	85	43	11	1	27	42	4.66	105	.283	.345	25	.160	-2	78	3	—	0.2
	Was A	15	9	.625	27	25	20	1	202.1	191	90	6	1	69	65	3.60	128	.249	.312	76-0-6	.171	-2	111	24	—	2.0
	Year	18	16	.529	40	35	25-1	2	279.2	276	133	17	2	96	107	3.89	120	.259	.321	101-0-6	.168	-4	101	30	—	2.2
1931	Was A	18	11	.621	44	26	13-1	2	234.1	255	117	13	1	72	85	3.88	111	.275	.328	88-0-3	.216	-1	99	12	—	1.0
1932	Was A	**26**	13	.667	50	**39**	21-3	1	**327**	319	136	17	0	77	103	3.33	130	.252	.295	122-0-5	.221	2*	98	37	—	3.8
1933	†Was A★	**24**	15	.615	**52**	35	17	4	299.1	311	140	14	3	81	110	3.97	105	.267	.316	102-0-8	.186	1	110	11	—	1.2
1934	Was A	4	10	.286	29	13	4	3	100.2	142	88	9	0	38	39	6.79	64	.326	.380	32-0-2	.219	1	116	-30	—	-3.4
	†Det A	5	1	.833	9	9	3-1	0	66.2	81	35	3	0	20	30	4.18	105	.295	.342	30	.133	-2	117	2	—	-0.1
	Year	9	11	.450	38	22	7-1	3	167.1	223	123	12	0	58	69	5.75	76	.314	.365	62-0-2	.177	-1	116	-27	—	-3.5
1935	†Det A	16	10	.615	33	32	16-2	0	241	269	127	16	4	67	59	4.26	98	.285	.335	93-0-5	.183	-2	118	-1	—	-0.5
1936	Det A	4	3	.571	9	7	1	0	44	64	42	5	0	21	10	8.39	59	.342	.409	20-0-1	.150	-1	135	-15	—	-1.8
Total	11	167	115	.592	402	292	150-16	22	2344.1	2453	1204	136	16	800	799	4.12	105	.270	.330	847-0-44	.194	-12	106	63	—	3.3

YEAR	TM LG	W	L	PCT	G	GS	CG-SHO	SV-BS	IP	H	R	HR	HB	BB-IB	SO	ERA	AERA	OAV	OOB	AB-HR-SH	AVG	PB	SUP	APR	DL	PW
CROWELL, JIM	James Everette; B5.14.1974 Minneapolis MN; BL/TL/6´4˝/(225–230); d9.12; Col Indianapolis																									
1997	Cin N	0	1	.000	2	1	0	0-0	6.1	12	7	2	0	5-0	3	9.95	43	.414	.500	2	.000	-0	108	-4	0	-0.5
2004	Phi N	0	0	ø	4	0	0	0-0	3	6	2	0	0	0-0	1	3.00	148	.333	.333	0	ø	0	—	0	0	0.0
2005	Fla N	0	0	ø	4	0	0	0-0	3.1	10	8	1	2	0-0	2	21.60	19	.526	.545	0	ø	0	—	-7	0	-0.3
Total	3	0	1	.000	10	1	0	0-0	12.2	28	17	3	2	5-0	6	11.37	37	.424	.473	2	.000	-0	108	-11	0	-0.8
CROWELL, CAP	Minot Joy; B9.5.1892 Roxbury MA; D9.30.1962 Central Falls RI; BR/TR/6´1˝/178; d6.23; Col Brown																									
1915	Phi A	2	6	.250	10	8	4	0	54.1	56	53	1	5	47	15	5.47	54	.292	.443	22	.227	-0	78	-18	—	-2.3
1916	Phi A	0	5	.000	9	6	1	0	39.2	43	33	0	2	34	15	4.99	57	.289	.427	12	.000	-2	57	-11	—	-1.4
Total	2	2	11	.154	19	14	5	0	94	99	86	1	7	81	30	5.27	55	.290	.436	34	.147	-2	69	-29	—	-3.7
CROWELL, BILLY	William Theodore; B11.6.1865 Cincinnati OH; D7.24.1935 Ft.Worth TX; BR/TR/5´8.5˝/160; d4.20																									
1887	Cle AA	14	31	.311	45	45	45-1	0	389.1	541	350	9	20	138	72	4.88	89	.327	.386	156	.141	-13	71	-17	—	-2.5
1888	Cle AA	5	13	.278	18	18	16	0	150.2	212	148	8	9	61	61	5.79	53	.320	.385	58	.086	-5	93	-39	—	-3.9
	Lou AA	0	1	.000	1	1	1	0	9	12	14	1	1	6	5	6.00	51	.308	.413	3	.000	-0	57	-3	—	-0.3
	Year	5	14	.263	19	19	17	0	159.2	224	162	9	10	67	66	5.81	53	.320	.387	61	.082	-5	91	-41	—	-4.2
Total	2	19	45	.297	64	64	62-1	0	549	765	512	18	30	205	138	5.15	77	.325	.386	217	.124	-18	76	-59	—	-6.7
CROWSON, WOODY	Thomas Woodrow; B9.9.1918 Fuquay Sprgs. (now Fuquay–Varina) NC; D8.14.1947 Mayodan NC; BR/TR/6´2˝/185; d4.17																									
1945	Phi A	0	0	ø	1	0	0	0	3	2	2	0	0	3	2	6.00	57	.200	.385	1	.000	-0	—	-1	0	0.0
CRUCETA, FRANCISCO	Francisco Alberto; B7.4.1981 LaVega, D.R.; BR/TR/6´2˝/(180–215); d9.21																									
2004	Cle A	0	1	.000	2	2	0	0-0	7.2	10	9	1	1	4-0	9	9.39	46	.303	.385	0	ø	0	107	-5	0	-0.5
2006	Sea A	0	0	ø	4	1	0	0-0	6.2	10	8	2	0	6-0	2	10.80	41	.370	.471	0	ø	0	235	-5	0	-0.2
Total	2	0	1	.000	6	3	0	0-0	14.1	20	17	3	1	10-0	11	10.05	44	.333	.425	0	ø	0	149	-10	0	-0.7
CRUDALE, MIKE	Michael Christopher; B1.3.1977 San Diego CA; BR/TR/6´0˝/205; [StLN99 24/732]; d4.10; Col Santa Clara																									
2002	†StL N	3	0	1.000	49	1	0	0-1	52.2	43	11	3	1	14-2	47	1.88	215	.228	.276	2	.000	-0	115	13	0	0.6
2003	StL N	0	1	.000	13	0	0	0-1	11.1	11	5	1	1	12-1	6	2.38	173	.250	.414	0	ø	0	—	1	0	0.1
	Mil N	0	0	ø	9	0	0	0-0	9.1	1	3	0	0	6-0	7	2.89	149	.036	.206	0	ø	0	—	2	0	0.1
	Year	0	1	.000	22	0	0	0-1	20.2	12	8	1	1	18-1	13	2.61	161	.167	.337	0	ø	0	—	3	0	0.2
Total	2	3	1	.750	71	1	0	0-2	73.1	55	19	4	2	32-3	60	2.09	196	.211	.295	2	.000	-0	115	16	0	0.8
CRUM, CAL	Clarence Newton; B7.27.1889 Cooks Mills IL; D12.7.1945 Tulsa OK; BR/TR/6´1˝/175; d5.4																									
1917	Bos N	0	0	ø	1	0	0	0	1	1	0	0	0	1	0	0.00	ø	.250	.400	0	ø	0	—	0	—	0.0
1918	Bos N	0	1	.000	1	1	0	0	2.1	6	4	0	1	3	0	15.43	17	.600	.714	1	.000	-0	56	-3	—	-0.5
Total	2	0	1	.000	2	1	0	0	3.1	7	4	0	1	4	0	10.80	24	.500	.632	1	.000	-0	56	-3	—	-0.5
CRUMPLER, ROY	Roy Maxton; B7.8.1896 Clinton NC; D10.6.1969 Fayetteville NC; BL/TL/6´1˝/195; d9.16																									
1920	Det A	1	0	1.000	2	2	1	0	13	17	13	2	1	11	2	5.54	67	.315	.439	9	.333	1*	245	-4	—	-0.1
1925	Phi N	0	0	ø	3	1	0	0	4.2	8	4	0	0	2	1	7.71	62	.381	.435	2	.000	-0	124	-1	—	-0.1
Total	2	1	0	1.000	5	3	1	0	17.2	25	17	2	1	13	3	6.11	65	.333	.438	11	.273	1	203	-5	—	-0.2
CRUTCHER, DICK	Richard Luther; B11.25.1889 Frankfort KY; D6.19.1952 Frankfort KY; BR/TR/5´9˝/148; d4.14																									
1914	Bos N	5	7	.417	33	15	5-1	0	158.2	169	73	4	6	66	48	3.46	80	.293	.371	54-0-1	.148	-1	100	-11	—	-0.8
1915	Bos N	2	2	.500	14	4	1	2	43.2	50	28	1	2	16	17	4.33	60	.309	.378	13-0-1	.231	1	115	-9	—	-0.8
Total	2	7	9	.438	47	19	6-1	2	202.1	219	101	5	8	82	65	3.65	75	.296	.373	67-0-2	.164	-0	103	-20	—	-1.6
CRUZ, JUAN	Juan Carlos; B10.15.1978 Bonao, D.R.; BR/TR/6´2˝/(155–165); d8.21																									
2001	Chi N	3	1	.750	8	8	0	0-0	44.2	40	16	4	2	17-1	39	3.22	130	.244	.322	16-0-2	.125	-1*	132	6	0	0.4
2002	Chi N	3	11	.214	45	9	0	1-3	97.1	84	56	11	8	59-4	81	3.98	102	.241	.356	14-0-2	.143	-0	76	-3	15	-0.5
2003	†Chi N	2	7	.222	25	6	0	0-1	61	66	44	7	7	28-0	65	6.05	72	.275	.365	12-0-1	.250	1	86	-11	0	-1.3
2004	†Atl N	6	2	.750	50	0	0	0-0	72	59	24	7	2	30-1	70	2.75	157	.224	.307	5	.200	1	—	13	0	1.3
2005	Oak A	0	3	.000	28	0	0	0-0	32.2	38	33	5	4	22-4	34	7.44	59	.290	.403	0	ø	0	—	-13	0	-1.0
2006	Ari N	5	6	.455	31	15	0	0-0	94.2	80	45	7	11	47-2	88	4.18	112	.230	.338	21-0-2	.000	-1	90	6	29	0.5
Total	6	19	30	.388	187	38	0	1-4	402.1	367	218	41	34	203-12	377	4.32	100	.245	.346	68-0-7	.118	-1	96	-2	44	-0.6
CRUZ, NELSON	Nelson; B9.13.1972 Puerto Plata, D.R.; BR/TR/6´1˝/185; d8.1																									
1997	Chi A	0	2	.000	19	0	0	0-0	26.1	29	19	6	0	9-1	23	6.49	68	.274	.330	0	ø	0	—	-5	0	-0.4
1999	Det A	2	5	.286	29	6	0	0-0	66.2	74	44	11	3	23-1	46	5.67	88	.281	.341	0	ø	0	90	-4	0	-0.3
2000	Det A	5	2	.714	27	0	0	0-1	41	39	14	4	3	13-3	34	3.07	160	.253	.320	1	.000	-0	—	9	0	1.3
2001	†Hou N	3	3	.500	66	0	0	2-2	82.1	72	41	11	9	24-4	75	4.15	111	.237	.310	6	.167	-0	—	4	0	0.3
2002	Hou N	2	6	.250	43	5	0	0-2	78.1	90	44	12	6	29-4	61	4.48	97	.284	.352	13-0-2	.000	-1	124	-2	15	-0.3
2003	Col N	3	5	.375	20	7	0	0-1	53.2	65	43	15	3	11-2	38	7.21	68	.301	.341	13-0-2	.154	-0	134	-11	77	-1.4
Total	6	15	23	.395	204	18	0	2-6	348.1	369	205	59	24	109-15	277	5.04	93	.271	.333	33-0-4	.091	-2	118	-9	92	-0.8
CRUZ, VICTOR	Victor Manuel (b Victor Manuel De La Cruz (Gil)); B12.24.1957 Rancho Viejo, D.R.; D9.26.2004 Santo Domingo, D.R.; BR/TR/5´9˝/(175–215); d6.24																									
1978	Tor A	7	3	.700	32	0	0	9-3	47.1	28	10	0	1	35-4	51	1.71	231	.179	.330	0	ø	0	—	11	0	2.4
1979	Cle A	3	9	.250	61	0	0	10-5	78.2	70	41	10	1	44-4	63	4.23	102	.244	.341	0	ø	0	—	0	0	0.0
1980	Cle A	6	7	.462	55	0	0	12-8	86	71	36	10	3	27-8	88	3.45	120	.229	.289	0	ø	0	—	6	0	1.0
1981	Pit N	1	1	.500	22	0	0	1-3	34	33	10	6	1	15-4	28	2.65	138	.264	.348	4-0-1	.000	-0	—	4	0	0.2
1983	Tex A	1	3	.250	17	0	0	5-2	25	16	7	2	1	10-3	18	1.44	281	.184	.270	0	ø	0	—	6	0	1.2
Total	5	18	23	.439	187	0	0	37-21	271	218	104	28	7	131-23	248	3.09	132	.226	.317	4-0-1	.000	-0	—	27	0	4.8
CUBILLAN, DARWIN	Darwin Harrikson (Salom); B11.15.1972 Bobures, Zulia, Venez.; BR/TR/6´2˝/(165–170); d5.20																									
2000	Tor A	1	0	1.000	7	0	0	0-0	15.2	20	14	5	1	11-0	14	8.04	63	.317	.427	1	.000	-0	—	-5	0	-0.2
	Tex A	0	0	ø	13	0	0	0-0	17.2	32	22	4	0	14-0	13	10.70	48	.400	.474	0	ø	0	—	-10	0	-0.5
	Year	1	0	1.000	20	0	0	0-0	33.1	52	36	9	1	25-0	27	9.45	54	.364	.453	1	.000	-0	—	-14	0	-0.7
2001	Mon N	0	0	ø	29	0	0	0-0	26.1	31	13	1	0	12-1	19	4.10	105	.295	.358	0	ø	0	—	1	0	0.0
2004	Bal A	0	0	ø	7	0	0	0-1	10	13	7	3	0	7-0	8	5.40	86	.302	.400	0	ø	0	—	-1	0	-0.1
Total	3	1	0	1.000	56	0	0	0-1	69.2	96	56	13	1	44-1	54	6.85	69	.330	.412	1	.000	-0	—	-15	0	-0.8
CUCCURULLO, COOKIE	Arthur Joseph; B2.8.1918 Asbury Park NJ; D1.23.1983 W.Orange NJ; BL/TL/5´10˝/168; d10.3																									
1943	Pit N	0	1	.000	1	1	0	0	7	10	7	0	0	3	3	6.43	54	.357	.419	0	ø	1	73	-3	0	-0.2
1944	Pit N	2	1	.667	32	4	0	4	106.1	110	65	5	3	44	31	4.06	91	.270	.346	38	.368	5*	152	-6	0	0.2
1945	Pit N	1	3	.250	29	4	0	1	56.2	68	41	2	1	34	17	5.24	75	.305	.399	14	.214	-0	70	-9	0	-0.6
Total	3	3	5	.375	62	9	0	5	170	188	113	7	4	81	51	4.55	83	.286	.367	52	.327	5	106	-18	0	-0.6
CUDWORTH, JIM	James Alaric "Cuddy"; B8.22.1858 Fairhaven MA; D12.21.1943 Middleboro MA; BR/TR/6´0˝/165; d7.27; ▲																									
1884	KC U	0	0	ø	2	1	1	0	17	19	16	1	—	3	6	4.24	53	.264	.293	116	.147	-1*	153	-4	—	-0.3
CUELLAR, CHARLIE	Jesus Patracis; B8.23.1917 Ybor City FL; D10.11.1994 Tampa FL; BR/TR/5´11˝/183; d7.2																									
1950	Chi A	0	0	ø	2	0	0	0	1.1	6	6	0	0	3	1	33.75	13	.600	.692	0	ø	0	—	-5	0	-0.2
CUELLAR, MIKE	Miguel Angel (Santana); B5.8.1937 Santa Clara, Cuba; BL/TL/5´11˝/(165–175); d4.18																									
1959	Cin N	0	0	ø	2	0	0	0	4	7	8	1	0	4-1	5	15.75	26	.368	.458	1	.000	-0	—	-5	0	-0.3
1964	StL N	5	5	.500	32	7	1	4	72	80	43	8	1	33-4	56	4.50	85	.288	.362	18	.000	-2	102	-5	0	-0.9
1965	Hou N	1	4	.200	25	4	0	2	56	55	24	3	1	21-4	46	3.54	95	.262	.330	12-0-1	.000	-1	52	-1	0	-0.1
1966	Hou N	12	10	.545	38	28	11-1	2	227.1	193	79	10	0	52-8	175	2.22	154	.229	.273	71-1-4	.113	-1	106	25	0	2.4
1967	Hou N★	16	11	.593	36	32	16-3	1	246.1	233	99	16	1	63-3	203	3.03	109	.248	.295	93-0-3	.140	1*	97	6	0	0.8
1968	Hou N	8	11	.421	28	24	11-2	1	170.2	152	60	8	1	45-7	133	2.74	108	.237	.286	57-1-3	.193	2	97	3	21	0.7
1969	†Bal A	23	11	.676	39	39	18-5	0-0	290.2	213	94	18	1	79-7	182	2.38	151	.204	**.260**	103-0-8	.117	-3	105	36	0	3.8
1970	†Bal A☆	**24**	8	**.750**	40	**40**	**21**-4	0-0	297.2	273	126	34	1	69-5	190	3.48	106	.242	.284	112-2-9	.089	-4*	127	8	0	0.2
1971	†Bal A★	20	9	.690	38	38	21-4	0-0	292.1	250	111	30	1	78-1	124	3.08	111	.234	.285	107-1-8	.103	-4	109	11	0	0.7
1972	Bal A	18	12	.600	35	35	17-4	0-0	248.1	197	78	21	0	71-4	132	2.57	121	.220	.276	87-2-7	.126	-1	105	15	0	1.8
1973	†Bal A	18	13	.581	38	38	17-2	0-0	267	265	120	29	0	84-2	140	3.27	115	.258	.313	0	ø	0	111	10	0	1.1

YEAR	TM LG	W	L	PCT	G	GS	CG-SHO	SV-BS	IP	H	R	HR	HB	BB-IB	SO	ERA	AERA	OAV	OOB	AB-HR-SH	AVG	PB	SUP	APR	DL	PW
1974	†Bal A☆	22	10	**.688**	38	38	20-5	0-0	269.1	253	106	17	2	86-4	106	3.11	112	.252	.310	0	ø	0	111	12	0	1.2
1975	Bal A	14	12	.538	36	36	17-5	0-0	256	229	112	17	1	84-5	105	3.66	97	.249	.310	0	ø	0	99	-3	0	-0.2
1976	Bal A	4	13	.235	26	19	2-1	1-0	107	129	63	8	2	50-5	32	4.96	66	.307	.379	0	ø	0	84	-20	0	-2.9
1977	Cal A	0	1	.000	2	1	0	0-1	3.1	9	7	2	0	3-1	3	18.90	21	.500	.571	0	ø	0	23	-5	0	-0.8
Total	15	185	130	.587	453	379	172-36	11-1	2808	2538	1130	222	12	822-61	1632	3.14	110	.243	.297	661-7-43	.115	-14	105	87	21	7.5
CUELLAR, BOBBY	Robert; B8.20.1952 Alice TX; BR/TR/5´11˝/190; [TexA74 29/594]; d9.9; C8; Col Texas																									
1977	Tex A	0	0	ø	4	0	0	0-0	6.2	4	1	1	0	2-0	3	1.35	302	.182	.250	0	ø	0	—	2	0	0.1
CUETO, BERT	Dagoberto (Concepcion); B8.14.1937 San Luis, Cuba; BR/TR/6´4˝/170; d6.18																									
1961	Min A	1	3	.250	7	5	0	0	21.1	27	24	7	1	10-0	5	7.17	59	.300	.376	5-0-2	.000	-0	138	-8	0	-1.3
CULLEN, JACK	John Patrick; B10.6.1939 Newark NJ; BR/TR/5´11˝/170; d9.9																									
1962	NY A	0	0	ø	2	0	0	1	3	2	0	0	0	2-0	2	0.00	ø	.182	.308	0	ø	0	—	1	0	0.1
1965	NY A	3	4	.429	12	9	2-1	0	59	59	22	2	0	21-2	25	3.05	112	.262	.324	20	.150	-0	72	3	0	0.3
1966	NY A	1	0	1.000	5	0	0	0	11.1	11	5	0	0	5-2	7	3.97	84	.256	.327	3	.000	-0	—	-1	0	-0.1
Total	3	4	4	.500	19	9	2-1	1	73.1	72	27	2	0	28-4	34	3.07	111	.258	.324	23	.130	-1	72	3	0	0.3
CULLOP, NICK	Norman Andrew; B9.17.1887 Chilhowie VA; D4.15.1961 Tazewell VA; BL/TL/5´11.5˝/172; d5.20																									
1913	Cle A	3	6	.333	23	8	4	0	97.2	105	58	3	3	35	30	4.42	69	.294	.362	31-0-3	.129	-1	98	-12	—	-1.1
1914	Cle A	0	1	.000	1	0	0	0	3.1	4	3	0	0	1	3	2.70	107	.364	.417	1	.000	-0	—	0	—	-0.1
	KC F	14	19	.424	44	36	22-4	1	295.2	256	116	6	12	87	149	2.34	119	.235	.299	99-0-4	.141	-4	84	9	—	0.5
1915	KC F	22	11	.667	44	36	22-3	2	302.1	278	105	8	9	67	111	2.44	108	.249	.297	96-0-9	.188	0	108	7	—	1.0
1916	NY A	13	6	.684	28	22	9	1	167	151	60	4	3	32	77	2.05	141	.243	.284	55-0-1	.109	-3	113	11	—	0.7
1917	NY A	5	9	.357	30	18	5-2	1	146.1	161	70	2	2	31	27	3.32	81	.307	.348	44-0-2	.159	-1	88	-9	—	-1.0
1921	StL A	0	2	.000	4	1	0	0	11.2	18	12	1	0	6	3	8.49	53	.340	.407	3	.000	-1	93	-5	—	-0.6
Total	6	57	54	.514	174	121	62-9	5	1024	973	424	24	29	259	400	2.73	102	.258	.311	329-0-19	.149	-10	97	1	—	-0.6
CULLOTON, BUD	Bernard Aloysius; B5.19.1897 Kingston NY; D11.9.1976 Kingston NY; BR/TR/5´11˝/180; d4.16; Col Fordham																									
1925	Pit N	0	1	.000	9	1	0	0	21	19	8	1	0	1	3	2.57	173	.241	.250	3-0-1	.000	-0	19	4	—	0.1
1926	Pit N	0	0	ø	4	0	0	0	3.2	3	4	0	0	6	1	7.36	53	.214	.450	0	ø	0	—	-1	—	-0.1
Total	2	0	1	.000	13	1	0	0	24.2	22	12	1	0	7	4	3.28	133	.237	.290	3-0-1	.000	-0	19	3	—	0.0
CULP, RAY	Raymond Leonard; B8.6.1941 Elgin TX; BR/TR/6´0˝/(197–200); d4.10																									
1963	Phi N★	14	11	.560	34	30	10-5	0	203.1	148	76	15	6	102-8	176	2.97	109	.206	.308	66-0-7	.136	-0	106	7	0	0.8
1964	Phi N	8	7	.533	30	19	3-1	0	135	139	77	15	5	56-4	96	4.13	84	.263	.337	44	.114	-1	112	-12	0	-1.4
1965	Phi N	14	10	.583	33	30	11-2	0	204.1	188	89	14	12	78-9	134	3.22	108	.243	.321	68-0-8	.088	-2	114	4	0	0.1
1966	Phi N	7	4	.636	34	12	1	1	110.2	106	66	19	7	53-4	100	5.04	71	.246	.337	26-0-5	.077	-2	100	-17	0	-1.8
1967	Chi N	8	11	.421	30	22	4-1	0	152.2	138	69	22	2	59-4	111	3.89	91	.239	.309	51-0-8	.098	-1	115	-4	0	-0.7
1968	Bos A	16	6	.727	35	30	11-6	0	216.1	166	79	18	9	82-8	190	2.91	108	.210	.291	70-0-7	.114	-1	109	6	0	0.4
1969	Bos A★	17	8	.680	32	32	9-2	0-0	227	195	103	25	6	79-6	172	3.81	100	.231	.299	79-1-6	.152	1	124	3	0	0.4
1970	Bos A	17	14	.548	33	33	15-1	0-0	251.1	211	104	22	11	91-8	197	3.04	131	.224	.299	97-0-5	.124	-3	104	22	0	2.2
1971	Bos A	14	16	.467	35	35	12-3	0-0	242.1	236	108	21	5	67-4	151	3.60	103	.253	.305	68-0-17	.118	-2	85	2	0	-0.1
1972	Bos A	5	8	.385	16	16	4-1	0-0	105	104	60	8	3	53-3	52	4.46	73	.260	.347	33-0-4	.212	1	128	-13	48	-1.6
1973	Bos A	2	6	.250	10	9	0	0-0	50.1	46	32	9	4	32-0	32	4.47	90	.247	.366	0	ø	0	76	-4	31	-0.6
Total	11	122	101	.547	322	268	80-22	1-0	1898.1	1677	863	188	70	752-58	1411	3.58	100	.235	.313	602-1-67	.123	-11	107	-6	79	-2.3
CULP, BILL	William Edward; B6.11.1887 Bellaire OH; D9.3.1969 Arnold PA; BB/TR/6´1.5˝/165; d9.8																									
1910	Phi N	0	0	ø	4	0	0	1	6.2	8	6	0	0	4	4	8.10	39	.333	.429	2	.000	-0	—	-3	—	-0.1
CULVER, GEORGE	George Raymond; B7.8.1943 Salinas CA; BR/TR/6´2˝/(175–185); d9.7; Col Bakersfield (CA) JC																									
1966	Cle A	0	2	.000	5	1	0	0	9.2	15	9	1	1	7-0	6	8.38	41	.357	.460	2	.000	-0	103	-5	0	-0.9
1967	Cle A	7	3	.700	53	1	0	3	75	71	40	2	6	31-9	41	3.96	82	.258	.344	4	.250	0	80	-7	0	-0.9
1968	Cin N	11	16	.407	42	35	5-2	2	226	229	95	8	14	84-7	114	3.23	98	.264	.336	66-0-11	.121	-1*	101	-3	0	-0.4
1969	Cin N	5	7	.417	32	13	0	4-0	101.1	117	55	8	9	52-6	58	4.26	88	.291	.383	31-0-2	.097	-2	91	-5	49	-0.8
1970	StL N	3	3	.500	11	7	2	0-0	56.2	64	31	6	1	24-4	23	4.61	90	.284	.355	17-0-1	.176	0	111	-2	0	-0.1
	Hou N	3	3	.500	32	0	0	3-0	45	44	17	1	3	21-2	31	3.20	122	.254	.343	4-0-1	.250	0	—	4	0	0.5
	Year	6	6	.500	43	7	2	3-0	101.2	108	48	7	4	45-6	54	3.98	101	.271	.350	21-0-2	.190	0	114	2	0	0.4
1971	Hou N	5	8	.385	59	0	0	7-2	95.1	89	33	4	2	38-10	57	2.64	127	.257	.331	11-0-3	.091	-1	—	7	0	1.0
1972	Hou N	6	2	.750	45	0	0	2-1	97.1	73	33	7	5	43-3	82	3.05	110	.212	.306	19-0-2	.158	0	—	5	0	0.5
1973	LA N	4	4	.500	28	0	0	2-2	42	45	15	4	1	21-6	23	3.00	116	.292	.376	4	.000	-0	—	3	0	0.6
	Phi N	3	1	.750	14	0	0	0-1	18.2	26	10	0	0	15-6	7	4.82	79	.342	.451	0	ø	0	—	-2	0	-0.3
	Year	7	5	.583	42	0	0	2-3	60.2	71	25	4	1	36-12	30	3.56	101	.309	.401	4	.000	-0	—	1	0	0.3
1974	Phi N	1	0	1.000	14	0	0	0-0	21.2	20	16	1	1	16-1	9	6.65	57	.267	.394	3	.000	-0	—	-6	0	-0.4
Total	9	48	49	.495	335	57	7-2	23-6	788.2	793	354	42	43	352-54	451	3.62	96	.266	.350	161-0-20	.124	-4	99	-11	49	-1.2
CUMBERLAND, JOHN	John Sheldon; B5.10.1947 Westbrook ME; BR/TL/6´0˝/190; d9.27; C7; Col Maine																									
1968	NY A	0	0	ø	1	0	0	0	2	3	4	1	0	1-0	1	9.00	32	.333	.400	0	ø	0	—	-2	0	-0.1
1969	NY A	0	0	ø	2	0	0	0-0	4	3	2	0	0	4-1	0	4.50	78	.231	.389	0	ø	0	—	0	0	0.0
1970	NY A	3	4	.429	15	8	1	0-0	64	62	31	9	0	15-3	38	3.94	91	.252	.292	17-0-3	.059	-1	78	-2	0	-0.4
	SF N	2	0	1.000	7	0	0	0-0	11	6	3	0	0	4-0	6	0.82	486	.158	.233	1	.000	-0	—	3	0	0.5
1971	†SF N	9	6	.600	45	21	5-2	2-1	185	153	66	22	0	55-6	65	2.92	117	.223	.280	59-0-1	.119	-2	103	13	0	0.6
1972	SF N	0	4	.000	9	6	0	0-0	25	38	29	6	0	7-0	8	8.64	41	.336	.372	9	.111	-0	114	-15	0	-2.1
	StL N	1	1	.500	14	1	0	0-0	21.2	23	17	6	0	7-0	7	6.65	52	.291	.341	5-0-1	.000	-1	77	-7	0	-0.7
	Year	1	5	.167	23	7	0	0-0	46.2	61	46	12	0	14-0	15	7.71	45	.318	.359	14-0-1	.071	-1	109	-22	0	-2.8
1974	Cal A	0	1	.000	17	0	0	0-1	21.2	24	9	2	0	10-2	12	3.74	93	.289	.362	0	ø	0	—	0	0	0.0
Total	6	15	16	.484	110	36	6-2	2-2	334.1	312	161	46	0	103-12	137	3.82	91	.246	.301	91-0-5	.099	-5	98	-10	0	-2.2
CUMMINGS, JOHN	John Russell; B5.10.1969 Torrance CA; BL/TL/6´3˝/200; [SeaA90 8/215]; d4.10; Col USC																									
1993	Sea A	0	6	.000	10	8	1	0-0	46.1	59	34	6	2	16-2	19	6.02	74	.316	.372	0	ø	0	62	-8	0	-0.9
1994	Sea A	2	4	.333	17	8	0	0-0	64	66	43	7	0	37-2	33	5.63	88	.270	.363	0	ø	0	84	-4	17	-0.3
1995	Sea A	0	0	ø	4	0	0	0-0	5.1	8	8	0	0	7-2	4	11.81	40	.400	.517	0	ø	0	—	-4	0	-0.2
	†LA N	3	1	.750	35	0	0	0-0	39	38	16	3	0	10-4	21	3.00	129	.250	.294	3	.000	-0	—	4	0	0.3
1996	LA N	0	1	.000	4	0	0	0-0	5.1	12	7	1	0	2-1	5	6.75	58	.462	.483	0	ø	0	—	-3	0	-0.4
	Det A	3	3	.500	21	0	0	0-1	31.2	36	20	3	2	20-3	24	5.12	100	.283	.387	0	ø	0	—	0	0	-0.1
1997	Det A	2	0	1.000	19	0	0	0-0	24.2	32	22	3	0	14-1	8	5.47	84	.311	.393	0	ø	0	—	-5	0	-0.3
Total	5	10	15	.400	110	16	1	0-1	216.1	251	150	23	4	106-15	114	5.33	86	.292	.369	3	.000	-0	75	-20	17	-1.9
CUMMINGS, STEVE	Steven Brent; B7.15.1964 Houston TX; BB/TR/6´2˝/200; [TorA86 2/54]; d6.24; Col Houston																									
1989	Tor A	2	0	1.000	5	2	0	0-0	21	18	9	1	1	11-0	8	3.00	126	.231	.333	0	ø	0	191	1	0	0.1
1990	Tor A	0	0	ø	6	2	0	0-0	12.1	22	7	4	1	5-0	4	5.11	78	.431	.491	0	ø	0	80	-1	0	-0.1
Total	2	2	0	1.000	11	4	0	0-0	33.1	40	16	5	2	16-0	12	3.78	102	.310	.395	0	ø	0	135	0	0	0.0
CUMMINGS, CANDY	William Arthur; B10.18.1848 Ware MA; D5.16.1924 Toledo OH; BR/TR/5´9˝/120; d4.22; HF1939																									
1872	Mut NA	33	20	.623	**55**	**55**	**53-3**	0	**497**	604	347	2	—	31	45	3.01	113	.272	.282	249	.209	-4	106	23	—	1.1
1873	Bal NA	28	14	.667	42	42	42-1	0	382	475	292	4	—	33	34	2.80	121	.274	.287	192	.250	2	123	28	—	2.1
1874	Phi NA	28	26	.519	54	54	52-3	0	483	616	386	4	—	18	61	1.96	113	.276	.282	231	.225	-4	110	16	—	0.7
1875	Har NA	35	12	.745	48	47	46-**7**	0	416	397	184	0	—	4	**82**	1.60	146	.235	.236	221	.199	-5*	111	**34**	—	2.7
1876	Har N	16	8	.667	24	24	24-5	0	216	215	97	0	—	14	26	1.67	142	.239	.251	105	.162	-8	109	15	—	0.5
1877	Cin N	5	14	.263	19	19	16	0	155.2	219	144	2	—	13	11	4.34	61	.315	.327	70	.200	0	106	-29	—	-2.6
Total	4NA	124	72	.633	199	198	193-14	0	1778	2092	1209	10	—	86	222	2.35	122	.266	.274	893	.219	-10	111	101	—	6.6
Total	2	21	22	.488	43	43	40-5	0	371.2	434	241	2	—	27	37	2.78	90	.272	.284	175	.177	-7	107	-14	—	-2.1

YEAR	TM LG	W	L	PCT	G	GS	CG-SHO	SV-BS	IP	H	R	HR	HB	BB-IB	SO	ERA	AERA	OAV	OOB	AB-HR-SH	AVG	PB	SUP	APR	DL	PW
Cunnane, Will	William Joseph; B4.24.1974 Suffern NY; BR/TR/6´2″/(175–200); d4.3																									
1997	SD N	6	3	.667	54	8	0	0-2	91.1	114	69	11	5	49-3	79	5.81	68	.305	.392	14-0-1	.357	3*	158	-22	0	-1.7
1998	SD N	0	0	ø	3	0	0	0-0	3	4	2	1	0	1-1	1	6.00	66	.308	.357	0	ø	0	—	-1	82	0.0
1999	SD N	2	1	.667	24	0	0	0-0	31	34	19	8	0	12-3	22	5.23	82	.293	.359	3	.000	-0	—	-3	0	-0.3
2000	SD N	1	1	.500	27	3	0	0-0	38.1	35	21	2	1	21-0	34	4.23	105	.241	.339	7	.143	0	138	1	0	0.0
2001	Mil N	0	3	.000	31	1	0	0-0	51.2	66	34	6	2	22-6	37	5.40	79	.320	.390	7	.000	-1*	65	-7	0	-0.4
2002	Chi N	1	1	.500	16	0	0	0-1	26.1	27	16	5	1	13-1	30	5.47	74	.270	.360	4	.250	0	—	-3	0	-0.2
2003	†Atl N	2	2	.500	20	0	0	3-0	20	14	6	2	0	6-2	20	2.70	156	.189	.250	0	ø	0	—	4	0	0.7
2004	Atl N	1	1	.500	9	0	0	0-1	12.1	18	10	3	1	4-1	11	7.30	59	.346	.390	0	ø	0	—	-4	0	-0.5
Total	8	13	12	.520	184	12	0	3-4	274	312	177	38	10	128-17	234	5.26	79	.289	.368	35-0-1	.200	2	142	-35	82	-2.4
Cunningham, Bruce	Bruce Lee; B9.29.1905 San Francisco CA; D3.8.1984 Hayward CA; BR/TR/5´10.5″/165; d5.7																									
1929	Bos N	4	6	.400	17	8	4	1	91.2	100	52	7	2	32	22	4.52	104	.282	.344	27-0-2	.148	-0*	58	2	—	0.2
1930	Bos N	5	6	.455	36	6	2	0	106.2	121	73	7	0	41	28	5.48	90	.289	.352	31	.194	0*	53	-7	—	-0.4
1931	Bos N	3	12	.200	33	16	6-1	1	136.2	157	74	7	2	54	32	4.48	85	.296	.363	42	.071	-4*	74	-9	—	-1.1
1932	Bos N	1	0	1.000	18	3	0	0	47	50	21	1	4	19	21	3.45	109	.281	.363	9	.222	2	157	2	—	0.3
Total	4	13	24	.351	104	33	12-1	2	382	428	220	22	8	146	103	4.64	93	.289	.356	109-0-2	.138	-2	70	-12	—	-1.0
Cunningham, Bert	Ellsworth Elmer; B11.25.1865 Wilmington DE; D5.14.1952 Cragmere DE; BR/TR/5´6″/187; d9.15; U1																									
1887	Bro AA	0	2	.000	3	3	3	0	23	26	22	0	4	13	8	5.09	85	.263	.371	8	.000	-1	44	-3	—	-0.2
1888	Bal AA	22	29	.431	51	51	50	0	453.1	412	275	8	30	157	186	3.39	88	.233	.307	177-1	.186	-2	88	-25	—	-2.5
1889	Bal AA	16	19	.457	39	33	29	1	279.1	306	245	11	15	141	140	4.87	81	.270	.358	131	.206	-3*	96	-25	—	-2.6
1890	Phi P	3	9	.250	14	11	11	0	108.2	133	103	0	7	67	33	5.22	82	.289	.387	52	.115	-4*	82	-11	—	-1.1
	Buf P	9	15	.375	25	25	24-2	0	211	251	190	8	6	134	78	5.84	70	.283	.381	101	.228	1*	79	-35	—	-2.6
	Year	12	24	.333	39	36	35-2	0	319.2	384	293	8	13	201	111	5.63	74	.285	.383	153	.190	-4	80	-42	—	-3.7
1891	Bal AA	11	14	.440	30	25	21	0	237.2	241	181	8	11	138	59	4.01	93	.254	.356	100-1	.150	-2*	115	-7	—	-0.7
1895	Lou N	11	16	.407	31	28	24-1	0	231	299	185	6	5	104	49	4.75	97	.309	.378	100	.300	6*	79	-5	—	0.2
1896	Lou N	7	14	.333	27	20	17	1	189.1	242	168	6	17	74	37	5.09	85	.308	.380	88-2-1	.250	3*	89	-18	—	-1.2
1897	Lou N	14	13	.519	30	28	26	0	242.2	294	152	3	14	72	49	4.15	103	.297	.353	97-2-5	.227	-1*	83	9	—	0.8
1898	Lou N	28	15	.651	44	42	41	0	362	387	174	8	20	65	34	3.16	114	.272	.313	140-1-0	.229	2	109	15	—	1.6
1899	Lou N	17	17	.500	39	37	33-1	0	323.2	385	188	4	15	75	36	3.84	100	.295	.340	154-2-4	.260	3*	108	7	—	1.1
1900	Chi N	4	3	.571	8	7	7	0	64	84	53	0	4	21	7	4.36	83	.316	.375	27	.148	-1	131	-6	—	-0.7
1901	Chi N	0	1	.000	1	1	1	0	9	11	6	0	0	3	2	5.00	65	.297	.350	1-0-2	.000	0	88	-1	—	-0.1
Total	12	142	167	.460	342	311	287-4	2	2734.2	3071	1942	62	148	1064	718	4.22	91	.277	.349	1176-9-12	.216	1	94	-105	—	-8.0
Cunningham, George	George Harold; B7.13.1894 Sturgeon Lake MN; D3.10.1972 Chattanooga TN; BR/TR/5´11″/185; d4.14																									
1916	Det A	7	10	.412	35	14	5	2	150.1	146	71	0	3	74	68	2.75	104	.269	.360	41-0-1	.268	5	126	-3	—	0.3
1917	Det A	2	7	.222	44	8	4	4	139	113	72	2	4	51	49	2.91	91	.227	.304	34-1-2	.176	1	150	-7	—	-0.4
1918	Det A	6	7	.462	27	14	10	1	140	131	68	0	5	38	39	3.15	84	.255	.312	112-0-4	.223	3*	97	-10	—	-0.5
1919	Det A	1	1	.500	17	0	0	1	47.2	54	36	0	5	15	11	4.91	65	.292	.361	23	.217	2*	—	-11	—	-0.3
Total	4	16	25	.390	123	36	19	8	477	444	247	2	17	178	167	3.13	89	.255	.330	210-1-7	.224	11	119	-31	—	-0.9
Cunningham, Mike	Mody; B6.14.1882 Lancaster SC; D12.10.1969 Lancaster SC; BR/TR/5´10.5″/175; d8.31; Col South Carolina																									
1906	Phi A	1	0	1.000	5	1	1	0	28	29	15	1	1	9	15	3.21	85	.271	.333	12	.333	1*	132	-2	—	0.0
Cuppy, Nig	George Joseph (b George Koppe); B7.3.1869 Logansport IN; D7.27.1922 Elkhart IN; BR/TR/5´7″/160; d4.16																									
1892	†Cle N	28	13	.683	47	42	38-1	1	376	333	175	9	10	121	103	2.51	135	.228	.292	168	.214	0*	113	37	—	3.7
1893	Cle N	17	10	.630	31	30	24	0	243.2	316	200	6	10	75	39	4.47	109	.305	.357	109	.248	1*	106	8	—	0.6
1894	Cle N	24	15	.615	43	33	29-**3**	0	316	381	246	11	10	128	65	4.56	120	.295	.363	135-0-1	.259	1*	91	26	—	2.4
1895	†Cle N	26	14	.650	47	40	36-1	2	353	384	210	9	8	95	91	3.54	141	.273	.323	140-0-4	.286	7	101	51	—	5.2
1896	†Cle N	25	14	.641	46	40	35-1	1	358	388	173	8	7	75	86	3.12	146	.274	.314	141-1-4	.270	6*	90	55	—	5.5
1897	Cle N	10	6	.625	19	17	13-1	0	138	150	69	3	5	26	23	3.20	140	.275	.314	55-0-1	.145	-4*	77	19	—	1.3
1898	Cle N	9	8	.529	18	15	13-1	0	128	147	62	4	6	25	27	3.30	110	.286	.327	48-0-2	.104	-4	76	6	—	0.2
1899	StL N	11	8	.579	21	21	18-1	0	171.2	203	89	3	5	26	25	3.15	127	.294	.324	70-0-2	.186	-3	104	15	—	1.2
1900	Bos N	8	4	.667	17	13	9	1	105.1	107	64	8	6	24	23	3.08	134	.263	.314	42	.262	1	117	7	—	0.8
1901	Bos A	4	6	.400	13	11	9	0	93.1	111	58	1	2	14	22	4.15	85	.292	.321	49-0-1	.204	0*	106	-5	—	-0.5
Total	10	162	98	.623	302	262	224-9	5	2283	2520	1346	62	69	609	504	3.48	127	.275	.325	957-1-15	.233	6	98	219	—	20.4
Curran, Sammy	Simon Francis; B10.30.1874 Dorchester MA; D5.19.1936 Dorchester MA; TL; d8.1; Col Tufts																									
1902	Bos N	0	0	ø	1	0	0	0	6.2	6	1	0	0	0	3	1.35	209	.240	.240	2	.000	-0	—	1	—	0.0
Currence, Lafayette	Delancy Lafayette; B12.3.1951 Rock Hill SC; BB/TL/5´11″/159; d7.24																									
1975	Mil A	0	2	.000	8	1	0	0-0	18.2	25	17	5	0	14-1	7	7.71	50	.316	.415	0	ø	0	114	-7	0	-0.7
Currie, Murphy	Archibald Murphy; B8.31.1893 Fayetteville NC; D6.22.1939 Asheboro NC; BR/TR/5´11.5″/185; d8.31																									
1916	StL N	0	0	ø	6	0	0	0	14.1	7	4	1	0	9	8	1.88	140	.149	.286	3	.000	-0	—	1	—	0.0
Currie, Clarence	Clarence Franklin; B12.30.1878 Windsor ON, Can.; D7.15.1941 Little Chute WI; BR/TR/5´10″/170; d4.25																									
1902	Cin N	3	4	.429	10	7	6-1	0	65.1	70	37	1	2	17	20	3.72	81	.273	.324	24-0-1	.083	-2	68	-4	—	-0.5
	StL N	7	5	.583	15	12	10-2	0	124.2	125	54	0	6	35	30	2.60	106	.261	.319	46-0-1	.196	-0*	81	2	—	0.3
	Year	10	9	.526	25	19	16-3	0	190	195	91	1	8	52	50	2.98	95	.265	.321	70-0-2	.157	-2	76	-5	—	-0.2
1903	StL N	4	12	.250	22	16	13-1	1	148	155	93	7	10	60	52	4.01	81	.281	.362	47-0-2	.085	-3	63	-8	—	-0.9
	Chi N	1	2	.333	6	3	2	1	33.1	35	25	1	3	9	9	2.97	106	.254	.313	12	.417	2	79	-2	—	0.0
	Year	5	14	.263	28	19	15-1	2	181.1	190	118	8	13	69	61	3.82	85	.275	.352	59-0-2	.153	-1	66	-16	—	-0.9
Total	2	15	23	.395	53	38	31-4	2	371.1	385	209	9	21	121	111	3.39	89	.270	.336	129-0-4	.155	-4	70	-12	—	-1.1
Currie, Bill	William Cleveland; B11.29.1928 Leary GA; BR/TR/6´0″/175; d4.13																									
1955	Was A	0	0	ø	3	0	0	0	4.1	7	7	3	1	2-0	2	12.46	31	.350	.435	0	ø	0	—	-4	0	-0.2
Curry, George	George James "Soldier Boy"; B12.21.1888 Bridgeport CT; D10.5.1963 West Haven CT; BR/TR/6´0″/185; d7.16																									
1911	StL A	0	3	.000	3	3	0	0	15.2	19	15	0	0	24	2	7.47	45	.339	.538	5	.000	-1	78	-6	—	-0.9
Curry, Steve	Stephen Thomas; B9.13.1965 Winter Park FL; BR/TR/6´6″/217; [BosA84 7/172]; d7.10; Col Manatee (FL) CC																									
1988	Bos A	0	1	.000	3	3	0	0-0	11	15	10	0	0	14-2	4	8.18	50	.357	.500	0	ø	0	133	-4	0	-0.3
Curry, Wes	Wesley; B4.1.1860 Wilmington DE; D5.19.1933 Philadelphia PA; d8.6; U6																									
1884	Ric AA	0	2	.000	2	2	2	0	16	15	14	2	1	3	1	5.06	66	.221	.264	8	.250	-0	55	-3	—	-0.3
Curtis, Cliff	Clifton Garfield; B7.3.1881 Delaware OH; D4.23.1943 Utica OH; BR/TR/6´2″/180; d8.23																									
1909	Bos N	4	5	.444	10	9	8-2	0	83	53	17	1	2	30	22	1.41	200	.191	.275	29	.034	-3	47	12	—	1.2
1910	Bos N	6	24	.200	43	37	12-2	2	251	251	154	9	12	124	75	3.55	94	.277	.371	82-0-2	.146	-4	68	-11	—	-1.3
1911	Bos N	1	8	.111	12	9	5	1	77	79	50	4	2	34	23	4.44	86	.265	.344	28-0-1	.250	-0	72	-5	—	-0.5
	Chi N	1	2	.333	4	1	0	0	7	7	4	0	3	5	4	3.86	86	.241	.405	2	.500	0	0	0	—	-0.1
	Phi N	2	1	.667	8	5	3-1	0	45	45	19	0	1	15	13	2.60	132	.260	.323	15-0-1	.267	0	87	3	—	0.2
	Year	4	11	.267	24	15	8-1	1	129	131	73	4	6	54	40	3.77	97	.262	.341	45-0-2	.267	0	72	-3	—	-0.4
1912	Phi N	2	5	.286	10	8	2	0	50	55	30	3	4	17	20	3.24	112	.286	.357	15	.000	-2	78	0	—	-0.1
	Bro N	4	7	.364	19	9	3	1	80	72	44	4	6	37	22	3.94	85	.250	.347	26-0-2	.308	1	102	-4	—	-0.4
	Year	6	12	.333	29	17	5	1	130	127	74	7	10	54	42	3.67	94	.265	.351	41-0-2	.195	-1	91	-5	—	-0.5
1913	Bro N	8	9	.471	30	16	6	2	151.2	145	75	1	7	55	57	3.26	101	.255	.328	49-0-5	.122	-3	93	-1	—	-0.4
Total	5	28	61	.315	136	94	39-5	6	744.2	707	393	22	37	317	236	3.31	101	.259	.344	246-0-11	.159	-10	76	-6	—	-1.4
Curtis, Jack	Jack Patrick; B1.11.1937 Rhodhiss NC; BL/TL/5´10″/(175–180); d4.22																									
1961	Chi N	10	13	.435	31	27	6	0	180.1	220	117	23	1	51-6	57	4.89	85	.303	.346	60-2-2	.167	3	90	-15	0	-1.3
1962	Chi N	0	2	.000	4	3	0	0	18	18	8	2	0	6-1	8	3.50	118	.277	.333	4	.250	0	42	1	0	0.1
	Mil N	4	4	.500	30	5	0	1	75.2	82	39	8	2	27-3	40	4.16	91	.282	.345	18	.222	2	120	-3	0	-0.1
	Year	4	6	.400	34	8	0	1	93.2	100	47	10	2	33-4	48	4.04	96	.281	.343	22	.227	2	91	-2	0	0.0

YEAR	TM LG	W	L	PCT	G	GS	CG-SHO	SV-BS	IP	H	R	HR	HB	BB-IB	SO	ERA	AERA	OAV	OOB	AB-HR-SH	AVG	PB	SUP	APR	DL	PW
1963	Cle A	0	0	ø	4	0	0	0	5	8	10	0	1	5-1	3	18.00	20	.348	.483	0	ø	0	—	-7	0	-0.4
Total	3	14	19	.424	69	35	6	1	279	328	174	33	4	89-11	108	4.84	84	.297	.349	82-2-2	.183	5	91	-24	0	-1.7
Curtis, John	John Duffield; B3.9.1948 Newton MA; BL/TL/6´2˝/(175–190); [BosA68 S1/10]; d8.13; Col Clemson																									
1970	Bos A	0	0	ø	1	0	0	0-0	2.1	4	4	1	0	1-0	1	11.57	34	.333	.385	0	ø	0	—	-2	0	-0.1
1971	Bos A	2	2	.500	5	3	1	0-1	26	30	9	3	0	6-1	19	3.12	120	.291	.330	9	.111	-0	64	2	0	0.2
1972	Bos A	11	8	.579	26	21	8-3	0-0	154.1	161	69	8	0	50-6	106	3.73	87	.271	.327	53-0-3	.094	-3*	100	-6	0	-1.0
1973	Bos A	13	13	.500	35	30	10-4	0-0	221.1	225	103	24	2	83-10	101	3.58	113	.264	.330	0	ø	0	91	8	0	0.9
1974	StL N	10	14	.417	33	29	5-2	1-0	195	199	91	15	2	83-6	89	3.78	95	.267	.340	63-0-6	.159	-1*	103	-3	0	-0.4
1975	StL N	8	9	.471	39	18	4	1-0	146.2	151	70	13	2	65-6	67	3.44	111	.268	.342	38-0-5	.211	2	90	4	0	0.8
1976	StL N	6	11	.353	37	15	3-1	1-0	134	139	68	11	0	65-10	52	4.50	80	.276	.357	35-0-5	.200	2*	74	-9	0	-1.0
1977	SF N	3	3	.500	43	9	1-1	1-2	77	95	48	5	1	48-9	47	5.49	72	.314	.406	13-0-3	.231	1*	120	-10	0	-0.6
1978	SF N	4	3	.571	46	0	0	1-2	63	60	31	1	0	29-8	38	3.71	93	.262	.336	2-0-1	.000	-0	—	-3	0	-0.3
1979	SF N	10	9	.526	27	18	3-2	0-0	120.2	121	62	15	0	42-7	85	4.18	84	.257	.316	34-0-6	.147	1*	89	-9	0	-1.3
1980	SD N	10	8	.556	30	27	6	0-0	187	184	84	9	2	67-13	71	3.51	97	.262	.328	62-0-5	.194	1*	98	-4	0	-0.2
1981	SD N	2	6	.250	28	8	0	0-1	66.2	70	41	11	1	30-2	31	5.13	63	.275	.349	13-0-1	.077	-1	127	-15	0	-1.7
1982	SD N	8	6	.571	26	18	1-1	0-0	116.1	121	62	15	1	46-0	54	4.10	84	.271	.340	37-0-4	.297	3	123	-10	0	-0.8
	Cal A	0	1	.000	8	0	0	1-1	12	16	8	0	0	3-2	10	6.00	68	.320	.358	0	ø	0	—	-2	0	-0.2
1983	Cal A	1	2	.333	37	3	0	5-3	90	89	44	5	2	40-11	36	3.80	107	.258	.334	0	ø	0	75	1	0	0.0
1984	Cal A	1	2	.333	17	0	0	0-0	28.2	30	16	4	0	11-1	18	4.40	91	.263	.325	0	ø	0	—	-2	82	-0.1
Total	15	89	97	.478	438	199	42-14	11-10	1641	1695	810	140	13	669-92	825	3.96	92	.270	.339	359-0-39	.175	4	97	-60	82	-5.8
Curtis, Vern	Vernon Eugene "Turk"; B5.24.1920 Cairo IL; D6.24.1992 Cairo IL; BR/TR/6´0˝/170; d9.6; Mil 1944–45																									
1943	Was A	0	0	ø	2	0	0	0	4	3	3	0	0	6	1	6.75	47	.200	.429	0	ø	0	—	-1	0	-0.1
1944	Was A	0	1	.000	3	1	0	0	9.2	8	3	0	0	3	2	2.79	117	.235	.297	2	.000	-0	0	1	0	0.0
1946	Was A	0	0	ø	11	0	0	0	16.1	19	13	1	0	10	7	7.16	47	.297	.392	2	.000	-0	—	-6	0	-0.3
Total	3	0	1	.000	16	1	0	0	30	30	19	1	0	19	10	5.70	58	.265	.371	4	.000	-1	0	-6	0	-0.4
Cushman, Ed	Edgar Leander; B3.27.1852 Eagleville OH; D9.26.1915 Erie PA; BR/TL/6´0˝/177; d7.6																									
1883	Buf N	3	3	.500	7	7	5	0	50.1	61	41	0	—	17	34	3.93	81	.285	.338	23	.217	-0	130	-4	—	-0.4
1884	Mil U	4	0	1.000	4	4	4-2	0	36	10	4	0	—	3	47	1.00	133	.082	.104	11	.091	-1	144	3	—	0.2
1885	Phi AA	3	7	.300	10	10	10	0	87	101	77	1	3	17	37	3.52	98	.269	.306	37	.189	-1	127	-4	—	-0.5
	NY AA	8	14	.364	22	22	22	0	191	158	105	2	3	33	133	2.78	112	.210	.246	69	.145	-1	72	4	—	0.2
	Year	11	21	.344	32	32	32	0	278	259	182	3	6	50	170	3.01	107	.229	.266	106	.160	-2	91	-3	—	-0.3
1886	NY AA	17	21	.447	38	38	37-2	0	325.2	278	180	6	1	99	167	3.12	105	.220	.277	126	.151	-6	82	7	—	0.1
1887	NY AA	10	15	.400	26	26	25	0	220	310	232	9	9	83	64	5.97	71	.325	.384	93	.247	3	97	-43	—	-3.1
1890	Tol AA	17	21	.447	40	38	34	1	315.2	346	208	5	10	107	125	4.19	94	.270	.331	130	.100	-9	101	-4	—	-1.5
Total	6	62	81	.434	147	145	137-4	1	1225.2	1264	847	23	26	359	607	3.86	92	.254	.308	489	.160	-16	96	-41	—	-5.0
Cushman, Harvey	Harvey Barnes; B7.10.1877 Rockland ME; D12.27.1920 Emsworth PA; d8.24; Col Maine																									
1902	Pit N	0	4	.000	4	4	3	0	25.2	30	31	0	2	31	12	7.36	37	.291	.463	10	.200	-0	50	-14	—	-1.7
Cvengros, Mike	Michael John; B12.1.1900 Pana IL; D8.2.1970 Hot Springs AR; BL/TL/5´8˝/159; d9.30																									
1922	NY N	0	1	.000	1	1	1	0	9	6	5	1	1	3	3	4.00	100	.194	.286	3	.000	-0	20	0	—	0.0
1923	Chi A	12	13	.480	40	26	14	3	214.1	216	110	6	13	107	86	4.41	90	.269	.364	74-0-4	.203	-1*	98	-5	—	-0.6
1924	Chi A	3	12	.200	26	15	2	0	105.2	119	80	5	3	67	36	5.88	70	.300	.405	30-0-1	.200	2	93	-20	—	-2.2
1925	Chi A	3	9	.250	22	11	4	0	104.2	109	56	7	3	55	32	4.30	97	.278	.371	33-0-3	.152	-1	105	-1	—	-0.2
1927	†Pit N	2	1	.667	23	4	0	1	53.2	55	25	3	1	24	21	3.35	123	.271	.351	19-0-1	.158	-0	114	4	—	0.2
1929	Chi N	5	4	.556	32	4	0	2	64	82	39	2	1	29	23	4.64	99	.319	.390	15	.400	2*	109	0	—	0.2
Total	6	25	40	.385	144	61	21	6	551.1	587	315	24	22	285	201	4.59	90	.282	.374	174-0-9	.201	1	98	-22	—	-2.6
Cyr, Eric	Eric; B2.11.1979 Montreal QC, Can.; BR/TL/6´4˝/200; [SDN98 30/892]; d6.23; Col Seminole St. (OK) JC																									
2002	SD N	0	1	.000	5	0	0	0-0	6	6	7	0	0	6-1	4	10.50	37	.286	.429	1	.000	-0	—	-4	31	-0.6
Czajkowski, Jim	James Mark; B12.18.1963 Parma OH; BB/TR/6´4˝/215; [AtlN86 29/711]; d7.29; Col North Alabama																									
1994	Col N	0	0	ø	5	0	0	0-0	8.2	9	4	2	3	6-1	2	4.15	120	.281	.439	0	ø	0	—	1	0	0.1
Daal, Omar	Omar Jesus (Cordero); B3.1.1972 Maracaibo, Zulia, Venez.; BL/TL/6´3˝/(160–204); d4.23; [DL 2004 Bal A 183]																									
1993	LA N	2	3	.400	47	0	0	0-1	35.1	36	20	5	0	21-3	19	5.09	76	.277	.373	0	ø	0	—	-4	0	-0.4
1994	LA N	0	0	ø	24	0	0	0-0	13.2	12	5	1	0	5-0	9	3.29	121	.245	.315	0	ø	0	—	1	0	0.1
1995	LA N	4	0	1.000	28	0	0	0-1	20	29	16	1	1	15-4	11	7.20	54	.354	.455	0	ø	0	—	-7	0	-1.2
1996	Mon N	4	5	.444	64	6	0	0-4	87.1	74	40	10	1	37-3	82	4.02	108	.228	.308	11	.000	-1	87	4	0	0.3
1997	Mon N	1	2	.333	33	0	0	1-2	30.1	48	35	4	2	15-3	16	9.79	43	.378	.448	5	.200	0	—	-18	0	-1.6
	Tor A	1	1	.500	9	3	0	0-0	27	34	13	3	0	6-0	28	4.00	115	.304	.339	0	ø	0	80	2	0	0.1
1998	Ari N	8	12	.400	33	23	3-1	0-0	162.2	146	60	12	3	51-3	132	2.88	149	.245	.305	46-0-5	.109	-1	68	24	19	2.8
1999	†Ari N	16	9	.640	32	32	2-1	0-0	214.2	188	92	21	7	79-3	148	3.65	127	.236	.308	69-0-6	.232	3	106	25	0	2.9
2000	Ari N	2	10	.167	20	16	0	0-0	96	127	88	17	7	42-11	45	7.22	66	.315	.385	27-1-3	.259	2	89	-27	0	-2.5
	Phi N	2	9	.182	12	12	0	0-0	71	81	40	9	2	30-0	51	4.69	98	.290	.362	18-0-2	.278	2	73	-1	0	0.2
	Year	4	19	.174	32	28	0	0-0	167	208	128	26	9	72-11	96	6.14	77	.305	.376	45-1-5	.267	5	82	-29	0	-2.3
2001	Phi N	13	7	.650	32	32	0	0-0	185.2	199	100	26	5	56-3	107	4.46	92	.273	.327	55-0-7	.236	3	116	-8	0	-0.5
2002	LA N	11	9	.550	39	23	0	0-0	161.1	142	73	20	4	54-3	105	3.90	100	.239	.304	39-1-8	.154	1	95	1	0	0.4
2003	Bal A	4	11	.267	19	17	0	0-0	93.2	134	69	11	2	30-1	53	6.34	73	.343	.390	0	ø	0	84	-17	74	-2.1
Total	11	68	78	.466	392	164	5-2	1-8	1198.2	1250	651	140	34	441-37	806	4.55	95	.271	.337	270-2-31	.196	10	94	-25	276	-1.5
D'Acquisto, John	John Francis; B12.24.1951 San Diego CA; BR/TR/6´2˝/(195–200); [SFN70 1/17]; d9.2																									
1973	SF N	1	1	.500	7	3	1	0-0	27.2	23	14	4	0	19-0	29	3.58	108	.219	.336	9	.000	-1	145	0	0	-0.1
1974	SF N	12	14	.462	38	36	5-1	0-0	215	182	101	13	6	124-7	167	3.77	101	.227	.334	71-1-2	.113	-1*	81	3	0	0.1
1975	SF N	2	4	.333	10	6	0	0-0	28	29	35	5	2	34-0	22	10.29	37	.264	.445	7	.000	-0	115	-19	100	-3.2
1976	SF N	3	8	.273	28	19	0	0-0	106	93	69	5	3	102-1	53	5.35	68	.243	.401	26-0-4	.269	2	94	-17	0	-1.5
1977	StL N	0	0	ø	3	2	0	0-0	8.1	5	4	0	1	10-0	9	4.32	90	.185	.410	2	.000	-0	137	0	21	0.0
	SD N	1	2	.333	17	12	0	0-0	44	49	41	3	1	47-0	45	6.95	51	.297	.451	6-0-2	.000	-0	116	-19	0	-1.2
	Year	1	2	.333	20	14	0	0-0	52.1	54	45	3	2	57-0	54	6.54	56	.281	.445	8-0-2	.000	-1	119	-20	0	-1.2
1978	SD N	4	3	.571	45	3	0	10-0	93	60	24	2	1	56-2	104	2.13	157	.185	.305	21	.190	1	54	14	0	1.4
1979	SD N	9	13	.409	51	11	1-1	2-4	133.2	140	83	15	3	86-6	97	4.92	72	.275	.380	31-0-3	.129	1	96	-22	0	-3.3
1980	SD N	2	3	.400	39	0	0	1-1	67	67	29	2	1	36-9	44	3.76	91	.270	.359	8-0-2	.000	-1	—	-2	0	-0.2
	Mon N	0	2	.000	11	0	0	2-1	20.2	14	7	0	0	9-0	15	2.18	167	.206	.295	0	ø	0	—	3	0	0.3
	Year	2	5	.286	50	0	0	3-2	87.2	81	36	2	1	45-9	59	3.39	102	.256	.345	8-0-2	.000	-1	—	1	0	0.1
1981	Cal A	0	0	ø	6	0	0	0-0	19.1	26	24	2	1	12-0	8	10.71	34	.338	.415	0	ø	0	—	-14	0	-0.7
1982	Oak A	0	1	.000	11	0	0	0-0	17	20	11	1	0	9-0	7	5.29	75	.290	.372	0	ø	0	—	-3	0	-0.1
Total	10	34	51	.400	266	92	7-2	15-6	779.2	708	442	52	19	544-25	600	4.56	80	.245	.365	181-1-13	.127	0	97	-76	121	-8.5
Dagenhard, John	John Douglas; B4.25.1917 Magnolia OH; D7.16.2001 Bolivar OH; BR/TR/6´2˝/195; d9.28; Col Ohio St.																									
1943	Bos N	1	0	1.000	2	1	1	0	11	9	2	0	2	4	2	0.00	ø	.225	.326	3-0-1	.000	-0	124	3	0	0.3
Daglia, Pete	Peter George; B2.28.1907 Napa CA; D3.11.1952 Willits CA; BR/TR/6´3˝/210; d6.8																									
1932	Chi A	2	4	.333	12	5	2	0	50	67	35	4	4	20	16	5.76	75	.324	.394	13-0-2	.077	-1	83	-6	—	-0.7
Dahl, Jay	Jay Steven; B12.6.1945 San Bernardino CA; D6.20.1965 Salisbury NC; BB/TL/5´10˝/178; d9.27																									
1963	Hou N	0	1	.000	1	1	0	0	2.2	7	7	0	0	0-0	0	16.88	19	.438	.438	0	ø	0	82	-5	0	-0.7
Dahlke, Jerry	Jerome Alexander "Joe"; B6.8.1929 Marathon WI; D9.3.2006 Batesville MS; BR/TR/6´0˝/180; d5.6																									
1956	Chi A	0	0	ø	5	0	0	0	2.1	5	5	0	0	6-0	1	19.29	21	.455	.647	0	ø	0	—	-4	0	-0.2

YEAR	TM LG	W	L	PCT	G	GS	CG-SHO	SV-BS	IP	H	R	HR	HB	BB-IB	SO	ERA	AERA	OAV	OOB	AB-HR-SH	AVG	PB	SUP	APR	DL	PW
DAIGLE, CASEY	Sean Casey; B4.4.1981 Lake Charles LA; BR/TR/6´5˝/(215–250); [AriN99 1/31]; d4.9																									
2004	Ari N	2	3	.400	10	10	0	0-0	49	63	41	9	2	27-3	17	7.16	64	.320	.405	17-0-1	.118	-0*	104	-12	0	-1.1
2006	Ari N	0	0	ø	10	0	0	0-0	12.1	14	5	1	0	6-0	7	3.65	128	.311	.385	1	.000	-0	—	2	0	0.1
Total	2	2	3	.400	20	10	0	0-0	61.1	77	46	10	2	33-3	24	6.46	71	.318	.401	18-0-1	.111	-0	104	-10	0	-1.0
DAILEY, SAM	Samuel Laurence; B3.31.1904 Oakford IL; D12.2.1979 Columbia MO; BL/TR/5´11˝/168; d7.4																									
1929	Phi N	2	2	.500	20	4	0	0	51.1	74	48	5	1	23	18	7.54	69	.349	.415	17	.059	-2	80	-12	—	-1.0
DAILEY, BILL	William Garland; B5.13.1935 Arlington VA; BR/TR/6´3˝/(185–195); d8.17																									
1961	Cle A	1	0	1.000	12	0	0	0	19	16	4	0	0	6-1	7	0.95	415	.232	.289	2	.000	-0	—	6	0	0.3
1962	Cle A	2	2	.500	27	0	0	1	42.2	43	18	0	2	17-4	24	3.59	108	.270	.341	3	.000	-0	—	2	0	0.1
1963	Min A	6	3	.667	66	0	0	21	108.2	80	26	9	0	19-5	72	1.99	183	.208	.244	21-1-1	.238	2	—	21	0	2.9
1964	Min A	1	2	.333	14	0	0	0	15.1	23	16	3	4	17-2	6	8.22	44	.377	.537	0	ø	0	—	-8	0	-1.4
Total	4	10	7	.588	119	0	0	22	185.2	162	64	12	6	59-12	109	2.76	135	.241	.304	26-1-1	.192	1	—	21	0	1.9
DAILY, ED	Edward M.; B9.7.1862 Providence RI; D10.21.1891 Washington DC; BR/TR/5´10.5˝/174; d5.4; b–Con; ▲																									
1885	Phi N	26	23	.531	50	50	49-4	0	440	370	212	12	—	90	140	2.21	126	.217	.256	184-1	.207	-0	82	29	—	2.6
1886	Phi N	16	9	.640	27	23	22-1	0	218	211	123	7	—	59	95	3.06	108	.242	.290	309-4	.227	3*	104	7	—	0.9
1887	Phi N	0	4	.000	6	5	4	0	41.1	52	52	2	0	25	7	7.19	59	.289	.376	106-1	.283	1*	101	-13	—	-0.8
	Was N	0	1	.000	1	1	1	0	7	5	6	0	0	6	3	7.71	52	.208	.367	311-2	.251	0*	48	-2	—	-0.2
	Year	0	5	.000	7	6	5	0	48.1	57	58	2	0	31	10	7.26	58	.279	.374	417-3	.259	1	92	-14	—	-1.0
1888	Was N	2	7	.222	9	8	8	0	73.2	88	69	7	3	19	20	4.89	57	.278	.325	453-7	.225	1*	77	-20	—	-1.8
1889	Col AA	0	0	ø	2	0	0	1	1.2	1	7	0	0	4	2	21.60	17	.167	.500	578-3	.256	0*	—	-4	—	-0.4
1890	Bro AA	10	14	.417	27	27	27	0	235.2	252	161	3	18	93	82	4.05	96	.265	.342	394-1	.239	3*	95	-2	—	0.3
	NY N	2	0	1.000	2	1	1	0	16	6	6	0	4	6	0	2.25	156	.113	.254	15	.133	-1*	72	3	—	0.2
	†Lou AA	6	3	.667	12	10	9-1	0	93	83	35	2	4	30	31	1.94	199	.232	.298	80	.250	2*	106	20	—	2.0
1891	Lou AA	4	8	.333	15	14	11	0	111.1	149	109	6	8	48	27	5.74	64	.310	.382	64	.250	2*	101	-26	—	-1.9
Total	7	66	69	.489	151	139	132-6	1	1237.2	1217	780	39	37	380	407	3.39	98	.246	.305	2494-19	.240	12	93	-8	—	0.9
DAILY, HUGH	Hugh Ignatius "One Arm" (b Harry Criss); B7.17.1847 , Ireland; BR/TR/6´2˝/180; d5.1																									
1882	Buf N	15	14	.517	29	29	29	0	255.2	246	165	7	—	70	116	2.99	98	.234	.282	110	.164	-6	103	-7	—	-1.4
1883	Cle N	23	19	.548	45	43	40-4	1	378.2	360	193	5	—	99	171	2.42	130	.243	.291	142	.127	-10	72	34	—	2.1
1884	CP U	27	27	.500	56	56	54-5	0	484.2	430	257	11	—	71	469	2.43	100	.222	.249	196	.219	-6*	78	0	—	-0.9
	Was U	1	1	.500	2	2	2	0	16	16	11	0	—	1	14	2.25	107	.242	.254	5	.000	-1	89	-1	—	-0.2
	Year	28	28	.500	58	58	56-5	0	500.2	446	268	11	—	72	**483**	2.43	100	.223	.250	201	.214	-7	79	-4	—	-1.1
1885	StL N	3	8	.273	11	11	10-1	0	91.1	92	72	5	—	44	31	3.94	70	.252	.333	35	.086	-3	71	-14	—	-1.6
1886	Was N	0	6	.000	6	6	6	0	49	69	60	2	—	40	15	7.35	44	.332	.440	16	.125	-1	69	-22	—	-1.9
1887	Cle AA	4	12	.250	16	16	16	0	139.2	181	108	1	3	44	30	3.67	118	.311	.362	58	.069	-8	77	8	—	0.0
Total	6	73	87	.456	165	163	157-10	1	1415	1394	866	31	3	369	846	2.92	101	.245	.291	562	.157	-34	80	-2	—	-3.9
DALCANTON, BRUCE	John Bruce; B6.15.1942 California PA; BR/TR/6´2˝/(205–230); d9.3; C5; Col California (PA)																									
1967	Pit N	2	1	.667	8	2	1	0	24	19	5	1	1	10-3	13	1.88	179	.211	.297	6	.333	1	65	4	0	0.6
1968	Pit N	1	1	.500	7	0	0	2	17	7	4	0	2	6-2	8	2.12	138	.127	.234	3-0-1	.000	-0	—	2	0	0.2
1969	Pit N	8	2	.800	57	0	0	5-1	86.1	79	34	3	0	49-12	56	3.34	104	.252	.351	10	.300	2	—	2	0	0.5
1970	Pit N	9	4	.692	41	6	1	1-3	84.2	94	48	7	1	39-8	53	4.57	87	.282	.356	16-0-1	.000	-1	178	-6	0	-1.0
1971	KC A	8	6	.571	25	22	2	0-0	141.1	144	63	8	0	44-0	58	3.44	100	.262	.315	46-0-6	.087	-3	105	-1	28	-0.5
1972	KC A	6	6	.500	35	16	1	2-0	132.1	135	54	7	1	29-6	75	3.40	90	.265	.304	41-0-5	.098	-2	124	-5	0	-0.7
1973	KC A	4	3	.571	32	3	1	3-3	97.1	108	60	8	4	46-12	38	4.81	86	.284	.367	0	ø	0	43	-8	0	-0.6
1974	KC A	8	10	.444	31	22	9-2	0-0	175.1	135	71	5	5	82-3	96	3.13	122	.211	.304	0	ø	0	110	13	0	1.3
1975	KC A	0	2	.000	4	2	0	0-0	8.2	23	18	0	1	7-0	5	15.58	25	.479	.554	0	ø	0	103	-11	0	-1.8
	Atl N	2	7	.222	26	9	0	3-3	67	63	33	2	6	24-1	38	3.36	113	.248	.321	19	.105	-1	77	2	0	0.1
1976	Atl N	3	5	.375	42	1	0	1-0	73.1	67	41	6	2	42-8	36	3.56	107	.244	.344	9-0-1	.222	0	70	-2	0	-0.1
1977	Chi A	0	2	.000	8	0	0	2-0	24	20	11	1	0	13-0	9	3.75	109	.230	.330	0	ø	0	—	1	89	0.1
Total	11	51	49	.510	316	83	15-2	19-10	931.1	894	442	48	23	391-55	485	3.67	99	.253	.329	150-0-14	.113	-3	106	-9	117	-1.9
DALE, GENE	Emmett Eugene; B6.16.1889 St.Louis MO; D3.20.1958 St.Louis MO; BR/TR/6´3˝/179; d9.19																									
1911	StL N	0	2	.000	5	2	0	0	14.2	13	12	0	2	16	13	6.75	50	.250	.443	5	.400	1	100	-5	—	-0.5
1912	StL N	0	5	.000	19	3	1	0	61.2	76	58	4	3	51	37	6.57	52	.311	.436	22	.273	1*	43	-19	—	-1.3
1915	Cin N	18	17	.514	49	35	20-4	3	296.2	256	115	6	6	107	104	2.46	116	.243	.316	91-0-8	.220	2	90	9	—	1.2
1916	Cin N	3	4	.429	17	5	2	0	69.2	80	44	3	2	33	23	5.17	50	.304	.386	21	.143	-0	98	-17	—	-1.7
Total	4	21	28	.429	90	45	23-4	3	442.2	425	229	13	13	207	177	3.60	81	.263	.352	139-0-8	.223	3	87	-32	—	-2.3
DALE, CARL	James Carl; B12.7.1972 Indianapolis IN; BR/TR/6´2˝/198; [StLN94 2/53]; d9.7; Col Winthrop																									
1999	Mil N	0	1	.000	4	0	0	0-0	4	8	9	2	1	6-0	4	20.25	23	.400	.556	0	ø	0	—	-7	0	-1.1
DALEY, BUD	Leavitt Leo; B10.7.1932 Orange CA; BL/TL/6´1˝/185; d9.10																									
1955	Cle A	0	1	.000	2	1	0	0	7	10	5	1	0	1-0	2	6.43	62	.333	.355	2	.000	-0	45	-2	0	-0.2
1956	Cle A	1	0	1.000	14	0	0	0	20.1	21	15	2	5	14-1	13	6.20	68	.273	.408	2-0-1	.000	-0	—	-4	0	-0.2
1957	Cle A	2	8	.200	34	10	1	2	87.1	99	59	6	10	40-4	54	4.43	84	.279	.367	20-0-2	.200	0	79	-11	0	-1.1
1958	KC A	3	2	.600	26	5	1	0	70.2	67	29	5	6	19-1	39	3.31	118	.249	.312	16-0-1	.125	-1	78	4	0	0.3
1959	KC A★	16	13	.552	39	29	12-2	1	216.1	212	90	24	11	62-2	125	3.16	127	.257	.317	78-0-5	.295	4	100	19	0	2.9
1960	KC A★	16	16	.500	37	35	13-1	0	231	234	129	27	10	96-3	126	4.56	87	.263	.339	75-0-6	.160	1	114	-13	0	-1.4
1961	KC A	4	8	.333	16	10	2	1	63.2	84	46	6	5	22-2	36	4.95	84	.319	.378	18-0-1	.111	-1	87	-8	0	-1.3
	†NY A	8	9	.471	23	17	7	0	129.2	127	63	17	4	51-6	83	3.96	94	.257	.330	45-0-2	.133	-1	119	-4	0	-0.6
	Year	12	17	.414	39	27	9	1	193.1	211	109	23	9	73-8	119	4.28	90	.278	.347	63-0-3	.127	-2	107	-12	0	-1.9
1962	†NY A	7	5	.583	43	6	0	4	105.1	105	47	8	5	21-0	55	3.59	104	.258	.301	27-0-1	.185	-0	147	2	0	0.2
1963	NY A	0	0	ø	1	0	0	1	1	2	0	0	0	0-0	0	0.00	ø	.667	.500	0	ø	0	—	0	149	0.1
1964	NY A	3	2	.600	13	3	0	1	35	37	19	3	4	25-1	16	4.63	78	.274	.400	8-0-1	.250	1	147	-4	0	-0.4
Total	10	60	64	.484	248	116	36-3	10	967.1	998	502	99	60	351-20	549	4.03	97	.266	.337	291-0-20	.192	3	107	-21	149	-1.7
DALEY, BILL	William; B6.27.1868 Poughkeepsie NY; D5.4.1922 Poughkeepsie NY; TL/5´7˝/140; d7.17																									
1889	Bos N	3	3	.500	9	7	4	0	48	34	29	1	2	43	40	4.31	97	.193	.357	20	.150	-1	94	1	—	0.1
1890	Bos P	18	7	**.720**	34	25	19-2	2	235	246	178	7	9	167	110	3.60	122	.258	.373	110-2	.155	-5*	113	12	—	0.5
1891	Bos AA	8	6	.571	19	11	10	2	126.2	119	76	6	7	81	68	2.98	117	.240	.354	59	.169	-3*	169	5	—	0.2
Total	3	29	16	.644	62	43	33-2	4	409.2	399	283	14	18	291	218	3.49	117	.245	.366	189-2	.159	-8	123	18	—	0.8
DALTON, MIKE	Michael Edward; B3.27.1963 Palo Alto CA; BR/TL/6´0˝/215; [BosA83 15/385]; d5.31; Col De Anza (CA) JC																									
1991	Det A	0	0	ø	4	0	0	0-0	8	12	3	2	0	2-0	4	3.38	124	.333	.368	0	ø	0	—	1	0	0.0
DALY, GEORGE	George Josephs "Pecks"; B7.28.1887 Buffalo NY; D12.12.1957 Buffalo NY; BR/TR/5´10.5˝/175; d9.26; Col St. Bonaventure																									
1909	NY N	0	3	.000	3	3	3	0	21	31	19	0	1	8	8	6.00	43	.341	.400	9	.111	-1	55	-7	—	-1.0
D'AMICO, JEFF	Jeffrey Charles; B12.27.1975 St.Petersburg FL; BR/TR/6´7˝/(245–255); [MilA93 1/23]; d6.28; [DL 1998 Mil N 181]																									
1996	Mil A	6	6	.500	17	17	0	0-0	86	88	53	21	0	31-0	53	5.44	95	.267	.327	0	ø	0	101	-1	0	-0.1
1997	Mil A	9	7	.563	23	23	1-1	0-0	135.2	139	81	25	8	43-2	94	4.71	98	.264	.327	4-0-1	.000	-0	92	-2	45	-0.3
1999	Mil N	0	0	ø	1	0	0	0-0	1	1	0	0	0	0-0	1	0.00	ø	.250	.250	0	ø	0	—	1	172	0.0
2000	Mil N	12	7	.632	23	23	1-1	0-0	162.1	143	55	14	6	46-5	101	2.66	174	.238	.297	44-1-6	.091	-1	76	34	24	3.5
2001	Mil N	2	4	.333	10	10	0	0-0	47.1	60	42	11	1	16-4	32	6.08	71	.306	.360	15	.067	0	110	-13	131	-1.3
2002	NY N	6	10	.375	29	22	1-1	0-0	145.2	152	84	20	3	37-8	101	4.94	80	.267	.313	37-0-5	.108	-1	105	-14	0	-1.5
2003	Pit N	9	16	.360	29	29	2-1	0-0	175.1	204	104	23	7	42-6	100	4.77	91	.291	.336	48-1-9	.125	1	94	-11	0	-1.3
2004	Cle A	1	2	.333	7	7	0	0-0	30.2	45	29	6	1	6-0	16	7.63	57	.333	.361	0	ø	0	143	-12	46	-0.9
Total	8	45	52	.464	139	131	5-4	0-0	784	832	448	120	26	221-25	498	4.61	97	.272	.324	148-2-21	.101	-1	97	-18	599	-1.9
D'AMICO, JEFF	Jeffrey Michael; B11.9.1974 Inglewood CA; BR/TR/6´3˝/200; [OakA93 2/67]; d6.3																									
2000	KC A	0	1	.000	7	1	0	0-0	13.2	19	14	2	0	15-1	9	9.22	57	.345	.486	0	ø	0	54	-5	0	-0.3

YEAR	TM LG	W	L	PCT	G	GS	CG-SHO	SV-BS	IP	H	R	HR	HB	BB-IB	SO	ERA	AERA	OAV	OOB	AB-HR-SH	AVG	PB	SUP	APR	DL	PW
Dammann, Bill	William Henry "Wee Willie"; B8.9.1872 Chicago IL; D12.6.1948 Lynnhaven VA; BL/TL/5´7˝/155; d4.24																									
1897	Cin N	6	4	.600	16	11	7-1	0	95	122	65	2	5	37	21	4.74	96	.309	.375	31	.161	-1	100	-1	—	-0.1
1898	Cin N	16	10	.615	35	22	16-2	2	224.2	277	132	3	7	67	51	3.61	106	.301	.353	82-0-1	.195	1	101	2	—	0.1
1899	Cin N	2	1	.667	9	5	3-1	1	48	74	30	0	1	11	2	4.88	80	.351	.386	18	.056	-2	143	-3	—	-0.3
Total	3	24	15	.615	60	38	26-4	3	367.2	473	227	5	13	115	74	4.06	99	.310	.363	131-0-1	.168	-1	106	-2	—	-0.3
Daneker, Pat	Patrick Rees; B1.14.1976 Williamsport PA; BR/TR/6´3˝/195; [ChiA97 5/159]; d7.2; Col Virginia																									
1999	Chi A	0	0	ø	3	2	0	0-0	15	14	8	1	0	6-0	5	4.20	118	.255	.323	2	.000	-0	151	1	0	0.0
Daney, Art	Arthur Lee (Also Known As Arthur Lee Whitehorn); B7.9.1904 Talihina OK; D3.11.1988 Phoenix AZ; BR/TR/5´11˝/165; d5.25																									
1928	Phi A	0	0	ø	1	0	0	0	1	1	0	0	0	0	0	0.00	ø	.250	.250	0	ø	0	—	0	—	0.0
Danforth, Dave	David Charles "Dauntless Dave"; B3.7.1890 Granger TX; D9.19.1970 Baltimore MD; BL/TL/6´0˝/167; d8.1; Col Baylor																									
1911	Phi A	4	1	.800	14	2	1	1	33.2	29	18	1	3	17	21	3.74	84	.240	.348	6-0-1	.167	0	126	-2	—	-0.3
1912	Phi A	0	0	ø	3	0	0	0	20.1	26	14	0	0	12	8	3.98	77	.338	.427	8	.250	0	—	-3	—	-0.1
1916	Chi A	6	5	.545	28	8	1	2	93.2	87	43	1	3	37	49	3.27	85	.259	.338	23-0-2	.087	-1	82	-4	—	-0.6
1917	†Chi A	11	6	.647	**50**	9	1-1	**9**	173	155	56	1	3	74	79	2.65	100	.244	.325	46-0-5	.130	0	96	5	—	0.4
1918	Chi A	6	15	.286	39	11	5	2	139	148	73	1	5	40	48	3.43	80	.288	.345	42-0-2	.143	-2	68	-13	—	-2.1
1919	Chi A	1	2	.333	15	1	0	1	41.2	58	44	1	1	20	17	7.78	41	.333	.405	9-0-1	.111	0	49	-21	—	-1.5
1922	StL A	5	2	.714	20	10	3	1	79.2	93	37	1	1	38	48	3.28	127	.304	.383	23	.087	-2	113	7	—	0.3
1923	StL A	16	14	.533	38	29	16	1	226.1	221	111	4	12	87	96	3.94	106	.262	.340	71-0-8	.211	2	100	9	—	1.3
1924	StL A	15	12	.556	41	27	12-1	4	219.2	246	126	16	3	69	65	4.51	100	.292	.348	76-0-6	.171	-2	91	1	—	-0.2
1925	StL A	7	9	.438	38	15	5	2	159	172	96	19	3	61	53	4.36	107	.284	.353	46-0-5	.174	-2	115	4	—	0.0
Total	10	71	66	.518	286	112	44-2	23	1186	1235	618	45	34	455	484	3.89	95	.277	.349	350-0-30	.160	-6	102	-17	—	-2.8
Daniel, Chuck	Charles Edward; B9.17.1933 Bluffton AR; BR/TR/6´2˝/190; d9.21; Col Ozarks																									
1957	Det A	0	0	ø	1	0	0	0	2.1	3	2	1	0	0-0	2	7.71	50	.333	.333	0	ø	0	—	-1	0	0.0
Daniels, Bennie	Bennie; B6.17.1932 Tuscaloosa AL; BL/TR/6´1.5˝/(190–214); d9.24; Col Compton (CA) CC																									
1957	Pit N	0	1	.000	1	1	0	0	7	5	2	0	0	3-0	2	1.29	295	.208	.296	2	.000	-0	0	2	0	0.2
1958	Pit N	0	3	.000	8	5	1	0	27.2	31	19	3	1	15-1	7	5.53	70	.290	.379	8	.125	-0	56	-5	0	-0.5
1959	Pit N	7	9	.438	34	12	0	1	100.2	115	69	9	2	39-6	67	5.45	71	.287	.351	29-1-0	.310	6*	83	-18	0	-2.0
1960	Pit N	1	3	.250	10	6	0	0	40.1	52	35	4	0	17-1	16	7.81	48	.311	.371	16	.188	-0	122	-17	0	-1.4
1961	Was A	12	11	.522	32	28	12-1	0	212	184	90	14	3	80-8	110	3.44	117	.237	.309	76-2-3	.197	3	96	15	0	1.9
1962	Was A	7	16	.304	44	21	3-1	2	161.1	172	98	14	2	68-5	66	4.85	83	.280	.351	46-1-4	.130	-1	78	-15	0	-1.8
1963	Was A	5	10	.333	35	24	6-1	1	168.2	163	90	19	1	58-9	88	4.38	85	.250	.310	46-0-6	.152	1*	93	-11	0	-0.6
1964	Was A	8	10	.444	33	24	3-2	0	163	147	75	20	0	64-8	73	3.70	100	.245	.314	47-1-4	.128	0	82	1	0	0.2
1965	Was A	5	13	.278	33	18	1	1	116.1	135	75	16	0	39-7	42	4.72	74	.290	.343	30-0-3	.133	0	70	-18	0	-2.6
Total	9	45	76	.372	230	139	26-5	5	997	1004	553	99	9	383-45	471	4.44	86	.264	.330	300-5-20	.170	9	85	-66	0	-6.6
Daniels, Charlie	Charles L.; B7.1.1861 Roxbury MA; D2.9.1938 Boston MA; d4.18																									
1884	Bos U	0	2	.000	2	2	2	0	16.2	20	14	0	—	2	12	4.32	55	.278	.297	11	.273	0*	108	-3	—	-0.3
Daniels, Pete	Peter J. "Smiling Pete"; B4.8.1864 Co. Cavan, Ireland; D2.13.1928 Indianapolis IN; BL/TL/5´8.5˝/160; d4.19																									
1890	Pit N	1	2	.333	4	4	3	0	28	40	29	1	3	12	8	7.07	47	.325	.399	12	.333	1	153	-11	—	-0.7
1898	StL N	1	6	.143	10	6	3	0	54.2	62	41	0	3	14	13	3.62	105	.283	.335	17	.176	0	62	-3	—	-0.3
Total	2	2	8	.200	14	10	6	0	82.2	102	70	1	6	26	21	4.79	76	.298	.358	29	.241	1	98	-14	—	-1.0
Darby, George	George William "Deacon"; B2.6.1869 Kansas City MO; D2.25.1937 Sacramento CA; BR/TR/5´10.5˝/160; d4.28																									
1893	Cin N	1	1	.500	4	3	2	0	29	41	32	2	3	18	6	7.76	62	.323	.419	10	.300	0	83	-9	—	-0.4
Darcy, Pat	Patrick Leonard; B5.12.1950 Troy OH; BL/TR/6´3˝/175; d9.12; Col Mesa (AZ) CC																									
1974	Cin N	1	0	1.000	6	2	0	0-0	17	17	7	2	0	8-1	14	3.71	94	.262	.342	3-0-1	.333	0	125	0	0	0.0
1975	†Cin N	11	5	.688	27	22	1	1-1	130.2	134	54	4	0	59-9	46	3.58	100	.269	.344	47-0-2	.085	-3	114	1	0	-0.2
1976	Cin N	2	3	.400	11	4	0	2-0	39	41	27	2	0	22-2	15	6.23	56	.279	.368	11-0-1	.182	1	164	-11	0	-1.3
Total	3	14	8	.636	44	28	1	3-1	186.2	192	88	8	0	89-12	75	4.15	86	.270	.349	61-0-4	.115	-2	122	-10	0	-1.5
Darensbourg, Vic	Victor Anthony; B11.13.1970 Los Angeles CA; BL/TL/5´10˝/(165–180); d4.1; Col Lewis–Clark St.; [DL 1995 Fla N 17]																									
1998	Fla N	0	7	.000	59	0	0	1-1	71	52	29	5	0	30-6	74	3.68	110	.207	.289	8	.000	-1*	—	5	0	0.3
1999	Fla N	0	1	.000	56	0	0	0-1	34.2	50	36	3	5	21-1	16	8.83	50	.340	.434	0	ø	0	—	-17	0	-0.8
2000	Fla N	5	3	.625	56	0	0	0-1	62	61	32	7	2	28-1	59	4.06	108	.260	.336	8	.250	0	—	2	0	0.3
2001	Fla N	1	2	.333	58	0	0	1-2	48.2	52	24	4	1	10-6	33	4.25	98	.277	.313	0	ø	0*	—	0	28	0.0
2002	Fla N	1	2	.333	42	0	0	0-0	48.1	61	34	10	2	26-4	33	6.14	64	.305	.385	1-0-1	.000	-0*	—	-12	0	-0.7
2003	Col N	0	0	ø	3	0	0	0-0	2.1	4	1	0	0	0-0	0	0.00	ø	.333	.333	0	ø	0	—	1	0	0.0
	Mon N	0	0	ø	6	0	0	0-0	6.2	13	8	2	0	1-0	4	10.80	41	.406	.424	1	.000	-0*	—	-4	0	-0.2
	Year	0	0	ø	9	0	0	0-0	9	17	9	2	0	1-0	4	8.00	57	.386	.400	1	.000	-0	—	-3	0	-0.2
2004	NY N	0	1	.000	5	0	0	0-0	5.2	10	5	1	0	2-0	1	7.94	54	.435	.444	0	ø	0	—	-2	0	-0.3
	Chi A	0	0	ø	2	0	0	0-0	1.1	1	0	0	0	1-0	1	0.00	ø	.333	.500	0	ø	0	—	1	0	0.0
2005	Det A	1	1	.500	22	0	0	0-0	22.1	24	7	2	0	7-2	9	2.82	152	.282	.330	0	ø	0	—	4	0	0.3
Total	8	8	17	.320	309	0	0	2-5	303	328	176	34	10	126-20	229	4.96	85	.279	.348	18-0-1	.111	-0	—	-22	45	-1.1
Darling, Ron	Ronald Maurice; B8.19.1960 Honolulu HI; BR/TR/6´3˝/(195–200); [TexA81 1/9]; d9.6; Col Yale																									
1983	NY N	1	3	.250	5	5	1	0-0	35.1	31	11	0	3	17-1	23	2.80	131	.248	.352	10-0-1	.100	-1	63	4	0	0.4
1984	NY N	12	9	.571	33	33	2-2	0-0	205.2	179	97	17	5	104-2	136	3.81	94	.235	.328	67-0-6	.149	-1*	109	-4	0	-0.3
1985	NY N☆	16	6	.727	36	35	4-2	0-0	248	214	93	21	3	114-1	167	2.90	121	.235	.321	76-0-13	.171	2*	104	15	0	1.7
1986	†NY N	15	6	.714	34	34	4-2	0-0	237	203	84	21	3	81-2	184	2.81	128	.234	.300	81-0-10	.099	-2	122	21	0	1.7
1987	NY N	12	8	.600	32	32	2	0-0	207.2	183	111	24	3	96-3	167	4.29	89	.233	.318	65-0-10	.123	0	119	-11	23	-0.7
1988	†NY N	17	9	.654	34	34	7-4	0-0	240.2	218	97	24	5	60-2	161	3.25	100	.245	.294	82-0-9	.220	6	115	1	0	0.8
1989	NY N	14	14	.500	33	33	4	0-0	217.1	214	100	19	3	70-7	153	3.52	94	.258	.314	73-2-5	.123	1*	105	-8	0	-0.9
1990	NY N	7	9	.438	33	18	1	0-0	126	135	73	20	5	44-4	99	4.50	84	.273	.336	31-0-5	.129	0*	105	-11	0	-1.3
1991	NY N	5	6	.455	17	17	0	0-0	102.1	96	50	9	6	28-1	58	3.87	95	.251	.310	34-0-5	.118	-0	97	-2	0	-0.3
	Mon N	0	2	.000	3	3	0	0-0	17	25	16	6	1	5-0	11	7.41	49	.333	.383	6-0-1	.167	0	90	-7	0	-0.7
	Year	5	8	.385	20	20	0	0-0	119.1	121	66	15	7	33-1	69	4.37	84	.265	.321	40-0-6	.125	-0	96	-10	0	-1.0
	Oak A	3	7	.300	12	12	0	0-0	75	64	34	7	2	38-2	60	4.08	94	.237	.331	0	ø	0	61	-1	0	-0.1
1992	†Oak A	15	10	.600	33	33	4-3	0-0	206.1	198	98	15	4	72-5	99	3.66	103	.253	.318	0	ø	0*	103	1	0	0.1
1993	Oak A	5	9	.357	31	29	3	0-0	178	198	107	22	5	72-5	95	5.16	80	.281	.349	0	ø	0*	116	-20	0	-1.4
1994	Oak A	10	11	.476	25	**25**	4	0-0	160	162	89	18	7	59-3	108	4.50	100	.267	.337	1	.000	-0*	89	-1	0	-0.1
1995	Oak A	4	7	.364	21	21	1	0-0	104	124	79	16	4	46-2	69	6.23	73	.296	.365	0	ø	0*	119	-21	0	-1.7
Total	13	136	116	.540	382	364	37-13	0-0	2360.1	2244	1139	239	59	906-40	1590	3.87	96	.252	.323	526-2-65	.144	5	107	-44	23	-2.8
Darnell, Bob	Robert Jack; B11.6.1930 Wewoka OK; D1.3.1995 Fredericksburg TX; BR/TR/5´10˝/175; d8.10																									
1954	Bro N	0	0	ø	6	1	0	0	14.1	15	7	2	0	7	5	3.14	130	.278	.361	2-0-1	.000	-0	131	1	0	0.0
1956	Bro N	0	0	ø	1	0	0	0	1.1	1	0	0	0	0-0	0	0.00	ø	.200	.200	0	ø	0	—	1	0	0.0
Total	2	0	0	ø	7	1	0	0	15.2	16	7	2	0	7-0	5	2.87	142	.271	.348	2-0-1	.000	-0	131	2	0	0.0
Darr, Mike	Michael Edward; B3.23.1956 Pomona CA; BR/TR/6´4˝/190; [BalA74 4/96]; d9.6																									
1977	Tor A	0	1	.000	1	1	0	0-0	1.1	3	5	1	1	4-0	1	33.75	13	.429	.667	0	ø	0	42	-4	0	-0.6
Darrow, George	George Oliver; B7.12.1903 Beloit KS; D3.24.1983 Sun City AZ; BL/TL/6´0˝/180; d4.22; Col Washburn Topeka																									
1934	Phi N	2	6	.250	17	8	2	1	49	57	37	4	4	28	14	5.51	86	.302	.403	15	.133	0	103	-5	—	-0.6
Darwin, Danny	Daniel Wayne; B10.25.1955 Bonham TX; BR/TR/6´3˝/(185–202); d9.8; b–Jeff; Col Grayson Co. (TX) JC																									
1978	Tex A	1	0	1.000	3	1	0	0-0	8.2	11	4	0	0	1-0	8	4.15	90	.324	.333	0	ø	0	96	0	0	0.0
1979	Tex A	4	4	.500	20	6	1	0-0	78	50	36	5	5	30-2	58	4.04	103	.186	.274	0	ø	0	138	3	0	0.2
1980	Tex A	13	4	.765	53	2	0	8-6	109.2	98	37	4	2	50-7	104	2.63	148	.243	.324	0	ø	0	150	16	21	2.5
1981	Tex A	9	9	.500	22	22	6-2	0-0	146	115	67	12	6	57-5	98	3.64	96	.218	.300	0	ø	0	121	-4	0	-0.5

YEAR	TM LG	W	L	PCT	G	GS	CG-SHO	SV-BS	IP	H	R	HR	HB	BB-IB	SO	ERA	AERA	OAV	OOB	AB-HR-SH	AVG	PB	SUP	APR	DL	PW
1982	Tex A	10	8	.556	56	1	0	7-7	89	95	38	6	2	37-8	61	3.44	113	.279	.349	0	ø	0	47	4	0	0.9
1983	Tex A	8	13	.381	28	26	9-2	0-0	183	175	86	9	3	62-3	92	3.49	116	.250	.310	0	ø	0	88	9	29	0.9
1984	Tex A	8	12	.400	35	32	5-1	0-0	223.2	249	110	19	4	54-2	123	3.94	106	.279	.322	0	ø	0	89	6	0	0.4
1985	Mil A	8	18	.308	39	29	11-1	2-0	217.2	212	112	34	4	65-4	125	3.80	110	.254	.308	0	ø	0	73	6	0	0.5
1986	Mil A	6	8	.429	27	14	5-1	0-1	130.1	120	62	13	3	35-1	80	3.52	124	.246	.297	0	ø	0	70	10	0	1.0
	Hou N	5	2	.714	12	8	1	0-0	54.1	50	19	3	0	9-0	40	2.32	156	.239	.267	16-0-2	.063	-1	114	6	0	0.7
1987	Hou N	9	10	.474	33	30	3-1	0-0	195.2	184	87	17	5	69-12	134	3.59	110	.246	.313	66-0-1	.182	2*	102	7	0	0.8
1988	Hou N	8	13	.381	44	20	3	3-0	192	189	86	20	7	48-9	129	3.84	87	.259	.307	56-1-2	.071	-1	99	-8	0	-0.9
1989	Hou N	11	4	.733	68	0	0	7-4	122	92	34	8	2	33-9	104	2.36	144	.212	.268	17	.118	-1	—	15	0	1.9
1990	Hou N	11	4	.733	48	17	3	2-2	162.2	136	42	11	4	31-4	109	**2.21**	**169**	.225	**.266**	38-0-3	.132	1*	97	29	0	2.6
1991	Bos A	3	6	.333	12	12	0	0-0	68	71	39	15	4	15-1	42	5.16	84	.263	.309	0	ø	0	74	-4	123	-0.5
1992	Bos A	9	9	.500	51	15	2	3-3	161.1	159	76	11	5	53-9	124	3.96	107	.257	.319	0	ø	0	79	7	0	0.7
1993	Bos A	15	11	.577	34	34	2-1	0-0	229.1	196	93	31	3	49-8	130	3.26	142	.230	**.272**	0	ø	0	87	33	0	3.5
1994	Bos A	7	5	.583	13	13	0	0-0	75.2	101	54	13	1	24-6	54	6.30	80	.317	.361	0	ø	0	119	-8	57	-1.1
1995	Tor A	1	8	.111	13	11	1	0-0	65	91	60	13	3	24-2	36	7.62	62	.340	.393	0	ø	0	64	-20	0	-2.2
	Tex A	2	2	.500	7	4	0	0-0	34	40	27	12	1	7-1	22	7.15	68	.292	.331	0	ø	0	135	-7	0	-0.7
	Year	3	10	.231	20	15	1	0-0	99	131	87	25	4	31-3	58	7.45	64	.323	.373	0	ø	0	83	-29	0	-2.9
1996	Pit N	7	9	.438	19	19	0	0-0	122.1	117	48	9	6	16-0	69	3.02	145	.253	.285	39-1-5	.205	2	80	17	0	2.4
	Hou N	3	2	.600	15	6	0	0-2	42.1	43	31	7	6	11-3	27	5.95	65	.267	.331	10-0-2	.100	-0	105	-10	0	-1.1
	Year	10	11	.476	34	25	0	0-2	164.2	160	79	16	12	27-3	96	3.77	113	.257	.297	49-1-7	.184	2	86	8	0	1.3
1997	Chi A	4	8	.333	21	17	1	0-0	113.1	130	60	21	1	31-1	62	4.13	107	.286	.329	3-0-1	.000	-0	92	3	0	0.3
	SF N	1	3	.250	10	7	0	0-0	44	51	26	5	1	14-0	30	4.91	84	.288	.342	15	.133	-0	118	-4	0	-0.3
1998	SF N	8	10	.444	33	25	0	0-0	148.2	176	97	23	3	49-4	81	5.51	73	.297	.352	45-0-4	.089	-2	115	-25	0	-2.8
Total	21	171	182	.484	716	371	53-9	32-25	3016.2	2951	1431	321	81	874-101	1942	3.84	106	.256	.310	305-2-20	.128	-0	95	81	230	9.2
DARWIN, JEFF	Jeffrey Scott; B7.6.1969 Sherman TX; BR/TR/6´3˝/180; [SeaA88 13/331]; d6.13; b–Danny; Col Alvin (TX) CC																									
1994	Sea A	0	0	ø	2	0	0	0-0	4	7	6	1	1	3-1	1	13.50	37	.389	.500	0	ø	0	—	-3	0	-0.2
1996	Chi A	0	1	.000	22	0	0	0-1	30.2	26	10	5	2	9-1	15	2.93	162	.232	.301	0	ø	0	—	7	0	0.3
1997	Chi A	0	1	.000	14	0	0	0-0	13.2	17	8	1	0	7-0	9	5.27	84	.298	.369	0	ø	0	—	-1	0	-0.1
Total	3	0	2	.000	38	0	0	0-1	48.1	50	24	7	3	19-2	25	4.47	105	.267	.343	0	ø	0	—	3	0	0.0
DASHNER, LEE	Lee Claire "Lefty"; B4.25.1887 Renault IL; D12.16.1959 ElDorado KS; BB/TL/5´11.5˝/192; d8.4																									
1913	Cle A	0	0	ø	1	0	0	0	1.2	0	1	0	0	0	2	5.40	56	.000	.000	0	ø	0	—	0	—	0.0
DASSO, FRANK	Francis Joseph Nicholas; B8.31.1917 Chicago IL; BR/TR/5´11.5˝/185; d4.22; Col American International																									
1945	Cin N	4	5	.444	16	12	6	0	95.2	89	50	9	0	53	39	3.67	102	.253	.351	31-0-4	.161	-1	99	-1	0	-0.2
1946	Cin N	0	0	ø	2	0	0	0	1	2	3	0	0	2	1	27.00	12	.400	.571	0	ø	0	—	-2	0	-0.1
Total	2	4	5	.444	18	12	6	0	96.2	91	53	9	0	55	40	3.91	96	.255	.354	31-0-4	.161	-1	99	-3	0	-0.3
DAUB, DAN	Daniel William "Mickey"; B1.12.1868 Middletown OH; D3.25.1951 Bradenton FL; BR/TR/5´10˝/160; d8.31; Col Denison																									
1892	Cin N	1	2	.333	4	3	2	0	25	23	10	0	2	13	7	2.88	113	.235	.336	7	.000	-1	39	2	—	0.1
1893	Bro N	6	6	.500	12	12	12	0	103	104	64	3	5	61	25	3.84	115	.254	.358	42	.190	-2	91	7	—	0.6
1894	Bro N	10	12	.455	34	27	15	0	224	291	209	7	18	91	45	6.11	81	.311	.383	95-0-4	.189	-6	103	-29	—	-2.4
1895	Bro N	10	10	.500	25	21	16	0	184.2	212	134	5	11	51	36	4.29	103	.284	.339	71	.197	-2	100	-5	—	-0.5
1896	Bro N	12	11	.522	32	24	18	0	225	255	120	4	8	63	53	3.60	115	.283	.335	84	.226	2	95	16	—	1.6
1897	Bro N	6	11	.353	19	16	11	0	137.2	180	117	8	10	48	19	6.08	67	.313	.376	49-0-2	.224	2	105	-28	—	-2.3
Total	6	45	52	.464	126	103	74	0	899.1	1065	654	27	54	327	185	4.75	93	.291	.357	348-0-6	.201	-6	98	-37	—	-2.9
DAUSS, HOOKS	George August (b George August Daus); B9.22.1889 Indianapolis IN; D7.27.1963 St.Louis MO; BR/TR/5´10.5˝/168; d9.28																									
1912	Det A	1	1	.500	2	2	2	0	17	11	7	0	3	9	7	3.18	103	.186	.324	4	.250	1	68	1	—	0.2
1913	Det A	13	12	.520	33	29	22-2	1	225	188	96	4	13	82	107	2.48	118	.231	.311	79-0-1	.177	3*	113	8	—	1.1
1914	Det A	19	15	.559	45	35	22-3	3	302	286	126	3	18	87	150	2.86	98	.257	.321	97-1-5	.216	6*	102	0	—	0.7
1915	Det A	24	13	.649	46	35	27-1	2	309.2	261	115	1	11	115	132	2.50	121	.235	.313	103-0-5	.146	0	125	17	—	2.6
1916	Det A	19	12	.613	39	29	18-1	4	238.2	220	102	2	16	90	95	3.21	89	.257	.339	72-1-4	.222	8	117	-6	—	0.1
1917	Det A	17	14	.548	37	31	22-6	2	270.2	243	105	3	7	87	102	2.43	109	.245	.311	87-0-3	.126	-1*	105	7	—	1.0
1918	Det A	12	16	.429	33	26	21-1	3	249.2	243	105	3	9	58	73	2.99	89	.263	.313	77-0-4	.182	3	103	-10	—	-0.6
1919	Det A	21	9	.700	34	32	22-2	0	256.1	262	125	9	5	63	73	3.55	90	.267	.315	97-0-5	.144	-3	146	-9	—	-1.0
1920	Det A	13	21	.382	38	32	18	0	270.1	308	158	11	8	84	82	3.56	105	.289	.345	83-0-3	.169	1	88	-1	—	0.5
1921	Det A	10	15	.400	32	28	16	1	233	275	141	11	13	81	68	4.33	99	.297	.362	88-1-2	.261	2	106	-2	—	0.3
1922	Det A	13	13	.500	39	25	12-1	4	218.2	251	123	7	6	59	78	4.20	92	.289	.339	72-1-3	.208	3	110	-9	—	-0.6
1923	Det A	21	13	.618	50	39	22-4	3	316	331	140	10	7	78	105	3.62	107	.272	.319	104-0-6	.231	5	118	14	—	1.9
1924	Det A	12	11	.522	40	10	5	6	131.1	155	78	6	1	40	44	4.59	90	.302	.354	38-0-2	.132	-2	109	-6	—	-1.0
1925	Det A	16	11	.593	35	30	16-1	1	228	238	110	11	4	85	58	3.16	136	.272	.339	81-1-0	.185	1	114	23	—	2.4
1926	Det A	12	6	.667	35	5	0	9	124.1	135	63	6	0	49	27	4.20	97	.287	.354	42-1-2	.238	4	112	1	—	0.5
Total	15	223	182	.551	538	388	245-22	39	3390.2	3407	1594	87	121	1067	1201	3.30	103	.266	.329	1124-6-45	.189	32	112	28	—	8.1
DAVENPORT, CLAUDE	Claude Edwin "Big Dave"; B5.28.1898 Runge TX; D6.13.1976 Corpus Christi TX; BR/TR/6´6˝/193; d10.2; b–Dave																									
1920	NY N	0	0	ø	1	0	0	0	2	2	1	1	0	1	0	4.50	67	.250	.333	1	.000	-0	—	0	—	0.0
DAVENPORT, DAVE	David W.; B2.20.1890 Alexandria LA; D10.16.1954 ElDorado AR; BR/TR/6´6˝/220; d4.17; b–Claude																									
1914	Cin N	2	2	.500	10	6	3-1	2	54	38	18	1	3	30	22	2.50	117	.202	.321	18-0-1	.111	-1	106	4	—	0.2
	StL F	8	13	.381	33	26	13-2	4	215.2	204	100	3	7	80	142	3.46	88	.251	.324	68-0-3	.088	-6	79	-7	—	-1.3
1915	StL F	22	18	.550	**55**	**46**	**30-10**	1	**392.2**	300	116	5	5	96	**229**	2.20	131	**.215**	.268	130-0-7	.092	-10	101	**28**	—	1.2
1916	StL A	12	11	.522	**59**	31	13-1	2	290.2	267	112	4	8	100	129	2.85	96	.256	.326	73-0-5	.137	3	105	0	—	0.2
1917	StL A	17	17	.500	47	**39**	20-2	2	280.2	273	137	5	8	105	100	3.08	84	.260	.331	92-0-4	.098	-6	107	-17	—	-2.7
1918	StL A	10	11	.476	31	22	12-2	1	180	182	84	0	7	69	60	3.25	84	.273	.347	52-1-5	.135	1	96	-10	—	-0.9
1919	StL A	2	11	.154	24	16	5	0	123.1	135	74	4	2	41	37	3.94	84	.280	.339	39-0-3	.077	-4	78	-10	—	-1.3
Total	6	73	83	.468	259	186	96-18	12	1537	1399	641	22	40	521	719	2.93	97	.248	.316	472-1-28	.104	-23	97	-12	—	-4.6
DAVENPORT, JOE	Joseph Jonathan; B3.24.1976 Chicago IL; BR/TR/6´5˝/(220–225); [TorA94 13/371]; d7.20																									
1999	Chi A	0	0	ø	3	0	0	0-0	1.2	1	0	0	0	2-0	0	0.00	ø	.200	.429	0	ø	0	—	1	0	0.0
2001	Col N	0	0	ø	7	0	0	0-0	10.1	8	7	1	0	7-0	8	3.48	153	.222	.349	1	1.000	0	—	1	0	0.1
Total	2	0	0	ø	10	0	0	0-0	12	9	7	1	0	9-0	8	3.00	176	.220	.360	1	1.000	0	—	2	0	0.1
DAVENPORT, LUM	Joubert Lum; B6.26.1900 Tucson AZ; D4.21.1961 Dallas TX; BL/TL/6´1˝/165; d5.2; Col Arizona																									
1921	Chi A	0	3	.000	13	2	0	0	35.1	41	35	1	1	32	9	6.88	62	.318	.457	17	.412	2*	158	-12	—	-0.7
1922	Chi A	1	1	.500	9	1	0	0	16.2	14	21	2	0	13	9	10.80	38	.233	.370	3	.000	-0*	188	-12	—	-1.2
1923	Chi A	0	0	ø	2	0	0	0	4.1	7	4	0	0	4	1	6.23	64	.438	.550	1-0-1	1.000	0	—	-1	—	0.0
1924	Chi A	0	0	ø	1	0	0	0	2	1	1	0	0	2	1	0.00	ø	.125	.300	0	ø	0	—	1	—	0.0
Total	4	1	4	.200	25	3	0	0	58.1	63	61	3	1	51	20	7.71	54	.296	.434	21-0-1	.381	2	168	-24	—	-1.9
DAVEY, MIKE	Michael Gerard; B6.2.1952 Spokane WA; BR/TL/6´2˝/190; [AtlN74*S2/32]; d8.13; Col Gonzaga																									
1977	Atl N	0	0	ø	16	0	0	2-0	16	19	9	1	0	9-4	7	5.06	88	.302	.389	1	.000	-0	—	0	0	0.0
1978	Atl N	0	0	ø	3	0	0	0-0	2.2	1	0	0	0	1-0	0	0.00	ø	.125	.222	0	ø	0	—	1	0	0.0
Total	2	0	0	ø	19	0	0	2-0	18.2	20	9	1	0	10-4	7	4.34	101	.282	.370	1	.000	-0	—	1	0	0.0
DAVEY, TOM	Thomas Joseph; B9.11.1973 Garden City MI; BR/TR/6´7˝/230; [TorA94 5/147]; d4.6; Col Henry Ford (MI) CC																									
1999	Tor A	1	1	.500	29	0	0	1-0	44	40	28	5	3	26-0	42	4.70	105	.241	.350	0	ø	0	—	0	0	0.0
	Sea A	1	0	1.000	16	0	0	0-0	21	22	13	0	4	14-1	17	4.71	102	.268	.400	0	ø	0	—	0	0	0.0
	Year	2	1	.667	45	0	0	1-0	65	62	41	5	7	40-1	59	4.71	104	.250	.367	0	ø	0	—	-1	0	0.0
2000	SD N	2	1	.667	11	0	0	0-1	12.2	12	1	0	0	2-0	6	0.71	627	.250	.280	0	ø	0	—	6	0	1.1
2001	SD N	2	4	.333	39	0	0	0-4	38	41	22	3	1	17-3	37	4.50	92	.272	.349	0	ø	0	—	-2	72	-0.2
2002	SD N	1	0	1.000	19	0	0	0-1	21	23	14	2	3	11-1	21	5.57	70	.287	.381	0	ø	0	—	-4	45	-0.2
Total	4	7	6	.538	114	0	0	1-6	136.2	138	78	10	11	70-5	123	4.41	101	.262	.357	0	ø	0	—	0	117	0.7

YEAR	TM LG	W	L	PCT	G	GS	CG-SHO	SV-BS	IP	H	R	HR	HB	BB-IB	SO	ERA	AERA	OAV	OOB	AB-HR-SH	AVG	PB	SUP	APR	DL	PW
Daviault, Ray	Raymond Joseph Robert; B5.27.1934 Montreal QC, Can.; BR/TR/6´1˝/170; d4.13																									
1962	NY N	1	5	.167	36	3	0	0	81	92	64	14	4	48-1	51	6.22	67	.288	.384	15	.067	-1	91	-16	0	-1.2
Davidson, Bob	Robert Banks; B1.6.1963 Bad Kurznach, West Germany; BR/TR/6´0˝/185; [NYA84 24/615]; d7.15; Col East Carolina																									
1989	NY A	0	0	ø	1	0	0	0-0	1	1	2	1	0	1-0	0	18.00	22	.250	.400	0	ø	0	—	-1	0	-0.1
Davidson, Ted	Thomas Eugene; B10.4.1939 Las Vegas NV; D9.1.2006 Bullhead City AZ; BR/TL/6´0˝/(180–192); d7.24; Col Hancock (CA) JC																									
1965	Cin N	4	3	.571	24	1	0	1	68.2	57	21	5	2	17-4	54	2.23	168	.233	.285	17-0-2	.000	-2	140	10	0	0.9
1966	Cin N	5	4	.556	54	0	0	4	85.1	82	41	11	1	23-2	54	3.90	100	.253	.302	12	.000	-1	—	0	0	-0.2
1967	Cin N	1	0	1.000	9	0	0	0	13	13	6	0	0	3-1	6	4.15	90	.250	.291	0	ø	0	—	0	62	0.0
1968	Cin N	1	0	1.000	23	0	0	0	21.2	27	15	3	0	7-0	7	6.23	51	.307	.358	2	.000	-0	—	-6	0	-0.4
	Atl N	0	0	ø	4	0	0	0	6.2	10	5	2	0	4-1	3	6.75	44	.345	.424	0	ø	0	—	-2	0	-0.1
	Year	1	0	1.000	27	0	0	0	28.1	37	20	5	0	11-1	10	6.35	49	.316	.375	2	.000	0	—	-9	0	-0.5
Total	4	11	7	.611	114	1	0	5	195.1	189	88	21	3	54-8	124	3.69	101	.256	.307	31-0-2	.000	-3	140	2	62	0.2
Davie, Jerry	Gerald Lee; B2.10.1933 Detroit MI; BR/TR/6´0˝/185; d4.14																									
1959	Det A	2	2	.500	11	5	1	0	36.2	40	25	8	4	17-1	20	4.17	97	.265	.351	10	.400	2	100	-3	0	-0.1
Davies, George	George Washington; B2.22.1868 Portage WI; D9.22.1906 Waterloo WI; ?/180; d8.18; Col Wisconsin–Madison																									
1891	Mil AA	7	5	.583	12	12	12-1	0	102	94	48	2	3	35	61	2.65	166	.237	.303	37	.243	1	67	18	—	1.8
1892	Cle N	10	16	.385	26	26	23	0	215.2	201	112	4	6	69	95	2.59	131	.237	.299	87	.138	-5	69	17	—	1.3
1893	Cle N	0	2	.000	3	3	1	0	15	28	25	1	0	10	3	11.40	43	.389	.463	6	.333	-0	110	-9	—	-0.8
	NY N	1	1	.500	5	1	1	0	36.1	41	31	1	0	13	7	6.19	75	.275	.333	12	.333	2	120	-4	—	0.0
	Year	1	3	.250	8	4	2	0	51.1	69	56	2	0	23	10	7.71	61	.312	.377	18	.333	2	115	-13	—	-0.8
Total	3	18	24	.429	46	42	37-1	0	369	364	216	8	9	127	166	3.32	116	.248	.312	142	.190	-3	73	22	—	2.3
Davies, Kyle	Hiram Kyle; B9.9.1983 Decatur GA; BR/TR/6´2˝/205; [AtlN01 4/135]; d5.21																									
2005	Atl N	7	6	.538	21	14	0	0-1	87.2	98	51	8	1	49-5	62	4.93	86	.280	.370	15-0-10	.200	1	116	-7	0	-0.9
2006	Atl N	3	7	.300	14	14	1	0-0	63.1	90	60	14	3	33-0	51	8.38	54	.332	.408	23-1-1	.043	-1	125	-25	108	-3.1
Total	2	10	13	.435	35	28	1	0-1	151	188	111	22	4	82-5	113	6.38	68	.303	.386	38-1-11	.105	-0	122	-32	108	-4.0
Davies, Chick	Lloyd Garrison; B3.6.1892 Peabody MA; D9.5.1973 Middletown CT; BL/TL/5´8˝/145; d7.11; Col Massachusetts; ▲																									
1914	Phi A	1	0	1.000	1	1	1	0	9	8	4	0	0	3	4	1.00	261	.258	.324	46-0-3	.239	0*	167	0	—	0.1
1915	Phi A	1	2	.333	4	2	0	0	15.1	20	16	0	1	12	2	8.80	33	.339	.458	132-0-5	.182	0*	125	-8	—	-1.3
1925	NY N	0	0	ø	2	1	0	0	7.1	13	8	0	0	4	5	6.14	66	.361	.425	6	.000	-0*	188	-3	—	-0.1
1926	NY N	2	4	.333	38	1	0	**6**	89	96	60	3	0	35	27	3.94	95	.277	.344	18	.222	1	44	-8	—	-0.5
Total	4	4	6	.400	45	5	1	6	120.2	137	88	3	1	54	38	4.48	80	.290	.364	202-0-8	.193	1	123	-19	—	-1.8
Davis, Curt	Curtis Benton "Coonskin"; B9.7.1903 Greenfield MO; D10.12.1965 Covina CA; BR/TR/6´2˝/185; d4.21																									
1934	Phi N	19	17	.528	**51**	31	18-3	5	274.1	283	114	14	7	60	99	2.95	160	.269	.313	95-1-7	.211	-2	71	43	—	5.7
1935	Phi N	16	14	.533	44	27	19-3	2	231	264	103	14	7	47	74	3.66	124	.285	.324	75-1-4	.173	-1*	70	23	—	2.8
1936	Phi N	2	4	.333	10	8	3	0	60.1	71	37	6	1	19	18	4.62	98	.291	.345	26	.154	-1*	94	0	—	-0.1
	Chi N★	11	9	.550	24	20	10	1	153	146	60	11	1	31	52	3.00	133	.251	.290	53-0-6	.151	-2	102	15	—	1.8
	Year	13	13	.500	34	28	13	1	213.1	217	97	17	2	50	70	3.46	120	.263	.307	79-0-6	.152	-3	99	17	—	1.7
1937	Chi N	10	5	.667	28	14	8	1	123.2	138	64	7	5	30	32	4.08	98	.286	.334	40-1-5	.300	4	122	-2	—	0.2
1938	StL N	12	8	.600	40	21	8-2	3	173.1	187	80	9	1	27	36	3.63	109	.272	.301	57-3-4	.228	2	99	8	—	1.1
1939	StL N☆	22	16	.579	49	31	13-3	7	248	279	121	18	3	48	70	3.63	113	.280	.315	105-1-7	.381	12*	108	10	—	2.8
1940	StL N	0	4	.000	14	7	0	1	54	73	34	4	1	19	12	5.17	77	.327	.383	19-0-1	.000	-2	65	-6	—	-0.6
	Bro N	8	7	.533	22	18	9	2	137	135	62	13	1	19	46	3.81	105	.256	.283	47-1-4	.128	-1	110	4	—	0.4
	Year	8	11	.421	36	25	9	3	191	208	96	17	2	38	58	4.19	95	.277	.314	66-1-5	.091	-3	97	-1	—	-0.2
1941	†Bro N	13	7	.650	28	16	10-5	2	154.1	141	58	6	2	27	50	2.97	123	.244	.280	59-2-5	.186	2*	137	12	0	1.9
1942	Bro N	15	6	.714	32	26	13-5	2	206	179	62	10	7	51	60	2.36	138	.233	.287	68-0-8	.176	-0	129	21	0	2.3
1943	Bro N	10	13	.435	31	21	8-2	3	164.1	182	85	8	2	39	47	3.78	89	.281	.324	55-0-4	.164	-1	123	-11	0	-1.4
1944	Bro N	10	11	.476	31	23	12-1	4	194	207	84	12	5	39	49	3.34	106	.270	.310	63-0-6	.159	-2	90	5	0	0.4
1945	Bro N	10	10	.500	24	18	10	0	149.2	171	66	9	3	21	39	3.25	116	.280	.308	51-1-2	.137	-1	101	9	0	1.0
1946	Bro N	0	0	ø	1	0	0	0	2	3	3	1	1	2	0	13.50	25	.375	.545	0	ø	0	—	-2	0	-0.1
Total	13	158	131	.547	429	281	141-24	33	2325	2459	1033	142	47	479	684	3.42	116	.270	.310	813-11-63	.203	7	100	129	0	18.2
Davis, Doug	Douglas; B9.21.1975 Sacramento CA; BR/TL/6´4˝/(185–215); [TexA96 10/293]; d8.9; Col San Francisco (CA) City																									
1999	Tex A	0	0	ø	2	0	0	0-0	2.2	12	10	3	0	0-0	3	33.75	15	.600	.600	0	ø	0	—	-8	0	-0.3
2000	Tex A	7	6	.538	30	13	1	0-3	98.2	109	61	14	3	58-3	66	5.38	95	.288	.383	0	ø	0	108	-1	0	-0.1
2001	Tex A	11	10	.524	30	30	1	0-0	186	220	103	14	3	69-1	115	4.45	107	.295	.354	3-0-1	.000	-0	99	4	0	0.3
2002	Tex A	3	5	.375	10	10	1-1	0-0	59.2	67	36	7	3	22-0	28	4.98	96	.290	.355	0	ø	0	89	-2	0	-0.2
2003	Tex A	0	0	ø	1	1	0	0-0	3	4	4	2	0	4-0	2	12.00	41	.308	.471	0	ø	0	93	-2	0	-0.1
	Tor A	4	6	.400	12	11	0	0-0	54	70	33	6	1	26-1	25	5.00	95	.318	.393	1	.000	-0	109	-1	0	-0.2
	Year	4	6	.400	13	12	0	0-0	57	74	37	8	1	30-1	27	5.37	89	.318	.398	1	.000	-0	108	-3	0	-0.3
	Mil N	3	2	.600	8	8	1	0-0	52.1	49	18	8	0	21-0	35	2.58	167	.247	.317	20-0-1	.100	-1	81	9	0	0.7
2004	Mil N	12	12	.500	34	34	0	0-0	207.1	192	84	14	7	79-3	166	3.39	130	.247	.320	64-0-6	.016	-6	85	24	0	1.9
2005	Mil N	11	11	.500	35	**35**	2-1	0-0	222.2	196	103	26	4	93-5	208	3.84	111	.235	.314	73-0-2	.137	-1	105	11	0	0.9
2006	Mil N	11	11	.500	34	34	1-1	0-0	203.1	206	118	19	5	102-1	159	4.91	91	.266	.352	65-0-11	.046	-4	111	-8	0	-1.2
Total	8	62	63	.496	196	176	7-3	0-3	1089.2	1125	570	113	26	474-14	807	4.35	104	.268	.344	226-0-21	.071	-13	100	26	0	1.7
Davis, Dixie	Frank Talmadge; B10.12.1890 Wilsons Mills NC; D2.4.1944 Raleigh NC; BR/TR/5´11˝/155; d7.12; Mil 1918																									
1912	Cin N	0	1	.000	7	0	0	0	26.2	25	17	0	1	16	12	2.70	124	.258	.368	10	.200	-0	—	0	—	-0.1
1915	Chi A	0	0	ø	2	0	0	0	3	2	0	0	1	2	2	0.00	ø	.250	.455	0	ø	0	—	1	—	0.1
1918	Phi N	0	2	.000	17	2	1	0	47	43	25	1	0	30	18	3.06	98	.247	.358	9	.000	-0*	101	-2	—	-0.2
1920	StL A	18	12	.600	38	31	22	0	269.1	250	117	10	7	149	85	3.17	123	.256	.359	94-0-7	.266	3	110	22	—	2.2
1921	StL A	16	16	.500	40	36	20-2	0	265.1	279	150	12	10	123	100	4.44	101	.281	.366	95-0-4	.211	-3	99	4	—	0.0
1922	StL A	11	6	.647	25	25	7-2	0	174.1	162	91	10	8	87	65	4.08	102	**.250**	.345	59-0-6	.136	-3	111	3	—	0.0
1923	StL A	4	6	.400	19	17	5-1	0	109.1	106	61	4	5	63	36	3.62	115	.259	.365	40-0-1	.250	0	77	3	—	0.2
1924	StL A	11	13	.458	29	24	11-5	0	160.1	159	84	9	6	72	45	4.10	110	.263	.347	46-0-7	.152	-2	85	8	—	0.7
1925	StL A	12	7	.632	35	22	9	1	180.1	192	121	10	6	106	58	4.59	102	.279	.380	64-0-5	.172	-4	108	-3	—	-0.6
1926	StL A	3	8	.273	27	7	2	1	83	93	56	7	1	40	39	4.66	92	.292	.372	24	.167	-0	76	-5	—	-0.6
Total	10	75	71	.514	239	164	77-10	2	1318.2	1311	722	63	45	688	460	3.97	107	.267	.362	441-0-30	.197	-10	99	31	—	1.7
Davis, George	George Allen "Iron"; B3.9.1890 Lancaster NY; D6.4.1961 Buffalo NY; BB/TR/5´10.5˝/175; d7.16; Col Williams																									
1912	NY A	1	4	.200	10	7	5	0	54	61	43	3	3	28	22	6.50	55	.293	.385	18	.111	-1	111	-12	—	-1.1
1913	Bos N	0	0	ø	2	0	0	0	8	7	5	1	0	5	3	4.50	73	.241	.353	2	.000	-0	—	-1	—	-0.1
1914	Bos N	3	3	.500	9	6	4-1	0	55.2	42	25	1	3	26	26	3.40	81	.215	.317	18	.167	0	117	-3	—	-0.4
1915	Bos N	3	3	.500	15	9	4	0	73.1	85	45	2	4	19	26	3.80	68	.304	.356	23-0-1	.261	1	134	-12	—	-0.8
Total	4	7	10	.412	36	22	13-1	0	191	195	118	7	10	78	77	4.48	66	.274	.354	61-0-1	.180	-0	122	-28	—	-2.4
Davis, Storm	George Earl; B12.26.1961 Dallas TX; BR/TR/6´4˝/(194–225); [BalA79 7/175]; d4.29																									
1982	Bal A	8	4	.667	29	8	1	0-1	100.2	96	40	8	0	28-4	67	3.49	117	.257	.304	0	ø	0	121	7	0	0.8
1983	†Bal A	13	7	.650	34	29	6-1	0-0	200.1	180	90	14	2	64-4	125	3.59	111	.238	.298	0	ø	0	121	9	0	0.7
1984	Bal A	14	9	.609	35	31	10-2	1-1	225	205	86	7	5	71-6	105	3.12	125	.247	.307	0	ø	0	98	21	0	1.9
1985	Bal A	10	8	.556	31	28	8-1	0-0	175	172	92	11	1	70-5	93	4.53	90	.256	.325	0	ø	0	121	-7	0	-0.7
1986	Bal A	9	12	.429	25	25	2	0-0	154	166	70	16	0	49-2	96	3.62	115	.275	.329	0	ø	0	86	9	18	1.1
1987	SD N	2	7	.222	21	10	0	0-0	62.2	70	48	5	2	36-6	37	6.18	64	.280	.372	16-0-1	.063	-1	71	-16	48	-2.0
	Oak A	1	1	.500	5	5	0	0-0	30.1	28	13	3	0	11-0	28	3.26	127	.241	.305	0	ø	0	140	3	0	0.1
1988	†Oak A	16	7	.696	33	33	1	0-0	201.2	211	86	16	1	91-2	127	3.70	103	.274	.349	0	ø	0	127	4	0	0.4
1989	†Oak A	19	7	.731	31	31	1	0-0	169.1	187	91	19	3	68-1	91	4.36	85	.288	.354	0	ø	0	137	-12	23	-1.7
1990	KC A	7	10	.412	21	20	0	0-0	112	129	66	9	0	35-1	62	4.74	81	.281	.330	0	ø	0	110	-10	37	-1.5
1991	KC A	3	9	.250	51	9	1-1	2-1	114.1	140	69	11	1	46-9	53	4.96	84	.306	.367	0	ø	0	81	-9	0	-1.0
1992	Bal A	7	3	.700	48	2	0	4-3	89.1	79	35	5	2	36-6	53	3.43	119	.244	.320	0	ø	0	56	7	15	0.8

YEAR	TM LG	W	L	PCT	G	GS	CG-SHO	SV-BS	IP	H	R	HR	HB	BB-IB	SO	ERA	AERA	OAV	OOB	AB-HR-SH	AVG	PB	SUP	APR	DL	PW
1993	Oak A	2	6	.250	19	8	0	0-0	62.2	68	45	5	2	33-2	37	6.18	67	.276	.364	0	ø	0	92	-14	0	-1.5
	Det A	0	2	.000	24	0	0	4-1	35.1	25	12	4	1	15-4	36	3.06	143	.198	.287	0	ø	0	—	6	0	0.4
	Year	2	8	.200	43	8	0	4-1	98	93	57	9	3	48-6	73	5.05	84	.250	.338	0	ø	0	90	-7	0	-1.1
1994	Det A	2	4	.333	35	0	0	0-1	48	36	23	3	0	34-7	38	3.56	138	.207	.335	0	ø	0	—	6	0	0.7
Total	13	113	96	.541	442	239	30-5	11-8	1780.2	1792	866	136	20	687-59	1048	4.02	100	.263	.330	16-0-1	.063	-1	110	4	141	-1.5
Davis, Jim	James Bennett; B9.15.1924 Red Bluff CA; D11.30.1995 San Mateo CA; BB/TL/6´0˝/180; d4.18																									
1954	Chi N	11	7	.611	46	12	2	4	127.2	114	57	12	3	51	58	3.52	119	.247	.321	32	.063	-1	99	9	0	1.1
1955	Chi N	7	11	.389	42	16	0	3	133.2	122	79	16	2	58-5	62	4.44	92	.246	.323	37-0-3	.027	-4	63	-8	0	-1.4
1956	Chi N	5	7	.417	46	11	2-1	2	120.1	116	56	11	6	59-4	66	3.66	103	.256	.347	28-0-3	.179	-0	68	2	0	0.2
1957	StL N	0	1	.000	10	0	0	1	13.2	18	8	1	0	6-0	5	5.27	75	.340	.400	1	.000	-0	—	-2	0	-0.1
	NY N	1	0	1.000	10	0	0	0	11	13	9	2	0	5-1	6	6.55	60	.283	.353	1	1.000	0	—	-3	0	-0.2
	Year	1	1	.500	20	0	0	1	24.2	31	17	3	0	11-1	11	5.84	68	.313	.378	2	.500	0	—	-5	0	-0.3
Total	4	24	26	.480	154	39	4-1	10	406.1	383	209	42	11	179-10	197	4.01	100	.253	.333	99-0-6	.091	-5	76	-2	0	-0.4
Davis, Jason	Jason Thomas; B5.8.1980 Chattanooga TN; BR/TR/6´6˝/(195–230); [CleA99 21/647]; d9.9; Col Cleveland St. (TN) CC																									
2002	Cle A	1	0	1.000	3	2	0	0-0	14.2	12	3	1	0	4-0	11	1.84	241	.218	.271	0	ø	0	83	4	0	0.3
2003	Cle A	8	11	.421	27	27	1	0-0	165.1	172	101	25	8	47-4	85	4.68	95	.273	.329	2-0-1	.000	-0*	89	-6	0	-0.6
2004	Cle A	2	7	.222	26	19	0	0-0	114.1	148	81	13	4	51-1	72	5.51	79	.311	.381	5-1-0	.200	1	109	-18	0	-1.0
2005	Cle A	4	2	.667	11	4	0	0-0	40.1	44	22	4	3	20-0	32	4.69	89	.282	.368	2-0-1	.000	-0	139	-2	0	-0.3
2006	Cle A	3	2	.600	39	0	0	1-2	55.1	67	28	1	3	14-2	37	3.74	116	.302	.346	0	ø	0	—	3	0	0.2
Total	5	18	22	.450	106	52	1	1-2	390	443	235	44	18	136-7	237	4.68	93	.288	.350	9-1-2	.111	1	100	-19	0	-1.4
Davis, Joel	Joel Clark; B1.30.1965 Jacksonville FL; BL/TR/6´5˝/205; [ChiA83 1/13]; d8.11																									
1985	Chi A	3	3	.500	12	11	1	0-0	71.1	71	34	6	1	26-0	37	4.16	104	.256	.320	0	ø	0	103	2	0	0.1
1986	Chi A	4	5	.444	19	19	1	0-0	105.1	115	64	9	1	51-0	54	4.70	92	.280	.359	0	ø	0	87	-5	0	-0.4
1987	Chi A	1	5	.167	13	9	1	0-1	55	56	35	7	0	29-1	25	5.73	81	.264	.351	0	ø	0	72	-5	0	-0.5
1988	Chi A	0	1	.000	5	2	0	0-0	16	21	12	4	0	5-0	10	6.75	59	.328	.371	0	ø	0	68	-4	0	-0.2
Total	4	8	14	.364	49	41	3	0-1	247.2	263	145	26	2	111-1	126	4.91	89	.273	.347	0	ø	0	87	-12	0	-1.0
Davis, Daisy	John Henry Albert; B11.28.1858 Boston MA; D11.5.1902 Lynn MA; TR/5´6.5˝/150; d5.6																									
1884	StL AA	10	12	.455	25	24	20-1	0	198.1	196	113	1	14	35	143	2.90	112	.249	.293	87	.172	-2	85	9	—	0.5
	Bos N	1	3	.250	4	4	3	0	31	50	36	2	—	8	13	7.84	37	.355	.389	16	.000	-3	87	-15	—	-1.5
1885	Bos N	5	6	.455	11	11	10-1	0	94.1	110	58	2	—	28	30	4.29	63	.280	.328	37	.189	-0	90	-11	—	-1.1
Total	2	16	21	.432	40	39	33-2	0	323.2	356	207	5	14	71	186	3.78	81	.269	.313	140	.157	-5	87	-17	—	-2.1
Davis, John	John Kirk; B1.5.1963 Chicago IL; BR/TR/6´7˝/215; [KCA81 7/178]; d7.24																									
1987	KC A	5	2	.714	27	0	0	2-1	43.2	29	13	0	2	26-4	24	2.27	203	.195	.315	0	ø	0	—	11	0	1.6
1988	Chi A	2	5	.286	34	1	0	1-3	63.2	77	58	5	4	50-10	37	6.64	60	.297	.413	0	ø	0	46	-20	0	-2.0
1989	Chi A	0	1	.000	4	0	0	1-0	6	5	4	2	0	2-0	5	4.50	85	.217	.280	0	ø	0	—	-1	0	-0.1
1990	SD N	0	1	.000	6	0	0	0-0	9.1	9	7	1	0	4-0	7	5.79	66	.257	.333	1	.000	-0	—	-2	0	-0.2
Total	4	7	9	.438	71	1	0	4-4	122.2	120	82	8	6	82-14	73	4.92	85	.258	.370	1	.000	-0	46	-12	0	-0.7
Davis, Bud	John Wilbur "Country"; B12.7.1895 Merry Point VA; D5.26.1967 Williamsburg VA; BL/TR/6´0˝/207; d4.19																									
1915	Phi A	0	2	.000	18	2	2	0	66.2	65	53	1	6	59	18	4.05	72	.273	.429	26	.308	2*	62	-13	—	-0.4
Davis, Lance	Johnny Lance; B9.1.1976 Winter Haven FL; BR/TL/6´0˝/167; [CinN95 16/447]; d6.16; [DL 2002 Cin N 26]																									
2001	Cin N	8	4	.667	20	20	1	0-0	106.1	124	60	12	1	34-0	53	4.74	97	.294	.348	33-0-4	.121	-1*	106	-1	0	-0.1
Davis, Kane	Kane Thomas; B6.25.1975 Ripley WV; BR/TR/6´3˝/(190–194); [PitN93 13/374]; d6.12; [DL 1998 Pit N 31]																									
2000	Cle A	0	3	.000	5	2	0	0-0	11	20	21	3	1	8-0	2	14.73	34	.385	.475	1	.000	-0	56	-13	0	-1.9
	Mil N	0	0	ø	3	0	0	0-0	4	7	3	1	1	5-0	2	6.75	68	.389	.542	0	ø	0	—	-1	0	0.0
2001	Col N	2	4	.333	57	0	0	0-5	68.1	66	36	11	1	32-4	47	4.35	123	.252	.331	5	.000	-1	—	6	29	0.4
2002	NY N	1	1	.500	16	0	0	0-0	14	15	11	2	1	11-2	24	7.07	56	.273	.397	0	ø	0	—	-4	140	-0.6
2005	Mil N	1	1	.500	15	0	0	0-2	16.2	10	6	2	0	10-0	11	2.70	157	.167	.286	0	ø	0	—	3	0	0.3
Total	4	4	9	.308	96	2	0	0-7	114	118	77	19	4	66-6	86	5.53	90	.264	.360	6	.000	-1	56	-9	200	-1.8
Davis, Mark	Mark William; B10.19.1960 Livermore CA; BL/TL/6´4˝/(180–215); [PhiN79*S1/1]; d9.12; C3; Col Chabot (CA) JC																									
1980	Phi N	0	0	ø	2	1	0	0-0	7	4	2	0	0	5-0	5	2.57	149	.160	.300	2	.500	0	164	1	0	0.1
1981	Phi N	1	4	.200	9	9	0	0-0	43	49	37	7	0	24-0	29	7.74	47	.299	.380	11-0-1	.091	-0	92	-17	0	-1.7
1983	SF N	6	4	.600	20	20	2-2	0-0	111	93	51	14	3	50-4	83	3.49	102	.227	.313	30-0-9	.133	0	125	0	0	0.1
1984	SF N	5	17	.227	46	27	1	0-2	174.2	201	113	25	5	54-12	124	5.36	66	.293	.344	46-0-6	.130	0	100	-34	0	-3.9
1985	SF N	5	12	.294	77	1	0	7-9	114.1	89	49	13	3	41-7	131	3.54	98	.219	.294	12-0-4	.250	1	51	0	0	0.1
1986	SF N	5	7	.417	67	2	0	4-3	84.1	63	33	6	1	34-7	90	2.99	118	.212	.291	8	.125	0	50	5	0	0.7
1987	SF N	4	5	.444	20	11	1	0-1	70.2	72	38	9	4	28-1	51	4.71	82	.273	.349	23-0-2	.217	2*	120	-6	0	-0.5
	SD N	5	3	.625	43	0	0	2-1	62.1	51	26	5	2	31-7	47	3.18	125	.224	.322	7	.286	0	—	5	0	0.7
	Year	9	8	.529	63	11	1	2-2	133	123	64	14	6	59-8	98	3.99	98	.250	.336	30-0-2	.233	2	118	0	0	0.2
1988	SD N★	5	10	.333	62	0	0	28-6	98.1	70	24	2	0	42-11	102	2.01	169	.199	.284	10-1-1	.200	1	—	16	0	3.6
1989	SD N★	4	3	.571	70	0	0	**44**-4	92.2	66	21	6	2	31-1	92	1.85	190	.200	.270	13	.000	-1	—	17	0	2.7
1990	KC A	2	7	.222	53	3	0	6-4	68.2	71	43	9	4	52-3	73	5.11	76	.259	.383	0	ø	0	118	-9	26	-1.2
1991	KC A	6	3	.667	29	5	0	1-1	62.2	55	36	6	1	39-0	47	4.45	93	.240	.347	0	ø	0	93	-3	63	-0.3
1992	KC A	1	3	.250	13	6	0	0-0	36.1	42	31	6	0	28-0	19	7.18	57	.294	.400	0	ø	0	112	-12	0	-1.1
	Atl N	1	0	1.000	14	0	0	0-0	16.2	22	13	3	1	13-2	15	7.02	52	.314	.424	1	.000	-0	—	-5	0	-0.3
1993	Phi N	1	2	.333	25	0	0	0-1	31.1	35	22	4	1	24-1	28	5.17	77	.273	.392	3	.333	0	—	-5	0	-0.4
	SD N	0	3	.000	35	0	0	4-2	38.1	44	15	6	0	20-6	42	3.52	117	.295	.376	1-0-1	.000	-0	—	3	0	0.3
	Year	1	5	.167	60	0	0	4-3	69.2	79	37	10	1	44-7	70	4.26	95	.285	.384	4-0-1	.250	0	—	-2	0	-0.1
1994	SD N	0	1	.000	20	0	0	0-0	16.1	20	18	4	0	13-1	15	8.82	47	.299	.412	0	ø	0	—	-9	0	-0.5
1997	Mil A	0	0	ø	19	0	0	0-1	16.1	21	10	4	1	5-0	14	5.51	84	.323	.380	0	ø	0	—	-1	0	0.0
Total	15	51	84	.378	624	85	4-2	96-35	1145	1068	582	129	28	534-63	1007	4.17	89	.249	.333	167-1-24	.156	4	107	-54	89	-1.6
Davis, Bob	Robert Edward; B9.11.1933 New York NY; D12.22.2001 New York NY; BR/TR/6´0˝/170; d7.26; Col Yale																									
1958	KC A	0	4	.000	8	4	0	0	31	45	28	5	2	12-0	22	7.84	50	.346	.410	6-0-1	.167	-0	75	-12	0	-1.3
1960	KC A	0	0	ø	21	0	0	1	32	31	15	1	1	22-1	28	3.66	109	.263	.383	4	.250	0	—	1	0	0.1
Total	2	0	4	.000	29	4	0	1	63	76	43	6	3	34-1	50	5.71	69	.306	.396	10-0-1	.200	-0	75	-11	0	-1.2
Davis, Ron	Ronald Gene; B8.6.1955 Houston TX; BR/TR/6´4˝/(196–207); [ChiN76*3/56]; d7.29; Col Blinn (TX) JC																									
1978	NY A	0	0	ø	4	0	0	0-0	2.1	3	4	0	0	3-0	0	11.57	32	.333	.500	0	ø	0	—	-2	0	-0.1
1979	NY A	14	2	.875	44	0	0	9-10	85.1	84	29	5	1	28-9	43	2.85	145	.262	.320	1	.000	-0	—	13	0	2.5
1980	†NY A	9	3	.750	53	0	0	7-2	131	121	50	9	5	32-3	65	2.95	134	.246	.296	1	.000	-0	—	14	0	1.4
1981	†NY A★	4	5	.444	43	0	0	6-2	73	47	22	6	0	25-3	83	2.71	133	.186	.256	0	ø	0	—	9	0	1.2
1982	Min A	3	9	.250	63	0	0	22-5	106	106	53	16	1	47-12	89	4.42	97	.261	.338	0	ø	0	—	0	0	-0.1
1983	Min A	5	8	.385	66	0	0	30-3	89	89	34	6	3	33-3	84	3.34	128	.266	.332	0	ø	0	—	10	0	1.9
1984	Min A	7	11	.389	64	0	0	29-14	83	79	44	11	2	41-9	74	4.55	93	.253	.338	0	ø	0	—	-2	0	-0.4
1985	Min A	2	6	.250	57	0	0	25-3	64.2	55	28	7	4	35-6	72	3.48	127	.230	.333	0	ø	0	—	6	0	1.1
1986	Min A	2	6	.250	36	0	0	2-4	38.2	55	42	7	4	29-8	30	9.08	48	.340	.449	0	ø	0	—	-19	0	-3.5
	Chi N	0	2	.000	17	0	0	0-0	20	31	18	3	0	3-0	10	7.65	53	.356	.374	2	.000	-0	—	-7	0	-0.7
1987	Chi N	0	0	ø	21	0	0	0-0	32.1	43	23	8	0	12-1	31	5.85	74	.328	.382	0	ø	0	—	-5	21	-0.3
	LA N	0	0	ø	4	0	0	0-0	4	7	4	0	1	6-2	1	6.75	59	.412	.560	0	ø	0	—	-2	0	-0.1
	Year	0	0	ø	25	0	0	0-0	36.1	50	27	8	1	18-3	32	5.94	72	.338	.408	0	ø	0	—	-6	0	-0.4
1988	SF N	1	1	.500	9	0	0	0-0	17.1	15	10	4	1	6-0	15	4.67	70	.234	.310	2	.000	-0	—	-3	0	-0.3
Total	11	47	53	.470	481	0	0	130-43	746.2	735	361	82	22	300-56	597	4.05	102	.260	.332	6	.000	-1	—	12	21	2.6
Davis, Peaches	Roy Thomas; B5.31.1905 Glen Rose TX; D4.28.1995 Duncan OK; BL/TR/6´3.5˝/190; d7.11																									
1936	Cin N	8	8	.500	26	15	5	5	125.2	139	62	7	2	36	32	3.58	107	.280	.331	43-0-1	.163	-1	101	2	—	0.2
1937	Cin N	11	13	.458	42	24	11-1	3	218	252	105	5	2	51	59	3.59	104	.295	.337	78-0-3	.128	-4	105	3	—	-0.3
1938	Cin N	7	12	.368	29	19	11-1	1	167.2	193	86	9	1	40	28	3.97	92	.290	.331	61-0-3	.246	1	98	-7	—	-0.7

YEAR	TM LG	W	L	PCT	G	GS	CG-SHO	SV-BS	IP	H	R	HR	HB	BB-IB	SO	ERA	AERA	OAV	OOB	AB-HR-SH	AVG	PB	SUP	APR	DL	PW
1939	Cin N	1	0	1.000	20	0	0	2	30.2	43	24	5	1	11	4	6.46	59	.341	.399	3	.333	0	—	-8	—	-0.4
Total	4	27	33	.450	117	58	27-2	11	542	627	277	26	6	138	123	3.87	96	.293	.337	185-0-7	.178	-4	101	-10	—	-1.2
Davis, Steve	Steven Kennon; B8.4.1960 San Antonio TX; BL/TL/6´1˝/(170–185); [TorA82 21/523]; d8.25; Col Texas A&M																									
1985	Tor A	2	1	.667	10	5	0	0-0	28	23	14	5	0	13-0	22	3.54	120	.223	.308	0	ø	0	133	1	0	0.1
1986	Tor A	0	0	ø	3	0	0	0-0	3.2	8	7	2	0	5-1	5	17.18	25	.471	.591	0	ø	0	—	-5	0	-0.2
1989	Cle A	1	1	.500	12	2	0	0-0	25.2	34	24	2	0	14-1	12	8.06	49	.318	.397	0	ø	0	102	-11	0	-0.7
Total	3	3	2	.600	25	7	0	0-0	57.1	65	45	9	0	32-2	39	6.44	64	.286	.373	0	ø	0	126	-15	0	-0.8
Davis, Tim	Timothy Howard; B7.14.1970 Marianna FL; BL/TL/5´11˝/165; [SeaA92 6/166]; d4.4; Col Florida St.; [DL 1998 Sea A 181]																									
1994	Sea A	2	2	.500	42	1	0	2-2	49.1	57	25	4	1	25-5	28	4.01	123	.295	.374	0	ø	0	205	5	0	0.4
1995	Sea A	2	1	.667	5	5	0	0-0	24	30	21	2	0	18-2	19	6.38	75	.306	.410	0	ø	0	141	-5	24	-0.5
1996	Sea A	2	2	.500	40	0	0	0-0	42.2	43	21	4	2	17-1	34	4.01	124	.259	.333	0	ø	0	—	4	45	0.3
1997	Sea A	0	0	ø	2	0	0	0-0	6.2	6	5	1	1	4-0	10	6.75	67	.231	.355	0	ø	0	—	-1	158	-0.1
Total	4	6	5	.545	89	6	0	2-2	122.2	136	72	11	4	64-8	91	4.62	106	.282	.367	0	ø	0	148	3	408	0.1
Davis, Wiley	Wiley Anderson; B8.1.1875 Seymour TN; D9.22.1942 Detroit MI; BR/TR/5´10˝/165; d4.18																									
1896	Cin N	1	1	.500	2	0	0	0	4.1	8	4	0	0	2	1	8.31	56	.400	.455	1	.000	0	—	-1	—	-0.2
Davis, Woody	Woodrow Wilson "Babe"; B4.25.1913 Nicholls GA; D7.18.1999 Jesup GA; BL/TR/6´1˝/200; d5.2; Col Brewton–Parker																									
1938	Det A	0	0	ø	2	0	0	0	6	3	1	0	0	4	1	1.50	333	.158	.304	1	.000	-0	—	2	—	0.1
Davison, Mike	Michael Lynn; B8.4.1945 Galesburg IL; BL/TL/6´1˝/(170–180); d10.1; Col Augsburg																									
1969	SF N	0	0	ø	1	0	0	0-0	2	2	1	0	0	0-0	2	4.50	78	.250	.250	0	ø	0	—	0	0	0.0
1970	SF N	3	5	.375	31	0	0	1-2	36	46	29	4	0	22-4	21	6.50	61	.324	.410	1	.000	0	—	-10	0	-1.9
Total	2	3	5	.375	32	0	0	1-2	38	48	30	4	0	22-4	23	6.39	62	.320	.402	1	.000	0	—	-10	0	-1.9
Davison, Scott	Scotty Ray; B10.16.1970 Inglewood CA; BR/TR/6´0˝/190; [MonN88 4/102]; d9.4																									
1995	Sea A	0	0	ø	3	0	0	0-0	4.1	7	3	1	0	1-0	3	6.23	77	.350	.381	0	ø	0	—	-1	0	0.0
1996	Sea A	0	0	ø	5	0	0	0-0	9	11	9	6	0	3-0	9	9.00	55	.297	.350	0	ø	0	—	-4	27	-0.2
Total	2	0	0	ø	8	0	0	0-0	13.1	18	12	7	0	4-0	12	8.10	61	.316	.361	0	ø	0	—	-5	27	-0.2
Dawley, Joey	Joseph Thomas; B9.19.1971 Riverside CA; BR/TR/6´4˝/205; [BalA92 28/772]; d9.29; Col Riverside (CA) CC																									
2002	Atl N	0	0	ø	1	0	0	0-0	0.1	0	0	0	0	0-0	1	0.00	ø	.000	.000	0	ø	0	—	0	0	0.0
2003	Atl N	0	0	ø	5	0	0	0-0	7	15	14	3	1	3-0	8	18.00	23	.405	.463	1	.000	-0	—	-10	0	-0.5
2004	Cle A	0	0	ø	2	2	0	0-0	8.1	7	5	1	0	7-0	8	5.40	80	.233	.378	0	ø	0	117	-1	120	0.0
Total	3	0	0	ø	8	2	0	0-0	15.2	22	19	4	1	10-0	17	10.91	39	.324	.418	1	.000	-0	117	-11	120	-0.5
Dawley, Bill	William Chester; B2.6.1958 Norwich CT; BR/TR/6´4˝/240; [CinN76 7/167]; d4.15																									
1983	Hou N★	6	6	.500	48	0	0	14-2	79.2	51	26	9	1	22-4	60	2.82	121	.185	.247	9	.222	0	—	7	0	1.2
1984	Hou N	11	4	.733	60	0	0	5-5	98	82	24	5	0	35-9	47	1.93	173	.234	.298	9-0-2	.333	2	—	17	0	2.8
1985	Hou N	5	3	.625	49	0	0	2-1	81	76	35	7	0	37-7	48	3.56	98	.259	.337	10	.200	0	—	0	18	0.1
1986	Chi A	0	7	.000	46	0	0	2-2	97.2	91	38	10	1	28-3	66	3.32	131	.247	.300	2	.000	-0	—	12	0	0.7
1987	StL N	5	8	.385	60	0	0	2-5	96.2	93	51	15	1	38-11	65	4.47	94	.259	.330	12-0-1	.167	0	—	-2	0	-0.2
1988	Phi N	0	2	.000	8	0	0	0-0	8.2	16	13	3	0	4-1	3	13.50	27	.381	.426	0	ø	0	—	-9	100	-1.6
1989	Oak A	0	0	ø	4	0	0	0-0	9	11	5	0	1	2-0	3	4.00	93	.297	.341	0	ø	0	—	-1	0	0.0
Total	7	27	30	.474	275	0	0	25-15	470.2	420	192	49	4	166-35	292	3.42	110	.243	.308	42-0-3	.214	2	—	24	118	3.0
Dawson, Joe	Ralph Fenton; B3.9.1897 Bow WA; D1.4.1978 Longview TX; BR/TR/5´11˝/182; d7.4																									
1924	Cle A	1	2	.333	4	4	0	0	20.1	24	17	0	1	21	7	6.64	64	.300	.451	7-0-1	.286	0	64	-5	—	-0.5
1927	†Pit N	3	7	.300	20	7	4	0	80.2	80	47	2	0	32	17	4.46	92	.268	.338	25-0-1	.200	-1	80	-3	—	-0.5
1928	Pit N	7	7	.500	31	7	1	3	128.2	116	54	5	1	56	36	3.29	124	.242	.322	43-0-1	.279	3	51	12	—	1.4
1929	Pit N	0	1	.000	4	0	0	0	8.2	13	9	2	0	3	2	8.31	57	.342	.390	2	.500	1	—	-3	—	-0.2
Total	4	11	17	.393	59	18	5	3	238.1	233	127	9	2	112	62	4.15	99	.260	.343	77-0-3	.260	3	65	1	—	0.2
Dawson, Rex	Rexford Paul; B2.10.1889 Skagit Co. WA; D10.20.1958 Indianapolis IN; BL/TR/6´0˝/185; d10.3																									
1913	Was A	0	0	ø	1	0	0	0	1	1	0	0	0	0	1	0.00	ø	.250	.250	0	ø	0	—	0	—	0.0
Day, Pea Ridge	Henry Clyde; B8.25.1899 Pea Ridge AR; D3.21.1934 Kansas City MO; BR/TR/6´0˝/190; d9.19																									
1924	StL N	1	1	.500	3	3	1	0	17.2	22	11	0	0	6	3	4.58	82	.306	.359	8	.125	-1	105	-2	—	-0.3
1925	StL N	2	4	.333	17	4	1	1	40	53	31	5	3	7	13	6.30	69	.325	.364	13	.154	-1	142	-8	—	-1.1
1926	Cin N	0	0	ø	4	0	0	0	7.1	13	13	1	0	2	2	7.36	50	.406	.441	2	.000	-0	—	-6	—	-0.3
1931	Bro N	2	2	.500	22	2	1	1	57.1	75	38	5	0	13	30	4.55	84	.315	.351	18	.222	0	56	-7	—	-0.5
Total	4	5	7	.417	46	9	3	2	122.1	163	93	11	3	28	48	5.30	75	.323	.362	41	.171	-2	114	-23	—	-2.2
Day, Zach	Stephen Zachary; B6.15.1978 Cincinnati OH; BR/TR/6´4˝/(185–215); [NYA96 5/149]; d6.15																									
2002	Mon N	4	1	.800	19	2	0	1-1	37.1	28	18	3	1	15-2	25	3.62	121	.207	.289	6-0-2	.167	0	116	2	0	0.4
2003	Mon N	9	8	.529	23	23	1-1	0-0	131.1	132	64	8	10	59-3	61	4.18	106	.262	.348	47-0-1	.043	-4	96	5	58	0.2
2004	Mon N	5	10	.333	19	19	1-1	0-0	116.2	117	53	13	4	45-7	61	3.93	117	.265	.337	29-1-3	.034	-2	55	9	79	0.9
2005	Was N	1	2	.333	12	5	0	0-0	36	41	29	4	1	25-3	16	6.75	61	.289	.396	8-0-1	.125	-0	78	-11	48	-0.8
	Col N	0	1	.000	5	3	0	0-1	11.1	20	11	2	0	7-1	7	7.15	65	.385	.458	3	.333	0	121	-3	16	-0.2
	Year	1	3	.250	17	8	0	0-1	47.1	61	40	6	1	32-4	23	6.85	62	.314	.412	11-0-1	.182	-0	97	-14	0	-1.0
2006	Col N	1	2	.333	3	3	0	0-0	13.1	22	17	3	1	10-1	6	10.80	44	.373	.465	5-0-1	.000	-1	154	-8	0	-1.3
	Was N	1	3	.250	5	5	0	0-0	26.2	29	15	2	2	11-1	13	4.73	92	.276	.356	7-0-1	.000	-1	63	-1	132	-0.2
	Year	2	5	.286	8	8	0	0-0	40	51	32	5	3	21-2	19	6.75	67	.311	.397	12-0-2	.000	-1	100	-10	0	-1.5
Total	5	21	27	.438	86	60	2-2	1-2	372.2	389	207	35	19	172-18	189	4.66	96	.270	.354	105-1-9	.057	-7	84	-7	333	-1.0
Day, Bill	William M.; B7.28.1867 Marcus Hook PA; D8.16.1923 Wilmington DE; TR/5´8˝/150; d8.20																									
1889	Phi N	0	3	.000	4	3	2	0	19	16	24	0	0	23	20	5.21	83	.222	.411	10	.000	-2	77	-4	—	-0.6
1890	Phi N	1	1	.500	4	2	2	0	23.2	26	16	0	0	12	9	3.04	120	.271	.352	10	.100	-1	78	1	—	-0.1
	Pit N	0	6	.000	6	6	6	0	50	66	50	1	1	24	10	5.22	63	.308	.381	23	.043	-4	73	-13	—	-1.4
	Year	1	7	.125	10	8	8	0	73.2	92	66	1	1	36	19	4.52	76	.297	.372	33	.061	-5	74	-13	—	-1.5
Total	2	1	10	.091	14	11	10	0	92.2	108	90	1	1	59	39	4.66	77	.283	.380	43	.047	-6	76	-16	—	-2.1
Dayley, Ken	Kenneth Grant; B2.25.1959 Jerome ID; BL/TL/6´0˝/(171–180); [AtlN80 1/3]; d5.13; Col Portland; [DL 1992 Tor A 182]																									
1982	Atl N	5	6	.455	20	11	0	0-0	71.1	79	39	9	0	25-2	34	4.54	81	.286	.340	20-0-1	.250	1	115	-6	0	-0.8
1983	Atl N	5	8	.385	24	16	0	0-0	104.2	100	59	12	2	39-2	70	4.30	90	.257	.326	32-0-5	.219	1*	116	-7	0	-0.7
1984	Atl N	0	3	.000	4	4	0	0-0	18.2	28	18	5	1	6-1	10	5.30	73	.341	.393	4	.500	1*	97	-5	0	-0.6
	StL N	0	2	.000	3	2	0	0-0	5	16	10	1	0	5-0	0	18.00	19	.615	.677	0-0-1	ø	0	76	-8	0	-1.3
	Year	0	5	.000	7	6	0	0-0	23.2	44	28	6	1	11-1	10	7.99	47	.407	.467	4-0-1	.500	1	90	-12	0	-1.9
1985	†StL N	4	4	.500	57	0	0	11-5	65.1	65	24	2	0	18-9	62	2.76	130	.263	.311	5	.400	1	—	5	0	1.0
1986	StL N	0	3	.000	31	0	0	5-2	38.2	42	19	1	1	11-3	33	3.26	113	.275	.325	5	.200	0*	—	0	85	0.1
1987	†StL N	9	5	.643	53	0	0	4-6	61	52	21	2	2	33-8	63	2.66	158	.234	.337	0	ø	0	—	10	45	1.9
1988	StL N	2	7	.222	54	0	0	5-3	55.1	48	20	2	1	19-7	38	2.77	127	.239	.306	4	.000	-0	—	4	35	0.7
1989	StL N	4	3	.571	71	0	0	12-5	75.1	63	26	3	0	30-10	40	2.87	128	.228	.303	5	.000	-1	—	7	0	0.7
1990	StL N	4	4	.500	58	0	0	2-5	73.1	63	32	5	0	30-7	51	3.56	108	.233	.305	6	.000	-1	—	3	0	0.2
1991	Tor A	0	0	ø	8	0	0	0-0	4.1	7	3	0	1	5-0	3	6.23	68	.368	.500	0	ø	0	—	-1	163	0.0
1993	Tor A	0	0	ø	2	0	0	0-0	0.2	1	2	0	0	4-0	2	0.00	ø	.333	.714	0	ø	0	—	-1	0	0.0
Total	11	33	45	.423	385	33	0	39-26	573.2	564	273	42	8	225-49	406	3.64	104	.261	.330	81-0-7	.210	3	112	1	510	1.2
Deagle, Ren	Lorenzo Burroughs; B6.26.1858 New York NY; D12.24.1936 Kansas City MO; BR/TR/5´9˝/190; d5.17																									
1883	Cin AA	10	8	.556	18	18	17-1	0	148	136	78	0	—	34	48	2.31	141	.229	.270	70	.129	-5*	91	14	—	0.9
1884	Cin AA	3	1	.750	4	4	4-1	0	34	38	26	0	1	9	12	5.03	66	.314	.366	13	.000	-2	86	-6	—	-0.7
	Lou AA	4	6	.400	12	12	8	0	87.1	81	43	0	7	13	23	2.58	120	.241	.284	45	.133	-3	83	6	—	0.3
	Year	7	7	.500	16	16	12-1	0	121.1	119	69	0	8	22	35	3.26	97	.260	.306	58	.103	-5	84	1	—	-0.4
Total	2	17	15	.531	34	34	29-2	0	269.1	255	147	0	8	56	83	2.74	117	.242	.286	128	.117	-9	87	14	—	0.5

YEAR	TM LG	W	L	PCT	G	GS	CG-SHO	SV-BS	IP	H	R	HR	HB	BB-IB	SO	ERA	AERA	OAV	OOB	AB-HR-SH	AVG	PB	SUP	APR	DL	PW
Deago, Roger	Roger I. (Villarreal); B6.21.1977 Monagrillo, Pan; BR/TL/5´10˝/180; d5.10																									
2003	SD N	0	1	.000	2	2	0	0-0	10.1	11	9	0	0	8-0	10	7.84	51	.282	.396	4	.000	-0	94	-4	0	-0.4
Deal, Cot	Ellis Fergason; B1.23.1923 Arapaho OK; BB/TR (BL 1947–48)/5´10.5˝/185; d9.11; C15																									
1947	Bos A	0	1	.000	5	2	0	0	12.2	20	13	0	0	7	6	9.24	42	.364	.435	4	.500	1*	125	-6	0	-0.4
1948	Bos A	1	0	1.000	4	0	0	0	4	3	0	0	0	3	2	0.00	ø	.200	.333	0	ø	0	—	2	0	0.4
1950	StL N	0	0	ø	3	0	0	0	1	3	5	0	0	2	1	18.00	24	.500	.625	0	ø	0	—	-3	0	-0.1
1954	StL N	2	3	.400	33	0	0	1	71.2	85	56	14	4	36	25	6.28	65	.297	.379	20-1-0	.100	0	—	-17	0	-1.0
Total	4	3	4	.429	45	2	0	1	89.1	111	74	14	4	48	34	6.55	63	.307	.390	24-1-0	.167	1	125	-24	0	-1.1
Dean, Chubby	Alfred Lovell; B8.24.1915 Mt.Airy NC; D12.21.1970 Riverside NJ; BL/TL/5´11˝/181; d4.14.1936; Mil 1943–46; ▲																									
1937	Phi A	1	0	1.000	2	1	0	0	9	7	4	0	0	6	4	4.00	118	.219	.342	309-2-7	.262	0*	148	1	—	0.1
1938	Phi A	2	1	.667	6	1	0	0	23	22	10	3	0	15	3	3.52	137	.250	.359	20	.300	2*	91	4	—	0.6
1939	Phi A	5	8	.385	54	1	0	7	116.2	132	93	8	0	80	39	5.25	90	.289	.395	77-0-3	.351	8*	37	-12	—	-0.4
1940	Phi A	6	13	.316	30	19	8-1	1	159.1	220	136	21	0	63	38	6.61	67	.324	.381	90-0-2	.289	4*	88	-36	—	-2.7
1941	Phi A	2	4	.333	18	7	2	0	75.2	90	53	9	0	35	22	6.19	68	.294	.367	37-0-1	.243	2*	71	-14	0	-0.7
	Cle A	1	4	.200	8	8	2	0	53.1	57	31	3	0	24	14	4.39	90	.282	.358	25-0-1	.160	0*	77	-4	0	-0.2
	Year	3	8	.273	26	15	4	0	129	147	84	12	0	59	36	5.44	75	.289	.363	62-0-2	.210	2	73	-16	0	-0.9
1942	Cle A	8	11	.421	27	22	8	1	172.2	170	83	7	0	66	46	3.81	91	.261	.329	101	.267	8*	87	-6	0	0.1
1943	Cle A	5	5	.500	17	9	3	0	76	83	46	1	1	34	29	4.50	69	.281	.358	46-0-1	.196	1*	157	-13	0	-1.5
Total	7	30	46	.395	162	68	23-1	9	685.2	781	456	52	1	323	195	5.08	79	.288	.364	705-2-15	.268	25	89	-80	0	-4.7
Dean, Dory	Charles Wilson; B11.6.1852 Cincinnati OH; D5.4.1935 Nashville TN; BR/TR; d6.22																									
1876	Cin N	4	26	.133	30	30	26	0	262.2	397	268	1	—	24	22	3.73	59	.322	.335	138	.261	1*	70	-48	—	-3.8
Dean, Harry	James Harry; B5.12.1915 Rockmart GA; D6.1.1960 Rockmart GA; BR/TR/6´4˝/185; d4.16; Col Oglethorpe																									
1941	Was A	0	0	ø	2	0	0	0	2	2	3	0	1	3	0	4.50	90	.250	.500	0	ø	0	—	-1	0	-0.1
Dean, Dizzy	Jay Hanna; B1.16.1910 Lucas AR; D7.17.1974 Reno NV; BR/TR/6´2˝/182; d9.28; C1; HF1953; b–Paul																									
1930	StL N	1	0	1.000	1	1	1	0	9	3	1	0	0	3	5	1.00	502	.103	.188	3	.333	0	52	4	—	0.5
1932	StL N	18	15	.545	46	33	16-**4**	2	**286**	280	122	14	5	102	**191**	3.30	119	.260	.327	97-2-8	.258	5*	91	20	—	2.5
1933	StL N	20	18	.526	**48**	34	**26**-3	4	293	279	113	11	5	64	**199**	3.04	114	.250	.293	105-1-3	.181	1*	107	15	—	1.7
1934	†StL N★	**30**	7	**.811**	50	33	24-**7**	7	311.2	288	110	14	6	75	**195**	2.66	159	.241	.289	118-2-7	.246	4*	119	51	—	**6.1**
1935	StL N★	**28**	12	.700	50	**36**	**29**-3	5	**325.1**	324	126	16	4	77	**190**	3.04	135	.256	.300	128-2-4	.234	4*	124	38	—	**4.5**
1936	StL N★	24	13	.649	**51**	34	**28**-2	**11**	**315**	310	128	21	3	53	195	3.17	124	.253	.285	121-0-3	.223	1	118	27	—	3.0
1937	StL N★	13	10	.565	27	25	17-4	1	197.1	200	76	9	2	33	120	2.69	148	.259	.291	66-1-9	.227	2	100	25	—	2.8
1938	†Chi N	7	1	.875	13	10	3-1	0	74.2	63	20	2	1	8	22	1.81	212	.226	.250	26-0-1	.192	-0	113	15	—	1.5
1939	Chi N	6	4	.600	19	13	7-2	0	96.1	98	40	4	1	17	27	3.36	117	.261	.294	34-0-2	.147	-1	119	7	—	0.5
1940	Chi N	3	3	.500	10	9	3	0	54	68	35	4	0	20	18	5.17	73	.306	.364	18-0-2	.222	0	93	-8	—	-0.8
1941	Chi N	0	0	ø	1	1	0	0	1	3	3	0	0	0	1	18.00	19	.429	.429	0	ø	0	193	-2	0	-0.1
1947	StL A	0	0	ø	1	1	0	0	4	3	0	0	0	1	0	0.00	ø	.231	.286	1	1.000	0	46	2	0	0.1
Total	12	150	83	.644	317	230	154-26	30	1967.1	1919	774	95	27	453	1163	3.02	130	.253	.298	717-8-39	.225	15	110	194	0	22.3
Dean, Paul	Paul Dee "Daffy"; B8.14.1913 Lucas AR; D3.17.1981 Springdale AR; BR/TR/6´0˝/175; d4.18; b–Dizzy																									
1934	†StL N	19	11	.633	39	26	16-5	2	233.1	225	96	19	5	52	150	3.43	123	.248	.292	83-0-3	.241	1	101	23	—	2.5
1935	StL N	19	12	.613	46	33	19-2	5	269.2	261	109	16	9	55	143	3.37	122	.249	.292	90-0-4	.133	-5	102	25	—	1.8
1936	StL N	5	5	.500	17	14	5	1	92	113	57	3	1	20	28	4.60	86	.300	.337	34-0-3	.059	-4	105	-8	—	-1.3
1937	StL N	0	0	ø	1	0	0	0	0	1	3	0	0	2	0	(3)	ø	1.000	1.000	0	ø	0	—	-3	—	-0.2
1938	StL N	3	1	.750	5	4	2-1	0	31	37	12	3	0	5	14	2.61	151	.298	.326	11	.182	-0	96	4	—	0.4
1939	StL N	0	1	.000	16	2	0	0	43	54	30	4	1	10	16	6.07	68	.310	.351	9-0-1	.111	-1	74	-8	—	-0.5
1940	NY N	4	4	.500	27	7	2	0	99.1	110	50	8	0	29	32	3.90	100	.281	.330	26-0-5	.115	-2	90	0	—	-0.3
1941	NY N	0	0	ø	5	0	0	0	5.2	8	2	0	0	3	3	3.18	116	.320	.393	0	ø	0	—	0	0	0.0
1943	StL A	0	0	ø	3	1	0	0	13.1	16	5	0	1	3	1	3.38	99	.296	.345	3	.000	-0	152	0	0	0.0
Total	9	50	34	.595	159	87	44-8	8	787.1	825	364	53	17	179	387	3.75	109	.266	.309	256-0-16	.156	-10	101	33	0	2.4
Dean, Wayland	Wayland Ogden; B6.20.1902 Richwood WV; D4.11.1930 Huntington WV; BB/TR/6´1˝/178; d4.17																									
1924	†NY N	6	12	.333	26	20	6	0	125.2	139	80	9	5	45	39	5.01	73	.280	.346	40-2-1	.200	1	106	-19	—	-2.2
1925	NY N	10	7	.588	33	14	6-1	1	151.1	169	98	13	4	50	53	4.64	87	.282	.342	51-1-0	.235	3	85	-13	—	-1.0
1926	Phi N	8	16	.333	33	26	15-1	0	203.2	245	136	9	3	89	52	4.91	84	.307	.379	102-3-3	.265	5*	84	-17	—	-1.3
1927	Phi N	0	1	.000	2	0	0	0	3	6	4	0	0	2	1	12.00	34	.500	.571	3	.667	1*	—	-2	—	-0.3
	Chi N	0	0	ø	2	0	0	0	2	0	0	0	1	2	2	0.00	ø	.000	.429	0	ø	0	—	1	—	0.1
	Year	0	1	.000	4	0	0	0	5	6	4	0	1	4	3	7.20	56	.375	.524	3	.667	1	—	-1	—	-0.2
Total	4	24	36	.400	96	60	27-2	1	485.2	559	318	31	13	188	147	4.87	82	.293	.360	196-6-4	.250	10	90	-50	—	-4.7
DeBarr, Dennis	Dennis Lee; B1.16.1953 Cheyenne WY; BL/TL/6´2˝/185; [DetA71 2/35]; d5.14																									
1977	Tor A	0	1	.000	14	0	0	0-1	21.1	29	14	1	0	8-0	10	5.91	72	.337	.385	0	ø	0	—	-3	0	-0.1
DeBerry, Joe	Joseph Gaddy; B11.29.1896 Mt.Gilead NC; D10.9.1944 Southern Pines NC; BL/TR/6´1˝/175; d8.24; Col North Carolina St.																									
1920	StL A	2	4	.333	10	7	3-1	0	54.2	65	35	2	2	20	12	4.94	79	.307	.372	18-0-2	.167	-1	87	-5	—	-0.5
1921	StL A	0	1	.000	10	1	0	0	12.1	15	9	0	0	10	1	6.57	68	.300	.417	2	.000	-0	75	-2	—	-0.2
Total	2	2	5	.286	20	8	3-1	0	67	80	44	2	2	30	13	5.24	77	.305	.381	20-0-2	.150	-1	85	-7	—	-0.7
DeBusschere, Dave	David Albert; B10.16.1940 Detroit MI; D5.14.2003 New York NY; BR/TR/6´6˝/225; d4.22; Mil 1964; Col Detroit Mercy																									
1962	Chi A	0	0	ø	12	0	0	0	18	5	7	1	1	23-1	8	2.00	195	.089	.358	0	ø	0	—	3	0	0.1
1963	Chi A	3	4	.429	24	10	1-1	0	84.1	80	35	9	4	34-1	53	3.09	113	.249	.327	22-0-2	.045	-2	89	3	0	0.1
Total	2	3	4	.429	36	10	1-1	0	102.1	85	42	10	5	57-2	61	2.90	123	.225	.333	22-0-2	.045	-2	89	6	0	0.2
Decatur, Art	Arthur Rue; B1.14.1894 Cleveland OH; D4.25.1966 Talladega AL; BR/TR/6´1˝/190; d4.15																									
1922	Bro N	3	4	.429	29	3	1	1	87.2	87	31	3	1	29	31	2.77	147	.265	.327	25-0-1	.080	-2	67	13	—	0.7
1923	Bro N	3	3	.500	36	5	2	3	97.2	101	44	3	2	32	25	2.58	150	.264	.325	21-0-1	.000	-3	64	**11**	—	0.3
1924	Bro N	10	9	.526	31	10	3	1	126.1	156	74	12	4	27	38	4.13	91	.308	.348	44	.114	-4	68	-7	—	-1.4
1925	Bro N	0	0	ø	1	0	0	0	1	3	2	0	0	0	0	18.00	23	.600	.600	0	ø	0	—	-1	—	-0.1
	Phi N	4	13	.235	25	15	4	2	128	170	87	13	2	35	31	5.27	91	.316	.360	41-0-4	.049	-5	71	-4	—	-1.0
	Year	4	13	.235	26	15	4	2	129	173	89	13	2	35	31	5.37	89	.319	.362	41-0-4	.049	-5	71	-5	—	-1.1
1926	Phi N	0	0	ø	2	1	0	0	3	6	3	0	0	2	0	6.00	69	.375	.444	1	.000	-0	40	-1	—	-0.1
1927	Phi N	3	5	.375	29	3	0	0	94.2	130	78	11	4	20	27	7.42	56	.334	.373	27-0-3	.222	0	48	-29	—	-2.2
Total	6	23	34	.404	153	37	10	7	538.1	653	319	42	13	145	152	4.51	92	.302	.349	159-0-9	.094	-14	68	-18	—	-3.8
Decker, Marty	Dee Martin; B6.7.1957 Upland CA; BR/TR/5´10˝/168; [PhiN80 23/582]; d9.20; Col Point Loma Nazarene																									
1983	SD N	0	0	ø	4	0	0	0-0	8.2	5	2	1	1	3-0	9	2.08	169	.167	.265	0	ø	0	—	2	0	0.1
Decker, Joe	George Henry; B6.16.1947 Storm Lake IA; D3.2.2003 Fraser MI; BR/TR/6´0˝/(175–180); [ChiN65 8/148]; d9.18																									
1969	Chi N	1	0	1.000	4	1	0	0-0	12.1	10	4	0	0	6-0	13	2.92	138	.222	.314	2	.000	-0	66	2	0	0.1
1970	Chi N	2	7	.222	24	17	1	0-1	108.2	108	64	12	4	56-3	79	4.64	97	.263	.354	34-1-2	.176	1	76	-2	0	-0.1
1971	Chi N	3	2	.600	21	4	0	0-0	45.2	62	24	2	0	25-3	37	4.73	83	.343	.418	8-0-1	.250	1*	62	-2	0	-0.1
1972	Chi N	1	0	1.000	5	1	0	0-0	12.2	9	3	1	0	4-0	7	2.13	179	.188	.250	2-0-3	.000	-0	348	2	0	0.1
1973	Min A	10	10	.500	29	24	6-3	0-0	170.1	167	87	12	4	88-0	109	4.17	95	.260	.350	0	ø	0	101	-2	0	-0.3
1974	Min A	16	14	.533	37	37	11-1	0-0	248.2	234	105	24	2	97-1	158	3.29	114	.252	.321	0	ø	0	89	11	0	1.2
1975	Min A	1	3	.250	10	7	1	0-0	26.1	25	25	2	0	36-0	8	8.54	45	.260	.462	0	ø	0	108	-12	49	-1.6
1976	Min A	2	7	.222	13	12	0	0-0	58	60	37	3	1	51-0	35	5.28	68	.273	.404	0	ø	0	105	-10	0	-1.3
1979	Sea A	0	1	.000	9	2	0	0-0	27.1	27	14	2	0	14-1	12	4.28	102	.255	.339	0	ø	0	83	0	0	0.1
Total	9	36	44	.450	152	105	19-4	0-1	710	702	363	58	11	377-8	458	4.17	95	.262	.353	46-1-6	.174	1	93	-13	49	-1.9

YEAR	TM LG	W	L	PCT	G	GS	CG-SHO	SV-BS	IP	H	R	HR	HB	BB-IB	SO	ERA	AERA	OAV	OOB	AB-HR-SH	AVG	PB	SUP	APR	DL	PW
DEDMON, JEFF	Jeffrey Linden; B3.4.1960 Torrance CA; BL/TR/6´2˝/200; [AtlN80 S1/5]; d9.2; Col West Los Angeles (CA) CC																									
1983	Atl N	0	0	ø	5	0	0	0-2	4	10	6	1	0	0-0	3	13.50	29	.455	.455	0	ø	0	—	-4	0	-0.2
1984	Atl N	4	3	.571	54	0	0	4-2	81	86	39	5	2	35-9	51	3.78	102	.277	.352	6-0-1	.000	-1	—	1	0	0.1
1985	Atl N	6	3	.667	60	0	0	0-4	86	84	52	5	1	49-14	41	4.08	94	.264	.363	9-0-1	.111	-0	—	-5	0	-0.3
1986	Atl N	6	6	.500	57	0	0	3-6	99.2	90	43	8	4	39-5	58	2.98	133	.242	.319	16-0-1	.125	-1	—	8	0	1.0
1987	Atl N	3	4	.429	53	3	0	4-5	89.2	82	46	8	1	42-1	40	3.91	111	.246	.327	16-0-3	.250	1	153	3	0	0.4
1988	Cle A	1	0	1.000	21	0	0	1-0	33.2	35	20	3	3	21-1	17	4.54	91	.276	.383	0	ø	0	—	-2	0	0.0
Total	6	20	16	.556	250	3	0	12-19	394	387	206	30	11	186-30	210	3.84	105	.261	.345	47-0-6	.149	-0	153	1	0	1.0
DEDRICK, JIM	James Michael; B4.4.1968 Los Angeles CA; BB/TR/6´0˝/185; [BalA90 33/890]; d8.12; Col Vanguard																									
1995	Bal A	0	0	ø	6	0	0	0-0	7.2	8	2	1	1	6-0	3	2.35	204	.308	.429	0	ø	0	—	2	0	0.1
DEEGAN, DUMMY	William Joseph; B11.16.1874 Bronx NY; D5.17.1957 Bronx NY; d8.3																									
1901	NY N	0	1	.000	2	1	1	0	17	27	17	0	0	6	8	6.35	52	.355	.402	5	.000	-1	43	-6	—	-0.3
DEERING, JOHN	John Thomas; B6.25.1879 Lynn MA; D2.15.1943 Beverly MA; BR/TR/6´0˝/180; d5.12																									
1903	Det A	3	4	.429	10	8	5	0	60.2	77	38	3	1	24	14	3.86	75	.308	.371	24-0-1	.333	2	83	-6	—	-0.5
	NY A	4	3	.571	9	7	6-1	0	60	59	33	0	1	18	14	3.75	83	.257	.313	23	.043	-3	92	-3	—	-0.7
	Year	7	7	.500	19	15	11-1	0	120.2	136	71	3	2	42	28	3.80	79	.283	.344	47-0-1	.191	-0	87	-10	—	-1.2
DEGERICK, MIKE	Michael Arthur; B4.1.1943 New York NY; BR/TR/6´2˝/180; d9.4; [DL 1963 Chi A 128]																									
1961	Chi A	0	0	ø	1	0	0	0	1.2	2	1	0	0	1-0	0	5.40	72	.400	.429	0	ø	0	—	0	0	0.0
1962	Chi A	0	0	ø	1	0	0	0	1	1	0	0	0	1-0	0	0.00	ø	.250	.400	0	ø	0	—	0	0	0.0
Total	2	0	0	ø	2	0	0	0	2.2	3	1	0	0	2-0	0	3.38	116	.333	.417	0	ø	0	—	0	128	0.0
DEHART, RICK	Rick Allen; B3.21.1970 Topeka KS; BL/TL/6´1˝/(180–190); d7.16; Col Washburn Topeka																									
1997	Mon N	2	1	.667	23	0	0	0-1	29.1	33	21	7	0	14-4	29	5.52	76	.292	.364	2	.000	-0	—	-5	0	-0.4
1998	Mon N	0	0	ø	26	0	0	1-1	28	34	22	3	0	13-1	14	4.82	87	.291	.359	0	ø	0	—	-4	0	-0.2
1999	Mon N	0	0	ø	3	0	0	0-0	1.2	6	4	2	0	3-1	1	21.60	21	.545	.643	0	ø	0	—	-3	0	-0.1
2003	KC A	0	2	.000	4	0	0	0-0	4	8	6	1	0	2-0	1	13.50	36	.421	.476	1	.000	-0	—	-3	0	-0.6
Total	4	2	3	.400	56	0	0	1-2	63	81	53	13	0	32-6	45	6.14	69	.312	.383	3	.000	-0	—	-15	0	-1.3
DEININGER, PEP	Otto Charles; B10.10.1877 Wasseralfingen, Germany; D9.25.1950 Boston MA; BL/TL/5´8.5˝/180; d4.26; ▲																									
1902	Bos A	0	0	ø	2	1	0	0	12	19	16	3	2	9	2	9.75	37	.358	.469	6	.333	1	101	-7	—	-0.2
DEJEAN, MIKE	Michel Dwain; B9.28.1970 Baton Rouge LA; BR/TR/6´2˝/(205–220); [NYA92 24/662]; d5.2; Col West Alabama																									
1997	Col N	5	0	1.000	55	0	0	2-2	67.2	74	34	4	3	24-2	38	3.99	129	.280	.346	3-0-1	.333	0*	—	7	21	0.5
1998	Col N	3	1	.750	59	1	0	2-1	74.1	78	29	4	1	24-1	27	3.03	171	.285	.340	5	.000	-1	124	14	26	0.6
1999	Col N	2	4	.333	56	0	0	0-4	61	83	61	13	2	32-8	31	8.41	69	.335	.411	2	.000	-0*	—	-14	18	-1.1
2000	Col N	4	4	.500	54	0	0	0-4	53.1	54	31	9	0	30-6	34	4.89	118	.269	.362	2	.000	-0	—	4	44	0.5
2001	Mil N	4	2	.667	75	0	0	2-2	84.1	75	31	4	9	39-7	68	2.77	155	.236	.332	3	.000	-0	—	13	0	0.9
2002	Mil N	1	5	.167	68	0	0	27-3	75	66	28	7	2	39-8	65	3.12	132	.237	.332	1	.000	-0	—	8	0	1.1
2003	Mil N	4	7	.364	58	0	0	18-8	64.2	69	38	12	1	27-7	58	4.87	89	.271	.339	0	ø	0	—	-4	0	-0.7
	StL N	1	1	.500	18	0	0	1-0	18	17	8	1	1	12-0	13	4.00	103	.262	.385	0	ø	0	—	0	0	0.1
	Year	5	8	.385	76	0	0	19-8	82.2	86	46	13	2	39-7	71	4.68	91	.269	.349	0	ø	0	—	-4	0	-0.6
2004	Bal A	0	5	.000	37	0	0	0-0	39.2	49	29	2	6	28-6	36	6.13	76	.308	.426	1	.000	-0	—	-6	0	-0.7
	NY N	0	0	ø	17	0	0	0-0	21.1	21	5	0	2	5-2	24	1.69	255	.256	.315	0	ø	0	—	6	37	0.3
2005	NY N	3	1	.750	28	0	0	0-0	25.2	36	19	3	1	18-2	17	6.31	65	.327	.423	0	ø	0*	—	-6	0	-0.8
	Col N	2	3	.400	38	0	0	0-3	36.2	26	14	0	2	12-1	35	3.19	146	.195	.268	0	ø	0	—	5	0	0.7
	Year	5	4	.556	66	0	0	0-3	62.1	62	33	3	3	30-3	52	4.48	99	.255	.341	0	ø	0	—	0	0	-0.1
2006	Col N	1	0	1.000	2	0	0	0-0	1.2	1	0	0	0	2-0	0	0.00	ø	.167	.375	0	ø	0	—	1	177	0.2
Total	10	30	33	.476	565	1	0	52-27	623.1	649	327	59	30	292-50	446	4.30	111	.271	.355	17-0-1	.059	-1	124	28	323	1.6
DEJESUS, JOSE	Jose Luis; B1.6.1965 Brooklyn NY; BR/TR/6´5˝/(175–223); d9.9; [DL 1993 Phi N 120]																									
1988	KC A	0	1	.000	2	1	0	0-0	2.2	6	10	0	0	5-1	2	27.00	15	.429	.579	0	ø	0	136	-7	0	-1.1
1989	KC A	0	0	ø	3	1	0	0-0	8	7	4	1	0	8-0	2	4.50	86	.241	.405	0	ø	0	70	0	0	0.0
1990	Phi N	7	8	.467	22	22	3-1	0-0	130	97	63	10	2	73-3	87	3.74	103	.210	.321	38-0-4	.079	-1	87	0	0	-0.1
1991	Phi N	10	9	.526	31	29	3	1-0	181.2	147	74	7	4	128-4	118	3.42	108	.224	.353	62-0-4	.129	-1	91	6	0	0.3
1994	KC A	3	1	.750	5	4	0	0-0	26.2	27	14	2	0	13-0	12	4.73	106	.276	.360	0	ø	0	96	1	0	0.2
Total	5	20	19	.513	63	57	6-1	1-0	349	284	165	20	6	227-8	221	3.84	100	.226	.346	100-0-8	.110	-2	90	0	120	-0.7
DE LA CRUZ, TOMMY	Tomas (Rivero); B9.18.1911 Marianao, Cuba; D9.6.1958 Havana, Cuba; BR/TR/6´2˝/168; d4.20																									
1944	Cin N	9	9	.500	34	20	9	1	191.1	170	73	9	1	45	65	3.25	108	.238	.284	58-0-4	.155	-0*	89	9	0	0.7
DE LA MAZA, ROLAND	Roland Robert (Suastegui); B11.11.1971 Granada Hills CA; BR/TR/6´2˝/195; [CleA93 15/419]; d9.26; Col Cal St.–Sacramento																									
1997	KC A	0	0	ø	1	0	0	0-0	2	1	1	1	0	1-0	1	4.50	105	.125	.222	0	ø	0	—	0	0	0.0
DELANEY, ART	Arthur Dewey "Swede" (b Arthur Dewey Helenius); B1.5.1895 Chicago IL; D5.2.1970 Hayward CA; BR/TR/5´10.5˝/178; d4.16																									
1924	StL N	1	0	1.000	8	1	1	0	20	19	4	0	0	6	2	1.80	210	.250	.305	7	.286	0	157	5	—	0.3
1928	Bos N	9	17	.346	39	22	8	2	192.1	197	100	11	1	56	45	3.79	103	.267	.319	63-0-1	.143	-3	80	2	—	0.0
1929	Bos N	3	5	.375	20	8	3-1	0	75	103	59	6	1	35	17	6.12	76	.336	.405	21-1-2	.143	0	86	-13	—	-1.1
Total	3	13	22	.371	67	31	12-1	2	287.1	319	163	17	2	97	64	4.26	96	.285	.343	91-1-3	.154	-2	84	-6	—	-0.8
DE LA ROSA, FRANCISCO	Francisco (Jimenez); B3.3.1966 LaRomana, D.R.; BB/TR/5´11˝/185; d9.7																									
1991	Bal A	0	0	ø	2	0	0	0-0	4	6	3	0	0	2-0	1	4.50	88	.353	.400	0	ø	0	—	-1	0	0.0
DE LA ROSA, JORGE	Jorge Alberto (Gonzalez); B4.5.1981 Monterrey, Nuevo Leon, Mexico; BL/TL/6´1˝/(190–210); d8.14																									
2004	Mil N	0	3	.000	5	5	0	0-0	22.2	29	20	1	1	14-0	5	6.35	69	.309	.393	6-0-1	.000	-1	80	-6	0	-0.7
2005	Mil N	2	2	.500	38	0	0	0-2	42.1	48	23	1	0	38-4	42	4.46	95	.289	.417	0	ø	0	—	-1	0	-0.1
2006	Mil N	2	2	.500	18	3	0	0-0	30.1	32	30	4	1	22-1	31	8.60	52	.269	.379	5	.000	-1	75	-13	45	-1.5
	KC A	3	4	.429	10	10	0	0-0	48.2	49	29	10	1	32-0	36	5.18	91	.263	.373	0	ø	0	90	-2	0	-0.3
Total	3	7	11	.389	71	18	0	0-2	144	158	102	16	3	106-5	114	5.88	76	.280	.391	11-0-1	.000	-1	87	-22	45	-2.6
DELCARMEN, MANNY	Manuel; B2.16.1982 Boston MA; BR/TR/6´2˝/190; [BosA00 2/62]; d7.26																									
2005	Bos A	0	0	ø	10	0	0	0-0	9	8	3	0	1	7-0	9	3.00	151	.242	.390	0	ø	0	—	2	0	0.1
2006	Bos A	2	0	1.000	50	0	0	0-4	53.1	68	32	2	2	17-2	45	5.06	92	.309	.363	0	ø	0	—	-2	0	-0.1
Total	2	2	0	1.000	60	0	0	0-4	62.1	76	35	2	3	24-2	54	4.76	98	.300	.367	0	ø	0	—	0	0	0.0
DELEON, JOSE	Jose (Chestaro); B12.20.1960 Rancho Viejo, D.R.; BR/TR/6´3˝/(210–226); [PitN79 3/62]; d7.23																									
1983	Pit N	7	3	.700	15	15	3-2	0-0	108	75	36	5	1	47-2	118	2.83	132	.196	.283	34-0-3	.059	-1	102	12	0	0.9
1984	Pit N	7	13	.350	30	28	5-1	0-1	192.1	147	86	10	3	92-5	153	3.74	97	.214	.307	59-0-4	.085	-4	78	-1	0	-0.6
1985	Pit N	2	19	.095	31	25	1	3-0	162.2	138	93	15	3	89-3	149	4.70	77	.231	.332	36-0-7	.056	-2	57	-19	0	-2.5
1986	Pit N	1	3	.250	9	1	0	1-0	16.1	17	16	2	1	17-3	11	8.27	47	.266	.427	1	.000	0	92	-7	0	-1.4
	Chi A	4	5	.444	13	13	1	0-0	79	49	30	7	4	42-0	68	2.96	147	.179	.296	0	ø	0	72	11	0	1.2
1987	Chi A	11	12	.478	33	31	2	0-0	206	177	106	24	10	97-4	153	4.02	115	.230	.322	0	ø	0	90	10	0	0.8
1988	StL N	13	10	.565	34	34	3-1	0-0	225.1	198	95	13	2	86-7	208	3.67	96	.237	.308	72-0-12	.139	-1*	96	0	0	-0.2
1989	StL N	16	12	.571	36	36	5-3	0-0	244.2	173	96	16	6	80-5	**201**	3.05	120	**.197**	.268	83-0-9	.096	-4	80	14	0	0.9
1990	StL N	7	19	.269	32	32	0	0-0	182.2	168	96	15	5	86-9	164	4.43	87	.246	.331	56-0-5	.107	-1	73	-9	0	-1.5
1991	StL N	5	9	.357	28	28	1	0-0	162.2	144	57	15	6	61-1	118	2.71	138	.239	.313	46-0-5	.043	-4	96	17	0	0.9
1992	StL N	2	7	.222	29	15	0	0-0	102.1	95	56	7	2	43-1	72	4.57	75	.245	.320	21-0-4	.048	-1	95	-13	0	-1.3
	Phi N	0	1	.000	3	3	0	0-0	15	16	7	0	0	5-0	7	3.00	117	.281	.339	5-0-1	.400	1	103	0	0	0.1
	Year	2	8	.200	32	18	0	0-0	117.1	111	63	7	2	48-1	79	4.37	79	.250	.322	26-0-5	.115	-0	97	-13	0	-1.2
1993	Phi N	3	0	1.000	24	3	0	0-1	47	39	25	5	5	27-3	34	3.26	122	.229	.348	6-0-1	.000	-1	91	1	0	0.0
	†Chi A	0	0	ø	11	0	0	0-1	10.1	5	2	2	1	3-0	6	1.74	242	.152	.243	0	ø	0	—	3	0	0.1
1994	Chi A	3	2	.600	42	0	0	2-2	67	48	28	5	6	31-5	67	3.36	140	.200	.301	0	ø	0	—	10	0	0.7
1995	Chi A	5	3	.625	38	0	0	0-5	67.2	60	41	10	6	28-2	53	5.19	86	.238	.323	0	ø	0	—	-5	0	-0.5

YEAR	TM LG	W	L	PCT	G	GS	CG-SHO	SV-BS	IP	H	R	HR	HB	BB-IB	SO	ERA	AERA	OAV	OOB	AB-HR-SH	AVG	PB	SUP	APR	DL	PW
	Mon N	0	1	.000	7	0	0	0-0	8.1	7	7	2	1	7-0	12	7.56	57	.233	.375	0-0-1	ø	0	—	-3	0	-0.3
Total	13	86	119	.420	415	264	21-7	6-10	1897.1	1556	877	153	62	841-50	1594	3.76	103	.224	.311	419-0-52	.091	-16	83	21	0	-2.7

DeLeon, Luis Luis Antonio (Tricoche); B8.19.1958 Ponce, PR; BR/TR/6´1˝/(153–160); d9.6

YEAR	TM LG	W	L	PCT	G	GS	CG-SHO	SV-BS	IP	H	R	HR	HB	BB-IB	SO	ERA	AERA	OAV	OOB	AB-HR-SH	AVG	PB	SUP	APR	DL	PW
1981	StL N	0	1	.000	10	0	0	0-0	15.1	11	4	1	0	3-2	8	2.35	154	.200	.241	1	.000	-0	—	2	0	0.1
1982	SD N	9	5	.643	61	0	0	15-8	102	77	25	10	1	16-9	60	2.03	169	.212	.246	11-0-1	.091	0	—	17	0	2.9
1983	SD N	6	6	.500	63	0	0	13-6	111	89	34	8	1	27-7	90	2.68	131	.224	.269	14-0-3	.143	0*	—	12	0	1.4
1984	SD N	2	2	.500	32	0	0	0-3	42.2	44	34	12	4	12-2	44	5.48	65	.256	.317	4-0-1	.000	-0	—	-11	95	-1.0
1985	SD N	0	3	.000	29	0	0	3-2	38.2	39	18	6	3	10-4	31	4.19	85	.267	.325	5	.200	0	—	-2	0	-0.2
1987	Bal A	0	2	.000	11	0	0	1-1	20.2	19	15	1	2	8-2	13	4.79	93	.253	.326	0	ø	0	—	-2	0	-0.2
1989	Sea A	0	0	ø	1	1	0	0-0	4	5	1	1	1	1-0	2	2.25	180	.313	.389	0	ø	0	157	1	0	0.0
Total	7	17	19	.472	207	1	0	32-20	334.1	284	131	39	12	77-26	248	3.12	114	.232	.280	35-0-5	.114	-0	157	17	95	3.0

Delhi, Flame Lee William; B11.5.1892 Harqua Hala AZ; D5.9.1966 Greenbrae CA; BR/TR/6´2.5˝/198; d4.16

YEAR	TM LG	W	L	PCT	G	GS	CG-SHO	SV-BS	IP	H	R	HR	HB	BB-IB	SO	ERA	AERA	OAV	OOB	AB-HR-SH	AVG	PB	SUP	APR	DL	PW
1912	Chi A	0	0	ø	1	0	0	0	3	7	6	0	0	3	2	9.00	36	.412	.500	0	ø	0	—	-3	—	-0.1

Dell, Wheezer William George; B6.11.1886 Tuscarora NV; D8.24.1966 Lone Pine CA; BR/TR/6´4˝/210; d4.22

YEAR	TM LG	W	L	PCT	G	GS	CG-SHO	SV-BS	IP	H	R	HR	HB	BB-IB	SO	ERA	AERA	OAV	OOB	AB-HR-SH	AVG	PB	SUP	APR	DL	PW
1912	StL N	0	0	ø	3	0	0	0	2.1	3	3	0	0	3	0	11.57	30	.188	.316	0	ø	0	—	-2	—	-0.1
1915	Bro N	11	10	.524	40	24	12-4	1	215	166	80	5	8	100	94	2.34	119	.218	.315	66-0-2	.152	-1	91	9	—	0.8
1916	†Bro N	8	9	.471	32	16	9-2	1	155	143	52	2	4	43	76	2.26	118	.256	.314	44-0-2	.091	-2	77	8	—	0.5
1917	Bro N	0	4	.000	17	4	0	1	58	55	35	3	2	25	28	3.72	75	.263	.347	16	.063	-2	108	-8	—	-0.8
Total	4	19	23	.452	92	44	21-6	3	430.1	367	170	10	14	171	198	2.55	108	.237	.319	126-0-4	.119	-5	88	7	—	0.4

Delock, Ike Ivan Martin; B11.11.1929 Highland Park MI; BR/TR/5´11˝/(175–178); d4.17

YEAR	TM LG	W	L	PCT	G	GS	CG-SHO	SV-BS	IP	H	R	HR	HB	BB-IB	SO	ERA	AERA	OAV	OOB	AB-HR-SH	AVG	PB	SUP	APR	DL	PW
1952	Bos A	4	9	.308	39	7	1-1	5	95	88	50	9	2	50	46	4.26	92	.245	.341	22-0-1	.045	-1	89	-3	0	-0.5
1953	Bos A	3	1	.750	23	1	0	1	48.2	60	27	2	2	20	22	4.44	95	.308	.378	10	.100	-1	42	-1	0	-0.2
1955	Bos A	9	7	.563	29	18	6	3	143.2	136	67	17	4	61-2	88	3.76	114	.247	.325	49-0-2	.143	-1	91	8	0	0.8
1956	Bos A	13	7	.650	48	8	1	9	128.1	122	65	12	5	80-3	105	4.21	110	.252	.359	29-0-7	.103	-2	67	7	0	0.9
1957	Bos A	9	8	.529	49	2	0	11	94	80	40	11	3	45-7	62	3.83	104	.230	.322	21	.048	-1	34	4	0	0.6
1958	Bos A	14	8	.636	31	19	9-1	2	160	155	66	13	0	56-6	82	3.37	119	.252	.314	48-0-5	.063	-4	90	12	0	1.1
1959	Bos A	11	6	.647	28	17	4	0	134.1	120	53	12	2	62-1	55	2.95	138	.236	.318	47-1-5	.064	-3	116	14	0	1.2
1960	Bos A	9	10	.474	24	23	3-1	0	129.1	145	77	21	4	52-3	49	4.73	85	.283	.353	43-0-6	.116	-3	104	-10	0	-1.6
1961	Bos A	6	9	.400	28	28	3-1	0	156	185	110	24	2	52-2	80	4.90	85	.293	.346	48-0-5	.104	-2	111	-17	0	-1.7
1962	Bos A	4	5	.444	17	13	4-2	0	86.1	89	39	10	0	24-2	49	3.75	110	.268	.315	23-0-4	.087	-1	73	4	39	0.2
1963	Bos A	1	2	.333	6	6	1	0	32	31	18	4	0	12-0	23	4.50	84	.246	.309	12	.000	-1	98	-3	0	-0.4
	Bal A	1	3	.250	7	5	0	0	30.1	25	17	7	0	16-1	11	5.04	69	.236	.336	9	.000	-1	56	-5	0	-0.7
	Year	2	5	.286	13	11	1	0	62.1	56	35	11	0	28-1	34	4.76	76	.241	.322	21	.000	-3	80	-7	0	-1.1
Total	11	84	75	.528	329	147	32-6	31	1238	1236	629	142	24	530-27	672	4.03	102	.259	.335	361-1-35	.086	-20	94	10	39	-0.3

de los Santos, Luis Luis; B11.1.1977 Santo Domingo, D.R.; BR/TR/6´2˝/216; d7.20; [DL 2000 NY A 181]

YEAR	TM LG	W	L	PCT	G	GS	CG-SHO	SV-BS	IP	H	R	HR	HB	BB-IB	SO	ERA	AERA	OAV	OOB	AB-HR-SH	AVG	PB	SUP	APR	DL	PW
2002	TB A	0	3	.000	3	3	0	0-0	14	24	19	5	3	4-0	7	11.57	39	.387	.437	0	ø	0	82	-11	0	-1.5

de los Santos, Ramon Ramon (Genero); B1.19.1949 Santo Domingo, D.R.; BL/TL/6´1˝/175; d8.21

YEAR	TM LG	W	L	PCT	G	GS	CG-SHO	SV-BS	IP	H	R	HR	HB	BB-IB	SO	ERA	AERA	OAV	OOB	AB-HR-SH	AVG	PB	SUP	APR	DL	PW
1974	Hou N	1	1	.500	12	0	0	0-0	12.1	11	6	0	0	9-4	7	2.19	159	.234	.351	0	ø	0	—	1	0	0.1

de los Santos, Valerio Valerio Lorenzo; B10.6.1972 Las Matas de Farfan, D.R.; BL/TL/6´2˝/(180–210); d7.31

YEAR	TM LG	W	L	PCT	G	GS	CG-SHO	SV-BS	IP	H	R	HR	HB	BB-IB	SO	ERA	AERA	OAV	OOB	AB-HR-SH	AVG	PB	SUP	APR	DL	PW
1998	Mil N	0	0	ø	13	0	0	0-0	21.2	11	7	4	0	2-0	18	2.91	149	.151	.173	0	ø	0	—	4	0	0.2
1999	Mil N	0	1	.000	7	0	0	0-0	8.1	12	6	1	1	7-0	5	6.48	71	.343	.465	0	ø	0	—	-1	156	-0.1
2000	Mil N	2	3	.400	66	2	0	0-1	73.2	72	43	15	1	33-7	70	5.13	90	.254	.333	6	.000	-1	70	-3	0	-0.2
2001	Mil N	0	0	ø	1	0	0	0-0	1	1	1	0	0	1-0	1	9.00	48	.250	.400	0	ø	0	—	0	187	0.0
2002	Mil N	2	3	.400	51	0	0	0-0	57.2	42	21	4	2	26-3	38	3.12	132	.211	.299	2-0-2	.000	0	—	7	0	0.5
2003	Mil N	3	3	.500	45	0	0	1-3	48	38	24	8	4	22-0	35	4.13	105	.225	.322	1	.000	-0	—	1	30	0.1
	Phi N	1	0	1.000	6	0	0	0-0	4	7	7	0	1	3-0	4	9.00	44	.389	.500	0	ø	0	—	-4	0	-0.7
	Year	4	3	.571	51	0	0	1-3	52	45	31	8	5	25-0	39	4.50	95	.241	.339	1	.000	-0	—	-3	0	-0.6
2004	Tor A	0	0	ø	17	0	0	0-1	11.2	11	8	0	0	10-2	10	6.17	79	.250	.382	0	ø	0	—	-1	120	-0.1
2005	Fla N	1	2	.333	27	0	0	0-1	22	25	15	4	2	12-3	16	6.14	65	.281	.379	0	ø	0	—	-5	0	-0.6
Total	8	9	12	.429	233	2	0	1-6	248	219	132	36	11	116-15	197	4.54	96	.240	.328	9-0-2	.000	-1	70	-2	493	-0.9

DelToro, Miguel Miguel; B6.22.1972 San Ignacio, Sonora, Mexico; D10.6.2001 Obregon, Sonora, Mexico; BR/TR/6´1˝/(160–180); d4.6

YEAR	TM LG	W	L	PCT	G	GS	CG-SHO	SV-BS	IP	H	R	HR	HB	BB-IB	SO	ERA	AERA	OAV	OOB	AB-HR-SH	AVG	PB	SUP	APR	DL	PW
1999	SF N	0	0	ø	14	0	0	0-0	23.2	24	11	5	0	11-0	20	4.18	102	.264	.343	4-0-1	.000	-0	—	1	0	0.0
2000	†SF N	2	0	1.000	9	1	0	0-0	17.1	17	10	3	2	6-2	16	5.19	84	.250	.329	2	.500	0	190	-1	0	-0.1
Total	2	2	0	1.000	23	1	0	0-0	41	41	21	8	2	17-2	36	4.61	93	.258	.337	6-0-1	.167	-0	190	0	0	-0.1

DeLucia, Rich Richard Anthony; B10.7.1964 Reading PA; BR/TR/6´0˝/(180–190); [SeaA86 6/141]; d9.8; Col Tennessee

YEAR	TM LG	W	L	PCT	G	GS	CG-SHO	SV-BS	IP	H	R	HR	HB	BB-IB	SO	ERA	AERA	OAV	OOB	AB-HR-SH	AVG	PB	SUP	APR	DL	PW
1990	Sea A	1	2	.333	5	5	1	0-0	36	30	9	2	0	9-0	20	2.00	199	.226	.275	0	ø	0	55	8	0	0.6
1991	Sea A	12	13	.480	32	31	0	0-0	182	176	107	31	4	78-4	98	5.09	81	.260	.333	0	ø	0	110	-17	0	-2.1
1992	Sea A	3	6	.333	30	11	0	1-2	83.2	100	55	13	2	35-1	66	5.49	73	.293	.361	0	ø	0	114	-13	27	-1.3
1993	Sea A	3	6	.333	30	1	0	0-4	42.2	46	24	5	1	23-3	48	4.64	96	.272	.361	0	ø	0	82	-1	24	-0.2
1994	Cin N	0	0	ø	8	0	0	0-0	10.2	9	6	4	0	5-0	15	4.22	99	.214	.298	0	ø	0	—	0	0	0.0
1995	StL N	8	7	.533	56	1	0	0-1	82.1	63	38	9	3	36-2	76	3.39	126	.213	.303	10-0-1	.200	0	84	7	0	1.2
1996	SF N	3	6	.333	56	0	0	0-2	61.2	62	44	8	3	31-6	55	5.84	71	.259	.349	4	.250	0	—	-11	58	-1.3
1997	SF N	0	0	ø	3	0	0	0-0	1.2	6	3	0	0	0-0	2	10.80	38	.500	.500	0	ø	0	—	-2	0	-0.1
	Ana A	6	4	.600	33	0	0	3-4	42.1	29	18	5	1	27-2	42	3.61	128	.204	.331	0	ø	0	—	5	49	0.9
1998	Ana A	2	6	.250	61	0	0	3-3	71.2	56	36	10	3	46-5	73	4.27	111	.221	.340	0	ø	0	—	4	0	0.4
1999	Cle A	0	1	.000	6	0	0	0-0	9.1	13	7	4	0	9-2	7	6.75	75	.317	.440	0	ø	0	—	-1	-0	-0.1
Total	10	38	51	.427	320	49	1	7-16	624	590	347	91	17	299-25	502	4.62	93	.251	.337	14-0-1	.214	1	100	-21	158	-2.0

Demarais, Fred Frederick; B11.1.1866 Montreal QC, Can.; D3.6.1919 Stamford CT; TR/5´9˝/168; d7.26

YEAR	TM LG	W	L	PCT	G	GS	CG-SHO	SV-BS	IP	H	R	HR	HB	BB-IB	SO	ERA	AERA	OAV	OOB	AB-HR-SH	AVG	PB	SUP	APR	DL	PW
1890	Chi N	0	0	ø	1	0	0	0	2	1	0	0	0	1	1	0.00	ø	.143	.250	2	.000	-0	—	1	—	0.0

Demaree, Al Albert Wentworth; B9.8.1884 Quincy IL; D4.30.1962 Los Angeles CA; BL/TR/6´0˝/170; d9.26

YEAR	TM LG	W	L	PCT	G	GS	CG-SHO	SV-BS	IP	H	R	HR	HB	BB-IB	SO	ERA	AERA	OAV	OOB	AB-HR-SH	AVG	PB	SUP	APR	DL	PW
1912	NY N	1	0	1.000	2	2	1-1	0	16	17	3	0	0	2	11	1.69	200	.288	.311	5	.000	-1	87	3	—	0.1
1913	†NY N	13	4	.765	31	25	11-2	2	199.2	176	65	4	5	38	76	2.21	141	.243	.286	66-0-1	.106	-3	106	21	—	1.2
1914	NY N	10	17	.370	38	29	13-2	0	224	219	97	3	8	77	89	3.09	86	.263	.331	68-0-2	.132	-2	116	-11	—	-1.6
1915	Phi N	14	11	.560	32	26	13-3	1	209.2	201	84	4	3	58	69	3.05	90	.260	.314	68-0-3	.176	0	112	-2	—	-0.5
1916	Phi N	19	14	.576	39	35	25-4	1	285	252	99	4	8	48	130	2.62	101	.242	.281	101-0-1	.109	-4	105	6	—	-0.2
1917	Chi N	5	9	.357	24	18	6-1	1	141.1	125	53	5	2	37	43	2.55	114	.244	.297	41-0-1	.122	-1	84	6	—	0.5
	NY N	4	5	.444	15	11	1	0	78.1	70	33	1	1	17	23	2.64	97	.239	.283	18-0-3	.111	-1	67	-3	—	-0.4
	Year	9	14	.391	39	29	7-1	1	219.2	195	86	6	3	54	66	2.58	108	.242	.292	59-0-4	.119	-2	78	2	—	0.1
1918	NY N	8	6	.571	26	14	8-2	1	142	143	56	5	2	25	39	2.47	106	.262	.297	47-0-4	.128	-3	152	0	—	-0.3
1919	Bos N	6	6	.500	25	13	6	3	128	147	66	8	1	35	34	3.80	75	.300	.348	42	.048	-5	111	-13	—	-1.8
Total	8	80	72	.526	232	173	84-15	9	1424	1350	556	34	30	337	514	2.77	100	.256	.304	456-0-15	.118	-20	107	7	—	-3.0

Demaria, Chris Chris Neil; B9.28.1980 Torrance CA; BB/TR/6´3˝/210; [PitN02 17/493]; d9.9; Col Cal St.–Long Beach

YEAR	TM LG	W	L	PCT	G	GS	CG-SHO	SV-BS	IP	H	R	HR	HB	BB-IB	SO	ERA	AERA	OAV	OOB	AB-HR-SH	AVG	PB	SUP	APR	DL	PW
2005	KC A	1	0	1.000	8	0	0	0-0	9	14	10	3	0	5-0	11	9.00	49	.359	.432	0	ø	0	—	-5	0	-0.4
2006	Mil N	0	1	.000	10	0	0	0-0	13.2	10	11	4	2	9-0	11	5.93	76	.200	.344	0	ø	0	—	-3	0	-0.2
Total	2	1	1	.500	18	0	0	0-0	22.2	24	21	7	2	14-0	22	7.15	62	.270	.381	0	ø	0	—	-8	0	-0.6

Demery, Larry Lawrence Calvin; B6.4.1953 Bakersfield CA; BR/TR/6´0˝/170; [PitN72*S7/107]; d6.2; Col Los Angeles (CA) City; [DL 1978 Pit N 58]

YEAR	TM LG	W	L	PCT	G	GS	CG-SHO	SV-BS	IP	H	R	HR	HB	BB-IB	SO	ERA	AERA	OAV	OOB	AB-HR-SH	AVG	PB	SUP	APR	DL	PW
1974	†Pit N	6	6	.500	19	15	2	0-0	95.1	95	47	12	0	51-5	51	4.25	82	.262	.351	33-0-3	.152	0*	132	-6	0	-0.7
1975	†Pit N	7	5	.583	45	8	1	4-1	114.2	95	40	7	3	43-6	59	2.90	123	.230	.305	24-0-2	.125	1*	166	10	0	1.1
1976	Pit N	10	7	.588	36	15	4-1	2-1	145	123	56	8	2	58-8	72	3.17	111	.234	.309	40-0-4	.125	-1*	92	7	0	0.7
1977	Pit N	6	5	.545	39	8	0	1-1	90.1	100	59	13	0	47-3	35	5.08	79	.279	.360	20	.150	-0*	94	-11	0	-1.3
Total	4	29	23	.558	139	46	7-1	7-3	445.1	413	202	40	5	199-22	217	3.72	98	.249	.328	117-0-9	.137	0	117	0	58	-0.2

YEAR	TM LG	W	L	PCT	G	GS	CG-SHO	SV-BS	IP	H	R	HR	HB	BB-IB	SO	ERA	AERA	OAV	OOB	AB-HR-SH	AVG	PB	SUP	APR	DL	PW
DeMiller, Harry	Harry; B11.12.1867 Wooster OH; D10.19.1928 Santa Ana CA; BR/TL; d8.20																									
1892	Chi N	1	1	.500	4	2	2	0	24	29	22	1	1	16	15	6.38	52	.287	.390	10	.300	1	105	-6	—	-0.3
DeMola, Don	Donald John; B7.5.1952 Glen Cove NY; BR/TR/6´2˝/180; [NYA70 7/160]; d4.13; [DL 1976 Mon N 157]																									
1974	Mon N	1	0	1.000	25	1	0	0-0	57.2	46	21	7	0	21-1	47	3.12	123	.223	.295	4	.000	-1	23	5	0	0.2
1975	Mon N	4	7	.364	60	0	0	1-1	97.2	92	47	8	4	42-4	63	4.15	93	.251	.333	8	.000	-1	—	-1	0	-0.4
Total	2	5	7	.417	85	1	0	1-1	155.1	138	68	15	4	63-5	110	3.77	103	.241	.320	12	.000	-1	23	4	157	-0.2
DeMott, Ben	Benyew Harrison; B4.2.1889 Green Village NJ; D7.5.1963 Somerville NJ; BR/TR/6´0˝/192; d8.12; Col Lafayette																									
1910	Cle A	0	3	.000	6	4	1	0	28.1	45	25	0	1	8	13	5.40	48	.388	.432	18	.167	-0*	58	-9	—	-0.9
1911	Cle A	0	1	.000	1	1	0	0	3.2	10	5	0	0	2	2	12.27	28	.588	.632	4	.000	-0*	21	-3	—	-0.4
Total	2	0	4	.000	7	5	1	0	32	55	30	0	1	10	15	6.19	43	.414	.458	22	.136	-0	51	-12	—	-1.3
Dempsey, Con	Cornelius Francis; B9.16.1922 San Francisco CA; D8.5.2006 Redwood City CA; BR/TR/6´4˝/190; d4.28; Col San Francisco																									
1951	Pit N	0	2	.000	3	2	0	0	7	11	7	2	0	4	3	9.00	47	.393	.469	1	.000	-0	31	-3	0	-0.6
Dempsey, Mark	Mark Steven; B12.17.1957 Dayton OH; BR/TR/6´6˝/215; [SFN80 26/646]; d9.4; Col Ohio St.																									
1982	SF N	0	0	ø	3	1	0	0-0	5.2	11	5	1	0	2-0	4	7.94	45	.440	.464	1	.000	-0	123	-2	0	-0.1
Dempster, Ryan	Ryan Scott; B5.3.1977 Sechelt BC, Can.; BR/TR/6´1˝/(195–215); [TexA95 3/66]; d5.23																									
1998	Fla N	1	5	.167	14	11	0	0-1	54.2	72	47	6	9	38-1	35	7.08	57	.336	.446	13-0-1	.000	-1	78	-19	0	-1.8
1999	Fla N	7	8	.467	25	25	0	0-0	147	146	77	21	6	93-2	126	4.71	93	.262	.370	49-0-1	.102	-2*	96	-2	0	-0.4
2000	Fla N☆	14	10	.583	33	33	2-1	0-0	226.1	210	102	30	5	97-7	209	3.66	120	.243	.322	77-0-4	.078	-4	90	19	0	1.3
2001	Fla N	15	12	.556	34	34	2-1	0-0	211.1	218	123	21	10	112-5	171	4.94	84	.269	.362	61-0-16	.049	-4	117	-18	0	-2.2
2002	Fla N	5	8	.385	18	18	3	0-0	120.1	126	66	12	7	55-1	87	4.79	82	.281	.366	34-0-4	.059	-2	122	-10	0	-1.1
	Cin N	5	5	.500	15	15	1	0-0	88.2	102	61	16	3	38-1	66	6.19	69	.293	.365	29-0-5	.207	1*	124	-15	0	-1.4
	Year	10	13	.435	33	33	4	0-0	209	228	127	28	10	93-2	153	5.38	76	.286	.365	63-0-9	.127	-1	123	-27	0	-2.5
2003	Cin N	3	7	.300	22	20	0	0-0	115.2	134	89	14	5	70-4	84	6.54	64	.293	.390	33-0-1	.030	-3*	100	-30	77	-2.5
2004	Chi N	1	1	.500	23	0	0	2-0	20.2	16	9	1	2	13-0	18	3.92	113	.208	.337	1	.000	-0	—	1	119	0.1
2005	Chi N	5	3	.625	63	6	0	33-2	92	83	35	4	4	49-7	89	3.13	140	.242	.343	14	.071	-1	65	12	0	1.6
2006	Chi N	1	9	.100	74	0	0	24-9	75	77	47	5	3	36-3	67	4.80	96	.262	.344	2	.000	-0	—	-3	0	-0.6
Total	9	57	68	.456	321	162	8-2	59-12	1151.2	1184	656	130	54	601-31	952	4.83	88	.268	.360	313-0-32	.077	-17	102	-65	196	-7.0
Denehy, Bill	William Francis; B3.31.1946 Middletown CT; BB/TR (BL 1971)/6´3˝/200; d4.16																									
1967	NY N	1	7	.125	15	8	0	0	53.2	51	38	8	0	29-2	35	4.70	72	.248	.338	9-0-2	.000	-1	26	-11	0	-1.5
1968	Was A	0	0	ø	3	0	0	0	2	4	3	0	0	4-1	1	9.00	32	.444	.615	0	ø	0	—	-2	0	-0.1
1971	Det A	0	3	.000	31	1	0	1-0	49	47	25	4	4	28-0	27	4.22	86	.250	.357	2-0-1	.000	1	25	-3	0	-0.1
Total	3	1	10	.091	49	9	0	1-0	104.2	102	66	12	4	61-3	63	4.56	77	.253	.355	11-0-3	.000	0	25	-16	0	-1.7
Denman, Brian	Brian John; B2.12.1956 Minneapolis MN; BR/TR/6´4˝/205; [BosA78*S1/13]; d8.22; Col Minnesota																									
1982	Bos A	3	4	.429	9	9	2-1	0-0	49	55	32	6	0	9-3	9	4.78	91	.282	.312	0	ø	0	95	-4	0	-0.5
Denney, Kyle	Kyle Dean; B7.27.1977 Prague OK; BR/TR/6´2˝/190; [CleA99 26/797]; d9.14; Col Oklahoma; [DL 2005 Cle A 35]																									
2004	Cle A	1	2	.333	4	4	0	0-0	16	32	17	3	0	8-0	13	9.56	45	.421	.471	0	ø	0	96	-9	0	-1.2
Dennis, Don	Donald Ray; B3.3.1942 Uniontown KS; BR/TR/6´2˝/190; d6.18; Col Emporia St.																									
1965	StL N	2	3	.400	41	0	0	6	55	47	17	3	1	16-11	29	2.29	168	.236	.294	5	.400	1	—	8	0	1.1
1966	StL N	4	2	.667	38	1	0	2	59.2	73	36	8	1	17-10	25	4.98	72	.302	.346	12	.083	-1	221	-9	0	-0.8
Total	2	6	5	.545	79	1	0	8	114.2	120	53	11	2	33-21	54	3.69	101	.272	.322	17	.176	-0	221	-1	0	0.3
Denny, John	John Allen; B11.8.1952 Prescott AZ; BR/TR/6´3˝/(180–190); [StLN70 29/679]; d9.12																									
1974	StL N	0	0	ø	2	0	0	0-0	2	3	2	0	0	0-0	1	0.00	ø	.273	.273	0	ø	0	—	0	0	0.0
1975	StL N	10	7	.588	25	24	3-2	0-0	136	149	73	5	3	51-6	72	3.97	96	.280	.344	44-0-6	.227	1*	95	-3	0	-0.2
1976	StL N	11	9	.550	30	30	8-3	0-0	207	189	71	11	8	74-3	74	**2.52**	**142**	.246	.318	67-0-7	.224	2	103	22	0	2.4
1977	StL N	8	8	.500	26	26	3-1	0-0	149.2	165	85	9	5	62-0	60	4.51	87	.281	.353	51-0-5	.098	-3	138	-10	37	-1.1
1978	StL N	14	11	.560	33	33	11-2	0-0	234	200	81	13	6	74-4	103	2.96	120	.238	.302	73-0-7	.178	2	105	19	0	2.7
1979	StL N	8	11	.421	31	31	5-2	0-0	206	206	116	24	3	100-7	99	4.85	79	.264	.349	70-0-8	.129	-1	104	-20	0	-1.7
1980	Cle A	8	6	.571	16	16	4-1	0-0	108.2	116	54	4	5	47-2	59	4.39	94	.284	.363	0	ø	0	89	-1	55	-0.1
1981	Cle A	10	6	.625	19	19	6-3	0-0	145.2	139	62	9	3	66-3	94	3.15	117	.254	.335	0	ø	0	103	6	0	0.9
1982	Cle A	6	11	.353	21	21	5	0-0	138.1	126	80	11	6	73-2	94	5.01	83	.240	.338	0	ø	0	95	-10	0	-1.1
	Phi N	0	2	.000	4	4	0	0-0	22.1	18	12	1	0	10-1	19	4.03	92	.217	.301	6	.167	0	30	-1	0	0.0
1983	†Phi N	**19**	6	**.760**	36	36	7-1	0-0	242.2	229	77	9	4	53-5	139	2.37	152	.250	.293	77-0-17	.169	0	112	**32**	0	3.4
1984	Phi N	7	7	.500	22	22	2	0-0	154.1	122	53	11	4	29-2	94	2.45	149	.214	.256	47-0-5	.191	0	103	19	60	1.9
1985	Phi N	11	14	.440	33	33	6-2	0-0	230.2	252	112	15	3	83-5	123	3.82	97	.282	.342	81-0-3	.123	-2	103	-3	0	-0.4
1986	Cin N	11	10	.524	27	27	2-1	0-0	171.1	179	89	15	4	56-9	115	4.20	92	.272	.331	54-0-5	.222	2	93	-6	0	-0.4
Total	13	123	108	.532	325	322	62-18	0-0	2148.2	2093	967	137	54	778-49	1146	3.59	105	.258	.325	570-0-63	.170	2	104	44	152	6.3
Dent, Eddie	Elliott Estill; B12.8.1887 Baltimore MD; D11.25.1974 Birmingham AL; BR/TR/6´1˝/190; d8.31																									
1909	Bro N	2	4	.333	6	5	4	0	42	47	23	2	0	15	17	4.29	60	.307	.369	15	.067	-1	119	-7	—	-1.0
1911	Bro N	2	1	.667	5	3	1	0	31.2	30	15	0	2	10	3	3.69	90	.256	.326	10	.100	-0	158	-1	—	-0.1
1912	Bro N	0	0	ø	1	0	0	0	1	4	4	0	0	1	1	36.00	9	.571	.625	1	.000	-0	—	-3	—	-0.2
Total	3	4	5	.444	12	8	5	0	74.2	81	42	2	2	26	21	4.46	65	.292	.357	26	.077	-2	133	-11	—	-1.3
Denzer, Roger	Roger "Peaceful Valley"; B10.5.1871 LeSueur MN; D9.18.1949 LeSueur MN; BL/TR/6´0˝/180; d4.24																									
1897	Chi N	2	8	.200	12	10	8	0	94.2	125	91	4	2	34	17	5.13	87	.315	.372	39	.154	-3	85	-10	—	-1.1
1901	NY N	2	6	.250	11	9	3-1	0	61.2	69	30	2	2	5	22	3.36	98	.280	.300	22	.091	-1	52	1	—	-0.1
Total	2	4	14	.222	23	19	11-1	0	156.1	194	121	6	4	39	39	4.43	90	.302	.345	61	.131	-4	70	-9	—	-1.2
DePaula, Jorge	Jorge; B11.10.1978 Sabana Grande, D.R.; BR/TR/6´1˝/160; d9.5																									
2003	NY A	0	0	ø	4	1	0	0-0	11.1	3	1	1	1	1-0	7	0.79	553	.083	.132	0	ø	0	42	5	0	0.2
2004	NY A	0	1	.000	3	1	0	0-0	9	9	6	2	0	4-0	2	5.00	92	.281	.342	0	ø	0	60	-1	170	-0.1
2005	NY A	0	0	ø	3	0	0	0-0	6.2	8	6	2	0	3-0	3	8.10	53	.296	.367	0	ø	0	—	-3	0	-0.1
Total	3	0	1	.000	10	2	0	0-0	27	20	13	5	1	8-0	12	4.00	111	.211	.274	0	ø	0	52	1	170	0.0
DePaula, Sean	Sean Michael; B11.7.1973 Newton MA; BR/TR/6´4˝/215; [CleA96 9/273]; d8.31; Col Wake Forest																									
1999	†Cle A	0	0	ø	11	0	0	0-0	11.2	8	6	0	0	3-0	18	4.63	110	.200	.256	0	ø	0	—	1	0	0.0
2000	Cle A	0	0	ø	13	0	0	0-2	16.2	20	11	3	0	14-2	16	5.94	84	.294	.410	0	ø	0	—	-1	65	0.0
2002	Cle A	1	1	.500	5	0	0	0-2	6.1	11	9	3	0	3-0	8	12.79	35	.367	.424	0	ø	0	—	-6	0	-1.0
Total	3	1	1	.500	29	0	0	0-4	34.2	39	26	6	0	20-2	42	6.75	73	.283	.371	0	ø	0	—	-6	65	-1.0
Derby, George	George H. "Jonah"; B7.6.1857 Webster MA; D7.4.1925 Philadelphia PA; BL/TR/6´0˝/175; d5.2																									
1881	Det N	29	26	.527	56	55	55-**9**	0	494.2	505	252	3	—	86	**212**	2.20	132	.251	.281	236	.186	-10*	99	**34**	—	**2.3**
1882	Det N	17	20	.459	40	39	38-3	0	362	386	267	8	—	81	182	3.26	90	.256	.294	149	.195	-6	84	-20	—	-2.1
1883	Buf N	2	10	.167	14	13	12	1	107.2	173	120	3	—	15	34	5.85	54	.334	.353	59	.237	-1*	92	-30	—	-2.5
Total	3	48	56	.462	110	107	105-12	1	964.1	1064	639	14	—	182	428	3.01	98	.263	.295	444	.196	-17	92	-16	—	-2.3
Derringer, Paul	Samuel Paul "Duke"; B10.17.1906 Springfield KY; D11.17.1987 Sarasota FL; BR/TR/6´3.5˝/205; d4.16; Col Georgetown																									
1931	†StL N	18	8	**.692**	35	23	15-4	2	211.2	225	88	9	4	65	134	3.36	117	.274	.330	72-0-6	.097	-6	99	15	—	1.1
1932	StL N	11	14	.440	39	30	14-1	0	233.1	296	133	6	2	67	78	4.05	97	.310	.356	73-0-3	.178	-0	92	-8	—	-0.8
1933	StL N	0	2	.000	3	2	1	0	17	24	11	0	1	9	3	4.24	82	.353	.436	5	.000	-1	12	-2	—	-0.3
	Cin N	7	25	.219	33	31	16-2	1	231	240	106	4	5	51	86	3.23	105	.271	.315	76-0-2	.184	-1	55	3	—	0.4
	Year	7	27	.206	36	33	17-2	1	248	264	117	4	6	60	89	3.30	103	.277	.324	81-0-2	.173	-2	53	-3	—	0.1
1934	Cin N	15	21	.417	47	31	18-1	4	261	297	129	8	4	59	122	3.59	114	.283	.323	92-0-3	.196	0	79	14	—	1.7
1935	Cin N★	22	13	.629	45	33	20-3	2	276.2	295	132	13	4	49	120	3.51	113	.271	.305	93-0-6	.140	-5	90	13	—	1.1
1936	Cin N	19	19	.500	**51**	**37**	13-2	5	282.1	331	147	11	4	42	121	4.02	95	.289	.316	90-0-7	.200	-1	110	-5	—	-0.7
1937	Cin N	10	14	.417	43	26	12-1	1	222.2	240	112	7	0	55	94	4.04	92	.271	.313	80-0-2	.200	1	116	-5	—	-0.4

YEAR	TM LG	W	L	PCT	G	GS	CG-SHO	SV-BS	IP	H	R	HR	HB	BB-IB	SO	ERA	AERA	OAV	OOB	AB-HR-SH	AVG	PB	SUP	APR	DL	PW
1938	Cin N☆	21	14	.600	41	**37**	**26**-4	3	**307**	315	110	20	0	49	132	2.93	124	.262	.291	119-2-4	.176	-0	114	28	—	2.9
1939	†Cin N★	25	7	**.781**	38	35	28-5	0	301	321	115	15	3	35	128	2.93	131	.272	.295	110-0-17	.209	0	134	30	—	2.9
1940	†Cin N★	20	12	.625	37	**37**	26-3	0	296.2	280	110	17	0	48	115	3.06	124	.246	**.276**	108-0-4	.167	-2	97	25	—	2.1
1941	Cin N★	12	14	.462	29	28	17-2	1	228.1	233	91	16	0	54	76	3.31	109	.266	.309	84-0-2	.155	-3	78	10	0	0.7
1942	Cin N✳	10	11	.476	29	27	13-1	0	208.2	203	83	4	4	49	68	3.06	107	.250	.296	68-0-6	.132	-2	81	7	0	0.3
1943	Chi N	10	14	.417	32	22	10-2	3	174	184	90	7	0	39	75	3.57	93	.264	.303	58-0-4	.224	1	99	-8	0	-1.2
1944	Chi N	7	13	.350	42	16	7	3	180	205	96	13	0	39	69	4.15	85	.284	.321	57-0-2	.158	-2	104	-11	0	-1.4
1945	†Chi N	16	11	.593	35	30	15-1	4	213.2	223	99	8	1	51	86	3.45	106	.265	.308	75-0-9	.200	0	97	4	0	0.4
Total	15	223	212	.513	579	445	251-32	29	3645	3912	1652	158	32	761	1507	3.46	108	.272	.310	1260-2-77	.175	-20	96	110	0	8.8
Derrington, Jim	Charles James "Blackie"; B11.29.1939 Compton CA; BL/TL/6´3˝/190; d9.30																									
1956	Chi A	0	1	.000	1	1	0	0	6	9	6	2	0	6-0	3	7.50	55	.375	.500	2	.500	0	130	-3	0	-0.3
1957	Chi A	0	1	.000	20	5	0	0	37	29	21	4	1	29-0	14	4.86	77	.216	.358	4-0-2	.000	-0	158	-4	0	-0.3
Total	2	0	2	.000	21	6	0	0	43	38	27	6	1	35-0	17	5.23	72	.241	.379	6-0-2	.167	0	153	-7	0	-0.6
Deshaies, Jim	James Joseph; B6.23.1960 Massena NY; BL/TL/6´4˝/(220–222); [NYA82 21/542]; d8.7; Col LeMoyne (NY)																									
1984	NY A	0	1	.000	2	2	0	0-0	7	14	9	1	0	7-0	5	11.57	33	.438	.525	0	ø	0	94	-6	0	-0.6
1985	Hou N	0	0	ø	2	0	0	0-0	3	1	0	0	0	0-0	2	0.00	ø	.100	.100	0	ø	0	—	1	0	0.1
1986	Hou N	12	5	.706	26	26	1-1	0-0	144	124	58	16	2	59-2	128	3.25	111	.234	.311	43-0-4	.047	-1	105	6	16	0.4
1987	Hou N	11	6	.647	26	25	1	0-0	152	149	81	22	0	57-7	104	4.62	85	.257	.322	53-0-4	.094	-0	107	-10	21	-1.0
1988	Hou N	11	14	.440	31	31	3-2	0-0	207	164	77	20	2	72-5	127	3.00	111	.218	.284	63-0-6	.048	-4	77	8	0	0.4
1989	Hou N	15	10	.600	34	34	6-3	0-0	225.2	180	80	15	4	79-8	153	2.91	117	.217	.287	75-0-9	.120	-2*	108	13	0	1.2
1990	Hou N	7	12	.368	34	34	2	0-0	209.1	186	93	21	8	84-9	119	3.78	99	.245	.322	63-0-7	.063	-4	95	2	0	-0.2
1991	Hou N	5	12	.294	28	28	1	0-0	161	156	90	19	1	72-5	98	4.98	71	.259	.336	41-0-8	.098	-1	86	-23	0	-2.3
1992	SD N	4	7	.364	15	15	0	0-0	96	92	40	6	1	33-2	46	3.28	110	.258	.321	29-0-5	.207	1	72	2	0	0.4
1993	Min A	11	13	.458	27	27	1	0-0	167.1	159	85	24	6	51-1	80	4.41	100	.254	.313	0	ø	0	84	2	0	0.2
	SF N	2	2	.500	5	4	0	0-0	17	24	9	2	1	6-0	5	4.24	93	.348	.408	5-0-1	.000	-1	103	-1	0	-0.2
1994	Min A	6	12	.333	25	**25**	0	0-0	130.1	170	109	30	2	54-0	78	7.39	67	.321	.382	0	ø	0	103	-32	0	-3.4
1995	Phi N	0	1	.000	2	2	0	0-0	5.1	15	12	3	0	1-0	6	20.25	21	.484	.500	1	.000	-0	75	-9	0	-1.1
Total	12	84	95	.469	257	253	15-6	0-0	1525	1434	743	179	27	575-39	951	4.14	91	.251	.320	373-0-44	.088	-12	95	-47	37	-6.1
DeShong, Jimmie	James Brooklyn; B11.30.1909 Harrisburg PA; D10.16.1993 Lower Paxton Twp. PA; BR/TR/5´11˝/165; d4.12																									
1932	Phi A	0	0	ø	6	0	0	0	10	17	14	3	1	9	5	11.70	39	.378	.491	3	.000	-0	—	-8	—	-0.4
1934	NY A	6	7	.462	31	12	6	3	133.2	126	71	6	2	56	40	4.11	99	.243	.319	42-0-4	.190	2	103	-1	—	0.1
1935	NY A	4	1	.800	29	3	0	3	69	64	30	6	2	33	30	3.26	124	.242	.331	14-0-2	.071	-1	121	6	—	0.4
1936	Was A	18	10	.643	34	31	16-2	2	223.2	255	135	11	3	96	59	4.63	103	.285	.356	79-0-8	.190	2*	128	4	—	0.5
1937	Was A	14	15	.483	37	34	20	1	264.1	290	161	15	3	124	86	4.90	90	.280	.359	94-0-4	.202	2	111	-10	—	-0.8
1938	Was A	5	8	.385	31	14	1	0	131.1	160	104	11	1	83	41	6.58	69	.310	.407	46-0-1	.261	3	106	-28	—	-2.0
1939	Was A	0	3	.000	7	6	1	0	40.2	56	45	7	0	31	12	8.63	50	.337	.442	15	.200	0	128	-21	—	-1.1
Total	7	47	44	.516	175	100	44-2	9	872.2	968	560	59	12	432	273	5.08	87	.281	.363	293-0-19	.198	7	117	-58	—	-3.3
DeSilva, John	John Reed; B9.30.1967 Fort Bragg CA; BR/TR/6´0˝/(193–195); [DetA89 8/213]; d8.15; Col Brigham Young																									
1993	Det A	0	0	ø	1	0	0	0-0	1	2	1	0	0	0-0	0	9.00	48	.667	.500	0	ø	0	—	0	0	0.0
	LA N	0	0	ø	3	0	0	0-0	5.1	6	4	0	0	1-0	6	6.75	57	.273	.304	0	ø	0	—	-2	0	-0.1
1995	Bal A	1	0	1.000	2	2	0	0-0	8.2	8	7	3	1	7-0	1	7.27	66	.258	.400	0	ø	0	195	-2	0	-0.2
Total	2	1	0	1.000	6	2	0	0-0	15	16	12	3	1	8-0	7	7.20	61	.286	.373	0	ø	0	195	-4	0	-0.3
DesJardien, Shorty	Paul Raymond; B8.24.1893 Coffeyville KS; D3.7.1956 Monrovia CA; BR/TR/6´4.5˝/205; d5.20; Col Chicago																									
1916	Cle A	0	0	ø	1	0	0	0	1	1	2	0	0	1	0	18.00	17	.200	.333	0	ø	0	—	-1	—	-0.1
Dessau, Rube	Frank Rolland; B3.29.1883 New Galilee PA; D5.6.1952 York PA; BB/TR/5´11˝/175; d9.22																									
1907	Bos N	0	1	.000	2	2	1	0	9.1	13	11	0	1	10	1	10.61	24	.394	.545	4	.000	-0	167	-7	—	-0.6
1910	Bro N	2	3	.400	19	0	0	1	51.1	67	48	0	5	29	24	5.79	52	.328	.424	15-0-1	.067	-1	—	-18	—	-1.8
Total	2	2	4	.333	21	2	1	1	60.2	80	59	0	6	39	25	6.53	45	.338	.443	19-0-1	.053	-1	167	-25	—	-2.4
Dessens, Elmer	Elmer (Jusaino); B1.13.1971 Hermosillo, Sonora, Mexico; BR/TR/6´0˝/(178–200); d6.24																									
1996	Pit N	0	2	.000	15	3	0	0-0	25	40	23	2	0	4-0	13	8.28	53	.385	.404	5	.400	1	62	-9	41	-0.6
1997	Pit N	0	0	ø	3	0	0	0-0	3.1	2	0	0	1	0-0	2	0.00	ø	.167	.231	0	ø	0	—	2	0	0.1
1998	Pit N	2	6	.250	43	5	0	0-1	74.2	90	50	10	0	25-2	43	5.67	75	.300	.351	8-0-3	.000	-1	52	-10	16	-1.0
2000	Cin N	11	5	.688	40	16	1	1-0	147.1	170	73	10	3	43-7	85	4.28	112	.296	.344	40-0-1	.100	-0	118	9	0	0.9
2001	Cin N	10	14	.417	34	34	1-1	0-0	205	221	103	32	1	56-1	128	4.48	102	.279	.325	57-0-10	.193	1*	86	7	0	0.7
2002	Cin N	7	8	.467	30	30	0	0-0	178	173	70	24	7	49-8	93	3.03	141	.257	.314	45-0-9	.200	1*	85	22	25	1.8
2003	Ari N	8	8	.500	34	30	0	0-0	175.2	212	107	22	4	57-6	113	5.07	91	.299	.354	46-0-10	.196	1*	104	-7	0	-0.5
2004	Ari N	1	6	.143	38	9	0	2-2	85.1	107	54	11	1	23-4	55	4.75	96	.301	.343	18-0-4	.167	1	106	-3	0	-0.1
	†LA N	1	0	1.000	12	1	0	0-1	19.2	16	7	4	0	8-0	18	3.20	129	.216	.293	4	.250	0	157	2	0	0.1
	Year	2	6	.250	50	10	0	2-3	105	123	61	15	1	31-4	73	4.46	101	.287	.334	22-0-4	.182	1	112	-1	0	0.0
2005	LA N	1	2	.333	28	7	0	0-0	65.2	63	30	6	1	19-2	37	3.56	117	.249	.301	10	.000	-1	97	4	56	0.1
2006	KC A	5	7	.417	43	0	0	2-5	54	63	31	4	1	13-6	36	4.50	104	.292	.333	0	ø	0	—	0	0	0.1
	LA N	0	1	.000	19	0	0	0-0	23	23	12	4	0	9-2	16	4.70	93	.258	.327	1	.000	-0	—	0	11	0.0
Total	10	46	59	.438	339	135	2-1	5-9	1056.2	1180	560	129	19	306-38	639	4.41	102	.284	.334	234-0-37	.167	3	95	17	149	1.6
Dettmer, John	John Franklin; B3.4.1970 Centreville IL; BR/TR/6´0˝/185; [TexA92 11/314]; d6.16; Col Missouri																									
1994	Tex A	0	6	.000	11	9	0	0-0	54	63	42	10	3	20-3	27	4.33	112	.286	.347	0	ø	0	95	-3	0	-0.2
1995	Tex A	0	0	ø	1	0	0	0-0	0.1	2	1	0	0	0-0	0	27.00	18	.667	.500	0	ø	0	—	-1	0	0.0
Total	2	0	6	.000	12	9	0	0-0	54.1	65	43	10	3	20-3	27	4.47	108	.291	.349	0	ø	0	95	-4	0	-0.2
Dettore, Tom	Thomas Anthony; B11.17.1947 Canonsburg PA; BL/TR/6´4˝/(197–200); [PitN68*S3/58]; d6.11																									
1973	Pit N	0	1	.000	12	1	0	0-0	22.2	33	19	1	3	14-4	13	5.96	59	.340	.435	4-0-1	.000	-0	25	-7	0	-0.4
1974	Chi N	3	5	.375	16	9	0	0-1	64.2	64	39	4	6	31-3	43	4.18	92	.255	.348	20-0-1	.250	1	152	-4	0	-0.2
1975	Chi N	5	4	.556	36	5	0	0-2	85.1	88	57	8	9	31-4	46	5.38	72	.270	.348	24	.250	1	68	-13	0	-1.2
1976	Chi N	0	1	.000	4	0	0	0-1	7	11	8	3	0	2-0	4	10.29	38	.355	.394	0	ø	0	—	-4	0	-0.5
Total	4	8	11	.421	68	15	0	0-4	179.2	196	123	16	18	78-11	106	5.21	73	.278	.362	48-0-2	.229	2	116	-28	0	-2.3
Deutsch, Mel	Melvin Elliott; B7.26.1915 Caldwell TX; D11.18.2001 Austin TX; BR/TR/6´4˝/215; d4.21; Col Texas																									
1946	Bos A	0	0	ø	3	0	0	0	6.1	7	5	1	0	3	2	5.68	64	.280	.357	2	.000	-0	—	-2	0	-0.1
Devens, Charlie	Charles; B1.1.1910 Milton MA; D8.13.2003 Scarborough ME; BR/TR/6´1˝/180; d9.24; Col Harvard																									
1932	NY A	1	0	1.000	1	1	1	0	9	6	2	0	0	7	4	2.00	204	.200	.351	2-0-1	.000	0	167	2	—	0.2
1933	NY A	3	3	.500	14	8	2	0	62	59	39	1	0	50	23	4.35	89	.250	.381	21-0-1	.095	-1	148	-5	—	-0.6
1934	NY A	1	0	1.000	1	1	1	0	11	9	3	0	0	5	4	1.64	248	.225	.311	2	.500	1	86	3	—	0.5
Total	3	5	3	.625	16	10	4	0	82	74	44	1	0	62	31	3.73	105	.242	.370	25-0-2	.120	0	143	0	—	0.1
Devine, Joey	Joseph Neal; B9.19.1983 Junction City KS; BR/TR/6´0˝/210; [AtlN05 1/27]; d8.20; Col North Carolina St.																									
2005	†Atl N	0	1	.000	5	0	0	0-0	5	6	7	2	0	5-1	3	12.60	34	.286	.423	1	.000	-0	—	-4	0	-0.8
2006	Atl N	0	0	ø	10	0	0	0-1	6.1	8	7	1	1	9-1	10	9.95	46	.308	.500	0	ø	0	—	-3	0	-0.2
Total	2	0	1	.000	15	0	0	0-1	11.1	14	14	3	1	14-2	13	11.12	40	.298	.468	1	.000	-0	—	-7	0	-1.0
Devine, Adrian	Paul Adrian; B12.2.1951 Galveston TX; BR/TR/6´4˝/(185–205); [AtlN70 2/45]; d6.27; [DL 1981 Tex A 32]																									
1973	Atl N	2	3	.400	24	1	0	4-1	32.1	45	24	6	2	12-3	15	6.40	62	.338	.399	4	.250	0	111	-7	0	-1.2
1975	Atl N	1	0	1.000	5	2	0	0-0	16.1	19	8	2	1	7-1	8	4.41	86	.284	.360	5	.000	-1	151	0	0	-0.1
1976	Atl N	5	6	.455	48	1	0	9-2	73	72	30	3	1	26-7	48	3.21	118	.255	.316	14-0-2	.000	-2	139	4	35	0.5
1977	Tex A	11	6	.647	56	2	0	15-4	105.2	102	43	8	4	31-11	67	3.58	114	.259	.316	0	ø	0	121	8	0	1.5
1978	Atl N	5	4	.556	31	6	0	3-1	65.1	84	45	3	0	25-5	26	5.92	68	.323	.380	11-0-1	.091	-1	108	-11	57	-1.5
1979	Atl N	1	2	.333	40	0	0	0-2	66.2	84	28	8	2	25-5	22	3.24	124	.311	.372	7	.000	-1	—	5	0	0.2
1980	Tex A	1	1	.500	13	0	0	0-0	28	49	22	4	1	9-1	8	4.82	81	.377	.415	0	ø	0	—	-5	86	-0.3
Total	7	26	22	.542	217	12	0	31-10	387.1	455	200	34	11	135-33	194	4.21	95	.296	.354	41-0-3	.049	-3	119	-6	210	-0.9

YEAR	TM LG	W	L	PCT	G	GS	CG-SHO	SV-BS	IP	H	R	HR	HB	BB-IB	SO	ERA	AERA	OAV	OOB	AB-HR-SH	AVG	PB	SUP	APR	DL	PW
DEVINEY, HAL	Harold John; B4.11.1893 Newton MA; D1.4.1933 Westwood MA; BR/TR; d7.30																									
1920	Bos A	0	0	ø	1	0	0	0	3	7	5	0	0	2	0	15.00	24	.500	.563	2	1.000	2	—	-4	—	0.0
DEVLIN, JIM	James Alexander; B6.6.1849 Philadelphia PA; D10.10.1883 Philadelphia PA; BR/TR/5´11˝/175; d4.21.1873; ▲																									
1875	Chi NA	7	16	.304	28	24	24	0	224	254	179	0	—	12	23	1.93	118	.256	.265	318	.289	7*	81	8	—	1.2
1876	Lou N	30	35	.462	**68**	**68**	**66**-5	0	**622**	566	309	3	—	37	**122**	1.56	174	.224	.235	298	.315	2	58	**67**	—	**6.2**
1877	Lou N	35	25	.583	**61**	**61**	**61**-4	0	**559**	617	288	4	—	41	141	2.25	**147**	.270	.283	268-1	.269	-2	82	**56**	—	**5.0**
Total	2	65	60	.520	129	129	127-9	0	1181	1183	597	7	—	78	263	1.89	159	.246	.258	566-1	.293	1	69	123	—	11.2
DEVLIN, JIM	James H.; B4.16.1866 Troy NY; D12.14.1900 Troy NY; TL/5´7˝/135; d6.28																									
1886	NY N	0	0	ø	1	0	0	1	2	3	5	0	—	4	2	18.00	18	.250	.438	1	.000	-0	—	-3	—	-0.3
1887	Phi N	0	2	.000	2	2	2	0	18	20	19	0	3	10	6	6.00	71	.267	.375	6	.333	0	122	-3	—	-0.2
1888	†StL AA	6	5	.545	11	11	10	0	90.1	82	54	3	8	20	45	3.19	102	.233	.289	37	.297	2	103	1	—	0.3
1889	StL AA	5	3	.625	9	8	5	0	60	56	38	0	7	24	37	2.40	176	.239	.328	26	.192	-2	101	8	—	0.7
Total	4	11	10	.524	23	21	17	1	170.1	161	116	3	18	58	90	3.38	109	.239	.316	70	.257	1	105	3	—	0.5
DEWALD, CHARLIE	Charles H.; B9.22.1867 Newark NJ; D8.22.1904 Cleveland OH; TL; d9.20																									
1890	Cle P	2	0	1.000	2	2	2	0	14	13	7	0	0	5	6	0.64	618	.236	.300	8	.375	1	108	4	—	0.5
DEWEY, MARK	Mark Alan; B1.3.1965 Grand Rapids MI; BR/TR/6´0˝/(185–216); [SFN87 23/594]; d8.24; Col Grand Valley St.																									
1990	SF N	1	1	.500	14	0	0	0-1	22.2	22	7	1	0	5-1	11	2.78	132	.259	.300	1	.000	0	—	3	0	0.2
1992	NY N	1	0	1.000	20	0	0	0-0	33.1	37	16	2	0	10-2	24	4.32	81	.280	.331	1	.000	-0	—	-2	0	-0.1
1993	Pit N	1	2	.333	21	0	0	7-5	26.2	14	8	0	3	10-1	14	2.36	173	.157	.257	0	ø	0	—	5	0	0.8
1994	Pit N	2	1	.667	45	0	0	1-1	51.1	61	22	4	3	19-3	30	3.68	119	.303	.371	1	1.000	0	—	4	15	0.3
1995	SF N	1	0	1.000	27	0	0	0-0	31.2	30	12	2	0	17-6	32	3.13	132	.254	.346	1	.000	-0	—	4	89	0.2
1996	SF N	6	3	.667	78	0	0	0-5	83.1	79	40	9	5	41-9	57	4.21	98	.257	.350	7	.000	-0	—	1	0	0.1
Total	6	12	7	.632	205	0	0	8-12	249	243	105	18	11	102-22	168	3.65	111	.261	.338	11	.091	0	—	15	104	1.5
DEWITT, MATT	Matthew Brian; B9.4.1977 San Bernardino CA; BR/TR/6´4˝/(210–220); [StLN95 10/267]; d6.20																									
2000	Tor A	1	0	1.000	8	0	0	0-0	13.2	20	13	4	2	9-0	6	8.56	59	.351	.456	0	ø	0	—	-5	39	-0.3
2001	Tor A	0	2	.000	16	0	0	0-0	19	22	8	2	1	10-5	13	3.79	121	.293	.384	0	ø	0	—	2	0	0.2
2002	SD N	0	1	.000	5	0	0	0-0	7.1	6	2	1	0	3-0	5	1.23	317	.231	.300	0	ø	0	—	2	150	0.2
Total	3	1	3	.250	29	0	0	0-0	40	48	23	7	3	22-5	24	4.95	93	.304	.397	0	ø	0	—	-1	189	0.1
DIAZ, CARLOS	Carlos Antonio; B1.7.1958 Kaneohe HI; BR/TL/6´0˝/(161–170); [SeaA79 S1/15]; d6.30; Col Hancock (CA) JC																									
1982	Atl N	3	2	.600	19	0	0	1-0	25.1	31	15	3	0	9-2	16	4.62	80	.307	.360	3	.000	-0	—	-3	0	-0.5
	NY N	0	0	ø	4	0	0	0-0	3.2	6	2	0	0	4-1	0	0.00	ø	.353	.476	0	ø	0	—	1	0	0.0
	Year	3	2	.600	23	0	0	1-0	29	37	17	3	0	13-3	16	4.03	91	.314	.379	3	.000	-0	—	-2	0	-0.5
1983	NY N	3	1	.750	54	0	0	2-1	83.1	62	22	1	1	35-13	64	2.05	179	.211	.294	5-0-1	.000	-0	—	15	0	0.8
1984	LA N	1	0	1.000	37	0	0	1-1	41	47	26	4	0	24-5	36	5.49	65	.285	.374	1-0-1	.000	-0	—	-8	0	-0.4
1985	†LA N	6	3	.667	46	0	0	0-1	79.1	70	28	7	0	18-6	73	2.61	134	.230	.272	4	.000	-0	—	8	0	0.8
1986	LA N	0	0	ø	19	0	0	0-1	25.1	33	14	2	0	7-2	18	4.26	81	.317	.357	1	.000	-0	—	-3	16	-0.1
Total	5	13	6	.684	179	0	0	4-4	258	249	107	17	1	97-29	207	3.21	112	.253	.318	14-0-2	.000	-1	—	10	16	0.6
DIAZ, FELIX	Felix Antonio; B7.27.1980 Las Matas de Farfan, D.R.; BR/TR/6´1˝/180; d5.13; [DL 2005 Chi A 32]																									
2004	Chi A	2	5	.286	18	7	0	0-0	49.1	62	38	13	3	16-1	33	6.75	70	.307	.362	1	.000	-0	98	-10	0	-1.2
DIAZ, JOSELO	Joselo (Soriano); B4.13.1980 San Pedro de Macoris, D.R.; BR/TR/6´0˝/240; d9.6																									
2006	KC A	0	0	ø	4	0	0	0-0	6.2	10	8	2	1	8-0	3	10.80	43	.345	.500	0	ø	0	—	-4	0	-0.2
DIBBLE, ROB	Robert Keith; B1.24.1964 Bridgeport CT; BL/TR/6´4˝/(220–235); [CinN83 S1/20]; d6.29; Col Florida Southern; [DL 1994 Cin N 130]																									
1988	Cin N	1	1	.500	37	0	0	0-1	59.1	43	12	2	1	21-5	59	1.82	196	.207	.279	2-0-2	.000	-0	—	12	0	0.5
1989	Cin N	10	5	.667	74	0	0	2-6	99	62	23	4	3	39-11	141	2.09	172	.176	.261	8	.000	-1	—	17	15	2.5
1990	†Cin N★	8	3	.727	68	0	0	11-6	98	62	22	3	1	34-3	136	1.74	226	.183	.255	7-0-3	.000	-1	—	**22**	0	2.8
1991	Cin N★	3	5	.375	67	0	0	31-5	82.1	67	32	5	0	25-2	124	3.17	120	.223	.280	2-0-1	.000	-0	—	6	0	0.9
1992	Cin N	3	5	.375	63	0	0	25-5	70.1	48	26	3	2	31-2	110	3.07	117	.193	.285	5	.400	1	—	4	10	0.8
1993	Cin N	1	4	.200	45	0	0	19-9	41.2	34	33	8	2	42-0	49	6.48	62	.225	.400	1	1.000	0	—	-12	48	-2.0
1995	Chi A	0	1	.000	16	0	0	1-0	14.1	7	10	1	3	27-2	16	6.28	71	.156	.481	0	ø	0	—	-3	0	-0.2
	Mil A	1	1	.500	15	0	0	0-1	12	9	11	1	0	19-0	10	8.25	61	.225	.444	0	ø	0	—	-4	0	-0.5
	Year	1	2	.333	31	0	0	1-1	26.1	16	21	2	3	46-2	26	7.18	66	.188	.464	0	ø	0	—	-7	0	-0.7
Total	7	27	25	.519	385	0	0	89-33	477	332	169	27	12	238-25	645	2.98	128	.197	.297	25-0-6	.120	-1	—	42	203	4.8
DIBUT, PEDRO	Pedro (Villafana); B11.18.1892 Cienfuegos, Cuba; D12.4.1979 Hialeah FL; BR/TR/5´8˝/190; d5.1																									
1924	Cin N	3	0	1.000	7	2	2	0	36.2	24	9	1	0	12	15	2.21	170	.188	.257	11-0-1	.273	1	203	7	—	0.7
1925	Cin N	0	0	ø	1	0	0	0	0	3	2	0	0	0	0	(2)	ø	1.000	1.000	0	ø	0	—	-2	—	-0.2
Total	2	3	0	1.000	8	2	2	0	36.2	27	11	1	0	12	15	2.70	139	.206	.273	11-0-1	.273	1	203	5	—	0.5
DICKERMAN, LEO	Leo Louis; B10.31.1896 DeSoto MO; D4.30.1982 Atkins AR; BR/TR/6´4˝/192; d4.21																									
1923	Bro N	8	12	.400	35	20	7-1	0	159.2	180	95	4	2	72	58	3.72	104	.283	.357	52-2-4	.250	3	112	-2	—	0.2
1924	Bro N	0	0	ø	7	2	0	0	19.2	20	16	0	2	16	9	5.49	68	.263	.404	6	.167	-0	181	-5	—	-0.2
	StL N	7	4	.636	18	13	8-1	0	119.2	108	43	6	0	51	28	2.41	157	.249	.328	39-0-3	.231	1	128	17	—	1.5
	Year	7	4	.636	25	15	8-1	0	139.1	128	59	6	2	67	37	2.84	133	.251	.340	45-0-3	.222	1	135	11	—	1.3
1925	StL N	4	11	.267	29	18	7-2	1	130.2	135	95	10	2	79	40	5.58	77	.273	.376	44-0-3	.114	-3	92	-18	—	-1.8
Total	3	19	27	.413	89	53	22-4	1	429.2	443	249	20	6	218	135	4.00	99	.270	.358	141-2-10	.199	1	112	-8	—	-0.3
DICKERSON, GEORGE	George Clark; B12.1.1892 Renner TX; D7.9.1938 Los Angeles CA; BR/TR/6´1˝/170; d8.2																									
1917	Cle A	0	0	ø	1	0	0	0	1	0	0	0	0	0	0	0.00	ø	.000	.000	0	ø	0	—	0	—	0.0
DICKEY, R.A.	Robert Alan; B10.29.1974 Nashville TN; BR/TR/6´3˝/(200–220); [TexA96 1/18]; d4.22; Col Tennessee																									
2001	Tex A	0	1	.000	4	0	0	0-0	12	13	9	3	0	7-1	4	6.75	71	.283	.377	0	ø	0	—	-2	0	-0.2
2003	Tex A	9	8	.529	38	13	1-1	1-0	116.2	135	68	16	5	38-5	94	5.09	98	.292	.350	1	1.000	0	89	0	0	0.0
2004	Tex A	6	7	.462	25	15	0	1-0	104.1	136	77	17	4	33-1	57	5.61	88	.311	.363	0	ø	0	100	-10	48	-1.0
2005	Tex A	1	2	.333	9	4	0	0-0	29.2	29	23	4	2	17-0	15	6.67	68	.254	.358	0	ø	0	91	-6	42	-0.5
2006	Tex A	0	1	.000	1	1	0	0-0	3.1	8	7	6	0	1-0	1	18.90	25	.471	.500	0	ø	0	121	-5	0	-0.7
Total	5	16	19	.457	77	33	1-1	2-0	266	321	184	46	11	96-7	171	5.72	86	.298	.359	1	1.000	0	95	-23	90	-2.4
DICKMAN, EMERSON	George Emerson; B11.12.1914 Buffalo NY; D4.27.1981 New York NY; BR/TR/6´2˝/175; d6.27; Mil 1941–42; Col Washington and Lee																									
1936	Bos A	0	0	ø	1	0	0	0	1	2	2	0	0	1	2	9.00	59	.400	.500	0	ø	0	—	-1	—	0.0
1938	Bos A	5	5	.500	32	11	3-1	0	104	117	74	9	4	54	22	5.28	93	.288	.377	35-1-2	.286	4	104	-5	—	-0.1
1939	Bos A	8	3	.727	48	1	0	5	113.2	126	70	10	3	43	46	4.43	107	.282	.349	36	.056	-4	317	2	—	-0.1
1940	Bos A	8	6	.571	35	9	2	3	100	121	74	15	4	38	40	6.03	75	.291	.356	28-0-2	.107	-2	109	-17	—	-2.1
1941	Bos A	1	1	.500	9	3	1	0	31	37	23	4	0	17	16	6.39	65	.301	.386	11	.091	-1	138	-6	0	-0.5
Total	5	22	15	.595	125	24	6-1	8	349.2	403	243	38	11	153	126	5.33	88	.288	.363	110-1-4	.145	-2	118	-27	0	-2.8
DICKSON, JIM	James Edward; B4.20.1938 Portland OR; BL/TR/6´1˝/185; d7.2; Col Clark (WA) CC																									
1963	Hou N	0	1	.000	13	0	0	2	14.2	22	13	0	0	2-0	6	6.14	51	.344	.353	1	.000	-0	—	-6	0	-0.6
1964	Cin N	1	0	1.000	4	0	0	0	5	8	4	0	0	5-1	6	7.20	50	.444	.542	0	ø	0	—	-2	0	-0.3
1965	KC A	3	2	.600	68	0	0	0	85.2	68	40	6	2	47-7	54	3.47	101	.220	.324	2	.000	-0	—	-1	0	-0.1
1966	KC A	1	0	1.000	24	1	0	1	37	37	28	4	0	23-2	20	5.35	63	.264	.366	4	.250	0	104	-9	0	-0.5
Total	4	5	3	.625	109	1	0	3	142.1	135	85	10	2	77-10	86	4.36	79	.254	.347	7	.143	-0	104	-18	0	-1.5
DICKSON, JASON	Jason Royce; B3.30.1973 London ON, Can.; BL/TR/6´0˝/(190–202); [CalA94 6/153]; d8.21; Col NE Oklahoma A&M JC; [DL 1999 Ana A 182]																									
1996	Cal A	1	4	.200	7	7	0	0-0	43.1	52	22	6	1	18-1	20	4.57	111	.306	.374	0	ø	0	63	3	0	0.3
1997	Ana A☆	13	9	.591	33	32	2-1	0-0	203.2	236	111	32	7	56-3	115	4.29	108	.289	.338	2	.000	-0	105	5	0	0.3
1998	Ana A	10	10	.500	27	18	0	0-0	122	147	89	17	6	41-1	61	6.05	78	.303	.359	4	.000	-0	98	-17	0	-2.4

YEAR	TM LG	W	L	PCT	G	GS	CG-SHO	SV-BS	IP	H	R	HR	HB	BB-IB	SO	ERA	AERA	OAV	OOB	AB-HR-SH	AVG	PB	SUP	APR	DL	PW
2000	Ana A	2	2	.500	6	6	0	0-0	28	39	20	5	1	7-0	18	6.11	85	.336	.379	0	ø	0	103	-3	153	-0.3
Total	4	26	25	.510	73	63	2-1	0-0	397	474	242	60	15	122-5	214	4.99	95	.299	.351	6	.000	-0	98	-12	335	-2.1
Dickson, Lance	Lance Michael; B10.19.1969 Fullerton CA; BR/TL/6´0˝/185; [ChiN90 1/23]; d8.9; Col Arizona																									
1990	Chi N	0	3	.000	3	3	0	0-0	13.2	20	12	2	0	4-1	4	7.24	56	.370	.407	3	.000	-0	66	-4	23	-0.8
Dickson, Murry	Murry Monroe; B8.21.1916 Tracy MO; D9.21.1989 Kansas City KS; BR/TR/5´10.5˝/(150–160); d9.30; Mil 1944–45																									
1939	StL N	0	0	ø	1	0	0	0	3.2	1	0	0	0	1	2	0.00	ø	.091	.167	1	.000	-0	—	2	—	0.1
1940	StL N	0	0	ø	1	1	0	0	1.2	5	4	0	0	1	0	16.20	25	.500	.545	0	ø	0	174	-2	—	-0.1
1942	StL N	6	3	.667	36	7	2	2	120.2	91	41	1	1	61	66	2.91	118	.216	.316	42-0-1	.190	-0*	137	9	0	0.7
1943	†StL N	8	2	.800	31	7	2	0	115.2	119	51	4	1	49	44	3.58	94	.269	.343	34-0-3	.265	1	101	-2	0	0.0
1946	†StL N	15	6	**.714**	47	19	12-2	1	184.1	160	71	8	4	56	82	2.88	120	.234	.295	65-0-1	.277	4	129	11	0	1.9
1947	StL N	13	16	.448	47	25	11-4	3	231.2	211	101	16	2	88	111	3.07	135	.243	.315	80-0-2	.213	1	87	23	0	2.8
1948	StL N	12	16	.429	42	29	11-1	1	252.1	257	121	39	0	85	113	4.14	99	.265	.325	96-0-4	.281	4*	107	1	0	0.5
1949	Pit N	12	14	.462	44	20	11-2	0	224.1	216	97	17	6	80	89	3.29	128	.255	.324	84-0-1	.202	0	94	19	0	2.3
1950	Pit N	10	15	.400	51	22	8	3	225	227	104	20	2	83	76	3.80	115	.260	.326	82	.256	3*	75	15	0	2.0
1951	Pit N	20	16	.556	45	35	19-3	2	288.2	294	151	32	6	101	112	4.02	105	.262	.327	110-1-4	.273	5*	101	5	0	1.3
1952	Pit N	14	21	.400	43	34	21-2	2	277.2	278	128	26	1	76	112	3.57	112	.261	.311	107-0-2	.224	2*	88	11	0	1.8
1953	Pit N★	10	19	.345	45	26	10-1	4	200.2	240	121	27	3	58	88	4.53	99	.298	.348	61-0-4	.115	-4	64	-4	0	-0.9
1954	Phi N	10	20	.333	40	31	12-4	3	226.1	256	107	31	2	73	64	3.78	107	.286	.339	79-0-4	.190	0	77	7	0	0.9
1955	Phi N	12	11	.522	36	28	12-4	0	216	190	98	27	4	82-8	92	3.50	113	.238	.309	82-1-3	.220	1	98	10	0	1.1
1956	Phi N	0	3	.000	3	3	0	0	23	20	15	1	0	12-1	1	5.09	73	.241	.337	9	.333	1	71	-4	0	-0.3
	StL N	13	8	.619	28	27	12-3	0	196.1	175	75	20	1	57-4	109	3.07	123	.240	.295	77-0-2	.247	4*	122	16	0	2.3
	Year	13	11	.542	31	30	12-3	0	219.1	195	90	21	1	69-5	110	3.28	115	.240	.300	86-0-2	.256	4	117	11	0	2.0
1957	StL N	5	3	.625	14	13	3-1	0	74	87	41	8	1	25-0	29	4.14	96	.296	.350	27	.222	1	135	-3	33	-0.1
1958	KC A	9	5	.643	27	9	3	1	99	99	42	12	2	31-4	46	3.27	119	.258	.317	35-1-2	.257	2*	102	6	0	1.1
	†NY A	1	2	.333	6	2	0	1	20.1	18	17	4	1	12-0	9	5.75	61	.237	.348	7	.286	0	127	-6	0	-0.8
	Year	10	7	.588	33	11	3	2	119.1	117	59	16	3	43-4	55	3.70	104	.255	.322	42-1-2	.262	2	106	0	0	0.3
1959	KC A	2	1	.667	38	0	0	0	71	85	46	9	0	27-1	36	4.94	81	.290	.349	17	.176	-1	—	-8	0	-0.4
Total	18	172	181	.487	625	338	149-27	23	3052.1	3029	1431	302	37	1058-18	1281	3.66	110	.260	.323	1095-3-33	.231	25	97	106	33	16.2
Dickson, Walt	Walter Raleigh "Hickory"; B12.3.1878 New Summerfield TX; D12.9.1918 Ardmore OK; BR/TR/5´11.5˝/175; d4.26																									
1910	NY N	1	0	1.000	12	1	0	0	29.2	31	19	1	0	9	9	5.46	54	.272	.325	4	.250	0	176	-6	—	-0.3
1912	Bos N	3	19	.136	36	20	9-1	1	189	233	123	2	3	61	47	3.86	93	.320	.375	60-0-3	.167	-1	85	-11	—	-1.1
1913	Bos N	6	7	.462	19	15	8	0	128	118	71	4	1	45	47	3.23	102	.249	.316	45-0-1	.178	-1	134	-1	—	-0.3
1914	Pit F	9	19	.321	40	32	19-3	1	256.2	262	117	5	2	74	63	3.16	91	.273	.327	83-0-5	.084	-8	82	-9	—	-1.8
1915	Pit F	7	5	.583	27	11	4	0	96.2	115	51	5	2	33	36	4.19	65	.316	.376	31-0-3	.129	-1	152	-14	—	-1.7
Total	5	26	50	.342	134	79	40-4	2	700	759	381	17	8	222	202	3.60	86	.288	.345	223-0-12	.135	-11	103	-41	—	-5.2
Diehl, George	George Krause; B2.25.1918 Emmaus PA; D8.24.1986 Kingsport TN; BR/TR/6´2˝/196; d4.19																									
1942	Bos N	0	0	ø	1	0	0	0	3.2	2	2	0	1	2	0	2.45	136	.167	.333	1	.000	-0	—	0	0	0.0
1943	Bos N	0	0	ø	1	0	0	0	4	4	2	0	0	3	1	4.50	76	.267	.389	1	.000	-0	—	0	0	0.0
Total	2	0	0	ø	2	0	0	0	7.2	6	4	0	1	5	1	3.52	96	.222	.364	2	.000	-0	—	0	0	0.0
Dierker, Larry	Lawrence Edward; B9.22.1946 Hollywood CA; BR/TR/6´4˝/(190–210); d9.22; Mil 1967; M5																									
1964	Hou N	0	1	.000	3	1	0	0	9	7	4	1	0	3-0	5	2.00	171	.219	.278	3	.000	-0	26	1	0	0.0
1965	Hou N	7	8	.467	26	19	1	0	146.2	135	69	16	3	37-4	109	3.50	96	.240	.288	50-1-4	.100	-1	88	-4	0	-0.6
1966	Hou N	10	8	.556	29	28	8-2	0	187	173	73	17	1	45-0	108	3.18	108	.240	.284	67-1-2	.149	1	95	7	17	0.7
1967	Hou N	6	5	.545	15	15	4	0	99	95	44	4	1	25-0	68	3.36	98	.252	.300	31-0-1	.226	2	95	-1	0	0.1
1968	Hou N	12	15	.444	32	32	10-1	0	233.2	206	95	14	8	89-12	161	3.31	89	.240	.314	73-0-9	.068	-3*	96	-9	0	-1.5
1969	Hou N★	20	13	.606	39	37	20-4	0-0	305.1	240	97	18	1	72-6	232	2.33	153	.214	**.261**	118-1-7	.144	-1	102	40	0	4.2
1970	Hou N	16	12	.571	37	36	17-2	1-0	269.2	263	124	31	6	82-4	191	3.87	101	.254	.311	92-0-9	.174	-0	113	3	0	0.2
1971	Hou N✳	12	6	.667	24	23	6-2	0-1	159	150	50	8	2	33-1	91	2.72	124	.248	.287	54-0-3	.074	-3	111	13	0	1.1
1972	Hou N	15	8	.652	31	31	12-5	0-0	214.2	209	87	14	5	51-0	115	3.40	99	.256	.301	78-0-6	.167	-0	140	0	0	-0.2
1973	Hou N	1	1	.500	14	3	0	0-1	27	27	14	3	2	13-0	18	4.33	84	.265	.356	4	.000	-0	73	-2	74	-0.2
1974	Hou N	11	10	.524	33	33	7-3	0-0	223.2	189	76	18	6	82-4	150	2.90	120	.232	.306	71-0-11	.197	1	90	18	0	1.7
1975	Hou N	14	16	.467	34	34	14-2	0-0	232	225	109	24	7	91-6	127	4.00	85	.260	.331	76-0-13	.092	-4	104	-15	0	-2.3
1976	Hou N	13	14	.481	28	28	7-4	0-0	187.2	171	85	9	6	72-6	112	3.69	87	.243	.317	64-1-3	.141	-1	109	-9	0	-1.3
1977	StL N	2	6	.250	11	9	0	0-0	39.1	40	21	7	2	16-0	6	4.58	85	.267	.343	8-0-2	.000	-1	48	-2	83	-0.5
Total	14	139	123	.531	356	329	106-25	1-2	2333.2	2130	948	184	50	711-43	1493	3.31	104	.243	.302	789-4-70	.136	-12	102	40	174	1.4
Dietrich, Bill	William John "Bullfrog"; B3.29.1910 Philadelphia PA; D6.20.1978 Philadelphia PA; BR/TR/6´0˝/185; d4.13; Col Villanova																									
1933	Phi A	0	1	.000	8	1	0	0	17	13	11	1	0	19	4	5.82	74	.236	.432	3	.333	1	20	-2	—	0.0
1934	Phi A	11	12	.478	39	23	14-4	3	207.2	201	121	12	3	114	88	4.68	94	.255	.351	72-1-4	.208	3*	81	-7	—	-0.4
1935	Phi A	7	13	.350	43	15	8-1	3	185.1	203	128	7	1	101	59	5.39	84	.276	.364	60-0-3	.083	-6*	82	-17	—	-2.2
1936	Phi A	4	6	.400	21	4	0	3	71.2	91	55	4	0	40	34	6.53	78	.305	.388	27-0-1	.111	-2	60	-9	—	-1.2
	Was A	0	1	.000	5	0	0	0	8.1	13	11	0	0	6	4	9.72	49	.351	.442	0	ø	0	—	-5	—	-0.5
	Chi A	4	4	.500	14	11	6-1	0	82.2	93	50	8	1	36	39	4.68	111	.284	.356	30-0-2	.267	1	97	4	—	0.3
	Year	8	11	.421	40	15	6-1	3	162.2	197	116	12	1	82	77	5.75	89	.297	.375	57-0-3	.193	-1	88	-9	—	-1.4
1937	Chi A	8	10	.444	29	20	7-1	1	143.1	162	93	15	0	72	62	4.90	94	.285	.366	44-0-3	.182	1	90	-6	—	-0.5
1938	Chi A	2	4	.333	8	7	1	0	48	49	33	7	0	31	11	5.44	90	.259	.364	16	.063	-1	67	-2	—	-0.4
1939	Chi A	7	8	.467	25	19	2	0	127.2	134	81	14	2	56	43	5.22	91	.272	.349	37-1-2	.216	2	88	-6	—	-0.4
1940	Chi A	10	6	.625	23	17	6-1	0	149.2	154	78	10	0	65	43	4.03	110	.266	.340	50-1-3	.240	3	89	7	—	0.8
1941	Chi A	5	8	.385	19	15	4-1	0	109.1	114	73	7	4	50	26	5.35	77	.263	.345	34-0-1	.088	0	92	-14	0	-1.4
1942	Chi A	6	11	.353	26	23	6	0	160	173	92	16	5	70	39	4.89	74	.277	.355	48-0-7	.104	-1	93	-19	0	-1.9
1943	Chi A	12	10	.545	26	26	12-2	0	186.2	180	72	4	2	53	52	2.80	119	.253	.307	56-1-6	.143	0	82	10	0	1.3
1944	Chi A	16	17	.485	36	36	15-2	0	246	269	132	15	2	68	70	3.62	95	.279	.328	77-1-8	.117	-3	90	-11	0	-1.7
1945	Chi A	7	10	.412	18	16	6-3	0	122.1	136	61	4	0	36	43	4.19	79	.279	.329	36-0-3	.167	0	109	-10	0	-1.2
1946	Chi A	3	3	.500	11	9	3	1	62	63	21	4	0	24	20	2.61	131	.267	.335	19	.053	-2	84	6	76	0.5
1947	Phi A	5	2	.714	11	9	2-1	0	60.2	48	24	0	2	40	18	3.12	122	.223	.350	16-0-4	.063	-2	116	4	0	0.3
1948	Phi A	1	2	.333	4	2	0	0	15.1	21	10	0	0	9	5	5.87	73	.356	.441	2	.000	-0	42	-2	0	-0.4
Total	16	108	128	.458	366	253	92-17	11	2003.2	2117	1146	128	22	890	660	4.48	92	.271	.348	627-5-47	.150	-5	87	-79	76	-9.0
Dietz, Dutch	Lloyd Arthur; B2.9.1912 Cincinnati OH; D10.29.1972 Beaumont TX; BR/TR/5´11.5˝/180; d4.26; Mil 1944–45; Col Western Michigan																									
1940	Pit N	0	1	.000	4	2	0	0	15.1	22	11	2	0	4	8	5.87	65	.355	.394	7	.143	-0*	148	-3	—	-0.2
1941	Pit N	7	2	.778	33	6	4-1	1	100.1	88	28	6	2	33	22	2.33	155	.233	.298	25-0-1	.160	-1	67	16	0	1.3
1942	Pit N	6	9	.400	40	13	3	3	134.1	139	67	8	1	57	35	3.95	86	.268	.342	35-0-2	.200	1	84	-7	0	-0.9
1943	Pit N	0	3	.000	8	0	0	0	9	12	6	0	1	4	4	6.00	58	.324	.405	0	ø	0*	—	-2	0	-0.3
	Phi N	1	1	.500	21	0	0	2	36	42	29	2	0	15	10	6.50	52	.292	.358	6	.167	0	—	-12	0	-0.8
	Year	1	4	.200	29	0	0	2	45	54	35	2	1	19	14	6.40	53	.298	.368	6	.167	0	—	-14	0	-1.1
Total	4	14	16	.467	106	21	7-1	6	295	303	141	18	4	113	79	3.87	90	.266	.334	73-0-3	.178	-0	85	-8	0	-0.9
Diggins, Ben	Benjamin Howard; B6.13.1979 Leoti KS; BR/TR/6´7˝/230; [LAN00 1/17]; d9.2; Col Arizona																									
2002	Mil N	0	4	.000	5	5	0	0-0	24	28	24	4	1	18-1	15	8.63	48	.298	.409	7-0-1	.143	-0	50	-12	0	-1.5
Diggs, Reese	Reese Wilson "Diggsy"; B9.22.1915 Mathews VA; D10.30.1978 Baltimore MD; BB/TR/6´2˝/180; d9.15																									
1934	Was A	1	2	.333	4	3	2	0	21.1	26	17	3	0	15	2	6.75	64	.313	.418	8-0-2	.250	0	155	-6	—	-0.6
DiLauro, Jack	Jack Edward; B5.3.1943 Akron OH; BB/TL/6´2˝/185; d5.15; Col Akron																									
1969	NY N	1	4	.200	23	4	0	1-1	63.2	50	19	4	0	18-5	27	2.40	152	.216	.269	12	.000	-1	67	9	0	0.5
1970	Hou N	1	3	.250	42	0	0	3-6	33.2	34	23	4	0	17-2	23	4.28	91	.262	.340	2	.000	-0*	—	-4	0	-0.5
Total	2	2	7	.222	65	4	0	4-7	97.1	84	42	8	0	35-7	50	3.05	123	.232	.295	14	.000	-2	67	5	0	0.0

YEAR	TM LG	W	L	PCT	G	GS	CG-SHO	SV-BS	IP	H	R	HR	HB	BB-IB	SO	ERA	AERA	OAV	OOB	AB-HR-SH	AVG	PB	SUP	APR	DL	PW
DILLARD, GORDON	Gordon Lee; B5.20.1964 Salinas CA; BL/TL/6´1˝/(180–190); [BalA86 14/357]; d8.12; Col Oklahoma St.																									
1988	Bal A	0	0	ø	2	1	0	0-0	3	3	2	1	0	4-0	2	6.00	66	.273	.467	0	ø	0	93	-1	0	0.0
1989	Phi N	0	0	ø	5	0	0	0-0	4	7	3	0	0	0-0	2	6.75	53	.368	.368	0	ø	0	—	-1	0	-0.1
Total	2	0	0	ø	7	1	0	0-0	7	10	5	1	0	4-0	4	6.43	58	.333	.412	0	ø	0	93	-2	0	-0.1
DILLINGER, HARLEY	Harley Hugh "Hoke","Lefty"; B10.30.1894 Pomeroy OH; D1.8.1959 Cleveland OH; BR/TL/5´11˝/175; d8.16; Col Rio Grande																									
1914	Cle A	0	1	.000	11	2	1	0	33.2	41	28	0	1	25	11	4.54	64	.325	.441	10	.000	-1	189	-7	—	-0.6
DILLMAN, BILL	William Howard; B5.25.1945 Trenton NJ; BR/TR/6´2˝/180; [BalA65 6/118]; d4.14; Col Wake Forest																									
1967	Bal A	5	9	.357	32	15	2-1	3	124	115	61	13	3	33-2	69	4.35	72	.249	.301	31-0-4	.161	-0*	87	-15	0	-1.8
1970	Mon N	2	3	.400	18	0	0	0-0	30.2	28	18	4	1	18-4	17	5.28	79	.255	.356	2	.000	-0	—	-3	0	-0.4
Total	2	7	12	.368	50	15	2-1	3-0	154.2	143	79	17	4	51-6	86	4.54	74	.250	.313	33-0-4	.152	-1	87	-18	0	-2.2
DILLON, STEVE	Stephen Edward; B3.20.1943 Yonkers NY; BL/TL/5´10˝/160; d9.5																									
1963	NY N	0	0	ø	1	0	0	0	1.2	3	2	0	0	0-0	1	10.80	32	.429	.429	0	ø	0	—	-1	0	-0.1
1964	NY N	0	0	ø	2	0	0	0	3	4	3	1	0	2-0	2	9.00	40	.333	.400	0	ø	0	—	-2	0	-0.1
Total	2	0	0	ø	3	0	0	0	4.2	7	5	1	0	2-0	3	9.64	37	.368	.409	0	ø	0	—	-3	0	-0.2
DIMICHELE, FRANK	Frank Lawrence; B2.16.1965 Philadelphia PA; BR/TL/6´3˝/205; [CalA85 15/381]; d4.8; Col CC of Philadelphia (PA)																									
1988	Cal A	0	0	ø	4	0	0	0-0	4.2	5	5	2	0	2-0	1	9.64	40	.263	.333	0	ø	0	—	-3	0	-0.1
DINARDO, LENNY	Leonard Edward; B9.19.1979 Miami FL; BL/TL/6´4˝/(190–195); [NYN01 3/102]; d4.23; Col Stetson																									
2004	Bos A	0	0	ø	22	0	0	0-0	27.2	34	17	1	2	12-1	21	4.23	115	.298	.372	0	ø	0	—	1	106	0.0
2005	Bos A	0	1	.000	8	1	0	0-0	14.2	13	6	1	0	5-1	15	1.84	247	.236	.295	0	ø	0	61	3	0	0.2
2006	Bos A	1	2	.333	13	6	0	0-0	39	61	35	6	1	20-1	17	7.85	60	.363	.432	1	.000	-0	128	-13	101	-0.8
Total	3	1	3	.250	43	7	0	0-0	81.1	108	58	8	3	37-3	53	5.53	85	.320	.389	1	.000	-0	116	-9	207	-0.6
DINGMAN, CRAIG	Craig Allen; B3.12.1974 Wichita KS; BR/TR/6´4˝/(195–230); [NYA93 36/1009]; d6.30; Col Hutchinson (KS) CC; [DL 2006 Det A 182]																									
2000	NY A	0	0	ø	10	0	0	0-0	11	18	8	1	0	3-0	8	6.55	73	.375	.412	0	ø	0	—	-2	0	-0.1
2001	Col N	0	0	ø	7	0	0	1-0	7.1	11	11	4	2	3-2	2	13.50	40	.355	.444	0	ø	0	—	-5	15	-0.2
2004	Det A	2	2	.500	24	0	0	0-2	29.1	33	22	3	4	22-3	16	6.75	66	.295	.421	0	ø	0	—	-7	0	-0.8
2005	Det A	2	3	.400	34	0	0	4-1	32	30	14	5	1	9-0	24	3.66	117	.259	.317	0	ø	0	—	2	0	0.3
Total	4	4	5	.444	75	0	0	5-3	79.2	92	55	13	7	37-5	50	6.10	74	.300	.385	0	ø	0	—	-12	197	-0.8
DINNEEN, BILL	William Henry "Big Bill"; B4.5.1876 Syracuse NY; D1.13.1955 Syracuse NY; BR/TR/6´1˝/190; d4.22; U29																									
1898	Was N	9	16	.360	29	27	22	0	218.1	238	140	6	16	88	83	4.00	92	.275	.353	80-0-1	.100	-4*	89	-9	—	-1.2
1899	Was N	14	20	.412	37	35	30	0	291	350	191	6	11	106	91	3.93	100	.297	.361	119-0-2	.303	5	94	-6	—	0.1
1900	Bos N	20	14	.588	40	37	33-1	0	320.2	304	161	11	9	105	107	3.12	133	.250	.314	125-0-6	.280	2*	98	**32**	—	**3.1**
1901	Bos N	15	18	.455	37	34	31	0	309.1	295	136	8	6	77	141	2.94	123	.250	.299	147-1-4	.211	0*	70	22	—	2.1
1902	Bos A	21	21	.500	42	42	39-2	0	371.1	348	155	9	8	99	136	2.93	122	.248	.302	141-0-2	.128	-6*	95	33	—	2.3
1903	†Bos A	21	13	.618	37	34	32-6	**2**	299	255	98	6	4	66	148	2.26	134	.230	.276	106-0-5	.160	-1	103	28	—	2.9
1904	Bos A	23	14	.622	37	37	37-5	0	335.2	283	115	8	2	63	153	2.20	122	.230	.268	120-0-4	.208	-0	105	17	—	1.7
1905	Bos A	12	14	.462	31	29	23-2	1	243.2	235	117	7	7	50	97	3.73	72	.255	.299	88-0-4	.148	-3	100	-22	—	-2.6
1906	Bos A	8	19	.296	28	27	22-1	0	218.2	209	101	4	1	52	60	2.92	94	.255	.300	63-0-3	.111	-1	67	-6	—	-1.0
1907	Bos A	0	4	.000	5	5	3	0	32.2	42	25	5	2	8	8	5.23	49	.313	.361	10	.000	-1	63	-9	—	-1.1
	StL A	7	10	.412	24	16	15-2	4	155.1	153	67	3	5	33	38	2.43	103	.260	.305	49-0-3	.204	2	97	-2	—	-0.2
	Year	7	14	.333	29	21	18-2	**4**	188	195	92	8	7	41	46	2.92	86	.270	.315	59-0-3	.169	1	89	-10	—	-1.3
1908	StL A	14	7	.667	27	16	11-2	0	167	133	52	2	4	53	39	2.10	114	.231	.300	59-0-1	.203	0	89	7	—	0.8
1909	StL A	6	7	.462	17	13	8-3	0	112	112	53	3	1	29	26	3.46	70	.267	.316	36-0-1	.194	2	90	-12	—	-1.1
Total	12	170	177	.490	391	352	306-24	7	3074.2	2957	1411	78	76	829	1127	3.01	107	.254	.308	1143-1-36	.192	-6	92	73	—	5.8
DIORIO, RON	Ronald Michael; B7.15.1946 Waterbury CT; BR/TR/6´6˝/(212–215); d8.9; Col New Haven																									
1973	Phi N	0	0	ø	23	0	0	1-0	19.1	18	5	1	0	6-4	11	2.33	164	.257	.312	0	ø	0	—	3	0	0.2
1974	Phi N	0	0	ø	2	0	0	0-0	1	2	2	1	0	1-0	0	18.00	21	.400	.500	0	ø	0	—	-1	0	-0.1
Total	2	0	0	ø	25	0	0	1-0	20.1	20	7	2	0	7-4	11	3.10	123	.267	.325	0	ø	0	—	2	0	0.1
DIPINO, FRANK	Frank Michael; B10.22.1956 Syracuse NY; BL/TL/6´0˝/(175–195); d9.14; Col St. Leo; [DL 1991 StL N 182]																									
1981	Mil A	0	0	ø	2	0	0	0-0	2.1	0	0	0	0	3-0	3	0.00	ø	.000	.300	0	ø	0	—	1	0	0.0
1982	Hou N	2	2	.500	6	6	0	0-0	28.1	32	20	1	0	11-1	25	6.04	55	.302	.361	8-0-1	.000	-1	102	-9	0	-1.1
1983	Hou N	3	4	.429	53	0	0	20-9	71.1	52	21	2	1	20-5	67	2.65	129	.205	.263	6	.167	1	—	8	0	1.3
1984	Hou N	4	9	.308	57	0	0	14-4	75.1	74	32	3	1	36-11	65	3.35	100	.260	.343	10	.000	-1	—	0	0	0.0
1985	Hou N	3	7	.300	54	0	0	6-2	76	69	44	7	2	43-6	49	4.03	87	.248	.350	12	.167	-0	—	-7	0	-1.0
1986	Hou N	1	3	.250	31	0	0	3-3	40.1	27	18	5	2	16-1	27	3.57	101	.189	.278	5	.200	0	—	0	0	0.0
	Chi N	2	4	.333	30	0	0	0-2	40	47	27	6	0	14-5	43	5.17	79	.297	.351	1	.000	-0	—	-5	0	-0.7
	Year	3	7	.300	61	0	0	3-5	80.1	74	45	11	2	30-6	70	4.37	88	.246	.315	6	.167	-0	—	-5	0	-0.7
1987	Chi N	3	3	.500	69	0	0	4-1	80	75	31	7	1	34-2	61	3.15	137	.252	.326	2-0-1	.500	0	—	10	0	0.8
1988	Chi N	2	3	.400	63	0	0	6-2	90.1	102	54	6	0	32-7	69	4.98	73	.285	.338	10-0-1	.100	-0	—	-12	0	-0.9
1989	StL N	9	0	1.000	67	0	0	0-3	88.1	73	26	6	0	20-7	44	2.45	150	.227	.269	13-0-1	.077	-1	—	12	0	1.1
1990	StL N	5	2	.714	62	0	0	3-2	81	92	45	8	1	31-12	49	4.56	85	.294	.352	4-0-1	.250	0	—	-6	0	-0.4
1992	StL N	0	0	ø	9	0	0	0-0	11	9	2	0	0	3-0	8	1.64	209	.220	.273	1	1.000	0	—	2	131	0.2
1993	KC A	1	1	.500	11	0	0	0-0	15.2	21	12	2	2	6-0	5	6.89	67	.328	.392	0	ø	0	—	-3	31	-0.4
Total	12	35	38	.479	514	6	0	56-28	700	673	332	53	10	269-57	515	3.83	97	.256	.324	72-0-5	.125	-2	102	-9	344	-1.1
DIPOTO, JERRY	Gerard Peter; B5.24.1968 Jersey City NJ; BR/TR/6´2˝/(200–207); [CleA89 3/71]; d5.11; Col Virginia Commonwealth; [DL 2001 Col N 151]																									
1993	Cle A	4	4	.500	46	0	0	11-6	56.1	57	21	0	1	30-7	41	2.40	183	.270	.361	0	ø	0	—	10	0	1.7
1994	Cle A	0	0	ø	7	0	0	0-0	15.2	26	14	1	1	10-0	9	8.04	59	.406	.468	0	ø	0	—	-5	70	-0.2
1995	NY N	4	6	.400	58	0	0	2-4	78.2	77	41	2	4	29-8	49	3.78	107	.267	.340	5-0-1	.000	-1	—	0	0	0.0
1996	NY N	7	2	.778	57	0	0	0-5	77.1	91	44	5	3	45-8	52	4.19	96	.298	.389	1	.000	-0	—	-3	0	-0.3
1997	Col N	5	3	.625	74	0	0	16-5	95.2	108	56	6	4	33-5	74	4.70	110	.288	.346	9	.111	-1	—	3	0	0.3
1998	Col N	3	4	.429	68	0	0	19-4	71.1	61	31	8	3	25-3	49	3.53	147	.232	.304	1	.000	0	—	10	0	1.4
1999	Col N	4	5	.444	63	0	0	1-0	86.2	91	44	10	3	44-4	69	4.26	136	.279	.365	5	.000	-0	—	12	0	1.0
2000	Col N	0	0	ø	17	0	0	0-1	13.2	16	6	1	0	5-2	9	3.95	147	.314	.362	1	.000	-0	—	2	138	0.1
Total	8	27	24	.529	390	0	0	49-25	495.1	527	257	33	19	221-37	352	4.05	119	.280	.356	22-0-1	.045	-2	—	29	359	4.0
DISCH, GEORGE	George Charles; B3.15.1879 Lincoln MO; D8.25.1950 Rapid City SD; TR/5´11˝/?; d8.8																									
1905	Det A	0	2	.000	8	3	1	0	47.2	43	19	1	2	8	14	2.64	103	.243	.283	19	.105	-1	52	1	—	-0.1
DISHMAN, GLENN	Glenelg Edward; B11.5.1970 Baltimore MD; BR/TL/6´1˝/195; d6.22; Col TCU																									
1995	SD N	4	8	.333	19	16	0	0-0	97	104	60	11	4	34-1	43	5.01	81	.278	.342	30-0-2	.200	0	108	-10	0	-1.0
1996	SD N	0	0	ø	3	0	0	0-0	2.1	3	2	0	0	1-0	0	7.71	52	.300	.364	0	ø	0	—	-1	0	0.0
	Phi N	0	0	ø	4	1	0	0-0	7	9	6	2	0	2-0	3	7.71	56	.321	.355	0-0-2	ø	0	188	-2	0	-0.1
	Year	0	0	ø	7	1	0	0-0	9.1	12	8	2	0	3-0	3	7.71	55	.316	.357	0-0-2	ø	0	191	-3	0	-0.1
1997	Det A	1	2	.333	7	4	0	0-0	29	30	18	4	2	8-0	20	5.28	88	.268	.323	0	ø	0	114	-2	0	-0.1
Total	3	5	10	.333	33	21	0	0-0	135.1	146	86	17	6	45-1	66	5.25	80	.279	.339	30-0-4	.200	0	113	-15	0	-1.2
DISTASO, ALEC	Alec John; B12.23.1948 Los Angeles CA; BR/TR/6´2˝/190; [ChiN67*1/1]; d4.20																									
1969	Chi N	0	0	ø	2	0	0	0-0	4.2	6	2	0	0	1-0	1	3.86	104	.316	.350	0	ø	0	—	0	0	0.0
DITMAR, ART	Arthur John; B4.3.1929 Winthrop MA; BR/TR/6´2˝/(185–197); d4.19																									
1954	Phi A	1	4	.200	14	5	0	0	39.1	50	35	4	1	36	14	6.41	61	.314	.442	8-0-1	.125	0	131	-12	0	-1.3
1955	KC A	12	12	.500	35	22	7-1	1	175.1	180	109	23	7	86-5	79	5.03	83	.270	.358	62-0-4	.210	-0	107	-16	0	-1.9
1956	KC A	12	22	.353	44	34	14-2	1	254.1	254	141	30	7	108-6	126	4.42	98	.262	.338	91-1-4	.143	-4	90	-3	0	-0.8
1957	†NY A	8	3	.727	46	11	0	6	127.1	128	55	9	2	35-1	64	3.25	110	.261	.312	35-0-1	.200	-0	115	4	0	0.3
1958	†NY A	9	8	.529	38	13	4	4	139.2	124	71	14	5	38-2	52	3.42	103	.237	.292	44-0-2	.250	2	143	-2	0	-0.2
1959	NY A	13	9	.591	38	25	7-1	1	202	156	75	17	8	52-2	96	2.90	126	.211	**.268**	76-1-1	.197	2	118	18	0	1.9
1960	†NY A	15	9	.625	34	28	8-1	0	200	195	77	25	1	56-1	65	3.06	117	.256	.308	69-0-3	.159	0*	117	13	0	1.4

YEAR	TM LG	W	L	PCT	G	GS	CG-SHO	SV-BS	IP	H	R	HR	HB	BB-IB	SO	ERA	AERA	OAV	OOB	AB-HR-SH	AVG	PB	SUP	APR	DL	PW
1961	NY A	2	3	.400	12	8	1	0	54.1	59	33	9	2	14-0	24	4.64	80	.285	.329	19	.053	-2	128	-7	0	-0.7
	KC A	0	5	.000	20	5	0	1	54	60	34	6	2	23-1	19	5.67	74	.286	.359	12-0-1	.167	-0	55	-6	0	-0.6
	Year	2	8	.200	32	13	1	1	108.1	119	67	15	4	37-1	43	5.15	77	.285	.344	31-0-1	.097	-2	96	-14	0	-1.3
1962	KC A	0	2	.000	6	5	0	0	21.2	31	19	1	2	13-1	13	6.65	64	.323	.411	6	.167	-0	97	-6	0	-0.5
Total	9	72	77	.483	287	156	41-5	14	1268	1237	649	138	37	461-19	552	3.98	97	.256	.324	422-2-17	.178	-3	110	-17	0	-2.4
DIVEN, FRANK	Frank Robert; B8.29.1859; D5.30.1914 Nutley NJ; TL; d5.9																									
1883	Bal AA	1	1	.500	2	2	1	0	11	15	15	0	—	1	3	7.36	47	.306	.320	9	.222	-0	174	-4	—	-0.5
DIXON, SONNY	John Craig; B11.5.1924 Charlotte NC; BB/TR/6´2.5˝/205; d4.20																									
1953	Was A	5	8	.385	43	6	3	3	120	123	57	13	2	31	40	3.75	104	.267	.316	26-0-2	.154	0	99	2	0	0.3
1954	Was A	1	2	.333	16	0	0	1	29.2	26	15	3	0	12	7	3.03	117	.236	.309	6	.000	-1	—	0	0	0.0
	Phi A	5	7	.417	38	6	1	4	107.1	136	63	8	3	27	42	4.86	80	.308	.349	28	.250	2	75	-10	0	-0.8
	Year	6	9	.400	**54**	6	1	5	137	162	78	11	3	39	49	4.47	86	.293	.341	34	.206	1	77	-10	0	-0.8
1955	KC A	0	0	ø	2	0	0	0	1.2	6	3	1	0	0-0	0	16.20	26	.545	.545	0	ø	0	—	-2	0	-0.1
1956	NY A	0	1	.000	3	0	0	1	4.1	5	3	0	0	5-1	1	2.08	186	.294	.455	1	.000	-0	—	0	0	0.0
Total	4	11	18	.379	102	12	4	9	263	296	141	25	5	75-1	90	4.17	93	.284	.334	61-0-2	.180	1	88	-10	0	-0.6
DIXON, KEN	Kenneth John; B10.17.1960 Monroe VA; BB/TR/5´11˝/(166–192); [BalA80 3/61]; d9.22																									
1984	Bal A	0	1	.000	2	2	0	0-0	13	14	6	1	0	4-0	8	4.15	94	.269	.321	0	ø	0	58	0	0	0.0
1985	Bal A	8	4	.667	34	18	3-1	1-0	162	144	68	20	2	64-7	108	3.67	111	.237	.311	0	ø	0*	117	9	0	0.6
1986	Bal A	11	13	.458	35	33	2	0-0	202.1	194	111	33	1	83-6	170	4.58	91	.249	.320	0	ø	0	94	-8	0	-0.9
1987	Bal A	7	10	.412	34	15	0	5-4	105	128	81	31	1	27-4	91	6.43	69	.292	.333	0	ø	0	108	-23	0	-3.2
Total	4	26	28	.481	105	68	5-1	6-4	482.1	480	266	85	4	178-17	377	4.66	90	.256	.320	0	ø	0	102	-22	0	-3.5
DIXON, STEVE	Steven Ross; B8.3.1969 Cincinnati OH; BL/TL/6´0˝/190; [StLN89 31/796]; d9.7; Col Kentucky																									
1993	StL N	0	0	ø	4	0	0	0-0	2.2	7	10	1	0	5-0	2	33.75	12	.538	.667	0	ø	0	—	-8	0	-0.4
1994	StL N	0	0	ø	2	0	0	0-0	2.1	3	6	0	0	8-0	1	23.14	18	.333	.611	0	ø	0	—	-5	0	-0.2
Total	2	0	0	ø	6	0	0	0-0	5	10	16	1	0	13-0	3	28.80	14	.455	.639	0	ø	0	—	-13	0	-0.6
DIXON, TOM	Thomas Earl; B4.23.1955 Orlando FL; BR/TR/5´11˝/(175–183); d7.30																									
1977	Hou N	1	0	1.000	9	4	1	0-0	30.1	40	12	0	1	7-0	15	3.26	111	.320	.361	7-0-3	.000	-1	154	1	0	0.0
1978	Hou N	7	11	.389	30	19	3-2	1-0	140	140	70	8	1	40-3	66	3.99	84	.265	.312	40-0-3	.100	-2	91	-12	0	-1.7
1979	Hou N	1	2	.333	19	1	0	0-1	25.2	39	23	2	0	15-1	9	6.66	53	.348	.425	1	1.000	1	126	-10	71	-1.0
1983	Mon N	0	1	.000	4	0	0	0-0	3.2	6	4	1	1	1-0	4	9.82	37	.375	.421	0	ø	0	—	-2	0	-0.5
Total	4	9	14	.391	62	24	4-2	1-1	199.2	225	109	11	3	63-4	94	4.33	79	.288	.338	48-0-6	.104	-2	103	-23	71	-3.2
DOAK, BILL	William Leopold "Spittin' Bill"; B1.28.1891 Pittsburgh PA; D11.26.1954 Bradenton FL; BR/TR/6´0.5˝/165; d9.1																									
1912	Cin N	0	0	ø	1	1	0	0	2	4	2	0	0	1	0	4.50	75	.444	.500	0	ø	0	240	0	—	0.0
1913	StL N	2	8	.200	15	12	5-1	1	93	79	42	4	5	39	51	3.10	104	.236	.325	31	.032	-3	39	0	—	-0.3
1914	StL N	19	6	.760	36	33	16-7	1	256	193	79	2	7	87	118	**1.72**	**162**	.216	.290	85-0-3	.118	-3	94	27	—	2.6
1915	StL N	16	18	.471	38	36	19-3	1	276	263	103	4	8	85	124	2.64	106	.261	.323	86-0-10	.174	1	102	6	—	1.3
1916	StL N	12	8	.600	29	26	11-2	0	192	177	76	5	3	55	82	2.63	101	.251	.308	62-0-4	.129	-2	114	0	—	-0.1
1917	StL N	16	20	.444	44	37	16-3	2	281.1	257	123	6	9	85	111	3.10	87	.250	.312	95-0-2	.126	-4	94	-16	—	-2.2
1918	StL N	9	15	.375	31	23	16-1	1	211	191	76	3	4	60	74	2.43	111	.249	.306	66-0-7	.182	1	87	7	—	1.2
1919	StL N	13	14	.481	31	29	13-3	0	202.2	182	87	5	2	55	69	3.11	90	.246	.299	64-0-5	.109	-4	93	-7	—	-1.1
1920	StL N	20	12	.625	39	37	20-5	1	270	256	94	7	6	80	90	2.53	118	.253	.312	88-0-8	.114	-6	105	15	—	1.1
1921	StL N	15	6	**.714**	32	29	13-1	1	208.2	224	85	3	4	37	83	**2.59**	142	.278	.313	70-0-10	.143	-3	118	21	—	1.7
1922	StL N	11	13	.458	37	29	8-2	2	180.1	222	127	12	3	69	73	5.54	70	.311	.374	54-0-7	.130	-3	125	-32	—	-3.8
1923	StL N	8	13	.381	30	26	7-2	0	185	199	85	4	3	69	53	3.26	120	.279	.346	67-0-3	.045	-9	96	12	—	0.5
1924	StL N	2	1	.667	11	1	0	3	22	25	8	0	0	14	7	3.27	116	.313	.415	5	.200	-0	67	2	—	0.3
	Bro N	11	5	.688	21	16	8-2	0	149.1	130	58	8	3	35	32	3.07	122	.239	.289	56-1-2	.179	-0	105	13	—	1.4
	Year	13	6	.684	32	17	8-2	3	171.1	155	66	8	3	49	39	3.10	121	.249	.307	61-1-2	.180	-1	102	14	—	1.7
1927	Bro N	11	8	.579	27	20	6-1	0	145	153	73	6	3	40	32	3.48	114	.271	.322	47-0-8	.128	-3	85	5	—	0.4
1928	Bro N	3	8	.273	28	12	4-1	3	99.1	104	51	1	5	35	12	3.26	122	.271	.340	27-0-1	.111	-2	50	6	—	0.5
1929	StL N	1	2	.333	3	2	0	0	9	17	15	1	0	5	3	12.00	39	.415	.478	2-0-1	.000	0	103	-8	—	-1.2
Total	16	169	157	.518	453	369	162-34	16	2782.2	2676	1184	71	65	851	1014	2.98	107	.259	.319	905-1-71	.127	-42	99	51	—	2.3
DOANE, WALT	Walter Rudolph; B3.12.1887 Bellevue ID; D10.19.1935 Coatesville PA; BL/TR/6´0˝/165; d9.20																									
1909	Cle A	0	1	.000	1	1	0	0	5	10	7	0	0	1	2	5.40	47	.400	.423	9	.111	-0*	110	-2	—	-0.4
1910	Cle A	0	0	ø	6	0	0	0	17.2	31	21	1	1	8	7	5.60	46	.413	.476	7	.286	1	—	-8	—	-0.4
Total	2	0	1	.000	7	1	0	0	22.2	41	28	1	1	9	9	5.56	46	.410	.464	16	.188	1	110	-10	—	-0.8
DOBB, JOHN	John Kenneth "Lefty"; B11.15.1901 Muskegon MI; D7.31.1991 Muskegon MI; BR/TL/6´2˝/180; d8.13; Col Central Michigan																									
1924	Chi A	0	0	ø	2	0	0	0	2	4	2	0	0	1	2	9.00	46	.400	.455	0	ø	0	—	-1	—	0.0
DOBENS, RAY	Raymond Joseph "Lefty"; B7.28.1906 Nashua NH; D4.21.1980 Stuart FL; BL/TL/5´8˝/175; d7.7; Col Holy Cross																									
1929	Bos A	0	0	ø	11	1	0	0	28.1	32	12	0	1	9	4	3.81	112	.302	.362	8-0-1	.375	1	197	2	—	0.1
DOBERNIC, JESS	Andrew Joseph; B11.20.1917 Mt.Olive IL; D7.16.1998 St.Louis MO; BR/TR/5´10˝/170; d7.2																									
1939	Chi A	0	1	.000	4	0	0	0	3.1	3	6	0	1	6	1	13.50	35	.231	.500	1	.000	-0	—	-3	—	-0.6
1948	Chi N	7	2	.778	54	0	0	1	85.2	67	33	8	1	40	48	3.15	124	.213	.303	10	.200	-0	—	8	0	0.7
1949	Chi N	0	0	ø	4	0	0	0	4	9	9	2	0	4	0	20.25	20	.450	.542	0	ø	0	—	-7	0	-0.3
	Cin N	0	0	ø	14	0	0	0	19.1	28	22	7	0	16	6	9.78	43	.329	.436	2	.000	0	—	-11	0	-0.5
	Year	0	0	ø	18	0	0	0	23.1	37	31	9	0	20	6	11.57	36	.352	.456	2	.000	0	—	-17	0	-0.8
Total	3	7	3	.700	76	0	0	1	112.1	107	70	17	2	66	55	5.21	76	.247	.349	13	.154	-0	—	-13	0	-0.7
DOBSON, CHUCK	Charles Thomas; B1.10.1944 Kansas City MO; BR/TR/6´4˝/200; d4.19; Col Kansas; [DL 1972 Oak A 17]																									
1966	KC A	4	6	.400	14	14	1	0	83.2	71	41	7	2	50-0	61	4.09	83	.234	.345	26-0-2	.115	-1	69	-5	63	-0.7
1967	KC A	10	10	.500	32	29	4-1	0	197.2	172	83	17	3	75-6	110	3.69	86	.233	.305	72-0-3	.181	0*	102	-7	0	-0.7
1968	Oak A	12	14	.462	35	34	11-3	0	225.1	197	91	20	4	80-10	168	3.00	94	.234	.302	75-0-6	.200	2	99	-7	0	-0.5
1969	Oak A	15	13	.536	35	35	11-1	0-0	235.1	244	111	16	1	80-2	137	3.86	89	.270	.328	79-0-9	.101	-3	113	-11	0	-1.7
1970	Oak A	16	15	.516	41	**40**	13-**5**	0-0	267	230	122	32	5	92-7	149	3.74	94	.229	.296	93-0-5	.118	-3	115	-6	0	-1.1
1971	Oak A	15	5	.750	30	30	7-1	0-0	189	185	84	24	1	71-6	100	3.81	87	.259	.326	66-0-5	.197	3	165	-8	27	-0.5
1973	Oak A	0	1	.000	1	1	0	0-0	2.1	6	4	1	0	2-0	3	7.71	46	.429	.500	0	ø	0	100	-2	0	-0.3
1974	Cal A	2	3	.400	5	5	2	0-0	30	39	19	3	0	13-1	16	5.70	61	.315	.380	0	ø	0	46	-6	0	-0.9
1975	Cal A	0	2	.000	9	2	0	0-0	28	30	26	5	2	13-1	14	6.75	53	.275	.349	0	ø	0	74	-11	0	-0.7
Total	9	74	69	.517	202	190	49-11	0-0	1258.1	1174	581	125	18	476-33	758	3.78	87	.247	.316	411-0-30	.153	-2	112	-63	107	-7.1
DOBSON, JOE	Joseph Gordon "Burrhead"; B1.20.1917 Durant OK; D6.23.1994 Jacksonville FL; BR/TR/6´2˝/(190–197); d4.26; Mil 1944–45																									
1939	Cle A	2	3	.400	35	3	0	1	78	87	56	3	1	51	27	5.88	75	.290	.395	18-0-1	.056	-2	87	-13	—	-0.9
1940	Cle A	3	7	.300	40	7	2-1	3	100	101	60	8	0	48	57	4.95	85	.268	.351	24	.125	-1	71	-7	—	-0.7
1941	Bos A	12	5	.706	27	18	7-1	0	134.1	136	70	8	2	67	69	4.49	93	.262	.349	47-1-3	.149	0	119	-1	0	-0.2
1942	Bos A	11	9	.550	30	23	10-3	0	182.2	155	73	9	2	68	72	3.30	113	.231	.303	69-0-5	.145	-1	92	10	0	1.0
1943	Bos A	7	11	.389	25	20	9-3	0	164.1	144	63	4	0	57	63	3.12	106	.239	.305	52-0-3	.096	-3	98	4	0	-0.1
1946	†Bos A	13	7	.650	32	24	9-1	0	166.2	148	72	11	1	68	91	3.24	113	.234	.309	50-0-6	.100	-2	119	6	0	0.5
1947	Bos A	18	8	.692	33	31	15-1	1	228.2	203	84	15	1	73	110	2.95	132	.238	**.299**	77-0-7	.208	1	110	23	0	2.6
1948	Bos A☆	16	10	.615	38	32	16-5	2	245.1	237	115	14	1	92	116	3.56	123	.253	.320	84-1-8	.202	1	124	19	0	1.8
1949	Bos A	14	12	.538	33	27	12-2	2	212.2	219	103	12	2	97	87	3.85	113	.269	.348	68-0-5	.147	-1	94	10	0	0.9
1950	Bos A	15	10	.600	39	27	12-1	4	206.2	217	103	15	0	81	81	4.18	117	.275	.343	70-0-8	.214	1	115	16	0	1.9
1951	Chi A	7	6	.538	28	21	6	3	146.2	136	68	17	0	51	67	3.62	111	.248	.312	46-0-7	.065	-6	131	7	0	0.0
1952	Chi A	14	10	.583	29	25	11-3	1	200.2	164	66	11	0	60	101	2.51	145	.222	.280	63-0-10	.190	0	90	24	0	2.7
1953	Chi A	5	5	.500	23	15	3-1	1	100.2	96	46	10	0	37	50	3.67	110	.249	.314	29-0-1	.069	-2	85	4	0	0.1
1954	Bos A	0	0	ø	2	0	0	0	2.2	5	2	0	0	1	1	6.75	61	.385	.429	0	ø	0	—	-1	0	0.0
Total	14	137	103	.571	414	273	112-22	18	2170	2048	981	137	10	851	992	3.62	112	.250	.322	697-2-64	.152	-15	107	101	0	9.6

YEAR	TM LG	W	L	PCT	G	GS	CG-SHO	SV-BS	IP	H	R	HR	HB	BB-IB	SO	ERA	AERA	OAV	OOB	AB-HR-SH	AVG	PB	SUP	APR	DL	PW
DOBSON, PAT	Patrick Edward; B2.12.1942 Depew NY; D11.22.2006 San Diego CA; BR/TR/6´3˝/190; d5.31; C8																									
1967	Det A	1	2	.333	28	1	0	0	49.1	38	20	6	2	27-1	34	2.92	112	.216	.324	5	.000	-1	80	1	0	0.0
1968	†Det A	5	8	.385	47	10	2-1	7	125	89	39	13	2	48-6	93	2.66	113	.200	.280	28-0-2	.143	0	90	5	0	0.7
1969	Det A	5	10	.333	49	9	1	9-4	105	100	48	10	1	39-5	64	3.60	105	.253	.316	22-0-2	.091	-1	118	1	0	0.1
1970	SD N	14	15	.483	40	34	8-1	1-0	251	257	126	28	4	78-13	185	3.76	107	.265	.320	71-0-19	.141	-0	110	4	0	0.3
1971	†Bal A	20	8	.714	38	37	18-4	1-0	282.1	248	104	24	2	63-2	187	2.90	118	.235	.278	91-0-13	.110	-3	132	15	0	1.0
1972	Bal A☆	16	18	.471	38	36	13-3	0-0	268.1	220	89	13	4	69-7	161	2.65	118	.224	.277	85-0-8	.141	-2	81	13	0	1.4
1973	Atl N	3	7	.300	12	10	1-1	0-0	57.2	73	33	1	1	19-5	23	4.99	79	.315	.362	15-0-3	.067	-1	60	-5	0	-0.9
	NY A	9	8	.529	22	21	6-1	0-0	142.1	150	72	22	2	34-8	70	4.17	89	.266	.309	0	ø	0	119	-6	0	-0.6
1974	NY A	19	15	.559	39	39	12-2	0-0	281	282	111	23	4	75-5	157	3.07	115	.262	.311	0	ø	0	90	15	0	1.7
1975	NY A	11	14	.440	33	30	7-1	0-0	207.2	205	105	21	1	83-10	129	4.07	91	.261	.330	0	ø	0	97	-8	0	-0.9
1976	Cle A	16	12	.571	35	35	6	0-0	217.1	226	98	13	2	65-7	117	3.48	101	.272	.323	0	ø	0	87	-1	0	-0.2
1977	Cle A	3	12	.200	33	17	0	1-0	133.1	155	94	23	1	65-7	81	6.14	65	.299	.376	0	ø	0	85	-29	0	-2.8
Total	11	122	129	.486	414	279	74-14	19-4	2120.1	2043	939	197	26	665-76	1301	3.54	101	.255	.312	317-0-47	.123	-8	99	5	0	-0.2
DOCKINS, GEORGE	George Woodrow "Lefty"; B5.5.1917 Clyde KS; D1.22.1997 Clyde KS; BL/TL/6´0˝/175; d5.5																									
1945	StL N	8	6	.571	31	12	5-2	0	126.1	132	53	4	0	38	33	3.21	117	.269	.321	34-0-4	.176	1	106	7	0	0.8
1947	Bro N	0	0	ø	4	0	0	0	5.1	10	7	2	0	2	1	11.81	35	.400	.444	1	.000	-0	—	-4	0	-0.2
Total	2	8	6	.571	35	12	5-2	0	131.2	142	60	6	0	40	34	3.55	106	.275	.327	35-0-4	.171	1	106	3	0	0.6
DODD, ROBERT	Robert Wayne; B3.14.1973 Kansas City KS; BL/TL/6´3˝/195; [PhiN94 14/394]; d5.28; Col Florida																									
1998	Phi N	1	0	1.000	4	0	0	0-0	5	7	6	1	1	1-0	4	7.20	60	.333	.360	0	ø	0	—	-2	0	-0.4
DODGE, SAM	Samuel Edward; B12.19.1889 Neath PA; D4.5.1966 Utica NY; BR/TR/6´1˝/170; d9.24																									
1921	Bos A	0	0	ø	1	0	0	0	1	1	1	0	0	1	0	9.00	47	.500	.667	0	ø	0	—	0	—	0.0
1922	Bos A	0	0	ø	3	0	0	0	6	11	6	0	0	3	3	4.50	91	.379	.438	2	.000	-0	—	-1	—	-0.1
Total	2	0	0	ø	4	0	0	0	7	12	7	0	0	4	3	5.14	80	.387	.457	2	.000	-0	—	-1	—	-0.1
DOE, FRED	Alfred George "Count"; B4.18.1864 Rockport MA; D10.4.1938 Quincy MA; BR/TR/5´10˝/165; d8.23																									
1890	Buf P	0	1	.000	1	1	1	0	6	10	10	0	0	7	2	12.00	34	.357	.486	2	.000	-0	0	-5	—	-0.5
	Pit P	0	0	ø	1	0	0	0	4	4	2	0	0	2	2	4.50	87	.250	.333	2	.500	0	—	0	—	0.0
	Year	0	1	.000	2	1	1	0	10	14	12	0	0	9	4	9.00	45	.318	.434	4	.250	-0	0	-4	—	-0.5
DOHENY, ED	Edwin Richard; B11.24.1873 Northfield VT; D12.29.1916 Medfield MA; BL/TL/5´10.5˝/165; d9.16																									
1895	NY N	0	3	.000	3	3	3	0	25.2	37	29	2	3	19	9	6.66	70	.333	.444	10	.100	-1	82	-6	—	-0.6
1896	NY N	6	7	.462	17	15	9	0	108.1	112	78	3	6	59	39	4.49	94	.265	.363	40	.150	-2	119	-4	—	-0.5
1897	NY N	4	4	.500	10	10	10	0	85	69	45	0	8	45	37	2.12	196	.220	.333	35	.200	-1	79	15	—	1.1
1898	NY N	7	19	.269	28	27	23	0	213	238	164	1	20	101	96	3.68	95	.280	.370	86-2-0	.163	-1	108	-15	—	-1.5
1899	NY N	14	17	.452	36	34	31-1	0	277.2	291	207	2	37	158	120	4.41	85	.269	.381	116	.233	-1	99	-26	—	-2.1
1900	NY N	4	14	.222	20	18	12	0	133.2	148	134	2	22	96	44	5.45	66	.280	.411	54	.222	-0	103	-31	—	-3.1
1901	NY N	2	5	.286	10	6	6	0	74	88	53	1	6	17	36	4.50	73	.293	.344	29-0-1	.345	3*	104	-10	—	-0.5
	Pit N	6	2	.750	11	10	6-1	0	76.2	68	36	1	5	22	28	2.00	164	.236	.302	26	.115	0	135	7	—	0.7
	Year	8	7	.533	21	16	12-1	0	150.2	156	89	2	11	39	64	3.23	102	.265	.323	55-0-1	.236	4	123	-2	—	0.2
1902	Pit N	16	4	.800	22	21	19-2	0	188.1	161	68	0	15	61	88	2.53	108	.231	.307	77-1-1	.156	-2	141	6	—	0.3
1903	Pit N	16	8	.667	27	25	22-2	2	222.2	209	122	1	19	89	75	3.19	101	.252	.338	91-0-1	.209	-0	125	0	—	0.2
Total	9	75	83	.475	184	169	141-6	2	1405	1421	936	13	141	667	572	3.73	94	.262	.358	564-3-3	.197	-4	112	-64	—	-6.0
DOHERTY, JOHN	John Harold; B6.11.1967 New York NY; BR/TR/6´4˝/(200–215); [DetA89 19/499]; d4.8; Col Concordia (NY)																									
1992	Det A	7	4	.636	47	11	0	3-1	116	131	61	4	4	25-5	37	3.88	103	.287	.328	0	ø	0	129	-2	19	-0.1
1993	Det A	14	11	.560	32	31	3-2	0-0	184.2	205	104	19	5	48-7	63	4.44	98	.286	.333	0	ø	0	114	-3	15	-0.4
1994	Det A	6	7	.462	18	17	2	0-0	101.1	139	75	13	3	26-6	28	6.48	76	.337	.374	0	ø	0	104	-15	33	-1.4
1995	Det A	5	9	.357	48	2	0	6-3	113	130	66	10	6	37-10	46	5.10	94	.288	.349	0	ø	0	87	-2	0	-0.2
1996	Bos A	0	0	ø	3	0	0	0-0	6.1	8	10	1	1	4-0	3	5.68	90	.276	.382	0	ø	0	—	-3	0	-0.1
Total	5	32	31	.508	148	61	5-2	9-4	521.1	613	316	47	19	140-28	177	4.87	92	.296	.344	0	ø	0	112	-25	67	-2.2
DOHMANN, SCOTT	Christopher Scott; B2.13.1978 New Orleans LA; BR/TR/6´1˝/(180–200); [ColN00 6/167]; d5.15; Col Louisiana–Lafayette																									
2004	Col N	0	3	.000	41	0	0	0-4	46	41	22	8	0	19-0	49	4.11	116	.236	.306	1-0-1	.000	0	—	3	0	0.2
2005	Col N	2	1	.667	32	0	0	0-3	31	33	21	6	0	19-1	35	6.10	76	.266	.364	1	.000	-0	—	-4	0	-0.4
2006	Col N	1	1	.500	27	0	0	1-1	24.2	26	18	4	2	15-2	22	6.20	77	.274	.384	1	.000	-0	—	-3	15	-0.3
	KC A	1	3	.250	21	0	0	0-1	23.2	33	21	5	2	18-5	22	7.99	59	.347	.461	0	ø	0	—	-8	0	-1.1
Total	3	4	8	.333	121	0	0	1-9	125.1	133	82	23	4	71-8	128	5.74	82	.273	.367	3-0-1	.000	-0	—	-12	15	-1.6
DOLAN, JOHN	John; B9.12.1867 Newport KY; D5.8.1948 Springfield OH; TR/5´10˝/170; d9.5																									
1890	Cin N	1	1	.500	2	2	2	0	18	17	13	3	1	10	9	4.50	79	.243	.346	8	.125	-1	80	-1	—	-0.2
1891	Col AA	12	11	.522	27	24	19	0	203.1	216	131	8	0	84	68	4.16	83	.263	.331	78-1	.090	-4*	92	-13	—	-1.5
1892	Was N	2	2	.500	5	4	3	0	37	39	26	0	1	15	8	4.38	74	.260	.331	13	.231	0	112	-3	—	-0.3
1893	StL N	0	1	.000	3	1	1	1	17.1	26	22	2	1	7	1	4.15	114	.338	.400	7-1	.143	0	74	-2	—	-0.1
1895	Chi N	0	1	.000	2	2	1	0	11	16	12	0	1	6	1	6.55	78	.333	.418	3	.000	-0	77	-2	—	-0.1
Total	5	15	16	.484	39	33	26	1	286.2	314	204	13	4	122	87	4.30	83	.269	.341	109-2	.110	-5	92	-21	—	-2.2
DOLAN, COZY	Patrick Henry; B12.3.1872 Cambridge MA; D3.29.1907 Louisville KY; BL/TL/5´10˝/160; d4.26; ▲																									
1895	Bos N	11	7	.611	25	21	18-3	1	198.1	215	142	11	14	67	47	4.27	119	.272	.340	83-0-1	.241	-1*	90	16	—	1.1
1896	Bos N	1	4	.200	6	5	3	0	41	55	44	1	3	27	14	4.83	94	.318	.419	14-0-2	.143	-1	122	-4	—	-0.5
1905	Bos N	0	1	.000	2	0	0	0	4	7	5	2	0	1	1	9.00	34	.368	.400	433-3-9	.275	1*	—	-2	—	-0.4
1906	Bos N	0	1	.000	2	0	0	0	12	12	6	1	0	6	7	4.50	60	.300	.391	549-0-13	.248	0*	—	-2	—	-0.1
Total	4	12	13	.480	35	26	21-3	1	255.1	289	197	15	17	101	69	4.44	109	.283	.357	1079-3-25	.257	-2	98	8	—	0.1
DOLL, ART	Arthur James "Moose"; B5.7.1913 Chicago IL; D4.28.1978 Calumet City IL; BR/TR/6´1˝/190; d9.21.1935																									
1936	Bos N	0	1	.000	1	1	0	0	8	11	3	1	1	2	2	3.38	114	.355	.412	2	.000	-0	44	1	—	0.0
1938	Bos N	0	0	ø	3	0	0	0	4	4	1	0	0	3	1	2.25	153	.286	.412	1	1.000	1	—	1	—	0.1
Total	2	0	1	.000	4	1	0	0	12	15	4	1	1	5	3	3.00	123	.333	.412	3	.333	0	44	2	—	0.1
DOMINGUEZ, JUAN	Juan Ramon; B5.18.1980 Sanchez Ramirez, D.R.; BR/TR/6´2˝/(180–195); d8.12																									
2003	Tex A	0	2	.000	6	3	0	0-0	16.1	16	14	5	0	12-0	13	7.16	69	.271	.389	0	ø	0	68	-4	0	-0.4
2004	Tex A	1	2	.333	4	4	0	0-0	23	25	11	2	2	5-0	14	3.91	126	.281	.330	0	ø	0	108	2	93	0.3
2005	Tex A	4	6	.400	22	10	0	0-1	70.1	78	37	11	2	25-0	45	4.22	108	.277	.338	0	ø	0	110	2	0	0.2
Total	3	5	10	.333	32	17	0	0-1	109.2	119	62	18	4	42-0	72	4.60	102	.277	.344	0	ø	0	102	0	93	0.1
DONAHUE, RED	Francis Rostell; B1.23.1873 Waterbury CT; D8.25.1913 Philadelphia PA; BR/TR/6´0˝/187; d5.6; Col Villanova																									
1893	NY N	0	0	ø	2	0	0	1	5	8	10	1	2	3	1	9.00	52	.348	.464	2	.000	-0	—	-3	—	-0.2
1895	StL N	0	1	.000	1	1	1	0	8	9	6	2	1	3	2	6.75	72	.281	.361	3	.000	-1	0	-1	—	-0.1
1896	StL N	7	24	.226	32	32	28	0	267	376	235	6	13	98	70	5.80	75	.329	.389	107-0-3	.159	-8*	78	-42	—	-4.2
1897	StL N	10	35	.222	46	42	**38**-1	1	348	485	306	16	22	106	64	6.13	72	.327	.380	155-1-4	.213	-3*	72	-57	—	-5.4
1898	Phi N	16	17	.485	35	35	33-1	0	284.1	327	165	7	14	80	57	3.55	97	.286	.340	112-0-7	.143	-7	105	-4	—	-0.9
1899	Phi N	21	8	.724	35	31	27-4	0	279	292	147	6	11	63	51	3.39	109	.269	.316	111-0-5	.180	-5	136	11	—	0.6
1900	Phi N	15	10	.600	32	24	21-2	0	240	299	144	6	9	50	41	3.60	100	.304	.344	90-0-5	.222	-1	123	-4	—	-0.5
1901	Phi N	20	13	.606	34	33	33-1	1	295.1	299	111	2	9	59	88	2.59	131	.261	.302	113-0-3	.097	-9	88	28	—	1.8
1902	StL A	22	11	.667	35	34	33-2	0	316.1	322	134	7	8	65	63	2.76	128	.264	.306	118-0-5	.093	-9	91	25	—	1.6
1903	StL A	8	7	.533	16	15	14	0	131	145	59	0	0	22	51	2.75	106	.279	.309	51-0-2	.157	-2	126	1	—	-0.1
	Cle A	7	9	.438	16	15	14-4	0	136.2	142	61	3	6	12	45	2.44	117	.267	.291	53-0-1	.151	-1	112	5	—	0.5
	Year	15	16	.484	32	30	28-4	0	267.2	287	120	3	6	34	96	2.59	111	.273	.300	104-0-3	.154	-3	119	4	—	0.4
1904	Cle A	19	14	.576	35	32	30-6	0	277	281	96	2	5	49	127	2.40	105	.264	.299	101-0-5	.168	-1	118	8	—	0.9
1905	Cle A	6	12	.333	20	18	14-1	0	137.2	132	68	2	5	25	45	3.40	77	.254	.295	53-0-3	.075	-5	93	-11	—	-1.8
1906	Det A	13	14	.481	28	28	26-3	0	241	260	96	1	8	54	82	2.73	101	.278	.323	81-0-5	.123	-4*	86	1	—	-0.4
Total	13	164	175	.484	367	340	312-25	3	2966.1	3377	1638	61	113	689	787	3.61	96	.286	.331	1150-1-48	.152	-56	97	-43	—	-8.2

YEAR	TM LG	W	L	PCT	G	GS	CG-SHO	SV-BS	IP	H	R	HR	HB	BB-IB	SO	ERA	AERA	OAV	OOB	AB-HR-SH	AVG	PB	SUP	APR	DL	PW
DONAHUE, DEACON	John Stephen Michael; B6.23.1920 Chicago IL; BR/TR/6´0˝/180; d9.16																									
1943	Phi N	0	0	ø	2	0	0	0	4	4	3	0	1	1	1	4.50	75	.235	.316	0	ø	0	—	-1	0	0.0
1944	Phi N	0	2	.000	6	0	0	0	9.1	18	8	0	0	2	2	7.71	47	.429	.455	1	.000	-0	—	-4	0	-0.7
Total	2	0	2	.000	8	0	0	0	13.1	22	11	0	1	3	3	6.75	52	.373	.413	1	.000	-0	—	-5	0	-0.7
DONALD, ATLEY	Richard Atley "Swampy"; B8.19.1910 Morton MS; D10.19.1992 West Monroe LA; BL/TR/6´1˝/186; d4.21; Col Louisiana Tech																									
1938	NY A	0	1	.000	2	2	0	0	12	7	8	0	1	14	6	5.25	86	.175	.400	6	.167	-0	78	-1	—	-0.1
1939	NY A	13	3	.813	24	20	11-2	1	153	144	74	12	0	60	55	3.71	118	.247	.317	60	.250	3	138	10	—	1.0
1940	NY A	8	3	.727	24	11	6-1	0	118.2	113	49	11	2	59	60	3.03	133	.249	.339	41-0-5	.146	-2	111	13	—	0.7
1941	†NY A	9	5	.643	22	20	10	0	159	141	69	11	3	69	71	3.57	110	.237	.320	62	.081	-4	117	8	0	0.2
1942	†NY A	11	3	.786	20	19	10-1	0	147.2	133	58	6	0	45	53	3.11	111	.239	.296	61-0-2	.148	-1	144	6	0	0.2
1943	NY A	6	4	.600	22	15	2	0	119.1	134	69	10	0	38	57	4.60	70	.276	.329	47-0-4	.128	-2	159	-18	0	-1.7
1944	NY A	13	10	.565	30	19	9	0	159	173	77	13	2	59	48	3.34	104	.280	.345	55-0-1	.182	-0	138	-1	0	-0.2
1945	NY A	5	4	.556	9	9	6-2	0	63.2	62	29	3	0	25	19	2.97	117	.248	.316	24-1-2	.208	0	126	2	0	0.1
Total	8	65	33	.663	153	115	54-6	1	932.1	907	433	66	8	369	369	3.52	107	.253	.325	356-1-14	.160	-7	132	19	0	0.2
DONALDS, ED	Edward Alexander "Erston"; B6.22.1885 Bidwell OH; D7.3.1950 Columbus OH; BR/TR/5´11˝/180; d9.1																									
1912	Cin N	1	0	1.000	1	0	0	0	4	7	2	0	0	0	1	4.50	75	.438	.438	1	.000	-0	—	0	—	-0.1
DONLIN, MIKE	Michael Joseph "Turkey Mike"; B5.30.1878 Peoria IL; D9.24.1933 Hollywood CA; BL/TL/5´9˝/170; d7.19; ▲																									
1899	StL N	0	1	.000	3	1	0	0	15.1	15	15	1	1	14	6	7.63	52	.254	.405	266-6-3	.323	1*	127	-5	—	-0.1
1902	Cin N	0	0	ø	1	0	0	0	1	1	0	0	0	0	0	0.00	ø	.250	.250	143	.287	0*	—	0	—	0.0
Total	2	0	1	.000	4	1	0	0	16.1	16	15	1	1	14	6	7.16	55	.254	.397	409-6-3	.311	1	127	-5	—	-0.1
DONNELLY, BRENDAN	Brendan Kevin; B7.4.1971 Washington DC; BR/TR/6´3˝/(205–240); [ChiA92 27/764]; d4.9; Col Mesa St.																									
2002	†Ana A	1	1	.500	46	0	0	1-2	49.2	32	13	2	2	19-3	54	2.17	206	.184	.270	0	ø	0	—	13	0	0.6
2003	Ana A★	2	2	.500	63	0	0	3-2	74	55	14	2	4	24-1	79	1.58	277	.200	.273	0	ø	0	—	24	0	1.2
2004	†Ana A	5	2	.714	40	0	0	0-0	42	34	14	5	1	15-0	56	3.00	149	.224	.294	0	ø	0	—	8	74	1.1
2005	†LA A	9	3	.750	65	0	0	0-5	65.1	60	30	9	2	19-3	53	3.72	115	.244	.302	1	.000	-0*	—	4	0	0.5
2006	LA A	6	0	1.000	62	0	0	0-1	64	58	32	8	4	28-3	53	3.94	113	.240	.326	0	ø	0	—	3	0	0.2
Total	5	23	8	.742	276	0	0	4-10	295	239	103	26	13	105-10	295	2.87	153	.219	.294	1	.000	-0	—	52	74	3.6
DONNELLY, ED	Edward "Big Ed","Ned" (b Edward O'Donnell); B7.29.1879 Hampton NY; D11.28.1957 Rutland VT; BR/TR/6´1˝/205; d9.19																									
1911	Bos N	3	2	.600	5	4	4-1	0	36.2	33	15	0	2	9	16	2.45	156	.236	.291	14	.071	-1	98	4	—	0.4
1912	Bos N	5	10	.333	37	18	10	0	184.1	225	127	10	5	72	67	4.35	82	.304	.370	69-0-4	.275	3*	83	-18	—	-0.9
Total	2	8	12	.400	42	22	14-1	0	221	258	142	10	7	81	83	4.03	90	.294	.358	83-0-4	.241	1	86	-14	—	-0.5
DONNELLY, ED	Edward Vincent; B12.10.1932 Allen MI; D12.25.1997 Houston TX; BR/TR/6´0˝/175; d8.1																									
1959	Chi N	1	1	.500	9	0	0	0	14.1	18	7	1	0	9-1	6	3.14	126	.305	.397	0	ø	0	—	1	0	0.1
DONNELLY, FRANK	Franklin Marion; B10.7.1869 Tamaroa IL; D2.3.1953 Canton IL; 5´6˝/180; d8.15																									
1893	Chi N	3	1	.750	7	5	3	**2**	42	51	42	1	4	17	6	5.36	86	.291	.367	18	.444	4	124	-5	—	-0.1
1894	Chi N	0	0	ø	1	0	0	0	4.2	6	8	0	0	8	1	15.43	37	.316	.519	1	.000	-0	—	-4	—	-0.1
Total	2	3	1	.750	8	5	3	2	46.2	57	50	1	4	25	7	6.36	74	.294	.386	19	.421	4	124	-9	—	-0.2
DONNELLY, BLIX	Sylvester Urban; B1.21.1914 Olivia MN; D6.20.1976 Olivia MN; BR/TR/5´10˝/178; d5.6																									
1944	†StL N	2	1	.667	27	4	2-1	2	76.1	61	26	2	2	34	45	2.12	166	.218	.307	16-0-2	.063	-1	119	10	0	0.5
1945	StL N	8	10	.444	31	23	9-4	2	166.1	157	79	10	6	87	76	3.52	106	.250	.346	54-0-6	.130	-2	101	2	0	-0.2
1946	StL N	1	2	.333	13	0	0	0	13.2	17	7	1	1	10	11	3.95	87	.347	.467	0	ø	0	—	-1	0	-0.1
	Phi N	3	4	.429	12	8	2	1	76.1	64	31	7	2	24	38	2.95	116	.220	.284	25	.280	2	90	3	0	0.5
	Year	4	6	.400	25	8	2	1	90	81	38	8	3	34	49	3.10	111	.238	.313	25	.280	2	90	3	0	0.4
1947	Phi N	4	6	.400	38	10	5-1	5	120.2	113	44	6	3	46	31	2.98	134	.265	.340	32-0-5	.063	-2	97	15	0	1.0
1948	Phi N	5	7	.417	26	19	8-1	2	131.2	125	65	13	0	49	46	3.69	107	.261	.330	45-0-1	.222	2	102	3	0	0.3
1949	Phi N	2	1	.667	23	10	1	0	78.1	84	50	7	1	40	36	5.06	78	.294	.382	23-0-1	.174	-1	123	-10	0	-0.7
1950	Phi N	2	4	.333	14	1	0	0	21	30	13	5	0	10	10	4.29	94	.330	.396	5	.200	-0	65	-1	0	-0.2
1951	Bos N	0	1	.000	6	0	0	0	7.1	8	6	1	1	6	3	7.36	50	.286	.429	1	.000	-0	—	-3	0	-0.3
Total	8	27	36	.429	190	75	27-7	12	691.2	659	321	52	16	306	296	3.49	109	.257	.340	201-0-15	.159	-1	104	18	0	0.8
DONOHUE, JIM	James Thomas; B10.31.1938 St.Louis MO; BR/TR/6´4˝/190; d4.11																									
1961	Det A	1	1	.500	14	0	0	1	20.1	23	10	2	0	15-2	20	3.54	116	.287	.400	1	.000	-0	—	1	0	0.1
	LA A	4	6	.400	38	7	0	5	100.1	93	48	16	0	50-4	79	4.31	105	.246	.332	27	.148	-1	84	5	0	0.3
	Year	5	7	.417	52	7	0	6	120.2	116	58	18	0	65-6	99	4.18	106	.253	.344	28	.143	-1	85	5	0	0.4
1962	LA A	1	0	1.000	12	1	0	0	24.1	22	14	4	2	11-0	14	3.70	104	.258	.349	4-0-1	.250	0	46	-1	0	0.0
	Min A	0	1	.000	6	1	0	1	10.1	12	8	2	0	6-0	3	6.97	59	.324	.419	2	.000	-0	109	-3	0	-0.3
	Year	1	1	.500	18	2	0	1	34.2	36	22	6	2	17-0	17	4.67	84	.277	.369	6-0-1	.167	0	80	-4	0	-0.3
Total	2	6	8	.429	70	9	0	7	155.1	152	80	24	2	82-6	116	4.29	101	.259	.350	34-0-1	.147	-1	84	2	0	0.1
DONOHUE, PETE	Peter Joseph; B11.5.1900 Athens TX; D2.23.1988 Ft.Worth TX; BR/TR/6´2˝/185; d7.1; Col TCU																									
1921	Cin N	7	6	.538	21	11	7	1	118.1	117	48	5	0	26	44	3.35	107	.263	.304	38-1-4	.211	1	98	6	—	0.8
1922	Cin N	18	9	**.667**	33	30	18-2	1	242	257	110	7	5	43	66	3.12	128	.276	.312	88-0-5	.182	-3	117	22	—	1.9
1923	Cin N	21	15	.583	42	36	19-2	3	274.1	304	138	3	10	68	84	3.38	114	.278	.326	96-1-4	.250	3	87	12	—	1.7
1924	Cin N	16	9	.640	35	31	16-3	0	222.1	248	100	9	9	36	72	3.60	105	.285	.321	73-1-4	.192	-0*	100	8	—	0.7
1925	Cin N	21	14	.600	42	**38**	**27**-3	2	**301**	310	122	3	2	49	78	3.08	133	.268	.299	109-1-7	.294	7*	97	38	—	4.6
1926	Cin N	**20**	14	.588	47	**36**	17-**5**	2	**285.2**	298	133	6	9	39	73	3.37	109	.268	.298	106-0-5	.311	9	112	9	—	1.7
1927	Cin N	6	16	.273	33	24	12-1	1	190.2	253	111	3	1	32	48	4.11	92	.328	.356	64-0-3	.250	1	91	-9	—	-0.8
1928	Cin N	7	11	.389	23	18	8	0	150	180	84	10	3	32	37	4.74	83	.309	.348	48-1-3	.146	-0	96	-10	—	-1.0
1929	Cin N	10	13	.435	32	24	7	0	177.2	243	123	12	4	51	30	5.42	84	.331	.377	60-0-4	.333	4	93	-18	—	-1.5
1930	Cin N	1	3	.250	8	5	2	1	34.1	53	24	0	1	13	4	6.29	77	.363	.419	10-0-1	.100	-1	76	-4	—	-0.5
	NY N	7	6	.538	18	11	4	1	86.2	135	65	6	2	18	26	6.13	77	.360	.392	33-1-2	.273	1	129	-12	—	-1.4
	Year	8	9	.471	26	16	6	2	121	188	89	6	3	31	30	6.17	77	.361	.400	43-1-3	.233	0	112	-18	—	-1.9
1931	NY N	0	1	.000	4	1	0	0	11.1	14	7	1	0	4	4	5.56	66	.311	.367	2	.000	-0	23	-2	—	-0.2
	Cle A	0	0	ø	2	0	0	0	5.1	9	6	1	0	5	4	8.44	55	.429	.538	2	.000	-0	—	-2	—	-0.1
1932	Bos A	0	1	.000	4	2	0	0	12.2	18	11	2	0	6	1	7.82	57	.340	.407	3	.000	-0	66	-4	—	-0.3
Total	12	134	118	.532	344	267	137-16	12	2112.1	2439	1082	68	46	422	571	3.87	103	.293	.330	732-6-42	.246	21	100	34	—	5.6
DONOSO, LINO	Lino (Galata); B9.23.1922 Havana, Cuba; D10.13.1990 Veracruz, Veracruz, Mexico; BL/TL/5´11˝/160; d6.18; Negro Lg 1947–49																									
1955	Pit N	4	6	.400	25	9	3	1	95	106	58	16	1	35-3	38	5.31	78	.287	.345	27-0-3	.185	-1	108	-10	0	-1.0
1956	Pit N	0	0	ø	3	0	0	0	1.2	2	0	0	0	1-0	1	0.00	ø	.250	.333	0	ø	0	—	1	0	0.0
Total	2	4	6	.400	28	9	3	1	96.2	108	58	16	1	36-3	39	5.21	79	.286	.345	27-0-3	.185	-1	108	-9	0	-1.0
DONOVAN, DICK	Richard Edward; B12.7.1927 Boston MA; D1.6.1997 Weymouth MA; BL/TR/6´3˝/(190–215); d4.24																									
1950	Bos N	0	2	.000	10	3	0	0	29.2	28	28	4	2	34	9	8.19	47	.255	.438	6	.167	1	115	-14	0	-0.7
1951	Bos N	0	0	ø	8	2	0	0	13.2	17	11	0	0	11	4	5.27	70	.298	.412	3	.333	1	264	-3	0	0.0
1952	Bos N	0	2	.000	7	2	0	1	13	18	10	1	2	12	6	5.54	65	.346	.485	3	.000	-0	25	-3	0	-0.5
1954	Det A	0	0	ø	2	0	0	0	6	9	7	1	0	5	2	10.50	35	.360	.438	1	.000	-0	—	-4	0	-0.2
1955	Chi A☆	15	9	.625	29	24	11-5	0	187	186	77	17	3	48-5	88	3.32	119	.261	.310	76-1-1	.224	5*	94	12	0	1.9
1956	Chi A	12	10	.545	34	31	14-3	0	234.2	212	99	22	6	59-6	120	3.64	113	.240	**.290**	90-3-1	.222	8*	117	15	0	2.1
1957	Chi A	16	6	**.727**	28	28	**16**-2	0	220.2	203	76	17	8	45-8	88	2.77	135	.247	.291	83-3-1	.145	2*	118	23	0	2.4
1958	Chi A	15	14	.517	34	34	16-4	0	248	240	92	23	7	53-5	127	3.01	121	.251	.295	80-0-2	.112	-1	81	18	0	1.8
1959	†Chi A	9	10	.474	31	29	5-1	0	179.2	171	84	15	5	58-3	71	3.66	103	.247	.308	61-1-3	.131	1	86	1	0	0.1
1960	Chi A	6	1	.857	33	8	0	3	78.2	87	49	13	0	25-3	30	5.38	70	.283	.333	23	.130	-0	114	-13	0	-1.1
1961	Was A★	10	10	.500	23	22	11-2	0	168.2	138	60	10	3	35-3	62	**2.40**	**167**	.224	**.267**	56-1-1	.179	2*	86	27	0	3.3
1962	Cle A★	20	10	.667	34	34	16-**5**	0	250.2	255	109	23	2	47-5	94	3.59	108	.263	.297	89-4-2	.180	6	107	10	0	1.6
1963	Cle A	11	13	.458	30	30	7-3	0	206	211	106	27	5	28-5	84	4.24	85	.265	.292	69-1-3	.130	-1*	102	-12	0	-1.5
1964	Cle A	7	9	.438	30	23	5	1	158.1	181	86	19	2	29-6	83	4.55	79	.290	.321	48-1-4	.146	3*	117	-15	0	-1.1

YEAR	TM LG	W	L	PCT	G	GS	CG-SHO	SV-BS	IP	H	R	HR	HB	BB-IB	SO	ERA	AERA	OAV	OOB	AB-HR-SH	AVG	PB	SUP	APR	DL	PW
1965	Cle A	1	3	.250	12	3	0	0	22.2	32	15	6	0	6-0	12	5.96	58	.333	.373	6	.000	-1	76	-5	0	-0.9
Total	15	122	99	.552	345	273	101-25	5	2017.1	1988	909	198	45	495-49	880	3.67	104	.258	.305	694-15-18	.163	24	102	37	0	7.2
DONOVAN, BILL	Willard Earl; B7.6.1916 Maywood IL; D9.25.1997 Maywood IL; BR/TL/6´2˝/198; d4.19; Mil 1943–45																									
1942	Bos N	3	6	.333	31	10	2	0	89.1	97	43	2	0	32	23	3.43	97	.283	.344	25-0-2	.240	1	75	-2	0	0.0
1943	Bos N	1	0	1.000	7	0	0	0	14.2	17	4	0	0	9	1	1.84	185	.304	.400	3	.333	0	—	2	0	0.2
Total	2	4	6	.400	38	10	2	0	104	114	47	2	0	41	24	3.20	105	.286	.352	28-0-2	.250	1	75	0	0	0.2
DONOVAN, BILL	William Edward "Wild Bill"; B10.13.1876 Lawrence MA; D12.9.1923 Forsyth NY; BR/TR/5´11˝/190; d4.22; M4/C1; ▲																									
1898	Was N	1	6	.143	17	7	6	0	88	88	74	0	7	69	36	4.30	85	.259	.394	103-2-1	.165	-1*	41	-11	—	-0.8
1899	Bro N	1	2	.333	5	2	2	1	25	35	22	0	0	13	11	4.32	91	.330	.403	13	.231	-0	110	-3	—	-0.3
1900	Bro N	1	2	.333	5	4	2	0	31	36	23	0	3	18	13	6.68	57	.290	.393	13	.000	-2	104	-7	—	-0.6
1901	Bro N	**25**	15	.625	**45**	38	36-2	**3**	351	324	151	1	8	152	226	2.77	121	.244	.325	135-2-8	.170	-1*	117	23	—	2.2
1902	Bro N	17	15	.531	35	33	30-4	1	297.2	250	122	1	7	111	170	2.78	99	.228	.303	161-1-2	.174	-0*	98	1	—	0.1
1903	Det A	17	16	.515	35	34	**34-4**	0	307	247	104	3	5	95	187	2.29	127	.220	.284	124-0-9	.242	4*	106	25	—	3.0
1904	Det A	16	16	.500	34	34	30-3	0	293	251	111	5	10	94	137	2.46	104	.232	.300	140-1-5	.271	5*	100	4	—	1.1
1905	Det A	18	15	.545	34	32	27-5	0	280.2	236	111	2	10	101	135	2.60	105	.230	.305	130-0-13	.192	1*	100	5	—	0.7
1906	Det A	9	15	.375	25	25	22	0	211.2	221	92	4	8	72	85	3.15	88	.272	.337	91-0-4	.121	-5*	76	-7	—	-1.3
1907	†Det A	25	4	**.862**	32	28	27-3	1	271	222	96	3	8	82	123	2.19	119	.226	.291	109-0-4	.266	7*	156	13	—	1.9
1908	†Det A	18	7	.720	29	28	25-6	0	242.2	210	78	2	6	53	141	2.08	116	.231	.278	82-0-1	.159	0*	122	11	—	0.8
1909	†Det A	8	7	.533	21	17	13-4	2	140.1	121	50	0	6	60	76	2.31	109	.235	.322	45-0-5	.200	1*	97	3	—	0.3
1910	Det A	17	7	.708	26	23	20-3	0	206.2	184	74	4	7	61	107	2.44	108	.243	.305	69-0-2	.145	-2	101	5	—	0.0
1911	Det A	10	9	.526	20	19	15-1	0	168.1	160	83	4	3	64	81	3.31	104	.250	.321	60-1-1	.200	3*	133	3	—	0.4
1912	Det A	1	0	1.000	3	1	0	0	10	5	2	0	1	2	6	0.90	362	.147	.216	13	.077	-1*	226	2	—	0.1
1915	NY A	0	3	.000	9	1	0	0	33.2	35	18	1	1	10	17	4.81	61	.278	.336	12	.083	-1*	99	-5	—	-0.6
1916	NY A	0	0	ø	1	0	0	0	1	1	0	0	0	1	0	0.00	ø	.250	.400	0	ø	0	—	0	—	0.0
1918	Det A	1	0	1.000	2	1	0	0	6	5	1	0	0	1	1	1.50	177	.227	.261	2	.500	0	198	1	—	0.2
Total	18	185	139	.571	378	327	289-35	8	2964.2	2631	1212	30	90	1059	1552	2.69	106	.239	.310	1302-7-55	.193	8	108	63	—	7.2
DOPSON, JOHN	John Robert; B7.14.1963 Baltimore MD; BL/TR/6´4˝/(205–235); [MonN82 2/45]; d9.4																									
1985	Mon N	0	2	.000	4	3	0	0-0	13	25	17	4	0	4-0	4	11.08	31	.379	.414	4	.000	0	51	-11	0	-1.3
1988	Mon N	3	11	.214	26	26	1	0-0	168.2	150	69	15	1	58-3	101	3.04	120	.235	.299	51-0-4	.059	-3	80	9	0	0.3
1989	Bos A	12	8	.600	29	28	2	0-0	169.1	166	84	14	2	69-0	95	3.99	103	.257	.328	0	ø	0	102	3	26	0.4
1990	Bos A	0	0	ø	4	4	0	0-0	17.2	13	7	2	0	9-0	9	2.04	201	.200	.293	0	ø	0	94	3	151	0.2
1991	Bos A	0	0	ø	1	0	0	0-0	1	2	2	0	0	1-0	0	18.00	24	.500	.500	0	ø	0	—	-1	148	-0.1
1992	Bos A	7	11	.389	25	25	0	0-0	141.1	159	78	17	2	38-2	55	4.08	104	.287	.334	0	ø	0	80	1	41	0.1
1993	Bos A	7	11	.389	34	28	1-1	0-0	155.2	170	93	16	2	59-12	89	4.97	93	.281	.343	0	ø	0	98	-4	0	-0.3
1994	Cal A	1	4	.200	21	5	0	1-1	58.2	67	41	6	3	26-3	33	6.14	80	.288	.365	0	ø	0	71	-7	50	-0.5
Total	8	30	47	.390	144	119	4-1	1-1	725.1	752	391	74	10	264-20	386	4.27	98	.268	.331	55-0-4	.055	-3	89	-7	416	-1.2
DORAN, JOHN	John F.; B1867 Chicago IL; TL/5´11˝/175; d4.11																									
1891	Lou AA	5	10	.333	15	14	12-1	0	126	160	111	3	13	75	55	5.43	67	.299	.398	53	.189	-2	78	-23	—	-2.2
DORGAN, MIKE	Michael Cornelius; B10.2.1853 Middletown CT; D4.26.1909 Hartford CT; BR/TR/5´9˝/180; d5.8.1877; M3; b–Jerry; ▲																									
1879	Syr N	0	0	ø	2	0	0	0	12	13	6	0	—	2	8	2.25	105	.260	.288	270-1	.267	0*	—	0	—	0.0
1880	Pro N	0	0	ø	1	0	0	0	8	4	3	0	—	0	2	1.13	196	.138	.138	321	.246	0*	—	1	—	0.1
1883	NY N	0	1	.000	1	1	1	0	7	8	7	0	—	6	3	3.86	80	.286	.412	261	.234	0*	35	-1	—	-0.1
1884	NY N	8	6	.571	14	14	12	0	113	98	84	5	—	51	90	3.50	85	.215	.294	341-1	.276	2*	130	-8	—	-0.6
Total	4	8	7	.533	18	15	13	0	140	123	100	5	—	59	103	3.28	88	.218	.293	1193-2	.256	3	126	-8	—	-0.6
DORISH, HARRY	Harry "Fritz"; B7.13.1921 Swoyersville PA; D12.31.2000 Wilkes–Barre PA; BR/TR/5´11˝/206; d4.15; C5																									
1947	Bos A	7	8	.467	41	9	2	2	136	149	80	6	1	54	50	4.70	83	.283	.351	35-0-4	.143	-1	94	-11	0	-1.3
1948	Bos A	0	1	.000	9	0	0	0	14.1	18	13	1	0	6	5	5.65	78	.281	.343	4	.250	-0	—	-3	0	-0.2
1949	Bos A	0	0	ø	5	0	0	0	7.2	7	2	1	0	1	5	2.35	186	.241	.267	0	ø	0	—	2	0	0.1
1950	StL A	4	9	.308	29	13	4	0	109	162	90	13	9	36	36	6.44	77	.337	.394	31-0-1	.161	0*	91	-16	0	-1.6
1951	Chi A	5	6	.455	32	4	2-1	0	96.2	101	50	6	0	31	29	3.54	114	.272	.328	31	.258	0	88	3	0	0.4
1952	Chi A	8	4	.667	39	1	1	**11**	91	66	28	4	1	42	47	2.47	148	.208	.303	22-0-2	.091	-1	72	**12**	0	1.8
1953	Chi A	10	6	.625	55	6	2	18	145.2	140	59	9	6	52	69	3.40	118	.254	.325	41-0-3	.171	-2	92	11	0	1.3
1954	Chi A	6	4	.600	37	6	2-1	6	109	88	35	9	1	29	48	2.72	137	.228	.282	27-0-2	.111	-2	106	13	0	1.0
1955	Chi A	2	0	1.000	13	0	0	1	17	16	4	0	0	9-1	6	1.59	249	.258	.352	3	.333	0	—	4	0	0.5
	Bal A	3	3	.500	35	1	0	6	65.2	58	25	5	1	28-2	22	3.15	121	.238	.318	10-0-1	.000	-1	0	6	0	0.5
	Year	5	3	.625	48	1	0	7	82.2	74	29	5	1	37-3	28	2.83	136	.242	.325	13-0-1	.077	-1	0	10	0	1.0
1956	Bal A	0	0	ø	13	0	0	0	19.2	22	10	3	0	3-0	4	4.12	95	.297	.316	0	ø	0	—	0	0	0.0
	Bos A	0	2	.000	15	0	0	0	22.2	23	10	1	0	10-1	11	3.57	129	.277	.351	0	ø	0	—	3	0	0.3
	Year	0	2	.000	28	0	0	0	42.1	45	20	4	0	13-1	15	3.83	112	.287	.335	0	ø	0	—	2	0	0.3
Total	10	45	43	.511	323	40	13-2	44	834.1	850	406	58	19	301-4	332	3.83	106	.267	.333	204-0-13	.157	-6	95	24	0	2.8
DORNER, GUS	Augustus; B8.18.1876 Chambersburg PA; D5.4.1956 Chambersburg PA; BR/TR/5´10˝/176; d9.17																									
1902	Cle A	3	1	.750	4	4	4-1	0	36	33	13	1	1	13	5	1.25	275	.244	.315	13-0-1	.385	2	63	7	—	1.0
1903	Cle A	3	5	.375	12	8	4-2	0	73.2	83	51	4	1	24	28	4.52	63	.283	.340	25-0-3	.080	-2	106	-12	—	-1.3
1906	Cin N	0	1	.000	2	1	1	0	15	16	5	0	1	4	5	1.20	230	.276	.333	5	.000	-1	26	2	—	0.0
	Bos N	8	25	.242	34	32	29	0	273.1	264	152	5	16	103	104	3.65	74	.260	.338	100-0-5	.140	-4	68	-28	—	-3.5
	Year	8	26	.235	36	33	30	0	288.1	280	157	5	17	107	109	3.53	76	.261	.338	105-0-5	.133	-5	66	-29	—	-3.5
1907	Bos N	12	16	.429	36	31	24-2	0	271.1	253	120	4	15	92	85	3.12	82	.255	.327	92-0-7	.130	-3	81	-15	—	-2.1
1908	Bos N	8	19	.296	38	28	14-3	0	216.1	176	120	3	15	77	41	3.54	68	.224	.305	67-0-5	.179	-1	103	-27	—	-3.3
1909	Bos N	1	2	.333	5	2	0	1	24.2	17	11	1	2	17	7	2.55	110	.198	.343	6-0-1	.167	-0	37	0	—	0.0
Total	6	35	69	.337	131	106	76-8	1	910.1	842	472	18	51	330	275	3.37	78	.250	.326	308-0-22	.149	-9	82	-73	—	-9.2
DORR, BERT	Charles Albert; B2.2.1862 NY; D6.16.1914 Dickinson NY; d8.24																									
1882	StL AA	2	6	.250	8	8	8	0	66	53	39	0	—	1	34	2.59	108	.205	.208	26	.154	-2	64	2	—	0.1
DORSETT, CAL	Calvin Leavelle "Preacher"; B6.10.1913 Lone Oak TX; D10.22.1970 Elk City OK; BR/TR/6´0˝/180; d8.19; Mil 1942–45																									
1940	Cle A	0	0	ø	1	0	0	0	1	1	1	1	0	0	0	9.00	47	.250	.250	0	ø	0	—	0	0	0.0
1941	Cle A	0	1	.000	5	2	0	0	11.1	21	15	0	0	10	5	10.32	38	.382	.477	2	.000	-0	88	-9	0	-0.6
1947	Cle A	0	0	ø	2	0	0	0	1.1	3	4	1	0	3	1	27.00	13	.500	.667	0-0-1	ø	0	—	-4	0	-0.2
Total	3	0	1	.000	8	2	0	0	13.2	25	20	2	0	13	6	11.85	33	.385	.487	2-0-1	.000	-0	88	-13	0	-0.8
DORSEY, JIM	James Edward; B8.2.1955 Oak Park IL; BR/TR/6´2˝/(190–200); [AnaA75*2/26]; d9.2; Col Los Angeles Valley (CA) JC																									
1980	Cal A	1	2	.333	4	4	0	0-0	15.2	25	16	2	1	8-0	8	9.19	43	.368	.436	0	ø	0	96	-8	0	-1.2
1984	Bos A	0	0	ø	2	0	0	0-0	2.2	6	3	0	0	2-0	4	10.13	42	.462	.533	0	ø	0	—	-1	0	-0.1
1985	Bos A	0	1	.000	2	1	0	0-0	5.1	12	12	2	0	10-1	2	20.25	21	.444	.595	0	ø	0	63	-9	0	-1.1
Total	3	1	3	.250	8	5	0	0-0	23.2	43	31	4	1	20-1	14	11.79	34	.398	.492	0	ø	0	88	-18	0	-2.4
DORSEY, JERRY	Michael Jeremiah; B1.1856 , Can; D11.3.1938 Auburn NY; BL; d7.9																									
1884	Bal U	0	1	.000	1	1	0	0	4	7	8	1	—	0	3	9.00	30	.368	.368	3	.000	-1	32	-3	—	-0.4
DOSCHER, JACK	John Henry Jr.; B7.27.1880 Troy NY; D5.27.1971 Park Ridge NJ; BL/TL/6´1˝/205; d7.2; f–Herm; Col Fordham																									
1903	Chi N	0	1	.000	1	1	0	0	3	6	5	0	1	2	5	12.00	26	.429	.529	1	.000	-0	43	-3	—	-0.4
	Bro N	0	0	ø	3	0	0	0	7	8	8	1	1	9	4	7.71	41	.296	.486	3	.000	-0	—	-3	—	-0.2
	Year	0	1	.000	4	1	0	0	10	14	13	1	2	11	9	9.00	35	.341	.500	4	.000	-1	42	-6	—	-0.6
1904	Bro N	0	0	ø	2	0	0	0	6.1	1	1	0	0	1	2	0.00	ø	.053	.100	2	.500	0	—	2	—	0.1
1905	Bro N	1	5	.167	12	7	6	0	71	60	34	1	3	30	33	3.17	91	.232	.318	24-0-1	.083	-2	78	-2	—	-0.4
1906	Bro N	0	1	.000	2	1	1	0	14	12	3	0	0	4	10	1.29	196	.250	.308	5	.000	-1	0	2	—	0.0
1908	Cin N	1	3	.250	7	4	3	0	44.1	31	19	1	3	22	7	1.83	126	.196	.306	15	.133	0	53	0	—	0.0
Total	5	2	10	.167	27	13	10	0	145.2	118	70	3	8	68	61	2.84	95	.225	.323	50-0-1	.100	-3	63	-4	—	-0.9

YEAR	TM LG	W	L	PCT	G	GS	CG-SHO	SV-BS	IP	H	R	HR	HB	BB-IB	SO	ERA	AERA	OAV	OOB	AB-HR-SH	AVG	PB	SUP	APR	DL	PW
DOTEL, OCTAVIO	Octavio Eduardo (Diaz); B11.25.1973 Santo Domingo, D.R.; BR/TR/6´0˝/(175–210); d6.26																									
1999	†NY N	8	3	.727	19	14	0	0-0	85.1	69	52	12	6	49-1	85	5.38	81	.226	.340	24-0-1	.125	1	122	-10	0	-1.0
2000	Hou N	3	7	.300	50	16	0	16-7	125	127	80	26	7	61-3	142	5.40	91	.265	.351	32-0-7	.031	-3	92	-6	0	-0.8
2001	†Hou N	7	5	.583	61	4	0	2-2	105	79	35	5	2	47-2	145	2.66	173	.205	.294	11-0-1	.091	-1	101	21	0	2.2
2002	Hou N	6	4	.600	83	0	0	6-4	97.1	58	21	7	4	27-2	118	1.85	234	.173	.239	1	.000	-0	—	**26**	0	2.6
2003	Hou N	6	4	.600	76	0	0	4-2	87	53	25	9	3	31-2	97	2.48	178	.172	.253	6	.000	-1	—	19	0	1.9
2004	Hou N	0	4	.000	32	0	0	14-3	34.2	27	15	4	1	15-4	50	3.12	140	.213	.299	0	ø	0	—	4	0	0.6
	Oak A	6	2	.750	45	0	0	22-6	50.2	41	23	9	3	18-3	72	4.09	113	.220	.298	0	ø	0	—	4	0	0.8
2005	Oak A	1	2	.333	15	0	0	7-4	15.1	10	6	2	0	11-2	16	3.52	124	.185	.323	0	ø	0	—	2	137	0.3
2006	NY A	0	0	ø	14	0	0	0-0	10	18	13	2	0	11-1	7	10.80	42	.383	.492	0	ø	0	—	-7	135	-0.3
Total	8	37	31	.544	395	34	0	71-28	610.1	482	270	76	26	270-20	732	3.75	121	.216	.305	74-0-9	.068	-4	108	53	272	6.3
DOTSON, RICHARD	Richard Elliott; B1.10.1959 Cincinnati OH; BR/TR/6´0˝/(185–205); [CalA77 1/7]; d9.4																									
1979	Chi A	2	0	1.000	5	5	1-1	0-0	24.1	28	13	0	0	6-0	13	3.70	115	.286	.321	0	ø	0	128	1	0	0.1
1980	Chi A	12	10	.545	33	32	8	0-0	198	185	105	20	6	87-2	109	4.27	95	.247	.328	0	ø	0*	99	-3	0	-0.3
1981	Chi A	9	8	.529	24	24	5-**4**	0-0	141	145	67	13	4	49-0	73	3.77	96	.270	.333	0	ø	0*	139	-2	0	-0.2
1982	Chi A	11	15	.423	34	31	3-1	0-0	196.2	219	97	19	5	73-4	109	3.84	106	.282	.345	0	ø	0	92	5	0	0.5
1983	†Chi A	22	7	**.759**	35	35	8-1	0-0	240	209	92	19	8	106-1	137	3.23	131	.240	.325	0	ø	0	127	27	0	3.3
1984	Chi A★	14	15	.483	32	32	14-1	0-0	245.2	216	110	24	7	103-5	120	3.59	117	.238	.317	0	ø	0*	92	14	0	1.6
1985	Chi A	3	4	.429	9	9	0	0-0	52.1	53	30	5	3	17-1	33	4.47	97	.261	.324	0	ø	0	65	-1	132	-0.2
1986	Chi A	10	17	.370	34	34	3-1	0-0	197	226	125	24	2	69-2	110	5.48	79	.289	.347	0	ø	0	81	-21	0	-2.5
1987	Chi A	11	12	.478	31	31	7-2	0-0	211.1	201	109	24	0	86-2	114	4.17	111	.249	.320	0	ø	0	78	9	0	0.9
1988	NY A	12	9	.571	32	29	4	0-0	171	178	103	27	4	72-3	77	5.00	79	.266	.338	0	ø	0	130	-20	17	-2.2
1989	NY A	2	5	.286	11	9	1	0-0	51.2	69	33	8	1	17-0	14	5.57	70	.317	.366	0	ø	0	101	-9	0	-1.0
	Chi A	3	7	.300	17	17	1	0-0	99.2	112	51	8	0	41-3	55	3.88	99	.282	.348	0	ø	0	99	-2	0	-0.2
	Year	5	12	.294	28	26	2	0-0	151.1	181	84	16	1	58-3	69	4.46	86	.294	.354	0	ø	0	99	-11	0	-1.2
1990	KC A	0	4	.000	8	7	0	0-0	28.2	43	29	3	0	14-1	9	8.48	46	.355	.410	0	ø	0	94	-14	0	-1.6
Total	12	111	113	.496	305	295	55-11	0-0	1857.1	1884	964	194	40	740-24	973	4.23	98	.264	.334	0	ø	0	101	-16	149	-1.8
DOTTER, GARY	Gary Richard; B8.7.1942 St.Louis MO; BL/TL/6´1˝/180; d9.10																									
1961	Min A	0	0	ø	2	0	0	0	6	6	6	0	0	4-1	2	9.00	47	.273	.357	1	.000	-0	—	-3	0	-0.1
1963	Min A	0	0	ø	2	0	0	0	2	0	0	0	0	0-0	2	0.00	ø	.000	.000	0	ø	0	—	1	0	0.1
1964	Min A	0	0	ø	3	0	0	0	4.1	3	2	1	0	3-0	6	2.08	172	.188	.316	0	ø	0	—	0	0	0.0
Total	3	0	0	ø	7	0	0	0	12.1	9	8	1	0	7-1	10	5.11	76	.205	.302	1	.000	-0	—	-2	0	0.0
DOTY, BABE	Elmer L.; B12.17.1867 Lyons NY; D11.20.1929 Toledo OH; BL/TR/6´0˝/160; d8.18																									
1890	Tol AA	1	0	1.000	1	1	1	0	9	9	1	0	0	1	4	1.00	395	.250	.270	3	.000	-0	85	3	—	0.3
DOUGHERTY, JIM	James E.; B3.8.1968 Brentwood NY; BR/TR/6´0˝/(210–225); [HouN90 26/703]; d4.27; Col North Carolina																									
1995	Hou N	8	4	.667	56	0	0	0-2	67.2	76	37	7	3	25-1	49	4.92	78	.292	.357	8-0-1	.125	-0	—	-6	0	-1.0
1996	Hou N	0	2	.000	12	0	0	0-1	13	14	14	2	1	11-1	6	9.00	43	.280	.413	0	ø	0	—	-8	0	-1.0
1998	Oak A	0	2	.000	9	0	0	0-1	12	17	11	2	1	7-0	3	8.25	56	.340	.431	0	ø	0	—	-4	0	-0.5
1999	Pit N	0	0	ø	2	0	0	0-0	2	3	3	0	0	3-0	1	9.00	51	.333	.500	0	ø	0	—	-1	0	0.0
Total	4	8	8	.500	79	0	0	0-4	94.2	110	65	11	5	46-2	59	5.99	66	.298	.380	8-0-1	.125	0	—	-19	0	-2.5
DOUGHERTY, TOM	Thomas James "Sugar Boy"; B5.30.1881 Chicago IL; D11.6.1953 Milwaukee WI; BL/TR/5´11.5˝/195; d4.24																									
1904	Chi A	1	0	1.000	1	0	0	0	2	0	0	0	0	0	0	0.00	ø	.000	.000	1	.000	-0	—	1	—	0.1
DOUGLAS, WHAMMY	Charles William; B2.17.1935 Carrboro NC; BR/TR/6´2˝/185; d7.29																									
1957	Pit N	3	3	.500	11	8	0	0	47	48	23	5	3	30-2	28	3.26	116	.270	.384	16	.063	-1	93	1	0	0.0
DOUGLAS, LARRY	Lawrence Howard; B6.5.1890 Jellico TN; D11.4.1949 Jellico TN; BR/TR/6´3˝/175; d6.17																									
1915	Bal F	1	0	1.000	2	0	0	0	3	3	1	0	0	2	1	3.00	96	.273	.385	0	ø	0	—	0	—	0.0
DOUGLAS, PHIL	Phillip Brooks "Shufflin' Phil"; B6.17.1890 Cedartown GA; D8.1.1952 Sequatchie TN; BR/TR/6´3˝/190; d8.30																									
1912	Chi A	0	1	.000	3	1	0	0	12.1	21	17	0	0	6	7	7.30	44	.382	.443	2-0-1	.000	-0	46	-7	—	-0.5
1914	Cin N	11	18	.379	45	25	13	1	239.1	186	111	7	11	92	121	2.56	115	.223	.308	73-0-4	.137	-2	91	5	—	0.2
1915	Cin N	1	5	.167	8	7	0	0	46.2	53	35	0	0	23	29	5.40	53	.299	.380	17	.118	-1	97	-12	—	-1.5
	Bro N	5	5	.500	20	13	5-1	0	116.2	104	45	1	5	17	63	2.62	106	.241	.278	39	.154	-1	101	2	—	0.1
	Chi N	1	1	.500	4	4	2-1	0	25	17	9	0	1	7	18	2.16	129	.187	.253	8	.000	-1	100	1	—	0.0
	Year	7	11	.389	32	24	7-2	0	188.1	174	89	1	6	47	110	3.25	86	.249	.301	64	.125	-3	100	-8	—	-1.4
1917	Chi N	14	20	.412	**51**	37	20-5	1	293.1	269	123	13	6	50	151	2.55	114	.250	.287	87-0-7	.126	-4	80	8	—	0.7
1918	†Chi N	10	9	.526	25	19	11-2	2	156.2	145	57	2	1	31	51	2.13	131	.246	.285	55-0-2	.255	1	90	9	—	1.4
1919	Chi N	10	6	.625	25	19	8-4	0	161.2	133	52	0	2	34	63	2.00	144	.230	.275	51-0-3	.157	-2	93	14	—	1.5
	NY N	2	4	.333	8	6	4	0	51.1	53	22	0	1	6	21	2.10	133	.264	.288	15-0-1	.000	-2	90	1	—	-0.1
	Year	12	10	.545	33	25	12-4	0	213	186	74	0	3	40	84	2.03	141	.238	.278	66-0-4	.121	-4	92	15	—	1.4
1920	NY N	14	10	.583	46	21	10-3	2	226	225	84	6	2	55	71	2.71	111	.263	.309	73-0-2	.151	-4	125	8	—	0.4
1921	†NY N	15	10	.600	40	27	13-**3**	2	221.2	266	119	17	2	55	55	4.22	87	.308	.351	81-1-5	.198	0	147	-13	—	-1.2
1922	NY N	11	4	.733	24	21	9-1	0	157.2	154	56	6	4	35	33	**2.63**	**152**	**.257**	**.302**	58-1-1	.207	1	115	25	—	2.1
Total	9	94	93	.503	299	200	95-20	8	1708.1	1626	730	52	35	411	683	2.80	111	.256	.305	559-2-26	.161	-16	105	41	—	3.1
DOUGLASS, SEAN	Sean Reed; B4.28.1979 Lancaster CA; BR/TR/6´6˝/(198–220); [BalA97 2/73]; d7.18																									
2001	Bal A	2	1	.667	4	4	0	0-0	20.1	21	12	3	1	11-0	17	5.31	81	.259	.351	0	ø	0	124	-2	0	-0.2
2002	Bal A	0	5	.000	15	8	0	0-0	53.1	58	41	10	2	35-2	44	6.08	71	.283	.391	0	ø	0	88	-12	0	-0.9
2003	Bal A	0	0	ø	3	0	0	0-0	8	14	12	2	1	6-0	3	13.50	34	.378	.477	0	ø	0	—	-7	0	-0.3
2004	Tor A	0	2	.000	14	3	0	0-0	38.2	37	27	6	2	28-4	36	6.28	78	.252	.374	0	ø	0	76	-5	0	-0.3
2005	Det A	5	5	.500	18	16	0	0-0	87.1	92	57	13	2	33-2	55	5.56	77	.276	.340	2	.000	-0	107	-12	0	-1.2
Total	5	7	13	.350	54	31	0	0-0	207.2	222	149	34	8	113-8	155	6.11	72	.276	.368	2	.000	-0	99	-38	0	-2.9
DOWD, SKIP	James Joseph; B2.16.1889 Holyoke MA; D12.20.1960 Holyoke MA; BR/TR/5´10.5˝/160; d7.5; Col Holy Cross																									
1910	Pit N	0	0	ø	1	0	0	0	2	4	4	0	1	2	1	0.00	ø	.400	.538	0	ø	0	—	-1	—	0.0
DOWLING, DAVE	David Barclay; B8.23.1942 Baton Rouge LA; BR/TL/6´2˝/(182–185); d10.3; Col California																									
1964	StL N	0	0	ø	1	0	0	0	1	2	0	0	0	0-0	0	0.00	ø	.400	.400	0	ø	0	—	0	0	0.0
1966	Chi N	1	0	1.000	1	1	1	0	9	10	2	0	0	0-0	3	2.00	184	.270	.270	2-0-2	.000	-0	167	2	0	0.2
Total	2	1	0	1.000	2	1	1	0	10	12	2	0	0	0-0	3	1.80	205	.286	.286	2-0-2	.000	-0	167	2	0	0.2
DOWLING, PETE	Henry Peter; B St.Louis MO; D6.30.1905 Hot Lake OR; BL/TL/5´11˝/165; d7.17																									
1897	Lou N	1	2	.333	4	4	2	0	26	39	30	0	6	8	3	5.88	72	.342	.414	10	.200	-0	121	-6	—	-0.5
1898	Lou N	13	20	.394	36	32	30	0	285.2	284	176	7	22	120	84	4.16	86	.257	.342	107-0-2	.196	1	85	-19	—	-1.7
1899	Lou N	13	17	.433	35	33	30	0	298.1	329	166	6	17	95	89	3.05	127	.279	.342	119-0-2	.227	-1	91	22	—	1.7
1901	Mil A	1	3	.250	10	4	3	1	49.2	71	49	1	4	14	25	5.62	64	.332	.384	19	.211	1	103	-12	—	-0.7
	Cle A	11	22	.333	33	30	28-2	0	256.1	269	160	1	15	104	99	3.86	92	.267	.344	99-1-1	.162	-4	71	-6	—	-1.0
	Year	12	25	.324	43	34	31-2	1	306	340	209	2	19	118	124	4.15	86	.278	.351	118-1-1	.169	-3	75	-21	—	-1.7
Total	4	39	64	.379	118	103	93-2	1	916	992	581	15	64	341	300	3.84	96	.274	.347	354-1-5	.198	-3	85	-21	—	-2.2
DOWNING, AL	Alphonso Erwin; B6.28.1941 Trenton NJ; BR/TL/5´11˝/(177–185); d7.19; Col Rider																									
1961	NY A	0	1	.000	5	1	0	0	9	7	8	0	1	12-0	12	8.00	46	.212	.426	1	.000	-0	48	-4	0	-0.4
1962	NY A	0	0	ø	1	0	0	0	1	0	0	0	0	0-0	1	0.00	ø	.000	.000	0	ø	0	—	0	0	0.0
1963	†NY A	13	5	.722	24	22	10-4	0	175.2	114	52	7	0	80-1	171	2.56	137	**.184**	.277	58-0-3	.103	-2	106	21	0	1.8
1964	†NY A	13	8	.619	37	35	11-1	2	244	201	104	18	0	120-5	**217**	3.47	104	.223	.312	85-0-4	.176	1*	107	4	0	0.4
1965	NY A	12	14	.462	35	32	8-2	0	212	185	92	16	2	105-2	179	3.40	100	.237	.326	74-1-6	.108	-1*	104	0	0	-0.1
1966	NY A	10	11	.476	30	30	1	0	200	178	90	23	1	79-3	152	3.56	94	.235	.307	70-0-5	.100	-2	109	-5	0	-0.9
1967	NY A★	14	10	.583	31	28	10-4	0	201.2	158	65	13	6	61-1	171	2.63	119	.217	.281	66-1-1	.121	1	88	13	0	1.7
1968	NY A	3	3	.500	15	12	1	0	61.1	54	24	7	1	20-2	40	3.52	83	.237	.299	17	.176	0	65	-2	31	-0.2
1969	NY A	7	5	.583	30	15	5-1	0-0	130.2	117	57	12	0	49-6	85	3.38	104	.240	.306	44-0-2	.136	-0	112	2	0	0.0

YEAR	TM LG	W	L	PCT	G	GS	CG-SHO	SV-BS	IP	H	R	HR	HB	BB-IB	SO	ERA	AERA	OAV	OOB	AB-HR-SH	AVG	PB	SUP	APR	DL	PW
1970	Oak A	3	3	.500	10	6	1	0-0	41	39	19	5	1	22-0	26	3.95	89	.252	.346	11-0-1	.182	-0	122	-1	0	-0.1
	Mil A	2	10	.167	17	16	1	0-0	94.1	79	47	8	3	59-2	53	3.34	113	.232	.346	24-0-7	.083	-2	58	1	0	0.0
	Year	5	13	.278	27	22	2	0-0	135.1	118	66	13	4	81-2	79	3.52	105	.238	.346	35-0-8	.114	-2	74	1	0	-0.1
1971	LA N	20	9	.690	37	36	12-**5**	0-0	262.1	245	93	16	3	84-3	136	2.68	122	.247	.307	92-0-8	.174	2	126	15	0	1.9
1972	LA N	9	9	.500	31	30	7-4	0-0	202.2	196	81	13	7	67-2	117	2.98	113	.254	.317	66-0-6	.121	-1	116	9	0	0.9
1973	LA N	9	9	.500	30	28	5-2	0-0	193	155	87	19	1	68-3	124	3.31	105	.219	.288	57-0-7	.088	-1	110	1	0	0.0
1974	†LA N	5	6	.455	21	16	1-1	0-1	98.1	94	52	7	3	45-0	63	3.66	94	.255	.338	29-0-3	.172	-0	132	-5	0	-0.5
1975	LA N	2	1	.667	22	6	0	1-2	74.2	59	31	6	2	28-1	39	2.89	118	.215	.292	16	.000	-1	103	3	0	0.1
1976	LA N	1	2	.333	17	3	0	0-0	46.2	43	21	3	0	18-1	30	3.86	88	.250	.318	6	.000	-1	52	-2	0	-0.2
1977	LA N	0	1	.000	12	1	0	0-0	20	22	15	4	0	16-0	23	6.75	57	.278	.400	1	.000	-0	115	-6	21	-0.3
Total	17	123	107	.535	405	317	73-24	3-3	2268.1	1946	938	177	31	933-32	1639	3.22	106	.232	.309	717-2-53	.127	-7	105	44	52	4.1
Downs, Dave	David Ralph; B6.21.1952 Logan UT; BR/TR/6´5˝/215; [PhiN70 6/128]; d9.2; b–Kelly																									
1972	Phi N	1	1	.500	4	4	1-1	0-0	23	25	7	1	1	3-0	5	2.74	132	.294	.326	8	.250	0	80	2	0	0.2
Downs, Kelly	Kelly Robert; B10.25.1960 Ogden UT; BR/TR/6´4˝/(200–205); [PhiN79 26/661]; d7.29; b–Dave																									
1986	SF N	4	4	.500	14	14	1	0-0	88.1	78	29	5	3	30-7	64	2.75	128	.236	.302	29	.172	0*	81	9	0	0.8
1987	†SF N	12	9	.571	41	28	4-3	1-0	186	185	83	14	4	67-11	137	3.63	106	.258	.324	56-0-7	.143	-0	94	5	0	0.2
1988	SF N	13	9	.591	27	26	6-3	0-0	168	140	67	11	3	47-8	118	3.32	98	.225	.279	54-0-4	.167	2	148	0	33	0.3
1989	†SF N	4	8	.333	18	15	0	0-0	82.2	82	47	7	1	26-4	49	4.79	71	.261	.316	22-0-3	.091	-1	80	-12	103	-1.8
1990	SF N	3	2	.600	13	9	0	0-0	63	56	26	2	2	20-4	31	3.43	107	.233	.297	13-0-3	.000	-1	93	2	123	0.0
1991	SF N	10	4	.714	45	11	0	0-2	111.2	99	59	12	3	53-9	62	4.19	86	.239	.326	23-0-2	.087	-1	73	-9	9	-1.1
1992	SF N	1	2	.333	19	7	0	0-0	62.1	65	27	4	3	24-0	33	3.47	96	.275	.347	14-0-2	.000	-1	97	-1	0	-0.3
	†Oak A	5	5	.500	18	13	0	0-0	82	72	36	4	4	46-3	38	3.29	115	.237	.341	0	ø	0	97	4	0	0.4
1993	Oak A	5	10	.333	42	12	0	0-1	119.2	135	80	14	2	60-8	66	5.64	73	.287	.368	0	ø	0	93	-21	0	-2.3
Total	8	57	53	.518	237	135	11-6	1-3	963.2	912	454	73	25	373-54	598	3.86	94	.250	.321	211-0-21	.123	-2	99	-23	268	-3.8
Downs, Scott	Scott Jeremy; B3.17.1976 Louisville KY; BL/TL/6´2˝/190; [ChiN97 3/94]; d4.9; Col Kentucky; [DL 2002 Mon N 71]																									
2000	Chi N	4	3	.571	18	18	0	0-0	94	117	59	13	5	37-1	63	5.17	89	.310	.375	26-0-4	.077	-1	116	-7	0	-0.6
	Mon N	0	0	ø	1	1	0	0-0	3	5	3	0	0	3-0	0	9.00	52	.385	.500	2	.000	-0	175	-1	53	-0.1
	Year	4	3	.571	19	19	0	0-0	97	122	62	13	5	40-1	63	5.29	87	.312	.380	28-0-4	.071	-1	119	-8	0	-0.7
2003	Mon N	0	1	.000	1	1	0	0-0	3	5	5	2	0	3-2	4	15.00	30	.357	.471	1	.000	-0	42	-3	0	-0.5
2004	Mon N	3	6	.333	12	12	1-1	0-0	63	79	47	9	3	23-2	38	5.14	89	.310	.372	15-0-6	.067	-1	83	-7	0	-0.9
2005	Tor A	4	3	.571	26	13	0	0-0	94	93	49	12	5	34-0	75	4.31	107	.253	.324	0	ø	0	98	3	0	0.2
2006	Tor A	6	2	.750	59	5	0	1-3	77	73	38	9	2	30-6	61	4.09	116	.249	.322	0	ø	0	131	5	0	0.6
Total	5	17	15	.531	117	50	1-1	1-3	334	372	201	45	15	130-11	241	4.80	96	.282	.351	44-0-10	.068	-2	104	-10	124	-1.3
Doyle, Jess	Jesse Herbert; B4.14.1898 Knoxville TN; D4.15.1961 Belleville IL; BR/TR/5´11˝/175; d4.14																									
1925	Det A	4	7	.364	45	3	0	8	118.1	158	83	6	5	50	31	5.93	73	.340	.410	33-2-0	.242	3	98	-18	—	-1.4
1926	Det A	0	0	ø	2	0	0	1	4.1	6	3	0	0	1	2	4.15	98	.316	.350	1-0-1	1.000	0	—	0	—	0.0
1927	Det A	0	0	ø	7	0	0	0	12.1	16	11	0	0	5	5	8.03	52	.314	.375	3	.333	0	—	-4	—	-0.2
1931	StL A	0	0	ø	1	0	0	0	1	3	3	0	0	1	0	27.00	17	.500	.571	0	ø	0	—	-2	—	-0.1
Total	4	4	7	.364	55	3	0	9	136	183	100	6	5	57	38	6.22	69	.338	.406	37-2-1	.270	4	98	-24	—	-1.7
Doyle, John	John Aloysius; B1858 Halifax NS (now Canada); D12.24.1915 Providence RI; TR/5´10˝/160; d7.26; Col Fordham																									
1882	StL AA	0	3	.000	3	3	3	0	24	41	33	0	—	3	5	2.63	107	.353	.370	11	.182	-0	24	-3	—	-0.4
Doyle, Slow Joe	Judd Bruce; B9.15.1881 Clay Center KS; D11.21.1947 Tannersville NY; BR/TR/5´8˝/150; d8.25																									
1906	NY A	2	1	.667	9	6	3-2	0	45.1	34	15	1	1	13	28	2.38	124	.211	.274	14	.214	-0	81	3	—	0.2
1907	NY A	11	11	.500	29	23	15-1	1	193.2	169	86	2	6	67	94	2.65	105	.237	.308	58-0-4	.138	-1	92	2	—	0.0
1908	NY A	1	1	.500	12	4	2-1	0	48	42	24	1	2	14	20	2.63	94	.235	.297	14	.214	0	110	-2	—	-0.1
1909	NY A	8	6	.571	17	15	8-3	0	125.2	103	49	3	2	37	57	2.58	98	.232	.294	42-0-2	.167	0	132	1	—	-0.1
1910	NY A	0	2	.000	3	2	1	0	12.1	19	13	0	1	5	6	8.03	33	.365	.431	4	.250	0	38	-6	—	-0.8
	Cin N	0	0	ø	5	0	0	0	11.1	16	19	0	0	11	4	6.35	46	.327	.450	3	.000	-0	—	-7	—	-0.4
Total	5	22	21	.512	75	50	29-7	1	436.1	383	206	7	12	147	209	2.85	95	.240	.308	135-0-6	.163	-1	101	-9	—	-1.2
Doyle, Paul	Paul Sinnott; B10.2.1939 Philadelphia PA; BL/TL/5´11˝/(170–172); d5.28																									
1969	†Atl N	2	0	1.000	36	0	0	4-3	39	31	9	4	0	16-3	25	2.08	174	.231	.307	3	.000	-0	—	7	0	0.5
1970	Cal A	3	1	.750	40	0	0	5-2	42	43	25	7	1	21-3	34	5.14	70	.267	.355	3	.000	-0	—	-6	0	-0.7
	SD N	0	2	.000	9	0	0	2-0	7	9	5	0	0	6-1	2	6.43	62	.360	.469	1	.000	-0	—	-2	0	-0.3
1972	Cal A	0	0	ø	2	0	0	0-0	2.1	2	0	0	0	3-0	4	0.00	ø	.250	.455	0	ø	0	—	1	0	0.1
Total	3	5	3	.625	87	0	0	11-5	90.1	85	39	11	1	46-7	65	3.79	96	.259	.348	7	.000	-1	—	0	0	-0.4
Doyle, Carl	William Carl; B7.30.1912 Knoxville TN; D9.4.1951 Knoxville TN; BR/TR/6´1˝/185; d8.5																									
1935	Phi A	2	7	.222	14	9	3	0	79.2	86	63	3	2	72	34	5.99	76	.282	.422	30	.133	-2	85	-13	—	-1.4
1936	Phi A	0	3	.000	8	6	1	0	38.2	66	53	4	5	29	12	10.94	47	.369	.469	15	.267	1	126	-24	—	-1.3
1939	Bro N	1	2	.333	5	1	1-1	1	17.2	8	5	1	0	7	7	1.02	395	.136	.227	6	.167	0	174	5	—	0.8
1940	Bro N	0	0	ø	3	0	0	1	5.2	18	17	3	4	6	4	27.00	15	.545	.651	1	1.000	1	—	-13	—	-0.5
	StL N	3	3	.500	21	5	1	0	81	99	57	7	6	41	44	5.89	68	.294	.380	30-1-0	.200	2	100	-14	—	-0.8
	Year	3	3	.500	24	5	1	1	86.2	117	74	10	10	47	48	7.27	55	.316	.407	31-1-0	.226	2	100	-28	—	-1.3
Total	4	6	15	.286	51	21	6-1	2	222.2	277	195	18	17	155	101	6.95	63	.303	.414	82-1-0	.195	1	109	-59	—	-3.2
Dozier, Tom	Thomas Dean; B9.5.1961 San Pablo CA; BR/TR/6´2˝/190; [StLN79 11/266]; d5.17																									
1986	Oak A	0	0	ø	4	0	0	0-0	6.1	6	6	1	0	5-1	4	5.68	69	.261	.367	0	ø	0	—	-2	0	-0.1
Dozier, Buzz	William Joseph; B8.31.1928 Waco TX; BR/TR/6´3˝/185; d9.12; Col Baylor																									
1947	Was A	0	0	ø	2	0	0	0	4.2	2	0	0	0	1	2	0.00	ø	.133	.188	1	.000	-0	—	2	0	0.1
1949	Was A	0	0	ø	2	0	0	0	6.1	12	8	0	0	6	1	11.37	37	.429	.529	2	.000	-0	—	-4	0	-0.2
Total	2	0	0	ø	4	0	0	0	11	14	8	0	0	7	3	6.55	62	.326	.420	3	.000	-0	—	-2	0	-0.1
Drabek, Doug	Douglas Dean; B7.25.1962 Victoria TX; BR/TR/6´1˝/(185–190); [ChiA83 11/279]; d5.30; Col Houston																									
1986	NY A	7	8	.467	27	21	0	0-0	131.2	126	64	13	3	50-1	76	4.10	101	.251	.322	0	ø	0	95	2	0	0.1
1987	Pit N	11	12	.478	29	28	1-1	0-0	176.1	165	86	22	0	46-2	120	3.88	107	.247	.294	59-0-7	.119	-1*	95	5	22	0.5
1988	Pit N	15	7	.682	33	32	3-1	0-0	219.1	194	83	21	6	50-4	127	3.08	112	.239	.286	76-0-5	.171	3	116	9	0	1.2
1989	Pit N	14	12	.538	35	34	8-5	0-0	244.1	215	83	21	3	69-3	123	2.80	121	.238	.293	77-0-6	.104	-2*	76	18	0	1.6
1990	†Pit N	**22**	6	**.786**	33	33	9-3	0-0	231.1	190	78	15	3	56-2	131	2.76	132	.225	.274	84-1-7	.214	5	133	25	0	3.6
1991	†Pit N	15	14	.517	35	35	5-2	0-0	234.2	245	92	16	3	62-6	142	3.07	117	.274	.321	84-0-4	.179	1*	109	14	0	1.8
1992	†Pit N	15	11	.577	34	34	10-4	0-0	256.2	218	84	17	6	54-8	177	2.77	125	.231	.274	89-0-8	.157	1*	103	21	0	2.2
1993	Hou N	9	18	.333	34	34	7-2	0-0	237.2	242	108	18	3	60-12	157	3.79	102	.267	.312	71-1-9	.085	-2	74	5	0	0.3
1994	Hou N★	12	6	.667	23	23	6-2	0-0	164.2	132	58	14	2	45-2	121	2.84	139	.220	.275	58-0-4	.241	3*	117	22	0	2.7
1995	Hou N	10	9	.526	31	**31**	2-1	0-0	185	205	104	18	8	54-4	143	4.77	81	.282	.337	60-0-8	.233	4*	118	-17	0	-1.1
1996	Hou N	7	9	.438	30	30	1	0-0	175.1	208	102	21	7	60-5	137	4.57	85	.298	.355	56-0-7	.179	0*	112	-16	16	-1.2
1997	Chi A	12	11	.522	31	31	0	0-0	169.1	170	109	30	4	69-5	85	5.74	77	.261	.334	1-0-1	.000	-0*	103	-21	0	-2.4
1998	Bal A	6	11	.353	23	21	1	0-0	108.2	138	90	20	5	29-2	55	7.29	62	.312	.355	1	.000	-0	114	-33	31	-4.0
Total	13	155	134	.536	398	387	53-21	0-0	2535	2448	1141	246	53	704-56	1594	3.73	102	.255	.308	716-2-66	.166	12	105	34	69	5.3
Drabowsky, Moe	Myron Walter; B7.21.1935 Ozanna, Poland; D6.10.2006 Little Rock AR; BR/TR/6´2˝/(190–212); d8.7; C2; Col Trinity (CT)																									
1956	Chi N	2	4	.333	9	7	3	0	51	37	19	1	2	39-3	36	2.47	153	.207	.353	16-0-2	.250	0	70	6	0	0.7
1957	Chi N	13	15	.464	36	33	12-2	0	239.2	214	103	22	10	94-6	170	3.53	110	.242	.319	82-1-3	.183	2	85	10	0	1.4
1958	Chi N	9	11	.450	22	20	4-1	0	125.2	118	73	19	5	73-4	77	4.51	87	.245	.349	45-0-3	.156	-1	110	-9	0	-1.4
1959	Chi N	5	10	.333	31	23	3-1	0	141.2	138	78	21	3	75-4	70	4.13	96	.251	.343	45	.111	-1	91	-6	0	-0.7
1960	Chi N	3	1	.750	32	7	0	1	50.1	71	44	3	1	23-0	26	6.44	59	.338	.397	6-0-1	.000	-1*	137	-16	0	-1.3
1961	Mil N	0	2	.000	16	0	0	2	25.1	26	15	4	1	18-3	5	4.62	81	.277	.391	4	.250	0	—	-3	0	-0.2
1962	Cin N	2	6	.250	23	10	1	1	83	84	49	13	6	31-0	56	4.99	81	.267	.340	17-0-1	.000	-2	74	-8	0	-0.9
	KC A	1	1	.500	10	3	0	0	28	29	20	8	1	10-0	19	5.14	82	.266	.328	6-0-1	.167	-0	120	-4	0	-0.3
1963	KC A	7	13	.350	26	22	9-2	0	174.1	135	62	16	8	64-2	109	3.05	128	.214	.294	62-2-3	.161	1	81	17	0	1.9

YEAR	TM LG	W	L	PCT	G	GS	CG-SHO	SV-BS	IP	H	R	HR	HB	BB-IB	SO	ERA	AERA	OAV	OOB	AB-HR-SH	AVG	PB	SUP	APR	DL	PW
1964	KC A	5	13	.278	53	21	1	1	168.1	176	103	24	8	72-5	119	5.29	72	.273	.350	43-0-1	.023	-4*	84	-24	0	-2.8
1965	KC A	1	5	.167	14	5	0	0	38.2	44	22	5	3	18-2	25	4.42	79	.291	.367	11	.091	-1	96	-4	0	-0.7
1966	†Bal A	6	0	1.000	44	3	0	7	96	62	31	10	1	29-5	98	2.81	118	.181	.246	22-0-1	.364	4	106	7	0	0.9
1967	Bal A	7	5	.583	43	0	0	12	95.1	66	21	7	2	25-3	96	1.60	196	.194	.252	20-0-3	.350	2	—	16	0	2.8
1968	Bal A	4	4	.500	45	0	0	7	61.1	35	17	3	4	25-5	46	1.91	153	.166	.266	7	.286	0	—	6	0	1.1
1969	KC A	11	9	.550	52	0	0	11-5	98	68	33	10	2	30-2	76	2.94	126	.190	.255	17-0-2	.235	1	—	10	0	2.2
1970	KC A	1	2	.333	24	0	0	2-4	35.2	28	13	3	2	12-3	38	3.28	114	.217	.288	4	.250	0	—	3	0	0.2
	†Bal A	4	2	.667	21	0	0	1-1	33.1	30	17	7	1	15-3	21	3.78	97	.233	.317	5-0-1	.000	-1	—	-1	0	-0.3
	Year	5	4	.556	45	0	0	3-5	69	58	30	10	3	27-6	59	3.52	105	.225	.302	9-0-1	.111	-0	—	2	0	-0.1
1971	StL N	6	1	.857	51	0	0	8-2	60.1	45	23	2	2	33-8	49	3.43	106	.207	.315	6	.167	-0	—	2	0	0.3
1972	StL N	1	1	.500	30	0	0	2-1	27.2	29	13	4	1	14-4	22	2.60	132	.259	.346	1	.000	-0	—	1	0	0.0
	Chi A	0	0	ø	7	0	0	0-0	7.1	6	2	0	0	2-0	4	2.45	127	.240	.296	1	.000	-0	—	1	0	0.0
Total	17	88	105	.456	589	154	33-6	55-13	1641	1441	758	182	63	702-62	1162	3.71	101	.236	.318	420-3-22	.162	-0	94	4	0	2.9

DRAGO, DICK Richard Anthony; B6.25.1945 Toledo OH; BR/TR/6´1˝/(186–200); d4.11; Col Detroit Mercy

YEAR	TM LG	W	L	PCT	G	GS	CG-SHO	SV-BS	IP	H	R	HR	HB	BB-IB	SO	ERA	AERA	OAV	OOB	AB-HR-SH	AVG	PB	SUP	APR	DL	PW
1969	KC A	11	13	.458	41	26	10-2	1-0	200.2	190	95	19	2	65-6	108	3.77	98	.248	.306	52-0-9	.058	-3	74	-1	0	-0.4
1970	KC A	9	15	.375	35	34	7-1	0-0	240	239	110	20	7	72-5	127	3.75	100	.266	.322	76-0-9	.053	-6	88	2	0	-0.5
1971	KC A	17	11	.607	35	34	15-4	0-0	241.1	251	84	14	9	46-1	109	2.98	115	.276	.315	77-0-7	.130	1	95	14	0	1.8
1972	KC A	12	17	.414	34	33	11-2	0-0	239.1	230	88	22	6	51-4	135	3.01	101	.254	.297	68-0-7	.059	-2*	82	1	0	-0.3
1973	KC A	12	14	.462	37	33	10-1	0-0	212.2	252	116	16	7	76-10	98	4.23	97	.300	.360	0	ø	0*	105	-5	0	-0.5
1974	Bos A	7	10	.412	33	18	8	3-1	175.2	165	71	17	5	56-9	90	3.48	110	.251	.313	0	ø	0	69	8	0	0.7
1975	†Bos A	2	2	.500	40	2	0	15-3	72.2	69	31	5	0	31-3	43	3.84	106	.247	.321	0	ø	0	184	3	0	0.3
1976	Cal A	7	8	.467	43	0	0	6-3	79.1	80	42	7	5	31-8	43	4.42	76	.264	.338	0	ø	0	—	-9	0	-1.8
1977	Cal A	0	1	.000	13	0	0	2-1	21	22	8	3	0	3-2	15	3.00	131	.272	.291	0	ø	0	—	2	0	0.1
	Bal A	6	3	.667	36	0	0	3-6	39.2	49	19	2	1	15-4	20	3.63	106	.308	.363	0	ø	0	—	0	0	0.0
	Year	6	4	.600	49	0	0	5-7	60.2	71	27	5	1	18-6	35	3.41	113	.296	.340	0	ø	0	—	3	0	0.1
1978	Bos A	4	4	.500	37	1	0	7-3	77.1	71	30	5	4	32-5	42	3.03	136	.246	.327	0	ø	0	218	8	0	1.0
1979	Bos A	10	6	.625	53	1	0	13-4	89	85	33	6	3	21-6	67	3.03	147	.254	.300	0	ø	0	387	13	0	2.6
1980	Bos A	7	7	.500	43	7	1	3-4	132.2	127	67	17	5	44-7	63	4.14	103	.251	.316	1	.000	-0	81	2	0	0.1
1981	Sea A	4	6	.400	39	0	0	5-3	53.2	71	33	4	0	15-5	27	5.53	70	.324	.361	0	ø	0	—	-8	0	-1.5
Total	13	108	117	.480	519	189	62-10	58-28	1875	1901	827	157	54	558-75	987	3.62	103	.266	.321	274-0-32	.077	-11	89	30	0	1.6

DRAHMAN, BRIAN Brian Stacy; B11.7.1966 Kenton KY; BR/TR/6´3˝/(205–231); [MilA86 S2/30]; d4.16; Col Miami–Dade Kendall (FL) CC

YEAR	TM LG	W	L	PCT	G	GS	CG-SHO	SV-BS	IP	H	R	HR	HB	BB-IB	SO	ERA	AERA	OAV	OOB	AB-HR-SH	AVG	PB	SUP	APR	DL	PW
1991	Chi A	3	2	.600	28	0	0	0-2	30.2	21	12	4	0	13-1	18	3.23	124	.193	.276	0	ø	0	—	3	0	0.4
1992	Chi A	0	0	ø	5	0	0	0-0	7	6	3	0	0	2-0	1	2.57	151	.222	.276	0	ø	0	—	1	0	0.0
1993	Chi A	0	0	ø	5	0	0	1-0	5.1	7	0	0	0	2-0	3	0.00	ø	.333	.391	0	ø	0	—	3	0	0.1
1994	Fla N	0	0	ø	9	0	0	0-0	13	15	9	2	0	6-1	7	6.23	71	.300	.362	0	ø	0	—	-2	0	-0.1
Total	4	3	2	.600	47	0	0	1-2	56	49	24	6	0	23-2	29	3.54	116	.237	.309	0	ø	0	—	5	0	0.4

DRAKE, LOGAN Logan Gaffney "L.G."; B12.26.1899 Spartanburg SC; D6.1.1940 Columbia SC; BR/TR/5´10.5˝/165; d9.21

YEAR	TM LG	W	L	PCT	G	GS	CG-SHO	SV-BS	IP	H	R	HR	HB	BB-IB	SO	ERA	AERA	OAV	OOB	AB-HR-SH	AVG	PB	SUP	APR	DL	PW
1922	Cle A	0	0	ø	1	0	0	0	3	4	1	0	0	2	1	3.00	134	.364	.462	1	.000	-0	—	0	—	0.0
1923	Cle A	0	0	ø	4	0	0	0	4.1	2	2	0	1	4	2	4.15	95	.133	.350	0	ø	0	—	0	—	0.0
1924	Cle A	0	1	.000	5	1	0	0	11.1	18	15	0	1	10	8	10.32	41	.400	.518	1	.000	-0	138	-7	—	-0.5
Total	3	0	1	.000	10	1	0	0	18.2	24	18	0	2	16	11	7.71	54	.338	.472	2	.000	-0	138	-7	—	-0.5

DRAKE, TOM Thomas Kendall; B8.7.1912 Birmingham AL; D7.2.1988 Birmingham AL; BR/TR/6´1˝/185; d4.24; Col Troy St.

YEAR	TM LG	W	L	PCT	G	GS	CG-SHO	SV-BS	IP	H	R	HR	HB	BB-IB	SO	ERA	AERA	OAV	OOB	AB-HR-SH	AVG	PB	SUP	APR	DL	PW
1939	Cle A	0	1	.000	8	1	0	0	15	23	18	2	2	19	1	9.00	49	.377	.537	2-0-1	.000	-0	160	-9	—	-0.5
1941	Bro N	1	1	.500	10	2	0	0	24.2	26	13	2	0	9	12	4.38	84	.280	.343	5	.400	0*	81	-1	0	-0.1
Total	2	1	2	.333	18	3	0	0	39.2	49	31	4	2	28	13	6.13	65	.318	.429	7-0-1	.286	0	109	-10	0	-0.6

DRAPER, MIKE Michael Anthony; B9.14.1966 Hagerstown MD; BR/TR/6´2˝/180; [NYA88 26/677]; d4.10; Col George Mason

YEAR	TM LG	W	L	PCT	G	GS	CG-SHO	SV-BS	IP	H	R	HR	HB	BB-IB	SO	ERA	AERA	OAV	OOB	AB-HR-SH	AVG	PB	SUP	APR	DL	PW
1993	NY N	1	1	.500	29	1	0	0-2	42.1	53	22	2	0	14-3	16	4.25	94	.327	.370	3	.667	1	224	-1	52	0.1

DRAVECKY, DAVE David Francis; B2.14.1956 Youngstown OH; BR/TL/6´1˝/(193–202); [PitN78 21/531]; d6.15; Col Youngstown St.

YEAR	TM LG	W	L	PCT	G	GS	CG-SHO	SV-BS	IP	H	R	HR	HB	BB-IB	SO	ERA	AERA	OAV	OOB	AB-HR-SH	AVG	PB	SUP	APR	DL	PW
1982	SD N	5	3	.625	31	10	0	2-0	105	86	37	8	1	33-3	59	2.57	133	.225	.288	23-0-4	.130	-0*	93	9	0	0.8
1983	SD N★	14	10	.583	28	28	9-1	0-0	183.2	181	78	18	3	44-4	74	3.58	98	.262	.307	61-0-6	.098	-1	100	0	0	-0.1
1984	†SD N	9	8	.529	50	14	3-2	8-2	156.2	125	53	12	4	51-0	71	2.93	123	.222	.289	41-0-5	.098	-1	123	13	0	1.4
1985	SD N	13	11	.542	34	31	7-2	0-0	214.2	200	79	18	1	57-5	105	2.93	121	.249	.299	69-0-6	.116	-0	88	15	0	1.5
1986	SD N	9	11	.450	26	26	3-1	0-0	161.1	149	68	17	1	54-7	87	3.07	119	.246	.307	50-1-6	.140	0*	84	8	0	1.0
1987	SD N	3	7	.300	30	10	1	0-0	79	71	39	10	3	31-4	60	3.76	106	.240	.315	18-0-2	.167	0*	80	1	0	0.1
	†SF N	7	5	.583	18	18	4-3	0-0	112.1	115	43	8	2	33-3	78	3.20	120	.272	.325	38-0-2	.132	0	111	9	0	1.0
	Year	10	12	.455	48	28	5-3	0-0	191.1	186	82	18	5	64-7	138	3.43	114	.259	.321	56-0-4	.143	1	99	11	0	1.1
1988	SF N	2	2	.500	7	7	1	0-0	37	33	19	4	0	8-0	19	3.16	103	.243	.279	10-0-3	.100	-0	101	-2	150	-0.2
1989	SF N	2	0	1.000	2	2	0	0-0	13	8	5	2	1	4-0	5	3.46	98	.182	.265	3	.333	1	92	0	176	0.1
Total	8	64	57	.529	226	146	28-9	10-2	1062.2	968	421	97	16	315-26	558	3.13	115	.245	.302	313-1-34	.121	-2	96	53	326	5.6

DREES, TOM Thomas Kent; B6.17.1963 Des Moines IA; BB/TL/6´6˝/210; [ChiA85 17/423]; d9.3; Col Creighton

YEAR	TM LG	W	L	PCT	G	GS	CG-SHO	SV-BS	IP	H	R	HR	HB	BB-IB	SO	ERA	AERA	OAV	OOB	AB-HR-SH	AVG	PB	SUP	APR	DL	PW
1991	Chi A	0	0	ø	4	0	0	0-0	7.1	10	10	4	0	6-0	2	12.27	33	.345	.444	0	ø	0	—	-6	0	-0.3

DREIFORT, DARREN Darren James; B5.3.1972 Wichita KS; BR/TR/6´2˝/(205–211); [LAN93 1/2]; d4.7; Col Wichita St.; [DL 1995 LA N 160, 2002 LA N 183, 2005 LA N 183]

YEAR	TM LG	W	L	PCT	G	GS	CG-SHO	SV-BS	IP	H	R	HR	HB	BB-IB	SO	ERA	AERA	OAV	OOB	AB-HR-SH	AVG	PB	SUP	APR	DL	PW
1994	LA N	0	5	.000	27	0	0	6-3	29	45	21	0	4	15-3	22	6.21	64	.357	.441	1-0-1	1.000	1*	—	-7	0	-1.3
1996	†LA N	1	4	.200	19	0	0	0-2	23.2	23	13	2	0	12-4	24	4.94	79	.256	.340	3	.000	-0*	—	-2	45	-0.4
1997	LA N	5	2	.714	48	0	0	4-3	63	45	21	3	1	34-2	63	2.86	137	.202	.308	7	.143	-0	—	8	36	1.0
1998	LA N	8	12	.400	32	26	1-1	0-0	180	171	84	12	10	57-2	168	4.00	101	.256	.321	49-1-5	.224	3*	91	3	0	0.8
1999	LA N	13	13	.500	30	29	1-1	0-0	178.2	177	105	20	7	76-2	140	4.79	91	.260	.340	62-1-4	.210	4	118	-9	0	-0.7
2000	LA N	12	9	.571	32	32	1-1	0-0	192.2	175	105	31	12	87-1	164	4.16	107	.238	.329	68-3-1	.162	3	117	3	0	0.8
2001	LA N	4	7	.364	16	16	0	0-0	94.2	89	62	11	6	47-0	91	5.13	80	.251	.347	33-1-3	.152	1	106	-13	100	-1.1
2003	LA N	4	4	.500	10	10	0	0-0	60.1	58	29	6	0	25-0	67	4.03	102	.250	.322	15-0-3	.133	0	59	1	123	0.2
2004	LA N	1	4	.200	60	0	0	1-3	50.2	43	25	5	0	36-2	63	4.44	93	.232	.354	1	.000	-0	—	-1	48	-0.1
Total	9	48	60	.444	274	113	3-3	11-11	872.2	826	465	90	40	389-16	802	4.36	96	.251	.336	239-6-17	.184	12	107	-17	878	-0.8

DREISEWERD, CLEM Clemens Johann "Steamboat"; B1.24.1916 Old Monroe MO; D9.11.2001 Ocean Springs MS; BL/TL/6´1.5˝/195; d8.29; Mil 1945

YEAR	TM LG	W	L	PCT	G	GS	CG-SHO	SV-BS	IP	H	R	HR	HB	BB-IB	SO	ERA	AERA	OAV	OOB	AB-HR-SH	AVG	PB	SUP	APR	DL	PW
1944	Bos A	2	4	.333	7	7	3	0	48.2	52	25	2	0	9	9	4.07	84	.268	.300	16-0-2	.188	0	95	-4	0	-0.4
1945	Bos A	0	1	.000	2	2	0	0	9.2	13	5	0	1	2	3	4.66	73	.325	.372	3	.000	-0	50	-1	0	-0.2
1946	†Bos A	4	1	.800	20	1	0	0	47.1	50	22	3	0	15	19	4.18	88	.276	.332	10-0-2	.000	-1	210	-1	0	-0.2
1948	StL A	0	2	.000	13	0	0	1	22.1	28	15	6	0	8	6	5.64	81	.318	.375	5	.000	-1	—	-2	0	-0.3
	NY N	0	0	ø	4	0	0	1	12.2	17	8	3	0	5	2	5.68	69	.321	.379	4	.250	1	—	-2	0	0.0
Total	4	6	8	.429	46	10	3	2	140.2	160	75	14	1	39	39	4.54	82	.288	.336	38-0-4	.105	-1	93	-10	0	-1.1

DRESE, RYAN Ryan Thomas; B4.5.1976 San Francisco CA; BR/TR/6´3˝/235; [CleA98 5/153]; d7.29; Col California

YEAR	TM LG	W	L	PCT	G	GS	CG-SHO	SV-BS	IP	H	R	HR	HB	BB-IB	SO	ERA	AERA	OAV	OOB	AB-HR-SH	AVG	PB	SUP	APR	DL	PW
2001	Cle A	1	2	.333	9	4	0	0-0	36.2	32	15	2	1	15-2	24	3.44	134	.242	.324	0	ø	0	91	5	0	0.3
2002	Cle A	10	9	.526	26	26	1	0-0	137.1	176	104	15	6	62-1	102	6.55	68	.317	.386	3-0-1	.000	0	113	-31	0	-3.3
2003	Tex A	2	4	.333	11	8	0	0-0	46	61	42	8	5	24-1	26	6.85	73	.314	.404	0	ø	0	123	-11	0	-1.2
2004	Tex A	14	10	.583	34	33	2	0-0	207.2	233	104	16	11	58-6	98	4.20	117	.285	.339	4	.500	1	97	17	0	1.8
2005	Tex A	4	6	.400	12	12	1	0-0	69.2	96	52	5	3	24-1	20	6.46	71	.334	.390	1	.000	-0	105	-13	0	-1.6
	Was N	3	6	.333	11	11	0	0-0	59.2	66	38	3	5	22-1	26	4.98	83	.283	.352	14-0-5	.071	-1*	79	-7	45	-1.1
2006	Was N	0	2	.000	2	2	0	0-0	8.2	9	8	0	0	8-0	5	5.19	84	.290	.436	3	.000	-0	63	-2	176	-0.4
Total	6	34	39	.466	105	96	4	0-0	565.2	673	363	49	31	213-12	301	5.31	87	.299	.365	25-0-6	.120	-0	101	-42	221	-5.5

DRESSENDORFER, KIRK Kirk Richard; B4.8.1969 Houston TX; BR/TR/5´11˝/190; [OakA90 1/36]; d4.13; Col Texas; [DL 1992 Oak A 182]

YEAR	TM LG	W	L	PCT	G	GS	CG-SHO	SV-BS	IP	H	R	HR	HB	BB-IB	SO	ERA	AERA	OAV	OOB	AB-HR-SH	AVG	PB	SUP	APR	DL	PW
1991	Oak A	3	3	.500	7	7	0	0-0	34.2	33	28	5	0	21-0	17	5.45	71	.244	.344	0	ø	0	156	-9	41	-1.3

DRESSER, BOB Robert Nicholson; B10.4.1878 Newton MA; D7.27.1924 Duxbury MA; BL/TL; d8.13

YEAR	TM LG	W	L	PCT	G	GS	CG-SHO	SV-BS	IP	H	R	HR	HB	BB-IB	SO	ERA	AERA	OAV	OOB	AB-HR-SH	AVG	PB	SUP	APR	DL	PW
1902	Bos N	0	1	.000	1	1	1	0	9	12	6	0	0	0	8	3.00	94	.316	.316	4	.250	0	24	-1	—	-0.1

YEAR	TM LG	W	L	PCT	G	GS	CG-SHO	SV-BS	IP	H	R	HR	HB	BB-IB	SO	ERA	AERA	OAV	OOB	AB-HR-SH	AVG	PB	SUP	APR	DL	PW
Dressler, Rob	Robert Alan; B2.2.1954 Portland OR; BR/TR/6´3˝/(175–195); [SFN72 1/19]; d9.7																									
1975	SF N	1	0	1.000	3	2	1	0-0	16.1	17	3	0	0	4-2	6	1.10	346	.274	.318	4	.000	-0	92	4	0	0.3
1976	SF N	3	10	.231	25	19	0	0-1	107.2	125	68	8	2	35-4	33	4.43	82	.291	.343	31-0-2	.129	-1	69	-11	0	-1.3
1978	StL N	0	1	.000	3	2	0	0-0	13	12	3	0	0	4-1	4	2.08	172	.267	.327	3-0-1	.000	-0	88	2	0	0.1
1979	Sea A	3	2	.600	21	11	2	0-0	104	134	61	11	0	22-3	36	4.93	89	.312	.344	0	ø	0	88	-5	0	-0.3
1980	Sea A	4	10	.286	30	14	3	0-0	149.1	161	75	14	3	33-7	50	3.98	105	.280	.318	0	ø	0	89	3	0	0.3
Total	5	11	23	.324	82	48	6	0-1	390.1	449	210	33	5	98-17	129	4.17	97	.291	.333	38-0-3	.105	-1	80	-7	0	-0.9
Drew, Tim	Timothy Andrew; B8.31.1978 Valdosta GA; BR/TR/6´1˝/(190–195); [CleA97 1/28]; d5.24; b–J.D. b–Stephen																									
2000	Cle A	1	0	1.000	3	3	0	0-0	9	17	12	1	1	8-0	5	10.00	50	.425	.510	0	ø	0	144	-6	0	-0.5
2001	Cle A	0	2	.000	8	6	0	0-0	35	51	39	9	4	16-0	15	7.97	58	.340	.413	0	ø	0	141	-15	0	-0.7
2002	Mon N	1	0	1.000	7	1	0	2-1	16	12	8	1	0	2-0	10	2.81	156	.200	.222	4	.000	-0	148	2	0	0.1
2003	Mon N	0	2	.000	6	1	0	0-0	8.2	12	12	3	0	8-1	3	12.46	36	.343	.444	1-0-1	.000	-0	106	-7	0	-1.2
2004	Atl N	0	0	ø	11	0	0	0-0	16	21	11	2	1	5-0	7	4.50	96	.318	.375	2	.000	0*	—	-1	15	0.0
Total	5	2	4	.333	35	11	0	2-1	84.2	113	82	16	6	39-1	40	7.02	65	.322	.392	7-0-1	.000	-0	144	-27	15	-2.3
Drews, Karl	Karl August; B2.22.1920 Staten Island NY; D8.15.1963 Dania FL; BR/TR/6´4˝/198; d9.8																									
1946	NY A	0	1	.000	3	1	0	0	6.1	6	6	0	1	6	4	8.53	40	.250	.419	1	.000	-0	199	-3	0	-0.5
1947	†NY A	6	6	.500	30	10	0	1	91.2	92	57	6	5	55	45	4.91	72	.264	.373	27-0-1	.037	-2	105	-16	0	-2.1
1948	NY A	2	3	.400	19	2	0	1	38	35	17	3	0	31	11	3.79	108	.248	.384	7-0-2	.000	-1	55	2	0	0.2
	StL A	3	2	.600	20	2	0	2	38	43	35	3	0	38	11	8.05	57	.289	.433	8	.000	-0	59	-13	0	-1.6
	Year	5	5	.500	39	4	0	3	76	78	52	6	0	69	22	5.92	73	.269	.409	15-0-2	.000	-1	58	-12	0	-1.4
1949	StL A	4	12	.250	31	23	3-1	0	139.2	180	113	11	9	66	35	6.64	68	.317	.397	46-0-1	.000	-5	75	-27	0	-3.1
1951	Phi N	1	0	1.000	5	3	1	0	23	29	16	2	4	7	13	6.26	61	.296	.367	8	.250	1	130	-6	0	-0.2
1952	Phi N	14	15	.483	33	30	15-5	0	228.2	213	79	13	4	52	96	2.72	135	.252	.298	82-0-2	.110	-2	76	25	0	2.9
1953	Phi N	9	10	.474	47	27	6	3	185.1	218	116	26	10	50	72	4.52	93	.293	.346	59-0-1	.119	-2	101	-10	0	-1.1
1954	Phi N	1	0	1.000	8	0	0	0	16	18	10	2	0	8	6	5.63	72	.300	.377	4	.000	-1	—	-2	0	-0.2
	Cin N	4	4	.500	22	9	1-1	0	60	79	44	6	2	19	29	6.00	70	.326	.376	12-0-1	.167	1	135	-11	0	-1.2
	Year	5	4	.556	30	9	1-1	0	76	97	54	8	2	27	35	5.92	70	.321	.376	16-0-1	.125	1	136	-14	0	-1.4
Total	8	44	53	.454	218	107	26-7	7	826.2	913	493	72	35	332	322	4.76	84	.284	.356	254-0-8	.083	-12	92	-61	0	-6.9
Dreyer, Steve	Steven William; B11.19.1969 Ames IA; BR/TR/6´3˝/(180–188); [TexA90 8/225]; d8.8; Col Northern Iowa; [DL 1995 Tex A 61]																									
1993	Tex A	3	3	.500	10	6	0	0-0	41	48	26	7	1	20-1	23	5.71	74	.291	.371	0	ø	0	143	-6	0	-0.7
1994	Tex A	1	1	.500	5	3	0	0-0	17.1	19	15	1	1	8-0	11	5.71	85	.271	.350	0	ø	0	158	-3	0	-0.3
Total	2	4	4	.500	15	9	0	0-0	58.1	67	41	8	2	28-1	34	5.71	77	.285	.365	0	ø	0	149	-9	61	-1.0
Driscoll, Denny	John F.; B11.19.1855 Lowell MA; D7.11.1886 Lowell MA; BL/TL/5´10.5˝/160; d7.1; ▲																									
1880	Buf N	1	3	.250	6	4	4	0	41.2	48	33	1	—	9	17	3.89	63	.270	.305	65	.154	-1*	95	-6	—	-0.6
1882	Pit AA	13	9	.591	23	23	23	0	201	162	73	0	—	12	59	**1.21**	**216**	.206	.218	80-1	.138	-2	101	27	—	2.1
1883	Pit AA	18	21	.462	41	40	35-1	0	336.1	427	239	3	—	39	79	3.99	82	.290	.309	148	.182	-5	111	-27	—	-2.5
1884	Lou AA	6	6	.500	13	13	10	0	102	110	69	3	2	7	16	3.44	90	.252	.267	48	.188	-1	126	-4	—	-0.4
Total	4	38	39	.494	83	80	72-1	0	681	747	414	7	2	67	171	3.08	97	.260	.277	341-1	.167	-10	110	-10	—	-1.4
Driscoll, Michael	Michael Columbus; B10.19.1892 N.Abington MA; D3.22.1953 Foxboro MA; BR/TR/5´11˝/160; d7.6; Col Maine																									
1916	Phi A	0	1	.000	1	0	0	0	5	6	5	0	0	2	0	5.40	53	.273	.333	2	.000	-0	—	-2	—	-0.3
Driskill, Travis	Travis Corey; B8.1.1971 Omaha NE; BR/TR/6´0˝/(185–215); [CleA93 4/111]; d4.26; Col Texas Tech																									
2002	Bal A	8	8	.500	29	19	0	0-0	132.2	150	78	21	8	48-1	78	4.95	88	.284	.351	3	.000	0	84	-9	0	-1.0
2003	Bal A	3	5	.375	20	0	0	1-0	48	62	35	8	1	9-2	33	6.00	77	.310	.340	1	.000	-0	—	-8	0	-1.1
2004	Col N	0	0	ø	5	0	0	0-1	8.1	13	6	0	0	3-0	6	6.48	73	.361	.410	1	.000	-0	—	-1	0	-0.1
2005	Hou N	0	0	ø	1	0	0	0-0	1	1	0	0	0	0-0	2	0.00	ø	.250	.250	0	ø	0	—	0	0	0.0
Total	4	11	13	.458	55	19	0	1-1	190	226	119	29	9	60-3	119	5.26	84	.294	.350	5	.000	-0	84	-18	0	-2.2
Drohan, Tom	Thomas F; B8.26.1887 Fall River MA; D9.17.1926 Kewanee IL; BR/TR/5´10˝/175; d5.1																									
1913	Was A	0	0	ø	2	0	0	0	2	5	2	1	0	0	2	9.00	33	.500	.500	0	ø	0	—	-1	—	-0.1
Drott, Dick	Richard Fred "Hummer"; B7.1.1936 Cincinnati OH; D8.16.1985 Glendale Heights IL; BR/TR/6´0˝/(180–185); d4.16																									
1957	Chi N	15	11	.577	38	32	7-3	0	229	200	107	22	7	129-2	170	3.58	108	.234	.337	80-0-3	.100	-5	107	5	0	0.0
1958	Chi N	7	11	.389	39	31	4	0	167.1	156	118	23	6	99-6	127	5.43	72	.245	.347	55-0-1	.273	3	121	-30	0	-2.5
1959	Chi N	1	2	.333	8	6	1-1	0	27.1	25	19	5	0	26-1	15	5.93	67	.245	.398	8	.125	-0	94	-6	31	-0.6
1960	Chi N	0	6	.000	23	9	0	0	55.1	63	49	7	3	42-0	32	7.16	53	.296	.409	10	.100	-1	83	-20	0	-2.0
1961	Chi N	1	4	.200	35	8	0	0	98	75	54	13	1	51-0	48	4.22	99	.215	.311	22	.273	1	69	-1	0	0.0
1962	Hou N	1	0	1.000	6	1	0	0	13	12	12	1	0	9-0	10	7.62	49	.240	.356	4	.000	-0	188	-6	0	-0.4
1963	Hou N	2	12	.143	27	14	2-1	0	97.2	95	61	13	6	49-2	58	4.98	63	.257	.349	23-0-1	.130	-1	49	-20	0	-2.8
Total	7	27	46	.370	176	101	14-5	0	687.2	626	420	84	23	405-11	460	4.78	80	.243	.347	202-0-5	.168	-2	99	-78	31	-8.3
Drucke, Louis	Louis Frank; B12.3.1888 Waco TX; D9.22.1955 Waco TX; BR/TR/6´1˝/188; d9.25; Col TCU																									
1909	NY N	2	1	.667	3	3	2	0	24	20	9	0	0	13	8	2.25	114	.227	.327	8-0-2	.125	-0	146	1	—	0.0
1910	NY N	12	10	.545	34	27	15	0	215.1	174	73	3	11	82	151	2.47	120	.228	.312	70-1-9	.214	4	115	15	—	2.0
1911	NY N	4	4	.500	15	10	4	0	75.2	83	39	1	8	41	42	4.04	83	.281	.384	23-0-1	.087	-1*	121	-4	—	-0.4
1912	NY N	0	0	ø	1	0	0	1	2	5	4	0	0	1	0	13.50	25	.417	.462	0	ø	0	—	-2	—	-0.2
Total	4	18	15	.545	53	40	21	1	317	282	125	4	19	137	201	2.90	105	.243	.333	101-1-12	.178	2	119	10	—	1.4
Druhot, Carl	Carl A. "Collie"; B9.1.1882 OH; D2.5.1918 Portland OR; BL/TL/5´7˝/150; d4.18																									
1906	Cin N	2	2	.500	4	3	1	0	25	27	17	0	2	7	14	4.32	64	.270	.330	9	.222	0	150	-4	—	-0.6
	StL N	6	7	.462	15	13	12-1	0	130.1	117	55	1	5	46	45	2.62	100	.238	.310	56-0-1	.232	1	105	-2	—	0.0
	Year	8	9	.471	19	16	13-1	0	155.1	144	72	1	7	53	59	2.90	91	.244	.313	65-0-1	.231	1	113	-7	—	-0.6
1907	StL N	0	1	.000	1	1	0	0	2.1	3	5	0	1	4	1	15.43	16	.600	.800	0	ø	0	57	-3	—	-0.5
Total	2	8	10	.444	20	17	13-1	0	157.2	147	77	1	8	57	60	3.08	86	.247	.321	65-0-1	.231	1	110	-9	—	-1.1
Drummond, Tim	Timothy Darnell; B12.24.1964 LaPlata MD; BR/TR/6´3˝/(170–195); [PitN83*12/272]; d9.12; Col CC of Southern Maryland																									
1987	Pit N	0	0	ø	6	0	0	0-0	6	5	3	0	0	3-0	5	4.50	93	.227	.320	1	.000	-0	—	0	0	0.0
1989	Min A	0	0	ø	8	0	0	1-0	16.1	16	7	0	2	8-1	9	3.86	108	.246	.347	0	ø	0	—	1	0	0.0
1990	Min A	3	5	.375	35	4	0	1-1	91	104	46	8	1	36-1	49	4.35	96	.295	.357	0	ø	0	38	-1	0	-0.1
Total	3	3	5	.375	49	4	0	2-1	113.1	125	56	8	3	47-2	63	4.29	97	.284	.354	1	.000	-0	38	0	0	-0.1
Drysdale, Don	Donald Scott; B7.23.1936 Van Nuys CA; D7.3.1993 Montreal QC, Can.; BR/TR/6´6˝/(189–220); d4.17; HF1984																									
1956	†Bro N	5	5	.500	25	12	2	0	99	95	35	9	3	31-3	55	2.64	150	.255	.315	26-1-2	.192	1*	89	13	0	1.4
1957	Bro N	17	9	.654	34	29	9-4	0	221	197	76	17	7	61-3	148	2.69	155	.236	.293	73-2-3	.123	-0*	108	**33**	0	**4.1**
1958	LA N	12	13	.480	44	29	6-1	0	211.2	214	107	21	14	72-6	131	4.17	98	.263	.331	66-7-3	.227	8*	90	0	0	0.9
1959	†LA N★	17	13	.567	44	36	15-**4**	2	270.2	237	113	26	18	93-9	**242**	3.46	122	.233	.308	91-4-8	.165	3*	86	23	0	2.9
1960	LA N	15	14	.517	41	36	15-5	2	269	214	93	27	10	72-5	**246**	2.84	140	.215	**.274**	83-0-9	.157	2	88	**33**	0	4.0
1961	LA N☆	13	10	.565	40	37	10-3	0	244	236	111	29	20	83-15	182	3.69	118	.254	.326	83-5-5	.193	4	91	17	0	1.8
1962	LA N★	**25**	9	.735	43	**41**	19-2	1	**314.1**	272	122	21	11	78-12	**232**	2.83	128	.230	.282	111-0-8	.198	5	137	27	0	3.3
1963	†LA N★	19	17	.528	42	**42**	17-3	0	315.1	287	114	25	10	57-13	251	2.63	115	.242	.282	96-0-6	.167	5	98	13	0	2.1
1964	LA N★	18	16	.529	40	**40**	21-5	0	**321.1**	242	91	15	10	68-9	237	2.18	148	.207	.255	110-1-14	.173	4	116	**41**	0	**5.0**
1965	†LA N★	23	12	.657	44	**42**	20-7	1	308.1	270	113	30	12	66-11	210	2.77	118	.232	.279	130-7-2	.300	22*	114	16	0	4.2
1966	†LA N	13	16	.448	40	40	11-3	0	273.2	279	114	21	17	45-8	177	3.42	96	.265	.304	106-2-2	.189	4*	97	-1	0	0.2
1967	LA N★	13	16	.448	38	38	9-3	0	282	269	101	19	8	60-19	196	2.74	113	.251	.295	93-0-2	.129	-0	81	10	0	1.2
1968	LA N★	14	12	.538	31	31	12-8	0	239	201	68	11	12	56-10	155	2.15	129	.231	.284	79-0-4	.177	1	91	17	0	2.3
1969	LA N	5	4	.556	12	12	1-1	0-0	62.2	71	34	9	2	13-0	24	4.45	75	.291	.327	22-0-1	.136	0	121	-8	47	-1.0
Total	14	209	166	.557	518	465	167-49	6-0	3432	3084	1292	280	154	855-123	2486	2.95	121	.239	.293	1169-29-69	.186	60	101	234	47	32.4

YEAR	TM LG	W	L	PCT	G	GS	CG-SHO	SV-BS	IP	H	R	HR	HB	BB-IB	SO	ERA	AERA	OAV	OOB	AB-HR-SH	AVG	PB	SUP	APR	DL	PW
Dubiel, Monk	Walter John; B2.12.1918 Hartford CT; D10.23.1969 Hartford CT; BR/TR/6´0˝/(190–196); d4.19																									
1944	NY A	13	13	.500	30	28	19-3	0	232	217	93	12	1	86	79	3.38	103	.248	.316	83-0-5	.181	-2*	93	7	0	0.5
1945	NY A	10	9	.526	26	20	9-1	0	151.1	157	88	9	0	62	45	4.64	75	.266	.335	58-1-4	.276	4	133	-18	0	-1.8
1948	Phi N	8	10	.444	37	17	6-2	4	150.1	139	84	13	1	58	42	3.89	101	.248	.320	42-0-4	.167	0*	93	-2	0	-0.3
1949	Chi N	6	9	.400	32	20	3-1	4	147.2	142	75	16	1	54	52	4.14	97	.250	.317	35-0-7	.286	3*	101	-1	0	0.3
1950	Chi N	6	10	.375	39	12	4-2	2	142.2	152	79	12	1	67	51	4.16	101	.270	.348	45-0-1	.200	1	96	0	0	0.2
1951	Chi N	2	2	.500	22	0	0	1	54.2	46	17	3	0	22	19	2.30	178	.232	.309	12	.000	-1	—	10	0	0.6
1952	Chi N	0	0	ø	1	0	0	0	0.2	1	0	0	0	0	1	0.00	ø	.333	.333	0	ø	0	—	0	0	0.0
Total	7	45	53	.459	187	97	41-9	11	879.1	854	436	65	4	349	289	3.87	98	.254	.325	275-1-21	.207	5	102	-4	0	-0.5
DuBois, Brian	Brian Andrew; B4.18.1967 Joliet IL; BL/TL/5´10˝/(165–170); [BalA85 4/99]; d8.17; [DL 1991 Bal A 182]																									
1989	Det A	0	4	.000	6	5	0	1-0	36	29	14	2	2	17-3	13	1.75	219	.218	.314	0	ø	0	38	6	0	0.6
1990	Det A	3	5	.375	12	11	0	0-0	58.1	70	37	9	1	22-1	34	5.09	78	.310	.368	0	ø	0	117	-8	0	-1.0
Total	2	3	9	.250	18	16	0	1-0	94.1	99	51	11	3	39-4	47	3.82	103	.276	.347	0	ø	0	93	-2	182	-0.4
DuBose, Eric	Eric Ladell; B5.15.1976 Bradenton FL; BL/TL/6´3˝/(215–235); [OakA97 1/21]; d9.19; Col Mississippi St.																									
2002	Bal A	0	0	ø	4	0	0	0-0	6	7	2	1	1	1-0	4	3.00	145	.304	.360	0	ø	0	—	1	0	0.0
2003	Bal A	3	6	.333	17	10	1	0-1	73.2	60	33	6	5	25-2	44	3.79	122	.222	.297	0	ø	0	48	7	0	0.7
2004	Bal A	4	6	.400	14	14	0	0-0	74.2	76	55	12	3	44-0	48	6.39	73	.263	.365	2	.000	-0	119	-13	106	-1.4
2005	Bal A	2	3	.400	15	3	0	0-0	29.1	28	21	4	1	19-0	17	5.52	80	.243	.356	0	ø	0	98	-4	0	-0.6
2006	Bal A	0	0	ø	2	0	0	0-0	4.2	10	5	2	0	3-0	2	9.64	47	.500	.565	0	ø	0	—	-3	0	-0.1
Total	5	9	15	.375	52	27	1	0-1	188.1	181	116	25	10	92-2	115	5.21	88	.252	.344	2	.000	-0	91	-12	106	-1.4
Dubuc, Jean	Jean Joseph Octave Arthur "Chauncey"; B9.15.1888 St.Johnsbury VT; D8.28.1958 Fort Myers FL; BR/TR/5´10.5˝/185; d6.25; C2; Col Notre Dame																									
1908	Cin N	5	6	.455	15	9	7-1	0	85.1	62	34	2	5	41	32	2.74	84	.205	.309	29-0-2	.138	-1	75	-3	—	-0.4
1909	Cin N	2	5	.286	19	5	2	1	71.1	72	58	0	4	46	19	3.66	71	.269	.384	18-0-1	.167	0	70	-13	—	-1.2
1912	Det A	17	10	.630	37	26	23-2	3	250	217	107	2	7	109	97	2.77	118	.235	.321	108-1-1	.269	6*	128	13	—	2.2
1913	Det A	15	14	.517	36	28	22-1	2	242.2	228	113	1	8	91	73	2.89	101	.254	.329	135-2-4	.267	5*	111	-1	—	1.3
1914	Det A	12	14	.462	36	27	15-2	1	224	216	124	3	6	76	70	3.46	81	.257	.324	124-1-4	.226	7*	117	-18	—	-1.0
1915	Det A	17	12	.586	39	33	22-5	2	258	231	116	5	10	88	74	3.21	94	.245	.316	112-0-3	.205	0*	115	-3	—	-0.2
1916	Det A	10	10	.500	36	16	8-1	1	170.1	134	66	1	5	84	40	2.96	97	.233	.336	78-0-2	.256	5*	106	0	—	0.8
1918	†Bos A	0	1	.000	2	1	1	0	10.2	11	5	1	0	5	1	4.22	64	.268	.348	6	.167	0*	84	-1	—	-0.1
1919	NY N	6	4	.600	36	5	1	3	132	119	49	4	2	37	32	2.66	105	.246	.303	42	.143	-1*	85	2	—	0.1
Total	9	84	76	.525	256	150	101-12	13	1444.1	1290	672	19	47	577	438	3.04	96	.245	.325	652-4-17	.230	21	113	-24	—	1.5
Duchscherer, Justin	Justin Craig; B11.19.1977 Aberdeen SD; BR/TR/6´3˝/(164–200); [BosA96 8/241]; d7.25																									
2001	Tex A	1	1	.500	5	2	0	0-0	14.2	24	20	5	4	4-0	11	12.27	39	.353	.421	0	ø	0	78	-11	0	-1.2
2003	Oak A	1	1	.500	4	3	0	0-0	16.1	17	7	1	2	3-0	15	3.31	139	.262	.314	0	ø	0	114	2	0	0.2
2004	Oak A	7	6	.538	53	0	0	0-2	96.1	85	37	13	5	32-6	59	3.27	141	.241	.312	0	ø	0	—	15	0	1.8
2005	Oak A☆	7	4	.636	65	0	0	5-2	85.2	67	25	7	2	19-3	85	2.21	199	.215	.263	0	ø	0	—	20	0	2.5
2006	†Oak A	2	1	.667	53	0	0	9-2	55.2	52	18	4	1	9-0	51	2.91	156	.244	.278	0	ø	0	—	11	47	0.9
Total	5	18	13	.581	180	5	0	14-6	268.2	245	107	30	14	67-9	221	3.35	135	.243	.298	0	ø	0	102	37	47	4.2
Duckworth, Brandon	Brandon J.; B1.23.1976 Salt Lake City UT; BR/TR/6´2˝/(185–215); d8.7; Col Cal St.–Fullerton																									
2001	Phi N	3	2	.600	11	11	0	0-0	69	57	29	2	6	29-5	40	3.52	117	.234	.326	22-0-2	.227	2	88	5	0	0.4
2002	Phi N	8	9	.471	30	29	0	0-0	163	167	103	26	7	69-5	167	5.41	71	.261	.338	48-0-6	.188	2	113	-29	0	-2.5
2003	Phi N	4	7	.364	24	18	0	0-0	93	98	58	12	10	44-3	68	4.94	81	.272	.366	27-0-1	.185	1	104	-12	21	-1.2
2004	Hou N	1	2	.333	19	6	0	0-0	39.1	55	30	11	0	13-3	23	6.86	64	.337	.384	9	.222	0	142	-10	0	-0.6
2005	Hou N	0	1	.000	7	2	0	0-0	16.1	24	20	4	5	7-1	10	11.02	38	.348	.439	3	.667	1	134	-12	0	-0.5
2006	KC A	1	5	.167	10	8	0	0-0	45.2	62	36	3	2	24-4	27	6.11	77	.332	.409	3-0-1	.333	1	80	-8	63	-0.8
Total	6	17	26	.395	101	74	0	0-0	426.1	463	276	58	30	186-21	335	5.43	75	.279	.359	112-0-10	.214	7	106	-66	84	-5.2
Duckworth, Jim	James Raymond; B5.24.1939 National City CA; BR/TR/6´4˝/(190–195); d4.13																									
1963	Was A	4	12	.250	37	15	2	0	120.2	131	89	13	10	67-3	66	6.04	61	.278	.373	27-0-3	.000	-3	93	-29	0	-3.8
1964	Was A	1	6	.143	30	2	0	3	56	52	37	9	3	25-4	56	4.34	85	.244	.332	9	.222	0	60	-6	35	-0.8
1965	Was A	2	2	.500	17	8	0	0	64	45	30	11	2	36-4	74	3.94	88	.202	.314	18-0-1	.000	-2	88	-2	0	-0.4
1966	Was A	0	3	.000	5	4	0	0	14.1	14	12	2	1	10-1	14	5.02	69	.259	.379	3	.000	-0	76	-4	19	-0.8
	KC A	0	2	.000	8	0	0	1	12	14	12	2	1	10-0	10	9.00	38	.292	.424	2	.000	-0	—	-7	0	-1.2
	Year	0	5	.000	13	4	0	1	26.1	28	24	4	2	20-1	24	6.84	50	.275	.400	5	.000	-1	77	-10	0	-2.0
Total	4	7	25	.219	97	29	2	4	267	256	180	37	17	148-12	220	5.26	69	.253	.355	59-0-4	.034	-5	87	-48	54	-7.0
Dudley, Clise	Elzie Clise; B8.8.1903 Graham NC; D1.12.1989 Moncks Corner SC; BL/TR/6´1˝/195; d4.18; Col South Carolina																									
1929	Bro N	6	14	.300	35	20	8-1	0	156.2	202	130	9	10	64	33	5.69	81	.315	.385	51-2-3	.098	-1*	75	-24	—	-2.5
1930	Bro N	2	4	.333	21	7	2	1	66.2	103	62	3	2	27	18	6.35	77	.371	.430	24	.208	-0	104	-13	—	-0.9
1931	Phi N	8	14	.364	30	24	8	0	179	206	95	10	6	56	50	3.52	121	.287	.343	84-0-1	.214	-0*	82	9	—	1.1
1932	Phi N	1	1	.500	13	0	0	1	17.2	23	14	3	0	8	5	7.13	62	.329	.397	14-1-0	.286	3*	—	-4	—	-0.2
1933	Pit N	0	0	ø	1	0	0	0	0.1	6	5	0	0	1	0	135.00	2	.857	.875	0	ø	0	—	-4	—	-0.2
Total	5	17	33	.340	100	51	18-1	2	420.1	540	306	25	18	156	106	5.03	90	.315	.378	173-3-4	.185	1	82	-36	—	-2.7
Dues, Hal	Hal Joseph; B9.22.1954 LaMarque TX; BR/TR/6´3˝/(185–190); d9.9; Col Mary Hardin–Baylor																									
1977	Mon N	1	1	.500	6	4	0	0-0	23	26	14	2	0	9-1	9	4.30	90	.265	.327	5-0-1	.000	-1	69	-2	0	-0.2
1978	Mon N	5	6	.455	25	12	1	1-0	99	85	29	5	4	42-4	36	2.36	151	.240	.326	31	.194	0	76	13	0	1.4
1980	Mon N	0	1	.000	6	1	0	0-0	12.1	17	9	1	0	4-1	2	6.57	55	.333	.382	3	.000	-0	98	-4	0	-0.3
Total	3	6	8	.429	37	17	1	1-0	134.1	128	52	8	4	55-6	47	3.08	118	.254	.332	39-0-1	.154	-1	76	7	0	0.9
Duff, Larry	Cecil Elba; B11.20.1896 Radersburg MT; D11.10.1969 Bend OR; BL/TR/6´1˝/175; d9.5																									
1922	Chi A	1	1	.500	3	1	0	0	12.2	16	7	1	0	3	7	4.97	82	.340	.380	5	.400	0	42	-1	—	-0.1
Duff, Matt	Matthew Clark; B10.6.1974 Clarksdale MS; BR/TR/6´1˝/192; d7.30; Col U. of Mississippi																									
2002	StL N	0	0	ø	7	0	0	0-0	5.2	3	3	0	0	8-2	4	4.76	85	.150	.393	0	ø	0	—	0	0	0.0
Duffalo, Jim	James Francis; B11.25.1935 Helvetia PA; BR/TR/6´1˝/180; d4.12																									
1961	SF N	5	1	.833	24	4	1	1	61.2	59	31	9	2	32-7	37	4.23	90	.257	.347	17-1-0	.294	3*	140	-2	0	0.0
1962	SF N	1	2	.333	24	2	0	0	42	42	27	3	0	23-3	29	3.64	104	.256	.344	6-0-1	.000	-0	104	-3	0	-0.3
1963	SF N	4	2	.667	34	5	0	2	75.1	56	26	3	2	37-6	55	2.87	112	.209	.307	18-0-1	.111	-1	81	4	31	0.3
1964	SF N	5	1	.833	35	3	1	3	74	57	25	9	2	31-4	55	2.92	122	.209	.293	14	.071	-1	82	6	31	0.4
1965	SF N	0	1	.000	2	0	0	0	0.1	1	1	0	0	2-0	0	27.00	13	.500	.750	0	ø	0	—	-1	0	-0.2
	Cin N	0	1	.000	22	0	0	0	44.1	33	21	3	5	30-2	34	3.45	109	.212	.351	8	.000	-1	—	1	0	0.0
	Year	0	2	.000	24	0	0	0	44.2	34	22	3	5	32-2	34	3.63	103	.215	.359	8	.000	-1	—	0	0	-0.2
Total	5	15	8	.652	141	14	2	6	297.2	248	131	27	11	155-22	210	3.39	106	.227	.326	63-1-2	.127	1	101	5	62	0.2
Duffie, John	John Brown; B10.4.1945 Greenwood SC; BR/TR/6´7˝/215; d9.18; Col Brewton–Parker																									
1967	LA N	0	2	.000	2	2	0	0	9.2	11	6	1	0	4-1	6	2.79	111	.282	.341	2	.000	-0	43	-1	0	-0.2
Duffy, Bernie	Bernard Allen; B8.18.1893 Vinson OK; D2.9.1962 Abilene TX; BR/TR/5´11˝/180; d9.20																									
1913	Pit N	0	0	ø	3	2	0	0	11.1	18	8	0	0	3	8	5.56	54	.360	.396	4	.250	0	87	-3	—	-0.1
Dugan, Dan	Daniel Phillip; B2.22.1907 Plainfield NJ; D6.25.1968 Green Brook NJ; BL/TL/6´1.5˝/187; d9.5; Col St. Louis																									
1928	Chi A	0	0	ø	1	0	0	0	0.1	0	0	0	0	0	0	0.00	ø	.000	.000	0	ø	0	—	0	—	0.0
1929	Chi A	1	4	.200	19	2	0	1	65	77	51	8	2	19	15	6.65	64	.300	.353	20-0-1	.150	-1	30	-14	—	-1.1
Total	2	1	4	.200	20	2	0	1	65.1	77	51	8	2	19	15	6.61	65	.298	.351	20-0-1	.150	-1	30	-14	—	-1.1
Dugan, Ed	Edward John; B1864 Brooklyn NY; TR; d8.5; b–Bill																									
1884	Ric AA	5	14	.263	20	20	20	0	166.1	196	137	5	2	15	60	4.49	74	.267	.284	70	.114	-4*	77	-23	—	-2.5

YEAR	TM LG	W	L	PCT	G	GS	CG-SHO	SV-BS	IP	H	R	HR	HB	BB-IB	SO	ERA	AERA	OAV	OOB	AB-HR-SH	AVG	PB	SUP	APR	DL	PW
DUGGLEBY, BILL	William James "Frosty Bill"; B3.16.1874 Utica NY; D8.30.1944 Redfield NY; TR; d4.21																									
1898	Phi N	3	3	.500	9	5	4	0	54	70	39	4	6	18	12	5.50	62	.311	.378	21-1-1	.238	2	149	-10	—	-0.6
1901	Phi N	20	12	.625	35	29	26-5	0	284.2	302	120	9	10	41	95	2.88	118	.270	.302	115-0-3	.165	-3	92	18	—	1.7
1902	Phi A	1	1	.500	2	2	2	0	17	19	9	0	0	4	4	3.18	116	.284	.324	7	.000	-1	78	1	—	0.0
	Phi N	11	17	.393	33	27	25	1	258.2	282	130	2	12	57	60	3.38	83	.277	.323	98-0-1	.173	-1	93	-15	—	-1.5
1903	Phi N	13	16	.448	36	30	28-3	2	264.1	318	162	4	12	79	57	3.75	87	.303	.358	104-0-3	.231	2	98	-18	—	-1.4
1904	Phi N	12	13	.480	32	27	22-2	1	223.2	265	138	3	11	53	55	3.78	71	.292	.338	82-2-2	.171	0	124	-26	—	-2.6
1905	Phi N	18	17	.514	38	36	27-1	0	289.1	270	116	10	13	83	75	2.46	119	.253	.315	101-1-3	.109	-2	102	12	—	1.2
1906	Phi N	13	19	.406	42	30	22-5	2	280.1	241	93	5	12	66	83	2.25	116	.227	.280	99-2-1	.141	-2*	80	14	—	1.5
1907	Phi N	0	2	.000	5	2	2	0	29	43	27	2	5	11	8	7.45	33	.371	.447	9	.111	0	103	-14	—	-0.8
	Pit N	2	2	.500	9	3	1-1	0	40.1	34	17	0	2	12	4	2.68	91	.239	.308	13	.154	-0	88	-1	—	0.0
	Year	2	4	.333	14	5	3-1	0	69.1	77	44	2	7	23	12	4.67	52	.298	.372	22	.136	0	94	-14	—	-0.8
Total	8	93	102	.477	241	191	159-17	6	1741.1	1844	851	39	83	424	453	3.18	93	.272	.323	649-6-14	.165	-4	99	-39	—	-2.5
DUKE, MARTIN	Martin F. "Duck" (b Martin F. Duck); B1867 Zanesville OH; D12.31.1898 Minneapolis MN; TL/5´8˝/157; d8.24																									
1891	Was AA	0	3	.000	4	3	2	0	23	36	33	0	0	19	5	7.43	50	.346	.447	9	.111	-1	44	-10	—	-0.9
DUKE, ZACH	Zachary Thomas; B4.19.1983 Clifton TX; BL/TL/6´2˝/(210–220); [PitN01 20/594]; d7.2																									
2005	Pit N	8	2	.800	14	14	0	0-0	84.2	79	20	3	2	23-2	58	1.81	235	.253	.308	28	.143	-0	97	22	23	2.6
2006	Pit N	10	15	.400	34	34	2-1	0-0	215.1	255	116	17	7	68-6	117	4.47	102	.302	.358	68-0-9	.191	2	84	3	0	0.7
Total	2	18	17	.514	48	48	2-1	0-0	300	334	136	20	9	91-8	175	3.72	121	.289	.344	96-0-9	.177	1	88	25	23	3.3
DUKES, JAN	Noble Jan; B8.16.1945 Cheyenne WY; BL/TL/5´11˝/(170–180); [TexA67*S1/8]; d9.6; Col Santa Clara																									
1969	Was A	0	2	.000	8	0	0	0-0	11	8	3	0	0	4-1	3	2.45	143	.216	.293	1	.000	0	—	2	0	0.3
1970	Was A	0	0	ø	5	0	0	0-0	6.2	6	3	0	1	1-0	4	2.70	134	.240	.286	1	.000	-0	—	0	0	0.0
1972	Tex A	0	0	ø	3	0	0	0-0	2.1	1	2	0	0	5-1	0	3.86	79	.167	.500	0	ø	0	—	-1	0	0.0
Total	3	0	2	.000	16	0	0	0-0	20	15	8	0	1	10-2	7	2.70	129	.221	.321	2	.000	0	—	1	0	0.3
DUKES, TOM	Thomas Earl; B8.31.1942 Knoxville TN; BR/TR/6´2˝/(185–200); d8.15																									
1967	Hou N	0	2	.000	17	0	0	1	23.2	25	14	2	2	11-1	23	5.32	62	.275	.362	2	.500	0	—	-4	0	-0.4
1968	Hou N	2	2	.500	43	0	0	4	52.2	62	31	3	2	28-12	37	4.27	69	.291	.376	4	.000	-0	—	-9	0	-0.9
1969	SD N	1	0	1.000	13	0	0	1-0	22.1	26	18	2	0	10-2	15	7.25	49	.295	.360	1	.000	-0	—	-8	0	-0.4
1970	SD N	1	6	.143	53	0	0	10-6	69	62	39	7	2	25-9	56	4.04	99	.246	.312	7	.000	-1	—	-2	32	-0.4
1971	†Bal A	1	5	.167	28	0	0	4-1	38.1	40	15	4	1	8-2	30	3.52	97	.263	.299	7	.143	0	—	0	21	0.0
1972	Cal A	0	1	.000	7	0	0	1-0	11	11	3	1	1	0-0	8	1.64	179	.262	.279	0	ø	0	—	1	47	0.1
Total	6	5	16	.238	161	0	0	21-7	217	226	120	19	8	82-26	169	4.35	80	.270	.335	21	.095	-1	—	-22	100	-2.0
DULIBA, BOB	Robert John "Ach"; B1.9.1935 Glen Lyon PA; BR/TR/5´10˝/(175–185); d8.11																									
1959	StL N	0	1	.000	11	0	0	1	22.2	19	7	2	0	12-1	14	2.78	153	.237	.330	4	.000	-0	—	4	0	0.2
1960	StL N	4	4	.500	27	0	0	0	40.2	49	20	6	0	16-4	23	4.20	97	.310	.367	5	.200	-0	—	0	72	0.0
1962	StL N	2	0	1.000	28	0	0	2	39.1	33	11	3	0	17-0	22	2.06	207	.239	.321	4	.000	-0	—	9	0	0.5
1963	LA A	1	1	.500	6	0	0	1	7.2	3	1	0	0	6-0	4	1.17	292	.125	.290	1	.000	-0	—	2	0	0.4
1964	LA A	6	4	.600	58	0	0	9	72.2	80	35	5	1	22-3	33	3.59	91	.287	.339	5-0-1	.000	-1	—	-3	0	-0.5
1965	Bos A	4	2	.667	39	0	0	1	64.1	60	31	6	0	22-7	27	3.78	99	.248	.308	7	.000	-0	—	0	0	-0.1
1967	KC A	0	0	ø	7	0	0	0	9.2	13	7	3	0	1-0	6	6.52	49	.342	.359	0	ø	0	—	-3	0	-0.2
Total	7	17	12	.586	176	0	0	14	257	257	112	25	1	96-15	129	3.47	108	.268	.332	26-0-1	.038	-2	—	9	72	0.3
DUMONT, GEORGE	George Henry "Pea Soup"; B11.13.1895 Minneapolis MN; D10.13.1956 Minneapolis MN; BR/TR/5´11˝/163; d9.14																									
1915	Was A	2	1	.667	6	4	3-2	0	40	23	17	0	2	12	18	2.02	147	.169	.247	12-0-2	.167	-0	80	2	—	0.1
1916	Was A	2	3	.400	17	5	2	1	53	37	25	0	1	17	21	3.06	91	.194	.263	14-0-1	.071	-0	125	-2	—	-0.3
1917	Was A	5	14	.263	37	23	8-2	2	204.2	171	76	3	6	76	65	2.55	103	.227	.303	58-0-2	.034	-5	67	2	—	-0.6
1918	Was A	1	1	.500	4	1	1	0	14	18	12	0	0	6	12	5.14	53	.295	.358	3	.333	1	0	-4	—	-0.4
1919	Bos A	0	4	.000	13	2	0	0	35.1	45	21	1	1	19	12	4.33	70	.326	.411	7	.000	-0	52	-6	—	-0.6
Total	5	10	23	.303	77	35	14-4	3	347	294	151	4	10	130	128	2.85	96	.230	.306	94-0-5	.064	-5	74	-8	—	-1.8
DUMOULIN, DAN	Daniel Lynn; B8.20.1953 Kokomo IN; BR/TR/6´0˝/(169–178); d9.5																									
1977	Cin N	0	0	ø	5	0	0	0-0	5.1	12	8	0	0	3-1	5	13.50	29	.462	.517	0	ø	0	—	-5	0	-0.3
1978	Cin N	1	0	1.000	3	0	0	0-0	5	7	1	0	1	3-1	2	1.80	197	.368	.478	0	ø	0	—	1	0	0.2
Total	2	1	0	1.000	8	0	0	0-0	10.1	19	9	0	1	6-2	7	7.84	48	.422	.500	0	ø	0	—	-4	0	-0.1
DUMOVICH, NICK	Nicholas; B1.2.1902 Sacramento CA; D12.12.1978 Laguna Hills CA; BL/TL/6´0˝/170; d4.20																									
1923	Chi N	3	5	.375	28	8	1	1	94	118	60	4	3	45	23	4.60	87	.319	.397	29	.241	1	98	-7	—	-0.4
DUNBAR, MATT	Matthew Marshall; B10.15.1968 Tallahassee FL; BL/TL/6´0˝/175; [NYA90 25/672]; d4.25; Col Florida St.																									
1995	Fla N	0	1	.000	8	0	0	0-0	7	12	9	0	1	11-3	5	11.57	37	.387	.558	0	ø	0	—	-5	0	-0.6
DUNCAN, COURTNEY	Courtney Demond; B10.9.1974 Mobile AL; BL/TR/6´0˝/185; [ChiN96 20/592]; d4.2; Col Grambling St.																									
2001	Chi N	3	3	.500	36	0	0	0-2	42.2	42	24	5	2	25-3	49	5.06	83	.259	.359	3	.000	0	—	-3	50	-0.4
2002	Chi N	0	0	ø	2	0	0	0-0	2.1	2	0	0	0	1-0	1	0.00	ø	.222	.300	0	ø	0	—	1	0	0.1
Total	2	3	3	.500	38	0	0	0-2	45	44	24	5	2	26-3	50	4.80	87	.257	.356	3	.000	0	—	-2	50	-0.3
DUNDON, ED	Edward Joseph "Dummy"; B7.10.1859 Columbus OH; D8.18.1893 Columbus OH; TR/6´0˝/170; d6.2; ▲																									
1883	Col AA	3	16	.158	20	19	16	0	166.2	213	153	7	—	38	31	4.48	69	.292	.327	93	.161	-3*	85	-30	—	-2.7
1884	Col AA	6	4	.600	11	9	7	0	81	85	55	9	0	15	37	3.78	80	.249	.281	86	.140	-1*	73	-8	—	-0.8
Total	2	9	20	.310	31	28	23	0	247.2	298	208	16	0	53	68	4.25	72	.278	.312	179	.151	-4	81	-38	—	-3.5
DUNEGAN, JIM	James William; B8.6.1947 Burlington IA; BR/TR/6´1˝/205; [ChiN67*2/21]; d5.28																									
1970	Chi N	0	2	.000	7	0	0	0-0	13.1	13	7	2	0	12-1	3	4.73	95	.277	.417	4	.250	0*	—	0	0	0.1
DUNHAM, WILEY	Harry Houston; B1.30.1877 Piketon OH; D1.16.1934 Cleveland OH; 6´1˝/180; d5.24																									
1902	StL N	2	3	.400	7	5	3	1	38	47	31	1	3	13	15	5.68	48	.303	.368	12	.083	-1	55	-11	—	-1.4
DUNKLE, DAVEY	Edward Perks; B8.30.1872 Philipsburg PA; D11.19.1941 Lock Haven PA; BB/TR/6´2˝/220; d8.28																									
1897	Phi N	5	2	.714	7	7	7	0	62	72	41	0	1	23	9	3.48	120	.288	.350	23-0-1	.174	-1	82	2	—	0.0
1898	Phi N	1	4	.200	12	7	4	0	68.1	83	70	1	9	38	21	6.98	49	.297	.399	28	.214	-0	133	-25	—	-1.5
1899	Was N	0	2	.000	4	2	2	0	26	46	34	3	1	14	9	10.04	39	.383	.452	11	.273	-0	18	-15	—	-0.9
1903	Chi A	4	4	.500	12	7	6	1	82	96	58	1	3	31	26	4.06	69	.291	.357	33	.303	2	98	-13	—	-1.1
	Was A	5	9	.357	14	13	10	0	108.1	111	60	4	4	33	51	4.24	74	.264	.324	41	.098	-4	58	-10	—	-1.6
	Year	9	13	.409	26	20	16	1	190.1	207	118	5	7	64	77	4.16	72	.276	.339	74	.189	-2	72	-23	—	-2.7
1904	Was A	2	9	.182	12	11	7	0	74.1	95	56	1	3	23	23	4.96	54	.311	.366	28	.143	-2*	85	-19	—	-2.6
Total	5	17	30	.362	61	47	36	1	421	503	319	10	21	162	139	5.02	65	.295	.364	164-0-1	.189	-4	82	-80	—	-7.7
DUNLEAVY, JACK	John Francis; B9.14.1879 Harrison NJ; D4.11.1944 S.Norwalk CT; BL/TL/5´6˝/167; d5.30; Col Amherst; ▲																									
1903	StL N	6	8	.429	14	13	9	0	102	101	59	2	8	57	51	4.06	80	.264	.371	193-0-7	.249	2*	91	-4	—	-0.3
1904	StL N	1	4	.200	7	5	5	0	55	63	32	4	1	23	28	4.42	61	.275	.344	172-1-1	.233	2*	82	-8	—	-0.5
Total	2	7	12	.368	21	18	14	0	157	164	91	6	9	80	79	4.18	73	.268	.361	365-1-8	.241	4	90	-12	—	-0.8
DUNN, JIM	James William "Bill"; B2.25.1931 Valdosta GA; D1.6.1999 Gadsden AL; BR/TR/6´0.5˝/185; d8.26; Col Alabama																									
1952	Pit N	0	0	ø	3	0	0	0	5.1	4	2	0	0	3	2	3.38	118	.190	.292	1	.000	-0	—	0	0	0.0
DUNN, JACK	John Joseph; B10.6.1872 Meadville PA; D10.22.1928 Towson MD; BR/TR/5´9˝/?; d5.6; ▲																									
1897	Bro N	14	9	.609	25	21	21	0	216.2	251	147	6	9	66	26	4.57	90	.288	.344	131-0-4	.221	-2*	116	-10	—	-1.0
1898	Bro N	16	21	.432	41	37	31	0	322.2	352	180	10	15	82	66	3.60	100	.275	.327	167-0-1	.246	1*	82	0	—	-0.1
1899	Bro N	23	13	.639	41	34	29-2	2	299.1	323	161	8	18	86	48	3.70	106	.275	.334	122-0-2	.246	0*	108	12	—	1.3
1900	Bro N	3	4	.429	10	7	5	0	63	88	48	1	4	28	6	5.57	69	.330	.401	26	.231	-0	93	-10	—	-0.9
	Phi N	5	5	.500	10	9	9-1	0	80	87	50	2	5	29	12	4.84	75	.276	.347	33	.303	1	59	-8	—	-0.7

YEAR	TM LG	W	L	PCT	G	GS	CG-SHO	SV-BS	IP	H	R	HR	HB	BB-IB	SO	ERA	AERA	OAV	OOB	AB-HR-SH	AVG	PB	SUP	APR	DL	PW
	Year	8	9	.471	20	16	14-1	0	143	175	98	3	9	57	18	5.16	72	.301	.372	59	.271	1	74	-16	—	-1.6
1901	Phi N	0	1	.000	2	2	0	0	4.2	11	16	0	2	7	1	21.21	16	.458	.606	1	1.000	1	219	-9	—	-1.2
	Bal A	3	3	.500	9	6	6	0	59.2	74	45	2	1	21	5	3.62	107	.301	.358	362-0-14	.249	0*	102	-1	—	0.0
1902	NY N	0	3	.000	3	2	2	0	26.2	28	14	0	0	12	6	3.71	76	.269	.345	342-0-19	.211	0*	24	-2	—	-0.1
1904	NY N	0	0	ø	1	0	0	1	4	3	3	1	0	3	1	4.50	61	.167	.286	181-1-5	.309	0*	—	-1	—	0.0
Total	7	64	59	.520	142	118	103-3	3	1076.2	1217	664	30	54	334	171	4.11	92	.283	.342	1365-1-45	.245	1	97	-29	—	-2.7
DUNN, SCOTT	Scott Allen; B5.23.1978 San Antonio TX; BR/TR/6´3˝/200; [CinN99 10/308]; d9.11																									
2004	Ana A	0	0	ø	3	0	0	0-0	3	7	3	0	0	1-0	2	9.00	50	.438	.471	0	ø	0	—	-1	0	-0.1
2006	TB A	1	0	1.000	7	0	0	0-1	7.2	17	10	2	2	4-0	4	11.74	40	.436	.511	0	ø	0	—	-5	0	-0.6
Total	2	1	0	1.000	10	0	0	0-1	10.2	24	13	2	2	5-0	6	10.97	42	.436	.500	0	ø	0	—	-6	0	-0.7
DUNNE, MIKE	Michael Dennis; B10.27.1962 South Bend IN; BR/TR/6´4˝/(200–221); [StLN84 1/7]; d6.5; Col Bradley; [DL 1993 Chi A 107]																									
1987	Pit N	13	6	.684	23	23	5-1	0-0	163.1	143	66	10	1	68-8	72	3.03	138	.240	.317	53-0-7	.094	-1	86	18	0	2.0
1988	Pit N	7	11	.389	30	28	1	0-0	170	163	88	15	5	88-3	70	3.92	88	.255	.345	46-0-7	.109	-1*	101	-11	22	-1.2
1989	Pit N	1	1	.500	3	3	0	0-0	14.1	21	12	1	1	9-1	4	7.53	45	.328	.419	4	.250	0	130	-6	0	-0.7
	Sea A	2	9	.182	15	15	1	0-0	85.1	104	61	7	2	37-1	38	5.27	77	.307	.373	0	ø	0	84	-13	0	-1.4
1990	SD N	0	3	.000	10	6	0	0-0	28.2	28	21	4	0	17-0	15	5.65	68	.241	.338	6	.000	-1	90	-6	91	-0.6
1992	Chi A	2	0	1.000	4	1	0	0-1	12.2	12	7	0	1	6-1	6	4.26	91	.255	.352	0	ø	0	94	-1	0	-0.1
Total	5	25	30	.455	85	76	7-1	0-1	474.1	471	255	37	10	225-14	205	4.08	94	.261	.344	109-0-14	.101	-1	92	-19	220	-2.0
DUNNING, ANDY	Andrew Jackson; B8.12.1871 New York NY; D6.21.1952 New York NY; BR/TR/6´0˝/175; d5.23																									
1889	Pit N	0	2	.000	2	2	2	0	18	20	19	1	0	16	4	7.00	54	.274	.404	7	.000	-1	63	-7	—	-0.6
1891	NY N	0	1	.000	1	1	0	0	2	3	5	1	0	3	1	4.50	71	.333	.500	0	ø	0	93	-1	—	-0.2
Total	2	0	3	.000	3	3	2	0	20	23	24	2	0	19	5	6.75	55	.280	.416	7	.000	-1	72	-8	—	-0.8
DUNNING, STEVE	Steven John; B5.15.1949 Denver CO; BR/TR/6´2˝/(200–205); [CleA70 1/2]; d6.14; Col Stanford																									
1970	Cle A	4	9	.308	19	17	0	0-1	94.1	93	55	16	4	54-3	77	4.96	81	.261	.362	31-0-3	.161	-1	86	-9	0	-1.1
1971	Cle A	8	14	.364	31	29	3-1	1-0	184	173	98	25	5	109-5	132	4.50	86	.254	.359	55-1-8	.182	1*	78	-10	0	-1.0
1972	Cle A	6	4	.600	16	16	1	0-0	105	98	39	16	0	43-8	52	3.26	100	.248	.321	33-3-3	.273	5*	88	1	0	0.7
1973	Cle A	0	2	.000	4	3	0	0-0	18	17	15	2	0	13-0	10	6.50	61	.250	.370	0	ø	0	83	-5	0	-0.5
	Tex A	2	6	.250	23	12	2	0-1	94.1	101	63	11	1	52-2	38	5.34	70	.275	.362	0	ø	0*	97	-16	0	-1.3
	Year	2	8	.200	27	15	2	0-1	112.1	118	78	13	1	65-2	48	5.53	69	.271	.364	0	ø	0	94	-23	0	-1.8
1974	Tex A	0	0	ø	1	0	0	0-0	2.1	3	5	2	0	3-1	1	19.29	19	.333	.500	0	ø	0	—	-4	0	-0.2
1976	Cal A	0	0	ø	4	0	0	0-0	6	9	9	2	0	6-1	4	7.50	45	.310	.417	0	ø	0	—	-4	0	-0.2
	Mon N	2	6	.250	32	7	1	0-0	91.1	93	50	6	2	33-4	72	4.14	91	.274	.338	15-0-3	.133	-0	74	-4	0	-0.3
1977	Oak A	1	0	1.000	6	0	0	0-0	18.1	17	8	2	0	10-1	4	3.93	103	.254	.351	0	ø	0	—	1	0	0.0
Total	7	23	41	.359	136	84	7-1	1-2	613.2	604	342	82	12	323-25	390	4.56	82	.261	.352	134-4-17	.194	6	84	-50	0	-3.9
DUPEE, FRANK	Frank Oliver; B4.29.1877 Monkton VT; D8.14.1956 W.Falmouth ME; TR/6´1˝/200; d8.24																									
1901	Chi A	0	1	.000	1	1	0	0	0	0	3	0	0	3	0	(3)	ø	ø	1.000	0	ø	0	78	-3	—	-0.2
DUPREE, MIKE	Michael Dennis; B5.29.1953 Kansas City KS; BR/TR/6´1˝/175; [SDN73*4/70]; d4.13; Col Fresno (CA) City																									
1976	SD N	0	0	ø	12	0	0	0-0	15.2	18	17	4	0	7-0	5	9.19	36	.286	.352	1	1.000	1	—	-10	0	-0.5
DURAN, ROBERTO	Roberto Alejandro; B3.6.1973 Moca, D.R.; BL/TL/6´0˝/(190–205); d7.6																									
1997	Det A	0	0	ø	13	0	0	0-0	10.2	7	9	0	3	15-0	11	7.59	61	.189	.446	0	ø	0	—	-3	0	-0.2
1998	Det A	0	1	.000	18	0	0	0-0	15.1	9	10	0	2	17-0	12	5.87	81	.170	.389	0	ø	0	—	-1	122	-0.1
Total	2	0	1	.000	31	0	0	0-0	26	16	19	0	5	32-0	23	6.58	71	.178	.414	0	ø	0	—	-4	122	-0.3
DURBIN, KID	Blaine Alphonsus; B9.10.1886 Lamar MO; D9.11.1943 Kirkwood MO; BL/TL/5´8˝/155; d4.24; ▲																									
1907	Chi N	0	1	.000	5	1	1	1	16.2	14	13	0	1	10	5	5.40	46	.233	.352	18	.333	1*	57	-5	—	-0.3
DURBIN, CHAD	Chad Griffin; B12.3.1977 Spring Valley IL; BB/TR/6´2˝/(175–200); [KCA96 3/79]; d9.26																									
1999	KC A	0	0	ø	1	0	0	0-0	2.1	1	0	0	0	1-0	3	0.00	ø	.125	.222	0	ø	0	—	1	0	0.1
2000	KC A	2	5	.286	16	16	0	0-0	72.1	91	71	14	0	43-1	37	8.21	64	.301	.385	0	ø	0	106	-23	0	-1.7
2001	KC A	9	16	.360	29	29	2	0-0	179	201	109	26	11	58-0	95	4.93	101	.288	.348	1-0-1	.000	-0	69	0	0	0.0
2002	KC A	0	1	.000	2	2	0	0-0	8.1	13	11	3	1	4-0	5	11.88	42	.342	.419	0	ø	0	74	-5	0	-0.5
2003	Cle A	0	1	.000	3	1	0	0-0	8.2	18	12	2	0	3-0	8	7.27	61	.429	.467	0	ø	0	146	-5	0	-0.4
2004	Cle A	5	6	.455	17	8	1	0-0	51.1	63	40	10	4	24-3	38	6.66	65	.301	.381	0	ø	0	99	-13	0	-2.3
	Ari N	1	1	.500	7	0	0	0-0	9.1	9	10	1	1	11-0	10	8.68	53	.237	.420	1	.000	-0	—	-4	0	-0.7
2006	Det A	0	0	ø	3	0	0	0-0	6	6	1	1	0	0-0	3	1.50	299	.250	.250	0	ø	0	—	2	0	0.1
Total	7	17	30	.362	78	56	3	0-0	337.1	402	254	57	17	144-4	199	6.14	80	.296	.367	2-0-1	.000	-0	86	-47	0	-5.4
DURBIN, J.D.	Joseph Adam; B2.24.1982 Portland OR; BR/TR/6´0˝/200; [MinA00 2/54]; d9.8																									
2004	Min A	0	1	.000	4	1	0	0-0	7.1	12	6	0	0	6-0	6	7.36	63	.387	.474	0	ø	0	140	-2	0	-0.2
DUREN, RYNE	Rinold George; B2.22.1929 Cazenovia WI; BR/TR/6´1˝/(194–197); d9.25																									
1954	Bal A	0	0	ø	1	0	0	0	2	3	3	0	0	1	2	9.00	40	.333	.400	0	ø	0	—	-2	0	-0.1
1957	KC A	0	3	.000	14	6	0	1	42.2	37	26	4	2	30-1	37	5.27	75	.236	.359	14	.071	-1	53	-5	0	-0.5
1958	†NY A☆	6	4	.600	44	1	0	**20**	75.2	40	20	4	7	43-1	87	2.02	175	.157	.296	13-0-4	.077	0	51	14	0	2.6
1959	NY A★	3	6	.333	41	0	0	14	76.2	49	18	6	3	43-2	96	1.88	194	.181	.300	14-0-3	.000	-1	—	16	0	2.4
1960	†NY A	3	4	.429	42	1	0	9	49	27	29	3	7	49-1	67	4.96	72	.160	.367	6-0-1	.000	-1	123	-7	0	-1.3
1961	NY A	0	1	.000	4	0	0	0	5	2	3	2	0	4-0	7	5.40	69	.125	.300	0	ø	0	—	-1	0	-0.2
	LA A☆	6	12	.333	40	14	1-1	2	99	87	70	13	3	75-1	108	5.18	87	.233	.361	25-0-1	.040	-2	90	-9	0	-1.6
	Year	6	13	.316	44	14	1-1	2	104	89	73	15	3	79-1	115	5.19	86	.229	.358	25-0-1	.040	-2	90	-10	0	-1.8
1962	LA A	2	9	.182	42	3	0	8	71.1	53	38	1	6	57-2	74	4.42	87	.206	.361	15-0-1	.067	-1	154	-3	0	-0.7
1963	Phi N	6	2	.750	33	7	1	2	87.1	65	33	6	5	52-1	84	3.30	98	.210	.332	21	.143	1*	118	1	0	0.1
1964	Phi N	0	0	ø	2	0	0	0	3	5	3	0	1	1-0	5	6.00	58	.357	.438	0	ø	0	—	-1	0	-0.1
	Cin N	0	2	.000	26	0	0	1	43.2	41	17	1	3	15-1	39	2.89	125	.248	.319	5	.000	-0	—	3	0	0.1
	Year	0	2	.000	28	0	0	1	46.2	46	20	1	4	16-1	44	3.09	117	.257	.328	5	.000	-0	—	2	0	0.0
1965	Phi N	0	0	ø	6	0	0	0	11	10	7	0	1	4-1	6	3.27	106	.270	.349	1	.000	-0	—	-1	0	0.0
	Was A	1	1	.500	16	0	0	0	23	24	17	0	3	18-4	18	6.65	52	.286	.421	0	ø	0	—	-7	0	-0.6
Total	10	27	44	.380	311	32	2-1	57	589.1	443	284	40	41	392-15	630	3.83	98	.209	.341	114-0-10	.061	-5	100	-2	0	0.1
DURHAM, DON	Donald Gary; B3.21.1949 Yosemite KY; BR/TR/6´0˝/165; [StLN70 7/159]; d7.16; Col Western Kentucky																									
1972	StL N	2	7	.222	10	8	1	0-0	47.2	42	28	1	0	22-5	35	4.34	79	.240	.318	14-2-0	.500	4*	48	-6	0	-0.6
1973	Tex A	0	4	.000	15	4	0	1-0	40.1	49	35	7	1	23-0	23	7.59	50	.304	.390	0	ø	0*	77	-16	0	-1.5
Total	2	2	11	.154	25	12	1	1-0	88	91	63	8	1	45-5	58	5.83	61	.271	.353	14-2-0	.500	4	58	-22	0	-2.1
DURHAM, ED	Edward Fant "Bull"; B8.17.1907 Chester SC; D4.27.1976 Chester SC; BL/TR/5´11˝/170; d4.19																									
1929	Bos A	1	0	1.000	14	1	0	0	22.1	34	24	2	0	14	6	9.27	46	.374	.457	4	.000	-0	39	-11	—	-0.5
1930	Bos A	4	15	.211	33	12	6-1	1	140	144	81	9	2	43	28	4.69	98	.270	.326	41-0-2	.098	-4	54	0	—	-0.4
1931	Bos A	8	10	.444	38	15	7-2	0	165.1	175	91	9	4	50	53	4.25	101	.266	.322	54-0-1	.056	-6*	64	0	—	-0.6
1932	Bos A	6	13	.316	34	22	4	0	175.1	187	90	13	4	49	52	3.80	118	.274	.327	57-0-1	.123	-3*	71	13	—	0.9
1933	Chi A	10	6	.625	24	21	6	0	138.2	137	74	12	5	46	65	4.48	95	.256	.320	46-0-8	.217	0	118	0	—	0.0
Total	5	29	44	.397	143	71	23-3	1	641.2	677	360	45	15	202	204	4.45	99	.271	.329	202-0-12	.119	-14	79	2	—	-0.6
DURHAM, JIM	James Garfield; B10.7.1881 Douglass KS; D5.7.1949 Coffeyville KS; BR/TR/6´0˝/175; d9.15; Col Southwestern (KS)																									
1902	Chi A	1	1	.500	3	3	3	0	20	21	15	0	0	16	3	5.85	58	.269	.394	15	.067	-1*	57	-5	—	-0.4
DURHAM, BULL	Louis Raphael (b Louis Raphael Staub); B6.27.1877 New Oxford PA; D6.28.1960 Bentley KS; BR/TR/5´10˝/?; d9.15																									
1904	Bro N	2	0	1.000	2	2	1	0	11	10	5	0	0	5	1	3.27	84	.250	.333	4	.250	0	213	0	—	-0.1
1907	Was A	0	0	ø	2	0	0	0	5	10	9	0	1	4	1	12.60	19	.417	.517	1	.000	-0	—	-5	—	-0.3
1908	NY N	0	0	ø	1	0	0	0	2	2	2	0	0	1	2	9.00	27	.250	.333	0	ø	0	—	-1	—	-0.1
1909	NY N	0	0	ø	4	0	0	1	11	15	8	0	0	2	2	3.27	78	.326	.354	2	.000	-0	—	-2	—	-0.1
Total	4	2	0	1.000	9	2	1	1	29	37	24	0	1	12	6	5.28	49	.314	.382	7	.143	-0	213	-8	—	-0.6

YEAR	TM LG	W	L	PCT	G	GS	CG-SHO	SV-BS	IP	H	R	HR	HB	BB-IB	SO	ERA	AERA	OAV	OOB	AB-HR-SH	AVG	PB	SUP	APR	DL	PW
Durning, Rich	Richard Knott; B10.10.1892 Louisville KY; D9.23.1948 Castle Point NY; BL/TL/6´2˝/178; d4.16																									
1917	Bro N	0	0	ø	1	0	0	0	1	0	0	0	0	0	0	0.00	ø	.000	.000	0	ø	0	—	0	—	0.0
1918	Bro N	0	0	ø	1	0	0	0	2	3	5	0	0	4	0	13.50	21	.375	.583	0	ø	0	—	-3	—	-0.1
Total	2	0	0	ø	2	0	0	0	3	3	5	0	0	4	0	9.00	31	.273	.467	0	ø	0	—	-3	—	-0.1
Durocher, Jayson	Jayson Paul; B8.18.1974 Hartford CT; BR/TR/6´3˝/195; [MonN93 9/258]; d6.11																									
2002	Mil N	1	1	.500	39	0	0	0-1	48	27	13	3	2	21-2	44	1.88	220	.164	.265	2	.000	-0	—	11	0	0.5
2003	Mil N	2	0	1.000	6	0	0	0-0	7.1	9	9	4	1	2-0	7	11.05	39	.300	.364	0	ø	0	—	-5	165	-0.9
Total	2	3	1	.750	45	0	0	0-1	55.1	36	22	7	3	23-2	51	3.09	134	.185	.279	2	.000	-0	—	6	165	-0.4
Duryea, Jesse	James Newton "Cyclone Jim"; B9.7.1859 Osage IA; D8.19.1942 Algona IA; BR/TR/5´10˝/175; d4.20																									
1889	Cin AA	32	19	.627	53	48	38-2	1	401	372	208	9	16	127	183	2.56	153	.238	.302	162	.272	6*	114	51	—	**5.7**
1890	Cin N	16	12	.571	33	32	29-2	0	274	270	148	11	8	60	108	2.92	122	.249	.294	99-1	.152	1	93	21	—	1.8
1891	Cin N	1	9	.100	10	10	8	0	77	101	67	4	7	25	23	5.38	63	.305	.366	32	.031	-5	71	-14	—	-1.8
	StL AA	1	1	.500	3	3	2	0	24	19	13	0	0	10	13	3.38	124	.211	.290	11	.364	1	99	3	—	0.2
1892	Cin N	2	5	.286	9	7	5	0	68	55	37	3	3	26	21	3.57	91	.212	.292	27	.111	-1	94	-1	—	-0.1
	Was N	3	11	.214	18	15	13-1	2	127	102	59	6	9	45	48	2.41	135	.211	.291	50	.120	-2	64	12	—	1.1
	Year	5	16	.238	27	22	18-1	2	195	157	96	9	12	71	69	2.82	116	.212	.291	77	.117	-3	73	12	—	1.0
1893	Was N	4	10	.286	17	15	9	0	117	182	137	8	13	56	20	7.54	61	.345	.420	47	.277	2	118	-36	—	-2.8
Total	5	59	67	.468	143	130	104-5	3	1088	1101	669	41	56	349	416	3.45	109	.254	.318	428-1	.201	3	100	36	—	4.1
Dusak, Erv	Ervin Frank "Four Sack"; B7.29.1920 Chicago IL; D11.6.1994 Glendale Heights IL; BR/TR/6´2˝/(183–185); d9.18.1941; Mil 1943–45; ▲																									
1948	StL N	0	0	ø	1	0	0	0	1	0	0	0	0	1	0	0.00	ø	.000	.250	311-6-5	.209	0*	—	0	0	0.0
1950	StL N	0	2	.000	14	2	0	1	36.1	27	17	2	1	27	16	3.72	116	.211	.353	12	.083	-0*	72	2	0	0.1
1951	StL N	0	0	ø	5	0	0	0	10	14	8	0	0	7	8	7.20	55	.333	.429	2-1-0	.500	1	—	-3	0	0.0
	Pit N	0	1	.000	3	1	0	0	6.2	10	10	2	1	9	2	12.15	35	.357	.526	39-1-0	.308	1*	84	-5	70	-0.6
	Year	0	1	.000	8	1	0	0	16.2	24	18	2	1	16	10	9.18	44	.343	.471	41-2-0	.317	2	87	-8	0	-0.6
Total	3	0	3	.000	23	3	0	1	54	51	35	4	2	44	26	5.33	79	.254	.393	364-8-5	.217	2	77	-6	70	-0.5
Duser, Carl	Carl Robert; B7.22.1932 Hazleton PA; BL/TL/6´1˝/(175–180); d9.15																									
1956	KC A	1	1	.500	2	2	0	0	6	14	6	0	0	2-0	5	9.00	48	.452	.485	3	.000	-0	134	-3	0	-0.5
1958	KC A	0	0	ø	1	0	0	0	2	5	1	0	0	1-1	0	4.50	87	.500	.545	0	ø	0	—	0	0	0.0
Total	2	1	1	.500	3	2	0	0	8	19	7	0	0	3-1	5	7.88	54	.463	.500	3	.000	-0	134	-3	0	-0.5
Dustal, Bob	Robert Andrew; B9.28.1935 Sayreville NJ; BR/TR/6´0˝/175; d4.9																									
1963	Det A	0	1	.000	7	0	0	0	6	10	9	0	0	5-1	4	9.00	42	.357	.455	0	ø	0	—	-4	0	-0.6
Duvall, Mike	Michael Alan; B10.11.1974 Warrenton VA; BR/TL/6´0˝/(185–200); [FlaN95 19/513]; d9.22; Col Potomac St. (WV) JC; [DL 2002 Min A 183]																									
1998	TB A	0	0	ø	3	0	0	0-0	4	4	3	0	0	2-0	1	6.75	71	.267	.353	0	ø	0	—	-1	0	0.0
1999	TB A	1	1	.500	40	0	0	0-1	40	46	21	5	2	27-1	18	4.05	123	.293	.401	0	ø	0	—	4	27	0.2
2000	TB A	0	0	ø	2	0	0	0-0	2.1	5	2	0	0	1-0	0	7.71	63	.455	.500	0	ø	0	—	-1	0	0.0
2001	Min A	0	0	ø	8	0	0	0-1	4.2	7	4	1	0	2-0	4	7.71	61	.368	.409	0	ø	0	—	-1	0	-0.1
Total	4	1	1	.500	53	0	0	0-2	51	62	30	6	2	32-1	23	4.76	103	.307	.403	0	ø	0	—	1	210	0.1
Duzen, Bill	William George; B2.21.1870 Buffalo NY; D3.11.1944 Buffalo NY; BR/TR/5´11˝/165; d9.21																									
1890	Buf P	0	2	.000	2	2	2	0	13	20	24	2	0	14	5	13.85	30	.339	.466	4	.250	1	89	-12	—	-1.0
Dwyer, Frank	John Francis; B3.25.1868 Lee MA; D2.4.1943 Pittsfield MA; BR/TR/5´8˝/145; d9.20; M1; Col Hobart and William Smith																									
1888	Chi N	4	1	.800	5	5	5-1	0	42	32	20	1	0	9	17	1.07	283	.198	.240	21	.190	-0	170	5	—	0.6
1889	Chi N	16	13	.552	32	30	27	0	276	307	177	14	7	72	63	3.59	116	.274	.321	135-1	.200	-2*	94	16	—	1.0
1890	Chi P	3	6	.333	12	6	6	1	69.1	98	71	4	0	25	17	6.23	70	.319	.370	53	.264	-0*	94	-11	—	-1.1
1891	Cin AA	13	19	.406	35	31	29-1	0	289	332	225	10	10	124	101	4.52	91	.279	.351	141	.284	3*	87	-1	—	0.2
	Mil AA	6	4	.600	10	10	10	0	86	92	41	2	4	21	27	2.20	199	.264	.314	40	.225	-1*	79	17	—	1.5
	Year	19	23	.452	45	41	39-1	0	375	424	266	12	14	145	128	3.98	104	.275	.343	181	.271	1	85	11	—	1.7
1892	StL N	2	8	.200	10	10	6	0	64	90	58	1	2	24	16	5.63	57	.319	.377	25	.080	-1	113	-18	—	-2.1
	Cin N	20	10	.667	34	28	25-3	1	268.1	262	101	6	5	49	47	2.31	141	.246	.282	132	.159	-4*	106	30	—	2.2
	Year	22	18	.550	44	38	31-3	1	332.1	352	159	7	7	73	63	2.95	110	.261	.302	157	.146	-6	107	19	—	0.1
1893	Cin N	18	15	.545	37	30	28-1	**2**	287.1	332	187	17	5	93	53	4.13	116	.281	.336	120-1	.200	-3*	96	18	—	1.4
1894	Cin N	19	21	.475	45	39	34-1	1	348	471	282	26	15	106	49	5.07	109	.320	.371	172-2-0	.267	1*	97	17	—	1.5
1895	Cin N	18	15	.545	37	31	23-2	0	280.1	355	191	10	14	74	46	4.24	117	.304	.353	113-1-1	.265	2	90	19	—	1.7
1896	Cin N	24	11	.686	36	34	30-3	1	288.2	321	144	8	11	60	57	3.15	147	.279	.321	110-0-3	.264	4	90	42	—	4.4
1897	Cin N	18	13	.581	37	31	22	0	247.1	315	142	5	11	56	41	3.78	120	.307	.350	94-0-7	.266	0	88	19	—	1.7
1898	Cin N	16	10	.615	31	28	24	0	240	257	117	3	16	42	29	3.04	126	.272	.314	85-0-1	.141	-4	86	18	—	1.2
1899	Cin N	0	5	.000	5	5	2	0	32.2	48	26	1	1	9	2	5.51	71	.340	.384	11	.364	1	48	-5	—	-0.6
Total	12	177	151	.540	366	318	271-12	6	2819	3312	1782	108	101	764	565	3.84	115	.286	.336	1252-5-12	.229	-7	93	166	—	13.6
Dyer, Eddie	Edwin Hawley; B10.11.1899 Morgan City LA; D4.20.1964 Houston TX; BL/TL/5´11.5˝/168; d7.8; M5; Col Rice; ▲																									
1922	StL N	0	0	ø	2	0	0	0	3.2	7	2	0	0	0	3	2.45	157	.412	.412	3	.333	1*	—	0	—	0.1
1923	StL N	2	1	.667	4	3	2-1	0	22	30	10	0	1	5	7	4.09	95	.333	.375	45-2-0	.267	0*	70	0	—	0.2
1924	StL N	8	11	.421	29	15	7-1	0	136.2	174	82	6	4	51	23	4.61	82	.331	.395	76-0-3	.237	1*	133	-12	—	-1.2
1925	StL N	4	3	.571	27	5	1	3	82.1	93	52	4	7	24	25	4.15	104	.278	.340	31-0-1	.097	-2*	137	-1	—	-0.3
1926	StL N	1	0	1.000	6	0	0	0	9.1	7	14	0	1	14	4	11.57	34	.219	.468	2	.500	0	—	-8	—	-0.7
1927	StL N	0	0	ø	1	0	0	0	2	5	4	1	0	2	1	18.00	22	.500	.583	0	ø	0	—	-3	—	-0.1
Total	6	15	15	.500	69	23	10-2	3	256	316	164	11	13	96	63	4.75	84	.313	.380	157-2-4	.223	1	124	-24	—	-2.0
Dyer, Mike	Michael Lawrence; B9.8.1966 Upland CA; BR/TR/6´3˝/(195–200); [MinA86*4/87]; d6.29; Col Citrus (CA) JC																									
1989	Min A	4	7	.364	16	12	1	0-0	71	74	43	2	2	37-0	37	4.82	86	.273	.362	0	ø	0	80	-6	0	-0.9
1994	Pit N	1	1	.500	14	0	0	4-2	15.1	15	12	1	3	12-4	13	5.87	75	.268	.411	1	.000	-0	—	-3	0	-0.5
1995	Pit N	4	5	.444	55	0	0	0-2	74.2	81	40	9	5	30-3	53	4.34	100	.281	.358	7-0-1	.571	1	—	0	0	0.2
1996	Mon N	5	5	.500	70	1	0	2-4	75.2	79	40	7	5	34-4	51	4.40	98	.277	.360	7	.000	-1	62	0	0	-0.1
Total	4	14	18	.438	155	13	1	6-8	236.2	249	135	19	15	113-11	154	4.60	93	.277	.364	15-0-1	.267	1	76	-9	0	-1.3
Dygert, Jimmy	James Henry "Sunny Jim"; B7.5.1884 Utica NY; D2.8.1936 New Orleans LA; BR/TR/5´10˝/158; d9.8																									
1905	Phi A	1	4	.200	6	3	2	0	35.1	41	20	2	2	11	24	4.33	61	.291	.351	15	.267	0	89	-5	—	-0.6
1906	Phi A	11	13	.458	35	25	15-4	0	213.2	175	88	1	10	91	106	2.70	101	.226	.316	74-1-2	.176	-0	95	2	—	0.1
1907	Phi A	21	8	.724	42	28	18-5	1	261.2	200	98	2	18	85	151	2.34	111	**.214**	.292	94-0-6	.128	-4	121	8	—	0.4
1908	Phi A	11	15	.423	41	28	15-5	1	238.2	184	95	3	11	97	164	2.87	89	.220	.309	75-0-5	.080	-6	77	-4	—	-1.0
1909	Phi A	9	5	.643	32	13	6-1	0	137.1	117	60	1	11	50	79	2.42	99	.242	.327	44-0-3	.205	0	156	-4	—	-0.4
1910	Phi A	4	4	.500	19	8	6-1	0	99.1	81	44	0	3	49	59	2.54	94	.231	.331	36	.083	-2	124	-2	—	-0.5
Total	6	57	49	.538	175	105	62-16	2	986	798	405	9	55	383	583	2.65	97	.227	.312	338-1-16	.139	-11	107	-5	—	-2.0
Dykhoff, Radhames	Radhames Alviro; B9.27.1974 Paradera, Aruba; BL/TL/6´0˝/160; d6.7																									
1998	Bal A	0	0	ø	1	0	0	0-0	1	2	2	0	0	1-0	1	18.00	25	.400	.500	0	ø	0	—	-1	0	-0.1
Earley, Arnold	Arnold Carl; B6.4.1933 Lincoln Park MI; D9.29.1999 Flint MI; BL/TL/6´1˝/(195–200); d9.27																									
1960	Bos A	0	1	.000	2	0	0	0	4	9	8	1	0	4-0	5	15.75	26	.429	.520	1	.000	0	—	-5	0	-0.8
1961	Bos A	2	4	.333	33	0	0	7	49.2	42	31	3	0	34-3	44	3.99	105	.226	.345	6	.000	-1	—	-1	0	-0.3
1962	Bos A	4	5	.444	38	3	0	5	68.1	76	53	8	1	46-1	59	5.80	71	.281	.384	10	.200	0	58	-14	0	-1.8
1963	Bos A	3	7	.300	53	4	0	1	115.2	124	73	13	8	43-8	97	4.75	80	.270	.342	18	.278	1	112	-14	0	-1.1
1964	Bos A	1	1	.500	25	3	1	1	50.1	51	17	3	1	18-0	45	2.68	144	.266	.332	9-0-1	.111	0	123	6	63	0.4
1965	Bos A	0	1	.000	57	0	0	0	74.1	79	42	5	3	29-8	47	3.63	103	.271	.338	6	.000	-0	—	-2	0	-0.1
1966	Chi N	2	1	.667	13	0	0	0	17.2	14	11	1	0	9-0	12	3.57	103	.226	.319	1-0-1	.000	-0	—	-1	0	-0.2
1967	Hou N	0	0	ø	2	0	0	0	1.1	5	5	1	0	1-0	1	27.00	12	.625	.667	0	ø	0	—	-4	0	-0.2
Total	8	12	20	.375	223	10	1	14	381.1	400	240	35	13	184-20	310	4.48	87	.269	.352	51-0-2	.157	0	98	-35	63	-4.1

YEAR	TM LG	W	L	PCT	G	GS	CG-SHO	SV-BS	IP	H	R	HR	HB	BB-IB	SO	ERA	AERA	OAV	OOB	AB-HR-SH	AVG	PB	SUP	APR	DL	PW
Earley, Tom	Thomas Francis Aloysius; B2.19.1917 Roxbury MA; D4.5.1988 Nantucket MA; BR/TR/6´0˝/180; d9.27; Mil 1943–44																									
1938	Bos N	1	0	1.000	2	1	1	0	11	8	9	2	1	1	4	3.27	105	.186	.222	4	.000	-1	99	-2	—	-0.2
1939	Bos N	1	4	.200	14	2	0	1	40	49	28	1	2	19	9	4.72	78	.304	.385	10	.300	1	59	-6	—	-0.7
1940	Bos N	2	0	1.000	4	1	1-1	0	16.1	16	7	1	2	3	5	3.86	96	.267	.323	5	.400	1	187	0	—	0.1
1941	Bos N	6	8	.429	33	13	6-1	3	138.2	120	52	9	3	46	54	2.53	141	.233	.300	47-0-2	.234	1*	93	14	0	1.5
1942	Bos N	6	11	.353	27	18	6	1	112.2	120	65	10	1	55	28	4.71	71	.276	.359	34-0-3	.118	-1	95	-16	0	-2.2
1945	Bos N	2	1	.667	11	2	1	0	41	36	22	4	0	19	4	4.61	83	.235	.320	14-0-1	.214	1*	166	-2	0	-0.1
Total	6	18	24	.429	91	37	15-2	5	359.2	349	183	27	9	143	104	3.78	94	.256	.330	114-0-6	.202	2	98	-12	0	-1.6
Earley, Bill	William Albert; B1.30.1956 Cincinnati OH; BR/TL/6´4˝/200; d9.22; Col Miami–Ohio																									
1986	StL N	0	0	ø	3	0	0	0-0	3	0	0	0	0	2-0	2	0.00	ø	.000	.182	0	ø	0	—	1	0	0.1
Earnshaw, George	George Livingston "Moose"; B2.15.1900 New York NY; D12.1.1976 Little Rock AR; BR/TR/6´4˝/210; d6.3; C2; Col Swarthmore																									
1928	Phi A	7	7	.500	26	22	7-3	1	158.1	143	81	7	1	100	117	3.81	105	.240	.351	57-0-5	.246	1	123	3	—	0.3
1929	†Phi A	**24**	8	.750	44	33	13-3	1	254.2	233	110	8	5	125	149	3.29	129	**.241**	.331	87-1-10	.172	-2	118	27	—	2.6
1930	†Phi A	22	13	.629	49	**39**	20-**3**	2	296	299	162	20	1	139	193	4.44	105	.266	.347	114-0-7	.228	1	118	10	—	1.0
1931	†Phi A	21	7	.750	43	30	23-3	6	281.2	255	130	16	3	75	152	3.67	122	.236	.288	114-2-3	.263	6	118	28	—	3.1
1932	Phi A	19	13	.594	36	33	21-1	0	245.1	262	147	28	4	94	109	4.77	95	.270	.336	91-0-11	.286	4	121	-9	—	-0.6
1933	Phi A	5	10	.333	21	18	4	0	117.2	153	93	8	1	58	37	5.97	72	.311	.385	44-0-2	.182	-0	133	-22	—	-2.3
1934	Chi A	14	11	.560	33	30	16-2	0	227	242	128	28	4	104	97	4.52	105	.270	.349	79-0-3	.203	-0	82	7	—	0.6
1935	Chi A	1	2	.333	3	3	0	0	18	26	19	2	0	11	8	9.00	51	.342	.425	7-0-1	.286	0	138	-8	—	-0.9
	Bro N	8	12	.400	25	22	6-2	0	166	175	87	14	0	53	72	4.12	96	.270	.325	60-0-1	.217	1	110	-1	—	0.0
1936	Bro N	4	9	.308	19	13	4-1	1	93	113	63	7	3	30	40	5.32	78	.297	.354	33-0-1	.242	0	81	-11	—	-1.2
	StL N	2	1	.667	20	6	1	1	57.2	80	43	4	3	20	28	6.40	62	.333	.392	18	.222	-0	122	-14	—	-0.7
	Year	6	10	.375	39	19	5-1	2	150.2	193	106	11	6	50	68	5.73	71	.311	.368	51-0-1	.235	0	93	-23	—	-1.9
Total	9	127	93	.577	319	249	115-18	12	1915.1	1981	1063	142	25	809	1002	4.38	100	.265	.339	704-3-44	.230	9	113	10	—	1.9
Easley, Logan	Kenneth Logan; B11.4.1961 Salt Lake City UT; BR/TR/6´1˝/185; [NYA81 20/519]; d4.9; Col Southern Idaho [JC]																									
1987	Pit N	1	1	.500	17	0	0	1-0	26.1	23	17	5	1	17-4	21	5.47	76	.242	.357	2	.000	-0	—	-3	0	-0.2
1989	Pit N	1	0	1.000	10	0	0	1-0	12.1	8	6	1	1	7-1	6	4.38	78	.190	.320	1	.000	-0	—	-1	0	-0.1
Total	2	2	1	.667	27	0	0	2-0	38.2	31	23	6	2	24-5	27	5.12	76	.226	.345	3	.000	-0	—	-4	0	-0.3
Eason, Mal	Malcolm Wayne "Kid"; B3.13.1879 Brookville PA; D4.16.1970 Douglas AZ; BR/TR/6´0˝/175; d10.1; U8; Col Grove City																									
1900	Chi N	1	0	1.000	1	1	1	0	9	9	2	0	0	3	2	1.00	361	.257	.316	3	.000	-1	77	3	—	0.2
1901	Chi N	8	17	.320	27	25	23-1	0	220.2	246	136	9	13	60	68	3.59	90	.280	.335	87-0-1	.138	-5	76	-10	—	-1.5
1902	Chi N	1	1	.500	2	2	2	0	18	21	7	0	0	2	4	1.00	271	.292	.311	5-0-1	.200	0	75	2	—	0.3
	Bos N	9	12	.429	27	27	20-2	0	213.1	249	100	4	12	61	51	2.91	97	.291	.347	72-0-6	.083	-6	94	-3	—	-1.0
	Year	10	13	.435	29	29	22-2	0	231.1	270	107	4	12	63	55	2.76	102	.291	.344	77-0-7	.091	-6	92	-2	—	-0.7
1903	Det A	2	5	.286	7	6	6-1	0	56.1	60	33	1	3	19	21	3.36	87	.271	.337	20	.100	-2	53	-4	—	-0.5
1905	Bro N	5	21	.192	27	27	20-3	0	207	230	128	5	5	72	64	4.30	67	.292	.355	81-0-2	.173	-1*	69	-29	—	-3.2
1906	Bro N	10	17	.370	34	26	18-3	1	227	212	109	1	9	74	64	3.25	78	.256	.323	88-0-1	.091	-4*	98	-19	—	-2.6
Total	6	36	73	.330	125	114	90-10	1	951.1	1027	515	20	42	291	274	3.42	84	.279	.339	356-0-11	.121	-19	82	-60	—	-8.3
East, Hugh	Gordon Hugh; B7.7.1919 Birmingham AL; D11.2.1981 Charleston SC; BR/TR/6´2˝/185; d9.13; Mil 1943–45																									
1941	NY N	1	1	.500	2	2	0	0	15.2	19	12	0	0	9	4	3.45	107	.297	.384	9	.222	0	138	-2	0	-0.2
1942	NY N	0	2	.000	4	1	0	0	7.1	15	16	1	0	7	2	9.82	34	.429	.524	2-1-0	.500	2	50	-8	0	-1.2
1943	NY N	1	3	.250	13	5	1	0	40.1	51	27	4	0	25	21	5.36	64	.298	.388	13	.077	-1*	64	-8	0	-0.9
Total	3	2	6	.250	19	8	1	0	63.1	85	55	5	0	41	27	5.40	65	.315	.405	24-1-0	.167	1	82	-18	0	-2.3
Easterly, Jamie	James Morris; B2.17.1953 Houston TX; BL/TL (BB 1974–76)/5´9˝/(170–180); [AtlN71 2/34]; d4.6																									
1974	Atl N	0	0	ø	3	0	0	0-0	2.2	6	7	0	0	4-0	0	16.88	23	.400	.526	0	ø	0	—	-4	0	-0.2
1975	Atl N	2	9	.182	21	13	0	0-0	68.2	73	47	5	2	42-2	34	4.98	76	.275	.375	18-0-3	.056	-2	91	-10	0	-1.6
1976	Atl N	1	1	.500	4	4	0	0-0	22	23	12	0	0	13-1	11	4.91	77	.280	.379	9	.111	-0	70	-2	0	-0.2
1977	Atl N	2	4	.333	22	5	0	1-0	58.2	72	46	5	3	30-4	37	6.14	72	.303	.386	15-0-2	.267	1*	92	-10	88	-0.9
1978	Atl N	3	6	.333	37	6	0	1-1	78	91	52	9	2	45-6	42	5.65	71	.299	.391	19-0-1	.211	0	85	-11	0	-1.1
1979	Atl N	0	0	ø	4	0	0	0-0	2.2	7	6	0	0	3-0	3	13.50	30	.467	.556	0	ø	0	—	-3	0	-0.2
1981	†Mil A	3	3	.500	44	0	0	4-3	62	46	23	0	0	34-4	31	3.19	109	.219	.321	0	ø	0	—	2	0	0.3
1982	Mil A	0	2	.000	28	0	0	2-1	30.2	39	19	6	0	15-0	16	4.70	82	.312	.380	0	ø	0	—	-4	51	-0.2
1983	Mil A	0	1	.000	12	0	0	1-1	11.2	14	7	0	2	10-1	6	3.86	98	.350	.491	1-0-1	.000	-0*	—	-1	0	-0.1
	Cle A	4	2	.667	41	0	0	3-4	57	69	25	4	2	22-4	39	3.63	118	.309	.375	0	ø	0	—	4	0	0.5
	Year	4	3	.571	53	0	0	4-5	68.2	83	32	4	4	32-5	45	3.67	114	.316	.395	1-0-1	.000	-0	—	4	0	0.4
1984	Cle A	3	1	.750	26	1	0	2-0	69.1	74	31	3	1	23-3	42	3.38	122	.273	.330	0	ø	0	88	5	74	0.3
1985	Cle A	4	1	.800	50	7	0	0-0	98.2	96	52	9	4	53-4	58	3.92	106	.264	.356	0	ø	0	159	1	0	0.0
1986	Cle A	0	2	.000	13	0	0	0-0	17.2	27	16	3	0	12-0	9	7.64	55	.365	.443	0	ø	0	—	-6	127	-0.6
1987	Cle A	1	1	.500	16	0	0	0-1	31.2	26	17	4	1	13-1	22	4.55	100	.218	.296	0	ø	0	—	1	125	0.0
Total	13	23	33	.411	321	36	0	14-11	611.1	663	360	48	17	319-30	350	4.62	88	.283	.368	62-0-7	.161	-1	101	-38	465	-4.0
Easton, Jack	John S.; B2.28.1867 Bridgeport OH; D11.28.1903 Steubenville OH; d9.23																									
1889	Col AA	1	0	1.000	4	1	1	1	18	13	8	0	3	21	7	3.50	104	.197	.411	7	.000	-1	120	1	—	0.0
1890	Col AA	15	14	.517	37	29	23	1	255.2	213	148	4	20	125	147	3.52	102	.220	.321	107	.178	0*	108	4	—	0.4
1891	Col AA	5	10	.333	18	16	13	0	135.1	145	111	3	15	59	52	4.52	76	.265	.352	63	.238	2*	86	-20	—	-1.5
	StL AA	3	2	.600	7	6	4	0	47.2	48	38	3	4	23	22	5.10	82	.253	.346	28	.179	-1*	108	-2	—	-0.3
	Col AA	0	2	.000	2	2	2	0	15	15	8	2	2	4	13	3.60	96	.250	.318	11	.000	-1*	18	0	—	-0.1
	Year	8	14	.364	27	24	19	0	198	208	157	8	21	86	87	4.59	79	.261	.348	102	.196	-0	88	-17	—	-1.9
1892	StL N	2	0	1.000	5	2	2	0	31	38	31	2	3	26	4	6.39	50	.290	.419	17	.176	-1	188	-11	—	-0.6
1894	Pit N	0	1	.000	3	1	1	0	19.2	26	16	0	3	4	1	4.12	127	.313	.367	5-0-2	.000	-1	54	1	—	-0.1
Total	5	26	29	.473	76	57	46	2	522.1	498	360	14	50	262	246	4.12	89	.243	.343	238-0-2	.176	-2	100	-27	—	-2.2
Eastwick, Rawly	Rawlins Jackson; B10.24.1950 Camden NJ; BR/TR/6´3˝/(172–180); [CinN69 3/62]; d9.12																									
1974	Cin N	0	0	ø	8	0	0	2-0	17.2	12	5	1	0	5-0	14	2.04	172	.188	.243	1	.000	-0	—	3	0	0.1
1975	†Cin N	5	3	.625	58	0	0	**22**-3	90	77	26	6	2	25-4	61	2.60	138	.229	.287	15-0-1	.067	-1	—	11	0	1.3
1976	†Cin N	11	5	.688	71	0	0	**26**-9	107.2	93	30	3	2	27-3	70	2.09	167	.232	.282	17-0-2	.000	-2	—	16	0	2.9
1977	Cin N	2	2	.500	23	0	0	7-2	43.1	40	14	3	0	8-1	17	2.91	135	.244	.279	6-0-1	.167	-0	—	5	0	0.6
	StL N	3	7	.300	41	1	0	4-2	53.2	74	34	6	0	21-3	30	4.70	83	.332	.385	5	.400	1	114	-6	0	-1.0
	Year	5	9	.357	64	1	0	11-4	97	114	48	9	0	29-4	47	3.90	101	.295	.341	11-0-1	.273	1	113	-1	0	-0.4
1978	NY A	2	1	.667	8	0	0	0-0	24.2	22	9	2	1	4-0	13	3.28	111	.232	.270	0	ø	0	—	2	0	0.2
	†Phi N	2	1	.667	22	0	0	0-2	40.1	31	21	5	0	18-2	14	4.02	90	.209	.292	3	.000	-0	—	-2	0	-0.2
1979	Phi N	3	6	.333	51	0	0	6-3	82.2	90	46	8	1	25-3	47	4.90	79	.284	.336	7	.000	-1	—	-8	0	-1.1
1980	KC A	0	1	.000	14	0	0	0-1	22	37	14	2	2	8-2	5	5.32	76	.363	.416	0	ø	0	—	-3	0	-0.1
1981	Chi N	0	1	.000	30	0	0	1-1	43.1	43	16	2	0	15-3	24	2.28	164	.264	.322	2	.000	-0	—	5	21	0.3
Total	8	28	27	.509	326	1	0	68-23	525.1	519	215	38	8	156-21	295	3.31	112	.258	.312	56-0-4	.071	-4	119	23	21	3.0
Eaton, Adam	Adam Thomas; B11.23.1977 Seattle WA; BR/TR/6´2˝/(190–200); [PhiN96 1/11]; d5.30																									
2000	SD N	7	4	.636	22	22	0	0-0	135	134	63	14	2	61-3	90	4.13	108	.260	.338	38	.289	5*	106	8	0	1.1
2001	SD N	8	5	.615	17	17	2	0-0	116.2	108	61	20	5	40-3	109	4.32	96	.241	.308	38-0-2	.105	-0*	114	-1	94	0.0
2002	SD N	1	1	.500	6	6	0	0-0	33.1	28	20	5	2	17-0	25	5.40	72	.235	.336	9	.111	-0	91	-5	154	-0.3
2003	SD N	9	12	.429	31	31	1	0-0	183	173	91	20	7	68-6	146	4.08	98	.246	.316	56-2-7	.196	5*	99	-3	15	0.4
2004	SD N	11	14	.440	33	33	0	0-0	199.1	204	113	28	10	52-3	153	4.61	86	.266	.318	64-0-5	.203	6*	109	-17	0	-1.3
2005	SD N	11	5	.688	24	22	0	0-0	128.2	140	70	14	5	44-6	100	4.27	92	.275	.335	46-0-3	.174	2*	128	-7	67	-0.7
2006	Tex A	7	4	.636	13	13	0	0-0	65	78	38	11	4	24-0	43	5.12	91	.299	.366	0	ø	0	127	-2	113	-0.4
Total	7	54	45	.545	146	144	3	0-0	861	865	456	112	35	306-21	666	4.40	93	.260	.327	251-2-17	.191	18	111	-27	443	-1.2
Eaton, Craig	Craig; B9.7.1954 Glendale OH; BR/TR/5´11˝/175; d9.5; Col Florida St.																									
1979	KC A	0	0	ø	5	0	0	0-0	10	8	3	0	0	3-2	4	2.70	158	.222	.282	0	ø	0	—	2	0	0.1

THE PITCHER REGISTER

YEAR	TM LG	W	L	PCT	G	GS	CG-SHO	SV-BS	IP	H	R	HR	HB	BB-IB	SO	ERA	AERA	OAV	OOB	AB-HR-SH	AVG	PB	SUP	APR	DL	PW
EATON, ZEB	Zebulon Vance "Red"; B2.2.1920 Cooleemee NC; D12.17.1989 W.Palm Beach FL; BR/TR/5´10˝/185; d4.18																									
1944	Det A	0	0	ø	6	0	0	0	15.2	19	12	2	0	8	4	5.74	62	.322	.403	10	.100	-1*	—	-4	0	-0.2
1945	†Det A	4	2	.667	17	3	0	0	53.1	48	28	0	3	40	15	4.05	87	.247	.384	32-2-0	.250	2*	40	-3	0	-0.1
Total	2	4	2	.667	23	3	0	0	69	67	40	2	3	48	19	4.43	80	.265	.388	42-2-0	.214	2	40	-7	0	-0.3
EAVE, GARY	Gary Louis; B7.22.1963 Monroe LA; BR/TR/6´4˝/190; [AtlN85 12/302]; d4.12; Col Grambling St.																									
1988	Atl N	0	0	ø	5	0	0	0-0	5	7	5	0	0	3-0	0	9.00	41	.333	.417	0	ø	0	—	-3	0	-0.1
1989	Atl N	2	0	1.000	3	3	0	0-0	20.2	15	3	0	1	12-0	9	1.31	280	.200	.318	6-0-1	.000	-1	81	5	0	0.4
1990	Sea A	0	3	.000	8	5	0	0-0	30	27	16	5	2	20-1	16	4.20	95	.241	.366	0	ø	0	87	-1	0	-0.1
Total	3	2	3	.400	16	8	0	0-0	55.2	49	24	5	3	35-1	25	3.56	108	.236	.354	6-0-1	.000	-1	85	1	0	0.2
EAVES, VALLIE	Vallie Ennis "Chief"; B9.6.1911 Allen OK; D4.19.1960 Norman OK; BR/TR/6´2.5˝/180; d9.12																									
1935	Phi A	1	2	.333	3	3	1	0	14	12	9	0	0	15	6	5.14	88	.240	.415	4	.000	-1	57	-1	—	-0.2
1939	Chi A	0	1	.000	2	1	1	0	11.2	11	7	1	1	8	5	4.63	102	.250	.377	6	.333	0	56	0	—	0.0
1940	Chi A	0	2	.000	5	3	0	0	18.2	22	16	2	1	24	11	6.75	66	.301	.480	5-0-1	.000	-1	73	-5	—	-0.5
1941	Chi N	3	3	.500	12	7	4	0	58.2	56	27	4	3	21	24	3.53	99	.253	.327	20-0-1	.100	-1	100	0	0	-0.2
1942	Chi N	0	0	ø	2	0	0	0	3	4	3	0	1	2	0	9.00	36	.308	.438	0	ø	0	—	-2	0	-0.1
Total	5	4	8	.333	24	14	6	0	106	105	62	7	6	70	46	4.58	86	.262	.379	35-0-2	.114	-3	82	-8	0	-1.0
EAYRS, EDDIE	Edwin; B11.10.1890 Blackstone MA; D11.30.1969 Warwick RI; BL/TL/5´7˝/160; d6.30; Col Brown; ▲																									
1913	Pit N	0	0	ø	2	0	0	0	8	8	6	0	0	6	5	2.25	134	.267	.389	6	.167	-0*	—	-1	—	-0.1
1920	Bos N	1	2	.333	7	3	0	0	26.1	36	18	1	2	12	7	5.47	56	.346	.424	244-1-6	.328	2*	69	-7	—	-0.5
1921	Bos N	0	0	ø	2	0	0	0	4.2	9	10	0	0	9	1	17.36	21	.391	.563	15	.067	-2*	—	-7	—	-0.5
Total	3	1	2	.333	11	3	0	0	39	53	34	1	2	27	13	6.23	50	.338	.441	265-1-6	.309	0	69	-15	—	-1.1
EBERT, DERRIN	Derrin Lee; B8.21.1976 Anaheim CA; BR/TL/6´3˝/200; [AtlN94 18/510]; d4.6																									
1999	Atl N	0	1	.000	5	0	0	1-0	8	9	5	2	0	5-1	4	5.63	79	.300	.400	1	.000	-0	—	-1	0	-0.1
ECCLES, HARRY	Harry Josiah "Bugs"; B7.9.1893 Kennedy NY; D6.2.1955 Jamestown NY; BL/TL/6´2˝/170; d9.13																									
1915	Phi A	0	1	.000	5	1	0	1	21	18	16	2	0	6	13	4.71	62	.240	.296	6	.167	-0	125	-4	—	-0.3
ECKENSTAHLER, ERIC	Eric Ryan; B12.17.1976 Waukegan IL; BL/TL/6´7˝/210; [DetA99 32/957]; d9.9; Col Illinois St.																									
2002	Det A	1	0	1.000	7	0	0	0-0	8	14	5	1	0	2-0	13	5.63	78	.378	.410	0	ø	0	—	-1	0	-0.1
2003	Det A	0	0	ø	20	0	0	0-0	15.2	9	6	0	2	15-1	12	2.87	153	.167	.366	0	ø	0	—	2	0	0.1
Total	2	1	0	1.000	27	0	0	0-0	23.2	23	11	1	2	17-1	25	3.80	115	.253	.382	0	ø	0	—	1	0	0.0
ECKERSLEY, DENNIS	Dennis Lee; B10.3.1954 Oakland CA; BR/TR/6´2˝/(175–195); [CleA72 3/50]; d4.12; HF2004																									
1975	Cle A	13	7	.650	34	24	6-2	2-1	186.2	147	61	16	7	90-8	152	2.60	146	.215	.310	0	ø	0	110	25	0	2.5
1976	Cle A	13	12	.520	36	30	9-3	1-0	199.1	155	82	13	5	78-2	200	3.43	102	.214	.293	0	ø	0	94	3	0	0.3
1977	Cle A★	14	13	.519	33	33	12-3	0-0	247.1	214	100	31	7	54-11	191	3.53	113	.231	**.276**	0	ø	0*	91	17	0	1.5
1978	Bos A	20	8	.714	35	35	16-3	0-0	268.1	258	99	30	7	71-8	162	2.99	138	.251	.302	0	ø	0	111	32	0	3.1
1979	Bos A	17	10	.630	33	33	17-2	0-0	246.2	234	89	29	6	59-4	150	2.99	**149**	.250	.297	0	ø	0	105	**39**	0	4.0
1980	Bos A	12	14	.462	30	30	8	0-0	197.2	188	101	25	2	44-7	121	4.28	100	.248	.289	0	ø	0	87	0	0	0.0
1981	Bos A	9	8	.529	23	23	8-2	0-0	154	160	82	9	3	35-2	79	4.27	92	.267	.308	0	ø	0	111	-5	0	-0.6
1982	Bos A★	13	13	.500	33	33	11-3	0-0	224.1	228	101	31	2	43-3	127	3.73	117	.261	.296	0	ø	0	79	15	0	1.5
1983	Bos A	9	13	.409	28	28	2	0-0	176.1	223	119	27	6	39-4	77	5.61	78	.303	.341	0	ø	0	78	-21	0	-2.3
1984	Bos A	4	4	.500	9	9	2	0-0	64.2	71	38	10	1	13-2	33	5.01	84	.284	.318	0	ø	0	119	-4	0	-0.4
	†Chi N	10	8	.556	24	24	2	0-0	160.1	152	59	11	4	36-7	81	3.03	129	.250	.294	55-0-1	.109	-3	99	15	0	1.3
1985	Chi N	11	7	.611	25	25	6-2	0-0	169.1	145	61	15	3	19-4	117	3.08	130	.229	.254	56-1-2	.125	0*	89	16	27	1.8
1986	Chi N	6	11	.353	33	32	1	0-0	201	226	109	21	3	43-3	137	4.57	89	.285	.320	69-2-2	.159	1	88	-10	0	-0.6
1987	Oak A	6	8	.429	54	2	0	16-4	115.2	99	41	11	3	17-3	113	3.03	137	.228	.260	0	ø	0	77	17	0	2.2
1988	†Oak A★	4	2	.667	60	0	0	**45**-8	72.2	52	20	5	1	11-2	70	2.35	162	.198	.230	0	ø	0	—	13	0	2.4
1989	†Oak A	4	0	1.000	51	0	0	33-6	57.2	32	10	5	1	3-0	55	1.56	237	.162	.175	0	ø	0	—	15	45	2.5
1990	†Oak A★	4	2	.667	63	0	0	48-2	73.1	41	9	2	0	4-1	73	0.61	609	.160	.172	0	ø	0	—	25	0	4.7
1991	Oak A★	5	4	.556	67	0	0	43-8	76	60	26	11	1	9-3	87	2.96	130	.208	.235	0	ø	0	—	8	0	1.7
1992	†Oak A★	7	1	.875	69	0	0	**51**-3	80	62	17	5	1	11-6	93	1.91	197	.211	.242	0	ø	0	—	18	0	3.8
1993	Oak A	2	4	.333	64	0	0	36-10	67	67	32	7	2	13-4	80	4.16	99	.261	.299	0	ø	0	—	0	0	0.0
1994	Oak A	5	4	.556	45	0	0	19-6	44.1	49	26	5	1	13-2	47	4.26	105	.275	.328	0	ø	0	—	0	0	-0.1
1995	Oak A	4	6	.400	52	0	0	29-9	50.1	53	29	5	1	11-0	40	4.83	94	.269	.308	0	ø	0	—	-2	0	-0.3
1996	†StL N	0	6	.000	63	0	0	30-4	60	65	26	8	4	6-2	49	3.30	129	.274	.300	1	.000	-0	—	5	25	0.9
1997	StL N	1	5	.167	57	0	0	36-7	53	49	24	9	2	8-0	45	3.91	107	.238	.273	0	ø	0	—	3	0	0.5
1998	†Bos A	4	1	.800	50	0	0	1-3	39.2	46	21	6	2	8-3	22	4.76	99	.291	.331	0	ø	0	—	1	53	0.1
Total	24	197	171	.535	1071	361	100-20	390-71	3285.2	3076	1382	347	75	738-91	2401	3.50	117	.246	.290	181-3-5	.133	-1	96	225	150	30.5
ECKERT, AL	Albert George "Obbie"; B5.17.1906 Milwaukee WI; D4.20.1974 Milwaukee WI; BL/TL/5´10˝/174; d4.21																									
1930	Cin N	0	1	.000	2	1	0	0	5	7	6	0	0	4	1	7.20	67	.304	.407	1	.000	-0	54	-2	—	-0.3
1931	Cin N	0	1	.000	14	1	0	0	18.2	26	20	3	0	9	5	9.16	41	.325	.393	3	.333	0	92	-11	—	-0.5
1935	StL N	0	0	ø	2	0	0	0	3	7	4	0	0	1	1	12.00	34	.467	.500	0	ø	0	—	-2	—	-0.1
Total	3	0	2	.000	18	2	0	0	26.2	40	30	3	0	14	7	9.11	44	.339	.409	4	.250	0	76	-15	—	-0.9
ECKERT, CHARLIE	Charles William "Buzz"; B8.8.1897 Philadelphia PA; D8.22.1986 Trevose PA; BR/TR/5´10.5˝/165; d9.18																									
1919	Phi A	0	1	.000	2	1	1	0	16	17	9	1	0	3	6	3.94	87	.270	.303	6	.167	-0	23	-1	—	-0.1
1920	Phi A	0	0	ø	2	0	0	0	5.2	8	3	0	1	1	1	4.76	84	.421	.476	1	.000	-0	—	0	—	0.0
1922	Phi A	0	2	.000	21	0	0	0	50	61	33	7	1	23	15	4.68	91	.319	.395	11	.091	-1	—	-3	—	-0.2
Total	3	0	3	.000	25	1	1	0	71.2	86	45	8	2	27	22	4.52	90	.315	.381	18	.111	-2	23	-4	—	-0.3
EDDY, CHRIS	Christopher Mark; B11.27.1969 Dallas TX; BL/TL/6´3˝/200; [KCA92 3/78]; d4.26; Col TCU																									
1995	Oak A	0	0	ø	6	0	0	0-0	3.2	7	3	0	2	2-0	2	7.36	62	.438	.550	0	ø	0	—	-1	0	0.0
EDDY, DON	Donald Eugene; B10.25.1946 Mason City IA; BR/TL/5´11˝/170; d9.7																									
1970	Chi A	0	0	ø	7	0	0	0-0	11.2	10	4	0	0	6-0	9	2.31	168	.244	.340	0	ø	0	—	2	0	0.1
1971	Chi A	0	2	.000	22	0	0	0-1	22.2	19	6	3	0	19-2	14	2.38	150	.232	.373	1	1.000	1	—	3	0	0.4
Total	2	0	2	.000	29	0	0	0-1	34.1	29	10	3	0	25-2	23	2.36	156	.236	.362	1	1.000	1	—	5	0	0.5
EDDY, STEVE	Steven Allen; B8.21.1957 Sterling IL; BR/TR/6´2˝/185; [AnaA75 19/433]; d6.13																									
1979	Cal A	1	1	.500	7	4	0	0-0	32.1	36	19	1	2	20-0	7	4.73	86	.290	.389	0	ø	0	128	-2	0	-0.1
EDELEN, JOE	Benny Joe; B9.16.1955 Durant OK; BR/TR/6´0˝/(165–180); [StLN73 1/12]; d4.18																									
1981	StL N	1	0	1.000	13	0	0	0-0	17.1	29	18	2	1	3-1	10	9.35	39	.367	.393	3	.333	0	—	-10	0	-0.5
	Cin N	1	0	1.000	5	0	0	0-0	12.2	5	1	1	0	0-0	5	0.71	493	.128	.128	2	.000	-0	—	4	0	0.3
	Year	2	0	1.000	18	0	0	0-0	30	34	19	3	1	3-1	15	5.70	63	.288	.309	5	.200	-0	—	-6	0	-0.2
1982	Cin N	0	0	ø	9	0	0	0-0	15.1	22	15	2	0	8-3	11	8.80	42	.344	.411	2	.500	0	—	-8	0	-0.4
Total	2	2	0	1.000	27	0	0	0-0	45.1	56	34	5	1	11-4	26	6.75	53	.308	.347	7	.286	0	—	-14	0	-0.6
EDELEN, ED	Edward Joseph "Doc"; B3.16.1912 Bryantown MD; D2.1.1982 LaPlata MD; BR/TR/6´0˝/191; d8.20; Col Mount St. Marys																									
1932	Was A	0	0	ø	2	0	0	0	1	0	3	0	0	6	0	27.00	16	.000	.600	0	ø	0	—	-2	—	-0.1
EDELMAN, JOHN	John Rogers; B7.27.1935 Philadelphia PA; BR/TR/6´3˝/185; d6.2; Col West Chester																									
1955	Mil N	0	0	ø	5	0	0	0	5.2	7	7	0	0	8-0	3	11.12	34	.304	.484	0	ø	0	—	-5	0	-0.2
EDEN, CHARLIE	Charles M.; B1.18.1855 Lexington KY; D9.17.1920 Cincinnati OH; BL/TL/?/168; d8.17.1877; ▲																									
1884	Pit AA	0	1	.000	2	1	1	0	12	12	9	1	1	3	3	6.00	55	.255	.314	122-1	.270	1*	91	-2	—	-0.1
1885	Pit AA	1	2	.333	4	1	0	0	15.2	22	13	0	0	3	5	5.17	62	.314	.342	405	.254	1*	92	-3	—	-0.4
Total	2	1	3	.250	6	2	1	0	27.2	34	22	1	1	6	8	5.53	59	.291	.331	527-1	.258	1	92	-5	—	-0.5

YEAR	TM LG	W	L	PCT	G	GS	CG-SHO	SV-BS	IP	H	R	HR	HB	BB-IB	SO	ERA	AERA	OAV	OOB	AB-HR-SH	AVG	PB	SUP	APR	DL	PW
EDENFIELD, KEN	Kenneth Edward; B3.18.1967 Jesup GA; BR/TR/6´1˝/(165–175); [CalA90 21/582]; d5.11; Col Western Kentucky																									
1995	Cal A	0	0	ø	7	0	0	0-0	12.2	15	7	1	0	5-0	6	4.26	111	.300	.357	0	ø	0	—	0	0	0.0
1996	Cal A	0	0	ø	2	0	0	0-0	4.1	10	5	2	1	2-0	4	10.38	49	.435	.500	0	ø	0	—	-2	0	-0.1
Total	2	0	0	ø	9	0	0	0-0	17	25	12	3	1	7-0	10	5.82	82	.342	.402	0	ø	0	—	-2	0	-0.1
EDENS, TOM	Thomas Patrick; B6.9.1961 Ontario OR; BR/TR/6´2˝/(185–190); [KCA83 14/361]; d6.2; Col Lewis–Clark St.																									
1987	NY N	0	0	ø	2	2	0	0-0	8	15	6	2	0	4-0	4	6.75	57	.417	.475	3	.000	-0	142	-2	0	-0.1
1990	Mil A	4	5	.444	35	6	0	2-0	89	89	52	8	4	33-3	40	4.45	87	.262	.331	0	ø	0	102	-6	0	-0.6
1991	Min A	2	2	.500	8	6	0	0-0	33	34	15	2	0	10-1	19	4.09	105	.256	.308	0	ø	0	107	1	0	0.2
1992	Min A	6	3	.667	52	0	0	3-2	76.1	65	26	1	2	36-3	57	2.83	144	.236	.329	0	ø	0	—	10	0	1.2
1993	Hou N	1	1	.500	38	0	0	0-1	49	47	17	4	0	19-7	21	3.12	124	.263	.332	1	.000	-0	—	5	31	0.3
1994	Hou N	4	1	.800	39	0	0	1-2	50	55	25	3	2	17-4	38	4.50	88	.289	.349	2-0-1	.000	-0	—	-2	0	-0.1
	Phi N	1	0	1.000	3	0	0	0-0	4	4	1	0	0	1-0	1	2.25	190	.267	.313	0	ø	0	—	1	0	0.2
	Year	5	1	.833	42	0	0	1-2	54	59	26	3	2	18-4	39	4.33	92	.288	.346	2-0-1	.000	-0	—	-1	0	0.1
1995	Chi N	1	0	1.000	5	0	0	0-0	3	6	3	0	0	3-0	2	6.00	70	.400	.500	0	ø	0	—	-1	0	-0.2
Total	7	19	12	.613	182	14	0	6-5	312.1	315	145	20	8	123-18	182	3.86	103	.266	.337	6-0-1	.000	-1	111	6	31	0.9
EDGE, BUTCH	Claude Lee; B7.18.1956 Houston TX; BR/TR/6´3˝/202; [MilA74 1/6]; d8.13																									
1979	Tor A	3	4	.429	9	9	1	0-0	51.2	60	32	6	1	24-1	19	5.23	84	.283	.357	0	ø	0	85	-4	0	-0.5
EDGERTON, BILL	William Albert; B8.16.1941 South Bend IN; BL/TL/6´2˝/185; d9.3																									
1966	KC A	0	1	.000	6	1	0	0	8.1	10	3	0	0	7-2	3	3.24	105	.303	.425	0-0-1	ø	0	26	0	0	0.1
1967	KC A	1	0	1.000	7	0	0	0	8.1	11	4	1	1	3-0	6	2.16	147	.324	.395	0	ø	0	—	0	0	0.0
1969	Sea A	0	1	.000	4	0	0	0-0	4	10	7	1	1	0-0	2	13.50	27	.455	.478	0	ø	0	—	-4	0	-0.8
Total	3	1	2	.333	17	1	0	0-0	20.2	31	14	2	2	10-2	11	4.79	70	.348	.426	0-0-1	ø	0	26	-4	0	-0.7
EDMONDSON, BRIAN	Brian Christopher; B1.29.1973 Fontana CA; BR/TR/6´2˝/175; [DetA91 3/78]; d4.2; [DL 2000 Fla N 181]																									
1998	Atl N	0	1	.000	10	0	0	0-1	16.2	14	10	2	0	8-1	8	4.32	96	.215	.301	2	.000	-0	—	-1	0	0.0
	Fla N	4	3	.571	43	0	0	0-2	59.1	62	28	8	3	29-4	32	3.79	107	.281	.367	10-0-1	.000	-1	—	2	0	0.0
	Year	4	4	.500	53	0	0	0-3	76	76	38	10	3	37-5	40	3.91	104	.266	.353	12-0-1	.000	-1	—	0	0	0.0
1999	Fla N	5	8	.385	68	0	0	1-5	94	106	65	11	6	44-5	58	5.84	75	.290	.370	11	.364	2	—	-15	0	-1.6
Total	2	9	12	.429	121	0	0	1-8	170	182	103	21	9	81-10	98	4.98	85	.280	.362	23-0-1	.174	0	—	-14	181	-1.6
EDMONDSON, GEORGE	George Henderson "Big Ed"; B5.18.1896 Waxahachie TX; D7.11.1973 Waco TX; BR/TR/6´1˝/179; d8.15																									
1922	Cle A	0	0	ø	2	0	0	0	2	4	2	0	0	0	0	9.00	45	.444	.444	0	ø	0	—	-1	—	0.0
1923	Cle A	0	0	ø	1	0	0	0	4	8	5	0	1	3	0	11.25	35	.444	.545	1	.000	-0	—	-3	—	-0.1
1924	Cle A	0	0	ø	5	1	0	0	8	10	8	1	0	5	3	9.00	47	.294	.385	3	.333	0	178	-3	—	-0.2
Total	3	0	0	ø	8	1	0	0	14	22	15	1	1	8	3	9.64	43	.361	.443	4	.250	-0	178	-7	—	-0.3
EDMONDSON, PAUL	Paul Michael; B2.12.1943 Kansas City KS; D2.13.1970 Santa Barbara CA; BR/TR/6´5˝/195; [ChiA65 12/421]; d6.20; Col Cal St.–Northridge																									
1969	Chi A	1	6	.143	14	13	1	0-1	87.2	72	36	5	4	39-4	46	3.70	104	.227	.316	29-0-1	.172	-1	62	3	0	0.3
EDMONDSON, BOB	Robert E.; B4.30.1879 Paris KY; D8.14.1931 Lawrence KS; BR/TR/5´11˝/185; d9.15; ▲																									
1906	Was A	0	1	.000	2	1	1	0	10	10	8	0	0	2	0	4.50	59	.263	.300	3	.333	0*	27	-3	—	-0.2
EDMONSTON, SAM	Samuel Sherwood "Big Sam"; B8.30.1883 Washington DC; D4.12.1979 Corpus Christi TX; BL/TL/5´11.5˝/185; d6.24; Col Georgetown																									
1907	Was A	0	0	ø	1	0	0	0	3	8	3	0	0	1	0	9.00	27	.500	.529	2	.000	-0	—	-2	—	-0.1
EDWARDS	; d9.11																									
1875	Atl NA	0	1	.000	1	1	0	0	2	4	6	0	—	0	0	4.50	46	.308	.308	5	.200	-0	102	-1	—	-0.2
EDWARDS, FOSTER	Foster Hamilton "Eddie"; B9.1.1903 Holstein IA; D1.4.1980 Orleans MA; BR/TR/6´3˝/175; d7.2; Col Dartmouth																									
1925	Bos N	0	0	ø	1	0	0	0	2	6	5	0	0	1	1	9.00	45	.545	.583	0	ø	0	—	-2	—	-0.1
1926	Bos N	2	0	1.000	3	3	1	0	25	20	4	0	0	13	4	0.72	492	.230	.330	9	.000	-2	55	8	—	0.4
1927	Bos N	2	8	.200	29	11	1	0	92	95	59	2	3	45	37	4.99	74	.274	.362	22-0-4	.045	-2*	85	-13	—	-1.5
1928	Bos N	2	1	.667	21	3	2	0	49.1	67	36	2	2	23	17	5.66	69	.327	.400	11-0-2	.091	-1	108	-9	—	-0.6
1930	NY A	0	0	ø	2	0	0	0	1.2	5	4	0	0	2	1	21.60	20	.500	.583	0	ø	0	—	-3	—	-0.1
Total	5	6	9	.400	56	17	4	0	170	193	108	4	5	84	60	4.76	79	.292	.377	42-0-6	.048	-5	84	-19	—	-1.9
EDWARDS, JIM JOE	James Corbette "Little Joe"; B12.14.1894 Banner MS; D1.19.1965 Sarepta MS; BR/TL/6´2˝/185; d5.14; Col Mississippi College																									
1922	Cle A	3	8	.273	25	7	0	0	92.2	113	56	1	5	40	44	4.47	90	.313	.389	23	.087	-2	58	-6	—	-0.9
1923	Cle A	10	10	.500	38	21	7-1	1	179.1	200	101	5	5	75	68	3.71	107	.286	.359	59-0-2	.119	-5	110	1	—	-0.4
1924	Cle A	4	3	.571	10	7	5-1	0	57	64	29	3	0	34	15	2.84	150	.305	.402	20-0-2	.150	-1	82	6	—	0.5
1925	Cle A	0	3	.000	13	3	1	0	36	60	44	0	1	23	12	8.25	54	.382	.464	9	.111	-1	101	-17	—	-1.2
	Chi A	1	2	.333	9	4	1-1	0	45.1	46	25	4	1	23	20	3.97	105	.263	.352	17	.176	-1	101	0	—	0.0
	Year	1	5	.167	22	7	2-1	0	81.1	106	69	4	2	46	32	5.86	73	.319	.405	26	.154	-2	101	-16	—	-1.2
1926	Chi A	6	9	.400	32	16	8-3	1	142	140	76	4	1	63	41	4.18	92	.264	.343	46-0-3	.109	-3	94	-5	—	-0.9
1928	Cin N	2	2	.500	18	1	0	2	32	43	29	1	0	20	11	7.59	52	.347	.438	10	.300	0	43	-12	—	-1.4
Total	6	26	37	.413	145	59	22-6	4	584.1	666	360	18	13	278	211	4.37	92	.295	.376	184-0-7	.130	-13	94	-33	—	-4.3
EDWARDS, SHERMAN	Sherman Stanley; B7.25.1909 Mt.Ida AR; D3.8.1992 ElDorado AR; BR/TR/6´0˝/165; d9.21																									
1934	Cin N	0	0	ø	1	0	0	0	3	4	1	0	0	1	1	3.00	136	.333	.385	1	.000	-0	—	0	—	0.0
EDWARDS, WAYNE	Wayne Maurice; B3.7.1964 Burbank CA; BL/TL/6´5˝/185; [ChiA85 10/241]; d9.11; Col Azusa Pacific																									
1989	Chi A	0	0	ø	7	0	0	0-0	7.1	7	3	1	0	3-0	9	3.68	104	.269	.333	0	ø	0	—	0	0	0.0
1990	Chi A	5	3	.625	42	5	0	2-0	95	81	39	6	3	41-2	63	3.22	119	.234	.319	0	ø	0	85	6	0	0.5
1991	Chi A	0	2	.000	13	0	0	0-0	23.1	22	14	2	0	17-3	12	3.86	104	.259	.375	0	ø	0	—	-1	0	-0.1
Total	3	5	5	.500	62	5	0	2-0	125.2	110	56	9	3	61-5	84	3.37	115	.241	.331	0	ø	0	85	5	0	0.4
EELLS, HARRY	Harry Archibald "Slippery"; B2.14.1880 Danbury IA; D12.7.1940 Los Angeles CA; BR/TR/6´1˝/195; d4.22																									
1906	Cle A	4	5	.444	14	8	6-1	0	86.1	77	39	1	3	48	35	2.61	100	.242	.347	32	.188	1	124	-1	—	0.0
EGAN, WISH	Aloysius Jerome; B6.16.1881 Evart MI; D4.13.1951 Detroit MI; BR/TR/6´3˝/185; d9.3																									
1902	Det A	0	2	.000	3	3	2	0	22	23	12	0	0	6	0	2.86	127	.271	.319	8	.250	-0	92	1	—	0.1
1905	StL N	6	15	.286	23	19	18	0	171.1	189	93	2	9	39	29	3.57	83	.285	.333	59-0-2	.102	-3	74	-12	—	-1.4
1906	StL N	2	9	.182	16	12	7	0	86.1	97	45	2	2	27	23	4.59	57	.278	.333	29-0-1	.069	-2	76	-14	—	-1.8
Total	3	8	26	.235	42	34	27	0	279.2	309	150	4	11	72	52	3.83	76	.282	.332	96-0-3	.104	-5	76	-25	—	-3.1
EGAN, JIM	James K. "Troy Terrier"; B1858 Derby CT; D9.26.1884 New Haven CT; TL; d5.15; ▲																									
1882	Tro N	4	6	.400	12	10	10	0	100	133	79	2	—	24	20	4.14	68	.315	.352	115	.200	-2*	116	-12	—	-1.1
EGAN, RIP	John Joseph; B7.9.1871 Philadelphia PA; D12.22.1950 Cranston RI; TR/5´11˝/168; d4.30; U9																									
1894	Was N	0	0	ø	1	0	0	0	5	8	6	1	0	2	2	10.80	49	.364	.417	3	.000	-0	—	-2	—	-0.1
EGAN, DICK	Richard Wallis; B3.24.1937 Berkeley CA; BL/TL/6´4˝/(193–195); d4.9; C2; Col Diablo Valley (CA) JC																									
1963	Det A	0	1	.000	20	0	0	0	21	25	12	4	0	3-0	16	5.14	73	.287	.311	0	ø	0	—	-3	0	-0.1
1964	Det A	0	0	ø	23	0	0	2	34.1	33	22	4	1	17-1	21	4.46	82	.246	.333	3	.000	-0	—	-5	0	-0.2
1966	Cal A	0	0	ø	11	0	0	0	14.1	17	7	2	0	6-2	11	4.40	76	.309	.365	1	.000	-0	—	-1	0	-0.1
1967	LA N	1	1	.500	20	0	0	0	31.2	34	25	3	4	15-4	20	6.25	50	.272	.368	1	.000	-0	—	-12	0	-0.8
Total	4	1	2	.333	74	0	0	2	101.1	109	66	13	5	41-7	68	5.15	67	.272	.344	5	.000	-1	—	-21	0	-1.2
EGLOFF, BRUCE	Bruce Edward; B4.10.1965 Denver CO; BR/TR/6´2˝/215; [CleA86 5/109]; d4.13; Col California–Santa Barbara; [DL 1992 Cle A 136]																									
1991	Cle A	0	0	ø	6	0	0	0-0	5.2	8	3	0	0	4-1	8	4.76	88	.333	.429	0	ø	0	—	0	0	0.0

YEAR	TM LG	W	L	PCT	G	GS	CG-SHO	SV-BS	IP	H	R	HR	HB	BB-IB	SO	ERA	AERA	OAV	OOB	AB-HR-SH	AVG	PB	SUP	APR	DL	PW
Ehmke, Howard	Howard Jonathan "Bob"; B4.24.1894 Silver Creek NY; D3.17.1959 Philadelphia PA; BR/TR/6´3˝/190; d4.12; Mil 1918																									
1915	Buf F	0	2	.000	18	2	0	0	53.2	69	46	2	5	25	18	5.53	51	.325	.409	12	.000	-2	100	-18	—	-1.1
1916	Det A	3	1	.750	5	4	4	0	37.1	34	16	0	0	15	15	3.13	91	.252	.327	14	.143	-1	152	-1	—	-0.1
1917	Det A	10	15	.400	35	25	13-4	2	206	174	84	3	5	88	90	2.97	89	.243	.330	69-0-1	.246	2	104	-2	—	0.1
1919	Det A	17	10	.630	33	31	20-2	0	248.2	255	114	5	6	107	79	3.18	100	.274	.353	91-0-3	.253	3	109	-1	—	0.4
1920	Det A	15	18	.455	38	33	23-2	3	268.1	250	132	8	13	124	98	3.25	115	.253	.344	105-0-2	.238	2	83	13	—	2.0
1921	Det A	13	14	.481	30	22	13-1	0	196.1	220	123	15	13	81	68	4.54	94	.286	.364	74-0-4	.284	2	114	-5	—	-0.4
1922	Det A	17	17	.500	45	29	16-1	1	279.2	299	146	12	23	101	108	4.22	92	.281	.356	102-0-4	.157	-4	95	-6	—	-1.0
1923	Bos A	20	17	.541	43	39	28-2	3	316.2	318	155	12	20	119	121	3.78	109	.272	.349	112-0-6	.223	-2	89	16	—	1.9
1924	Bos A	19	17	.528	45	36	26-4	4	**315**	324	139	9	11	81	119	3.46	126	.265	.316	126-0-4	.222	-2*	94	33	—	3.4
1925	Bos A	9	20	.310	34	31	**22**	1	260.2	285	141	8	11	85	95	3.73	122	.285	.348	88-0-6	.148	-5	61	21	—	1.7
1926	Bos A	3	10	.231	14	14	7-1	0	97.1	115	69	3	4	45	38	5.46	75	.303	.382	34-0-1	.147	-1	103	-15	—	-1.7
	Phi A	12	4	.750	20	18	10-1	0	147.1	125	54	1	4	50	55	2.81	148	.232	.302	46-0-9	.152	-2*	92	23	—	2.1
	Year	15	14	.517	34	32	17-2	0	244.2	240	123	4	8	95	93	3.86	107	.261	.336	80-0-10	.150	-3	97	7	—	0.4
1927	Phi A	12	10	.545	30	27	10-1	0	189.2	200	103	13	14	60	68	4.22	101	.281	.349	68-0-3	.206	-1	93	2	—	0.2
1928	Phi A	9	8	.529	23	18	5-1	0	139.1	135	65	6	4	44	34	3.62	111	.254	.316	46-0-10	.239	1	109	7	—	0.9
1929	†Phi A	7	2	.778	11	8	2	0	54.2	48	24	2	1	15	20	3.29	129	.233	.288	19	.105	-2	100	6	—	0.6
1930	Phi A	0	1	.000	3	1	0	0	10	22	13	4	3	2	4	11.70	40	.458	.509	3	.333	0	18	-7	—	-0.5
Total	15	166	166	.500	427	338	199-20	14	2820.2	2873	1424	103	137	1042	1030	3.75	104	.271	.343	1009-0-53	.208	-10	94	66	—	8.5
Ehret, Red	Philip Sydney; B8.31.1868 Louisville KY; D7.28.1940 Cincinnati OH; BR/TR/6´0˝/175; d7.7; ▲																									
1888	KC AA	3	2	.600	7	6	5	0	52	58	30	1	3	22	12	3.98	85	.272	.349	63	.190	-1*	137	-1	—	-0.1
1889	Lou AA	10	29	.256	45	38	35-1	0	364	441	287	11	18	115	135	4.80	80	.290	.347	258-1	.252	2*	73	-28	—	-2.0
1890	†Lou AA	25	14	.641	43	38	35-4	2	359	351	182	5	17	79	174	2.53	152	.248	.296	146	.212	-3	99	50	—	4.1
1891	Lou AA	13	13	.500	26	24	23-2	0	220.2	225	150	2	11	70	76	3.47	105	.255	.318	91	.242	1	100	-2	—	-0.1
1892	Pit N	16	20	.444	39	36	32	0	316	290	183	7	22	83	101	2.65	124	.234	.294	132	.258	3*	94	16	—	1.6
1893	Pit N	18	18	.500	39	35	32-**4**	0	314.1	322	203	3	23	115	70	3.44	132	.257	.331	136-1	.176	-6*	95	29	—	2.1
1894	Pit N	19	21	.475	46	38	31-1	0	346.2	441	269	12	10	128	102	5.14	102	.306	.367	135-0-10	.170	-11	87	3	—	-0.7
1895	StL N	6	19	.240	37	32	18	0	231.2	360	223	11	10	88	55	6.02	80	.349	.405	96-1-3	.219	-3	98	-32	—	-2.7
1896	Cin N	18	14	.563	34	33	29-2	0	276.2	298	147	5	9	74	60	3.42	135	.273	.324	102-1-5	.196	-3	91	34	—	2.8
1897	Cin N	8	10	.444	34	19	11	2	184.1	256	135	3	13	47	43	4.78	95	.326	.374	66-0-2	.197	-3	84	-6	—	-0.7
1898	Lou N	3	7	.300	12	10	9	0	89	130	72	3	3	20	20	5.76	62	.338	.375	40	.225	1*	89	-20	—	-1.8
Total	11	139	167	.454	362	309	260-14	4	2754.1	3172	1881	63	139	841	848	4.02	105	.282	.339	1265-4-20	.217	-22	92	43	—	2.5
Ehrhardt, Rube	Welton Claude; B11.20.1894 Beecher IL; D4.27.1980 Chicago Heights IL; BR/TR/6´2˝/190; d7.18																									
1924	Bro N	5	3	.625	15	9	6-2	0	83.2	71	27	5	1	17	13	2.26	166	.232	.275	29-0-1	.138	-2	103	14	—	0.9
1925	Bro N	10	14	.417	36	25	12	1	207.2	239	134	10	3	62	47	5.03	83	.293	.345	71-1-2	.211	2	113	-17	—	-1.3
1926	Bro N	2	5	.286	44	1	0	4	97	101	52	5	0	35	25	3.90	98	.275	.338	24-0-2	.250	0	109	-1	—	-0.1
1927	Bro N	3	7	.300	46	3	2	2	95.2	90	46	3	3	37	22	3.57	111	.264	.341	24	.250	1	86	4	—	0.6
1928	Bro N	1	3	.250	28	2	1	2	54	74	36	1	1	27	12	4.67	85	.352	.429	14	.286	0	64	-4	—	-0.2
1929	Cin N	1	2	.333	24	1	1-1	1	49.1	58	29	2	1	22	9	4.74	96	.305	.380	11	.182	-0	172	-1	—	-0.1
Total	6	22	34	.393	193	41	22-3	10	587.1	633	324	26	9	200	128	4.15	97	.284	.345	173-1-5	.214	1	109	-5	—	-0.2
Eibel, Hack	Henry Hack; B12.6.1893 Brooklyn NY; D10.16.1945 Macon GA; BL/TL/5´11˝/220; d6.13.1912; ▲																									
1920	Bos A	0	0	ø	3	0	0	0	10.1	10	4	0	0	3	5	3.48	105	.270	.325	43-0-1	.186	-0*	—	0	—	0.0
Eichelberger, Juan	Juan Tyrone; B10.21.1953 St.Louis MO; BR/TR/6´3˝/(195–205); [SDN75*S1/19]; d9.7; Col California																									
1978	SD N	0	0	ø	3	0	0	0-0	3.1	4	4	0	0	2-0	2	10.80	31	.267	.353	0	ø	0	—	-3	0	-0.1
1979	SD N	1	1	.500	3	3	1	0-0	21	15	10	1	0	11-1	12	3.43	103	.211	.313	5-0-1	.400	1	75	0	0	0.1
1980	SD N	4	2	.667	15	13	0	0-0	88.2	73	41	8	1	55-4	43	3.65	94	.233	.348	27-0-4	.111	-1	133	-3	21	-0.3
1981	SD N	8	8	.500	25	24	3-1	0-0	141.1	136	60	5	3	74-5	81	3.50	93	.259	.351	46-0-6	.087	-3	104	-4	0	-0.7
1982	SD N	7	14	.333	31	24	8	0-0	177.2	171	98	23	2	72-5	74	4.20	82	.251	.321	55-0-5	.091	-2	103	-18	21	-2.1
1983	Cle A	4	11	.267	28	15	2	0-1	134	132	80	10	2	59-3	56	4.90	87	.259	.336	0	ø	0	85	-9	0	-0.9
1988	Atl N	2	0	1.000	20	0	0	0-0	37.1	44	19	3	0	10-2	13	3.86	95	.297	.333	3	.000	-0	—	-1	0	0.0
Total	7	26	36	.419	125	79	14-1	0-1	603.1	575	312	50	8	283-20	281	4.10	87	.254	.336	136-0-16	.103	-4	102	-38	42	-4.0
Eichhorn, Mark	Mark Anthony; B11.21.1960 San Jose CA; BR/TR/6´3˝/(185–210); [TorA79*2/30]; d8.30; Col Cabrillo (CA) JC; [DL 1995 Bal A 160]																									
1982	Tor A	0	3	.000	7	7	0	0-0	38	40	28	4	0	14-1	16	5.45	83	.260	.318	0	ø	0	78	-5	0	-0.4
1986	Tor A	14	6	.700	69	0	0	10-3	157	105	32	8	7	45-14	166	1.72	247	.191	.260	0	ø	0	—	**44**	15	**5.8**
1987	Tor A	10	6	.625	**89**	0	0	4-2	127.2	110	47	14	6	52-13	96	3.17	143	.234	.315	0	ø	0	—	20	0	2.4
1988	Tor A	0	3	.000	37	0	0	1-0	66.2	79	32	3	6	27-4	28	4.18	95	.304	.381	0	ø	0	—	-1	0	0.0
1989	Atl N	5	5	.500	45	0	0	0-2	68.1	70	36	6	1	19-8	49	4.35	84	.275	.323	2-0-1	.000	-0	—	-4	0	-0.5
1990	Cal A	2	5	.286	60	0	0	13-3	84.2	98	36	2	6	23-0	69	3.08	125	.289	.341	0	ø	0	—	6	0	0.7
1991	Cal A	3	3	.500	70	0	0	1-3	81.2	63	21	2	2	13-1	49	1.98	208	.219	.255	0	ø	0	—	19	0	1.4
1992	Cal A	2	4	.333	42	0	0	2-4	56.2	51	19	2	0	18-8	42	2.38	169	.238	.294	0	ø	0	—	9	0	1.0
	†Tor A	2	0	1.000	23	0	0	0-0	31	35	15	1	2	7-0	19	4.35	94	.285	.328	0	ø	0	—	0	0	0.0
	Year	4	4	.500	65	0	0	2-4	87.2	86	34	3	2	25-8	61	3.08	132	.255	.306	0	ø	0	—	9	0	1.0
1993	†Tor A	3	1	.750	54	0	0	0-2	72.2	76	26	3	3	22-7	47	2.72	161	.272	.330	0	ø	0	—	12	0	0.7
1994	Bal A	6	5	.545	43	0	0	1-4	71	62	19	1	5	19-4	35	2.15	235	.240	.301	0	ø	0	—	**21**	0	3.0
1996	Cal A	1	2	.333	24	0	0	0-2	30.1	36	17	3	2	11-3	24	5.04	100	.308	.371	0	ø	0	—	1	103	0.1
Total	11	48	43	.527	563	7	0	32-25	885.2	825	328	49	40	270-63	640	3.00	142	.249	.311	2-0-1	.000	-0	78	122	278	14.2
Eiland, Dave	David William; B7.5.1966 Dade City FL; BR/TR/6´3˝/(205–210); [NYA87 7/185]; d8.3; Col South Florida																									
1988	NY A	0	0	ø	3	3	0	0-0	12.2	15	9	6	2	4-0	7	6.39	62	.294	.368	0	ø	0	161	-3	0	-0.1
1989	NY A	1	3	.250	6	6	0	0-0	34.1	44	25	5	2	13-3	11	5.77	67	.328	.391	0	ø	0	105	-7	0	-0.8
1990	NY A	2	1	.667	5	5	0	0-0	30.1	31	14	2	0	5-0	16	3.56	112	.254	.283	0	ø	0	146	1	0	0.1
1991	NY A	2	5	.286	18	13	0	0-0	72.2	87	51	10	3	23-1	18	5.33	78	.302	.356	0	ø	0	73	-11	45	-1.0
1992	SD N	0	2	.000	7	7	0	0-0	27	33	21	1	0	5-0	10	5.67	63	.287	.317	9-1-1	.111	1	101	-7	105	-0.4
1993	SD N	0	3	.000	10	9	0	0-0	48.1	58	33	5	1	17-1	14	5.21	79	.297	.353	12-0-3	.083	-1	94	-6	0	-0.4
1995	NY A	1	1	.500	4	1	0	0-0	10	16	10	1	1	3-1	6	6.30	73	.348	.392	0	ø	0	161	-3	0	-0.5
1998	TB A	0	1	.000	1	1	0	0-0	2.2	6	6	0	0	3-0	1	20.25	24	.429	.529	0	ø	0	19	-4	0	-0.6
1999	TB A	4	8	.333	21	15	0	0-1	80.1	98	59	8	3	27-1	53	5.60	89	.294	.349	1-0-1	.000	-0	85	-7	30	-0.8
2000	TB A	2	3	.400	17	10	0	0-0	54.2	77	46	8	4	18-0	17	7.24	68	.326	.381	0	ø	0	82	-13	76	-0.9
Total	10	12	27	.308	92	70	0	0-1	373	465	274	46	16	118-7	153	5.74	76	.303	.356	22-1-5	.091	-0	93	-60	256	-5.4
Eilers, Dave	David Louis; B12.3.1936 Oldenburg TX; BR/TR/5´11˝/(180–190); d7.27																									
1964	Mil N	0	0	ø	6	0	0	0	7.2	11	5	1	1	1-1	1	4.70	75	.333	.351	0	ø	0	—	-1	0	-0.1
1965	Mil N	0	0	ø	6	0	0	0	3.2	8	5	1	0	0-0	1	12.27	29	.421	.421	0	ø	0	—	-3	0	-0.2
	NY N	1	1	.500	11	0	0	2	18	20	11	2	2	4-3	9	4.00	88	.274	.325	1	1.000	0	—	-2	0	-0.2
	Year	1	1	.500	17	0	0	2	21.2	28	16	3	2	4-3	10	5.40	65	.304	.343	1	1.000	0	—	-5	0	-0.4
1966	NY N	1	1	.500	23	0	0	0	34.2	39	18	7	1	7-2	14	4.67	78	.287	.326	1	.000	-0	—	-3	0	-0.1
1967	Hou N	6	4	.600	35	0	0	1	59.1	68	29	3	3	17-7	27	3.94	84	.296	.349	7-0-2	.000	-1	—	-4	0	-0.7
Total	4	8	6	.571	81	0	0	3	123.1	146	68	14	7	29-13	52	4.45	78	.297	.342	9-0-2	.111	-0	—	-13	0	-1.3
Einertson, Darrell	Darrell Lee; B9.4.1972 Rhinelander WI; BR/TR/6´2˝/190; [NYA95 11/310]; d4.15; Col Iowa Wesleyan; [DL 1999 NY A 104, 2001 NY A 190]																									
2000	NY A	0	0	ø	11	0	0	0-0	12.2	16	9	1	0	4-0	3	3.55	134	.302	.345	0	ø	0	—	0	26	0.0
Eischen, Joey	Joseph Raymond; B5.25.1970 West Covina CA; BL/TL/6´1˝/(190–215); [TexA89 4/92]; d6.19; Col Pasadena (CA) City																									
1994	Mon N	0	0	ø	1	0	0	0-0	0.2	4	4	0	1	0-0	1	54.00	8	.667	.714	0	ø	0	—	-3	0	-0.2
1995	LA N	0	0	ø	17	0	0	0-0	20.1	19	9	1	2	11-1	15	3.10	125	.232	.337	1	.000	-0	—	1	0	0.1
1996	LA N	0	1	.000	28	0	0	0-0	43.1	48	25	4	4	20-4	36	4.78	82	.282	.369	6	.000	-1	—	-4	0	-0.3
	Det A	1	1	.500	24	0	0	0-2	25	27	11	3	0	14-3	15	3.24	157	.284	.373	0	ø	0	—	5	0	0.3
1997	Cin N	0	0	ø	1	0	0	0-0	1.1	2	2	0	0	1-0	2	6.75	63	.333	.429	1	.000	-0	—	-1	105	0.0
2001	Mon N	0	1	.000	24	0	0	0-2	29.2	29	17	4	1	16-1	19	4.85	89	.257	.354	0	ø	0	—	-2	0	-0.1
2002	Mon N	6	1	.857	59	0	0	2-1	53.2	43	11	1	2	18-5	51	1.34	326	.224	.294	8	.125	0	—	16	0	2.1

YEAR	TM LG	W	L	PCT	G	GS	CG-SHO	SV-BS	IP	H	R	HR	HB	BB-IB	SO	ERA	AERA	OAV	OOB	AB-HR-SH	AVG	PB	SUP	APR	DL	PW
2003	Mon N	2	2	.500	70	0	0	1-3	53	57	27	7	3	13-1	40	3.06	145	.282	.335	4	.250	0*	—	5	0	0.4
2004	Mon N	0	1	.000	21	0	0	0-1	18.1	16	10	2	1	8-2	17	3.93	117	.232	.316	3-0-1	.667	1*	—	1	120	0.1
2005	Was N	2	1	.667	57	0	0	0-1	36.1	34	14	1	6	19-7	30	3.22	128	.252	.364	3-0-1	.333	0*	—	4	60	0.3
2006	Was N	0	1	.000	22	0	0	0-1	14.2	18	18	2	1	19-5	18	8.59	51	.295	.458	2-0-1	.000	-0	—	-8	124	-0.5
Total	10	11	9	.550	324	0	0	3-11	296.1	297	148	25	21	139-29	244	3.67	118	.263	.352	28-0-3	.179	0	—	14	409	2.2
Eisenhart, Jake	Jacob Henry; B10.3.1922 Perkasie PA; D12.20.1987 Huntingdon PA; BL/TL/6´3.5˝/195; d6.10; Col Juniata																									
1944	Cin N	0	0	ø	1	0	0	0	0.1	0	0	0	0	1	0	0.00	ø	.000	.500	0	ø	0	—	0	0	0.0
Eisenstat, Harry	Harry; B10.10.1915 Brooklyn NY; D3.21.2003 Beachwood OH; BL/TL/5´11˝/185; d5.19; Mil 1943–46																									
1935	Bro N	0	1	.000	2	0	0	0	4.2	9	8	0	0	2	2	13.50	29	.429	.478	1	.000	-0	—	-5	—	-0.7
1936	Bro N	1	2	.333	5	2	1	0	14.1	22	17	1	0	6	5	5.65	73	.344	.400	3	.333	0	72	-5	—	-0.8
1937	Bro N	3	3	.500	13	5	0	0	47.2	61	28	2	1	11	12	3.97	102	.308	.348	11-0-1	.000	-1	68	0	—	-0.1
1938	Det A	9	6	.600	32	9	5	4	125.1	131	60	7	1	29	37	3.73	134	.266	.308	36-0-5	.139	-1	78	16	—	1.6
1939	Det A	2	2	.500	10	2	1	0	29.2	39	24	3	0	9	6	6.98	70	.315	.361	8-0-1	.375	1	162	-5	—	-0.5
	Cle A	6	7	.462	26	11	4-1	2	103.2	109	45	8	0	23	38	3.30	133	.265	.304	32-0-2	.250	1	80	12	—	1.4
	Year	8	9	.471	36	13	5-1	2	133.1	148	69	11	0	32	44	4.12	110	.277	.317	40-0-3	.275	1	93	6	—	0.9
1940	Cle A	1	4	.200	27	3	0	4	71.2	78	25	6	0	12	27	3.14	134	.282	.311	22	.273	1	76	**11**	—	0.8
1941	Cle A	1	1	.500	21	0	0	2	34	43	16	2	2	16	11	4.24	93	.312	.391	6	.333	1	—	0	0	0.0
1942	Cle A	2	1	.667	29	1	0	2	47.2	58	19	1	0	6	19	2.45	140	.304	.325	4	.250	0	25	4	0	0.3
Total	8	25	27	.481	165	33	11-1	14	478.2	550	242	30	4	114	157	3.84	114	.287	.328	123-0-9	.211	1	83	28	0	2.0
Eiteljorge, Ed	Edward Henry; B10.14.1871 Berlin, Germany; D12.5.1942 Greencastle IN; BR/TR/6´2˝/190; d5.2; Col DePauw																									
1890	Chi N	0	1	.000	1	1	0	0	2	5	7	0	0	1	1	22.50	16	.455	.500	1	.000	-0	155	-4	—	-0.5
1891	Was AA	1	5	.167	8	7	6	0	61.1	79	67	3	9	41	23	6.16	61	.303	.415	26	.192	-1	86	-15	—	-1.1
Total	2	1	6	.143	9	8	6	0	63.1	84	74	3	9	42	24	6.68	56	.309	.418	27	.185	-1	94	-19	—	-1.6
Elarton, Scott	Vincent Scott; B2.23.1976 Lamar CO; BR/TR/6´7˝/(240–260); [HouN94 1/25]; d6.20; [DL 2002 Col N 183]																									
1998	†Hou N	2	1	.667	28	2	0	2-1	57	40	21	5	1	20-0	56	3.32	122	.196	.270	7-0-3	.000	-1	159	6	0	0.2
1999	†Hou N	9	5	.643	42	15	0	1-3	124	111	55	8	4	43-0	121	3.48	127	.238	.306	26-0-7	.192	0*	108	12	0	1.1
2000	Hou N	17	7	.708	30	30	2	0-0	192.2	198	117	29	6	84-1	131	4.81	102	.263	.339	63-0-6	.159	-0	126	0	19	-0.1
2001	Hou N	4	8	.333	20	20	0	0-0	109.2	126	88	26	6	49-1	76	7.14	64	.290	.368	30-0-5	.067	-1	124	-27	14	-2.5
	Col N	0	2	.000	4	4	0	0-0	23	20	17	8	0	10-1	11	6.65	80	.233	.313	8	.125	-0	65	-2	35	-0.2
	Year	4	10	.286	24	24	0	0-0	132.2	146	105	34	6	59-2	87	7.06	67	.280	.359	38-0-5	.079	-1	112	-28	0	-2.7
2003	Col N	4	4	.500	11	10	0	0-0	51.2	73	46	13	4	20-3	20	6.27	78	.329	.388	14-0-1	.071	-1	117	-10	31	-1.3
2004	Col N	0	6	.000	8	8	0	0-0	41.1	57	45	8	0	20-1	23	9.80	49	.328	.391	9-0-4	.222	0	100	-20	0	-2.2
	Cle A	3	5	.375	21	21	1-1	0-0	117.1	107	62	25	4	42-2	80	4.53	96	.240	.309	3	.333	0	94	-1	0	-0.1
2005	Cle A	11	9	.550	31	31	1	0-0	181.2	189	100	32	6	48-1	103	4.61	90	.267	.315	2	.000	-0	103	-8	0	-0.9
2006	KC A	4	9	.308	20	20	0	0-0	114.2	117	73	26	6	52-1	49	5.34	88	.267	.351	3-0-1	.333	1	87	-8	77	-0.7
Total	8	54	56	.491	215	161	4-1	3-4	1013	1038	624	180	37	388-11	670	5.13	89	.264	.333	165-0-27	.139	-2	108	-58	359	-6.7
Elder, Dave	David Matthew; B9.23.1975 Atlanta GA; BR/TR/6´0˝/180; [TexA97 4/137]; d7.24; Col Georgia Tech																									
2002	Cle A	0	2	.000	15	0	0	0-0	23	18	10	1	1	14-3	23	3.13	142	.220	.333	0	ø	0	—	3	0	0.2
2003	Cle A	1	1	.500	4	0	0	0-1	2.1	5	5	2	0	4-0	3	19.29	23	.417	.563	0	ø	0	—	-4	140	-0.6
Total	2	1	3	.250	19	0	0	0-1	25.1	23	15	3	1	18-3	26	4.62	96	.245	.365	0	ø	0	—	-1	140	-0.4
Elder, Heinie	Henry Knox; B8.23.1890 Seattle WA; D11.13.1958 Long Beach CA; BL/TL/6´2˝/200; d7.7; Col Minnesota																									
1913	Det A	0	0	ø	1	0	0	0	3.1	4	3	0	0	5	0	8.10	36	.286	.474	1	.000	-0	—	-1	—	-0.1
Eldred, Cal	Calvin John; B11.24.1967 Cedar Rapids IA; BR/TR/6´4˝/(215–240); [MilA89 1/17]; d9.24; Col Iowa																									
1991	Mil A	2	0	1.000	3	3	0	0-0	16	20	9	2	0	6-0	10	4.50	89	.299	.356	0	ø	0	99	-1	0	-0.1
1992	Mil A	11	2	.846	14	14	2-1	0-0	100.1	76	21	4	2	23-0	62	1.79	216	.207	.257	0	ø	0	133	24	0	3.2
1993	Mil A	16	16	.500	36	**36**	8-1	0-0	**258**	232	120	32	10	91-5	180	4.01	108	.239	.308	0	ø	0	97	12	0	1.3
1994	Mil A	11	11	.500	25	**25**	6	0-0	179	158	96	23	4	84-0	98	4.68	109	.236	.322	0	ø	0	85	10	0	1.1
1995	Mil A	1	1	.500	4	4	0	0-0	23.2	24	10	4	1	10-0	18	3.42	147	.261	.340	0	ø	0	97	4	140	0.3
1996	Mil A	4	4	.500	15	15	0	0-0	84.2	82	43	8	4	38-0	50	4.46	116	.259	.342	0	ø	0	101	8	104	0.6
1997	Mil A	13	15	.464	34	34	1-1	0-0	202	207	118	31	9	89-0	122	4.99	93	.266	.346	3-0-1	.000	-0	93	-5	0	-0.8
1998	Mil N	4	8	.333	23	23	0	0-0	133	157	82	14	4	61-3	86	4.80	90	.297	.372	32-0-5	.125	-0*	109	-9	63	-0.8
1999	Mil N	2	8	.200	20	15	0	0-0	82	101	75	19	1	46-0	60	7.79	59	.297	.379	24-0-4	.083	-1*	108	-28	60	-2.8
2000	Chi A	10	2	.833	20	20	2-1	0-0	112	103	61	12	5	59-0	97	4.58	110	.243	.342	4	.250	1	122	7	73	0.7
2001	Chi A	0	1	.000	2	2	0	0-0	6	12	9	1	3	3-1	6	13.50	35	.429	.529	0	ø	0	109	-5	179	-0.6
2003	StL N	7	4	.636	62	0	0	8-6	67.1	62	32	9	4	31-4	67	3.74	110	.248	.337	2	.500	0*	—	2	0	0.3
2004	†StL N	4	2	.667	52	0	0	1-2	67	71	31	11	1	17-1	54	3.76	113	.276	.321	5-0-1	.000	-1	—	4	0	0.2
2005	†StL N	1	0	1.000	31	1	0	0-1	37	35	9	3	2	18-3	29	2.19	192	.259	.353	2	.000	-0	135	9	62	0.4
Total	14	86	74	.538	341	192	19-4	9-9	1368	1340	716	173	50	576-17	939	4.42	103	.257	.334	72-0-11	.111	-1	104	32	681	3.0
Eller, Hod	Horace Owen; B7.5.1894 Muncie IN; D7.18.1961 Indianapolis IN; BR/TR/5´11.5˝/185; d4.16																									
1917	Cin N	10	5	.667	37	11	7-1	1	152.1	131	60	2	3	37	77	2.36	111	.239	.290	45-0-3	.133	-2	149	4	—	0.1
1918	Cin N	16	12	.571	37	22	14	1	217.2	205	71	1	6	59	84	2.36	113	.253	.309	70-0-5	.157	-2	82	9	—	0.7
1919	†Cin N	19	9	.679	38	30	16-7	2	248.1	216	80	7	4	50	137	2.39	116	.238	.281	93-1-1	.280	7	137	12	—	2.1
1920	Cin N	13	12	.520	35	23	15-1	0	210.1	208	79	6	5	52	76	2.95	103	.266	.315	87-0-2	.253	1*	93	6	—	0.7
1921	Cin N	2	2	.500	13	3	0	1	34.1	46	23	3	0	15	7	4.98	72	.322	.386	13	.231	0	138	-5	—	-0.6
Total	5	60	40	.600	160	89	52-9	5	863	806	313	19	18	213	381	2.62	108	.253	.303	308-1-11	.221	5	113	26	—	3.0
Ellingsen, Bruce	Harold Bruce; B4.26.1949 Pocatello ID; BL/TL/6´0˝/180; [LAN67 63/944]; d7.4																									
1974	Cle A	1	1	.500	16	2	0	0-1	42	45	21	5	0	17-4	16	3.21	113	.278	.339	0	ø	0	97	0	0	0.0
Elliott, Claud	Claud Judson "Chaucer","Old Pardee"; B11.17.1876 Pardeeville WI; D6.21.1923 Pardeeville WI; BR/TR/6´0˝/190; d4.16																									
1904	Cin N	3	1	.750	9	6	4-1	0	57.2	53	25	1	4	23	19	2.97	99	.247	.331	24-1-0	.208	1	131	1	—	0.1
	NY N	0	1	.000	3	1	1	0	15	21	14	2	0	3	8	3.00	91	.328	.358	5	.200	0	0	-3	—	-0.2
	Year	3	2	.600	12	7	5-1	0	72.2	74	39	3	4	26	27	2.97	97	.265	.337	29-1-0	.207	1	116	-2	—	-0.1
1905	NY N	0	1	.000	10	2	2	**6**	38	41	20	3	1	12	20	4.03	73	.270	.327	16	.188	-0	62	-3	—	-0.2
Total	2	3	3	.500	22	9	7-1	6	110.2	115	59	6	5	38	47	3.33	87	.267	.333	45-1-0	.200	1	106	-5	—	-0.3
Elliott, Donnie	Donald Glenn; B9.20.1968 Pasadena TX; BR/TR/6´4˝/225; [PhiN87 7/182]; d4.23																									
1994	SD N	0	1	.000	30	1	0	0-1	33	31	12	3	1	21-2	24	3.27	126	.250	.363	1-0-1	.000	-0	176	4	33	0.2
1995	SD N	0	0	ø	1	0	0	0-0	2	2	0	0	0	1-0	3	0.00	ø	.250	.333	0	ø	0	—	1	146	0.0
Total	2	0	1	.000	31	1	0	0-1	35	33	12	3	1	22-2	27	3.09	134	.250	.361	1-0-1	.000	-0	176	5	179	0.2
Elliott, Hal	Harold William; B5.29.1899 Mt.Clemens MI; D4.25.1963 Honolulu HI; BR/TR/6´1.5˝/170; d4.19; Col Michigan																									
1929	Phi N	3	7	.300	40	8	2	2	114.1	146	94	5	0	59	32	6.06	86	.313	.390	30	.167	-1	84	-13	—	-1.0
1930	Phi N	6	11	.353	**48**	11	2	0	117.1	191	120	7	1	58	37	7.67	71	.382	.447	32-0-1	.094	-3	77	-27	—	-3.2
1931	Phi N	0	2	.000	16	4	0	2	33	46	36	5	1	19	8	9.55	44	.338	.423	9	.111	-0	136	-15	—	-1.0
1932	Phi N	2	4	.333	16	7	0	0	57.2	70	45	5	0	38	13	5.77	76	.297	.394	18	.167	-0	95	-8	—	-0.9
Total	4	11	24	.314	120	30	4	4	322.1	453	295	22	2	174	90	6.95	73	.338	.415	89-0-1	.135	-5	88	-63	—	-6.1
Elliott, Glenn	Herbert Glenn "Lefty"; B11.11.1919 Sapulpa OK; D7.27.1969 Portland OR; BB/TL/5´10˝/170; d4.17; Col Oregon St.																									
1947	Bos N	0	1	.000	11	0	0	1	19	18	10	4	0	11	8	4.74	82	.269	.372	2-0-1	.500	0	—	-1	0	0.0
1948	Bos N	1	0	1.000	1	1	0	0	3	5	1	0	0	1	2	3.00	128	.357	.400	2	.000	-0	254	0	0	0.0
1949	Bos N	3	4	.429	22	6	1	0	68.1	70	35	7	0	27	15	3.95	96	.269	.338	17-0-1	.059	-1	74	-2	0	-0.2
Total	3	4	5	.444	34	7	1	1	90.1	93	46	11	0	39	25	4.08	93	.273	.347	21-0-2	.095	-1	99	-3	0	-0.2
Elliott, Jumbo	James Thomas; B10.22.1900 St.Louis MO; D1.7.1970 Terre Haute IN; BR/TL/6´3˝/235; d4.21																									
1923	StL A	0	0	ø	1	0	0	0	1	1	3	0	0	3	0	27.00	15	.333	.667	0	ø	0	—	-2	—	-0.1
1925	Bro N	0	2	.000	3	1	0	0	10.2	17	14	0	1	9	3	8.44	50	.362	.474	4	.000	-1	61	-6	—	-0.9
1927	Bro N	6	13	.316	30	21	12-2	3	188.1	188	82	5	1	60	99	3.30	120	.269	.327	64-0-1	.141	-1	80	14	—	1.0

YEAR	TM LG	W	L	PCT	G	GS	CG-SHO	SV-BS	IP	H	R	HR	HB	BB-IB	SO	ERA	AERA	OAV	OOB	AB-HR-SH	AVG	PB	SUP	APR	DL	PW
1928	Bro N	9	14	.391	41	21	7-2	1	192	194	106	8	6	64	74	3.89	102	.268	.332	68-3-0	.176	2	117	2	—	0.3
1929	Bro N	1	2	.333	6	3	0	0	19	21	17	2	1	16	7	6.63	70	.280	.413	4	.250	0	69	-4	—	-0.5
1930	Bro N	10	7	.588	35	21	6-2	1	198.1	204	100	16	5	70	59	3.95	124	.271	.337	68-1-1	.147	-2	101	23	—	1.4
1931	Phi N	**19**	14	.576	**52**	30	12-2	5	249	288	138	15	4	83	99	4.27	100	.287	.344	90-0-2	.122	-6	92	1	—	-0.8
1932	Phi N	11	10	.524	39	22	8	0	166	210	115	14	2	47	62	5.42	81	.300	.346	61	.197	-1	111	-16	—	-1.9
1933	Phi N	6	10	.375	35	21	6	2	161.2	188	89	8	3	49	43	3.84	99	.295	.348	52-0-2	.231	0*	95	-3	—	-0.5
1934	Phi N	0	1	.000	3	1	0	0	5.1	8	7	0	1	4	1	10.13	47	.333	.448	1	.000	-0	18	-3	—	-0.4
	Bos N	1	1	.500	7	3	0	0	15.1	19	16	2	1	9	6	5.87	65	.284	.377	4	.250	0	105	-6	—	-0.6
	Year	1	2	.333	10	4	0	0	20.2	27	23	2	2	13	7	6.97	58	.297	.396	5	.200	0	80	-8	—	-1.0
Total	10	63	74	.460	252	144	51-8	12	1206.2	1338	687	70	25	414	453	4.24	100	.283	.344	416-4-6	.163	-8	97	0	—	-3.0

Ellis, Dock Dock Phillip; B3.11.1945 Los Angeles CA; BB/TR/6´3˝/(185–203); d6.18

YEAR	TM LG	W	L	PCT	G	GS	CG-SHO	SV-BS	IP	H	R	HR	HB	BB-IB	SO	ERA	AERA	OAV	OOB	AB-HR-SH	AVG	PB	SUP	APR	DL	PW
1968	Pit N	6	5	.545	26	10	2	0	104.1	82	35	4	1	38-4	52	2.50	117	.213	.285	29-0-3	.069	-1*	122	5	0	0.3
1969	Pit N	11	17	.393	35	33	8-2	0-0	218.2	206	101	14	4	76-7	173	3.58	97	.250	.314	68-0-7	.088	-3*	84	-4	0	-0.8
1970	†Pit N	13	10	.565	30	30	9-4	0-0	201.2	194	81	9	10	87-11	128	3.21	123	.257	.340	70-0-4	.100	-3*	90	17	21	1.5
1971	†Pit N★	19	9	.679	31	31	11-2	0-0	226.2	207	93	15	2	63-5	137	3.06	111	.239	.290	79-0-10	.203	2*	150	6	0	0.9
1972	†Pit N	15	7	.682	25	25	4-1	0-0	163.1	156	60	6	3	33-4	96	2.70	123	.253	.292	59-0-1	.153	-1*	128	10	0	1.2
1973	Pit N	12	14	.462	28	28	3-1	0-0	192	176	86	7	6	55-7	122	3.05	116	.240	.297	65-0-6	.108	-3*	92	5	0	0.5
1974	Pit N	12	9	.571	26	26	9	0-0	176.2	163	71	13	7	41-5	91	3.16	110	.242	.291	56-0-5	.214	3*	110	7	0	1.0
1975	†Pit N	8	9	.471	27	24	5-2	0-0	140	163	69	9	3	43-9	69	3.79	95	.292	.342	36-0-7	.111	0*	93	-3	0	-0.4
1976	†NY A	17	8	.680	32	32	8-1	0-0	211.2	195	83	14	4	76-1	65	3.19	107	.247	.312	0	ø	0	96	6	0	0.5
1977	NY A	1	1	.500	3	3	1	0-0	19.2	18	9	1	0	8-0	5	1.83	217	.237	.306	0	ø	0	98	3	0	0.2
	Oak A	1	5	.167	7	7	0	0-0	26	35	33	5	1	14-0	11	9.69	42	.315	.394	0	ø	0	83	-17	0	-2.7
	Tex A	10	6	.625	23	22	7-1	1-0	167.1	158	60	13	0	42-1	90	2.90	140	.254	.297	0	ø	0	106	22	0	1.9
	Year	12	12	.500	33	32	8-1	1-0	213	211	102	19	1	64-1	106	3.63	112	.260	.312	0	ø	0	100	8	0	-0.6
1978	Tex A	9	7	.563	22	22	3	0-0	141.1	131	81	15	2	46-0	45	4.20	89	.245	.305	0	ø	0	120	-10	0	-1.0
1979	Tex A	1	5	.167	10	9	0	0-0	46.2	64	34	5	0	16-2	10	5.98	69	.323	.372	0	ø	0	109	-9	0	-1.0
	NY N	3	7	.300	17	14	1	0-0	85	110	60	9	1	34-10	41	6.04	62	.320	.377	26-0-1	.077	-1	126	-20	0	-2.2
	Pit N	0	0	ø	3	1	0	0-0	7	9	2	1	0	2-0	1	2.57	152	.346	.393	1	.000	-0	136	1	0	0.0
	Year	3	7	.300	20	15	1	0-0	92	119	62	10	1	36-10	42	5.77	65	.322	.378	27-0-1	.074	-2	127	-19	0	-2.2
Total	12	138	119	.537	345	317	71-14	1-0	2128	2067	958	140	44	674-66	1136	3.46	104	.255	.313	489-0-44	.133	-7	107	19	21	-0.1

Ellis, Jim James Russell; B3.25.1945 Tulare CA; BR/TL/6´2˝/(170–185); d8.11

YEAR	TM LG	W	L	PCT	G	GS	CG-SHO	SV-BS	IP	H	R	HR	HB	BB-IB	SO	ERA	AERA	OAV	OOB	AB-HR-SH	AVG	PB	SUP	APR	DL	PW
1967	Chi N	1	1	.500	8	1	0	0	16.2	20	7	1	0	9-1	8	3.24	109	.313	.397	5-0-1	.200	0	74	0	0	0.1
1969	StL N	0	0	ø	2	1	0	0-0	5.1	7	1	0	0	3-1	0	1.69	213	.318	.400	0-0-1	ø	0	148	1	0	0.1
Total	2	1	1	.500	10	2	0	0-0	22	27	8	1	0	12-2	8	2.86	124	.314	.398	5-0-2	.200	0	111	1	0	0.2

Ellis, Robert Robert Randolph; B12.15.1970 Baton Rouge LA; BR/TR/6´5˝/220; [ChiA90 3/77]; d9.12; Col Northwestern Louisiana

YEAR	TM LG	W	L	PCT	G	GS	CG-SHO	SV-BS	IP	H	R	HR	HB	BB-IB	SO	ERA	AERA	OAV	OOB	AB-HR-SH	AVG	PB	SUP	APR	DL	PW
1996	Cal A	0	0	ø	3	0	0	0-0	5	0	0	0	0	4-0	5	0.00	ø	.000	.211	0	ø	0	—	3	0	0.1
2001	Ari N	6	5	.545	19	17	0	0-0	92	106	61	12	4	34-2	41	5.77	80	.293	.354	26-0-1	.154	-0	108	-10	67	-1.1
2002	LA N	0	1	.000	3	0	0	0-0	2.2	6	3	1	0	0-0	0	10.13	38	.462	.462	0	ø	0	—	-2	0	-0.4
2003	Tex A	1	1	.500	4	4	0	0-0	18.1	26	17	7	1	10-0	8	8.35	60	.342	.416	0	ø	0	135	-6	0	-0.5
Total	4	7	7	.500	29	21	0	0-0	118	138	81	20	5	48-2	54	6.03	78	.296	.362	26-0-1	.154	-0	113	-15	67	-1.9

Ellis, Sammy Samuel Joseph; B2.11.1941 Youngstown OH; BL/TR/6´1˝/(175–181); d4.14; C12; Col Mississippi St.

YEAR	TM LG	W	L	PCT	G	GS	CG-SHO	SV-BS	IP	H	R	HR	HB	BB-IB	SO	ERA	AERA	OAV	OOB	AB-HR-SH	AVG	PB	SUP	APR	DL	PW
1962	Cin N	2	2	.500	8	4	0	0	28	29	25	6	1	29-0	27	6.75	60	.269	.424	10	.200	-0	125	-9	0	-1.1
1964	Cin N	10	3	.769	52	5	2	14	122.1	101	38	9	1	28-2	125	2.57	140	.223	.269	24-0-3	.083	-0	165	14	0	1.9
1965	Cin N☆	22	10	.688	44	39	15-2	2	263.2	222	119	22	6	104-4	183	3.79	99	.226	.303	96-0-7	.125	-1	131	1	0	-0.2
1966	Cin N	12	19	.387	41	36	7	0	221	226	135	35	3	78-8	154	5.29	74	.264	.324	70-0-9	.114	-2*	98	-29	0	-4.1
1967	Cin N	8	11	.421	32	27	8-1	0	175.2	197	86	18	4	67-7	80	3.84	98	.286	.351	49-0-6	.082	-2	101	-2	0	-0.5
1968	Cal A	9	10	.474	42	24	3	2	164	150	80	22	6	56-4	93	3.95	74	.244	.310	44-0-7	.045	-3	116	-19	0	-2.7
1969	Chi A	0	3	.000	10	5	0	0-0	29.1	42	20	6	1	16-2	15	5.83	66	.336	.415	6-0-1	.167	0	106	-6	0	-0.5
Total	7	63	58	.521	229	140	35-3	18-0	1004	967	503	118	22	378-27	677	4.15	88	.253	.321	299-0-33	.104	-8	114	-50	0	-7.2

Ellison, George George Russell; B1.24.1897 San Francisco CA; D1.20.1978 San Francisco CA; BR/TR/6´3˝/185; d8.21; Col California

YEAR	TM LG	W	L	PCT	G	GS	CG-SHO	SV-BS	IP	H	R	HR	HB	BB-IB	SO	ERA	AERA	OAV	OOB	AB-HR-SH	AVG	PB	SUP	APR	DL	PW
1920	Cle A	0	0	ø	1	0	0	0	1	0	0	0	0	2	1	0.00	ø	.000	.400	0	ø	0	—	0	—	0.0

Ellsworth, Dick Richard Clark; B3.22.1940 Lusk WY; BL/TL/6´4˝/(180–200); d6.22; s–Steve; Col Fresno (CA) City

YEAR	TM LG	W	L	PCT	G	GS	CG-SHO	SV-BS	IP	H	R	HR	HB	BB-IB	SO	ERA	AERA	OAV	OOB	AB-HR-SH	AVG	PB	SUP	APR	DL	PW
1958	Chi N	0	1	.000	1	1	0	0	2.1	4	4	0	1	3-0	0	15.43	25	.364	.533	1	.000	-0	46	-3	0	-0.4
1960	Chi N	7	13	.350	31	27	6	0	176.2	170	83	12	2	72-8	94	3.72	102	.257	.329	48-0-6	.042	-3	86	1	0	-0.1
1961	Chi N	10	11	.476	37	31	7-1	0	186.2	213	90	23	3	48-3	91	3.86	108	.292	.337	56-0-5	.036	-5	86	8	0	0.5
1962	Chi N	9	20	.310	37	33	6	1	208.2	241	131	23	5	77-6	113	5.09	81	.291	.354	62-0-2	.113	1	80	-19	0	-2.2
1963	Chi N	22	10	.688	37	37	19-4	0	290.2	223	75	14	2	75-7	185	2.11	**167**	.210	.262	94-0-8	.096	-2	98	44	0	**5.0**
1964	Chi N☆	14	18	.438	37	36	16-1	0	256.2	267	129	34	3	71-9	148	3.75	99	.266	.315	87-0-6	.046	-5	92	-6	0	-1.1
1965	Chi N	14	15	.483	36	34	8	1	222.1	227	108	22	4	57-7	130	3.81	97	.265	.312	73-0-6	.096	-2	92	-2	0	-0.3
1966	Chi N	8	22	.267	38	37	9	0	269.1	321	150	28	5	51-5	144	3.98	92	.294	.326	90-0-5	.156	-0	92	-14	0	-1.4
1967	Phi N	6	7	.462	32	21	3-1	0	125.1	152	75	6	5	36-10	45	4.38	78	.306	.357	37-0-4	.108	-1	126	-15	0	-1.5
1968	Bos A	16	7	.696	31	28	10-1	0	196	196	74	16	7	37-3	106	3.03	104	.260	.300	72-0-5	.056	-5	129	3	0	-0.2
1969	Bos A	0	0	ø	2	2	0	0-0	12	16	5	1	0	4-0	4	3.75	102	.320	.370	3-0-1	.000	-0	81	0	0	0.0
	Cle A	6	9	.400	34	22	3-1	0-0	135	162	73	10	5	40-10	48	4.13	92	.301	.353	45-0-1	.133	-1	99	-6	0	-0.7
	Year	6	9	.400	36	24	3-1	0-0	147	178	78	11	5	44-10	52	4.10	93	.302	.354	48-0-2	.125	-2	98	-5	0	-0.7
1970	Cle A	3	3	.500	29	1	0	2-2	43.2	49	23	4	1	14-2	13	4.53	88	.299	.354	4	.000	-0	156	-2	0	-0.3
	Mil A	0	0	ø	14	0	0	1-0	15.2	11	3	0	1	3-0	9	1.72	219	.196	.250	0-0-1	ø	0	—	4	0	0.2
	Year	3	3	.500	43	1	0	3-2	59.1	60	26	4	2	17-2	22	3.79	104	.273	.328	4-0-1	.000	-0	158	2	0	-0.1
1971	Mil A	0	1	.000	11	0	0	0-0	14.2	22	10	1	1	7-1	10	4.91	71	.361	.423	1	.000	-0	—	-3	0	-0.2
Total	13	115	137	.456	407	310	87-9	5-2	2155.2	2274	1033	194	45	595-71	1140	3.72	100	.272	.322	673-0-50	.088	-25	96	-10	0	-2.7

Ellsworth, Steve Steven Clark; B7.30.1960 Chicago IL; BR/TR/6´8˝/220; [BosA81 S1/9]; d4.7; f–Dick; Col Cal St.–Northridge

YEAR	TM LG	W	L	PCT	G	GS	CG-SHO	SV-BS	IP	H	R	HR	HB	BB-IB	SO	ERA	AERA	OAV	OOB	AB-HR-SH	AVG	PB	SUP	APR	DL	PW
1988	Bos A	1	6	.143	8	7	0	0-0	36	47	29	7	1	16-1	16	6.75	61	.315	.383	0	ø	0	117	-10	0	-1.6

Elston, Don Donald Ray; B4.6.1929 Campbellstown OH; D1.2.1995 Arlington Heights IL; BR/TR/6´0˝/(165–170); d9.17

YEAR	TM LG	W	L	PCT	G	GS	CG-SHO	SV-BS	IP	H	R	HR	HB	BB-IB	SO	ERA	AERA	OAV	OOB	AB-HR-SH	AVG	PB	SUP	APR	DL	PW
1953	Chi N	0	1	.000	2	1	0	0	5	11	8	1	0	0	2	14.40	31	.458	.458	1	.000	-0	80	-5	0	-0.7
1957	Bro N	0	0	ø	1	0	0	0	1	1	0	0	0	0-0	1	0.00	ø	.250	.250	0	ø	0	—	0	0	0.0
	Chi N	6	7	.462	39	14	2	8	144	139	61	15	5	55-4	102	3.56	109	.259	.332	37-0-2	.108	-2	76	6	0	0.4
	Year	6	7	.462	40	14	2	8	145	140	61	15	5	55-4	103	3.54	109	.259	.331	37-0-2	.108	-2	76	7	0	0.4
1958	Chi N	9	8	.529	**69**	0	0	10	97	75	35	9	1	39-10	84	2.88	136	.214	.291	14-0-1	.357	1	—	**11**	0	2.3
1959	Chi N★	10	8	.556	**65**	0	0	13	97.2	77	40	11	3	46-7	82	3.32	119	.218	.310	19-0-3	.211	0	—	7	0	1.4
1960	Chi N	8	9	.471	60	0	0	11	127	109	57	17	4	55-8	85	3.40	111	.231	.312	24-0-2	.125	-1	—	4	0	0.4
1961	Chi N	6	7	.462	58	0	0	8	93.1	108	64	11	6	45-12	59	5.59	75	.297	.381	11-0-3	.182	-0	—	-13	0	-1.8
1962	Chi N	4	8	.333	57	0	0	8	66.1	57	25	6	1	32-7	37	2.44	170	.247	.338	8	.000	-1	—	10	0	1.9
1963	Chi N	4	1	.800	51	0	0	4	70	57	26	6	2	21-3	41	2.83	124	.226	.290	4-0-1	.000	-0	—	5	0	0.3
1964	Chi N	2	5	.286	48	0	0	1	54.1	68	38	4	3	34-12	26	5.30	70	.330	.422	6	.167	-0	—	-10	0	-1.2
Total	9	49	54	.476	450	15	2	63	755.2	702	354	80	25	327-63	519	3.69	106	.251	.332	124-0-12	.153	-3	77	15	0	3.0

Elvira, Narciso Narciso Chicho (Delgado); B10.29.1967 Tlalixcoyan, Veracruz, Mexico; BL/TL/5´10˝/160; d9.9

YEAR	TM LG	W	L	PCT	G	GS	CG-SHO	SV-BS	IP	H	R	HR	HB	BB-IB	SO	ERA	AERA	OAV	OOB	AB-HR-SH	AVG	PB	SUP	APR	DL	PW
1990	Mil A	0	0	ø	4	0	0	0-0	5	6	3	0	0	5-0	6	5.40	72	.300	.440	0	ø	0	—	-1	0	0.0

Ely, Harry Harry; d9.24

YEAR	TM LG	W	L	PCT	G	GS	CG-SHO	SV-BS	IP	H	R	HR	HB	BB-IB	SO	ERA	AERA	OAV	OOB	AB-HR-SH	AVG	PB	SUP	APR	DL	PW
1892	Bal N	0	1	.000	1	1	1	0	7	14	9	0	2	7	0	7.71	44	.400	.523	3	.000	-0	0	-3	—	-0.3

Ely, Bones William Frederick; B6.7.1863 N.Girard PA; D1.10.1952 Berkeley CA; BR/TR/6´1˝/155; d6.19; ▲

YEAR	TM LG	W	L	PCT	G	GS	CG-SHO	SV-BS	IP	H	R	HR	HB	BB-IB	SO	ERA	AERA	OAV	OOB	AB-HR-SH	AVG	PB	SUP	APR	DL	PW
1884	Buf N	0	1	.000	1	1	0	0	5	17	15	1	—	5	4	14.40	22	.500	.564	4	.000	-1	34	-6	—	-0.7
1886	Lou AA	0	4	.000	6	4	4	**1**	44	53	47	0	0	26	28	5.32	68	.280	.367	32	.156	-1*	94	-7	—	-0.6
1890	Syr AA	0	0	ø	1	0	0	0	2	7	5	0	0	0	0	22.50	16	.538	.538	496	.262	0*	—	-4	—	-0.1
1894	StL N	0	0	ø	1	0	0	0	1	0	0	0	0	3	0	0.00	ø	.000	.500	510-12-13	.306	0*	—	1	—	0.0
Total	4	0	5	.000	9	5	4	1	52	77	67	1	0	34	32	6.75	54	.322	.407	1042-12-13	.279	-1	82	-16	—	-1.4

YEAR	TM LG	W	L	PCT	G	GS	CG-SHO	SV-BS	IP	H	R	HR	HB	BB-IB	SO	ERA	AERA	OAV	OOB	AB-HR-SH	AVG	PB	SUP	APR	DL	PW
EMBREE, ALAN	Alan Duane; B1.23.1970 The Dalles OR; BL/TL/6´2˝/(185–190); [CleA89 5/125]; d9.15; [DL 1993 Cle A 124]																									
1992	Cle A	0	2	.000	4	4	0	0-0	18	19	14	3	1	8-0	12	7.00	56	.271	.346	0	ø	0	87	-5	0	-0.5
1995	†Cle A	3	2	.600	23	0	0	1-0	24.2	23	16	2	0	16-0	23	5.11	92	.253	.358	0	ø	0	—	-1	0	-0.2
1996	†Cle A	1	1	.500	24	0	0	0-0	31	30	26	10	0	21-3	33	6.39	77	.259	.364	0	ø	0	—	-6	37	-0.3
1997	†Atl N	3	1	.750	66	0	0	0-0	46	36	13	1	2	20-2	45	2.54	165	.221	.312	0	ø	0	—	9	0	0.7
1998	Atl N	1	0	1.000	20	0	0	0-1	18.2	23	14	2	0	10-0	19	4.34	96	.307	.384	1	.000	-0	—	-2	0	-0.1
	Ari N	3	2	.600	35	0	0	1-1	35	33	18	5	1	13-0	24	4.11	104	.248	.320	0	ø	0	—	0	0	0.1
	Year	4	2	.667	55	0	0	1-2	53.2	56	32	7	1	23-0	43	4.19	101	.269	.343	1	.000	0	—	-2	0	0.0
1999	SF N	3	2	.600	68	0	0	0-3	58.2	42	22	6	3	26-2	53	3.38	127	.200	.295	0	ø	0	—	7	0	0.5
2000	†SF N	3	5	.375	63	0	0	2-3	60	62	34	4	3	25-2	49	4.95	88	.274	.347	0	ø	0	—	-3	0	-0.4
2001	SF N	0	2	.000	22	0	0	0-1	20	34	26	7	2	10-2	25	11.25	36	.374	.434	1	.000	-0	—	-16	20	-1.4
	Chi A	1	2	.333	39	0	0	0-2	34	31	21	7	1	7-0	34	5.03	93	.242	.281	0	ø	0	—	-1	0	-0.1
2002	SD N	3	4	.429	36	0	0	0-2	28.2	23	7	2	0	9-2	38	1.26	309	.211	.271	0	ø	0	—	8	0	1.6
	Bos A	1	2	.333	32	0	0	2-3	33.1	24	12	4	1	11-1	43	2.97	151	.203	.273	0	ø	0	—	6	15	0.5
2003	†Bos A	4	1	.800	65	0	0	1-1	55	49	26	5	0	16-3	45	4.25	110	.241	.294	0	ø	0	—	4	20	0.3
2004	†Bos A	2	2	.500	71	0	0	0-1	52.1	49	28	7	1	11-1	37	4.13	118	.244	.284	0	ø	0	—	4	0	0.3
2005	Bos A	1	4	.200	43	0	0	1-2	37.2	42	33	8	1	11-2	30	7.65	59	.284	.333	0	ø	0	—	-12	0	-1.4
	NY A	1	1	.500	24	0	0	0-0	14.1	20	14	2	1	3-1	8	7.53	57	.328	.364	0	ø	0	—	-6	0	-0.7
	Year	2	5	.286	67	0	0	1-2	52	62	47	10	2	14-3	38	7.62	59	.297	.342	0	ø	0	—	-17	0	-2.1
2006	†SD N	4	3	.571	73	0	0	0-0	52.1	50	21	4	0	15-2	53	3.27	127	.249	.297	1	.000	-0	—	5	15	0.6
Total	13	34	36	.486	708	4	0	8-20	619.2	590	345	79	17	232-23	571	4.58	96	.252	.319	3	.000	-0	87	-9	231	-0.5
EMBREE, RED	Charles Willard; B8.30.1917 ElMonte CA; D9.24.1996 Eugene OR; BR/TR/6´0˝/165; d9.10; Def 1943; Col Citrus (CA) JC																									
1941	Cle A	0	1	.000	1	1	0	0	4	7	3	0	1	3	4	6.75	58	.438	.550	1	.000	-0	88	-1	0	-0.2
1942	Cle A	3	4	.429	19	6	2	0	63	58	31	0	2	31	44	3.86	89	.242	.333	15-0-1	.133	-0	66	-3	0	-0.3
1944	Cle A	0	1	.000	3	1	0	0	3.1	2	5	0	0	5	4	13.50	24	.167	.412	0	ø	0	25	-4	0	-0.7
1945	Cle A	4	4	.500	8	8	5-1	0	70	56	17	3	0	26	42	1.93	168	.215	.287	21-0-4	.143	-1	105	11	0	1.3
1946	Cle A	8	12	.400	28	26	8	0	200	170	86	15	2	79	87	3.47	95	.227	.302	70-0-7	.186	1	100	-3	0	-0.2
1947	Cle A	8	10	.444	27	21	6	0	162.2	137	65	13	1	67	56	3.15	110	.233	.313	52-0-6	.173	-1*	116	5	0	0.4
1948	NY A	5	3	.625	20	8	4	0	76.2	77	37	6	1	30	25	3.76	109	.261	.331	27	.148	-1	133	2	0	0.0
1949	StL A	3	13	.188	35	19	4	1	127.1	146	90	13	3	89	24	5.37	84	.294	.405	37-0-3	.162	-1*	89	-11	0	-1.4
Total	8	31	48	.392	141	90	29-1	1	707	653	334	50	10	330	286	3.72	98	.246	.331	223-0-21	.166	-4	102	-4	0	-1.1
EMBREY, SLIM	Charles Akin; B8.17.1901 Columbia TN; D10.10.1947 Nashville TN; BR/TR/6´2˝/184; d10.1; Col Vanderbilt																									
1923	Chi A	0	0	ø	1	0	0	0	2.2	7	6	0	0	2	1	10.13	39	.500	.563	0	ø	0	—	-3	—	-0.1
EMIG, CHARLIE	Charles Henry; B4.5.1875 Cincinnati OH; D10.2.1975 Oklahoma City OK; BR/TL; d9.4																									
1896	Lou N	0	1	.000	1	1	1	0	8	12	17	1	3	7	1	7.88	55	.343	.489	3	.000	-1	49	-5	—	-0.4
EMMERICH, SLIM	William Peter; B9.29.1919 Allentown PA; D9.17.1998 Allentown PA; BR/TR/6´1˝/170; d5.14																									
1945	NY N	4	4	.500	31	7	1	0	100	111	55	8	1	33	27	4.86	80	.278	.334	25-0-4	.120	-2	84	-8	0	-0.7
1946	NY N	0	0	ø	2	0	0	0	4	6	2	1	0	0	1	4.50	76	.400	.400	0	ø	0	—	0	0	0.0
Total	2	4	4	.500	33	7	1	0	104	117	57	9	1	33	28	4.85	80	.282	.336	25-0-4	.120	-2	84	-8	0	-0.7
EMSLIE, BOB	Robert Daniel; B1.27.1859 Guelph ON, Can.; D4.26.1943 St.Thomas ON, Can.; BR/TR/5´11˝/180; d7.25; U35																									
1883	Bal AA	9	13	.409	24	23	21-1	0	201.1	188	149	3	—	41	62	3.17	110	.231	.268	97	.165	-3*	78	4	—	0.1
1884	Bal AA	32	17	.653	50	50	50-4	0	455.1	419	241	5	14	88	264	2.75	126	.224	.264	195	.190	-5*	96	36	—	2.8
1885	Bal AA	3	10	.231	13	13	11	0	107	131	87	0	5	30	27	4.29	76	.298	.350	51	.235	0	112	-14	—	-1.3
	Phi AA	0	4	.000	4	4	3	0	28.2	37	30	1	0	6	9	6.28	55	.291	.323	12	.083	-1	107	-6	—	-0.7
	Year	3	14	.176	17	17	14	0	135.2	168	117	1	5	36	36	4.71	70	.297	.344	63	.206	-1	111	-22	—	-2.0
Total	3	44	44	.500	91	90	85-5	0	792.1	775	507	9	19	165	362	3.19	108	.239	.279	355	.186	-9	94	20	—	0.9
ENCARNACION, LUIS	Luis Martin Lora (b Luis Martin Lora (Encarnacion)); B10.20.1963 Santo Domingo, D.R.; BR/TR/5´10˝/180; d7.27																									
1990	KC A	0	0	ø	4	0	0	0-0	10.1	14	10	1	0	4-0	8	7.84	49	.311	.367	0	ø	0	—	-5	0	-0.2
ENDERS, TREVOR	Trevor Hale; B12.22.1974 Milwaukee WI; BR/TL/6´1˝/214; d9.2; Col Houston Baptist																									
2000	TB A	0	1	.000	9	0	0	0-1	9.1	14	13	2	0	5-0	5	10.61	46	.359	.432	0	ø	0	—	-6	0	-0.5
ENGEL, JOE	Joseph William; B3.12.1893 Washington DC; D6.12.1969 Chattanooga TN; BR/TL/6´1.5˝/183; d5.30; Col Mount St. Marys																									
1912	Was A	2	5	.286	17	10	2	1	75	70	41	2	4	50	29	3.96	84	.253	.375	17-0-1	.059	-1	102	-3	—	-0.3
1913	Was A	8	9	.471	36	24	6-2	0	164.2	124	75	2	11	85	70	3.06	97	.218	.331	49-0-1	.061	-5	93	-2	—	-0.8
1914	Was A	7	5	.583	35	15	1	3	124.1	108	53	2	5	75	41	2.97	95	.254	.372	28-0-2	.107	1	123	-2	—	-0.2
1915	Was A	0	3	.000	11	3	0	0	33.2	30	15	0	3	19	9	3.21	93	.261	.380	6	.000	-1	57	0	—	-0.1
1917	Cin N	0	1	.000	1	1	1	0	8	12	8	0	0	6	2	5.63	47	.353	.450	3	.000	-0	0	-3	—	-0.3
1919	Cle A	0	0	ø	1	0	0	0	0	0	3	0	0	3	0	(2)	ø	ø	1.000	0	ø	0	—	-2	—	-0.2
1920	Was A	0	0	ø	1	0	0	0	1.2	0	4	0	1	4	0	21.60	17	.000	.556	1	.000	-0*	—	-3	—	-0.2
Total	7	17	23	.425	102	53	10-2	4	407.1	344	199	6	24	242	151	3.38	88	.242	.361	104-0-4	.067	-6	99	-15	—	-2.1
ENGEL, STEVE	Steven Michael; B12.31.1961 Cincinnati OH; BR/TL/6´3˝/216; [ChiN83 5/112]; d7.30; Col Eastern Kentucky																									
1985	Chi N	1	5	.167	11	8	1	1-0	51.2	61	36	10	0	26-1	29	5.57	72	.298	.375	16-1-0	.188	1	91	-9	0	-0.8
ENGLE, RICK	Richard Douglas; B4.7.1957 Corbin KY; BR/TL/5´11.5˝/180; d9.2																									
1981	Mon N	0	0	ø	1	0	0	0-0	2	6	4	0	0	1-0	2	18.00	20	.500	.538	0	ø	0	—	-3	0	-0.1
ENNIS, JOHN	John Wayne; B10.17.1979 Montrose CO; BR/TR/6´5˝/220; [AtlN98 14/431]; d4.10																									
2002	Atl N	0	0	ø	1	1	0	0-0	4	5	2	0	0	3-0	1	4.50	90	.385	.471	1	.000	-0	114	0	0	0.0
2004	Det A	0	0	ø	12	0	0	1-1	16	20	16	3	0	5-0	13	8.44	53	.290	.333	0	ø	0	—	-7	0	-0.4
Total	2	0	0	ø	13	1	0	1-1	20	25	18	3	0	8-0	14	7.65	57	.305	.359	1	.000	-0	114	-7	0	-0.4
ENRIGHT, JACK	Jackson Percy; B11.29.1895 Fort Worth TX; D8.18.1975 Pompano Beach FL; BR/TR/5´11˝/177; d9.26																									
1917	NY A	0	1	.000	1	1	0	0	5	5	5	0	0	3	1	5.40	50	.294	.400	1	.000	-0	27	-2	—	-0.3
ENYART, TERRY	Terry Gene; B10.10.1950 Ironton OH; BR/TL/6´2˝/190; d6.17; Col Chipola (FL) JC																									
1974	Mon N	0	0	ø	2	0	0	0-0	1.2	4	6	0	0	4-0	2	16.20	24	.444	.615	0	ø	0	—	-3	0	-0.2
ENZMANN, JOHNNY	John "Gentleman John"; B3.4.1890 Brooklyn NY; D3.14.1984 Riverhead NY; BR/TR/5´10˝/165; d7.10																									
1914	Bro N	1	0	1.000	7	1	0	0	19	21	16	1	3	8	5	4.74	60	.300	.395	6	.000	-1	275	-4	—	-0.3
1918	Cle A	5	7	.417	30	14	8	2	136.2	130	44	2	5	29	38	2.37	127	.263	.310	47-0-2	.149	-2	86	10	—	0.7
1919	Cle A	3	2	.600	14	4	2	0	55.1	67	29	0	2	8	13	2.28	147	.312	.342	15-0-1	.133	-0	111	2	—	0.1
1920	Phi N	2	3	.400	16	2	1	0	58.2	79	40	1	5	16	35	3.84	89	.320	.373	24	.167	1*	115	-5	—	-0.4
Total	4	11	12	.478	67	21	11	2	269.2	297	129	4	15	61	91	2.84	111	.289	.338	92-0-3	.141	-3	102	3	—	0.1
EPPERLY, AL	Albert Paul "Tub","Pard"; B5.7.1918 Glidden IA; D4.14.2003 McFarland MI; BL/TR/6´2˝/194; d4.25																									
1938	Chi N	2	0	1.000	9	4	1	0	27	28	11	1	0	15	10	3.67	104	.264	.355	8	.250	1	243	1	—	0.2
1950	Bro N	0	0	ø	5	0	0	0	9	14	8	1	0	5	3	5.00	82	.378	.452	0	ø	0	—	-2	0	-0.1
Total	2	2	0	1.000	14	4	1	0	36	42	19	2	0	20	13	4.00	97	.294	.380	8	.250	1	243	-1	0	0.1
ERARDI, GREG	Joseph Gregory; B5.31.1954 Syracuse NY; BR/TR/6´1˝/190; [MilA72 24/552]; d9.6																									
1977	Sea A	0	1	.000	5	0	0	0-0	9	12	8	3	0	6-1	5	6.00	69	.300	.391	0	ø	0	—	-2	0	-0.2
ERAUTT, EDDIE	Edward Lorenz Sebastian; B9.26.1924 Portland OR; BR/TR/6´0˝/(186–190); d4.16; b–Joe																									
1947	Cin N	4	9	.308	36	10	2	0	119	146	78	5	2	53	43	5.07	81	.307	.379	29-0-3	.069	-1	77	-14	0	-1.4
1948	Cin N	0	0	ø	2	0	0	0	3	3	2	0	0	1	0	6.00	65	.250	.308	0	ø	0	—	-1	0	0.0
1949	Cin N	4	11	.267	39	9	1	1	112.2	99	53	9	3	61	43	3.36	125	.247	.351	23-0-1	.174	0	47	8	0	1.0
1950	Cin N	4	2	.667	33	2	1	1	65.1	82	48	9	6	22	35	5.65	75	.307	.373	13-0-1	.154	0	83	-11	0	-0.9
1951	Cin N	0	0	ø	30	0	0	0	39.1	50	31	4	3	23	20	5.72	71	.314	.411	3	.000	-0	—	-8	0	-0.4

YEAR	TM LG	W	L	PCT	G	GS	CG-SHO	SV-BS	IP	H	R	HR	HB	BB-IB	SO	ERA	AERA	OAV	OOB	AB-HR-SH	AVG	PB	SUP	APR	DL	PW
1953	Cin N	0	0	ø	4	0	0	0	4.2	11	3	1	0	3	1	5.79	75	.500	.560	1	.000	-0	—	-1	0	0.0
	StL N	3	1	.750	20	1	0	0	35.2	43	25	6	2	16	15	6.31	67	.299	.377	6-0-1	.167	-0	84	-7	0	-0.7
	Year	3	1	.750	24	1	0	0	40.1	54	28	7	2	19	16	6.25	68	.325	.401	7-0-1	.143	-0	84	-8	0	-0.7
Total	6	15	23	.395	164	22	4	2	379.2	434	240	34	16	179	157	4.86	86	.293	.376	75-0-6	.120	-2	66	-34	0	-2.4
Erdos, Todd	Todd Michael; B11.21.1973 Washington PA; BR/TR/6´1˝/(190–204); [SDN92 9/253]; d6.8																									
1997	SD N	2	0	1.000	11	0	0	0-0	13.2	17	9	1	2	4-0	13	5.27	75	.293	.359	1	.000	-0	—	-2	0	-0.3
1998	NY A	0	0	ø	2	0	0	0-0	2	5	2	0	0	1-1	0	9.00	49	.500	.545	0	ø	0	—	-1	0	-0.1
1999	NY A	0	0	ø	4	0	0	0-0	7	5	4	2	0	4-0	4	3.86	123	.192	.290	0	ø	0	—	0	0	0.0
2000	NY A	0	0	ø	14	0	0	1-0	25	31	14	2	1	11-0	18	5.04	95	.304	.377	1	.000	-0	—	0	0	0.0
	SD N	0	0	ø	22	0	0	1-1	29.2	32	24	5	6	17-1	16	6.67	67	.271	.379	1	.000	-0	—	-7	0	-0.4
2001	Bos A	0	0	ø	10	0	0	0-0	16.1	15	9	2	3	8-1	7	4.96	89	.263	.366	0	ø	0	—	-1	0	0.0
Total	5	2	0	1.000	63	0	0	2-1	93.2	105	62	12	12	45-3	58	5.57	80	.283	.372	3	.000	-0	—	-11	0	-0.8
Ericks, John	John Edward; B6.16.1967 Tinley Park IL; BR/TR/6´7˝/(250–255); [StLN88 1/22]; d6.24; Col Illinois																									
1995	Pit N	3	9	.250	19	18	1	0-0	106	108	59	7	2	50-4	80	4.58	95	.263	.343	31-0-6	.097	-2	72	-2	0	-0.5
1996	Pit N	4	5	.444	28	4	0	8-2	46.2	56	35	11	0	19-2	46	5.79	76	.292	.354	5	.000	-1	72	-8	0	-1.6
1997	Pit N	1	0	1.000	10	0	0	6-1	9.1	7	3	1	0	4-0	6	1.93	222	.200	.282	0	ø	0	—	2	153	0.4
Total	3	8	14	.364	57	22	1	14-3	162	171	97	19	2	73-6	132	4.78	91	.268	.343	36-0-6	.083	-2	72	-8	153	-1.7
Erickson, Don	Don Lee; B12.13.1931 Springfield IL; BR/TR/6´0˝/175; d9.1; Col Western Illinois																									
1958	Phi N	0	1	.000	9	0	0	1	11.2	11	7	3	0	9-1	9	4.63	86	.244	.364	1	.000	-0	—	-1	0	-0.1
Erickson, Eric	Eric George Adolph; B3.13.1895 Goteborg, Sweden; D5.19.1965 Jamestown NY; BR/TR/6´2˝/190; d10.6; Mil 1918																									
1914	NY N	0	1	.000	1	1	0	0	5	8	7	0	0	3	3	0.00	ø	.364	.440	1	.000	-0	0	-1	—	-0.3
1916	Det A	0	0	ø	8	0	0	0	16	13	6	0	1	8	7	2.81	102	.220	.324	4	.000	-1	—	0	—	-0.1
1918	Det A	4	5	.444	12	9	8	1	94.1	81	32	2	3	29	48	2.48	107	.240	.306	33-0-1	.121	-3	97	2	—	-0.2
1919	Det A	0	2	.000	3	2	0	0	14.2	17	17	0	1	10	4	6.75	47	.293	.406	5	.200	-0	123	-7	—	-0.8
	Was A	6	11	.353	20	15	7-1	0	132	130	69	7	7	63	86	3.95	81	.254	.344	48-0-4	.146	-1	111	-8	—	-1.2
	Year	6	13	.316	23	17	7-1	0	146.2	147	86	7	8	73	90	4.23	76	.258	.351	53-0-4	.151	-2	112	-16	—	-2.0
1920	Was A	12	16	.429	39	27	12	1	239.1	231	142	13	11	128	87	3.84	97	.264	.365	83-1-8	.277	4	107	-8	—	-0.6
1921	Was A	8	10	.444	32	22	9-3	0	179	181	90	7	9	65	71	3.62	114	.269	.341	60-0-3	.150	-3	71	9	—	0.3
1922	Was A	4	12	.250	30	17	6-2	2	141.2	144	95	8	3	73	61	4.96	78	.279	.372	45-0-1	.133	-2	80	-18	—	-2.1
Total	7	34	57	.374	145	93	42-6	4	822	805	458	37	35	379	367	3.85	93	.264	.352	279-1-17	.179	-6	92	-31	—	-5.0
Erickson, Hal	Harold James; B7.17.1919 Portland OR; BR/TR/6´5˝/230; d4.14																									
1953	Det A	0	1	.000	18	0	0	1	32.1	43	23	4	2	10	19	4.73	86	.323	.379	4	.000	-1	—	-4	0	-0.3
Erickson, Paul	Paul Walford "Li'L Abner"; B12.14.1915 Zion IL; D4.5.2002 Fond Du Lac WI; BR/TR/6´2˝/200; d6.29																									
1941	Chi N	5	7	.417	32	15	7-1	1	141	126	70	2	2	64	85	3.70	95	.234	.318	46-1-1	.152	0	100	-4	0	-0.3
1942	Chi N	1	6	.143	18	7	1	0	63	70	40	4	0	41	26	5.43	59	.288	.391	21	.143	-1	60	-14	0	-1.5
1943	Chi N	1	3	.250	15	4	0	0	42.2	47	32	4	2	22	24	6.12	55	.280	.370	15	.200	0	172	-12	0	-1.1
1944	Chi N	5	9	.357	33	15	5-3	1	124.1	113	59	5	0	67	82	3.55	100	.243	.338	36-1-0	.056	-1	93	0	0	-0.1
1945	†Chi N	7	4	.636	28	9	3	3	108.1	94	41	5	7	48	53	3.32	110	.233	.325	32-0-4	.156	0	147	7	0	0.7
1946	Chi N	9	7	.563	32	14	5-1	0	137	119	46	2	3	65	70	2.43	137	.232	.321	40-0-6	.050	-4	105	13	0	0.9
1947	Chi N	7	12	.368	40	20	6	1	174	179	90	17	5	93	82	4.34	91	.268	.362	60-1-0	.250	3	85	-4	0	-0.1
1948	Chi N	0	0	ø	3	0	0	0	5.2	7	5	0	0	6	4	6.35	61	.292	.433	1	.000	-0	—	-2	0	-0.1
	Phi N	2	0	1.000	4	2	0	0	17.1	19	10	2	0	17	5	5.19	76	.292	.439	7	.143	-0	112	-2	0	-0.2
	NY N	0	0	ø	2	0	0	0	1	0	0	0	0	2	1	0.00	ø	.000	.400	0	ø	0	—	0	0	0.0
	Year	2	0	1.000	9	2	0	0	24	26	15	2	0	25	10	5.25	75	.283	.436	8	.125	-0	113	-3	0	-0.3
Total	8	37	48	.435	207	86	27-5	6	814.1	774	393	41	19	425	432	3.86	93	.250	.345	258-3-11	.147	-2	101	-18	0	-1.8
Erickson, Ralph	Ralph Lief; B6.25.1902 Dubois ID; D6.27.2002 Chandler AZ; BL/TL/6´1˝/175; d9.11; Col Idaho St.																									
1929	Pit N	0	0	ø	1	0	0	0	1	2	3	0	0	2	0	27.00	18	.500	.667	0	ø	0	—	-2	—	-0.1
1930	Pit N	1	0	1.000	7	0	0	0	14	21	12	1	0	10	2	7.07	70	.375	.470	4	.250	-0	—	-3	—	-0.2
Total	2	1	0	1.000	8	0	0	0	15	23	15	1	0	12	2	8.40	59	.383	.486	4	.250	-0	—	-5	—	-0.3
Erickson, Roger	Roger Farrell; B8.30.1956 Springfield IL; BR/TR/6´3˝/(180–199); [MinA77 3/67]; d4.6; Col New Orleans																									
1978	Min A	14	13	.519	37	37	14	0-0	265.2	268	129	19	8	79-1	121	3.96	97	.263	.319	0	ø	0	105	-2	0	-0.2
1979	Min A	3	10	.231	24	21	0	0-0	123	154	86	17	1	48-1	47	5.63	78	.310	.368	0	ø	0	91	-17	0	-1.6
1980	Min A	7	13	.350	32	27	7	0-0	191.1	198	83	13	4	56-0	97	3.25	135	.268	.320	0	ø	0*	70	20	0	2.0
1981	Min A	3	8	.273	14	14	1	0-0	91.1	93	48	7	0	31-4	44	3.84	103	.262	.316	0	ø	0	63	-1	47	-0.1
1982	Min A	4	3	.571	7	7	2	0-0	40.2	56	29	6	1	12-1	12	4.87	88	.326	.369	0	ø	0	119	-5	0	-0.7
	NY A	4	5	.444	16	11	0	1-0	70.2	86	36	5	0	17-1	37	4.46	90	.301	.334	0	ø	0	78	-2	28	-0.3
	Year	8	8	.500	23	18	2	1-0	111.1	142	65	11	1	29-2	49	4.61	89	.310	.347	0	ø	0	95	-7	0	-1.0
1983	NY A	0	1	.000	5	0	0	0-0	16.2	13	8	1	0	8-1	7	4.32	91	.213	.304	0	ø	0	—	0	0	0.0
Total	6	35	53	.398	135	117	24	1-0	799.1	868	419	68	14	251-9	365	4.13	99	.277	.331	0	ø	0	88	-7	75	-0.9
Erickson, Scott	Scott Gavin; B2.2.1968 Long Beach CA; BR/TR/6´4˝/(222–234); [MinA89 4/112]; d6.25; Col Arizona; [DL 2001 Bal A 190, 2003 Bal A 183]																									
1990	Min A	8	4	.667	19	17	1	0-0	113	108	49	9	5	51-4	53	2.87	145	.256	.342	0	ø	0	112	11	0	1.1
1991	†Min A	**20**	8	**.714**	32	32	5-3	0-0	204	189	80	13	6	71-3	108	3.18	135	.248	.314	0	ø	0	115	24	15	3.1
1992	Min A	13	12	.520	32	32	5-3	0-0	212	197	86	18	8	83-3	101	3.40	120	.252	.328	0	ø	0	87	16	0	1.9
1993	Min A	8	19	.296	34	34	1	0-0	218.2	266	138	17	10	71-1	116	5.19	85	.305	.359	0	ø	0	91	-19	13	-1.9
1994	Min A	8	11	.421	23	23	2-1	0-0	144	173	95	15	9	59-0	104	5.44	91	.299	.370	0	ø	0	85	-8	16	-0.8
1995	Min A	4	6	.400	15	15	0	0-0	87.2	102	61	11	4	32-0	45	5.95	81	.291	.356	0	ø	0	101	-10	0	-0.9
	Bal A	9	4	.692	17	16	7-2	0-0	108.2	111	47	7	1	35-0	61	3.89	123	.273	.330	0	ø	0	122	12	0	1.4
	Year	13	10	.565	32	31	7-2	0-0	196.1	213	108	18	5	67-0	106	4.81	100	.281	.342	0	ø	0	111	1	0	0.5
1996	†Bal A	13	12	.520	34	34	6	0-0	222.1	262	137	21	11	66-4	100	5.02	99	.297	.352	0	ø	0	103	-4	0	-0.2
1997	†Bal A	16	7	.696	34	33	3-2	0-0	221.2	218	100	16	5	61-5	131	3.69	120	.257	.309	2-0-2	.000	0	103	17	0	1.7
1998	Bal A	16	13	.552	36	**36**	**11**-2	0-0	**251.1**	284	125	23	13	69-4	186	4.01	114	.281	.334	2-0-1	.000	1	108	11	0	1.4
1999	Bal A	15	12	.556	34	34	6-**3**	0-0	230.1	244	127	27	11	99-4	106	4.81	98	.280	.358	6-0-1	.000	-1	96	0	0	0.0
2000	Bal A	5	8	.385	16	16	1	0-0	92.2	127	81	14	5	48-0	41	7.87	60	.330	.406	5	.400	1*	92	-31	97	-3.3
2002	Bal A	5	12	.294	29	28	3-1	0-0	160.2	192	109	20	8	68-2	74	5.55	78	.303	.374	4	.000	-0	94	-23	0	-2.1
2004	NY N	0	1	.000	2	2	0	0-0	8	15	9	1	0	4-0	3	7.88	55	.395	.452	3	.000	-0	162	-4	87	-0.4
	Tex A	1	3	.250	4	4	0	0-0	19	23	13	2	0	16-0	6	6.16	80	.307	.415	0	ø	0	94	-2	0	-0.3
2005	LA N	1	4	.200	19	8	0	0-0	55.1	62	37	12	4	25-0	15	6.02	69	.288	.370	13-0-1	.154	-0	102	-10	0	-0.8
2006	NY A	0	0	ø	9	0	0	0-0	11.1	13	12	2	3	7-2	2	7.94	57	.283	.411	0	ø	0	—	-5	0	-0.2
Total	15	142	136	.511	389	364	51-17	0-0	2360.2	2586	1306	228	103	865-32	1252	4.59	99	.282	.348	35-0-5	.114	0	100	-25	601	-0.3
Errickson, Dick	Richard Merriwell "Lief"; B3.5.1912 Vineland NJ; D11.28.1999 Vineland NJ; BL/TR/6´1˝/175; d4.27																									
1938	Bos N	9	7	.563	34	10	6-1	6	122.2	113	53	1	2	56	40	3.15	109	.246	.330	35-0-5	.114	-1	106	3	—	0.4
1939	Bos N	6	9	.400	28	11	3	1	128.1	143	63	6	1	54	33	4.00	92	.293	.365	44-0-2	.227	1	75	-3	—	-0.2
1940	Bos N	12	13	.480	34	29	17-3	4	236.1	241	91	8	1	90	34	3.16	118	.270	.338	83-0-5	.157	-2	87	16	—	1.5
1941	Bos N	6	12	.333	38	23	5-2	1	165.2	192	100	12	4	62	45	4.78	75	.287	.351	45-0-4	.178	-0	85	-21	0	-2.1
1942	Bos N	2	5	.286	21	4	0	1	59.1	76	34	8	0	20	15	5.01	67	.309	.361	16-0-1	.125	-1	82	-9	0	-1.2
	Chi N	1	1	.500	13	0	0	0	24	39	12	1	1	8	9	4.13	78	.411	.462	5	.000	-1	—	-2	0	-0.2
	Year	3	6	.333	34	4	0	1	83.1	115	46	9	1	28	24	4.75	69	.337	.389	21-0-1	.095	-1	83	-11	0	-1.4
Total	5	36	47	.434	168	77	31-6	13	736.1	804	353	36	9	290	176	3.85	93	.282	.350	228-0-17	.162	-5	87	-16	0	-1.8
Erskine, Carl	Carl Daniel "Oisk"; B12.13.1926 Anderson IN; BR/TR/5´10˝/(165–170); d7.25																									
1948	Bro N	6	3	.667	17	9	3	0	64	51	28	5	1	35	29	3.23	124	.231	.339	21	.095	-2	109	5	0	0.4
1949	†Bro N	8	1	.889	22	3	2	0	79.2	68	44	6	2	51	49	4.63	89	.235	.354	26-0-2	.115	-2	179	-4	0	-0.6
1950	Bro N	7	6	.538	22	13	3	1	103	109	56	15	1	35	50	4.72	87	.273	.333	37-0-1	.243	2	121	-6	0	-0.6
1951	Bro N	16	12	.571	46	19	7	4	189.2	206	105	23	2	78	95	4.46	88	.280	.351	61-0-3	.131	-2	130	-12	0	-1.9
1952	†Bro N	14	6	.700	33	26	10-4	2	206.2	167	72	17	2	71	131	2.70	135	.220	.289	66-0-7	.152	-0*	116	20	0	2.0
1953	†Bro N	20	6	**.769**	39	33	16-4	3	246.2	213	106	21	3	95	187	3.54	120	.230	.304	93-0-7	.215	0*	138	20	0	1.8

YEAR	TM LG	W	L	PCT	G	GS	CG-SHO	SV-BS	IP	H	R	HR	HB	BB-IB	SO	ERA	AERA	OAV	OOB	AB-HR-SH	AVG	PB	SUP	APR	DL	PW
1954	Bro N★	18	15	.545	38	37	12-2	1	260.1	239	128	31	4	92	166	4.15	98	.243	.310	88-0-5	.159	-1*	94	0	0	-0.1
1955	†Bro N	11	8	.579	31	29	7-2	1	194.2	185	89	29	0	64-3	84	3.79	107	.253	.312	74-1-0	.203	-0*	98	8	0	0.6
1956	†Bro N	13	11	.542	31	28	8-1	0	186.1	189	92	25	1	57-5	95	4.25	93	.264	.317	66-0-5	.121	-3*	95	-3	0	-0.7
1957	Bro N	5	3	.625	15	7	1	0	66	62	27	8	0	20-1	26	3.55	118	.248	.301	22	.091	-2*	88	5	0	0.4
1958	LA N	4	4	.500	31	9	2-1	0	98.1	115	61	14	0	35-3	54	5.13	80	.297	.353	27-0-1	.037	-3*	105	-10	0	-1.0
1959	LA N	0	3	.000	10	3	0	1	23.1	33	22	5	0	13-1	15	7.71	55	.320	.397	7	.000	-1	70	-8	0	-1.1
Total	12	122	78	.610	335	216	71-14	13	1718.2	1637	830	199	16	646-13	981	4.00	101	.252	.320	588-1-31	.156	-13	111	15	0	-0.8
ESCARREGA, CHICO	Ernesto (Acosta); B12.27.1949 Los Mochis, Sinaloa, Mexico; BR/TR/5´11˝/185; d4.26																									
1982	Chi A	1	3	.250	38	2	0	1-1	73.2	73	33	3	0	16-2	33	3.67	111	.263	.299	0	ø	0	56	4	0	0.2
ESCOBAR, KELVIM	Kelvim Jose (Bolivar); B4.11.1976 LaGuaira, Vargas, Venez.; BR/TR/6´1˝/(195–230); d6.29																									
1997	Tor A	3	2	.600	27	0	0	14-3	31	28	12	1	0	19-2	36	2.90	158	.237	.343	0	ø	0	—	5	0	1.0
1998	Tor A	7	3	.700	22	10	0	0-1	79.2	72	37	5	0	35-0	72	3.73	125	.237	.313	0	ø	0	124	8	20	0.8
1999	Tor A	14	11	.560	33	30	1	0-0	174	203	118	19	10	81-2	129	5.69	87	.293	.371	1	.000	-0	109	-14	0	-1.7
2000	Tor A	10	15	.400	43	24	3-1	2-1	180	186	118	26	3	85-3	142	5.35	94	.267	.347	7	.000	-1	78	-6	0	-0.8
2001	Tor A	6	8	.429	59	11	1-1	0-0	126	93	51	8	3	52-5	121	3.50	131	.204	.287	0	ø	0	90	16	0	1.4
2002	Tor A	5	7	.417	76	0	0	38-8	78	75	39	10	5	44-6	85	4.27	108	.246	.350	0	ø	0	—	3	0	0.6
2003	Tor A	13	9	.591	41	26	1-1	4-1	180.1	189	94	15	9	78-3	159	4.29	111	.270	.348	6	.167	-0	84	9	0	1.0
2004	†Ana A	11	12	.478	33	33	0	0-0	208.1	192	91	21	7	76-2	191	3.93	114	.244	.314	2	.000	-0	81	16	0	1.5
2005	†LA A	3	2	.600	16	7	0	1-0	59.2	45	21	4	2	21-1	63	3.02	142	.207	.283	1-0-1	.000	-0	111	9	126	0.6
2006	LA A	11	14	.440	30	30	1	0-0	189.1	192	93	17	4	50-2	147	3.61	123	.264	.314	4	.000	-0	79	15	15	1.6
Total	10	83	83	.500	380	171	7-3	59-14	1306.1	1275	674	126	43	541-26	1145	4.26	109	.255	.331	21-0-1	.048	-2	90	61	161	6.0
ESHELMAN, VAUGHN	Vaughn Michael; B5.22.1969 Philadelphia PA; BL/TL/6´3˝/(210–215); [BalA91 4/108]; d5.2; Col Houston; [DL 1998 TB A 181]																									
1995	Bos A	6	3	.667	23	14	0	0-0	81.2	86	47	3	1	36-0	41	4.85	100	.272	.346	0	ø	0	107	1	52	0.0
1996	Bos A	6	3	.667	39	10	0	0-0	87.2	112	79	13	2	58-4	59	7.08	72	.311	.405	0	ø	0	127	-19	26	-1.6
1997	Bos A	3	3	.500	21	6	0	0-1	42.2	58	32	3	2	17-5	18	6.33	74	.330	.391	4	.250	0	118	-7	0	-0.9
Total	3	15	9	.625	83	30	0	0-1	212	256	158	19	5	111-9	118	6.07	81	.300	.380	4	.250	0	116	-25	259	-2.5
ESPER, DUKE	Charles H. (b Charles Esbacher); B7.28.1868 Salem NJ; D8.31.1910 Philadelphia PA; TL/5´11.5˝/185; d4.18																									
1890	Phi AA	8	9	.471	18	16	14-1	0	143.2	176	99	1	5	67	61	4.89	79	.292	.368	61	.295	4	107	-12	—	-0.7
	Pit N	0	2	.000	2	2	2	0	17	18	16	0	1	10	9	5.29	62	.265	.367	7	.143	-1	10	-4	—	-0.4
	Phi N	5	0	1.000	5	5	4	0	41	40	22	1	0	16	18	3.07	119	.247	.315	19	.158	-1	131	3	—	0.2
	Year	5	2	.714	7	7	6	0	58	58	38	1	1	26	27	3.72	95	.252	.331	26	.154	-2	99	-2	—	-0.2
1891	Phi N	20	15	.571	39	36	25-1	1	296	302	185	8	7	121	108	3.56	96	.254	.327	123	.220	1	102	-8	—	-0.6
1892	Phi N	11	6	.647	21	18	14	1	160.1	171	84	2	1	60	45	3.42	95	.262	.325	70-1	.243	2*	112	0	—	0.1
	Pit N	2	0	1.000	3	3	1	0	18.1	18	13	0	0	12	5	5.40	61	.247	.353	9	.000	-1	179	-3	—	-0.4
	Year	13	6	.684	24	21	15	1	178.2	189	97	2	1	72	50	3.63	90	.261	.328	79-1	.215	0	121	0	—	-0.3
1893	Was N	12	28	.300	42	36	34	0	334.1	442	277	14	12	156	78	4.71	98	.309	.381	143	.287	7	87	-10	—	-0.2
1894	Was N	5	10	.333	18	14	7	0	116	177	132	8	2	39	24	7.45	71	.346	.395	54-1-0	.259	1*	98	-20	—	-1.6
	†Bal N	10	2	.833	16	9	8	2	101	107	56	1	1	36	25	3.92	139	.269	.331	45	.222	-1	117	18	—	1.5
	Year	15	12	.556	34	23	15	2	217	284	188	9	3	75	49	5.81	92	.312	.367	99-1-0	.242	0	105	-6	—	-0.1
1895	†Bal N	10	12	.455	34	25	16-1	1	218.1	248	132	2	0	79	39	3.92	122	.281	.341	90-0-2	.178	-6	98	19	—	0.8
1896	Bal N	14	5	.737	20	18	14-1	0	155.2	168	80	3	2	39	19	3.58	119	.273	.319	66-0-1	.197	-2	95	14	—	1.1
1897	StL N	1	6	.143	8	8	7	0	61.1	95	51	5	1	12	8	5.28	83	.351	.380	25	.320	1	63	-6	—	-0.4
1898	StL N	3	5	.375	10	8	6	0	64.2	86	49	1	0	22	14	5.98	63	.316	.367	27	.370	2*	66	-11	—	-1.0
Total	9	101	100	.502	236	198	152-4	5	1727.2	2048	1196	46	32	669	453	4.39	96	.288	.351	739-2-3	.241	5	97	-20	—	-1.6
ESPINOSA, NINO	Arnulfo Acevedo (b Arnulfo Acevedo (Espinosa)); B8.15.1953 Villa Altagracia, D.R.; D12.24.1987 Villa Altagracia, D.R.; BR/TR/6´1˝/(165–186); d9.13																									
1974	NY N	0	0	ø	2	1	0	0-0	9	12	5	1	0	0-0	2	5.00	72	.324	.324	2	.500	0	73	-1	0	0.0
1975	NY N	0	1	.000	2	0	0	0-0	3	8	6	0	0	1-0	2	18.00	20	.471	.500	0	ø	0	—	-5	0	-0.8
1976	NY N	4	4	.500	12	5	0	0-0	41.2	41	21	3	0	13-3	30	3.67	91	.265	.316	9-0-1	.000	-1	63	-2	0	-0.5
1977	NY N	10	13	.435	32	29	7-1	0-0	200	188	82	17	5	55-5	105	3.42	111	.249	.304	62-0-7	.129	-2	86	9	0	0.8
1978	NY N	11	15	.423	32	32	6-1	0-0	203.2	230	117	24	3	75-10	76	4.73	75	.292	.352	67-0-7	.209	2	108	-27	0	-2.7
1979	Phi N	14	12	.538	33	33	8-3	0-0	212	211	94	20	3	65-8	88	3.65	106	.262	.318	72-0-4	.194	2*	82	5	0	0.6
1980	Phi N	3	5	.375	12	12	1	0-0	76.1	73	36	9	2	19-2	13	3.77	101	.250	.298	26-0-3	.115	-1*	82	0	83	-0.1
1981	Phi N	2	5	.286	14	14	2	0-0	73.2	98	52	11	1	24-2	22	6.11	60	.333	.378	20-0-3	.200	-0	113	-18	0	-1.6
	Tor A	0	0	ø	1	0	0	0-0	1	4	1	0	0	0-0	0	9.00	44	.667	.667	0	ø	0	—	0	0	0.0
Total	8	44	55	.444	140	126	24-5	0-0	820.1	865	414	85	14	252-30	338	4.17	89	.275	.329	258-0-25	.171	0	92	-39	83	-4.3
ESPOSITO, MIKE	Michael Anthony; B9.27.1981 Los Angeles CA; BR/TR/6´0˝/190; [ColN02 12/351]; d9.21; Col Arizona St.																									
2005	Col N	0	2	.000	3	3	0	0-0	14.2	21	11	3	0	9-1	5	6.75	69	.333	.417	5-0-1	.200	-0	61	-3	0	-0.3
ESSER, MARK	Mark Gerald; B4.1.1956 Erie PA; BR/TL/6´1˝/190; [ChiA77*8/160]; d4.22; Col Miami–Dade North (FL) CC																									
1979	Chi A	0	0	ø	2	0	0	0-0	1.2	2	3	0	0	4-0	1	16.20	26	.286	.545	0	ø	0	—	-2	0	-0.1
ESSICK, BILL	William Earl "Vinegar Bill"; B12.18.1880 Grand Ridge IL; D10.12.1951 Los Angeles CA; TR/5´10˝/175; d9.12; Col Knox																									
1906	Cin N	2	2	.500	6	4	3	0	39.1	39	18	1	2	16	16	2.97	93	.273	.354	13-0-2	.077	-1	106	-1	—	-0.2
1907	Cin N	0	2	.000	3	2	2	0	21.2	23	15	0	1	8	7	2.91	89	.274	.344	8	.000	-1	41	-2	—	-0.3
Total	2	2	4	.333	9	6	5	0	61	62	33	1	3	24	23	2.95	91	.273	.350	21-0-2	.048	-2	85	-3	—	-0.5
ESTELLE, DICK	Richard Henry; B1.18.1942 Lakewood NJ; BB/TL/6´2˝/187; d9.4																									
1964	SF N	1	2	.333	6	6	0	0	41.2	39	15	3	0	23-0	23	3.02	118	.247	.341	15-0-1	.067	-1	107	3	0	0.1
1965	SF N	0	0	ø	6	1	0	0	11.1	12	6	0	1	8-1	6	3.97	91	.261	.375	1	.000	0	146	-1	0	0.0
Total	2	1	2	.333	12	7	0	0	53	51	21	3	1	31-1	29	3.23	111	.250	.349	16-0-1	.063	-0	112	2	0	0.1
ESTES, SHAWN	Aaron Shawn; B2.18.1973 San Bernardino CA; BR/TL/6´2˝/(185–220); [SeaA91 1/11]; d9.16																									
1995	SF N	0	3	.000	3	3	0	0-0	17.1	16	14	2	1	5-0	14	6.75	61	.229	.289	5	.000	-1	36	-5	0	-0.7
1996	SF N	3	5	.375	11	11	0	0-0	70	63	30	3	2	39-3	60	3.60	115	.243	.347	19-0-6	.158	-0*	91	5	0	0.5
1997	†SF N★	19	5	.792	32	32	3-2	0-0	201	162	80	12	8	100-2	181	3.18	130	.223	.323	68-1-7	.147	1*	122	21	6	2.5
1998	SF N	7	12	.368	25	25	1-1	0-0	149.1	150	89	14	5	80-6	136	5.06	80	.269	.364	42-0-8	.190	1*	91	-17	55	-1.7
1999	SF N	11	11	.500	32	32	1-1	0-0	203	209	121	21	5	112-2	159	4.92	87	.268	.362	61-0-10	.164	2*	117	-16	0	-1.1
2000	†SF N	15	6	.714	30	30	4-2	0-0	190.1	194	99	11	3	108-1	136	4.26	102	.275	.371	68-1-11	.206	4*	156	2	13	0.8
2001	SF N	9	8	.529	27	27	0	0-0	159	151	78	11	5	77-7	109	4.02	102	.253	.339	42-0-6	.071	-2	96	1	30	0.0
2002	NY N	4	9	.308	23	23	1-1	0-0	132.2	133	70	12	5	66-9	92	4.55	87	.267	.356	35-1-5	.086	-1*	86	-7	0	-0.7
	Cin N	1	3	.250	6	6	0	0-0	28	38	24	1	4	17-0	17	7.71	55	.345	.444	8-0-2	.000	-1	119	-9	0	-1.1
	Year	5	12	.294	29	29	1-1	0-0	160.2	171	94	13	9	83-9	109	5.10	79	.281	.373	43-1-7	.070	-2	93	-18	0	-1.8
2003	Chi N	8	11	.421	29	28	1-1	0-0	152.1	182	113	20	1	83-1	103	5.73	76	.305	.387	39-1-9	.179	2*	103	-26	0	-2.5
2004	Col N	15	8	.652	34	34	1	0-0	202	223	133	30	11	105-5	117	5.84	82	.291	.380	72-0-7	.236	2*	105	-20	0	-1.8
2005	Ari N	7	8	.467	21	21	2	0-0	123.2	132	70	15	4	45-0	63	4.80	92	.280	.345	29-0-2	.069	-2	82	-4	65	-0.5
2006	SD N	0	1	.000	1	1	0	0-0	6	5	3	0	1	3-0	4	4.50	92	.217	.333	1	.000	0	22	0	179	0.0
Total	12	99	90	.524	274	273	14-8	0-0	1634.2	1658	924	152	55	840-36	1191	4.71	91	.269	.359	489-4-73	.157	6	107	-75	348	-6.3
ESTOCK, GEORGE	George John; B11.2.1924 Stirling NJ; BR/TR/6´0˝/185; d4.21																									
1951	Bos N	0	1	.000	37	1	0	3	60.1	56	33	2	0	37	11	4.33	85	.258	.366	7-0-1	.286	1	0	-5	0	-0.1
ESTRADA, CHUCK	Charles Leonard; B2.15.1938 San Luis Obispo CA; BR/TR/6´1˝/(175–185); d4.21; C6																									
1960	Bal A★	**18**	11	.621	36	25	12-1	2	208.2	162	87	18	15	101-3	144	3.58	106	**.218**	.319	64-0-9	.141	-0	105	8	0	1.0
1961	Bal A	15	9	.625	33	31	6-1	0	212	159	91	19	10	132-0	160	3.69	104	**.207**	.329	70-0-9	.114	-3	116	7	0	0.3
1962	Bal A	9	17	.346	34	33	6	0	223.1	199	112	24	10	121-16	165	3.83	97	.240	.341	66-1-8	.152	-0*	81	-5	0	-0.7
1963	Bal A	3	2	.600	8	7	0	0	31.1	26	17	2	1	19-0	16	4.60	76	.226	.336	10-0-2	.100	-1	121	-4	100	-0.6
1964	Bal A	3	2	.600	17	6	0	0	54.2	62	34	8	2	21-5	32	5.27	68	.282	.348	14-0-2	.143	-0*	162	-10	41	-0.9
1966	Chi N	1	1	.500	9	1	0	0	12.1	16	12	2	1	5-0	3	7.30	50	.314	.379	3	.000	-0	167	-5	0	-0.8
1967	NY N	1	2	.333	9	2	0	0	22	28	24	5	1	17-1	15	9.41	36	.326	.442	5	.000	-1	0*	-14	0	-1.7
Total	7	50	44	.532	146	105	24-2	2	764.1	652	377	78	40	416-25	535	4.07	92	.232	.336	232-1-30	.129	-5	103	-23	141	-3.4

YEAR	TM LG	W	L	PCT	G	GS	CG-SHO	SV-BS	IP	H	R	HR	HB	BB-IB	SO	ERA	AERA	OAV	OOB	AB-HR-SH	AVG	PB	SUP	APR	DL	PW
Estrada, Horacio	Horacio (Jimenez); B10.19.1975 San Joaquin, Venezuela; BL/TL/6´1˝/(160–192); d5.4																									
1999	Mil N	0	0	ø	4	0	0	0-0	7.1	10	6	4	0	4-0	5	7.36	63	.313	.389	2	.000	-0	—	-2	0	-0.1
2000	Mil N	3	0	1.000	7	4	0	0-0	24.1	30	18	5	2	20-4	13	6.29	73	.300	.423	7-0-1	.143	-0	179	-4	0	-0.4
2001	Col N	1	1	.500	4	0	0	0-0	4.1	8	7	1	1	1-0	4	14.54	37	.400	.455	0	ø	0	—	-3	90	-0.6
Total	3	4	1	.800	15	4	0	0-0	36	48	31	10	3	25-4	22	7.50	63	.316	.420	9-0-1	.111	-0	179	-9	90	-1.1
Estrada, Oscar	Oscar; B2.15.1904 Havana, Cuba; D1.2.1978 Havana, Cuba; BL/TL/5´8˝/160; d4.21																									
1929	StL A	0	0	ø	1	0	0	0	1	1	0	0	0	1	0	0.00	ø	.250	.400	0	ø	0	—	0	—	0.0
Estrella, Leo	Leoncio (Ramirez); B2.20.1975 Puerto Plata, D.R.; BR/TR/6´1˝/(180–190); d7.18																									
2000	Tor A	0	0	ø	2	0	0	0-0	4.2	9	3	1	0	0-0	3	5.79	87	.450	.429	0	ø	0	—	0	0	0.0
2003	Mil N	7	3	.700	58	0	0	3-5	66	75	32	10	3	21-5	25	4.36	99	.290	.346	0	ø	0	—	1	0	0.2
2004	SF N	0	0	ø	2	0	0	0-0	1.1	8	4	0	0	1-0	0	27.00	16	.727	.692	0	ø	0	—	-3	0	-0.2
Total	3	7	3	.700	62	0	0	3-5	72	92	39	11	3	22-5	28	4.88	90	.317	.366	0	ø	0	—	-2	0	0.0
Etherton, Seth	Seth Michael; B10.17.1976 Laguna Beach CA; BR/TR/6´1˝/200; [AnaA98 1/18]; d5.26; Col USC; [DL 2002 Cin N 69]																									
2000	Ana A	5	1	.833	11	11	0	0-0	60.1	68	38	16	1	22-0	32	5.52	94	.278	.338	2	.000	0	114	-1	57	-0.1
2003	Cin N	2	4	.333	7	7	0	0-0	30	39	23	4	3	15-1	17	6.90	60	.322	.401	7-0-3	.143	-0	77	-8	0	-1.4
2005	Oak A	1	1	.500	3	3	0	0-0	17.2	16	13	4	0	5-0	10	6.62	66	.235	.284	0	ø	0	134	-4	0	-0.4
2006	KC A	1	1	.500	2	2	0	0-0	7.2	10	9	3	0	6-0	4	9.39	50	.313	.400	0	ø	0	70	-4	0	-0.7
Total	4	9	7	.563	23	23	0	0-0	115.2	133	83	27	4	48-1	63	6.30	75	.285	.352	9-0-3	.111	-0	102	-17	126	-2.6
Ettles, Mark	Mark Edward; B10.30.1966 Perth, Western Australia, Australia; BR/TR/6´0˝/185; [DetA89 33/863]; d6.5; Col West Florida																									
1993	SD N	1	0	1.000	14	0	0	0-0	18	23	16	4	0	4-1	9	6.50	64	.307	.333	2	.000	-0	—	-5	0	-0.3
Eubank, John	John Franklin "Honest John"; B9.9.1872 Servia IN; D11.3.1958 Bellevue MI; BR/TR/6´2˝/215; d9.19																									
1905	Det A	1	0	1.000	3	2	0	0	17.1	13	12	0	1	3	1	2.08	132	.210	.258	14	.357	1*	194	-1	—	0.0
1906	Det A	4	10	.286	24	12	7-1	2	135	147	69	0	8	35	38	3.53	78	.280	.335	63-0-2	.206	0*	69	-11	—	-1.1
1907	Det A	3	3	.500	15	8	4-1	0	81	88	40	0	0	20	17	2.67	98	.279	.322	31	.129	-1	110	-2	—	-0.3
Total	3	8	13	.381	42	22	11-2	2	233.1	248	121	0	9	58	56	3.12	87	.275	.325	108-0-2	.204	-1	96	-14	—	-1.4
Eubanks, Uel	Uel Melvin "Poss"; B2.14.1903 Quinlan TX; D11.21.1954 Dallas TX; BR/TR/6´3˝/175; d7.20																									
1922	Chi N	0	0	ø	2	0	0	0	1.2	5	9	0	0	4	1	27.00	16	.556	.692	1	1.000	1	—	-5	—	-0.2
Eufemia, Frank	Frank Anthony; B12.23.1959 Bronx NY; BR/TR/5´11˝/185; [MinA82 18/448]; d5.21; Col Ramapo																									
1985	Min A	4	2	.667	39	0	0	2-0	61.2	56	27	7	0	21-7	30	3.79	117	.250	.310	0	ø	0	—	5	0	0.5
Evans, Bart	Bart Steven; B12.30.1970 Springfield MO; BR/TR/6´2˝/210; [KCA92 9/246]; d6.16; Col Missouri St.																									
1998	KC A	0	0	ø	8	0	0	0-0	9	7	3	1	0	0-0	7	2.00	243	.206	.206	0	ø	0	—	2	31	0.1
Evans, Chick	Charles Franklin; B10.15.1889 Arlington VT; D9.2.1916 Schenectady NY; BR/TR; d9.19																									
1909	Bos N	0	3	.000	4	3	1	0	21.2	25	16	0	0	14	11	4.57	62	.305	.406	9	.000	-1	50	-4	—	-0.6
1910	Bos N	1	1	.500	13	1	0	2	31	28	20	1	3	27	12	5.23	64	.275	.439	10	.100	-1	22	-4	—	-0.4
Total	2	1	4	.200	17	4	1	2	52.2	53	36	1	3	41	23	4.96	63	.288	.425	19	.053	-2	41	-8	—	-1.0
Evans, Roy	Roy; B3.19.1874 Knoxville TN; D8.15.1915 Galveston TX; BR/TR/6´0˝/180; d5.15; Col Emporia St.																									
1897	StL N	0	0	ø	3	0	0	0	13	33	27	1	0	13	4	9.69	45	.471	.554	3	.000	0	—	-10	—	-0.4
	Lou N	5	4	.556	9	8	6	0	59.1	66	40	4	8	24	20	4.10	104	.280	.366	23	.130	-2	94	2	—	0.0
	Year	5	4	.556	12	8	6	0	72.1	99	67	5	8	37	24	5.10	84	.324	.410	26	.115	-2	93	-10	—	-0.4
1898	Was N	3	3	.500	7	6	4	0	50.2	50	27	0	7	25	11	3.38	109	.256	.361	19	.053	-2	94	2	—	-0.1
1899	Was N	3	4	.429	7	7	6	0	54	60	40	1	0	25	27	5.67	69	.280	.356	20-0-2	.200	-1	100	-8	—	-0.8
1902	NY N	8	13	.381	23	17	17	0	176	186	87	2	9	58	48	3.17	89	.271	.336	54-0-4	.148	-1	54	-5	—	-0.5
	Bro N	5	6	.455	13	11	11-2	0	97.1	91	42	0	2	33	35	2.68	103	.247	.313	34	.265	2	58	0	—	0.1
	Year	13	19	.406	36	28	28-2	0	273.1	277	129	2	11	91	83	3.00	93	.263	.328	88-0-4	.193	1	56	-8	—	-0.4
1903	Bro N	5	9	.357	15	12	9	0	110	121	75	1	7	41	42	3.27	98	.297	.371	29-0-4	.172	0	58	-7	—	-0.8
	StL A	0	4	.000	7	7	4	0	54	66	30	1	3	14	24	4.17	70	.300	.350	19-0-1	.105	-1	60	-6	—	-0.5
Total	5	29	43	.403	84	68	57-2	0	614.1	673	368	10	36	233	211	3.66	88	.281	.353	201-0-11	.159	-4	72	-32	—	-3.0
Evans, Red	Russell Edison; B11.12.1906 Chicago IL; D6.14.1982 Lakeview AR; BR/TR/5´11˝/168; d4.24																									
1936	Chi A	0	3	.000	17	0	0	1	47.1	70	46	4	0	22	19	7.61	68	.338	.402	15	.133	-1*	—	-12	—	-0.7
1939	Bro N	1	8	.111	24	6	0	1	64.1	74	43	4	0	26	28	5.18	78	.284	.348	13-0-2	.308	1	29	-9	—	-0.9
Total	2	1	11	.083	41	6	0	2	111.2	144	89	8	0	48	47	6.21	73	.308	.372	28-0-2	.214	-0	29	-21	—	-1.6
Evans, Jake	Uriah L. P. "Bloody Jake"; B9.22.1856 Baltimore MD; D1.16.1907 Baltimore MD; TR/5´8˝/154; d5.1.1879; ▲																									
1880	Tro N	0	0	ø	1	0	0	0	4	11	8	0	—	0	0	13.50	19	.524	.524	180	.256	0*	—	-4	—	-0.1
1882	Wor N	0	1	.000	1	1	1	0	8	13	10	1	—	0	2	5.63	55	.317	.317	334	.213	-0*	119	-2	—	-0.2
1883	Cle N	0	0	ø	1	0	0	0	3	0	0	0	—	0	1	0.00	ø	.000	.000	332	.238	0*	—	-1	—	0.1
Total	3	0	1	.000	3	1	1	0	15	24	18	1	—	0	3	6.60	45	.338	.338	846	.232	-0	119	-5	—	-0.2
Evans, Art	William Arthur; B8.3.1911 Elvins MO; D1.8.1952 Wichita KS; BB/TL/6´1.5˝/181; d6.20																									
1932	Chi A	0	0	ø	7	0	0	0	18	19	9	1	0	10	6	3.00	144	.257	.345	5	.000	-0	—	2	—	0.1
Evans, Bill	William James; B2.10.1893 Reidsville NC; D12.21.1946 Burlington NC; BR/TR/6´0˝/175; d8.13; Mil 1918; Col North Carolina St.																									
1916	Pit N	2	5	.286	13	7	3	0	63	57	27	2	3	16	21	3.00	89	.249	.306	20-0-1	.150	-1	56	-2	—	-0.2
1917	Pit N	0	4	.000	8	2	1	0	26.2	24	14	0	1	14	5	3.38	84	.231	.328	9	.111	-0	27	-2	—	-0.3
1919	Pit N	0	4	.000	7	3	2	0	36.2	41	25	1	0	18	15	5.65	53	.297	.378	11-0-1	.000	-1	44	-10	—	-1.1
Total	3	2	13	.133	28	12	6	0	126.1	122	66	3	4	48	41	3.85	73	.259	.333	40-0-2	.100	-2	47	-14	—	-1.6
Evans, Bill	William Lawrence; B3.25.1919 Quanah TX; D11.30.1983 Grand Junction CO; BR/TR/6´2˝/180; d4.21																									
1949	Chi A	0	1	.000	4	0	0	0	6.1	6	6	0	0	8	1	7.11	59	.261	.452	1	.000	-0	—	-2	0	-0.3
1951	Bos A	0	0	ø	9	0	0	0	15.1	15	8	0	0	8	3	4.11	109	.268	.359	4	.000	-1	—	1	0	-0.1
Total	2	0	1	.000	13	0	0	0	21.2	21	14	0	0	16	4	4.98	88	.266	.389	5	.000	-1	—	-1	0	-0.4
Eveland, Dana	Dana James; B10.29.1983 Olympia WA; BL/TL/6´1˝/(220–250); [MilN02 16/469]; d7.16; Col Canyons (CA) [JC]																									
2005	Mil N	1	1	.500	27	0	0	1-1	31.2	40	21	2	1	18-3	23	5.97	71	.317	.404	1-0-1	.000	-0	—	-5	0	-0.3
2006	Mil N	0	3	.000	9	5	0	0-1	27.2	39	25	4	5	16-2	32	8.13	55	.331	.429	7-0-1	.000	-1	90	-10	0	-1.0
Total	2	1	4	.200	36	5	0	1-2	59.1	79	46	6	6	34-5	55	6.98	63	.324	.416	8-0-2	.000	-1	90	-15	0	-1.3
Everitt, Leon	Edward Leon; B1.12.1947 Marshall TX; BL/TR/6´1.5˝/180; [LAN65 10/303]; d4.21																									
1969	SD N	0	1	.000	5	0	0	0-0	15.2	18	14	4	1	12-1	11	8.04	45	.300	.425	3	.000	-0*	—	-7	0	-0.4
Eversgerd, Bryan	Bryan David; B2.11.1969 Centralia IL; BR/TL/6´1˝/190; d4.30; Col Kaskaskia (IL) CC																									
1994	StL N	2	3	.400	40	1	0	0-1	67.2	75	36	8	2	20-1	47	4.52	94	.295	.349	6-0-2	.000	-1	64	-2	0	-0.2
1995	Mon N	0	0	ø	25	0	0	0-0	21	22	13	2	1	9-2	8	5.14	84	.268	.340	1	.000	-0	—	-2	0	-0.1
1997	Tex A	0	2	.000	3	0	0	0-0	1.1	5	3	0	0	3-0	2	20.25	24	.556	.667	0	ø	0	—	-2	0	-0.4
1998	StL N	0	0	ø	8	0	0	0-0	6	9	7	1	1	2-0	4	9.00	47	.346	.387	0	ø	0	—	-3	0	-0.2
Total	4	2	5	.286	76	1	0	0-1	96	111	59	11	4	34-3	61	5.16	83	.299	.359	7-0-2	.000	-1	64	-9	0	-0.9
Ewing, Bob	George Lemuel "Long Bob"; B4.24.1873 New Hampshire OH; D6.20.1947 Wapakoneta OH; BR/TR/6´1.5˝/170; d4.19																									
1902	Cin N	5	6	.455	15	12	10	0	117.2	126	67	1	3	47	44	2.98	101	.274	.345	71	.169	-1*	125	-2	—	-0.4
1903	Cin N	14	13	.519	29	28	27-1	1	246.2	254	127	3	10	64	104	2.77	128	.265	.317	95-0-1	.253	4*	93	17	—	2.3
1904	Cin N	11	13	.458	26	24	22	0	212	198	85	3	4	58	99	2.46	119	.253	.308	97-1-0	.258	5*	92	11	—	1.7
1905	Cin N	20	11	.645	40	34	30-4	0	311.2	284	125	5	11	79	164	2.51	132	.246	.301	122-0-5	.262	4*	113	27	—	2.9
1906	Cin N	13	14	.481	33	32	26-2	0	287.2	248	98	4	2	60	145	2.38	116	.238	.281	101-1-1	.139	-3	87	15	—	1.0
1907	Cin N	17	19	.472	41	37	32-2	0	332.2	279	104	2	7	85	147	1.73	150	.231	.286	123-1-10	.154	-1*	100	26	—	2.6
1908	Cin N	17	15	.531	37	32	23-4	3	293.2	247	105	5	5	57	95	2.21	105	.241	.284	94-0-4	.149	0	100	3	—	0.2
1909	Cin N	11	12	.478	31	29	14-2	0	218.1	195	94	1	6	63	86	2.43	107	.238	.298	73-0-5	.110	-4	105	2	—	-0.4

YEAR	TM LG	W	L	PCT	G	GS	CG-SHO	SV-BS	IP	H	R	HR	HB	BB-IB	SO	ERA	AERA	OAV	OOB	AB-HR-SH	AVG	PB	SUP	APR	DL	PW
1910	Phi N	16	14	.533	34	32	20-4	0	255.1	235	110	5	7	86	102	3.00	104	.251	.318	90-0-4	.222	2	106	5	—	0.6
1911	Phi N	0	1	.000	4	3	1	0	24	29	25	2	0	14	12	7.88	44	.309	.398	6-0-1	.333	0	138	-11	—	-0.5
1912	StL N	0	0	ø	1	1	0	0	1.1	2	0	0	0	1	0	0.00	ø	.333	.429	0	ø	0	86	1	—	0.0
Total	11	124	118	.512	291	264	205-19	4	2301	2097	940	31	55	614	998	2.49	116	.247	.302	872-3-31	.195	7	102	94	—	10.0
EWING, JOHN	John "Long John"; B6.1.1863 Cincinnati OH; D4.23.1895 Denver CO; TR/6´1˝/168; d6.18.1883; b–Buck																									
1888	Lou AA	8	13	.381	21	21	21-2	0	191	175	105	3	8	34	87	2.83	109	.235	.276	79	.203	-2	78	8	—	0.6
1889	Lou AA	6	30	.167	40	39	37-1	0	331	407	296	6	14	147	155	4.87	79	.293	.367	134	.172	-6*	64	-37	—	-3.3
1890	NY P	18	12	.600	35	31	27-1	2	267.1	294	196	6	16	104	145	4.24	107	.267	.339	114-2	.211	-3	92	10	—	0.6
1891	NY N	21	8	**.724**	33	30	28-5	0	269.1	237	118	2	11	105	138	**2.27**	141	.227	.305	113	.204	-2	108	30	—	2.5
Total	4	53	63	.457	129	121	113-9	2	1058.2	1113	715	17	49	390	525	3.68	101	.260	.329	440-2	.195	-12	85	11	—	0.4
EWING, BUCK	William; B10.17.1859 Hoagland OH; D10.20.1906 Cincinnati OH; BR/TR/5´10˝/188; d9.9.1880; M7; HF1939; b–John; ▲																									
1882	Tro N	0	0	ø	1	0	0	0	1	2	1	0	—	1	0	9.00	31	.400	.500	328-2	.271	0*	—	0	—	0.0
1884	NY N	0	1	.000	1	1	1	0	8	7	3	0	—	4	3	1.13	265	.241	.333	382-3	.277	0*	36	1	—	0.2
1885	NY N	0	1	.000	1	0	0	0	2	4	4	0	—	3	0	4.50	59	.444	.583	342-6	.304	0*	—	-1	—	-0.2
1888	†NY N	0	0	ø	2	0	0	0	7	8	9	1	1	4	6	2.57	107	.174	.255	415-6	.306	1*	—	-1	—	0.0
1889	†NY N	2	0	1.000	3	2	2	0	20	23	14	0	0	8	12	4.05	97	.280	.344	407-4	.327	2*	136	0	—	0.1
1890	NY P	0	1	.000	1	1	1	0	9	11	5	1	0	3	2	4.00	114	.289	.341	352-8	.338	0*	27	1	—	0.1
Total	6	2	3	.400	9	4	4	0	47	55	36	2	1	23	23	3.45	105	.263	.339	2226-29	.305	4	86	0	—	0.2
EYRE, SCOTT	Scott Alan; B5.30.1972 Inglewood CA; BL/TL/6´1˝/(190–215); [TexA91 9/248]; d8.1; b–Willie; Col Southern Idaho [JC]																									
1997	Chi A	4	4	.500	11	11	0	0-0	60.2	62	36	11	1	31-1	36	5.04	87	.267	.353	2	.500	0	91	-4	0	-0.4
1998	Chi A	3	8	.273	33	17	0	0-0	107	114	78	24	2	64-0	73	5.38	85	.271	.368	3	.000	-0	100	-13	0	-1.1
1999	Chi A	1	1	.500	21	0	0	0-0	25	38	22	6	1	15-2	17	7.56	65	.339	.419	0	ø	0	—	-7	26	-0.5
2000	Chi A	1	1	.500	13	1	0	0-0	19	29	15	3	1	12-0	16	6.63	76	.372	.452	0	ø	0	93	-3	0	-0.3
2001	Tor A	1	2	.333	17	0	0	2-1	15.2	15	6	1	1	7-2	16	3.45	133	.263	.348	0	ø	0	—	2	0	0.4
2002	Tor A	2	4	.333	49	3	0	0-1	63.1	69	37	4	0	29-7	51	4.97	93	.278	.349	0	ø	0	127	-2	0	-0.2
	†SF N	0	0	ø	21	0	0	0-0	11.1	11	4	0	0	7-1	7	1.59	249	.256	.360	0	ø	0	—	2	0	0.1
2003	†SF N	2	1	.667	74	0	0	1-2	57	60	23	4	1	26-0	35	3.32	128	.268	.343	2	.500	0	—	6	0	0.3
2004	SF N	2	2	.500	83	0	0	1-4	52.2	43	26	8	0	27-3	49	4.10	106	.219	.310	2	.000	-0	—	1	18	0.1
2005	SF N	2	2	.500	**86**	0	0	0-2	68.1	48	21	3	4	26-0	65	2.63	161	.200	.286	2	.000	0	—	12	0	0.6
2006	Chi N	1	3	.250	74	0	0	0-3	61.1	61	25	11	0	30-4	73	3.38	136	.265	.345	1	.000	-0	—	8	16	0.5
Total	10	19	28	.404	482	32	0	4-13	541.1	550	293	75	11	274-20	438	4.39	102	.264	.349	12	.167	0	101	2	60	-0.5
EYRE, WILLIE	William Mays; B7.21.1978 Fountain Valley CA; BR/TR/6´2˝/205; [MinA99 23/689]; d4.6; b–Scott; Col Eastern Utah JC																									
2006	Min A	1	0	1.000	42	0	0	0-0	59.1	75	36	8	6	22-4	26	5.31	86	.309	.376	1	.000	-0	—	-4	0	-0.2
EYRICH, GEORGE	George Lincoln; B3.3.1925 Reading PA; BR/TR/5´11˝/175; d6.13; Mil 1943–46																									
1943	Phi N	0	0	ø	9	0	0	0	18.2	27	8	1	0	9	5	3.38	100	.342	.409	2	.000	-0	—	0	0	0.0
FABER, RED	Urban Clarence; B9.6.1888 Cascade IA; D9.25.1976 Chicago IL; BB/TR/6´2˝/180; d4.17; Mil 1918; C3; HF1964; Col Loras																									
1914	Chi A	10	9	.526	40	19	11-2	**4**	181.1	154	77	3	12	64	88	2.68	100	.239	.319	55-0-2	.145	2	100	0	—	0.3
1915	Chi A	24	14	.632	**50**	32	21-2	2	299.2	264	118	3	11	99	182	2.55	117	.240	.309	84-0-12	.131	2	134	12	—	1.9
1916	Chi A	17	9	.654	35	25	15-3	1	205.1	167	67	1	5	61	87	2.02	137	.228	.292	63-0-4	.095	-3	102	15	—	1.7
1917	†Chi A	16	13	.552	41	29	16-3	3	248	224	92	1	10	85	84	1.92	138	.247	.319	69-0-8	.058	-4	113	13	—	1.2
1918	Chi A	4	1	.800	11	9	5-1	1	80.2	70	23	3	0	23	26	1.23	223	.245	.301	24-0-2	.042	-2	98	10	—	0.5
1919	Chi A	11	9	.550	25	20	9	0	162.1	185	92	7	8	45	45	3.83	83	.287	.341	54-0-3	.185	-0	112	-14	—	-1.6
1920	Chi A	23	13	.639	40	**39**	28-2	1	319	332	136	8	4	88	108	2.99	126	.277	.328	104-0-6	.106	-4	124	24	—	2.0
1921	Chi A	25	15	.625	43	39	**32**-4	1	330.2	293	107	10	7	87	124	**2.48**	**171**	**.242**	**.297**	108-0-8	.148	-4	84	**64**	—	**6.8**
1922	Chi A	21	17	.553	43	38	**31**-4	2	**352**	334	128	10	6	83	148	**2.81**	**145**	.252	**.299**	125-0-10	.200	-2	89	**47**	—	4.6
1923	Chi A	14	11	.560	32	31	15-2	0	232.1	233	114	6	6	62	91	3.41	116	.259	.311	69-1-8	.217	3*	100	10	—	1.4
1924	Chi A	9	11	.450	21	20	9	0	161.1	173	78	5	2	58	47	3.85	107	.282	.346	54-0-2	.148	-2	106	7	—	0.4
1925	Chi A	12	11	.522	34	32	16-1	0	238	266	117	8	2	59	71	3.78	110	.289	.333	77-0-6	.104	-4	106	10	—	0.5
1926	Chi A	15	9	.625	27	25	13-1	0	184.2	203	84	3	2	57	65	3.56	109	.281	.335	60-0-6	.150	-0	110	7	—	0.6
1927	Chi A	4	7	.364	18	15	6	0	110.2	131	64	2	5	41	39	4.55	89	.312	.380	37-0-5	.270	2	77	-5	—	-0.2
1928	Chi A	13	9	.591	27	27	16-2	0	201.1	223	98	11	4	68	43	3.75	108	.286	.347	70-1-4	.114	-3	94	7	—	0.4
1929	Chi A	13	13	.500	31	31	15-1	0	234	241	119	10	9	61	68	3.88	110	.273	.327	78-1-4	.128	-3	87	11	—	0.8
1930	Chi A	8	13	.381	29	26	10	1	169	188	101	7	5	49	62	4.21	110	.283	.337	49-0-5	.041	-5	83	7	—	0.3
1931	Chi A	10	14	.417	44	19	5-1	1	184	210	96	11	3	57	49	3.82	112	.285	.339	53-0-4	.075	-3	70	8	—	0.6
1932	Chi A	2	11	.154	42	5	0	6	106	123	61	0	1	38	26	3.74	116	.290	.350	18-0-4	.222	3	118	5	—	0.8
1933	Chi A	3	4	.429	36	2	0	5	86.1	92	41	2	1	28	18	3.44	123	.275	.332	18-0-1	.000	-3	50	7	—	0.3
Total	20	254	213	.544	669	483	273-29	28	4086.2	4106	1813	111	103	1213	1471	3.15	119	.266	.323	1269-3-104	.134	-31	100	245	—	23.3
FACE, ROY	Elroy Leon; B2.20.1928 Stephentown NY; BR/TR (BB 1960–69)/5´8˝/155; d4.16																									
1953	Pit N	6	8	.429	41	13	2	0	119	145	90	19	2	30	56	6.58	68	.297	.340	30-0-4	.133	-1*	81	-23	0	-2.5
1955	Pit N	5	7	.417	42	10	4	5	125.2	128	58	10	0	40-4	84	3.58	115	.268	.323	26-0-3	.115	-1*	58	7	0	0.5
1956	Pit N	12	13	.480	**68**	3	0	6	135.1	131	57	16	1	42-15	96	3.52	107	.256	.313	26-0-1	.192	-0*	86	5	0	1.0
1957	Pit N	4	6	.400	59	1	0	10	93.2	97	41	9	1	24-5	53	3.07	123	.270	.311	16-0-1	.125	-1	70	6	0	0.6
1958	Pit N	5	2	.714	57	0	0	**20**	84	77	30	6	0	22-6	47	2.89	134	.244	.293	7-0-2	.000	-1	—	9	0	1.2
1959	Pit N★	18	1	**.947**	57	0	0	10	93.1	91	29	5	1	25-8	69	2.70	143	.266	.315	13-0-1	.231	0*	—	14	0	2.8
1960	†Pit N★	10	8	.556	**68**	0	0	24	114.2	93	39	11	0	29-9	72	2.90	129	.226	.274	17-0-2	.412	2	—	11	0	2.6
1961	Pit N★	6	12	.333	62	0	0	**17**	92	94	44	12	1	10-4	55	3.82	105	.267	.287	11	.273	0	—	2	0	0.5
1962	Pit N	8	7	.533	63	0	0	**28**	91	74	23	7	1	18-7	45	1.88	209	.231	.270	12-0-1	.083	-1	—	**20**	0	4.1
1963	Pit N	3	9	.250	56	0	0	16	69.2	75	33	6	3	19-11	41	3.23	102	.285	.338	8	.250	0	—	-1	0	-0.1
1964	Pit N	3	3	.500	55	0	0	4	79.2	82	48	11	1	27-10	63	5.20	68	.269	.324	4	.000	-0	—	-13	0	-1.1
1965	Pit N	5	2	.714	16	0	0	0	20.1	20	6	1	0	7-5	19	2.66	132	.263	.321	1	.000	-0	—	2	105	0.5
1966	Pit N	6	6	.500	54	0	0	18	70	68	24	9	1	24-5	67	2.70	132	.262	.325	11-0-1	.000	-1	—	7	0	1.3
1967	Pit N	7	5	.583	61	0	0	17	74.1	62	23	5	0	22-11	41	2.42	139	.230	.286	6	.000	-1	—	8	0	1.6
1968	Pit N	2	4	.333	43	0	0	13	52	46	17	3	2	7-2	34	2.60	113	.238	.271	4-0-1	.000	-0	—	2	0	0.3
	Det A	0	0	ø	2	0	0	0	1	2	0	0	0	1-1	1	0.00	ø	.500	.600	0	ø	0	—	0	0	0.0
1969	Mon N	4	2	.667	44	0	0	5-1	59.1	62	29	11	0	15-3	34	3.94	94	.263	.307	2-0-1	.500	0	—	-1	0	-0.1
Total	16	104	95	.523	848	27	6	193-1	1375	1347	591	141	14	362-106	877	3.48	109	.260	.308	194-0-18	.160	-4	81	55	105	13.2
FAETH, TONY	Anthony Joseph; B7.9.1893 Aberdeen SD; D12.22.1982 St.Paul MN; BR/TR/6´0˝/180; d8.10																									
1919	Cle A	0	0	ø	6	0	0	0	18.1	13	4	0	0	10	7	0.49	682	.224	.338	4	.000	-1	—	5	—	0.2
1920	Cle A	0	0	ø	13	0	0	0	25	31	19	0	1	20	14	4.32	88	.333	.456	5	.000	-1	—	-3	—	-0.2
Total	2	0	0	ø	19	0	0	0	43.1	44	23	0	1	30	21	2.70	134	.291	.412	9	.000	-1	—	2	—	0.0
FAGAN, EVERETT	Everett Joseph; B1.13.1918 Pottersville NJ; D2.16.1983 Morristown NJ; BR/TR/6´0˝/195; d4.24; Mil 1943–46																									
1943	Phi A	2	6	.250	18	2	0	3	37.1	41	28	4	2	14	9	6.27	54	.283	.354	7	.000	-0	124	-11	0	-2.2
1946	Phi A	0	1	.000	20	0	0	0	45	47	27	2	3	24	12	4.80	74	.264	.361	14	.286	1	—	-6	0	-0.2
Total	2	2	7	.222	38	2	0	3	82.1	88	55	6	5	38	21	5.47	64	.272	.358	21	.190	1	124	-17	0	-2.4
FAGAN, BILL	William A. "Clinkers"; B2.15.1869 Troy NY; D3.21.1930 Troy NY; TL/5´11˝/165; d9.15																									
1887	NY AA	1	4	.200	6	6	6	0	45	55	34	1	2	24	12	4.00	106	.306	.393	21	.143	-2	50	0	—	-0.1
1888	KC AA	5	11	.313	17	17	15	0	142.1	179	148	4	1	75	49	5.69	59	.296	.375	65	.215	-1*	92	-34	—	-2.9
Total	2	6	15	.286	23	23	21	0	187.1	234	182	5	3	99	61	5.28	68	.298	.379	86	.198	-3	80	-34	—	-3.0
FAHEY, FRANK	Francis Raymond; B1.22.1896 Milford MA; D3.19.1954 Boston MA; BB/TR/6´1˝/190; d4.25; Col Catholic America; ▲																									
1918	Phi A	0	0	ø	3	0	0	0	9	5	7	0	1	14	1	6.00	49	.200	.500	17-0-1	.176	-0*	—	-3	—	-0.2
FAHR, JERRY	Gerald Warren; B12.9.1924 Marmaduke AR; BR/TR/6´5˝/185; d4.29																									
1951	Cle A	0	0	ø	5	0	0	0	5.2	11	3	0	0	2	0	4.76	80	.500	.542	0	ø	0	—	0	0	0.0

YEAR	TM LG	W	L	PCT	G	GS	CG-SHO	SV-BS	IP	H	R	HR	HB	BB-IB	SO	ERA	AERA	OAV	OOB	AB-HR-SH	AVG	PB	SUP	APR	DL	PW
Fahrer, Pete	Clarence Willie; B3.10.1890 Holgate OH; D6.10.1967 Fremont MI; BL/TR/6´0˝/190; d8.17																									
1914	Cin N	0	0	ø	5	0	0	0	8	8	3	0	0	4	2	1.13	260	.308	.400	1	.000	-0	—	1	—	0.1
Fairbank, Jim	James Lee "Lee","Smoky"; B3.17.1881 Deansboro NY; D12.27.1955 Utica NY; BR/TR/5´9.5˝/175; d9.18																									
1903	Phi A	1	1	.500	4	1	1	0	24	33	14	1	0	12	10	4.88	63	.327	.398	10	.100	-1	164	-4	—	-0.3
1904	Phi A	0	1	.000	3	1	1	0	17	19	14	0	2	13	6	6.35	42	.284	.415	6	.000	-1	0	-6	—	-0.4
Total	2	1	2	.333	7	2	2	0	41	52	28	1	2	25	16	5.49	53	.310	.405	16	.063	-1	86	-10	—	-0.7
Faircloth, Rags	James Lamar; B8.19.1892 Kenton TN; D10.5.1953 Tucson AZ; BR/TR/5´11˝/160; d5.6; Col Mississippi St.																									
1919	Phi N	0	0	ø	2	0	0	0	2	5	2	0	0	0	0	9.00	36	.625	.625	0	ø	0	—	-1	—	-0.1
Fajardo, Hector	Hector (Nabaratte); B11.16.1970 Sahuayo, Michoacan, Mexico; BR/TR/6´4˝/(185–200); d8.10; [DL 1992 Tex A 112]																									
1991	Pit N	0	0	ø	2	2	0	0-0	6.1	10	7	0	0	7-0	8	9.95	36	.357	.486	3	.000	-0	187	-4	0	-0.2
	Tex A	0	2	.000	4	3	0	0-0	19	25	13	2	1	4-0	15	5.68	71	.329	.357	0	ø	0	113	-3	0	-0.3
1993	Tex A	0	0	ø	1	0	0	0-0	0.2	0	0	0	0	0-0	1	0.00	ø	.000	.000	0	ø	0	—	0	148	0.0
1994	Tex A	5	7	.417	18	12	0	0-0	83.1	95	67	15	2	26-0	45	6.91	70	.284	.336	0	ø	0	76	-17	0	-1.9
1995	Tex A	0	0	ø	5	0	0	0-0	15	19	13	2	1	5-0	9	7.80	62	.311	.373	0	ø	0	—	-4	0	-0.2
Total	4	5	9	.357	30	17	0	0-0	124.1	149	100	19	4	42-0	78	6.95	67	.297	.352	3	.000	-0	91	-28	260	-2.6
Falcone, Pete	Peter Frank; B10.1.1953 Brooklyn NY; BL/TL/6´2˝/(180–185); [SFN73 S1/4]; d4.13; Col Kingsborough (NY) CC																									
1975	SF N	12	11	.522	34	32	3-1	0-0	190	171	97	16	4	111-7	131	4.17	91	.244	.348	65-0-4	.062	-5	92	-6	0	-1.2
1976	StL N	12	16	.429	32	32	9-2	0-0	212	173	87	12	2	93-1	138	3.23	111	.222	.303	62-0-12	.129	-2	84	8	0	0.7
1977	StL N	4	8	.333	27	22	1-1	1-0	124	130	79	19	3	61-3	75	5.44	72	.273	.355	41-0-4	.244	2	124	-19	0	-1.5
1978	StL N	2	7	.222	19	14	0	0-0	75	94	52	9	2	48-2	28	5.76	62	.319	.414	21-0-2	.238	1	86	-17	0	-1.8
1979	NY N	6	14	.300	33	31	1-1	0-0	184	194	91	24	1	76-10	113	4.16	89	.276	.343	52-0-5	.173	0	82	-7	0	-0.9
1980	NY N	7	10	.412	37	23	1	1-0	157.1	163	89	16	2	58-9	109	4.52	80	.269	.332	41-0-6	.146	-1	115	-16	0	-1.8
1981	NY N	5	3	.625	35	9	3-1	1-0	95.1	84	32	3	0	36-4	56	2.55	139	.241	.308	22-1-0	.182	1	117	10	0	0.9
1982	NY N	8	10	.444	40	23	3	2-1	171	159	82	24	1	71-4	101	3.84	96	.252	.326	53-0-2	.113	-2	85	-2	0	-0.6
1983	Atl N	9	4	.692	33	15	2	0-0	106.2	102	47	14	1	60-2	59	3.63	107	.256	.352	26-0-5	.115	-1	120	3	0	0.1
1984	Atl N	5	7	.417	35	16	2-1	2-1	120	115	61	15	0	57-3	55	4.13	93	.252	.333	33-0-3	.212	1	99	-3	0	-0.2
Total	10	70	90	.438	325	217	25-7	7-2	1435.1	1385	717	152	16	671-45	865	4.07	91	.257	.337	416-1-43	.149	-6	98	-49	0	-6.3
Falk, Chet	Chester Emanuel "Spot"; B5.15.1905 Austin TX; D1.7.1982 Austin TX; BL/TL/6´2˝/170; d4.20; b–Bibb; Col Texas																									
1925	StL A	0	0	ø	13	0	0	0	25	38	26	2	0	17	7	8.28	56	.362	.451	8	.625	2*	—	-9	—	-0.2
1926	StL A	4	4	.500	18	8	3	0	74	95	53	1	6	27	7	5.35	80	.338	.408	31	.194	-1*	115	-8	—	-0.9
1927	StL A	1	0	1.000	9	0	0	0	15.2	25	18	1	0	10	2	5.74	76	.352	.432	5	.200	-0	—	-5	—	-0.3
Total	3	5	4	.556	40	8	3	0	114.2	158	97	4	6	54	16	6.04	73	.346	.422	44	.273	1	115	-22	—	-1.4
Falkenberg, Cy	Frederick Peter; B12.17.1879 Chicago IL; D4.15.1961 San Francisco CA; BR/TR/6´5˝/180; d4.21; Col Illinois																									
1903	Pit N	1	5	.167	10	6	3	0	56	65	43	0	2	32	24	3.86	84	.295	.390	21-0-1	.190	-0	90	-6	—	-0.5
1905	Was A	7	2	.778	12	10	6-2	0	75.1	71	41	1	5	31	35	3.82	69	.251	.335	32	.125	-2	209	-8	—	-1.1
1906	Was A	14	20	.412	40	36	30-2	1	298.2	277	136	1	13	108	178	2.86	92	.249	.323	106-1-4	.170	1	118	-9	—	-0.8
1907	Was A	6	17	.261	32	24	17-1	1	233.2	195	105	0	8	77	108	2.35	103	.229	.299	86	.140	-3*	99	-3	—	-0.6
1908	Was A	6	2	.750	17	8	5-1	0	82.2	70	29	2	2	21	34	1.96	117	.236	.291	27-0-1	.222	0	150	2	—	0.3
	Cle A	2	4	.333	8	7	2	0	46.1	52	25	1	2	10	17	3.88	62	.284	.328	17	.118	-1	135	-6	—	-0.9
	Year	8	6	.571	25	15	7-1	0	129	122	54	3	4	31	51	2.65	88	.254	.305	44-0-1	.182	-1	143	-4	—	-0.6
1909	Cle A	10	9	.526	24	18	13-2	0	165	135	56	0	5	50	82	2.40	107	.231	.297	52-0-3	.173	-1	69	5	—	.7
1910	Cle A	14	13	.519	37	29	18-3	1	256.2	246	114	3	8	75	107	2.95	88	.261	.320	82-0-3	.183	-0	85	-9	—	-0.8
1911	Cle A	8	5	.615	15	13	7	1	106.2	117	56	0	3	24	46	3.29	104	.282	.326	40-0-5	.175	-1*	102	0	—	-0.1
1913	Cle A	23	10	.697	39	36	23-6	0	276	238	85	2	5	88	166	2.22	137	.237	.302	84-0-6	.119	-2	97	27	—	2.9
1914	Ind F	25	16	.610	**49**	**43**	33-**9**	3	**377.1**	332	127	5	5	89	**236**	2.22	141	.236	.284	125-0-12	.168	-3	109	33	—	3.2
1915	New F	9	11	.450	25	21	14	1	172	175	78	6	9	47	76	3.24	79	.268	.326	57-0-5	.053	-7	105	-11	—	-1.9
	Bro F	3	3	.500	7	7	5-1	0	48	31	15	1	1	12	20	1.50	181	.189	.249	15-0-1	.067	-1	59	5	—	0.4
	Year	12	14	.462	32	28	19-1	1	220	206	93	7	10	59	96	2.86	91	.252	.311	72-0-6	.056	-8	93	-7	—	-1.5
1917	Phi A	2	6	.250	15	8	4	0	80.2	86	53	1	0	26	35	3.35	82	.293	.350	27-0-2	.185	0	72	-9	—	-0.7
Total	12	130	123	.514	330	266	180-27	8	2275	2090	963	23	68	690	1164	2.68	103	.248	.311	771-1-43	.152	-21	104	11	—	0.1
Falkenborg, Brian	Brian Thomas; B1.18.1978 Newport Beach CA; BR/TR/6´6˝/(190–225); [BalA96 2/51]; d10.1; [DL 2000 Bal A 181]																									
1999	Bal A	0	0	ø	2	0	0	0-0	3	2	0	0	0	2-0	1	0.00	ø	.200	.333	0	ø	0	—	2	0	0.1
2004	LA N	1	0	1.000	6	0	0	0-0	14.1	19	14	2	3	9-0	11	7.53	55	.322	.437	2	.000	0	—	-6	19	-0.4
2005	SD N	0	0	ø	10	0	0	0-0	11	17	11	2	0	5-1	10	8.18	48	.347	.407	0	ø	0	—	-6	0	-0.3
2006	StL N	0	1	.000	5	0	0	0-0	6.1	5	2	0	1	0-0	5	2.84	153	.217	.250	1	.000	-0	—	1	0	0.2
Total	4	1	1	.500	23	0	0	0-0	34.2	43	27	4	4	16-1	27	6.23	67	.305	.391	3	.000	0	—	-9	200	-0.4
Fallenstein, Ed	Edward Joseph "Jack" (b Edward Joseph Valestin); B12.22.1908 Newark NJ; D11.24.1971 Orange NJ; BR/TR/6´3˝/180; d4.16																									
1931	Phi N	0	0	ø	24	0	0	0	41.2	56	37	2	0	26	15	7.13	60	.333	.423	5	.200	0	—	-11	—	-0.5
1933	Bos N	2	1	.667	9	4	1-1	0	35	43	23	1	1	13	5	3.60	85	.305	.368	8-0-1	.375	1*	122	-6	—	-0.3
Total	2	2	1	.667	33	4	1-1	0	76.2	99	60	3	1	39	20	5.52	67	.320	.398	13-0-1	.308	1	122	-17	—	-0.8
Fallon, Bob	Robert Joseph; B2.18.1960 Bronx NY; BL/TL/6´3˝/211; [ChiA79 S1/5]; d4.26; Col Miami–Dade North (FL) CC																									
1984	Chi A	0	0	ø	3	3	0	0-0	14.2	12	7	0	0	11-0	10	3.68	114	.235	.371	0	ø	0	130	1	0	0.0
1985	Chi A	0	0	ø	10	0	0	0-0	16	25	11	5	0	9-2	17	6.19	70	.362	.430	0	ø	0	—	-3	0	-0.1
Total	2	0	0	ø	13	3	0	0-0	30.2	37	18	5	0	20-2	27	4.99	86	.308	.404	0	ø	0	130	-2	0	-0.1
Falteisek, Steve	Steven James; B1.28.1972 Mineola NY; BR/TR/6´2˝/200; [MonN92 10/267]; d7.22; Col South Alabama																									
1997	Mon N	0	0	ø	5	0	0	0-0	8	8	4	0	1	3-0	2	3.38	124	.286	.353	2-0-1	.000	-0	—	0	0	0.0
1999	Mil N	0	0	ø	10	0	0	0-0	12	18	10	3	0	3-0	5	7.50	61	.375	.404	1	.000	-0*	—	-3	0	-0.2
Total	2	0	0	ø	15	0	0	0-0	20	26	14	3	1	6-0	7	5.85	76	.342	.384	3-0-1	.000	-0	—	-3	0	-0.2
Fannin, Cliff	Clifford Bryson "Mule"; B5.13.1924 Louisa KY; D12.11.1966 Sandusky OH; BL/TR/6´0˝/(170–175); d9.2																									
1945	StL A	0	0	ø	5	0	0	0	10.1	8	3	0	0	5	5	2.61	135	.222	.317	1	.000	-0	—	1	0	0.0
1946	StL A	5	2	.714	27	7	4-1	2	86.2	76	37	4	1	42	52	3.01	124	.236	.326	31	.161	-1	128	5	0	0.3
1947	StL A	6	8	.429	26	18	6-2	1	145.2	134	70	10	1	77	77	3.58	108	.245	.340	46-0-4	.196	-0	94	3	0	0.2
1948	StL A	10	14	.417	34	29	10-3	1	213.2	198	106	14	1	104	102	4.17	109	.245	.332	65-0-6	.169	-0*	94	10	0	0.9
1949	StL A	8	14	.364	30	25	5	1	143	177	106	15	0	93	57	6.17	73	.308	.404	55-0-1	.164	-2*	92	-21	0	-3.0
1950	StL A	5	9	.357	25	16	3	1	102	116	82	18	0	58	42	6.53	76	.280	.369	34	.176	-2*	87	-15	0	-1.9
1951	StL A	0	2	.000	7	1	0	0	15.1	20	16	7	0	5	11	6.46	68	.317	.368	4	.250	-0*	202	-5	0	-0.5
1952	StL A	0	2	.000	10	2	0	0	16.1	34	25	5	0	9	6	12.67	31	.453	.512	1	.000	0*	67	-14	0	-1.5
Total	8	34	51	.400	164	98	28-6	6	733	763	445	73	3	393	352	4.85	89	.269	.358	237-0-11	.173	-5	96	-36	0	-5.5
Fanning, Jack	John Jacob; B1863 S.Orange NJ; D6.10.1917 Aberdeen WA; TR/5´9˝/163; d9.20																									
1889	Ind N	0	1	.000	1	1	0	0	1	3	3	0	0	2	0	18.00	23	.500	.625	1	.000	-0	161	-2	—	-0.2
1894	Phi N	1	3	.250	6	4	2	0	34.1	54	52	4	2	22	7	8.91	58	.353	.441	14	.143	-1	100	-17	—	-1.3
Total	2	1	4	.200	7	5	2	0	35.1	57	55	4	2	24	7	9.17	56	.358	.449	15	.133	-1	108	-19	—	-1.5
Fanok, Harry	Harry Michael "The Flame Thrower"; B5.11.1940 Whippany NJ; BB/TR/6´0˝/180; d4.16																									
1963	StL N	2	1	.667	12	0	0	1	25.2	24	16	3	1	21-1	25	5.26	67	.255	.387	5	.400	1	—	-4	0	-0.4
1964	StL N	0	0	ø	4	0	0	0	7.2	5	6	0	0	3-0	10	5.87	65	.179	.250	1	.000	-0	—	-2	0	-0.1
Total	2	2	1	.667	16	0	0	1	33.1	29	22	3	1	24-1	35	5.40	67	.238	.358	6	.333	1	—	-6	0	-0.5
Fanovich, Frank	Frank Joseph "Lefty"; B1.11.1922 New York NY; BL/TL/5´11˝/185; d4.25																									
1949	Cin N	0	2	.000	29	1	0	0	43.1	44	31	2	2	28	27	5.40	77	.257	.368	4	.000	-0	42	-6	0	-0.3
1953	Phi A	0	3	.000	26	3	0	0	61.2	62	41	5	6	37	37	5.55	77	.273	.389	11	.182	-0	69	-8	0	-0.5
Total	2	0	5	.000	55	4	0	0	105	106	72	7	8	65	64	5.49	77	.266	.380	15	.133	-1	63	-14	0	-0.8

YEAR	TM LG	W	L	PCT	G	GS	CG-SHO	SV-BS	IP	H	R	HR	HB	BB-IB	SO	ERA	AERA	OAV	OOB	AB-HR-SH	AVG	PB	SUP	APR	DL	PW
Fansler, Stan	Stanley Robert; B2.12.1965 Elkins WV; BR/TR/5´11˝/185; [PitN83 2/36]; d9.6																									
1986	Pit N	0	3	.000	5	5	0	0-0	24	20	12	2	0	15-0	13	3.75	104	.247	.361	6-0-1	.167	-0	55	0	0	0.0
Fanwell, Harry	Harry Clayton; B10.16.1886 Patapsco MD; D7.15.1965 Baltimore MD; BR/TR/6´0˝/175; d7.23																									
1910	Cle A	2	9	.182	17	11	5-1	0	92	87	52	0	6	38	30	3.62	71	.260	.347	30-0-1	.033	-3	47	-10	—	-1.5
Farmer, Ed	Edward Joseph; B10.18.1949 Evergreen Park IL; BR/TR/6´5˝/(205–212); [CleA67 5/91]; d6.9																									
1971	Cle A	5	4	.556	43	4	0	4-1	78.2	77	42	9	3	41-3	48	4.35	89	.263	.356	14-0-1	.071	-1	64	-4	0	-0.6
1972	Cle A	2	5	.286	46	1	0	7-2	61.1	51	32	10	1	27-6	33	4.40	74	.231	.316	7-0-1	.143	-0	136	-7	0	-1.0
1973	Cle A	0	2	.000	16	0	0	1-1	17.1	25	12	4	0	5-0	10	4.67	85	.325	.361	0	ø	0	—	-2	0	-0.3
	Det A	3	0	1.000	24	0	0	2-0	45	52	26	3	2	27-0	28	5.00	82	.292	.389	0	ø	0	—	-4	0	-0.3
	Year	3	2	.600	40	0	0	3-1	62.1	77	38	7	2	32-0	38	4.91	83	.302	.381	0	ø	0	—	-6	0	-0.6
1974	Phi N	2	1	.667	14	3	0	0-0	31	41	32	5	0	27-0	20	8.42	45	.323	.433	9	.111	-1	130	-15	0	-1.4
1977	Bal A	0	0	ø	1	0	0	0-0	0	1	1	0	0	1-0	0	(1)	ø	1.000	1.000	0	ø	0	—	-1	0	-0.1
1978	Mil A	1	0	1.000	3	0	0	1-0	11	7	1	1	0	4-0	6	0.82	464	.175	.250	0	ø	0	—	4	0	0.4
1979	Tex A	2	0	1.000	11	2	0	0-1	33	30	21	2	2	19-2	25	4.36	95	.252	.359	0	ø	0	164	-2	0	-0.1
	Chi A	3	7	.300	42	3	0	14-3	81.1	66	36	2	1	34-8	48	2.43	175	.219	.299	0	ø	0	57	12	0	1.8
	Year	5	7	.417	53	5	0	14-4	114.1	96	57	4	3	53-10	73	2.99	141	.229	.317	0	ø	0	99	10	0	1.7
1980	Chi A★	7	9	.438	64	0	0	30-11	99.2	92	37	6	1	56-11	54	3.34	122	.244	.343	0	ø	0	—	10	0	2.2
1981	Chi A	3	3	.500	42	0	0	10-5	52.2	53	33	5	1	34-1	42	4.61	78	.262	.368	0	ø	0	—	-7	0	-1.0
1982	Phi N	2	6	.250	47	4	0	6-3	76	66	44	2	0	50-11	58	4.86	76	.234	.347	11-0-2	.000	-1	107	-9	0	-1.1
1983	Phi N	0	6	.000	12	3	0	0-0	26.2	35	22	2	1	20-8	16	6.08	59	.307	.412	6-0-1	.167	-0	65	-8	41	-1.5
	Oak A	0	0	ø	5	1	0	0-0	10.1	15	4	1	0	0-0	7	3.48	112	.366	.357	0	ø	0	187	1	0	0.0
Total	11	30	43	.411	370	21	0	75-27	624	611	343	52	12	345-50	395	4.30	90	.257	.352	47-0-5	.085	-3	99	-32	41	-3.0
Farmer, Howard	Howard Earl; B11.18.1966 Gary IN; BR/TR/6´3˝/190; [MonN87 7/174]; d7.2; b–Mike; Col Jackson St.; [DL 1991 Mon N 44]																									
1990	Mon N	0	3	.000	6	4	0	0-0	23	26	18	9	0	10-1	14	7.04	52	.302	.371	5-0-1	.400	1	135	-8	0	-0.8
Farmer, Mike	Michael Anthony; B7.3.1968 Gary IN; BB/TL/6´1˝/193; d5.4; b–Howard; Col Jackson St.																									
1996	Col N	0	1	.000	7	4	0	0-0	28	32	25	8	0	13-0	16	7.71	68	.286	.360	10	.400	1	151	-6	0	-0.2
Farnsworth, Jeff	Jeffrey Ellis; B10.6.1975 Wichita KS; BR/TR/6´2˝/190; [SeaA96 2/57]; d4.3; Col Okaloosa–Walton (FL) CC																									
2002	Det A	2	3	.400	44	0	0	0-1	70	100	47	6	2	29-8	28	5.79	76	.338	.399	0	ø	0	—	-10	0	-0.6
Farnsworth, Kyle	Kyle Lynn; B4.14.1976 Wichita KS; BR/TR/6´4˝/(215–240); [ChiN94 47/1290]; d4.29; Col Abraham Baldwin (GA) JC																									
1999	Chi N	5	9	.357	27	21	1-1	0-0	130	140	80	28	3	52-1	70	5.05	90	.271	.340	35-0-6	.086	-1	111	-7	0	-0.8
2000	Chi N	2	9	.182	46	5	0	1-5	77	90	58	14	4	50-8	74	6.43	71	.291	.392	14-0-2	.071	-1	104	-16	0	-2.0
2001	Chi N	4	6	.400	76	0	0	2-1	82	65	26	8	1	29-2	107	2.74	153	.213	.282	2	.000	-0	—	14	0	1.5
2002	Chi N	4	6	.400	45	0	0	1-6	46.2	53	47	9	1	24-7	46	7.33	55	.293	.370	1	.000	-0	—	-20	55	-3.7
2003	†Chi N	3	2	.600	77	0	0	0-3	76.1	53	31	6	0	36-1	92	3.30	132	.196	.289	1	.000	-0	—	9	0	0.5
2004	Chi N	4	5	.444	72	0	0	0-4	66.2	67	39	10	2	33-1	78	4.72	94	.260	.348	1	.000	-0	—	-3	15	-0.3
2005	Det A	1	1	.500	46	0	0	6-2	42.2	29	12	1	1	20-0	55	2.32	184	.192	.289	0	ø	0	—	9	0	0.6
	†Atl N	0	0	ø	26	0	0	10-0	27.1	15	6	4	2	7-0	32	1.98	214	.161	.235	0	ø	0	—	7	0	0.5
2006	†NY A	3	6	.333	72	0	0	6-4	66	62	34	8	1	28-3	75	4.36	104	.243	.318	0	ø	0	—	2	0	0.2
Total	8	26	44	.371	487	26	1-1	26-25	614.2	574	333	88	15	279-23	629	4.44	99	.245	.328	54-0-8	.074	-3	115	-5	70	-3.5
Farr, Jim	James Alfred; B5.18.1956 Waverly NY; BR/TR/6´1˝/195; [TexA78 29/675]; d9.7; Col Penn St.																									
1982	Tex A	0	0	ø	5	0	0	0-0	18	20	8	0	0	7-2	6	2.50	155	.278	.338	0	ø	0	—	2	0	0.1
Farr, Steve	Steven Michael; B12.12.1956 LaPlata MD; BR/TR/5´11˝/(190–206); d5.16; Col American																									
1984	Cle A	3	11	.214	31	16	0	1-1	116	106	61	14	5	46-3	83	4.58	90	.245	.323	0	ø	0	68	-4	15	-0.4
1985	†KC A	2	1	.667	16	3	0	1-0	37.2	34	15	2	2	20-4	36	3.11	135	.245	.344	0	ø	0	94	4	0	0.3
1986	KC A	8	4	.667	56	0	0	8-1	109.1	90	39	10	4	39-8	83	3.13	137	.228	.302	0	ø	0	—	15	0	1.7
1987	KC A	4	3	.571	47	0	0	1-4	91	97	47	9	2	44-4	88	4.15	111	.270	.350	0	ø	0	—	5	0	0.2
1988	KC A	5	4	.556	62	1	0	20-6	82.2	74	25	5	2	30-6	72	2.50	160	.240	.309	0	ø	0	45	14	0	2.0
1989	KC A	2	5	.286	51	2	0	18-4	63.1	75	35	5	1	22-5	56	4.12	94	.296	.351	0	ø	0	82	-3	23	-0.5
1990	KC A	13	7	.650	57	6	1-1	1-1	127	99	32	6	5	48-9	94	1.98	195	.220	.301	0	ø	0	67	**27**	0	4.1
1991	NY A	5	5	.500	60	0	0	23-6	70	57	19	4	5	20-3	60	2.19	191	.219	.288	0	ø	0	—	15	0	2.9
1992	NY A	2	2	.500	50	0	0	30-6	52	34	10	2	2	19-0	37	1.56	254	.186	.267	0	ø	0	—	14	18	2.3
1993	NY A	2	2	.500	49	0	0	25-6	47	44	22	8	2	28-4	39	4.21	99	.253	.356	0	ø	0	—	1	17	0.2
1994	Cle A	1	1	.500	19	0	0	4-2	15.1	17	12	3	2	15-1	12	5.28	90	.279	.430	0	ø	0	—	-2	6	-0.3
	Bos A	1	0	1.000	11	0	0	0-1	13	24	9	2	0	3-0	8	6.23	81	.407	.435	0	ø	0	—	-1	9	-0.1
	Year	2	1	.667	30	0	0	4-3	28.1	41	21	5	2	18-1	20	5.72	85	.342	.433	0	ø	0	—	-3	0	-0.4
Total	11	48	45	.516	509	28	1-1	132-38	824.1	751	326	70	32	334-47	668	3.25	128	.244	.322	0	ø	0	70	85	88	12.4
Farrell, John	John Edward; B8.4.1962 Monmouth Beach NJ; BR/TR/6´4˝/210; [CleA84 2/32]; d8.18; Col Oklahoma St.; [DL 1992 Cal A 182]																									
1987	Cle A	5	1	.833	10	9	1	0-0	69	68	29	7	5	22-1	28	3.39	135	.256	.323	0	ø	0	131	9	0	0.7
1988	Cle A	14	10	.583	31	30	4	0-0	210.1	216	106	15	9	67-3	92	4.24	98	.269	.330	0	ø	0	96	-1	23	-0.1
1989	Cle A	9	14	.391	31	31	7-2	0-0	208	196	97	14	7	71-4	132	3.63	110	.244	.309	0	ø	0	84	6	13	0.5
1990	Cle A	4	5	.444	17	17	1	0-0	96.2	108	49	10	1	33-1	44	4.28	92	.286	.344	0	ø	0	102	-3	88	-0.3
1993	Cal A	3	12	.200	21	17	0	0-0	90.2	110	74	22	7	44-3	45	7.35	62	.301	.385	0	ø	0	78	-23	0	-3.2
1994	Cal A	1	2	.333	3	3	0	0-0	13	16	14	2	1	8-0	10	9.00	55	.308	.410	0	ø	0	87	-6	0	-0.9
1995	Cle A	0	0	ø	1	0	0	0-0	4.2	7	4	0	0	0-0	4	3.86	122	.368	.350	0	ø	0	—	0	0	0.0
1996	Det A	0	2	.000	2	2	0	0-0	6.1	11	10	2	1	5-0	0	14.21	36	.407	.515	0	ø	0	73	-6	0	-0.9
Total	8	36	46	.439	116	109	13-2	0-0	698.2	732	383	72	31	250-12	355	4.56	92	.270	.336	0	ø	0	93	-24	306	-4.2
Farrell, Kerby	Major Kerby; B9.3.1913 Leapwood TN; D12.17.1975 Nashville TN; BL/TL/5´11˝/172; d4.24; M1/C6; Col Freed–Hardeman; ▲																									
1943	Bos N	0	1	.000	5	0	0	0	23	24	11	1	0	9	4	4.30	79	.276	.344	280-0-7	.268	1*	—	-1	0	0.0
Farrell, Turk	Richard Joseph; B4.8.1934 Boston MA; D6.10.1977 Great Yarmouth, England; BR/TR/6´4˝/(192–220); d9.21																									
1956	Phi N	0	1	.000	1	1	0	0	4.1	6	6	0	1	3-0	0	12.46	30	.353	.476	1-0-1	.000	-0	71	-4	0	-0.6
1957	Phi N	10	2	.833	52	0	0	10	83.1	74	29	2	2	36-9	54	2.38	160	.242	.323	9-1-0	.111	0	—	11	0	1.9
1958	Phi N★	8	9	.471	54	0	0	11	94	84	41	7	0	40-7	73	3.35	118	.244	.320	24	.208	0	—	6	0	1.0
1959	Phi N	1	6	.143	38	0	0	6	57	61	30	9	0	25-7	31	4.74	87	.288	.354	6-0-1	.167	-0	—	-2	0	-0.3
1960	Phi N	10	6	.625	59	0	0	11	103.1	88	36	3	4	29-6	70	2.70	144	.239	.298	15-0-2	.200	1	—	13	0	2.2
1961	Phi N	2	1	.667	5	0	0	0	9.2	10	8	3	1	6-1	10	6.52	63	.270	.386	2	.500	0	—	-3	0	-0.5
	LA N	6	6	.500	50	0	0	10	89	107	56	12	1	43-14	80	5.06	86	.296	.371	18-0-3	.000	-2	—	-6	0	-1.2
	Year	8	7	.533	55	0	0	10	98.2	117	64	15	2	49-15	90	5.20	83	.294	.373	20-0-3	.050	-2	—	-9	0	-1.7
1962	Hou N★	10	20	.333	43	29	11-2	4	241.2	210	91	21	5	55-2	203	3.02	124	.233	.279	78-2-3	.179	2	64	22	0	2.7
1963	Hou N	14	13	.519	34	26	12	1	202.1	161	76	12	2	35-2	141	3.02	104	.219	.255	63-0-3	.143	1	71	4	0	0.7
1964	Hou N★	11	10	.524	32	27	7	0	198.1	196	80	21	3	52-4	117	3.27	105	.261	.308	69-0-2	.072	-3	96	5	0	0.1
1965	Hou N★	11	11	.500	33	29	8-3	1	208.1	202	94	18	3	35-8	122	3.50	96	.252	.284	74-0-2	.135	-1	99	-4	0	-0.6
1966	Hou N	6	10	.375	32	21	3	2	152.2	167	84	23	0	28-4	101	4.60	74	.278	.307	48-1-1	.146	-0	87	-18	0	-1.9
1967	Hou N	1	0	1.000	7	0	0	0	11.2	11	7	0	1	7-1	10	4.63	72	.244	.358	1	.000	-0	—	-2	0	-0.2
	Phi N	9	6	.600	50	1	0	12	92	76	26	6	1	15-5	68	2.05	166	.228	.258	19-0-1	.105	-0	52	13	0	2.5
	Year	10	6	.625	57	1	0	12	103.2	87	33	6	2	22-6	78	2.34	145	.230	.271	20-0-1	.100	-0	52	11	0	2.3
1968	Phi N	4	6	.400	54	0	0	12	82.2	83	40	7	2	32-6	57	3.48	86	.271	.340	6	.167	-0	—	-6	0	-1.0
1969	Phi N	3	4	.429	46	0	0	3-3	74.1	92	33	8	1	27-6	40	4.00	89	.307	.364	3-0-1	.000	-0	—	-2	0	-0.3
Total	14	106	111	.488	590	134	41-5	83-3	1704.2	1628	737	152	27	468-82	1177	3.45	103	.254	.304	436-4-20	.135	-3	80	27	0	4.5
Fass, Fred	Frederick Peter; B10.30.1859 Milwaukee WI; D7.5.1930 Burnt Mill CO; d7.11																									
1887	Ind N	0	1	.000	4	2	1	**1**	15.2	25	22	1	2	8	0	10.34	40	.347	.427	11	.182	-1	94	-9	—	-0.5

FASSERO, JEFF Jeffrey Joseph; B1.5.1963 Springfield IL; BL/TL/6´1˝/(195–200); [StLN84 22/554]; d5.4; Col U. of Mississippi

YEAR	TM LG	W	L	PCT	G	GS	CG-SHO	SV-BS	IP	H	R	HR	HB	BB-IB	SO	ERA	AERA	OAV	OOB	AB-HR-SH	AVG	PB	SUP	APR	DL	PW
1991	Mon N	2	5	.286	51	0	0	8-3	55.1	39	17	1	1	17-1	42	2.44	149	.196	.263	3-0-2	.000	0	—	7	0	1.1
1992	Mon N	8	7	.533	70	0	0	1-6	85.2	81	35	1	2	34-6	63	2.84	123	.249	.322	7-0-1	.143	0	—	4	0	0.7
1993	Mon N	12	5	.706	56	15	1	1-2	149.2	119	50	7	0	54-0	140	2.29	183	.216	.284	32-0-5	.063	-2	78	**28**	0	2.8
1994	Mon N	8	6	.571	21	21	1	0-0	138.2	119	54	13	1	40-4	119	2.99	142	.229	.285	44-0-9	.068	-2	92	18	18	1.6
1995	Mon N	13	14	.481	30	30	1	0-0	189	207	102	15	2	74-3	164	4.33	99	.283	.348	57-0-8	.070	-3	95	-2	0	-0.5
1996	Mon N	15	11	.577	34	34	5-1	0-0	231.2	217	95	20	3	55-3	222	3.30	131	.244	.289	64-0-14	.094	-1	89	25	0	2.7
1997	†Sea A	16	9	.640	35	**35**	2-1	0-0	234.1	226	108	21	3	84-6	189	3.61	126	.249	.312	5	.200	0	113	21	0	2.1
1998	Sea A	13	12	.520	32	32	7	0-0	224.2	223	115	33	10	66-2	176	3.97	118	.259	.316	3	.000	-0	103	15	12	1.4
1999	Sea A	4	14	.222	30	24	0	0-0	139	188	123	34	4	73-3	101	7.38	65	.321	.397	7	.000	-1	106	-41	0	-4.1
	†Tex A	1	0	1.000	7	3	0	0-0	17.1	20	12	1	0	10-0	13	5.71	91	.286	.370	0	ø	0	126	-1	0	-0.1
	Year	5	14	.263	37	27	0	0-0	156.1	208	135	35	4	83-3	114	7.20	67	.318	.394	7	.000	-1	109	-41	0	-4.2
2000	Bos A	8	8	.500	38	23	0	0-0	130	153	72	16	1	50-2	97	4.78	105	.296	.358	2-0-1	.000	-0	94	5	15	0.5
2001	Chi N	4	4	.500	82	0	0	12-5	73.2	66	31	6	1	23-5	79	3.42	122	.235	.293	2	.000	-0	—	6	0	0.8
2002	Chi N	5	6	.455	57	0	0	0-1	51	65	37	5	3	22-5	44	6.18	66	.313	.385	3	.333	0	—	-12	0	-2.2
	†StL N	3	0	1.000	16	0	0	0-2	18	16	6	4	0	5-0	12	3.00	134	.232	.284	0	ø	0	—	2	0	0.4
	Year	8	6	.571	73	0	0	0-3	69	81	43	9	3	27-5	56	5.35	76	.292	.360	3	.333	0	—	-10	0	-1.8
2003	StL N	1	7	.125	62	6	0	3-3	77.2	93	51	17	2	34-4	55	5.68	73	.296	.368	9-0-1	.000	-1	129	-13	0	-1.4
2004	Col N	3	8	.273	40	12	0	0-0	111	136	73	9	4	44-5	59	5.51	86	.306	.368	21-0-2	.190	-0	107	-9	0	-0.7
	Ari N	0	0	ø	1	0	0	0-0	1	0	0	0	0	0-0	1	0.00	ø	.000	.000	0	ø	0	—	0	0	0.0
	Year	3	8	.273	41	12	0	0-0	112	136	73	9	4	44-5	60	5.46	87	.304	.366	21-0-2	.190	-0	107	-6	0	-0.7
2005	SF N	4	7	.364	48	6	0	0-2	91	92	48	7	0	31-1	60	4.05	105	.268	.326	13-0-1	.000	-1	44	0	0	0.0
2006	SF N	1	1	.500	10	1	0	0-0	15	23	13	4	0	8-0	7	7.80	57	.365	.431	4-0-1	.250	0	208	-5	0	-0.6
Total	16	121	124	.494	720	242	17-2	25-24	2033.2	2083	1042	214	37	724-50	1643	4.11	107	.264	.327	276-0-45	.083	-11	102	48	45	4.5

FAST, DARCY Darcy Rae; B3.10.1947 Dallas OR; BL/TL/6´3˝/195; d6.15; Mil 1969; Col Warner Pacific

YEAR	TM LG	W	L	PCT	G	GS	CG-SHO	SV-BS	IP	H	R	HR	HB	BB-IB	SO	ERA	AERA	OAV	OOB	AB-HR-SH	AVG	PB	SUP	APR	DL	PW
1968	Chi N	0	1	.000	8	1	0	0	10	8	6	1	0	8-0	10	5.40	58	.216	.348	3	.000	-0	110	-2	0	-0.2

FASZHOLZ, JACK John Edward "Preacher"; B4.11.1927 St.Louis MO; BR/TR/6´3˝/205; d4.25

YEAR	TM LG	W	L	PCT	G	GS	CG-SHO	SV-BS	IP	H	R	HR	HB	BB-IB	SO	ERA	AERA	OAV	OOB	AB-HR-SH	AVG	PB	SUP	APR	DL	PW
1953	StL N	0	0	ø	4	1	0	0	11.2	16	9	3	1	1	7	6.94	61	.327	.353	3	.000	-0	126	-3	0	-0.2

FAUL, BILL William Alvan; B4.21.1940 Cincinnati OH; D2.21.2002 Cincinnati OH; BR/TR/5´10˝/(183–190); d9.19; Col Cincinnati

YEAR	TM LG	W	L	PCT	G	GS	CG-SHO	SV-BS	IP	H	R	HR	HB	BB-IB	SO	ERA	AERA	OAV	OOB	AB-HR-SH	AVG	PB	SUP	APR	DL	PW
1962	Det A	0	0	ø	1	0	0	0	1.2	4	6	1	1	3-0	2	32.40	13	.444	.615	0	ø	0	—	-5	0	-0.2
1963	Det A	5	6	.455	28	10	2	1	97	93	55	14	4	48-3	64	4.64	81	.251	.340	27-0-1	.148	0	93	-9	0	-1.0
1964	Det A	0	0	ø	1	1	0	0	5	5	6	2	0	2-0	1	10.80	34	.250	.318	2	.000	-0	146	-4	0	-0.2
1965	Chi N	6	6	.500	17	16	5-3	0	96.2	83	43	12	3	18-0	59	3.54	104	.232	.274	30	.100	-1	84	2	0	0.1
1966	Chi N	1	4	.200	17	6	1	0	51.1	47	31	12	4	18-1	32	5.08	72	.242	.318	13	.000	-2	44	-7	0	-0.8
1970	SF N	0	0	ø	7	0	0	1-0	9.2	15	9	1	0	6-2	6	7.45	53	.357	.438	0	ø	0	—	-4	0	-0.2
Total	6	12	16	.429	71	33	8-3	2-0	261.1	247	150	42	12	95-6	164	4.72	79	.249	.320	72-0-1	.097	-2	81	-27	0	-2.3

FAULKNER, JIM James Leroy "Lefty"; B7.27.1899 Beatrice NE; D6.1.1962 W.Palm Beach FL; BB/TL (BL 1927)/6´3˝/190; d9.15

YEAR	TM LG	W	L	PCT	G	GS	CG-SHO	SV-BS	IP	H	R	HR	HB	BB-IB	SO	ERA	AERA	OAV	OOB	AB-HR-SH	AVG	PB	SUP	APR	DL	PW
1927	NY N	1	0	1.000	3	1	0	0	9.2	13	4	0	1	5	2	3.72	104	.317	.404	2	.500	1	243	0	—	0.1
1928	NY N	9	8	.529	38	8	3	2	117.1	131	61	5	3	41	32	3.53	111	.289	.351	39-0-2	.231	1	84	2	—	0.3
1930	Bro N	0	0	ø	2	1	0	1	0.1	2	3	1	0	1	0	81.00	6	.667	.750	0	ø	0	266	-3	—	-0.4
Total	3	10	8	.556	43	10	3	3	127.1	146	68	6	4	47	34	3.75	104	.293	.359	41-0-2	.244	2	124	-1	—	0.0

FAUSETT, BUCK Robert Shaw "Leaky"; B4.8.1908 Sheridan AR; D5.2.1994 College Station TX; BL/TR/5´10˝/170; d4.18; Col Texas A&M–Commerce; ▲

YEAR	TM LG	W	L	PCT	G	GS	CG-SHO	SV-BS	IP	H	R	HR	HB	BB-IB	SO	ERA	AERA	OAV	OOB	AB-HR-SH	AVG	PB	SUP	APR	DL	PW
1944	Cin N	0	0	ø	2	0	0	0	10.2	13	8	0	2	7	3	5.91	59	.295	.415	31-0-1	.097	-0*	—	-3	0	-0.2

FAUST, CHARLIE Charles Victor "Victory"; B10.9.1880 Marion KS; D6.18.1915 Fort Steilacoom WA; BR/TR/6´2˝/?; d10.7

YEAR	TM LG	W	L	PCT	G	GS	CG-SHO	SV-BS	IP	H	R	HR	HB	BB-IB	SO	ERA	AERA	OAV	OOB	AB-HR-SH	AVG	PB	SUP	APR	DL	PW
1911	NY N	0	0	ø	2	0	0	0	2	2	1	0	0	0	0	4.50	75	.250	.250	0	ø	0	—	0	—	0.0

FAUVER, CLAY Clayton King "Cayt"; B8.1.1872 N.Eaton OH; D3.3.1942 Chatsworth GA; BB/TR/5´10˝/?; d9.7; Col Oberlin

YEAR	TM LG	W	L	PCT	G	GS	CG-SHO	SV-BS	IP	H	R	HR	HB	BB-IB	SO	ERA	AERA	OAV	OOB	AB-HR-SH	AVG	PB	SUP	APR	DL	PW
1899	Lou N	1	0	1.000	1	1	1	0	9	11	4	0	0	2	1	0.00	ø	.297	.333	4	.000	-1	75	3	—	0.2

FEAR, VERN Luvern Carl; B8.21.1924 Everly IA; D9.6.1976 Spencer IA; BB/TR/6´0˝/170; d8.3

YEAR	TM LG	W	L	PCT	G	GS	CG-SHO	SV-BS	IP	H	R	HR	HB	BB-IB	SO	ERA	AERA	OAV	OOB	AB-HR-SH	AVG	PB	SUP	APR	DL	PW
1952	Chi N	0	0	ø	4	0	0	0	8	9	7	1	1	3	4	7.88	49	.290	.371	1	.000	-0	—	-3	0	-0.2

FEE, JACK John; B12.23.1867 Carbondale PA; D3.3.1913 Carbondale PA; d9.14

YEAR	TM LG	W	L	PCT	G	GS	CG-SHO	SV-BS	IP	H	R	HR	HB	BB-IB	SO	ERA	AERA	OAV	OOB	AB-HR-SH	AVG	PB	SUP	APR	DL	PW
1889	Ind N	2	2	.500	7	3	2	0	40	39	29	2	6	31	10	4.27	98	.248	.392	21	.143	-2	96	-1	—	-0.2

FEIERABEND, RYAN Ryan Robert; B8.22.1985 Cleveland OH; BL/TL/6´3˝/190; [SeaA03 3/86]; d9.13

YEAR	TM LG	W	L	PCT	G	GS	CG-SHO	SV-BS	IP	H	R	HR	HB	BB-IB	SO	ERA	AERA	OAV	OOB	AB-HR-SH	AVG	PB	SUP	APR	DL	PW
2006	Sea A	0	1	.000	4	2	0	0-0	17	15	7	3	0	7-0	11	3.71	119	.231	.306	0	ø	0	128	2	0	0.1

FELDMAN, HARRY Harry; B11.10.1919 New York NY; D3.16.1962 Fort Smith AR; BR/TR/6´0˝/175; d9.10

YEAR	TM LG	W	L	PCT	G	GS	CG-SHO	SV-BS	IP	H	R	HR	HB	BB-IB	SO	ERA	AERA	OAV	OOB	AB-HR-SH	AVG	PB	SUP	APR	DL	PW
1941	NY N	1	1	.500	3	3	1-1	0	20.1	21	10	0	0	6	9	3.98	93	.280	.333	6-0-1	.167	0	115	0	0	-0.1
1942	NY N	7	1	.875	31	6	2-1	0	114	100	46	5	1	73	49	3.16	106	.236	.350	39-1-1	.282	3	121	3	0	0.5
1943	NY N	4	5	.444	31	10	1	0	104.2	114	59	7	4	58	49	4.30	80	.279	.374	30	.133	-1*	79	-11	0	-1.0
1944	NY N	11	13	.458	40	27	8-1	2	205.1	214	120	18	2	91	70	4.16	88	.266	.342	73-0-3	.205	0*	110	-14	0	-1.6
1945	NY N	12	13	.480	35	30	10-3	1	217.2	213	92	14	1	69	74	3.27	120	.251	.308	72-1-0	.097	-3*	77	14	0	1.1
1946	NY N	0	2	.000	3	2	0	0	4	9	8	1	0	3	3	18.00	19	.474	.545	1	.000	-0	25	-6	0	-1.0
Total	6	35	35	.500	143	78	22-6	3	666	671	335	45	8	300	254	3.80	96	.260	.339	221-2-5	.172	-1	93	-14	0	-2.1

FELDMAN, SCOTT Scott Wayne; B2.7.1983 Kailua HI; BL/TR/6´5˝/(210–225); [TexA03 30/886]; d8.31; Col San Mateo (CA) JC

YEAR	TM LG	W	L	PCT	G	GS	CG-SHO	SV-BS	IP	H	R	HR	HB	BB-IB	SO	ERA	AERA	OAV	OOB	AB-HR-SH	AVG	PB	SUP	APR	DL	PW
2005	Tex A	0	1	.000	8	0	0	0-0	9.1	9	1	0	0	2-1	4	0.96	472	.257	.297	0	ø	0	—	4	0	0.3
2006	Tex A	0	2	.000	36	0	0	0-1	41.1	42	19	4	4	10-0	30	3.92	119	.266	.324	0	ø	0	—	4	0	0.2
Total	2	0	3	.000	44	0	0	0-1	50.2	51	20	4	4	12-1	34	3.38	138	.264	.319	0	ø	0	—	8	0	0.5

FELICIANO, PEDRO Pedro Juan (Molina); B8.25.1976 Rio Piedras, PR; BL/TL/5´11˝/(165–185); [LAN95 31/863]; d9.4

YEAR	TM LG	W	L	PCT	G	GS	CG-SHO	SV-BS	IP	H	R	HR	HB	BB-IB	SO	ERA	AERA	OAV	OOB	AB-HR-SH	AVG	PB	SUP	APR	DL	PW
2002	NY N	0	0	ø	6	0	0	0-0	6	9	5	0	0	1-0	4	7.50	53	.360	.385	0	ø	0	—	-2	0	-0.1
2003	NY N	0	0	ø	23	0	0	0-0	48.1	52	21	5	3	21-3	43	3.35	125	.269	.349	3-0-1	.000	-0	—	4	0	0.2
2004	NY N	1	1	.500	22	0	0	0-0	18.1	14	12	2	1	12-0	14	5.40	80	.209	.333	0	ø	0	—	-2	0	-0.2
2006	†NY N	7	2	.778	64	0	0	0-3	60.1	56	15	4	3	20-1	54	2.09	210	.248	.313	3	.000	-0	—	16	0	2.1
Total	4	8	3	.727	115	0	0	0-3	133	131	53	11	7	54-4	115	3.25	132	.256	.333	6-0-1	.000	-0	—	16	0	2.0

FELIX, HARRY Harry; B1870 Brooklyn NY; D10.17.1961 Miami FL; BR/TR/5´7.5˝/160; d10.5

YEAR	TM LG	W	L	PCT	G	GS	CG-SHO	SV-BS	IP	H	R	HR	HB	BB-IB	SO	ERA	AERA	OAV	OOB	AB-HR-SH	AVG	PB	SUP	APR	DL	PW
1901	NY N	0	0	ø	1	0	0	0	2	3	0	0	0	0	0	0.00	ø	.333	.333	1	.000	-0	—	1	—	0.0
1902	Phi N	1	3	.250	9	5	3	0	45	61	37	1	0	11	10	5.60	50	.323	.360	37-0-3	.135	-1*	53	-13	—	-1.1
Total	2	1	3	.250	10	5	3	0	47	64	37	1	0	11	10	5.36	53	.323	.359	38-0-3	.132	-1	53	-12	—	-1.1

FELLER, BOB Robert William Andrew "Rapid Robert" (b Robert William Feller); B11.3.1918 Van Meter IA; BR/TR/6´0˝/185; d7.19; Mil 1942–45; HF1962

YEAR	TM LG	W	L	PCT	G	GS	CG-SHO	SV-BS	IP	H	R	HR	HB	BB-IB	SO	ERA	AERA	OAV	OOB	AB-HR-SH	AVG	PB	SUP	APR	DL	PW
1936	Cle A	5	3	.625	14	8	5	1	62	52	29	1	4	47	76	3.34	151	.229	.371	22-0-1	.136	-2	109	11	—	1.0
1937	Cle A	9	7	.563	26	19	9	1	148.2	116	68	4	2	106	150	3.39	136	.218	.351	53	.170	-1	80	19	—	1.7
1938	Cle A☆	17	11	.607	39	36	20-2	1	277.2	225	136	13	7	208	**240**	4.08	114	**.220**	.356	94-0-9	.181	2	104	21	—	1.8
1939	Cle A★	**24**	9	.727	39	35	**24**-4	1	**296.2**	227	105	13	3	142	**246**	2.85	154	**.210**	.303	99-0-6	.212	5	114	**54**	—	**6.0**
1940	Cle A★	**27**	11	.711	**43**	**37**	**31-4**	4	**320.1**	245	102	13	5	118	**261**	**2.61**	161	**.210**	**.285**	115-2-6	.157	1	99	**61**	—	**6.8**
1941	Cle A★	**25**	13	.658	**44**	**40**	28-**6**	2	**343**	284	129	15	5	194	**260**	3.15	125	.226	.332	120-1-10	.150	2	108	34	0	3.6
1945	Cle A	5	3	.625	9	9	7-1	0	72	50	21	1	2	35	59	2.50	130	.192	.293	25-0-1	.160	-0	111	7	0	0.7
1946	Cle A★	**26**	15	.634	**48**	**42**	**36-10**	4	**371.1**	277	101	11	3	153	**348**	2.18	152	.208	.291	124-0-8	.129	-2	80	50	0	5.4
1947	Cle A✳	**20**	11	.645	42	**37**	20-**5**	3	**299**	230	97	17	4	127	**196**	2.68	130	.215	.300	98-0-8	.184	3	105	**29**	0	3.2
1948	†Cle A✳	19	15	.559	44	**38**	18-2	3	280.1	255	123	20	2	116	**164**	3.56	114	.241	.317	95-0-9	.095	-8	109	17	0	1.0
1949	Cle A	15	14	.517	36	28	15	0	211	198	104	18	1	84	108	3.75	106	.248	.320	72-2-7	.236	4	95	3	0	0.5
1950	Cle A★	16	11	.593	35	34	16-3	0	247	230	105	20	5	103	119	3.43	126	.247	.325	83-2-8	.120	-2	99	27	0	2.1
1951	Cle A	**22**	8	**.733**	33	32	16-4	0	249.2	239	105	22	7	95	111	3.50	108	.253	.325	81-0-10	.123	-4	125	11	0	0.6
1952	Cle A	9	13	.409	30	30	11	0	191.2	219	124	13	3	83	81	4.74	71	.288	.360	60-1-3	.117	1	152	-36	0	-3.5
1953	Cle A	10	7	.588	25	25	10-1	0	175.2	163	78	16	3	60	60	3.59	105	.251	.317	56-0-8	.107	-2	124	4	0	0.2

YEAR	TM LG	W	L	PCT	G	GS	CG-SHO	SV-BS	IP	H	R	HR	HB	BB-IB	SO	ERA	AERA	OAV	OOB	AB-HR-SH	AVG	PB	SUP	APR	DL	PW
1954	Cle A	13	3	.813	19	19	9-1	0	140	127	53	13	3	39	59	3.09	119	.239	.292	48-0-3	.188	1	128	10	0	1.1
1955	Cle A	4	4	.500	25	11	2-1	0	83	71	43	7	1	31-2	25	3.47	115	.235	.305	21-0-3	.048	-2	93	2	0	-0.1
1956	Cle A	0	4	.000	19	4	2	1	58	63	34	7	0	23-4	18	4.97	85	.280	.344	16	.000	-2	69	-4	0	-0.5
Total	18	266	162	.621	570	484	279-44	21	3827	3271	1557	224	60	1764-6	2581	3.25	122	.231	.319	1282-8-100	.151	-7	107	320	0	31.6

FELTON, TERRY Terry Lane; B10.29.1957 Texarkana AR; BR/TR/6´1˝/(180–185); [MinA76 2/34]; d9.28

YEAR	TM LG	W	L	PCT	G	GS	CG-SHO	SV-BS	IP	H	R	HR	HB	BB-IB	SO	ERA	AERA	OAV	OOB	AB-HR-SH	AVG	PB	SUP	APR	DL	PW
1979	Min A	0	0	ø	1	0	0	0-0	2	0	0	0	0	0-0	1	0.00	ø	.000	.000	0	ø	0	—	1	0	0.0
1980	Min A	0	3	.000	5	4	0	0-0	17.2	20	18	2	1	9-1	14	7.13	61	.286	.370	0	ø	0	56	-6	0	-0.8
1981	Min A	0	0	ø	1	0	0	0-0	1.1	4	6	1	0	2-0	1	40.50	10	.500	.600	0	ø	0	—	-5	0	-0.2
1982	Min A	0	13	.000	48	6	0	3-3	117.1	99	71	18	4	76-8	92	4.99	86	.230	.348	0	ø	0	50	-9	0	-1.1
Total	4	0	16	.000	55	10	0	3-3	138.1	123	95	21	5	87-9	108	5.53	77	.240	.352	0	ø	0	53	-19	0	-2.1

FENNER, HOD Horace Alfred; B7.12.1897 Martin MI; D11.20.1954 Detroit MI; BR/TR/5´10.5˝/165; d9.9; Col Kalamazoo

YEAR	TM LG	W	L	PCT	G	GS	CG-SHO	SV-BS	IP	H	R	HR	HB	BB-IB	SO	ERA	AERA	OAV	OOB	AB-HR-SH	AVG	PB	SUP	APR	DL	PW
1921	Chi A	0	0	ø	2	1	0	0	7	14	6	0	0	3	1	7.71	55	.452	.500	2	.000	-0	394	-2	—	-0.2

FERENS, STAN Stanley "Lefty"; B3.5.1915 Wendel PA; D10.7.1994 Hempfield Twp. PA; BB/TL/5´11˝/170; d6.10

YEAR	TM LG	W	L	PCT	G	GS	CG-SHO	SV-BS	IP	H	R	HR	HB	BB-IB	SO	ERA	AERA	OAV	OOB	AB-HR-SH	AVG	PB	SUP	APR	DL	PW
1942	StL A	3	4	.429	19	3	1	0	69	76	31	2	0	21	23	3.78	98	.279	.331	21-0-1	.143	-1	192	1	0	0.0
1946	StL A	2	9	.182	34	6	1	0	88	100	60	3	3	38	28	4.50	83	.293	.369	24-0-2	.167	-1	77	-10	0	-1.3
Total	2	5	13	.278	53	9	2	0	157	176	91	5	3	59	51	4.18	89	.287	.353	45-0-3	.156	-1	115	-9	0	-1.3

FERGUSON, GEORGE Cecil "George" or "Cecil"; B8.19.1883 Ellsworth IN; D9.5.1943 Montverde FL; BR/TR/5´10˝/165; d4.19

YEAR	TM LG	W	L	PCT	G	GS	CG-SHO	SV-BS	IP	H	R	HR	HB	BB-IB	SO	ERA	AERA	OAV	OOB	AB-HR-SH	AVG	PB	SUP	APR	DL	PW
1906	NY N	2	0	1.000	22	1	1-1	**7**	52.1	43	22	1	2	24	32	2.58	101	.229	.322	15	.333	2	56	0	—	0.3
1907	NY N	3	2	.600	15	5	4	1	64	63	32	2	5	20	37	2.11	118	.266	.336	18-0-1	.056	-1	138	-2	—	-0.3
1908	Bos N	11	11	.500	37	21	13-3	0	208	168	72	1	8	84	98	2.47	98	.230	.316	65-0-3	.169	1*	113	2	—	0.1
1909	Bos N	5	23	.179	36	30	19-3	0	226.2	235	121	2	12	83	87	3.73	76	.282	.355	73-0-1	.205	1	65	-18	—	-1.9
1910	Bos N	7	7	.500	26	14	10-1	0	123	110	56	3	7	58	40	3.80	87	.254	.351	40-1-2	.175	-1	85	0	—	-0.1
1911	Bos N	1	3	.250	6	3	0	0	24	40	29	3	0	12	4	9.75	39	.388	.452	7	.286	1	52	-12	—	-1.5
Total	6	29	46	.387	142	74	47-8	8	698	659	332	12	34	281	298	3.34	83	.261	.343	218-1-7	.188	3	86	-30	—	-3.4

FERGUSON, CHARLIE Charles Augustus; B5.10.1875 Okemos MI; D5.17.1931 Sault Ste.Marie MI; TR/5´11˝/?; d9.20

YEAR	TM LG	W	L	PCT	G	GS	CG-SHO	SV-BS	IP	H	R	HR	HB	BB-IB	SO	ERA	AERA	OAV	OOB	AB-HR-SH	AVG	PB	SUP	APR	DL	PW
1901	Chi N	0	0	ø	1	0	0	0	2	1	0	0	0	2	0	0.00	ø	.143	.333	1	.000	-0	—	1	—	0.0

FERGUSON, CHARLIE Charles J.; B4.17.1863 Charlottesville VA; D4.29.1888 Philadelphia PA; BB/TR/6´0˝/165; d5.1

YEAR	TM LG	W	L	PCT	G	GS	CG-SHO	SV-BS	IP	H	R	HR	HB	BB-IB	SO	ERA	AERA	OAV	OOB	AB-HR-SH	AVG	PB	SUP	APR	DL	PW
1884	Phi N	21	25	.457	50	47	46-2	1	416.2	443	297	13	—	93	194	3.54	84	.253	.291	203	.246	7*	98	-21	—	-1.2
1885	Phi N	26	20	.565	48	45	45-5	0	405	345	197	5	—	81	197	2.22	126	.219	.257	235-1	.306	17*	104	26	—	4.3
1886	Phi N	30	9	.769	48	45	43-4	**2**	395.2	317	145	11	—	69	212	1.98	166	.210	.244	261-2	.253	12*	101	**59**	—	**6.5**
1887	Phi N	22	10	.688	37	33	31-2	**1**	297.1	297	154	13	11	47	125	3.00	142	.254	.289	264-3	.337	14*	106	40	—	4.7
Total	4	99	64	.607	183	170	165-13	4	1514.2	1402	793	42	11	290	728	2.67	122	.233	.270	963-6	.288	49	102	104	—	14.3

FERGUSON, ALEX James Alexander; B2.16.1897 Montclair NJ; D4.26.1976 Sepulveda CA; BR/TR/6´0˝/180; d8.16; Mil 1918

YEAR	TM LG	W	L	PCT	G	GS	CG-SHO	SV-BS	IP	H	R	HR	HB	BB-IB	SO	ERA	AERA	OAV	OOB	AB-HR-SH	AVG	PB	SUP	APR	DL	PW
1918	NY A	0	0	ø	1	0	0	0	1.2	2	0	0	0	2	1	0.00	ø	.333	.500	1	.000	-0	—	1	—	0.0
1921	NY A	3	1	.750	17	4	1	1	56.1	64	40	4	4	27	9	5.91	72	.296	.385	19	.211	-1	118	-8	—	-0.6
1922	Bos A	9	16	.360	39	27	10-1	2	198.1	201	108	5	6	62	44	4.31	95	.265	.326	65-0-6	.092	-6	69	-3	—	-1.0
1923	Bos A	9	13	.409	34	27	11	0	198.1	229	115	5	9	67	72	4.04	102	.297	.360	62-0-6	.097	-5	77	1	—	-0.6
1924	Bos A	14	17	.452	41	32	15	2	237.2	259	115	6	6	108	78	3.79	115	.286	.366	86-0-8	.140	-6	78	17	—	1.4
1925	Bos A	0	2	.000	5	4	0	1	15.2	22	22	6	1	5	5	10.91	42	.314	.368	4	.000	-0	88	-10	—	-1.1
	NY A	4	2	.667	21	6	0	1	54.1	83	57	3	2	42	20	7.79	55	.358	.460	15-0-2	.133	-1	135	-23	—	-2.1
	†Was A	5	1	.833	7	6	3	0	55.1	52	22	2	2	23	24	3.25	130	.256	.338	20-0-4	.050	-3	126	7	—	0.3
	Year	9	5	.643	33	16	3	2	125.1	157	101	11	5	70	49	6.18	69	.311	.400	39-0-6	.077	-4	120	-24	—	-2.9
1926	Was A	3	4	.429	19	4	0	1	47.2	69	51	4	3	18	16	7.74	50	.343	.405	11-0-1	.182	-0	136	-23	—	-2.8
1927	Phi N	8	16	.333	31	31	16	0	227	280	132	15	6	65	73	4.84	85	.313	.363	70-0-10	.100	-5	85	-15	—	-1.8
1928	Phi N	5	10	.333	34	19	5-1	2	134.2	168	91	14	6	52	51	5.88	73	.315	.382	39-0-2	.026	-4	118	-19	—	-2.2
1929	Phi N	1	2	.333	5	4	1	0	12.2	19	18	2	0	10	3	12.08	43	.345	.446	4	.000	-1	50	-8	—	-1.4
	Bro N	0	1	.000	3	2	0	0	2	7	7	2	0	1	1	22.50	21	.583	.615	1	1.000	0	189	-4	—	-0.7
	Year	1	3	.250	8	6	1	0	14.2	26	25	4	0	11	4	13.50	38	.388	.474	5	.200	-0	91	-13	—	-2.1
Total	10	61	85	.418	257	166	62-2	10	1241.2	1455	778	68	45	482	397	4.93	85	.299	.368	397-0-39	.106	-33	90	-87	—	-12.6

FERGUSON, BOB Robert Lester; B4.18.1919 Birmingham AL; BR/TR/6´1.5˝/180; d4.29

YEAR	TM LG	W	L	PCT	G	GS	CG-SHO	SV-BS	IP	H	R	HR	HB	BB-IB	SO	ERA	AERA	OAV	OOB	AB-HR-SH	AVG	PB	SUP	APR	DL	PW
1944	Cin N	0	3	.000	9	2	0	1	16	24	17	3	2	10	9	9.00	39	.358	.456	3	.333	0	84	-9	0	-1.6

FERGUSON, BOB Robert Vavasour; B1.31.1845 Brooklyn NY; D5.3.1894 Brooklyn NY; BB/TR/5´9.5˝/149; d5.18; M16/U10; ▲

YEAR	TM LG	W	L	PCT	G	GS	CG-SHO	SV-BS	IP	H	R	HR	HB	BB-IB	SO	ERA	AERA	OAV	OOB	AB-HR-SH	AVG	PB	SUP	APR	DL	PW
1871	Mut NA	0	0	ø	1	0	0	0	1	8	9	0	—	0	0	27.00	14	.571	.571	158	.241	-0*	—	-3	—	-0.1
1873	Atl NA	0	1	.000	4	1	1	0	19.1	41	30	2	—	2	0	5.59	57	.383	.394	228	.259	1*	47	-6	—	-0.2
1874	Atl NA	0	1	.000	1	1	1	0	9	12	10	0	—	3	0	4.00	51	.273	.319	245	.261	0*	99	-1	—	-0.1
1875	Har NA	0	0	ø	1	0	0	0	2	9	7	1	—	0	0	22.50	10	.600	.600	366	.240	0*	—	-3	—	-0.1
1877	Har N	1	1	.500	3	2	2	0	25	38	15	0	—	2	1	3.96	61	.352	.364	254	.256	0*	140	-2	—	-0.1
1883	Phi N	0	0	ø	1	0	0	0	1	2	2	0	—	0	0	9.00	34	.286	.286	329	.258	0*	—	-1	—	0.0
Total	4NA	0	2	.000	7	2	2	0	31.1	70	56	3	—	5	0	6.89	41	.389	.405	997	.250	1	69	-13	—	-0.5
Total	2	1	1	.500	4	2	2	0	26	40	17	0	—	2	1	4.15	59	.348	.359	583	.257	0	139	-3	—	-0.1

FERMIN, RAMON Ramon Antonio (Ventura); B11.25.1972 San Francisco de Macoris, D.R.; BR/TR/6´3˝/180; d8.6

YEAR	TM LG	W	L	PCT	G	GS	CG-SHO	SV-BS	IP	H	R	HR	HB	BB-IB	SO	ERA	AERA	OAV	OOB	AB-HR-SH	AVG	PB	SUP	APR	DL	PW
1995	Oak A	0	0	ø	1	0	0	0-0	1.1	4	2	0	0	1-0	0	13.50	34	.500	.556	0	ø	0	—	-1	0	-0.1

FERNANDEZ, ALEX Alexander; B8.13.1969 Miami Beach FL; BR/TR/6´1˝/(205–225); [ChiA90 1/4]; d8.2; Col Miami; [DL 1998 Fla N 181, 2001 Fla N 190]

YEAR	TM LG	W	L	PCT	G	GS	CG-SHO	SV-BS	IP	H	R	HR	HB	BB-IB	SO	ERA	AERA	OAV	OOB	AB-HR-SH	AVG	PB	SUP	APR	DL	PW
1990	Chi A	5	5	.500	13	13	3	0-0	87.2	89	40	6	3	34-0	61	3.80	101	.265	.338	0	ø	0	89	1	0	0.0
1991	Chi A	9	13	.409	34	32	2	0-0	191.2	186	100	16	2	88-2	145	4.51	89	.259	.337	0	ø	0	83	-9	0	-0.9
1992	Chi A	8	11	.421	29	29	4-2	0-0	187.2	199	100	21	8	50-3	95	4.27	91	.270	.322	0	ø	0	113	-9	0	-0.7
1993	†Chi A	18	9	.667	34	34	3-1	0-0	247.1	221	95	27	6	67-5	169	3.13	135	.240	.295	0	ø	0	112	31	0	3.2
1994	Chi A	11	7	.611	24	24	4-3	0-0	170.1	163	83	25	1	50-4	122	3.86	122	.250	.302	0	ø	0	118	16	0	1.6
1995	Chi A	12	8	.600	30	30	5-2	0-0	203.2	200	98	19	0	65-7	159	3.80	118	.255	.310	0	ø	0	114	14	0	1.2
1996	Chi A	16	10	.615	35	35	6-1	0-0	258	248	110	34	7	72-4	200	3.45	138	.253	.307	0	ø	0	97	38	0	3.4
1997	†Fla N	17	12	.586	32	32	5-1	0-0	220.2	193	93	25	4	69-2	183	3.59	113	.238	.299	66-0-7	.152	3*	102	13	0	2.1
1999	Fla N	7	8	.467	24	24	1	0-0	141	135	60	10	4	41-1	91	3.38	129	.252	.307	43-3-3	.233	4*	86	15	57	2.0
2000	Fla N	4	4	.500	8	8	0	0-0	52.1	59	25	7	0	16-1	27	4.13	106	.292	.342	17	.118	1*	86	2	135	0.4
Total	10	107	87	.552	263	261	33-10	0-0	1760.1	1693	804	190	35	552-29	1252	3.74	115	.254	.312	126-3-10	.175	8	102	112	563	12.3

FERNANDEZ, SID Charles Sidney; B10.12.1962 Honolulu HI; BL/TL/6´1˝/(205–230); [LAN81 3/73]; d9.20

YEAR	TM LG	W	L	PCT	G	GS	CG-SHO	SV-BS	IP	H	R	HR	HB	BB-IB	SO	ERA	AERA	OAV	OOB	AB-HR-SH	AVG	PB	SUP	APR	DL	PW
1983	LA N	0	1	.000	2	1	0	0-0	6	7	4	0	1	7-0	9	6.00	60	.280	.455	1	1.000	0	73	-1	0	-0.1
1984	NY N	6	6	.500	15	15	0	0-0	90	74	40	8	0	34-3	62	3.50	102	.226	.295	28-0-3	.179	-0	109	1	0	0.0
1985	NY N	9	9	.500	26	26	3	0-0	170.1	108	56	14	2	80-3	180	2.80	125	**.181**	.279	52-0-7	.212	2	102	15	0	1.7
1986	†NY N★	16	6	.727	32	31	2-1	1-0	204.1	161	82	13	2	91-1	200	3.52	102	.216	.300	68-0-6	.162	1	128	5	0	0.6
1987	NY N★	12	8	.600	28	27	3-1	0-0	156	130	75	16	8	67-8	134	3.81	101	.224	.310	43-0-10	.163	1*	123	0	18	0.0
1988	†NY N	12	10	.545	31	31	1-1	0-0	187	127	69	15	6	70-1	189	3.03	108	**.191**	.271	56-0-7	.250	6	109	7	0	1.2
1989	NY N	14	5	.737	35	32	6-2	0-0	219.1	157	73	21	6	75-3	198	2.83	116	.198	.271	71-1-10	.211	4	126	14	0	1.5
1990	NY N	9	14	.391	30	30	2-1	0-0	179.1	130	79	18	5	67-4	181	3.46	109	**.200**	.277	58-0-5	.190	1	101	5	0	0.6
1991	NY N	1	3	.250	8	8	0	0-0	44	36	18	4	0	9-0	31	2.86	128	.222	.262	13-0-1	.154	0	92	3	101	0.3
1992	NY N	14	11	.560	32	32	5-2	0-0	214.2	162	67	12	4	67-4	193	2.73	129	.210	.273	74-0-7	.203	2	112	21	0	2.6
1993	NY N	5	6	.455	18	18	1-1	0-0	119.2	82	42	17	3	36-0	81	2.93	137	.192	.260	32-0-8	.094	-1	84	16	89	1.1
1994	Bal A	6	6	.500	19	19	2	0-0	115.1	109	66	27	2	46-2	95	5.15	98	.248	.320	0	ø	0	101	0	29	-0.1
1995	Bal A	0	4	.000	8	7	0	0-0	28	36	26	9	0	17-2	31	7.39	65	.305	.390	0	ø	0	100	-9	23	-1.0
	Phi N	6	1	.857	11	11	0	0-0	64.2	48	25	11	1	21-0	79	3.34	126	.200	.267	23-0-1	.043	-2	109	7	0	0.4
1996	Phi N	3	6	.333	11	11	0	0-0	63	50	25	5	1	26-2	77	3.43	126	.215	.294	19-0-2	.105	0	68	7	122	0.9
1997	Hou N	1	0	1.000	1	1	0	0-0	5	4	2	1	0	2-0	3	3.60	111	.211	.286	1	.000	-0	138	0	109	0.1
Total	15	114	96	.543	307	300	25-9	1-0	1866.2	1421	749	191	41	715-33	1743	3.36	111	.209	.286	539-1-67	.182	14	109	91	491	9.8

FERNANDEZ, JARED Jared Wade; B2.2.1972 Salt Lake City UT; BR/TR/6´2˝/(223–235); d9.19; Col Cal St.–Fresno

YEAR	TM LG	W	L	PCT	G	GS	CG-SHO	SV-BS	IP	H	R	HR	HB	BB-IB	SO	ERA	AERA	OAV	OOB	AB-HR-SH	AVG	PB	SUP	APR	DL	PW
2001	Cin N	0	1	.000	5	2	0	0-0	12.1	13	9	1	2	6-0	5	4.38	105	.265	.368	2	.000	-0	70	-1	0	-0.1
2002	Cin N	1	3	.250	14	8	0	0-0	50.2	59	31	5	3	24-1	36	4.44	96	.294	.374	10-0-2	.200	0	100	-2	0	-0.1
2003	Hou N	3	3	.500	12	6	0	0-0	38.1	37	17	2	2	12-2	19	3.99	111	.259	.323	9-0-1	.000	-1	74	2	0	0.3
2004	Hou N	0	0	ø	2	1	0	0-0	1	6	6	0	0	5-0	0	54.00	8	.750	.786	0	ø	0	212	-5	0	-0.2
2006	Mil N	0	0	ø	4	0	0	0-0	6.1	11	7	2	0	1-0	1	9.95	45	.367	.387	0	ø	0	—	-4	0	-0.2
Total	5	4	7	.364	37	17	0	0-0	108.2	126	70	10	7	48-3	61	5.05	87	.292	.369	21-0-3	.095	-1	94	-10	0	-0.3

FERNANDEZ, OSVALDO Osvaldo; B11.4.1968 Holguin, Cuba; BR/TR/6´2˝/(190–193); d4.5; [DL 1998 SF N 181]

YEAR	TM LG	W	L	PCT	G	GS	CG-SHO	SV-BS	IP	H	R	HR	HB	BB-IB	SO	ERA	AERA	OAV	OOB	AB-HR-SH	AVG	PB	SUP	APR	DL	PW
1996	SF N	7	13	.350	30	28	2	0-0	171.2	193	95	20	10	57-4	106	4.61	90	.286	.348	57-0-5	.088	-3*	79	-7	0	-1.0
1997	SF N	3	4	.429	11	11	0	0-0	56.1	74	39	9	0	15-2	31	4.95	83	.314	.353	17-0-2	.000	-1*	102	-7	126	-0.9
2000	Cin N	4	3	.571	15	14	1	0-0	79.2	69	33	6	2	31-2	36	3.62	132	.238	.313	22-0-5	.091	-1	95	11	55	0.7
2001	Cin N	5	6	.455	20	14	0	0-1	79.1	103	62	8	0	33-3	35	6.92	66	.316	.376	19-0-3	.053	-1	88	-17	0	-2.0
Total	4	19	26	.422	76	67	3	0-1	387	439	229	43	12	136-11	208	4.93	88	.287	.348	115-0-15	.070	-7	88	-20	362	-3.2

FERRARESE, DON Donald Hugh; B6.19.1929 Oakland CA; BR/TL/5´9˝/(160–170); d4.11; Col St. Marys (CA)

YEAR	TM LG	W	L	PCT	G	GS	CG-SHO	SV-BS	IP	H	R	HR	HB	BB-IB	SO	ERA	AERA	OAV	OOB	AB-HR-SH	AVG	PB	SUP	APR	DL	PW
1955	Bal A	0	0	ø	6	0	0	0	9	8	3	0	0	11-0	5	3.00	127	.276	.463	1	.000	-0	—	1	0	0.0
1956	Bal A	4	10	.286	36	14	3-1	2	102	86	60	8	3	64-0	81	5.03	78	.229	.342	28	.036	-3	81	-12	0	-1.7
1957	Bal A	1	1	.500	8	2	0	0	19	14	13	1	0	12-1	13	4.74	76	.200	.317	3	.000	-0	137	-4	0	-0.4
1958	Cle A	3	4	.429	28	10	2	1	94.2	91	45	4	1	46-2	62	3.71	98	.254	.340	26	.115	-1	91	-1	0	-0.3
1959	Cle A	5	3	.625	15	10	4	0	76	58	29	6	1	51-2	45	3.20	115	.219	.346	27-0-1	.259	2	105	5	0	0.7
1960	Chi A	0	1	.000	5	0	0	0	4	8	8	2	0	9-0	4	18.00	21	.400	.586	2	.500	0	—	-6	0	-1.1
1961	Phi N	5	12	.294	42	14	3-1	1	138.2	120	64	14	1	68-4	89	3.76	108	.234	.325	35-0-4	.171	-1*	72	5	0	0.4
1962	Phi N	0	1	.000	5	0	0	0	6.2	9	8	1	0	3-0	6	8.10	48	.310	.364	1	1.000	0	—	-4	0	-0.4
	StL N	1	4	.200	38	0	0	1	56.2	55	19	2	1	31-4	45	2.70	158	.270	.367	5-1-0	.200	1	—	9	0	0.9
	Year	1	5	.167	43	0	0	1	63.1	64	27	3	1	34-4	51	3.27	129	.275	.367	6-1-0	.333	1	—	6	0	0.5
Total	8	19	36	.345	183	50	12-2	5	506.2	449	249	38	7	295-13	350	4.00	98	.241	.345	128-1-5	.156	-2	86	-7	0	-1.9

FERRARI, ANTHONY Anthony Michael; B6.22.1978 San Francisco CA; BL/TL/5´9˝/160; [MonN00 44/1300]; d6.7; Col Lewis–Clark St.

YEAR	TM LG	W	L	PCT	G	GS	CG-SHO	SV-BS	IP	H	R	HR	HB	BB-IB	SO	ERA	AERA	OAV	OOB	AB-HR-SH	AVG	PB	SUP	APR	DL	PW
2003	Mon N	0	0	ø	4	0	0	0-0	4	4	3	1	1	5-1	1	6.75	66	.267	.476	0	ø	0	—	-1	0	0.0

FERRAZZI, BILL William Joseph; B4.19.1907 W.Quincy MA; D8.10.1993 Gainesville FL; BR/TR/6´2.5˝/200; d9.7; Col Florida

YEAR	TM LG	W	L	PCT	G	GS	CG-SHO	SV-BS	IP	H	R	HR	HB	BB-IB	SO	ERA	AERA	OAV	OOB	AB-HR-SH	AVG	PB	SUP	APR	DL	PW
1935	Phi A	1	2	.333	3	2	0	0	7	7	5	0	0	5	0	5.14	88	.269	.387	1	.000	0	76	-1	—	-0.1

FERREIRA, TONY Anthony Ross; B10.4.1962 Riverside CA; BL/TL/6´1˝/160; [KCA81 2/49]; d9.17

YEAR	TM LG	W	L	PCT	G	GS	CG-SHO	SV-BS	IP	H	R	HR	HB	BB-IB	SO	ERA	AERA	OAV	OOB	AB-HR-SH	AVG	PB	SUP	APR	DL	PW
1985	KC A	0	0	ø	2	0	0	0-0	5.2	6	5	0	0	2-0	5	7.94	53	.273	.333	0	ø	0	—	-2	0	-0.1

FERRELL, WES Wesley Cheek; B2.2.1908 Greensboro NC; D12.9.1976 Sarasota FL; BR/TR/6´2˝/195; d9.9; b–Rick; ▲

YEAR	TM LG	W	L	PCT	G	GS	CG-SHO	SV-BS	IP	H	R	HR	HB	BB-IB	SO	ERA	AERA	OAV	OOB	AB-HR-SH	AVG	PB	SUP	APR	DL	PW
1927	Cle A	0	0	ø	1	0	0	0	1	3	3	0	0	2	0	27.00	16	.600	.714	0	ø	0	—	-2	—	-0.1
1928	Cle A	0	2	.000	2	2	1	0	16	15	5	0	0	5	4	2.25	184	.242	.299	4	.250	1	0	3	—	0.5
1929	Cle A	21	10	.677	43	25	18-1	5	242.2	256	112	7	3	109	100	3.60	124	.279	.358	93-1-3	.237	4*	105	24	—	3.3
1930	Cle A	25	13	.658	43	35	25-1	3	296.2	299	141	14	0	106	143	3.31	146	.262	.325	118-0-3	.297	8*	113	46	—	5.9
1931	Cle A	22	12	.647	40	35	**27**-2	3	276.1	276	134	9	3	130	123	3.75	123	.255	.336	116-9-2	.319	17*	111	27	—	5.0
1932	Cle A	23	13	.639	38	34	26-3	1	287.2	299	141	17	0	104	105	3.66	130	.264	.326	128-2-6	.242	5*	90	32	—	4.0
1933	Cle A☆	11	12	.478	28	26	16-1	0	201	225	108	8	2	70	41	4.21	106	.282	.341	140-7-1	.271	7*	97	7	—	1.8
1934	Bos A	14	5	.737	26	23	17-3	1	181	205	87	4	0	49	67	3.63	132	.282	.327	78-4-3	.282	8*	106	22	—	2.8
1935	Bos A	**25**	14	.641	41	**38**	**31**-3	0	**322.1**	336	149	16	3	108	110	3.52	135	.267	.326	150-7-8	.347	20*	101	41	—	**6.8**
1936	Bos A	20	15	.571	39	**38**	**28**-3	0	**301**	330	160	11	6	119	106	4.19	127	.274	.343	135-5-5	.267	11*	89	36	—	4.4
1937	Bos A	3	6	.333	12	11	5	0	73.1	111	66	14	1	34	31	7.61	62	.348	.412	33-1-1	.364	6*	134	-21	—	-1.4
	Was A☆	11	13	.458	25	24	21	0	207.2	214	111	11	2	88	92	3.94	112	.265	.339	106-0-2	.255	5*	87	10	—	1.5
	Year	14	19	.424	37	35	**26**	0	**281**	325	177	25	3	122	123	4.90	92	.289	.360	139-1-3	.281	11	103	-11	—	0.1
1938	Was A	13	8	.619	23	22	9	0	149	193	111	12	1	68	36	5.92	76	.311	.380	49-1-6	.224	7*	119	-23	—	-1.9
	NY A	2	2	.500	5	4	1	0	30	52	33	6	0	18	7	8.10	56	.388	.461	12	.167	0	121	-13	—	-1.2
	Year	15	10	.600	28	26	10	0	179	245	144	18	1	86	43	6.28	72	.325	.394	61-1-6	.213	7	119	-39	—	-3.1
1939	NY A	1	2	.333	3	3	1	0	19.1	14	10	2	0	17	6	4.66	94	.219	.383	8	.125	-0	47	0	—	0.0
1940	Bro N	0	0	ø	1	0	0	0	4	4	3	0	1	4	4	6.75	59	.250	.429	2	.000	-0*	—	-1	—	-0.1
1941	Bos N	2	1	.667	4	3	1	0	14	13	8	1	1	9	10	5.14	69	.241	.359	4-1-0	.500	2	103	-2	0	-0.2
Total	15	193	128	.601	374	323	227-17	13	2623	2845	1382	132	23	1040	985	4.04	117	.275	.343	1176-38-40	.280	100	102	186	0	31.1

FERRICK, TOM Thomas Jerome; B1.6.1915 New York NY; D10.15.1996 Lima PA; BR/TR/6´2.5˝/220; d4.19; Mil 1943–45; C12

YEAR	TM LG	W	L	PCT	G	GS	CG-SHO	SV-BS	IP	H	R	HR	HB	BB-IB	SO	ERA	AERA	OAV	OOB	AB-HR-SH	AVG	PB	SUP	APR	DL	PW
1941	Phi A	8	10	.444	36	4	2-1	7	119.1	130	61	8	0	33	30	3.77	111	.275	.322	44	.205	1	134	4	0	0.9
1942	Cle A	3	2	.600	31	2	2	3	81.1	56	20	3	0	32	28	1.99	173	.200	.282	19-0-1	.211	0	186	**14**	0	1.1
1946	Cle A	0	0	ø	9	0	0	1	18	25	12	3	0	4	9	5.00	66	.321	.354	3	.667	1	—	-4	0	-0.1
	StL A	4	1	.800	25	1	0	5	32.1	26	13	1	0	5	13	2.78	134	.224	.256	4	.000	-1	69	3	0	0.5
	Year	4	1	.800	34	1	0	6	50.1	51	25	4	0	9	22	3.58	100	.263	.296	7	.286	1	72	-1	0	0.4
1947	Was A	1	7	.125	31	0	0	9	60	57	24	1	0	20	23	3.15	118	.256	.317	10	.100	-1	—	4	0	0.6
1948	Was A	2	5	.286	37	0	0	10	73.2	75	37	3	0	38	34	4.15	105	.261	.348	15	.067	-1	—	2	0	0.2
1949	StL A	6	4	.600	50	0	0	6	104.1	102	51	9	1	41	34	3.88	117	.258	.329	21-0-2	.143	-1*	—	8	0	0.7
1950	StL A	1	3	.250	16	0	0	2	24	24	15	2	0	7	6	4.13	120	.267	.320	4	.250	-0	—	1	0	0.2
	†NY A	8	4	.667	30	0	0	9	56.2	49	26	5	0	22	20	3.65	118	.233	.306	14-0-1	.143	0	—	4	0	0.8
	Year	9	7	.563	46	0	0	11	80.2	73	41	7	0	29	26	3.79	118	.243	.310	18-0-1	.167	0	—	5	0	1.0
1951	NY A	1	1	.500	9	0	0	1	12	21	12	4	0	7	3	7.50	51	.389	.459	1-0-1	1.000	1	—	-6	0	-0.8
	Was A	2	0	1.000	22	0	0	2	41.2	36	16	3	0	7	17	2.38	172	.234	.267	7-0-1	.286	0	—	6	0	0.4
	Year	3	1	.750	31	0	0	3	53.2	57	28	7	0	14	20	3.52	115	.274	.320	8-0-2	.375	1	—	1	0	-0.4
1952	Was A	4	3	.571	27	0	0	1	50.2	53	19	2	0	11	28	3.02	118	.273	.312	5-0-1	.200	1	—	3	0	0.6
Total	9	40	40	.500	323	7	4-1	56	674	654	306	44	1	227	245	3.47	117	.256	.317	147-0-7	.184	1	137	39	0	5.1

FERRIS, BOB Robert Eugene; B5.7.1955 Arlington VA; BR/TR/6´6˝/225; [AnaA76 2/30]; d9.12; Col Maryland

YEAR	TM LG	W	L	PCT	G	GS	CG-SHO	SV-BS	IP	H	R	HR	HB	BB-IB	SO	ERA	AERA	OAV	OOB	AB-HR-SH	AVG	PB	SUP	APR	DL	PW
1979	Cal A	0	0	ø	2	0	0	0-0	6	5	2	1	0	3-1	2	1.50	272	.217	.308	0	ø	0	—	1	0	0.1
1980	Cal A	0	2	.000	5	3	0	0-0	15.1	23	13	2	0	9-0	4	5.87	67	.354	.432	0	ø	0	83	-4	0	-0.5
Total	2	0	2	.000	7	3	0	0-0	21.1	28	15	3	0	12-1	6	4.64	86	.318	.400	0	ø	0	83	-3	0	-0.4

FERRISS, DAVE David Meadow "Boo"; B12.5.1921 Shaw MS; BL/TR/6´2˝/208; d4.29; C5; Col Mississippi St.

YEAR	TM LG	W	L	PCT	G	GS	CG-SHO	SV-BS	IP	H	R	HR	HB	BB-IB	SO	ERA	AERA	OAV	OOB	AB-HR-SH	AVG	PB	SUP	APR	DL	PW
1945	Bos A✶	21	10	.677	35	31	26-5	2	264.2	263	101	6	7	85	94	2.96	115	.264	.327	120-1-1	.267	11*	118	13	0	3.0
1946	†Bos A☆	25	6	**.806**	40	35	26-6	3	274	274	109	14	3	71	106	3.25	113	.259	.308	115-0-2	.209	2*	144	13	0	1.8
1947	Bos A	12	11	.522	33	28	14-1	0	218.1	241	106	14	7	92	64	4.04	96	.287	.362	99	.273	7*	113	-1	0	0.5
1948	Bos A	7	3	.700	31	9	1	3	115.1	127	71	7	7	61	30	5.23	84	.286	.381	37-0-2	.243	2	135	-9	0	-0.6
1949	Bos A	0	0	ø	4	0	0	0	6.2	7	3	1	1	4	1	4.05	108	.292	.414	1	1.000	1	—	0	73	0.1
1950	Bos A	0	0	ø	1	0	0	0	1	2	2	0	0	1	1	18.00	27	.500	.600	0	ø	0	—	-1	0	-0.1
Total	6	65	30	.684	144	103	67-12	8	880	914	392	42	25	314	296	3.64	103	.272	.338	372-1-5	.250	23	126	15	73	4.7

FERRY, CY Alfred Joseph; B9.27.1878 Hudson NY; D9.27.1938 Pittsfield MA; BR/TR/6´1˝/170; d5.12; b–Jack; Col Manhattan

YEAR	TM LG	W	L	PCT	G	GS	CG-SHO	SV-BS	IP	H	R	HR	HB	BB-IB	SO	ERA	AERA	OAV	OOB	AB-HR-SH	AVG	PB	SUP	APR	DL	PW
1904	Det A	0	1	.000	3	1	1	0	13	12	9	0	1	11	4	6.23	41	.245	.393	6	.333	1	196	-4	—	-0.2
1905	Cle A	0	0	ø	1	1	0	0	2	3	3	1	2	0	2	13.50	19	.333	.455	1	.000	-0	135	-2	—	-0.1
Total	2	0	1	.000	4	2	1	0	15	15	12	1	3	11	6	7.20	36	.259	.403	7	.286	1	167	-6	—	-0.3

FERRY, JACK John Francis; B4.7.1887 Pittsfield MA; D8.29.1954 Pittsfield MA; BR/TR/5´11˝/175; d9.4; b–Cy; Col Seton Hall

YEAR	TM LG	W	L	PCT	G	GS	CG-SHO	SV-BS	IP	H	R	HR	HB	BB-IB	SO	ERA	AERA	OAV	OOB	AB-HR-SH	AVG	PB	SUP	APR	DL	PW
1910	Pit N	1	2	.333	6	3	2	0	31	26	10	0	1	8	12	2.32	133	.230	.287	9-0-2	.333	1	48	3	—	0.4
1911	Pit N	6	4	.600	26	8	4-1	3	85.2	83	35	3	2	27	32	3.15	109	.260	.322	29-0-2	.310	3*	148	4	—	0.7
1912	Pit N	2	0	1.000	11	3	1-1	1	39	33	21	1	1	23	10	3.00	109	.234	.345	13	.077	-1	142	-1	—	-0.1
1913	Pit N	1	0	1.000	4	0	0	0	5	4	3	0	0	2	2	5.40	56	.286	.375	0	ø	0	—	-1	—	-0.2
Total	4	10	6	.625	47	14	7-2	4	160.2	146	69	4	4	60	56	3.02	110	.249	.323	51-0-4	.255	3	127	5	—	0.8

THE PITCHER REGISTER

FERSON, ALEX Alexander "Colonel"; B7.14.1866 Philadelphia PA; D12.5.1957 Boston MA; BR/TR/5´9˝/165; d5.4

YEAR	TM LG	W	L	PCT	G	GS	CG-SHO	SV-BS	IP	H	R	HR	HB	BB-IB	SO	ERA	AERA	OAV	OOB	AB-HR-SH	AVG	PB	SUP	APR	DL	PW
1889	Was N	17	17	.500	36	34	28-1	0	288.1	319	199	9	12	105	85	3.90	101	.272	.339	114	.114	-5	83	0	—	-0.5
1890	Buf P	1	7	.125	10	10	7	0	71	88	66	5	1	40	13	5.45	75	.291	.376	32	.219	1*	104	-11	—	-0.7
1892	Bal N	0	1	.000	2	1	1	0	9	17	13	1	0	6	8	11.00	31	.386	.460	4	.000	-1	55	-6	—	-0.5
Total	3	18	25	.419	48	45	36-1	0	368.1	424	278	15	13	151	106	4.37	91	.279	.350	150	.133	-5	88	-17	—	-1.7

FETTE, LOU Louis Henry William; B3.15.1907 Alma MO; D1.3.1981 Warrensburg MO; BR/TR/6´1.5˝/200; d4.26; Col Missouri Valley

YEAR	TM LG	W	L	PCT	G	GS	CG-SHO	SV-BS	IP	H	R	HR	HB	BB-IB	SO	ERA	AERA	OAV	OOB	AB-HR-SH	AVG	PB	SUP	APR	DL	PW
1937	Bos N	20	10	.667	35	33	23-**5**	0	259	243	93	5	4	81	70	2.88	124	.251	.311	92-0-7	.239	3*	103	23	—	2.8
1938	Bos N	11	13	.458	33	32	17-3	1	239.2	235	95	11	4	79	83	3.15	109	.258	.320	85-0-2	.188	0	89	10	—	1.0
1939	Bos N★	10	10	.500	27	26	11-**6**	0	146	123	62	7	1	61	35	2.96	125	.229	.309	49-0-4	.061	-4	87	10	—	0.9
1940	Bos N	0	5	.000	7	5	0	0	32.1	38	23	0	1	18	2	5.57	67	.302	.393	8-0-1	.375	1	56	-7	—	-0.8
	Bro N	0	0	ø	2	0	0	0	3	3	0	0	0	2	0	0.00	ø	.300	.417	0	ø	0	—	1	—	0.1
	Year	0	5	.000	9	5	0	0	35.1	41	23	0	1	20	2	5.09	73	.301	.395	8-0-1	.375	1	56	-5	—	-0.7
1945	Bos N	0	2	.000	5	1	0	0	11	16	10	1	1	7	4	5.73	67	.356	.453	2	.000	-0	0	-3	0	-0.5
Total	5	41	40	.506	109	97	51-14	1	691	658	283	24	11	248	194	3.15	113	.253	.321	236-0-14	.186	-0	91	34	0	3.5

FETTERS, MIKE Michael Lee; B12.19.1964 Van Nuys CA; BR/TR/6´4˝/(200–230); [CalA86 1/27]; d9.1; Col Pepperdine

YEAR	TM LG	W	L	PCT	G	GS	CG-SHO	SV-BS	IP	H	R	HR	HB	BB-IB	SO	ERA	AERA	OAV	OOB	AB-HR-SH	AVG	PB	SUP	APR	DL	PW
1989	Cal A	0	0	ø	1	0	0	0-0	3.1	5	4	1	0	1-0	4	8.10	47	.333	.375	0	ø	0	—	-2	0	-0.1
1990	Cal A	1	1	.500	26	2	0	1-0	67.2	77	33	9	2	20-0	35	4.12	93	.287	.341	0	ø	0	261	-1	0	0.0
1991	Cal A	2	5	.286	19	4	0	0-1	44.2	53	29	4	3	28-2	24	4.84	85	.305	.410	0	ø	0	94	-5	0	-0.7
1992	Mil A	5	1	.833	50	0	0	2-3	62.2	38	15	3	7	24-2	43	1.87	207	.185	.290	0	ø	0	—	14	16	1.3
1993	Mil A	3	3	.500	45	0	0	0-0	59.1	59	29	4	2	22-4	23	3.34	129	.278	.344	0	ø	0	—	4	0	0.4
1994	Mil A	1	4	.200	42	0	0	17-3	46	41	16	0	1	27-5	31	2.54	200	.243	.345	0	ø	0	—	12	0	1.8
1995	Mil A	0	3	.000	40	0	0	22-5	34.2	40	16	3	0	20-4	33	3.38	149	.286	.373	0	ø	0	—	5	15	0.9
1996	Mil A	3	3	.500	61	0	0	32-6	61.1	65	28	4	1	26-4	53	3.38	154	.274	.343	0	ø	0	—	11	0	1.8
1997	Mil A	1	5	.167	51	0	0	6-5	70.1	62	30	4	1	33-3	62	3.45	134	.244	.329	0	ø	0	—	9	31	0.8
1998	Oak A	1	6	.143	48	0	0	5-3	47.1	48	26	3	1	21-2	34	3.99	116	.258	.333	0	ø	0	—	2	20	0.4
	Ana A	1	2	.333	12	0	0	0-1	11.1	14	8	2	0	4-0	9	5.56	85	.304	.360	0	ø	0	—	-1	0	-0.2
	Year	2	8	.200	60	0	0	5-4	58.2	62	34	5	1	25-2	43	4.30	108	.267	.338	0	ø	0	—	1	0	0.2
1999	Bal A	1	0	1.000	27	0	0	0-3	31	35	23	5	2	22-2	22	5.81	81	.278	.393	0	ø	0	—	-5	86	-0.2
2000	LA N	6	2	.750	51	0	0	5-2	50	35	18	7	2	25-2	40	3.24	137	.205	.313	0	ø	0	—	8	21	1.3
2001	LA N	2	1	.667	34	0	0	1-2	29.2	33	23	6	1	13-0	26	6.07	68	.273	.341	0	ø	0	—	-7	15	-0.7
	Pit N	1	1	.500	20	0	0	8-1	17.2	16	9	1	3	13-1	11	4.58	98	.235	.381	0	ø	0	—	0	0	0.0
	Year	3	2	.600	54	0	0	9-3	47.1	49	32	7	4	26-1	37	5.51	77	.259	.356	0	ø	0	—	-7	0	-0.7
2002	Pit N	1	0	1.000	32	0	0	0-1	30.1	25	13	3	1	18-1	29	3.26	129	.219	.328	0	ø	0	—	3	0	0.1
	†Ari N	2	3	.400	33	0	0	0-1	24.2	28	18	1	2	19-5	24	5.11	88	.292	.415	0	ø	0	—	-3	0	-0.5
	Year	3	3	.500	65	0	0	0-2	55	53	31	4	3	37-6	53	4.09	106	.252	.369	0	ø	0	—	0	0	-0.4
2003	Min A	0	0	ø	5	0	0	0-0	6	2	0	0	1	1-0	1	0.00	ø	.100	.182	0	ø	0	—	3	170	0.1
2004	Ari N	0	1	.000	23	0	0	1-0	18.2	23	22	2	1	14-2	14	8.68	53	.299	.404	0	ø	0	—	-9	0	-0.5
Total	16	31	41	.431	620	6	0	100-37	716.2	699	360	62	31	351-39	518	3.86	116	.259	.348	0	ø	0	134	38	374	6.0

FICK, JOHN John Ralph; B5.18.1921 Baltimore MD; D6.9.1958 Somers Point NJ; BL/TL/5´10˝/150; d7.29

YEAR	TM LG	W	L	PCT	G	GS	CG-SHO	SV-BS	IP	H	R	HR	HB	BB-IB	SO	ERA	AERA	OAV	OOB	AB-HR-SH	AVG	PB	SUP	APR	DL	PW
1944	Phi N	0	0	ø	4	0	0	0	5.1	3	2	0	1	3	2	3.38	107	.150	.292	0	ø	0	—	0	0	0.0

FIDRYCH, MARK Mark Steven "The Bird"; B8.14.1954 Worcester MA; BR/TR/6´3˝/(170–175); [DetA74 10/232]; d4.20

YEAR	TM LG	W	L	PCT	G	GS	CG-SHO	SV-BS	IP	H	R	HR	HB	BB-IB	SO	ERA	AERA	OAV	OOB	AB-HR-SH	AVG	PB	SUP	APR	DL	PW
1976	Det A★	19	9	.679	31	29	**24**-4	0-0	250.1	217	76	12	3	53-3	97	**2.34**	**159**	.235	.277	0	ø	0	85	**36**	0	**4.5**
1977	Det A★	6	4	.600	11	11	7-1	0-0	81	82	29	2	1	12-2	42	2.89	149	.269	.295	0	ø	0	95	12	118	1.4
1978	Det A	2	0	1.000	3	3	2	0-0	22	17	6	1	0	5-0	10	2.45	159	.213	.259	0	ø	0	146	4	135	0.4
1979	Det A	0	3	.000	4	4	0	0-0	14.2	23	17	3	1	9-2	5	10.43	42	.371	.458	0	ø	0	99	-9	157	-1.3
1980	Det A	2	3	.400	9	9	1	0-0	44.1	58	35	5	1	20-2	16	5.68	73	.309	.376	0	ø	0*	147	-10	0	-0.9
Total	5	29	19	.604	58	56	34-5	0-0	412.1	397	163	23	6	99-9	170	3.10	126	.255	.300	0	ø	0	102	33	410	4.1

FIEBER, CLARENCE Clarence Thomas "Lefty"; B9.4.1913 San Francisco CA; D8.20.1985 Redwood City CA; BL/TL/6´4˝/187; d5.18; Col San Francisco

YEAR	TM LG	W	L	PCT	G	GS	CG-SHO	SV-BS	IP	H	R	HR	HB	BB-IB	SO	ERA	AERA	OAV	OOB	AB-HR-SH	AVG	PB	SUP	APR	DL	PW
1932	Chi A	1	0	1.000	3	0	0	0	5.1	6	1	0	0	3	1	1.69	256	.273	.360	0	ø	0	—	2	—	0.3

FIELD, JIM James C.; B4.24.1863 Philadelphia PA; D5.13.1953 Atlantic City NJ; 6´1˝/170; d6.2.1883; ▲

YEAR	TM LG	W	L	PCT	G	GS	CG-SHO	SV-BS	IP	H	R	HR	HB	BB-IB	SO	ERA	AERA	OAV	OOB	AB-HR-SH	AVG	PB	SUP	APR	DL	PW
1890	Roc AA	1	0	1.000	2	1	1	1	9.2	7	4	0	1	4	2	2.79	128	.194	.293	188-4	.202	1*	189	1	—	0.1

FIELD, NATE Nathan Patrick; B12.11.1975 Denver CO; BR/TR/6´2˝/(185–205); d4.12; Col Fort Hays St.

YEAR	TM LG	W	L	PCT	G	GS	CG-SHO	SV-BS	IP	H	R	HR	HB	BB-IB	SO	ERA	AERA	OAV	OOB	AB-HR-SH	AVG	PB	SUP	APR	DL	PW
2002	KC A	0	0	ø	5	0	0	0-0	5	8	5	2	0	3-1	3	9.00	55	.364	.440	0	ø	0	—	-2	0	-0.1
2003	KC A	1	1	.500	19	0	0	0-0	21.2	19	10	3	1	14-1	19	4.15	116	.235	.351	0	ø	0	—	2	0	0.2
2004	KC A	2	3	.400	43	0	0	3-2	44.1	40	25	5	2	19-2	30	4.26	109	.240	.321	0	ø	0	—	1	54	0.1
2005	KC A	0	0	ø	7	0	0	0-0	6.2	13	7	1	0	5-2	4	9.45	46	.433	.514	0	ø	0	—	-4	0	-0.2
2006	Col N	1	1	.500	14	0	0	0-1	9	9	4	2	0	5-1	14	4.00	120	.257	.350	0	ø	0	—	1	0	0.2
Total	5	4	5	.444	88	0	0	3-3	86.2	89	51	13	3	46-7	70	4.88	97	.266	.357	0	ø	0	—	-2	54	0.2

FIENE, LOU Louis Henry "Big Finn"; B12.29.1884 Ft.Dodge IA; D12.22.1964 Chicago IL; BR/TR/6´0˝/175; d5.7

YEAR	TM LG	W	L	PCT	G	GS	CG-SHO	SV-BS	IP	H	R	HR	HB	BB-IB	SO	ERA	AERA	OAV	OOB	AB-HR-SH	AVG	PB	SUP	APR	DL	PW
1906	Chi A	1	1	.500	6	2	1	0	31	35	17	0	4	9	12	2.90	87	.287	.356	10	.200	0	57	-2	—	-0.1
1907	Chi A	0	1	.000	6	1	1	1	26	30	17	0	2	7	15	4.15	58	.291	.348	11	.182	-0*	113	-6	—	-0.3
1908	Chi A	0	1	.000	1	1	1	0	9	9	7	0	0	1	3	4.00	58	.257	.278	3	.000	-0	30	-2	—	-0.3
1909	Chi A	2	5	.286	13	6	4	0	72	75	37	1	5	18	24	4.13	57	.284	.341	29-0-1	.069	-2*	65	-11	—	-1.2
Total	4	3	8	.273	26	10	7	1	138	149	78	1	11	35	54	3.85	62	.284	.342	53-0-1	.113	-2	64	-21	—	-1.9

FIFE, DANNY Danny Wayne; B10.5.1949 Harrisburg IL; BR/TR/6´3˝/(175–190); d8.18; Col Michigan

YEAR	TM LG	W	L	PCT	G	GS	CG-SHO	SV-BS	IP	H	R	HR	HB	BB-IB	SO	ERA	AERA	OAV	OOB	AB-HR-SH	AVG	PB	SUP	APR	DL	PW
1973	Min A	3	2	.600	10	7	1	0-0	51.2	54	26	2	3	29-0	18	4.35	91	.270	.369	0	ø	0	129	-1	0	-0.1
1974	Min A	0	0	ø	4	0	0	0-0	4.2	10	11	0	1	4-0	3	17.36	22	.417	.517	0	ø	0	—	-7	0	-0.4
Total	2	3	2	.600	14	7	1	0-0	56.1	64	37	2	4	33-0	21	5.43	73	.286	.385	0	ø	0	129	-8	0	-0.5

FIFIELD, JACK John Proctor; B10.5.1871 Enfield NH; D11.27.1939 Syracuse NY; BR/TR/5´11˝/160; d4.28

YEAR	TM LG	W	L	PCT	G	GS	CG-SHO	SV-BS	IP	H	R	HR	HB	BB-IB	SO	ERA	AERA	OAV	OOB	AB-HR-SH	AVG	PB	SUP	APR	DL	PW
1897	Phi N	5	18	.217	27	26	21	0	210.2	263	163	8	9	80	38	5.51	76	.303	.368	77-2-2	.234	3	88	-28	—	-2.0
1898	Phi N	11	9	.550	21	21	18-2	0	171.1	170	91	2	18	60	31	3.31	104	.257	.336	64-0-3	.109	-4	123	3	—	-0.2
1899	Phi N	3	8	.273	14	11	9-1	1	92.2	110	64	0	4	36	8	4.08	90	.294	.362	35	.257	1	106	-5	—	-0.4
	Was N	2	4	.333	6	6	6	0	47	73	44	1	2	17	12	6.13	64	.353	.407	20	.200	-0*	123	-11	—	-1.1
	Year	5	12	.294	20	17	15-1	1	139.2	183	108	1	6	53	20	4.77	79	.315	.378	55	.236	1	112	-15	—	-1.5
Total	3	21	39	.350	68	64	54-3	1	521.2	616	362	11	33	193	89	4.59	83	.292	.360	196-2-5	.194	-0	105	-41	—	-3.7

FIGGEMEIER, FRANK Frank Y.; B4.22.1873 St.Louis MO; D4.15.1915 St.Louis MO; d9.25

YEAR	TM LG	W	L	PCT	G	GS	CG-SHO	SV-BS	IP	H	R	HR	HB	BB-IB	SO	ERA	AERA	OAV	OOB	AB-HR-SH	AVG	PB	SUP	APR	DL	PW
1894	Phi N	0	1	.000	1	1	1	0	8	12	14	1	3	4	2	11.25	46	.343	.452	3-0-1	.333	0	97	-6	—	-0.4

FIGUEROA, ED Eduardo (Padilla); B10.14.1948 Ciales, PR; BR/TR/6´1˝/(174–194); d4.9

YEAR	TM LG	W	L	PCT	G	GS	CG-SHO	SV-BS	IP	H	R	HR	HB	BB-IB	SO	ERA	AERA	OAV	OOB	AB-HR-SH	AVG	PB	SUP	APR	DL	PW
1974	Cal A	2	8	.200	25	12	5-1	0-0	105.1	119	46	3	4	36-2	49	3.67	94	.294	.355	0	ø	0	80	-1	0	-0.1
1975	Cal A	16	13	.552	33	32	16-2	0-0	244.2	213	96	14	5	84-6	139	2.91	123	.233	.299	0	ø	0	100	17	0	2.0
1976	†NY A	19	10	.655	34	34	14-4	0-0	256.2	237	101	13	3	94-0	119	3.02	113	.246	.312	0	ø	0	132	9	0	0.8
1977	†NY A	16	11	.593	32	32	12-2	0-0	239.1	228	102	19	3	75-1	104	3.57	111	.252	.308	0	ø	0	103	13	0	1.2
1978	†NY A	20	9	.690	35	35	12-2	0-0	253	233	96	22	3	77-4	92	2.99	122	.248	.305	0	ø	0	111	19	0	2.0
1979	NY A	4	6	.400	16	16	4-1	0-0	104.2	109	49	6	0	35-1	42	4.13	100	.275	.333	0	ø	0	98	2	88	0.1
1980	NY A	3	3	.500	15	9	0	1-0	58	90	47	3	1	24-2	16	6.98	57	.363	.417	0	ø	0	103	-18	0	-1.6
	Tex A	0	7	.000	8	8	0	0-0	39.2	62	29	9	0	12-0	9	5.90	66	.365	.400	0	ø	0	58	-9	0	-1.3
	Year	3	10	.231	23	17	0	1-0	97.2	152	76	12	1	36-2	25	6.54	60	.364	.410	0	ø	0	82	-26	0	-2.9
1981	Oak A	0	0	ø	2	1	0	0-0	8.1	8	5	1	0	6-0	1	5.40	65	.258	.378	0	ø	0	102	-2	0	-0.1
Total	8	80	67	.544	200	179	63-12	1-0	1309.2	1299	571	90	19	443-16	571	3.51	105	.261	.322	0	ø	0	105	30	88	3.0

FIGUEROA, NELSON Nelson; B5.18.1974 Brooklyn NY; BB/TR/6´1˝/(155–180); [NYN95 30/833]; d6.3; Col Brandeis

YEAR	TM LG	W	L	PCT	G	GS	CG-SHO	SV-BS	IP	H	R	HR	HB	BB-IB	SO	ERA	AERA	OAV	OOB	AB-HR-SH	AVG	PB	SUP	APR	DL	PW
2000	Ari N	0	1	.000	3	3	0	0-0	15.2	17	13	4	0	5-0	7	7.47	64	.283	.328	3-0-1	.333	0	115	-4	0	-0.2
2001	Phi N	4	5	.444	19	13	0	0-0	89	95	40	8	7	37-3	61	3.94	104	.275	.357	24-0-1	.250	2	109	3	0	0.3
2002	Mil N	1	7	.125	30	11	0	0-0	93	96	59	18	4	37-6	51	5.03	82	.270	.342	15-0-4	.133	-0	108	-11	15	-0.9

YEAR	TM LG	W	L	PCT	G	GS	CG-SHO	SV-BS	IP	H	R	HR	HB	BB-IB	SO	ERA	AERA	OAV	OOB	AB-HR-SH	AVG	PB	SUP	APR	DL	PW
2003	Pit N	2	1	.667	12	3	0	0-0	35.1	28	13	8	2	13-2	23	3.31	131	.220	.299	7	.000	-1	101	4	0	0.2
2004	Pit N	0	3	.000	10	3	0	0-0	28.1	32	18	4	0	11-1	10	5.72	76	.302	.368	7	.143	-0	71	-4	0	-0.4
Total	5	7	17	.292	74	33	0	0-0	261.1	268	143	42	13	103-12	152	4.65	91	.270	.343	56-0-6	.179	1	105	-12	15	-1.0
Fikac, Jeremy	Jeremy Joseph; B4.8.1975 Shiner TX; BR/TR/6´2˝/185; [SDN98 19/562]; d8.16; Col Southwest Texas																									
2001	SD N	2	0	1.000	23	0	0	0-2	26.1	15	6	2	1	5-1	19	1.37	303	.165	.216	0	ø	0	—	8	0	0.5
2002	SD N	4	7	.364	65	0	0	0-6	69	74	50	13	3	34-8	66	5.35	73	.267	.351	2	.000	-0	—	-14	0	-2.1
2003	Oak A	0	1	.000	14	0	0	0-0	16	14	8	4	3	11-1	9	4.50	102	.246	.394	0	ø	0	—	1	0	0.0
2004	Mon N	1	2	.333	19	0	0	0-0	25	26	16	5	0	13-4	22	5.40	85	.274	.358	0	ø	0	—	-2	0	-0.2
Total	4	7	10	.412	121	0	0	0-8	136.1	129	80	24	7	63-14	116	4.49	92	.248	.336	2	.000	-0	—	-7	0	-1.8
File, Bob	Robert Michael; B1.28.1977 Philadelphia PA; BR/TR/6´4˝/(210–215); [TorA98 19/561]; d4.14; Col Philadelphia; [DL 2003 Tor A 142]																									
2001	Tor A	5	3	.625	60	0	0	0-2	74.1	57	28	6	7	29-8	38	3.27	140	.220	.314	0	ø	0	—	11	0	1.1
2002	Tor A	0	1	.000	5	0	0	0-0	3.1	8	7	0	0	2-0	2	18.90	24	.471	.526	0	ø	0	—	-5	44	-0.9
2004	Tor A	1	0	1.000	24	0	0	0-0	33.2	45	19	4	2	12-2	15	4.81	102	.331	.383	1	.000	-0	—	0	40	0.0
Total	3	6	4	.600	89	0	0	0-2	111.1	110	54	10	9	43-10	55	4.20	111	.267	.345	1	.000	-0	—	6	226	0.2
Filer, Tom	Thomas Carson; B12.1.1956 Philadelphia PA; BR/TR/6´1˝/(195–200); d6.8; Col LaSalle; [DL 1986 Tor A 182]																									
1982	Chi N	1	2	.333	8	8	0	0-0	40.2	50	25	5	0	18-2	15	5.53	68	.301	.370	12-0-1	.083	-1	88	-6	0	-0.4
1985	Tor A	7	0	1.000	11	9	0	0-0	48.2	38	21	6	0	18-0	24	3.88	109	.222	.295	0	ø	0	155	3	15	0.3
1988	Mil A	5	8	.385	19	16	2-1	0-0	101.2	108	54	8	1	33-4	39	4.43	91	.281	.333	0	ø	0	98	-4	0	-0.3
1989	Mil A	7	3	.700	13	13	0	0-0	72.1	74	30	6	4	23-1	20	3.61	107	.271	.337	0	ø	0*	130	3	35	0.5
1990	Mil A	2	3	.400	7	4	0	0-0	22	26	17	2	0	9-0	8	6.14	63	.289	.354	0	ø	0	47	-5	93	-1.0
1992	NY N	0	1	.000	9	1	0	0-0	22	18	8	2	0	6-2	9	2.05	171	.222	.276	3	.000	-0	26	2	0	0.1
Total	6	22	17	.564	67	51	2-1	0-0	307.1	314	155	29	5	107-9	115	4.25	93	.269	.331	15-0-1	.067	-1	111	-7	325	-0.8
Files, Eddie	Charles Edward; B5.19.1883 Portland ME; D5.10.1954 Cornish ME; BR/TR; d10.3; Col Bowdoin																									
1908	Phi A	0	0	ø	2	0	0	0	9	8	7	0	2	3	6	6.00	43	.286	.394	3	.000	-0	—	-3	—	-0.2
Filley, Marc	Marcus Lucius; B2.28.1912 Lansingburgh NY; D1.20.1995 Yarmouth ME; BR/TR/5´11˝/172; d4.19; Col Williams																									
1934	Was A	0	0	ø	1	0	0	0	0.1	2	1	0	0	0	0	27.00	16	.667	.667	0	ø	0	—	-1	—	0.0
Fillingim, Dana	Dana; B11.6.1893 Columbus GA; D2.3.1961 Tuskegee AL; BL/TR/5´10˝/175; d8.2; Mil 1918																									
1915	Phi A	0	5	.000	8	4	1	0	39.1	42	25	0	1	32	17	3.43	85	.313	.449	12-0-1	.167	-0	62	-4	—	-0.5
1918	Bos N	7	6	.538	14	13	10-4	0	113	99	37	0	5	28	29	2.23	120	.243	.300	42-0-1	.214	0	104	6	—	0.7
1919	Bos N	6	13	.316	32	18	9	2	186.1	185	80	2	2	39	50	3.38	85	.270	.312	65-0-4	.246	1	79	-8	—	-0.5
1920	Bos N	12	21	.364	37	31	22-2	0	272	292	123	8	3	79	66	3.11	98	.287	.340	92-0-1	.174	-2*	75	-5	—	-0.5
1921	Bos N	15	10	.600	44	23	11-**3**	1	239.2	249	108	10	2	56	54	3.45	106	.272	.316	85-2-1	.247	5*	107	5	—	0.9
1922	Bos N	5	9	.357	25	12	5-1	2	117	143	74	6	1	37	25	4.54	88	.311	.363	38-0-1	.158	-2	75	-7	—	-0.9
1923	Bos N	1	9	.100	35	12	1	0	100.1	141	74	6	1	36	27	5.20	77	.345	.399	31-0-1	.226	1*	69	-15	—	-1.2
1925	Phi N	1	0	1.000	5	1	0	0	8.2	19	12	0	0	6	2	10.38	46	.432	.500	3	.000	0	230	-5	—	-0.4
Total	8	47	73	.392	200	114	59-10	5	1076.1	1170	533	32	15	313	270	3.56	93	.287	.340	368-2-10	.209	4	86	-33	—	-2.4
Filson, Pete	William Peter; B9.28.1958 Darby PA; BB/TL/6´2˝/(175–195); [NYA79 9/233]; d5.15; Col Temple																									
1982	Min A	0	2	.000	5	3	0	0-0	12.1	17	12	2	0	8-1	10	8.76	49	.321	.397	0	ø	0	71	-5	0	-0.7
1983	Min A	4	1	.800	26	8	0	1-0	90	87	34	9	1	29-0	49	3.40	126	.252	.310	0	ø	0	90	10	21	0.4
1984	Min A	6	5	.545	55	7	0	1-2	118.2	106	56	14	3	54-7	59	4.10	103	.238	.323	0	ø	0	98	3	0	0.2
1985	Min A	4	5	.444	40	6	1	2-1	95.2	93	42	13	0	30-4	42	3.67	121	.251	.305	0	ø	0	92	8	0	0.7
1986	Min A	0	0	ø	4	0	0	0-0	6.1	13	4	1	1	2-0	4	5.68	76	.406	.457	0	ø	0	—	-1	0	0.0
	Chi A	0	1	.000	3	1	0	0-0	11.2	14	9	4	0	5-0	4	6.17	70	.286	.352	0	ø	0	42	-2	0	-0.2
	Year	0	1	.000	7	1	0	0-0	18	27	13	5	1	7-0	8	6.00	72	.333	.393	0	ø	0	42	-3	0	-0.2
1987	NY A	1	0	1.000	7	2	0	0-0	22	26	10	2	1	9-1	10	3.27	136	.299	.371	0	ø	0	72	2	0	0.1
1990	KC A	0	4	.000	8	7	0	0-0	35	42	31	6	2	13-0	9	5.91	65	.282	.345	0	ø	0	71	-10	53	-1.0
Total	7	15	18	.455	148	34	1	4-3	391.2	398	198	51	8	150-13	187	4.18	102	.260	.327	0	ø	0	83	5	74	-0.5
Finch, Joel	Joel D; B8.20.1956 South Bend IN; BR/TR/6´2˝/175; [BosA74 9/212]; d6.12																									
1979	Bos A	0	3	.000	15	7	0	0-0	57.1	65	31	5	1	25-3	25	4.87	92	.289	.361	1	.000	-0	79	-1	0	0.0
Fincher, Bill	William Allen; B5.26.1894 Atlanta GA; D5.7.1946 Shreveport LA; BR/TR/6´1˝/180; d4.23																									
1916	StL A	0	1	.000	12	1	0	0	21	22	11	0	0	7	5	2.14	128	.282	.341	4	.250	0	55	0	—	0.1
Fine, Tommy	Thomas Morgan; B10.10.1914 Cleburne TX; D1.10.2005 Little Elm TX; BB/TR/6´0˝/180; d4.26; Col Baylor																									
1947	Bos A	1	2	.333	9	7	1	0	36	41	24	0	1	19	10	5.50	71	.285	.372	9-0-2	.333	1	124	-6	0	-0.3
1950	StL A	0	1	.000	14	0	0	0	36.2	53	38	6	0	25	6	8.10	61	.342	.433	12	.333	1*	—	-12	0	-0.4
Total	2	1	3	.250	23	7	1	0	72.2	94	62	6	1	44	16	6.81	65	.314	.404	21-0-2	.333	2	124	-18	0	-0.7
Fingers, Rollie	Roland Glen; B8.25.1946 Steubenville OH; BR/TR/6´4˝/(180–200); d9.15; HF1992; Col Chaffey (CA) JC; [DL 1983 Mil A 182]																									
1968	Oak A	0	0	ø	1	0	0	0	1.1	4	4	1	1	1-0	0	27.00	10	.571	.667	0	ø	0	—	-4	0	-0.2
1969	Oak A	6	7	.462	60	8	1-1	12-6	119	116	60	13	4	41-5	61	3.71	93	.257	.323	25-0-3	.200	0	135	-6	0	-0.7
1970	Oak A	7	9	.438	45	19	1	2-1	148	137	65	13	2	48-5	79	3.65	97	.250	.310	39-1-4	.103	-0	89	-1	0	-0.1
1971	†Oak A	4	6	.400	48	8	2-1	17-3	129.1	94	46	14	8	30-3	98	2.99	111	.207	.266	33-0-5	.212	1	88	6	0	0.8
1972	†Oak A	11	9	.550	65	0	0	21-5	111.1	85	35	8	1	32-7	113	2.51	114	.212	.271	19-1-1	.316	3	—	5	0	1.3
1973	†Oak A★	7	8	.467	62	2	0	22-5	126.2	107	41	5	4	39-6	110	1.92	186	.226	.288	1	.000	-0	25	20	0	3.0
1974	†Oak A★	9	5	.643	**76**	0	0	18-7	119	104	41	5	1	29-6	95	2.65	126	.240	.282	0	ø	0	—	10	0	1.6
1975	†Oak A☆	10	6	.625	**75**	0	0	24-8	126.2	95	43	13	6	33-5	115	2.98	122	.213	.274	1	.000	-0*	—	12	0	1.9
1976	Oak A☆	13	11	.542	70	0	0	20-14	134.2	118	40	3	7	40-10	113	2.47	136	.243	.304	0	ø	0	—	15	0	3.2
1977	SD N	8	9	.471	**78**	0	0	**35**-11	132.1	123	47	12	1	36-12	113	2.99	120	.248	.298	20-0-1	.050	-2	—	11	0	1.7
1978	SD N★	6	13	.316	67	0	0	**37**-10	107.1	84	33	4	1	29-12	72	2.52	133	.212	.265	12-0-2	.167	-0	—	11	0	2.4
1979	SD N	9	9	.500	54	0	0	13-10	83.2	91	47	7	1	37-8	65	4.52	78	.281	.351	12-0-1	.083	-1	—	-9	0	-2.0
1980	SD N	11	9	.550	66	0	0	23-6	103	101	35	3	0	32-13	69	2.80	122	.263	.315	18-0-1	.278	2	—	8	0	1.8
1981	†Mil A★	6	3	.667	47	0	0	**28**-6	78	55	9	3	1	13-5	61	1.04	334	.198	.235	0	ø	0	—	**23**	0	**4.6**
1982	Mil A★	5	6	.455	50	0	0	29-6	79.2	63	23	5	1	20-5	71	2.60	148	.220	.268	0	ø	0	—	13	0	2.6
1984	Mil A	1	2	.333	33	0	0	23-3	46	38	13	5	0	13-2	40	1.96	199	.213	.267	0	ø	0	—	9	69	1.5
1985	Mil A	1	6	.143	47	0	0	17-8	55.1	59	33	9	0	19-5	24	5.04	83	.272	.329	0	ø	0	—	-4	0	-0.7
Total	17	114	118	.491	944	37	4-2	341-109	1701.1	1474	615	123	39	492-109	1299	2.90	120	.235	.292	180-2-18	.172	2	95	119	251	22.7
Fink, Herman	Herman Adam; B8.22.1911 Concord NC; D8.24.1980 Salisbury NC; BR/TR/6´2˝/198; d9.16																									
1935	Phi A	0	3	.000	5	3	0	0	15.2	18	19	0	1	10	2	9.19	49	.290	.397	5	.200	-0	57	-8	—	-1.2
1936	Phi A	8	16	.333	34	24	9	3	188.2	222	126	18	0	78	53	5.39	95	.294	.360	64	.125	-4	65	-5	—	-0.9
1937	Phi A	2	1	.667	28	3	1	1	80	82	43	6	1	35	18	4.05	116	.263	.339	24	.208	-1	99	6	—	0.2
Total	3	10	20	.333	67	30	10	4	284.1	322	188	24	2	123	73	5.22	95	.285	.356	93	.151	-5	68	-7	—	-1.9
Finlayson, Pembroke	Pembroke; B7.31.1888 Cheraw SC; D3.6.1912 Brooklyn NY; BR/TR/5´6˝/140; d6.6																									
1908	Bro N	0	0	ø	1	0	0	0	0.1	0	5	0	0	4	0	135.00	2	.000	.800	0	ø	0	—	-4	—	-0.2
1909	Bro N	0	0	ø	1	0	0	0	7	7	4	0	0	4	2	5.14	50	.212	.297	3	.000	-0	—	-2	—	-0.1
Total	2	0	0	ø	2	0	0	0	7.1	7	9	0	0	8	2	11.05	23	.206	.357	3	.000	-0	—	-6	—	-0.3
Finley, Chuck	Charles Edward; B11.26.1962 Monroe LA; BL/TL/6´6˝/(212–226); [CalA85*S1/4]; d5.29; Col Louisiana–Monroe																									
1986	†Cal A	3	1	.750	25	0	0	0-0	46.1	40	17	2	1	23-1	37	3.30	125	.235	.330	0	ø	0	—	5	0	0.5
1987	Cal A	2	7	.222	35	3	0	0-2	90.2	102	54	7	3	43-3	63	4.67	93	.287	.367	0	ø	0	141	-4	0	-0.3
1988	Cal A	9	15	.375	31	31	2	0-0	194.1	191	95	15	6	82-7	111	4.17	93	.263	.339	0	ø	0	91	-4	0	-0.5
1989	Cal A☆	16	9	.640	29	29	9-1	0-0	199.2	171	64	13	2	82-0	156	2.57	149	.233	.311	0	ø	0	91	28	24	3.2
1990	Cal A★	18	9	.667	32	32	7-2	0-0	236	210	77	17	2	81-3	177	2.40	160	.243	.308	0	ø	0	107	36	0	4.0
1991	Cal A	18	9	.667	34	34	4-2	0-0	227.1	205	102	23	8	101-1	171	3.80	108	.244	.330	0	ø	0	106	10	0	0.9
1992	Cal A	7	12	.368	31	31	4-1	0-0	204.1	212	99	24	3	98-2	124	3.96	101	.277	.358	0	ø	0	92	1	16	-0.1
1993	Cal A	16	14	.533	35	35	**13**-2	0-0	251.1	243	108	22	6	82-1	187	3.15	144	.253	.314	0	ø	0	80	33	0	3.5

YEAR	TM LG	W	L	PCT	G	GS	CG-SHO	SV-BS	IP	H	R	HR	HB	BB-IB	SO	ERA	AERA	OAV	OOB	AB-HR-SH	AVG	PB	SUP	APR	DL	PW
1994	Cal A	10	10	.500	25	**25**	7-2	0-0	**183.1**	178	95	21	3	71-0	148	4.32	114	.260	.329	0	ø	0	79	11	0	1.0
1995	Cal A☆	15	12	.556	32	32	2-1	0-0	203	192	106	20	7	93-1	195	4.21	112	.249	.333	0	ø	0	112	10	0	1.0
1996	†Cal A★	15	16	.484	35	35	4-1	0-0	238	241	124	27	11	94-5	215	4.16	121	.263	.336	0	ø	0	69	23	0	2.5
1997	Ana A	13	6	.684	25	25	3-1	0-0	164	152	79	20	5	65-0	155	4.23	109	.248	.323	6	.000	-1	106	9	54	0.8
1998	Ana A	11	9	.550	34	34	1-1	0-0	223.1	210	97	20	6	109-1	212	3.39	140	.246	.334	4	.000	-0	84	31	0	2.4
1999	Ana A	12	11	.522	33	33	1	0-0	213.1	197	117	23	8	94-2	200	4.43	110	.246	.330	4-0-1	.000	-0	90	9	0	0.8
2000	Cle A☆	16	11	.593	34	34	3	0-0	218	211	108	23	2	101-3	189	4.17	120	.256	.337	7	.000	-1	111	19	0	1.9
2001	†Cle A	8	7	.533	22	22	1	0-0	113.2	131	78	14	2	35-0	96	5.54	83	.290	.341	0	ø	0	114	-12	62	-1.4
2002	Cle A	4	11	.267	18	18	1	0-0	105.1	114	56	6	0	48-3	91	4.44	100	.284	.356	4	.000	-0	65	0	0	0.0
	†StL N	7	4	.636	14	14	1-1	0-0	85.1	69	41	7	1	30-3	83	3.80	106	.219	.288	28-0-5	.107	-1	113	1	0	0.0
Total	17	200	173	.536	524	467	63-15	0-2	3197.1	3069	1517	304	76	1332-36	2610	3.85	116	.255	.331	53-0-6	.057	-4	94	206	156	20.2
FINNERAN, HAPPY	Joseph Ignatius "Smokey Joe"; B10.29.1890 E.Orange NJ; D2.3.1942 Orange NJ; BR/TR/5´10.5˝/169; d8.20																									
1912	Phi N	0	2	.000	14	4	0	1	46.1	50	27	2	1	10	10	2.53	144	.282	.324	10	.200	0	86	2	—	0.1
1913	Phi N	0	0	ø	3	0	0	0	5	12	7	0	0	2	0	7.20	46	.462	.500	3	.667	1	—	-3	—	0.0
1914	Bro F	12	11	.522	27	23	13-2	1	175.1	153	77	6	6	60	54	3.18	90	.237	.308	55-0-4	.127	-4	92	-4	—	-1.1
1915	Bro F	10	12	.455	37	24	12-1	2	215.1	197	90	2	9	87	68	2.80	97	.249	.331	74	.149	-4*	91	-2	—	-0.7
1918	Det A	0	2	.000	5	2	0	1	13.2	22	17	0	0	8	2	9.88	27	.393	.469	3	.000	-0*	170	-11	—	-1.5
	NY A	3	6	.333	23	13	4	0	114.1	134	52	7	2	35	34	3.78	75	.305	.359	39-0-1	.231	1	123	-9	—	-0.7
	Year	3	8	.273	28	15	4	1	128	156	69	7	2	43	36	4.43	63	.315	.372	42-0-1	.214	0	129	-18	—	-2.2
Total	5	25	33	.431	109	66	29-3	5	570	568	270	17	18	202	168	3.30	87	.266	.335	184-0-5	.168	-6	99	-27	—	-3.9
FINNVOLD, GAR	Anders Gar; B3.11.1968 Boynton Beach FL; BR/TR/6´5˝/195; [BosA90 6/173]; d5.10; Col Florida St.																									
1994	Bos A	0	4	.000	8	8	0	0-0	36.1	45	27	4	3	15-0	17	5.94	85	.304	.377	0	ø	0	78	-4	48	-0.4
FIORE, TONY	Anthony James; B10.12.1971 Oak Park IL; BR/TR/6´4˝/210; [PhiN92 28/781]; d8.27; Col Triton (IL) JC																									
2000	TB A	1	1	.500	11	0	0	0-1	15	21	16	3	2	9-2	8	8.40	58	.333	.432	0	ø	0	—	-6	0	-0.7
2001	TB A	0	0	ø	3	0	0	0-0	3.1	4	2	0	1	1-0	3	5.40	83	.308	.400	0	ø	0	—	0	0	0.0
	Min A	0	1	.000	4	0	0	0-0	6.1	5	4	0	0	2-0	5	5.68	82	.208	.269	0	ø	0	—	-1	0	-0.1
	Year	0	1	.000	7	0	0	0-0	9.2	9	6	0	1	3-0	8	5.59	83	.243	.317	0	ø	0	—	-1	0	-0.1
2002	†Min A	10	3	.769	48	2	0	0-0	91	74	32	10	5	43-4	55	3.16	141	.224	.320	3	.000	-0	135	14	0	1.8
2003	Min A	1	1	.500	21	0	0	0-0	36	32	25	5	3	21-1	23	5.50	82	.242	.352	1	.000	-0	—	-5	0	-0.2
Total	4	12	6	.667	87	2	0	0-1	151.2	136	79	18	11	76-7	94	4.39	103	.242	.340	4	.000	-0	135	2	0	0.8
FIREOVID, STEVE	Stephen John; B6.6.1957 Bryan OH; BB/TR/6´2˝/(195–210); [SDN78 7/161]; d9.6; Col Miami–Ohio																									
1981	SD N	0	1	.000	5	4	0	0-0	26.1	30	8	2	0	7-0	11	2.73	119	.294	.336	7	.143	-0	82	2	0	0.1
1983	SD N	0	0	ø	3	0	0	0-0	5	4	2	0	0	2-0	1	1.80	195	.235	.316	0	ø	0	—	1	0	0.0
1984	Phi N	0	0	ø	6	0	0	0-0	5.2	4	1	0	0	0-0	3	1.59	230	.200	.200	0	ø	0	—	1	0	0.1
1985	Chi A	0	0	ø	4	0	0	0-0	7	17	4	0	0	2-0	2	5.14	85	.472	.500	0	ø	0	—	0	0	0.0
1986	Sea A	2	0	1.000	10	1	0	0-0	21	28	11	1	1	4-0	10	4.29	100	.333	.371	0	ø	0	43	0	0	0.0
1992	Tex A	1	0	1.000	3	0	0	0-0	6.2	10	5	0	0	4-2	0	4.05	94	.370	.452	0	ø	0	—	-1	0	-0.1
Total	6	3	1	.750	31	5	0	0-0	71.2	93	31	3	1	19-2	27	3.39	110	.325	.368	7	.143	-0	67	3	0	0.1
FIRTH, TED	John E.; B5.6.1855 Lowell MA; D6.23.1902 Tewksbury MA; d8.15																									
1884	Ric AA	0	1	.000	1	1	1	0	9	14	13	0	0	5	0	8.00	41	.326	.396	3	.333	0	55	-5	—	-0.4
FISCHER, CARL	Charles William; B11.5.1905 Medina NY; D12.10.1963 Medina NY; BR/TL/6´0˝/180; d7.19																									
1930	Was A	1	1	.500	8	4	1	1	33.1	37	22	0	2	18	21	4.86	95	.285	.380	9	.000	-1	93	-2	—	-0.2
1931	Was A	13	9	.591	46	23	7	3	191	207	98	12	2	80	96	4.38	98	.273	.344	66-0-5	.121	-5	103	3	—	-0.3
1932	Was A	3	2	.600	12	7	1-1	1	50.2	57	30	4	0	31	23	4.97	87	.282	.378	15-0-2	.200	1	169	-3	—	-0.3
	StL A	3	7	.300	24	11	4	0	97	122	65	12	0	45	35	5.57	87	.310	.380	34-0-3	.265	0	69	-5	—	-0.4
	Year	6	9	.400	36	18	5-1	1	147.2	179	95	16	0	76	58	5.36	87	.300	.379	49-0-5	.245	1	104	-6	—	-0.7
1933	Det A	11	15	.423	35	22	9	3	182.2	176	86	5	3	84	93	3.55	122	.251	.334	62-0-4	.145	-3	73	15	—	1.5
1934	Det A	6	4	.600	20	15	4-1	1	95	107	50	5	1	38	39	4.36	101	.288	.356	31-0-5	.065	-3	119	2	—	-0.2
1935	Det A	0	1	.000	3	1	0	0	12	16	8	2	1	5	7	6.00	69	.320	.393	2	.000	-0	62	-2	—	-0.2
	Chi A	5	5	.500	24	11	3-1	0	88.2	102	67	7	2	39	31	6.19	75	.283	.356	21-0-2	.190	-0	80	-14	—	-1.4
	Year	5	6	.455	27	12	3-1	0	100.2	118	75	9	3	44	38	6.17	74	.287	.360	23-0-2	.174	-1	79	-16	—	-1.6
1937	Cle A	0	1	.000	2	0	0	0	0.2	2	2	0	0	1	1	27.00	17	.667	.750	0	ø	0	—	-2	—	-0.3
	Was A	4	5	.444	17	11	2	2	72	74	43	6	0	31	30	4.38	101	.270	.344	22-0-2	.136	-1	106	0	—	-0.2
	Year	4	6	.400	19	11	2	2	72.2	76	45	6	0	32	31	4.58	97	.274	.350	22-0-2	.136	-1	106	-2	—	-0.5
Total	7	46	50	.479	191	105	31-3	11	823	900	471	53	11	372	376	4.63	96	.277	.354	262-0-23	.145	-12	96	-8	—	-2.0
FISCHER, HANK	Henry William "Bulldog"; B1.11.1940 Yonkers NY; BR/TR/6´0˝/(185–190); d4.16; Col Seton Hall																									
1962	Mil N	2	3	.400	29	0	0	4	37.1	43	27	4	0	20-1	29	5.30	72	.291	.373	4	.000	-0	—	-7	0	-1.1
1963	Mil N	4	3	.571	31	6	1	0	74.1	74	46	8	5	28-4	72	4.96	65	.262	.333	19-0-2	.105	-0	219	-15	0	-1.4
1964	Mil N	11	10	.524	37	28	9-5	2	168.1	177	95	17	3	39-5	99	4.01	88	.265	.308	52-0-4	.154	1*	117	-14	0	-1.6
1965	Mil N	8	9	.471	31	19	2	0	122.2	126	61	18	3	39-5	79	3.89	91	.270	.329	37-0-2	.108	-1*	80	-6	0	-1.0
1966	Atl N	2	3	.400	14	8	0	0	48.1	55	23	3	1	14-1	22	3.91	93	.296	.343	13-0-2	.000	-2	73	-1	0	-0.3
	Cin N	0	6	.000	11	9	0	0	38	53	31	3	3	15-0	24	6.63	59	.331	.394	11	.091	-1	100	-11	0	-1.6
	Year	2	9	.182	25	17	0	0	86.1	108	54	6	4	29-1	46	5.11	73	.312	.367	24-0-2	.042	-2	88	-13	0	-1.9
	Bos A	2	3	.400	6	5	1	0	31	35	12	4	1	11-1	26	2.90	131	.287	.351	9	.222	0	46	3	0	0.5
1967	Bos A	1	2	.333	9	2	1	1	26.2	24	15	3	1	8-0	18	2.36	148	.229	.289	7-0-1	.143	-0	137	0	73	0.0
Total	6	30	39	.435	168	77	14-5	7	546.2	587	310	60	17	174-17	369	4.23	84	.275	.332	152-0-11	.118	-3	104	-51	73	-6.5
FISCHER, JEFF	Jeffrey Thomas; B8.17.1963 W.Palm Beach FL; BR/TR/6´3˝/(180–185); [MonN85 7/166]; d6.19; Col Florida																									
1987	Mon N	0	1	.000	4	2	0	0-0	13.2	21	14	3	0	5-0	6	8.56	50	.362	.400	5	.200	0	149	-6	0	-0.4
1989	LA N	0	0	ø	2	0	0	0-0	3.1	7	5	1	0	0-0	2	13.50	25	.438	.438	0	ø	0	—	-4	0	-0.2
Total	2	0	1	.000	6	2	0	0-0	17	28	19	4	0	5-0	8	9.53	43	.378	.407	5	.200	0	149	-10	0	-0.6
FISCHER, RUBE	Reuben Walter; B9.19.1916 Carlock SD; D7.16.1997 Green Bay WI; BR/TR/6´4˝/190; d9.12																									
1941	NY N	1	0	1.000	2	1	1	0	11	10	3	0	0	6	9	2.45	151	.238	.333	3	.333	0	161	2	0	0.2
1943	NY N	5	10	.333	22	17	4	1	130.2	140	69	4	2	59	47	4.61	75	.281	.360	43-1-1	.256	3	71	-14	0	-1.2
1944	NY N	6	14	.300	38	18	2-1	2	128.2	128	83	7	6	87	39	5.18	71	.266	.384	40-0-2	.125	-2	93	-19	0	-3.0
1945	NY N	3	8	.273	31	4	0	1	76.2	90	55	6	1	49	27	5.63	69	.288	.387	19-1-0	.211	2	92	-15	0	-1.7
1946	NY N	1	2	.333	15	1	0	0	35.2	48	32	3	0	21	14	6.31	55	.316	.399	9	.111	-1	124	-12	0	-1.0
Total	5	16	34	.320	108	41	7-1	4	382.2	416	242	20	9	222	136	5.10	71	.280	.377	114-2-3	.193	2	86	-58	0	-6.7
FISCHER, TODD	Todd Richard; B9.15.1960 Columbus OH; BR/TR/5´10˝/170; d5.29; Col Edison (FL) CC																									
1986	Cal A	0	0	ø	9	0	0	0-0	17	18	8	4	0	8-2	7	4.24	98	.286	.361	0	ø	0	—	0	0	0.0
FISCHER, BILL	William Charles; B10.11.1930 Wausau WI; BR/TR/6´0˝/(190–195); d4.21; C14																									
1956	Chi A	0	0	ø	3	0	0	0	1.2	6	4	0	0	1-0	2	21.60	19	.545	.583	0	ø	0	—	-3	0	-0.1
1957	Chi A	7	8	.467	33	11	3-1	1	124	139	50	1	3	35-6	48	3.48	107	.291	.342	40-0-3	.150	-2	91	5	0	0.3
1958	Chi A	2	3	.400	17	3	0	0	36.1	43	28	6	0	13-1	16	6.69	54	.301	.357	7-0-1	.143	-0	82	-12	0	-1.4
	Det A	2	4	.333	22	0	0	2	30.2	46	34	6	0	13-2	16	7.63	53	.362	.415	1-0-1	.000	0	—	-13	0	-2.5
	Was A	0	3	.000	3	3	0	0	21	24	9	1	1	5-1	10	3.86	99	.320	.366	5	.200	0	16	0	0	0.1
	Year	4	10	.286	42	6	0	2	88	113	71	13	1	31-4	42	6.34	60	.328	.381	13-0-2	.154	0	47	-25	0	-3.8
1959	Was A	9	11	.450	34	29	6-1	0	187.1	211	98	16	4	43-2	62	4.28	92	.281	.321	54-0-7	.130	-2	106	-5	0	-0.5
1960	Was A	3	5	.375	20	7	1	0	77	85	45	7	0	17-2	31	4.91	79	.281	.318	19-1-2	.158	1	65	-7	0	-0.5
	Det A	5	3	.625	20	6	1	0	55	50	23	6	0	18-3	24	3.44	115	.244	.301	11-0-2	.364	2	111	3	0	0.7
	Year	8	8	.500	40	13	2	0	132	135	68	13	0	35-5	55	4.30	91	.266	.311	30-1-4	.233	3	87	-4	0	0.2
1961	Det A	3	2	.600	26	1	0	3	46.2	54	28	10	0	17-2	18	5.01	82	.292	.351	7	.000	-1	86	-4	0	-0.5
	KC A	1	0	1.000	15	0	0	2	21	26	9	1	0	6-0	12	3.86	108	.321	.364	2-0-1	.000	-0	—	1	0	0.1
	Year	4	2	.667	41	1	0	5	67.2	80	37	11	0	23-2	30	4.66	89	.301	.355	9-0-1	.000	-1	86	-3	0	-0.4
1962	KC A	4	12	.250	34	16	5	2	127.2	150	61	16	1	8-2	38	3.95	107	.293	.302	38-0-1	.105	-2	67	4	0	0.2
1963	KC A	9	6	.600	45	2	0	3	95.2	86	44	13	3	29-5	34	3.57	109	.242	.302	15-0-3	.067	-0	171	2	0	0.3

YEAR	TM LG	W	L	PCT	G	GS	CG-SHO	SV-BS	IP	H	R	HR	HB	BB-IB	SO	ERA	AERA	OAV	OOB	AB-HR-SH	AVG	PB	SUP	APR	DL	PW
1964	Min A	0	1	.000	9	0	0	0	7.1	16	6	2	0	5-3	2	7.36	49	.471	.525	0	ø	0	—	-3	0	-0.3
Total	9	45	58	.437	281	78	16-2	13	831.1	936	439	85	12	210-29	313	4.34	91	.287	.330	199-1-21	.136	-4	90	-32	0	-4.1

FISHEL, LEO Leo; B12.13.1877 Babylon NY; D5.19.1960 Hempstead NY; BR/TR/6´0˝/175; d5.3; Col Columbia

YEAR	TM LG	W	L	PCT	G	GS	CG-SHO	SV-BS	IP	H	R	HR	HB	BB-IB	SO	ERA	AERA	OAV	OOB	AB-HR-SH	AVG	PB	SUP	APR	DL	PW
1899	NY N	0	1	.000	1	1	1	0	9	9	7	0	2	6	6	6.00	63	.257	.395	4	.250	-0	58	-2	—	-0.1

FISHER, BRIAN Brian Kevin; B3.18.1962 Honolulu HI; BR/TR/6´4˝/210; [AtlN80 2/29]; d5.7

YEAR	TM LG	W	L	PCT	G	GS	CG-SHO	SV-BS	IP	H	R	HR	HB	BB-IB	SO	ERA	AERA	OAV	OOB	AB-HR-SH	AVG	PB	SUP	APR	DL	PW
1985	NY A	4	4	.500	55	0	0	14-4	98.1	77	32	4	0	29-3	85	2.38	170	.216	.273	0	ø	0	—	17	0	1.8
1986	NY A	9	5	.643	62	0	0	6-9	96.2	105	61	14	1	37-2	67	4.93	84	.277	.341	0	ø	0	—	-9	0	-1.4
1987	Pit N	11	9	.550	37	26	6-3	0-0	185.1	185	99	27	4	72-7	117	4.52	92	.262	.332	58-2-5	.190	4	99	-5	0	-0.2
1988	Pit N	8	10	.444	33	22	1-1	1-1	146.1	157	78	13	5	57-4	66	4.61	75	.277	.345	42-0-2	.048	-2	115	-17	15	-2.2
1989	Pit N	0	3	.000	9	3	0	1-0	17	25	17	2	0	10-3	8	7.94	43	.329	.402	5	.000	-1	78	-9	101	-1.5
1990	Hou N	0	0	ø	4	0	0	0-0	5	9	5	1	0	0-0	1	7.20	52	.409	.375	0	ø	0	—	-2	0	-0.1
1992	Sea A	4	3	.571	22	14	0	1-0	91.1	80	49	9	1	47-2	26	4.53	88	.234	.326	0	ø	0	114	-5	0	-0.3
Total	7	36	34	.514	222	65	7-4	23-14	640	638	341	70	11	252-21	370	4.39	90	.261	.330	105-2-7	.124	2	105	-30	116	-3.9

FISHER, CHAUNCEY Chauncey Burr "Peach","Whoa Bill"; B1.8.1872 Anderson IN; D4.27.1939 Los Angeles CA; BR/TR/5´11˝/175; d9.20; b–Tom

YEAR	TM LG	W	L	PCT	G	GS	CG-SHO	SV-BS	IP	H	R	HR	HB	BB-IB	SO	ERA	AERA	OAV	OOB	AB-HR-SH	AVG	PB	SUP	APR	DL	PW
1893	Cle N	0	2	.000	2	2	2	0	18	26	18	0	0	9	9	5.50	89	.329	.398	8	.250	-0	79	-1	—	-0.1
1894	Cle N	0	2	.000	3	2	0	0	11	22	17	0	1	5	0	11.45	48	.407	.467	4	.000	-1	52	-6	—	-0.7
	Cin N	2	8	.200	12	12	11	0	100	153	123	4	1	46	17	7.47	74	.347	.410	47-1-0	.213	-2	67	-22	—	-1.6
	Year	2	10	.167	15	14	11	0	111	175	140	4	2	51	17	7.86	70	.354	.416	51-1-0	.196	-3	65	-28	—	-2.3
1896	Cin N	10	7	.588	27	15	13-2	2	159.2	199	111	9	5	36	25	4.45	104	.303	.344	57-0-4	.246	0	122	2	—	0.1
1897	Bro N	9	7	.563	20	13	11-1	1	149	184	96	5	2	43	31	4.23	97	.301	.349	59-0-1	.203	-1	153	-2	—	-0.3
1901	NY N	0	0	ø	1	1	0	0	4	11	9	0	0	2	1	15.75	21	.500	.542	2	.000	-0	279	-5	—	-0.3
	StL N	0	0	ø	1	0	0	0	3	7	5	0	0	1	0	15.00	21	.438	.471	1	.000	-0	—	-3	—	-0.2
	Year	0	0	ø	2	1	0	0	7	18	14	0	0	3	1	15.43	21	.474	.512	3	.000	-0	284	-8	—	-0.5
Total	5	21	26	.447	66	45	37-3	3	444.2	602	379	18	9	142	83	5.44	85	.320	.371	178-1-5	.213	-4	111	-37	—	-3.1

FISHER, CLARENCE Clarence Henry; B8.27.1898 Letart WV; D11.2.1965 Point Pleasant WV; BR/TR/6´0˝/174; d9.14; Col Rio Grande

YEAR	TM LG	W	L	PCT	G	GS	CG-SHO	SV-BS	IP	H	R	HR	HB	BB-IB	SO	ERA	AERA	OAV	OOB	AB-HR-SH	AVG	PB	SUP	APR	DL	PW
1919	Was A	0	0	ø	2	0	0	0	4	8	6	0	0	3	1	13.50	24	.421	.500	0	ø	0	—	-4	—	-0.2
1920	Was A	0	1	.000	2	0	0	0	3.2	5	4	0	0	5	0	9.82	38	.714	.833	1	.000	-0	—	-2	—	-0.4
Total	2	0	1	.000	4	0	0	0	7.2	13	10	0	0	8	1	11.74	29	.500	.618	1	.000	-0	—	-6	—	-0.6

FISHER, DON Donald Raymond; B2.6.1916 Cleveland OH; D7.29.1973 Mayfield Heights OH; BR/TR/6´0˝/210; d8.25

YEAR	TM LG	W	L	PCT	G	GS	CG-SHO	SV-BS	IP	H	R	HR	HB	BB-IB	SO	ERA	AERA	OAV	OOB	AB-HR-SH	AVG	PB	SUP	APR	DL	PW
1945	NY N	1	0	1.000	2	1	1-1	0	18	12	4	0	2	7	4	2.00	196	.190	.292	7	.143	-0	22	4	0	0.2

FISHER, EDDIE Eddie Gene; B7.16.1936 Shreveport LA; BR/TR/6´2.5˝/200; d6.22; Col Oklahoma

YEAR	TM LG	W	L	PCT	G	GS	CG-SHO	SV-BS	IP	H	R	HR	HB	BB-IB	SO	ERA	AERA	OAV	OOB	AB-HR-SH	AVG	PB	SUP	APR	DL	PW
1959	SF N	2	6	.250	17	5	0	1	40	57	37	8	1	8-0	15	7.87	48	.339	.369	8	.000	-1	75	-17	0	-3.0
1960	SF N	1	0	1.000	3	1	1	0	12.2	11	5	2	0	2-0	7	3.55	98	.244	.260	5	.600	1	279	0	0	0.2
1961	SF N	0	2	.000	15	1	0	1	33.2	36	23	7	0	9-3	16	5.35	71	.267	.313	7	.143	0	442	-6	0	-0.4
1962	Chi A	9	5	.643	57	12	2-1	5	182.2	169	74	17	1	45-1	88	3.10	126	.245	.291	46-0-8	.130	-0	116	14	0	1.1
1963	Chi A	9	8	.529	33	15	2-1	0	120.2	114	57	14	2	28-2	67	3.95	89	.244	.286	36-0-1	.139	-1	110	-5	0	-0.7
1964	Chi A	6	3	.667	59	2	0	9	125	86	43	13	3	32-3	74	3.02	114	.192	.249	18-0-1	.167	-0	206	8	0	0.7
1965	Chi A★	15	7	.682	**82**	0	0	24	165.1	118	51	13	2	43-8	90	2.40	133	.205	.259	29-0-1	.138	0	—	15	0	2.5
1966	Chi A	1	3	.250	23	0	0	6	35.1	27	11	1	1	17-1	18	2.29	138	.214	.310	2	.000	-0	—	4	0	0.5
	Bal A	5	3	.625	44	0	0	13	71.2	60	26	4	2	19-1	39	2.64	126	.226	.280	13	.154	0	—	4	0	0.7
	Year	6	6	.500	**67**	0	0	19	107	87	37	5	3	36-2	57	2.52	130	.222	.290	15	.133	-0	—	8	0	1.2
1967	Bal A	4	3	.571	46	0	0	1	89.2	82	40	7	4	26-3	53	3.61	87	.245	.304	5-0-2	.200	0	—	-5	0	-0.4
1968	Cle A	4	2	.667	54	0	0	4	94.2	87	36	8	2	17-3	42	2.85	104	.248	.283	12	.000	-1	—	1	0	0.0
1969	Cal A	3	2	.600	52	1	0	2-0	96.2	100	46	9	1	28-3	47	3.63	96	.272	.322	13-0-2	.000	-1	101	-2	0	-0.3
1970	Cal A	4	4	.500	67	2	0	8-4	130.1	117	51	15	2	35-1	74	3.04	119	.239	.291	11-0-3	.091	-1	123	8	0	0.5
1971	Cal A	10	8	.556	57	3	0	3-2	119	92	46	11	2	50-5	82	2.72	119	.211	.293	16-0-1	.063	-1	147	5	0	0.7
1972	Cal A	4	5	.444	43	1	0	4-2	81.1	73	35	6	0	31-3	32	3.76	78	.247	.314	17	.118	-1	30	-6	0	-0.9
	Chi A	0	1	.000	6	4	0	0-0	22.1	31	13	1	0	9-0	10	4.43	70	.348	.404	7	.000	-1	121	-3	0	-0.3
	Year	4	6	.400	49	5	0	4-2	103.2	104	48	7	0	40-3	42	3.91	76	.271	.335	24	.083	-1	107	-10	0	-1.2
1973	Chi A	6	7	.462	26	16	2	0-0	110.2	135	64	12	3	38-1	57	4.88	81	.301	.358	0	ø	0	107	-9	0	-1.0
	StL N	2	1	.667	6	0	0	0-0	7	3	1	1	1	1-0	1	1.29	286	.125	.192	1	1.000	0	—	2	0	0.5
Total	15	85	70	.548	690	63	7-2	81-8	1538.2	1398	659	149	27	438-38	812	3.41	101	.243	.297	246-0-19	.122	-5	127	8	0	0.4

FISHER, ED Edward Fredrick; B10.31.1876 Wayne MI; D7.24.1951 Spokane WA; BR/TR/6´2˝/200; d9.5

YEAR	TM LG	W	L	PCT	G	GS	CG-SHO	SV-BS	IP	H	R	HR	HB	BB-IB	SO	ERA	AERA	OAV	OOB	AB-HR-SH	AVG	PB	SUP	APR	DL	PW
1902	Det A	0	0	ø	1	0	0	0	4	4	0	0	0	1	0	0.00	ø	.267	.313	2	.000	-0	—	2	—	0.0

FISHER, FRITZ Frederick Brown; B11.28.1941 Adrian MI; BL/TL/6´1˝/180; d4.19; Col Michigan

YEAR	TM LG	W	L	PCT	G	GS	CG-SHO	SV-BS	IP	H	R	HR	HB	BB-IB	SO	ERA	AERA	OAV	OOB	AB-HR-SH	AVG	PB	SUP	APR	DL	PW
1964	Det A	0	0	ø	1	0	0	0	0.1	2	4	0	0	2-0	1	108.00	3	.667	.800	0	ø	0	—	-4	0	-0.2

FISHER, HARRY Harry Devereux; B1.3.1926 Newbury ON, Can.; D9.20.1981 Waterloo ON, Can.; BL/TR/6´0˝/180; d9.16.1951; ▲

YEAR	TM LG	W	L	PCT	G	GS	CG-SHO	SV-BS	IP	H	R	HR	HB	BB-IB	SO	ERA	AERA	OAV	OOB	AB-HR-SH	AVG	PB	SUP	APR	DL	PW
1952	Pit N	1	2	.333	8	3	0	0	18.1	17	14	4	2	13	5	6.87	58	.266	.405	15	.333	1*	74	-5	0	-0.6

FISHER, J. J.; B Philadelhia PA; d7.17

YEAR	TM LG	W	L	PCT	G	GS	CG-SHO	SV-BS	IP	H	R	HR	HB	BB-IB	SO	ERA	AERA	OAV	OOB	AB-HR-SH	AVG	PB	SUP	APR	DL	PW
1884	Phi U	1	7	.125	8	8	8	0	70.2	76	49	0	—	13	42	3.57	65	.257	.288	36	.222	-0*	69	-10	—	-1.0
1885	Buf N	0	1	.000	1	1	1	0	9	10	9	0	—	2	4	5.00	60	.256	.293	4	.000	-1	95	-2	—	-0.2
Total	2	1	8	.111	9	9	9	0	79.2	86	58	0	—	15	46	3.73	64	.257	.289	40	.200	-1	72	-12	—	-1.2

FISHER, JACK John Howard "Fat Jack"; B3.4.1939 Frostburg MD; BR/TR/6´2˝/(210–215); d4.14

YEAR	TM LG	W	L	PCT	G	GS	CG-SHO	SV-BS	IP	H	R	HR	HB	BB-IB	SO	ERA	AERA	OAV	OOB	AB-HR-SH	AVG	PB	SUP	APR	DL	PW
1959	Bal A	1	6	.143	27	7	1-1	2	88.2	76	36	7	1	38-1	52	3.05	124	.230	.307	23	.130	-1	57	6	0	0.4
1960	Bal A	12	11	.522	40	20	8-3	2	197.2	174	87	13	2	78-4	99	3.41	111	.241	.315	60-1-4	.183	2	110	8	0	1.1
1961	Bal A	10	13	.435	36	25	10-1	1	196	205	104	17	4	75-3	118	3.90	99	.270	.335	56-0-10	.089	-2	94	-5	0	-0.9
1962	Bal A	7	9	.438	32	25	4	1	152	173	101	23	2	56-3	81	5.09	73	.284	.345	49-0-3	.102	-1*	128	-27	30	-2.6
1963	SF N	6	10	.375	36	12	2	1	116	132	77	12	5	38-3	57	4.58	70	.284	.342	29-0-2	.103	1	106	-22	0	-2.8
1964	NY N	10	17	.370	40	34	8-1	0	227.2	256	124	23	10	56-0	115	4.23	85	.283	.330	76-0-2	.158	1	105	-17	0	-1.8
1965	NY N	8	24	.250	43	36	10	1	253.2	252	121	22	4	68-6	116	3.94	90	.259	.309	78-0-4	.154	0	69	-9	0	-0.9
1966	NY N	11	14	.440	38	33	10-2	0	230	229	108	26	8	54-2	127	3.68	99	.260	.308	67-0-6	.090	-2	84	-1	0	-0.1
1967	NY N	9	18	.333	39	30	7-1	0	220.1	251	121	21	4	64-10	117	4.70	72	.287	.336	70-0-6	.100	-2	77	-28	0	-3.3
1968	Chi A	8	13	.381	35	28	2	0	180.2	176	68	14	7	48-4	80	2.99	101	.257	.310	53-0-5	.113	-1	62	2	0	0.0
1969	Cin N	4	4	.500	34	15	0	1-0	113	137	77	15	5	30-3	55	5.50	68	.295	.344	33-0-3	.121	-1	129	-20	0	-1.6
Total	11	86	139	.382	400	265	62-9	9-0	1975.2	2061	1024	193	52	605-39	1017	4.06	88	.269	.325	594-1-45	.125	-6	92	-113	30	-12.5

FISHER, MAURICE Maurice Wayne; B2.16.1931 Uniondale IN; BR/TR/6´5˝/200; d4.16

YEAR	TM LG	W	L	PCT	G	GS	CG-SHO	SV-BS	IP	H	R	HR	HB	BB-IB	SO	ERA	AERA	OAV	OOB	AB-HR-SH	AVG	PB	SUP	APR	DL	PW
1955	Cin N	0	0	ø	1	0	0	0	2.2	5	2	1	0	2-0	1	6.75	63	.385	.467	1	.000	-0	—	-1	0	0.0

FISHER, RAY Ray Lyle "Pick"; B10.4.1887 Middlebury VT; D11.3.1982 Ann Arbor MI; BR/TR/5´11.5˝/180; d7.2; Mil 1918; Col Middlebury

YEAR	TM LG	W	L	PCT	G	GS	CG-SHO	SV-BS	IP	H	R	HR	HB	BB-IB	SO	ERA	AERA	OAV	OOB	AB-HR-SH	AVG	PB	SUP	APR	DL	PW
1910	NY A	5	3	.625	17	7	3	1	92.1	95	41	0	3	18	42	2.92	91	.274	.315	29-0-1	.103	-2	101	-3	—	-0.3
1911	NY A	10	11	.476	29	22	8-2	0	171.2	178	85	3	5	55	99	3.25	111	.269	.330	59-1-3	.119	-3	88	6	—	0.5
1912	NY A	2	8	.200	17	13	5	0	90.1	107	70	2	2	32	47	5.88	61	.312	.374	31-0-3	.065	-4	74	-17	—	-1.9
1913	NY A	12	16	.429	43	31	14-1	1	246.1	244	113	3	9	71	92	3.18	94	.263	.321	79-0-6	.278	3	84	-3	—	0.1
1914	NY A	10	12	.455	29	26	17-2	1	209	177	65	2	4	61	86	2.28	121	.241	.303	65-0-5	.138	-2	78	12	—	1.2
1915	NY A	18	11	.621	30	28	20-4	0	247.2	219	82	7	5	62	97	2.11	139	.243	.295	83-0-4	.108	-5	100	19	—	1.7
1916	NY A	11	8	.579	31	21	9-1	2	179	191	81	4	4	51	56	3.17	91	.285	.339	62-0-1	.177	1	113	-6	—	-0.6
1917	NY A	8	9	.471	23	18	12-3	0	144	126	49	3	2	43	64	2.19	123	.243	.304	50-1-2	.180	-0	89	7	—	0.9
1919	†Cin N	14	5	.737	26	20	12-5	1	174.1	141	55	4	1	38	41	2.17	128	.226	.271	59-0-2	.271	3	136	12	—	1.9
1920	Cin N	10	11	.476	33	21	10-1	1	201	189	86	5	8	50	56	2.73	111	.249	.302	70-0-3	.243	1	113	4	—	0.6
Total	10	100	94	.515	278	207	110-19	7	1755.2	1667	727	33	43	481	680	2.82	106	.257	.312	587-2-30	.179	-8	97	31	—	4.1

FISHER, TOM Thomas Chalmers "Red"; B11.1.1880 Anderson IN; D9.3.1972 Anderson IN; BR/TR/5´10.5˝/185; d4.17; b–Chauncey

YEAR	TM LG	W	L	PCT	G	GS	CG-SHO	SV-BS	IP	H	R	HR	HB	BB-IB	SO	ERA	AERA	OAV	OOB	AB-HR-SH	AVG	PB	SUP	APR	DL	PW
1904	Bos N	6	16	.273	31	21	19-2	0	214	257	165	5	10	82	84	4.25	65	.302	.370	99-2-0	.212	3*	78	-42	—	-3.7

YEAR	TM LG	W	L	PCT	G	GS	CG-SHO	SV-BS	IP	H	R	HR	HB	BB-IB	SO	ERA	AERA	OAV	OOB	AB-HR-SH	AVG	PB	SUP	APR	DL	PW
FISHER, TOM	Thomas Gene; B4.4.1942 Cleveland OH; BR/TR/6´0˝/190; d9.20; Col Ohio U.																									
1967	Bal A	0	0	ø	2	0	0	0	3.1	2	0	0	0	2-0	1	0.00	ø	.182	.308	0	ø	0	—	1	0	0.1
FISHER, CHEROKEE	William Charles; B12.1845 Philadelphia PA; D9.26.1912 New York NY; BR/TR/5´9˝/164; d5.6; ▲																									
1871	Rok NA	4	16	.200	24	24	22-**1**	0	213	295	257	3	—	31	15	4.35	94	.281	.302	123-1	.228	-3*	89	-3	—	-0.2
1872	Bal NA	10	1	.909	19	11	9-1	1	110	93	78	0	—	11	20	**1.80**	**205**	**.197**	**.216**	225-1	.231	-1*	172	19	—	1.2
1873	Ath NA	3	4	.429	13	5	5	2	84.1	90	73	1	—	10	14	**1.81**	**197**	**.231**	**.250**	253-1	.261	1*	75	10	—	0.6
1874	Har NA	13	23	.361	39	35	31	0	322.1	416	277	1	—	13	25	2.32	100	.277	.284	241	.224	-4*	98	1	—	-0.3
1875	Phi NA	22	19	.537	41	41	36-2	0	358	345	189	6	—	9	18	1.99	115	.229	.233	177	.232	-1	99	13	—	0.9
1876	Cin N	4	20	.167	28	24	22	0	229.1	294	206	6	—	6	29	3.02	73	.285	.289	129	.248	-1*	60	-26	—	-2.2
1878	Pro N	0	1	.000	1	1	1	0	9	14	12	0	—	0	2	4.00	55	.304	.304	3	.000	-0	79	-3	—	-0.2
Total	5NA	52	63	.452	136	116	103-4	3	1087.2	1239	874	11	—	74	92	2.52	115	.252	.263	1019-3	.237	-8	102	40	—	2.2
Total	2	4	21	.160	29	25	23	0	238.1	308	218	6	—	6	31	3.06	72	.285	.289	132	.242	-2	61	-29	—	-2.4
FISKE, MAX	Maximilian Patrick "Ski"; B10.12.1888 Chicago IL; D5.25.1928 Chicago IL; BR/TR/5´11˝/185; d4.19																									
1914	Chi F	12	12	.500	38	22	7	0	198	161	84	7	7	59	87	3.14	85	.231	.298	68-0-1	.235	1*	105	-8	—	-0.9
FITTERY, PAUL	Paul Clarence; B10.10.1887 Lebanon PA; D1.28.1974 Cartersville GA; BB/TL/5´8.5˝/156; d9.5																									
1914	Cin N	0	2	.000	8	4	2	0	43.2	41	20	0	1	12	21	3.09	95	.246	.300	17-0-1	.059	-1*	79	0	—	-0.2
1917	Phi N	1	1	.500	17	2	1	0	55.2	69	36	1	5	27	13	4.53	62	.317	.404	22-0-1	.091	-1*	188	-10	—	-0.5
Total	2	1	3	.250	25	6	3	0	99.1	110	56	1	6	39	34	3.90	73	.286	.360	39-0-2	.077	-2	116	-10	—	-0.7
FITZGERALD, BRIAN	Brian Michael; B12.26.1974 Woodbridge VA; BL/TL/5´11˝/175; [SeaA96 20/597]; d4.17; Col VPI																									
2002	Sea A	0	0	ø	6	0	0	0-0	6.1	11	8	2	1	2-0	3	8.53	51	.344	.389	0	ø	0	—	-4	0	-0.2
FITZGERALD, JOHN	John Francis; B9.15.1933 Brooklyn NY; BL/TL/6´3˝/190; d9.28																									
1958	SF N	0	0	ø	1	1	0	0	3	1	1	1	0	1-0	3	3.00	127	.111	.200	1	.000	-0	165	0	0	0.0
FITZGERALD, JOHN	John H.; B5,30.1870 Natick MA; D3.31.1921 Boston MA; d7.18																									
1891	Bos AA	1	1	.500	6	3	2	1	32	49	32	2	2	11	16	5.63	62	.340	.395	14	.071	-2	89	-8	—	-0.5
FITZGERALD, JOHN	John J.; B1866; D12.20.1892 Waterbury CT; d4.18																									
1890	Roc AA	3	8	.273	11	11	8-1	0	78	77	51	0	6	45	35	4.04	88	.250	.357	31	.194	-0	91	-3	—	-0.4
FITZGERALD, WARREN	Warren Bartholomew; B4.1868 PA; D11.7.1930 Phoenix AZ; TL/5´9˝/162; d6.4																									
1891	Lou AA	14	17	.452	32	31	28-3	0	267	265	157	5	12	89	110	3.34	110	.250	.316	108-1	.176	1*	84	8	—	0.6
1892	Lou N	1	3	.250	4	4	4	0	34	45	27	2	1	11	3	4.24	72	.306	.358	15	.133	-0	98	-5	—	-0.5
Total	2	15	20	.429	36	35	32-3	0	301	310	184	7	13	100	113	3.44	104	.257	.321	123-1	.171	0	86	3	—	0.1
FITZKE, PAUL	Robert Paul "Bob" (b Frederick Herman Fitzke); B7.30.1900 LaCrosse WI; D6.30.1950 Sacramento CA; BR/TR/5´11.5˝/185; d9.1; Col Idaho																									
1924	Cle A	0	0	ø	1	0	0	0	4	5	2	0	0	3	1	4.50	95	.313	.421	1	.000	-0	—	0	—	0.0
FITZMORRIS, AL	Alan James; B3.21.1946 Buffalo NY; BB/TR/6´2˝/(185–200); d9.8																									
1969	KC A	1	1	.500	7	0	0	2-0	10.2	9	5	1	0	4-0	3	4.22	88	.237	.310	1	.000	-0	—	0	0	-0.1
1970	KC A	8	5	.615	43	11	2	1-1	117.2	112	60	14	0	52-6	47	4.44	84	.254	.330	31	.290	4*	178	-6	0	-0.2
1971	KC A	7	5	.583	36	15	2-1	0-1	127.1	112	61	6	1	55-2	53	4.17	83	.245	.324	44-0-2	.250	2	135	-8	0	-0.5
1972	KC A	2	5	.286	38	2	0	3-1	101	99	46	10	1	28-5	51	3.74	81	.252	.303	23	.174	1*	102	-8	0	-0.4
1973	KC A	8	3	.727	15	13	3-1	0-0	89	88	29	5	0	25-3	26	2.83	145	.259	.309	0	ø	0	95	13	0	1.6
1974	KC A	13	6	.684	34	27	9-4	1-1	190	189	73	8	0	63-10	53	2.79	137	.260	.317	0	ø	0	98	19	0	2.0
1975	KC A	16	12	.571	35	35	11-3	0-0	242	239	104	16	5	76-6	78	3.57	108	.262	.320	0	ø	0	106	10	0	1.1
1976	KC A	15	11	.577	35	33	8-2	0-0	220.1	227	89	6	2	56-6	80	3.06	114	.273	.316	0	ø	0*	90	10	0	1.3
1977	Cle A	6	10	.375	29	21	1	0-0	133	164	87	12	1	53-4	54	5.41	74	.306	.367	0	ø	0	108	-20	0	-2.1
1978	Cle A	0	1	.000	7	0	0	0-0	14.1	19	10	3	1	7-2	5	6.28	60	.333	.415	0	ø	0	—	-3	34	-0.2
	Cal A	1	0	1.000	9	2	0	0-0	31.2	26	9	2	0	14-3	8	1.71	213	.236	.317	0	ø	0	186	6	0	0.3
	Year	1	1	.500	16	2	0	0-0	46	45	19	5	1	21-5	13	3.13	118	.269	.351	0	ø	0	183	3	0	0.1
Total	10	77	59	.566	288	159	36-11	7-4	1277	1284	573	83	11	433-47	458	3.65	101	.265	.324	99-0-2	.242	7	111	13	34	2.8
FITZSIMMONS, FREDDIE	Frederick Landis "Fat Freddie"; B7.28.1901 Mishawaka IN; D11.18.1979 Yucca Valley CA; BR/TR/5´11˝/185; d8.12; M3/C14																									
1925	NY N	6	3	.667	10	8	6-1	0	74.2	70	25	4	0	18	17	2.65	152	.248	.293	29-0-1	.310	2	120	13	—	1.7
1926	NY N	14	10	.583	37	26	12	0	219	224	90	7	4	58	48	2.88	130	.272	.322	86-0-1	.128	-6	117	19	—	1.3
1927	NY N	17	10	.630	42	31	14-1	3	244.2	260	127	15	4	67	78	3.72	104	.275	.325	87-0-8	.207	-0	128	0	—	0.1
1928	NY N	20	9	.690	40	32	16-1	1	261.1	264	119	13	4	65	67	3.68	106	.268	.316	94-0-5	.191	1	103	9	—	1.0
1929	NY N	15	11	.577	37	30	14-4	1	221.2	242	122	14	2	66	55	4.10	112	.285	.338	82-0-2	.183	-2	135	11	—	1.1
1930	NY N	19	7	**.731**	41	29	17-1	1	224.1	230	125	26	1	59	76	4.25	111	.266	.314	83-2-5	.265	5	148	12	—	1.8
1931	NY N	18	11	.621	35	33	19-4	0	253.2	242	111	16	0	62	78	3.05	121	.251	.296	92-4-3	.228	9	130	15	—	2.9
1932	NY N	11	11	.500	35	31	11	0	237.2	287	132	18	3	83	65	4.43	84	.299	.356	86-2-6	.221	4	139	-16	—	-0.6
1933	†NY N	16	11	.593	36	**35**	13-1	0	251.2	243	106	14	2	72	65	2.90	111	.251	.305	95-2-3	.200	3	110	6	—	1.2
1934	NY N	18	14	.563	38	37	14-3	1	263.1	266	114	12	1	51	73	3.04	127	.261	.297	95-2-2	.232	5	105	22	—	3.2
1935	NY N	4	8	.333	18	15	6-**4**	0	94	104	43	7	1	22	23	4.02	96	.281	.323	31-0-2	.258	1	81	0	—	0.2
1936	†NY N	10	7	.588	28	17	7-1	2	141	147	58	6	0	39	35	3.32	117	.274	.323	47-0-5	.149	-2	96	10	—	1.0
1937	NY N	2	2	.500	6	4	1-1	0	27.1	28	14	3	0	8	13	4.61	84	.272	.324	10-1-1	.300	2	144	-1	—	0.0
	Bro N	4	8	.333	13	13	4	0	90.2	91	47	2	1	32	29	4.27	95	.263	.327	30-0-1	.167	-1	72	0	—	0.0
	Year	6	10	.375	19	17	5-1	0	118	119	61	5	1	40	42	4.35	92	.265	.327	40-1-2	.200	1	89	-2	—	0.0
1938	Bro N	11	8	.579	27	26	12-3	0	202.2	205	83	8	3	43	38	3.02	129	.261	.302	70-0-4	.171	-1	98	18	—	1.8
1939	Bro N	7	9	.438	27	20	5	3	151.1	178	79	6	3	28	44	3.87	104	.293	.327	47-1-3	.234	3	76	0	—	0.6
1940	Bro N	16	2	**.889**	20	18	11-4	1	134.1	120	43	5	1	25	35	2.81	142	.233	.269	47-0-4	.106	-2	121	19	—	2.3
1941	†Bro N	6	1	.857	13	12	3-1	0	82.2	78	33	3	2	26	19	2.07	177	.245	.305	28-0-1	.143	-0	106	10	0	0.9
1942	Bro N	0	0	ø	1	1	0	0	3	6	5	1	0	1	0	15.00	22	.400	.438	2	.500	0	154	-4	0	-0.1
1943	Bro N	3	4	.429	9	7	1	0	44.2	50	29	6	1	21	12	5.44	62	.281	.360	14-0-1	.071	-1	97	-10	0	-1.4
Total	19	217	146	.598	513	425	186-30	13	3223.2	3335	1505	186	33	846	870	3.51	111	.268	.316	1155-14-58	.200	21	115	133	0	19.0
FLAHERTY, PATSY	Patrick Joseph; B6.29.1876 Mansfield PA; D1.23.1968 Alexandria LA; BL/TL/5´8˝/165; d9.8; ▲																									
1899	Lou N	2	3	.400	5	4	4	0	39	41	21	0	1	5	5	2.31	167	.270	.297	24	.208	1*	75	5	—	0.5
1900	Pit N	0	0	ø	4	1	0	0	22	30	16	0	5	9	5	6.14	59	.323	.411	9	.111	-1	152	-4	—	-0.2
1903	Chi A	11	25	.306	40	34	29-2	1	293.2	338	173	9	14	50	65	3.74	75	.288	.324	102-0-3	.137	-3	80	-29	—	-3.4
1904	Chi A	1	2	.333	5	5	4	0	43	36	19	1	1	10	14	2.09	117	.228	.278	12	.333	2	134	0	—	0.3
	Pit N	19	9	.679	29	28	28-5	0	242	210	81	3	11	59	54	2.05	134	.232	.287	104-2-4	.212	5*	135	16	—	2.8
1905	Pit N	10	10	.500	27	20	15	1	187.2	197	87	2	6	49	44	3.50	86	.272	.324	76-0-1	.197	2*	125	-8	—	-0.5
1907	Bos N	12	15	.444	27	25	23	0	217	197	90	4	7	59	34	2.70	95	.248	.306	115-2-0	.191	2*	95	-5	—	-0.2
1908	Bos N	12	18	.400	31	31	21	0	244	221	109	6	8	81	50	3.25	74	.236	.303	86-0-5	.140	-0*	94	-17	—	-2.0
1910	Phi N	0	0	ø	1	0	0	0	0.1	1	4	0	0	1	0	0.00	ø	.333	.500	2	.500	0*	—	-1	—	-0.1
1911	Bos N	0	2	.000	4	2	1	0	14	21	15	0	3	8	0	7.07	54	.350	.451	94-2-1	.287	1*	98	-5	—	-0.5
Total	9	67	84	.444	173	150	125-7	2	1302.2	1292	615	25	56	331	271	3.10	89	.259	.312	624-6-14	.197	10	104	-48	—	-3.3
FLANAGAN, MIKE	Michael Kendall; B12.16.1951 Manchester NH; BL/TL/6´0˝/(185–199); [BalA73 7/159]; d9.5; C2; Col Massachusetts																									
1975	Bal A	0	1	.000	2	1	0	0-0	9.2	9	4	0	0	6-1	7	2.79	127	.250	.357	0	ø	0	50	0	0	0.1
1976	Bal A	3	5	.375	20	10	4	0-0	85	83	41	7	0	33-0	56	4.13	80	.260	.326	0	ø	0	101	-7	0	-0.6
1977	Bal A	15	10	.600	36	33	15-2	1-0	235	235	100	17	2	70-5	149	3.64	105	.266	.318	0	ø	0	106	7	0	0.7
1978	Bal A☆	19	15	.559	40	**40**	17-2	0-0	281.1	271	128	22	3	87-2	167	4.03	88	.257	.314	0	ø	0	109	-10	0	-1.2
1979	†Bal A	**23**	9	.719	39	38	16-**5**	0-0	265.2	245	107	23	3	70-1	190	3.08	131	.245	.296	0	ø	0	110	27	0	3.0
1980	Bal A	16	13	.552	37	37	12-2	0-0	251.1	278	121	27	2	71-3	128	4.12	96	.287	.333	0	ø	0*	101	-3	0	-0.2
1981	Bal A	9	6	.600	20	20	3-2	0-0	116	108	55	11	2	37-1	72	4.19	87	.244	.305	0	ø	0	102	-4	0	-0.5
1982	Bal A	15	11	.577	36	35	11-1	0-0	236	233	110	24	4	76-5	103	3.97	102	.259	.317	0	ø	0	105	3	0	0.3
1983	†Bal A	12	4	.750	20	20	3-1	0-0	125.1	135	53	10	2	31-2	50	3.30	121	.278	.321	0	ø	0	118	9	81	1.0
1984	Bal A	13	13	.500	34	34	10-2	0-0	226.2	213	103	24	1	81-5	115	3.53	111	.250	.314	0	ø	0	99	8	0	0.9
1985	Bal A	4	5	.444	15	15	1	0-0	86	101	49	14	2	28-0	42	5.13	79	.297	.352	0	ø	0	89	-8	103	-0.7

YEAR	TM LG	W	L	PCT	G	GS	CG-SHO	SV-BS	IP	H	R	HR	HB	BB-IB	SO	ERA	AERA	OAV	OOB	AB-HR-SH	AVG	PB	SUP	APR	DL	PW
1986	Bal A	7	11	.389	29	28	2	0-1	172	179	95	15	1	66-4	96	4.24	98	.270	.334	0	ø	0	89	-4	19	-0.4
1987	Bal A	3	6	.333	16	16	4	0-0	94.2	102	57	9	0	36-1	50	4.94	90	.278	.342	0	ø	0	103	-5	60	-0.4
	Tor A	3	2	.600	7	7	0	0-0	49.1	46	15	3	0	15-3	43	2.37	191	.237	.292	0	ø	0	78	11	0	1.0
	Year	6	8	.429	23	23	4	0-0	144	148	72	12	0	51-4	93	4.06	110	.264	.325	0	ø	0	95	6	0	0.6
1988	Tor A	13	13	.500	34	34	2-1	0-0	211	220	106	23	6	80-1	99	4.18	95	.271	.339	0	ø	0	115	-4	0	-0.4
1989	†Tor A	8	10	.444	30	30	1-1	0-0	171.2	186	82	10	5	47-0	47	3.93	96	.283	.331	0	ø	0	105	-2	0	-0.1
1990	Tor A	2	2	.500	5	5	0	0-0	20.1	28	14	3	0	8-0	5	5.31	75	.329	.387	0	ø	0	147	-4	0	-0.6
1991	Bal A	2	7	.222	64	1	0	3-2	98.1	84	27	6	3	25-6	55	2.38	167	.236	.289	0	ø	0	69	18	0	1.7
1992	Bal A	0	0	ø	42	0	0	0-0	34.2	50	34	3	5	23-1	17	8.05	51	.338	.438	0	ø	0	—	-15	0	-0.7
Total	18	167	143	.539	526	404	101-19	4-3	2770	2806	1301	251	41	890-41	1491	3.90	101	.266	.323	0	ø	0	104	17	263	2.9
Flanigan, Ray	Raymond Arthur; B1.8.1923 Morgantown WV; D3.28.1993 Baltimore MD; BR/TR/6´0˝/190; d9.20																									
1946	Cle A	0	1	.000	3	1	0	0	9	11	12	1	0	8	2	11.00	30	.289	.413	2	.500	1	78	-8	0	-0.7
Flanigan, Tom	Thomas Anthony; B9.6.1934 Cincinnati OH; BR/TL/6´3˝/(175–185); d4.14																									
1954	Chi A	0	0	ø	2	0	0	0	1.2	1	0	0	0	1	0	0.00	ø	.200	.286	0	ø	0	—	1	0	0.0
1958	StL N	0	0	ø	1	0	0	0	1	2	1	1	0	1-0	0	9.00	46	.500	.600	0	ø	0	—	0	0	0.0
Total	2	0	0	ø	3	0	0	0	2.2	3	1	1	0	2-0	0	3.38	115	.333	.417	0	ø	0	—	1	0	0.0
Flater, Jack	John William; B9.22.1883 Sandymount MD; D3.20.1970 Westminster MD; BR/TR/5´10˝/175; d9.18																									
1908	Phi A	1	3	.250	5	3	3	0	39.1	35	15	0	2	12	8	2.06	124	.252	.320	15-0-1	.133	-0	62	1	—	0.2
Flavin, John	John Thomas; B5.7.1942 Albany CA; BL/TL/6´2˝/208; d8.25																									
1964	Chi N	0	1	.000	5	1	0	0	4.2	11	7	0	0	3-1	5	13.50	28	.500	.538	1	.000	-0	95	-5	0	-0.9
Fleet, Frank	Frank H.; B1848 New York NY; D6.13.1900 New York NY; d10.18; ▲																									
1871	Mut NA	0	1	.000	1	1	1	0	9	20	21	0	—	3	0	10.00	38	.370	.404	6	.333	0	73	-6	—	-0.3
1873	Res NA	0	3	.000	3	3	2	0	24	57	47	0	—	0	1	5.25	67	.404	.404	89	.258	0*	53	-3	—	-0.2
1875	StL NA	2	1	.667	3	3	3	0	27	33	17	0	—	3	3	3.33	60	.277	.295	16	.063	-1*	140	-3	—	-0.3
	Atl NA	0	1	.000	2	1	1	0	15.1	26	20	0	—	0	0	4.70	44	.333	.333	111	.225	-0*	118	-4	—	-0.2
	Year	2	2	.500	5	4	4	0	42.1	59	37	0	—	3	3	3.83	53	.299	.310	127	.205	-1	134	-7	—	-0.5
Total	3NA	2	6	.250	9	8	7	0	75.1	136	105	0	—	6	4	5.02	54	.347	.357	222	.230	-1	90	-16	—	-1.0
Fleming, Dave	David Anthony; B11.7.1969 Jackson Heights NY; BL/TL/6´3˝/200; [SeaA90 3/79]; d8.6; Col Georgia																									
1991	Sea A	1	0	1.000	9	3	0	0-0	17.2	19	13	3	3	3-0	11	6.62	63	.284	.342	0	ø	0	132	-4	0	-0.2
1992	Sea A	17	10	.630	33	33	7-4	0-0	228.1	225	95	13	4	60-3	112	3.39	118	.257	.306	0	ø	0	97	15	0	1.7
1993	Sea A	12	5	.706	26	26	1-1	0-0	167.1	189	84	15	6	67-6	75	4.36	103	.290	.357	0	ø	0	106	3	48	0.4
1994	Sea A	7	11	.389	23	23	0	0-0	117	152	93	17	1	65-4	65	6.46	76	.311	.391	0	ø	0	104	-19	0	-2.3
1995	Sea A	1	5	.167	16	7	1	0-1	48	57	44	15	0	34-3	26	7.50	64	.294	.394	0	ø	0	100	-14	0	-1.5
	KC A	0	1	.000	9	5	0	0-0	32	27	17	4	2	19-1	14	3.66	131	.229	.343	0	ø	0	54	3	0	0.1
	Year	1	6	.143	25	12	1	0-1	80	84	61	19	2	53-4	40	5.96	80	.269	.375	0	ø	0	81	-13	0	-1.4
Total	5	38	32	.543	116	97	9-5	0-1	610.1	669	346	67	16	248-17	303	4.67	94	.279	.349	0	ø	0	101	-16	48	-1.8
Fleming, Bill	Leslie Fletchard; B7.31.1913 Rowland CA; D6.4.2006 Reno NV; BR/TR/6´0˝/190; d8.21; Mil 1945; Col St. Marys (CA)																									
1940	Bos A	1	2	.333	10	6	1	0	46.1	53	27	4	2	20	24	4.86	93	.290	.366	13-0-2	.000	-2	94	-2	—	-0.3
1941	Bos A	1	1	.500	16	1	0	1	41.1	32	21	4	0	24	20	3.92	106	.212	.320	9	.222	1	125	1	0	0.1
1942	Chi N	5	6	.455	33	14	4-2	2	134.1	117	51	9	3	63	59	3.01	106	.230	.318	39-0-1	.051	-4	79	4	0	-0.1
1943	Chi N	0	1	.000	11	0	0	0	32.1	41	24	2	3	12	12	6.40	52	.311	.381	8	.000	-1	—	-10	0	-0.6
1944	Chi N	9	10	.474	39	18	9-1	0	158.1	163	74	6	1	62	42	3.13	113	.269	.337	53-0-4	.170	-1*	104	4	0	0.4
1946	Chi N	0	1	.000	14	1	0	0	29.1	37	23	2	1	12	10	6.14	54	.301	.368	3	.000	-0	26	-9	0	-0.5
Total	6	16	21	.432	123	40	14-3	3	442	443	220	27	10	193	167	3.79	94	.260	.339	125-0-7	.104	-7	94	-12	0	-1.0
Flener, Huck	Gregory Alan; B2.25.1969 Austin TX; BB/TL/5´11˝/(185–190); [TorA90 9/258]; d9.14; Col Cal St.–Fullerton																									
1993	Tor A	0	0	ø	6	0	0	0-0	6.2	7	3	0	0	4-1	2	4.05	108	.269	.367	0	ø	0	—	0	0	0.0
1996	Tor A	3	2	.600	15	11	0	0-0	70.2	68	40	9	1	33-1	44	4.58	109	.251	.330	0	ø	0	89	3	0	0.2
1997	Tor A	0	1	.000	8	1	0	0-0	17.1	40	19	3	0	6-0	9	9.87	47	.444	.474	0	ø	0	60	-9	0	-0.5
Total	3	3	3	.500	29	12	0	0-0	94.2	115	62	12	1	43-2	55	5.51	89	.297	.365	0	ø	0	88	-6	0	-0.3
Fletcher, Van	Alfred Vanoide; B8.6.1924 East Bend NC; BR/TR/6´2˝/185; d4.12																									
1955	Det A	0	0	ø	9	0	0	0	12	13	10	1	0	2-1	4	3.00	128	.260	.288	0	ø	0	—	-1	0	0.0
Fletcher, Paul	Edward Paul; B1.14.1967 Gallipolis OH; BR/TR/6´1˝/(185–193); [PhiN88 40/1029]; d7.11; Col West Virginia St.																									
1993	Phi N	0	0	ø	1	0	0	0-0	0.1	0	0	0	0	0-0	0	0.00	ø	.000	.000	0	ø	0	—	0	0	0.0
1995	Phi N	1	0	1.000	10	0	0	0-0	13.1	15	8	2	1	9-2	10	5.40	78	.288	.397	0	ø	0	—	-1	0	-0.1
1996	Oak A	0	0	ø	1	0	0	0-0	1.1	6	3	0	0	1-0	0	20.25	25	.667	.700	0	ø	0	—	-2	0	-0.1
Total	3	1	0	1.000	12	0	0	0-0	15	21	11	2	1	10-2	10	6.60	65	.339	.432	0	ø	0	—	-3	0	-0.2
Fletcher, Sam	Samuel Scott; B2.21.1881 Bedford PA; TR/6´2˝/210; d10.6																									
1909	Bro N	0	1	.000	1	1	1	0	9	13	8	0	0	2	5	8.00	32	.351	.385	3	.000	-0	108	-4	—	-0.4
1912	Cin N	0	0	ø	2	0	0	0	9.2	15	15	1	0	11	3	12.10	28	.366	.500	4	.500	1	—	-8	—	-0.3
Total	2	0	1	.000	3	1	1	0	18.2	28	23	1	0	13	8	10.13	30	.359	.451	7	.286	0	108	-12	—	-0.7
Fletcher, Tom	Thomas Wayne; B6.28.1942 Elmira NY; BB/TL/6´0˝/170; d9.12; s–Darrin; Col Illinois																									
1962	Det A	0	0	ø	1	0	0	0	2	2	0	0	0	2-0	1	0.00	ø	.250	.400	0	ø	0	—	1	0	0.0
Flinn, John	John Richard; B9.2.1954 Merced CA; BR/TR/6´0˝/(175–180); [BalA73*S2/39]; d5.6; Col Los Angeles Valley (CA) JC																									
1978	Bal A	1	1	.500	13	0	0	0-1	15.2	24	18	3	0	13-3	8	8.04	44	.348	.446	0	ø	0	—	-10	0	-1.1
1979	Bal A	0	0	ø	4	0	0	0-0	2.2	2	0	0	0	1-0	0	0.00	ø	.222	.273	0	ø	0	—	1	0	0.1
1980	Mil A	2	1	.667	20	1	0	2-1	37	31	20	3	0	20-2	15	3.89	101	.220	.313	0	ø	0	320	-1	0	-0.1
1982	Bal A	2	0	1.000	5	0	0	0-0	13.2	13	3	1	0	3-1	13	1.32	308	.260	.302	0	ø	0	—	4	0	0.5
Total	4	5	2	.714	42	1	0	2-2	69	70	41	7	0	37-6	36	4.17	92	.260	.345	0	ø	0	320	-6	0	-0.6
Flitcraft, Hilly	Hildreth Milton; B8.21.1923 Woodstown NJ; D4.2.2003 Boulder CO; BL/TL/6´2˝/180; d8.31; Col Rutgers																									
1942	Phi N	0	0	ø	3	0	0	0	3.1	6	4	0	0	2	1	8.10	41	.429	.500	0	ø	0	—	-2	0	-0.1
Flohr, Mort	Moritz Herman "Dutch"; B8.15.1911 Canisteo NY; D6.2.1994 Hornell NY; BL/TL/6´0˝/173; d6.8; Col Duke																									
1934	Phi A	0	2	.000	14	3	0	0	30.2	34	21	3	1	33	6	5.87	75	.296	.456	12	.333	1*	73	-5	—	-0.1
Florence, Don	Donald Emery; B3.16.1967 Manchester NH; BR/TL/6´0˝/195; d8.8; Col Crowder (MO) CC																									
1995	NY N	3	0	1.000	14	0	0	0-1	12	17	3	0	0	6-0	5	1.50	269	.340	.411	1	.000	-0	—	3	0	0.6
Flores, Jesse	Jesse (Sandoval); B11.2.1914 Guadalajara, Jalisco, Mexico; D12.17.1991 Orange CA; BR/TR/5´10˝/175; d4.16																									
1942	Chi N	0	1	.000	4	0	0	0	5.1	5	5	1	0	2	6	3.38	95	.227	.292	0	ø	0	—	-1	0	-0.2
1943	Phi A	12	14	.462	31	27	13	0	231.1	208	88	13	5	70	113	3.11	109	.240	.301	80-0-5	.175	-0	82	9	0	1.0
1944	Phi A	9	11	.450	27	25	11-2	0	185.2	172	75	8	4	49	65	3.39	103	.245	.298	64-0-6	.172	-0	92	5	0	0.4
1945	Phi A	7	10	.412	29	24	9-4	1	191.1	180	79	6	4	63	52	3.43	100	.250	.314	61-0-7	.148	-2	103	2	0	-0.2
1946	Phi A	9	7	.563	29	15	8-4	1	155	147	51	8	1	38	48	2.32	153	.249	.295	44-0-5	.250	3	85	19	0	2.2
1947	Phi A	4	13	.235	28	20	4	0	151.1	139	72	10	0	59	41	3.39	112	.244	.315	44-0-2	.227	1	59	4	0	0.4
1950	Cle A	3	3	.500	28	2	1-1	4	53	53	24	3	1	25	27	3.74	116	.261	.345	11	.000	-2	73	4	0	0.2
Total	7	44	59	.427	176	113	46-11	6	973	904	394	49	15	306	352	3.18	112	.246	.307	304-0-25	.181	-0	84	42	0	3.8
Flores, Randy	Randy Alan; B7.31.1975 Bellflower CA; BL/TL/6´0˝/180; [NYA97 9/289]; d4.23; b–Ron; Col USC																									
2002	Tex A	0	0	ø	20	0	0	1-1	12	11	7	2	0	8-2	7	4.50	106	.268	.373	0	ø	0	—	0	0	0.0
	Col N	0	2	.000	8	2	0	0-0	17	29	19	5	3	8-1	7	9.53	50	.382	.460	4	.000	-0	108	-8	0	-0.8
2004	StL N	1	0	1.000	9	1	0	0-0	14	13	3	0	3	3-1	7	1.93	221	.265	.339	2	.000	-0	196	4	0	0.2
2005	†StL N	3	1	.750	50	0	0	1-2	41.2	37	22	5	3	13-0	43	3.46	121	.240	.306	1	.000	-0	—	2	15	0.1

YEAR	TM LG	W	L	PCT	G	GS	CG-SHO	SV-BS	IP	H	R	HR	HB	BB-IB	SO	ERA	AERA	OAV	OOB	AB-HR-SH	AVG	PB	SUP	APR	DL	PW
2006	†StL N	1	1	.500	65	0	0	0-1	41.2	49	29	5	1	22-3	40	5.62	77	.290	.373	0	ø	0	—	-7	0	-0.3
Total	4	5	4	.556	152	3	0	2-4	126.1	139	80	17	10	54-7	104	4.92	89	.284	.363	7	.000	-1	141	-9	15	-0.8
Flores, Ron	Ronald Joel; B8.9.1979 Whittier CA; BL/TL/5´11˝/(190–200); [OakA00 29/870]; d6.17; b–Randy; Col USC																									
2005	Oak A	0	0	ø	11	0	0	0-0	8.2	8	1	1	0	0-0	6	1.04	422	.235	.235	0	ø	0	—	3	0	0.2
2006	Oak A	1	2	.333	25	0	0	1-0	29.2	28	11	3	0	10-2	20	3.34	136	.255	.311	1	.000	-0	—	4	0	0.4
Total	2	1	2	.333	36	0	0	1-0	38.1	36	12	4	0	10-2	26	2.82	160	.250	.295	1	.000	-0	—	7	0	0.6
Florie, Bryce	Bryce Bettencourt; B5.21.1970 Charleston SC; BR/TR/5´11˝/(190–195); [SDN88 5/110]; d7.17																									
1994	SD N	0	0	ø	9	0	0	0-0	9.1	8	1	0	0	3-0	8	0.96	429	.242	.297	0	ø	0	—	3	0	0.2
1995	SD N	2	2	.500	47	0	0	1-3	68.2	49	30	8	4	38-3	68	3.01	135	.202	.319	2	.000	-0	—	7	0	0.3
1996	SD N	2	2	.500	39	0	0	0-1	49.1	45	24	1	6	27-3	51	4.01	100	.239	.351	3	.000	-0	—	0	0	0.0
	Mil A	0	1	.000	15	0	0	0-2	19	20	16	3	0	13-2	12	6.63	78	.270	.371	0	ø	0	—	-3	0	-0.2
1997	Mil A	4	4	.500	32	8	0	0-1	75	74	43	4	3	42-2	53	4.32	107	.262	.360	0	ø	0	87	1	18	0.0
1998	Det A	8	9	.471	42	16	0	0-0	133	141	80	16	4	59-6	97	4.80	99	.275	.354	3-0-1	.333	1	72	-2	27	-0.1
1999	Det A	2	1	.667	27	3	0	0-0	51.1	61	31	6	1	20-2	40	4.56	110	.292	.355	1	.000	-0	93	1	31	0.0
	Bos A	2	0	1.000	14	2	0	0-0	30	33	19	2	1	15-3	25	4.80	104	.282	.366	0	ø	0	140	0	0	0.0
	Year	4	1	.800	41	5	0	0-0	81.1	94	50	8	2	35-5	65	4.65	107	.288	.359	1	.000	-0	112	1	0	0.0
2000	Bos A	0	4	.000	29	0	0	1-1	49.1	57	30	5	1	19-6	34	4.56	110	.294	.355	0	ø	0	—	1	91	0.2
2001	Bos A	0	1	.000	7	0	0	0-0	8.2	12	11	1	0	7-3	7	11.42	39	.316	.422	0	ø	-0	—	-6	87	-0.6
Total	8	20	24	.455	261	29	0	2-8	493.2	500	285	46	20	243-30	395	4.47	104	.265	.352	9-0-1	.111	0	85	2	254	-0.2
Flowers, Ben	Bennett; B6.15.1927 Wilson NC; BR/TR/6´4˝/195; d9.29																									
1951	Bos A	0	0	ø	1	0	0	0	3	2	0	0	0	1	2	0.00	ø	.200	.273	1	.000	-0	—	1	0	0.0
1953	Bos A	1	4	.200	32	6	1-1	3	79.1	87	39	6	1	24	36	3.86	109	.280	.333	19-0-1	.158	-0	74	3	0	0.2
1955	Det A	0	0	ø	4	0	0	0	6	5	4	1	0	2-0	2	6.00	64	.238	.292	1	.000	-0	—	-1	0	-0.1
	StL N	1	0	1.000	4	4	0	0	27.1	27	12	1	0	12-0	19	3.62	112	.255	.328	10	.100	-1	104	1	0	0.0
1956	StL N	1	1	.500	3	3	0	0	11.2	15	9	1	0	5-1	5	6.94	54	.341	.392	3	.000	-0	147	-4	0	-0.5
	Phi N	0	2	.000	32	0	0	0	41	54	29	9	1	10-1	22	5.71	65	.331	.369	2	.000	0	—	-9	0	-0.4
	Year	1	3	.250	35	3	0	0	52.2	69	38	10	1	15-2	27	5.98	62	.333	.374	5	.000	-0	149	-13	0	-0.9
Total	4	3	7	.300	76	13	1-1	3	168.1	190	93	18	2	54-2	86	4.49	90	.290	.343	36-0-1	.111	-2	100	-9	0	-0.8
Flowers, Wes	Charles Wesley; B8.13.1913 Vanndale AR; D12.31.1988 Wynne AR; BL/TL/6´1.5˝/190; d8.8																									
1940	Bro N	1	1	.500	5	2	0	0	21	23	10	2	3	10	8	3.43	117	.299	.400	5	.200	-0	54	1	—	0.1
1944	Bro N	1	1	.500	9	1	0	0	17.1	26	17	3	1	13	3	7.79	46	.333	.435	5	.600	1	212	-8	0	-0.7
Total	2	2	2	.500	14	3	0	0	38.1	49	27	5	4	23	11	5.40	70	.316	.418	10	.400	1	105	-7	0	-0.6
Floyd, Gavin	Gavin Christopher; B1.27.1983 Annapolis MD; BR/TR/6´4˝/225; [PhiN01 1/4]; d9.3																									
2004	Phi N	2	0	1.000	6	4	0	0-0	28.1	25	11	1	5	16-0	24	3.49	127	.240	.368	10	.000	-1	115	3	0	0.1
2005	Phi N	1	2	.333	7	4	0	0-0	26	30	31	5	3	16-2	17	10.04	43	.283	.389	9	.111	-0	109	-16	0	-1.5
2006	Phi N	4	3	.571	11	11	1-1	0-0	54.1	70	48	14	3	32-3	34	7.29	64	.315	.401	23	.043	-2	109	-15	0	-1.7
Total	3	7	5	.583	24	19	1-1	0-0	108.2	125	90	20	11	64-5	75	6.96	65	.289	.390	42	.048	-3	111	-28	0	-3.1
Flynn, Carney	Cornelius Francis Xavier; B1.23.1875 Cincinnati OH; D2.10.1947 Cincinnati OH; BL/TL/5´11˝/165; d7.17																									
1894	Cin N	0	2	.000	2	1	0	0	7.2	16	15	4	1	10	4	17.61	31	.421	.551	3	.000	-1	115	-8	—	-1.0
1896	NY N	0	2	.000	3	2	1	0	10.2	18	22	0	5	8	4	11.81	36	.367	.500	4-1-0	.500	2	177	-10	—	-1.1
	Was N	0	1	.000	4	1	1	0	20	43	31	0	2	10	3	8.55	52	.430	.491	8	.250	-0	97	-9	—	-0.4
	Year	0	3	.000	7	3	2	0	30.2	61	53	0	7	18	7	9.68	45	.409	.494	12-1-0	.333	1	147	-21	—	-1.5
Total	2	0	5	.000	9	4	2	0	38.1	77	68	4	8	28	11	11.27	41	.412	.507	15-1-0	.267	1	140	-27	—	-2.5
Flynn, Jocko	John A.; B6.30.1864 Lawrence MA; D12.31.1907 Lawrence MA; BR/TR/5´6.5˝/143; d5.1																									
1886	Chi N	23	6	**.793**	32	29	28-2	1	257	207	127	9	—	63	146	2.24	161	.210	.257	205-4	.200	1*	122	32	—	3.3
Flythe, Stu	Stuart McGuire; B12.5.1911 Conway NC; D10.18.1963 Durham NC; BR/TR/6´2˝/175; d5.31; Col North Carolina St.																									
1936	Phi A	0	0	ø	17	3	0	0	39.1	49	63	4	3	61	14	13.04	39	.302	.500	15	.267	0	172	-33	—	-1.4
Fodge, Gene	Gene Arlan "Suds"; B7.9.1931 South Bend IN; BR/TR/6´0˝/170; d4.20																									
1958	Chi N	1	1	.500	16	4	1	0	39.2	47	22	5	0	11-3	15	4.76	82	.296	.337	7-0-1	.000	-1	132	-3	0	-0.2
Fogarty, Jim	James G.; B2.12.1864 San Francisco CA; D5.20.1891 Philadelphia PA; BR/TR/5´10.5˝/180; d5.1; M1; b–Joe; Col St. Marys (CA); ▲																									
1884	Phi N	0	0	ø	1	0	0	0	1	2	2	0	—	0	1	0.00	ø	.333	.333	378-1	.212	0*	—	0	—	0.0
1886	Phi N	0	1	.000	1	0	0	0	6	7	6	0	—	0	4	0.00	ø	.250	.250	280-3	.293	0*	—	0	—	0.1
1887	Phi N	0	0	ø	1	0	0	0	3	3	4	0	0	1	0	9.00	47	.200	.250	495-8	.261	0*	—	-1	—	-0.1
1889	Phi N	0	0	ø	4	0	0	0	4	4	4	0	0	2	0	9.00	48	.250	.333	499-3	.259	1*	—	-1	—	-0.1
Total	4	0	1	.000	7	0	0	0	14	16	16	0	0	3	5	4.50	84	.246	.279	1652-15	.254	2	—	-2	—	-0.1
Fogg, Josh	Joshua Smith; B12.13.1976 Lynn MA; BR/TR/6´2˝/205; [ChiA98 3/89]; d9.2; Col Florida																									
2001	Chi A	0	0	ø	11	0	0	0-0	13.1	10	3	0	1	3-1	17	2.03	230	.208	.264	0	ø	0	—	4	0	0.2
2002	Pit N	12	12	.500	33	33	0	0-0	194.1	199	102	28	8	69-12	113	4.35	96	.267	.334	58-0-2	.121	-2*	80	-3	0	-0.5
2003	Pit N	10	9	.526	26	26	1	0-0	142	166	90	22	9	40-0	71	5.26	82	.293	.347	42-0-7	.190	1	122	-15	35	-1.7
2004	Pit N	11	10	.524	32	32	0	0-0	178.1	193	98	17	8	66-8	82	4.64	93	.283	.351	53-0-11	.075	-3	99	-5	0	-0.8
2005	Pit N	6	11	.353	34	28	0	0-0	169.1	196	106	27	6	53-11	85	5.05	84	.291	.346	47-0-6	.106	-1	94	-16	0	-1.6
2006	Col N	11	9	.550	31	31	1-1	0-0	172	206	115	24	6	60-13	93	5.49	87	.299	.358	51-0-15	.098	-1*	102	-13	0	-1.4
Total	6	50	51	.495	167	150	2-1	0-0	869.1	970	514	118	38	291-45	461	4.89	90	.285	.346	251-0-41	.116	-7	99	-48	35	-5.8
Foley, Curry	Charles Joseph; B1.14.1856 Milltown, Ireland; D10.20.1898 Boston MA; TL/5´10˝/160; d5.13; ▲																									
1879	Bos N	9	9	.500	21	16	16-1	0	161.2	175	111	1	—	15	57	2.51	99	.252	.268	146	.315	5*	77	-7	—	-0.3
1880	Bos N	14	14	.500	36	28	21-1	0	238	264	150	1	—	40	68	3.89	58	.274	.303	332-2	.292	8*	105	-35	—	-2.8
1881	Buf N	3	4	.429	10	6	2	0	41	70	48	1	—	5	2	5.27	53	.337	.352	375-1	.256	1*	107	-12	—	-1.5
1882	Buf N	0	0	ø	1	0	0	0	1	2	2	0	—	0	0	18.00	16	.333	.333	341-3	.305	0*	—	-1	—	-0.1
1883	Buf N	1	0	1.000	1	0	0	0	1	0	0	0	—	4	0	0.00	ø	.000	.667	111	.270	0*	—	0	—	0.1
Total	5	27	27	.500	69	50	39-2	0	442.2	511	311	3	—	64	127	3.54	68	.273	.297	1305-6	.286	14	95	-55	—	-4.6
Foley, John	John J; B10.25.1857 Brattleboro VT; TL; d9.18																									
1885	Pro N	0	1	.000	1	1	1	0	8	6	7	0	—	5	2	4.50	60	.188	.297	2	.000	0	63	-2	—	-0.2
Folkers, Rich	Richard Nevin; B10.17.1946 Waterloo IA; BL/TL/6´2˝/180; [NYN67 S1/20]; d6.10																									
1970	NY N	0	2	.000	16	1	0	2-2	29.1	36	21	6	0	25-4	15	6.44	63	.313	.433	6	.333	0	88	-7	0	-0.4
1972	StL N	1	0	1.000	9	0	0	0-1	13.1	12	5	0	0	5-0	7	3.38	102	.240	.309	1	.000	-0	—	0	0	0.0
1973	StL N	4	4	.500	34	9	1	3-0	82.1	74	34	10	3	34-4	44	3.61	102	.239	.319	20-0-1	.100	-1	93	2	0	0.1
1974	StL N	6	2	.750	55	0	0	2-2	90	65	31	4	2	38-10	57	3.00	120	.207	.292	10-0-1	.100	-1	—	7	0	0.5
1975	SD N	6	11	.353	45	15	4	0-1	142	155	70	8	1	39-3	87	4.18	84	.278	.323	36-0-4	.167	1	90	-7	0	-0.7
1976	SD N	2	3	.400	33	3	0	0-0	59.2	67	39	10	2	25-8	26	5.28	62	.279	.348	4-0-1	.000	-0	62	-14	0	-1.1
1977	Mil A	0	1	.000	3	0	0	0-1	6.1	7	7	2	0	4-1	6	4.26	96	.269	.367	0	ø	0	—	-2	0	-0.2
Total	7	19	23	.452	195	28	5	7-7	423	416	207	40	8	170-30	242	4.11	87	.258	.329	77-0-7	.143	-1	88	-21	0	-1.8
Fontenot, Joe	Joseph Daniel; B3.20.1977 Scott LA; BR/TR/6´2˝/185; [SFN95 1/16]; d5.23; [DL 1999 Fla N 27]																									
1998	Fla N	0	7	.000	8	8	0	0-0	42.2	56	34	5	5	20-1	24	6.33	64	.320	.403	10-0-1	.000	-1	51	-12	87	-1.6
Fontenot, Ray	Silton Ray; B8.8.1957 Lake Charles LA; BL/TL/6´0˝/175; [TexA79 34/815]; d6.30; Col McNeese St.																									
1983	NY A	8	2	.800	15	15	3-1	0-0	97.1	101	41	3	1	25-0	27	3.33	119	.266	.313	0	ø	0	132	7	0	0.6
1984	NY A	8	9	.471	35	24	0	0-0	169.1	189	77	8	3	58-4	85	3.61	106	.290	.349	0	ø	0	100	3	0	0.3
1985	Chi N	6	10	.375	38	23	0	0-1	154.2	177	86	23	0	45-4	70	4.36	92	.294	.342	41-0-4	.049	-3	92	-7	0	-1.0
1986	Chi N	3	5	.375	42	0	0	2-1	56	57	30	5	0	21-3	24	3.86	106	.266	.332	6	.167	-0	—	0	0	-0.1
	Min A	0	0	ø	15	0	0	0-0	16.1	27	19	3	2	4-0	10	9.92	44	.360	.407	1	.000	-0	—	-9	0	-0.4
Total	4	25	26	.490	145	62	3-1	2-2	493.2	551	253	42	6	153-11	216	4.03	98	.287	.340	48-0-4	.063	-4	104	-6	0	-0.6

YEAR	TM LG	W	L	PCT	G	GS	CG-SHO	SV-BS	IP	H	R	HR	HB	BB-IB	SO	ERA	AERA	OAV	OOB	AB-HR-SH	AVG	PB	SUP	APR	DL	PW
Foor, Jim	James Emerson; B1.13.1949 St.Louis MO; BL/TL/6´2˝/170; [DetA67 1/15]; d4.9																									
1971	Det A	0	0	ø	3	0	0	0-0	1	2	2	0	0	4-0	2	18.00	20	.400	.667	0	ø	0	—	-1	0	-0.1
1972	Det A	1	0	1.000	7	0	0	0-0	3.2	6	6	1	0	6-1	2	14.73	22	.353	.522	0	ø	0	—	-4	0	-0.9
1973	Pit N	0	0	ø	3	0	0	0-0	1.1	2	0	0	0	1-1	1	0.00	ø	.286	.375	0	ø	0	—	1	0	0.0
Total	3	1	0	1.000	13	0	0	0-0	6	10	8	1	0	11-2	5	12.00	28	.345	.525	0	ø	0	—	-4	0	-1.0
Foppert, Jesse	Jesse William; B7.10.1980 Reading PA; BR/TR/6´6˝/210; [SFN01 2/74]; d4.14; Col San Francisco																									
2003	SF N	8	9	.471	23	21	0	0-0	111	103	69	16	3	69-4	101	5.03	85	.249	.354	37	.081	-1	100	-11	39	-1.6
2004	SF N	0	0	ø	1	0	0	0-0	1	1	0	0	0	0-0	2	0.00	ø	.250	.250	0	ø	0	—	0	136	0.0
2005	SF N	0	0	ø	3	2	0	0-0	10.1	11	7	2	1	13-0	6	5.23	81	.297	.472	0	ø	0	122	-1	29	-0.1
Total	3	8	9	.471	27	23	0	0-0	122.1	115	76	18	4	82-4	109	5.00	85	.253	.364	37	.081	-1	102	-12	204	-1.7
Force, Davy	David W. "Wee Davy","Tom Thumb"; B7.27.1849 New York NY; D6.21.1918 Englewood NJ; BR/TR/5´4˝/130; d5.5.1871; ▲																									
1873	Bal NA	1	1	.500	3	1	1	0	18	23	20	0	—	1	0	2.50	136	.258	.267	233	.365	1*	154	0	—	0.1
1874	Chi NA	0	0	ø	1	0	0	0	7	22	24	4	—	0	0	15.43	14	.431	.431	294	.313	0*	—	-8	—	-0.3
Total	2NA	1	1	.500	4	1	1	0	25	45	44	4	—	1	0	6.12	50	.321	.326	527	.336	2	161	-8	—	-0.2
Ford, Ben	Benjamin Cooper; B8.15.1975 Cedar Rapids IA; BR/TR/6´7˝/(200–230); [NYA94 20/563]; d8.20; Col Indian Hills (IA) CC																									
1998	Ari N	0	0	ø	8	0	0	0-0	10	13	12	2	2	3-0	5	9.90	43	.295	.367	0	ø	0	—	-6	0	-0.3
2000	NY A	0	1	.000	4	2	0	0-0	11	14	11	1	3	7-0	5	9.00	53	.333	.462	0	ø	0	88	-5	0	-0.4
2004	Mil N	1	1	.500	19	0	0	0-3	24	25	17	4	2	10-0	13	6.38	69	.269	.349	0	ø	0	—	-4	47	-0.3
Total	3	1	2	.333	31	2	0	0-3	45	52	40	7	7	20-0	23	7.80	57	.291	.382	0	ø	0	88	-15	47	-1.0
Ford, Dave	David Alan; B12.29.1956 Cleveland OH; BR/TR/6´4˝/(195–210); [BalA75 1/23]; d9.2																									
1978	Bal A	1	0	1.000	2	1	0	0-0	15	10	0	0	0	2-0	5	0.00	ø	.196	.226	0	ø	0	25	6	0	0.4
1979	Bal A	2	1	.667	9	2	0	2-1	30	23	7	2	0	7-0	7	2.10	193	.219	.265	0	ø	0	123	7	0	0.8
1980	Bal A	1	3	.250	25	3	1	1-0	69.2	66	34	11	2	13-2	22	4.26	93	.251	.291	0	ø	0	60	-1	0	-0.1
1981	Bal A	1	2	.333	15	2	0	0-0	40	61	33	2	0	10-2	12	6.52	56	.359	.390	0	ø	0	74	-13	0	-0.9
Total	4	5	6	.455	51	8	1	3-1	154.2	160	74	15	2	32-4	46	4.02	96	.272	.310	0	ø	0	76	-1	0	0.2
Ford, Whitey	Edward Charles "The Chairman of the Board"; B10.21.1928 New York NY; BL/TL/5´10˝/(175–185); d7.1; Mil 1951–52; C4; HF1974																									
1950	†NY A	9	1	.900	20	12	7-2	1	112	87	39	7	2	52	59	2.81	153	.216	.309	36-0-4	.194	0	131	19	0	1.5
1953	†NY A	18	6	.750	32	30	11-3	0	207	187	77	13	4	110	110	3.00	123	.245	.344	75-0-1	.267	6*	151	18	0	2.5
1954	NY A★	16	8	.667	34	28	11-3	1	210.2	170	72	10	1	101	125	2.82	122	.227	.317	62-0-7	.161	2	116	17	0	2.1
1955	†NY A★	**18**	7	.720	39	33	**18**-5	2	253.2	188	83	20	1	113-7	137	2.63	143	.208	.296	86-1-3	.163	2	119	34	0	3.4
1956	†NY A★	19	6	**.760**	31	30	18-2	1	225.2	187	70	13	4	84-3	141	**2.47**	156	.228	.301	78-0-5	.218	3	110	38	0	4.6
1957	†NY A	11	5	.688	24	17	5	0	129.1	114	46	10	1	53-3	84	2.57	139	.237	.313	42-0-5	.143	-1	132	14	0	1.6
1958	†NY A☆	14	7	.667	30	29	15-**7**	1	219.1	174	62	14	3	62-3	145	**2.01**	**176**	.217	**.276**	73-0-5	.205	2	114	**37**	0	**3.9**
1959	NY A★	16	10	.615	35	29	9-2	1	204	194	82	13	1	89-5	114	3.04	120	.250	.327	65-1-3	.231	7	109	13	0	2.6
1960	†NY A★	12	9	.571	33	29	8-**4**	0	192.2	168	76	15	1	65-5	85	3.08	116	.235	.297	53-0-4	.151	2	109	11	0	1.5
1961	†NY A★	**25**	4	**.862**	39	**39**	11-3	0	**283**	242	108	23	1	92-3	209	3.21	116	.229	.291	96-0-5	.177	3	135	19	0	2.1
1962	†NY A	17	8	.680	38	37	7	0	257.2	243	90	22	4	69-1	160	2.90	129	.246	.296	85-0-3	.118	-1	107	27	0	2.7
1963	†NY A	**24**	7	**.774**	38	**37**	13-3	1	**269.1**	240	94	26	2	56-3	189	2.74	128	.241	.281	92-1-5	.141	0	116	22	0	2.5
1964	†NY A☆	17	6	.739	39	36	12-8	1	244.2	212	67	10	2	57-3	172	2.13	170	.230	.276	67-0-7	.119	1	101	39	0	3.9
1965	NY A	16	13	.552	37	36	9-2	1	244.1	241	97	22	1	50-2	162	3.24	105	.258	.296	82-0-6	.183	2*	100	6	0	1.0
1966	NY A	2	5	.286	22	9	0	0	73	79	33	8	0	24-6	43	2.47	135	.277	.330	18	.000	-2	85	3	60	0.2
1967	NY A	2	4	.333	7	7	2-1	0	44	40	11	2	0	9-0	21	1.64	191	.247	.285	13-0-2	.154	-0	92	7	0	1.1
Total	16	236	106	.690	498	438	156-45	10	3170.1	2766	1107	228	28	1086-44	1956	2.75	133	.235	.300	1023-3-65	.173	27	115	324	60	37.2
Ford, Gene	Eugene Matthew; B6.23.1912 Ft.Dodge IA; D9.7.1970 Emmetsburg IA; BR/TR/6´2˝/195; d6.17; Col Iowa																									
1936	Bos N	0	0	ø	1	0	0	0	2	2	1	0	0	0	0	4.50	85	.250	.250	0	ø	0	—	0	—	0.0
1938	Chi A	0	0	ø	4	0	0	0	14	21	16	1	0	12	2	10.29	48	.350	.458	6	.167	-0	—	-7	—	-0.3
Total	2	0	0	ø	5	0	0	0	16	23	17	1	0	12	2	9.56	50	.338	.438	6	.167	-0	—	-7	—	-0.3
Ford, Gene	Eugene Wyman; B4.16.1881 Milton NS, Can.; D8.23.1973 Dunedin FL; BR/TR/6´0˝/170; d5.5; b–Russ																									
1905	Det A	0	1	.000	7	1	1	0	35	51	30	0	2	14	20	5.66	48	.340	.404	10-0-1	.000	-1	26	-11	—	-0.6
Ford, Matt	Matthew Lee; B4.8.1981 Plantation FL; BB/TL/6´1˝/170; [TorA99 3/103]; d4.2																									
2003	Mil N	0	3	.000	25	4	0	0-0	43.2	46	23	5	1	21-0	26	4.33	100	.264	.345	7	.143	0	103	0	70	0.0
Ford, Wenty	Percival Edmund Wentworth; B11.25.1946 Nassau, Bahamas; D7.8.1980 Nassau, Bahamas; BR/TR/5´11˝/165; d9.10																									
1973	Atl N	1	2	.333	4	2	1	0-0	16.1	17	10	3	1	8-0	4	5.51	72	.279	.366	5	.400	1	145	-2	0	-0.3
Ford, Russ	Russell William; B4.25.1883 Brandon MB, Can.; D1.24.1960 Rockingham NC; BR/TR/5´11˝/175; d4.28; b–Gene																									
1909	NY A	0	0	ø	1	0	0	0	3	4	4	0	3	4	2	9.00	28	.333	.579	1	.000	-0	—	-2	—	-0.1
1910	NY A	26	6	.813	36	33	29-8	1	299.2	194	69	4	8	70	209	1.65	161	.188	.245	96-0-6	.208	4	102	34	—	4.2
1911	NY A	22	11	.667	37	33	26-1	0	281.1	251	119	3	4	76	158	2.27	158	.237	.291	102-0-4	.196	-2	99	30	—	3.0
1912	NY A	13	21	.382	36	35	30	0	291.2	317	165	11	5	79	112	3.55	101	.280	.329	112-1-7	.286	5*	92	0	—	0.6
1913	NY A	12	18	.400	33	28	15-1	2	237	244	101	9	4	58	72	2.66	113	.277	.324	74-0-2	.162	0	77	7	—	0.7
1914	Buf F	21	6	**.778**	35	26	19-5	**6**	247.1	190	63	11	7	41	123	1.82	**163**	.214	.254	78-0-4	.128	-3	92	30	—	3.0
1915	Buf F	5	9	.357	21	15	7	0	127.1	140	74	7	3	48	34	4.52	62	.285	.352	43-0-3	.279	3*	100	-22	—	-1.9
Total	7	99	71	.582	199	170	126-15	9	1487.1	1340	595	45	34	376	710	2.59	121	.244	.296	506-1-26	.209	6	94	77	—	9.5
Ford, Tom	Thomas Walter; B1866 Chattanooga TN; D5.27.1917 Chattanooga TN; 5´10.5˝/155; d5.6																									
1890	Col AA	0	0	ø	1	0	0	0	2	0	0	0	0	3	0	0.00	ø	.000	.333	1	.000	-0	—	1	—	0.0
	Bro AA	0	6	.000	7	6	6	0	49	70	60	2	0	32	12	5.14	76	.326	.413	30	.033	-3*	92	-12	—	-1.2
	Year	0	6	.000	8	6	6	0	51	70	60	2	0	35	12	4.94	79	.317	.410	31	.032	-3	92	-14	—	-1.2
Ford, Bill	William Brown; B10.14.1915 Buena Vista PA; D4.6.1994 Jefferson PA; 6´2˝/200; d9.27; Col Penn St.																									
1936	Bos N	0	0	ø	1	1	0	0	0	0	3	0	0	3	0	(3)	ø	ø	1.000	0	ø	0	155	-3	—	-0.3
Fordham, Tom	Thomas James; B2.20.1974 San Diego CA; BL/TL/6´2˝/205; [ChiA93 11/313]; d8.19; Col Grossmont (CA) JC																									
1997	Chi A	0	1	.000	7	1	0	0-1	17.1	17	13	2	1	10-2	10	6.23	71	.266	.364	0	ø	0	104	-3	0	-0.2
1998	Chi A	1	2	.333	29	5	0	0-0	48	51	36	7	1	42-0	23	6.75	68	.279	.414	1	.000	-0	89	-10	0	-0.5
Total	2	1	3	.250	36	6	0	0-1	65.1	68	49	9	2	52-2	33	6.61	69	.275	.401	1	.000	-0	92	-13	0	-0.7
Foreman, Happy	August G.; B7.20.1897 Memphis TN; D2.13.1953 New York NY; BL/TL/5´7˝/160; d9.3																									
1924	Chi A	0	0	ø	3	0	0	0	4	7	3	0	0	4	1	2.25	183	.467	.579	2	.000	-0*	—	0	—	0.0
1926	Bos A	0	0	ø	3	0	0	0	7.1	3	3	0	0	5	3	3.68	111	.130	.286	2	.000	-0	—	1	—	0.0
Total	2	0	0	ø	6	0	0	0	11.1	10	6	0	0	9	4	3.18	129	.263	.404	4	.000	-1	—	1	—	0.0
Foreman, Frank	Francis Isaiah "Monkey"; B5.1.1863 Baltimore MD; D11.19.1957 Baltimore MD; BL/TL/6´0˝/160; d5.15; b–Brownie																									
1884	CP U	1	2	.333	3	3	1	0	18	23	17	0	—	2	10	4.00	61	.291	.309	11	.091	-2	70	-3	—	-0.6
	KC U	0	1	.000	1	1	1	0	8	17	12	0	—	2	5	5.63	40	.405	.432	3	.000	-1	57	-4	—	-0.4
	Year	1	3	.250	4	4	2	0	26	40	29	0	—	4	15	4.50	53	.331	.352	14	.071	-2	68	-8	—	-1.0
1885	Bal AA	2	1	.667	3	3	2	0	27	33	32	0	1	9	11	6.00	54	.284	.341	14	.286	1	218	-9	—	-0.7
1889	Bal AA	23	21	.523	51	48	43-5	0	414	364	257	8	40	137	180	3.52	112	.229	.306	181-1	.144	-10*	83	24	—	0.9
1890	Cin N	13	10	.565	25	24	20	0	198.1	201	139	6	20	89	57	3.95	90	.254	.345	75-1	.133	-0	110	-6	—	-0.7
1891	Was AA	18	20	.474	43	41	39-1	1	345.1	381	245	9	43	142	170	3.73	100	.271	.355	153-4	.222	9*	87	-1	—	0.8
1892	Was N	2	4	.333	11	7	4	0	60	53	39	3	5	37	16	3.30	99	.227	.345	28-1	.464	8	117	-1	—	0.6
	Bal N	0	3	.000	4	3	2	0	25	40	29	4	1	11	5	6.84	50	.348	.409	23	.174	0*	80	-8	—	-0.7
	Year	2	7	.222	15	10	6	0	85	93	68	7	6	48	21	4.34	76	.267	.366	51-1	.333	8	105	-9	—	-0.1
1893	NY N	0	1	.000	2	1	0	0	5.2	19	17	1	1	10	0	27.00	17	.528	.638	3	.000	-1	90	-11	—	-1.2
1895	Cin N	11	14	.440	32	27	19	1	219	253	142	11	15	92	55	4.11	121	.285	.362	94-2-1	.309	5	85	19	—	1.9
1896	Cin N	14	7	.667	27	22	17	1	185.2	212	110	2	8	62	33	3.97	116	.285	.346	74-0-5	.243	-1	115	13	—	1.0
1901	Bos A	0	1	.000	1	1	1	0	8	8	9	1	2	2	1	9.00	39	.258	.343	4	.000	-1	77	-4	—	-0.4

YEAR	TM LG	W	L	PCT	G	GS	CG-SHO	SV-BS	IP	H	R	HR	HB	BB-IB	SO	ERA	AERA	OAV	OOB	AB-HR-SH	AVG	PB	SUP	APR	DL	PW
	Bal A	12	6	.667	24	22	18-1	1	191.1	225	120	2	6	58	41	3.67	105	.290	.344	80-0-1	.325	5	121	4	—	0.6
	Year	12	7	.632	25	23	19-1	1	199.1	233	129	3	8	60	42	3.88	99	.288	.344	84-0-1	.310	4	119	-1	—	0.2
1902	Bal A	0	2	.000	2	2	2	0	16.1	28	18	0	0	6	2	6.06	62	.378	.425	7	.429	1	76	-5	—	-0.3
Total	11	96	93	.508	229	205	169-7	4	1721.2	1857	1186	47	142	659	586	3.97	100	.268	.344	750-9-7	.224	13	97	8	—	0.8
Foreman, Brownie	John Davis; B8.6.1875 Baltimore MD; D10.10.1926 Baltimore MD; BL/TL/5´8˝/150; d7.18; b–Frank																									
1895	Pit N	8	6	.571	19	16	12	2	139.2	131	83	0	19	64	54	3.22	140	**.244**	.346	46-0-1	.065	-6	100	18	—	1.0
1896	Pit N	3	3	.500	9	9	5	0	61.2	73	55	4	8	35	18	6.57	64	.292	.396	20	.150	0	120	-15	—	-1.0
	Cin N	1	3	.250	4	4	3-1	0	23	41	30	2	2	16	9	11.35	41	.383	.472	10	.200	-0	69	-13	—	-1.5
	Year	4	6	.400	13	13	8-1	0	84.2	114	85	6	10	51	27	7.87	55	.319	.419	30	.167	-0	104	-27	—	-2.5
Total	2	12	12	.500	32	29	20-1	2	224.1	245	168	6	29	115	81	4.97	89	.274	.375	76-0-1	.105	-6	101	-10	—	-1.5
Forman, Bill	William Orange; B10.10.1886 Venango PA; D10.2.1958 Uniontown PA; BB/TR/5´11˝/180; d9.20																									
1909	Was A	0	2	.000	2	2	1	0	11	8	8	0	2	7	2	4.91	50	.211	.362	3	.333	0	44	-3	—	-0.4
1910	Was A	0	0	ø	1	0	0	0	0.2	1	1	0	0	0	0	13.50	18	.333	.333	0	ø	0	—	-1	—	0.0
Total	2	0	2	.000	3	2	1	0	11.2	9	9	0	2	7	2	5.40	45	.220	.360	3	.333	1	44	-4	—	-0.4
Fornieles, Mike	Jose Miguel (Torres); B1.18.1932 Havana, Cuba; D2.11.1998 St.Petersburg FL; BR/TR/5´11˝/(155–172); d9.2																									
1952	Was A	2	2	.500	4	2	2-1	0	26.1	13	4	1	0	11	12	1.37	260	.143	.235	10	.000	-1	86	7	0	0.9
1953	Chi A	8	7	.533	39	16	5	3	153	160	68	8	2	61	72	3.59	112	.270	.340	41-0-9	.098	-3	121	7	0	0.5
1954	Chi A	1	2	.333	15	6	0	1	42	41	24	4	0	14	18	4.29	87	.252	.309	11-0-1	.273	0*	146	-3	0	-0.2
1955	Chi A	6	3	.667	26	9	2	2	86.1	84	37	12	2	29-3	23	3.86	102	.255	.317	29-0-2	.103	-2*	115	2	0	0.0
1956	Chi A	0	1	.000	6	0	0	0	15.2	22	9	1	0	6-1	6	4.60	89	.306	.354	5-0-1	.200	0	—	-1	0	0.0
	Bal A	4	7	.364	30	11	1-1	1	111	109	59	7	0	25-2	53	3.97	99	.266	.306	30-0-1	.167	-1*	58	-3	0	-0.3
	Year	4	8	.333	36	11	1-1	1	126.2	131	68	8	0	31-3	59	4.05	97	.272	.313	35-0-2	.171	-1	57	-4	0	-0.3
1957	Bal A	2	6	.250	15	4	1-1	0	57	57	30	4	0	17-2	43	4.26	84	.257	.308	18-0-1	.278	1*	81	-5	0	-0.5
	Bos A	8	7	.533	25	18	7-1	2	125.1	136	61	7	3	38-3	64	3.52	113	.271	.324	44-0-2	.136	-2*	123	4	0	0.2
	Year	10	13	.435	40	22	8-2	2	182.1	193	91	11	3	55-5	107	3.75	103	.267	.319	62-0-3	.177	-1	118	-2	0	-0.3
1958	Bos A	4	6	.400	37	7	1	1	110.2	123	62	10	6	33-0	49	4.96	81	.284	.339	29	.207	-0	90	-8	0	-0.7
1959	Bos A	5	3	.625	46	0	0	11	82	77	29	6	1	29-3	54	3.07	132	.254	.318	19	.158	-1	—	9	0	1.1
1960	Bos A	10	5	.667	**70**	0	0	**14**	109	86	38	6	6	49-7	64	2.64	153	.219	.312	15-0-2	.400	2	—	15	0	2.6
1961	Bos A★	9	8	.529	57	2	1	15	119.1	121	65	18	2	54-7	70	4.68	89	.265	.341	32-1-1	.156	0	74	-4	0	-0.5
1962	Bos A	3	6	.333	42	1	0	5	82.1	96	57	14	8	37-4	36	5.36	77	.303	.385	16-0-1	.188	-0	0	-12	0	-1.3
1963	Bos A	0	0	ø	9	0	0	0	14	16	10	0	0	5-0	5	6.43	59	.286	.339	3	.333	1	—	-4	0	-0.1
	Min A	1	1	.500	11	0	0	0	22.2	24	14	0	2	13-0	7	4.76	76	.273	.371	6	.167	0	—	-3	0	-0.2
	Year	1	1	.500	20	0	0	0	36.2	40	24	0	2	18-0	12	5.40	68	.278	.359	9	.222	1	—	-6	0	-0.3
Total	12	63	64	.496	432	76	20-4	55	1156.2	1165	567	98	32	421-32	576	3.96	100	.263	.329	308-1-21	.169	-6	104	1	0	1.5
Forsch, Ken	Kenneth Roth; B9.8.1946 Sacramento CA; BR/TR/6´4˝/(195–215); [HouN68 18/399]; d9.7; b–Bob; Col Oregon St.; [DL 1985 Cal A 182]																									
1970	Hou N	1	2	.333	4	4	1	0-0	24	28	15	1	0	5-0	13	5.63	69	.298	.333	6-0-3	.000	-1	132	-4	0	-0.5
1971	Hou N	8	8	.500	33	23	7-2	0-0	188.1	162	60	8	4	53-5	131	2.53	133	.230	.287	59-0-3	.136	-1	88	17	0	1.2
1972	Hou N	6	8	.429	30	24	1	0-0	156.1	163	75	19	0	62-1	113	3.91	86	.273	.339	41-0-7	.146	-1	82	-10	0	-1.1
1973	Hou N	9	12	.429	46	26	5	4-3	201.1	197	101	18	4	74-7	149	4.20	87	.257	.323	62-0-5	.065	-4	119	-12	0	-1.7
1974	Hou N	8	7	.533	70	0	0	10-9	103.1	98	38	3	4	37-13	48	2.79	125	.255	.322	7-0-1	.000	-1	—	7	0	1.1
1975	Hou N	4	8	.333	34	9	2	2-2	109	114	42	9	2	30-3	54	3.22	105	.277	.325	22-0-3	.045	-1	83	2	53	0.2
1976	Hou N★	4	3	.571	52	0	0	19-7	92	76	23	5	2	26-7	49	2.15	150	.226	.284	11-0-2	.091	-0	—	13	0	1.6
1977	Hou N	5	8	.385	42	5	0	8-2	86	80	32	2	2	28-6	45	2.72	133	.246	.308	13-0-1	.077	-1	39	8	0	1.2
1978	Hou N	10	6	.625	52	6	4-2	7-4	133.1	136	44	2	1	37-13	71	2.70	124	.268	.315	27-0-2	.185	0	81	10	0	1.3
1979	Hou N	11	6	.647	26	24	10-2	0-0	177.2	155	67	14	0	35-2	58	3.04	116	.236	**.273**	58-0-6	.138	0	113	10	34	1.1
1980	†Hou N	12	13	.480	32	32	6-3	0-0	222.1	230	90	15	7	41-1	84	3.20	103	.266	.303	77-0-6	.234	4	97	3	0	0.8
1981	Cal A★	11	7	.611	20	20	10-**4**	0-0	153	143	54	7	4	27-2	55	2.88	127	.250	.286	0	ø	0	117	14	0	1.7
1982	Cal A	13	11	.542	37	35	12-4	0-0	228	225	108	25	11	57-2	73	3.87	106	.258	.309	0	ø	0	106	5	0	0.3
1983	Cal A	11	12	.478	31	31	11-1	0-0	219.1	226	107	21	4	61-6	81	4.06	100	.266	.317	0	ø	0	112	1	0	0.0
1984	Cal A	1	1	.500	2	2	1	0-0	16.1	14	4	2	0	3-0	10	2.20	181	.237	.274	0	ø	0	34	3	173	0.5
1986	Cal A	0	1	.000	10	0	0	1-1	17	24	21	4	2	10-0	13	9.53	43	.343	.429	0	ø	0	—	-11	0	-0.7
Total	16	114	113	.502	521	241	70-18	51-28	2127.1	2071	881	155	47	586-68	1047	3.37	107	.257	.309	383-0-39	.136	-5	103	56	442	7.0
Forsch, Bob	Robert Herbert; B1.13.1950 Sacramento CA; BR/TR/6´4˝/(185–215); [StLN68 26/594]; d7.7; b–Ken																									
1974	StL N	7	4	.636	19	14	5-2	0-1	100	84	38	5	1	34-4	39	2.97	122	.230	.295	29-0-6	.241	1*	124	7	0	0.9
1975	StL N	15	10	.600	34	34	7-4	0-0	230	213	89	14	3	70-8	108	2.86	133	.244	.300	78-1-6	.308	9*	97	22	0	3.5
1976	StL N	8	10	.444	33	32	2	0-1	194	209	112	17	3	71-8	76	3.94	91	.277	.339	62-1-9	.177	1*	114	-14	0	-1.1
1977	StL N	20	7	.741	35	35	8-2	0-0	217.1	210	97	20	3	69-2	95	3.48	112	.251	.310	72-0-12	.167	0	107	9	0	1.0
1978	StL N	11	17	.393	34	34	7-3	0-0	233.2	205	110	15	5	97-9	114	3.70	96	.238	.316	83-1-5	.181	3	87	-3	0	0.0
1979	StL N	11	11	.500	33	32	7-1	0-0	218.2	215	102	16	3	52-1	92	3.83	100	.262	.304	73-0-4	.110	-0	99	1	0	0.1
1980	StL N	11	10	.524	31	31	8	0-0	214.2	225	102	12	4	33-6	87	3.77	99	.273	.301	78-3-9	.295	9*	129	-1	0	1.0
1981	StL N	10	5	.667	20	20	1	0-0	124.1	106	47	7	4	29-3	41	3.18	114	.232	.281	41-0-6	.122	-1	110	6	0	0.6
1982	†StL N	15	9	.625	36	34	6-2	1-0	233	238	95	16	4	54-7	69	3.48	106	.268	.310	73-0-14	.205	3	104	7	0	0.9
1983	StL N	10	12	.455	34	30	6-2	0-0	187	190	104	23	3	54-2	56	4.28	85	.266	.317	54-1-7	.241	4*	98	-14	0	-1.1
1984	StL N	2	5	.286	16	11	1	0-0	52.1	64	38	6	0	19-0	21	6.02	58	.303	.358	16-0-1	.250	1	76	-14	94	-1.6
1985	†StL N	9	6	.600	34	19	3-1	2-0	136	132	63	11	2	47-4	48	3.90	92	.258	.322	45-1-2	.244	4	117	-3	0	0.0
1986	StL N	14	10	.583	33	33	3	0-0	230	211	91	19	2	68-11	104	3.25	114	.247	.301	76-2-11	.171	3*	104	12	0	1.5
1987	†StL N	11	7	.611	33	30	2-1	0-0	179	189	90	15	4	45-4	89	4.32	97	.273	.318	57-2-11	.298	8*	121	-1	0	0.7
1988	StL N	9	4	.692	30	12	1-1	0-0	108.2	111	51	8	1	38-8	40	3.73	95	.270	.330	25-0-5	.280	2*	97	-3	0	-0.2
	Hou N	1	4	.200	6	6	0	0-0	27.2	42	22	2	2	6-1	14	6.51	51	.359	.385	7-0-1	.143	0	62	-10	0	-1.5
	Year	10	8	.556	36	18	1-1	0-0	136.1	153	73	10	3	44-9	54	4.29	81	.290	.342	32-0-6	.250	2	85	-12	0	-1.7
1989	Hou N	4	5	.444	37	15	0	0-0	108.1	133	68	10	1	46-6	40	5.32	64	.303	.367	24-0-6	.167	-0	107	-22	0	-1.8
Total	16	168	136	.553	498	422	67-19	3-2	2794.2	2777	1319	216	45	832-84	1133	3.76	98	.261	.315	893-12-115	.213	47	106	-21	94	2.9
Forster, Scott	Scott Christian; B10.27.1971 Philadelphia PA; BR/TL/6´1˝/194; [MonN94 6/168]; d6.18; Col James Madison																									
2000	Mon N	0	1	.000	42	0	0	0-0	32	28	31	5	2	25-1	23	7.88	60	.230	.362	0	ø	0	—	-11	0	-0.5
Forster, Terry	Terry Jay; B1.14.1952 Sioux Falls SD; BL/TL/6´3˝/(185–230); [ChiA70 2/30]; d4.11																									
1971	Chi A	2	3	.400	45	3	0	1-0	49.2	46	23	5	1	23-3	48	3.99	89	.241	.323	5	.400	1	75	-1	0	0.0
1972	Chi A	6	5	.545	62	0	0	29-6	100	75	31	0	3	44-3	104	2.25	139	.208	.296	19-0-2	.526	4*	—	8	0	2.1
1973	Chi A	6	11	.353	51	12	4	16-3	172.2	174	69	7	0	78-6	120	3.23	122	.266	.342	1	.000	-0*	68	14	0	1.8
1974	Chi A	7	8	.467	59	1	0	**24**-10	134.1	120	57	6	8	48-3	105	3.62	104	.245	.319	0	ø	0	24	4	0	0.7
1975	Chi A	3	3	.500	17	1	0	4-3	37	30	12	0	0	24-4	32	2.19	178	.236	.358	0	ø	0	136	6	101	1.2
1976	Chi A	2	12	.143	29	16	1	1-0	111.1	126	61	7	1	41-4	70	4.37	82	.288	.350	0	ø	0	82	-11	0	-1.2
1977	Pit N	6	4	.600	33	6	0	1-2	87.1	90	47	7	2	32-3	58	4.43	91	.269	.332	26-0-1	.346	3*	77	-3	0	-0.1
1978	†LA N	5	4	.556	47	0	0	22-4	65.1	56	19	2	0	23-4	46	1.93	182	.233	.300	8-0-1	.500	2	—	10	0	2.4
1979	LA N	1	2	.333	17	0	0	2-0	16.1	18	11	0	0	11-4	8	5.51	66	.295	.397	0	ø	0	—	-3	100	-0.6
1980	LA N	0	0	ø	9	0	0	0-0	11.2	10	4	0	0	4-0	2	3.09	113	.222	.286	0	ø	0	—	1	123	0.1
1981	†LA N	0	1	.000	21	0	0	0-1	30.2	37	14	1	0	15-3	17	4.11	80	.308	.385	2	.000	-0	—	-2	0	-0.1
1982	LA N	5	6	.455	56	0	0	3-2	83	66	38	3	4	31-9	52	3.04	114	.221	.298	2	.000	-0	—	1	0	0.2
1983	Atl N	3	2	.600	56	0	0	13-3	79.1	60	19	3	2	31-9	54	2.16	179	.217	.301	8-0-1	.500	2	—	15	0	1.6
1984	Atl N	2	0	1.000	25	0	0	5-0	26.2	30	9	1	0	7-3	10	2.70	143	.297	.339	3	.667	1	—	3	79	0.4
1985	Atl N	2	3	.400	46	0	0	1-2	59.1	49	22	7	0	28-4	37	2.28	169	.222	.307	4-0-1	.000	-0	—	8	0	0.6
1986	Cal A	4	1	.800	41	0	0	5-3	41	47	18	2	3	17-1	28	3.51	118	.297	.374	0	ø	0	—	3	55	0.4
Total	16	54	65	.454	614	39	5	127-39	1105.2	1034	454	51	24	457-63	791	3.23	115	.251	.327	78-0-6	.397	11	77	53	458	9.5
Fortugno, Tim	Timothy Shawn; B4.11.1962 Clinton MA; BL/TL/6´1˝/185; d7.20; Col Vanguard																									
1992	Cal A	1	1	.500	14	5	1-1	1-0	41.2	37	24	5	0	19-0	31	5.18	78	.236	.316	0	ø	0	127	-4	0	-0.2
1994	Cin N	1	0	1.000	25	0	0	0-0	30	32	14	2	3	14-0	29	4.20	100	.288	.380	3	.333	0	—	1	0	0.1
1995	Chi A	1	3	.250	37	0	0	0-1	38.2	30	24	7	0	19-2	24	5.59	80	.213	.302	0	ø	0	—	-4	0	-0.3
Total	3	3	4	.429	76	5	1-1	1-1	110.1	99	62	14	3	52-2	84	5.06	84	.242	.329	3	.333	0	127	-7	0	-0.4

YEAR	TM LG	W	L	PCT	G	GS	CG-SHO	SV-BS	IP	H	R	HR	HB	BB-IB	SO	ERA	AERA	OAV	OOB	AB-HR-SH	AVG	PB	SUP	APR	DL	PW
Fortunato, Bartolome	Bartolome; B8.24.1974 Santo Domingo, D.R.; BR/TR/6´1˝/195; d6.29; [DL 2005 NY N 183]																									
2004	TB A	0	0	ø	3	0	0	0-0	7.1	10	3	1	0	2-0	5	3.68	127	.357	.400	0	ø	0	—	1	0	0.0
	NY N	1	0	1.000	15	0	0	1-1	18.2	14	8	2	0	13-0	20	3.86	111	.203	.329	0	ø	0	—	1	0	0.1
2006	NY N	1	0	1.000	2	0	0	0-0	3	7	9	2	1	2-0	0	27.00	16	.467	.556	0	ø	0	—	-7	15	-1.1
Total	2	2	0	1.000	20	0	0	1-1	29	31	20	5	1	17-0	25	6.21	71	.277	.377	0	ø	0	—	-5	198	-1.0
Fortune, Gary	Garrett Reese; B10.11.1894 High Point NC; D9.23.1955 Washington DC; BB/TR/5´11.5˝/176; d10.5																									
1916	Phi N	0	1	.000	1	1	0	0	5	2	2	0	0	4	3	3.60	74	.118	.286	2	.000	-0	28	0	—	-0.1
1918	Phi N	0	2	.000	5	2	1	0	31	41	30	2	1	19	10	8.13	37	.333	.427	10	.200	0	114	-14	—	-0.8
1920	Bos A	0	2	.000	14	3	1	0	41.2	46	32	0	0	23	10	5.83	63	.282	.371	12	.167	-0	94	-11	—	-0.6
Total	3	0	5	.000	20	6	2	0	77.2	89	64	2	1	46	23	6.61	51	.294	.389	24	.167	-0	89	-25	—	-1.5
Fosnow, Jerry	Gerald Eugene; B9.21.1940 Deshler OH; BR/TL/6´4˝/195; d6.29																									
1964	Min A	0	1	.000	7	0	0	0	10.2	13	13	3	0	8-0	9	10.97	33	.302	.404	0	ø	0	—	-8	0	-0.7
1965	Min A	3	3	.500	29	0	0	2	46.2	33	29	7	1	25-2	35	4.44	80	.193	.299	5	.000	-1	—	-5	0	-0.7
Total	2	3	4	.429	36	0	0	2	57.1	46	42	10	1	33-2	44	5.65	63	.215	.321	5	.000	-1	—	-13	0	-1.4
Foss, Larry	Larry Curtis; B4.18.1936 Castleton KS; BR/TR/6´2˝/195; d9.18; Col Wichita St.																									
1961	Pit N	1	1	.500	3	3	0	0	15.1	15	11	3	2	11-0	9	5.87	68	.273	.406	6	.167	-0	96	-3	0	-0.4
1962	NY N	0	1	.000	5	1	0	0	11.2	17	6	2	1	7-0	3	4.63	90	.362	.446	1	.000	-0	126	0	0	0.0
Total	2	1	2	.333	8	4	0	0	27	32	17	5	3	18-0	12	5.33	76	.314	.424	7	.143	-0	103	-3	0	-0.4
Fossas, Tony	Emilio Antonio (Morejon); B9.23.1957 Havana, Cuba; BL/TL/6´0˝/(187–198); [TexA79 12/303]; d5.15; Col South Florida																									
1988	Tex A	0	0	ø	5	0	0	0-0	5.2	11	3	0	0	2-0	0	4.76	86	.423	.464	0	ø	0	—	0	0	0.0
1989	Mil A	2	2	.500	51	0	0	1-2	61	57	27	3	1	22-7	42	3.54	109	.256	.321	0	ø	0	—	2	0	0.2
1990	Mil A	2	3	.400	32	0	0	0-2	29.1	44	23	5	0	10-2	24	6.44	60	.331	.375	0	ø	0	—	-8	0	-1.2
1991	Bos A	3	2	.600	64	0	0	1-1	57	49	27	3	3	28-9	29	3.47	125	.236	.335	0	ø	0	—	4	0	0.4
1992	Bos A	1	2	.333	60	0	0	2-1	29.2	31	9	1	1	14-3	19	2.43	175	.279	.365	0	ø	0	—	6	0	0.6
1993	Bos A	1	1	.500	71	0	0	0-2	40	38	28	4	2	15-4	39	5.17	90	.242	.314	0	ø	0	—	-3	0	-0.1
1994	Bos A	2	0	1.000	44	0	0	1-0	34	35	18	6	1	15-1	31	4.76	106	.263	.342	0	ø	0	—	2	0	0.1
1995	StL N	3	0	1.000	58	0	0	0-0	36.2	28	6	1	1	10-3	40	1.47	291	.214	.273	0	ø	0	—	12	0	0.8
1996	†StL N	0	4	.000	65	0	0	2-5	47	43	19	7	0	21-3	36	2.68	158	.231	.308	1	.000	-0	—	6	0	0.5
1997	StL N	2	7	.222	71	0	0	0-1	51.2	62	32	7	1	26-3	41	3.83	109	.298	.377	0	ø	0	—	-1	0	-0.1
1998	Sea A	0	3	.000	23	0	0	0-1	11.1	19	11	1	0	6-0	10	8.74	54	.404	.463	0	ø	0	—	-5	0	-0.8
	Chi N	0	0	ø	8	0	0	0-0	4	8	4	0	0	6-0	6	9.00	49	.421	.560	0	ø	0	—	-2	0	-0.1
	Tex A	1	0	1.000	10	0	0	0-0	7.1	3	0	0	0	4-0	7	0.00	ø	.120	.241	0	ø	0	—	4	0	0.4
1999	NY A	0	0	ø	5	0	0	0-0	1	6	4	1	0	1-1	0	36.00	13	.667	.700	0	ø	0	—	-3	0	-0.2
Total	12	17	24	.415	567	0	0	7-15	415.2	434	211	39	10	180-36	324	3.90	110	.269	.344	1	.000	-0	—	14	0	0.5
Fossum, Casey	Casey Paul; B1.6.1978 Cherry Hill NJ; BL/TL/6´1˝/160; [BosA99 1/48]; d7.28; Col Texas A&M																									
2001	Bos A	3	2	.600	13	7	0	0-0	44.1	44	26	4	6	20-1	26	4.87	91	.259	.355	0	ø	0	119	-2	0	-0.2
2002	Bos A	5	4	.556	43	12	0	1-0	106.2	113	56	12	4	30-0	101	3.46	129	.268	.320	0	ø	0	97	7	0	0.5
2003	Bos A	6	5	.545	19	14	0	1-0	79	82	55	9	4	34-0	63	5.47	85	.270	.348	0	ø	0*	137	-8	39	-0.9
2004	Ari N	4	15	.211	27	27	0	0-0	142	171	111	31	10	63-5	117	6.65	69	.302	.379	42-0-3	.095	-2*	65	-28	40	-3.3
2005	TB A	8	12	.400	36	25	0	0-1	162.2	170	100	21	18	60-3	128	4.92	89	.266	.343	2-0-1	.000	-0	87	-10	0	-1.1
2006	TB A	6	6	.500	25	25	0	0-0	130	136	89	18	12	63-3	88	5.33	87	.265	.356	2	.000	-0	120	-12	15	-0.9
Total	6	32	44	.421	163	110	0	2-1	664.2	716	437	95	54	270-12	523	5.20	87	.274	.351	46-0-4	.087	-3	99	-53	94	-5.9
Foster, Alan	Alan Benton; B12.8.1946 Pasadena CA; BR/TR/6´0˝/(176–180); [LAN65 2/28]; d4.25																									
1967	LA N	0	1	.000	4	2	0	0	16.2	10	4	0	0	3-0	15	2.16	143	.169	.210	4	.000	-0	28	2	0	0.1
1968	LA N	1	1	.500	3	3	0	0	15.2	11	4	1	0	2-0	10	1.72	161	.200	.228	4-0-1	.250	0	63	2	0	0.3
1969	LA N	3	9	.250	24	15	2-2	0-0	102.2	119	55	11	4	29-4	59	4.38	76	.290	.341	27-0-3	.074	-1	93	-12	0	-1.4
1970	LA N	10	13	.435	33	33	7-1	0-0	198.2	200	104	22	2	81-2	83	4.26	90	.264	.334	64-0-8	.109	-2	112	-10	0	-1.2
1971	Cle A	8	12	.400	36	26	3	0-0	181.2	158	93	19	4	82-5	97	4.16	93	.232	.316	51-0-7	.039	-4*	69	-6	0	-1.3
1972	Cal A	0	1	.000	8	0	0	0-1	12.2	12	8	3	2	6-0	11	4.97	59	.245	.351	0	ø	0	—	-3	0	-0.2
1973	StL N	13	9	.591	35	29	6-2	0-0	203.2	195	82	17	5	63-3	106	3.14	117	.254	.313	68-0-5	.191	1	107	12	0	1.2
1974	StL N	7	10	.412	31	25	5-1	0-0	162.1	167	81	16	3	61-7	78	3.88	93	.268	.335	48-0-7	.167	-1*	94	-6	0	-0.7
1975	SD N	3	1	.750	17	4	1	0-0	44.2	41	14	1	0	21-5	20	2.42	145	.244	.326	11	.091	-1*	94	6	71	0.4
1976	SD N	3	6	.333	26	11	2	0-0	86.2	75	36	9	1	35-2	22	3.22	102	.235	.311	18-0-3	.056	-0*	73	0	0	0.0
Total	10	48	63	.432	217	148	26-6	0-1	1025.1	988	481	99	21	383-28	501	3.74	97	.254	.322	295-0-34	.119	-8	94	-15	71	-2.8
Foster, Ed	Eddy Lee "Slim"; B GA; D3.1.1929 Montgomery AL; BR/TR/6´1˝/?; d7.31																									
1908	Cle A	1	0	1.000	6	1	1	2	21	16	5	1	2	12	11	2.14	111	.229	.357	6	.000	-0	143	1	—	0.0
Foster, Rube	George; B1.5.1888 Lehigh OK; D3.1.1976 Bokoshe OK; BR/TR/5´7.5˝/170; d4.10																									
1913	Bos A	3	3	.500	19	8	4-1	0	68.1	64	35	1	4	28	36	3.16	93	.252	.336	21	.095	-1*	88	-2	—	-0.3
1914	Bos A	14	8	.636	32	27	17-5	0	211.2	164	68	2	7	52	89	1.70	158	.218	.274	63-0-5	.175	0*	89	18	—	2.0
1915	†Bos A	19	8	.704	37	33	21-5	1	255.1	217	83	3	10	86	82	2.11	131	.237	.310	83-1-9	.277	7*	105	19	—	2.9
1916	†Bos A	14	7	.667	33	19	9-3	2	182.1	173	73	0	4	86	53	3.06	90	.263	.352	62-0-2	.177	0*	98	-5	—	-0.4
1917	Bos A	8	7	.533	17	16	9-1	0	124.2	108	43	0	4	53	34	2.53	102	.243	.329	41-0-3	.268	2	110	2	—	0.5
Total	5	58	33	.637	138	103	60-15	3	842.1	726	302	6	29	305	294	2.36	116	.240	.316	270-1-19	.215	9	99	32	—	4.7
Foster, Kris	John Kristian; B8.30.1974 Riverdale NJ; BR/TR/6´1˝/200; [MonN92 39/1079]; d8.3; Col Edison (FL) CC; [DL 2000 LA N 181]																									
2001	Bal A	0	0	ø	7	0	0	0-0	10	9	4	1	0	8-0	8	2.70	160	.231	.362	0	ø	0	—	2	0	0.1
Foster, John	John Norman; B5.17.1978 Stockton CA; BL/TL/6´0˝/200; [AtlN99 25/774]; d4.24; Col Lewis–Clark St.; [DL 2006 Atl N 182]																									
2002	Atl N	1	0	1.000	5	0	0	0-0	5	6	6	3	1	6-0	6	10.80	37	.286	.464	0	ø	0	—	-4	43	-0.6
2003	Mil N	2	0	1.000	23	0	0	0-2	21	30	11	5	1	8-2	16	4.71	92	.341	.398	0	ø	0	—	-1	0	-0.1
2005	†Atl N	4	2	.667	62	0	0	1-1	34.2	27	17	3	2	19-0	32	4.15	102	.213	.324	0	ø	0	—	0	0	0.1
Total	3	7	2	.778	90	0	0	1-3	60.2	63	34	11	4	33-2	54	4.90	87	.267	.365	0	ø	0	—	-5	225	-0.6
Foster, Kevin	Kevin Christopher; B1.13.1969 Evanston IL; BR/TR/6´1˝/(160–175); [MonN87 29/746]; d9.12; Col Kishwaukee (IL) CC																									
1993	Phi N	0	1	.000	2	1	0	0-0	6.2	13	11	3	0	7-0	6	14.85	27	.394	.500	2	.000	-0	23	-8	0	-0.8
1994	Chi N	3	4	.429	13	13	0	0-0	81	70	31	7	1	35-1	75	2.89	146	.234	.315	27-0-3	.074	-2	81	11	0	0.6
1995	Chi N	12	11	.522	30	28	0	0-0	167.2	149	90	32	6	65-4	146	4.51	93	.240	.315	60-1-5	.250	5*	117	-4	0	-0.1
1996	Chi N	7	6	.538	17	16	1	0-0	87	98	63	16	2	35-3	53	6.21	70	.288	.354	27-0-3	.296	5*	103	-16	0	-1.5
1997	Chi N	10	7	.588	26	25	1	0-0	146.1	141	79	27	2	66-4	118	4.61	94	.255	.333	47-0-11	.128	-1*	106	-4	15	-0.6
1998	Chi N	0	0	ø	3	0	0	0-0	3.1	8	6	1	0	2-0	3	16.20	27	.500	.500	0	ø	0	—	-4	70	-0.2
2001	Tex A	0	1	.000	9	0	0	0-0	17.2	21	14	2	3	10-0	16	6.62	72	.309	.415	0	ø	0	—	-3	0	-0.2
Total	7	32	30	.516	100	83	2	0-0	509.2	500	294	88	14	220-12	417	4.86	88	.259	.336	163-1-22	.190	7	104	-28	85	-2.8
Foster, Larry	Larry Lynn; B12.24.1937 Lansing MI; BL/TR/6´0˝/180; d9.18; Col Michigan St.																									
1963	Det A	0	0	ø	1	0	0	0	2	4	3	0	0	1-0	1	13.50	28	.364	.417	0	ø	0	—	-2	0	-0.1
Foster, Steve	Stephen Eugene; B8.16.1966 Dallas TX; BR/TR/6´0˝/180; [CinN88 12/306]; d8.22; Col Texas–Arlington; [DL 1994 Cin N 131]																									
1991	Cin N	0	0	ø	11	0	0	0-0	14	7	5	1	0	4-0	11	1.93	197	.143	.208	0	ø	0	—	2	0	0.1
1992	Cin N	1	1	.500	31	1	0	2-1	50	52	16	4	0	13-1	34	2.88	125	.275	.319	5	.200	0	25	5	0	0.3
1993	Cin N	2	2	.500	17	0	0	0-0	25.2	23	8	1	1	5-2	16	1.75	230	.235	.279	0-0-1	ø	0	—	5	134	0.7
Total	3	3	3	.500	59	1	0	2-1	89.2	82	29	6	1	22-3	61	2.41	156	.244	.291	5-0-1	.200	0	25	12	265	1.1
Foucault, Steve	Steven Raymond; B10.3.1949 Duluth MN; BL/TR/6´0˝/(180–205); [TexA69 43/910]; d4.7; Col South Georgia JC																									
1973	Tex A	2	4	.333	32	0	0	8-6	55.2	54	26	6	3	31-4	28	3.88	97	.262	.364	0	ø	0	—	0	59	0.0
1974	Tex A	8	9	.471	69	0	0	12-8	144.1	123	51	8	5	40-5	106	2.24	160	.234	.291	0	ø	0	—	17	0	2.3
1975	Tex A	8	4	.667	59	0	0	10-9	107	96	57	10	4	55-15	56	4.12	92	.249	.344	0	ø	0	—	-4	0	-0.6
1976	Tex A	8	8	.500	46	0	0	5-5	75.2	68	31	9	4	25-7	41	3.33	108	.249	.318	0	ø	0	—	3	0	0.7
1977	Det A	7	7	.500	44	0	0	13-5	74.1	64	29	7	0	17-4	58	3.15	137	.226	.270	0	ø	0	—	9	0	1.8

YEAR	TM LG	W	L	PCT	G	GS	CG-SHO	SV-BS	IP	H	R	HR	HB	BB-IB	SO	ERA	AERA	OAV	OOB	AB-HR-SH	AVG	PB	SUP	APR	DL	PW
1978	Det A	2	4	.333	24	0	0	4-0	37.1	48	18	1	1	21-4	18	3.13	124	.324	.405	0	ø	0	—	1	0	0.2
	KC A	0	0	ø	3	0	0	0-0	2.1	5	1	0	0	1-1	0	3.86	99	.417	.462	0	ø	0	—	0	0	0.0
	Year	2	4	.333	27	0	0	4-0	39.2	53	19	1	1	22-5	18	3.18	123	.331	.409	0	ø	0	—	2	0	0.2
Total	6	35	36	.493	277	0	0	52-33	496.2	458	213	41	17	190-40	307	3.21	118	.250	.323	0	ø	0	—	26	59	4.4

Foulke, Keith Keith Charles; B10.19.1972 San Diego CA; BR/TR/6´0˝/(195–210); [SFN94 9/256]; d5.21; Col Lewis–Clark St.

YEAR	TM LG	W	L	PCT	G	GS	CG-SHO	SV-BS	IP	H	R	HR	HB	BB-IB	SO	ERA	AERA	OAV	OOB	AB-HR-SH	AVG	PB	SUP	APR	DL	PW
1997	SF N	1	5	.167	11	8	0	0-1	44.2	60	41	9	4	18-1	33	8.26	50	.324	.396	13-0-2	.154	-0	70	-19	0	-2.0
	Chi A	3	0	1.000	16	0	0	3-2	28.2	28	11	4	0	5-1	21	3.45	128	.255	.284	0	ø	0	—	4	0	0.4
1998	Chi A	3	2	.600	54	0	0	1-1	65.1	51	31	9	4	20-3	57	4.13	111	.213	.283	0	ø	0	—	4	31	0.3
1999	Chi A	3	3	.500	67	0	0	9-4	105.1	72	28	11	3	21-4	123	2.22	222	.188	.235	2	.000	-0	—	**32**	0	2.0
2000	†Chi A	3	1	.750	72	0	0	34-5	88	66	31	9	2	22-2	91	2.97	171	.207	.261	0	ø	0	—	21	0	2.1
2001	Chi A	4	9	.308	72	0	0	42-3	81	57	21	3	8	22-1	75	2.33	200	.199	.274	0	ø	0	—	**21**	0	4.2
2002	Chi A	2	4	.333	65	0	0	11-3	77.2	65	26	7	2	13-2	58	2.90	156	.225	.263	1	.000	-0	—	14	0	1.3
2003	†Oak A★	9	1	.900	72	0	0	**43**-5	86.2	57	21	10	7	20-2	88	2.08	221	.184	.249	0	ø	0	—	24	0	4.8
2004	†Bos A	5	3	.625	72	0	0	32-7	83	63	22	8	6	15-5	79	2.17	225	.206	.254	0	ø	0	—	24	0	3.8
2005	Bos A	5	5	.500	43	0	0	15-4	45.2	53	30	8	5	18-1	34	5.91	77	.288	.365	0	ø	0	—	-6	58	-1.1
2006	Bos A	3	1	.750	44	0	0	0-0	49.2	52	24	9	2	7-0	36	4.35	107	.271	.298	0	ø	0	—	2	67	0.1
Total	10	41	34	.547	588	8	0	190-35	755.2	624	286	87	43	181-22	695	3.30	142	.223	.279	16-0-2	.125	-1	70	121	156	15.9

Fournier, Henry Julius Henry "Frenchy"; B8.8.1865 Syracuse NY; D12.8.1945 Detroit MI; TL; d8.22

YEAR	TM LG	W	L	PCT	G	GS	CG-SHO	SV-BS	IP	H	R	HR	HB	BB-IB	SO	ERA	AERA	OAV	OOB	AB-HR-SH	AVG	PB	SUP	APR	DL	PW
1894	Cin N	1	3	.250	6	4	4	0	45	71	51	4	2	20	5	5.40	103	.353	.417	19	.105	-3	73	-4	—	-0.4

Foutz, Dave David Luther "Scissors"; B9.7.1856 Carroll Co. MD; D3.5.1897 Waverly MD; BR/TR/6´2˝/161; d7.29; M4; b–Frank; ▲

YEAR	TM LG	W	L	PCT	G	GS	CG-SHO	SV-BS	IP	H	R	HR	HB	BB-IB	SO	ERA	AERA	OAV	OOB	AB-HR-SH	AVG	PB	SUP	APR	DL	PW
1884	StL AA	15	6	.714	25	25	19-2	0	206.2	167	100	7	9	36	95	2.18	150	.212	.255	119	.227	1*	100	22	—	2.2
1885	†StL AA	33	14	.702	47	46	46-2	0	407.2	351	200	8	18	92	147	2.63	125	.227	.278	238	.248	5*	114	29	—	3.5
1886	†StL AA	**41**	16	**.719**	59	57	55-11	**1**	504	418	216	5	10	144	283	**2.11**	**163**	.216	.274	414-3	.280	11*	112	71	—	**7.6**
1887	†StL AA	25	12	.676	40	38	36-1	0	339.1	369	244	7	10	90	94	3.87	117	.258	.306	423-4	.357	15*	123	16	—	2.4
1888	Bro AA	12	7	.632	23	19	19	0	176	146	85	3	5	35	73	2.51	119	.218	.262	563-3	.277	6*	92	10	—	1.5
1889	†Bro AA	3	0	1.000	12	4	3	0	59.2	70	50	2	0	19	21	4.37	85	.283	.335	553-6	.275	3*	158	-7	—	-0.1
1890	†Bro N	2	1	.667	5	2	2	**2**	29	29	10	0	1	6	4	1.86	185	.252	.295	509-5	.303	2*	46	5	—	0.6
1891	Bro N	3	2	.600	6	5	5	0	52	51	24	1	1	16	14	3.29	100	.246	.304	521-2	.257	1*	98	2	—	0.3
1892	Bro N	13	8	.619	27	20	17	1	203	210	119	3	4	63	56	3.41	93	.256	.313	220-1	.186	0*	122	-9	—	-0.6
1893	Bro N	0	0	ø	6	0	0	0	18	28	17	2	0	8	3	7.50	59	.346	.404	557-7	.246	1*	—	-5	—	-0.1
1894	Bro N	0	0	ø	1	0	0	0	2	4	3	0	0	1	0	13.50	37	.400	.455	297-0-8	.303	0*	—	-2	—	-0.1
Total	11	147	66	.690	251	216	202-16	4	1997.1	1843	1068	38	58	510	790	2.84	124	.235	.286	4414-31-8	.276	45	113	132	—	17.2

Fowler, Jesse Jesse Peter "Pete"; B10.30.1898 Spartanburg SC; D9.23.1973 Columbia SC; BR/TL/5´10.5˝/158; d7.29; b–Art

YEAR	TM LG	W	L	PCT	G	GS	CG-SHO	SV-BS	IP	H	R	HR	HB	BB-IB	SO	ERA	AERA	OAV	OOB	AB-HR-SH	AVG	PB	SUP	APR	DL	PW
1924	StL N	1	1	.500	13	3	0	0	32.2	28	21	0	2	18	5	4.41	86	.226	.333	9	.222	0	82	-3	—	-0.2

Fowler, Art John Arthur; B7.3.1922 Converse SC; BR/TR/5´11˝/(180–185); d4.17; C15; b–Jesse

YEAR	TM LG	W	L	PCT	G	GS	CG-SHO	SV-BS	IP	H	R	HR	HB	BB-IB	SO	ERA	AERA	OAV	OOB	AB-HR-SH	AVG	PB	SUP	APR	DL	PW
1954	Cin N	12	10	.545	40	29	8-1	0	227.2	256	112	20	4	85	93	3.83	109	.286	.348	60-0-12	.100	-1	90	7	0	0.4
1955	Cin N	11	10	.524	46	28	8-3	2	207.2	198	96	20	1	63-3	94	3.90	109	.250	.303	60-0-7	.200	-0	83	10	0	0.9
1956	Cin N	11	11	.500	45	23	8	1	177.2	191	92	15	0	35-3	86	4.05	98	.278	.311	48-0-5	.146	-0	92	-3	0	-0.3
1957	Cin N	3	0	1.000	33	7	1	0	87.2	111	65	11	2	24-2	45	6.47	64	.310	.355	17-0-3	.176	0	156	-20	0	-1.0
1959	LA N	3	4	.429	36	0	0	2	61	70	39	8	0	23-7	47	5.31	80	.294	.350	12-0-1	.083	-1	—	-6	0	-0.8
1961	LA A	5	8	.385	53	3	0	11	89	68	42	12	0	29-3	78	3.64	124	.209	.272	13-0-3	.077	-1	72	7	0	1.0
1962	LA A	4	3	.571	48	0	0	5	77	67	25	6	1	25-3	38	2.81	138	.234	.296	11	.273	1	—	11	0	1.1
1963	LA A	5	3	.625	57	0	0	10	89.1	70	26	5	0	19-8	53	2.42	142	.219	.260	9-0-2	.222	0	—	11	0	1.3
1964	LA A	0	2	.000	4	0	0	1	7	8	8	2	1	5-2	5	10.29	32	.296	.424	1	.000	-0	—	-5	0	-1.0
Total	9	54	51	.514	362	90	25-4	32	1024	1039	505	99	9	308-31	539	4.03	102	.265	.317	231-0-33	.152	-2	94	12	0	1.6

Fowler, Dick Richard John; B3.30.1921 Toronto ON, Can.; D5.22.1972 Oneonta NY; BR/TR/6´4.5˝/(195–215); d9.13; Mil 1943–45

YEAR	TM LG	W	L	PCT	G	GS	CG-SHO	SV-BS	IP	H	R	HR	HB	BB-IB	SO	ERA	AERA	OAV	OOB	AB-HR-SH	AVG	PB	SUP	APR	DL	PW
1941	Phi A	1	2	.333	4	3	1	0	24	26	11	4	0	8	8	3.38	124	.289	.347	9	.000	-1	131	2	0	0.1
1942	Phi A	6	11	.353	31	17	4	1	140	159	90	13	0	45	38	4.95	76	.287	.341	50-0-1	.160	-1*	65	-17	0	-2.1
1945	Phi A	1	2	.333	7	3	2-1	0	37.1	41	21	1	0	18	21	4.82	71	.283	.362	18	.444	3*	33	-5	0	0.0
1946	Phi A	9	16	.360	32	28	14-1	0	205.2	213	101	16	2	75	89	3.28	108	.263	.327	71-0-2	.183	-1	75	0	0	-0.1
1947	Phi A	12	11	.522	36	31	16-3	0	227.1	210	77	12	3	85	75	2.81	136	.249	.319	82-0-4	.171	-3	105	26	0	2.1
1948	Phi A	15	8	.652	29	26	16-2	2	204.2	221	93	15	4	76	50	3.78	113	.281	.348	82-1-4	.171	-2	113	12	0	0.9
1949	Phi A	15	11	.577	31	28	15-4	1	213.2	210	108	13	2	115	43	3.75	110	.262	.357	77-0-2	.234	3	102	5	0	0.9
1950	Phi A	1	5	.167	11	9	2	0	66.2	75	52	7	3	56	15	6.48	70	.300	.434	26	.192	-1	59	-14	0	-1.1
1951	Phi A	5	11	.313	22	22	4	0	125	141	89	11	1	72	29	5.62	76	.291	.384	42-0-1	.190	-0	96	-19	0	-2.1
1952	Phi A	1	2	.333	18	3	1	0	58.2	71	43	4	4	28	14	6.44	61	.302	.386	15	.000	-2	44	-13	0	-0.8
Total	10	66	79	.455	221	170	75-11	4	1303	1367	685	96	19	578	382	4.11	97	.273	.351	472-1-14	.186	-6	92	-23	0	-2.2

Fowlkes, Alan Alan Kim; B8.8.1958 Brawley CA; BR/TR/6´2˝/190; [SFN80 10/241]; d4.7; Col Cal Poly–Pomona; [DL 1983 SF N 17]

YEAR	TM LG	W	L	PCT	G	GS	CG-SHO	SV-BS	IP	H	R	HR	HB	BB-IB	SO	ERA	AERA	OAV	OOB	AB-HR-SH	AVG	PB	SUP	APR	DL	PW
1982	SF N	4	2	.667	21	15	1	0-0	85	111	55	12	5	24-3	50	5.19	69	.321	.366	26-0-2	.115	-1	108	-15	0	-1.1
1985	Cal A	0	0	ø	2	0	0	0-0	7	8	7	4	0	4-0	5	9.00	46	.276	.364	0	ø	0	—	-3	39	-0.2
Total	2	4	2	.667	23	15	1	0-0	92	119	62	16	5	28-3	55	5.48	66	.317	.365	26-0-2	.115	-1	108	-18	56	-1.3

Fox, Chad Chad Douglas; B9.3.1970 Coronado CA; BR/TR/6´3˝/(175–210); [CinN92 23/633]; d7.13; Col Tarleton St.; [DL 2000 Mil N 181]

YEAR	TM LG	W	L	PCT	G	GS	CG-SHO	SV-BS	IP	H	R	HR	HB	BB-IB	SO	ERA	AERA	OAV	OOB	AB-HR-SH	AVG	PB	SUP	APR	DL	PW
1997	Atl N	0	1	.000	30	0	0	0-1	27.1	24	12	4	0	16-0	28	3.29	128	.231	.333	0	ø	0	—	2	0	0.1
1998	Mil N	1	4	.200	49	0	0	0-2	57	56	27	4	1	20-0	64	3.95	110	.260	.326	3-0-1	.000	-0	—	3	52	0.1
1999	Mil N	0	0	ø	6	0	0	0-0	6.2	11	8	1	1	4-0	12	10.80	43	.355	.444	1	.000	-0	—	-4	166	-0.2
2001	Mil N	5	2	.714	65	0	0	2-2	66.2	44	16	6	5	36-7	80	1.89	227	.181	.298	3	.000	-0	—	18	0	1.7
2002	Mil N	1	0	1.000	3	0	0	0-0	4.2	6	3	0	0	5-1	3	5.79	71	.316	.458	0	ø	0	—	-1	175	-0.2
2003	Bos A	1	2	.333	17	0	0	3-2	18	19	10	2	1	17-2	19	4.50	104	.264	.407	0	ø	0	—	0	62	0.0
	†Fla N	2	1	.667	21	0	0	0-0	25.1	16	6	1	0	14-2	27	2.13	192	.190	.294	0	ø	0	—	6	0	0.6
2004	Fla N	0	1	.000	12	0	0	0-2	10.2	9	8	1	1	8-0	17	6.75	61	.225	.367	0	ø	0	—	-3	159	-0.2
2005	Chi N	0	0	ø	11	0	0	1-0	8	8	6	2	0	8-0	11	6.75	65	.276	.421	0	ø	0	—	-2	160	-0.1
Total	8	10	11	.476	214	0	0	6-9	224.1	193	96	21	9	128-12	261	3.57	120	.231	.336	7-0-1	.000	-1	—	19	955	1.8

Fox, Henry Henry (b Henry Fuchs); B11.18.1873 Scranton PA; D6.6.1927 Scranton PA; d9.4

YEAR	TM LG	W	L	PCT	G	GS	CG-SHO	SV-BS	IP	H	R	HR	HB	BB-IB	SO	ERA	AERA	OAV	OOB	AB-HR-SH	AVG	PB	SUP	APR	DL	PW
1902	Phi N	0	0	ø	1	0	0	1	1	2	3	0	0	1	1	18.00	16	.400	.500	0	ø	0	—	-2	—	-0.3

Fox, Howie Howard Francis; B3.1.1921 Coburg OR; D10.9.1955 San Antonio TX; BR/TR/6´3˝/(195–210); d9.28; Col Oregon

YEAR	TM LG	W	L	PCT	G	GS	CG-SHO	SV-BS	IP	H	R	HR	HB	BB-IB	SO	ERA	AERA	OAV	OOB	AB-HR-SH	AVG	PB	SUP	APR	DL	PW
1944	Cin N	0	0	ø	2	0	0	0	2.1	2	0	0	0	0	0	0.00	ø	.222	.222	1	.000	-0	—	1	0	0.0
1945	Cin N	8	13	.381	45	15	7	0	164.1	169	102	6	6	77	54	4.93	76	.268	.353	46-0-5	.283	3	93	-21	0	-1.9
1946	Cin N	0	0	ø	4	0	0	0	5	12	13	2	0	5	1	18.00	19	.462	.548	0	ø	0	—	-9	0	-0.4
1948	Cin N	6	9	.400	34	24	5	1	171	185	100	11	1	62	63	4.53	86	.280	.343	60-0-1	.200	1*	93	-13	0	-0.8
1949	Cin N	6	19	.240	38	30	9	0	215	221	120	13	4	77	60	3.98	105	.265	.330	72-0-6	.236	2*	79	0	0	0.4
1950	Cin N	11	8	.579	34	22	10-1	1	187	196	97	14	2	85	64	4.33	98	.269	.347	63-1-3	.175	-0*	88	0	0	0.1
1951	Cin N	9	14	.391	40	30	9-4	2	228	239	105	16	2	69	57	3.83	107	.272	.326	70-1-8	.114	-2	74	10	0	0.7
1952	Phi N	2	7	.222	13	11	2	0	62	70	41	8	0	26	16	5.08	72	.287	.356	21-0-3	.048	-2	120	-10	0	-1.4
1954	Bal A	1	2	.333	38	0	0	2	73.2	80	33	2	2	34	27	3.67	98	.289	.366	16	.250	1	—	0	0	0.1
Total	9	43	72	.374	248	132	42-5	6	1108.1	1174	611	72	17	435	342	4.33	92	.274	.343	349-2-26	.189	2	87	-42	0	-3.2

Fox, John John Joseph; B2.7.1859 Roxbury MA; D4.18.1893 Boston MA; d6.2

YEAR	TM LG	W	L	PCT	G	GS	CG-SHO	SV-BS	IP	H	R	HR	HB	BB-IB	SO	ERA	AERA	OAV	OOB	AB-HR-SH	AVG	PB	SUP	APR	DL	PW
1881	Bos N	6	8	.429	17	16	12	0	124.1	144	90	0	—	39	30	3.33	80	.279	.329	118	.178	-4*	85	-11	—	-1.3
1883	Bal AA	6	13	.316	20	19	18	0	165.1	209	140	2	—	32	49	4.03	86	.289	.320	92	.152	-4*	82	-9	—	-1.1
1884	Pit AA	1	6	.143	7	7	7	0	59	76	59	2	3	16	22	5.64	59	.291	.339	25	.240	0*	60	-15	—	-1.3
1886	Was N	0	1	.000	1	1	1	0	8	11	13	0	—	11	3	9.00	36	.314	.478	3	.333	0	57	-5	—	-0.4
Total	4	13	28	.317	45	43	38	0	356.2	440	302	4	3	98	104	4.16	76	.287	.331	238	.176	-7	79	-40	—	-4.1

YEAR	TM LG	W	L	PCT	G	GS	CG-SHO	SV-BS	IP	H	R	HR	HB	BB-IB	SO	ERA	AERA	OAV	OOB	AB-HR-SH	AVG	PB	SUP	APR	DL	PW
FOX, TERRY	Terrence Edward; B7.31.1935 Chicago IL; BR/TR/6´0˝/175; d9.4																									
1960	Mil N	0	0	ø	5	0	0	0	8.1	6	5	0	0	6-0	5	4.32	79	.200	.333	1	.000	-0	—	-1	0	-0.1
1961	Det A	5	2	.714	39	0	0	12	57.1	42	12	6	3	16-1	32	1.41	290	.200	.265	12-0-1	.167	-0	—	16	0	2.6
1962	Det A	3	1	.750	44	0	0	16	58	48	13	2	1	16-6	23	1.71	238	.227	.283	8-0-1	.250	2*	—	15	0	2.1
1963	Det A	8	6	.571	46	0	0	11	80.1	81	37	9	2	20-5	35	3.59	104	.263	.310	11-0-1	.091	-0	—	1	0	0.2
1964	Det A	4	3	.571	32	0	0	5	61	77	26	4	1	16-1	28	3.39	108	.316	.357	12	.250	1	—	1	0	0.3
1965	Det A	6	4	.600	42	0	0	10	77.2	59	26	7	3	31-2	34	2.78	125	.214	.298	15-0-4	.000	-1	—	6	0	0.9
1966	Det A	0	1	.000	4	0	0	1	10	9	8	3	0	2-0	6	6.30	55	.243	.282	3	.000	-0	—	-3	0	-0.4
	Phi N	3	2	.600	36	0	0	4	44.1	57	22	3	2	17-8	22	4.47	80	.322	.384	3-0-1	.000	-0*	—	-3	0	-0.4
Total	7	29	19	.604	248	0	0	59	397	379	149	34	12	124-23	185	2.99	125	.254	.314	65-0-8	.123	1	—	32	0	5.2
FOXEN, BILL	William Aloysius; B5.31.1879 Tenafly NJ; D4.17.1937 Brooklyn NY; BL/TL/5´11.5˝/165; d5.5; Col St. Peters																									
1908	Phi N	7	7	.500	22	16	10-2	0	147.1	126	45	2	8	53	52	1.95	124	.240	.319	53-0-1	.094	-3	113	7	—	0.5
1909	Phi N	3	7	.300	18	7	5-1	0	83.1	65	40	0	4	32	37	3.35	78	.219	.303	24-1-0	.208	3	65	-6	—	-0.1
1910	Phi N	5	5	.500	16	9	5	0	77.2	73	30	2	3	40	33	2.55	123	.268	.368	23-0-1	.174	-1	71	5	—	0.6
	Chi N	0	0	ø	2	0	0	0	5	7	5	0	0	3	2	9.00	32	.350	.435	2	.000	-0	—	-3	—	-0.2
	Year	5	5	.500	18	9	5	0	82.2	80	35	2	3	43	35	2.94	106	.274	.373	25-0-1	.160	-1	72	1	—	0.4
1911	Chi N	1	1	.500	3	1	0	0	13	12	6	0	0	12	6	2.08	159	.255	.407	4	.250	1	113	1	—	0.3
Total	4	16	20	.444	61	33	20-3	0	326.1	283	126	4	15	140	130	2.56	104	.244	.333	106-1-2	.142	0	90	4	—	1.1
FOXX, JIMMIE	James Emory "Beast","Double X"; B10.22.1907 Sudlersville MD; D7.21.1967 Miami FL; BR/TR/6´0˝/195; d5.1.1925; C1; HF1951; ▲																									
1939	Bos A☆	0	0	ø	1	0	0	0	1	0	0	0	0	0	1	0.00	ø	.000	.000	467-35-5	.360	1*	—	1	—	0.0
1945	Phi N	1	0	1.000	9	2	0	0	22.2	13	4	0	1	14	10	1.59	241	.171	.308	224-7-1	.268	2*	77	6	0	0.4
Total	2	1	0	1.000	10	2	0	0	23.2	13	4	0	1	14	11	1.52	254	.165	.298	691-42-6	.330	3	77	7	0	0.4
FOYTACK, PAUL	Paul Eugene; B11.16.1930 Scranton PA; BR/TR/5´11˝/(175–185); d4.21																									
1953	Det A	0	0	ø	6	0	0	0	9.2	15	12	1	1	9	7	11.17	36	.375	.500	1	.000	-0	—	-7	0	-0.4
1955	Det A	0	1	.000	22	1	0	0	49.2	48	29	4	0	36-3	38	5.26	73	.259	.375	11	.091	-1	139	-6	0	-0.4
1956	Det A	15	13	.536	43	33	16-1	1	256	211	114	24	2	142-4	184	3.59	115	.226	.327	90-0-6	.122	-6	122	16	0	0.9
1957	Det A	14	11	.560	38	27	8-1	1	212	175	79	19	4	104-12	118	3.14	123	.226	.318	63-0-12	.222	1	81	17	0	1.9
1958	Det A	15	13	.536	39	33	16-2	1	230	198	98	23	3	77-1	135	3.44	117	.233	.298	75-0-7	.240	2	97	14	0	1.8
1959	Det A	14	14	.500	39	**37**	11-2	1	240.1	239	137	34	2	64-3	110	4.64	87	.259	.307	81-0-6	.111	-4	106	-12	0	-1.7
1960	Det A	2	11	.154	28	13	1	2	96.2	108	70	11	0	49-3	38	6.14	64	.286	.366	25-0-2	.280	2*	96	-21	35	-2.4
1961	Det A	11	10	.524	32	20	6	0	169.2	152	81	27	2	56-0	89	3.93	104	.238	.300	54-1-6	.222	2	112	5	0	0.6
1962	Det A	10	7	.588	29	21	5-1	0	143.2	145	80	18	1	86-2	63	4.39	93	.259	.358	42-0-2	.143	-1	105	-5	0	-0.7
1963	Det A	0	1	.000	9	0	0	1	17.2	18	18	4	0	8-0	7	8.66	43	.265	.338	4	.000	-0	—	-9	0	-0.6
	LA A	5	5	.500	25	8	0	0	70.1	68	35	9	0	29-6	37	3.71	92	.255	.326	15-0-2	.267	1*	84	-3	0	-0.3
	Year	5	6	.455	34	8	0	1	88	86	53	13	0	37-6	44	4.70	74	.257	.328	19-0-2	.211	1	83	-13	0	-0.9
1964	LA A	0	1	.000	2	0	0	0	2.1	4	4	2	0	2-1	1	15.43	21	.364	.462	0	ø	0	—	-3	0	-0.6
Total	11	86	87	.497	312	193	63-7	7	1498	1381	757	176	15	662-35	827	4.14	97	.246	.324	461-1-43	.178	-3	103	-14	35	-1.9
FRAILING, KEN	Kenneth Douglas; B1.19.1948 Marion WI; BL/TL/6´0˝/190; [ChiA66 5/98]; d9.1; [DL 1977 Chi N 96]																									
1972	Chi A	1	0	1.000	4	0	0	0-0	3	3	1	1	0	1-0	1	3.00	104	.250	.308	0	ø	0	—	0	0	0.0
1973	Chi A	0	0	ø	10	0	0	0-0	18.1	18	6	1	1	7-0	15	1.96	201	.254	.325	0	ø	0	—	3	0	0.2
1974	Chi N	6	9	.400	55	16	1	1-1	125.1	150	65	11	1	43-10	71	3.88	99	.296	.351	31-0-4	.258	1*	87	-1	0	0.0
1975	Chi N	2	5	.286	41	0	0	1-1	53	61	37	6	2	26-2	39	5.43	71	.293	.374	7-0-1	.143	0	—	-9	0	-1.0
1976	Chi N	1	2	.333	6	3	0	0-0	18.2	20	7	0	0	5-0	10	2.41	161	.274	.316	3-0-1	.000	-0	45	2	20	0.3
Total	5	10	16	.385	116	19	1	2-2	218.1	252	116	19	4	82-12	136	3.96	97	.290	.351	41-0-6	.220	1	80	-5	116	-0.5
FRANCE, OSSIE	Osman Beverly "O. B."; B10.4.1858 Greensburg OH; D5.2.1947 Akron OH; BL/TL/5´8˝/155; d7.14																									
1890	Chi N	0	0	ø	1	0	0	0	2	3	3	0	0	2	0	13.50	27	.333	.455	1	.000	-0	—	-2	—	-0.1
FRANCIS, EARL	Earl Coleman; B7.14.1935 Slab Fork WV; D7.3.2002 Pittsburgh PA; BR/TR/6´2˝/(208–215); d6.30																									
1960	Pit N	1	0	1.000	7	0	0	0	18	14	5	0	1	4-0	8	2.00	188	.222	.275	5	.000	-1	—	3	0	0.1
1961	Pit N	2	8	.200	23	15	0	0	102.2	110	60	4	1	47-7	53	4.21	95	.274	.348	28	.107	-1	88	-5	0	-0.5
1962	Pit N	9	8	.529	36	23	5-1	0	176	153	68	8	2	83-10	121	3.07	128	.235	.322	61-1-3	.164	1	92	18	0	1.7
1963	Pit N	4	6	.400	33	13	0	0	97.1	107	59	6	4	43-11	72	4.53	73	.284	.361	26	.308	3*	82	-13	0	-1.0
1964	Pit N	0	1	.000	2	1	0	0	6.1	7	7	2	1	1-0	6	8.53	41	.269	.321	1	.000	-0	0	-4	0	-0.5
1965	StL N	0	0	ø	2	0	0	0	5.1	7	4	1	0	3-2	3	5.06	76	.318	.385	1	.000	-0	—	-1	0	-0.1
Total	6	16	23	.410	103	52	5-1	0	405.2	398	203	21	9	181-30	263	3.77	100	.258	.337	122-1-3	.172	2	87	-2	0	-0.3
FRANCIS, JEFF	Jeffrey William; B1.8.1981 Vancouver BC, Can.; BL/TL/6´5˝/(200–205); [ColN02 1/9]; d8.25; Col British Columbia																									
2004	Col N	3	2	.600	7	7	0	0-0	36.2	42	22	8	1	13-1	32	5.15	92	.286	.346	10-0-4	.000	-1	112	-1	0	-0.3
2005	Col N	14	12	.538	33	33	0	0-0	183.2	228	119	26	8	70-5	128	5.68	82	.311	.372	58-0-6	.103	-1	116	-17	0	-2.2
2006	Col N	13	11	.542	32	32	1-1	0-0	199	187	101	18	13	69-15	117	4.16	115	.250	.322	61-0-9	.115	-0	105	13	0	1.4
Total	3	30	25	.545	72	72	1-1	0-0	419.1	457	242	52	22	152-21	277	4.91	96	.281	.347	129-0-19	.101	-2	110	-5	0	-1.1
FRANCIS, RAY	Ray James; B3.8.1893 Sherman TX; D7.6.1934 Atlanta GA; BL/TL/6´1.5˝/182; d4.18																									
1922	Was A	7	18	.280	39	26	15-2	2	225	265	136	7	6	66	64	4.28	90	.303	.356	78-0-3	.167	-2	85	-13	—	-1.5
1923	Det A	5	8	.385	33	6	0	1	79.1	95	51	2	4	28	27	4.42	87	.308	.374	21	.143	-2*	96	-7	—	-1.2
1925	NY A	0	0	ø	4	0	0	0	4.2	5	4	0	1	3	1	7.71	55	.278	.409	0	ø	0	—	-2	—	-0.1
	Bos A	0	2	.000	6	4	0	0	28	44	29	3	1	13	4	7.71	59	.373	.439	8	.125	-0	79	-9	—	-0.5
	Year	0	2	.000	10	4	0	0	32.2	49	33	3	2	16	5	7.71	58	.360	.435	8	.125	-0	79	-11	—	-0.6
Total	3	12	28	.300	82	36	15-2	3	337	409	220	12	12	110	96	4.65	84	.310	.368	107-0-3	.159	-4	86	-31	—	-3.3
FRANCISCO, FRANK	Franklin; B9.11.1979 Santo Domingo, D.R.; BR/TR/6´2˝/(180–235); d5.14; [DL 2005 Tex A 183]																									
2004	Tex A	5	1	.833	45	0	0	0-3	51.1	36	19	4	3	28-2	60	3.33	148	.198	.313	0	ø	0	—	9	0	0.9
2006	Tex A	0	1	.000	8	0	0	0-0	7.1	8	4	2	0	2-0	6	4.91	95	.267	.313	0	ø	0	—	0	77	0.0
Total	2	5	2	.714	53	0	0	0-3	58.2	44	23	6	3	30-2	66	3.53	139	.208	.313	0	ø	0	—	9	260	0.9
FRANCO, JOHN	John Anthony; B9.17.1960 Brooklyn NY; BL/TL/5´10˝/(170–188); [LAN81 5/125]; d4.24; Col St. Johns; [DL 2002 NY N 183]																									
1984	Cin N	6	2	.750	54	0	0	4-5	79.1	74	28	3	2	36-4	55	2.61	145	.256	.338	3-0-1	.000	-0	—	9	0	0.9
1985	Cin N	12	3	.800	67	0	0	12-3	99	83	27	5	1	40-8	61	2.18	174	.234	.313	6-0-2	.333	0	—	**17**	0	3.0
1986	Cin N☆	6	6	.500	74	0	0	29-9	101	90	40	7	2	44-12	84	2.94	131	.242	.323	4	.000	-0	—	9	0	1.5
1987	Cin N★	8	5	.615	68	0	0	32-9	82	76	26	6	0	27-6	61	2.52	167	.245	.304	2	.000	-0	—	15	0	2.9
1988	Cin N	6	6	.500	70	0	0	**39**-3	86	60	18	3	0	27-3	46	1.57	227	.198	.263	1	.000	-0	—	**18**	0	4.0
1989	Cin N☆	4	8	.333	60	0	0	32-7	80.2	77	35	3	0	36-8	60	3.12	115	.258	.334	3	.333	0	—	3	0	0.7
1990	NY N★	5	3	.625	55	0	0	**33**-6	67.2	66	22	4	0	21-2	56	2.53	149	.252	.306	5	.000	-1	—	9	0	1.9
1991	NY N	5	9	.357	52	0	0	30-5	55.1	61	27	2	1	18-4	45	2.93	125	.271	.328	1	.000	-0	—	2	0	0.4
1992	NY N	6	2	.750	31	0	0	15-2	33	24	6	1	0	11-2	20	1.64	214	.209	.273	1	.000	-0	—	7	73	1.7
1993	NY N	4	3	.571	35	0	0	10-7	36.1	46	24	6	1	19-3	29	5.20	77	.313	.393	1	.000	-0	—	-5	43	-0.9
1994	NY N	1	4	.200	47	0	0	**30**-6	50	47	20	2	1	19-0	42	2.70	155	.244	.313	3	.000	-0	—	7	0	1.3
1995	NY N	5	3	.625	48	0	0	29-7	51.2	48	17	4	0	17-2	41	2.44	166	.251	.311	0	ø	0	—	9	0	1.8
1996	NY N	4	3	.571	51	0	0	28-8	54	54	15	2	0	21-0	48	1.83	220	.260	.328	1	.000	-0	—	13	0	2.6
1997	NY N	5	3	.625	59	0	0	36-6	60	49	18	3	1	20-2	53	2.55	157	.226	.293	0	ø	0	—	11	0	2.2
1998	NY N	0	8	.000	61	0	0	38-8	64.2	66	28	4	4	29-7	59	3.62	114	.267	.347	2	.000	-0	—	3	0	0.8
1999	†NY N	0	2	.000	46	0	0	19-2	40.2	40	14	1	2	19-1	41	2.88	151	.255	.341	0	ø	0	—	7	63	0.8
2000	†NY N	5	4	.556	62	0	0	4-0	55.2	46	24	6	2	26-6	56	3.40	129	.221	.314	1	.000	-0	—	6	0	0.9
2001	NY N	6	2	.750	58	0	0	2-5	53.1	55	25	8	2	19-2	50	4.05	100	.264	.330	0	ø	0	—	1	0	0.1
2003	NY N	0	3	.000	38	0	0	2-1	34.1	35	11	5	1	13-2	16	2.62	160	.265	.333	0	ø	0	—	6	61	0.6
2004	NY N	2	7	.222	52	0	0	0-1	46	46	28	6	1	24-2	36	5.28	81	.258	.346	0	ø	0	—	-4	0	-0.7
2005	Hou N	0	1	.000	31	0	0	0-1	15	23	13	0	1	9-2	16	7.20	59	.343	.429	0	ø	0	—	-5	0	-0.3
Total	21	90	87	.508	1119	0	0	424-101	1245.2	1166	466	81	22	495-78	975	2.89	137	.249	.322	34-0-3	.088	-2	—	138	423	26.2

YEAR	TM LG	W	L	PCT	G	GS	CG-SHO	SV-BS	IP	H	R	HR	HB	BB-IB	SO	ERA	AERA	OAV	OOB	AB-HR-SH	AVG	PB	SUP	APR	DL	PW
Frankhouse, Fred	Frederick Meloy; B4.9.1904 Port Royal PA; D8.17.1989 Mifflintown PA; BR/TR/5´11˝/175; d9.7																									
1927	StL N	5	1	.833	6	6	5-1	0	50	41	18	2	1	16	20	2.70	146	.218	.283	20-0-1	.250	0*	133	7	—	0.8
1928	StL N	3	2	.600	21	10	1	1	84	91	47	6	5	36	29	3.96	101	.277	.358	27-0-2	.185	1*	133	-1	—	0.1
1929	StL N	7	2	.778	30	10	6	1	133.1	149	70	9	4	43	37	4.12	113	.289	.349	52-1-2	.288	4*	140	8	—	0.9
1930	StL N	2	3	.400	8	1	0	0	19.2	31	16	1	0	11	4	7.32	69	.373	.447	5	.000	-1*	17	-4	—	-0.7
	Bos N	7	6	.538	27	11	3-1	0	110.2	138	72	13	2	43	30	5.61	88	.313	.377	39-0-1	.359	4	82	-6	—	-0.2
	Year	9	9	.500	35	12	3-1	0	130.1	169	88	14	2	54	34	5.87	84	.323	.388	44-0-1	.318	3	76	-10	—	-0.9
1931	Bos N	8	8	.500	26	15	6	1	127.1	125	64	4	3	43	50	4.03	94	.252	.315	40-0-1	.150	-0	71	-3	—	-0.3
1932	Bos N	4	6	.400	37	6	3	0	108.2	113	56	7	3	45	35	3.56	106	.278	.355	30-0-2	.100	-1*	101	0	—	0.0
1933	Bos N	16	15	.516	43	30	14-2	2	244.2	249	97	12	3	77	83	3.16	97	.267	.324	80-0-7	.237	4	102	-2	—	0.4
1934	Bos N★	17	9	.654	37	30	13-2	1	233.2	239	102	10	4	77	78	3.20	120	.262	.322	85-0-7	.200	2	114	14	—	1.6
1935	Bos N	11	15	.423	40	29	10-1	0	230.2	278	147	12	6	81	64	4.76	80	.293	.352	76-0-1	.263	6	109	-29	—	-1.9
1936	Bro N	13	10	.565	41	31	9-1	2	234.1	236	112	18	3	89	84	3.65	113	.257	.325	91-0-1	.143	-4*	93	13	—	0.8
1937	Bro N	10	13	.435	33	25	9-1	0	179.1	214	104	8	4	78	64	4.27	95	.297	.369	58-0-7	.190	-0*	105	-4	—	-0.3
1938	Bro N	3	5	.375	30	8	2-1	0	93.2	92	48	6	4	44	32	4.04	97	.256	.344	26-0-3	.154	-1*	71	-1	—	-0.1
1939	Bos N	0	2	.000	23	0	0	4	38	37	16	3	1	18	12	2.61	142	.253	.339	7	.000	-1	—	3	—	0.1
Total	13	106	97	.522	402	212	81-10	12	1888	2033	969	111	43	701	622	3.92	100	.275	.341	636-1-35	.208	12	102	-5	—	1.2
Franklin, Wayne	Gary Wayne; B3.9.1974 Wilmington DE; BL/TL/6´2˝/(195–205); [LAN96 36/1078]; d7.24; Col Maryland–Baltimore Co.																									
2000	Hou N	0	0	ø	25	0	0	0-0	21.1	24	14	2	4	12-1	21	5.48	89	.282	.388	2	.000	-0	—	-1	0	-0.1
2001	Hou N	0	0	ø	11	0	0	0-0	12	17	9	4	0	9-0	9	6.75	68	.333	.433	0	ø	0	—	-2	0	-0.1
2002	Mil N	2	1	.667	4	4	0	0-0	24	16	8	1	0	17-1	17	2.63	157	.188	.324	6	.000	-0	62	4	0	0.5
2003	Mil N	10	13	.435	36	34	1-1	0-0	194.2	201	129	36	10	94-2	116	5.50	78	.268	.355	59-0-12	.169	-0	113	-26	0	-2.7
2004	SF N	2	1	.667	43	2	0	0-1	50.2	55	37	11	3	22-2	40	6.39	68	.281	.359	3	.333	1	161	-10	20	-0.5
2005	NY A	0	1	.000	13	0	0	0-3	12.2	11	12	1	1	8-0	10	6.39	67	.239	.357	0	ø	0	—	-4	0	-0.3
2006	Atl N	0	0	ø	11	0	0	0-0	7.2	8	6	2	0	6-2	3	7.04	64	.296	.400	0	ø	0	—	-2	0	-0.1
Total	7	14	16	.467	143	40	1-1	0-4	323	332	215	57	18	168-8	216	5.54	79	.268	.360	70-0-12	.157	-0	109	-41	20	-3.3
Franklin, Jack	Jack Wilford; B10.20.1919 Paris IL; D11.15.1991 Panama City FL; BR/TR/5´11.5˝/170; d6.12; Col Illinois																									
1944	Bro N	0	0	ø	1	0	0	0	2	2	3	1	2	4	0	13.50	26	.250	.571	0	ø	0	—	-2	0	-0.1
Franklin, Jay	John William; B3.16.1953 Arlington VA; BR/TR/6´2˝/185; [SDN71 1/2]; d9.4																									
1971	SD N	0	1	.000	3	1	0	0-0	5.2	5	5	3	0	4-0	4	6.35	52	.250	.375	1	.000	-0	53	-2	0	-0.3
Franklin, Ryan	Ryan Ray; B3.5.1973 Fort Smith AR; BR/TR/6´3˝/(165–190); [SeaA92 23/642]; d5.15; Col Seminole St. (OK) JC																									
1999	Sea A	0	0	ø	6	0	0	0-0	11.1	10	6	2	1	8-1	6	4.76	101	.238	.373	0	ø	0	—	0	0	0.0
2001	Sea A	5	1	.833	38	0	0	0-1	78.1	76	32	13	4	24-4	60	3.56	120	.250	.311	0	ø	0	—	7	0	0.5
2002	Sea A	7	5	.583	41	12	0	0-1	118.2	117	62	14	5	22-1	65	4.02	107	.255	.294	0	ø	0	81	1	17	0.1
2003	Sea A	11	13	.458	32	32	2-1	0-0	212	199	93	34	9	61-3	99	3.57	121	.251	.310	4-0-1	.250	0	99	17	0	1.6
2004	Sea A	4	16	.200	32	32	2-1	0-0	200.1	224	116	33	10	61-1	104	4.90	91	.285	.340	3-0-1	.000	0	76	-10	0	-0.9
2005	Sea A	8	15	.348	32	30	2-1	0-0	190.2	212	110	28	7	62-4	93	5.10	82	.280	.339	4	.000	-0	75	-19	0	-2.0
2006	Phi N	1	5	.167	46	0	0	0-1	53	59	28	10	4	17-4	25	4.58	102	.280	.343	2	.000	-0	—	1	0	0.1
	Cin N	5	2	.714	20	0	0	0-2	24.1	27	14	3	0	16-6	18	4.44	106	.297	.398	2	.000	-0	—	0	0	0.0
	Year	6	7	.462	66	0	0	0-3	77.1	86	42	13	4	33-10	43	4.54	103	.285	.361	4	.000	-0	—	1	0	0.1
Total	7	41	57	.418	247	106	6-3	0-5	888.2	924	461	137	40	271-24	470	4.35	100	.268	.327	15-0-2	.067	-0	83	-3	17	-0.6
Frascatore, John	John Vincent; B2.4.1970 Ozone Park NY; BR/TR/6´1˝/(200–228); [StLN91 24/623]; d7.21; Col Long Island–C.W.Post																									
1994	StL N	0	1	.000	1	1	0	0-0	3.1	7	6	2	0	2-0	2	16.20	26	.438	.500	1	.000	-0	21	-4	0	-0.6
1995	StL N	1	1	.500	14	4	0	0-0	32.2	39	19	3	2	16-1	21	4.41	97	.298	.380	7-0-1	.000	-1	95	-1	0	-0.1
1997	StL N	5	2	.714	59	0	0	0-4	80	74	25	5	6	33-5	58	2.47	169	.247	.329	3	.000	-0	—	15	0	1.1
1998	StL N	3	4	.429	69	0	0	0-2	95.2	95	48	11	3	36-3	49	4.14	102	.256	.326	6	.167	-0	—	1	0	0.0
1999	Ari N	1	4	.200	26	0	0	0-1	33	31	16	6	1	12-4	15	4.09	113	.256	.326	0	ø	0	—	2	0	0.2
	Tor A	7	1	.875	33	0	0	1-1	37	42	16	5	1	9-4	22	3.41	145	.292	.333	0	ø	0	—	6	0	1.1
2000	Tor A	2	4	.333	60	0	0	0-5	73	87	51	14	7	33-2	30	5.42	93	.301	.381	0	ø	0	—	-4	0	-0.3
2001	Tor A	1	0	1.000	12	0	0	0-1	16.1	16	4	4	0	4-1	9	2.20	208	.246	.290	0	ø	0	—	4	0	0.3
Total	7	20	17	.541	274	5	0	1-14	371	391	185	50	20	145-20	206	4.00	112	.272	.344	17-0-1	.059	-1	78	19	0	1.7
Fraser, Chick	Charles Carrolton; B8.26.1873 Chicago IL; D5.8.1940 Wendell ID; BR/TR/5´10.5˝/188; d4.19; C1																									
1896	Lou N	12	27	.308	43	38	36	1	349.1	396	282	9	29	166	91	4.87	89	.283	.371	146	.151	-9*	89	-19	—	-2.2
1897	Lou N	15	19	.441	36	34	32	0	294.1	334	226	11	22	139	70	4.04	106	.283	.369	115-2-2	.157	-5*	92	0	—	-0.2
1898	Lou N	7	17	.292	26	26	20-1	0	203	230	157	4	23	100	58	5.32	67	.283	.378	78-0-3	.167	-2	93	-39	—	-3.6
	Cle N	2	3	.400	6	6	6	0	42	49	34	2	6	12	19	5.57	65	.290	.358	16	.250	0	101	-8	—	-0.7
	Year	9	20	.310	32	32	26-1	0	245	279	191	6	29	112	77	5.36	67	.284	.374	94-0-3	.181	-2	94	-42	—	-4.3
1899	Phi N	21	12	.636	35	33	29-4	0	270.2	278	146	1	22	85	68	3.36	110	.265	.333	117-0-1	.179	-2*	123	10	—	0.9
1900	Phi N	15	9	.625	29	26	22-1	0	223.1	250	117	7	11	93	58	3.14	115	.282	.358	85-0-5	.259	4	106	9	—	1.2
1901	Phi A	22	16	.579	40	37	35-2	0	331	344	210	6	32	132	110	3.81	99	.265	.347	139-0-5	.187	-3*	103	-5	—	-0.7
1902	Phi N	12	13	.480	27	26	24-3	0	224	238	115	2	15	74	97	3.42	82	.272	.339	86	.174	0*	81	-14	—	-1.4
1903	Phi N	12	17	.414	31	29	26-1	1	250	260	160	8	16	97	104	4.50	73	.267	.344	93-1-2	.204	4*	94	-30	—	-2.3
1904	Phi N	14	24	.368	42	36	32-2	1	302	287	164	5	11	100	127	3.25	82	.246	.311	110-0-5	.155	-1*	88	-18	—	-2.1
1905	Bos N	14	21	.400	39	37	35-2	0	334.1	320	174	8	15	149	130	3.28	94	.254	.340	156-0-3	.224	3*	83	-10	—	-0.5
1906	Cin N	10	20	.333	31	28	25-2	0	236	221	92	1	8	80	58	2.67	103	.259	.329	82-0-4	.171	-1	78	4	—	0.5
1907	Chi N	8	5	.615	22	15	9-2	1	138.1	112	51	1	3	46	41	2.28	110	.229	.299	45-0-3	.067	-3	80	3	—	0.0
1908	Chi N	11	9	.550	26	17	11-2	2	162.2	141	71	4	6	61	66	2.27	104	.244	.323	50-0-5	.120	-2	130	-5	—	-0.6
1909	Chi N	0	0	ø	1	0	0	0	3	2	1	0	0	4	1	0.00	ø	.222	.462	1	.000	-0	—	1	—	0.0
Total	14	175	212	.452	434	388	342-22	6	3364	3462	2000	69	219	1338	1098	3.67	92	.266	.345	1319-3-38	.178	-15	95	-121	—	-11.7
Fraser, Willie	William Patrick; B5.26.1964 New York NY; BR/TR/6´1˝/(200–208); [CalA85 1/15]; d9.10; Col Concordia (NY)																									
1986	Cal A	0	0	ø	1	1	0	0-0	4.1	6	4	0	0	1-0	2	8.31	50	.353	.368	0	ø	0	154	-2	0	-0.1
1987	Cal A	10	10	.500	36	23	5-1	1-0	176.2	160	85	26	6	63-3	106	3.92	110	.240	.310	0	ø	0	99	9	0	0.8
1988	Cal A	12	13	.480	34	32	2	0-0	194.2	203	129	33	9	80-7	86	5.41	72	.267	.340	0	ø	0	109	-34	0	-3.7
1989	Cal A	4	7	.364	44	0	0	2-1	91.2	80	33	6	5	23-4	46	3.24	118	.235	.291	0	ø	0	—	8	0	0.9
1990	Cal A	5	4	.556	45	0	0	2-3	76	69	29	4	0	24-3	32	3.08	125	.241	.297	0	ø	0	—	7	0	0.7
1991	Tor A	0	2	.000	13	1	0	0-0	26.1	33	20	4	3	11-2	12	6.15	69	.303	.382	0	ø	0	173	-6	0	-0.4
	StL N	3	3	.500	35	0	0	0-0	49.1	44	28	9	3	21-3	25	4.93	76	.242	.325	2	.000	-0	—	-6	0	-0.7
1994	Fla N	2	0	1.000	9	0	0	0-0	12.1	20	9	1	0	6-3	7	5.84	76	.370	.426	0	ø	0	—	-2	0	-0.3
1995	Mon N	2	1	.667	22	0	0	2-0	25.2	25	17	6	3	9-1	12	5.61	77	.248	.327	2	.000	-0	—	-3	0	-0.4
Total	8	38	40	.487	239	57	7-1	7-4	657	640	354	89	29	238-26	328	4.47	90	.254	.323	4	.000	-0	107	-29	0	-3.2
Frasier, Vic	Victor Patrick (b Victor Patrick Frazier); B8.5.1904 Ruston LA; D1.10.1977 Jacksonville TX; BR/TR/6´0˝/182; d4.18																									
1931	Chi A	13	15	.464	46	29	13-2	4	254	258	156	11	5	127	87	4.46	95	.259	.345	86-0-3	.209	1	97	-8	—	-0.7
1932	Chi A	3	13	.188	29	21	4	0	146	180	121	14	4	70	33	6.23	69	.297	.374	44-0-5	.091	-3	94	-30	—	-2.8
1933	Chi A	1	1	.500	10	1	0	0	20.1	32	22	2	0	11	4	8.85	48	.368	.439	4	.000	-1	100	-10	—	-0.8
	Det A	5	5	.500	20	14	4	0	104.1	129	85	9	1	59	26	6.64	65	.312	.399	37-0-4	.189	-0	116	-24	—	-1.9
	Year	6	6	.500	30	15	4	0	124.2	161	107	11	1	70	30	7.00	61	.321	.406	41-0-4	.171	-1	115	-34	—	-2.7
1934	Det A	1	3	.250	8	2	0	0	22.2	30	19	0	1	12	11	5.96	74	.313	.394	7	.286	0	169	-5	—	-0.6
1937	Bos N	0	0	ø	3	0	0	0	8	12	7	1	0	1	2	5.63	64	.364	.382	1	.000	-0	—	-3	—	-0.1
1939	Chi A	0	1	.000	10	1	0	0	23.2	45	27	0	0	11	7	10.27	46	.405	.459	7	.286	0	37	-13	—	-0.6
Total	6	23	38	.377	126	68	21-2	4	579	686	437	37	11	291	170	5.77	75	.293	.373	186-0-12	.177	-3	101	-93	—	-7.5
Frasor, Jason	Jason Andrew; B8.9.1977 Chicago IL; BR/TR/5´10˝/170; [DetA99 33/987]; d4.16; Col Southern Illinois																									
2004	Tor A	4	6	.400	63	0	0	17-2	68.1	64	31	4	2	36-3	54	4.08	120	.251	.345	0	ø	0	—	7	0	1.2
2005	Tor A	3	5	.375	67	0	0	1-2	74.2	67	31	8	3	28-2	62	3.25	141	.247	.323	0	ø	0	—	10	0	0.9
2006	Tor A	3	2	.600	51	0	0	0-1	50	47	24	8	2	17-1	51	4.32	110	.244	.307	0	ø	0	—	3	0	0.3
Total	3	10	13	.435	181	0	0	18-5	193	178	86	20	7	81-6	167	3.82	124	.248	.327	0	ø	0	—	20	0	2.4

YEAR	TM LG	W	L	PCT	G	GS	CG-SHO	SV-BS	IP	H	R	HR	HB	BB-IB	SO	ERA	AERA	OAV	OOB	AB-HR-SH	AVG	PB	SUP	APR	DL	PW
Frazier, George	George Allen; B10.13.1954 Oklahoma City OK; BR/TR/6´5˝/(200–205); [MilA76 9/196]; d5.25; Col Oklahoma																									
1978	StL N	0	3	.000	14	0	0	0-0	22	22	14	2	0	6-2	8	4.09	87	.250	.292	3	.333	0	—	-2	0	-0.3
1979	StL N	2	4	.333	25	0	0	0-2	32.1	35	19	3	1	12-2	14	4.45	86	.278	.343	1	.000	-0	—	-3	0	-0.5
1980	StL N	1	4	.200	22	0	0	3-4	23	24	10	2	0	7-3	11	2.74	137	.273	.326	0	ø	0	—	2	0	0.3
1981	†NY A	0	1	.000	16	0	0	3-0	27.2	26	7	1	0	11-2	17	1.63	222	.245	.316	0	ø	0	—	6	0	0.3
1982	NY A	4	4	.500	63	0	0	1-1	111.2	103	51	7	5	39-5	69	3.47	116	.252	.321	0	ø	0	—	6	0	0.4
1983	NY A	4	4	.500	61	0	0	8-2	115.1	94	44	5	3	45-4	78	3.43	115	.227	.300	0	ø	0	—	9	0	0.7
1984	Cle A	3	2	.600	22	0	0	1-2	44.1	45	19	3	0	14-4	24	3.65	113	.259	.314	0	ø	0	—	3	0	0.2
	†Chi N	6	3	.667	37	0	0	3-1	63.2	53	30	4	1	26-8	58	4.10	95	.221	.296	7	.286	0	—	0	0	-0.1
1985	Chi N	7	8	.467	51	0	0	2-2	76	88	57	11	3	52-9	46	6.39	63	.299	.409	6	.000	-1	—	-17	0	-3.3
1986	Chi N	2	4	.333	35	0	0	0-0	51.2	63	36	5	1	34-4	41	5.40	75	.310	.407	4	.000	-0	—	-8	0	-1.0
	Min A	1	1	.500	15	0	0	6-3	26.2	23	13	2	0	16-1	25	4.39	99	.232	.331	0	ø	0	—	0	0	0.1
1987	†Min A	5	5	.500	54	0	0	2-5	81.1	77	49	9	2	51-4	58	4.98	93	.258	.359	0	ø	0	—	-3	0	-0.4
Total	10	35	43	.449	415	0	0	29-22	675.2	653	349	54	16	313-48	449	4.20	97	.257	.338	21	.143	-1	—	-7	0	-3.6
Frederick, Kevin	Kevin Albert Francis; B11.4.1976 Evanston IL; BL/TR/6´1˝/(208–210); [MinA98 34/1009]; d7.15; Col Creighton																									
2002	Min A	0	0	ø	8	0	0	0-0	11.2	13	13	3	0	10-0	5	10.03	45	.283	.411	0	ø	0	—	-7	0	-0.3
2004	Tor A	0	2	.000	22	0	0	0-1	28.2	32	21	4	1	16-1	22	6.59	74	.283	.368	0	ø	0	—	-5	0	-0.3
Total	2	0	2	.000	30	0	0	0-1	40.1	45	34	7	1	26-1	27	7.59	63	.283	.381	0	ø	0	—	-12	0	-0.6
Fredrickson, Scott	Scott Eric; B8.19.1967 Manchester NH; BR/TR/6´3˝/215; [SDN90 14/390]; d4.29; Col Texas; [DL 1994 Col N 131]																									
1993	Col N	0	1	.000	25	0	0	0-0	29	33	25	3	1	17-2	20	6.21	77	.287	.378	3	.000	-0	—	-5	0	-0.3
Freeman, Buck	Alexander Vernon; B7.5.1893 Mart TX; D2.21.1953 Fort Sam Houston TX; BB/TR/5´10˝/167; d4.13																									
1921	Chi N	9	10	.474	38	20	6	3	177.1	189	96	12	8	70	42	4.11	93	.281	.356	53-0-1	.208	0	102	-7	—	-0.7
1922	Chi N	0	1	.000	11	1	0	1	25.2	47	28	0	2	10	10	8.77	48	.412	.468	8	.125	-0	78	-12	—	-0.5
Total	2	9	11	.450	49	21	6	4	203	236	124	12	10	80	52	4.70	82	.300	.372	61-0-1	.197	-0	100	-19	—	-1.2
Freeman, Harvey	Harvey Bayard "Buck"; B12.22.1897 Mottville MI: D1.10.1970 Kalamazoo MI; BR/TR/5´10˝/160; d7.10; Col Western Michigan																									
1921	Phi A	1	4	.200	18	4	2	0	48	65	50	2	5	35	5	7.69	58	.346	.461	12-0-1	.083	-2	70	-16	—	-1.5
Freeman, Hersh	Hershell Baskin "Buster"; B7.1.1928 Gadsden AL; D1.17.2004 Orlando FL; BR/TR/6´3˝/(220–228); d9.10; Col Alabama																									
1952	Bos A	1	0	1.000	4	1	1	0	13.2	13	5	1	1	5	5	3.29	120	.260	.339	4	.500	1	66	1	0	0.2
1953	Bos A	1	4	.200	18	2	0	0	39	50	31	2	0	17	15	5.54	76	.316	.383	11	.091	-1	21	-7	0	-0.9
1955	Bos A	0	0	ø	2	0	0	0	1.2	1	0	0	0	1-1	1	0.00	ø	.200	.333	0	ø	0	—	1	0	0.0
	Cin N	7	4	.636	52	0	0	11	91.2	94	31	3	2	30-6	37	2.16	196	.276	.335	18-1-0	.167	1*	—	**18**	0	2.5
1956	Cin N	14	5	.737	64	0	0	18	108.2	112	44	2	1	34-11	50	3.40	117	.274	.329	18	.056	-1	—	7	0	1.4
1957	Cin N	7	2	.778	52	0	0	8	83.2	90	49	14	3	14-4	36	4.52	91	.277	.308	10	.200	0	—	-5	0	-0.6
1958	Cin N	0	0	ø	3	0	0	0	7.2	4	3	0	0	5-0	7	3.52	118	.154	.281	1	.000	-0	—	1	0	0.0
	Chi N	0	1	.000	9	0	0	0	13	23	13	3	0	3-0	7	8.31	47	.354	.382	1	.000	-0	—	-6	0	-0.4
	Year	0	1	.000	12	0	0	0	20.2	27	16	3	0	8-0	14	6.53	61	.297	.350	2	.000	-0	—	-5	0	-0.4
Total	6	30	16	.652	204	3	1	37	359	387	176	25	7	109-22	158	3.74	110	.281	.334	63-1-0	.143	-0	36	10	0	2.2
Freeman, Jimmy	Jimmy Lee; B6.29.1951 Carlsbad NM; BL/TL/6´4˝/(175–180); [AtlN69 6/130]; d9.1																									
1972	Atl N	2	2	.500	6	6	1	0-0	36	40	26	5	0	22-1	18	6.00	63	.278	.373	13	.077	-0*	120	-8	0	-0.8
1973	Atl N	0	2	.000	13	5	0	1-2	37.1	50	33	7	0	25-1	20	7.71	51	.327	.417	13	.154	-0*	142	-13	0	-0.8
Total	2	2	4	.333	19	11	1	1-2	73.1	90	59	12	0	47-2	38	6.87	57	.303	.396	26	.115	-1	130	-21	0	-1.6
Freeman, Buck	John Frank; B10.30.1871 Catasauqua PA; D6.25.1949 Wilkes–Barre PA; BL/TL/5´9˝/169; d6.27; ▲																									
1891	Was AA	3	2	.600	5	4	4	0	44	35	32	0	4	33	28	3.89	96	.211	.355	18	.222	0	96	-1	—	0.0
1899	Was N	0	0	ø	2	0	0	0	7	15	13	3	3	3	0	7.71	51	.429	.512	588-25-5	.318	1*	—	-5	—	-0.2
Total	2	3	2	.600	7	4	4	0	51	50	45	3	7	36	28	4.41	85	.249	.381	606-25-5	.315	1	96	-6	—	-0.2
Freeman, Julie	Julius Benjamin; B11.7.1868 MO; D6.10.1921 St.Louis MO; BR; d10.10																									
1888	StL AA	0	1	.000	1	1	0	0	6.1	7	5	0	1	4	1	4.26	77	.269	.387	3	.333	0	71	-1	—	-0.1
Freeman, Mark	Mark Price; B12.7.1930 Memphis TN; D2.21.2006 Rancho Mirage CA; BR/TR/6´4˝/220; d4.18; Col Louisiana St.																									
1959	KC A	0	0	ø	3	0	0	0	3.2	6	6	0	0	3-0	1	9.82	41	.375	.450	0	ø	0	—	-3	0	-0.1
	NY A	0	0	ø	1	1	0	0	7	6	2	0	1	2-0	4	2.57	142	.240	.310	2	.000	-0	48	1	0	0.0
	Year	0	0	ø	4	1	0	0	10.2	12	8	0	1	5-0	5	5.06	74	.293	.367	2	.000	-0	47	-2	0	-0.1
1960	Chi N	3	3	.500	30	8	1	1	76.2	70	51	10	5	33-3	50	5.63	67	.240	.325	20-0-1	.150	-0	146	-14	0	-1.2
Total	2	3	3	.500	34	9	1	1	87.1	82	59	10	6	38-3	55	5.56	68	.246	.331	22-0-1	.136	-1	135	-16	0	-1.3
Freeman, Marvin	Marvin; B4.10.1963 Chicago IL; BR/TR/6´7˝/(200–222); [PhiN84 2/49]; d9.16; Col Jackson St.																									
1986	Phi N	2	0	1.000	3	3	0	0-0	16	6	4	0	0	10-0	8	2.25	173	.120	.262	6-0-1	.000	-1	160	3	0	0.3
1988	Phi N	2	3	.400	11	11	0	0-0	51.2	55	36	2	1	43-2	37	6.10	59	.276	.406	14-0-3	.214	0	101	-12	0	-1.1
1989	Phi N	0	0	ø	1	1	0	0-0	3	2	2	0	0	5-0	0	6.00	60	.182	.438	2	.000	-0	197	-1	160	-0.1
1990	Phi N	0	2	.000	16	3	0	1-0	32.1	34	21	5	3	14-2	26	5.57	69	.264	.349	7	.000	-1	86	-6	0	-0.4
	Atl N	1	0	1.000	9	0	0	0-0	15.2	7	3	0	2	3-0	12	1.72	234	.130	.203	0	ø	0	—	4	0	0.2
	Year	1	2	.333	25	3	0	1-0	48	41	24	5	5	17-2	38	4.31	91	.224	.307	7	.000	-1	85	-1	0	-0.2
1991	Atl N	1	0	1.000	34	0	0	1-0	48	37	19	2	2	13-1	34	3.00	129	.214	.275	7	.000	-1	—	4	50	0.1
1992	†Atl N	7	5	.583	58	0	0	3-3	64.1	61	26	7	1	29-7	41	3.22	114	.251	.332	4	.500	1	—	3	15	0.6
1993	Atl N	2	0	1.000	21	0	0	0-0	23.2	24	16	1	1	10-2	25	6.08	67	.261	.340	0-0-2	ø	0	—	-5	64	-0.4
1994	Col N	10	2	.833	19	18	0	0-0	112.2	113	39	10	5	23-2	67	2.80	178	.262	.306	36-1-3	.111	-0	97	23	0	2.3
1995	Col N	3	7	.300	22	18	0	0-1	94.2	122	64	15	2	41-1	61	5.89	91	.318	.384	23-1-6	.087	-1	88	-3	19	-0.4
1996	Col N	7	9	.438	26	23	0	0-1	129.2	151	100	21	6	57-1	71	6.04	86	.294	.370	41-0-4	.122	-2	112	-12	0	-1.4
	Chi A	0	0	ø	1	1	0	0-0	2	4	3	0	0	1-0	1	13.50	35	.364	.417	0	ø	0	253	-2	0	-0.1
Total	10	35	28	.556	221	78	0	5-5	593.2	616	333	63	23	249-18	383	4.64	98	.269	.345	140-2-19	.114	-5	111	-4	308	-0.4
Freeze, Jake	Carl Alexander; B4.25.1900 Huntington AR; D4.9.1983 San Angelo TX; BR/TR/5´8˝/150; d7.1; Col Baylor																									
1925	Chi A	0	0	ø	2	0	0	0	3.2	5	7	1	0	3	1	2.45	169	.333	.444	1	.000	-0	—	-2	—	-0.1
Freisleben, Dave	David James; B10.31.1951 Coraopolis PA; BR/TR/5´11˝/(195–205); [SDN71 5/98]; d4.26																									
1974	SD N	9	14	.391	33	31	6-2	0-0	211.2	194	100	13	7	112-9	130	3.66	98	.241	.338	64-0-9	.172	2	85	-3	0	-0.1
1975	SD N	5	14	.263	36	27	4-1	0-0	181	206	102	11	7	82-9	77	4.28	82	.289	.366	48-0-6	.083	-1	76	-16	0	-1.6
1976	SD N	10	13	.435	34	24	6-3	1-0	172	163	73	10	5	66-7	81	3.51	94	.248	.320	37-0-9	.189	1	67	-3	0	-0.1
1977	SD N	7	9	.438	33	23	1	0-0	138.2	140	86	21	2	71-9	72	4.61	78	.266	.353	37-0-2	.135	0	111	-19	0	-2.0
1978	SD N	0	3	.000	12	4	0	0-0	26.2	41	22	3	0	15-3	16	6.08	55	.363	.427	6-0-1	.000	-1	87	-9	0	-1.0
	Cle A	1	4	.200	12	10	0	0-0	44.1	52	37	4	2	31-1	19	7.11	53	.299	.405	0	ø	0	102	-15	0	-1.5
1979	Tor A	2	3	.400	42	2	0	3-2	91	101	57	5	2	53-3	35	4.95	89	.294	.388	0	ø	0	62	-6	0	-0.3
Total	6	34	60	.362	202	121	17-6	4-2	865.1	897	477	67	25	430-41	430	4.30	84	.269	.355	192-0-27	.141	2	84	-71	0	-6.6
Freitas, Tony	Antonio; B5.5.1908 Mill Valley CA; D3.14.1994 Orangevale CA; BR/TL/5´8˝/161; d5.31																									
1932	Phi A	12	5	.706	23	18	10-1	0	150.1	150	68	11	4	48	31	3.83	118	.263	.325	54-0-8	.148	-1	136	12	—	1.2
1933	Phi A	2	4	.333	19	9	2	1	64.1	90	56	8	2	24	15	7.27	59	.337	.396	16-0-2	.063	-1	130	-19	—	-1.6
1934	Cin N	6	12	.333	30	18	5	1	152.2	194	80	6	3	25	37	4.01	102	.311	.341	47-0-1	.191	0*	73	3	—	0.5
1935	Cin N	5	10	.333	31	18	5	2	143.2	174	95	6	2	38	51	4.57	87	.295	.340	46-0-4	.130	-0	90	-13	—	-1.2
1936	Cin N	0	2	.000	4	0	0	0	7	6	2	0	0	2	1	1.29	297	.240	.296	2	.000	-0	—	2	—	0.3
Total	5	25	33	.431	107	63	22-1	4	518	614	301	31	11	137	135	4.48	94	.296	.343	165-0-15	.145	-2	105	-15	—	-0.8
French, Larry	Lawrence Herbert; B11.1.1907 Visalia CA; D2.9.1987 San Diego CA; BR/TL (BB 1934, 1940–42)/6´1˝/195; d4.18; Mil 1943–45																									
1929	Pit N	7	5	.583	30	13	6	1	123	130	78	10	3	62	49	4.90	97	.276	.364	42-0-1	.190	-1	107	-2	—	-0.1
1930	Pit N	17	18	.486	42	35	21-3	1	274.2	325	163	20	6	89	90	4.36	114	.295	.351	91-0-11	.242	1	88	16	—	1.6
1931	Pit N	15	13	.536	39	33	20-1	1	275.2	301	127	9	1	70	73	3.26	118	.278	.322	95-0-6	.179	-1	97	16	—	1.4
1932	Pit N	18	16	.529	**47**	33	19-3	4	274.1	301	127	17	1	62	72	3.02	126	.276	.316	92-0-4	.207	1	96	19	—	2.1
1933	Pit N	18	13	.581	47	**35**	21-5	1	291.1	290	106	9	5	55	88	2.72	122	.257	.294	101-0-3	.149	-2	92	21	—	1.8

YEAR	TM LG	W	L	PCT	G	GS	CG-SHO	SV-BS	IP	H	R	HR	HB	BB-IB	SO	ERA	AERA	OAV	OOB	AB-HR-SH	AVG	PB	SUP	APR	DL	PW
1934	Pit N	12	18	.400	49	34	16-3	1	263.2	299	135	8	3	59	103	3.58	115	.281	.321	84-0-10	.190	-0	96	9	—	0.8
1935	†Chi N	17	10	.630	42	30	16-**4**	2	246.1	279	94	10	2	44	90	2.96	133	.286	.318	85-0-9	.141	-4	104	28	—	2.5
1936	Chi N	18	9	.667	43	28	16-**4**	3	252.1	262	103	16	6	54	104	3.39	118	.266	.308	85-0-10	.212	0	100	18	—	1.6
1937	Chi N	16	10	.615	42	28	11-4	0	208	229	106	17	1	65	100	3.98	100	.274	.327	71-0-4	.127	-4	104	-1	—	-0.5
1938	†Chi N	10	19	.345	43	27	10-3	0	201.1	210	95	17	1	62	83	3.80	101	.271	.326	62-0-6	.210	2	79	1	—	0.5
1939	Chi N	15	8	.652	36	21	10-2	1	194	205	80	7	1	50	98	3.29	120	.269	.314	73-1-4	.192	1	104	15	—	1.8
1940	Chi N★	14	14	.500	40	33	18-3	2	246	240	93	12	4	64	107	3.29	114	.256	.306	85-0-4	.165	1	102	18	—	2.2
1941	Chi N	5	14	.263	26	18	6-1	0	138	161	88	10	2	43	60	4.63	76	.285	.338	47-0-3	.191	1	78	-19	0	-2.3
	†Bro N	0	0	ø	6	1	0	0	15.2	16	6	1	1	4	8	3.45	106	.267	.323	4	.250	0	116	1	0	0.1
	Year	5	14	.263	32	19	6-1	0	153.2	177	94	11	3	47	68	4.51	78	.283	.336	51-0-3	.196	1	80	-20	0	-2.2
1942	Bro N	15	4	**.789**	38	14	8-4	0	147.2	127	39	1	5	36	62	1.83	178	.233	.287	40-0-9	.300	4	109	22	0	3.3
Total	14	197	171	.535	570	383	198-40	17	3152	3375	1440	164	42	819	1187	3.44	114	.272	.320	1057-1-84	.188	0	96	162	0	16.8
FRENCH, BILL	William; B Baltimore MD; d4.14; ▲																									
1873	Mar NA	0	1	.000	1	1	1	0	9	30	27	0	—	0	0	12.00	28	.462	.462	18	.222	-0*	77	-7	—	-0.4
FREY, BENNY	Benjamin Rudolph; B4.6.1906 Dexter MI; D11.1.1937 Spring Arbor Twp. MI; BR/TR/5´10˝/165; d9.18																									
1929	Cin N	1	2	.333	3	3	2	0	24	29	12	2	0	8	1	4.13	111	.302	.356	8-0-1	.375	1	83	1	—	0.3
1930	Cin N	11	18	.379	44	28	14-2	1	245	295	145	15	3	62	43	4.70	103	.305	.349	88-0-3	.284	4	63	4	—	1.1
1931	Cin N	8	12	.400	34	17	7-1	2	133.2	166	76	2	2	36	19	4.92	76	.319	.365	44-0-1	.318	4	80	-14	—	-1.3
1932	StL N	0	2	.000	2	0	0	0	3	6	5	0	0	2	0	12.00	33	.600	.667	1	.000	-0	—	-3	—	-0.5
	Cin N	4	10	.286	28	15	5	0	131.1	159	72	10	1	30	27	4.32	89	.299	.338	44	.205	-0	93	-5	—	-0.3
	Year	4	12	.250	30	15	5	0	134.1	165	77	10	1	32	27	4.49	86	.305	.345	45	.200	-0	93	-9	—	-0.8
1933	Cin N	6	4	.600	37	9	1-1	0	132	144	67	4	0	21	12	3.82	89	.281	.309	42-0-1	.262	3*	79	-5	—	0.1
1934	Cin N	11	16	.407	39	30	12-2	2	245.1	288	118	10	2	42	33	3.52	116	.289	.319	82-0-2	.171	-0*	88	15	—	1.7
1935	Cin N	6	10	.375	38	13	3-1	2	114.1	164	100	6	4	32	24	6.85	58	.335	.381	32-0-3	.344	4	105	-35	—	-3.8
1936	Cin N	10	8	.556	31	12	5	0	131.1	164	73	5	0	30	20	4.25	90	.296	.332	44-0-2	.250	2*	92	-6	—	-0.6
Total	8	57	82	.410	256	127	49-7	7	1160	1415	668	54	12	263	179	4.50	90	.303	.341	385-0-13	.255	17	83	-48	—	-3.3
FREY, STEVE	Steven Francis; B7.29.1963 Meadowbrook PA; BR/TL/5´9˝/170; [NYA83 15/379]; d5.10; Col Bucks Co. (PA) CC																									
1989	Mon N	3	2	.600	20	0	0	0-0	21.1	29	15	4	1	11-1	15	5.48	65	.326	.398	0	ø	0	—	-5	0	-1.0
1990	Mon N	8	2	.800	51	0	0	9-0	55.2	44	15	4	1	29-6	29	2.10	175	.219	.318	1	.000	-0	—	10	21	1.9
1991	Mon N	0	1	.000	31	0	0	1-1	39.2	43	31	3	1	23-4	21	4.99	73	.281	.374	2	.000	0	—	-9	0	-0.5
1992	Cal A	4	2	.667	51	0	0	4-1	45.1	39	18	6	2	22-3	24	3.57	112	.238	.330	0	ø	0	—	3	16	0.4
1993	Cal A	2	3	.400	55	0	0	13-3	48.1	41	20	1	3	26-1	22	2.98	152	.230	.337	0	ø	0	—	7	0	1.0
1994	SF N	1	0	1.000	44	0	0	0-3	31	37	17	6	2	15-3	20	4.94	82	.322	.397	0	ø	0	—	-2	0	-0.1
1995	SF N	0	1	.000	9	0	0	0-0	6.1	7	6	1	0	2-0	5	4.26	97	.280	.321	0	ø	0	—	-1	0	-0.2
	Sea A	0	3	.000	13	0	0	0-0	11.1	16	7	0	1	6-1	7	4.76	100	.356	.434	0	ø	0	—	0	20	0.0
	Phi N	0	0	ø	9	0	0	1-0	10.2	3	1	1	0	2-1	2	0.84	500	.091	.143	1	.000	-0	—	4	0	0.2
1996	Phi N	0	1	.000	31	0	0	0-0	34.1	38	19	4	0	18-3	12	4.72	91	.295	.376	0	ø	0	—	-1	0	0.0
Total	8	18	15	.545	314	0	0	28-8	304	297	149	30	11	154-23	157	3.76	107	.262	.351	4	.000	-0	—	6	57	1.7
FRICANO, MARION	Marion John; B7.15.1923 Brant NY; D5.18.1976 Tijuana, Baja California, Mexico; BR/TR/6´0˝/170; d9.6; Col Cortland																									
1952	Phi A	1	0	1.000	2	0	0	0	5	5	1	0	0	1	0	1.80	220	.238	.273	0-0-1	ø	0	—	1	0	0.2
1953	Phi A	9	12	.429	39	23	10	0	211	206	105	21	6	90	67	3.88	110	.257	.337	69-0-3	.145	-3*	83	6	0	0.2
1954	Phi A	5	11	.313	37	20	4	1	151.2	163	98	17	4	64	43	5.16	76	.275	.347	41-0-6	.098	-3*	89	-21	0	-2.4
1955	KC A	0	0	ø	10	0	0	0	20	19	9	2	0	9-0	5	3.15	133	.253	.333	3	.667	1	—	2	0	0.2
Total	4	15	23	.395	88	43	14	1	387.2	393	213	40	10	164-0	115	4.32	96	.264	.340	113-0-10	.142	-5	85	-12	0	-1.8
FRIDAY, SKIPPER	Grier William; B10.26.1897 Gastonia NC; D8.25.1962 Gastonia NC; BR/TR/5´11˝/170; d6.17																									
1923	Was A	0	1	.000	7	2	1	0	30	35	27	2	2	22	9	6.90	55	.313	.434	9	.222	0	99	-11	—	-0.4
FRIED, CY	Arthur Edwin; B7.23.1897 San Antonio TX; D10.10.1970 San Antonio TX; BL/TL/5´11.5˝/150; d9.17																									
1920	Det A	0	0	ø	2	0	0	0	1.2	3	4	0	0	4	0	16.20	23	.500	.700	0	ø	0	—	-2	—	-0.1
FRIEDRICHS, BOB	Robert George; B8.30.1906 Cincinnati OH; D4.15.1997 Jasper IN; BR/TR/5´11.5˝/165; d5.17; Col Holy Cross																									
1932	Was A	0	0	ø	2	0	0	0	4	4	5	0	1	7	2	11.25	38	.250	.500	1	.000	-0	—	-3	—	-0.2
FRIEND, DANNY	Daniel Sebastian; B4.18.1873 Cincinnati OH; D6.1.1942 Chillicothe OH; BL/TL/5´9˝/175; d9.10																									
1895	Chi N	2	2	.500	5	5	5	0	41	50	27	5	3	14	10	5.27	97	.296	.360	17-0-1	.235	-1	92	2	—	0.0
1896	Chi N	18	14	.563	36	33	28-1	0	290.2	298	196	11	39	139	86	4.74	96	.263	.363	126-1-4	.238	-1*	78	0	—	-0.2
1897	Chi N	12	11	.522	24	24	23	0	203	244	144	5	17	86	58	4.52	99	.295	.373	88-0-1	.284	2*	94	1	—	0.2
1898	Chi N	0	2	.000	2	2	2	0	17	20	15	1	1	10	4	5.29	68	.290	.387	7	.286	0	79	-3	—	-0.1
Total	4	32	29	.525	67	64	58-1	0	551.2	612	382	22	60	249	158	4.71	96	.279	.368	238-1-6	.256	0	85	0	—	-0.1
FRIEND, BOB	Robert Bartmess "Warrior"; B11.24.1930 Lafayette IN; BR/TR/6´0˝/(190–200); d4.28; Col Purdue																									
1951	Pit N	6	10	.375	34	22	3-1	0	149.2	173	94	12	0	68	41	4.27	99	.293	.366	44-0-1	.091	-2	104	-6	0	-0.7
1952	Pit N	7	17	.292	35	23	6-1	0	185	186	96	15	3	84	75	4.18	95	.258	.338	52-0-7	.058	-4	74	-3	0	-0.8
1953	Pit N	8	11	.421	32	24	8	0	170.2	193	103	18	3	57	66	4.90	91	.286	.344	52-0-3	.135	-2	99	-7	0	-0.9
1954	Pit N	7	12	.368	35	20	4-2	2	170.1	204	106	16	1	58	73	5.07	83	.302	.355	51-1-1	.275	5	93	-14	0	-1.0
1955	Pit N	14	9	.609	44	20	9-2	2	200.1	178	80	18	2	52-4	98	**2.83**	**145**	.242	.291	61-0-6	.164	-2	88	**25**	0	2.7
1956	Pit N★	17	17	.500	49	**42**	19-4	3	**314.1**	310	137	25	2	85-18	166	3.46	109	.258	.306	97-1-11	.165	-1	91	11	0	1.0
1957	Pit N	14	18	.438	40	**38**	17-3	0	**277**	273	121	28	1	68-8	143	3.38	112	.257	.301	87-0-6	.184	1	89	13	0	1.4
1958	Pit N★	**22**	14	.611	38	**38**	16-1	0	274	299	120	25	4	61-11	135	3.68	105	.281	.320	94-0-10	.106	-4	106	8	0	0.6
1959	Pit N	8	19	.296	35	35	7-2	0	234.2	267	129	19	7	52-9	104	4.03	96	.283	.324	73-0-12	.164	0	90	-9	0	-0.9
1960	†Pit N★	18	12	.600	38	37	16-4	1	275.2	266	97	18	0	45-10	183	3.00	125	.251	.280	88-0-11	.068	-5	106	25	0	2.0
1961	Pit N	14	19	.424	41	35	10-1	1	236	271	119	16	3	45-10	108	3.85	104	.289	.322	79-0-9	.139	-3	80	2	0	-0.2
1962	Pit N	18	14	.563	39	36	13-**5**	1	261.2	280	99	23	2	53-10	144	3.06	129	.273	.309	91-0-8	.121	-3	92	27	0	2.8
1963	Pit N	17	16	.515	39	38	12-4	0	268.2	236	87	13	5	44-9	144	2.34	141	.233	.267	86-0-10	.105	-3	88	27	0	2.9
1964	Pit N	13	18	.419	35	35	13-3	0	240.1	253	98	10	4	50-12	128	3.33	105	.271	.309	71-0-11	.070	-3	81	6	0	0.4
1965	Pit N	8	12	.400	34	34	8-2	0	222	221	89	17	8	47-7	74	3.24	108	.260	.304	71-0-6	.042	-5	91	9	0	0.2
1966	NY A	1	4	.200	12	8	0	0	44.2	61	25	2	0	9-1	22	4.84	69	.330	.359	11-0-3	.000	-1	70	-7	0	-0.8
	NY N	5	8	.385	22	12	2-1	1	86	101	52	11	1	16-6	30	4.40	83	.289	.321	29-0-5	.034	-3	111	-9	0	-1.6
Total	16	197	230	.461	602	497	163-36	11	3611	3772	1652	286	46	894-115	1734	3.58	107	.269	.313	1137-2-120	.121	-36	92	98	0	7.1
FRIES, PETE	Peter Martin; B10.30.1857 Scranton PA; D7.29.1937 Chicago IL; BL/TL/5´8˝/160; d8.10																									
1883	Col AA	0	3	.000	3	3	3	0	25	34	31	1	—	14	7	6.48	48	.304	.381	10	.300	1	125	-10	—	-0.7
FRILL, JOHN	John Edmond; B4.3.1879 Reading PA; D9.28.1918 Westerly RI; BR/TL/5´10.5˝/170; d4.16																									
1910	NY A	2	2	.500	10	5	3-1	1	48.1	55	33	1	1	5	27	4.47	59	.289	.311	18-0-1	.111	-1	111	-9	—	-0.9
1912	StL A	0	1	.000	3	3	0	0	4.1	16	11	1	1	1	2	20.77	16	.571	.600	2	.500	0	163	-7	—	-1.2
	Cin N	1	0	1.000	3	2	0	0	15	19	11	0	2	1	4	6.00	56	.345	.379	4	.250	0	87	-3	—	-0.2
Total	2	3	3	.500	16	10	3-1	1	67.2	90	55	2	4	7	33	5.85	49	.330	.356	24-0-1	.167	-1	125	-19	—	-2.3
FRISELLA, DANNY	Daniel Vincent "Bear"; B3.4.1946 San Francisco CA; D1.1.1977 Phoenix AZ; BL/TR/6´0˝/(190–195); [NYN66 S3/49]; d7.27; Col Washington St.																									
1967	NY N	1	6	.143	14	11	0	0	74	68	32	6	0	33-1	51	3.41	100	.249	.325	23	.087	-1	54	0	0	-0.1
1968	NY N	2	4	.333	19	4	0	2	50.2	53	23	5	0	17-0	47	3.91	77	.270	.326	12	.083	-1	72	-4	0	-0.6
1969	NY N	0	0	ø	3	0	0	0-0	4.2	8	4	1	0	3-0	5	7.71	47	.381	.458	1	.000	-0	—	-2	0	-0.1
1970	NY N	8	3	.727	30	1	0	1-1	65.2	49	23	4	0	34-11	54	3.02	135	.204	.302	13-0-1	.308	1	110	8	0	1.4
1971	NY N	8	5	.615	53	0	0	12-3	90.2	76	28	6	3	30-9	93	1.99	173	.227	.295	13-0-1	.231	1	—	12	0	2.2
1972	NY N	5	8	.385	39	0	0	9-4	67.1	63	31	8	0	20-5	46	3.34	101	.243	.296	7	.286	0	—	-1	0	-0.1
1973	Atl N	1	2	.333	42	0	0	8-8	45	40	27	5	1	23-2	27	4.20	94	.241	.332	2	.500	0	—	-2	56	-0.2
1974	Atl N	3	4	.429	36	1	0	6-4	41.2	37	26	4	0	28-8	27	5.18	73	.240	.357	1	.000	0	115	-6	0	-1.1
1975	SD N	1	6	.143	65	0	0	9-2	97.2	86	36	7	2	51-16	67	3.13	112	.242	.335	5	.200	0	—	6	0	0.5
1976	StL N	0	0	ø	18	0	0	1-0	22.2	19	10	3	0	13-1	11	3.97	90	.232	.330	1	.000	-0	—	0	0	0.0

YEAR	TM LG	W	L	PCT	G	GS	CG-SHO	SV-BS	IP	H	R	HR	HB	BB-IB	SO	ERA	AERA	OAV	OOB	AB-HR-SH	AVG	PB	SUP	APR	DL	PW
	Mil A	5	2	.714	32	0	0	9-3	49.1	30	16	4	1	34-5	43	2.74	128	.175	.314	0	ø	0	—	5	0	0.9
Total	10	34	40	.459	351	17	0	57-25	609.1	529	256	53	7	286-58	471	3.32	107	.235	.320	78-0-2	.179	1	63	16	56	2.8
Frisk, Emil	John Emil; B10.15.1874 Kalkaska MI; D1.27.1922 Seattle WA; BL/TR/6´1˝/190; d9.2; ▲																									
1899	Cin N	3	6	.333	9	9	9	0	68.1	81	52	1	6	17	17	3.95	99	.295	.349	25	.280	1	100	-4	—	-0.3
1901	Det A	5	4	.556	11	7	6	0	74.2	94	60	1	2	26	22	4.34	89	.304	.362	48-1-0	.313	2*	130	-5	—	-0.1
Total	2	8	10	.444	20	16	15	0	143	175	112	2	8	43	39	4.15	93	.300	.356	73-1-0	.301	3	113	-9	—	-0.4
Fritz, Charlie	Charles Cornelius; B6.13.1882 Mobile AL; D7.30.1943 Mobile AL; TL; d10.5																									
1907	Phi A	0	0	ø	1	1	0	0	3	0	1	0	1	3	1	3.00	87	.000	.333	1	.000	-0	104	0	—	0.0
Froats, Bill	William John; B10.20.1930 New York NY; D2.9.1998 Minneapolis MN; BL/TL/6´0˝/180; d4.22; Col Notre Dame																									
1955	Det A	0	0	ø	1	0	0	0	2	0	0	0	0	2-0	0	0.00	ø	.000	.333	0	ø	0	—	1	0	0.1
Frock, Sam	Samuel William; B12.23.1882 Baltimore MD; D11.3.1925 Baltimore MD; BR/TR/6´0˝/168; d9.21																									
1907	Bos N	1	2	.333	5	3	3-1	0	33.1	28	17	1	2	11	12	2.97	86	.243	.320	14	.071	-1	149	-2	—	-0.4
1909	Pit N	2	1	.667	8	4	3	1	36.1	44	19	0	3	4	11	2.48	110	.299	.331	14	.143	-1	161	-1	—	-0.1
1910	Pit N	0	0	ø	1	0	0	0	2	2	4	0	1	2	1	4.50	69	.400	.625	0	ø	0	—	-1	—	-0.1
	Bos N	12	19	.387	45	29	13-2	2	255.1	245	133	8	4	91	170	3.21	104	.262	.330	84-0-5	.190	-3	75	1	—	-0.1
	Year	12	19	.387	46	29	13-2	2	257.1	247	137	8	5	93	171	3.22	103	.263	.333	84-0-5	.190	-3	75	-4	—	-0.2
1911	Bos N	0	1	.000	4	1	1	0	16	29	18	0	1	5	8	5.63	68	.426	.473	5	.200	-0	39	-4	—	-0.3
Total	4	15	23	.395	63	37	20-3	3	343	348	191	9	11	113	202	3.23	99	.274	.339	117-0-5	.171	-5	87	-7	—	-1.0
Frohwirth, Todd	Todd Gerard; B9.28.1962 Milwaukee WI; BR/TR/6´4˝/(190–205); [PhiN84 13/335]; d8.10; Col Northwest Missouri																									
1987	Phi N	1	0	1.000	10	0	0	0-0	11	12	0	0	0	2-0	9	0.00	ø	.293	.326	1-0-1	.000	-0	—	5	0	0.4
1988	Phi N	1	2	.333	12	0	0	0-1	12	16	11	2	0	11-6	11	8.25	44	.327	.443	0	ø	0	—	-5	0	-1.1
1989	Phi N	1	0	1.000	45	0	0	0-1	62.2	56	26	4	3	18-0	39	3.59	100	.240	.302	1-0-1	.000	-0	—	1	0	0.0
1990	Phi N	0	1	.000	5	0	0	0-0	1	3	2	0	0	6-2	1	18.00	21	.500	.750	0	ø	0	—	-1	0	-0.3
1991	Bal A	7	3	.700	51	0	0	3-2	96.1	64	24	2	1	29-3	77	1.87	212	.190	.255	0	ø	0	—	**22**	0	2.4
1992	Bal A	4	3	.571	65	0	0	4-3	106	97	33	4	3	41-4	58	2.46	165	.247	.323	0	ø	0	—	17	0	1.3
1993	Bal A	6	7	.462	70	0	0	3-4	96.1	91	47	7	3	44-8	50	3.83	118	.256	.342	0	ø	0	—	6	0	0.8
1994	Bos A	0	3	.000	22	0	0	1-0	26.2	40	36	3	2	17-2	13	10.80	47	.339	.431	0	ø	0	—	-17	0	-1.6
1996	Cal A	0	0	ø	4	0	0	0-0	5.2	10	11	1	1	4-0	1	11.12	45	.370	.455	0	ø	0	—	-5	0	-0.2
Total	9	20	19	.513	284	0	0	11-11	417.2	389	190	23	13	172-25	259	3.60	115	.250	.328	2-0-2	.000	-0	—	23	0	1.7
Fromme, Art	Arthur Henry; B9.3.1883 Quincy IL; D8.24.1956 Los Angeles CA; BR/TR/6´0˝/178; d9.14																									
1906	StL N	1	2	.333	3	3	3-1	0	25	19	6	0	1	10	11	1.44	183	.221	.309	9	.222	0	28	3	—	0.4
1907	StL N	5	13	.278	23	16	13-2	0	145.2	138	73	3	4	67	67	2.90	86	.256	.343	55-0-2	.182	1	73	-7	—	-0.8
1908	StL N	5	13	.278	20	14	9-2	0	116	102	59	1	2	50	62	2.72	87	.218	.296	36-0-2	.139	-1	72	-6	—	-1.1
1909	Cin N	19	13	.594	37	34	22-4	2	279.1	195	84	2	3	101	126	1.90	137	.201	.278	94-0-6	.191	2	97	23	—	3.2
1910	Cin N	3	4	.429	11	5	1	0	49.1	44	22	2	1	39	10	2.92	100	.260	.402	15-0-1	.133	-1	77	0	—	0.0
1911	Cin N	10	11	.476	38	26	11-1	0	208	190	111	8	16	79	107	3.46	96	.248	.331	74-0-4	.189	-1	93	-4	—	-0.5
1912	Cin N	16	18	.471	43	37	23-3	0	296	285	126	7	11	88	120	2.74	123	.260	.321	103-0-5	.087	-9	88	20	—	1.1
1913	Cin N	1	4	.200	9	7	2	0	56	55	30	1	3	21	24	4.18	78	.274	.351	21	.143	-0	63	-4	—	-0.4
	NY N	11	6	.647	26	12	3	0	112.1	112	58	5	2	29	50	4.01	78	.260	.310	35-0-3	.171	-0	84	-8	—	-1.1
	Year	12	10	.545	35	19	5	0	168.1	167	88	6	5	50	74	4.06	78	.264	.323	56-0-3	.161	-1	76	-10	—	-1.5
1914	NY N	9	5	.643	38	12	3-1	2	138	142	57	7	7	44	57	3.20	83	.283	.349	31-0-3	.226	1	124	-7	—	-0.4
1915	NY N	0	1	.000	4	1	0	0	12.1	15	11	1	0	2	4	5.84	44	.306	.333	3	.333	1	87	-5	—	-0.3
Total	10	80	90	.471	252	167	90-14	4	1438	1297	637	37	50	530	638	2.90	100	.246	.320	476-0-26	.162	-8	88	5	—	0.1
Frost, Dave	Carl David; B11.17.1952 Long Beach CA; BR/TR/6´6˝/(220–235); [ChiA74 18/412]; d9.11; Col Stanford																									
1977	Chi A	1	1	.500	4	3	0	0-0	23.2	30	9	0	1	3-0	15	3.04	134	.323	.343	0	ø	0	95	3	0	0.2
1978	Cal A	5	4	.556	11	10	2-1	0-0	80.1	71	24	6	2	24-3	30	2.58	141	.240	.298	0	ø	0	59	11	0	1.2
1979	†Cal A	16	10	.615	36	33	12-2	1-0	239.1	226	108	17	5	77-4	107	3.57	114	.251	.311	0	ø	0	129	13	0	1.2
1980	Cal A	4	8	.333	15	15	2	0-0	78.1	97	53	8	2	21-1	28	5.29	75	.308	.352	0	ø	0	93	-13	58	-1.7
1981	Cal A	1	8	.111	12	9	0	0-0	47.1	44	30	3	1	19-0	16	5.51	67	.250	.323	0	ø	0	68	-8	0	-1.4
1982	KC A	6	6	.500	21	14	0	0-0	81.2	103	53	7	3	30-0	26	5.51	74	.313	.372	0	ø	0	105	-12	44	-1.6
Total	6	33	37	.471	99	84	16-3	1-0	550.2	571	277	41	14	174-8	222	4.10	97	.271	.327	0	ø	0	103	-6	102	-2.1
Fruto, Emiliano	Emiliano; B6.6.1984 Cartagena, Colombia; BR/TR/6´3˝/235; d5.14																									
2006	Sea A	2	2	.500	23	0	0	1-1	36	34	24	4	2	24-1	34	5.50	80	.246	.364	0	ø	0	—	-5	0	-0.5
Fry, Johnson	Johnson "Jay"; B11.21.1901 Huntington WV; D4.7.1959 Carmi IL; BR/TR/6´1˝/150; d8.24; Col Marshall																									
1923	Cle A	0	0	ø	1	0	0	0	3.2	6	5	0	0	4	0	12.27	32	.353	.476	1	1.000	1	—	-3	—	-0.1
Frye, Charlie	Charles Andrew; B7.17.1914 Hickory NC; D5.25.1945 Hickory NC; BR/TR/6´1˝/175; d7.28																									
1940	Phi N	0	6	.000	15	5	1	0	50.1	58	32	3	0	26	18	4.65	84	.291	.373	19-1-0	.263	1*	27	-5	—	-0.4
Fryman, Woodie	Woodrow Thompson; B4.15.1940 Ewing KY; BR/TL/6´2˝/(197–225); d4.15																									
1966	Pit N	12	9	.571	36	28	9-3	1	181.2	182	86	13	1	47-9	105	3.81	94	.261	.308	63-0-4	.159	-1	107	-5	0	-0.7
1967	Pit N	3	8	.273	28	18	3-1	1	113.1	121	67	12	4	44-3	74	4.05	83	.276	.344	34-0-1	.118	-1	104	-12	0	-1.2
1968	Phi N☆	12	14	.462	34	32	10-5	0	213.2	198•	78	12	6	64-2	151	2.78	108	.246	.305	71-0-7	.085	-2	106	4	0	0.2
1969	Phi N	12	15	.444	36	35	10-1	0-0	228.1	243	123	15	11	89-3	150	4.41	81	.270	.343	76-1-8	.118	-2	109	-21	0	-2.4
1970	Phi N	8	6	.571	27	20	4-3	0-1	127.2	122	61	11	1	43-2	97	4.09	98	.253	.313	39-0-3	.128	-2	107	0	34	-0.2
1971	Phi N	10	7	.588	37	17	3-2	2-2	149.1	133	61	7	3	46-1	104	3.38	105	.242	.301	37-0-5	.189	0	101	4	0	0.6
1972	Phi N	4	10	.286	23	17	3-2	1-0	119.2	131	64	15	2	39-9	69	4.36	83	.279	.335	33-1-2	.152	1	99	-9	0	-0.9
	†Det A	10	3	.769	16	14	6-1	0-0	113.2	93	31	6	7	31-3	72	2.06	154	.220	.284	40-0-4	.125	-2	114	13	0	1.3
1973	Det A	6	13	.316	34	29	1	0-0	169.2	200	106	23	3	64-5	119	5.36	76	.294	.356	0	ø	0	83	-21	0	-2.0
1974	Det A	6	9	.400	27	22	4-1	0-0	141.2	120	73	16	4	67-2	92	4.32	89	.233	.324	0	ø	0	84	-5	0	-0.6
1975	Mon N	9	12	.429	38	20	7-3	3-4	157	141	69	10	5	68-7	118	3.32	116	.239	.323	49-0-5	.204	1	76	7	0	1.2
1976	Mon N☆	13	13	.500	34	32	4-2	2-0	216.1	218	89	14	9	76-7	123	3.37	112	.263	.328	64-0-11	.109	-3	88	10	0	0.9
1977	Cin N	5	5	.500	17	12	0	1-0	75.1	83	45	13	2	45-2	57	5.38	73	.292	.390	22-0-3	.318	2	109	-10	0	-1.0
1978	Chi N	2	4	.333	13	9	0	0-1	55.2	64	37	6	0	37-5	28	5.17	78	.309	.407	16-0-3	.063	-1	74	-7	0	-0.7
	Mon N	5	7	.417	19	17	4-3	1-0	94.2	93	39	4	3	37-1	53	3.61	99	.260	.334	34-0-2	.059	-2	108	1	0	-0.1
	Year	7	11	.389	32	26	4-3	1-1	150.1	157	76	10	3	74-6	81	4.19	89	.278	.362	50-0-5	.060	-3	95	-7	0	-0.8
1979	Mon N	3	6	.333	44	0	0	10-1	58	52	25	4	3	22-4	44	2.79	133	.248	.328	7	.000	-1	—	4	0	0.7
1980	Mon N	7	4	.636	61	0	0	17-6	80	61	23	1	2	30-9	59	2.25	161	.209	.285	12-0-2	.167	-0	—	12	0	2.1
1981	†Mon N	5	3	.625	35	0	0	7-8	43	38	16	1	1	14-1	25	1.88	189	.247	.308	3-0-2	.667	1	—	5	0	1.2
1982	Mon N	9	4	.692	60	0	0	12-6	69.2	66	36	3	1	26-4	46	3.75	99	.259	.326	9-0-1	.222	0	—	-2	0	-0.2
1983	Mon N	0	3	.000	6	0	0	0-1	3	8	7	1	0	1-0	1	21.00	17	.571	.600	0	ø	0	—	-5	144	-1.0
Total	18	141	155	.476	625	322	68-27	58-30	2411.1	2367	1136	187	68	890-79	1587	3.77	96	.259	.327	609-2-63	.138	-12	98	-37	178	-2.8
Fuchs, Charlie	Charles Thomas; B11.18.1912 Union Hill NJ; D6.10.1969 Weehawken NJ; BB/TR/5´8˝/168; d4.17																									
1942	Det A	3	3	.500	9	4	1-1	0	36.2	43	27	5	1	19	15	6.63	60	.285	.368	13	.077	-1	76	-8	0	-1.2
1943	Phi N	2	7	.222	17	9	4-1	1	77.2	76	40	4	3	34	12	4.29	79	.266	.350	22-0-3	.091	-2	87	-7	0	-1.0
	StL A	0	0	ø	13	0	0	0	35.2	42	22	4	1	11	9	4.04	82	.294	.348	7	.000	-1	—	-4	0	-0.3
1944	Bro N	1	0	1.000	8	0	0	0	15.2	25	16	2	1	9	5	5.74	62	.347	.427	1	.000	0	—	-6	0	-0.3
Total	3	6	10	.375	47	13	5-2	1	165.2	186	105	15	6	73	41	4.89	72	.285	.363	43-0-3	.070	-4	84	-25	0	-2.8
Fuentes, Brian	Brian Christopher; B8.9.1975 Merced CA; BL/TL/6´4˝/(220–230); [SeaA95 25/678]; d6.2; Col Merced (CA) JC																									
2001	Sea A	1	1	.500	10	0	0	0-1	11.2	6	6	2	3	8-0	10	4.63	92	.171	.362	0	ø	0	—	0	0	0.0
2002	Col N	2	0	1.000	31	0	0	0-0	26.2	25	14	4	3	13-0	38	4.73	100	.250	.347	0	ø	0	—	1	0	0.0
2003	Col N	3	3	.500	75	0	0	4-2	75.1	64	24	7	6	34-2	82	2.75	178	.231	.325	1	.000	-0	—	16	0	1.3
2004	Col N	2	4	.333	47	0	0	0-1	44.2	46	30	5	4	19-6	48	5.64	84	.269	.356	0	ø	0	—	-4	69	-0.5
2005	Col N☆	2	5	.286	78	0	0	31-3	74.1	59	25	6	10	34-4	91	2.91	160	.218	.326	0	ø	0	—	13	0	2.1

YEAR	TM LG	W	L	PCT	G	GS	CG-SHO	SV-BS	IP	H	R	HR	HB	BB-IB	SO	ERA	AERA	OAV	OOB	AB-HR-SH	AVG	PB	SUP	APR	DL	PW
2006	Col N★	3	4	.429	66	0	0	30-6	65.1	50	25	8	6	26-4	73	3.44	139	.209	.301	0	ø	0	—	10	0	1.8
Total	6	13	17	.433	307	0	0	65-13	298	250	124	32	32	134-16	342	3.62	131	.229	.328	1	.000	-0	—	36	69	4.7

FUENTES, MIGUEL Miguel (Pinet); B5.10.1946 Loiza Aldea, PR; D1.29.1970 Loiza Aldea, PR; BR/TR/6´0˝/165; d9.1

YEAR	TM LG	W	L	PCT	G	GS	CG-SHO	SV-BS	IP	H	R	HR	HB	BB-IB	SO	ERA	AERA	OAV	OOB	AB-HR-SH	AVG	PB	SUP	APR	DL	PW
1969	Sea A	1	3	.250	8	4	1	0-0	26	29	15	1	0	16-1	14	5.19	70	.284	.381	6-0-2	.333	0	79	-4	0	-0.5

FUHR, OSCAR Oscar Lawrence; B8.22.1893 Defiance MO; D3.27.1975 Dallas TX; BL/TL/6´0.5˝/176; d4.19

YEAR	TM LG	W	L	PCT	G	GS	CG-SHO	SV-BS	IP	H	R	HR	HB	BB-IB	SO	ERA	AERA	OAV	OOB	AB-HR-SH	AVG	PB	SUP	APR	DL	PW
1921	Chi N	0	0	ø	1	0	0	0	4	11	9	1	0	0	2	9.00	42	.500	.500	1	.000	-0	—	-4	—	-0.2
1924	Bos A	3	6	.333	23	10	4-1	0	80.1	100	71	1	5	39	30	5.94	74	.310	.392	22-0-1	.182	-1	133	-17	—	-1.6
1925	Bos A	0	6	.000	39	5	0	0	91.1	138	83	7	3	30	27	6.60	69	.364	.415	20	.250	0	129	-20	—	-1.0
Total	3	3	12	.200	63	15	4-1	0	175.2	249	163	9	8	69	59	6.35	70	.344	.407	43-0-1	.209	-1	131	-41	—	-2.8

FULCHINO, JEFF Jeffrey Joseph; B11.26.1979 Titusville FL; BR/TR/6´5˝/250; [FlaN01 8/242]; d6.22; Col Connecticut

YEAR	TM LG	W	L	PCT	G	GS	CG-SHO	SV-BS	IP	H	R	HR	HB	BB-IB	SO	ERA	AERA	OAV	OOB	AB-HR-SH	AVG	PB	SUP	APR	DL	PW
2006	Fla N	0	0	ø	1	0	0	0-0	0.1	0	0	0	0	1-0	0	0.00	ø	.000	.500	0	ø	0	—	0	0	0.0

FULGHAM, JOHN John Thomas; B6.9.1956 St.Louis MO; BR/TR/6´2˝/205; [StLN76 S1/15]; d6.19; Col Miami; [DL 1981 StL N 180]

YEAR	TM LG	W	L	PCT	G	GS	CG-SHO	SV-BS	IP	H	R	HR	HB	BB-IB	SO	ERA	AERA	OAV	OOB	AB-HR-SH	AVG	PB	SUP	APR	DL	PW
1979	StL N	10	6	.625	20	19	10-2	0-0	146	123	47	10	3	26-3	75	2.53	151	.227	.266	42-0-11	.143	1*	90	20	0	2.2
1980	StL N	4	6	.400	15	14	4-1	0-0	85.1	66	33	7	1	32-1	48	3.38	111	.219	.295	27-0-3	.000	-3*	82	5	45	0.2
Total	2	14	12	.538	35	33	14-3	0-0	231.1	189	80	17	4	58-4	123	2.84	133	.224	.276	69-0-14	.087	-2	87	25	225	2.4

FULLER, ED Edward Ashton; B3.22.1868 Washington DC; D3.16.1935 Hyattsville MD; BR/TR/6´0˝/158; d7.17

YEAR	TM LG	W	L	PCT	G	GS	CG-SHO	SV-BS	IP	H	R	HR	HB	BB-IB	SO	ERA	AERA	OAV	OOB	AB-HR-SH	AVG	PB	SUP	APR	DL	PW
1886	Was N	0	1	.000	2	1	1	0	13	15	12	0	—	5	3	6.92	47	.375	.444	7	.143	-0	76	-4	—	-0.3

FULLERTON, CURT Curtis Hooper; B9.13.1898 Ellsworth ME; D1.9.1975 Winthrop MA; BL/TR/6´0˝/162; d4.14

YEAR	TM LG	W	L	PCT	G	GS	CG-SHO	SV-BS	IP	H	R	HR	HB	BB-IB	SO	ERA	AERA	OAV	OOB	AB-HR-SH	AVG	PB	SUP	APR	DL	PW
1921	Bos A	0	1	.000	4	1	1	0	15.1	22	17	3	1	10	4	8.80	48	.355	.452	4	.000	-0	118	-8	—	-0.5
1922	Bos A	1	4	.200	31	3	0	0	64.1	70	40	4	5	35	17	5.46	75	.290	.391	8	.250	1	103	-7	—	-0.3
1923	Bos A	2	15	.118	37	15	6	1	143.1	167	108	9	6	71	37	5.09	81	.300	.385	37-0-1	.297	2	51	-17	—	-1.7
1924	Bos A	7	12	.368	33	20	9	2	152	166	93	1	6	73	33	4.32	101	.283	.368	42-0-2	.071	-3	77	-1	—	-0.5
1925	Bos A	0	3	.000	4	2	0	0	22.2	22	11	1	2	9	3	3.18	143	.259	.344	10-0-1	.200	-0	46	3	—	0.4
1933	Bos A	0	2	.000	6	2	2	0	25.1	36	24	1	1	13	10	8.53	51	.364	.442	9	.222	0	39	-10	—	-0.6
Total	6	10	37	.213	115	43	18	3	423	483	293	19	21	211	104	5.11	83	.296	.384	110-0-4	.182	-1	68	-40	—	-3.2

FULTON, BILL William David; B10.22.1963 Pittsburgh PA; BR/TR/6´3˝/195; [NYA83 S2/35]; d9.12; Col Pensacola (FL) JC

YEAR	TM LG	W	L	PCT	G	GS	CG-SHO	SV-BS	IP	H	R	HR	HB	BB-IB	SO	ERA	AERA	OAV	OOB	AB-HR-SH	AVG	PB	SUP	APR	DL	PW
1987	NY A	1	0	1.000	3	0	0	0-0	4.2	9	6	4	1	1-0	2	11.57	38	.409	.458	0	ø	0	—	-4	0	-0.6

FULTZ, AARON Richard Aaron; B9.4.1973 Memphis TN; BL/TL/6´0˝/(196–210); [SFN92 6/159]; d4.5; Col North Florida CC

YEAR	TM LG	W	L	PCT	G	GS	CG-SHO	SV-BS	IP	H	R	HR	HB	BB-IB	SO	ERA	AERA	OAV	OOB	AB-HR-SH	AVG	PB	SUP	APR	DL	PW
2000	†SF N	5	2	.714	58	0	0	1-2	69.1	67	38	8	3	28-0	62	4.67	93	.263	.336	6-0-1	.333	1	—	-2	0	0.0
2001	SF N	3	1	.750	66	0	0	1-1	71	70	40	9	1	21-3	67	4.56	90	.258	.310	5	.400	1	—	-4	0	-0.1
2002	†SF N	2	2	.500	43	0	0	0-1	41.1	47	22	4	3	19-3	31	4.79	82	.294	.377	1	.000	-0*	—	-3	0	-0.3
2003	Tex A	1	3	.250	64	0	0	0-0	67.1	75	43	9	2	27-7	53	5.21	95	.287	.356	0	ø	0	—	-2	18	-0.1
2004	Min A	3	3	.500	55	0	0	1-3	50	50	28	5	1	23-2	37	5.04	92	.267	.344	0	ø	0	—	-1	0	-0.1
2005	Phi N	4	0	1.000	62	0	0	0-1	72.1	47	21	6	5	23-2	54	2.24	194	.186	.266	3	.333	0	—	16	0	0.9
2006	Phi N	3	1	.750	66	1	0	0-2	71.1	80	39	7	2	28-8	62	4.54	103	.288	.350	4	.000	-0	217	1	0	0.1
Total	7	21	12	.636	414	1	0	3-10	442.2	436	231	48	17	169-25	366	4.37	102	.262	.332	19-0-1	.263	1	217	5	18	0.4

FUNK, FRANK Franklin Ray; B8.30.1935 Washington DC; BR/TR/6´0˝/180; d9.3; C11

YEAR	TM LG	W	L	PCT	G	GS	CG-SHO	SV-BS	IP	H	R	HR	HB	BB-IB	SO	ERA	AERA	OAV	OOB	AB-HR-SH	AVG	PB	SUP	APR	DL	PW
1960	Cle A	4	2	.667	9	0	0	1	31.2	27	8	3	0	9-3	18	1.99	188	.248	.305	9	.111	-0	—	6	0	1.2
1961	Cle A	11	11	.500	56	0	0	11	92.1	79	35	9	4	31-6	64	3.31	119	.234	.303	17	.059	-1	—	8	0	1.5
1962	Cle A	2	1	.667	47	0	0	6	80.2	62	35	11	4	32-1	49	3.24	120	.212	.293	15	.067	-1	—	5	0	0.1
1963	Mil N	3	3	.500	25	0	0	0	43.2	42	14	3	1	13-3	19	2.68	120	.258	.315	4	.000	-0*	—	3	0	0.3
Total	4	20	17	.541	137	0	0	18	248.1	210	92	26	9	85-13	150	3.01	125	.233	.302	45	.067	-3	—	22	0	3.1

FUNK, TOM Thomas James; B3.13.1962 Kansas City MO; BL/TL/6´2˝/210; [HouN83 28/691]; d7.24; Col Northwest Missouri

YEAR	TM LG	W	L	PCT	G	GS	CG-SHO	SV-BS	IP	H	R	HR	HB	BB-IB	SO	ERA	AERA	OAV	OOB	AB-HR-SH	AVG	PB	SUP	APR	DL	PW
1986	Hou N	0	0	ø	8	0	0	0-0	8.1	10	6	1	0	6-0	2	6.48	56	.286	.390	1	.000	-0	—	-2	0	-0.1

FUSSELBACK, EDDIE Edward L.; B7.17.1856 Philadelphia PA; D4.14.1926 Philadelphia PA; BR/5´6˝/156; d5.3; ▲

YEAR	TM LG	W	L	PCT	G	GS	CG-SHO	SV-BS	IP	H	R	HR	HB	BB-IB	SO	ERA	AERA	OAV	OOB	AB-HR-SH	AVG	PB	SUP	APR	DL	PW
1882	StL AA	1	2	.333	4	2	2	1	23	34	24	0	—	2	3	4.70	60	.321	.333	136	.228	0*	119	-4	—	-0.5

FUSSELL, CHRIS Christopher Wren; B5.19.1976 Oregon OH; BR/TR/6´2˝/(200–201); [BalA94 9/251]; d9.15

YEAR	TM LG	W	L	PCT	G	GS	CG-SHO	SV-BS	IP	H	R	HR	HB	BB-IB	SO	ERA	AERA	OAV	OOB	AB-HR-SH	AVG	PB	SUP	APR	DL	PW
1998	Bal A	0	1	.000	3	2	0	0-0	9.2	11	9	1	0	9-1	8	8.38	54	.306	.435	0	ø	0	82	-4	0	-0.3
1999	KC A	0	5	.000	17	8	0	2-0	56	72	51	9	5	36-3	37	7.39	69	.329	.428	0	ø	0	101	-14	0	-1.1
2000	KC A	5	3	.625	20	9	0	0-0	70	76	52	18	2	44-2	46	6.30	83	.286	.385	2	.000	-0	126	-8	60	-0.8
Total	3	5	9	.357	40	19	0	2-0	135.2	159	112	28	7	89-6	91	6.90	74	.305	.407	2	.000	-0	111	-26	60	-2.2

FUSSELL, FRED Frederick Morris "Moonlight Ace"; B10.7.1895 Sheridan MO; D10.23.1966 Syracuse NY; BL/TL/5´10˝/155; d9.23

YEAR	TM LG	W	L	PCT	G	GS	CG-SHO	SV-BS	IP	H	R	HR	HB	BB-IB	SO	ERA	AERA	OAV	OOB	AB-HR-SH	AVG	PB	SUP	APR	DL	PW
1922	Chi N	1	1	.500	3	2	1	0	19	24	11	0	0	8	4	4.74	89	.333	.400	6	.000	-1	78	-1	—	-0.1
1923	Chi N	3	5	.375	28	2	1	3	76.1	90	51	2	3	31	38	5.54	72	.298	.369	20	.200	-0	62	-11	—	-1.0
1928	Pit N	8	9	.471	28	20	9-2	1	159.2	183	79	6	1	41	43	3.61	113	.295	.340	58-0-1	.121	-3	108	7	—	0.2
1929	Pit N	2	2	.500	21	3	0	1	39.2	68	42	8	1	8	18	8.62	55	.389	.418	16-2-0	.250	2	171	-16	—	-1.2
Total	4	14	17	.452	80	27	11-2	5	294.2	365	183	16	5	88	103	4.86	85	.312	.363	100-2-1	.150	-2	110	-21	—	-2.1

FYHRIE, MIKE Michael Edwin; B12.9.1969 Long Beach CA; BR/TR/6´2˝/(190–203); [KCA91 12/314]; d9.14; Col UCLA

YEAR	TM LG	W	L	PCT	G	GS	CG-SHO	SV-BS	IP	H	R	HR	HB	BB-IB	SO	ERA	AERA	OAV	OOB	AB-HR-SH	AVG	PB	SUP	APR	DL	PW
1996	NY N	0	1	.000	2	0	0	0-0	2.1	4	4	0	0	3-0	0	15.43	26	.364	.500	0	ø	0	—	-3	0	-0.5
1999	Ana A	0	4	.000	16	7	0	0-0	51.2	61	32	8	0	21-1	26	5.05	97	.286	.349	0	ø	0	71	-1	0	-0.1
2000	Ana A	0	0	ø	32	0	0	0-0	52.2	54	14	4	0	15-4	43	2.39	216	.269	.315	0	ø	0	—	16	23	0.7
2001	Chi N	0	2	.000	15	0	0	0-0	15	16	7	1	0	7-0	6	4.20	100	.281	.359	2	.000	-0	—	0	73	0.0
	Oak A	0	0	ø	3	0	0	0-0	5	2	0	0	0	1-0	5	0.00	ø	.125	.176	0	ø	0	—	2	0	0.1
2002	Oak A	2	4	.333	16	4	0	0-0	48.2	46	25	3	4	20-1	29	4.44	101	.246	.332	0	ø	0	140	1	0	0.1
Total	5	2	11	.154	84	11	0	0-0	175.1	183	82	16	4	67-6	109	4.00	119	.267	.334	2	.000	-0	94	15	96	0.3

GABBARD, KASON Kason Ronald; B4.8.1982 Oxford OH; BL/TL/6´3˝/200; [BosA00 29/872]; d7.22; Col Indian River (FL) CC

YEAR	TM LG	W	L	PCT	G	GS	CG-SHO	SV-BS	IP	H	R	HR	HB	BB-IB	SO	ERA	AERA	OAV	OOB	AB-HR-SH	AVG	PB	SUP	APR	DL	PW
2006	Bos A	1	3	.250	7	4	0	0-0	25.2	24	11	0	0	16-0	15	3.51	133	.255	.364	0	ø	0	45	3	0	0.4

GABLER, FRANK Frank Harold "The Great Gabbo"; B11.6.1911 E.Highlands CA; D11.1.1967 Long Beach CA; BR/TR/6´1˝/175; d4.19

YEAR	TM LG	W	L	PCT	G	GS	CG-SHO	SV-BS	IP	H	R	HR	HB	BB-IB	SO	ERA	AERA	OAV	OOB	AB-HR-SH	AVG	PB	SUP	APR	DL	PW
1935	NY N	2	1	.667	26	1	0	0	60	79	43	6	0	20	24	5.70	68	.315	.365	16	.125	-1	154	-13	—	-0.7
1936	†NY N	9	8	.529	43	14	5	6	161.2	170	62	11	3	34	46	3.12	125	.274	.315	48-0-6	.208	2	110	16	—	1.7
1937	NY N	0	0	ø	6	0	0	0	9	20	14	1	0	2	3	10.00	39	.455	.478	0	ø	0	—	-7	—	-0.3
	Bos N	4	7	.364	19	9	2-1	2	76	84	45	7	0	16	19	5.09	70	.283	.319	22	.182	0	72	-12	—	-1.5
	Year	4	7	.364	25	9	2-1	2	85	104	59	8	0	18	22	5.61	64	.305	.340	22	.182	0	71	-18	—	-1.8
1938	Bos N	0	0	ø	1	0	0	0	0.1	3	3	0	0	1	0	81.00	4	1.000	1.000	0	ø	0	—	-3	—	-0.1
	Chi A	1	7	.125	18	7	3	0	69.1	101	74	12	1	34	17	9.09	54	.348	.418	21	.238	0	85	-28	—	-2.5
Total	4	16	23	.410	113	31	10-1	8	376.1	457	241	37	4	107	109	5.26	76	.303	.351	107-0-6	.196	1	95	-47	—	-3.4

GABLER, JOHN John Richard "Gab"; B10.2.1930 Kansas City MO; BB/TR/6´2˝/(165–175); d9.18

YEAR	TM LG	W	L	PCT	G	GS	CG-SHO	SV-BS	IP	H	R	HR	HB	BB-IB	SO	ERA	AERA	OAV	OOB	AB-HR-SH	AVG	PB	SUP	APR	DL	PW
1959	NY A	1	1	.500	3	1	0	0	19.1	21	6	1	1	10-0	11	2.79	130	.284	.376	6	.000	-1	24	2	0	0.1
1960	NY A	3	3	.500	21	4	0	1	52	46	27	2	0	32-1	19	4.15	86	.242	.348	11-0-1	.091	-0	86	-3	0	-0.4
1961	Was A	3	8	.273	29	9	0	4	92.2	104	61	5	1	37-3	33	4.86	83	.283	.349	25	.200	1*	47	-10	0	-1.0
Total	3	7	12	.368	53	14	0	5	164	171	94	8	2	79-4	63	4.39	87	.271	.352	42-0-1	.143	-0	56	-11	0	-1.3

GABLES, KEN Kenneth Harlin "Coral"; B1.31.1919 Walnut Grove MO; D1.2.1960 Walnut Grove MO; BR/TR/5´11˝/210; d4.18

YEAR	TM LG	W	L	PCT	G	GS	CG-SHO	SV-BS	IP	H	R	HR	HB	BB-IB	SO	ERA	AERA	OAV	OOB	AB-HR-SH	AVG	PB	SUP	APR	DL	PW
1945	Pit N	11	7	.611	29	16	6	1	138.2	139	69	5	4	46	49	4.15	95	.256	.319	39-0-3	.103	-3	117	0	0	-0.4
1946	Pit N	2	4	.333	32	7	0	1	100.2	113	64	3	1	52	39	5.27	67	.281	.365	24-0-2	.250	1	80	-17	0	-0.9
1947	Pit N	0	0	ø	1	0	0	0	0.1	3	2	1	0	0	0	54.00	8	.750	.750	0	ø	0	—	-2	0	-0.1
Total	3	13	11	.542	62	23	6	2	239.2	255	135	9	5	98	88	4.69	80	.269	.340	63-0-5	.159	-1	108	-19	0	-1.4

GADDY, JOHN John Wilson "Sheriff"; B2.5.1914 Wadesboro NC; D5.3.1966 Albemarle NC; BR/TR/6´0.5˝/182; d9.27; Col Wake Forest

YEAR	TM LG	W	L	PCT	G	GS	CG-SHO	SV-BS	IP	H	R	HR	HB	BB-IB	SO	ERA	AERA	OAV	OOB	AB-HR-SH	AVG	PB	SUP	APR	DL	PW
1938	Bro N	2	0	1.000	2	2	1	0	13	13	3	0	1	4	3	0.69	564	.255	.321	6	.000	-1	130	4	—	0.5

YEAR	TM LG	W	L	PCT	G	GS	CG-SHO	SV-BS	IP	H	R	HR	HB	BB-IB	SO	ERA	AERA	OAV	OOB	AB-HR-SH	AVG	PB	SUP	APR	DL	PW
GAFF, BRENT	Brent Allen; B10.5.1958 Fort Wayne IN; BR/TR/6´2˝/(185–200); [NYN77 6/146]; d7.7; [DL 1985 NY N 182]																									
1982	NY N	0	3	.000	7	5	0	0-0	31.2	41	22	3	1	10-0	14	4.55	81	.323	.374	8-0-1	.000	-0	77	-4	0	-0.4
1983	NY N	1	0	1.000	4	0	0	0-0	10.1	18	9	0	0	1-1	4	6.10	60	.360	.365	3	.000	-0	—	-3	0	-0.3
1984	NY N	3	2	.600	47	0	0	1-0	84.1	77	39	4	1	36-11	42	3.63	98	.247	.320	6	.000	-1	—	0	0	-0.1
Total	3	4	5	.444	58	5	0	1-0	126.1	136	70	7	2	47-12	60	4.06	89	.278	.338	17-0-1	.000	-1	77	-7	182	-0.8
GAGNE, ERIC	Eric Serge; B1.7.1976 Montreal QC, Can.; BR/TR/6´2˝/(195–235); d9.7; Col Seminole St. (OK) JC																									
1999	LA N	1	1	.500	5	5	0	0-0	30	18	8	3	0	15-0	30	2.10	207	.175	.280	10	.200	0	72	8	0	0.4
2000	LA N	4	6	.400	20	19	0	0-0	101.1	106	62	20	3	60-1	79	5.15	86	.270	.368	28-0-6	.143	-1	102	-7	0	-0.7
2001	LA N	6	7	.462	33	24	0	0-0	151.2	144	90	24	16	46-1	130	4.75	87	.251	.320	44-1-6	.136	2	119	-13	0	-0.9
2002	LA N★	4	1	.800	77	0	0	52-4	82.1	55	18	6	2	16-4	114	1.97	198	.189	.235	1	.000	-0	—	19	0	3.3
2003	LA N★	2	3	.400	77	0	0	**55**-0	82.1	37	12	2	3	20-2	137	1.20	343	.133	.199	0	ø	0	—	**28**	0	4.9
2004	†LA N★	7	3	.700	70	0	0	45-2	82.1	53	24	5	5	22-3	114	2.19	189	.181	.248	3	.000	-0	—	17	0	3.4
2005	LA N	1	0	1.000	14	0	0	8-0	13.1	10	4	2	0	3-0	22	2.70	154	.200	.245	0	ø	0	—	2	153	0.4
2006	LA N	0	0	ø	2	0	0	1-0	2	0	0	0	1	1-0	3	0.00	ø	.000	.250	0	ø	0	—	1	174	0.1
Total	8	25	21	.543	298	48	0	161-6	545.1	423	218	62	30	183-11	629	3.27	127	.213	.287	86-1-12	.140	0	111	55	327	10.9
GAGUS, CHARLIE	Charles Frederick (b Charles Frederick Geggus); B3.25.1862 San Francisco CA; D1.16.1917 San Francisco CA; 5´7.5˝/150; d8.7; Col St. Marys (CA)																									
1884	Was U	10	9	.526	23	21	19	0	177.1	143	100	2	—	38	156	2.54	95	.206	.247	154	.247	-1*	98	-5	—	-0.6
GAILLARD, EDDIE	Julian Edward; B8.13.1970 Camden NJ; BR/TR/6´1˝/(180–200); [DetA93 13/361]; d8.11; Col Florida Southern																									
1997	Det A	1	0	1.000	16	0	0	1-1	20.1	16	12	2	0	10-2	12	5.31	87	.211	.295	0	ø	0	—	-1	0	-0.1
1998	TB A	0	0	ø	6	0	0	0-0	7.2	4	5	3	0	3-0	5	5.87	82	.148	.233	0	ø	0	—	-1	95	0.0
1999	TB A	1	0	1.000	8	0	0	0-0	8.2	12	9	1	1	4-0	7	2.08	239	.324	.405	0	ø	0	—	0	0	0.0
Total	3	2	0	1.000	30	0	0	1-1	36.2	32	26	6	1	17-2	24	4.66	102	.229	.313	0	ø	0	—	-2	95	-0.1
GAINES, NEMO	Willard Roland; B12.23.1897 Alexandria VA; D1.26.1979 Warrenton VA; BL/TL/6´0˝/180; d6.26; Col Navy																									
1921	Was A	0	0	ø	4	0	0	0	4.2	5	0	0	0	2	1	0.00	ø	.294	.368	1	.000	-0	—	2	—	0.1
GAISER, FRED	Frederick Jacob; B8.31.1885 Stuttgart, Germany; D10.9.1918 Trenton NJ; TR; d9.3																									
1908	StL N	0	0	ø	1	0	0	0	2.1	4	2	0	0	3	2	7.71	31	.444	.583	1	.000	-0	—	-1	—	-0.1
GAJKOWSKI, STEVE	Stephen Robert; B12.30.1969 Seattle WA; BR/TR/6´2˝/185; [CleA90 18/487]; d5.25; Col Bellevue (WA) CC																									
1998	Sea A	0	0	ø	9	0	0	0-0	8.2	14	8	3	2	4-0	3	7.27	64	.389	.476	0	ø	0	—	-3	0	-0.1
GAKELER, DAN	Daniel Michael; B5.1.1964 Mt.Holly NJ; BR/TR/6´6˝/210; [BosA84*S1/3]; d6.9; Col Mercer Co. (NJ) CC; [DL 1992 Det A 182]																									
1991	Det A	1	4	.200	31	7	0	2-2	73.2	73	52	5	1	39-6	43	5.74	73	.256	.345	0	ø	0	100	-13	0	-0.8
GALASSO, BOB	Robert Joseph; B1.13.1952 Connellsville PA; BL/TR/6´1˝/205; d7.24																									
1977	Sea A	0	6	.000	11	7	0	0-0	35	57	36	8	3	8-0	21	9.00	46	.365	.402	0	ø	0	62	-17	0	-2.4
1979	Mil A	3	1	.750	31	0	0	3-3	51.1	64	30	5	0	26-3	28	4.38	96	.299	.372	0	ø	0	—	-2	0	-0.2
1981	Sea A	1	1	.500	13	1	0	1-0	31.2	32	19	2	0	13-1	14	4.83	80	.264	.331	0	ø	0	23	-3	0	-0.2
Total	3	4	8	.333	55	8	0	4-3	118	153	85	15	3	47-4	63	5.87	70	.312	.371	0	ø	0	58	-22	0	-2.8
GALE, RICH	Richard Blackwell; B1.19.1954 Littleton NH; BR/TR/6´7˝/225; [KCA75 5/105]; d4.30; C2; Col New Hampshire																									
1978	KC A	14	8	.636	31	30	9-3	0-0	192.1	171	78	10	3	100-3	88	3.09	124	.244	.339	0	ø	0	110	15	0	1.5
1979	KC A	9	10	.474	34	31	2-1	0-0	181.2	197	131	19	4	99-4	103	5.65	76	.278	.366	0	ø	0	126	-28	0	-2.5
1980	†KC A	13	9	.591	32	28	6-1	1-1	190.2	169	90	16	2	78-2	97	3.92	103	.239	.315	0	ø	0	110	4	0	0.4
1981	KC A	6	6	.500	19	15	2	0-0	101.2	107	63	14	2	38-0	47	5.40	67	.270	.335	0	ø	0	86	-18	0	-2.0
1982	SF N	7	14	.333	33	29	2	0-1	170.1	193	91	9	5	81-11	102	4.23	85	.294	.370	48-1-1	.125	1	79	-12	0	-1.2
1983	Cin N	4	6	.400	33	7	0	1-0	89.2	103	64	8	1	43-8	53	5.82	66	.286	.362	20-1-1	.150	1	96	-19	0	-1.9
1984	Bos A	2	3	.400	13	4	0	0-0	43.2	57	27	6	1	18-0	28	5.56	76	.315	.380	0	ø	0	129	-5	0	-0.5
Total	7	55	56	.495	195	144	21-5	2-2	970	997	544	82	18	457-28	518	4.54	86	.269	.349	68-2-2	.132	2	106	-63	0	-6.2
GALEHOUSE, DENNY	Dennis Ward; B12.7.1911 Marshallville OH; D10.12.1998 Doylestown OH; BR/TR/6´1˝/195; d4.30; Def 1944																									
1934	Cle A	0	0	ø	1	0	0	0	1	2	3	0	0	1	0	18.00	25	.500	.600	0	ø	0	—	-2	—	-0.1
1935	Cle A	1	0	1.000	5	1	1	0	13	16	14	1	1	9	8	9.00	50	.314	.426	4	.250	-0	135	-6	—	-0.4
1936	Cle A	8	7	.533	36	15	5	1	148.1	161	86	5	2	68	71	4.85	104	.280	.358	47-0-1	.170	-0	95	6	—	0.4
1937	Cle A	9	14	.391	36	29	7	3	200.2	238	114	11	1	83	78	4.57	101	.302	.369	72-0-2	.208	-1	80	2	—	0.1
1938	Cle A	7	8	.467	36	12	5-1	3	114	119	62	12	1	65	66	4.34	107	.275	.371	39	.154	-1	104	4	—	0.3
1939	Bos A	9	10	.474	30	18	6-1	0	146.2	160	84	6	1	52	68	4.54	104	.276	.337	47-0-4	.064	-3	77	4	—	0.1
1940	Bos A	6	6	.500	25	20	5	0	120	155	77	10	0	41	53	5.18	87	.313	.366	39-0-7	.077	-4	109	-9	—	-1.1
1941	StL A	9	10	.474	30	24	11-2	0	190.1	183	85	10	4	68	61	3.64	118	.253	.320	68-0-5	.191	-0	86	14	0	1.3
1942	StL A	12	12	.500	32	28	12-3	1	192.1	193	91	5	4	79	75	3.60	103	.262	.337	72-0-4	.194	1	115	2	0	0.3
1943	StL A	11	11	.500	31	28	14-2	1	224	217	80	8	1	74	114	2.77	120	.255	.315	72-0-8	.125	-3	106	13	0	0.8
1944	†StL A	9	10	.474	24	19	6-2	0	153	162	64	6	1	44	80	3.12	115	.266	.316	48-0-4	.063	-4	82	7	0	0.3
1946	StL A	8	12	.400	30	24	11-2	0	180	194	82	9	0	52	90	3.65	102	.273	.322	55-0-6	.091	-3	88	3	0	-0.2
1947	StL A	1	3	.250	9	4	0	1	32.1	42	26	3	0	16	11	6.12	63	.311	.384	8-0-2	.000	-1	114	-8	0	-1.0
	Bos A	11	7	.611	21	21	11-3	0	149	150	60	7	0	34	38	3.32	117	.260	.301	52-0-9	.096	-4	117	10	0	0.6
	Year	12	10	.545	30	25	11-3	1	181.1	192	86	10	0	50	49	3.82	102	.269	.317	60-0-11	.083	-5	117	2	0	-0.4
1948	Bos A	8	8	.500	27	15	6-1	3	137.1	152	68	10	2	46	38	4.00	110	.282	.341	42-0-3	.167	-0	95	6	0	0.5
1949	Bos A	0	0	ø	2	0	0	0	2	4	3	1	0	3	0	13.50	32	.400	.538	0	ø	0	—	-2	0	-0.1
Total	15	109	118	.480	375	258	100-17	13	2004	2148	999	104	18	735	851	3.97	105	.275	.338	665-0-55	.138	-25	95	44	0	1.8
GALLAGHER, DOUG	Douglas Eugene; B2.21.1940 Fremont OH; BR/TL/6´3.5˝/195; d4.9																									
1962	Det A	0	4	.000	9	2	0	1	25	31	18	2	0	15-1	14	4.68	87	.290	.371	6	.333	1	132	-3	0	-0.4
GALLAGHER, ED	Edward Michael "Lefty"; B11.28.1910 Dorchester MA; D12.22.1981 Hyannis MA; BB/TL/6´2˝/197; d7.8; Col Boston College																									
1932	Bos A	0	3	.000	9	3	0	0	23.2	30	36	3	0	28	6	12.55	36	.323	.479	5	.000	-1	38	-20	—	-1.9
GALLAGHER, BILL	William John; B Philadelphia PA; TL; d5.2; ▲																									
1883	Bal AA	0	5	.000	7	5	4	0	51.2	79	57	0	—	6	19	5.40	64	.331	.347	61	.164	-1*	89	-10	—	-0.8
1884	Phi U	1	2	.333	3	3	3	0	25	32	29	3	—	4	12	3.24	71	.291	.316	11	.091	-2	92	-7	—	-0.7
Total	2	1	7	.125	10	8	7	0	76.2	111	86	3	—	10	31	4.70	66	.318	.337	72	.153	-2	90	-17	—	-1.5
GALLIA, BERT	Melvin Allys; B10.14.1891 Beeville TX; D3.19.1976 Devine TX; BR/TR/6´0˝/165; d9.4; Col St. Marys (TX)																									
1912	Was A	0	0	ø	2	0	0	0	2	0	0	0	0	3	0	0.00	ø	.000	.333	0	ø	0	—	1	—	0.0
1913	Was A	1	5	.167	31	4	0	3	96	85	66	2	7	46	46	4.13	72	.232	.329	23	.087	-2	69	-15	—	-1.1
1914	Was A	0	0	ø	2	0	0	0	6	3	4	0	0	4	4	4.50	63	.120	.241	2	.000	-0	—	-1	—	-0.1
1915	Was A	17	11	.607	43	29	14-3	1	259.2	220	90	2	4	64	130	2.29	130	.234	.286	85-0-3	.165	-2	97	20	—	1.8
1916	Was A	17	13	.567	49	31	13-1	2	283.2	278	109	3	8	99	120	2.76	101	.266	.334	93-0-4	.194	1	111	2	—	0.1
1917	Was A	9	13	.409	42	23	9-1	1	207.2	191	92	1	4	93	84	2.99	88	.258	.344	67-0-2	.209	2*	100	-9	—	-0.8
1918	StL A	8	6	.571	19	17	10-1	0	124	126	63	1	6	61	48	3.48	79	.268	.359	46-0-1	.130	-3	115	-10	—	-1.5
1919	StL A	12	14	.462	34	25	14-1	1	222.1	220	109	10	8	92	83	3.60	92	.264	.343	72-1-4	.153	-2	99	-5	—	-0.6
1920	StL A	0	1	.000	2	1	0	0	3.2	8	7	0	0	3	0	7.36	53	.400	.478	1	.000	-0	81	-3	—	-0.5
	Phi N	2	6	.250	18	5	1	2	72	79	48	2	3	29	35	4.50	76	.287	.362	23-0-1	.174	-1*	60	-9	—	-1.1
Total	9	66	69	.489	242	135	61-7	10	1277	1210	588	21	40	494	550	3.14	94	.256	.332	412-1-15	.167	-7	100	-29	—	-3.8
GALLIVAN, PHIL	Philip Joseph; B5.29.1907 Seattle WA; D11.24.1969 St.Paul MN; BR/TR/6´0˝/170; d4.21																									
1931	Bro N	0	1	.000	6	1	0	0	15.1	23	11	2	0	7	1	5.28	72	.354	.417	3	.000	-0	22	-3	—	-0.1
1932	Chi A	1	3	.250	13	3	1	0	33.1	49	32	4	1	24	12	7.56	57	.338	.435	8	.375	1	79	-11	—	-1.0
1934	Chi A	4	7	.364	35	7	3	1	126.2	155	97	14	1	64	55	5.61	84	.295	.373	40-0-3	.225	1	110	-14	—	-1.0
Total	3	5	11	.313	54	11	4	1	175.1	227	140	20	2	95	68	5.95	77	.309	.389	51-0-3	.235	1	95	-28	—	-2.1

YEAR	TM LG	W	L	PCT	G	GS	CG-SHO	SV-BS	IP	H	R	HR	HB	BB-IB	SO	ERA	AERA	OAV	OOB	AB-HR-SH	AVG	PB	SUP	APR	DL	PW
GALLO, MIKE	Michael Dwain; B4.2.1977 Long Beach CA; BL/TL/6´0˝/(170–175); [HouN99 5/173]; d7.2; Col Cal St.–Long Beach																									
2003	Hou N	1	0	1.000	32	0	0	0-1	30	28	10	3	1	10-2	16	3.00	147	.267	.328	2	.000	-0	—	5	0	0.3
2004	†Hou N	2	0	1.000	69	0	0	0-1	49.1	55	27	12	6	20-7	34	4.74	92	.284	.367	1	.000	-0	—	-2	0	-0.1
2005	†Hou N	0	1	.000	36	0	0	0-2	20.1	18	6	1	2	10-2	12	2.66	159	.250	.353	0	ø	0	—	4	0	0.2
2006	Hou N	1	2	.333	23	0	0	0-1	16.1	28	11	3	2	7-1	7	6.06	74	.400	.463	1	.000	-0	—	-2	0	-0.4
Total	4	4	3	.571	160	0	0	0-5	116	129	54	19	11	47-12	69	4.11	106	.293	.370	4	.000	-0	—	5	0	0.0
GALVEZ, BALVINO	Balvino (Jerez); B3.31.1964 San Pedro de Macoris, D.R.; BR/TR/6´0˝/180; d5.7																									
1986	LA N	0	1	.000	10	0	0	0-2	20.2	19	10	3	0	12-2	11	3.92	88	.241	.341	2	.000	-0	—	-1	0	-0.1
GALVIN, JIM	James Francis "Pud", "Gentle Jeems","The Little Steam Engine"; B12.25.1856 St.Louis MO; D3.7.1902 Pittsburgh PA; BR/TR/5´8˝/190; d5.22; M1/U1; HF1965																									
1875	StL NA	4	2	.667	8	7	7	1	62	53	37	0	—	1	8	**1.16**	**173**	.209	.212	46	.130	-1*	105	3	—	0.2
1879	Buf N	37	27	.578	66	66	65-6	0	593	585	299	3	—	31	136	2.28	115	.243	.253	265	.249	5*	85	20	—	2.5
1880	Buf N	20	35	.364	58	54	46-5	0	458.2	528	281	5	—	32	128	2.71	91	.273	.284	241	.212	-4*	86	-14	—	-1.7
1881	Buf N	28	24	.538	56	53	48-5	0	474	546	250	4	—	46	136	2.37	117	.274	.291	236	.212	-1*	103	18	—	2.0
1882	Buf N	28	23	.549	52	51	48-3	0	445.1	476	255	8	—	40	162	3.17	93	.256	.272	206	.214	-5*	109	-8	—	-1.2
1883	Buf N	46	29	.613	**76**	**75**	**72-5**	0	**656.1**	676	367	9	—	50	279	2.72	117	.251	.265	322-1	.220	-4*	106	31	—	2.4
1884	Buf N	46	22	.676	72	72	71-**12**	0	636.1	566	254	23	—	63	369	1.99	158	.227	.246	274	.179	-14	103	81	—	6.3
1885	Buf N	13	19	.406	33	32	31-3	1	284	356	204	8	—	37	93	4.09	73	.292	.313	122-1	.189	-2	94	-30	—	-2.7
	Pit AA	3	7	.300	11	11	9	0	88.1	97	64	2	0	7	27	3.67	88	.266	.280	38	.105	-4	82	-6	—	-0.8
1886	Pit AA	29	21	.580	50	50	49-2	0	434.2	457	229	3	7	75	72	2.67	127	.263	.296	194	.253	2	114	31	—	3.2
1887	Pit N	28	21	.571	49	48	47-3	0	440.2	490	259	12	11	67	76	3.29	117	.269	.299	193-2	.212	-2	98	20	—	1.9
1888	Pit N	23	25	.479	50	50	49-6	0	437.1	446	190	9	8	53	107	2.63	100	.255	.280	175-1	.143	-6	83	5	—	0.1
1889	Pit N	23	16	.590	41	40	38-4	0	341	392	230	19	10	78	77	4.17	90	.280	.323	150	.187	-1	109	-19	—	-1.7
1890	Pit P	12	13	.480	26	25	23-1	0	217	275	192	3	9	49	35	4.35	90	.296	.337	97	.206	-1	102	-16	—	-1.2
1891	Pit N	15	14	.517	33	30	23-2	0	246.2	256	143	9	13	62	46	2.88	114	.258	.310	109	.165	-4	106	14	—	0.9
1892	Pit N	5	6	.455	12	12	10	0	96	104	51	0	0	28	29	2.63	126	.265	.314	41	.122	-3	109	6	—	0.3
	StL N	5	6	.455	12	12	10	0	92	102	47	4	3	26	27	3.23	99	.270	.322	39	.051	-5	89	0	—	-0.5
	Year	10	12	.455	24	24	20	0	188	206	98	4	3	54	56	2.92	111	.268	.318	80	.087	-7	99	9	—	-0.2
Total	14	361	308	.540	697	681	639-57	1	5941.1	6352	3315	121	61	744	1799	2.87	108	.261	.284	2702-5	.202	-47	99	133	—	9.8
GALVIN, LOU	Louis J.; B4.1862 St.Paul MN; D6.17.1895; d10.1																									
1884	StP U	0	2	.000	3	3	3	0	25	21	18	0	—	10	17	2.88	46	.212	.284	9	.222	-0	64	-8	—	-0.5
GAMBLE, BOB	Robert J.; B2.6.1867 Philadelphia PA; TR/5´10˝/155; d5.2																									
1888	Phi AA	0	1	.000	1	1	1	0	9	10	10	0	0	3	2	8.00	37	.270	.325	3	.333	0	19	-4	—	-0.3
GANDARILLAS, GUS	Gustavo; B7.19.1971 Coral Gables FL; BR/TR/6´0˝/183; [MinA92 3/94]; d7.17; Col Miami																									
2001	Mil N	0	0	ø	16	0	0	0-0	19.2	25	13	2	0	10-3	7	5.49	78	.321	.398	0	ø	0	—	-3	0	-0.1
GANNON, GUSSIE	James Edward; B11.26.1873 Erie PA; D4.12.1966 Erie PA; BL/TL/5´11˝/154; d6.15																									
1895	Pit N	0	0	ø	1	0	0	0	5	7	4	0	0	2	0	1.80	250	.333	.391	2	.000	-0	—	1	—	0.0
GANNON, JOE	Michael Joseph; B2.22.1877 St.Louis MO; D3.19.1931 St.Louis MO; d8.28																									
1898	StL N	0	1	.000	1	1	1	0	9	13	13	0	1	5	2	11.00	34	.333	.422	3	.000	-1	37	-6	—	-0.5
GARAGOZZO, KEITH	Keith John; B10.25.1969 Camden NJ; BL/TL/6´0˝/170; [NYA91 9/230]; d4.5; Col Delaware																									
1994	Min A	0	0	ø	7	0	0	0-0	9.1	9	10	3	0	13-2	3	9.64	51	.273	.468	0	ø	0	—	-4	0	-0.2
GARBER, GENE	Henry Eugene; B11.13.1947 Lancaster PA; BR/TR/5´10˝/(165–175); [PitN65 12/387]; d6.17																									
1969	Pit N	0	0	ø	2	1	0	0-0	5	6	3	3	0	1-0	3	5.40	64	.333	.368	1	.000	-0	102	-1	0	-0.1
1970	Pit N	0	3	.000	14	0	0	0-3	22.1	22	13	4	2	10-1	7	5.24	76	.275	.366	3	.667	1	—	-3	0	-0.2
1972	Pit N	0	0	ø	4	0	0	0-0	6.1	7	5	3	0	3-0	3	7.11	47	.269	.345	1	.000	-0	—	-2	0	-0.1
1973	KC A	9	9	.500	48	8	4	11-5	152.2	164	78	14	2	49-15	60	4.24	97	.283	.338	0	ø	0*	71	-1	0	-0.1
1974	KC A	1	2	.333	17	0	0	1-2	28	35	21	3	1	13-9	14	4.82	79	.313	.389	0	ø	0	—	-4	0	-0.5
	Phi N	4	0	1.000	34	0	0	4-3	48	39	15	1	1	31-15	27	2.06	184	.236	.357	3	.000	-0	—	8	0	0.7
1975	Phi N	10	12	.455	**71**	0	0	14-6	110	104	48	13	2	27-11	69	3.60	105	.254	.302	12-0-1	.167	-0	—	3	0	0.5
1976	†Phi N	9	3	.750	59	0	0	11-3	92.2	78	33	4	4	30-8	92	2.82	127	.228	.295	7-0-3	.286	1	—	7	0	1.3
1977	†Phi N	8	6	.571	64	0	0	19-6	103.1	82	30	6	2	23-8	78	2.35	171	.220	.268	10	.000	-1	—	19	0	3.1
1978	Phi N	2	1	.667	22	0	0	3-1	38.2	26	6	1	3	11-3	24	1.40	259	.191	.267	3	.000	-0	—	10	0	0.9
	Atl N	4	4	.500	43	0	0	22-4	78.1	58	26	11	2	13-3	61	2.53	159	.204	.244	11	.091	-0	—	11	0	1.8
	Year	6	5	.545	65	0	0	25-5	117	84	32	12	5	24-6	85	2.15	181	.200	.252	14	.071	-1	—	**20**	0	2.7
1979	Atl N	6	16	.273	68	0	0	25-8	106	121	66	10	5	24-9	56	4.33	93	.283	.326	10-0-2	.300	1	—	-6	0	-1.0
1980	Atl N	5	5	.500	68	0	0	7-2	82.1	95	42	6	0	24-5	51	3.83	96	.288	.335	2	.500	0	—	-3	0	-0.2
1981	Atl N	4	6	.400	35	0	0	2-3	58.2	49	23	2	0	20-9	34	2.61	135	.214	.277	5	.000	-1	—	4	97	0.8
1982	†Atl N	8	10	.444	69	0	0	30-8	119.1	100	40	4	2	32-16	68	2.34	158	.231	.285	15-0-2	.133	0	—	15	0	3.2
1983	Atl N	4	5	.444	43	0	0	9-8	60.2	72	37	8	2	23-7	45	4.60	84	.300	.358	3	.000	0	—	-6	32	-0.9
1984	Atl N	3	6	.333	62	0	0	11-5	106	103	45	7	2	24-9	55	3.06	126	.254	.294	14-0-1	.143	-0	—	7	0	0.7
1985	Atl N	6	6	.500	59	0	0	1-2	97.1	98	41	8	2	25-8	66	3.61	107	.263	.313	5-0-1	.200	0	—	4	0	0.5
1986	Atl N	5	5	.500	61	0	0	24-5	78	76	23	3	1	20-7	56	2.54	156	.260	.309	6-0-1	.167	0	—	12	0	2.3
1987	Atl N	8	10	.444	49	0	0	10-6	69.1	87	39	7	1	28-10	48	4.41	98	.311	.372	4	.000	-0	—	-1	0	-0.1
	KC A	0	0	ø	13	0	0	8-0	14.1	13	5	1	1	1-0	3	2.51	183	.245	.273	0	ø	0	—	3	0	0.4
1988	KC A	0	4	.000	26	0	0	6-2	32.2	29	15	4	2	13-2	20	3.58	112	.238	.321	0	ø	0	—	1	0	0.2
Total	19	96	113	.459	931	9	4	218-82	1510	1464	654	123	37	445-155	940	3.34	116	.257	.312	115-0-11	.148	-0	76	77	129	13.2
GARBER, BOB	Robert Mitchell; B9.10.1928 Hunker PA; D6.7.1999 Redwood City CA; BR/TR/6´1˝/190; d5.13																									
1956	Pit N	0	0	ø	2	0	0	0	4	3	1	1	0	3-1	3	2.25	168	.200	.333	0	ø	0	—	1	0	0.0
GARCES, RICH	Richard Aron (Mendoza) "El Guapo"; B5.18.1971 Maracay, Aragua, Venez.; BR/TR/6´0˝/(215–255); d9.18																									
1990	Min A	0	0	ø	5	0	0	2-0	5.2	4	2	0	0	4-0	1	1.59	262	.200	.333	0	ø	0	—	1	0	0.1
1993	Min A	0	0	ø	3	0	0	0-0	4	4	2	0	0	2-0	3	0.00	ø	.250	.333	0	ø	0	—	1	0	0.0
1995	Chi N	0	0	ø	7	0	0	0-0	11	11	6	0	0	3-0	6	3.27	127	.256	.304	1	.000	-0	—	0	0	0.0
	Fla N	0	2	.000	11	0	0	0-1	13.1	14	9	1	0	8-2	16	5.40	80	.264	.361	0	ø	0	—	-2	0	-0.2
	Year	0	2	.000	18	0	0	0-1	24.1	25	15	1	0	11-2	22	4.44	96	.260	.336	1	.000	-0	—	-1	0	-0.2
1996	Bos A	3	2	.600	37	0	0	0-2	44	42	26	5	0	33-5	55	4.91	104	.251	.366	0	ø	0	—	1	63	0.2
1997	Bos A	0	1	.000	12	0	0	0-2	13.2	14	9	2	1	9-0	12	4.61	101	.255	.364	0	ø	0	—	-1	46	0.0
1998	Bos A	1	1	.500	30	0	0	1-2	46	36	19	6	2	27-3	34	3.33	142	.213	.327	0	ø	0	—	7	95	0.3
1999	†Bos A	5	1	.833	30	0	0	2-1	40.2	25	9	1	0	18-1	33	1.55	322	.171	.262	0	ø	0	—	15	0	2.0
2000	Bos A	8	1	.889	64	0	0	1-4	74.2	64	28	7	1	23-5	69	3.25	154	.229	.286	0	ø	0	—	15	0	1.5
2001	Bos A	6	1	.857	62	0	0	1-1	67	55	32	6	4	25-1	51	3.90	114	.219	.299	2	.000	-0	—	4	16	0.4
2002	Bos A	0	1	.000	26	0	0	0-0	21.1	21	20	4	3	12-2	16	7.59	59	.273	.379	0	ø	0	—	-7	23	-0.3
Total	10	23	10	.697	287	0	0	7-13	341.1	290	162	32	11	164-19	296	3.74	127	.227	.317	3	.000	-0	—	34	243	4.0
GARCIA, MIKE	Edward Miguel "The Big Bear"; B11.17.1923 San Gabriel CA; D1.13.1986 Fairview Park OH; BR/TR/6´1˝/(200–218); d10.3																									
1948	Cle A	0	0	ø	1	0	0	0	2	3	0	0	0	0	1	0.00	ø	.333	.333	0	ø	0	—	1	0	0.1
1949	Cle A	14	5	.737	41	20	8-5	2	175.2	154	51	6	2	60	94	**2.36**	**169**	.241	.308	51-1-8	.235	3	81	34	0	3.7
1950	Cle A	11	11	.500	33	29	11	0	184	191	88	15	0	74	76	3.86	112	.266	.334	65-0-5	.200	-1	111	11	0	1.1
1951	Cle A	20	13	.606	47	30	15-1	6	254	239	101	10	3	82	118	3.15	120	.246	.307	85-1-9	.212	2	97	20	0	2.6
1952	Cle A☆	22	11	.667	46	**36**	19-**6**	4	292.1	284	93	9	7	87	143	2.37	141	.253	.310	95-0-10	.137	-2	116	33	0	3.7
1953	Cle A★	18	9	.667	38	35	21-3	0	271.2	260	106	18	3	81	134	3.25	116	.250	.307	96-0-6	.250	4	107	18	0	2.1
1954	†Cle A✳	19	8	.704	45	34	13-**5**	5	258.2	220	85	6	2	71	129	**2.64**	**139**	.229	**.282**	81-0-6	.136	-2	89	**31**	0	3.0
1955	Cle A	11	13	.458	38	31	6-2	3	210.2	230	101	17	3	56-6	120	4.02	99	.278	.326	69-0-3	.217	2	101	2	0	0.4
1956	Cle A	11	12	.478	35	30	8-4	0	197.2	213	93	18	5	74-5	119	3.78	111	.272	.338	61-0-8	.115	-3	104	10	0	0.6
1957	Cle A	12	8	.600	38	27	9-1	0	211.1	221	98	14	6	73-6	110	3.75	99	.269	.331	75-0-3	.160	-1	117	1	0	-0.2
1958	Cle A	1	0	1.000	6	1	0	0	8	15	10	2	1	7-0	2	9.00	41	.395	.500	1	.000	-0	123	-5	0	-0.6
1959	Cle A	3	6	.333	29	8	1	1	72	72	39	4	0	31-3	49	4.00	92	.265	.340	14	.071	-1	138	-4	0	-0.6

YEAR	TM LG	W	L	PCT	G	GS	CG-SHO	SV-BS	IP	H	R	HR	HB	BB-IB	SO	ERA	AERA	OAV	OOB	AB-HR-SH	AVG	PB	SUP	APR	DL	PW
1960	Chi A	0	0	ø	15	0	0	2	17.2	23	9	2	0	10-0	8	4.58	82	.338	.423	3	.333	0	—	-1	0	0.0
1961	Was A	0	1	.000	16	0	0	0	19	23	14	1	1	13-3	14	4.74	85	.287	.385	0	ø	0	—	-3	0	-0.2
Total	14	142	97	.594	428	281	111-27	23	2174.2	2148	888	122	33	719-23	1117	3.27	117	.257	.318	696-2-58	.182	1	105	148	0	15.7
GARCIA, FREDDY	Freddy Antonio; B6.10.1975 Caracas, Distrito Capital, Venez.; BR/TR/6´4˝/(235–250); d4.7																									
1999	Sea A	17	8	.680	33	33	2-1	0-0	201.1	205	96	18	10	90-4	170	4.07	118	.263	.345	4-0-2	.250	0*	120	18	0	1.9
2000	†Sea A	9	5	.643	21	20	0	0-0	124.1	112	62	16	2	64-4	79	3.91	123	.241	.335	3-0-3	.667	1	111	11	0	1.1
2001	†Sea A★	18	6	.750	34	34	4-3	0-0	**238.2**	199	88	16	5	69-6	163	**3.05**	139	**.225**	.283	7-0-2	.143	-0	109	34	0	3.2
2002	Sea A★	16	10	.615	34	34	1	0-0	223.2	227	110	30	6	63-3	181	4.39	98	.260	.311	6-0-1	.333	1	108	1	0	0.2
2003	Sea A	12	14	.462	33	33	1	0-0	201.1	196	109	31	11	71-2	144	4.51	96	.255	.323	5	.200	0	93	-5	0	-0.6
2004	Sea A	4	7	.364	15	15	1	0-0	107	96	39	8	2	32-1	82	3.20	140	.236	.294	4	.000	-0	48	16	0	1.6
	Chi A	9	4	.692	16	16	0	0-0	103	96	53	14	5	32-2	102	4.46	106	.247	.311	0	ø	0	102	3	0	0.4
	Year	13	11	.542	31	31	1	0-0	210	192	92	22	7	64-3	184	3.81	120	.241	.302	4	.000	-0	77	20	0	2.0
2005	†Chi A	14	8	.636	33	33	2	0-0	228	225	102	26	3	60-2	146	3.87	117	.259	.307	7-0-2	.000	-1	113	18	0	1.5
2006	Chi A	17	9	.654	33	33	1	0-0	216.1	228	116	32	7	48-3	135	4.53	103	.267	.309	5-0-1	.200	0	115	4	0	0.3
Total	8	116	71	.620	252	251	12-4	0-0	1643.2	1584	775	191	51	529-27	1202	4.01	113	.252	.313	41-0-11	.195	1	106	100	0	9.6
GARCIA, JOSE	Jose Luis; B1.7.1985 Dejabon, D.R.; BR/TR/5´11˝/165; d9.11																									
2006	Fla N	0	0	ø	5	0	0	0-0	11	10	6	1	0	5-0	8	4.91	87	.233	.313	2	.500	0	—	0	0	0.0
GARCIA, MIKE	Michael R.; B5.11.1968 Riverside CA; BR/TR/6´2˝/220; [DetA89 55/1362]; d9.10; Col Riverside (CA) CC																									
1999	Pit N	1	0	1.000	7	0	0	0-0	7	2	1	1	0	3-0	9	1.29	358	.091	.200	0	ø	0	—	3	0	0.3
2000	Pit N	0	2	.000	13	0	0	0-1	11.1	21	15	1	0	7-1	9	11.12	42	.429	.475	3	.333	0	—	-8	0	-1.1
Total	2	1	2	.333	20	0	0	0-1	18.1	23	16	2	0	10-1	18	7.36	63	.324	.393	3	.333	0	—	-5	0	-0.8
GARCIA, MIGUEL	Miguel Angel (Sifontes); B4.3.1967 Caracas, Distrito Capital, Venez.; BL/TL/5´11˝/170; d4.30																									
1987	Cal A	0	0	ø	1	0	0	0-0	1.2	3	4	0	0	3-0	0	16.20	27	.375	.545	0	ø	0	—	-3	0	-0.1
	Pit N	0	0	ø	1	0	0	0-0	0.2	0	0	0	0	0-0	0	0.00	ø	.000	.000	0	ø	0	—	0	0	0.0
1988	Pit N	0	0	ø	1	0	0	0-0	2	3	2	1	1	2-0	2	4.50	77	.375	.500	0	ø	0	—	-1	0	0.0
1989	Pit N	0	2	.000	11	0	0	0-0	16	25	15	2	0	7-3	9	8.44	40	.357	.416	1	1.000	0	—	-8	0	-0.9
Total	3	0	2	.000	14	0	0	0-0	20.1	31	21	3	1	12-3	11	8.41	42	.352	.431	1	1.000	0	—	-12	0	-1.0
GARCIA, RALPH	Ralph; B12.14.1948 Los Angeles CA; BR/TR/6´0˝/195; d9.26; Col Nevada–Las Vegas																									
1972	SD N	0	0	ø	3	0	0	0-0	5	4	1	0	0	3-2	3	1.80	184	.211	.318	0	ø	0	—	1	0	0.1
1974	SD N	0	0	ø	8	0	0	0-0	10.1	15	8	1	0	7-2	9	6.10	59	.357	.431	0	ø	0	—	-3	0	-0.1
Total	2	0	0	ø	11	0	0	0-0	15.1	19	9	1	0	10-4	12	4.70	75	.311	.397	0	ø	0	—	-2	0	0.0
GARCIA, RAMON	Ramon (Garcia); B3.5.1924 LaEsperanza, Cuba; BR/TR/5´10˝/170; d4.19																									
1948	Was A	0	0	ø	4	0	0	0	3.2	11	7	0	1	4	2	17.18	25	.524	.615	1	1.000	0	—	-5	0	-0.2
GARCIA, RAMON	Ramon Antonio (Fortunato); B12.9.1969 Guanare, Portuguesa, Venez.; BR/TR/6´2˝/200; d5.31; [DL 1998 Hou N 181]																									
1991	Chi A	4	4	.500	16	15	0	0-0	78.1	79	50	13	2	31-2	40	5.40	74	.269	.340	0	ø	0	130	-12	0	-1.0
1996	Mil A	4	4	.500	37	2	0	4-3	75.2	84	58	17	6	21-3	40	6.66	78	.287	.342	0	ø	0	116	-11	0	-1.0
1997	†Hou N	9	8	.529	42	20	1-1	1-0	158.2	155	71	20	9	52-1	120	3.69	109	.262	.330	36-0-7	.111	-0	124	6	0	0.6
Total	3	17	16	.515	95	37	1-1	5-3	312.2	318	179	50	17	104-6	200	4.84	88	.270	.335	36-0-7	.111	-0	120	-17	181	-1.4
GARCIA, REYNALDO	Reynaldo; B4.15.1974 Nagua, D.R.; BR/TR/6´3˝/170; d7.19; [DL 2004 Bos A 183]																									
2002	Tex A	0	0	ø	3	0	0	0-0	2	7	7	3	0	1-0	2	31.50	15	.538	.571	0	ø	0	—	-5	0	-0.2
2003	Tex A	0	0	ø	17	0	0	0-0	18	19	18	6	2	14-0	15	9.00	55	.275	.407	0	ø	0	—	-7	0	-0.3
Total	2	0	0	ø	20	0	0	0-0	20	26	25	9	2	15-0	17	11.25	44	.317	.430	0	ø	0	—	-12	183	-0.5
GARCIA, ROSMAN	Rosman Jose; B1.3.1979 Maracay, Aragua, Venezuela; BR/TR/6´2˝/(160–215); d4.19																									
2003	Tex A	1	2	.333	46	0	0	0-2	46.1	63	33	4	2	23-0	25	6.02	83	.320	.395	0	ø	0	—	-5	0	-0.3
2004	Tex A	0	0	ø	4	0	0	0-0	6.2	9	5	1	0	5-0	5	5.40	91	.310	.400	0	ø	0	—	-1	0	0.0
Total	2	1	2	.333	50	0	0	0-2	53	72	38	5	2	28-0	30	5.94	84	.319	.395	0	ø	0	—	-6	0	-0.3
GARDINER, ART	Arthur Cecil; B12.26.1899 Brooklyn NY; D10.21.1954 Copiague NY; BR/TR; d9.25																									
1923	Phi N	0	0	ø	1	0	0	0	0	1	0	0	0	1	0	(0)	ø	1.000	1.000	0	ø	0	—	0	—	0.0
GARDINER, MIKE	Michael James; B10.19.1965 Sarnia ON, Can.; BB/TR/6´0˝/(185–200); [SeaA87 18/449]; d9.8; Col Indiana St.																									
1990	Sea A	0	2	.000	5	3	0	0-0	12.2	22	17	1	2	5-0	6	10.66	37	.379	.439	0	ø	0	92	-9	0	-1.2
1991	Bos A	9	10	.474	22	22	0	0-0	130	140	79	18	0	47-2	91	4.85	89	.274	.333	0	ø	0	103	-8	18	-1.0
1992	Bos A	4	10	.286	28	18	0	0-0	130.2	126	78	12	2	58-2	79	4.75	89	.253	.330	0	ø	0	70	-6	0	-0.6
1993	Mon N	2	3	.400	24	2	0	0-1	38	40	28	3	1	19-2	21	5.21	80	.268	.349	4	.000	-0	140	-5	0	-0.6
	Det A	0	0	ø	10	0	0	0-1	11.1	12	5	0	0	7-1	4	3.97	110	.279	.380	0	ø	0	—	1	0	0.0
1994	Det A	2	2	.500	38	1	0	5-1	58.2	53	35	10	0	23-5	31	4.14	119	.233	.302	0	ø	0	168	3	0	0.1
1995	Det A	0	0	ø	9	0	0	0-1	12.1	27	20	5	0	2-1	7	14.59	33	.458	.460	0	ø	0	—	-12	105	-0.6
Total	6	17	27	.386	136	46	0	5-4	393.2	420	262	49	5	161-13	239	5.21	84	.272	.339	4	.000	-0	91	-36	123	-3.9
GARDNER, CHRIS	Christopher John; B3.30.1969 Long Beach CA; BR/TR/6´0˝/175; [HouN88 6/142]; d9.10																									
1991	Hou N	1	2	.333	5	4	0	0-0	24.2	19	12	5	0	14-1	12	4.01	88	.218	.327	5	.000	-0	76	-1	0	-0.1
GARDNER, GID	Franklin Washington; B5.6.1859 Boston MA; D8.1.1914 Cambridge MA; ?/165; d8.23; ▲																									
1879	Tro N	0	2	.000	2	2	2	0	14	27	21	0	—	0	3	5.79	43	.365	.365	6	.167	-0	37	-5	—	-0.5
1880	Cle N	1	8	.111	9	9	9	0	77	80	53	2	—	20	21	2.57	91	.254	.299	32	.188	-0*	58	-4	—	-0.4
1883	Bal AA	1	0	1.000	2	0	0	0	7	9	7	1	—	1	2	5.14	68	.290	.313	161-1	.273	1*	—	-1	—	-0.1
1884	CP U	0	1	.000	1	1	0	0	6	10	8	0	—	1	4	6.00	40	.345	.367	149	.255	0*	18	-2	—	-0.3
1885	Bal AA	0	1	.000	1	1	1	0	9	16	13	2	1	6	3	10.00	33	.372	.460	170	.218	0*	36	-6	—	-0.4
Total	5	2	12	.143	15	13	12	0	113	142	102	5	1	28	33	3.90	64	.289	.328	518-1	.243	0	49	-18	—	-1.7
GARDNER, HARRY	Harry Ray; B6.1.1887 Quincy MI; D8.2.1961 Canby OR; BR/TR/6´2˝/180; d4.17																									
1911	Pit N	1	1	.500	13	3	2	2	42	39	25	2	2	20	24	4.50	76	.244	.335	14	.214	0	95	-4	—	-0.3
1912	Pit N	0	0	ø	1	0	0	0	0.1	3	6	0	0	1	0	0.00	ø	.500	.571	0	ø	0	—	-2	—	-0.1
Total	2	1	1	.500	14	3	2	2	42.1	42	31	2	2	21	24	4.46	77	.253	.344	14	.214	0	95	-6	—	-0.4
GARDNER, JIM	James Anderson; B10.4.1874 Pittsburgh PA; D4.24.1905 Pittsburgh PA; TR; d6.20																									
1895	Pit N	8	2	.800	11	10	8	0	85.1	99	53	1	6	27	31	2.64	171	.286	.348	34	.265	1	120	13	—	1.2
1897	Pit N	5	5	.500	14	11	8	0	95.1	115	72	4	9	32	35	5.19	80	.296	.363	76-1-2	.158	-1*	88	-10	—	-0.8
1898	Pit N	10	13	.435	25	22	19-1	0	185.1	179	96	3	8	48	41	3.21	111	.252	.306	91-0-2	.154	-2*	71	6	—	0.3
1899	Pit N	1	0	1.000	6	3	0	0	32.1	52	37	1	0	13	2	7.52	51	.361	.414	13	.231	1	164	-13	—	-0.6
1902	Chi N	1	2	.333	3	3	2	0	25	23	12	0	0	10	6	2.88	94	.245	.317	10	.200	0	101	0	—	0.0
Total	5	25	22	.532	59	49	37-1	0	423.1	468	270	9	23	130	115	3.85	100	.278	.338	224-1-4	.179	-1	93	-4	—	0.1
GARDNER, MARK	Mark Allan; B3.1.1962 Los Angeles CA; BR/TR/6´1˝/(190–224); [MonN85 8/192]; d5.16; C4; Col Cal St.–Fresno																									
1989	Mon N	0	3	.000	7	4	0	0-0	26.1	26	16	2	2	11-1	21	5.13	70	.250	.333	6-0-1	.167	-0	56	-4	0	-0.5
1990	Mon N	7	9	.438	27	26	3-3	0-0	152.2	129	62	13	9	61-5	135	3.42	108	.230	.312	44-0-8	.114	-1	93	5	14	0.5
1991	Mon N	9	11	.450	27	27	0	0-0	168.1	139	78	17	4	75-1	107	3.85	95	.230	.318	55-0-4	.091	-3	87	-3	36	-0.7
1992	Mon N	12	10	.545	33	30	0	0-0	179.2	179	91	15	9	60-2	132	4.36	80	.259	.324	50-0-8	.140	1	107	-16	0	-1.8
1993	KC A	4	6	.400	17	16	0	0-0	91.2	92	65	17	4	36-0	54	6.19	75	.271	.342	0	ø	0	81	-14	51	-1.4
1994	Fla N	4	4	.500	20	14	0	0-0	92.1	97	53	14	1	30-2	57	4.87	91	.276	.331	25-0-4	.040	-2	97	-3	19	-0.4
1995	Fla N	5	5	.500	39	11	1-1	1-0	102.1	109	60	14	5	43-5	87	4.49	96	.272	.350	21-0-4	.190	-0	101	-4	0	-0.4
1996	SF N	12	7	.632	30	28	4-1	0-0	179.1	200	105	28	8	57-3	145	4.42	94	.283	.341	68-0-8	.162	0*	131	-8	18	-0.8
1997	SF N	12	9	.571	30	30	2-1	0-0	180.1	188	92	28	1	57-6	136	4.29	96	.272	.326	61-0-3	.115	-2*	100	-2	0	-0.3
1998	SF N	13	6	.684	33	33	4-2	0-0	212	203	106	29	6	65-5	151	4.33	93	.253	.311	73-0-4	.164	1	131	-6	0	-0.3
1999	SF N	5	11	.313	29	21	1	0-1	139	142	103	27	8	57-2	86	6.47	66	.267	.341	39-1-6	.103	0	116	-33	22	-3.1
2000	†SF N	11	7	.611	30	20	0	0-0	149	155	72	16	5	42-2	92	4.05	107	.270	.322	43-0-7	.116	-2	82	6	0	0.3

YEAR	TM LG	W	L	PCT	G	GS	CG-SHO	SV-BS	IP	H	R	HR	HB	BB-IB	SO	ERA	AERA	OAV	OOB	AB-HR-SH	AVG	PB	SUP	APR	DL	PW
2001	SF N	5	5	.500	23	15	0	0-0	91.2	93	57	17	3	34-3	53	5.40	76	.263	.330	21-0-4	.000	-2	95	-13	56	-1.4
Total	13	99	93	.516	345	275	15-8	1-1	1764.2	1752	960	237	65	628-37	1256	4.56	89	.261	.327	506-1-61	.123	-9	103	-95	216	-10.3

GARDNER, GLENN Miles Glenn; B1.25.1916 Burnsville NC; D7.7.1964 Rochester NY; BR/TR/5´11˝/180; d7.19

YEAR	TM LG	W	L	PCT	G	GS	CG-SHO	SV-BS	IP	H	R	HR	HB	BB-IB	SO	ERA	AERA	OAV	OOB	AB-HR-SH	AVG	PB	SUP	APR	DL	PW
1945	StL N	3	1	.750	17	4	2-1	1	54.2	50	21	2	0	27	20	3.29	114	.242	.329	21-0-1	.333	2	130	4	0	0.4

GARDNER, ROB Richard Frank; B12.19.1944 Binghamton NY; BR/TL/6´1˝/(165–185); d9.1

YEAR	TM LG	W	L	PCT	G	GS	CG-SHO	SV-BS	IP	H	R	HR	HB	BB-IB	SO	ERA	AERA	OAV	OOB	AB-HR-SH	AVG	PB	SUP	APR	DL	PW
1965	NY N	0	2	.000	5	4	0	0	28	23	13	4	0	7-0	19	3.21	110	.217	.265	7-0-1	.000	-1	62	0	0	0.0
1966	NY N	4	8	.333	41	17	3	1	133.2	147	82	15	3	64-4	74	5.12	71	.285	.366	41-0-1	.171	-0*	87	-19	0	-1.7
1967	Chi N	0	2	.000	18	5	0	0	31.2	33	14	2	0	6-0	16	3.98	89	.260	.289	6	.000	-0	89	-1	0	-0.1
1968	Cle A	0	0	ø	5	0	0	0	2.2	5	3	0	0	2-0	6	6.75	44	.417	.467	0	ø	0	—	-1	0	-0.1
1970	NY A	1	0	1.000	1	1	0	0-0	7.1	8	4	2	0	4-0	6	4.91	73	.276	.364	3	.333	1	150	-1	0	0.0
1971	Oak A	0	0	ø	4	1	0	0-0	7.2	8	2	1	0	3-0	5	2.35	142	.267	.333	2	.500	0	135	1	0	0.1
	NY A	0	0	ø	2	0	0	0-0	3	3	1	0	0	2-0	2	3.00	110	.273	.385	0	ø	0	—	0	0	0.0
	Year	0	0	ø	6	1	0	0-0	10.2	11	3	1	0	5-0	7	2.53	131	.268	.348	2	.500	0	135	1	0	0.1
1972	NY A	8	5	.615	20	14	1	0-1	97	91	43	9	0	28-3	58	3.06	98	.243	.295	28-0-5	.107	-1	110	-3	0	-0.6
1973	Oak A	0	0	ø	3	0	0	0-0	7.1	10	4	2	0	4-0	2	4.91	73	.370	.452	0	ø	0	—	-1	0	-0.1
	Mil A	1	1	.500	10	0	0	1-0	12.2	17	14	0	1	13-1	5	9.95	38	.327	.470	0	ø	0	—	-8	0	-1.2
	Year	1	1	.500	13	0	0	1-0	20	27	18	2	1	17-1	7	8.10	46	.342	.464	0	ø	0	—	-9	0	-1.3
Total	8	14	18	.438	109	42	4	2-1	331	345	180	35	4	133-8	193	4.35	78	.269	.338	87-0-7	.138	-2	94	-33	0	-3.7

GARDNER, LEE Terrence Lee; B1.16.1975 Hartland MI; BR/TR/6´0˝/(210–219); d5.24; Col Central Michigan

YEAR	TM LG	W	L	PCT	G	GS	CG-SHO	SV-BS	IP	H	R	HR	HB	BB-IB	SO	ERA	AERA	OAV	OOB	AB-HR-SH	AVG	PB	SUP	APR	DL	PW
2002	TB A	1	1	.500	12	0	0	0-2	13.1	12	11	3	3	8-0	8	4.05	112	.235	.359	0	ø	0	—	-1	0	-0.2
2005	TB A	0	0	ø	5	0	0	0-0	7.1	12	9	2	0	2-0	4	4.91	90	.353	.378	0	ø	0	—	-2	0	-0.1
Total	2	1	1	.500	17	0	0	0-2	20.2	24	20	5	3	10-0	12	4.35	103	.282	.366	0	ø	0	—	-3	0	-0.3

GARDNER, WES Wesley Brian; B4.29.1961 Benton AR; BR/TR/6´4˝/(195–205); [NYN82 22/551]; d7.29; Col Central Arkansas

YEAR	TM LG	W	L	PCT	G	GS	CG-SHO	SV-BS	IP	H	R	HR	HB	BB-IB	SO	ERA	AERA	OAV	OOB	AB-HR-SH	AVG	PB	SUP	APR	DL	PW
1984	NY N	1	1	.500	21	0	0	1-2	25.1	34	19	0	0	8-2	19	6.39	56	.321	.365	1	.000	-0	—	-7	0	-0.6
1985	NY N	0	2	.000	9	0	0	0-0	12	18	14	1	0	8-2	11	5.25	67	.375	.456	0	ø	0	—	-5	0	-0.8
1986	Bos A	0	0	ø	1	0	0	0-0	1	1	1	0	0	0-0	1	9.00	47	.333	.250	0	ø	0	—	0	175	0.0
1987	Bos A	3	6	.333	49	1	0	10-2	89.2	98	55	17	2	42-7	70	5.42	84	.279	.358	0	ø	0	80	-7	0	-0.8
1988	†Bos A	8	6	.571	36	18	1	2-0	149	119	61	17	3	64-2	106	3.50	118	.220	.302	0	ø	0	98	11	15	1.0
1989	Bos A	3	7	.300	22	16	0	0-0	86	97	64	10	1	47-7	81	5.97	69	.287	.372	0	ø	0	116	-17	57	-1.7
1990	Bos A	3	7	.300	34	9	0	0-2	77.1	77	43	6	2	35-0	58	4.89	84	.259	.339	0	ø	0	74	-5	30	-0.6
1991	SD N	0	1	.000	14	0	0	1-0	20.1	27	16	1	0	12-1	9	7.08	54	.310	.394	2	.000	-0	—	-6	0	-0.4
	KC A	0	0	ø	3	0	0	0-0	5.2	5	4	0	0	2-0	3	1.59	261	.208	.269	0	ø	0	—	0	0	0.0
Total	8	18	30	.375	189	44	1	14-6	466.1	476	277	52	8	218-21	358	4.90	85	.265	.344	3	.000	-0	99	-36	277	-3.9

GARDNER, BILL William A.; B9.1868 Baltimore MD; d8.9

YEAR	TM LG	W	L	PCT	G	GS	CG-SHO	SV-BS	IP	H	R	HR	HB	BB-IB	SO	ERA	AERA	OAV	OOB	AB-HR-SH	AVG	PB	SUP	APR	DL	PW
1887	Bal AA	0	1	.000	3	2	1	0	13	23	20	0	1	10	3	11.08	37	.426	.523	11	.273	0*	124	-9	—	-0.5

GARFIELD, BILL William Milton; B10.26.1867 Sheffield OH; D12.16.1941 Danville IL; BR/TR/5´11.5˝/160; d7.10; Col Oberlin

YEAR	TM LG	W	L	PCT	G	GS	CG-SHO	SV-BS	IP	H	R	HR	HB	BB-IB	SO	ERA	AERA	OAV	OOB	AB-HR-SH	AVG	PB	SUP	APR	DL	PW
1889	Pit N	0	2	.000	4	2	2	0	29	45	35	2	1	17	4	7.76	48	.344	.423	13	.000	-2	81	-14	—	-0.8
1890	Cle N	1	7	.125	9	8	7	0	70	91	64	3	8	35	16	4.89	73	.304	.392	26	.154	-1	42	-12	—	-1.1
Total	2	1	9	.100	13	10	9	0	99	136	99	5	9	52	20	5.73	64	.316	.401	39	.103	-3	50	-26	—	-1.9

GARIBALDI, BOB Robert Roy; B3.3.1942 Stockton CA; BL/TR/6´4˝/210; d7.15; Col Santa Clara

YEAR	TM LG	W	L	PCT	G	GS	CG-SHO	SV-BS	IP	H	R	HR	HB	BB-IB	SO	ERA	AERA	OAV	OOB	AB-HR-SH	AVG	PB	SUP	APR	DL	PW
1962	SF N	0	0	ø	9	0	0	1	12.1	13	7	1	0	5-0	9	5.11	74	.265	.327	1	.000	-0	—	-1	0	-0.1
1963	SF N	0	1	.000	4	0	0	1	8	8	2	0	1	4-2	4	1.13	284	.276	.382	1	.000	-0	—	2	0	0.2
1966	SF N	0	0	ø	1	0	0	0	1	1	0	0	0	0-0	0	0.00	ø	.250	.250	0	ø	0	—	0	0	0.0
1969	SF N	0	1	.000	1	1	0	0-0	5	6	4	0	0	2-0	1	1.80	195	.316	.381	2	.000	-0	101	0	0	-0.1
Total	4	0	2	.000	15	1	0	2-0	26.1	28	13	1	1	11-2	14	3.08	116	.277	.351	4	.000	-0	101	1	0	0.0

GARIBAY, DANIEL Daniel (Bravo); B2.14.1973 Maneadero, Baja California, Mexico; BL/TL/5´8˝/160; d4.9

YEAR	TM LG	W	L	PCT	G	GS	CG-SHO	SV-BS	IP	H	R	HR	HB	BB-IB	SO	ERA	AERA	OAV	OOB	AB-HR-SH	AVG	PB	SUP	APR	DL	PW
2000	Chi N	2	8	.200	30	8	0	0-2	74.2	88	54	9	1	39-1	46	6.03	76	.299	.376	15-0-4	.133	-1	65	-13	0	-1.4

GARLAND, JON Jon Steven; B9.27.1979 Valencia CA; BR/TR/6´6˝/(205–215); [ChiN97 1/10]; d7.4

YEAR	TM LG	W	L	PCT	G	GS	CG-SHO	SV-BS	IP	H	R	HR	HB	BB-IB	SO	ERA	AERA	OAV	OOB	AB-HR-SH	AVG	PB	SUP	APR	DL	PW
2000	Chi A	4	8	.333	15	13	0	0-0	69.2	82	55	10	1	40-0	42	6.46	78	.292	.380	0	ø	0	101	-10	14	-1.4
2001	Chi A	6	7	.462	35	16	0	1-0	117	123	59	16	4	55-2	61	3.69	126	.277	.358	2	.000	-0	86	9	0	0.9
2002	Chi A	12	12	.500	33	33	1-1	0-0	192.2	188	109	23	9	83-1	112	4.58	98	.258	.340	2-0-1	.000	-0	85	-2	0	-0.3
2003	Chi A	12	13	.480	32	32	0	0-0	191.2	188	103	28	4	74-1	108	4.51	102	.260	.329	2-0-1	.000	0	100	2	0	0.3
2004	Chi A	12	11	.522	34	33	1	0-0	217	223	125	34	4	76-2	113	4.89	96	.269	.332	4-0-1	.250	0	98	-4	0	-0.3
2005	†Chi A★	18	10	.643	32	32	3-**3**	0-0	221	212	93	26	7	47-3	115	3.50	129	.255	.298	2	.500	0	93	24	0	2.9
2006	Chi A	18	7	.720	33	32	1-1	0-0	211.1	247	112	26	6	41-4	112	4.51	104	.294	.328	5-1-2	.200	1	113	4	0	0.6
Total	7	82	68	.547	214	191	6-5	1-0	1220.1	1263	656	163	35	416-13	663	4.44	104	.270	.332	17-1-5	.176	1	97	23	14	2.7

GARLAND, LOU Louis Lyman; B7.16.1905 Archie MO; D8.30.1990 Idaho Falls ID; BR/TR/6´2.5˝/200; d8.31

YEAR	TM LG	W	L	PCT	G	GS	CG-SHO	SV-BS	IP	H	R	HR	HB	BB-IB	SO	ERA	AERA	OAV	OOB	AB-HR-SH	AVG	PB	SUP	APR	DL	PW
1931	Chi A	0	2	.000	7	2	0	0	16.2	30	24	2	1	14	4	10.26	41	.400	.500	3	.000	-0	109	-12	—	-1.1

GARLAND, WAYNE Marcus Wayne; B10.26.1950 Nashville TN; BR/TR/6´0˝/(190–205); [BalA69 S1/5]; d9.13; Col Gulf Coast (FL) CC

YEAR	TM LG	W	L	PCT	G	GS	CG-SHO	SV-BS	IP	H	R	HR	HB	BB-IB	SO	ERA	AERA	OAV	OOB	AB-HR-SH	AVG	PB	SUP	APR	DL	PW
1973	Bal A	0	1	.000	4	1	0	0-0	16	14	8	1	0	7-0	10	3.94	96	.233	.313	0	ø	0	47	0	0	0.0
1974	†Bal A	5	5	.500	20	6	0	1-0	91	68	37	5	3	26-3	40	2.97	117	.211	.272	0	ø	0	97	4	0	0.4
1975	Bal A	2	5	.286	29	1	0	4-1	87.1	80	37	7	1	31-6	46	3.71	96	.252	.316	0	ø	0	124	-1	0	-0.1
1976	Bal A	20	7	.741	38	25	14-4	1-1	232.1	224	81	10	6	64-9	113	2.67	123	.255	.306	0	ø	0	107	15	0	1.8
1977	Cle A	13	19	.406	38	38	21-1	0-0	282.2	281	130	23	2	88-8	118	3.60	111	.261	.316	0	ø	0	94	11	0	1.1
1978	Cle A	2	3	.400	6	6	0	0-0	29.2	43	27	6	1	16-1	13	7.89	48	.347	.423	0	ø	0	103	-13	153	-1.7
1979	Cle A	4	10	.286	18	14	2	0-0	94.2	120	70	11	3	34-2	40	5.23	82	.318	.371	0	ø	0	75	-14	60	-1.8
1980	Cle A	6	9	.400	25	20	4-1	0-0	150.1	163	85	18	6	48-2	55	4.61	90	.276	.334	0	ø	0	118	-8	0	-0.8
1981	Cle A	3	7	.300	12	10	2-1	0-0	56	89	40	8	0	14-0	15	5.79	64	.374	.399	0	ø	0	76	-13	0	-2.0
Total	9	55	66	.455	190	121	43-7	6-2	1040	1082	515	89	22	328-31	450	3.89	97	.272	.327	0	ø	0	98	-19	213	-3.1

GARMAN, MIKE Michael Douglas; B9.16.1949 Caldwell ID; BR/TR/6´3˝/(198–215); [BosA67 1/3]; d9.22

YEAR	TM LG	W	L	PCT	G	GS	CG-SHO	SV-BS	IP	H	R	HR	HB	BB-IB	SO	ERA	AERA	OAV	OOB	AB-HR-SH	AVG	PB	SUP	APR	DL	PW
1969	Bos A	1	0	1.000	2	2	0	0-0	12.1	13	6	0	0	10-0	10	4.38	87	.277	.404	5	.400	1	116	0	0	0.0
1971	Bos A	1	1	.500	3	3	0	0-0	18.2	15	8	3	1	9-1	6	3.86	97	.217	.313	6	.333	0	104	0	0	0.0
1972	Bos A	0	1	.000	3	1	0	0-0	3.1	4	4	1	0	2-0	1	10.80	30	.286	.375	0	ø	0	82	-2	0	-0.5
1973	Bos A	0	0	ø	12	0	0	0-0	22	32	15	1	0	15-3	9	5.32	76	.352	.439	0	ø	0	—	-3	0	-0.2
1974	StL N	7	2	.778	64	0	0	6-3	81.2	66	26	4	2	27-10	45	2.64	137	.227	.297	10-0-1	.100	-1	—	9	0	1.1
1975	StL N	3	8	.273	66	0	0	10-6	79	73	31	3	1	48-23	48	2.39	159	.245	.347	2	.000	-0	—	9	0	1.4
1976	Chi N	2	4	.333	47	2	0	1-1	76.1	79	48	7	3	35-8	37	4.95	78	.273	.351	7	.000	-1	23	-8	0	-0.7
1977	†LA N	4	4	.500	49	0	0	12-5	62.2	60	20	7	2	22-5	29	2.73	141	.254	.323	7	.000	-1	—	8	0	1.2
1978	LA N	0	1	.000	10	0	0	0-1	16.1	15	8	3	0	3-0	5	4.41	80	.259	.295	0	ø	0	—	-1	0	-0.1
	Mon N	4	6	.400	47	0	0	13-6	61.1	54	32	5	0	31-8	23	4.40	81	.238	.327	5	.000	-1	—	-5	0	-1.1
	Year	4	7	.364	57	0	0	13-7	77.2	69	40	8	0	34-8	28	4.40	81	.242	.321	5	.000	-1	—	-7	0	-1.2
Total	9	22	27	.449	303	8	0	42-22	433.2	411	198	34	9	202-58	213	3.63	103	.254	.337	42-0-1	.119	-2	83	7	0	1.1

GARONI, WILLIE William; B7.28.1877 Ft.Lee NJ; D9.9.1914 Ft.Lee NJ; BR/TR/6´1˝/165; d9.7

YEAR	TM LG	W	L	PCT	G	GS	CG-SHO	SV-BS	IP	H	R	HR	HB	BB-IB	SO	ERA	AERA	OAV	OOB	AB-HR-SH	AVG	PB	SUP	APR	DL	PW
1899	NY N	0	1	.000	3	1	1	0	10	12	7	0	0	2	2	4.50	83	.300	.333	4	.000	-1	77	-1	—	-0.1

GARRELTS, SCOTT Scott William; B10.30.1961 Urbana IL; BR/TR/6´4˝/(195–210); [SFN79 1/15]; d10.2; [DL 1992 SF N 177]

YEAR	TM LG	W	L	PCT	G	GS	CG-SHO	SV-BS	IP	H	R	HR	HB	BB-IB	SO	ERA	AERA	OAV	OOB	AB-HR-SH	AVG	PB	SUP	APR	DL	PW
1982	SF N	0	0	ø	1	0	0	0-0	2	3	3	0	0	2-0	4	13.50	27	.333	.455	0	ø	0	—	-2	0	-0.1
1983	SF N	2	2	.500	5	5	1-1	0-0	35.2	33	11	4	2	19-4	16	2.52	141	.254	.358	9-0-3	.222	0	65	4	0	0.5
1984	SF N	2	3	.400	21	3	0	0-1	43	45	33	6	1	34-1	32	5.65	63	.274	.398	10	.100	-0	217	-11	0	-1.3
1985	SF N☆	9	6	.600	74	0	0	13-8	105.2	76	37	2	3	58-12	106	2.30	151	.198	.306	9	.222	1	—	12	0	2.1
1986	SF N	13	9	.591	53	18	2	10-6	173.2	144	65	17	2	74-11	125	3.11	114	.231	.311	45-1-7	.178	2*	90	10	0	1.6
1987	†SF N	11	7	.611	64	0	0	12-10	106.1	70	41	10	0	55-4	127	3.22	120	.192	.297	10	.200	1*	—	8	0	1.5
1988	SF N	5	9	.357	65	0	0	13-6	98	80	42	3	2	46-10	86	3.58	91	.226	.317	13	.077	-1	—	-3	0	-0.5

YEAR	TM LG	W	L	PCT	G	GS	CG-SHO	SV-BS	IP	H	R	HR	HB	BB-IB	SO	ERA	AERA	OAV	OOB	AB-HR-SH	AVG	PB	SUP	APR	DL	PW
1989	†SF N	14	5	.737	30	29	2-1	0-0	193.1	149	58	11	0	46-3	119	**2.28**	148	.212	**.258**	66-0-2	.136	1*	120	23	16	2.3
1990	SF N	12	11	.522	31	31	4-2	0-0	182	190	91	16	3	70-8	80	4.15	88	.272	.339	66	.061	-3*	94	-10	0	-1.6
1991	SF N	1	1	.500	8	3	0	0-0	19.2	25	14	5	0	9-0	8	6.41	56	.313	.378	4-0-1	.000	-0*	200	-6	141	-0.6
Total	10	69	53	.566	352	89	9-4	48-31	959.1	815	395	74	13	413-53	703	3.29	107	.232	.313	232-1-13	.125	-1	107	25	334	3.9

GARRETT, CLARENCE Clarence Raymond "Laz"; B3.6.1891 Reader WV; D2.11.1977 Moundsville WV; BR/TR/6´5.5˝/185; d9.13; Col West Liberty St.

YEAR	TM LG	W	L	PCT	G	GS	CG-SHO	SV-BS	IP	H	R	HR	HB	BB-IB	SO	ERA	AERA	OAV	OOB	AB-HR-SH	AVG	PB	SUP	APR	DL	PW
1915	Cle A	2	2	.500	4	4	2	0	23.1	19	13	1	1	6	5	2.31	132	.224	.283	8	.000	-0	102	0	—	0.1

GARRETT, GREG Gregory; B3.12.1947 Atascadero CA; D6.7.2003 Newhall CA; BB/TL/6´0˝/200; d4.24; Col Washington St.

YEAR	TM LG	W	L	PCT	G	GS	CG-SHO	SV-BS	IP	H	R	HR	HB	BB-IB	SO	ERA	AERA	OAV	OOB	AB-HR-SH	AVG	PB	SUP	APR	DL	PW
1970	Cal A	5	6	.455	32	7	0	0-0	74.2	48	23	6	1	44-9	53	2.65	137	.190	.309	15-0-1	.067	-1	88	9	0	1.2
1971	Cin N	0	1	.000	2	1	0	0-0	8.2	7	1	0	0	10-0	2	1.04	325	.250	.447	3	.333	0	0	2	0	0.3
Total	2	5	7	.417	34	8	0	0-0	83.1	55	24	6	1	54-9	55	2.48	145	.196	.324	18-0-1	.111	-1	77	11	0	1.5

GARRISON, CLIFF Clifford William; B8.13.1906 Bellemont OK; D8.25.1994 Woodland CA; BR/TR/6´0˝/180; d4.16

YEAR	TM LG	W	L	PCT	G	GS	CG-SHO	SV-BS	IP	H	R	HR	HB	BB-IB	SO	ERA	AERA	OAV	OOB	AB-HR-SH	AVG	PB	SUP	APR	DL	PW
1928	Bos A	0	0	ø	6	0	0	0	16	22	15	2	0	6	0	7.88	52	.361	.418	3	.000	-0	—	-6	—	-0.3

GARRY, JIM James Thomas; B9.21.1869 Great Barrington MA; D1.13.1917 Pittsfield MA; BL/TL/5´10˝/165; d5.2

YEAR	TM LG	W	L	PCT	G	GS	CG-SHO	SV-BS	IP	H	R	HR	HB	BB-IB	SO	ERA	AERA	OAV	OOB	AB-HR-SH	AVG	PB	SUP	APR	DL	PW
1893	Bos N	0	1	.000	1	0	0	0	1	5	8	0	0	4	2	63.00	8	.625	.750	1	.000	-0	—	-6	—	-0.7

GARVER, NED Ned Franklin; B12.25.1925 Ney OH; BR/TR/5´10.5˝/180; d4.28

YEAR	TM LG	W	L	PCT	G	GS	CG-SHO	SV-BS	IP	H	R	HR	HB	BB-IB	SO	ERA	AERA	OAV	OOB	AB-HR-SH	AVG	PB	SUP	APR	DL	PW
1948	StL A	7	11	.389	38	24	7	5	198	200	92	14	1	95	75	3.41	134	.268	.352	66-1-9	.288	4*	78	20	0	2.2
1949	StL A	12	17	.414	41	32	16-1	3	223.2	245	126	14	3	102	70	3.98	114	.277	.354	75-0-4	.187	1*	78	9	0	1.2
1950	StL A	13	18	.419	37	31	**22**-2	0	260	264	120	18	4	108	85	3.39	**146**	.264	.338	91-1-7	.286	4*	75	**39**	0	**4.9**
1951	StL A★	20	12	.625	33	30	**24**-1	0	246	237	114	17	5	96	84	3.73	118	.255	.328	95-1-5	.305	7*	97	17	0	2.9
1952	StL A	7	10	.412	21	21	7-2	0	148.2	130	67	14	4	55	60	3.69	106	.235	.309	49-0-1	.184	0*	76	5	0	0.6
	Det A	1	0	1.000	1	1	1	0	9	9	2	1	0	3	3	2.00	190	.265	.324	2	.000	0	92	2	0	0.3
	Year	8	10	.444	22	22	8-2	0	157.2	139	69	15	4	58	63	3.60	109	.237	.310	51-0-1	.176	0	77	7	0	0.9
1953	Det A	11	11	.500	30	26	13	1	198.1	228	107	16	2	66	69	4.45	91	.290	.347	72-1-4	.153	-1	93	-7	0	-0.8
1954	Det A	14	11	.560	35	32	16-3	1	246.1	216	93	20	4	62	93	2.81	131	.236	.286	79-0-5	.165	-0*	106	22	0	2.2
1955	Det A	12	16	.429	33	32	16-1	0	230.2	251	115	21	5	67-10	83	3.98	97	.279	.330	76-1-3	.224	5	111	-3	0	0.1
1956	Det A	0	2	.000	6	3	1	0	17.2	15	10	2	1	13-0	6	4.08	101	.234	.367	5	.000	-0	79	0	61	-0.1
1957	KC A	6	13	.316	24	23	6-1	0	145.1	120	72	13	5	55-5	61	3.84	103	.223	.298	44-0-2	.182	0	82	1	0	0.1
1958	KC A	12	11	.522	31	28	10-3	1	201	192	97	24	2	66-8	72	4.03	97	.244	.303	69-0-4	.174	0	103	-2	0	0.2
1959	KC A	10	13	.435	32	30	9-2	1	201.1	214	94	22	3	42-0	61	3.71	108	.270	.308	71-2-4	.282	6	104	7	0	1.4
1960	KC A	4	9	.308	28	15	5-2	0	122.1	110	57	15	2	35-2	50	3.83	104	.240	.293	27-0-4	.074	-1	65	3	0	0.2
1961	LA A	0	3	.000	12	2	0	0	29	40	18	2	0	16-0	9	5.59	81	.348	.427	6-0-1	.000	-1	29	-2	0	-0.2
Total	14	129	157	.451	402	330	153-18	12	2477.1	2471	1184	213	41	881-25	881	3.73	112	.260	.325	827-7-53	.218	24	89	111	61	15.2

GARVIN, JERRY Theodore Jared; B10.21.1955 Oakland CA; BL/TL/6´3˝/(190–195); [MinA74*S1/11]; d4.10; Col Merced (CA) JC

YEAR	TM LG	W	L	PCT	G	GS	CG-SHO	SV-BS	IP	H	R	HR	HB	BB-IB	SO	ERA	AERA	OAV	OOB	AB-HR-SH	AVG	PB	SUP	APR	DL	PW
1977	Tor A	10	18	.357	34	34	12-1	0-0	244.2	247	127	33	4	85-5	127	4.19	101	.264	.326	0	ø	0	76	2	0	0.5
1978	Tor A	4	12	.250	26	22	3	0-1	144.2	189	92	20	4	48-4	67	5.54	71	.319	.372	0	ø	0	88	-23	0	-2.1
1979	Tor A	0	1	.000	8	1	0	0-1	22.2	15	9	2	2	10-0	14	2.78	158	.197	.300	0	ø	0	165	3	89	0.2
1980	Tor A	4	7	.364	61	0	0	8-5	82.2	70	23	6	0	27-7	52	2.29	189	.233	.296	0	ø	0	—	18	0	2.6
1981	Tor A	1	2	.333	35	4	0	0-1	53	46	20	3	0	23-4	25	3.40	117	.240	.318	0	ø	0	62	4	0	0.2
1982	Tor A	1	1	.500	32	4	0	0-1	58.1	81	48	10	1	26-2	35	7.25	62	.335	.400	0	ø	0	106	-14	0	-0.6
Total	6	20	41	.328	196	65	15-1	8-9	606	648	319	74	11	219-22	320	4.43	95	.277	.340	0	ø	0	82	-10	89	0.8

GARVIN, NED Virgil Lee; B1.1.1874 Navasota TX; D6.16.1908 Fresno CA; BR/TR/6´3.5˝/160; d7.13

YEAR	TM LG	W	L	PCT	G	GS	CG-SHO	SV-BS	IP	H	R	HR	HB	BB-IB	SO	ERA	AERA	OAV	OOB	AB-HR-SH	AVG	PB	SUP	APR	DL	PW
1896	Phi N	0	1	.000	2	1	1	0	13	19	13	0	0	7	4	7.62	57	.339	.413	6	.000	-1	132	-4	—	-0.3
1899	Chi N	9	13	.409	24	23	22-4	0	199	202	101	1	12	42	69	2.85	132	.263	.311	71-0-5	.155	-5	102	19	—	1.3
1900	Chi N	10	18	.357	30	28	25-1	0	246.1	225	126	4	18	63	107	2.41	150	.243	.304	91	.154	-5	73	28	—	2.4
1901	Mil A	8	20	.286	37	27	22-1	1	257.1	258	155	4	14	90	122	3.46	104	.258	.328	93-0-4	.108	-9	63	2	—	-0.5
1902	Chi A	10	10	.500	23	19	16-2	0	175.1	169	68	3	8	43	55	2.21	153	.254	.307	59-0-1	.153	-2	76	19	—	1.8
	Bro N	1	1	.500	2	2	2-1	0	18	15	3	0	0	4	7	1.00	277	.227	.271	7	.143	-0	98	3	—	0.4
1903	Bro N	15	18	.455	38	34	30-2	2	298	277	163	2	13	84	154	3.08	104	.248	.308	106-0-5	.075	-8	109	-1	—	-0.6
1904	Bro N	5	15	.250	23	22	16-2	0	181.2	141	81	6	6	78	86	1.68	163	.218	.308	63-0-3	.127	-4	66	12	—	1.1
	NY A	0	1	.000	2	2	0	0	12	14	4	0	0	2	8	2.25	121	.292	.320	4	.000	-1	53	1	—	0.0
Total	7	58	97	.374	181	158	134-13	3	1400.2	1320	714	20	71	413	612	2.72	125	.249	.312	500-0-18	.122	-35	83	79	—	5.6

GARZA, MATT Matthew Scott; B11.26.1983 Selma CA; BR/TR/6´4˝/185; [MinA05 1/25]; d8.11; Col Fresno St.

YEAR	TM LG	W	L	PCT	G	GS	CG-SHO	SV-BS	IP	H	R	HR	HB	BB-IB	SO	ERA	AERA	OAV	OOB	AB-HR-SH	AVG	PB	SUP	APR	DL	PW
2006	Min A	3	6	.333	10	9	0	0-0	50	62	33	6	0	23-0	38	5.76	79	.301	.366	0	ø	0	76	-6	0	-0.9

GASPAR, HARRY Harry Lambert; B4.28.1883 Kingsley IA; D5.14.1940 Orange CA; BR/TR/6´0˝/180; d4.21

YEAR	TM LG	W	L	PCT	G	GS	CG-SHO	SV-BS	IP	H	R	HR	HB	BB-IB	SO	ERA	AERA	OAV	OOB	AB-HR-SH	AVG	PB	SUP	APR	DL	PW
1909	Cin N	19	11	.633	44	29	19-4	2	260	228	97	0	9	57	65	2.01	129	.242	.291	82-0-10	.122	-3	103	14	—	1.0
1910	Cin N	15	17	.469	48	31	16-4	**7**	275	257	103	6	15	75	74	2.59	113	.255	.317	87-0-1	.115	-3	100	14	—	1.2
1911	Cin N	11	17	.393	44	32	11-2	4	253.2	272	112	9	14	69	76	3.30	100	.283	.340	85-0-1	.153	-2	92	6	—	0.3
1912	Cin N	1	3	.250	7	6	2-1	0	36.2	38	21	0	1	16	13	4.17	81	.277	.357	12	.250	0	127	-3	—	-0.2
Total	4	46	48	.489	143	98	48-11	13	825.1	795	333	15	39	217	228	2.69	110	.261	.318	266-0-12	.135	-9	100	31	—	2.3

GASSAWAY, CHARLIE Charles Cason "Sheriff"; B8.12.1918 Gassaway TN; D1.15.1992 Miami FL; BL/TL/6´2.5˝/210; d9.25

YEAR	TM LG	W	L	PCT	G	GS	CG-SHO	SV-BS	IP	H	R	HR	HB	BB-IB	SO	ERA	AERA	OAV	OOB	AB-HR-SH	AVG	PB	SUP	APR	DL	PW
1944	Chi N	0	1	.000	2	2	0	0	11.2	20	11	3	0	10	7	7.71	46	.385	.484	4	.250	0	95	-5	0	-0.3
1945	Phi A	4	7	.364	24	11	4	0	118	114	59	4	2	55	50	3.74	92	.252	.336	39	.154	-2	72	-5	0	-0.7
1946	Cle A	1	1	.500	13	6	0	0	50.2	54	25	2	4	26	23	3.91	85	.273	.368	15	.067	-1	99	-4	0	-0.3
Total	3	5	9	.357	39	19	4	0	180.1	188	95	9	6	91	80	4.04	84	.268	.357	58	.138	-3	83	-14	0	-1.3

GASSNER, DAVE David K.; B12.14.1978 Hortonville WI; BR/TL/6´2˝/190; [TorA01 24/721]; d4.16; Col Purdue; [DL 2006 Min A 121]

YEAR	TM LG	W	L	PCT	G	GS	CG-SHO	SV-BS	IP	H	R	HR	HB	BB-IB	SO	ERA	AERA	OAV	OOB	AB-HR-SH	AVG	PB	SUP	APR	DL	PW
2005	Min A	1	0	1.000	2	2	0	0-0	7.2	9	7	1	0	1-0	2	5.87	75	.281	.294	0	ø	0	169	-2	0	-0.2

GASTON, MILT Nathaniel Milton; B1.27.1896 Ridgefield Park NJ; D4.26.1996 Barnstable MA; BR/TR (BB 1933)/6´1˝/185; d4.20; b–Alex

YEAR	TM LG	W	L	PCT	G	GS	CG-SHO	SV-BS	IP	H	R	HR	HB	BB-IB	SO	ERA	AERA	OAV	OOB	AB-HR-SH	AVG	PB	SUP	APR	DL	PW
1924	NY A	5	3	.625	29	2	0	1	86	92	48	3	6	44	24	4.50	92	.286	.382	27-0-2	.222	-1	51	-3	—	-0.4
1925	StL A	15	14	.517	42	29	16	1	238.2	284	146	8	5	101	84	4.41	106	.305	.376	80-1-6	.262	2	102	4	—	0.6
1926	StL A	10	18	.357	32	28	14-1	0	214.1	227	116	13	4	101	39	4.33	99	.283	.366	78-1-2	.167	-2	79	2	—	0.0
1927	StL A	13	17	.433	37	30	21	1	254	275	177	18	3	100	77	5.00	87	.281	.350	96-3-5	.260	5	102	-20	—	-1.4
1928	Was A	6	12	.333	28	22	8-3	0	148.2	179	102	3	0	53	45	5.51	73	.302	.360	49-0-4	.143	-3	108	-23	—	-2.5
1929	Bos A	12	19	.387	39	28	20-1	2	243.2	265	121	15	3	81	83	3.73	115	.289	.348	78-1-4	.192	0	76	14	—	1.6
1930	Bos A	13	20	.394	38	34	20-2	2	273	272	138	15	0	98	99	3.92	117	.259	.323	98-0-5	.204	-4	81	20	—	1.8
1931	Bos A	2	13	.133	23	18	4	0	119	137	76	4	0	41	33	4.46	96	.291	.348	38-0-1	.158	-2	60	-6	—	-0.8
1932	Chi A	7	17	.292	28	25	7-1	1	166.2	183	101	10	1	73	44	4.00	108	.279	.352	60	.233	2	80	3	—	0.6
1933	Chi A	8	12	.400	30	25	7-1	0	167	177	106	9	1	60	39	4.85	87	.272	.334	52-0-2	.154	-0	84	-11	—	-1.1
1934	Chi A	6	19	.240	29	28	10-1	0	194	247	146	16	1	84	48	5.85	81	.313	.379	68-0-1	.147	-3	77	-23	—	-2.5
Total	11	97	164	.372	355	269	127-10	8	2105	2338	1277	114	24	836	615	4.55	97	.287	.355	724-6-32	.200	-5	85	-43	—	-4.1

GASTON, WELCOME Welcome Thornburg; B12.19.1874 Senecaville OH; D12.13.1944 Columbus OH; TL; d10.6

YEAR	TM LG	W	L	PCT	G	GS	CG-SHO	SV-BS	IP	H	R	HR	HB	BB-IB	SO	ERA	AERA	OAV	OOB	AB-HR-SH	AVG	PB	SUP	APR	DL	PW
1898	Bro N	1	1	.500	2	2	2	0	16	17	9	0	0	9	0	2.81	127	.270	.361	8	.125	-0	178	1	—	0.0
1899	Bro N	0	0	ø	1	0	0	0	3	3	1	0	1	4	0	3.00	130	.250	.471	1	1.000	1	—	0	—	0.1
Total	2	1	1	.500	3	2	2	0	19	20	10	0	1	13	0	2.84	128	.267	.382	9	.222	1	178	1	—	0.1

GASTRIGHT, HANK Henry Carl (b Henry Carl Gastreich); B3.29.1865 Covington KY; D10.9.1937 Cold Spring KY; BR/TR/6´2˝/190; d4.19

YEAR	TM LG	W	L	PCT	G	GS	CG-SHO	SV-BS	IP	H	R	HR	HB	BB-IB	SO	ERA	AERA	OAV	OOB	AB-HR-SH	AVG	PB	SUP	APR	DL	PW
1889	Col AA	10	16	.385	32	26	21	0	222.2	255	175	8	5	104	115	4.57	79	.279	.355	94	.181	-4	76	-24	—	-2.4
1890	Col AA	30	14	.682	48	45	41-4	0	401.1	312	204	8	18	135	199	2.94	122	.208	.281	169	.213	3	131	30	—	2.7
1891	Col AA	12	19	.387	35	33	28-1	0	283.2	280	196	7	11	136	109	3.78	91	.249	.336	117	.197	2	105	-16	—	-1.1
1892	Was N	3	3	.500	11	8	6	0	79.2	94	54	3	3	38	32	5.08	64	.282	.361	29	.138	0*	136	-10	—	-0.6
1893	Pit N	3	1	.750	9	5	3	0	59	74	54	3	3	39	12	6.25	73	.297	.399	24	.042	-4	120	-10	—	-0.7
	Bos N	12	4	.750	19	18	16	0	156	179	117	9	9	76	27	5.13	96	.279	.364	68	.191	-3*	105	-1	—	-0.4
	Year	15	5	**.750**	28	23	19	0	215	253	171	12	12	115	39	5.44	89	.284	.374	92	.152	-6	108	-4	—	-1.1
1894	Bro N	2	6	.250	16	8	6-1	2	93	135	85	1	6	55	20	6.39	78	.335	.422	41	.171	-3	112	-13	—	-1.0

YEAR	TM LG	W	L	PCT	G	GS	CG-SHO	SV-BS	IP	H	R	HR	HB	BB-IB	SO	ERA	AERA	OAV	OOB	AB-HR-SH	AVG	PB	SUP	APR	DL	PW
1896	Cin N	0	0	ø	1	0	0	0	6	8	6	0	0	1	0	4.50	103	.320	.346	2	.000	-0	—	-1	—	-0.1
Total	7	72	63	.533	171	143	121-6	2	1301.1	1337	891	39	55	584	514	4.20	92	.258	.339	544	.186	-8	110	-45	—	-3.6
Gatewood, Aubrey	Aubrey Lee; B11.17.1938 Little Rock AR; BR/TR/6´1˝/170; d9.11; Col Arkansas St.																									
1963	LA A	1	1	.500	4	3	1	0	24	12	5	0	0	16-0	13	1.50	228	.148	.283	8	.000	-1	69	5	0	0.3
1964	LA A	3	3	.500	15	7	0	0	60.1	59	18	4	1	12-1	25	2.24	147	.258	.295	20	.100	-1*	85	8	0	0.6
1965	Cal A	4	5	.444	46	3	0	0	92	91	41	5	1	37-3	37	3.42	99	.266	.336	14	.214	1	43	-1	0	0.0
1970	Atl N	0	0	ø	3	0	0	0-0	2	4	6	0	1	2-1	0	4.50	95	.364	.500	0	ø	0	—	-2	0	-0.1
Total	4	8	9	.471	68	13	1	0-0	178.1	166	70	9	3	67-5	75	2.78	122	.250	.318	42	.119	-1	70	10	0	0.8
Gaudin, Chad	Chad Edward; B3.24.1983 Metairie LA; BR/TR/5´10˝/(165–170); [TBA01 34/1009]; d8.1																									
2003	TB A	2	0	1.000	15	3	0	0-0	40	37	18	4	1	16-0	23	3.60	127	.240	.312	0	ø	0	114	4	0	0.2
2004	TB A	1	2	.333	26	4	0	0-1	42.2	59	27	4	4	16-4	30	4.85	96	.337	.397	1-0-1	.000	-0*	104	-2	0	-0.1
2005	Tor A	1	3	.250	5	3	0	0-0	13	31	19	6	1	6-0	12	13.15	35	.470	.514	0	ø	0	87	-11	0	-1.8
2006	†Oak A	4	2	.667	55	0	0	2-1	64	51	24	3	1	42-2	36	3.09	147	.222	.341	0	ø	0	—	10	0	0.8
Total	4	8	7	.533	101	10	0	2-2	159.2	178	88	17	7	80-6	101	4.51	102	.285	.367	1-0-1	.000	-0	103	1	0	-0.9
Gaw, Chippy	George Joseph; B3.13.1892 W.Newton MA; D5.26.1968 Boston MA; BR/TR/5´11˝/180; d4.20; Col Tufts																									
1920	Chi N	1	1	.500	6	1	0	0	13	16	9	1	1	3	4	4.85	66	.320	.370	4	.250	-0	74	-2	—	-0.4
Gear, Dale	Dale Dudley; B2.2.1872 Lone Elm KS; D9.23.1951 Topeka KS; BR/TR/5´11˝/165; d8.15; Col Kansas; ▲																									
1896	Cle N	0	2	.000	3	2	2	0	23	35	23	1	2	6	6	5.48	83	.347	.394	15	.400	2*	102	-3	—	-0.1
1901	Was A	4	11	.267	24	16	14-1	1	163	199	100	9	4	22	35	4.03	91	.297	.324	199-0-2	.236	0*	78	-5	—	-0.3
Total	2	4	13	.235	27	18	16-1	1	186	234	123	10	6	28	41	4.21	90	.304	.333	214-0-2	.248	2	81	-8	—	-0.4
Gearin, Dinty	Dennis John; B10.15.1897 Providence RI; D3.11.1959 Providence RI; BL/TL/5´4˝/148; d8.6																									
1923	†NY N	1	1	.500	6	2	1	0	24	23	11	1	0	10	9	3.38	113	.264	.340	7	.286	0	65	1	—	0.1
1924	NY N	1	2	.333	6	3	2	0	29	30	9	3	0	16	4	2.48	148	.275	.368	9	.333	0*	154	4	—	0.4
	Bos N	0	1	.000	1	1	0	0	0	3	5	0	0	2	0	(5)	ø	1.000	1.000	0	ø	0	178	-5	—	-0.4
	Year	1	3	.250	7	4	2	0	29	33	14	3	0	18	4	4.03	91	.295	.392	9	.333	0	162	-1	—	0.0
Total	2	2	4	.333	13	6	3	0	53	56	25	4	0	28	13	3.74	100	.281	.370	16	.313	1	127	0	—	0.1
Geary, Geoff	Geoffrey Michael; B8.26.1976 Buffalo NY; BR/TR/6´0˝/(165–180); [PhiN98 15/434]; d8.27; Col Oklahoma																									
2003	Phi N	0	0	ø	5	0	0	0-0	6	8	3	0	0	3-0	3	4.50	88	.333	.407	0	ø	0	—	0	0	0.0
2004	Phi N	1	0	1.000	33	0	0	0-0	44.2	52	29	8	3	16-3	30	5.44	81	.292	.357	1	.000	-0	—	-5	0	-0.3
2005	Phi N	2	1	.667	40	0	0	0-1	58	54	29	5	1	21-4	42	3.72	117	.247	.310	6	.167	-0	—	2	15	0.1
2006	Phi N	7	1	.875	81	0	0	1-3	91.1	103	34	6	6	20-4	60	2.96	159	.286	.333	5	.200	1	—	16	0	1.4
Total	4	10	2	.833	159	0	0	1-4	200	217	95	19	10	60-11	135	3.78	119	.278	.334	12	.167	0	—	13	15	1.2
Geary, Bob	Robert Norton "Speed"; B5.10.1891 Cincinnati OH; D1.3.1980 Cincinnati OH; BR/TR/5´11˝/168; d4.25; Mil 1918																									
1918	Phi A	2	5	.286	16	7	6-2	4	87	94	37	0	3	31	22	2.69	109	.289	.357	27-0-1	.148	-1	81	1	—	0.0
1919	Phi A	0	3	.000	9	2	1	0	32.1	32	22	1	0	18	9	4.73	72	.264	.360	10	.500	2	69	-5	—	-0.2
1921	Cin N	1	1	.500	10	1	0	0	29	38	17	1	0	2	10	4.34	82	.333	.345	8	.250	0	138	-2	—	-0.2
Total	3	3	9	.250	35	10	7-2	4	148.1	164	76	2	3	51	41	3.46	92	.293	.355	45-0-1	.244	1	83	-6	—	-0.4
Gebhard, Bob	Robert Henry; B1.3.1943 Lamberton MN; BR/TR/6´2˝/210; [MinA65 15/547]; d8.2; C1; Col Iowa																									
1971	Min A	1	2	.333	17	0	0	0-0	18	17	6	0	1	11-3	13	3.00	118	.243	.354	0	ø	0	—	1	0	0.3
1972	Min A	0	1	.000	13	0	0	1-0	21	36	29	3	2	13-2	13	8.57	37	.371	.447	0	ø	0	—	-14	0	-0.8
1974	Mon N	0	0	ø	1	0	0	0-0	2	5	1	1	0	0-0	0	4.50	86	.500	.500	0	ø	0	—	0	0	0.0
Total	3	1	3	.250	31	0	0	1-0	41	58	36	4	3	24-5	26	5.93	57	.328	.413	0	ø	0	—	-13	0	-0.5
Gebrian, Pete	Peter "Gabe"; B8.10.1923 Bayonne NJ; D5.6.2005 Stuart FL; BR/TR/6´0˝/170; d5.6																									
1947	Chi A	2	3	.400	27	4	0	5	66.1	61	40	7	2	33	17	4.48	82	.247	.340	13-0-1	.000	-2	48	-7	0	-0.8
Geddes, Jim	James Lee; B3.23.1949 Columbus OH; BR/TR/6´2˝/190; d4.28; Col Ohio St.																									
1972	Chi A	0	0	ø	5	1	0	0-0	10.1	12	9	1	1	10-0	3	6.97	45	.293	.442	1-0-1	.000	-0*	170	-4	0	-0.3
1973	Chi A	0	0	ø	6	1	0	0-0	15.2	14	6	0	3	14-0	7	2.87	138	.255	.431	0	ø	0	45	2	0	0.1
Total	2	0	0	ø	11	2	0	0-0	26	26	15	1	4	24-0	10	4.50	80	.271	.435	1-0-1	.000	-0	98	-2	0	-0.2
Gedney, Count	Alfred W.; B5.10.1849 Brooklyn NY; D3.26.1922 Hackensack NJ; 5´9˝/140; d4.27.1872; ▲																									
1875	Mut NA	1	0	1.000	2	1	1	0	11	7	4	0	—	1	2	0.82	285	.167	.186	267	.206	-0*	136	1	—	0.1
Gee, Johnny	John Alexander "Whiz"; B12.7.1915 Syracuse NY; D1.23.1988 Cortland NY; BL/TL/6´9˝/225; d9.17; Def 1945; Col Michigan																									
1939	Pit N	1	2	.333	3	3	1	0	19.2	20	17	0	0	10	16	4.12	93	.253	.337	6	.000	-1	83	-4	—	-0.5
1941	Pit N	0	2	.000	3	2	0	0	7.1	10	10	0	0	5	2	6.14	59	.294	.385	3	.333	0	106	-4	0	-0.7
1943	Pit N	4	4	.500	15	10	2	0	82	89	42	5	0	27	18	4.28	81	.280	.336	26-0-2	.115	-1	122	-4	0	-0.6
1944	Pit N	0	0	ø	4	0	0	0	11.1	20	10	0	0	5	3	7.15	52	.377	.431	2	.500	0	—	-4	0	-0.2
	NY N	0	0	ø	4	0	0	0	4.2	5	1	0	0	0	3	0.00	ø	.263	.263	0	ø	0	—	1	0	0.1
	Year	0	0	ø	8	0	0	0	16	25	11	0	0	5	6	5.06	73	.347	.390	2	.500	0	—	-2	0	-0.1
1945	NY N	0	0	ø	2	0	0	1	3	5	3	0	0	2	1	9.00	43	.385	.467	1	.000	-0	—	-1	0	-0.1
1946	NY N	2	4	.333	13	6	1	0	47.1	60	27	3	2	15	22	3.99	86	.308	.363	13-0-1	.231	0	46	-4	0	-0.5
Total	6	7	12	.368	44	21	4	1	175.1	209	110	8	2	64	65	4.41	80	.294	.354	51-0-3	.157	-1	93	-20	0	-2.5
Gehring, Henry	Henry; B1.24.1881 St.Paul MN; D4.18.1912 Kansas City MO; BR/TR; d7.16																									
1907	Was A	3	7	.300	15	9	8-2	0	87	92	44	1	1	14	31	3.31	73	.274	.305	44-1-0	.205	3*	93	-8	—	-0.7
1908	Was A	0	1	.000	3	1	0	0	5	9	8	0	2	2	0	14.40	16	.450	.542	5	.600	2*	90	-6	—	-0.7
Total	2	3	8	.273	18	10	8-2	0	92	101	52	1	3	16	31	3.91	62	.284	.320	49-1-0	.245	5	93	-14	—	-1.4
Gehrman, Paul	Paul Arthur "Dutch"; B5.3.1912 Marquam OR; D10.23.1986 Bend OR; BR/TR/6´0˝/195; d9.15																									
1937	Cin N	0	1	.000	2	1	0	0	9.1	11	8	0	0	5	1	2.89	129	.282	.364	3	.000	-0	116	-1	—	-0.1
Geis, Bill	William J. (b William J. Geiss); B7.15.1858 Chicago IL; D9.18.1924 Chicago IL; 5´10˝/164; d7.19; b–Emil; ▲																									
1882	Bal AA	4	9	.308	13	13	10-1	0	95.2	84	73	2	—	22	10	4.80	57	.220	.263	41	.146	-2	59	-16	—	-1.9
1884	Det N	0	0	ø	1	0	0	0	5	14	16	0	0	2	1	14.40	20	.424	.457	283-2	.177	-0*	—	-7	—	-0.3
Total	2	4	9	.308	14	13	10-1	0	100.2	98	89	2	—	24	11	5.27	52	.237	.279	324-2	.173	-2	59	-23	—	-2.2
Geisel, Dave	John David; B1.18.1955 Windber PA; BL/TL/6´3˝/(205–210); [ChiN73 5/112]; d6.13																									
1978	Chi N	1	0	1.000	18	1	0	0-0	23.1	27	12	0	0	11-4	15	4.24	95	.278	.352	3	.000	-0	89	0	0	-0.1
1979	Chi N	0	0	ø	7	0	0	0-0	15	10	1	0	1	4-1	5	0.60	693	.189	.259	1	.000	-0	—	5	0	0.3
1981	Chi N	2	0	1.000	11	2	0	0-1	16	11	3	0	0	10-1	7	0.56	666	.204	.318	3	.000	-0	118	5	0	0.5
1982	Tor A	1	1	.500	16	2	0	0-0	31.2	32	15	6	2	17-2	22	3.98	113	.260	.359	0	ø	0	81	2	0	0.1
1983	Tor A	0	3	.000	47	0	0	5-3	52.1	47	28	4	2	31-5	50	4.64	94	.240	.349	0	ø	0	—	-1	0	-0.1
1984	Sea A	1	1	.500	20	3	0	3-0	43.1	47	22	2	2	9-3	28	4.15	97	.273	.314	0	ø	0	97	-1	0	-0.1
1985	Sea A	0	0	ø	12	0	0	0-0	27	35	21	3	0	15-3	17	6.33	67	.310	.391	0	ø	0	—	-6	0	-0.3
Total	7	5	5	.500	131	8	0	8-4	208.2	209	102	15	7	97-19	144	4.01	105	.259	.342	7	.000	-1	94	4	0	0.3
Geishert, Vern	Vernon William; B1.10.1946 Madison WI; BR/TR/6´1˝/195; [AnaA66*2/26]; d8.26; Col Wisconsin–Madison																									
1969	Cal A	1	1	.500	11	3	0	1-0	31	32	18	4	1	7-3	18	4.65	75	.267	.308	9	.000	-1	143	-4	0	-0.3
Geiss, Emil	Emil August; B3.20.1867 Chicago IL; D10.4.1911 Chicago IL; BR/TR/5´11˝/170; d5.18; b–Bill; ▲																									
1887	Chi N	0	1	.000	1	1	1	0	9	17	11	0	0	3	4	8.00	56	.395	.435	12	.083	-1*	58	-3	—	-0.2
Gelnar, John	John Richard; B6.25.1943 Granite OK; BR/TR/6´1.5˝/(185–190); d8.4; Col Oklahoma																									
1964	Pit N	0	0	ø	7	0	0	0	9	11	5	2	0	1-0	4	5.00	70	.314	.333	0	ø	0	—	-1	0	-0.1
1967	Pit N	0	1	.000	10	1	0	0	19	30	18	4	2	11-1	5	8.05	42	.375	.453	6	.167	0	104	-9	0	-0.5
1969	Sea A	3	10	.231	39	10	0	3-2	108.2	103	49	7	5	26-5	69	3.31	110	.250	.299	19-0-3	.053	-2*	61	2	0	0.1
1970	Mil A	4	3	.571	53	0	0	4-2	92.1	98	46	7	5	23-5	48	4.19	90	.277	.326	12	.083	-1	—	-3	0	-0.3

YEAR	TM LG	W	L	PCT	G	GS	CG-SHO	SV-BS	IP	H	R	HR	HB	BB-IB	SO	ERA	AERA	OAV	OOB	AB-HR-SH	AVG	PB	SUP	APR	DL	PW
1971	Mil A	0	0	ø	2	0	0	0-0	1.1	3	2	0	0	1-0	0	13.50	26	.429	.500	0	ø	0	—	-1	0	-0.1
Total	5	7	14	.333	111	11	0	7-4	230.1	245	120	20	12	62-11	126	4.18	88	.276	.328	37-0-3	.081	-2	64	-12	0	-0.9

GENEWICH, JOE Joseph Edward; B1.15.1897 Elmira NY; D12.21.1985 Lockport NY; BR/TR/6´0˝/174; d9.3

YEAR	TM LG	W	L	PCT	G	GS	CG-SHO	SV-BS	IP	H	R	HR	HB	BB-IB	SO	ERA	AERA	OAV	OOB	AB-HR-SH	AVG	PB	SUP	APR	DL	PW
1922	Bos N	0	2	.000	6	2	1	0	23	29	19	2	0	11	4	7.04	57	.319	.392	6	.167	-0	102	-7	—	-0.5
1923	Bos N	13	14	.481	43	24	12-1	1	227.1	272	110	15	7	46	54	3.72	107	.303	.341	77-0-1	.247	2	83	9	—	1.2
1924	Bos N	10	19	.345	34	27	11-2	1	200.1	258	136	4	8	65	43	5.21	73	.329	.386	60-0-5	.167	-2	72	-32	—	-4.0
1925	Bos N	12	10	.545	34	21	10	0	169	185	87	4	6	41	34	3.99	100	.279	.327	55-0-4	.273	1	94	2	—	0.3
1926	Bos N	8	16	.333	37	26	12-2	2	216	239	114	6	6	63	59	3.88	92	.288	.342	67-0-5	.164	-1	88	-10	—	-1.1
1927	Bos N	11	8	.579	40	19	7	1	181	199	93	7	2	54	38	3.83	97	.279	.332	57-0-3	.193	-1	93	-3	—	-0.4
1928	Bos N	3	7	.300	13	11	4	0	80.2	88	43	14	3	18	15	4.13	95	.280	.325	26-0-4	.038	-3	77	-1	—	-0.4
	NY N	11	4	.733	26	18	10-2	3	158.1	136	62	10	1	54	37	3.18	123	.232	.298	64-0-2	.203	-1	112	14	—	1.2
	Year	14	11	.560	39	29	14-2	3	239	224	105	24	4	72	52	3.50	112	.249	.307	90-0-6	.156	-4	99	12	—	0.8
1929	NY N	3	7	.300	21	9	1	1	85	133	70	9	1	30	19	6.78	68	.359	.409	32	.375	3*	104	-19	—	-1.6
1930	NY N	2	5	.286	18	9	3	3	61	71	44	6	1	20	13	5.61	84	.297	.354	20-0-1	.150	-1*	92	-6	—	-0.6
Total	9	73	92	.442	272	166	71-7	12	1401.2	1610	778	77	35	402	316	4.29	91	.293	.345	464-0-25	.207	-4	89	-53	—	-5.9

GENTRY, GARY Gary Edward; B10.6.1946 Phoenix AZ; BR/TR/6´0˝/(165–183); [NYN67 S3/60]; d4.10; Col Arizona St.

YEAR	TM LG	W	L	PCT	G	GS	CG-SHO	SV-BS	IP	H	R	HR	HB	BB-IB	SO	ERA	AERA	OAV	OOB	AB-HR-SH	AVG	PB	SUP	APR	DL	PW
1969	†NY N	13	12	.520	35	35	6-3	0-0	233.2	192	94	24	5	81-5	154	3.43	107	.222	.291	74-0-7	.081	-4	90	8	0	0.5
1970	NY N	9	9	.500	32	29	5-2	1-1	188.1	155	88	19	9	86-7	134	3.68	110	.224	.316	59-0-5	.068	-2	100	7	0	0.3
1971	NY N	12	11	.522	32	31	8-3	0-0	203.1	167	84	16	6	82-8	155	3.23	106	.224	.304	68-0-6	.074	-5	92	4	0	-0.2
1972	NY N	7	10	.412	32	26	3	0-0	164	153	82	20	6	75-5	120	4.01	85	.250	.334	48-0-3	.104	-1	94	-11	0	-1.1
1973	Atl N	4	6	.400	16	14	3	1-0	86.2	74	37	7	1	35-3	42	3.43	116	.231	.305	30-0-3	.233	1*	100	5	34	0.5
1974	Atl N	0	0	ø	3	1	0	0-0	6.2	4	1	1	1	2-0	0	1.35	281	.167	.259	1	.000	-0	46	2	164	0.1
1975	Atl N	1	1	.500	7	2	0	0-1	20	25	14	3	0	8-1	10	4.95	76	.313	.371	5-0-1	.000	-1	46	-3	0	-0.3
Total	7	46	49	.484	157	138	25-8	2-2	902.2	770	400	90	28	369-29	615	3.56	103	.231	.310	285-0-25	.095	-12	94	12	198	-0.2

GENTRY, RUFE James Ruffus; B5.18.1918 Daisy Station (now Ogburn) NC; D7.3.1997 Winston–Salem NC; BR/TR/6´1˝/180; d9.10; b–Harvey

YEAR	TM LG	W	L	PCT	G	GS	CG-SHO	SV-BS	IP	H	R	HR	HB	BB-IB	SO	ERA	AERA	OAV	OOB	AB-HR-SH	AVG	PB	SUP	APR	DL	PW
1943	Det A	1	3	.250	4	4	2	0	29.1	30	12	2	2	12	8	3.68	96	.268	.349	10	.000	-1	60	0	0	-0.1
1944	Det A	12	14	.462	37	30	10-3	0	203.2	211	104	9	4	108	68	4.24	84	.273	.365	76-0-2	.197	-1	85	-10	0	-1.2
1946	Det A	0	0	ø	2	0	0	0	3	4	5	0	0	7	1	15.00	24	.333	.579	0	ø	0	—	-3	0	-0.2
1947	Det A	0	0	ø	1	0	0	0	0.1	1	3	0	0	2	0	81.00	5	.500	.750	0	ø	0	—	-3	0	-0.1
1948	Det A	0	0	ø	4	0	0	0	6.2	5	2	0	1	5	1	2.70	162	.208	.367	1	1.000	0	—	1	0	0.1
Total	5	13	17	.433	48	34	12-3	0	243	251	126	11	7	134	78	4.37	82	.272	.368	87-0-2	.184	-1	82	-15	0	-1.5

GEORGE, CHRIS Christopher Coleman; B9.16.1979 Houston TX; BL/TL/6´2˝/200; [KCA98 1/31]; d7.26

YEAR	TM LG	W	L	PCT	G	GS	CG-SHO	SV-BS	IP	H	R	HR	HB	BB-IB	SO	ERA	AERA	OAV	OOB	AB-HR-SH	AVG	PB	SUP	APR	DL	PW
2001	KC A	4	8	.333	13	13	1	0-0	74	83	48	14	0	18-0	32	5.59	89	.288	.326	0	ø	0	93	-4	0	-0.5
2002	KC A	0	4	.000	6	6	0	0-0	27.1	37	17	2	1	8-0	13	5.60	89	.325	.371	0	ø	0	84	-1	32	-0.1
2003	KC A	9	6	.600	18	18	0	0-0	93.2	120	75	22	3	44-2	39	7.11	68	.309	.380	1-0-2	1.000	0	106	-21	0	-2.6
2004	KC A	1	2	.333	10	7	0	0-0	42.1	60	39	1	0	25-1	15	7.23	65	.331	.411	2	.000	0	82	-13	0	-0.7
Total	4	14	20	.412	47	44	1	0-0	237.1	300	179	39	4	95-3	99	6.48	75	.309	.369	3-0-2	.333	1	96	-39	32	-3.9

GEORGE, CHRIS Christopher Sean; B9.24.1966 Pittsburgh PA; BR/TR/6´2˝/200; [MilA88 7/185]; d10.1; Col Kent St.

YEAR	TM LG	W	L	PCT	G	GS	CG-SHO	SV-BS	IP	H	R	HR	HB	BB-IB	SO	ERA	AERA	OAV	OOB	AB-HR-SH	AVG	PB	SUP	APR	DL	PW
1991	Mil A	0	0	ø	2	1	0	0-0	6	8	2	0	0	0-0	2	3.00	133	.333	.320	0	ø	0	46	1	0	0.0

GEORGE, LEFTY Thomas Edward; B8.13.1886 Pittsburgh PA; D5.13.1955 York PA; BL/TL/6´0˝/155; d4.14

YEAR	TM LG	W	L	PCT	G	GS	CG-SHO	SV-BS	IP	H	R	HR	HB	BB-IB	SO	ERA	AERA	OAV	OOB	AB-HR-SH	AVG	PB	SUP	APR	DL	PW
1911	StL A	4	9	.308	27	13	6-1	0	116.1	136	81	3	9	51	23	4.18	81	.256	.332	44-0-2	.114	-3	82	-12	—	-1.5
1912	Cle A	0	5	.000	11	5	2	0	44.1	69	38	1	2	18	18	4.87	70	.373	.434	14-0-1	.214	1	74	-9	—	-0.8
1915	Cin N	2	2	.500	5	3	2-1	0	28	24	12	1	5	8	11	3.86	74	.242	.330	12	.333	2*	78	-2	—	0.0
1918	Bos N	1	5	.167	9	5	4	0	54.1	56	23	0	3	21	22	2.32	116	.281	.359	22	.091	-2*	90	0	—	0.0
Total	4	7	21	.250	52	26	14-2	0	243	285	154	5	19	98	74	3.85	82	.281	.355	92-0-3	.152	-2	82	-23	—	-2.3

GEORGE, BILL William M.; B1.27.1865 Bellaire OH; D8.23.1916 Wheeling WV; BR/TL/5´8˝/165; d5.11

YEAR	TM LG	W	L	PCT	G	GS	CG-SHO	SV-BS	IP	H	R	HR	HB	BB-IB	SO	ERA	AERA	OAV	OOB	AB-HR-SH	AVG	PB	SUP	APR	DL	PW
1887	NY N	3	9	.250	13	13	10	0	108	126	112	1	14	89	49	5.25	72	.292	.429	53	.170	-4	146	-23	—	-2.0
1888	†NY N	2	1	.667	4	3	3-1	0	33.2	18	9	0	1	11	26	1.34	205	.149	.226	39-1	.231	1*	164	5	—	0.5
1889	Col AA	0	0	ø	2	0	0	0	8	11	13	1	0	3	3	7.88	46	.314	.368	17	.235	-0*	—	-5	—	-0.2
Total	3	5	10	.333	19	16	13-1	0	149.2	155	134	2	15	103	78	4.51	78	.264	.387	109-1	.202	-3	149	-23	—	-1.7

GEORGY, OSCAR Oscar John; B11.25.1916 New Orleans LA; D1.15.1999 New Orleans LA; BR/TR/6´3.5˝/180; d6.4

YEAR	TM LG	W	L	PCT	G	GS	CG-SHO	SV-BS	IP	H	R	HR	HB	BB-IB	SO	ERA	AERA	OAV	OOB	AB-HR-SH	AVG	PB	SUP	APR	DL	PW
1938	NY N	0	0	ø	1	0	0	0	1	2	2	0	0	1	0	18.00	21	.400	.500	0	ø	0	—	-1	—	-0.1

GERARD, DAVE David Frederick; B8.6.1936 New York NY; D10.10.2001 Newtown PA; BR/TR/6´2˝/205; d4.10

YEAR	TM LG	W	L	PCT	G	GS	CG-SHO	SV-BS	IP	H	R	HR	HB	BB-IB	SO	ERA	AERA	OAV	OOB	AB-HR-SH	AVG	PB	SUP	APR	DL	PW
1962	Chi N	2	3	.400	39	0	0	3	58.2	67	40	10	1	28-5	30	4.91	84	.289	.365	8	.375	1	—	-6	0	-0.5

GERBERMAN, GEORGE George Alois; B3.8.1942 ElCampo TX; BR/TR/6´0˝/175; d9.23

YEAR	TM LG	W	L	PCT	G	GS	CG-SHO	SV-BS	IP	H	R	HR	HB	BB-IB	SO	ERA	AERA	OAV	OOB	AB-HR-SH	AVG	PB	SUP	APR	DL	PW
1962	Chi N	0	0	ø	1	1	0	0	5.1	3	1	1	0	5-0	1	1.69	246	.158	.333	1	.000	0	21	1	0	0.1

GERHARDT, RUSTY Allen Russell; B8.13.1950 Baltimore MD; BB/TL/5´9˝/174; d7.27; Col Clemson

YEAR	TM LG	W	L	PCT	G	GS	CG-SHO	SV-BS	IP	H	R	HR	HB	BB-IB	SO	ERA	AERA	OAV	OOB	AB-HR-SH	AVG	PB	SUP	APR	DL	PW
1974	SD N	2	1	.667	23	1	0	1-0	35.2	44	28	1	2	17-5	22	7.07	51	.308	.384	6	.167	-0	73	-12	0	-1.1

GERHEAUSER, AL Albert "Lefty"; B6.24.1917 St.Louis MO; D5.28.1972 Springfield MO; BL/TL/6´3˝/190; d4.24

YEAR	TM LG	W	L	PCT	G	GS	CG-SHO	SV-BS	IP	H	R	HR	HB	BB-IB	SO	ERA	AERA	OAV	OOB	AB-HR-SH	AVG	PB	SUP	APR	DL	PW
1943	Phi N	10	19	.345	38	31	11-2	0	215	222	108	10	2	70	92	3.60	94	.263	.321	71-0-1	.113	-3	92	-9	0	-1.5
1944	Phi N	8	16	.333	30	29	10-2	0	182.2	210	102	8	1	65	66	4.58	79	.285	.344	65-1-1	.231	3*	77	-17	0	-1.7
1945	Pit N	5	10	.333	32	14	5	1	140.1	170	72	5	1	54	55	3.91	101	.304	.366	48	.250	3	107	1	0	0.4
1946	Pit N	2	2	.500	35	3	1	0	81.2	92	42	2	1	25	32	3.97	89	.286	.339	21	.333	2*	97	-4	0	0.1
1948	StL A	0	3	.000	14	2	0	0	23.1	32	23	0	1	10	10	7.33	62	.317	.384	6	.333	0	50	-8	0	-0.8
Total	5	25	50	.333	149	79	27-4	1	643	726	347	25	6	224	255	4.13	88	.283	.342	211-1-2	.209	5	88	-37	0	-3.5

GERKIN, STEVE Stephen Paul "Splinter"; B11.19.1912 Grafton WV; D11.9.1978 Bay Pines FL; BR/TR/6´1˝/162; d5.13

YEAR	TM LG	W	L	PCT	G	GS	CG-SHO	SV-BS	IP	H	R	HR	HB	BB-IB	SO	ERA	AERA	OAV	OOB	AB-HR-SH	AVG	PB	SUP	APR	DL	PW
1945	Phi A	0	12	.000	21	12	3	0	102	112	49	4	3	27	25	3.62	95	.285	.336	34-0-1	.059	-4	70	-3	0	-0.7

GERMAN, FRANKLYN Franklyn Miguel (Made); B1.20.1980 San Cristobal, D.R.; BR/TR/6´6˝/(245–270); d9.7

YEAR	TM LG	W	L	PCT	G	GS	CG-SHO	SV-BS	IP	H	R	HR	HB	BB-IB	SO	ERA	AERA	OAV	OOB	AB-HR-SH	AVG	PB	SUP	APR	DL	PW
2002	Det A	1	0	1.000	7	0	0	1-0	6.2	3	0	0	1	2-1	6	0.00	ø	.150	.261	0	ø	0	—	3	0	0.5
2003	Det A	2	4	.333	45	0	0	5-2	44.2	47	32	5	2	45-3	41	6.04	72	.273	.427	0	ø	0	—	-8	0	-1.1
2004	Det A	1	0	1.000	16	0	0	0-1	14.2	17	15	4	0	11-1	8	7.36	61	.279	.389	1	.000	-0	—	-6	0	-0.4
2005	Det A	4	0	1.000	58	0	0	1-2	59	63	26	7	7	34-4	38	3.66	117	.284	.388	0	ø	0	—	4	0	0.2
2006	Fla N	0	0	ø	12	0	0	0-1	12	7	4	1	1	14-2	6	3.00	143	.171	.393	0	ø	0	—	2	20	0.1
Total	5	8	4	.667	138	0	0	7-6	137	137	77	17	11	106-11	99	4.60	94	.266	.397	1	.000	-0	—	-5	20	-0.7

GERMAN, LES Lester Stanley; B6.1.1869 Baltimore MD; D6.10.1934 Germantown MD; BR/TR/5´8˝/165; d8.27

YEAR	TM LG	W	L	PCT	G	GS	CG-SHO	SV-BS	IP	H	R	HR	HB	BB-IB	SO	ERA	AERA	OAV	OOB	AB-HR-SH	AVG	PB	SUP	APR	DL	PW
1890	Bal AA	5	11	.313	17	16	15	0	132.1	147	95	2	13	54	37	4.83	84	.273	.353	51	.118	-2	75	-10	—	-1.2
1893	NY N	8	8	.500	20	18	14	0	152	162	109	6	9	70	35	4.14	112	.265	.349	74	.311	2*	98	6	—	0.6
1894	NY N	9	8	.529	24	16	11	1	143	186	139	7	12	68	21	5.54	95	.311	.392	60-0-2	.300	0	114	-6	—	-0.4
1895	NY N	7	11	.389	25	18	16	0	178.1	243	159	7	9	78	36	5.96	78	.320	.390	111-2-1	.261	3*	99	-23	—	-1.4
1896	NY N	0	0	ø	1	0	0	0	2.2	9	6	0	0	1	0	13.50	31	.529	.556	1	.000	-0	—	-3	—	-0.1
	Was N	2	20	.091	28	20	14	1	166.2	240	174	6	5	74	20	6.32	70	.334	.400	70-1-0	.229	0*	84	-32	—	-3.0
	Year	2	20	.091	29	20	14	1	169.1	249	180	6	5	75	20	6.43	69	.339	.404	71-1-0	.225	-0	84	-41	—	-3.1
1897	Was N	3	5	.375	15	5	4	0	83.2	117	74	2	7	33	2	5.59	78	.328	.395	44-0-1	.341	2*	92	-10	—	-0.5
Total	6	34	63	.351	130	93	74	2	858.2	1104	756	30	55	378	151	5.45	84	.307	.381	411-3-4	.260	5	95	-78	—	-6.0

GERMANO, JUSTIN Justin William; B8.6.1982 Pasadena CA; BR/TR/6´1˝/(190–205); [SDN00 13/379]; d5.22

YEAR	TM LG	W	L	PCT	G	GS	CG-SHO	SV-BS	IP	H	R	HR	HB	BB-IB	SO	ERA	AERA	OAV	OOB	AB-HR-SH	AVG	PB	SUP	APR	DL	PW
2004	SD N	1	2	.333	7	5	0	0-0	21.1	31	24	2	0	14-0	16	8.86	45	.341	.425	7-0-1	.000	-1	113	-13	0	-1.5
2006	Cin N	0	1	.000	2	1	0	0-0	6.2	8	4	1	1	3-1	8	5.40	87	.296	.387	2-0-1	.000	-0	59	0	0	-0.1
Total	2	1	3	.250	9	6	0	0-0	28	39	28	3	1	17-1	24	8.04	51	.331	.416	9-0-2	.000	-1	101	-13	0	-1.6

GERNER, ED Edwin Frederick "Lefty"; B7.22.1897 Philadelphia PA; D5.15.1970 Philadelphia PA; BL/TL/5´8.5˝/175; d5.14

YEAR	TM LG	W	L	PCT	G	GS	CG-SHO	SV-BS	IP	H	R	HR	HB	BB-IB	SO	ERA	AERA	OAV	OOB	AB-HR-SH	AVG	PB	SUP	APR	DL	PW
1919	Cin N	1	0	1.000	5	1	0	0	17	22	10	0	2	3	2	3.18	87	.333	.380	6	.167	0*	230	-2	—	-0.1

YEAR	TM LG	W	L	PCT	G	GS	CG-SHO	SV-BS	IP	H	R	HR	HB	BB-IB	SO	ERA	AERA	OAV	OOB	AB-HR-SH	AVG	PB	SUP	APR	DL	PW
GERVAIS, LEFTY	Lucien Edward; B7.6.1890 Grover WI; D10.19.1950 Los Angeles CA; BL/TL/5´10˝/165; d4.17																									
1913	Bos N	0	1	.000	5	2	1	0	15.2	18	11	0	0	4	1	5.74	57	.383	.431	5	.000	-0*	80	-3	—	-0.2
GESSNER, CHARLIE	Charles R.; B12.1863 Philadelphia PA; D5.25.1922 Washington DC; 5´8˝/?; d7.19																									
1886	Phi AA	0	1	.000	1	1	1	0	8	13	14	0	2	5	0	9.00	39	.351	.455	4	.250	-0	136	-5	—	-0.4
GETTEL, AL	Allen Jones; B9.17.1917 Norfolk VA; D4.8.2005 Norfolk VA; BR/TR/6´3.5˝/200; d4.20																									
1945	NY A	9	8	.529	27	17	9	3	154.2	141	70	11	7	53	67	3.90	89	.243	.314	57-0-2	.281	2	93	-4	0	-0.3
1946	NY A	6	7	.462	26	11	5-2	0	103	89	40	6	2	40	54	2.97	116	.229	.305	32-0-3	.125	-2	81	5	0	0.5
1947	Cle A	11	10	.524	31	21	9-2	0	149	122	54	12	3	62	64	3.20	109	.229	.313	51-0-2	.294	4*	93	7	0	1.4
1948	Cle A	0	1	.000	5	2	0	0	7.2	15	15	2	1	10	4	17.61	23	.385	.520	3	.000	-0	211	-11	0	-1.2
	Chi A	8	10	.444	22	19	7	1	148	154	76	7	4	60	49	4.01	106	.268	.342	54-0-3	.241	0*	96	3	0	0.3
	Year	8	11	.421	27	21	7	1	155.2	169	91	9	5	70	53	4.68	91	.276	.355	57-0-3	.228	-0	106	-8	0	-0.9
1949	Chi A	2	5	.286	19	7	1-1	1	63	69	48	12	2	26	22	6.43	65	.283	.357	18	.167	-0	95	-15	0	-1.5
	Was A	0	2	.000	16	1	0	1	34.2	43	24	4	0	24	7	5.45	78	.314	.416	8	.000	-1	105	-5	0	-0.3
	Year	2	7	.222	35	8	1-1	2	97.2	112	72	16	2	50	29	6.08	69	.294	.379	26	.115	-1	96	-20	0	-1.8
1951	NY N	1	2	.333	30	1	0	0	57.1	52	37	12	0	25	36	4.87	80	.240	.318	12	.083	-1	158	-6	0	-0.4
1955	StL N	1	0	1.000	8	0	0	0	17	26	18	6	0	10-0	7	9.00	45	.361	.429	6	.500	1	—	-9	0	-0.4
Total	7	38	45	.458	184	79	31-5	6	734.1	711	382	72	19	310-0	310	4.28	88	.255	.334	241-0-10	.228	3	96	-35	0	-1.9
GETTIG, CHARLIE	Charles Henry; B12.1870 Baltimore MD; D4.11.1935 Baltimore MD; BR/5´10˝/172; d8.5; ▲																									
1896	NY N	1	0	1.000	4	1	1	1	14	20	17	0	2	8	5	9.64	44	.333	.429	9	.333	1*	253	-7	—	-0.4
1897	NY N	1	1	.500	3	2	2	0	19	23	23	0	2	9	7	5.21	80	.295	.382	75	.200	0*	120	-4	—	-0.3
1898	NY N	6	3	.667	17	8	7	0	115	141	72	1	8	39	14	3.83	91	.299	.363	196-0-1	.250	2*	186	-4	—	0.0
1899	NY N	7	8	.467	18	15	12	0	128	161	102	3	4	54	25	4.43	85	.307	.376	97-0-3	.247	1*	104	-15	—	-1.2
Total	4	15	12	.556	42	26	22	1	276	345	214	4	16	110	51	4.50	82	.304	.374	377-0-4	.241	4	136	-30	—	-1.9
GETZIEN, CHARLIE	Charles H. "Pretzels"; B2.14.1864 , Germany; D6.19.1932 Chicago IL; BR/TR/5´10˝/172; d8.13																									
1884	Det N	5	12	.294	17	17	17-1	0	147.1	118	73	2	—	25	107	1.95	148	.204	.237	55	.109	-4	61	13	—	0.9
1885	Det N	12	25	.324	37	37	37-1	0	330	360	222	8	—	92	110	3.03	94	.264	.311	137	.212	-1*	96	-10	—	-1.1
1886	Det N	30	11	.732	43	43	42-1	0	386.2	388	203	6	—	85	172	3.03	110	.250	.288	165	.176	-3	121	11	—	0.5
1887	†Det N	29	13	**.690**	43	42	41-2	0	366.2	373	217	24	2	106	135	3.73	109	.254	.305	156-1	.186	-2	109	14	—	1.0
1888	Det N	19	25	.432	46	46	45-2	0	404	411	225	13	8	54	202	3.05	92	.251	.279	167-1	.246	9	107	-9	—	-0.2
1889	Ind N	18	22	.450	45	44	36	1	349	395	256	27	9	100	139	4.54	92	.277	.328	139-2	.180	2	94	-16	—	-1.3
1890	Bos N	23	17	.575	40	40	39-4	0	350	342	201	5	3	82	140	3.19	118	.248	.291	147-2	.231	5*	88	•17	—	1.9
1891	Bos N	4	5	.444	11	9	7	0	89	112	62	4	0	23	29	3.84	95	.296	.337	41-1	.171	1*	82	-1	—	0.1
	Cle N	0	1	.000	1	1	1	0	9	12	9	1	0	4	4	8.00	43	.308	.372	4	.000	-1	52	-3	—	-0.3
	Year	4	6	.400	12	10	8	0	98	124	71	5	0	27	33	4.22	86	.297	.340	45-1	.156	0	79	-3	—	-0.2
1892	StL N	5	8	.385	13	13	12	0	108	159	87	5	6	31	32	5.67	56	.329	.377	45-1	.200	0	81	-26	—	-2.4
Total	9	145	139	.511	296	292	277-11	1	2539.2	2670	1555	95	28	602	1070	3.46	99	.259	.302	1056-8	.198	7	99	-10	—	-0.9
GEYER, RUBE	Jacob Bowman; B3.26.1884 Allegheny (now part of Pittsburgh) PA; D10.12.1962 Ford Twp. MN; BR/TR/5´10˝/170; d4.24																									
1910	StL N	0	1	.000	4	0	0	0	4	5	3	0	0	3	5	4.50	66	.294	.400	1	.000	-0	—	-1	—	-0.2
1911	StL N	9	6	.600	29	11	7-1	0	148.2	141	80	7	6	56	46	3.27	103	.259	.335	57-0-2	.228	1	103	-2	—	-0.2
1912	StL N	7	14	.333	41	18	5	0	181	191	110	4	4	84	61	3.28	104	.288	.371	53-0-1	.208	-0	70	-3	—	-0.3
1913	StL N	1	5	.167	30	4	2	1	78.2	83	57	6	2	38	21	5.26	61	.282	.368	22-0-1	.091	-2	76	-19	—	-1.6
Total	4	17	26	.395	104	33	14-1	1	412.1	420	250	17	12	181	133	3.67	92	.276	.358	133-0-4	.195	-1	82	-25	—	-2.3
GHELFI, TONY	Anthony Paul; B8.23.1961 LaCrosse WI; BR/TR/6´3˝/185; [PhiN80*1/14]; d9.1; [DL 1984 Phi N 107]																									
1983	Phi N	1	1	.500	3	3	0	0-0	14.1	15	5	2	0	6-0	14	3.14	115	.268	.339	4	.250	0	57	1	0	0.2
GIALLOMBARDO, BOB	Robert Paul; B5.20.1937 Brooklyn NY; BL/TL/6´0˝/175; d6.21																									
1958	LA N	1	1	.500	6	5	0	0	26.1	29	14	3	0	15-0	14	3.76	109	.284	.376	6-0-3	.167	-0*	92	0	0	0.0
GIARD, JOE	Joseph Oscar "Peco"; B10.7.1898 Ware MA; D7.10.1956 Worcester MA; BL/TL/5´10.5˝/170; d4.18																									
1925	StL A	10	5	.667	30	21	9-4	0	160.2	179	96	13	5	87	43	5.04	93	.295	.388	53-0-3	.057	-6	98	-1	—	-0.6
1926	StL A	3	10	.231	22	15	2	0	90	113	81	7	1	67	18	7.00	61	.318	.428	29-0-3	.276	0	94	-24	—	-2.9
1927	NY A	0	0	ø	16	0	0	0	27	38	25	1	0	19	10	8.00	48	.352	.449	7	.286	0	—	-12	—	-0.5
Total	3	13	15	.464	68	36	11-4	0	277.2	330	202	21	6	173	71	5.96	75	.309	.408	89-0-6	.146	-6	97	-37	—	-4.0
GIBBON, JOE	Joseph Charles; B4.10.1935 Hickory MS; BR/TL (BB 1967–68)/6´4˝/(200–210); d4.17; Col U. of Mississippi																									
1960	†Pit N	4	2	.667	27	9	0	0	80.1	87	40	5	0	31-5	60	4.03	93	.277	.341	19-0-4	.211	1	115	-3	0	-0.1
1961	Pit N	13	10	.565	30	29	7-3	0	195.1	185	85	16	4	57-4	145	3.32	120	.251	.306	59-0-10	.136	-2*	107	13	0	1.2
1962	Pit N	3	4	.429	19	8	0	0	57	53	29	4	0	24-3	26	3.63	108	.250	.324	17-0-1	.176	-0	112	1	0	0.1
1963	Pit N	5	12	.294	37	22	5	1	147.1	147	61	7	5	54-15	110	3.30	100	.258	.326	43-0-3	.093	-2*	87	1	0	0.0
1964	Pit N	10	7	.588	28	24	3	0	146.2	145	66	10	6	54-10	97	3.68	95	.262	.331	47-0-5	.255	3*	118	-2	0	0.2
1965	Pit N	4	9	.308	31	15	1	1	105.2	85	57	7	4	34-6	63	4.51	78	.221	.288	26-0-2	.115	-0	101	-10	0	-1.1
1966	SF N	4	6	.400	37	10	1	1	81	86	41	4	2	16-1	48	3.67	100	.275	.310	15	.200	0	96	-1	0	0.0
1967	SF N	6	2	.750	28	10	3-1	1	82	65	31	4	3	33-4	63	3.07	107	.220	.302	24-0-1	.042	-1	142	3	0	0.2
1968	SF N.	1	2	.333	29	0	0	1	40	33	10	3	2	19-4	22	1.57	187	.234	.331	1	.000	-0	—	5	0	0.5
1969	SF N	1	3	.250	16	0	0	2-1	20	15	10	1	1	13-4	9	3.60	98	.211	.341	3	.000	-0	—	0	0	-0.1
	Pit N	5	1	.833	35	0	0	9-0	51.1	38	14	5	2	17-2	35	1.93	181	.208	.281	5-0-2	.000	-1	—	8	0	1.3
	Year	6	4	.600	51	0	0	11-1	71.1	53	24	6	3	30-6	44	2.40	146	.209	.299	8-0-2	.000	-1	—	8	0	1.2
1970	†Pit N	0	1	.000	41	0	0	5-1	41	44	25	2	2	24-8	26	4.83	82	.280	.380	3	.000	-0	—	-4	24	-0.2
1971	Cin N	5	6	.455	50	0	0	11-4	64.1	54	25	3	1	32-11	34	2.94	115	.239	.332	1-0-1	.000	-0	—	2	0	0.5
1972	Cin N	0	0	ø	2	0	0	0-0	0.1	3	2	1	0	1-1	1	54.00	6	.750	.800	0	ø	0	—	-2	0	-0.1
	Hou N	0	0	ø	9	0	0	0-0	7.1	13	9	2	1	5-2	4	9.82	34	.394	.487	0	ø	0	—	-6	0	-0.3
	Year	0	0	ø	11	0	0	0-0	7.2	16	11	3	1	6-3	5	11.74	29	.432	.523	0	ø	0	—	-7	0	-0.4
Total	13	61	65	.484	419	127	20-4	32-6	1119.2	1053	505	74	33	414-80	743	3.52	102	.251	.321	263-0-29	.144	-3	109	5	24	2.1
GIBSON, NORWOOD	Norwood Ringold "Gibby"; B3.11.1877 Peoria IL; D7.7.1959 Peoria IL; BR/TR/5´10˝/165; d4.29; Col Notre Dame																									
1903	Bos A	13	9	.591	24	21	17-2	0	183.1	166	95	2	7	65	76	3.19	95	.241	.313	64-0-5	.266	5*	96	-4	—	-0.1
1904	Bos A	17	14	.548	33	32	29-1	0	273	216	111	8	4	81	112	2.21	121	.219	.281	92-0-5	.065	-6	91	8	—	0.0
1905	Bos A	4	7	.364	23	17	9	0	134	118	77	9	5	55	67	3.69	73	.238	.321	42-0-2	.095	-2	97	-16	—	-1.6
1906	Bos A	0	2	.000	5	2	1	0	18.2	25	21	2	0	7	3	5.30	52	.325	.381	5	.200	0	13	-7	—	-0.7
Total	4	34	32	.515	85	72	56-3	0	609	525	304	21	16	208	258	2.93	95	.233	.303	203-0-12	.138	-4	92	-19	—	-2.4
GIBSON, PAUL	Paul Marshall; B1.4.1960 Southampton NY; BR/TL/6´0˝/(165–195); [CinN78*3/70]; d4.8																									
1988	Det A	4	2	.667	40	1	0	0-2	92	83	33	6	2	34-8	50	2.93	131	.240	.307	0	ø	0	190	10	0	0.6
1989	Det A	4	8	.333	45	13	0	0-2	132	129	71	11	6	57-12	77	4.64	83	.259	.339	0	ø	0	76	-9	0	-0.8
1990	Det A	5	4	.556	61	0	0	3-3	97.1	99	36	10	1	44-12	56	3.05	130	.269	.344	0	ø	0	—	10	0	0.9
1991	Det A	5	7	.417	68	0	0	8-5	96	112	51	10	3	48-8	52	4.59	91	.297	.379	0	ø	0	—	-3	0	-0.4
1992	NY N	0	1	.000	43	1	0	0-0	62	70	37	7	0	25-0	49	5.23	67	.287	.352	6-0-1	.000	-0	103	-11	33	-0.6
1993	NY N	1	1	.500	8	0	0	0-1	8.2	14	6	1	0	2-0	12	5.19	77	.350	.381	0	ø	0	—	-1	0	-0.2
	NY A	2	0	1.000	20	0	0	0-0	35.1	31	15	4	0	9-0	25	3.06	137	.238	.282	0	ø	0	—	4	0	0.2
1994	NY A	1	1	.500	30	0	0	0-2	29	26	17	5	1	17-3	21	4.97	93	.236	.338	0	ø	0	—	-1	22	-0.1
1996	NY A	0	0	ø	4	0	0	0-0	4.1	6	3	1	0	0-0	3	6.23	79	.316	.316	0	ø	0	—	-1	0	0.0
Total	8	22	24	.478	319	15	0	11-15	556.2	570	269	55	13	236-43	345	4.07	97	.267	.341	6-0-1	.000	-0	83	-2	55	-0.4
GIBSON, BOB	Robert (b Pack Robert Gibson); B11.9.1935 Omaha NE; BR/TR/6´1.5˝/(185–195); d4.15; C5; HF1981; Col Creighton																									
1959	StL N	3	5	.375	13	9	2-1	0	75.2	77	35	4	1	39-2	48	3.33	127	.273	.360	26-0-1	.115	-1*	61	5	0	0.4
1960	StL N	3	6	.333	27	12	2	0	86.2	97	61	7	1	48-6	69	5.61	73	.284	.371	28-0-1	.179	-0*	92	-14	0	-1.3
1961	StL N	13	12	.520	35	27	10-2	1	211.1	186	91	13	6	119-7	166	3.24	136	.239	.342	66-1-3	.197	2*	81	24	0	2.9
1962	StL N★	15	13	.536	32	30	15-**5**	1	233.2	174	84	15	10	95-9	208	2.85	**150**	.204	.291	76-2-6	.263	6*	84	34	0	**4.7**
1963	StL N	18	9	.667	36	33	14-2	0	254.2	224	110	19	13	96-1	204	3.39	105	.233	.309	87-3-5	.207	7*	116	5	0	1.2
1964	†StL N	19	12	.613	40	36	17-2	1	287.1	250	106	25	9	86-9	245	3.01	127	.232	.293	96-0-6	.156	1	94	27	0	2.9

YEAR	TM LG	W	L	PCT	G	GS	CG-SHO	SV-BS	IP	H	R	HR	HB	BB-IB	SO	ERA	AERA	OAV	OOB	AB-HR-SH	AVG	PB	SUP	APR	DL	PW
1965	StL N★	20	12	.625	38	36	20-6	1	299	243	110	34	11	103-6	270	3.07	125	.222	.293	104-5-8	.240	8*	107	25	0	3.5
1966	StL N✳	21	12	.636	35	35	20-**5**	0	280.1	210	90	20	5	78-5	225	2.44	147	.207	.265	100-1-7	.200	3*	81	35	0	4.4
1967	†StL N★	13	7	.650	24	24	10-2	0	175.1	151	62	10	3	40-3	147	2.98	110	.231	.278	60-0-6	.133	1*	125	8	50	1.0
1968	†StL N☆	22	9	.710	34	34	28-**13**	0	304.2	198	49	11	7	62-6	**268**	**1.12**	**258**	**.184**	**.233**	94-0-7	.170	4*	91	**60**	0	**7.6**
1969	StL N★	20	13	.606	35	35	**28**-4	0-0	314	251	84	12	10	95-7	269	2.18	165	.219	.283	118-1-5	.246	8*	88	**50**	0	**6.3**
1970	StL N★	**23**	7	**.767**	34	34	23-3	0-0	294	262	111	13	4	88-9	274	3.12	133	.237	.293	109-2-6	.303	12*	108	34	0	**4.5**
1971	StL N	16	13	.552	31	31	20-**5**	0-0	245.2	215	96	14	7	76-11	185	3.04	120	.232	.294	87-2-2	.172	2	99	14	20	1.8
1972	StL N★	19	11	.633	34	34	23-4	0-0	278	226	83	14	3	88-11	208	2.46	139	.224	.286	103-5-2	.194	7	99	31	0	4.4
1973	StL N	12	10	.545	25	25	13-1	0-0	195	159	71	12	3	57-6	142	2.77	133	.224	.281	65-2-2	.185	2	96	18	43	2.2
1974	StL N	11	13	.458	33	33	9-1	0-0	240	236	111	24	5	104-14	129	3.83	94	.259	.335	81-0-1	.210	3	108	-4	0	-0.2
1975	StL N	3	10	.231	22	14	1	2-1	109	120	66	10	4	62-6	60	5.04	75	.287	.382	28-0-4	.179	0	86	-12	0	-1.3
Total	17	251	174	.591	528	482	255-56	6-1	3884.1	3279	1420	257	102	1336-118	3117	2.91	127	.228	.297	1328-24-72	.206	65	97	340	113	45.0

GIBSON, BOB Robert Louis; B6.19.1957 Philadelphia PA; BR/TR/6´0˝/195; d4.13; Col Bloomsburg

YEAR	TM LG	W	L	PCT	G	GS	CG-SHO	SV-BS	IP	H	R	HR	HB	BB-IB	SO	ERA	AERA	OAV	OOB	AB-HR-SH	AVG	PB	SUP	APR	DL	PW
1983	Mil A	3	4	.429	27	7	0	2-3	80.2	71	40	6	1	46-2	46	3.90	97	.237	.334	0	ø	0	96	-2	0	-0.2
1984	Mil A	2	5	.286	18	9	1-1	0-0	69	61	43	10	0	47-2	54	4.96	79	.236	.352	0	ø	0	101	-8	0	-0.7
1985	Mil A	6	7	.462	41	1	0	11-3	92.1	86	44	10	1	49-3	53	3.90	108	.260	.353	0	ø	0	43	4	0	0.5
1986	Mil A	1	2	.333	11	1	0	0-0	26.2	23	18	3	0	23-1	11	4.73	92	.232	.374	0	ø	0	125	-2	0	-0.2
1987	NY N	0	0	ø	1	0	0	0-0	1	0	0	0	0	1-0	2	0.00	ø	.000	.250	0	ø	0	—	0	0	0.0
Total	5	12	18	.400	98	18	1-1	13-6	269.2	241	145	29	2	166-8	166	4.24	95	.243	.349	0	ø	0	94	-8	0	-0.6

GIBSON, ROBERT Robert Murray; B8.20.1869 Duncansville PA; D12.19.1949 Pittsburgh PA; BR/TR/6´3˝/185; d6.4; Col Penn St.

YEAR	TM LG	W	L	PCT	G	GS	CG-SHO	SV-BS	IP	H	R	HR	HB	BB-IB	SO	ERA	AERA	OAV	OOB	AB-HR-SH	AVG	PB	SUP	APR	DL	PW
1890	Chi N	1	0	1.000	1	1	1	0	9	6	1	0	0	2	1	0.00	ø	.182	.229	4	.000	-0	17	3	—	0.3
	Pit N	0	3	.000	3	3	2	0	12	24	38	0	3	23	3	17.25	19	.400	.581	13	.231	-0	153	-21	—	-2.5
	Year	1	3	.250	4	4	3	0	21	30	39	0	3	25	4	9.86	35	.323	.479	17	.176	-1	114	-17	—	-2.2

GIBSON, SAM Samuel Braxton; B8.5.1899 King NC; D1.31.1983 High Point NC; BL/TR/6´2˝/198; d4.19; Col Catawba

YEAR	TM LG	W	L	PCT	G	GS	CG-SHO	SV-BS	IP	H	R	HR	HB	BB-IB	SO	ERA	AERA	OAV	OOB	AB-HR-SH	AVG	PB	SUP	APR	DL	PW
1926	Det A	12	9	.571	35	24	16-2	2	196.1	199	94	6	6	75	61	3.48	117	.269	.341	72-0-1	.250	2*	93	12	—	1.3
1927	Det A	11	12	.478	33	26	11	0	184.2	201	113	9	8	86	76	3.80	111	.285	.369	66-0-3	.212	-1	126	2	—	0.1
1928	Det A	5	8	.385	20	18	5-1	0	119.2	155	83	4	7	52	29	5.42	76	.322	.396	42-0-1	.286	2	102	-15	—	-1.3
1930	NY A	0	1	.000	2	2	0	0	6	14	11	1	0	6	3	15.00	29	.424	.513	3	.333	0	260	-7	—	-0.8
1932	NY N	4	8	.333	41	5	1-1	3	81.2	107	51	7	2	30	39	4.85	77	.322	.382	19-0-1	.263	0	82	-10.	—	-1.3
Total	5	32	38	.457	131	75	33-4	5	588.1	676	352	27	23	249	208	4.28	95	.295	.370	202-0-6	.248	3	112	-18	—	-2.0

GICK, GEORGE George Edward; B10.18.1915 Dunnington IN; BB/TR/6´0˝/190; d10.3

YEAR	TM LG	W	L	PCT	G	GS	CG-SHO	SV-BS	IP	H	R	HR	HB	BB-IB	SO	ERA	AERA	OAV	OOB	AB-HR-SH	AVG	PB	SUP	APR	DL	PW
1937	Chi A	0	0	ø	1	0	0	1	2	0	0	0	0	0	1	0.00	ø	.000	.000	0	ø	0	—	1	—	0.1
1938	Chi A	0	0	ø	1	0	0	0	1	0	0	0	1	0	1	0.00	ø	.000	.250	0	ø	0	—	1	—	0.0
Total	2	0	0	ø	2	0	0	1	3	0	0	0	1	0	2	0.00	ø	.000	.100	0	ø	0	—	2	—	0.1

GIDEON, BRETT Byron Brett; B8.8.1963 Ozona TX; BR/TR/6´2˝/195; [PitN85 6/138]; d7.5; Col Mary Hardin–Baylor

YEAR	TM LG	W	L	PCT	G	GS	CG-SHO	SV-BS	IP	H	R	HR	HB	BB-IB	SO	ERA	AERA	OAV	OOB	AB-HR-SH	AVG	PB	SUP	APR	DL	PW
1987	Pit N	1	5	.167	29	0	0	3-3	36.2	34	22	6	1	10-3	31	4.66	89	.243	.298	1	1.000	1	—	-2	0	-0.3
1989	Mon N	0	0	ø	4	0	0	0-0	4.2	5	1	1	0	5-1	2	1.93	185	.294	.455	0	ø	0	—	1	0	0.0
1990	Mon N	0	0	ø	1	0	0	0-0	1	2	1	0	0	4-1	0	9.00	41	.500	.750	0	ø	0	—	-1	176	0.0
Total	3	1	5	.167	34	0	0	3-3	42.1	41	24	7	1	19-5	33	4.46	92	.255	.337	1	1.000	1	—	-2	176	-0.3

GIDEON, JIM James Leslie; B9.26.1953 Taylor TX; BR/TR/6´3˝/190; [TexA75 1/17]; d9.14; Col Texas

YEAR	TM LG	W	L	PCT	G	GS	CG-SHO	SV-BS	IP	H	R	HR	HB	BB-IB	SO	ERA	AERA	OAV	OOB	AB-HR-SH	AVG	PB	SUP	APR	DL	PW
1975	Tex A	0	0	ø	1	1	0	0-0	5.2	7	6	1	0	5-0	2	7.94	48	.292	.414	0	ø	0	210	-3	0	-0.1

GIEBELL, FLOYD Floyd George; B12.10.1909 Pennsboro WV; D4.28.2004 Wilkesboro NC; BL/TR/6´2.5˝/172; d4.21; Col Salem International

YEAR	TM LG	W	L	PCT	G	GS	CG-SHO	SV-BS	IP	H	R	HR	HB	BB-IB	SO	ERA	AERA	OAV	OOB	AB-HR-SH	AVG	PB	SUP	APR	DL	PW
1939	Det A	1	1	.500	9	0	0	0	15.1	19	7	1	0	12	9	2.93	167	.317	.431	2-0-1	.000	-0	—	3	—	0.2
1940	Det A	2	0	1.000	2	2	2-1	0	18	14	2	2	0	4	11	1.00	476	.206	.250	6-0-1	.000	-1	139	7	—	0.7
1941	Det A	0	0	ø	17	2	0	0	34.1	45	29	3	0	26	10	6.03	75	.313	.418	6-0-1	.333	0	162	-6	0	-0.3
Total	3	3	1	.750	28	4	2-1	0	67.2	78	38	6	0	42	30	3.99	117	.287	.382	14-0-3	.143	-1	149	4	0	0.6

GIEL, PAUL Paul Robert; B2.29.1932 Winona MN; D5.22.2002 Minneapolis MN; BR/TR/5´11˝/(180–185); d7.10; Mil 1956–57; Col Minnesota

YEAR	TM LG	W	L	PCT	G	GS	CG-SHO	SV-BS	IP	H	R	HR	HB	BB-IB	SO	ERA	AERA	OAV	OOB	AB-HR-SH	AVG	PB	SUP	APR	DL	PW
1954	NY N	0	0	ø	6	0	0	0	4.1	8	4	0	0	2	4	8.31	49	.421	.455	0	ø	0	—	-2	0	-0.1
1955	NY N	4	4	.500	34	2	0	0	82.1	70	36	8	2	50-5	47	3.39	119	.233	.345	19-0-1	.053	-2	55	6	0	0.3
1958	SF N	4	5	.444	29	9	0	0	92	89	56	12	2	55-4	55	4.70	81	.259	.363	27-0-4	.074	-2	86	-10	0	-1.0
1959	Pit N	0	0	ø	4	0	0	0	7.2	17	12	0	0	6-1	3	14.09	27	.472	.548	0	ø	0	—	-8	0	-0.4
1960	Pit N	2	0	1.000	16	0	0	0	33	35	25	3	0	15-1	21	5.73	65	.276	.350	7-0-1	.000	-1	—	-8	0	-0.6
1961	Min A	1	0	1.000	12	0	0	0	19.1	24	27	6	0	17-1	14	9.78	43	.289	.406	2	.500	0*	—	-13	0	-0.6
	KC A	0	0	ø	1	0	0	0	1.2	6	7	1	0	3-0	1	37.80	11	.600	.692	0	ø	0	—	-6	0	-0.2
	Year	1	0	1.000	13	0	0	0	21	30	34	7	0	20-1	15	12.00	35	.323	.439	2	.500	0	—	-18	0	-0.8
Total	6	11	9	.550	102	11	0	0	240.1	249	167	30	4	148-12	145	5.39	73	.271	.372	55-0-6	.073	-4	79	-41	0	-2.6

GIGGIE, BOB Robert Thomas; B8.13.1933 Dorchester MA; BR/TR/6´1˝/(195–200); d4.18

YEAR	TM LG	W	L	PCT	G	GS	CG-SHO	SV-BS	IP	H	R	HR	HB	BB-IB	SO	ERA	AERA	OAV	OOB	AB-HR-SH	AVG	PB	SUP	APR	DL	PW
1959	Mil N	1	0	1.000	13	0	0	1	20	24	10	2	0	10-0	15	4.05	87	.316	.395	1	.000	-0	—	-1	0	0.0
1960	Mil N	0	0	ø	3	0	0	0	4.1	5	2	0	0	4-1	5	4.15	83	.278	.409	0	ø	0	—	0	0	0.0
	KC A	1	0	1.000	10	0	0	0	18.2	24	12	1	0	15-2	8	5.79	69	.333	.443	2	.000	-0	—	-3	0	-0.2
1962	KC A	1	1	.500	4	2	0	0	14.1	17	11	5	1	3-0	4	6.28	67	.293	.339	4	.000	-0	74	-3	0	-0.4
Total	3	3	1	.750	30	2	0	1	57.1	70	35	8	1	32-3	32	5.18	74	.313	.399	7	.000	-1	74	-7	0	-0.6

GILBERT, BILL Alfred Gideon; B3.13.1868 Havre de Grace MD; D12.17.1927 Havre de Grace MD; 6´0˝/180; d9.15

YEAR	TM LG	W	L	PCT	G	GS	CG-SHO	SV-BS	IP	H	R	HR	HB	BB-IB	SO	ERA	AERA	OAV	OOB	AB-HR-SH	AVG	PB	SUP	APR	DL	PW
1892	Bal N	0	1	.000	2	1	1	0	14	14	15	1	0	17	5	5.79	59	.250	.425	6	.333	1	37	-4	—	-0.2

GILBERT, JOE Joe Dennis; B4.20.1952 Jasper TX; BR/TL/6´1˝/163; [MonN70 9/201]; d4.30

YEAR	TM LG	W	L	PCT	G	GS	CG-SHO	SV-BS	IP	H	R	HR	HB	BB-IB	SO	ERA	AERA	OAV	OOB	AB-HR-SH	AVG	PB	SUP	APR	DL	PW
1972	Mon N	0	1	.000	22	0	0	0-0	33	41	31	3	0	18-3	25	8.45	42	.306	.386	3	.000	-0	—	-16	0	-0.9
1973	Mon N	1	2	.333	21	0	0	1-0	29	30	18	1	0	19-1	17	4.97	77	.270	.374	2	.000	0	—	-3	0	-0.3
Total	2	1	3	.250	43	0	0	1-0	62	71	49	4	0	37-4	42	6.82	54	.290	.380	5	.000	-0	—	-19	0	-1.2

GILBRETH, BILL William Freeman; B9.3.1947 Abilene TX; BL/TL/6´0˝/180; [DetA69 3/67]; d6.25; Col Abilene Christian

YEAR	TM LG	W	L	PCT	G	GS	CG-SHO	SV-BS	IP	H	R	HR	HB	BB-IB	SO	ERA	AERA	OAV	OOB	AB-HR-SH	AVG	PB	SUP	APR	DL	PW
1971	Det A	2	1	.667	9	5	2	0-0	30	28	17	4	2	21-1	14	4.80	76	.264	.395	11	.182	-0	119	-4	0	-0.3
1972	Det A	0	0	ø	2	0	0	0-0	5	10	9	1	0	4-0	2	16.20	20	.476	.519	1	.000	-0	—	-7	0	-0.3
1974	Cal A	0	0	ø	3	0	0	0-1	1.1	2	2	0	0	1-0	0	13.50	26	.400	.429	0	ø	0	—	-1	0	-0.1
Total	3	2	1	.667	14	5	2	0-1	36.1	40	28	5	2	26-1	16	6.69	53	.303	.417	12	.167	-0	119	-12	0	-0.7

GILFILLAN, JASON Jason Edward; B8.31.1976 Shelby NC; BR/TR/6´5˝/220; [KCA97 12/361]; d5.16; Col Charleston (SC)/Limestone

YEAR	TM LG	W	L	PCT	G	GS	CG-SHO	SV-BS	IP	H	R	HR	HB	BB-IB	SO	ERA	AERA	OAV	OOB	AB-HR-SH	AVG	PB	SUP	APR	DL	PW
2003	KC A	2	0	1.000	13	0	0	0-1	16.1	22	14	3	1	10-1	12	7.71	62	.310	.402	0	ø	0	—	-4	0	-0.5

GILKS, BOB Robert James; B7.2.1864 Cincinnati OH; D8.21.1944 Brunswick GA; BR/TR/5´8˝/178; d8.25; ▲

YEAR	TM LG	W	L	PCT	G	GS	CG-SHO	SV-BS	IP	H	R	HR	HB	BB-IB	SO	ERA	AERA	OAV	OOB	AB-HR-SH	AVG	PB	SUP	APR	DL	PW
1887	Cle AA	7	5	.583	13	13	12-1	0	108	104	66	1	9	42	28	3.08	141	.245	.326	83	.313	2*	98	15	—	1.5
1888	Cle AA	0	2	.000	4	2	2	**1**	21	26	23	1	1	8	3	8.14	38	.292	.357	484-1	.229	0*	103	-9	—	-0.7
1890	Cle N	2	2	.500	4	3	3	0	31.2	34	17	0	4	9	5	4.26	84	.266	.333	544	.213	-0*	70	0	—	-0.1
Total	3	9	9	.500	21	18	17-1	1	160.2	164	106	2	14	59	36	3.98	101	.256	.332	1111-1	.228	2	96	6	—	0.7

GILL, ED Edward James; B8.7.1895 Somerville MA; D10.10.1995 Brockton MA; BL/TR/5´10˝/165; d7.5; Col Holy Cross

YEAR	TM LG	W	L	PCT	G	GS	CG-SHO	SV-BS	IP	H	R	HR	HB	BB-IB	SO	ERA	AERA	OAV	OOB	AB-HR-SH	AVG	PB	SUP	APR	DL	PW
1919	Was A	1	1	.500	16	2	0	0	37.1	38	25	0	2	21	7	4.82	67	.260	.361	7	.000	-1	110	-6	—	-0.4

GILL, GEORGE George Lloyd; B2.13.1909 Catchings MS; D2.21.1999 Jackson MS; BR/TR/6´1˝/185; d5.4; Col Mississippi College

YEAR	TM LG	W	L	PCT	G	GS	CG-SHO	SV-BS	IP	H	R	HR	HB	BB-IB	SO	ERA	AERA	OAV	OOB	AB-HR-SH	AVG	PB	SUP	APR	DL	PW
1937	Det A	11	4	.733	31	10	4-1	1	127.2	146	74	11	1	42	40	4.51	104	.285	.340	50-0-1	.140	-3	130	2	—	-0.1
1938	Det A	12	9	.571	24	23	13-1	0	164	195	82	15	2	50	30	4.12	121	.296	.348	57-0-5	.105	-4	98	16	—	1.3
1939	Det A	0	1	.000	3	1	0	0	8.2	14	8	1	0	3	1	8.31	59	.368	.415	2	.000	-0	72	-3	—	-0.3
	StL A	1	12	.077	27	11	5	0	95	139	89	10	3	34	24	7.11	68	.343	.398	26-0-1	.154	-2	86	-24	—	-2.7
	Year	1	13	.071	30	12	5	0	103.2	153	97	11	3	37	25	7.21	68	.345	.400	28-0-1	.143	-2	85	-27	—	-3.0
Total	3	24	26	.480	85	45	22-2	1	395.1	494	253	37	6	129	95	5.05	96	.306	.360	135-0-7	.126	-9	102	-9	—	-1.8

YEAR	TM LG	W	L	PCT	G	GS	CG-SHO	SV-BS	IP	H	R	HR	HB	BB-IB	SO	ERA	AERA	OAV	OOB	AB-HR-SH	AVG	PB	SUP	APR	DL	PW
Gill, Haddie	Harold Edward; B1.23.1899 Brockton MA; D8.1.1932 Brockton MA; BL/TL/5´11˝/165; d8.16; Col Holy Cross																									
1923	Cin N	0	0	ø	1	0	0	0	1	1	0	0	0	1	1	0.00	ø	.333	.500	0	ø	0	—	0	—	0.0
Gillenwater, Claral	Claral Lewis; B5.20.1900 Sims IN; D2.26.1978 Bradenton FL; BR/TR/6´0˝/187; d8.20																									
1923	Chi A	1	3	.250	5	3	1-1	0	21.1	28	15	2	1	6	2	5.48	72	.337	.389	6-0-1	.000	-1	56	-3	—	-0.6
Gilles, Tom	Thomas Bradford; B7.2.1962 Peoria IL; BR/TR/6´1˝/185; [NYA84 47/834]; d6.7; Col Indiana St.																									
1990	Tor A	1	0	1.000	2	0	0	0-0	1.1	2	1	0	0	0-0	1	6.75	59	.333	.333	0	ø	0	—	0	0	-0.1
Gillespie, Duke	John Patrick "Silent John"; B2.25.1900 Oakland CA; D2.15.1954 Vallejo CA; BR/TR/5´11.5˝/172; d4.12																									
1922	Cin N	3	3	.500	31	4	1	0	77.2	84	43	2	4	29	21	4.52	88	.294	.367	15-0-1	.133	-1	153	-2	—	-0.2
Gillespie, Bob	Robert William "Bunch"; B10.8.1919 Columbus OH; D11.4.2001 Winston–Salem NC; BR/TR/6´4˝/187; d5.11																									
1944	Det A	0	1	.000	7	0	0	0	11	7	8	0	0	12	4	6.55	54	.194	.396	2	.000	-0	—	-3	0	-0.3
1947	Chi A	5	8	.385	25	17	1	0	118	133	71	4	1	53	36	4.73	77	.291	.366	33	.061	-3	90	-13	0	-1.5
1948	Chi A	0	4	.000	25	6	1	0	72	81	45	3	1	33	19	5.13	83	.287	.364	16-0-1	.000	-2	53	-7	0	-0.5
1950	Bos A	0	0	ø	1	0	0	0	1.1	2	3	1	0	4	0	20.25	24	.333	.600	0	ø	0	—	-2	0	-0.1
Total	4	5	13	.278	58	23	2	0	202.1	223	127	8	2	102	59	5.07	76	.286	.369	51-0-1	.039	-5	78	-25	0	-2.4
Gilliford, Paul	Paul Gant "Gorilla"; B1.12.1945 Bryn Mawr PA; BR/TL/5´11˝/210; d9.20																									
1967	Bal A	0	0	ø	2	0	0	0	3	6	4	1	0	1-0	2	12.00	26	.429	.467	0	ø	0	—	-3	0	-0.1
Gilligan, Jack	John Patrick (b John Peter Gilgen); B10.18.1885 Chicago IL; D11.19.1980 Modesto CA; BB/TR/6´0˝/190; d9.16																									
1909	StL A	1	2	.333	3	3	3	0	23	28	19	1	2	9	4	5.48	44	.315	.390	9-0-1	.111	-1	58	-8	—	-1.0
1910	StL A	0	3	.000	9	5	2	0	39.1	37	21	0	1	28	10	3.66	68	.253	.377	15	.200	-0	119	-4	—	-0.3
Total	2	1	5	.167	12	8	5	0	62.1	65	40	1	3	37	14	4.33	57	.277	.382	24-0-1	.167	-1	97	-12	—	-1.3
Gillpatrick, George	George Fred; B2.28.1875 Holden MO; D12.15.1941 Kansas City MO; BR/TR/6´0˝/210; d5.22																									
1898	StL N	0	2	.000	7	3	1	0	35	42	38	0	2	19	12	6.94	55	.296	.387	16	.125	-2	87	-12	—	-0.7
Gilmore, Frank	Frank T. "Shadow"; B4.27.1864 Webster MA; D7.21.1929 Hartford CT; BR/5´11.5˝/164; d9.11																									
1886	Was N	4	4	.500	9	9	9-1	0	75	57	35	3	—	22	75	2.52	128	.200	.257	29	.000	-4	80	5	—	0.1
1887	Was N	7	20	.259	28	27	27-1	0	234.2	247	172	7	13	92	114	3.87	104	.262	.336	93	.065	-11	59	1	—	-1.0
1888	Was N	1	9	.100	12	11	10	0	95.2	131	101	4	7	29	23	6.59	42	.323	.378	41	.024	-5*	115	-39	—	-3.6
Total	3	12	33	.267	49	47	46-2	0	405.1	435	308	14	20	143	212	4.26	84	.266	.333	163	.043	-20	73	-33	—	-4.5
Gilmore, Len	Leonard Preston "Meow"; B11.3.1917 Fairview Park IN; BR/TR/6´3˝/175; d10.1; Col Indiana (PA)																									
1944	Pit N	0	1	.000	1	1	1	0	8	13	7	2	0	0	0	7.88	47	.361	.361	2	.000	-0	23	-3	0	-0.3
Gilroy, John	John M.; B10.26.1869 Washington DC; D8.4.1897 Norfolk VA; d8.30																									
1895	Was N	1	4	.200	8	4	2	0	41.1	63	48	3	4	24	2	6.53	74	.344	.431	29	.241	-1*	82	-8	—	-0.7
1896	Was N	0	0	ø	1	0	0	0	2	0	0	0	0	1	0	0.00	ø	.000	.143	1	.000	-0	—	1	—	0.0
Total	2	1	4	.200	9	4	2	0	43.1	63	48	3	4	25	2	6.23	77	.333	.422	30	.233	-1	82	-7	—	-0.7
Gilson, Hal	Harold "Lefty"; B2.9.1942 Los Angeles CA; BR/TL/6´5˝/195; d4.14; Col San Jose (CA) City																									
1968	StL N	0	2	.000	13	0	0	2	21.2	27	11	1	0	11-1	19	4.57	63	.310	.388	4-0-1	.000	-0	—	-3	0	-0.5
	Hou N	0	0	ø	2	0	0	0	3.2	7	4	0	1	1-1	1	7.36	40	.412	.474	0	ø	0*	—	-2	0	-0.1
	Year	0	2	.000	15	0	0	2	25.1	34	15	1	1	12-2	20	4.97	58	.327	.402	4-0-1	.000	-0	—	-6	0	-0.6
Ging, Billy	William Joseph; B11.7.1872 Elmira NY; D9.14.1950 Elmira NY; BR/TR/5´10˝/170; d9.25																									
1899	Bos N	1	0	1.000	1	1	1	0	8	5	1	0	0	5	2	1.13	370	.179	.303	2-0-1	.000	-0	35	3	—	0.2
Gingras, Joe	Joseph Elzead John; B1.10.1894 New York NY; D9.6.1947 Jersey City NJ; BR/TR/6´2˝/188; d6.18																									
1915	KC F	0	0	ø	2	0	0	0	4	6	3	0	0	1	2	6.75	39	.353	.389	1	.000	-0	—	-2	—	-0.1
Ginter, Matt	Matthew Shane; B12.24.1977 Lexington KY; BR/TR/6´2˝/(215–220); [ChiA99 1/22]; d9.1; Col Mississippi St.																									
2000	Chi A	1	0	1.000	7	0	0	0-1	9.1	18	14	5	0	7-0	6	13.50	37	.409	.481	0	ø	0	—	-8	0	-0.7
2001	Chi A	1	0	1.000	20	0	0	0-0	39.2	34	23	2	7	14-2	24	5.22	89	.238	.329	0	ø	0	—	-1	0	-0.1
2002	Chi A	1	0	1.000	33	0	0	1-0	54.1	59	34	6	1	21-0	37	4.47	101	.278	.343	0	ø	0	—	-2	0	-0.1
2003	Chi A	0	0	ø	3	0	0	0-0	3.1	2	5	1	2	1-0	0	13.50	34	.182	.357	0	ø	0	—	-3	0	-0.1
2004	NY N	1	3	.250	15	14	0	0-0	69.1	82	41	8	5	20-5	38	4.54	95	.289	.345	14-0-3	.214	1	97	-3	23	-0.1
2005	Det A	0	1	.000	14	1	0	0-0	35	49	25	6	2	9-1	15	6.17	69	.340	.385	0	ø	0	65	-7	0	-0.3
Total	6	4	4	.500	92	15	0	1-1	211	244	142	28	17	72-8	120	5.46	82	.291	.356	14-0-3	.214	1	92	-24	23	-1.4
Girard, Charlie	Charles August; B12.16.1884 Brooklyn NY; D8.6.1936 Brooklyn NY; BR/TR/5´10˝/175; d9.14																									
1910	Phi N	1	2	.333	7	1	0	1	26.2	33	26	2	2	12	11	6.41	49	.308	.388	8	.125	-0	95	-10	—	-1.1
Gissell, Chris	Christopher Odell; B1.4.1978 Tacoma WA; BR/TR/6´5˝/210; [ChiN96 4/112]; d8.22																									
2004	Col N	0	1	.000	5	1	0	0-0	8.2	20	14	4	0	3-0	11	14.54	33	.465	.489	1	.000	-0	59	-8	0	-0.8
Giusti, Dave	David John; B11.27.1939 Seneca Falls NY; BR/TR/5´11˝/(190–195); d4.13; Col Syracuse																									
1962	Hou N	2	3	.400	22	5	0	0	73.2	82	49	7	0	30-1	43	5.62	66	.280	.346	24-0-1	.292	3*	117	-14	0	-0.6
1964	Hou N	0	0	ø	8	0	0	0	25.2	24	10	1	0	8-1	16	3.16	108	.253	.308	7	.286	1	—	1	0	0.2
1965	Hou N	8	7	.533	38	13	4-1	3	131.1	132	67	13	1	46-11	92	4.32	78	.259	.319	35-1-3	.171	2	96	-13	0	-1.1
1966	Hou N	15	14	.517	34	33	9-4	0	210	215	112	23	5	54-3	131	4.20	81	.260	.309	74-0-6	.230	5*	117	-19	0	-1.9
1967	Hou N	11	15	.423	37	33	8-1	1	221.2	231	114	20	3	58-4	157	4.18	79	.265	.311	84-3-2	.155	3*	119	-20	0	-2.0
1968	Hou N	11	14	.440	37	34	12-2	1	251	226	95	15	4	67-7	186	3.19	93	.239	.291	82-0-5	.183	2*	79	-4	0	-0.1
1969	StL N	3	7	.300	22	12	2-1	0-0	99.2	96	46	7	1	37-2	62	3.61	99	.255	.321	25-0-1	.200	1	51	-1	21	0.1
1970	†Pit N	9	3	.750	66	1	0	26-6	103	98	38	7	0	39-9	85	3.06	129	.259	.325	16-0-1	.188	2	159	11	0	1.9
1971	†Pit N	5	6	.455	58	0	0	**30**-6	86	79	31	5	1	31-8	55	2.93	116	.241	.305	17	.059	-1	—	5	0	0.8
1972	†Pit N	7	4	.636	54	0	0	22-5	74.2	59	18	3	0	20-6	54	1.93	172	.219	.271	10-0-1	.000	-1	—	12	0	2.6
1973	Pit N★	9	2	.818	67	0	0	20-6	98.2	89	31	9	0	37-13	64	2.37	149	.241	.308	13-0-2	.308	1	—	13	0	1.9
1974	†Pit N	7	5	.583	64	2	0	12-6	105.2	101	43	2	0	40-11	53	3.32	105	.258	.323	9-0-1	.111	-0	63	3	0	0.4
1975	†Pit N	5	4	.556	61	0	0	17-6	91.2	79	38	3	0	42-17	38	2.95	122	.237	.320	10-0-4	.300	1	—	5	0	0.8
1976	Pit N	5	4	.556	40	0	0	6-2	58.1	59	31	5	0	27-9	24	4.32	82	.267	.345	4	.000	-0	—	-5	36	-0.8
1977	Oak A	3	3	.500	40	0	0	6-1	60.1	54	22	4	0	20-5	28	2.98	135	.245	.308	0	ø	0	—	8	0	0.9
	Chi N	0	2	.000	20	0	0	1-1	25.1	30	19	2	0	14-2	15	6.04	73	.297	.379	2	.000	-0	—	-4	0	-0.4
Total	15	100	93	.518	668	133	35-9	145-39	1716.2	1654	764	126	15	570-109	1103	3.60	96	.253	.313	412-4-27	.187	18	96	-22	57	2.7
Givens, Brian	Brian Allen; B11.6.1965 Lompoc CA; BR/TL/6´6˝/220; [NYN84*10/234]; d6.24; Col Trinidad St. (CO) JC																									
1995	Mil A	5	7	.417	19	19	0	0-0	107.1	116	71	11	3	54-0	73	4.95	101	.275	.360	0	ø	0	99	-2	0	-0.3
1996	Mil A	1	3	.250	4	4	0	0-0	14	32	22	3	0	7-0	10	12.86	40	.438	.481	0	ø	0	94	-12	32	-1.7
Total	2	6	10	.375	23	23	0	0-0	121.1	148	93	14	3	61-0	83	5.86	86	.299	.378	0	ø	0	98	-14	32	-2.0
Gladding, Fred	Fred Earl; B6.28.1936 Flat Rock MI; BL/TR/6´0˝/(220–225); d7.1; C3																									
1961	Det A	1	0	1.000	8	0	0	0	16.1	18	7	1	2	11-1	11	3.31	124	.286	.397	3	.000	-0	—	1	0	0.0
1962	Det A	0	0	ø	6	0	0	0	5	3	0	0	0	2-0	4	0.00	ø	.176	.263	0	ø	0	—	2	0	0.1
1963	Det A	1	1	.500	22	0	0	7	27.1	19	6	1	0	14-1	24	1.98	189	.198	.297	1	.000	-0	—	6	0	0.7
1964	Det A	7	4	.636	42	0	0	7	67.1	57	23	7	2	27-4	59	3.07	119	.233	.312	9	.000	-1	—	5	0	0.9
1965	Det A	6	2	.750	46	0	0	5	70	63	22	6	4	29-5	43	2.83	123	.239	.323	7-0-1	.000	-1	—	6	0	0.6
1966	Det A	5	0	1.000	51	0	0	2	74	62	33	6	1	29-6	57	3.28	106	.230	.306	2	.000	-0	—	0	0	0.0
1967	Det A	6	4	.600	42	1	0	12	77	62	20	6	4	19-0	64	1.99	164	.227	.286	18-0-1	.000	-2	27	10	0	1.5
1968	Hou N	0	0	ø	7	0	0	2	4.1	8	7	0	1	3-1	2	14.54	20	.421	.500	0	ø	0	—	-5	125	-0.6
1969	Hou N	4	8	.333	57	0	0	**29**-6	72.2	83	39	2	1	27-6	40	4.21	84	.289	.352	10	.100	-1	—	-5	0	-1.1
1970	Hou N	7	4	.636	63	0	0	18-4	71	84	39	4	3	24-8	46	4.06	96	.293	.352	6-0-1	.000	-1	—	-3	0	-0.6
1971	Hou N	4	5	.444	48	0	0	12-4	51.1	51	17	0	7	22-7	17	2.10	160	.268	.362	2	.000	-0	—	6	0	1.1
1972	Hou N	5	6	.455	42	0	0	14-2	48.2	38	16	1	2	12-5	18	2.77	121	.222	.278	5-0-1	.000	-1	—	3	0	0.6

THE PITCHER REGISTER

YEAR	TM LG	W	L	PCT	G	GS	CG-SHO	SV-BS	IP	H	R	HR	HB	BB-IB	SO	ERA	AERA	OAV	OOB	AB-HR-SH	AVG	PB	SUP	APR	DL	PW
1973	Hou N	2	0	1.000	16	0	0	1-2	16	18	8	4	0	4-1	9	4.50	81	.290	.333	0	ø	0	—	-1	0	-0.1
Total	13	48	34	.585	450	1	0	109-18	601	566	237	38	27	223-45	394	3.13	113	.252	.325	63-0-4	.016	-6	27	25	125	3.1
GLADE, FRED	Frederick Monroe "Lucky"; B1.25.1876 Dubuque IA; D11.21.1934 Grand Island NE; BR/TR/6´0˝/190; d5.27																									
1902	Chi N	0	1	.000	1	1	1	0	8	13	11	0	1	3	3	9.00	30	.361	.425	3	.333	1	50	-5	—	-0.4
1904	StL A	18	15	.545	35	34	30-6	1	289	248	101	2	13	58	156	2.27	109	.233	.281	102-0-3	.186	1	87	6	—	1.0
1905	StL A	6	25	.194	32	32	28-2	0	275	257	109	3	11	58	127	2.81	90	.249	.296	98	.092	-6	69	-3	—	-0.8
1906	StL A	15	14	.517	35	32	28-4	1	266.2	215	91	4	10	59	96	2.36	109	.224	.276	95-0-2	.137	-4	100	11	—	0.7
1907	StL A	13	9	.591	24	22	18-2	0	202	187	81	2	9	45	71	2.67	94	.248	.298	73-0-2	.205	2	121	-3	—	-0.3
1908	NY A	0	4	.000	5	5	2	0	32	30	18	0	4	14	11	4.22	59	.275	.378	10	.000	-1	66	-5	—	-0.7
Total	6	52	68	.433	132	126	107-14	2	1072.2	950	411	11	48	237	464	2.62	97	.240	.291	381-0-7	.150	-7	91	1	—	-0.5
GLAISER, JOHN	John Burke "Bert"; B7.28.1894 Yoakum TX; D3.7.1959 Houston TX; BL/TR/5´8˝/165; d4.20; Col St. Edwards																									
1920	Det A	0	0	ø	9	1	0	1	17	23	12	1	1	8	3	6.35	59	.354	.432	3	.000	-0	171	-4	—	-0.1
GLASS, TOM	Thomas Joseph; B4.29.1898 Greensboro NC; D12.15.1981 Greensboro NC; BR/TR/6´3˝/170; d6.12																									
1925	Phi A	1	0	1.000	2	0	0	0	5	9	4	0	0	0	2	5.40	86	.409	.409	2-0-1	.000	-0	—	-1	—	-0.1
GLAUBER, KEITH	Keith Harris; B1.18.1972 Brooklyn NY; BR/TR/6´2˝/190; [StLN94 42/1169]; d9.8; Col Montclair St.																									
1998	Cin N	0	0	ø	3	0	0	0-0	7.2	6	2	0	0	1-0	4	2.35	183	.214	.226	2	.000	-0	—	2	154	0.0
2000	Cin N	0	0	ø	4	0	0	0-0	7.1	5	3	0	1	2-0	4	3.68	129	.185	.267	1	.000	-0	—	1	0	0.0
Total	2	0	0	ø	7	0	0	0-0	15	11	5	0	1	3-0	8	3.00	151	.200	.246	3	.000	-0	—	3	154	0.0
GLAVENICH, LUKE	Luke Frank; B1.17.1893 Jackson CA; D5.22.1935 Stockton CA; BR/TR/5´9.5˝/189; d4.12; Col St. Marys (CA)																									
1913	Cle A	0	0	ø	1	0	0	0	1	3	5	0	0	3	1	9.00	34	.500	.667	0	ø	0	—	-2	—	-0.1
GLAVINE, TOM	Thomas Michael; B3.25.1966 Concord MA; BL/TL/6´1˝/(175–190); [AtlN84 2/47]; d8.17; b–Mike																									
1987	Atl N	2	4	.333	9	9	0	0-0	50.1	55	34	5	3	33-4	20	5.54	78	.279	.386	16	.125	-0	86	-6	0	-0.6
1988	Atl N	7	17	.292	34	34	1	0-0	195.1	201	111	12	8	63-7	84	4.56	80	.270	.329	60-0-8	.183	1*	96	-18	0	-1.9
1989	Atl N	14	8	.636	29	29	6-4	0-0	186	172	88	20	2	40-3	90	3.68	99	.243	.283	67-0-4	.149	0*	127	-1	0	0.0
1990	Atl N	10	12	.455	33	33	1	0-0	214.1	232	111	18	1	78-10	129	4.28	94	.281	.343	62-0-7	.113	0*	94	-4	0	-0.2
1991	†Atl N★	**20**	11	.645	34	34	**9**-1	0-0	246.2	201	83	17	2	69-6	192	2.55	152	.222	.277	74-0-15	.230	4*	106	**33**	0	**4.9**
1992	†Atl N★	**20**	8	.714	33	33	7-**5**	0-0	225	197	81	6	2	70-7	129	2.76	133	.235	.293	77-0-9	.247	4*	114	20	0	3.0
1993	†Atl N☆	**22**	6	.786	36	**36**	4-2	0-0	239.1	236	91	16	2	90-7	120	3.20	127	.259	.327	81-0-11	.173	1	122	24	0	2.7
1994	Atl N	13	9	.591	25	25	2	0-0	165.1	173	76	10	1	70-10	140	3.97	109	.268	.338	56-0-9	.179	1*	114	8	0	1.2
1995	†Atl N	16	7	.696	29	29	3-1	0-0	198.2	182	76	9	5	66-0	127	3.08	140	.246	.310	63-1-8	.222	3	91	26	0	3.3
1996	†Atl N★	15	10	.600	36	**36**	1	0-0	235.1	222	91	14	0	85-7	181	2.98	149	.249	.314	76-0-15	.289	6*	89	35	0	4.4
1997	†Atl N☆	14	7	.667	33	33	5-2	0-0	240	197	86	20	4	79-9	152	2.96	142	.226	.292	63-0-17	.222	4	104	34	0	3.2
1998	†Atl N★	**20**	6	.769	33	33	4-3	0-0	229.1	202	67	13	2	74-2	157	2.47	168	.238	.300	71-0-14	.239	3	114	45	0	5.6
1999	†Atl N	14	11	.560	35	**35**	2	0-0	234	259	115	18	4	83-14	138	4.12	109	.287	.346	65-0-7	.138	-0*	106	11	0	1.3
2000	†Atl N★	**21**	9	.700	35	**35**	4-2	0-0	241	222	101	24	4	65-6	152	3.40	133	.244	.296	68-0-14	.147	1*	110	30	0	3.5
2001	†Atl N	16	7	.696	35	**35**	1-1	0-0	219.1	213	92	24	2	97-10	116	3.57	121	.261	.338	57-0-17	.140	0	107	20	0	2.1
2002	†Atl N☆	18	11	.621	36	**36**	2-1	0-0	224.2	210	85	21	8	78-8	127	2.96	136	.252	.320	68-0-13	.103	-2*	100	26	0	3.1
2003	NY N	9	14	.391	32	32	0	0-0	183.1	205	94	21	2	66-7	82	4.52	93	.288	.348	53-0-10	.151	0*	76	-5	0	-0.3
2004	NY N★	11	14	.440	33	33	1-1	0-0	212.1	204	94	20	0	70-10	109	3.60	119	.252	.308	54-0-8	.204	4*	91	17	0	2.4
2005	NY N	13	13	.500	33	33	2-1	0-0	211.1	227	88	12	3	61-5	105	3.53	117	.279	.330	64-0-5	.203	1	94	15	0	2.0
2006	†NY N✳	15	7	.682	32	32	0	0-0	198	202	94	22	6	62-7	131	3.82	115	.267	.325	53-0-10	.170	2	113	12	0	1.6
Total	20	290	191	.603	635	635	55-24	0-0	4149.2	4012	1758	322	61	1399-139	2481	3.46	120	.256	.317	1248-1-201	.186	34	103	322	0	41.3
GLAZE, RALPH	Daniel Ralph; B3.13.1881 Denver CO; D10.31.1968 Atascadero CA; BR/TR/5´9˝/165; d6.1; Col Dartmouth																									
1906	Bos A	4	6	.400	19	10	7	0	123	110	58	4	5	32	56	3.59	77	.242	.299	55-0-1	.182	0*	107	-8	—	-0.6
1907	Bos A	9	13	.409	32	21	11-1	0	182.1	150	75	4	4	48	68	2.32	111	.227	.283	61-1-2	.180	0	97	3	—	0.1
1908	Bos A	2	2	.500	10	3	2	0	34.2	43	24	1	0	5	13	3.38	73	.253	.274	13	.077	-1	111	-5	—	-0.7
Total	3	15	21	.417	61	34	20-1	0	340	303	157	9	9	85	137	2.89	91	.236	.288	129-1-3	.171	-1	102	-10	—	-1.2
GLAZNER, WHITEY	Charles Franklin; B9.17.1893 Sycamore AL; D6.6.1989 Orlando FL; BR/TR/5´9˝/165; d9.26																									
1920	Pit N	0	0	ø	2	0	0	0	8.2	9	3	0	0	2	1	3.12	103	.300	.344	3	.000	-0	—	0	—	-0.1
1921	Pit N	14	5	.737	36	25	15	1	234	214	88	5	12	58	88	2.77	139	**.250**	.306	76-0-6	.132	-3	96	26	—	1.4
1922	Pit N	11	12	.478	34	26	10-1	1	193	238	118	9	2	52	77	4.38	93	.309	.354	65-1-5	.246	3	86	-9	—	-0.6
1923	Pit N	2	1	.667	7	4	1-1	1	30	29	18	5	0	11	8	3.30	122	.250	.315	12-1-0	.333	2	149	0	—	0.2
	Phi N	7	14	.333	28	23	12-2	1	161.1	195	104	11	6	63	51	4.69	98	.304	.371	53-0-1	.170	-1	81	-2	—	-0.2
	Year	9	15	.375	35	27	13-3	2	191.1	224	122	16	6	74	59	4.47	101	.296	.363	65-1-1	.200	1	90	-5	—	0.0
1924	Phi N	7	16	.304	35	24	8-2	0	156.2	210	108	14	4	63	41	5.92	75	.339	.403	51-0-3	.157	-4	69	-18	—	-2.5
Total	5	41	48	.461	142	102	46-6	4	783.2	895	439	44	24	249	266	4.21	99	.295	.353	260-2-15	.181	-3	86	-3	—	-1.8
GLEASON, JOE	Joseph Paul; B7.9.1895 Phelps NY; D9.8.1990 Phelps NY; BR/TR/5´10.5˝/175; d9.11																									
1920	Was A	0	0	ø	3	0	0	0	8	14	13	2	1	6	2	13.50	28	.326	.420	2	.000	1	—	-8	—	-0.3
1922	Was A	2	2	.500	8	5	3	0	40.2	53	26	3	1	18	12	4.65	83	.319	.389	14	.143	-0	141	-4	—	-0.4
Total	2	2	2	.500	11	5	3	0	48.2	67	39	5	2	24	14	6.10	63	.321	.396	16	.125	0	141	-12	—	-0.7
GLEASON, BILL	William; B1868 Cleveland OH; D12.2.1893 Cleveland OH; d4.24																									
1890	Cle P	0	1	.000	1	1	0	0	4	14	16	1	0	6	0	27.00	15	.538	.625	2	.000	-0	230	-9	—	-1.0
GLEASON, KID	William J.; B10.26.1866 Camden NJ; D1.2.1933 Philadelphia PA; BB/TR/5´7˝/158; d4.20; M5/C16; b–Harry; ▲																									
1888	Phi N	7	16	.304	24	23	23	0	199.2	199	112	11	12	53	89	2.84	105	.252	.309	83	.205	0	84	0	—	-0.1
1889	Phi N	9	15	.375	29	21	15	1	205	242	177	8	9	97	64	5.58	78	.285	.365	99	.253	2*	92	-23	—	-1.9
1890	Phi N	38	17	.691	60	55	54-6	**2**	506	479	253	8	15	167	222	2.63	139	.242	.306	224	.210	-6*	94	51	—	4.0
1891	Phi N	24	22	.522	53	44	40-1	1	418	431	237	11	13	165	100	3.51	97	.256	.328	214	.248	6*	93	-2	—	0.2
1892	StL N	20	24	.455	47	45	43-2	0	400	389	244	11	10	151	133	3.33	96	.245	.314	233-3	.215	8*	112	-16	—	-0.4
1893	StL N	21	22	.488	48	45	37-1	1	380.1	436	276	18	10	187	86	4.61	103	.279	.360	199	.256	4*	93	11	—	1.3
1894	StL N	2	6	.250	8	8	6	0	58	75	50	2	3	21	9	6.05	90	.310	.372	28	.250	-0*	60	-2	—	-0.2
	†Bal N	15	5	.750	21	20	19	0	172	224	111	3	3	44	35	4.45	123	.312	.354	86-0-4	.349	4*	109	19	—	1.9
	Year	17	11	.607	29	28	25	0	230	299	161	5	6	65	44	4.85	112	.311	.359	114-0-4	.325	4	95	21	—	1.7
1895	†Bal N	2	4	.333	9	5	3	1	50.1	77	51	4	3	21	6	6.97	68	.345	.409	421-0-6	.309	2*	185	-12	—	-1.0
Total	8	138	131	.513	299	266	240-10	6	2389.1	2552	1511	76	78	906	744	3.79	103	.265	.333	1587-3-10	.258	20	98	26	—	3.8
GLEATON, JERRY DON	Jerry Don; B9.14.1957 Brownwood TX; BL/TL/6´3˝/(210–215); [TexA79 1/17]; d7.11; Col Texas																									
1979	Tex A	0	1	.000	5	2	0	0-0	9.2	15	7	0	1	2-0	2	6.52	64	.375	.409	0	ø	0	66	-2	0	-0.2
1980	Tex A	0	0	ø	5	0	0	0-0	7	5	2	0	0	4-0	2	2.57	151	.208	.300	0	ø	0	—	1	0	0.1
1981	Sea A	4	7	.364	20	13	1	0-0	85.1	88	50	10	2	38-2	31	4.75	82	.273	.350	0	ø	0	125	-8	0	-0.9
1982	Sea A	0	0	ø	3	0	0	0-0	4.2	7	7	3	1	2-0	1	13.50	32	.333	.417	0	ø	0	—	-4	0	-0.2
1984	Chi A	1	2	.333	11	1	0	2-1	18.1	20	12	2	1	6-0	4	3.44	122	.286	.333	0	ø	0	0	0	0	-0.1
1985	Chi A	1	0	1.000	31	0	0	1-1	29.2	37	19	3	0	13-3	22	5.76	75	.316	.382	0	ø	0	—	-4	0	-0.2
1987	KC A	4	4	.500	48	0	0	5-2	50.2	38	28	4	0	28-3	44	4.26	108	.216	.319	0	ø	0	—	1	0	0.3
1988	KC A	0	4	.000	42	0	0	3-1	38	33	17	2	3	17-1	29	3.55	113	.232	.327	0	ø	0	—	2	0	0.2
1989	KC A	0	0	ø	15	0	0	0-0	14.1	20	10	0	0	6-0	9	5.65	69	.345	.394	0	ø	0	—	-3	0	-0.1
1990	Det A	1	3	.250	57	0	0	13-3	82.2	62	27	5	3	25-2	56	2.94	135	.213	.279	0	ø	0	—	10	0	0.7
1991	Det A	3	2	.600	47	0	0	2-1	75.1	74	37	7	0	39-8	47	4.06	103	.269	.355	0	ø	0	—	1	38	0.1
1992	Pit N	1	0	1.000	23	0	0	0-2	31.2	34	16	4	0	19-3	18	4.26	81	.283	.379	2-0-1	.000	0	—	-3	0	-0.1
Total	12	15	23	.395	307	16	1	26-11	447.1	433	232	40	11	199-22	265	4.25	96	.261	.340	2-0-1	.000	0	106	-9	38	-0.4
GLENDON, MARTIN	Martin J.; B2.8.1877 Milwaukee WI; D11.6.1950 Norwood Park IL; BR/TR/5´8˝/165; d4.18																									
1902	Cin N	0	1	.000	1	1	0	0	3	5	5	0	0	4	0	12.00	25	.357	.500	1	.000	-0	45	-2	—	-0.4
1903	Cle A	1	2	.333	3	3	3	0	27.2	20	9	0	0	7	9	0.98	292	.202	.255	8-0-1	.000	-1	117	5	—	0.4
Total	2	1	3	.250	4	4	3	0	30.2	25	14	0	0	11	9	2.05	140	.221	.290	9-0-1	.000	-1	99	3	—	0.0

YEAR	TM LG	W	L	PCT	G	GS	CG-SHO	SV-BS	IP	H	R	HR	HB	BB-IB	SO	ERA	AERA	OAV	OOB	AB-HR-SH	AVG	PB	SUP	APR	DL	PW
GLENN, BOB	Burdette; B6.16.1894 W.Sunbury PA; D6.3.1977 Richmond CA; BR/TR; d7.27; Col Michigan																									
1920	StL N	0	0	ø	2	0	0	0	2	2	0	0	0	0	0	0.00	ø	.222	.222	0	ø	0	—	1	—	0.0
GLIATTO, SAL	Salvador Michael; B5.7.1902 Chicago IL; D11.2.1995 Tyler TX; BB/TR/5´8.5˝/150; d4.19																									
1930	Cle A	0	0	ø	8	0	0	2	15	21	15	1	2	9	7	6.60	73	.328	.427	2	.000	-0*	—	-3	—	-0.2
GLINATSIS, GEORGE	George; B6.29.1969 Youngstown OH; BR/TR/6´4˝/195; [SeaA91 32/838]; d7.18; Col Cincinnati																									
1994	Sea A	0	1	.000	2	2	0	0-0	5.1	9	8	2	0	6-0	1	13.50	37	.429	.536	0	ø	0	84	-5	0	-0.6
GLOVER, GARY	John Gary; B12.3.1976 Cleveland OH; BR/TR/6´5˝/(205–220); [TorA94 15/427]; d9.30																									
1999	Tor A	0	0	ø	1	0	0	0-0	1	0	0	0	0	1-0	0	0.00	ø	.000	.333	0	ø	0	—	1	0	0.0
2001	Chi A	5	5	.500	46	11	0	0-1	100.1	98	61	16	4	32-3	63	4.93	94	.252	.314	0	ø	0	90	-3	0	-0.3
2002	Chi A	7	8	.467	41	22	0	1-0	138.1	136	86	21	7	52-1	70	5.20	87	.253	.326	1	.000	-0	124	-10	0	-0.9
2003	Chi A	1	0	1.000	24	0	0	0-0	35.2	43	18	3	2	14-2	23	4.54	101	.305	.369	0	ø	0	—	1	0	0.0
	Ana A	1	0	1.000	18	0	0	0-0	27	34	15	3	1	8-1	14	5.00	88	.315	.361	0	ø	0	—	-1	0	-0.1
	Year	2	0	1.000	42	0	0	0-0	62.2	77	33	6	3	22-3	37	4.74	95	.309	.366	0	ø	0	—	0	0	-0.1
2004	Mil N	2	1	.667	4	3	0	0-0	18	18	9	2	2	8-1	8	3.50	125	.265	.350	7	.000	-1	113	1	0	0.1
2005	Mil N	5	4	.556	15	11	0	0-0	64.2	74	41	10	2	20-0	58	5.57	76	.288	.342	20-0-3	.100	-0	117	-8	0	-1.0
Total	6	21	18	.538	149	47	0	1-1	385	403	230	55	18	135-8	236	5.03	90	.268	.333	28-0-3	.071	-1	113	-19	0	-2.2
GLYNN, ED	Edward Paul; B6.3.1953 Flushing NY; BR/TL/6´2˝/(170–180); d9.19																									
1975	Det A	0	2	.000	3	1	0	0-0	14.2	11	8	1	0	8-0	8	4.30	94	.220	.322	0	ø	0	0	0	0	0.0
1976	Det A	1	3	.250	5	4	1	0-0	23.2	22	18	3	0	20-1	17	6.08	61	.265	.396	0	ø	0	112	-6	0	-0.9
1977	Det A	2	1	.667	8	3	0	0-0	27.1	36	17	3	0	12-1	13	5.27	82	.316	.372	0	ø	0	153	-2	0	-0.2
1978	Det A	0	0	ø	10	0	0	0-0	14.2	11	5	3	0	4-0	9	3.07	127	.208	.259	0	ø	0	—	2	0	0.1
1979	NY N	1	4	.200	46	0	0	7-4	60	57	22	3	2	40-10	32	3.00	124	.259	.372	4	.000	-0	—	5	0	0.4
1980	NY N	3	3	.500	38	0	0	1-1	52.1	49	26	5	0	23-4	32	4.13	87	.246	.321	6-0-2	.000	-1	—	-3	21	-0.3
1981	Cle A	0	0	ø	4	0	0	0-0	7.2	5	1	0	0	4-0	4	1.17	314	.192	.300	0	ø	0	—	2	0	0.1
1982	Cle A	5	2	.714	47	0	0	4-4	49.2	43	27	6	0	30-5	54	4.17	100	.232	.336	0	ø	0	—	-1	0	-0.1
1983	Cle A	0	2	.000	11	0	0	0-1	12.1	22	11	2	0	6-0	13	5.84	73	.373	.424	0	ø	0	—	-3	0	-0.4
1985	Mon N	0	0	ø	3	0	0	0-0	2.1	5	5	0	0	4-0	2	19.29	18	.455	.600	0	ø	0	—	-4	0	-0.2
Total	10	12	17	.414	175	8	1	12-10	264.2	261	140	26	2	151-21	184	4.25	91	.261	.354	10-0-2	.000	-1	118	-10	21	-1.5
GLYNN, RYAN	Ryan David; B11.1.1974 Portsmouth VA; BR/TR/6´3˝/(195–200); [TexA95 4/94]; d5.16; Col VMI																									
1999	Tex A	2	4	.333	13	10	0	0-0	54.2	71	46	10	1	35-0	39	7.24	71	.316	.408	1	.000	-0	133	-12	0	-1.1
2000	Tex A	5	7	.417	16	16	0	0-0	88.2	107	65	15	3	41-2	33	5.58	91	.293	.369	2	.000	-0	82	-6	30	-0.7
2001	Tex A	1	5	.167	12	9	0	0-0	46	59	38	7	0	26-1	15	7.04	68	.309	.388	0	ø	0	78	-11	29	-1.2
2004	Tor A	1	0	1.000	6	2	0	0-0	20	19	9	4	3	8-1	14	4.05	121	.250	.341	0	ø	0	189	2	0	0.1
2005	Oak A	0	4	.000	5	3	0	0-0	17	24	16	5	0	7-0	15	6.88	64	.320	.378	1	.000	-0	70	-5	0	-0.9
Total	5	9	20	.310	52	40	0	0-0	226.1	280	174	41	7	117-4	116	6.24	80	.300	.381	4	.000	-0	99	-32	59	-3.8
GOAR, JOT	Joshua Mercer; B1.31.1870 New Lisbon IN; D4.4.1947 New Castle IN; BR/TR/5´9˝/160; d4.18																									
1896	Pit N	0	1	.000	3	0	0	0	13.1	36	33	1	1	8	3	16.88	25	.486	.542	6	.167	-1	—	-19	—	-1.0
1898	Cin N	0	0	ø	1	0	0	0	2	4	3	0	0	1	0	9.00	43	.400	.455	0	ø	0	—	-1	—	0.0
Total	2	0	1	.000	4	0	0	0	15.1	40	36	1	1	9	3	15.85	26	.476	.532	6	.167	-1	—	-20	—	-1.0
GOBBLE, JIMMY	Billy James; B7.19.1981 Bristol TN; BL/TL/6´3˝/(190–205); [KCA99 1/43]; d8.3																									
2003	KC A	4	5	.444	9	9	0	0-0	52.2	56	32	8	4	15-0	31	4.61	104	.271	.328	0	ø	0	72	0	0	-0.1
2004	KC A	9	8	.529	25	24	1	0-0	148	157	94	24	3	43-0	49	5.35	87	.270	.320	2	.000	-0	103	-10	0	-1.0
2005	KC A	1	1	.500	28	4	0	0-0	53.2	64	34	9	1	30-4	38	5.70	77	.299	.386	0	ø	0	132	-7	0	-0.4
2006	KC A	4	6	.400	60	6	0	2-2	84	95	51	12	1	29-1	80	5.14	91	.282	.341	0-0-1	ø	0	87	-4	0	-0.4
Total	4	18	20	.474	122	43	1	2-2	338.1	372	211	53	9	117-5	198	5.24	89	.278	.337	2-0-1	.000	-0	97	-21	0	-1.9
GOETZ, GEORGE	George Burt; B Greencastle PA; 6´2˝/180; d6.17																									
1889	Bal AA	1	0	1.000	1	1	0	0	9	12	6	0	0	0	2	4.00	99	.308	.308	4	.000	-1	157	0	—	0.0
GOETZ, JOHN	John Hardy; B10.24.1937 Goetzville MI; BR/TR/6´0˝/185; d4.16; Col Western Michigan																									
1960	Chi N	0	0	ø	4	0	0	0	6.1	10	9	2	0	4-1	6	12.79	30	.370	.452	1	.000	-0	—	-6	0	-0.3
GOGOLEWSKI, BILL	William Joseph; B10.26.1947 Oshkosh WI; BL/TR/6´4˝/(185–195); [TexA65 13/468]; d9.3																									
1970	Was A	2	2	.500	8	5	0	0-0	33.2	33	18	2	1	25-1	19	4.81	75	.260	.386	7-0-2	.000	-0	64	-4	0	-0.4
1971	Was A	6	5	.545	27	17	4-1	0-0	124.1	112	39	5	2	39-6	70	2.75	123	.241	.301	32-0-4	.156	0	98	11	0	1.0
1972	Tex A	4	11	.267	36	21	2-1	2-0	150.2	136	74	9	6	58-9	95	4.24	72	.239	.315	40-0-2	.125	-1	83	-16	0	-1.8
1973	Tex A	3	6	.333	49	1	0	6-2	123.2	139	67	10	1	48-16	77	4.22	89	.286	.348	0	ø	0	95	-7	0	-0.4
1974	Cle A	0	0	ø	5	0	0	0-0	13.2	15	7	1	1	2-0	3	4.61	79	.283	.321	0	ø	0	—	-1	0	0.0
1975	Chi A	0	0	ø	19	0	0	2-1	55	61	35	5	1	28-3	37	5.24	74	.292	.377	0	ø	0	—	-8	54	-0.4
Total	6	15	24	.385	144	44	6-2	10-3	501	496	240	32	12	200-35	301	4.02	86	.260	.332	79-0-8	.127	-1	82	-25	54	-2.0
GOHR, GREG	Gregory James; B10.29.1967 Santa Clara CA; BR/TR/6´3˝/205; [DetA89 1/21]; d4.7; Col Santa Clara																									
1993	Det A	0	0	ø	16	0	0	0-1	22.2	26	15	1	2	14-2	23	5.96	73	.289	.393	0	ø	0	—	-3	0	-0.2
1994	Det A	2	2	.500	8	6	0	0-0	34	36	19	3	0	21-1	21	4.50	109	.263	.358	0	ø	0	68	1	21	0.1
1995	Det A	1	0	1.000	10	0	0	0-0	10.1	9	1	0	0	3-0	12	0.87	553	.243	.300	0	ø	0	—	4	129	0.4
1996	Det A	4	8	.333	17	16	0	0-0	91.2	129	76	24	3	34-2	60	7.17	71	.328	.383	0	ø	0	81	-19	25	-2.0
	Cal A	1	1	.500	15	0	0	1-0	24	34	20	7	0	10-0	15	7.50	67	.337	.393	0	ø	0	—	-5	0	-0.4
	Year	5	9	.357	32	16	0	1-0	115.2	163	96	31	3	44-2	75	7.24	70	.330	.385	0	ø	0	81	-25	0	-2.4
Total	4	8	11	.421	66	22	0	1-1	182.2	234	131	35	5	82-5	131	6.21	80	.309	.377	0	ø	0	79	-22	175	-2.1
GOLDEN, JIM	James Edward; B3.20.1936 Eldon MO; BL/TR/6´0˝/175; d9.30																									
1960	LA N	1	0	1.000	1	1	0	0	7	6	5	1	0	4-0	4	6.43	62	.240	.333	3	.333	0	156	-2	0	-0.1
1961	LA N	1	1	.500	28	0	0	1	42	52	30	7	0	20-2	18	5.79	75	.306	.377	3	.000	-0	—	-6	0	-0.4
1962	Hou N	7	11	.389	37	18	5-2	1	152.2	163	84	13	0	50-4	88	4.07	92	.270	.324	54-0-3	.222	4*	108	-8	0	-0.4
1963	Hou N	0	1	.000	3	1	0	0	6.1	12	4	0	0	2-0	5	5.68	55	.429	.467	0	ø	0	0	-2	0	-0.2
Total	4	9	13	.409	69	20	5-2	1	208	233	123	21	0	76-6	115	4.54	85	.282	.340	60-0-3	.217	4	103	-18	0	-1.1
GOLDEN, MIKE	Michael Henry; B9.11.1851 Shirley MA; D1.11.1929 Rockford IL; BR/TR/5´8˝/168; d5.4; ▲																									
1875	Wes NA	1	12	.077	13	13	13	0	113	111	88	0	—	12	20	1.83	133	.225	.243	46	.130	-4	50	7	—	0.3
	Chi NA	6	7	.462	14	14	12-1	0	119	129	95	0	—	8	14	1.89	120	.247	.258	155	.258	1*	95	5	—	0.4
	Year	7	19	.269	27	27	25-1	0	232	240	183	0	—	20	34	1.86	126	.236	.251	201	.229	-3	73	1	—	0.7
1878	Mil N	3	13	.188	22	18	15	0	161	217	171	1	—	33	52	4.14	63	.295	.325	214	.206	-2*	79	-22	—	-1.8
GOLDEN, ROY	Roy Kramer; B7.12.1888 Madisonville OH; D10.4.1961 Norwood OH; BR/TR/6´1˝/195; d9.7																									
1910	StL N	2	3	.400	7	6	3	0	42.2	44	28	3	2	33	31	4.43	67	.286	.418	15-0-2	.267	1	92	-7	—	-0.7
1911	StL N	4	9	.308	30	25	6	0	148.2	127	90	6	5	129	81	5.02	67	.240	.394	44-0-1	.114	-1	125	-21	—	-1.7
Total	2	6	12	.333	37	31	9	0	191.1	171	118	9	7	162	112	4.89	67	.250	.399	59-0-3	.153	-1	119	-28	—	-2.4
GOLDSMITH, FRED	Fredrick Ernest; B5.15.1852 New Haven CT; D3.28.1939 Berkley MI; BR/TR/6´1˝/195; d10.23.1875; U2																									
1879	Tro N	2	4	.333	8	7	7	0	63	61	38	0	—	1	31	1.57	159	.237	.240	38	.237	0*	69	4	—	0.4
1880	Chi N	21	3	**.875**	26	24	22-4	1	210.1	189	80	2	—	18	90	1.75	138	.233	.247	142	.261	2*	123	15	—	1.7
1881	Chi N	24	13	.649	39	39	37-5	0	330	328	166	4	—	44	76	2.59	106	.247	.271	158	.241	3*	131	9	—	1.2
1882	Chi N	28	17	.622	45	45	45-4	0	405	377	192	7	—	38	109	2.42	119	.236	.254	183	.230	-2	129	23	—	1.8
1883	Chi N	25	19	.568	46	45	40-2	0	383.1	456	256	14	—	39	82	3.15	105	.277	.294	235-1	.221	-1*	108	10	—	0.8
1884	Chi N	9	11	.450	21	21	20-1	0	188	245	140	11	—	29	34	4.26	74	.298	.322	81-2	.136	-2*	125	-15	—	-1.6
	Bal AA	3	1	.750	4	4	3	0	30	29	12	0	1	2	11	2.70	128	.238	.256	14	.143	-0	87	3	—	0.4
Total	6	112	68	.622	189	185	174-16	1	1609.2	1685	884	38	1	171	433	2.73	107	.256	.275	851-3	.224	-2	120	49	—	4.7

YEAR	TM LG	W	L	PCT	G	GS	CG-SHO	SV-BS	IP	H	R	HR	HB	BB-IB	SO	ERA	AERA	OAV	OOB	AB-HR-SH	AVG	PB	SUP	APR	DL	PW
Goldsmith, Hal	Harold Eugene; B8.18.1898 Peconic NY; D10.20.1985 Riverhead NY; BR/TR/6´0˝/174; d6.23; Col St. Lawrence																									
1926	Bos N	5	7	.417	19	15	5	0	101	135	62	2	1	28	16	4.37	81	.333	.377	38-0-1	.211	0	119	-12	—	-1.1
1927	Bos N	1	3	.250	22	5	1	1	71.2	83	34	4	0	26	13	3.52	106	.289	.348	21-0-1	.238	0	128	1	—	0.1
1928	Bos N	0	0	ø	4	0	0	0	8.1	14	5	2	0	1	1	3.24	121	.359	.375	2	.000	-0	—	0	—	0.0
1929	StL N	0	0	ø	2	0	0	0	4	3	3	1	0	1	0	6.75	69	.214	.267	1	.000	-0	—	-1	—	-0.1
Total	4	6	10	.375	47	20	6	1	185	235	104	9	1	56	30	4.04	90	.315	.364	62-0-2	.210	0	120	-12	—	-1.1
Goldstein, Izzy	Isidore; B6.6.1908 Odessa, Russia; D9.24.1993 Delray Beach FL; BB/TR/6´0˝/160; d4.24																									
1932	Det A	3	2	.600	16	6	2	0	56.1	63	42	2	3	41	14	4.47	105	.276	.393	17	.294	1	82	-2	—	-0.1
Goltz, Dave	David Allan; B6.23.1949 Pelican Rapids MN; BR/TR/6´4˝/(200–215); [MinA67 5/97]; d7.18																									
1972	Min A	3	3	.500	15	11	2	1-0	91	75	30	5	0	26-3	38	2.67	120	.224	.278	29-0-3	.103	-1	98	6	0	0.3
1973	Min A	6	4	.600	32	10	1	1-1	106.1	138	68	11	2	32-1	65	5.25	76	.318	.363	0	ø	0	133	-13	0	-1.1
1974	Min A	10	10	.500	28	24	5-1	1-0	174.1	192	81	14	7	45-1	89	3.25	115	.282	.330	0	ø	0	109	5	0	0.6
1975	Min A	14	14	.500	32	32	15-1	0-0	243	235	112	18	6	72-2	128	3.67	104	.255	.312	0	ø	0	96	5	0	0.6
1976	Min A	14	14	.500	36	35	13-4	0-0	249.1	239	113	14	5	91-4	133	3.36	106	.254	.320	0	ø	0*	97	4	0	0.4
1977	Min A	**20**	11	.645	39	**39**	19-2	0-0	303	284	129	23	2	91-4	186	3.36	119	.247	.303	0	ø	0*	124	20	0	1.8
1978	Min A	15	10	.600	29	29	13-2	0-0	220.1	209	72	12	1	67-1	116	2.49	154	.253	.307	0	ø	0	91	31	0	3.5
1979	Min A	14	13	.519	36	35	12-1	0-0	250.2	282	124	22	1	69-3	132	4.16	106	.288	.334	0	ø	0	96	7	0	0.7
1980	LA N	7	11	.389	35	27	2-2	1-1	171.1	198	91	12	0	59-3	91	4.31	81	.299	.353	47-0-7	.128	0	111	-17	0	-1.6
1981	†LA N	2	7	.222	26	8	0	1-4	77	83	35	4	0	25-3	48	4.09	81	.288	.343	17-0-2	.059	-1	118	-6	0	-0.7
1982	LA N	0	1	.000	2	1	0	0-0	3.2	6	4	0	0	0-0	3	4.91	71	.353	.353	1	.000	-0	76	-1	0	-0.3
	†Cal A	8	5	.615	28	7	1	3-0	86	82	43	4	1	32-1	49	4.08	100	.252	.317	0	ø	0	127	0	21	-0.1
1983	Cal A	0	6	.000	15	6	0	0-2	63.2	81	48	10	1	37-2	27	6.22	65	.315	.399	0	ø	0	97	-15	0	-1.3
Total	12	113	109	.509	353	264	83-13	8-8	2039.2	2104	950	149	26	646-28	1105	3.69	104	.269	.325	94-0-12	.106	-1	105	26	21	2.8
Gomes, Wayne	Wayne Maurice; B1.15.1973 Hampton VA; BR/TR/6´2˝/(220–227); [PhiN93 1/4]; d6.13; Col Old Dominion																									
1997	Phi N	5	1	.833	37	0	0	0-1	42.2	45	26	4	1	24-0	24	5.27	80	.274	.370	2	.000	0	—	-4	0	-0.6
1998	Phi N	9	6	.600	71	0	0	1-7	93.1	94	48	9	3	35-4	86	4.24	102	.258	.328	2	.000	-0	—	0	0	0.0
1999	Phi N	5	5	.500	73	0	0	19-5	74	70	38	5	2	56-2	58	4.26	110	.255	.381	1	.000	-0	—	3	0	0.4
2000	Phi N	4	6	.400	65	0	0	7-4	73.2	72	41	6	3	35-3	49	4.40	104	.262	.347	0	ø	0	—	1	31	0.0
2001	Phi N	4	3	.571	42	0	0	1-4	48	51	23	4	1	22-4	35	4.31	95	.276	.351	1	1.000	1	—	0	20	0.0
	SF N	2	0	1.000	13	0	0	0-0	15	21	14	3	0	7-2	17	8.40	49	.350	.412	0	ø	0	—	-7	15	-0.8
	Year	6	3	.667	55	0	0	1-4	63	72	37	7	1	29-6	52	5.29	78	.294	.366	1	1.000	1	—	-7	0	-0.8
2002	Bos A	1	2	.333	20	0	0	1-0	21.1	20	11	2	3	12-2	15	4.64	96	.241	.357	0	ø	0	—	0	0	0.0
Total	6	30	23	.566	321	0	0	29-21	368	373	201	33	13	191-17	284	4.60	96	.265	.356	6	.167	1	—	-7	66	-1.0
Gomez, Pat	Patrick Alexander; B3.17.1968 Roseville CA; BL/TL/5´11˝/185; [ChiN86 4/90]; d4.6																									
1993	SD N	1	2	.333	27	1	0	0-0	31.2	35	19	2	0	19-4	26	5.12	81	.292	.378	5	.000	-1*	87	-3	100	-0.3
1994	SF N	0	1	.000	26	0	0	0-0	33.1	23	14	2	0	20-1	14	3.78	107	.211	.328	2-0-1	.000	-0	—	2	0	0.0
1995	SF N	0	0	ø	18	0	0	0-0	14	16	8	2	0	12-1	15	5.14	80	.276	.400	1	.000	-0	—	-1	101	-0.1
Total	3	1	3	.250	71	1	0	0-0	79	74	41	6	0	51-6	55	4.56	90	.258	.363	8-0-1	.000	-1	87	-2	201	-0.4
Gomez, Ruben	Ruben (Colon); B7.13.1927 Arroyo, PR; D7.26.2004 Carolina, PR; BR/TR/6´0˝/(170–175); d4.17																									
1953	NY N	13	11	.542	29	26	13-3	0	204	166	89	17	4	101	113	3.40	126	.218	.313	72-0-6	.208	-0*	81	20	0	2.2
1954	†NY N	17	9	.654	37	32	10-4	0	221.2	202	85	20	7	109	106	2.88	140	.244	.336	81-2-4	.173	0*	104	27	0	3.0
1955	NY N	9	10	.474	33	31	9-3	1	185.1	207	103	20	7	63-6	79	4.56	88	.285	.345	60-0-4	.300	4*	103	-9	0	-0.3
1956	NY N	7	17	.292	40	31	4-2	0	196.1	191	108	19	9	77-8	76	4.58	83	.259	.334	60-0-1	.183	-0*	84	-15	0	-1.6
1957	NY N	15	13	.536	38	36	16-1	0	238.1	233	110	28	5	71-10	92	3.78	104	.254	.309	87-1-4	.184	1*	103	5	0	0.9
1958	SF N	10	12	.455	42	30	8-1	1	207.2	204	107	21	8	77-3	112	4.38	87	.261	.330	70-0-4	.200	1*	126	-10	0	-0.7
1959	Phi N	3	8	.273	20	12	2-1	1	72.1	90	55	12	0	24-2	37	6.10	67	.300	.350	17-0-3	.176	0*	82	-15	0	-2.0
1960	Phi N	0	3	.000	22	1	0	1	52.1	68	37	7	1	9-2	24	5.33	73	.321	.344	12-0-1	.083	-1	273	-9	0	-0.6
1962	Cle A	1	2	.333	15	4	0	1	45.1	50	23	5	2	25-3	21	4.37	89	.292	.383	13	.231	0*	104	-2	0	-0.1
	Min A	1	1	.500	6	2	1	0	19.1	17	11	3	0	11-2	8	4.66	88	.254	.354	5	.000	-0	87	-1	0	-0.1
	Year	2	3	.400	21	6	1	1	64.2	67	34	8	2	36-5	29	4.45	88	.282	.375	18	.167	-0	98	-3	0	-0.2
1967	Phi N	0	0	ø	7	0	0	0	11.1	8	6	2	0	7-3	9	3.97	86	.211	.333	0	ø	0	—	-1	0	0.0
Total	10	76	86	.469	289	205	63-15	5	1454	1436	734	154	43	574-39	677	4.09	97	.259	.331	477-3-27	.199	6	100	-10	0	0.7
Gomez, Lefty	Vernon Louis "Goofy"; B11.26.1908 Rodeo CA; D2.17.1989 Greenbrae CA; BL/TL/6´2˝/173; d4.29; Def 1943; HF1972																									
1930	NY A	2	5	.286	15	6	2	1	60	66	41	12	1	28	22	5.55	78	.280	.358	20-0-3	.150	-2	120	-7	—	-0.8
1931	NY A	21	9	.700	40	26	17-1	3	243	206	88	7	4	85	150	2.67	149	.226	.295	83-0-4	.133	-3	126	36	—	3.6
1932	†NY A	24	7	.774	37	31	21-1	1	265.1	266	140	23	2	105	176	4.21	97	.259	.329	104-0-5	.173	-1	145	-2	—	-0.5
1933	NY A★	16	10	.615	35	30	14-4	2	234.2	218	108	16	0	106	**163**	3.18	122	.240	.319	80-0-5	.112	-3	107	15	—	1.0
1934	NY A★	**26**	5	**.839**	38	33	**25-6**	1	**281.2**	223	86	12	0	96	**158**	**2.33**	174	**.215**	**.282**	99-0-13	.131	-3	125	**59**	—	5.5
1935	NY A★	12	15	.444	34	30	15-2	1	246	223	104	18	2	86	138	3.18	127	.242	.309	83-0-7	.120	-6	96	26	—	1.8
1936	†NY A☆	13	7	.650	31	30	10	0	188.2	184	104	6	1	122	105	4.39	106	.254	.362	69-0-8	.145	-3	117	6	—	0.2
1937	†NY A★	**21**	11	.656	34	34	25-**6**	0	278.1	233	88	10	1	93	**194**	**2.33**	191	**.223**	.287	105-0-5	.200	-1	106	**67**	—	**6.8**
1938	†NY A★	18	12	.600	32	32	20-**4**	0	239	239	110	7	1	99	129	3.35	135	.260	.332	86-0-9	.151	-2	107	31	—	3.2
1939	†NY A☆	12	8	.600	26	26	14-2	0	198	173	80	11	3	84	102	3.41	128	.235	.316	73-0-4	.151	-2	100	24	—	1.9
1940	NY A	3	3	.500	9	5	0	0	27.1	37	20	2	1	18	14	6.59	61	.325	.421	9	.000	-1	139	-7	—	-1.4
1941	NY A	15	5	**.750**	23	23	8-2	0	156.1	151	76	10	1	103	76	3.74	105	.250	.360	59-0-4	.153	-1	128	3	0	0.1
1942	NY A	6	4	.600	13	13	2	0	80	67	42	4	2	65	41	4.27	80	.237	.383	33-0-1	.152	-1	153	-7	0	-1.0
1943	Was A	0	1	.000	1	1	0	0	4.2	4	4	0	0	5	0	5.79	55	.250	.429	1	.000	-0	26	-2	0	-0.3
Total	14	189	102	.649	368	320	173-28	9	2503	2290	1091	138	19	1095	1468	3.34	125	.242	.321	904-0-68	.147	-30	117	242	0	20.1
Gonzales, Joe	Joe Madrid "Smokey"; B3.19.1915 San Francisco CA; D11.16.1996 Torrance CA; BR/TR/5´9˝/175; d8.25; Col USC																									
1937	Bos A	1	2	.333	8	2	2	0	31	37	16	1	0	11	11	4.35	109	.291	.348	10-0-1	.000	-2	73	2	—	0.0
Gonzales, Vince	Wenceslao (O'Reilly); B9.28.1925 Quivican, Cuba; D3.11.1981 Ciudad Del Carmen, Campeche, Mexico; BL/TL/6´1˝/165; d4.13																									
1955	Was A	0	0	ø	1	0	0	0	2	6	6	0	0	3-0	1	27.00	14	.500	.600	0	ø	0	—	-5	0	-0.2
Gonzalez, Dicky	Dicky Angel; B12.21.1978 Bayamon, PR; BR/TR/5´11˝/170; [NYN96 16/468]; d5.1																									
2001	NY N	3	2	.600	16	7	0	0-0	59	72	33	4	1	17-3	31	4.88	83	.306	.347	20-0-1	.100	-1	137	-5	0	-0.4
2004	TB A	0	0	ø	4	0	0	0-0	7.1	9	5	1	0	2-0	7	6.14	76	.310	.344	0	ø	0	—	-1	0	0.0
Total	2	3	2	.600	20	7	0	0-0	66.1	81	38	5	1	19-3	38	5.02	82	.307	.347	20-0-1	.100	-1	137	-6	0	-0.4
Gonzalez, Edgar	Edgardo Gerardo (Elizondo); B2.23.1983 San Nicolas de los Garza, Nuevo Leon, Mexico; BR/TR/6´0˝/(215–225); d6.1																									
2003	Ari N	2	1	.667	9	2	0	0-1	18.1	28	10	3	0	7-2	14	4.91	94	.368	.417	4-0-1	.250	0	132	0	0	0.0
2004	Ari N	0	9	.000	10	10	0	0-0	46.1	72	49	15	5	18-4	31	9.32	49	.362	.426	13-0-1	.154	-0	59	-21	0	-3.1
2005	Ari N	0	0	ø	1	0	0	0-0	0.1	2	4	1	0	2-0	1	108.00	4	.667	.800	0	ø	0	—	-4	0	-0.2
2006	Ari N	3	4	.429	11	5	0	0-0	42.2	45	20	7	3	9-0	28	4.22	111	.273	.320	13	.077	-1	75	3	0	0.3
Total	4	5	14	.263	31	17	0	0-1	107.2	147	83	26	8	36-6	74	6.85	67	.332	.390	30-0-2	.133	-1	72	-22	0	-3.0
Gonzalez, Enrique	Enrique Cesar; B8.6.1982 Ciudad Bolivar, Bolivar, Venezuela; BR/TR/5´10˝/210; d5.28																									
2006	Ari N	3	7	.300	22	18	0	0-0	106.1	114	71	14	4	34-0	66	5.67	82	.275	.334	32-0-3	.281	2*	89	-11	0	-0.7
Gonzalez, Gabe	Gabriel; B5.24.1972 Long Beach CA; BB/TL/6´1˝/150; [FlaN95 16/429]; d4.1; Col Cal St.–Long Beach																									
1998	Fla N	0	0	ø	3	0	0	0-0	1	1	1	0	1	1-0	0	9.00	45	.333	.600	0	ø	0	—	-1	0	0.0
Gonzalez, Jeremi	Geremis Segundo (Acosta); B1.8.1975 Maracaibo, Zulia, Venezuela; BR/TR/6´2˝/(180–220); d5.27; [DL 2000 Chi N 186]																									
1997	Chi N	11	9	.550	23	23	1-1	0-0	144	126	73	16	2	69-5	93	4.25	102	.236	.323	40-0-8	.100	-1	98	1	0	0.0
1998	Chi N	7	7	.500	20	20	1-1	0-0	110	124	72	13	3	41-5	70	5.32	83	.281	.344	32-0-8	.188	0*	111	-12	65	-1.3
2003	TB A	6	11	.353	25	25	2	0-0	156.1	131	71	18	12	69-1	97	3.91	117	.228	.319	6	.000	-1	71	13	0	1.1
2004	TB A	0	5	.000	11	8	0	0-0	50.1	72	42	9	3	20-0	22	6.97	67	.346	.406	0	ø	0	67	-12	0	-1.0
2005	†Bos A	2	1	.667	28	3	0	0-0	56	64	39	7	2	16-2	28	6.11	74	.288	.336	0	ø	0	109	-9	0	-0.4
2006	NY N	0	0	ø	3	3	0	0-0	14	21	12	4	0	6-1	8	7.71	57	.362	.415	3-0-2	.000	0	133	-5	0	-0.2

THE PITCHER REGISTER

YEAR	TM LG	W	L	PCT	G	GS	CG-SHO	SV-BS	IP	H	R	HR	HB	BB-IB	SO	ERA	AERA	OAV	OOB	AB-HR-SH	AVG	PB	SUP	APR	DL	PW
	Mil N	4	2	.667	21	1	0	0-1	42	50	31	6	2	17-1	36	5.14	87	.298	.365	5	.000	-1	103	-5	0	-0.7
	Year	4	2	.667	24	4	0	0-1	56	71	43	10	2	23-2	44	5.79	77	.314	.378	8-0-2	.000	-0	124	-10	0	-0.9
Total	6	30	35	.462	131	83	4-2	0-1	572.2	588	340	73	24	238-15	354	4.93	91	.267	.341	86-0-18	.116	-2	91	-29	251	-2.5
GONZALEZ, GERMAN	German Jose (Caraballo); B3.7.1962 Rio Caribe, Sucre, Venez.; BR/TR/6´0˝/170; d8.5																									
1988	Min A	0	0	ø	16	0	0	1-0	21.1	20	8	4	1	8-1	19	3.38	121	.244	.319	0	ø	0	—	2	0	0.1
1989	Min A	3	2	.600	22	0	0	0-0	29	32	17	2	4	11-1	25	4.66	89	.274	.353	0	ø	0	—	-2	38	-0.3
Total	2	3	2	.600	38	0	0	1-0	50.1	52	25	6	5	19-2	44	4.11	100	.261	.339	0	ø	0	—	0	38	-0.2
GONZALEZ, JULIO	Julio Enrique (Herrera); B12.20.1920 Banes, Cuba; D2.15.1991 Banes, Cuba; BR/TR/5´11˝/150; d8.9																									
1949	Was A	0	0	ø	13	0	0	0	34.1	33	20	3	1	27	5	4.72	90	.256	.389	5	.200	0	—	-2	0	0.0
GONZALEZ, LARIEL	Lariel Alfonso; B5.25.1976 San Cristobal, D.R.; BR/TR/6´4˝/228; d9.22																									
1998	Col N	0	0	ø	1	0	0	0-0	1	0	0	0	0	0-0	0	0.00	ø	.000	.000	0	ø	0	—	0	0	0.0
GONZALEZ, MIKE	Michael Vela; B5.23.1978 Corpus Christi TX; BR/TL/6´2˝/(200–220); [PitN97 30/902]; d8.11; Col San Jacinto (TX) JC																									
2003	Pit N	0	1	.000	16	0	0	0-0	8.1	7	7	4	0	6-0	6	7.56	57	.233	.351	0	ø	0	—	-3	0	-0.3
2004	Pit N	3	1	.750	47	0	0	1-3	43.1	32	7	2	1	6-0	55	1.25	348	.201	.235	1	1.000	1	—	15	0	1.3
2005	Pit N	1	3	.250	51	0	0	3-0	50	35	15	2	1	31-2	58	2.70	157	.197	.316	0	ø	0	—	9	54	0.8
2006	Pit N	3	4	.429	54	0	0	24-0	54	42	13	1	2	31-2	64	2.17	211	.213	.325	1	.000	-0	—	15	38	2.9
Total	4	7	9	.438	168	0	0	28-3	155.2	116	42	9	4	74-4	183	2.37	185	.206	.300	2	.500	1	—	36	92	4.7
GOOD, ANDREW	Andrew Richard; B9.19.1979 San Diego CA; BR/TR/6´3˝/(170–210); [AriN98 8/253]; d4.18																									
2003	Ari N	4	2	.667	16	10	0	0-0	66.1	74	42	15	3	16-3	42	5.29	87	.281	.325	16-0-4	.125	-1	89	-4	0	-0.4
2004	Ari N	1	2	.333	17	2	0	0-0	40.2	43	25	8	3	13-0	26	5.31	86	.272	.335	5	.000	-1	81	-2	87	-0.2
2005	Det A	0	0	ø	2	0	0	0-0	5	4	3	1	0	1-0	7	5.40	79	.211	.250	0	ø	0	—	-1	0	0.0
Total	3	5	4	.556	35	12	0	0-0	112	121	70	24	6	30-3	75	5.30	86	.275	.326	21-0-4	.095	-1	88	-7	87	-0.6
GOOD, RALPH	Ralph Nelson "Holy"; B4.25.1886 Monticello ME; D11.24.1965 Waterville ME; BR/TR/6´0˝/165; d7.1; Col Colby																									
1910	Bos N	0	0	ø	2	0	0	0	9	6	4	0	2	2	4	2.00	166	.188	.278	3	.000	-0	—	1	—	0.0
GOOD, WILBUR	Wilbur David "Lefty"; B9.28.1885 Punxsutawney PA; D12.30.1963 Brooksville FL; BL/TL/5´11.5˝/180; d8.18; ▲																									
1905	NY A	0	2	.000	5	2	0	0	19	18	17	1	0	14	13	4.74	62	.250	.372	8	.375	1	24	-4	—	-0.4
GOODALL, HERB	Herbert Frank; B3.10.1870 Mansfield PA; D1.20.1938 Mansfield PA; BR/TR/5´9˝/180; d4.29																									
1890	Lou AA	8	5	.615	18	13	8-1	**4**	109	94	73	2	10	51	46	3.39	114	.225	.324	45	.422	6*	103	5	—	1.1
GOODELL, JOHN	John Henry William "Lefty"; B4.5.1907 Muskogee OK; D9.21.1993 Mesquite TX; BR/TL/5´10˝/165; d4.19																									
1928	Chi A	0	0	ø	2	0	0	0	3	6	6	0	1	2	0	18.00	23	.500	.600	0	ø	0	—	-4	—	-0.2
GOODEN, DOC	Dwight Eugene "Doctor K"; B11.16.1964 Tampa FL; BR/TR/6´3˝/(190–210); [NYN82 1/5]; d4.7																									
1984	NY N★	17	9	.654	31	31	7-3	0-0	218	161	72	7	2	73-2	**276**	2.60	137	**.202**	**.269**	70-0-10	.200	1	92	**24**	0	3.0
1985	NY N☆	**24**	4	.857	35	35	**16**-8	0-0	**276.2**	198	51	13	2	69-4	**268**	**1.53**	**229**	.201	.254	93-1-9	.226	6	123	**63**	0	**7.6**
1986	†NY N★	17	6	.739	33	33	12-2	0-0	250	197	92	17	4	80-3	200	2.84	126	.215	.278	81-0-13	.086	-3	115	20	0	1.6
1987	NY N	15	7	**.682**	25	25	7-3	0-0	179.2	162	68	11	2	53-2	148	3.21	120	.244	.299	64-0-5	.219	2	119	15	60	1.9
1988	†NY N★	18	9	.667	34	34	10-3	0-0	248.1	242	98	8	6	57-4	175	3.19	102	.256	.301	90-1-9	.178	2	152	3	0	0.9
1989	NY N	9	4	.692	19	17	0	1-0	118.1	93	42	9	2	47-2	101	2.89	114	.211	.288	40-0-3	.200	2	96	6	62	0.8
1990	NY N	19	7	.731	34	34	2-1	0-0	232.2	229	106	10	7	70-3	223	3.83	98	.258	.314	75-1-14	.187	4*	141	0	0	0.5
1991	NY N	13	7	.650	27	27	3-1	0-0	190	185	80	12	3	56-2	150	3.60	102	.257	.311	63-1-8	.238	4	123	4	44	0.9
1992	NY N	10	13	.435	31	31	3	0-0	206	197	93	11	3	70-7	145	3.67	95	.255	.317	72-1-4	.264	6*	84	-4	21	0.3
1993	NY N	12	15	.444	29	29	7-2	0-0	208.2	188	89	16	9	61-1	149	3.45	116	.242	.302	70-2-6	.200	4*	91	14	0	2.2
1994	NY N	3	4	.429	7	7	0	0-0	41.1	46	32	9	1	15-1	40	6.31	66	.282	.346	12-0-4	.167	-0	112	-10	48	-1.3
1996	NY A	11	7	.611	29	29	1-1	0-0	170.2	169	101	19	9	88-4	126	5.01	99	.259	.352	0	ø	0	94	-1	0	-0.1
1997	†NY A	9	5	.643	20	19	0	0-0	106.1	116	61	14	7	53-1	66	4.91	91	.283	.373	4	.000	-0	100	-4	70	-0.5
1998	†Cle A	8	6	.571	23	23	0	0-0	134	135	59	13	9	51-0	83	3.76	127	.262	.337	2	.000	-0	84	15	53	1.4
1999	Cle A	3	4	.429	26	22	0	0-0	115	127	90	18	9	67-3	88	6.26	81	.282	.382	2-1-0	.500	2	140	-16	28	-0.6
2000	Hou N	0	0	ø	1	1	0	0-0	4	6	4	1	0	3-0	1	9.00	55	.353	.450	1	.000	-0	150	-2	0	-0.1
	TB A	2	3	.400	8	8	0	0-0	36.2	47	32	14	3	20-0	23	6.63	74	.315	.407	0	ø	0	86	-8	0	-0.9
	†NY A	4	2	.667	18	5	0	2-0	64.1	66	28	8	0	21-3	31	3.36	142	.266	.321	2	.000	-0	110	9	0	0.8
	Year	6	5	.545	26	13	0	2-0	101	113	60	22	3	41-3	54	4.54	106	.285	.354	2	.000	-0	96	2	0	-0.1
Total	16	194	112	.634	430	410	68-24	3-0	2800.2	2564	1198	210	78	954-42	2293	3.51	111	.244	.309	741-8-85	.196	29	113	128	386	18.4
GOODWIN, ART	Arthur Ingram; B2.27.1877 Whiteley Twnshp PA; D6.19.1943 Franklin Twp. PA; TR/5´8˝/195; d10.7																									
1905	NY A	0	0	ø	1	0	0	0	0.1	2	4	0	0	2	0	81.00	4	.667	.800	0	ø	0	—	-3	—	-0.1
GOODWIN, CLYDE	Clyde Samuel; B11.12.1886 Athens OH; D10.12.1963 Dayton OH; BR/TR/5´11˝/145; d9.18; Col Purdue																									
1906	Was A	0	2	.000	4	3	1	0	22.1	20	16	0	1	13	9	4.43	59	.244	.354	5-0-1	.200	-0	118	-5	—	-0.4
GOODWIN, JIM	James Patrick; B8.15.1926 St.Louis MO; BL/TL/6´1˝/170; d4.24																									
1948	Chi A	0	0	ø	8	1	0	1	10.1	9	11	0	1	12	3	8.71	49	.237	.431	2	.500	0	85	-5	0	-0.2
GOODWIN, MARV	Marvin Mardo; B1.16.1891 Gordonsville VA; D10.21.1925 Houston TX; BR/TR/5´11˝/168; d9.7; Mil 1918																									
1916	Was A	0	0	ø	3	0	0	0	5.2	5	4	0	0	3	1	3.18	88	.217	.308	1	.000	-0	—	-1	—	-0.1
1917	StL N	6	4	.600	14	12	6-3	0	85.1	70	33	1	0	19	38	2.21	122	.222	.266	23-0-5	.174	-0	100	1	—	0.2
1919	StL N	11	9	.550	33	17	7	0	179	163	66	3	8	33	48	2.51	111	.245	.289	60-0-1	.200	1*	127	5	—	0.6
1920	StL N	3	8	.273	32	12	3	1	116.1	153	79	1	5	28	23	4.95	60	.314	.357	35-0-3	.200	-0	119	-26	—	-2.5
1921	StL N	1	2	.333	14	4	1	1	36.1	47	21	1	1	9	7	3.72	99	.315	.358	6-0-3	.000	-1	157	-1	—	-0.1
1922	StL N	0	0	ø	2	0	0	0	4	3	1	0	0	3	0	2.25	172	.250	.400	0	ø	0	—	1	—	0.1
1925	Cin N	0	2	.000	4	3	2	0	20.2	26	14	2	1	5	4	4.79	86	.317	.364	4-0-1	.250	0	62	-2	—	-0.1
Total	7	21	25	.457	102	48	19-3	2	447.1	467	218	8	15	100	121	3.30	90	.269	.315	129-0-13	.186	0	117	-23	—	-1.9
GORDINIER, RAY	Raymond Cornelius "Gordy"; B4.11.1892 Rochester NY; D11.15.1960 Rochester NY; BB/TR/5´8.5˝/170; d9.17																									
1921	Bro N	1	0	1.000	3	3	0	0	12	10	8	0	0	8	4	5.25	74	.227	.346	4	.250	0	134	-2	—	-0.1
1922	Bro N	0	0	ø	5	0	0	0	11.1	13	11	3	0	8	5	8.74	47	.289	.396	2	.000	-0	—	-5	—	-0.3
Total	2	1	0	1.000	8	3	0	0	23.1	23	19	3	0	16	9	6.94	57	.258	.371	6	.167	-0	134	-7	—	-0.4
GORDON, DON	Donald Thomas; B10.10.1959 New York NY; BR/TR/6´1˝/(175–185); [DetA82 31/769]; d4.10; Col South Carolina																									
1986	Tor A	0	1	.000	14	0	0	1-1	21.2	28	20	1	1	8-1	13	7.06	60	.311	.366	0	ø	0	—	-7	0	-0.4
1987	Tor A	0	0	ø	5	0	0	0-0	11	8	5	2	0	3-0	3	4.09	111	.200	.256	0	ø	0	—	1	0	0.0
	Cle A	0	3	.000	21	0	0	1-0	39.2	49	31	3	4	12-3	20	4.08	112	.295	.353	0	ø	0	—	-2	0	-0.1
	Year	0	3	.000	26	0	0	1-0	50.2	57	36	5	4	15-3	23	4.09	112	.277	.335	0	ø	0	—	-3	0	-0.1
1988	Cle A	3	4	.429	38	0	0	1-2	59.1	65	33	5	3	19-3	20	4.40	94	.284	.341	0	ø	0	—	-2	0	-0.2
Total	3	3	8	.273	78	0	0	3-3	131.2	150	89	11	8	42-7	56	4.72	92	.286	.343	0	ø	0	—	-10	0	-0.7
GORDON, TOM	Thomas; B11.18.1967 Sebring FL; BR/TR/5´9˝/(160–195); [KCA86 6/157]; d9.8; [DL 2000 Bos A 181]																									
1988	KC A	0	2	.000	5	2	0	0-0	15.2	16	9	1	0	7-0	18	5.17	78	.267	.343	0	ø	0	57	-2	0	-0.2
1989	KC A	17	9	.654	49	16	1-1	1-6	163	122	67	10	1	86-4	153	3.64	106	.210	.311	0	ø	0	85	7	0	1.2
1990	KC A	12	11	.522	32	32	6-1	0-0	195.1	192	99	17	3	99-1	175	3.73	104	.257	.346	0	ø	0	115	0	0	0.0
1991	KC A	9	14	.391	45	14	1	1-3	158	129	76	16	4	87-6	167	3.87	107	.221	.324	0	ø	0*	99	5	0	0.7
1992	KC A	6	10	.375	40	11	0	0-2	117.2	116	67	9	4	55-4	98	4.59	89	.258	.340	0	ø	0	87	-7	20	-0.9
1993	KC A	12	6	.667	48	14	2	1-5	155.2	125	65	11	1	77-5	143	3.58	129	.223	.315	0	ø	0	103	17	0	1.9
1994	KC A	11	7	.611	24	24	0	0-0	155.1	136	79	15	3	87-3	126	4.35	116	.237	.336	0	ø	0	87	13	0	1.3
1995	KC A	12	12	.500	31	31	2	0-0	189	204	110	12	4	89-4	119	4.43	108	.279	.355	0	ø	0*	88	3	16	0.4
1996	Bos A	12	9	.571	34	34	4-1	0-0	215.2	249	143	28	4	105-5	171	5.59	91	.284	.359	0	ø	0	130	-8	0	-0.6
1997	Bos A	6	10	.375	42	25	2-1	11-2	182.2	155	85	10	3	78-1	159	3.74	124	.226	.306	0	ø	0	96	17	0	1.5
1998	†Bos A★	7	4	.636	73	0	0	**46**-1	79.1	55	24	2	0	25-1	78	2.72	174	.191	.254	0	ø	0	—	18	0	3.5
1999	†Bos A	0	2	.000	21	0	0	11-2	17.2	17	11	2	1	12-2	24	5.60	89	.246	.366	0	ø	0	—	-1	129	-0.1

YEAR	TM LG	W	L	PCT	G	GS	CG-SHO	SV-BS	IP	H	R	HR	HB	BB-IB	SO	ERA	AERA	OAV	OOB	AB-HR-SH	AVG	PB	SUP	APR	DL	PW
2001	Chi N	1	2	.333	47	0	0	27-4	45.1	32	18	4	1	16-1	67	3.38	124	.188	.262	0	ø	0	—	5	30	0.7
2002	Chi N	1	1	.500	19	0	0	0-0	23.2	27	12	1	1	10-1	31	3.42	118	.293	.369	0	ø	0	—	1	93	0.1
	Hou N	0	2	.000	15	0	0	0-0	19	15	7	2	0	6-2	17	3.32	130	.217	.280	1	.000	-0	—	2	0	0.2
	Year	1	3	.250	34	0	0	0-0	42.2	42	19	3	1	16-3	48	3.38	124	.261	.331	1	.000	-0	—	3	0	0.3
2003	Chi A	7	6	.538	66	0	0	12-5	74	57	29	4	4	31-3	91	3.16	145	.213	.301	0	ø	0	—	11	0	2.1
2004	†NY A★	9	4	.692	80	0	0	4-6	89.2	56	23	5	1	23-5	96	2.21	208	.180	.237	1	.000	-0	—	**24**	0	3.3
2005	†NY A	5	4	.556	79	0	0	2-7	80.2	59	25	8	0	29-4	69	2.57	168	.203	.272	0	ø	0	—	16	0	1.7
2006	Phi N★	3	4	.429	59	0	0	34-5	59.1	53	23	9	1	22-4	68	3.34	140	.233	.303	0	ø	0	—	9	21	1.8
Total	18	130	119	.522	809	203	18-4	150-48	2036.2	1815	972	166	36	944-56	1870	3.91	115	.238	.322	2	.000	-0	103	130	490	18.6
Gorecki, Rick	Richard John; B8.27.1973 Evergreen Park IL; BR/TR/6´3˝/167; [LAN91 19/507]; d9.10; [DL 1996 LA N 182, 1999 TB A 182]																									
1997	LA N	1	0	1.000	4	1	0	0-0	6	9	10	3	0	6-1	6	15.00	26	.346	.469	0-0-1	ø	0	212	-7	0	-1.0
1998	TB A	1	2	.333	3	3	0	0-0	16.2	15	9	1	0	10-0	7	4.86	99	.259	.357	0	ø	0	58	0	163	0.0
Total	2	2	2	.500	7	4	0	0-0	22.2	24	19	4	0	16-1	13	7.54	60	.286	.392	0-0-1	ø	0	92	-7	527	-1.0
Gorin, Charlie	Charles Perry; B2.6.1928 Waco TX; BL/TL/5´10˝/165; d5.29; Col Texas																									
1954	Mil N	0	1	.000	5	0	0	0	9.2	5	3	0	0	6	12	1.86	200	.152	.282	3	.000	-0	—	2	0	0.1
1955	Mil N	0	0	ø	2	0	0	0	0.1	1	2	0	0	3-0	0	54.00	7	.500	.800	0	ø	0	—	-2	0	-0.1
Total	2	0	1	.000	7	0	0	0	10	6	5	0	0	9-0	12	3.60	103	.171	.341	3	.000	-0	—	0	0	0.0
Gorman, Jack	John F. "Stooping Jack"; B1859 St.Louis MO; D9.9.1889 St.Louis MO; d7.1.1883; ▲																									
1884	Pit AA	1	2	.333	3	3	3	0	25	22	20	0	1	5	10	4.68	71	.212	.255	27	.148	-0*	91	-4	—	-0.4
Gorman, Tom	Thomas Aloysius; B1.4.1925 New York NY; D12.26.1992 Valley Stream NY; BR/TR/6´1˝/(190–200); d7.16																									
1952	†NY A	6	2	.750	12	6	1-1	1	60.2	63	34	8	2	22	31	4.60	72	.272	.340	23	.087	-1	127	-9	0	-1.2
1953	†NY A	4	5	.444	40	1	0	6	77	65	32	5	6	32	38	3.39	109	.226	.317	15-0-1	.133	-1	48	3	0	0.3
1954	NY A	0	0	ø	23	0	0	2	36.2	30	14	1	1	14	31	2.21	156	.222	.300	4	.000	-1	—	4	0	0.1
1955	KC A	7	6	.538	57	0	0	18	109	98	48	11	4	36-5	46	3.55	118	.246	.311	24-0-1	.083	-1	—	7	0	0.8
1956	KC A	9	10	.474	52	13	1	3	171.1	168	83	23	2	68-7	56	3.83	113	.258	.329	39-0-1	.051	-4	77	9	0	0.5
1957	KC A	5	9	.357	38	12	3-1	3	124.2	125	59	18	1	33-7	66	3.83	103	.261	.307	33-0-1	.121	-2	83	2	0	0.0
1958	KC A	4	4	.500	50	1	0	8	89.2	86	41	8	3	20-0	44	3.51	111	.258	.305	17	.118	-1	46	3	0	0.1
1959	KC A	1	0	1.000	17	0	0	1	20.1	24	21	3	1	14-0	9	7.08	57	.293	.398	0	ø	0	—	-8	0	-0.5
Total	8	36	36	.500	289	33	5-2	42	689.1	659	332	77	20	239-19	321	3.77	105	.254	.320	155-0-4	.090	-10	86	11	0	0.1
Gorman, Tom	Thomas David "Big Tom"; B3.16.1919 New York NY; D8.11.1986 Closter NJ; BR/TL/6´2˝/200; d9.14; U26																									
1939	NY N	0	0	ø	4	0	0	0	5	7	4	0	0	1	2	7.20	55	.350	.381	1	.000	-0	—	-2	—	-0.1
Gorman, Tom	Thomas Patrick; B12.16.1957 Portland OR; BL/TL/6´4˝/(195–200); [MonN80 4/99]; d9.2; Col Gonzaga																									
1981	Mon N	0	0	ø	9	0	0	0-0	15	12	7	0	1	6-2	13	4.20	85	.222	.306	0	ø	0	—	-1	0	0.0
1982	Mon N	1	0	1.000	5	0	0	0-0	7	8	4	0	0	4-0	6	5.14	72	.286	.364	0	ø	0	—	-1	0	-0.1
	NY N	0	1	.000	3	1	0	0-0	9.1	8	1	0	0	0-0	7	0.96	381	.235	.235	1-0-1	.000	-0	24	3	0	0.3
	Year	1	1	.500	8	1	0	0-0	16.1	16	5	0	0	4-0	13	2.76	134	.258	.299	1-0-1	.000	-0	24	2	0	0.2
1983	NY N	1	4	.200	25	4	0	0-0	49.1	45	29	3	0	15-4	30	4.93	75	.245	.299	4-0-1	.250	0	48	-6	0	-0.6
1984	NY N	6	0	1.000	36	0	0	0-2	57.2	51	20	6	1	13-3	40	2.97	120	.238	.284	3	.000	-0	—	5	0	0.4
1985	NY N	4	4	.500	34	2	0	0-3	52.2	56	32	8	0	18-2	32	5.13	68	.277	.335	5-0-1	.000	-1	126	-9	0	-1.3
1986	Phi N	0	1	.000	8	0	0	0-0	11.2	21	10	0	0	5-1	8	7.71	51	.382	.426	1	.000	-0	—	-4	0	-0.3
1987	SD N	0	0	ø	6	0	0	0-0	11	11	5	1	0	5-0	8	4.09	97	.262	.340	0	ø	0	—	0	37	0.0
Total	7	12	10	.545	126	7	0	0-5	213.2	212	108	18	2	66-12	144	4.34	84	.261	.315	14-0-3	.071	-1	66	-13	37	-1.6
Gormley, Joe	Joseph; B12.20.1866 Summit Hill PA; D7.2.1950 Summit Hill PA; BL/TL; d6.16																									
1891	Phi N	0	1	.000	1	1	1	0	8	10	8	0	0	5	2	5.63	61	.294	.385	4	.000	-1	53	-2	—	-0.2
Gornicki, Hank	Henry Frank; B1.14.1911 Niagara Falls NY; D2.16.1996 Riviera Beach FL; BR/TR/6´1˝/145; d4.17; Mil 1944–45																									
1941	StL N	1	0	1.000	4	1	1-1	0	11.1	6	4	0	1	9	6	3.18	118	.158	.333	4	.250	0	135	1	0	0.1
	Chi N	0	0	ø	1	0	0	0	2	3	1	0	0	0	2	4.50	78	.375	.375	0	ø	0	—	0	0	0.0
	Year	1	0	1.000	5	1	1-1	0	13.1	9	5	0	1	9	8	3.38	110	.196	.339	4	.250	0	137	1	0	0.1
1942	Pit N	5	6	.455	25	14	7-2	2	112	89	45	2	1	40	48	2.57	132	.215	.286	35-1-2	.114	-1	113	7	0	0.5
1943	Pit N	9	13	.409	42	18	4-1	4	147	165	86	10	2	47	63	3.98	87	.286	.342	40-0-2	.175	-1	80	-10	0	-1.5
1946	Pit N	0	0	ø	7	0	0	0	12.2	12	10	0	0	11	4	3.55	99	.255	.397	3	.000	-0	—	-2	0	-0.1
Total	4	15	19	.441	79	33	12-4	6	285	275	146	12	4	107	123	3.38	102	.254	.323	82-1-4	.146	-2	96	-4	0	-1.0
Gorsica, Johnny	John Joseph Perry (b John Joseph Perry Gorczyca); B3.29.1915 Bayonne NJ; D12.16.1998 Charlottesville VA; BR/TR/6´2˝/180; d4.22; Mil 1945–46; Col West Virginia																									
1940	†Det A	7	7	.500	29	20	5-2	0	160	170	85	10	4	57	68	4.33	110	.272	.337	62-1-1	.194	0	102	9	—	0.9
1941	Det A	9	11	.450	33	21	8-1	2	171	193	98	14	2	55	59	4.47	102	.281	.336	57-0-3	.298	4	75	1	0	0.7
1942	Det A	3	2	.600	28	0	0	4	53	63	31	2	3	26	19	4.75	83	.310	.397	10-0-1	.100	-0*	—	-3	0	-0.2
1943	Det A	4	5	.444	35	4	1	5	96.1	88	43	3	2	40	45	3.36	105	.247	.327	23-0-2	.174	0*	84	1	0	0.3
1944	Det A	6	14	.300	34	19	8-1	4	162	192	88	5	4	32	47	4.11	87	.296	.333	52	.135	-1*	88	-9	0	-1.0
1946	Det A	0	0	ø	14	0	0	1	23.2	28	13	5	0	11	14	4.56	80	.301	.375	3	.667	1	—	-2	0	0.0
1947	Det A	2	0	1.000	31	0	0	1	57.2	44	27	5	2	26	20	3.75	101	.208	.300	10	.200	0	—	0	0	0.1
Total	7	31	39	.443	204	64	22-4	17	723.2	778	385	44	17	247	272	4.18	98	.276	.338	217-1-7	.207	4	91	-3	0	0.8
Gorzelanny, Tom	Thomas Stephen; B7.12.1982 Evergreen Park IL; BL/TL/6´2˝/210; [PitN03 2/45]; d9.20; Col Triton (IL) JC																									
2005	Pit N	0	1	.000	3	1	0	0-0	6	10	8	1	0	3-0	3	12.00	35	.357	.419	1-0-1	.000	-0	89	-5	0	-0.6
2006	Pit N	2	5	.286	11	11	0	0-0	61.2	50	29	3	4	31-2	40	3.79	121	.226	.327	19-0-1	.000	-2	77	5	29	0.4
Total	2	2	6	.250	14	12	0	0-0	67.2	60	37	4	4	34-2	43	4.52	101	.241	.337	20-0-2	.000	-2	78	0	29	-0.2
Gosling, Mike	Michael F.; B9.23.1980 Madison WI; BL/TL/6´2˝/210; [AriN01 2/66]; d9.9; Col Stanford																									
2004	Ari N	1	1	.500	6	4	0	0-0	25.1	26	13	5	2	13-1	14	4.62	99	.274	.373	6-0-1	.000	-0	71	1	0	0.0
2005	Ari N	0	3	.000	13	5	0	0-0	32.1	40	20	2	0	19-2	14	4.45	99	.301	.388	6-0-1	.000	-1	94	-1	0	-0.2
2006	Cin N	0	0	ø	1	0	0	0-0	1.1	1	2	1	1	1-0	1	13.50	35	.200	.429	0	ø	0	—	-1	0	-0.1
Total	3	1	4	.200	20	9	0	0-0	59	67	35	8	3	33-3	29	4.73	95	.288	.383	12-0-2	.000	-1	83	-1	0	-0.3
Gossage, Rich	Richard Michael "Goose"; B7.5.1951 Colorado Springs CO; BR/TR/6´3˝/(180–226); [ChiA70 9/204]; d4.16																									
1972	Chi A	7	1	.875	36	1	0	2-0	80	72	44	2	4	44-3	57	4.27	73	.247	.351	16-0-1	.000	-2	57	-11	0	-1.4
1973	Chi A	0	4	.000	20	4	1	0-0	49.2	57	44	9	3	37-2	33	7.43	53	.311	.427	0	ø	0*	23	-18	0	-1.3
1974	Chi A	4	6	.400	39	3	0	1-1	89.1	92	45	4	2	47-7	64	4.13	91	.272	.361	0	ø	0	78	-3	0	-0.3
1975	Chi A★	9	8	.529	62	0	0	**26**-5	141.2	99	32	3	5	70-15	130	1.84	211	.201	.306	0	ø	0	—	**31**	0	5.1
1976	Chi A☆	9	17	.346	31	29	15	1-1	224	214	104	16	9	90-3	135	3.94	91	.254	.330	0	ø	0	75	-8	0	-0.9
1977	Pit N★	11	9	.550	72	0	0	26-10	133	78	27	9	2	49-6	151	1.62	248	.170	.250	23-0-1	.217	1	—	**34**	0	**6.4**
1978	†NY A★	10	11	.476	63	0	0	**27**-10	134.1	87	41	9	2	59-8	122	2.01	182	.187	.277	0	ø	0	—	**22**	0	4.3
1979	NY A	5	3	.625	36	0	0	18-3	58.1	48	18	5	0	19-4	41	2.62	157	.227	.291	0	ø	0	—	10	79	1.9
1980	†NY A★	6	2	.750	64	0	0	**33**-4	99	74	29	5	1	37-3	103	2.27	174	.211	.285	0	ø	0	—	19	0	2.8
1981	†NY A✳	3	2	.600	32	0	0	20-3	46.2	22	6	2	1	14-1	48	0.77	469	.141	.215	0	ø	0	—	14	0	3.0
1982	NY A☆	4	5	.444	56	0	0	30-9	93	63	23	5	0	28-5	102	2.23	181	.196	.259	0	ø	0	—	20	0	3.2
1983	NY A	13	5	.722	57	0	0	22-13	87.1	82	27	5	1	25-5	90	2.27	174	.248	.298	0	ø	0	—	16	0	3.1
1984	†SD N★	10	6	.625	62	0	0	25-11	102.1	75	34	6	1	36-4	84	2.90	124	.204	.275	22-0-2	.182	0	—	9	0	1.8
1985	SD N★	5	3	.625	50	0	0	26-6	79	64	21	1	1	17-1	52	1.82	195	.226	.269	11	.000	-1	—	14	24	2.2
1986	SD N	5	7	.417	45	0	0	21-11	64.2	69	36	8	2	20-0	63	4.45	82	.273	.326	7	.000	-1	—	-6	0	-1.3
1987	SD N	5	4	.556	40	0	0	11-6	52	47	18	4	0	19-6	44	3.12	127	.244	.307	4	.000	-0	—	6	19	1.1
1988	Chi N	4	4	.500	46	0	0	13-10	43.2	50	23	3	3	15-5	30	4.33	84	.291	.356	1	.000	-0	—	-3	15	-0.7
1989	SF N	2	1	.667	31	0	0	4-1	43.2	32	16	2	0	27-3	24	2.68	126	.212	.328	1	.000	-0	—	3	0	0.2
	NY A	1	0	1.000	11	0	0	1-0	14.1	14	6	0	1	3-1	6	3.77	103	.275	.327	0	ø	0	—	0	0	0.0
1991	Tex A	4	2	.667	44	0	0	1-4	40.1	33	16	4	3	16-1	28	3.57	113	.228	.317	0	ø	0	—	3	51	0.4
1992	Oak A	0	2	.000	30	0	0	0-1	38	32	13	5	2	19-4	26	2.84	133	.230	.327	0	ø	0	—	4	78	0.2
1993	Oak A	4	5	.444	39	0	0	1-3	47.2	49	24	6	1	26-2	40	4.53	91	.266	.357	0	ø	0	—	-1	26	-0.3

YEAR	TM LG	W	L	PCT	G	GS	CG-SHO	SV-BS	IP	H	R	HR	HB	BB-IB	SO	ERA	AERA	OAV	OOB	AB-HR-SH	AVG	PB	SUP	APR	DL	PW
1994	Sea A	3	0	1.000	36	0	0	1-0	47.1	44	23	6	3	15-1	29	4.18	118	.251	.318	0	ø	0	—	5	0	0.2
Total	22	124	107	.537	1002	37	16	310-112	1809.1	1497	670	119	47	732-90	1502	3.01	126	.228	.308	85-0-4	.106	-3	66	160	292	29.7
GOTT, JIM	James William; B8.3.1959 Hollywood CA; BR/TR/6´4˝/(200–230); [StLN77 4/84]; d4.9																									
1982	Tor A	5	10	.333	30	23	1-1	0-0	136	134	76	15	3	66-0	82	4.43	102	.255	.340	0	ø	0	64	0	0	0.0
1983	Tor A	9	14	.391	34	30	6-1	0-1	176.2	195	103	15	5	68-5	121	4.74	92	.280	.347	0	ø	0	97	-7	0	-0.9
1984	Tor A	7	6	.538	35	12	1-1	2-3	109.2	93	54	7	3	49-3	73	4.02	103	.233	.317	0	ø	0	97	1	0	0.1
1985	SF N	7	10	.412	26	26	2	0-0	148.1	144	73	10	1	51-3	78	3.88	89	.254	.315	51-3-4	.196	4	97	-7	0	-0.2
1986	SF N	0	0	ø	9	2	0	1-0	13	16	12	0	0	13-2	9	7.62	46	.314	.446	3	.000	0	177	-6	150	-0.3
1987	SF N	1	0	1.000	30	3	0	0-1	56	53	32	4	2	32-5	63	4.50	86	.244	.345	10-1-0	.100	1	165	-5	0	-0.2
	Pit N	0	2	.000	25	0	0	13-3	31	28	11	0	0	8-2	27	1.45	287	.233	.281	1	.000	-0	—	7	0	0.9
	Year	1	2	.333	55	3	0	13-4	87	81	43	4	2	40-7	90	3.41	116	.240	.324	11-1-0	.091	0	160	3	0	0.7
1988	Pit N	6	6	.500	67	0	0	34-6	77.1	68	30	9	2	22-5	76	3.49	99	.243	.300	1	.000	-0	—	1	0	0.2
1989	Pit N	0	0	ø	1	0	0	0-0	0.2	1	0	0	0	1-0	1	0.00	ø	.333	.500	0	ø	0	—	0	178	0.0
1990	LA N	3	5	.375	50	0	0	3-2	62	59	27	5	0	34-7	44	2.90	127	.257	.347	1	.000	-0	—	4	46	0.4
1991	LA N	4	3	.571	55	0	0	2-3	76	63	28	5	1	32-7	73	2.96	122	.223	.304	2-0-1	.500	0	—	6	0	0.6
1992	LA N	3	3	.500	68	0	0	6-1	88	72	27	4	1	41-13	75	2.45	141	.225	.314	2	.500	0	—	10	0	0.9
1993	LA N	4	8	.333	62	0	0	25-4	77.2	71	23	6	1	17-5	67	2.32	167	.248	.291	1	.000	-0	—	14	0	2.8
1994	LA N	5	3	.625	37	0	0	2-5	36.1	46	24	3	3	20-4	29	5.94	67	.322	.413	0	ø	0	—	-7	35	-1.4
1995	Pit N	2	4	.333	25	0	0	3-0	31.1	38	26	2	1	12-2	19	6.03	72	.288	.349	1	.000	-0	—	-7	91	-1.2
Total	14	56	74	.431	554	96	10-3	91-29	1120	1081	546	85	23	466-63	837	3.87	101	.254	.329	73-4-5	.178	5	96	4	500	1.7
GOULAIT, TED	Theodore Lee; B8.12.1889 St.Clair MI; D7.15.1936 St.Clair MI; BR/TR/5´9.5˝/172; d9.28																									
1912	NY N	0	0	ø	1	1	1	0	7	11	6	0	0	4	6	6.43	53	.367	.441	2-0-1	.500	0	130	-2	—	-0.1
GOULD, AL	Albert Frank "Pudgy"; B1.20.1893 Muscatine IA; D8.8.1982 San Jose CA; BR/TR/5´6.5˝/160; d7.11																									
1916	Cle A	5	6	.455	30	9	6-1	1	106.2	101	37	0	3	40	41	2.53	119	.256	.329	29-0-3	.103	-2	112	6	—	0.4
1917	Cle A	4	4	.500	27	7	1	0	94	95	44	1	3	52	24	3.64	78	.281	.382	24-0-1	.208	1	109	-5	—	-0.3
Total	2	9	10	.474	57	16	7-1	1	200.2	196	81	1	6	92	65	3.05	96	.267	.354	53-0-4	.151	-1	111	1	—	0.1
GOWELL, LARRY	Lawrence Clyde; B5.2.1948 Lewiston ME; BR/TR/6´2˝/190; [NYA67 4/61]; d9.21																									
1972	NY A	0	1	.000	2	1	0	0-0	7	3	1	0	0	2-0	7	1.29	233	.143	.208	1	1.000	1	0	1	0	0.3
GOZZO, MAURO	Mauro Paul; B3.7.1966 New Britain CT; BR/TR/6´3˝/(210–212); [NYN84 13/315]; d8.8																									
1989	Tor A	4	1	.800	9	3	0	0-1	31.2	35	19	1	1	9-1	10	4.83	79	.289	.338	0	ø	0	159	-4	0	-0.5
1990	Cle A	0	0	ø	2	0	0	0-0	3	2	0	0	0	2-0	2	0.00	ø	.182	.308	0	ø	0	—	1	0	0.1
1991	Cle A	0	0	ø	2	2	0	0-0	4.2	9	10	0	0	7-0	3	19.29	22	.450	.571	0	ø	0	164	-7	0	-0.3
1992	Min A	0	0	ø	2	0	0	0-0	1.2	7	5	2	0	0-0	1	27.00	15	.583	.583	0	ø	0	—	-4	0	-0.2
1993	NY N	0	1	.000	10	0	0	1-0	14	11	5	1	0	5-1	6	2.57	156	.212	.281	0	ø	0	—	2	0	0.1
1994	NY N	3	5	.375	23	8	0	0-1	69	86	48	5	1	28-10	33	4.83	87	.304	.363	16-0-1	.250	1	120	-8	0	-0.7
Total	6	7	7	.500	48	13	0	1-2	124	150	87	9	2	51-12	55	5.30	76	.301	.363	16-0-1	.250	1	136	-20	0	-1.5
GRABOW, JOHN	John William; B11.4.1978 Arcadia CA; BL/TL/6´2˝/(190–210); [PitN97 3/92]; d9.14																									
2003	Pit N	0	0	ø	5	0	0	0-0	5	6	3	0	0	0-0	9	3.60	120	.273	.273	0	ø	0	—	0	0	0.0
2004	Pit N	2	5	.286	68	0	0	1-6	61.2	81	39	8	0	28-7	64	5.11	85	.323	.389	1	.000	-0	—	-6	0	-0.5
2005	Pit N	2	3	.400	63	0	0	0-1	52	46	31	6	2	25-2	42	4.85	88	.238	.332	0	ø	0	—	-4	0	-0.3
2006	Pit N	4	2	.667	72	0	0	0-2	69.2	68	34	7	3	30-3	66	4.13	111	.260	.339	1	.000	-0	—	4	0	0.3
Total	4	8	10	.444	208	0	0	1-9	188.1	201	107	21	5	83-12	181	4.64	95	.276	.352	2	.000	-0	—	-6	0	-0.5
GRABOWSKI, AL	Alfons Francis; B9.4.1901 Syracuse NY; D10.29.1966 Memphis NY; BL/TL/5´11.5˝/175; d9.11; b–Reggie																									
1929	StL N	3	2	.600	6	6	4-2	0	50	44	18	0	0	8	22	2.52	185	.227	.257	16-0-1	.250	2	97	11	—	1.2
1930	StL N	6	4	.600	33	8	1	1	107	120	66	7	3	49	43	4.79	105	.290	.369	33	.364	3*	122	3	—	0.4
Total	2	9	6	.600	39	14	5-2	1	157	164	84	7	3	57	65	4.07	120	.270	.335	49-0-1	.327	4	111	14	—	1.6
GRABOWSKI, REGGIE	Reginald John; B7.16.1907 Syracuse NY; D4.2.1955 Syracuse NY; BR/TR/6´0.5˝/185; d4.15; b–Al																									
1932	Phi N	2	2	.500	14	2	0	0	34.1	38	18	2	2	22	15	3.67	120	.273	.380	6-0-1	.000	-1	95	2	—	0.1
1933	Phi N	1	3	.250	10	5	4-1	0	48	38	13	4	1	10	9	2.44	157	.220	.266	16	.125	-1	52	7	—	0.5
1934	Phi N	1	3	.250	27	5	0	0	65.1	114	72	13	3	23	13	9.23	51	.384	.433	18-0-1	.056	-2	88	-26	—	-1.6
Total	3	4	8	.333	51	12	4-1	0	147.2	190	103	19	6	55	37	5.73	76	.312	.375	40-0-2	.075	-3	75	-17	—	-1.0
GRACE, MIKE	Michael James; B6.20.1970 Joliet IL; BR/TR/6´4˝/(210–224); [PhiN91 10/265]; d9.1; Col Bradley																									
1995	Phi N	1	1	.500	2	2	0	0-0	11.1	10	4	0	0	4-0	7	3.18	133	.238	.304	2-0-2	.000	-0	43	1	0	0.2
1996	Phi N	7	2	.778	12	12	1-1	0-0	80	72	33	9	1	16-1	49	3.49	124	.238	.279	29-0-1	.138	-0	101	8	119	0.9
1997	Phi N	3	2	.600	6	6	1-1	0-0	39	32	16	3	1	10-1	26	3.46	122	.230	.285	12	.083	-1	95	3	85	0.3
1998	Phi N	4	7	.364	21	15	0	0-0	90.1	116	61	10	8	30-1	46	5.48	79	.312	.375	23-0-3	.087	-1	108	-12	0	-1.4
1999	Phi N	1	4	.200	27	5	0	0-0	55	80	48	5	6	30-0	28	7.69	61	.346	.430	7-0-3	.000	-1	63	-17	0	-1.3
Total	5	16	16	.500	68	40	2-2	0-0	275.2	310	162	27	16	90-3	156	4.96	88	.285	.348	73-0-9	.096	-2	94	-17	204	-1.3
GRACESQUI, FRANKLYN	Franklyn Benjamin; B8.20.1979 Santo Domingo, D.R.; BB/TL/6´5˝/210; [TorA98 21/621]; d4.29																									
2004	Fla N	0	1	.000	7	0	0	1-0	4	6	5	0	2	3-0	1	11.25	37	.333	.478	0	ø	0	—	-3	0	-0.6
GRAFF, JOHN	John J.; B11.1866 Washington DC; D4.2.1932 Washington DC; d7.19																									
1893	Was N	0	1	.000	2	1	1	0	12	21	21	2	1	13	4	11.25	41	.368	.493	5	.200	-0	60	-9	—	-0.5
GRAHAM, SKINNY	Kyle; B8.14.1899 Oak Grove AL; D12.1.1973 Oak Grove AL; BR/TR/6´2˝/172; d9.3																									
1924	Bos N	0	4	.000	5	4	1	0	33	33	14	0	0	11	15	3.82	100	.287	.349	7-0-2	.000	-1	17	1	—	0.0
1925	Bos N	7	12	.368	34	23	5	1	157	177	90	6	3	62	32	4.41	91	.296	.365	44-0-7	.136	-2	81	-6	—	-0.9
1926	Bos N	3	3	.500	15	4	1	0	36.1	54	32	3	2	19	7	7.93	45	.370	.449	12	.167	-1	153	-16	—	-2.3
1929	Det A	1	3	.250	13	6	2	1	51.2	70	41	2	3	33	7	5.57	77	.340	.438	19-1-0	.105	-1	183	-8	—	-0.7
Total	4	11	22	.333	67	37	9	2	278	334	177	11	8	125	61	5.02	79	.314	.390	82-1-9	.122	-5	100	-29	—	-3.9
GRAHAM, OSCAR	Oscar Marion; B7.20.1878 Plattsmouth NE; D10.15.1931 Moline IL; BL/TL/6´0.5˝/180; d4.16																									
1907	Was A	4	9	.308	20	14	6	0	104	116	66	3	10	29	44	3.98	61	.284	.347	48-1-1	.229	3*	128	-18	—	-1.8
GRAHAM, BILL	William Albert; B1.21.1937 Flemingsburg KY; D10.26.2006 Flemingsburg KY; BR/TR/6´3˝/(210–217); d10.2; Col Florida																									
1966	Det A	0	0	ø	1	0	0	0	2	2	0	0	0	0-0	2	0.00	ø	.250	.250	0	ø	0	—	1	0	0.0
1967	NY N	1	2	.333	5	3	1	0	27.1	20	10	3	0	11-0	14	2.63	129	.200	.279	8	.125	-0	43	2	0	0.1
Total	2	1	2	.333	6	3	1	0	29.1	22	10	3	0	11-0	16	2.45	138	.204	.277	8	.125	-0	43	3	0	0.1
GRAHAME, BILL	William James; B7.22.1884 Owosso MI; D2.15.1936 Holt MI; TL/6´0˝/?; d4.18																									
1908	StL A	6	7	.462	21	13	7	0	117.1	104	46	0	12	32	47	2.30	104	.240	.310	42-0-2	.119	-3	83	0	—	-0.3
1909	StL A	8	14	.364	34	21	13-3	1	187.1	171	78	3	5	60	82	3.12	77	.256	.322	63	.159	-0	86	-12	—	-1.4
1910	StL A	0	8	.000	9	6	1	0	43	46	31	2	4	13	12	3.56	70	.297	.366	13	.154	-0	41	-7	—	-1.3
Total	3	14	29	.326	64	40	21-3	1	347.2	321	155	5	21	105	141	2.90	83	.256	.323	118-0-2	.144	-3	78	-19	—	-3.0
GRAHE, JOE	Joseph Milton; B8.14.1967 W.Palm Beach FL; BR/TR/6´0˝/(185–200); [CalA89 2/39]; d8.4; Col Miami																									
1990	Cal A	3	4	.429	8	8	0	0-0	43.1	51	30	3	3	23-1	25	4.98	77	.293	.385	0	ø	0	101	-7	0	-0.9
1991	Cal A	3	7	.300	18	10	1	0-0	73	84	43	2	3	33-0	40	4.81	86	.288	.365	0	ø	0	64	-6	0	-0.7
1992	Cal A	5	6	.455	46	7	0	21-3	94.2	85	37	5	6	39-2	39	3.52	114	.246	.329	0	ø	0	107	7	0	1.0
1993	Cal A	4	1	.800	45	0	0	11-2	56.2	54	22	5	2	25-4	31	2.86	159	.251	.331	0	ø	0	—	9	40	1.1
1994	Cal A	2	5	.286	40	0	0	13-6	43.1	68	33	5	6	18-4	26	6.65	74	.362	.428	0	ø	0	—	-8	0	-1.4
1995	Col N	4	3	.571	17	9	0	0-0	56.2	69	42	6	3	27-2	27	5.08	106	.301	.378	12-0-6	.417	1	99	-1	45	0.0
1999	Phi N	1	4	.200	13	5	0	0-0	32.2	40	16	1	3	17-0	16	3.86	121	.308	.392	7	.143	0	43	2	0	0.3
Total	7	22	30	.423	187	39	1	45-11	400.1	451	223	27	26	182-13	204	4.41	101	.287	.366	19-0-6	.316	1	85	-4	85	-0.6

YEAR	TM LG	W	L	PCT	G	GS	CG-SHO	SV-BS	IP	H	R	HR	HB	BB-IB	SO	ERA	AERA	OAV	OOB	AB-HR-SH	AVG	PB	SUP	APR	DL	PW
GRAMAN, ALEX	Alex Joseph; B11.17.1977 Huntingburg IN; BL/TL/6´4˝/210; [NYA99 3/111]; d4.20; Col Indiana St.																									
2004	NY A	0	0	ø	3	2	0	0-0	5	14	11	1	0	2-0	4	19.80	23	.500	.516	0	ø	0	181	-8	0	-0.4
2005	NY A	0	0	ø	2	0	0	0-0	1.1	3	2	1	0	2-1	0	13.50	32	.429	.556	0	ø	0	—	-1	0	-0.1
Total	2	0	0	ø	5	2	0	0-0	6.1	17	13	2	0	4-1	4	18.47	25	.486	.525	0	ø	0	181	-9	0	-0.5
GRAMLY, TOMMY	Bert Thomas; B4.19.1945 Dallas TX; BR/TR/6´3˝/175; [CleA66 S4/75]; d4.18; Col TCU																									
1968	Cle A	0	1	.000	3	0	0	0	3.1	3	1	0	0	2-2	1	2.70	110	.250	.357	0	ø	0*	—	0	0	0.0
GRAMPP, HANK	Henry Eckhard; B9.28.1903 New York NY; D3.24.1986 New York NY; BR/TR/6´1˝/185; d6.21																									
1927	Chi N	0	0	ø	2	0	0	0	3	4	3	0	0	1	3	9.00	43	.333	.385	0	ø	0	—	-2	—	-0.1
1929	Chi N	0	1	.000	1	1	0	0	2	4	6	0	1	3	0	27.00	17	.500	.667	0	ø	0	57	-5	—	-0.6
Total	2	0	1	.000	3	1	0	0	5	8	9	0	1	4	3	16.20	26	.400	.520	0	ø	0	57	-7	—	-0.7
GRANGER, JEFF	Jeffrey Adam; B12.16.1971 San Pedro CA; BR/TL/6´4˝/200; [KCA93 1/5]; d9.16; Col Texas A&M																									
1993	KC A	0	0	ø	1	0	0	0-0	1	3	3	0	0	2-0	1	27.00	17	.500	.625	0	ø	0	—	-2	0	-0.1
1994	KC A	0	1	.000	2	2	0	0-0	9.1	13	8	2	0	6-0	3	6.75	74	.325	.404	0	ø	0	73	-2	0	-0.2
1996	KC A	0	0	ø	15	0	0	0-0	16.1	21	13	3	2	10-0	11	6.61	76	.313	.412	0	ø	0	—	-3	0	-0.1
1997	Pit N	0	0	ø	9	0	0	0-0	5	10	10	3	0	8-1	4	18.00	24	.417	.563	0	ø	0	—	-7	0	-0.3
Total	4	0	1	.000	27	2	0	0-0	31.2	47	34	8	2	26-1	19	9.09	54	.343	.449	0	ø	0	73	-14	0	-0.7
GRANGER, WAYNE	Wayne Allan; B3.15.1944 Springfield MA; BR/TR/6´2˝/(165–170); d6.5; Col Springfield																									
1968	†StL N	4	2	.667	34	0	0	4	44	40	14	2	2	12-3	27	2.25	129	.238	.297	5	.200	0	—	3	0	0.5
1969	Cin N	9	6	.600	**90**	0	0	27-10	144.2	143	64	10	7	40-14	68	2.80	134	.262	.316	21-0-3	.095	-0	—	10	0	1.4
1970	†Cin N	6	5	.545	67	0	0	**35**-4	84.2	79	33	5	1	27-8	38	2.66	152	.252	.311	10	.100	-1	—	11	0	2.3
1971	Cin N	7	6	.538	**70**	0	0	11-0	100	94	39	8	1	28-7	51	3.33	101	.251	.303	7-1-1	.143	1	—	1	0	0.4
1972	Min A	4	6	.400	63	0	0	19-6	89.2	83	42	7	2	28-6	45	3.01	107	.243	.303	10	.200	0	—	0	0	-0.1
1973	StL N	2	4	.333	33	0	0	5-4	46.2	50	29	3	2	21-7	14	4.24	87	.284	.363	3	.000	-0	—	-5	0	-0.7
	NY A	0	1	.000	7	0	0	0-0	15.1	19	7	1	1	3-1	10	1.76	211	.279	.319	0	ø	0	—	2	0	0.1
1974	Chi A	0	0	ø	5	0	0	0-0	7.2	16	8	1	0	3-0	4	8.22	46	.432	.475	0	ø	0	—	-4	0	-0.2
1975	Hou N	2	5	.286	55	0	0	5-3	74	76	39	7	4	23-7	30	3.65	93	.264	.324	9	.000	-1	—	-5	0	-0.6
1976	Mon N	1	0	1.000	27	0	0	2-2	32	32	15	3	2	16-4	16	3.66	103	.264	.355	3-0-2	.000	-0	—	0	0	0.0
Total	9	35	35	.500	451	0	0	108-29	638.2	632	290	47	22	201-57	303	3.14	113	.260	.319	68-1-6	.103	-1	—	13	0	3.1
GRANT, GEORGE	George Addison; B1.6.1903 E.Tallassee AL; D3.25.1986 Montgomery AL; BR/TR/5´11.5˝/175; d9.17; Col Auburn																									
1923	StL A	0	0	ø	4	0	0	0	8.2	15	7	0	0	3	2	5.19	80	.395	.439	2	.000	-0	—	-1	—	-0.1
1924	StL A	1	2	.333	22	2	0	0	51.1	69	43	4	1	25	11	6.31	72	.325	.399	13	.000	-2	75	-10	—	-0.7
1925	StL A	0	2	.000	12	0	0	0	16.1	26	15	2	0	8	7	6.06	77	.400	.466	4	.250	-0	—	-3	—	-0.3
1927	Cle A	4	6	.400	25	3	2	1	74.2	85	46	1	0	40	19	4.46	94	.300	.387	21-0-2	.095	-2	146	-3	—	-0.5
1928	Cle A	10	8	.556	28	18	6-1	0	155.1	196	102	7	2	76	39	5.04	82	.319	.395	60-0-2	.183	-2*	91	-14	—	-1.4
1929	Cle A	0	2	.000	12	0	0	0	24	41	29	2	0	23	5	10.50	42	.414	.525	2	.000	-0	—	-14	—	-0.9
1931	Pit N	0	0	ø	11	0	0	0	17	28	16	0	1	7	6	7.41	52	.364	.424	2	.000	-0	—	-6	—	-0.3
Total	7	15	20	.429	114	23	8-1	1	347.1	460	258	16	4	182	89	5.65	75	.331	.410	104-0-4	.135	-8	95	-51	—	-4.2
GRANT, JIM	James Ronald; B8.4.1894 Coalville IA; D11.30.1985 Des Moines IA; BR/TL/5´11˝/180; d4.21																									
1923	Phi N	0	0	ø	2	0	0	0	4	10	8	0	1	4	0	13.50	34	.588	.682	1	.000	-0	—	-4	—	-0.2
GRANT, MUDCAT	James Timothy "Jim"; B8.13.1935 Lacoochee FL; BR/TR/6´1˝/(184–195); d4.17																									
1958	Cle A	10	11	.476	44	28	11-1	4	204	173	93	20	1	104-5	111	3.84	95	.228	.317	66-0-4	.076	-4*	106	-3	0	-0.8
1959	Cle A	10	7	.588	38	19	6-1	3	165.1	140	80	23	2	81-4	85	4.14	89	.232	.323	55-1-1	.200	1*	100	-6	0	-0.5
1960	Cle A	9	8	.529	33	19	5	0	159.2	147	88	26	2	78-4	75	4.40	85	.243	.330	57-0-1	.281	4*	133	-12	0	-0.8
1961	Cle A	15	9	.625	35	35	11-3	0	244.2	207	118	32	3	109-3	146	3.86	102	.227	.310	88-1-5	.170	1*	123	2	0	0.3
1962	Cle A	7	10	.412	26	23	6-1	0	149.2	128	75	24	0	81-4	90	4.27	91	.233	.330	53-0-1	.151	-0*	99	-5	0	-0.5
1963	Cle A☆	13	14	.481	38	32	10-2	1	229.1	213	107	30	4	87-3	157	3.69	98	.243	.312	69-1-7	.188	3*	100	-2	0	-0.1
1964	Cle A	3	4	.429	13	9	1	0	62	82	41	11	1	25-2	43	5.95	60	.324	.384	22-2-1	.273	4*	112	-14	0	-1.0
	Min A	11	9	.550	26	23	10-1	1	166	162	73	21	0	36-2	75	2.82	127	.248	.286	60-0-2	.167	0*	139	9	0	1.0
	Year	14	13	.519	39	32	11-1	1	228	244	114	32	1	61-4	118	3.67	98	.270	.314	82-2-3	.195	4	132	-5	0	0.0
1965	†Min A★	**21**	7	**.750**	41	39	14-**6**	0	270.1	252	107	34	0	61-2	142	3.30	108	.247	.287	97-0-5	.155	2*	135	12	0	1.4
1966	Min A	13	13	.500	35	35	10-3	0	249	248	104	23	6	49-2	110	3.25	111	.260	.298	78-0-10	.192	2	96	9	0	1.3
1967	Min A	5	6	.455	27	14	2	0	95.1	121	56	10	1	17-0	50	4.72	73	.315	.343	28-0-2	.179	0	131	-12	0	-1.4
1968	LA N	6	4	.600	37	4	1	3	95	77	29	1	6	19-3	35	2.08	133	.226	.275	31-1-0	.129	0*	94	6	0	0.8
1969	Mon N	1	6	.143	11	10	1	0-0	50.2	64	33	7	1	14-1	20	4.80	77	.299	.343	16	.125	-1	91	-7	0	-0.9
	StL N	7	5	.583	30	3	1	7-2	63.1	62	31	9	2	22-8	35	4.12	87	.252	.319	17-0-2	.294	2*	82	-3	0	-0.5
	Year	8	11	.421	41	13	2	7-2	114	126	64	16	3	36-9	55	4.42	82	.274	.330	33-0-2	.212	1	90	-10	0	-1.4
1970	Oak A	6	2	.750	72	0	0	24-1	123.1	104	26	8	3	30-8	54	1.82	193	.235	.287	9-0-5	.222	2	—	**26**	0	2.8
	Pit N	2	1	.667	8	0	0	0-1	12	8	3	2	0	2-0	4	2.25	176	.190	.227	2	.000	-0	—	2	0	0.5
1971	Pit N	5	3	.625	42	0	0	7-4	75	79	32	8	1	28-8	22	3.60	94	.274	.340	8	.250	1	—	-1	0	0.0
	†Oak A	1	0	1.000	15	0	0	3-1	27.1	25	9	3	0	6-0	13	1.98	168	.243	.284	3-0-2	.333	0	—	3	0	0.2
Total	14	145	119	.549	571	293	89-18	53-9	2442	2292	1105	292	33	849-59	1267	3.63	100	.248	.311	759-6-48	.178	16	115	4	0	1.8
GRANT, MARK	Mark Andrew; B10.24.1963 Aurora IL; BR/TR/6´2˝/(195–215); [SFN81 1/10]; d4.27; [DL 1991 Atl N 182]																									
1984	SF N	1	4	.200	11	10	0	1-0	53.2	56	40	6	1	19-0	32	6.37	55	.272	.332	17-0-2	.000	-2	110	-16	19	-1.5
1986	SF N	0	1	.000	4	1	0	0-0	10	6	4	0	0	5-0	5	3.60	98	.176	.282	1-0-1	.000	-0	25	0	0	0.0
1987	SF N	1	2	.333	16	8	0	1-0	61	66	29	6	1	21-5	32	3.54	109	.282	.342	12-0-3	.083	-0	94	1	0	0.0
	SD N	6	7	.462	17	17	2-1	0-0	102.1	104	59	16	0	52-3	58	4.66	85	.263	.348	32-0-3	.094	-1*	87	-8	0	-1.0
	Year	7	9	.438	33	25	2-1	1-0	163.1	170	88	22	1	73-8	90	4.24	92	.270	.346	44-0-6	.091	-1	89	-7	0	-1.0
1988	SD N	2	8	.200	33	11	0	0-1	97.2	97	41	14	2	36-6	61	3.69	92	.268	.334	16-0-4	.000	-1	62	-2	0	-0.3
1989	SD N	8	2	.800	50	0	0	2-1	116.1	105	45	11	3	32-6	69	3.33	105	.248	.304	20-0-1	.050	-0	—	4	0	0.3
1990	SD N	1	1	.500	26	0	0	0-1	39	47	23	5	0	19-8	29	4.85	79	.305	.375	2	.500	0	—	-4	0	-0.1
	Atl N	1	2	.333	33	1	0	3-2	52.1	61	30	4	1	18-3	40	4.64	87	.293	.349	4	.250	1	90	-3	0	-0.2
	Year	2	3	.400	59	1	0	3-3	91.1	108	53	9	1	37-11	69	4.73	84	.298	.360	6	.333	1	91	-7	0	-0.3
1992	Sea A	2	4	.333	23	10	0	0-0	81	100	39	6	2	22-2	42	3.89	103	.311	.357	0	ø	0	103	1	0	0.0
1993	Hou N	0	0	ø	6	0	0	0-0	11	11	4	0	0	5-2	6	0.82	474	.275	.348	0	ø	0	—	3	0	0.2
	Col N	0	1	.000	14	0	0	1-1	14.1	23	20	4	0	6-1	8	12.56	38	.377	.426	0	ø	0	—	-10	34	-0.7
	Year	0	1	.000	20	0	0	1-1	25.1	34	24	4	0	11-3	14	7.46	59	.337	.395	0	ø	0	—	-8	0	-0.5
Total	8	22	32	.407	233	58	2-1	8-6	638.2	676	334	72	10	235-36	382	4.31	87	.277	.341	104-0-14	.067	-3	89	-34	235	-3.3
GRAPENTHIN, RICK	Richard Ray; B4.16.1958 Linn Grove IA; BR/TR/6´2˝/(190–210); d5.3; Col Indiana St.																									
1983	Mon N	0	1	.000	1	0	0	0-0	4	4	4	2	0	1-0	3	9.00	40	.267	.313	1	.000	-0	—	-2	0	-0.4
1984	Mon N	1	2	.333	13	1	0	2-0	23	19	9	3	0	7-0	9	3.52	98	.235	.289	5	.200	0	77	0	0	0.1
1985	Mon N	0	0	ø	5	0	0	0-0	7	13	11	0	1	8-2	4	14.14	24	.394	.512	1	1.000	0	—	-8	0	-0.4
Total	3	1	3	.250	19	1	0	2-0	34	36	24	5	1	16-2	16	6.35	55	.279	.356	7	.286	0	77	-10	0	-0.7
GRASMICK, LOU	Louis Junior; B9.11.1924 Baltimore MD; BR/TR/6´0˝/195; d4.22																									
1948	Phi N	0	0	ø	2	0	0	0	5	3	4	1	0	8	2	7.20	55	.176	.440	1	1.000	0	—	-2	0	0.0
GRATE, DON	Donald "Buckeye"; B8.27.1923 Greenfield OH; BR/TR/6´2.5˝/180; d7.6; Col Ohio St.																									
1945	Phi N	0	1	.000	4	2	0	0	8.1	18	16	0	0	12	6	17.28	22	.439	.566	3	.000	-0*	55	-11	0	-1.1
1946	Phi N	1	0	1.000	3	0	0	0	8	4	1	0	0	2	2	1.13	305	.160	.222	1	.000	0	—	2	0	0.3
Total	2	1	1	.500	7	2	0	0	16.1	22	17	0	0	14	8	9.37	39	.333	.450	4	.000	-0	55	-9	0	-0.8
GRATER, MARK	Mark Anthony; B1.19.1964 Rochester PA; BR/TR/5´10˝/205; [StLN86 23/594]; d6.12; Col Florida International																									
1991	StL N	0	0	ø	3	0	0	0-0	3	5	0	0	0	2-0	0	0.00	ø	.385	.467	0	ø	0	—	1	0	0.1
1993	Det A	0	0	ø	6	0	0	0-0	5	6	3	0	0	4-1	4	5.40	81	.286	.400	0	ø	0	—	0	0	0.0
Total	2	0	0	ø	9	0	0	0-0	8	11	3	0	0	6-1	4	3.38	122	.324	.425	0	ø	0	—	1	0	0.1

YEAR	TM LG	W	L	PCT	G	GS	CG-SHO	SV-BS	IP	H	R	HR	HB	BB-IB	SO	ERA	AERA	OAV	OOB ○	AB-HR-SH	AVG	PB	SUP	APR	DL	PW
Graterol, Beiker	Beiker; B11.9.1974 Lara, Venezuela; BR/TR/6´2˝/165; d4.9																									
1999	Det A	0	1	.000	1	1	0	0-0	4	4	7	3	0	4-1	2	15.75	32	.250	.400	0	ø	0	56	-4	0	-0.6
Graves, Danny	Daniel Peter; B8.7.1973 Saigon, South Vietnam; BR/TR/5´11˝/(185–200); [CleA94 4/101]; d7.13; Col Miami																									
1996	Cle A	2	0	1.000	15	0	0	0-1	29.2	29	18	2	0	10-0	22	4.55	107	.246	.302	0	ø	0	—	0	0	0.0
1997	Cle A	0	0	ø	5	0	0	0-0	11.1	15	8	2	0	9-0	4	4.76	99	.326	.429	0	ø	0	—	-1	0	-0.1
	Cin N	0	0	ø	10	0	0	0-0	14.2	26	14	0	0	11-1	7	6.14	70	.413	.493	1	.000	-0	—	-4	0	-0.2
1998	Cin N	2	1	.667	62	0	0	8-0	81.1	76	31	6	2	28-4	44	3.32	129	.251	.314	4	.000	-0	—	9	0	0.4
1999	Cin N	8	7	.533	75	0	0	27-9	111	90	42	10	2	49-4	69	3.08	152	.227	.314	5	.000	-1	—	19	0	3.1
2000	Cin N★	10	5	.667	66	0	0	30-5	91.1	81	31	8	3	42-7	53	2.56	186	.243	.330	2-1-0	.500	2	—	21	0	4.3
2001	Cin N	6	5	.545	66	0	0	32-7	80.1	83	41	7	4	18-6	49	4.15	111	.268	.314	4-1-0	.250	1	—	4	0	0.9
2002	Cin N	7	3	.700	68	4	0	32-7	98.2	99	37	7	3	25-9	58	3.19	134	.264	.311	6-0-2	.000	-1*	43	12	0	1.9
2003	Cin N	4	15	.211	30	26	2-1	2-0	169	204	108	30	7	41-6	60	5.33	78	.298	.343	54-0-3	.111	-2*	88	-22	0	-2.3
2004	Cin N☆	1	6	.143	68	0	0	41-9	68.1	77	39	12	2	13-6	40	3.95	109	.282	.317	0	ø	0	—	0	15	-0.1
2005	Cin N	1	1	.500	20	0	0	10-2	18.1	30	18	4	0	12-3	8	7.36	58	.357	.433	0	ø	0	—	-7	0	-1.3
	NY N	0	0	ø	20	0	0	0-0	20.1	29	17	5	3	8-1	12	5.75	72	.337	.412	0	ø	0	—	-5	0	-0.3
	Year	1	1	.500	40	0	0	10-2	38.2	59	35	9	3	20-4	20	6.52	64	.347	.423	0	ø	0	—	-12	0	-1.6
2006	Cle A	2	1	.667	13	0	0	0-1	14	18	12	3	0	5-1	3	5.79	75	.305	.354	0	ø	0	—	-3	0	-0.6
Total	11	43	44	.494	518	30	2-1	182-41	808.1	857	416	96	26	271-48	429	4.05	109	.274	.334	76-2-5	.105	-2	77	23	15	5.7
Gray, Charlie	Charles A.; B6.1864 Indianapolis IN; D6.1.1900 Indianapolis IN; d4.23																									
1890	Pit N	1	4	.200	5	4	3	0	31	48	35	0	1	24	10	7.55	44	.343	.442	15	.200	-0	43	-14	—	-1.6
Gray, Dave	David Alexander; B1.7.1943 Ogden UT; BR/TR/6´1˝/195; d6.14; Col Weber St.																									
1964	Bos A	0	0	ø	9	1	0	0	13	18	20	3	0	20-0	17	9.00	43	.321	.494	1	1.000	0	138	-9	0	-0.4
Gray, Chummy	George Edward; B7.17.1873 Rockland ME; D8.14.1913 Rockland ME; TR/5´11.5˝/163; d9.14																									
1899	Pit N	3	3	.500	9	7	6	0	70.2	85	35	1	4	24	9	3.44	111	.297	.360	26	.038	-3	81	4	—	0.1
Gray, Jeff	Jeffrey Edward; B4.10.1963 Richmond VA; BR/TR/6´1˝/(185–190); d6.21; Col Florida St.; [DL 1992 Bos A 182]																									
1988	Cin N	0	0	ø	5	0	0	0-0	9.1	12	4	0	0	4-2	5	3.86	93	.333	.381	1-0-1	.000	-0	—	0	0	0.0
1990	†Bos A	2	4	.333	41	0	0	9-3	50.2	53	27	3	1	15-3	50	4.44	92	.268	.321	0	ø	0	—	-1	0	-0.2
1991	Bos A	2	3	.400	50	0	0	1-3	61.2	39	17	7	1	10-4	41	2.34	185	.181	.219	0	ø	0	—	13	70	1.0
Total	3	4	7	.364	96	0	0	10-6	121.2	104	48	10	2	29-9	96	3.33	125	.231	.278	1-0-1	.000	-0	—	12	252	0.8
Gray, Johnny	John Leonard; B12.11.1926 W.Palm Beach FL; BR/TR/6´4˝/(216–226); d7.18; Col Rollins																									
1954	Phi A	3	12	.200	18	16	5	0	105	111	83	10	0	91	51	6.51	60	.273	.406	34-0-1	.029	-4*	66	-28	0	-3.7
1955	KC A	0	3	.000	8	5	0	0	26.2	28	23	2	1	24-0	11	6.41	65	.277	.417	8	.125	-0	85	-7	0	-0.8
1957	Cle A	1	3	.250	7	3	1-1	0	20	21	17	1	0	13-1	3	5.85	64	.288	.395	4-0-1	.000	-1	72	-6	0	-1.0
1958	Phi N	0	0	ø	15	0	0	0	17.1	12	9	3	0	14-3	10	4.15	95	.222	.377	1	.000	-0	—	0	0	0.0
Total	4	4	18	.182	48	24	6-1	0	169	172	132	16	1	142-4	75	6.18	64	.271	.404	47-0-2	.043	-5	71	-41	0	-5.5
Gray, Dolly	Samuel David "Sam"; B10.15.1897 Van Alstyne TX; D4.16.1953 McKinney TX; BR/TR/5´11˝/175; d4.19																									
1924	Phi A	8	7	.533	34	19	8-2	2	151.2	169	95	5	6	89	54	3.98	108	.284	.383	57	.175	-2	98	-1	—	-0.4
1925	Phi A	16	8	.667	32	28	14-4	3	203.2	199	90	11	3	63	80	3.27	142	.260	.319	67-0-2	.179	-2	106	29	—	2.7
1926	Phi A	11	12	.478	38	18	5	0	150.2	164	81	9	4	50	82	3.64	114	.279	.340	51-0-5	.216	1	97	7	—	1.0
1927	Phi A	9	6	.600	37	13	3-1	3	133.1	153	79	4	4	51	49	4.59	93	.295	.362	42-0-3	.190	-1	123	-4	—	-0.5
1928	StL A	20	12	.625	35	31	21-2	3	262.2	256	119	11	1	86	102	3.19	132	.260	.320	101-1-4	.188	-2	100	24	—	2.7
1929	StL A	18	15	.545	43	**37**	23-**4**	1	**305**	336	142	18	1	96	109	3.72	119	.285	.340	103-0-9	.184	-2	88	24	—	2.0
1930	StL A	4	15	.211	27	24	7	0	167.2	215	133	17	4	52	51	6.28	78	.316	.368	54-0-1	.204	-2	73	-25	—	-2.3
1931	StL A	11	24	.314	43	**37**	13	2	258	323	187	20	4	54	88	5.09	91	.297	.332	79-1-5	.177	-1	76	-17	—	-2.0
1932	StL A	7	12	.368	52	18	7-3	4	206.2	250	126	9	1	53	79	4.53	107	.294	.336	62-0-1	.210	-0	77	5	—	0.4
1933	StL A	7	4	.636	38	6	0	4	112	131	55	7	1	45	36	4.10	114	.301	.368	32-0-1	.219	1	94	7	—	0.8
Total	10	111	115	.491	379	231	101-16	22	1951.1	2196	1107	111	29	639	730	4.18	108	.286	.343	648-2-31	.191	-10	91	49	—	4.4
Gray, Ted	Ted Glenn; B12.31.1924 Detroit MI; BB/TL (BR 1946)/5´11˝/(160–175); d5.15																									
1946	Det A	0	2	.000	3	2	0	1	11.2	17	12	4	0	5	5	8.49	43	.340	.400	3	.000	-0	129	-6	0	-0.9
1948	Det A	6	2	.750	26	11	3-1	0	85.1	73	43	2	3	72	60	4.22	104	.236	.385	29-0-2	.241	1	117	3	0	0.2
1949	Det A	10	10	.500	34	27	8-3	1	195	163	83	11	5	103	96	3.51	119	.227	.328	63-0-3	.127	-3*	96	15	0	1.2
1950	Det A★	10	7	.588	27	21	7	1	149.1	139	85	22	2	72	102	4.40	107	.248	.335	50-0-4	.140	-2	102	3	0	0.0
1951	Det A	7	14	.333	34	28	9-1	1	197.1	194	103	17	6	95	131	4.06	103	.256	.343	63-0-4	.143	-3*	77	1	0	-0.2
1952	Det A	12	17	.414	35	32	13-2	0	224	212	118	21	3	101	138	4.14	92	.249	.331	76-0-8	.171	-2*	73	-9	0	-1.2
1953	Det A	10	15	.400	30	28	8	0	176	166	102	25	7	76	115	4.60	88	.252	.336	61-0-1	.230	2*	83	-11	0	-1.2
1954	Det A	3	5	.375	19	10	2	0	72	70	48	8	2	56	29	5.38	69	.268	.395	22	.045	-2	93	-13	0	-1.6
1955	Chi A	0	0	ø	2	1	0	0	3	9	6	0	0	2-0	1	18.00	22	.500	.550	0	ø	0	180	-4	0	-0.2
	Cle A	0	0	ø	2	0	0	0	2	5	4	1	0	2-0	1	18.00	22	.455	.538	0	ø	0	—	-3	0	-0.1
	NY A	0	0	ø	1	1	0	0	3	3	1	0	0	0-0	1	3.00	125	.300	.273	1	.000	-0	190	0	0	0.0
	Bal A	1	2	.333	9	1	0	0	15.1	21	19	3	0	11-1	8	8.22	46	.344	.438	2	.000	-0	93	-9	0	-1.5
	Year	1	2	.333	14	3	0	0	23.1	38	30	4	0	15-1	11	9.64	40	.380	.453	3	.000	-0	154	-16	0	-1.8
Total	9	59	74	.444	222	162	50-7	4	1134	1072	624	114	28	595-1	687	4.37	94	.251	.346	370-0-22	.159	-10	90	-33	0	-5.5
Gray, Dolly	William Denton; B12.4.1878 Houghton MI; D4.3.1956 Yuba City CA; BL/TL/6´2˝/160; d4.13																									
1909	Was A	5	19	.208	36	26	19	0	218	210	123	1	9	77	87	3.59	68	.258	.329	89-0-1	.146	-1*	81	-29	—	-3.2
1910	Was A	8	19	.296	34	29	21-3	0	229	216	106	3	10	65	84	2.63	95	.249	.309	85-0-1	.247	4*	74	-6	—	-0.2
1911	Was A	2	13	.133	28	15	6	0	121	160	90	4	3	40	42	5.06	65	.331	.385	44	.227	1	85	-21	—	-2.1
Total	3	15	51	.227	98	70	46-3	0	568	586	319	8	22	182	213	3.52	75	.271	.333	218-0-2	.202	3	79	-56	—	-5.5
Grba, Eli	Eli; B8.9.1934 Chicago IL; BR/TR/6´2˝/(204–208); d7.10																									
1959	NY A	2	5	.286	19	6	0	0	50.1	52	44	6	0	39-0	23	6.44	57	.269	.387	14-0-1	.214	1	109	-18	0	-2.0
1960	†NY A	6	4	.600	24	9	1	1	80.2	65	45	9	2	46-3	32	3.68	97	.226	.333	21-1-3	.238	2*	90	-4	0	-0.3
1961	LA A	11	13	.458	40	30	8	2	211.2	197	119	26	7	114-10	105	4.25	106	.242	.339	64-2-8	.234	4*	103	3	0	0.7
1962	LA A	8	9	.471	40	29	1	1	176.1	185	101	19	2	75-5	90	4.54	85	.267	.338	58-1-3	.207	3*	110	-12	0	-0.8
1963	LA A	1	2	.333	12	1	0	0	17.1	14	9	2	1	10-1	5	4.67	73	.222	.333	3	.000	-0*	130	-2	0	-0.3
Total	5	28	33	.459	135	75	10	4	536.1	513	318	62	12	284-19	255	4.48	90	.250	.342	160-4-15	.219	10	106	-33	0	-2.7
Greason, John	John A.; B7.29.1851 Washington DC; D7.22.1889 Washington DC; TL; d8.27																									
1873	Was NA	1	6	.143	7	7	7	0	63	113	90	3	—	10	5	5.86	60	.359	.378	27	.148	-2	52	-13	—	-1.0
Greason, Bill	William Henry "Booster"; B9.3.1924 Atlanta GA; BR/TR/5´10˝/170; d5.31; Negro Lg 1948–51																									
1954	StL N	0	1	.000	3	2	0	0	4	8	8	4	0	4	2	13.50	30	.421	.522	1	.000	-0	130	-5	0	-0.8
Green, Chris	Christopher De Wayne; B9.5.1960 Los Angeles CA; BL/TL/6´2˝/214; [PitN79 4/94]; d4.17																									
1984	Pit N	0	0	ø	4	0	0	0-0	3	5	2	0	0	1-0	3	6.00	61	.417	.429	0	ø	0	—	-1	0	0.0
Green, Jason	David Jason; B6.5.1975 Port Hope ON, Can.; BR/TR/6´1˝/205; [HouN93 30/840]; d7.23; Col Chipola (FL) JC																									
2000	Hou N	1	1	.500	14	0	0	0-0	17.2	15	16	3	1	20-1	19	6.62	74	.234	.424	1	.000	-0	—	-4	0	-0.4
Green, Ed	Edward M.; B1850 Philadelphia PA; d4.22																									
1890	Phi AA	7	15	.318	25	22	20-1	1	191	267	184	4	6	94	56	5.80	67	.321	.393	126	.119	-4*	69	-43	—	-3.9
Green, Fred	Fred Allen; B9.14.1933 Titusville NJ; D12.22.1996 Titusville NJ; BR/TL/6´4˝/190; d4.15; s–Gary																									
1959	Pit N	1	2	.333	17	1	0	1	37.1	37	16	2	0	15-8	20	3.13	123	.259	.327	6	.000	-1	0	2	0	0.1
1960	†Pit N	8	4	.667	45	0	0	3	70	61	26	4	1	33-8	49	3.21	117	.243	.328	8-2-0	.375	3	—	5	0	1.1
1961	Pit N	0	0	ø	13	0	0	0	20.2	27	16	2	0	9-2	4	4.79	83	.321	.387	3	.000	-0	—	-3	0	-0.2
1962	Was A	0	1	.000	5	0	0	0	7	7	6	3	0	6-1	2	6.43	63	.250	.382	0	ø	0	—	-2	0	-0.3

YEAR	TM LG	W	L	PCT	G	GS	CG-SHO	SV-BS	IP	H	R	HR	HB	BB-IB	SO	ERA	AERA	OAV	OOB	AB-HR-SH	AVG	PB	SUP	APR	DL	PW
1964	Pit N	0	0	ø	8	0	0	0	7.1	10	1	1	0	0-0	2	1.23	286	.323	.313	0	ø	0	—	2	0	0.1
Total	5	9	7	.563	88	1	0	4	142.1	142	65	12	1	63-19	77	3.48	110	.264	.339	17-2-0	.176	2	0	4	0	0.8
Green, Dallas	George Dallas; B8.4.1934 Newport DE; BL/TR/6´5˝/210; d6.18; M8; Col Delaware																									
1960	Phi N	3	6	.333	23	10	5-1	0	108.2	100	54	10	2	44-4	51	4.06	96	.248	.321	34-0-2	.206	0*	75	-2	0	-0.1
1961	Phi N	2	4	.333	42	10	1-1	1	128	160	77	8	2	47-6	51	4.85	84	.315	.372	33-0-1	.152	0	102	-11	0	-0.5
1962	Phi N	6	6	.500	37	10	2	1	129.1	145	58	10	5	43-6	58	3.83	101	.289	.350	32-0-3	.063	-1*	84	2	0	0.2
1963	Phi N	7	5	.583	40	14	4	2	120	134	53	10	2	38-8	68	3.23	100	.286	.339	35	.086	-1*	103	-1	0	-0.2
1964	Phi N	2	1	.667	25	0	0	0	42	63	31	4	2	14-0	21	5.79	60	.362	.414	3	.000	-0*	—	-11	0	-0.8
1965	Was A	0	0	ø	6	2	0	0	14.1	14	6	0	0	3-0	6	3.14	111	.241	.279	4	.000	-0	139	0	0	0.0
1966	NY N	0	0	ø	4	0	0	0	5	6	3	2	0	2-1	1	5.40	67	.333	.400	0	ø	0	—	-1	0	0.0
1967	Phi N	0	0	ø	8	0	0	0	15	25	16	2	1	6-2	12	9.00	38	.362	.421	1	.000	-0	—	-9	0	-0.4
Total	8	20	22	.476	185	46	12-2	4	562.1	647	298	46	14	197-27	268	4.26	88	.294	.353	142-0-6	.120	-3	93	-33	0	-1.8
Green, Harvey	Harvey George "Buck"; B2.9.1915 Kenosha WI; D7.24.1970 Franklin LA; BB/TR/6´2.5˝/185; d9.12																									
1935	Bro N	0	0	ø	2	0	0	0	1	2	1	0	1	3	0	9.00	44	.400	.667	0	ø	0	—	0	—	0.0
Green, Sean	Sean William; B4.20.1979 Louisville KY; BR/TR/6´6˝/230; [ColN00 12/347]; d5.2; Col Louisville																									
2006	Sea A	0	0	ø	24	0	0	0-1	32	34	16	2	2	13-1	15	4.50	98	.279	.355	0	ø	0	—	0	50	0.0
Green, Steve	Steve; B1.26.1978 Greenfield Park QC, Can.; BR/TR/6´2˝/195; [AnaA97 10/297]; d4.7; Col Fort Scott (KS) CC; [DL 2002 Ana A 183]																									
2001	Ana A	0	0	ø	1	1	0	0-0	6	4	2	0	0	6-0	4	3.00	155	.190	.370	0	ø	0	40	1	0	0.1
Green, Tyler	Tyler Scott; B2.18.1970 Springfield OH; BR/TR/6´5˝/(185–210); [PhiN91 1/10]; d4.9; Col Wichita St.; [DL 1996 Phi N 182, 1999 Phi N 80]																									
1993	Phi N	0	0	ø	3	2	0	0-0	7.1	16	9	1	0	5-0	7	7.36	54	.444	.512	2-0-1	.000	-0	147	-4	0	-0.2
1995	Phi N★	8	9	.471	26	25	4-2	0-0	140.2	157	86	15	4	66-3	85	5.31	79	.290	.367	44-1-8	.182	2*	113	-15	0	-1.4
1997	Phi N	4	4	.500	14	14	0	0-0	76.2	72	50	8	1	45-4	58	4.93	85	.247	.347	26-0-1	.308	3	109	-8	62	-0.5
1998	Phi N	6	12	.333	27	27	0	0-0	159.1	142	97	23	9	85-1	113	5.03	86	.239	.340	41-0-6	.146	-0	92	-13	31	-1.4
Total	4	18	25	.419	70	68	4-2	0-0	384	387	242	47	14	201-8	263	5.16	83	.265	.356	113-1-16	.195	4	105	-40	355	-3.5
Greene, Tommy	Ira Thomas; B4.6.1967 Lumberton NC; BR/TR/6´5˝/(219–227); [AtlN85 1/14]; d9.10																									
1989	Atl N	1	2	.333	4	4	1-1	0-0	26.1	22	12	5	0	6-1	17	4.10	89	.234	.275	10	.100	-1	54	-1	0	-0.1
1990	Atl N	1	0	1.000	5	2	0	0-0	12.1	14	11	3	1	9-0	4	8.03	50	.286	.407	1-0-1	.000	-0	123	-5	0	-0.4
	Phi N	2	3	.400	10	7	0	0-0	39	36	20	5	0	17-1	17	4.15	93	.247	.325	11-0-2	.182	0	57	-1	0	-0.1
	Year	3	3	.500	15	9	0	0-0	51.1	50	31	8	1	26-1	21	5.08	77	.256	.347	12-0-3	.167	0	72	-6	0	-0.5
1991	Phi N	13	7	.650	36	27	3-2	0-0	207.2	177	85	19	3	66-4	154	3.38	109	.230	.290	71-2-3	.268	7*	101	7	0	1.3
1992	Phi N	3	3	.500	13	12	0	0-0	64.1	75	39	5	0	34-2	39	5.32	66	.291	.371	24	.125	-1	116	-12	111	-1.1
1993	†Phi N	16	4	.800	31	30	7-2	0-0	200	175	84	12	3	62-3	167	3.42	116	.233	.291	72-2-6	.222	6*	136	14	15	1.8
1994	Phi N	2	0	1.000	7	7	0	0-0	35.2	37	20	5	0	22-0	28	4.54	94	.272	.371	13-0-1	.385	2	149	-1	99	0.2
1995	Phi N	0	5	.000	11	6	0	0-0	33.2	45	32	6	3	20-0	24	8.29	51	.319	.412	8-0-1	.000	-0	68	-14	112	-1.8
1997	Hou N	0	1	.000	2	2	0	0-0	9	10	7	2	0	5-0	11	7.00	57	.286	.375	3-0-1	.333	1	138	-3	81	-0.2
Total	8	38	25	.603	119	97	11-5	0-0	628	591	310	62	10	241-11	461	4.14	93	.249	.317	213-4-15	.221	14	112	-16	418	-0.4
Greene, June	Julius Foust; B6.25.1899 Ramseur NC; D3.19.1974 Glendora CA; BL/TR/6´2.5˝/185; d4.20; ▲																									
1928	Phi N	0	0	ø	1	0	0	0	2	5	2	0	0	0	0	9.00	47	.556	.556	6-0-1	.500	2*	—	-1	—	0.2
1929	Phi N	0	0	ø	5	0	0	0	13.2	33	32	2	3	9	4	19.76	26	.465	.542	19	.211	0*	—	-19	—	-0.8
Total	2	0	0	ø	6	0	0	0	15.2	38	34	2	3	9	4	18.38	28	.475	.543	25-0-1	.280	2	—	-20	—	-0.6
Greene, Nelson	Nelson George "Lefty"; B9.20.1899 Philadelphia PA; D5.6.1983 Lebanon PA; BL/TL/6´0˝/185; d4.28; Col Villanova																									
1924	Bro N	0	1	.000	4	1	0	0	9	14	6	1	0	2	3	4.00	94	.350	.381	1	.000	-0	45	-1	—	-0.1
1925	Bro N	2	0	1.000	11	0	0	1	22	45	28	4	0	7	4	10.64	39	.417	.452	7	.286	0	—	-15	—	-1.2
Total	2	2	1	.667	15	1	0	1	31	59	34	5	0	9	7	8.71	47	.399	.433	8	.250	-0	45	-16	—	-1.3
Greene, Rick	Richard Douglas; B1.2.1971 Fort Knox KY; BR/TR/6´5˝/200; [DetA92 1/16]; d6.19; Col Louisiana St.																									
1999	Cin N	0	0	ø	1	0	0	0-0	5.2	7	4	2	0	1-0	3	4.76	99	.292	.320	2	.000	-0	—	0	0	0.0
Greenfield, Kent	Kent; B7.1.1902 Guthrie KY; D3.14.1978 Guthrie KY; BR/TR/6´1˝/180; d9.28																									
1924	NY N	0	1	.000	1	1	0	0	3	9	8	1	0	1	1	15.00	24	.500	.526	0	ø	0	139	-5	—	-0.7
1925	NY N	12	8	.600	29	20	12	0	171.2	195	86	4	2	64	66	3.88	104	.288	.352	62-0-3	.081	-6	85	4	—	-0.2
1926	NY N	13	12	.520	39	28	8-1	1	222.2	206	111	17	5	82	74	3.96	95	.251	.322	65-0-3	.092	-5	90	-3	—	-0.9
1927	NY N	2	2	.500	12	1	0	0	20	39	25	3	2	13	4	9.45	41	.411	.491	2-0-1	.000	-0	110	-13	—	-2.1
	Bos N	11	14	.440	27	26	11-1	0	190	203	92	3	5	59	59	3.84	97	.282	.341	64-0-7	.172	-2	82	-1	—	-0.3
	Year	13	16	.448	39	27	11-1	0	210	242	117	6	7	72	63	4.37	85	.297	.359	66-0-8	.167	-2	83	-13	—	-2.4
1928	Bos N	3	11	.214	32	20	5	0	143.2	173	100	6	5	60	30	5.32	73	.307	.378	38-0-7	.053	-4	88	-22	—	-2.2
1929	Bos N	0	0	ø	6	2	0	0	15.2	33	19	1	2	15	7	10.91	43	.465	.568	5	.000	-1	140	-10	—	-0.5
	Bro N	0	0	ø	6	0	0	0	8.2	13	8	1	0	3	1	8.31	56	.382	.432	1	.000	-0*	—	-3	—	-0.1
	Year	0	0	ø	12	2	0	0	24.1	46	27	2	2	18	8	9.99	47	.438	.528	6	.000	-1	140	-13	—	-0.6
Total	6	41	48	.461	152	98	36-2	1	775.1	871	449	36	21	297	242	4.54	85	.290	.358	237-0-21	.101	-18	88	-53	—	-7.0
Greenig, John	John A.; B1848 Philadelphia PA; D7.28.1913 Philadelphia PA; TR; d5.9																									
1888	Was N	0	1	.000	1	1	1	0	9	17	13	2	0	4	2	11.00	25	.405	.457	3	.000	-0	44	-7	—	-0.6
Greenwood, Bob	Robert Chandler "Greenie"; B3.13.1928 Cananea, Sonora, Mexico; D9.1.1994 Hayward CA; BR/TR/6´5˝/190; d4.21; Col St. Marys (CA)																									
1954	Phi N	1	2	.333	11	4	0	0	36.2	28	16	2	0	18	9	3.19	127	.209	.301	9-0-1	.000	-1*	99	3	0	0.2
1955	Phi N	0	0	ø	1	0	0	0	2.1	7	4	1	0	0-0	0	15.43	26	.500	.500	1	.000	-0	—	-3	0	-0.1
Total	2	1	2	.333	12	4	0	0	39	35	20	3	0	18-0	9	3.92	103	.236	.317	10-0-1	.000	-1	99	0	0	0.1
Greer, Kenny	Kenneth William; B5.12.1967 Boston MA; BR/TR/6´2˝/(210–215); [NYA88 10/261]; d9.29; Col Massachusetts																									
1993	NY N	1	0	1.000	1	0	0	0-0	1	0	0	0	0	0-0	2	0.00	ø	.000	.000	0	ø	0	—	0	0	0.1
1995	SF N	0	2	.000	8	0	0	0-1	12	15	12	3	1	5-2	7	5.25	79	.288	.356	1	.000	-0	—	-3	0	-0.5
Total	2	1	2	.333	9	0	0	0-1	13	15	12	3	1	5-2	9	4.85	85	.273	.339	1	.000	-0	—	-3	0	-0.4
Gregg, Dave	David Charles "Highpockets"; B3.14.1891 Chehalis WA; D11.12.1965 Clarkston WA; BR/TR/6´1˝/185; d6.15; b–Vean																									
1913	Cle A	0	0	ø	1	0	0	0	1	2	2	0	1	0	0	18.00	17	.400	.500	0	ø	0	—	-1	—	-0.1
Gregg, Hal	Harold Dana "Skeets"; B7.11.1921 Anaheim CA; D5.13.1991 Bishop CA; BR/TR/6´3.5˝/195; d8.18																									
1943	Bro N	0	3	.000	5	4	0	0	18.2	21	21	2	0	21	7	9.64	35	.304	.467	2-0-1	.000	0	88	-12	0	-1.6
1944	Bro N	9	16	.360	39	31	6	2	197.2	201	142	12	9	137	92	5.46	65	.258	.376	68-0-4	.206	-0*	117	-43	0	-4.9
1945	Bro N✱	18	13	.581	42	34	13-2	2	254.1	221	116	5	8	120	139	3.47	108	.232	.323	91-1-8	.220	3	106	11	0	1.6
1946	Bro N	6	4	.600	26	16	4-1	2	117.1	103	46	3	1	44	54	2.99	113	.236	.308	32-0-6	.125	-1	95	5	0	0.2
1947	†Bro N	4	5	.444	37	16	2-1	1	104.1	115	79	6	4	55	59	5.87	70	.272	.361	34	.265	2	107	-20	0	-1.4
1948	Pit N	2	4	.333	22	8	1	1	74.1	72	40	3	3	34	25	4.60	88	.255	.342	22-1-2	.273	2	131	-3	0	-0.1
1949	Pit N	1	1	.500	8	1	0	0	18.2	20	10	1	1	8	9	3.38	125	.303	.387	5-0-2	.000	-0	126	1	0	0.0
1950	Pit N	0	1	.000	5	1	0	0	5.1	10	10	2	1	7	3	13.50	32	.400	.545	1	.000	-0	60	-5	0	-0.8
1952	NY N	0	1	.000	16	4	1	1	36.1	42	22	7	2	17	13	4.71	79	.286	.367	8	.125	-0	138	-4	0	-0.3
Total	9	40	48	.455	200	115	27-4	9	827	805	486	41	29	443	401	4.54	82	.253	.350	263-2-23	.205	4	110	-70	0	-7.3
Gregg, Kevin	Kevin Marschall; B6.20.1978 Corvallis OR; BB/TR/6´6˝/(200–235); [OakA96 15/435]; d8.9																									
2003	Ana A	2	0	1.000	5	3	0	0-0	24.2	18	9	3	1	8-0	14	3.28	133	.205	.278	0	ø	0	49	3	0	0.2
2004	†Ana A	5	2	.714	55	0	0	1-1	87.2	86	43	6	3	28-3	84	4.21	106	.255	.314	0	ø	0	—	3	0	0.1
2005	†LA A	1	2	.333	33	2	0	0-1	64.1	70	37	8	3	29-2	52	5.04	85	.273	.353	0	ø	0	119	-5	0	-0.2
2006	LA A	3	4	.429	32	3	0	0-0	78.1	88	41	10	2	21-0	71	4.14	108	.279	.326	3	.000	-0	85	3	0	0.1
Total	4	11	8	.579	125	8	0	1-2	255	262	130	27	9	86-5	221	4.31	102	.263	.325	3	.000	-0	79	4	0	0.2

YEAR	TM LG	W	L	PCT	G	GS	CG-SHO	SV-BS	IP	H	R	HR	HB	BB-IB	SO	ERA	AERA	OAV	OOB	AB-HR-SH	AVG	PB	SUP	APR	DL	PW
Gregg, Vean	Sylveanus Augustus; B4.13.1885 Chehalis WA; D7.29.1964 Aberdeen WA; BR/TL/6´1˝/185; d4.12; b–Dave; Col South Dakota St.																									
1911	Cle A	23	7	.767	34	26	22-5	0	244.2	172	67	2	10	86	125	**1.80**	**189**	**.205**	.286	85-0-5	.165	-4	93	43	—	4.6
1912	Cle A	20	13	.606	37	34	26-1	2	271.1	242	99	4	10	90	184	2.59	132	.246	.316	97-0-8	.175	-3	94	27	—	2.8
1913	Cle A	20	13	.606	44	34	23-3	3	285.2	258	103	2	13	124	166	2.24	136	.250	.338	99-0-4	.131	-4	93	22	—	1.9
1914	Cle A	9	3	.750	17	12	6-1	0	96.2	88	46	0	3	48	56	3.07	94	.251	.347	34-0-1	.176	1	120	-2	—	-0.2
	Bos A	3	4	.429	12	9	4	0	68.1	71	39	0	0	37	24	3.95	68	.283	.375	19-0-2	.211	0	117	-9	—	-0.9
	Year	12	7	.632	29	21	10-1	0	165	159	85	0	3	85	80	3.44	82	.265	.358	53-0-3	.189	1	119	-11	—	-1.1
1915	Bos A	4	2	.667	18	9	3-1	3	75	71	37	2	5	32	43	3.36	83	.260	.348	20-0-2	.350	2	137	-5	—	-0.2
1916	Bos A	2	5	.286	21	7	3	0	77.2	71	30	0	3	30	41	3.01	92	.259	.339	18	.111	-1	94	-1	—	-0.2
1918	Phi A	9	14	.391	30	25	17-3	2	199.1	180	85	4	5	67	63	3.12	94	.251	.320	71-0-1	.169	-3	75	-2	—	-0.6
1925	Was A	2	2	.500	26	5	1	2	74.1	87	41	3	2	38	18	4.12	103	.318	.404	14-0-4	.214	0	143	1	—	0.0
Total	8	92	63	.594	239	161	105-14	12	1393	1240	547	17	51	552	720	2.70	117	.248	.329	457-0-27	.171	-12	97	74	—	7.2
Gregory, Frank	Frank Ernst; B7.25.1888 Spring Valley Twp. WI; D11.5.1955 Beloit WI; BR/TR/5´11˝/185; d9.5																									
1912	Cin N	2	0	1.000	4	2	1	0	15.2	19	12	0	1	7	4	4.60	73	.297	.375	5	.200	0	109	-3	—	-0.3
Gregory, Lee	Grover Leroy; B6.2.1938 Bakersfield CA; BL/TL/6´1˝/180; d4.17; Col Cal St.–Fresno																									
1964	Chi N	0	0	ø	11	0	0	0	18	23	8	3	0	5-2	8	3.50	106	.333	.373	13	.077	0*	—	0	0	0.0
Gregory, Howie	Howard Watterson; B11.18.1886 Hannibal MO; D5.30.1970 Tulsa OK; BL/TR/6´0˝/175; d4.16																									
1911	StL A	0	1	.000	3	1	0	0	7	11	5	0	0	4	1	5.14	66	.393	.469	2	.000	-0	21	-1	—	-0.2
Gregory, Paul	Paul Edwin "Pop"; B6.9.1908 Tomnolen MS; D9.16.1999 Southaven MS; BR/TR/6´2˝/180; d4.20; Col Mississippi St.																									
1932	Chi A	5	3	.625	33	9	3	0	117.2	125	75	8	2	51	39	4.51	96	.273	.348	38-0-3	.079	-3	105	-3	—	-0.3
1933	Chi A	4	11	.267	23	17	5	0	103.2	124	75	10	1	47	18	4.95	86	.296	.368	35-0-1	.143	-1	93	-11	—	-1.4
Total	2	9	14	.391	56	26	8	0	221.1	249	150	18	3	98	57	4.72	91	.284	.358	73-0-4	.110	-4	97	-14	—	-1.7
Greif, Bill	William Briley; B4.25.1950 Ft.Stockton TX; BR/TR/6´5˝/(195–196); [HouN68 3/43]; d7.19																									
1971	Hou N	1	1	.500	7	3	0	0-0	16	18	10	1	2	8-0	14	5.06	67	.290	.384	3	.333	0	105	-3	0	-0.3
1972	SD N	5	16	.238	34	22	2-1	2-1	125.1	143	86	18	8	47-4	91	5.60	59	.287	.353	33-0-5	.030	-3	69	-32	0	-5.2
1973	SD N	10	17	.370	36	31	9-3	1-0	199.1	181	88	20	5	62-12	120	3.21	110	.246	.306	61-0-2	.098	-2	77	5	0	0.4
1974	SD N	9	19	.321	43	35	7-1	1-1	226	244	126	17	14	95-11	137	4.66	77	.279	.356	56-0-9	.071	-2*	86	-25	0	-2.9
1975	SD N	4	6	.400	59	1	0	9-3	72	74	44	7	5	38-17	43	3.88	90	.269	.366	1-0-1	.000	-0	201	-6	0	-1.1
1976	SD N	1	3	.250	5	5	0	0-0	22.1	27	20	2	0	11-0	5	8.06	41	.297	.369	8	.000	-1	139	-11	0	-1.7
	StL N	1	5	.167	47	0	0	6-0	54.2	60	28	5	2	26-5	32	4.12	87	.290	.367	4	.000	0	—	-3	0	-0.4
	Year	2	8	.200	52	5	0	6-0	77	87	48	7	2	37-5	37	5.26	67	.292	.367	12	.000	-1	131	-13	0	-2.1
Total	6	31	67	.316	231	97	18-5	19-5	715.2	747	402	70	36	287-49	442	4.41	79	.272	.345	166-0-17	.072	-7	83	-75	0	-11.2
Greinke, Zack	Donald Zackary; B10.21.1983 Orlando FL; BR/TR/6´2˝/(175–200); [KCA02 1/6]; d5.22																									
2004	KC A	8	11	.421	24	24	0	0-0	145	143	64	26	8	26-3	100	3.97	117	.255	.297	2	.000	-0	80	14	0	1.6
2005	KC A	5	17	.227	33	33	2	0-0	183	233	125	23	13	53-0	114	5.80	75	.309	.362	2-1-0	.500	1	82	-28	0	-2.7
2006	KC A	1	0	1.000	3	0	0	0-0	6.1	7	3	1	0	3-2	5	4.26	110	.280	.357	0	ø	0	—	0	79	0.1
Total	3	14	28	.333	60	57	2	0-0	334.1	383	192	50	21	82-5	219	4.98	91	.286	.335	4-1-0	.250	1	81	-14	79	-1.0
Greisinger, Seth	Seth Adam; B7.29.1975 Kansas City KS; BR/TR/6´4˝/200; [DetA96 1/6]; d6.3; Col Virginia; [DL 2001 Det A 190]																									
1998	Det A	6	9	.400	21	21	0	0-0	130	142	79	17	4	48-2	66	5.12	93	.282	.346	4	.250	0	75	-5	0	-0.5
2002	Det A	2	2	.500	8	8	0	0-0	37.2	46	26	4	1	13-2	14	6.21	70	.303	.359	0	ø	0	85	-6	0	-0.6
2004	Min A	2	5	.286	12	9	0	0-0	51	68	40	12	2	15-1	36	6.18	75	.319	.366	0	ø	0	71	-10	0	-1.1
2005	Atl N	0	0	ø	1	1	0	0-0	5	7	2	1	0	1-0	2	3.60	117	.350	.381	2	.000	-0	45	0	0	0.0
Total	4	10	16	.385	42	39	0	0-0	223.2	263	147	34	7	77-5	118	5.51	84	.296	.354	6	.167	-0	75	-21	190	-2.2
Grevell, Bill	William Joseph; B3.5.1898 Williamstown NJ; D6.21.1923 Philadelphia PA; BR/TR/5´11˝/170; d5.14																									
1919	Phi A	0	0	ø	5	2	0	0	12	15	20	0	1	18	3	14.25	24	.306	.500	5	.000	-1	183	-12	—	-0.6
Griffeth, Lee	Leon Clifford; B5.20.1925 Carmel NY; BB/TL/5´11.5˝/180; d6.25; Col Duke																									
1946	Phi A	0	0	ø	10	0	0	0	15.1	13	7	1	2	6	4	2.93	121	.232	.328	1	.000	0	—	1	0	0.0
Griffin, Hank	James Linton "Pepper"; B7.11.1886 Whitehouse TX; D2.11.1950 Terrell TX; BR/TR/6´0˝/165; d5.5																									
1911	Chi N	0	0	ø	1	1	0	0	1	1	2	1	0	3	1	18.00	18	.250	.571	0	ø	0	45	-1	—	-0.1
	Bos N	0	6	.000	15	6	1	0	82.2	96	70	3	6	34	30	5.23	73	.305	.383	30	.233	-0	92	-14	—	-0.9
	Year	0	6	.000	16	7	1	0	83.2	97	72	4	6	37	31	5.38	71	.304	.387	30	.233	-0	84	-15	—	-1.0
1912	Bos N	0	0	ø	3	0	0	0	1.2	3	5	0	1	3	0	27.00	13	.750	.875	0	ø	0	—	-4	—	-0.2
Total	2	0	6	.000	19	7	1	0	85.1	100	77	4	7	40	31	5.80	66	.310	.397	30	.233	-0	84	-19	—	-1.2
Griffin, Marty	Martin John; B9.2.1901 San Francisco CA; D11.19.1951 Los Angeles CA; BR/TR/6´2˝/200; d7.25																									
1928	Bos A	0	3	.000	11	3	0	0	37.2	42	21	0	0	17	9	5.02	82	.300	.376	13	.308	1*	27	-2	—	-0.1
Griffin, Mike	Michael Leroy; B6.26.1957 Colusa CA; BR/TR/6´5˝/(195–210); [TexA76 3/60]; d9.17																									
1979	NY A	0	0	ø	3	0	0	1-0	4.1	5	2	0	0	2-0	5	4.15	99	.313	.389	0	ø	0	—	0	0	0.0
1980	NY A	2	4	.333	13	9	0	0-0	54	64	36	6	1	23-2	25	4.83	82	.287	.353	0	ø	0	123	-7	0	-0.7
1981	NY A	0	0	ø	2	0	0	0-0	4.1	5	1	0	0	0-0	4	2.08	174	.278	.278	0	ø	0	—	1	0	0.1
	Chi N	2	5	.286	16	9	0	1-0	52	64	27	4	0	9-0	20	4.50	83	.302	.327	13-0-2	.154	-0	66	-3	0	-0.4
1982	SD N	0	1	.000	7	0	0	0-0	10.1	9	4	0	0	3-0	4	3.48	98	.237	.293	1	.000	-0	—	0	0	0.0
1987	Bal A	3	5	.375	23	6	1	1-1	74.1	78	39	9	3	33-3	42	4.36	102	.269	.347	0	ø	0	51	1	0	0.1
1989	Cin N	0	0	ø	3	0	0	0-0	4.1	10	6	0	0	3-2	1	12.46	29	.500	.520	1	1.000	0	—	-4	0	-0.1
Total	6	7	15	.318	67	24	1	3-1	203.2	235	115	19	4	73-7	101	4.60	88	.288	.346	15-0-2	.200	-0	82	-12	0	-1.0
Griffin, Pat	Patrick Richard; B5.6.1893 Niles OH; D6.7.1927 Youngstown OH; BR/TR/6´2˝/180; d7.23																									
1914	Cin N	0	0	ø	1	0	0	0	1	3	3	0	0	2	0	9.00	33	.750	.833	0	ø	0	—	-1	—	0.0
Griffin, Tom	Thomas James; B2.22.1948 Los Angeles CA; BR/TR/6´3˝/(200–210); [HouN66*1/4]; d4.10																									
1969	Hou N	11	10	.524	31	31	6-3	0-0	188.1	156	80	19	7	93-4	200	3.54	101	.220	.317	62-2-4	.145	2	113	3	0	0.5
1970	Hou N	3	13	.188	23	20	2-1	0-0	111.1	118	72	9	3	72-1	72	5.74	68	.275	.381	33-0-4	.061	-2	89	-20	0	-2.7
1971	Hou N	0	6	.000	10	6	0	0-1	37.2	44	22	4	2	20-1	29	4.78	70	.288	.375	9	.111	-0	44	-6	0	-0.9
1972	Hou N	5	4	.556	39	5	1-1	3-3	94.1	92	39	7	3	38-5	83	3.24	104	.258	.333	25-1-3	.280	3	110	0	0	0.4
1973	Hou N	4	6	.400	25	12	4	0-0	99.2	83	51	10	2	46-6	69	4.15	88	.229	.316	28-1-4	.107	0	91	-6	25	-0.5
1974	Hou N	14	10	.583	34	34	8-3	0-0	211	202	97	14	5	89-7	110	3.54	99	.250	.326	68-2-9	.294	8*	128	-3	0	0.6
1975	Hou N	3	8	.273	17	13	3-1	0-0	79.1	89	52	11	2	46-5	56	5.33	64	.288	.384	22-0-2	.136	-0	92	-19	89	-2.3
1976	Hou N	5	3	.625	20	2	0	0-0	41.2	44	29	4	1	37-2	33	6.05	53	.278	.412	5-0-1	.000	-0	96	-13	0	-2.2
	SD N	4	3	.571	11	11	2	0-0	70.1	56	27	0	1	42-1	36	2.94	112	.222	.333	26-0-3	.077	-2*	90	3	0	0.0
	Year	9	6	.600	31	13	2	0-0	112	100	56	4	2	79-3	69	4.10	80	.244	.365	31-0-4	.065	-2	91	-10	0	-2.2
1977	SD N	6	9	.400	38	20	0	0-0	151.1	144	88	17	5	88-8	79	4.46	80	.254	.356	45-2-3	.133	1*	112	-17	0	-1.4
1978	Cal A	3	4	.429	24	4	0	0-0	56	63	39	8	1	31-2	35	4.02	90	.279	.364	0	ø	0	93	-8	0	-0.8
1979	SF N	5	6	.455	59	3	0	2-2	94.1	83	46	9	4	46-8	82	3.91	89	.237	.331	14-0-1	.071	-1	42	-5	0	-0.5
1980	SF N	5	1	.833	42	4	0	0-0	107.2	80	35	8	8	49-6	79	2.76	127	.212	.312	18-1-2	.111	0*	95	10	0	0.6
1981	SF N	8	8	.500	22	22	3-1	0-0	129.1	121	62	8	7	57-8	83	3.76	91	.249	.335	41-1-6	.195	2	98	-6	0	-0.4
1982	Pit N	1	3	.250	6	4	0	0-0	22.1	32	23	5	1	15-2	8	8.87	42	.330	.425	9	.222	0	106	-12	0	-1.6
Total	14	77	94	.450	401	191	29-10	5-6	1494.2	1407	762	133	52	769-66	1054	4.07	86	.249	.343	405-10-42	.163	12	103	-99	114	-11.2
Griffith, Clark	Clark Calvin "The Old Fox"; B11.20.1869 Clear Creek MO; D10.27.1955 Washington DC; BR/TR/5´6.5˝/156; d4.11; M20; HF1946																									
1891	StL AA	11	8	.579	27	17	12	2	186.1	195	122	8	15	58	68	3.33	126	.260	.326	77-1	.156	-3	106	15	—	0.9
	Bos AA	3	1	.750	7	4	3	0	40	47	33	3	5	15	20	5.62	62	.283	.360	23-1	.174	2*	161	-8	—	-0.4
	Year	14	9	.609	34	21	15	2	226.1	242	155	11	20	73	88	3.74	109	.264	.332	100-2	.160	-1	115	9	—	0.5
1893	Chi N	1	2	.333	4	2	2	0	19.2	24	14	1	1	5	9	5.03	92	.293	.341	11	.182	-1	113	0	—	-0.1
1894	Chi N	21	14	.600	36	30	28	0	261.1	328	193	12	14	85	71	4.92	114	.303	.362	142	.232	-0*	107	25	—	2.3
1895	Chi N	26	14	.650	42	41	39	0	353	434	228	11	22	91	79	3.93	130	.298	.348	144-1-2	.319	5*	93	40	—	3.9

YEAR	TM LG	W	L	PCT	G	GS	CG-SHO	SV-BS	IP	H	R	HR	HB	BB-IB	SO	ERA	AERA	OAV	OOB	AB-HR-SH	AVG	PB	SUP	APR	DL	PW
1896	Chi N	23	11	.676	36	35	35	0	317.2	370	189	3	12	70	81	3.54	128	.289	.331	135-1-2	.267	3*	86	29	—	2.7
1897	Chi N	21	18	.538	41	38	**38**-1	1	343.2	410	231	3	17	86	102	3.72	120	.293	.342	162-0-3	.235	3*	90	20	—	2.2
1898	Chi N	24	10	.706	38	38	36-4	0	325.2	305	105	1	20	64	97	**1.88**	**191**	.246	.294	122-0-2	.164	-2	106	**63**	—	5.9
1899	Chi N	22	14	.611	38	38	35	0	319.2	329	163	5	14	65	73	2.79	134	.266	.310	120-0-4	.258	6*	113	31	—	3.9
1900	Chi N	14	13	.519	30	30	27-**4**	0	248	245	126	6	16	51	61	3.05	118	.258	.306	95-1-1	.253	5	79	20	—	2.2
1901	Chi A	24	7	**.774**	35	30	26-**5**	1	266.2	275	114	4	4	50	67	2.67	131	.263	.299	89-2-3	.303	14	142	29	—	4.2
1902	Chi A	15	9	.625	28	24	20-3	0	213	247	117	11	16	47	51	4.18	81	.290	.339	92-0-3	.217	2*	105	-15	—	-1.3
1903	NY A	14	11	.560	25	24	22-2	0	213	201	92	3	6	33	69	2.70	116	.249	.283	69-1-2	.159	2	76	8	—	1.0
1904	NY A	7	5	.583	16	11	8-1	0	100.1	91	40	3	4	16	36	2.87	94	.243	.281	42-0-1	.143	-1	112	-1	—	-0.2
1905	NY A	9	6	.600	25	7	4-2	1	101.2	82	30	1	1	15	46	1.68	174	.223	.255	32-0-2	.219	1*	76	12	—	1.8
1906	NY A	2	2	.500	17	2	1	2	59.2	58	30	0	4	15	16	3.02	98	.258	.316	18-0-2	.111	-1	146	-2	—	-0.1
1907	NY A	0	0	ø	4	0	0	0	8.1	15	16	0	0	6	5	8.64	32	.395	.477	2	.000	-0*	—	-6	—	-0.3
1909	Cin N	0	1	.000	1	1	1	0	6	11	8	0	0	2	3	6.00	43	.379	.419	2	.000	-0	27	-3	—	-0.4
1912	Was A	0	0	ø	1	0	0	0	0	1	1	1	0	0	0	(1)	ø	1.000	1.000	1	.000	-0	—	-1	—	-0.1
1913	Was A	0	0	ø	1	0	0	0	1	1	0	0	0	0	0	0.00	ø	.250	.250	1	1.000	1	—	0	—	0.1
1914	Was A	0	0	ø	1	0	0	1	1	1	0	0	0	0	1	0.00	ø	.250	.250	1	1.000	1	—	0	—	0.1
Total	20	237	146	.619	453	372	337-22	8	3385.2	3670	1852	76	171	774	955	3.31	121	.274	.322	1380-8-27	.233	35	101	256	—	28.3
Griffith, Frank	Frank Wesley; B11.18.1872 Gilman IL; D12.8.1908 Waterman IL; BL/TL; d8.13; Col Northwestern																									
1892	Chi N	0	1	.000	1	1	0	0	4	3	5	1	0	6	3	11.25	30	.200	.429	1	.000	-0	38	-3	—	-0.4
1894	Cle N	1	2	.333	7	6	3	0	42.1	64	62	5	9	37	15	9.99	55	.344	.474	24-0-1	.333	2	125	-19	—	-0.8
Total	2	1	3	.250	8	7	3	0	46.1	67	67	6	9	43	18	10.10	52	.333	.470	25-0-1	.320	2	114	-22	—	-1.2
Griffiths, Jeremy	Jeremy Richard; B3.22.1978 Fairview OH; BR/TR/6´6˝/(235–240); [NYN99 3/106]; d6.5; Col Toledo																									
2003	NY N	1	4	.200	9	6	0	0-0	41	57	34	5	2	19-2	25	7.02	60	.328	.400	9-0-1	.000	-1	89	-13	0	-1.4
2004	Hou N	0	0	ø	1	1	0	0-0	4.1	4	5	1	0	3-0	5	10.38	42	.235	.350	1	.000	0	212	-3	0	-0.1
Total	2	1	4	.200	10	7	0	0-0	45.1	61	39	6	2	22-2	30	7.35	57	.319	.395	10-0-1	.000	-0	108	-16	0	-1.5
Griggs, Hal	Harold Lloyd; B8.24.1928 Shannon GA; D5.10.2005 Tucson AZ; BR/TR/6´0˝/170; d4.18																									
1956	Was A	1	6	.143	34	12	1	1	98.2	120	82	14	1	76-2	48	6.02	72	.307	.415	16-0-2	.000	-1*	72	-21	0	-1.4
1957	Was A	0	1	.000	2	2	0	0	13.2	11	5	1	0	7-0	12	3.29	118	.229	.327	4	.250	0	46	1	0	0.1
1958	Was A	3	11	.214	32	21	3	0	137	138	91	20	2	74-1	69	5.52	69	.262	.353	41-0-2	.122	-2	85	-26	0	-2.6
1959	Was A	2	8	.200	37	10	2-1	2	97.2	103	63	8	1	52-4	43	5.25	75	.270	.356	18	.056	-2	59	-13	0	-1.5
Total	4	6	26	.188	105	45	6-1	3	347	372	241	43	4	209-7	172	5.50	73	.276	.372	79-0-4	.089	-5	73	-59	0	-5.4
Grilli, Guido	Guido John; B1.9.1939 Memphis TN; BL/TL/6´0˝/188; d4.12; Col Memphis																									
1966	Bos A	0	1	.000	6	0	0	0	4.2	5	6	1	0	9-0	4	7.71	49	.278	.519	2	.500	0	—	-2	0	-0.4
	KC A	0	1	.000	16	0	0	1	15.2	19	15	0	3	11-4	8	6.89	49	.302	.429	0	ø	0	—	-7	0	-0.5
	Year	0	2	.000	22	0	0	1	20.1	24	21	1	3	20-4	12	7.08	49	.296	.452	2	.500	0	—	-9	0	-0.9
Grilli, Jason	Jason Michael; B11.11.1976 Royal Oak MI; BR/TR/6´4˝/(185–225); [SFN97 1/4]; d5.11; f–Steve; Col Seton Hall																									
2000	Fla N	1	0	1.000	1	1	0	0-0	6.2	11	4	0	2	2-0	3	5.40	81	.379	.455	2	.500	0	105	-1	0	0.0
2001	Fla N	2	2	.500	6	5	0	0-0	26.2	30	18	6	2	11-0	17	6.08	69	.297	.377	7-1-2	.286	1	120	-5	0	-0.5
2004	Chi A	2	3	.400	8	8	1	0-0	45	52	38	11	3	20-0	26	7.40	64	.294	.373	0	ø	0	121	-13	0	-1.1
2005	Det A	1	1	.500	3	2	0	0-0	16	14	6	1	0	6-0	5	3.38	127	.255	.323	0	ø	0	97	2	0	0.2
2006	†Det A	2	3	.400	51	0	0	0-0	62	61	31	6	5	25-3	31	4.21	107	.261	.340	0	ø	0	—	2	0	0.1
Total	5	8	9	.471	69	16	1	0-0	156.1	168	97	24	12	64-3	82	5.41	83	.282	.360	9-1-2	.333	2	117	-15	0	-1.3
Grilli, Steve	Stephen Joseph; B5.2.1949 Brooklyn NY; BR/TR/6´2˝/170; d9.19; s–Jason; Col Gannon																									
1975	Det A	0	0	ø	3	0	0	0-0	6.2	3	2	0	0	6-1	5	1.35	299	.136	.310	0	ø	0	—	2	0	0.1
1976	Det A	3	1	.750	36	0	0	3-1	66	63	43	5	5	41-5	36	4.64	80	.258	.369	0	ø	0	—	-8	0	-0.4
1977	Det A	1	2	.333	30	2	0	0-0	72.2	71	42	8	3	49-2	49	4.83	89	.265	.383	0	ø	0	63	-3	0	-0.2
1979	Tor A	0	0	ø	1	0	0	0-0	2.1	1	0	0	0	0-0	1	0.00	ø	.143	.143	0	ø	0	—	1	0	0.1
Total	4	4	3	.571	70	2	0	3-1	147.2	138	87	13	8	96-8	91	4.51	90	.255	.371	0	ø	0	63	-8	0	-0.4
Grim, Bob	Robert Anton; B3.8.1930 New York NY; D10.23.1996 Shawnee KS; BR/TR/6´1˝/185; d4.18																									
1954	NY A	20	6	.769	37	20	8-1	0	199	175	78	9	3	85	108	3.26	106	.244	.322	70-1-7	.143	-1	141	6	0	0.5
1955	†NY A	7	5	.583	26	11	1-1	4	92.1	81	49	9	3	42-2	63	4.19	89	.238	.321	25-0-4	.120	-1	134	-5	47	-0.7
1956	NY A	6	1	.857	26	6	1	5	74.2	64	27	3	2	31-0	48	2.77	139	.235	.317	16-0-1	.063	-0	123	9	0	0.8
1957	†NY A★	12	8	.600	46	0	0	**19**	72	60	22	5	0	36-5	52	2.63	137	.239	.330	9-1-3	.111	1	—	9	0	2.0
1958	NY A	0	1	.000	11	0	0	0	16.1	12	10	3	1	10-0	11	5.51	64	.211	.338	1-0-1	.000	-0	—	-3	0	-0.2
	KC A	7	6	.538	26	14	5-1	0	113.2	118	54	7	3	41-4	54	3.56	110	.269	.334	32-0-3	.188	-0	87	2	0	0.1
	Year	7	7	.500	37	14	5-1	0	130	130	64	10	4	51-4	65	3.81	101	.263	.335	33-0-4	.182	-1	88	0	0	-0.1
1959	KC A	6	10	.375	40	9	3-1	4	125.1	124	69	10	3	57-6	65	4.09	98	.260	.341	32-1-6	.094	-1	125	-3	0	-0.5
1960	Cle A	0	1	.000	3	0	0	0	2.1	6	3	0	0	1-0	2	11.57	32	.500	.538	0	ø	0	—	-2	0	-0.4
	Cin N	2	2	.500	26	0	0	2	30.1	32	18	3	0	10-2	22	4.45	86	.274	.321	1	.000	-0	—	-3	0	-0.4
	StL N	1	0	1.000	15	0	0	0	20.2	22	7	1	0	9-1	15	3.05	134	.272	.337	1	.000	-0	—	3	0	0.1
	Year	3	2	.600	41	0	0	2	51	54	25	4	0	19-3	37	3.88	101	.273	.327	2	.000	-0	—	0	0	-0.3
1962	KC A	0	1	.000	12	0	0	3	13	14	9	0	0	8-2	3	6.23	68	.292	.393	2	.000	-0	—	-2	0	-0.3
Total	8	61	41	.598	268	60	18-4	37	759.2	708	346	50	15	330-22	443	3.61	104	.252	.330	189-3-25	.127	-4	122	11	47	1.0
Grimes, Burleigh	Burleigh Arland "Ol' Stubblebeard"; B8.18.1893 Emerald WI; D12.6.1985 Clear Lake WI; BR/TR/5´10˝/175; d9.10; M2/C1; HF1964																									
1916	Pit N	2	3	.400	6	5	4	0	45.2	40	19	1	0	10	20	2.36	114	.241	.284	17-0-1	.176	-0	78	1	—	0.0
1917	Pit N	3	16	.158	37	17	8-1	0	194	186	101	5	6	70	72	3.53	80	.260	.331	69-0-4	.232	2*	67	-17	—	-1.3
1918	Bro N	19	9	.679	**40**	30	19-7	1	270	210	94	3	4	76	113	2.13	131	.216	.276	90-0-6	.200	0*	91	16	—	1.9
1919	Bro N	10	11	.476	25	21	13-1	0	181.1	179	97	2	7	60	82	3.47	86	.256	.321	69-0-2	.246	1*	107	-12	—	-1.1
1920	†Bro N	23	11	**.676**	40	33	25-5	2	303.2	271	101	5	4	67	131	2.22	144	.238	.282	111-0-6	.306	10*	116	30	—	4.9
1921	Bro N	**22**	13	.629	37	35	**30**-2	0	302.1	313	120	6	5	76	**136**	2.83	138	.274	.322	114-1-4	.237	2	92	**33**	—	**4.0**
1922	Bro N	17	14	.548	36	34	18-1	1	259	324	159	17	7	84	99	4.76	85	.308	.363	93-0-4	.237	4	104	-17	—	-1.1
1923	Bro N	21	18	.538	39	**38**	**33**-2	0	**327**	356	165	9	11	100	119	3.58	108	.280	.338	126-0-7	.238	3*	104	11	—	1.8
1924	Bro N	22	13	.629	38	**36**	**30**-1	1	**310.2**	351	161	15	6	91	135	3.82	98	.287	.339	124-0-3	.298	6*	114	-3	—	0.6
1925	Bro N	12	19	.387	33	31	19	0	246.2	305	164	15	7	102	73	5.04	83	.309	.377	96-1-2	.250	5*	109	-23	—	-1.5
1926	Bro N	12	13	.480	30	29	18-1	0	225.1	238	114	4	5	88	64	3.71	103	.276	.346	81-0-3	.222	1*	95	2	—	0.5
1927	NY N	19	8	.704	39	34	15-2	2	259.2	274	116	12	4	87	102	3.54	109	.276	.337	96-0-5	.188	-0	117	11	—	1.3
1928	Pit N	**25**	14	.641	**48**	**37**	**28-4**	3	**330.2**	311	146	11	9	77	97	2.99	136	.248	.297	131-0-5	.321	11	138	32	—	4.9
1929	Pit N	17	7	.708	33	29	18-2	2	232.2	245	108	11	4	70	62	3.13	**152**	.269	.324	91-0-2	.286	6	118	36	—	4.0
1930	Bos N	3	5	.375	11	9	1	0	49	72	53	4	3	22	15	7.35	67	.353	.424	16-0-2	.188	-0	112	-17	—	-2.0
	†StL N	13	6	.684	22	19	10-1	0	152.1	174	66	5	4	43	58	3.01	166	.293	.345	57-0-3	.263	2*	122	31	—	3.6
	Year	16	11	.593	33	28	11-1	0	201.1	246	119	9	7	65	73	4.07	123	.308	.366	73-0-5	.247	2	118	13	—	1.6
1931	†StL N	17	9	.654	29	28	17-3	0	212.1	240	97	11	10	59	67	3.65	108	.286	.340	76-0-9	.184	-2	112	8	—	0.8
1932	†Chi N	6	11	.353	30	18	5-1	1	141.1	174	89	8	1	50	36	4.78	79	.297	.354	44-0-5	.250	1	104	-17	—	-1.6
1933	Chi N	3	6	.333	17	7	3-1	3	69.2	71	29	2	1	29	12	3.49	94	.277	.353	20-0-2	.150	-1	109	0	—	-0.1
	StL N	0	1	.000	4	3	0	1	13.2	15	13	1	1	8	4	5.27	66	.263	.364	5	.200	0	144	-4	—	-0.4
	Year	3	7	.300	21	10	3-1	4	83.1	86	42	3	2	37	16	3.78	87	.275	.355	25-0-2	.160	-0	121	-5	—	-0.5
1934	StL N	2	1	.667	4	0	0	0	7.2	5	3	1	0	2	1	3.52	120	.179	.233	0-0-1	ø	0	—	1	—	0.2
	NY A	1	2	.333	10	0	0	1	18	22	11	0	1	14	5	5.50	74	.319	.440	2	.000	-0	—	-2	—	-0.3
	Pit N	1	2	.333	8	4	0	0	27.1	36	24	0	1	10	9	7.24	57	.310	.370	7	.143	-0	73	-9	—	-0.8
Total	19	270	212	.560	616	497	314-35	18	4180	4412	2050	148	101	1295	1512	3.53	107	.273	.331	1535-2-76	.248	52	109	91	—	18.3
Grimes, John	John Thomas; B4.17.1869 Woodstock MD; D1.17.1964 San Francisco CA; BR/TR/5´11˝/160; d7.28																									
1897	StL N	0	2	.000	3	1	1	0	19.2	24	23	0	6	8	4	5.95	74	.300	.404	7	.286	1	81	-5	—	-0.2
Grimsley, Jason	Jason Alan; B8.7.1967 Cleveland TX; BR/TR/6´3˝/(180–205); [PhiN85 10/252]; d9.8																									
1989	Phi N	1	3	.250	4	4	0	0-0	18.1	19	13	2	0	19-1	7	5.89	61	.268	.422	5-0-2	.000	-1	62	-4	0	-0.8
1990	Phi N	3	2	.600	11	11	0	0-0	57.1	47	21	1	2	43-0	41	3.30	117	.227	.364	16-0-3	.188	0*	104	4	0	0.5
1991	Phi N	1	7	.125	12	12	0	0-0	61	54	34	4	3	41-3	42	4.87	76	.242	.364	17	.059	-1	73	-7	77	-0.8

YEAR	TM LG	W	L	PCT	G	GS	CG-SHO	SV-BS	IP	H	R	HR	HB	BB-IB	SO	ERA	AERA	OAV	OOB	AB-HR-SH	AVG	PB	SUP	APR	DL	PW
1993	Cle A	3	4	.429	10	6	0	0-0	42.1	52	26	3	1	20-1	27	5.31	82	.302	.378	0	ø	0	53	-4	0	-0.5
1994	Cle A	5	2	.714	14	13	1	0-0	82.2	91	47	7	6	34-1	59	4.57	104	.283	.360	0	ø	0	122	2	0	0.1
1995	Cle A	0	0	ø	15	2	0	1-0	34	37	24	4	2	32-1	25	6.09	78	.289	.433	0	ø	0	108	-5	0	-0.2
1996	Cal A	5	7	.417	35	20	2-1	0-0	130.1	150	110	14	13	74-5	82	6.84	74	.286	.385	0	ø	0	101	-26	0	-1.8
1999	†NY A	7	2	.778	55	0	0	1-3	75	66	39	7	4	40-5	49	3.60	131	.231	.330	0	ø	0	—	7	0	0.7
2000	†NY A	3	2	.600	63	4	0	1-3	96.1	100	58	10	5	42-1	53	5.04	95	.268	.345	1	.000	1	138	-3	0	-0.1
2001	KC A	1	5	.167	73	0	0	0-7	80.1	71	32	8	2	28-5	61	3.02	164	.241	.311	0	ø	0	—	15	0	1.0
2002	KC A	4	7	.364	70	0	0	1-2	71.1	64	32	4	1	37-8	59	3.91	128	.236	.330	0	ø	0	—	8	18	1.1
2003	KC A	2	6	.250	76	0	0	0-7	75	88	47	6	5	36-5	58	5.16	93	.299	.379	0	ø	0	—	-3	0	-0.2
2004	KC A	3	3	.500	32	0	0	0-3	26.2	24	11	1	1	15-3	18	3.38	138	.238	.342	0	ø	0	—	4	0	0.8
	Bal A	2	4	.333	41	0	0	0-6	36.1	37	25	3	2	20-3	21	4.21	111	.261	.358	0	ø	0	—	-1	0	-0.1
	Year	5	7	.417	73	0	0	0-9	63	61	36	4	3	35-6	39	3.86	121	.251	.351	0	ø	0	—	3	0	0.7
2005	Bal A	1	2	.333	22	0	0	0-3	22	24	15	5	0	9-2	10	5.73	77	.289	.355	0	ø	0	—	-3	117	-0.4
2006	Ari N	1	2	.333	19	0	0	0-0	27.2	30	15	4	0	8-2	10	4.88	96	.280	.330	4	.000	-0	—	0	0	-0.1
Total	15	42	58	.420	552	72	3-1	4-34	936.2	954	549	83	47	498-46	622	4.77	98	.265	.359	43-0-5	.093	-1	94	-16	212	-0.8

GRIMSLEY, ROSS Ross Albert I; B6.4.1922 Americus KS; D2.6.1994 Memphis TN; BL/TL/6´0˝/175; d9.3; s–Ross

YEAR	TM LG	W	L	PCT	G	GS	CG-SHO	SV-BS	IP	H	R	HR	HB	BB-IB	SO	ERA	AERA	OAV	OOB	AB-HR-SH	AVG	PB	SUP	APR	DL	PW
1951	Chi A	0	0	ø	7	0	0	0	14	12	8	1	0	10	8	3.86	105	.235	.361	2-0-1	.000	-0	—	0	0	-0.1

GRIMSLEY, ROSS Ross Albert II; B1.7.1950 Topeka KS; BL/TL/6´3˝/(195–200); [CinN69*S1/17]; d5.16; f–Ross; Col Jackson St. (TN) CC; [DL 1981 Cle A 48]

YEAR	TM LG	W	L	PCT	G	GS	CG-SHO	SV-BS	IP	H	R	HR	HB	BB-IB	SO	ERA	AERA	OAV	OOB	AB-HR-SH	AVG	PB	SUP	APR	DL	PW
1971	Cin N	10	7	.588	26	26	6-3	0-0	161.1	151	67	15	2	43-2	67	3.57	95	.250	.301	51-0-6	.118	-1	118	-3	0	-0.4
1972	†Cin N	14	8	.636	30	28	4-1	1-0	197.2	194	73	18	0	50-8	79	3.05	106	.260	.305	66-0-11	.121	-2	114	5	0	0.3
1973	†Cin N	13	10	.565	38	36	8-1	1-0	242.1	245	96	24	0	68-11	90	3.23	107	.266	.315	82-0-8	.061	-6*	102	6	0	-0.2
1974	†Bal A	18	13	.581	40	39	17-4	1-0	295.2	267	111	26	3	76-9	158	3.07	113	.244	.292	0	ø	0	101	16	0	1.6
1975	Bal A	10	13	.435	35	32	8-1	0-0	197	210	95	29	1	47-1	89	4.07	87	.276	.317	0	ø	0	90	-12	0	-1.2
1976	Bal A	8	7	.533	28	19	2	0-0	136.2	143	66	8	1	35-2	41	3.95	83	.270	.315	0	ø	0	129	-10	0	-1.1
1977	Bal A	14	10	.583	34	34	11-2	0-0	218.1	230	105	24	1	74-2	53	3.96	97	.277	.335	0	ø	0	98	-4	0	-0.2
1978	Mon N☆	20	11	.645	36	36	19-3	0-0	263	237	103	17	2	67-6	84	3.05	117	.243	.291	90-0-11	.144	-1	106	13	0	1.5
1979	Mon N	10	9	.526	32	27	2	0-1	151.1	199	102	18	3	41-1	42	5.35	69	.322	.363	55-0-3	.200	1	115	-27	0	-2.9
1980	Mon N	2	4	.333	11	7	0	0-0	41.1	61	31	5	1	12-1	11	6.31	57	.351	.385	9	.222	0	84	-12	0	-1.4
	Cle A	4	5	.444	14	11	2	0-0	74.2	103	63	11	1	24-1	18	6.75	61	.331	.376	0	ø	0	114	-22	0	-2.2
1982	Bal A	1	2	.333	21	0	0	0-2	60	65	35	7	0	22-5	18	5.25	77	.283	.343	0	ø	0	—	-7	0	-0.3
Total	11	124	99	.556	345	295	79-15	3-3	2039.1	2105	947	202	15	559-49	750	3.81	93	.270	.318	353-0-39	.127	-10	106	-57	48	-6.5

GRINER, DAN Donald Dexter "Rusty"; B3.7.1888 Centerville TN; D6.3.1950 Bishopville SC; BL/TR/6´1.5˝/200; d8.17*

YEAR	TM LG	W	L	PCT	G	GS	CG-SHO	SV-BS	IP	H	R	HR	HB	BB-IB	SO	ERA	AERA	OAV	OOB	AB-HR-SH	AVG	PB	SUP	APR	DL	PW
1912	StL N	3	4	.429	12	7	2	0	54	59	35	3	3	15	20	3.17	108	.278	.335	13	.077	-0	89	-1	—	-0.2
1913	StL N	10	22	.313	34	34	18-1	0	225	279	150	12	10	66	79	5.08	64	.312	.366	81-0-2	.259	5	91	-46	—	-5.0
1914	StL N	9	13	.409	37	17	11-2	2	179	163	66	3	3	57	74	2.51	111	.254	.318	55-0-3	.255	4	70	7	—	1.4
1915	StL N	5	11	.313	37	17	9-3	3	150.1	137	59	4	8	46	46	2.81	99	.259	.328	52-0-2	.269	4*	78	1	—	0.5
1916	StL N	0	0	ø	4	0	0	1	11	15	5	0	1	3	3	4.09	65	.341	.396	4	.250	0	—	-1	—	-0.1
1918	Bro N	1	5	.167	11	6	3-1	0	54.1	47	16	0	7	15	22	2.15	129	.267	.348	14	.071	-1*	50	4	—	0.4
Total	6	28	55	.337	135	81	43-7	6	673.2	700	331	22	32	202	244	3.49	86	.280	.342	219-0-7	.237	12	83	-36	—	-3.0

GRISSOM, LEE Lee Theo; B10.23.1907 Sherman TX; D10.4.1998 Corning CA; BB/TL (BR 1934, 37)/6´3˝/200; d9.2; Mil 1942–45; b–Marv

YEAR	TM LG	W	L	PCT	G	GS	CG-SHO	SV-BS	IP	H	R	HR	HB	BB-IB	SO	ERA	AERA	OAV	OOB	AB-HR-SH	AVG	PB	SUP	APR	DL	PW
1934	Cin N	0	1	.000	4	1	0	0	7	13	12	0	0	7	4	15.43	26	.382	.488	1	.000	-0	42	-8	—	-0.9
1935	Cin N	1	1	.500	3	3	1	0	21	31	10	0	0	4	13	3.86	103	.333	.361	7-0-1	.000	-1	114	1	—	0.0
1936	Cin N	1	1	.500	6	4	0	0	24.1	33	18	1	0	9	13	6.29	61	.320	.375	9	.000	-1	133	-6	—	-0.5
1937	Cin N★	12	17	.414	50	30	14-**5**	6	223.2	193	89	7	4	93	149	3.26	114	.232	.313	64-0-6	.109	-3*	74	15	—	1.5
1938	Cin N	2	3	.400	14	7	0	0	51	60	38	4	2	22	16	5.29	69	.300	.375	16	.188	-0	76	-11	—	-1.0
1939	†Cin N	9	7	.563	33	21	3	0	153.2	145	77	14	1	56	53	4.10	93	.249	.316	47-0-3	.085	-2	114	-3	—	-0.6
1940	NY A	0	0	ø	5	0	0	0	4.2	4	0	0	0	2	1	0.00	ø	.250	.333	0	ø	0	—	2	—	0.1
	Bro N	2	5	.286	14	10	3-1	0	73.2	59	30	3	0	34	56	2.81	142	.215	.302	23	.217	0	52	7	—	0.6
1941	Bro N	0	0	ø	4	1	0	1	11.1	10	3	2	0	8	5	2.38	154	.238	.360	2-0-1	.500	0	232	2	0	0.1
	Phi N	2	13	.133	29	18	2	0	131.1	120	69	4	2	70	74	3.97	93	.242	.338	36-0-3	.167	-1	84	-5	0	-0.6
	Year	2	13	.133	33	19	2	1	142.2	130	72	6	2	78	79	3.85	96	.242	.340	38-0-4	.184	-0	92	-3	0	-0.5
Total	8	29	48	.377	162	95	23-6	7	701.2	668	346	35	9	305	384	3.89	97	.250	.329	205-0-14	.127	-8	88	-6	0	-1.3

GRISSOM, MARV Marvin Edward; B3.31.1918 Los Molinos CA; D9.19.2005 Red Bluff CA; BR/TR/6´3˝/(195–205); d9.10; C15; b–Lee

YEAR	TM LG	W	L	PCT	G	GS	CG-SHO	SV-BS	IP	H	R	HR	HB	BB-IB	SO	ERA	AERA	OAV	OOB	AB-HR-SH	AVG	PB	SUP	APR	DL	PW
1946	NY N	0	2	.000	4	3	0	0	18.2	17	11	1	1	13	9	4.34	79	.254	.383	5	.200	-0	75	-2	0	-0.2
1949	Det A	2	4	.333	27	2	0	0	39.1	56	32	6	1	34	17	6.41	65	.335	.450	9	.222	1	140	-10	0	-1.3
1952	Chi A	12	10	.545	28	24	7-1	0	166	156	79	6	3	79	97	3.74	98	.250	.337	53-0-8	.151	-1	101	-3	0	-0.5
1953	Bos A	2	6	.250	13	11	1-1	0	59.1	61	34	5	1	30	31	4.70	89	.266	.354	18-0-2	.000	-3	109	-2	0	-0.6
	NY N	4	2	.667	21	7	3	0	84.1	83	40	6	1	31	46	3.95	109	.255	.321	27-0-1	.074	-2	140	4	0	0.2
1954	†NY N★	10	7	.588	56	3	1-1	19	122.1	100	37	13	7	50	64	2.35	171	.226	.312	32-0-2	.156	-1	74	23	0	3.7
1955	NY N	5	4	.556	55	0	0	8	89.1	76	35	6	6	41-5	49	2.92	138	.237	.332	13-0-1	.154	-1	—	10	0	1.1
1956	NY N	1	1	.500	43	2	0	7	80.2	71	15	3	1	16-3	49	1.56	242	.241	.279	11	.091	-0	70	**20**	0	1.0
1957	NY N	4	4	.500	55	0	0	14	82.2	74	36	6	2	23-6	51	2.61	151	.243	.300	12	.167	0	—	8	0	1.1
1958	SF N	7	5	.583	51	0	0	10	65.1	71	34	11	5	26-7	46	3.99	95	.287	.367	9-0-1	.000	-1	—	-2	0	-0.4
1959	StL N	0	0	ø	3	0	0	0	2	6	5	2	0	0-0	0	22.50	19	.500	.500	0	ø	0	—	-4	36	-0.2
Total	10	47	45	.511	356	52	12-3	58	810	771	358	65	28	343-21	459	3.41	115	.254	.334	189-0-15	.122	-7	105	42	36	3.9

GROB, CONNIE Conrad George; B11.9.1932 Cross Plains WI; D9.28.1997 Madison WI; BL/TR/6´0.5˝/180; d4.22

YEAR	TM LG	W	L	PCT	G	GS	CG-SHO	SV-BS	IP	H	R	HR	HB	BB-IB	SO	ERA	AERA	OAV	OOB	AB-HR-SH	AVG	PB	SUP	APR	DL	PW
1956	Was A	4	5	.444	37	1	0	1	79.1	121	79	14	1	26-1	27	7.83	55	.353	.396	18-0-1	.333	1	82	-30	0	-2.7

GRODZICKI, JOHNNY John "Grod"; B2.26.1917 Nanticoke PA; D5.2.1998 Daytona Beach FL; BR/TR/6´1.5˝/200; d4.18; Mil 1942–46; C1

YEAR	TM LG	W	L	PCT	G	GS	CG-SHO	SV-BS	IP	H	R	HR	HB	BB-IB	SO	ERA	AERA	OAV	OOB	AB-HR-SH	AVG	PB	SUP	APR	DL	PW
1941	StL N	2	1	.667	5	1	0	0	13.1	6	7	0	0	11	10	1.35	279	.130	.298	2-0-1	.000	0	90	2	0	0.4
1946	StL N	0	0	ø	3	0	0	0	4	4	5	1	0	4	2	9.00	38	.250	.400	0	ø	0	—	-3	63	-0.1
1947	StL N	0	1	.000	16	0	0	0	23.1	21	17	5	0	19	8	5.40	77	.253	.392	1	.000	-0	—	-4	0	-0.2
Total	3	2	2	.500	24	1	0	0	40.2	31	29	6	0	34	20	4.43	89	.214	.363	3-0-1	.000	0	90	-5	63	0.1

GROMEK, STEVE Stephen Joseph; B1.15.1920 Hamtramck MI; D3.12.2002 Clinton Twp. MI; BB/TR/6´2˝/(180–195); d8.18

YEAR	TM LG	W	L	PCT	G	GS	CG-SHO	SV-BS	IP	H	R	HR	HB	BB-IB	SO	ERA	AERA	OAV	OOB	AB-HR-SH	AVG	PB	SUP	APR	DL	PW
1941	Cle A	1	1	.500	9	2	1	2	23.1	25	12	0	0	11	19	4.24	93	.266	.343	6	.167	-0	143	-1	0	-0.1
1942	Cle A	2	0	1.000	14	0	0	0	44.1	46	24	2	0	23	14	3.65	94	.267	.354	15	.333	3	—	-2	0	0.1
1943	Cle A	0	0	ø	3	0	0	0	4	6	4	0	0	0	4	9.00	35	.353	.353	2	1.000	1	—	-2	0	0.0
1944	Cle A	10	9	.526	35	21	12-2	1	203.2	160	74	5	3	70	115	2.56	129	**.219**	.290	73-0-5	.260	5*	102	15	0	1.7
1945	Cle A✶	19	9	.679	33	30	21-3	1	251	229	80	6	4	66	101	2.55	128	.243	.295	91-0-3	.231	3*	101	21	0	2.6
1946	Cle A	5	15	.250	29	21	5-2	4	153.2	159	79	20	3	47	75	4.33	76	.264	.321	56	.196	0*	75	-16	0	-2.0
1947	Cle A	3	5	.375	29	7	0	4	84.1	77	43	8	1	36	39	3.74	93	.240	.318	22	.318	2*	127	-5	0	-0.3
1948	†Cle A	9	3	.750	38	9	4-1	2	130	109	52	10	6	51	50	2.84	143	.226	.307	41-0-1	.146	-1	106	16	0	1.2
1949	Cle A	4	6	.400	27	12	3	0	92	86	41	8	2	40	22	3.33	120	.250	.332	24-0-2	.167	-0	107	6	0	0.5
1950	Cle A	10	7	.588	31	13	4-1	0	113.1	94	50	10	3	36	43	3.65	119	.226	.292	38-0-2	.158	-2	90	10	0	1.1
1951	Cle A	7	4	.636	27	8	4	1	107.1	98	41	6	4	29	40	2.77	137	.238	.295	27-0-1	.296	3	123	12	0	1.4
1952	Cle A	7	7	.500	29	13	3-1	1	122.2	109	55	14	2	28	65	3.67	91	.232	.278	30-0-3	.100	-0*	108	-3	0	-0.5
1953	Cle A	1	1	.500	5	1	0	0	11	11	4	0	1	3	8	3.27	115	.268	.333	2-0-1	.000	-0	24	1	0	0.1
	Det A	6	8	.429	19	17	6-1	1	125.2	138	70	17	8	36	59	4.51	90	.276	.335	41-0-5	.073	-4	94	-6	0	-1.1
	Year	7	9	.438	24	18	6-1	1	136.2	149	74	17	9	39	67	4.41	92	.275	.334	43-0-6	.070	-4	90	-6	0	-1.0
1954	Det A	18	16	.529	36	32	17-4	1	252.2	236	85	26	12	57	102	2.74	135	.246	.294	79-0-10	.190	2	84	28	0	**3.7**
1955	Det A	13	10	.565	28	25	8-2	0	181	183	89	26	9	37-5	73	3.98	97	.261	.305	54-0-4	.167	4	138	-2	0	0.1
1956	Det A	8	6	.571	40	13	4	4	141	142	74	25	9	47-7	64	4.28	96	.263	.329	27-0-3	.148	2	83	-2	0	-0.1
1957	Det A	0	1	.000	15	1	0	1	23.2	32	16	3	1	13-3	11	6.08	63	.333	.414	2	.000	-0	69	-5	0	-0.3
Total	17	123	108	.532	447	225	92-17	23	2064.2	1940	893	186	68	630-15	904	3.41	108	.247	.308	630-0-40	.197	15	101	65	0	8.1

GROOM, BOB Robert; B9.12.1884 Belleville IL; D2.19.1948 Belleville IL; BR/TR/6´2˝/175; d4.13

YEAR	TM LG	W	L	PCT	G	GS	CG-SHO	SV-BS	IP	H	R	HR	HB	BB-IB	SO	ERA	AERA	OAV	OOB	AB-HR-SH	AVG	PB	SUP	APR	DL	PW
1909	Was A	7	26	.212	44	31	17-1	0	260.2	218	114	2	13	105	131	2.87	85	.229	.314	88-0-7	.091	-6*	60	-12	—	-2.0
1910	Was A	12	17	.414	34	30	22-3	0	257.2	244	117	8	9	77	98	2.76	90	.260	.322	92-0-3	.120	-6	81	-8	—	-1.6
1911	Was A	13	17	.433	37	32	20-2	2	254.2	280	148	9	8	67	135	3.82	86	.282	.332	82-0-6	.134	-4	81	-13	—	-1.7

YEAR	TM LG	W	L	PCT	G	GS	CG-SHO	SV-BS	IP	H	R	HR	HB	BB-IB	SO	ERA	AERA	OAV	OOB	AB-HR-SH	AVG	PB	SUP	APR	DL	PW
1912	Was A	24	13	.649	43	40	28-2	1	316	287	133	3	5	94	179	2.62	127	.246	.305	103-0-12	.117	-7	105	25	—	1.8
1913	Was A	16	16	.500	37	36	17-4	0	264.1	258	118	8	5	81	156	3.23	91	.261	.320	92-0-5	.163	1	95	-5	—	-0.5
1914	StL F	13	20	.394	42	34	23-1	1	280.2	281	141	9	4	75	167	3.24	94	.262	.312	94-0-1	.160	-3	77	-10	—	-1.5
1915	StL F	11	11	.500	37	26	11-4	2	209	200	93	6	2	73	111	3.27	88	.261	.327	66-0-3	.152	-2	86	-9	—	-1.2
1916	StL A	13	9	.591	41	26	8-1	4	217.1	174	82	1	3	98	92	2.57	107	.226	.315	63-0-6	.111	-2	121	4	—	0.3
1917	StL A	8	19	.296	38	28	11-4	3	232.2	193	80	3	5	95	82	2.94	88	.233	.315	72-0-3	.111	-4	77	0	—	-0.5
1918	Cle A	2	2	.500	14	5	0	0	43.1	70	42	0	1	18	8	7.06	43	.380	.438	12-0-1	.083	-1	125	-17	—	-1.6
Total	10	119	150	.442	367	288	157-22	13	2336.1	2205	1068	49	55	783	1159	3.10	93	.255	.320	764-0-47	.128	-34	88	-45	—	-8.5
Groom, Buddy	Wedsel Gary; B7.10.1965 Dallas TX; BL/TL/6´2˝/(200–208); [ChiA87 12/297]; d6.20; Col Mary Hardin–Baylor																									
1992	Det A	0	5	.000	12	7	0	1-1	38.2	48	28	4	0	22-4	15	5.82	69	.320	.402	0	ø	0	75	-8	0	-1.0
1993	Det A	0	2	.000	19	3	0	0-0	36.2	48	25	4	2	13-5	15	6.14	71	.322	.375	0	ø	0	113	-6	0	-0.3
1994	Det A	0	1	.000	40	0	0	1-0	32	31	14	4	2	13-2	27	3.94	125	.256	.331	0	ø	0	—	4	0	0.1
1995	Det A	1	3	.250	23	4	0	1-2	40.2	55	35	6	2	26-4	23	7.52	64	.322	.413	0	ø	0	102	-11	0	-1.0
	Fla N	1	2	.333	14	0	0	0-0	15	26	12	2	0	6-0	12	7.20	60	.400	.451	0	ø	0	—	-4	0	-0.7
1996	Oak A	5	0	1.000	72	1	0	2-2	77.1	85	37	8	3	34-3	57	3.84	129	.281	.360	0	ø	0	56	9	0	0.5
1997	Oak A	2	2	.500	78	0	0	3-2	64.2	75	38	9	0	24-1	45	5.15	89	.292	.347	0	ø	0	—	-3	0	-0.2
1998	Oak A	3	1	.750	75	0	0	0-6	57.1	62	30	4	1	20-1	36	4.24	109	.274	.332	0	ø	0	—	3	0	0.1
1999	Oak A	3	2	.600	**76**	0	0	0-3	46	48	29	1	1	18-5	32	5.09	93	.274	.345	0	ø	0	—	-2	0	-0.1
2000	Bal A	6	3	.667	70	0	0	4-7	59.1	63	37	5	0	21-2	44	4.85	97	.275	.329	0	ø	0	—	-2	0	-0.3
2001	Bal A	1	4	.200	70	0	0	11-2	66	64	28	4	1	9-0	54	3.55	122	.252	.279	0	ø	0	—	6	0	0.6
2002	Bal A	3	2	.600	70	0	0	2-2	62	44	11	4	2	12-3	48	1.60	272	.196	.243	0	ø	0	—	20	0	1.5
2003	Bal A	1	3	.250	60	0	0	1-2	45.1	58	27	7	3	14-2	34	5.36	86	.309	.364	0	ø	0	—	-3	0	-0.2
2004	Bal A	4	1	.800	60	0	0	0-2	52.2	67	30	6	1	16-1	32	4.78	98	.309	.356	0	ø	0	—	0	0	-0.1
2005	NY A	1	0	1.000	24	0	0	0-0	25.2	32	14	3	3	7-2	13	4.91	88	.305	.362	0	ø	0	—	-1	0	-0.1
	Ari N	0	1	.000	23	0	0	1-0	15.1	19	8	2	0	5-1	7	4.70	94	.302	.348	0	ø	0	—	0	0	0.0
Total	14	31	32	.492	786	15	0	27-31	734.2	825	403	73	21	260-36	494	4.64	99	.285	.345	0	ø	0	85	2	0	-1.2
Gross, Don	Donald John; B6.30.1931 Weidman MI; BL/TL/5´11˝/(184–190); d7.21; Col Michigan St.																									
1955	Cin N	4	5	.444	17	11	2-1	0	67.1	79	33	11	1	16-0	33	4.14	102	.298	.337	19-0-3	.158	-1	97	2	0	0.1
1956	Cin N	3	0	1.000	19	7	2	0	69.1	69	25	4	1	20-2	47	1.95	204	.257	.309	19	.105	-1	114	11	0	0.6
1957	Cin N	7	9	.438	43	16	5	1	148.1	152	75	21	3	33-3	73	4.31	95	.264	.304	46-0-6	.109	-2	100	-2	0	-0.5
1958	Pit N	5	7	.417	40	3	0	7	74.2	67	37	5	1	38-7	59	3.98	97	.241	.333	18-0-1	.056	-1	124	-1	0	-0.3
1959	Pit N	1	1	.500	21	0	0	2	33	28	16	3	1	10-3	15	3.55	109	.228	.289	2-0-1	.000	-0	—	1	0	0.1
1960	Pit N	0	0	ø	5	0	0	0	5.1	5	2	1	0	0-0	3	3.38	111	.238	.238	0	ø	0	—	0	0	0.0
Total	6	20	22	.476	145	37	9-1	10	398	400	188	45	7	117-15	230	3.73	108	.261	.314	104-0-11	.106	-5	106	11	0	0.0
Gross, Kevin	Kevin Frank; B6.8.1961 Downey CA; BR/TR/6´5˝/(203–227); [PhiN81*S1/11]; d6.25; Col California Lutheran																									
1983	Phi N	4	6	.400	17	17	1-1	0-0	96	100	46	13	3	35-3	66	3.56	101	.265	.332	33-0-1	.091	-1	98	0	0	-0.1
1984	Phi N	8	5	.615	44	14	1	1-2	129	140	66	8	5	44-4	84	4.12	89	.277	.339	30-0-2	.067	-2	91	-5	0	-0.6
1985	Phi N	15	13	.536	38	31	6-2	0-1	205.2	194	86	11	7	81-6	151	3.41	109	.251	.326	65-1-8	.138	0*	80	8	0	1.1
1986	Phi N	12	12	.500	37	36	7-2	0-0	241.2	240	115	28	8	94-2	154	4.02	97	.259	.331	80-1-9	.188	3	103	0	0	0.3
1987	Phi N	9	16	.360	34	33	3-1	0-0	200.2	205	107	26	10	87-7	110	4.35	99	.267	.347	63-1-8	.190	2	75	-1	0	0.0
1988	Phi N★	12	14	.462	33	33	5-1	0-0	231.2	209	101	18	11	89-5	162	3.69	98	.239	.315	75-0-8	.173	1	89	0	0	0.1
1989	Mon N	11	12	.478	31	31	4-3	0-0	201.1	188	105	20	6	88-6	158	4.38	81	.247	.329	64-0-6	.141	1	89	-16	0	-1.7
1990	Mon N	9	12	.429	31	26	2-1	0-0	163.1	171	86	9	4	65-7	111	4.57	80	.272	.340	50-1-7	.200	4*	90	-15	22	-1.5
1991	LA N	10	11	.476	46	10	0	3-3	115.2	123	55	10	2	50-6	95	3.58	101	.275	.348	25-0-2	.280	2*	95	-1	0	0.1
1992	LA N	8	13	.381	34	30	4-3	0-0	204.2	182	82	11	3	77-10	158	3.17	110	.241	.311	63-0-3	.095	-1	89	8	0	0.6
1993	LA N	13	13	.500	33	32	3	0-0	202.1	224	110	15	5	74-7	150	4.14	93	.281	.344	64-1-8	.203	4	119	-8	0	-0.3
1994	LA N	9	7	.563	25	23	1	1-0	157.1	162	64	11	2	43-2	124	3.60	111	.263	.313	47-1-4	.149	1	80	9	0	1.0
1995	Tex A	9	15	.375	31	30	4	0-0	183.2	200	124	27	8	89-8	106	5.54	87	.279	.362	0	ø	0	92	-15	0	-1.6
1996	Tex A	11	8	.579	28	19	1	0-0	129.1	151	78	19	4	50-2	78	5.22	101	.293	.355	0	ø	0	101	2	36	0.2
1997	Ana A	2	1	.667	12	3	0	0-0	25.1	30	20	4	1	20-1	20	6.75	68	.313	.429	1	.000	-0	133	-6	0	-0.6
Total	15	142	158	.473	474	368	42-14	5-6	2487.2	2519	1245	230	79	986-76	1727	4.11	95	.264	.335	660-6-66	.161	13	93	-40	58	-3.0
Gross, Kip	Kip Lee; B8.24.1964 Scottsbluff NE; BR/TR/6´2˝/(190–195); [NYN86 4/102]; d4.21; Col Nebraska																									
1990	Cin N	0	0	ø	5	0	0	0-0	6.1	6	3	0	0	2-0	3	4.26	93	.273	.320	0	ø	0	—	0	0	0.0
1991	Cin N	6	4	.600	29	9	1	0-0	85.2	93	43	8	0	40-2	40	3.47	110	.279	.355	22-0-3	.091	-1	129	1	0	-0.1
1992	LA N	1	1	.500	16	1	0	0-0	23.2	32	14	1	0	10-1	14	4.18	83	.323	.385	2-0-1	1.000	1	209	-2	0	-0.1
1993	LA N	0	0	ø	10	0	0	0-0	15	13	1	0	0	4-0	12	0.60	644	.236	.288	0	ø	0	—	6	0	0.3
1999	Bos A	0	2	.000	11	1	0	0-1	12.2	15	11	3	3	8-2	9	7.82	64	.294	.413	0	ø	0	168	-3	18	-0.4
2000	Hou N	0	1	.000	2	1	0	0-0	4.1	9	8	2	0	2-0	3	10.38	47	.429	.478	1	.000	-0	19	-4	0	-0.6
Total	6	7	8	.467	73	12	1	0-1	147.2	168	80	14	3	66-5	81	3.90	100	.289	.362	25-0-4	.160	-0	130	-2	18	-0.9
Grossman, Harley	Harley Joseph; B5.5.1930 Evansville IN; D9.5.2003 Evansville IN; BR/TR/6´0˝/170; d4.22; Col Ball St.																									
1952	Was A	0	0	ø	1	0	0	0	0.1	2	2	1	0	0	0	54.00	7	.667	.667	0	ø	0	—	-2	0	-0.1
Groth, Ernie	Ernest John "Dango"; B12.24.1884 Cedarburg WI; D5.23.1950 Milwaukee WI; BR/TR/5´11˝/175; d9.6																									
1904	Chi N	0	2	.000	3	2	2	1	16	22	13	1	1	6	9	5.63	47	.310	.372	6	.000	-1	26	-5	—	-0.7
Groth, Ernest	Ernest William; B5.3.1922 Beaver Falls PA; D12.27.2004 Beaver PA; BR/TR/5´9˝/185; d9.11																									
1947	Cle A	0	0	ø	2	0	0	0	1.1	0	0	0	0	1	1	0.00	ø	.000	.250	0	ø	0	—	1	0	0.0
1948	Cle A	0	0	ø	1	0	0	0	1	1	1	0	0	2	0	9.00	45	.250	.500	0	ø	0*	—	-1	0	0.0
1949	Chi A	0	1	.000	3	0	0	0	5	2	3	2	1	3	1	5.40	77	.125	.300	0	ø	0	—	-1	0	-0.1
Total	3	0	1	.000	6	0	0	0	7.1	3	4	2	1	6	2	4.91	82	.130	.333	0	ø	0	—	-1	0	-0.1
Grott, Matt	Matthew Allen; B12.5.1967 LaPorte IN; BL/TL/6´1˝/205; d5.4; Col Phoenix (AZ) JC																									
1995	Cin N	0	0	ø	2	0	0	0-0	1.2	6	4	1	0	0-0	2	21.60	19	.545	.545	0	ø	0	—	-3	0	-0.1
Grove, Orval	Orval Leroy; B8.29.1919 Mineral KS; D4.20.1992 Carmichael CA; BR/TR/6´3˝/196; d5.28																									
1940	Chi A	0	0	ø	3	0	0	0	6	4	2	0	0	4	1	3.00	147	.182	.308	1	.000	-0	—	1	—	0.0
1941	Chi A	0	0	ø	2	0	0	0	7	9	8	2	0	5	5	10.29	40	.321	.424	2	.000	-0	—	-4	0	-0.2
1942	Chi A	4	6	.400	12	8	4	0	66.1	77	47	1	1	33	21	5.16	70	.283	.363	22-1-3	.227	1	62	-13	0	-1.5
1943	Chi A	15	9	.625	32	25	18-3	2	216.1	192	84	9	4	72	76	2.75	122	.239	.304	66-0-7	.182	2	109	12	0	1.6
1944	Chi A☆	14	15	.483	34	33	11-2	0	234.2	237	112	11	8	71	105	3.72	92	.263	.322	77-0-4	.104	-3	81	-6	0	-0.8
1945	Chi A	14	12	.538	33	30	16-4	1	217	233	100	12	5	68	54	3.44	96	.273	.330	71-0-2	.099	-4	101	-5	0	-0.9
1946	Chi A	8	13	.381	33	26	10-1	0	205.1	213	96	10	3	78	60	3.02	113	.272	.340	65-0-3	.108	-2	102	5	0	0.3
1947	Chi A	6	8	.429	25	19	6-1	0	135.2	158	78	10	4	70	33	4.44	82	.296	.382	48-0-1	.146	-0	93	-12	0	-1.1
1948	Chi A	2	10	.167	32	11	1	1	87.2	110	64	6	3	42	18	6.16	69	.315	.393	21-0-1	.095	-2	64	-17	0	-2.1
1949	Chi A	0	0	ø	1	0	0	0	0.2	4	4	1	1	1	1	54.00	8	.667	.750	0	ø	0	—	-3	0	-0.2
Total	10	63	73	.463	207	152	66-11	4	1176.2	1237	595	62	29	444	374	3.78	93	.272	.340	373-1-21	.129	-9	92	-42	0	-4.9
Grove, Lefty	Robert Moses; B3.6.1900 Lonaconing MD; D5.22.1975 Norwalk OH; BL/TL/6´3˝/190; d4.14; HF1947																									
1925	Phi A	10	12	.455	45	18	5	1	197	207	120	11	5	131	**116**	4.75	98	.278	.390	65-0-2	.123	-6	91	0	—	-0.5
1926	Phi A	13	13	.500	45	33	20-1	6	258	227	97	6	6	101	**194**	**2.51**	**166**	.244	.322	81-0-9	.099	-5	96	44	—	3.7
1927	Phi A	20	13	.606	51	28	14-1	9	262.1	251	116	6	2	79	**174**	3.19	134	.252	.309	80-2-9	.125	-3	110	28	—	3.0
1928	Phi A	**24**	8	.750	39	31	24-4	4	261.2	228	93	10	1	64	**183**	2.58	156	.229	.277	88-1-5	.170	1	110	**41**	—	**4.7**
1929	†Phi A	20	6	**.769**	42	**37**	19-2	4	275.1	278	104	8	3	81	**170**	**2.81**	**151**	.262	.316	102-1-8	.216	1	139	**43**	—	3.6
1930	†Phi A	**28**	5	**.848**	**50**	32	22-2	**9**	291	273	101	8	5	60	**209**	**2.54**	**184**	**.247**	**.288**	110-2-4	.200	0	125	**66**	—	**6.9**
1931	†Phi A	**31**	4	**.886**	41	30	**27-4**	5	288.2	249	84	10	1	62	**175**	**2.06**	**218**	.229	**.271**	115-0-4	.200	-2	103	**74**	—	**8.2**
1932	Phi A	25	10	.714	44	30	**27-4**	7	291.2	269	101	13	1	79	188	**2.84**	**159**	.241	**.292**	107-4-4	.168	0	115	**54**	—	**5.9**
1933	Phi A★	**24**	8	**.750**	45	28	**21**-2	6	275.1	280	113	12	4	83	114	3.20	134	.261	.316	105-1-4	.086	-7	109	35	—	3.1
1934	Bos A	8	8	.500	22	12	5	0	109.1	149	84	5	1	32	43	6.50	74	.320	.365	37-1-3	.162	-0	88	-15	—	-1.9
1935	Bos A☆	20	12	.625	35	30	23-2	1	273	269	105	6	3	65	121	**2.70**	**176**	.257	.302	89-1-6	.079	-5	76	**55**	—	5.5
1936	Bos A★	17	12	.586	35	30	22-**6**	2	253.1	237	90	14	4	65	130	**2.81**	**189**	.246	**.297**	80-0-12	.138	-3	78	**67**	—	**6.6**
1937	Bos A☆	17	9	.654	32	32	21-3	0	262	269	101	9	1	83	153	3.02	157	.261	.317	91-0-6	.143	-3	92	49	—	3.9

YEAR	TM LG	W	L	PCT	G	GS	CG-SHO	SV-BS	IP	H	R	HR	HB	BB-IB	SO	ERA	AERA	OAV	OOB	AB-HR-SH	AVG	PB	SUP	APR	DL	PW
1938	Bos A★	14	4	.778	24	21	12-1	1	163.2	169	65	8	1	52	99	**3.08**	**160**	.263	.319	54-0-7	.148	-1	110	33	—	3.0
1939	Bos A☆	15	4	**.789**	23	23	17-2	0	191	180	63	8	1	58	81	**2.54**	**186**	.249	.305	67-1-9	.134	-1*	96	45	—	3.7
1940	Bos A	7	6	.538	22	21	9-1	0	153.1	159	73	20	1	50	62	3.99	113	.269	.328	53-1-5	.151	-1*	96	9	—	0.5
1941	Bos A	7	7	.500	21	21	10	0	134	155	84	8	2	42	54	4.37	95	.287	.340	45-0-6	.111	-1	125	-6	0	-0.8
Total	17	300	141	.680	616	457	298-35	55	3940.2	3849	1594	162	42	1187	2266	3.06	148	.255	.311	1369-15-103	.148	-37	104	622	0	59.1
GROVER, CHARLIE	Charles Byrd "Bugs"; B6.20.1890 Gallipolis OH; D5.24.1971 Emmett Twp. MI; BL/TR/6´1.5˝/185; d9.9																									
1913	Det A	0	0	ø	2	1	0	0	10.2	9	4	0	0	7	2	3.38	86	.273	.400	3-0-1	.000	-0	51	0	—	0.0
GRUBBS, TOM	Thomas Dillard "Judge"; B2.22.1894 Mt.Sterling KY; D1.28.1986 Lexington KY; BR/TR/6´2˝/165; d10.3; Col Kentucky																									
1920	NY N	0	1	.000	1	1	0	0	5	9	4	0	0	0	0	7.20	42	.409	.409	1	.000	-0	26	-2	—	-0.3
GRUBER, HENRY	Henry John; B12.14.1863 Hamden CT; D9.26.1932 New Haven CT; BR/TR/5´9˝/155; d7.28																									
1887	Det N	4	3	.571	7	7	7	0	62.1	63	29	3	0	21	12	2.74	149	.262	.322	24	.167	1	118	9	—	0.7
1888	Det N	11	14	.440	27	25	25-3	0	240	196	121	8	4	41	71	2.29	122	.213	.249	92	.141	-1	91	9	—	0.7
1889	Cle N	7	16	.304	25	23	23	1	205	198	125	6	8	94	74	3.64	111	.246	.331	69	.101	-1	75	8	—	0.6
1890	Cle P	22	23	.489	48	44	39-1	0	383.1	464	352	15	15	204	110	4.27	93	.286	.371	163	.221	6*	99	-15	—	-0.7
1891	Cle N	17	22	.436	44	40	35-1	0	348.2	407	258	10	7	119	79	4.13	84	.281	.338	141-1	.163	1*	96	-16	—	-1.2
Total	5	61	78	.439	151	139	129-5	1	1239.1	1328	885	42	34	479	346	3.67	99	.264	.332	489-1	.170	5	94	-5	—	0.1
GRUNDT, KEN	Kenneth Allan; B8.26.1969 Melrose Park IL; BL/TL/6´4˝/195; [SFN91 53/1354]; d8.8; Col Missouri Southern																									
1996	Bos A	0	0	ø	1	0	0	0-0	0.1	1	1	0	0	0-0	0	27.00	19	.500	.500	0	ø	0	—	-1	0	0.0
1997	Bos A	0	0	ø	2	0	0	0-0	3	5	3	0	0	0-0	0	9.00	52	.357	.357	0	ø	0	—	-1	0	-0.1
Total	2	0	0	ø	3	0	0	0-0	3.1	6	4	0	0	0-0	0	10.80	44	.375	.375	0	ø	0	—	-2	0	-0.1
GRUNWALD, AL	Alfred Henry "Stretch"; B2.13.1930 Los Angeles CA; BL/TL/6´4˝/(180–200); d4.18																									
1955	Pit N	0	0	ø	3	0	0	0	7.2	7	4	1	0	7-0	2	4.70	88	.241	.389	4	.500	1	—	0	0	0.0
1959	KC A	0	1	.000	6	1	0	1	11.1	18	14	1	0	11-1	9	7.94	50	.360	.475	4	.000	-1*	88	-6	0	-0.6
Total	2	0	1	.000	9	1	0	1	19	25	18	2	0	18-1	11	6.63	61	.316	.443	8	.250	0	88	-6	0	-0.6
GRYBOSKI, KEVIN	Kevin John; B11.15.1973 Wilkes–Barre PA; BR/TR/6´5˝/(220–255); [SeaA95 16/426]; d4.13; Col Wilkes																									
2002	†Atl N	2	1	.667	57	0	0	0-2	51.2	50	20	6	5	37-5	33	3.48	116	.256	.388	0	ø	0	—	4	27	0.2
2003	†Atl N	6	4	.600	64	0	0	0-4	44.1	44	22	3	2	23-6	32	3.86	109	.272	.369	1	.000	-0	—	1	23	0.2
2004	†Atl N	3	2	.600	69	0	0	2-2	50.2	54	22	2	0	23-4	24	2.84	152	.280	.356	0	ø	0	—	6	0	0.6
2005	Atl N	0	0	ø	31	0	0	0-2	21.1	24	10	0	2	12-3	8	2.95	143	.300	.396	0	ø	0	—	2	15	0.1
	Tex A	1	1	.500	11	0	0	0-0	9.2	17	15	1	1	8-2	2	11.17	41	.378	.481	0	ø	0	—	-8	0	-1.3
2006	Was N	0	0	ø	6	0	0	0-1	5.2	14	11	3	1	2-0	4	14.29	31	.452	.500	0	ø	0	—	-7	0	-0.3
Total	5	12	8	.600	238	0	0	2-11	183.1	203	100	15	11	105-20	103	4.07	103	.288	.387	1	.000	-0	—	-2	65	-0.5
GRZANICH, MIKE	Michael Edward; B8.24.1972 Canton IL; BR/TR/6´1˝/180; [HouN92 19/517]; d5.14; Col Parkland (IL) JC																									
1998	Hou N	0	0	ø	1	0	0	0-0	1	1	2	0	0	2-0	1	18.00	23	.333	.500	0	ø	0	—	-2	0	-0.1
GRZENDA, JOE	Joseph Charles; B6.8.1937 Scranton PA; BR/TL/6´2˝/(170–180); d4.26																									
1961	Det A	1	0	1.000	4	0	0	0	5.2	9	5	2	0	2-1	0	7.94	52	.375	.423	1	1.000	0	—	-2	0	-0.3
1964	KC A	0	2	.000	20	0	0	0	25	34	15	2	1	13-2	17	5.40	71	.324	.400	2	.000	-0	—	-4	0	-0.2
1966	KC A	0	2	.000	21	0	0	0	22	28	8	1	0	12-3	14	3.27	104	.337	.412	1	.000	-0	—	1	0	0.1
1967	NY N	0	0	ø	11	0	0	0	16.2	14	4	0	1	8-4	9	2.16	157	.237	.333	1	.000	-0	—	2	0	0.1
1969	†Min A	4	1	.800	38	0	0	3-1	48.2	52	23	4	1	17-4	24	3.88	94	.281	.343	5	.000	0	—	-1	0	0.0
1970	Was A	3	6	.333	49	3	0	6-1	84.2	86	52	8	3	34-9	38	5.00	72	.267	.341	12	.000	-1	181	-13	0	-1.6
1971	Was A	5	2	.714	46	0	0	5-3	70.1	54	19	2	1	17-7	56	1.92	176	.217	.266	7-0-2	.143	-0	—	11	0	1.2
1972	StL N	1	0	1.000	30	0	0	0-0	35	46	24	1	3	17-8	15	5.66	61	.326	.410	1	.000	-0	—	-8	0	-0.4
Total	8	14	13	.519	219	3	0	14-5	308	323	150	20	10	120-38	173	4.00	88	.277	.346	30-0-2	.067	-2	181	-14	0	-1.1
GUANTE, CECILIO	Cecilio (Magallane); B2.1.1960 Villa Mella, D.R.; BR/TR/6´3˝/(185–205); d5.1																									
1982	Pit N	0	0	ø	10	0	0	0-0	27	28	16	1	2	5-0	26	3.33	112	.264	.299	5	.000	-1	—	-1	0	-0.1
1983	Pit N	2	6	.250	49	0	0	9-0	100.1	90	45	5	2	46-6	82	3.32	113	.241	.325	22	.091	-1	—	3	0	0.1
1984	Pit N	2	3	.400	27	0	0	2-1	41.1	32	12	3	2	16-2	30	2.61	139	.224	.305	4-0-1	.000	-0	—	5	17	0.6
1985	Pit N	4	6	.400	63	0	0	5-7	109	84	34	5	5	40-9	92	2.72	133	.214	.293	17	.059	-1	—	12	0	1.0
1986	Pit N	5	2	.714	52	0	0	4-4	78	65	32	11	3	29-3	63	3.35	116	.225	.300	1	.000	-0	—	5	29	0.3
1987	NY A	3	2	.600	23	0	0	1-1	44	42	30	8	1	20-0	46	5.73	77	.247	.323	0	ø	0	—	-6	84	-0.7
1988	NY A	5	6	.455	56	0	0	11-6	75	59	25	10	5	22-3	61	2.88	138	.213	.282	0	ø	0	—	10	0	1.5
	Tex A	0	0	ø	7	0	0	1-0	4.2	8	1	1	0	4-1	4	1.93	213	.400	.500	0	ø	0	—	1	0	0.1
	Year	5	6	.455	63	0	0	12-6	79.2	67	26	11	5	26-4	65	2.82	141	.226	.298	0	ø	0	—	11	0	1.6
1989	Tex A	6	6	.500	50	0	0	2-3	69	66	35	7	4	36-10	69	3.91	102	.249	.343	0	ø	0	—	0	15	0.0
1990	Cle A	2	3	.400	26	1	0	0-3	46.2	38	26	10	3	18-4	30	5.01	79	.220	.301	0	ø	0	69	-4	0	-0.4
Total	9	29	34	.460	363	1	0	35-25	595	512	256	61	27	236-38	503	3.48	111	.232	.310	49-0-1	.061	-3	69	25	145	2.4
GUARDADO, EDDIE	Edward Adrian; B10.2.1970 Stockton CA; BR/TL/6´0˝/(190–205); [MinA90 21/570]; d6.13; Col San Joaquin Delta (CA) JC																									
1993	Min A	3	8	.273	19	16	0	0-0	94.2	123	68	13	1	36-2	46	6.18	71	.319	.376	0	ø	0	86	-17	0	-1.7
1994	Min A	0	2	.000	4	4	0	0-0	17	26	16	3	0	4-0	8	8.47	58	.351	.375	0	ø	0	65	-6	0	-0.6
1995	Min A	4	9	.308	51	5	0	2-3	91.1	99	54	13	0	45-2	71	5.12	94	.280	.356	0	ø	0	35	-2	0	-0.3
1996	Min A	6	5	.545	**83**	0	0	4-3	73.2	61	45	12	3	33-4	74	5.25	98	.228	.316	0	ø	0	—	-1	0	-0.1
1997	Min A	0	4	.000	69	0	0	1-0	46	45	23	7	2	17-2	54	3.91	119	.251	.322	0	ø	0	—	3	0	0.3
1998	Min A	3	1	.750	79	0	0	0-4	65.2	66	34	10	0	28-6	53	4.52	106	.265	.332	0	ø	0	—	3	0	0.1
1999	Min A	2	5	.286	63	0	0	2-2	48	37	24	6	2	25-4	50	4.50	115	.222	.328	0	ø	0	—	4	38	0.6
2000	Min A	7	4	.636	70	0	0	9-2	61.2	55	27	14	1	25-3	52	3.94	134	.238	.313	0	ø	0	—	9	0	1.6
2001	Min A	7	1	.875	67	0	0	12-2	66.2	47	27	5	1	23-4	67	3.51	133	.197	.268	0	ø	0	—	8	15	1.1
2002	†Min A★	1	3	.250	68	0	0	**45**-6	67.2	53	22	9	1	18-2	70	2.93	153	.215	.269	0	ø	0	—	12	0	2.1
2003	†Min A★	3	5	.375	66	0	0	41-4	65.1	50	22	7	0	14-2	60	2.89	155	.207	.249	0	ø	0	—	12	0	2.3
2004	Sea A	2	2	.500	41	0	0	18-7	45.1	31	14	8	1	14-0	45	2.78	161	.194	.261	1	.000	-0	—	9	64	1.4
2005	Sea A	2	3	.400	58	0	0	36-5	56.1	52	23	7	0	15-3	48	2.72	154	.239	.285	0	ø	0	—	7	0	1.3
2006	Sea A	1	3	.250	28	0	0	5-3	23	29	14	8	0	11-1	22	5.48	80	.309	.381	0	ø	0	—	-2	0	-0.4
	Cin N	0	0	ø	15	0	0	8-2	14	15	5	2	1	2-1	17	1.29	367	.278	.310	0	ø	0	—	4	43	0.4
Total	14	41	55	.427	781	25	0	183-43	836.1	789	418	124	13	310-36	737	4.26	110	.250	.316	1	.000	-0	70	43	160	8.1
GUBICZA, MARK	Mark Steven; B8.14.1962 Philadelphia PA; BR/TR/6´5˝/(210–230); [KCA81 2/34]; d4.6																									
1984	KC A	10	14	.417	29	29	4-2	0-0	189	172	90	13	5	75-0	111	4.05	100	.243	.317	0	ø	0	89	1	0	0.2
1985	†KC A	14	10	.583	29	28	0	0-0	177.1	160	88	14	5	77-0	99	4.06	103	.238	.319	0	ø	0	100	3	0	0.5
1986	KC A	12	6	.667	35	24	3-2	0-0	180.2	155	77	8	5	84-2	118	3.64	117	.233	.321	0	ø	0	113	14	15	1.4
1987	KC A	13	18	.419	35	35	10-2	0-0	241.2	231	114	18	6	120-3	166	3.98	115	.259	.347	0	ø	0	81	19	0	2.3
1988	KC A★	20	8	.714	35	35	8-4	0-0	269.2	237	94	11	6	83-3	183	2.70	148	.234	.294	0	ø	0	112	37	0	3.9
1989	KC A★	15	11	.577	36	**36**	8-2	0-0	255	252	100	10	5	63-8	173	3.04	128	.259	.305	0	ø	0	102	22	0	2.2
1990	KC A	4	7	.364	16	16	2	0-0	94	101	48	5	4	38-4	71	4.50	86	.283	.355	0	ø	0	97	-4	95	-0.4
1991	KC A	9	12	.429	26	26	0	0-0	133	168	90	10	6	42-1	89	5.68	73	.308	.361	0	ø	0	92	-20	36	-2.6
1992	KC A	7	6	.538	18	18	2-1	0-0	111.1	110	47	8	1	36-3	81	3.72	110	.259	.316	0	ø	0	91	6	86	0.6
1993	KC A	5	8	.385	49	6	0	2-1	104.1	128	61	2	2	43-8	80	4.66	99	.307	.370	0	ø	0	86	-2	0	-0.3
1994	KC A	7	9	.438	22	22	0	0-0	130	158	74	11	0	26-5	59	4.50	112	.301	.331	0	ø	0	90	6	0	0.7
1995	KC A	12	14	.462	33	**33**	3-2	0-0	213.1	222	97	21	6	62-2	81	3.75	128	.272	.326	0	ø	0	77	24	0	2.7
1996	KC A	4	12	.250	19	19	2-1	0-0	119.1	132	70	22	7	34-0	55	5.13	98	.284	.339	0	ø	0	68	0	86	0.0
1997	Ana A	0	1	.000	2	2	0	0-0	4.2	13	13	2	0	3-0	5	25.07	18	.481	.533	0	ø	0	110	-10	170	-1.3
Total	14	132	136	.493	384	329	42-16	2-1	2223.1	2239	1063	155	58	786-39	1371	3.96	109	.264	.327	0	ø	0	92	96	488	9.9
GUDAT, MARV	Marvin John; B8.27.1903 Goliad TX; D3.1.1954 Los Angeles CA; BL/TL/5´11˝/162; d5.21; Col UCLA; ▲																									
1929	Cin N	1	1	.500	7	2	2	0	26.2	29	12	0	0	4	0	3.38	135	.282	.308	10	.200	-0*	48	3	—	0.1
1932	†Chi N	0	0	ø	1	0	0	0	1	1	0	0	0	0	2	0.00	ø	.250	.250	94-1-1	.255	0*	—	0	—	0.0
Total	2	1	1	.500	8	2	2	0	27.2	30	12	0	0	4	2	3.25	139	.280	.306	104-1-1	.250	-0	48	3	—	0.1

YEAR	TM LG	W	L	PCT	G	GS	CG-SHO	SV-BS	IP	H	R	HR	HB	BB-IB	SO	ERA	AERA	OAV	OOB	AB-HR-SH	AVG	PB	SUP	APR	DL	PW
GUERRIER, MATT	Matthew Olson; B8.2.1978 Cleveland OH; BR/TR/6´3˝/(185–194); [ChiA99 10/309]; d6.17; Col Kent St.																									
2004	Min A	0	1	.000	9	2	0	0-0	19	22	13	5	1	6-0	11	5.68	81	.293	.354	1	.000	-0	80	-2	0	-0.1
2005	Min A	0	3	.000	43	0	0	0-0	71.2	71	29	6	3	24-5	46	3.39	129	.259	.325	1	.000	-0	—	8	0	0.5
2006	†Min A	1	0	1.000	39	1	0	1-0	69.2	78	29	9	0	21-0	37	3.36	136	.287	.333	0	ø	0	144	9	53	0.4
Total	3	1	4	.200	91	3	0	1-0	160.1	171	71	20	4	51-5	94	3.65	123	.275	.332	2	.000	-0	104	15	53	0.8
GUESE, WHITEY	Theodore; B1.24.1872 New Bremen OH; D4.8.1951 Wapakoneta OH; BR/TR/6´0.5˝/200; d7.13																									
1901	Cin N	1	4	.200	6	5	4	0	44.1	62	48	5	3	14	11	6.09	53	.328	.383	15	.200	1	137	-17	—	-1.5
GUETTERMAN, LEE	Arthur Lee; B11.22.1958 Chattanooga TN; BL/TL/6´8˝/(225–235); [SeaA81 4/80]; d9.12; Col Liberty																									
1984	Sea A	0	0	ø	3	0	0	0-0	4.1	9	2	0	0	2-0	2	4.15	97	.450	.500	0	ø	0	—	0	0	0.0
1986	Sea A	0	4	.000	41	4	1	0-3	76	108	67	7	4	30-3	38	7.34	58	.347	.406	0	ø	0	112	-24	0	-1.2
1987	Sea A	11	4	.733	25	17	2-1	0-0	113.1	117	60	13	2	35-2	42	3.81	124	.267	.320	0	ø	0	106	8	0	1.0
1988	NY A	1	2	.333	20	2	0	0-1	40.2	49	21	2	1	14-0	15	4.65	85	.306	.364	0	ø	0	23	-2	0	-0.2
1989	NY A	5	5	.500	70	0	0	13-0	103	98	31	6	0	26-9	51	2.45	159	.258	.304	0	ø	0	—	17	0	2.0
1990	NY A	11	7	.611	64	0	0	2-5	93	80	37	6	0	26-7	48	3.39	118	.236	.288	0	ø	0	—	7	15	1.3
1991	NY A	3	4	.429	64	0	0	6-3	88	91	42	6	3	25-5	35	3.68	113	.268	.320	0	ø	0	—	3	0	0.3
1992	NY A	1	1	.500	15	0	0	0-0	22.2	35	24	5	0	13-3	5	9.53	41	.354	.421	0	ø	0	—	-13	0	-1.0
	NY N	3	4	.429	43	0	0	2-1	43.1	57	28	5	1	14-5	15	5.82	60	.324	.371	2	.000	-0	—	-10	0	-1.6
1993	StL N	3	3	.500	40	0	0	1-3	46	41	18	1	2	16-5	19	2.93	137	.240	.309	2	.500	1	—	5	0	0.6
1995	Sea A	0	0	ø	23	0	0	1-1	17	21	13	1	3	11-0	11	6.88	69	.300	.417	0	ø	0	—	-3	0	-0.1
1996	Sea A	0	2	.000	17	0	0	0-0	11	11	8	0	0	10-2	6	4.09	122	.275	.420	0	ø	0	—	0	0	0.0
Total	11	38	36	.514	425	23	3-1	25-17	658.1	717	351	52	16	222-41	287	4.33	96	.282	.340	4	.250	0	111	-12	15	1.1
GUIDRY, RON	Ronald Ames; B8.28.1950 Lafayette LA; BL/TL/5´11˝/(157–170); [NYA71 3/65]; d7.27; C1; Col Louisiana–Lafayette; [DL 1989 NY A 78]																									
1975	NY A	0	1	.000	10	1	0	0-0	15.2	15	6	0	1	9-0	15	3.45	108	.259	.362	0	ø	0	95	1	0	0.0
1976	†NY A	0	0	ø	7	0	0	0-0	16	20	12	1	0	4-0	12	5.63	61	.294	.333	0	ø	0	—	-4	0	-0.2
1977	†NY A	16	7	.696	31	25	9-5	1-0	210.2	174	72	12	0	65-2	176	2.82	141	.224	.283	0	ø	0*	107	28	0	2.9
1978	†NY A★	**25**	3	**.893**	35	35	16-**9**	0-0	273.2	187	61	13	1	72-1	248	**1.74**	**210**	**.193**	**.249**	0	ø	0*	116	**60**	0	**6.4**
1979	NY A★	18	8	.692	33	30	15-2	2-0	236.1	203	83	20	0	71-0	201	**2.78**	148	.236	.292	0	ø	0*	100	35	0	3.6
1980	†NY A	17	10	.630	37	29	5-3	1-1	219.2	215	97	19	1	80-1	166	3.56	111	.260	.322	0	ø	0	118	11	0	1.3
1981	†NY A	11	5	.688	23	21	0	0-0	127	100	41	12	1	26-0	104	2.76	131	.214	**.256**	0	ø	0	98	13	0	1.7
1982	NY A☆	14	8	.636	34	33	6-1	0-0	222	216	104	22	1	69-3	162	3.81	106	.254	.309	0	ø	0	124	5	0	0.4
1983	NY A✳	21	9	.700	31	31	**21**-3	0-0	250.1	232	99	26	2	60-3	156	3.42	116	.244	.288	0	ø	0*	105	18	0	2.1
1984	NY A	10	11	.476	29	28	5-1	0-0	195.2	223	102	24	2	44-3	127	4.51	85	.287	.323	0	ø	0*	109	-13	18	-1.2
1985	NY A	**22**	6	**.786**	34	33	11-2	0-0	259	243	104	28	0	42-3	143	3.27	124	.248	.277	0	ø	0	125	24	0	2.3
1986	NY A	9	12	.429	30	30	5	0-0	192.1	202	94	28	1	38-2	140	3.98	104	.265	.300	0	ø	0	89	4	24	0.3
1987	NY A	5	8	.385	22	17	2	0-0	117.2	111	50	14	1	38-3	96	3.67	121	.248	.307	0	ø	0	86	11	0	1.0
1988	NY A	2	3	.400	12	10	0	0-0	56	57	28	7	2	15-3	32	4.18	95	.259	.311	0	ø	0*	94	-1	100	-0.1
Total	14	170	91	.651	368	323	95-26	4-1	2392	2198	953	226	13	633-24	1778	3.29	120	.244	.292	0	ø	0	108	192	220	20.5
GUINN, SKIP	Drannon Eugene; B10.25.1944 St.Charles MO; BR/TL/5´10˝/(170–180); d5.7; Col Santa Monica (CA) City																									
1968	Atl N	0	0	ø	3	0	0	0	5	3	2	0	0	3-0	4	3.60	83	.167	.286	0	ø	0*	—	0	0	0.0
1969	Hou N	1	2	.333	28	0	0	0-2	27	34	22	3	1	21-2	33	6.67	53	.304	.412	3	.000	-0	—	-9	0	-0.9
1971	Hou N	0	0	ø	4	0	0	1-0	4.2	1	0	0	0	3-1	3	0.00	ø	.067	.222	0	ø	0	—	2	0	0.1
Total	3	1	2	.333	35	0	0	1-2	36.2	38	24	3	1	27-3	40	5.40	64	.262	.377	3	.000	-0	—	-7	0	-0.8
GUISE, LEFTY	Witt Orison; B9.18.1908 Driggs AR; D8.13.1968 Little Rock AR; BL/TL/6´2˝/172; d9.3; Col Florida																									
1940	Cin N	0	0	ø	2	0	0	0	7.2	8	2	0	1	5	1	1.17	323	.296	.424	3	.333	0	—	2	—	0.1
GULLETT, DON	Donald Edward; B1.6.1951 Lynn KY; BR/TL/6´0˝/(187–190); [CinN69 1/14]; d4.10; C13; [DL 1979 NY A 180, 1980 NY A 180]																									
1970	†Cin N	5	2	.714	44	2	0	6-0	77.2	54	23	4	0	44-6	76	2.43	166	.196	.306	19	.211	1	89	14	0	1.5
1971	Cin N	16	6	**.727**	35	31	4-3	0-3	217.2	196	73	14	2	64-6	107	2.65	128	.242	.298	75-0-5	.120	-2*	94	16	0	1.2
1972	†Cin N	9	10	.474	31	16	2	2-2	134.2	127	61	15	1	43-5	96	3.94	82	.250	.309	38-0-5	.211	2	128	-9	0	-1.2
1973	†Cin N	18	8	.692	45	30	7-4	2-0	228.1	198	95	24	3	69-8	153	3.51	98	.232	.290	64-0-7	.188	3*	128	0	0	0.3
1974	Cin N	17	11	.607	36	35	10-3	0-1	243	201	93	22	2	88-8	183	3.04	115	.222	.291	80-0-10	.237	4*	131	13	0	1.8
1975	†Cin N	15	4	**.789**	22	22	8-3	0-0	159.2	127	49	11	2	56-4	98	2.42	148	.218	.287	62-0-3	.226	3	126	19	62	2.6
1976	†Cin N	11	3	.786	23	20	4	1-0	126	119	48	8	0	48-3	64	3.00	117	.253	.321	44-0-6	.182	-0*	131	6	0	0.7
1977	†NY A	14	4	.778	22	22	7-1	0-0	158.1	137	67	14	1	69-1	116	3.58	111	.232	.312	0	ø	0	131	8	24	0.8
1978	NY A	4	2	.667	8	8	2	0-0	44.2	46	19	3	1	20-1	28	3.63	101	.269	.347	0	ø	0	129	1	98	0.1
Total	9	109	50	.686	266	186	44-14	11-6	1390	1205	528	115	12	501-42	921	3.11	114	.233	.301	382-0-36	.194	10	123	68	544	7.8
GULLICKSON, BILL	William Lee; B2.20.1959 Marshall MN; BR/TR/6´3˝/(198–225); [MonN77 1/2]; d9.26																									
1979	Mon N	0	0	ø	1	0	0	0-0	1	2	0	0	0	0-0	0	0.00	ø	.500	.500	0	ø	0	—	0	0	0.0
1980	Mon N	10	5	.667	24	19	5-2	0-0	141	127	53	6	2	50-2	120	3.00	121	.238	.303	40-0-10	.175	0	111	10	0	1.0
1981	†Mon N	7	9	.438	22	22	3-2	0-0	157.1	142	54	3	4	34-4	115	2.80	127	.239	.283	46-0-4	.152	-0	87	13	0	1.3
1982	Mon N	12	14	.462	34	34	6	0-0	236.2	231	101	25	4	61-2	155	3.57	103	.254	.302	82-0-9	.122	-2	107	6	0	0.2
1983	Mon N	17	12	.586	34	34	10-1	0-0	242.1	230	108	19	4	59-4	120	3.75	97	.251	.297	82-1-9	.134	1	113	-2	0	-0.1
1984	Mon N	12	9	.571	32	32	3	0-0	226.2	230	100	27	1	37-7	100	3.61	96	.265	.294	73-0-6	.110	-2	105	-3	18	-0.8
1985	Mon N	14	12	.538	29	29	4-1	0-0	181.1	187	78	8	1	47-9	68	3.52	98	.271	.315	64-0-4	.188	2	91	-1	21	0.0
1986	Cin N	15	12	.556	37	37	6-2	0-0	244.2	245	103	24	2	60-10	121	3.38	114	.264	.306	79-0-9	.076	-4	98	12	0	0.7
1987	Cin N	10	11	.476	27	27	3-1	0-0	165	172	99	33	2	39-6	89	4.85	87	.267	.308	53-1-4	.208	2	101	-12	0	-1.2
	NY A	4	2	.667	8	8	1	0-0	48	46	29	7	1	11-1	28	4.88	91	.253	.296	0	ø	0	123	-3	0	-0.3
1990	Hou N	10	14	.417	32	32	2-1	0-0	193.1	221	100	21	2	61-14	73	3.82	98	.287	.338	57-1-7	.158	2	88	-5	0	-0.6
1991	Det A	**20**	9	.690	35	**35**	4	0-0	226.1	256	109	22	4	44-13	91	3.90	107	.288	.321	0-0-1	ø	0	124	6	0	0.5
1992	Det A	14	13	.519	34	34	4-1	0-0	221.2	228	109	35	0	50-5	64	4.34	92	.267	.305	0	ø	0	116	-6	0	-0.6
1993	Det A	13	9	.591	28	28	2	0-0	159.1	186	106	28	3	44-3	70	5.37	81	.291	.336	0	ø	0	121	-18	35	-2.1
1994	Det A	4	5	.444	21	19	1	0-0	115.1	156	79	24	4	25-2	65	5.93	83	.322	.360	0	ø	0	130	-10	0	-0.6
Total	14	162	136	.544	398	390	54-11	0-0	2560	2659	1228	282	34	622-82	1279	3.93	98	.268	.311	576-3-63	.141	-2	108	-13	74	-2.6
GUMBERT, AD	Addison Courtney; B10.10.1868 Pittsburgh PA; D4.23.1925 Pittsburgh PA; BR/TR/5´10˝/200; d9.15; b–Billy																									
1888	Chi N	3	3	.500	6	6	5	0	48.2	44	24	0	5	10	16	3.14	96	.234	.291	24	.333	2*	111	1	—	0.2
1889	Chi N	16	13	.552	31	28	25-2	0	246.1	258	148	16	14	76	91	3.62	115	.262	.323	153-7	.288	11*	112	17	—	2.4
1890	Bos P	23	12	.657	39	33	27-1	0	277.1	338	189	18	11	86	81	3.96	111	.288	.342	145-3	.241	5*	115	15	—	1.8
1891	Chi N	17	11	.607	32	31	24-1	0	256.1	282	149	5	10	90	73	3.58	93	.269	.332	105	.305	12*	103	-4	—	0.8
1892	Chi N	22	19	.537	46	45	39	0	382.2	399	220	11	14	107	118	3.41	97	.258	.312	178-1	.236	4*	100	0	—	0.4
1893	Pit N	11	7	.611	22	20	16-2	0	162.2	207	119	5	5	78	40	5.15	88	.301	.376	95	.221	1*	121	-6	—	-0.4
1894	Pit N	15	14	.517	38	32	26	0	271	376	245	14	6	85	67	6.04	87	.325	.374	114-1-1	.298	6*	103	-25	—	-1.4
1895	Bro N	11	16	.407	33	26	20	1	234	288	183	11	12	69	45	5.08	87	.298	.352	97-2-0	.361	11*	102	-23	—	-1.0
1896	Bro N	0	4	.000	5	4	2	0	31	34	18	2	0	11	3	3.77	109	.276	.336	11	.182	-0	43	1	—	0.2
	Phi N	5	3	.625	11	10	7-1	0	77.1	99	55	0	4	23	14	4.54	95	.308	.362	34-1-1	.265	1	132	-2	—	-0.1
	Year	5	7	.417	16	14	9-1	0	108.1	133	73	2	4	34	17	4.32	99	.300	.355	45-1-1	.244	1	107	-1	—	0.1
Total	9	123	102	.547	263	235	191-7	1	1987.1	2325	1350	82	81	635	548	4.28	96	.284	.341	956-15-2	.274	53	107	-26	—	2.9
GUMBERT, HARRY	Harry Edwards "Gunboat"; B11.5.1909 Elizabeth PA; D1.4.1995 Wimberley TX; BR/TR/6´2˝/185; d9.12; Mil 1945																									
1935	NY N	1	2	.333	6	3	1	0	23.2	35	27	1	0	10	11	6.08	63	.330	.388	8	.000	-1	73	-10	—	-1.1
1936	†NY N	11	3	.786	39	15	3	0	140.2	157	77	7	2	54	52	3.90	100	.281	.346	44	.250	2	121	-3	—	0.1
1937	†NY N	10	11	.476	34	24	10-1	1	200.1	194	92	11	4	62	65	3.68	106	.257	.317	72-1-2	.181	-1	95	6	—	0.8
1938	NY N	15	13	.536	38	33	14-1	0	235.2	238	114	13	7	84	84	4.01	94	.261	.328	84-0-3	.155	-3*	93	-3	—	-0.2
1939	NY N	18	11	.621	36	34	14-2	0	243.2	257	132	21	1	81	81	4.32	91	.271	.329	90-0-6	.200	-0*	107	-10	—	-0.8
1940	NY N	12	14	.462	35	30	14-2	2	237	230	110	17	3	81	77	3.76	103	.252	.316	87-1-2	.195	2	86	5	—	0.8
1941	NY N	1	1	.500	5	5	1	0	32.1	34	20	3	0	18	9	4.45	83	.266	.356	12-0-1	.167	-0	129	-3	0	-0.2
	StL N	11	5	.688	33	17	8-3	1	144.1	139	52	7	1	30	53	2.74	137	.251	.291	53-2-1	.321	6*	94	16	0	2.4
	Year	12	6	.667	38	22	9-3	1	176.2	173	72	10	1	48	62	3.06	123	.254	.304	65-2-2	.292	5	102	12	0	2.2
1942	†StL N	9	5	.643	38	19	5	5	163	156	67	3	1	59	52	3.26	105	.250	.315	54-0-1	.111	-2	115	4	0	0.4

YEAR	TM LG	W	L	PCT	G	GS	CG-SHO	SV-BS	IP	H	R	HR	HB	BB-IB	SO	ERA	AERA	OAV	OOB	AB-HR-SH	AVG	PB	SUP	APR	DL	PW
1943	StL N	10	5	.667	21	19	7-2	0	133	115	46	4	0	32	40	2.84	118	.237	.284	45-0-6	.156	-2	97	9	0	0.9
1944	StL N	4	2	.667	10	7	3	1	61.1	60	23	1	0	19	16	2.49	141	.258	.313	21	.190	-0	102	6	0	0.6
	Cin N	10	8	.556	24	19	11-2	2	155.1	157	61	7	2	40	40	3.30	106	.262	.310	52-0-5	.096	-2	96	6	0	0.5
	Year	14	10	.583	34	26	14-2	3	216.2	217	84	8	2	59	56	3.07	114	.261	.311	73-0-5	.123	-2	98	13	0	1.1
1946	Cin N	6	8	.429	36	10	5	4	119	112	48	8	1	42	44	3.25	103	.248	.314	32-0-1	.250	1	67	2	0	0.4
1947	Cin N	10	10	.500	46	0	0	10	90.1	88	42	3	0	47	43	3.89	106	.260	.351	22-0-2	.273	1	—	3	0	0.7
1948	Cin N	10	8	.556	**61**	0	0	**17**	106.1	123	50	5	0	34	25	3.47	113	.291	.344	25-1-1	.040	-1	—	4	0	0.7
1949	Cin N	4	3	.571	29	0	0	2	40.2	58	28	5	1	8	12	5.53	76	.341	.374	2	.000	-0	—	-6	0	-0.9
	Pit N	1	4	.200	16	0	0	3	27.2	30	20	5	0	18	5	5.86	72	.270	.372	4	.250	0	—	-5	0	-0.8
	Year	5	7	.417	45	0	0	5	68.1	88	48	10	1	26	17	5.66	74	.313	.373	6	.167	-0	—	-10	0	-1.7
1950	Pit N	0	0	ø	1	0	0	0	1.2	3	3	0	0	2	0	5.40	81	.333	.455	1	1.000	0	—	-1	0	0.0
Total	15	143	113	.559	508	235	96-13	48	2156	2186	1012	121	23	721	709	3.68	102	.263	.323	708-5-31	.184	-2	98	20	0	4.3

GUMBERT, BILLY William Skeen; B8.8.1865 Pittsburgh PA; D4.13.1946 Pittsburgh PA; BR/TR/6´1.5˝/200; d6.19; b–Ad

YEAR	TM LG	W	L	PCT	G	GS	CG-SHO	SV-BS	IP	H	R	HR	HB	BB-IB	SO	ERA	AERA	OAV	OOB	AB-HR-SH	AVG	PB	SUP	APR	DL	PW
1890	Pit N	4	6	.400	10	10	8	0	79.1	96	71	0	8	31	18	5.22	63	.290	.365	37-1	.243	3	134	-18	—	-1.4
1892	Pit N	3	2	.600	6	3	2	0	39.2	30	15	0	1	23	3	1.36	242	.201	.312	18	.111	-1*	64	7	—	0.7
1893	Lou N	0	0	ø	1	1	0	0	0.2	2	6	0	0	5	0	27.00	16	.500	.778	1	1.000	1	175	-3	—	-0.1
Total	3	7	8	.467	17	14	10	0	119.2	128	92	0	9	59	21	4.06	81	.264	.355	56-1	.214	3	124	-14	—	-0.8

GUMPERT, DAVE David Lawrence; B5.5.1958 South Haven MI; BR/TR/6´1˝/190; d7.25; Col Aquinas

YEAR	TM LG	W	L	PCT	G	GS	CG-SHO	SV-BS	IP	H	R	HR	HB	BB-IB	SO	ERA	AERA	OAV	OOB	AB-HR-SH	AVG	PB	SUP	APR	DL	PW
1982	Det A	0	0	ø	5	1	0	1-1	2	7	6	1	0	2-0	0	27.00	15	.700	.750	0	ø	0	89	-5	0	-0.5
1983	Det A	0	2	.000	26	0	0	2-0	44.1	43	16	1	0	7-3	14	2.64	150	.257	.281	0	ø	0	—	6	0	0.3
1985	Chi N	1	0	1.000	9	0	0	0-0	10.1	12	7	0	0	7-1	4	3.48	115	.279	.365	1	.000	-0	—	-1	26	-0.1
1986	Chi N	2	0	1.000	38	0	0	2-2	59.2	60	32	4	1	28-7	45	4.37	93	.267	.349	5	.000	-1	—	-2	0	-0.2
1987	KC A	0	0	ø	8	0	0	0-0	19.1	27	16	3	0	6-0	13	6.05	76	.333	.375	0	ø	0	—	-4	0	-0.2
Total	5	3	2	.600	86	1	0	5-3	135.2	149	77	9	1	50-11	76	4.31	95	.283	.342	6	.000	-1	89	-6	26	-0.7

GUMPERT, RANDY Randall Pennington; B1.23.1918 Monocacy PA; BR/TR/6´3˝/205; d6.13; Mil 1943–45; C1

YEAR	TM LG	W	L	PCT	G	GS	CG-SHO	SV-BS	IP	H	R	HR	HB	BB-IB	SO	ERA	AERA	OAV	OOB	AB-HR-SH	AVG	PB	SUP	APR	DL	PW
1936	Phi A	1	2	.333	22	3	2	2	62.1	74	42	2	0	32	9	4.76	107	.295	.375	22	.273	0	46	0	—	0.0
1937	Phi A	0	0	ø	10	1	0	0	12	16	17	1	1	15	5	12.00	39	.333	.500	3	.333	0	111	-9	—	-0.4
1938	Phi A	0	2	.000	4	2	0	0	12.1	24	18	1	0	10	1	10.95	44	.393	.479	4	.250	0	91	-8	—	-0.9
1946	NY A	11	3	.786	33	12	4	1	132.2	113	44	8	0	32	63	2.31	150	.229	.276	47-0-1	.128	-2	151	15	0	1.2
1947	NY A	4	1	.800	24	6	2	0	56.1	71	36	4	0	28	25	5.43	65	.311	.387	14-0-2	.071	-1*	108	-12	0	-1.1
1948	NY A	1	0	1.000	15	0	0	0	25	27	10	0	1	6	12	2.88	142	.267	.315	0	ø	0	—	3	0	0.1
	Chi A	2	6	.250	16	11	6-1	0	97.1	103	43	6	2	13	31	3.79	112	.275	.303	29-0-3	.138	-2	50	6	0	0.2
	Year	3	6	.333	31	11	6-1	0	122.1	130	53	6	3	19	43	3.60	117	.273	.305	29-0-3	.138	-2	51	9	0	0.3
1949	Chi A	13	16	.448	34	32	18-3	1	234	223	111	22	1	83	78	3.81	110	.253	.318	84-0-6	.190	-1	92	10	0	1.0
1950	Chi A	5	12	.294	40	17	6-1	0	155.1	165	87	15	4	58	48	4.75	94	.275	.343	42-0-4	.071	-4*	73	-2	0	-0.6
1951	Chi A☆	9	8	.529	33	16	7-1	2	141.2	156	74	20	1	34	45	4.32	93	.272	.314	45-0-4	.333	3*	128	-2	0	-0.1
1952	Bos A	1	0	1.000	10	1	0	1	19.2	15	11	1	1	5	6	4.12	96	.205	.266	5	.000	-1	66	-1	0	-0.1
	Was A	4	9	.308	20	12	2	0	104	112	55	12	5	30	29	4.24	84	.273	.330	34-0-3	.206	0	110	-8	0	-0.9
	Year	5	9	.357	30	13	2	1	123.2	127	66	13	6	35	35	4.22	86	.262	.320	39-0-3	.179	-0	106	-8	0	-1.0
Total	10	51	59	.464	261	113	47-6	7	1052.2	1099	548	92	16	346	352	4.17	98	.268	.328	329-0-23	.182	-8	96	-8	0	-1.6

GUNDERSON, ERIC Eric Andrew; B3.29.1966 Portland OR; BR/TL/6´0˝/(175–195); [SFN87 2/48]; d4.11; Col Portland St.

YEAR	TM LG	W	L	PCT	G	GS	CG-SHO	SV-BS	IP	H	R	HR	HB	BB-IB	SO	ERA	AERA	OAV	OOB	AB-HR-SH	AVG	PB	SUP	APR	DL	PW
1990	SF N	1	2	.333	7	4	0	0-0	19.2	24	14	2	0	11-1	14	5.49	67	.293	.376	6	.000	-1	80	-5	0	-0.7
1991	SF N	0	0	ø	2	0	0	1-0	3.1	6	4	0	0	1-0	2	5.40	67	.353	.389	0	ø	0	—	-2	0	-0.1
1992	Sea A	2	1	.667	9	0	0	0-0	9.1	12	12	1	1	5-3	2	8.68	46	.324	.400	0	ø	0	—	-6	0	-1.1
1994	NY N	0	0	ø	14	0	0	0-0	9	5	0	0	0	4-0	4	0.00	ø	.185	.290	0	ø	0	—	4	0	0.2
1995	NY N	1	1	.500	30	0	0	0-3	24.1	25	10	2	1	8-3	19	3.70	109	.269	.330	0	ø	0	—	1	0	0.2
	Bos A	2	1	.667	19	0	0	0-0	12.1	13	7	0	2	9-1	9	5.11	95	.295	.429	0	ø	0	—	0	0	0.0
1996	Bos A	0	1	.000	28	0	0	0-0	17.1	21	17	5	2	8-2	7	8.31	61	.300	.378	0	ø	0	—	-6	0	-0.3
1997	Tex A	2	1	.667	60	0	0	1-3	49.2	45	19	5	2	15-3	31	3.26	149	.241	.300	0	ø	0	—	9	20	0.4
1998	Tex A	0	3	.000	68	1	0	0-2	67.2	88	43	13	1	19-4	41	5.19	94	.315	.358	0	ø	0	38	-2	0	-0.1
1999	Tex A	0	0	ø	11	0	0	0-0	10	20	8	1	0	2-0	6	7.20	72	.417	.431	0	ø	0	—	-2	149	-0.1
2000	Tor A	0	1	.000	6	0	0	0-0	6.1	15	6	0	1	2-1	2	7.11	71	.455	.486	0	ø	0	—	-2	0	-0.2
Total	10	8	11	.421	254	5	0	2-8	229	274	140	29	10	84-18	137	4.95	93	.299	.359	6	.000	-0	60	-11	169	-1.8

GUNKEL, RED Woodward William; B4.15.1894 Sheffield IL; D4.19.1954 Chicago IL; BB/TR/5´8˝/158; d6.18; Col Illinois

YEAR	TM LG	W	L	PCT	G	GS	CG-SHO	SV-BS	IP	H	R	HR	HB	BB-IB	SO	ERA	AERA	OAV	OOB	AB-HR-SH	AVG	PB	SUP	APR	DL	PW
1916	Cle A	0	0	ø	1	0	0	0	1	0	2	0	1	1	1	0.00	ø	.000	.500	0	ø	0	—	0	—	0.0

GURA, LARRY Lawrence Cyril; B11.26.1947 Joliet IL; BB/TL (BR 1970–72)/6´1˝/(170–185); [ChiN69 2/40]; d4.30; Col Arizona St.

YEAR	TM LG	W	L	PCT	G	GS	CG-SHO	SV-BS	IP	H	R	HR	HB	BB-IB	SO	ERA	AERA	OAV	OOB	AB-HR-SH	AVG	PB	SUP	APR	DL	PW
1970	Chi N	1	3	.250	20	3	1	1-1	38	35	18	6	1	23-3	21	3.79	119	.254	.364	10-0-1	.000	-1	146	3	0	0.2
1971	Chi N	0	0	ø	6	0	0	1-0	3	6	3	0	0	1-1	2	6.00	66	.400	.438	1	.000	-0	—	-1	0	-0.1
1972	Chi N	0	0	ø	7	0	0	0-0	12.1	11	5	3	0	3-1	13	3.65	104	.250	.298	1	.000	-0	—	0	0	0.0
1973	Chi N	2	4	.333	21	7	0	0-1	64.2	79	39	10	1	11-0	43	4.87	81	.296	.325	15-0-2	.200	0*	118	-6	0	-0.4
1974	NY A	5	1	.833	8	8	4-2	0-0	56	54	17	2	0	12-1	17	2.41	147	.248	.287	0	ø	0	124	7	0	0.8
1975	NY A	7	8	.467	26	20	5	0-0	151.1	173	65	13	3	41-1	65	3.51	106	.295	.342	0	ø	0	81	4	0	0.4
1976	†KC A	4	0	1.000	20	2	1-1	1-0	62.2	47	20	4	1	20-3	22	2.30	153	.213	.274	0	ø	0	88	8	22	0.6
1977	†KC A	8	5	.615	52	6	1-1	10-6	106.1	108	43	8	1	28-4	46	3.13	129	.265	.310	0	ø	0	108	10	0	1.4
1978	†KC A	16	4	.800	35	26	8-2	0-0	221.2	183	73	13	4	60-3	81	2.72	141	.229	.283	0	ø	0	104	29	0	2.6
1979	KC A	13	12	.520	39	33	7-1	0-1	233.2	226	137	29	7	73-4	85	4.47	96	.253	.312	0	ø	0	116	-7	0	-0.6
1980	†KC A☆	18	10	.643	36	36	16-4	0-0	283.1	272	107	20	5	76-6	113	2.95	137	.255	.304	0	ø	0	115	33	0	3.1
1981	†KC A	11	8	.579	23	23	12-2	0-0	172.1	139	61	11	4	35-0	61	2.72	133	.223	.265	0	ø	0	91	16	0	1.8
1982	KC A	18	12	.600	37	37	8-3	0-0	248	251	124	31	6	64-2	98	4.03	101	.261	.309	0	ø	0	111	1	0	0.2
1983	KC A	11	18	.379	34	31	5	0-0	200.1	220	119	23	8	76-6	57	4.90	84	.284	.347	0	ø	0*	80	-16	0	-1.8
1984	KC A	12	9	.571	31	25	3	0-0	168.2	175	102	26	4	67-3	68	5.18	78	.269	.338	0	ø	0	129	-19	0	-2.0
1985	KC A	0	0	ø	3	0	0	1-0	4.1	7	6	1	0	4-0	2	12.46	34	.368	.478	0	ø	0	—	-4	0	-0.2
	Chi N	0	3	.000	5	4	0	0-0	20.1	34	19	4	1	6-0	7	8.41	48	.370	.414	6	.000	-0	88	-8	0	-1.0
Total	16	126	97	.565	403	261	71-16	14-9	2047	2020	958	204	46	600-38	801	3.76	106	.260	.313	33-0-3	.091	-2	106	50	22	5.0

GUTH, CHARLIE Charles J.; B1856 Chicago IL; D7.5.1883 Cambridge MA; d9.30

YEAR	TM LG	W	L	PCT	G	GS	CG-SHO	SV-BS	IP	H	R	HR	HB	BB-IB	SO	ERA	AERA	OAV	OOB	AB-HR-SH	AVG	PB	SUP	APR	DL	PW
1880	Chi N	1	0	1.000	1	1	1	0	9	12	8	0	—	1	7	5.00	48	.293	.310	4	.250	0	204	-2	—	-0.2

GUTHRIE, JEREMY Jeremy Shane; B4.8.1979 Roseburg OR; BR/TR/6´1˝/200; [CleA02 1/22]; d8.28; Col Brigham Young/Stanford

YEAR	TM LG	W	L	PCT	G	GS	CG-SHO	SV-BS	IP	H	R	HR	HB	BB-IB	SO	ERA	AERA	OAV	OOB	AB-HR-SH	AVG	PB	SUP	APR	DL	PW
2004	Cle A	0	0	ø	6	0	0	0-0	11.2	9	6	1	1	6-0	7	4.63	94	.214	.327	0	ø	0	—	0	0	0.0
2005	Cle A	0	0	ø	1	0	0	0-0	6	9	4	2	0	2-0	3	6.00	69	.360	.393	0	ø	0	—	-1	0	0.0
2006	Cle A	0	0	ø	9	1	0	0-0	19.1	24	15	2	2	15-1	14	6.98	62	.316	.441	0	ø	0	131	-5	0	-0.2
Total	3	0	0	ø	16	1	0	0-0	37	42	25	5	3	23-1	24	6.08	71	.294	.400	0	ø	0	131	-6	0	-0.2

GUTHRIE, MARK Mark Andrew; B9.22.1965 Buffalo NY; BR/TL/6´4˝/(196–215); [MinA87 7/165]; d7.25; Col Louisiana St.

YEAR	TM LG	W	L	PCT	G	GS	CG-SHO	SV-BS	IP	H	R	HR	HB	BB-IB	SO	ERA	AERA	OAV	OOB	AB-HR-SH	AVG	PB	SUP	APR	DL	PW
1989	Min A	2	4	.333	13	8	0	0-0	57.1	66	32	7	1	21-1	38	4.55	91	.292	.348	0	ø	0	68	-3	0	-0.3
1990	Min A	7	9	.438	24	21	3-1	0-0	144.2	154	65	8	1	39-3	101	3.79	110	.276	.325	0	ø	0	92	7	0	0.7
1991	†Min A	7	5	.583	41	12	0	2-0	98	116	52	11	1	41-2	72	4.32	99	.303	.369	0	ø	0*	117	-1	0	-0.1
1992	Min A	2	3	.400	54	0	0	5-2	75	59	27	7	0	23-7	76	2.88	142	.215	.274	0	ø	0	—	9	0	0.7
1993	Min A	2	1	.667	22	0	0	0-1	21	20	11	2	0	16-2	15	4.71	94	.267	.387	0	ø	0	—	0	128	0.0
1994	Min A	4	2	.667	50	2	0	1-2	51.1	65	43	8	2	18-2	38	6.14	80	.316	.366	0	ø	0	103	-9	0	-0.9
1995	Min A	5	3	.625	36	0	0	0-2	42.1	47	22	5	1	16-3	48	4.46	108	.290	.358	0	ø	0	—	2	0	0.3
	†LA N	0	2	.000	24	0	0	0-0	19.2	19	11	1	1	9-2	19	3.66	106	.241	.326	1	.000	-0	—	0	0	0.0
1996	†LA N	2	3	.400	66	0	0	1-2	73	65	21	3	1	22-2	56	2.22	176	.240	.295	3	.000	-0	—	15	0	0.9
1997	LA N	1	4	.200	62	0	0	1-3	69.1	71	44	12	0	30-6	42	5.32	73	.271	.342	4-0-1	.250	0	—	-11	0	-0.7
1998	LA N	2	1	.667	53	0	0	0-1	54	56	26	3	2	24-1	45	3.50	115	.267	.347	1	.000	-0	—	2	0	0.1
1999	Bos A	1	1	.500	46	0	0	2-0	46.1	50	32	9	2	20-3	36	5.83	86	.275	.348	0	ø	0	—	-3	20	-0.2
	Chi N	0	2	.000	11	0	0	0-0	12.1	7	6	1	0	4-2	9	3.65	125	.171	.244	0	ø	0	—	1	0	0.1
2000	Chi N	2	3	.400	19	0	0	0-0	18.2	17	11	1	1	10-4	17	4.82	95	.258	.350	2	.000	-0	—	-1	0	-0.2
	TB A	1	1	.500	34	0	0	0-3	32	33	18	4	0	18-5	26	4.50	109	.262	.354	0	ø	0	—	1	0	0.1

YEAR	TM LG	W	L	PCT	G	GS	CG-SHO	SV-BS	IP	H	R	HR	HB	BB-IB	SO	ERA	AERA	OAV	OOB	AB-HR-SH	AVG	PB	SUP	APR	DL	PW
	Tor A	0	2	.000	23	0	0	0-1	20.2	20	12	3	1	9-0	20	4.79	105	.263	.345	0	ø	0	—	1	0	0.0
	Year	1	3	.250	57	0	0	0-4	52.2	53	30	7	1	27-5	46	4.61	107	.262	.351	0	ø	0	—	2	0	0.1
2001	†Oak A	6	2	.750	54	0	0	1-2	52.1	49	29	7	4	20-1	52	4.47	102	.249	.326	0	ø	0	—	0	0	0.0
2002	NY N	5	3	.625	68	0	0	1-1	48	35	13	3	1	19-3	44	2.44	162	.207	.289	2	.000	-0	—	9	0	1.4
2003	†Chi N	2	3	.400	65	0	0	0-1	42.2	40	14	6	3	22-4	24	2.74	158	.260	.359	1	.000	-0	—	8	21	0.8
Total	15	51	54	.486	765	43	3-1	14-21	978.2	989	489	101	22	381-53	778	4.05	106	.266	.335	14-0-1	.071	-1	94	27	169	2.7
GUZMAN, ANGEL	Angel Moises; B12.14.1981 Caracas, Venezuela; BR/TR/6´3˝/195; d4.26																									
2006	Chi N	0	6	.000	15	10	0	0-0	56	68	48	9	6	37-1	60	7.39	62	.308	.416	12-0-4	.167	0	64	-16	0	-1.4
GUZMAN, JOHNNY	Dionini Ramon (Estrella); B1.21.1971 Hatillo Palma, D.R.; BR/TL/5´10˝/155; d6.8																									
1991	Oak A	1	0	1.000	5	0	0	0-0	5	11	5	0	0	2-0	3	9.00	43	.500	.542	0	ø	0	—	-3	0	-0.5
1992	Oak A	0	0	ø	2	0	0	0-0	3	8	4	0	1	0-0	0	12.00	31	.471	.500	0	ø	0	—	-3	0	-0.1
Total	2	1	0	1.000	7	0	0	0-0	8	19	9	0	1	2-0	3	10.13	38	.487	.524	0	ø	0	—	-6	0	-0.6
GUZMAN, DOMINGO	Domingo Serrano; B4.5.1975 San Cristobal, D.R.; BR/TR/6´0˝/210; d9.9																									
1999	SD N	0	1	.000	7	0	0	0-0	5	13	12	1	0	3-2	4	21.60	20	.464	.516	0	ø	0	—	-10	0	-1.5
2000	SD N	0	0	ø	1	0	0	0-0	1	1	1	0	2	1-0	0	9.00	49	.333	.667	0	ø	0	—	0	0	0.0
Total	2	0	1	.000	8	0	0	0-0	6	14	13	1	2	4-2	4	19.50	22	.452	.541	0	ø	0	—	-10	0	-1.5
GUZMAN, GERALDO	Geraldo Moreno (Suarez); B11.28.1972 Tenares, D.R.; BR/TR/6´2˝/(180–186); d7.6																									
2000	Ari N	5	4	.556	13	10	0	0-1	60.1	66	36	8	2	22-0	52	5.37	89	.286	.352	19-0-3	.000	-2	125	-2	0	-0.6
2001	Ari N	0	0	ø	4	0	0	0-0	9.1	7	4	2	0	3-1	4	2.89	160	.206	.270	1	.000	-0	—	1	12	0.0
Total	2	5	4	.556	17	10	0	0-1	69.2	73	40	10	2	25-1	56	5.04	95	.275	.341	20-0-3	.000	-2	125	-1	12	-0.6
GUZMAN, JOSE	Jose Alberto (Mirabal); B4.9.1963 Santa Isabel, PR; BR/TR/6´2˝/(185–195); d9.10; [DL 1990 Tex A 122, 1995 Chi N 160, 1996 Chi N 84]																									
1985	Tex A	3	2	.600	5	5	0	0-0	32.2	27	13	3	0	14-1	24	2.76	155	.214	.293	0	ø	0	85	4	0	0.6
1986	Tex A	9	15	.375	29	29	2	0-0	172.1	199	101	23	6	60-2	87	4.54	95	.293	.353	0	ø	0	80	-5	0	-0.7
1987	Tex A	14	14	.500	37	30	6	0-0	208.1	196	115	30	3	82-0	143	4.67	97	.251	.322	0	ø	0	94	0	0	0.1
1988	Tex A	11	13	.458	30	30	6-2	0-0	206.2	180	99	20	5	82-3	157	3.70	111	.231	.306	0	ø	0	88	8	0	0.8
1991	Tex A	13	7	.650	25	25	5-1	0-0	169.2	152	67	10	4	84-1	125	3.08	132	.239	.330	0	ø	0	111	17	0	2.0
1992	Tex A	16	11	.593	33	33	5	0-0	224	229	103	17	4	73-0	179	3.66	105	.268	.326	0	ø	0	108	4	0	0.5
1993	Chi N	12	10	.545	30	30	2-1	0-0	191	188	98	25	3	74-6	163	4.34	93	.258	.327	63-0-9	.111	-3	120	-5	0	-0.8
1994	Chi N	2	2	.500	4	4	0	0-0	19.2	22	20	1	1	13-0	11	9.15	46	.289	.396	8	.000	-1	113	-10	108	-1.5
Total	8	80	74	.519	193	186	26-4	0-0	1224.1	1193	616	129	26	482-13	889	4.05	102	.256	.327	71-0-9	.099	-3	100	13	474	1.0
GUZMAN, JUAN	Juan Andres (Correa); B10.28.1966 Santo Domingo, D.R.; BR/TR/5´11˝/(190–195); d6.7; [DL 2001 TB A 159]																									
1991	†Tor A	10	3	.769	23	23	1	0-0	138.2	98	53	6	4	66-0	123	2.99	141	.197	.294	0	ø	0	104	17	0	1.4
1992	†Tor A★	16	5	.762	28	28	1	0-0	180.2	135	56	6	1	72-2	165	2.64	156	.207	.286	0	ø	0	99	29	25	3.2
1993	†Tor A	14	3	.824	33	33	2-1	0-0	221	211	107	17	3	110-2	194	3.99	110	.252	.338	0	ø	0	129	10	0	0.5
1994	Tor A	12	11	.522	25	**25**	2	0-0	147.1	165	102	20	3	76-1	124	5.68	86	.282	.364	0	ø	0	117	-14	0	-1.8
1995	Tor A	4	14	.222	24	24	3	0-0	135.1	151	101	13	3	73-6	94	6.32	75	.281	.369	0	ø	0	68	-21	39	-2.4
1996	Tor A	11	8	.579	27	27	4-1	0-0	187.2	158	68	20	7	53-3	165	**2.93**	**171**	**.228**	**.289**	0	ø	0	75	43	15	3.8
1997	Tor A	3	6	.333	13	13	0	0-0	60	48	42	14	2	31-0	52	4.95	93	.213	.312	0	ø	0	79	-5	104	-0.6
1998	Tor A	6	12	.333	22	22	2	0-0	145	133	83	19	6	65-1	113	4.41	106	.239	.324	2	.000	-0	83	2	0	0.1
	Bal A	4	4	.500	11	11	0	0-0	66	60	34	4	2	33-1	55	4.23	108	.241	.332	0	ø	0	95	2	0	0.1
	Year	10	16	.385	33	33	2	0-0	211	193	117	23	8	98-2	168	4.35	106	.240	.326	2	.000	-0	86	4	0	0.2
1999	Bal A	5	9	.357	21	21	1-1	0-0	122.2	124	63	18	3	65-3	95	4.18	112	.264	.356	6	.167	-0	89	6	0	0.6
	Cin N	6	3	.667	12	12	1	0-0	77.1	70	33	10	1	21-3	60	3.03	155	.238	.290	26-0-3	.115	-1	124	12	0	1.1
2000	TB A	0	1	.000	1	1	0	0-0	1.2	7	8	2	0	2-0	3	43.20	11	.636	.692	0	ø	0	96	-7	176	-0.8
Total	10	91	79	.535	240	240	17-3	0-0	1483.1	1360	750	149	35	667-22	1243	4.08	113	.243	.325	34-0-3	.118	-1	97	74	518	5.2
GUZMAN, SANTIAGO	Santiago Donovan (b Santiago Donovan (Guzman)); B7.25.1949 San Pedro de Macoris, D.R.; BR/TR/6´2˝/180; d9.30																									
1969	StL N	0	1	.000	1	1	0	0-0	7.1	9	4	2	0	3-1	7	4.91	73	.321	.387	3	.333	0	74	-1	0	-0.1
1970	StL N	1	1	.500	8	3	1	0-0	13.2	14	12	1	0	13-0	9	7.24	57	.275	.422	5	.200	-0	166	-4	0	-0.6
1971	StL N	0	0	ø	2	1	0	0-0	10	6	1	0	0	2-0	13	0.00	ø	.162	.205	1-0-1	.000	-0	146	3	0	0.2
1972	StL N	0	0	ø	1	0	0	0-0	1	1	1	1	0	0-0	0	9.00	38	.250	.250	0	ø	0	—	-1	0	0.0
Total	4	1	2	.333	12	5	1	0-0	32	30	18	4	0	18-1	29	4.50	85	.250	.348	9-0-1	.222	0	149	-3	0	-0.5
HAAS, BRUNO	Bruno Philip "Boon"; B5.5.1891 Worcester MA; D6.5.1952 Sarasota FL; BB/TL/5´10˝/180; d6.23; Col Dean (MA) JC																									
1915	Phi A	0	1	.000	6	2	1	0	14.1	23	27	0	0	28	7	11.93	25	.404	.600	18	.056	-1*	150	-15	—	-0.9
HAAS, MOOSE	Bryan Edmund; B4.22.1956 Baltimore MD; BR/TR/6´0˝/170; [MilA74 2/30]; d9.8																									
1976	Mil A	0	1	.000	5	2	0	0-0	16	12	8	0	0	12-0	9	3.94	89	.207	.338	0	ø	0	75	-1	0	0.0
1977	Mil A	10	12	.455	32	32	6	0-0	197.2	195	104	21	2	84-8	113	4.33	95	.261	.334	0	ø	0*	89	-4	0	-0.5
1978	Mil A	2	3	.400	7	6	2	1-0	30.2	33	22	6	0	8-0	32	6.16	62	.273	.315	0	ø	0	181	-7	142	-1.1
1979	Mil A	11	11	.500	29	28	8-1	0-0	184.2	198	112	26	0	59-2	95	4.78	88	.275	.327	0	ø	0	113	-13	0	-1.4
1980	Mil A	16	15	.516	33	33	14-3	0-0	252.1	246	96	25	1	56-6	146	3.10	126	.258	.297	0	ø	0	81	25	0	2.8
1981	†Mil A	11	7	.611	24	22	5	0-1	137.1	146	69	10	1	40-4	64	4.46	78	.275	.324	0	ø	0	119	-14	0	-1.7
1982	†Mil A	11	8	.579	32	27	3	1-0	193.1	232	101	15	3	39-4	104	4.47	86	.302	.334	0	ø	0	130	-12	0	-1.1
1983	Mil A	13	3	.813	25	25	7-3	0-0	179	170	66	12	1	42-5	75	3.27	116	.251	.294	0	ø	0*	118	14	0	1.1
1984	Mil A	9	11	.450	31	30	4	0-0	189.1	205	91	15	0	43-3	84	3.99	98	.279	.316	0	ø	0	87	0	0	0.1
1985	Mil A	8	8	.500	27	26	6-1	0-0	161.2	165	85	21	1	25-3	78	3.84	109	.260	.287	0	ø	0	97	4	0	0.2
1986	Oak A	7	2	.778	12	12	1	0-0	72.1	58	23	4	1	19-1	40	2.74	142	.218	.271	0	ø	0	173	11	65	1.2
1987	Oak A	2	2	.500	9	9	0	0-0	40.2	57	29	7	0	9-0	13	5.75	72	.335	.367	0	ø	0	134	-8	127	-0.6
Total	12	100	83	.546	266	252	56-8	2-1	1655	1717	806	162	10	436-36	853	4.01	98	.269	.314	0	ø	0	108	-5	334	-1.0
HAAS, DAVID	Robert David; B10.19.1965 Independence MO; BR/TR/6´1˝/200; [DetA88 15/395]; d9.8; Col Wichita St.																									
1991	Det A	1	0	1.000	11	0	0	0-1	10.2	8	8	1	1	12-3	6	6.75	62	.242	.438	0	ø	0	—	-3	0	-0.2
1992	Det A	5	3	.625	12	11	1-1	0-0	61.2	68	30	8	1	16-1	29	3.94	101	.276	.323	0	ø	0	110	0	0	0.0
1993	Det A	1	2	.333	20	0	0	0-0	28	45	20	9	0	8-5	17	6.11	71	.375	.411	0	ø	0	—	-5	112	-0.4
Total	3	7	5	.583	43	11	1-1	0-1	100.1	121	58	18	2	36-9	52	4.84	85	.303	.361	0	ø	0	110	-8	112	-0.6
HABENICHT, BOB	Robert Julius "Hobby"; B2.13.1926 St.Louis MO; D12.24.1980 Richmond VA; BR/TR/6´2˝/185; d4.17; Col St. Louis																									
1951	StL N	0	0	ø	3	0	0	0	5	5	4	0	0	9	1	7.20	55	.278	.519	1	.000	0	—	-2	0	-0.1
1953	StL A	0	0	ø	1	0	0	0	1.2	1	1	0	1	1	1	5.40	78	.167	.375	0	ø	0	—	0	0	0.0
Total	2	0	0	ø	4	0	0	0	6.2	6	5	0	1	10	2	6.75	60	.250	.486	1	.000	0	—	-2	0	-0.1
HABYAN, JOHN	John Gabriel; B1.29.1964 Bay Shore NY; BR/TR/6´2˝/(178–198); [BalA82 3/78]; d9.29; [DL 1989 Bal A 67]																									
1985	Bal A	1	0	1.000	2	0	0	0-0	2.2	3	1	0	0	0-0	2	0.00	ø	.250	.250	0	ø	0	—	1	0	0.2
1986	Bal A	1	3	.250	6	5	0	0-0	26.1	24	17	3	0	18-2	14	4.44	94	.250	.365	0	ø	0	61	-2	0	-0.3
1987	Bal A	6	7	.462	27	13	0	1-0	116.1	110	67	20	2	40-1	64	4.80	93	.248	.311	0	ø	0	82	-4	0	-0.4
1988	Bal A	1	0	1.000	7	0	0	0-0	14.2	22	10	2	0	4-0	4	4.30	92	.355	.382	0	ø	0	—	-2	0	-0.1
1990	NY A	0	0	ø	6	0	0	0-1	8.2	10	2	0	1	2-0	4	2.08	192	.294	.351	0	ø	0	—	2	0	0.1
1991	NY A	4	2	.667	66	0	0	2-2	90	73	28	2	2	20-2	70	2.30	181	.225	.274	0	ø	0	—	17	0	1.1
1992	NY A	5	6	.455	56	0	0	7-5	72.2	84	32	6	2	21-5	44	3.84	103	.295	.344	0	ø	0	—	2	0	0.3
1993	NY A	2	1	.667	36	0	0	1-2	42.1	45	20	5	0	16-2	29	4.04	104	.276	.337	0	ø	0	—	1	0	0.1
	KC A	0	0	ø	12	0	0	0-0	14	14	7	1	0	4-2	10	4.50	103	.259	.310	0	ø	0	—	0	0	0.0
	Year	2	1	.667	48	0	0	1-2	56.1	59	27	6	0	20-4	39	4.15	103	.272	.331	0	ø	0	—	2	0	0.1
1994	StL N	1	0	1.000	52	0	0	1-2	47.1	50	17	2	0	20-8	46	3.23	131	.275	.347	0	ø	0	—	6	22	0.3
1995	StL N	3	2	.600	31	0	0	0-1	40.2	32	18	0	1	15-4	35	2.88	149	.222	.298	2	.000	-0	—	5	0	0.5
	Cal A	1	2	.333	28	0	0	0-1	32.2	36	16	2	1	12-0	25	4.13	114	.279	.340	0	ø	0	—	2	0	0.1
1996	Col N	1	1	.500	19	0	0	0-0	24	34	19	4	1	14-1	25	7.13	73	.347	.430	3	.000	-0	—	-3	0	-0.3
Total	11	26	24	.520	348	18	0	12-14	532.1	537	254	47	10	186-27	372	3.85	112	.265	.327	5	.000	-0	78	25	89	1.6

YEAR	TM LG	W	L	PCT	G	GS	CG-SHO	SV-BS	IP	H	R	HR	HB	BB-IB	SO	ERA	AERA	OAV	OOB	AB-HR-SH	AVG	PB	SUP	APR	DL	PW
Hacker, Warren	Warren Louis; B11.21.1924 Marissa IL; D5.22.2002 Lenzburg IL; BR/TR/6´1˝/(180–185); d9.24																									
1948	Chi N	0	1	.000	3	1	0	0	3	7	7	0	0	3	0	21.00	19	.438	.526	0	ø	0	68	-5	0	-0.9
1949	Chi N	5	8	.385	30	12	3	0	125.2	141	68	7	4	53	40	4.23	95	.283	.356	38	.184	-1*	82	-3	0	-0.3
1950	Chi N	0	1	.000	5	3	1	1	15.1	20	11	3	0	8	5	5.28	80	.313	.389	5	.000	-1	77	-2	0	-0.2
1951	Chi N	0	0	ø	2	0	0	0	1.1	3	2	0	1	0	2	13.50	30	.500	.571	0	ø	0	—	-1	0	-0.1
1952	Chi N	15	9	.625	33	20	12-5	1	185	144	56	17	1	31	84	2.58	149	**.212**	**.247**	58-0-6	.121	-2*	88	27	0	3.1
1953	Chi N	12	19	.387	39	32	9	2	221.2	225	123	35	3	54	106	4.38	101	.254	.299	78-0-5	.218	0*	92	2	0	0.2
1954	Chi N	6	13	.316	39	18	4-1	2	158.2	157	89	28	4	37	80	4.25	99	.257	.299	55-0-3	.236	1*	99	-3	0	-0.3
1955	Chi N	11	15	.423	35	30	13	3	213	202	112	38	2	43-7	80	4.27	96	.245	.282	72	.250	2	79	-4	0	-0.4
1956	Chi N	3	13	.188	34	24	4	0	168	190	103	28	1	44-11	65	4.66	81	.285	.327	54-0-1	.148	-2	97	-18	0	-1.8
1957	Cin N	3	2	.600	15	6	0	0	43.1	50	26	5	3	13-3	18	5.19	79	.294	.347	8	.125	-0	111	-4	0	-0.5
	Phi N	4	4	.500	20	10	1	0	74	72	40	10	1	18-2	33	4.50	85	.257	.303	23-0-1	.261	1	88	-5	0	-0.4
	Year	7	6	.538	35	16	1	0	117.1	122	66	15	4	31-5	51	4.76	82	.271	.320	31-0-1	.226	1	97	-9	0	-0.9
1958	Phi N	0	1	.000	9	1	0	0	17	24	17	2	0	8-1	4	7.41	53	.329	.395	1	.000	-0	45	-7	0	-0.4
1961	Chi A	3	3	.500	42	0	0	8	57.1	62	26	8	1	8-1	40	3.77	104	.272	.297	9	.111	-1	—	1	0	0.0
Total	12	62	89	.411	306	157	47-6	17	1283.1	1297	680	181	21	320-25	557	4.21	96	.259	.305	401-0-16	.195	-2	90	-22	0	-2.0
Hackett, Jim	James Joseph "Sunny Jim"; B10.1.1877 Jacksonville IL; D3.28.1961 Douglas MI; BR/TR/6´2˝/185; d9.14; ▲																									
1902	StL N	0	3	.000	4	3	3	0	30.1	46	26	0	1	16	7	6.23	44	.348	.423	21	.286	1*	107	-10	—	-0.8
1903	StL N	1	3	.250	7	6	5	1	48.1	47	28	0	3	18	21	3.72	88	.249	.324	351-0-2	.228	1*	86	-1	—	0.0
Total	2	1	6	.143	11	9	8	1	78.2	93	54	0	4	34	28	4.69	65	.290	.365	372-0-2	.231	2	93	-11	—	-0.8
Hackman, Luther	Luther Gean; B10.10.1974 Columbus MS; BR/TR/6´4˝/(195–200); [ColN94 6/154]; d9.1																									
1999	Col N	1	2	.333	5	3	0	0-0	16	26	19	5	0	12-0	10	10.69	54	.371	.463	5	.200	-0	74	-6	0	-0.9
2000	StL N	0	0	ø	1	0	0	0-0	2.2	4	3	0	1	4-1	0	10.13	46	.400	.600	0	ø	0	—	-1	0	-0.1
2001	StL N	1	2	.333	35	0	0	1-2	35.2	28	18	7	2	14-0	24	4.29	101	.212	.297	1-0-2	.000	-0	—	0	38	0.0
2002	StL N	5	4	.556	43	6	0	0-1	81	90	42	7	4	39-3	46	4.11	98	.287	.366	16	.063	-1	149	-2	0	-0.3
2003	SD N	2	2	.500	65	0	0	0-2	76.2	78	51	7	8	36-2	48	5.17	78	.261	.354	2	.000	-0	—	-12	0	-0.6
Total	5	9	10	.474	149	9	0	1-5	212	226	133	26	15	105-6	128	5.09	83	.274	.363	24-0-2	.083	-1	130	-21	38	-1.9
Haddix, Harvey	Harvey "The Kitten"; B9.18.1925 Medway OH; D1.8.1994 Springfield OH; BL/TL/5´9.5˝/(160–170); d8.20; C14																									
1952	StL N	2	2	.500	7	6	3	0	42	31	18	4	2	10	31	2.79	133	.201	.259	14	.214	0*	148	3	0	0.3
1953	StL N☆	20	9	.690	36	33	19-**6**	1	253	220	97	24	4	69	163	3.06	139	.232	.287	97-1-3	.289	10*	122	33	0	4.5
1954	StL N✳	18	13	.581	43	35	13-3	4	259.2	247	114	26	3	77	184	3.57	115	.249	.303	93	.194	3*	120	17	0	2.2
1955	StL N★	12	16	.429	37	30	9-2	1	208	216	111	27	5	62-7	150	4.46	91	.268	.322	73-1-1	.164	0	89	-9	0	-0.9
1956	StL N	1	0	1.000	4	4	1-1	0	23.2	28	15	3	0	10-0	16	5.32	71	.298	.362	9	.222	1*	175	-4	0	-0.1
	Phi N	12	8	.600	31	26	11-2	2	206.2	196	98	23	6	55-9	154	3.48	107	.247	.299	93	.237	4*	121	3	0	0.7
	Year	13	8	.619	35	30	12-3	2	230.1	224	113	26	6	65-9	170	3.67	102	.253	.306	102	.235	5	128	-3	0	0.6
1957	Phi N	10	13	.435	27	25	8-1	0	170.2	176	84	18	1	39-4	136	4.06	94	.264	.303	68-0-2	.309	7*	80	-4	0	0.1
1958	Cin N	8	7	.533	29	26	8-1	0	184	191	79	28	7	43-7	110	3.52	118	.268	.314	61-1-6	.180	3*	102	12	0	1.2
1959	Pit N	12	12	.500	31	29	14-2	0	224.1	189	88	26	2	49-12	149	3.13	124	.228	**.271**	83-0-1	.145	-0	94	19	0	1.9
1960	†Pit N	11	10	.524	29	28	4	1	172.1	189	87	13	1	38-8	101	3.97	94	.277	.315	67	.254	4	110	-6	0	-0.1
1961	Pit N	10	6	.625	29	22	5-2	0	156	159	72	15	2	41-6	99	4.10	97	.266	.313	56-0-5	.143	0*	124	2	0	0.2
1962	Pit N	9	6	.600	28	20	4	0	141.1	146	74	17	2	42-6	101	4.20	94	.264	.318	52-1-0	.250	4	94	-3	0	0.1
1963	Pit N	3	4	.429	49	1	0	1	70	67	27	7	4	20-4	70	3.34	99	.256	.314	11	.182	1*	105	1	0	0.2
1964	Bal A	5	5	.500	49	0	0	10	89.2	68	26	4	2	23-8	90	2.31	155	.211	.265	19-0-2	.000	-2	—	13	0	1.5
1965	Bal A	3	2	.600	24	0	0	1	33.2	31	22	5	2	23-6	21	3.48	100	.248	.371	2	.000	-0	—	-3	0	-0.4
Total	14	136	113	.546	453	285	99-20	21	2235	2154	1012	240	43	601-77	1575	3.63	108	.252	.303	798-4-20	.212	35	109	74	0	11.4
Haddock, George	George Silas "Gentleman George"; B12.25.1866 Portsmouth NH; D4.18.1926 Boston MA; BR/TR/5´11˝/155; d9.27																									
1888	Was N	0	2	.000	2	2	2	0	16	9	8	0	1	2	3	2.25	123	.148	.188	5	.200	0	55	0	—	0.1
1889	Was N	11	19	.367	33	31	30	0	276.1	299	203	10	9	123	106	4.20	94	.268	.346	112-2	.223	7*	94	-9	—	0.0
1890	Buf P	9	26	.257	35	34	31	0	290.2	366	307	15	14	149	123	5.76	71	.295	.377	146	.247	7*	97	-62	—	-4.1
1891	Bos AA	34	11	.756	51	47	37-**5**	1	379.2	330	172	8	14	137	169	2.49	140	.226	.299	185-3	.243	9*	128	45	—	5.3
1892	Bro N	29	13	.690	46	44	39-3	1	381.1	340	.190	11	14	163	153	3.14	101	.229	.311	158	.177	-1*	111	2	—	0.2
1893	Bro N	8	9	.471	23	20	12	0	151	193	145	10	7	89	37	5.60	79	.302	.393	85-1	.282	4*	102	-24	—	-1.7
1894	Phi N	4	3	.571	10	7	5	0	56	63	46	0	1	34	7	5.79	89	.281	.378	29	.172	-1	116	-3	—	-0.3
	Was N	0	4	.000	4	4	4	0	29	50	40	2	1	17	1	8.69	61	.373	.447	16	.188	-1*	87	-9	—	-0.8
	Year	4	7	.364	14	11	9	0	85	113	86	2	2	51	8	6.78	77	.316	.404	45	.178	-1	106	-13	—	-1.1
Total	7	95	87	.522	204	189	160-8	2	1580	1650	1111	56	61	714	599	4.07	93	.259	.340	736-6	.227	25	108	-60	—	-1.3
Hadley, Bump	Irving Darius; B7.5.1904 Lynn MA; D2.15.1963 Lynn MA; BR/TR/5´11˝/190; d4.20; Col Brown																									
1926	Was A	0	0	ø	1	0	0	0	3	6	5	0	0	2	0	12.00	32	.429	.500	0	ø	0	—	-3	—	-0.1
1927	Was A	14	6	.700	30	27	13	0	198.2	177	72	2	9	86	60	2.85	142	.244	.332	70-0-2	.271	2	107	28	—	2.7
1928	Was A	12	13	.480	33	31	16-3	0	231.2	236	105	4	8	100	80	3.54	113	.268	.348	81-0-3	.210	1	99	13	—	1.4
1929	Was A	6	16	.273	37	27	7-1	0	195.1	196	139	10	5	85	98	5.62	75	.263	.342	62-0-4	.097	-4	97	-28	—	-2.9
1930	Was A	15	11	.577	42	34	15-1	2	260.1	242	123	6	6	105	162	3.73	123	.247	.323	93-0-1	.226	1	99	25	—	2.2
1931	Was A	11	10	.524	**55**	11	2-1	8	179.2	145	81	4	1	92	124	3.06	140	**.218**	.314	54-0-5	.167	-1	82	21	—	2.3
1932	Chi A	1	1	.500	3	2	1	1	18.2	17	8	2	0	8	13	3.86	112	.262	.342	6	.167	-0	39	2	—	0.2
	StL A	13	20	.394	40	33	12-1	1	229.2	244	160	21	8	163	132	5.53	88	.274	.391	78-0-6	.282	4	94	-14	—	-1.4
	Year	14	21	.400	43	35	13-1	2	248.1	261	168	23	8	171	145	5.40	89	.273	.388	84-0-6	.274	4	92	-10	—	-1.2
1933	StL A	15	20	.429	45	36	19-2	3	**316.2**	309	152	17	3	141	149	3.92	119	.256	.335	109-0-6	.156	-4	75	25	—	2.0
1934	StL A	10	16	.385	39	32	7-2	1	213	212	120	14	6	127	79	4.35	115	.257	.361	64-0-6	.203	-1	67	15	—	1.4
1935	Was A	10	15	.400	35	32	13	0	230.1	268	143	18	4	102	77	4.92	88	.292	.366	77-0-7	.195	1	110	-17	—	-1.3
1936	†NY A	14	4	.778	31	17	8-1	1	173.2	194	97	12	1	89	74	4.35	107	.283	.366	68-0-4	.235	2	129	5	—	0.6
1937	†NY A	11	8	.579	29	25	6	0	178.1	199	122	16	3	83	70	5.30	84	.281	.358	65	.169	1	127	-16	—	-1.4
1938	NY A	9	8	.529	29	17	8-1	1	167.1	165	79	13	3	66	61	3.60	126	.254	.325	54-0-3	.093	-1	113	18	—	1.6
1939	†NY A	12	6	.667	26	18	7-1	2	154	132	62	10	3	85	65	2.98	146	.237	.342	62-0-2	.177	-1	98	23	—	2.4
1940	NY A	3	5	.375	25	2	0	2	80	88	62	4	1	52	39	5.74	70	.276	.379	27-0-2	.111	-1	44	-19	—	-1.7
1941	NY N	1	0	1.000	3	2	0	0	13	19	10	1	0	9	4	6.23	59	.345	.438	3-0-1	.000	-0	161	-3	0	-0.3
	Phi A	4	6	.400	25	9	1	3	102.1	131	69	13	2	47	31	5.01	84	.310	.381	31-0-1	.129	-1	83	-11	0	-1.0
Total	16	161	165	.494	528	355	135-14	25	2945.2	2980	1609	167	63	1442	1318	4.24	105	.263	.350	1004-0-53	.189	-1	97	64	0	6.7
Haefner, Mickey	Milton Arnold; B10.9.1912 Lenzburg IL; D1.3.1995 New Athens IL; BL/TL/5´8˝/160; d4.22																									
1943	Was A	11	5	.688	36	13	8-1	6	165.1	126	56	4	4	60	65	2.29	140	.208	.283	45-0-7	.133	0	138	15	0	1.6
1944	Was A	12	15	.444	31	28	18-3	1	228	221	94	7	4	71	86	3.04	107	.251	.310	70-0-8	.157	-1	91	6	0	0.7
1945	Was A	16	14	.533	37	28	19-1	3	238.1	226	103	10	7	69	83	3.47	89	.247	.305	82-0-6	.244	4	102	-6	0	-0.3
1946	Was A	14	11	.560	33	27	17-2	1	227.2	220	86	10	5	80	85	2.85	118	.251	.317	74-0-4	.203	4	97	14	0	1.9
1947	Was A	10	14	.417	31	28	14-4	1	193	195	86	8	4	85	77	3.64	102	.264	.343	59-0-3	.136	-1	59	3	0	0.1
1948	Was A	5	13	.278	28	20	4	0	147.2	151	86	7	6	61	45	4.02	108	.265	.342	43-0-1	.163	-1	58	0	0	0.0
1949	Was A	5	5	.500	19	12	4-1	0	91.2	85	51	7	2	53	23	4.42	96	.249	.353	25-0-3	.200	1*	86	-2	0	0.0
	Chi A	4	6	.400	14	12	4-1	1	80.1	84	40	9	5	41	17	4.37	95	.275	.370	23-0-6	.261	2	75	0	0	0.2
	Year	9	11	.450	33	24	8-2	1	172	169	91	16	7	94	40	4.40	96	.261	.361	48-0-9	.229	2	81	-2	0	0.2
1950	Chi A	1	6	.143	24	9	2	0	70.2	83	49	11	2	45	17	5.73	78	.299	.400	20-0-3	.200	0	80	-9	0	-0.8
	Bos N	0	2	.000	8	2	1	0	24	23	15	3	0	12	10	5.63	68	.247	.333	7-0-1	.286	1	92	-4	0	-0.2
Total	8	78	91	.462	261	179	91-13	13	1466.2	1414	666	76	39	577	508	3.50	102	.252	.326	448-0-42	.188	8	86	17	0	3.2
Haeger, Charlie	Charles Wallis; B9.19.1983 Livonia MI; BR/TR/6´1˝/200; [ChiA01 25/763]; d5.10																									
2006	Chi A	1	1	.500	7	1	0	1-0	18.1	12	10	0	0	13-0	19	3.44	136	.182	.316	0	ø	0	101	1	0	0.2
Hafford, Leo	Leo Edgar; B9.17.1883 Somerville MA; D10.1.1911 Willimantic CT; TR/6´0˝/170; d4.15; Col Tufts																									
1906	Cin N	1	1	.500	3	1	1	0	19	13	9	0	1	11	5	0.95	291	.191	.313	9	.222	-0	212	2	—	0.1
Hafner, Frank	Francis R.; B8.14.1867 Hannibal MO; D3.2.1957 Hannibal MO; TR; d5.5																									
1888	KC AA	0	2	.000	2	2	2	0	18	24	23	2	1	16	5	7.00	48	.308	.432	6	.000	-1	69	-7	—	-0.6

YEAR	TM LG	W	L	PCT	G	GS	CG-SHO	SV-BS	IP	H	R	HR	HB	BB-IB	SO	ERA	AERA	OAV	OOB	AB-HR-SH	AVG	PB	SUP	APR	DL	PW
HAGAN, ART	Arthur Charles; B3.17.1863 Providence RI; D3.25.1936 Providence RI; TR; d6.30																									
1883	Phi N	1	14	.067	17	16	15	0	137	207	151	2	—	33	39	5.45	57	.342	.376	59	.102	-5	75	-39	—	-3.5
	Buf N	0	2	.000	2	2	1	0	15	17	12	0	—	6	7	3.60	88	.270	.333	7	.000	-1	51	-1	—	-0.2
	Year	1	16	.059	19	18	16	0	152	224	163	2	—	39	46	5.27	59	.335	.371	66	.091	-7	72	-33	—	-3.7
1884	Buf N	1	2	.333	3	3	3	0	26	53	38	1	—	4	4	5.88	54	.384	.401	13	.308	0	135	-9	—	-0.7
Total	2	2	18	.100	22	21	19	0	178	277	201	3	—	43	50	5.36	58	.343	.376	79	.127	-6	81	-49	—	-4.4
HAGEMAN, CASEY	Kurt Moritz; B5.12.1887 Mt.Oliver PA; D4.1.1964 New Bedford PA; BL/TR/5´10.5˝/186; d9.18; Col Geneva																									
1911	Bos A	0	2	.000	2	2	2	0	17	16	8	2	1	5	8	2.12	155	.262	.328	4	.000	-0	33	2	—	0.1
1912	Bos A	0	0	ø	2	1	0	0	1.1	5	5	0	0	3	1	27.00	13	.500	.615	0	ø	0	174	-3	—	-0.1
1914	StL N	2	4	.333	12	7	2	0	55.1	43	24	0	5	20	21	2.44	115	.215	.302	16	.125	-1	84	1	—	0.1
	Chi N	1	1	.500	16	1	0	1	46.2	44	26	0	3	12	17	3.47	80	.254	.314	15	.467	3	103	-3	—	0.1
	Year	3	5	.375	28	8	2	1	102	87	50	0	8	32	38	2.91	96	.233	.308	31	.290	2	87	-1	—	0.2
Total	3	3	7	.300	32	11	4	1	120.1	108	63	2	9	40	47	3.07	93	.243	.318	35	.257	2	86	-3	—	0.2
HAGEN, KEVIN	Kevin Eugene; B3.8.1960 Renton WA; BR/TR/6´2˝/185; [StLN80*4/94]; d6.4; Col Bellevue (WA) CC																									
1983	StL N	2	2	.500	9	4	0	0-0	22.1	34	15	0	0	7-0	7	4.84	76	.362	.406	5	.000	-1	73	-3	0	-0.6
1984	StL N	1	0	1.000	4	0	0	0-0	7.1	9	2	0	0	1-0	2	2.45	143	.300	.323	0	ø	0	—	1	0	0.1
Total	2	3	2	.600	13	4	0	0-0	29.2	43	17	0	0	8-0	9	4.25	85	.347	.386	5	.000	-1	73	-2	0	-0.5
HAGERMAN, RIP	Zerah Zequiel; B6.20.1888 Lyndon KS; D1.30.1930 Albuquerque NM; BR/TR/6´2˝/200; d4.16																									
1909	Chi N	4	4	.500	13	7	4-1	0	79	64	29	0	2	28	32	1.82	139	.225	.298	23	.130	-0	79	4	—	0.4
1914	Cle A	9	15	.375	37	26	12-3	0	198	189	98	3	5	118	112	3.09	93	.265	.374	61-0-2	.016	-5	80	-5	—	-1.3
1915	Cle A	6	14	.300	29	22	7	0	151	156	85	4	6	77	69	3.52	87	.277	.370	38-0-2	.105	-2	86	-8	—	-1.4
1916	Cle A	0	0	ø	2	0	0	0	3.2	5	6	1	2	2	1	12.27	25	.333	.474	1	.000	-0	—	-3	—	-0.2
Total	4	19	33	.365	81	55	23-4	0	431.2	414	218	8	15	225	214	3.09	93	.263	.360	123-0-4	.065	-9	83	-12	—	-2.5
HAHN, NOODLES	Frank George; B4.29.1879 Nashville TN; D2.6.1960 Candler NC; BL/TL/5´9˝/160; d4.18																									
1899	Cin N	23	8	.742	38	34	32-4	0	309	280	128	3	10	68	**145**	2.68	146	.242	.289	109-0-4	.147	-4	98	41	—	2.9
1900	Cin N	16	20	.444	39	37	29-**4**	0	311.1	306	145	4	7	89	**132**	3.27	112	.256	.312	115-2-3	.209	0	85	18	—	1.7
1901	Cin N	22	19	.537	42	42	**41**-2	0	**375.1**	370	159	12	9	69	**239**	2.71	118	.256	.294	141-0-4	.170	-1	95	21	—	2.0
1902	Cin N	23	12	.657	36	36	35-6	0	321	282	97	2	6	58	142	1.77	170	.236	.275	119-0-1	.185	0*	99	41	—	4.4
1903	Cin N	22	12	.647	34	34	34-5	0	296	297	125	3	8	47	127	2.52	141	.262	.297	112-0-4	.161	-2	101	32	—	3.1
1904	Cin N	16	18	.471	35	34	33-2	0	297.2	258	101	3	7	35	98	2.06	143	.234	.262	99-0-3	.172	1	70	27	—	3.2
1905	Cin N	5	3	.625	13	8	5-1	0	77	85	44	0	2	9	17	2.81	118	.272	.297	24-0-2	.167	-1	101	2	—	0.0
1906	NY A	3	2	.600	6	6	3-1	0	42	38	22	0	3	6	17	3.86	77	.245	.287	12	.333	1	113	-3	—	-0.3
Total	8	130	94	.580	243	231	212-25	0	2029.1	1916	821	27	52	381	917	2.55	133	.249	.289	731-2-21	.176	-5	92	179	—	17.0
HAHN, FRED	Frederick Aloys; B2.16.1929 Nyack NY; D8.16.1984 Valhalla NY; BR/TL/6´3˝/174; d4.19																									
1952	StL N	0	0	ø	1	0	0	0	2	2	2	0	0	1	0	0.00	ø	.250	.333	0	ø	0	—	0	0	0.0
HAID, HAL	Harold Augustine; B12.21.1897 Barberton OH; D8.13.1952 Los Angeles CA; BR/TR/5´10.5˝/150; d9.5; Col Belmont Abbey																									
1919	StL A	0	0	ø	1	0	0	0	2	5	5	0	0	3	1	18.00	18	.556	.667	0	ø	0	—	-3	—	-0.1
1928	StL N	2	2	.500	27	0	0	**5**	47	39	24	1	1	11	21	2.30	174	.218	.267	8	.375	1	—	5	—	0.6
1929	StL N	9	9	.500	38	14	8	4	154.2	171	90	8	5	66	41	4.07	115	.284	.360	49-0-3	.082	-4	101	6	—	0.2
1930	StL N	3	2	.600	20	0	0	2	33	38	17	1	3	14	13	4.09	123	.297	.379	3	.000	-0*	—	4	—	0.5
1931	Bos N	0	2	.000	27	0	0	1	56	59	36	3	3	16	20	4.50	84	.263	.321	8	.125	-1	—	-6	—	-0.3
1933	Chi A	0	0	ø	6	0	0	0	14.2	18	15	2	2	13	7	7.98	53	.310	.452	4	.250	0	—	-6	—	-0.3
Total	6	14	15	.483	119	14	8	12	307.1	330	187	15	14	123	103	4.16	106	.275	.349	72-0-3	.125	-3	101	0	—	0.6
HAINES, JESSE	Jesse Joseph "Pop"; B7.22.1893 Clayton OH; D8.5.1978 Dayton OH; BR/TR/6´0˝/190; d7.20; C1; HF1970																									
1918	Cin N	0	0	ø	1	0	0	0	5	5	1	0	0	1	2	1.80	148	.294	.333	1	1.000	0	—	1	—	0.1
1920	StL N	13	20	.394	**47**	37	19-4	2	301.2	303	136	9	9	80	120	2.98	100	.270	.324	108-1-4	.176	-1*	109	-5	—	-0.9
1921	StL N	18	12	.600	37	29	13-**3**	0	244.1	261	112	15	8	56	84	3.50	105	.286	.333	94-0-4	.181	-3*	141	7	—	0.5
1922	StL N	11	9	.550	29	26	11-2	0	183	207	103	10	4	45	62	3.84	101	.284	.329	72-0-1	.167	-2*	101	-3	—	-0.4
1923	StL N	20	13	.606	37	36	23-1	0	266	283	125	7	5	75	73	3.11	125	.275	.328	99-0-4	.202	-2	97	18	—	1.8
1924	StL N	8	19	.296	35	31	16-1	0	222.2	275	129	14	5	66	69	4.41	86	.309	.360	74-0-6	.189	-2	91	-15	—	-1.9
1925	StL N	13	14	.481	29	25	15	0	207	234	116	11	1	52	63	4.57	95	.290	.334	74-0-3	.176	-2	95	-2	—	-0.5
1926	†StL N	13	4	.765	33	20	14-3	1	183	186	76	10	2	48	46	3.25	120	.265	.314	61-0-2	.213	-1	112	14	—	1.0
1927	StL N	24	10	.706	38	36	**25-6**	1	300.2	273	114	11	5	77	89	2.72	145	.245	.297	114-0-4	.202	-1	98	39	—	4.1
1928	†StL N	20	8	.714	33	28	20-1	0	240.1	238	98	14	6	72	77	3.18	126	.266	.324	87-0-7	.184	-1	116	23	—	2.2
1929	StL N	13	10	.565	28	25	12	0	179.2	230	123	21	2	73	59	5.71	82	.313	.376	69-1-3	.159	-3	108	-18	—	-2.2
1930	†StL N	13	8	.619	29	24	14	1	182	215	107	15	1	54	68	4.30	117	.298	.348	65-0-4	.246	1	108	12	—	1.1
1931	StL N	12	3	.800	19	17	8-2	0	122.1	134	48	2	0	28	27	3.02	131	.278	.318	45-0-4	.133	-2	133	12	—	1.0
1932	StL N	3	5	.375	20	10	4-1	0	85.1	116	51	4	1	16	27	4.75	83	.326	.357	27-1-4	.185	0	83	-7	—	-0.6
1933	StL N	9	6	.600	32	10	5	1	115.1	113	46	3	1	37	37	2.50	139	.252	.311	30-0-1	.067	-2*	93	9	—	0.8
1934	†StL N	4	4	.500	37	6	0	1	90	86	42	6	4	19	17	3.50	121	.262	.311	19-0-1	.158	-1	126	**6**	—	0.5
1935	StL N	6	5	.545	30	11	3	2	115.1	110	49	4	1	28	24	3.59	114	.252	.299	33-0-2	.273	1	116	8	—	0.8
1936	StL N	7	5	.583	25	9	4	1	99.1	110	44	4	1	21	19	3.90	101	.284	.323	30-0-5	.167	-1	117	3	—	0.2
1937	StL N	3	3	.500	16	6	2	0	65.2	81	36	5	1	23	18	4.52	88	.303	.361	22	.182	-0	101	-3	—	-0.3
Total	19	210	158	.571	555	386	208-24	10	3208.2	3460	1556	165	57	871	981	3.64	108	.280	.330	1124-3-59	.186	-22	108	99	—	7.3
HAISLIP, JIM	James Clifton "Slim"; B8.4.1891 Farmersville TX; D1.22.1970 Dallas TX; BR/TR/6´1˝/186; d8.27; Col TCU																									
1913	Phi N	0	0	ø	1	0	0	0	3	4	4	0	0	3	0	6.00	56	.400	.538	1	.000	-0	—	-1	—	-0.1
HALAMA, JOHN	John Thadeuz; B2.22.1972 Brooklyn NY; BL/TL/6´5˝/(200–215); [HouN94 23/640]; d4.2; Col St. Francis (NY)																									
1998	Hou N	1	1	.500	6	6	0	0-0	32.1	37	21	0	2	13-0	21	5.85	69	.296	.361	10-0-1	.000	-0	106	-6	0	-0.4
1999	Sea A	11	10	.524	38	24	1-1	0-0	179	193	88	20	7	56-3	105	4.22	113	.281	.338	5	.200	1	93	13	0	1.4
2000	†Sea A	14	9	.609	30	30	1-1	0-0	166.2	206	108	19	2	56-0	87	5.08	95	.308	.361	2-0-1	.500	0	114	-8	0	-0.9
2001	†Sea A	10	7	.588	31	17	0	0-0	110.1	132	69	18	6	26-0	50	4.73	90	.296	.340	1-0-1	.000	-0	139	-9	0	-1.1
2002	Sea A	6	5	.545	31	10	0	0-0	101	112	45	9	1	33-5	70	3.56	121	.281	.336	0	ø	0	131	8	0	0.8
2003	Oak A	3	5	.375	35	13	0	0-0	108.2	117	68	18	2	36-2	51	4.22	109	.268	.325	0	ø	0	107	-1	0	0.0
2004	TB A	7	6	.538	34	14	0	0-0	118.2	134	68	17	10	27-3	59	4.70	99	.284	.334	3	.000	-0	98	0	0	-0.1
2005	Bos A	1	1	.500	30	1	0	0-0	43.2	56	33	5	7	9-3	26	6.18	73	.299	.353	0	ø	0	102	-8	0	-0.4
	Was N	0	3	.000	10	3	0	0-0	21.1	23	11	1	0	8-0	11	4.64	89	.277	.337	5	.200	0	15	-1	0	-0.1
2006	Bal A	3	1	.750	17	1	0	0-1	29.1	38	20	6	0	13-2	12	6.14	74	.325	.389	0	ø	0	292	-5	0	-0.5
Total	9	56	48	.538	262	119	2-2	0-1	911	1048	531	113	37	277-18	492	4.65	98	.290	.343	26-0-3	.115	0	111	-17	0	-1.3
HALBRITER, ED	Edward L.; B2.2.1860 Auburn NY; D8.9.1936 Los Angeles CA; d5.23																									
1882	Phi AA	0	1	.000	1	1	1	0	8	17	12	1	—	4	4	7.88	36	.405	.457	4	.000	-1	146	-4	—	-0.4
HALE, DAD	Ray Luther; B2.18.1880 Allegan MI; D2.1.1946 Allegan MI; BR/TR/5´10˝/180; d4.21																									
1902	Bos N	1	3	.250	8	5	3	0	40	57	38	1	1	16	11	6.07	47	.333	.394	14	.000	-1	104	-14	—	-1.3
	Bal A	0	1	.000	3	2	1	0	14	21	14	0	1	6	6	4.50	84	.344	.412	6	.000	-1	124	-2	—	-0.2
Total	1	1	4	.200	11	7	4	0	54	78	52	1	2	22	17	5.67	54	.336	.398	20	.000	-2	110	-16	—	-1.5
HALICKI, ED	Edward Louis; B10.4.1950 Newark NJ; BR/TR/6´7˝/(220–230); [SFN72 24/564]; d7.8; Col Monmouth																									
1974	SF N	1	8	.111	16	11	2	0-0	74.1	84	49	6	2	31-8	40	4.24	90	.275	.341	25-1-2	.240	1	69	-6	0	-0.6
1975	SF N	9	13	.409	24	23	7-2	0-0	159.2	143	76	6	3	59-7	153	3.49	109	.240	.307	53-0-5	.113	-2	82	3	0	0.2
1976	SF N	12	14	.462	32	31	8-4	0-0	186.1	171	86	10	2	61-7	130	3.62	101	.246	.308	53-0-7	.170	1	83	2	0	0.3
1977	SF N	16	12	.571	37	37	7-2	0-0	257.2	241	105	27	7	70-5	168	3.32	119	.244	.298	85-2-5	.176	3	97	20	0	2.2
1978	SF N	9	10	.474	29	28	9-4	1-0	199	166	74	11	7	45-9	105	2.85	122	.221	**.270**	66-0-8	.136	-2	102	12	28	0.8
1979	SF N	5	8	.385	33	19	3-1	0-0	125.2	134	82	12	3	47-8	81	4.58	76	.266	.330	34-0-2	.206	1	97	-21	29	-1.8
1980	SF N	0	0	ø	11	2	0	0-0	25	29	15	5	0	10-1	14	5.40	65	.293	.355	6	.167	-0	102	-4	0	-0.2
	Cal A	3	1	.750	10	6	0	0-0	35.1	39	22	5	0	11-0	16	4.84	82	.279	.327	0	ø	0	113	-4	34	-0.4
Total	7	55	66	.455	192	157	36-13	1-0	1063	1007	509	82	24	334-45	707	3.62	102	.247	.306	322-3-29	.165	3	92	2	91	0.5

YEAR	TM LG	W	L	PCT	G	GS	CG-SHO	SV-BS	IP	H	R	HR	HB	BB-IB	SO	ERA	AERA	OAV	OOB	AB-HR-SH	AVG	PB	SUP	APR	DL	PW
Hall, Drew	Andrew Clark; B3.27.1963 Louisville KY; BL/TL/6´4˝/(205–220); [ChiN84 1/3]; d9.14; Col Morehead St.																									
1986	Chi N	1	2	.333	5	4	1	1-0	23.2	24	12	3	0	10-0	21	4.56	89	.267	.340	7	.143	0	109	-1	0	-0.1
1987	Chi N	1	1	.500	21	0	0	0-1	32.2	40	31	4	0	14-0	20	6.89	63	.308	.370	4	.000	-0	—	-10	0	-0.6
1988	Chi N	1	1	.500	19	0	0	1-2	22.1	26	20	4	1	9-2	22	7.66	48	.295	.360	1	.000	0	—	-9	0	-0.8
1989	Tex A	2	1	.667	38	0	0	0-0	58.1	42	24	3	3	33-1	45	3.70	108	.207	.325	0	ø	0	—	3	0	0.2
1990	Mon N	4	7	.364	42	0	0	3-2	58.1	52	35	6	0	29-5	40	5.09	72	.242	.327	4-0-1	.000	-0	—	-9	45	-1.7
Total	5	9	12	.429	125	4	1	5-5	195.1	184	122	20	4	95-8	148	5.21	75	.253	.339	16-0-1	.063	-1	109	-26	45	-3.0
Hall, Charley	Charles Louis "Sea Lion" (b Carlos Luis Hall); B7.27.1884 Ventura CA; D12.6.1943 Ventura CA; BL/TR/6´1˝/187; d7.12																									
1906	Cin N	4	8	.333	14	9	9-1	1	95	86	56	1	8	50	49	3.32	83	.258	.368	47-0-1	.128	-1*	94	-8	—	-1.1
1907	Cin N	4	2	.667	11	8	5	0	68	51	22	0	4	43	25	2.51	103	.226	.359	26-0-1	.269	1*	110	2	—	0.3
1909	Bos A	6	4	.600	11	7	3	0	59.2	59	24	0	3	17	27	2.56	98	.271	.332	19-0-2	.158	-1	109	-1	—	-0.2
1910	Bos A	12	9	.571	35	16	13	2	188.2	142	68	6	9	73	95	1.91	134	.207	.292	82-0-5	.207	3*	100	10	—	1.6
1911	Bos A	8	7	.533	32	10	6	**4**	146.1	149	79	3	5	72	83	3.75	87	.279	.370	64-1-6	.141	-1*	134	-3	—	-0.5
1912	†Bos A	15	8	.652	34	20	9-2	2	191	178	85	3	4	70	83	3.02	113	.257	.329	75-1-3	.267	5	120	8	—	1.4
1913	Bos A	5	4	.556	35	4	2	2	105	97	67	1	5	46	48	3.43	86	.238	.322	42-0-1	.214	1	76	-10	—	-0.8
1916	StL N	0	4	.000	10	5	2	1	42.2	45	27	1	0	14	15	5.48	48	.280	.337	14	.143	-1	68	-11	—	-1.1
1918	Det A	0	1	.000	6	1	0	0	13.1	14	10	1	0	6	2	6.75	39	.269	.345	2	.000	-0	0	-5	—	-0.4
Total	9	54	47	.535	188	80	49-3	12	909.2	821	438	16	38	391	427	3.09	95	.248	.334	371-2-19	.197	7	107	-18	—	-0.8
Hall, Bert	Herbert Earl; B10.15.1889 Portland OR; D7.18.1948 Seattle WA; BR/TR/5´10˝/178; d8.21																									
1911	Phi N	0	1	.000	7	1	0	0	18	19	11	0	1	13	8	4.00	86	.297	.423	3	.333	0	218	-1	—	-0.1
Hall, Herb	Herbert Silas "Iron Duke"; B6.5.1893 Steeleville IL; D7.1.1970 Fresno CA; BB/TR/6´4˝/220; d4.28																									
1918	Det A	0	0	ø	3	0	0	0	6	12	11	0	2	7	1	15.00	18	.500	.636	1	.000	-0	—	-8	—	-0.4
Hall, John	John Sylvester; B1.9.1924 Muskogee OK; D1.17.1995 Midwest City OK; BR/TR/6´2.5˝/170; d4.21																									
1948	Bro N	0	0	ø	3	0	0	0	4.1	4	3	1	0	2	2	6.23	64	.267	.353	0	ø	0	—	-1	0	0.0
Hall, Josh	Joshua Alan; B12.16.1980 Lynchburg VA; BR/TR/6´2˝/190; [CinN98 7/200]; d8.2; [DL 2004 Cin N 183]																									
2003	Cin N	0	2	.000	6	5	0	0-0	24.2	33	22	4	0	15-1	18	6.57	63	.314	.397	6-0-1	.167	-0	85	-8	0	-0.6
Hall, Marc	Marcus; B8.12.1887 Joplin MO; D2.24.1915 Joplin MO; BR/TR/6´1.5˝/190; d8.20																									
1910	StL A	1	7	.125	8	7	5	0	46.1	50	33	0	3	31	25	4.27	58	.289	.406	15	.067	-2	77	-9	—	-1.5
1913	Det A	10	12	.455	30	21	8-1	0	165	154	79	1	2	79	69	3.27	89	.259	.348	45-0-7	.089	-3	98	-5	—	-0.9
1914	Det A	4	6	.400	25	8	1	0	90.1	88	38	1	0	27	18	2.69	104	.267	.322	23	.043	-2	88	1	—	-0.2
Total	3	15	25	.375	63	36	14-1	0	301.2	292	150	2	5	137	112	3.25	87	.266	.350	83-0-7	.072	-7	92	-13	—	-2.6
Hall, Darren	Michael Darren; B7.14.1964 Marysville OH; BR/TR/6´3˝/(205–207); [TorA86 28/706]; d4.30; Col Dallas Baptist; [DL 1999 Chi A 182]																									
1994	Tor A	2	3	.400	30	0	0	17-3	31.2	26	12	3	1	14-1	28	3.41	143	.226	.315	0	ø	0	—	6	0	1.1
1995	Tor A	0	2	.000	17	0	0	3-1	16.1	21	9	2	0	9-0	11	4.41	108	.309	.390	0	ø	0	—	1	85	0.1
1996	LA N	0	2	.000	9	0	0	0-1	12	13	9	2	0	5-0	12	6.00	65	.271	.340	0	ø	0	—	-3	137	-0.4
1997	LA N	3	2	.600	63	0	0	2-3	54.2	58	15	3	0	26-7	39	2.30	170	.283	.362	0	ø	0	—	11	0	1.0
1998	LA N	0	3	.000	11	0	0	0-1	11.1	17	14	2	1	5-0	8	10.32	39	.347	.411	0	ø	0	—	-8	139	-1.5
Total	5	5	12	.294	130	0	0	22-9	126	135	59	12	2	59-8	98	3.93	108	.278	.358	0	ø	0	—	7	543	0.3
Hall, Dick	Richard Wallace; B9.27.1930 St.Louis MO; BR/TR/6´6˝/(199–220); d4.15.1952; Col Swarthmore; ▲																									
1955	Pit N	6	6	.500	15	13	4	1	94.1	92	43	8	2	28-4	46	3.91	105	.253	.308	40-1-1	.175	1*	88	4	0	0.5
1956	Pit N	0	7	.000	19	9	1	1	62.1	64	36	8	0	21-3	27	4.76	79	.270	.327	29	.345	2*	62	-6	41	-0.3
1957	Pit N	0	0	ø	8	0	0	0	10	17	12	4	1	5-1	7	10.80	35	.362	.434	1	.000	-0*	—	-7	30	-0.4
1959	Pit N	0	0	ø	2	1	0	0	8.2	12	5	1	0	1-1	3	3.12	124	.333	.342	2	.000	-0	92	0	0	0.0
1960	KC A	8	13	.381	29	28	9-1	0	182.1	183	96	28	3	38-4	79	4.05	98	.261	.299	56-0-8	.107	-2*	97	-3	0	-0.6
1961	Bal A	7	5	.583	29	13	4-2	4	122.1	102	47	10	0	30-5	92	3.09	124	.227	.273	36-0-4	.139	-0*	103	11	0	1.0
1962	Bal A	6	6	.500	43	6	1	6	118.1	102	31	9	0	19-2	71	2.28	162	.230	.261	24-0-2	.167	1*	80	21	0	2.4
1963	Bal A	5	5	.500	47	3	0	12	111.2	91	39	12	4	16-6	74	2.98	116	.224	.258	28-1-2	.464	6*	102	7	0	1.5
1964	Bal A	9	1	.900	45	0	0	7	87.2	58	19	8	0	16-5	52	1.85	193	.188	.226	16-0-3	.125	-0	—	17	0	2.2
1965	Bal A	11	8	.579	48	0	0	12	93.2	84	34	8	0	11-7	79	3.07	113	.243	.265	15-0-2	.333	3*	—	6	0	1.4
1966	Bal A	6	2	.750	32	0	0	7	66	59	30	8	3	8-4	44	3.95	84	.233	.263	12-0-4	.167	0	—	-4	0	-0.5
1967	Phi N	10	8	.556	48	1	1	8	86	83	28	5	2	12-8	49	2.20	155	.255	.286	14-0-2	.071	-1	103	10	0	2.2
1968	Phi N	4	1	.800	32	0	0	0	46	53	26	6	1	5-3	31	4.89	61	.296	.316	3	.333	0	—	-9	0	-0.9
1969	†Bal A	5	2	.714	39	0	0	6-2	65.2	49	14	3	1	9-6	31	1.92	187	.213	.244	7-0-2	.286	1	—	13	0	1.7
1970	†Bal A	10	5	.667	32	0	0	3-4	61.1	51	25	8	0	6-2	30	3.08	119	.229	.247	12-0-1	.083	-1	—	3	0	0.5
1971	†Bal A	6	6	.500	27	0	0	1-3	43.1	52	27	4	1	11-9	26	4.98	68	.302	.342	5-0-1	.400	1	—	-8	0	-1.6
Total	16	93	75	.554	495	74	20-3	68-9	1259.2	1152	512	130	18	236-70	741	3.32	111	.244	.280	300-2-32	.203	10	97	55	71	9.1
Hall, Bob	Robert Louis; B12.22.1923 Swissvale PA; D3.12.1983 St.Petersburg FL; BR/TR/6´2˝/195; d4.23																									
1949	Bos N	6	4	.600	31	6	2	0	74.1	77	40	7	1	41	43	4.36	87	.272	.366	22	.364	3	109	-4	0	-0.4
1950	Bos N	0	2	.000	21	4	0	0	50.1	58	43	8	2	33	22	6.97	55	.293	.399	12	.083	-1	172	-18	0	-0.9
1953	Pit N	3	12	.200	37	17	6-1	1	152	172	99	17	1	72	68	5.39	83	.286	.364	38-1-1	.158	0	74	-13	0	-1.1
Total	3	9	18	.333	89	27	8-1	1	276.2	307	182	32	4	146	133	5.40	77	.284	.371	72-1-1	.208	2	95	-35	0	-2.4
Hall, Tom	Tom Edward; B11.23.1947 Thomasville NC; BL/TL/6´0˝/(146–155); [MinA66*3/53]; d6.9; Col Riverside (CA) CC																									
1968	Min A	2	1	.667	8	4	0	0	29.2	27	15	1	1	12-2	18	2.43	127	.239	.317	9-0-1	.000	-1*	127	0	0	-0.1
1969	†Min A	8	7	.533	31	18	5-2	0-1	140.2	129	63	12	0	50-4	92	3.33	109	.243	.308	43-0-3	.186	1*	108	3	0	0.3
1970	†Min A	11	6	.647	52	11	1	4-0	155.1	94	46	11	2	66-4	184	2.55	145	.173	.262	44-0-6	.182	-0*	112	22	0	2.3
1971	Min A	4	7	.364	48	11	0	9-1	129.2	104	54	13	0	58-5	137	3.33	106	.216	.297	34-0-1	.265	2*	97	3	0	0.5
1972	†Cin N	10	1	.909	47	7	1-1	8-0	124.1	77	43	13	2	56-1	134	2.61	124	.173	.268	30-0-3	.100	-1	125	8	0	0.6
1973	†Cin N	8	5	.615	54	7	0	8-6	103.2	74	43	13	0	48-10	96	3.47	99	.202	.293	22	.045	-2*	117	0	0	-0.3
1974	Cin N	3	1	.750	40	1	0	1-1	64	54	32	9	0	30-0	48	4.08	86	.232	.317	5-0-3	.000	-1	225	-4	0	-0.3
1975	Cin N	0	0	ø	2	0	0	0-0	2	2	0	0	0	2-0	3	0.00	ø	.250	.400	0	ø	0	—	1	0	0.0
	NY N	4	3	.571	34	4	0	1-1	60.2	58	39	10	3	31-3	48	4.75	74	.254	.348	5-0-1	.400	1*	138	-10	0	-1.0
	Year	4	3	.571	36	4	0	1-1	62.2	60	39	10	3	33-3	51	4.60	76	.254	.350	5-0-1	.400	1	138	-8	0	-1.0
1976	NY N	1	1	.500	5	0	0	0-0	4.2	5	3	0	0	5-2	5	5.79	58	.250	.400	0	ø	0	—	-1	0	-0.2
	†KC A	1	1	.500	31	0	0	1-0	30.1	28	19	4	0	18-1	25	4.45	79	.246	.346	0	ø	0*	—	-4	0	-0.2
1977	KC A	0	0	ø	6	0	0	0-1	7.2	4	3	2	0	6-0	10	3.52	115	.154	.313	0	ø	0	—	1	0	0.0
Total	10	52	33	.612	358	63	7-3	32-11	852.2	656	360	88	8	382-32	797	3.27	107	.211	.297	192-0-18	.161	-1	114	19	0	1.6
Hall, Bill	William Bernard "Beanie"; B2.22.1894 Charleston WV; D8.15.1947 Newport KY; BR/TR/6´2˝/250; d7.4																									
1913	Bro N	0	0	ø	3	0	0	0	4.2	4	3	0	1	5	3	5.79	57	.267	.476	1	.000	-0	—	-1	—	-0.1
Halla, John	John Arthur; B5.13.1884 St.Louis MO; D9.30.1947 ElSegundo CA; BL/TL/5´11˝/175; d8.18																									
1905	Cle A	0	0	ø	3	0	0	0	12.2	12	6	0	1	0	4	2.84	92	.250	.265	5	.200	-0	—	-1	—	0.0
Halladay, Roy	Harry Leroy; B5.14.1977 Denver CO; BR/TR/6´6˝/(205–230); [TorA95 1/17]; d9.20																									
1998	Tor A	1	0	1.000	2	2	1	0-0	14	9	4	2	0	2-0	13	1.93	242	.176	.208	0	ø	0	90	4	0	0.3
1999	Tor A	8	7	.533	36	18	1-1	1-0	149.1	156	76	19	4	79-1	82	3.92	126	.270	.359	2-0-1	.000	-0	83	14	0	1.2
2000	Tor A	4	7	.364	19	13	0	0-0	67.2	107	87	14	2	42-0	44	10.64	47	.357	.435	0	.000	0	112	-41	0	-4.8
2001	Tor A	5	3	.625	17	16	1-1	0-0	105.1	97	41	3	1	25-0	96	3.16	145	.241	.287	1-0-1	.000	-0	82	16	0	1.1
2002	Tor A★	19	7	.731	34	34	2-1	0-0	**239.1**	223	93	10	7	62-6	168	2.93	158	.244	.297	6	.000	-1	104	39	0	4.0
2003	Tor A☆	**22**	7	**.759**	36	**36**	**9-2**	0-0	**266**	253	111	26	9	32-1	204	3.25	146	.247	.275	9	.111	-0	108	40	0	4.2
2004	Tor A	8	8	.500	21	21	1-1	0-0	133	140	66	13	1	39-1	95	4.20	117	.272	.323	6	.000	-1	87	10	81	1.0
2005	Tor A✳	12	4	.750	19	19	**5**-2	0-0	141.2	118	39	11	7	18-2	108	2.41	190	.225	.260	2	.000	-0	83	33	86	3.7
2006	Tor A★	16	5	**.762**	32	32	4	0-0	220	208	82	19	5	34-5	132	3.19	148	.251	.283	3	.000	-0	110	38	0	3.3
Total	9	95	48	.664	216	191	24-8	1-0	1336.1	1311	599	117	36	333-16	942	3.62	131	.255	.304	29-0-2	.034	-2	98	153	167	14.0

YEAR	TM LG	W	L	PCT	G	GS	CG-SHO	SV-BS	IP	H	R	HR	HB	BB-IB	SO	ERA	AERA	OAV	OOB	AB-HR-SH	AVG	PB	SUP	APR	DL	PW
HALLAHAN, BILL	William Anthony "Wild Bill"; B8.4.1902 Binghamton NY; D7.8.1981 Binghamton NY; BR/TL/5´10.5˝/170; d4.16																									
1925	StL N	1	0	1.000	6	0	0	0	15.1	14	6	0	0	11	8	3.52	123	.259	.385	3	.333	0	—	-2	—	0.1
1926	†StL N	1	4	.200	19	3	0	0	56.2	45	27	1	1	32	28	3.65	107	.260	.379	16	.250	0	78	**2**	—	0.1
1929	StL N	4	4	.500	20	12	5	0	93.2	94	51	6	0	60	52	4.42	106	.269	.376	26-0-2	.154	-1	83	3	—	0.2
1930	†StL N	15	9	.625	35	32	13-2	2	237.1	233	135	15	0	126	**177**	4.66	108	.260	.351	81-0-11	.123	-6	100	13	—	0.5
1931	†StL N	**19**	9	.679	37	30	16-3	4	248.2	242	102	10	1	112	**159**	3.29	120	.259	.339	81-0-10	.099	-4	125	19	—	1.5
1932	StL N	12	7	.632	25	22	13-1	1	176.1	169	79	10	0	69	108	3.11	126	.253	.323	56-0-4	.214	2*	96	12	—	1.4
1933	StL N★	16	13	.552	36	32	16-2	0	244.1	245	114	6	0	98	93	3.50	99	.260	.330	80-0-6	.150	-0*	107	-2	—	-0.4
1934	†StL N	8	12	.400	32	26	10-2	0	162.2	195	93	2	0	66	70	4.26	99	.294	.358	55-0-4	.182	-1	109	-2	—	-0.4
1935	StL N	15	8	.652	40	23	8-2	1	181.1	196	91	7	1	57	73	3.42	120	.275	.329	56-1-4	.143	-2	123	8	—	0.8
1936	StL N	2	2	.500	9	6	1	0	37	58	28	4	0	17	16	6.32	62	.360	.421	9-0-3	.556	3	151	-9	—	-0.6
	Cin N	5	9	.357	23	19	5-2	0	135	150	78	3	1	57	32	4.33	88	.287	.359	47-1-1	.191	1	99	-9	—	-0.6
	Year	7	11	.389	32	25	6-2	0	172	208	106	7	1	74	48	4.76	81	.305	.373	56-1-4	.250	3	112	-15	—	-1.2
1937	Cin N	3	9	.250	21	9	2	0	63	90	52	3	2	29	18	6.14	61	.345	.414	21-0-1	.095	-1	90	-18	—	-2.9
1938	Phi N	1	8	.111	21	10	1	0	89	107	59	4	2	45	22	5.46	71	.295	.376	26	.192	-0	59	-14	—	-1.2
Total	12	102	94	.520	324	224	90-14	8	1740.1	1838	915	71	8	779	856	4.03	102	.274	.351	557-2-46	.162	-9	105	5	—	-1.5
HALLETT, JACK	Jack Price; B11.13.1914 Toledo OH; D6.11.1982 Toledo OH; BR/TR/6´4˝/215; d9.13; Mil 1943–45																									
1940	Chi A	1	1	.500	2	2	1	0	14	15	10	1	1	6	9	6.43	69	.273	.355	5	.400	0	139	-2	—	-0.2
1941	Chi A	5	5	.500	22	6	3	0	74.2	96	57	7	3	38	25	6.03	68	.306	.386	26-0-1	.154	0	116	-16	0	-1.7
1942	Pit N	0	1	.000	3	3	2	0	22.1	23	12	0	0	8	16	4.84	70	.274	.337	8-1-0	.375	2	91	-3	0	0.0
1943	Pit N	1	2	.333	9	4	2-1	0	47.2	36	11	0	1	11	11	1.70	205	.212	.264	14	.286	2	98	9	0	0.7
1946	Pit N	5	7	.417	35	9	3-1	0	115	107	48	0	0	39	64	3.29	107	.267	.332	26-0-2	.231	0	40	4	0	0.4
1948	NY N	0	0	ø	2	0	0	0	4	3	3	0	0	4	3	4.50	87	.214	.389	1	.000	-0	—	-1	0	0.0
Total	6	12	16	.429	73	24	11-2	0	277.2	280	141	8	5	106	128	4.05	92	.270	.340	80-1-3	.237	4	86	-9	0	-0.8
HALLSTROM, CHARLIE	Charles E. "Swedish Wonder"; B1.22.1864 Jonkoping, Sweden; D5.6.1949 Chicago IL; d9.23																									
1885	Pro N	0	1	.000	1	1	1	0	9	18	16	3	—	6	0	11.00	24	.409	.480	4	.000	-1	169	-8	—	-0.6
HALSEY, BRAD	Bradford Alexander; B2.14.1981 Houston TX; BL/TL/6´1˝/(180–185); [NYA02 8/246]; d6.19; Col Texas																									
2004	NY A	1	3	.250	8	7	0	0-0	32	41	26	4	2	14-0	25	6.47	71	.306	.375	2	.500	0	124	-7	0	-0.7
2005	Ari N	8	12	.400	28	26	0	0-0	160	191	101	20	9	39-3	82	4.61	96	.300	.347	48-0-6	.063	-2	100	-8	0	-1.1
2006	Oak A	5	4	.556	52	7	0	0-0	94.1	108	53	11	5	46-7	53	4.67	97	.288	.371	0	ø	0	101	-2	0	-0.1
Total	3	14	19	.424	88	40	0	0-0	286.1	340	180	35	16	99-10	160	4.84	93	.297	.359	50-0-6	.080	-2	104	-17	0	-1.9
HAMANN, DOC	Elmer Joseph; B12.21.1900 New Ulm MN; D1.11.1973 Milwaukee WI; BR/TR/6´1˝/180; d9.21																									
1922	Cle A	0	0	ø	1	0	0	0	0	3	6	0	1	3	0	(6)	ø	1.000	1.000	0	ø	0	—	-6	—	-0.4
HAMBRIGHT, ROGER	Roger Dee; B3.26.1949 Sunnyside WA; BR/TR/5´10˝/180; [NYA67 67/955]; d7.19																									
1971	NY A	3	1	.750	18	0	0	2-0	26.2	22	13	5	0	10-2	14	4.39	75	.224	.294	2	.500	0	—	-3	0	-0.4
HAMELS, COLE	Colbert Richard; B12.27.1983 San Diego CA; BL/TL/6´4˝/195; [PhiN02 1/17]; d5.12																									
2006	Phi N	9	8	.529	23	23	0	0-0	132.1	117	66	19	3	48-4	145	4.08	115	.237	.304	44-0-2	.114	-0	114	8	18	1.0
HAMILL, JOHN	John Alexander Charles; B12.18.1860 New York NY; D12.6.1911 Bristol RI; BR/TR/5´8˝/158; d5.1																									
1884	Was AA	2	17	.105	19	19	18-1	0	156.2	197	158	8	5	43	50	4.48	68	.287	.333	71	.099	-3*	95	-28	—	-2.9
HAMILTON, DAVE	David Edward; B12.13.1947 Seattle WA; BL/TL/6´0˝/(180–190); [OakA66 5/82]; d5.29																									
1972	†Oak A	6	6	.500	25	14	1	0-0	101.1	94	34	7	1	31-2	55	2.93	97	.249	.304	26-0-1	.154	2	115	1	0	0.3
1973	Oak A	6	4	.600	16	11	1	0-0	69.2	74	37	8	1	24-0	34	4.39	81	.274	.334	0	ø	0	100	-6	0	-0.8
1974	Oak A	7	4	.636	29	18	1-1	0-0	117	104	45	10	5	48-3	69	3.15	106	.241	.322	0	ø	0	114	4	0	0.3
1975	Oak A	1	2	.333	11	4	0	0-0	35.2	42	19	4	0	18-1	20	4.04	90	.290	.366	0	ø	0	60	-2	0	-0.1
	Chi A	6	5	.545	30	1	0	6-2	69.2	63	23	4	0	29-2	51	2.84	137	.246	.322	0	ø	0	68	8	0	1.5
	Year	7	7	.500	41	5	0	6-2	105.1	105	42	8	0	47-3	71	3.25	117	.262	.338	0	ø	0	60	7	0	1.4
1976	Chi A	6	6	.500	45	1	0	10-3	90.1	81	38	4	4	45-6	62	3.59	99	.243	.335	0	ø	0	172	0	0	0.0
1977	Chi A	4	5	.444	55	0	0	9-6	67.1	71	33	6	0	33-4	45	3.61	113	.270	.344	0	ø	0	—	2	0	0.4
1978	StL N	0	0	ø	13	0	0	0-1	14	16	13	5	0	6-0	8	6.43	55	.296	.367	1	.000	-0	—	-5	0	-0.3
	Pit N	0	2	.000	16	0	0	1-1	26.1	23	16	2	0	12-2	15	3.42	109	.221	.302	6	.000	-1	—	-1	0	-0.2
	Year	0	2	.000	29	0	0	1-2	40.1	39	29	7	0	18-2	23	4.46	82	.247	.324	7	.000	-1	—	-7	0	-0.5
1979	Oak A	3	4	.429	40	7	1	5-1	82.2	80	42	5	1	43-2	52	3.70	110	.261	.349	0	ø	0	67	2	0	0.2
1980	Oak A	0	3	.000	21	1	0	0-0	30	44	39	6	3	28-2	23	11.40	33	.344	.466	0	ø	0	94	-25	0	-2.1
Total	9	39	41	.488	301	57	4-1	31-14	704	692	339	61	15	317-24	434	3.85	93	.259	.338	33-0-1	.121	1	95	-22	0	-0.8
HAMILTON, EARL	Earl Andrew; B7.19.1891 Gibson City IL; D11.17.1968 Anaheim CA; BL/TL/5´8˝/160; d4.14; Mil 1918																									
1911	StL A	5	12	.294	32	17	10-1	0	177	191	103	4	4	69	55	3.97	85	.284	.354	56-0-1	.107	-1	99	-9	—	-0.8
1912	StL A	11	14	.440	41	26	17-1	2	249.2	228	117	2	9	86	139	3.24	102	.248	.319	73-0-6	.178	-0	56	4	—	0.3
1913	StL A	13	12	.520	31	24	19-3	1	217.1	197	95	3	9	83	101	2.57	114	.244	.321	74-0-2	.135	-2	100	5	—	0.3
1914	StL A	16	18	.471	44	35	20-5	2	302.1	265	111	5	10	100	111	2.50	108	.239	.307	85-0-7	.176	4	85	8	—	1.3
1915	StL A	9	17	.346	35	28	13-1	0	204	203	98	4	12	69	63	2.87	100	.274	.346	62-0-2	.113	-2	85	-2	—	-0.6
1916	StL A	0	0	ø	1	0	0	0	4	4	5	0	0	4	0	9.00	31	.250	.400	0	ø	0	—	-3	—	-0.2
	Det A	1	2	.333	5	5	3	0	37.1	34	14	0	4	22	7	2.65	108	.254	.375	13	.077	-1	121	1	—	0.0
	StL A	5	7	.417	22	12	3	0	91.1	97	44	2	2	26	25	3.05	90	.284	.339	24	.000	-1	90	-5	—	-0.8
	Year	6	9	.400	28	17	6	0	132.2	135	63	2	6	52	32	3.12	89	.275	.352	37	.027	-2	99	-7	—	-1.0
1917	StL A	0	9	.000	27	8	2	1	83	86	46	1	2	41	19	3.14	83	.274	.361	19-0-2	.368	3	38	-7	—	-0.5
1918	Pit N	6	0	1.000	6	6	6-1	0	54	47	7	0	0	13	20	0.83	344	.242	.290	21	.286	1	141	12	—	1.6
1919	Pit N	8	11	.421	28	19	9-1	1	160.1	167	73	3	5	49	39	3.31	91	.280	.340	52-0-1	.135	-2	83	-7	—	-1.0
1920	Pit N	10	13	.435	39	23	12	3	230.1	223	99	2	2	69	74	3.24	99	.258	.314	67-0-7	.149	-3	94	0	—	-0.3
1921	Pit N	13	15	.464	35	30	12-2	0	225	237	103	5	8	58	59	3.36	114	.272	.323	75-0-5	.160	-0	95	11	—	1.3
1922	Pit N	11	7	.611	33	14	9-1	2	160	183	84	6	1	40	34	3.99	102	.296	.339	58-0-3	.155	-2	126	2	—	0.0
1923	Pit N	7	9	.438	28	15	5	1	141	148	67	6	1	42	42	3.77	106	.271	.324	52-0-1	.173	-2	83	5	—	0.4
1924	Phi N	0	1	.000	3	0	0	0	6	9	9	0	1	2	2	10.50	42	.391	.462	2	.000	-0	—	-4	—	-0.5
Total	14	115	147	.439	410	262	140-16	13	2342.2	2319	1075	43	70	773	790	3.16	102	.265	.329	733-0-37	.153	-9	89	11	—	0.5
HAMILTON, JACK	Jack Edwin; B12.25.1938 Burlington IA; BR/TR/6´0˝/200; d4.13																									
1962	Phi N	9	12	.429	41	26	4-1	2	182	185	115	18	5	107-8	101	5.09	76	.268	.366	54-0-5	.056	-4	97	-25	0	-2.8
1963	Phi N	2	1	.667	19	1	0	1	30	22	19	3	0	17-2	23	5.40	60	.200	.307	3	.000	-0	27	-7	0	-0.7
1964	Det A	0	1	.000	5	1	0	0	15	24	17	2	1	8-0	5	8.40	44	.364	.434	3	.000	-0	49	-9	33	-0.5
1965	Det A	1	1	.500	4	1	0	0	4.1	6	7	1	0	4-0	3	14.54	24	.316	.417	0	ø	0	76	-5	0	-0.9
1966	NY N	6	13	.316	57	13	3-1	13	148.2	138	89	13	5	88-4	93	3.93	92	.248	.354	38-0-1	.132	-1	102	-11	0	-1.6
1967	NY N	2	0	1.000	17	1	0	1	31.1	24	15	2	1	16-5	22	3.73	91	.205	.306	5-1-0	.200	1	233	-1	0	0.0
	Cal A	9	6	.600	26	20	0	0	119.1	104	47	6	1	63-3	74	3.24	97	.239	.334	38-0-2	.158	-0	110	0	0	-0.1
1968	Cal A	3	1	.750	21	2	1	2	38	34	15	0	0	15-1	18	3.32	88	.246	.316	7	.143	-0	105	-1	0	-0.2
1969	Cle A	0	2	.000	20	0	0	1-2	30.2	37	17	2	0	23-4	13	4.40	86	.316	.426	2	.000	-0	—	-2	0	-0.2
	Chi A	0	3	.000	8	0	0	0-0	12.1	23	16	1	0	7-3	5	11.68	33	.411	.476	0	ø	0	—	-10	0	-1.8
	Year	0	5	.000	28	0	0	1-2	43	60	33	3	0	30-7	18	6.49	59	.347	.441	2	.000	-0	—	-11	0	-2.0
Total	8	32	40	.444	218	65	8-2	20-2	611.2	597	357	48	13	348-30	357	4.53	78	.259	.356	150-1-8	.107	-6	102	-71	33	-8.8
HAMILTON, JOEY	Johns Joseph; B9.9.1970 Statesboro GA; BR/TR/6´4˝/(220–240); [SDN91 1/8]; d5.24; Col Georgia Southern																									
1994	SD N	9	6	.600	16	16	1-1	0-0	108.2	98	40	7	6	29-3	61	2.98	139	.241	.300	40-0-5	.000	-4	103	14	0	1.4
1995	SD N	6	9	.400	31	30	2-2	0-0	204.1	189	89	17	11	56-5	123	3.08	132	.246	.305	65-0-5	.108	-2	98	19	0	1.0
1996	†SD N	15	9	.625	34	33	3-1	0-0	211.2	206	100	19	9	83-3	184	4.17	97	.256	.330	68-1-11	.162	1	100	1	0	0.2
1997	SD N	12	7	.632	31	29	1	0-0	192.2	199	100	22	12	69-2	124	4.25	92	.271	.340	54-2-9	.130	1	121	-7	23	-0.6
1998	†SD N	13	13	.500	34	34	0	0-0	217.1	220	113	15	8	106-10	147	4.27	93	.267	.353	71-1-2	.141	0*	82	-8	0	-0.9
1999	Tor A	7	8	.467	22	18	0	0-0	98	118	73	13	3	39-0	56	6.52	76	.298	.364	2	.000	-0	107	-15	40	-1.9
2000	Tor A	2	1	.667	6	6	0	0-0	33	28	13	3	2	12-0	15	3.55	142	.233	.311	0	ø	0	115	6	137	0.4

YEAR	TM LG	W	L	PCT	G	GS	CG-SHO	SV-BS	IP	H	R	HR	HB	BB-IB	SO	ERA	AERA	OAV	OOB	AB-HR-SH	AVG	PB	SUP	APR	DL	PW
2001	Tor A	5	8	.385	22	22	0	0-0	122.1	170	88	17	3	38-1	82	5.89	78	.339	.384	3	.333	1	101	-18	0	-1.5
	Cin N	1	2	.333	4	4	0	0-0	17.1	23	12	3	1	6-0	10	6.23	74	.329	.390	5	.000	-1	70	-2	0	-0.4
2002	Cin N	4	10	.286	39	17	0	1-1	124.2	136	78	11	6	50-2	85	5.27	81	.279	.351	28-0-4	.250	2	96	-12	44	-1.1
2003	Cin N	0	0	ø	3	0	0	0-0	10.2	21	15	3	0	5-0	7	12.66	33	.404	.456	3	.000	-0	—	-10	0	-0.5
Total	10	74	73	.503	242	209	7-4	1-1	1340.2	1408	721	130	61	493-26	894	4.44	94	.273	.341	339-4-36	.127	-2	101	-32	244	-3.9

HAMILTON, STEVE Steve Absher; B11.30.1935 Columbia KY; D12.2.1997 Morehead KY; BL/TL/6´7˝/(190–196); d4.23; C1; Col Morehead St.

YEAR	TM LG	W	L	PCT	G	GS	CG-SHO	SV-BS	IP	H	R	HR	HB	BB-IB	SO	ERA	AERA	OAV	OOB	AB-HR-SH	AVG	PB	SUP	APR	DL	PW
1961	Cle A	0	0	ø	2	0	0	0	3	2	1	0	0	3-0	4	3.00	131	.200	.385	1	1.000	0	—	0	0	0.1
1962	Was A	3	8	.273	41	10	1	2	107.1	103	51	10	3	39-5	83	3.77	107	.248	.317	26-0-3	.077	-1*	88	2	0	0.2
1963	Was A	0	1	.000	3	0	0	0	2	5	3	0	0	2-0	1	13.50	27	.556	.583	0	ø	0	—	-2	0	-0.4
	†NY A	5	1	.833	34	0	0	5	62.1	49	19	3	1	24-2	63	2.60	135	.220	.296	14-0-5	.286	1	—	7	0	1.0
	Year	5	2	.714	37	0	0	5	64.1	54	22	3	1	26-2	64	2.94	120	.233	.309	14-0-5	.286	1	—	5	0	0.6
1964	†NY A	7	2	.778	30	3	1	3	60.1	55	24	6	0	15-0	49	3.28	110	.246	.289	20	.200	1*	164	2	0	0.4
1965	NY A	3	1	.750	46	1	0	5	58.1	47	12	2	0	16-5	51	1.39	245	.214	.265	6	.167	0	103	12	0	1.0
1966	NY A	8	3	.727	44	3	1-1	3	90	69	32	8	3	22-3	57	3.00	111	.218	.273	19-0-2	.053	-2	62	4	0	0.3
1967	NY A	2	4	.333	44	0	0	4	62	57	25	7	1	23-4	55	3.48	90	.250	.320	9-0-1	.111	-0	—	-1	0	-0.2
1968	NY A	2	2	.500	40	0	0	11	50.2	37	13	0	1	13-4	42	2.13	137	.211	.268	3	.000	0	—	5	0	0.7
1969	NY A	3	4	.429	38	0	0	2-2	57	39	22	7	0	21-5	39	3.32	106	.194	.269	5	.000	-1	—	2	0	0.2
1970	NY A	4	3	.571	35	0	0	3-1	45.1	36	16	3	1	16-5	33	2.78	129	.222	.294	6	.000	-1	—	4	0	0.6
	Chi A	0	0	ø	3	0	0	0-0	3	4	2	0	0	1-0	3	6.00	65	.333	.385	0	ø	0	—	-1	0	0.0
	Year	4	3	.571	38	0	0	3-1	48.1	40	18	3	1	17-5	36	2.98	121	.230	.301	6	.000	-1	—	4	0	0.6
1971	†SF N	2	2	.500	39	0	0	4-3	44.2	29	15	4	1	11-6	38	3.02	113	.186	.238	2	.000	-0	—	3	0	0.3
1972	Chi N	1	0	1.000	22	0	0	0-0	17	24	9	1	1	8-3	13	4.76	80	.333	.398	1	.000	-0	—	-1	0	-0.1
Total	12	40	31	.563	421	17	3-1	42-6	663	556	244	51	12	214-42	531	3.05	115	.229	.293	112-0-11	.125	-2	106	36	0	4.1

HAMLIN, LUKE Lewis Dennison "Hot Potato"; B7.3.1904 Ferris Center MI; D2.18.1978 Clare MI; BL/TR/6´2˝/168; d9.18

YEAR	TM LG	W	L	PCT	G	GS	CG-SHO	SV-BS	IP	H	R	HR	HB	BB-IB	SO	ERA	AERA	OAV	OOB	AB-HR-SH	AVG	PB	SUP	APR	DL	PW
1933	Det A	1	0	1.000	3	3	0	0	16.2	20	11	3	0	10	10	4.86	89	.294	.385	5-0-1	.400	1	118	-1	—	0.0
1934	Det A	2	3	.400	20	5	1	1	75.1	87	48	11	0	44	30	5.38	82	.289	.380	26-0-3	.231	-0	174	-7	—	-0.4
1937	Bro N	11	13	.458	39	25	11-1	1	185.2	183	96	4	0	48	93	3.59	113	.252	.298	59-0-5	.186	-1*	85	7	—	0.6
1938	Bro N	12	15	.444	44	30	10-3	6	237.1	243	111	14	2	65	97	3.68	106	.263	.313	78-0-4	.141	-3	92	7	—	0.3
1939	Bro N	20	13	.606	40	**36**	19-2	0	269.2	255	115	27	0	54	88	3.64	111	.248	.285	103-1-6	.126	-5	102	15	—	0.9
1940	Bro N	9	8	.529	33	25	9-2	0	182.1	183	77	17	2	34	91	3.06	131	.256	.292	58-0-8	.086	-4*	79	15	—	0.6
1941	Bro N	8	8	.500	30	20	5-1	1	136	139	75	14	2	41	58	4.24	87	.261	.316	41-0-3	.146	-1	130	-9	0	-1.1
1942	Pit N	4	4	.500	23	14	6-1	0	112	128	58	3	1	19	38	3.94	86	.281	.312	37-0-3	.243	1	115	-7	0	-0.5
1944	Phi A	6	12	.333	29	23	9-2	0	190	204	94	13	3	38	58	3.74	93	.271	.309	56-0-4	.232	3	88	-6	0	-0.5
Total	9	73	76	.490	261	181	70-12	9	1405	1442	685	106	10	353	563	3.77	103	.262	.308	463-1-37	.164	-8	99	14	0	-0.1

HAMM, PETE Peter Whitfield; B9.20.1947 Buffalo NY; BR/TR/6´5˝/210; [MinA67 S9/156]; d7.29; Col Stanford

YEAR	TM LG	W	L	PCT	G	GS	CG-SHO	SV-BS	IP	H	R	HR	HB	BB-IB	SO	ERA	AERA	OAV	OOB	AB-HR-SH	AVG	PB	SUP	APR	DL	PW
1970	Min A	0	2	.000	10	0	0	0-0	16.1	17	10	3	0	7-1	3	5.51	67	.262	.333	1	.000	-0	—	-3	0	-0.3
1971	Min A	2	4	.333	13	8	1	0-0	44	55	33	7	1	18-1	16	6.75	52	.309	.372	11-0-1	.273	1	127	-14	0	-1.6
Total	2	2	6	.250	23	8	1	0-0	60.1	72	43	10	1	25-2	19	6.41	56	.296	.362	12-0-1	.250	1	127	-17	0	-1.9

HAMMAKER, ATLEE Charlton Atlee; B1.24.1958 Carmel CA; BB/TL/6´3˝/(195–204); [KCA79 1/21]; d8.13; Col East Tennessee; [DL 1986 SF N 182]

YEAR	TM LG	W	L	PCT	G	GS	CG-SHO	SV-BS	IP	H	R	HR	HB	BB-IB	SO	ERA	AERA	OAV	OOB	AB-HR-SH	AVG	PB	SUP	APR	DL	PW
1981	KC A	1	3	.250	10	6	0	0-0	39	44	24	2	0	12-1	11	5.54	65	.286	.335	0	ø	0	95	-7	0	-0.7
1982	SF N	12	8	.600	29	27	4-1	0-0	175	189	86	16	2	28-8	102	4.11	87	.278	.307	59-0-1	.068	-4	96	-8	0	-1.2
1983	SF N★	10	9	.526	23	23	8-3	0-0	172.1	147	57	9	3	32-12	127	**2.25**	**158**	.228	**.266**	59-0-3	.102	-1	88	23	26	2.4
1984	SF N	2	0	1.000	6	6	0	0-0	33	32	10	2	0	9-1	24	2.18	162	.256	.301	11	.182	1	113	5	113	0.4
1985	SF N	5	12	.294	29	29	1-1	0-0	170.2	161	81	17	0	47-5	100	3.74	93	.247	.295	47-0-6	.085	-3	86	-5	0	-0.7
1987	†SF N	10	10	.500	31	27	2	0-0	168.1	159	73	22	3	57-10	107	3.58	107	.248	.312	57-0-2	.123	-1	114	6	24	0.5
1988	SF N	9	9	.500	43	17	3-1	5-2	144.2	136	68	11	3	41-9	65	3.73	87	.248	.302	33-0-4	.121	-0	91	-8	0	-0.9
1989	†SF N	6	6	.500	28	9	0	0-1	76.2	78	34	5	1	23-2	30	3.76	90	.271	.323	19-0-4	.368	2	128	-2	77	-0.1
1990	SF N	4	5	.444	25	6	0	0-0	67.1	69	33	7	0	21-4	28	4.28	86	.273	.324	17-0-1	.059	-1	119	-4	23	-0.6
	SD N	0	4	.000	9	1	0	0-0	19.1	16	11	1	0	6-1	16	4.66	82	.213	.272	2	.500	0	118	-2	0	-0.3
	Year	4	9	.308	34	7	0	0-0	86.2	85	44	8	0	27-5	44	4.36	85	.259	.312	19-0-1	.105	-0	119	-5	0	-0.9
1991	SD N	0	1	.000	1	1	0	0-0	4.2	8	7	0	0	3-0	1	5.79	66	.364	.440	1	.000	-0	24	-3	143	-0.4
1994	Chi A	0	0	ø	2	0	0	0-0	1.1	1	0	0	0	0-0	1	0.00	ø	.200	.200	0	ø	0	—	1	0	0.0
1995	Chi A	0	0	ø	13	0	0	0-0	6.1	11	9	2	1	8-1	3	12.79	35	.393	.541	0	ø	0	—	-6	0	-0.3
Total	12	59	67	.468	249	152	18-6	5-3	1078.2	1051	493	94	13	287-54	615	3.66	97	.255	.304	305-0-21	.118	-7	99	-10	588	-1.9

HAMMEL, JASON Jason Aaron; B9.2.1982 Greenville SC; BR/TR/6´6˝/200; [TBA02 10/284]; d4.11; Col Treasure Valley (OR) CC

YEAR	TM LG	W	L	PCT	G	GS	CG-SHO	SV-BS	IP	H	R	HR	HB	BB-IB	SO	ERA	AERA	OAV	OOB	AB-HR-SH	AVG	PB	SUP	APR	DL	PW
2006	TB A	0	6	.000	9	9	0	0-0	44	61	38	7	1	21-0	32	7.77	60	.333	.399	0	ø	0	76	-13	0	-1.4

HAMMOND, CHRIS Christopher Andrew; B1.21.1966 Atlanta GA; BL/TL/6´1˝/(190–210); [CinN86*6/148]; d7.16; b–Steve; Col Alabama–Birmingham

YEAR	TM LG	W	L	PCT	G	GS	CG-SHO	SV-BS	IP	H	R	HR	HB	BB-IB	SO	ERA	AERA	OAV	OOB	AB-HR-SH	AVG	PB	SUP	APR	DL	PW
1990	Cin N	0	2	.000	3	3	0	0-0	11.1	13	9	2	0	12-1	4	6.35	62	.302	.455	3	.000	-0	91	-3	0	-0.5
1991	Cin N	7	7	.500	20	18	0	0-0	99.2	92	51	4	2	48-3	50	4.06	94	.250	.339	34-0-1	.353	5	77	-3	36	0.1
1992	Cin N	7	10	.412	28	26	0	0-0	147.1	149	75	13	3	55-6	79	4.21	86	.266	.333	44-1-3	.136	2*	90	-10	0	-0.8
1993	Fla N	11	12	.478	32	32	1	0-0	191	207	106	18	1	66-2	108	4.66	94	.277	.336	63-2-5	.190	4*	86	-5	0	-0.1
1994	Fla N	4	4	.500	13	13	1-1	0-0	73.1	79	30	5	1	23-1	40	3.07	145	.281	.336	22-0-3	.136	0	87	10	53	0.9
1995	Fla N	9	6	.600	25	24	3-2	0-0	161	157	73	17	9	47-2	126	3.80	113	.256	.315	48-1-5	.271	5	111	9	34	1.4
1996	Fla N	5	8	.385	38	9	0	0-0	81	104	65	14	4	27-3	50	6.56	63	.315	.370	15-0-2	.067	-1	105	-22	35	-3.1
1997	Bos A	3	4	.429	29	8	0	1-1	65.1	81	45	5	2	27-4	48	5.92	79	.310	.375	0	ø	0	121	-8	93	-0.7
1998	Fla N	0	2	.000	3	3	0	0-0	13.2	20	11	3	1	8-0	8	6.59	62	.357	.446	5	.200	0	68	-4	0	-0.5
2002	†Atl N	7	2	.778	63	0	0	0-2	76	53	15	1	1	31-9	63	0.95	427	.195	.278	1	.000	0	—	24	0	2.7
2003	†NY A	3	2	.600	62	0	0	1-3	63	65	23	5	2	11-0	45	2.86	154	.270	.304	0	ø	0	—	11	0	0.7
2004	Oak A	4	1	.800	41	0	0	1-2	53.2	56	21	4	3	13-1	34	2.68	172	.277	.326	0	ø	0	—	10	45	0.8
2005	SD N	5	1	.833	55	0	0	0-3	58.2	51	25	9	2	14-0	34	3.84	102	.229	.278	3	.000	-0	—	2	20	0.1
2006	Cin N	1	1	.500	29	0	0	0-2	28.2	36	23	5	0	5-0	23	6.91	68	.303	.331	0	ø	0	—	-6	0	-0.4
Total	14	66	62	.516	441	136	5-3	3-13	1123.2	1163	572	105	31	387-32	712	4.14	101	.269	.332	238-4-19	.202	15	93	5	316	0.6

HAMNER, GRANNY Granville Wilbur; B4.26.1927 Richmond VA; D9.12.1993 Philadelphia PA; BR/TR/5´10˝/(160–185); d9.14.1944; Mil 1945; b–Garvin; ▲

YEAR	TM LG	W	L	PCT	G	GS	CG-SHO	SV-BS	IP	H	R	HR	HB	BB-IB	SO	ERA	AERA	OAV	OOB	AB-HR-SH	AVG	PB	SUP	APR	DL	PW
1956	Phi N	0	1	.000	3	1	0	0	8.1	10	4	0	0	2-0	4	4.32	86	.294	.333	401-4-3	.224	1*	71	0	0	0.0
1957	Phi N	0	0	ø	1	0	0	0	1	1	0	0	0	0-0	1	0.00	ø	.250	.250	502-10-7	.227	0*	—	0	0	0.0
1962	KC A	0	1	.000	3	0	0	0	4	10	6	0	0	6-1	0	9.00	47	.476	.593	0	ø	0	—	-3	0	-0.5
Total	3	0	2	.000	7	1	0	0	13.1	21	10	0	0	8-1	5	5.40	72	.356	.433	903-14-10	.226	1	71	-3	0	-0.5

HAMNER, RALPH Ralph Conant "Bruz"; B9.12.1916 Gibsland LA; D5.22.2001 Little Rock AR; BR/TR/6´3˝/165; d4.28

YEAR	TM LG	W	L	PCT	G	GS	CG-SHO	SV-BS	IP	H	R	HR	HB	BB-IB	SO	ERA	AERA	OAV	OOB	AB-HR-SH	AVG	PB	SUP	APR	DL	PW
1946	Chi A	2	7	.222	25	7	1	1	71.1	80	47	2	5	39	29	4.42	77	.276	.371	18-0-2	.167	0	54	-10	0	-1.2
1947	Chi N	1	2	.333	3	3	2	0	25	24	10	0	0	16	14	2.52	157	.267	.377	8	.125	-0	52	3	0	0.3
1948	Chi N	5	9	.357	27	17	5	0	111.1	110	63	12	5	69	53	4.69	83	.259	.369	33-1-1	.182	1	106	-8	0	-0.7
1949	Chi N	0	2	.000	6	1	0	0	12.1	22	13	2	1	8	3	8.76	46	.407	.492	2-0-1	.000	-0	44	-6	0	-0.8
Total	4	8	20	.286	61	28	8	1	220	236	133	16	11	132	99	4.58	82	.275	.378	61-1-4	.164	0	86	-21	0	-2.4

HAMPSON, JUSTIN Justin Michael; B5.24.1980 Belleville IL; BL/TL/6´1˝/200; [ColN99 28/850]; d9.10; Col Southwestern Illinois CC

YEAR	TM LG	W	L	PCT	G	GS	CG-SHO	SV-BS	IP	H	R	HR	HB	BB-IB	SO	ERA	AERA	OAV	OOB	AB-HR-SH	AVG	PB	SUP	APR	DL	PW
2006	Col N	1	0	1.000	5	1	0	0-1	12	19	10	3	1	5-0	9	7.50	64	.352	.417	3-0-1	.000	-0	385	-3	0	-0.2

HAMPTON, MIKE Michael William; B9.9.1972 Brooksville FL; BR/TL/5´10˝/(180–195); [SeaA90 6/161]; d4.17; [DL 2006 Atl N 182]

YEAR	TM LG	W	L	PCT	G	GS	CG-SHO	SV-BS	IP	H	R	HR	HB	BB-IB	SO	ERA	AERA	OAV	OOB	AB-HR-SH	AVG	PB	SUP	APR	DL	PW
1993	Sea A	1	3	.250	13	3	0	1-0	17	28	20	3	0	17-3	8	9.53	47	.368	.479	0	ø	0	89	-10	0	-1.7
1994	Hou N	2	1	.667	44	0	0	0-1	41.1	46	19	4	2	16-1	24	3.70	107	.282	.354	1	.000	-0	—	1	0	0.1
1995	Hou N	9	8	.529	24	24	0	0-0	150.2	141	73	13	4	49-3	115	3.35	115	.247	.308	48-0-4	.146	1	130	5	29	0.6
1996	Hou N	10	10	.500	27	27	2-1	0-0	160.1	175	79	12	3	49-1	101	3.59	108	.280	.333	42-0-7	.238	4*	116	2	0	0.7
1997	†Hou N	15	10	.600	34	34	7-2	0-0	223	217	105	16	2	77-2	139	3.83	104	.257	.318	73-0-10	.137	1	123	5	0	0.8
1998	†Hou N	11	7	.611	32	32	1-1	0-0	211.2	227	92	18	5	81-1	137	3.36	121	.278	.344	61-0-7	.262	7	110	14	18	2.0
1999	†Hou N★	**22**	4	**.846**	34	34	3-2	0-0	239	206	86	12	5	101-2	177	2.90	153	.241	.322	74-0-5	.311	11	140	41	0	**5.3**
2000	†NY N	15	10	.600	33	33	3-1	0-0	217.2	194	89	10	8	99-5	151	3.14	139	.241	.328	73-0-4	.274	6*	115	29	0	3.7
2001	Col N★	14	13	.519	32	32	2-1	0-0	203	236	138	31	8	85-7	122	5.41	99	.296	.367	79-7-5	.291	8*	105	-4	0	0.6
2002	Col N	7	15	.318	30	30	0	0-0	178.2	228	135	24	7	91-4	74	6.15	77	.313	.390	64-3-1	.344	7*	87	-25	0	-1.9

YEAR	TM LG	W	L	PCT	G	GS	CG-SHO	SV-BS	IP	H	R	HR	HB	BB-IB	SO	ERA	AERA	OAV	OOB	AB-HR-SH	AVG	PB	SUP	APR	DL	PW
2003	†Atl N	14	8	.636	31	31	1	0-0	190	186	91	14	1	78-4	110	3.84	109	.255	.326	60-2-9	.183	5*	115	8	20	1.5
2004	†Atl N	13	9	.591	29	29	1	0-0	172.1	198	86	15	1	65-3	87	4.28	101	.290	.351	64-2-4	.172	3*	106	3	0	0.7
2005	Atl N	5	3	.625	12	12	1-1	0-0	69.1	74	28	5	0	18-0	27	3.50	121	.281	.326	25-1-3	.320	3	149	6	107	1.0
Total	13	138	101	.577	375	321	21-9	1-1	2074	2156	1041	177	46	826-36	1272	3.97	109	.271	.341	664-15-59	.242	54	115	75	356	13.4
Hamulack, Tim	Timothy William; B11.14.1976 Ithaca NY; BR/TL/6´4˝/220; [HouN95 32/893]; d9.2; Col Montgomery (MD) CC																									
2005	NY N	0	0	ø	6	0	0	0-0	2.1	7	6	3	0	1-1	2	23.14	18	.583	.571	0	ø	0	—	-5	0	-0.2
2006	LA N	0	3	.000	33	0	0	0-0	34	36	28	7	2	22-1	34	6.35	69	.265	.375	1	.000	-0	—	-8	0	-0.6
Total	2	0	3	.000	39	0	0	0-0	36.1	43	34	10	2	23-2	36	7.43	59	.291	.391	1	.000	-0	—	-13	0	-0.8
Hancock, Josh	Joshua Morgan; B4.11.1978 Cleveland MS; BR/TR/6´3˝/(205–217); [BosA98 5/145]; d9.10; Col Auburn																									
2002	Bos A	0	1	.000	3	1	0	0-0	7.1	5	3	1	0	2-0	6	3.68	122	.200	.259	0	ø	0	41	1	0	0.1
2003	Phi N	0	0	ø	2	0	0	0-0	3	2	1	0	0	0-0	4	3.00	132	.182	.182	0	ø	0	—	0	0	0.0
2004	Phi N	0	1	.000	4	2	0	0-0	9	13	9	3	0	3-0	5	9.00	49	.333	.381	2	.000	-0	105	-4	0	-0.4
	Cin N	5	1	.833	12	9	0	0-0	54.2	60	34	14	1	25-2	31	4.45	97	.273	.347	15-0-1	.133	0	127	-3	0	-0.3
	Year	5	2	.714	16	11	0	0-0	63.2	73	43	17	1	28-2	36	5.09	85	.282	.352	17-0-1	.118	0	123	-6	0	-0.7
2005	Cin N	1	0	1.000	11	0	0	0-0	14	11	4	1	0	1-0	5	1.93	221	.208	.222	0	ø	0	—	3	151	0.2
2006	†StL N	3	3	.500	62	0	0	1-2	77	70	37	9	1	23-2	50	4.09	106	.241	.295	6-0-1	.000	-0	—	2	0	0.1
Total	5	9	6	.600	94	12	0	1-2	165	161	88	28	2	54-4	101	4.25	102	.252	.310	23-0-2	.087	-0	116	-1	151	-0.3
Hancock, Lee	Leland David; B6.27.1967 N.Hollywood CA; BL/TL/6´4˝/(220–225); [SeaA88 4/97]; d9.3; Col Cal Poly–San Luis Obispo																									
1995	Pit N	0	0	ø	11	0	0	0-0	14	10	3	0	0	2-0	6	1.93	226	.192	.222	0	ø	0	—	4	0	0.2
1996	Pit N	0	0	ø	13	0	0	0-0	18.1	21	18	5	2	10-3	13	6.38	69	.276	.375	0	ø	0	—	-5	0	-0.2
Total	2	0	0	ø	24	0	0	0-0	32.1	31	21	5	2	12-3	19	4.45	98	.242	.317	0	ø	0	—	-1	0	0.0
Hancock, Ryan	Ryan Lee; B11.11.1971 Santa Clara CA; BR/TR/6´2˝/220; [CalA93 2/45]; d6.8; Col Brigham Young																									
1996	Cal A	4	1	.800	11	4	0	0-0	27.2	34	23	2	2	17-1	19	7.48	68	.306	.408	1	1.000	0	115	-6	0	-0.9
Hand, Rich	Richard Allen; B7.10.1948 Bellevue WA; BR/TR/6´1˝/(185–195); [CleA69 S1/1]; d4.9; Col Puget Sound																									
1970	Cle A	6	13	.316	35	25	3-1	3-0	159.2	132	71	27	4	69-3	110	3.83	105	.228	.313	41-0-5	.146	-1	82	4	0	0.3
1971	Cle A	2	6	.250	15	12	0	0-0	60.2	74	43	6	4	38-1	26	5.79	67	.311	.413	16-0-2	.125	-0*	116	-12	32	-1.5
1972	Tex A	10	14	.417	30	28	2-1	0-0	170.2	139	66	12	3	103-8	109	3.32	92	.226	.336	52-0-3	.154	1	95	-2	0	-0.2
1973	Tex A	2	3	.400	8	7	1	0-0	41.2	49	29	2	2	19-5	14	5.40	70	.290	.363	0	ø	0	92	-8	0	-0.8
	Cal A	4	3	.571	16	6	0	0-0	54.2	58	29	5	1	21-0	19	3.62	99	.274	.336	0	ø	0	91	-2	25	-0.2
	Year	6	6	.500	24	13	1	0-0	96.1	107	58	7	3	40-5	33	4.39	83	.281	.348	0	ø	0	92	-11	0	-1.0
Total	4	24	39	.381	104	78	6-2	3-0	487.1	452	238	52	14	250-17	278	4.01	89	.249	.341	109-0-10	.147	-1	93	-20	57	-2.4
Handiboe, Jim	James Edward "Nick"; B7.17.1866 Columbus OH; D11.8.1942 Columbus OH; BR/TR/5´11˝/160; d5.28																									
1886	Pit AA	7	7	.500	14	14	12-1	0	114	82	65	1	12	33	83	3.32	102	.195	.273	44	.114	-2	94	3	—	0.0
Handrahan, Vern	James Vernon; B11.27.1938 Charlottetown PE, Can.; BL/TR/6´2˝/185; d4.14																									
1964	KC A	0	1	.000	18	1	0	0	35.2	33	24	9	2	25-0	18	6.06	63	.252	.377	9	.222	0	23	-7	0	-0.4
1966	KC A	0	1	.000	16	1	0	1	25.1	20	12	5	1	15-1	18	4.26	80	.227	.343	3	.000	-0	26	-2	0	-0.1
Total	2	0	2	.000	34	2	0	1	61	53	36	14	3	40-1	36	5.31	69	.242	.364	12	.167	-0	24	-9	0	-0.5
Hands, Bill	William Alfred; B5.6.1940 Hackensack NJ; BR/TR/6´2˝/(185–195); d6.3																									
1965	SF N	0	2	.000	4	2	0	0	6	13	11	0	0	6-2	5	16.50	22	.433	.528	1	.000	-0	36	-8	0	-1.4
1966	Chi N	8	13	.381	41	26	0	2	159	168	91	17	5	59-6	93	4.58	80	.272	.338	49-0-4	.041	-3	110	-15	0	-2.1
1967	Chi N	7	8	.467	49	11	3-1	6	150	134	46	9	2	48-15	84	2.46	144	.239	.301	38-0-4	.105	-1	95	17	0	1.7
1968	Chi N	16	10	.615	38	34	11-4	0	258.2	221	91	26	6	36-0	148	2.89	109	.231	.262	82-0-7	.061	-5	109	8	0	0.2
1969	Chi N	20	14	.588	41	41	18-3	0-0	300	268	102	21	6	73-8	181	2.49	161	.237	.286	98-0-11	.092	-5	80	42	0	4.3
1970	Chi N	18	15	.545	39	38	12-2	1-0	265	278	121	20	4	76-8	170	3.70	122	.269	.321	75-0-9	.133	1	99	22	0	2.8
1971	Chi N	12	18	.400	36	35	14-1	0-0	242.1	248	112	27	2	50-6	128	3.42	115	.260	.297	72-0-9	.083	-3	89	9	0	0.7
1972	Chi N	11	8	.579	32	28	6-3	0-0	189	168	73	12	2	47-7	96	3.00	127	.237	.285	57-0-4	.018	-4	111	15	0	0.9
1973	Min A	7	10	.412	39	15	3-1	2-3	142	138	69	14	2	41-2	78	3.49	114	.252	.305	0	ø	0	90	5	0	0.5
1974	Min A	4	5	.444	35	10	0	3-4	115.1	130	57	9	4	25-0	74	4.45	84	.284	.326	0	ø	0	99	-5	0	-0.5
	Tex A	2	0	1.000	2	2	1-1	0-0	14	11	3	0	0	3-0	4	1.93	186	.208	.250	0	ø	0	123	3	0	0.4
	Year	6	5	.545	37	12	1-1	3-4	129.1	141	60	9	4	28-0	78	4.18	89	.276	.319	0	ø	0	103	-4	0	-0.1
1975	Tex A	6	7	.462	18	18	4-1	0-0	109.2	118	58	12	3	28-1	67	4.02	94	.271	.318	0	ø	0	123	-4	38	-0.4
Total	11	111	110	.502	374	260	72-17	14-7	1951	1895	834	167	36	492-55	1128	3.35	114	.253	.301	472-0-48	.078	-20	99	89	38	7.1
Haney, Chris	Christopher Deane; B11.16.1968 Baltimore MD; BL/TL/6´3˝/(185–210); [MonN90 2/51]; d6.21; f–Larry; Col North Carolina–Charlotte																									
1991	Mon N	3	7	.300	16	16	0	0-0	84.2	94	49	6	1	43-1	51	4.04	90	.280	.362	27-0-2	.074	-2	79	-7	0	-0.8
1992	Mon N	2	3	.400	9	6	1-1	0-0	38	40	25	6	4	10-0	27	5.45	64	.270	.327	9-0-1	.222	0*	143	-8	0	-1.0
	KC A	2	3	.400	7	7	1-1	0-0	42	35	18	5	0	16-2	27	3.86	106	.226	.293	0	ø	0	51	2	0	0.1
1993	KC A	9	9	.500	23	23	1-1	0-0	124	141	87	13	3	53-2	65	6.02	77	.286	.356	0	ø	0	96	-17	0	-2.1
1994	KC A	2	2	.500	6	6	0	0-0	28.1	36	25	2	1	11-1	18	7.31	69	.333	.387	0	ø	0	113	-7	0	-0.7
1995	KC A	3	4	.429	16	13	1	0-0	81.1	78	35	7	2	33-0	31	3.65	131	.262	.335	0	ø	0	69	10	81	0.8
1996	KC A	10	14	.417	35	35	4-1	0-0	228	267	136	29	6	51-0	115	4.70	107	.291	.330	0	ø	0	82	4	0	0.3
1997	KC A	1	2	.333	8	3	0	0-0	24.2	29	16	1	2	5-2	16	4.38	108	.290	.333	0	ø	0	71	0	131	0.0
1998	KC A	6	6	.500	33	12	0	0-1	97.1	125	78	18	5	36-0	51	7.03	69	.316	.371	0	ø	0	99	-20	16	-2.0
	Chi N	0	0	ø	5	0	0	0-0	5	3	4	2	0	1-0	4	7.20	61	.167	.211	0	ø	0	—	-1	0	-0.1
1999	Cle A	0	2	.000	13	4	0	0-0	40.1	43	22	3	3	16-0	22	4.69	109	.270	.348	0	ø	0	82	2	0	0.1
2000	Cle A	0	0	ø	1	0	0	0-0	1	1	1	0	0	1-0	0	9.00	56	.333	.400	0	ø	0	—	0	0	0.0
2002	Bos A	0	0	ø	24	0	0	1-0	30	32	14	2	4	10-2	15	4.20	107	.274	.343	0	ø	0	—	2	0	0.1
Total	11	38	52	.422	196	125	8-4	1-1	824.2	924	510	94	31	286-10	442	5.07	91	.284	.344	36-0-3	.111	-1	86	-40	228	-5.3
Hankins, Don	Donald Wayne; B2.9.1902 Pendleton IN; D5.16.1963 Winston–Salem NC; BR/TR/6´3˝/183; d4.23																									
1927	Det A	2	1	.667	20	1	0	2	42.2	67	39	1	0	13	10	6.33	67	.383	.426	7	.143	-1	119	-10	—	-0.8
Hankinson, Frank	Frank Edward; B4.29.1856 New York NY; D4.5.1911 Palisades Park NJ; BR/TR/5´11˝/168; d5.1; ▲																									
1878	Chi N	0	1	.000	1	1	1	0	9	11	9	0	—	0	4	6.00	40	.282	.282	240-1	.267	0*	108	-2	—	-0.2
1879	Chi N	15	10	.600	26	25	25-2	0	230.2	248	134	0	—	27	69	2.50	103	.255	.275	171	.181	-4*	92	1	—	-0.1
1880	Cle N	1	1	.500	4	2	2	1	25	20	10	0	—	3	8	1.08	217	.215	.240	263-1	.209	-0*	74	3	—	0.2
1885	NY AA	0	0	ø	1	0	0	0	2	2	1	1	0	1	0	4.50	69	.250	.333	362-2	.224	0*	—	0	—	0.0
Total	4	16	12	.571	32	28	28-2	1	266.2	281	154	1	0	31	81	2.50	102	.252	.273	1036-4	.223	-4	92	2	—	-0.1
Hanley, Jim	James Patrick; B10.13.1885 Providence RI; D5.1.1961 Elmhurst NY; BR/TL/5´11˝/165; d7.3; Col Manhattan																									
1913	NY A	0	0	ø	1	0	0	0	4	5	3	0	0	4	2	6.75	44	.313	.450	1	.000	-0	—	-1	—	-0.1
Hanna, Preston	Preston Lee; B9.10.1954 Pensacola FL; BR/TR/6´1˝/(180–185); [AtlN72 1/11]; d9.13																									
1975	Atl N	0	0	ø	4	0	0	0-0	5.2	7	1	0	2	5-0	2	1.59	238	.304	.467	0	ø	0	—	1	0	0.1
1976	Atl N	0	0	ø	5	0	0	0-0	8	11	5	0	0	4-0	3	4.50	84	.333	.405	1	.000	-0	—	-1	0	-0.1
1977	Atl N	2	6	.250	17	9	1	1-0	60	69	40	6	2	34-1	37	4.95	90	.285	.378	14-0-1	.071	-0	80	-4	0	-0.4
1978	Atl N	7	13	.350	29	28	0	0-0	140.1	132	89	10	3	93-5	90	5.13	79	.251	.362	49-1-2	.184	1	81	-14	0	-1.8
1979	Atl N	1	1	.500	6	4	0	0-0	24.1	27	11	1	0	15-1	15	2.96	136	.284	.382	6	.000	-0	61	2	94	0.2
1980	Atl N	2	0	1.000	32	2	0	0-0	79.1	63	28	3	3	44-4	35	3.18	116	.224	.331	14	.143	0	109	6	0	0.3
1981	Atl N	2	1	.667	20	1	0	0-0	35.1	45	27	2	0	23-2	22	6.37	55	.341	.425	4	.250	0	25	-11	21	-0.7
1982	Atl N	3	0	1.000	20	1	0	0-0	36	36	15	3	0	28-2	17	3.75	98	.277	.405	5	.400	1	96	1	0	0.1
	Oak A	0	4	.000	23	2	1	0-0	48.1	54	34	3	1	33-1	32	5.59	71	.287	.389	0	ø	0	35	-9	0	-0.7
Total	8	17	25	.405	156	47	2	1-0	437.1	444	250	28	11	279-16	253	4.61	86	.269	.374	93-1-3	.161	1	80	-29	115	-3.0
Hannahs, Gerry	Gerald Ellis; B3.6.1953 Binghamton NY; BL/TL/6´3˝/(200–208); d9.8; Col Arkansas																									
1976	Mon N	2	0	1.000	3	3	0	0-0	16	20	14	2	0	12-0	10	6.75	56	.323	.421	8	.375	1	164	-5	0	-0.5
1977	Mon N	1	5	.167	8	7	0	0-0	37	43	27	7	0	17-0	21	4.86	79	.291	.364	7-0-2	.000	-0	72	-6	0	-0.9
1978	LA N	0	0	ø	1	0	0	0-0	2	3	2	0	0	0-0	5	9.00	39	.333	.333	0	ø	0	—	-1	0	-0.1

YEAR	TM LG	W	L	PCT	G	GS	CG-SHO	SV-BS	IP	H	R	HR	HB	BB-IB	SO	ERA	AERA	OAV	OOB	AB-HR-SH	AVG	PB	SUP	APR	DL	PW
1979	LA N	0	2	.000	4	2	0	1-0	16	10	8	2	0	13-1	6	3.38	107	.175	.324	4	.250	0	49	0	0	0.0
Total	4	3	7	.300	16	12	0	1-0	71	76	51	11	0	42-1	42	5.07	75	.275	.368	19-0-2	.211	1	92	-12	0	-1.5
HANNAN, JIM	James John; B1.7.1940 Jersey City NJ; BR/TR/6´3˝/(200–205); d4.17; Col Notre Dame																									
1962	Was A	2	4	.333	42	3	0	4	68	56	27	6	0	49-4	39	3.31	122	.230	.355	11	.091	-1	118	6	0	0.5
1963	Was A	2	2	.500	13	2	0	0	27.2	23	18	2	0	17-0	14	4.88	76	.228	.336	6	.000	-0	72	-4	0	-0.5
1964	Was A	4	7	.364	49	7	0	3	106	108	60	13	0	45-4	67	4.16	89	.266	.338	20-0-1	.150	-1	75	-7	0	-0.8
1965	Was A	1	1	.500	4	1	1-1	0	14.2	18	8	0	1	6-1	5	4.91	71	.340	.417	3-0-1	.000	-0	227	-2	0	-0.3
1966	Was A	3	9	.250	30	18	2	0	114	125	58	9	3	59-5	68	4.26	81	.288	.374	30-0-2	.067	-2	86	-9	0	-1.1
1967	Was A	1	1	.500	8	2	0	0	21.2	28	14	3	1	7-0	14	5.40	59	.315	.367	4	.000	-0	41	-5	0	-0.5
1968	Was A	10	6	.625	25	22	4-1	0	140.1	147	53	4	4	50-1	75	3.01	97	.272	.338	47-0-3	.064	-2	104	-1	0	-0.4
1969	Was A	7	6	.538	35	28	1-1	0-1	158.1	138	73	17	2	91-2	72	3.64	96	.238	.342	52-0-3	.115	-2	92	-2	0	-0.4
1970	Was A	9	11	.450	42	17	1-1	0-0	128	119	65	17	1	54-8	61	4.01	90	.250	.326	31-0-2	.129	-1	87	-6	21	-0.9
1971	Det A	1	0	1.000	7	0	0	0-0	11	7	4	1	1	7-0	6	3.27	111	.189	.333	2	.000	-0	—	1	0	0.1
	Mil A	1	1	.500	21	1	0	0-1	32.1	38	23	7	1	21-4	17	5.01	70	.295	.395	3	.000	-0	180	-6	0	-0.4
	Year	2	1	.667	28	1	0	0-1	43.1	45	27	8	2	28-4	23	4.57	77	.271	.381	5	.000	-1	178	-6	0	-0.3
Total	10	41	48	.461	276	101	9-4	7-2	822	807	403	79	14	406-29	438	3.88	90	.261	.348	209-0-12	.091	-9	91	-35	21	-4.7
HANNING, LOY	Loy Vernon; B10.18.1917 Bunker MO; D6.24.1986 Washington MO; BR/TR/6´2˝/175; d9.20																									
1939	StL A	0	1	.000	4	1	0	0	10	6	5	1	0	4	8	3.60	135	.158	.238	1	.000	-0	91	1	—	0.1
1942	StL A	1	1	.500	11	0	0	0	17.1	26	15	2	1	12	9	7.79	48	.356	.453	4	.250	0	—	-7	0	-0.7
Total	2	1	2	.333	15	1	0	0	27.1	32	20	3	1	16	17	6.26	66	.288	.383	5	.200	-0	91	-6	0	-0.6
HANSACK, DEVERN	Devern M.; B2.5.1978 Pearl Lagoon, Nicaragua; BR/TR/6´2˝/180; d9.23																									
2006	Bos A	1	1	.500	2	2	1-1	0-0	10	6	3	2	0	1-0	8	2.70	173	.171	.194	0	ø	0	121	2	0	0.4
HANSELL, GREG	Gregory Michael; B3.12.1971 Bellflower CA; BR/TR/6´5˝/(215–224); [BosA89 10/267]; d4.28																									
1995	LA N	0	1	.000	20	0	0	0-1	19.1	29	17	5	2	6-1	13	7.45	52	.349	.402	0	ø	0	—	-8	0	-0.4
1996	Min A	3	0	1.000	50	0	0	3-1	74.1	83	48	14	2	31-1	46	5.69	90	.285	.356	0	ø	0	—	-4	0	-0.2
1997	Mil A	0	0	ø	3	0	0	0-0	4.2	5	5	1	1	1-0	5	9.64	48	.263	.333	0	ø	0	—	-2	0	-0.1
1999	Pit N	1	3	.250	33	0	0	0-3	39.1	42	20	5	3	11-3	34	3.89	118	.280	.339	2	.000	-0	—	3	0	0.2
Total	4	4	4	.500	106	0	0	3-5	137.2	159	90	25	8	49-5	98	5.56	86	.293	.358	2	.000	-0	—	-11	0	-0.5
HANSEN, ANDY	Andrew Viggo "Swede"; B11.12.1924 Lake Worth FL; D2.2.2002 Lake Worth FL; BR/TR/6´3˝/190; d6.30; Mil 1945–46																									
1944	NY N	3	3	.500	23	4	0	1	52.2	63	39	3	3	32	15	6.49	56	.301	.402	12	.167	0*	86	-14	0	-1.4
1945	NY N	4	3	.571	23	13	4	3	92.2	98	52	7	2	28	37	4.66	84	.273	.329	25-0-4	.000	-3	103	-7	0	-0.7
1947	NY N	1	5	.167	27	9	1	0	82.1	78	45	8	0	38	18	4.37	93	.248	.330	21	.190	-0	77	-3	0	-0.2
1948	NY N	5	3	.625	36	9	3	1	100	96	40	4	0	36	27	2.97	133	.255	.320	20-0-3	.050	-0	138	10	0	0.7
1949	NY N	2	6	.250	33	2	0	1	66.1	58	35	7	0	28	26	4.61	86	.234	.312	12-0-1	.000	-1	133	-2	0	-0.3
1950	NY N	0	1	.000	31	1	0	3	57	64	37	8	1	26	19	5.53	74	.279	.355	7-0-2	.000	-1	151	-8	0	-0.5
1951	Phi N	3	1	.750	24	0	0	0	39	34	14	4	1	7	11	2.54	152	.228	.268	3	.333	1	—	5	0	0.6
1952	Phi N	5	6	.455	43	0	0	4	77.1	76	36	6	3	27	18	3.26	112	.259	.328	11-0-2	.182	1	—	2	0	0.4
1953	Phi N	0	2	.000	30	1	0	3	51.1	60	30	6	1	24	17	4.03	104	.296	.373	7	.286	0	0	-1	0	0.0
Total	9	23	30	.434	270	39	8	16	618.2	627	328	53	11	246	188	4.22	93	.263	.335	118-0-12	.102	-3	105	-18	0	-1.4
HANSEN, CRAIG	Craig R.; B11.15.1983 Glen Cove NY; BR/TR/6´6˝/185; [BosA05 1/26]; d9.19; Col St. John's																									
2005	Bos A	0	0	ø	4	0	0	0-1	3	6	2	1	0	1-0	3	6.00	76	.429	.438	0	ø	0	—	0	0	0.0
2006	Bos A	2	2	.500	38	0	0	0-2	38	46	32	5	4	15-0	30	6.63	70	.305	.376	0	ø	0	—	-9	0	-0.8
Total	2	2	2	.500	42	0	0	0-3	41	52	34	6	4	16-0	33	6.59	71	.315	.381	0	ø	0	—	-9	0	-0.8
HANSEN, SNIPE	Roy Emil Frederick; B2.21.1907 Chicago IL; D9.11.1978 Chicago IL; BB/TL (BL 1930)/6´3˝/195; d7.5																									
1930	Phi N	0	7	.000	22	9	1	0	84.1	123	76	8	2	38	25	6.72	81	.364	.431	27	.111	-2	71	-12	—	-1.0
1932	Phi N	10	10	.500	39	23	5	2	191	215	103	13	6	51	56	3.72	118	.278	.328	63-0-4	.127	-4	104	8	—	0.4
1933	Phi N	6	14	.300	32	22	8	1	168.1	199	103	12	4	30	47	4.44	86	.294	.328	58-0-2	.155	-3*	91	-12	—	-1.7
1934	Phi N	6	12	.333	50	16	5-2	3	151	194	112	15	3	61	40	5.42	87	.307	.371	43	.233	-0	99	-13	—	-1.3
1935	Phi N	0	1	.000	2	1	0	0	4.1	8	7	0	0	5	0	12.46	36	.421	.542	2	.000	-0	94	-3	—	-0.6
	StL A	0	1	.000	10	0	0	0	26.2	44	28	2	1	9	8	8.78	55	.364	.412	7	.143	-1	—	-10	—	-0.5
Total	5	22	45	.328	155	71	19-2	6	625.2	783	429	50	16	194	176	5.01	90	.306	.358	200-0-6	.155	-10	93	-42	—	-4.7
HANSEN, ROY	Roy Inglof "Ing"; B3.6.1898 Beloit WI; D2.9.1977 Beloit WI; BR/TR/6´0˝/165; d5.28																									
1918	Was A	1	0	1.000	5	0	0	0	9	10	4	0	1	3	2	3.00	91	.278	.350	0	ø	0	—	0	—	0.0
HANSFORD, FRANK	Frank Cicero; B12.26.1874 DuQuoin IL; D12.14.1952 Fort Scott KS; TL/6´0˝/180; d6.9																									
1898	Bro N	0	0	ø	1	0	0	0	7	10	4	0	0	5	0	3.86	93	.333	.429	3	.000	-1	—	0	—	-0.1
HANSON, OLLIE	Earl Sylvester; B1.19.1896 Holbrook MA; D8.19.1951 Clifton NJ; BR/TR/5´11˝/178; d4.27																									
1921	Chi N	0	2	.000	2	2	1	0	9	9	7	0	1	6	2	7.00	55	.265	.390	3	.000	-0	86	-3	—	-0.5
HANSON, ERIK	Erik Brian; B5.18.1965 Kinnelon NJ; BR/TR/6´6˝/(205–215); [SeaA86 2/36]; d9.5; Col Wake Forest																									
1988	Sea A	2	3	.400	6	6	0	0-0	41.2	35	17	4	1	12-1	36	3.24	129	.230	.291	0	ø	0	65	4	0	0.4
1989	Sea A	9	5	.643	17	17	1	0-0	113.1	103	44	7	5	32-1	75	3.18	127	.243	.304	0	ø	0	94	11	71	1.3
1990	Sea A	18	9	.667	33	33	5-1	0-0	236	205	88	15	2	68-6	211	3.24	123	.232	.287	0	ø	0	94	23	0	2.5
1991	Sea A	8	8	.500	27	27	2-1	0-0	174.2	182	82	16	2	56-2	143	3.81	109	.269	.323	0	ø	0	103	6	40	0.4
1992	Sea A	8	17	.320	31	30	6-1	0-0	186.2	209	110	14	7	57-1	112	4.82	83	.287	.341	0	ø	0	83	-17	20	-2.0
1993	Sea A	11	12	.478	31	30	7	0-0	215	215	91	17	5	60-6	163	3.47	129	.263	.315	0	ø	0*	85	22	0	2.2
1994	Cin N	5	5	.500	22	21	0	0-0	122.2	137	60	10	3	23-3	101	4.11	102	.283	.317	39-0-2	.154	-1	107	2	3	0.1
1995	†Bos A☆	15	5	.750	29	29	1-1	0-0	186.2	187	94	17	1	59-0	139	4.24	115	.258	.311	0	ø	0	108	14	0	1.2
1996	Tor A	13	17	.433	35	35	4-1	0-0	214.2	243	143	26	2	102-2	156	5.41	93	.289	.365	0	ø	0	82	-10	0	-1.2
1997	Tor A	0	0	ø	3	2	0	0-0	15	15	13	3	0	6-0	18	7.80	59	.254	.323	0	ø	0	120	-5	160	-0.2
1998	Tor A	0	3	.000	11	8	0	0-0	49	73	34	10	1	29-1	21	6.24	75	.348	.429	0	ø	0	80	-7	12	-0.3
Total	11	89	84	.514	245	238	26-5	0-0	1555.1	1604	776	139	29	504-23	1175	4.15	105	.267	.325	39-0-2	.154	-1	93	43	306	4.4
HANYZEWSKI, ED	Edward Michael; B9.18.1920 Union Mills IN; D10.8.1991 Fargo ND; BR/TR/6´1˝/200; d5.12; Col Notre Dame																									
1942	Chi N	1	1	.500	6	1	0	0	19	17	9	2	0	8	6	3.79	84	.254	.333	5	.200	-0	26	-1	0	-0.1
1943	Chi N	8	7	.533	33	16	3	0	130	120	54	2	2	45	55	2.56	130	.243	.309	41-0-2	.049	-4	97	7	0	0.4
1944	Chi N	2	5	.286	14	7	3	0	58.1	61	33	6	1	20	19	4.47	79	.261	.322	17	.059	-1	71	-5	0	-0.5
1945	Chi N	0	0	ø	2	1	0	0	4.2	7	4	1	0	1	0	5.79	63	.350	.381	1	.000	0	116	-1	0	0.0
1946	Chi N	1	0	1.000	3	0	0	0	6	8	3	0	1	5	1	4.50	74	.348	.483	1	.000	-0	—	-1	0	-0.1
Total	5	12	13	.480	58	25	6	0	218	213	103	11	4	79	81	3.30	102	.254	.321	65-0-2	.062	-5	88	-1	0	-0.3
HARANG, AARON	Aaron Michael; B5.9.1978 San Diego CA; BR/TR/6´7˝/(240–270); [TexA99 6/195]; d5.25; Col San Diego St.																									
2002	Oak A	5	4	.556	16	15	0	0-0	78.1	78	44	7	3	45-2	64	4.83	93	.261	.359	3	.000	-0	92	-2	0	-0.2
2003	Oak A	1	3	.250	7	6	0	0-0	30.1	41	19	5	0	9-0	16	5.34	86	.331	.373	1	.000	-0	84	-2	0	-0.3
	Cin N	4	3	.571	9	9	0	0-0	46	48	28	6	1	10-0	26	5.28	79	.271	.314	17	.059	-1	110	-5	0	-0.8
2004	Cin N	10	9	.526	28	28	1-1	0-0	161	177	90	26	5	53-5	125	4.86	88	.279	.337	57-0-4	.070	-4	106	-8	24	-1.2
2005	Cin N	11	13	.458	32	32	1	0-0	211.2	217	93	22	8	51-3	163	3.83	111	.267	.315	74-0-4	.027	-7	99	12	0	0.4
2006	Cin N	**16**	11	.593	36	**35**	**6**-2	0-0	234.1	242	109	28	8	56-8	**216**	3.76	125	.269	.315	74-0-5	.108	-3	94	23	0	2.1
Total	5	47	43	.522	128	125	8-3	0-0	761.2	803	383	94	25	224-18	610	4.28	104	.273	.327	226-0-13	.066	-15	98	18	24	0.0
HARDEN, RICH	James Richard; B11.30.1981 Victoria BC, Can.; BL/TR/6´1˝/(180–195); [OakA00 17/510]; d7.21; Col Central Arizona JC																									
2003	†Oak A	5	4	.556	15	13	0	0-0	74.2	72	38	5	1	40-1	67	4.46	103	.259	.351	0	ø	0	105	2	0	0.3
2004	Oak A	11	7	.611	31	31	0	0-0	189.2	171	90	16	3	81-6	167	3.99	116	.242	.320	5	.000	-0	101	14	0	1.1
2005	Oak A	10	5	.667	22	19	2-1	0-0	128	93	42	7	2	43-0	121	2.53	173	.201	.271	0	ø	0	98	25	38	2.7
2006	†Oak A	4	0	1.000	9	9	0	0-0	46.2	31	22	5	1	26-0	49	4.24	107	.191	.304	0	ø	0	141	2	146	0.2
Total	4	30	16	.652	77	72	2-1	0-0	439	367	192	33	7	190-7	404	3.67	124	.228	.310	5	.000	-0	106	43	184	4.3

YEAR	TM LG	W	L	PCT	G	GS	CG-SHO	SV-BS	IP	H	R	HR	HB	BB-IB	SO	ERA	AERA	OAV	OOB	AB-HR-SH	AVG	PB	SUP	APR	DL	PW
Harder, Mel	Melvin Leroy "Chief"; B10.15.1909 Beemer NE; D10.20.2002 Chardon OH; BR/TR/6´1˝/195; d4.24; M2/C23																									
1928	Cle A	0	2	.000	23	1	0	1	49	64	42	4	0	32	15	6.61	63	.335	.430	8	.000	-1	82	-12	—	-0.8
1929	Cle A	1	0	1.000	11	0	0	0	17.2	24	15	2	3	5	4	5.60	79	.333	.400	1	.000	-0	—	-3	—	-0.2
1930	Cle A	11	10	.524	36	19	7	2	175.1	205	108	9	4	68	45	4.21	115	.295	.361	63-0-2	.143	-4	106	9	—	0.5
1931	Cle A	13	14	.481	40	24	9	1	194	229	119	8	6	72	63	4.36	106	.289	.352	75-0-4	.253	1	101	3	—	0.4
1932	Cle A	15	13	.536	39	32	17-1	0	254.2	277	125	9	3	68	90	3.75	127	.272	.319	94-0-2	.181	-0	103	27	—	2.7
1933	Cle A	15	17	.469	43	31	14-2	4	253	254	113	10	3	67	81	2.95	**151**	.259	.309	84-1-2	.190	-1*	57	**35**	—	**4.4**
1934	Cle A★	20	12	.625	44	29	17-**6**	4	255.1	246	97	6	7	81	91	2.61	**174**	.254	.316	87-0-9	.161	-1	92	50	—	**5.7**
1935	Cle A★	22	11	.667	42	35	17-4	2	287.1	313	120	6	0	53	95	3.29	137	.275	.307	102-2-7	.206	-1	89	39	—	4.1
1936	Cle A★	15	15	.500	36	30	13	1	224.2	294	155	13	6	71	84	5.17	97	.313	.365	80-0-6	.138	-4	88	-6	—	-1.0
1937	Cle A★	15	12	.556	38	30	13	2	233.2	269	127	9	4	86	95	4.28	108	.288	.350	86-0-7	.174	-1	105	9	—	0.8
1938	Cle A	17	10	.630	38	29	15-2	4	240	257	115	16	5	62	102	3.83	121	.271	.319	88-0-2	.114	-5*	87	23	—	1.8
1939	Cle A	15	9	.625	29	26	12-1	1	208	213	89	15	3	64	67	3.50	126	.269	.326	72-1-6	.139	-2	99	23	—	2.1
1940	Cle A	12	11	.522	31	25	5	0	186.1	200	96	16	5	59	76	4.06	104	.278	.337	62-0-5	.177	-1	98	4	—	0.4
1941	Cle A	5	4	.556	15	10	1	1	68.2	76	43	8	2	37	21	5.24	75	.279	.370	25	.080	-2	99	-10	0	-1.2
1942	Cle A	13	14	.481	29	29	13-4	0	198.2	179	83	8	3	82	74	3.44	100	.240	.317	67-0-3	.119	-3	77	3	0	0.1
1943	Cle A	8	7	.533	19	18	6-1	0	135.1	126	57	7	1	61	40	3.06	102	.254	.337	47-0-4	.213	2	110	-1	59	0.1
1944	Cle A	12	10	.545	30	27	12-2	0	196.1	211	95	5	3	69	64	3.71	89	.278	.341	74-0-2	.216	1	120	-9	0	-0.9
1945	Cle A	3	7	.300	11	11	2	0	76	93	37	3	0	23	16	3.67	88	.303	.352	25-0-3	.080	-2	76	-4	0	-0.7
1946	Cle A	5	4	.556	13	12	4-1	0	92.1	85	37	4	0	31	21	3.41	97	.249	.311	35	.086	-2	95	0	0	-0.3
1947	Cle A	6	4	.600	15	15	4-1	0	80	91	41	3	1	27	17	4.50	77	.289	.347	28-0-5	.179	0	141	-8	0	-1.0
Total	20	223	186	.545	582	433	181-25	23	3426.1	3706	1714	161	59	1118	1161	3.80	113	.276	.334	1203-4-69	.165	-27	94	172	59	17.0
Hardin, Jim	James Warren; B8.6.1943 Morris Chapel TN; D3.9.1991 Key West FL; BR/TR/6´0˝/(170–176); d6.23; Col Memphis																									
1967	Bal A	8	3	.727	19	14	5-2	0	111	85	30	5	3	27-0	64	2.27	139	.211	.266	37-0-1	.135	-0	122	12	0	1.1
1968	Bal A	18	13	.581	35	35	16-2	0	244	188	79	20	10	70-5	160	2.51	117	.212	.277	82-0-11	.085	-3	97	11	0	1.1
1969	Bal A	6	7	.462	30	20	3-1	1-1	137.2	128	62	18	6	43-7	64	3.60	100	.248	.311	45-2-4	.156	1	120	0	0	0.0
1970	Bal A	6	5	.545	36	19	3-2	1-1	145.1	150	60	13	1	26-3	78	3.53	104	.267	.299	45-0-2	.067	-2	101	4	0	0.0
1971	Bal A	0	0	ø	6	0	0	0-0	5.2	12	5	0	0	3-1	3	4.76	72	.480	.536	0	ø	0	—	-2	0	-0.1
	NY A	0	2	.000	12	3	0	0-0	28.1	35	19	3	1	9-3	14	5.08	65	.313	.366	4	.000	-0	127	-6	27	-0.5
	Year	0	2	.000	18	3	0	0-0	34	47	24	3	1	12-4	17	5.03	66	.343	.397	4	.000	-0	127	-8	0	-0.6
1972	Atl N	5	2	.714	26	9	1	2-1	79.2	93	47	11	2	24-4	25	4.41	86	.287	.337	21-1-3	.095	1	140	-6	0	-0.5
Total	6	43	32	.573	164	100	28-7	4-3	751.2	691	302	70	23	202-23	408	3.18	105	.244	.299	234-3-21	.103	-3	111	13	27	1.1
Harding, Charlie	Charles Harold "Slim"; B1.3.1891 Nashville TN; D10.30.1971 Bold Spring TN; BR/TR/6´2.5˝/172; d9.18																									
1913	Det A	0	0	ø	1	0	0	0	2	3	1	0	0	1	0	4.50	65	.375	.444	0	ø	0	—	0	—	0.0
Hardy, Alex	David Alexander "Dooney"; B1877 Toronto ON, Can.; D4.22.1940 Toronto ON, Can.; BR/TL/5´10.5˝/175; d9.4																									
1902	Chi N	2	2	.500	4	4	4-1	0	35	29	19	0	0	12	12	3.60	75	.227	.293	14	.214	0	151	-2	—	-0.2
1903	Chi N	1	1	.500	3	3	1	0	12.2	21	10	0	1	7	4	6.39	49	.375	.453	6	.167	0	129	-3	—	-0.4
Total	2	3	3	.500	7	7	5-1	0	47.2	50	29	0	1	19	16	4.34	65	.272	.343	20	.200	1	144	-5	—	-0.6
Hardy, Red	Francis Joseph; B1.6.1923 Marmarth ND; D8.15.2003 Phoenix AZ; BR/TR/5´11˝/175; d6.20; Col St. Thomas (MN)																									
1951	NY N	0	0	ø	2	0	0	0	1.1	4	1	0	1	1	0	6.75	58	.571	.667	0	ø	0	—	0	0	0.0
Hardy, Harry	Harry; B11.5.1875 Steubenville OH; D9.4.1943 Steubenville OH; BL/TL/5´6˝/155; d9.26																									
1905	Was A	1	1	.500	3	2	2	0	24	20	9	0	0	6	10	1.88	141	.227	.277	9	.111	-1	67	1	—	0.0
1906	Was A	0	3	.000	5	3	2	0	20	35	27	0	0	12	4	9.00	29	.385	.456	6	.000	-1	64	-14	—	-1.7
Total	2	1	4	.200	8	5	4	0	44	55	36	0	0	18	14	5.11	52	.307	.371	15	.067	-2	65	-13	—	-1.7
Hardy, Larry	Howard Lawrence; B1.10.1948 Goose Creek TX; BR/TR/5´10˝/180; [SDN70 23/536]; d4.28; C7; Col Texas																									
1974	SD N	9	4	.692	76	1	0	2-4	101.2	129	58	9	0	44-14	57	4.69	77	.317	.380	10	.000	-1	73	-12	0	-1.5
1975	SD N	0	0	ø	3	0	0	0-0	2.2	8	6	3	0	2-0	3	13.50	26	.500	.556	0	ø	0	—	-4	0	-0.2
1976	Hou N	0	0	ø	15	0	0	3-0	21.2	34	19	2	0	10-2	10	7.06	46	.362	.423	2	.000	-0	—	-10	0	-0.5
Total	3	9	4	.692	94	1	0	5-4	126	171	83	14	0	56-16	70	5.29	67	.331	.393	12	.000	-1	73	-26	0	-2.2
Hardy, Jack	John Graydon; B10.8.1959 St.Petersburg FL; BR/TR/6´2˝/175; [ChiA81 21/526]; d5.23; Col St. Thomas (FL)																									
1989	Chi A	0	0	ø	5	0	0	0-0	12.1	14	9	1	1	5-0	4	6.57	58	.286	.357	0	ø	0	—	-3	0	-0.1
Haren, Danny	Daniel John; B9.17.1980 Monterey Park CA; BR/TR/6´5˝/220; [StLN01 2/72]; d6.30; Col Pepperdine																									
2003	StL N	3	7	.300	14	14	0	0-0	72.2	84	44	9	5	22-0	43	5.08	81	.293	.351	25-0-1	.080	-0*	93	-8	0	-1.1
2004	†StL N	3	3	.500	14	5	0	0-0	46	45	23	4	2	17-2	32	4.50	95	.265	.335	12-0-2	.000	-1	100	0	0	-0.2
2005	Oak A	14	12	.538	34	34	3	0-0	217	212	101	26	6	53-5	163	3.73	117	.255	.303	5	.400	1	118	15	0	1.6
2006	†Oak A	14	13	.519	34	**34**	2	0-0	223	224	109	31	10	45-6	176	4.12	110	.258	.301	7	.000	-1	87	10	0	1.0
Total	4	34	35	.493	96	87	5	0-0	558.2	565	277	70	23	137-13	414	4.12	107	.262	.311	49-0-3	.082	-1	101	17	0	1.3
Hargan, Steve	Steven Lowell; B9.8.1942 Ft.Wayne IN; BR/TR/6´3˝/(170–180); d8.3																									
1965	Cle A	4	3	.571	17	8	1	2	60.1	55	26	2	1	28-2	37	3.43	101	.246	.331	19-0-2	.053	-1	107	0	0	-0.1
1966	Cle A	13	10	.565	38	21	7-3	0	192	173	60	9	1	45-8	132	2.48	138	.241	.286	58-0-3	.121	-2	81	20	0	2.2
1967	Cle A☆	14	13	.519	30	29	15-**6**	0	223	180	79	9	3	72-7	141	2.62	125	.224	.288	67-1-7	.164	1	84	14	0	1.9
1968	Cle A	8	15	.348	32	27	4-2	0	158.1	139	81	11	5	81-8	78	4.15	72	.241	.336	51-0-1	.176	1	86	-19	0	-2.7
1969	Cle A	5	14	.263	32	23	1-1	0-0	143.2	145	95	14	3	81-9	76	5.70	67	.265	.359	44-0-1	.159	-1*	69	-25	0	-3.0
1970	Cle A	11	3	.786	23	19	8-1	0-0	142.2	101	47	14	3	53-0	72	2.90	138	.201	.279	45-0-8	.111	-2*	99	17	22	1.5
1971	Cle A	1	13	.071	37	16	1	1-1	113.1	138	83	18	6	56-5	52	6.19	63	.304	.387	32-0-1	.063	-3	84	-25	48	-3.3
1972	Cle A	0	3	.000	12	1	0	0-0	20	23	16	1	0	15-2	10	5.85	56	.291	.392	3	.000	-0	27	-6	0	-0.9
1974	Tex A	12	9	.571	37	27	8-2	0-0	186.2	202	103	15	5	48-4	98	3.95	91	.275	.320	0	ø	0	96	-12	0	-1.2
1975	Tex A	9	10	.474	33	26	8-1	0-1	189.1	203	96	17	6	62-7	93	3.80	99	.275	.334	0	ø	0	101	-2	0	-0.1
1976	Tex A	8	8	.500	35	8	2-1	1-2	124.1	127	63	8	3	38-3	63	3.62	99	.261	.317	0	ø	0	70	-3	0	-0.4
1977	Tor A	1	3	.250	6	5	1	0-0	29.1	36	17	2	0	14-2	11	5.22	81	.308	.382	0	ø	0	76	-2	0	-0.2
	Tex A	1	0	1.000	6	0	0	0-0	12.1	22	13	2	0	5-0	10	8.76	47	.393	.429	0	ø	0	—	-6	0	-0.4
	Year	2	3	.400	12	5	1	0-0	41.2	58	30	4	0	19-2	21	6.26	67	.335	.397	0	ø	0	77	-8	0	-0.6
	Atl N	0	3	.000	16	5	0	0-0	36.2	49	31	3	0	16-1	18	6.87	65	.325	.385	6	.000	-1	112	-8	0	-0.6
Total	12	87	107	.448	354	215	56-17	4-4	1632	1593	810	125	36	614-58	891	3.92	91	.257	.326	325-1-23	.129	-7	88	-57	70	-7.3
Hargesheimer, Alan	Alan Robert; B11.21.1954 Chicago IL; BR/TR/6´3˝/(195–200); d7.14; Col Northeastern Illinois																									
1980	SF N	4	6	.400	15	13	0	0-0	75	82	38	3	0	32-2	40	4.32	81	.285	.355	22-0-1	.182	1	90	-6	0	-0.6
1981	SF N	1	2	.333	6	3	0	0-0	18.2	20	9	1	1	9-2	6	4.34	78	.299	.385	5-0-1	.200	0	70	-1	0	-0.2
1983	Chi N	0	0	ø	5	0	0	0-0	4	6	4	0	0	2-0	5	9.00	42	.375	.444	0	ø	0	—	-2	0	-0.1
1986	KC A	0	1	.000	5	1	0	0-0	13	18	9	1	1	7-2	4	6.23	69	.340	.426	0	ø	0	191	-2	14	-0.2
Total	4	5	9	.357	31	17	0	0-0	110.2	126	60	5	2	50-6	55	4.72	76	.297	.372	27-0-2	.185	1	92	-11	14	-1.1
Harikkala, Tim	Timothy Allan; B7.15.1971 W.Palm Beach FL; BR/TR/6´2˝/185; [SeaA92 34/950]; d5.27; Col Florida Atlantic																									
1995	Sea A	0	0	ø	1	0	0	0-0	3.1	7	6	1	0	1-0	1	16.20	29	.412	.444	0	ø	0	—	-4	0	-0.2
1996	Sea A	0	1	.000	1	1	0	0-0	4.1	4	6	1	1	2-0	1	12.46	40	.250	.368	0	ø	0	37	-3	0	-0.5
1999	Bos A	1	1	.500	7	0	0	0-0	13	15	9	0	1	6-1	7	6.23	80	.306	.393	0	ø	0	—	-1	0	-0.2
2004	Col N	6	6	.500	55	0	0	0-7	62.2	55	34	10	1	23-5	30	4.74	100	.235	.304	3-0-1	.000	-0	—	0	0	0.0
2005	Oak A	0	0	ø	8	0	0	0-0	12.2	16	9	3	0	4-0	7	6.39	68	.308	.357	0	ø	0	—	-2	0	-0.1
Total	5	7	8	.467	72	1	0	0-7	96	97	64	15	3	36-6	46	5.91	81	.264	.333	3-0-1	.000	-0	37	-10	0	-1.0
Harkey, Mike	Michael Anthony; B10.25.1966 San Diego CA; BR/TR/6´5˝/(220–235); [ChiN87 1/4]; d9.5; C1; Col Cal St.–Fullerton																									
1988	Chi N	0	3	.000	5	5	0	0-0	34.2	33	14	0	2	15-3	18	2.60	140	.248	.333	11-0-2	.091	-1	58	3	0	0.1
1990	Chi N	12	6	.667	27	27	2-1	0-0	173.2	153	71	14	7	59-8	94	3.26	125	.234	.303	56-0-8	.250	3	97	14	15	1.7
1991	Chi N	0	2	.000	4	4	0	0-0	18.2	21	11	3	0	6-1	15	5.30	74	.273	.321	5	.400	1	121	-2	163	-0.1
1992	Chi N	4	0	1.000	7	7	0	0-0	38	34	13	4	1	15-0	21	1.89	192	.243	.316	15	.267	1*	135	5	105	0.7
1993	Chi N	10	10	.500	28	28	1	0-0	157.1	187	100	17	3	43-4	67	5.26	77	.305	.349	54-0-5	.093	-2	103	-21	31	-2.6
1994	Col N	1	6	.143	24	13	0	0-0	91.2	125	61	10	1	35-4	39	5.79	86	.336	.393	22-0-4	.182	-1	70	-6	0	-0.4

YEAR	TM LG	W	L	PCT	G	GS	CG-SHO	SV-BS	IP	H	R	HR	HB	BB-IB	SO	ERA	AERA	OAV	OOB	AB-HR-SH	AVG	PB	SUP	APR	DL	PW
1995	Oak A	4	6	.400	14	12	0	0-0	66	75	46	12	3	31-0	28	6.27	72	.292	.372	0	ø	0	81	-11	0	-1.4
	Cal A	4	3	.571	12	8	1	0-0	61.1	80	32	12	1	16-2	28	4.55	104	.311	.351	0	ø	0	84	2	0	0.1
	Year	8	9	.471	26	20	1	0-0	127.1	155	78	24	4	47-2	56	5.44	85	.302	.362	0	ø	0	82	-10	0	-1.3
1997	LA N	1	0	1.000	10	0	0	0-0	14.2	12	8	3	0	5-0	6	4.30	91	.211	.274	1-0-2	.000	-0	—	-1	0	-0.1
Total	8	36	36	.500	131	104	4-1	0-0	656	720	356	75	18	225-22	316	4.49	95	.281	.341	164-0-21	.183	1	93	-17	314	-2.0
Harkins, John	John Joseph "Pa"; B4.12.1859 New Brunswick NJ; D11.20.1940 New Brunswick NJ; BR/TR/6´1˝/205; d5.2; Col Rutgers																									
1884	Cle N	12	32	.273	46	45	42-3	0	391	399	300	7	—	108	192	3.68	86	.249	.297	229	.205	-4*	71	-21	—	-2.3
1885	Bro AA	14	20	.412	34	34	33-1	0	293	303	224	7	7	56	141	3.75	88	.250	.287	159-1	.264	5*	101	-19	—	-1.1
1886	Bro AA	15	16	.484	34	33	33	0	292.1	286	203	6	5	114	118	3.60	97	.244	.313	142-1	.225	3*	90	-3	—	0.2
1887	Bro AA	10	14	.417	24	24	22	0	199	262	184	6	5	77	36	6.02	72	.309	.369	98	.235	-0*	95	-30	—	-2.6
1888	Bal AA	0	1	.000	1	1	1	0	8	12	12	0	0	3	2	6.75	44	.333	.385	3	.000	-0	136	-4	—	-0.4
Total	5	51	83	.381	139	137	131-4	0	1183.1	1262	923	26	17	358	489	4.09	85	.259	.312	631-2	.228	4	88	-77	—	-6.2
Harkness, Spec	Frederick Harvey; B12.13.1887 Los Angeles CA; D5.16.1952 Compton CA; BR/TR/5´11˝/180; d6.13																									
1910	Cle A	10	7	.588	26	16	6-1	1	136.1	132	61	2	3	55	60	3.04	85	.268	.345	50-0-1	.140	-1	94	-6	—	-0.9
1911	Cle A	2	2	.500	12	6	3	0	53.1	62	36	1	0	21	25	4.22	81	.310	.376	19	.316	1	162	-5	—	-0.3
Total	2	12	9	.571	38	22	9-1	1	189.2	194	97	3	3	76	85	3.37	84	.280	.354	69-0-1	.188	-0	115	-11	—	-1.2
Harley, Dick	Henry Risk; B8.18.1874 Springfield OH; D5.16.1961 Springfield OH; BR/TR; d4.15																									
1905	Bos N	2	5	.286	9	4	4-1	0	65.2	72	45	5	1	19	19	4.66	67	.286	.338	22-0-1	.045	-2	35	-11	—	-1.1
Harman, Bill	William Bell; B1.2.1919 Bridgewater VA; BR/TR/6´4˝/200; d6.17; Mil 1942; Col Virginia; ▲																									
1941	Phi N	0	0	ø	5	0	0	0	13	15	8	0	0	8	3	4.85	76	.319	.418	14	.071	-0*	—	-2	0	-0.2
Harmon, Bob	Robert Green "Hickory Bob"; B10.15.1887 Liberal MO; D11.27.1961 Monroe LA; BB/TR/6´0˝/187; d6.23																									
1909	StL N	6	11	.353	21	17	10	0	159	155	85	6	4	65	48	3.68	69	.265	.342	51-0-4	.255	4	94	-19	—	-1.5
1910	StL N	13	15	.464	43	33	15	2	236	227	128	1	7	133	87	4.46	67	.258	.360	76-0-4	.184	2	129	-31	—	-3.1
1911	StL N	23	16	.590	51	**41**	28-2	4	348	290	155	10	7	181	144	3.13	108	.235	.336	111-0-9	.153	0	98	10	—	1.2
1912	StL N	18	18	.500	43	34	15-3	0	268	284	156	4	3	116	73	3.93	87	.281	.357	99-0-2	.232	1*	93	-11	—	-1.1
1913	StL N	8	21	.276	42	27	16-1	2	273.1	291	135	6	6	99	66	3.92	83	.286	.353	92-0-3	.261	5*	72	-18	—	-1.2
1914	Pit N	13	17	.433	37	30	19-2	3	245	226	84	4	7	55	61	2.53	105	.252	.300	86-1-5	.140	-1*	64	5	—	0.4
1915	Pit N	16	17	.485	37	32	25-5	1	269.2	242	106	6	3	62	86	2.50	109	.247	.294	95-0-3	.147	1*	100	4	—	0.7
1916	Pit N	8	11	.421	31	17	10-2	0	172.2	175	78	4	1	39	62	2.81	95	.267	.309	55	.109	-3*	103	-5	—	-0.6
1918	Pit N	2	7	.222	16	9	5	0	82.1	76	30	3	0	12	7	2.62	109	.254	.283	27-0-1	.148	-1*	79	3	—	0.2
Total	9	107	133	.446	321	240	143-15	12	2054	1966	957	44	38	762	634	3.33	90	.260	.331	692-1-31	.184	7	94	-62	—	-5.0
Harnisch, Pete	Peter Thomas; B9.23.1966 Commack NY; BB/TR (BR 2000)/6´0˝/(195–228); [BalA87 1/27]; d9.13; Col Fordham; [DL 2002 Col N 183]																									
1988	Bal A	0	2	.000	2	2	0	0-0	13	13	8	1	0	9-1	10	5.54	71	.260	.373	0	ø	0	70	-2	0	-0.2
1989	Bal A	5	9	.357	18	17	2	0-0	103.1	97	55	10	5	64-3	70	4.62	83	.249	.358	0	ø	0	82	-9	0	-1.1
1990	Bal A	11	11	.500	31	31	3	0-0	188.2	189	96	17	1	86-5	122	4.34	88	.261	.339	0	ø	0	115	-10	0	-1.2
1991	Hou N★	12	9	.571	33	33	4-2	0-0	216.2	169	71	14	5	83-3	172	2.70	131	**.212**	.288	62-0-7	.097	-1	88	21	0	1.7
1992	Hou N	9	10	.474	34	34	0	0-0	206.2	182	92	18	5	64-3	164	3.70	92	.233	.294	67-0-5	.164	2	120	-7	0	-0.5
1993	Hou N	16	9	.640	33	33	5-**4**	0-0	217.2	171	84	20	6	79-5	185	2.98	130	**.214**	.289	67-0-10	.104	-1	108	21	0	1.9
1994	Hou N	8	5	.615	17	17	1	0-0	95	100	59	13	3	39-1	62	5.40	73	.269	.341	35-0-2	.171	1*	136	-14	38	-1.6
1995	NY N	2	8	.200	18	18	0	0-0	110	111	55	13	3	24-4	82	3.68	110	.261	.301	33-0-3	.091	-2	98	2	61	-0.1
1996	NY N	8	12	.400	31	31	2-1	0-0	194.2	195	103	30	7	61-5	114	4.21	96	.260	.318	55-0-10	.091	-2*	103	-3	13	-0.6
1997	NY N	0	1	.000	6	5	0	0-0	25.2	35	24	5	1	11-1	12	8.06	50	.327	.388	8-0-1	.000	-1	124	-11	122	-0.6
	Mil A	1	1	.500	4	3	0	0-0	14	13	9	1	0	12-0	10	5.14	90	.245	.385	0	ø	0	46	-1	0	-0.1
1998	Cin N	14	7	.667	32	32	2-1	0-0	209	176	79	24	6	64-4	157	3.14	137	.228	.291	66-0-9	.106	-3	115	26	0	2.0
1999	Cin N	16	10	.615	33	33	2-2	0-0	198.1	190	86	25	5	57-2	120	3.68	128	.252	.306	66-1-8	.152	0	110	23	0	2.6
2000	Cin N	8	6	.571	22	22	3-1	0-0	131	133	76	23	1	46-1	71	4.74	101	.261	.321	43-1-6	.186	1*	85	0	54	0.1
2001	Cin N	1	3	.250	7	7	0	0-0	35.1	48	29	9	1	17-0	17	6.37	72	.318	.384	11-0-1	.273	1*	101	-7	153	-0.6
Total	14	111	103	.519	321	318	24-11	0-0	1959	1822	926	223	49	716-38	1368	3.89	103	.245	.313	513-2-62	.129	-6	105	29	624	1.7
Harper, Jack	Charles William; B4.2.1878 Galloway PA; D9.30.1950 Jamestown NY; BR/TR/6´0˝/178; d9.18																									
1899	Cle N	1	4	.200	5	5	5	0	37	44	33	3	3	12	14	3.89	95	.295	.360	11	.182	1	102	-5	—	-0.4
1900	StL N	0	1	.000	1	1	0	0	3	4	7	0	0	2	0	12.00	30	.308	.400	1	.000	-0	114	-3	—	-0.5
1901	StL N	23	13	.639	39	37	28-1	0	308.2	294	158	7	16	99	128	3.62	88	.249	.316	116-1-3	.172	1	128	-13	—	-1.2
1902	StL A	15	11	.577	29	26	20-2	0	222.1	224	131	8	8	81	74	4.13	85	.262	.332	83-0-3	.205	-0	89	-14	—	-1.3
1903	Cin N	8	9	.471	17	15	13	0	135	143	87	2	10	70	45	4.33	82	.271	.367	56	.250	2*	97	-7	—	-0.5
1904	Cin N	23	9	.719	35	35	31-6	0	293.2	262	113	2	9	85	125	2.30	128	.234	.293	113-0-3	.159	-2	127	19	—	1.5
1905	Cin N	9	13	.409	26	23	15-1	1	179.1	189	116	2	8	69	70	3.86	86	.271	.344	60-0-4	.167	1	105	-10	—	-1.1
1906	Cin N	1	4	.200	5	5	3	0	36.2	38	23	1	2	20	10	4.17	66	.286	.387	11-0-1	.273	1	90	-5	—	-0.6
	Chi N	0	0	ø	1	1	0	0	1	0	0	0	0	0	0	0.00	ø	.000	.000	0	ø	0	304	0	—	0.0
	Year	1	4	.200	6	6	3	0	37.2	38	23	1	2	20	10	4.06	68	.279	.380	11-0-1	.273	1	124	-5	—	-0.6
Total	8	80	64	.556	158	148	115-10	1	1216.2	1198	668	25	56	438	466	3.55	92	.256	.327	451-1-14	.186	3	111	-38	—	-4.1
Harper, George	George B.; B8.17.1866 Milwaukee WI; D12.11.1931 Stockton CA; BR/TR/5´10˝/165; d7.11																									
1894	Phi N	6	6	.500	12	9	7	0	86.1	128	84	3	2	49	24	5.32	97	.340	.418	40	.150	-4	127	-7	—	-0.9
1896	Bro N	4	8	.333	16	11	7	0	86	106	72	4	3	39	22	5.55	74	.300	.375	37	.162	0	96	-13	—	-1.3
Total	2	10	14	.417	28	20	14	0	172.1	234	156	7	5	88	46	5.43	85	.321	.397	77	.156	-4	110	-20	—	-2.2
Harper, Harry	Harry Clayton; B4.24.1895 Hackensack NJ; D4.23.1963 New York NY; BL/TL/6´2˝/165; d6.27																									
1913	Was A	0	0	ø	4	0	0	0	12.2	10	11	1	1	5	9	3.55	83	.213	.302	4	.250	0	—	-2	—	-0.1
1914	Was A	2	1	.667	23	3	1	2	57	45	29	1	5	35	50	3.47	81	.211	.336	12	.250	0	95	-4	—	-0.3
1915	Was A	4	4	.500	19	10	5-2	2	86.1	66	26	1	1	40	54	1.77	168	.222	.317	25-0-2	.000	-4	81	10	—	0.5
1916	Was A	14	10	.583	36	34	13-2	0	249.2	209	82	4	8	101	149	2.45	114	.235	.319	87-0-1	.207	1	95	11	—	1.0
1917	Was A	11	12	.478	31	31	10-4	0	179.1	145	85	1	5	106	99	3.01	87	.230	.345	60-0-2	.117	-3	117	-10	—	-1.8
1918	Was A	11	10	.524	35	32	14-3	1	244	182	77	1	8	104	78	2.18	125	.212	.303	82-0-3	.134	-4*	103	17	—	0.8
1919	Was A	6	21	.222	35	31	8	0	208	220	119	3	8	97	87	3.72	86	.284	.370	65-0-2	.169	-2	72	-14	—	-1.9
1920	Bos A	5	14	.263	27	22	11-1	0	162.2	163	73	9	2	66	71	3.04	120	.275	.349	50-0-2	.120	-3	58	8	—	0.4
1921	†NY A	4	3	.571	8	7	4	0	52.2	52	23	3	2	25	22	3.76	113	.263	.351	16	.125	-1	76	4	—	0.3
1923	Bro N	0	1	.000	1	1	0	0	3.2	8	6	2	0	3	4	14.73	26	.421	.500	1	.000	-0	127	-4	—	-0.6
Total	10	57	76	.429	219	171	66-12	5	1256	1100	531	26	40	582	623	2.87	105	.244	.335	402-0-12	.147	-16	88	16	—	-1.7
Harper, Jack	John Wesley; B8.5.1893 Hendricks WV; D6.18.1927 Halstead KS; BR/TR/5´11˝/180; d4.17; Col Marshall																									
1915	Phi A	0	0	ø	3	0	0	0	8.2	5	4	0	0	1	3	3.12	94	.161	.188	2	.000	-0	—	0	—	0.0
Harper, Travis	Travis Boyd; B5.21.1976 Harrisonburg VA; BL/TR/6´4˝/(187–193); [BosA97 3/101]; d8.4; Col James Madison																									
2000	TB A	1	2	.333	6	5	1-1	0-0	32	30	17	5	1	15-0	14	4.78	102	.244	.329	0	ø	0	100	1	0	0.1
2001	TB A	0	2	.000	2	2	0	0-0	7	15	11	5	0	3-0	2	7.71	58	.455	.500	0	ø	0	21	-4	0	-0.7
2002	TB A	5	9	.357	37	7	0	1-1	85.2	101	54	14	9	27-3	60	5.46	83	.289	.352	0	ø	0	70	-8	0	-1.2
2003	TB A	4	8	.333	61	0	0	1-5	93	86	45	9	6	31-8	64	3.77	121	.252	.323	0	ø	0	—	7	0	0.8
2004	TB A	6	2	.750	52	0	0	0-1	78.2	69	37	8	7	23-3	59	3.89	120	.234	.303	0	ø	0	—	7	0	0.6
2005	TB A	4	6	.400	52	0	0	0-3	73.1	88	57	14	1	24-9	40	6.75	65	.304	.358	1	.000	-0	—	-17	0	-2.1
2006	TB A	2	0	1.000	30	0	0	0-2	42	62	27	6	2	13-1	32	4.93	95	.348	.397	0	ø	0	—	-2	60	-0.1
Total	7	22	29	.431	240	14	1-1	2-12	411.2	451	248	61	26	136-24	271	4.94	93	.280	.344	1	.000	-0	75	-16	60	-2.6
Harper, Bill	William Homer "Blue Sleeve"; B6.14.1889 Bertrand MO; D6.17.1951 Somerville TN; BB/TR/6´1˝/180; d6.10																									
1911	StL A	0	0	ø	2	0	0	0	8	9	9	0	1	4	6	6.75	50	.300	.400	3	.000	-0	—	-3	—	-0.2
Harrell, Slim	Oscar Martin; B7.31.1890 Grandview TX; D4.30.1971 Hillsboro TX; BR/TR/6´3˝/180; d6.21; Col Baylor																									
1912	Phi A	0	0	ø	1	0	0	0	3	4	0	0	0	0	1	0.00	ø	.364	.364	1	.000	-0	—	1	—	0.0

YEAR	TM LG	W	L	PCT	G	GS	CG-SHO	SV-BS	IP	H	R	HR	HB	BB-IB	SO	ERA	AERA	OAV	OOB	AB-HR-SH	AVG	PB	SUP	APR	DL	PW
Harrell, Ray	Raymond James "Cowboy"; B2.16.1912 Petrolia TX; D1.28.1984 Alexandria LA; BR/TR/6´1˝/185; d4.16																									
1935	StL N	1	1	.500	11	1	0	0	29.2	39	26	4	0	11	13	6.67	61	.320	.376	4-0-1	.000	-1	124	-9	—	-0.6
1937	StL N	3	7	.300	35	15	1-1	1	96.2	99	73	7	2	59	41	5.87	68	.263	.366	22-0-2	.045	-2	110	-19	—	-2.0
1938	StL N	2	3	.400	32	3	1	2	63	78	37	6	3	29	32	4.86	81	.308	.386	10	.000	-1	143	-4	—	-0.5
1939	Chi N	0	2	.000	4	2	0	0	17.1	29	16	2	0	6	5	8.31	47	.387	.432	5	.000	-1	33	-7	—	-0.8
	Phi N	3	7	.300	22	10	4	0	94.2	101	77	6	4	56	35	5.42	74	.270	.371	26	.115	-1	54	-20	—	-2.0
	Year	3	9	.250	26	12	4	0	112	130	93	8	4	62	40	5.87	68	.290	.381	31	.097	-2	51	-27	—	-2.8
1940	Pit N	0	0	ø	3	0	0	0	3.1	5	5	0	0	2	3	8.10	47	.333	.412	0	ø	0	—	-2	—	-0.1
1945	NY N	0	0	ø	12	0	0	0	25.1	34	22	1	1	14	7	4.97	79	.343	.430	5	.200	1	—	-6	0	-0.2
Total	6	9	20	.310	119	31	6-1	3	330	385	256	26	10	177	136	5.70	70	.293	.381	72-0-3	.069	-5	91	-67	0	-6.2
Harrelson, Bill	William Charles; B11.17.1945 Tahlequah OK; BB/TR/6´5˝/195; d7.31; Col Bakersfield (CA) JC																									
1968	Cal A	1	6	.143	10	5	1	0	33.2	28	23	4	1	26-0	22	5.08	57	.226	.359	10	.100	-0	60	-9	0	-1.8
Harriger, Denny	Dennis Scott; B7.21.1969 Kittanning PA; BR/TR/5´11˝/185; [NYN87 18/472]; d6.16																									
1998	Det A	0	3	.000	4	2	0	0-0	12	17	12	1	0	8-2	3	6.75	70	.327	.417	0	ø	0	98	-4	0	-0.6
Harrington, Andy	Andrew Francis; B11.13.1888 Wakefield MA; D11.12.1938 Malden MA; BR/TR/6´0˝/193; d9.8; Col Boston College																									
1913	Cin N	0	0	ø	1	0	0	0	4	6	5	0	0	1	1	9.00	36	.353	.389	2	.500	0	—	-2	—	-0.1
Harrington, Bill	William Womble; B10.3.1927 Sanford NC; BR/TR/5´11˝/160; d4.16; Mil 1953–55																									
1953	Phi A	0	0	ø	1	0	0	0	2	5	3	0	0	0	0	13.50	32	.500	.500	0	ø	0	—	-2	0	-0.1
1955	KC A	3	3	.500	34	1	0	2	76.2	69	41	6	2	41-4	26	4.11	102	.246	.339	17	.118	-1	21	0	0	-0.1
1956	KC A	2	2	.500	23	1	0	1	37.2	40	27	3	0	26-1	14	6.45	67	.274	.384	7-0-2	.000	-1	144	-7	0	-0.8
Total	3	5	5	.500	58	2	0	3	116.1	114	71	9	2	67-5	40	5.03	84	.261	.357	24-0-2	.083	-1	84	-9	0	-1.0
Harris, Ben	Ben Franklin; B12.17.1889 Donelson TN; D4.29.1927 St.Louis MO; BR/TR/6´0˝/220; d4.19																									
1914	KC F	7	7	.500	31	14	5	1	154	179	89	7	6	41	40	4.09	68	.303	.354	45-0-3	.200	1	102	-22	—	-1.7
1915	KC F	0	0	ø	1	0	0	0	2	1	0	0	0	0	0	0.00	ø	.143	.143	0	ø	0	—	1	—	0.0
Total	2	7	7	.500	32	14	5	1	156	180	89	7	6	41	40	4.04	69	.301	.352	45-0-3	.200	1	102	-21	—	-1.7
Harris, Lum	Chalmer Luman; B1.17.1915 New Castle AL; D11.11.1996 Pell City AL; BR/TR/6´1˝/180; d4.19; Mil 1945; M8/C14																									
1941	Phi A	4	4	.500	33	10	5	2	131.2	134	77	16	2	51	49	4.78	88	.260	.329	40-0-2	.275	2	101	-7	0	-0.3
1942	Phi A	11	15	.423	26	20	10-1	0	166	146	80	14	1	70	60	3.74	101	.234	.313	62-0-1	.161	-2	66	1	0	0.0
1943	Phi A	7	21	.250	32	27	15-1	1	216.1	241	122	17	3	63	55	4.20	81	.279	.330	70-0-4	.171	-1	71	-22	0	-2.7
1944	Phi A	10	9	.526	23	22	12-2	0	174.1	193	70	8	0	26	33	3.30	105	.281	.308	59-0-2	.169	-1	77	6	0	0.5
1946	Phi A	3	14	.176	34	12	4	0	125.1	153	78	11	0	48	33	5.24	68	.308	.369	36-1-4	.222	1	75	-20	0	-2.2
1947	Was A	0	0	ø	3	0	0	0	6.1	7	2	0	0	7	2	2.84	131	.318	.483	1	.000	-0	—	1	0	0.1
Total	6	35	63	.357	151	91	46-4	3	820	874	429	66	6	265	232	4.16	88	.273	.329	268-1-13	.190	-0	75	-41	0	-4.6
Harris, Bubba	Charles; B2.15.1926 Sulligent AL; BR/TR/6´4˝/204; d4.29																									
1948	Phi A	5	2	.714	45	0	0	5	93.2	89	51	2	1	35	32	4.13	104	.249	.317	24-0-2	.125	-1	—	0	0	-0.1
1949	Phi A	1	1	.500	37	0	0	3	84.1	92	57	12	1	42	18	5.44	75	.286	.370	24-0-3	.125	-2	—	-12	0	-0.7
1951	Phi A	0	0	ø	3	0	0	0	4	4	4	0	1	5	2	9.00	48	.250	.455	0	ø	0	—	-2	0	-0.1
	Cle A	0	0	ø	2	0	0	0	4	5	2	0	0	4	1	4.50	84	.333	.474	0	ø	0	—	0	0	0.0
	Year	0	0	ø	5	0	0	0	8	9	6	0	1	9	3	6.75	60	.290	.463	0	ø	0	—	-2	0	-0.1
Total	3	6	3	.667	87	0	0	8	186	190	114	14	3	86	53	4.84	87	.267	.349	48-0-5	.125	-3	—	-14	0	-0.9
Harris, Greg	Greg Allen; B11.2.1955 Lynwood CA; BB/TR (TB 1995p)/6´0˝/(165–175); d5.20; Col Long Beach (CA) City																									
1981	NY N	3	5	.375	16	14	0	1-0	68.2	65	36	8	2	28-2	54	4.46	79	.245	.321	22	.182	0*	108	-5	0	-0.6
1982	Cin N	2	6	.250	34	10	1	1-0	91.1	96	56	12	2	37-1	67	4.83	76	.274	.344	18	.167	-0*	84	-12	0	-1.0
1983	Cin N	0	0	ø	1	0	0	0-0	1	2	3	0	1	3-2	1	27.00	14	.500	.750	1	.000	-0	—	-2	0	-0.1
1984	Mon N	0	1	.000	15	0	0	2-0	17.2	10	4	0	2	7-1	15	2.04	170	.172	.284	1	.000	-0	—	3	0	0.2
	†SD N	2	1	.667	19	1	0	1-0	36.2	28	14	3	2	18-0	30	2.70	133	.209	.306	8	.375	1	172	3	0	0.4
	Year	2	2	.500	34	1	0	3-0	54.1	38	18	3	4	25-1	45	2.48	143	.198	.299	9	.333	1	174	6	0	0.6
1985	Tex A	5	4	.556	58	0	0	11-4	113	74	35	7	5	43-3	111	2.47	173	.186	.273	0	ø	0	—	21	0	2.0
1986	Tex A	10	8	.556	73	0	0	20-11	111.1	103	40	12	1	42-6	95	2.83	153	.251	.318	0	ø	0	—	18	0	3.2
1987	Tex A	5	10	.333	42	19	0	0-4	140.2	157	92	18	4	56-3	106	4.86	93	.281	.349	0	ø	0	124	-8	0	-0.7
1988	Phi N	4	6	.400	66	1	0	1-1	107	80	34	7	4	52-14	71	2.36	153	.209	.309	9-0-1	.333	1	98	13	0	1.3
1989	Phi N	2	2	.500	44	0	0	1-0	75.1	64	34	7	2	43-7	51	3.58	100	.234	.340	6-0-1	.167	1	—	0	0	0.1
	Bos A	2	2	.500	15	0	0	0-1	28	21	12	1	0	15-2	25	2.57	160	.208	.308	0	ø	0	—	3	0	0.4
1990	†Bos A	13	9	.591	34	30	1	0-0	184.1	186	90	13	6	77-7	117	4.00	102	.265	.338	0	ø	0	99	2	0	0.4
1991	Bos A	11	12	.478	53	21	1	2-3	173	157	79	13	5	69-5	127	3.85	112	.243	.318	0	ø	0	79	10	0	1.3
1992	Bos A	4	9	.308	70	2	1	4-6	107.2	82	38	6	4	60-11	73	2.51	170	.215	.324	0	ø	0	32	18	0	2.1
1993	Bos A	6	7	.462	**80**	0	0	8-10	112.1	95	55	7	10	60-14	103	3.77	123	.232	.341	0	ø	0	—	9	0	1.1
1994	Bos A	3	4	.429	35	0	0	2-4	45.2	60	44	8	1	23-6	44	8.28	61	.321	.396	0	ø	0	—	-15	0	-1.9
	NY A	0	1	.000	3	0	0	0-1	5	4	5	1	2	3-1	4	5.40	85	.222	.375	0	ø	0	—	-1	0	-0.2
	Year	3	5	.375	38	0	0	2-5	50.2	64	49	9	3	26-7	48	7.99	63	.312	.394	0	ø	0	—	-16	0	-2.1
1995	Mon N	2	3	.400	45	0	0	0-1	48.1	45	18	6	1	16-1	47	2.61	165	.245	.308	3	.333	1	—	8	0	0.7
Total	15	74	90	.451	703	98	4	54-46	1467	1329	689	129	54	652-86	1141	3.69	113	.243	.327	68-0-2	.221	3	98	65	0	8.7
Harris, Greg	Gregory Wade; B12.1.1963 Greensboro NC; BR/TR/6´2˝/(187–195); [SDN85 10/258]; d9.19; Col Elon																									
1988	SD N	2	0	1.000	3	1	1	0-0	18	13	3	0	0	3-0	15	1.50	227	.200	.235	7	.000	-1	235	4	0	0.4
1989	SD N	8	9	.471	56	8	0	6-2	135	106	43	8	2	52-9	106	2.60	135	.215	.291	19-0-4	.053	-1	95	14	0	1.9
1990	SD N	8	8	.500	73	0	0	9-7	117.1	92	35	6	4	49-13	97	2.30	167	.220	.303	12-0-1	.083	-0	—	19	0	2.8
1991	SD N	9	5	.643	20	20	3-2	0-0	133	116	42	16	1	27-6	95	2.23	171	.233	.273	36-0-7	.083	-2	86	20	72	1.9
1992	SD N	4	8	.333	20	20	1	0-0	118	113	62	13	2	35-2	66	4.12	87	.252	.307	31-0-5	.129	1	98	-8	81	-0.7
1993	SD N	10	9	.526	22	22	4	0-0	152	151	65	18	3	39-6	83	3.67	113	.257	.306	53-0-4	.170	1	95	10	0	1.4
	Col N	1	8	.111	13	13	0	0-0	73.1	88	62	15	4	30-3	40	6.50	74	.299	.370	20-0-1	.050	-2	70	-13	0	-1.5
	Year	11	17	.393	35	35	4	0-0	225.1	239	127	33	7	69-9	123	4.59	95	.271	.328	73-0-5	.137	-0	85	-5	0	-0.1
1994	Col N	3	12	.200	29	19	1	1-0	130	154	99	22	5	52-4	82	6.65	75	.300	.366	40-0-4	.175	-0	67	-19	0	-1.8
1995	Min A	0	5	.000	7	6	0	0-0	32.2	50	35	5	0	16-0	21	8.82	55	.355	.415	0	ø	0	74	-14	0	-1.6
Total	8	45	64	.413	243	109	10-2	16-9	909.1	883	446	103	21	303-43	605	3.98	102	.255	.317	218-0-26	.119	-3	87	13	153	2.8
Harris, Herb	Herbert Benjamin "Hub","Lefty"; B4.24.1913 Chicago IL; D1.18.1991 Crystal Lake IL; BL/TL/6´1˝/175; d7.21; Col Northwestern																									
1936	Phi N	0	0	ø	4	0	0	0	7	14	8	0	1	5	0	10.29	44	.438	.526	1	.000	-0	—	-3	—	-0.2
Harris, Pep	Hernando Petrocelli; B9.23.1972 Lancaster SC; BR/TR/6´2˝/(185–253); [CleA91 7/190]; d8.14; [DL 1999 Ana A 182]																									
1996	Cal A	2	0	1.000	11	3	0	0-0	32.1	31	16	4	3	17-2	20	3.90	130	.254	.349	0	ø	0	171	4	0	0.2
1997	Ana A	5	4	.556	61	0	0	0-3	79.2	82	33	7	2	38-6	56	3.62	128	.274	.356	0	ø	0	—	10	0	1.0
1998	Ana A	3	1	.750	49	0	0	0-1	60	55	32	7	0	23-4	34	4.35	109	.239	.307	0	ø	0	—	2	18	0.2
Total	3	10	5	.667	121	3	0	0-4	172	168	81	18	5	78-12	110	3.92	121	.258	.338	0	ø	0	171	16	200	1.4
Harris, Jeff	Jeffrey Austin; B7.4.1974 Alameda CA; BR/TR/6´1˝/190; [MinA95 28/772]; d8.2; Col San Francisco																									
2005	Sea A	2	5	.286	11	8	0	0-0	53.2	48	27	9	3	20-2	25	4.19	100	.238	.313	0	ø	0	91	0	0	-0.1
2006	Sea A	0	0	ø	3	0	0	0-0	3.1	3	2	0	0	0-0	1	5.40	82	.250	.250	0	ø	0	—	0	0	0.0
Total	2	2	5	.286	14	8	0	0-0	57	51	29	9	3	20-2	26	4.26	98	.238	.310	0	ø	0	91	0	0	-0.1
Harris, Joe	Joseph White; B2.1.1882 Melrose MA; D4.12.1966 Melrose MA; BR/TR/6´1˝/198; d9.22																									
1905	Bos A	1	2	.333	3	3	3	0	23	16	6	0	0	8	14	2.35	115	.198	.270	9	.111	-1	52	2	—	0.1
1906	Bos A	2	21	.087	30	24	20-1	2	235	211	130	5	7	67	99	3.52	78	.243	.303	81-0-1	.160	-2	44	-22	—	-2.0
1907	Bos A	0	7	.000	12	5	3	0	59	57	28	0	1	13	24	3.05	84	.256	.300	21	.190	-0	58	-3	—	-0.3
Total	3	3	30	.091	45	32	26-1	2	317	284	164	5	8	88	137	3.35	81	.242	.300	111-0-1	.162	-3	47	-23	—	-2.2

YEAR	TM LG	W	L	PCT	G	GS	CG-SHO	SV-BS	IP	H	R	HR	HB	BB-IB	SO	ERA	AERA	OAV	OOB	AB-HR-SH	AVG	PB	SUP	APR	DL	PW
HARRIS, MICKEY	Maurice Charles; B1.30.1917 New York NY; D4.15.1971 Farmington MI; BL/TL/6´0˝/(185–195); d4.23; Mil 1942–45																									
1940	Bos A	4	2	.667	13	9	3	0	68.1	83	40	8	2	26	36	5.00	90	.292	.356	22-0-1	.273	2	119	-3	—	0.0
1941	Bos A	8	14	.364	35	22	11-1	1	194	189	86	6	2	86	111	3.25	128	.250	.328	55-0-4	.109	2	114	18	0	2.0
1946	†Bos A☆	17	9	.654	34	30	15	0	222.2	236	105	18	3	76	131	3.64	101	.268	.329	78-0-5	.231	4	121	-1	0	0.2
1947	Bos A	5	4	.556	15	6	1	0	51.2	42	20	3	0	23	35	2.44	159	.225	.310	12-0-1	.417	3	95	6	0	1.4
1948	Bos A	7	10	.412	20	17	6-1	0	113.2	120	73	10	1	59	42	5.30	83	.273	.360	32-0-2	.063	-1	94	-11	0	-1.5
1949	Bos A	2	3	.400	7	6	2	0	37.2	53	26	3	1	20	14	5.02	87	.323	.400	12-0-2	.083	-1	113	-4	0	-0.5
	Was A	2	12	.143	23	19	4	0	129	151	82	8	0	55	54	5.16	82	.292	.360	39-0-2	.205	1	69	-12	0	-1.0
	Year	4	15	.211	30	25	6	0	166.2	204	108	11	1	75	68	5.13	83	.299	.369	51-0-4	.176	1	79	-16	0	-1.5
1950	Was A	5	9	.357	**53**	0	0	**15**	98	93	56	9	1	46	41	4.78	94	.247	.330	17	.235	1	—	-1	0	-0.2
1951	Was A	6	8	.429	41	0	0	4	87.1	87	45	6	1	43	47	3.81	107	.260	.347	16-0-1	.188	0	—	1	0	0.2
1952	Was A	0	0	ø	1	0	0	0	1	1	1	1	0	0	0	9.00	40	.250	.250	0	ø	0	—	-1	0	0.0
	Cle A	3	0	1.000	29	0	0	1	46.2	42	26	6	1	21	23	4.63	72	.249	.335	5	.200	-0	—	-6	0	-0.4
	Year	3	0	1.000	30	0	0	1	47.2	43	27	7	1	21	23	4.72	71	.249	.333	5	.200	-0	—	-7	0	-0.4
Total	9	59	71	.454	271	109	42-2	21	1050	1097	560	78	12	455	534	4.18	98	.267	.342	288-0-18	.188	11	104	-14	0	0.2
HARRIS, REGGIE	Reginald Allen; B8.12.1968 Waynesboro VA; BR/TR/6´1˝/(180–217); [BosA87 1/26]; d7.4																									
1990	Oak A	1	0	1.000	16	1	0	0-0	41.1	25	16	5	2	21-1	31	3.48	107	.176	.287	0	ø	0	97	2	85	0.1
1991	Oak A	0	0	ø	2	0	0	0-0	3	5	4	0	0	3-1	2	12.00	32	.455	.533	0	ø	0	—	-3	0	-0.1
1996	Bos A	0	0	ø	4	0	0	0-1	4.1	7	6	2	1	5-0	4	12.46	41	.389	.542	0	ø	0	—	-3	0	-0.1
1997	Phi N	1	3	.250	50	0	0	0-0	54.1	55	33	1	5	43-1	45	5.30	80	.263	.395	0	ø	0	—	-6	0	-0.4
1998	Hou N	0	0	ø	6	0	0	0-0	6	6	4	1	0	2-0	2	6.00	68	.261	.308	0	ø	0	—	-1	0	-0.1
1999	Mil N	0	0	ø	8	0	0	0-0	12	8	4	1	2	7-0	11	3.00	153	.186	.321	1	.000	-0	—	2	0	0.1
Total	6	2	3	.400	86	1	0	0-1	121	106	67	10	10	81-3	95	4.91	84	.238	.361	1	.000	-0	97	-9	85	-0.5
HARRIS, BOB	Robert Arthur; B5.1.1915 Gillette WY; D8.8.1989 North Platte NE; BR/TR/6´0˝/185; d9.19; Mil 1943–45; Col Western Nebraska CC																									
1938	Det A	1	0	1.000	3	1	1	0	10	14	9	0	0	4	7	7.20	69	.318	.375	3	.333	0	176	-2	—	-0.1
1939	Det A	1	1	.500	5	1	0	0	18	18	8	4	0	8	9	4.00	122	.269	.347	5	.400	0	90	2	—	0.2
	StL A	3	12	.200	28	16	6	0	126	162	88	5	0	71	48	5.71	85	.321	.405	37-0-2	.189	-0*	67	-10	—	-0.9
	Year	4	13	.235	33	17	6	0	144	180	96	9	0	79	57	5.50	89	.315	.398	42-0-2	.214	-0	68	-8	—	-0.7
1940	StL A	11	15	.423	35	28	8-1	1	193.2	225	120	24	3	85	49	4.93	93	.290	.362	60-0-5	.250	3	86	-7	—	-0.5
1941	StL A	12	14	.462	34	29	9-2	1	186.2	237	117	18	2	85	57	5.21	83	.312	.383	61-0-14	.115	-3	104	-16	0	-2.2
1942	StL A	1	5	.167	6	6	0	0	33.2	37	24	2	0	17	9	5.61	66	.268	.348	10-0-2	.000	-1	69	-7	0	-1.1
	Phi A	1	5	.167	16	8	2-1	0	78	77	31	5	0	24	26	2.88	131	.253	.308	26	.269	1	79	7	0	0.7
	Year	2	10	.167	22	14	2-1	0	111.2	114	55	7	0	41	35	3.71	101	.258	.321	36-0-2	.194	0	75	0	0	-0.4
Total	5	30	52	.366	127	89	26-4	2	646	770	397	58	5	294	205	4.96	89	.297	.370	202-0-23	.193	1	87	-33	0	-3.9
HARRIS, GENE	Tyrone Eugene; B12.5.1964 Sebring FL; BR/TR/5´11˝/(190–195); [MonN86 5/122]; d4.5; Col Tulane																									
1989	Mon N	1	1	.500	11	0	0	0-2	20	16	11	1	0	10-0	11	4.95	72	.242	.338	1-0-1	.000	-0	—	-2	0	-0.2
	Sea A	1	4	.200	10	6	0	1-0	33.1	47	27	3	1	15-1	14	6.48	62	.353	.414	0	ø	0*	97	-9	65	-1.2
1990	Sea A	1	2	.333	25	0	0	0-1	38	31	25	5	1	30-5	43	4.74	84	.217	.352	0	ø	0	—	-4	0	-0.3
1991	Sea A	0	0	ø	8	0	0	1-0	13.1	15	8	1	0	10-3	6	4.05	102	.273	.385	0	ø	0	—	-1	0	0.0
1992	Sea A	0	0	ø	8	0	0	0-0	9	8	7	3	0	6-0	6	7.00	57	.235	.350	0	ø	0	—	-3	0	-0.2
	SD N	0	2	.000	14	1	0	0-0	21.1	15	8	0	1	9-0	19	2.95	122	.195	.287	3	.333	0*	126	1	0	0.1
1993	SD N	6	6	.500	59	0	0	23-8	59.1	57	27	3	1	37-8	39	3.03	136	.254	.360	1	.000	-0	—	5	0	1.1
1994	SD N	1	1	.500	13	0	0	0-3	12.1	21	11	2	0	8-2	9	8.03	51	.389	.468	1	.000	-0	—	-5	0	-0.7
	Det A	0	0	ø	11	0	0	1-1	11.1	13	10	1	1	4-1	10	7.15	69	.271	.340	0	ø	0	—	-3	55	-0.1
1995	Phi N	2	2	.500	21	0	0	0-1	19	19	9	2	0	8-0	9	4.26	99	.260	.333	0	ø	0	—	0	0	0.1
	Bal A	0	0	ø	3	0	0	0-1	4	4	2	0	0	1-0	4	4.50	106	.267	.313	0	ø	0	—	0	99	0.0
Total	7	12	18	.400	183	7	0	26-17	241	246	145	21	5	138-20	170	4.71	86	.267	.363	6-0-1	.167	-0	99	-21	219	-1.4
HARRIS, BUDDY	Walter Francis; B12.5.1948 Philadelphia PA; BR/TR/6´7˝/250; [HouN68 S1/15]; d9.10; Col Miami																									
1970	Hou N	0	0	ø	2	0	0	0-0	6.1	6	4	3	0	0-0	2	5.68	69	.240	.240	1	.000	-0	—	-1	0	-0.1
1971	Hou N	1	1	.500	20	0	0	0-0	30.2	33	22	3	0	16-1	21	6.46	52	.275	.358	2	.000	-0	—	-10	0	-0.7
Total	2	1	1	.500	22	0	0	0-0	37	39	26	6	0	16-1	23	6.32	55	.269	.340	3	.000	-0	—	-11	0	-0.8
HARRIS, BILL	William Milton; B6.23.1900 Wylie TX; D8.21.1965 Charlotte NC; BR/TR/6´1˝/180; d4.22																									
1923	Cin N	3	2	.600	22	3	1	0	69.2	79	42	3	3	18	18	5.17	75	.292	.342	17-0-1	.353	1	71	-7	—	-0.3
1924	Cin N	0	0	ø	3	0	0	0	7	10	7	0	0	2	5	9.00	42	.323	.364	1	1.000	0	—	-4	—	-0.1
1931	Pit N	2	2	.500	4	4	3-1	0	31	21	6	0	0	9	10	0.87	442	.194	.256	11	.091	-1	67	9	—	1.2
1932	Pit N	10	9	.526	37	17	4	2	168	178	84	6	6	38	63	3.64	105	.271	.317	55	.182	-1	88	3	—	0.2
1933	Pit N	4	4	.500	31	0	0	5	58.2	68	28	1	1	14	19	3.22	103	.289	.332	9	.000	-1	—	0	—	-0.2
1934	Pit N	0	0	ø	11	1	0	0	19	28	15	2	1	7	8	6.63	62	.350	.409	2	.500	0	231	-5	—	-0.2
1938	Bos A	5	5	.500	13	11	5-1	1	80.1	83	39	5	1	21	26	4.03	122	.268	.316	28-0-2	.214	-0	115	9	—	0.9
Total	7	24	22	.522	121	36	13-2	8	433.2	467	221	17	12	109	149	3.92	101	.276	.324	123-0-3	.203	-1	102	5	—	1.5
HARRIS, BILL	William Thomas; B12.3.1931 Duguayville NB, Can.; BL/TR/5´8˝/(185–187); d9.27																									
1957	Bro N	0	1	.000	1	1	0	0	7	9	3	1	0	1-0	3	3.86	108	.321	.345	2	.500	0	42	0	0	0.1
1959	LA N	0	0	ø	1	0	0	0	1.2	0	0	0	0	3-1	0	0.00	ø	.000	.375	0	ø	0	—	1	0	0.0
Total	2	0	1	.000	2	1	0	0	8.2	9	3	1	0	4-1	3	3.12	134	.273	.351	2	.500	0	42	1	0	0.1
HARRISON, BOB	Robert Lee; B9.22.1930 St.Louis MO; BL/TR/5´11˝/178; d9.23																									
1955	Bal A	0	0	ø	1	0	0	0	2	3	2	0	0	4-0	0	9.00	42	.500	.700	0	ø	0	—	-1	0	-0.1
1956	Bal A	0	0	ø	1	1	0	0	1.2	3	3	0	0	5-0	0	16.20	24	.375	.615	0	ø	0	136	-2	0	-0.1
Total	2	0	0	ø	2	1	0	0	3.2	6	5	0	0	9-0	0	12.27	31	.429	.652	0	ø	0	136	-3	0	-0.2
HARRISON, RORIC	Roric Edward; B9.20.1946 Los Angeles CA; BR/TR/6´3˝/(191–200); d4.18; Col Santa Monica (CA) City																									
1972	Bal A	3	4	.429	39	2	0	4-1	94	68	24	2	4	34-9	62	2.30	136	.209	.291	17-1-1	.118	1	99	10	0	0.9
1973	Atl N	11	8	.579	38	22	3	5-2	177.1	161	90	15	3	98-6	130	4.16	95	.242	.339	54-2-5	.056	-2*	134	-3	0	-0.5
1974	Atl N	6	11	.353	20	20	3	0-0	126	148	70	12	3	49-1	46	4.71	81	.294	.358	38-3-6	.184	2	90	-11	70	-1.2
1975	Atl N	3	4	.429	15	7	2	1-0	54.2	58	33	7	0	19-1	22	4.77	79	.266	.324	15	.200	1	83	-5	0	-0.6
	Cle A	7	7	.500	19	19	4	0-0	126	137	71	9	4	46-4	52	4.79	80	.275	.338	0	ø	0	107	-11	0	-1.2
1978	Min A	0	1	.000	9	0	0	0-0	12	18	10	0	0	11-0	7	7.50	51	.346	.453	0	ø	0	—	-4	0	-0.3
Total	5	30	35	.462	140	70	12	10-3	590	590	298	45	14	257-21	319	4.24	88	.261	.338	124-6-12	.121	2	111	-24	70	-2.9
HARRISON, TOM	Thomas James; B1.18.1945 Trail BC, Can.; BR/TR/6´3˝/200; d5.7																									
1965	KC A	0	0	ø	1	0	0	0	1	2	1	0	0	1-0	0	9.00	39	.667	.750	0	ø	0*	—	-1	0	0.0
HARRISS, SLIM	William Jennings Bryan; B12.11.1896 Brownwood TX; D9.19.1963 Temple TX; BR/TR/6´6˝/180; d4.19; Col Howard Payne																									
1920	Phi A	9	14	.391	31	25	11-1	0	192	226	111	5	5	57	60	4.08	99	.305	.359	66-0-3	.106	-7	70	2	—	-0.3
1921	Phi A	11	16	.407	39	28	14	2	227.2	258	136	16	9	73	92	4.27	104	.290	.350	81-0-5	.148	-7	84	4	—	-0.3
1922	Phi A	9	20	.310	47	32	13	3	229.2	262	148	19	3	94	102	5.02	85	.290	.359	74-0-4	.176	-4	99	-17	—	-2.2
1923	Phi A	10	16	.385	46	28	9	6	209.1	221	114	9	2	95	89	4.00	103	.280	.359	61-0-5	.066	-8	85	3	—	-0.2
1924	Phi A	6	10	.375	36	12	4-1	2	123	138	78	5	3	62	45	4.68	92	.291	.377	42	.167	-3	62	-6	—	-0.8
1925	Phi A	19	12	.613	46	**33**	15-2	1	252.2	263	118	8	6	95	95	3.49	133	.268	.336	88-1-7	.205	-3	105	31	—	3.2
1926	Phi A	3	5	.375	12	10	2	0	57	66	34	0	0	22	13	4.11	102	.289	.352	17-0-1	.059	-2	81	0	—	-0.2
	Bos A	6	10	.375	21	18	6-1	0	113	135	66	0	2	33	34	4.46	91	.311	.362	34-0-1	.206	-0	84	-5	—	-0.6
	Year	9	15	.375	33	28	8-1	0	170	201	100	0	2	55	47	4.34	95	.304	.359	51-0-2	.157	-2	83	-6	—	-0.8
1927	Bos A	14	21	.400	44	27	11-1	1	217.2	253	127	8	9	66	77	4.18	101	.298	.355	66-0-6	.121	-5	75	-2	—	-0.7
1928	Bos A	8	11	.421	27	15	4-1	1	128.1	141	74	5	2	33	37	4.63	89	.287	.335	36-0-5	.139	-3	64	-6	—	-1.1
Total	9	95	135	.413	349	228	89-7	16	1750.1	1963	1006	75	41	630	644	4.25	100	.290	.354	565-1-37	.145	-40	84	4	—	-3.2

YEAR	TM LG	W	L	PCT	G	GS	CG-SHO	SV-BS	IP	H	R	HR	HB	BB-IB	SO	ERA	AERA	OAV	OOB	AB-HR-SH	AVG	PB	SUP	APR	DL	PW
HARRIST, EARL	Earl "Irish"; B8.20.1919 Dubach LA; D9.7.1998 Simsboro LA; BR/TR/6´0˝/178; d8.18																									
1945	Cin N	2	4	.333	14	5	1	0	62.1	60	30	2	1	27	15	3.61	104	.249	.327	15-0-3	.000	-2	59	0	0	-0.2
1947	Chi A	3	8	.273	33	4	0	5	93.2	85	48	3	3	49	55	3.56	103	.248	.347	24-0-2	.208	-0	97	-1	0	-0.1
1948	Chi A	1	3	.250	11	1	0	0	23	23	17	4	3	13	14	5.87	73	.267	.382	4	.000	-1	127	-4	0	-0.7
	Was A	3	3	.500	23	4	0	0	60.2	70	35	1	3	37	21	4.60	94	.293	.394	18	.167	-1	73	-2	0	-0.3
	Year	4	6	.400	34	5	0	0	83.2	93	52	5	6	50	35	4.95	87	.286	.391	22	.136	-2	84	-6	0	-1.0
1952	StL A	2	8	.200	36	9	1	5	116.2	119	61	7	10	47	49	4.01	98	.269	.352	31-0-4	.097	-2	67	-2	0	-0.4
1953	Chi A	1	0	1.000	7	0	0	0	8.1	9	7	1	0	5	1	7.56	53	.290	.389	1	.000	-0	—	-3	0	-0.3
	Det A	0	2	.000	8	1	0	0	18.2	25	19	2	0	15	7	8.68	47	.333	.444	3	.000	-0	22	-9	0	-0.8
	Year	1	2	.333	15	1	0	0	27	34	26	3	0	20	8	8.33	49	.321	.429	4	.000	-0	22	-12	0	-1.1
Total	5	12	28	.300	132	24	2	10	383.1	391	217	20	20	193	162	4.34	90	.268	.361	96-0-9	.115	-7	72	-21	0	-2.8
HARSHMAN, JACK	John Elvin; B7.12.1927 San Diego CA; BL/TL/6´2˝/(185–190); d9.16.1948																									
1952	NY N	0	2	.000	2	2	0	0	6.1	12	10	2	0	6	6	14.21	26	.429	.529	2	.000	-0*	48	-7	0	-1.0
1954	Chi A	14	8	.636	35	21	9-4	1	177	157	61	7	5	96	134	2.95	127	.238	.339	56-2-3	.143	3*	106	17	0	2.4
1955	Chi A	11	7	.611	32	23	9	0	179.1	144	74	16	4	97-3	116	3.36	117	.224	.327	60-2-5	.183	4	122	11	0	1.3
1956	Chi A	15	11	.577	34	30	15-4	0	226.2	183	85	14	3	102-4	143	3.10	132	.221	.305	71-6-4	.169	6*	98	26	0	3.3
1957	Chi A	8	8	.500	30	26	6	1	151.1	142	78	16	5	82-2	83	4.10	91	.250	.344	45-2-2	.222	5	108	-8	0	-0.3
1958	Bal A	12	15	.444	34	29	17-3	4	236.1	204	89	20	3	75-1	161	2.89	124	.231	.292	82-6-1	.195	8*	67	17	0	3.3
1959	Bal A	0	6	.000	14	8	0	0	47.1	58	39	6	2	28-5	24	6.85	55	.319	.409	10-1-0	.200	1*	67	-16	0	-1.5
	Bos A	2	3	.400	8	2	0	0	24.2	29	19	2	0	10-0	14	6.57	62	.284	.348	7-0-1	.143	0*	54	-6	0	-1.1
	Cle A	5	1	.833	13	6	5-1	1	66	46	21	6	0	13-0	35	2.59	142	.179	.218	34	.206	2*	128	9	0	1.0
	Year	7	10	.412	35	16	5-1	1	138	133	79	14	2	51-5	73	4.76	79	.246	.311	51-1-1	.196	3	87	-14	0	-1.6
1960	Cle A	2	4	.333	15	8	0	0	54.1	50	32	7	0	30-2	25	3.98	94	.243	.333	17-0-2	.176	-0	106	-4	86	-0.4
Total	8	69	65	.515	217	155	61-12	7	1169.1	1025	508	96	22	539-17	741	3.50	109	.235	.320	384-19-18	.182	29	98	39	86	7.0
HARSTAD, OSCAR	Oscar Theander; B5.24.1892 Parkland WA; D11.14.1985 Corvallis OR; BR/TR/6´0˝/174; d4.23																									
1915	Cle A	3	5	.375	32	7	4	1	82	81	45	1	1	35	35	3.40	90	.270	.348	16-0-1	.125	-1	102	-4	—	-0.4
HART, BILLY	Robert Lee; B5.16.1866 Palmyra MO; D5.14.1944 Hannibal MO; 5´8˝/?; d7.13																									
1890	StL AA	12	8	.600	26	24	20	0	201.1	188	111	6	16	66	95	3.67	118	.240	.312	78-1	.192	-1*	92	17	—	1.1
HART, BILL	William Franklin; B7.19.1865 Louisville KY; D9.19.1936 Cincinnati OH; TR/5´10˝/163; d7.26; U2																									
1886	Phi AA	9	13	.409	22	22	22-2	0	186	183	144	7	7	66	78	3.19	110	.234	.299	73	.137	-5	79	-2	—	-0.6
1887	Phi AA	1	2	.333	3	3	3	0	26	28	22	1	1	17	4	4.50	95	.272	.380	13	.077	-2	99	-2	—	-0.3
1892	Bro N	9	12	.429	28	23	16-2	1	195	188	109	3	7	96	65	3.28	97	.243	.332	125-2	.192	.3*	97	-5	—	-0.1
1895	Pit N	14	17	.452	36	29	24	1	261.2	293	186	4	15	135	85	4.75	95	.279	.369	106-0-3	.236	-2	88	-1	—	0.0
1896	StL N	12	29	.293	42	41	37	0	336	411	271	11	15	141	65	5.12	85	.299	.370	161-0-4	.186	-5*	72	-31	—	-3.0
1897	StL N	9	27	.250	39	38	31	0	294.2	395	292	10	16	148	67	6.26	70	.318	.398	156-2-0	.250	-1*	76	-62	—	-5.4
1898	Pit N	5	9	.357	16	15	13-1	1	125	141	81	4	7	44	19	4.82	74	.282	.348	50	.240	0	64	-14	—	-1.3
1901	Cle A	7	11	.389	20	19	16	0	157.2	180	109	3	10	57	48	3.77	94	.283	.352	64-0-1	.219	-2	83	-7	—	-0.7
Total	8	66	120	.355	206	190	162-5	3	1582	1819	1214	43	78	704	431	4.65	86	.282	.359	748-4-8	.207	-14	80	-124	—	-11.4
HARTENSTEIN, CHUCK	Charles Oscar "Twiggy"; B5.26.1942 Seguin TX; BR/TR/5´11˝/165; d9.11.1965; C4; Col Texas																									
1966	Chi N	0	0	ø	5	0	0	0	9.1	8	2	0	1	3-0	4	1.93	191	.222	.300	0	ø	0	—	2	0	0.1
1967	Chi N	9	5	.643	45	0	0	10	73	74	27	4	1	17-7	20	3.08	115	.278	.321	16-0-1	.063	-1	—	4	0	0.7
1968	Chi N	2	4	.333	28	0	0	1	35.2	41	19	3	1	11-2	17	4.54	69	.291	.346	2	.000	-0	—	-5	0	-0.9
1969	Pit N	5	4	.556	56	0	0	10-3	95.2	84	42	9	4	27-3	44	3.95	88	.241	.300	14-0-1	.071	-1	—	-3	0	-0.3
1970	Pit N	1	1	.500	17	0	0	1-0	23.2	25	15	3	0	8-4	14	4.56	87	.278	.333	1	.000	-0	—	-2	0	-0.2
	StL N	0	0	ø	6	0	0	0-1	13.1	24	13	1	0	5-0	9	8.78	47	.375	.414	2	.000	0	—	-6	0	-0.3
	Year	1	1	.500	23	0	0	1-1	37	49	28	4	0	13-4	23	6.08	66	.318	.367	3	.000	-0	—	-8	0	-0.5
	Bos A	0	3	.000	17	0	0	1-2	19	21	17	6	1	12-5	12	8.05	49	.288	.395	2	.000	0	—	-7	0	-1.1
1977	Tor A	0	2	.000	13	0	0	0-1	27.1	40	22	8	1	6-0	15	6.59	65	.348	.385	0	ø	0	—	-7	0	-0.4
Total	6	17	19	.472	187	0	0	23-7	297	317	157	34	9	89-21	135	4.52	81	.280	.335	37-0-2	.054	-2	—	-24	0	-2.4
HARTER, FRANK	Franklin Pierce "Chief"; B9.19.1886 Keyesport IL; D4.14.1959 Breese IL; BR/TR/5´11˝/165; d8.31																									
1912	Cin N	1	2	.333	6	3	1	0	29.1	25	16	1	0	11	12	3.07	110	.234	.305	11	.091	-1	44	0	—	-0.1
1913	Cin N	1	1	.500	17	2	0	0	46.2	47	23	3	0	19	10	3.86	84	.272	.344	14	.143	-1	116	-2	—	-0.2
1914	Ind F	1	2	.333	6	1	1	0	24.2	33	12	0	0	7	8	4.01	78	.330	.374	8	.000	-1	154	-1	—	-0.3
Total	3	3	5	.375	29	6	2	0	100.2	105	51	4	0	37	30	3.67	89	.276	.341	33	.091	-3	86	-3	—	-0.6
HARTGRAVES, DEAN	Dean Charles; B8.12.1966 Bakersfield CA; BR/TL/6´0˝/185; [HouN87 20/522]; d5.3; Col Cal St.–Fresno																									
1995	Hou N	2	0	1.000	40	0	0	0-3	36.1	30	14	2	0	16-2	24	3.22	120	.227	.309	2-0-1	.000	-0	—	3	0	0.1
1996	Hou N	0	0	ø	19	0	0	0-0	19	18	11	1	1	16-3	16	5.21	74	.257	.398	0-0-1	ø	0	—	-2	0	-0.1
	Atl N	1	0	1.000	20	0	0	0-0	18.2	16	10	3	1	7-0	14	4.34	103	.232	.308	1	.000	-0	—	0	0	0.0
	Year	1	0	1.000	39	0	0	0-0	37.2	34	21	4	2	23-3	30	4.78	87	.245	.355	1-0-1	.000	-0	—	-2	0	-0.1
1998	SF N	0	0	ø	5	0	0	0-0	5.2	10	7	1	0	4-0	4	9.53	42	.385	.438	0	ø	0	—	-4	0	-0.2
Total	3	3	0	1.000	84	0	0	0-3	79.2	74	42	7	2	43-5	58	4.41	91	.249	.343	3-0-2	.000	-0	—	-3	0	-0.2
HARTLEY, MIKE	Michael Edward; B8.31.1961 Hawthorne CA; BR/TR/6´1˝/(185–197); d9.10; Col Grossmont (CA) JC																									
1989	LA N	0	1	.000	5	0	0	0-1	6	2	1	0	0	0-0	4	1.50	229	.100	.100	1	.000	-0	—	1	0	0.2
1990	LA N	6	3	.667	32	6	1-1	1-1	79.1	58	32	7	2	30-2	76	2.95	125	.200	.279	13-0-3	.077	-1	82	6	0	0.5
1991	LA N	2	0	1.000	40	0	0	1-0	57	53	29	7	3	37-7	44	4.42	82	.245	.362	4	.000	-0	—	-4	0	-0.3
	Phi N	2	1	.667	18	0	0	1-2	26.1	21	11	4	3	10-1	19	3.76	98	.219	.312	1	.000	-0	—	0	0	0.0
	Year	4	1	.800	58	0	0	2-2	83.1	74	40	11	6	47-8	63	4.21	86	.237	.347	5	.000	-1	—	-4	0	-0.3
1992	Phi N	7	6	.538	46	0	0	0-4	55	54	23	5	2	23-6	53	3.44	102	.255	.332	4	.000	-0*	—	0	37	0.0
1993	Min A	1	2	.333	53	0	0	1-2	81	86	38	4	7	36-3	57	4.00	110	.281	.363	0	ø	0	—	4	0	0.1
1995	Bos A	0	0	ø	5	0	0	0-0	7	8	7	1	2	2-0	2	9.00	54	.308	.375	0	ø	0	—	-3	0	-0.1
	Bal A	1	0	1.000	3	0	0	0-0	7	5	1	0	0	1-0	4	1.29	372	.217	.250	0	ø	0	—	3	0	0.4
	Year	1	0	1.000	8	0	0	0-0	14	13	8	1	2	3-0	6	5.14	94	.265	.321	0	ø	0	—	0	0	0.3
Total	6	19	13	.594	202	6	1-1	4-10	318.2	287	142	28	19	139-19	259	3.70	105	.241	.328	23-0-3	.043	-2	82	7	37	0.8
HARTMAN, CHARLIE	Charles Otto; B8.10.1888 Los Angeles CA; D10.22.1960 Los Angeles CA; TL; d6.24																									
1908	Bos A	0	0	ø	1	0	0	0	2	1	1	0	0	2	1	4.50	55	.143	.333	0	ø	0	—	0	—	0.0
HARTMAN, BOB	Robert Louis; B8.28.1937 Kenosha WI; BR/TL/5´11˝/(185–195); d4.26																									
1959	Mil N	0	0	ø	3	0	0	0	1.2	6	5	0	0	2-0	1	27.00	13	.545	.615	0	ø	0	—	-4	0	-0.2
1962	Cle A	0	1	.000	8	2	0	0	17.1	14	10	1	0	8-0	11	3.12	124	.209	.289	7	.000	-1	104	0	0	-0.1
Total	2	0	1	.000	11	2	0	0	19	20	15	1	0	10-0	12	5.21	74	.256	.337	7	.000	-1	104	-4	0	-0.3
HARTRANFT, RAY	Raymond Joseph; B9.19.1890 Quakertown PA; D2.10.1955 Spring City PA; BL/TL/6´1˝/195; d6.16																									
1913	Phi N	0	0	ø	1	0	0	0	1	3	1	0	0	1	1	9.00	37	.500	.571	0	ø	0	—	-1	—	0.0
HARTSOCK, JEFF	Jeffrey Roger; B11.19.1966 Fairfield OH; BR/TR/6´0˝/190; [LAN88 7/166]; d9.12; Col North Carolina St.																									
1992	Chi N	0	0	ø	4	0	0	0-0	9.1	15	7	2	0	4-0	6	6.75	54	.375	.422	2	.000	-0	—	-3	0	-0.2
HARTUNG, CLINT	Clinton Clarence "Floppy","The Hondo Hurricane"; B8.10.1922 Hondo TX; BR/TR/6´4˝/(200–215); d4.15; ▲																									
1947	NY N	9	7	.563	23	20	8-1	0	138	140	76	15	2	69	54	4.57	89	.263	.350	94-4-0	.309	9*	107	-6	0	0.3
1948	NY N	8	8	.500	36	19	6-2	1	153.1	146	89	15	5	72	42	4.75	83	.258	.347	56	.179	2*	123	-11	0	-0.9
1949	NY N	9	11	.450	33	25	8	0	154.2	156	98	17	4	86	48	5.00	80	.260	.357	63-4-0	.190	4*	114	-16	0	-1.4
1950	NY N	3	3	.500	20	8	1	0	65.1	87	56	10	2	44	23	6.61	62	.326	.425	43-3-0	.302	4*	108	-19	0	-1.0
Total	4	29	29	.500	112	72	23-3	1	511.1	529	319	57	13	271	167	5.02	80	.269	.361	256-11-0	.250	19	114	-52	0	-3.0

YEAR	TM LG	W	L	PCT	G	GS	CG-SHO	SV-BS	IP	H	R	HR	HB	BB-IB	SO	ERA	AERA	OAV	OOB	AB-HR-SH	AVG	PB	SUP	APR	DL	PW
HARTZELL, PAUL	Paul Franklin; B11.2.1953 Bloomsburg PA; BR/TR/6´5˝/200; [AnaA75 10/217]; d4.10; Col Lehigh																									
1976	Cal A	7	4	.636	37	15	7-2	2-1	166	166	64	6	10	43-5	51	2.77	121	.266	.321	0	ø	0	119	9	0	0.6
1977	Cal A	8	12	.400	41	23	6	4-0	189.1	200	92	14	4	38-6	79	3.57	110	.274	.309	0	ø	0	97	6	0	0.6
1978	Cal A	6	10	.375	54	12	5	6-2	157	168	67	8	5	41-9	55	3.44	106	.278	.328	0	ø	0	72	4	0	0.4
1979	Min A	6	10	.375	28	26	4	0-0	163	193	102	18	4	44-4	44	5.36	82	.301	.346	0	ø	0	92	-15	25	-1.2
1980	Bal A	0	2	.000	6	0	0	0-0	17.2	22	14	3	0	9-2	5	6.62	60	.310	.387	0	ø	0	—	-5	0	-0.5
1984	Mil A	0	1	.000	4	1	0	0-0	10.1	17	11	0	0	6-0	3	7.84	50	.370	.426	0	ø	0	70	-5	0	-0.4
Total	6	27	39	.409	170	77	22-2	12-3	703.1	766	350	49	23	181-26	237	3.90	98	.282	.329	0	ø	0	97	-6	25	-0.5
HARVEY, BRYAN	Bryan Stanley; B6.2.1963 Soddy–Daisy TN; BR/TR/6´2˝/(190–215); d5.16; Col North Carolina–Charlotte; [DL 1996 Cal A 182, 1997 Atl N 96]																									
1987	Cal A	0	0	ø	3	0	0	0-0	5	6	0	0	0	2-0	3	0.00	ø	.300	.364	0	ø	0	—	2	0	0.1
1988	Cal A	7	5	.583	50	0	0	17-6	76	59	22	4	1	20-6	67	2.13	182	.214	.267	0	ø	0	—	14	0	2.6
1989	Cal A	3	3	.500	51	0	0	25-7	55	36	21	6	0	41-1	78	3.44	111	.183	.321	0	ø	0	—	3	0	0.6
1990	Cal A	4	4	.500	54	0	0	25-6	64.1	45	24	4	0	35-6	82	3.22	119	.201	.304	0	ø	0	—	6	0	1.0
1991	Cal A☆	2	4	.333	67	0	0	**46**-6	78.2	51	20	6	1	17-3	101	1.60	257	.178	.225	0	ø	0	—	20	0	3.4
1992	Cal A	0	4	.000	25	0	0	13-3	28.2	22	12	4	0	11-1	34	2.83	142	.208	.275	0	ø	0	—	3	111	0.5
1993	Fla N★	1	5	.167	59	0	0	45-4	69	45	14	4	0	13-2	73	1.70	258	.186	.222	0	ø	0	—	19	0	3.7
1994	Fla N	0	0	ø	12	0	0	6-0	10.1	12	6	1	0	4-0	10	5.23	85	.279	.340	0	ø	0	—	-1	92	-0.1
1995	Fla N	0	0	ø	1	0	0	0-0	0	2	3	1	0	1-0	0	(3)	ø	1.000	1.000	0	ø	0	—	-3	156	-0.2
Total	9	17	25	.405	322	0	0	177-32	387	278	122	30	2	144-19	448	2.49	162	.199	.271	0	ø	0	—	63	637	11.6
HARVEY, ZAZA	Ervin King; B1.5.1879 Saratoga CA; D6.3.1954 Santa Monica CA; BL/TL/6´0˝/190; d5.3; ▲																									
1900	Chi N	0	0	ø	1	0	0	0	4	3	0	0	0	1	0	0.00	ø	.214	.267	3	.000	-1*	—	2	—	0.0
1901	Chi A	3	7	.300	16	9	5	1	92	91	59	2	5	34	27	3.62	96	.255	.328	40-0-2	.250	2*	108	-2	—	0.1
Total	2	3	7	.300	17	9	5	1	96	94	59	2	5	35	27	3.47	101	.253	.326	43-0-2	.233	2	108	0	—	0.1
HARVILLE, CHAD	Chad Ashley; B9.16.1976 Selmer TN; BR/TR/5´9˝/(180–186); [OakA97 2/63]; d6.23; Col Memphis																									
1999	Oak A	0	2	.000	15	0	0	0-0	14.1	18	11	2	0	10-1	15	6.91	69	.310	.406	0	ø	0	—	-3	0	-0.4
2001	Oak A	0	0	ø	3	0	0	0-0	3	2	0	0	0	0-0	2	0.00	ø	.182	.182	0	ø	0	—	1	69	0.1
2003	Oak A	1	0	1.000	21	0	0	1-0	21.2	25	15	3	1	17-1	18	5.82	79	.294	.413	0	ø	0	—	-3	0	-0.2
2004	Oak A	0	0	ø	3	0	0	0-0	2.2	2	1	0	0	1-0	0	3.38	137	.200	.273	0	ø	0	—	0	0	0.0
	†Hou N	3	2	.600	56	0	0	0-4	53	54	35	8	2	26-2	46	4.75	92	.260	.347	1	.000	-0	—	-4	25	-0.4
2005	Hou N	0	2	.000	37	0	0	0-1	38.1	36	21	7	4	24-1	33	4.46	95	.254	.372	1	.000	-0	—	-1	0	-0.1
	Bos A	0	1	.000	8	0	0	0-0	7	7	5	1	1	3-0	3	6.43	71	.269	.367	0	ø	0	—	-1	0	-0.1
2006	TB A	0	2	.000	32	0	0	1-1	41	44	27	5	0	22-2	30	5.93	79	.277	.363	0	ø	0	—	-5	0	-0.1
Total	6	4	9	.308	175	0	0	2-6	181	188	115	26	8	103-7	147	5.22	86	.269	.367	2	.000	-0	—	-16	94	-1.2
HASEGAWA, SHIGETOSHI	Shigetoshi; B8.1.1968 Kobe, Japan; BR/TR/5´11˝/(160–180); d4.5																									
1997	Ana A	3	7	.300	50	7	0	0-1	116.2	118	60	14	3	46-6	83	3.93	117	.269	.339	0	ø	0	91	7	0	0.6
1998	Ana A	8	3	.727	61	0	0	5-2	97.1	86	37	14	2	32-2	73	3.14	151	.241	.302	0	ø	0	—	17	0	1.8
1999	Ana A	4	6	.400	64	1	0	2-3	77	80	45	14	2	34-2	44	4.91	100	.276	.352	0	ø	0	0	0	0	0.0
2000	Ana A	10	5	.667	66	0	0	9-9	95.2	100	42	11	2	38-6	59	3.48	148	.270	.339	1	.000	-0	—	16	0	2.4
2001	Ana A	5	6	.455	46	0	0	0-6	55.2	52	28	5	2	20-5	41	4.04	115	.248	.316	0	ø	0	—	3	41	0.5
2002	Sea A	8	3	.727	53	0	0	1-4	70.1	60	26	4	2	30-8	39	3.20	135	.238	.323	0	ø	0	—	9	0	1.3
2003	Sea A★	2	4	.333	63	0	0	16-1	73	62	12	5	0	18-3	32	1.48	293	.235	.284	0	ø	0	—	25	0	2.8
2004	Sea A	4	6	.400	68	0	0	0-5	68	67	42	5	2	31-4	46	5.16	87	.260	.339	0	ø	0	—	-6	0	-0.7
2005	Sea A	1	3	.250	46	0	0	0-1	66.2	66	31	4	3	16-1	30	4.18	100	.259	.307	0	ø	0	—	1	0	0.1
Total	9	45	43	.511	517	8	0	33-32	720.1	691	323	76	18	265-37	447	3.70	125	.256	.324	1	.000	-0	80	72	41	8.8
HASH, HERB	Herbert Howard; B2.13.1911 Woolwine VA; BR/TR/6´1˝/180; d4.19; Col Richmond																									
1940	Bos A	7	7	.500	34	12	3-1	3	120	123	68	11	5	84	36	4.95	91	.266	.385	40-0-3	.175	-0*	103	-4	—	-0.4
1941	Bos A	1	0	1.000	4	0	0	1	8.1	7	5	1	0	7	3	5.40	77	.226	.368	2	.000	-0	—	-1	67	-0.1
Total	2	8	7	.533	38	12	3-1	4	128.1	130	73	12	5	91	39	4.98	90	.264	.384	42-0-3	.167	-1	103	-5	67	-0.5
HASSLER, ANDY	Andrew Earl; B10.18.1951 Texas City TX; BL/TL/6´5˝/(215–220); [AnaA69 25/579]; d5.30																									
1971	Cal A	0	3	.000	6	4	0	0-0	18.2	25	10	0	1	15-2	13	3.86	84	.333	.446	5-0-1	.000	-1	48	-2	0	-0.3
1973	Cal A	0	4	.000	7	4	1	0-0	31.2	33	23	0	3	19-0	19	3.69	97	.262	.369	0	ø	0	81	-4	0	-0.5
1974	Cal A	7	11	.389	23	22	10-2	1-0	162	132	64	10	9	79-2	76	2.61	133	.225	.325	0	ø	0	103	12	0	1.4
1975	Cal A	3	12	.200	30	18	6-1	0-0	133.1	158	94	12	6	53-0	82	5.94	60	.303	.369	0	ø	0	100	-34	0	-3.2
1976	Cal A	0	6	.000	14	4	0	0-0	47.1	50	31	3	0	17-2	16	5.13	65	.284	.342	0	ø	0	72	-10	0	-1.1
	†KC A	5	6	.455	19	14	4-1	0-1	99.2	89	37	2	0	39-0	45	2.89	121	.242	.311	0	ø	0	79	7	0	0.8
	Year	5	12	.294	33	18	4-1	0-1	147	139	68	5	0	56-2	61	3.61	96	.256	.321	0	ø	0	78	-3	0	-0.3
1977	†KC A	9	6	.600	29	27	3-1	0-0	156.1	166	88	7	5	75-3	83	4.20	96	.270	.352	0	ø	0*	126	-5	28	-0.4
1978	KC A	1	4	.200	11	9	1	0-0	58.1	76	36	1	2	24-0	26	4.32	89	.317	.381	0	ø	0	110	-5	34	-0.4
	Bos A	2	1	.667	13	2	0	1-0	30	38	13	0	0	13-2	23	3.00	137	.302	.367	0	ø	0	142	3	0	0.3
	Year	3	5	.375	24	11	1	1-0	88.1	114	49	1	2	37-2	49	3.87	101	.311	.376	0	ø	0	114	-2	0	-0.1
1979	Bos A	1	2	.333	8	0	0	0-0	15.1	23	17	0	1	7-0	7	8.80	51	.365	.431	0	ø	0	—	-7	0	-1.2
	NY N	4	5	.444	29	8	1	4-0	80.1	74	35	5	0	42-8	53	3.70	100	.252	.344	22	.000	-2	80	1	0	-0.1
1980	Pit N	0	0	ø	6	0	0	0-0	11.2	9	6	2	0	4-0	4	3.86	96	.243	.310	2	.000	-0	—	0	0	0.0
	Cal A	5	1	.833	41	0	0	10-2	83	67	25	8	1	37-8	75	2.49	159	.214	.298	0	ø	0	—	14	0	1.3
1981	Cal A	4	3	.571	42	0	0	5-2	75.2	72	29	8	0	33-8	44	3.21	114	.262	.339	0	ø	0	—	5	0	0.5
1982	†Cal A	2	1	.667	54	0	0	4-2	71.1	58	24	5	4	40-5	38	2.78	147	.232	.343	0	ø	0	—	10	0	0.6
1983	Cal A	0	5	.000	42	0	0	4-3	36.1	42	22	2	0	17-8	20	5.45	74	.302	.378	0	ø	0	—	-5	0	-0.6
1984	StL N	1	0	1.000	3	0	0	0-0	2.1	4	3	2	0	2-1	1	11.57	30	.364	.462	0	ø	0	—	-2	0	-0.4
1985	StL N	0	1	.000	10	0	0	0-0	10	9	5	0	0	4-0	5	1.80	199	.225	.289	0	ø	0	—	1	0	0.1
Total	14	44	71	.383	387	112	26-5	29-10	1123.1	1125	562	67	32	520-49	630	3.83	98	.264	.346	29-0-1	.000	-3	100	-21	62	-3.2
HASTINGS, CHARLIE	Charles Morton; B11.11.1870 Ironton OH; D8.3.1934 Parkersburg WV; 5´11˝/179; d5.3																									
1893	Cle N	4	5	.444	15	9	6	1	92	128	81	5	5	33	14	4.70	104	.320	.379	39	.179	0*	100	0	—	0.0
1896	Pit N	5	10	.333	17	13	9	1	104	126	86	1	7	44	19	5.88	71	.296	.372	37	.216	-0	79	-18	—	-1.9
1897	Pit N	5	4	.556	16	10	9	0	118	138	84	3	7	47	42	4.58	91	.289	.362	43-1-1	.233	3	108	-6	—	-0.1
1898	Pit N	4	10	.286	19	13	12	0	137.1	142	76	2	10	52	40	3.41	104	.265	.341	43-0-1	.233	2	64	1	—	0.3
Total	4	18	29	.383	67	45	36	2	451.1	534	327	11	29	176	115	4.55	91	.291	.362	162-1-2	.216	5	87	-23	—	-1.7
HASTY, BOB	Robert Keller; B5.3.1896 Canton GA; D5.28.1972 Dallas GA; BR/TR/6´3˝/210; d9.11																									
1919	Phi A	0	2	.000	2	2	1	0	12	15	10	1	0	4	5	5.25	65	.306	.358	3-0-1	.333	0	46	-3	—	-0.4
1920	Phi A	1	3	.250	19	4	1	0	71.2	91	53	5	0	28	12	5.02	80	.323	.384	24	.250	0	94	-7	—	-0.2
1921	Phi A	5	16	.238	35	22	9	0	179.1	238	120	8	2	40	46	4.87	92	.331	.368	68-0-1	.294	2	63	-8	—	-0.5
1922	Phi A	9	14	.391	28	26	14-1	0	192.1	225	110	20	3	41	33	4.26	100	.298	.336	75-1-0	.200	-2	95	-1	—	-0.3
1923	Phi A	13	15	.464	44	36	10-1	1	243.1	274	146	11	9	72	56	4.44	93	.291	.347	88-0-6	.193	-3	82	-8	—	-1.1
1924	Phi A	1	3	.250	18	4	0	0	52.2	57	36	4	1	30	15	5.64	76	.282	.378	13	.077	-1	59	-7	—	-0.5
Total	6	29	53	.354	146	94	35-2	1	751.1	900	475	49	15	215	167	4.65	91	.305	.355	271-1-8	.221	-3	80	-34	—	-3.0
HATFIELD, GIL	Gilbert "Colonel"; B1.27.1855 Hoboken NJ; D5.26.1921 Hoboken NJ; TR/5´9.5˝/168; d9.24.1885; b–John; ▲																									
1889	NY N	2	4	.333	6	5	5	0	52	53	43	2	1	25	28	3.98	99	.256	.339	125-1	.184	-0*	163	-2	—	-0.2
1890	NY P	1	1	.500	3	0	0	1	7.2	8	8	1	1	4	3	3.52	129	.258	.361	287-2	.279	0*	—	0	—	0.0
1891	Was AA	0	0	ø	4	0	0	0	18	29	28	1	0	14	3	11.00	34	.349	.443	500-1	.256	1*	—	-12	—	-0.5
Total	3	3	5	.375	13	5	5	1	77.2	90	79	4	2	43	34	5.56	71	.280	.369	912-4	.253	1	163	-14	—	-0.7
HATHAWAY, HILLY	Hillary Houston; B9.12.1969 Jacksonville FL; BL/TL/6´4˝/195; [CalA89 35/903]; d9.8; Col Manatee (FL) CC																									
1992	Cal A	0	0	ø	2	1	0	0-0	5.2	8	5	1	0	3-0	1	7.94	51	.333	.393	0	ø	0	91	-2	0	-0.1
1993	Cal A	4	3	.571	11	11	0	0-0	57.1	71	35	6	5	26-1	11	5.02	90	.326	.405	0	ø	0	98	-3	24	-0.3
Total	2	4	3	.571	13	12	0	0-0	63	79	40	7	5	29-1	12	5.29	85	.326	.404	0	ø	0	97	-5	24	-0.4

YEAR	TM LG	W	L	PCT	G	GS	CG-SHO	SV-BS	IP	H	R	HR	HB	BB-IB	SO	ERA	AERA	OAV	OOB	AB-HR-SH	AVG	PB	SUP	APR	DL	PW
Hathaway, Ray	Ray Wilson; B10.13.1916 Greenville OH; BR/TR/6´0˝/165; d4.20																									
1945	Bro N	0	1	.000	4	1	0	0	9	11	7	1	0	6	3	4.00	94	.297	.395	2	.000	-0	68	-1	0	-0.1
Hatten, Joe	Joseph Hilarian; B11.7.1916 Bancroft IA; D12.16.1988 Redding CA; BR/TL/6´0˝/176; d4.21																									
1946	Bro N	14	11	.560	42	30	13-1	2	222	207	79	10	7	110	85	2.84	119	.253	.347	79-0-4	.076	-6	107	15	0	0.9
1947	†Bro N	17	8	.680	42	32	11-3	0	225.1	211	95	9	5	105	76	3.63	114	.252	.339	83-0-3	.205	0	104	16	0	1.8
1948	Bro N	13	10	.565	42	30	11-1	0	208.2	228	93	9	3	94	73	3.58	112	.283	.360	63-0-8	.206	1*	112	11	0	1.4
1949	†Bro N	12	8	.600	37	29	11-2	2	187.1	194	102	15	2	69	58	4.18	98	.271	.337	67-0-3	.179	-1*	122	-5	0	-0.6
1950	Bro N	2	2	.500	23	8	2-1	0	68.2	82	45	10	0	31	29	4.59	89	.294	.365	18-0-1	.111	-1*	97	-7	0	-0.5
1951	Bro N	1	0	1.000	11	6	0	0	49.1	55	25	3	0	21	22	4.56	86	.281	.350	15-0-1	.133	-1	139	-2	0	-0.2
	Chi N	2	6	.250	23	6	1	0	75.1	82	48	8	1	37	23	5.14	80	.281	.364	17-0-1	.235	0	58	-8	0	-0.8
	Year	3	6	.333	34	12	1	0	124.2	137	73	11	1	58	45	4.91	82	.281	.358	32-0-2	.188	-1	97	-9	0	-1.0
1952	Chi N	4	4	.500	13	8	2	0	50.1	65	35	6	1	25	15	6.08	63	.314	.391	15-0-1	.067	-1*	75	-10	0	-1.5
Total	7	65	49	.570	233	149	51-8	4	1087	1124	522	70	19	492	381	3.87	101	.271	.351	357-0-22	.160	-8	107	10	0	0.5
Hatter, Clyde	Clyde Melno; B8.7.1908 Poplar Hill KY; D10.16.1937 Yosemite KY; BR/TL/5´11˝/170; d4.23; Col Eastern Kentucky																									
1935	Det A	0	0	ø	8	2	0	0	33.1	44	33	2	1	30	15	7.56	55	.319	.444	10-0-1	.300	0	156	-14	—	-0.6
1937	Det A	1	0	1.000	3	0	0	0	9.1	17	12	0	1	11	4	11.57	40	.415	.547	3	.000	-0	—	-6	—	-0.5
Total	2	1	0	1.000	11	2	0	0	42.2	61	45	2	2	41	19	8.44	51	.341	.468	13-0-1	.231	0	156	-20	—	-1.1
Haughey, Chris	Christopher Francis "Bud"; B10.3.1925 Astoria NY; BR/TR/6´1˝/180; d10.3; Mil 1944–45																									
1943	Bro N	0	1	.000	1	0	0	0	7	5	6	0	0	10	0	3.86	87	.238	.484	3	.000	-0	—	-2	0	-0.2
Haught, Gary	Gary Allen; B9.29.1970 Tacoma WA; BB/TR/6´1˝/180; [OakA92 22/620]; d7.16; Col Louisiana–Lafayette																									
1997	Oak A	0	0	ø	6	0	0	0-0	11.1	12	9	3	2	6-0	11	7.15	64	.279	.385	0	ø	0	—	-3	0	-0.1
Haugstad, Phil	Philip Donald; B2.23.1924 Black River Falls WI; D10.21.1998 Black River Falls WI; BR/TR/6´2˝/165; d9.1																									
1947	Bro N	1	0	1.000	6	1	0	0	12.2	14	4	1	0	4	4	2.84	145	.298	.353	2	.000	-0	43	2	0	0.1
1948	Bro N	0	0	ø	1	0	0	0	1	1	0	0	0	0	0	0.00	ø	.333	.333	0	ø	0	—	0	0	0.0
1951	Bro N	0	1	.000	21	1	0	0	30.2	28	25	4	3	24	22	6.46	61	.233	.374	1	.000	0	270	-9	0	-0.4
1952	Cin N	0	0	ø	9	0	0	0	12	8	9	1	1	13	2	6.75	56	.190	.393	1	.000	-0	—	-4	0	-0.2
Total	4	1	1	.500	37	2	0	0	56.1	51	38	6	4	41	28	5.59	70	.241	.374	4	.000	-0	157	-11	0	-0.5
Hausman, Tom	Thomas Matthew; B3.31.1953 Mobridge SD; BR/TR/6´5˝/(190–200); [MilA71 10/224]; d4.26																									
1975	Mil A	3	6	.333	29	9	1	0-0	112	110	57	7	6	47-7	46	4.10	94	.258	.338	0	ø	0	76	-2	0	-0.1
1976	Mil A	0	0	ø	3	0	0	0-0	3.1	3	2	0	0	3-1	1	5.40	65	.250	.400	0	ø	0	—	-1	0	0.0
1978	NY N	3	3	.500	10	10	0	0-0	51.2	58	28	6	1	9-1	16	4.70	75	.287	.318	17-0-1	.176	0	94	-6	0	-0.6
1979	NY N	2	6	.250	19	10	1	2-1	78.2	65	25	6	4	19-1	33	2.75	135	.226	.282	26-0-1	.115	-1	69	9	0	0.8
1980	NY N	6	5	.545	55	4	0	1-0	122	125	63	12	3	26-8	53	3.98	91	.266	.307	16-0-1	.063	-1	87	-6	0	-0.6
1981	NY N	0	1	.000	20	0	0	0-0	33	28	8	2	0	7-1	13	2.18	162	.235	.273	2	.000	0	—	6	58	0.3
1982	NY N	1	2	.333	21	0	0	0-0	36.2	44	26	4	2	6-1	16	4.42	83	.295	.323	2	.000	-0	—	-5	85	-0.4
	Atl N	0	0	ø	3	0	0	0-0	3.2	6	2	0	0	4-2	2	4.91	75	.500	.588	0	ø	0	—	0	0	0.0
	Year	1	2	.333	24	0	0	0-0	40.1	50	28	4	2	10-3	18	4.46	82	.311	.348	2	.000	-0	—	-6	0	-0.4
Total	7	15	23	.395	160	33	2	3-1	441	439	211	37	16	121-22	180	3.80	97	.262	.315	63-0-3	.111	-2	80	-5	143	-0.6
Hausmann, Clem	Clemens Raymond; B8.17.1919 Houston TX; D8.29.1972 Baytown TX; BR/TR/5´9˝/165; d4.28																									
1944	Bos A	4	7	.364	32	12	3	2	137	139	55	6	3	69	43	3.42	99	.266	.355	38-0-1	.079	-3	74	2	0	-0.1
1945	Bos A	5	7	.417	31	13	4-2	2	125	131	77	5	2	60	30	5.04	68	.270	.352	39	.103	-3	65	-21	0	-2.1
1949	Phi A	0	0	ø	1	0	0	0	1	0	1	0	0	2	0	9.00	46	.000	.500	0	ø	0	—	0	0	0.0
Total	3	9	14	.391	64	25	7-2	4	263	270	133	11	5	131	73	4.21	81	.267	.354	77-0-1	.091	-5	69	-19	0	-2.2
Havens, Brad	Bradley David; B11.17.1959 Highland Park MI; BL/TL/6´1˝/(180–196); [CalA77 8/189]; d6.5																									
1981	Min A	3	6	.333	14	12	1-1	0-0	78	76	33	6	1	24-4	43	3.58	110	.257	.314	0	ø	0	61	4	0	0.4
1982	Min A	10	14	.417	33	32	4-1	0-1	208.2	201	112	32	0	80-4	129	4.31	99	.250	.317	0	ø	0	85	-3	0	-0.4
1983	Min A	5	8	.385	16	14	1	0-0	80.1	110	75	11	0	38-3	40	8.18	52	.333	.393	0	ø	0	111	-31	0	-4.0
1985	Bal A	0	1	.000	8	1	0	0-0	14.1	20	14	4	0	10-1	19	8.79	46	.333	.429	0	ø	0	45	-7	0	-0.4
1986	Bal A	3	3	.500	46	0	0	1-1	71	64	37	7	0	29-1	57	4.56	91	.248	.323	0	ø	0	—	-2	0	-0.1
1987	LA N	0	0	ø	31	1	0	1-1	35.1	30	18	2	1	23-11	23	4.33	92	.227	.346	2	.000	-0	91	-1	26	-0.1
1988	LA N	0	0	ø	9	0	0	0-0	9.2	15	5	1	0	4-0	8	4.66	72	.357	.404	1	.000	-0	—	-1	0	0.0
	Cle A	2	3	.400	28	0	0	1-1	57.1	62	22	7	0	17-3	30	3.14	132	.273	.321	0	ø	0	—	6	0	0.5
1989	Cle A	0	0	ø	7	0	0	0-0	13.1	18	6	3	0	7-2	6	4.05	98	.353	.417	0	ø	0	—	0	0	0.0
	Det A	1	2	.333	13	1	0	0-1	22.2	28	14	3	3	14-2	15	5.56	69	.308	.409	0	ø	0	0	-4	0	-0.4
	Year	1	2	.333	20	1	0	0-1	36	46	20	6	3	21-4	21	5.00	78	.324	.412	0	ø	0	0	-3	0	-0.4
Total	8	24	37	.393	205	61	6-2	3-5	590.2	624	336	76	5	246-31	370	4.81	86	.272	.341	3	.000	-0	86	-39	26	-4.5
Hawblitzel, Ryan	Ryan Wade; B4.30.1971 West Palm Beach FL; BR/TR/6´2˝/185; [ChiN90 2/63]; d6.9																									
1996	Col N	0	1	.000	8	0	0	0-0	15	18	12	2	0	6-0	7	6.00	87	.290	.348	1	.000	-0	—	-1	0	-0.1
Hawk, Ed	Edward; B2.22.1888 Exeter MO; D3.26.1936 Neosho MO; BL/TR/5´11˝/175; d9.7																									
1911	StL A	0	4	.000	5	4	4	0	37.2	38	18	1	4	8	14	3.35	101	.253	.309	13	.154	-1	16	1	—	0.0
Hawke, Bill	William Victor "Dick"; B4.28.1870 Elsmere DE; D12.11.1902 Wilmington DE; BR/TR/5´8.5˝/169; d7.28																									
1892	StL N	5	5	.500	14	11	10-1	0	97.1	108	59	2	8	45	55	3.70	86	.270	.355	45	.089	-4*	103	-6	—	-0.9
1893	StL N	0	1	.000	1	1	0	0	5.1	9	9	0	0	3	1	5.06	93	.360	.429	3	.333	0	74	-2	—	-0.2
	Bal N	11	16	.407	29	29	22-1	0	225	248	175	8	9	108	69	4.76	100	.271	.354	93-1	.172	-4	90	-2	—	-0.5
	Year	11	17	.393	30	30	22-1	0	230.1	257	184	8	9	111	70	4.77	100	.274	.356	96-1	.177	-4	89	2	—	-0.7
1894	†Bal N	16	9	.640	32	25	17	3	206	264	174	9	12	78	68	5.81	94	.308	.374	92-1-5	.304	2	112	-7	—	-0.5
Total	3	32	31	.508	76	66	49-2	3	533.2	629	417	19	29	234	193	4.98	95	.286	.363	233-2-5	.210	-7	101	-17	—	-2.1
Hawkins, La Troy	La Troy; B12.21.1972 Gary IN; BR/TR/6´5˝/(193–215); [MinA91 7/180]; d4.29																									
1995	Min A	2	3	.400	6	6	1	0-0	27	39	29	3	1	12-0	9	8.67	56	.339	.397	0	ø	0	93	-12	0	-1.6
1996	Min A	1	1	.500	7	6	0	0-0	26.1	42	24	8	0	9-0	24	8.20	63	.372	.415	0	ø	0	129	-8	0	-0.5
1997	Min A	6	12	.333	20	20	0	0-0	103.1	134	71	19	4	47-0	58	5.84	80	.317	.389	1	.000	-0	86	-13	0	-1.8
1998	Min A	7	14	.333	33	33	0	0-0	190.1	227	126	27	5	61-1	105	5.25	91	.299	.350	1	.000	-0	90	-13	0	-1.1
1999	Min A	10	14	.417	33	33	1	0-0	174.1	238	136	29	1	60-2	103	6.66	78	.323	.373	2	.000	-0	80	-26	0	-3.0
2000	Min A	2	5	.286	66	0	0	14-0	87.2	85	34	7	1	32-1	59	3.39	155	.256	.322	1	.000	-0	—	18	0	1.7
2001	Min A	1	5	.167	62	0	0	28-9	51.1	59	34	3	1	39-3	36	5.96	78	.291	.401	0	ø	0	—	-6	0	-1.2
2002	†Min A	6	0	1.000	65	0	0	0-3	80.1	63	23	5	0	15-1	63	2.13	210	.217	.253	0	ø	0	—	20	0	1.3
2003	†Min A	9	3	.750	74	0	0	2-6	77.1	69	20	4	1	15-1	75	1.86	242	.239	.278	0-0-1	ø	0	—	21	0	3.0
2004	Chi N	5	4	.556	77	0	0	25-9	82	72	27	10	2	14-5	69	2.63	168	.233	.269	0	ø	0	—	15	0	2.2
2005	Chi N	1	4	.200	21	0	0	4-4	19	18	9	4	0	7-0	13	3.32	132	.250	.316	0	ø	0	—	1	0	0.3
	SF N	1	4	.200	45	0	0	2-5	37.1	40	18	3	0	17-3	30	4.10	104	.272	.345	0	ø	0	—	1	24	0.1
	Year	2	8	.200	66	0	0	6-9	56.1	58	27	7	0	24-3	43	3.83	112	.265	.336	0	ø	0	—	2	0	0.4
2006	Bal A	3	2	.600	60	0	0	0-4	60.1	73	30	4	0	15-3	27	4.48	101	.300	.338	0	ø	0	—	1	0	0.1
Total	12	54	71	.432	569	98	2	75-40	1016.2	1159	581	126	16	343-20	671	4.75	100	.287	.343	5-0-1	.000	-1	91	-1	24	-0.5
Hawkins, Andy	Melton Andrew; B1.21.1960 Waco TX; BR/TR/6´3˝/(200–223); [SDN78 1/5]; d7.17																									
1982	SD N	2	5	.286	15	10	1	0-0	63.2	66	33	4	2	27-3	25	4.10	84	.274	.345	15-0-3	.000	-2	124	-5	0	-0.7
1983	SD N	5	7	.417	21	19	4-1	0-0	119.2	106	50	8	5	48-4	59	2.93	120	.244	.324	31-0-6	.065	-1	86	5	0	0.4
1984	†SD N	8	9	.471	36	22	2-1	0-0	146	143	90	13	2	72-2	77	4.68	77	.254	.339	41-0-3	.195	0	122	-20	0	-2.1
1985	SD N	18	8	.692	33	33	5-2	0-0	228.2	229	88	18	4	65-8	69	3.15	113	.267	.317	77-0-13	.078	-4	112	12	0	0.8
1986	SD N	10	8	.556	37	35	3-1	0-0	209.1	218	111	24	5	75-7	117	4.30	85	.268	.332	67-0-6	.149	-1	113	-14	0	-1.3
1987	SD N	3	10	.231	24	20	0	0-0	117.2	131	71	16	2	49-2	51	5.05	79	.287	.356	32-0-5	.156	-0	112	-13	34	-1.3
1988	SD N	14	11	.560	33	33	4-2	0-0	217.2	196	88	16	6	76-4	91	3.35	102	.244	.312	62-0-10	.113	-2	83	2	0	-0.1
1989	NY A	15	15	.500	34	34	5-2	0-0	208.1	238	127	23	6	76-6	98	4.80	81	.290	.354	0	ø	0	98	-23	0	-3.0
1990	NY A	5	12	.294	28	26	2-1	0-0	157.2	156	101	20	2	82-3	74	5.37	74	.260	.349	0	ø	0	86	-22	0	-2.2

YEAR	TM LG	W	L	PCT	G	GS	CG-SHO	SV-BS	IP	H	R	HR	HB	BB-IB	SO	ERA	AERA	OAV	OOB	AB-HR-SH	AVG	PB	SUP	APR	DL	PW
1991	NY A	0	2	.000	4	3	0	0-0	12.2	23	15	5	0	6-0	5	9.95	42	.383	.439	0	ø	0	88	-8	0	-0.9
	Oak A	4	4	.500	15	14	1	0-0	77	68	41	5	5	36-0	40	4.79	80	.237	.329	0	ø	0	120	-7	0	-0.7
	Year	4	6	.400	19	17	1	0-0	89.2	91	56	10	5	42-0	45	5.52	71	.262	.348	0	ø	0	115	-14	0	-1.6
Total	10	84	91	.480	280	249	27-10	0-0	1558.1	1574	815	152	39	612-39	706	4.22	87	.265	.335	325-0-46	.117	-8	104	-93	34	-11.1
Hawkins, Wynn	Wynn Firth "Hawk"; B2.20.1936 E.Palestine OH; BR/TR/6´3˝/190; d4.22																									
1960	Cle A	4	4	.500	15	9	1	0	66	68	32	10	1	39-2	39	4.23	88	.269	.366	20-0-1	.100	-1	86	-2	0	-0.3
1961	Cle A	7	9	.438	30	21	3-1	1	133	139	72	16	2	59-1	51	4.06	97	.270	.344	37-0-3	.108	-2	95	-4	0	-0.6
1962	Cle A	1	0	1.000	3	0	0	0	3.2	9	5	1	0	1-0	0	7.36	53	.429	.455	0	ø	0	—	-2	0	-0.4
Total	3	12	13	.480	48	30	4-1	1	202.2	216	109	27	3	99-3	90	4.17	93	.274	.354	57-0-4	.105	-2	93	-8	0	-1.3
Hawley, Pink	Emerson Pink; B12.5.1872 Beaver Dam WI; D9.19.1938 Beaver Dam WI; BL/TR/5´10˝/185; d8.13																									
1892	StL N	6	14	.300	20	20	18	0	166.1	160	116	4	11	63	63	3.19	100	.243	.319	71-1	.169	-2	86	-10	—	-1.3
1893	StL N	5	17	.227	31	24	21	1	227	249	184	5	20	103	73	4.60	103	.270	.356	91	.286	7	80	1	—	0.5
1894	StL N	19	27	.413	53	41	36	0	392.2	481	306	14	21	149	120	4.90	111	.298	.365	163-2-5	.264	2	73	20	—	1.8
1895	Pit N	31	22	.585	**56**	50	44-**4**	1	**444.1**	449	242	7	33	122	142	3.18	142	.258	.319	185-5-3	.308	14*	93	66	—	**7.4**
1896	Pit N	22	21	.512	49	43	37-2	0	378	382	197	2	28	157	137	3.57	118	.260	.343	163-1-3	.239	2*	82	29	—	2.9
1897	Pit N	18	18	.500	40	39	33	0	311.1	362	221	7	26	94	88	4.80	87	.288	.350	130	.231	-2	87	-19	—	-1.8
1898	Cin N	27	11	.711	43	37	32-3	0	331	357	163	5	22	91	69	3.37	114	.273	.331	130-1-5	.185	-4	90	18	—	1.1
1899	Cin N	14	17	.452	34	29	25	1	250.1	289	161	7	20	65	46	4.24	92	.289	.344	101	.218	-1	108	-9	—	-1.1
1900	NY N	18	18	.500	41	38	**34**-2	0	329.1	377	204	7	20	89	80	3.53	103	.287	.341	123-1-4	.203	-2	104	2	—	0.2
1901	Mil A	7	14	.333	26	23	17	0	182.1	228	133	3	9	41	50	4.59	78	.302	.346	73-0-4	.260	2*	77	-18	—	-1.4
Total	10	167	179	.483	393	344	297-11	3	3012.2	3334	1927	61	210	974	868	3.96	107	.277	.342	1230-11-24	.241	15	87	80	—	8.3
Hawley, Scott	Marvin Hiram; B Painesville OH; D4.28.1904 Alliance OH; d9.22																									
1894	Bos N	0	1	.000	1	1	1	0	7	10	6	0	2	7	1	7.71	74	.333	.487	3	.000	-1	50	-1	—	-0.1
Haydel, Hal	John Harold; B7.9.1944 Houma LA; BR/TR/6´0˝/190; d9.7																									
1970	Min A	2	0	1.000	4	0	0	0-0	9	7	3	2	0	4-0	4	3.00	123	.226	.306	3-1-0	.667	2	—	1	0	0.4
1971	Min A	4	2	.667	31	0	0	1-2	40	33	19	3	2	20-1	29	4.27	83	.243	.346	3	.333	0	—	-2	0	-0.3
Total	2	6	2	.750	35	0	0	1-2	49	40	22	5	2	24-1	33	4.04	88	.240	.338	6-1-0	.500	2	—	-1	0	0.1
Hayden, Lefty	Eugene Franklin; B4.14.1935 San Francisco CA; BL/TL/6´2˝/175; d6.26																									
1958	Cin N	0	0	ø	3	0	0	0	3.2	5	2	0	0	1-0	3	4.91	84	.313	.353	0	ø	0	—	0	0	0.0
Hayes, Ben	Ben Joseph; B8.4.1957 Niagara Falls NY; BR/TR/6´1˝/180; d6.25; Col South Florida																									
1982	Cin N	2	0	1.000	26	0	0	2-1	45.2	37	12	3	0	22-5	38	1.97	186	.219	.307	4-0-2	.000	-0	—	8	0	0.3
1983	Cin N	4	6	.400	60	0	0	7-3	69.1	82	53	8	1	37-6	44	6.49	59	.301	.381	5	.000	-1	—	-19	0	-2.9
Total	2	6	6	.500	86	0	0	9-4	115	119	65	11	1	59-11	82	4.70	80	.270	.353	9-0-2	.000	-1	—	-11	0	-2.6
Hayes, Jim	James Millard "Whitey"; B2.25.1912 Montevallo AL; D11.27.1993 Decatur GA; BL/TR/6´1˝/168; d7.13																									
1935	Was A	2	4	.333	7	4	1	0	28	38	28	0	0	23	9	8.36	52	.322	.433	8-0-2	.250	-0	90	-12	—	-2.0
Hayner, Fred	Fred Ames; B11.3.1871 Janesville WI; D1.14.1929 Lake Forest IL; 6´0˝/160; d8.19																									
1890	Pit N	0	0	ø	1	0	0	0	4	7	9	2	0	5	1	13.50	24	.368	.500	2	.000	-0	—	-5	—	-0.2
Haynes, Heath	Heath Burnett; B11.30.1968 Wheeling WV; BR/TR/6´0˝/180; d6.1; Col Western Kentucky																									
1994	Mon N	0	0	ø	4	0	0	0-0	3.2	3	1	0	0	3-0	1	0.00	ø	.231	.353	0	ø	0	—	1	0	0.1
Haynes, Jimmy	Jimmy Wayne; B9.5.1972 LaGrange GA; BR/TR/6´4˝/(175–220); [BalA91 7/186]; d9.13																									
1995	Bal A	2	1	.667	4	3	0	0-0	24	11	6	2	0	12-1	22	2.25	212	.136	.247	0	ø	0	97	7	0	0.8
1996	Bal A	3	6	.333	26	11	0	1-0	89	122	84	14	2	58-1	65	8.29	60	.333	.422	0	ø	0	118	-31	0	-2.5
1997	Oak A	3	6	.333	13	13	0	0-0	73.1	74	38	7	2	40-1	65	4.42	104	.262	.354	2	.000	-0	88	2	0	0.2
1998	Oak A	11	9	.550	33	33	1-1	0-0	194.1	229	124	25	5	88-4	134	5.09	91	.298	.370	3	.000	0	118	-10	0	-0.9
1999	Oak A	7	12	.368	30	25	0	0-0	142	158	112	21	2	80-3	93	6.34	75	.282	.370	4-0-1	.000	-0	89	-26	0	-2.9
2000	Mil N	12	13	.480	33	33	0	0-0	199.1	228	128	21	7	100-7	88	5.33	87	.295	.378	64-0-5	.125	-1	97	-15	0	-1.6
2001	Mil N	8	17	.320	31	29	0	0-0	172.2	182	98	20	4	78-17	112	4.85	89	.279	.356	52-0-5	.154	0*	88	-9	34	-1.1
2002	Cin N	15	10	.600	34	34	0	0-0	196.2	210	97	21	3	81-4	126	4.12	104	.278	.348	61-0-10	.164	-0*	87	5	0	0.5
2003	Cin N	2	12	.143	18	18	1	0-0	94.1	118	74	14	3	57-3	49	6.30	66	.311	.404	23-0-7	.261	1	94	-24	95	-2.8
2004	Cin N	0	3	.000	5	4	0	0-0	15	26	17	3	2	7-0	8	9.60	45	.382	.455	4	.000	-0	81	-9	0	-1.4
Total	10	63	89	.414	227	203	2-1	1-0	1200.2	1358	778	148	30	601-41	762	5.37	84	.290	.371	213-0-28	.150	-1	96	-110	129	-11.7
Haynes, Joe	Joseph Walton; B9.21.1917 Lincolnton GA; D1.6.1967 Hopkins MN; BR/TR/6´2.5˝/(185–190); d4.24; C3																									
1939	Was A	8	12	.400	27	20	10-1	0	173	186	118	10	1	78	64	5.36	81	.276	.352	67-0-2	.209	0	90	-20	—	-1.9
1940	Was A	3	6	.333	22	7	1	0	63.1	85	50	4	1	34	23	6.54	64	.327	.407	19-0-1	.105	-2	114	-16	—	-2.0
1941	Chi A	0	0	ø	8	0	0	0	28	30	13	0	0	11	18	3.86	106	.280	.347	11	.273	0	—	1	0	0.1
1942	Chi A	8	5	.615	**40**	1	1	6	103	88	37	6	3	47	35	2.62	137	.234	.324	28-0-1	.179	0	95	10	0	1.4
1943	Chi A	7	2	.778	35	2	1	3	109.1	114	51	2	2	32	37	2.96	113	.263	.316	34	.265	2	126	1	0	0.3
1944	Chi A	5	6	.455	33	12	8	2	154.1	148	55	5	0	43	44	2.57	134	.254	.306	50-0-1	.200	1	67	14	0	1.2
1945	Chi A	5	5	.500	14	13	8-1	1	104	92	44	5	1	29	34	3.55	94	.237	.291	40	.175	-2*	126	-1	0	-0.3
1946	Chi A	7	9	.438	32	23	9	2	177.1	203	80	14	4	60	60	3.76	91	.289	.349	57-0-3	.246	3	88	-2	0	0.2
1947	Chi A	14	6	.700	29	22	7-2	0	182	174	65	5	2	61	50	**2.42**	**151**	.250	.312	65-0-1	.262	2	86	22	0	2.6
1948	Chi A☆	9	10	.474	27	22	6	0	149.2	167	79	13	2	52	40	3.97	107	.284	.344	50-0-3	.160	-1	77	2	0	0.0
1949	Was A	2	9	.182	37	10	0	2	96.1	106	77	6	3	55	19	6.26	68	.283	.380	25	.240	1	93	-21	0	-2.1
1950	Was A	7	5	.583	27	10	1-1	0	101.2	124	73	14	5	46	15	5.84	77	.305	.382	35-0-1	.200	1	119	-14	0	-1.2
1951	Was A	1	4	.200	26	3	1	2	73	85	46	9	1	37	18	4.56	90	.290	.372	21-1-1	.333	2	130	-6	0	-0.2
1952	Was A	0	3	.000	22	2	0	3	66	70	35	2	1	35	18	4.50	79	.275	.364	19	.105	-1	86	-6	0	-0.4
Total	14	76	82	.481	379	147	53-5	21	1581	1672	823	95	26	620	475	4.01	96	.272	.342	521-1-14	.213	7	94	-36	0	-2.3
Hayward, Ray	Raymond Alton; B4.27.1961 Enid OK; BL/TL/6´1˝/(190–194); [SDN83 1/10]; d9.20; Col Oklahoma																									
1986	SD N	0	2	.000	3	3	0	0-0	10	16	12	1	0	4-0	6	9.00	41	.340	.392	4	.000	-0*	106	-6	0	-1.0
1987	SD N	0	0	ø	4	0	0	0-0	6	12	11	3	0	3-0	2	16.50	24	.444	.500	1	.000	-0	—	-8	0	-0.4
1988	Tex A	4	6	.400	12	12	1-1	0-0	62.2	63	44	6	0	35-0	37	5.46	75	.276	.367	0	ø	0	87	-10	57	-1.3
Total	3	4	8	.333	19	15	1-1	0-0	78.2	91	67	10	0	42-0	45	6.75	60	.301	.382	5	.000	-1	90	-24	57	-2.7
Haywood, Bill	William Kiernan; B4.21.1937 Colon, Pan; BR/TR/6´3˝/205; d7.28; Col North Carolina																									
1968	Was A	0	0	ø	14	0	0	0	23	27	16	1	2	12-0	10	4.70	62	.314	.406	0	ø	0	—	-6	0	-0.3
Head, Ed	Edward Marvin; B1.25.1918 Selma LA; D1.31.1980 Bastrop LA; BR/TR/6´1˝/175; d7.27; Mil 1944–45																									
1940	Bro N	1	2	.333	13	5	2	0	39.1	40	21	0	0	18	13	4.12	97	.260	.337	11	.182	-0*	113	-1	—	-0.2
1942	Bro N	10	6	.625	36	15	5-1	4	136.2	118	60	11	3	47	78	3.56	92	.231	.300	39-0-4	.333	4	124	-3	0	0.0
1943	Bro N	9	10	.474	47	18	7-3	6	169.2	166	75	8	0	66	83	3.66	92	.250	.318	46-0-9	.152	-2	111	-4	0	-0.6
1944	Bro N	4	3	.571	9	8	5-1	0	63.1	54	21	2	0	19	17	2.70	132	.232	.290	19-0-4	.263	1	86	7	0	0.8
1946	Bro N	3	2	.600	13	7	3-1	1	56	56	24	3	0	24	17	3.21	105	.267	.342	16	.313	2	109	1	0	0.2
Total	5	27	23	.540	118	53	22-6	11	465	434	201	24	3	174	208	3.48	98	.245	.314	131-0-17	.244	5	111	0	0	0.2
Head, Ralph	Ralph; B8.30.1893 Tallapoosa GA; D10.8.1962 Muscadine AL; BR/TR/5´10˝/175; d4.18																									
1923	Phi N	2	9	.182	35	13	5	0	132.1	185	111	13	1	57	24	6.66	69	.341	.404	42	.071	-5	91	-23	—	-2.1
Healey, Tom	Thomas F.; B1853 Cranston RI; D2.6.1891 Lewiston ME; TR; d6.13																									
1878	Pro N	0	3	.000	3	3	3	0	24	27	17	1	—	7	2	3.00	74	.278	.327	9	.222	0	40	-2	—	-0.2
	Ind N	6	4	.600	11	10	9	1	89	98	50	1	—	13	18	2.22	91	.270	.295	45	.178	-1*	92	-3	—	-0.3
	Year	6	7	.462	14	13	12	**1**	113	125	67	2	—	20	20	2.39	87	.272	.302	54	.185	-1	79	-4	—	-0.5

YEAR	TM LG	W	L	PCT	G	GS	CG-SHO	SV-BS	IP	H	R	HR	HB	BB-IB	SO	ERA	AERA	OAV	OOB	AB-HR-SH	AVG	PB	SUP	APR	DL	PW
HEALY, JOHN	John J. "Egyptian","Long John"; B10.27.1866 Cairo IL; D3.16.1899 St.Louis MO; BR/TR/6´2˝/158; d9.11																									
1885	StL N	1	7	.125	8	8	8	0	66	54	37	0	—	20	32	3.00	92	.210	.267	24	.042	-3	26	-2	—	-0.5
1886	StL N	17	23	.425	43	41	39-3	0	353.2	315	213	5	—	118	213	2.88	112	.230	.291	145	.097	-12	83	12	—	0.0
1887	Ind N	12	29	.293	41	41	40-3	0	341	415	292	24	15	108	75	5.17	80	.294	.350	138-3	.174	-4	74	-37	—	-3.6
1888	Ind N	12	24	.333	37	37	36-1	0	321.1	347	199	13	15	87	124	3.89	76	.267	.320	131-1	.229	4	102	-32	—	-2.6
1889	Was N	1	11	.083	13	12	10	0	101	139	111	2	5	38	49	6.24	63	.318	.379	45-1	.222	1	84	-27	—	-2.1
	Chi N	1	4	.200	5	5	5	0	46	48	35	4	4	18	22	4.50	92	.261	.340	20	.100	-2	77	-1	—	-0.3
	Year	2	15	.118	18	17	15	0	147	187	146	6	9	56	71	5.69	70	.301	.367	65-1	.185	-1	82	-30	—	-2.4
1890	Tol AA	22	21	.512	46	46	44-2	0	389	326	201	5	24	127	225	2.89	137	.221	.293	156-1	.218	7*	76	40	—	4.3
1891	Bal AA	8	10	.444	23	22	19	0	170.1	179	124	6	5	57	54	3.75	99	.261	.322	64	.141	-2	102	-1	—	-0.5
1892	Bal N	3	6	.333	9	8	5	0	68.1	82	51	4	2	21	24	4.74	72	.286	.339	27	.222	0	90	-7	—	-0.7
	Lou N	1	1	.500	2	2	2	0	18.1	15	7	0	0	5	4	1.96	156	.214	.267	7	.286	1	82	2	—	0.3
	Year	4	7	.364	11	10	7	0	86.2	97	58	4	2	26	28	4.15	81	.272	.325	34	.235	1	89	-5	—	-0.4
Total	8	78	136	.364	227	222	208-9	0	1875	1920	1270	63	70	599	822	3.84	94	.257	.318	757-6	.174	-9	83	-53	—	-5.7
HEARD, CHARLIE	Charles; B1.30.1872 Philadelphia PA; D2.20.1945 Philadelphia PA; BR/TR/6´2˝/190; d7.14; ▲																									
1890	Pit N	0	6	.000	6	6	5	0	44	75	65	5	2	32	13	8.39	39	.364	.454	43	.186	-1*	67	-27	—	-2.5
HEARD, JAY	Jehosie; B1.17.1920 Athens GA; D11.18.1999 Birmingham AL; BL/TL/5´7˝/155; d4.24; Negro Lg 1945–58																									
1954	Bal A	0	0	ø	2	0	0	0	3.1	6	5	1	0	3	2	13.50	27	.375	.474	0	ø	0	—	-4	0	-0.2
HEARN, BUNNY	Charles Bunn; B5.21.1891 Chapel Hill NC; D10.10.1959 Wilson NC; BL/TL/5´11˝/190; d9.17; Col Elon																									
1910	StL N	1	3	.250	5	5	4	0	39	49	22	2	1	16	14	5.08	59	.322	.391	15-1-0	.133	-0	130	-7	—	-0.6
1911	StL N	0	0	ø	2	0	0	0	2.2	7	4	1	0	0	1	13.50	25	.538	.538	1	.000	-0	—	-3	—	-0.1
1913	NY N	1	1	.500	2	2	1	0	13	13	6	0	0	7	8	2.77	113	.277	.370	5	.400	1	96	0	—	0.1
1915	Pit F	6	11	.353	29	17	8-1	0	175.2	187	74	6	2	37	49	3.38	80	.285	.326	53-0-2	.189	-0	68	-10	—	-1.0
1918	Bos N	5	6	.455	17	12	9-1	0	126.1	119	43	2	0	29	30	2.49	108	.256	.300	45-0-1	.178	-1	68	4	—	0.3
1920	Bos N	0	3	.000	11	4	2	0	43	54	34	3	1	11	9	5.65	54	.329	.375	14	.143	-1	84	-13	—	-0.9
Total	6	13	24	.351	66	40	24-2	0	399.2	429	183	14	4	100	111	3.56	78	.287	.333	133-1-3	.180	-2	80	-29	—	-2.2
HEARN, BUNNY	Elmer Lafayette; B1.13.1904 Brooklyn NY; D3.31.1974 Venice FL; BL/TL/5´8˝/160; d4.13																									
1926	Bos N	4	9	.308	34	12	3	2	117.1	121	63	2	0	56	40	4.22	84	.276	.358	30-0-2	.100	-2	102	-9	—	-1.0
1927	Bos N	0	2	.000	8	0	0	0	12.2	16	9	0	0	9	5	4.26	87	.327	.431	5	.400	1	—	-2	—	-0.2
1928	Bos N	1	0	1.000	7	0	0	0	10	6	8	0	1	8	8	6.30	62	.167	.333	1	.000	-0	—	-3	—	-0.2
1929	Bos N	2	0	1.000	10	1	0	0	18.1	18	10	2	0	9	12	4.42	106	.277	.365	2-0-1	.000	0	112	1	—	0.1
Total	4	7	11	.389	59	13	3	2	158.1	161	90	4	1	82	65	4.38	85	.273	.363	38-0-3	.132	-2	101	-13	—	-1.3
HEARN, JIM	James Tolbert; B4.11.1921 Atlanta GA; D6.10.1998 Boca Grande FL; BR/TR/6´3˝/(200–205); d4.17; Col Georgia Tech																									
1947	StL N	12	7	.632	37	21	4-1	1	162	151	67	9	1	63	57	3.22	128	.248	.319	55-0-2	.145	-1	111	16	0	1.5
1948	StL N	8	6	.571	34	13	3	1	89.2	92	44	9	2	35	27	4.22	97	.271	.342	25-0-1	.200	-0*	88	0	0	-0.2
1949	StL N	1	3	.250	17	4	0	0	42	48	27	3	2	23	18	5.14	81	.294	.388	10	.100	-0	79	-4	0	-0.4
1950	StL N	0	1	.000	6	0	0	0	9	12	11	1	0	6	4	10.00	43	.333	.429	1	1.000	0	—	-5	0	-0.5
	NY N	11	3	.786	16	16	11-5	0	125	72	33	8	0	38	54	1.94	211	.169	.237	44-0-2	.136	-0	113	29	0	3.2
	Year	11	4	.733	22	16	11-**5**	0	134	84	44	9	0	44	58	**2.49**	165	.182	.253	45-0-2	.156	0	113	23	0	2.7
1951	†NY N	17	9	.654	34	34	11	0	211.1	204	102	21	2	82	66	3.62	108	.251	.321	74-1-9	.162	-0	124	6	0	0.9
1952	NY N☆	14	7	.667	37	34	11-1	1	223.2	208	113	16	5	97	89	3.78	98	.245	.326	77-3-5	.182	4	128	-3	0	0.3
1953	NY N	9	12	.429	36	32	6	0	196.2	206	111	22	3	84	77	4.53	95	.266	.341	66-0-6	.136	0*	110	-4	0	-0.3
1954	NY N	8	8	.500	29	18	3-2	1	130	137	71	10	2	66	45	4.15	97	.272	.357	45-1-5	.111	-1	119	-3	0	-0.3
1955	NY N	14	16	.467	39	33	11-1	0	226.2	225	107	27	3	66-7	86	3.73	108	.260	.312	77-4-4	.156	1*	95	8	0	1.2
1956	NY N	5	11	.313	30	19	2	1	129.1	124	74	17	3	44-4	66	3.97	95	.254	.317	41	.098	-3*	76	-7	0	-1.1
1957	Phi N	5	1	.833	36	4	1	3	74	79	35	7	2	18-4	46	3.65	104	.274	.320	17-0-1	.000	-2	150	1	0	-0.1
1958	Phi N	5	3	.625	39	1	0	0	73.1	88	45	6	0	27-6	33	4.17	95	.292	.348	14	.000	-1	91	-5	0	-0.6
1959	Phi N	0	2	.000	6	0	0	0	11	15	7	2	0	6-1	1	5.73	72	.333	.412	2	.000	0	—	-2	0	-0.2
Total	13	109	89	.551	396	229	63-10	8	1703.2	1661	847	158	25	655-22	669	3.81	105	.255	.325	548-9-35	.141	-3	110	27	0	3.4
HEATH, SPENCER	Spencer Paul; B11.5.1893 Chicago IL; D1.25.1930 Chicago IL; BB/TR/6´0˝/170; d5.4																									
1920	Chi A	0	0	ø	4	0	0	0	7	19	12	1	0	2	0	15.43	24	.475	.500	3	.000	-1	—	-8	—	-0.4
HEATHCOCK, JEFF	Ronald Jeffrey; B11.18.1959 Covina CA; BR/TR/6´4˝/195; [HouN80 S1/1]; d9.3; Col Oral Roberts																									
1983	Hou N	2	1	.667	6	3	0	1-0	28	19	14	1	1	4-0	12	3.21	107	.181	.216	6-0-3	.000	-1	120	0	0	-0.1
1985	Hou N	3	1	.750	14	7	1	1-0	56.1	50	25	9	1	13-0	25	3.36	104	.239	.286	16	.063	0	192	1	0	0.1
1987	Hou N	4	2	.667	19	2	0	1-1	42.2	44	15	4	1	9-1	15	3.16	124	.277	.314	10-0-1	.000	-1	81	4	0	0.5
1988	Hou N	0	5	.000	17	1	0	0-0	31	33	25	2	1	16-6	12	5.81	57	.275	.360	3	.000	-0	0	-10	0	-1.5
Total	4	9	9	.500	56	13	1	3-1	158	146	79	16	4	42-7	64	3.76	95	.246	.297	35-0-4	.029	-2	142	-5	0	-1.0
HEATHCOTT, MIKE	Michael Joseph; B5.16.1969 Chicago IL; BR/TR/6´3˝/180; [ChiA91 13/358]; d8.28; Col Creighton																									
1998	Chi A	0	0	ø	1	0	0	0-0	3	2	1	0	0	1-0	3	3.00	153	.182	.250	0	ø	0	—	1	0	0.0
HEATON, NEAL	Neal; B3.3.1960 South Ozone Park NY; BL/TL/6´1˝/(195–205); [CleA81 2/39]; d9.3; Col Miami																									
1982	Cle A	0	2	.000	8	4	0	0-0	31	32	21	1	0	16-0	14	5.23	79	.260	.340	0	ø	0	44	-4	0	-0.2
1983	Cle A	11	7	.611	39	16	4-3	7-2	149.1	157	79	11	1	44-10	75	4.16	103	.269	.319	0	ø	0	101	1	0	0.0
1984	Cle A	12	15	.444	38	34	4-1	0-0	198.2	231	128	21	0	75-5	75	5.21	79	.293	.350	0	ø	0	109	-24	0	-2.9
1985	Cle A	9	17	.346	36	33	5-1	0-1	207.2	244	119	19	7	80-2	82	4.90	85	.298	.362	0	ø	0	85	-14	0	-1.6
1986	Cle A	3	6	.333	12	12	2	0-0	74.1	73	42	8	1	34-4	24	4.24	99	.254	.335	0	ø	0	96	-2	0	-0.2
	Min A	4	9	.308	21	17	3	1-0	124.1	128	60	18	1	47-4	66	3.98	109	.273	.337	0	ø	0	65	5	0	0.5
	Year	7	15	.318	33	29	5	1-0	198.2	201	102	26	2	81-8	90	4.08	105	.266	.336	0	ø	0	77	4	0	0.3
1987	Mon N	13	10	.565	32	32	3-1	0-0	193.1	207	103	25	3	37-3	105	4.52	94	.273	.308	67-0-6	.209	2	102	-2	0	-0.1
1988	Mon N	3	10	.231	32	11	0	2-0	97.1	98	54	14	3	43-5	43	4.99	73	.271	.351	21-0-4	.143	-0	100	-10	21	-1.4
1989	Pit N	6	7	.462	42	18	1	0-1	147.1	127	55	12	6	55-12	67	3.05	111	.233	.309	42-0-2	.214	1*	96	6	0	0.6
1990	Pit N☆	12	9	.571	30	24	0	0-1	146	143	66	17	2	38-1	68	3.45	106	.263	.311	43-0-3	.047	-2*	106	2	0	0.1
1991	Pit N	3	3	.500	42	1	0	0-1	68.2	72	37	6	4	21-2	34	4.33	83	.275	.334	14	.286	2*	25	-5	0	-0.3
1992	KC A	3	1	.750	31	0	0	0-2	41	43	21	5	1	22-2	29	4.17	98	.274	.361	0	ø	0	—	-1	0	-0.1
	Mil A	0	0	ø	1	0	0	0-0	1	0	0	0	0	1-0	2	0.00	ø	.000	.250	0	ø	0	—	0	0	0.0
	Year	3	1	.750	32	0	0	0-2	42	43	21	5	1	23-2	31	4.07	100	.269	.358	0	ø	0	—	0	0	0.0
1993	NY A	1	0	1.000	18	0	0	0-0	27	34	19	6	3	11-1	15	6.00	70	.301	.375	0	ø	0	—	-5	0	-0.2
Total	12	80	96	.455	382	202	22-6	10-8	1507	1589	804	163	32	524-51	699	4.37	92	.273	.334	187-0-15	.171	2	96	-53	21	-5.8
HEAVERLO, DAVE	David Wallace; B8.25.1950 Ellensburg WA; BR/TR/6´1˝/(195–220); [SFN73*S1/23]; d4.14; Col Central Washington																									
1975	SF N	3	1	.750	42	0	0	1-1	64	62	18	2	1	31-4	35	2.39	159	.262	.348	4	.500	1	—	10	0	0.7
1976	SF N	4	4	.500	61	0	0	1-2	75	85	45	2	2	15-3	40	4.44	82	.289	.324	3	.333	0	—	-7	0	-0.6
1977	SF N	5	1	.833	56	0	0	1-1	98.2	92	36	10	3	21-8	58	2.55	155	.251	.294	5-0-2	.000	-0	—	14	0	0.8
1978	Oak A	3	6	.333	69	0	0	10-3	130	141	56	11	3	41-9	71	3.25	112	.281	.333	0	ø	0	—	6	0	0.6
1979	Oak A	4	11	.267	62	0	0	9-8	85.2	97	42	7	4	42-18	40	4.20	97	.294	.376	1	.000	-0	—	0	0	0.0
1980	Sea A	6	3	.667	60	0	0	4-5	78.2	75	37	9	5	35-12	42	3.89	107	.253	.338	0	ø	0	—	3	0	0.2
1981	Oak A	1	0	1.000	6	0	0	0-1	5.2	7	1	0	0	3-1	2	1.59	222	.292	.370	0	ø	0	—	1	0	0.2
Total	7	26	26	.500	356	0	0	26-21	537.2	559	235	41	18	188-55	288	3.41	113	.273	.335	13-0-2	.231	0	—	27	0	1.9
HEBERT, WALLY	Wallace Andrew "Preacher"; B8.21.1907 Lake Charles LA; D12.8.1999 Westlake LA; BL/TL/6´1˝/195; d5.1																									
1931	StL A	6	7	.462	23	13	5	0	103	128	70	11	3	43	26	5.07	91	.306	.375	43-0-1	.209	-1	116	-5	—	-0.7
1932	StL A	1	12	.077	35	15	2	1	108.1	145	99	6	2	45	29	6.48	75	.322	.386	34-0-2	.353	2	74	-21	—	-1.9
1933	StL A	4	6	.400	33	10	3	0	88.1	114	58	4	1	35	19	5.30	88	.308	.369	23-0-4	.391	3	71	-6	—	-0.3
1943	Pit N	10	11	.476	34	23	12-1	0	184	197	75	3	2	45	41	2.98	117	.272	.316	59-0-5	.220	1*	101	10	0	1.4
Total	4	21	36	.368	125	61	22-1	1	483.2	584	302	24	8	168	115	4.63	91	.298	.355	159-0-12	.270	5	92	-22	0	-1.5
HEBSON, BRYAN	Bryan McCall; B3.12.1976 Columbus GA; BR/TR/6´5˝/210; [MonN97 1/44]; d7.6; Col Auburn																									
2003	Mon N	0	0	ø	2	0	0	0-0	2	4	3	1	1	1-0	1	13.50	33	.444	.500	0	ø	0	—	-2	0	-0.1

YEAR	TM LG	W	L	PCT	G	GS	CG-SHO	SV-BS	IP	H	R	HR	HB	BB-IB	SO	ERA	AERA	OAV	OOB	AB-HR-SH	AVG	PB	SUP	APR	DL	PW
HECKER, GUY	Guy Jackson; B4.3.1856 Youngsville PA; D12.3.1938 Wooster OH; BR/TR/6´0˝/190; d5.2; M1/U1; ▲																									
1882	Lou AA	6	6	.500	13	11	10	0	104	75	49	0	—	5	33	1.30	191	**.188**	**.199**	340-3	.276	4*	100	11	—	1.6
1883	Lou AA	28	23	.549	53	52	51-3	0	469	526	298	4	—	75	164	3.34	90	.266	.292	332-1	.271	12*	101	-24	—	-0.8
1884	Lou AA	**52**	20	.722	**75**	**73**	**72**-6	0	**670.2**	526	230	4	16	56	**385**	**1.80**	**172**	.204	**.226**	316-4	.297	28*	98	103	—	**12.9**
1885	Lou AA	30	23	.566	53	53	51-2	0	480	454	252	6	18	54	209	2.18	148	.237	.265	297-2	.273	9*	102	51	—	6.0
1886	Lou AA	26	23	.531	49	48	45-2	0	420.2	390	273	6	10	118	133	2.87	127	.231	.285	343-4	.341	18*	131	31	—	4.8
1887	Lou AA	18	12	.600	34	32	32-2	1	285.1	325	214	9	10	50	58	4.16	105	.272	.307	370-4	.319	11*	119	9	—	1.8
1888	Lou AA	8	17	.320	26	25	25	0	223.1	251	154	5	10	43	63	3.39	91	.274	.313	211	.227	2*	94	-5	—	-0.2
1889	Lou AA	5	13	.278	19	16	15	0	151.1	215	145	7	5	47	33	5.59	69	.324	.373	327-1	.284	4*	98	-26	—	-1.9
1890	Pit N	2	9	.182	14	12	11	0	119.2	160	111	9	3	44	32	5.11	65	.311	.368	340	.226	2*	75	-27	—	-1.7
Total	9	175	146	.545	336	322	312-15	1	2924	2922	1726	50	72	492	1110	2.93	113	.247	.281	2876-19	.282	90	106	123	—	22.5
HEDGPETH, HARRY	Harry Malcolm; B9.4.1888 Fayetteville NC; D7.30.1966 Richmond VA; BL/TL/6´1.5˝/194; d10.3; Col North Carolina																									
1913	Was A	0	0	ø	1	0	0	1	1	1	0	0	0	0	0	0.00	ø	.250	.250	0	ø	0	—	0	—	0.1
HEDLUND, MIKE	Michael David "Red"; B8.11.1946 Dallas TX; BR/TR (BB 1965–68)/6´1˝/(182–190); d5.8																									
1965	Cle A	0	0	ø	6	0	0	0	5.1	6	4	0	0	5-1	4	5.06	69	.286	.407	1	.000	-0	—	-1	61	-0.1
1968	Cle A	0	0	ø	3	0	0	0	1.2	6	2	0	1	2-0	0	10.80	28	.545	.643	0	ø	0	—	-1	0	-0.1
1969	KC A	3	6	.333	34	16	1	2-0	125	123	53	8	1	40-2	74	3.24	114	.259	.314	33-0-1	.152	-1	87	5	0	0.4
1970	KC A	2	3	.400	9	0	0	0-0	15	18	13	6	0	7-0	5	7.20	52	.300	.373	4-0-1	.000	-0	—	-5	14	-1.1
1971	KC A	15	8	.652	32	30	7-1	0-0	205.2	168	68	15	1	72-1	76	2.71	127	.227	.295	68-0-5	.088	-4	89	17	0	1.6
1972	KC A	5	7	.417	29	16	1	0-0	113	119	67	10	4	41-1	52	4.78	64	.275	.341	32-0-3	.188	-0	127	-23	0	-2.3
Total	6	25	24	.510	113	62	9-1	2-0	465.2	440	207	39	7	167-5	211	3.56	96	.253	.318	138-0-10	.123	-5	97	-8	75	-1.6
HEFFNER, BOB	Robert Frederic; B9.13.1938 Allentown PA; BR/TR/6´4˝/(198–210); d6.19																									
1963	Bos A	4	9	.308	20	19	3-1	0	124.2	131	61	15	2	36-1	77	4.26	89	.267	.318	43-0-2	.116	-1*	74	-5	0	-0.6
1964	Bos A	7	9	.438	55	10	1-1	6	158.2	152	81	20	3	44-6	112	4.08	94	.251	.305	44-1-1	.159	0	113	-4	0	-0.4
1965	Bos A	0	2	.000	27	1	0	0	49	59	42	9	1	18-1	42	7.16	52	.304	.364	6-0-1	.000	-1	188	-16	0	-0.9
1966	Cle A	0	1	.000	5	1	0	0	13	12	6	1	0	3-0	7	3.46	99	.240	.283	1	.000	0	51	0	0	0.0
1968	Cal A	0	0	ø	7	0	0	0	8	6	2	0	0	6-1	3	2.25	130	.240	.375	0	ø	0	—	1	0	0.1
Total	5	11	21	.344	114	31	4-2	6	353.1	360	192	45	6	107-9	241	4.51	84	.264	.319	94-1-4	.128	-1	90	-24	0	-1.8
HEFLIN, BRONSON	Bronson Wayne; B8.29.1971 Clarksville TN; BR/TR/6´3˝/200; [PhiN94 37/1038]; d8.1; Col Tennessee																									
1996	Phi N	0	0	ø	3	0	0	0-0	6.2	11	7	1	0	3-0	4	6.75	64	.367	.412	0	ø	0	—	-2	0	-0.1
HEFLIN, RANDY	Randolph Rutherford; B9.11.1918 Fredericksburg VA; D8.17.1999 Fredericksburg VA; BL/TR/6´0˝/185; d6.9																									
1945	Bos A	4	10	.286	20	14	6-2	0	102	102	52	3	4	61	39	4.06	84	.272	.380	35-0-1	.086	-3	73	-7	0	-1.2
1946	Bos A	0	1	.000	5	1	0	0	14.2	16	5	0	1	12	6	2.45	149	.296	.433	3	.667	1	210	2	0	0.2
Total	2	4	11	.267	25	15	6-2	0	116.2	118	57	3	5	73	45	3.86	89	.275	.387	38-0-1	.132	-2	83	-5	0	-1.0
HEHL, JAKE	Herman Charles; B12.10.1899 Brooklyn NY; D7.4.1961 Brooklyn NY; BR/TR/5´11˝/180; d6.20																									
1918	Bro N	0	0	ø	1	0	0	0	1	0	0	0	1	0	0	0.00	ø	.000	.250	0	ø	0	—	0	—	0.0
HEILMAN, AARON	Aaron Michael; B11.12.1978 Logansport IN; BR/TR/6´5˝/220; [NYN01 1/18]; d6.26; Col Notre Dame																									
2003	NY N	2	7	.222	14	13	0	0-0	65.1	79	53	13	3	41-2	51	6.75	62	.300	.397	22	.045	-2	79	-19	0	-2.3
2004	NY N	1	3	.250	5	5	0	0-0	28	27	17	4	0	13-0	22	5.46	79	.257	.339	7-0-3	.000	-1	86	-3	0	-0.4
2005	NY N	5	3	.625	53	7	1-1	5-1	108	87	40	6	6	37-4	106	3.17	131	.223	.299	14-0-2	.000	-1	95	12	0	0.9
2006	†NY N	4	5	.444	74	0	0	0-5	87	73	37	5	3	28-2	73	3.62	121	.231	.298	0	ø	0	—	8	0	0.8
Total	4	12	18	.400	146	25	1-1	5-6	288.1	266	147	28	12	119-8	252	4.34	98	.247	.328	43-0-5	.023	-4	84	-2	0	-1.0
HEIMACH, FRED	Frederick Amos "Lefty"; B1.27.1901 Camden NJ; D6.1.1973 Ft.Myers FL; BL/TL/6´0˝/175; d10.1																									
1920	Phi A	0	1	.000	1	1	0	0	5	13	9	0	0	1	0	14.40	28	.542	.560	1	.000	-0	59	-5	—	-0.6
1921	Phi A	1	0	1.000	1	1	1-1	0	9	7	0	0	0	1	1	0.00	ø	.226	.250	4	.250	-0	75	4	—	0.6
1922	Phi A	7	11	.389	37	19	7	1	171.2	220	117	18	3	63	47	5.03	85	.316	.375	60-0-3	.250	2	86	-15	—	-1.1
1923	Phi A	6	12	.333	40	19	10	0	208.1	238	120	14	6	69	63	4.32	95	.292	.352	118-1-5	.254	2*	75	-4	—	0.0
1924	Phi A	14	12	.538	40	26	10	0	198	243	122	2	4	60	60	4.73	91	.306	.357	90-0-3	.322	6*	101	-9	—	-0.3
1925	Phi A	0	1	.000	10	0	0	0	20.1	24	10	2	1	9	6	3.98	117	.312	.391	6	.167	-0*	—	2	—	0.1
1926	Phi A	1	0	1.000	13	1	0	0	31.2	28	14	1	0	5	8	2.84	147	.239	.270	10	.100	-1*	121	4	—	0.2
	Bos A	2	9	.182	20	13	6	0	102	119	72	5	0	42	17	5.65	72	.303	.370	44-0-1	.295	2*	88	-16	—	-1.1
	Year	3	9	.250	33	14	6	0	133.2	147	86	6	0	47	25	4.98	82	.288	.348	54-0-1	.259	2	90	-13	—	-0.9
1928	NY A	2	3	.400	13	9	5	0	68	66	30	3	1	16	25	3.31	114	.250	.295	30-0-1	.167	-1*	143	4	—	0.1
1929	NY A	11	6	.647	35	10	3-3	4	134.2	141	72	4	3	29	26	4.01	96	.272	.314	49-1-0	.184	1*	107	-2	—	-0.1
1930	Bro N	0	2	.000	9	0	0	1	7.1	14	5	0	0	3	1	4.91	100	.424	.472	4	.250	-0*	—	0	—	0.0
1931	Bro N	9	7	.563	31	10	7-1	1	135.1	145	66	6	1	23	43	3.46	110	.274	.306	61	.197	1*	81	3	—	0.6
1932	Bro N	9	4	.692	36	15	7	0	167.2	203	85	7	6	28	30	3.97	96	.299	.333	55-1-3	.164	1*	103	-3	—	-0.1
1933	Bro N	0	1	.000	10	3	0	0	29.2	49	33	2	2	11	7	10.01	32	.374	.431	10	.200	-0	138	-20	—	-1.0
Total	13	62	69	.473	296	127	56-5	7	1288.2	1510	755	64	27	360	334	4.46	90	.296	.346	542-3-16	.236	12	96	-57	—	-2.7
HEIMUELLER, GORMAN	Gorman John; B9.24.1955 Los Angeles CA; BL/TL/6´4˝/195; d7.12; Col Cal Poly–San Luis Obispo																									
1983	Oak A	3	5	.375	16	14	2-1	0-0	83.2	93	43	8	1	29-2	31	4.41	88	.286	.346	0	ø	0	98	-4	0	-0.2
1984	Oak A	0	1	.000	6	0	0	0-0	14.2	21	14	2	0	7-1	3	6.14	62	.344	.400	0	ø	0	—	-5	0	-0.3
Total	2	3	6	.333	22	14	2-1	0-0	98.1	114	57	10	1	36-3	34	4.67	83	.295	.354	0	ø	0	98	-9	0	-0.5
HEINKEL, DON	Donald Elliott; B10.20.1959 Racine WI; BL/TR/6´0˝/185; [DetA82 30/752]; d4.7; Col Wichita St.																									
1988	Det A	0	0	ø	21	0	0	1-0	36.1	30	17	4	1	12-1	30	3.96	97	.219	.285	0	ø	0	—	0	49	0.0
1989	StL N	1	1	.500	7	5	0	0-0	26.1	40	19	2	0	7-0	16	5.81	63	.348	.379	6-0-2	.000	-0	101	-6	134	-0.4
Total	2	1	1	.500	28	5	0	1-0	62.2	70	36	6	1	19-1	46	4.74	80	.278	.327	6-0-2	.000	-0	101	-6	183	-0.4
HEINTZELMAN, KEN	Kenneth Alphonse; B10.14.1915 Peruque MO; D8.14.2000 St.Peters MO; BR/TL/5´11.5˝/(175–185); d10.3; Mil 1943–45; s–Tom																									
1937	Pit N	1	0	1.000	1	1	1	0	9	6	3	0	1	3	4	2.00	193	.207	.303	4	.000	-1	89	2	—	0.1
1938	Pit N	0	0	ø	1	0	0	0	2	1	2	0	0	3	1	9.00	42	.167	.444	0	ø	0	—	-1	—	0.0
1939	Pit N	1	1	.500	17	2	1-1	0	35.2	35	23	2	0	18	18	5.05	76	.250	.335	9	.222	0	102	-5	—	-0.2
1940	Pit N	8	8	.500	39	16	5-2	3	165	193	86	7	4	65	71	4.47	85	.292	.359	54-0-3	.167	-1*	104	-8	—	-0.7
1941	Pit N	11	11	.500	35	24	13-2	0	196	206	91	8	1	83	81	3.44	105	.272	.345	63-0-5	.127	-2	110	4	0	0.2
1942	Pit N	8	11	.421	27	18	5-3	0	130	143	69	9	0	63	39	4.57	74	.281	.361	35-0-2	.086	-2	79	-13	0	-2.0
1946	Pit N	8	12	.400	32	24	6-2	1	157.2	165	84	7	0	86	57	3.77	94	.271	.362	44-0-6	.136	-1	91	-7	0	-0.8
1947	Pit N	0	0	ø	2	1	0	0	4	9	11	2	0	6	2	20.25	21	.409	.536	0	ø	0	167	-7	0	-0.3
	Phi N	7	10	.412	24	19	8	1	136	144	72	12	2	46	55	4.04	99	.277	.338	43-0-6	.116	-2	92	-1	0	-0.5
	Year	7	10	.412	26	20	8	1	140	153	83	14	2	52	57	4.50	89	.282	.347	43-0-6	.116	-2	96	-9	0	-0.8
1948	Phi N	6	11	.353	27	16	5-2	2	130	117	66	10	1	45	57	4.29	92	.241	.307	37-0-6	.135	-1	77	-2	0	-0.4
1949	Phi N	17	10	.630	33	32	15-**5**	0	250	239	96	19	1	93	65	3.02	130	.255	.323	83-0-5	.157	-1	88	25	0	2.3
1950	†Phi N	3	9	.250	23	17	4-1	0	125.1	122	66	10	0	54	39	4.09	99	.250	.325	38-0-3	.053	-3	86	-1	0	-0.5
1951	Phi N	6	12	.333	35	12	3	2	118.1	119	61	13	4	53	55	4.18	92	.267	.350	28-0-3	.107	-1	67	-5	0	-0.8
1952	Phi N	1	3	.250	23	1	0	1	42.2	41	16	1	0	12	20	3.16	115	.266	.319	2-0-3	.000	-0	49	3	0	0.2
Total	13	77	98	.440	319	183	66-18	10	1501.2	1540	746	100	14	630	564	3.93	96	.267	.341	440-0-42	.127	-16	90	-16	0	-3.4
HEISE, CLARENCE	Clarence Edward "Lefty"; B8.7.1907 Topeka KS; D5.30.1999 Winter Park FL; BL/TL/5´10˝/172; d4.22																									
1934	StL N	0	0	ø	1	0	0	0	2	3	3	1	0	0	1	4.50	94	.300	.300	0	ø	0	—	-1	—	0.0
HEISE, JIM	James Edward; B10.2.1932 Scottdale PA; BR/TR/6´1˝/185; d6.29; Col West Virginia																									
1957	Was A	0	3	.000	8	2	0	0	19	25	19	2	0	16-1	8	8.05	48	.329	.441	4	.000	-0	46	-9	0	-1.2
HEISER, ROY	Le Roy Barton; B6.22.1942 Baltimore MD; BR/TR/6´4˝/190; d9.2; Col Maryland																									
1961	Was A	0	0	ø	3	0	0	0	5.2	6	5	1	1	9-0	1	6.35	63	.261	.485	2	.000	-0	—	-2	0	-0.1

YEAR	TM LG	W	L	PCT	G	GS	CG-SHO	SV-BS	IP	H	R	HR	HB	BB-IB	SO	ERA	AERA	OAV	OOB	AB-HR-SH	AVG	PB	SUP	APR	DL	PW
HEISERMAN, RICK	Richard Michael; B2.22.1973 Atlantic IA; BR/TR/6´7˝/225; [CleA94 3/73]; d5.23; Col Creighton																									
1999	StL N	0	0	ø	3	0	0	0-0	4.1	8	4	2	0	4-0	4	8.31	55	.400	.500	1	.000	-0	—	-2	0	-0.1
HEISMANN, CRESE	Christian Ernest; B4.16.1880 Cincinnati OH; D11.19.1951 Cincinnati OH; BL/TL/6´0˝/150; d9.25																									
1901	Cin N	0	1	.000	3	2	1	0	13.2	18	9	1	3	6	6	5.93	54	.316	.409	5	.400	1	33	-3	—	-0.1
1902	Cin N	2	1	.667	5	3	2	0	33	33	18	1	5	10	15	2.45	122	.260	.338	14	.214	0	204	1	—	0.1
	Bal A	0	3	.000	3	3	2	0	16	20	17	1	2	12	2	8.44	45	.308	.430	7	.143	-1	76	-6	—	-0.9
Total	2	2	5	.286	11	8	5	0	62.2	71	44	3	10	28	23	4.74	69	.285	.380	26	.231	1	113	-8	—	-0.9
HEITMANN, HARRY	Henry Anton; B10.6.1896 Albany NY; D12.15.1958 Brooklyn NY; BR/TR/6´0˝/175; d7.27; Mil 1918																									
1918	Bro N	0	1	.000	1	1	0	0	0	4	4	0	0	0	0	(4)	ø	1.000	1.000	0	ø	0	190	-3	—	-0.3
HELD, MEL	Melvin Nicholas "Country"; B4.12.1929 Edon OH; BR/TR/6´1˝/178; d4.27																									
1956	Bal A	0	0	ø	4	0	0	0	7	7	4	1	0	3-1	4	5.14	76	.318	.385	0	ø	0	—	-1	0	0.0
HELLING, RICK	Ricky Allen; B12.15.1970 Devils Lake ND; BR/TR/6´3˝/(215–255); [TexA92 1/22]; d4.10; Col Stanford																									
1994	Tex A	3	2	.600	9	9	1-1	0-0	52	62	34	14	0	18-0	25	5.88	82	.295	.351	0	ø	0	108	-4	0	-0.4
1995	Tex A	0	2	.000	3	3	0	0-0	12.1	17	11	2	2	8-0	5	6.57	74	.340	.435	0	ø	0	71	-3	0	-0.4
1996	Tex A	1	2	.333	6	2	0	0-0	20.1	23	17	7	0	9-0	16	7.52	70	.280	.348	0	ø	0	70	-4	0	-0.5
	Fla N	2	1	.667	5	4	0	0-0	27.2	14	6	2	0	7-0	26	1.95	211	.143	.200	9	.111	-0	60	7	0	0.7
1997	Fla N	2	6	.250	31	8	0	0-1	76	61	38	12	4	48-2	53	4.38	93	.232	.351	11-0-1	.091	-1	82	-2	0	-0.3
	Tex A	3	3	.500	10	8	0	0-0	55	47	29	5	2	21-0	46	4.58	106	.235	.311	3	.000	-0	85	2	0	0.1
1998	†Tex A	**20**	7	.741	33	33	4-2	0-0	216.1	209	109	27	1	78-6	164	4.41	111	.253	.314	5-0-1	.200	0	112	14	0	1.3
1999	†Tex A	13	11	.542	35	**35**	3	0-0	219.1	228	127	41	6	85-5	131	4.84	107	.272	.340	2	.000	-0	100	7	0	0.5
2000	Tex A	16	13	.552	35	**35**	0	0-0	217	212	122	29	9	99-2	146	4.48	114	.252	.334	5	.000	-1	103	13	0	1.3
2001	Tex A	12	11	.522	34	34	2-1	0-0	215.2	256	134	38	4	63-2	154	5.17	92	.297	.344	4	.000	-0	109	-10	0	-1.1
2002	†Ari N	10	12	.455	30	30	0	0-0	175.2	180	94	31	6	48-6	120	4.51	100	.264	.316	46-0-6	.043	-2	98	0	22	-0.3
2003	Bal A	7	8	.467	24	24	0	0-0	138.2	156	90	30	12	40-0	86	5.71	81	.286	.347	1	.000	-0	115	-15	0	-1.5
	†Fla N	1	0	1.000	11	0	0	0-0	16.1	11	1	1	0	5-0	12	0.55	745	.193	.258	2	.500	1	—	7	0	0.4
2005	Mil N	3	1	.750	15	7	0	0-0	49	39	13	2	2	18-1	42	2.39	178	.219	.296	13-0-1	.000	-1	67	11	0	0.6
2006	Mil N	0	2	.000	20	2	0	0-1	35	25	17	6	0	15-0	32	4.11	109	.202	.284	3	.000	-0	10	2	70	0.0
Total	12	93	81	.534	301	234	10-4	0-2	1526.1	1540	842	247	48	562-24	1058	4.68	102	.263	.329	104-0-9	.058	-5	102	25	92	0.4
HELMBOLD, HORACE	Horace; B Philadelphia PA; D11.18.1939 Lake Lure NC; d10.11																									
1890	Phi AA	0	1	.000	1	1	1	0	7	17	15	0	0	6	3	14.14	27	.447	.523	3	.000	-1	69	-8	—	-0.7
HEMAN, RUSS	Russell Frederick; B2.10.1933 Olive CA; BR/TR/6´4˝/200; d4.20																									
1961	Cle A	0	0	ø	6	0	0	1	10	8	4	0	1	8-0	4	3.60	109	.216	.370	1	.000	-0	—	1	0	0.0
	LA A	0	0	ø	6	0	0	0	10	4	3	1	1	2-0	2	1.80	251	.125	.189	1	.000	-0	—	2	0	0.1
	Year	0	0	ø	12	0	0	1	20	12	7	1	2	10-0	6	2.70	156	.174	.289	2	.000	-0	—	3	0	0.1
HEMMING, GEORGE	George Earl "Old Wax Figger"; B12.15.1868 Carrollton OH; D6.3.1930 Springfield MA; BR/TR/5´11˝/170; d4.21																									
1890	Cle P	0	1	.000	3	1	1	0	21	25	23	1	2	19	3	6.86	58	.284	.422	11	.182	-1	61	-5	—	-0.2
	Bro P	8	4	.667	19	11	11	3	123	117	86	3	3	59	32	3.80	117	.240	.325	57	.158	-4	88	9	—	0.4
	Year	8	5	.615	22	12	12	**3**	144	142	109	4	5	78	35	4.25	103	.247	.341	68	.162	-5	87	3	—	0.2
1891	Bro N	8	15	.348	27	22	19-1	1	199.2	231	173	11	11	84	83	4.96	67	.279	.353	82	.159	-1	109	-37	—	-3.3
1892	Cin N	0	1	.000	1	0	0	0	6	10	6	1	0	2	0	7.50	44	.357	.400	3	.333	0	—	-2	—	-0.3
	Lou N	2	2	.500	4	4	4	0	35	36	25	1	0	17	12	4.63	66	.255	.335	13	.077	-1	98	-5	—	-0.5
	Year	2	3	.400	5	4	4	0	41	46	31	2	0	19	12	5.05	61	.272	.346	16	.125	-1	97	-7	—	-0.8
1893	Lou N	18	17	.514	41	32	32-1	1	332	369	245	7	15	175	79	5.10	86	.273	.363	158	.203	-2*	96	-26	—	-2.0
1894	Lou N	13	19	.406	35	32	32-1	1	294.1	358	213	7	9	133	66	4.37	117	.297	.371	131-2-0	.252	2*	73	26	—	2.1
	†Bal N	4	0	1.000	6	6	4	0	45.1	48	22	0	2	26	4	3.57	153	.268	.367	21	.286	1	97	10	—	0.7
	Year	17	19	.472	41	38	36-1	1	339.2	406	235	7	11	159	70	4.27	121	.293	.370	152-2-0	.257	3	77	33	—	2.8
1895	Bal N	20	13	.606	34	31	26-1	0	262.1	288	155	10	6	96	43	4.05	118	.275	.339	117-1-1	.282	3*	96	22	—	2.2
1896	Bal N	15	6	.714	25	21	20-3	0	202	233	113	9	3	54	33	4.19	102	.287	.333	97-0-2	.258	4*	149	8	—	0.8
1897	Lou N	3	4	.429	9	8	7	0	67	80	59	5	1	25	7	5.10	84	.294	.356	28	.179	-1*	77	-7	—	-0.6
Total	8	91	82	.526	204	168	156-7	6	1587.2	1795	1120	55	52	690	362	4.53	98	.279	.353	718-3-3	.223	-0	97	-7	—	-0.7
HENDERSON, BERNIE	Bernard "Barnyard"; B4.12.1899 Douglassville TX; D6.6.1966 Linden TX; BR/TR/5´9˝/175; d9.5; Col Texas A&M																									
1921	Cle A	0	1	.000	2	1	0	0	3	5	5	0	0	0	1	9.00	47	.333	.333	1	.000	0*	78	-2	—	-0.4
HENDERSON, ED	Edward Johnson (b Eugene Johnson Ball); B12.25.1884 Newark NJ; D1.15.1964 New York NY; BL/TL/5´9˝/168; d5.15																									
1914	Pit F	0	1	.000	6	1	1	0	16	14	8	2	0	8	4	3.94	73	.241	.333	3	.000	-0	0	-2	—	-0.1
	Ind F	1	0	1.000	2	1	1	0	10	8	7	0	3	4	1	4.50	69	.229	.357	4	.000	-1	110	-2	—	-0.2
	Year	1	1	.500	8	2	2	0	26	22	15	2	3	12	5	4.15	71	.237	.343	7	.000	-1	58	-3	—	-0.3
HENDERSON, HARDIE	James Harding; B10.31.1862 Philadelphia PA; D2.6.1903 Philadelphia PA; BR/TR/?/200; d5.2; U2																									
1883	Phi N	0	1	.000	1	1	1	0	9	26	24	0	—	2	2	19.00	16	.481	.500	8	.250	0*	104	-14	—	-0.8
	Bal AA	10	32	.238	45	42	38	0	358.1	383	315	4	—	87	145	4.02	87	.256	.297	191-1	.162	-6*	82	-22	—	-2.5
1884	Bal AA	27	23	.540	52	52	50-4	0	439.1	382	235	9	16	116	346	2.62	132	.216	.271	203	.227	2*	94	37	—	3.9
1885	Bal AA	25	35	.417	61	61	59	0	539.1	539	311	7	19	117	263	3.19	102	.253	.298	229-1	.223	3	91	3	—	0.7
1886	Bal AA	3	15	.167	19	19	19	0	171.1	188	147	0	9	66	88	4.62	74	.252	.320	68	.235	2	102	-25	—	-1.7
	Bro AA	10	4	.714	14	14	14	0	124	112	82	2	0	51	49	2.90	120	.232	.306	50	.180	-1	132	5	—	0.3
	Year	13	19	.406	33	33	33	0	295.1	300	229	2	9	117	137	3.90	88	.244	.314	118	.212	1	115	-20	—	-1.4
1887	Bro AA	5	8	.385	13	12	12	0	111.2	127	85	3	5	63	28	3.95	109	.281	.375	41	.122	-3	107	2	—	-0.1
1888	Pit N	1	3	.250	5	5	4	0	35.1	43	31	0	2	20	9	5.35	49	.289	.380	18	.278	1	149	-11	—	-0.9
Total	6	81	121	.401	210	206	197-4	0	1788.1	1800	1230	25	51	522	930	3.50	98	.247	.302	808-2	.204	-2	96	-25	—	-1.1
HENDERSON, JOE	Joseph Lee; B7.4.1946 Lake Cormorant MS; BL/TR/6´2˝/195; [AnaA65 5/87]; d6.7; [DL 1969 Cal A 4]																									
1974	Chi A	1	0	1.000	5	3	0	0-0	15	21	15	2	0	11-0	12	8.40	45	.328	.427	1	.000	-0	165	-7	0	-0.4
1976	Cin N	2	0	1.000	4	0	0	0-0	11	9	1	0	0	8-3	7	0.00	ø	.225	.354	0	ø	0	—	4	0	0.8
1977	Cin N	0	2	.000	7	0	0	0-0	9	17	13	2	0	6-0	8	12.00	33	.386	.460	1	.000	-0	—	-8	0	-1.5
Total	3	3	2	.600	16	3	0	0-0	35	47	29	4	0	25-3	27	6.69	56	.318	.416	2	.000	-0	165	-11	4	-1.1
HENDERSON, ROD	Rodney Wood; B3.11.1971 Greensburg KY; BR/TR/6´4˝/(193–195); [MonN92 2/41]; d4.19; Col Kentucky; [DL 1995 Mon N 160]																									
1994	Mon N	0	1	.000	3	2	0	0-0	6.2	9	9	1	0	7-0	3	9.45	45	.333	.471	1	.000	-0	129	-4	0	-0.5
1998	Mil N	0	0	ø	2	0	0	0-0	3.2	5	4	2	1	0-0	1	9.82	44	.313	.353	0	ø	0	—	-2	0	-0.1
Total	2	0	1	.000	5	2	0	0-0	10.1	14	13	3	1	7-0	4	9.58	45	.326	.431	1	.000	-0	129	-6	160	-0.6
HENDERSON, BILL	William Maxwell; B11.4.1901 Pensacola FL; D10.6.1966 Pensacola FL; BR/TR/6´0˝/190; d6.20																									
1930	NY A	0	0	ø	3	0	0	0	8	7	6	1	0	4	2	4.50	96	.250	.344	2	.500	0	—	-1	—	0.0
HENDLEY, BOB	Charles Robert; B4.30.1939 Macon GA; BR/TL/6´2˝/195; d6.23																									
1961	Mil N	5	7	.417	19	13	3	0	97	96	46	8	0	39-2	44	3.90	96	.262	.332	31-0-2	.032	-3	100	-2	0	-0.4
1962	Mil N	11	13	.458	35	29	7-2	1	200	188	90	17	0	59-2	112	3.60	105	.247	.299	59-1-3	.119	1*	98	5	0	0.7
1963	Mil N	9	9	.500	41	24	7-3	3	169.1	153	80	16	1	64-4	105	3.93	82	.244	.312	47-0-5	.106	-1*	133	-12	0	-1.3
1964	SF N	10	11	.476	30	29	4-1	0	163.1	161	71	18	2	59-9	104	3.64	98	.258	.322	47-0-5	.106	-1	92	0	0	-0.2
1965	SF N	0	0	ø	8	2	0	0	15	27	22	6	1	13-2	8	12.60	29	.397	.500	3	.000	-0	158	-14	0	-0.7
	Chi N	4	4	.500	18	10	2	0	62	59	39	9	1	25-0	38	4.35	85	.244	.317	14-0-3	.000	-1	102	-6	0	-0.8
	Year	4	4	.500	26	12	2	0	77	86	61	15	2	38-2	46	5.96	62	.277	.360	17-0-3	.000	-2	111	-21	0	-1.5
1966	Chi N	4	5	.444	43	6	0	7	89.2	98	46	10	0	39-6	65	3.91	94	.285	.353	18	.167	1	124	-3	0	-0.2
1967	Chi N	2	0	1.000	7	0	0	1	12.1	17	10	4	0	3-0	10	6.57	54	.315	.351	6	.000	-1	—	-4	0	-0.7
	NY N	3	3	.500	15	13	2	0	70.2	65	35	11	1	28-4	36	3.44	99	.241	.312	18-0-4	.111	-0	92	-2	0	-0.3
	Year	5	3	.625	22	13	2	1	83	82	45	15	1	31-4	46	3.90	87	.253	.318	24-0-4	.083	-1	91	-6	0	-1.0
Total	7	48	52	.480	216	126	25-6	12	879.1	864	439	99	6	329-29	522	3.97	90	.257	.323	243-1-22	.095	-6	104	-38	0	-3.9

YEAR	TM LG	W	L	PCT	G	GS	CG-SHO	SV-BS	IP	H	R	HR	HB	BB-IB	SO	ERA	AERA	OAV	OOB	AB-HR-SH	AVG	PB	SUP	APR	DL	PW
Hendricks, Ed	Edward "Big Ed"; B6.20.1885 Zeeland MI; D11.28.1930 Jackson MI; BL/TL/6´3˝/200; d9.15																									
1910	NY N	0	1	.000	4	1	1	1	12	12	7	0	0	4	2	3.75	79	.261	.320	4	.000	-1	25	-1	—	-0.2
Hendrickson, Ben	Benjamin John; B2.4.1981 St. Cloud MN; BR/TR/6´4˝/190; [MilN99 10/304]; d6.2																									
2004	Mil N	1	8	.111	10	9	0	0-0	46.1	58	33	6	4	20-1	29	6.22	71	.310	.385	16-0-1	.125	-1	56	-8	0	-1.4
2006	Mil N	0	2	.000	4	3	0	0-0	12	21	17	0	0	9-0	8	12.00	37	.382	.462	3	.000	0	130	-10	0	-1.2
Total	2	1	10	.091	14	12	0	0-0	58.1	79	50	6	4	29-1	37	7.41	60	.326	.403	19-0-1	.105	-1	75	-18	0	-2.6
Hendrickson, Don	Donald William; B7.14.1913 Kewanna IN; D1.19.1977 Norfolk VA; BR/TR/6´2˝/204; d7.4																									
1945	Bos N	4	8	.333	37	2	1	5	73.1	74	46	8	1	39	14	4.91	78	.261	.353	18	.167	-0	210	-8	0	-1.4
1946	Bos N	0	1	.000	2	0	0	0	2	4	2	0	0	2	2	4.50	76	.364	.462	1	.000	-0	—	-1	0	-0.1
Total	2	4	9	.308	39	2	1	5	75.1	78	48	8	1	41	16	4.90	78	.265	.357	19	.158	-0	210	-9	0	-1.5
Hendrickson, Mark	Mark Allan; B6.23.1974 Mount Vernon WA; BL/TL/6´9˝/230; [TorA97 20/599]; d8.6; Col Washington St.																									
2002	Tor A	3	0	1.000	16	4	0	0-1	36.2	25	11	1	2	12-3	21	2.45	188	.202	.279	0	ø	0	105	8	0	0.6
2003	Tor A	9	9	.500	30	30	1-1	0-0	158.1	207	111	24	0	40-3	76	5.51	86	.317	.352	4-1-0	.250	1	130	-15	0	-1.3
2004	TB A	10	15	.400	32	30	2	0-0	183.1	211	113	21	7	46-5	87	4.81	97	.285	.330	5	.200	0	76	-5	0	-0.5
2005	TB A	11	8	.579	31	31	1	0-0	178.1	227	126	24	2	49-1	89	5.90	75	.311	.353	7	.143	-0	110	-28	16	-2.5
2006	TB A	4	8	.333	13	13	1-1	0-0	89.2	81	42	10	2	34-0	51	3.81	122	.241	.312	0	ø	0	62	8	18	1.0
	†LA N	2	7	.222	18	12	0	0-0	75	92	45	7	2	28-0	48	4.68	94	.299	.360	19-0-2	.000	-1	63	-4	0	-0.5
Total	5	39	47	.453	140	120	5-2	0-1	721.1	843	448	87	15	209-12	372	4.98	92	.291	.339	35-1-2	.086	-0	97	-36	34	-3.2
Hendrix, Claude	Claude Raymond; B4.13.1889 Olathe KS; D3.22.1944 Allentown PA; BR/TR/6´0˝/195; d6.7; Col Wichita St.																									
1911	Pit N	4	6	.400	22	12	6-1	1	118.2	85	52	1	1	53	57	2.73	126	.204	.295	41-1-0	.098	-1	89	7	—	0.6
1912	Pit N	24	9	**.727**	39	32	25-4	1	288.2	256	110	6	9	105	176	2.59	126	.246	.320	121-1-2	.322	16*	121	21	—	4.0
1913	Pit N	14	15	.483	42	25	17-2	3	241	216	95	3	5	89	138	2.84	106	.248	.321	99-1-2	.273	10*	111	6	—	1.8
1914	Chi F	**29**	10	.744	**49**	37	**34**-6	5	362	262	91	6	5	77	189	1.69	157	**.203**	**.251**	130-2-6	.231	5*	118	**42**	—	**5.4**
1915	Chi F	16	15	.516	40	31	26-5	4	285	256	120	7	2	84	107	3.00	84	.241	.298	113-4-3	.265	12*	125	-15	—	-0.7
1916	Chi N	8	16	.333	36	24	15-3	2	218	193	81	4	6	67	117	2.68	108	.242	.306	80-1-2	.200	2*	70	6	—	1.1
1917	Chi N	10	12	.455	40	21	13-1	1	215	202	94	3	4	72	81	2.60	112	.257	.322	86-0-4	.256	3*	106	4	—	0.8
1918	†Chi N	20	7	**.741**	32	27	21-3	0	233	229	87	2	5	54	86	2.78	100	.259	.305	91-3-5	.264	8*	140	4	—	1.5
1919	Chi N	10	14	.417	33	25	15-2	0	206.1	208	79	3	9	42	69	2.62	110	.266	.311	78-1-0	.192	-0*	86	6	—	0.7
1920	Chi N	9	12	.429	27	23	12	0	203.2	216	101	6	3	54	72	3.58	90	.273	.322	83-0-1	.181	-2*	108	-8	—	-0.9
Total	10	144	116	.554	360	257	184-27	17	2371.1	2123	910	41	49	697	1092	2.65	110	.243	.303	922-14-25	.241	52	109	73	—	14.3
Henion, Lafayette	Lafayette Marion; B6.7.1899 Eureka CA; D7.22.1955 San Luis Obispo CA; BR/TR/5´11˝/154; d9.10																									
1919	Bro N	0	0	ø	1	0	0	0	3	2	2	0	0	2	2	6.00	50	.200	.333	1	.000	-0	—	-1	—	-0.1
Henke, Tom	Thomas Anthony; B12.21.1957 Kansas City MO; BR/TR/6´5˝/(215–230); [TexA80 S4/67]; d9.10; Col East Central (MO) JC																									
1982	Tex A	1	0	1.000	8	0	0	0-1	15.2	14	2	0	1	8-2	9	1.15	338	.246	.348	0	ø	0	—	5	0	0.3
1983	Tex A	1	0	1.000	8	0	0	1-0	16	16	6	1	0	4-0	17	3.38	120	.262	.308	0	ø	0	—	2	0	0.1
1984	Tex A	1	1	.500	25	0	0	2-2	28.1	36	21	0	1	20-2	25	6.35	66	.313	.407	0	ø	0	—	-6	0	-0.5
1985	†Tor A	3	3	.500	28	0	0	13-1	40	29	12	4	0	8-2	42	2.02	209	.206	.245	0	ø	0	—	9	0	1.8
1986	Tor A	9	5	.643	63	0	0	27-8	91.1	63	39	6	1	32-4	118	3.35	127	.191	.261	0	ø	0	—	8	0	1.5
1987	Tor A★	0	6	.000	72	0	0	**34**-8	94	62	27	10	0	25-3	128	2.49	182	.188	.242	0	ø	0	—	**22**	0	2.9
1988	Tor A	4	4	.500	52	0	0	25-4	68	60	23	6	2	24-3	66	2.91	136	.237	.306	0	ø	0	—	9	0	1.5
1989	†Tor A	8	3	.727	64	0	0	20-4	89	66	20	5	2	25-4	116	1.92	197	.205	.264	0	ø	0	—	20	0	3.1
1990	Tor A	2	4	.333	61	0	0	32-6	74.2	58	18	8	1	19-2	75	2.17	183	.213	.266	0	ø	0	—	15	0	2.2
1991	†Tor A	0	2	.000	49	0	0	32-3	50.1	33	13	4	0	11-2	53	2.32	182	.184	.232	0	ø	0	—	11	35	1.5
1992	†Tor A	3	2	.600	57	0	0	34-3	55.2	40	19	5	0	22-2	46	2.26	182	.197	.272	0	ø	0	—	9	0	1.7
1993	Tex A	5	5	.500	66	0	0	40-7	74.1	55	25	7	1	27-3	79	2.91	144	.205	.278	0	ø	0	—	12	0	2.3
1994	Tex A	3	6	.333	37	0	0	15-6	38	33	16	6	0	12-0	39	3.79	128	.232	.290	0	ø	0	—	5	31	1.0
1995	StL N★	1	1	.500	52	0	0	36-2	54.1	42	11	2	0	18-0	48	1.82	235	.209	.274	1	.000	-0	—	15	0	2.3
Total	14	41	42	.494	642	0	0	311-55	789.2	607	252	64	9	255-29	861	2.67	157	.211	.275	1	.000	-0	—	136	66	21.7
Henley, Weldon	Weldon; B10.25.1880 Jasper GA; D11.16.1960 Palatka FL; BR/TR/6´0˝/175; d4.23; Col Georgia Tech																									
1903	Phi A	12	10	.545	29	21	13-1	0	186.1	186	108	3	12	67	86	3.91	78	.259	.333	68-0-1	.132	-3*	124	-18	—	-2.3
1904	Phi A	15	17	.469	36	34	31-5	0	295.2	245	126	3	19	76	130	2.53	106	.226	.289	108-0-3	.222	2	117	2	—	0.6
1905	Phi A	4	11	.267	25	19	13-1	0	183.2	155	74	4	9	67	82	2.60	102	.231	.309	65-0-2	.169	-1	97	2	—	0.3
1907	Bro N	1	5	.167	7	7	5	0	56	54	31	2	1	21	11	3.05	77	.273	.345	20-0-2	.200	1*	83	-6	—	-0.5
Total	4	32	43	.427	97	81	62-7	0	721.2	640	339	12	41	231	309	2.94	93	.240	.310	261-0-8	.184	-2	112	-20	—	-1.9
Henn, Sean	Sean Michael; B4.23.1981 Fort Worth TX; BR/TL/6´5˝/200; [NYA00 26/788]; d5.4; Col McLennan (TX) JC																									
2005	NY A	0	3	.000	3	3	0	0-0	11.1	18	16	3	0	11-0	3	11.12	39	.360	.475	0	ø	0	108	-9	0	-1.4
2006	NY A	0	1	.000	4	1	0	0-0	9.1	11	5	2	1	5-0	7	4.82	94	.297	.386	0	ø	0	42	0	0	0.0
Total	2	0	4	.000	7	4	0	0-0	20.2	29	21	5	1	16-0	10	8.27	53	.333	.438	0	ø	0	90	-9	0	-1.4
Henneman, Mike	Michael Alan; B12.11.1961 St.Charles MO; BR/TR/6´4˝/(195–210); [DetA84 4/104]; d5.11; Col Oklahoma St.																									
1987	†Det A	11	3	.786	55	0	0	7-4	96.2	86	36	8	3	30-5	75	2.98	143	.238	.300	1	.000	-0	—	15	0	2.0
1988	Det A	9	6	.600	65	0	0	22-7	91.1	72	23	7	2	24-10	58	1.87	205	.218	.273	0	ø	0	—	**20**	15	3.9
1989	Det A☆	11	4	.733	60	0	0	8-4	90	84	46	4	5	51-15	69	3.70	104	.251	.355	0	ø	0	—	0	21	-0.1
1990	Det A	8	6	.571	69	0	0	22-6	94.1	90	36	4	3	33-12	50	3.05	130	.253	.320	0	ø	0	—	9	0	1.6
1991	Det A	10	2	.833	60	0	0	21-3	84.1	81	29	2	0	34-8	61	2.88	145	.258	.326	0	ø	0	—	12	16	2.1
1992	Det A	2	6	.250	60	0	0	24-4	77.1	75	36	6	0	20-10	58	3.96	101	.256	.299	0	ø	0	—	1	0	0.1
1993	Det A	5	3	.625	63	0	0	24-5	71.2	69	28	4	2	32-8	58	2.64	165	.251	.331	0	ø	0	—	12	0	1.8
1994	Det A	1	3	.250	30	0	0	8-5	34.2	43	27	5	2	17-7	27	5.19	95	.297	.376	0	ø	0	—	-3	20	-0.4
1995	Det A	0	1	.000	29	0	0	18-2	29.1	24	5	0	0	9-1	24	1.53	314	.222	.282	0	ø	0	—	11	0	1.5
	Hou N	0	1	.000	21	0	0	8-1	21	21	7	1	2	4-1	19	3.00	129	.266	.310	0	ø	0	—	3	0	0.3
1996	†Tex A	0	7	.000	49	0	0	31-6	42	41	28	6	0	17-5	34	5.79	91	.258	.326	0	ø	0	—	-2	0	-0.4
Total	10	57	42	.576	561	0	0	193-47	732.2	686	301	47	19	271-82	533	3.21	131	.249	.318	1	.000	-0	—	78	72	12.4
Hennessey, Brad	Brad Martin; B2.7.1980 Toledo OH; BR/TR/6´2˝/(185–195); [SFN01 1/21]; d8.7; Col Youngstown St.																									
2004	SF N	2	2	.500	7	7	0	0-0	34.1	42	24	2	0	15-1	25	4.98	87	.294	.358	13	.231	1	190	-4	0	-0.3
2005	SF N	5	8	.385	21	21	0	0-0	118.1	127	63	15	4	52-3	64	4.64	91	.276	.353	39-2-2	.231	3	73	-4	0	-0.1
2006	SF N	5	6	.455	34	12	0	1-0	99.1	92	53	12	10	42-1	42	4.26	104	.250	.341	27-0-3	.222	1*	90	1	0	0.1
Total	3	12	16	.429	62	40	0	1-0	252	261	140	29	14	109-5	131	4.54	96	.269	.349	79-2-5	.228	5	99	-7	0	-0.3
Hennessey, George	George "Three Star"; B10.28.1907 Slatington PA; D1.15.1988 Princeton NJ; BR/TR/5´10˝/168; d9.2																									
1937	StL A	0	1	.000	5	0	0	0	7	15	8	2	0	6	4	10.29	47	.500	.583	0-0-1	ø	0	—	-4	—	-0.4
1942	Phi N	1	1	.500	5	1	0	0	17	11	5	1	0	10	2	2.65	125	.180	.296	5	.000	-1	25	2	0	0.1
1945	Chi N	0	0	ø	2	0	0	0	3.2	7	3	0	0	1	2	7.36	50	.438	.471	0	ø	0	—	-1	0	-0.1
Total	3	1	2	.333	12	1	0	0	27.2	33	16	3	0	17	8	5.20	72	.308	.403	5-0-1	.000	-1	25	-3	0	-0.4
Hennigan, Phil	Phillip Winston; B4.10.1946 Jasper TX; BR/TR/5´11.5˝/(180–195); [CleA66*4/60]; d9.2; Col Sam Houston St.																									
1969	Cle A	2	1	.667	9	0	0	0-2	16.1	14	6	0	1	4-1	10	3.31	115	.241	.297	2	.000	-0	—	1	0	0.2
1970	Cle A	6	3	.667	42	1	0	3-0	71.2	69	34	7	4	44-6	43	4.02	100	.263	.376	7-0-2	.143	1	222	0	0	0.2
1971	Cle A	4	3	.571	57	0	0	14-2	82	80	45	13	3	51-4	69	4.94	78	.261	.365	6-0-2	.000	-0	—	-7	0	-0.9
1972	Cle A	5	3	.625	38	1	0	6-0	67.1	54	20	8	2	18-4	44	2.67	122	.226	.281	12	.083	-0	81	5	33	0.7
1973	NY N	0	4	.000	30	0	0	3-1	43.1	50	30	6	1	16-6	22	6.23	59	.289	.353	3	.333	0	—	-11	0	-1.1
Total	5	17	14	.548	176	2	0	26-5	280.2	267	135	34	11	133-21	188	4.26	87	.257	.344	30-0-4	.100	1	155	-12	33	-0.9
Henning, Pete	Ernest Herman; B12.28.1887 Crown Point IN; D11.4.1939 Dyer IN; BR/TR/5´11˝/185; d4.17																									
1914	KC F	5	10	.333	28	14	7	2	138	153	88	5	7	58	45	4.83	58	.291	.369	44	.182	0	129	-29	—	-2.8
1915	KC F	9	15	.375	40	20	15-1	2	207	181	88	5	3	76	73	3.17	83	.235	.307	68-0-4	.206	-1	72	-10	—	-1.2
Total	2	14	25	.359	68	34	22-1	4	345	334	176	10	10	134	118	3.83	70	.258	.332	112-0-4	.196	-0	96	-39	—	-4.0

YEAR	TM LG	W	L	PCT	G	GS	CG-SHO	SV-BS	IP	H	R	HR	HB	BB-IB	SO	ERA	AERA	OAV	OOB	AB-HR-SH	AVG	PB	SUP	APR	DL	PW
HENNINGER, RICK	Richard Lee; B1.11.1948 Hastings NE; BR/TR/6´6˝/220; [TexA68 S1/16]; d9.3; Col Missouri																									
1973	Tex A	1	0	1.000	6	2	0	0-0	23	23	8	1	0	11-0	6	2.74	137	.261	.333	0	ø	0	131	3	0	0.1
HENNIS, RANDY	Randall Philip; B12.16.1965 Clearlake CA; BR/TR/6´6˝/220; [HouN87 2/54]; d9.17; Col UCLA																									
1990	Hou N	0	0	ø	3	1	0	0-0	9.2	1	0	0	1	3-0	4	0.00	ø	.033	.147	2	.000	-0	73	4	0	0.2
HENRIQUEZ, OSCAR	Oscar Eduardo; B1.28.1974 LaGuaira, Vargas, Venez.; BR/TR/6´6˝/220; d9.7																									
1997	Hou N	0	1	.000	4	0	0	0-0	4	2	2	0	1	3-0	3	4.50	89	.167	.375	0	ø	0	—	0	0	0.0
1998	Fla N	0	0	ø	15	0	0	0-0	20	26	22	4	1	12-0	19	8.55	47	.306	.390	1	.000	-0	—	-11	0	-0.6
2002	Det A	1	1	.500	30	0	0	2-0	28	19	14	5	1	15-4	23	4.50	97	.196	.307	0	ø	0	—	0	10	0.0
Total	3	1	2	.333	49	0	0	2-0	52	47	38	9	3	30-4	45	6.06	70	.242	.348	1	.000	-0	—	-11	10	-0.6
HENRY, DWAYNE	Dwayne Allen; B2.16.1962 Elkton MD; BR/TR/6´3˝/(205–230); [TexA80 2/40]; d9.7																									
1984	Tex A	0	1	.000	3	0	0	0-1	4.1	5	4	0	0	7-0	2	8.31	50	.294	.500	0	ø	0	—	-2	0	-0.3
1985	Tex A	2	2	.500	16	0	0	3-3	21	16	7	0	0	7-0	20	2.57	166	.211	.274	0	ø	0	—	4	0	0.7
1986	Tex A	1	0	1.000	19	0	0	0-0	19.1	14	11	1	1	22-0	17	4.66	93	.209	.402	0	ø	0	—	-1	38	0.0
1987	Tex A	0	0	ø	5	0	0	0-1	10	12	10	2	0	9-0	7	9.00	50	.293	.420	0	ø	0	—	-4	0	-0.2
1988	Tex A	0	1	.000	11	0	0	1-1	10.1	15	10	1	3	9-1	10	8.71	47	.326	.458	0	ø	0	—	-5	0	-0.5
1989	Atl N	0	2	.000	12	0	0	1-1	12.2	12	6	2	0	5-1	16	4.26	86	.250	.321	0	ø	0	—	0	0	-0.1
1990	Atl N	2	2	.500	34	0	0	0-1	38.1	41	26	3	0	25-0	34	5.63	72	.273	.375	0	ø	0	—	-6	0	-0.6
1991	Hou N	3	2	.600	52	0	0	2-0	67.2	51	25	7	2	39-7	51	3.19	111	.219	.333	1	.000	-0	—	3	0	0.2
1992	Cin N	3	3	.500	60	0	0	0-2	83.2	59	31	4	1	44-6	72	3.33	108	.199	.301	4	.250	0	—	4	0	0.3
1993	Cin N	0	1	.000	3	0	0	0-0	4.2	6	8	0	0	4-1	2	3.86	105	.273	.385	1	.000	-0	—	-3	0	-0.5
	Sea A	2	1	.667	31	1	0	2-0	54	56	40	6	2	35-4	35	6.67	67	.273	.378	0	ø	0	330	-11	30	-0.7
1995	Det A	1	0	1.000	10	0	0	5-0	8.2	11	6	0	0	10-2	9	6.23	77	.306	.457	0	ø	0	—	-1	0	-0.2
Total	11	14	15	.483	256	1	0	14-10	334.2	298	184	26	9	216-22	275	4.65	85	.241	.354	6	.167	-0	330	-22	68	-1.9
HENRY, EARL	Earl Clifford "Hook"; B6.10.1917 Roseville OH; D12.10.2002 Zanesville OH; BL/TL/5´11˝/172; d9.23																									
1944	Cle A	1	1	.500	2	2	1	0	17.2	18	9	0	0	3	5	4.58	72	.269	.300	5	.000	-0*	101	-2	0	-0.2
1945	Cle A	0	3	.000	15	1	0	0	21.2	20	13	0	1	20	10	5.40	60	.253	.410	4	.500	1*	105	-5	0	-0.5
Total	2	1	4	.200	17	3	1	0	39.1	38	22	0	1	23	15	5.03	65	.260	.365	9	.222	0	103	-7	0	-0.7
HENRY, BUTCH	Floyd Bluford; B10.7.1968 ElPaso TX; BL/TL/6´1˝/(195–205); [CinN87 15/388]; d4.9; [DL 1996 Bos A 182]																									
1992	Hou N	6	9	.400	28	28	2-1	0-0	165.2	185	81	16	1	41-7	96	4.02	84	.285	.325	54-1-5	.148	1	89	-12	0	-0.9
1993	Col N	2	8	.200	20	15	1	0-0	84.2	117	66	14	1	24-2	39	6.59	73	.331	.370	22-0-2	.091	-1	82	-13	0	-1.5
	Mon N	1	1	.500	10	1	0	0-0	18.1	18	10	1	0	4-0	8	3.93	106	.250	.286	2-0-1	.000	-0	129	0	0	0.0
	Year	3	9	.250	30	16	1	0-0	103	135	76	15	1	28-2	47	6.12	76	.317	.356	24-0-3	.083	-2	85	-13	0	-1.5
1994	Mon N	8	3	.727	24	15	0	1-0	107.1	97	30	10	2	20-1	70	2.43	174	.241	.278	31-0-5	.290	3	103	22	0	2.5
1995	Mon N	7	9	.438	21	21	1-1	0-0	126.2	133	47	11	2	28-3	60	2.84	151	.275	.315	42-0-5	.048	-4	77	18	47	1.9
1997	Bos A	7	3	.700	36	5	0	6-2	84.1	89	36	6	0	19-2	51	3.52	132	.277	.315	0-0-1	ø	0	75	10	49	1.3
1998	Bos A	0	0	ø	2	2	0	0-0	9	8	4	2	1	3-0	6	4.00	118	.235	.316	0	ø	0	138	1	174	0.1
1999	Sea A	2	0	1.000	7	4	0	0-0	25	30	15	1	2	10-0	15	5.04	95	.303	.375	0	ø	0	209	-1	126	-0.1
Total	7	33	33	.500	148	91	4-2	7-2	621	677	289	61	9	149-15	345	3.83	109	.280	.322	151-1-19	.139	-2	93	25	578	3.3
HENRY, DUTCH	Frank John; B5.12.1902 Cleveland OH; D8.23.1968 Cleveland OH; BL/TL/6´1˝/175; d9.16																									
1921	StL A	0	0	ø	1	0	0	0	2	2	1	0	0	0	1	4.50	100	.250	.250	1	1.000	0	—	0	—	0.0
1922	StL A	0	0	ø	4	0	0	0	5	7	3	0	0	5	3	5.40	77	.280	.400	0	ø	0	—	0	—	0.0
1923	Bro N	4	6	.400	17	9	5-2	0	94.1	105	55	9	2	28	28	3.91	99	.281	.334	35	.229	1	82	-1	—	-0.1
1924	Bro N	1	2	.333	16	4	0	0	46	69	33	0	0	15	11	5.67	66	.352	.398	20	.250	1	192	-9	—	-0.5
1927	NY N	11	6	.647	45	15	7-1	4	163.2	184	93	6	0	31	40	4.23	91	.278	.311	55-0-1	.236	1	137	-8	—	-0.7
1928	NY N	3	6	.333	17	8	4	1	64	82	36	4	1	25	23	3.80	103	.325	.388	19	.158	-1	100	-1	—	-0.2
1929	NY N	5	6	.455	27	9	4	1	101.1	129	52	10	1	31	27	3.82	120	.316	.366	28-0-1	.250	2	133	8	—	0.9
	Chi A	1	0	1.000	2	1	1	0	15	20	12	1	0	7	2	6.00	71	.308	.375	7	.143	0	276	-3	—	-0.2
1930	Chi A	2	17	.105	35	16	4	0	155	211	116	12	4	48	35	4.88	95	.331	.381	51	.235	1	62	-9	—	-0.7
Total	8	27	43	.386	164	62	25-3	6	646.1	809	401	42	8	190	170	4.39	95	.308	.356	216-0-2	.231	6	108	-23	—	-1.5
HENRY, JIM	James Francis; B6.26.1910 Danville VA; D8.15.1976 Memphis TN; BR/TR/6´2˝/175; d4.23																									
1936	Bos A	5	1	.833	21	8	2	0	76.1	75	43	10	2	40	36	4.60	116	.255	.348	26	.115	-1*	108	6	—	0.3
1937	Bos A	1	0	1.000	3	2	1	0	15.1	15	9	2	0	11	8	5.28	90	.263	.382	5	.000	-0	101	0	—	-0.1
1939	Phi N	0	1	.000	9	1	0	1	23	24	13	3	1	8	7	5.09	79	.276	.344	5	.000	-1	218	-2	—	-0.2
Total	3	6	2	.750	33	11	3	1	114.2	114	65	15	3	59	51	4.79	104	.260	.352	36	.083	-2	117	4	—	0.0
HENRY, JOHN	John Michael; B9.2.1863 Springfield MA; D6.11.1939 Hartford CT; TL; d8.13; ▲																									
1884	Cle N	1	4	.200	5	5	5-1	0	42	46	39	2	—	26	23	3.64	87	.257	.351	26	.154	-1*	27	-4	—	-0.4
1885	Bal AA	2	7	.222	9	9	9	0	71	71	55	0	2	13	31	4.31	76	.247	.284	34	.265	1*	60	-8	—	-0.6
1886	Was N	1	3	.250	4	4	4	0	27.2	35	27	1	—	15	19	4.23	76	.285	.362	14	.357	1	99	-5	—	-0.5
Total	3	4	14	.222	18	18	18-1	0	140.2	152	121	3	2	54	73	4.09	79	.258	.322	74	.243	1	59	-17	—	-1.5
HENRY, DOUG	Richard Douglas; B12.10.1963 Sacramento CA; BR/TR/6´4˝/(185–205); [MilA85 8/185]; d7.15; Col Arizona St.																									
1991	Mil A	2	1	.667	32	0	0	15-1	36	16	4	1	0	14-1	28	1.00	399	.133	.221	0	ø	0	—	12	0	1.8
1992	Mil A	1	4	.200	68	0	0	29-4	65	64	34	6	0	24-4	52	4.02	96	.256	.319	0	ø	0	—	-2	0	-0.3
1993	Mil A	4	4	.500	54	0	0	17-7	55	67	37	7	3	25-8	38	5.56	78	.300	.373	0	ø	0	—	-7	0	-1.3
1994	Mil A	2	3	.400	25	0	0	0-0	31.1	32	17	7	1	23-1	20	4.60	110	.271	.394	1	.000	-0	—	2	24	0.2
1995	NY N	3	6	.333	51	0	0	4-3	67	48	23	7	1	25-6	62	2.96	137	.198	.274	1-0-1	1.000	0	—	9	0	1.2
1996	NY N	2	8	.200	58	0	0	9-5	75	82	48	7	1	36-6	58	4.68	86	.273	.350	5	.000	-1	—	-7	0	-1.1
1997	†SF N	4	5	.444	75	0	0	3-3	70.2	70	45	5	1	41-6	69	4.71	87	.261	.358	4	.000	-0	—	-6	0	-0.9
1998	†Hou N	8	2	.800	59	0	0	2-3	71	55	25	9	0	35-5	59	3.04	133	.216	.307	4-0-1	.000	-0	—	9	0	1.1
1999	†Hou N	2	3	.400	35	0	0	2-2	40.2	45	24	8	3	24-0	36	4.65	95	.281	.385	1	.000	-0	—	-2	66	-0.2
2000	Hou N	1	3	.250	45	0	0	1-1	53	39	26	10	3	28-2	46	4.42	111	.204	.314	1	.000	-0	—	4	0	0.2
	†SF N	3	1	.750	27	0	0	0-2	25.1	18	10	2	1	21-1	16	2.49	175	.214	.374	0	ø	0	—	4	0	0.6
	Year	4	4	.500	72	0	0	1-3	78.1	57	36	12	4	49-3	62	3.79	125	.207	.333	1	.000	-0	—	8	0	0.8
2001	KC A	2	2	.500	53	0	0	0-2	75.2	75	53	14	3	45-2	57	6.07	82	.262	.365	0	ø	0	—	-7	0	-0.4
Total	11	34	42	.447	582	0	0	82-33	665.2	611	346	83	17	341-42	541	4.19	103	.245	.337	17-0-2	.059	-1	—	9	90	0.9
HENRY, BILL	William Francis; B2.15.1942 Long Beach CA; BL/TL/6´3˝/195; d9.13; Col Seton Hall																									
1966	NY A	0	0	ø	2	0	0	0	3	0	0	0	0	2-0	3	0.00	ø	.000	.200	0	ø	0	—	1	0	0.1
HENRY, BILL	William Rodman; B10.15.1927 Alice TX; BL/TL/6´2˝/(175–195); d4.17; Col Houston																									
1952	Bos A	5	4	.556	13	10	5	0	76.2	75	40	7	2	36	23	3.87	102	.254	.339	31	.258	2*	120	-1	0	0.1
1953	Bos A	5	5	.500	21	12	4-1	1	85.2	86	39	4	4	33	56	3.26	129	.260	.334	32	.188	-0	95	7	0	0.7
1954	Bos A	3	7	.300	24	13	3-1	0	95.2	104	56	9	1	49	38	4.52	91	.270	.351	34	.118	-1*	96	-4	0	-0.6
1955	Bos A	2	4	.333	17	7	0	0	59.2	56	28	7	0	21-2	23	3.32	129	.247	.306	19	.105	-1	112	5	0	0.3
1958	Chi N	5	4	.556	44	0	0	6	81.1	63	27	8	1	17-6	58	2.88	136	.214	.259	17	.235	1	—	11	0	1.4
1959	Chi N	9	8	.529	**65**	0	0	12	134.1	111	42	19	1	26-3	115	2.68	147	.227	.264	31-0-1	.194	0	—	**20**	0	2.7
1960	Cin N★	1	5	.167	51	0	0	17	67.2	62	25	8	4	20-5	58	3.19	120	.247	.313	8	.000	-1	—	5	0	0.7
1961	†Cin N	2	1	.667	47	0	0	16	53.1	50	18	8	0	15-4	53	2.19	185	.244	.294	5	.000	-1*	—	10	0	1.1
1962	Cin N	4	2	.667	40	0	0	11	37.1	40	21	5	1	20-5	35	4.58	88	.280	.365	3	.333	0	—	-2	0	-0.4
1963	Cin N	1	3	.250	47	0	0	14	52	55	30	4	1	11-2	45	4.15	81	.279	.316	6-0-1	.167	-0	—	-6	0	-0.8
1964	Cin N	2	2	.500	37	0	0	6	52	31	9	2	3	12-4	28	0.87	418	.170	.231	6	.500	1*	—	14	0	1.6
1965	Cin N	2	0	1.000	3	0	0	0	5	3	0	0	0	1-0	5	0.00	ø	.176	.222	0	ø	0	—	2	0	0.4
	SF N	2	2	.500	35	0	0	4	42	40	18	2	1	8-3	35	3.64	99	.248	.287	5	.200	0	—	0	0	0.0
	Year	4	2	.667	38	0	0	4	47	43	18	2	1	9-3	40	3.26	111	.242	.280	5	.200	0	—	2	0	0.4
1966	SF N	1	1	.500	35	0	0	1	22	15	6	3	1	10-3	15	2.45	149	.190	.286	2	.000	-0	—	3	0	0.3
1967	SF N	2	0	1.000	28	1	0	2	21.2	16	5	1	2	9-4	23	2.08	158	.198	.290	1	.000	-0	27	3	0	0.4
1968	SF N	0	2	.000	7	1	0	0	5	4	3	0	1	3-1	0	5.40	55	.250	.400	0	ø	0	29	-1	0	-0.2

YEAR	TM LG	W	L	PCT	G	GS	CG-SHO	SV-BS	IP	H	R	HR	HB	BB-IB	SO	ERA	AERA	OAV	OOB	AB-HR-SH	AVG	PB	SUP	APR	DL	PW
	Pit N	0	0	ø	10	0	0	0	16.2	29	18	2	2	3-1	9	8.10	36	.382	.420	3	.000	-0	—	-10	0	-0.6
	Year	0	2	.000	17	1	0	0	21.2	33	21	2	3	6-2	9	7.48	39	.359	.416	3	.000	-0	30	-12	0	-0.8
1969	Hou N	0	0	ø	3	0	0	0-0	5	2	1	0	0	2-0	2	0.00	ø	.111	.200	0	ø	0	—	2	0	0.1
Total	16	46	50	.479	527	44	12-2	90-0	913	842	386	89	25	296-43	621	3.26	119	.244	.306	203-0-2	.177	-0	106	58	0	7.2
Henshaw, Roy	Roy Knikelbine; B7.29.1911 Chicago IL; D6.8.1993 LaGrange IL; BR/TL/5´8˝/155; d4.15; Col Chicago																									
1933	Chi N	2	1	.667	21	0	0	0	38.2	32	22	0	2	20	16	4.19	78	.230	.335	10	.200	-0	—	-4	—	-0.4
1935	†Chi N	13	5	.722	31	18	7-3	1	142.2	135	60	6	4	68	53	3.28	120	.249	.337	51-0-5	.255	2	118	11	—	1.2
1936	Chi N	6	5	.545	39	14	6-2	1	129.1	152	67	8	5	56	69	3.97	100	.296	.370	44-0-2	.136	-2	102	-1	—	-0.5
1937	Bro N	5	12	.294	42	16	5	2	156.1	176	110	14	4	69	98	5.07	80	.278	.352	48-0-4	.167	-2*	77	-18	—	-1.9
1938	StL N	5	11	.313	27	15	4	0	130	132	63	7	1	48	34	4.02	99	.266	.332	41-0-1	.220	-0	84	2	—	0.2
1942	Det A	2	4	.333	23	2	0	1	61.2	63	32	3	1	27	24	4.09	97	.269	.347	12	.083	-1	32	0	0	-0.1
1943	Det A	0	2	.000	26	3	0	2	71.1	75	35	2	3	33	33	3.79	93	.276	.360	18	.111	-1	160	-2	0	-0.2
1944	Det A	0	0	ø	7	1	0	0	12.1	17	12	0	0	6	10	8.76	41	.315	.383	5	.000	-1	117	-6	0	-0.4
Total	8	33	40	.452	216	69	22-5	7	742.1	782	401	40	20	327	337	4.16	94	.271	.349	229-0-12	.179	-5	98	-18	0	-2.1
Hensiek, Phil	Philip Frank "Sid"; B10.13.1901 St.Louis MO; D2.21.1972 St.Louis MO; BR/TR/6´0˝/160; d8.15																									
1935	Was A	0	3	.000	6	1	0	1	13	21	15	2	0	9	6	9.69	45	.356	.441	3	.667	1	80	-8	—	-1.2
Hensley, Chuck	Charles Floyd; B3.11.1959 Tulare CA; BL/TL/6´3˝/190; [DetA80 10/252]; d5.10; Col California																									
1986	SF N	0	0	ø	11	0	0	1-1	7.1	5	2	2	0	2-0	6	2.45	144	.179	.233	0	ø	0	—	1	0	0.1
Hensley, Clay	Clayton Allen; B8.31.1979 Tomball TX; BR/TR/5´11˝/190; [SFN02 8/247]; d7.20; Col Lamar																									
2005	†SD N	1	1	.500	24	1	0	0-0	47.2	33	12	0	0	17-2	28	1.70	231	.195	.266	6	.167	0	24	12	0	0.6
2006	†SD N	11	12	.478	37	29	1-1	0-1	187	174	82	15	3	76-7	122	3.71	112	.250	.326	48-0-5	.083	-1*	92	10	0	1.0
Total	2	12	13	.480	61	30	1-1	0-1	234.2	207	94	15	3	93-9	150	3.30	124	.240	.314	54-0-5	.093	-1	91	22	0	1.6
Hensley, Matt	Matthew Davis; B8.18.1978 San Diego CA; BR/TR/6´2˝/220; [AnaA00 10/290]; d5.4; Col Grossmont (CA) JC; [DL 2005 Ala A 183]																									
2004	Ana A	0	2	.000	16	0	0	0-0	27.2	32	15	5	2	7-1	30	4.88	92	.294	.345	1	.000	-0	—	-1	0	0.0
Hentgen, Pat	Patrick George; B11.13.1968 Detroit MI; BR/TR/6´2˝/(195–200); [TorA86 5/133]; d9.3																									
1991	Tor A	0	0	ø	3	1	0	0-0	7.1	5	2	1	2	3-0	3	2.45	172	.208	.345	0	ø	0	65	1	0	0.1
1992	Tor A	5	2	.714	28	2	0	0-1	50.1	49	30	7	0	32-5	39	5.36	77	.254	.357	0	ø	0	44	-6	47	-0.7
1993	†Tor A☆	19	9	.679	34	32	3	0-0	216.1	215	103	27	7	74-0	122	3.87	113	.258	.322	0	ø	0	120	12	0	1.3
1994	Tor A★	13	8	.619	24	24	6-3	0-0	174.2	158	74	21	3	59-1	147	3.40	143	.240	.305	0	ø	0	89	27	0	2.9
1995	Tor A	10	14	.417	30	30	2	0-0	200.2	236	129	24	5	90-6	135	5.11	93	.290	.363	0	ø	0	91	-9	0	-1.0
1996	Tor A	20	10	.667	35	35	**10-3**	0-0	**265.2**	238	105	20	5	94-3	177	3.22	156	.241	.308	0	ø	0	103	**53**	0	**5.2**
1997	Tor A★	15	10	.600	35	**35**	**9-3**	0-0	**264**	253	116	31	7	71-2	160	3.68	125	.254	.308	7	.000	-1	96	28	0	2.3
1998	Tor A	12	11	.522	29	29	0	0-0	177.2	208	109	28	5	69-1	94	5.17	90	.293	.357	5-0-1	.000	-1	109	-9	0	-1.0
1999	Tor A	11	12	.478	34	34	1	0-0	199	225	115	32	3	65-1	118	4.79	103	.286	.338	6	.167	-0	97	3	0	0.3
2000	†StL N	15	12	.556	33	33	1-1	0-0	194.1	202	107	24	3	89-4	118	4.72	98	.276	.353	60-0-8	.133	-1	119	1	0	-0.1
2001	Bal A	2	3	.400	9	9	1	0-0	62.1	51	25	7	0	19-3	33	3.47	124	.221	.279	0	ø	0	76	7	144	0.5
2002	Bal A	0	4	.000	4	4	0	0-0	22	31	20	6	0	10-0	11	7.77	56	.337	.398	0	ø	0	48	-8	161	-1.1
2003	Bal A	7	8	.467	28	22	1	1-0	160.2	150	74	25	5	58-1	100	4.09	113	.247	.316	5	.000	-1	65	11	0	0.8
2004	Tor A	2	9	.182	18	16	0	0-0	80.1	90	67	16	4	42-2	33	6.95	71	.283	.366	1	.000	-0	63	-18	0	-2.0
Total	14	131	112	.539	344	306	34-10	1-1	2075.1	2111	1076	269	49	775-29	1290	4.32	109	.264	.331	84-0-9	.107	-3	97	93	352	7.5
Hepler, Bill	William Lewis; B9.25.1945 Covington VA; BL/TL/6´0˝/160; d4.23																									
1966	NY N	3	3	.500	37	3	0	0	69	71	30	3	3	51-6	25	3.52	103	.274	.397	14-0-1	.214	0	65	1	0	0.1
Herbel, Ron	Ronald Samuel; B1.16.1938 Denver CO; D1.20.2000 Tacoma WA; BR/TR/6´1˝/(175–195); d9.10; Col Northern Colorado																									
1963	SF N	0	0	ø	2	0	0	0	1.1	1	1	0	0	1-0	1	6.75	47	.200	.333	0	ø	0	—	0	0	0.0
1964	SF N	9	9	.500	40	22	7-2	1	161	162	65	7	3	61-9	98	3.07	116	.259	.327	47-0-5	.000	-4*	94	7	0	0.4
1965	SF N	12	9	.571	47	21	1	1	170.2	172	80	16	3	47-7	106	3.85	94	.261	.311	49-0-2	.020	-4	107	-3	0	-0.7
1966	SF N	4	5	.444	32	18	0	1	129.2	149	70	15	2	39-9	55	4.16	88	.291	.343	38	.026	-4	119	-7	0	-0.9
1967	SF N	4	5	.444	42	11	1-1	1	125.2	125	54	10	2	35-10	52	3.08	107	.268	.320	28-0-3	.107	0	66	1	0	0.3
1968	SF N	0	0	ø	28	2	0	0	43	55	26	5	1	15-8	18	3.35	88	.309	.364	3	.000	-0	103	-5	0	-0.3
1969	SF N	4	1	.800	39	4	2	1-0	87.1	92	43	7	1	23-5	34	4.02	87	.275	.320	17-0-1	.000	-2	221	-4	0	-0.4
1970	SD N	7	5	.583	64	1	0	9-6	111	114	69	14	4	39-5	53	4.95	81	.266	.330	13	.000	-1	22	-12	0	-1.5
	NY N	2	2	.500	12	0	0	1-1	13	14	3	1	0	2-1	8	1.38	293	.275	.302	0	ø	0	—	4	0	0.7
	Year	9	7	.563	**76**	1	0	10-7	124	128	72	15	4	41-6	61	4.57	88	.267	.327	13	.000	-1	22	-8	0	-0.8
1971	Atl N	0	1	.000	25	0	0	1-0	51.2	61	31	6	4	23-1	22	5.23	71	.300	.381	11	.091	-1	—	-7	0	-0.4
Total	9	42	37	.532	331	79	11-3	16-7	894.1	945	442	81	20	285-55	447	3.82	94	.273	.330	206-0-11	.029	-15	105	-26	0	-2.8
Herbert, Ernie	Earn Albert "Tex"; B1.30.1887 Breckenridge MO; D1.13.1968 Dallas TX; BR/TR/5´10˝/165; d7.27																									
1913	Cin N	0	0	ø	6	0	0	0	17.1	12	12	0	1	5	5	2.08	156	.179	.247	4	.250	0	—	0	—	0.0
1914	StL F	1	0	1.000	18	1	0	1	50.1	56	33	2	4	27	24	3.58	85	.293	.392	13	.538	2*	45	-6	—	-0.2
1915	StL F	1	0	1.000	11	1	1	0	48	48	21	1	3	18	23	3.38	85	.253	.327	18	.278	1*	122	-2	—	0.0
Total	3	2	0	1.000	35	2	1	1	115.2	116	66	3	8	50	52	3.27	92	.259	.344	35	.371	4	70	-8	—	-0.2
Herbert, Fred	Frederick (b Herbert Frederick Kemman); B3.4.1887 LaGrange IL; D5.29.1963 Tice FL; BR/TR/6´0˝/185; d9.25																									
1915	NY N	1	1	.500	2	2	1	0	17	12	5	0	0	4	6	1.06	242	.197	.246	6	.167	-0	87	2	—	0.2
Herbert, Ray	Raymond Ernest; B12.15.1929 Detroit MI; BR/TR/5´11˝/185; d8.27; Mil 1951–52																									
1950	Det A	1	2	.333	8	3	1	1	22.1	20	11	1	0	12	5	3.63	129	.244	.340	7	.286	0	90	2	0	0.3
1951	Det A	4	0	1.000	5	0	0	0	12.2	8	2	0	0	9	9	1.42	294	.190	.333	4	.000	-0	—	4	0	0.8
1953	Det A	4	6	.400	43	3	0	6	87.2	109	58	5	0	46	37	5.24	78	.308	.387	19	.158	-0	102	-12	0	-1.2
1954	Det A	3	6	.333	42	4	0	0	84.1	114	64	6	2	50	44	5.87	63	.334	.419	17-1-0	.176	2	101	-21	0	-1.8
1955	KC A	1	8	.111	23	11	2	0	87.2	99	65	10	1	40-9	30	6.26	67	.292	.361	21-0-1	.190	0*	81	-18	0	-1.5
1958	KC A	8	8	.500	42	16	5	3	175	161	76	20	4	55-3	108	3.50	112	.248	.309	52-0-2	.192	1	79	7	0	0.9
1959	KC A	11	11	.500	37	26	10-2	1	183.2	196	108	24	1	62-4	99	4.85	83	.275	.330	57-1-3	.211	2	99	-14	0	-1.4
1960	KC A	14	15	.483	37	33	14	1	252.2	256	106	17	7	72-6	122	3.28	121	.267	.320	76-0-9	.171	1	78	18	0	2.3
1961	KC A	3	6	.333	13	12	1	0	83.2	103	56	10	2	30-1	34	5.38	78	.303	.360	28-0-2	.107	-1	79	-10	0	-1.0
	Chi A	9	6	.600	21	20	4	0	137.2	142	69	15	0	36-2	50	4.05	97	.265	.308	53-2-1	.226	4	98	-2	0	0.2
	Year	12	12	.500	34	32	5	0	221.1	245	125	25	2	66-3	84	4.55	88	.280	.328	81-2-3	.185	3	91	-13	0	-0.8
1962	Chi A★	20	9	**.690**	35	35	12-2	0	236.2	228	90	13	1	74-4	115	3.27	119	.255	.310	82-2-3	.195	5	109	19	0	2.9
1963	Chi A	13	10	.565	33	33	14-**7**	0	224.2	230	86	12	2	35-5	105	3.24	108	.265	.295	63-1-10	.222	6	115	9	0	1.7
1964	Chi A	6	7	.462	20	19	1-1	0	111.2	117	50	14	2	17-2	40	3.47	100	.275	.303	36-0-2	.139	-1	93	-1	38	-0.2
1965	Phi N	5	8	.385	25	19	4-1	1	130.2	162	60	13	1	19-2	51	3.86	90	.309	.333	41-0-4	.268	3	92	-4	0	0.0
1966	Phi N	2	5	.286	23	2	0	2	50.1	55	26	7	1	14-2	15	4.29	84	.293	.341	13	.077	-1	73	-4	0	-0.6
Total	14	104	107	.493	407	236	68-13	15	1881.1	2000	927	167	24	571-40	864	4.01	96	.276	.328	569-7-37	.192	20	95	-27	38	1.4
Heredia, Felix	Felix (Perez); B6.18.1975 Santa Cruz de Barahona, D.R.; BL/TL/6´0˝/(165–185); d8.9																									
1996	Fla N	1	1	.500	21	0	0	0-0	16.2	21	8	1	0	10-1	10	4.32	95	.313	.397	0	ø	0	—	0	0	0.0
1997	†Fla N	5	3	.625	56	0	0	0-1	56.2	53	30	3	5	30-1	54	4.29	95	.241	.342	2-0-1	.500	0	—	-2	0	-0.3
1998	Fla N	0	3	.000	41	2	0	2-1	41	38	30	1	1	32-2	38	5.49	74	.241	.368	3	.000	-0	91	-8	0	-0.6
	†Chi N	3	0	1.000	30	0	0	0-2	17.2	19	9	1	0	6-1	16	4.08	108	.279	.338	0	ø	0	—	0	0	0.0
	Year	3	3	.500	71	2	0	2-3	58.2	57	39	2	1	38-3	54	5.06	82	.252	.360	3	.000	-0	88	-8	0	-0.6
1999	Chi N	3	1	.750	69	0	0	1-6	52	56	35	7	1	25-2	50	4.85	94	.272	.347	4	.500	1	—	-4	0	-0.2
2000	Chi N	7	3	.700	74	0	0	2-3	58.2	46	31	6	2	33-4	52	4.76	96	.220	.329	2	.000	-0	—	0	0	-0.1
2001	Chi N	2	2	.500	48	0	0	0-3	35	45	27	6	2	16-1	28	6.17	68	.315	.384	1	.000	-0	—	-8	30	-0.9
2002	Tor A	1	2	.333	53	0	0	0-2	52.1	51	29	5	2	26-3	31	3.61	128	.256	.345	0	ø	0	—	3	0	0.2
2003	Cin N	5	2	.714	57	0	0	1-3	72	61	27	9	2	28-5	41	3.00	139	.228	.304	3	.333	0	—	9	0	0.8
	†NY A	0	1	.000	12	0	0	0-1	15	13	5	1	0	5-2	4	1.20	366	.228	.290	0	ø	0	—	4	0	0.3
2004	†NY A	1	1	.500	47	0	0	0-1	38.2	44	28	5	2	20-0	25	6.28	73	.278	.365	0	ø	0	—	-7	30	-0.3

YEAR	TM LG	W	L	PCT	G	GS	CG-SHO	SV-BS	IP	H	R	HR	HB	BB-IB	SO	ERA	AERA	OAV	OOB	AB-HR-SH	AVG	PB	SUP	APR	DL	PW
2005	NY N	0	0	ø	3	0	0	0-0	2.2	1	0	0	1	1-0	2	0.00	ø	.125	.300	0	ø	0	—	1	167	0.1
Total	10	28	19	.596	511	2	0	6-23	458.1	448	259	45	18	232-22	351	4.42	98	.255	.344	15-0-1	.267	1	85	-12	227	-1.0
HEREDIA, GIL	Gilbert; B10.26.1965 Nogales AZ; BR/TR/6´1˝/(190–221); [SFN87 9/230]; d9.1; Col Arizona																									
1991	SF N	0	2	.000	7	4	0	0-0	33	27	14	4	0	7-2	13	3.82	94	.233	.274	7	.429	1	88	0	0	0.1
1992	SF N	2	3	.400	13	4	0	0-0	30	32	20	3	1	16-1	15	5.40	62	.278	.371	6-0-1	.167	0	81	-7	0	-1.2
	Mon N	0	0	ø	7	1	0	0-0	14.2	12	3	1	0	4-0	7	1.84	189	.250	.302	3	.000	-0	26	3	0	0.1
	Year	2	3	.400	20	5	0	0-0	44.2	44	23	4	1	20-1	22	4.23	80	.270	.351	9-0-1	.111	-0	70	-4	0	-1.1
1993	Mon N	4	2	.667	20	9	1	2-1	57.1	66	28	4	2	14-2	40	3.92	106	.293	.339	13-0-4	.154	-0	110	2	0	0.3
1994	Mon N	6	3	.667	39	3	0	0-0	75.1	85	34	7	2	13-3	62	3.46	122	.281	.311	16	.313	1	136	6	0	0.7
1995	Mon N	5	6	.455	40	18	0	1-2	119	137	60	7	5	21-1	74	4.31	100	.291	.326	33-0-5	.182	-0	95	1	0	0.1
1996	Tex A	2	5	.286	44	0	0	1-3	73.1	91	50	12	1	14-2	43	5.89	89	.301	.332	0	ø	0	—	-4	0	-0.4
1998	Oak A	3	3	.500	8	6	0	0-0	42.2	43	14	4	3	3-0	27	2.74	169	.256	.282	0	ø	0	60	9	0	1.2
1999	Oak A	13	8	.619	33	33	1	0-0	200.1	228	119	22	8	34-4	117	4.81	99	.283	.318	6-0-1	.000	-0	113	-2	0	-0.2
2000	†Oak A	15	11	.577	32	32	2	0-0	198.2	214	106	24	4	66-5	101	4.12	118	.274	.332	2-0-1	.500	0	105	14	0	1.6
2001	Oak A	7	8	.467	24	18	0	0-0	109.2	144	75	27	2	29-3	48	5.58	82	.316	.357	3	.333	0	110	-12	0	-1.3
Total	10	57	51	.528	267	128	4	4-6	954	1079	523	115	28	221-23	547	4.46	102	.285	.327	89-0-12	.213	2	104	10	0	1.0
HEREDIA, UBALDO	Ubaldo Jose (Martinez); B5.4.1956 Ciudad Bolivar, Bolivar, Venez.; BR/TR/6´2˝/180; d5.12																									
1987	Mon N	0	1	.000	2	2	0	0-0	10	10	6	2	1	3-1	6	5.40	79	.263	.333	2	.000	-0	106	-1	0	-0.1
HEREDIA, WILSON	Wilson; B3.30.1972 LaRomana, D.R.; BR/TR/6´0˝/175; d4.27; [DL 1996 Fla N 182]																									
1995	Tex A	0	1	.000	6	0	0	0-0	12	9	5	2	0	15-2	6	3.75	129	.225	.429	0	ø	0	—	2	0	0.1
1997	Tex A	1	0	1.000	10	0	0	0-0	19.2	14	9	2	0	16-0	8	3.20	152	.197	.337	0	ø	0	—	3	0	0.1
Total	2	1	1	.500	16	0	0	0-0	31.2	23	14	4	0	31-2	14	3.41	142	.207	.372	0	ø	0	—	5	182	0.2
HERGES, MATT	Matthew Tyler; B4.1.1970 Champaign IL; BL/TR/6´0˝/(200–210); d8.3; Col Illinois St.																									
1999	LA N	0	2	.000	17	0	0	0-2	24.1	24	13	5	1	8-0	18	4.07	107	.255	.320	1	.000	-0	—	0	0	0.0
2000	LA N	11	3	.786	59	4	0	1-2	110.2	100	43	7	6	40-5	75	3.17	140	.249	.323	13-0-1	.077	-1	57	16	0	1.8
2001	LA N	9	8	.529	75	0	0	1-7	99.1	97	39	8	8	46-12	76	3.44	120	.259	.350	9-0-1	.444	1	—	9	0	1.5
2002	Mon N	2	5	.286	62	0	0	6-8	64.2	80	33	10	2	26-8	50	4.04	109	.305	.370	1	.000	0	—	2	0	0.2
2003	SD N	2	2	.500	40	0	0	3-2	44	40	16	2	2	20-2	40	2.86	140	.244	.325	1	.000	-0	—	5	0	0.5
	†SF N	1	0	1.000	27	0	0	0-1	35	28	11	1	1	9-0	28	2.31	184	.219	.273	2	.500	0	—	7	0	0.4
	Year	3	2	.600	67	0	0	3-3	79	68	27	3	3	29-2	68	2.62	157	.233	.303	3	.333	0	—	13	0	0.9
2004	SF N	4	5	.444	70	0	0	23-8	65.1	90	44	8	3	21-4	39	5.23	83	.338	.388	0	ø	0	—	-8	0	-1.4
2005	Ari N	0	0	ø	7	0	0	0-0	8	12	12	4	1	5-0	3	13.50	33	.343	.429	0	ø	0	—	-7	0	-0.4
	SF N	1	1	.500	21	0	0	0-0	21	23	11	2	0	7-1	6	4.71	90	.287	.341	0	ø	0	—	-1	0	-0.1
	Year	1	1	.500	28	0	0	0-0	29	35	23	6	1	12-1	9	7.14	60	.304	.369	0	ø	0	—	-8	0	-0.5
2006	Fla N	2	3	.400	66	0	0	0-4	71	94	42	5	3	28-5	36	4.31	99	.321	.385	0	ø	0	—	-2	0	-0.2
Total	8	32	29	.525	444	4	0	34-34	543.1	588	264	52	27	210-37	371	3.89	110	.280	.350	27-0-2	.222	1	57	21	0	2.3
HERMAN, ART	Arthur; B5.11.1871 Louisville KY; D9.20.1955 Los Angeles CA; d6.29																									
1896	Lou N	4	6	.400	14	12	9	0	94.1	122	73	4	2	36	13	5.63	77	.310	.371	36	.139	-4	89	-8	—	-1.0
1897	Lou N	0	1	.000	3	2	1	0	18	23	14	1	0	5	4	4.00	107	.307	.350	6	.333	1	125	0	—	0.2
Total	2	4	7	.364	17	14	10	0	112.1	145	87	5	2	41	17	5.37	81	.310	.368	42	.167	-2	94	-8	—	-0.8
HERMANSON, DUSTIN	Dustin Michael; B12.21.1972 Springfield OH; BR/TR/6´3˝/(195–205); [SDN94 1/3]; d5.8; Col Kent St.																									
1995	SD N	3	1	.750	26	0	0	0-0	31.2	35	26	8	1	22-1	19	6.82	60	.280	.392	0	ø	0	—	-9	0	-1.0
1996	SD N	1	0	1.000	8	0	0	0-0	13.2	18	15	3	0	4-0	11	8.56	47	.340	.367	0	ø	0	—	-8	0	-0.5
1997	Mon N	8	8	.500	32	28	1-1	0-0	158.1	134	68	15	1	66-2	136	3.69	113	.234	.311	48-1-5	.104	-0	89	11	0	0.9
1998	Mon N	14	11	.560	32	30	1	0-0	187	163	80	21	3	56-3	154	3.13	134	.234	.292	52-1-5	.115	2	91	20	15	2.7
1999	Mon N	9	14	.391	34	34	0	0-0	216.1	225	110	20	7	69-4	145	4.20	106	.271	.330	64-0-8	.047	-5	79	9	0	0.3
2000	Mon N	12	14	.462	38	30	2-1	4-3	198	226	128	26	4	75-5	94	4.77	99	.290	.352	55-0-8	.145	-1	88	-7	0	-0.8
2001	†StL N	14	13	.519	33	33	0	0-0	192.1	195	106	34	8	73-3	123	4.45	97	.264	.335	62-0-5	.081	-3*	108	-4	0	-0.9
2002	Bos A	1	1	.500	12	1	0	0-1	22	35	19	3	0	7-0	13	7.77	58	.354	.393	0	ø	0	248	-7	139	-0.6
2003	StL N	1	2	.333	23	0	0	1-5	29.2	35	18	4	1	14-2	12	5.46	76	.315	.394	0	ø	0	—	-4	0	-0.3
	†SF N	2	1	.667	9	6	0	0-0	39	35	14	5	2	10-2	27	3.00	142	.238	.294	11-0-3	.000	-1	103	5	16	0.2
	Year	3	3	.500	32	6	0	1-5	68.2	70	32	9	3	24-4	39	4.06	103	.271	.338	11-0-3	.000	-1	104	2	0	-0.1
2004	SF N	6	9	.400	47	18	0	17-3	131	132	71	15	3	46-5	102	4.53	96	.262	.323	30-0-6	.100	-1	127	-2	17	-0.5
2005	†Chi A	2	4	.333	57	0	0	34-5	57.1	46	17	4	1	17-4	33	2.04	221	.222	.284	0	ø	0	—	14	0	2.7
2006	Chi A	0	0	ø	6	0	0	0-0	6.2	6	3	2	1	1-1	5	4.05	115	.240	.296	0	ø	0	—	1	155	0.0
Total	12	73	78	.483	357	180	4-2	56-17	1283	1285	675	160	32	460-32	874	4.21	104	.263	.328	322-2-40	.093	-8	96	19	342	2.2
HERNAIZ, JESUS	Jesus Rafael (Rodriguez); B1.8.1945 Santurce, PR; BR/TR/6´2˝/170; d6.14																									
1974	Phi N	2	3	.400	27	0	0	1-3	41.1	53	31	6	0	25-1	16	5.88	65	.323	.411	2	.000	-0	—	-10	0	-1.1
HERNANDEZ, ADRIAN	Adrian; B3.25.1975 Havana, Cuba; BR/TR/6´1˝/(180–185); d4.21																									
2001	NY A	0	3	.000	6	3	0	0-0	22	15	10	7	2	10-1	10	3.68	121	.190	.297	0	ø	0	42	2	0	0.2
2002	NY A	0	1	.000	2	1	0	0-0	6	10	8	2	0	6-0	9	12.00	36	.357	.471	0	ø	0	64	-5	0	-0.6
2004	Mil N	0	2	.000	6	1	0	0-1	16	20	18	1	0	14-0	14	8.44	52	.294	.410	4-0-1	.000	-0	127	-8	0	-0.8
Total	3	0	6	.000	14	5	0	0-1	44	45	36	10	2	30-1	33	6.55	67	.257	.370	4-0-1	.000	-0	63	-11	0	-1.2
HERNANDEZ, CARLOS	Carlos E.; B4.22.1980 Guacara, Carabobo, Venez.; BL/TL/5´10˝/(145–200); d8.18; [DL 2003 Hou N 183]																									
2001	Hou N	1	0	1.000	3	3	0	0-0	17.2	11	2	1	0	7-0	17	1.02	451	.177	.261	5-0-1	.200	0	74	7	0	0.4
2002	Hou N	7	5	.583	23	21	0	0-0	111	112	56	11	3	61-5	93	4.38	99	.261	.357	35-0-4	.171	-0*	90	0	47	0.1
2004	Hou N	1	3	.250	9	9	0	0-0	42	50	31	11	5	23-0	26	6.43	68	.303	.398	12-0-4	.083	-1	120	-9	0	-0.8
Total	3	9	8	.529	35	33	0	0-0	170.2	173	89	23	8	91-5	136	4.54	96	.264	.359	52-0-9	.154	-1	96	-2	230	-0.3
HERNANDEZ, LIVAN	Eisler Livan; B2.20.1975 Villa Clara, Cuba; BR/TR/6´2˝/(220–245); d9.24; b–Orlando																									
1996	Fla N	0	0	ø	1	0	0	0-0	3	3	0	0	0	2-0	2	0.00	ø	.273	.385	1	1.000	0	—	1	0	0.1
1997	†Fla N	9	3	.750	17	17	0	0-0	96.1	81	39	5	3	38-1	72	3.18	128	.229	.304	29-0-3	.172	1	126	9	0	1.2
1998	Fla N	10	12	.455	33	33	9	0-0	234.1	265	133	37	6	104-8	162	4.72	86	.289	.363	82-0-1	.195	2*	103	-17	0	-1.2
1999	Fla N	5	9	.357	20	20	2	0-0	136	161	78	17	2	55-3	97	4.76	92	.294	.358	45-2-1	.289	5	97	-6	0	0.1
	SF N	3	3	.500	10	10	0	0-0	63.2	66	32	6	0	21-2	47	4.38	98	.267	.322	18-0-6	.222	1*	92	0	0	0.2
	Year	8	12	.400	30	30	2	0-0	199.2	227	110	23	2	76-5	144	4.64	94	.286	.347	63-2-7	.270	6	95	-6	0	0.3
2000	†SF N	17	11	.607	33	33	5-2	0-0	240	254	114	22	4	73-3	165	3.75	116	.273	.325	89-1-9	.236	5*	110	15	0	2.2
2001	SF N	13	15	.464	34	34	2	0-0	226.2	266	143	24	3	85-7	138	5.24	78	.297	.355	81-1-4	.296	8*	97	-30	0	-2.2
2002	†SF N	12	16	.429	33	33	5-3	0-0	216	233	113	19	4	71-5	134	4.38	90	.283	.340	64-0-10	.234	4*	102	-10	0	-0.6
2003	Mon N	15	10	.600	33	33	**8**	0-0	**233.1**	225	92	27	10	57-3	178	3.20	139	.253	.304	74-0-6	.189	0	109	31	0	3.4
2004	Mon N☆	11	15	.423	35	**35**	**9**-2	0-0	**255**	234	105	26	10	83-9	186	3.60	128	.248	.314	81-1-15	.247	5*	72	30	0	3.7
2005	Was N★	15	10	.600	35	**35**	2	0-0	**246.1**	268	116	25	13	84-14	147	3.98	103	.284	.348	82-2-14	.244	6	96	4	0	1.2
2006	Was N	9	8	.529	24	24	0	0-0	146.2	176	94	22	2	52-4	89	5.34	82	.298	.353	45-1-9	.267	5*	98	-16	0	-1.0
	Ari N	4	5	.444	10	10	0	0-0	69.1	70	31	7	2	26-2	39	3.76	124	.266	.336	23-0-4	.087	-1*	77	7	0	0.7
	Year	13	13	.500	34	34	0	0-0	216	246	125	29	4	78-6	128	4.83	92	.288	.348	68-1-13	.206	4	91	-8	0	-0.3
Total	11	123	117	.512	318	317	42-7	0-0	2166.2	2302	1090	237	59	751-61	1456	4.18	102	.275	.337	714-8-82	.234	43	98	18	0	7.8
HERNANDEZ, FELIX	Felix Abraham (Garcia); B4.8.1986 Valencia, Carabobo, Venezuela; BR/TR/6´3˝/(170–230); d8.4																									
2005	Sea A	4	4	.500	12	12	0	0-0	84.1	61	26	5	2	23-0	77	2.67	156	.203	.263	0	ø	0	74	15	0	1.4
2006	Sea A	12	14	.462	31	31	2-1	0-0	191	195	105	23	6	60-2	176	4.52	97	.262	.321	4-0-1	.000	-0	95	-4	0	-0.4
Total	2	16	18	.471	43	43	2-1	0-0	275.1	256	131	28	8	83-2	253	3.96	110	.245	.304	4-0-1	.000	-0	89	11	0	1.0
HERNANDEZ, FERNANDO	Fernando; B6.16.1971 Santiago, D.R.; BR/TR/6´2˝/185; d4.3																									
1997	Det A	0	0	ø	2	0	0	0-0	1.1	5	6	0	1	3-1	2	40.50	11	.556	.692	0	ø	0	—	-5	0	-0.2

YEAR	TM LG	W	L	PCT	G	GS	CG-SHO	SV-BS	IP	H	R	HR	HB	BB-IB	SO	ERA	AERA	OAV	OOB	AB-HR-SH	AVG	PB	SUP	APR	DL	PW
HERNANDEZ, XAVIER	Francis Xavier; B8.16.1965 Port Arthur TX; BL/TR/6´2˝/(185–195); [TorA86 4/107]; d6.4; Col Louisiana–Lafayette																									
1989	Tor A	1	0	1.000	7	0	0	0-0	22.2	25	15	2	1	8-0	7	4.76	80	.278	.337	0	ø	0	—	-3	0	-0.2
1990	Hou N	2	1	.667	34	1	0	0-1	62.1	60	34	8	4	24-5	24	4.62	81	.256	.331	3	.333	0*	48	-5	0	-0.3
1991	Hou N	2	7	.222	32	6	0	3-3	63	66	34	6	0	32-7	55	4.71	75	.263	.345	10-0-1	.000	-0	42	-7	23	-1.1
1992	Hou N	9	1	.900	77	0	0	7-3	111	81	31	5	3	42-7	96	2.11	161	.200	.279	9	.000	-1	—	15	0	1.4
1993	Hou N	4	5	.444	72	0	0	9-8	96.2	75	37	6	1	28-3	101	2.61	149	.212	.269	5-0-2	.000	-1	—	12	0	1.1
1994	NY A	4	4	.500	31	0	0	6-2	40	48	27	7	2	21-3	37	5.85	79	.300	.384	0	ø	0	—	-5	15	-0.9
1995	†Cin N	7	2	.778	59	0	0	3-1	90	95	47	8	4	31-1	84	4.60	91	.273	.338	8	.000	-1	—	-3	0	-0.4
1996	Cin N	0	0	ø	3	0	0	0-0	3.1	8	6	2	0	2-0	3	13.50	32	.471	.526	0	ø	0	—	-4	0	-0.2
	Hou N	5	5	.500	58	0	0	6-4	74.2	69	39	11	2	26-5	78	4.22	92	.245	.310	2-0-1	.000	-0	—	-3	0	-0.4
	Year	5	5	.500	61	0	0	6-4	78	77	45	13	2	28-5	81	4.62	84	.258	.322	2-0-1	.000	-0	—	-7	0	-0.6
1997	Tex A	0	4	.000	44	0	0	0-1	49.1	51	27	7	2	22-4	36	4.56	107	.262	.341	0	ø	0	—	2	58	0.1
1998	Tex A	6	6	.500	46	0	0	1-5	58	43	27	5	1	30-1	41	3.57	137	.207	.307	0	ø	0	—	7	35	1.3
Total	10	40	35	.533	463	7	0	35-28	671	621	324	67	20	266-36	562	3.90	102	.244	.318	37-0-4	.027	-3	39	6	131	0.4
HERNANDEZ, EVELIO	Gregorio Evelio (Lopez); B12.24.1931 Guanabacoa, Cuba; BR/TR/6´1˝/195; d9.12																									
1956	Was A	1	1	.500	4	4	1	0	22.2	24	12	2	0	8-0	9	4.76	91	.276	.333	11	.182	-0	103	0	0	-0.1
1957	Was A	0	0	ø	14	2	0	0	36	38	18	2	0	20-1	15	4.25	92	.268	.356	6	.000	-1	115	-1	0	-0.2
Total	2	1	1	.500	18	6	1	0	58.2	62	30	4	0	28-1	24	4.45	91	.271	.347	17	.118	-1	110	-1	0	-0.3
HERNANDEZ, WILLIE	Guillermo (Villanueva); B11.14.1954 Aguada, PR; BL/TL/6´3˝/(180–186); d4.9																									
1977	Chi N	8	7	.533	67	1	0	4-7	110	94	42	11	1	28-9	78	3.03	146	.234	.284	16-0-3	.063	-1	20	15	0	2.0
1978	Chi N	8	2	.800	54	0	0	3-1	59.2	57	26	6	1	35-7	38	3.77	107	.263	.363	1	.000	-0*	—	2	0	0.4
1979	Chi N	4	4	.500	51	2	0	0-0	79	85	50	8	4	39-12	53	5.01	83	.281	.364	8-0-1	.250	0*	128	-7	0	-0.6
1980	Chi N	1	9	.100	53	7	0	0-2	108.1	115	58	8	2	45-4	75	4.40	90	.276	.347	19-0-1	.211	0	48	-4	0	-0.2
1981	Chi N	0	0	ø	12	0	0	2-0	13.2	14	7	0	0	8-2	13	3.95	95	.280	.367	0	ø	0*	—	0	0	0.0
1982	Chi N	4	6	.400	75	0	0	10-2	75	74	26	3	1	24-11	54	3.00	126	.268	.326	3-0-1	.000	-0	—	7	0	1.2
1983	Chi N	1	0	1.000	11	1	0	1-0	19.2	16	8	0	0	6-1	18	3.20	119	.222	.282	2	.500	0	139	1	0	0.1
	†Phi N	8	4	.667	63	0	0	7-3	95.2	93	39	9	1	26-7	75	3.29	109	.254	.305	13	.385	2	—	4	0	0.7
	Year	9	4	.692	74	1	0	8-3	115.1	109	47	9	1	32-8	93	3.28	111	.249	.301	15	.400	2	146	4	0	0.8
1984	†Det A★	9	3	.750	**80**	0	0	32-1	140.1	96	30	6	4	36-8	112	1.92	206	.194	.252	0	ø	0	—	**34**	0	**4.3**
1985	Det A★	8	10	.444	74	0	0	31-9	106.2	82	38	13	1	14-2	76	2.70	152	.210	.236	1	.000	-0	—	16	0	3.1
1986	Det A☆	8	7	.533	64	0	0	24-6	88.2	87	35	13	5	21-1	77	3.55	117	.251	.301	0	ø	0	—	8	0	1.6
1987	†Det A	3	4	.429	45	0	0	8-5	49	53	27	8	0	20-7	30	3.67	116	.276	.340	0	ø	0	—	1	50	0.2
1988	Det A	6	5	.455	63	0	0	10-5	67.2	50	24	8	4	31-6	59	3.06	126	.208	.306	0	ø	0	—	7	0	1.3
1989	Det A	2	2	.500	32	0	0	15-2	31.1	36	21	4	1	16-2	30	5.74	67	.293	.379	0	ø	0	—	-6	69	-1.2
Total	13	70	63	.526	744	11	0	147-43	1044.2	952	431	97	25	349-79	788	3.38	119	.245	.308	63-0-6	.206	1	69	78	119	12.9
HERNANDEZ, JEREMY	Jeremy Stuart; B7.6.1966 Burbank CA; BR/TR/6´6˝/(195–210); [StLN87 2/46]; d9.2; Col Cal St.–Northridge																									
1991	SD N	0	0	ø	9	0	0	2-0	14.1	8	1	0	0	5-0	9	0.00	ø	.157	.232	2	.000	-0	—	5	0	0.3
1992	SD N	1	4	.200	26	0	0	1-1	36.2	39	17	4	1	11-5	25	4.17	86	.291	.338	2	.000	-0	—	-2	0	-0.2
1993	SD N	0	2	.000	21	0	0	0-0	34.1	41	19	2	0	7-1	26	4.72	88	.301	.333	1	.000	-0	—	-1	0	-0.1
	Cle A	6	5	.545	49	0	0	8-5	77.1	75	33	12	0	27-6	44	3.14	139	.261	.320	0	ø	0	—	9	0	1.3
1994	Fla N	3	3	.500	21	0	0	9-3	23.1	16	9	0	2	14-3	13	2.70	165	.205	.337	1	.000	-0	—	4	70	0.7
1995	Fla N	0	0	ø	7	0	0	0-1	7	12	9	2	1	3-1	5	11.57	37	.400	.457	1	.000	-0	—	-5	114	-0.3
Total	5	10	14	.417	133	0	0	20-10	193	191	88	20	4	67-16	122	3.64	114	.267	.327	7	.000	-1	—	10	184	1.7
HERNANDEZ, MANNY	Manuel Antonio (Montas); B5.7.1961 LaRomana, D.R.; BR/TR/6´0˝/150; d6.5																									
1986	Hou N	2	3	.400	9	4	0	0-0	27.2	33	15	2	0	12-3	9	3.90	92	.306	.372	6-0-1	.000	-1	62	-2	0	-0.3
1987	Hou N	0	4	.000	6	3	0	0-0	21.2	25	15	1	1	5-1	12	5.40	73	.301	.341	5	.000	-1	84	-4	0	-0.7
1989	NY N	0	0	ø	1	0	0	0-0	1	0	0	0	0	0-0	1	0.00	ø	.000	.000	0	ø	0	—	0	0	0.0
Total	3	2	7	.222	16	7	0	0-0	50.1	58	30	3	1	17-4	22	4.47	84	.299	.353	11-0-1	.000	-1	72	-6	0	-1.0
HERNANDEZ, ORLANDO	Orlando P. "El Duque"; B10.11.1965 Villa Clara, Cuba; BR/TR/6´2˝/(190–220); d6.3; b–Livan; [DL 2003 Mon N 183]																									
1998	†NY A	12	4	.750	21	21	3-1	0-0	141	113	53	11	6	52-1	131	3.13	140	.222	.299	7-0-1	.000	-1	146	20	0	2.1
1999	†NY A★	17	9	.654	33	33	2-1	0-0	214.1	187	108	24	8	87-2	157	4.12	115	.233	.311	3	.333	0	105	15	0	1.6
2000	†NY A	12	13	.480	29	29	3	0-0	195.2	186	104	34	6	51-2	141	4.51	106	.247	.298	9-0-1	.000	-1	82	7	22	0.7
2001	†NY A	4	7	.364	17	16	0	0-0	94.2	90	51	19	5	42-1	77	4.85	92	.248	.333	0	ø	0	70	-2	87	-0.2
2002	†NY A	8	5	.615	24	22	0	1-0	146	131	63	17	8	36-2	113	3.64	119	.236	.289	0	ø	0	107	13	42	1.1
2004	†NY A	8	2	.800	15	15	0	0-0	84.2	73	31	9	5	36-0	84	3.30	139	.230	.318	0	ø	0	110	13	103	1.4
2005	†Chi A	9	9	.500	24	22	0	1-0	128.1	137	77	18	12	50-1	91	5.12	88	.275	.352	3	.333	0	89	-7	50	-0.8
2006	Ari N	2	4	.333	9	9	0	0-0	45.2	52	32	8	4	20-3	52	6.11	77	.292	.376	11-0-2	.273	1	103	-6	0	-0.6
	NY N	9	7	.563	20	20	1	0-0	116.2	103	58	14	8	41-2	112	4.09	107	.236	.310	35-0-5	.143	-0	102	4	0	0.5
	Year	11	11	.500	29	29	1	0-0	162.1	155	90	22	12	61-5	164	4.66	96	.252	.329	46-0-7	.174	1	102	-3	0	-0.1
Total	8	81	60	.574	192	187	9-2	2-0	1167	1072	577	154	62	415-14	958	4.19	109	.243	.314	68-0-9	.147	0	101	57	487	5.8
HERNANDEZ, RAMON	Ramon (Gonzalez); B8.31.1940 Carolina, PR; BB/TL/5´9˝/(165–170); d4.11																									
1967	Atl N	0	2	.000	46	0	0	5	51.2	60	27	5	2	14-3	28	4.18	79	.296	.345	4	.000	-0	—	-5	0	-0.3
1968	Chi N	0	0	ø	8	0	0	0	9	14	11	1	1	0-0	3	9.00	35	.350	.366	0	ø	0	—	-6	0	-0.3
1971	Pit N	0	1	.000	10	0	0	4-0	12.1	5	1	0	0	2-1	7	0.73	466	.122	.163	2	.500	0	—	4	0	0.7
1972	†Pit N	5	0	1.000	53	0	0	14-1	70	50	14	3	3	22-2	47	1.67	199	.194	.264	12	.167	0	—	14	0	1.7
1973	Pit N	4	5	.444	59	0	0	11-1	89.2	71	27	5	4	25-8	64	2.41	146	.218	.282	8	.125	0	—	12	0	1.5
1974	†Pit N	5	2	.714	58	0	0	2-3	68.2	68	21	3	2	18-8	33	2.75	126	.258	.310	4	.250	1	—	7	0	0.8
1975	†Pit N	7	2	.778	46	0	0	5-3	64	62	21	0	0	28-14	43	2.95	121	.252	.325	6-0-2	.000	-0	—	6	0	1.0
1976	Pit N	2	2	.500	37	0	0	3-3	43	42	17	3	1	16-5	17	3.56	99	.262	.326	3	.000	-0	—	1	0	0.0
	Chi N	0	0	ø	2	0	0	0-0	1.2	2	0	0	0	0-0	1	0.00	ø	.333	.333	0	ø	0	—	1	0	0.0
	Year	2	2	.500	39	0	0	3-3	44.2	44	17	3	1	16-5	18	3.43	103	.265	.326	3	.000	-0	—	2	0	0.0
1977	Chi N	0	0	ø	6	0	0	1-0	7.2	11	9	1	0	3-0	4	8.22	54	.306	.359	1	.000	-0	—	-3	0	-0.2
	Bos A	0	1	.000	12	0	0	1-0	12.2	14	10	2	1	7-1	8	5.68	79	.280	.379	0	ø	0	—	-2	0	-0.2
Total	9	23	15	.605	337	0	0	46-11	430.1	399	158	23	14	135-42	255	3.03	115	.245	.307	40-0-2	.125	1	—	29	0	4.7
HERNANDEZ, ROBERTO	Roberto Manuel (Rodriguez); B11.11.1964 Santurce, PR; BR/TR/6´4˝/(220–250); [CalA86 1/16]; d9.2; Col South Carolina–Aiken																									
1991	Chi A	1	0	1.000	9	3	0	0-0	15	18	15	1	0	7-0	6	7.80	51	.290	.362	0	ø	0	153	-7	0	-0.4
1992	Chi A	7	3	.700	43	0	0	12-4	71	45	15	4	4	20-1	68	1.65	236	.180	.249	0	ø	0	—	18	0	2.9
1993	†Chi A	3	4	.429	70	0	0	38-6	78.2	66	21	6	0	20-1	71	2.29	184	.228	.276	0	ø	0	—	18	0	2.9
1994	Chi A	4	4	.500	45	0	0	14-6	47.2	44	29	5	1	19-1	50	4.91	96	.238	.311	0	ø	0	—	-1	0	-0.3
1995	Chi A	3	7	.300	60	0	0	32-10	59.2	63	30	9	3	28-4	84	3.92	114	.266	.351	0	ø	0	—	3	0	0.6
1996	Chi A★	6	5	.545	72	0	0	38-8	84.2	65	21	2	0	38-5	85	1.91	249	.208	.292	0	ø	0	—	27	0	5.1
1997	Chi A	5	1	.833	46	0	0	27-4	48	38	15	5	1	24-4	47	2.44	181	.216	.312	0	ø	0	—	11	0	2.1
	†SF N	5	2	.714	28	0	0	4-4	32.2	29	9	2	0	14-1	35	2.48	166	.238	.316	2	.500	0	—	7	0	1.3
1998	TB A	2	6	.250	67	0	0	26-9	71.1	55	33	5	5	41-4	55	4.04	119	.212	.330	0	ø	0	—	6	0	1.0
1999	TB A	2	3	.400	72	0	0	43-4	73.1	68	27	1	4	33-1	69	3.07	162	.244	.329	0	ø	0	—	16	0	2.5
2000	TB A	4	7	.364	68	0	0	32-8	73.1	76	33	9	3	23-1	61	3.19	154	.272	.331	0	ø	0	—	12	0	2.2
2001	KC A	5	6	.455	63	0	0	28-6	67.2	69	34	7	1	26-3	46	4.12	120	.266	.336	0	ø	0	—	6	0	1.1
2002	KC A	1	3	.250	53	0	0	26-7	52	62	29	6	3	12-2	39	4.33	115	.300	.345	0	ø	0	—	2	32	0.4
2003	†Atl N	5	3	.625	66	0	0	0-4	60	61	36	10	3	43-7	45	4.35	97	.263	.385	0	ø	0	—	-3	35	-0.3
2004	Phi N	3	5	.375	63	0	0	0-4	56.2	66	39	9	1	29-3	44	4.76	93	.297	.379	0	ø	0	—	-5	15	-0.6
2005	NY N	8	6	.571	67	0	0	4-6	69.2	57	20	5	2	28-4	61	2.58	160	.228	.309	0	ø	0	—	13	0	2.6
2006	Pit N	0	3	.000	46	0	0	2-3	43	46	24	3	1	24-7	33	2.93	156	.264	.355	0	ø	0	—	4	0	0.2
	†NY N	0	0	ø	22	0	0	0-0	20.2	15	8	2	0	8-1	15	3.48	126	.208	.287	0	ø	0	—	2	0	0.1
	Year	0	3	.000	68	0	0	2-3	63.2	61	32	5	1	32-8	48	3.11	145	.248	.336	0	ø	0	—	6	0	0.3
Total	16	64	68	.485	960	3	0	326-93	1025	943	438	91	32	437-50	914	3.32	137	.244	.324	2	.500	0	153	129	82	23.4

YEAR	TM LG	W	L	PCT	G	GS	CG-SHO	SV-BS	IP	H	R	HR	HB	BB-IB	SO	ERA	AERA	OAV	OOB	AB-HR-SH	AVG	PB	SUP	APR	DL	PW
Hernandez, Rudy	Rudolph Albert (Fuentes); B12.10.1931 Santiago, D.R.; BR/TR/6´3˝/(185–190); d7.3																									
1960	Was A	4	1	.800	21	0	0	0	34.2	34	24	2	1	21-3	22	4.41	88	.262	.366	6-0-1	.167	-0*	—	-4	0	-0.5
1961	Was A	0	1	.000	7	0	0	0	9	8	5	0	0	3-0	4	3.00	134	.250	.306	0	ø	0	—	0	0	0.1
Total	2	4	2	.667	28	0	0	0	43.2	42	29	2	1	24-3	26	4.12	95	.259	.354	6-0-1	.167	-0	—	-4	0	-0.4
Hernandez, Runelvys	Runelvys Antonio; B4.27.1978 Santo Domingo, D.R.; BR/TR/6´3˝/(185–250); d7.15; [DL 2004 KC A 183]																									
2002	KC A	4	4	.500	12	12	0	0-0	74.1	79	36	8	1	22-0	45	4.36	114	.273	.324	0	ø	0	105	6	0	0.6
2003	KC A	7	5	.583	16	16	0	0-0	91.2	87	51	9	6	37-0	48	4.61	104	.249	.328	0	ø	0	102	2	98	0.2
2005	KC A	8	14	.364	29	29	0	0-0	159.2	172	101	18	7	70-0	88	5.52	79	.277	.353	5	.000	-1	77	-18	15	-2.2
2006	KC A	6	10	.375	21	21	1-1	0-0	109.2	145	87	22	6	48-0	50	6.48	72	.327	.394	0	ø	0	89	-22	0	-2.6
Total	4	25	33	.431	78	78	1-1	0-0	435.1	483	275	57	20	177-0	231	5.38	87	.284	.354	5	.000	-1	90	-32	296	-4.0
Herndon, Junior	Harry Francis; B9.11.1978 Liberal KS; BR/TR/6´1˝/190; [SDN97 9/290]; d8.2																									
2001	SD N	2	6	.250	12	8	0	0-0	42.2	55	34	5	3	25-5	14	6.33	66	.322	.417	12-0-1	.000	-1	75	-11	0	-1.8
Herrell, Walt	Walter William "Reds"; B2.19.1889 Rockville MD; D1.23.1949 Front Royal VA; 5´10.5˝/?; d6.10																									
1911	Was A	0	0	ø	1	0	0	0	2	5	4	0	0	2	0	18.00	18	.556	.636	1	.000	-0	—	-3	—	-0.1
Herrera, Alex	Alexander Jose; B11.5.1979 Maracaibo, Zulia, Venezuela; BL/TL/5´11˝/175; d9.13																									
2002	Cle A	0	0	ø	5	0	0	0-0	5.1	3	0	0	0	1-0	5	0.00	ø	.158	.200	0	ø	0	—	3	0	0.1
2003	Cle A	0	0	ø	10	0	0	0-0	7	7	7	3	0	8-1	6	9.00	49	.250	.417	0	ø	0	—	-3	0	-0.2
Total	2	0	0	ø	15	0	0	0-0	12.1	10	7	3	0	9-1	11	5.11	87	.213	.339	0	ø	0	—	0	0	-0.1
Herrera, Bobby	Procopio Rodriguez "Tito" (b Procopio Rodriguez (Herrera)); B7.26.1926 Nuevo Laredo, Tamaulipas, Mexico; BR/TR/6´0˝/184; d4.19																									
1951	StL A	0	0	ø	3	0	0	0	2.1	6	7	2	1	4	1	27.00	16	.462	.611	0	ø	0	—	-5	0	-0.2
Herriage, Troy	William Troy "Dutch"; B12.20.1930 Tipton OK; BR/TR/6´1˝/170; d4.25																									
1956	KC A	1	13	.071	31	16	1	0	103	135	83	16	6	64-6	59	6.64	65	.321	.414	25-0-2	.120	-1*	63	-24	0	-3.0
Herrin, Tom	Thomas Edward; B9.12.1929 Shreveport LA; D11.29.1999 Homer LA; BR/TR/6´3˝/190; d4.13; Col Louisiana Tech																									
1954	Bos A	1	2	.333	14	1	0	0	28.1	34	23	2	0	22	8	7.31	56	.315	.424	8	.125	-0	0	-8	0	-0.7
Herring, Art	Arthur L "Red","Sandy"; B3.10.1906 Altus OK; D12.2.1995 Marion IN; BR/TR/5´7˝/168; d9.12																									
1929	Det A	2	1	.667	4	4	2	0	32	38	17	0	1	19	15	4.78	90	.302	.397	14	.214	1	103	0	—	0.1
1930	Det A	3	3	.500	23	6	1	0	77.2	97	54	2	3	36	16	5.33	90	.315	.392	23-0-2	.130	-2	89	-4	—	-0.5
1931	Det A	7	13	.350	35	16	9	1	165	186	95	8	8	67	64	4.31	106	.281	.355	55-0-3	.200	-1	93	4	—	0.5
1932	Det A	1	2	.333	12	0	0	2	22.1	25	18	2	1	15	12	5.24	90	.284	.394	4	.000	-0	—	-2	—	-0.3
1933	Det A	1	2	.333	24	3	1	0	61	61	34	6	1	20	20	3.84	112	.264	.325	13	.077	-1	171	2	—	0.0
1934	Bro N	2	4	.333	14	4	2	0	49.1	63	36	2	0	29	15	6.20	63	.307	.393	14	.143	1	111	-11	—	-1.1
1939	Chi A	0	0	ø	7	0	0	0	14.1	13	9	2	1	5	8	5.65	84	.250	.328	4	.000	-0	—	-1	—	-0.1
1944	Bro N	3	4	.429	12	6	3-1	1	55.1	59	28	3	1	17	19	3.42	104	.277	.333	15-0-3	.200	0	122	-1	0	0.0
1945	Bro N	7	4	.636	22	15	7-2	2	124	103	60	11	3	43	34	3.48	108	.222	.292	42-0-4	.095	-2*	126	4	0	0.1
1946	Bro N	7	2	.778	35	2	0	5	86	91	39	2	1	29	34	3.35	101	.277	.338	22-0-1	.182	0	76	0	0	0.1
1947	Pit N	1	3	.250	11	0	0	2	10.2	18	11	3	0	4	6	8.44	50	.360	.407	2	.000	-0	—	-5	0	-0.9
Total	11	34	38	.472	199	56	25-3	13	697.2	754	401	41	20	284	243	4.32	96	.276	.349	208-0-13	.149	-4	110	-14	0	-2.1
Herring, Herb	Herbert Lee; B7.22.1891 Danville AR; D4.22.1964 Tucson AZ; BR/TR/5´11˝/178; d9.4																									
1912	Was A	0	0	ø	1	0	0	0	1	1	0	0	0	1	0	0.00	ø	.250	.400	0	ø	0	—	0	—	0.0
Herring, Bill	William Francis "Smoke"; B10.31.1893 New York NY; D9.10.1962 Honesdale PA; BR/TR/6´3˝/185; d6.26																									
1915	Bro F	0	0	ø	3	0	0	0	3	5	6	1	1	2	3	15.00	18	.385	.500	0	ø	0	—	-4	—	-0.2
Herrmann, Leroy	Leroy George; B2.27.1906 Steward IL; D7.3.1972 Livermore CA; BR/TR/5´10˝/185; d7.30																									
1932	Chi N	2	1	.667	7	0	0	0	12.2	18	9	0	0	9	5	6.39	59	.346	.443	2	.500	0	—	-3	—	-0.6
1933	Chi N	0	1	.000	9	1	0	1	21	26	19	3	4	8	4	5.57	59	.299	.384	6	.167	-0	102	-7	—	-0.4
1935	Cin N	3	5	.375	29	8	2	0	108	124	53	9	8	31	30	3.58	111	.297	.357	30	.267	1	117	4	—	0.4
Total	3	5	7	.417	45	9	2	1	141.2	168	81	12	12	48	39	4.13	93	.302	.370	38	.263	1	117	-6	—	-0.6
Herrmann, Marty	Martin John "Lefty"; B1.10.1893 Oldenburg IN; D9.11.1956 Cincinnati OH; BL/TL/5´10˝/150; d7.10; gs–Ed																									
1918	Bro N	0	0	ø	1	0	0	0	1	0	0	0	0	1	0	0.00	ø	.000	.250	0	ø	0	—	0	—	0.0
Hershey, Frank	Frank; B12.13.1877 Gorham NY; D12.15.1949 Canandaigua NY; TR/5´10˝/175; d4.20																									
1905	Bos N	0	1	.000	1	1	0	0	4	5	4	0	0	2	1	6.75	46	.313	.389	1	.000	-0	47	-2	—	-0.3
Hershiser, Orel	Orel Leonard; B9.16.1958 Buffalo NY; BR/TR/6´3˝/(190–198); [LAN79 17/440]; d9.1; C4; Col Bowling Green																									
1983	LA N	0	0	ø	8	0	0	1-0	8	7	6	1	0	6-0	5	3.38	107	.233	.361	0	ø	0	—	-1	0	0.0
1984	LA N	11	8	.579	45	20	8-**4**	2-2	189.2	160	65	9	4	50-8	150	2.66	134	.225	.278	50-0-8	.200	2	103	19	0	2.1
1985	†LA N	19	3	**.864**	36	34	9-5	0-0	239.2	179	72	8	6	68-5	157	2.03	173	.206	.267	76-0-10	.197	3*	114	37	0	3.8
1986	LA N	14	14	.500	35	35	8-1	0-0	231.1	213	112	13	5	86-11	153	3.85	90	.243	.312	71-0-10	.239	4*	96	-11	0	-0.8
1987	LA N★	16	16	.500	37	35	10-1	1-0	**264.2**	247	105	17	9	74-5	190	3.06	130	.247	.304	90-0-10	.211	4*	92	26	0	**3.5**
1988	†LA N★	**23**	8	.742	35	34	**15-8**	1-0	**267**	208	73	18	4	73-10	178	2.26	148	.213	.269	85-0-19	.129	-0*	107	**35**	0	**4.5**
1989	LA N☆	15	15	.500	35	33	8-4	0-0	**256.2**	226	75	9	3	77-14	178	2.31	148	.240	.298	77-0-10	.182	3	85	**32**	0	**4.4**
1990	LA N	1	1	.500	4	4	0	0-0	25.1	26	12	1	1	4-0	16	4.26	86	.260	.295	7-0-1	.000	-1	92	-1	160	-0.1
1991	LA N	7	2	.778	21	21	0	0-0	112	112	43	3	5	32-6	73	3.46	104	.259	.316	31-0-4	.258	3	140	5	51	0.8
1992	LA N	10	15	.400	33	33	1	0-0	210.2	209	101	15	8	69-13	130	3.67	94	.257	.320	68-0-6	.221	4*	81	-5	0	0.0
1993	LA N	12	14	.462	33	33	5-1	0-0	215.2	201	106	17	7	72-13	141	3.59	108	.246	.311	73-0-8	.356	10*	106	4	0	1.6
1994	LA N	6	6	.500	21	21	1	0-0	135.1	146	67	15	2	42-6	72	3.79	105	.279	.333	44-0-3	.205	2*	114	1	0	0.3
1995	†Cle A	16	6	.727	26	26	1-1	0-0	167.1	151	76	21	5	51-1	111	3.87	122	.244	.304	0	ø	0	108	17	15	2.1
1996	†Cle A	15	9	.625	33	33	1	0-0	206	238	115	21	12	58-4	125	4.24	115	.287	.341	0	ø	0	113	11	0	1.3
1997	†Cle A	14	6	.700	32	32	1	0-0	195.1	199	105	26	11	69-2	107	4.47	105	.272	.340	3-0-1	.000	-0	109	5	15	0.5
1998	SF N	11	10	.524	34	34	0	0-0	202	200	105	22	13	85-7	126	4.41	91	.259	.341	66-0-8	.152	1	99	-8	0	-0.6
1999	†NY N	13	12	.520	32	32	0	0-0	179	175	92	14	11	77-2	89	4.58	95	.260	.342	62-0-3	.145	-1	97	-4	0	-0.4
2000	LA N	1	5	.167	10	6	0	0-1	24.2	42	36	5	11	14-1	13	13.14	34	.389	.493	7	.000	-1	86	-23	0	-3.6
Total	18	204	150	.576	510	466	68-25	5-3	3130.1	2939	1366	235	117	1007-108	2014	3.48	112	.248	.312	810-0-101	.201	32	104	139	241	19.4
Hesketh, Joe	Joseph Thomas; B2.15.1959 Lackawanna NY; BL/TL/6´2˝/(170–173); [MonN80 2/50]; d8.7																									
1984	Mon N	2	2	.500	11	5	1-1	1-0	45	38	12	2	0	15-3	32	1.80	192	.233	.294	10	.100	0	97	8	0	0.7
1985	Mon N	10	5	.667	25	25	2-1	0-0	155.1	125	52	10	0	45-2	113	2.49	138	.222	.279	44-0-5	.091	-1*	94	15	44	1.3
1986	Mon N	6	5	.545	15	15	0	0-0	82.2	92	46	11	2	31-4	67	5.01	75	.283	.347	23-0-3	.000	-2	94	-9	94	-1.3
1987	Mon N	0	0	ø	18	0	0	1-0	28.2	23	12	2	2	15-3	31	3.14	136	.211	.317	4-0-1	.000	-0	—	3	0	0.1
1988	Mon N	4	3	.571	60	0	0	9-2	72.2	63	30	1	0	35-9	64	2.85	128	.242	.328	2	.000	0	—	5	0	0.7
1989	Mon N	6	4	.600	43	0	0	3-1	48.1	54	34	5	0	26-6	44	5.77	62	.292	.376	2	.500	0	—	-11	21	-2.3
1990	Mon N	1	0	1.000	2	0	0	0-0	3	2	0	0	0	2-1	3	0.00	ø	.200	.333	0	ø	0	—	1	0	0.3
	Atl N	0	2	.000	31	0	0	5-4	31	30	23	5	1	12-0	21	5.81	69	.248	.319	1	.000	-0	—	-6	0	-0.6
	Year	1	2	.333	33	0	0	5-4	34	32	23	5	1	14-1	24	5.29	76	.244	.320	1	.000	-0	—	-5	0	-0.3
	Bos A	0	4	.000	12	2	0	0-0	25.2	37	12	2	0	11-1	26	3.51	117	.333	.393	0	ø	0	11	1	0	0.2
1991	Bos A	12	4	.750	39	17	0	0-0	153.1	142	59	19	0	53-3	104	3.29	132	.250	.313	0	ø	0	103	18	0	1.8
1992	Bos A	8	9	.471	30	25	1	1-0	148.2	162	84	15	2	58-9	104	4.36	98	.276	.339	0	ø	0	93	-2	0	-0.2
1993	Bos A	3	4	.429	28	5	0	1-0	53.1	62	35	4	0	29-4	34	5.06	92	.294	.376	0	ø	0	80	-3	45	-0.3
1994	Bos A	8	5	.615	25	20	0	0-0	114	117	70	9	2	46-3	83	4.26	118	.267	.334	0	ø	0	99	5	0	0.4
Total	11	60	47	.561	339	114	4-2	21-7	961.2	947	469	85	9	378-48	726	3.78	108	.259	.328	86-0-9	.070	-2	96	25	204	0.8
Hess, Otto	Otto C.; B10.10.1878 Bern, Switzerland; D2.25.1926 Tucson AZ; BL/TL/6´1˝/170; d8.3; ▲																									
1902	Cle A	2	4	.333	7	4	4	0	43.2	67	42	0	1	23	13	5.98	58	.351	.423	14	.071	-1	104	-12	—	-1.3
1904	Cle A	8	7	.533	21	16	15-4	0	151.1	134	60	2	5	31	64	1.67	152	.238	.284	100-0-1	.120	-3*	102	8	—	0.4
1905	Cle A	10	15	.400	26	25	22-4	0	213.2	179	97	1	9	72	109	3.16	83	.229	.302	173-2-3	.254	5*	88	-11	—	-0.7

YEAR	TM LG	W	L	PCT	G	GS	CG-SHO	SV-BS	IP	H	R	HR	HB	BB-IB	SO	ERA	AERA	OAV	OOB	AB-HR-SH	AVG	PB	SUP	APR	DL	PW
1906	Cle A	20	17	.541	43	36	33-7	**3**	333.2	274	104	4	24	85	167	1.83	143	.227	.291	154-0-1	.201	1*	109	28	—	3.3
1907	Cle A	6	6	.500	17	14	7	1	93.1	84	37	1	12	37	36	2.89	87	.243	.337	30-0-1	.133	0*	94	-1	—	-0.2
1908	Cle A	0	0	ø	4	0	0	0	7	11	6	0	0	1	2	5.14	46	.407	.429	14	.000	-1*	—	-2	—	-0.2
1912	Bos N	12	17	.414	33	31	21	0	254	270	142	3	15	90	80	3.76	95	.283	.354	94-0-6	.245	3	103	-5	—	-0.3
1913	Bos N	7	17	.292	29	27	19-2	0	218.1	231	123	13	7	70	80	3.83	86	.279	.340	83-2-4	.313	8*	104	-10	—	-0.2
1914	Bos N	5	6	.455	14	11	7-1	1	89	89	39	2	5	33	24	3.03	91	.271	.347	47-1-2	.234	1*	116	-3	—	-0.1
1915	Bos N	0	1	.000	4	1	1	0	14	16	13	0	2	6	5	3.86	67	.286	.375	5	.400	1*	115	-4	—	-0.2
Total	10	70	90	.438	198	165	129-18	5	1418	1355	663	26	80	448	580	2.98	98	.257	.324	714-5-18	.216	14	103	-12	—	0.5

HESSELBACHER, GEORGE George Edward; B1.18.1895 Philadelphia PA; D2.18.1980 Rydal PA; BR/TR/6´2˝/175; d6.29; Col Penn St.

YEAR	TM LG	W	L	PCT	G	GS	CG-SHO	SV-BS	IP	H	R	HR	HB	BB-IB	SO	ERA	AERA	OAV	OOB	AB-HR-SH	AVG	PB	SUP	APR	DL	PW
1916	Phi A	0	4	.000	6	4	2	0	26	37	33	3	0	22	6	7.27	39	.349	.461	8	.125	-0	86	-15	—	-1.8

HESTERFER, LARRY Lawrence; B6.9.1878 Newark NJ; D9.22.1943 Cedar Grove NJ; BR/TL/5´8˝/145; d9.5

YEAR	TM LG	W	L	PCT	G	GS	CG-SHO	SV-BS	IP	H	R	HR	HB	BB-IB	SO	ERA	AERA	OAV	OOB	AB-HR-SH	AVG	PB	SUP	APR	DL	PW
1901	NY N	0	1	.000	1	1	1	0	6	15	15	0	0	3	2	7.50	44	.469	.514	2	.000	0	150	-6	—	-0.6

HETKI, JOHNNY John Edward; B5.12.1922 Leavenworth KS; BR/TR/6´1˝/(190–205); d9.14

YEAR	TM LG	W	L	PCT	G	GS	CG-SHO	SV-BS	IP	H	R	HR	HB	BB-IB	SO	ERA	AERA	OAV	OOB	AB-HR-SH	AVG	PB	SUP	APR	DL	PW
1945	Cin N	1	2	.333	5	2	2	0	32.2	28	13	1	0	11	9	3.58	105	.235	.300	11	.091	-1	79	1	0	0.1
1946	Cin N	6	6	.500	32	11	4	1	126.1	121	44	3	1	31	41	2.99	112	.253	.300	33-0-5	.333	3	88	7	0	1.0
1947	Cin N	3	4	.429	37	5	2	0	96	110	72	7	1	48	33	5.81	71	.287	.368	27	.222	1	69	-19	0	-1.1
1948	Cin N	0	1	.000	3	0	0	0	6.2	8	7	0	0	3	3	9.45	41	.286	.355	1	.000	0	—	-4	0	-0.5
1950	Cin N	1	2	.333	22	1	0	0	53	53	33	9	3	27	21	5.09	83	.265	.361	9-0-2	.222	0	42	-5	0	-0.2
1952	StL A	0	1	.000	3	1	0	0	9.1	15	7	2	0	2	4	3.86	101	.357	.386	1	.000	0	67	-1	0	-0.1
1953	Pit N	3	6	.333	54	2	0	3	118.1	120	60	9	1	33	37	3.95	113	.266	.318	24-0-1	.208	1	80	6	0	0.6
1954	Pit N	4	4	.500	58	1	0	9	83	102	53	11	0	30	27	4.99	84	.297	.349	9-0-1	.222	-0	21	-7	0	-0.8
Total	8	18	26	.409	214	23	8	13	525.1	557	289	42	6	185	175	4.39	91	.272	.334	115-0-9	.235	5	72	-22	0	-1.0

HETZEL, ERIC Eric Paul; B9.25.1963 Crowley LA; BR/TR/6´3˝/(175–180); [BosA85 S1/1]; d7.1; Col Louisiana St.

YEAR	TM LG	W	L	PCT	G	GS	CG-SHO	SV-BS	IP	H	R	HR	HB	BB-IB	SO	ERA	AERA	OAV	OOB	AB-HR-SH	AVG	PB	SUP	APR	DL	PW
1989	Bos A	2	3	.400	12	11	0	0-0	50.1	61	39	7	2	28-1	33	6.26	66	.296	.382	0	ø	0	132	-11	21	-1.0
1990	Bos A	1	4	.200	9	8	0	0-0	35	39	28	3	1	21-0	20	5.91	69	.281	.377	0	ø	0	72	-8	0	-1.0
Total	2	3	7	.300	21	19	0	0-0	85.1	100	67	10	3	49-1	53	6.12	67	.290	.380	0	ø	0	107	-19	21	-2.0

HEUSSER, ED Edward Burlton "The Wild Elk of the Wasatch"; B5.7.1909 Salt Lake Co. UT; D3.1.1956 Aurora CO; BB/TR (BR 1935–36, 38)/6´0.5˝/187; d4.25

YEAR	TM LG	W	L	PCT	G	GS	CG-SHO	SV-BS	IP	H	R	HR	HB	BB-IB	SO	ERA	AERA	OAV	OOB	AB-HR-SH	AVG	PB	SUP	APR	DL	PW
1935	StL N	5	5	.500	33	11	2	2	123.1	125	50	5	2	27	39	2.92	140	.263	.305	34-0-1	.118	-1	90	14	—	0.9
1936	StL N	7	3	.700	42	3	0	3	104.1	130	73	6	4	38	26	5.43	73	.310	.373	26-1-0	.269	3	72	-18	—	-1.4
1938	Phi N	0	0	ø	1	0	0	0	1	2	3	1	0	1	0	27.00	14	.400	.500	0	ø	0	—	-2	—	-0.1
1940	Phi A	6	13	.316	41	6	2	5	110	144	84	11	2	42	39	4.99	89	.308	.368	30-1-1	.167	1	119	-11	—	-1.6
1943	Cin N	4	3	.571	26	10	2-1	0	91	97	40	4	0	23	28	3.46	96	.275	.319	27-0-1	.185	-1	120	-2	0	-0.3
1944	Cin N	13	11	.542	30	23	17-4	2	192.2	165	59	9	1	42	42	**2.38**	**146**	.231	.275	69-0-1	.217	1	68	25	0	3.1
1945	Cin N	11	16	.407	31	30	18-4	1	223	248	105	10	3	60	56	3.71	101	.280	.328	77-1-5	.247	4	73	1	0	0.6
1946	Cin N	7	14	.333	29	21	9-1	2	167.2	167	68	11	1	39	47	3.22	104	.260	.304	53-0-4	.208	2	83	4	0	0.5
1948	Phi N	3	2	.600	33	0	0	3	74	89	46	9	0	28	22	4.99	79	.299	.359	19	.158	-1	—	-8	0	-0.6
Total	9	56	67	.455	266	104	50-10	18	1087	1167	528	66	13	300	299	3.69	101	.274	.324	335-3-13	.206	8	81	3	0	1.1

HEVING, JOE Joseph William; B9.2.1900 Covington KY; D4.11.1970 Covington KY; BR/TR/6´1˝/185; d4.29; b–Johnnie

YEAR	TM LG	W	L	PCT	G	GS	CG-SHO	SV-BS	IP	H	R	HR	HB	BB-IB	SO	ERA	AERA	OAV	OOB	AB-HR-SH	AVG	PB	SUP	APR	DL	PW
1930	NY N	7	5	.583	41	2	0	6	89.2	109	57	7	1	27	37	5.22	91	.309	.360	22-0-2	.227	-0	120	-3	—	-0.3
1931	NY N	1	6	.143	22	0	0	3	42.1	48	27	4	2	11	26	4.89	76	.277	.328	8-0-2	.125	-0	—	-6	—	-0.9
1933	Chi A	7	5	.583	40	6	3-1	6	118	113	50	6	2	27	47	2.67	159	.249	.295	38-0-1	.211	0	50	17	—	1.8
1934	Chi A	1	7	.125	33	2	0	4	88	133	85	12	3	48	40	7.26	65	.343	.419	27	.185	1	92	-25	—	-1.9
1937	Cle A	8	4	.667	40	0	0	5	72.2	92	53	6	2	30	35	4.83	95	.311	.378	19-0-2	.263	0	—	-5	—	-0.7
1938	Cle A	1	1	.500	3	0	0	0	6	10	8	0	0	5	0	9.00	52	.370	.469	1	.000	-0	—	-4	—	-0.6
	Bos A	8	1	.889	16	11	7-1	2	82	94	35	5	1	22	34	3.73	132	.283	.330	30-0-3	.133	-2	135	12	—	1.2
	Year	9	2	.818	19	11	7-1	2	88	104	43	5	1	27	34	4.09	120	.290	.341	31-0-3	.129	-2	135	9	—	0.6
1939	Bos A	11	3	.786	46	5	1	7	107	124	65	8	2	34	43	3.70	128	.295	.350	32-0-3	.188	-1	116	6	—	0.6
1940	Bos A	12	7	.632	39	7	4	3	119	129	63	7	3	42	55	4.01	112	.272	.335	40-0-2	.200	0	179	4	—	0.6
1941	Cle A	5	2	.714	27	3	2-1	5	70.2	63	21	2	1	31	18	2.29	172	.240	.323	15-0-1	.000	-1	73	13	0	1.4
1942	Cle A	5	3	.625	27	2	0	3	46.1	52	28	4	2	25	13	4.86	71	.278	.369	7-0-1	.000	-1	62	-7	0	-1.3
1943	Cle A	1	1	.500	30	1	0	9	72	58	23	1	2	34	34	2.75	113	.230	.326	14-0-2	.071	-0	54	4	0	0.3
1944	Cle A	8	3	.727	**63**	1	0	10	119.2	106	42	2	2	41	46	1.96	169	.239	.307	22-0-2	.182	-1	25	14	0	1.4
1945	Bos N	1	0	1.000	3	0	0	0	5.1	5	2	0	1	3	1	3.38	114	.294	.429	1-0-1	.000	-0	—	0	0	0.1
Total	13	76	48	.613	430	40	17-3	63	1038.2	1136	559	64	24	380	429	3.90	108	.279	.344	276-0-22	.170	-4	120	20	0	1.7

HEWITT, JAKE Charles Jacob; B6.6.1870 Maidsville WV; D5.18.1959 Morgantown WV; BL/TL/5´7˝/150; d8.6; Col West Virginia

YEAR	TM LG	W	L	PCT	G	GS	CG-SHO	SV-BS	IP	H	R	HR	HB	BB-IB	SO	ERA	AERA	OAV	OOB	AB-HR-SH	AVG	PB	SUP	APR	DL	PW
1895	Pit N	1	0	1.000	4	2	1	2	13	13	6	0	1	2	4	4.15	108	.255	.296	6	.167	-1	103	2	—	0.1

HEYDEMAN, GREG Gregory George; B1.2.1952 Carmel CA; BR/TR/6´0˝/205; d9.2; Col Monterey Peninsula (CA) JC

YEAR	TM LG	W	L	PCT	G	GS	CG-SHO	SV-BS	IP	H	R	HR	HB	BB-IB	SO	ERA	AERA	OAV	OOB	AB-HR-SH	AVG	PB	SUP	APR	DL	PW
1973	LA N	0	0	ø	1	0	0	0-0	2	2	1	0	1	1-0	1	4.50	77	.222	.364	0	ø	0	—	0	0	0.0

HIBBARD, GREG James Gregory; B9.13.1964 New Orleans LA; BL/TL/6´0˝/(180–190); [KCA86 16/417]; d5.31; Col Alabama; [DL 1995 Sea A 160, 1996 Sea A 183, 1997 Sea A 181]

YEAR	TM LG	W	L	PCT	G	GS	CG-SHO	SV-BS	IP	H	R	HR	HB	BB-IB	SO	ERA	AERA	OAV	OOB	AB-HR-SH	AVG	PB	SUP	APR	DL	PW
1989	Chi A	6	7	.462	23	23	2	0-0	137.1	142	58	5	2	41-0	55	3.21	120	.268	.321	0	ø	0	109	8	0	0.8
1990	Chi A	14	9	.609	33	33	3-1	0-0	211	202	80	11	6	55-2	92	3.16	122	.255	.305	0	ø	0	85	17	0	1.7
1991	Chi A	11	11	.500	32	29	5	0-0	194	196	107	23	2	57-1	71	4.31	93	.266	.320	0	ø	0	114	-10	0	-1.0
1992	Chi A	10	7	.588	31	28	0	1-0	176	187	92	17	7	57-2	69	4.40	88	.277	.337	0	ø	0	102	-9	0	-0.7
1993	Chi N	15	11	.577	31	31	1	0-0	191	209	96	19	3	47-9	82	3.96	102	.286	.327	65-0-3	.092	-3*	104	0	20	-0.3
1994	Sea A	1	5	.167	15	14	0	0-0	80.2	115	78	11	2	31-1	39	6.69	74	.328	.383	0	ø	0	100	-20	49	-1.2
Total	6	57	50	.533	165	158	11-1	1-0	990	1051	511	86	22	288-15	408	4.05	99	.275	.327	65-0-3	.092	-3	102	-14	593	-0.7

HIBBARD, JOHN John Denison; B12.2.1864 Chicago IL; D11.17.1937 Hollywood CA; TL; d7.31; Col Michigan

YEAR	TM LG	W	L	PCT	G	GS	CG-SHO	SV-BS	IP	H	R	HR	HB	BB-IB	SO	ERA	AERA	OAV	OOB	AB-HR-SH	AVG	PB	SUP	APR	DL	PW
1884	Chi N	1	1	.500	2	2	2-1	0	17	18	10	1	—	9	4	2.65	118	.300	.391	7	.000	-1	102	1	—	0.0

HICKERSON, BRYAN Bryan David; B10.13.1963 Bemidji MN; BL/TL/6´2˝/(190–203); [MinA86 7/169]; d7.25; Col Minnesota

YEAR	TM LG	W	L	PCT	G	GS	CG-SHO	SV-BS	IP	H	R	HR	HB	BB-IB	SO	ERA	AERA	OAV	OOB	AB-HR-SH	AVG	PB	SUP	APR	DL	PW
1991	SF N	2	2	.500	17	6	0	0-0	50	53	20	3	0	17-3	43	3.60	100	.275	.333	12-0-1	.000	-1	92	1	0	-0.1
1992	SF N	5	3	.625	61	1	0	0-5	87.1	74	31	7	1	21-2	68	3.09	108	.236	.282	4	.000	-0	190	3	0	0.2
1993	SF N	7	5	.583	47	15	0	0-0	120.1	137	58	14	1	39-3	69	4.26	92	.291	.344	28-0-4	.143	-0	119	-3	0	-0.4
1994	SF N	4	8	.333	28	14	0	1-0	98.1	118	60	20	1	38-6	59	5.40	75	.301	.363	27-0-2	.185	1	104	-13	0	-1.3
1995	Chi N	2	3	.400	38	0	0	1-2	31.2	36	28	3	0	15-4	28	6.82	61	.283	.359	2	.500	1	—	-10	0	-1.3
	Col N	1	0	1.000	18	0	0	0-1	16.2	33	24	5	1	13-1	12	11.88	45	.407	.495	1-0-1	1.000	1	—	-9	0	-0.4
	Year	3	3	.500	56	0	0	1-3	48.1	69	52	8	1	28-5	40	8.57	54	.332	.414	3-0-1	.667	1	—	-20	0	-1.7
Total	5	21	21	.500	209	36	0	2-8	404.1	451	221	52	4	143-19	279	4.72	82	.286	.345	74-0-8	.149	0	112	-31	0	-3.3

HICKEY, JIM James Robert "Sid"; B10.22.1920 N.Abington MA; D9.20.1997 Manchester CT; BR/TR/6´1˝/204; d4.25; Mil 1944–45

YEAR	TM LG	W	L	PCT	G	GS	CG-SHO	SV-BS	IP	H	R	HR	HB	BB-IB	SO	ERA	AERA	OAV	OOB	AB-HR-SH	AVG	PB	SUP	APR	DL	PW
1942	Bos N	0	1	.000	1	1	0	0	1.1	4	4	1	0	2	0	20.25	16	.500	.600	1	.000	-0	25	-3	0	-0.5
1944	Bos N	0	0	ø	8	0	0	0	9.1	15	9	0	1	5	3	4.82	79	.366	.447	1	.000	-0	—	-2	0	-0.1
Total	2	0	1	.000	9	1	0	0	10.2	19	13	1	1	7	3	6.75	56	.388	.474	2	.000	-0	25	-5	0	-0.6

HICKEY, JACK John William; B11.3.1881 Minneapolis MN; D12.28.1941 Seattle WA; BR/TL/5´10˝/170; d4.16

YEAR	TM LG	W	L	PCT	G	GS	CG-SHO	SV-BS	IP	H	R	HR	HB	BB-IB	SO	ERA	AERA	OAV	OOB	AB-HR-SH	AVG	PB	SUP	APR	DL	PW
1904	Cle A	0	1	.000	2	2	1	0	12.1	14	13	0	0	11	5	7.30	35	.286	.417	5	.000	-1	141	-6	—	-0.5

HICKEY, KEVIN Kevin John; B2.25.1957 Chicago IL; BL/TL/6´1˝/(170–201); d4.14

YEAR	TM LG	W	L	PCT	G	GS	CG-SHO	SV-BS	IP	H	R	HR	HB	BB-IB	SO	ERA	AERA	OAV	OOB	AB-HR-SH	AVG	PB	SUP	APR	DL	PW
1981	Chi A	0	2	.000	41	0	0	3-0	44.1	38	22	3	1	18-5	17	3.65	99	.232	.308	0	ø	0	—	-1	0	0.0
1982	Chi A	4	4	.500	60	0	0	6-2	78	73	32	4	2	30-6	38	3.00	136	.256	.327	0	ø	0	—	8	0	1.0
1983	Chi A	1	2	.333	23	0	0	5-3	20.2	23	14	5	0	11-2	8	5.23	81	.264	.347	0	ø	0	—	-3	33	-0.5
1989	Bal A	2	3	.400	51	0	0	2-0	49.1	38	16	3	1	23-4	28	2.92	131	.220	.315	0	ø	0	—	6	0	0.5
1990	Bal A	1	3	.250	37	0	0	1-0	26.1	26	16	3	0	13-2	17	5.13	75	.265	.348	0	ø	0	—	-4	0	-0.6
1991	Bal A	1	0	1.000	19	0	0	0-1	14	15	14	3	0	6-0	10	9.00	44	.278	.339	0	ø	0	—	-8	0	-0.5
Total	6	9	14	.391	231	0	0	17-6	232.2	213	114	21	4	101-19	118	3.91	100	.247	.326	0	ø	0	—	-2	33	-0.1

YEAR	TM LG	W	L	PCT	G	GS	CG-SHO	SV-BS	IP	H	R	HR	HB	BB-IB	SO	ERA	AERA	OAV	OOB	AB-HR-SH	AVG	PB	SUP	APR	DL	PW
HICKMAN, CHARLIE	Charles Taylor "Cheerful Charlie","Piano Legs"; B3.4.1876 Taylortown (Dunkard Twp.) PA; D4.19.1934 Morgantown WV; BR/TR/5´9˝/180; d9.8; Col West Virginia; ▲																									
1897	†Bos N	0	0	ø	2	0	0	1	7.2	10	5	0	0	5	0	5.87	76	.313	.405	3-1-0	.667	2	—	-1	—	0.1
1898	Bos N	1	2	.333	6	3	3-1	2	33	22	8	0	0	13	9	2.18	169	.188	.269	58-0-1	.259	0*	83	6	—	0.6
1899	Bos N	6	0	1.000	11	9	5-2	1	66.1	52	38	3	8	40	14	4.48	93	.216	.346	63-0-1	.397	6*	167	0	—	0.3
1901	NY N	3	5	.375	9	9	6	0	65	76	42	1	3	26	11	4.57	72	.290	.361	406-4-0	.278	2*	64	-7	—	-0.5
1902	Cle A	0	1	.000	1	1	1	0	8	11	8	0	1	5	1	7.88	44	.324	.425	426-8-8	.378	1*	146	-3	—	-0.3
1907	Was A	0	0	ø	1	0	0	0	5	4	4	0	0	5	2	3.60	67	.222	.391	198-1-1	.278	0*	—	-1	—	0.0
Total	6	10	8	.556	30	22	15-3	4	185	175	105	4	12	94	37	4.28	86	.249	.347	1154-14-11	.321	11	117	-6	—	0.2
HICKMAN, ERNIE	Ernest P.; B1856 E.St.Louis IL; D11.19.1891 E.St.Louis IL; d6.7																									
1884	KC U	4	13	.235	17	17	15	0	137.1	172	146	5	—	36	68	4.52	49	.287	.328	72	.167	-5*	67	-41	—	-4.1
HICKMAN, JESSE	Jesse Owens; B2.18.1939 Lecompte LA; BR/TR/6´2˝/186; d6.5; Col Louisiana																									
1965	KC A	0	1	.000	12	0	0	0	15.1	9	10	3	0	8-0	16	5.87	59	.184	.293	0	ø	0*	—	-3	0	-0.2
1966	KC A	0	0	ø	1	0	0	0	1	0	0	0	0	1-0	0	0.00	ø	.000	.333	0	ø	0	—	0	0	0.0
Total	2	0	1	.000	13	0	0	0	16.1	9	10	3	0	9-0	16	5.51	63	.176	.295	0	ø	0	—	-3	0	-0.2
HIGBE, KIRBY	Walter Kirby; B4.8.1915 Columbia SC; D5.6.1985 Columbia SC; BR/TR/5´11˝/190; d10.3; Mil 1944–45																									
1937	Chi N	1	0	1.000	1	0	0	0	5	4	3	1	0	1	2	5.40	74	.182	.217	3	.000	-0	—	-1	—	-0.2
1938	Chi N	0	0	ø	2	2	0	0	10	10	6	1	0	6	4	5.40	71	.263	.364	3	.000	-0	111	-1	—	-0.1
1939	Chi N	2	1	.667	9	2	0	0	22.2	12	9	0	0	22	16	3.18	124	.158	.347	7-0-1	.286	1	177	2	—	0.3
	Phi N	10	14	.417	34	26	14-1	2	187.1	208	113	10	10	101	79	4.85	83	.283	.378	66-0-6	.167	-2	92	-17	—	-2.3
	Year	12	15	.444	43	28	14-1	2	210	220	122	10	10	123	95	4.67	86	.272	.374	73-0-7	.178	-2	98	-14	—	-2.0
1940	Phi N☆	14	19	.424	41	36	20-1	1	283	242	126	12	3	121	**137**	3.72	105	.232	.313	103-0-3	.165	-2	77	8	—	0.7
1941	†Bro N	**22**	9	.710	**48**	**39**	19-2	3	298	244	123	17	6	132	121	3.14	117	.220	.306	112-0-6	.188	1	126	17	0	1.4
1942	Bro N	16	11	.593	38	32	13-2	0	221.2	180	89	17	2	106	115	3.25	100	.223	.315	77-0-7	.104	-4	127	2	0	-0.3
1943	Bro N	13	10	.565	35	27	8-1	0	185	189	81	4	5	95	108	3.70	91	.264	.354	65-1-4	.138	-2	95	-5	0	-0.8
1946	Bro N★	17	8	.680	42	29	11-3	1	210.2	178	82	6	1	107	134	3.03	111	.229	.323	77-0-6	.130	-4	121	9	0	0.7
1947	Bro N	2	0	1.000	4	3	0	0	15.2	18	9	0	1	12	10	5.17	80	.295	.419	5	.200	0	171	-1	0	-0.1
	Pit N	11	17	.393	46	30	10-1	5	225	204	108	22	3	110	99	3.72	113	.240	.329	72-1-6	.139	-1	90	11	0	1.0
	Year	13	17	.433	50	33	10-1	5	240.2	222	117	22	4	122	109	3.81	111	.243	.335	77-1-6	.143	-1	97	10	0	0.9
1948	Pit N	8	7	.533	56	8	3	10	158	140	75	11	3	83	86	3.36	121	.240	.337	48-1-0	.208	1	82	8	0	0.8
1949	Pit N	0	2	.000	7	1	0	0	15.1	25	24	2	0	12	5	13.50	31	.379	.474	3	.000	-0	126	-15	0	-1.5
	NY N	2	0	1.000	37	2	0	2	80.1	72	42	11	1	41	38	3.47	115	.242	.335	15	.067	-0	122	2	0	0.0
	Year	2	2	.500	44	3	0	2	95.2	97	66	13	1	53	43	5.08	79	.266	.361	18	.056	-1	124	-12	0	-1.5
1950	NY N	0	3	.000	18	1	0	0	34.2	37	19	2	0	30	17	4.93	83	.285	.419	4	.250	0	129	-2	0	-0.1
Total	12	118	101	.539	418	238	98-11	24	1952.1	1763	909	116	35	979	971	3.69	102	.241	.333	660-3-39	.153	-14	104	17	0	-0.5
HIGGINBOTHAM, IRV	Irving Clinton; B4.26.1882 Homer NE; D6.12.1959 Seattle WA; BR/TR/6´1˝/196; d8.11																									
1906	StL N	1	4	.200	7	6	4	0	47.1	50	23	1	1	11	14	3.23	81	.266	.310	18	.222	0	46	-3	—	-0.3
1908	StL N	3	8	.273	19	11	7-1	0	107	113	51	0	3	33	38	3.20	74	.270	.328	38-0-1	.132	-1	81	-8	—	-1.0
1909	StL N	1	0	1.000	3	1	1	0	11.1	5	3	0	0	2	2	1.59	159	.143	.189	3	.000	-0	138	1	—	0.0
	Chi N	5	2	.714	19	6	4	1	78	64	32	0	3	20	32	2.19	116	.213	.269	26-0-1	.231	1	202	1	—	0.1
	Year	6	2	.750	22	7	5	1	89.1	69	35	0	3	22	34	2.12	120	.205	.260	29-0-1	.207	0	193	2	—	0.1
Total	3	10	14	.417	48	24	16-1	1	243.2	232	109	1	7	66	86	2.81	88	.246	.300	85-0-2	.176	-1	106	-9	—	-1.2
HIGGINS, DENNIS	Dennis Dean; B8.4.1939 Jefferson City MO; BR/TR/6´4˝/(180–198); d4.12																									
1966	Chi A	1	0	1.000	42	1	0	5	93	66	27	9	5	33-4	86	2.52	126	.202	.283	17	.176	0	195	9	0	0.5
1967	Chi A	1	2	.333	9	0	0	0	12.1	13	9	0	3	10-0	8	5.84	53	.271	.426	1	.000	-0	—	-4	79	-0.8
1968	Was A	4	4	.500	59	0	0	13	99.2	81	40	9	3	46-9	66	3.25	90	.226	.313	15-0-1	.133	-0	—	-3	0	-0.5
1969	Was A	10	9	.526	55	0	0	16-10	85.1	79	42	7	3	56-7	71	3.48	101	.252	.364	11-0-1	.091	-1	—	-2	0	-0.5
1970	Cle A	4	6	.400	58	0	0	11-2	90.1	82	43	8	2	54-8	82	3.99	101	.248	.356	12-0-1	.250	1	—	0	0	0.1
1971	StL N	1	0	1.000	3	0	0	0-0	7	6	3	0	0	2-0	6	3.86	94	.240	.286	1	.000	-0	—	0	0	0.0
1972	StL N	1	2	.333	15	1	0	1-0	22.2	19	14	0	0	22-0	20	3.97	86	.226	.387	1	.000	-0	103	-3	0	-0.4
Total	7	22	23	.489	241	2	0	46-12	410.1	346	178	33	16	223-28	339	3.42	99	.233	.335	58-0-3	.155	0	144	-3	79	-1.6
HIGGINS, EDDIE	Thomas Edward "Doc","Irish"; B3.18.1888 Nevada IL; D2.14.1959 Elgin IL; BR/TR/6´0.5˝/174; d5.14																									
1909	StL N	3	3	.500	16	5	5	0	66	68	36	4	1	17	15	4.50	56	.273	.322	21	.190	-0	55	-11	—	-1.0
1910	StL N	0	1	.000	2	0	0	0	10.1	15	8	0	0	7	1	4.35	68	.349	.440	5	.400	1*	—	-2	—	-0.1
Total	2	3	4	.429	18	5	5	0	76.1	83	44	4	1	24	16	4.48	58	.284	.341	26	.231	1	55	-13	—	-1.1
HIGH, ED	Edward Thomas "Lefty"; B10.26.1873 Baltimore MD; D2.10.1926 Baltimore MD; TL; d7.4																									
1901	Det A	1	0	1.000	4	1	1	0	18	21	9	0	1	6	4	3.50	110	.288	.350	7	.000	-1	88	1	—	0.0
HIGUERA, TEDDY	Teodoro Valenzuela (Valenzuela); B11.9.1958 Los Mochis, Sinaloa, Mexico; BB/TL/5´10˝/(178–180); d4.23; [DL 1992 Mil A 182]																									
1985	Mil A	15	8	.652	32	30	7-2	0-0	212.1	186	105	22	3	63-0	127	3.90	108	.235	.290	0	ø	0	96	7	0	0.6
1986	Mil A★	20	11	.645	34	34	15-4	0-0	248.1	226	84	26	3	74-5	207	2.79	156	.241	.296	0	ø	0	83	43	0	5.1
1987	Mil A	18	10	.643	35	35	14-3	0-0	261.2	236	120	24	2	87-2	240	3.85	120	.241	.301	0	ø	0	109	22	0	2.0
1988	Mil A	16	9	.640	31	31	8-1	0-0	227.1	168	66	15	6	59-4	192	2.45	163	.207	**.263**	0	ø	0	96	**40**	0	4.4
1989	Mil A	9	6	.600	22	22	2-1	0-0	135.1	125	56	9	4	48-2	91	3.46	112	.248	.316	0	ø	0	98	7	28	0.6
1990	Mil A	11	10	.524	27	27	4-1	0-0	170	167	80	16	3	50-2	129	3.76	103	.256	.310	0	ø	0	102	3	15	0.3
1991	Mil A	3	2	.600	7	6	0	0-0	36.1	37	18	2	1	10-0	33	4.46	90	.262	.314	0	ø	0	137	-1	144	-0.1
1993	Mil A	1	3	.250	8	8	0	0-0	30	43	24	4	1	16-2	27	7.20	60	.333	.408	0	ø	0	117	-9	131	-1.0
1994	Mil A	1	5	.167	17	12	0	0-0	58.2	74	55	13	2	36-0	35	7.06	72	.311	.403	0	ø	0	89	-14	0	-1.1
Total	9	94	64	.595	213	205	50-12	0-0	1380	1262	608	131	25	443-17	1081	3.61	117	.243	.303	0	ø	0	99	98	500	10.8
HILCHER, WHITEY	Walter Frank; B2.28.1909 Chicago IL; D11.21.1962 Minneapolis MN; BR/TR/6´0˝/174; d9.17; Col Alabama																									
1931	Cin N	0	1	.000	2	1	0	0	12	16	5	0	1	4	5	3.00	125	.320	.382	4	.000	-1	69	1	—	0.0
1932	Cin N	0	3	.000	11	2	0	0	18.2	24	19	3	0	10	4	7.71	50	.316	.395	3	.333	1	76	-8	—	-1.0
1935	Cin N	2	0	1.000	4	2	1-1	0	19.1	19	6	0	0	5	9	2.79	142	.264	.312	6	.167	-0	75	3	—	0.3
1936	Cin N	1	2	.333	14	1	0	0	35	44	31	3	1	14	10	6.17	62	.299	.364	8	.000	-1	178	-11	—	-0.9
Total	4	3	6	.333	31	6	1-1	0	85	103	61	6	2	33	28	5.29	73	.299	.363	21	.095	-2	92	-15	—	-1.6
HILDEBRAND, ORAL	Oral Clyde; B4.7.1907 Indianapolis IN; D9.8.1977 Southport IN; BR/TR/6´3˝/175; d9.8; Col Butler																									
1931	Cle A	2	1	.667	5	2	2	0	26.2	25	16	0	3	13	6	4.39	105	.243	.345	11	.182	-1	64	0	—	0.0
1932	Cle A	8	6	.571	27	15	7	0	129.1	124	69	7	0	62	49	3.69	129	.249	.333	48-0-3	.146	-3	84	12	—	0.7
1933	Cle A☆	16	11	.593	36	31	15-**6**	1	220.1	205	110	8	1	88	90	3.76	118	.245	.318	84	.190	-1	93	16	—	1.6
1934	Cle A	11	9	.550	33	28	10-1	1	198	225	112	14	3	99	72	4.50	101	.282	.364	76-0-4	.171	-1	124	3	—	0.1
1935	Cle A	9	8	.529	34	20	8	5	171.1	171	85	12	3	63	49	3.94	114	.263	.331	55-0-6	.164	-2	97	11	—	0.8
1936	Cle A	10	11	.476	36	21	9	4	174.2	197	107	10	4	83	65	4.90	103	.283	.362	63-0-2	.190	0	116	4	—	0.4
1937	StL A	8	17	.320	30	27	12-1	1	201.1	228	127	18	3	87	75	5.14	94	.284	.356	70-0-9	.200	-1	90	-6	—	-0.7
1938	StL A	8	10	.444	23	23	10	0	163	194	104	18	3	73	66	5.69	87	.297	.370	59-0-4	.254	1*	82	-8	—	-0.7
1939	†NY A	10	4	.714	21	15	7-1	2	126.2	102	44	11	1	41	50	3.06	143	.219	.284	44-0-3	.182	-1	113	21	—	2.0
1940	NY A	1	1	.500	13	0	0	0	19.1	19	7	1	1	14	5	1.86	217	.268	.395	3	.000	-0	—	4	—	0.3
Total	10	83	78	.516	258	182	80-9	13	1430.2	1490	781	99	22	623	527	4.35	107	.267	.343	513-0-31	.187	-9	99	57	—	4.5
HILGENDORF, TOM	Thomas Eugene; B3.10.1942 Clinton IA; BB/TL/6´1˝/(175–190); d8.15																									
1969	StL N	0	0	ø	6	0	0	2-1	6.1	3	1	0	0	2-0	2	1.42	252	.150	.217	1	1.000	1	—	2	0	0.2
1970	StL N	0	4	.000	23	0	0	3-0	20.2	22	11	0	0	13-5	13	3.92	106	.272	.368	1	.000	-0	—	0	0	0.0
1972	Cle A	3	1	.750	19	5	1	0-2	47	51	16	4	2	21-7	25	2.68	122	.283	.361	13	.077	-1	147	3	0	0.2
1973	Cle A	5	3	.625	48	1	1	6-2	94.2	87	38	9	3	36-6	58	3.14	126	.242	.316	0	ø	0	45	8	0	0.8
1974	Cle A	4	3	.571	35	0	0	3-3	48.1	58	26	6	1	17-6	23	4.84	75	.302	.353	0	ø	0	—	-5	0	-0.7
1975	Phi N	7	3	.700	53	0	0	0-2	96.2	81	32	6	1	38-3	52	2.14	176	.230	.303	12-0-2	.250	1	—	14	0	1.5
Total	6	19	14	.576	184	6	2	14-10	313.2	302	124	25	7	127-27	173	3.04	123	.255	.327	27-0-2	.185	1	114	22	0	2.0

YEAR	TM LG	W	L	PCT	G	GS	CG-SHO	SV-BS	IP	H	R	HR	HB	BB-IB	SO	ERA	AERA	OAV	OOB	AB-HR-SH	AVG	PB	SUP	APR	DL	PW
Hiljus, Erik	Erik Kristian; B12.25.1972 Los Angeles CA; BR/TR/6´5˝/230; [NYN91 4/121]; d9.10																									
1999	Det A	0	0	ø	6	0	0	0-0	8.2	7	5	2	0	5-0	1	5.19	96	.241	.343	0	ø	0	—	0	0	0.0
2000	Det A	0	0	ø	3	0	0	0-0	3.2	5	3	1	0	1-0	2	7.36	67	.333	.375	0	ø	0	—	-1	0	0.0
2001	†Oak A	5	0	1.000	16	11	0	0-0	66	70	29	7	0	21-1	67	3.41	134	.263	.316	0	ø	0	161	8	0	0.5
2002	Oak A	3	3	.500	9	9	0	0-0	45.2	52	36	11	0	21-1	29	6.50	69	.284	.356	0	ø	0	94	-10	0	-1.1
Total	4	8	3	.727	34	20	0	0-0	124	134	73	21	0	48-2	99	4.79	95	.272	.335	0	ø	0	130	-3	0	-0.6
Hill, Carmen	Carmen Proctor "Specs","Bunker"; B10.1.1895 Royalton MN; D1.1.1990 Indianapolis IN; BR/TR/6´1˝/180; d8.24																									
1915	Pit N	2	1	.667	8	3	2-1	0	47	42	8	0	2	13	24	1.15	238	.255	.317	13	.154	0	91	8	—	0.6
1916	Pit N	0	0	ø	2	0	0	0	6.1	11	10	0	1	5	5	8.53	31	.611	.708	0	ø	0	—	-5	—	-0.2
1918	Pit N	2	3	.400	6	4	3	0	43.2	24	11	0	0	17	15	1.24	232	.160	.246	12-0-1	.167	0	79	6	—	0.9
1919	Pit N	0	0	ø	4	0	0	0	5	12	6	0	0	1	1	9.00	33	.480	.500	0	ø	0	—	-3	—	-0.2
1922	NY N	2	1	.667	8	4	0	0	28.1	33	15	0	0	5	6	4.76	84	.295	.325	11	.182	-0	112	-1	—	-0.1
1926	Pit N	3	3	.500	6	6	4-1	0	39.2	42	17	2	2	9	8	3.40	116	.288	.338	17	.176	-1	123	3	—	0.4
1927	†Pit N	22	11	.667	43	31	22-2	3	277.2	260	125	12	4	80	95	3.24	127	.249	.305	104-0-3	.212	2*	107	22	—	2.6
1928	Pit N	16	10	.615	36	31	16-1	2	237	229	110	16	4	81	73	3.53	115	.259	.324	86-0-4	.233	2	107	14	—	1.4
1929	Pit N	2	3	.400	27	3	0	3	79	94	45	4	0	35	28	3.99	120	.297	.366	28	.036	-3	85	5	—	0.0
	StL N	0	0	ø	3	1	0	0	8.2	10	10	2	1	8	1	8.31	56	.303	.452	3	.000	-0	262	-4	—	-0.2
	Year	2	3	.400	30	4	0	3	87.2	104	55	6	1	43	29	4.41	108	.297	.376	31	.032	-4	128	1	—	-0.2
1930	StL N	0	1	.000	4	2	0	0	14.2	12	12	2	0	13	8	7.36	68	.240	.397	3	.333	0	122	-3	—	-0.2
Total	10	49	33	.598	147	85	47-5	8	787	769	369	38	14	267	264	3.44	116	.261	.326	277-0-8	.191	-0	109	42	—	5.0
Hill, Red	Clifford Joseph; B1.20.1893 Marshall TX; D8.11.1938 ElPaso TX; BB/TL; d4.21																									
1917	Phi A	0	0	ø	1	0	0	0	2.2	5	4	0	0	1	0	6.75	41	.385	.429	0	ø	0	—	-2	—	-0.1
Hill, Dave	David Burnham; B11.11.1937 New Orleans LA; BR/TL/6´2˝/170; d8.22; Col Northwestern																									
1957	KC A	0	0	ø	2	0	0	0	2.1	6	7	3	0	3-0	1	27.00	15	.462	.563	0	ø	0	—	-5	0	-0.3
Hill, Garry	Garry Alton; B11.3.1946 Rutherfordton NC; BR/TR/6´2˝/195; [AtlN67 S1/8]; d6.12; Col North Carolina																									
1969	Atl N	0	1	.000	1	1	0	0-0	2.1	6	4	1	0	1-0	2	15.43	23	.462	.500	0	ø	0	147	-3	0	-0.5
Hill, Herbert	Herbert Lee; B8.19.1891 Hutchins TX; D9.1.1970 Farmers Branch TX; BR/TR/5´11.5˝/175; d7.17																									
1915	Cle A	0	0	ø	1	0	0	0	2	1	0	0	0	2	0	0.00	ø	.250	.500	0	ø	0	—	1	—	0.0
Hill, Jeremy	Jeremy Dee; B8.8.1977 Dallas TX; BR/TR/5´10˝/200; [KCA96 5/139]; d9.7																									
2002	KC A	0	1	.000	10	0	0	0-0	9.1	8	4	1	0	8-1	7	3.86	129	.235	.372	0	ø	0	—	1	0	0.1
2003	KC A	0	0	ø	1	0	0	0-0	1	1	0	0	0	0-0	0	0.00	ø	.250	.250	0	ø	0	—	1	0	0.0
Total	2	0	1	.000	11	0	0	0-0	10.1	9	4	1	0	8-1	7	3.48	143	.237	.362	0	ø	0	—	2	0	0.1
Hill, Ken	Kenneth Wade; B12.14.1965 Lynn MA; BR/TR/6´2˝/(175–215); d9.3; Col Massachusetts Liberal Arts																									
1988	StL N	0	1	.000	4	1	0	0-0	14	16	9	0	0	6-0	6	5.14	68	.286	.355	3	.000	-0	50	-3	35	-0.2
1989	StL N	7	15	.318	33	33	2-1	0-0	196.2	186	92	9	5	99-6	112	3.80	97	.252	.342	59-0-8	.153	-0	92	-3	0	-0.3
1990	StL N	5	6	.455	17	14	1	0-0	78.2	79	49	7	1	33-1	58	5.49	70	.264	.334	19-0-5	.211	1	102	-12	0	-1.4
1991	StL N	11	10	.524	30	30	0	0-0	181.1	147	76	15	6	67-4	121	3.57	105	.224	.299	50-0-7	.100	-1	92	5	21	0.4
1992	Mon N	16	9	.640	33	33	3-3	0-0	218	187	76	13	3	75-4	150	2.68	130	.230	.297	62-1-10	.177	5	100	17	0	2.7
1993	Mon N	9	7	.563	28	28	2	0-0	183.2	163	84	7	6	74-7	90	3.23	129	.238	.315	52-0-14	.115	-1*	98	16	21	1.4
1994	Mon N★	**16**	5	.762	23	23	2-1	0-0	154.2	145	61	12	6	44-7	85	3.32	128	.248	.304	48-0-16	.146	-0*	124	17	0	2.2
1995	StL N	6	7	.462	18	18	0	0-0	110.1	125	71	16	0	45-4	50	5.06	85	.286	.351	31-0-5	.194	0	98	-9	0	-0.9
	†Cle A	4	1	.800	12	11	1	0-0	74.2	77	36	5	1	32-0	48	3.98	119	.268	.343	0	ø	0	136	6	0	0.4
1996	†Tex A	16	10	.615	35	35	7-**3**	0-0	250.2	250	110	19	6	95-3	170	3.63	145	.263	.332	0	ø	0	102	42	0	3.9
1997	Tex A	5	8	.385	19	19	0	0-0	111	129	69	11	2	56-3	68	5.19	94	.298	.376	0	ø	0	88	-3	23	-0.2
	Ana A	4	4	.500	12	12	1	0-0	79	65	34	8	1	39-0	38	3.65	127	.223	.315	2-0-1	.500	1	83	9	0	0.9
	Year	9	12	.429	31	31	1	0-0	190	194	103	19	3	95-3	106	4.55	105	.268	.352	2-0-1	.500	1	86	4	0	0.7
1998	Ana A	9	6	.600	19	19	0	0-0	103	123	60	6	3	47-0	57	4.98	95	.311	.384	1	.000	-0	98	-2	78	-0.1
1999	Ana A	4	11	.267	26	22	0	0-0	128.1	129	72	14	4	76-1	76	4.77	103	.270	.369	3	.000	-0	80	3	35	0.3
2000	Ana A	5	7	.417	16	16	0	0-0	78.2	102	59	16	2	53-1	50	6.52	79	.323	.415	3-0-1	.333	0	89	-10	48	-1.2
	Chi A	0	1	.000	2	1	0	0-0	3	5	8	0	0	6-0	0	24.00	21	.455	.611	0	ø	0	93	-6	0	-0.8
	Year	5	8	.385	18	17	0	0-0	81.2	107	67	16	2	59-1	50	7.16	72	.327	.424	3-0-1	.333	0	89	-15	0	-2.0
2001	TB A	0	1	.000	5	0	0	0-1	7.1	10	11	4	1	5-2	2	12.27	37	.333	.444	0	ø	0	—	-6	0	-0.7
Total	14	117	109	.518	332	315	19-8	0-1	1973	1938	977	162	47	852-43	1181	4.06	107	.260	.337	333-1-67	.150	4	98	61	261	6.4
Hill, Milt	Milton Giles; B8.22.1965 Atlanta GA; BR/TR/6´0˝/180; [CinN87 28/726]; d8.1; Col Georgia College																									
1991	Cin N	1	1	.500	22	0	0	0-1	33.1	36	14	1	0	8-2	20	3.78	101	.295	.331	1	.000	-0	—	1	0	0.0
1992	Cin N	0	0	ø	14	0	0	1-0	20	15	9	1	1	5-2	10	3.15	114	.211	.269	0	ø	-0	—	0	0	0.0
1993	Cin N	3	0	1.000	19	0	0	0-0	28.2	34	18	5	0	9-1	23	5.65	71	.301	.344	2	.000	-0	—	-4	0	-0.5
1994	Atl N	0	0	ø	10	0	0	0-0	11.1	18	10	3	0	6-1	10	7.94	54	.367	.436	0	ø	0	—	-4	0	-0.2
	Sea A	1	0	1.000	13	0	0	0-0	23.2	30	19	4	0	11-3	16	6.46	76	.306	.373	0	ø	0	—	-4	0	-0.2
Total	4	5	1	.833	78	0	0	1-1	117	133	70	14	1	39-9	79	5.08	81	.294	.345	3	.000	-0	—	-11	0	-0.9
Hill, Rich	Richard Joseph; B3.11.1980 Boston MA; BL/TL/6´5˝/205; [ChiN02 4/112]; d6.15; Col Michigan																									
2005	Chi N	0	2	.000	10	4	0	0-0	23.2	25	24	3	1	17-1	21	9.13	48	.260	.377	6	.333	0	65	-11	0	-0.8
2006	Chi N	6	7	.462	17	16	2-1	0-0	99.1	83	51	16	2	39-1	90	4.17	110	.227	.303	30-0-3	.100	-1	74	4	0	0.4
Total	2	6	9	.400	27	20	2-1	0-0	123	108	75	19	3	56-2	111	5.12	89	.234	.319	36-0-3	.139	-0	72	-7	0	-0.4
Hill, Shawn	Shawn Richard; B4.28.1981 Mississauga ON, Can.; BR/TR/6´2˝/185; [MonN00 6/165]; d6.29																									
2004	Mon N	1	2	.333	3	3	0	0-0	9	17	16	1	1	7-0	10	16.00	29	.415	.490	2-0-1	.000	-0	88	-10	0	-1.5
2006	Was N	1	3	.250	6	6	0	0-0	36.2	43	20	2	3	12-2	16	4.66	94	.297	.360	6-0-2	.167	-0	67	-1	95	0.0
Total	2	2	5	.286	9	9	0	0-0	45.2	60	36	3	4	19-2	26	6.90	64	.323	.392	8-0-3	.125	-0	74	-11	95	-1.5
Hill, Bill	William Cicero "Still Bill"; B8.2.1874 Chattanooga TN; D1.28.1938 Cincinnati OH; BL/TL/6´1˝/201; d4.18; b–Hugh																									
1896	Lou N	9	28	.243	43	39	32	2	319.2	353	229	14	18	155	104	4.31	101	.278	.364	116-0-4	.207	-5	73	2	—	-0.1
1897	Lou N	7	17	.292	27	26	20-1	0	199	209	127	6	17	69	55	3.62	118	.268	.341	74-0-2	.095	-8	81	13	—	0.6
1898	Cin N	13	14	.481	33	32	26-2	0	262	261	146	3	17	119	75	3.98	96	.258	.346	98	.133	-7	94	0	—	-0.6
1899	Cle N	3	6	.333	11	10	7	0	72.1	96	67	0	4	39	26	6.97	53	.318	.403	31	.129	-2	88	-23	—	-2.3
	Bal N	3	4	.429	8	7	6	0	61	64	35	1	3	18	17	3.25	122	.269	.328	24	.292	1	122	4	—	0.4
	Bro N	1	0	1.000	2	1	1	1	11	11	3	0	0	6	3	0.82	478	.262	.354	5	.600	2	258	3	—	0.5
	Year	7	10	.412	21	18	14	1	144.1	171	105	1	7	63	46	4.93	78	.294	.370	60	.233	0	111	-13	—	-1.4
Total	4	36	69	.343	124	115	92-3	3	925	994	607	24	59	406	280	4.16	99	.273	.355	348-0-6	.167	-20	85	-1	—	-1.5
Hillebrand, Homer	Homer Hiller Henry; B10.10.1879 Freeport IL; D1.20.1974 Elsinore (now Lake Elsinore) CA; BR/TL/5´8˝/165; d4.24; Col Princeton; ▲																									
1905	Pit N	5	2	.714	10	6	4	1	60.2	43	20	0	2	19	37	2.82	107	.198	.269	110-0-4	.236	1*	124	3	—	0.4
1906	Pit N	3	2	.600	7	5	4-1	0	53	42	19	1	1	21	32	2.21	121	.220	.300	21	.238	1	125	2	—	0.4
1908	Pit N	0	0	ø	1	0	0	0	1	1	0	0	0	0	1	0.00	ø	.333	.333	0	ø	0	—	0	—	0.0
Total	3	8	4	.667	18	11	8-1	1	114.2	86	39	1	3	40	70	2.51	113	.209	.284	131-0-4	.237	2	125	5	—	0.8
Hillegas, Shawn	Shawn Patrick; B8.21.1964 Dos Palos CA; BR/TR/6´2˝/(208–223); [LAN84*S1/4]; d8.9; Col Middle Georgia JC																									
1987	LA N	4	3	.571	12	10	0	0-0	58	52	27	5	0	31-0	51	3.57	112	.241	.335	14-0-1	.000	-1	100	2	0	0.1
1988	LA N	3	4	.429	11	10	0	0-0	56.2	54	26	5	3	17-1	30	4.13	81	.250	.311	15-0-2	.133	0	85	-4	0	-0.5
	Chi A	3	2	.600	6	6	0	0-0	40	30	16	4	1	18-0	26	3.15	127	.207	.295	0	ø	0	87	4	0	0.4
1989	Chi A	7	11	.389	50	13	0	3-0	119.2	132	67	12	3	51-4	76	4.74	81	.279	.352	0	ø	0	102	-11	0	-1.5
1990	Chi A	0	0	ø	7	0	0	0-0	11.1	4	1	0	0	5-1	5	0.79	484	.111	.214	0	ø	0	—	4	0	0.2
1991	Cle A	3	4	.429	51	3	0	7-2	83	67	42	7	2	46-7	66	4.34	96	.223	.324	0	ø	0	73	0	0	0.0
1992	NY A	1	8	.111	21	9	1-1	0-0	78.1	96	52	12	0	33-1	46	5.51	72	.306	.369	0	ø	0	72	-13	0	-1.4
	Oak A	0	0	ø	5	0	0	0-0	7.2	8	5	1	0	4-1	3	2.35	161	.276	.364	0	ø	0	—	0	0	0.0
	Year	1	8	.111	26	9	1-1	0-0	86	104	57	13	0	37-2	49	5.23	75	.303	.368	0	ø	0	72	-12	0	-1.4

YEAR	TM LG	W	L	PCT	G	GS	CG-SHO	SV-BS	IP	H	R	HR	HB	BB-IB	SO	ERA	AERA	OAV	OOB	AB-HR-SH	AVG	PB	SUP	APR	DL	PW
1993	Oak A	3	6	.333	18	11	0	0-0	60.2	78	48	8	4	33-1	29	6.97	59	.317	.404	0	ø	0	111	-19	0	-2.3
Total	7	24	38	.387	181	62	1-1	10-2	515.1	521	284	54	13	238-16	332	4.61	85	.264	.344	29-0-3	.069	-1	93	-37	0	-5.0

HILLER, FRANK Frank Walter "Dutch"; B7.13.1920 Irvington NJ; D1.10.1987 West Chester PA; BR/TR/6´0˝/200; d5.25; Col Lafayette

YEAR	TM LG	W	L	PCT	G	GS	CG-SHO	SV-BS	IP	H	R	HR	HB	BB-IB	SO	ERA	AERA	OAV	OOB	AB-HR-SH	AVG	PB	SUP	APR	DL	PW
1946	NY A	0	2	.000	3	1	0	0	11.1	13	7	2	0	6	4	4.76	72	.295	.380	4-0-1	.250	0	75	-2	0	-0.3
1948	NY A	5	2	.714	22	5	1	0	62.1	59	29	8	1	30	25	4.04	101	.244	.330	16-0-1	.375	2	133	1	0	0.3
1949	NY A	0	2	.000	4	0	0	1	7.2	9	5	0	0	7	3	5.87	69	.290	.421	2	.500	0	—	-1	0	-0.2
1950	Chi N	12	5	.706	38	17	9-2	1	153	153	68	16	4	32	55	3.53	119	.258	.300	44-0-4	.114	-3	96	12	0	1.0
1951	Chi N	6	12	.333	24	21	6-2	1	141.1	147	83	17	9	31	50	4.84	85	.268	.317	48-0-1	.125	-2	88	-10	0	-1.3
1952	Cin N	5	8	.385	28	15	6-1	1	124.1	129	67	7	6	37	50	4.63	81	.271	.331	30-0-7	.167	1*	124	-11	0	-1.0
1953	NY N	2	1	.667	19	1	0	0	33.2	43	29	6	4	15	10	6.15	70	.303	.385	4	.500	1	104	-8	0	-0.5
Total	7	30	32	.484	138	60	22-5	4	533.2	553	288	56	24	158	197	4.42	92	.266	.325	148-0-14	.176	-1	103	-19	0	-2.0

HILLER, JOHN John Frederick; B4.8.1943 Toronto ON, Can.; BR/TL/6´0˝/(165–195); d9.6

YEAR	TM LG	W	L	PCT	G	GS	CG-SHO	SV-BS	IP	H	R	HR	HB	BB-IB	SO	ERA	AERA	OAV	OOB	AB-HR-SH	AVG	PB	SUP	APR	DL	PW
1965	Det A	0	0	ø	5	0	0	1	6	5	0	0	0	1-0	4	0.00	ø	.227	.261	0	ø	0	—	2	0	0.1
1966	Det A	0	0	ø	1	0	0	0	2	2	2	0	0	2-0	1	9.00	39	.286	.400	0	ø	0	—	-1	0	-0.1
1967	Det A	4	3	.571	23	6	2-2	3	65	57	20	4	0	9-0	49	2.63	124	.233	.259	15-0-1	.133	-0	80	5	0	0.6
1968	†Det A	9	6	.600	39	12	4-1	2	128	92	37	9	0	51-4	78	2.39	126	.200	.279	37	.081	-2	123	9	0	0.9
1969	Det A	4	4	.500	40	8	1-1	4-3	99.1	97	50	13	1	44-2	74	3.99	94	.257	.334	21-0-2	.286	2*	100	-3	0	-0.1
1970	Det A	6	6	.500	47	5	1-1	3-3	104	82	39	12	2	46-4	89	3.03	124	.219	.302	23-0-1	.000	-2	71	8	0	0.7
1972	†Det A	1	2	.333	24	3	1	3-0	44.1	39	13	4	3	13-2	26	2.03	156	.232	.299	4	.000	-0	93	5	0	0.4
1973	Det A	10	5	.667	**65**	0	0	**38**-4	125.1	89	21	7	0	39-7	124	1.44	285	.198	.260	0	ø	0	—	**35**	0	**6.7**
1974	Det A☆	17	14	.548	59	0	0	13-9	150	127	51	10	3	62-19	134	2.64	145	.231	.309	0	ø	0	—	18	0	3.9
1975	Det A	2	3	.400	36	0	0	14-5	70.2	52	20	6	0	36-4	87	2.17	187	.205	.300	0	ø	0	—	14	37	1.6
1976	Det A	12	8	.600	56	1	1-1	13-13	121	93	37	7	2	67-9	117	2.38	157	.219	.323	1	.000	-0	118	17	0	3.2
1977	Det A	8	14	.364	45	8	3	7-9	124	120	59	15	1	61-8	115	3.56	121	.258	.342	0	ø	0	70	8	0	1.4
1978	Det A	9	4	.692	51	0	0	15-7	92.1	64	27	6	0	35-4	74	2.34	167	.202	.277	0	ø	0	—	15	21	2.6
1979	Det A	4	7	.364	43	0	0	9-7	79.1	83	47	14	0	55-7	46	5.22	83	.274	.382	0	ø	0	—	-6	34	-0.9
1980	Det A	1	0	1.000	11	0	0	0-0	30.2	38	15	3	0	14-1	18	4.40	94	.309	.374	0	ø	0	—	0	0	0.0
Total	15	87	76	.534	545	43	13-6	125-60	1242	1040	438	110	12	535-71	1036	2.83	134	.229	.309	101-0-4	.109	-4	87	126	92	21.0

HILLMAN, DAVE Darius Dutton; B9.14.1927 Dungannon VA; BR/TR/5´11˝/168; d4.30

YEAR	TM LG	W	L	PCT	G	GS	CG-SHO	SV-BS	IP	H	R	HR	HB	BB-IB	SO	ERA	AERA	OAV	OOB	AB-HR-SH	AVG	PB	SUP	APR	DL	PW
1955	Chi N	0	0	ø	25	3	0	0	57.2	63	36	10	1	25-0	23	5.31	77	.283	.352	10-0-1	.100	0*	182	-7	0	-0.3
1956	Chi N	0	2	.000	2	2	0	0	12.1	11	7	0	0	5-0	6	2.19	172	.216	.286	4	.000	-1	35	1	0	0.1
1957	Chi N	6	11	.353	32	14	1	1	103.1	115	52	13	0	37-2	53	4.35	89	.280	.338	24-0-2	.000	-2*	86	-4	0	-0.8
1958	Chi N	4	8	.333	31	16	3	1	125.2	132	57	12	0	31-4	65	3.15	124	.265	.305	41-0-2	.146	-1*	85	8	0	0.6
1959	Chi N	8	11	.421	39	24	4-1	0	191	178	84	17	1	43-3	88	3.53	112	.248	.290	60-0-4	.150	1*	87	8	0	0.9
1960	Bos A	0	3	.000	16	3	0	0	36.2	41	27	6	0	12-1	14	5.65	72	.281	.333	6-0-1	.000	-0	80	-7	58	-0.5
1961	Bos A	3	2	.600	28	1	0	0	78	70	26	8	0	23-0	39	2.77	151	.242	.296	17-0-2	.000	-2	42	12	0	0.6
1962	Cin N	0	0	ø	2	0	0	0	3.2	8	4	0	0	1-0	0	9.82	41	.421	.450	0	ø	0	—	-2	0	-0.1
	NY N	0	0	ø	13	1	0	1	15.2	21	12	5	1	8-0	8	6.32	66	.333	.405	1	.000	-0	42	-3	0	-0.2
	Year	0	0	ø	15	1	0	1	19.1	29	16	5	1	9-0	8	6.98	59	.354	.415	1	.000	-0	42	-5	0	-0.3
Total	8	21	37	.362	188	64	8-1	3	624	639	305	71	3	185-10	296	3.87	103	.264	.315	163-0-12	.098	-5	86	6	58	0.3

HILLMAN, ERIC John Eric; B4.27.1966 Gary IN; BL/TL/6´10˝/225; [NYN87 16/420]; d5.18; Col Eastern Illinois

YEAR	TM LG	W	L	PCT	G	GS	CG-SHO	SV-BS	IP	H	R	HR	HB	BB-IB	SO	ERA	AERA	OAV	OOB	AB-HR-SH	AVG	PB	SUP	APR	DL	PW
1992	NY N	2	2	.500	11	8	0	0-0	52.1	67	31	9	2	10-2	16	5.33	66	.318	.353	13-0-5	.077	-1	90	-9	0	-0.8
1993	NY N	2	9	.182	27	22	3-1	0-0	145	173	83	12	4	24-2	60	3.97	101	.299	.326	44-0-6	.159	-0	95	-3	0	-0.3
1994	NY N	0	3	.000	11	6	0	0-0	34.2	45	30	9	2	11-3	20	7.79	54	.321	.377	8-0-1	.000	-1	91	-12	0	-1.0
Total	3	4	14	.222	49	36	3-1	0-0	232	285	144	30	8	45-7	96	4.85	81	.306	.340	65-0-12	.123	-2	93	-24	0	-2.1

HILSEY, CHARLIE Charles T.; B3.23.1864 Philadelphia PA; D10.31.1918 Philadelphia PA; 5´7˝/180; d9.27

YEAR	TM LG	W	L	PCT	G	GS	CG-SHO	SV-BS	IP	H	R	HR	HB	BB-IB	SO	ERA	AERA	OAV	OOB	AB-HR-SH	AVG	PB	SUP	APR	DL	PW
1883	Phi N	0	3	.000	3	3	3	0	26	36	26	0	—	4	8	5.54	56	.305	.328	10	.100	-1	41	-7	—	-0.7
1884	Phi AA	2	1	.667	3	3	3	0	27	29	19	0	0	5	10	4.67	73	.257	.288	24	.208	0*	172	-3	—	-0.2
Total	2	2	4	.333	6	6	6	0	53	65	45	0	0	9	18	5.09	64	.281	.308	34	.176	-1	105	-10	—	-0.9

HILTON, HOWARD Howard James; B1.3.1964 Oxnard CA; BR/TR/6´3˝/230; [StLN85 22/566]; d4.9; Col Arkansas

YEAR	TM LG	W	L	PCT	G	GS	CG-SHO	SV-BS	IP	H	R	HR	HB	BB-IB	SO	ERA	AERA	OAV	OOB	AB-HR-SH	AVG	PB	SUP	APR	DL	PW
1990	StL N	0	0	ø	2	0	0	0-0	3	2	0	0	0	3-0	2	0.00	ø	.182	.357	0	ø	0	—	1	0	0.1

HINCHLIFFE, BRETT Brett; B7.21.1974 Detroit MI; BR/TR/6´5˝/190; [SeaA92 16/446]; d4.5

YEAR	TM LG	W	L	PCT	G	GS	CG-SHO	SV-BS	IP	H	R	HR	HB	BB-IB	SO	ERA	AERA	OAV	OOB	AB-HR-SH	AVG	PB	SUP	APR	DL	PW
1999	Sea A	0	4	.000	11	4	0	0-0	30.2	41	31	10	4	21-0	14	8.80	54	.323	.434	0	ø	0	63	-13	0	-1.4
2000	Ana A	0	0	ø	2	0	0	0-0	1.2	1	1	0	0	1-0	0	5.40	96	.167	.286	0	ø	0	—	0	0	0.0
2001	NY N	0	1	.000	1	1	0	0-0	2	9	8	2	1	1-0	2	36.00	11	.643	.688	1	.000	-0	183	-7	0	-0.9
Total	3	0	5	.000	14	5	0	0-0	34.1	51	40	12	5	23-0	16	10.22	47	.347	.451	1	.000	-0	82	-20	0	-2.3

HINDS, SAM Samuel Russell; B7.11.1953 Frederick MD; BR/TR/6´6˝/210; d5.21; Col Broward (FL) CC

YEAR	TM LG	W	L	PCT	G	GS	CG-SHO	SV-BS	IP	H	R	HR	HB	BB-IB	SO	ERA	AERA	OAV	OOB	AB-HR-SH	AVG	PB	SUP	APR	DL	PW
1977	Mil A	0	3	.000	29	1	0	2-1	72.1	72	42	5	2	40-3	46	4.73	87	.266	.355	0	ø	0	0	-5	0	-0.3

HINRICHS, PAUL Paul Edwin "Herky"; B8.31.1925 Marengo IA; BR/TR/6´0˝/180; d5.16; Col Concordia (TX)

YEAR	TM LG	W	L	PCT	G	GS	CG-SHO	SV-BS	IP	H	R	HR	HB	BB-IB	SO	ERA	AERA	OAV	OOB	AB-HR-SH	AVG	PB	SUP	APR	DL	PW
1951	Bos A	0	0	ø	4	0	0	0	3.1	7	8	1	0	4	1	21.60	21	.412	.524	0	ø	0	—	-5	0	-0.3

HINRICHS, DUTCH William Louis; B4.27.1889 Orange CA; D8.18.1972 Kingsburg CA; BR/TR/6´3˝/195; d6.25; Col Occidental

YEAR	TM LG	W	L	PCT	G	GS	CG-SHO	SV-BS	IP	H	R	HR	HB	BB-IB	SO	ERA	AERA	OAV	OOB	AB-HR-SH	AVG	PB	SUP	APR	DL	PW
1910	Was A	0	1	.000	3	0	0	1	7	10	7	0	0	3	5	2.57	97	.357	.419	4	.000	-1	—	-1	—	-0.3

HINSLEY, JERRY Jerry Dean; B4.9.1945 Hugo OK; BR/TR/5´11˝/165; d4.18

YEAR	TM LG	W	L	PCT	G	GS	CG-SHO	SV-BS	IP	H	R	HR	HB	BB-IB	SO	ERA	AERA	OAV	OOB	AB-HR-SH	AVG	PB	SUP	APR	DL	PW
1964	NY N	0	2	.000	9	2	0	0	15.1	21	17	0	0	7-0	11	8.22	44	.313	.373	1	.000	-0	61	-8	0	-1.0
1967	NY N	0	0	ø	2	0	0	0	5	6	2	0	0	4-0	3	3.60	94	.316	.435	0	ø	0	—	0	0	0.0
Total	2	0	2	.000	11	2	0	0	20.1	27	19	0	0	11-0	14	7.08	50	.314	.388	1	.000	-0	61	-8	0	-1.0

HINTON, RICH Richard Michael; B5.22.1947 Tucson AZ; BL/TL/6´2˝/(170–185); [ChiA69 S3/62]; d7.17; Col Arizona

YEAR	TM LG	W	L	PCT	G	GS	CG-SHO	SV-BS	IP	H	R	HR	HB	BB-IB	SO	ERA	AERA	OAV	OOB	AB-HR-SH	AVG	PB	SUP	APR	DL	PW
1971	Chi A	3	4	.429	18	2	0	0-2	24.1	27	12	1	1	6-1	15	4.44	80	.310	.358	1-0-2	.000	-0	63	-1	0	-0.3
1972	NY A	1	0	1.000	7	3	0	0-0	16.2	20	11	2	0	8-2	13	4.86	62	.299	.364	3	.000	-0	158	-4	0	-0.3
	Tex A	0	1	.000	5	0	0	0-0	11.1	7	10	1	0	10-1	4	2.38	128	.171	.327	2	.500	1	—	-2	0	-0.1
	Year	1	1	.500	12	3	0	0-0	28	27	21	3	0	18-3	17	3.86	78	.250	.349	5	.200	1	157	-6	0	-0.4
1975	Chi A	1	0	1.000	15	0	0	0-1	37.1	41	22	2	0	15-1	30	4.82	81	.270	.331	0	ø	0	—	-4	0	-0.1
1976	Cin N	1	2	.333	12	1	0	0-1	17.2	30	15	4	0	11-3	8	7.64	46	.380	.451	1	.000	-0	201	-7	0	-1.2
1978	Chi A	2	6	.250	29	4	2	1-2	80.2	78	38	5	2	28-2	48	4.02	95	.261	.326	0	ø	0	124	-1	0	-0.1
1979	Chi A	1	2	.333	16	2	0	2-0	41.2	57	30	4	2	8-1	27	6.05	70	.331	.362	0	ø	0	53	-7	0	-0.5
	Sea A	0	2	.000	14	1	0	0-1	20	23	14	4	2	5-1	7	5.40	81	.284	.337	0	ø	0	41	-2	0	-0.2
	Year	1	4	.200	30	3	0	2-1	61.2	80	44	8	4	13-2	34	5.84	74	.316	.354	0	ø	0	49	-10	0	-0.7
Total	6	9	17	.346	116	13	2	3-7	249.2	283	152	23	7	91-12	152	4.87	78	.289	.350	7-0-2	.143	0	103	-28	0	-2.8

HIPPAUF, HERB Herbert August; B5.9.1939 New York NY; D7.17.1995 Santa Clara CA; BR/TL/6´0˝/180; d4.27; Col Pasadena (CA) City

YEAR	TM LG	W	L	PCT	G	GS	CG-SHO	SV-BS	IP	H	R	HR	HB	BB-IB	SO	ERA	AERA	OAV	OOB	AB-HR-SH	AVG	PB	SUP	APR	DL	PW
1966	Atl N	0	1	.000	3	0	0	0	2.2	6	5	0	0	1-0	1	13.50	27	.462	.500	0	ø	0	—	-3	0	-0.6

HIRSH, JASON Jason Michael; B2.20.1982 Santa Monica CA; BR/TR/6´8˝/250; [HouN03 2/59]; d8.12; Col California Lutheran

YEAR	TM LG	W	L	PCT	G	GS	CG-SHO	SV-BS	IP	H	R	HR	HB	BB-IB	SO	ERA	AERA	OAV	OOB	AB-HR-SH	AVG	PB	SUP	APR	DL	PW
2006	Hou N	3	4	.429	9	9	0	0-0	44.2	48	32	11	3	22-2	29	6.04	74	.267	.354	15-0-2	.000	-2	114	-8	0	-1.1

HISNER, HARLEY Harley Parnell; B11.6.1926 Maples IN; BR/TR/6´1˝/185; d9.30

YEAR	TM LG	W	L	PCT	G	GS	CG-SHO	SV-BS	IP	H	R	HR	HB	BB-IB	SO	ERA	AERA	OAV	OOB	AB-HR-SH	AVG	PB	SUP	APR	DL	PW
1951	Bos A	0	1	.000	1	1	0	0	6	7	3	0	0	4	3	4.50	99	.292	.393	2	.500	0	0	0	0	0.0

HITCHCOCK, STERLING Sterling Alex; B4.29.1971 Fayetteville NC; BL/TL/6´1˝/(192–205); [NYA89 9/233]; d9.11

YEAR	TM LG	W	L	PCT	G	GS	CG-SHO	SV-BS	IP	H	R	HR	HB	BB-IB	SO	ERA	AERA	OAV	OOB	AB-HR-SH	AVG	PB	SUP	APR	DL	PW
1992	NY A	0	2	.000	3	3	0	0-0	13	23	12	2	1	6-0	6	8.31	48	.377	.441	0	ø	0	123	-6	0	-0.7
1993	NY A	1	2	.333	6	6	0	0-0	31	32	18	4	1	14-1	26	4.65	90	.271	.348	0	ø	0	117	-2	0	-0.2
1994	NY A	4	1	.800	23	5	1	2-0	49.1	48	24	3	0	29-1	37	4.20	110	.265	.355	0	ø	0	100	3	0	0.2
1995	†NY A	11	10	.524	27	27	4-1	0-0	168.1	155	91	22	5	68-1	121	4.70	98	.245	.319	0	ø	0	98	0	0	-0.2
1996	Sea A	13	9	.591	35	35	0	0-0	196.2	245	131	27	7	73-4	132	5.35	93	.309	.368	0	ø	0	104	-11	0	-1.0
1997	SD N	10	11	.476	32	28	1	0-0	161	172	102	24	4	55-2	106	5.20	76	.276	.337	50-0-8	.100	-1	112	-24	27	-2.8

YEAR	TM LG	W	L	PCT	G	GS	CG-SHO	SV-BS	IP	H	R	HR	HB	BB-IB	SO	ERA	AERA	OAV	OOB	AB-HR-SH	AVG	PB	SUP	APR	DL	PW
1998	†SD N	9	7	.563	39	27	2-1	1-1	176.1	169	83	29	9	48-2	158	3.93	101	.251	.308	50-0-5	.140	-1	110	1	0	-0.1
1999	SD N	12	14	.462	33	33	1	0-0	205.2	202	99	29	5	76-6	194	4.11	104	.254	.320	61-0-7	.082	-3	95	6	0	0.4
2000	SD N	1	6	.143	11	11	0	0-0	65.2	69	38	12	5	26-1	61	4.93	90	.267	.345	22-0-1	.000	-3	88	-3	127	-0.5
2001	SD N	2	1	.667	3	3	0	0-0	19	22	9	1	1	3-0	15	3.32	125	.275	.310	8	.125	-0	186	1	94	0.2
	†NY A	4	4	.500	10	9	1	0-0	51.1	67	37	5	2	18-0	28	6.49	68	.315	.367	0	ø	0	120	-10	0	-1.3
2002	NY A	1	2	.333	20	2	0	0-0	39.1	57	29	4	1	15-3	31	5.49	79	.326	.380	0	ø	0	139	-6	68	-0.4
2003	NY A	1	3	.250	27	1	0	0-0	49.2	57	33	6	0	18-3	36	5.44	81	.285	.341	0	ø	0	105	-6	0	-0.4
	StL N	5	1	.833	8	6	0	0-0	38	34	17	8	1	14-1	32	3.79	109	.238	.308	12-0-2	.083	-1	99	1	0	0.1
2004	SD N	0	3	.000	4	4	0	0-0	21.1	22	15	5	0	8-0	14	6.33	62	.265	.330	7	.000	-1	65	-5	121	-0.7
Total	13	74	76	.493	281	200	10-2	3-1	1285.2	1374	738	181	42	471-25	997	4.80	91	.273	.337	210-0-23	.090	-9	105	-61	437	-7.4
HITT, BRUCE	Bruce Smith; B3.14.1897 Comanche TX; D11.10.1973 Portland OR; BR/TR/6´1˝/190; d9.23; Mil 1918																									
1917	StL N	0	0	ø	2	0	0	0	4	7	6	1	0	1	1	9.00	30	.368	.400	1	.000	-0	—	-3	—	-0.2
HITT, ROY	Roy Wesley "Rhino"; B6.22.1884 Carleton NE; D2.8.1956 Pomona CA; BL/TL/5´10˝/200; d4.27																									
1907	Cin N	6	10	.375	21	18	14-2	0	153.1	143	76	2	12	56	63	3.40	76	.258	.339	56-0-1	.179	-0	107	-11	—	-1.2
HITTLE, LLOYD	Lloyd Eldon "Red"; B2.21.1924 Lodi CA; BR/TL/5´10.5˝/164; d6.12																									
1949	Was A	5	7	.417	36	9	3-2	0	109	123	62	2	0	57	32	4.21	101	.285	.369	28-0-2	.143	-2	61	-1	0	-0.3
1950	Was A	2	4	.333	11	4	1	0	43.1	60	27	1	0	17	9	4.98	90	.326	.383	13-0-1	.077	-1	55	-2	0	-0.3
Total	2	7	11	.389	47	13	4-2	0	152.1	183	89	3	0	74	41	4.43	98	.298	.373	41-0-3	.122	-3	59	-3	0	-0.6
HOBAUGH, ED	Edward Russell; B6.27.1934 Kittanning PA; BR/TR/6´0˝/176; d4.19; Col Michigan St.																									
1961	Was A	7	9	.438	26	18	3	0	126.1	142	68	12	1	64-3	67	4.42	91	.281	.362	41-0-5	.098	-2*	92	-4	0	-0.7
1962	Was A	2	1	.667	26	2	0	1	69.1	66	36	9	0	25-2	37	3.76	107	.258	.320	12	.167	0	88	0	0	0.0
1963	Was A	0	0	ø	9	1	0	0	16	20	13	3	2	6-2	11	6.19	60	.308	.368	2-1-0	.500	2	192	-4	0	-0.1
Total	3	9	10	.474	61	21	3	1	211.2	228	117	24	3	95-7	115	4.34	92	.276	.350	55-1-5	.127	-1	96	-8	0	-0.8
HOBBIE, GLEN	Glen Frederick; B4.24.1936 Witt IL; BR/TR/6´2˝/(195–198); d9.20																									
1957	Chi N	0	0	ø	2	0	0	0	4.1	6	5	0	0	5-0	3	10.38	37	.333	.458	2	.000	-0	—	-3	0	-0.2
1958	Chi N	10	6	.625	55	16	2-1	2	168.1	163	80	13	7	93-8	91	3.74	105	.252	.352	48-0-1	.146	-2	106	3	0	0.3
1959	Chi N	16	13	.552	46	33	10-3	0	234	204	105	15	6	106-1	138	3.69	107	.236	.322	79-0-3	.114	-3	106	7	0	0.6
1960	Chi N	16	20	.444	46	36	16-4	1	258.2	253	130	27	9	101-7	134	3.97	95	.256	.328	86-1-1	.151	1	92	-5	0	-0.4
1961	Chi N	7	13	.350	36	29	7-2	2	198.2	207	113	26	6	54-7	103	4.26	98	.268	.319	66-2-3	.167	2	105	-3	0	0.1
1962	Chi N	5	14	.263	42	23	5	0	162	198	112	18	3	62-8	87	5.22	79	.304	.365	49-0-1	.122	-1	85	-20	0	-2.2
1963	Chi N	7	10	.412	36	24	4-1	0	165.1	172	80	17	6	49-2	94	3.92	90	.270	.327	50-0-3	.080	-2	94	-6	0	-0.9
1964	Chi N	0	3	.000	8	4	0	0	27.1	39	29	4	1	10-1	14	7.90	47	.325	.382	5	.000	0	65	-13	0	-1.2
	StL N	1	2	.333	13	5	1	1	44.1	41	23	4	1	15-1	18	4.26	89	.241	.305	13-1-1	.154	1	125	-1	0	0.0
	Year	1	5	.167	21	9	1	1	71.2	80	52	8	2	25-2	32	5.65	67	.276	.336	18-1-1	.111	1	98	-14	0	-1.2
Total	8	62	81	.434	284	170	45-11	6	1263	1283	677	124	39	495-35	682	4.20	93	.264	.335	398-4-13	.131	-5	98	-41	0	-3.9
HOBBS, JACK	John Douglas; B11.11.1956 Philadelphia PA; BR/TL/6´3˝/190; [SeaA78 7/162]; d8.31; Col Lynchburg																									
1981	Min A	0	0	ø	4	0	0	0-0	5.2	5	2	0	2	6-1	1	3.18	124	.238	.448	0	ø	0	—	1	0	0.0
HOCH, HARRY	Harry Keller; B1.9.1887 Woodside DE; D10.26.1981 Lewes DE; BR/TR/5´10.5˝/165; d4.16; Col Kutztown																									
1908	Phi N	2	1	.667	3	3	2	0	26	20	10	0	2	13	4	2.77	88	.211	.318	5-0-3	.200	1	126	-1	—	0.0
1914	StL A	0	2	.000	15	2	1	0	54	55	31	1	2	27	13	3.00	90	.284	.377	18	.056	-2	13	-4	—	-0.3
1915	StL A	0	4	.000	12	3	1	0	40	52	49	2	3	26	9	7.20	40	.311	.413	10-0-1	.200	0	17	-21	—	-1.8
Total	3	2	7	.222	30	8	4	0	120	127	90	3	7	66	26	4.35	62	.279	.378	33-0-4	.121	-1	54	-26	—	-2.1
HOCKENBERY, CHUCK	Charles Marion; B12.15.1950 LaCrosse WI; BB/TR/6´1˝/165; d7.4																									
1975	Cal A	0	5	.000	16	4	0	1-0	41	48	27	3	3	19-2	15	5.27	68	.296	.378	0	ø	0	37	-8	0	-0.9
HOCKETTE, GEORGE	George Edward "Lefty"; B4.7.1908 Perth MS; D1.20.1974 Plantation FL; BL/TL/6´0˝/174; d9.17																									
1934	Bos A	2	1	.667	3	3	3-2	0	27.1	22	5	3	0	6	14	1.65	292	.218	.262	11	.273	0	72	9	—	1.0
1935	Bos A	2	3	.400	23	4	0	0	61	83	43	6	1	12	11	5.16	92	.329	.362	14-0-3	.143	-1	91	-3	—	-0.1
Total	2	4	4	.500	26	7	3-2	0	88.1	105	48	9	1	18	25	4.08	117	.297	.333	25-0-3	.200	-0	83	6	—	0.9
HODGE, SHOVEL	Clarence Clemet; B7.6.1893 Clayton AL; D12.31.1967 Ft.Walton Beach FL; BL/TR/6´4˝/190; d9.6																									
1920	Chi A	1	1	.500	4	2	1	0	19.2	15	14	0	0	12	5	2.29	165	.224	.342	6	.000	-1	53	0	—	-0.1
1921	Chi A	6	8	.429	36	10	5	2	142.2	191	118	7	5	54	25	6.56	65	.335	.397	52-0-3	.327	3	116	-37	—	-2.6
1922	Chi A	7	6	.538	35	8	2	1	139	154	73	3	2	65	37	4.14	98	.300	.381	58-0-3	.207	-1	91	-2	—	-0.2
Total	3	14	15	.483	75	20	8	3	301.1	360	205	10	7	131	67	5.17	80	.313	.387	116-0-6	.250	1	100	-39	—	-2.9
HODGE, ED	Ed Oliver; B4.19.1958 Bellflower CA; BL/TL/6´2˝/192; [MinA79*5/114]; d5.1; Col Cerritos (CA) JC																									
1984	Min A	4	3	.571	25	15	0	0-0	100	116	59	13	1	29-1	59	4.77	89	.291	.338	0	ø	0	107	-6	0	-0.5
HODGES, KEVIN	Kevin Jon; B6.24.1973 Houston TX; BR/TR/6´4˝/200; [KCA91 8/210]; d4.24																									
2000	Sea A	0	0	ø	13	0	0	0-0	17.1	18	10	4	2	12-0	7	5.19	93	.310	.438	0	ø	0	—	0	0	0.0
HODGES, TREY	Trey Alan; B6.29.1978 Houston TX; BR/TR/6´3˝/187; [AtlN00 17/520]; d9.10; Col Louisiana St.																									
2002	Atl N	2	0	1.000	4	0	0	0-0	11.2	16	7	2	1	2-0	6	5.40	75	.348	.373	3	.000	-0	—	-1	0	-0.3
2003	Atl N	3	3	.500	52	1	0	0-2	65.2	69	38	11	3	31-7	66	4.66	90	.268	.350	5-0-1	.000	-1	134	-3	17	-0.3
Total	2	5	3	.625	56	1	0	0-2	77.1	85	45	13	4	33-7	72	4.77	88	.281	.354	8-0-1	.000	-1	134	-4	17	-0.6
HODKEY, ELI	Aloysius Joseph; B11.3.1917 Lorain OH; D8.30.2005 Lorain OH; BL/TL/6´4˝/185; d9.12																									
1946	Phi N	0	1	.000	2	1	0	0	4.1	9	6	0	0	5	0	12.46	28	.391	.500	2	.000	-0	50	-4	0	-0.7
HODNETT, CHARLIE	Charles; B1861 IA; D4.25.1890 St.Louis MO; d5.3																									
1883	StL AA	2	2	.500	4	4	3	0	32	28	10	1	—	7	6	1.41	248	.220	.261	11	.182	-0	45	7	—	0.7
1884	StL U	12	2	.857	14	14	12-1	0	121	121	56	0	—	16	41	2.01	119	.243	.267	58	.207	-0*	174	5	—	0.1
Total	2	14	4	.778	18	18	15-1	0	153	149	66	1	—	23	47	1.88	138	.239	.266	69	.203	-0	144	12	—	0.8
HODSON, GEORGE	George S. (b George S. Hodgdon); B6.1870 PA; D1.9.1924 San Rafael CA; BR/TR/5´7˝/150; d8.9																									
1894	Bos N	4	4	.500	12	11	8	0	74	103	66	4	5	35	12	5.84	97	.326	.402	30	.100	-4	101	0	—	-0.4
1895	Phi N	1	2	.333	4	2	1	0	17	27	23	4	0	9	6	9.53	50	.355	.424	5	.000	-1	52	-8	—	-1.0
Total	2	5	6	.455	16	13	9	0	91	130	89	8	5	44	18	6.53	84	.332	.406	35	.086	-5	95	-8	—	-1.4
HOEFT, BILLY	William Frederick; B5.17.1932 Oshkosh WI; BL/TL/6´3˝/(177–205); d4.18																									
1952	Det A	2	7	.222	34	10	1	4	125	123	66	14	5	63	67	4.32	88	.260	.353	40-0-1	.150	-1	99	-6	0	-0.5
1953	Det A	9	14	.391	29	27	9	2	197.2	223	113	24	4	58	90	4.83	84	.283	.335	64-0-3	.172	0*	97	-14	0	-1.5
1954	Det A	7	15	.318	34	25	10-4	1	175	180	93	22	4	59	114	4.58	81	.266	.327	52	.192	4*	78	-14	0	-1.2
1955	Det A☆	16	7	.696	32	29	17-**7**	0	220	187	75	17	6	75-1	133	2.99	129	.229	.296	82-0-4	.207	3*	129	25	0	2.7
1956	Det A	20	14	.588	38	34	18-4	0	248	276	127	22	5	104-12	172	4.06	101	.287	.356	80-0-5	.250	6*	108	1	0	0.6
1957	Det A	9	11	.450	34	28	10-1	1	207	188	85	15	5	69-2	111	3.48	111	.244	.308	67-3-5	.149	2*	85	10	0	1.0
1958	Det A	10	9	.526	36	21	6	3	143	148	70	15	1	49-3	94	4.15	97	.268	.326	44-0-1	.273	3*	103	0	0	0.2
1959	Det A	1	1	.500	2	2	0	0	9	6	5	0	1	4-0	2	5.00	81	.188	.297	3-0-2	.333	0*	65	-1	0	-0.1
	Bos A	0	3	.000	5	3	0	0	17.2	22	12	1	1	8-1	8	5.60	72	.319	.383	3	.000	-0*	80	-3	0	-0.4
	Bal A	1	1	.500	16	3	0	0	41	50	29	6	0	19-3	30	5.71	66	.307	.375	12	.250	1	70	-9	0	-0.4
	Year	2	5	.286	23	8	0	0	67.2	78	46	7	2	31-4	40	5.59	70	.295	.368	18-0-2	.222	0	74	-12	0	-0.9
1960	Bal A	2	1	.667	19	0	0	0	18.2	18	10	2	0	14-1	14	4.34	88	.240	.360	1	.000	-0	—	-1	0	-0.1
1961	Bal A	7	4	.636	35	12	3-1	3	138	106	37	7	1	55-3	100	2.02	190	.216	.295	39-0-2	.179	1	90	**28**	0	2.4
1962	Bal A	4	8	.333	57	4	0	7	113.2	103	62	7	1	43-5	73	4.59	81	.243	.311	19-0-1	.158	3	91	-10	0	-0.8
1963	SF N	2	0	1.000	23	0	0	4	24.1	26	12	5	0	10-2	8	4.44	72	.271	.340	1-0-1	1.000	1	—	-3	77	-0.2
1964	Mil N	4	0	1.000	42	0	0	4	73.1	76	35	9	1	18-6	47	3.80	93	.271	.318	9-0-3	.222	1	—	-2	0	0.0
1965	Chi N	2	2	.500	29	2	1	1	51.1	41	21	3	0	20-2	44	2.81	131	.215	.285	11	.273	1	83	4	0	0.3
1966	Chi N	1	2	.333	36	0	0	3	41	43	28	4	1	14-3	30	4.61	80	.264	.326	4	.250	0	—	-6	0	-0.4

YEAR	TM LG	W	L	PCT	G	GS	CG-SHO	SV-BS	IP	H	R	HR	HB	BB-IB	SO	ERA	AERA	OAV	OOB	AB-HR-SH	AVG	PB	SUP	APR	DL	PW
	SF N	0	2	.000	4	0	0	0	3.2	4	3	0	0	3-1	3	7.36	50	.250	.368	0	ø	0	—	-1	0	-0.3
	Year	1	4	.200	40	0	0	3	44.2	47	31	4	1	17-4	33	4.84	76	.263	.330	4	.250	0	—	-8	0	-0.7
Total	15	97	101	.490	505	200	75-17	33	1847.1	1820	883	173	36	685-45	1140	3.94	98	.259	.325	531-3-28	.202	24	100	-2	77	1.3
HOELSKOETTER, ART	Arthur William "Holley","Hoss" (aka Arthur William Hostetter); B9.30.1882 St.Louis MO; D8.3.1954 St.Louis MO; BR/TR/6´2˝/?; d9.10; ▲																									
1905	StL N	0	1	.000	1	1	1	0	6	6	6	1	0	5	4	1.50	199	.273	.407	83-0-2	.241	0*	73	-1	—	-0.1
1906	StL N	1	4	.200	12	3	2	0	58.1	53	37	1	1	34	20	4.63	57	.240	.344	317-0-7	.224	1*	129	-12	—	-0.9
1907	StL N	0	0	ø	2	0	0	0	11	9	16	0	2	10	8	5.73	44	.209	.382	397-2-8	.247	0*	—	-6	—	-0.3
Total	3	1	5	.167	15	4	3	0	75.1	68	59	2	3	49	32	4.54	58	.238	.355	797-2-17	.237	1	117	-19	—	-1.3
HOERNER, JOE	Joseph Walter; B11.12.1936 Dubuque IA; D10.4.1996 Hermann MO; BR/TL/6´1˝/(180–200); d9.27																									
1963	Hou N	0	0	ø	1	0	0	0	3	2	0	0	0	0-0	2	0.00	ø	.182	.182	1	.000	-0	—	1	0	0.1
1964	Hou N	0	0	ø	7	0	0	0	11	13	11	3	0	6-1	4	4.91	70	.310	.380	1	.000	-0	—	-4	0	-0.2
1966	StL N	5	1	.833	57	0	0	13	76	57	16	5	4	21-8	63	1.54	233	.212	.274	8-1-3	.125	1	—	17	0	2.0
1967	†StL N	4	4	.500	57	0	0	15	66	52	25	5	1	20-6	50	2.59	127	.225	.283	11-0-2	.182	0	—	4	0	0.6
1968	†StL N	8	2	.800	47	0	0	17	49	34	9	2	0	12-4	42	1.47	197	.192	.241	6-0-1	.000	-1	—	8	0	1.8
1969	StL N	2	3	.400	45	0	0	15-2	53.1	44	18	5	1	9-4	35	2.87	125	.230	.263	5	.000	-1	—	5	0	0.7
1970	Phi N☆	9	5	.643	44	0	0	9-3	57.2	53	20	5	1	20-7	39	2.65	152	.247	.307	10	.200	1	—	8	0	1.7
1971	Phi N	4	5	.444	49	0	0	9-5	73	57	19	6	1	21-3	57	1.97	180	.215	.272	10	.100	-1	—	12	0	1.8
1972	Phi N	0	2	.000	15	0	0	3-4	21.2	21	6	2	1	5-5	12	2.08	174	.259	.297	1-0-1	.000	-0	—	3	0	0.4
	Atl N	1	3	.250	25	0	0	2-6	23.1	34	18	4	1	8-2	19	6.56	58	.351	.394	4	.000	-0	—	-6	0	-1.2
	Year	1	5	.167	40	0	0	5-10	45	55	24	6	2	13-7	31	4.40	84	.309	.350	5-0-1	.000	-1	—	-3	0	-0.8
1973	Atl N	2	2	.500	20	0	0	2-3	12.2	17	9	1	0	4-0	10	6.39	62	.333	.382	0	ø	0	—	-3	46	-0.6
	KC A	2	0	1.000	22	0	0	4-2	19.1	28	11	0	0	13-5	15	5.12	80	.329	.418	0	ø	0	—	-2	0	-0.2
1974	KC A	2	3	.400	30	0	0	2-3	35.1	32	15	3	4	12-5	24	3.82	100	.244	.320	0	ø	0	—	1	0	0.1
1975	Phi N	0	0	ø	25	0	0	0-0	21	25	6	3	1	8-2	20	2.57	147	.298	.358	2	.000	-0	—	3	32	0.1
1976	Tex A	0	4	.000	41	0	0	8-3	35	41	22	3	0	19-6	15	5.14	70	.315	.395	0	ø	0	—	-6	0	-0.9
1977	Cin N	0	0	ø	8	0	0	0-2	5.2	9	8	3	3	3-1	5	12.71	31	.375	.469	0	ø	0	—	-5	0	-0.3
Total	14	39	34	.534	493	0	0	99-33	563	519	213	50	18	181-59	412	2.99	120	.249	.309	59-1-7	.102	-1	—	36	78	5.9
HOERST, LEFTY	Frank Joseph; B8.11.1917 Philadelphia PA; D2.18.2000 Maple Shade NJ; BL/TL/6´3˝/192; d4.26; Mil 1943–45; Col LaSalle																									
1940	Phi N	1	0	1.000	6	0	0	0	12	12	7	1	0	8	3	5.25	74	.250	.357	2	.000	-0	—	-1	—	-0.1
1941	Phi N	3	10	.231	37	11	1	0	105.2	111	70	7	1	50	33	5.20	71	.275	.357	22-0-2	.182	0	58	-17	0	-1.8
1942	Phi N	4	16	.200	33	22	5	1	150.2	162	99	11	1	78	52	5.20	64	.271	.357	46-0-3	.152	-0	70	-31	0	-3.7
1946	Phi N	1	6	.143	18	7	2	0	68.1	77	42	4	1	36	17	4.61	74	.288	.375	17-0-2	.059	-1	96	-9	0	-1.1
1947	Phi N	1	1	.500	4	1	0	0	11.1	19	12	1	0	3	0	7.94	50	.358	.393	4	.500	1	66	-5	0	-0.7
Total	5	10	33	.233	98	41	8	1	348	381	230	24	3	175	105	5.17	68	.279	.362	91-0-7	.154	-1	70	-63	0	-7.4
HOEY, JIM	James Urban; B12.30.1982 Trenton NJ; BR/TR/6´6˝/200; [BalA03 13/374]; d8.23; Col Rider																									
2006	Bal A	0	1	.000	12	0	0	0-1	9.2	14	11	1	2	5-0	6	10.24	44	.359	.438	0	ø	0	—	-6	0	-0.5
HOFF, CHET	Chester Cornelius "Red"; B5.8.1891 Ossining NY; D9.17.1998 Daytona Beach FL; BL/TL/5´9˝/162; d9.6																									
1911	NY A	0	1	.000	5	1	0	0	20.2	21	8	0	0	7	10	2.18	165	.262	.322	7	.286	0	80	3	—	0.2
1912	NY A	0	1	.000	5	1	0	0	15.2	20	14	0	0	6	14	6.89	52	.303	.361	5	.200	-0	82	-4	—	-0.3
1913	NY A	0	0	ø	2	0	0	0	3	0	0	0	0	1	2	0.00	ø	.000	.111	1	.000	-0	—	1	—	0.0
1915	StL A	2	2	.500	11	3	2	0	43.2	26	16	0	1	24	23	1.24	232	.169	.285	17	.176	-1	76	5	—	0.4
Total	4	2	4	.333	23	5	2	0	83	67	38	0	1	38	49	2.49	127	.218	.305	30	.200	-1	78	5	—	0.3
HOFFER, BILL	William Leopold "Chick","Wizard"; B11.8.1870 Cedar Rapids IA; D7.21.1959 Cedar Rapids IA; BR/TR/5´9˝/155; d4.26																									
1895	†Bal N	31	6	**.838**	41	38	32-**4**	0	314	296	146	9	19	124	80	3.21	148	.245	.325	126-0-3	.214	-3	122	56	—	4.6
1896	†Bal N	25	7	**.781**	35	35	32-3	0	309	317	151	1	12	95	93	3.38	127	.263	.323	125-0-3	.304	11	128	35	—	3.9
1897	†Bal N	22	11	.667	38	33	29-1	0	303.1	350	188	5	17	104	62	4.30	97	.287	.351	139-1-2	.237	2*	110	2	—	0.2
1898	Bal N	0	4	.000	4	4	4	0	34.1	62	44	0	1	16	5	7.34	49	.387	.446	24	.208	0*	164	-16	—	-1.3
	Pit N	3	0	1.000	4	3	3	0	31	26	7	0	0	15	11	1.74	204	.226	.315	11	.091	-1	66	7	—	0.5
	Year	3	4	.429	8	7	7	0	65.1	88	51	0	1	31	16	4.68	76	.320	.391	35	.171	-0	122	-9	—	-0.8
1899	Pit N	8	10	.444	23	19	15-2	0	163.2	169	98	5	10	64	44	3.63	105	.266	.343	91	.198	-1*	112	1	—	0.0
1901	Cle A	3	8	.273	16	10	10	**3**	99	113	78	2	1	35	19	4.55	78	.283	.343	44	.136	-1*	86	-12	—	-1.2
Total	6	92	46	.667	161	142	125-10	3	1254.1	1333	712	22	60	453	314	3.75	112	.270	.339	560-1-8	.229	6	118	73	—	6.7
HOFFMAN, FRANK	Frank J. "The Texas Wonder"; B Houston TX; TR/5´9.5˝/163; d8.13																									
1888	KC AA	3	9	.250	12	12	12	0	104	102	71	3	6	42	38	2.77	122	.248	.326	39	.154	-1	67	1	—	0.0
HOFFMAN, GUY	Guy Alan; B7.9.1956 Ottawa IL; BL/TL/5´9˝/(175–185); d7.4; Col Bradley																									
1979	Chi A	0	5	.000	24	0	0	2-1	30.1	30	18	0	1	23-5	18	5.34	80	.261	.388	0	ø	0	—	-2	0	-0.4
1980	Chi A	1	0	1.000	23	1	0	1-0	37.2	38	12	1	0	17-2	24	2.63	154	.268	.344	0	ø	0	88	6	0	0.3
1983	Chi A	1	0	1.000	11	0	0	0-0	6	14	5	1	0	2-0	2	7.50	56	.483	.500	0	ø	0	—	-2	0	-0.3
1986	Chi N	6	2	.750	32	8	1	0-0	84	92	37	6	2	29-7	47	3.86	106	.288	.348	15-0-3	.067	-1*	109	3	0	0.1
1987	Cin N	9	10	.474	36	22	0	0-0	158.2	160	83	20	4	49-5	87	4.37	97	.265	.322	45-0-3	.111	-2	106	-2	0	-0.4
1988	Tex A	0	0	ø	11	0	0	0-0	22.1	22	14	5	1	8-0	9	5.24	78	.247	.313	0	ø	0	—	-2	0	-0.1
Total	6	17	17	.500	137	31	1	3-1	339	356	169	33	8	128-19	187	4.25	98	.274	.341	60-0-6	.100	-2	107	1	0	-0.8
HOFFMAN, TREVOR	Trevor William; B10.13.1967 Bellflower CA; BR/TR/6´0˝/(200–215); [CinN89 11/290]; d4.6; b–Glenn; Col Arizona																									
1993	Fla N	2	2	.500	28	0	0	2-1	35.2	24	13	5	0	19-7	26	3.28	133	.185	.287	2	.000	-0	—	4	0	0.5
	SD N	2	4	.333	39	0	0	3-2	54.1	56	30	5	1	20-6	53	4.31	96	.264	.325	5	.200	0	—	-1	0	-0.1
	Year	4	6	.400	67	0	0	5-3	90	80	43	10	1	39-13	79	3.90	108	.234	.310	7	.143	-0	—	3	0	0.4
1994	SD N	4	4	.500	47	0	0	20-3	56	39	16	4	0	20-6	68	2.57	161	.193	.263	3-0-1	.000	-0	—	11	0	2.0
1995	SD N	7	4	.636	55	0	0	31-7	53.1	48	25	10	0	14-3	52	3.88	105	.235	.284	2	.500	1	—	2	0	0.4
1996	†SD N	9	5	.643	70	0	0	42-7	88	50	23	6	2	31-5	111	2.25	179	.161	.240	8-0-1	.000	-1	—	19	0	3.7
1997	SD N	6	4	.600	70	0	0	37-7	81.1	59	25	9	0	24-4	111	2.66	148	.200	.259	3	.333	0	—	13	0	2.5
1998	†SD N★	4	2	.667	66	0	0	**53**-1	73	41	12	2	1	21-2	86	1.48	268	.165	.232	3	.000	-0	—	22	0	4.4
1999	SD N★	2	3	.400	64	0	0	40-3	67.1	48	23	5	0	15-2	73	2.14	200	.197	.240	3	.333	1	—	15	0	2.5
2000	SD N★	4	7	.364	70	0	0	43-7	72.1	61	29	7	0	11-4	85	2.99	149	.224	.250	0	ø	0	—	11	0	2.1
2001	SD N	3	4	.429	62	0	0	43-3	60.1	48	25	10	1	21-2	63	3.43	121	.216	.285	4	.000	-0	—	5	0	1.0
2002	SD N★	2	5	.286	61	0	0	38-3	59.1	52	20	2	1	18-2	69	2.73	142	.234	.292	0	ø	0	—	8	0	1.6
2003	SD N	0	0	ø	9	0	0	0-0	9	7	2	1	0	3-0	11	2.00	200	.212	.278	0	ø	0	—	2	156	0.1
2004	SD N	3	3	.500	55	0	0	41-4	54.2	42	14	5	0	8-1	53	2.30	171	.211	.242	0	ø	0	—	12	0	2.3
2005	†SD N	1	6	.143	60	0	0	43-3	57.2	52	23	3	1	12-1	54	2.97	132	.234	.273	0	ø	0	—	5	0	1.1
2006	†SD N★	0	2	.000	65	0	0	**46**-5	63	48	16	6	1	13-1	50	2.14	194	.205	.250	0	ø	0	—	15	0	2.5
Total	14	49	55	.471	821	0	0	482-56	885.1	675	296	80	8	250-46	965	2.71	151	.208	.264	33-0-2	.121	-1	—	143	156	26.6
HOFFMAN, BILL	William Joseph; B3.3.1918 Philadelphia PA; D5.14.2004 Roxborough PA; BL/TL/5´9˝/170; d8.13																									
1939	Phi N	0	0	ø	3	0	0	0	6	8	9	2	3	7	1	13.50	30	.333	.529	1	.000	-0	—	-6	—	-0.3
HOFFORD, JOHN	John William; B5.25.1863 Philadelphia PA; D12.16.1915 Philadelphia PA; d9.26																									
1885	Pit AA	0	3	.000	3	3	3	0	25	28	16	1	0	9	21	3.60	89	.275	.333	8	.125	-1	61	-1	—	-0.1
1886	Pit AA	3	6	.333	9	9	9	0	81	88	66	1	2	40	25	4.33	78	.261	.343	34	.294	3	91	-9	—	-0.5
Total	2	3	9	.250	12	12	12	0	106	116	82	2	2	49	46	4.16	80	.264	.341	42	.262	2	84	-10	—	-0.6
HOGAN, GEORGE	George Augustine; B9.25.1885 Marion OH; D2.22.1922 Bartlesville OK; BR/TR/6´0˝/160; d4.18; b–Willie																									
1914	KC F	0	1	.000	4	1	0	0	13	12	9	1	1	7	7	4.15	67	.255	.364	4	.000	-1	74	-2	—	-0.2
HOGAN, EDDIE	Robert Edward; B4.6.1862 St.Louis MO; D1.22.1932 Yucaipa CA; 5´7˝/153; d7.5																									
1882	StL AA	0	1	.000	1	1	1	0	8	10	7	0	—	0	4	1.13	249	.286	.286	3	.333	0	73	0	—	0.0

YEAR	TM LG	W	L	PCT	G	GS	CG-SHO	SV-BS	IP	H	R	HR	HB	BB-IB	SO	ERA	AERA	OAV	OOB	AB-HR-SH	AVG	PB	SUP	APR	DL	PW
Hogg, Brad	Carter Bradley; B3.26.1889 Buena Vista GA; D4.2.1935 Buena Vista GA; BR/TR/6´0˝/185; d9.1; Col Mercer																									
1911	Bos N	0	3	.000	8	3	2	1	25.2	33	20	0	1	14	8	6.66	57	.337	.425	9-0-1	.444	1	118	-6	—	-0.5
1912	Bos N	1	1	.500	10	1	0	1	31	37	32	2	2	16	12	6.97	51	.308	.399	11	.091	-1	164	-11	—	-0.8
1915	Chi N	1	0	1.000	2	2	1-1	0	13	12	3	1	1	6	0	2.08	134	.245	.339	3-0-1	.000	-0	120	1	—	0.1
1918	Phi N	13	13	.500	29	25	17-3	1	228	201	83	3	6	61	81	2.53	119	.245	.302	79-0-4	.228	3*	80	10	—	1.8
1919	Phi N	5	12	.294	22	19	13	0	150.1	163	85	7	5	55	48	4.43	73	.292	.360	60-0-1	.283	3*	86	-17	—	-1.6
Total	5	20	29	.408	71	50	33-4	3	448	446	223	13	15	152	149	3.70	85	.271	.338	162-0-7	.247	5	87	-23	—	-1.0
Hogg, Bill	William Johnston "Buffalo Bill"; B9.11.1881 Port Huron MI; D12.8.1909 New Orleans LA; BR/TR/6´0˝/200; d4.25																									
1905	NY A	9	13	.409	39	22	9-3	1	205	178	104	1	13	101	125	3.20	92	.236	.336	67-0-1	.060	-6	79	-6	—	-1.5
1906	NY A	14	13	.519	28	25	15-3	0	206	171	77	5	12	72	107	2.93	101	.229	.307	72-0-5	.125	-5	97	4	—	-0.2
1907	NY A	10	8	.556	25	21	13	0	166.2	173	84	3	6	83	64	3.08	91	.270	.359	60-1-5	.183	-0*	101	-5	—	-0.6
1908	NY A	4	16	.200	24	21	6	0	152.1	155	89	4	4	63	72	3.01	82	.262	.337	43-0-1	.093	-3	63	-13	—	-2.1
Total	4	37	50	.425	116	89	43-6	1	730	677	354	13	35	319	368	3.06	92	.248	.334	242-1-12	.116	-14	86	-20	—	-4.4
Hogsett, Chief	Elon Chester; B11.2.1903 Brownell KS; D7.17.2001 Hays KS; BL/TL/6´0˝/190; d9.18																									
1929	Det A	1	2	.333	4	4	2-1	0	28.2	34	10	0	1	9	9	2.83	152	.312	.370	10	.200	-0	84	5	—	0.4
1930	Det A	9	8	.529	33	17	4	1	146	174	102	9	9	63	54	5.42	88	.300	.377	58-1-0	.293	3	83	-9	—	-0.6
1931	Det A	3	9	.250	22	12	5	2	112.1	150	80	8	5	33	47	5.93	77	.324	.375	47	.234	0	94	-13	—	-1.1
1932	Det A	11	9	.550	47	15	7	7	178	201	97	8	5	66	56	3.54	133	.286	.351	57-2-4	.246	3*	87	17	—	2.2
1933	Det A	6	10	.375	45	2	0	9	116	137	78	7	4	56	39	4.50	96	.296	.377	38	.211	-0	128	-6	—	-0.8
1934	†Det A	3	2	.600	26	0	0	3	50.1	61	34	4	1	19	23	4.29	102	.303	.367	13	.231	-0	—	-2	—	-0.2
1935	†Det A	6	6	.500	40	0	0	5	96.2	109	45	1	5	49	39	3.54	118	.288	.377	23-2-0	.261	2	—	7	—	1.1
1936	Det A	0	1	.000	3	0	0	0	4	8	7	1	0	1	1	9.00	55	.400	.429	0	ø	0	—	-3	—	-0.4
	StL A	13	15	.464	39	29	10	1	215.1	278	153	15	15	90	67	5.52	97	.310	.383	70-0-2	.143	-2*	88	-4	—	-0.6
	Year	13	16	.448	42	29	10	1	219.1	286	160	16	15	91	68	5.58	96	.312	.384	70-0-2	.143	-2	88	-6	—	-1.0
1937	StL A	6	19	.240	37	26	8-1	2	177.1	245	144	19	5	75	68	6.29	77	.328	.393	62-1-0	.210	0*	56	-29	—	-3.3
1938	Was A	5	6	.455	31	9	1	3	91	107	73	12	8	36	33	6.03	75	.292	.368	23	.304	3*	102	-17	—	-1.4
1944	Det A	0	0	ø	3	0	0	0	6.1	7	6	1	2	4	5	0.00	ø	.250	.382	2	.000	-0	—	0	0	0.0
Total	11	63	87	.420	330	114	37-2	33	1222	1511	829	85	60	501	441	5.02	94	.305	.376	403-6-6	.226	8	84	-54	0	-4.7
Hogue, Cal	Calvin Grey; B10.24.1927 Dayton OH; D8.5.2005 Kettering OH; BR/TR/6´0˝/(185–195); d7.15																									
1952	Pit N	1	8	.111	19	12	3	0	83.2	79	56	7	4	68	34	4.84	82	.258	.399	24-0-1	.250	1	71	-10	0	-0.9
1953	Pit N	1	1	.500	3	2	2	0	19	19	13	4	1	16	10	5.21	86	.250	.387	5-0-1	.000	-1	100	-2	0	-0.2
1954	Pit N	0	1	.000	3	2	0	0	11	11	6	1	0	12	7	4.91	85	.282	.442	3-0-1	.000	-0	75	0	0	-0.1
Total	3	2	10	.167	25	16	5	0	113.2	109	75	12	5	96	51	4.91	83	.259	.402	32-0-3	.188	0	75	-12	0	-1.2
Hogue, Bobby	Robert Clinton; B4.5.1921 Miami FL; D12.22.1987 Miami FL; BR/TR/5´10˝/195; d4.24																									
1948	Bos N	8	2	.800	40	1	0	2	86.1	88	34	4	2	19	43	3.23	119	.265	.309	21-0-7	.095	-1	162	6	0	0.5
1949	Bos N	2	2	.500	33	0	0	3	72	78	30	4	2	25	23	3.13	121	.280	.343	21-0-3	.286	1	—	5	0	0.5
1950	Bos N	3	5	.375	36	1	0	7	62.2	69	35	8	4	31	15	5.03	77	.280	.370	13-0-1	.231	1	115	-6	0	-0.7
1951	Bos N	0	0	ø	3	0	0	0	5	4	3	1	0	3	0	5.40	68	.235	.350	2	.500	0	—	-1	0	0.0
	StL A	1	1	.500	18	0	0	1	29.2	31	17	1	0	23	11	5.16	85	.279	.403	3	.667	1	—	-2	0	0.1
	†NY A	1	0	1.000	7	0	0	0	7.1	4	0	0	0	3	2	0.00	ø	.174	.269	0	ø	0	—	3	0	0.4
	Year	2	1	.667	25	0	0	1	37	35	17	1	0	26	13	4.14	104	.261	.381	3	.667	1	—	2	0	0.5
1952	NY A	3	5	.375	27	0	0	4	47.1	52	30	6	1	25	12	5.32	62	.294	.384	11	.273	0	—	-11	0	-1.8
	StL A	0	1	.000	8	1	0	0	16.1	10	5	1	0	13	2	2.76	142	.179	.333	2	.000	-0	22	2	0	0.1
	Year	3	6	.333	35	1	0	4	63.2	62	35	7	1	38	14	4.66	74	.266	.371	13	.231	0	25	-7	0	-1.7
Total	5	18	16	.529	172	3	0	17	326.2	336	154	25	9	142	108	3.97	96	.271	.350	73-0-11	.233	3	101	-4	0	-0.9
Holborow, Wally	Walter Albert; B11.30.1913 New York NY; D7.14.1986 Ft.Lauderdale FL; BR/TR/5´11˝/187; d9.27																									
1944	Was A	0	0	ø	1	0	0	0	3	0	0	0	0	2	1	0.00	ø	.000	.182	0	ø	0	—	1	0	0.1
1945	Was A	1	1	.500	15	1	1-1	0	31.1	20	9	0	0	16	14	2.30	135	.189	.295	2-0-2	.000	-0	110	3	0	0.1
1948	Phi A	1	2	.333	5	1	1	0	17.1	32	12	1	0	7	3	5.71	75	.421	.470	4-0-1	.500	1	147	-3	0	-0.2
Total	3	2	3	.400	21	2	2-1	0	51.2	52	21	1	0	25	18	3.31	106	.272	.356	6-0-3	.333	1	137	1	0	0.0
Holcombe, Ken	Kenneth Edward; B8.23.1918 Burnsville NC; BR/TR/5´11.5˝/169; d4.27																									
1945	NY A	3	3	.500	23	2	0	0	55.1	43	19	2	0	27	20	1.79	194	.226	.323	15	.133	-1	74	7	0	0.7
1948	Cin N	0	0	ø	2	0	0	0	2.1	3	2	0	0	0	2	7.71	51	.300	.300	0	ø	0	—	-1	0	0.0
1950	Chi A	3	10	.231	24	15	5	1	96	122	68	10	0	45	37	4.59	98	.307	.378	32-0-2	.156	-2	87	-7	0	-1.0
1951	Chi A	11	12	.478	28	23	12-2	0	159.1	142	69	9	1	68	39	3.78	107	.241	.321	44-0-10	.250	1	77	9	0	1.3
1952	Chi A	0	5	.000	7	7	1	0	35	38	24	3	2	18	12	6.17	59	.286	.379	10-0-1	.000	-1	58	-9	0	-1.2
	StL A	0	2	.000	12	1	0	0	21	20	10	1	0	9	7	3.86	101	.263	.341	3	.333	0	0	0	0	0.1
	Year	0	7	.000	19	8	1	0	56	58	34	4	2	27	19	5.30	71	.278	.366	13-0-1	.077	-1	49	-8	0	-1.1
1953	Bos A	1	0	1.000	3	0	0	1	6	9	4	0	0	3	1	6.00	70	.333	.400	2-0-1	.000	-0	—	-1	0	-0.2
Total	6	18	32	.360	99	48	18-2	2	375	377	196	25	3	170	118	3.98	101	.265	.345	106-0-14	.179	-3	77	-2	0	-0.3
Holdridge, David	David Allen; B2.5.1969 Wayne MI; BR/TR/6´3˝/190; [CalA87 1/31]; d8.8																									
1998	Sea A	0	0	ø	7	0	0	0-0	6.2	6	3	0	0	4-0	6	4.05	116	.231	.323	0	ø	0	—	1	0	0.0
Holdsworth, Fred	Fredrick William; B5.29.1952 Detroit MI; BR/TR/6´1˝/(185–190); [DetA70 21/507]; d7.27																									
1972	Det A	0	1	.000	2	2	0	0-0	7	13	10	0	0	2-0	5	12.86	25	.419	.441	3	.333	0	154	-7	0	-0.8
1973	Det A	0	1	.000	5	2	0	0-0	14.2	13	11	3	0	6-0	9	6.75	61	.236	.311	0	ø	0	87	-4	0	-0.2
1974	Det A	0	3	.000	8	5	0	0-0	35.2	40	20	4	1	14-3	16	4.29	89	.286	.355	0	ø	0	51	-2	0	-0.2
1976	Bal A	4	1	.800	16	0	0	2-2	39.2	24	9	0	0	13-1	24	2.04	161	.179	.250	0	ø	0	—	6	0	0.8
1977	Bal A	0	1	.000	12	0	0	0-1	14.1	17	11	0	1	16-2	4	6.28	61	.333	.479	0	ø	0	—	-4	31	-0.3
	Mon N	3	3	.500	14	6	0	0-0	42.1	35	17	6	0	18-0	21	3.19	121	.230	.306	10	.000	-1	108	3	0	0.3
1978	Mon N	0	0	ø	6	0	0	0-0	8.2	16	10	3	0	8-3	3	7.27	49	.381	.480	0	ø	0	—	-5	55	-0.2
1980	Mil A	0	0	ø	9	0	0	0-0	19.2	24	12	2	0	9-0	12	4.58	86	.286	.355	0	ø	0	—	-2	0	-0.1
Total	7	7	10	.412	72	15	0	2-3	182	182	100	18	2	86-9	94	4.40	84	.264	.344	13	.077	-1	92	-15	86	-0.7
Holland, Al	Alfred Willis; B8.16.1952 Roanoke VA; BR/TL/5´11˝/(200–213); d9.5; Col North Carolina A&T																									
1977	Pit N	0	0	ø	2	0	0	0-0	2.1	4	2	0	0	0-0	1	7.71	52	.400	.400	0	ø	0	—	-1	0	0.0
1979	SF N	0	0	ø	3	0	0	0-0	7	3	0	0	0	5-0	7	0.00	ø	.125	.276	0	ø	0	—	3	0	0.1
1980	SF N	5	3	.625	54	0	0	7-4	82.1	71	21	2	1	34-8	65	1.75	201	.233	.308	5-0-2	.200	1	—	15	0	1.9
1981	SF N	7	5	.583	47	3	0	7-1	100.2	87	31	4	2	44-11	78	2.41	141	.233	.314	16-0-5	.063	-1	78	11	0	1.3
1982	SF N	7	3	.700	58	7	0	5-0	129.2	115	56	12	1	40-6	97	3.33	108	.231	.288	34-0-3	.059	-3	109	3	24	0.0
1983	†Phi N	8	4	.667	68	0	0	25-7	91.2	63	26	8	0	30-12	100	2.26	160	.188	.254	7-0-1	.000	-1	—	14	25	2.4
1984	Phi N☆	5	10	.333	68	0	0	29-7	98.1	82	38	14	1	30-6	61	3.39	108	.225	.283	5	.000	-1	—	5	0	0.9
1985	Phi N	0	1	.000	3	0	0	1-0	4	5	2	0	0	4-2	1	4.50	83	.333	.450	0	ø	0	—	0	0	0.0
	Pit N	1	3	.250	38	0	0	4-4	58.2	48	22	5	0	17-6	47	3.38	108	.227	.281	5-0-1	.400	2	—	3	0	0.3
	Year	1	4	.200	41	0	0	5-4	62.2	53	24	5	0	21-8	48	3.45	105	.235	.295	5-0-1	.400	2	—	3	0	0.3
	Cal A	0	1	.000	15	0	0	0-1	24.1	17	4	4	0	10-1	14	1.48	279	.193	.276	0	ø	0	—	7	0	0.4
1986	NY A	1	0	1.000	25	1	0	0-1	40.2	44	29	5	0	9-2	37	5.09	81	.268	.301	0	ø	0	263	-6	15	-0.3
1987	NY A	0	0	ø	3	0	0	0-0	6.1	9	10	1	0	9-0	5	14.21	31	.321	.486	0	ø	0	—	-7	56	-0.3
Total	10	34	30	.531	384	11	0	78-25	646	548	241	55	5	232-54	513	2.98	122	.227	.293	72-0-12	.083	-2	116	47	120	6.7
Holland, Mul	Howard Arthur; B1.6.1903 Franklin VA; D2.16.1969 Winchester VA; BR/TR/6´4˝/185; d5.25; Col Virginia																									
1926	Cin N	0	0	ø	3	0	0	0	6.2	3	1	0	0	5	0	1.35	273	.136	.296	2	.500	0	—	2	—	0.2
1927	NY N	1	0	1.000	2	0	0	0	2	0	0	0	0	3	0	0.00	ø	.000	.333	0	ø	0	—	1	—	0.2
1929	StL N	0	1	.000	8	0	0	0	14.1	13	15	3	1	7	5	9.42	50	.232	.328	4	.250	0	—	-7	—	-0.4
Total	3	1	1	.500	13	0	0	0	23	16	16	3	1	15	5	6.26	69	.190	.320	6	.333	1	—	-4	—	0.0
Holland, Bill	William David "Dutch"; B6.4.1915 Varina (now Fuquay–Varina) NC; D4.5.1997 Goldsboro NC; BL/TL/6´1˝/190; d9.17; Col East Carolina																									
1939	Was A	0	1	.000	3	0	0	0	4	6	5	1	0	5	2	11.25	39	.400	.550	0	ø	0	—	-3	—	-0.5

YEAR	TM LG	W	L	PCT	G	GS	CG-SHO	SV-BS	IP	H	R	HR	HB	BB-IB	SO	ERA	AERA	OAV	OOB	AB-HR-SH	AVG	PB	SUP	APR	DL	PW
Holley, Ed	Edward Edgar; B7.23.1899 Benton KY; D10.26.1986 Paducah KY; BR/TR/6´1.5˝/195; d5.24																									
1928	Chi N	0	0	ø	13	1	0	0	31	31	15	1	2	16	10	3.77	102	.265	.363	5	.000	-0	154	0	—	0.0
1932	Phi N	11	14	.440	34	30	16-2	0	228	247	114	15	6	55	87	3.95	112	.273	.319	91-0-2	.132	-6	85	11	—	0.4
1933	Phi N	13	15	.464	30	28	12-3	0	206.2	219	93	18	13	62	56	3.53	108	.273	.335	74-0-2	.162	-2	83	7	—	0.5
1934	Phi N	1	8	.111	15	13	2	0	72.2	85	62	10	4	31	14	7.18	66	.294	.370	24	.208	-1*	91	-15	—	-1.7
	Pit N	0	3	.000	5	4	0	0	9.1	20	16	1	2	6	2	15.43	27	.426	.509	2	1.000	2	126	-11	—	-1.6
	Year	1	11	.083	20	17	2	0	82	105	78	11	6	37	16	8.12	57	.313	.391	26	.269	1	97	-24	—	-3.3
Total	4	25	40	.385	97	76	30-5	0	547.2	602	300	45	27	170	169	4.40	95	.279	.339	196-0-4	.158	-8	89	-8	—	-2.4
Holling, Carl	Carl Theodore; B7.9.1896 Dixon CA; D7.18.1962 Santa Rosa CA; BR/TR/6´1˝/172; d4.19																									
1921	Det A	3	7	.300	35	11	4	4	136	162	95	8	4	58	38	4.30	99	.305	.378	48-0-2	.271	1	98	-6	—	-0.2
1922	Det A	1	1	.500	5	1	0	0	9.1	21	16	1	2	5	2	15.43	25	.525	.596	2	.000	-0*	88	-11	—	-1.7
Total	2	4	8	.333	40	12	4	4	145.1	183	111	9	6	63	40	5.02	85	.320	.394	50-0-2	.260	1	97	-17	—	-1.9
Hollingsworth, Al	Albert Wayne "Boots"; B2.25.1908 St.Louis MO; D4.28.1996 Austin TX; BL/TL/6´0˝/174; d4.16; C2																									
1935	Cin N	6	13	.316	38	22	8	0	173.1	165	90	5	1	76	89	3.89	102	.243	.321	54-0-3	.148	-2*	76	1	—	-0.1
1936	Cin N	9	10	.474	29	25	9	0	184	204	97	4	5	66	76	4.16	92	.281	.345	73-1-1	.315	7*	108	-6	—	0.1
1937	Cin N	9	15	.375	43	24	11-1	5	202.1	224	108	8	2	73	74	3.91	95	.278	.339	76	.250	3*	110	-6	—	-0.3
1938	Cin N	2	2	.500	9	4	1	0	34	43	28	2	0	12	13	7.15	51	.307	.362	12	.250	1	139	-12	—	-1.1
	Phi N	5	16	.238	24	21	11-1	0	174.1	177	89	4	0	77	80	3.82	102	.264	.340	67-0-1	.224	-0	78	0	—	-0.1
	Year	7	18	.280	33	25	12-1	0	208.1	220	117	6	0	89	93	4.36	88	.272	.344	79-0-1	.228	1	87	-11	—	-1.2
1939	Phi N	1	9	.100	15	10	3	0	60	78	48	2	0	27	24	5.85	69	.317	.385	20	.100	-1	92	-14	—	-2.1
	Bro N	1	2	.333	8	5	1	0	27.1	33	17	1	1	11	11	5.27	76	.311	.381	8-0-1	.125	-1*	95	-3	—	-0.3
	Year	2	11	.154	23	15	4	0	87.1	111	65	3	1	38	35	5.67	71	.315	.384	28-0-1	.107	-2	93	-16	—	-2.4
1940	Was A	1	0	1.000	3	2	0	0	18	18	12	0	0	11	7	5.50	76	.261	.363	6	.167	0	158	-2	—	-0.1
1942	StL A	10	6	.625	33	18	7-1	4	161	173	70	4	2	52	60	2.96	125	.272	.329	56-0-1	.179	0*	138	10	0	1.0
1943	StL A	6	13	.316	35	20	9-1	3	154	169	81	7	2	51	63	4.21	79	.281	.339	50-0-2	.140	-1*	91	-14	0	-1.9
1944	†StL A	5	7	.417	26	10	3-2	1	92.2	108	51	3	1	37	22	4.47	81	.291	.357	28	.071	-2	65	-7	0	-1.1
1945	StL A	12	9	.571	26	22	15-1	1	173.1	164	60	4	0	68	64	2.70	130	.251	.322	61-1-3	.197	1*	88	15	0	2.0
1946	StL A	0	0	ø	5	0	0	0	11	23	8	1	0	4	3	6.55	57	.411	.450	2	.000	-0	—	-3	0	-0.2
	Chi A	3	2	.600	21	2	0	1	55	63	29	2	0	22	22	4.58	74	.288	.353	12-0-2	.000	-1	63	-5	0	-0.6
	Year	3	2	.600	26	2	0	1	66	86	37	3	0	26	25	4.91	71	.313	.372	14-0-2	.000	-1	62	-9	0	-0.8
Total	11	70	104	.402	315	185	78-7	15	1520.1	1642	788	47	14	587	608	3.99	93	.275	.341	525-2-14	.196	3	97	-46	0	-4.8
Hollingsworth, Bonnie	John Burnette; B12.26.1895 Jacksboro TN; D1.4.1990 Knoxville TN; BR/TR/5´10˝/170; d5.30																									
1922	Pit N	0	0	ø	9	0	0	0	13.2	17	14	0	1	8	7	7.90	52	.315	.413	0	ø	0	—	-6	—	-0.3
1923	Was A	3	7	.300	17	8	1	0	72.2	72	43	3	3	50	26	4.09	92	.272	.393	22	.091	-1	77	-4	—	-0.6
1924	Bro N	1	0	1.000	3	1	1	0	8.2	8	6	0	0	10	7	6.23	60	.267	.450	3	.000	-1	91	-2	—	-0.2
1928	Bos N	0	2	.000	7	2	0	0	22.1	30	19	2	0	13	10	5.24	75	.341	.426	6	.167	-0	130	-5	—	-0.4
Total	4	4	9	.308	36	11	2	0	117.1	127	82	5	4	81	50	4.91	78	.291	.406	31	.097	-2	87	-17	—	-1.5
Hollins, Jessie	Jessie Edward; B1.27.1970 Conroe TX; BR/TR/6´3˝/190; [ChiN88 40/1027]; d9.19; [DL 1993 Chi N 182, 1994 Chi N 123]																									
1992	Chi N	0	0	ø	4	0	0	0-0	4.2	8	7	1	0	5-0	0	13.50	27	.400	.481	0	ø	0	—	-5	0	-0.2
Hollison, John	John Henry "Swede"; B5.3.1870 Chicago IL; D8.19.1969 Chicago IL; BR/TL/5´8˝/162; d8.13																									
1892	Chi N	0	0	ø	1	0	0	0	4	1	1	1	0	0	2	2.25	148	.077	.077	3	.000	-0	—	1	—	0.0
Holloman, Bobo	Alva Lee; B3.7.1923 Thomaston GA; D5.1.1987 Athens GA; BR/TR/6´2˝/207; d4.18																									
1953	StL A	3	7	.300	22	10	1-1	0	65.1	69	41	2	1	50	25	5.23	80	.275	.397	19-0-3	.105	-2	72	-6	0	-1.0
Holloway, Jim	James Madison; B9.22.1908 Plaquemine LA; D4.15.1997 Baton Rouge LA; BR/TR/6´1˝/165; d5.17																									
1929	Phi N	0	0	ø	3	0	0	0	4.2	10	7	2	0	5	1	13.50	38	.455	.556	1	1.000	0	—	-4	—	-0.1
Holloway, Ken	Kenneth Eugene (b Kenneth Eugene Hollaway); B8.8.1897 Barwick GA; D9.25.1968 Thomasville GA; BR/TR/6´0˝/185; d8.27; Col Georgia																									
1922	Det A	0	0	ø	1	0	0	0	1	1	1	0	0	0	1	0.00	ø	.250	.250	0	ø	0	—	0	—	0.0
1923	Det A	11	10	.524	42	24	7-1	1	194	232	117	12	10	75	55	4.45	87	.302	.372	65-0-3	.123	-5	106	-14	—	-1.8
1924	Det A	14	6	.700	49	13	5	3	181.1	209	105	6	6	61	46	4.07	101	.299	.361	58-0-2	.190	-1	118	-1	—	-0.2
1925	Det A	13	4	.765	38	14	6	2	157.2	170	90	8	2	67	29	4.62	93	.282	.356	48-0-4	.229	-0	120	-4	—	-0.5
1926	Det A	4	6	.400	36	12	3	2	139	192	94	2	8	42	43	5.12	79	.343	.397	46-0-1	.239	0	126	-15	—	-1.0
1927	Det A	11	12	.478	36	23	11-1	6	183.1	210	103	10	4	61	36	4.07	103	.299	.359	62-0-6	.129	-5	94	3	—	-0.1
1928	Det A	4	8	.333	30	11	5	2	120.1	137	67	2	5	32	32	4.34	95	.291	.343	33-0-5	.121	-2	69	-2	—	-0.3
1929	Cle A	6	5	.545	25	11	6-2	0	119	118	52	2	2	37	32	3.03	147	.264	.323	41	.171	-2	74	16	—	1.1
1930	Cle A	1	1	.500	12	2	0	2	30	49	32	5	0	14	8	8.40	57	.374	.434	12-0-2	.000	-2	98	-10	—	-0.8
	NY A	0	0	ø	16	0	0	0	34.1	52	23	3	0	8	11	5.24	82	.374	.408	13	.231	-0	—	-3	—	-0.2
	Year	1	1	.500	28	2	0	2	64.1	101	55	8	0	22	19	6.72	68	.374	.421	25-0-2	.120	-3	104	-15	—	-1.0
Total	9	64	52	.552	285	110	43-4	18	1160	1370	684	50	37	397	293	4.40	95	.303	.364	378-0-23	.167	-18	101	-30	—	-3.8
Holly, Jeff	Jeffrey Owen; B3.1.1953 San Pedro CA; BL/TL/6´5˝/(210–215); [ChiA71 17/390]; d5.1																									
1977	Min A	2	3	.400	18	5	0	0-0	48.1	57	37	8	1	12-0	32	6.89	58	.300	.343	0	ø	0	131	-14	0	-1.3
1978	Min A	1	1	.500	15	1	0	0-0	35.1	28	15	1	0	18-3	12	3.57	108	.222	.313	0	ø	0	70	1	0	0.1
1979	Min A	0	0	ø	6	0	0	0-0	6.1	10	7	0	0	3-0	5	7.11	62	.385	.419	0	ø	0	—	-3	0	-0.1
Total	3	3	4	.429	39	6	0	0-0	90	95	59	9	1	33-3	49	5.60	71	.278	.338	0	ø	0	121	-16	0	-1.3
Holman, Brad	Bradley Thomas; B2.9.1968 Kansas City MO; BR/TR/6´5˝/200; [KCA90 35/947]; d7.4; b–Brian; Col Auburn–Montgomery																									
1993	Sea A	1	3	.250	19	0	0	3-0	36.1	27	17	1	5	16-2	17	3.72	120	.208	.318	0	ø	0	—	3	19	0.3
Holman, Brian	Brian Scott; B1.25.1965 Denver CO; BR/TR/6´4˝/(185–190); [MonN83 1/16]; d6.25; b–Brad; [DL 1992 Sea A 182, 1993 Sea A 182]																									
1988	Mon N	4	8	.333	18	16	1-1	0-0	100.1	101	39	3	0	34-2	58	3.23	113	.264	.323	28-0-4	.107	-1*	69	5	0	0.5
1989	Mon N	1	2	.333	10	3	0	0-0	31.2	34	18	2	1	15-0	23	4.83	74	.270	.350	8	.125	-0	108	-4	0	-0.4
	Sea A	8	10	.444	23	22	6-2	0-0	159.2	160	68	9	6	62-6	82	3.44	117	.261	.333	0	ø	0	91	11	0	1.2
1990	Sea A	11	11	.500	28	28	3	0-0	189.2	188	92	17	6	66-2	121	4.03	99	.260	.324	1	.000	-0	87	1	0	0.0
1991	Sea A	13	14	.481	30	30	5-3	0-0	195.1	199	86	16	10	77-0	108	3.69	112	.268	.343	0	ø	0	77	10	0	1.4
Total	4	37	45	.451	109	99	15-6	0-0	676.2	682	303	47	23	254-10	392	3.71	107	.263	.333	37-0-4	.108	-1	82	23	364	2.7
Holman, Scott	Randy Scott; B9.18.1958 Santa Paula CA; BR/TR/6´1˝/(190–194); d9.20; Col Ventura (CA) JC																									
1980	NY N	0	0	ø	4	0	0	0-0	7	6	2	0	0	1-1	3	1.29	281	.250	.269	0	ø	0	—	1	0	0.1
1982	NY N	2	1	.667	4	4	1	0-0	26.2	23	10	2	0	7-0	11	2.36	156	.232	.280	9-0-1	.222	0	78	3	0	0.4
1983	NY N	1	7	.125	35	10	0	0-0	101	90	48	7	1	52-8	44	3.74	98	.242	.333	23-0-2	.217	0	70	-1	0	0.1
Total	3	3	8	.273	43	14	1	0-0	134.2	119	60	9	1	60-9	58	3.34	110	.240	.320	32-0-3	.219	1	72	3	0	0.6
Holman, Shawn	Shawn Leroy; B11.10.1964 Sewickley PA; BR/TR/6´2˝/186; [PitN82 14/347]; d9.5																									
1989	Det A	0	0	ø	5	0	0	0-0	10	8	2	0	0	11-1	9	1.80	213	.211	.380	0	ø	0	—	2	0	0.1
Holmes, Darren	Darren Lee; B4.25.1966 Asheville NC; BR/TR/6´0˝/(199–203); [LAN84 16/415]; d9.1																									
1990	LA N	0	1	.000	14	0	0	0-0	17.1	15	10	1	0	11-3	19	5.19	71	.238	.342	0	ø	0	—	-2	0	-0.1
1991	Mil A	1	4	.200	40	0	0	3-3	76.1	90	43	6	1	27-1	59	4.72	85	.295	.351	0	ø	0	—	-6	15	-0.4
1992	Mil A	4	4	.500	41	0	0	6-2	42.1	35	12	1	2	11-4	31	2.55	152	.224	.284	0	ø	0	—	7	0	1.4
1993	Col N	3	3	.500	62	0	0	25-4	66.2	56	31	6	2	20-1	60	4.05	118	.222	.285	0	ø	0	—	6	0	0.8
1994	Col N	0	3	.000	29	0	0	3-5	28.1	35	25	5	1	24-4	33	6.35	78	.313	.435	1	.000	-0	—	-5	46	-0.6
1995	†Col N	6	1	.857	68	0	0	14-4	66.2	59	26	3	1	28-3	61	3.24	166	.237	.313	1-0-3	.000	-0	—	12	0	1.7
1996	Col N	5	4	.556	62	0	0	1-7	77	78	41	8	1	28-2	73	3.97	131	.259	.323	2	.000	-0	—	7	0	0.7
1997	Col N	9	2	.818	42	6	0	3-1	89.1	113	58	12	0	36-3	70	5.34	97	.314	.373	19-1-3	.158	-0	149	-2	15	-0.2
1998	NY A	0	3	.000	34	0	0	2-1	51.1	53	19	4	2	14-3	31	3.33	132	.270	.321	0	ø	0	—	7	36	0.4
1999	†Ari N	4	3	.571	44	0	0	0-2	48.2	50	21	3	1	25-8	35	3.70	125	.262	.350	2	.000	-0	—	5	45	0.6
2000	Ari N	0	0	ø	4	0	0	1-0	2.1	5	3	0	0	1-0	2	11.57	41	.455	.462	0	ø	0	—	-2	0	-0.1
	StL N	0	1	.000	5	0	0	0-1	8.1	12	9	2	1	3-0	5	9.72	48	.364	.410	1	.000	-0	—	-4	0	-0.4

YEAR	TM LG	W	L	PCT	G	GS	CG-SHO	SV-BS	IP	H	R	HR	HB	BB-IB	SO	ERA	AERA	OAV	OOB	AB-HR-SH	AVG	PB	SUP	APR	DL	PW
	Bal A	0	0	ø	5	0	0	0-0	4.2	13	13	3	0	5-0	6	25.07	19	.481	.563	0	ø	0	—	-11	0	-0.5
	Ari N	0	0	ø	4	0	0	0-0	4	7	3	1	1	0-0	3	6.75	71	.389	.421	0	ø	0	—	-1	0	0.0
	Year	0	1	.000	13	0	0	1-1	14.2	24	15	3	2	4-0	10	9.20	51	.387	.423	1-0	.000	-0	—	-7	0	-0.5
2002	†Atl N	2	2	.500	55	0	0	1-1	54.2	41	12	3	2	12-4	47	1.81	223	.210	.262	2	.000	-0	—	14	20	1.0
2003	Atl N	1	2	.333	48	0	0	0-1	42	47	22	5	0	11-0	46	4.29	98	.280	.322	0	ø	0	—	0	52	0.0
Total	13	35	33	.515	557	6	0	59-32	680	709	348	63	15	256-36	581	4.25	109	.269	.334	28-1-6	.107	-1	149	25	229	4.3

Holmes, Chick Elwood Marter; B3.22.1896 Beverly NJ; D4.15.1954 Camden NJ; TR; d6.27

YEAR	TM LG	W	L	PCT	G	GS	CG-SHO	SV-BS	IP	H	R	HR	HB	BB-IB	SO	ERA	AERA	OAV	OOB	AB-HR-SH	AVG	PB	SUP	APR	DL	PW
1918	Phi A	0	0	ø	2	0	0	0	2	4	5	0	1	1	0	13.50	22	.400	.500	0	ø	0	—	-3	—	-0.1

Holmes, Jim James Scott; B8.2.1882 Lawrenceburg KY; D3.10.1960 Jacksonville FL; d9.8

YEAR	TM LG	W	L	PCT	G	GS	CG-SHO	SV-BS	IP	H	R	HR	HB	BB-IB	SO	ERA	AERA	OAV	OOB	AB-HR-SH	AVG	PB	SUP	APR	DL	PW
1906	Phi A	0	1	.000	3	1	0	0	9	10	11	0	1	8	1	4.00	68	.286	.432	5	.600	1	106	-3	—	-0.2
1908	Bro N	1	4	.200	13	1	1	0	40	37	19	0	3	20	10	3.37	69	.270	.375	13	.077	-1	150	-4	—	-0.7
Total	2	1	5	.167	16	2	1	0	49	47	30	0	4	28	11	3.49	69	.273	.387	18	.222	0	132	-7	—	-0.9

Holmes, Ducky James William; B1.28.1869 Des Moines IA; D8.6.1932 Truro IA; BL/TR/5´6˝/170; d8.8; ▲

YEAR	TM LG	W	L	PCT	G	GS	CG-SHO	SV-BS	IP	H	R	HR	HB	BB-IB	SO	ERA	AERA	OAV	OOB	AB-HR-SH	AVG	PB	SUP	APR	DL	PW
1895	Lou N	1	0	1.000	2	1	1	0	14	16	11	1	1	4	0	5.79	80	.281	.339	161-3-3	.373	1*	138	-1	—	0.0
1896	Lou N	0	1	.000	2	1	0	0	12	26	23	0	0	8	3	7.50	58	.433	.500	141-0-4	.270	0*	213	-7	—	-0.4
Total	2	1	1	.500	4	2	1	0	26	42	34	1	1	12	3	6.58	68	.359	.423	302-3-7	.325	1	174	-8	—	-0.4

Holshouser, Herm Herman Alexander; B1.20.1907 Rockwell NC; D7.26.1994 Concord NC; BR/TR/6´0˝/170; d4.15; Col North Carolina

YEAR	TM LG	W	L	PCT	G	GS	CG-SHO	SV-BS	IP	H	R	HR	HB	BB-IB	SO	ERA	AERA	OAV	OOB	AB-HR-SH	AVG	PB	SUP	APR	DL	PW
1930	StL A	0	1	.000	25	1	0	1	62.1	103	63	8	3	28	37	7.80	63	.376	.439	16	.125	-1	211	-20	—	-0.9

Holt, Chris Christopher Michael; B9.18.1971 Dallas TX; BR/TR/6´4˝/205; [HouN92 3/69]; d9.1; Col Navarro (TX) JC; [DL 1998 Hou N 181]

YEAR	TM LG	W	L	PCT	G	GS	CG-SHO	SV-BS	IP	H	R	HR	HB	BB-IB	SO	ERA	AERA	OAV	OOB	AB-HR-SH	AVG	PB	SUP	APR	DL	PW
1996	Hou N	0	1	.000	4	0	0	0-0	4.2	5	3	0	0	3-1	0	5.79	67	.263	.364	1	.000	-0	—	-1	0	-0.2
1997	Hou N	8	12	.400	33	32	0	0-0	209.2	211	98	17	8	61-4	95	3.52	114	.263	.320	67-0-9	.090	-3	94	9	0	0.4
1999	†Hou N	5	13	.278	32	26	0	1-1	164	193	92	12	8	57-1	115	4.66	95	.303	.363	45-0-7	.067	-2	89	-4	0	-0.7
2000	Hou N	8	16	.333	34	32	3-1	0-0	207	247	131	22	8	75-2	136	5.35	92	.303	.363	60-0-5	.100	-2	101	-8	0	-1.0
2001	Det A	7	9	.438	30	22	1	0-0	151.1	197	102	18	8	57-5	80	5.77	77	.319	.381	4	.250	0	105	-21	0	-1.8
Total	5	28	51	.354	133	112	4-1	1-1	736.2	853	426	69	32	253-13	426	4.76	93	.295	.355	177-0-21	.090	-7	97	-25	181	-3.3

Holtgrave, Vern Lavern George "Woody"; B10.18.1942 Aviston IL; BR/TR/6´1˝/185; d9.26

YEAR	TM LG	W	L	PCT	G	GS	CG-SHO	SV-BS	IP	H	R	HR	HB	BB-IB	SO	ERA	AERA	OAV	OOB	AB-HR-SH	AVG	PB	SUP	APR	DL	PW
1965	Det A	0	0	ø	1	0	0	0	3	4	2	0	0	2-0	2	6.00	58	.308	.400	0	ø	0	—	-1	0	0.0

Holton, Brian Brian John; B11.29.1959 McKeesport PA; BR/TR/6´0˝/(193–196); [LAN78*1/22]; d9.9; Col Louisburg (NC) JC

YEAR	TM LG	W	L	PCT	G	GS	CG-SHO	SV-BS	IP	H	R	HR	HB	BB-IB	SO	ERA	AERA	OAV	OOB	AB-HR-SH	AVG	PB	SUP	APR	DL	PW
1985	LA N	1	1	.500	3	0	0	0-0	4	9	7	0	0	1-0	1	9.00	39	.450	.476	0	ø	0	—	-3	0	-0.6
1986	LA N	2	3	.400	12	3	0	0-1	24.1	28	13	1	1	6-2	24	4.44	78	.292	.337	5	.000	-1	51	-3	0	-0.5
1987	LA N	3	2	.600	53	1	0	2-1	83.1	87	39	11	0	32-11	58	3.89	102	.269	.332	5	.200	0	114	2	0	0.1
1988	†LA N	7	3	.700	45	0	0	1-0	84.2	69	19	1	1	26-7	49	1.70	197	.228	.289	10	.000	-1	—	16	0	1.8
1989	Bal A	5	7	.417	39	12	0	0-1	116.1	140	63	11	1	39-1	51	4.02	95	.300	.352	0	ø	0	111	-6	0	-0.6
1990	Bal A	2	3	.400	33	0	0	0-1	58	68	31	7	0	21-6	27	4.50	85	.292	.348	0	ø	0	—	-4	0	-0.3
Total	6	20	19	.513	185	16	0	3-4	370.2	401	172	31	3	125-27	210	3.62	103	.278	.334	20	.050	-1	101	2	0	-0.1

Holtz, Mike Michael James; B10.10.1972 Arlington VA; BL/TL/5´9˝/(175–188); [CalA94 17/461]; d7.11; Col Clemson

YEAR	TM LG	W	L	PCT	G	GS	CG-SHO	SV-BS	IP	H	R	HR	HB	BB-IB	SO	ERA	AERA	OAV	OOB	AB-HR-SH	AVG	PB	SUP	APR	DL	PW
1996	Cal A	3	3	.500	30	0	0	0-0	29.1	21	11	1	3	19-2	31	2.45	206	.204	.341	0	ø	0	—	7	0	1.3
1997	Ana A	3	4	.429	66	0	0	2-6	43.1	38	21	7	2	15-4	40	3.32	139	.228	.296	1	.000	-0	—	5	0	0.7
1998	Ana A	2	2	.500	53	0	0	1-1	30.1	38	16	0	1	15-1	29	4.75	100	.322	.397	0	ø	0	—	1	0	0.1
1999	Ana A	2	3	.400	28	0	0	0-0	22.1	26	20	3	2	15-1	17	8.06	61	.295	.410	0	ø	0	—	-7	16	-1.3
2000	Ana A	3	4	.429	61	0	0	0-0	41	37	26	4	2	18-2	40	5.05	102	.248	.331	0	ø	0	—	0	0	0.0
2001	Ana A	1	2	.333	63	0	0	0-1	37	40	24	5	2	15-4	38	4.86	96	.274	.348	0	ø	0	—	-2	19	-0.1
2002	Oak A	0	0	ø	16	0	0	0-1	14	24	11	3	1	9-0	7	6.43	70	.358	.442	0	ø	0	—	-3	0	-0.1
	SD N	2	2	.500	33	0	0	0-3	21	18	14	2	1	21-3	19	4.71	82	.237	.396	2	.000	-0	—	-3	0	-0.5
2006	Bos A	0	0	ø	3	0	0	0-0	1.2	3	3	0	1	4-0	2	16.20	29	.429	.667	0	ø	0	—	-2	30	-0.1
Total	8	16	20	.444	353	0	0	3-12	240	245	146	25	15	131-17	223	4.76	99	.266	.362	3	.000	-0	—	-4	65	-0.0

Holtzman, Ken Kenneth Dale; B11.3.1945 St.Louis MO; BR/TL/6´2˝/(175–198); [ChiN65 4/61]; d9.4; Mil 1967; Col Illinois

YEAR	TM LG	W	L	PCT	G	GS	CG-SHO	SV-BS	IP	H	R	HR	HB	BB-IB	SO	ERA	AERA	OAV	OOB	AB-HR-SH	AVG	PB	SUP	APR	DL	PW
1965	Chi N	0	0	ø	3	0	0	0	4	2	4	1	0	3-0	3	2.25	164	.143	.294	0	ø	0	—	-1	0	0.0
1966	Chi N	11	16	.407	34	33	9	0	220.2	194	104	27	4	68-6	171	3.79	97	.235	.295	73-0-6	.123	-3	87	-1	0	-0.5
1967	Chi N	9	0	1.000	12	12	3	0	92.2	76	31	11	2	44-7	62	2.53	140	.222	.314	35-0-6	.200	1	165	9	0	1.0
1968	Chi N	11	14	.440	34	32	6-3	1	215	201	89	17	6	76-7	151	3.35	94	.248	.316	80-0-1	.125	-2*	99	-4	0	-0.7
1969	Chi N	17	13	.567	39	39	12-6	0-0	261.1	248	117	18	5	93-8	176	3.58	112	.247	.313	100-1-5	.150	-1	110	12	0	1.1
1970	Chi N	17	11	.607	39	38	15-1	0-0	287.2	271	125	30	3	94-6	202	3.38	133	.248	.307	105-0-8	.200	1*	105	31	0	3.0
1971	Chi N	9	15	.375	30	29	9-3	0-1	195	213	108	18	2	64-7	143	4.48	88	.276	.331	69-1-2	.130	-1	89	-10	0	-1.3
1972	†Oak A☆	19	11	.633	39	37	16-4	0-1	265.1	232	83	23	4	52-6	134	2.51	114	.236	.276	90-0-11	.178	2*	139	11	0	1.5
1973	†Oak A★	21	13	.618	40	40	16-4	0-0	297.1	275	109	22	4	66-5	157	2.97	120	.243	.286	0	ø	0*	114	23	0	2.5
1974	†Oak A	19	17	.528	39	38	9-3	0-0	255.1	273	111	14	3	51-3	117	3.07	109	.272	.308	0	ø	0	107	4	0	0.6
1975	†Oak A	18	14	.563	39	38	13-2	0-0	266.1	217	111	16	7	108-1	122	3.14	116	.222	.301	2	.000	-0	104	13	0	1.7
1976	Bal A	5	4	.556	13	13	6-1	0-0	97.2	100	34	4	1	35-2	25	2.86	115	.271	.333	0	ø	0	96	5	0	0.5
	NY A	9	7	.563	21	21	10-2	0-0	149	165	74	14	0	35-0	41	4.17	82	.283	.322	0	ø	0	114	-11	0	-1.1
	Year	14	11	.560	34	34	16-3	0-0	246.2	265	108	18	1	70-2	66	3.65	92	.278	.326	0	ø	0	107	-6	0	-0.6
1977	NY A	2	3	.400	18	11	0	0-0	71.2	105	55	7	1	24-2	14	5.78	69	.362	.410	0	ø	0	120	-17	0	-0.9
1978	NY A	1	0	1.000	5	3	0	0-0	17.2	21	8	2	0	9-0	3	4.08	90	.313	.395	0	ø	0	115	0	0	0.0
	Chi N	0	3	.000	23	6	0	2-0	53	61	40	10	1	35-3	36	6.11	66	.286	.388	10-0-1	.200	0	92	-11	0	-0.6
1979	Chi N	6	9	.400	23	20	3-2	0-0	117.2	133	70	15	6	53-7	44	4.59	91	.287	.366	43	.233	2*	95	-6	21	-0.6
Total	15	174	150	.537	451	410	127-31	3-2	2867.1	2787	1273	249	49	910-70	1601	3.49	105	.255	.313	607-2-40	.163	-1	108	47	21	6.2

Holzemer, Mark Mark Harold; B8.20.1969 Littleton CO; BL/TL/6´0˝/(165–185); [CalA87 4/109]; d8.21; Col Seminole St. (OK) JC

YEAR	TM LG	W	L	PCT	G	GS	CG-SHO	SV-BS	IP	H	R	HR	HB	BB-IB	SO	ERA	AERA	OAV	OOB	AB-HR-SH	AVG	PB	SUP	APR	DL	PW
1993	Cal A	0	3	.000	5	4	0	0-0	23.1	34	24	2	3	13-0	10	8.87	51	.340	.431	0	ø	0	81	-10	0	-1.0
1995	Cal A	0	1	.000	12	0	0	0-0	8.1	11	6	1	1	7-1	5	5.40	87	.306	.432	0	ø	0	—	-1	0	-0.1
1996	Cal A	1	0	1.000	25	0	0	0-0	24.2	35	28	7	3	8-1	20	8.76	58	.327	.387	0	ø	0	—	-11	83	-0.5
1997	Sea A	0	0	ø	14	0	0	1-0	9	9	6	0	0	8-0	7	6.00	76	.250	.386	0	ø	0	—	-1	0	0.0
1998	Oak A	1	0	1.000	13	0	0	0-0	9.2	13	6	1	1	3-0	3	5.59	83	.333	.386	0	ø	0	—	-1	0	-0.1
2000	Phi N	0	1	.000	25	0	0	0-1	25.2	36	23	4	1	8-1	19	7.71	59	.336	.388	1	.000	-0	—	-9	15	-0.4
Total	6	2	5	.286	94	4	0	1-1	100.2	138	93	15	9	47-3	64	7.69	61	.325	.402	1	.000	-0	81	-33	98	-2.1

Honeycutt, Rick Frederick Wayne; B6.29.1954 Chattanooga TN; BL/TL/5´11˝/(185–195); [PitN76 17/405]; d8.24; C1; Col Tennessee

YEAR	TM LG	W	L	PCT	G	GS	CG-SHO	SV-BS	IP	H	R	HR	HB	BB-IB	SO	ERA	AERA	OAV	OOB	AB-HR-SH	AVG	PB	SUP	APR	DL	PW
1977	Sea A	0	1	.000	10	3	0	0-0	29	26	16	7	3	11-2	17	4.34	95	.239	.320	0	ø	0	72	-1	0	-0.1
1978	Sea A	5	11	.313	26	24	4-1	0-0	134.1	150	81	12	3	49-5	50	4.89	79	.285	.345	0	ø	0	95	-15	37	-1.5
1979	Sea A	11	12	.478	33	28	8-1	0-0	194	201	103	22	6	67-7	83	4.04	108	.268	.331	0	ø	0	89	5	0	0.4
1980	Sea A☆	10	17	.370	30	30	9-1	0-0	203.1	221	99	22	3	60-7	79	3.94	106	.280	.330	0	ø	0	69	5	0	0.6
1981	Tex A	11	6	.647	20	20	8-2	0-0	127.2	120	49	12	0	17-1	40	3.31	105	.246	.272	0	ø	0	110	4	0	0.5
1982	Tex A	5	17	.227	30	26	4-1	0-1	164	201	103	20	3	54-4	64	5.27	74	.305	.356	0	ø	0	79	-25	0	-2.8
1983	Tex A★	14	8	.636	25	25	5-2	0-0	174.2	168	59	9	6	37-2	56	**2.42**	**167**	.262	.306	0	ø	0	100	29	0	3.8
	†LA N	2	3	.400	9	7	1	0-0	39	46	26	6	2	13-4	18	5.77	63	.297	.359	12-0-2	.083	-1	115	-8	0	-0.9
1984	LA N	10	9	.526	29	28	6-2	0-0	183.2	180	72	11	2	51-11	75	2.84	125	.258	.308	56-0-9	.143	-0	88	13	0	1.4
1985	†LA N	8	12	.400	31	25	1	1-0	142	141	71	9	1	49-7	67	3.42	102	.261	.321	38-0-8	.132	0*	94	-2	0	-0.1
1986	LA N	11	9	.550	32	28	0	0-0	171	164	71	9	3	45-4	100	3.32	105	.249	.300	43-0-6	.070	0	104	3	0	0.5
1987	LA N	2	12	.143	27	20	1-1	0-0	115.2	133	74	10	2	45-4	92	4.59	87	.278	.343	30-0-3	.233	2	59	-12	0	-1.0
	Oak A	1	4	.200	7	4	0	0-0	23.2	25	17	3	2	9-0	10	5.32	78	.275	.343	0	ø	0	88	-4	0	-0.7
1988	†Oak A	3	2	.600	55	0	0	7-2	79.2	74	36	6	3	25-2	47	3.50	109	.253	.312	0	ø	0	—	2	0	0.2
1989	†Oak A	2	2	.500	64	0	0	12-4	76.2	56	26	5	1	26-3	52	2.35	158	.207	.277	0	ø	0	—	11	0	0.9
1990	†Oak A	2	2	.500	63	0	0	7-3	63.1	46	23	2	1	22-2	38	2.70	138	.204	.272	2	.000	-0*	—	7	0	0.5
1991	Oak A	2	4	.333	43	0	0	0-4	37.2	37	16	3	2	20-3	26	3.58	108	.261	.358	0	ø	0	—	1	69	0.2
1992	†Oak A	1	4	.200	54	0	0	3-4	39	41	19	2	3	10-3	32	3.69	102	.272	.327	0	ø	0	—	0	0	0.0
1993	Oak A	1	4	.200	52	0	0	1-2	41.2	30	18	2	1	20-6	21	2.81	147	.211	.305	0	ø	0	—	4	39	0.5
1994	Tex A	1	2	.333	42	0	0	1-1	25	37	21	4	2	9-1	18	7.20	67	.349	.410	0	ø	0	—	-6	23	-0.6

YEAR	TM LG	W	L	PCT	G	GS	CG-SHO	SV-BS	IP	H	R	HR	HB	BB-IB	SO	ERA	AERA	OAV	OOB	AB-HR-SH	AVG	PB	SUP	APR	DL	PW
1995	Oak A	5	1	.833	49	0	0	2-3	44.2	37	13	5	1	9-0	21	2.42	187	.231	.275	0	ø	0	—	11	0	1.3
	NY A	0	0	ø	3	0	0	0-0	1	2	3	1	0	1-0	0	27.00	17	.400	.500	0	ø	0	—	-2	0	-0.1
	Year	5	1	.833	52	0	0	2-3	45.2	39	16	6	1	10-0	21	2.96	153	.236	.282	0	ø	0	—	8	0	1.2
1996	†StL N	2	1	.667	61	0	0	4-3	47.1	42	15	3	0	7-3	30	2.85	149	.240	.265	1	.000	1	—	8	0	0.7
1997	StL N	0	0	ø	2	0	0	0-0	2	5	3	0	0	1-0	2	13.50	31	.500	.545	0	ø	0	—	-2	147	-0.1
Total	21	109	143	.433	797	268	47-11	38-27	2160	2183	1034	185	50	657-81	1038	3.72	104	.264	.320	182-0-28	.132	2	88	26	315	3.6

HOOD, DON Donald Harris; B10.16.1949 Florence SC; BL/TL/6´2˝/(180–190); [BalA69 1/17]; d7.16

YEAR	TM LG	W	L	PCT	G	GS	CG-SHO	SV-BS	IP	H	R	HR	HB	BB-IB	SO	ERA	AERA	OAV	OOB	AB-HR-SH	AVG	PB	SUP	APR	DL	PW
1973	†Bal A	3	2	.600	8	4	1-1	1-0	32.1	31	17	1	1	6-0	18	3.90	97	.256	.295	0	ø	0	71	-1	0	-0.2
1974	Bal A	1	1	.500	20	2	0	1-1	57.1	47	26	1	0	20-1	26	3.45	101	.223	.289	0	ø	0*	63	0	0	0.0
1975	Cle A	6	10	.375	29	19	2	0-0	135.1	136	76	16	0	57-6	51	4.39	87	.268	.340	0	ø	0*	88	-9	0	-1.0
1976	Cle A	3	5	.375	33	6	0	1-0	77.2	89	46	5	4	41-3	32	4.87	72	.296	.386	0	ø	0*	71	-11	0	-1.1
1977	Cle A	2	1	.667	41	5	1	0-2	105	87	42	3	4	49-7	62	3.00	133	.224	.317	0	ø	0*	72	11	0	0.5
1978	Cle A	5	6	.455	36	19	1	0-0	154.2	166	82	13	1	77-5	73	4.48	85	.278	.357	0	ø	0	110	-10	0	-0.6
1979	Cle A	1	0	1.000	13	0	0	1-1	22	13	9	1	1	14-1	7	3.68	117	.169	.304	0	ø	0	—	2	0	0.1
	NY A	3	1	.750	27	6	0	1-0	67.1	62	24	3	2	30-1	22	3.07	134	.252	.333	0	ø	0	132	9	0	0.5
	Year	4	1	.800	40	6	0	2-1	89.1	75	33	4	3	44-2	29	3.22	129	.232	.326	0	ø	0	131	11	0	0.6
1980	StL N	4	6	.400	33	8	1	0-1	82.1	90	39	2	2	34-5	35	3.39	111	.288	.359	20-0-2	.200	-0*	125	1	0	0.2
1982	KC A	4	0	1.000	30	3	0	1-1	66.2	71	31	7	2	22-1	31	3.51	116	.276	.333	0	ø	0	111	3	0	0.2
1983	KC A	2	3	.400	27	0	0	0-1	47.2	48	20	5	2	14-2	17	2.27	181	.273	.328	0	ø	0	—	7	21	0.7
Total	10	34	35	.493	297	72	6-1	6-7	848.1	840	412	57	19	364-32	374	3.79	102	.263	.339	20-0-2	.200	-0	98	2	21	-0.7

HOOD, WALLY Wallace James Jr.; B9.24.1925 Los Angeles CA; D6.16.2001 Glendale CA; BR/TR/6´1˝/190; d9.23; f-Wally; Col USC

YEAR	TM LG	W	L	PCT	G	GS	CG-SHO	SV-BS	IP	H	R	HR	HB	BB-IB	SO	ERA	AERA	OAV	OOB	AB-HR-SH	AVG	PB	SUP	APR	DL	PW
1949	NY A	0	0	ø	2	0	0	0	2.1	0	0	0	0	1	2	0.00	ø	.000	.143	0	ø	0	—	1	0	0.1

HOOK, CHRIS Christopher Wayne; B8.4.1968 San Diego CA; BR/TR/6´5˝/230; d4.30; Col Northern Kentucky

YEAR	TM LG	W	L	PCT	G	GS	CG-SHO	SV-BS	IP	H	R	HR	HB	BB-IB	SO	ERA	AERA	OAV	OOB	AB-HR-SH	AVG	PB	SUP	APR	DL	PW
1995	SF N	5	1	.833	45	0	0	0-0	52.1	55	33	7	3	29-3	40	5.50	75	.274	.369	3	.000	-0	—	-7	0	-0.8
1996	SF N	0	1	.000	10	0	0	0-0	13.1	16	13	3	2	14-2	4	7.43	56	.308	.464	2	.500	0	—	-5	0	-0.3
Total	2	5	2	.714	55	0	0	0-0	65.2	71	46	10	5	43-5	44	5.89	70	.281	.390	5	.200	0	—	-12	0	-1.1

HOOK, JAY James Wesley; B11.18.1936 Waukegan IL; BL/TR/6´2˝/(182–185); d9.3; Col Northwestern

YEAR	TM LG	W	L	PCT	G	GS	CG-SHO	SV-BS	IP	H	R	HR	HB	BB-IB	SO	ERA	AERA	OAV	OOB	AB-HR-SH	AVG	PB	SUP	APR	DL	PW
1957	Cin N	0	1	.000	3	2	0	0	10	6	7	0	0	8-0	6	4.50	91	.176	.326	3	.000	-0	86	-1	0	-0.1
1958	Cin N	0	1	.000	1	1	0	0	3	3	4	2	0	2-0	5	12.00	35	.250	.357	1	.000	-0	22	-2	0	-0.4
1959	Cin N	5	5	.500	17	15	4	0	79	79	46	10	3	39-1	37	5.13	79	.266	.356	24-0-2	.125	-1*	100	-7	0	-0.9
1960	Cin N	11	18	.379	36	33	10-2	0	222	222	119	31	5	73-7	103	4.50	85	.263	.323	72-0-6	.083	-3	106	-14	0	-2.0
1961	Cin N	1	3	.250	22	5	0	0	62.2	83	55	14	5	22-2	36	7.76	52	.322	.382	15	.133	-1	100	-23	0	-1.4
1962	NY N	8	19	.296	37	34	13	0	213.2	230	137	31	8	71-4	113	4.84	86	.273	.332	69-0-6	.203	2*	88	-15	0	-1.5
1963	NY N	4	14	.222	41	20	3	1	152.2	168	104	21	9	53-2	89	5.48	64	.281	.346	38-0-2	.237	2	86	-29	0	-3.1
1964	NY N	0	1	.000	3	2	0	0	9.2	17	10	2	0	7-0	5	9.31	38	.395	.471	3	.000	-0	74	-5	0	-0.5
Total	8	29	62	.319	160	112	30-2	1	752.2	808	482	111	30	275-16	394	5.23	75	.276	.341	225-0-16	.151	-2	94	-96	0	-9.9

HOOKER, BUCK William Edward; B8.28.1880 Richmond VA; D7.2.1929 Richmond VA; TR/5´6˝/?; d9.5

YEAR	TM LG	W	L	PCT	G	GS	CG-SHO	SV-BS	IP	H	R	HR	HB	BB-IB	SO	ERA	AERA	OAV	OOB	AB-HR-SH	AVG	PB	SUP	APR	DL	PW
1902	Cin N	0	1	.000	1	1	1	0	8	11	5	1	0	0	0	4.50	67	.324	.324	3	.000	-0	68	-1	—	-0.2
1903	Cin N	0	0	ø	1	0	0	0	2.1	2	0	0	0	2	0	0.00	ø	.250	.400	1	.000	-0*	—	1	—	0.0
Total	2	0	1	.000	2	1	1	0	10.1	13	5	1	0	2	0	3.48	90	.310	.341	4	.000	-1	68	0	—	-0.2

HOOPER, BOB Robert Nelson; B5.30.1922 Leamington ON, Can.; D3.17.1980 New Brunswick NJ; BR/TR/5´11˝/195; d4.19; Col Montclair St.

YEAR	TM LG	W	L	PCT	G	GS	CG-SHO	SV-BS	IP	H	R	HR	HB	BB-IB	SO	ERA	AERA	OAV	OOB	AB-HR-SH	AVG	PB	SUP	APR	DL	PW
1950	Phi A	15	10	.600	45	20	3	5	170.1	181	108	15	1	91	58	5.02	91	.272	.361	56-1-4	.125	-2	132	-10	0	-1.3
1951	Phi A	12	10	.545	38	23	9	5	189	192	98	13	3	61	64	4.38	98	.267	.327	72-1-2	.208	-1	103	0	0	-0.1
1952	Phi A	8	15	.348	43	14	4	6	144.1	158	100	13	4	68	40	5.18	76	.279	.361	41-2-3	.195	1	60	-21	0	-2.9
1953	Cle A	5	4	.556	43	0	0	7	69.1	50	37	4	2	38	16	4.02	93	.206	.318	12	.083	-1	—	-3	0	-0.5
1954	Cle A	0	0	ø	17	0	0	2	34.2	39	22	3	1	16	12	4.93	74	.289	.364	5	.000	-1	—	-5	0	-0.3
1955	Cin N	0	2	.000	8	0	0	0	13	20	12	2	0	6-0	6	7.62	56	.357	.419	1	.000	-0	—	-4	0	-0.6
Total	6	40	41	.494	194	57	16	25	620.2	640	377	50	11	280-0	196	4.80	87	.268	.348	187-4-9	.166	-4	106	-43	0	-5.7

HOOTEN, LEON Michael Leon; B4.4.1948 Downey CA; BR/TR/5´11˝/180; d4.13; Col Arizona

YEAR	TM LG	W	L	PCT	G	GS	CG-SHO	SV-BS	IP	H	R	HR	HB	BB-IB	SO	ERA	AERA	OAV	OOB	AB-HR-SH	AVG	PB	SUP	APR	DL	PW
1974	Oak A	0	0	ø	6	0	0	0-0	8.1	6	3	1	1	4-0	1	3.24	103	.207	.314	0	ø	0	—	0	0	0.0

HOOTON, BURT Burt Carlton; B2.7.1950 Greenville TX; BR/TR/6´1˝/(190–210); [ChiN71 D1/2]; d6.17; C5; Col Texas

YEAR	TM LG	W	L	PCT	G	GS	CG-SHO	SV-BS	IP	H	R	HR	HB	BB-IB	SO	ERA	AERA	OAV	OOB	AB-HR-SH	AVG	PB	SUP	APR	DL	PW
1971	Chi N	2	0	1.000	3	3	2-1	0-0	21.1	8	5	2	0	10-0	22	2.11	187	.111	.220	7	.000	-1	98	4	0	0.3
1972	Chi N	11	14	.440	33	31	9-3	0-1	218.1	201	78	13	1	81-7	132	2.80	136	.246	.313	72-1-5	.125	-1	85	22	0	2.4
1973	Chi N	14	17	.452	42	34	9-2	0-1	239.2	248	107	12	4	73-7	134	3.68	107	.270	.325	70-0-5	.129	-0	95	8	0	0.8
1974	Chi N	7	11	.389	48	21	3-1	1-2	176.1	214	112	16	3	51-6	94	4.80	80	.299	.344	50-0-7	.060	-4	108	-18	0	-1.9
1975	Chi N	0	2	.000	3	3	0	0-0	11	18	12	2	0	4-0	5	8.18	47	.383	.431	3	.000	-0	76	-5	0	-0.8
	LA N	18	7	.720	31	30	12-4	0-0	223.2	172	76	16	0	64-2	148	2.82	122	.210	.265	70-1-13	.129	1	115	17	0	1.8
	Year	18	9	.667	34	33	12-4	0-0	234.2	190	88	18	0	68-2	153	3.07	112	.219	.274	73-1-13	.123	0	111	13	0	1.0
1976	LA N	11	15	.423	33	33	8-4	0-0	226.2	203	93	16	1	60-6	116	3.26	105	.241	.290	62-0-13	.097	-2	99	3	0	0.0
1977	†LA N	12	7	.632	32	31	6-2	1-0	223.1	184	74	14	3	60-5	153	2.62	147	.225	.279	67-0-14	.164	-0	107	30	0	2.4
1978	†LA N	19	10	.655	32	32	10-3	0-0	236	196	74	17	0	61-4	104	2.71	130	.226	.275	67-0-18	.149	1	94	25	0	3.1
1979	LA N	11	10	.524	29	29	12-1	0-0	212	191	85	11	2	63-4	129	2.97	122	.244	.298	75-0-8	.147	-1*	117	14	0	1.2
1980	LA N	14	8	.636	34	33	4-2	1-0	206.2	194	90	22	0	64-1	118	3.66	95	.249	.305	64-1-14	.063	-3	108	-3	0	-0.7
1981	†LA N★	11	6	.647	23	23	5-4	0-0	142.1	124	42	3	2	33-2	74	2.28	145	.237	.281	42-0-7	.190	2	104	15	0	2.1
1982	LA N	4	7	.364	21	21	2-2	0-0	120.2	130	57	5	2	33-2	51	4.03	86	.275	.325	35-1-6	.086	-1	98	-6	69	-0.6
1983	LA N	9	8	.529	33	27	2	0-0	160	156	86	21	2	59-4	87	4.22	86	.254	.319	50-0-4	.160	1	112	-9	0	-0.8
1984	LA N	3	6	.333	54	6	0	4-1	110	109	43	5	0	43-6	62	3.44	104	.263	.331	14-0-3	.071	-1	79	4	0	0.2
1985	Tex A	5	8	.385	29	20	2	0-0	124	149	78	18	0	40-2	62	5.23	82	.297	.346	0	ø	0	85	-12	0	-1.2
Total	15	151	136	.526	480	377	86-29	7-5	2652	2497	1112	193	20	799-58	1491	3.38	108	.250	.304	748-4-117	.123	-9	101	89	69	8.3

HOOVER, JOHN John Nicklaus; B11.22.1962 Fresno CA; BR/TR/6´2˝/195; [BalA84 1/25]; d5.23; Col Cal St.–Fresno

YEAR	TM LG	W	L	PCT	G	GS	CG-SHO	SV-BS	IP	H	R	HR	HB	BB-IB	SO	ERA	AERA	OAV	OOB	AB-HR-SH	AVG	PB	SUP	APR	DL	PW
1990	Tex A	0	0	ø	2	0	0	0-0	4.2	8	6	0	0	3-0	0	11.57	34	.364	.440	0	ø	0	—	-4	0	-0.2

HOOVER, DICK Richard Lloyd; B12.11.1925 Columbus OH; D4.12.1981 Lake Placid FL; BL/TL/6´0˝/170; d4.16

YEAR	TM LG	W	L	PCT	G	GS	CG-SHO	SV-BS	IP	H	R	HR	HB	BB-IB	SO	ERA	AERA	OAV	OOB	AB-HR-SH	AVG	PB	SUP	APR	DL	PW
1952	Bos N	0	0	ø	2	0	0	0	4.2	8	4	1	0	3	0	7.71	47	.348	.423	0	ø	0	—	-2	0	-0.1

HOPE, JOHN John Alan; B12.21.1970 Ft.Lauderdale FL; BR/TR/6´3˝/(195–206); [PitN89 2/59]; d8.29

YEAR	TM LG	W	L	PCT	G	GS	CG-SHO	SV-BS	IP	H	R	HR	HB	BB-IB	SO	ERA	AERA	OAV	OOB	AB-HR-SH	AVG	PB	SUP	APR	DL	PW
1993	Pit N	0	2	.000	7	7	0	0-0	38	47	19	2	2	8-3	8	4.03	102	.313	.354	13	.077	-1	116	0	0	-0.1
1994	Pit N	0	0	ø	9	0	0	0-0	14	18	12	1	2	4-0	6	5.79	76	.310	.375	3	.333	0	—	-3	0	-0.1
1995	Pit N	0	0	ø	3	0	0	0-0	2.1	8	8	0	3	4-0	2	30.86	14	.615	.714	0	ø	0	—	-6	0	-0.3
1996	Pit N	1	3	.250	5	4	0	0-0	19.1	17	18	5	2	11-1	13	6.98	63	.243	.357	5-0-1	.200	-0	82	-6	0	-0.9
Total	4	1	5	.167	24	11	0	0-0	73.2	90	57	8	9	27-4	29	5.99	71	.309	.382	21-0-1	.143	-1	103	-15	0	-1.4

HOPE, SAM Samuel Everett; B12.4.1878 Brooklyn NY; D6.30.1946 Greenport NY; BR/TR/5´10˝/?; d8.5

YEAR	TM LG	W	L	PCT	G	GS	CG-SHO	SV-BS	IP	H	R	HR	HB	BB-IB	SO	ERA	AERA	OAV	OOB	AB-HR-SH	AVG	PB	SUP	APR	DL	PW
1907	Phi A	0	0	ø	1	0	0	0	0.1	3	1	0	0	0	0	0.00	ø	.750	.750	0	ø	0	—	0	—	0.0

HOPKINS, PAUL Paul Henry; B9.25.1904 Chester CT; D1.2.2004 Middletown CT; BR/TR/6´0˝/175; d9.29; Col Colgate

YEAR	TM LG	W	L	PCT	G	GS	CG-SHO	SV-BS	IP	H	R	HR	HB	BB-IB	SO	ERA	AERA	OAV	OOB	AB-HR-SH	AVG	PB	SUP	APR	DL	PW
1927	Was A	1	0	1.000	2	1	0	0	9	13	6	1	0	4	5	5.00	81	.361	.425	3	.667	1	185	-1	—	0.0
1929	Was A	0	1	.000	7	0	0	0	16.1	15	5	1	0	9	5	2.20	192	.250	.348	3	.000	-1	—	4	—	0.1
	StL A	0	0	ø	2	0	0	0	2	0	0	0	0	2	1	0.00	ø	.000	.286	0	ø	0	—	1	—	0.0
	Year	0	1	.000	9	0	0	0	18.1	15	5	1	0	11	6	1.96	217	.231	.342	3	.000	-1	—	5	—	0.1
Total	2	1	1	.500	11	1	0	0	27.1	28	11	2	0	15	11	2.96	142	.277	.371	6	.333	1	185	4	—	0.1

HOPPER, LEFTY Clarence Franklin; B5.27.1875 Jersey City NJ; D9.27.1959 San Diego CA; TL/6´0˝/?; d10.10

YEAR	TM LG	W	L	PCT	G	GS	CG-SHO	SV-BS	IP	H	R	HR	HB	BB-IB	SO	ERA	AERA	OAV	OOB	AB-HR-SH	AVG	PB	SUP	APR	DL	PW
1898	Bro N	0	2	.000	2	2	2	0	11	14	11	0	0	5	5	4.91	73	.304	.373	4	.000	-1	59	-3	—	-0.4

HOPPER, JIM James McDaniel; B9.1.1919 Charlotte NC; D1.23.1982 Charlotte NC; BR/TR/6´1˝/175; d4.21

YEAR	TM LG	W	L	PCT	G	GS	CG-SHO	SV-BS	IP	H	R	HR	HB	BB-IB	SO	ERA	AERA	OAV	OOB	AB-HR-SH	AVG	PB	SUP	APR	DL	PW
1946	Pit N	0	1	.000	2	1	0	0	4	6	5	1	0	3	1	11.25	31	.316	.409	0	ø	0	49	-3	0	-0.5

YEAR	TM LG	W	L	PCT	G	GS	CG-SHO	SV-BS	IP	H	R	HR	HB	BB-IB	SO	ERA	AERA	OAV	OOB	AB-HR-SH	AVG	PB	SUP	APR	DL	PW
Hopper, Bill	William Booth "Bird Dog"; B8.26.1891 Jackson TN; D1.14.1965 Allen Park MI; BR/TR/6´0˝/175; d9.11; Col Union (TN)																									
1913	StL N	0	3	.000	3	3	2	0	24	20	14	2	3	8	3	3.75	86	.230	.316	8	.375	1	39	-2	—	-0.1
1914	StL N	0	0	ø	3	0	0	0	5	6	3	0	0	5	1	3.60	78	.286	.423	0	ø	0	—	0	—	0.0
1915	Was A	0	1	.000	13	0	0	1	31.1	39	23	0	1	16	8	4.60	65	.348	.434	5	.200	0	—	-6	—	-0.3
Total	3	0	4	.000	19	3	2	1	60.1	65	40	2	4	29	12	4.18	73	.295	.387	13	.308	1	39	-8	—	-0.4
Horan, John	Patrick J.; B1863 , Ireland; 5´10.5˝/160; d5.17																									
1884	CP U	3	6	.333	13	10	9	0	98	94	73	0	—	24	55	3.49	70	.236	.279	68	.088	-6*	91	-11	—	-1.4
Horgan, Joe	Joseph Paul; B6.7.1977 Sacramento CA; BL/TL/6´1˝/200; [CleA96 11/333]; d6.12; Col Sacramento (CA) City																									
2004	Mon N	4	1	.800	47	0	0	2-1	40	35	18	5	3	22-3	30	3.15	146	.230	.339	4	.250	0	—	5	0	0.6
2005	Was N	0	0	ø	8	0	0	0-0	6	19	15	0	1	4-0	5	21.00	20	.514	.558	0	ø	0	—	-12	0	-0.6
Total	2	4	1	.800	55	0	0	2-1	46	54	33	5	4	26-3	35	5.48	83	.286	.382	4	.250	0	—	-7	0	0.0
Horlen, Joe	Joel Edward; B8.14.1937 San Antonio TX; BR/TR/6´0˝/(170–175); d9.4; Col Oklahoma St.																									
1961	Chi A	1	3	.250	5	4	0	0	17.2	25	15	2	0	13-0	11	6.62	59	.338	.437	7-0-1	.000	-1	107	-6	0	-1.1
1962	Chi A	7	6	.538	20	19	5-1	0	108.2	108	62	10	2	43-2	63	4.89	80	.262	.333	38-0-4	.053	-3	120	-11	62	-1.3
1963	Chi A	11	7	.611	33	21	3	0	124	122	50	10	2	55-8	61	3.27	107	.261	.339	40-0-2	.225	1	121	4	0	0.7
1964	Chi A	13	9	.591	32	28	9-2	0	210.2	142	54	11	4	55-4	138	1.88	184	**.190**	**.248**	69-0-8	.159	-1	75	37	0	4.0
1965	Chi A	13	13	.500	34	34	7-4	0	219	203	88	16	3	39-9	125	2.88	111	.245	.279	68-0-8	.132	0	95	4	0	0.5
1966	Chi A	10	13	.435	37	29	4-2	1	211	185	64	14	6	53-11	124	2.43	130	.233	.285	60-0-4	.067	-4*	83	20	0	2.2
1967	Chi A☆	19	7	**.731**	35	35	13-**6**	0	258	188	66	13	4	58-4	103	**2.06**	**151**	.203	**.253**	83-0-8	.169	1*	107	**34**	0	**3.8**
1968	Chi A	12	14	.462	35	35	4-1	0	223.2	197	75	16	14	70-7	102	2.37	127	.238	.307	67-0-5	.104	-1*	72	14	0	1.6
1969	Chi A	13	16	.448	36	35	7-2	0-1	235.2	237	105	20	5	77-10	121	3.78	102	.261	.321	77-0-7	.182	-1	80	2	0	0.1
1970	Chi A	6	16	.273	28	26	4	0-0	172.1	198	99	18	4	41-4	77	4.86	80	.287	.330	52-0-5	.115	-2	71	-15	35	-1.7
1971	Chi A	8	9	.471	34	18	3	2-1	137.1	150	72	12	5	30-2	82	4.26	84	.284	.325	40-0-2	.100	-2*	117	-8	27	-1.2
1972	†Oak A	3	4	.429	32	6	0	1-0	84	74	33	3	4	20-4	58	3.00	95	.236	.291	17	.176	-0	88	-2	0	-0.2
Total	12	116	117	.498	361	290	59-18	4-2	2002	1829	783	145	53	554-65	1065	3.11	109	.243	.299	618-0-54	.134	-12	92	73	124	7.4
Horne, Trader	Berlyn Dale "Sonny"; B4.12.1899 Bachman OH; D2.3.1983 Franklin OH; BB/TR/5´9˝/155; d4.24																									
1929	Chi N	1	1	.500	11	1	0	0	23	24	20	3	0	21	6	5.09	91	.273	.413	5-0-1	.400	0	76	-3	—	-0.2
Horner, Jack	William Frank; B9.21.1863 Baltimore MD; D7.14.1910 New Orleans LA; BR; d5.7																									
1894	Bal N	0	1	.000	2	1	1	1	11	15	12	0	1	7	2	9.00	61	.319	.418	6	.167	-0	91	-3	—	-0.3
Horsey, Hanson	Hanson; B11.26.1889 Galena MD; D12.1.1949 Millington MD; BR/TR/5´11˝/165; d4.27																									
1912	Cin N	0	0	ø	1	0	0	0	4	14	10	0	0	3	0	22.50	15	.609	.654	2	.000	-0	—	-7	—	-0.3
Horsman, Vince	Vincent Stanley Joseph; B3.9.1967 Halifax NS, Can.; BR/TL/6´2˝/180; d9.5																									
1991	Tor A	0	0	ø	4	0	0	0-0	4	2	0	0	0	3-1	2	0.00	ø	.167	.333	0	ø	0	—	2	0	0.1
1992	Oak A	2	1	.667	58	0	0	1-1	43.1	39	13	3	0	21-4	18	2.49	151	.252	.339	0	ø	0	—	7	0	0.4
1993	Oak A	2	0	1.000	40	0	0	0-0	25	25	15	2	3	15-1	17	5.40	77	.255	.371	0	ø	0	—	-3	0	-0.2
1994	Oak A	0	1	.000	33	0	0	0-0	29.1	29	17	2	1	11-2	20	4.91	91	.266	.331	0	ø	0	—	-1	0	0.0
1995	Min A	0	0	ø	6	0	0	0-0	9	12	8	2	0	4-1	4	7.00	69	.333	.390	0	ø	0	—	-2	0	-0.1
Total	5	4	2	.667	141	0	0	1-1	110.2	107	53	9	4	54-9	61	4.07	102	.261	.349	0	ø	0	—	3	0	0.2
Horstmann, Oscar	Oscar Theodore; B6.2.1891 Alma MO; D5.11.1977 Salina KS; BR/TR/5´11˝/165; d4.18; Mil 1918																									
1917	StL N	9	4	.692	35	11	4-1	1	138.2	111	67	5	4	54	50	3.44	78	.225	.307	46-0-2	.196	1	132	-13	—	-1.2
1918	StL N	0	2	.000	9	2	0	0	23	29	18	0	0	14	6	5.48	49	.349	.443	4	.000	-0	70	-7	—	-0.6
1919	StL N	0	1	.000	6	2	0	0	15	14	6	0	0	12	5	3.00	93	.264	.400	2-0-1	.500	0	114	0	—	0.0
Total	3	9	7	.563	50	15	4-1	1	176.2	154	91	5	4	80	61	3.67	74	.245	.334	52-0-3	.192	1	121	-20	—	-1.8
Horton, Elmer	Elmer Edward "Herky Jerky"; B9.4.1869 Hamilton OH; D7.17.1918 Newark OH; d9.24																									
1896	Pit N	0	2	.000	2	2	2	0	15	22	18	0	1	9	3	9.60	44	.338	.427	7	.000	-1	68	-8	—	-0.8
1898	Bro N	0	1	.000	1	1	1	0	9	16	13	0	0	6	0	10.00	36	.381	.458	4	.250	-0	59	-6	—	-0.5
Total	2	0	3	.000	3	3	3	0	24	38	31	0	1	15	3	9.75	41	.355	.439	11	.091	-1	66	-14	—	-1.3
Horton, Ricky	Ricky Neal; B7.30.1959 Poughkeepsie NY; BL/TL/6´2˝/195; [StLN80 4/93]; d4.7; Col Virginia																									
1984	StL N	9	4	.692	37	18	1-1	1-1	125.2	140	53	14	1	39-2	76	3.44	102	.285	.337	31-0-6	.065	-2*	125	1	0	0.1
1985	†StL N	3	2	.600	49	3	0	1-1	89.2	84	30	5	3	34-13	59	2.91	123	.251	.324	16-0-2	.063	-0	107	8	0	0.5
1986	StL N	4	3	.571	42	9	1	3-0	100.1	77	25	7	1	26-7	49	2.24	165	.218	.271	18-0-2	.056	0	67	18	30	1.4
1987	†StL N	8	3	.727	67	6	0	7-1	125	127	58	15	0	42-10	55	3.82	110	.263	.321	29	.172	0*	90	5	0	0.6
1988	Chi A	6	10	.375	52	9	1	2-1	109.1	120	64	6	5	36-4	28	4.86	82	.291	.349	0	ø	0	99	-9	0	-1.1
	†LA N	1	1	.500	12	0	0	0-2	9	11	7	2	0	2-0	8	5.00	67	.306	.333	0	ø	0	—	-2	0	-0.5
1989	LA N	0	0	ø	23	0	0	0-1	26.2	35	15	1	1	11-2	12	5.06	68	.343	.405	1	.000	-0	—	-4	0	-0.2
	StL N	0	3	.000	11	8	0	0-0	45.2	50	24	2	3	10-2	14	4.73	77	.282	.328	11-0-2	.273	1	60	-4	0	-0.1
	Year	0	3	.000	34	8	0	0-1	72.1	85	39	3	4	21-4	26	4.85	74	.305	.357	12-0-2	.250	1	62	-8	0	-0.3
1990	StL N	1	1	.500	32	0	0	1-1	42	52	25	3	1	22-7	18	4.93	78	.315	.397	4-0-1	.000	-0	—	-5	0	-0.2
Total	7	32	27	.542	325	53	3-1	15-8	673.1	696	301	55	15	222-47	319	3.76	101	.273	.331	110-0-13	.109	-1	94	8	30	0.5
Hoskins, Dave	David Taylor; B8.3.1925 Greenwood MS; D4.2.1970 Flint MI; BL/TR/6´1˝/180; d4.18; Negro Lg 1942–49																									
1953	Cle A	9	3	.750	26	7	3	1	112.2	102	57	9	4	38	55	3.99	94	.243	.312	58-1-1	.259	4*	162	-4	0	0.1
1954	Cle A	0	1	.000	14	1	0	0	26.2	29	10	3	0	10	9	3.04	121	.284	.342	8	.000	-1*	312	2	0	0.0
Total	2	9	4	.692	40	8	3	1	139.1	131	67	12	4	48	64	3.81	98	.251	.318	66-1-1	.227	3	181	-2	0	0.1
Host, Gene	Eugene Earl "Twinkles","Slick"; B1.1.1933 Leeper PA; D8.20.1998 Nashville TN; BB/TL/5´11˝/(190–195); d9.16																									
1956	Det A	0	0	ø	1	1	0	0	4.2	9	4	2	0	2-0	5	7.71	53	.409	.458	2	.000	-0	173	-2	0	-0.1
1957	KC A	0	2	.000	11	2	0	0	23.2	29	19	5	0	14-0	9	7.23	55	.315	.398	5	.000	-1	90	-7	0	-0.6
Total	2	0	2	.000	12	3	0	0	28.1	38	23	7	0	16-0	14	7.31	55	.333	.409	7	.000	-1	119	-9	0	-0.7
Houck, Byron	Byron Simon "Duke"; B8.28.1891 Prosper MN; D6.17.1969 Santa Cruz CA; BR/TR/6´0˝/175; d5.15; Col Oregon																									
1912	Phi A	8	8	.500	30	17	10	1	180.2	148	79	1	12	74	75	2.94	105	.234	.326	62-0-4	.065	-7	144	3	—	-0.5
1913	Phi A	14	6	.700	41	19	4-1	0	176	147	93	3	6	122	71	4.14	67	.237	.368	60-0-5	.083	-4	127	-26	—	-3.1
1914	Phi A	0	0	ø	3	3	0	0	11	14	9	0	0	6	4	3.27	80	.318	.400	3	.333	0	195	-3	—	-0.1
	Bro F	2	6	.250	17	9	3	0	92	95	48	4	2	43	45	3.13	92	.272	.355	30-1-1	.233	2	95	-5	—	-0.3
1918	StL A	2	4	.333	27	2	0	2	71.2	58	24	0	0	29	29	2.39	115	.225	.303	20	.150	-1	96	**3**	—	0.2
Total	4	26	24	.520	118	50	17-1	3	531.1	462	253	8	20	274	224	3.30	87	.243	.344	175-1-10	.114	-9	130	-28	—	-3.8
Hough, Charlie	Charles Oliver; B1.5.1948 Honolulu HI; BR/TR/6´2˝/(190–195); [LAN66 8/159]; d8.12; C4																									
1970	LA N	0	0	ø	8	0	0	2-0	17	18	11	7	0	11-0	8	5.29	73	.265	.367	3	.333	0	—	-3	0	-0.1
1971	LA N	0	0	ø	4	0	0	0-0	4.1	3	3	1	0	3-0	4	4.15	78	.200	.333	0	ø	0	—	-1	0	0.0
1972	LA N	0	0	ø	2	0	0	0-0	2.2	2	1	0	1	2-0	4	3.38	99	.200	.385	0	ø	0	—	0	0	0.0
1973	LA N	4	2	.667	37	0	0	5-2	71.2	52	24	3	6	45-2	70	2.76	126	.207	.338	14-0-1	.214	0	—	7	0	0.6
1974	†LA N	9	4	.692	49	0	0	1-2	96	65	45	12	4	40-2	63	3.75	91	.196	.285	12-0-3	.000	-1	—	-3	0	-0.5
1975	LA N	3	7	.300	38	0	0	4-2	61	43	25	3	8	34-0	34	2.95	116	.195	.323	6-0-1	.333	1	—	2	0	0.4
1976	LA N	12	8	.600	77	0	0	18-4	142.2	102	43	6	8	77-3	81	2.21	154	.200	.314	21	.286	2	—	**17**	0	**3.1**
1977	†LA N	6	12	.333	70	1	0	22-5	127.1	98	53	10	7	70-6	105	3.32	116	.213	.323	22-1-0	.182	1	46	7	0	1.2
1978	†LA N	5	5	.500	55	0	0	7-4	93.1	69	38	6	5	48-4	66	3.28	107	.205	.313	12	.333	1	—	3	0	0.5
1979	LA N	7	5	.583	42	14	0	0-1	151.1	152	88	16	8	66-2	76	4.76	76	.264	.346	38-0-5	.158	-0	145	-18	0	-1.3
1980	LA N	1	3	.250	19	1	0	1-0	32.1	37	21	4	2	21-0	25	5.57	62	.291	.392	2	.500	0	103	-7	0	-0.9
	Tex A	2	2	.500	16	2	2-1	0-0	61.1	54	30	2	3	37-2	47	3.96	98	.240	.353	0	ø	0	127	0	0	0.0
1981	Tex A	4	1	.800	21	5	2	1-1	82	61	30	4	3	31-1	69	2.96	117	.207	.289	0	ø	0	124	5	0	0.2
1982	Tex A	16	13	.552	34	34	12-2	0-0	228	217	111	21	7	72-5	128	3.95	98	.251	.313	0	ø	0	101	-2	0	-0.2
1983	Tex A	15	13	.536	34	33	11-3	0-0	252	219	96	22	3	95-0	152	3.18	127	.238	.309	0	ø	0	92	27	0	3.0
1984	Tex A	16	14	.533	36	**36**	**17**-1	0-0	266	260	127	26	9	94-3	164	3.76	111	.255	.322	0	ø	0	94	12	0	1.4
1985	Tex A	14	16	.467	34	34	14-1	0-0	250.1	198	102	23	7	83-1	141	3.31	129	.215	.283	0	ø	0	77	25	0	2.9

YEAR	TM LG	W	L	PCT	G	GS	CG-SHO	SV-BS	IP	H	R	HR	HB	BB-IB	SO	ERA	AERA	OAV	OOB	AB-HR-SH	AVG	PB	SUP	APR	DL	PW
1986	Tex A★	17	10	.630	33	33	7-2	0-0	230.1	188	115	32	9	89-2	146	3.79	114	.221	.301	0	ø	0	105	11	29	1.1
1987	Tex A	18	13	.581	40	**40**	13	0-0	**285.1**	238	159	36	19	124-1	223	3.79	119	.223	.311	0	ø	0	106	13	0	1.4
1988	Tex A	15	16	.484	34	34	10	0-0	252	202	111	20	12	126-1	174	3.32	124	.221	.321	0	ø	0	80	19	0	2.3
1989	Tex A	10	13	.435	30	30	5-1	0-0	182	168	97	28	6	95-2	94	4.35	92	.245	.340	0	ø	0	90	-6	15	-0.7
1990	Tex A	12	12	.500	32	32	5	0-0	218.2	190	108	24	11	119-2	114	4.07	97	.235	.338	0	ø	0	102	-2	0	-0.2
1991	Chi A	9	10	.474	31	29	4-1	0-0	199.1	167	98	21	11	94-0	107	4.02	99	.229	.320	0	ø	0	96	-1	7	-0.1
1992	Chi A	7	12	.368	27	27	4	0-0	176.1	160	88	19	7	66-2	76	3.93	99	.239	.311	0	ø	0	87	-2	0	-0.3
1993	Fla N	9	16	.360	34	34	0	0-0	204.1	202	109	20	8	71-2	126	4.27	102	.259	.325	63-0-4	.032	-5	62	1	0	-0.4
1994	Fla N	5	9	.357	21	21	1-1	0-0	113.2	118	74	17	10	52-1	65	5.15	86	.274	.359	33-0-4	.121	-1	77	-8	16	-1.0
Total	25	216	216	.500	858	440	107-13	61-21	3801.1	3283	1807	383	174	1665-44	2362	3.75	107	.233	.319	226-1-18	.146	-2	95	96	67	12.4
Houlton, D.J.	Dennis Sean; B8.12.1979 Fullerton CA; BR/TR/6´4˝/220; [HouN01 11/326]; d4.9; Col Pacific (CA)																									
2005	LA N	6	9	.400	35	19	0	0-0	129	145	79	21	8	52-3	90	5.16	80	.289	.362	30-0-2	.100	-0	67	-14	0	-1.5
House, Craig	Craig Michael; B7.8.1977 Naha A.F.B., Okinawa; BR/TR/6´2˝/210; [ColN99 12/370]; d8.6; Col Memphis																									
2000	Col N	1	1	.500	16	0	0	0-0	13.2	13	11	3	2	17-0	8	7.24	80	.265	.464	0	ø	0	—	-1	0	-0.2
House, Pat	Patrick Lory; B9.1.1940 Boise ID; BL/TL/6´3˝/185; d9.6; Col Wyoming																									
1967	Hou N	1	0	1.000	6	0	0	1	4	3	2	0	1	0-0	2	4.50	74	.214	.267	0	ø	0	—	0	0	-0.1
1968	Hou N	1	1	.500	18	0	0	0	16.1	21	15	0	2	6-3	6	7.71	38	.323	.392	0	ø	0	—	-8	21	-1.0
Total	2	2	1	.667	24	0	0	1	20.1	24	17	0	3	6-3	8	7.08	43	.304	.371	0	ø	0	—	-8	21	-1.1
House, Tom	Thomas Ross; B4.29.1947 Seattle WA; BL/TL/5´11˝/(175–190); [AtlN67 S3/48]; d6.23; C8; Col USC																									
1971	Atl N	1	0	1.000	11	1	0	0-0	20.2	20	8	2	1	3-0	11	3.05	122	.263	.296	5	.400	1	143	1	0	0.1
1972	Atl N	0	0	ø	8	0	0	2-0	9.1	7	3	1	1	6-0	7	2.89	131	.226	.368	1	.000	-0	—	1	0	0.0
1973	Atl N	4	2	.667	52	0	0	4-2	67.1	58	37	13	2	31-7	42	4.68	85	.243	.326	10-0-2	.200	0	—	-4	0	-0.4
1974	Atl N	6	2	.750	56	0	0	11-5	102.2	74	26	5	3	27-8	64	1.93	197	.203	.261	10-0-3	.400	1	—	20	0	2.2
1975	Atl N	7	7	.500	58	0	0	11-4	79.1	79	39	2	2	36-10	36	3.18	119	.262	.342	9	.111	-0	—	3	0	0.6
1976	Bos A	1	3	.250	36	0	0	4-2	43.2	39	22	4	2	19-4	27	4.33	90	.241	.324	0	ø	0	—	-1	20	-0.1
1977	Bos A	1	0	1.000	8	0	0	0-0	7.2	15	11	0	0	6-0	6	12.91	35	.405	.488	0	ø	0	—	-6	0	-0.7
	Sea A	4	5	.444	26	11	1	1-0	89.1	94	42	12	4	19-2	39	3.93	106	.268	.310	0	ø	0	63	3	23	0.2
	Year	5	5	.500	34	11	1	1-0	97	109	53	12	4	25-2	45	4.64	90	.281	.329	0	ø	0	63	-3	0	-0.5
1978	Sea A	5	4	.556	34	9	3	0-0	116	130	70	10	5	35-2	29	4.66	83	.289	.339	0	ø	0	127	-11	0	-0.8
Total	8	29	23	.558	289	21	4	33-13	536	516	258	49	20	182-33	261	3.79	103	.256	.320	35-0-5	.257	1	94	6	43	1.1
House, Fred	Willard Edwin; B10.3.1890 Cabool MO; D11.16.1923 Kansas City MO; BR/TR/6´3˝/190; d4.22																									
1913	Det A	1	2	.333	19	2	0	0	53.2	64	40	1	2	17	16	5.20	56	.328	.388	10	.000	-1	127	-12	—	-0.7
Houseman, Frank	Frank; B , Netherlands; d9.2																									
1886	Bal AA	0	1	.000	1	1	1	0	8	6	3	0	1	1	5	3.38	101	.182	.229	4	.250	-0	35	1	—	0.1
Houser, Joe	Joseph William; B7.3.1891 Steubenville OH; D1.3.1953 Orlando FL; BL/TL/5´9.5˝/160; d4.24																									
1914	Buf F	0	1	.000	7	2	0	0	23	21	16	1	0	20	6	5.48	54	.250	.394	7	.143	-0*	127	-6	—	-0.3
Houtteman, Art	Arthur Joseph; B8.7.1927 Detroit MI; D5.6.2003 Rochester Hills MI; BR/TR/6´2˝/(188–191); d4.29; Mil 1951																									
1945	Det A	0	2	.000	13	0	0	0	25.1	27	17	1	1	11	9	5.33	66	.270	.348	5	.000	-1	—	-4	0	-0.4
1946	Det A	0	1	.000	1	1	0	0	8	15	8	1	0	0	2	9.00	41	.385	.385	2-0-1	.500	0	164	-4	0	-0.4
1947	Det A	7	2	.778	23	9	7-2	0	110.2	106	51	6	1	36	58	3.42	110	.247	.306	40	.300	2	123	3	0	0.4
1948	Det A	2	16	.111	43	20	4	10	164.1	186	101	11	2	52	74	4.66	94	.287	.342	56-0-1	.196	-2	69	-7	0	-0.8
1949	Det A	15	10	.600	34	25	13-2	0	203.2	227	101	19	5	59	85	3.71	112	.282	.335	78-0-2	.244	1*	108	7	0	1.1
1950	Det A★	19	12	.613	41	34	21-**4**	4	274.2	257	112	29	8	99	88	3.54	132	.251	.322	93-0-11	.151	-3	100	38	0	3.7
1952	Det A	8	20	.286	35	28	10-2	1	221	218	116	19	5	65	109	4.36	87	.253	.309	69-0-6	.101	-4*	71	-11	0	-1.7
1953	Det A	2	6	.250	16	9	3-1	1	68.2	87	50	11	4	29	28	5.90	69	.309	.381	19-1-2	.158	0	80	-14	0	-1.4
	Cle A	7	7	.500	22	13	6-1	3	109	113	56	4	5	25	40	3.80	99	.269	.318	34-0-2	.147	-1*	133	-3	0	-0.4
	Year	9	13	.409	38	22	9-2	4	177.2	200	106	15	9	54	68	4.61	84	.285	.344	53-1-4	.151	-1	111	-18	0	-1.8
1954	†Cle A	15	7	.682	32	25	11-1	0	188	198	80	14	3	59	68	3.35	110	.273	.328	65-1-8	.277	5	131	7	0	1.3
1955	Cle A	10	6	.625	35	12	3-1	0	124.1	126	63	15	2	44-1	53	3.98	100	.265	.328	38-0-4	.158	-1	89	0	0	0.1
1956	Cle A	2	2	.500	22	4	0	1	46.2	60	39	5	4	31-2	19	6.56	64	.317	.417	12-0-1	.167	-1*	95	-12	0	-1.0
1957	Cle A	0	0	ø	3	0	0	0	4	6	3	1	0	3-0	3	6.75	55	.353	.450	0	ø	0	—	-1	0	-0.1
	Bal A	0	0	ø	5	1	0	0	6.2	20	13	0	0	3-0	3	17.55	20	.513	.548	2	.500	0	149	-10	0	-0.5
	Year	0	0	ø	8	1	0	0	10.2	26	16	1	0	6-0	6	13.50	27	.464	.516	2	.500	0	147	-12	0	-0.6
Total	12	87	91	.489	325	181	78-14	20	1555	1646	810	136	40	516-3	639	4.14	99	.272	.333	513-2-38	.193	-4	99	-11	0	-0.1
Hovlik, Ed	Edward Charles; B8.20.1891 Cleveland OH; D3.19.1955 Painesville OH; BR/TR/6´0˝/180; d7.14																									
1918	Was A	2	1	.667	8	2	1	0	28	25	10	0	0	10	10	1.29	212	.272	.343	8	.125	-1	207	3	—	0.2
1919	Was A	0	0	ø	3	0	0	0	5.2	12	10	0	0	9	3	12.71	25	.480	.618	2	.000	-0	—	-6	—	-0.3
Total	2	2	1	.667	11	2	1	0	33.2	37	20	0	0	19	13	3.21	88	.316	.412	10	.100	-1	207	-3	—	-0.1
Hovlik, Joe	Joseph (b Joseph Havlik); B8.16.1884 , Czechoslovakia; D11.3.1951 Oxford Junction IA; BR/TR/5´10.5˝/194; d7.10																									
1909	Was A	0	0	ø	3	0	0	0	6	13	10	0	1	3	1	4.50	54	.419	.486	2	.000	0	—	-3	—	-0.1
1910	Was A	0	0	ø	1	0	0	0	1.2	6	5	0	1	0	0	16.20	15	.500	.538	0	ø	0	—	-3	—	-0.1
1911	Chi A	2	0	1.000	12	3	1-1	0	47	47	21	1	0	20	24	3.06	105	.257	.330	13	.077	-0	104	1	—	0.1
Total	3	2	0	1.000	16	3	1-1	0	54.2	66	36	1	2	23	25	3.62	86	.292	.363	15	.067	-0	104	-5	—	-0.1
Howard, Ben	Benjamin Richard; B1.15.1979 Danville IL; BR/TR/6´2˝/(190–220); [SDN97 2/78]; d4.28																									
2002	SD N	0	1	.000	3	2	0	0-0	10.2	13	11	4	0	14-1	10	9.28	42	.302	.466	4-0-1	.000	-0	72	-6	0	-0.5
2003	SD N	1	3	.250	6	6	0	0-0	34.2	31	17	10	0	15-1	24	3.63	110	.235	.313	11	.091	-1	86	1	0	0.0
2004	Fla N	1	1	.500	31	0	0	0-0	37.2	37	23	6	1	21-3	33	5.50	75	.261	.355	3	.000	-0	—	-5	0	-0.3
Total	3	2	5	.286	40	8	0	0-0	83	81	51	20	1	50-5	67	5.20	78	.256	.356	18-0-1	.056	-1	81	-10	0	-0.8
Howard, Bruce	Bruce Ernest; B3.23.1943 Salisbury MD; BB/TR/6´2˝/(172–185); d9.4; s–David; Col Villanova																									
1963	Chi A	2	1	.667	7	0	0	1	17	12	7	0	0	14-0	9	2.65	132	.207	.361	4	.250	0	—	1	0	0.2
1964	Chi A	2	1	.667	3	3	1-1	0	22.1	10	2	0	1	8-1	17	0.81	429	.139	.235	8	.000	-1	69	7	0	0.9
1965	Chi A	9	8	.529	30	22	1-1	0	148	123	61	13	1	72-5	120	3.47	92	.224	.315	41-0-6	.146	2	106	-3	0	-0.2
1966	Chi A	9	5	.643	27	21	4-2	0	149	110	48	14	1	44-2	85	2.30	138	.202	.262	43-0-2	.070	-1	95	14	0	1.2
1967	Chi A	3	10	.231	30	17	1	0	112.2	102	55	9	3	52-1	76	3.43	90	.240	.325	28-0-3	.179	1	68	-6	0	-0.5
1968	Bal A	0	2	.000	10	5	0	0	31	30	16	2	2	26-2	19	3.77	78	.268	.406	7-1-2	.286	2	71	-3	0	0.0
	Was A	1	4	.200	13	7	0	0	48.2	62	30	7	0	23-2	23	5.36	54	.330	.401	16	.000	-2	68	-12	22	-1.3
	Year	1	6	.143	23	12	0	0	79.2	92	46	9	2	49-4	42	4.74	62	.307	.403	23-1-2	.087	0	70	-15	0	-1.3
Total	6	26	31	.456	120	75	7-4	1	528.2	449	219	45	8	239-13	349	3.18	99	.231	.316	147-1-13	.116	2	87	-2	22	0.3
Howard, Chris	Christian; B11.18.1965 Lynn MA; BR/TL/6´0˝/185; d9.21; Col Miami; [DL 1996 Tex A 182]																									
1993	Chi A	1	0	1.000	3	0	0	0-0	2.1	2	0	0	0	3-1	1	0.00	ø	.286	.500	0	ø	0	—	1	0	0.2
1994	Bos A	1	0	1.000	37	0	0	1-1	39.2	35	17	5	0	12-4	22	3.63	139	.233	.287	0	ø	0	—	6	0	0.3
1995	Tex A	0	0	ø	4	0	0	0-0	4	3	0	0	0	1-0	2	0.00	ø	.231	.267	0	ø	0	—	2	0	0.1
Total	3	2	0	1.000	44	0	0	1-1	46	40	17	5	0	16-5	25	3.13	159	.235	.296	0	ø	0	—	9	182	0.6
Howard, Earl	Earl Nycum; B6.25.1893 Everett PA; D4.4.1937 Everett PA; BR/TR/6´1˝/160; d4.18																									
1918	StL N	0	0	ø	1	0	0	0	2	0	0	0	0	2	0	0.00	ø	.000	.286	0	ø	0	—	1	—	0.1
Howard, Fred	Fred Irving; B9.2.1956 Portland ME; BR/TR/6´3˝/190; [ChiA76*6/110]; d5.26; Col Maine																									
1979	Chi A	1	5	.167	28	6	0	0-0	68	73	34	5	1	32-2	36	3.57	119	.283	.357	0	ø	0	92	4	0	0.3
Howard, Lee	Lee Vincent; B11.11.1923 Staten Island NY; BL/TL/6´2˝/175; d9.22																									
1946	Pit N	0	1	.000	3	2	1	0	13.1	14	3	0	0	9	6	2.03	174	.286	.397	5	.000	-1	24	2	0	0.1
1947	Pit N	0	0	ø	2	0	0	0	2.2	4	1	1	0	0	2	3.38	125	.333	.333	0	ø	0	—	0	0	0.0
Total	2	0	1	.000	5	2	1	0	16	18	4	1	0	9	8	2.25	162	.295	.386	5	.000	-1	24	2	0	0.1

YEAR	TM LG	W	L	PCT	G	GS	CG-SHO	SV-BS	IP	H	R	HR	HB	BB-IB	SO	ERA	AERA	OAV	OOB	AB-HR-SH	AVG	PB	SUP	APR	DL	PW
HOWE, CAL	Calvin Earl; B11.27.1924 Rock Falls IL; BL/TL/6´3˝/230; d9.26																									
1952	Chi N	0	0	ø	1	0	0	0	2	0	0	0	0	1	2	0.00	ø	.000	.143	0	ø	0	—	1	0	0.0
HOWE, LES	Lester Curtis "Lucky"; B8.24.1895 Brooklyn NY; D7.16.1976 Woodmere NY; BR/TR/5´11.5˝/170; d8.18																									
1923	Bos A	1	0	1.000	12	2	0	0	30	23	10	0	1	7	7	2.40	171	.211	.265	6	.000	-1	111	6	—	0.2
1924	Bos A	1	0	1.000	4	0	0	0	7.1	11	6	1	1	2	3	7.36	59	.423	.483	2	.500	0	—	-2	—	-0.2
Total	2	2	0	1.000	16	2	0	0	37.1	34	16	1	2	9	10	3.38	123	.252	.308	8	.125	-1	111	4	—	0.0
HOWE, STEVE	Steven Roy; B3.10.1958 Pontiac MI; D4.28.2006 Coachella CA; BL/TL/6´1˝/(180–198); [LAN79 1/16]; d4.11; Col Michigan																									
1980	LA N	7	9	.438	59	0	0	17-9	84.2	83	33	1	2	22-10	39	2.66	131	.256	.305	11	.091	-1	—	5	0	1.2
1981	†LA N	5	3	.625	41	0	0	8-2	54	51	17	2	0	18-7	32	2.50	132	.254	.309	1	.000	0	—	5	0	0.8
1982	LA N★	7	5	.583	66	0	0	13-9	99.1	87	27	3	0	17-11	49	2.08	167	.240	.272	7-0-1	.000	-1	—	15	0	2.1
1983	LA N	4	7	.364	46	0	0	18-5	68.2	55	15	2	1	12-7	52	1.44	250	.217	.253	8	.125	0	—	16	32	3.4
1985	LA N	1	1	.500	19	0	0	3-0	22	30	17	2	1	5-2	11	4.91	71	.319	.353	0	ø	0	—	-5	0	-0.5
	Min A	2	3	.400	13	0	0	0-3	19	28	16	1	0	7-2	10	6.16	72	.333	.372	0	ø	0	—	-4	0	-0.8
1987	Tex A	3	3	.500	24	0	0	1-2	31.1	33	15	2	3	8-1	19	4.31	105	.280	.341	0	ø	0	—	2	0	0.3
1991	NY A	3	1	.750	37	0	0	3-0	48.1	39	12	1	3	7-2	34	1.68	249	.222	.262	0	ø	0	—	12	22	1.1
1992	NY A	3	0	1.000	20	0	0	6-1	22	9	7	1	0	3-1	12	2.45	161	.122	.154	0	ø	0	—	3	0	0.6
1993	NY A	3	5	.375	51	0	0	4-3	50.2	58	31	7	3	10-4	19	4.97	84	.297	.338	0	ø	0	—	-5	29	-0.7
1994	NY A	3	0	1.000	40	0	0	15-4	40	28	8	2	0	7-1	18	1.80	256	.194	.232	0	ø	0	—	13	18	1.8
1995	†NY A	6	3	.667	56	0	0	2-1	49	66	29	7	4	17-3	28	4.96	93	.324	.383	0	ø	0	—	-2	0	-0.3
1996	NY A	0	1	.000	25	0	0	1-1	17	19	12	1	1	6-3	5	6.35	78	.284	.351	0	ø	0	—	-2	0	-0.1
Total	12	47	41	.534	497	0	0	91-40	606	586	239	32	18	139-54	328	3.03	129	.255	.300	27-0-1	.074	-1	—	53	101	8.9
HOWELL, HARRY	Harry Taylor; B11.14.1876 NJ; D5.22.1956 Spokane WA; BR/TR/5´9˝/?; d10.10; U1																									
1898	Bro N	2	0	1.000	2	2	2	0	18	15	11	0	1	11	2	5.00	72	.224	.342	8-0-1	.250	0	188	-2	—	-0.1
1899	Bal N	13	8	.619	28	25	21	1	209.1	248	126	1	10	69	58	3.91	101	.294	.355	82-0-3	.146	-3	103	3	—	-0.1
1900	†Bro N	6	5	.545	21	10	7-2	0	110.1	131	69	4	3	36	26	3.75	102	.294	.351	42-1-0	.286	4*	88	-1	—	0.3
1901	Bal A	14	21	.400	37	34	32-1	0	294.2	333	188	5	7	79	93	3.67	106	.281	.330	188-2-4	.218	1*	94	6	—	0.6
1902	Bal A	9	15	.375	26	23	19-1	0	199	243	136	5	7	48	33	4.12	92	.301	.346	347-2-8	.268	5*	93	-8	—	-0.1
1903	NY A	9	6	.600	25	15	13	0	155.2	140	79	4	6	44	62	3.53	89	.240	.300	106-1-3	.217	2*	119	-5	—	-0.1
1904	StL A	13	21	.382	34	33	32-2	0	299.2	254	99	1	13	60	122	2.19	113	.230	.278	113-1-4	.221	5*	81	10	—	2.4
1905	StL A	15	22	.405	38	37	**35**-4	0	323	252	109	2	12	101	198	1.98	129	.217	.286	135-1-1	.193	3*	91	19	—	3.6
1906	StL A	15	14	.517	35	33	30-6	1	276.2	233	98	1	10	61	140	2.11	122	.231	.282	103-0-3	.126	-3	113	14	—	1.6
1907	StL A	16	15	.516	42	35	26-2	3	316.1	258	112	3	8	88	118	1.93	130	.225	.285	114-2-9	.237	6*	94	14	—	2.6
1908	StL A	18	18	.500	41	32	27-2	1	324.1	279	103	1	17	70	117	1.89	127	.240	.293	120-1-1	.183	1	94	16	—	2.2
1909	StL A	1	1	.500	10	3	0	0	37.1	42	21	0	3	8	16	3.13	77	.294	.344	34-0-3	.176	0*	136	-5	—	-0.2
1910	StL A	0	0	ø	1	0	0	0	3.1	7	7	0	0	2	1	10.80	23	.467	.529	2	.000	-0	—	-3	—	-0.2
Total	13	131	146	.473	340	282	244-20	6	2567.2	2435	1158	27	97	677	986	2.74	108	.252	.307	1394-11-40	.217	21	98	58	—	12.5
HOWELL, J.P.	James Phillip; B4.25.1983 Modesto CA; BL/TL/6´0˝/175; [KCA04 1/31]; d6.11; Col Texas																									
2005	KC A	3	5	.375	15	15	0	0-0	72.2	73	55	9	6	39-0	54	6.19	71	.264	.363	3	.000	-0	106	-15	0	-1.4
2006	TB A	1	3	.250	8	8	0	0-0	42.1	52	25	4	3	14-0	33	5.10	91	.310	.369	0	ø	-0	101	-1	0	-0.1
Total	2	4	8	.333	23	23	0	0-0	115	125	80	13	9	53-0	87	5.79	77	.281	.365	3	.000	-0	104	-16	0	-1.5
HOWELL, JAY	Jay Canfield; B11.26.1955 Miami FL; BR/TR/6´3˝/(200–220); [CinN76 31/668]; d8.10; Col Colorado																									
1980	Cin N	0	0	ø	5	0	0	0-0	3.1	8	5	0	1	0-0	1	13.50	26	.471	.474	0	ø	0	—	-4	0	-0.2
1981	Chi N	2	0	1.000	10	2	0	0-0	22.1	23	13	3	2	10-2	10	4.84	77	.277	.365	2-0-2	.000	0	166	-2	0	-0.1
1982	NY A	2	3	.400	6	6	0	0-0	28	42	25	1	0	13-0	21	7.71	52	.341	.399	0	ø	0	147	-11	0	-1.5
1983	NY A	1	5	.167	19	12	2	0-0	82	89	53	7	3	35-0	61	5.38	73	.275	.346	0	ø	0	98	-13	30	-0.8
1984	NY A	9	4	.692	61	1	0	7-2	103.2	86	33	5	0	34-3	109	2.69	142	.223	.284	0	ø	0	189	14	0	1.9
1985	Oak A☆	9	8	.529	63	0	0	29-7	98	98	32	5	1	31-3	68	2.85	136	.261	.316	0	ø	0	—	13	0	2.6
1986	Oak A	3	6	.333	38	0	0	16-4	53.1	53	23	3	1	23-4	42	3.38	115	.262	.339	0	ø	0	—	3	18	0.6
1987	Oak A★	3	4	.429	36	0	0	16-8	44.1	48	30	6	1	21-1	35	5.89	71	.277	.355	0	ø	0	—	-8	41	-1.5
1988	†LA N	5	3	.625	50	0	0	21-6	65	44	16	1	1	21-2	70	2.08	161	.188	.255	2	.000	-0	—	10	16	1.8
1989	LA N★	5	3	.625	56	0	0	28-4	79.2	60	15	3	0	22-6	55	1.58	217	.211	.266	3	.000	-0	—	17	0	2.8
1990	LA N	5	5	.500	45	0	0	16-8	66	59	17	5	6	20-3	59	2.18	169	.242	.315	2	.000	-0	—	12	24	2.3
1991	LA N	6	5	.545	44	0	0	16-2	51	39	19	3	1	11-3	40	3.18	114	.213	.259	0	ø	0	—	3	33	0.7
1992	LA N	1	3	.250	41	0	0	4-2	46.2	41	9	2	1	18-5	36	1.54	225	.230	.303	0	ø	0	—	10	42	1.1
1993	Atl N	3	3	.500	54	0	0	0-3	58.1	48	16	3	0	16-4	37	2.31	175	.229	.278	0	ø	0	—	11	0	1.1
1994	Tex A	4	1	.800	40	0	0	2-3	43	44	29	10	1	16-2	22	5.44	89	.262	.324	0	ø	0	—	-3	0	-0.3
Total	15	58	53	.523	568	21	2	155-49	844.2	782	335	57	19	291-38	666	3.34	115	.246	.310	9-0-2	.000	-1	126	52	204	10.5
HOWELL, KEN	Kenneth; B11.28.1960 Detroit MI; BR/TR/6´3˝/(200–230); [LAN82 3/73]; d6.25; Col Tuskegee; [DL 1991 Phi N 182, 1992 Phi N 182]																									
1984	LA N	5	5	.500	32	1	0	6-4	51.1	51	21	1	1	9-4	54	3.33	107	.267	.298	5-0-1	.000	-1	0	2	0	0.3
1985	†LA N	4	7	.364	56	0	0	12-3	86	66	41	8	0	35-3	85	3.77	93	.208	.287	4	.000	-0	—	-2	0	-0.3
1986	LA N	6	12	.333	62	0	0	12-9	97.2	86	48	7	3	63-9	104	3.87	90	.239	.354	5	.000	-1	—	-5	0	-1.1
1987	LA N	3	4	.429	40	2	0	1-5	55	54	32	7	0	29-2	60	4.91	81	.265	.356	4	.250	0	136	-5	0	-0.6
1988	LA N	0	1	.000	4	1	0	0-0	12.2	16	10	0	0	4-1	12	6.39	52	.320	.370	1-0-1	.000	-0	53	-4	72	-0.3
1989	Phi N	12	12	.500	33	32	1-1	0-0	204	155	84	11	2	86-6	164	3.44	104	.215	.297	65-0-10	.092	-2	100	5	0	0.3
1990	Phi N	8	7	.533	18	18	2	0-0	106.2	106	60	12	3	49-6	70	4.64	83	.260	.343	30-0-8	.067	-1	92	-9	83	-1.3
Total	7	38	48	.442	245	54	3-1	31-21	613.1	534	296	46	9	275-31	549	3.95	92	.237	.320	114-0-20	.079	-5	98	-18	519	-3.0
HOWELL, DIXIE	Millard; B1.7.1920 Harold KY; D3.18.1960 Hollywood FL; BL/TR/6´2˝/(198–210); d9.14																									
1940	Cle A	0	0	ø	3	0	0	0	5	2	1	0	0	4	2	1.80	234	.143	.333	0	ø	0	—	1	—	0.1
1949	Cin N	0	1	.000	5	1	0	0	13.1	21	12	3	0	8	7	8.10	52	.362	.439	9	.111	-0*	84	-5	0	-0.3
1955	Chi A	8	3	.727	35	0	0	9	73.2	70	27	1	0	25-5	25	2.93	135	.250	.308	21-0-1	.381	2	—	8	0	1.6
1956	Chi A	5	6	.455	34	1	0	4	64.1	79	39	3	2	36-10	28	4.62	89	.309	.398	17-2-0	.235	2	130	-5	0	-0.6
1957	Chi A	6	5	.545	37	0	0	6	68.1	64	25	6	0	30-4	37	3.29	113	.255	.332	27-3-0	.185	4*	—	4	0	1.2
1958	Chi A	0	0	ø	1	0	0	0	1.2	0	0	0	0	0-0	0	0.00	ø	.000	.000	0	ø	0	—	1	0	0.0
Total	6	19	15	.559	115	2	0	19	226.1	236	104	13	2	103-19	99	3.78	104	.273	.350	74-5-1	.243	8	113	4	0	2.0
HOWELL, ROLAND	Roland Boatner "Billiken"; B1.3.1892 Napoleonville LA; D3.31.1973 Baton Rouge LA; BR/TR/6´4˝/210; d6.14; Col Louisiana St.																									
1912	StL N	0	0	ø	3	0	0	0	1.2	5	5	0	0	5	0	27.00	13	.556	.714	0	ø	0	—	-4	—	-0.2
HOWRY, BOB	Bobby Dean; B8.4.1973 Phoenix AZ; BL/TR/6´5˝/(215–220); [SFN94 5/144]; d6.21; Col McNeese St.																									
1998	Chi A	0	3	.000	44	0	0	9-2	54.1	37	20	7	2	19-2	51	3.15	146	.194	.270	0	ø	0	—	9	0	0.7
1999	Chi A	5	3	.625	69	0	0	28-6	67.2	58	34	8	3	38-3	80	3.59	138	.229	.336	0	ø	0	—	8	0	1.3
2000	†Chi A	2	4	.333	65	0	0	7-5	71	54	26	6	4	29-2	60	3.17	160	.216	.303	0	ø	0	—	15	0	1.3
2001	Chi A	4	5	.444	69	0	0	5-6	78.2	85	41	11	4	30-9	64	4.69	99	.279	.348	0	ø	0	—	1	0	0.1
2002	Chi A	2	2	.500	47	0	0	0-0	50.2	45	22	7	3	17-2	31	3.91	115	.245	.313	0	ø	0	—	4	0	0.3
	Bos A	1	3	.250	20	0	0	0-1	18	22	15	2	2	4-2	14	5.00	90	.306	.350	0	ø	0	—	-3	0	-0.5
	Year	3	5	.375	67	0	0	0-1	68.2	67	37	9	5	21-4	45	4.19	107	.262	.323	0	ø	0	—	-2	0	-0.2
2003	Bos A	0	0	ø	4	0	0	0-1	4.1	11	6	1	0	3-1	4	12.46	37	.478	.519	0	ø	0	—	-3	38	-0.2
2004	Cle A	4	2	.667	37	0	0	0-2	42.2	37	14	5	2	12-0	39	2.74	158	.228	.288	0	ø	0	—	8	0	1.0
2005	Cle A	7	4	.636	79	0	0	3-2	73	49	23	4	0	16-1	48	2.47	169	.191	.237	1	.000	-0	—	14	0	1.9
2006	Chi N	4	5	.444	84	0	0	5-4	76.2	70	28	8	3	17-4	71	3.17	145	.245	.291	1	1.000	0	—	13	0	1.5
Total	9	29	31	.483	518	0	0	57-29	537	468	229	59	23	185-26	462	3.52	131	.236	.305	2	.500	0	—	66	38	7.4
HOY, PETER	Peter Alexander; B6.29.1966 Brockville ON, Can.; BL/TR/6´7˝/220; [BosA88 33/849]; d4.11; Col LeMoyne (NY)																									
1992	Bos A	0	0	ø	5	0	0	0-1	3.2	8	3	0	0	2-1	2	7.36	58	.471	.526	0	ø	0	—	-1	0	0.0
HOYLE, TEX	Roland Edison; B7.17.1921 Carbondale PA; D7.4.1994 Carbondale PA; BR/TR/6´4˝/170; d4.18																									
1952	Phi A	0	0	ø	3	0	0	0	2.1	9	7	2	0	1	1	27.00	15	.563	.588	0	ø	0	—	-5	0	-0.2

YEAR	TM LG	W	L	PCT	G	GS	CG-SHO	SV-BS	IP	H	R	HR	HB	BB-IB	SO	ERA	AERA	OAV	OOB	AB-HR-SH	AVG	PB	SUP	APR	DL	PW
Hoyt, La Marr	Dewey La Marr; B1.1.1955 Columbia SC; BR/TR/6´1˝/(190–244); [NYA73 5/109]; d9.14																									
1979	Chi A	0	0	ø	2	0	0	0-0	3	2	0	0	0	0-0	0	0.00	ø	.200	.200	0	ø	0	—	1	0	0.1
1980	Chi A	9	3	.750	24	13	3-1	0-0	112.1	123	66	8	2	41-3	55	4.57	89	.281	.340	0	ø	0*	93	-6	0	-0.7
1981	Chi A	9	3	.750	43	1	0	10-1	90.2	80	40	10	3	28-1	60	3.57	101	.240	.303	0	ø	0	0	1	0	0.1
1982	Chi A	**19**	15	.559	39	32	14-2	0-1	239.2	248	104	17	2	48-3	124	3.53	115	.266	.301	0	ø	0	119	16	0	2.1
1983	†Chi A	**24**	10	.706	36	36	11-1	0-0	260.2	236	115	27	1	31-4	148	3.66	115	.238	**.260**	0	ø	0	115	16	0	2.2
1984	Chi A	13	18	.419	34	34	11-1	0-0	235.2	244	127	31	5	43-3	126	4.47	94	.266	.301	0	ø	0*	85	-6	0	-0.7
1985	SD N★	16	8	.667	31	31	8-3	0-0	210.1	210	85	20	2	20-2	83	3.47	103	.261	.280	64-0-12	.063	-4	112	5	0	0.1
1986	SD N	8	11	.421	35	25	1	0-1	159	170	100	27	3	68-8	85	5.15	71	.276	.350	46-0-3	.130	-1	105	-26	0	-2.9
Total	8	98	68	.590	244	172	48-8	10-3	1311.1	1313	637	140	18	279-24	681	3.99	99	.260	.300	110-0-15	.091	-5	106	1	0	0.3
Hoyt, Waite	Waite Charles "Schoolboy"; B9.9.1899 Brooklyn NY; D8.25.1984 Cincinnati OH; BR/TR/6´0˝/180; d7.24; HF1969																									
1918	NY N	0	0	ø	1	0	0	0	1	0	0	0	0	0	2	0.00	ø	.000	.000	1	.000	-0	—	0	—	0.0
1919	Bos A	4	6	.400	13	11	6-1	0	105.1	99	42	1	0	22	28	3.25	93	.262	.303	38-0-2	.132	-3	83	-1	—	-0.3
1920	Bos A	6	6	.500	22	11	6-2	1	121.1	123	72	2	1	47	45	4.38	83	.270	.339	43-0-2	.116	-3	103	-11	—	-1.3
1921	†NY A	19	13	.594	43	32	21-1	3	282.1	301	121	3	5	81	102	3.09	137	.276	.329	99-0-9	.222	-2	102	35	—	3.3
1922	†NY A	19	12	.613	37	31	17-3	0	265	271	114	13	9	76	95	3.43	117	.269	.326	92-0-3	.217	1	94	19	—	2.0
1923	†NY A	17	9	.654	37	28	19-1	1	238.2	227	97	9	4	66	60	3.02	131	.253	.307	84-0-6	.190	-2	91	21	—	1.8
1924	NY A	18	13	.581	46	32	14-2	4	247	295	117	8	3	76	71	3.79	110	.300	.352	75-0-12	.133	-5	96	11	—	0.7
1925	NY A	11	14	.440	46	30	17-1	6	243	283	124	14	1	78	86	4.00	107	.292	.346	79-0-8	.304	6	95	8	—	1.3
1926	†NY A	16	12	.571	40	28	12-1	4	217.2	224	112	4	2	62	79	3.85	100	.264	.316	76-0-7	.211	-0	115	1	—	-0.1
1927	†NY A	**22**	7	**.759**	36	32	23-3	1	256.1	242	90	10	4	54	86	2.63	146	.251	.294	99-0-9	.222	0	145	38	—	3.8
1928	†NY A	23	7	.767	42	31	19-3	**8**	273	279	118	16	1	60	67	3.36	112	.272	.313	109-0-3	.257	2	146	15	—	1.6
1929	NY A	10	9	.526	30	25	12	1	201.2	219	115	9	3	69	57	4.24	91	.279	.339	76-0-8	.224	1	134	-9	—	-0.7
1930	NY A	2	2	.500	8	7	2	0	47.2	64	27	7	0	9	10	4.53	95	.317	.346	16-0-1	.063	-2	137	0	—	-0.2
	Det A	9	8	.529	26	20	8-1	4	135.2	176	89	7	2	47	25	4.78	100	.313	.368	46-0-2	.196	-2	81	-1	—	-0.5
	Year	11	10	.524	34	27	10-1	4	183.1	240	116	14	2	56	35	4.71	99	.314	.363	62-0-3	.161	-4	95	-1	—	-0.7
1931	Det A	3	8	.273	16	12	5	0	92	124	70	2	2	32	10	5.87	78	.319	.374	30	.133	-2	71	-12	—	-1.4
	†Phi A	10	5	.667	16	14	9-2	0	111	130	60	9	0	37	30	4.22	107	.298	.353	43-0-2	.302	3	109	4	—	0.7
	Year	13	13	.500	32	26	14-2	0	203	254	130	11	2	69	40	4.97	91	.308	.363	73-0-2	.233	0	91	-7	—	-0.7
1932	Bro N	1	3	.250	8	4	0	1	26.2	38	27	3	0	12	7	7.76	49	.342	.407	6	.000	-1	61	-12	—	-1.6
	NY N	5	7	.417	18	12	3	0	97.1	103	43	6	5	25	29	3.42	109	.275	.328	31-0-2	.097	-2	83	4	—	0.3
	Year	6	10	.375	26	16	3	1	124	141	70	9	5	37	36	4.35	86	.290	.347	37-0-2	.081	-3	77	-8	—	-1.3
1933	Pit N	5	7	.417	36	8	4-1	4	117	118	45	3	1	19	44	2.92	114	.262	.293	32	.156	-1	66	6	—	0.6
1934	Pit N	15	6	.714	48	17	8-3	5	190.2	184	75	6	2	43	105	2.93	141	.252	.296	56-0-2	.179	-1	95	23	—	2.3
1935	Pit N	7	11	.389	39	11	5	6	164	187	72	8	1	27	63	3.40	121	.285	.315	54-0-3	.259	2	75	15	—	1.7
1936	Pit N	7	5	.583	22	9	6	1	116.2	115	44	5	3	20	37	2.70	150	.255	.291	39-0-2	.154	-1	81	16	—	1.5
1937	Pit N	1	2	.333	11	0	0	2	28	31	14	3	0	6	21	4.50	86	.270	.306	12	.083	-1	—	-1	—	-0.2
	Bro N	7	7	.500	27	19	10-1	0	167	180	83	5	0	30	44	3.23	125	.270	.301	48-0-8	.083	-2	93	11	—	0.6
	Year	8	9	.471	38	19	10-1	2	195	211	97	8	0	36	65	3.42	117	.270	.302	60-0-8	.083	-3	94	9	—	0.4
1938	Bro N	0	3	.000	6	1	0	0	16.1	24	9	1	0	5	3	4.96	79	.333	.377	3	.000	-0	43	-1	—	-0.2
Total	21	237	182	.566	674	425	226-26	52	3762.1	4037	1780	154	49	1003	1206	3.59	112	.276	.325	1287-0-91	.198	-17	104	179	—	15.7
Hrabosky, Al	Alan Thomas "The Mad Hungarian"; B7.21.1949 Oakland CA; BR/TL/5´11˝/(180–185); [StLN69*1/19]; d6.16; Mil 1971; Col Fullerton (CA) JC																									
1970	StL N	2	1	.667	16	1	0	0-1	19	22	10	2	0	7-1	12	4.74	88	.286	.345	3	.000	-0	65	-1	0	-0.2
1971	StL N	0	0	ø	1	0	0	0-0	2	2	0	0	0	0-0	2	0.00	ø	.250	.250	0	ø	0	—	1	0	0.0
1972	StL N	1	0	1.000	5	0	0	0-0	7	2	0	0	0	3-0	9	0.00	ø	.087	.185	1	.000	-0	—	3	0	0.4
1973	StL N	2	4	.333	44	0	0	5-1	56	45	15	2	2	21-6	57	2.09	176	.220	.297	4-0-1	.000	-0	—	10	0	1.1
1974	StL N	8	1	.889	65	0	0	9-4	88.1	71	34	3	1	38-7	82	2.95	122	.221	.302	13-0-1	.308	1*	—	6	0	0.8
1975	StL N	13	3	.813	65	0	0	**22**-6	97.1	72	27	3	1	33-8	82	1.66	228	.205	.273	15-0-3	.200	1	—	**20**	0	4.2
1976	StL N	8	6	.571	68	0	0	13-4	95.1	89	42	5	4	39-9	73	3.30	108	.252	.328	7-0-3	.000	0	—	2	0	0.4
1977	StL N	6	5	.545	65	0	0	10-6	86.1	82	44	12	3	41-7	68	4.38	89	.256	.340	8	.000	-1	—	-3	0	-0.6
1978	†KC A	8	7	.533	58	0	0	20-3	75	52	24	6	1	35-2	60	2.88	133	.200	.290	0	ø	0	—	9	0	2.0
1979	KC A	9	4	.692	58	0	0	11-2	65	67	31	3	1	41-10	39	3.74	114	.272	.377	0	ø	0	—	4	0	0.7
1980	Atl N	4	2	.667	45	0	0	3-3	59.2	50	27	8	0	31-5	31	3.62	102	.223	.313	1	.000	-0	—	0	0	-0.1
1981	Atl N	1	1	.500	24	0	0	1-0	33.2	24	5	1	0	9-1	13	1.07	330	.207	.260	1	.000	-0	—	9	26	0.5
1982	Atl N	2	1	.667	31	0	0	3-2	37.1	41	25	5	0	17-2	20	5.54	67	.285	.354	3	.333	0	—	-7	21	-0.7
Total	13	64	35	.646	545	1	0	97-32	722	619	284	50	13	315-58	548	3.10	122	.234	.314	56-0-8	.143	0	65	53	47	8.5
Hubbell, Carl	Carl Owen "King Carl","The Meal Ticket"; B6.22.1903 Carthage MO; D11.21.1988 Scottsdale AZ; BR/TL (BB 1928–29, 31–32)/6´0˝/170; d7.26; HF1947																									
1928	NY N	10	6	.625	20	14	8-1	1	124	117	49	7	3	21	37	2.83	138	.248	.284	47-0-1	.106	-3	101	13	—	1.4
1929	NY N	18	11	.621	39	35	19-1	1	268	273	128	17	6	67	106	3.69	124	.265	.313	93-0-7	.129	-6	116	28	—	2.2
1930	NY N	17	12	.586	37	32	17-3	2	241.2	263	120	11	11	58	117	3.87	122	.278	.327	86-0-10	.151	-5	104	25	—	1.9
1931	NY N	14	12	.538	36	30	21-4	3	248	211	88	14	4	67	155	2.65	139	**.227**	**.282**	83-0-6	.241	4	100	30	—	**3.4**
1932	NY N	18	11	.621	40	32	22	2	284	260	96	20	4	40	137	2.50	148	.238	**.268**	108-1-4	.241	4	107	40	—	**4.7**
1933	†NY N★	**23**	12	.657	45	33	22-**10**	5	**308.2**	256	69	6	3	47	156	**1.66**	**193**	.227	**.260**	109-1-5	.183	1	75	**55**	—	**7.3**
1934	NY N★	21	12	.636	49	35	**25**-5	**8**	313	286	100	17	2	37	118	**2.30**	**168**	.239	**.263**	117-0-3	.197	-1	103	**55**	—	5.9
1935	NY N☆	23	12	.657	42	35	24-1	0	302.2	314	125	27	3	49	150	3.27	118	.263	.294	109-1-2	.239	4	104	21	—	2.8
1936	†NY N★	**26**	6	**.813**	42	34	25-3	3	304	265	81	7	5	57	123	**2.31**	**169**	.236	**.276**	110-0-10	.227	1	92	**60**	—	**6.2**
1937	†NY N★	**22**	8	**.733**	39	32	18-4	4	261.2	261	108	18	3	55	**159**	3.20	122	.257	.298	97-0-3	.216	1	115	20	—	2.2
1938	NY N☆	13	10	.565	24	22	13-1	1	179	171	70	16	2	33	104	3.07	123	.249	**.285**	58-0-10	.155	-2	96	15	—	1.5
1939	NY N	11	9	.550	29	18	10	2	154	150	60	11	2	24	62	2.75	143	.249	**.280**	53-1-3	.151	-1	77	18	—	2.1
1940	NY N★	11	12	.478	31	28	11-2	0	214.1	220	102	22	2	59	86	3.65	106	.259	.309	81-0-2	.185	-0	111	5	—	0.5
1941	NY N☆	11	9	.550	26	22	11-1	1	164	169	73	10	2	53	75	3.57	104	.266	.325	57-0-2	.140	-2	90	3	0	0.0
1942	NY N☆	11	8	.579	24	20	11	0	157.1	158	75	17	1	34	61	3.95	85	.259	.299	60-0-3	.183	-0	124	-7	0	-0.9
1943	NY N	4	4	.500	12	11	3	0	66	87	36	7	0	24	31	4.91	70	.322	.378	20-0-4	.200	-0	116	-9	0	-1.0
Total	16	253	154	.622	535	433	260-36	33	3590.1	3461	1380	227	53	725	1677	2.98	130	.251	.291	1288-4-75	.191	-5	102	372	0	40.2
Hubbell, Bill	Wilbert William; B6.17.1897 San Francisco CA; D8.3.1980 Lakewood CO; BR/TR/6´1.5˝/195; d9.24; Col Idaho																									
1919	NY N	1	1	.500	2	2	2	0	18.1	19	4	0	2	2	3	1.96	143	.260	.299	8	.125	-1	128	2	—	0.2
1920	NY N	0	1	.000	14	0	0	2	30	26	12	2	1	15	8	2.10	143	.239	.336	5	.200	-0	—	2	—	0.1
	Phi N	9	9	.500	24	18	9-1	2	150	176	77	3	4	42	26	3.84	89	.301	.352	53-0-2	.132	-3	83	-5	—	-1.0
	Year	9	10	.474	38	18	9-1	4	180	202	89	5	5	57	34	3.55	94	.291	.349	58-0-2	.138	-3	85	-5	—	-0.9
1921	Phi N	9	16	.360	36	30	15-1	2	220.1	269	146	18	3	38	43	4.33	98	.306	.337	75-1-1	.160	-2	83	-3	—	-0.4
1922	Phi N	7	15	.318	35	26	11-1	1	189	257	136	14	4	41	33	5.00	93	.317	.353	70-0-2	.171	-2	85	-6	—	-0.7
1923	Phi N	1	6	.143	22	5	1	0	55	102	70	13	2	17	8	8.35	55	.394	.435	17-0-2	.235	0*	79	-22	—	-2.3
1924	Phi N	10	9	.526	36	22	9-2	2	179	233	103	9	2	45	30	4.83	92	.324	.365	59-0-3	.220	-1	107	-3	—	-0.3
1925	Phi N	0	0	ø	2	0	0	0	2.2	5	4	0	0	1	0	0.00	ø	.385	.429	1-0-1	.000	-0	—	0	—	0.0
	Bro N	3	6	.333	33	5	3	1	86.2	120	59	8	2	24	16	5.30	79	.337	.382	20-0-1	.150	0	77	-10	—	-0.8
	Year	3	6	.333	35	5	3	1	89.1	125	63	8	2	25	16	5.14	82	.339	.384	21-0-2	.143	0	76	-9	—	-0.8
Total	7	40	63	.388	204	108	50-5	10	931	1207	611	67	20	225	167	4.68	89	.317	.359	308-1-12	.172	-8	90	-45	—	-5.2
Huber, Jon	Jonathan Lloyd; B7.7.1981 Sacramento CA; BR/TR/6´2˝/195; [SDN00 5/139]; d8.30																									
2006	Sea A	2	1	.667	16	0	0	0-0	16.2	10	3	0	0	6-1	11	1.08	408	.172	.250	0	ø	0	—	6	0	1.0
Huckleberry, Earl	Earl Eugene; B5.23.1910 Konawa OK; D2.25.1999 Seminole OK; BR/TR/5´11˝/165; d9.13																									
1935	Phi A	1	0	1.000	1	1	0	0	6.2	8	7	1	0	4	2	9.45	48	.296	.387	3	.000	-0	363	-3	—	-0.3
Hudek, John	John Raymond; B8.8.1966 Tampa FL; BB/TR/6´1˝/(200–210); [ChiA88 10/249]; d4.23; Col Florida Southern																									
1994	Hou N★	0	2	.000	42	0	0	16-2	39.1	24	14	5	1	18-2	39	2.97	133	.174	.270	0	ø	0	—	5	0	0.5
1995	Hou N	2	2	.500	19	0	0	7-2	20	19	12	3	0	5-0	29	5.40	72	.247	.293	1	1.000	1	—	-3	101	-0.5
1996	Hou N	2	0	1.000	15	0	0	2-0	16	12	5	2	0	5-2	14	2.81	138	.207	.270	0	ø	0	—	2	105	0.3
1997	Hou N	1	3	.250	40	0	0	4-4	40.2	38	27	8	3	33-2	36	5.98	67	.252	.396	0	ø	0	—	-8	0	-0.8
1998	NY N	1	4	.200	28	0	0	0-0	27	23	13	2	2	19-3	28	4.00	103	.237	.367	0	ø	0	—	0	0	0.0
	Cin N	4	2	.667	30	0	0	0-1	37	27	14	6	2	28-1	40	2.43	176	.206	.348	3-0-1	.000	-0	—	6	0	0.8

YEAR	TM LG	W	L	PCT	G	GS	CG-SHO	SV-BS	IP	H	R	HR	HB	BB-IB	SO	ERA	AERA	OAV	OOB	AB-HR-SH	AVG	PB	SUP	APR	DL	PW
	Year	5	6	.455	58	0	0	0-1	64	50	27	8	4	47-4	68	3.09	136	.219	.356	3-0-1	.000	-0	—	6	0	0.8
1999	Cin N	0	1	.000	2	0	0	0-1	1	4	3	1	0	3-0	0	27.00	17	.667	.778	0	ø	0	—	-2	0	-0.4
	Atl N	0	1	.000	15	0	0	0-0	16.2	21	14	1	1	11-0	18	6.48	69	.296	.393	1	.000	-0	—	-4	44	-0.2
	Year	0	2	.000	17	0	0	0-1	17.2	25	17	2	1	14-0	18	7.64	59	.325	.430	1	.000	-0	—	-7	0	-0.6
	Tor A	0	0	ø	3	0	0	0-0	3.2	8	5	1	0	1-0	2	12.27	40	.471	.474	0	ø	0	—	-3	0	-0.1
Total	6	10	15	.400	194	0	0	29-10	201.1	176	107	29	9	123-10	206	4.43	93	.236	.347	5-0-1	.200	0	—	-7	250	-0.4
HUDLIN, WILLIS	George Willis "Ace"; B5.23.1906 Wagoner OK; D8.5.2002 Little Rock AR; BR/TR/6´0˝/190; d8.15; Mil 1944; C3																									
1926	Cle A	1	3	.250	8	2	1	0	32.1	25	13	1	2	13	6	2.78	146	.227	.320	8-0-1	.125	0	83	4	—	0.5
1927	Cle A	18	12	.600	43	30	18-1	0	264.2	291	132	3	11	83	65	4.01	105	.283	.343	96-1-6	.250	2	105	9	—	1.2
1928	Cle A	14	14	.500	42	26	10	7	220.1	231	114	7	7	90	62	4.04	103	.279	.355	72-0-2	.194	-0	97	5	—	0.7
1929	Cle A	17	15	.531	40	33	22-2	1	280.1	299	122	7	1	73	60	3.34	133	.272	.318	97-0-8	.196	-3	81	34	—	3.5
1930	Cle A	13	16	.448	37	33	13-1	1	216.2	255	133	12	1	76	60	4.57	106	.293	.351	73-0-3	.219	-1	101	7	—	0.9
1931	Cle A	15	14	.517	44	34	15-1	4	254.1	313	155	14	1	88	83	4.60	100	.301	.356	100-0-2	.200	1	112	1	—	0.3
1932	Cle A	12	8	.600	33	21	12	2	181.2	204	108	10	1	59	65	4.71	101	.278	.332	64-0-3	.203	1	114	3	—	0.4
1933	Cle A	5	13	.278	34	17	6	1	147.1	161	85	7	3	61	44	3.97	112	.275	.346	41-1-5	.146	-1	72	5	—	0.6
1934	Cle A	15	10	.600	36	26	15-1	4	195	210	109	8	5	65	58	4.75	96	.277	.338	68-1-5	.206	3	108	1	—	0.6
1935	Cle A	15	11	.577	36	29	14-3	5	231.2	252	107	8	3	61	45	3.69	122	.277	.324	86-1-1	.279	6*	113	22	—	2.8
1936	Cle A	1	5	.167	27	7	1	0	64	112	74	1	2	31	20	9.00	56	.397	.460	18	.111	-1	80	-28	—	-2.0
1937	Cle A	12	11	.522	35	23	10-2	2	175.2	213	106	8	2	43	31	4.10	112	.295	.337	59-0-5	.169	-1	96	4	—	0.5
1938	Cle A	8	8	.500	29	15	8	1	127	158	80	13	2	45	27	4.89	95	.303	.361	43-0-2	.116	-2	119	-4	—	-0.6
1939	Cle A	9	10	.474	27	20	7	3	143	175	85	6	1	42	28	4.91	90	.303	.352	48-1-3	.188	1	88	-7	—	-0.5
1940	Cle A	2	1	.667	4	4	2	0	23.2	31	13	3	0	2	8	4.94	85	.316	.330	8	.125	-0	115	-1	—	-0.1
	Was A	1	2	.333	8	6	1	0	37.1	50	33	9	2	5	9	6.51	64	.314	.343	10-0-2	.100	-1	133	-11	—	-0.8
	StL A	0	1	.000	6	1	0	0	11.1	19	16	0	0	8	4	11.12	41	.358	.443	2	.500	0	77	-8	—	-0.5
	Year	3	4	.429	18	11	3	0	72.1	100	62	12	2	15	21	6.72	63	.323	.358	20-0-2	.150	-1	120	-20	—	-1.4
	NY N	0	1	.000	1	1	0	0	5	9	6	1	0	1	1	10.80	36	.409	.435	1	.000	-0	22	-3	—	-0.5
1944	StL A	0	1	.000	1	0	0	0	2	3	2	0	0	0	1	4.50	80	.300	.300	0	ø	0	—	-1	0	-0.1
Total	16	158	156	.503	491	328	155-11	31	2613.1	3011	1493	118	44	846	677	4.41	102	.289	.345	894-5-48	.201	4	101	32	0	6.9
HUDSON, CHARLIE	Charles; B8.18.1949 Ada OK; BL/TL/6´3˝/185; [NYN67 10/184]; d5.21																									
1972	StL N	1	0	1.000	12	0	0	0-0	12.1	10	8	0	1	7-0	4	5.11	67	.233	.353	0	ø	0	—	-2	0	-0.2
1973	Tex A	4	2	.667	25	4	1-1	1-1	62.1	59	35	3	0	31-2	34	4.62	81	.254	.335	0	ø	0	89	-5	47	-0.5
1975	Cal A	0	1	.000	3	1	0	0-0	5.2	7	6	0	0	4-0	0	9.53	38	.304	.407	0	ø	0	98	-4	0	-0.5
Total	3	5	3	.625	40	5	1-1	1-1	80.1	76	49	3	1	42-2	38	5.04	73	.255	.343	0	ø	0	92	-11	47	-1.2
HUDSON, CHARLES	Charles Lynn; B3.16.1959 Ennis TX; BB/TR (BR 1983, 84p)/6´3˝/185; [PhiN81 12/305]; d5.31; Col Prairie View A&M																									
1983	†Phi N	8	8	.500	26	26	3	0-0	169.1	158	73	13	0	53-6	101	3.35	108	.248	.304	54-0-5	.093	-2*	125	5	0	0.2
1984	Phi N	9	11	.450	30	30	1-1	0-0	173.2	181	101	12	2	52-4	94	4.04	91	.265	.316	56-0-4	.089	-2	97	-11	22	-1.5
1985	Phi N	8	13	.381	38	26	3	0-0	193	188	92	23	1	74-7	122	3.78	98	.252	.319	57-0-3	.140	-1	116	-1	0	-0.3
1986	Phi N	7	10	.412	33	23	0	0-0	144	165	87	20	0	58-1	82	4.94	79	.291	.355	43-0-7	.047	-3*	90	-14	0	-1.9
1987	NY A	11	7	.611	35	16	6-2	0-0	154.2	137	63	19	3	57-1	100	3.61	123	.239	.308	0	ø	0	109	16	0	1.6
1988	NY A	6	6	.500	28	12	1	2-0	106.1	93	53	9	4	36-4	58	4.49	89	.235	.301	0	ø	0	117	-4	34	-0.4
1989	Det A	1	5	.167	18	7	0	0-0	66.2	75	49	14	2	31-3	23	6.35	60	.288	.367	0	ø	0*	98	-17	30	-1.4
Total	7	50	60	.455	208	140	14-3	2-0	1007.2	997	518	110	12	361-26	580	4.14	93	.258	.321	210-0-19	.095	-8	107	-26	86	-3.7
HUDSON, HAL	Hal Campbell "Bud","Lefty"; B5.4.1927 Grosse Pointe MI; BL/TL/5´10˝/175; d4.20																									
1952	StL A	0	0	ø	3	0	0	0	5.2	9	8	0	0	6	0	12.71	31	.360	.484	1	.000	-0	—	-5	0	-0.3
	Chi A	0	0	ø	2	0	0	0	4	7	2	0	0	1	4	2.25	162	.389	.421	0	ø	0	—	0	0	0.0
	Year	0	0	ø	5	0	0	0	9.2	16	10	0	0	7	4	8.38	45	.372	.460	1	.000	-0	—	-5	0	-0.3
1953	Chi A	0	0	ø	1	0	0	0	0.2	0	0	0	0	0	0	0.00	ø	.000	.000	0	ø	0	—	0	0	0.0
Total	2	0	0	ø	6	0	0	0	10.1	16	10	0	0	7	4	7.84	49	.364	.451	1	.000	-0	—	-5	0	-0.3
HUDSON, JESSE	Jesse James; B7.22.1948 Mansfield LA; BL/TL/6´2˝/170; d9.19																									
1969	NY N	0	0	ø	1	0	0	0-0	2	2	1	0	0	2-0	3	4.50	81	.250	.400	0	ø	0	—	0	0	0.0
HUDSON, JOE	Joseph Paul; B9.29.1970 Philadelphia PA; BR/TR/6´1˝/(175–180); [BosA92 27/758]; d6.10; Col West Virginia																									
1995	†Bos A	0	1	.000	39	0	0	1-3	46	53	21	2	2	23-1	29	4.11	118	.301	.386	0	ø	0	—	5	0	0.2
1996	Bos A	3	5	.375	36	0	0	1-4	45	57	35	4	0	32-4	19	5.40	94	.318	.418	0	ø	0	—	-3	0	-0.5
1997	Bos A	3	1	.750	26	0	0	0-0	35.2	39	16	1	4	14-2	14	3.53	132	.289	.373	0	ø	0	—	4	0	0.4
1998	Mil N	0	0	ø	1	0	0	0-0	0.1	2	6	0	0	4-1	0	162.00	3	1.000	.857	0	ø	0	—	-5	0	-0.2
Total	4	6	7	.462	102	0	0	2-7	127	151	78	7	6	73-8	62	4.82	101	.307	.400	0	ø	0	—	1	0	-0.1
HUDSON, LUKE	Luke Stephen; B5.2.1977 Fountain Valley CA; BR/TR/6´3˝/195; [ColN98 4/120]; d7.1; Col Tennessee																									
2002	Cin N	0	0	ø	3	0	0	0-0	6	5	5	1	0	6-0	7	4.50	95	.227	.393	0-0-1	ø	0	—	-1	0	-0.1
2004	Cin N	4	2	.667	9	9	0	0-0	48.1	36	16	3	2	25-1	38	2.42	178	.208	.312	16	.125	-0	98	9	0	1.0
2005	Cin N	6	9	.400	19	16	0	0-0	84.2	83	62	14	11	50-2	53	6.38	67	.268	.384	25-0-2	.320	3*	119	-18	67	-2.5
2006	KC A	7	6	.538	26	15	0	0-1	102	109	62	7	4	38-1	64	5.12	92	.276	.343	0	ø	0	114	-4	0	-0.5
Total	4	17	17	.500	57	40	0	0-1	241	233	145	25	17	119-4	162	5.00	89	.259	.353	41-0-3	.244	3	112	-14	67	-2.1
HUDSON, NAT	Nathaniel P.; B1.12.1859 Chicago IL; D3.14.1928 Chicago IL; BR/TR; d4.18																									
1886	†StL AA	16	10	.615	29	27	25	**1**	234.1	224	122	3	2	62	100	3.03	113	.243	.293	150	.233	1*	119	15	—	1.3
1887	StL AA	4	4	.500	9	9	7	0	67	91	57	2	4	20	15	4.97	91	.305	.357	48	.250	0*	89	-3	—	-0.3
1888	StL AA	25	10	**.714**	39	37	36-5	0	333	283	155	8	15	59	130	2.54	128	.222	.264	196-2	.255	5*	120	28	—	2.9
1889	StL AA	3	2	.600	9	5	4	0	60	71	47	2	4	15	13	4.20	101	.285	.336	52-1	.250	0*	82	0	—	0.0
Total	4	48	26	.649	86	78	72-5	1	694.1	669	381	15	25	156	258	3.08	114	.244	.291	446-3	.247	6	113	40	—	3.9
HUDSON, REX	Rex Haughton; B8.11.1953 Tulsa OK; BB/TR/5´11˝/165; d7.27																									
1974	LA N	0	0	ø	1	0	0	0-0	2	6	5	2	0	0-0	0	22.50	15	.500	.500	0	ø	0	—	-4	0	-0.2
HUDSON, SID	Sidney Charles; B1.3.1915 Coalfield TN; BR/TR/6´4˝/180; d4.18; Mil 1943–45; C14																									
1940	Was A	17	16	.515	38	31	19-3	1	252	272	149	20	3	81	96	4.57	91	.274	.330	93-0-2	.237	2	93	-11	—	-1.0
1941	Was A★	13	14	.481	33	33	17-3	0	249.2	242	124	12	1	97	108	3.46	117	.253	.322	86-0-6	.186	-0	95	12	0	1.3
1942	Was A☆	10	17	.370	35	31	19-1	2	239.1	266	140	9	5	70	72	4.36	84	.276	.328	89-0-2	.213	1*	94	-20	0	-1.7
1946	Was A	8	11	.421	31	15	6-1	1	142.1	160	75	9	4	37	35	3.60	93	.280	.328	43-0-1	.279	3	89	-7	0	-0.5
1947	Was A	6	9	.400	20	17	5-1	0	106	113	66	8	1	58	37	5.60	66	.272	.363	39	.308	2	73	-18	0	-2.0
1948	Was A	4	16	.200	39	29	4	1	182	217	128	11	6	107	53	5.88	74	.299	.394	59-0-3	.237	2	77	-28	0	-2.2
1949	Was A	8	17	.320	40	27	11-2	1	209	234	117	11	5	91	54	4.22	101	.283	.357	67-0-5	.239	2	74	-1	0	0.2
1950	Was A	14	14	.500	30	30	17	0	237.2	261	129	17	6	98	75	4.09	110	.284	.356	93-0-3	.215	-1*	92	9	0	0.9
1951	Was A	5	12	.294	23	19	8	0	138.2	168	90	8	4	52	43	5.13	80	.302	.365	44-0-1	.273	2*	71	-17	0	-1.5
1952	Was A	3	4	.429	7	7	6	0	62.2	59	22	4	0	29	24	2.73	130	.257	.340	24-0-1	.167	-0	77	6	0	0.7
	Bos A	7	9	.438	21	18	7	0	134.1	145	64	9	7	36	50	3.62	109	.276	.330	46	.174	-1	89	3	0	0.5
	Year	10	13	.435	28	25	13	0	197	204	86	13	7	65	74	3.34	114	.270	.333	70-0-1	.171	-1	86	10	0	1.2
1953	Bos A	6	9	.400	30	17	4	2	156	164	65	13	4	49	60	3.52	120	.269	.327	50-0-2	.140	-2	80	14	0	1.0
1954	Bos A	3	4	.429	33	5	0	5	71.1	83	43	5	2	30	27	4.42	93	.296	.363	13	.154	-1	77	-3	0	-0.4
Total	12	104	152	.406	380	279	123-11	13	2181	2384	1212	136	48	835	734	4.28	95	.278	.345	746-0-26	.220	9	85	-61	0	-4.7
HUDSON, TIM	Timothy Adam; B7.14.1975 Columbus GA; BR/TR/6´1˝/(160–170); [OakA97 6/185]; d6.8; Col Auburn																									
1999	Oak A	11	2	.846	21	21	1	0-0	136.1	121	56	8	4	62-2	132	3.23	146	.237	.323	4	.250	1*	125	23	0	2.0
2000	†Oak A★	**20**	6	**.769**	32	32	2-2	0-0	202.1	169	100	24	7	82-5	169	4.14	117	.227	.306	3	.000	-0*	118	18	0	1.9
2001	†Oak A	18	9	.667	35	**35**	3	0-0	235	216	100	20	6	71-5	181	3.37	135	.245	.303	8	.000	-1*	96	29	0	3.1
2002	†Oak A	15	9	.625	34	34	4-2	0-0	238.1	237	87	19	8	62-9	152	2.98	150	.263	.314	5	.200	1	91	39	0	3.8
2003	†Oak A	16	7	.696	34	34	3-**2**	0-0	240	197	84	15	10	61-9	162	2.70	170	.223	.280	3	.333	0	111	48	0	4.5
2004	Oak A✶	12	6	.667	27	27	3-**2**	0-0	188.2	194	82	8	12	44-3	103	3.53	131	.267	.318	3	.000	-0	87	22	45	1.9
2005	†Atl N	14	9	.609	29	29	2	0-0	192	194	79	20	9	65-5	115	3.52	120	.265	.332	65-0-4	.138	0	105	15	32	1.9

YEAR	TM LG	W	L	PCT	G	GS	CG-SHO	SV-BS	IP	H	R	HR	HB	BB-IB	SO	ERA	AERA	OAV	OOB	AB-HR-SH	AVG	PB	SUP	APR	DL	PW
2006	Atl N	13	12	.520	35	**35**	2-1	0-0	218.1	235	129	25	9	79-10	141	4.86	93	.273	.340	63-0-14	.095	-2	121	-8	0	-1.0
Total	8	119	60	.665	247	247	20-9	0-0	1651	1563	717	139	65	526-48	1155	3.53	129	.250	.314	154-0-18	.117	-2	106	186	77	18.1
Huenke, Al	Albert Alfred; B6.26.1891 New Bremen OH; D9.20.1974 St.Marys OH; BR/TR/6´0˝/175; d10.6																									
1914	NY N	0	0	ø	1	0	0	0	2	2	1	0	0	0	2	4.50	59	.250	.250	1	.000	-0	—	0	—	0.0
Huffman, Phil	Phillip Lee; B6.20.1958 Freeport TX; BR/TR/6´2˝/180; [SFN77 2/36]; d4.10																									
1979	Tor A	6	18	.250	31	31	2-1	0-0	173	220	130	25	0	68-0	56	5.77	76	.304	.361	0	ø	0	86	-28	0	-3.2
1985	Bal A	0	0	ø	2	1	0	0-0	4.2	7	8	1	0	5-1	2	15.43	26	.350	.480	0	ø	0	201	-6	0	-0.3
Total	2	6	18	.250	33	32	2-1	0-0	177.2	227	138	26	0	73-1	58	6.03	73	.305	.365	0	ø	0	89	-34	0	-3.5
Hughes, Ed	Edward J.; B10.5.1880 Chicago IL; D10.14.1927 McHenry IL; BR/TR/6´1˝/180; d8.29.1902; b–Tom																									
1905	Bos A	3	2	.600	6	4	2	0	33.1	38	27	0	1	9	8	4.59	59	.288	.338	14	.214	-0	144	-9	—	-1.2
1906	Bos A	0	0	ø	2	0	0	0	10	15	7	0	0	3	3	5.40	51	.349	.391	3	.000	-0	—	-2	—	-0.2
Total	2	3	2	.600	8	4	2	0	43.1	53	34	0	1	12	11	4.78	57	.303	.351	17	.176	-1	144	-11	—	-1.4
Hughes, Jay	James Jay; B1.22.1874 Sacramento CA; D6.2.1924 Sacramento CA; BR/TR/?/185; d4.18; b–Mickey																									
1898	Bal N	23	12	.657	38	35	31-5	0	300.2	268	152	4	18	100	81	3.20	112	.237	.309	164-2-3	.226	4*	126	14	—	1.9
1899	Bro N	**28**	6	**.824**	35	35	30-3	0	291.2	250	121	6	14	119	99	2.68	146	.231	.316	107-0-2	.252	5	119	40	—	4.6
1901	Bro N	17	12	.586	31	29	24	0	250.2	265	125	3	12	102	96	3.27	103	.269	.345	91-0-5	.176	-1	125	4	—	0.3
1902	Bro N	15	10	.600	30	29	26	0	245	223	114	3	9	51	92	2.87	97	.243	.289	91-1-1	.209	4*	104	-5	—	0.0
Total	4	83	40	.675	134	128	111-8	0	1088	1006	512	16	53	372	368	3.00	114	.245	.315	453-3-11	.219	13	120	53	—	6.8
Hughes, Jim	James Michael; B7.2.1951 Los Angeles CA; BR/TR/6´3˝/185; [MinA69 33/760]; d9.14																									
1974	Min A	0	2	.000	2	2	1	0-0	10.1	8	8	2	0	4-0	8	5.23	72	.216	.293	0	ø	0	47	-2	0	-0.4
1975	Min A	16	14	.533	37	34	12-2	0-0	249.2	241	119	17	13	127-3	130	3.82	100	.255	.350	0	ø	0	99	1	0	0.2
1976	Min A	9	14	.391	37	26	3	0-0	177	190	113	17	8	73-2	87	4.98	72	.281	.354	0	ø	0	116	-27	0	-3.2
1977	Min A	0	0	ø	2	0	0	0-0	4.1	4	1	0	0	1-0	1	2.08	192	.250	.278	0	ø	0	—	1	0	0.0
Total	4	25	30	.455	78	62	16-2	0-0	441.1	443	241	36	21	205-5	226	4.30	87	.265	.350	0	ø	0	104	-27	0	-3.4
Hughes, Jim	James Robert; B3.21.1923 Chicago IL; D8.13.2001 Palos Heights IL; BR/TR/6´1˝/(185–200); d9.13																									
1952	Bro N	2	1	.667	6	0	0	0	18.2	16	4	0	0	11	8	1.45	252	.235	.342	4-0-1	.000	-0	—	4	0	0.6
1953	†Bro N	4	3	.571	48	0	0	9	85.2	80	33	6	1	41	49	3.47	123	.245	.332	14-0-1	.286	1	—	9	0	0.9
1954	Bro N	8	4	.667	**60**	0	0	**24**	86.2	76	36	7	0	44	58	3.22	127	.239	.326	16-0-1	.188	-0	—	8	0	1.3
1955	Bro N	0	2	.000	24	0	0	6	42.2	41	22	10	0	19-1	20	4.22	96	.256	.333	10	.000	-2	—	0	0	-0.2
1956	Bro N	0	0	ø	5	0	0	0	12	10	7	3	0	4-1	8	5.25	76	.233	.298	2	.000	-0	—	-1	0	-0.1
	Chi N	1	3	.250	25	1	0	0	45.1	43	35	4	4	30-5	20	5.16	73	.259	.379	7	.286	1	70	-9	0	-0.7
	Year	1	3	.250	30	1	0	0	57.1	53	42	7	4	34-6	28	5.18	74	.254	.364	9	.222	0	69	-11	0	-0.8
1957	Chi A	0	0	ø	4	0	0	0	5	12	6	0	0	3-0	2	10.80	35	.462	.517	0	ø	0	—	-4	0	-0.2
Total	6	15	13	.536	172	1	0	39	296	278	143	30	5	152-7	165	3.83	106	.251	.341	53-0-3	.170	-1	66	7	0	1.6
Hughes, Mickey	Michael J.; B10.25.1866 New York NY; D4.10.1931 Jersey City NJ; TR/5´6˝/165; d4.22; b–Jay																									
1888	Bro AA	25	13	.658	40	40	40-2	0	363	281	163	5	6	98	159	2.13	140	.206	.262	139	.137	-7	105	31	—	2.1
1889	†Bro AA	9	8	.529	20	17	13	0	153	172	120	6	7	86	54	4.35	86	.275	.369	68	.176	-3	135	-16	—	-1.6
1890	Bro N	4	4	.500	9	8	6	0	66.1	77	46	1	4	30	22	5.16	67	.281	.360	26	.038	-4	89	-8	—	-1.1
	Phi AA	1	3	.250	6	5	4	0	41.1	64	56	0	5	21	15	5.44	71	.344	.425	16	.125	-1	73	-14	—	-1.1
Total	3	39	28	.582	75	70	63-2	0	623.2	594	385	12	22	235	250	3.22	102	.243	.314	249	.137	-14	109	-7	—	-1.7
Hughes, Dick	Richard Henry; B2.13.1938 Stephens AR; BR/TR/6´3˝/(193–200); d9.11; Col Arkansas																									
1966	StL N	2	1	.667	6	2	1-1	1	21	12	4	0	2	7-3	20	1.71	209	.162	.253	5-0-1	.400	1	98	5	0	0.8
1967	†StL N	16	6	**.727**	37	27	12-3	3	222.1	164	72	22	5	48-6	161	2.67	123	**.203**	**.251**	78-0-4	.128	-1*	101	17	0	1.4
1968	†StL N	2	2	.500	25	5	0	4	63.2	45	25	7	0	21-3	49	3.53	82	.202	.269	15-0-1	.000	-1	150	-3	22	-0.3
Total	3	20	9	.690	68	34	13-4	8	307	221	101	29	7	76-12	230	2.79	116	.200	.255	98-0-6	.122	-2	108	19	22	1.9
Hughes, Tom	Thomas Edward; B9.13.1934 Ancon, Canal Zone; BL/TR/6´2˝/180; d9.13																									
1959	StL N	0	2	.000	2	2	0	0	4	9	9	2	0	2-0	2	15.75	27	.409	.458	1	.000	-0	32	-5	0	-0.9
Hughes, Tom	Thomas James "Long Tom"; B11.29.1878 Chicago IL; D2.8.1956 Chicago IL; BR/TR/6´1˝/175; d9.7; b–Ed																									
1900	Chi N	1	1	.500	3	3	3	0	21	31	14	0	1	7	12	5.14	70	.341	.394	6	.000	-0	77	-2	—	-0.2
1901	Chi N	10	23	.303	37	35	32-1	0	308.1	309	166	4	17	115	225	3.24	100	.259	.333	118-0-4	.119	-8*	89	1	—	-0.8
1902	Bal A	7	5	.583	13	13	12-1	0	108.1	120	57	2	2	32	45	3.90	97	.281	.334	43-0-4	.140	-2	119	2	—	0.0
	Bos A	3	3	.500	9	8	4	0	49.1	51	31	0	1	24	15	3.28	109	.267	.352	30	.367	2*	136	0	—	0.2
	Year	10	8	.556	22	21	16-1	0	157.2	171	88	2	3	56	60	3.71	100	.277	.340	73-0-4	.233	0	125	2	—	0.2
1903	†Bos A	20	7	.741	33	31	25-5	0	244.2	232	95	5	9	60	112	2.57	118	.249	.301	93-1-4	.280	7	132	13	—	1.9
1904	NY A	7	11	.389	19	18	12-1	0	136.1	141	72	3	5	48	75	3.70	73	.268	.334	54-0-2	.241	1*	105	-13	—	-1.7
	Was A	3	12	.200	16	14	14	0	124.1	133	67	4	6	34	48	3.47	77	.274	.330	57-1-2	.228	3*	73	-12	—	-1.0
	Year	10	23	.303	35	32	26-1	0	260.2	274	139	7	11	82	123	3.59	75	.271	.332	111-1-4	.234	4	91	-23	—	-2.7
1905	Was A	17	20	.459	39	35	26-6	0	291.1	239	113	3	10	79	149	2.35	113	.225	.285	104-1-1	.212	4	104	8	—	1.3
1906	Was A	7	17	.292	30	24	18-1	0	204	230	118	5	3	81	90	3.62	73	.287	.355	66-1-2	.212	3	84	-24	—	-2.6
1907	Was A	7	14	.333	34	23	18-2	**4**	211	206	104	1	12	47	102	3.11	78	.258	.309	80-1-3	.237	3*	94	-16	—	-1.2
1908	Was A	18	15	.545	43	31	24-3	4	276.1	224	91	3	6	77	165	2.21	103	.227	.287	87-0-8	.195	2	81	6	—	1.0
1909	Was A	4	7	.364	22	13	7-2	1	120.1	113	56	1	5	33	77	2.69	90	.246	.303	36-0-3	.083	-2	98	-6	—	-0.7
1911	Was A	11	17	.393	34	27	17-2	0	223	251	128	7	4	77	86	3.47	95	.288	.348	81-1-2	.185	-1	90	-6	—	-0.9
1912	Was A	13	10	.565	31	26	11-1	0	196	201	99	8	6	78	108	2.94	113	.270	.344	67-0-3	.194	1	102	6	—	0.7
1913	Was A	4	12	.250	36	12	4	6	129.2	129	81	6	15	61	59	4.30	69	.265	.365	36-0-1	.111	-1	84	-19	—	-2.4
Total	13	132	174	.431	399	313	227-25	15	2644	2610	1292	52	102	853	1368	3.09	93	.260	.324	958-6-39	.198	12	99	-62	—	-6.4
Hughes, Tom	Thomas L. "Salida Tom"; B1.28.1884 Coal Creek CO; D11.1.1961 Los Angeles CA; BR/TR/6´2˝/175; d9.18																									
1906	NY A	1	0	1.000	3	1	1	0	15	11	8	2	0	1	5	4.20	71	.208	.222	5	.200	0	121	-1	—	-0.1
1907	NY A	2	0	1.000	4	3	2	0	27	16	10	0	2	11	10	2.67	105	.174	.276	7-0-1	.143	-0	121	1	—	0.0
1909	NY A	7	8	.467	24	15	9-2	2	118.2	109	42	3	4	37	69	2.65	95	.249	.313	39-1-1	.128	0	104	2	—	0.2
1910	NY A	7	9	.438	23	15	11	1	151.2	153	77	2	3	37	64	3.50	76	.271	.320	55-0-2	.164	-1	89	-12	—	-1.3
1914	Bos N	2	0	1.000	2	2	1	0	17	14	7	0	0	4	11	2.65	104	.226	.273	7	.000	-1	156	0	—	-0.1
1915	Bos N	16	14	.533	**50**	25	17-4	**9**	280.1	208	88	4	11	58	171	2.12	122	.213	.265	90-1-5	.100	-3	72	16	—	1.3
1916	Bos N	16	3	**.842**	40	13	7-1	5	161	121	46	2	8	51	97	2.35	106	.215	.290	52-0-2	.192	2	123	6	—	1.0
1917	Bos N	5	3	.625	11	8	6-2	0	74	54	21	1	3	30	40	1.95	131	.216	.307	24-0-1	.000	-3*	118	5	—	0.2
1918	Bos N	0	2	.000	3	3	1	0	18.1	17	10	1	0	6	9	3.44	78	.250	.311	6-1-0	.333	1	66	-2	—	0.0
Total	9	56	39	.589	160	85	55-9	17	863	703	309	15	31	235	476	2.56	102	.229	.291	285-3-12	.130	-4	97	15	—	1.2
Hughes, Tommy	Thomas Owen; B10.7.1919 Wilkes–Barre PA; D11.28.1990 Wilkes–Barre PA; BR/TR/6´1˝/190; d4.19; Mil 1943–45																									
1941	Phi N	9	14	.391	34	24	5-2	0	170	187	106	12	4	82	59	4.45	83	.280	.362	55-0-4	.200	0*	74	-18	0	-2.0
1942	Phi N	12	18	.400	40	31	19	1	253	224	105	8	0	99	77	3.06	108	.238	.310	80-0-7	.100	-5*	61	4	0	0.1
1946	Phi N	6	9	.400	29	13	3-2	1	111	123	64	5	1	44	34	4.38	78	.281	.349	31-0-2	.097	-1	58	-12	0	-1.7
1947	Phi N	4	11	.267	29	15	4-1	1	127	121	52	5	0	59	44	3.47	115	.265	.350	40-0-1	.050	-4*	57	10	0	0.7
1948	Cin N	0	4	.000	12	4	0	0	27	43	28	3	0	24	7	9.00	43	.364	.472	7	.143	-0	28	-14	0	-1.8
Total	5	31	56	.356	144	87	31-5	3	688	698	355	33	5	308	221	3.92	91	.266	.344	213-0-14	.117	-10	62	-30	0	-4.7
Hughes, Travis	Travis Wade; B5.25.1978 Newton KS; BR/TR/6´5˝/(235–240); [TexA97 19/587]; d9.26; Col Cowley Co. (KS) CC																									
2004	Tex A	0	0	ø	2	0	0	0-0	1.1	4	2	0	0	2-0	4	13.50	37	.500	.600	0	ø	0	—	-1	0	-0.1
2005	Was N	1	1	.500	14	0	0	0-1	13	18	8	4	1	8-1	8	5.54	74	.333	.429	0	ø	0	—	-2	0	-0.3
2006	Was N	0	0	ø	8	0	0	0-0	11.1	13	8	2	3	6-1	4	6.35	69	.310	.423	1	1.000	0	—	-2	0	-0.1
Total	3	1	1	.500	24	0	0	0-1	25.2	35	18	6	4	16-2	16	6.31	68	.337	.440	1	1.000	0	—	-5	0	-0.5
Hughes, Vern	Vernon Alexander "Lefty"; B4.15.1893 Etna PA; D9.26.1961 Sewickley PA; BL/TL/5´10˝/155; d7.6																									
1914	Bal F	0	0	ø	3	0	0	0	5.2	5	4	0	0	3	0	3.18	95	.250	.348	1	.000	-0	—	-1	—	-0.1

YEAR	TM LG	W	L	PCT	G	GS	CG-SHO	SV-BS	IP	H	R	HR	HB	BB-IB	SO	ERA	AERA	OAV	OOB	AB-HR-SH	AVG	PB	SUP	APR	DL	PW
HUGHES, BILL	William Nesbert; B11.18.1896 Philadelphia PA; D2.25.1963 Birmingham AL; BR/TR/5´10.5˝/155; d9.15																									
1921	Pit N	0	0	ø	1	0	0	0	2	3	1	0	1	1	2	4.50	85	.375	.500	0	ø	0	—	0	—	0.0
HUGHES, BILL	William R.; B11.25.1866 Blandinsville IL; D8.25.1943 Santa Ana CA; BL/TL; d9.28.1884; ▲																									
1885	Phi AA	0	2	.000	2	2	2	0	16.2	18	17	0	2	10	4	4.86	71	.269	.380	16	.188	0*	137	-2	—	-0.2
HUGHEY, JIM	James Ulysses "Coldwater Jim"; B3.8.1869 Wakeshma MI; D3.29.1945 Coldwater MI; TR/6´0˝/?; d9.29																									
1891	Mil AA	1	0	1.000	2	1	1	0	15	18	6	0	0	3	9	3.00	146	.286	.318	7	.143	-1	113	3	—	0.1
1893	Chi N	0	1	.000	2	2	1	0	9	14	16	0	1	3	4	11.00	42	.341	.400	2	.000	0	113	-6	—	-0.4
1896	Pit N	6	8	.429	25	14	11	0	155	171	108	3	7	67	48	4.99	84	.278	.355	65	.215	-1	121	-12	—	-1.0
1897	Pit N	6	10	.375	25	17	13	1	149.1	193	115	3	7	45	38	5.06	82	.310	.364	63-0-1	.127	-5	93	-15	—	-1.7
1898	StL N	7	24	.226	35	33	31	0	283.2	325	169	2	11	71	74	3.93	96	.285	.333	97-1-3	.113	-5	66	-3	—	-0.8
1899	Cle N	4	30	.118	36	34	32	0	283	403	244	9	22	88	54	5.41	68	.334	.389	111-0-3	.162	-5	76	-59	—	-6.0
1900	StL N	5	7	.417	20	12	11	0	112.2	147	90	4	6	40	23	5.19	70	.314	.375	41	.171	0	97	-18	—	-1.6
Total	7	29	80	.266	145	113	100	1	1007.2	1271	748	21	54	317	250	4.87	80	.306	.363	386-1-7	.153	-17	85	-110	—	-11.4
HUGHSON, TEX	Cecil Carlton; B2.9.1916 Buda TX; D8.6.1993 San Marcos TX; BR/TR/6´3˝/198; d4.16; Mil 1944–45; Col Texas																									
1941	Bos A	5	3	.625	12	8	4	0	61	70	30	3	1	13	22	4.13	101	.289	.328	17-0-3	.059	-1	86	1	0	0.1
1942	Bos A☆	**22**	6	.786	38	30	**22**-4	4	**281**	258	92	10	1	75	**113**	2.59	144	.245	.296	102-0-7	.176	1	123	**35**	0	3.7
1943	Bos A★	12	15	.444	35	32	**20**-4	2	266	242	87	23	2	73	114	2.64	126	.247	.300	86-0-10	.105	-4	85	20	0	1.6
1944	Bos A★	18	5	**.783**	28	23	19-2	5	203.1	172	57	4	2	41	112	2.26	151	.225	**.267**	66-0-10	.152	-1	140	27	0	3.1
1946	†Bos A	20	11	.645	39	35	21-6	3	278	252	89	15	2	51	172	2.75	133	.238	.274	91-0-10	.132	-2	90	30	0	3.0
1947	Bos A	12	11	.522	29	26	13-3	0	189.1	173	86	17	2	71	119	3.33	117	.244	.314	61-0-4	.033	-6	95	8	0	0.3
1948	Bos A	3	1	.750	15	0	0	0	19.1	21	14	0	0	7	6	5.12	86	.276	.337	2-0-1	.000	-0	—	-2	0	-0.5
1949	Bos A	4	2	.667	29	2	0	3	77.2	82	49	5	1	41	35	5.33	82	.268	.356	22-0-4	.045	-3	113	-7	0	-0.9
Total	8	96	54	.640	225	156	99-19	17	1375.2	1270	504	77	11	372	693	2.94	125	.245	.297	447-0-49	.119	-15	103	112	0	10.4
HUISMAN, JUSTIN	Justin Ray; B4.16.1979 Harvey IL; BR/TR/6´1˝/195; [ColN00 15/437]; d4.25; Col Mississippi																									
2004	KC A	0	0	ø	14	0	0	1-0	25	36	20	3	1	8-3	13	6.84	68	.336	.388	0	ø	0	—	-6	0	-0.3
HUISMAN, RICK	Richard Allen; B5.17.1969 Oak Park IL; BR/TR/6´3˝/(200–210); [SFN90 3/94]; d9.4; Col Lewis; [DL 1997 KC A 66]																									
1995	KC A	0	0	ø	7	0	0	0-0	9.2	14	8	2	0	1-0	12	7.45	64	.333	.349	0	ø	0	—	-3	0	-0.1
1996	KC A	2	1	.667	22	0	0	1-0	29.1	25	15	4	0	18-2	23	4.60	109	.231	.336	0	ø	0	—	2	0	0.2
Total	2	2	1	.667	29	0	0	1-0	39	39	23	6	0	19-2	35	5.31	94	.260	.339	0	ø	0	—	-1	66	0.1
HUISMANN, MARK	Mark Lawrence; B5.11.1958 Littleton CO; BR/TR/6´3˝/(195–205); d8.16; Col Colorado St.																									
1983	KC A	2	1	.667	13	0	0	0-1	30.2	29	20	1	0	17-3	20	5.58	74	.250	.343	0	ø	0	—	-4	0	-0.4
1984	†KC A	3	3	.500	38	0	0	3-1	75	84	38	7	1	21-3	54	4.20	96	.286	.330	0	ø	0	—	-1	0	-0.1
1985	KC A	1	0	1.000	9	0	0	0-0	18.2	14	4	1	0	3-0	9	1.93	217	.219	.246	0	ø	0	—	5	0	0.2
1986	KC A	0	1	.000	10	0	0	1-2	17.1	18	8	1	0	6-0	13	4.15	103	.269	.324	0	ø	0	—	1	0	0.1
	Sea A	3	3	.500	36	1	0	4-3	80	80	39	18	1	19-0	59	3.71	115	.256	.299	0	ø	0	64	4	0	0.3
	Year	3	4	.429	46	1	0	5-5	97.1	98	47	19	1	25-0	72	3.79	113	.259	.304	0	ø	0	64	5	0	0.4
1987	Sea A	0	0	ø	6	0	0	0-0	14.2	10	10	1	2	4-0	15	4.91	97	.196	.276	0	ø	0	—	-1	0	0.0
	Cle A	2	3	.400	20	0	0	2-2	35.1	38	22	6	0	8-0	23	5.09	90	.271	.307	0	ø	0	—	-2	0	-0.2
	Year	2	3	.400	26	0	0	2-2	50	48	32	7	2	12-0	38	5.04	92	.251	.298	0	ø	0	—	-3	0	-0.2
1988	Det A	1	0	1.000	5	0	0	0-0	5.1	6	3	0	0	2-1	6	5.06	76	.286	.348	0	ø	0	—	-1	0	-0.1
1989	Bal A	0	0	ø	8	0	0	1-1	11.1	13	8	0	0	0-0	13	6.35	60	.277	.271	0	ø	0	—	-3	113	-0.1
1990	Pit N	1	0	1.000	2	0	0	0-0	3	6	5	2	1	1-0	2	9.00	41	.462	.533	0	ø	0	—	-3	0	-0.5
1991	Pit N	0	0	ø	5	0	0	0-0	5	7	6	0	0	2-1	5	7.20	50	.304	.360	0	ø	0	—	-3	0	-0.1
Total	9	13	11	.542	152	1	0	11-10	296.1	305	163	37	5	83-8	219	4.40	95	.266	.314	0	ø	0	65	-8	113	-0.9
HULIHAN, HARRY	Harry Joseph; B4.18.1899 Rutland VT; D9.11.1980 Rutland VT; BR/TL/5´11˝/170; d8.16; Col Middlebury																									
1922	Bos N	2	3	.400	7	6	2	0	40	40	23	0	4	26	16	3.15	127	.274	.398	13-0-1	.154	-0	115	2	—	0.1
HULVEY, HANK	James Hensel; B7.18.1897 Mount Sidney VA; D4.9.1982 Mount Sidney VA; BB/TR/6´0˝/180; d9.5; Col Shenandoah																									
1923	Phi A	0	1	.000	1	1	0	0	7	10	6	1	0	2	2	7.71	53	.357	.400	2	.500	0	60	-2	—	-0.2
HUMBER, PHILIP	Philip Gregory; B12.21.1982 Nacogdoches TX; BR/TR/6´4˝/210; [NYN04 1/3]; d9.24; Col Rice																									
2006	NY N	0	0	ø	2	0	0	0-0	2	0	0	0	0	1-0	2	0.00	ø	.000	.143	0	ø	0	—	1	0	0.0
HUME, TOM	Thomas Hubert; B3.29.1953 Cincinnati OH; BR/TR/6´1˝/(175–185); [CinN72*S1/16]; d5.25; C11; Col Manatee (FL) CC																									
1977	Cin N	3	3	.500	14	5	0	0-0	43	54	36	5	0	17-3	22	7.12	55	.305	.364	10-1-2	.200	1	122	-15	0	-1.7
1978	Cin N	8	11	.421	42	23	3	1-2	174	198	89	12	4	50-9	90	4.14	86	.289	.339	45-0-8	.067	-3*	108	-11	0	-1.4
1979	†Cin N	10	9	.526	57	12	2	17-3	163	162	54	12	0	33-9	80	2.76	**134**	.262	.295	46-0-1	.174	0	106	18	0	2.4
1980	Cin N	9	10	.474	78	0	0	25-10	137	121	44	6	3	38-14	68	2.56	138	.240	.296	16-0-1	.188	1	—	14	0	2.6
1981	Cin N	9	4	.692	51	0	0	13-5	67.2	63	27	7	1	31-9	27	3.46	101	.259	.343	4	.000	-0	—	1	0	0.2
1982	Cin N★	2	6	.250	46	0	0	17-2	63.2	57	24	2	1	21-8	22	3.11	118	.245	.306	5	.000	-1	—	4	69	0.6
1983	Cin N	3	5	.375	48	0	0	9-3	66	66	40	8	3	41-11	34	4.77	80	.264	.369	5-0-1	.000	-1	—	-7	25	-1.0
1984	Cin N	4	13	.235	54	8	0	3-4	113.1	142	83	14	1	41-9	59	5.64	67	.309	.363	22	.136	-0	64	-24	0	-3.4
1985	Cin N	3	5	.375	56	0	0	3-2	80	65	33	7	3	35-5	50	3.26	116	.224	.313	5	.000	-1	—	4	0	0.4
1986	Phi N	4	1	.800	48	1	0	4-1	94.1	89	37	5	3	34-5	51	2.77	141	.252	.317	11-0-5	.000	-1	137	10	30	0.5
1987	Phi N	1	4	.200	38	6	0	0-1	70.2	75	48	10	4	41-5	29	5.60	77	.277	.377	15	.200	0	112	-9	0	-0.5
	Cin N	1	0	1.000	11	0	0	0-0	13.1	14	6	0	1	2-0	4	4.05	104	.292	.321	0	ø	0	—	1	0	0.0
	Year	2	4	.333	49	6	0	0-1	84	89	54	10	5	43-5	33	5.36	80	.279	.369	15	.200	0	113	-9	0	-0.5
Total	11	57	71	.445	543	55	5	92-33	1086	1106	521	88	24	384-87	536	3.85	97	.268	.330	184-1-18	.120	-4	103	-14	124	-1.3
HUMPHREY, BILL	Byron William; B6.17.1911 Vienna MO; D2.13.1992 Springfield MO; BR/TR/6´0˝/180; d4.24																									
1938	Bos A	0	0	ø	2	0	0	0	2	5	2	0	0	1	0	9.00	55	.500	.545	0	ø	0	—	-1	—	0.0
HUMPHREYS, BOB	Robert William; B8.18.1935 Covington VA; BR/TR/5´11˝/(168–170); d9.8; Col Hampden–Sydney																									
1962	Det A	0	1	.000	4	0	0	1	5	8	4	3	0	2-0	3	7.20	57	.381	.435	0	ø	0	—	-1	0	-0.3
1963	StL N	0	1	.000	9	0	0	0	10.2	11	8	4	1	7-1	8	5.06	70	.282	.404	0	ø	0	—	-2	31	-0.2
1964	†StL N	2	0	1.000	28	0	0	2	42.2	32	14	3	1	15-3	36	2.53	150	.213	.287	4-0-2	.250	1	—	6	0	0.4
1965	Chi N	2	0	1.000	41	0	0	0	65.2	59	25	6	2	27-6	38	3.15	117	.244	.322	3-0-1	.000	-0	—	5	0	0.2
1966	Was A	7	3	.700	58	1	0	3	111.2	91	38	6	4	28-5	88	2.82	123	.229	.285	12-0-5	.167	1	229	9	0	0.9
1967	Was A	6	2	.750	48	2	0	4	105.2	93	54	13	2	41-3	54	4.17	76	.238	.310	15-0-2	.133	1	69	-11	0	-0.9
1968	Was A	5	7	.417	56	0	0	2	92.2	78	40	13	0	30-2	56	3.69	79	.233	.293	5-0-1	.400	1	—	-7	0	-0.8
1969	Was A	3	3	.500	47	0	0	5-0	79.2	69	37	3	1	38-2	43	3.05	115	.233	.320	13	.077	-1	—	1	0	0.1
1970	Was A	0	0	ø	5	0	0	0-0	6.2	4	2	1	0	9-0	6	1.35	267	.200	.448	0	ø	0	—	1	0	0.1
	Mil A	2	4	.333	23	1	0	3-2	45.2	37	18	3	2	22-3	32	3.15	120	.222	.314	9-0-1	.000	-1	71	3	0	0.3
	Year	2	4	.333	28	1	0	3-2	52.1	41	20	4	2	31-3	38	2.92	128	.219	.332	9-0-1	.000	-1	71	5	0	0.4
Total	9	27	21	.563	319	4	0	20-2	566	482	240	55	13	219-25	364	3.36	102	.234	.309	61-0-12	.131	1	110	4	31	-0.2
HUMPHRIES, BERT	Albert; B9.26.1880 California PA; D9.21.1945 Orlando FL; BR/TR/5´11.5˝/182; d4.16																									
1910	Phi N	0	0	ø	5	0	0	2	9.2	13	8	0	1	3	3	4.66	67	.317	.378	2	.000	0	—	-2	—	-0.1
1911	Phi N	3	1	.750	11	5	2	1	41	56	25	1	6	10	13	4.17	83	.339	.398	15	.333	3	161	-3	—	-0.1
	Cin N	4	3	.571	14	7	3	0	65	62	25	3	6	18	16	2.35	141	.266	.335	16-0-2	.063	-1	101	6	—	0.6
	Year	7	4	.636	25	12	5	1	106	118	50	4	12	28	29	3.06	110	.296	.361	31-0-2	.194	2	127	2	—	0.5
1912	Cin N	9	11	.450	30	15	9-1	2	158.2	162	77	6	8	36	58	3.23	104	.270	.319	51-0-2	.137	-2	74	3	—	0.1
1913	Chi N	16	4	**.800**	28	20	13-2	1	181	169	70	10	2	24	61	2.69	118	.250	.277	62-0-4	.194	1	143	10	—	1.1
1914	Chi N	10	11	.476	34	21	8-2	0	171	162	80	5	2	37	62	2.68	104	.250	.293	55-0-3	.236	2*	96	1	—	0.4
1915	Chi N	8	13	.381	31	22	10-4	3	171.2	183	69	6	5	23	45	2.31	120	.280	.309	46-0-6	.174	0	72	4	—	0.4
Total	6	50	43	.538	153	90	45-9	9	798	807	354	31	30	151	258	2.79	110	.267	.309	247-0-17	.186	3	101	19	—	2.4

YEAR	TM LG	W	L	PCT	G	GS	CG-SHO	SV-BS	IP	H	R	HR	HB	BB-IB	SO	ERA	AERA	OAV	OOB	AB-HR-SH	AVG	PB	SUP	APR	DL	PW
Humphries, Johnny	John William; B6.23.1915 Clifton Forge VA; D6.24.1965 New Orleans LA; BR/TR/6´1˝/185; d5.8; Col North Carolina																									
1938	Cle A	9	8	.529	**45**	6	1	6	103.1	105	69	6	1	63	56	5.23	89	.264	.367	29-0-2	.103	-1	76	-7	—	-1.2
1939	Cle A	2	4	.333	15	1	0	2	28.1	30	30	0	1	32	12	8.26	53	.294	.467	7	.000	-1	60	-13	—	-2.3
1940	Cle A	0	2	.000	19	1	1	1	33.2	35	35	5	2	29	17	8.29	51	.269	.410	6-0-1	.000	-1	21	-16	—	-0.9
1941	Chi A	4	2	.667	14	6	4-4	1	73.1	63	18	2	1	22	25	1.84	223	.230	.290	23-0-1	.087	-1	39	18	0	1.3
1942	Chi A	12	12	.500	28	28	17-2	0	228.1	227	85	9	7	59	71	2.68	134	.257	.309	80-0-3	.225	5	104	21	0	2.6
1943	Chi A	11	11	.500	28	27	8-2	0	188.1	198	86	7	6	54	51	3.30	101	.268	.322	69	.290	5	93	-1	0	0.5
1944	Chi A	8	10	.444	30	20	8	1	169	170	75	9	4	57	42	3.67	93	.267	.331	53-0-3	.189	0	80	-1	0	-0.3
1945	Chi A	6	14	.300	22	21	10-1	1	153	172	83	11	3	48	33	4.24	78	.282	.337	54-0-3	.148	-3	84	-16	0	-2.3
1946	Phi N	0	0	ø	10	1	0	0	24.2	24	17	1	1	9	10	4.01	85	.258	.330	8	.250	0	75	-3	0	-0.2
Total	9	52	63	.452	211	111	49-9	12	1002	1024	498	50	26	373	317	3.78	97	.265	.334	329-0-13	.191	4	84	-18	0	-2.8
Hunt, Ben	Benjamin Franklin "High Pockets"; B11.10.1888 Eufaula OK; D9.27.1927 Greybull WY; BL/TL/6´5˝/190; d8.24																									
1910	Bos A	2	3	.400	7	7	3	0	46.2	45	22	4	0	20	19	4.05	63	.266	.344	18-0-1	.056	-2	105	-5	—	-0.7
1913	StL N	0	1	.000	2	1	0	0	8	6	5	0	1	9	6	3.38	96	.240	.457	2	.000	-0	23	-1	—	-0.1
Total	2	2	4	.333	9	8	3	0	54.2	51	27	4	1	29	25	3.95	67	.263	.362	20-0-1	.050	-2	93	-6	—	-0.8
Hunt, Ken	Kenneth Raymond; B12.14.1938 Ogden UT; BR/TR/6´4˝/225; d4.16; Col Brigham Young																									
1961	†Cin N	9	10	.474	29	22	4	0	136.1	130	70	13	6	66-1	75	3.96	103	.257	.348	39-0-3	.179	0	95	1	0	0.0
Hunter, George	George Henry; B7.8.1887 Buffalo NY; D1.11.1968 Harrisburg PA; BB/TL/5´8.5˝/165; d5.4; twb–Bill; ▲																									
1909	Bro N	4	10	.286	16	13	10	0	113.1	104	48	2	3	38	43	2.46	105	.254	.322	123-0-2	.228	2*	87	-1	—	0.2
Hunter, Catfish	James Augustus "Jim"; B4.8.1946 Hertford NC; D9.9.1999 Hertford NC; BR/TR/6´0˝/(190–202); d5.13; HF1987																									
1965	KC A	8	8	.500	32	20	3-2	0	133	124	68	21	2	46-5	82	4.26	82	.246	.309	40-0-6	.150	-1	103	-10	0	-1.3
1966	KC A☆	9	11	.450	30	25	4	0	176.2	158	87	17	2	64-4	103	4.02	84	.239	.306	59-0-3	.153	1	95	-11	36	-1.3
1967	KC A★	13	17	.433	35	35	13-5	0	259.2	209	91	16	2	84-6	196	2.81	113	.219	.283	92-2-2	.196	4*	91	11	0	1.5
1968	Oak A	13	13	.500	36	34	11-2	1	234	210	99	29	4	69-10	172	3.35	84	.238	.295	82-1-8	.232	5*	126	-14	0	-1.2
1969	Oak A	12	15	.444	38	35	10-3	0-0	247	210	99	34	5	85-1	150	3.35	103	.234	.302	85-1-1	.224	4*	93	4	0	0.8
1970	Oak A★	18	14	.563	40	**40**	9-1	0-0	262.1	253	124	32	9	74-3	178	3.81	93	.250	.304	90-1-6	.200	4*	106	-8	0	-0.7
1971	†Oak A	21	11	.656	37	37	16-4	0-0	273.2	225	103	27	4	80-7	181	2.96	112	.223	.281	103-1-4	.350	13*	111	11	0	2.5
1972	†Oak A☆	21	7	**.750**	38	37	16-5	0-0	295.1	200	74	21	3	70-6	191	2.04	140	.189	.241	105-0-9	.219	3*	123	29	0	3.1
1973	†Oak A★	21	5	**.808**	36	36	11-3	0-0	256.1	222	105	39	1	69-1	124	3.34	107	.232	.282	1	1.000	1*	138	9	0	0.7
1974	†Oak A★	**25**	12	.676	41	41	23-6	0-0	318.1	268	97	25	4	46-2	143	**2.49**	134	.229	**.258**	0	ø	0	121	35	0	3.9
1975	NY A★	**23**	14	.622	39	39	**30**-7	0-0	**328**	248	107	25	5	83-4	177	2.58	144	**.208**	**.261**	0	ø	0	110	42	0	4.4
1976	†NY A★	17	15	.531	36	36	21-2	0-0	298.2	268	126	28	3	68-5	173	3.53	97	.241	.283	1	.000	-0	116	-2	0	-0.3
1977	†NY A	9	9	.500	22	22	8-1	0-0	143.1	137	83	29	3	47-3	52	4.71	84	.250	.310	0	ø	0	127	-12	21	-1.4
1978	†NY A	12	6	.667	21	20	5-1	0-0	118	98	49	16	1	35-0	56	3.58	102	.226	.283	0	ø	0	119	3	44	0.4
1979	NY A	2	9	.182	19	19	1	0-0	105	128	68	15	1	34-0	34	5.31	78	.312	.361	0	ø	0	87	-14	0	-1.3
Total	15	224	166	.574	500	476	181-42	1-0	3449.1	2958	1380	374	49	954-57	2012	3.26	104	.231	.285	658-6-39	.226	33	112	73	101	9.8
Hunter, Jim	James Mac Gregor; B6.22.1964 Jersey City NJ; BR/TR/6´3˝/205; [MonN85 S1/10]; d5.17; Col Georgia																									
1991	Mil A	0	5	.000	8	6	0	0-0	31	45	26	3	4	17-0	14	7.26	55	.349	.437	0	ø	0	88	-11	0	-1.4
Hunter, Rich	Richard Thomas; B9.25.1974 Pasadena CA; BR/TR/6´1˝/185; [PhiN93 14/384]; d4.6																									
1996	Phi N	3	7	.300	14	14	0	0-0	69.1	84	54	10	5	33-2	32	6.49	66	.303	.382	18-0-4	.167	0*	82	-16	0	-1.8
Hunter, Bill	Willard Mitchell "Hawk"; B3.8.1934 Newark NJ; BR/TL/6´2˝/180; d4.16																									
1962	LA N	0	0	ø	1	0	0	0	2	6	10	1	0	4-0	1	40.50	9	.545	.625	0	ø	0	—	-9	0	-0.4
	NY N	1	6	.143	27	6	1	0	63	67	41	9	1	34-0	40	5.57	75	.270	.360	13	.231	0	66	-7	0	-0.7
	Year	1	6	.143	28	6	1	0	65	73	51	10	1	38-0	41	6.65	63	.282	.375	13	.231	0	67	-16	0	-1.1
1964	NY N	3	3	.500	41	0	0	5	49	54	25	4	2	9-1	22	4.41	81	.284	.322	1-0-2	1.000	0	—	-3	0	-0.4
Total	2	4	9	.308	69	6	1	5	114	127	76	14	3	47-1	63	5.68	69	.283	.353	14-0-2	.286	1	71	-19	0	-1.5
Huntzinger, Walt	Walter Henry "Shakes"; B2.6.1899 Pottsville PA; D8.11.1981 Upper Darby PA; BR/TR/6´0˝/150; d9.29; Col Penn																									
1923	NY N	0	1	.000	2	1	0	0	8	9	7	0	0	1	2	7.88	49	.290	.313	2	.000	-0	22	-3	—	-0.4
1924	NY N	1	1	.500	12	2	0	1	32.1	41	19	3	0	9	6	4.45	82	.318	.362	8	.500	1	58	-3	—	-0.1
1925	NY N	5	1	.833	26	1	0	0	64.1	68	30	3	0	17	19	3.50	115	.281	.328	11	.091	-1	230	**4**	—	0.2
1926	StL N	0	4	.000	9	4	2	0	34	35	19	4	0	14	9	4.24	92	.267	.338	8	.000	-1	75	-1	—	-0.2
	Chi N	1	1	.500	11	0	0	2	28.2	26	8	0	3	8	4	0.94	408	.260	.333	7	.143	-1	—	7	—	0.5
	Year	1	5	.167	20	4	2	2	62.2	61	27	4	3	22	13	2.73	142	.264	.336	15	.067	-2	75	6	—	0.3
Total	4	7	8	.467	60	8	2	3	167.1	179	83	10	3	49	40	3.60	108	.283	.337	36	.167	-1	83	4	—	0.0
Hurd, Tom	Thomas Carr "Whitey"; B5.27.1924 Danville VA; D9.5.1982 Waterloo IA; BR/TR/5´9˝/155; d7.30																									
1954	Bos A	2	0	1.000	16	0	0	1	29.2	21	11	2	0	12	14	3.03	135	.198	.277	3	.333	0	—	3	0	0.3
1955	Bos A	8	6	.571	43	0	0	5	80.2	72	32	7	1	38-10	48	3.01	142	.242	.326	14-0-1	.071	-1	—	10	0	1.6
1956	Bos A	3	4	.429	40	0	0	5	76	84	52	5	3	47-2	34	5.33	87	.289	.386	12-0-1	.500	2	—	-5	0	-0.4
Total	3	13	10	.565	99	0	0	11	186.1	177	95	14	4	97-12	96	3.96	111	.255	.345	29-0-2	.276	1	—	8	0	1.5
Hurst, Bruce	Bruce Vee; B3.24.1958 St.George UT; BL/TL/6´3˝/(185–220); [BosA76 1/22]; d4.12																									
1980	Bos A	2	2	.500	12	7	0	0-0	30.2	39	33	4	2	16-0	16	9.10	47	.307	.388	0	ø	0	144	-15	0	-1.7
1981	Bos A	2	0	1.000	5	5	0	0-0	23	23	11	1	1	12-2	11	4.30	91	.258	.346	0	ø	0	115	0	0	0.0
1982	Bos A	3	7	.300	28	19	0	0-0	117	161	87	16	3	40-2	53	5.77	76	.333	.383	0	ø	0	95	-19	0	-1.4
1983	Bos A	12	12	.500	33	32	6-2	0-0	211.1	241	102	22	3	62-5	115	4.09	108	.290	.340	0	ø	0	93	9	0	1.0
1984	Bos A	12	12	.500	33	33	9-2	0-0	218	232	106	25	6	88-3	136	3.92	107	.271	.341	0	ø	0	104	7	0	0.8
1985	Bos A	11	13	.458	35	31	6-1	0-3	229.1	243	123	31	3	70-4	189	4.51	96	.273	.327	0	ø	0	126	-4	0	-0.3
1986	†Bos A	13	8	.619	25	25	11-4	0-0	174.1	169	63	18	3	50-2	167	2.99	140	.256	.310	0	ø	0	91	24	45	2.7
1987	Bos A☆	15	13	.536	33	33	15-3	0-0	238.2	239	124	35	1	76-5	190	4.41	104	.262	.317	0	ø	0	96	5	0	0.6
1988	†Bos A	18	6	.750	33	32	7-1	0-0	216.2	222	98	21	2	65-1	166	3.66	113	.264	.316	0	ø	0	133	10	16	1.1
1989	SD N	15	11	.577	33	33	**10**-2	0-0	244.2	214	84	16	0	66-7	179	2.69	131	.237	.288	70-0-8	.071	-2	94	22	0	2.2
1990	SD N	11	9	.550	33	33	9-**4**	0-0	223.2	188	85	21	1	63-5	162	3.14	122	.228	.284	67-0-7	.090	-2	89	18	0	1.4
1991	SD N	15	8	.652	31	31	4	0-0	221.2	201	89	17	3	59-3	141	3.29	116	.241	.292	67-0-12	.134	-1	103	13	0	1.2
1992	SD N	14	9	.609	32	32	6-4	0-0	217.1	223	96	22	0	51-3	131	3.85	93	.267	.308	69-0-9	.159	1*	109	-3	0	-0.2
1993	SD N	0	1	.000	2	2	0	0-0	4.1	9	7	0	0	3-0	3	12.46	33	.409	.480	0-0-1	ø	0	120	-4	101	-0.7
	Col N	0	1	.000	3	3	0	0-0	8.2	6	5	1	0	3-0	6	5.19	92	.194	.265	1	.000	-0	107	0	42	0.0
	Year	0	2	.000	5	5	0	0-0	13	15	12	1	0	6-0	9	7.62	60	.283	.356	1-0-1	.000	-0	110	-4	0	-0.7
1994	Tex A	2	1	.667	8	8	0	0-0	38	53	30	8	0	16-0	24	7.11	68	.342	.394	0	ø	0	152	-8	0	-0.5
Total	15	145	113	.562	379	359	83-23	0-3	2417.1	2463	1143	258	28	740-42	1689	3.92	104	.265	.319	274-0-37	.113	-3	106	55	204	6.2
Hurst, James	James Lavon; B6.1.1967 Plantation FL; BL/TL/6´0˝/170; [CleA89 32/827]; d4.4; Col Florida Southern																									
1994	Tex A	0	0	ø	8	0	0	0-0	10.2	17	12	1	0	8-1	5	10.13	48	.362	.446	0	ø	0	—	-6	0	-0.3
Hurst, Jonathan	Jonathan; B10.20.1966 New York NY; BR/TR/6´3˝/(175–190); [TexA87 4/103]; d6.9; Col Spartanburg Methodist (SC) JC																									
1992	Mon N	1	1	.500	3	3	0	0-0	16.1	18	10	1	1	7-0	4	5.51	63	.281	.361	4-0-2	.000	-0	95	-3	0	-0.4
1994	NY N	0	1	.000	7	0	0	0-1	10	15	14	5	0	5-0	6	12.60	33	.341	.400	0	ø	0	—	-9	0	-0.7
Total	2	1	2	.333	10	3	0	0-1	26.1	33	24	6	1	12-0	10	8.20	46	.306	.377	4-0-2	.000	-0	95	-12	0	-1.1
Hurst, Bill	William Hansel; B4.28.1970 Miami Beach FL; BR/TR/6´7˝/215; [StLN89 20/510]; d9.18; Col Central Florida CC; [DL 1997 Fla N 30]																									
1996	Fla N	0	0	ø	2	0	0	0-0	2	3	0	0	0	1-0	1	0.00	ø	.333	.400	0	ø	0	—	1	0	0.0
Hurtado, Edwin	Edwin Amilgar; B2.1.1970 Barquisimeto, Lara, Venez.; BR/TR/6´3˝/215; d5.22																									
1995	Tor A	5	2	.714	14	10	1	0-0	77.2	81	50	11	5	40-3	33	5.45	87	.275	.367	0	ø	0	133	-5	0	-0.4
1996	Sea A	2	5	.286	16	4	0	2-1	47.2	61	42	10	0	30-3	36	7.74	64	.324	.408	0	ø	0	84	-14	29	-1.6
1997	Sea A	1	2	.333	13	1	0	0-0	19	25	19	5	2	15-0	10	9.00	50	.329	.447	0	ø	0	142	-9	0	-1.1
Total	3	8	9	.471	43	15	1	2-1	144.1	167	111	26	7	85-6	79	6.67	72	.299	.392	0	ø	0	120	-28	29	-3.1

YEAR	TM LG	W	L	PCT	G	GS	CG-SHO	SV-BS	IP	H	R	HR	HB	BB-IB	SO	ERA	AERA	OAV	OOB	AB-HR-SH	AVG	PB	SUP	APR	DL	PW
Husted, Bill	William J.; B10.19.1866 Gloucester NJ; D5.17.1941 Gloucester NJ; d4.29																									
1890	Phi P	5	10	.333	18	17	12	0	129	148	105	2	5	67	33	4.88	88	.276	.361	56	.107	-6	97	-6	—	-1.0
Husting, Bert	Berthold Juneau "Pete"; B3.6.1878 Fond Du Lac WI; D9.3.1948 Milwaukee WI; BR/TR/5´10.5˝/185; d8.16; Col Wisconsin–Madison																									
1900	Pit N	0	0	ø	2	0	0	0	8	10	5	2	1	5	7	5.63	65	.303	.410	3	.000	-1	—	-1	—	-0.1
1901	Mil A	9	15	.375	34	26	19	1	217.1	234	151	5	13	95	67	4.27	84	.272	.353	94-1-4	.202	-1*	113	-15	—	-1.3
1902	Bos A	0	1	.000	1	1	1	0	8	15	15	0	0	8	4	9.00	40	.395	.500	4	.250	1	80	-6	—	-0.5
	Phi A	14	5	.737	32	27	17-1	0	204	240	126	7	9	91	44	3.79	97	.293	.370	82-0-4	.159	-3	142	-4	—	-0.5
	Year	14	6	.700	33	28	18-1	0	212	255	141	7	9	99	48	3.99	92	.298	.377	86-0-4	.163	-2	140	-9	—	-1.0
Total	3	23	21	.523	69	54	37-1	1	437.1	499	297	14	23	199	122	4.16	87	.285	.366	183-1-8	.180	-4	126	-26	—	-2.4
Hutchings, Johnny	John Richard Joseph; B4.14.1916 Chicago IL; D4.27:1963 Indianapolis IN; BB/TR/6´2˝/250; d4.26																									
1940	†Cin N	2	1	.667	19	4	0	0	54	53	21	3	1	18	18	3.50	108	.260	.323	13	.154	0	75	3	—	0.1
1941	Cin N	0	0	ø	8	0	0	0	11	12	6	0	0	4	5	4.09	88	.279	.340	0	ø	0	—	-1	0	0.0
	Bos N	1	6	.143	36	7	1-1	2	95.2	110	59	6	4	22	36	4.14	86	.287	.333	27-0-1	.148	0	75	-9	0	-0.6
	Year	1	6	.143	44	7	1-1	2	106.2	122	65	6	4	26	41	4.13	86	.286	.333	27-0-1	.148	0	75	-10	0	-0.6
1942	Bos N	1	0	1.000	20	3	0	0	65.2	66	33	2	2	34	27	4.39	76	.260	.352	20	.050	-2	101	-6	0	-0.6
1944	Bos N	1	4	.200	14	7	1	1	56.2	55	30	3	1	26	26	3.97	96	.252	.335	15	.067	-1	75	-1	0	-0.2
1945	Bos N	7	6	.538	57	12	3-2	3	185	173	87	21	4	75	99	3.75	102	.244	.320	54-0-1	.241	2	138	3	0	0.4
1946	Bos N	0	1	.000	1	1	0	0	3	5	3	1	0	1	1	9.00	38	.357	.400	1	.000	-0	25	-2	0	-0.3
Total	6	12	18	.400	155	34	5-3	6	471	474	239	36	12	180	212	3.96	93	.260	.330	130-0-2	.162	-1	99	-13	0	-1.2
Hutchinson, Chad	Chad Martin; B2.21.1977 Boulder CO; BR/TR/6´5˝/230; [StLN98 2/48]; d4.4; Col Stanford																									
2001	StL N	0	0	ø	3	0	0	0-0	4	9	11	3	1	6-0	2	24.75	17	.450	.593	1	.000	-0	—	-9	0	-0.4
Hutchinson, Fred	Frederick Charles; B8.12.1919 Seattle WA; D11.12.1964 Bradenton FL; BL/TR/6´2˝/200; d5.2; Mil 1942–45; M12																									
1939	Det A	3	6	.333	13	12	3	0	84.2	95	56	9	0	51	22	5.21	94	.287	.382	34	.382	3	89	-2	—	0.1
1940	†Det A	3	7	.300	17	10	1	0	76	85	52	6	2	26	32	5.68	84	.281	.342	30	.267	0	91	-6	—	-0.6
1946	Det A	14	11	.560	28	26	16-3	2	207	184	78	14	0	66	138	3.09	118	.236	.295	89-0-2	.315	8*	112	14	0	2.7
1947	Det A	18	10	.643	33	25	18-3	2	219.2	211	84	14	2	61	113	3.03	124	.251	.304	106-2-1	.302	11*	104	18	0	3.7
1948	Det A	13	11	.542	33	28	15	0	221	223	119	32	1	48	92	4.32	101	.258	**.297**	112-1-2	.205	4*	103	2	0	0.8
1949	Det A	15	7	.682	33	21	9-4	1	188.2	167	70	18	1	52	54	2.96	141	.237	**.290**	73-0-4	.247	4*	118	25	0	3.3
1950	Det A	17	8	.680	39	26	10-1	0	231.2	269	119	18	5	48	71	3.96	118	.290	.329	95-0-4	.326	10*	126	15	0	2.5
1951	Det A★	10	10	.500	31	20	9-2	2	188.1	204	84	12	2	27	53	3.68	113	.275	.302	85-0-2	.188	-2*	98	11	0	1.0
1952	Det A	2	1	.667	12	1	0	0	37.1	40	16	4	1	9	12	3.38	113	.276	.323	18	.056	-1*	69	2	0	0.1
1953	Det A	0	0	ø	3	0	0	0	9.2	9	3	0	0	0	4	2.79	146	.243	.243	6-1-0	.167	0*	—	1	0	0.1
Total	10	95	71	.572	242	169	81-13	7	1464	1487	681	127	14	388	591	3.73	113	.262	.311	648-4-15	.264	39	108	80	0	13.7
Hutchinson, Ira	Ira Kendall; B8.31.1910 Chicago IL; D8.21.1973 Chicago IL; BR/TR/5´10.5˝/180; d9.24																									
1933	Chi A	0	0	ø	1	1	0	0	4	7	6	1	0	3	2	13.50	31	.368	.455	2	.500	0	161	-4	—	-0.1
1937	Bos N	4	6	.400	31	8	1	0	91.2	99	44	4	1	35	29	3.73	96	.286	.353	26-0-1	.115	-1	78	-2	—	-0.3
1938	Bos N	9	8	.529	36	12	4-1	4	151	150	58	3	4	61	38	2.74	125	.258	.332	52-0-2	.173	-1	80	11	—	1.2
1939	Bro N	5	2	.714	41	1	0	1	105.2	103	54	9	1	51	46	4.34	93	.265	.352	27-0-1	.037	-3	217	-2	—	-0.4
1940	StL N	4	2	.667	20	2	1	1	63.1	68	27	3	0	19	19	3.13	128	.271	.322	18-0-1	.222	0	120	5	—	0.5
1941	StL N	1	5	.167	29	0	0	5	46.2	32	23	3	2	19	19	3.86	98	.196	.288	8	.250	0	—	0	0	0.0
1944	Bos N	9	7	.563	40	8	1-1	1	119.2	136	59	8	3	53	22	4.21	91	.296	.373	29-0-2	.138	-1	104	-2	0	-0.3
1945	Bos N	2	3	.400	11	0	0	1	28.2	33	18	2	1	8	4	5.02	76	.277	.328	9-0-1	.000	-1	—	-3	0	-0.7
Total	8	34	33	.507	209	32	7-2	13	610.2	628	289	33	12	249	179	3.76	100	.270	.344	171-0-8	.140	-7	94	3	0	-0.1
Hutchison, Bill	William Forrest "Wild Bill"; B12.17.1859 New Haven CT; D3.19.1926 Kansas City MO; BR/TR/5´9˝/175; d6.10; Col Yale																									
1884	KC U	1	1	.500	2	2	2	0	17	14	11	0	—	1	5	2.65	84	.209	.221	8	.250	-0	143	-1	—	-0.1
1889	Chi N	16	17	.485	37	36	33-3	0	318	306	206	11	8	117	136	3.54	118	.246	.315	133-1	.158	-5	90	19	—	1.3
1890	Chi N	**42**	25	.627	**71**	**66**	**65**-5	**2**	**603**	505	315	20	13	199	289	2.70	136	.220	.286	261-2	.203	-4	90	51	—	4.5
1891	Chi N	**44**	19	.698	**66**	**58**	**56**-4	1	**561**	508	283	26	7	178	261	2.81	119	.232	.292	243-2	.185	-1*	101	29	—	2.4
1892	Chi N	**36**	36	.500	**75**	**70**	**67**-5	1	**622**	571	316	11	13	190	**314**	2.76	120	.234	.293	263-1	.217	3*	79	36	—	4.0
1893	Chi N	16	24	.400	44	40	38-2	0	348.1	420	266	9	13	156	80	4.75	97	.289	.364	162	.253	1*	97	-4	—	-0.3
1894	Chi N	14	16	.467	37	34	28	0	279	374	257	9	18	140	60	6.03	93	.318	.399	136-6-2	.309	6*	97	-6	—	-0.1
1895	Chi N	13	21	.382	38	35	30-2	0	291	371	218	13	13	129	85	4.73	108	.306	.378	126	.198	-7	72	11	—	0.3
1897	StL N	1	4	.200	6	5	2	0	40	55	41	5	2	22	5	6.07	72	.324	.407	18	.278	1	55	-8	—	-0.7
Total	9	183	163	.529	376	346	321-21	4	3079.1	3124	1913	104	87	1132	1235	3.59	111	.255	.323	1350-12-2	.216	-6	90	127	—	11.3
Hutson, Herb	George Herbert; B7.17.1949 Savannah GA; BR/TR/6´2˝/219; d4.10; Col Georgia Southern																									
1974	Chi N	0	2	.000	20	2	0	0-0	28.2	24	15	3	1	15-1	22	3.45	111	.233	.325	2	.000	-0	11	0	27	0.0
Hutton, Mark	Mark Steven; B2.6.1970 South Adelaide, South Australia, Australia; BR/TR/6´6˝/(225–240); d7.23																									
1993	NY A	1	1	.500	7	4	0	0-0	22	24	17	2	1	17-0	12	5.73	73	.293	.412	0	ø	0	137	-5	0	-0.4
1994	NY A	0	0	ø	2	0	0	0-0	3.2	4	3	0	0	0-0	1	4.91	94	.250	.250	0	ø	0	—	-1	0	0.0
1996	NY A	0	2	.000	12	2	0	0-0	30.1	32	19	3	1	18-1	25	5.04	98	.269	.364	0	ø	0	37	-1	44	-0.1
	Fla N	5	1	.833	13	9	0	0-0	56.1	47	23	6	3	18-0	31	3.67	112	.222	.291	19-1-1	.316	2	95	4	0	0.6
1997	Fla N	3	1	.750	32	0	0	0-2	47.2	50	24	7	2	19-3	29	3.78	107	.286	.357	0	ø	0	—	0	0	0.1
	Col N	0	1	.000	8	1	0	0-1	12.2	22	10	3	4	7-0	10	7.11	73	.407	.500	3	.000	-0	71	-2	0	-0.2
	Year	3	2	.600	40	1	0	0-3	60.1	72	34	10	6	26-3	39	4.48	96	.314	.392	3	.000	-0	86	-2	0	-0.1
1998	Cin N	0	1	.000	10	2	0	0-0	17	24	14	2	1	17-0	3	7.41	58	.348	.483	1	1.000	0	54	-5	37	-0.2
Total	5	9	7	.563	84	18	0	0-3	189.2	203	110	23	12	96-4	111	4.75	91	.279	.368	23-1-1	.304	3	90	-10	81	-0.2
Hyde, Dick	Richard Elde; B8.3.1928 Hindsboro IL; BR/TR/5´11˝/170; d4.23; Col Illinois																									
1955	Was A	0	0	ø	3	0	0	0	2	2	1	0	0	1-1	1	4.50	85	.286	.375	0	ø	0	—	0	0	0.0
1957	Was A	4	3	.571	52	2	0	1	109.1	104	54	4	7	56-7	46	4.12	95	.261	.356	18	.167	-0	92	-2	0	-0.1
1958	Was A	10	3	.769	53	0	0	18	103	82	26	1	2	35-7	49	1.75	218	.220	.288	18-0-3	.000	-2	—	**21**	0	3.4
1959	Was A	2	5	.286	37	0	0	4	54.1	56	34	5	2	27-3	29	4.97	79	.269	.354	6-0-1	.000	-1	—	-6	0	-0.8
1960	Was A	0	1	.000	9	0	0	0	8.2	11	4	2	1	5-1	4	4.15	94	.355	.459	0	ø	0	—	0	0	0.0
1961	Bal A	1	2	.333	15	0	0	0	21	18	14	1	1	13-3	15	5.57	69	.228	.344	1	1.000	0	—	-4	0	-0.4
Total	6	17	14	.548	169	2	0	23	298.1	273	133	13	13	137-22	144	3.56	109	.249	.336	43-0-4	.093	-2	92	9	0	2.1
Hyndman, Jim	James Harvey; B7.9.1866 Hamilton ON, Can.; D1.16.1934 Alamosa CO; d7.23																									
1886	Phi AA	0	1	.000	1	1	0	0	2	5	10	1	1	5	1	27.00	13	.455	.647	4	.000	-1	288	-5	—	-0.6
Hynes, Pat	Patrick J.; B3.12.1884 St.Louis MO; D3.12.1907 St.Louis MO; TL; d9.27; ▲																									
1903	StL N	0	1	.000	1	1	1	0	9	10	6	0	0	6	1	4.00	82	.294	.400	3	.000	-0	62	-1	—	-0.1
1904	StL A	1	0	1.000	5	2	1	0	26	35	21	1	0	7	6	6.23	40	.321	.362	254-0-6	.236	0*	187	-10	—	-0.5
Total	2	1	1	.500	6	3	2	0	35	45	27	1	0	13	7	5.66	47	.315	.372	257-0-6	.233	0	140	-11	—	-0.6
Iburg, Ham	Herman Edward; B10.30.1873 San Francisco CA; D2.11.1945 San Francisco CA; BR/TR/5´11˝/165; d4.17																									
1902	Phi N	11	18	.379	30	29	20-1	0	236	286	141	1	11	62	106	3.89	72	.299	.349	87	.138	-5*	94	-28	—	-3.5
Ignasiak, Gary	Gary Raymond; B9.1.1949 Anchorville MI; BR/TL/5´11˝/175; [DetA67 36/673]; d9.20; b–Mike																									
1973	Det A	0	0	ø	3	0	0	0-0	4.2	5	2	0	0	3-0	4	3.86	106	.278	.364	0	ø	0	—	0	0	0.0
Ignasiak, Mike	Michael James; B3.12.1966 Mt.Clemens MI; BB/TR/5´11˝/(175–190); [MilA88 8/211]; d8.22; b–Gary; Col Michigan																									
1991	Mil A	2	1	.667	4	1	0	0-0	12.2	7	8	2	0	8-0	10	5.68	70	.163	.294	0	ø	0	92	-2	28	-0.4
1993	Mil A	1	1	.500	27	0	0	0-2	37	32	17	2	2	21-4	28	3.65	118	.241	.350	0	ø	0	—	3	0	0.1
1994	Mil A	3	1	.750	23	5	0	0-1	47.2	51	25	5	1	13-2	24	4.53	112	.276	.325	0	ø	0	65	3	9	0.2
1995	Mil A	4	1	.800	25	0	0	0-1	39.2	51	27	5	2	23-3	26	5.90	85	.325	.411	0	ø	0	—	-3	35	-0.4
Total	4	10	4	.714	79	6	0	0-4	137	141	77	14	5	65-9	88	4.80	99	.272	.356	0	ø	0	71	1	72	-0.5

YEAR	TM LG	W	L	PCT	G	GS	CG-SHO	SV-BS	IP	H	R	HR	HB	BB-IB	SO	ERA	AERA	OAV	OOB	AB-HR-SH	AVG	PB	SUP	APR	DL	PW
ILSLEY, BLAISE	Blaise Francis; B4.9.1964 Alpena MI; BL/TL/6´1˝/195; [HouN85 4/92]; d4.4; Col Indiana St.																									
1994	Chi N	0	0	ø	10	0	0	0-0	15	25	13	2	0	9-2	9	7.80	54	.385	.459	1	.000	-0	—	-5	19	-0.3
IMLAY, DOC	Harry Miller; B1.12.1889 Allentown NJ; D10.7.1948 Bordentown NJ; BR/TR/5´11˝/168; d7.7; Col Penn																									
1913	Phi N	0	0	ø	9	0	0	0	13.2	19	13	1	0	7	7	7.24	46	.358	.433	3	.000	-0	—	-5	—	-0.3
INGERSOLL, BOB	Robert Randolph; B1.8.1883 Rapid City SD; D1.13.1927 Minneapolis MN; BR/TR/5´11.5˝/175; d4.23																									
1914	Cin N	0	0	ø	4	0	0	0	6	5	2	0	1	5	2	3.00	98	.250	.423	1	1.000	0	—	0	—	0.1
INKS, BERT	Albert John; B1.27.1871 Ligonier IN; D10.3.1941 Ligonier IN; BL/TL/6´3˝/175; d9.2																									
1891	Bro N	3	10	.231	13	13	11-1	0	96.1	99	70	2	6	43	47	4.02	82	.256	.339	35	.286	2	74	-8	—	-0.7
1892	Bro N	4	2	.667	9	8	4-1	0	58	48	34	0	4	33	25	3.88	82	.216	.328	25	.400	3	155	-4	—	0.0
	Was N	1	2	.333	3	3	3	0	21	29	27	0	2	10	11	5.14	63	.315	.394	10	.300	1	136	-6	—	-0.6
	Year	5	4	.556	12	11	7-1	0	79	77	61	0	6	43	36	4.22	76	.245	.347	35	.371	4	150	-9	—	-0.6
1894	Bal N	9	4	.692	22	14	10	1	133	181	108	4	11	54	30	5.55	99	.321	.391	57-0-1	.316	2*	95	-1	—	0.0
	Lou N	2	6	.250	8	8	8	0	59.2	87	70	2	1	34	8	6.49	79	.336	.415	27	.444	3	83	-11	—	-0.8
	Year	11	10	.524	30	22	18	1	192.2	268	178	6	12	88	38	5.84	92	.326	.399	84-0-1	.357	5	91	-10	—	-0.8
1895	Lou N	7	20	.259	28	27	21	0	205.1	294	197	3	15	78	42	6.40	72	.331	.394	84-0-1	.250	-0	81	-35	—	-3.1
1896	Phi N	0	1	.000	3	1	0	0	10.1	21	13	1	1	5	2	7.84	55	.412	.474	5	.200	-0	66	-4	—	-0.4
	Cin N	1	1	.500	3	3	2	0	20	21	13	0	1	9	2	4.50	103	.269	.352	7	.000	-1	62	0	—	-0.1
	Year	1	2	.333	6	4	2	0	30.1	42	26	1	2	14	4	5.64	80	.326	.400	12	.083	-1	63	-3	—	-0.5
Total	5	27	46	.370	89	77	59-2	1	603.2	780	532	12	41	266	167	5.52	81	.307	.382	250-0-2	.300	9	89	-69	—	-5.7
INNIS, JEFF	Jeffrey David; B7.5.1962 Decatur IL; BR/TR/6´0˝/(168–180); [NYN83 13/318]; d5.16; Col Illinois																									
1987	NY N	0	1	.000	17	1	0	0-0	25.2	29	9	5	1	4-1	28	3.16	121	.279	.312	3	.000	-0	71	3	0	0.1
1988	NY N	1	1	.500	12	0	0	0-0	19	19	6	0	0	2-1	14	1.89	172	.250	.266	0	ø	0	—	2	0	0.2
1989	NY N	0	1	.000	29	0	0	0-0	39.2	38	16	2	1	8-0	16	3.18	104	.255	.296	2	.000	-0	—	0	0	0.0
1990	NY N	1	3	.250	18	0	0	1-1	26.1	19	9	4	1	10-3	12	2.39	157	.209	.288	0-0-1	ø	0	—	4	0	0.5
1991	NY N	0	2	.000	69	0	0	0-3	84.2	66	30	2	0	23-6	47	2.66	138	.219	.270	2	.000	-0	—	9	0	0.6
1992	NY N	6	9	.400	76	0	0	1-3	88	85	32	4	6	36-4	39	2.86	122	.266	.347	2	.000	-0	—	6	0	1.1
1993	NY N	2	3	.400	67	0	0	3-2	76.2	81	39	5	6	38-12	36	4.11	98	.278	.372	0-0-2	ø	0	—	0	0	0.0
Total	7	10	20	.333	288	1	0	5-9	360	337	141	22	15	121-27	192	3.05	120	.253	.319	9-0-3	.000	-1	71	24	0	2.5
IOTT, HOOKS	Clarence Eugene; B12.3.1919 Mountain Grove MO; D8.17.1980 St.Petersburg FL; BB/TL/6´2˝/200; d9.6; Mil 1943–45																									
1941	StL A	0	0	ø	2	0	0	0	2	2	2	0	0	1	1	9.00	48	.250	.333	0	ø	0	—	-1	0	0.0
1947	StL A	0	1	.000	4	0	0	0	8.1	15	16	4	0	14	6	16.20	24	.375	.537	2	.000	-0	—	-10	0	-1.0
	NY N	3	8	.273	20	9	2-1	0	71.1	67	50	3	1	52	46	5.93	69	.251	.375	21-0-2	.143	1	132	-13	0	-1.6
Total	2	3	9	.250	26	9	2-1	0	81.2	84	68	7	1	67	53	7.05	58	.267	.397	23-0-2	.130	1	132	-24	0	-2.6
IRABU, HIDEKI	Hideki; B5.5.1969 Hyogo, Japan; BR/TR/6´4˝/(240–250); d7.10																									
1997	NY A	5	4	.556	13	9	0	0-0	53.1	69	47	15	1	20-0	56	7.09	63	.311	.367	1	.000	-0	144	-16	0	-2.2
1998	NY A	13	9	.591	29	28	2-1	0-0	173	148	79	27	9	76-1	126	4.06	108	.233	.321	4-0-1	.250	0	105	8	0	0.8
1999	†NY A	11	7	.611	32	27	2-1	0-0	169.1	180	98	26	6	46-0	133	4.84	98	.267	.317	4-0-2	.000	-0	144	-1	0	-0.2
2000	Mon N	2	5	.286	11	11	0	0-0	54.2	77	45	9	1	14-0	42	7.24	65	.339	.377	16-0-2	.125	-1	108	-13	124	-1.4
2001	Mon N	0	2	.000	3	3	0	0-0	16.2	22	9	3	0	3-0	18	4.86	89	.314	.338	3	.000	-0	36	-1	139	-0.1
2002	Tex A	3	8	.273	38	2	0	16-4	47	51	30	11	1	16-2	30	5.74	83	.279	.337	0	ø	0	68	-4	79	-0.7
Total	6	34	35	.493	126	80	4-2	16-4	514	547	308	91	18	175-3	405	5.15	89	.272	.333	28-0-5	.107	-1	120	-27	342	-3.8
IRVINE, DARYL	Daryl Keith; B11.15.1964 Harrisonburg VA; BR/TR/6´3˝/195; [BosA85*S1/20]; d4.28; Col Ferrum																									
1990	Bos A	1	1	.500	11	0	0	0-0	17.1	15	10	0	0	10-3	9	4.67	88	.246	.338	0	ø	0	—	-1	0	-0.1
1991	Bos A	0	0	ø	9	0	0	0-0	18	25	13	2	2	9-1	8	6.00	72	.321	.404	0	ø	0	—	-3	67	-0.1
1992	Bos A	3	4	.429	21	0	0	0-3	28	31	20	1	2	14-2	10	6.11	70	.287	.370	0	ø	0	—	-5	0	-0.9
Total	3	4	5	.444	41	0	0	0-3	63.1	71	43	3	4	33-6	27	5.68	74	.287	.372	0	ø	0	—	-9	67	-1.1
IRWIN, BILL	William Franklin "Phil"; B9.16.1859 Neville OH; D8.7.1933 Ft.Thomas KY; BR/TR/6´0˝/195; d8.30																									
1886	Cin AA	0	2	.000	2	2	2	0	17	18	19	2	0	8	6	5.82	60	.247	.321	6	.000	-0	59	-5	—	-0.4
ISBELL, FRANK	William Frank "Bald Eagle"; B8.21.1875 Delevan NY; D7.15.1941 Wichita KS; BL/TR/5´11˝/190; d5.1; ▲																									
1898	Chi N	4	7	.364	13	9	7	0	81	86	54	0	7	42	16	3.56	101	.270	.368	159-0-6	.233	-0*	101	-1	—	-0.1
1901	Chi A	0	0	ø	1	0	0	0	1	2	1	0	0	0	0	9.00	39	.400	.400	556-3-13	.257	0*	—	0	—	0.0
1902	Chi A	0	0	ø	1	1	0	0	1	3	2	0	0	1	1	9.00	38	.500	.571	515-4-23	.252	0*	212	-1	—	0.0
1906	†Chi A	0	0	ø	1	0	0	0	2	1	0	0	0	0	2	0.00	ø	.143	.143	549-0-31	.279	0*	—	1	—	0.0
1907	Chi A	0	0	ø	1	0	0	1	0.1	0	0	0	0	0	0	0.00	ø	.000	.000	486-0-24	.243	0*	—	0	—	0.0
Total	5	4	7	.364	17	10	7	1	85.1	92	57	0	7	43	19	3.59	99	.273	.367	2265-7-97	.257	1	112	-1	—	-0.1
ISHII, KAZUHISA	Kazuhisa; B9.9.1973 Tokyo, Japan; BL/TL/6´0˝/(187–215); d4.6																									
2002	LA N	14	10	.583	28	28	0	0-0	154	137	82	20	4	106-3	143	4.27	91	.240	.360	50-0-4	.100	-2	112	-8	21	-1.3
2003	LA N	9	7	.563	27	27	0	0-0	147	129	72	16	6	101-4	140	3.86	107	.238	.363	34-0-9	.029	-3	82	3	31	0.0
2004	LA N	13	8	.619	31	31	2-2	0-0	172	155	97	21	4	98-2	99	4.71	88	.246	.348	55-1-6	.127	-1	128	-12	0	-1.5
2005	NY N	3	9	.250	19	16	0	0-0	91	87	59	13	3	49-3	53	5.14	80	.257	.354	25-0-4	.200	0	93	-12	28	-1.3
Total	4	39	34	.534	105	102	2-2	0-0	564	508	310	70	17	354-12	435	4.44	92	.244	.356	164-1-23	.110	-5	106	-29	80	-4.1
ISRINGHAUSEN, JASON	Jason Derik; B9.7.1972 Brighton IL; BR/TR/6´3˝/(196–230); [NYN91 44/1157]; d7.17; Col Lewis & Clark (IL) CC; [DL 1998 NY N 181]																									
1995	NY N	9	2	.818	14	14	1	0-0	93	88	29	6	2	31-2	55	2.81	144	.254	.317	27-0-4	.148	1	96	15	0	1.7
1996	NY N	6	14	.300	27	27	2-1	0-0	171.2	190	103	13	8	73-5	114	4.77	84	.284	.357	51-2-2	.255	6	90	-14	19	-0.8
1997	NY N	2	2	.500	6	6	0	0-0	29.2	40	27	3	1	22-0	25	7.58	53	.336	.438	7-0-1	.143	-0	150	-12	148	-1.3
1999	NY N	1	3	.250	13	5	0	1-0	39.1	43	29	7	2	22-2	31	6.41	68	.279	.374	12-0-1	.083	-0	135	-10	0	-0.9
	Oak A	0	1	.000	20	0	0	8-0	25.1	21	6	2	1	12-2	20	2.13	222	.223	.318	0	ø	0	—	8	0	0.7
2000	†Oak A★	6	4	.600	66	0	0	33-7	69	67	34	6	3	32-5	57	3.78	128	.252	.338	0	ø	0	—	8	0	1.4
2001	†Oak A	4	3	.571	65	0	0	34-9	71.1	54	24	5	0	23-5	74	2.65	172	.203	.266	0	ø	0	—	15	0	2.4
2002	†StL N	3	2	.600	60	0	0	32-5	65.1	46	22	0	1	18-1	68	2.48	163	.199	.257	0	ø	0	—	10	0	1.6
2003	StL N	0	1	.000	40	0	0	22-3	42	31	14	2	0	18-1	41	2.36	175	.200	.283	2	.500	1	—	7	72	0.9
2004	†StL N	4	2	.667	74	0	0	**47**-7	75.1	55	27	5	2	23-4	71	2.87	149	.199	.265	3	.333	0	—	11	0	2.1
2005	†StL N☆	1	2	.333	63	0	0	39-4	59	43	14	4	1	27-5	51	2.14	196	.202	.293	0	ø	0	—	14	16	2.4
2006	StL N	4	8	.333	59	0	0	33-10	58.1	47	25	10	3	38-3	52	3.55	123	.222	.344	0	ø	0	—	5	0	1.0
Total	11	40	44	.476	507	52	3-1	249-45	799.1	725	354	63	24	339-35	659	3.59	118	.242	.321	102-2-8	.206	7	100	57	436	11.2
IZQUIERDO, HANSEL	Hansel; B1.2.1977 Havana, Cuba; BR/TR/6´2˝/205; [FlaN95 7/177]; d4.21																									
2002	Fla N	2	0	1.000	20	2	0	0-0	29.2	33	17	2	5	21-3	20	4.55	86	.289	.413	2	.000	-0	71	-3	0	-0.2
JACKSON, AL	Alvin Neill; B12.26.1935 Waco TX; BL/TL/5´10˝/(165–173); d6.1; C8; Col Wiley																									
1959	Pit N	0	0	ø	8	3	0	0	18	30	14	1	0	8-3	13	6.50	60	.405	.463	5	.200	0	239	-5	0	-0.3
1961	Pit N	1	0	1.000	3	2	1	0	23.2	20	10	2	0	4-1	15	3.42	117	.233	.267	8	.000	-1*	167	2	0	0.0
1962	NY N	8	20	.286	36	33	12-4	0	231.1	244	132	16	5	78-5	118	4.40	95	.273	.333	73-0-6	.068	-5*	83	-5	0	-0.7
1963	NY N	13	17	.433	37	34	11	1	227	237	128	25	12	84-2	142	3.96	88	.267	.336	79-0-3	.203	2*	82	-15	0	-1.6
1964	NY N	11	16	.407	40	31	11-3	1	213.1	229	115	18	4	60-3	112	4.26	84	.272	.323	72-1-2	.153	2*	72	-16	0	-1.6
1965	NY N	8	20	.286	37	31	7-3	1	205.1	217	111	17	8	61-4	120	4.34	81	.271	.328	60-0-8	.117	-1*	64	-17	0	-2.2
1966	StL N	13	15	.464	36	30	11-3	0	232.2	222	82	18	3	45-10	90	2.51	143	.250	.288	74-0-5	.176	2*	75	25	0	3.5
1967	StL N	9	4	.692	38	11	1-1	1	107	117	61	7	1	29-5	43	3.95	83	.279	.322	31-0-1	.258	2*	172	-12	0	-1.0
1968	NY N	3	7	.300	25	9	0	3	92.2	88	42	5	2	17-6	59	3.69	82	.249	.285	28-0-1	.250	1*	86	-7	0	-0.6
1969	NY N	0	0	ø	9	0	0	0-0	11	18	13	1	1	4-0	10	10.64	34	.353	.397	1	.000	-0	—	-8	0	-0.4
	Cin N	1	0	1.000	33	0	0	3-0	27.1	27	17	5	3	17-3	16	5.27	71	.260	.376	4	.250	0	—	-4	0	-0.2
	Year	1	0	1.000	42	0	0	3-0	38.1	45	30	6	4	21-3	26	6.81	55	.290	.383	5	.200	0	—	-11	0	-0.6
Total	10	67	99	.404	302	184	54-14	10-0	1389.1	1449	725	115	39	407-42	738	3.98	91	.268	.322	435-1-26	.159	3	86	-62	0	-5.1

JACKSON, HERBERT Herbert; TR; d8.11

YEAR	TM LG	W	L	PCT	G	GS	CG-SHO	SV-BS	IP	H	R	HR	HB	BB-IB	SO	ERA	AERA	OAV	OOB	AB-HR-SH	AVG	PB	SUP	APR	DL	PW
1905	Det A	0	2	.000	2	2	1	0	11	14	12	1	0	7	3	5.73	48	.311	.404	4	.250	0	39	-4	—	-0.6

JACKSON, DANNY Danny Lynn; B1.5.1962 San Antonio TX; BR/TL/6´0˝/(190–220); [KCA82*S1/1]; d9.11; Col Oklahoma

YEAR	TM LG	W	L	PCT	G	GS	CG-SHO	SV-BS	IP	H	R	HR	HB	BB-IB	SO	ERA	AERA	OAV	OOB	AB-HR-SH	AVG	PB	SUP	APR	DL	PW
1983	KC A	1	1	.500	4	3	0	0-0	19	26	12	1	0	6-0	9	5.21	79	.325	.372	0	ø	0	111	-2	0	-0.2
1984	KC A	2	6	.250	15	11	1	0-0	76	84	41	4	5	35-0	40	4.26	95	.285	.370	0	ø	0	81	-3	0	-0.3
1985	†KC A	14	12	.538	32	32	4-3	0-0	208	209	94	7	6	76-2	114	3.42	122	.261	.328	0	ø	0	82	15	0	1.7
1986	KC A	11	12	.478	32	27	4-1	1-0	185.2	177	83	13	4	79-1	115	3.20	134	.256	.334	0	ø	0	62	17	14	1.9
1987	KC A	9	18	.333	36	34	11-2	0-1	224	219	115	11	7	109-1	152	4.02	114	.258	.344	0	ø	0	67	13	0	1.3
1988	Cin N☆	**23**	8	.742	35	35	**15**-6	0-0	260.2	206	86	13	2	71-6	161	2.73	131	.218	.273	90-0-8	.144	-0	114	24	0	3.0
1989	Cin N	6	11	.353	20	20	1	0-0	115.2	122	78	10	1	57-7	70	5.60	64	.271	.351	36-0-4	.222	1*	87	-23	56	-3.0
1990	†Cin N	6	6	.500	22	21	0	0-0	117.1	119	54	11	2	40-4	76	3.61	110	.266	.325	37-0-4	.054	-2*	87	3	54	0.0
1991	Chi N	1	5	.167	17	14	0	0-0	70.2	89	59	8	1	48-4	31	6.75	58	.309	.407	23-0-2	.087	-1	119	-21	94	-1.8
1992	Chi N	4	9	.308	19	19	0	0-0	113	117	59	5	3	48-3	51	4.22	86	.270	.343	36-0-4	.083	-2	79	-7	0	-1.0
	†Pit N	4	4	.500	15	15	0	0-0	88.1	94	40	1	1	29-3	46	3.36	103	.276	.330	24-0-5	.083	-1	120	-1	0	-0.2
	Year	8	13	.381	34	34	0	0-0	201.1	211	99	6	4	77-6	97	3.84	93	.272	.337	60-0-9	.083	-3	96	-9	0	-1.2
1993	†Phi N	12	11	.522	32	32	2-1	0-0	210.1	214	105	12	4	80-2	120	3.77	105	.263	.329	65-0-12	.077	-2	116	3	0	0.0
1994	Phi N★	14	6	.700	25	25	4-1	0-0	179.1	183	71	13	2	46-1	129	3.26	131	.266	.312	57-0-9	.158	1*	123	21	0	2.3
1995	StL N	2	12	.143	19	19	2-1	0-0	100.2	120	82	10	6	48-1	52	5.90	73	.303	.381	31-0-4	.161	0	83	-21	69	-2.4
1996	†StL N	1	1	.500	13	4	0	0-0	36.1	33	18	3	1	16-1	27	4.46	95	.243	.325	9-0-1	.333	1	117	0	124	0.2
1997	StL N	1	2	.333	4	4	0	0-0	18.2	26	17	3	2	8-1	13	7.71	54	.347	.414	7	.143	-0	105	-7	49	-0.9
	SD N	1	7	.125	13	9	0	0-0	49	72	47	8	3	20-2	19	7.53	52	.353	.413	13-0-1	.077	-0	91	-22	0	-2.9
	Year	2	9	.182	17	13	0	0-0	67.2	98	64	11	5	28-3	32	7.58	53	.351	.413	20-0-1	.100	-1	96	-29	0	-3.8
Total	15	112	131	.461	353	324	44-15	1-1	2072.2	2110	1061	133	50	816-39	1225	4.01	100	.266	.336	428-0-54	.126	-6	93	-11	460	-2.3

JACKSON, DARRELL Darrell Preston; B4.3.1956 Los Angeles CA; BB/TL/5´10˝/(143–151); [MinA77 9/223]; d6.16; Col Arizona St.

YEAR	TM LG	W	L	PCT	G	GS	CG-SHO	SV-BS	IP	H	R	HR	HB	BB-IB	SO	ERA	AERA	OAV	OOB	AB-HR-SH	AVG	PB	SUP	APR	DL	PW
1978	Min A	4	6	.400	19	15	1-1	0-0	92.1	89	53	9	2	48-1	54	4.48	86	.256	.347	0	ø	0	90	-7	0	-0.7
1979	Min A	4	4	.500	24	8	1	0-1	69.1	89	36	5	1	26-0	43	4.28	103	.319	.377	0	ø	0*	106	1	0	0.1
1980	Min A	9	9	.500	32	25	1	1-0	172	161	81	15	2	69-2	90	3.87	113	.250	.323	0	ø	0*	81	10	0	1.0
1981	Min A	3	3	.500	14	5	0	0-0	32.2	35	16	1	1	19-2	26	4.41	90	.282	.382	0	ø	0	50	-1	96	-0.2
1982	Min A	0	5	.000	13	7	0	0-0	44.2	51	33	6	1	24-3	16	6.25	68	.297	.384	0	ø	0	37	-9	52	-0.9
Total	5	20	27	.426	102	60	3-1	1-1	411	425	219	36	7	186-8	229	4.38	96	.272	.349	0	ø	0	79	-6	148	-0.7

JACKSON, EDWIN Edwin; B9.9.1983 Neu–Ulm, West Germany; BR/TR/6´3˝/190; [LAN01 6/190]; d9.9

YEAR	TM LG	W	L	PCT	G	GS	CG-SHO	SV-BS	IP	H	R	HR	HB	BB-IB	SO	ERA	AERA	OAV	OOB	AB-HR-SH	AVG	PB	SUP	APR	DL	PW
2003	LA N	2	1	.667	4	3	0	0-0	22	17	6	2	1	11-1	19	2.45	168	.221	.322	6-0-1	.000	-0	68	4	0	0.5
2004	LA N	2	1	.667	8	5	0	0-0	24.2	31	20	7	0	11-1	16	7.30	57	.307	.375	4-0-2	.250	0	157	-8	60	-0.8
2005	LA N	2	2	.500	7	6	0	0-0	28.2	31	22	2	1	17-0	13	6.28	66	.272	.366	10	.200	0*	117	-7	0	-0.8
2006	TB A	0	0	ø	23	1	0	0-0	36.1	42	27	2	1	25-0	27	5.45	85	.292	.395	0	ø	0	101	-4	0	-0.2
Total	4	6	4	.600	42	15	0	0-0	111.2	121	75	13	3	64-2	75	5.48	79	.278	.370	20-0-3	.150	0	116	-15	60	-1.3

JACKSON, GRANT Grant Dwight "Buck"; B9.28.1942 Fostoria OH; BB/TL (BL 1971–79)/6´0˝/(180–204); d9.3; C4; Col Bowling Green

YEAR	TM LG	W	L	PCT	G	GS	CG-SHO	SV-BS	IP	H	R	HR	HB	BB-IB	SO	ERA	AERA	OAV	OOB	AB-HR-SH	AVG	PB	SUP	APR	DL	PW
1965	Phi N	1	1	.500	6	2	0	0	13.2	17	11	4	0	5-0	15	7.24	48	.304	.361	4	.000	-0	101	-5	0	-0.7
1966	Phi N	0	0	ø	2	0	0	0	1.2	2	1	0	0	3-0	0	5.40	67	.333	.556	0	ø	0	—	0	0	0.0
1967	Phi N	2	3	.400	43	4	0	1	84.1	86	40	3	2	43-7	83	3.84	89	.267	.352	15	.133	-0	103	-3	0	-0.3
1968	Phi N	1	6	.143	33	6	1	1	61	59	28	4	0	20-3	49	2.95	102	.248	.302	10-0-1	.300	1*	149	-2	0	-0.1
1969	Phi N☆	14	18	.438	38	35	13-4	1-0	253	237	114	16	5	92-3	180	3.34	107	.249	.316	86-1-6	.140	-0*	87	2	0	0.2
1970	Phi N	5	15	.250	32	23	1	0-0	149.2	170	94	17	1	61-3	104	5.29	76	.288	.354	44-0-1	.091	-2*	49	-21	0	-2.6
1971	†Bal A	4	3	.571	29	9	0	0-0	77.2	72	31	7	2	20-5	51	3.13	109	.249	.299	22-1-0	.091	0	105	2	0	0.2
1972	Bal A	1	1	.500	32	0	0	8-0	41	33	14	1	0	9-0	34	2.63	118	.217	.261	4	.000	-0	—	2	0	0.1
1973	†Bal A	8	0	1.000	45	0	0	9-2	80.1	54	18	5	0	24-4	47	1.90	198	.198	.260	0	ø	0	—	17	0	2.1
1974	†Bal A	6	4	.600	49	0	0	12-7	66.2	48	19	7	1	22-4	56	2.57	136	.198	.265	0	ø	0	—	8	0	1.5
1975	Bal A	4	3	.571	41	0	0	7-1	48.1	42	18	3	1	21-6	39	3.35	106	.241	.322	0	ø	0	—	2	0	0.3
1976	Bal A	1	1	.500	13	0	0	3-0	19.1	19	11	1	2	9-2	14	5.12	64	.268	.361	0	ø	0	—	-4	0	-0.5
	†NY A	6	0	1.000	21	2	1-1	1-0	58.2	38	11	1	1	16-0	25	1.69	202	.186	.244	0	ø	0	206	12	0	1.2
	Year	7	1	.875	34	2	1-1	4-0	78	57	22	2	3	25-2	39	2.54	133	.207	.276	0	ø	0	208	9	0	0.7
1977	Pit N	5	3	.625	49	2	0	4-2	91	81	44	11	1	39-8	41	3.86	104	.240	.318	18	.333	2	111	1	0	0.3
1978	Pit N	7	5	.583	60	0	0	5-3	77.1	89	32	5	1	32-9	45	3.26	115	.298	.362	12	.250	1	—	4	0	0.8
1979	†Pit N	8	5	.615	72	0	0	14-5	82	67	32	9	2	35-5	39	2.96	132	.230	.311	9	.000	-1	—	8	0	1.3
1980	Pit N	8	4	.667	61	0	0	9-3	71	71	24	4	0	20-3	31	2.92	127	.275	.322	10	.000	-1	—	7	0	1.1
1981	Pit N	1	2	.333	35	0	0	4-2	32.1	30	10	1	0	10-3	17	2.51	146	.248	.301	2	.000	-0	—	4	0	0.4
	Mon N	1	0	1.000	10	0	0	0-0	10.2	14	9	2	0	9-2	4	7.59	47	.333	.451	0	ø	0	—	-4	0	-0.4
	Year	2	2	.500	45	0	0	4-2	43	44	19	3	0	19-5	21	3.77	96	.270	.342	2	.000	-0	—	0	0	0.0
1982	KC A	3	1	.750	20	0	0	0-2	38.1	42	27	7	2	21-4	15	5.17	79	.271	.363	0	ø	0	—	-6	0	-0.6
	Pit N	0	0	ø	1	0	0	0-0	0.2	1	1	1	0	0-0	0	13.50	28	.333	.333	0	ø	0	—	-1	0	0.0
Total	18	86	75	.534	692	83	16-5	79-27	1358.2	1272	589	109	21	511-71	889	3.46	105	.251	.318	236-2-8	.136	-2	85	23	0	4.3

JACKSON, JOHN John Lewis; B7.15.1909 Philadelphia PA; D10.22.1956 Somers Point NJ; BR/TR/6´2˝/180; d6.20; Col Penn

YEAR	TM LG	W	L	PCT	G	GS	CG-SHO	SV-BS	IP	H	R	HR	HB	BB-IB	SO	ERA	AERA	OAV	OOB	AB-HR-SH	AVG	PB	SUP	APR	DL	PW
1933	Phi N	2	2	.500	10	7	1	0	54	74	42	3	5	35	11	6.00	64	.329	.430	21	.143	-1	112	-11	—	-1.0

JACKSON, LARRY Lawrence Curtis; B6.2.1931 Nampa ID; D8.28.1990 Boise ID; BR/TR/6´2˝/(175–190); d4.17; Col Boise St.

YEAR	TM LG	W	L	PCT	G	GS	CG-SHO	SV-BS	IP	H	R	HR	HB	BB-IB	SO	ERA	AERA	OAV	OOB	AB-HR-SH	AVG	PB	SUP	APR	DL	PW
1955	StL N	9	14	.391	37	25	4-1	2	177.1	189	93	25	9	72-11	88	4.31	94	.277	.351	57-0-1	.053	-6	86	-5	0	-1.2
1956	StL N	2	2	.500	51	1	0	9	85.1	75	44	5	1	45-8	50	4.11	92	.240	.337	11	.091	-0	70	-3	0	-0.1
1957	StL N★	15	9	.625	41	22	6-2	1	210.1	196	84	21	4	57-8	96	3.47	114	.248	.301	72-0-3	.181	0	99	14	0	1.8
1958	StL N★	13	13	.500	49	23	11-1	8	198	211	93	21	10	51-11	124	3.68	112	.272	.324	60-0-2	.150	-2*	101	8	0	0.7
1959	StL N	14	13	.519	40	37	12-3	0	256	271	103	13	4	64-3	145	3.30	128	.270	.315	80-0-7	.112	-3*	88	25	0	2.1
1960	StL N★	18	13	.581	43	**38**	14-3	0	**282**	277	123	22	3	70-4	171	3.48	118	.257	.302	95-0-5	.211	2*	96	17	0	1.8
1961	StL N	14	11	.560	33	28	12-3	0	211	203	99	20	4	56-5	113	3.75	117	.252	.301	74-0-6	.176	0*	93	16	0	1.8
1962	StL N	16	11	.593	36	35	11-2	0	252.1	267	121	25	6	64-6	112	3.75	114	.269	.316	89-0-5	.169	2	104	13	0	1.5
1963	Chi N★	14	18	.438	37	37	13-4	0	275	256	102	11	6	54-3	153	2.55	137	.245	.284	87-0-9	.195	2	79	23	0	3.1
1964	Chi N	**24**	11	.686	40	38	19-3	0	297.2	265	114	17	1	58-8	148	3.14	118	.235	.272	114-0-5	.175	1	110	18	0	2.5
1965	Chi N	14	21	.400	39	39	12-4	0	257.1	268	126	28	5	57-8	131	3.85	96	.267	.309	86-1-4	.128	1*	81	-3	0	-0.2
1966	Chi N	0	2	.000	3	2	0	0	8	14	13	3	0	4-0	5	13.50	27	.368	.429	3	.000	-0	12	-8	0	-1.3
	Phi N	15	13	.536	35	33	12-5	0	247	243	93	22	5	58-5	107	2.99	120	.259	.305	89-1-5	.146	-0*	93	16	0	1.8
	Year	15	15	.500	38	35	12-**5**	0	255	257	106	25	5	62-5	112	3.32	108	.264	.310	92-1-5	.141	-1	88	6	0	0.5
1967	Phi N	13	15	.464	40	37	11-4	0	261.2	242	111	17	6	54-11	139	3.10	110	.241	.283	87-0-4	.161	0*	89	6	0	0.9
1968	Phi N	13	17	.433	34	34	12-2	0	243.2	229	86	9	4	60-15	127	2.77	108	.248	.296	85-0-2	.141	-0*	91	6	0	0.8
Total	14	194	183	.515	558	429	149-37	20	3262.2	3206	1405	259	68	824-106	1709	3.40	113	.256	.304	1089-2-58	.156	-5	93	143	0	16.0

JACKSON, MIKE Michael Ray; B12.22.1964 Houston TX; BR/TR/6´0˝/(185–225); [PhiN84*S2/44]; d8.11; Col Hill (TX) JC; [DL 2000 Phi N 177]

YEAR	TM LG	W	L	PCT	G	GS	CG-SHO	SV-BS	IP	H	R	HR	HB	BB-IB	SO	ERA	AERA	OAV	OOB	AB-HR-SH	AVG	PB	SUP	APR	DL	PW
1986	Phi N	0	0	ø	9	0	0	0-1	13.1	12	5	2	2	4-1	3	3.38	116	.250	.333	0	ø	0	—	1	0	0.0
1987	Phi N	3	10	.231	55	7	0	1-1	109.1	88	55	16	3	56-6	93	4.20	102	.219	.316	17-0-3	.118	-0	105	2	15	0.1
1988	Sea A	6	5	.545	62	0	0	4-7	99.1	74	37	10	2	43-10	76	2.63	159	.209	.291	0	ø	0	—	14	0	1.6
1989	Sea A	4	6	.400	65	0	0	7-3	99.1	81	43	8	6	54-6	94	3.17	127	.223	.332	0	ø	0	—	8	0	0.8
1990	Sea A	5	7	.417	63	0	0	3-9	77.1	64	42	8	2	44-12	69	4.54	88	.229	.333	0	ø	0	—	-4	0	-0.5
1991	Sea A	7	7	.500	72	0	0	14-8	88.2	64	35	5	6	34-11	74	3.25	128	.201	.290	0	ø	0	—	9	0	1.4
1992	SF N	6	6	.500	67	0	0	2-1	82	76	35	7	4	33-10	80	3.73	89	.252	.331	2	.000	-0	—	-3	0	-0.4
1993	SF N	6	6	.500	**81**	0	0	1-5	77.1	58	28	7	3	24-6	70	3.03	130	.204	.272	3	.667	2	—	8	16	1.3
1994	SF N	3	2	.600	36	0	0	4-2	42.1	23	8	4	2	11-0	51	1.49	273	.164	.234	1-0-1	.000	-0	—	12	51	1.5
1995	†Cin N	6	1	.857	40	0	0	2-2	49	38	13	5	1	19-1	41	2.39	175	.213	.291	4	.250	0	—	10	41	1.4
1996	Sea A	1	1	.500	73	0	0	6-2	72	61	32	11	6	24-3	70	3.63	137	.225	.301	0	ø	0	—	11	0	0.5
1997	†Cle A	2	5	.286	71	0	0	15-2	75	59	33	3	4	29-5	74	3.24	145	.215	.297	0	ø	0	—	10	0	1.3
1998	†Cle A	1	1	.500	69	0	0	40-5	64	43	11	4	4	13-0	55	1.55	309	.195	.252	0	ø	0	—	**23**	0	3.0
1999	†Cle A	3	4	.429	72	0	0	39-4	68.2	60	32	11	2	26-1	55	4.06	125	.232	.304	0	ø	0	—	8	0	1.5
2001	†Hou N	5	3	.625	67	0	0	4-5	69	68	36	14	2	22-3	46	4.70	98	.260	.319	1	.000	-0	—	1	0	0.0
2002	†Min A	2	3	.400	58	0	0	0-2	55	59	20	5	4	13-3	29	3.27	136	.284	.333	0	ø	0	—	8	23	0.7

YEAR	TM LG	W	L	PCT	G	GS	CG-SHO	SV-BS	IP	H	R	HR	HB	BB-IB	SO	ERA	AERA	OAV	OOB	AB-HR-SH	AVG	PB	SUP	APR	DL	PW
2004	Chi A	2	0	1.000	45	0	0	0-0	46.2	55	27	7	3	15-2	26	5.01	94	.294	.351	0	ø	0	—	-1	0	-0.1
Total	17	62	67	.481	1005	7	0	142-59	1188.1	983	492	127	56	464-80	1006	3.42	126	.226	.306	28-0-4	.179	1	105	117	323	14.1
JACKSON, MIKE	Michael Warren; B3.27.1946 Paterson NJ; BL/TL/6´3˝/(185–190); d5.10																									
1970	Phi N	1	1	.500	5	0	0	0-0	6.1	6	1	0	0	4-0	4	1.42	283	.286	.400	1	1.000	0	—	2	0	0.4
1971	StL N	0	0	ø	1	0	0	0-0	0.2	1	0	0	0	1-0	0	0.00	ø	.333	.500	1	.000	-0	—	0	0	0.0
1972	KC A	1	2	.333	7	3	0	0-0	19.2	24	14	0	0	14-1	15	6.41	48	.320	.422	5-0-1	.000	-1	87	-7	0	-1.0
1973	KC A	0	0	ø	9	0	0	0-0	22.1	25	17	3	1	20-1	13	6.85	60	.301	.438	0	ø	0	—	-6	0	-0.3
	Cle A	0	0	ø	1	0	0	0-0	0.2	1	0	0	0	0-0	1	0.00	ø	.333	.333	0	ø	0	—	0	0	0.0
	Year	0	0	ø	10	0	0	0-0	23	26	17	3	1	20-1	14	6.65	62	.302	.435	0	ø	0	—	-5	0	-0.3
Total	4	2	3	.400	23	3	0	0-0	49.2	57	32	3	1	39-2	33	5.80	63	.308	.427	7-0-1	.143	-0	87	-11	0	-0.9
JACKSON, ROY LEE	Roy Lee; B5.1.1954 Opelika AL; BR/TR/6´2˝/(190–223); d9.13; Col Tuskegee																									
1977	NY N	0	2	.000	4	4	0	0-0	24	25	16	2	3	15-1	13	6.00	63	.263	.377	6-0-1	.000	-1	94	-5	0	-0.5
1978	NY N	0	0	ø	4	2	0	0-0	12.2	21	13	2	2	6-0	6	9.24	38	.429	.500	3	.667	1	89	-7	0	-0.3
1979	NY N	1	0	1.000	8	0	0	0-1	16.1	11	4	1	1	5-0	10	2.20	169	.200	.279	1	1.000	0	—	3	0	0.2
1980	NY N	1	7	.125	24	8	1	1-0	70.2	78	37	4	0	20-4	58	4.20	86	.287	.331	16	.188	0*	102	-5	0	-0.5
1981	Tor A	1	2	.333	39	0	0	7-1	62	65	23	5	1	25-7	27	2.61	152	.275	.346	0	ø	0	—	8	0	0.6
1982	Tor A	8	8	.500	48	2	0	6-5	97	77	37	7	2	31-4	71	3.06	147	.218	.281	0	ø	0	111	14	0	2.3
1983	Tor A	8	3	.727	49	0	0	7-5	92	92	48	6	3	41-2	48	4.50	97	.267	.344	0	ø	0	—	0	0	0.0
1984	Tor A	7	8	.467	54	0	0	10-7	86	73	40	12	1	31-4	58	3.56	116	.230	.299	0	ø	0	—	4	0	0.8
1985	SD N	2	3	.400	22	2	0	2-0	40	32	13	4	1	13-1	28	2.70	132	.224	.289	5-0-1	.000	-1	62	4	0	0.5
1986	Min A	0	1	.000	28	0	0	1-0	58.1	57	29	7	3	16-0	32	3.86	113	.256	.308	0	ø	0	—	2	0	0.1
Total	10	28	34	.452	280	18	1	34-19	559	531	260	50	17	203-23	351	3.77	108	.254	.322	31-0-2	.194	1	88	18	0	3.2
JACKSON, ZACH	Zachary Thomas; B5.13.1983 Greensburg PA; BL/TL/6´5˝/220; [TorA04 1/32]; d6.4; Col Texas A&M																									
2006	Mil N	2	2	.500	8	7	0	0-0	38.1	48	26	6	4	14-0	22	5.40	83	.304	.373	9-0-4	.111	-0	109	-4	0	-0.5
JACOBS, TONY	Anthony Robert; B8.5.1925 Dixmoor IL; D12.21.1980 Nashville TN; BB/TR/5´9˝/150; d9.19																									
1948	Chi N	0	0	ø	1	0	0	0	2	3	1	1	0	0	2	4.50	87	.333	.333	0	ø	0	—	0	0	0.0
1955	StL N	0	0	ø	1	0	0	0	2	6	4	1	0	1-0	1	18.00	23	.500	.538	1	.000	-0	—	-3	0	-0.1
Total	2	0	0	ø	2	0	0	0	4	9	5	2	0	1-0	3	11.25	35	.429	.455	1	.000	-0	—	-3	0	-0.1
JACOBS, ART	Arthur Edward; B8.28.1902 Luckey OH; D6.8.1967 Inglewood CA; BL/TL/5´10˝/170; d6.18																									
1939	Cin N	0	0	ø	1	0	0	1	1	2	1	0	0	1	0	9.00	43	.400	.500	0	ø	0	—	-1	—	-0.1
JACOBS, BUCKY	Newton Smith; B3.21.1913 Altavista VA; D6.15.1990 Richmond VA; BR/TR/5´11˝/155; d6.27; Col Richmond																									
1937	Was A	1	1	.500	11	1	0	0	22.1	26	12	0	0	11	8	4.84	92	.295	.374	5	.000	-1	39	0	—	-0.1
1939	Was A	0	0	ø	2	0	0	0	3	1	0	0	0	0	1	0.00	ø	.100	.100	0	ø	0	—	2	—	0.1
1940	Was A	0	1	.000	9	0	0	0	15	16	11	1	2	9	6	6.00	69	.271	.386	1-0-1	.000	-0	—	-3	—	-0.1
Total	3	1	2	.333	22	1	0	0	40.1	43	23	1	2	20	15	4.91	88	.274	.363	6-0-1	.000	-1	39	-1	—	-0.1
JACOBS, ELMER	William Elmer; B8.10.1892 Salem MO; D2.10.1958 Salem MO; BR/TR/6´0˝/165; d4.23																									
1914	Phi N	1	3	.250	14	7	1	0	50.2	65	38	2	3	20	17	4.80	61	.342	.413	14	.000	-2	104	-9	—	-0.8
1916	Pit N	6	10	.375	34	17	8	0	153	151	70	2	4	38	46	2.94	91	.258	.308	40-0-1	.075	-2	95	-5	—	-0.8
1917	Pit N	6	19	.240	38	25	10-1	2	227.1	214	87	3	5	76	58	2.81	101	.262	.329	67-0-3	.179	-1	69	1	—	0.1
1918	Pit N	0	1	.000	8	4	0	0	23.1	31	18	0	0	14	2	5.79	50	.344	.433	7	.286	0	151	-7	—	-0.3
	Phi N	9	5	.643	18	14	12-4	1	123	91	39	3	4	42	33	2.41	124	.210	.285	38-0-2	.158	-1	94	8	—	0.8
	Year	9	6	.600	26	18	12-4	1	146.1	122	57	3	4	56	35	2.95	101	.233	.312	45-0-2	.178	-1	106	2	—	0.5
1919	Phi N	6	10	.375	17	15	13	0	128.2	150	66	5	6	44	37	3.85	84	.304	.368	45-0-1	.178	-1	86	-8	—	-1.0
	StL N	3	6	.333	17	8	4-1	1	85.1	81	30	2	5	25	31	2.53	110	.264	.329	23-0-1	.348	3	89	3	—	0.7
	Year	9	16	.360	34	23	17-1	1	214	231	96	7	11	69	68	3.32	92	.289	.353	68-0-2	.235	2	87	-5	—	-0.3
1920	StL N	4	8	.333	23	9	1	1	77.2	91	56	2	5	33	21	5.21	57	.296	.374	26-0-3	.192	-0	105	-20	—	-2.8
1924	Chi N	11	12	.478	38	22	13-1	1	190.1	181	93	9	2	72	50	3.74	104	.258	.329	54-0-6	.111	-4	92	4	—	0.1
1925	Chi N	2	3	.400	18	4	1-1	1	55.2	63	37	9	1	22	19	5.17	84	.274	.340	13	.231	-0	112	-5	—	-0.4
1927	Chi A	2	4	.333	25	8	2-1	0	74.1	105	49	3	4	37	22	4.60	88	.354	.432	20-0-4	.150	-1	95	-6	—	-0.5
Total	9	50	81	.382	250	133	65-9	7	1189.1	1223	583	40	39	423	336	3.55	91	.275	.343	347-0-21	.161	-8	91	-44	—	-4.9
JACOBSON, BEANY	Albert Leonard (b Albin Leonard Jacobson); B6.5.1881 Port Washington WI; D1.31.1933 Decatur IL; BL/TL/6´0˝/170; d4.30																									
1904	Was A	5	23	.179	33	30	23-1	0	253.2	276	135	6	3	57	75	3.55	75	.278	.319	88-0-1	.091	-6	66	-24	—	-3.0
1905	Was A	7	8	.467	22	17	12	0	144.1	139	83	1	5	35	50	3.30	80	.255	.305	44	.159	1	96	-13	—	-1.3
1906	StL A	9	9	.500	24	15	12	0	155	146	68	3	4	27	53	2.50	103	.252	.290	55-0-1	.091	-4	93	0	—	-0.5
1907	StL A	1	6	.143	7	7	6	0	57.1	55	28	1	0	26	16	2.98	84	.255	.335	18-0-1	.222	-0	54	-4	—	-0.5
	Bos A	0	0	ø	2	1	0	0	2	2	3	0	0	3	1	9.00	29	.250	.455	0	ø	0	52	-1	—	-0.1
	Year	1	6	.143	9	8	6	0	59.1	57	31	1	0	29	17	3.19	79	.254	.340	18-0-1	.222	-0	54	-5	—	-0.6
Total	4	22	46	.324	88	70	53-1	0	612.1	618	317	11	12	148	195	3.19	82	.264	.311	205-0-3	.117	-9	78	-42	—	-5.4
JACOBUS, LARRY	Stuart Louis; B12.13.1894 Cincinnati OH; D8.19.1965 N.College Hill OH; BB/TR/6´2˝/186; d7.15																									
1918	Cin N	0	1	.000	5	0	0	0	17.1	25	12	0	0	1	8	5.71	47	.368	.377	5	.000	-1	—	-5	—	-0.4
JACOME, JASON	Jason James; B11.24.1970 Tulsa OK; BL/TL/6´1˝/(155–185); [NYN91 12/329]; d7.2; Col Pima (AZ) CC																									
1994	NY N	4	3	.571	8	8	1-1	0-0	54	54	17	3	0	17-2	30	2.67	157	.269	.324	16-0-1	.063	-1	76	10	0	1.1
1995	NY N	0	4	.000	5	5	0	0-0	21	33	24	3	1	15-0	11	10.29	39	.359	.450	7-0-1	.000	-1	112	-14	0	-2.0
	KC A	4	6	.400	15	14	1	0-0	84	101	52	15	1	21-2	39	5.36	90	.300	.340	0	ø	0	98	-4	0	-0.3
1996	KC A	0	4	.000	49	2	0	1-3	47.2	67	27	5	2	22-5	32	4.72	107	.337	.408	0	ø	0	129	2	0	0.2
1997	KC A	0	0	ø	7	0	0	0-0	6.2	13	7	2	1	5-1	3	9.45	50	.448	.543	0	ø	0	—	-3	0	-0.1
	Cle A	2	0	1.000	21	4	0	0-1	42.2	45	26	8	0	15-4	24	5.27	89	.269	.328	0	ø	0	112	-2	0	-0.1
	Year	2	0	1.000	28	4	0	0-1	49.1	58	33	10	1	20-5	27	5.84	81	.296	.362	0	ø	0	112	-5	0	-0.2
1998	Cle A	0	1	.000	1	1	0	0-0	5	10	8	2	0	3-0	2	14.40	33	.435	.500	0	ø	0	78	-5	0	-0.6
Total	5	10	18	.357	106	34	2-1	1-4	261	323	161	38	5	98-14	141	5.34	87	.308	.368	23-0-2	.043	-2	97	-16	0	-1.8
JACQUEZ, PAT	Patrick Thomas; B4.23.1947 Stockton CA; BR/TR/6´0˝/200; [ChiN67*S4/67]; d4.18; s–Thomas; Col Santa Clara																									
1971	Chi A	0	0	ø	2	0	0	0-0	2	4	1	0	0	2-0	1	4.50	79	.444	.500	1	.000	-0	—	0	0	0.0
JACQUEZ, THOMAS	Thomas Patrick; B12.29.1975 Stockton CA; BL/TL/6´2˝/195; [PhiN97 6/176]; d9.9; f–Pat; Col UCLA																									
2000	Phi N	0	0	ø	9	0	0	1-0	7.1	10	9	2	0	3-1	6	11.05	42	.333	.382	0	ø	0	—	-5	0	-0.2
JAECKEL, JAKE	Paul Henry; B4.1.1942 E.Los Angeles CA; BR/TR/5´10˝/180; d9.19																									
1964	Chi N	1	0	1.000	4	0	0	1	8	4	0	0	0	3-0	2	0.00	ø	.160	.250	1	.000	-0	—	3	0	0.5
JAEGER, CHARLIE	Charles Thomas; B4.17.1875 Ottawa IL; D9.27.1942 Ottawa IL; BR/TR; d9.9																									
1904	Det A	3	3	.500	8	6	5	0	49	49	29	0	6	15	13	2.57	99	.261	.335	17	.059	-2	65	-3	—	-0.6
JAEGER, JOE	Joseph Peter "Zip"; B3.3.1895 St.Cloud MN; D12.13.1963 Hampton IA; BR/TR/6´1˝/190; d7.28																									
1920	Chi N	0	0	ø	2	0	0	0	3	6	6	0	0	4	0	12.00	27	.500	.625	1	.000	-0	—	-3	—	-0.2
JAKUCKI, SIG	Sigmund "Jack"; B8.20.1909 Camden NJ; D5.28.1979 Galveston TX; BR/TR/6´2.5˝/198; d8.30																									
1936	StL A	0	3	.000	7	2	0	0	20.2	32	22	2	1	12	9	8.71	62	.348	.429	6	.000	-1	90	-7	—	-0.8
1944	†StL A	13	9	.591	35	24	12-4	3	198	211	89	17	3	54	67	3.55	101	.268	.318	73-1-2	.151	-2*	109	3	0	0.2
1945	StL A	12	10	.545	30	24	15-1	2	192.1	188	84	9	1	65	55	3.51	100	.257	.318	70-2-3	.186	0	105	1	0	0.1
Total	3	25	22	.532	72	50	27-5	5	411	431	195	28	5	131	131	3.79	96	.268	.325	149-3-5	.161	-2	106	-3	0	-0.5
JAMERSON, LEFTY	Charles Dewey "Charlie"; B1.26.1900 Enfield IL; D8.4.1980 Mocksville NC; BL/TL/6´1˝/195; d8.16; Col Arkansas																									
1924	Bos A	0	0	ø	1	0	0	0	1	1	2	0	0	3	0	18.00	24	.250	.571	0	ø	0	—	-1	—	-0.1

YEAR	TM LG	W	L	PCT	G	GS	CG-SHO	SV-BS	IP	H	R	HR	HB	BB-IB	SO	ERA	AERA	OAV	OOB	AB-HR-SH	AVG	PB	SUP	APR	DL	PW
JAMES, CHUCK	Charles Hamilton; B11.9.1981 Atlanta GA; BL/TL/6´0˝/190; [AtlN02 20/605]; d9.28; Col Chattahoochee Valley (AL) CC																									
2005	Atl N	0	0	ø	2	0	0	0-0	5.2	4	1	0	0	3-0	5	1.59	266	.200	.304	1	1.000	0	—	2	0	0.1
2006	Atl N	11	4	.733	25	18	0	0-0	119	101	54	20	6	47-2	91	3.78	120	.232	.310	35-0-4	.029	-3	117	10	32	0.8
Total	2	11	4	.733	27	18	0	0-0	124.2	105	55	20	6	50-2	96	3.68	123	.230	.310	36-0-4	.056	-2	117	12	32	0.9
JAMES, DELVIN	Delvin Dewayne; B1.3.1978 Nacogdoches TX; BR/TR/6´4˝/222; [TBA96 14/424]; d4.16																									
2002	TB A	0	3	.000	8	6	0	0-0	34.1	40	25	5	1	15-1	17	6.55	69	.301	.373	0	ø	0	58	-7	35	-0.5
JAMES, JEFF	Jeffrey Lynn "Jesse"; B9.29.1941 Indianapolis IN; D5.7.2006 Indianapolis IN; BR/TR/6´3˝/(196–200); d4.13; Col Indiana St.																									
1968	Phi N	4	4	.500	29	13	1-1	0	115.2	112	61	8	4	46-2	83	4.28	70	.256	.330	33-0-1	.121	-1	102	-16	0	-1.2
1969	Phi N	2	2	.500	6	5	1	0-0	31.2	36	20	5	0	14-1	21	5.40	66	.288	.357	11	.182	-0	104	-6	0	-0.7
Total	2	6	6	.500	35	18	2-1	0-0	147.1	148	81	13	4	60-3	104	4.52	69	.263	.336	44-0-1	.136	-1	104	-22	0	-1.9
JAMES, JOHNNY	John Phillip; B7.23.1933 Bonners Ferry ID; BL/TR/5´10˝/160; d9.6; Col USC																									
1958	NY A	0	0	ø	1	0	0	0	3	2	0	0	0	4-0	1	0.00	ø	.250	.500	1	.000	-0	—	1	0	0.1
1960	NY A	5	1	.833	28	0	0	2	43.1	38	22	3	3	26-2	29	4.36	82	.248	.362	3	.000	-0	—	-3	0	-0.4
1961	NY A	0	0	ø	1	0	0	0	1.1	1	0	0	0	0-0	2	0.00	ø	.250	.250	0	ø	0	—	1	0	0.0
	LA A	0	2	.000	36	3	0	0	71.1	66	44	12	2	54-1	41	5.30	85	.246	.375	13	.000	-1*	85	-4	0	-0.3
	Year	0	2	.000	37	3	0	0	72.2	67	44	12	2	54-1	43	5.20	86	.246	.374	13	.000	-1	85	-4	0	-0.3
Total	3	5	3	.625	66	3	0	2	119	107	66	15	5	84-3	73	4.76	87	.247	.373	17	.000	-2	93	-5	0	-0.6
JAMES, MIKE	Michael Elmo; B8.15.1967 Ft.Walton Beach FL; BR/TR/6´3˝/(180–205); [LAN87 43/1064]; d4.29; Col Lurleen Wallace St. (AL) JC; [DL 1999 Ana A 155]																									
1995	Cal A	3	0	1.000	46	0	0	1-1	55.2	49	27	6	3	26-2	36	3.88	121	.238	.332	0	ø	0	—	5	21	0.2
1996	Cal A	5	5	.500	69	0	0	1-5	81	62	27	7	10	42-7	65	2.67	189	.214	.329	0	ø	0	—	21	0	2.2
1997	Ana A	5	5	.500	58	0	0	7-6	62.2	69	32	3	5	28-4	57	4.31	107	.283	.367	0	ø	0	—	2	24	0.4
1998	Ana A	0	0	ø	11	0	0	0-0	14	10	3	0	0	7-0	12	1.93	246	.208	.309	0	ø	0	—	4	146	0.2
2000	†StL N	2	2	.500	51	0	0	2-3	51.1	40	22	7	3	24-2	41	3.16	147	.219	.318	1	.000	-0*	—	7	24	0.5
2001	StL N	1	2	.333	40	0	0	0-0	38	43	24	5	5	17-2	26	5.21	83	.293	.382	1	.000	-0	—	-4	56	-0.3
2002	Col N	0	0	ø	13	0	0	0-0	11.1	12	9	2	1	5-0	10	5.56	85	.267	.353	0	ø	0	—	-1	0	-0.1
Total	7	16	14	.533	288	0	0	11-15	314	285	144	30	27	149-17	247	3.67	129	.245	.342	2	.000	-0	—	34	426	3.1
JAMES, RICK	Richard Lee; B10.11.1947 Sheffield AL; BR/TR/6´2.5˝/200; [ChiN65 1/6]; d9.20																									
1967	Chi N	0	1	.000	3	1	0	0	4.2	9	8	1	0	2-0	2	13.50	26	.529	.550	1	.000	-0	74	-5	0	-0.9
JAMES, BOB	Robert Harvey; B8.15.1958 Glendale CA; BR/TR/6´4˝/(215–230); [MonN76 1/9]; d9.7																									
1978	Mon N	0	1	.000	4	1	0	0-0	4	4	4	1	0	4-0	3	9.00	40	.267	.421	0	ø	0	101	-2	0	-0.4
1979	Mon N	0	0	ø	2	0	0	0-0	2	2	3	0	0	3-1	1	13.50	28	.250	.455	0	ø	0	—	-2	0	-0.1
1982	Mon N	0	0	ø	7	0	0	0-0	9	10	6	0	0	8-1	11	6.00	62	.294	.409	0	ø	0	—	-2	0	-0.1
	Det A	0	2	.000	12	1	0	0-1	19.2	22	13	4	0	8-0	20	5.03	81	.278	.345	0	ø	0	156	-2	0	-0.2
1983	Det A	0	0	ø	4	0	0	0-0	4	5	5	2	0	3-0	4	11.25	35	.313	.421	0	ø	0	—	-3	0	-0.2
	Mon N	1	0	1.000	27	0	0	7-0	50	37	17	3	3	23-2	56	2.88	126	.210	.312	7	.286	0	—	4	0	0.3
1984	Mon N	6	6	.500	62	0	0	10-9	96	92	47	6	4	45-7	91	3.66	95	.251	.333	14	.143	-0	—	-4	0	-0.6
1985	Chi A	8	7	.533	69	0	0	32-9	110	90	31	5	2	23-4	88	2.13	204	.226	.268	0	ø	0	—	**25**	0	4.5
1986	Chi A	5	4	.556	49	0	0	14-8	58.1	61	36	8	4	23-3	32	5.25	83	.268	.340	0	ø	0	—	-5	49	-0.9
1987	Chi A	4	6	.400	43	0	0	10-2	54	54	32	10	4	17-6	34	4.67	99	.256	.321	0	ø	0	—	-1	36	-0.2
Total	8	24	26	.480	279	2	0	73-29	407	377	194	39	17	157-24	340	3.80	106	.246	.319	21	.190	0	123	8	85	2.1
JAMES, LEFTY	William A.; B7.1.1889 Glen Roy OH; D5.3.1933 Glen Roy OH; BL/TL/5´11.5˝/175; d4.13																									
1912	Cle A	0	1	.000	3	1	0	1	6	8	9	0	2	4	2	7.50	45	.348	.483	3	.000	-0	22	-3	—	-0.6
1913	Cle A	2	3	.400	11	4	3	0	39	42	27	0	3	9	18	3.00	101	.275	.327	13-0-1	.231	-0	116	-3	—	-0.4
1914	Cle A	0	3	.000	17	6	1	0	50.2	44	23	0	2	32	16	3.20	90	.251	.373	12	.000	-1	97	-1	—	-0.1
Total	3	2	7	.222	31	11	4	1	95.2	94	59	0	7	45	36	3.39	88	.268	.362	28-0-1	.107	-1	96	-7	—	-1.1
JAMES, BILL	William Henry "Big Bill"; B1.20.1887 Detroit MI; D5.25.1942 Venice CA; BB/TR/6´4˝/195; d6.12																									
1911	Cle A	2	4	.333	8	6	4	0	51.2	58	37	1	2	32	21	4.88	70	.284	.387	17-0-1	.059	-1	99	-8	—	-0.9
1912	Cle A	0	0	ø	3	0	0	0	13.2	15	11	0	0	9	5	4.61	74	.288	.393	3-0-1	.000	-0	—	-2	—	-0.2
1914	StL A	15	14	.517	44	35	20-3	1	284	269	121	4	6	109	109	2.85	95	.257	.330	89-0-4	.112	-3	97	-4	—	-0.5
1915	StL A	6	10	.375	34	22	8	1	170.1	155	89	2	7	92	58	3.59	80	.255	.359	42-0-6	.190	1	86	-11	—	-0.8
	Det A	7	3	.700	11	9	3-1	0	67	57	26	1	0	33	24	2.42	125	.243	.336	21-0-1	.286	2	110	4	—	0.8
	Year	13	13	.500	45	31	11-1	1	237.1	212	115	3	7	125	82	3.26	89	.251	.352	63-0-7	.222	2	93	-10	—	0.0
1916	Det A	8	12	.400	30	20	8	1	151.2	141	76	1	11	79	61	3.68	78	.255	.360	44-0-6	.068	-3	90	-12	—	-2.0
1917	Det A	13	10	.565	34	23	10-2	1	198	163	71	2	12	96	62	2.09	127	.229	.330	57-0-2	.211	2	108	11	—	1.6
1918	Det A	6	11	.353	19	18	8-1	0	122	127	68	3	5	68	42	3.76	71	.279	.379	46	.109	-3	97	-17	—	-2.4
1919	Det A	1	0	1.000	2	1	0	0	9.1	12	6	0	0	7	3	5.79	55	.324	.432	4	.250	0	343	-2	—	-0.2
	Bos A	3	5	.375	13	7	4	0	72.2	74	42	2	3	39	12	4.09	74	.280	.379	21-0-3	.143	-1	100	-10	—	-1.0
	†Chi A	3	2	.600	5	5	3-2	0	39.1	39	12	0	2	14	11	2.52	126	.281	.355	14-0-1	.143	-1	103	4	—	0.3
	Year	7	7	.500	20	13	7-2	0	121.1	125	60	2	5	60	26	3.71	83	.284	.376	39-0-4	.154	-2	121	-8	—	-0.9
Total	8	64	71	.474	203	146	68-9	4	1179.2	1110	559	16	48	578	408	3.20	88	.258	.352	358-0-25	.142	-8	99	-47	—	-5.3
JAMES, BILL	William Lawrence "Seattle Bill"; B3.12.1892 Iowa Hill CA; D3.10.1971 Oroville CA; BR/TR/6´3˝/196; d4.17; Col St. Marys (CA)																									
1913	Bos N	6	10	.375	24	14	10-1	0	135.2	134	75	4	7	57	73	2.79	118	.264	.347	47-0-2	.255	1	59	2	—	0.4
1914	†Bos N	26	7	**.788**	46	37	30-4	3	332.1	261	91	7	13	118	156	1.90	145	.225	.304	129-0-5	.256	4*	118	**31**	—	**3.6**
1915	Bos N	5	4	.556	13	9	4	0	68.1	68	28	3	2	22	23	3.03	86	.269	.332	21-0-1	.048	-2*	128	-2	—	-0.4
1919	Bos N	0	0	ø	1	0	0	0	5.1	6	2	0	0	2	1	3.38	85	.273	.333	2	.000	-0	—	0	—	0.0
Total	4	37	21	.638	84	60	44-5	3	541.2	469	196	14	22	199	253	2.28	126	.242	.319	199-0-8	.231	4	104	31	—	3.6
JAMIESON, CHARLIE	Charles Devine "Cuckoo"; B2.7.1893 Paterson NJ; D10.27.1969 Paterson NJ; BL/TL/5´8.5˝/165; d9.20.1915; ▲																									
1916	Was A	0	0	ø	1	0	0	0	4	2	2	0	0	3	2	4.50	62	.143	.294	145-0-5	.248	0*	—	-1	—	0.0
1917	Was A	0	0	ø	1	0	0	0	2.1	10	10	0	0	2	1	38.57	7	.625	.667	35	.171	0*	—	-8	—	-0.4
1918	Phi A	2	1	.667	5	2	1	0	23	24	17	0	2	13	2	4.30	68	.261	.364	416-0-1	.202	0*	103	-4	—	-0.5
1919	Cle A	0	0	ø	4	1	0	0	13	12	9	0	0	8	0	5.54	60	.250	.357	17	.353	0*	141	-2	—	0.0
1922	Cle A	0	0	ø	2	0	0	0	5.2	7	3	0	0	4	2	3.18	126	.318	.423	567-3-14	.323	1*	—	0	—	0.0
Total	5	2	1	.667	13	3	1	0	48	55	41	0	2	30	7	6.19	51	.286	.388	1180-3-20	.267	2	115	-15	—	-0.9
JANESKI, JERRY	Gerard Joseph; B4.18.1946 Pasadena CA; BR/TR/6´4˝/(200–205); d4.10; Col Cal St.–Los Angeles																									
1970	Chi A	10	17	.370	35	35	4-1	0-0	205.2	247	125	22	5	63-10	79	4.77	81	.300	.351	66-0-7	.076	-4	106	-20	0	-2.7
1971	Was A	1	5	.167	23	10	0	1-1	61.2	72	38	5	3	34-4	19	4.96	68	.304	.395	14-0-2	.214	1	88	-11	0	-1.0
1972	Tex A	0	1	.000	4	1	0	0-0	12.2	11	5	0	0	7-0	7	2.84	107	.229	.321	2	.000	-0	29	0	0	0.0
Total	3	11	23	.324	62	46	4-1	1-1	280	330	168	27	8	104-14	105	4.72	79	.298	.360	82-0-9	.098	-4	102	-31	0	-3.7
JANSEN, LARRY	Lawrence Joseph; B7.16.1920 Verboort OR; BR/TR/6´2˝/190; d4.17; C14																									
1947	NY N	21	5	**.808**	42	30	20-1	1	248	241	102	23	1	57	104	3.16	129	.262	.306	86-0-9	.186	-0	126	24	0	2.2
1948	NY N	18	12	.600	42	36	15-4	2	277	283	125	25	3	54	126	3.61	109	.265	.303	95-0-7	.137	-2	115	12	0	1.1
1949	NY N	15	16	.484	37	35	17-3	0	259.2	271	130	36	2	62	113	3.85	104	.263	.306	97-0-6	.165	-0	114	5	0	0.6
1950	NY N★	19	13	.594	40	35	21-**5**	3	275	238	106	31	1	55	161	3.01	136	.232	**.271**	96-1-9	.167	-0	101	33	0	3.6
1951	†NY N☆	**23**	11	.676	39	34	18-3	0	278.2	254	102	26	3	56	145	3.04	129	.239	.279	96-0-12	.094	-5	101	31	0	3.2
1952	NY N	11	11	.500	34	27	8-1	2	167.1	183	91	16	6	47	74	4.09	91	.281	.335	45-0-6	.178	3	103	-8	0	-0.6
1953	NY N	11	16	.407	36	26	6	1	184.2	185	96	24	2	55	88	4.14	104	.256	.311	60-0-3	.133	-1	99	4	0	0.3
1954	NY N	2	2	.500	13	7	0	0	40.2	57	32	5	1	15	15	5.98	68	.337	.388	14	.286	1	98	-9	0	-0.6
1956	Cin N	2	3	.400	8	7	2	1	34.2	39	20	5	1	9-1	16	5.19	77	.281	.327	11	.000	-1	133	-4	0	-0.6
Total	9	122	89	.578	291	237	107-17	10	1765.2	1751	804	191	20	410-1	842	3.58	112	.258	.302	600-1-52	.150	-6	109	88	0	9.2
JANSSEN, CASEY	Robert Casey; B9.17.1981 Orange CA; BR/TR/6´4˝/205; [TorA04 4/117]; d4.27; Col UCLA																									
2006	Tor A	6	10	.375	19	17	0	0-0	94	103	58	12	7	21-3	44	5.07	93	.275	.323	1	.000	-0	81	-4	0	-0.5

YEAR	TM LG	W	L	PCT	G	GS	CG-SHO	SV-BS	IP	H	R	HR	HB	BB-IB	SO	ERA	AERA	OAV	OOB	AB-HR-SH	AVG	PB	SUP	APR	DL	PW
Janzen, Marty	Martin Thomas; B5.31.1973 Homestead FL; BR/TR/6´3˝/200; d5.12																									
1996	Tor A	4	6	.400	15	11	0	0-0	73.2	95	65	16	2	38-3	47	7.33	68	.317	.394	0	ø	0	99	-18	0	-2.0
1997	Tor A	2	1	.667	12	0	0	0-0	25	23	11	4	0	13-0	17	3.60	128	.250	.343	0	ø	0	—	3	0	0.3
Total	2	6	7	.462	27	11	0	0-0	98.2	118	76	20	2	51-3	64	6.39	77	.301	.382	0	ø	0	99	-15	0	-1.7
Jarvis, Kevin	Kevin Thomas; B8.1.1969 Lexington KY; BL/TR/6´2˝/200; [CinN91 21/561]; d4.6; Col Wake Forest																									
1994	Cin N	1	1	.500	6	3	0	0-0	17.2	22	14	4	0	5-0	10	7.13	59	.301	.346	4-0-2	.250	0	145	-5	0	-0.5
1995	Cin N	3	4	.429	19	11	1-1	0-0	79	91	56	13	3	32-2	33	5.70	73	.292	.358	21-0-1	.143	-0	114	-14	0	-1.1
1996	Cin N	8	9	.471	24	20	2-1	0-0	120.1	152	93	17	2	43-5	63	5.98	72	.305	.361	36-0-8	.167	-0	107	-24	0	-2.9
1997	Cin N	0	1	.000	9	0	0	1-0	13.1	21	16	4	1	7-0	12	10.13	42	.344	.420	1	.000	-0	—	-8	0	-0.7
	Min A	0	0	ø	6	2	0	0-0	13	23	18	4	0	8-0	9	12.46	37	.371	.443	0	ø	0	157	-10	0	-0.5
	Det A	0	3	.000	17	3	0	0-0	41.2	55	28	9	0	14-0	27	5.40	86	.318	.367	0	ø	0	46	-4	19	-0.3
	Year	0	3	.000	23	5	0	0-0	54.2	78	46	13	0	22-0	36	7.08	65	.332	.388	0	ø	0	91	-15	0	-0.8
1999	Oak A	0	1	.000	4	1	0	0-0	14	28	19	6	1	6-0	11	11.57	41	.418	.467	0	ø	0	59	-10	46	-0.6
2000	Col N	3	4	.429	24	19	0	0-0	115	138	83	26	4	33-3	60	5.95	97	.300	.351	34-0-3	.088	-2*	119	-2	34	-0.3
2001	SD N	12	11	.522	32	32	1-1	0-0	193.1	189	107	37	5	49-4	133	4.79	87	.254	.303	61-1-5	.180	4*	113	-11	0	-0.6
2002	SD N	2	4	.333	7	7	0	0-0	35	36	19	5	1	10-1	24	4.37	89	.269	.322	9-0-1	.333	2	68	-2	149	-0.2
2003	SD N	4	8	.333	16	16	0	0-0	92	113	65	15	2	32-5	49	5.87	68	.304	.358	22-0-3	.136	1*	88	-21	75	-2.1
2004	Sea A	1	0	1.000	8	0	0	0-0	13	20	12	4	0	5-0	7	8.31	54	.345	.397	0	ø	0	—	-5	0	-0.3
	Col N	0	0	ø	2	0	0	0-0	2	6	6	1	0	4-2	0	27.00	18	.600	.714	0	ø	0	—	-4	0	-0.2
2005	StL N	0	1	.000	4	0	0	0-1	3.1	3	5	1	2	3-0	2	13.50	31	.250	.471	0	ø	0	—	-3	0	-0.6
2006	Ari N	0	1	.000	5	1	0	0-0	11.1	18	15	2	1	5-0	6	11.91	39	.360	.414	0	ø	0	79	-8	0	-0.6
	Bos A	0	1	.000	4	3	0	0-0	16.2	22	12	1	1	6-1	7	4.86	96	.324	.382	0	ø	0	101	-1	0	-0.1
Total	12	34	49	.410	187	118	4-3	1-1	780.2	937	568	149	23	262-23	453	6.03	74	.297	.353	188-1-23	.160	4	107	-132	323	-11.6
Jarvis, Ray	Raymond Arnold; B5.10.1946 Providence RI; BR/TR/6´2˝/(185–198); [BosA65 11/370]; d4.15																									
1969	Bos A	5	6	.455	29	12	2	1-0	100.1	105	59	8	3	43-1	36	4.75	80	.274	.349	29-0-3	.069	-2	110	-9	21	-1.1
1970	Bos A	0	1	.000	15	0	0	0-1	16	17	12	1	2	14-1	8	3.94	101	.274	.418	0-0-1	ø	0	—	-2	0	-0.1
Total	2	5	7	.417	44	12	2	1-1	116.1	122	71	9	5	57-2	44	4.64	83	.274	.359	29-0-4	.069	-2	110	-11	21	-1.2
Jarvis, Pat	Robert Patrick; B3.18.1941 Carlyle IL; BR/TR/5´10.5˝/180; d8.4; Col Murray St.																									
1966	Atl N	6	2	.750	10	9	3-1	0	62.1	46	16	1	1	12-2	41	2.31	157	.206	.250	22-0-1	.000	-2	150	10	0	1.0
1967	Atl N	15	10	.600	32	30	7-1	0	194	195	86	15	4	62-14	118	3.66	91	.260	.317	71-0-3	.085	-3	105	-6	0	-1.1
1968	Atl N	16	12	.571	34	34	14-1	0	256	202	82	15	2	50-5	157	2.60	115	.214	.252	85-0-10	.141	0	102	12	0	1.3
1969	†Atl N	13	11	.542	37	33	4-1	0-0	217.1	204	113	25	1	73-7	123	4.43	82	.246	.306	71-0-5	.113	-3	110	-17	0	-2.0
1970	Atl N	16	16	.500	36	34	11-1	0-1	254	240	110	21	0	72-5	173	3.61	119	.247	.296	82-0-11	.183	-0	83	20	0	2.4
1971	Atl N	6	14	.300	35	23	3-3	1-0	162.1	162	81	16	3	51-11	68	4.10	91	.261	.320	47-0-4	.106	-2	88	-5	0	-0.8
1972	Atl N	11	7	.611	37	6	0	2-1	98.2	94	50	7	0	44-7	56	4.10	93	.260	.337	24-0-3	.125	-0	132	-3	0	-0.5
1973	Mon N	2	1	.667	28	0	0	0-1	39.1	37	21	6	1	16-4	19	3.20	119	.250	.325	3	.000	-0	—	1	33	0.0
Total	8	85	73	.538	249	169	42-8	3-3	1284	1180	559	106	12	380-55	755	3.58	101	.243	.298	405-0-37	.121	-10	101	12	33	0.3
Jasper, Hi	Henry W.; B11.15.1880 St.Louis MO; D5.22.1937 St.Louis MO; BR/TR/5´11˝/180; d4.19																									
1914	Chi A	1	0	1.000	16	0	0	0	32.1	22	22	0	1	20	19	3.34	80	.210	.341	5	.000	-1	—	-4	—	-0.2
1915	Chi A	0	1	.000	3	2	1	0	15.2	8	8	2	0	9	15	4.60	65	.157	.283	7	.286	0	98	-2	—	0.0
1916	StL N	5	6	.455	21	9	2	1	107	97	54	0	7	42	37	3.28	81	.254	.339	33-1-0	.212	1	97	-8	—	-0.7
1919	Cle A	4	5	.444	12	10	5	0	82.2	83	41	1	0	28	25	3.59	93	.269	.330	29-0-2	.103	-2	117	-1	—	-0.3
Total	4	10	12	.455	52	21	8	1	237.2	210	125	3	8	99	96	3.48	84	.248	.333	74-1-2	.162	-2	110	-15	—	-1.2
Jaster, Larry	Larry Edward; B1.13.1944 Midland MI; BL/TL/6´3.5˝/(190–205); d9.17																									
1965	StL N	3	0	1.000	4	3	3	0	28	21	5	1	0	7-0	10	1.61	239	.206	.255	10-0-1	.200	0	144	7	0	0.8
1966	StL N	11	5	.688	26	21	6-**5**	0	151.2	124	57	17	5	45-5	92	3.26	110	.227	.290	45-1-2	.178	1	83	8	0	0.9
1967	†StL N	9	7	.563	34	23	2-1	3	152.1	141	57	12	2	44-6	87	3.01	109	.244	.297	50-0-1	.100	-1*	109	5	0	0.3
1968	†StL N	9	13	.409	31	21	3-1	0	153.2	153	63	13	6	38-5	70	3.51	82	.262	.311	43-1-6	.140	0	73	-8	0	-1.2
1969	Mon N	1	6	.143	24	11	1	0-0	77	95	60	17	2	28-6	39	5.49	67	.302	.359	19	.421	3	81	-17	0	-1.2
1970	Atl N	1	1	.500	14	0	0	0-2	22.1	33	18	5	0	8-0	9	6.85	63	.359	.402	3	.000	-0	—	-6	0	-0.4
1972	Atl N	1	1	.500	5	1	0	0-0	12.1	12	7	4	0	8-0	6	5.11	74	.267	.377	1	.000	-0	23	-1	0	-0.2
Total	7	35	33	.515	138	80	15-7	3-2	597.1	579	267	69	15	178-22	313	3.65	93	.256	.312	171-2-10	.170	3	89	-12	0	-1.0
Javery, Al	Alva William "Beartracks"; B6.5.1918 Worcester MA; D8.16.1977 Putnam CT; BR/TR/6´3˝/183; d4.23																									
1940	Bos N	2	4	.333	29	4	1	1	83.1	99	62	2	2	36	42	5.51	68	.293	.364	23-0-1	.087	-1	76	-19	—	-1.5
1941	Bos N	10	11	.476	34	23	9-1	1	160.2	181	88	5	6	65	54	4.31	83	.283	.355	58-0-1	.103	-4	102	-12	0	-1.8
1942	Bos N	12	16	.429	42	**37**	19-5	0	261	251	106	8	3	78	85	3.03	110	.251	.307	86-0-9	.105	-5	81	7	0	0.3
1943	Bos N★	17	16	.515	41	35	19-5	0	**303**	288	130	13	4	99	134	3.21	106	.248	.309	104-0-11	.163	-3	84	7	0	0.6
1944	Bos N☆	10	19	.345	40	33	11-3	3	254	248	119	12	2	118	137	3.54	108	.262	.345	79-0-4	.152	-3	71	7	0	0.4
1945	Bos N	2	7	.222	17	14	2-1	0	77.1	92	59	4	0	51	18	6.28	61	.295	.394	29	.207	-0	95	-19	0	-1.9
1946	Bos N	0	1	.000	2	1	0	0	3.1	5	5	0	0	5	0	13.50	25	.417	.588	1	.000	-0	125	-3	0	-0.6
Total	7	53	74	.417	205	147	61-15	5	1142.2	1164	569	44	17	452	470	3.80	94	.264	.335	380-0-26	.137	-15	84	-32	0	-4.5
Jay, Joey	Joseph Richard; B8.15.1935 Middletown CT; BB/TR (BR 1953)/6´4˝/(200–228); d7.21																									
1953	Mil N	1	0	1.000	3	1	1-1	0	10	6	0	0	0	5	4	0.00	ø	.188	.297	3	.000	-0	68	5	0	0.4
1954	Mil N	1	0	1.000	15	1	0	0	18	21	13	2	1	16	13	6.50	57	.304	.437	0	ø	0	96	-5	0	-0.3
1955	Mil N	0	0	ø	12	1	0	0	19	23	11	2	0	13-2	3	4.74	79	.324	.419	3	.667	1	190	-2	0	0.0
1957	Mil N	0	0	ø	1	0	0	1	0.2	0	0	0	0	0-0	0	0.00	ø	.000	.000	0	ø	0	—	0	0	0.1
1958	Mil N	7	5	.583	18	12	6-3	0	96.2	60	25	8	1	43-3	74	2.14	164	.177	.271	32-0-1	.094	-1	70	17	0	1.9
1959	Mil N	6	11	.353	34	19	4-1	0	136.1	130	71	11	5	64-6	88	4.09	87	.248	.334	35-0-1	.086	-1	101	-9	0	-1.1
1960	Mil N	9	8	.529	32	11	3	1	133.1	128	60	10	6	59-5	90	3.24	106	.254	.336	45-0-3	.156	0	131	0	0	0.0
1961	†Cin N☆	**21**	10	.677	34	34	14-**4**	0	247.1	217	102	25	5	92-1	157	3.53	115	.236	.308	89-0-2	.090	-5	95	18	0	1.4
1962	Cin N	21	14	.600	39	37	16-4	0	273	269	121	26	4	100-5	155	3.76	107	.260	.325	90-2-7	.167	3	97	11	0	1.5
1963	Cin N	7	18	.280	30	22	4-1	1	170	172	91	19	3	73-2	116	4.29	78	.266	.340	50-0-2	.160	0	75	-17	0	-2.4
1964	Cin N	11	11	.500	34	23	10	2	183	167	75	17	3	36-6	134	3.39	107	.245	.284	53-0-5	.057	-3	87	6	0	0.3
1965	Cin N	9	8	.529	37	24	4-1	1	155.2	150	83	21	4	63-0	102	4.22	89	.252	.324	49-0-4	.041	-3	113	-8	0	-1.2
1966	Cin N	6	2	.750	12	10	1-1	0	73.2	78	33	8	3	23-1	44	3.91	100	.275	.335	26-0-2	.115	-1	108	1	0	-0.1
	Atl N	0	4	.000	9	8	0	1	29.2	39	29	4	1	20-3	19	7.89	46	.315	.405	8	.125	-0	94	-14	0	-1.7
	Year	6	6	.500	21	18	1-1	1	103.1	117	62	12	4	43-4	63	5.05	76	.287	.358	34-0-2	.118	-1	101	-13	0	-1.8
Total	13	99	91	.521	310	203	63-16	7	1546.1	1460	714	153	36	607-34	999	3.77	99	.251	.323	483-2-27	.114	-10	97	3	0	-1.2
Jean, Domingo	Domingo (Luisa); B1.9.1969 San Pedro de Macoris, D.R.; BR/TR/6´2˝/175; d8.8																									
1993	NY A	1	1	.500	10	6	0	0-0	40.1	37	20	7	0	19-1	20	4.46	94	.237	.318	0	ø	0	106	0	0	0.0
Jeffcoat, George	George Edward; B12.24.1913 New Brookland (now West Columbia) SC; D10.13.1978 Leesville SC; BR/TR/5´11.5˝/175; d4.20; b–Hal; Col South Carolina																									
1936	Bro N	5	6	.455	40	5	3	3	95.2	84	58	7	8	63	46	4.52	92	.239	.366	23-0-1	.130	-1	78	-4	—	-0.6
1937	Bro N	1	3	.250	21	3	1-1	0	54.1	58	33	4	1	27	29	5.13	79	.274	.358	12	.000	-2	85	-4	—	-0.5
1939	Bro N	0	0	ø	1	0	0	0	2	2	0	0	0	0	1	0.00	ø	.286	.286	0	ø	0	—	1	—	0.0
1943	Bos N	1	2	.333	8	1	0	0	17.2	15	10	1	0	10	10	3.06	112	.217	.316	4-0-1	.500	1	124	0	0	0.0
Total	4	7	11	.389	70	9	4-1	3	169.2	159	101	12	9	100	86	4.51	89	.248	.358	39-0-2	.128	-2	85	-7	0	-1.1
Jeffcoat, Hal	Harold Bentley; B9.6.1924 W.Columbia SC; BR/TR/5´10.5˝/(185–198); d4.20.1948; b–George; ▲																									
1954	Chi N	5	6	.455	43	3	1	7	104	110	63	12	4	58	35	5.19	81	.276	.368	31-1-0	.258	2*	85	-9	0	-0.7
1955	Chi N	8	6	.571	50	1	0	6	100.2	107	46	5	4	53-12	32	2.95	139	.276	.367	23-1-2	.174	1*	65	8	0	1.3
1956	Cin N	8	2	.800	38	16	2	2	171	189	79	12	5	55-4	55	3.84	104	.281	.337	54-0-3	.148	-1*	112	3	0	0.2
1957	Cin N	12	13	.480	37	31	10-1	0	207	236	117	29	7	46-7	63	4.52	91	.294	.335	69-4-8	.203	6*	111	-11	0	-0.6
1958	Cin N	6	8	.429	49	0	0	9	75	76	34	8	2	26-8	35	3.72	111	.268	.329	9	.556	2*	—	3	0	0.9
1959	Cin N	0	1	.000	17	0	0	1	21.2	21	8	3	0	10-2	12	3.32	122	.253	.333	1	1.000	1	—	2	0	0.2
	StL N	0	1	.000	11	0	0	0	17.2	33	18	4	0	9-2	7	9.17	46	.402	.462	3	.000	-0*	—	-8	0	-0.4

YEAR	TM LG	W	L	PCT	G	GS	CG-SHO	SV-BS	IP	H	R	HR	HB	BB-IB	SO	ERA	AERA	OAV	OOB	AB-HR-SH	AVG	PB	SUP	APR	DL	PW
	Year	0	2	.000	28	0	0	1	39.1	54	26	7	0	19-4	19	5.95	70	.327	.397	4	.250	0	—	-6	0	-0.2
Total	6	39	37	.513	245	51	13-1	25	697	772	365	73	22	257-35	239	4.22	97	.285	.349	190-6-13	.211	10	109	-12	0	0.9
Jeffcoat, Mike	James Michael; B8.3.1959 Pine Bluff AR; BL/TL/6´2˝/(185–192); [CleA80 13/322]; d8.21; Col Louisiana Tech																									
1983	Cle A	1	3	.250	11	2	0	0-0	32.2	32	13	1	1	13-1	9	3.31	129	.256	.331	0	ø	0	21	3	0	0.4
1984	Cle A	5	2	.714	63	1	0	1-5	75.1	82	28	7	1	24-7	41	2.99	138	.281	.330	0	ø	0	285	9	0	0.8
1985	Cle A	0	0	ø	9	0	0	0-0	9.2	8	5	1	0	6-1	4	2.79	149	.235	.333	0	ø	0	—	1	0	0.1
	SF N	0	2	.000	19	1	0	0-0	22	27	13	4	2	6-3	10	5.32	65	.307	.361	1	.000	0	230	-4	0	-0.3
1987	Tex A	0	1	.000	2	2	0	0-0	7	11	10	4	0	4-0	1	12.86	35	.355	.429	0	ø	0	91	-6	0	-0.6
1988	Tex A	0	2	.000	5	2	0	0-0	10	19	13	1	2	5-1	5	11.70	35	.432	.510	0	ø	0	22	-7	0	-1.2
1989	Tex A	9	6	.600	22	22	2-2	0-0	130.2	139	65	7	4	33-0	64	3.58	111	.270	.317	0	ø	0	110	3	0	0.4
1990	Tex A	5	6	.455	44	12	1	5-5	110.2	122	57	12	2	28-5	58	4.47	88	.283	.328	0	ø	0	83	-4	42	-0.5
1991	Tex A	5	3	.625	70	0	0	1-4	79.2	104	46	8	4	25-3	43	4.63	87	.320	.372	1	1.000	1	—	-5	0	-0.4
1992	Tex A	0	1	.000	6	3	0	0-0	19.2	28	17	2	0	5-0	6	7.32	52	.350	.379	0	ø	0	143	-7	99	-0.4
1994	Fla N	0	0	ø	4	0	0	0-0	2.2	4	3	2	0	0-0	1	10.13	44	.364	.333	0	ø	0	—	-1	0	-0.1
Total	10	25	26	.490	255	45	3-2	7-14	500	576	270	49	16	149-21	242	4.37	92	.292	.342	2	.500	1	102	-18	141	-1.8
Jefferson, Jesse	Jesse Harrison; B3.3.1949 Midlothian VA; BR/TR/6´3˝/(192–215); [BalA68 4/70]; d6.23																									
1973	Bal A	6	5	.545	18	15	3	0-0	100.2	104	53	15	0	46-1	52	4.11	92	.267	.342	0	ø	0	115	-4	0	-0.4
1974	Bal A	1	0	1.000	20	2	0	0-0	57.1	55	30	2	0	38-2	31	4.40	79	.261	.371	0	ø	0	190	-5	0	-0.3
1975	Bal A	0	2	.000	4	0	0	0-0	7.2	5	3	0	0	8-2	4	2.35	151	.227	.433	0	ø	0	—	1	0	0.2
	Chi A	5	9	.357	22	21	1	0-0	107.2	100	69	11	2	94-1	67	5.10	76	.249	.391	0	ø	0	82	-15	0	-1.7
	Year	5	11	.313	26	21	1	0-0	115.1	105	72	11	2	102-3	71	4.92	79	.248	.394	0	ø	0	83	-13	0	-1.5
1976	Chi A	2	5	.286	19	9	0	0-0	62.1	86	62	4	2	42-0	30	8.52	42	.339	.429	0	ø	0	115	-33	0	-3.1
1977	Tor A	9	17	.346	33	33	8	0-0	217	224	123	23	1	83-4	114	4.31	99	.269	.332	0	ø	0	78	-4	0	-0.4
1978	Tor A	7	16	.304	31	30	9-2	0-0	211.2	214	109	28	3	86-5	97	4.38	90	.267	.337	0	ø	0	75	-9	0	-0.9
1979	Tor A	2	10	.167	34	10	2	1-2	116	150	75	19	2	45-2	43	5.51	80	.328	.387	0	ø	0	56	-12	0	-1.0
1980	Tor A	4	13	.235	29	18	2-2	0-0	121.2	130	78	12	2	52-2	53	5.47	79	.281	.353	0	ø	0	64	-13	0	-1.5
	Pit N	1	0	1.000	1	1	0	0-0	6.2	3	1	0	0	2-0	4	1.35	273	.143	.217	1-0-1	.000	-0	73	2	0	0.3
1981	Cal A	2	4	.333	26	5	0	0-2	77	80	39	4	2	24-4	27	3.62	101	.269	.322	0	ø	0	39	-1	0	-0.1
Total	9	39	81	.325	237	144	25-4	1-4	1085.2	1151	642	118	14	520-23	522	4.81	83	.277	.356	1-0-1	.000	-0	81	-93	0	-8.9
Jenkins, Fergie	Ferguson Arthur; B12.13.1942 Chatham ON, Can.; BR/TR/6´5˝/(195–210); d9.10; C2; HF1991																									
1965	Phi N	2	1	.667	7	0	0	1	12.1	7	3	2	0	2-0	10	2.19	158	.159	.196	1	.000	-0	—	2	0	0.4
1966	Phi N	0	0	ø	1	0	0	0	2.1	3	2	0	0	1-1	2	3.86	93	.273	.333	0	ø	0	—	0	0	0.0
	Chi N	6	8	.429	60	12	2-1	5	182	147	75	24	3	51-11	148	3.31	111	.219	.275	51-1-3	.137	1	100	8	0	0.6
	Year	6	8	.429	61	12	2-1	5	184.1	150	77	24	3	52-12	150	3.32	111	.220	.276	51-1-3	.137	1	100	6	0	0.6
1967	Chi N★	20	13	.606	38	38	**20**-3	0	289.1	230	101	30	4	83-8	236	2.80	127	.217	.276	93-0-8	.151	1*	101	22	0	2.8
1968	Chi N	20	15	.571	40	**40**	20-3	0	308	255	96	26	3	65-7	260	2.63	120	.222	.265	100-1-6	.160	2	92	19	0	2.5
1969	Chi N	21	15	.583	43	**42**	23-7	1-0	311.1	284	122	27	8	71-15	**273**	3.21	125	.242	.289	108-1-4	.139	-1	93	27	0	3.0
1970	Chi N	22	16	.579	40	39	**24**-3	0-1	313	265	128	30	7	60-6	274	3.39	133	.224	**.264**	113-3-10	.124	-3	98	37	0	3.9
1971	Chi N★	**24**	13	.649	39	**39**	**30**-3	0-0	**325**	304	114	29	5	37-6	263	2.77	142	.246	.269	115-6-8	.243	10	92	36	0	5.6
1972	Chi N☆	20	12	.625	36	36	23-5	0-0	289.1	253	111	32	7	62-7	184	3.20	119	.234	.278	109-1-3	.183	1	105	20	0	2.5
1973	Chi N	14	16	.467	38	38	7-2	0-0	271	267	133	35	4	57-10	170	3.89	102	.259	.298	84-0-7	.119	-1	88	1	0	0.1
1974	Tex A	**25**	12	.676	41	41	**29**-6	0-0	328.1	286	117	27	8	45-3	225	2.82	127	.232	.262	2	.500	0	102	28	0	3.2
1975	Tex A	17	18	.486	37	37	22-4	0-0	270	261	130	37	9	56-7	157	3.93	96	.251	.294	0	ø	0	105	-2	0	-0.2
1976	Bos A	12	11	.522	30	29	12-2	0-0	209	201	85	20	5	43-6	142	3.27	119	.253	.292	0	ø	0	97	14	0	1.5
1977	Bos A	10	10	.500	28	28	11-1	0-0	193	190	91	30	0	36-2	105	3.68	122	.257	.290	0	ø	0	103	13	0	1.3
1978	Tex A	18	8	.692	34	30	16-4	0-0	249	228	92	21	3	41-2	157	3.04	123	.245	.278	0	ø	0	118	22	0	2.3
1979	Tex A	16	14	.533	37	37	10-3	0-0	259	252	127	40	3	81-6	164	4.07	102	.256	.311	0	ø	0	115	5	0	0.7
1980	Tex A	12	12	.500	29	29	12	0-0	198	190	90	22	4	52-8	129	3.77	103	.250	.299	0	ø	0	108	5	0	0.6
1981	Tex A	5	8	.385	19	16	1	0-0	106	122	55	14	0	40-4	63	4.50	77	.290	.351	0	ø	0	113	-11	0	-1.2
1982	Chi N	14	15	.483	34	34	4-1	0-0	217.1	221	92	19	5	68-2	134	3.15	120	.264	.319	67-0-12	.149	-1	104	12	0	1.3
1983	Chi N	6	9	.400	33	29	1-1	0-1	167.1	176	89	19	6	46-5	96	4.30	89	.275	.327	53-0-5	.245	3	94	-9	0	-0.5
Total	19	284	226	.557	664	594	267-49	7-2	4500.2	4142	1853	484	84	997-116	3192	3.34	115	.243	.287	896-13-66	.165	13	101	249	0	30.4
Jenkins, Jack	Warren Washington; B12.22.1942 Covington VA; D6.18.2002 Tampa FL; BR/TR/6´2˝/(195–205); d9.13; Col Lincoln Memorial																									
1962	Was A	0	1	.000	3	1	1	0	13.1	12	6	4	0	7-0	10	4.05	100	.245	.339	4	.000	-0	22	0	0	0.0
1963	Was A	0	2	.000	4	2	0	0	12.1	16	8	2	0	12-0	5	5.84	64	.340	.475	3	.333	0	48	-2	0	-0.3
1969	LA N	0	0	ø	1	0	0	0-0	1	0	0	0	0	0-0	1	0.00	ø	.000	.000	0	ø	0	—	0	0	0.0
Total	3	0	3	.000	8	3	1	0-0	26.2	28	14	6	0	19-0	16	4.73	82	.283	.398	7	.143	-0	38	-2	0	-0.3
Jenks, Bobby	Robert Scott; B3.14.1981 Mission Hills CA; BR/TR/6´3˝/(270–280); [AnaA00 5/140]; d7.6; [DL 2004 Ana A 68]																									
2005	†Chi A	1	1	.500	32	0	0	6-2	39.1	34	15	3	1	15-3	50	2.75	165	.225	.299	0	ø	0	—	7	0	0.5
2006	Chi A☆	3	4	.429	67	0	0	41-4	69.2	66	32	5	2	31-10	80	4.00	117	.253	.334	0	ø	0	—	6	0	1.0
Total	2	4	5	.444	99	0	0	47-6	109	100	47	8	3	46-13	130	3.55	130	.243	.322	0	ø	0	—	13	68	1.5
Jennings, Jason	Jason Ryan; B7.17.1978 Dallas TX; BL/TR/6´2˝/(235–245); [ColN99 1/16]; d8.23; Col Baylor																									
2001	Col N	4	1	.800	7	7	1-1	0-0	39.1	42	21	2	1	19-0	26	4.58	117	.276	.358	15-1-1	.267	1	124	3	0	0.5
2002	Col N	16	8	.667	32	32	0	0-0	185.1	201	102	26	8	70-2	127	4.52	105	.280	.349	62-0-2	.306	5	100	4	0	0.9
2003	Col N	12	13	.480	32	32	1	0-0	181.1	212	115	20	5	88-7	119	5.11	96	.299	.377	54-0-5	.222	2*	95	-5	0	-0.5
2004	Col N	11	12	.478	33	33	0	0-0	201	241	125	27	7	101-14	133	5.51	86	.299	.381	71-1-5	.239	3*	102	-14	0	-1.1
2005	Col N	6	9	.400	20	20	1	0-0	122	130	73	11	5	62-4	75	5.02	93	.274	.361	38-0-4	.158	-0*	84	-5	74	-0.5
2006	Col N	9	13	.409	32	32	3-2	0-0	212	206	94	17	3	85-7	142	3.78	127	.257	.329	62-0-10	.129	-1	85	24	0	2.0
Total	6	58	56	.509	156	156	6-3	0-0	941	1032	530	103	29	425-34	622	4.74	101	.282	.359	302-2-27	.219	10	95	7	74	1.3
Jensen, Ryan	Larry Ryan; B9.17.1975 Salt Lake City UT; BR/TR/6´0˝/(205–245); [SFN96 8/222]; d5.19; Col Southern Utah																									
2001	SF N	1	2	.333	10	7	0	0-0	42.1	44	21	5	4	25-0	26	4.25	96	.268	.378	12	.167	0	110	0	0	0.0
2002	SF N	13	8	.619	32	30	1	0-0	171.2	183	93	21	5	66-4	105	4.51	88	.278	.345	56-0-9	.107	-2	121	-11	0	-1.4
2003	SF N	0	0	ø	6	2	0	0-0	13.1	21	16	6	1	5-0	3	10.80	39	.404	.450	5	.400	1	242	-9	29	-0.4
2005	KC A	3	2	.600	9	3	0	0-1	25.1	31	20	4	2	7-1	18	7.11	62	.298	.348	1	.000	-0	106	-7	0	-1.2
Total	4	17	12	.586	57	42	1	0-1	252.2	279	150	36	12	103-5	152	5.06	80	.285	.357	74-0-9	.135	-1	124	-27	29	-3.0
Jensen, Willie	William Christian; B11.17.1889 Philadelphia PA; D3.27.1917 Philadelphia PA; BL/TR/5´11.5˝/170; d9.10																									
1912	Det A	1	2	.333	5	4	1	0	33	43	23	1	2	18	8	4.91	66	.339	.429	11	.000	-2	130	-6	—	-0.6
1914	Phi A	0	1	.000	1	1	1	0	9	7	4	1	0	2	1	2.00	131	.226	.273	2	.000	0	84	0	—	0.0
Total	2	1	3	.250	6	5	2	0	42	50	27	2	2	20	9	4.29	73	.316	.400	13	.000	-2	123	-6	—	-0.6
Jerzembeck, Mike	Michael Joseph; B5.18.1972 Queens NY; BR/TR/6´1˝/185; [NYA93 5/141]; d8.8; Col North Carolina; [DL 1999 NY A 182]																									
1998	NY A	0	1	.000	3	2	0	0-0	6.1	9	9	2	0	4-0	1	12.79	34	.346	.419	0	ø	0	127	-6	0	-0.7
Jester, Virgil	Virgil Milton; B7.23.1927 Denver CO; BR/TR/5´11˝/188; d6.18; Col Northern Colorado																									
1952	Bos N	3	5	.375	19	8	4-1	0	73	80	31	5	1	23	25	3.33	108	.283	.339	19-0-2	.211	1	86	2	0	0.2
1953	Mil N	0	0	ø	2	0	0	0	2	4	5	1	0	4	0	22.50	17	.400	.571	0	ø	0	—	-4	0	-0.2
Total	2	3	5	.375	21	8	4-1	0	75	84	36	6	1	27	25	3.84	94	.287	.349	19-0-2	.211	1	86	-2	0	0.0
Jimenez, Cesar	Cesar Enrique; B11.12.1984 Cumana, Venezuela; BL/TL/5´11˝/180; d9.11																									
2006	Sea A	0	0	ø	4	1	0	0-0	7.1	13	12	4	0	4-0	3	14.73	30	.382	.447	0	ø	0	214	-8	0	-0.4
Jimenez, German	German (Camarena); B12.5.1962 Santiago Ixcuintla, Nayarit, Mexico; BL/TL/5´11˝/200; d6.28																									
1988	Atl N	1	6	.143	15	9	0	0-0	55.2	65	39	4	1	12-0	26	5.01	73	.294	.326	17	.059	-1	73	-10	0	-1.3
Jimenez, Jason	Jason Jon; B1.10.1976 Modesto CA; BR/TL/6´2˝/205; [TBA97 28/864]; d6.3; Col San Jose St.																									
2002	TB A	0	0	ø	5	0	0	0-0	6.2	9	4	2	0	1-0	5	5.40	84	.333	.345	0	ø	0	—	0	0	0.0
	Det A	0	0	ø	1	0	0	0-0	0.2	3	4	0	0	1-0	0	27.00	16	.500	.571	0	ø	0	—	-3	0	-0.1
	Year	0	0	ø	6	0	0	0-0	7.1	12	8	2	0	2-0	5	7.36	61	.364	.389	0	ø	0	—	-3	0	-0.1

YEAR	TM LG	W	L	PCT	G	GS	CG-SHO	SV-BS	IP	H	R	HR	HB	BB-IB	SO	ERA	AERA	OAV	OOB	AB-HR-SH	AVG	PB	SUP	APR	DL	PW
JIMENEZ, JOSE	Jose; B7.7.1973 San Pedro de Macoris, D.R.; BR/TR/6´3˝/(170–230); d9.9																									
1998	StL N	3	0	1.000	4	3	0	0-0	21.1	22	8	0	0	8-0	12	2.95	142	.262	.323	6-0-2	.000	-1	146	3	0	0.3
1999	StL N	5	14	.263	29	28	2-2	0-1	163	173	114	16	11	71-2	113	5.85	79	.275	.356	53-0-2	.094	-3*	81	-21	0	-2.2
2000	Col N	5	2	.714	72	0	0	24-6	70.2	63	27	4	3	28-6	44	3.18	182	.239	.316	4-0-1	.500	0	—	16	0	2.4
2001	Col N	6	1	.857	56	0	0	17-5	55	56	27	6	0	22-4	37	4.09	130	.264	.332	1	.000	-0	—	6	43	1.1
2002	Col N	2	10	.167	74	0	0	41-6	73.1	76	34	7	3	11-4	47	3.56	133	.265	.297	0	ø	0	—	7	0	1.6
2003	Col N	2	10	.167	63	7	0	20-3	101.2	137	62	7	6	32-5	45	5.22	94	.322	.375	17-0-2	.176	-0	63	-3	0	-0.4
2004	Cle A	1	7	.125	31	0	0	8-3	36.1	45	37	6	4	14-2	21	8.42	52	.296	.371	0	ø	0	—	-18	25	-3.1
Total	7	24	44	.353	329	38	2-2	110-24	521.1	572	309	46	27	186-23	319	4.92	99	.278	.344	81-0-7	.123	-3	78	-10	68	-0.3
JIMENEZ, JUAN	Juan Antonio (Martes); B3.8.1949 LaTorre, D.R.; BR/TR/6´1˝/165; d9.9																									
1974	Pit N	0	0	ø	4	0	0	0-0	4	6	4	0	0	2-0	2	6.75	52	.353	.421	0	ø	0	—	-2	0	-0.1
JIMENEZ, MIGUEL	Miguel Anthony; B8.19.1969 New York NY; BR/TR/6´2˝/205; [OakA91 12/333]; d9.12; Col Fordham																									
1993	Oak A	1	0	1.000	5	4	0	0-0	27	27	12	5	1	16-0	13	4.00	103	.262	.367	0	ø	0	128	1	0	0.0
1994	Oak A	1	4	.200	8	7	0	0-0	34	38	33	9	1	32-2	22	7.41	61	.275	.413	0	ø	0	117	-13	0	-1.4
Total	2	2	4	.333	13	11	0	0-0	61	65	45	14	2	48-2	35	5.90	73	.270	.394	0	ø	0	122	-12	0	-1.4
JIMENEZ, UBALDO	Ubaldo; B1.22.1984 Nagua, D.R.; BR/TR/6´4˝/200; d9.26																									
2006	Col N	0	0	ø	2	1	0	0-0	7.2	5	4	1	0	3-0	3	3.52	136	.185	.267	3	.333	0	96	1	0	0.1
JODIE, BRETT	Brett Paul; B3.25.1977 Columbia SC; BR/TR/6´4˝/208; [NYA98 6/187]; d7.20; Col South Carolina																									
2001	NY A	0	1	.000	1	1	0	0-0	2	7	6	3	0	1-0	0	27.00	16	.583	.615	0	ø	0	83	-5	0	-0.7
	SD N	0	1	.000	7	2	0	0-0	23.1	19	12	7	0	12-1	13	4.63	90	.229	.326	4	.000	-0	22	-1	0	-0.1
Total	1	0	2	.000	8	3	0	0-0	25.1	26	18	10	0	13-1	13	6.39	65	.274	.361	4	.000	-0	44	-6	0	-0.8
JOHN, TOMMY	Thomas Edward; B5.22.1943 Terre Haute IN; BR/TL/6´3˝/(180–203); d9.6; [DL 1975 LA N 175]																									
1963	Cle A	0	2	.000	6	3	0	0	20.1	23	10	1	0	6-1	9	2.21	164	.284	.330	6	.000	-1	74	1	0	0.0
1964	Cle A	2	9	.182	25	14	2-1	0	94.1	97	53	10	0	35-4	65	3.91	92	.262	.324	24-0-3	.208	0	101	-7	0	-0.7
1965	Chi A	14	7	.667	39	27	6-1	3	183.2	162	67	12	2	58-6	126	3.09	103	.237	.298	59-1-6	.169	2	133	4	0	0.9
1966	Chi A	14	11	.560	34	33	10-**5**	0	223	195	76	13	7	57-4	138	2.62	121	.235	.289	69-2-4	.145	2	89	15	0	2.0
1967	Chi A	10	13	.435	31	29	9-**6**	0	178.1	143	62	12	5	47-7	110	2.47	126	.219	.275	51-0-5	.157	-0	76	12	27	1.9
1968	Chi A★	10	5	.667	25	25	5-1	0	177.1	135	45	10	12	49-4	117	1.98	153	.212	.280	62-1-5	.194	2	110	21	39	2.5
1969	Chi A	9	11	.450	33	33	6-2	0-0	232.1	230	91	16	1	90-10	128	3.25	118	.261	.329	79-0-1	.114	-1	80	14	0	1.4
1970	Chi A	12	17	.414	37	37	10-3	0-0	269.1	253	117	19	9	101-16	138	3.27	118	.251	.323	84-0-9	.202	1*	86	15	0	1.9
1971	Chi A	13	16	.448	38	35	10-3	0-0	229.1	244	115	17	5	58-5	131	3.61	99	.274	.318	69-0-9	.145	-1	90	-4	0	-0.6
1972	LA N	11	5	.688	29	29	4-1	0-0	186.2	172	68	14	3	40-1	117	2.89	116	.244	.286	63-0-7	.159	-1	108	12	0	1.1
1973	LA N	16	7	**.696**	36	31	4-2	0-0	218	202	88	16	4	50-2	116	3.10	112	.246	.291	74-0-7	.203	2	118	9	0	1.5
1974	LA N	13	3	.813	22	22	5-3	0-0	153	133	51	4	1	42-0	78	2.59	133	.235	.287	51-0-9	.118	-1	128	15	78	1.5
1976	LA N	10	10	.500	31	31	6-2	0-0	207	207	76	7	0	61-4	91	3.09	110	.261	.312	64-0-10	.109	-2	90	9	0	0.5
1977	†LA N	20	7	.741	31	31	11-3	0-0	220.1	225	82	12	3	50-3	123	2.78	139	.267	.310	79-1-6	.177	1	118	24	0	3.0
1978	†LA N☆	17	10	.630	33	30	7	1-0	213	230	95	11	5	53-7	124	3.30	107	.271	.317	66-0-12	.121	-1	124	3	0	0.3
1979	NY A☆	21	9	.700	37	36	17-3	0-0	276.1	268	109	9	4	65-1	111	2.96	139	.260	.305	0	ø	0	105	32	0	3.3
1980	†NY A★	22	9	.710	36	36	16-**6**	0-0	265.1	270	115	13	6	56-1	78	3.43	116	.268	.309	0	ø	0	119	16	0	1.8
1981	†NY A	9	8	.529	20	20	7	0-0	140.1	135	50	10	3	39-2	50	2.63	137	.256	.309	0	ø	0	92	14	65	1.7
1982	NY A	10	10	.500	30	26	9-2	0-0	186.2	190	84	11	3	34-1	54	3.66	110	.266	.299	0	ø	0	102	8	0	0.9
	†Cal A	4	2	.667	7	7	1	0-0	35	49	18	4	0	5-0	14	3.86	106	.336	.358	0	ø	0	102	0	0	0.0
	Year	14	12	.538	37	33	10-2	0-0	221.2	239	102	15	3	39-1	68	3.69	109	.278	.309	0	ø	0	102	8	0	0.9
1983	Cal A	11	13	.458	34	34	9	0-0	234.2	287	126	20	2	49-5	65	4.33	93	.304	.337	0	ø	0	94	-8	0	-0.7
1984	Cal A	7	13	.350	32	29	4-1	0-0	181.1	223	97	15	4	56-3	47	4.52	88	.306	.356	0	ø	0	96	-10	0	-0.9
1985	Cal A	2	4	.333	12	6	0	0-0	38.1	51	22	3	1	15-1	17	4.70	88	.329	.387	0	ø	0	77	-2	0	-0.3
	Oak A	2	6	.250	11	11	0	0-0	48	66	37	6	1	13-0	8	6.19	63	.332	.372	0	ø	0	72	-13	0	-1.8
	Year	4	10	.286	23	17	0	0-0	86.1	117	59	9	2	28-1	25	5.53	72	.331	.379	0	ø	0	74	-15	0	-2.1
1986	NY A	5	3	.625	13	10	1	0-0	70.2	73	27	8	2	15-1	28	2.93	141	.275	.316	0	ø	0	94	9	60	1.0
1987	NY A	13	6	.684	33	33	3-1	0-0	187.2	212	95	12	6	47-7	63	4.03	110	.288	.335	0	ø	0	120	6	0	0.5
1988	NY A	9	8	.529	35	32	0	0-0	176.1	221	96	11	6	46-4	81	4.49	88	.308	.354	0	ø	0	111	-10	0	-0.8
1989	NY A	2	7	.222	10	10	0	0-0	63.2	87	45	6	3	22-2	18	5.80	67	.336	.392	0	ø	0	72	-13	0	-1.5
Total	26	288	231	.555	760	700	162-46	4-0	4710.1	4783	2017	302	98	1259-102	2245	3.34	111	.265	.315	900-5-93	.157	1	102	172	444	20.4
JOHNS, AUGIE	Augustus Francis "Lefty"; B9.10.1899 St.Louis MO; D9.12.1975 San Antonio TX; BL/TL/5´8.5˝/170; d4.16																									
1926	Det A	6	4	.600	35	14	3-1	1	112.2	117	77	6	5	69	40	5.35	76	.271	.377	28-0-3	.143	-1	110	-14	—	-1.3
1927	Det A	0	0	ø	1	0	0	0	1	1	1	0	0	1	1	9.00	47	.333	.500	0	ø	0	—	0	—	0.0
Total	2	6	4	.600	36	14	3-1	1	113.2	118	78	6	5	70	41	5.38	75	.271	.378	28-0-3	.143	-1	110	-14	—	-1.3
JOHNS, DOUG	Douglas Alan; B12.19.1967 South Bend IN; BR/TL/6´2˝/(185–195); [OakA90 16/451]; d7.8; Col Virginia																									
1995	Oak A	5	3	.625	11	9	1-1	0-0	54.2	44	32	5	5	26-1	25	4.61	98	.226	.330	0	ø	0	87	-1	0	-0.1
1996	Oak A	6	12	.333	40	23	1	1-1	158	187	112	21	6	69-5	71	5.98	83	.297	.370	0	ø	0*	116	-18	0	-1.5
1998	Bal A	3	3	.500	31	10	0	1-0	86.2	108	46	9	4	32-2	34	4.57	100	.321	.381	2	1.000	1	114	0	15	0.2
1999	Bal A	6	4	.600	32	5	0	0-0	86.2	81	45	9	8	25-2	50	4.47	105	.248	.311	1	.000	-0	67	3	0	0.3
Total	4	20	22	.476	114	47	2-1	2-1	386	420	235	44	23	152-10	180	5.13	93	.282	.354	3	.667	1	106	-16	15	-1.1
JOHNS, OLLIE	Oliver Tracy; B8.21.1879 Trenton OH; D6.17.1961 Hamilton OH; BL/TL; d9.24																									
1905	Cin N	1	0	1.000	4	1	1	1	18	31	22	1	0	4	8	3.50	94	.369	.398	5-0-1	.200	-0	175	-4	—	-0.3
JOHNSON, ABE	Abraham; B Chicago IL; d7.16																									
1893	Chi N	0	0	ø	1	0	0	1	1	2	4	0	1	2	0	36.00	13	.400	.625	0	ø	0	—	-3	—	-0.4
JOHNSON, ADAM	Adam Bryant; B7.12.1979 San Jose CA; BR/TR/6´2˝/210; [MinA00 1/2]; d7.16; Col Cal St.–Fullerton																									
2001	Min A	1	2	.333	7	4	0	0-0	25	32	25	6	5	13-0	17	8.28	56	.323	.424	2	.000	-0	69	-10	0	-1.0
2003	Min A	0	1	.000	2	0	0	0-0	1.1	8	8	1	0	1-0	0	47.25	10	.667	.692	0	ø	0	—	-7	0	-1.0
Total	2	1	3	.250	9	4	0	0-0	26.1	40	33	7	5	14-0	17	10.25	45	.360	.450	2	.000	-0	69	-17	0	-2.0
JOHNSON, RANKIN	Adam Rankin Jr.; B3.1.1917 Hayden AZ; D2.11.2006 Williamsport PA; BR/TR/6´3˝/177; d4.17; Mil 1942–45; f–Rankin																									
1941	Phi A	1	0	1.000	7	0	0	0	10	14	10	0	0	3	0	3.60	116	.326	.370	1	.000	-0	—	-2	0	-0.1
JOHNSON, RANKIN	Adam Rankin Sr. "Tex"; B2.4.1888 Burnet TX; D7.2.1972 Williamsport PA; BR/TR/6´1.5˝/185; d4.20; s–Rankin																									
1914	Bos A	3	9	.250	16	13	4-2	0	99.1	92	41	2	3	34	24	3.08	87	.265	.336	30-0-2	.133	-1	52	-2	—	-0.5
	Chi F	9	5	.643	16	14	12-2	0	120	88	29	5	4	29	60	**1.58**	169	.209	.267	37	.108	-3	70	15	—	1.3
1915	Chi F	2	4	.333	11	6	3	1	57	58	34	2	1	23	19	4.42	57	.270	.343	22	.045	-2	153	-12	—	-1.6
	Bal F	7	11	.389	23	19	12-2	1	150.2	143	68	3	1	58	62	3.35	86	.255	.326	51-0-3	.157	-2	94	-6	—	-1.1
	Year	9	15	.375	34	25	15-2	2	207.2	201	102	5	2	81	81	3.64	76	.259	.331	73-0-3	.123	-4	107	-17	—	-2.7
1918	StL N	1	1	.500	6	1	0	0	23	20	10	0	0	7	4	2.74	99	.263	.325	4-0-2	.250	0	28	0	—	0.0
Total	3	22	30	.423	72	53	31-6	2	450	401	182	12	9	151	169	2.92	93	.248	.315	144-0-7	.125	-8	83	-5	—	-1.9
JOHNSON, ART	Arthur Gilbert; B2.15.1897 Warren PA; D6.7.1982 Sarasota FL; BB/TL/6´1˝/167; d9.18																									
1927	NY N	0	0	ø	1	0	0	0	3	1	1	0	0	1	0	0.00	ø	.125	.222	0	ø	0	—	1	—	0.0
JOHNSON, ART	Arthur Henry "Lefty"; B7.16.1916 Winchester MA; BL/TL/6´2˝/185; d9.22; Mil 1942–45; [DL 1946 Bos N 108]																									
1940	Bos N	0	1	.000	2	1	0	0	6	10	7	0	1	3	1	10.50	35	.345	.424	1	.000	-0	23	-4	—	-0.6
1941	Bos N	7	15	.318	43	18	6	1	183.1	189	92	7	5	71	70	3.53	101	.270	.342	55-0-5	.145	-2*	65	-2	0	-0.4
1942	Bos N	0	0	ø	4	0	0	0	6.1	4	1	0	1	5	0	1.42	235	.190	.370	1	.000	-0	—	1	0	0.1
Total	3	7	16	.304	49	19	6	1	195.2	203	100	7	7	79	71	3.68	97	.271	.346	57-0-5	.140	-2	63	-5	108	-0.9

YEAR	TM LG	W	L	PCT	G	GS	CG-SHO	SV-BS	IP	H	R	HR	HB	BB-IB	SO	ERA	AERA	OAV	OOB	AB-HR-SH	AVG	PB	SUP	APR	DL	PW
JOHNSON, BEN	Benjamin Franklin; B5.16.1931 Greenwood SC; BR/TR/6´2˝/190; d9.6																									
1959	Chi N	0	0	ø	4	2	0	0	16.2	17	5	1	0	4-0	6	2.16	183	.262	.304	4-0-1	.000	-0	113	3	0	0.1
1960	Chi N	2	1	.667	17	0	0	1	29.1	39	21	3	1	11-0	9	4.91	77	.355	.408	2-0-1	.000	-0	—	-5	0	-0.5
Total	2	2	1	.667	21	2	0	1	46	56	26	4	1	15-0	15	3.91	98	.320	.371	6-0-2	.000	-1	113	-2	0	-0.4
JOHNSON, CHET	Chester Lillis "Chesty Chet"; B8.1.1917 Redmond WA; D4.10.1983 Seattle WA; BL/TL/6´0˝/175; d9.12; b–Earl; Col Washington																									
1946	StL A	0	0	ø	5	3	0	0	18	20	12	0	0	13	8	5.00	75	.286	.398	6	.000	-1	184	-3	0	-0.2
JOHNSON, BART	Clair Barth; B1.3.1950 Torrance CA; BR/TR/6´5˝/195; [ChiA68 S1/2]; d9.8; [DL 1975 Chi A 175]																									
1969	Chi A	1	3	.250	4	3	0	0-0	22.1	22	11	2	0	6-0	18	3.22	119	.259	.308	6	.167	0	84	0	0	0.1
1970	Chi A	4	7	.364	18	15	2-1	0-0	89.2	92	53	11	2	46-2	71	4.82	81	.268	.358	29-0-2	.276	2	98	-8	0	-0.7
1971	Chi A	12	10	.545	53	16	4	14-5	178	148	67	9	6	111-6	153	2.93	122	.227	.342	57-0-3	.193	0	124	13	0	1.8
1972	Chi A	0	3	.000	9	0	0	1-1	13.2	18	20	2	1	13-2	9	9.22	34	.327	.464	1	.000	-0	—	-11	0	-2.2
1973	Chi A	3	3	.500	22	9	0	0-0	80.2	76	39	6	2	40-0	56	4.13	96	.252	.338	0	ø	0	103	0	0	0.0
1974	Chi A	10	4	.714	18	18	8-2	0-0	121.2	105	42	6	1	32-2	76	2.74	137	.229	.280	0	ø	0	89	13	0	1.4
1976	Chi A	9	16	.360	32	32	8-3	0-0	211.1	231	115	19	1	62-1	91	4.73	75	.282	.329	0	ø	0	75	-24	0	-2.6
1977	Chi A	4	5	.444	29	4	0	2-1	92	114	48	5	2	38-3	46	4.01	102	.302	.365	0	ø	0	105	0	0	0.0
Total	8	43	51	.457	185	97	22-6	17-7	809.1	806	395	60	15	348-16	520	3.94	95	.261	.336	93-0-5	.215	3	93	-17	175	-2.2
JOHNSON, CONNIE	Clifford; B12.27.1922 Stone Mountain GA; D11.28.2004 Kansas City MO; BR/TR/6´4˝/(190–200); d4.17; Negro Lg 1940–50 Mil 1943–45																									
1953	Chi A	4	4	.500	14	10	2-1	0	60.2	55	27	4	2	38	44	3.56	113	.238	.351	20-0-1	.050	-2*	102	3	0	0.1
1955	Chi A	7	4	.636	17	16	5-2	0	99	95	40	5	1	52-0	72	3.45	114	.251	.342	33-0-2	.152	-1*	110	6	0	0.4
1956	Chi A	0	1	.000	5	2	0	0	12.1	11	5	1	0	7-0	6	3.65	112	.234	.333	3	.000	-0	43	1	0	0.0
	Bal A	9	10	.474	26	25	9-2	0	183.2	165	79	12	1	62-3	130	3.43	114	.239	.301	58-0-6	.259	3	90	10	0	1.2
	Year	9	11	.450	31	27	9-2	0	196	176	84	13	1	69-3	136	3.44	114	.239	.303	61-0-6	.246	3	86	11	0	1.2
1957	Bal A	14	11	.560	35	30	14-3	0	242	212	93	17	3	66-1	177	3.20	112	.235	.287	89-0-6	.135	-4	116	11	0	0.5
1958	Bal A	6	9	.400	26	17	4	1	118.1	116	58	13	0	32-3	68	3.88	93	.260	.309	34-0-1	.206	1	82	-5	0	-0.5
Total	5	40	39	.506	123	100	34-8	1	716	654	302	52	7	257-7	497	3.44	109	.243	.309	237-0-16	.169	-3	100	26	0	1.7
JOHNSON, DANE	Dane Edward; B2.10.1963 Coral Gables FL; BR/TR/6´5˝/205; [TorA84 2/48]; d5.30; Col St. Thomas (FL)																									
1994	Chi A	2	1	.667	15	0	0	0-0	12.1	16	9	2	0	11-1	7	6.57	71	.327	.443	0	ø	0	—	-2	0	-0.4
1996	Tor A	0	0	ø	10	0	0	0-0	9	5	3	0	0	5-0	7	3.00	167	.161	.278	0	ø	0	—	2	0	0.1
1997	Oak A	4	1	.800	38	0	0	2-2	45.2	49	28	4	2	31-4	43	4.53	101	.272	.378	0	ø	0	—	-1	0	-0.2
Total	3	6	2	.750	63	0	0	2-2	67	70	40	6	2	47-5	57	4.70	99	.269	.379	0	ø	0	—	-1	0	-0.5
JOHNSON, DAVE	David Charles; B10.4.1948 Abilene TX; BR/TR/6´1˝/(180–183); [BalA67 5/99]; d7.2																									
1974	Bal A	2	2	.500	11	0	0	2-0	15.1	17	5	1	0	5-3	6	2.93	119	.274	.328	0	ø	0	—	1	0	0.3
1975	Bal A	0	1	.000	6	0	0	0-2	8.2	8	4	0	0	7-1	4	4.15	85	.250	.385	0	ø	0	—	0	0	-0.1
1977	Min A	2	5	.286	30	6	0	0-1	72.2	86	42	7	5	23-1	33	4.58	87	.299	.358	0	ø	0	109	-5	0	-0.5
1978	Min A	0	2	.000	6	1	0	0-0	12	15	11	1	0	9-0	7	7.50	51	.313	.421	0	ø	0	47	-5	0	-0.7
Total	4	4	10	.286	53	7	0	2-3	108.2	126	62	9	5	44-5	50	4.64	83	.293	.364	0	ø	0	103	-9	0	-1.0
JOHNSON, DAVE	David Wayne; B10.24.1959 Baltimore MD; BR/TR/5´11˝/(175–183); d5.29; Col CC of Baltimore (MD)																									
1987	Pit N	0	0	ø	5	0	0	0-0	6.1	13	7	1	0	2-0	4	9.95	42	.448	.484	0	ø	0	—	-4	0	-0.2
1989	Bal A	4	7	.364	14	14	4	0-0	89.1	90	44	11	4	28-1	26	4.23	90	.265	.325	0	ø	0	71	-4	0	-0.5
1990	Bal A	13	9	.591	30	29	3	0-0	180	196	83	30	3	43-2	68	4.10	93	.280	.321	0	ø	0	104	-3	20	-0.5
1991	Bal A	4	8	.333	22	14	0	0-0	84	127	68	18	4	24-3	38	7.07	56	.349	.394	0	ø	0	90	-29	68	-3.4
1993	Det A	1	1	.500	6	0	0	0-0	8.1	13	13	3	2	5-1	7	12.96	34	.342	.435	0	ø	0	—	-8	115	-1.3
Total	5	22	25	.468	77	57	7	0-0	368	439	215	63	-13	102-7	143	5.11	76	.298	.347	0	ø	0	92	-48	203	-5.9
JOHNSON, DON	Donald Roy; B11.12.1926 Portland OR; BR/TR/6´3˝/(190–200); d4.20																									
1947	NY A	4	3	.571	15	8	2	0	54.1	57	26	2	1	23	16	3.64	97	.270	.345	13-0-4	.000	-2	128	-2	0	-0.4
1950	NY A	1	0	1.000	8	0	0	0	18	35	21	2	0	12	9	10.00	43	.398	.470	3	.000	-0	—	-12	0	-0.6
	StL A	5	6	.455	25	12	4-1	1	96	126	72	14	1	55	31	6.09	81	.325	.410	29-0-3	.069	-3	77	-10	0	-1.3
	Year	6	6	.500	33	12	4-1	1	114	161	93	16	1	67	40	6.71	72	.338	.421	32-0-3	.063	-4	79	-21	0	-1.9
1951	StL A	0	1	.000	6	3	0	0	15	27	26	4	1	18	8	12.60	35	.391	.523	3-0-1	.333	0	108	-14	0	-0.8
	Was A	7	11	.389	21	20	8-1	0	143.2	138	67	9	2	58	52	3.95	104	.255	.329	47-0-6	.085	-5	93	4	0	-0.1
	Year	7	12	.368	27	23	8-1	0	158.2	165	93	13	3	76	60	4.76	87	.270	.354	50-0-7	.100	-5	96	-10	0	-0.9
1952	Was A	0	5	.000	29	6	0	2	69	80	41	4	4	33	37	4.43	80	.287	.370	13-0-2	.077	-1	74	-8	0	-0.7
1954	Chi A	8	7	.533	46	16	3-3	7	144	129	53	14	0	43	68	3.13	119	.243	.298	35-0-7	.029	-3	96	11	0	0.8
1955	Bal A	2	4	.333	31	5	0	1	68	89	46	4	0	35-2	27	5.82	65	.333	.404	10	.000	-1	70	-14	0	-1.2
1958	SF N	0	1	.000	17	0	0	1	23	31	19	2	2	8-1	14	6.26	61	.323	.383	2-0-1	.000	-0	—	-7	0	-0.4
Total	7	27	38	.415	198	70	17-5	12	631	712	371	55	11	285-3	262	4.78	84	.288	.363	155-0-24	.058	-16	93	-52	0	-4.7
JOHNSON, EARL	Earl Douglas "Lefty"; B4.2.1919 Redmond WA; D12.3.1994 Seattle WA; BL/TL/6´3˝/190; d7.20; Mil 1942–45; b–Chet; Col St. Marys (CA)																									
1940	Bos A	6	2	.750	17	10	2	0	70.1	69	33	0	2	39	26	4.09	110	.260	.359	27	.074	-3*	107	4	—	0.2
1941	Bos A	4	5	.444	17	12	4	0	93.2	90	57	4	3	51	46	4.52	92	.247	.344	34-0-3	.294	2	125	-4	0	-0.1
1946	†Bos A	5	4	.556	29	5	0	3	80	78	39	5	2	39	40	3.71	99	.250	.337	22-0-1	.227	2	61	-1	0	0.1
1947	Bos A	12	11	.522	45	17	6-3	8	142.1	129	63	7	2	62	65	2.97	131	.246	.328	44-0-2	.273	1*	68	10	0	1.9
1948	Bos A	10	4	.714	35	3	1	5	91.1	98	49	7	0	42	45	4.53	97	.276	.353	31-0-1	.097	-3	137	-1	0	-0.3
1949	Bos A	3	6	.333	19	3	0	0	49.1	65	45	1	4	29	20	7.48	58	.327	.422	11	.000	-1	75	-16	0	-2.6
1950	Bos A	0	0	ø	11	0	0	0	13.2	18	11	0	1	8	6	7.24	68	.333	.429	2	.000	-0	—	-3	0	-0.1
1951	Det A	0	0	ø	6	0	0	1	5.2	9	5	0	0	2	2	6.35	66	.375	.423	0	ø	0	—	-2	0	-0.1
Total	8	40	32	.556	179	50	13-3	17	546.1	556	302	24	14	272	250	4.30	96	.265	.353	171-0-7	.187	-2	95	-13	0	-1.0
JOHNSON, WALT	Ellis Walter; B12.8.1892 Minneapolis MN; D1.14.1965 Minneapolis MN; BR/TR/6´0.5˝/180; d9.22																									
1912	Chi A	0	0	ø	3	0	0	0	11.2	11	6	0	1	7	7	3.86	83	.262	.380	3	.000	-0	—	-1	—	-0.1
1915	Chi A	0	0	ø	1	0	0	0	2	3	2	0	0	0	3	9.00	33	.333	.333	0	ø	0	—	-1	—	-0.1
1917	Phi A	0	2	.000	4	2	0	0	13.2	15	12	0	0	5	8	7.24	38	.294	.357	1	.000	0	78	-5	—	-0.7
Total	3	0	2	.000	8	2	0	0	27.1	29	20	0	1	12	18	5.93	50	.284	.365	4	.000	0	78	-7	—	-0.9
JOHNSON, ERNIE	Ernest Thorwald; B6.16.1924 Brattleboro VT; BR/TR/6´4˝/(195–200); d4.28																									
1950	Bos N	2	0	1.000	16	1	0	0	20.2	37	21	1	0	13	15	6.97	55	.394	.467	2	.500	0	344	-9	0	-0.6
1952	Bos N	6	3	.667	29	10	2-1	1	92	100	53	8	2	31	45	4.11	88	.270	.329	22-0-4	.091	-0	155	-8	0	-0.7
1953	Mil N	4	3	.571	36	1	0	0	81	79	34	4	3	22	36	2.67	147	.263	.320	14-0-1	.071	-1	23	9	0	0.6
1954	Mil N	5	2	.714	40	4	1	2	99.1	77	34	11	1	34	68	2.81	133	.219	.289	13-0-5	.231	0	138	11	0	0.9
1955	Mil N	5	7	.417	40	2	0	4	92	81	38	5	2	55-8	43	3.42	110	.240	.348	20-0-1	.100	-1	95	4	0	0.4
1956	Mil N	4	3	.571	36	0	0	6	51	54	21	9	1	21-2	26	3.71	93	.270	.341	4	.250	0	—	0	0	0.1
1957	†Mil N	7	3	.700	30	0	0	4	65	67	29	9	1	26-5	44	3.88	90	.265	.335	17-1-1	.353	3	—	-2	0	0.1
1958	Mil N	3	1	.750	15	0	0	1	23.1	35	21	4	1	10-3	13	8.10	43	.357	.418	2	.000	0	—	-12	0	-1.9
1959	Bal A	4	1	.800	31	1	0	1	50.1	57	32	6	3	19-2	29	4.11	92	.286	.353	6	.333	0	47	-5	0	-0.4
Total	9	40	23	.635	273	19	3-1	19	574.2	587	283	57	14	231-20	319	3.77	98	.266	.338	100-1-12	.180	2	142	-12	0	-1.5
JOHNSON, FRED	Frederick Edward "Deacon","Cactus"; B3.10.1894 Tolar TX; D6.14.1973 Kerrville TX; BR/TR/6´0˝/185; d9.27																									
1922	NY N	0	2	.000	2	2	1	0	18	20	8	3	0	1	8	4.00	100	.294	.304	4-0-1	.000	-1	31	1	—	0.0
1923	NY N	2	0	1.000	3	2	1	0	17	11	8	2	0	7	5	4.24	90	.177	.261	6	.000	-1	108	0	—	-0.1
1938	StL A	3	7	.300	17	6	3	3	69	91	50	7	1	27	24	5.61	89	.316	.377	25-0-1	.240	-0	112	-6	—	-0.8
1939	StL A	0	1	.000	5	2	1	0	14	23	12	0	0	9	2	6.43	76	.383	.464	4-0-1	.000	-1	100	-3	—	-0.2
Total	4	5	10	.333	27	12	6	3	118	145	78	12	1	44	39	5.26	88	.303	.363	39-0-3	.154	-2	96	-8	—	-1.1
JOHNSON, CHIEF	George Howard "Murphy","Big Murph"; B3.30.1886 Winnebago NE; D6.12.1922 Des Moines IA; BR/TR/5´11.5˝/190; d4.16																									
1913	Cin N	14	16	.467	44	31	13-3	0	269	251	137	8	7	86	107	3.01	108	.256	.320	88-1-3	.114	-3	95	1	—	-0.1
1914	Cin N	0	0	ø	1	1	0	0	4	6	4	0	0	2	1	6.75	43	.333	.400	0	ø	0	122	-2	—	-0.1
	KC F	9	10	.474	20	19	12-2	0	134	157	76	2	4	33	78	3.16	88	.298	.345	49-1-1	.122	-2	117	-11	—	-1.8
1915	KC F	17	17	.500	46	34	19-4	2	281.1	253	121	5	8	71	118	2.75	96	.242	.295	87-1-4	.126	-3	103	-8	—	-1.2
Total	3	40	43	.482	111	85	44-9	2	688.1	667	338	15	19	192	304	2.95	98	.259	.315	224-3-8	.121	-7	103	-20	—	-3.2

YEAR	TM LG	W	L	PCT	G	GS	CG-SHO	SV-BS	IP	H	R	HR	HB	BB-IB	SO	ERA	AERA	OAV	OOB	AB-HR-SH	AVG	PB	SUP	APR	DL	PW
JOHNSON, HANK	Henry Ward; B5.21.1906 Bradenton FL; D8.20.1982 Bradenton FL; BR/TR (BB 1933)/5´11.5˝/175; d4.17																									
1925	NY A	1	3	.250	24	4	2-1	0	67	88	58	3	8	37	25	6.85	62	.319	.414	17-0-2	.059	-1	99	-19	—	-1.0
1926	NY A	0	0	ø	1	0	0	1	1	2	2	0	0	2	0	18.00	21	.400	.571	0	ø	0	—	-1	—	-0.2
1928	NY A	14	9	.609	31	22	10-1	0	199	188	107	16	12	104	110	4.30	88	.250	.351	79-1-4	.241	2	122	-10	—	-0.9
1929	NY A	3	3	.500	12	8	2	0	42.2	37	28	5	0	39	24	5.06	76	.237	.390	14-0-2	.071	-1*	123	-6	—	-0.8
1930	NY A	14	11	.560	44	15	7-1	2	175.1	177	112	12	2	104	115	4.67	92	.265	.366	64-1-5	.266	5*	130	-9	—	-0.5
1931	NY A	13	8	.619	40	23	8	4	196.1	176	114	13	1	102	106	4.72	84	.234	.326	77-0-1	.195	2	145	-16	—	-1.5
1932	NY A	2	2	.500	5	4	2	0	31.1	34	18	7	0	15	27	4.88	83	.266	.343	13	.231	0*	131	-2	—	-0.2
1933	Bos A	8	6	.571	25	21	7	1	155.1	156	84	13	3	74	65	4.06	108	.263	.348	52-0-2	.231	3*	93	5	—	0.7
1934	Bos A	6	8	.429	31	14	7-1	1	124.1	162	95	12	5	53	66	5.36	90	.316	.385	43-0-1	.233	1	92	-10	—	-0.9
1935	Bos A	2	1	.667	13	2	0	1	31	41	21	3	0	14	14	5.52	86	.331	.399	8-0-1	.000	-1	119	-2	—	-0.3
1936	Phi A	0	2	.000	3	3	0	0	11.2	16	16	4	1	10	6	7.71	66	.296	.415	4-0-1	.250	-0	75	-5	—	-0.7
1939	Cin N	0	3	.000	20	0	0	1	31.1	30	10	1	0	13	10	2.01	191	.268	.344	5	.400	1	—	6	—	0.5
Total	12	63	56	.529	249	116	45-4	11	1066.1	1107	665	89	32	567	568	4.75	88	.268	.361	376-2-19	.215	9	116	-69	—	-5.8
JOHNSON, JIM	James Brian; B11.3.1945 Muskegon MI; D12.6.1987 North Muskegon MI; BL/TL/5´11˝/175; [SFN67 S3/56]; d4.13; Col Western Michigan																									
1970	SF N	1	0	1.000	3	0	0	0-0	6.2	8	6	0	0	5-1	2	8.10	49	.320	.419	2	.000	0	—	-3	0	-0.3
JOHNSON, JIM	James Robert; B6.27.1983 Johnson City NY; BR/TR/6´5˝/225; [BalA01 5/143]; d7.29																									
2006	Bal A	0	1	.000	1	1	0	0-0	3	9	8	1	1	3-0	0	24.00	19	.563	.619	0	ø	0	229	-6	0	-0.8
JOHNSON, JASON	Jason Michael; B10.27.1973 Santa Barbara CA; BR/TR/6´6˝/(215–235); d8.27																									
1997	Pit N	0	0	ø	3	0	0	0-0	6	10	4	2	0	1-0	3	6.00	71	.400	.407	1	.000	-0	—	-1	0	-0.1
1998	TB A	2	5	.286	13	13	0	0-0	60	74	38	9	3	27-0	36	5.70	84	.306	.381	2	.000	-0	85	-5	86	-0.5
1999	Bal A	8	7	.533	22	21	0	0-0	115.1	120	74	16	3	55-0	71	5.46	86	.266	.347	2	.000	-0	117	-10	0	-1.1
2000	Bal A	1	10	.091	25	13	0	0-0	107.2	119	95	21	4	61-2	79	7.02	67	.278	.369	3-0-2	.000	-0	77	-32	0	-2.6
2001	Bal A	10	12	.455	32	32	2	0-0	196	194	109	28	13	77-3	114	4.09	106	.257	.334	3	.333	1	91	0	0	-0.1
2002	Bal A	5	14	.263	22	22	1	0-0	131.1	141	68	19	6	41-2	97	4.59	95	.276	.335	3	.000	-0	68	-2	60	-0.3
2003	Bal A	10	10	.500	32	32	0	0-0	189.2	216	100	22	10	80-8	118	4.18	110	.283	.358	5	.200	0	96	6	0	0.5
2004	Det A	8	15	.348	33	33	2-1	0-0	196.2	222	121	22	5	60-3	125	5.13	87	.284	.334	3-0-1	.000	-0	81	-15	0	-1.6
2005	Det A	8	13	.381	33	33	1	0-0	210	233	117	23	6	49-4	93	4.54	94	.285	.328	2-1-0	.500	1	102	-7	0	-0.5
2006	Cle A	3	8	.273	14	14	0	0-0	77	108	55	10	2	22-0	32	5.96	73	.341	.380	0	ø	0	112	-14	0	-1.6
	Bos A	0	4	.000	6	6	0	0-0	29.1	41	26	3	2	13-0	18	7.36	63	.331	.397	1	.000	-0	84	-9	0	-1.0
	Year	3	12	.200	20	20	0	0-0	106.1	149	81	13	4	35-0	50	6.35	70	.338	.385	1	.000	-0	103	-23	0	-2.6
	Cin N	0	0	ø	4	0	0	0-0	8.2	11	5	1	1	0-0	4	3.12	151	.297	.316	0	ø	0	—	1	0	0.0
Total	10	55	98	.359	239	219	6-1	0-0	1327.2	1489	812	176	55	486-22	790	4.99	90	.283	.348	25-1-3	.120	1	92	-88	146	-8.9
JOHNSON, JERRY	Jerry Michael; B12.3.1943 Miami FL; BR/TR/6´3˝/(190–200); d7.17																									
1968	Phi N	4	4	.500	16	11	2	0	80.2	82	33	5	2	29-2	40	3.24	93	.264	.328	25-0-1	.080	-0	87	-2	0	-0.2
1969	Phi N	6	13	.316	33	21	4-2	1-2	147.1	151	76	18	3	57-11	82	4.28	83	.268	.335	43-0-3	.209	2	78	-11	0	-1.2
1970	StL N	2	0	1.000	7	0	0	1-1	11.1	6	4	1	0	3-0	5	3.18	131	.146	.205	1	.000	0	—	1	0	0.3
	SF N	3	4	.429	33	1	0	3-2	65.1	67	39	5	1	38-2	44	4.27	93	.266	.364	15	.067	-1	90	-4	0	-0.6
	Year	5	4	.556	40	1	0	4-3	76.2	73	43	6	1	41-2	49	4.11	97	.249	.343	16	.063	-1	90	-3	0	-0.3
1971	†SF N	12	9	.571	67	0	0	18-5	109	93	42	9	1	48-9	85	2.97	115	.230	.310	13-0-1	.154	-0	—	6	0	1.3
1972	SF N	8	6	.571	48	0	0	8-6	73.1	73	40	4	0	40-10	57	4.42	79	.261	.350	9-0-1	.000	-1	—	-7	0	-1.5
1973	Cle A	5	6	.455	39	1	0	5-6	59.2	70	48	7	0	39-8	45	6.18	64	.299	.396	0	ø	0	90	-15	0	-2.8
1974	Hou N	2	1	.667	34	0	0	0-0	45	47	26	2	0	24-7	32	4.80	73	.276	.360	1	.000	-0	—	-6	0	-0.4
1975	SD N	3	1	.750	21	4	0	0-0	54	60	37	3	0	31-3	18	5.17	68	.282	.368	12	.083	-0	119	-10	0	-0.8
1976	SD N	1	3	.250	24	1	0	0-0	39	39	27	0	0	26-6	27	5.31	62	.260	.367	3	.000	-0	27	-10	0	-1.0
1977	Tor A	2	4	.333	43	0	0	5-2	86	91	50	9	0	54-4	54	4.60	92	.279	.375	0	ø	0	—	-3	0	-0.3
Total	10	48	51	.485	365	39	6-2	41-24	770.2	779	422	63	7	389-62	489	4.31	84	.265	.348	122-0-6	.123	-2	80	-61	0	-7.2
JOHNSON, JOHNNY	John Clifford "Swede"; B9.29.1914 Belmore OH; D6.26.1991 Iron Mountain MI; BL/TL/6´0˝/182; d4.19; Col Eastern Michigan; [DL 1946 Chi A 119]																									
1944	NY A	0	2	.000	22	1	0	3	26.2	25	14	0	1	24	11	4.05	86	.243	.391	6	.500	1	24	-2	0	-0.1
1945	Chi A	3	0	1.000	29	0	0	4	69.2	85	39	2	1	35	38	4.26	78	.306	.385	14-0-1	.286	2	—	-8	0	-0.2
Total	2	3	2	.600	51	1	0	7	96.1	110	53	2	2	59	49	4.20	80	.289	.387	20-0-1	.350	3	24	-10	119	-0.3
JOHNSON, YOUNGY	John Gottfred; B7.22.1873 San Francisco CA; D8.28.1936 Berkeley CA; TR; d4.29																									
1897	Phi N	1	2	.333	5	2	1	0	29	39	24	0	2	12	7	4.66	90	.320	.390	13	.077	-2	93	-3	—	-0.4
1899	NY N	0	0	ø	1	0	0	0	2	0	0	0	0	2	1	0.00	ø	.000	.250	1	.000	-0	—	1	—	0.0
Total	2	1	2	.333	6	2	1	0	31	39	24	0	2	14	8	4.35	96	.305	.382	14	.071	-2	93	-2	—	-0.4
JOHNSON, JOHN HENRY	John Henry; B8.21.1956 Houston TX; BL/TL/6´2˝/(185–210); [SFN74 15/355]; d4.10																									
1978	Oak A	11	10	.524	33	30	7-2	0-0	186	164	81	18	0	82-6	91	3.39	108	.238	.317	0	ø	0*	108	7	0	0.6
1979	Oak A	2	8	.200	14	13	1	0-0	84.2	89	45	13	1	36-0	50	4.36	93	.269	.341	0	ø	0	65	-2	0	-0.3
	Tex A	2	6	.250	17	12	1	0-0	82.1	79	50	12	1	36-3	46	4.92	84	.255	.330	0	ø	0	87	-7	0	-0.6
	Year	4	14	.222	31	25	2	0-0	167	168	95	25	2	72-3	96	4.63	89	.262	.335	0	ø	0	76	-9	0	-0.9
1980	Tex A	2	2	.500	33	0	0	4-3	38.2	27	12	2	1	15-4	44	2.33	167	.199	.281	0	ø	0	—	7	0	0.8
1981	Tex A	3	1	.750	24	0	0	2-1	23.2	19	7	2	1	6-1	8	2.66	131	.232	.283	0	ø	0	—	3	0	0.5
1983	Bos A	3	2	.600	34	1	0	1-1	53.1	58	28	3	1	20-4	51	3.71	118	.283	.342	0	ø	0	21	2	0	0.2
1984	Bos A	1	2	.333	30	3	0	1-0	63.2	64	26	7	0	27-1	57	3.53	119	.260	.333	0	ø	0	65	6	15	0.3
1986	Mil A	2	1	.667	19	0	0	1-0	44	43	15	2	0	10-1	42	2.66	164	.251	.293	0	ø	0	—	8	0	0.5
1987	Mil A	0	1	.000	10	2	0	0-0	26.1	42	30	1	0	18-1	18	9.57	48	.365	.451	0	ø	0	99	-14	16	-0.6
Total	8	26	33	.441	214	61	9-2	9-5	602.2	585	294	60	5	250-21	407	3.90	103	.256	.328	0	ø	0	88	10	31	1.4
JOHNSON, JOHN	John Louis (b John Louis Mercer); B11.18.1869 Pekin IL; D1.28.1941 Kansas City MO; TL/5´10˝/165; d9.11																									
1894	Phi N	1	1	.500	4	3	2	0	32.2	44	30	3	1	15	10	6.06	85	.319	.390	16-0-1	.188	-1	166	-3	—	-0.2
JOHNSON, JONATHAN	Jonathan Kent; B7.16.1974 LaGrange GA; BR/TR/6´0˝/180; [TexA95 1/7]; d9.27; Col Florida St.																									
1998	Tex A	0	0	ø	1	1	0	0-0	4.1	5	4	0	0	5-0	3	8.31	59	.313	.455	0	ø	0	228	-1	0	-0.1
1999	Tex A	0	0	ø	1	0	0	0-0	3	9	5	0	1	2-0	3	15.00	34	.529	.571	0	ø	0	—	-3	0	-0.1
2000	Tex A	1	1	.500	15	0	0	0-0	29	34	23	3	6	19-2	23	6.21	82	.291	.410	0	ø	0	—	-4	0	-0.2
2001	Tex A	0	0	ø	5	0	0	0-0	10.1	13	11	2	1	7-1	11	9.58	50	.317	.404	0	ø	0	—	-5	0	-0.2
2002	SD N	1	2	.333	16	0	0	0-0	15.1	15	8	2	1	5-1	21	4.11	95	.250	.318	0	ø	0	—	-1	0	-0.1
2003	Hou N	0	1	.000	4	3	0	0-0	15.1	20	11	2	0	15-3	7	5.87	75	.323	.449	4	.000	-0	64	-2	0	-0.2
Total	6	2	4	.333	42	4	0	0-0	77.1	96	62	9	9	53-7	68	6.63	70	.307	.413	4	.000	-0	105	-16	0	-0.9
JOHNSON, JOE	Joseph Richard; B10.30.1961 Brookline MA; BR/TR/6´2˝/(195–200); [AtlN82 2/37]; d7.25; Col Maine																									
1985	Atl N	4	4	.500	15	14	1	0-0	85.2	95	44	9	3	24-5	34	4.10	94	.285	.336	23-0-3	.043	-1	98	-2	0	-0.3
1986	Atl N	6	7	.462	17	15	2	0-0	87	101	58	8	2	35-4	49	4.97	80	.289	.357	26-0-2	.115	-1	98	-11	0	-1.4
	Tor A	7	2	.778	16	15	0	0-0	88	94	39	3	3	22-1	39	3.89	109	.281	.327	0	ø	0	104	5	0	0.4
1987	Tor A	3	5	.375	14	14	0	0-0	66.2	77	44	10	2	18-0	27	5.13	88	.289	.338	0	ø	0	99	-6	0	-0.6
Total	3	20	18	.526	62	58	3	0-0	327.1	367	185	30	10	99-10	149	4.48	92	.286	.340	49-0-5	.082	-2	100	-14	0	-1.9
JOHNSON, JOSH	Joshua Michael; B1.31.1984 Minneapolis MN; BL/TR/6´7˝/240; [FlaN02 4/113]; d9.10																									
2005	Fla N	0	0	ø	4	1	0	0-0	12.1	11	5	0	1	10-0	10	3.65	110	.256	.407	4	.250	0	118	1	0	0.1
2006	Fla N	12	7	.632	31	24	0	0-1	157	136	63	14	4	68-6	133	3.10	138	.236	.321	42-0-6	.095	-1	124	20	0	2.2
Total	2	12	7	.632	35	25	0	0-1	169.1	147	68	14	5	78-6	143	3.14	136	.237	.328	46-0-6	.109	-1	124	21	0	2.3
JOHNSON, KEN	Kenneth Travis; B6.16.1933 W.Palm Beach FL; BR/TR/6´4˝/(200–222); d9.13																									
1958	KC A	0	0	ø	2	0	0	0	2.1	6	7	1	0	3-0	1	27.00	14	.429	.529	0	ø	0	—	-5	0	-0.3
1959	KC A	1	1	.500	2	2	0	0	11	11	6	2	0	5-0	8	4.09	98	.268	.340	3	.000	-0	132	0	0	-0.1
1960	KC A	5	10	.333	42	6	2	3	120.1	120	68	16	7	45-6	83	4.26	93	.263	.336	30-0-3	.167	-1	85	-5	0	-0.6
1961	KC A	0	4	.000	6	1	0	0	9.1	11	11	2	0	7-0	4	10.61	39	.297	.409	1	.000	-0	0	-6	0	-1.0
	†Cin N	6	2	.750	15	11	3-1	1	83	71	33	11	2	22-1	42	3.25	125	.229	.283	25-0-1	.240	1	105	8	0	0.8
1962	Hou N	7	16	.304	33	31	5-1	0	197	195	100	18	7	46-1	178	3.84	97	.257	.302	52-0-9	.077	-3	71	-3	0	-0.6

THE PITCHER REGISTER

YEAR	TM LG	W	L	PCT	G	GS	CG-SHO	SV-BS	IP	H	R	HR	HB	BB-IB	SO	ERA	AERA	OAV	OOB	AB-HR-SH	AVG	PB	SUP	APR	DL	PW
1963	Hou N	11	17	.393	37	32	6-1	1	224	204	86	12	8	50-4	148	2.65	119	.242	.290	74-0-5	.068	-4*	77	9	0	0.8
1964	Hou N	11	16	.407	35	35	7-1	0	218	209	100	15	7	44-6	117	3.63	94	.250	.291	76-1-4	.079	-2	75	-5	0	-0.6
1965	Hou N	3	2	.600	8	8	1	0	51.2	52	25	4	4	11-1	28	4.18	80	.267	.315	18	.111	-0	111	-4	0	-0.3
	Mil N	13	8	.619	29	26	8-1	2	179.2	165	75	15	3	37-7	123	3.21	110	.240	.280	61-0-3	.115	-2	108	5	0	0.2
	Year	16	10	.615	37	34	9-1	2	231.1	217	100	19	7	48-8	151	3.42	102	.246	.288	79-0-3	.114	-2	108	1	0	-0.1
1966	Atl N	14	8	.636	32	31	11-2	0	215.2	213	89	24	0	46-6	105	3.30	110	.262	.300	70-1-10	.143	0	114	8	0	0.8
1967	Atl N	13	9	.591	29	29	6	0	210.1	191	78	19	7	38-8	85	2.74	121	.244	.284	71-0-6	.127	-0	121	12	0	1.1
1968	Atl N	5	8	.385	31	16	1	0	135	145	58	10	9	25-10	57	3.47	86	.279	.323	40-0-3	.175	-0	81	-6	0	-0.7
1969	Atl N	0	1	.000	9	2	0	1-1	29	32	17	4	0	9-1	20	4.97	73	.283	.328	6	.000	-0	73	-4	0	-0.2
	NY A	1	2	.333	12	0	0	0-0	26	19	11	1	0	11-2	21	3.46	102	.202	.286	3	.000	-0	—	0	0	0.1
	Chi N	1	2	.333	9	1	0	1-1	19	17	8	2	0	13-3	18	2.84	141	.230	.345	4-0-1	.000	-0	44	2	0	0.2
1970	Mon N	0	0	ø	3	0	0	0-0	6	9	6	1	2	1-0	4	7.50	55	.321	.387	0	ø	0	—	-2	0	-0.1
Total	13	91	106	.462	334	231	50-7	9-2	1737.1	1670	778	157	56	413-56	1042	3.46	101	.253	.301	534-2-45	.114	-12	92	4	0	-0.5

JOHNSON, KEN Kenneth Wandersee "Hook"; B1.14.1923 Topeka KS; D4.6.2004 Wichita KS; BL/TL/6´1˝/185; d9.18

YEAR	TM LG	W	L	PCT	G	GS	CG-SHO	SV-BS	IP	H	R	HR	HB	BB-IB	SO	ERA	AERA	OAV	OOB	AB-HR-SH	AVG	PB	SUP	APR	DL	PW
1947	StL N	1	0	1.000	2	1	1	0	10	2	1	0	1	5	8	0.00	ø	.063	.211	4	.500	1	64	4	0	0.5
1948	StL N	2	4	.333	13	4	0	0	45.1	43	27	1	1	30	20	4.76	86	.262	.379	20	.300	2*	60	-4	0	-0.3
1949	StL N	0	1	.000	14	2	0	0	33.2	29	28	1	3	35	18	6.42	65	.250	.435	8	.250	0*	106	-8	0	-0.3
1950	StL N	0	0	ø	2	0	0	0	2	1	1	0	0	3	1	0.00	ø	.167	.444	0	ø	0	—	0	0	0.0
	†Phi N	4	1	.800	14	8	3-1	0	60.2	61	32	3	1	43	32	4.01	101	.260	.376	19	.158	-0*	126	0	0	0.0
	Year	4	1	.800	16	8	3-1	0	62.2	62	33	3	1	46	33	3.88	105	.257	.378	19	.158	-0	126	0	0	0.0
1951	Phi N	5	8	.385	20	18	4-3	0	106.1	103	56	8	3	68	58	4.57	84	.259	.371	35-0-1	.143	-1*	74	-7	0	-0.9
1952	Det A	0	0	ø	9	1	0	0	11.1	12	11	1	0	11	10	6.35	60	.273	.418	3	.333	0	183	-4	0	-0.2
Total	6	12	14	.462	74	34	8-4	0	269.1	251	156	14	9	195	147	4.58	87	.252	.379	89-0-1	.213	1	90	-19	0	-1.2

JOHNSON, LLOYD Lloyd William "Eppa"; B12.24.1910 Santa Rosa CA; D10.8.1980 Stockton CA; BL/TL/6´4˝/204; d4.21

YEAR	TM LG	W	L	PCT	G	GS	CG-SHO	SV-BS	IP	H	R	HR	HB	BB-IB	SO	ERA	AERA	OAV	OOB	AB-HR-SH	AVG	PB	SUP	APR	DL	PW
1934	Pit N	0	0	ø	1	0	0	0	1	1	0	0	0	0	0	0.00	ø	.333	.333	0	ø	0	—	0	—	0.0

JOHNSON, MARK Mark J.; B5.2.1975 Dayton OH; BR/TR/6´3˝/226; [HouN96 1/19]; d4.7; Col Hawaii–Manoa

YEAR	TM LG	W	L	PCT	G	GS	CG-SHO	SV-BS	IP	H	R	HR	HB	BB-IB	SO	ERA	AERA	OAV	OOB	AB-HR-SH	AVG	PB	SUP	APR	DL	PW
2000	Det A	0	1	.000	9	3	0	0-0	24	25	23	3	1	16-1	11	7.50	65	.266	.365	0	ø	0	134	-7	35	-0.3

JOHNSON, MIKE Michael Keith; B10.3.1975 Edmonton AL, Can.; BL/TR/6´2˝/(170–180); [TorA93 17/490]; d4.6

YEAR	TM LG	W	L	PCT	G	GS	CG-SHO	SV-BS	IP	H	R	HR	HB	BB-IB	SO	ERA	AERA	OAV	OOB	AB-HR-SH	AVG	PB	SUP	APR	DL	PW
1997	Bal A	0	1	.000	14	5	0	2-0	39.2	52	36	12	1	16-2	29	7.94	56	.317	.377	0	ø	0	117	-15	0	-0.7
	Mon N	2	5	.286	11	11	0	0-0	50	54	34	8	0	21-2	28	5.94	70	.277	.344	13-0-2	.077	-1	86	-9	0	-1.1
1998	Mon N	0	2	.000	2	2	0	0-0	7.1	16	12	4	1	2-0	4	14.73	29	.432	.475	3	.333	0	109	-8	0	-1.1
1999	Mon N	0	0	ø	3	1	0	0-0	8.1	12	8	2	0	7-1	6	8.64	52	.324	.432	4	.250	0	289	-3	0	-0.1
2000	Mon N	5	6	.455	41	13	0	0-0	101.1	107	73	18	9	53-1	70	6.39	74	.269	.366	22-0-3	.182	0	118	-16	0	-1.4
2001	Mon N	0	0	ø	10	0	0	0-2	11.1	13	6	3	2	4-0	10	4.76	91	.295	.380	1	.000	-0	—	0	0	0.0
Total	5	7	14	.333	81	32	0	2-2	218	254	169	47	13	103-6	147	6.85	65	.290	.371	43-0-5	.163	-0	111	-51	0	-4.4

JOHNSON, MIKE Michael Norton; B3.2.1951 Slayton MN; BR/TR/6´1˝/185; d7.25

YEAR	TM LG	W	L	PCT	G	GS	CG-SHO	SV-BS	IP	H	R	HR	HB	BB-IB	SO	ERA	AERA	OAV	OOB	AB-HR-SH	AVG	PB	SUP	APR	DL	PW
1974	SD N	0	2	.000	18	0	0	0-0	21.1	29	13	1	1	15-5	15	4.64	77	.326	.421	0	ø	0	—	-3	0	-0.3

JOHNSON, RANDY Randall David "The Big Unit"; B9.10.1963 Walnut Creek CA; BR/TL/6´10˝/(225–232); [MonN85 2/36]; d9.15; Col USC

YEAR	TM LG	W	L	PCT	G	GS	CG-SHO	SV-BS	IP	H	R	HR	HB	BB-IB	SO	ERA	AERA	OAV	OOB	AB-HR-SH	AVG	PB	SUP	APR	DL	PW
1988	Mon N	3	0	1.000	4	4	1	0-0	26	23	8	3	0	7-0	25	2.42	150	.225	.275	9	.111	-0	152	3	0	0.3
1989	Mon N	0	4	.000	7	6	0	0-0	29.2	29	25	2	0	26-1	26	6.67	53	.264	.393	7-0-2	.143	-0	79	-10	0	-1.2
	Sea A	7	9	.438	22	22	2	0-0	131	118	75	11	3	70-1	104	4.40	92	.244	.338	0	ø	0	91	-6	0	-0.6
1990	Sea A☆	14	11	.560	33	33	5-2	0-0	219.2	174	103	26	5	120-2	194	3.65	109	.216	.319	0	ø	0	95	7	0	0.7
1991	Sea A	13	10	.565	33	33	2-1	0-0	201.1	151	96	15	12	152-0	228	3.98	104	.213	.358	0	ø	0	103	4	0	0.4
1992	Sea A	12	14	.462	31	31	6-2	0-0	210.1	154	104	13	18	144-1	**241**	3.77	106	**.206**	.344	0	ø	0	90	2	16	0.2
1993	Sea A★	19	8	.704	35	34	10-3	1-0	255.1	185	97	22	16	99-1	**308**	3.24	138	**.203**	.290	0	ø	0*	104	35	0	3.5
1994	Sea A★	13	6	.684	23	23	**9-4**	0-0	172	132	65	14	6	72-2	**204**	3.19	154	.216	.304	0	ø	0	103	34	0	3.5
1995	†Sea A★	18	2	**.900**	30	30	6-3	0-0	214.1	159	65	12	6	65-1	**294**	**2.48**	**193**	**.201**	**.266**	0	ø	0	108	**54**	0	**4.6**
1996	Sea A	5	0	1.000	14	8	0	1-1	61.1	48	27	8	2	25-0	85	3.67	136	.211	.294	0	ø	0	121	9	119	0.7
1997	†Sea A★	20	4	**.833**	30	29	5-2	0-0	213	147	60	20	10	77-2	291	2.28	199	**.194**	.277	0	ø	0	90	53	0	5.6
1998	Sea A	9	10	.474	23	23	6-2	0-0	160	146	90	19	11	60-0	213	4.33	108	.240	.319	7	.143	-0	97	3	0	0.4
	†Hou N	10	1	.909	11	11	4-4	0-0	84.1	57	12	4	3	26-1	116	1.28	317	.191	.261	32-0-3	.063	-2	99	28	0	3.5
1999	†Ari N★	17	9	.654	35	**35**	**12**-2	0-0	**271.2**	207	86	30	9	70-3	**364**	**2.48**	**186**	.208	.266	97-0-7	.124	-3	101	**62**	0	5.1
2000	Ari N★	19	7	**.731**	35	**35**	**8-3**	0-0	248.2	202	89	23	6	76-1	**347**	2.64	**182**	.224	.288	83-0-5	.157	-0	79	**53**	0	5.0
2001	†Ari N★	21	6	.778	35	34	3-2	0-0	249.2	181	74	19	18	71-2	**372**	**2.49**	**186**	.203	.274	80-0-7	.100	-3	103	**56**	0	**5.4**
2002	†Ari N☆	**24**	5	**.828**	35	35	**8**-4	0-0	**260**	197	78	26	13	71-1	**334**	**2.32**	**193**	**.208**	.273	89-0-6	.135	-2	114	**55**	0	**5.7**
2003	Ari N	6	8	.429	18	18	1-1	0-0	114	125	61	16	8	27-3	125	4.26	108	.280	.330	36-1-2	.194	1	83	4	98	0.4
2004	Ari N★	16	14	.533	35	**35**	4-2	0-0	245.2	177	88	18	10	44-1	**290**	2.60	**175**	**.197**	**.241**	80-0-3	.125	-1	72	**47**	0	**5.3**
2005	†NY A	17	8	.680	34	34	4	0-0	225.2	207	102	32	12	47-2	211	3.79	114	.243	.291	8	.000	-1	121	14	0	1.3
2006	†NY A	17	11	.607	33	33	2	0-0	205	194	125	28	10	60-1	172	5.00	91	.250	.309	6	.167	-0	131	-12	0	-1.3
Total	19	280	147	.656	556	546	98-37	2-1	3798.2	3013	1530	361	178	1409-26	4544	3.22	139	.217	.296	534-1-35	.127	-13	100	495	233	48.5

JOHNSON, BOB Robert Dale; B4.25.1943 Aurora IL; BL/TR/6´4˝/(210–220); d9.19; Col Bradley

YEAR	TM LG	W	L	PCT	G	GS	CG-SHO	SV-BS	IP	H	R	HR	HB	BB-IB	SO	ERA	AERA	OAV	OOB	AB-HR-SH	AVG	PB	SUP	APR	DL	PW
1969	NY N	0	0	ø	2	0	0	1-0	1.2	1	0	0	0	1-0	1	0.00	ø	.167	.286	0	ø	0	—	1	0	0.1
1970	KC A	8	13	.381	40	26	10-1	4-2	214	178	82	18	11	82-4	206	3.07	122	.228	.307	57-0-8	.105	-1	80	17	0	1.4
1971	†Pit N	9	10	.474	31	27	7-1	0-0	174.2	170	73	19	7	55-8	101	3.45	99	.259	.321	48-0-4	.063	-1	95	0	0	-0.2
1972	†Pit N	4	4	.500	31	11	1	3-1	115.2	98	40	14	4	46-8	79	2.96	112	.231	.309	35-0-1	.143	-0	114	7	0	0.4
1973	Pit N	4	2	.667	50	2	0	4-0	92	98	41	12	5	34-7	68	3.62	97	.276	.346	14-0-1	.000	-1	138	0	0	-0.3
1974	Cle A	3	4	.429	14	10	0	0-0	72	75	42	12	3	37-5	36	4.38	83	.273	.362	0	ø	0	126	-7	0	-0.6
1977	Atl N	0	1	.000	15	0	0	0-0	22.1	24	18	7	2	14-1	16	7.25	61	.270	.377	3	.333	0	—	-5	0	-0.3
Total	7	28	34	.452	183	76	18-2	12-3	692.1	644	296	82	32	269-33	507	3.48	102	.249	.325	157-0-14	.096	-4	97	13	0	0.5

JOHNSON, ROY Roy "Hardrock"; B10.1.1895 Madill OK; D1.10.1986 Scottsdale AZ; BR/TR/6´0˝/185; d8.7; M1/C15

YEAR	TM LG	W	L	PCT	G	GS	CG-SHO	SV-BS	IP	H	R	HR	HB	BB-IB	SO	ERA	AERA	OAV	OOB	AB-HR-SH	AVG	PB	SUP	APR	DL	PW
1918	Phi A	1	5	.167	10	8	3	0	50	47	32	0	2	34	12	3.42	86	.254	.376	15	.067	-2	77	-5	—	-0.8

JOHNSON, JING Russell Conwell; B10.9.1894 Parker Ford PA; D12.6.1950 Pottstown PA; BR/TR/5´9˝/172; d6.27; Mil 1918; Col Ursinus

YEAR	TM LG	W	L	PCT	G	GS	CG-SHO	SV-BS	IP	H	R	HR	HB	BB-IB	SO	ERA	AERA	OAV	OOB	AB-HR-SH	AVG	PB	SUP	APR	DL	PW
1916	Phi A	2	9	.182	12	12	8	0	84.1	90	46	3	0	39	25	3.74	76	.288	.368	27-1-1	.074	-1	88	-8	—	-0.9
1917	Phi A	9	12	.429	34	23	13	0	191	184	76	3	5	56	55	2.78	99	.260	.319	59-0-3	.203	2*	101	2	—	0.5
1919	Phi A	9	15	.375	34	25	12	0	202	222	106	8	3	62	67	3.61	95	.291	.346	72-1-4	.194	0*	82	-5	—	-0.3
1927	Phi A	4	2	.667	17	3	2	0	51.2	42	20	2	4	16	16	3.48	122	.235	.312	12-0-3	.167	-0	130	6	—	0.6
1928	Phi A	0	0	ø	3	0	0	0	10.2	13	8	1	0	5	3	5.06	79	.310	.383	4	.500	1	—	-2	—	0.0
Total	5	24	38	.387	100	63	35	0	539.2	551	256	17	12	178	166	3.35	95	.275	.338	174-2-11	.184	2	91	-7	—	-0.1

JOHNSON, SI Silas Kenneth; B10.5.1906 Danway IL; D5.12.1994 Sheridan IL; BR/TR/5´11.5˝/185; d5.2; Mil 1943–45

YEAR	TM LG	W	L	PCT	G	GS	CG-SHO	SV-BS	IP	H	R	HR	HB	BB-IB	SO	ERA	AERA	OAV	OOB	AB-HR-SH	AVG	PB	SUP	APR	DL	PW
1928	Cin N	0	0	ø	3	0	0	0	10.1	9	5	0	0	5	1	4.35	91	.250	.341	4	.250	0	—	0	—	0.0
1929	Cin N	0	0	ø	1	0	0	0	2	2	1	0	0	1	0	4.50	101	.250	.333	0	ø	0	—	0	—	0.0
1930	Cin N	3	1	.750	35	3	0	0	78.1	86	54	5	4	31	47	4.94	98	.286	.360	17	.235	-0	157	-3	—	-0.2
1931	Cin N	11	19	.367	42	33	14	0	262.1	273	131	5	6	74	95	3.77	99	.269	.323	87-0-3	.149	-3	77	-2	—	-0.7
1932	Cin N	13	15	.464	42	27	14-2	2	245	246	109	8	2	57	94	3.27	118	.259	.302	80-0-2	.125	-4	77	16	—	1.2
1933	Cin N	7	18	.280	34	28	14-4	1	211.1	212	101	7	3	54	51	3.49	97	.263	.312	72-0-3	.042	-7	63	-2	—	-1.0
1934	Cin N	7	22	.241	46	31	9	3	215.2	264	150	15	7	84	89	5.22	78	.297	.362	72	.139	-3	76	-26	—	-3.4
1935	Cin N	5	11	.313	30	20	4-1	0	130	155	106	14	3	59	40	6.23	64	.293	.367	41-0-1	.024	-4	78	-32	—	-3.7
1936	Cin N	0	0	ø	2	0	0	0	4	7	6	1	0	0	2	13.50	28	.368	.368	0	ø	0	—	-4	—	-0.2
	StL N	5	3	.625	12	9	3-1	0	61.2	82	30	4	1	11	21	4.38	90	.314	.344	21-0-1	.190	-0	100	-1	—	-0.2
	Year	5	3	.625	14	9	3-1	0	65.2	89	36	5	1	11	23	4.93	80	.318	.346	21-0-1	.190	-0	101	-4	—	-0.4
1937	StL N	12	12	.500	38	21	12-1	1	192.1	222	92	14	1	43	64	3.32	120	.292	.330	65-0-3	.138	-3	109	11	—	0.8
1938	StL N	0	3	.000	6	3	0	0	15.2	27	17	0	0	6	4	7.47	53	.380	.429	1-0-1	.000	-0	43	-6	—	-1.0
1940	Phi N	5	14	.263	37	14	5	1	138.1	145	81	13	2	42	58	4.88	80	.268	.323	43-0-2	.140	-2	62	-13	—	-1.9
1941	Phi N	5	12	.294	39	21	6-1	2	163.1	207	91	8	1	54	80	4.52	82	.309	.362	47-0-2	.149	-2	71	-13	0	-1.5
1942	Phi N	8	19	.296	39	26	10-1	0	195.1	198	96	6	1	72	78	3.69	90	.266	.332	58-0-5	.103	-4	66	-10	0	-1.8
1943	Phi N	8	3	.727	21	14	9-1	2	113	110	48	4	0	25	46	3.27	103	.252	.292	33-0-3	.182	0	122	1	0	0.1

YEAR	TM LG	W	L	PCT	G	GS	CG-SHO	SV-BS	IP	H	R	HR	HB	BB-IB	SO	ERA	AERA	OAV	OOB	AB-HR-SH	AVG	PB	SUP	APR	DL	PW
1946	Phi N	0	0	ø	1	0	0	0	3	7	4	1	0	0	2	3.00	114	.538	.538	1	1.000	0	—	-1	0	0.0
	Bos N	6	5	.545	28	12	5-1	1	127	134	47	8	4	35	41	2.76	124	.272	.325	37-0-4	.135	-2	121	9	0	0.5
	Year	6	5	.545	29	12	5-1	1	130	141	51	9	4	35	43	2.77	124	.279	.330	38-0-4	.158	-1	121	8	0	0.5
1947	Bos N	6	8	.429	36	10	3	2	112.2	124	57	7	1	34	27	4.23	92	.275	.327	30	.033	-3	97	-3	0	-0.5
Total	17	101	165	.380	492	272	108-13	15	2281.1	2510	1226	120	36	687	840	4.09	92	.279	.333	709-0-30	.123	-37	82	-79	0	-13.5
Johnson, Syl	Sylvester W (Born Sylvester Johnson); B12.31.1900 Portland OR; D2.20.1985 Portland OR; BR/TR/5´11˝/180; d4.24; C4																									
1922	Det A	7	3	.700	29	8	3	1	97	99	52	7	4	30	29	3.71	105	.273	.336	36-0-1	.222	-0	183	0	—	-0.1
1923	Det A	12	7	.632	37	18	7	0	176.1	181	82	12	3	47	93	3.98	97	.274	.325	62-1-2	.161	-1	106	2	—	-0.1
1924	Det A	5	4	.556	29	9	2	3	104	117	63	8	5	42	55	4.93	83	.287	.360	34-0-2	.206	-0	107	-7	—	-0.6
1925	Det A	0	2	.000	6	0	0	0	13	11	7	1	0	10	5	3.46	124	.250	.389	3	.000	-1	—	1	—	0.1
1926	StL N	0	3	.000	19	6	1	1	49	54	27	3	2	15	10	4.22	92	.297	.357	12	.000	-2	68	-2	—	-0.3
1927	StL N	0	0	ø	2	0	0	0	3	3	2	1	0	0	2	6.00	66	.250	.250	0	ø	0	—	0	—	0.0
1928	†StL N	8	4	.667	34	6	2	3	120	117	53	6	4	33	66	3.90	103	.259	.315	38	.158	-0	92	5	—	0.4
1929	StL N	13	7	.650	42	19	12-3	3	182.1	186	88	11	7	56	80	3.60	129	.265	.325	60-1-3	.117	-2	95	20	—	1.4
1930	†StL N	12	10	.545	32	24	9-2	2	187.2	215	105	13	4	38	92	4.65	108	.293	.332	70-0-1	.214	-0	113	11	—	0.9
1931	†StL N	11	9	.550	32	24	12-2	2	186	186	73	9	2	29	82	3.00	131	.255	.286	60-0-1	.233	2	103	18	—	1.9
1932	StL N	5	14	.263	32	22	7	2	164.2	199	103	14	4	35	70	4.92	80	.299	.338	51-0-3	.196	-1	93	-17	—	-1.9
1933	StL N	3	3	.500	35	1	0	3	84	89	45	7	3	16	28	4.29	81	.271	.311	21-0-1	.238	0	144	-6	—	-0.6
1934	Cin N	0	0	ø	2	0	0	0	6.2	9	6	2	0	0	0	2.70	151	.310	.310	2-1-0	.500	1	—	0	—	0.1
	Phi N	5	9	.357	42	10	4-3	3	133.2	122	58	14	1	24	54	3.50	135	.242	.277	41-0-2	.195	-1	86	16	—	1.4
	Year	5	9	.357	44	10	4-3	3	140.1	131	64	16	1	24	54	3.46	136	.245	.279	43-1-2	.209	1	86	16	—	1.5
1935	Phi N	10	8	.556	37	18	8-1	6	174.2	182	79	15	3	31	89	3.56	128	.265	.299	58-1-6	.241	1	88	18	—	1.8
1936	Phi N	5	7	.417	39	8	1	7	111	129	60	10	3	29	48	4.30	106	.288	.335	36	.250	-0	105	**5**	—	0.4
1937	Phi N	4	10	.286	32	15	4	3	138	155	81	19	2	22	46	5.02	86	.288	.318	48-0-2	.146	-3	72	-7	—	-1.0
1938	Phi N	2	7	.222	22	6	2	0	83	87	43	4	0	11	21	4.23	92	.267	.291	29-0-1	.034	-3	47	-2	—	-0.6
1939	Phi N	8	8	.500	22	13	6	2	111	112	50	10	1	15	37	3.81	105	.264	.291	33-0-4	.152	-1	84	4	—	0.3
1940	Phi N	2	2	.500	17	2	2	2	40.2	37	22	6	0	5	13	4.20	93	.236	.259	8-0-1	.000	-1	123	-2	—	-0.3
Total	19	112	117	.489	542	209	82-11	43	2165.2	2290	1099	172	48	488	920	4.06	104	.273	.316	702-4-30	.181	-10	98	57	—	3.2
Johnson, Tom	Thomas Raymond; B4.2.1951 St.Paul MN; BR/TR/6´1˝/185; d9.10																									
1974	Min A	2	0	1.000	4	0	0	1-0	7	4	1	0	0	0-0	4	0.00	ø	.167	.167	0	ø	0	—	2	0	0.5
1975	Min A	1	2	.333	18	0	0	3-2	38.2	40	23	4	2	21-4	17	4.19	91	.263	.356	0	ø	0	—	-3	0	-0.2
1976	Min A	3	1	.750	18	1	0	0-0	48.1	44	14	2	0	8-1	37	2.61	137	.243	.275	0	ø	0	74	6	0	0.5
1977	Min A	16	7	.696	71	0	0	15-7	146.2	152	57	11	5	47-8	87	3.13	127	.272	.329	0	ø	0	—	14	0	2.4
1978	Min A	1	4	.200	18	0	0	3-1	32.2	42	22	2	2	17-4	21	5.51	70	.318	.399	0	ø	0	—	-6	72	-0.9
Total	5	23	14	.622	129	1	0	22-10	273.1	282	117	19	9	93-17	166	3.39	114	.269	.330	0	ø	0	74	13	72	2.3
Johnson, Tyler	Tyler James; B6.7.1981 Columbia MO; BB/TL/6´2˝/180; [StLN00 34/1013]; d9.6; Col Moorpark (CA) JC																									
2005	StL N	0	0	ø	5	0	0	0-1	2.2	3	0	0	0	3-0	4	0.00	ø	.300	.462	0	ø	0	—	1	0	0.1
2006	†StL N	2	4	.333	56	0	0	0-2	36.1	33	21	5	4	23-2	37	4.95	88	.244	.368	1	.000	-0	—	-2	0	-0.4
Total	2	2	4	.333	61	0	0	0-3	39	36	21	5	4	26-2	41	4.62	94	.248	.375	1	.000	-0	—	-1	0	-0.3
Johnson, Vic	Victor Oscar; B8.3.1920 Eau Claire WI; D5.10.2005 Eau Claire WI; BR/TL/6´0˝/160; d5.3																									
1944	Bos A	0	3	.000	7	5	0	0	27.1	42	22	0	0	15	7	6.26	54	.362	.435	10	.000	-1	123	-9	0	-1.0
1945	Bos A	6	4	.600	26	9	4-1	2	85.1	90	41	4	2	46	21	4.01	85	.276	.369	30	.167	-1	100	-5	0	-0.6
1946	Cle A	0	1	.000	9	1	0	0	13.2	20	14	1	0	8	3	9.22	36	.357	.438	2	.000	-0	52	-9	0	-0.6
Total	3	6	8	.429	42	15	4-1	2	126.1	152	77	5	2	69	31	5.06	67	.305	.392	42	.119	-3	105	-23	0	-2.2
Johnson, Walter	Walter Perry "Barney","The Big Train"; B11.6.1887 Humboldt KS; D12.10.1946 Washington DC; BR/TR/6´1˝/200; d8.2; M7; HF1937																									
1907	Was A	5	9	.357	14	12	11-2	0	110.1	100	35	1	2	20	71	1.88	129	.244	.282	36	.111	-2	58	7	—	0.5
1908	Was A	14	14	.500	36	30	23-6	1	256.1	194	75	0	11	53	160	1.65	139	.211	.262	79-0-5	.165	3	79	17	—	2.1
1909	Was A	13	25	.342	40	36	27-4	1	296.1	247	112	1	15	84	164	2.22	110	.221	.284	101-1-3	.129	-3	52	4	—	0.1
1910	Was A	25	17	.595	**45**	**42**	**38**-8	1	**370**	262	92	1	13	76	**313**	1.36	183	.205	.257	137-2-1	.175	1	104	43	—	5.5
1911	Was A	25	13	.658	40	37	**36-6**	1	322.1	292	119	8	8	70	207	1.90	173	.238	.283	128-1-6	.234	3*	106	**43**	—	5.4
1912	Was A	33	12	.733	50	37	34-7	2	369	259	89	2	16	76	**303**	**1.39**	**240**	**.196**	**.248**	144-2-6	.264	9*	102	**77**	—	**10.6**
1913	Was A	**36**	7	**.837**	48	36	**29-11**	2	**346**	232	56	9	9	38	**243**	**1.14**	**258**	**.190**	**.220**	134-2-1	.261	10*	97	**70**	—	**10.9**
1914	Was A	**28**	18	.609	**51**	**40**	**33-9**	1	**371.2**	287	88	3	11	74	**225**	1.72	164	.217	.265	136-3-5	.221	8*	89	**45**	—	**7.2**
1915	Was A	**27**	13	.675	47	**39**	**35-7**	4	**336.2**	258	83	1	19	56	**203**	1.55	**192**	.214	**.260**	147-2-5	.231	6*	94	**51**	—	**7.4**
1916	Was A	**25**	20	.556	48	38	**36**-3	1	**369.2**	290	105	0	9	82	**228**	1.90	147	.220	.270	142-1-4	.225	8*	88	35	—	5.2
1917	Was A	23	16	.590	47	34	30-8	3	326	248	105	3	14	68	**188**	2.21	119	.211	.263	130-0-2	.254	10*	102	15	—	3.1
1918	Was A	**23**	13	.639	39	29	29-**8**	3	326	241	71	2	8	70	**162**	**1.27**	**215**	.210	**.260**	150-1-4	.267	6*	92	**51**	—	**7.6**
1919	Was A	20	14	.588	39	29	27-**7**	2	290.1	235	73	0	7	51	**147**	**1.49**	**216**	**.219**	**.259**	125-1-4	.192	2*	90	**52**	—	**6.7**
1920	Was A	8	10	.444	21	15	12-4	3	143.2	135	68	5	5	27	78	3.13	119	.245	.286	64-1-2	.266	4*	67	8	—	1.3
1921	Was A	17	14	.548	35	32	25-1	1	264	265	122	7	2	92	**143**	3.51	117	.263	.326	111-0-2	.270	4*	103	19	—	2.3
1922	Was A	15	16	.484	41	31	23-4	4	280	283	115	8	7	99	105	2.99	129	.267	.334	108-1-2	.204	-1*	77	28	—	2.8
1923	Was A	17	12	.586	42	34	18-3	4	261	263	112	9	20	73	**130**	3.48	108	.269	.333	93-0-6	.194	1	94	14	—	1.4
1924	†Was A	**23**	7	**.767**	38	**38**	20-**6**	0	277.2	233	97	10	10	77	**158**	**2.72**	148	**.224**	**.284**	113-1-2	.283	7*	117	**44**	—	**4.9**
1925	†Was A	20	7	.741	30	29	16-3	0	229	217	95	7	7	78	108	3.07	138	**.250**	.317	97-2-6	.433	17*	126	30	—	**4.6**
1926	Was A	15	16	.484	33	33	22-2	0	260.2	259	120	13	5	73	125	3.63	107	.263	.317	103-1-3	.194	1*	108	8	—	0.7
1927	Was A	5	6	.455	18	15	7-1	0	107.2	113	70	7	7	26	48	5.10	80	.278	.332	46-2-1	.348	6*	96	-12	—	-0.4
Total	21	417	279	.599	802	666	531-110	34	5914.1	4913	1902	97	205	1363	3509	2.17	147	.227	.279	2324-24-70	.235	99	96	649	—	89.9
Johnson, Bill	William Charles; B10.6.1960 Wilmington DE; BR/TR/6´5˝/205; d9.6																									
1983	Chi N	1	0	1.000	10	0	0	0-0	12.1	17	6	0	0	3-1	4	4.38	87	.347	.377	0	ø	0	—	0	0	0.0
1984	Chi N	0	0	ø	4	0	0	0-0	5.1	4	1	0	0	1-1	3	1.69	232	.235	.278	0	ø	0	—	1	0	0.1
Total	2	1	0	1.000	14	0	0	0-0	17.2	21	7	0	0	4-2	7	3.57	108	.318	.352	0	ø	0	—	1	0	0.1
Johnson, Jeff	William Jeffrey; B8.4.1966 Durham NC; BR/TL/6´3˝/(200–206); [NYA88 6/157]; d6.5; Col North Carolina–Charlotte																									
1991	NY A	6	11	.353	23	23	0	0-0	127	156	89	15	6	33-1	62	5.95	70	.305	.351	0	ø	0	90	-24	0	-2.6
1992	NY A	2	3	.400	13	8	0	0-0	52.2	71	44	4	2	23-0	14	6.66	59	.329	.395	0	ø	0	104	-16	0	-1.4
1993	NY A	0	2	.000	2	2	0	0-0	2.2	12	10	1	0	2-0	0	30.38	14	.600	.636	0	ø	0	44	-8	0	-1.2
Total	3	8	16	.333	38	33	0	0-0	182.1	239	143	20	8	58-1	76	6.52	63	.320	.372	0	ø	0	90	-48	0	-5.2
Johnston, Joel	Joel Raymond; B3.8.1967 West Chester PA; BR/TR/6´4˝/(220–234); [KCA88 3/75]; d9.5; Col Penn St.																									
1991	KC A	1	0	1.000	13	0	0	0-0	22.1	9	1	0	0	9-3	21	0.40	1029	.120	.214	0	ø	0	—	9	0	0.5
1992	KC A	0	0	ø	5	0	0	0-0	2.2	3	4	2	0	2-0	0	13.50	30	.273	.385	0	ø	0	—	-3	0	-0.1
1993	Pit N	2	4	.333	33	0	0	2-1	53.1	38	20	7	0	19-5	31	3.38	121	.203	.277	6-0-1	.333	1	—	5	0	0.6
1994	Pit N	0	0	ø	4	0	0	0-0	3.1	14	12	0	2	4-0	5	29.70	15	.583	.667	0	ø	0	—	-9	0	-0.4
1995	Bos A	0	1	.000	4	0	0	0-0	4	2	5	1	1	3-0	4	11.25	43	.143	.333	0	ø	0	—	-3	0	-0.5
Total	5	3	5	.375	59	0	0	2-1	85.2	66	42	10	3	37-8	61	4.31	96	.212	.302	6-0-1	.333	1	—	-1	0	0.1
Johnston, Mike	Michael Charles; B3.30.1979 Philadelphia PA; BL/TL/6´2˝/(215–225); [PitN98 20/598]; d4.7; Col Garrett (MD) CC																									
2004	Pit N	0	3	.000	24	0	0	0-1	22.2	29	16	2	2	15-1	18	4.37	99	.315	.422	0	ø	0	—	-2	41	-0.2
2005	Pit N	0	0	ø	1	0	0	0-0	1	4	4	2	0	0-0	2	36.00	12	.571	.571	0	ø	0	—	-3	0	-0.2
Total	2	0	3	.000	25	0	0	0-1	23.2	33	20	4	2	15-1	20	5.70	76	.333	.431	0	ø	0	—	-5	41	-0.4
Johnstone, John	John William; B11.25.1968 Liverpool NY; BR/TR/6´3˝/(195–210); [NYN87 20/524]; d9.3; [DL 2001 SF N 190]																									
1993	Fla N	0	2	.000	7	0	0	0-0	10.2	16	8	1	0	7-0	5	5.91	74	.340	.426	0	ø	0	—	-2	0	-0.3
1994	Fla N	1	2	.333	17	0	0	0-0	21.1	23	20	4	1	16-5	23	5.91	75	.264	.385	0-0-1	ø	0	—	-5	0	-0.6
1995	Fla N	0	0	ø	4	0	0	0-0	4.2	7	2	1	0	2-1	3	3.86	111	.333	.391	0	ø	0	—	0	147	0.0
1996	Hou N	1	0	1.000	9	0	0	0-0	13	17	8	2	0	5-0	5	5.54	70	.321	.367	0	ø	0	—	-2	0	-0.2
1997	SF N	0	0	ø	10	0	0	0-0	16.2	12	4	0	4	6-0	14	2.16	191	.218	.324	2	.000	-0	—	4	0	0.2
	Oak A	0	0	ø	5	0	0	0-0	6.1	7	2	0	0	7-0	4	2.84	162	.292	.438	0	ø	0	—	1	0	0.1
	SF N	0	0	ø	3	0	0	0-0	2	3	3	1	0	1-0	1	13.50	31	.333	.400	0	ø	0	—	-2	0	-0.1
1998	SF N	6	5	.545	70	0	0	0-1	88	72	32	10	1	38-8	86	3.07	131	.224	.303	2-0-1	.000	-0	—	10	0	1.0

YEAR	TM LG	W	L	PCT	G	GS	CG-SHO	SV-BS	IP	H	R	HR	HB	BB-IB	SO	ERA	AERA	OAV	OOB	AB-HR-SH	AVG	PB	SUP	APR	DL	PW
1999	SF N	4	6	.400	62	0	0	3-4	65.2	48	24	8	1	20-5	56	2.60	164	.203	.267	0	ø	0	—	11	0	1.6
2000	SF N	3	4	.429	47	0	0	0-3	50	64	35	11	2	13-2	37	6.30	69	.322	.362	2	.000	-0	—	-10	45	-1.2
Total	8	15	19	.441	234	0	0	3-8	278.1	269	138	38	9	115-21	234	4.01	105	.255	.329	6-0-2	.000	-1	—	5	382	0.5
JOINER, ROY	Roy Merrill "Pop"; B10.30.1906 Red Bluff CA; D12.26.1989 Red Bluff CA; BL/TL/6´0˝/170; d4.30																									
1934	Chi N	0	1	.000	20	2	0	0	34	61	33	3	0	8	9	8.21	47	.391	.421	10	.200	-0	100	-16	—	-0.8
1935	Chi N	0	0	ø	2	0	0	0	3.1	6	4	0	0	2	0	5.40	73	.429	.500	1	.000	-0	—	-1	—	-0.1
1940	NY N	3	2	.600	30	2	0	1	53	66	26	8	5	17	25	3.40	114	.308	.373	11-0-1	.273	1	67	2	—	0.2
Total	3	3	3	.500	52	4	0	1	90.1	133	63	11	5	27	34	5.28	74	.346	.397	22-0-1	.227	0	84	-15	—	-0.7
JOLLY, DAVE	David "Gabby"; B10.14.1924 Stony Point NC; D5.27.1963 Durham NC; BR/TR/6´0˝/(160–165); d5.9																									
1953	Mil N	0	1	.000	24	0	0	0	38.1	34	16	4	1	27	23	3.52	111	.239	.365	2	.500	1	—	3	0	0.2
1954	Mil N	11	6	.647	47	1	0	10	111.1	87	36	6	2	64	62	2.43	154	.215	.321	31-1-2	.290	3*	24	17	0	3.0
1955	Mil N	2	3	.400	36	0	0	1	58.1	58	42	6	1	51-7	23	5.71	66	.258	.396	6	.167	0	—	-14	0	-1.0
1956	Mil N	2	3	.400	29	0	0	7	45.2	39	21	7	0	35-4	20	3.74	92	.228	.356	4-0-1	.000	-0	—	-1	0	-0.2
1957	Mil N	1	1	.500	23	0	0	1	37.2	37	22	4	3	21-0	27	5.02	70	.264	.367	5	.600	1	—	-6	0	-0.2
Total	5	16	14	.533	159	1	0	19	291.1	255	137	27	7	198-11	155	3.77	98	.236	.354	48-1-3	.292	5	24	-1	0	1.8
JONES, COWBOY	Albert Edward "Bronco"; B8.23.1874 Golden CO; D2.9.1958 Inglewood CA; BL/TL/5´11˝/160; d6.24																									
1898	Cle N	4	4	.500	9	9	7	0	72	76	44	0	4	29	26	3.00	121	.269	.345	28-0-1	.071	-3	100	2	—	-0.2
1899	StL N	6	5	.545	12	12	9	0	85.1	111	51	1	6	22	28	3.59	111	.314	.364	29-0-1	.172	0	80	3	—	0.5
1900	StL N	13	19	.406	39	36	29-3	0	292.2	334	185	10	19	82	68	3.54	103	.286	.343	117-0-3	.179	-3	106	-2	—	-0.3
1901	StL N	2	6	.250	10	9	7	0	76.1	97	51	4	3	22	25	4.48	71	.307	.358	27-0-1	.148	0	114	-12	—	-0.9
Total	4	25	34	.424	70	66	52-3	0	526.1	618	331	15	32	155	147	3.61	100	.292	.349	201-0-6	.159	-5	101	-9	—	-0.9
JONES, ALEX	Alexander; B12.25.1869 Pittsburgh PA; D4.4.1941 Woodville PA; BL/TL/5´6˝/135; d9.25																									
1889	Pit N	1	0	1.000	1	1	1	0	9	7	5	0	0	1	10	3.00	125	.206	.229	5	.200	0	143	1	—	0.1
1892	Lou N	5	11	.313	18	16	13-1	0	146.2	130	90	3	9	56	44	3.31	93	.228	.307	55	.145	-1	84	-5	—	-0.5
	Was N	0	3	.000	4	4	3	0	27	33	23	0	2	14	7	4.00	81	.289	.377	11	.273	0	44	-3	—	-0.3
	Year	5	14	.263	22	20	16-1	0	173.2	163	113	3	11	70	51	3.42	91	.238	.319	66	.167	-1	76	-7	—	-0.8
1894	Phi N	1	0	1.000	1	1	1	0	9	10	4	0	0	0	2	2.00	257	.278	.278	4	.250	-0	83	3	—	0.2
1903	Det A	0	1	.000	2	2	0	0	8.2	19	15	0	0	6	2	12.46	23	.432	.500	4	.000	-1	184	-8	—	-0.8
Total	4	7	15	.318	26	24	18-1	0	200.1	199	137	3	11	77	65	3.73	86	.249	.324	79	.165	-1	86	-12	—	-1.3
JONES, AL	Alfornia; B2.10.1959 Charleston MS; BR/TR/5´11˝/165; [ChiA81 13/318]; d8.6; Col Alcorn St.																									
1983	Chi A	0	0	ø	2	0	0	0-0	2.1	3	1	0	0	2-0	2	3.86	110	.375	.500	0	ø	0	—	0	0	0.0
1984	Chi A	1	1	.500	20	0	0	5-1	20.1	23	10	3	1	11-0	15	4.43	95	.299	.385	0	ø	0	—	0	0	0.0
1985	Chi A	1	0	1.000	5	0	0	0-0	6	3	2	0	0	3-0	2	1.50	290	.167	.286	0	ø	0	—	1	134	0.2
Total	3	2	1	.667	27	0	0	5-1	28.2	29	13	3	1	16-0	19	3.77	112	.282	.377	0	ø	0	—	1	134	0.2
JONES, ART	Arthur Lennox; B2.7.1906 Kershaw SC; D11.25.1980 Columbia SC; BR/TR/6´0˝/165; d4.23; Col Furman																									
1932	Bro N	0	0	ø	1	0	0	0	1	2	2	0	0	1	0	18.00	21	.667	.750	0	ø	0	—	-1	—	-0.1
JONES, BARRY	Barry Louis; B2.15.1963 Centerville IN; BR/TR/6´4˝/(210–225); [PitN84 3/69]; d7.18; Col Indiana																									
1986	Pit N	3	4	.429	26	0	0	3-4	37.1	29	16	3	0	21-2	29	2.89	134	.215	.318	5-0-1	.200	0	—	3	0	0.6
1987	Pit N	2	4	.333	32	0	0	1-3	43.1	55	34	6	0	23-6	28	5.61	74	.314	.390	3	.000	-0	—	-9	0	-1.1
1988	Pit N	1	1	.500	42	0	0	2-3	56.1	57	21	3	1	21-6	31	3.04	114	.271	.335	5	.000	-0	—	3	0	0.1
	Chi A	2	2	.500	17	0	0	1-0	26	15	7	3	0	17-1	17	2.42	165	.170	.302	0	ø	0	—	5	0	0.8
1989	Chi A	3	2	.600	22	0	0	1-0	30.1	22	12	2	1	8-0	17	2.37	162	.208	.265	0	ø	0	—	4	112	0.6
1990	Chi A	11	4	.733	65	0	0	1-7	74	62	20	2	1	33-7	45	2.31	166	.235	.317	0	ø	0	—	13	0	2.6
1991	Mon N	4	9	.308	**77**	0	0	13-8	88.2	76	35	8	1	33-8	46	3.35	109	.246	.318	1-0-1	.000	-0	—	4	0	0.7
1992	Phi N	5	6	.455	44	0	0	0-6	54.1	65	30	3	2	24-4	19	4.64	76	.305	.378	2	.000	-0	—	-6	0	-1.2
	NY N	2	0	1.000	17	0	0	1-0	15.1	20	16	0	0	11-3	11	9.39	37	.317	.413	0	ø	0	—	-9	0	-1.2
	Year	7	6	.538	61	0	0	1-6	69.2	85	46	3	2	35-7	30	5.68	62	.308	.386	2	.000	-0	—	-16	0	-2.4
1993	Chi A	0	1	.000	6	0	0	0-0	7.1	14	8	2	0	3-0	7	8.59	49	.412	.459	0	ø	0	—	-4	0	-0.4
Total	8	33	33	.500	348	0	0	23-31	433	415	199	32	6	194-37	250	3.66	103	.260	.338	16-0-2	.063	-1	—	4	112	1.5
JONES, CALVIN	Calvin Douglas; B9.26.1963 Compton CA; BR/TR/6´3˝/185; [SeaA84*1/1]; d6.14; Col California–Riverside																									
1991	Sea A	2	2	.500	27	0	0	2-1	46.1	33	14	0	1	29-5	42	2.53	164	.209	.335	0	ø	0	—	8	0	0.7
1992	Sea A	3	5	.375	38	1	0	0-2	61.2	50	39	8	2	47-1	49	5.69	70	.226	.361	0	ø	0	91	-10	0	-1.2
Total	2	5	7	.417	65	1	0	2-3	108	83	53	8	3	76-6	91	4.33	94	.219	.351	0	ø	0	91	-2	0	-0.5
JONES, DEACON	Carroll Elmer; B12.20.1892 Arcadia KS; D12.28.1952 Pittsburg KS; BR/TR/6´1˝/174; d9.23																									
1916	Det A	0	0	ø	1	0	0	0	7	7	3	0	0	5	2	2.57	111	.269	.387	2	.000	-0	—	0	—	0.0
1917	Det A	4	4	.500	24	6	2	0	77	69	34	0	6	26	28	2.92	91	.256	.334	15-0-2	.000	-1	131	-2	—	-0.2
1918	Det A	3	2	.600	21	4	1	0	67	60	35	0	1	38	15	3.09	86	.244	.347	25	.200	-0*	198	-6	—	-0.4
Total	3	7	6	.538	46	10	3	0	151	136	72	0	7	69	45	2.98	89	.251	.343	42-0-2	.119	-1	158	-8	—	-0.6
JONES, BUMPUS	Charles Leander; B1.1.1870 Cedarville OH; D6.25.1938 Xenia OH; BR/TR; d10.15																									
1892	Cin N	1	0	1.000	1	1	1	0	9	0	1	0	0	4	3	0.00	ø	.000	.129	2	.000	-0	19	3	—	0.3
1893	Cin N	1	3	.250	6	5	2	0	28.2	37	37	1	5	23	6	10.05	48	.303	.433	16	.250	1	88	-14	—	-1.3
	NY N	0	1	.000	1	1	0	0	4	5	5	0	1	10	1	11.25	41	.294	.571	0	ø	0	30	-2	—	-0.3
	Year	1	4	.200	7	6	2	0	32.2	42	42	1	6	33	7	10.19	47	.302	.455	16	.250	1	78	-14	—	-1.6
Total	2	2	4	.333	8	7	3	0	41.2	42	43	1	6	37	10	7.99	56	.253	.407	18	.222	1	73	-13	—	-1.3
JONES, DALE	Dale Eldon "Nubs"; B12.17.1918 Marquette NE; D11.8.1980 Orlando FL; BR/TR/6´1˝/172; d9.7; Mil 1942–45; Col Wayne State (NE)																									
1941	Phi N	0	1	.000	2	1	0	0	8.1	13	11	0	0	6	2	7.56	49	.342	.432	3	.333	0	138	-5	0	-0.4
JONES, JACK	Daniel Albion "Jumping Jack"; B10.23.1860 Litchfield CT; D10.19.1936 Wallingford CT; TR; d7.9; Col Yale																									
1883	Det N	6	5	.545	12	12	9-1	0	92.2	103	63	0	—	19	33	3.50	89	.259	.293	42	.190	-2	78	-3	—	-0.5
	Phi AA	5	2	.714	7	7	7	0	65	58	38	1	—	6	28	2.63	135	.223	.241	25	.240	-0	95	6	—	0.5
Total	1	11	7	.611	19	19	16-1	0	157.2	161	101	1	—	25	61	3.14	104	.245	.273	67	.209	-2	84	3	—	0.0
JONES, DICK	Decatur Poindexter; B5.22.1902 Meadville MS; D8.2.1994 Burlingame CA; BL/TR/6´0˝/184; d9.11																									
1926	Was A	2	1	.667	4	3	1	0	21	20	10	0	0	11	3	4.29	90	.263	.356	10-0-1	.200	-0*	123	0	—	-0.1
1927	Was A	0	0	ø	2	0	0	0	3.1	8	11	0	0	5	1	21.60	19	.444	.565	0	ø	0	—	-7	—	-0.3
Total	2	2	1	.667	6	3	1	0	24.1	28	21	0	0	16	4	6.66	58	.298	.400	10-0-1	.200	-0	123	-7	—	-0.4
JONES, DOUG	Douglas Reid; B6.24.1957 Lebanon IN; BR/TR/6´2˝/(170–225); [MilA78*3/59]; d4.9; Col Butler																									
1982	Mil A	0	0	ø	4	0	0	0-0	2.2	5	3	1	0	1-0	1	10.13	38	.385	.429	0	ø	0	—	-2	0	-0.1
1986	Cle A	1	0	1.000	11	0	0	1-1	18	18	5	0	1	6-1	12	2.50	167	.257	.321	0	ø	0	—	4	0	0.2
1987	Cle A	6	5	.545	49	0	0	8-4	91.1	101	45	4	6	24-5	87	3.15	145	.281	.332	0	ø	0	—	10	0	1.3
1988	Cle A★	3	4	.429	51	0	0	37-6	83.1	69	26	1	2	16-3	72	2.27	182	.218	.260	0	ø	0	—	15	0	2.5
1989	Cle A★	7	10	.412	59	0	0	32-9	80.2	76	25	4	1	13-4	65	2.34	170	.251	.279	0	ø	0	—	14	0	2.9
1990	Cle A☆	5	5	.500	66	0	0	43-8	84.1	66	26	5	2	22-4	55	2.56	154	.218	.274	0	ø	0	—	13	0	2.5
1991	Cle A	4	8	.333	36	4	0	7-5	63.1	87	42	7	0	17-5	48	5.54	75	.320	.357	0	ø	0	99	-9	0	-1.6
1992	Hou N★	11	8	.579	80	0	0	36-6	111.2	96	29	5	5	17-5	93	1.85	183	.235	.274	4	.000	-0	—	18	0	3.9
1993	Hou N	4	10	.286	71	0	0	26-8	85.1	102	46	7	5	21-6	66	4.54	85	.298	.344	0	ø	0	—	-5	0	-1.1
1994	Phi N★	2	4	.333	47	0	0	27-2	54	55	14	2	0	6-0	38	2.17	198	.255	.275	1	1.000	0	—	**13**	0	2.5
1995	Bal A	0	4	.000	52	0	0	22-3	46.2	55	30	6	2	16-2	42	5.01	95	.286	.348	0	ø	0	—	-2	0	-0.4
1996	Chi N	2	2	.500	28	0	0	2-5	32.1	41	20	4	1	7-4	26	5.01	87	.306	.345	0	ø	0	—	-2	0	-0.3
	Mil A	5	0	1.000	24	0	0	1-3	31.2	31	13	3	2	13-2	34	3.41	152	.254	.331	0	ø	0	—	6	0	0.8
1997	Mil A	6	6	.500	75	0	0	36-2	80.1	62	20	4	3	9-1	82	2.02	230	.215	.242	0	ø	0	—	23	17	4.5
1998	Mil N	3	4	.429	46	0	0	12-8	54	65	32	15	4	11-1	43	5.17	84	.298	.339	2	.000	-0	—	-4	0	-0.6
	†Cle A	1	2	.333	23	0	0	1-1	31.1	34	12	2	0	6-3	28	3.45	139	.279	.305	0	ø	0	—	5	0	0.5
1999	Oak A	5	5	.500	70	0	0	10-6	104	106	43	10	3	24-3	63	3.55	133	.267	.311	0	ø	0	—	15	0	1.5

YEAR	TM LG	W	L	PCT	G	GS	CG-SHO	SV-BS	IP	H	R	HR	HB	BB-IB	SO	ERA	AERA	OAV	OOB	AB-HR-SH	AVG	PB	SUP	APR	DL	PW
2000	†Oak A	4	2	.667	54	0	0	2-0	73.1	86	34	6	2	18-4	54	3.93	124	.292	.334	0	ø	0	—	8	5	0.6
Total	16	69	79	.466	846	4	0	303-77	1128.1	1155	465	86	39	247-53	909	3.30	130	.264	.307	7	.143	0	99	120	22	19.6
Jones, Earl	Earl Leslie "Lefty"; B6.11.1919 Fresno CA; D1.24.1989 Fresno CA; BL/TL/5´10.5˝/190; d7.6																									
1945	StL A	0	0	ø	10	0	0	1	28.1	18	10	0	0	18	13	2.54	139	.184	.310	10-1-0	.200	1	—	3	0	0.2
Jones, Elijah	Elijah Albert "Bumpus"; B1.27.1882 Oxford MI; D4.29.1943 Pontiac MI; BR/TR/5´11.5˝/?; d4.13																									
1907	Det A	0	1	.000	4	1	1	1	16	23	15	0	1	4	9	5.06	51	.338	.384	4	.000	-1	104	-5	—	-0.4
1909	Det A	1	1	.500	2	2	0	0	10	10	3	0	0	0	2	2.70	93	.278	.278	4	.250	0	154	0	—	0.0
Total	2	1	2	.333	6	3	1	1	26	33	18	0	1	4	11	4.15	62	.317	.349	8	.125	-0	133	-5	—	-0.4
Jones, Gary	Gareth Howell; B6.12.1945 Huntington Park CA; BL/TL/6´0˝/(185–191); d9.25; b–Steve; Col Whittier																									
1970	NY A	0	0	ø	2	0	0	0-0	2	3	0	0	0	1-0	2	0.00	ø	.375	.444	0	ø	0	—	1	0	0.0
1971	NY A	0	0	ø	12	0	0	0-0	14	19	14	1	0	7-1	10	9.00	37	.317	.382	1	.000	-0	—	-8	0	-0.5
Total	2	0	0	ø	14	0	0	0-0	16	22	14	1	0	8-1	12	7.88	42	.324	.390	1	.000	-0	—	-7	0	-0.5
Jones, Gordon	Gordon Bassett; B4.2.1930 Portland OR; D4.25.1994 Lodi CA; BR/TR/6´0˝/(185–190); d8.6; C2																									
1954	StL N	4	4	.500	11	10	4-2	0	81	78	25	3	1	19	48	2.00	206	.248	.292	24-0-4	.125	-1	74	17	0	1.5
1955	StL N	1	4	.200	15	9	0	0	57	66	38	10	1	28-5	46	5.84	70	.286	.363	14-0-3	.071	-1	88	-10	0	-0.9
1956	StL N	0	2	.000	5	1	0	0	11.1	14	9	2	0	5-0	6	5.56	68	.311	.380	2	.000	-0	116	-3	0	-0.4
1957	NY N	0	1	.000	10	0	0	0	11.2	16	9	1	1	3-1	5	6.17	64	.320	.364	2	.500	0	—	-3	0	-0.2
1958	SF N	3	1	.750	11	1	0	1	30.1	33	11	2	1	5-1	8	2.37	161	.284	.320	7	.000	-1	188	4	0	0.5
1959	SF N	3	2	.600	31	0	0	2	43.2	45	23	6	1	19-5	29	4.33	88	.280	.355	4-0-1	.000	-0	—	-2	0	-0.3
1960	Bal A	1	1	.500	29	0	0	2	55	59	28	9	1	13-1	30	4.42	86	.281	.324	5	.400	1	—	-3	0	-0.1
1961	Bal A	0	0	ø	3	0	0	1	5	5	3	3	0	0-0	4	5.40	71	.250	.250	0	ø	0	—	-1	0	0.0
1962	KC A	3	2	.600	21	0	0	6	32.2	31	23	10	0	14-1	28	6.34	67	.252	.324	5-0-1	.000	-1	—	-6	0	-1.2
1964	Hou N	0	1	.000	34	0	0	0	50	58	24	3	0	14-2	28	4.14	83	.290	.333	4	.250	0	—	-3	0	-0.2
1965	Hou N	0	0	ø	1	0	0	0	1	0	0	0	0	0-0	0	0.00	ø	.000	.000	0	ø	0	—	0	0	0.0
Total	11	15	18	.455	171	21	4-2	12	378.2	405	193	49	6	120-16	232	4.16	94	.275	.330	67-0-9	.119	-3	90	-10	0	-1.3
Jones, Greg	Greg Alan; B11.15.1976 Clearwater FL; BR/TR/6´2˝/(190–195); [AnaA96 42/1253]; d7.30; Col Pasco–Hernando (FL) CC; [DL 2004 Ana A 64]																									
2003	Ana A	0	0	ø	18	0	0	0-0	27.2	29	15	3	2	14-0	28	4.88	90	.261	.354	0	ø	0	—	-1	0	-0.1
2005	LA A	0	0	ø	6	0	0	0-0	5.1	7	4	2	0	2-0	6	6.75	63	.318	.375	0	ø	0	—	-1	0	-0.1
2006	LA A	0	0	ø	5	0	0	0-0	6	8	5	1	0	2-0	1	6.00	74	.348	.357	0	ø	0	—	-1	0	-0.1
Total	3	0	0	ø	29	0	0	0-0	39	44	24	6	2	18-0	35	5.31	82	.282	.358	0	ø	0	—	-3	64	-0.3
Jones, Henry	Henry "Baldy"; B Pittsburgh PA; TR/?/150; d4.22																									
1890	Pit N	2	1	.667	5	4	2	0	31	35	25	1	0	14	13	3.48	95	.276	.348	9	.222	-0	110	-3	—	-0.3
Jones, Jimmy	James Condia; B4.20.1964 Dallas TX; BR/TR/6´2˝/(175–191); [SDN82 1/3]; d9.21																									
1986	SD N	2	0	1.000	3	3	1-1	0-0	18	10	6	1	0	3-0	15	2.50	147	.164	.203	6	.167	-0	114	2	0	0.2
1987	SD N	9	7	.563	30	22	2-1	0-0	145.2	154	85	14	5	54-2	51	4.14	96	.270	.336	49-1-8	.163	1*	114	-7	0	-0.5
1988	SD N	9	14	.391	29	29	3	0-0	179	192	98	14	3	44-3	82	4.12	82	.277	.319	55-1-9	.164	2*	95	-18	0	-1.9
1989	NY A	2	1	.667	11	6	0	0-0	48	56	29	7	2	16-1	25	5.25	74	.293	.352	0	ø	0	167	-6	0	-0.3
1990	NY A	1	2	.333	17	7	0	0-0	50	72	42	8	1	23-0	25	6.30	63	.344	.405	0	ø	0	104	-14	0	-0.8
1991	Hou N	6	8	.429	26	22	1-1	0-0	135.1	143	73	9	3	51-3	88	4.39	80	.270	.336	38-0-2	.184	2	91	-13	47	-1.0
1992	Hou N	10	6	.625	25	23	0	0-0	139.1	135	64	13	5	39-3	69	4.07	83	.258	.313	36-0-9	.167	2*	111	-8	36	-0.7
1993	Mon N	4	1	.800	12	6	0	0-0	39.2	47	34	6	0	9-0	21	6.35	66	.285	.322	9-0-3	.111	0	173	-10	34	-1.0
Total	8	43	39	.524	153	118	7-3	0-0	755	809	431	72	19	239-12	376	4.46	82	.275	.331	193-2-31	.166	7	110	-74	117	-6.0
Jones, Jim	James Tilford "Sheriff"; B12.25.1876 London KY; D5.6.1953 London KY; BR/TR/5´10˝/162; d6.29; Col Centre; ▲																									
1897	Lou N	0	0	ø	1	0	0	0	6.2	19	22	1	2	5	0	18.90	23	.500	.578	4	.250	1*	—	-11	—	-0.4
1901	NY N	0	1	.000	1	1	1	0	5	6	6	0	0	2	3	10.80	31	.300	.364	91	.209	0*	107	-3	—	-0.4
Total	2	0	1	.000	2	1	1	0	11.2	25	28	1	2	7	3	15.43	25	.431	.507	95	.211	1	107	-14	—	-0.8
Jones, Jeff	Jeffrey Allen; B7.29.1956 Detroit MI; BR/TR/6´3˝/(205–210); [OakA77 13/329]; d4.10; C5; Col Bowling Green																									
1980	Oak A	1	3	.250	35	0	0	5-3	44.1	32	21	2	1	26-2	34	2.84	134	.204	.316	0	ø	0	—	3	0	0.3
1981	†Oak A	4	1	.800	33	0	0	3-1	61	51	27	7	3	40-7	43	3.39	104	.233	.355	0	ø	0	—	0	0	0.0
1982	Oak A	3	1	.750	18	2	0	0-1	37	44	29	6	1	26-1	18	5.11	77	.306	.415	0	ø	0	150	-7	0	-0.7
1983	Oak A	1	1	.500	13	1	0	0-1	29.2	43	19	7	2	8-1	14	5.76	67	.339	.387	0	ø	0	93	-5	0	-0.3
1984	Oak A	0	3	.000	13	0	0	0-0	33	31	14	4	0	12-1	19	3.55	106	.258	.323	0	ø	0	—	1	64	0.1
Total	5	9	9	.500	112	3	0	8-6	205	201	110	26	7	112-12	128	3.95	95	.262	.358	0	ø	0	136	-8	64	-0.6
Jones, Broadway	Jesse Frank; B11.15.1898 Millsboro DE; D9.7.1977 Lewes DE; BR/TR/5´9˝/154; d7.4																									
1923	Phi N	0	0	ø	3	0	0	0	8	5	8	0	0	7	1	9.00	51	.185	.353	2	.500	0	—	-3	—	-0.1
Jones, Johnny	John Paul "Admiral"; B8.25.1892 Arcadia LA; D6.5.1980 Ruston LA; BR/TR/6´1˝/151; d4.24																									
1919	NY N	0	0	ø	2	0	0	1	6.2	9	4	0	1	3	3	5.40	52	.310	.394	3	.000	-0	—	-2	—	-0.1
1920	Bos N	1	0	1.000	3	1	0	0	9.2	16	7	1	0	5	6	6.52	47	.372	.438	4	.250	1	206	-3	—	-0.2
Total	2	1	0	1.000	5	1	0	1	16.1	25	11	1	1	8	9	6.06	49	.347	.420	7	.143	0	206	-5	—	-0.3
Jones, Stacy	Joseph Stacy; B5.26.1967 Gadsden AL; BR/TR/6´6˝/(225–230); [BalA88 3/61]; d7.30; Col Auburn																									
1991	Bal A	0	0	ø	4	1	0	0-0	11	11	6	1	0	5-0	10	4.09	97	.256	.327	0	ø	0	184	0	0	0.0
1996	Chi A	0	0	ø	2	0	0	0-0	2	0	0	0	0	1-0	1	0.00	ø	.000	.143	0	ø	0	—	1	0	0.0
Total	2	0	0	ø	6	1	0	0-0	13	11	6	1	0	6-0	11	3.46	118	.224	.304	0	ø	0	184	1	0	0.0
Jones, Ken	Kenneth Frederick "Broadway"; B4.13.1903 Dover NJ; D5.15.1991 Hartford CT; BR/TR/6´3˝/193; d5.19; Col Georgetown																									
1924	Det A	0	0	ø	1	0	0	0	2	1	0	0	0	1	0	0.00	ø	.143	.250	0	ø	0	—	1	—	0.0
1930	Bos N	0	1	.000	8	1	0	0	19.2	28	16	1	0	4	4	5.95	83	.359	.390	5	.200	-0	71	-3	—	-0.1
Total	2	0	1	.000	9	1	0	0	21.2	29	16	1	0	5	4	5.40	90	.341	.378	5	.200	-0	71	-2	—	-0.1
Jones, Marcus	Marcus Ray; B3.29.1975 Bellflower CA; BR/TR/6´5˝/235; [OakA97 3/95]; d7.17; Col Cal St.–Long Beach																									
2000	Oak A	0	0	ø	1	1	0	0-0	2.1	5	4	1	0	3-0	1	15.43	31	.417	.533	2	.000	-0	213	-3	0	-0.1
Jones, Mike	Michael; B7.6.1865 Hamilton ON, Can.; D3.24.1894 Hamilton ON, Can.; BL/TL/5´11.5˝/168; d8.1																									
1890	Lou AA	2	0	1.000	3	3	2	0	22	21	12	2	0	9	6	3.27	118	.244	.316	9	.444	2	180	2	—	0.3
Jones, Mike	Michael Carl; B7.30.1959 Penfield NY; BL/TL/6´6˝/(226–230); [KCA77 1/21]; d9.6; [DL 1982 KC A 182]																									
1980	KC A	0	1	.000	3	1	0	0-0	4.2	6	7	0	0	5-1	2	11.57	35	.333	.478	0	ø	0	0	-4	0	-0.7
1981	†KC A	6	3	.667	12	11	0	0-0	75.2	74	30	7	2	28-0	29	3.21	112	.256	.324	0	ø	0	131	3	0	0.4
1984	†KC A	2	3	.400	23	12	0	0-0	81	86	48	10	1	36-1	43	4.89	83	.270	.343	0	ø	0	99	-8	0	-0.5
1985	KC A	3	3	.500	33	1	0	0-0	64	62	40	6	0	39-4	32	4.78	87	.257	.353	0	ø	0	65	-5	0	-0.4
Total	4	11	10	.524	71	25	0	0-0	225.1	228	125	23	3	108-6	106	4.43	89	.263	.343	0	ø	0	105	-14	182	-1.2
Jones, Odell	Odell; B1.13.1953 Tulare CA; BR/TR/6´3˝/(174–195); d9.11																									
1975	Pit N	0	0	ø	2	0	0	0-0	3	1	0	0	0	0-0	2	0.00	ø	.100	.100	0	ø	0	—	1	0	0.1
1977	Pit N	3	7	.300	34	15	1	0-1	108	118	63	14	3	31-2	66	5.08	79	.278	.330	28	.143	-1	84	-10	0	-1.0
1978	Pit N	2	0	1.000	3	1	0	0-0	9	7	3	0	0	4-0	10	2.00	187	.206	.289	1	.000	-0	120	1	0	0.3
1979	Sea A	3	11	.214	25	19	3	0-0	118.2	151	90	16	3	58-8	72	6.07	72	.317	.390	0	ø	0	93	-22	0	-2.3
1981	Pit N	4	5	.444	13	8	0	0-0	54.1	51	23	3	0	23-6	30	3.31	110	.250	.325	10-0-3	.200	-0	76	2	0	0.3
1983	Tex A	3	6	.333	42	0	0	10-5	67	56	28	4	2	22-1	50	3.09	131	.223	.289	0	ø	0	—	6	21	0.9
1984	Tex A	2	4	.333	33	0	0	2-3	59.1	62	28	7	2	23-3	28	3.64	115	.281	.351	0	ø	0	—	3	0	0.3
1986	Bal A	2	2	.500	21	0	0	0-0	49.1	58	22	4	0	23-6	32	3.83	109	.305	.373	0	ø	0	—	2	0	0.2
1988	Mil A	5	0	1.000	28	2	0	1-0	80.2	75	47	8	1	29-6	48	4.35	92	.251	.313	0	ø	0	125	-5	0	-0.3
Total	9	24	35	.407	201	45	4	13-9	549.1	579	304	56	11	213-32	338	4.42	92	.275	.341	39-0-3	.154	-1	90	-22	21	-1.5

YEAR	TM LG	W	L	PCT	G	GS	CG-SHO	SV-BS	IP	H	R	HR	HB	BB-IB	SO	ERA	AERA	OAV	OOB	AB-HR-SH	AVG	PB	SUP	APR	DL	PW
Jones, Oscar Oscar Lafayette “Flip Flap”; B10.22.1879 Carter Co. MO; D3.16.1953 Fort Worth TX; BR/TR/5´7˝/163; d4.20																										
1903	Bro N	19	14	.576	38	36	31-4	0	324.1	320	159	4	19	77	95	2.94	109	.260	.313	125-0-3	.256	3	105	7	—	0.7
1904	Bro N	17	25	.405	46	41	38	0	377	387	175	7	17	92	96	2.75	100	.270	.321	137-0-4	.175	-1	86	0	—	-0.5
1905	Bro N	8	15	.348	29	20	14	1	174	197	121	6	9	56	66	4.66	62	.285	.347	65-0-1	.200	-0*	85	-33	—	-4.0
Total	3	44	54	.449	113	97	83-4	1	875.1	904	455	17	45	225	257	3.20	92	.269	.324	327-0-8	.211	2	94	-26	—	-3.8
Jones, Percy Percy Lee; B10.28.1899 Harwood TX; D3.18.1979 Dallas TX; BR/TL/5´11.5˝/175; d8.6																										
1920	Chi N	0	0	ø	4	0	0	0	7	15	10	1	1	3	0	11.57	28	.455	.514	2	.000	-0	—	-6	—	-0.3
1921	Chi N	3	5	.375	32	3	1	0	98.2	116	57	2	4	39	46	4.56	84	.295	.365	27	.222	-0	72	-8	—	-0.6
1922	Chi N	8	9	.471	44	24	7-2	1	162	197	104	10	5	68	45	4.78	88	.314	.385	47-0-4	.085	-4	94	-11	—	-1.3
1925	Chi N	6	6	.500	28	13	6-1	0	124	123	74	12	5	71	60	4.65	93	.263	.366	39-0-1	.154	-3	87	-5	—	-0.5
1926	Chi N	12	7	.632	30	20	10-2	2	160.1	151	64	3	5	90	80	3.09	125	.256	.359	50-0-4	.260	3	87	14	—	1.8
1927	Chi N	7	8	.467	30	11	5-1	0	112.2	123	67	3	6	72	37	4.07	95	.285	.394	40-0-1	.350	3	84	-6	—	-0.3
1928	Chi N	10	6	.625	39	19	9-1	3	154	167	80	4	7	56	41	4.03	95	.288	.358	56-0-2	.196	-0	130	-3	—	-0.3
1929	Bos N	7	15	.318	35	22	11-1	0	188.1	219	112	15	4	84	69	4.64	101	.298	.373	61-0-4	.148	-3*	72	0	—	-0.2
1930	Pit N	0	1	.000	9	2	0	0	19	26	20	3	3	11	3	6.63	75	.329	.430	2	.000	-0	105	-5	—	-0.3
Total	9	53	57	.482	251	114	49-8	6	1026	1137	588	53	40	494	381	4.34	95	.289	.374	324-0-16	.194	-5	92	-30	—	-2.0
Jones, Randy Randall Leo; B1.12.1950 Fullerton CA; BR/TL/6´0˝/180; [SDN72 5/97]; d6.16; Col Chapman																										
1973	SD N	7	6	.538	20	19	6-1	0-0	139.2	129	58	13	1	37-9	77	3.16	111	.241	.289	48-0-4	.167	-0	95	5	0	0.5
1974	SD N	8	22	.267	40	34	4-1	2-0	208.1	217	118	16	5	78-12	124	4.45	81	.270	.336	65-0-3	.154	-1*	74	-21	0	-2.8
1975	SD N★	20	12	.625	37	36	18-6	0-0	285	242	94	17	0	56-9	103	**2.24**	**156**	.232	.269	83-0-17	.133	-1*	94	37	0	4.5
1976	SD N★	**22**	14	.611	40	**40**	**25**-5	0-0	**315.1**	274	109	15	4	50-9	93	2.74	120	.234	**.265**	103-0-15	.058	-6	115	21	0	2.2
1977	SD N	6	12	.333	27	25	1	0-0	147.1	173	85	12	0	36-10	44	4.58	78	.291	.329	43-0-4	.116	-1*	73	-17	41	-1.8
1978	SD N	13	14	.481	37	36	7-2	0-1	253	263	104	6	0	64-20	71	2.88	116	.272	.314	82-0-6	.183	1*	95	9	0	1.1
1979	SD N	11	12	.478	39	39	6	0-0	263	257	120	17	3	64-10	112	3.63	97	.259	.304	86-0-7	.174	0*	93	-3	0	0.0
1980	SD N	5	13	.278	24	24	4-3	0-0	154.1	165	71	14	0	29-5	53	3.91	88	.276	.309	45-0-7	.067	-3*	78	-8	26	-1.0
1981	NY N	1	8	.111	13	12	0	0-0	59.1	65	48	8	1	38-1	14	4.85	73	.274	.373	17-0-1	.118	-1	73	-13	23	-1.7
1982	NY N	7	10	.412	28	20	2-1	0-0	107.2	130	68	11	4	51-3	44	4.60	80	.304	.380	27-0-2	.148	0	90	-13	0	-1.7
Total	10	100	123	.448	305	285	73-19	2-1	1933	1915	875	129	18	503-88	735	3.42	102	.260	.306	599-0-66	.132	-12	90	-3	90	-0.7
Jones, Bobby Robert Joseph; B2.10.1970 Fresno CA; BR/TR/6´4˝/(210–225); [NYN91 1/36]; d8.14; Col Cal St.–Fresno																										
1993	NY N	2	4	.333	9	9	0	0-0	61.2	61	35	6	2	22-3	35	3.65	110	.262	.327	20-0-2	.050	-2	95	0	0	-0.2
1994	NY N	12	7	.632	24	24	1-1	0-0	160	157	75	10	4	56-9	80	3.15	133	.257	.322	46-0-8	.109	-2	91	13	0	1.3
1995	NY N	10	10	.500	30	30	3-1	0-0	195.2	209	107	20	7	53-6	127	4.19	96	.274	.325	56-0-18	.161	-1	113	-6	0	-0.6
1996	NY N	12	8	.600	31	31	3-1	0-0	195.2	219	102	26	3	46-6	116	4.42	91	.288	.329	60-0-9	.117	-1	113	-5	0	-0.5
1997	NY N★	15	9	.625	30	30	2-1	0-0	193.1	177	88	24	2	63-3	125	3.63	110	.242	.303	62-0-4	.129	-0	103	8	0	0.9
1998	NY N	9	9	.500	30	30	0	0-0	195.1	192	94	23	8	53-2	115	4.05	102	.262	.316	48-0-12	.188	1	99	1	0	0.2
1999	NY N	3	3	.500	12	9	0	0-0	59.1	69	37	3	2	11-0	31	5.61	77	.295	.328	16-1-1	.313	2	115	-8	109	-0.5
2000	†NY N	11	6	.647	27	27	1	0-0	154.2	171	90	25	5	49-3	85	5.06	86	.281	.336	44-0-7	.045	-2	121	-10	30	-1.2
2001	SD N	8	19	.296	33	33	1	0-0	195	250	137	37	4	38-6	113	5.12	81	.305	.335	57-0-2	.140	0	88	-28	0	-3.2
2002	SD N	7	8	.467	19	18	0	0-0	108	134	68	20	1	21-1	60	5.50	71	.300	.331	33-0-1	.152	-1	103	-18	59	-2.2
Total	10	89	83	.517	245	241	11-4	0-0	1518.2	1639	833	194	38	412-39	887	4.36	94	.276	.325	442-1-64	.133	-5	104	-53	198	-6.0
Jones, Bobby Robert Mitchell; B4.11.1972 Orange NJ; BR/TL/6´0˝/(170–185); [MilA91 44/1140]; d5.18; Col Chipola (FL) JC; [DL 2001 NY N 190]																										
1997	Col N	1	1	.500	4	4	0	0-0	19.1	30	18	2	0	12-0	5	8.38	62	.380	.447	5-0-1	.200	0	98	-5	0	-0.4
1998	Col N	7	8	.467	35	20	1	0-0	141.1	153	87	12	6	66-0	109	5.22	99	.282	.362	45-0-5	.178	-1	95	0	0	-0.1
1999	Col N	6	10	.375	30	20	0	0-0	112.1	132	91	24	6	77-0	74	6.33	91	.292	.399	27-0-4	.148	-1	79	-8	0	-1.0
2000	NY N	0	1	.000	11	1	0	0-0	21.2	18	11	2	3	14-1	20	4.15	105	.222	.354	2-0-1	.500	1	168	1	0	0.1
2002	NY N	0	0	ø	12	0	0	0-0	17	20	11	3	1	11-2	11	5.29	75	.299	.405	0	ø	0*	—	-3	0	-0.1
	SD N	0	0	ø	4	2	0	0-0	9.2	10	7	1	0	7-0	7	6.52	60	.270	.378	2-0-1	.000	-0	155	-3	0	-0.2
	Year	0	0	ø	16	2	0	0-0	26.2	30	18	4	1	18-2	18	5.74	68	.288	.395	2-0-1	.000	-0	153	-5	0	-0.3
2004	Bos A	0	1	.000	9	3	0	0-0	3.1	3	2	1	0	8-1	3	5.40	90	.273	.579	0	ø	0	—	0	0	0.0
Total	6	14	21	.400	99	47	1	0-0	324.2	366	227	45	16	195-4	229	5.77	91	.288	.386	81-0-12	.173	-2	94	-18	190	-1.7
Jones, Sam Samuel “Toothpick Sam”; B12.14.1925 Stewartsville OH; D11.5.1971 Morgantown WV; BR/TR/6´4˝/200; d9.22; Negro Lg 1946–48																										
1951	Cle A	0	1	.000	2	1	0	0	8.2	4	2	0	0	5	4	2.08	182	.143	.273	2	.000	-0	23	2	0	0.2
1952	Cle A	2	3	.400	14	4	0	1	36	38	30	6	4	37	28	7.25	46	.270	.434	10	.100	-1	98	-15	0	-2.0
1955	Chi N★	14	20	.412	36	34	12-4	0	241.2	175	118	22	14	185-5	**198**	4.10	100	**.206**	.355	77-0-5	.182	-2	76	2	0	0.0
1956	Chi N	9	14	.391	33	28	8-2	0	188.2	155	93	21	8	115-6	**176**	3.91	96	.221	.337	57-0-10	.175	0	93	-2	0	-0.3
1957	StL N	12	9	.571	28	27	10-2	0	182.2	164	77	17	6	71-1	154	3.60	110	.239	.315	63-0-4	.159	-1	103	9	0	0.9
1958	StL N	14	13	.519	35	35	14-2	0	250	204	95	23	6	107-5	**225**	2.88	143	.223	.307	90-0-2	.100	-6	85	**31**	0	2.5
1959	SF N★	**21**	15	.583	50	35	16-**4**	4	270.2	232	99	18	8	109-6	209	**2.83**	135	**.228**	.306	85-0-11	.129	-2	102	30	0	**3.6**
1960	SF N	18	14	.563	39	35	13-3	0	234	200	112	18	4	91-5	190	3.19	109	.230	.305	80-0-7	.200	1	104	2	0	0.3
1961	SF N	8	8	.500	37	17	2	1	128.1	134	72	12	8	57-7	105	4.49	85	.264	.347	36-0-5	.139	-1	107	-10	0	-1.3
1962	Det A	2	4	.333	30	6	1	1	81.1	77	39	13	2	35-1	73	3.65	111	.254	.330	21-1-0	.095	-1	66	3	0	0.1
1963	StL N	2	0	1.000	11	0	0	2	11	15	12	0	0	5-1	8	9.00	39	.319	.385	1	.000	0	—	-6	0	-1.2
1964	Bal A	0	0	ø	7	0	0	0	10.1	5	3	1	0	5-0	6	2.61	137	.152	.263	0	ø	0	—	1	0	0.1
Total	12	102	101	.502	322	222	76-17	9	1643.1	1403	752	151	60	822-<u>37</u>	1376	3.59	108	.230	.326	522-1-44	.149	-11	93	47	0	2.9
Jones, Sam Samuel Pond “Sad Sam”; B7.26.1892 Woodsfield OH; D7.6.1966 Barnesville OH; BR/TR/6´0˝/170; d6.13																										
1914	Cle A	0	0	ø	1	0	0	0	3.1	2	1	0	0	2	0	2.70	107	.200	.333	2	.500	0	—	0	—	0.0
1915	Cle A	4	9	.308	48	9	2	4	145.2	131	78	0	1	63	42	3.65	84	.252	.334	32-0-3	.156	-0	82	-8	—	-0.7
1916	Bos A	0	1	.000	12	0	0	1	27	25	14	0	0	10	7	3.67	76	.272	.343	6	.333	0*	—	-3	—	-0.1
1917	Bos A	0	1	.000	9	1	0	1	16.1	15	9	1	0	6	5	4.41	59	.259	.328	4-0-1	.000	-1	56	-3	—	-0.3
1918	†Bos A	16	5	**.762**	24	21	16-5	0	184	151	66	1	8	70	44	2.25	119	.230	.312	57-0-3	.175	2	114	7	—	1.0
1919	Bos A	12	20	.375	35	31	21-5	1	245	258	120	4	7	95	67	3.75	81	.278	.350	81-0-5	.136	-0	103	-19	—	-2.2
1920	Bos A	13	16	.448	37	33	21-3	0	274	302	143	9	4	79	86	3.94	93	.288	.340	92-0-5	.217	1*	88	-10	—	-0.9
1921	Bos A	23	16	.590	40	38	25-**5**	1	298.2	318	122	1	6	78	98	3.22	131	.279	.329	100-2-2	.240	5*	79	34	—	4.3
1922	†NY A	13	13	.500	45	28	20	**8**	260	270	132	16	3	76	81	3.67	109	.275	.329	87-1-4	.264	8	97	6	—	1.4
1923	†NY A	21	8	.724	39	27	18-3	4	243	239	114	11	6	69	68	3.63	109	.257	.312	85-0-3	.224	2	136	6	—	0.9
1924	NY A	9	6	.600	36	21	8-3	3	178.2	187	85	6	1	76	53	3.63	115	.276	.350	51-1-6	.176	-0	82	10	—	0.7
1925	NY A	15	21	.417	43	31	14-1	2	246.2	267	147	14	3	104	92	4.63	92	.281	.354	80-0-10	.162	-3*	84	-10	—	-1.5
1926	†NY A	9	8	.529	39	23	6-1	5	161	186	104	6	4	80	69	4.98	77	.298	.381	49-0-5	.204	1*	124	-19	—	-1.9
1927	StL A	8	14	.364	30	26	11	0	189.2	211	121	13	3	102	72	4.32	101	.282	.371	55	.109	-2*	88	-3	—	-0.6
1928	Was A	17	7	.708	30	27	19-4	0	224.2	209	89	5	3	78	63	2.84	141	.252	.319	79-2-9	.253	6*	111	27	—	3.3
1929	Was A	9	9	.500	24	24	8-1	0	153.2	156	80	5	3	49	36	3.92	108	.264	.324	51-0-3	.157	0*	99	5	—	0.5
1930	Was A	15	7	.682	25	25	14-1	0	183.1	195	95	4	3	61	60	4.07	113	.277	.337	61-0-4	.148	-1*	126	11	—	0.9
1931	Was A	9	10	.474	25	24	8-1	1	148	185	88	10	4	47	58	4.32	99	.304	.358	48-0-6	.313	4*	97	-2	—	0.2
1932	Chi A	10	15	.400	30	28	10	0	200.1	217	123	9	3	75	64	4.22	102	.270	.335	57-0-8	.193	2*	93	0	—	0.3
1933	Chi A	10	12	.455	27	25	11-2	0	176.2	181	80	13	4	65	60	3.36	126	.265	.333	58-0-1	.155	-0*	79	17	—	1.8
1934	Chi A	8	12	.400	27	26	11-1	0	183.1	217	120	16	2	60	60	5.11	93	.289	.343	60-0-4	.200	2*	100	-7	—	-0.5
1935	Chi A	8	7	.533	21	19	7	0	140	162	77	8	1	51	38	4.05	114	.284	.343	48-0-3	.167	0*	109	6	—	0.6
Total	22	229	217	.513	647	487	250-36	31	3883	4084	2008	152	69	1396	1223	3.84	104	.274	.339	1243-6-85	.197	25	100	45	—	7.2
Jones, Sheldon Sheldon Leslie “Available”; B2.2.1922 Tecumseh NE; D4.18.1991 Greenville NC; BR/TR/6´0˝/(180–190); d9.9																										
1946	NY N	1	2	.333	6	4	1	0	28	21	10	4	1	17	24	3.21	107	.208	.328	8	.250	0	44	1	0	0.2
1947	NY N	2	2	.500	15	6	0	0	55.2	51	27	2	3	29	24	3.88	105	.250	.352	16-0-1	.125	-1	116	1	0	-0.1
1948	NY N	16	8	.667	55	21	8-1	5	201.1	204	89	16	6	90	82	3.35	117	.263	.344	64-0-9	.203	1	124	13	0	1.6
1949	NY N	15	12	.556	42	27	11-1	0	207.1	198	93	19	10	88	79	3.34	119	.248	.331	66-0-6	.121	-3	99	14	0	1.3
1950	NY N	13	16	.448	40	28	11-2	2	199	188	114	26	7	90	97	4.61	89	.249	.335	57-0-10	.105	-2	93	-11	0	-1.7
1951	†NY N	6	11	.353	41	12	2	4	120.1	119	77	12	4	52	58	4.26	92	.260	.340	31	.097	-1	73	-9	0	-1.3
1952	Bos N	1	4	.200	39	1	0	1	70	81	45	7	1	31	40	4.76	76	.286	.359	8-0-1	.125	-0	74	-11	0	-0.8
1953	Chi N	0	2	.000	22	2	0	0	38.1	47	24	3	5	16	9	5.40	82	.299	.382	7	.000	-1	60	-3	0	-0.2
Total	8	54	57	.486	260	101	33-4	12	920	909	479	89	37	413	413	3.96	100	.258	.342	257-0-27	.136	-7	98	-5	0	-1.0

YEAR	TM LG	W	L	PCT	G	GS	CG-SHO	SV-BS	IP	H	R	HR	HB	BB-IB	SO	ERA	AERA	OAV	OOB	AB-HR-SH	AVG	PB	SUP	APR	DL	PW
Jones, Sherman	Sherman Jarvis "Roadblock"; B2.10.1935 Winton NC; BL/TR/6´4˝/(195–210); d8.2																									
1960	SF N	1	1	.500	16	0	0	1	32	37	17	3	1	11-1	10	3.09	112	.291	.353	7	.286	0	—	0	0	0.0
1961	†Cin N	1	1	.500	24	2	0	2	55	51	32	6	2	27-6	32	4.42	92	.256	.340	11	.182	0	76	-3	0	-0.1
1962	NY N	0	4	.000	8	3	0	0	23.1	31	22	3	2	8-2	11	7.71	54	.326	.373	7	.429	1	70	-8	0	-1.0
Total	3	2	6	.250	48	5	0	3	110.1	119	71	12	5	46-9	53	4.73	83	.283	.351	25	.280	1	77	-11	0	-1.1
Jones, Steve	Steven Howell; B4.22.1941 Huntington Park CA; BL/TL/5´10˝/175; d8.15; b–Gary; Col Whittier																									
1967	Chi A	2	2	.500	11	3	0	0	25.2	21	13	1	0	12-0	17	4.21	74	.223	.311	4	.250	0	84	-3	0	-0.4
1968	Was A	1	2	.333	7	0	0	0	10.2	8	8	3	0	7-0	11	5.91	49	.205	.326	1	.000	-0	—	-4	0	-0.8
1969	KC A	2	3	.400	20	4	0	0-0	44.2	45	25	3	3	24-2	31	4.23	87	.260	.358	8	.125	0	126	-3	0	-0.3
Total	3	5	7	.417	38	7	0	0-0	81	74	46	7	3	43-2	59	4.44	77	.242	.340	13	.154	1	111	-10	0	-1.5
Jones, Rick	Thomas Fredrick; B4.16.1955 Jacksonville FL; BL/TL/6´5˝/(180–200); [BosA73 5/113]; d4.18																									
1976	Bos A	5	3	.625	24	14	1	0-0	104.1	133	48	6	1	26-1	45	3.36	115	.311	.348	0	ø	0	113	4	0	0.3
1977	Sea A	1	4	.200	10	10	0	0-0	42.1	47	25	10	0	37-2	16	5.10	81	.283	.414	0	ø	0	98	-4	62	-0.4
1978	Sea A	0	2	.000	3	2	0	0-0	12.1	17	8	1	0	7-0	11	5.84	66	.315	.393	0	ø	0	47	-2	0	-0.3
Total	3	6	9	.400	37	26	1	0-0	159	197	81	17	1	70-3	72	4.02	99	.304	.370	0	ø	0	102	-2	62	-0.4
Jones, Tim	Timmothy Byron; B1.24.1954 Sacramento CA; BB/TR/6´5˝/200; [PitN72 4/95]; d9.4																									
1977	Pit N	1	0	1.000	3	1	0	0-0	10	4	0	0	0	3-0	5	0.00	ø	.118	.189	2	.000	-0	111	4	0	0.4
Jones, Todd	Todd Barton Givin; B4.24.1968 Marietta GA; BL/TR/6´3˝/(200–230); [HouN89 1/27]; d7.7; Col Jacksonville St.																									
1993	Hou N	1	2	.333	27	0	0	2-1	37.1	28	14	4	1	15-2	25	3.13	124	.214	.297	0	ø	0	—	4	0	0.3
1994	Hou N	5	2	.714	48	0	0	5-4	72.2	52	23	3	1	26-4	63	2.72	145	.202	.277	5	.400	1	—	11	0	1.1
1995	Hou N	6	5	.545	68	0	0	15-5	99.2	89	38	8	6	52-17	96	3.07	126	.237	.336	5	.200	0	—	10	0	1.2
1996	Hou N	6	3	.667	51	0	0	17-6	57.1	61	30	5	5	32-6	44	4.40	88	.274	.375	1	.000	-0	—	-3	49	-0.6
1997	Det A	5	4	.556	68	0	0	31-5	70	60	29	3	1	35-2	70	3.09	150	.231	.320	0	ø	0	—	10	0	1.9
1998	Det A	1	4	.200	65	0	0	28-4	63.1	58	38	7	2	36-4	57	4.97	96	.249	.347	0	ø	0	—	-1	0	-0.2
1999	Det A	4	4	.500	65	0	0	30-5	66.1	64	30	7	1	35-1	64	3.80	132	.259	.352	0	ø	0	—	9	0	1.5
2000	Det A★	2	4	.333	67	0	0	**42**-4	64	67	28	6	1	25-1	67	3.52	140	.276	.344	0	ø	0	—	10	0	1.7
2001	Det A	4	5	.444	45	0	0	11-6	48.2	60	31	6	0	22-1	39	4.62	96	.303	.368	0	ø	0	—	-3	0	-0.5
	Min A	1	0	1.000	24	0	0	2-2	19.1	27	8	3	0	7-0	15	3.26	143	.333	.386	0	ø	0	—	3	0	0.2
	Year	5	5	.500	69	0	0	13-8	68	87	39	9	0	29-1	54	4.24	106	.312	.373	0	ø	0	—	0	0	-0.3
2002	Col N	1	4	.200	79	0	0	1-2	82.1	84	43	10	3	28-3	73	4.70	101	.269	.332	3	.000	-0	—	2	0	0.1
2003	Col N	1	4	.200	33	1	0	0-5	39.1	61	39	8	1	18-0	28	8.24	59	.361	.421	2	.000	-0	96	-13	0	-1.4
	†Bos A	2	1	.667	26	0	0	0-0	29.1	32	19	2	0	13-2	31	5.52	84	.269	.338	0	ø	0	—	-2	0	-0.2
2004	Cin N	8	2	.800	51	0	0	1-5	57	49	25	4	1	25-2	37	3.79	114	.243	.322	0	ø	0	—	4	0	0.5
	Phi N	3	3	.500	27	0	0	1-1	25.1	35	14	3	5	8-3	22	4.97	89	.330	.400	0	ø	0	—	-1	0	-0.2
	Year	11	5	.688	78	0	0	2-6	82.1	84	39	7	6	33-5	59	4.15	105	.273	.348	0	ø	0	—	3	0	0.3
2005	Fla N	1	5	.167	68	0	0	40-5	73	61	19	2	3	14-2	62	2.10	191	.230	.276	3	.333	0	—	16	0	2.9
2006	†Det A	2	6	.250	62	0	0	37-6	64	70	31	4	3	11-3	28	3.94	114	.276	.312	0	ø	0	—	4	16	0.7
Total	14	53	58	.477	874	1	0	263-66	969	958	459	85	34	402-53	821	3.91	113	.261	.336	19	.211	1	96	60	65	9.0
Jonnard, Claude	Claude Alfred; B11.23.1897 Nashville TN; D8.27.1959 Nashville TN; BR/TR/6´1˝/165; d10.1; twb–Bubber																									
1921	NY N	0	0	ø	1	0	0	1	4	4	0	0	0	0	7	0.00	ø	.267	.267	1	.000	-0	—	2	—	0.1
1922	NY N	6	1	.857	33	0	0	**5**	96	96	45	7	3	28	44	3.84	104	.272	.331	24-0-2	.042	-3	—	4	—	0.0
1923	†NY N	4	3	.571	**45**	1	1	**5**	96	105	45	6	0	35	45	3.28	116	.279	.340	26-0-1	.038	-3	86	4	—	-0.1
1924	†NY N	3	5	.375	34	3	1	5	89.2	80	33	2	2	24	40	2.41	152	.229	.282	22-0-1	.045	-3	123	**11**	—	0.7
1926	StL A	0	2	.000	12	3	0	1	36	46	29	1	0	24	13	6.00	71	.313	.409	7-0-1	.000	-1	79	-7	—	-0.4
1929	Chi N	0	1	.000	12	2	0	0	27.2	41	27	4	1	11	11	7.48	62	.320	.379	10	.200	1	76	-9	—	-0.3
Total	6	13	12	.520	137	9	2	17	349.1	372	179	20	6	122	160	3.79	104	.272	.334	90-0-5	.056	-9	94	5	—	-0.0
Jordan, Charlie	Charles T. "Kid"; B10.4.1871 Philadelphia PA; D6.1.1928 Hazleton PA; d7.31																									
1896	Phi N	0	0	ø	2	0	0	0	4.2	9	4	0	0	2	3	7.71	56	.409	.458	2	.500	0	—	-1	—	0.0
Jordan, Harry	Harry James; B2.14.1873 Pittsburgh PA; D3.1.1920 Pittsburgh PA; d9.25																									
1894	Pit N	1	0	1.000	1	1	1	0	9	10	7	0	1	2	1	4.00	131	.278	.333	3	.000	-0	135	1	—	0.0
1895	Pit N	0	2	.000	2	2	2	0	17	24	15	0	1	6	4	4.24	106	.329	.387	7	.286	-0	87	-1	—	-0.1
Total	2	1	2	.333	3	3	3	0	26	34	22	0	2	8	5	4.15	115	.312	.370	10	.200	-0	105	0	—	-0.1
Jordan, Milt	Milton Mignot; B5.24.1927 Mineral Springs PA; D5.13.1993 Ithaca NY; BR/TR/6´2.5˝/207; d4.16																									
1953	Det A	0	1	.000	8	1	0	0	17	26	13	3	0	5	4	5.82	70	.366	.408	2	.500	0	153	-4	0	-0.1
Jordan, Niles	Niles Chapman; B12.1.1925 Lyman WA; BL/TL/5´11˝/(165–180); d8.26																									
1951	Phi N	2	3	.400	5	5	2-1	0	36.2	35	15	4	0	8	11	3.19	121	.250	.291	13	.077	-1	55	2	0	0.2
1952	Cin N	0	1	.000	3	1	0	0	6.1	14	7	1	0	3	2	9.95	38	.452	.500	1-0-1	.000	-0	47	-4	0	-0.5
Total	2	2	4	.333	8	6	2-1	0	43	49	22	5	0	11	13	4.19	92	.287	.330	14-0-1	.071	-1	54	-2	0	-0.3
Jordan, Rip	Raymond Willis "Lanky"; B9.28.1889 Portland ME; D6.5.1960 Meriden CT; BL/TR/6´0˝/172; d6.25																									
1912	Chi A	0	0	ø	4	0	0	0	12.1	13	8	2	1	3	1	5.11	63	.289	.347	4	.000	-1	—	-2	—	-0.2
1919	Was A	0	0	ø	1	1	0	0	4	6	5	1	0	2	2	11.25	29	.353	.421	1	.000	-0	171	-3	—	-0.2
Total	2	0	0	ø	5	1	0	0	16.1	19	13	3	1	5	3	6.61	48	.306	.368	5	.000	-1	171	-5	—	-0.4
Jordan, Ricardo	Ricardo; B6.27.1970 Boynton Beach FL; BL/TL/5´11˝/(175–190); [TorA90 37/995]; d6.23; Col Miami–Dade Kendall (FL) CC																									
1995	Tor A	1	0	1.000	15	0	0	1-0	15	18	11	3	2	13-1	10	6.60	72	.305	.434	0	ø	0	—	-3	0	-0.2
1996	Phi N	2	2	.500	26	0	0	0-0	25	18	6	0	0	12-0	17	1.80	240	.202	.294	1	.000	-0	—	7	0	0.9
1997	NY N	1	2	.333	22	0	0	0-0	27	31	17	1	2	15-2	19	5.33	75	.304	.397	1	.000	-0	—	-4	0	-0.4
1998	Cin N	1	0	1.000	6	0	0	0-0	3.1	4	9	2	0	7-0	1	24.30	18	.308	.524	0	ø	0	—	-7	0	-1.2
Total	4	5	4	.556	69	0	0	1-0	70.1	71	43	6	4	47-3	47	5.25	82	.270	.381	2	.000	-0	—	-7	0	-0.9
Jorgens, Orville	Orville Edward; B6.4.1908 Rockford IL; D1.11.1992 Colorado Springs CO; BR/TR/6´1˝/180; d4.19; b–Art																									
1935	Phi N	10	15	.400	**53**	24	6	2	188.1	216	129	12	8	96	57	4.83	94	.283	.370	62-0-3	.097	-5	105	-8	—	-1.3
1936	Phi N	8	8	.500	39	21	4	0	167.1	196	110	16	7	69	58	4.79	95	.290	.361	60-0-2	.200	-1	105	-4	—	-0.4
1937	Phi N	3	4	.429	52	9	1	3	140.2	159	83	12	5	68	34	4.41	98	.298	.383	35-0-1	.143	-1	93	-3	—	-0.2
Total	3	21	27	.438	144	54	11	5	496.1	571	322	40	20	233	149	4.70	95	.290	.370	157-0-6	.146	-7	104	-15	—	-1.9
Joseph, Kevin	Kevin John; B8.1.1976 Camp Hill PA; BR/TR/6´4˝/200; [SFN97 6/178]; d8.1; Col Rice																									
2002	StL N	0	1	.000	11	0	0	0-0	11	16	7	1	2	6-0	2	4.91	82	.364	.462	0	ø	0	—	-1	0	-0.1
Joss, Addie	Adrian; B4.12.1880 Woodland WI; D4.14.1911 Toledo OH; BR/TR/6´3˝/185; d4.26; HF1978; Col Wisconsin–Madison																									
1902	Cle A	17	13	.567	32	29	28-**5**	0	269.1	225	120	2	13	75	106	2.77	124	.228	.291	103-0-7	.117	-5*	102	23	—	2.0
1903	Cle A	18	13	.581	32	31	31-3	0	283.2	232	105	3	9	37	120	2.19	130	.223	**.256**	114-0-1	.193	0*	105	22	—	2.5
1904	Cle A	14	10	.583	25	24	20-5	0	192.1	160	51	0	7	30	83	**1.59**	159	.227	.266	76-0-3	.132	-4*	114	20	—	2.2
1905	Cle A	20	12	.625	33	32	31-3	0	286	246	90	4	11	46	132	2.01	131	.234	.273	97-0-6	.134	-0*	101	18	—	2.3
1906	Cle A	21	9	.700	34	31	28-9	1	282	220	81	3	3	43	106	1.72	152	.218	.252	100-0-10	.210	2*	110	28	—	3.5
1907	Cle A	**27**	11	.711	42	38	34-6	2	338.2	279	100	3	7	54	127	1.83	137	.227	.263	114-0-6	.114	-5	94	27	—	3.0
1908	Cle A	24	11	.686	42	35	29-9	2	325	232	77	2	2	30	130	**1.16**	**205**	**.197**	**.218**	97-0-3	.155	2	87	38	—	5.0
1909	Cle A	14	13	.519	33	28	24-4	0	242.2	198	71	0	4	31	67	1.71	150	.226	.255	80-1-2	.100	-3	76	21	—	2.1
1910	Cle A	5	5	.500	13	12	9-1	0	107.1	96	35	2	2	18	49	2.26	114	.245	.282	36-0-1	.111	-1	67	5	—	0.4
Total	9	160	97	.623	286	260	234-45	5	2327	1888	730	19	58	364	920	1.89	142	.223	.260	817-1-39	.144	-14	96	202	—	23.0
Journell, Jimmy	James Richard; B12.29.1977 Springfield OH; BR/TR/6´4˝/(200–210); [StLN99 4/132]; d6.29; Col Illinois																									
2003	StL N	0	0	ø	7	0	0	0-0	9	10	7	0	0	11-0	8	6.00	69	.278	.438	0	ø	0	—	-2	19	-0.1
2005	StL N	0	1	.000	5	0	0	0-0	4.1	6	6	1	0	5-0	5	10.38	40	.333	.478	0	ø	0	—	-3	0	-0.6
Total	2	0	1	.000	12	0	0	0-0	13.1	16	13	1	0	16-0	13	7.43	56	.296	.451	0	ø	0	—	-5	19	-0.7

YEAR	TM LG	W	L	PCT	G	GS	CG-SHO	SV-BS	IP	H	R	HR	HB	BB-IB	SO	ERA	AERA	OAV	OOB	AB-HR-SH	AVG	PB	SUP	APR	DL	PW
Joyce, Mike	Michael Lewis; B2.12.1941 Detroit MI; BR/TR/6´2˝/195; d7.2; Col Michigan																									
1962	Chi A	2	1	.667	25	1	0	2	43.1	40	17	2	0	14-2	9	3.32	118	.247	.305	7	.429	1	137	3	0	0.3
1963	Chi A	0	0	ø	6	0	0	0	10.2	13	10	1	0	8-2	7	8.44	42	.289	.396	0-0-1	ø	0	—	-5	0	-0.3
Total	2	2	1	.667	31	1	0	2	54	53	27	3	0	22-4	16	4.33	88	.256	.326	7-0-1	.429	1	137	-2	0	0.0
Joyce, Dick	Richard Edward; B11.18.1943 Portland ME; BL/TL/6´5˝/225; d9.3; Col Holy Cross																									
1965	KC A	0	1	.000	5	3	0	0	13	12	7	0	0	4-0	7	2.77	126	.240	.291	4	.000	-0	84	0	0	-0.1
Joyce, Bob	Robert Emmett; B1.14.1915 Stockton CA; D12.10.1981 San Francisco CA; BR/TR/6´1˝/180; d5.4																									
1939	Phi A	3	5	.375	30	6	1	0	107.2	156	91	13	1	37	25	6.69	70	.337	.387	35-0-1	.086	-3	53	-22	—	-1.5
1946	NY N	3	4	.429	14	7	2	0	60.2	79	43	3	0	20	24	5.34	64	.315	.365	19-1-1	.158	0	139	-13	0	-1.3
Total	2	6	9	.400	44	13	3	0	168.1	235	134	16	1	57	49	6.20	69	.329	.380	54-1-2	.111	-3	89	-35	0	-2.8
Judd, Mike	Michael Galen; B6.30.1975 San Diego CA; BR/TR/6´1˝/(200–217); [NYA95 9/254]; d9.28; Col Grossmont (CA) JC																									
1997	LA N	0	0	ø	1	0	0	0-0	2.2	4	0	0	0	0-0	4	0.00	ø	.364	.364	1	.000	-0	—	1	0	0.0
1998	LA N	0	0	ø	7	0	0	0-0	11.1	19	19	4	1	9-1	14	15.09	27	.373	.475	1	.000	-0	—	-14	0	-0.6
1999	LA N	3	1	.750	7	4	0	0-0	28	30	17	4	1	12-0	22	5.46	80	.280	.358	5-0-3	.000	-0	111	-3	0	-0.4
2000	LA N	0	1	.000	1	1	0	0-0	4	4	7	2	1	3-0	5	15.75	28	.250	.400	1-0-1	1.000	0	124	-5	0	-0.6
2001	TB A	1	0	1.000	8	2	0	0-0	20	19	14	2	1	10-0	11	4.05	111	.250	.333	0	ø	0	154	-1	15	-0.1
	Tex A	0	1	.000	4	1	0	0-0	9	15	10	2	0	5-0	5	8.00	60	.357	.426	1	.000	-0	78	-4	0	-0.3
	Year	1	1	.500	12	3	0	0-0	29	34	24	4	1	15-0	16	5.28	87	.288	.365	1	.000	-0	128	-4	0	-0.4
Total	5	4	3	.571	28	8	0	0-0	75	91	67	14	4	39-1	61	7.20	61	.300	.384	9-0-4	.111	-0	121	-26	15	-2.0
Judd, Ralph	Ralph Wesley; B12.7.1901 Perrysburg OH; D5.6.1957 Lapeer MI; BL/TR/5´10˝/170; d10.2																									
1927	Was A	0	0	ø	1	0	0	1	4	8	3	0	0	2	2	6.75	60	.400	.455	1	.000	-0	—	-1	—	-0.1
1929	NY N	3	0	1.000	18	0	0	0	50.2	49	19	4	0	11	21	2.66	172	.261	.302	14	.000	-2	—	10	—	0.3
1930	NY N	0	0	ø	2	0	0	0	7.2	13	8	0	0	3	0	5.87	81	.394	.444	3	.000	-1	—	-2	—	-0.1
Total	3	3	0	1.000	21	0	0	1	62.1	70	30	4	0	16	23	3.32	138	.290	.335	18	.000	-3	—	7	—	0.1
Judd, Oscar	Thomas William Oscar "Ossie"; B2.14.1908 London ON, Can.; D12.27.1995 Ingersoll ON, Can.; BL/TL/6´0.5˝/180; d4.16																									
1941	Bos A	0	0	ø	7	0	0	1	12.1	15	12	1	0	10	5	8.76	48	.300	.417	4	.500	2*	—	-5	0	-0.1
1942	Bos A	8	10	.444	31	19	11	2	150.1	135	72	3	2	90	70	3.89	96	.239	.346	67-2-3	.269	6*	133	-2	0	0.4
1943	Bos A☆	11	6	.647	23	20	8-1	0	155.1	131	58	2	3	69	53	2.90	114	.230	.317	54-0-3	.259	4*	89	6	0	1.1
1944	Bos A	1	1	.500	9	6	1	0	30	30	16	1	0	15	9	3.60	94	.261	.346	11	.182	1*	188	-2	0	-0.1
1945	Bos A	0	1	.000	2	1	0	0	6.1	10	8	1	0	3	5	8.53	40	.333	.394	2	.500	0	50	-4	0	-0.5
	Phi N	5	4	.556	23	9	3-1	2	82.2	80	47	3	1	40	36	3.81	101	.254	.340	30-0-1	.267	3*	64	-1	0	0.2
1946	Phi N	11	12	.478	30	24	12-1	2	173.1	169	86	6	1	90	65	3.53	97	.260	.350	79-1-4	.316	8*	95	-5	0	0.5
1947	Phi N	4	15	.211	32	19	8-1	0	146.2	155	86	6	3	69	54	4.60	87	.279	.361	64	.188	2*	73	-10	0	-0.8
1948	Phi N	0	2	.000	4	1	0	0	14.1	19	14	1	0	11	7	6.91	57	.317	.423	6	.167	0	90	-5	0	-0.6
Total	8	40	51	.440	161	99	43-4	7	771.1	744	399	24	10	397	304	3.90	93	.256	.347	317-3-11	.262	26	98	-28	0	0.1
Juden, Jeff	Jeffrey Daniel; B1.19.1971 Salem MA; BR/TR/6´8˝/(245–265); [HouN89 1/12]; d9.15																									
1991	Hou N	0	2	.000	4	3	0	0-0	18	19	14	3	0	7-1	11	6.00	59	.275	.329	5	.000	-1	59	-5	0	-0.6
1993	Hou N	0	1	.000	2	0	0	0-0	5	4	3	1	0	4-1	7	5.40	72	.222	.348	0	ø	0	—	-1	0	-0.1
1994	Phi N	1	4	.200	6	5	0	0-0	27.2	29	25	4	1	12-0	22	6.18	69	.276	.350	9-0-2	.111	-0	72	-7	0	-1.1
1995	Phi N	2	4	.333	13	10	1	0-0	62.2	53	31	6	5	31-0	47	4.02	105	.235	.335	18-1-3	.056	-1	94	1	0	0.0
1996	SF N	4	0	1.000	36	0	0	0-0	41.2	39	23	7	1	20-2	35	4.10	101	.250	.335	3	.000	-0	—	0	0	-0.1
	Mon N	1	0	1.000	22	0	0	0-0	32.2	22	12	1	4	14-0	26	2.20	197	.188	.294	0-0-1	ø	0	—	6	0	0.3
	Year	5	0	1.000	58	0	0	0-0	74.1	61	35	8	5	34-2	61	3.27	129	.223	.317	3-0-1	.000	-0	—	6	0	0.2
1997	Mon N	11	5	.688	22	22	3	0-0	130	125	64	17	9	57-2	107	4.22	99	.255	.341	43-0-2	.140	0	119	1	0	0.1
	†Cle A	0	1	.000	8	5	0	0-0	31.1	32	21	6	1	15-0	29	5.46	86	.264	.345	0	ø	0	94	-3	0	-0.1
1998	Mil N	7	11	.389	24	24	2	0-0	138.1	149	91	20	10	66-0	109	5.53	78	.277	.363	41-0-3	.122	-1	100	-17	0	-2.1
	Ana A	1	3	.250	8	6	0	0-0	40	33	32	7	2	18-0	39	6.75	70	.217	.308	0	ø	0	91	-8	0	-0.7
1999	NY A	0	1	.000	2	1	0	0-0	5.2	5	9	1	1	3-0	9	1.59	298	.200	.310	0	ø	0	39	-2	0	-0.2
Total	8	27	32	.458	147	76	6	0-0	533	510	325	73	34	247-6	441	4.81	89	.253	.341	119-1-11	.109	-3	99	-35	0	-4.6
Judson, Howie	Howard Kolls; B2.16.1926 Hebron IL; BR/TR/6´1˝/195; d4.22; Col Illinois																									
1948	Chi A	4	5	.444	40	5	1	8	107.1	102	60	7	3	56	38	4.78	89	.255	.351	29-0-4	.103	-2*	98	-5	0	-0.6
1949	Chi A	1	14	.067	26	12	3	1	108	114	65	13	1	70	36	4.58	91	.274	.380	31-0-3	.065	-3	61	-6	0	-1.0
1950	Chi A	2	3	.400	46	3	1	0	112	105	53	10	2	63	34	3.94	114	.252	.353	20-0-4	.100	-1	94	8	0	0.2
1951	Chi A	5	6	.455	27	14	3	1	121.2	124	67	9	2	55	43	3.77	107	.264	.343	33-0-5	.121	-2	108	0	0	-0.2
1952	Chi A	0	1	.000	21	0	0	1	34	30	17	4	0	22	15	4.24	86	.244	.359	4	.000	-0	—	-2	0	-0.1
1953	Cin N	0	1	.000	10	6	0	0	38.2	58	28	8	0	11	11	5.59	78	.341	.381	9	.111	1	137	-6	0	-0.2
1954	Cin N	5	7	.417	37	8	0	3	93.1	86	47	9	3	42	27	3.95	106	.251	.335	24	.083	-2	104	2	0	0.0
Total	7	17	37	.315	207	48	8	14	615	619	337	60	11	319	204	4.29	98	.265	.355	150-0-16	.093	-9	97	-9	0	-1.9
Julio, Jorge	Jorge Dandys; B3.3.1979 Caracas Distrito Capital, Venezuela; BR/TR/6´1˝/(190–235); d4.26																									
2001	Bal A	1	1	.500	18	0	0	0-1	21.1	25	13	2	1	9-0	22	3.80	114	.287	.361	0	ø	0	—	0	0	0.0
2002	Bal A	5	6	.455	67	0	0	25-6	68	55	22	5	2	27-3	55	1.99	219	.213	.292	0	ø	0	—	16	0	3.0
2003	Bal A	0	7	.000	64	0	0	36-8	61.2	60	36	10	2	34-4	52	4.38	105	.256	.354	0	ø	0	—	0	0	-0.1
2004	Bal A	2	5	.286	65	0	0	22-4	69	59	35	11	3	39-4	70	4.57	102	.228	.332	0	ø	0	—	2	0	0.3
2005	Bal A	3	5	.375	67	0	0	0-2	71.2	76	50	14	2	24-4	58	5.90	75	.269	.327	0	ø	0	—	-11	0	-1.1
2006	NY N	1	2	.333	18	0	0	1-0	21.1	21	15	4	1	10-1	33	5.06	87	.247	.333	1	.000	-0	—	-3	0	-0.4
	Ari N	1	2	.333	44	0	0	15-4	44.2	31	20	6	0	25-1	55	3.83	122	.190	.298	0	ø	0	—	4	0	0.5
	Year	2	4	.333	62	0	0	16-4	66	52	35	10	1	35-2	88	4.23	108	.210	.310	1	.000	-0	—	2	0	0.1
Total	6	13	28	.317	343	0	0	99-25	357.2	327	191	52	11	168-17	345	4.20	107	.239	.325	1	.000	-0	—	8	0	2.2
Junge, Eric	Eric Debari; B1.5.1977 Manhasset NY; BR/TR/6´5˝/215; [LAN99 11/344]; d9.11; Col Bucknell; [DL 2004 Phi N 37]																									
2002	Phi N	2	0	1.000	4	1	0	0-0	12.2	14	3	0	0	5-0	11	1.42	270	.286	.352	3	.000	-0	97	3	0	0.5
2003	Phi N	0	0	ø	6	0	0	0-0	7.2	5	3	1	0	1-0	5	3.52	113	.185	.214	0	ø	0	—	1	0	0.0
Total	2	2	0	1.000	10	1	0	0-0	20.1	19	6	1	0	6-0	16	2.21	176	.250	.305	3	.000	-0	97	4	37	0.5
Jungels, Ken	Kenneth Peter "Curly"; B6.23.1916 Aurora IL; D9.9.1975 West Bend WI; BR/TR/6´1˝/180; d9.15																									
1937	Cle A	0	0	ø	2	0	0	0	3	3	1	0	0	1	0	0.00	ø	.273	.333	0	ø	0	—	1	—	0.0
1938	Cle A	1	0	1.000	9	0	0	0	15.1	21	16	1	2	18	7	8.80	53	.339	.500	5	.000	-1	—	-7	—	-0.4
1940	Cle A	0	0	ø	2	0	0	0	3.1	3	1	0	0	1	1	2.70	156	.273	.333	1	.000	-0	—	1	—	0.0
1941	Cle A	0	0	ø	6	0	0	0	13.2	17	12	4	1	8	6	7.24	54	.293	.388	2	.000	-0	—	-5	0	-0.3
1942	Pit N	0	0	ø	6	0	0	0	13.2	12	11	0	0	4	7	6.59	51	.235	.291	2	.500	0*	—	-4	0	-0.2
Total	5	1	0	1.000	25	0	0	0	49	56	41	5	3	32	21	6.80	60	.290	.399	10	.100	-1	—	-14	0	-0.9
Jurewicz, Mike	Michael Allen; B9.20.1945 Buffalo NY; BB/TL/6´3˝/205; d9.7																									
1965	NY A	0	0	ø	2	0	0	0	2.1	5	2	0	0	1-0	2	7.71	44	.417	.462	0	ø	0	—	-1	0	-0.1
Jurisich, Al	Alvin Joseph; B8.25.1921 New Orleans LA; D11.3.1981 New Orleans LA; BR/TR/6´2˝/193; d4.26																									
1944	†StL N	7	9	.438	30	14	5-2	1	130	102	53	7	5	65	53	3.39	104	.221	.323	45-0-1	.178	-1	78	4	0	0.3
1945	StL N	3	3	.500	27	6	1	0	71.2	61	45	7	1	41	42	5.15	73	.232	.338	23	.087	-2	143	-10	0	-1.0
1946	Phi N	4	3	.571	13	10	2-1	1	68.1	71	30	9	1	31	34	3.69	93	.263	.341	23-0-2	.130	-0	95	-1	0	-0.2
1947	Phi N	1	7	.125	34	12	5	3	118.1	110	69	15	1	52	48	4.94	81	.258	.340	31-0-4	.032	-3	81	-10	0	-1.0
Total	4	15	22	.405	104	42	13-3	5	388.1	344	197	38	8	189	177	4.24	87	.242	.334	122-0-7	.115	-6	92	-17	0	-1.9
Justis, Walt	Walter Newton "Smoke"; B8.17.1883 Moores Hill IN; D10.4.1941 Greendale IN; BR/TR/5´11.5˝/195; d7.12																									
1905	Det A	0	0	ø	2	0	0	0	3.1	4	3	0	1	6	0	8.10	34	.308	.550	0	ø	0	—	-2	—	-0.1
Juul, Herold	Earl Herold; B5.21.1893 Chicago IL; D1.4.1942 Chicago IL; BR/TR/5´9.5˝/150; d4.24; b–Herb																									
1914	Bro F	0	3	.000	9	3	0	0	29	26	24	0	1	31	16	6.21	46	.248	.423	9	.222	-0	80	-10	—	-0.9

Juul, Herb Herbert Victor; B2.2.1886 Chicago IL; D11.14.1928 Chicago IL; BL/TL/5´11˝/150; d7.11; b–Herold; Col Illinois

YEAR	TM LG	W	L	PCT	G	GS	CG-SHO	SV-BS	IP	H	R	HR	HB	BB-IB	SO	ERA	AERA	OAV	OOB	AB-HR-SH	AVG	PB	SUP	APR	DL	PW
1911	Cin N	0	0	ø	1	0	0	0	4	3	2	0	0	4	2	4.50	74	.231	.412	2	.000	-0*	—	0	—	-0.1

Kaat, Jim James Lee; B11.7.1938 Zeeland MI; BL/TL/6´4˝/(190–227); d8.2; C2; Col Hope

YEAR	TM LG	W	L	PCT	G	GS	CG-SHO	SV-BS	IP	H	R	HR	HB	BB-IB	SO	ERA	AERA	OAV	OOB	AB-HR-SH	AVG	PB	SUP	APR	DL	PW
1959	Was A	0	2	.000	3	2	0	0	5	7	9	1	2	4-0	2	12.60	31	.350	.481	1	.000	-0	56	-5	0	-0.9
1960	Was A	1	5	.167	13	9	0	0	50	48	39	8	5	31-2	25	5.58	70	.255	.370	14	.143	-1	88	-10	0	-1.1
1961	Min A	9	17	.346	36	29	8-1	0	200.2	188	105	12	11	82-1	122	3.90	109	.248	.329	63-0-3	.238	3*	75	5	0	1.1
1962	Min A☆	18	14	.563	39	35	16-**5**	1	269	243	106	23	18	75-5	173	3.14	130	.243	.305	100-1-0	.180	3*	99	27	0	3.8
1963	Min A	10	10	.500	31	27	7-1	1	178.1	195	96	24	9	38-1	105	4.19	87	.274	.318	61-1-1	.131	-0*	126	-11	0	-1.0
1964	Min A	17	11	.607	36	34	13	1	243	231	100	23	9	60-5	171	3.22	111	.251	.301	83-3-3	.169	5*	117	10	0	1.8
1965	†Min A	18	11	.621	45	**42**	7-2	2	264.1	267	121	25	5	63-6	154	2.83	126	.258	.302	93-1-3	.247	6*	116	11	0	2.1
1966	Min A★	**25**	13	.658	41	**41**	**19**-3	0	**304.2**	271	114	29	3	55-4	205	2.75	131	.235	.270	118-2-1	.195	4*	103	25	0	3.6
1967	Min A	16	13	.552	42	38	13-2	0	263.1	269	110	21	9	42-2	211	3.04	114	.260	.294	99-1-1	.172	3*	96	9	0	1.4
1968	Min A	14	12	.538	30	29	9-2	0	208	192	78	16	3	40-0	130	2.94	105	.243	.278	77	.156	0*	101	4	21	0.6
1969	Min A	14	13	.519	40	32	10	1-1	242.1	252	114	23	9	75-15	139	3.49	104	.265	.322	87-2-2	.207	6*	103	1	0	0.7
1970	†Min A	14	10	.583	45	34	4-1	0-1	230.1	244	110	26	3	58-8	120	3.56	104	.273	.316	76-1-4	.197	3*	113	2	0	0.7
1971	Min A	13	14	.481	39	38	15-4	0-0	260.1	275	104	16	6	47-9	137	3.32	107	.268	.302	93-0-7	.161	-0*	108	8	0	0.8
1972	Min A	10	2	.833	15	15	5	0-0	113.1	94	36	6	0	20-2	64	2.06	156	.227	.260	45-2-1	.289	5*	114	12	83	2.0
1973	Min A	11	12	.478	29	28	7-2	0-0	181.2	206	101	26	4	39-1	93	4.41	90	.282	.321	0	ø	0*	108	-8	0	-1.0
	Chi A	4	1	.800	7	7	3-1	0-0	42.2	44	23	4	0	4-0	16	4.22	94	.260	.277	0	ø	0	152	-1	0	-0.2
	Year	15	13	.536	36	35	10-3	0-0	224.1	250	124	30	4	43-1	109	4.37	91	.278	.313	0	ø	0	116	-11	0	-1.2
1974	Chi A	21	13	.618	42	39	15-3	0-0	277.1	263	106	18	6	63-3	142	2.92	128	.250	.293	1	.000	-0	92	23	0	2.6
1975	Chi A★	20	14	.588	43	41	12-1	0-0	303.2	321	121	20	9	77-0	142	3.11	125	.274	.321	0	ø	0	99	23	0	2.4
1976	†Phi N	12	14	.462	38	35	7-1	0-1	227.2	241	95	21	0	32-3	83	3.48	103	.274	.298	79-1-1	.177	2*	106	3	0	0.4
1977	Phi N	6	11	.353	35	27	2	0-0	160.1	211	100	20	2	40-6	55	5.39	75	.320	.360	53-0-1	.189	1*	108	-21	0	-1.9
1978	Phi N	8	5	.615	26	24	2-1	0-0	140.1	150	67	9	5	32-6	48	4.10	88	.280	.322	48-0-1	.146	-1	112	-6	0	-0.7
1979	Phi N	1	0	1.000	3	1	0	0-0	8.1	9	4	1	0	5-2	2	4.32	90	.281	.378	1	.000	0	160	0	0	0.0
	NY A	2	3	.400	40	1	0	2-2	58.1	64	29	4	2	14-2	23	3.86	107	.287	.329	0	ø	0	110	1	0	0.0
1980	NY A	0	1	.000	4	0	0	0-0	5	8	5	0	0	4-2	1	7.20	55	.381	.462	0	ø	0	—	-2	0	-0.3
	StL N	8	7	.533	49	14	6-1	4-1	129.2	140	61	6	0	33-11	36	3.82	98	.281	.322	35-1-4	.143	0	119	-1	0	-0.1
1981	StL N	6	6	.500	41	1	0	4-5	53	60	25	2	0	17-8	8	3.40	107	.299	.345	8	.375	1	98	0	0	0.2
1982	†StL N	5	3	.625	62	2	0	2-2	75	79	40	6	2	23-9	35	4.08	90	.276	.328	12	.000	-1	96	-4	0	-0.5
1983	StL N	0	0	ø	24	0	0	0-1	34.2	48	19	5	0	10-3	19	3.89	94	.327	.367	4-0-1	.000	-0	—	-2	0	-0.1
Total	25	283	237	.544	898	625	180-31	18-14	4530.1	4620	2038	395	122	1083-116	2461	3.45	107	.264	.309	1251-16-34	.185	41	105	93	104	16.4

Kahler, George George Runnells "Krum"; B9.6.1889 Athens OH; D2.7.1924 Battle Creek MI; BR/TR/6´0˝/183; d8.13; Col Ohio U.

YEAR	TM LG	W	L	PCT	G	GS	CG-SHO	SV-BS	IP	H	R	HR	HB	BB-IB	SO	ERA	AERA	OAV	OOB	AB-HR-SH	AVG	PB	SUP	APR	DL	PW
1910	Cle A	6	4	.600	12	12	8-2	0	95.1	80	35	0	4	46	38	1.60	161	.237	.335	35	.143	-2	110	6	—	0.4
1911	Cle A	9	8	.529	30	17	10	1	154.1	153	78	1	13	66	97	3.27	104	.270	.360	54-0-3	.167	-2	91	2	—	-0.1
1912	Cle A	12	19	.387	41	32	17-3	1	246.1	263	135	1	11	121	104	3.69	92	.291	.382	80-0-1	.112	-5	75	-6	—	-1.4
1913	Cle A	5	11	.313	24	15	5	0	117.2	118	56	1	4	32	43	3.14	97	.269	.324	33-0-3	.061	-3	86	-1	—	-0.7
1914	Cle A	0	1	.000	2	1	1	0	14	17	10	0	0	7	3	3.86	75	.309	.387	5	.000	-0	152	-2	—	-0.2
Total	5	32	43	.427	109	77	41-5	2	627.2	631	314	3	32	272	285	3.17	101	.274	.359	207-0-7	.121	-13	86	-1	—	-2.0

Kainer, Don Donald Wayne; B9.3.1955 Houston TX; BR/TR/6´3˝/200; [TexA77 13/321]; d9.6; Col Texas

YEAR	TM LG	W	L	PCT	G	GS	CG-SHO	SV-BS	IP	H	R	HR	HB	BB-IB	SO	ERA	AERA	OAV	OOB	AB-HR-SH	AVG	PB	SUP	APR	DL	PW
1980	Tex A	0	0	ø	4	3	0	0-0	19.2	22	7	0	3	9-1	10	1.83	213	.289	.386	0	ø	0	100	4	0	0.3

Kaiser, Don Clyde Donald "Tiger"; B2.3.1935 Byng OK; BR/TR/6´5˝/195; d7.20; Col East Central

YEAR	TM LG	W	L	PCT	G	GS	CG-SHO	SV-BS	IP	H	R	HR	HB	BB-IB	SO	ERA	AERA	OAV	OOB	AB-HR-SH	AVG	PB	SUP	APR	DL	PW
1955	Chi N	0	0	ø	11	0	0	0	18.1	20	11	2	1	5-0	11	5.40	76	.274	.329	2	.000	-0	—	-2	0	-0.2
1956	Chi N	4	9	.308	27	22	5-1	0	150.1	144	69	15	1	52-8	74	3.59	105	.247	.308	47	.043	-5	75	3	0	-0.3
1957	Chi N	2	6	.250	20	13	1	0	72	91	48	4	0	28-3	23	5.00	77	.316	.372	19	.105	-1	82	-10	0	-1.0
Total	3	6	15	.286	58	35	6-1	0	240.2	255	128	21	2	85-11	108	4.15	92	.270	.329	68	.059	-6	78	-9	0	-1.5

Kaiser, Jeff Jeffrey Patrick; B7.24.1960 Wyandotte MI; BR/TL/6´3˝/(195–205); [OakA82 10/262]; d4.11; Col Western Michigan

YEAR	TM LG	W	L	PCT	G	GS	CG-SHO	SV-BS	IP	H	R	HR	HB	BB-IB	SO	ERA	AERA	OAV	OOB	AB-HR-SH	AVG	PB	SUP	APR	DL	PW
1985	Oak A	0	0	ø	15	0	0	0-1	16.2	25	32	6	1	20-2	10	14.58	27	.342	.479	0	ø	0	—	-22	0	-1.0
1987	Cle A	0	0	ø	2	0	0	0-0	3.1	4	6	1	1	3-0	2	16.20	28	.286	.444	0	ø	0	—	-4	22	-0.2
1988	Cle A	0	0	ø	3	0	0	0-0	2.2	2	0	0	0	1-0	0	0.00	ø	.286	.333	0	ø	0	—	1	0	0.1
1989	Cle A	0	1	.000	6	0	0	0-1	3.2	5	5	1	0	5-0	4	7.36	54	.313	.455	0	ø	0	—	-2	0	-0.4
1990	Cle A	0	0	ø	5	0	0	0-0	12.2	16	5	2	0	7-1	9	3.55	111	.308	.383	0	ø	0	—	1	58	0.0
1991	Det A	0	1	.000	10	0	0	2-0	5	6	5	1	0	5-2	4	9.00	46	.286	.423	0	ø	0	—	-2	0	-0.5
1993	Cin N	0	0	ø	3	0	0	0-0	3.1	4	1	0	0	2-1	4	2.70	149	.286	.375	0	ø	0	—	1	0	0.0
	NY N	0	0	ø	6	0	0	0-0	4.2	6	6	1	0	3-0	5	11.57	35	.353	.429	0	ø	0	—	-4	20	-0.2
	Year	0	0	ø	9	0	0	0-0	8	10	7	1	0	5-1	9	7.88	51	.323	.405	0	ø	0	—	-3	0	-0.2
Total	7	0	2	.000	50	0	0	2-2	52	68	60	12	2	46-6	38	9.17	44	.318	.433	0	ø	0	—	-31	100	-2.2

Kaiser, Bob Robert Thomas; B4.29.1950 Cincinnati OH; BB/TL/5´10˝/180; [CleA68 3/46]; d9.3

YEAR	TM LG	W	L	PCT	G	GS	CG-SHO	SV-BS	IP	H	R	HR	HB	BB-IB	SO	ERA	AERA	OAV	OOB	AB-HR-SH	AVG	PB	SUP	APR	DL	PW
1971	Cle A	0	0	ø	5	0	0	0-0	6	8	3	2	2	3-0	4	4.50	86	.333	.448	0	ø	0	—	0	0	0.0

Kaiserling, George George; B5.12.1893 Steubenville OH; D3.2.1918 Steubenville OH; BR/TR/6´0˝/175; d4.20

YEAR	TM LG	W	L	PCT	G	GS	CG-SHO	SV-BS	IP	H	R	HR	HB	BB-IB	SO	ERA	AERA	OAV	OOB	AB-HR-SH	AVG	PB	SUP	APR	DL	PW
1914	Ind F	17	10	.630	37	33	20-1	0	275.1	288	119	8	17	72	75	3.11	100	.274	.330	98-0-3	.112	-6	121	2	—	-0.7
1915	New F	15	15	.500	41	29	16-5	2	261.1	246	90	1	9	73	75	2.24	114	.257	.316	79-0-9	.152	-2	104	10	—	0.7
Total	2	32	25	.561	78	62	36-6	2	536.2	534	209	9	26	145	150	2.68	106	.266	.323	177-0-12	.130	-8	115	12	—	0.0

Kalfass, Bill William Philip "Lefty"; B3.3.1916 New York NY; D9.8.1968 Brooklyn NY; BR/TL/6´3.5˝/190; d9.15; Col Columbia

YEAR	TM LG	W	L	PCT	G	GS	CG-SHO	SV-BS	IP	H	R	HR	HB	BB-IB	SO	ERA	AERA	OAV	OOB	AB-HR-SH	AVG	PB	SUP	APR	DL	PW
1937	Phi A	1	0	1.000	3	1	1	0	12	10	4	0	0	10	9	3.00	157	.233	.377	4	.000	-1	185	3	—	0.1

Kallio, Rudy Rudolph; B12.14.1892 Portland OR; D4.6.1979 Newport OR; BR/TR/5´10˝/160; d4.25

YEAR	TM LG	W	L	PCT	G	GS	CG-SHO	SV-BS	IP	H	R	HR	HB	BB-IB	SO	ERA	AERA	OAV	OOB	AB-HR-SH	AVG	PB	SUP	APR	DL	PW
1918	Det A	8	13	.381	30	22	10-2	0	181.1	178	91	0	1	76	70	3.62	73	.261	.336	56-0-4	.161	-1*	109	-20	—	-2.3
1919	Det A	0	0	ø	12	1	0	1	22.1	28	15	0	1	8	3	5.64	57	.326	.389	4	.000	-1	147	-5	—	-0.3
1925	Bos A	1	4	.200	7	4	0	0	18.2	28	18	0	1	9	2	7.71	59	.364	.437	6	.333	0	97	-6	—	-0.9
Total	3	9	17	.346	49	27	10-2	1	222.1	234	124	0	3	93	75	4.17	69	.277	.351	66-0-4	.167	-1	111	-31	—	-3.5

Kamieniecki, Scott Scott Andrew; B4.19.1964 Mt.Clemens MI; BR/TR/6´0˝/(195–200); [NYA86 14/366]; d6.18; Col Michigan

YEAR	TM LG	W	L	PCT	G	GS	CG-SHO	SV-BS	IP	H	R	HR	HB	BB-IB	SO	ERA	AERA	OAV	OOB	AB-HR-SH	AVG	PB	SUP	APR	DL	PW
1991	NY A	4	4	.500	9	9	0	0-0	55.1	54	24	8	3	22-1	34	3.90	107	.256	.333	0	ø	0	80	3	65	0.4
1992	NY A	6	14	.300	28	28	4	0-0	188	193	100	13	5	74-9	88	4.36	91	.269	.340	0	ø	0	103	-9	23	-0.9
1993	NY A	10	7	.588	30	20	2	1-0	154.1	163	73	17	3	59-7	72	4.08	103	.277	.343	0	ø	0	98	3	0	0.4
1994	NY A	8	6	.571	22	16	1	0-0	117.1	115	53	13	3	59-5	71	3.76	122	.261	.350	0	ø	0	134	12	0	1.2
1995	†NY A	7	6	.538	17	16	1	0-0	89.2	83	43	8	3	49-1	43	4.01	115	.246	.346	0	ø	0	99	6	70	0.7
1996	NY A	1	2	.333	7	5	0	0-1	22.2	36	30	6	2	19-1	15	11.12	45	.364	.475	0	ø	0	135	-16	84	-1.5
1997	†Bal A	10	6	.625	30	30	0	0-0	179.1	179	83	20	4	67-2	109	4.01	110	.261	.328	2	.000	-0	99	10	0	0.8
1998	Bal A	2	6	.250	12	11	0	0-0	54.2	67	41	7	4	26-0	25	6.75	67	.313	.394	0	ø	0	72	-13	117	-1.5
1999	Bal A	2	4	.333	43	3	0	2-0	56.1	52	32	4	4	29-2	39	4.95	95	.250	.348	0	ø	0	86	-1	33	0.0
2000	Cle A	1	3	.250	26	0	0	0-0	33.1	42	22	6	1	20-5	29	5.67	88	.311	.404	0	ø	0	—	-2	0	-0.2
	Atl N	2	1	.667	26	0	0	2-0	24.2	22	18	3	0	22-1	17	5.47	82	.239	.386	0	ø	0	—	-3	0	-0.4
Total	10	53	59	.473	250	138	8	5-1	975.2	1006	519	105	32	446-34	542	4.52	97	.270	.351	2	.000	-0	101	-10	392	-1.0

Kammeyer, Bob Robert Lynn; B12.2.1950 Kansas City KS; D1.27.2003 Sacramento CA; BR/TR/6´4˝/210; [NYA72 21/492]; d7.3; Col Stanford

YEAR	TM LG	W	L	PCT	G	GS	CG-SHO	SV-BS	IP	H	R	HR	HB	BB-IB	SO	ERA	AERA	OAV	OOB	AB-HR-SH	AVG	PB	SUP	APR	DL	PW
1978	NY A	0	0	ø	7	0	0	0-0	21.2	24	15	1	2	6-0	11	5.82	63	.276	.327	0	ø	0	—	-5	0	-0.2
1979	NY A	0	0	ø	1	0	0	0-0	0	7	8	2	1	0-0	0	(8)	ø	1.000	1.000	0	ø	0	—	-8	0	-0.6
Total	2	0	0	ø	8	0	0	0-0	21.2	31	23	3	3	6-0	11	9.14	40	.330	.377	0	ø	0	—	-13	0	-0.8

Kamp, Ike Alphonse Francis; B9.5.1900 Roxbury MA; D2.25.1955 Boston MA; BB/TL/6´0˝/170; d9.16; Col Boston College

YEAR	TM LG	W	L	PCT	G	GS	CG-SHO	SV-BS	IP	H	R	HR	HB	BB-IB	SO	ERA	AERA	OAV	OOB	AB-HR-SH	AVG	PB	SUP	APR	DL	PW
1924	Bos N	0	1	.000	1	1	0	0	7	9	5	0	0	5	4	5.14	74	.360	.467	1-0-1	.000	-0	67	-1	—	-0.1
1925	Bos N	2	4	.333	24	4	1	0	58.1	68	38	0	0	35	20	5.09	79	.301	.395	12-0-1	.167	-0	116	-7	—	-0.6
Total	2	2	5	.286	25	5	1	0	65.1	77	43	0	0	40	24	5.10	78	.307	.402	13-0-2	.154	-0	106	-8	—	-0.7

YEAR	TM LG	W	L	PCT	G	GS	CG-SHO	SV-BS	IP	H	R	HR	HB	BB-IB	SO	ERA	AERA	OAV	OOB	AB-HR-SH	AVG	PB	SUP	APR	DL	PW
Kane, Harry	Harry "Klondike" (b Harry Cohen); B7.27.1883 Hamburg AR; D9.15.1932 Portland OR; BL/TL; d8.8																									
1902	StL A	0	1	.000	4	1	1	0	23	34	21	2	0	16	7	5.48	64	.343	.435	9	.111	-1	82	-6	—	-0.4
1903	Det A	0	2	.000	3	3	2	0	18	26	22	0	1	8	10	8.50	34	.338	.407	7	.143	-0	106	-10	—	-0.9
1905	Phi N	1	1	.500	2	2	2-1	0	17	12	6	0	0	8	12	1.59	184	.203	.299	6-0-1	.167	-0	74	2	—	0.2
1906	Phi N	1	3	.250	6	3	2	0	28	28	16	0	3	18	14	3.86	68	.255	.374	8-0-1	.000	-1	74	-3	—	-0.5
Total	4	2	7	.222	15	9	7-1	0	86	100	65	2	4	50	43	4.81	62	.290	.386	30-0-2	.100	-2	83	-17	—	-1.6
Kantlehner, Erv	Erving Leslie "Peanuts"; B7.31.1892 San Jose CA; D2.3.1990 Santa Barbara CA; BL/TL/6´0˝/190; d4.17; Col Santa Clara																									
1914	Pit N	3	2	.600	21	5	3-2	0	67	51	33	1	3	39	26	3.09	86	.218	.337	15	.067	-0	108	-5	—	-0.4
1915	Pit N	5	12	.294	29	18	10-1	3	163	135	60	1	4	58	64	2.26	121	.230	.304	52-0-1	.288	3	73	6	—	1.0
1916	Pit N	5	15	.250	34	21	7-2	2	165	151	72	1	4	57	49	3.16	85	.249	.317	46	.174	-0	64	-7	—	-0.8
	Phi N	0	0	ø	3	0	0	0	4	7	4	0	0	3	2	9.00	29	.500	.588	0	ø	0	—	-2	—	-0.1
	Year	5	15	.250	37	21	7-2	2	169	158	76	1	4	60	51	3.30	81	.254	.324	46	.174	-0	64	-10	—	-0.9
Total	3	13	29	.310	87	44	20-5	5	399	344	169	3	11	157	141	2.84	95	.239	.318	113-0-1	.212	2	72	-8	—	-0.3
Karchner, Matt	Matthew Dean; B6.28.1967 Berwick PA; BR/TR/6´4˝/(210–220); [KCA89 8/205]; d7.18; Col Bloomsburg																									
1995	Chi A	4	2	.667	31	0	0	0-0	32	33	8	2	1	12-2	24	1.69	265	.275	.336	0	ø	0	—	10	0	1.6
1996	Chi A	7	4	.636	50	0	0	1-8	59.1	61	42	10	2	41-8	46	5.76	83	.266	.377	0	ø	0	—	-7	50	-1.2
1997	Chi A	3	1	.750	52	0	0	15-1	52.2	50	18	4	0	26-4	30	2.91	152	.258	.344	0	ø	0	—	10	0	1.1
1998	Chi A	2	4	.333	32	0	0	11-4	36.2	33	21	2	5	19-6	30	5.15	89	.243	.348	0	ø	0	—	-1	31	-0.2
	†Chi N	3	1	.750	29	0	0	0-3	28	30	18	6	2	14-2	22	5.14	86	.263	.354	0	ø	0	—	-3	0	-0.3
1999	Chi N	1	0	1.000	16	0	0	0-1	18	16	5	3	2	9-0	9	2.50	183	.235	.342	0	ø	0	—	4	138	0.2
2000	Chi N	1	1	.500	13	0	0	0-0	14.2	19	11	3	0	11-0	5	6.14	75	.311	.411	0-0-1	ø	0	—	-3	0	-0.3
Total	6	21	13	.618	223	0	0	27-17	241.1	242	123	30	12	132-22	166	4.21	108	.262	.357	0-0-1	ø	0	—	10	219	0.9
Kardow, Paul	Paul Otto "Tex"; B9.19.1915 Humble TX; D4.27.1968 San Antonio TX; BR/TR/6´6˝ /210; d7.1																									
1936	Cle A	0	0	ø	2	0	0	0	2	1	1	0	0	2	0	4.50	112	.167	.375	0	ø	0	—	0	—	0.0
Karger, Ed	Edwin "Loose"; B5.6.1883 San Angelo TX; D9.9.1957 Delta CO; BL/TL/5´11˝/185; d4.15																									
1906	Pit N	2	3	.400	6	2	0	0	28	21	11	0	2	9	8	1.93	139	.204	.281	11	.091	-1	95	1	—	0.3
	StL N	5	16	.238	25	20	17	1	191.2	193	85	0	7	43	73	2.72	97	.271	.319	73-1-0	.233	4	73	-5	—	0.0
	Year	7	19	.269	31	22	17	1	219.2	214	96	0	9	52	81	2.62	100	.263	.314	84-1-0	.214	3	75	-4	—	0.3
1907	StL N	15	19	.441	39	32	29-6	1	314	257	102	2	10	65	137	2.04	123	.223	.270	112-2-4	.179	1	65	17	—	2.4
1908	StL N	4	9	.308	22	15	9-1	0	141.1	148	77	1	2	50	34	3.06	77	.260	.322	54	.241	3*	70	-12	—	-0.8
1909	Cin N	1	3	.250	9	5	1	0	34.1	26	22	0	2	30	8	4.46	58	.217	.382	11	.273	2	156	-6	—	-0.5
	Bos A	5	2	.714	12	6	3	0	68	71	29	0	3	22	17	3.18	79	.273	.337	24-0-1	.125	-0	132	-3	—	-0.4
1910	Bos A	11	7	.611	27	25	16-1	1	183.1	162	75	5	5	53	81	3.19	80	.230	.289	68-2-3	.294	6	142	-6	—	-0.1
1911	Bos A	5	8	.385	25	18	6-1	0	131	134	70	4	4	42	57	3.37	97	.272	.334	47-1-2	.234	3	109	1	—	0.4
Total	6	48	67	.417	165	123	81-9	3	1091.2	1012	471	12	35	314	415	2.79	94	.246	.305	400-6-10	.220	18	99	-13	—	1.3
Karl, Andy	Anton Andrew; B4.8.1914 Mt.Vernon NY; D4.8.1989 LaJolla CA; BR/TR/6´1.5˝/175; d4.24; Col Manhattan																									
1943	Bos A	1	1	.500	11	0	0	1	26	31	11	0	0	13	6	3.46	96	.310	.389	7	.286	0	—	0	0	0.1
	Phi N	1	2	.333	9	2	0	0	26.2	44	22	0	0	11	4	7.09	48	.383	.437	8	.250	1*	63	-10	0	-0.9
1944	Phi N	3	2	.600	38	0	0	2	89	76	32	1	1	21	26	2.33	155	.237	.287	15	.200	1*	—	**11**	0	0.7
1945	Phi N	8	8	.500	**67**	2	1	**15**	180.2	175	80	7	3	50	51	2.99	128	.253	.306	49	.143	-2	88	**15**	0	1.3
1946	Phi N	3	7	.300	39	0	0	5	65.1	84	37	6	1	22	15	4.96	69	.321	.375	10-0-2	.100	-0	—	-9	0	-1.5
1947	Bos N	2	3	.400	27	0	0	3	35	41	18	2	0	13	5	3.86	101	.318	.380	6	.167	-0	—	0	0	0.0
Total	5	18	23	.439	191	4	1	26	422.2	451	200	16	5	130	107	3.51	104	.279	.334	95-0-2	.168	-0	75	7	0	-0.3
Karl, Scott	Randall Scott; B8.9.1971 Fontana CA; BL/TL/6´2˝/(195–209); [MilA92 6/164]; d5.4; Col Hawaii–Manoa																									
1995	Mil A	6	7	.462	25	18	1	0-0	124	141	65	10	3	50-6	59	4.14	121	.288	.356	0	ø	0	93	10	0	0.9
1996	Mil A	13	9	.591	32	32	3-1	0-0	207.1	220	124	29	11	72-0	121	4.86	107	.271	.336	0	ø	0	108	6	0	0.5
1997	Mil A	10	13	.435	32	32	1	0-0	193.1	212	103	23	4	67-1	119	4.47	104	.279	.339	4	.000	-0	79	5	0	0.5
1998	Mil N	10	11	.476	33	33	0	0-0	192.1	219	104	21	4	66-4	102	4.40	99	.290	.349	56-0-9	.071	-2*	87	-2	0	-0.3
1999	Mil N	11	11	.500	33	33	0	0-0	197.2	246	121	21	8	69-4	74	4.78	96	.312	.370	60-2-12	.183	3	88	-7	0	-0.2
2000	Col N	2	3	.400	17	9	0	0-0	65.2	95	56	14	3	33-3	29	7.68	76	.343	.415	14-0-2	.286	1	102	-10	20	-0.5
	Ana A	2	2	.500	6	4	0	0-0	21.2	31	21	2	0	12-0	9	6.65	78	.337	.413	0	ø	0	82	-5	0	-0.8
Total	6	54	56	.491	178	161	5-1	0-0	1002	1164	594	120	33	369-18	513	4.81	100	.293	.356	134-2-23	.142	1	91	-3	20	0.1
Karns, Bill	William Arthur; B12.28.1875 Richmond IA; D11.15.1941 Seattle WA; BL/TL; d8.14																									
1901	Bal A	1	0	1.000	3	1	1	0	17	30	18	0	0	9	5	6.35	61	.380	.443	7-0-1	.143	-1*	175	-4	—	-0.3
Karnuth, Jason	Jason Andre; B5.15.1976 LaGrange IL; BR/TR/6´2˝/190; [StLN97 8/254]; d4.20; Col Illinois St.																									
2001	StL N	0	0	ø	4	0	0	0-0	5	6	1	1	1	4-0	1	1.80	240	.316	.458	0	ø	0	—	1	0	0.1
2005	Det A	0	0	ø	3	0	0	0-0	1.2	2	1	0	0	0-0	0	5.40	79	.286	.286	0	ø	0	—	0	0	0.0
Total	2	0	0	ø	7	0	0	0-0	6.2	8	2	1	1	4-0	1	2.70	160	.308	.419	0	ø	0	—	1	0	0.1
Karp, Ryan	Ryan Jason; B4.5.1970 Los Angeles CA; BL/TL/6´4˝/(205–217); [NYA92 9/242]; d6.23; Col Florida International																									
1995	Phi N	0	0	ø	1	0	0	0-0	2	1	1	0	0	3-0	2	4.50	94	.143	.400	0	ø	0	—	0	0	0.0
1997	Phi N	1	1	.500	15	1	0	0-1	15	12	12	2	2	9-0	18	5.40	78	.218	.348	0	ø	0	131	-3	0	-0.4
Total	2	1	1	.500	16	1	0	0-1	17	13	13	2	2	12-0	20	5.29	80	.210	.355	0	ø	0	131	-3	0	-0.4
Karpel, Herb	Herbert "Lefty"; B12.27.1917 Brooklyn NY; D1.24.1995 San Diego CA; BL/TL/5´9.5˝/180; d4.19																									
1946	NY A	0	0	ø	2	0	0	0	1.2	4	2	0	0	0	0	10.80	32	.500	.500	0	ø	0	—	-1	0	-0.1
Karr, Benn	Benjamin Joyce "Baldy"; B11.28.1893 Mt.Pleasant MS; D12.8.1968 Memphis TN; BL/TR/6´0˝/175; d4.20																									
1920	Bos A	3	8	.273	26	2	0	1	91.2	109	55	3	1	24	21	4.81	76	.304	.349	75-1-1	.280	6*	54	-11	—	-0.7
1921	Bos A	8	7	.533	26	7	5	0	117.2	123	53	8	1	38	37	3.67	115	.283	.342	62-0-4	.258	1*	96	8	—	1.0
1922	Bos A	5	12	.294	41	13	7	1	183.1	212	115	10	5	45	41	4.47	92	.302	.348	98-0-1	.214	-1*	107	-11	—	-1.0
1925	Cle A	11	12	.478	32	24	12-1	0	197.2	248	127	8	6	80	41	4.78	92	.317	.385	92-1-7	.261	4*	98	-9	—	-0.4
1926	Cle A	5	6	.455	30	7	4	1	113.1	137	72	9	6	41	23	5.00	81	.291	.355	45-0-1	.222	2*	119	-11	—	-0.7
1927	Cle A	3	3	.500	22	5	1	2	76.2	92	49	5	1	32	17	5.05	83	.315	.385	20-0-1	.200	1	87	-6	—	-0.3
Total	6	35	48	.422	177	58	29-1	5	780.1	921	471	43	20	260	180	4.60	90	.303	.362	392-2-15	.245	12	101	-40	—	-2.1
Karsay, Steve	Stefan Andrew; B3.24.1972 Flushing NY; BR/TR/6´3˝/(185–215); [TorA90 1/22]; d8.17; [DL 1995 Oak A 160, 2003 NY A 183]																									
1993	Oak A	3	3	.500	8	8	0	0-0	49	49	23	4	2	16-1	33	4.04	102	.258	.319	0	ø	0	92	1	0	0.0
1994	Oak A	1	1	.500	4	4	1	0-0	28	26	8	1	1	8-0	15	2.57	175	.252	.310	0	ø	0	123	7	108	0.4
1997	Oak A	3	12	.200	24	24	0	0-0	132.2	166	92	20	9	47-3	92	5.77	80	.304	.366	0	ø	0*	82	-17	54	-1.7
1998	Cle A	0	2	.000	11	1	0	0-0	24.1	31	16	3	2	6-1	13	5.92	81	.310	.355	0	ø	0	19	-2	0	-0.2
1999	†Cle A	10	2	.833	50	3	0	1-2	78.2	71	29	6	2	30-3	68	2.97	171	.247	.320	0	ø	0	153	17	52	2.3
2000	Cle A	5	9	.357	72	0	0	20-9	76.2	79	33	5	3	25-4	66	3.76	133	.266	.327	1	.000	-0	—	11	0	2.1
2001	Cle A	0	1	.000	31	0	0	1-0	43.1	29	6	1	0	8-2	44	1.25	368	.188	.227	0	ø	0	—	16	0	0.8
	†Atl N	3	4	.429	43	0	0	7-4	44.2	44	21	4	1	17-8	39	3.43	126	.265	.332	2	.000	-0	—	3	0	0.6
2002	†NY A	6	4	.600	78	0	0	12-4	88.1	87	33	7	2	30-14	65	3.26	133	.258	.320	1	.000	-0	—	12	0	1.5
2004	NY A	0	0	ø	7	0	0	0-0	6.2	5	3	2	0	2-0	4	2.70	170	.217	.259	0	ø	0	—	1	155	0.0
2005	NY A	0	0	ø	6	0	0	0-0	6	10	5	0	0	2-1	5	6.00	72	.385	.414	0	ø	0	—	-1	0	-0.1
	Tex A	0	1	.000	14	0	0	0-0	15.2	26	14	2	0	5-0	9	7.47	61	.366	.403	0	ø	0	—	-5	0	-0.3
	Year	0	1	.000	20	0	0	0-0	21.2	36	19	2	0	7-1	14	7.06	63	.371	.406	0	ø	0	—	-6	0	-0.4
2006	Oak A	1	0	1.000	9	0	0	0-0	9.1	13	6	4	1	3-1	5	5.79	78	.351	.405	0	ø	0	—	-1	0	-0.1
Total	11	32	39	.451	357	40	1	41-19	603.1	636	289	59	23	199-38	458	4.01	115	.272	.332	4	.000	-0	91	42	712	5.3
Karstens, Jeff	Jeffrey Wayne; B9.24.1982 San Diego CA; BR/TR/6´3˝/175; [NYA03 19/574]; d8.22; Col Texas Tech																									
2006	NY A	2	1	.667	8	6	0	0-0	42.2	40	20	6	1	11-2	16	3.80	119	.242	.291	0	ø	0	121	3	0	0.2
Kashiwada, Takashi	Takashi; B5.14.1971 Tokyo, Japan; BL/TL/5´11˝/165; d5.1																									
1997	NY N	3	1	.750	35	0	0	0-2	31.1	35	15	4	3	18-0	19	4.31	93	.289	.389	1	.000	-0	—	0	0	0.0

Katoll, Jack John "Big Jack"; B6.24.1872 , Germany; D6.18.1955 Woodstock IL; BR/TR/5´11˝/195; d9.9

YEAR	TM LG	W	L	PCT	G	GS	CG-SHO	SV-BS	IP	H	R	HR	HB	BB-IB	SO	ERA	AERA	OAV	OOB	AB-HR-SH	AVG	PB	SUP	APR	DL	PW
1898	Chi N	0	1	.000	2	1	1	0	11	8	4	0	0	1	3	0.82	438	.200	.220	4	.000	-1	59	3	—	0.1
1899	Chi N	1	1	.500	2	2	2	0	18	17	15	0	1	4	1	6.00	62	.250	.301	7	.000	-1	125	-4	—	-0.4
1901	Chi A	11	10	.524	27	25	19	0	208	231	126	3	11	53	59	2.81	124	.278	.330	80-1-1	.125	-4	107	8	—	0.3
1902	Chi A	0	0	ø	1	0	0	0	1	1	0	0	0	0	2	0.00	ø	.250	.250	1	.000	-0	—	0	—	0.0
	Bal A	5	10	.333	15	13	13	0	123	175	106	5	2	32	25	4.02	94	.334	.375	57	.175	-0*	76	-12	—	-1.0
	Year	5	10	.333	16	13	13	0	124	176	106	5	2	32	27	3.99	94	.333	.374	58	.172	-0	76	-12	—	-1.0
Total	4	17	22	.436	47	41	35	0	361	432	251	8	14	90	90	3.32	109	.294	.341	149-1-1	.134	-6	97	-5	—	-1.0

Katz, Bob Robert Clyde; B1.30.1911 Lancaster PA; D12.14.1962 St.Joseph MI; BR/TR/5´11.5˝/190; d5.12

YEAR	TM LG	W	L	PCT	G	GS	CG-SHO	SV-BS	IP	H	R	HR	HB	BB-IB	SO	ERA	AERA	OAV	OOB	AB-HR-SH	AVG	PB	SUP	APR	DL	PW
1944	Cin N	0	1	.000	6	2	0	0	18.1	17	9	0	0	7	4	3.93	89	.254	.324	4	.000	-1	60	-1	0	-0.1

Kaufman, Curt Curt Gerrard; B7.19.1957 Omaha NE; BR/TR/6´2˝/175; d9.10; Col Iowa St.

YEAR	TM LG	W	L	PCT	G	GS	CG-SHO	SV-BS	IP	H	R	HR	HB	BB-IB	SO	ERA	AERA	OAV	OOB	AB-HR-SH	AVG	PB	SUP	APR	DL	PW
1982	NY A	1	0	1.000	7	0	0	0-0	8.2	9	5	2	0	6-1	1	5.19	78	.265	.375	0	ø	0	—	-1	0	-0.1
1983	NY A	0	0	ø	4	0	0	0-0	8.2	10	3	0	0	4-0	8	3.12	127	.303	.359	0	ø	0	—	1	0	0.0
1984	Cal A	2	3	.400	29	1	0	1-0	69	68	37	13	0	20-4	41	4.57	88	.254	.302	0	ø	0	136	-4	0	-0.2
Total	3	3	3	.500	40	1	0	1-0	86.1	87	45	15	0	30-5	50	4.48	89	.260	.316	0	ø	0	136	-4	0	-0.3

Kaufmann, Tony Anthony Charles; B12.16.1900 Chicago IL; D6.4.1982 Elgin IL; BR/TR/5´11˝/165; d9.23; C4; ▲

YEAR	TM LG	W	L	PCT	G	GS	CG-SHO	SV-BS	IP	H	R	HR	HB	BB-IB	SO	ERA	AERA	OAV	OOB	AB-HR-SH	AVG	PB	SUP	APR	DL	PW
1921	Chi N	1	0	1.000	2	1	1	1	13	12	6	0	0	3	6	4.15	92	.240	.283	5	.400	1	280	0	—	0.1
1922	Chi N	7	13	.350	37	14	4-1	3	153	161	81	15	5	57	45	4.06	103	.273	.343	45-1-5	.200	1*	100	3	—	0.4
1923	Chi N	14	10	.583	33	24	18-2	3	206.1	209	97	14	11	67	72	3.10	129	.264	.330	74-2-2	.216	3	106	16	—	2.0
1924	Chi N	16	11	.593	34	26	16-3	0	208.1	218	104	21	4	66	79	4.02	97	.272	.330	76-1-0	.316	6*	95	0	—	0.5
1925	Chi N	13	13	.500	31	23	14-2	2	196	221	107	9	7	77	49	4.50	96	.292	.363	78-2-1	.192	1	97	-1	—	0.0
1926	Chi N	9	7	.563	26	22	14-1	2	169.2	169	71	6	6	44	52	3.02	127	.262	.316	60-1-2	.250	2*	103	14	—	1.4
1927	Chi N	3	3	.500	9	6	3	0	53.1	75	44	8	4	19	21	6.41	60	.338	.400	16-1-2	.313	3	125	-15	—	-1.1
	Phi N	0	3	.000	5	5	1	0	18.2	37	25	2	0	8	4	10.61	39	.425	.474	7-1-0	.143	0*	87	-13	—	-1.5
	StL N	0	0	ø	1	0	0	0	0.1	4	3	0	0	1	0	81.00	5	1.000	1.000	0	ø	0	—	-3	—	-0.1
	Year	3	6	.333	15	11	4	0	72.1	116	72	10	4	28	25	7.84	50	.371	.429	23-2-2	.261	3	108	-29	—	-2.7
1928	StL N	0	0	ø	4	1	0	0	4.2	8	5	1	1	4	2	9.64	41	.444	.565	0	ø	0*	85	-3	—	-0.1
1930	StL N	0	1	.000	2	1	0	0	10.1	15	9	2	0	4	2	7.84	64	.357	.413	3	.333	0	139	-3	—	-0.2
1931	StL N	1	1	.500	15	1	0	1	49	65	34	3	1	17	13	6.06	65	.319	.374	18	.111	-1*	131	-10	—	-0.6
1935	StL N	0	0	ø	3	0	0	0	3.2	4	1	0	0	1	0	2.45	167	.286	.333	0	ø	0*	—	1	—	0.0
Total	11	64	62	.508	202	124	71-9	12	1086.1	1198	587	81	39	368	345	4.18	97	.284	.347	382-9-12	.236	17	102	-14	—	0.8

Kaye, Justin Justin Malcolm; B6.9.1976 Fort Lauderdale FL; BR/TR/6´4˝/195; [SeaA95 19/510]; d5.9

YEAR	TM LG	W	L	PCT	G	GS	CG-SHO	SV-BS	IP	H	R	HR	HB	BB-IB	SO	ERA	AERA	OAV	OOB	AB-HR-SH	AVG	PB	SUP	APR	DL	PW
2002	Sea A	0	0	ø	3	0	0	0-0	3	6	4	0	0	1-0	3	12.00	36	.429	.467	0	ø	0	—	-3	0	-0.1

Kazmir, Scott Scott Edward; B1.24.1984 Houston TX; BL/TL/6´0˝/(170–190); [NYN02 1/15]; d8.23

YEAR	TM LG	W	L	PCT	G	GS	CG-SHO	SV-BS	IP	H	R	HR	HB	BB-IB	SO	ERA	AERA	OAV	OOB	AB-HR-SH	AVG	PB	SUP	APR	DL	PW
2004	TB A	2	3	.400	8	7	0	0-0	33.1	33	22	4	2	21-0	41	5.67	82	.256	.368	0	ø	0	93	-3	0	-0.4
2005	TB A	10	9	.526	32	32	0	0-0	186	172	90	12	10	100-3	174	3.77	117	.248	.347	1	.000	-0	87	11	0	0.9
2006	TB A★	10	8	.556	24	24	1-1	0-0	144.2	132	59	15	2	52-3	163	3.24	144	.240	.305	3	.000	-0	79	21	48	2.3
Total	3	22	20	.524	64	63	1-1	0-0	364	337	171	31	14	173-6	378	3.73	121	.245	.333	4	.000	-0	85	29	48	2.8

Keagle, Greg Gregory Charles; B6.28.1971 Corning NY; BR/TR/6´1˝/(185–195); [SDN93 6/170]; d4.1; Col Florida International

YEAR	TM LG	W	L	PCT	G	GS	CG-SHO	SV-BS	IP	H	R	HR	HB	BB-IB	SO	ERA	AERA	OAV	OOB	AB-HR-SH	AVG	PB	SUP	APR	DL	PW
1996	Det A	3	6	.333	26	6	0	0-0	87.2	104	76	13	9	68-5	70	7.39	69	.298	.418	0	ø	0	79	-21	45	-1.7
1997	Det A	3	5	.375	11	10	0	0-0	45.1	58	33	9	5	18-0	33	6.55	70	.309	.382	1	.000	-0	90	-8	0	-1.2
1998	Det A	0	5	.000	9	7	0	0-0	38.2	46	26	5	4	20-0	25	5.59	85	.295	.389	0	ø	0	84	-3	0	-0.4
Total	3	6	16	.273	46	23	0	0-0	171.2	208	135	27	18	106-5	128	6.76	72	.300	.402	1	.000	-0	83	-32	45	-3.3

Kealey, Steve Steven William; B5.13.1947 Torrance CA; BR/TR/6´0˝/(175–185); d9.9; Col El Camino (CA) JC

YEAR	TM LG	W	L	PCT	G	GS	CG-SHO	SV-BS	IP	H	R	HR	HB	BB-IB	SO	ERA	AERA	OAV	OOB	AB-HR-SH	AVG	PB	SUP	APR	DL	PW
1968	Cal A	0	1	.000	6	0	0	0	10	10	3	0	0	5-2	4	2.70	108	.256	.341	0	ø	0	—	0	0	0.0
1969	Cal A	2	0	1.000	15	3	1-1	0-0	36.2	48	18	4	1	13-1	17	3.93	89	.322	.380	9	.000	-1	110	-2	0	-0.2
1970	Cal A	1	0	1.000	17	0	0	1-0	21.2	19	11	2	0	6-2	14	4.15	87	.260	.305	4	.250	0	—	-1	0	-0.1
1971	Chi A	2	2	.500	54	1	0	6-0	77.1	69	40	10	0	26-6	50	3.84	93	.239	.299	10-1-1	.200	1	101	-3	0	-0.1
1972	Chi A	3	2	.600	40	0	0	4-2	57.1	50	21	4	0	12-1	37	3.30	95	.234	.273	3	.000	-0	—	0	0	-0.1
1973	Chi A	0	0	ø	7	0	0	0-0	11.1	23	22	2	0	7-1	4	15.09	26	.418	.469	0	ø	0	—	-14	73	-0.7
Total	6	8	5	.615	139	4	1-1	11-2	214.1	219	115	22	1	69-13	126	4.28	80	.267	.322	26-1-1	.115	-0	110	-20	73	-1.2

Keas, Ed Edward James; B2.2.1863 Dubuque IA; D1.12.1940 Dubuque IA; d8.25

YEAR	TM LG	W	L	PCT	G	GS	CG-SHO	SV-BS	IP	H	R	HR	HB	BB-IB	SO	ERA	AERA	OAV	OOB	AB-HR-SH	AVG	PB	SUP	APR	DL	PW
1888	Cle AA	3	3	.500	6	6	6	0	51	53	28	1	1	12	18	2.29	135	.259	.303	23	.087	-2	106	3	—	0.1

Keating, Ray Raymond Herbert; B7.21.1893 Bridgeport CT; D12.28.1963 Sacramento CA; BR/TR/5´11˝/185; d9.12; Col Niagara

YEAR	TM LG	W	L	PCT	G	GS	CG-SHO	SV-BS	IP	H	R	HR	HB	BB-IB	SO	ERA	AERA	OAV	OOB	AB-HR-SH	AVG	PB	SUP	APR	DL	PW
1912	NY A	0	3	.000	6	5	3	0	35.2	36	27	0	1	18	21	5.80	62	.265	.355	16	.375	1	119	-6	—	-0.3
1913	NY A	6	12	.333	28	21	9-2	0	151.1	147	77	3	2	51	83	3.21	93	.256	.318	43-0-3	.070	-3	80	-5	—	-1.0
1914	NY A	8	11	.421	34	25	14	0	210	198	94	1	5	67	109	2.96	93	.253	.316	71-0-3	.169	-0*	102	-8	—	-0.5
1915	NY A	3	6	.333	11	10	8-1	0	79.1	66	41	3	3	45	37	3.63	81	.228	.337	26	.154	-1	109	-7	—	-0.7
1916	NY A	5	6	.455	14	11	6	0	91	91	42	4	2	37	35	3.07	94	.272	.349	29-0-1	.241	1	116	-3	—	-0.1
1918	NY A	2	2	.500	15	6	1	0	48.1	39	27	0	2	30	16	3.91	72	.238	.362	16-0-1	.188	-0	84	-6	—	-0.5
1919	Bos N	7	11	.389	22	14	9-1	0	136	129	61	2	2	45	48	2.98	96	.261	.325	46-1-3	.152	-1*	78	-4	—	-0.5
Total	7	31	51	.378	130	92	50-4	0	751.2	706	369	13	17	293	349	3.29	88	.254	.329	247-1-11	.170	-2	97	-39	—	-3.6

Keating, Bob Robert M.; B9.22.1862 Springfield MA; D1.19.1922 Springfield MA; BL/TL/6´4˝/190; d8.27

YEAR	TM LG	W	L	PCT	G	GS	CG-SHO	SV-BS	IP	H	R	HR	HB	BB-IB	SO	ERA	AERA	OAV	OOB	AB-HR-SH	AVG	PB	SUP	APR	DL	PW
1887	Bal AA	0	1	.000	1	1	1	0	9	16	16	0	0	6	0	11.00	37	.372	.449	4	.250	-0	31	-7	—	-0.4

Keck, Cactus Frank Joseph; B1.13.1899 St.Louis MO; D2.6.1981 Kirkwood MO; BR/TR/5´11˝/170; d5.26

YEAR	TM LG	W	L	PCT	G	GS	CG-SHO	SV-BS	IP	H	R	HR	HB	BB-IB	SO	ERA	AERA	OAV	OOB	AB-HR-SH	AVG	PB	SUP	APR	DL	PW
1922	Cin N	7	6	.538	27	15	5-1	1	131	138	71	4	5	29	27	3.37	119	.276	.322	44-0-3	.159	-1	105	5	—	0.1
1923	Cin N	3	6	.333	35	6	1	2	87	84	49	5	3	32	16	3.72	104	.254	.325	17-0-1	.059	-1	106	0	—	-0.1
Total	2	10	12	.455	62	21	6-1	3	218	222	120	9	8	61	43	3.51	112	.267	.323	61-0-4	.131	-2	106	5	—	0.0

Keefe, Dave David Edwin; B1.9.1897 Williston VT; D2.4.1978 Kansas City MO; BL/TR/5´9˝/165; d4.21; Mil 1918; C10

YEAR	TM LG	W	L	PCT	G	GS	CG-SHO	SV-BS	IP	H	R	HR	HB	BB-IB	SO	ERA	AERA	OAV	OOB	AB-HR-SH	AVG	PB	SUP	APR	DL	PW
1917	Phi A	1	0	1.000	3	0	0	0	5	5	4	0	0	4	1	1.80	153	.278	.409	1	.000	-0	—	0	—	-0.1
1919	Phi A	0	1	.000	1	1	1	0	9	8	4	0	0	3	5	4.00	86	.242	.306	3	.000	-0	46	0	—	-0.1
1920	Phi A	6	7	.462	31	13	7-1	0	130.1	129	60	2	6	30	41	2.97	136	.262	.313	40-0-1	.250	-0*	58	14	—	1.3
1921	Phi A	2	9	.182	44	12	4	1	173	214	126	19	5	64	68	4.68	95	.311	.374	57	.175	-3	94	-10	—	-0.9
1922	Cle A	0	0	ø	18	1	0	0	36.1	47	30	2	0	12	11	6.19	65	.333	.386	6	.333	1	106	-9	—	-0.4
Total	5	9	17	.346	97	27	12-1	1	353.2	403	224	23	11	113	126	4.15	101	.294	.352	107-0-1	.206	-3	76	-5	—	-0.2

Keefe, George George W.; B1.7.1867 Washington DC; D8.24.1935 Washington DC; BL/TL/5´9˝/168; d7.30

YEAR	TM LG	W	L	PCT	G	GS	CG-SHO	SV-BS	IP	H	R	HR	HB	BB-IB	SO	ERA	AERA	OAV	OOB	AB-HR-SH	AVG	PB	SUP	APR	DL	PW
1886	Was N	0	3	.000	4	4	4	0	31.1	28	22	0	—	15	5	5.17	62	.233	.319	14	.000	-2	109	-5	—	-0.6
1887	Was N	0	1	.000	1	1	1	0	8	16	20	1	2	4	0	9.00	45	.364	.440	3	.000	-1	16	-7	—	-0.5
1888	Was N	6	7	.462	13	13	13-1	0	114	87	55	2	4	43	52	2.84	98	.206	.286	42	.214	1	70	-1	—	0.2
1889	Was N	8	18	.308	30	27	24	0	230	266	182	6	4	143	90	5.13	77	.281	.378	98	.163	-2	84	-23	—	-2.2
1890	Buf P	6	16	.273	25	22	22	0	196	280	229	11	5	138	55	6.52	63	.321	.417	79	.203	1	87	-58	—	-4.2
1891	Was AA	0	3	.000	5	4	4	1	37	44	42	0	1	17	11	2.68	140	.286	.360	14	.143	-0	62	-3	—	-0.2
Total	6	20	48	.294	78	71	68-1	1	616.1	721	550	20	16	360	213	5.05	74	.282	.374	250	.172	-3	82	-97	—	-7.5

Keefe, John John Thomas; B5.5.1867 Fitchburg MA; D8.9.1937 Fitchburg MA; TL; d4.28; Col Holy Cross

YEAR	TM LG	W	L	PCT	G	GS	CG-SHO	SV-BS	IP	H	R	HR	HB	BB-IB	SO	ERA	AERA	OAV	OOB	AB-HR-SH	AVG	PB	SUP	APR	DL	PW
1890	Syr AA	17	24	.415	43	41	36-2	0	352.1	355	234	9	25	148	120	4.32	82	.254	.336	157	.191	-5	90	-34	—	-3.4

Keefe, Bobby Robert Francis; B6.16.1882 Folsom CA; D12.6.1964 Sacramento CA; BR/TR/5´11˝/155; d4.15; Col Santa Clara

YEAR	TM LG	W	L	PCT	G	GS	CG-SHO	SV-BS	IP	H	R	HR	HB	BB-IB	SO	ERA	AERA	OAV	OOB	AB-HR-SH	AVG	PB	SUP	APR	DL	PW
1907	NY A	3	5	.375	19	3	0	3	57.2	60	18	1	1	20	20	2.50	112	.270	.333	19	.053	-2	32	3	—	0.4
1911	Cin N	12	13	.480	39	26	15	3	234.1	196	88	7	3	76	105	2.69	123	.229	.294	70-0-5	.086	-2	96	19	—	1.4
1912	Cin N	1	3	.250	17	6	0	2	68.2	78	52	0	4	33	29	5.24	64	.289	.375	18-0-2	.167	-1	65	-14	—	-0.8
Total	3	16	21	.432	75	35	15	8	360.2	334	158	8	8	129	154	3.14	103	.248	.317	107-0-7	.093	-5	86	8	—	1.0

YEAR	TM LG	W	L	PCT	G	GS	CG-SHO	SV-BS	IP	H	R	HR	HB	BB-IB	SO	ERA	AERA	OAV	OOB	AB-HR-SH	AVG	PB	SUP	APR	DL	PW
KEEFE, TIM Timothy John "Smiling Tim","Sir Timothy"; B1.1.1857 Cambridge MA; D4.23.1933 Cambridge MA; BR/TR/5´10.5˝/185; d8.6; U3; HF1964																										
1880	Tro N	6	6	.500	12	12	12	0	105	68	27	0	—	16	39	**0.86**	**294**	**.178**	**.212**	43	.233	-0	67	16	—	1.8
1881	Tro N	18	27	.400	45	45	45-4	0	403	434	241	4	—	83	103	3.24	91	.270	.305	152	.230	4*	87	-12	—	-0.7
1882	Tro N	17	26	.395	43	42	41-1	0	376	367	221	4	—	78	111	2.49	114	.243	.280	189-1	.228	5*	89	11	—	1.8
1883	NY AA	41	27	.603	**68**	**68**	**68**-5	0	**619**	488	244	6	—	108	**359**	2.41	138	**.203**	**.237**	259	.220	4*	83	61	—	6.0
1884	†NY AA	37	17	.685	58	58	56-4	0	483	380	196	5	15	71	334	2.25	138	**.204**	.239	210-3	.238	12*	112	46	—	5.5
1885	NY N	32	13	.711	46	46	45-7	0	400	300	154	6	—	102	227	**1.58**	**170**	.203	.255	166	.163	-1*	123	46	—	4.5
1886	NY N	**42**	20	.677	**64**	**64**	**62**-2	0	**535**	479	250	9	—	102	297	2.56	125	.231	.267	205-1	.171	1	119	39	—	3.8
1887	NY N	35	19	.648	56	56	54-2	0	476.2	428	256	11	11	108	189	3.12	121	**.230**	**.276**	191-2	.220	8	105	39	—	4.2
1888	†NY N	**35**	12	**.745**	51	51	48-**8**	0	434.1	317	143	5	12	90	**335**	**1.74**	**157**	**.196**	.243	181-2	.127	-6	108	**53**	—	4.7
1889	†NY N	28	13	.683	47	45	39-3	1	364	319	216	9	18	151	225	3.36	117	**.229**	.312	149	.154	-4	109	24	—	1.9
1890	NY P	17	11	.607	30	30	23-1	0	229	225	137	6	8	89	89	3.38	134	.246	.318	92-2	.109	-5	105	28	—	2.2
1891	NY N	2	5	.286	8	7	4	0	55	70	57	1	4	27	30	5.24	61	.299	.381	21	.095	-1	117	-13	—	-1.3
	Phi N	3	6	.333	11	10	9	1	78.1	82	55	2	4	30	34	3.91	87	.259	.331	29	.172	0	79	-5	—	-0.5
	Year	5	11	.313	19	17	13	1	133.1	152	112	3	8	57	64	4.45	75	.276	.353	50	.140	-1	94	-15	—	-1.8
1892	Phi N	19	16	.543	39	38	31-2	0	313.1	279	142	4	13	98	136	2.36	138	.229	.293	117-1	.085	-7	98	26	—	1.8
1893	Phi N	10	7	.588	22	22	17	0	178	202	131	3	13	80	56	4.40	104	.277	.359	79	.228	0	133	-1	—	-0.1
Total	14	342	225	.603	600	594	554-39	2	5049.2	4438	2470	75	98	1233	2564	2.63	125	.226	.275	2083-12	.187	11	104	358	—	35.6
KEEGAN, ED Edward Charles; B7.8.1939 Camden NJ; BR/TR/6´3˝/(158–165); d8.24																										
1959	Phi N	0	3	.000	3	3	0	0	9	19	18	2	1	13-0	3	18.00	23	.432	.569	3	.000	-0	44	-12	0	-1.8
1961	KC A	0	0	ø	6	0	0	1	6	6	5	0	0	5-0	3	4.50	93	.261	.393	0	ø	0	—	-1	0	0.0
1962	Phi N	0	0	ø	4	0	0	0	8	6	2	1	1	5-0	5	2.25	172	.214	.353	0	ø	0*	—	2	0	0.1
Total	3	0	3	.000	13	3	0	1	23	31	25	3	2	23-0	11	9.00	45	.326	.467	3	.000	-0	44	-11	0	-1.7
KEEGAN, BOB Robert Charles "Smiley"; B8.4.1920 Rochester NY; D6.20.2001 Rochester NY; BR/TR/6´2.5˝/207; d5.24; Col Bucknell																										
1953	Chi A	7	5	.583	22	11	4-2	1	98.2	80	34	4	2	33	32	2.74	147	.223	.293	28-0-2	.321	2	96	14	38	1.8
1954	Chi A★	16	9	.640	31	27	14-2	2	209.2	211	84	16	1	82	61	3.09	121	.266	.334	75-0-1	.120	-2*	114	13	0	1.2
1955	Chi A	2	5	.286	18	11	1	0	58.2	83	39	4	1	28-1	29	5.83	68	.336	.400	18-0-2	.333	2	102	-11	31	-1.0
1956	Chi A	5	7	.417	20	16	4	0	105.1	119	56	15	2	35-2	32	3.93	104	.286	.342	32-0-4	.125	-1	100	0	0	-0.2
1957	Chi A	10	8	.556	30	20	6-2	2	142.2	131	62	22	2	37-2	36	3.53	106	.243	.292	39-0-10	.103	-1	106	3	0	0.1
1958	Chi A	0	2	.000	14	2	0	0	29.2	44	25	9	0	18-4	8	6.07	60	.358	.437	4-0-1	.000	-1	124	-10	0	-0.6
Total	6	40	36	.526	135	87	29-6	5	644.2	668	300	70	8	233-9	198	3.66	105	.270	.332	196-0-20	.163	-2	106	9	69	1.3
KEELEY, BURT Burton Elwood "Speed"; B11.2.1879 Wilmington IL; D5.3.1952 Ely MN; BR/TR/5´9˝/170; d4.18; Col Notre Dame																										
1908	Was A	6	11	.353	28	15	12-1	1	169	173	87	3	4	48	68	2.98	77	.259	.313	49-0-6	.102	-3*	102	-15	—	-1.8
1909	Was A	0	0	ø	2	0	0	0	7	12	13	0	1	1	0	11.57	21	.364	.400	2	.500	0	—	-7	—	-0.3
Total	2	6	11	.353	30	15	12-1	1	176	185	100	3	5	49	68	3.32	69	.264	.317	51-0-6	.118	-3	102	-22	—	-2.1
KEEN, VIC Howard Victor; B3.16.1899 Bel Air MD; D12.10.1976 Salisbury MD; BR/TR/5´9˝/165; d8.13; Col Maryland																										
1918	Phi A	0	1	.000	1	1	0	0	8	9	3	1	0	1	1	3.38	87	.300	.323	1-0-1	.000	-0	77	0	—	0.0
1921	Chi N	0	3	.000	5	4	1	0	25	29	17	0	1	9	9	4.68	82	.319	.386	5-0-1	.000	-0	59	-3	—	-0.4
1922	Chi N	1	2	.333	7	2	2	1	34.2	36	20	4	1	10	11	3.89	108	.275	.331	12-0-1	.333	1	78	0	—	0.1
1923	Chi N	12	8	.600	35	17	10	1	177	169	70	8	5	57	46	3.00	133	.255	.319	53-0-8	.151	-3	85	20	—	1.7
1924	Chi N	15	14	.517	40	28	15	3	234.2	242	112	17	4	80	75	3.80	103	.272	.335	77-0-4	.156	-4	89	5	—	0.0
1925	Chi N	2	6	.250	30	8	1	1	83.1	125	61	8	0	41	19	6.26	69	.359	.427	25-0-1	.240	0	115	-15	—	-1.2
1926	†StL N	10	9	.526	26	21	12-1	0	152	179	89	15	1	42	29	4.56	86	.295	.342	53-0-2	.057	-6	110	-10	—	-1.7
1927	StL N	2	1	.667	21	0	0	0	33.2	39	21	3	2	8	12	4.81	82	.293	.343	4	.250	0	—	-3	—	-0.2
Total	8	42	44	.488	165	81	41-1	6	748.1	828	393	56	14	248	202	4.11	97	.287	.346	230-0-18	.148	-12	94	-6	—	-1.7
KEENAN, KID Harry Leon; B1875 Louisville KY; D6.11.1903 Covington KY; TR/5´2˝/?; d8.11																										
1891	Cin AA	0	1	.000	1	1	1	0	8	6	9	0	1	4	5	0.00	ø	.200	.314	4	.500	0	46	1	—	0.2
KEENAN, JIM James William; B2.10.1858 New Haven CT; D9.21.1926 Cincinnati OH; BR/TR/5´10˝/186; d5.17.1875; ▲																										
1884	Ind AA	0	0	ø	1	0	0	0	3	2	1	0	0	0	0	3.00	110	.182	.182	249-3	.293	0*	—	0	—	0.0
1885	Cin AA	0	0	ø	1	0	0	0	8	7	2	0	0	1	0	1.13	290	.233	.258	132-1	.265	0*	—	2	—	0.1
1886	Cin AA	0	1	.000	2	0	0	0	8	8	5	0	0	3	2	3.38	104	.258	.324	148-3	.270	0*	—	0	—	0.0
Total	3	0	1	.000	4	0	0	0	19	17	8	0	0	4	2	2.37	142	.236	.276	529-7	.280	1	—	2	—	0.1
KEENAN, JIMMIE James William "Sparkplug"; B5.25.1898 Avon NY; D6.5.1980 Seminole FL; BL/TL/5´7˝/155; d9.9																										
1920	Phi N	0	0	ø	1	0	0	0	3	3	1	0	0	1	2	3.00	114	.333	.400	1	.000	-0	—	0	—	0.0
1921	Phi N	1	2	.333	15	2	0	0	32.1	48	31	3	1	15	7	6.68	63	.364	.432	9	.000	-1	29	-7	—	-0.7
Total	2	1	2	.333	16	2	0	0	35.1	51	32	3	1	16	9	6.37	65	.362	.430	10	.000	-2	29	-7	—	-0.7
KEENER, JEFF Jeffrey Bruce; B1.14.1959 Pana IL; BL/TR/6´0˝/(170–175); [StLN81 7/163]; d6.8; Col Kentucky																										
1982	StL N	1	1	.500	19	0	0	0-0	22.1	19	8	1	0	19-4	25	1.61	228	.235	.373	0	ø	0	—	3	0	0.3
1983	StL N	0	0	ø	4	0	0	0-0	4.1	6	4	0	1	1-0	4	8.31	44	.333	.381	0	ø	0	—	-2	0	-0.1
Total	2	1	1	.500	23	0	0	0-0	26.2	25	12	1	1	20-4	29	2.70	136	.253	.374	0	ø	0	—	1	0	0.2
KEENER, JOE Joseph Donald; B4.21.1953 San Pedro CA; BR/TR/6´4˝/185; d9.18; Col Antelope Valley (CA) JC																										
1976	Mon N	0	1	.000	2	2	0	0-0	4.1	7	7	0	1	8-0	1	10.38	36	.389	.593	1-0-1	.000	-0	94	-3	0	-0.6
KEENER, HARRY Joshua Harry "Beans"; B9.1869 Easton PA; D3.5.1912 Easton PA; TR; d6.27																										
1896	Phi N	3	11	.214	16	13	11	0	113.1	144	102	5	9	39	28	5.88	73	.307	.371	51	.314	2	94	-20	—	-1.6
KEETON, RICKEY Rickey; B3.18.1957 Cincinnati OH; BR/TR/6´2˝/190; [MilA78 3/60]; d5.27; Col Southern Illinois																										
1980	Mil A	2	2	.500	5	5	0	0-0	28.1	35	15	4	0	9-0	8	4.76	82	.307	.352	0	ø	0	96	-2	0	-0.2
1981	Mil A	1	0	1.000	17	0	0	0-0	35.1	47	21	4	0	11-4	9	5.09	68	.329	.374	0	ø	0	—	-7	0	-0.3
Total	2	3	2	.600	22	5	0	0-0	63.2	82	36	8	0	20-4	17	4.95	74	.319	.364	0	ø	0	96	-9	0	-0.5
KEFFER, FRANK Charles Franklin; B7.1861 Bradford PA; d4.19																										
1890	Syr AA	1	1	.500	2	1	1	0	16	15	13	0	0	9	4	5.63	63	.242	.338	7	.143	-1	76	-4	—	-0.4
KEHN, CHET Chester Lawrence; B10.30.1921 San Diego CA; D4.5.1984 San Diego CA; BR/TR/5´11˝/168; d4.30; Mil 1943–45																										
1942	Bro N	0	0	ø	3	1	0	0	7.2	8	6	2	0	4	3	7.04	46	.267	.353	2	1.000	1	283	-3	0	0.0
KEIFER, KATSY Sherman Carl; B9.3.1891 California PA; D2.19.1927 Outwood KY; BB/TL; d10.8																										
1914	Ind F	1	0	1.000	1	1	1	0	9	6	2	0	0	2	2	2.00	156	.194	.242	3	.333	0	88	1	—	0.2
KEISLER, RANDY Randy Dean; B2.24.1976 Richards TX; BL/TL/6´3˝/190; [NYA98 2/67]; d9.10; Col Louisiana St.; [DL 2002 NY A 183]																										
2000	NY A	1	0	1.000	4	1	0	0-0	10.2	16	14	1	0	8-0	6	11.81	40	.364	.462	0	ø	0	118	-8	0	-0.6
2001	NY A	1	2	.333	10	10	0	0-0	50.2	52	36	12	0	34-0	36	6.22	71	.259	.364	2	.000	-0	142	-9	0	-0.5
2003	SD N	0	1	.000	2	2	0	0-0	6	7	9	3	1	7-0	5	12.00	33	.292	.455	2	.000	-0*	117	-6	0	-0.7
2005	Cin N	2	1	.667	24	4	0	0-0	56	64	45	10	1	28-2	43	6.27	68	.277	.356	15-1-0	.267	2	122	-14	25	-0.4
2006	Oak A	0	0	ø	11	0	0	0-0	10	14	5	3	0	2-1	5	4.50	101	.350	.381	0	ø	0	—	0	0	0.0
Total	5	4	4	.500	51	17	0	0-0	133.1	153	109	29	2	79-3	95	6.82	64	.283	.375	19-1-0	.211	2	133	-37	208	-2.2
KEKICH, MIKE Michael Dennis; B4.2.1945 San Diego CA; BR/TL/6´1˝/(196–206); d6.9																										
1965	LA N	0	1	.000	5	1	0	0	10.1	10	12	2	0	13-0	9	9.58	34	.263	.451	2-0-1	.000	-0	80	-8	0	-0.7
1968	LA N	2	10	.167	25	20	1-1	0	115	116	54	9	1	46-0	84	3.91	71	.267	.336	37-0-2	.081	-2	78	-14	0	-1.6
1969	NY A	4	6	.400	28	13	1	1-0	105	91	58	11	2	49-5	66	4.54	78	.236	.323	27-0-3	.111	-1	72	-11	0	-1.2
1970	NY A	6	3	.667	26	14	1	0-0	98.2	103	59	12	1	55-3	63	4.83	74	.267	.358	32-0-2	.094	-1	109	-13	22	-1.3
1971	NY A	10	9	.526	37	24	3	0-0	170.1	167	89	13	4	82-11	93	4.07	81	.257	.341	52-0-8	.154	-0	116	-16	0	-1.6
1972	NY A	10	13	.435	29	28	2	0-0	175.1	172	77	13	4	76-5	78	3.70	81	.263	.343	59-0-6	.136	-1	106	-12	0	-1.7
1973	NY A	1	1	.500	5	4	0	0-0	14.2	20	15	1	2	14-0	4	9.20	40	.351	.486	0	ø	0	144	-8	0	-0.9
	Cle A	1	4	.200	16	6	0	0-0	50	73	47	6	0	35-0	26	7.02	56	.349	.437	0	ø	0*	83	-18	0	-1.6

YEAR	TM LG	W	L	PCT	G	GS	CG-SHO	SV-BS	IP	H	R	HR	HB	BB-IB	SO	ERA	AERA	OAV	OOB	AB-HR-SH	AVG	PB	SUP	APR	DL	PW
	Year	2	5	.286	21	10	0	0-0	64.2	93	62	7	2	49-0	30	7.52	52	.350	.449	0	ø	0	105	-26	0	-2.5
1975	Tex A	0	0	ø	23	0	0	2-2	31.1	33	16	2	0	21-2	19	3.73	101	.282	.388	0	ø	0	—	0	0	0.0
1977	Sea A	5	4	.556	41	2	0	3-1	90	90	58	11	3	51-3	55	5.60	74	.265	.363	0	ø	0	22	-12	24	-1.2
Total	9	39	51	.433	235	112	8-1	6-3	860.2	875	485	80	17	442-29	497	4.59	73	.268	.355	209-0-22	.120	-5	94	-112	46	-11.8
Kelb, George	George Francis "Pugger","Lefty"; B7.17.1870 Toledo OH; D10.20.1936 Toledo OH; BL/TL; d4.17																									
1898	Cle N	0	1	.000	3	1	1	0	16.1	23	17	0	4	1	8	4.41	82	.329	.373	5	.200	-0	20	-3	—	-0.2
Kelleher, Hal	Harold Joseph; B6.24.1913 Philadelphia PA; D8.27.1989 Cape May Court House NJ; BR/TR/6´0˝/165; d9.17																									
1935	Phi N	2	0	1.000	3	3	2-1	0	25	26	7	0	1	12	12	1.80	252	.260	.345	8	.375	1	56	6	—	0.6
1936	Phi N	0	5	.000	14	4	1	0	44	60	38	2	3	29	13	5.32	85	.331	.432	12	.167	-0	33	-5	—	-0.6
1937	Phi N	2	4	.333	27	2	1	0	58.1	72	51	3	7	31	20	6.63	65	.308	.404	17	.176	-0*	20	-15	—	-1.3
1938	Phi N	0	0	ø	6	0	0	0	7.1	16	15	0	0	9	4	18.41	21	.432	.543	2	.500	0	—	-11	—	-0.5
Total	4	4	9	.308	50	9	4-1	0	134.2	174	111	5	11	81	49	5.95	74	.315	.413	39	.231	0	39	-25	—	-1.8
Keller, Kris	Kristopher Shane; B3.1.1978 Williamsport PA; BR/TR/6´2˝/225; [DetA96 4/101]; d5.24; [DL 2002 Atl N 4]																									
2002	Det A	0	0	ø	1	0	0	0-0	1	2	3	1	0	3-0	1	27.00	16	.400	.625	0	ø	0	—	-2	25	-0.1
Keller, Ron	Ronald Lee; B6.3.1943 Indianapolis IN; BR/TR/6´2˝/200; [MinA65 8/143]; d7.9; Mil 1968; Col Indiana																									
1966	Min A	0	0	ø	2	0	0	0	5.1	7	4	1	0	1-0	1	5.06	71	.318	.348	1	.000	-0*	—	-1	0	-0.1
1968	Min A	0	1	.000	7	1	0	0	16	18	6	2	1	4-1	11	2.81	110	.305	.354	1	.000	-0*	28	0	0	0.0
Total	2	0	1	.000	9	1	0	0	21.1	25	10	3	1	5-1	12	3.38	95	.309	.352	2	.000	-0	28	-1	0	-0.1
Kellett, Al	Alfred Henry; B10.30.1901 Red Bank NJ; D7.14.1960 New York NY; BR/TR/6´3˝/200; d6.29; Col Columbia																									
1923	Phi A	0	1	.000	5	0	0	0	10	11	9	0	0	8	1	6.30	65	.282	.404	3	.333	0	—	-3	—	-0.2
1924	Bos A	0	0	ø	1	0	0	0	0	0	2	0	0	2	0	(2)	ø	ø	1.000	0	ø	0	—	-2	—	-0.2
Total	2	0	1	.000	6	0	0	0	10	11	11	0	0	10	1	8.10	51	.282	.429	3	.333	0	—	-5	—	-0.4
Kelley, Harry	Harry Leroy; B2.13.1906 Parkin AR; D3.23.1958 Parkin AR; BR/TR/5´9.5˝/170; d4.16																									
1925	Was A	1	1	.500	6	1	0	0	16	30	23	0	0	12	7	9.00	47	.405	.488	4	.000	-1	40	-10	—	-1.0
1926	Was A	0	0	ø	7	1	0	0	10	17	10	0	1	8	6	8.10	48	.405	.510	1	.000	-0	131	-5	—	-0.2
1936	Phi A	15	12	.556	35	27	20-1	3	235.1	250	112	21	2	75	82	3.86	132	.275	.332	91-0-7	.198	-1*	91	34	—	3.1
1937	Phi A	13	21	.382	41	29	14	0	205	267	154	16	3	79	68	5.36	88	.306	.365	71-0-1	.225	1	78	-18	—	-2.3
1938	Phi A	0	2	.000	4	3	0	0	8	17	16	0	0	10	3	16.88	29	.436	.551	2	.000	-0	67	-10	—	-1.5
	Was A	9	8	.529	38	14	7-2	1	148.1	162	90	12	1	46	44	4.49	100	.276	.330	48-0-1	.250	1	103	-1	—	0.0
	Year	9	10	.474	42	17	7-2	1	156.1	179	106	12	1	56	47	5.12	88	.286	.346	50-0-1	.240	1	97	-13	—	-1.5
1939	Was A	4	3	.571	15	3	2	1	53.2	69	32	2	3	14	20	4.70	93	.314	.363	15-0-2	.267	1	88	-2	—	-0.2
Total	6	42	47	.472	146	78	43-3	5	676.1	812	437	51	10	244	230	4.86	98	.296	.356	232-0-11	.216	0	88	-12	—	-2.1
Kelley, Dick	Richard Anthony; B1.8.1940 Boston MA; D12.11.1991 Northridge CA; BR/TL/6´0˝/(174–175); d4.15; [DL 1970 SD N 23]																									
1964	Mil N	0	0	ø	2	0	0	0	2	2	4	0	0	3-0	2	18.00	20	.250	.455	0	ø	0	—	-3	32	-0.2
1965	Mil N	1	1	.500	21	4	0	0	45	37	15	5	0	20-2	31	3.00	117	.226	.310	8	.000	-1*	81	3	0	0.1
1966	Atl N	7	5	.583	20	13	2-2	0	81	75	36	6	3	21-2	50	3.22	113	.247	.301	28-0-1	.036	-3	112	2	0	0.0
1967	Atl N	2	9	.182	39	9	1-1	2	98	88	48	8	1	42-7	75	3.77	88	.247	.324	16-0-2	.250	1	85	-5	0	-0.4
1968	Atl N	2	4	.333	31	11	1-1	1	98.1	86	36	4	1	45-2	73	2.75	109	.238	.323	23-0-1	.043	-1	63	2	0	0.1
1969	SD N	4	8	.333	27	23	1-1	0-1	136	113	60	11	5	61-8	96	3.57	100	.230	.320	47-0-1	.106	-2	75	0	0	-0.1
1971	SD N	2	3	.400	48	1	0	2-3	59.2	52	26	5	4	23-5	42	3.47	96	.232	.312	3	.333	0	213	0	0	0.0
Total	7	18	30	.375	188	61	5-5	5-4	520	453	225	39	14	215-26	369	3.39	100	.237	.317	125-0-5	.096	-5	87	-1	55	-0.5
Kelley, Tom	Thomas Henry; B1.5.1944 Manchester CT; BR/TR/6´0˝/(180–191); d5.5																									
1964	Cle A	0	0	ø	6	0	0	0	9.2	9	9	1	1	9-2	7	5.59	64	.237	.396	0	ø	0	—	-3	0	-0.2
1965	Cle A	2	1	.667	4	4	1	0	30	19	8	3	0	13-0	31	2.40	145	.186	.278	9-0-1	.222	0	95	4	0	0.5
1966	Cle A	4	8	.333	31	7	1	0	95.1	97	55	14	0	42-1	64	4.34	79	.264	.336	28	.143	-1	92	-11	0	-1.5
1967	Cle A	0	0	ø	1	0	0	0	1	0	0	0	0	2-0	0	0.00	ø	.000	.500	0	ø	0	—	0	0	0.0
1971	Atl N	9	5	.643	28	20	5	0-0	143	140	56	8	1	69-6	68	2.96	126	.262	.347	43-0-2	.047	-4	94	10	0	0.5
1972	Atl N	5	7	.417	27	14	2-1	0-1	116.1	122	65	12	0	65-4	59	4.56	83	.272	.363	34-0-2	.088	-2	98	-9	0	-1.2
1973	Atl N	0	1	.000	7	0	0	0-0	12.2	13	5	0	0	7-3	5	2.84	140	.289	.370	2	.000	-0	—	1	0	0.1
Total	7	20	22	.476	104	45	9-1	0-1	408	400	198	38	2	207-16	234	3.75	98	.260	.347	116-0-5	.095	-6	95	-8	0	-1.8
Kellner, Alex	Alexander Raymond; B8.26.1924 Tucson AZ; D5.3.1996 Tucson AZ; BR/TL/6´0˝/(190–215); d4.29; b–Walt																									
1948	Phi A	0	0	ø	13	1	0	0	23	21	20	0	2	16	14	7.83	55	.239	.368	5	.000	-1	211	-8	0	-0.5
1949	Phi A☆	20	12	.625	38	27	19	1	245	243	120	18	2	129	94	3.75	110	.261	.352	92-0-4	.217	1	120	8	0	1.1
1950	Phi A	8	20	.286	36	29	15	2	225.1	253	157	28	2	112	85	5.47	83	.282	.363	80	.200	-1	78	-25	0	-2.8
1951	Phi A	11	14	.440	33	29	11-1	2	209.2	218	118	20	4	93	94	4.46	96	.272	.350	79-0-2	.228	-1	97	-6	0	-0.7
1952	Phi A	12	14	.462	34	33	14-2	0	231.1	223	124	21	4	86	105	4.36	91	.252	.321	82-1-4	.207	0	100	-8	0	-0.9
1953	Phi A	11	12	.478	25	25	14-2	0	201.2	210	98	8	4	51	81	3.93	109	.269	.317	69-0-5	.217	1	81	7	0	0.7
1954	Phi A	6	17	.261	27	27	8-1	0	173.2	204	118	16	6	88	69	5.39	72	.301	.381	55-0-5	.182	-0	70	-28	0	-3.2
1955	KC A	11	8	.579	30	24	6-3	0	162.2	164	81	18	5	60-2	75	4.20	99	.265	.332	56-0-2	.214	2	87	1	0	0.3
1956	KC A	7	4	.636	20	17	5	0	91.2	103	49	15	2	33-3	44	4.32	100	.289	.351	30-0-3	.200	-0*	76	0	0	0.0
1957	KC A	6	5	.545	28	21	3	0	132.2	141	65	18	2	41-3	72	4.27	93	.278	.332	47-3-1	.234	4	98	-2	0	0.3
1958	KC A	0	2	.000	7	6	0	0	33.2	40	24	5	0	8-0	22	5.88	66	.315	.353	11-0-2	.091	-0*	84	-7	0	-0.4
	Cin N	7	3	.700	18	7	4	0	82	74	24	8	3	20-1	42	2.30	180	.243	.294	28	.357	3	93	15	0	2.0
1959	StL N	2	1	.667	12	4	0	0	37	31	17	9	1	10-2	19	3.16	134	.220	.275	9	.222	0	95	3	76	0.2
Total	12	101	112	.474	321	250	99-9	5	1849.1	1925	1015	184	37	747-11	816	4.41	95	.270	.342	643-4-28	.215	7	90	-50	76	-3.9
Kellner, Walt	Walter Joseph; B4.26.1929 Tucson AZ; D6.19.2006 Tucson AZ; BR/TR/6´0˝/(198–200); d9.6; b–Alex; Col Arizona																									
1952	Phi A	0	0	ø	1	0	0	0	4	4	3	0	0	3	2	6.75	59	.250	.368	1	.000	-0	—	-1	0	-0.1
1953	Phi A	0	0	ø	2	0	0	0	3	1	2	0	1	4	4	6.00	71	.111	.429	0	ø	0	—	0	0	0.0
Total	2	0	0	ø	3	0	0	0	7	5	5	0	1	7	6	6.43	64	.200	.394	1	.000	-0	—	-1	0	-0.1
Kellogg, Al	Albert C.; B9.9.1886 Providence RI; D7.21.1953 Portland OR; TL/6´3˝/208; d9.25																									
1908	Phi A	0	2	.000	3	3	2	0	17	20	19	1	1	9	8	5.82	44	.294	.385	8	.125	-0	89	-7	—	-0.7
Kellum, Win	Winford Ansley; B4.11.1876 Waterford ON, Can.; D8.10.1951 Big Rapids MI; BB/TL/5´10˝/190; d4.26																									
1901	Bos A	2	3	.400	6	6	5	0	48	61	42	3	3	7	8	6.38	55	.305	.338	18	.167	-1	124	-13	—	-1.0
1904	Cin N	15	10	.600	31	24	22-1	2	224.2	206	98	1	10	46	70	2.60	113	.244	.291	82-0-3	.159	2*	135	7	—	1.0
1905	StL N	3	3	.500	11	7	5-1	0	74	70	30	1	1	10	19	2.92	102	.255	.283	25-0-1	.200	1	132	1	—	0.3
Total	3	20	16	.556	48	37	32-2	2	346.2	337	170	5	14	63	97	3.19	95	.255	.297	125-0-4	.168	2	133	-5	—	0.3
Kelly, Bryan	Bryan Keith; B2.24.1959 Silver Spring MD; BR/TR/6´2˝/195; [DetA81 6/146]; d9.2; Col Alabama																									
1986	Det A	1	2	.333	6	4	0	0-0	20	21	11	4	0	10-1	18	4.50	93	.269	.352	0	ø	0	125	-1	0	-0.1
1987	Det A	0	1	.000	5	0	0	0-0	10.2	12	6	2	0	7-4	10	5.06	84	.286	.388	0	ø	0	—	-1	0	-0.1
Total	2	1	3	.250	11	4	0	0-0	30.2	33	17	6	0	17-5	28	4.70	89	.275	.365	0	ø	0	125	-2	0	-0.2
Kelly, Ed	Edward Leo; B12.10.1888 Pawtucket RI; D11.4.1928 Red Lodge MT; BR/TR/5´11.5˝/173; d4.14																									
1914	Bos A	0	0	ø	3	0	0	0	2.1	1	1	0	0	1	4	0.00	ø	.100	.182	1	.000	-0	—	0	—	0.0
Kelly, Herb	Herbert Barrett "Moke"; B6.4.1892 Mobile AL; D5.18.1973 Torrance CA; BL/TL/5´9˝/160; d9.25; Col Notre Dame																									
1914	Pit N	0	2	.000	5	2	2	0	25.2	24	11	0	0	7	6	2.45	108	.253	.304	9	.222	0	40	0	—	0.0
1915	Pit N	1	1	.500	5	1	0	0	11	10	9	0	1	4	6	4.09	67	.250	.333	2	.500	1	54	-3	—	-0.3
Total	2	1	3	.250	10	3	2	0	36.2	34	20	0	1	11	12	2.95	91	.252	.313	11	.273	1	45	-3	—	-0.3
Kelly, Mike	Michael J.; B11.9.1902 St.Louis MO; D4.26.1982 Modesto CA; BR/TR/6´1˝/178; d9.3																									
1926	Phi N	0	0	ø	4	0	0	0	6.2	9	7	0	1	4	2	9.45	44	.346	.452	3	.000	-0	—	-3	—	-0.2

YEAR	TM LG	W	L	PCT	G	GS	CG-SHO	SV-BS	IP	H	R	HR	HB	BB-IB	SO	ERA	AERA	OAV	OOB	AB-HR-SH	AVG	PB	SUP	APR	DL	PW
KELLY, KING	Michael Joseph; B12.31.1857 Troy NY; D11.8.1894 Boston MA; BR/TR/5´10˝/170; d5.1.1878; M3; HF1945; ▲																									
1880	Chi N	0	0	ø	1	0	0	0	3	3	2	0	—	1	1	0.00	ø	.250	.308	344-1	.291	0*	—	0	—	0.0
1883	Chi N	0	0	ø	1	0	0	0	1	1	0	0	—	0	1	0.00	ø	.333	.333	428-3	.255	0*	—	0	—	0.0
1884	Chi N	0	1	.000	2	0	0	0	5.1	12	11	2	—	2	1	8.44	37	.400	.438	452-13	.354	1*	—	-3	—	-0.4
1887	Bos N	1	0	1.000	3	0	0	0	13	17	16	1	0	14	0	3.46	118	.298	.437	484-8	.322	1*	—	-2	—	-0.1
1890	Bos P	1	0	1.000	1	0	0	0	2	1	1	0	0	2	2	4.50	98	.143	.333	340-4	.326	0*	—	0	—	0.0
1891	Cin AA	0	1	.000	3	0	0	0	15.1	21	15	2	1	7	0	5.28	77	.313	.387	283-1	.297	1*	—	-1	—	0.0
1892	†Bos N	0	0	ø	1	0	0	0	6	8	4	0	3	4	0	1.50	234	.308	.455	281-2	.189	0*	—	0	—	0.0
Total	7	2	2	.500	12	0	0	0	45.2	63	49	5	4	30	4	4.14	92	.312	.411	2612-32	.296	4	—	-6	—	-0.5
KELLY, REN	Reynolds Joseph; B11.18.1899 San Francisco CA; D8.24.1963 Millbrae CA; BR/TR/6´0˝/183; d9.18; b–George																									
1923	Phi A	0	0	ø	1	0	0	0	7	7	3	0	0	4	1	2.57	160	.259	.355	3	.000	-0	—	1	—	0.0
KELLY, BOB	Robert Edward; B10.4.1927 Cleveland OH; BR/TR/6´0˝/(175–185); d5.4; Col Case Western Reserve																									
1951	Chi N	7	4	.636	35	11	4	0	123.2	130	70	8	1	55	48	4.66	88	.275	.352	31-0-3	.161	-1	106	-7	0	-0.6
1952	Chi N	4	9	.308	31	15	3-2	0	125.1	114	62	7	3	46	50	3.59	107	.236	.306	37-0-1	.216	0	99	1	0	0.2
1953	Chi N	0	1	.000	14	0	0	0	17	27	19	2	1	9	6	9.53	47	.375	.451	1	.000	-0	—	-8	0	-0.4
	Cin N	1	2	.333	28	5	0	2	66.1	71	36	7	0	26	29	4.34	100	.276	.343	17-0-1	.118	-1	131	0	0	-0.1
	Year	1	3	.250	42	5	0	2	83.1	98	55	9	1	35	35	5.40	81	.298	.367	18-0-1	.111	-1	131	-9	0	-0.5
1958	Cin N	0	0	ø	2	1	0	0	2	3	1	0	0	3-1	1	4.50	92	.500	.667	0	ø	0	87	0	0	0.0
	Cle A	0	2	.000	13	3	0	0	27.2	29	18	4	1	13-0	12	5.20	70	.282	.368	4	.250	0	115	-5	0	-0.3
Total	4	12	18	.400	123	35	7-2	2	362	374	206	28	6	152-1	146	4.50	90	.268	.343	90-0-5	.178	-1	106	-19	0	-1.2
KELSO, BILL	William Eugene; B2.19.1940 Kansas City MO; BR/TR/6´4˝/(210–215); d7.31; Col Whitworth																									
1964	LA A	2	0	1.000	10	1	1-1	0	23.2	19	6	3	1	9-0	21	2.28	144	.218	.299	6	.000	-0	54	3	0	0.2
1966	Cal A	1	1	.500	5	0	0	0	11.1	11	3	1	1	6-1	11	2.38	141	.244	.346	1	.000	-0	—	1	0	0.2
1967	Cal A	5	3	.625	69	1	0	11	112	85	41	6	4	63-10	91	2.97	106	.219	.329	19-0-2	.105	-1	28	3	0	0.2
1968	Cin N	4	1	.800	35	0	0	1	54.1	56	26	6	3	15-5	39	3.98	80	.277	.325	8	.000	-1	—	-4	0	-0.5
Total	4	12	5	.706	119	2	1-1	12	201.1	171	76	16	9	93-16	162	3.13	102	.237	.325	34-0-2	.059	-2	41	3	0	0.1
KEMMERER, RUSS	Russell Paul "Rusty","Dutch"; B11.1.1931 Pittsburgh PA; BR/TR/6´3˝/(200–210); d6.27; Col Pittsburgh																									
1954	Bos A	5	3	.625	19	9	2-1	0	75.1	71	35	4	2	41	37	3.82	108	.257	.352	21-0-2	.143	-0	79	3	0	0.3
1955	Bos A	1	1	.500	7	2	0	0	17.1	18	14	3	0	15-1	13	7.27	59	.269	.402	3	.000	-0	145	-5	0	-0.5
1957	Bos A	0	0	ø	1	0	0	0	4	5	2	0	0	2-1	1	4.50	89	.333	.389	1	.000	-0	—	0	0	0.0
	Was A	7	11	.389	39	26	6	0	172.1	214	110	20	2	71-4	81	4.96	79	.309	.373	45-2-7	.067	-1	122	-23	0	-2.3
	Year	7	11	.389	40	26	6	0	176.1	219	112	20	2	73-5	82	4.95	79	.310	.373	46-2-7	.065	-1	122	-23	0	-2.3
1958	Was A	6	15	.286	40	30	6	0	224.1	234	122	25	4	74-5	111	4.61	83	.270	.327	69-0-2	.159	-2	82	-19	0	-1.8
1959	Was A	8	17	.320	37	28	8	0	206	221	116	20	4	71-3	89	4.50	87	.276	.335	60-0-5	.133	-1	81	-12	0	-1.4
1960	Was A	0	2	.000	3	3	0	0	17.1	18	15	2	1	10-0	10	7.79	50	.269	.367	4-0-1	.000	-0	98	-6	0	-0.6
	Chi A	6	3	.667	36	7	2-1	2	120.2	111	45	5	1	45-4	76	2.98	127	.248	.315	29-0-7	.000	-3	147	11	0	0.5
	Year	6	5	.545	39	10	2-1	2	138	129	60	7	2	55-4	86	3.59	106	.250	.322	33-0-8	.000	-3	132	4	0	-0.1
1961	Chi A	3	3	.500	47	2	0	2	96.2	102	53	10	0	26-1	35	4.38	89	.278	.323	15	.200	1	136	-5	0	-0.2
1962	Chi A	2	1	.667	20	0	0	0	28	30	14	3	0	11-1	17	3.86	101	.270	.336	2-0-1	.500	1	—	0	0	0.1
	Hou N	5	3	.625	36	2	0	3	68	72	34	10	3	15-1	23	4.10	91	.272	.318	9	.333	1	0	-2	0	-0.1
1963	Hou N	0	0	ø	17	0	0	1	36.2	48	28	1	0	8-0	12	5.65	56	.320	.350	7	.286	0	—	-11	0	-0.5
Total	9	43	59	.422	302	109	24-2	8	1066.2	1144	588	103	17	389-21	505	4.46	86	.277	.339	265-2-25	.128	-5	97	-69	0	-6.5
KEMNER, DUTCH	Herman John; B3.4.1899 Quincy IL; D1.16.1988 Quincy IL; BR/TR/5´10.5˝/175; d4.19																									
1929	Cin N	0	0	ø	9	0	0	1	15.1	19	13	0	0	8	10	7.63	60	.328	.409	4	.250	0	—	-5	—	-0.2
KENNA, ED	Edward Benninghaus "The Pitching Poet"; B10.17.1877 Charleston WV; D3.22.1912 Grant FL; TR/6´0˝/180; d5.5; Col West Virginia																									
1902	Phi A	1	1	.500	2	1	1	0	17	19	15	1	1	11	5	5.29	69	.284	.392	8	.125	-0	118	-3	—	-0.3
KENNEDY, JOE	Joseph Darley; B5.24.1979 LaMesa CA; BR/TL/6´4˝/(225–245); [TBA98 8/252]; d6.6; Col Grossmont (CA) JC																									
2001	TB A	7	8	.467	20	20	0	0-0	117.2	122	63	16	3	34-0	78	4.44	102	.269	.321	4	.250	0	83	2	0	0.3
2002	TB A	8	11	.421	30	30	5-1	0-0	196.2	204	114	23	16	55-0	109	4.53	100	.269	.328	7	.429	1	96	-3	0	-0.3
2003	TB A	3	12	.200	32	22	1-1	1-1	133.2	167	101	19	11	47-1	77	6.13	75	.303	.364	0	ø	0	80	-24	38	-2.2
2004	Col N	9	7	.563	27	27	1	0-0	162.1	163	68	17	8	67-12	117	3.66	130	.265	.342	48-0-4	.125	-1	92	18	38	1.6
2005	Col N	4	8	.333	16	16	0	0-0	92	128	81	12	6	44-4	52	7.04	66	.334	.406	29-0-5	.172	-0	94	-24	0	-2.6
	Oak A	4	5	.444	19	8	0	0-2	60.2	64	33	8	1	20-2	45	4.45	98	.267	.324	0	ø	0	92	0	0	-0.1
2006	†Oak A	4	1	.800	39	0	0	1-2	35	34	10	1	1	13-3	29	2.31	196	.254	.324	0	ø	0	—	9	95	1.1
Total	6	39	52	.429	183	123	7-2	2-5	798	882	470	96	46	280-22	507	4.79	96	.281	.346	88-0-9	.170	-0	90	-22	171	-2.2
KENNEDY, VERN	Lloyd Vernon; B3.20.1907 Kansas City MO; D1.28.1993 Mendon MO; BL/TR/6´0˝/175; d9.18																									
1934	Chi A	0	2	.000	3	3	1	0	19.1	21	8	1	0	9	7	3.72	127	.300	.380	7	.286	0	25	3	—	0.3
1935	Chi A	11	11	.500	31	25	16-2	1	211.2	211	110	17	4	95	65	3.91	118	.262	.343	73-0-7	.247	1	94	14	—	1.4
1936	Chi A☆	21	9	.700	35	34	20-1	0	274.1	282	167	13	3	147	99	4.63	112	.268	.360	113-0-6	.283	5*	111	14	—	1.7
1937	Chi A	14	13	.519	32	30	15-1	0	221	238	150	16	3	124	114	5.09	90	.273	.366	87-2-3	.230	2	116	-14	—	-1.2
1938	Det A☆	12	9	.571	33	26	11	2	190.1	215	123	13	1	113	53	5.06	99	.287	.381	79-0-7	.291	3*	105	-3	—	0.0
1939	Det A	0	3	.000	4	4	1	0	21	25	15	4	1	9	9	6.43	76	.301	.376	7	.286	0	59	-2	—	-0.2
	StL A	9	17	.346	33	27	12-1	0	191.2	229	130	18	1	115	55	5.73	85	.297	.389	67-0-10	.149	-2*	94	-14	—	-1.8
	Year	9	20	.310	37	31	13-1	0	212.2	254	145	22	2	124	64	5.80	84	.297	.388	74-0-10	.162	-2	89	-17	—	-2.0
1940	StL A	12	17	.414	34	32	18	0	222.1	263	149	18	3	122	70	5.59	82	.298	.385	84-2-3	.298	6*	105	-21	—	-1.5
1941	StL A	2	4	.333	6	6	2	0	45	44	27	5	0	27	6	4.40	98	.259	.360	15-0-1	.400	2	91	-1	0	0.1
	Was A	1	7	.125	17	7	2	0	66.1	77	49	5	2	39	22	5.70	71	.297	.393	21	.143	-1*	61	-12	0	-1.3
	Year	3	11	.214	23	13	4	0	111.1	121	76	10	2	66	28	5.17	80	.282	.380	36-0-1	.250	2	75	-13	0	-1.2
1942	Cle A	4	8	.333	28	12	4	1	108	99	57	1	1	50	37	4.08	84	.244	.328	30-0-2	.200	1*	70	-8	0	-0.7
1943	Cle A	10	7	.588	28	17	8-1	0	146.2	130	47	4	2	59	63	2.45	127	.242	.319	52-0-8	.231	1*	99	11	0	1.5
1944	Cle A	2	5	.286	12	10	2	0	59	66	36	0	0	37	17	5.03	66	.289	.389	23	.087	-2*	89	-11	0	-1.3
	Phi N	1	5	.167	12	7	3	0	55.1	60	31	3	0	20	23	4.23	85	.269	.329	21-0-2	.286	1*	113	-4	0	-0.3
1945	Phi N	0	3	.000	12	3	0	0	36	43	29	2	0	14	13	5.50	70	.297	.358	11	.182	0*	133	-7	0	-0.5
	Cin N	5	12	.294	24	20	11-1	1	157.2	170	74	10	3	69	38	4.00	94	.280	.356	53-0-1	.226	2	66	-2	0	0.1
	Year	5	15	.250	36	23	11-1	1	193.2	213	103	12	3	83	51	4.28	88	.283	.356	64-0-1	.219	2	75	-10	0	-0.4
Total	12	104	132	.441	344	263	126-7	5	2025.2	2173	1202	130	24	1049	691	4.67	94	.277	.363	743-4-50	.244	19	98	-57	0	-3.7
KENNEDY, MONTE	Montia Calvin; B5.11.1922 Amelia VA; D3.1.1997 Midlothian VA; BR/TL/6´2˝/185; d4.18																									
1946	NY N	9	10	.474	38	27	10-1	1	186.2	153	80	14	4	116	71	3.42	101	.224	.340	64-0-2	.234	2	100	2	0	0.4
1947	NY N	9	12	.429	34	24	9	0	148.1	158	90	8	4	88	60	4.85	84	.272	.372	48-0-1	.167	-1	116	-13	0	-1.6
1948	NY N	3	9	.250	25	16	7-1	0	114.1	118	64	10	3	57	63	4.01	98	.264	.351	31-0-2	.129	-1*	69	-3	0	-0.4
1949	NY N	12	14	.462	38	32	14-4	1	223.1	208	105	13	3	100	95	3.43	116	.242	.323	83-1-5	.145	-1*	106	12	0	1.1
1950	NY N	5	4	.556	36	17	5	2	114.1	120	65	14	3	53	41	4.72	87	.269	.351	36-0-2	.056	-3	96	-7	0	-0.8
1951	†NY N	1	2	.333	29	5	1	0	68	68	25	0	0	31	22	2.25	174	.270	.350	15-0-3	.200	0	81	11	0	0.5
1952	NY N	3	4	.429	31	6	2-1	0	83.1	73	37	6	2	31	48	3.02	122	.230	.303	22-0-1	.091	-1*	112	4	0	0.2
1953	NY N	0	0	ø	18	0	0	0	22.2	30	18	2	1	19	11	7.15	60	.337	.459	2	.000	-0*	—	-6	0	-0.3
Total	8	42	55	.433	249	127	48-7	4	961	928	484	67	20	495	411	3.84	101	.253	.344	301-1-16	.153	-5	100	0	0	-0.9
KENNEDY, TED	Theodore A.; B2.7.1865 Henry IL; D10.31.1907 St.Louis MO; BL/TR/5´8˝/178; d6.12																									
1885	Chi N	7	2	.778	9	9	8	0	78.2	91	54	5	—	28	36	3.43	88	.288	.346	36	.083	-4	146	-3	—	-0.6
1886	Phi AA	5	15	.250	20	19	19	0	172.2	197	143	4	8	65	68	4.53	77	.272	.339	68	.044	-9	81	-17	—	-2.2
	Lou AA	0	4	.000	4	4	4	0	32	53	43	1	1	16	14	5.34	68	.351	.417	13	.077	-1	82	-7	—	-0.8
	Year	5	19	.208	24	23	23	0	204.2	250	186	5	9	81	82	4.66	76	.286	.353	81	.049	-10	81	-29	—	-3.0
Total	2	12	21	.364	33	32	31	0	283.1	341	240	10	9	109	118	4.32	78	.287	.351	117	.060	-14	98	-27	—	-3.6

YEAR	TM LG	W	L	PCT	G	GS	CG-SHO	SV-BS	IP	H	R	HR	HB	BB-IB	SO	ERA	AERA	OAV	OOB	AB-HR-SH	AVG	PB	SUP	APR	DL	PW
KENNEDY, BILL	William Aulton "Lefty"; B3.14.1921 Carnesville GA; D4.9.1983 Seattle WA; BL/TL/6´2˝/(195–210); d4.26																									
1948	Cle A	1	0	1.000	6	3	0	0	11.1	16	14	0	0	13	12	11.12	37	.333	.475	3-0-1	.667	1	200	-9	0	-0.5
	StL A	7	8	.467	26	20	3	0	132	132	82	10	5	104	77	4.70	97	.259	.389	44-0-3	.250	1	93	-4	0	-0.4
	Year	8	8	.500	32	23	3	0	143.1	148	96	10	5	117	89	5.21	87	.265	.397	47-0-4	.277	2	105	-12	0	-0.9
1949	StL A	4	11	.267	48	16	2	1	153.2	172	97	12	3	73	69	4.69	97	.285	.365	40-0-2	.150	-2	88	-4	0	-0.5
1950	StL A	0	0	ø	1	0	0	0	2	1	1	0	0	2	1	0.00	ø	.143	.333	0	ø	0	—	1	0	0.0
1951	StL A	1	5	.167	19	5	1	0	56	76	37	4	1	37	29	5.79	76	.332	.427	16	.125	-2	85	-7	0	-0.7
1952	Chi A	2	2	.500	**47**	1	0	5	70.2	54	27	4	1	38	46	2.80	130	.213	.318	13-0-1	.231	0	24	6	0	0.4
1953	Bos A	0	0	ø	16	0	0	2	24.1	24	13	2	1	17	14	3.70	114	.255	.375	2-0-1	.500	0	—	1	0	0.1
1956	Cin N	0	0	ø	1	0	0	0	2	6	4	1	0	0-0	0	18.00	22	.667	.600	0	ø	0	—	-3	0	-0.1
1957	Cin N	0	2	.000	8	0	0	3	12.2	16	9	1	1	5-1	8	6.39	64	.314	.379	2	.000	0	—	-3	0	-0.5
Total	8	15	28	.349	172	45	6	11	464.2	497	284	34	12	289-1	256	4.73	92	.275	.379	120-0-8	.208	-1	98	-22	0	-2.2
KENNEDY, BILL	William Gorman; B12.22.1918 Alexandria VA; D8.20.1995 Alexandria VA; BL/TL/6´1˝/175; d5.1; Mil 1943–45																									
1942	Was A	0	1	.000	8	2	1	2	18	21	18	1	0	10	4	8.00	46	.296	.383	4	.000	-1	82	-8	0	-0.6
1946	Was A	1	2	.333	21	2	0	3	39	40	29	1	0	29	18	6.00	56	.270	.390	8-0-1	.125	-0	102	-11	0	-1.0
1947	Was A	0	0	ø	2	0	0	0	6.2	10	8	1	0	5	1	8.10	46	.370	.469	2	.000	-0	—	-4	0	-0.2
Total	3	1	3	.250	31	4	1	5	63.2	71	55	3	0	44	23	6.79	51	.289	.397	14-0-1	.071	-1	93	-23	0	-1.8
KENNEDY, BRICKYARD	William Park; B10.7.1867 Bellaire OH; D9.23.1915 Bellaire OH; BR/TR/5´11˝/160; d4.26																									
1892	Bro N	13	8	.619	26	21	18	1	191	189	115	3	4	95	108	3.86	82	.248	.334	85	.165	-1	117	-14	—	-1.4
1893	Bro N	25	20	.556	46	44	40-2	1	382.2	376	238	15	7	168	107	3.72	119	.249	.327	157	.248	2	90	28	—	2.9
1894	Bro N	24	20	.545	48	41	34	2	360.2	445	291	15	11	149	107	4.92	101	.300	.368	161-0-6	.304	4	105	-3	—	0.1
1895	Bro N	19	12	.613	40	34	27-2	1	288.2	341	199	14	7	95	41	5.05	87	.289	.346	131-0-1	.305	4*	112	-17	—	-1.0
1896	Bro N	17	20	.459	42	38	28-1	1	305.2	334	211	12	12	130	76	4.42	93	.276	.352	122-0-4	.189	-7	85	-10	—	-1.4
1897	Bro N	18	20	.474	44	40	36-2	1	343.1	370	206	6	8	149	81	3.91	105	.273	.348	147-1-2	.272	4*	90	7	—	1.0
1898	Bro N	16	22	.421	40	39	38	0	339.1	360	183	12	5	123	73	3.37	106	.270	.334	135-0-1	.252	3	84	6	—	1.1
1899	Bro N	22	9	.710	40	33	27-2	2	277.1	297	133	11	3	86	55	2.79	140	.273	.329	109-0-1	.248	4	101	31	—	3.3
1900	Bro N	20	13	.606	42	35	26-2	0	292	316	160	5	8	111	75	3.91	98	.276	.344	123-0-2	.301	7*	112	2	—	0.9
1901	Bro N	3	5	.375	14	8	6	0	85.1	80	40	1	1	24	28	3.06	110	.246	.300	36	.167	-1	98	3	—	0.1
1902	NY N	1	4	.200	6	6	4-1	0	38.2	44	25	0	0	16	9	3.96	71	.286	.353	15	.267	1	65	-5	—	-0.5
1903	†Pit N	9	6	.600	18	15	10-1	0	125.1	130	62	0	2	57	39	3.45	94	.277	.357	58-0-2	.362	8*	135	0	—	0.7
Total	12	187	159	.540	406	354	294-13	9	3030	3282	1863	94	68	1203	799	3.96	103	.273	.343	1279-1-19	.261	27	99	28	—	5.8
KENNEY, ART	Arthur Joseph; B4.29.1916 Milford MA; BL/TL/6´0˝/175; d7.1; Col Holy Cross																									
1938	Bos N	0	0	ø	2	0	0	0	2.1	3	4	0	0	8	2	15.43	22	.300	.611	0	ø	0	—	-3	—	-0.1
KENSING, LOGAN	Logan French; B7.3.1982 San Antonio TX; BR/TR/6´1˝/185; [FlaN03 2/53]; d9.10																									
2004	Fla N	0	3	.000	5	3	0	0-0	13.2	19	15	5	1	9-0	7	9.88	42	.345	.439	2-0-1	.000	-0	53	-9	0	-1.5
2005	Fla N	0	0	ø	3	0	0	0-0	5.2	11	7	2	0	3-0	4	11.12	36	.407	.452	0	ø	0	—	-4	130	-0.2
2006	Fla N	1	3	.250	37	0	0	1-6	37.2	30	19	6	3	19-2	45	4.54	94	.221	.329	1	.000	-0*	—	0	56	0.0
Total	3	1	6	.143	45	3	0	1-6	57	60	41	13	4	31-2	56	6.47	65	.275	.373	3-0-1	.000	-0	53	-13	186	-1.7
KENT, ED	Edward C.; B1859 NY; BR/TR/5´6.5˝/152; d8.14																									
1884	Tol AA	0	1	.000	1	1	1	0	9	14	11	0	1	3	4	6.00	57	.298	.353	4	.000	-1	124	-3	—	-0.2
KENT, MAURY	Maurice Allen; B9.17.1885 Marshalltown IA; D4.19.1966 Iowa City IA; BR/TR/6´0˝/168; d4.15; Col Iowa																									
1912	Bro N	5	5	.500	20	9	2-1	0	93	107	74	3	1	46	24	4.84	69	.296	.377	35	.229	1	122	-18	—	-1.5
1913	Bro N	0	0	ø	3	0	0	0	7.1	5	2	0	0	3	1	2.45	134	.192	.276	3	.000	-0*	—	1	—	0.0
Total	2	5	5	.500	23	9	2-1	0	100.1	112	76	3	1	49	25	4.66	72	.289	.371	38	.211	1	122	-17	—	-1.5
KENT, STEVE	Steven Patrick; B10.3.1978 Frankfurt, West Germany; BB/TL/5´11˝/170; [SeaA99 9/275]; d4.4; Col Florida International																									
2002	TB A	0	2	.000	34	0	0	1-1	57.1	67	41	6	3	38-0	41	5.65	80	.294	.399	0	ø	0	—	-8	0	-0.4
KEOUGH, MATT	Matthew Lon; B7.3.1955 Pomona CA; BR/TR/6´3˝/(175–190); [OakA73 7/167]; d9.3; f-Marty																									
1977	Oak A	1	3	.250	7	6	0	0-0	42.2	39	25	4	1	22-0	23	4.85	83	.247	.341	0	ø	0*	74	-3	0	-0.3
1978	Oak A★	8	15	.348	32	32	6	0-0	197.1	178	90	9	4	85-2	108	3.24	113	.241	.322	0	ø	0*	74	7	0	0.9
1979	Oak A	2	17	.105	30	28	7-1	0-0	176.2	220	115	18	7	78-2	95	5.04	80	.315	.385	0	ø	0	66	-21	0	-1.9
1980	Oak A	16	13	.552	34	32	20-2	0-1	250	218	94	24	5	94-3	121	2.92	131	.236	.308	0	ø	0	94	25	0	2.6
1981	†Oak A	10	6	.625	19	19	10-2	0-0	140.1	125	56	11	0	45-0	60	3.40	104	.239	.298	0	ø	0	121	3	0	0.2
1982	Oak A	11	18	.379	34	34	10-2	0-0	209.1	233	144	38	5	101-1	75	5.72	69	.284	.362	0	ø	0	101	-40	0	-4.8
1983	Oak A	2	3	.400	14	4	0	0-0	44	50	29	7	0	31-1	28	5.52	70	.284	.388	0	ø	0	105	-8	0	-0.8
	NY A	3	4	.429	12	12	0	0-0	55.2	59	42	12	2	20-0	26	5.17	76	.266	.331	0	ø	0	125	-11	0	-1.2
	Year	5	7	.417	26	16	0	0-0	99.2	109	71	19	2	51-1	54	5.33	74	.274	.357	0	ø	0	120	-19	0	-2.0
1985	StL N	0	1	.000	4	1	0	0-0	10	10	5	0	1	4-1	10	4.50	79	.278	.366	2	.000	-0	74	-1	0	-0.1
1986	Chi N	2	2	.500	19	2	0	0-1	29	36	17	4	1	12-2	19	4.97	82	.316	.386	5	.400	1	44	-3	0	-0.2
	Hou N	3	2	.600	10	5	0	0-0	35	22	14	5	1	18-2	25	3.09	117	.180	.289	11	.364	1	134	2	0	0.4
	Year	5	4	.556	29	7	0	0-1	64	58	31	9	2	30-4	44	3.94	97	.246	.335	16	.375	2	103	0	0	0.2
Total	9	58	84	.408	215	175	53-7	0-2	1190	1190	631	132	27	510-14	590	4.17	92	.262	.338	18	.333	2	92	-50	0	-5.2
KEPPEL, BOBBY	Robert Griffin; B6.11.1982 St.Louis MO; BR/TR/6´5˝/205; [NYN00 1/36]; d5.25																									
2006	KC A	0	4	.000	8	6	0	0-0	34.1	45	21	6	1	15-2	20	5.50	85	.326	.391	2	.000	-0	47	-2	0	-0.2
KEPSHIRE, KURT	Kurt David; B7.3.1959 Bridgeport CT; BL/TR/6´1˝/(180–195); [CinN79 25/639]; d7.4; Col New Haven																									
1984	StL N	6	5	.545	17	16	2-2	0-0	109	100	47	7	0	44-4	71	3.30	106	.249	.321	36-0-5	.056	-2	109	1	0	-0.2
1985	StL N	10	9	.526	32	29	0	0-0	153.1	155	89	16	0	71-3	67	4.75	75	.264	.339	51-0-7	.118	-1	122	-19	0	-2.3
1986	StL N	0	1	.000	2	1	0	0-0	8	8	4	2	0	4-0	6	4.50	82	.258	.343	1-0-1	.000	-0	48	-1	0	-0.1
Total	3	16	15	.516	51	46	2-2	0-0	270.1	263	140	25	0	119-7	144	4.16	85	.258	.332	88-0-13	.091	-3	116	-19	0	-2.6
KERFELD, CHARLIE	Charles Patrick; B9.28.1963 Knob Noster MO; BR/TR/6´6˝/(225–257); [HouN82 S1/5]; d7.27; Col Yavapai (AZ) JC; [DL 1988 Hou N 17]																									
1985	Hou N	4	2	.667	11	6	0	0-0	44.1	44	22	2	0	25-2	30	4.06	86	.268	.359	14-0-2	.000	-1	110	-2	0	-0.5
1986	†Hou N	11	2	.846	61	0	0	7-5	93.2	71	32	5	2	42-3	77	2.59	139	.213	.299	9	.111	-0	—	10	18	1.4
1987	Hou N	0	2	.000	21	0	0	0-0	29.2	34	22	3	1	21-2	17	6.67	59	.309	.421	3	.000	-0	—	-8	51	-0.5
1990	Hou N	0	2	.000	5	0	0	0-0	3.1	9	6	0	0	6-1	4	16.20	23	.529	.652	0	ø	0	—	-4	0	-0.8
	Atl N	3	1	.750	25	0	0	2-0	30.2	31	22	2	0	23-3	27	5.58	72	.270	.386	0	ø	0	—	-5	15	-0.7
	Year	3	3	.500	30	0	0	2-0	34	40	28	2	0	29-4	31	6.62	61	.303	.423	0	ø	0	—	-9	0	-1.5
Total	4	18	9	.667	123	6	0	9-5	201.2	189	104	12	3	117-11	155	4.20	88	.256	.354	26-0-2	.038	-2	110	-9	101	-1.1
KERIAZAKOS, GUS	Constantine Nicholas; B7.28.1931 W.Orange NJ; D5.4.1996 Hilton Head SC; BR/TR/6´3˝/187; d10.1																									
1950	Chi A	0	1	.000	1	1	0	0	2.1	7	5	0	0	5	1	19.29	23	.500	.632	1	1.000	0	121	-4	0	-0.5
1954	Was A	2	3	.400	22	3	2	0	59.2	59	29	4	0	30	33	3.77	94	.262	.346	15-0-2	.067	-1	99	-2	30	-0.2
1955	KC A	0	1	.000	5	1	0	0	11.2	15	16	4	0	7-0	8	12.34	34	.333	.415	3	.000	-0	149	-9	0	-0.7
Total	3	2	5	.286	28	5	2	0	73.2	81	50	8	0	42-0	42	5.62	65	.285	.374	19-0-2	.105	-1	120	-15	30	-1.4
KERKSIECK, BILL	Wayman William; B12.6.1913 Ulm AR; D3.11.1970 Stuttgart AR; BR/TR/6´1˝/183; d6.21; Col Arkansas–Monticello																									
1939	Phi N	0	2	.000	23	2	1	0	62.2	81	52	13	0	32	13	7.18	56	.328	.405	12	.083	-0*	33	-20	—	-1.0
KERN, JIM	James Lester; B3.15.1949 Gladwin MI; BR/TR/6´5˝/(185–205); d9.6																									
1974	Cle A	0	1	.000	4	3	1	0-0	15.1	16	9	1	0	14-1	11	4.70	78	.262	.395	0	ø	0	105	-2	0	-0.1
1975	Cle A	1	2	.333	13	7	0	0-0	71.2	60	31	5	5	45-3	55	3.77	101	.233	.356	0	ø	0	99	2	0	0.1
1976	Cle A	10	7	.588	50	2	0	15-1	117.2	91	38	2	5	50-7	111	2.37	148	.222	.309	0	ø	0	112	13	0	2.3
1977	Cle A★	8	10	.444	60	0	0	18-9	92	85	39	3	6	47-8	91	3.42	117	.260	.359	0	ø	0	—	6	0	1.2
1978	Cle A★	10	10	.500	58	0	0	13-4	99.1	77	36	4	3	58-7	95	3.08	123	.224	.338	1	.000	-0	—	9	0	1.8
1979	Tex A★	13	5	.722	71	0	0	29-9	143	99	35	5	2	62-6	136	1.57	264	.199	.288	0	ø	-0	—	**39**	0	**6.3**
1980	Tex A	3	11	.214	38	1	0	2-7	63.1	65	38	4	2	45-10	40	4.83	81	.279	.392	0	ø	0	0	-6	27	-1.2
1981	Tex A	1	2	.333	23	0	0	6-0	30	21	10	0	1	22-3	20	2.70	129	.204	.346	0	ø	0	—	3	33	0.4

YEAR	TM LG	W	L	PCT	G	GS	CG-SHO	SV-BS	IP	H	R	HR	HB	BB-IB	SO	ERA	AERA	OAV	OOB	AB-HR-SH	AVG	PB	SUP	APR	DL	PW
1982	Cin N	3	5	.375	50	0	0	2-4	76	61	27	3	2	48-14	43	2.84	129	.222	.338	7	.000	-0	—	7	0	0.7
	Chi A	2	1	.667	13	1	0	3-1	28	20	16	3	0	12-0	23	5.14	79	.204	.288	0	ø	0	89	-2	0	-0.3
1983	Chi A	0	0	ø	1	0	0	0-0	0.2	1	1	0	0	0-0	0	0.00	ø	.333	.333	0	ø	0	—	0	180	0.0
1984	Phi N	0	1	.000	8	0	0	0-0	13.1	20	16	3	0	10-1	8	10.13	36	.339	.435	1	.000	-0	—	-9	0	-0.6
	Mil A	1	0	1.000	6	0	0	0-0	4.2	6	0	0	0	3-0	4	0.00	ø	.300	.391	0	ø	0	—	2	0	0.4
1985	Mil A	0	1	.000	5	0	0	0-0	11	14	8	1	0	5-1	3	6.55	64	.318	.388	0	ø	0	—	-2	0	-0.2
1986	Cle A	1	1	.500	16	0	0	0-1	27.1	34	28	1	3	23-0	11	7.90	53	.298	.429	0	ø	0	—	-12	0	-0.7
Total	13	53	57	.482	416	14	1	88-36	793.1	670	332	35	29	444-61	651	3.32	116	.235	.341	9	.000	-1	93	48	240	10.1

KERR, DICKIE Richard Henry; B7.3.1893 St.Louis MO; D5.4.1963 Houston TX; BL/TL/5´7˝/155; d4.25

YEAR	TM LG	W	L	PCT	G	GS	CG-SHO	SV-BS	IP	H	R	HR	HB	BB-IB	SO	ERA	AERA	OAV	OOB	AB-HR-SH	AVG	PB	SUP	APR	DL	PW
1919	†Chi A	13	7	.650	39	17	10-1	0	212.1	208	78	2	2	64	79	2.88	110	.259	.316	68-0-9	.250	5	119	10	—	1.5
1920	Chi A	21	9	.700	45	27	19-3	**5**	253.2	266	116	7	4	72	72	3.37	112	.278	.331	90-0-4	.156	-4*	105	10	—	0.8
1921	Chi A	19	17	.528	44	37	25-3	1	308.2	357	182	12	11	96	80	4.72	90	.295	.352	105-0-5	.238	5*	89	-15	—	-1.0
1925	Chi A	0	1	.000	12	2	0	0	36.2	45	23	3	1	18	4	5.15	81	.304	.383	12-0-1	.333	1*	91	-4	—	-0.1
Total	4	53	34	.609	140	83	54-7	6	811.1	876	399	24	18	250	235	3.84	99	.281	.338	275-0-19	.218	7	101	1	—	1.2

KERRIGAN, JOE Joseph Thomas; B1.30.1954 Philadelphia PA; BR/TR/6´5˝/(210–222); [MonN74*1/10]; d7.9; M1/C17; Col Temple

YEAR	TM LG	W	L	PCT	G	GS	CG-SHO	SV-BS	IP	H	R	HR	HB	BB-IB	SO	ERA	AERA	OAV	OOB	AB-HR-SH	AVG	PB	SUP	APR	DL	PW
1976	Mon N	2	6	.250	38	0	0	1-2	56.2	63	27	3	2	23-5	22	3.81	99	.289	.362	2	.000	-0	—	0	0	0.0
1977	Mon N	3	5	.375	66	0	0	11-5	89.1	80	37	4	3	33-3	43	3.22	120	.241	.310	8-0-2	.000	-1	—	6	0	0.5
1978	Bal A	3	1	.750	26	2	0	3-0	71.2	75	44	10	2	36-5	41	4.77	74	.273	.361	0	ø	0	114	-11	0	-0.6
1980	Bal A	0	0	ø	1	0	0	0-0	2.1	3	1	0	0	0-0	1	3.86	103	.273	.273	0	ø	0	—	0	0	0.0
Total	4	8	12	.400	131	2	0	15-7	220	221	109	17	7	92-13	107	3.89	96	.264	.340	10-0-2	.000	-1	114	-5	0	-0.1

KERSHNER, JASON Jason Ashley; B12.19.1976 Scottsdale AZ; BL/TL/6´2˝/(165–185); [PhiN95 12/325]; d7.25

YEAR	TM LG	W	L	PCT	G	GS	CG-SHO	SV-BS	IP	H	R	HR	HB	BB-IB	SO	ERA	AERA	OAV	OOB	AB-HR-SH	AVG	PB	SUP	APR	DL	PW
2002	SD N	0	1	.000	15	0	0	0-0	18.2	15	14	2	2	10-0	11	5.79	67	.217	.333	0-0-1	ø	0	—	-5	0	-0.2
	Tor A	0	0	ø	10	0	0	1-1	5.1	5	2	1	0	4-1	7	1.69	274	.227	.346	0	ø	0	—	1	0	0.1
2003	Tor A	3	3	.500	40	0	0	0-1	54	43	21	5	2	15-2	32	3.17	150	.217	.275	0	ø	0	—	9	0	0.9
2004	Tor A	0	1	.000	24	2	0	0-0	22.1	30	16	3	0	8-0	15	6.04	81	.316	.369	0	ø	0	85	-3	0	-0.1
Total	3	3	5	.375	89	2	0	1-2	100.1	93	53	11	4	37-3	65	4.22	109	.242	.313	0-0-1	ø	0	85	2	0	0.7

KESTER, RICK Richard Lee; B7.7.1946 Iola KS; BR/TR/6´0˝/190; d8.18; Col UCLA

YEAR	TM LG	W	L	PCT	G	GS	CG-SHO	SV-BS	IP	H	R	HR	HB	BB-IB	SO	ERA	AERA	OAV	OOB	AB-HR-SH	AVG	PB	SUP	APR	DL	PW
1968	Atl N	0	0	ø	5	0	0	0	6.1	8	4	0	0	3-0	9	5.68	53	.308	.379	0	ø	0	—	-2	0	-0.1
1969	Atl N	0	0	ø	1	0	0	0-0	2	5	3	1	0	0-0	2	13.50	27	.455	.455	0	ø	0	—	-2	0	-0.1
1970	Atl N	0	0	ø	15	0	0	0-0	32.1	36	24	3	0	19-0	20	5.57	77	.283	.374	9	.000	-1	—	-5	0	-0.4
Total	3	0	0	ø	21	0	0	0-0	40.2	49	31	4	0	22-0	31	5.98	68	.299	.380	9	.000	-1	—	-9	0	-0.6

KETCHUM, GUS Augustus Franklin; B3.21.1897 Royse City TX; D9.6.1980 Oklahoma City OK; BR/TR/5´9.5˝/170; d8.7

YEAR	TM LG	W	L	PCT	G	GS	CG-SHO	SV-BS	IP	H	R	HR	HB	BB-IB	SO	ERA	AERA	OAV	OOB	AB-HR-SH	AVG	PB	SUP	APR	DL	PW
1922	Phi A	0	1	.000	6	0	0	0	16	19	12	2	1	8	4	5.63	76	.302	.389	4	.000	-1	—	-2	—	-0.2

KEUPPER, HENRY Henry John; B6.24.1887 Staunton IL; D8.14.1960 Marion IL; BL/TL/6´1˝/185; d4.19

YEAR	TM LG	W	L	PCT	G	GS	CG-SHO	SV-BS	IP	H	R	HR	HB	BB-IB	SO	ERA	AERA	OAV	OOB	AB-HR-SH	AVG	PB	SUP	APR	DL	PW
1914	StL F	8	20	.286	42	25	12-1	0	213	256	132	3	4	49	70	4.27	71	.291	.332	68-0-4	.250	2	86	-29	—	-3.1

KEY, JIMMY James Edward; B4.22.1961 Huntsville AL; BR/TL/6´1˝/(175–190); [TorA82 3/56]; d4.6; Col Clemson

YEAR	TM LG	W	L	PCT	G	GS	CG-SHO	SV-BS	IP	H	R	HR	HB	BB-IB	SO	ERA	AERA	OAV	OOB	AB-HR-SH	AVG	PB	SUP	APR	DL	PW
1984	Tor A	4	5	.444	63	0	0	10-7	62	70	37	8	1	32-8	44	4.65	89	.286	.369	0	ø	0	—	-4	0	-0.6
1985	†Tor A★	14	6	.700	35	32	3	0-0	212.2	188	77	22	2	50-1	85	3.00	141	.237	.282	0	ø	0*	100	29	0	2.8
1986	Tor A	14	11	.560	36	35	4-2	0-0	232	222	98	24	3	74-1	141	3.57	119	.256	.315	0	ø	0	109	19	0	2.0
1987	Tor A	17	8	.680	36	36	8-1	0-0	261	210	93	24	2	66-6	161	**2.76**	**164**	**.221**	**.272**	0	ø	0	93	48	0	4.3
1988	Tor A	12	5	.706	21	21	2-2	0-0	131.1	127	55	13	5	30-2	65	3.29	120	.250	.296	0	ø	0	106	9	75	1.1
1989	†Tor A	13	14	.481	33	33	5-1	0-0	216	226	99	18	3	27-2	118	3.88	98	.270	.292	0	ø	0	96	0	15	0.1
1990	Tor A	13	7	.650	27	27	0	0-0	154.2	169	79	20	1	22-2	88	4.25	93	.281	.304	0	ø	0	113	-5	30	-0.6
1991	†Tor A★	16	12	.571	33	33	2-2	0-0	209.1	207	84	12	3	44-3	125	3.05	138	.254	.293	0	ø	0	91	24	0	3.2
1992	†Tor A	13	13	.500	33	33	4-2	0-0	216.2	205	88	24	4	59-0	117	3.53	116	.248	.298	0	ø	0	111	15	0	1.8
1993	NY A★	18	6	**.750**	34	34	4-2	0-0	236.2	219	84	26	1	43-1	173	3.00	139	.246	.279	0	ø	0	127	33	0	3.1
1994	NY A★	**17**	4	.810	25	**25**	1	0-0	168	177	68	10	3	52-0	97	3.27	141	.273	.329	0	ø	0	134	25	0	2.9
1995	NY A	1	2	.333	5	5	0	0-0	30.1	40	20	3	0	6-1	14	5.64	82	.323	.351	0	ø	0	129	-3	138	-0.3
1996	†NY A	12	11	.522	30	30	0	0-0	169.1	171	93	21	2	58-1	116	4.68	106	.266	.326	0	ø	0	95	5	30	0.7
1997	†Bal A✳	16	10	.615	34	34	1-1	0-0	212.1	210	90	24	5	82-1	141	3.43	129	.261	.331	2-0-1	.000	-0	98	23	0	2.5
1998	Bal A	6	3	.667	25	11	0	0-1	79.1	77	39	5	3	23-0	53	4.20	108	.258	.316	0	ø	0	93	3	68	0.3
Total	15	186	117	.614	470	389	34-13	10-8	2591.2	2518	1104	254	38	668-29	1538	3.51	122	.255	.303	2-0-1	.000	-0	105	221	356	23.3

KEYSER, BRIAN Brian Lee; B10.31.1966 Castro Valley CA; BR/TR/6´1˝/180; [ChiA89 19/485]; d6.2; Col Stanford

YEAR	TM LG	W	L	PCT	G	GS	CG-SHO	SV-BS	IP	H	R	HR	HB	BB-IB	SO	ERA	AERA	OAV	OOB	AB-HR-SH	AVG	PB	SUP	APR	DL	PW
1995	Chi A	5	6	.455	23	10	0	0-1	92.1	114	53	10	2	27-1	48	4.97	90	.306	.354	0	ø	0	83	-4	0	-0.4
1996	Chi A	1	2	.333	28	0	0	1-1	59.2	78	35	3	0	28-8	19	4.98	96	.328	.394	0	ø	0	—	-1	0	0.0
Total	2	6	8	.429	51	10	0	1-2	152	192	88	13	2	55-9	67	4.97	92	.314	.370	0	ø	0	83	-5	0	-0.4

KIDA, MASAO Masao; B9.12.1968 Tokyo, Japan; BR/TR/6´2˝/(209–210); d4.5

YEAR	TM LG	W	L	PCT	G	GS	CG-SHO	SV-BS	IP	H	R	HR	HB	BB-IB	SO	ERA	AERA	OAV	OOB	AB-HR-SH	AVG	PB	SUP	APR	DL	PW
1999	Det A	1	0	1.000	49	0	0	1-0	64.2	73	48	6	4	30-3	50	6.26	80	.289	.368	0	ø	0	—	-9	28	-0.4
2000	Det A	0	0	ø	2	0	0	0-0	2.2	5	3	1	0	0-0	0	10.13	48	.385	.385	0	ø	0	—	-1	0	-0.1
2003	LA N	0	1	.000	3	2	0	0-0	12	15	5	0	0	3-0	8	3.00	137	.300	.340	4	.250	0	45	1	0	0.1
2004	LA N	0	0	ø	3	0	0	0-0	4.2	4	0	0	1	1-0	5	0.00	ø	.235	.316	0	ø	0	—	2	0	0.1
	Sea A	0	0	ø	7	0	0	0-0	9.2	15	9	1	1	5-0	5	8.38	53	.366	.447	0	ø	0	—	-4	0	-0.2
2005	Sea A	0	0	ø	1	0	0	0-0	2	2	1	1	0	0-0	0	4.50	93	.250	.250	0	ø	0	—	0	0	0.0
Total	5	1	1	.500	65	2	0	1-0	95.2	114	66	9	6	39-3	68	5.83	82	.298	.369	4	.250	0	45	-11	28	-0.5

KIECKER, DANA Dana Ervin; B2.25.1961 Sleepy Eye MN; BR/TR/6´3˝/(180–195); [BosA83 8/203]; d4.12; Col St. Cloud St.

YEAR	TM LG	W	L	PCT	G	GS	CG-SHO	SV-BS	IP	H	R	HR	HB	BB-IB	SO	ERA	AERA	OAV	OOB	AB-HR-SH	AVG	PB	SUP	APR	DL	PW
1990	†Bos A	8	9	.471	32	25	0	0-0	152	145	74	7	9	54-2	93	3.97	103	.253	.325	0	ø	0	94	2	0	0.3
1991	Bos A	2	3	.400	18	5	0	0-0	40.1	56	34	6	2	23-4	21	7.36	59	.344	.429	0	ø	0	135	-12	55	-1.2
Total	2	10	12	.455	50	30	0	0-0	192.1	201	108	13	11	77-6	114	4.68	89	.273	.349	0	ø	0	101	-10	55	-0.9

KIEFER, JOE Joseph William "Harlem Joe","Smoke"; B7.19.1899 W.Leyden NY; D7.5.1975 Utica NY; BR/TR/5´11˝/190; d10.1

YEAR	TM LG	W	L	PCT	G	GS	CG-SHO	SV-BS	IP	H	R	HR	HB	BB-IB	SO	ERA	AERA	OAV	OOB	AB-HR-SH	AVG	PB	SUP	APR	DL	PW
1920	Chi A	0	1	.000	2	1	0	0	4.2	7	8	0	1	5	1	15.43	24	.333	.481	2	.000	-0	148	-5	—	-0.8
1925	Bos A	0	2	.000	2	2	0	0	15	20	12	0	1	9	4	6.00	76	.351	.448	4	.000	-1	46	-2	—	-0.3
1926	Bos A	0	2	.000	11	1	0	0	30	29	19	2	2	16	4	4.80	85	.266	.370	7	.143	-0	41	-3	—	-0.1
Total	3	0	5	.000	15	4	0	0	49.2	56	39	2	4	30	9	6.16	68	.299	.407	13	.077	-1	70	-10	—	-1.2

KIEFER, MARK Mark Andrew; B11.13.1968 Orange CA; BR/TR/6´4˝/(175–184); [MilA87 21/539]; d9.20; b–Steve; Col Fullerton (CA) JC

YEAR	TM LG	W	L	PCT	G	GS	CG-SHO	SV-BS	IP	H	R	HR	HB	BB-IB	SO	ERA	AERA	OAV	OOB	AB-HR-SH	AVG	PB	SUP	APR	DL	PW
1993	Mil A	0	0	ø	6	0	0	1-1	9.1	3	0	0	1	5-0	7	0.00	ø	.097	.243	0	ø	0	—	4	0	0.2
1994	Mil A	1	0	1.000	7	0	0	0-0	10.2	15	12	4	0	8-0	8	8.44	60	.357	.442	0	ø	0	—	-4	0	-0.3
1995	Mil A	4	1	.800	24	0	0	0-0	49.2	37	20	6	0	27-2	41	3.44	146	.203	.306	0	ø	0	—	8	0	0.7
1996	Mil A	0	0	ø	7	0	0	0-0	10	15	9	1	0	5-1	5	8.10	64	.366	.426	0	ø	0	—	-3	0	-0.1
Total	4	5	1	.833	44	0	0	1-1	79.2	70	41	11	1	45-3	61	4.29	116	.236	.336	0	ø	0	—	5	0	0.5

KIELY, JOHN John Francis; B10.4.1964 Boston MA; BR/TR/6´3˝/(210–215); d7.26; Col Bridgewater St. (MA)

YEAR	TM LG	W	L	PCT	G	GS	CG-SHO	SV-BS	IP	H	R	HR	HB	BB-IB	SO	ERA	AERA	OAV	OOB	AB-HR-SH	AVG	PB	SUP	APR	DL	PW
1991	Det A	0	1	.000	7	0	0	0-0	6.2	13	11	0	1	9-2	1	14.85	28	.448	.575	0	ø	0	—	-7	0	-0.9
1992	Det A	4	2	.667	39	0	0	0-1	55	44	14	2	0	28-3	18	2.13	188	.224	.317	0	ø	0	—	11	0	1.3
1993	Det A	0	2	.000	8	0	0	0-0	11.2	13	11	2	1	13-5	5	7.71	56	.295	.466	0	ø	0	—	-4	0	-0.6
Total	3	4	5	.444	54	0	0	0-1	73.1	70	36	4	2	50-10	24	4.17	98	.260	.375	0	ø	0	—	0	0	-0.2

KIELY, LEO Leo Patrick "Kiki"; B11.30.1929 Hoboken NJ; D1.18.1984 Montclair NJ; BL/TL/6´2˝/(180–185); d6.27; Mil 1952–53

YEAR	TM LG	W	L	PCT	G	GS	CG-SHO	SV-BS	IP	H	R	HR	HB	BB-IB	SO	ERA	AERA	OAV	OOB	AB-HR-SH	AVG	PB	SUP	APR	DL	PW
1951	Bos A	7	7	.500	17	16	4	0	113.1	106	48	9	2	39	46	3.34	134	.251	.317	35	.143	-1*	75	13	0	1.4
1954	Bos A	5	8	.385	28	19	4-1	0	131	153	74	12	1	58	59	3.50	117	.295	.365	50-1-1	.180	0	91	2	0	0.2
1955	Bos A	3	3	.500	33	4	0	6	90	91	31	5	0	37-5	36	2.80	153	.269	.341	26-0-1	.192	-0	93	14	0	1.1
1956	Bos A	2	2	.500	23	0	0	3	31.1	47	25	1	2	14-5	9	5.17	89	.362	.429	6	.167	-0	—	-3	0	-0.5
1958	Bos A	5	2	.714	47	0	0	12	81	77	31	3	2	18-3	26	3.00	134	.254	.299	13-0-2	.000	-2	—	9	0	0.9
1959	Bos A	3	3	.500	41	0	0	7	55.2	67	26	8	1	18-3	30	4.20	97	.299	.352	8	.000	-1	—	0	0	0.0

YEAR	TM LG	W	L	PCT	G	GS	CG-SHO	SV-BS	IP	H	R	HR	HB	BB-IB	SO	ERA	AERA	OAV	OOB	AB-HR-SH	AVG	PB	SUP	APR	DL	PW
1960	KC A	1	2	.333	20	0	0	1	20.2	21	4	1	1	5-0	6	1.74	229	.266	.318	1	.000	0	—	5	0	0.9
Total	7	26	27	.491	209	39	8-1	29	523	562	239	39	9	189-16	212	3.37	125	.279	.342	139-1-4	.144	-4	86	40	0	4.0
Kieschnick, Brooks	Michael Brooks; B6.6.1972 Robstown TX; BL/TR/6´4˝/(220–250); [ChiN93 1/10]; d4.3.1996; Col Texas; ▲																									
2003	Mil N	1	1	.500	42	0	0	0-0	53	66	32	5	6	13-4	39	5.26	82	.299	.354	70-7-0	.300	8*	—	-5	0	0.7
2004	Mil N	1	1	.500	32	0	0	0-1	43	44	19	6	0	13-3	28	3.77	117	.262	.315	63-1-0	.270	6*	—	3	25	0.8
Total	2	2	2	.500	74	0	0	0-1	96	110	51	11	6	26-7	67	4.59	95	.283	.337	133-8-0	.286	14	—	-2	25	1.5
Kile, Darryl	Darryl Andrew; B12.2.1968 Garden Grove CA; D6.22.2002 Chicago IL; BR/TR/6´5˝/(185–212); [HouN87 30/782]; d4.8; Col Chaffey (CA) JC																									
1991	Hou N	7	11	.389	37	22	0	0-1	153.2	144	81	16	6	84-4	100	3.69	96	.246	.344	38-0-4	.000	-3	105	-8	0	-1.3
1992	Hou N	5	10	.333	22	22	2	0-0	125.1	124	61	8	4	63-4	90	3.95	86	.261	.348	32-0-5	.156	1	82	-8	0	-1.0
1993	Hou N☆	15	8	.652	32	26	4-2	0-0	171.2	152	73	12	15	69-1	141	3.51	110	.239	.324	53-1-8	.094	-1	121	8	0	0.9
1994	Hou N	9	6	.600	24	24	0	0-0	147.2	153	84	13	9	82-6	105	4.57	87	.275	.375	47-0-9	.149	1	123	-11	0	-0.9
1995	Hou N	4	12	.250	25	21	0	0-0	127	114	81	5	12	73-2	113	4.96	78	.240	.353	36-0-5	.111	0	105	-18	0	-1.8
1996	Hou N	12	11	.522	35	33	4	0-0	219	233	113	16	16	97-8	219	4.19	93	.276	.359	73-0-7	.137	1*	113	-8	0	-0.6
1997	†Hou N☆	19	7	.731	34	34	6-4	0-0	255.2	208	87	19	10	94-2	205	2.57	156	.225	.300	89-0-10	.124	0	110	40	0	4.0
1998	Col N	13	17	.433	36	**35**	4-1	0-0	230.1	257	141	28	7	96-4	158	5.20	100	.287	.358	71-0-9	.254	2*	87	0	0	0.3
1999	Col N	8	13	.381	32	32	1	0-0	190.2	225	150	33	6	109-5	116	6.61	88	.298	.387	52-0-8	.135	-2	88	-14	0	-1.5
2000	†StL N★	20	9	.690	34	34	5-1	0-0	232.1	215	109	33	13	58-1	192	3.91	119	.247	.301	73-0-8	.123	0	97	20	0	2.2
2001	†StL N	16	11	.593	34	34	2-1	0-0	227.1	228	83	22	11	65-3	179	3.09	140	.265	.322	71-1-5	.127	1	85	32	0	3.6
2002	StL N	5	4	.556	14	14	0	0-0	84.2	82	36	9	8	28-1	50	3.72	108	.257	.330	22-0-3	.091	-1	98	4	0	0.3
Total	12	133	119	.528	359	331	28-9	0-1	2165.1	2135	1099	214	117	918-41	1668	4.12	104	.260	.341	657-2-81	.132	-1	100	37	0	4.2
Kilgus, Paul	Paul Nelson; B2.2.1962 Bowling Green KY; BL/TL/6´1˝/(175–190); [TexA84 43/821]; d6.7; Col Kentucky; [DL 1994 StL N 131]																									
1987	Tex A	2	7	.222	25	12	0	0-0	89.1	95	45	14	2	31-2	42	4.13	109	.271	.334	0	ø	0	86	5	0	0.4
1988	Tex A	12	15	.444	32	32	5-3	0-0	203.1	190	105	18	10	71-2	88	4.16	99	.243	.313	0	ø	0	88	-1	0	0.0
1989	†Chi N	6	10	.375	35	23	0	2-0	145.2	164	90	9	5	49-6	61	4.39	86	.283	.342	41-0-4	.073	-3	97	-13	0	-1.7
1990	Tor A	0	0	ø	11	0	0	0-0	16.1	19	11	2	1	7-1	7	6.06	65	.306	.370	0	ø	0	—	-3	0	-0.2
1991	Bal A	0	2	.000	38	0	0	1-0	62	60	38	8	3	24-2	32	5.08	78	.256	.328	0	ø	0	—	-8	0	-0.3
1993	StL N	1	0	1.000	22	1	0	1-0	28.2	18	2	1	1	8-1	21	0.63	642	.180	.248	5	.200	0	22	11	69	0.6
Total	6	21	34	.382	163	68	5-3	4-0	545.1	546	291	52	22	190-14	251	4.19	97	.259	.325	46-0-4	.087	-2	90	-9	200	-1.2
Kilkenny, Mike	Michael David; B4.11.1945 Bradford ON, Can.; BR/TL/6´3.5˝/(165–175); d4.11																									
1969	Det A	8	6	.571	39	15	6-4	2-0	128.1	99	54	13	4	63-1	97	3.37	112	.211	.309	37-0-3	.054	-3	103	5	0	0.3
1970	Det A	7	6	.538	36	21	3	0-1	129	141	77	10	2	70-0	105	5.16	73	.279	.368	39-0-4	.077	-3*	91	-17	0	-1.8
1971	Det A	4	5	.444	30	11	2	1-0	86.1	83	52	8	2	44-3	47	5.00	72	.247	.337	24-0-1	.083	-2	76	-13	23	-1.5
1972	Det A	0	0	ø	1	0	0	0-0	1	1	1	1	0	0-0	0	9.00	35	.250	.250	0	ø	0	—	-1	0	0.0
	Oak A	0	0	ø	1	0	0	0-0	1	0	0	0	0	0-0	0	0.00	ø	.000	.000	0	ø	0	—	0	0	0.0
	SD N	0	0	ø	5	0	0	0-0	4.1	7	4	1	0	3-0	5	8.31	40	.350	.435	0	ø	0	—	-2	0	-0.1
	Cle A	4	1	.800	22	7	1	1-0	58	51	23	5	0	39-4	44	3.41	96	.237	.353	14-0-2	.071	-1	81	0	0	-0.1
	Year	4	1	.800	24	7	1	1-0	60	52	27	6	0	39-4	44	3.45	94	.234	.348	14-2	.071	-1	81	-1	0	-0.2
1973	Cle A	0	0	ø	5	0	0	0-0	2	5	5	1	1	5-0	3	22.50	18	.455	.647	0	ø	0	—	-4	0	-0.2
Total	5	23	18	.561	139	54	12-4	4-1	410	387	216	39	9	224-8	301	4.43	83	.248	.344	114-0-10	.070	-8	91	-32	23	-3.4
Killeen, Evans	Evans Henry; B2.27.1936 Brooklyn NY; BR/TR/6´0˝/195; d9.7																									
1959	KC A	0	0	ø	4	0	0	0	5.2	4	3	0	0	4-0	1	4.76	84	.211	.348	0	ø	0	—	0	0	0.0
Killeen, Henry	Henry F.; B5.1872 Troy NY; D10.16.1916 Waterbury CT; 5´9˝/150; d9.11																									
1891	Cle N	0	1	.000	1	1	1	0	8.2	11	8	1	0	8	3	6.23	56	.297	.422	3	.000	-0	34	-2	—	-0.2
Killen, Frank	Frank Bissell "Lefty"; B11.30.1870 Pittsburgh PA; D12.3.1939 Pittsburgh PA; BL/TL/6´1˝/200; d8.27																									
1891	Mil AA	7	4	.636	11	11	11-2	0	96.2	73	42	1	3	51	38	1.68	262	.202	.306	35	.229	1	126	22	—	2.3
1892	Was N	29	26	.527	60	52	46-2	0	459.2	448	286	15	20	182	147	3.31	98	.245	.321	186-4	.199	10*	90	-2	—	1.0
1893	Pit N	**36**	14	.720	55	48	38-2	0	415	401	235	12	15	140	99	3.64	125	.246	.312	171-4	.275	14	125	46	—	5.5
1894	Pit N	14	11	.560	28	28	20-1	0	204	261	148	3	5	86	62	4.50	117	.308	.375	80-0-1	.262	0	99	13	—	1.1
1895	Pit N	5	5	.500	13	11	6	0	95	113	77	2	1	57	25	5.49	82	.291	.383	38	.342	4*	83	-8	—	-0.2
1896	Pit N	**30**	18	.625	**52**	**50**	**44-5**	0	**432.1**	476	244	7	14	119	134	3.41	123	.277	.329	173-2-3	.231	9*	117	29	—	3.4
1897	Pit N	17	23	.425	42	41	**38**-1	0	337.1	417	246	4	8	76	99	4.46	94	.301	.341	129-1-0	.248	5	83	-16	—	-1.1
1898	Pit N	10	11	.476	23	23	17	0	177.2	201	106	3	11	41	48	3.75	95	.283	.332	65-0-4	.262	2*	93	-5	—	-0.3
	Was N	6	9	.400	17	16	15	0	128.1	149	80	4	2	29	43	3.58	102	.288	.328	55	.273	3*	110	-1	—	0.2
	Year	16	20	.444	40	39	32	0	306	350	186	7	13	70	91	3.68	98	.285	.330	120-0-4	.267	5	100	-5	—	-0.1
1899	Was N	0	2	.000	2	2	1	0	12	18	11	0	1	4	3	6.00	65	.346	.404	5	.200	-0	64	-3	—	-0.4
	Bos N	7	5	.583	12	12	11	0	99.1	108	65	3	3	26	23	4.26	98	.276	.326	41	.171	-2	101	-2	—	-0.4
	Year	7	7	.500	14	14	12	0	111.1	126	76	3	4	30	26	4.45	93	.284	.335	46	.174	-3	96	-2	—	-0.8
1900	Chi N	3	3	.500	6	6	6	0	54	65	31	1	2	11	4	4.67	77	.297	.336	20-0-1	.150	-1	96	-2	—	-0.2
Total	10	164	131	.556	321	300	253-13	0	2511.1	2730	1571	55	85	822	725	3.78	109	.272	.332	998-11-9	.241	44	104	71	—	10.9
Killian, Ed	Edwin Henry "Twilight Ed"; B11.12.1876 Racine WI; D7.18.1928 Detroit MI; BL/TL/5´11˝/170; d8.25																									
1903	Cle A	3	4	.429	9	8	7-3	0	61.2	61	24	1	4	13	18	2.48	115	.257	.307	28	.179	-1*	113	3	—	0.3
1904	Det A	15	20	.429	40	34	32-4	0	331.2	293	118	0	17	93	124	2.44	104	.238	.301	126-0-2	.143	-3	89	8	—	0.2
1905	Det A	23	14	.622	39	37	33-**8**	0	313.1	263	108	0	13	102	110	2.27	120	.230	.300	118-0-7	.271	6	90	17	—	2.6
1906	Det A	10	6	.625	21	16	14	2	149.2	165	71	0	5	54	47	3.43	81	.283	.348	53-0-3	.170	-1	133	-9	—	-1.2
1907	†Det A	25	13	.658	42	34	29-3	0	314	286	103	2	11	91	96	1.78	147	.245	.306	122-0-3	.320	10*	104	25	—	4.2
1908	†Det A	12	9	.571	27	23	15	1	180.2	170	78	3	8	53	47	2.99	81	.252	.314	73	.137	-3*	118	-8	—	-1.1
1909	Det A	11	9	.550	25	19	14-3	1	173.1	150	45	1	6	49	54	1.71	147	.236	.297	62-0-3	.161	-1	97	15	—	1.7
1910	Det A	4	3	.571	11	9	5-1	0	74	75	38	2	6	27	20	3.04	87	.268	.345	27-0-1	.148	-1	150	-5	—	-0.6
Total	8	103	78	.569	214	180	149-22	4	1598.1	1463	585	9	70	482	516	2.38	110	.246	.310	609-0-19	.209	6	105	46	—	6.1
Killilay, Jack	John William; B5.24.1887 Leavenworth KS; D10.21.1968 Tulsa OK; BR/TR/5´11˝/165; d5.13																									
1911	Bos A	4	2	.667	14	7	1	0	61	65	26	0	10	36	28	3.54	93	.302	.425	24	.042	-2	116	2	—	-0.1
Kilroy, Matt	Matthew Aloysius "Matches"; B6.21.1866 Philadelphia PA; D3.2.1940 Philadelphia PA; BL/TL/5´9˝/175; d4.17; b–Mike																									
1886	Bal AA	29	34	.460	**68**	**68**	**66**-5	0	583	476	350	10	19	182	**513**	3.37	102	.210	.274	218	.174	-5	76	3	—	0.1
1887	Bal AA	**46**	19	.708	**69**	**69**	**66-6**	0	**589.1**	585	326	9	20	157	217	3.07	134	.253	.306	239	.247	9*	113	**72**	—	**7.2**
1888	Bal AA	17	21	.447	40	40	35-2	0	321	347	224	5	23	79	135	4.04	74	.266	.319	145	.179	-0*	100	-40	—	-3.8
1889	Bal AA	29	25	.537	59	56	**55**-5	0	480.2	476	283	8	27	142	217	2.85	139	.250	.312	208-1	.274	10*	89	49	—	5.7
1890	Bos P	9	15	.375	30	27	18	1	217.2	268	161	14	15	87	48	4.26	103	.290	.361	93	.215	-0*	98	4	—	0.3
1891	Cin AA	1	4	.200	7	6	4	0	45.1	51	42	1	8	19	6	2.98	137	.274	.366	20	.150	-1*	73	2	—	0.1
1892	Was N	1	1	.500	4	3	2	0	26.1	20	11	0	2	15	1	2.39	136	.202	.319	10	.200	-0	45	3	—	0.3
1893	Lou N	3	2	.600	5	5	5-1	0	35	57	41	2	4	23	4	9.00	49	.354	.447	16	.438	3	105	-17	—	-1.3
1894	Lou N	0	5	.000	8	7	3	0	37	46	34	2	2	20	11	3.89	131	.301	.389	17	.118	-2	97	2	—	0.1
1898	Chi N	6	7	.462	13	11	10	0	100.1	119	67	2	11	30	18	4.31	83	.292	.357	96-0-2	.229	2*	108	-5	—	-0.3
Total	10	141	133	.515	303	292	264-19	1	2435.2	2445	1539	53	131	754	1170	3.47	109	.252	.314	1062-1-2	.222	15	95	73	—	8.4
Kilroy, Mike	Michael Joseph; B11.4.1872 Philadelphia PA; D10.2.1960 Philadelphia PA; BR/TR/5´11˝/180; d9.1; b–Matt																									
1888	Bal AA	0	1	.000	1	1	1	0	9	12	9	1	0	5	1	8.00	37	.308	.386	4	.000	-1	0	-4	—	-0.4
1891	Phi N	0	2	.000	3	1	0	0	10	15	14	1	2	4	3	9.90	34	.333	.412	5	.400	1	175	-6	—	-0.8
Total	2	0	3	.000	4	2	1	0	19	27	23	2	2	9	4	9.00	36	.321	.400	9	.222	0	92	-10	—	-1.2
Kim, Byung-Hyun	Byung-Hyun; B1.19.1979 Kwangju, South Korea; BR/TR/5´11˝/(175–180); d5.29																									
1999	Ari N	1	2	.333	25	0	0	1-3	27.1	20	15	2	5	20-2	31	4.61	100	.211	.375	1	.000	-0	—	0	44	0.0
2000	Ari N	6	6	.500	61	1	0	14-6	70.2	52	39	9	9	46-5	111	4.46	108	.200	.336	3	.000	-0	115	2	0	0.3
2001	†Ari N	5	6	.455	78	0	0	19-4	98	58	32	10	8	44-3	113	2.94	158	.173	.284	6	.167	-0	—	18	0	2.6
2002	†Ari N★	8	3	.727	72	0	0	36-6	84	64	20	5	6	26-2	92	2.04	220	.208	.281	2	.500	0	—	21	0	4.3
2003	Ari N	1	5	.167	7	7	0	0-0	43	34	17	6	4	15-0	33	3.56	130	.214	.298	13-0-2	.154	-0	52	5	27	0.8
	†Bos A	8	5	.615	49	5	0	16-3	79.1	70	38	6	8	18-3	69	3.18	147	.230	.288	7	.286	0	182	10	0	1.8

YEAR	TM LG	W	L	PCT	G	GS	CG-SHO	SV-BS	IP	H	R	HR	HB	BB-IB	SO	ERA	AERA	OAV	OOB	AB-HR-SH	AVG	PB	SUP	APR	DL	PW
2004	Bos A	2	1	.667	7	3	0	0-0	17.1	17	15	1	2	7-1	6	6.23	78	.258	.338	0	ø	0	120	-3	25	-0.4
2005	Col N	5	12	.294	40	22	0	0-2	148	156	82	17	14	71-8	115	4.86	96	.275	.366	38-0-4	.079	-2	78	-2	0	-0.4
2006	Col N	8	12	.400	27	27	0	0-0	155	179	103	18	8	61-8	129	5.57	86	.295	.364	50-0-6	.160	-0	96	-12	27	-1.4
Total	8	44	52	.458	366	65	0	86-24	722.2	650	361	74	64	308-32	699	4.15	113	.241	.330	120-0-12	.142	-2	94	39	123	7.6

KIM, SUN-WOO Sun-Woo; B9.4.1977 Inchon, South Korea; BR/TR/6´2˝/(180–190); d6.15

YEAR	TM LG	W	L	PCT	G	GS	CG-SHO	SV-BS	IP	H	R	HR	HB	BB-IB	SO	ERA	AERA	OAV	OOB	AB-HR-SH	AVG	PB	SUP	APR	DL	PW
2001	Bos A	0	2	.000	20	2	0	0-0	41.2	54	27	1	4	21-5	27	5.83	76	.312	.399	0	ø	0	94	-5	0	-0.3
2002	Bos A	2	0	1.000	15	2	0	0-0	29	34	24	5	1	7-0	18	7.45	60	.288	.328	0	ø	0	145	-8	0	-0.5
	Mon N	1	0	1.000	4	3	0	0-0	20.1	18	2	0	1	7-2	11	0.89	495	.250	.325	8	.250	0	134	8	0	0.4
2003	Mon N	0	1	.000	4	3	0	0-0	14	24	13	6	4	8-0	5	8.36	53	.407	.500	3	.000	-0	113	-5	0	-0.4
2004	Mon N	4	6	.400	43	17	0	0-0	135.2	145	80	17	13	55-11	87	4.58	100	.275	.356	28-0-4	.214	1	100	-1	0	0.0
2005	Was N	1	2	.333	12	2	0	0-0	29.1	41	20	3	2	8-2	17	6.14	67	.336	.381	4-0-2	.000	-0	195	-6	0	-0.6
	Col N	5	1	.833	12	8	1-1	0-0	53.1	56	26	7	1	13-0	38	4.22	110	.268	.313	15-0-4	.133	-1	101	3	0	0.2
	Year	6	3	.667	24	10	1-1	0-0	82.2	97	46	10	3	21-2	55	4.90	91	.293	.338	19-0-6	.105	-1	120	-3	0	-0.4
2006	Col N	0	0	ø	6	0	0	0-0	7	17	15	2	1	8-0	4	19.29	25	.500	.578	1	1.000	1	—	-10	35	-0.4
	Cin N	0	1	.000	2	1	0	0-0	6.2	7	4	3	0	0-0	4	5.40	87	.259	.250	1	.000	-0	39	0	0	-0.1
	Year	0	1	.000	8	1	0	0-0	13.2	24	19	5	1	8-0	8	12.51	38	.393	.452	2	.500	1	39	-10	0	-0.5
Total	6	13	13	.500	118	38	1-1	0-0	337	396	211	44	27	127-20	211	5.31	85	.295	.365	60-0-10	.183	0	109	-24	35	-1.7

KIMBALL, NEWT Newell W.; B3.27.1915 Logan UT; D3.22.2001 Las Vegas NV; BR/TR/6´2.5˝/190; d5.7

YEAR	TM LG	W	L	PCT	G	GS	CG-SHO	SV-BS	IP	H	R	HR	HB	BB-IB	SO	ERA	AERA	OAV	OOB	AB-HR-SH	AVG	PB	SUP	APR	DL	PW
1937	Chi N	0	0	ø	2	0	0	0	5	12	8	1	0	1	0	10.80	37	.444	.464	1	.000	-0	—	-4	—	-0.2
1938	Chi N	0	0	ø	1	0	0	0	1	3	1	0	0	0	1	9.00	43	.500	.500	0	ø	0	—	-1	—	0.0
1940	Bro N	3	1	.750	21	0	0	1	33.2	29	15	2	0	15	21	3.21	125	.238	.321	5	.000	-1	—	2	—	0.2
	StL N	1	0	1.000	2	1	1	0	14	11	5	1	0	6	6	2.57	155	.208	.288	6	.333	1	109	2	—	0.2
	Year	4	1	.800	23	1	1	1	47.2	40	20	3	0	21	27	3.02	132	.229	.311	11	.182	0	109	4	—	0.4
1941	Bro N	3	1	.750	15	5	1	1	52	43	22	0	0	29	17	3.63	101	.225	.327	14	.214	0	93	1	0	0.1
1942	Bro N	2	0	1.000	14	1	0	0	29.1	27	13	0	1	19	8	3.68	89	.265	.385	5	.200	-0	232	-1	0	-0.1
1943	Bro N	1	1	.500	5	0	0	1	11	9	2	0	0	5	2	1.64	205	.214	.298	3	.000	-0	—	2	0	0.4
	Phi N	1	6	.143	34	6	2	2	89.2	85	47	4	1	42	33	4.12	82	.253	.338	16-0-2	.188	1	101	-7	0	-0.5
	Year	2	7	.222	39	6	2	3	100.2	94	49	4	1	47	35	3.84	88	.249	.333	19-0-2	.158	1	101	-5	0	-0.1
Total	6	11	9	.550	94	13	4	5	235.2	219	113	8	2	117	88	3.78	94	.249	.339	50-0-2	.180	1	107	-6	0	0.1

KIMBER, SAM Samuel Jackson; B10.29.1852 Philadelphia PA; D11.7.1925 Philadelphia PA; BR/TR/5´10.5˝/165; d5.1

YEAR	TM LG	W	L	PCT	G	GS	CG-SHO	SV-BS	IP	H	R	HR	HB	BB-IB	SO	ERA	AERA	OAV	OOB	AB-HR-SH	AVG	PB	SUP	APR	DL	PW
1884	Bro AA	18	20	.474	41	41	41-4	0	361.1	364	240	6	15	72	122	3.81	87	.247	.289	142	.148	-5	94	-18	—	-2.0
1885	Pro N	0	1	.000	1	1	1	0	8	15	13	1	—	5	4	11.25	24	.405	.476	3	.000	-0	21	-6	—	-0.5
Total	2	18	21	.462	42	42	42-4	0	369.1	379	253	7	15	77	126	3.97	83	.251	.294	145	.145	-6	92	-24	—	-2.5

KIMBERLIN, HARRY Harry Lydle "Murphy","Mule Trader"; B3.13.1909 Sullivan MO; D12.31.1999 Poplar Bluff MO; BR/TR/6´3˝/175; d7.11

YEAR	TM LG	W	L	PCT	G	GS	CG-SHO	SV-BS	IP	H	R	HR	HB	BB-IB	SO	ERA	AERA	OAV	OOB	AB-HR-SH	AVG	PB	SUP	APR	DL	PW
1936	StL A	0	0	ø	13	0	0	0	20	24	13	3	0	16	4	5.40	100	.296	.412	1	.000	-0	—	0	—	0.0
1937	StL A	0	2	.000	3	2	1	0	15.1	16	13	2	0	9	5	2.35	206	.254	.347	5	.200	0	63	0	—	0.1
1938	StL A	0	0	ø	1	1	1	0	8	8	3	1	0	3	1	3.38	147	.286	.355	1-0-2	.000	-0	53	2	—	0.0
1939	StL A	1	2	.333	17	3	0	0	41	59	35	6	2	19	11	5.49	89	.326	.396	9	.333	0	42	-6	—	-0.3
Total	4	1	4	.200	34	6	2	0	84.1	107	64	12	2	47	21	4.70	106	.303	.388	16-0-2	.250	0	50	-4	—	-0.2

KIME, HAL Harold Lee "Lefty"; B3.15.1898 W.Salem OH; D5.16.1939 Columbus OH; BL/TL/5´9˝/160; d6.19; Col Ohio St.

YEAR	TM LG	W	L	PCT	G	GS	CG-SHO	SV-BS	IP	H	R	HR	HB	BB-IB	SO	ERA	AERA	OAV	OOB	AB-HR-SH	AVG	PB	SUP	APR	DL	PW
1920	StL N	0	0	ø	4	0	0	0	7	9	4	0	1	2	1	2.57	116	.333	.400	1	.000	-0	—	0	—	0.0

KIMSEY, CHAD Clyde Elias; B8.6.1906 Copperhill TN; D12.3.1942 Pryor OK; BL/TR/6´2˝/200; d4.21

YEAR	TM LG	W	L	PCT	G	GS	CG-SHO	SV-BS	IP	H	R	HR	HB	BB-IB	SO	ERA	AERA	OAV	OOB	AB-HR-SH	AVG	PB	SUP	APR	DL	PW
1929	StL A	3	6	.333	24	3	1	1	64.1	83	42	2	0	19	13	5.04	88	.340	.388	30-2-1	.267	3*	57	-5	—	-0.2
1930	StL A	6	10	.375	42	4	1	1	113.1	139	87	8	2	45	32	6.35	77	.312	.377	70-2-0	.343	7*	79	-16	—	-1.1
1931	StL A	4	6	.400	42	1	0	7	94.1	121	60	1	2	27	27	4.39	106	.312	.360	37-2-1	.270	5*	109	**1**	—	0.7
1932	StL A	4	2	.667	33	0	0	3	78.1	85	45	3	0	33	13	4.02	121	.281	.352	18	.333	1*	—	5	—	0.5
	Chi A	1	1	.500	7	0	0	2	11	8	4	0	1	5	6	2.45	176	.211	.318	2	.000	-0	—	2	—	0.5
	Year	5	3	.625	40	0	0	5	89.1	93	49	3	1	38	19	3.83	125	.274	.348	20	.300	1	—	**8**	—	1.0
1933	Chi A	4	1	.800	28	2	0	0	96	124	67	7	4	36	19	5.53	77	.318	.381	33	.152	-2	120	-12	—	-0.7
1936	Det A	2	3	.400	22	0	0	3	52	58	36	2	1	29	11	4.85	102	.284	.376	16	.313	2	—	-1	—	0.1
Total	6	24	29	.453	198	10	2	17	509.1	618	341	23	10	194	121	5.07	92	.307	.371	206-6-2	.282	16	83	-26	—	-0.2

KINDER, ELLIS Ellis Raymond "Old Folks"; B7.26.1914 Atkins AR; D10.16.1968 Jackson TN; BR/TR/6´0˝/(185–195); d4.30

YEAR	TM LG	W	L	PCT	G	GS	CG-SHO	SV-BS	IP	H	R	HR	HB	BB-IB	SO	ERA	AERA	OAV	OOB	AB-HR-SH	AVG	PB	SUP	APR	DL	PW
1946	StL A	3	3	.500	33	7	1	1	86.2	78	35	8	0	36	59	3.32	112	.241	.318	19-0-2	.053	-1	95	5	0	0.1
1947	StL A	8	15	.348	34	26	10-2	1	194.1	201	105	11	0	82	110	4.49	86	.264	.336	62-0-4	.129	-4	67	-11	0	-1.7
1948	Bos A	10	7	.588	28	22	10-1	0	178	183	84	10	2	63	53	3.74	117	.266	.330	62-0-3	.097	-4	122	12	0	0.4
1949	Bos A	23	6	**.793**	43	30	19-**6**	4	252	251	103	21	2	99	138	3.36	130	.260	.330	92-0-9	.130	-4	134	27	0	2.2
1950	Bos A	14	12	.538	48	23	11-1	9	207	212	105	23	1	78	95	4.26	115	.263	.328	71-1-4	.183	-1	136	14	0	1.4
1951	Bos A	11	2	.846	**63**	2	1	**14**	127	108	42	8	0	46	84	2.55	175	.230	.298	34	.118	-3	149	**24**	0	2.5
1952	Bos A	5	6	.455	23	10	4	4	97.2	85	33	11	1	28	50	2.58	153	.234	.290	32	.000	-4	53	13	105	1.1
1953	Bos A	10	6	.625	**69**	0	0	**27**	107	84	30	8	2	38	39	1.85	227	.215	.288	29-0-1	.379	3	—	**25**	0	**5.2**
1954	Bos A	8	8	.500	48	2	0	15	107	106	47	7	0	36	67	3.62	114	.260	.318	27-0-5	.185	0	172	6	0	1.0
1955	Bos A	5	5	.500	43	0	0	18	66.2	57	22	4	1	15-4	31	2.84	151	.229	.274	12-0-1	.250	0	—	11	0	2.1
1956	StL N	2	0	1.000	22	0	0	6	25.2	23	11	3	0	9-3	4	3.51	108	.245	.305	2	.000	-0	—	1	0	0.0
	Chi A	3	1	.750	29	0	0	3	29.2	33	10	2	0	8-0	19	2.73	150	.277	.318	2	.000	-0	—	5	0	0.6
1957	Chi A	0	0	ø	1	0	0	0	1	0	0	0	0	1-1	0	0.00	ø	.000	.250	0	ø	0	—	0	0	0.0
Total	12	102	71	.590	484	122	56-10	102	1479.2	1421	627	116	9	539-8	749	3.43	125	.252	.318	444-1-29	.142	-19	112	132	105	14.9

KING, SILVER Charles Frederick (b Charles Frederick Koenig); B1.11.1868 St.Louis MO; D5.21.1938 St.Louis MO; BR/TR/6´0˝/170; d9.28

YEAR	TM LG	W	L	PCT	G	GS	CG-SHO	SV-BS	IP	H	R	HR	HB	BB-IB	SO	ERA	AERA	OAV	OOB	AB-HR-SH	AVG	PB	SUP	APR	DL	PW
1886	KC N	1	3	.250	5	5	5	0	39	43	35	1	—	9	23	4.85	78	.243	.280	22	.045	-2*	58	-5	—	-0.5
1887	†StL AA	32	12	.727	46	44	43-2	0	390	401	231	4	17	109	128	3.78	120	.260	.316	222	.207	-4*	107	36	—	2.4
1888	†StL AA	**45**	20	.692	**66**	**64**	**64-6**	0	**584.2**	435	203	6	30	76	258	**1.63**	**200**	.200	**.237**	207-1	.208	9	89	**95**	—	**10.2**
1889	StL AA	35	16	.686	56	53	47-2	1	458	462	257	15	21	125	188	3.14	134	.254	.309	189	.228	1	117	52	—	4.4
1890	Chi P	30	22	.577	56	**56**	48-**4**	0	461	420	233	5	15	163	185	**2.69**	**161**	**.232**	.301	185-1	.168	-6*	84	**82**	—	**6.6**
1891	Pit N	14	29	.326	48	44	40-3	1	384.1	382	243	7	18	144	160	3.11	105	.250	.321	148	.169	-1*	71	11	—	0.8
1892	NY N	22	24	.478	51	47	45-1	0	410.1	392	250	15	21	171	170	3.29	98	.242	.322	163-2	.209	6	104	-2	—	0.3
1893	NY N	3	4	.429	7	7	4	0	49	69	58	4	2	26	13	8.63	54	.322	.401	17	.176	1	124	-18	—	-1.6
	Cin N	5	6	.455	17	15	8-1	1	105	119	69	2	7	56	30	4.89	98	.277	.369	37	.162	-0	80	2	—	0.1
	Year	8	10	.444	24	22	12-1	1	154	188	127	6	9	82	43	6.08	78	.292	.380	54	.167	1	94	-11	—	-1.5
1896	Was N	10	7	.588	22	16	12	1	145.1	179	106	3	4	43	35	4.09	108	.300	.351	58-0-3	.276	3	129	5	—	0.6
1897	Was N	6	9	.400	23	19	12	1	154	196	118	7	11	45	32	4.79	91	.307	.363	57	.193	0*	121	-5	—	-0.3
Total	10	203	152	.572	397	370	328-19	6	3180.2	3098	1803	69	146	967	1222	3.18	122	.247	.308	1305-4-3	.198	7	98	253	—	23.0

KING, CLYDE Clyde Edward; B5.23.1924 Goldsboro NC; BB/TR/6´1˝/(175–185); d6.21; M5/C8; Col North Carolina

YEAR	TM LG	W	L	PCT	G	GS	CG-SHO	SV-BS	IP	H	R	HR	HB	BB-IB	SO	ERA	AERA	OAV	OOB	AB-HR-SH	AVG	PB	SUP	APR	DL	PW
1944	Bro N	2	1	.667	14	3	1	0	43.2	42	18	1	1	12	14	3.09	115	.256	.311	10-0-1	.200	-0	79	2	0	0.0
1945	Bro N	5	5	.500	42	2	0	3	112.1	131	64	8	0	48	29	4.09	92	.295	.364	32-0-2	.125	-2*	68	-4	0	-0.5
1947	Bro N	6	5	.545	29	9	2	0	87.2	85	34	11	0	29	31	2.77	149	.252	.311	26-0-1	.115	-1	121	12	0	1.2
1948	Bro N	0	1	.000	9	0	0	0	12.1	14	11	3	1	6	5	8.03	50	.286	.375	2	.000	-0	—	-5	0	-0.4
1951	Bro N	14	7	.667	48	3	1	6	121.1	118	64	15	3	50	33	4.15	94	.263	.341	29-0-4	.138	0	217	-4	0	-0.7
1952	Bro N	2	0	1.000	23	0	0	0	42.2	56	25	5	1	12	17	5.06	72	.318	.365	5	.000	-1	—	-6	0	-0.3
1953	Cin N	3	6	.333	35	4	0	2	76	78	47	15	2	32	21	5.21	84	.271	.348	10-0-1	.000	-1	118	-6	0	-0.7
Total	7	32	25	.561	200	21	4	11	496	524	263	58	8	189	150	4.14	95	.275	.343	114-0-9	.114	-4	126	-11	0	-1.4

KING, CURTIS Curtis Albert; B10.25.1970 Norristown PA; BR/TR/6´5˝/(200–205); [StLN94 5/138]; d8.1; Col Philadelphia

YEAR	TM LG	W	L	PCT	G	GS	CG-SHO	SV-BS	IP	H	R	HR	HB	BB-IB	SO	ERA	AERA	OAV	OOB	AB-HR-SH	AVG	PB	SUP	APR	DL	PW
1997	StL N	4	2	.667	30	0	0	0-3	29.1	38	14	0	1	11-0	13	2.76	152	.325	.379	1	.000	-0	—	3	0	0.5
1998	StL N	2	0	1.000	36	0	0	2-6	51	50	20	5	3	20-4	28	3.53	119	.262	.338	5	.000	-1	—	5	0	0.2
1999	StL N	0	0	ø	2	0	0	0-0	1	3	2	0	0	0-0	1	18.00	26	.500	.500	0	ø	0	—	-1	72	-0.1
Total	3	6	2	.750	68	0	0	2-9	81.1	91	36	5	4	31-4	42	3.43	123	.290	.356	6	.000	-1	—	7	72	0.6

YEAR	TM LG	W	L	PCT	G	GS	CG-SHO	SV-BS	IP	H	R	HR	HB	BB-IB	SO	ERA	AERA	OAV	OOB	AB-HR-SH	AVG	PB	SUP	APR	DL	PW
KING, ERIC	Eric Steven; B4.10.1964 Oxnard CA; BR/TR/6´2˝/(180–218); d5.15																									
1986	Det A	11	4	.733	33	16	3-1	3-2	138.1	108	54	11	8	63-3	79	3.51	119	.216	.312	0	ø	0	123	13	0	1.3
1987	†Det A	6	9	.400	55	4	0	9-6	116	111	67	15	4	60-10	89	4.89	87	.251	.343	0	ø	0	59	-7	0	-0.7
1988	Det A	4	1	.800	23	5	0	3-0	68.2	60	28	5	5	34-2	45	3.41	113	.233	.332	0	ø	0	142	4	0	0.3
1989	Chi A	9	10	.474	25	25	1-1	0-0	159.1	144	69	13	4	64-1	72	3.39	113	.244	.320	0	ø	0	113	7	37	0.8
1990	Chi A	12	4	.750	25	25	2-2	0-0	151	135	59	10	6	40-0	70	3.28	117	.237	.293	0	ø	0	110	10	31	0.9
1991	Cle A	6	11	.353	25	24	2-1	0-0	150.2	166	83	7	3	44-4	59	4.60	91	.279	.328	0	ø	0	100	-6	45	-0.7
1992	Det A	4	6	.400	17	14	0	1-0	79.1	90	47	12	1	28-1	45	5.22	77	.285	.343	0	ø	0	113	-9	79	-1.1
Total	7	52	45	.536	203	113	8-5	16-8	863.1	814	407	73	31	333-21	459	3.97	101	.249	.322	0	ø	0	109	12	192	0.8
KING, KEVIN	Kevin Ray; B2.11.1969 Atwater CA; BL/TL/6´4˝/(170–200); [SeaA90 7/188]; d9.2; Col Oklahoma																									
1993	Sea A	0	1	.000	13	0	0	0-1	11.2	9	8	3	1	4-1	8	6.17	72	.231	.304	0	ø	0	—	-2	0	-0.2
1994	Sea A	0	2	.000	19	0	0	0-1	15.1	21	13	0	1	17-3	6	7.04	70	.333	.481	0	ø	0	—	-3	0	-0.3
1995	Sea A	0	0	ø	2	0	0	0-0	3.2	7	5	0	1	1-0	3	12.27	39	.412	.450	0	ø	0	—	-3	0	-0.1
Total	3	0	3	.000	34	0	0	0-2	30.2	37	26	3	3	22-4	17	7.34	65	.311	.422	0	ø	0	—	-8	0	-0.6
KING, NELLIE	Nelson Joseph; B3.15.1928 Shenandoah PA; BR/TR/6´6˝/185; d4.15																									
1954	Pit N	0	0	ø	4	0	0	0	7	10	5	0	0	1	3	5.14	81	.400	.367	0	ø	0	—	-1	0	0.0
1955	Pit N	1	3	.250	17	4	0	0	54.1	60	24	2	2	14-3	21	2.98	138	.286	.332	12-0-2	.000	-2	76	5	0	0.2
1956	Pit N	4	1	.800	38	0	0	5	60	54	24	8	1	19-5	25	3.15	120	.241	.302	6-0-2	.000	-1	—	4	0	0.3
1957	Pit N	2	1	.667	36	0	0	1	52	69	27	7	2	16-6	23	4.50	84	.337	.387	5-0-1	.000	-1	—	-3	0	-0.2
Total	4	7	5	.583	95	4	0	6	173.1	193	80	17	5	50-14	72	3.58	109	.291	.340	23-0-5	.000	-3	76	5	0	0.3
KING, RAY	Raymond Keith; B1.15.1974 Chicago IL; BL/TL/6´1˝/(225–240); [CinN95 8/223]; d5.21; Col Lambuth																									
1999	Chi N	0	0	ø	10	0	0	0-0	10.2	11	8	2	1	10-0	5	5.91	77	.289	.449	1	.000	-0	—	-2	0	-0.1
2000	Mil N	3	2	.600	36	0	0	0-1	28.2	18	7	1	0	10-1	19	1.26	368	.180	.252	0	ø	0	—	10	0	1.5
2001	Mil N	0	4	.000	82	0	0	1-3	55	49	22	5	1	25-7	49	3.60	119	.241	.325	2	.000	-0	—	5	0	0.4
2002	Mil N	3	2	.600	76	0	0	0-1	65	61	24	5	3	24-6	50	3.05	135	.255	.328	0	ø	0	—	8	15	0.7
2003	†Atl N	3	4	.429	80	0	0	0-1	59	46	30	3	1	27-2	43	3.51	120	.213	.301	0	ø	0	—	3	0	0.3
2004	†StL N	5	2	.714	86	0	0	0-1	62	43	19	1	3	24-0	40	2.61	163	.197	.285	2	.000	-0	—	12	0	1.2
2005	StL N	4	4	.500	77	0	0	0-6	40	46	17	4	3	16-0	23	3.37	124	.293	.367	0	ø	0	—	4	0	0.6
2006	Col N	1	4	.200	67	0	0	1-1	44.2	56	26	6	2	20-0	23	4.43	108	.327	.398	1	.000	-0	—	1	0	0.1
Total	8	19	22	.463	514	0	0	2-14	365	330	153	27	14	156-16	252	3.28	132	.246	.328	6	.000	-1	—	41	15	4.7
KINGMAN, BRIAN	Brian Paul; B7.27.1954 Los Angeles CA; BR/TR/6´2˝/(190–200); d6.28; Col California–Santa Barbara																									
1979	Oak A	8	7	.533	18	17	5-1	0-1	112.2	113	59	10	3	33-1	58	4.31	94	.258	.313	0	ø	0	95	-2	0	-0.4
1980	Oak A	8	20	.286	32	30	10-1	0-0	211.1	209	105	21	4	82-5	116	3.83	99	.256	.325	0	ø	0	67	-2	0	-0.4
1981	†Oak A	3	6	.333	18	15	3-1	0-0	100.1	112	48	10	4	32-2	52	3.95	89	.286	.345	0	ø	0	92	-5	0	-0.5
1982	Oak A	4	12	.250	23	20	3	1-0	122.2	131	64	11	7	57-0	46	4.48	88	.279	.360	0	ø	0	84	-5	0	-0.8
1983	SF N	0	0	ø	3	0	0	0-0	4.2	10	6	0	0	1-0	1	7.71	46	.417	.440	0	ø	0	—	-3	0	-0.2
Total	5	23	45	.338	94	82	21-3	1-1	551.2	575	282	52	18	205-8	273	4.13	93	.269	.336	0	ø	0	82	-17	0	-2.3
KINNEY, DENNIS	Dennis Paul; B2.26.1952 Toledo OH; BL/TL/6´1˝/(170–190); [CleA70 10/225]; d4.9																									
1978	Cle A	0	2	.000	18	0	0	5-2	38.2	37	21	3	1	14-1	19	4.42	86	.259	.325	0	ø	0	—	-3	0	-0.2
	SD N	0	1	.000	7	0	0	0-1	7	6	5	3	0	4-0	2	6.43	52	.222	.323	1	.000	-0	—	-2	0	-0.3
1979	SD N	0	0	ø	13	0	0	0-0	18	17	8	2	1	8-3	11	3.50	101	.250	.338	1	.000	-0	—	0	0	0.0
1980	SD N	4	6	.400	50	0	0	1-2	82.2	79	45	3	1	37-15	40	4.25	81	.252	.331	12-0-1	.083	-0	—	-9	0	-1.1
1981	Det A	0	0	ø	6	0	0	0-0	3.2	5	4	0	0	4-1	3	9.82	39	.313	.450	0	ø	0	—	-2	0	-0.1
1982	Oak A	0	0	ø	3	0	0	0-0	4.1	9	4	1	0	4-0	0	8.31	48	.474	.565	0	ø	0	—	-2	0	-0.1
Total	5	4	9	.308	97	0	0	6-5	154.1	153	87	12	3	71-20	75	4.55	78	.261	.341	14-0-1	.071	-1	—	-18	0	-1.8
KINNEY, JOSH	Joshua Thomas; B3.31.1979 Coudersport PA; BR/TR/6´1˝/195; d7.3; Col Quincy (IL)																									
2006	†StL N	0	0	ø	21	0	0	0-0	25	17	9	3	1	8-0	22	3.24	134	.189	.263	0	ø	0	—	3	0	0.2
KINNEY, MATT	Matthew John; B12.16.1976 Bangor ME; BR/TR/6´5˝/(215–230); [BosA95 6/158]; d8.18																									
2000	Min A	2	2	.500	8	8	0	0-0	42.1	41	26	7	0	25-1	24	5.10	103	.261	.355	0	ø	0	98	1	0	0.0
2002	Min A	2	7	.222	14	12	0	0-0	66	78	39	13	1	33-0	45	4.64	96	.295	.371	2	.000	-0	64	-2	50	-0.3
2003	Mil N	10	13	.435	33	31	1	0-0	190.2	201	121	27	6	80-4	152	5.19	83	.272	.343	55-0-5	.036	-4	104	-20	0	-2.4
2004	Mil N	3	4	.429	32	6	0	0-0	62.1	77	41	8	2	23-1	52	5.78	76	.301	.359	9-0-1	.222	0	113	-8	0	-0.8
	KC A	0	1	.000	11	0	0	0-0	16.1	27	14	3	2	7-1	21	7.16	65	.365	.429	0	ø	0	—	-4	0	-0.2
2005	SF N	2	0	1.000	5	1	0	0-1	12	18	8	2	1	6-0	3	6.00	71	.383	.463	3	.333	0	156	-2	0	-0.3
Total	5	19	27	.413	103	58	1	0-1	389.2	442	249	60	12	174-7	297	5.29	84	.287	.359	69-0-6	.072	-4	97	-35	50	-4.0
KINNEY, WALT	Walter William; B9.9.1893 Denison TX; D7.1.1971 Escondido CA; BL/TL/6´2˝/186; d7.26																									
1918	Bos A	0	0	ø	5	0	0	0	15	5	3	0	2	8	4	1.80	149	.106	.263	5	.000	-1*	—	2	—	0.0
1919	Phi A	9	15	.375	43	21	13	2	202.2	199	110	7	8	91	97	3.64	94	.262	.347	88-1-2	.284	5*	73	-7	—	0.2
1920	Phi A	2	4	.333	10	8	5-1	0	61	59	38	3	1	28	19	3.10	130	.261	.345	26	.346	2*	109	3	—	0.5
1923	Phi A	0	1	.000	5	1	0	0	12	11	13	0	0	9	9	7.50	55	.229	.351	6-1-0	.167	1	201	-5	—	-0.3
Total	4	11	20	.355	63	30	18-1	2	290.2	274	164	10	11	136	129	3.59	99	.254	.343	125-2-2	.280	7	90	-7	—	0.4
KINNUNEN, MIKE	Michael John; B4.1.1958 Seattle WA; BL/TL/6´1˝/(185–205); [MinA79 10/245]; d6.12; Col Washington St.																									
1980	Min A	0	0	ø	21	0	0	0-0	24.2	29	18	1	1	9-1	8	5.11	86	.290	.348	0	ø	0	—	-3	0	-0.1
1986	Bal A	0	0	ø	9	0	0	0-0	7	8	6	1	0	5-0	1	6.43	65	.308	.419	0	ø	0	—	-2	0	-0.1
1987	Bal A	0	0	ø	18	0	0	0-0	20	27	14	3	0	16-1	14	4.95	90	.338	.443	0	ø	0	—	-2	0	-0.1
Total	3	0	0	ø	48	0	0	0-0	51.2	64	38	5	1	30-2	23	5.23	84	.311	.396	0	ø	0	—	-7	0	-0.3
KINSELLA, ED	Edward William "Rube"; B1.15.1880 Lexington IL; D1.17.1976 Bloomington IL; BR/TR/6´1.5˝/175; d9.16; Col Illinois St.																									
1905	Pit N	0	1	.000	3	2	2	0	17	19	6	0	1	3	11	2.65	113	.292	.333	3	.000	-0	36	1	—	0.0
1910	StL A	1	3	.250	10	5	2	0	50	62	30	0	2	16	10	3.78	65	.321	.379	12-0-1	.250	2	114	-7	—	-0.3
Total	2	1	4	.200	13	7	4	0	67	81	36	0	3	19	21	3.49	75	.314	.368	15-0-1	.200	2	90	-6	—	-0.3
KINZER, MATT	Matthew Roy; B6.17.1963 Indianapolis IN; BR/TR/6´2˝/210; [StLN84 2/35]; d5.18; Col Purdue																									
1989	StL N	0	2	.000	8	1	0	0-0	13.1	25	20	3	0	4-2	8	12.83	29	.403	.433	1-0-1	.000	-0	97	-12	0	-1.6
1990	Det A	0	0	ø	1	0	0	0-0	1.2	3	3	0	0	3-0	1	16.20	25	.375	.545	0	ø	0	—	-2	30	-0.1
Total	2	0	2	.000	9	1	0	0-0	15	28	23	3	0	7-2	9	13.20	28	.400	.449	1-0-1	.000	-0	97	-14	30	-1.7
KINZY, HARRY	Harry Hersel "Slim"; B7.19.1910 Hallsville TX; D6.22.2003 Ft.Worth TX; BR/TR/6´4˝/185; d6.8; Col TCU																									
1934	Chi A	0	1	.000	13	2	1	0	34.1	38	23	1	4	31	12	4.98	95	.290	.440	10	.300	1	83	-1	—	0.0
KIPP, FRED	Fred Leo; B10.1.1931 Piqua KS; BL/TL/6´4˝/(180–200); d9.10; Col Emporia St.																									
1957	Bro N	0	0	ø	1	0	0	0	4	6	4	2	0	0-0	3	9.00	46	.333	.333	1	.000	-0	—	-2	0	-0.1
1958	LA N	6	6	.500	40	9	0	0	102.1	107	60	16	1	45-7	58	5.01	82	.273	.349	36	.250	1*	80	-8	0	-0.7
1959	LA N	0	0	ø	2	0	0	0	2.2	2	0	0	0	3-1	1	0.00	ø	.222	.417	0	ø	0	—	1	0	0.1
1960	NY A	0	1	.000	4	0	0	0	4.1	4	3	0	0	0-0	2	6.23	57	.250	.250	0	ø	0	—	-1	0	-0.2
Total	4	6	7	.462	47	9	0	0	113.1	119	67	18	1	48-8	64	5.08	80	.274	.346	37	.243	1	80	-10	0	-0.9
KIPPER, BOB	Robert Wayne; B7.8.1964 Aurora IL; BR/TL/6´2˝/(175–200); [CalA82 1/8]; d4.12; C1																									
1985	Cal A	0	1	.000	2	1	0	0-0	3.1	7	8	1	0	3-0	0	21.60	19	.467	.500	0	ø	0	199	-6	0	-0.9
	Pit N	1	2	.333	5	4	0	0-0	24.2	21	16	4	0	7-0	13	5.11	71	.221	.272	8-0-2	.250	0	91	-4	0	-0.4
1986	Pit N	6	8	.429	20	19	0	0-0	114	123	60	17	2	34-3	81	4.03	97	.271	.323	33-0-3	.030	-3*	83	-3	64	-0.7
1987	Pit N	5	9	.357	24	20	1-1	0-0	110.2	117	74	25	2	52-4	83	5.94	70	.271	.350	33-0-3	.242	2*	97	-18	0	-1.8
1988	Pit N	2	6	.250	50	0	0	0-0	65	54	33	7	2	26-4	39	3.74	92	.234	.313	4-0-1	.000	-0	—	-3	0	-0.3
1989	Pit N	3	4	.429	52	0	0	4-4	83	55	29	5	0	33-6	58	2.93	116	.188	.267	9-0-1	.111	-0	—	5	32	0.4
1990	Pit N	5	2	.714	41	1	0	3-1	62.2	44	24	7	3	26-1	35	3.02	121	.195	.283	7	.143	-0	272	4	28	0.5
1991	†Pit N	2	2	.500	52	0	0	4-2	60	66	34	7	0	22-3	38	4.65	77	.276	.335	1-0-1	.000	-0	—	-7	0	-0.6

YEAR	TM LG	W	L	PCT	G	GS	CG-SHO	SV-BS	IP	H	R	HR	HB	BB-IB	SO	ERA	AERA	OAV	OOB	AB-HR-SH	AVG	PB	SUP	APR	DL	PW
1992	Min A	3	3	.500	25	0	0	0-2	38.2	40	23	8	3	14-3	22	4.42	92	.268	.343	0	ø	0	—	-2	0	-0.3
Total	8	27	37	.422	271	45	1-1	11-9	562	527	301	81	12	217-24	369	4.34	87	.247	.317	95-0-11	.137	-1	102	-34	124	-4.1
KIPPER, THORNTON	Thornton John; B9.27.1928 Bagley WI; D3.29.2006 Scottsdale AZ; BR/TR/6´3˝/190; d6.7; Col Wisconsin–Madison																									
1953	Phi N	3	3	.500	20	3	0	0	45.2	59	26	8	0	12	15	4.73	89	.319	.360	11-0-2	.091	-1	35	-2	0	-0.3
1954	Phi N	0	0	ø	11	0	0	1	13.2	22	13	0	1	12	5	7.90	51	.379	.493	2	.000	-0	—	-6	0	-0.3
1955	Phi N	0	1	.000	24	0	0	0	39.2	47	23	4	1	22-4	15	4.99	80	.301	.389	3	.333	0	—	-4	0	-0.2
Total	3	3	4	.429	55	3	0	1	99	128	62	12	2	46-4	35	5.27	78	.321	.393	16-0-2	.125	-1	35	-12	0	-0.8
KIRBY, CLAY	Clayton Laws; B6.25.1948 Washington DC; D10.11.1991 Arlington VA; BR/TR/6´3˝/(170–185); [StLN66 3/47]; d4.11																									
1969	SD N	7	20	.259	35	35	2	0-0	215.2	204	108	18	6	100-13	113	3.80	94	.252	.337	66-0-2	.061	-2	74	-8	0	-1.3
1970	SD N	10	16	.385	36	34	6-1	0-0	214.2	198	118	29	9	120-5	154	4.53	89	.248	.348	74-0-3	.149	-0	91	-11	0	-1.3
1971	SD N	15	13	.536	38	36	13-2	0-0	267.1	213	99	20	3	103-14	231	2.83	118	.216	.291	86-0-5	.093	-3*	87	16	0	1.2
1972	SD N	12	14	.462	34	34	9-2	0-0	238.2	197	87	21	2	116-11	175	3.13	106	.226	.317	74-0-6	.068	-4*	82	8	0	0.4
1973	SD N	8	18	.308	34	31	4-2	0-0	191.2	214	122	30	1	66-7	129	4.79	73	.282	.338	54-0-11	.093	-3*	100	-30	0	-3.9
1974	Cin N	12	9	.571	36	35	7-1	0-0	230.2	210	97	15	2	91-3	160	3.28	107	.242	.313	74-0-8	.095	-3	114	5	0	0.0
1975	Cin N	10	6	.625	26	19	1	0-0	110.2	113	63	13	5	54-3	48	4.72	76	.263	.351	32-0-4	.188	1	137	-15	0	-1.9
1976	Mon N	1	8	.111	22	15	0	0-0	78.2	81	61	10	2	63-1	51	5.72	66	.273	.399	18-0-6	.056	-1	100	-17	0	-1.9
Total	8	75	104	.419	261	239	42-8	0-0	1548	1430	755	156	30	713-57	1061	3.84	92	.246	.329	478-0-45	.098	-15	96	-52	0	-8.7
KIRBY, JOHN	John F.; B1.13.1865 St.Louis MO; D10.6.1931 St.Louis MO; TR/5´8˝/172; d8.1																									
1884	KC U	0	1	.000	2	2	1	0	11	13	10	0	—	2	1	4.09	55	.277	.306	7	.143	-1	86	-3	—	-0.2
1885	StL N	5	8	.385	14	14	14	0	129.1	118	66	0	—	44	46	3.55	77	.241	.303	50	.060	-6	82	-6	—	-1.1
1886	StL N	11	26	.297	41	41	38-1	0	325	329	222	9	—	134	129	3.30	98	.252	.322	136	.110	-9*	81	-4	—	-1.3
1887	Ind N	1	6	.143	8	8	5	0	62	70	64	3	2	43	7	6.10	68	.272	.381	29	.138	-2	78	-13	—	-1.3
	Cle AA	0	5	.000	5	5	5	0	41	62	53	1	2	28	6	9.00	48	.339	.432	18	.167	-1	38	-16	—	-1.3
1888	KC AA	1	4	.200	5	5	5	0	43	48	36	0	1	7	11	4.19	81	.273	.304	16	.063	-2	24	-4	—	-0.6
Total	5	18	50	.265	75	75	68-1	0	611.1	640	451	13	5	258	200	4.09	80	.260	.332	256	.105	-21	74	-46	—	-5.8
KIRBY, LA RUE	La Rue; B12.30.1889 Eureka MI; D6.10.1961 Lansing MI; BB/TR/6´0˝/185; d8.7; ▲																									
1912	NY N	1	0	1.000	3	1	1	0	11	13	7	1	1	6	2	5.73	59	.295	.392	5	.200	0	152	-2	—	-0.1
1915	StL F	0	0	ø	1	0	0	0	7	7	5	1	0	2	7	5.14	56	.269	.321	178-0-9	.213	0*	—	-2	—	-0.1
Total	2	1	0	1.000	4	1	1	0	18	20	12	2	1	8	9	5.50	58	.286	.367	183-0-9	.213	0	152	-4	—	-0.2
KIRCHER, MIKE	Michael Andrew (b Wolfgang Andrew Kerscher); B9.30.1897 Rochester NY; D6.26.1972 Rochester NY; BB/TR/6´0˝/180; d8.8																									
1919	Phi A	0	0	ø	2	0	0	0	8	15	8	0	0	3	2	7.88	44	.429	.474	3	.000	-0	—	-3	—	-0.2
1920	StL N	2	1	.667	9	3	1	0	36.2	50	23	0	2	5	5	5.40	55	.333	.363	11	.273	0	88	-8	—	-0.7
1921	StL N	0	1	.000	3	0	0	0	3.1	4	3	0	1	1	2	8.10	45	.364	.462	0	ø	0	—	-1	—	-0.3
Total	3	2	2	.500	14	3	1	0	48	69	34	0	3	9	9	6.00	52	.352	.389	14	.214	-0	88	-12	—	-1.2
KIRK, BILL	William Partlemore; B7.19.1935 Coatesville PA; BL/TL/6´0˝/165; d9.23																									
1961	KC A	0	0	ø	1	1	0	0	3	6	4	2	0	1-0	3	12.00	35	.375	.412	0	ø	0	106	-2	0	-0.1
KIRKWOOD, DON	Donald Paul; B9.24.1949 Pontiac MI; BR/TR/6´3˝/(175–192); d9.13; Col Oakland																									
1974	Cal A	0	0	ø	3	0	0	0-0	7.1	12	8	0	0	6-0	4	8.59	40	.375	.474	0	ø	0	—	-4	0	-0.2
1975	Cal A	6	5	.545	44	2	0	7-5	84	85	38	6	0	28-2	49	3.11	115	.270	.323	0	ø	0*	98	3	0	0.3
1976	Cal A	6	12	.333	28	26	4	0-0	157.2	167	91	12	1	57-9	78	4.62	72	.278	.337	0	ø	0	94	-23	0	-2.3
1977	Cal A	1	0	1.000	13	0	0	1-2	17.2	20	12	3	0	9-3	10	5.09	77	.290	.372	0	ø	0	—	-3	0	-0.1
	Chi A	1	1	.500	16	0	0	0-0	40	49	27	3	1	10-2	24	5.17	79	.310	.349	0	ø	0	—	-5	0	-0.3
	Year	2	1	.667	29	0	0	1-2	57.2	69	39	6	1	19-5	34	5.15	78	.304	.356	0	ø	0	—	-8	0	-0.4
1978	Tor A	4	5	.444	16	9	3	0-0	68	76	36	6	0	25-1	29	4.24	93	.289	.348	0	ø	0*	86	-3	80	-0.3
Total	5	18	23	.439	120	37	7	8-7	374.2	409	212	30	2	135-17	194	4.37	83	.284	.342	0	ø	0	89	-35	80	-2.9
KIRSCH, HARRY	Harry Louis "Casey"; B10.17.1887 Pittsburgh PA; D12.25.1925 Philadelphia PA; BR/TR/5´11˝/170; d4.16																									
1910	Cle A	0	0	ø	2	0	0	0	3	5	2	0	0	1	5	6.00	43	.385	.429	0	ø	0	—	-1	—	-0.1
KISER, GARLAND	Garland Routhard; B7.8.1968 Charlotte NC; BL/TL/6´3˝/190; [PhiN86 24/604]; d9.9																									
1991	Cle A	0	0	ø	7	0	0	0-0	4.2	7	5	0	1	4-0	3	9.64	43	.368	.500	0	ø	0	—	-3	0	-0.1
KISINGER, RUBE	Charles Samuel; B12.13.1876 Adrian MI; D7.17.1941 Huron OH; BR/TR/6´0˝/190; d9.10; Col Adrian																									
1902	Det A	2	3	.400	5	5	5	0	43.1	48	20	0	3	14	7	3.12	117	.281	.346	19	.158	-1	71	3	—	0.2
1903	Det A	7	9	.438	16	14	13-2	0	118.2	118	58	0	2	27	33	2.96	98	.259	.303	47	.128	-3	67	-1	—	-0.4
Total	2	9	12	.429	21	19	18-2	0	162	166	78	0	5	41	40	3.00	103	.265	.315	66	.136	-4	68	2	—	-0.2
KISON, BRUCE	Bruce Eugene; B2.18.1950 Pasco WA; BR/TR/6´4˝/(170–180); [PitN68 14/309]; d7.4; C8																									
1971	†Pit N	6	5	.545	18	13	2-1	0-0	95.1	93	40	6	6	36-5	60	3.40	100	.259	.335	31-0-1	.065	-1	120	0	0	-0.1
1972	†Pit N	9	7	.563	32	18	6-1	3-2	152	123	61	11	9	69-2	102	3.26	102	.220	.316	53-0-2	.189	2	123	2	5	0.4
1973	Pit N	3	0	1.000	7	7	0	0-0	43.2	36	17	4	1	24-3	26	3.09	114	.232	.339	12	.083	0	129	2	16	0.2
1974	†Pit N	9	8	.529	40	16	1	2-2	129	123	64	8	11	57-7	71	3.49	100	.247	.335	37-0-2	.108	-0	125	-3	0	-0.4
1975	†Pit N	12	11	.522	33	29	6	0-0	192	160	89	10	4	92-9	89	3.23	111	.227	.317	59-0-10	.119	-2*	107	4	0	0.4
1976	Pit N	14	9	.609	31	29	6-1	1-0	193	180	83	10	3	52-4	98	3.08	115	.247	.297	59-0-8	.203	4	109	6	0	1.2
1977	Pit N	9	10	.474	33	32	3-1	0-0	193	209	113	25	6	55-6	122	4.90	82	.278	.328	69-1-3	.261	5*	114	-16	0	-1.0
1978	Pit N	6	6	.500	28	11	0	0-1	96	81	40	3	5	39-0	62	3.19	117	.229	.311	29-1-0	.138	1	88	5	39	0.7
1979	†Pit N	13	7	.650	33	25	3-1	0-1	172.1	157	70	13	4	45-5	105	3.19	123	.246	.298	55-1-7	.145	-0*	101	13	0	1.5
1980	Cal A	3	6	.333	13	13	2-1	0-0	73.1	73	46	5	3	32-2	28	4.91	81	.264	.344	0	ø	0	120	-9	116	-0.9
1981	Cal A	1	1	.500	11	4	0	0-0	44	40	18	8	0	14-1	19	3.48	106	.241	.300	0	ø	0	79	1	122	0.1
1982	†Cal A	10	5	.667	33	16	3-1	1-0	142	120	54	15	5	44-3	86	3.17	129	.226	.291	0	ø	0	129	14	0	1.5
1983	Cal A	11	5	.688	26	17	4-1	2-1	126.2	128	59	13	4	43-4	83	4.05	100	.264	.328	0	ø	0	111	2	28	0.2
1984	Cal A	4	5	.444	20	7	0	2-1	65.1	72	42	10	6	28-3	66	5.37	74	.280	.362	0	ø	0	110	-10	65	-1.3
1985	Bos A	5	3	.625	22	9	0	1-1	92	98	43	9	1	32-4	56	4.11	105	.274	.332	0	ø	0	112	3	22	0.4
Total	15	115	88	.567	380	246	36-8	12-9	1809.2	1693	839	150	68	662-58	1073	3.66	103	.248	.319	404-3-33	.163	8	113	14	413	2.9
KISSINGER, BILL	William Francis "Shang"; B8.15.1871 Dayton KY; D4.20.1929 Cincinnati OH; BR/TR/5´11˝/185; d5.30; ▲																									
1895	Bal N	1	0	1.000	2	2	1	0	11.1	18	11	0	0	2	3	3.97	120	.353	.377	5	.200	-0	120	-1	—	-0.1
	StL N	4	12	.250	24	14	9	0	140.2	222	145	8	8	51	31	6.72	72	.352	.408	97-0-1	.247	-2*	64	-28	—	-2.4
	Year	5	12	.294	26	16	10	0	152	240	156	8	8	53	34	6.51	74	.352	.406	102-0-1	.245	-2	71	-27	—	-2.5
1896	StL N	2	9	.182	20	12	11	1	136	209	136	5	8	55	22	6.49	67	.349	.411	73-0-2	.301	1*	69	-32	—	-1.8
1897	StL N	0	4	.000	7	4	2	0	31.1	51	50	2	8	15	5	11.49	38	.362	.451	39	.333	2*	61	-22	—	-1.8
Total	3	7	25	.219	53	32	23	1	319.1	500	342	15	24	123	61	6.99	66	.352	.413	214-0-3	.280	1	69	-83	—	-6.1
KITSON, FRANK	Frank R.; B9.11.1869 Hopkins MI; D4.14.1930 Allegan MI; BL/TR/5´11˝/165; d5.19																									
1898	Bal N	8	5	.615	17	13	13-1	0	119.1	123	71	0	8	35	32	3.24	110	.265	.327	86	.314	4*	92	2	—	0.5
1899	Bal N	22	16	.579	40	37	34-2	0	326.2	327	144	6	12	65	75	2.78	142	.260	.303	134-0-1	.201	-2*	81	42	—	3.9
1900	†Bro N	15	13	.536	40	30	21-2	**4**	253.1	283	152	12	9	56	55	4.19	92	.282	.326	109-0-1	.294	5*	106	-7	—	-0.4
1901	Bro N	19	11	.633	38	32	26-5	2	280.2	312	135	9	10	67	127	2.98	112	.279	.326	133-1-1	.263	5*	104	10	—	1.4
1902	Bro N	19	13	.594	32	31	29-3	0	268.2	256	105	4	7	52	109	2.85	97	.251	.292	116-1-1	.276	8*	107	2	—	1.1
1903	Det A	15	16	.484	31	28	28-2	0	257.2	277	112	8	5	38	102	2.58	113	.274	.303	116-0-5	.181	-1*	118	8	—	0.7
1904	Det A	9	13	.409	26	24	19	0	199.2	211	100	7	7	38	69	3.07	83	.272	.312	72-1-1	.208	1*	110	-13	—	-1.3
1905	Det A	12	14	.462	33	27	21-3	1	225.2	230	120	3	11	57	78	3.47	79	.266	.319	87	.184	-1	80	-17	—	-2.1
1906	Was A	6	14	.300	30	21	15-1	0	197	196	97	2	6	57	59	3.65	72	.262	.320	90-1-0	.244	8*	101	-18	—	-0.8
1907	Was A	0	3	.000	5	3	2	0	32	41	20	1	2	9	11	3.94	61	.313	.366	10	.100	-0	84	-5	—	-0.6
	NY A	4	0	1.000	12	4	3	0	61	75	31	0	4	17	14	3.10	90	.305	.360	25-0-1	.280	1	163	-2	—	-0.1
	Year	4	3	.571	17	7	5	0	93	116	51	1	6	26	25	3.39	79	.308	.362	35-0-1	.229	0	130	-7	—	-0.7
Total	10	129	118	.522	304	250	211-19	7	2221.2	2331	1087	52	81	491	731	3.18	99	.270	.315	978-4-11	.240	27	100	2	—	2.3

YEAR	TM LG	W	L	PCT	G	GS	CG-SHO	SV-BS	IP	H	R	HR	HB	BB-IB	SO	ERA	AERA	OAV	OOB	AB-HR-SH	AVG	PB	SUP	APR	DL	PW
KLAERNER, HUGO	Hugo Emil "Dutch"; B10.15.1908 Fredericksburg TX; D2.3.1982 Fredericksburg TX; BR/TR/5´11˝/190; d9.10																									
1934	Chi A	0	2	.000	3	3	1	0	17.1	24	21	4	0	16	9	10.90	43	.329	.449	6	.333	1	98	-10	—	-0.7
KLAGES, FRED	Frederick Albert Anthony; B10.31.1943 Ambridge PA; BR/TR/6´2˝/(180–185); d9.11																									
1966	Chi A	1	0	1.000	3	3	0	0	15.2	9	4	0	0	7-0	6	1.72	184	.167	.262	6	.500	1	102	3	0	0.3
1967	Chi A	4	4	.500	11	9	0	0	44.2	43	19	6	1	16-1	17	3.83	81	.256	.323	12-0-1	.000	-1*	94	-2	0	-0.5
Total	2	5	4	.556	14	12	0	0	60.1	52	23	6	1	23-1	23	3.28	95	.234	.308	18-0-1	.167	-0	96	1	0	-0.2
KLAWITTER, AL	Albert Hermann "Dutch"; B3.29.1889 Wilkes–Barre PA; D5.2.1950 Milwaukee WI; BR/TR/5´11.5˝/187; d9.20																									
1909	NY N	1	1	.500	6	3	2	1	27	24	11	1	0	13	6	2.00	128	.247	.336	9	.333	1	173	1	—	0.3
1910	NY N	0	0	ø	1	0	0	0	1	2	1	0	0	2	0	9.00	33	.400	.571	0	ø	0	—	-1	—	0.0
1913	Det A	1	2	.333	8	3	1	0	32	39	25	0	0	15	10	5.91	49	.307	.380	11	.000	-2	144	-9	—	-0.9
Total	3	2	3	.400	15	6	3	1	60	65	37	1	0	30	16	4.20	66	.284	.367	20	.150	-0	157	-9	—	-0.6
KLAWITTER, TOM	Thomas Carl; B6.24.1958 LaCrosse WI; BR/TL/6´2˝/195; [LAN80 19/477]; d4.14; Col Wisconsin–La Crosse																									
1985	Min A	0	0	ø	7	2	0	0-0	9.1	7	7	2	0	13-0	5	6.75	66	.226	.455	0	ø	0	154	-2	100	-0.1
KLEINE, HAL	Harold John; B6.8.1923 St.Louis MO; D12.10.1957 St.Louis MO; BL/TL/6´2˝/193; d4.26																									
1944	Cle A	1	2	.333	11	6	1	0	40.2	38	29	0	0	36	13	5.75	57	.248	.392	14-0-1	.143	-1*	110	-11	0	-0.8
1945	Cle A	0	0	ø	3	0	0	0	7	8	4	0	0	7	5	3.86	84	.286	.429	3	.333	1	—	-1	0	0.0
Total	2	1	2	.333	14	6	1	0	47.2	46	33	0	0	43	18	5.48	60	.254	.397	17-0-1	.176	-0	110	-12	0	-0.8
KLEINHANS, TED	Theodore Otto (b Traugott Otto Kleinhans); B4.8.1899 Deer Park WI; D7.24.1985 Redington Beach FL; BR/TL/6´0˝/170; d4.20																									
1934	Phi N	0	0	ø	5	0	0	0	6	11	8	1	0	3	2	9.00	52	.379	.438	1	.000	-0	—	-3	—	-0.1
	Cin N	2	6	.250	24	9	0	0	80	107	63	2	1	38	23	5.74	71	.321	.392	23-0-2	.130	-1*	61	-15	—	-1.3
	Year	2	6	.250	29	9	0	0	86	118	71	3	1	41	25	5.97	69	.326	.396	24-0-2	.125	-1	60	-19	—	-1.4
1936	NY A	1	1	.500	19	0	0	1	29.1	36	25	0	0	23	10	5.83	80	.300	.413	6	.167	-0	—	-6	—	-0.4
1937	Cin N	1	2	.333	7	3	1	0	27.1	29	13	1	1	12	13	2.30	162	.271	.350	8	.250	0	85	2	—	0.2
1938	Cin N	0	0	ø	1	0	0	0	1	2	1	0	0	0	0	9.00	41	.400	.400	0	ø	0	—	-1	—	0.0
Total	4	4	9	.308	56	12	1	1	143.2	185	110	4	2	76	48	5.26	79	.311	.391	38-0-2	.158	-1	64	-23	—	-1.6
KLEINKE, NUB	Norbert George; B5.19.1911 Fond Du Lac WI; D3.16.1950 Off Marin Coast CA; BR/TR/6´1˝/170; d4.25																									
1935	StL N	0	0	ø	4	2	0	0	12.2	19	8	1	0	3	5	4.97	82	.358	.393	2	.000	-0	155	-1	—	-0.1
1937	StL N	1	1	.500	5	2	1	0	20.2	25	14	0	0	7	9	4.79	83	.321	.376	8	.000	-1	141	-2	—	-0.3
Total	2	1	1	.500	9	4	1	0	33.1	44	22	1	0	10	14	4.86	83	.336	.383	10	.000	-1	149	-3	—	-0.4
KLEPFER, ED	Edward Lloyd "Big Ed"; B3.17.1888 Summerville PA; D8.9.1950 Tulsa OK; BR/TR/6´0˝/185; d7.4; Mil 1918; Col Penn St.																									
1911	NY A	0	0	ø	2	0	0	0	4	5	3	0	0	2	4	6.75	53	.250	.318	1	.000	-0	—	-1	—	-0.1
1913	NY A	0	1	.000	8	1	0	0	24.2	38	22	2	2	12	10	7.66	39	.376	.452	6	.167	0	0	-10	—	-0.5
1915	Chi A	1	0	1.000	3	2	1	0	12.2	11	4	0	0	5	3	2.84	105	.234	.308	3	.000	-0	122	1	—	0.0
	Cle A	1	6	.143	8	7	2	0	43	47	25	0	0	11	13	2.09	146	.283	.328	12-0-1	.167	-0	79	1	—	0.1
	Year	2	6	.250	11	9	3	0	55.2	58	29	0	0	16	16	2.26	134	.272	.323	15-0-1	.133	-0	88	1	—	0.1
1916	Cle A	6	6	.500	31	13	4-1	2	143	136	52	0	4	46	62	2.52	119	.262	.327	40-0-2	.025	-4	79	8	—	0.2
1917	Cle A	14	4	.778	41	27	9	1	213	208	84	0	0	55	66	2.37	120	.264	.312	62-0-5	.032	-6	109	8	—	-0.1
1919	Cle A	0	0	ø	5	0	0	0	7.1	12	14	1	0	6	7	7.36	45	.375	.474	1	.000	-0	—	-5	—	-0.3
Total	6	22	17	.564	98	50	16-1	3	447.2	457	204	3	6	137	165	2.81	104	.273	.330	125-0-8	.048	-11	95	2	—	-0.7
KLIEMAN, ED	Edward Frederick "Specs","Babe"; B3.21.1918 Norwood OH; D11.15.1979 Homosassa FL; BR/TR/6´1˝/190; d9.24																									
1943	Cle A	0	1	.000	1	1	1	0	9	8	1	0	0	5	2	1.00	311	.286	.394	3	.000	-0	0	2	0	0.2
1944	Cle A	11	13	.458	47	19	5-1	5	178.1	185	73	4	7	70	44	3.38	98	.274	.348	57-0-2	.105	-3	125	1	0	-0.2
1945	Cle A	5	8	.385	38	12	4-1	4	126.1	123	60	3	4	49	33	3.85	84	.261	.336	40-1-2	.200	1	76	-8	0	-0.6
1946	Cle A	0	0	ø	9	0	0	0	15	18	13	0	0	10	2	6.60	50	.290	.389	1	.000	-0	—	-6	0	-0.4
1947	Cle A	5	4	.556	**58**	0	0	**17**	92	78	32	5	2	39	21	3.03	115	.231	.315	19-0-1	.105	-1	—	6	0	0.8
1948	†Cle A	3	2	.600	44	0	0	4	79.2	62	26	3	2	46	18	2.60	156	.229	.345	14	.143	-0	—	**14**	0	0.9
1949	Was A	0	0	ø	2	0	0	0	3	8	6	0	0	3	1	18.00	24	.500	.579	1	1.000	0	—	-4	0	-0.2
	Chi A	2	0	1.000	18	0	0	3	33	33	15	2	0	15	9	3.00	139	.273	.353	8-0-2	.250	0	—	3	0	0.3
	Year	2	0	1.000	20	0	0	3	36	41	21	2	0	18	10	4.25	98	.299	.381	9-0-2	.333	1	—	-1	0	0.1
1950	Phi A	0	0	ø	5	0	0	0	5.2	10	6	0	2	2	0	9.53	48	.357	.438	1	.000	-0	—	-3	0	-0.2
Total	8	26	28	.481	222	32	10-2	33	542	525	232	17	17	239	130	3.49	100	.261	.345	144-1-7	.146	-3	100	5	0	0.6
KLIMKOWSKI, RON	Ronald Bernard; B3.1.1944 Jersey City NJ; BR/TR/6´2˝/(186–195); d9.15; Col Morehead St.																									
1969	NY A	0	0	ø	3	1	0	0-0	14	6	1	0	0	5-1	3	0.64	548	.130	.212	3	.000	-0	0	5	0	0.2
1970	NY A	6	7	.462	45	3	1-1	1-1	98.1	80	36	7	3	33-7	40	2.65	135	.223	.293	19-0-4	.053	-2	133	9	0	1.0
1971	Oak A	2	2	.500	26	0	0	2-0	45.1	37	19	3	1	23-8	25	3.38	99	.220	.316	5	.400	1	—	0	0	0.1
1972	NY A	0	3	.000	16	2	0	1-0	31.1	32	15	3	1	15-7	11	4.02	74	.271	.356	6	.000	-1	30	-3	0	-0.4
Total	4	8	12	.400	90	6	1-1	4-1	189	155	71	13	5	76-23	79	2.90	118	.224	.304	33-0-4	.091	-2	78	11	0	0.9
KLINE, BOB	Robert George "Junior"; B12.9.1909 Enterprise OH; D3.16.1987 Westerville OH; BR/TR/6´3˝/200; d9.17																									
1930	Bos A	0	0	ø	1	0	0	0	1	1	0	0	0	0	0	0.00	ø	.333	.333	0	ø	0	—	1	—	0.0
1931	Bos A	5	5	.500	28	10	3	0	98	110	54	3	3	35	25	4.41	98	.298	.364	27-0-1	.333	2	102	-1	—	0.3
1932	Bos A	11	13	.458	47	19	4-1	2	172	203	117	10	1	76	31	5.28	85	.294	.365	54-0-4	.130	-3	78	-13	—	-1.7
1933	Bos A	7	8	.467	46	8	1	4	127	127	70	5	6	67	16	4.54	97	.265	.362	34-0-3	.176	-1	104	0	—	0.1
1934	Phi A	6	2	.750	20	0	0	1	39.2	50	34	6	0	13	14	6.35	69	.314	.366	9-0-1	.333	1	—	-10	—	-1.5
	Was A	1	0	1.000	6	0	0	0	4	10	8	0	1	4	1	15.75	27	.500	.600	0	ø	0	—	-5	—	-0.9
	Year	7	2	.778	26	0	0	1	43.2	60	42	6	1	17	15	7.21	61	.335	.396	9-0-1	.333	1	—	-15	—	-2.4
Total	5	30	28	.517	148	37	8-1	7	441.2	501	283	24	11	195	87	5.05	87	.291	.367	124-0-9	.202	-1	90	-28	—	-3.7
KLINE, RON	Ronald Lee; B3.9.1932 Callery PA; D6.22.2002 Callery PA; BR/TR/6´3˝/(190–210); d4.21; Mil 1953–54																									
1952	Pit N	0	7	.000	27	11	0	0	78.2	74	55	3	6	66	27	5.49	73	.253	.401	19	.000	-2	67	-13	0	-1.3
1955	Pit N	6	13	.316	36	19	2-1	2	136.2	161	78	13	5	53-5	48	4.15	99	.298	.363	38-0-1	.132	-2*	60	-3	0	-0.5
1956	Pit N	14	18	.438	44	39	9-2	2	264	263	110	26	5	81-8	125	3.38	112	.263	.319	79-0-5	.127	-3	80	13	0	1.2
1957	Pit N	9	16	.360	40	31	11-2	0	205	214	107	27	1	61-6	88	4.04	94	.268	.319	66-0-3	.061	-6	79	-6	0	-1.3
1958	Pit N	13	16	.448	32	32	11-2	0	237.1	220	96	25	0	92-14	109	3.53	110	.252	.321	74-0-9	.027	-6*	74	13	0	0.8
1959	Pit N	11	13	.458	33	29	7	0	186	186	95	23	2	70-9	91	4.26	91	.263	.329	59-0-5	.136	-2*	99	-6	0	-0.9
1960	StL N	4	9	.308	34	17	1	1	117.2	133	86	21	0	43-5	54	6.04	68	.284	.341	35-0-1	.143	-2	75	-23	0	-2.4
1961	LA A	3	6	.333	26	12	0	1	104.2	119	62	16	1	44-5	70	4.90	92	.288	.357	31-0-3	.097	-2	83	-3	0	-0.4
	Det A	5	3	.625	10	8	3-1	0	56.1	53	25	3	0	17-1	27	2.72	151	.245	.297	18-0-3	.167	0	92	6	0	0.8
	Year	8	9	.471	36	20	3-1	1	161	172	87	19	1	61-6	97	4.14	106	.273	.336	49-0-6	.122	-2	86	2	0	0.4
1962	Det A	3	6	.333	36	4	0	2	77.1	88	40	9	2	28-2	47	4.31	94	.284	.347	16-0-1	.125	-1	27	-1	0	-0.2
1963	Was A	3	8	.273	62	1	0	17	93.2	85	36	3	3	30-7	49	2.79	133	.249	.312	11	.091	-0	72	8	0	1.2
1964	Was A	10	7	.588	61	0	0	14	81.1	81	29	4	2	21-9	40	2.32	159	.262	.310	6-0-2	.167	0	—	10	0	2.2
1965	Was A	7	6	.538	74	0	0	**29**	99.1	106	36	7	2	32-14	52	2.63	132	.275	.329	7-0-3	.000	-1	—	8	0	1.4
1966	Was A	6	4	.600	63	0	0	23	90.1	79	32	12	0	17-7	46	2.39	145	.237	.274	6	.167	0	—	8	0	1.3
1967	Min A	7	1	.875	54	0	0	5	71.2	71	33	10	1	15-7	36	3.77	92	.261	.302	5-0-1	.000	-1	—	-2	0	-0.3
1968	Pit N	12	5	.706	56	0	0	7	112.2	94	26	3	2	31-11	48	1.68	174	.234	.291	16-0-1	.000	-1	—	**15**	0	2.5
1969	Pit N	1	3	.250	20	0	0	3-2	31	37	23	3	1	5-2	15	5.81	60	.296	.326	5-0-1	.000	-1	—	-9	0	-1.3
	SF N	0	2	.000	7	0	0	0-2	11	16	6	1	0	6-3	7	4.09	86	.364	.440	0	ø	0	—	-1	0	-0.1
	Year	1	5	.167	27	0	0	3-4	42	53	29	4	1	11-5	22	5.36	65	.314	.357	5-0-1	.000	-1	—	-9	0	-1.4
	Bos A	0	1	.000	16	0	0	1-1	17	24	11	4	0	17-3	7	4.76	80	.329	.451	0	ø	0	—	-2	0	-0.1
1970	Atl N	0	0	ø	5	0	0	1-0	6.1	9	5	4	0	2-0	3	7.11	60	.321	.367	0	ø	0	—	-2	0	-0.1
Total	17	114	144	.442	736	203	44-8	108-5	2078	2113	991	217	33	731-118	989	3.75	101	.266	.329	491-0-39	.092	-28	81	10	0	2.5
KLINE, STEVE	Steven Jack; B10.6.1947 Wenatchee WA; BR/TR/6´3˝/(196–205); [NYA66 7/130]; d7.10; [DL 1975 Cle A 175]																									
1970	NY A	6	6	.500	16	15	5	0-0	100.1	99	42	8	0	24-3	49	3.41	105	.254	.296	28-0-4	.179	1	88	3	0	0.5
1971	NY A	12	13	.480	31	30	15-1	0-0	222.1	206	87	21	0	37-7	81	2.96	111	.244	.275	66-0-5	.136	-0	95	7	0	0.9
1972	NY A	16	9	.640	32	32	11-4	0-0	236.1	210	79	11	10	44-6	58	2.40	125	.237	.279	76-0-12	.092	-3	101	13	0	1.2

YEAR	TM LG	W	L	PCT	G	GS	CG-SHO	SV-BS	IP	H	R	HR	HB	BB-IB	SO	ERA	AERA	OAV	OOB	AB-HR-SH	AVG	PB	SUP	APR	DL	PW
1973	NY A	4	7	.364	14	13	2-1	0-0	74	76	39	5	1	31-3	19	4.01	92	.270	.342	0	ø	0	85	-3	92	-0.4
1974	NY A	2	2	.500	4	4	0	0-0	26	26	12	3	1	5-0	6	3.46	102	.263	.305	0	ø	0	99	0	0	0.0
	Cle A	3	8	.273	16	11	1	0-0	71	70	44	9	4	31-2	17	5.07	72	.266	.350	0	ø	0	64	-11	46	-1.4
	Year	5	10	.333	20	15	1	0-0	97	96	56	12	5	36-2	23	4.64	78	.265	.338	0	ø	0	73	-12	0	-1.4
1977	Atl N	0	0	ø	16	0	0	1-0	20.1	21	15	4	0	12-3	10	6.64	67	.259	.355	0	ø	0	—	-4	0	-0.2
Total	6	43	45	.489	129	105	34-6	1-0	750.1	708	318	61	16	184-24	240	3.26	103	.249	.297	170-0-21	.124	-2	91	5	313	0.6
Kline, Steve	Steven James; B8.22.1972 Sunbury PA; BB/TL/6´2˝/(200–240); [CleA93 8/223]; d4.2; Col West Virginia																									
1997	Cle A	3	1	.750	20	1	0	0-2	26.1	42	19	6	1	13-1	17	5.81	81	.365	.434	0	ø	0	59	-3	0	-0.5
	Mon N	1	3	.250	26	0	0	0-1	26.1	31	18	4	1	10-3	20	6.15	68	.304	.365	1	.000	-0	—	-5	0	-0.7
1998	Mon N	3	6	.333	78	0	0	1-1	71.2	62	25	4	3	41-7	76	2.76	152	.228	.333	4-0-1	.000	-0	—	11	0	1.3
1999	Mon N	7	4	.636	**82**	0	0	0-2	69.2	56	32	8	3	33-6	69	3.75	119	.218	.313	1-0-1	.000	-0	—	6	16	0.9
2000	Mon N	1	5	.167	**83**	0	0	14-4	82.1	88	36	8	3	27-2	64	3.50	135	.278	.340	2	.000	-0	—	11	0	1.0
2001	†StL N	3	3	.500	**89**	0	0	9-1	75	53	16	3	4	29-7	54	1.80	240	.203	.288	2	.500	0	—	21	0	2.0
2002	†StL N	2	1	.667	66	0	0	6-2	58.1	54	23	3	1	21-2	41	3.39	119	.251	.318	1	.000	-0	—	5	32	0.3
2003	StL N	5	5	.500	78	0	0	3-4	63.2	56	29	5	3	30-5	31	3.82	108	.237	.328	2-0-1	.500	1	—	2	0	0.4
2004	†StL N	2	2	.500	67	0	0	3-1	50.1	37	12	3	4	17-4	35	1.79	238	.209	.291	0-0-1	ø	0	—	13	32	1.1
2005	Bal A	2	4	.333	67	0	0	0-3	61	59	34	11	0	30-5	36	4.28	103	.257	.340	0	ø	0	—	0	0	0.1
2006	SF N	4	3	.571	72	0	0	1-0	51.2	53	24	3	1	26-3	33	3.66	121	.275	.362	0	ø	0	—	4	0	0.5
Total	10	33	37	.471	728	1	0	37-21	636.1	591	268	58	24	277-45	476	3.42	127	.249	.331	13-0-4	.154	0	59	65	80	6.4
Kling, Bill	William; B1.14.1867 Kansas City MO; D8.26.1934 Kansas City MO; BL/TR/6´0˝/190; d8.13; b–Johnny																									
1891	Phi N	4	2	.667	12	7	4	0	75	91	61	2	2	32	26	4.32	79	.289	.358	31	.194	1*	153	-10	—	-0.6
1892	Bal N	0	2	.000	2	2	0	0	11	17	16	1	2	7	7	11.45	30	.340	.441	4	.250	1	111	-7	—	-0.8
1895	Lou N	0	0	ø	1	0	0	0	1	0	0	0	0	1	0	0.00	ø	.000	.250	1	.000	-0	—	1	—	0.0
Total	3	4	4	.500	15	9	4	0	87	108	77	3	4	40	33	5.17	66	.293	.369	36	.194	1	143	-16	—	-1.4
Klingenbeck, Scott	Scott Edward; B2.3.1971 Cincinnati OH; BR/TR/6´2˝/205; [BalA92 5/128]; d6.2; Col Ohio St.																									
1994	Bal A	1	0	1.000	1	1	0	0-0	7	6	4	1	1	4-1	5	3.86	131	.240	.355	0	ø	0	200	0	0	0.1
1995	Bal A	2	2	.500	6	5	0	0-0	31.1	32	17	6	0	18-0	15	4.88	98	.269	.365	0	ø	0	97	0	0	0.0
	Min A	0	2	.000	18	4	0	0-0	48.1	69	48	16	4	24-0	27	8.57	56	.338	.416	0	ø	0	92	-19	0	-0.9
	Year	2	4	.333	24	9	0	0-0	79.2	101	65	22	4	42-0	42	7.12	67	.313	.397	0	ø	0	95	-19	0	-0.9
1996	Min A	1	1	.500	10	3	0	0-1	28.2	42	28	5	1	10-0	15	7.85	65	.339	.390	0	ø	0	169	-9	0	-0.5
1998	Cin N	1	3	.250	4	4	0	0-0	22.2	26	17	6	1	7-0	13	5.96	72	.286	.340	6	.000	-1	75	-5	0	-0.7
Total	4	5	8	.385	39	17	0	0-1	138	175	114	34	7	63-1	75	6.91	69	.311	.385	6	.000	-1	110	-33	0	-2.0
Klinger, Bob	Robert Harold; B6.4.1908 Allenton MO; D8.19.1977 Villa Ridge MO; BR/TR/6´0˝/180; d4.19; Mil 1944–45																									
1938	Pit N	12	5	.706	28	21	10-1	1	159.1	152	63	7	6	42	58	2.99	127	.253	.308	60-0-1	.167	-2	119	14	—	1.2
1939	Pit N	14	17	.452	37	33	10-2	0	225	251	120	11	3	81	64	4.36	88	.284	.346	84-0-1	.202	0	112	-11	—	-1.2
1940	Pit N	8	13	.381	39	22	3	3	142	196	102	5	5	53	48	5.39	71	.329	.388	42-0-1	.143	-2	85	-26	—	-3.6
1941	Pit N	9	4	.692	35	9	3	4	116.2	127	58	5	1	30	36	3.93	92	.276	.322	32-0-1	.250	2	123	-3	0	-0.1
1942	Pit N	8	11	.421	37	19	8-1	1	152.2	151	69	6	3	45	58	3.24	104	.252	.307	40-0-5	.200	1	107	0	0	0.3
1943	Pit N	11	8	.579	33	25	14-3	0	195	185	77	6	0	58	65	2.72	128	.252	.307	65-0-4	.246	3	121	15	0	1.7
1946	†Bos A	3	2	.600	28	1	0	**9**	57	49	16	1	1	25	16	2.37	155	.238	.323	16-0-3	.313	1	47	8	0	1.1
1947	Bos A	1	1	.500	28	0	0	5	42	42	20	5	1	24	12	3.86	101	.253	.351	9-0-2	.111	-1	—	0	0	-0.1
Total	8	66	61	.520	265	130	48-7	23	1089.2	1153	525	46	20	358	357	3.68	100	.271	.331	348-0-18	.204	3	110	-3	0	-0.7
Klink, Joe	Joseph Charles; B2.3.1962 Johnstown PA; BL/TL/5´11˝/(170–175); [NYN83 36/801]; d4.9; Col St. Thomas (FL); [DL 1992 Oak A 182]																									
1987	Min A	0	1	.000	12	0	0	0-0	23	37	18	4	0	11-0	17	6.65	70	.359	.417	0	ø	0	—	-5	0	-0.2
1990	†Oak A	0	0	ø	40	0	0	1-0	39.2	34	9	1	0	18-0	19	2.04	183	.233	.317	0	ø	0	—	8	0	0.4
1991	Oak A	10	3	.769	62	0	0	2-2	62	60	30	4	5	21-5	34	4.35	89	.259	.333	0	ø	0	—	-3	35	-0.5
1993	Fla N	0	2	.000	59	0	0	0-0	37.2	37	22	0	0	24-4	22	5.02	87	.266	.367	2-0-1	.000	-0	—	-2	0	-0.2
1996	Sea A	0	0	ø	3	0	0	0-0	2.1	3	1	1	0	1-0	2	3.86	129	.300	.364	0	ø	0	—	0	0	0.0
Total	5	10	6	.625	176	0	0	3-2	164.2	171	80	10	5	75-9	94	4.26	95	.271	.352	2-0-1	.000	-0	—	-2	217	-0.5
Klippstein, Johnny	John Calvin; B10.17.1927 Washington DC; D10.10.2003 Elgin IL; BR/TR/6´1˝/(170–190); d5.3																									
1950	Chi N	2	9	.182	33	11	3	1	104.2	112	69	9	4	64	51	5.25	80	.279	.383	33-1-0	.333	4*	80	-11	0	-0.6
1951	Chi N	6	6	.500	35	11	1-1	2	123.2	125	71	10	6	53	56	4.29	95	.263	.344	37-1-0	.108	-2	65	-5	0	-0.6
1952	Chi N	9	14	.391	41	25	7-2	3	202.2	208	110	17	6	89	110	4.44	87	.265	.344	63-1-7	.175	1	83	-11	0	-1.0
1953	Chi N	10	11	.476	48	19	5	6	167.2	169	115	15	8	107	113	4.83	92	.258	.369	58-1-3	.155	-1	88	-11	0	-1.5
1954	Chi N	4	11	.267	36	21	4	1	148	155	104	13	4	96	69	5.29	79	.272	.373	45-0-2	.133	-2	101	-20	0	-2.0
1955	Cin N	9	10	.474	39	14	3-2	0	138	120	66	13	4	60-5	68	3.39	125	.233	.317	31-0-4	.065	-2	90	10	0	1.0
1956	Cin N	12	11	.522	37	29	11	1	211	219	103	26	10	82-13	86	4.09	97	.275	.346	71-0-8	.099	-4	110	-1	0	-0.5
1957	Cin N	8	11	.421	46	18	3-1	3	146	146	84	17	3	68-6	99	5.05	81	.261	.342	41-0-2	.073	-3	86	-12	0	-1.8
1958	Cin N	3	2	.600	12	4	0	1	33	37	20	5	1	14-1	22	4.91	84	.285	.356	8-0-1	.125	-0	76	-3	0	-0.5
	LA N	3	5	.375	45	0	0	9	90	81	40	12	2	44-8	73	3.80	108	.248	.338	20-0-1	.050	-2	—	4	0	0.2
	Year	6	7	.462	57	4	0	10	123	118	60	17	3	58-9	95	4.10	100	.259	.343	28-0-2	.071	-2	76	1	0	-0.3
1959	†LA N	4	0	1.000	28	0	0	2	45.2	48	31	8	2	33-5	30	5.91	72	.276	.392	7	.143	-0	—	-7	0	-0.6
1960	Cle A	5	5	.500	49	0	0	**14**	74.1	53	30	8	1	35-3	46	2.91	129	.205	.302	14-0-2	.143	-0	—	6	0	1.0
1961	Was A	2	2	.500	42	1	0	0	71.2	83	59	13	4	43-1	41	6.78	59	.297	.395	7	.143	-0	66	-21	0	-1.0
1962	Cin N	7	6	.538	40	7	0	4	108.2	113	66	13	4	64-5	67	4.47	90	.278	.377	24-1-1	.125	0	72	-8	0	-0.8
1963	Phi N	5	6	.455	49	1	0	8	112	80	28	3	3	46-9	86	1.93	168	.204	.291	26-0-2	.038	-2	53	16	0	1.6
1964	Phi N	2	1	.667	11	0	0	1	22.1	22	10	6	2	8-1	13	4.03	86	.250	.327	4	.000	-0	—	-1	0	-0.1
	Min A	0	4	.000	33	0	0	2	45.2	44	12	4	1	20-7	39	1.97	181	.260	.340	2	.000	0	—	8	0	0.8
1965	†Min A	9	3	.750	56	0	0	5	76.1	59	22	8	3	31-4	59	2.24	159	.217	.302	8-0-2	.000	-1	—	11	0	1.7
1966	Min A	1	1	.500	26	0	0	3	39.2	35	15	2	2	20-2	26	3.40	106	.238	.335	3	.000	-0	—	2	0	0.1
1967	Det A	0	0	ø	5	0	0	0	6.2	6	4	1	0	1-0	4	5.40	60	.250	.269	0	ø	0	—	-1	0	-0.1
Total	18	101	118	.461	711	161	37-6	66	1967.2	1915	1059	203	70	978-70	1158	4.24	94	.258	.347	502-5-35	.125	-14	92	-55	0	-4.7
Klobedanz, Fred	Frederick Augustus "Duke"; B6.13.1871 Waterbury CT; D4.12.1940 Waterbury CT; BL/TL/5´11˝/190; d8.20																									
1896	Bos N	6	4	.600	10	9	9	0	80.2	69	41	5	7	31	26	3.01	151	.229	.316	41-2-0	.317	2*	115	14	—	1.5
1897	†Bos N	26	7	**.788**	38	37	30-2	0	309.1	344	198	13	23	125	92	4.60	97	.279	.357	148-1-3	.324	9*	129	2	—	0.8
1898	Bos N	19	10	.655	35	33	25	0	270.2	281	168	13	12	99	51	3.89	95	.266	.336	127-3-6	.213	0*	116	-8	—	-0.8
1899	Bos N	1	4	.200	5	5	4	0	33.1	39	22	2	2	9	8	4.86	86	.291	.345	11-1-0	.182	1	69	-2	—	-0.1
1902	Bos N	1	0	1.000	1	1	1	0	8	9	1	0	1	2	4	1.13	251	.281	.343	2-0-1	.500	1	289	2	—	0.3
Total	5	53	25	.679	89	85	69-2	0	702	742	430	33	45	266	181	4.12	101	.269	.343	329-7-10	.277	13	120	8	—	1.7
Klopp, Stan	Stanley Harold "Betz"; B12.22.1910 Womelsdorf PA; D3.11.1980 Robesonia PA; BR/TR/6´1.5˝/180; d4.29																									
1944	Bos N	1	2	.333	24	0	0	0	46.1	47	36	1	0	33	17	4.27	89	.272	.388	7	.286	0	—	-6	0	-0.4
Knackert, Brent	Brent Bradley; B8.1.1969 Los Angeles CA; BR/TR/6´3˝/(185–195); [ChiA87 2/37]; d4.10																									
1990	Sea A	1	1	.500	24	2	0	0-0	37.1	50	28	5	2	21-2	28	6.51	61	.313	.395	0	ø	0	57	-9	0	-0.5
1996	Bos A	0	1	.000	8	0	0	0-0	10	16	12	1	0	7-1	5	9.00	57	.356	.434	0	ø	0	—	-5	0	-0.3
Total	2	1	2	.333	32	2	0	0-0	47.1	66	40	6	2	28-3	33	7.04	60	.322	.403	0	ø	0	57	-14	0	-0.8
Knapp, Chris	Robert Christian; B9.16.1953 Cherry Point NC; BR/TR/6´5˝/200; [ChiA75 1/11]; d9.4; Col Central Michigan																									
1975	Chi A	0	0	ø	2	0	0	0-0	2	2	1	0	0	4-0	3	4.50	86	.250	.500	0	ø	0	—	0	0	0.0
1976	Chi A	3	1	.750	11	6	1	0-0	52.1	54	31	5	1	32-1	41	4.82	74	.273	.375	0	ø	0	131	-7	0	-0.5
1977	Chi A	12	7	.632	27	26	4	0-0	146.1	166	90	16	7	61-1	103	4.80	85	.283	.355	0	ø	0	116	-12	0	-1.4
1978	Cal A	14	8	.636	30	29	6	0-0	188.1	178	94	25	2	67-6	126	4.21	86	.250	.313	0	ø	0	112	-10	0	-1.2
1979	†Cal A	5	5	.500	20	18	3	0-0	98	109	73	8	2	35-1	36	5.51	74	.275	.334	0	ø	0	155	-19	52	-1.6
1980	Cal A	2	11	.154	32	20	1	1-0	117.1	133	83	18	8	51-1	46	6.14	65	.289	.365	0	ø	0	95	-26	0	-2.6
Total	6	36	32	.529	122	99	15	1-0	604.1	642	372	72	20	250-10	355	4.99	78	.272	.344	0	ø	0	119	-74	52	-7.3

YEAR	TM LG	W	L	PCT	G	GS	CG-SHO	SV-BS	IP	H	R	HR	HB	BB-IB	SO	ERA	AERA	OAV	OOB	AB-HR-SH	AVG	PB	SUP	APR	DL	PW
Knauss, Frank	Frank H.; B1868 Cleveland OH; BL/TL/5´10˝/170; d6.25																									
1890	Col AA	17	12	.586	37	34	28-3	2	275.2	206	131	3	21	106	148	2.81	128	**.202**	.290	106-1	.226	5	111	26	—	2.7
1891	Cle N	0	3	.000	3	3	1	0	15	23	29	2	4	8	6	7.20	48	.338	.438	6	.167	-0	115	-8	—	-1.1
1892	Cin N	0	0	ø	1	0	0	0	8	13	9	0	0	5	2	3.38	97	.351	.429	3	.333	0	—	-2	—	0.0
1894	Cle N	0	1	.000	2	2	1	0	11	7	9	0	3	14	2	5.73	96	.179	.429	4-0-1	.000	-1	129	0	—	0.0
1895	NY N	0	0	ø	1	1	0	0	3.2	9	7	0	0	2	1	17.18	27	.450	.500	1	.000	-0	153	-4	—	-0.2
Total	5	17	16	.515	44	40	30-3	2	313.1	258	185	5	28	135	159	3.30	111	.218	.312	120-1-1	.217	4	115	12	—	1.4
Kneisch, Rudy	Rudolph Frank; B4.10.1899 Baltimore MD; D4.6.1965 Baltimore MD; BR/TL/5´10.5˝/175; d9.21																									
1926	Det A	0	1	.000	2	2	1	0	17	18	7	2	2	6	4	2.65	153	.273	.351	5	.000	-1	73	2	—	0.1
Knell, Phil	Philip Louis; B3.12.1865 San Francisco CA; D6.5.1944 Santa Monica CA; BR/TL/5´7.5˝/154; d7.6																									
1888	Pit N	1	2	.333	3	3	3	0	26.1	20	19	1	5	18	15	3.76	70	.217	.374	11	.091	-1	77	-4	—	-0.5
1890	Phi P	22	11	.667	35	31	30-2	0	286.2	287	199	10	28	166	99	3.83	112	.249	.358	132-1	.220	-1*	124	14	—	1.1
1891	Col AA	28	27	.509	58	52	47-**5**	0	462	363	228	4	54	226	228	2.92	118	**.209**	.319	215	.158	-9*	84	30	—	2.2
1892	Was N	9	13	.409	22	21	17-1	0	170	156	114	4	11	76	74	3.65	89	.234	.323	68	.118	-5	90	-6	—	-1.1
	Phi N	5	5	.500	11	9	7	0	80	87	47	0	11	35	43	4.05	80	.266	.357	34	.088	-3	100	-5	—	-0.8
	Year	14	18	.438	33	30	24-1	0	250	243	161	4	22	111	117	3.78	86	.245	.334	102	.108	-7	93	-9	—	-1.9
1894	Pit N	0	0	ø	1	0	0	0	7	11	9	0	1	6	0	11.57	45	.355	.474	3	.000	-1	—	-4	—	-0.2
	Lou N	7	21	.250	32	28	25	0	247	330	237	8	14	104	67	5.32	96	.317	.387	113-1-1	.274	0	73	-12	—	-1.0
	Year	7	21	.250	33	28	25	0	254	341	246	8	15	110	67	5.49	93	.318	.389	116-1-1	.267	-0	73	-20	—	-1.2
1895	Lou N	0	6	.000	10	6	3	0	56.2	75	66	3	6	21	19	6.51	71	.314	.383	26	.231	0	108	-14	—	-1.0
	Cle N	7	5	.583	20	13	9	0	116.2	149	100	7	6	53	30	5.40	92	.306	.381	55-0-1	.200	-3	105	-5	—	-0.6
	Year	7	11	.389	30	19	12	0	173.1	224	166	10	12	74	49	5.76	85	.309	.382	81-0-1	.210	-3	106	-19	—	-1.6
Total	6	79	90	.467	192	163	141-8	0	1452.1	1478	1019	37	136	705	575	4.05	99	.256	.351	657-2-2	.187	-20	94	-6	—	-1.9
Knepper, Charlie	Charles; B2.18.1871 Anderson IN; D2.6.1946 Muncie IN; BR/TR/6´4˝/190; d5.26																									
1899	Cle N	4	22	.154	27	26	26	0	219.2	307	190	11	15	77	43	5.78	64	.329	.390	89	.135	-5	74	-51	—	-4.9
Knepper, Bob	Robert Wesley; B5.25.1954 Akron OH; BL/TL/6´2˝/(190–210); [SFN72 2/43]; d9.10																									
1976	SF N	1	2	.333	4	4	0	0-0	25	26	9	0	0	7-1	11	3.24	112	.277	.327	9	.111	-0	79	2	0	0.2
1977	SF N	11	9	.550	27	27	6-2	0-0	166	151	73	14	3	72-2	100	3.36	117	.242	.321	55-0-5	.182	1	102	10	0	1.3
1978	SF N	17	11	.607	36	35	16-**6**	0-0	260	218	85	10	4	85-11	147	2.63	132	.229	.292	79-0-8	.063	-3	92	25	0	2.2
1979	SF N	9	12	.429	34	34	6-2	0-0	207.1	241	117	30	3	77-8	123	4.64	75	.289	.350	66-1-9	.182	3*	121	-27	0	-2.1
1980	SF N	9	16	.360	35	33	8-1	0-0	215.1	242	114	15	8	61-10	103	4.10	86	.281	.333	66-0-9	.152	-0	95	-15	0	-1.5
1981	†Hou N★	9	5	.643	22	22	6-5	0-0	156.2	128	41	5	4	38-1	75	2.18	150	.226	.278	47-1-5	.149	1	78	21	0	2.0
1982	Hou N	5	15	.250	33	29	4	1-0	180	193	100	14	3	60-4	108	4.45	75	.278	.335	52-0-6	.058	-2	85	-24	0	-2.6
1983	Hou N	6	13	.316	35	29	4-3	0-0	203	202	93	12	4	71-3	125	3.19	107	.261	.323	66-1-4	.182	3	90	1	0	0.5
1984	Hou N	15	10	.600	35	34	11-3	0-0	233.2	223	93	26	1	55-5	140	3.20	105	.251	.295	76-1-6	.171	4	126	6	0	1.0
1985	Hou N	15	13	.536	37	37	4	0-0	241	253	119	21	3	54-5	131	3.55	98	.271	.310	78-1-8	.141	0*	103	-6	0	-0.7
1986	†Hou N	17	12	.586	40	38	8-**5**	0-0	258	232	100	19	4	62-13	143	3.14	115	.242	.289	91-0-4	.099	-3*	103	14	0	1.3
1987	Hou N	8	17	.320	33	31	1	0-0	177.2	226	118	26	4	54-3	76	5.27	75	.313	.362	51-0-9	.098	-1	95	-29	0	-3.5
1988	Hou N★	14	5	.737	27	27	3-2	0-0	175	156	70	13	2	67-2	103	3.14	106	.243	.314	48-0-14	.125	-1	123	3	0	0.4
1989	Hou N	4	10	.286	22	20	0	0-1	113	135	78	12	2	60-4	45	5.89	58	.303	.386	31-1-2	.226	5	100	-30	0	-2.7
	SF N	3	2	.600	13	6	1-1	0-0	52	55	20	4	1	15-2	19	3.46	98	.270	.318	12-0-1	.083	1	105	1	0	0.1
	Year	7	12	.368	35	26	1-1	0-1	165	190	98	16	3	75-6	64	5.13	66	.292	.365	43-1-3	.186	6	101	-30	0	-2.6
1990	SF N	3	3	.500	12	7	0	0-0	44.1	56	28	7	1	19-4	24	5.68	64	.311	.376	13	.231	1	166	-9	0	-1.0
Total	15	146	155	.485	445	413	78-30	1-1	2708	2737	1258	228	47	857-78	1473	3.68	95	.264	.321	840-6-90	.137	7	103	-57	0	-5.1
Knerr, Lou	Wallace Luther; B8.21.1921 Strasburg PA; D3.23.1980 Denver PA; BR/TR/6´1˝/210; d4.17; Col Muhlenberg																									
1945	Phi A	5	11	.313	27	17	5	0	130	142	77	6	1	74	41	4.22	81	.283	.376	47-0-1	.191	-1*	72	-14	0	-1.8
1946	Phi A	3	16	.158	30	22	6	0	148.1	171	95	13	1	67	58	5.40	66	.288	.361	50-0-1	.180	0	75	-26	0	-3.0
1947	Was A	0	0	ø	6	0	0	0	9	17	13	1	0	8	5	11.00	34	.405	.500	1	1.000	0	—	-8	0	-0.3
Total	3	8	27	.229	63	39	11	0	287.1	330	185	20	2	149	104	5.04	69	.290	.373	98-0-2	.194	-1	73	-48	0	-5.1
Knetzer, Elmer	Elmer Ellsworth "Baron"; B7.22.1885 Carrick PA; D10.3.1975 Pittsburgh PA; BR/TR/5´10˝/180; d9.11																									
1909	Bro N	1	3	.250	5	4	3	0	35.2	33	22	2	0	22	7	3.03	86	.252	.359	12	.000	-2	61	-4	—	-0.6
1910	Bro N	7	5	.583	20	15	10-3	0	132.2	122	63	1	1	60	56	3.19	95	.255	.339	38-0-3	.053	-3	121	-3	—	-0.6
1911	Bro N	11	12	.478	35	20	11-3	0	204	202	101	1	1	93	66	3.49	96	.277	.359	62-0-5	.097	-4	85	-4	—	-0.8
1912	Bro N	7	9	.438	33	16	4-1	0	140.1	135	86	6	4	70	61	4.55	74	.254	.345	37-0-4	.135	-1	112	-15	—	-1.6
1914	Pit F	20	12	.625	37	30	20-3	1	272	257	123	9	2	88	146	2.88	100	.254	.315	91-0-9	.099	-8	113	-5	—	-1.4
1915	Pit F	18	14	.563	41	33	22-3	3	279	256	105	5	1	89	120	2.58	105	.251	.311	91-0-8	.132	-6	106	1	—	-0.6
1916	Bos N	0	2	.000	2	0	0	0	5	11	9	0	0	2	2	7.20	35	.524	.565	0	ø	0	—	-4	—	-0.7
	Cin N	5	12	.294	36	16	12	1	171.1	161	76	6	3	48	70	2.89	90	.252	.307	52-0-4	.154	-1*	92	-8	—	-0.8
	Year	5	14	.263	38	16	12	1	176.1	172	85	6	3	50	72	3.01	86	.261	.316	52-0-4	.154	-1	92	-12	—	-1.5
1917	Cin N	0	0	ø	11	0	0	1	27.1	29	18	0	2	12	7	2.96	88	.282	.368	3	.000	-0	—	-3	—	-0.2
Total	8	69	69	.500	220	134	82-13	6	1267.1	1206	603	30	14	484	535	3.15	93	.258	.330	386-0-33	.109	-24	104	-45	—	-7.3
Knight, Lon	Alonzo P.; B6.16.1853 Philadelphia PA; D4.23.1932 Philadelphia PA; BR/TR/5´11.5˝/165; d9.4; M2/U3; ▲																									
1875	Ath NA	6	5	.545	13	13	12	0	107	114	73	0	—	12	15	2.27	105	.259	.278	47	.128	-3	86	-2	—	-0.3
1876	Phi N	10	22	.313	34	32	27	0	282	383	288	0	—	34	12	2.62	93	.297	.315	240	.250	-1*	128	-17	—	-1.5
1884	Phi AA	0	1	.000	2	1	1	0	14	24	19	0	1	4	2	9.00	38	.348	.392	484-1	.271	0*	125	-8	—	-0.4
1885	Phi AA	0	0	ø	1	0	0	0	5	4	1	0	0	2	1	1.80	191	.211	.286	119	.210	-0*	—	1	—	0.1
	Pro N	0	0	ø	1	0	0	0	4	4	4	1	—	4	1	6.75	40	.235	.381	81	.160	-0*	—	-1	—	-0.1
Total	3	10	23	.303	38	33	28	0	305	415	312	1	1	44	16	2.95	84	.297	.319	924-1	.248	-1	128	-25	—	-1.9
Knight, Brandon	Brandon Michael; B10.1.1975 Oxnard CA; BL/TR/6´0˝/170; [TexA95 14/374]; d6.5; Col Ventura (CA) JC																									
2001	NY A	0	0	ø	4	0	0	0-0	10.2	18	12	5	0	3-0	7	10.13	44	.367	.404	0	ø	0	—	-6	0	-0.3
2002	NY A	0	0	ø	7	0	0	0-0	8.2	11	12	2	0	5-0	7	11.42	38	.306	.390	0	ø	0	—	-7	0	-0.3
Total	2	0	0	ø	11	0	0	0-0	19.1	29	24	7	0	8-0	14	10.71	41	.341	.398	0	ø	0	—	-13	0	-0.6
Knight, Jack	Elmer Russell; B1.12.1895 Pittsboro MS; D7.30.1976 San Antonio TX; BL/TR/6´0˝/175; d9.20; Col Millsaps																									
1922	StL N	0	0	ø	1	1	0	0	4	9	4	0	0	3	1	9.00	43	.474	.545	2	.500	0	274	-2	—	-0.1
1925	Phi N	7	6	.538	33	11	4	3	105.1	161	100	14	1	36	19	6.84	70	.354	.402	44	.205	-1*	135	-22	—	-2.4
1926	Phi N	3	12	.200	35	15	5	2	142.2	206	122	14	0	48	29	6.62	63	.347	.396	56-2-2	.214	0*	86	-35	—	-2.9
1927	Bos N	0	0	ø	3	0	0	0	3	6	5	0	0	2	0	15.00	25	.429	.500	0	ø	0	—	-4	—	-0.1
Total	4	10	18	.357	72	27	9	5	255	382	231	28	1	89	49	6.85	64	.353	.403	102-2-2	.216	0	114	-63	—	-5.5
Knight, George	George Henry; B11.24.1855 Lakeville CT; D10.4.1912 Lakeville CT; d9.28																									
1875	NH NA	1	0	1.000	1	1	1	0	9	12	6	0	—	0	0	3.00	69	.293	.293	4	.000	-1	136	0	—	-0.1
Knight, Joe	Jonah William "Quiet Joe"; B9.28.1859 Port Stanley ON, Can.; D10.16.1938 Lynhurst ON, Can.; BL/TL/5´11˝/185; d5.16; ▲																									
1884	Phi N	2	4	.333	6	6	6	0	51	66	53	2	—	21	8	5.47	55	.293	.354	24	.250	1	68	-12	—	-1.0
Knolls, Oscar	Oscar Edward; B12.18.1883 Valparaiso IN; D7.1.1946 Chicago IL; TR/6´2˝/190; d5.1																									
1906	Bro N	0	0	ø	2	0	0	0	6.2	13	5	0	0	2	3	4.05	62	.382	.417	1-0-1	1.000	1	—	-2	—	0.0
Knott, Eric	Eric James; B9.23.1974 Harvey IL; BL/TL/6´0˝/188; [AriN96 24/725]; d9.1; Col Stetson																									
2001	Ari N	0	1	.000	3	1	0	0-0	4.2	8	9	0	2	0-0	4	1.93	240	.348	.400	1	.000	-0	100	-2	0	-0.4
2003	Mon N	1	2	.333	13	1	0	0-0	19.1	23	12	2	0	6-0	17	5.12	87	.295	.341	5	.000	-1	21	-1	0	-0.2
Total	2	1	3	.250	16	2	0	0-0	24	31	21	2	2	6-0	21	4.50	99	.307	.355	6	.000	-1	63	-3	0	-0.6
Knott, Jack	John Henry; B3.2.1907 Dallas TX; D10.13.1981 Brownwood TX; BR/TR/6´2.5˝/200; d4.13; Mil 1942–45; Col SMU																									
1933	StL A	1	8	.111	20	9	0	0	82.2	88	51	11	2	33	19	5.01	93	.269	.340	23-0-1	.304	1	75	-3	—	-0.2
1934	StL A	10	3	.769	45	10	2	4	138	149	86	17	1	67	56	4.96	101	.278	.359	30-0-3	.133	-1	82	2	—	0.1
1935	StL A	11	8	.579	48	19	7-2	**7**	187.2	219	119	8	1	78	45	4.60	104	.287	.353	61-0-8	.115	-5	95	0	—	-0.4

YEAR	TM LG	W	L	PCT	G	GS	CG-SHO	SV-BS	IP	H	R	HR	HB	BB-IB	SO	ERA	AERA	OAV	OOB	AB-HR-SH	AVG	PB	SUP	APR	DL	PW
1936	StL A	9	17	.346	47	23	9	6	192.2	272	174	15	4	93	60	7.29	74	.330	.401	57-0-8	.070	-5	89	-37	—	-4.5
1937	StL A	8	18	.308	38	22	8	2	191.1	220	117	25	5	91	74	4.89	99	.291	.370	57-0-4	.140	-4	76	-1	—	-0.6
1938	StL A	1	2	.333	7	4	0	0	30	35	19	3	0	15	8	4.80	104	.285	.362	10-0-1	.100	-1	84	0	—	-0.1
	Chi A	5	10	.333	20	18	9	0	131	135	70	8	0	54	35	4.05	121	.271	.342	40-0-7	.125	-2	68	12	—	0.9
	Year	6	12	.333	27	22	9	0	161	170	89	11	0	69	43	4.19	117	.273	.346	50-0-8	.120	-3	71	11	—	0.8
1939	Chi A	11	6	.647	25	23	8	0	149.2	157	71	13	1	41	56	4.15	114	.269	.318	53-0-5	.151	-3	92	12	—	0.8
1940	Chi A	11	9	.550	25	23	4-2	0	158	166	88	12	2	52	44	4.56	97	.265	.324	57-0-4	.088	-4	98	0	—	-0.4
1941	Phi A	13	11	.542	27	26	11	0	194.1	212	108	20	2	81	54	4.40	95	.279	.350	65-0-5	.077	-3	109	-4	0	-0.9
1942	Phi A	2	10	.167	20	14	4	0	95.1	127	84	7	1	36	31	5.57	68	.310	.367	29-0-2	.138	-1	78	-24	0	-2.6
1946	Phi A	0	1	.000	3	1	0	0	6.1	7	4	1	1	1	2	5.68	62	.280	.333	0-0-1	ø	0	0	-1	0	-0.2
Total	11	82	103	.443	325	192	62-4	19	1557	1787	991	140	20	642	484	4.97	95	.287	.355	482-0-49	.120	-29	87	-44	0	-8.1
Knotts, Gary	Gary Everett; B2.12.1977 Decatur AL; BR/TR/6´4˝/(230–235); [FlaN95 11/289]; d7.28; Col NW Alabama CG; [DL 2005 Det A 185]																									
2001	Fla N	0	1	.000	2	1	0	0-0	6	7	4	1	2	1-0	9	6.00	69	.280	.357	2	.500	0	67	-1	0	-0.1
2002	Fla N	3	1	.750	28	0	0	0-1	30.2	21	15	6	1	16-0	21	4.40	89	.193	.299	1	.000	-0	—	-1	0	-0.2
2003	Det A	3	8	.273	20	18	0	0-0	95.1	111	70	14	4	47-0	51	6.04	73	.288	.367	1	.000	-0	81	-18	0	-1.7
2004	Det A	7	6	.538	36	19	0	2-0	135.1	142	83	20	4	58-3	81	5.25	85	.267	.343	3-0-1	.333	1	113	-11	16	-0.9
Total	4	13	16	.448	86	38	0	2-1	267.1	281	172	41	11	122-3	162	5.45	80	.267	.348	7-0-1	.286	1	98	-31	201	-2.9
Knouff, Ed	Edward "Fred"; B6.1868 Philadelphia PA; D9.14.1900 Philadelphia PA; BR/TR/?/160; d7.1; ▲																									
1885	Phi AA	7	6	.538	14	13	12	0	106	103	76	0	9	44	43	3.65	94	.228	.309	48	.188	-2	111	-1	—	-0.2
1886	Bal AA	0	1	.000	1	1	1	0	9	2	5	0	3	5	8	2.00	171	.067	.263	3	.000	-0	17	1	—	0.1
1887	Bal AA	2	6	.250	9	9	6	0	63	79	79	0	13	41	27	7.57	54	.295	.413	31	.290	0	123	-23	—	-1.9
	StL AA	4	2	.667	6	6	6-1	0	50	40	34	0	3	36	18	4.50	101	.225	.364	56	.179	-1*	103	1	—	0.0
	Year	6	8	.429	15	15	12-1	0	113	119	113	0	16	77	45	6.21	69	.267	.393	87	.218	-1	114	-17	—	-1.9
1888	StL AA	5	4	.556	9	9	9	0	81	66	45	0	8	37	25	2.67	122	.214	.314	31	.097	-2	93	4	—	0.1
	Cle AA	0	1	.000	2	2	1	0	9	8	2	0	1	3	2	1.00	309	.229	.308	6	.167	0	66	2	—	0.3
	Year	5	5	.500	11	11	10	0	90	74	47	0	9	40	27	2.50	130	.216	.314	37	.108	-2	88	7	—	0.4
1889	Phi AA	2	0	1.000	3	3	2	0	25	37	17	2	1	9	5	3.96	96	.333	.388	12	.250	0	131	0	—	0.0
Total	5	20	20	.500	44	43	37-1	0	343	335	258	2	38	175	128	4.17	89	.242	.344	187	.187	-4	106	-16	—	-1.6
Knowles, Darold	Darold Duane; B12.9.1941 Brunswick MO; BL/TL/6´0˝/(175–190); d4.18; Mil 1968–69; C3; Col Missouri																									
1965	Bal A	0	1	.000	5	1	0	0	14.2	14	15	2	3	10-2	12	9.20	38	.250	.391	4	.000	-0	0	-8	0	-0.5
1966	Phi N	6	5	.545	69	0	0	13	100.1	98	38	4	7	46-10	88	3.05	118	.260	.347	16	.250	0	—	6	0	1.0
1967	Was A	6	8	.429	61	1	0	14	113.1	91	37	5	4	52-12	85	2.70	117	.228	.319	16	.063	-1	0	7	0	1.1
1968	Was A	1	1	.500	32	0	0	4	41.1	38	11	0	1	12-2	37	2.18	134	.241	.293	4-0-1	.250	1	—	4	0	0.4
1969	Was A★	9	2	.818	53	0	0	13-9	84.1	73	25	8	4	31-3	59	2.24	156	.236	.311	13	.077	0	—	12	0	2.0
1970	Was A	2	14	.125	71	0	0	27-11	119.1	100	36	4	4	58-16	71	2.04	177	.231	.325	20-0-2	.050	-1	—	19	0	3.2
1971	Was A	2	2	.500	12	0	0	2-2	15.1	17	6	2	0	6-1	16	3.52	96	.266	.329	2	.000	-0	—	0	0	0.0
	†Oak A	5	2	.714	43	0	0	7-3	52.2	40	22	3	3	16-4	40	3.59	93	.221	.289	8-0-1	.125	-0	—	-1	0	-0.1
	Year	7	4	.636	55	0	0	9-5	68	57	28	5	3	22-5	56	3.57	93	.233	.299	10-0-1	.100	-1	—	-1	0	-0.1
1972	Oak A	5	1	.833	54	0	0	11-3	65.2	49	12	1	0	37-4	36	1.37	208	.212	.319	12-0-1	.250	1	—	11	6	1.8
1973	†Oak A	6	8	.429	52	5	1-1	9-5	99	87	44	7	3	49-3	46	3.09	115	.246	.338	0	ø	0*	130	3	0	0.6
1974	Oak A	3	3	.500	45	1	0	3-2	53.1	61	29	6	2	35-3	18	4.22	79	.296	.397	0	ø	0	211	-6	0	-0.6
1975	Chi N	6	9	.400	58	0	0	15-7	88.1	107	61	3	3	36-9	63	5.81	67	.298	.364	15-0-2	.067	-1	—	-16	0	-3.1
1976	Chi N	5	7	.417	58	0	0	9-8	71.2	61	30	6	2	22-4	39	2.89	135	.242	.302	7-0-2	.143	1	—	6	0	1.3
1977	Tex A	5	2	.714	42	0	0	4-4	50.1	50	22	3	2	23-2	14	3.22	127	.272	.354	0	ø	0	—	4	11	0.6
1978	Mon N	3	3	.500	60	0	0	6-3	72	63	20	5	0	30-3	34	2.38	150	.250	.323	6-0-1	.167	-0	—	10	0	1.1
1979	StL N	2	5	.286	48	0	0	6-4	48.2	54	27	5	0	17-7	22	4.07	94	.277	.333	2	.000	-0	—	-2	0	-0.4
1980	StL N	0	1	.000	2	0	0	0-1	1.2	3	2	1	0	0-0	1	10.80	35	.375	.375	0	ø	0	—	-1	0	-0.2
Total	16	66	74	.471	765	8	1-1	143-62	1092	1006	437	65	38	480-85	681	3.12	113	.250	.332	125-0-10	.120	-2	107	48	17	8.2
Knowlson, Tom	Thomas Herbert "Doc"; B4.23.1895 Pittsburgh PA; D4.11.1943 Miami Shores FL; BB/TR/5´11˝/178; d7.3																									
1915	Phi A	4	6	.400	18	9	8	0	100.2	99	53	1	6	60	24	3.49	84	.273	.386	36	.083	-3	91	-6	—	-0.9
Knowlton, Bill	William Young; B8.18.1892 Philadelphia PA; D2.25.1944 Philadelphia PA; BR/TR; d9.3																									
1920	Phi A	0	1	.000	1	1	0	0	5.2	9	9	0	3	3	5	4.76	84	.346	.469	2	.000	-0	99	-2	—	-0.3
Knudsen, Kurt	Kurt David; B2.20.1967 Arlington Heights IL; BR/TR/6´3˝/200; [DetA88 9/239]; d5.16; Col Miami																									
1992	Det A	2	3	.400	48	1	0	5-2	70.2	70	39	9	1	41-9	51	4.58	87	.264	.362	0	ø	0	69	-5	0	-0.4
1993	Det A	3	2	.600	30	0	0	2-2	37.2	41	22	9	4	16-2	29	4.78	91	.281	.361	0	ø	0	—	-2	31	-0.2
1994	Det A	1	0	1.000	4	0	0	0-1	5.1	7	8	2	0	11-1	1	13.50	36	.304	.529	0	ø	0	—	-5	0	-0.7
Total	3	6	5	.545	82	1	0	7-5	113.2	118	69	20	5	68-12	81	5.07	82	.272	.373	0	ø	0	69	-12	31	-1.3
Knudson, Mark	Mark Richard; B10.28.1960 Denver CO; BR/TR/6´5˝/(200–215); [HouN82 3/69]; d7.8; Col Colorado St.																									
1985	Hou N	0	2	.000	2	2	0	0-0	11	21	11	0	0	3-0	4	9.00	39	.429	.462	2	.000	0	63	-6	21	-0.8
1986	Hou N	1	5	.167	9	7	0	0-0	42.2	48	23	5	1	15-5	20	4.22	85	.279	.340	10-0-3	.000	-1	106	-3	0	-0.5
	Mil A	0	1	.000	4	1	0	0-0	17.2	22	15	7	0	5-1	9	7.64	57	.286	.329	0	ø	0	21	-5	0	-0.3
1987	Mil A	4	4	.500	15	8	1	0-1	62	88	46	7	0	14-1	26	5.37	86	.331	.358	0	ø	0	104	-8	0	-0.9
1988	Mil A	0	0	ø	5	0	0	0-0	16	17	3	1	0	2-0	7	1.13	356	.279	.302	0	ø	0	—	5	0	0.2
1989	Mil A	8	5	.615	40	7	1	0-2	123.2	110	50	15	3	29-2	47	3.35	115	.237	.286	0	ø	0	158	8	0	0.7
1990	Mil A	10	9	.526	30	27	4-2	0-0	168.1	187	84	14	3	40-1	56	4.12	94	.282	.321	0	ø	0	96	-2	0	-0.3
1991	Mil A	1	3	.250	12	7	0	0-0	35	54	33	8	1	15-0	23	7.97	50	.355	.409	0	ø	0	118	-15	36	-1.5
1993	Col N	0	0	ø	4	0	0	0-0	5.2	16	14	4	0	5-0	3	22.24	22	.471	.538	1	.000	-0	—	-9	0	-0.4
Total	8	24	29	.453	121	59	6-2	0-3	482	563	279	61	8	128-10	195	4.72	84	.290	.334	13-0-3	.000	-1	105	-35	57	-3.8
Kobel, Kevin	Kevin Richard; B10.2.1953 Buffalo NY; BR/TL/6´1˝/183; [MilA71 11/248]; d9.8																									
1973	Mil A	0	1	.000	2	1	0	0-0	8.1	9	8	2	0	8-0	4	8.64	44	.273	.415	0	ø	0	70	-4	0	-0.4
1974	Mil A	6	14	.300	34	24	3-2	0-1	169.1	166	84	16	2	54-1	74	3.99	91	.258	.314	0	ø	0	80	-8	0	-0.8
1976	Mil A	0	1	.000	3	0	0	0-1	4	6	5	3	1	3-1	1	11.25	31	.375	.476	0	ø	0	—	-3	0	-0.6
1978	NY N	5	6	.455	32	11	1	0-1	108.1	95	42	9	2	30-9	51	2.91	122	.239	.291	25-0-4	.160	0	88	6	0	0.6
1979	NY N	6	8	.429	30	27	1-1	0-0	161.2	169	74	14	3	46-4	67	3.51	106	.274	.325	46-0-9	.196	0	78	2	24	0.3
1980	NY N	1	4	.200	14	1	0	0-0	24.1	36	21	5	0	11-3	8	7.03	51	.353	.416	2	.000	-0	74	-9	0	-1.7
Total	6	18	34	.346	115	64	5-3	0-3	476	481	234	49	8	152-18	205	3.88	94	.266	.322	73-0-13	.178	0	80	-16	24	-2.6
Koch, Alan	Alan Goodman; B3.25.1938 Decatur AL; BR/TR/6´4˝/195; d7.26; Col Auburn																									
1963	Det A	1	1	.500	7	1	0	0	10	21	12	3	1	9-0	5	10.80	35	.467	.564	3	.667	1*	71	-7	0	-1.1
1964	Det A	0	0	ø	3	0	0	0	4	6	3	1	0	3-0	1	6.75	54	.375	.474	0	ø	0	—	-1	0	-0.1
	Was A	3	10	.231	32	14	1	0	114	110	64	18	3	43-2	67	4.89	76	.253	.320	32-0-3	.250	2	87	-12	0	-1.1
	Year	3	10	.231	35	14	1	0	118	116	67	19	3	46-2	68	4.96	75	.258	.325	32-0-3	.250	2	88	-13	0	-1.2
Total	2	4	11	.267	42	15	1	0	128	137	79	22	4	55-2	73	5.41	68	.277	.349	35-0-3	.286	3	86	-20	0	-2.3
Koch, Billy	William Christopher; B12.14.1974 Rockville Centre NY; BR/TR/6´3˝/(205–220); [TorA96 1/4]; d5.5; Col Clemson																									
1999	Tor A	0	5	.000	56	0	0	31-4	63.2	55	26	5	3	30-5	57	3.39	145	.235	.328	1	.000	-0	—	11	0	1.6
2000	Tor A	9	3	.750	68	0	0	33-5	78.2	78	28	6	2	18-4	60	2.63	191	.258	.304	1	.000	-0	—	19	0	3.6
2001	Tor A	2	5	.286	69	0	0	36-8	69.1	69	39	7	6	33-7	55	4.80	95	.265	.356	0	ø	0	—	-1	0	-0.2
2002	†Oak A	11	4	.733	**84**	0	0	44-6	93.2	73	38	7	4	46-6	93	3.27	137	.214	.314	0	ø	0	—	12	0	2.5
2003	Chi A	5	5	.500	55	0	0	11-4	53	59	36	10	1	28-1	42	5.77	80	.281	.364	0	ø	0	—	-7	21	-1.3
2004	Chi A	1	1	.500	24	0	0	8-3	23.1	24	15	3	2	16-4	25	5.40	87	.255	.368	0	ø	0	—	-2	0	-0.3
	Fla N	1	2	.333	23	0	0	0-0	25.2	21	10	3	0	20-0	25	3.51	117	.226	.360	0	ø	0	—	2	0	0.2
Total	6	29	25	.537	379	0	0	163-30	407.1	379	192	41	18	191-27	357	3.89	120	.247	.335	2	.000	-0	—	34	21	6.1

YEAR	TM LG	W	L	PCT	G	GS	CG-SHO	SV-BS	IP	H	R	HR	HB	BB-IB	SO	ERA	AERA	OAV	OOB	AB-HR-SH	AVG	PB	SUP	APR	DL	PW
KOECHER, DICK	Richard Finlay "Highpockets"; B3.30.1926 Philadelphia PA; BL/TL/6´5˝/196; d9.29; Col Temple																									
1946	Phi N	0	1	.000	1	1	0	0	2.2	7	3	0	0	1	2	10.13	34	.467	.500	1	.000	-0	25	-2	0	-0.3
1947	Phi N	0	2	.000	3	2	1	0	17	20	12	1	1	10	4	4.76	84	.299	.397	4	.000	-1	22	-2	0	-0.3
1948	Phi N	0	1	.000	3	0	0	0	6	4	2	0	0	3	2	3.00	132	.235	.350	0	ø	0	—	1	0	0.1
Total	3	0	4	.000	7	3	1	0	25.2	31	17	1	1	14	8	4.91	80	.313	.404	5	.000	-1	22	-3	0	-0.5
KOENIG, MARK	Mark Anthony; B7.19.1904 San Francisco CA; D4.22.1993 Willows CA; BB/TR/6´0˝/180; d9.8.1925; ▲																									
1930	Det A	0	1	.000	2	1	0	0	9	11	10	0	1	8	6	10.00	48	.314	.455	267-1-13	.240	0*	89	-4	—	-0.4
1931	Det A	0	0	ø	3	0	0	0	7	7	5	0	0	11	3	6.43	71	.280	.500	364-1-2	.253	0*	—	-1	—	0.0
Total	2	0	1	.000	5	1	0	0	16	18	15	0	1	19	9	8.44	56	.300	.475	631-2-15	.247	0	89	-5	—	-0.4
KOENIGSMARK, WILL	Willis Thomas; B2.27.1896 Waterloo IL; D7.1.1972 Waterloo IL; BR/TR/6´4˝/180; d9.10																									
1919	StL N	0	0	ø	1	0	0	0	0	2	2	0	0	1	0	(2)	ø	1.000	1.000	0	ø	0	—	-2	—	-0.2
KOESTNER, ELMER	Elmer Joseph "Bob"; B11.30.1885 Piper City IL; D10.27.1959 Fairbury IL; BR/TR/6´1.5˝/175; d4.23																									
1910	Cle A	5	10	.333	27	13	8-1	2	145	145	76	0	6	63	44	3.04	85	.282	.367	48-0-6	.313	2	106	-10	—	-0.8
1914	Chi N	0	0	ø	4	0	0	0	6.1	6	5	0	0	4	6	2.84	98	.261	.370	1	.000	-0	—	-1	—	-0.1
	Cin N	0	0	ø	5	1	0	0	18.1	18	15	0	0	9	6	4.42	66	.265	.351	5	.400	1	171	-4	—	-0.1
	Year	0	0	ø	9	1	0	0	24.2	24	20	0	0	13	12	4.01	72	.264	.356	6	.333	1	173	-4	—	-0.2
Total	2	5	10	.333	36	14	8-1	2	169.2	169	96	0	6	76	56	3.18	83	.279	.365	54-0-6	.315	3	110	-15	—	-1.0
KOHLMAN, JOE	Joseph James "Blackie"; B1.28.1913 Philadelphia PA; D3.16.1974 Philadelphia PA; BR/TR/6´0˝/160; d9.26																									
1937	Was A	1	0	1.000	2	2	1	0	13	15	7	0	0	3	3	4.15	107	.283	.321	5	.200	-0	108	0	—	0.0
1938	Was A	0	0	ø	7	0	0	0	14.1	12	10	1	0	11	5	6.28	72	.240	.377	3	.000	-0	—	-2	—	-0.1
Total	2	1	0	1.000	9	2	1	0	27.1	27	17	1	0	14	8	5.27	85	.262	.350	8	.125	-1	108	-2	—	-0.1
KOHLMEIER, RYAN	Ryan Lyle; B6.25.1977 Salina KS; BR/TR/6´2˝/(197–223); [BalA96 14/411]; d7.29; Col Butler Co. (KS) CC																									
2000	Bal A	0	1	.000	25	0	0	13-1	26.1	30	9	1	0	15-2	17	2.39	197	.291	.378	0	ø	0	—	6	0	0.7
2001	Bal A	1	2	.333	34	1	0	6-4	40.2	48	33	13	2	19-2	29	7.30	59	.291	.371	0	ø	0	0	-12	0	-1.1
Total	2	1	3	.250	59	1	0	19-5	67	78	42	14	2	34-4	46	5.37	83	.291	.374	0	ø	0	0	-6	0	-0.4
KOLB, BRANDON	Brandon Charles; B11.20.1973 Oakland CA; BR/TR/6´1˝/190; [SDN95 4/89]; d5.12; Col Texas Tech																									
2000	SD N	0	1	.000	11	0	0	0-1	14	16	8	0	0	11-1	12	4.50	99	.296	.409	1	.000	-0	—	0	0	0.0
2001	Mil N	0	0	ø	10	0	0	0-0	9.2	16	16	6	0	8-0	8	13.03	33	.372	.453	1	.000	-0	—	-10	0	-0.5
Total	2	0	1	.000	21	0	0	0-1	23.2	32	24	6	0	19-1	20	7.99	55	.330	.429	2	.000	-0	—	-10	0	-0.5
KOLB, DAN	Daniel Lee; B3.29.1975 Sterling IL; BR/TR/6´4˝/(185–240); [TexA95 6/150]; d6.4; Col Illinois St.																									
1999	Tex A	2	1	.667	16	0	0	0-0	31	33	18	2	1	15-0	15	4.65	111	.268	.353	0	ø	0	—	1	1	0.1
2000	Tex A	0	0	ø	1	0	0	0-0	0.2	5	5	0	0	2-0	0	67.50	8	.833	.778	0	ø	0	—	-4	127	-0.2
2001	Tex A	0	0	ø	17	0	0	0-0	15.1	15	8	2	0	10-1	15	4.70	102	.259	.362	0	ø	0	—	0	101	0.0
2002	Tex A	3	6	.333	34	0	0	1-3	32	27	17	1	1	22-2	20	4.22	114	.227	.347	0	ø	0	—	1	107	0.3
2003	Mil N	1	2	.333	37	0	0	21-2	41.1	34	10	2	1	19-3	39	1.96	220	.221	.310	0	ø	0	—	11	0	1.6
2004	Mil N★	0	4	.000	64	0	0	39-5	57.1	50	22	3	3	15-1	21	2.98	147	.234	.292	0	ø	0	—	8	0	1.5
2005	Atl N	3	8	.273	65	0	0	11-7	57.2	78	39	5	1	29-5	39	5.93	71	.329	.403	1	.000	-0	—	-10	0	-2.1
2006	Mil N	2	2	.500	53	0	0	1-2	48.1	53	28	4	1	20-1	26	4.84	93	.282	.349	0	ø	0	—	-2	0	-0.2
Total	8	11	23	.324	287	0	0	73-19	283.2	295	147	19	8	132-13	175	4.31	105	.268	.349	1	.000	-0	—	5	336	1.0
KOLB, EDDIE	Edward William; B7.20.1880 Cincinnati OH; D10.1.1949 Calgary AL, Can.; BR/TR; d10.15																									
1899	Cle N	0	1	.000	1	1	1	0	8	18	19	0	1	5	1	10.13	36	.439	.511	4	.250	-0	59	-8	—	-0.6
KOLP, RAY	Raymond Carl "Jockey"; B10.1.1894 New Berlin (now North Canton) OH; D7.29.1967 Cincinnati OH; BR/TR/5´10.5˝/187; d4.16																									
1921	StL A	8	7	.533	37	18	5-1	0	166.2	208	111	12	0	51	43	4.97	90	.314	.363	55-0-8	.127	-5*	109	-9	—	-1.2
1922	StL A	14	4	.778	32	18	9-1	0	169.2	199	89	10	5	36	54	3.93	106	.292	.332	57-0-11	.298	5	153	5	—	0.7
1923	StL A	5	12	.294	34	17	11-1	1	171.1	178	91	11	6	54	44	3.89	107	.273	.335	54-0-5	.111	-4	70	4	—	-0.1
1924	StL A	5	7	.417	25	12	5-1	0	96.2	131	65	4	4	25	29	5.68	79	.329	.375	30-0-2	.200	-0	76	-9	—	-1.0
1927	Cin N	3	3	.500	24	5	2-1	3	82.1	86	38	5	1	29	28	3.06	124	.278	.342	30-0-1	.200	-0	90	5	—	0.4
1928	Cin N	13	10	.565	44	23	12-1	3	209	219	87	9	4	55	61	3.19	124	.280	.330	70-1-4	.214	3	98	17	—	2.0
1929	Cin N	8	10	.444	30	16	4-1	0	145.1	151	75	8	1	39	27	4.03	113	.278	.328	49-0-4	.163	-2	82	8	—	0.8
1930	Cin N	7	12	.368	37	19	5-2	3	168.1	180	86	10	0	34	40	4.22	114	.278	.314	49-1-1	.245	1	58	13	—	1.4
1931	Cin N	4	9	.308	30	10	2	1	107	144	66	8	4	39	24	4.96	75	.332	.392	32-0-3	.125	-1	96	-14	—	-1.6
1932	Cin N	6	10	.375	32	18	7-2	1	159.2	176	80	13	3	27	42	3.89	99	.280	.313	49-0-2	.184	-1	84	1	—	-0.1
1933	Cin N	6	9	.400	30	14	4	3	150.1	168	73	7	1	23	28	3.53	96	.290	.318	45-0-3	.156	-1	81	-2	—	-0.2
1934	Cin N	0	2	.000	28	2	0	3	61.2	78	36	1	2	12	19	4.52	90	.312	.348	12	.083	-1	53	-2	—	-0.1
Total	12	79	95	.454	383	172	66-11	18	1688	1918	897	98	31	424	439	4.08	102	.292	.338	532-2-44	.184	-7	91	17	—	1.0
KOLSTAD, HAL	Harold Everette; B6.1.1935 Rice Lake WI; BR/TR/5´9˝/190; d4.22; Col San Jose St.																									
1962	Bos A	0	2	.000	27	2	0	2	61.1	65	44	11	2	35-1	36	5.43	76	.269	.363	18-0-2	.056	-2	97	-10	0	-0.6
1963	Bos A	0	2	.000	7	0	0	0	11	16	16	4	2	6-0	6	13.09	29	.340	.436	1-0-1	.000	-0	—	-10	0	-1.6
Total	2	0	4	.000	34	2	0	2	72.1	81	60	15	4	41-1	42	6.59	62	.280	.375	19-0-3	.053	-2	97	-20	0	-2.2
KOMINE, SHANE	Shane Kenji; B10.18.1980 Honolulu HI; BR/TR/5´9˝/175; [OakA02 9/278]; d7.30; Col Nebraska																									
2006	Oak A	0	0	ø	2	2	0	0-0	9	10	5	3	0	8-1	1	5.00	91	.270	.400	0	ø	0	135	0	0	0.0
KOMIYAMA, SATORU	Satoru; B9.15.1965 Chiba, Japan; BR/TR/6´0˝/195; d4.4																									
2002	NY N	0	3	.000	25	0	0	0-0	43.1	53	29	7	3	12-4	33	5.61	71	.301	.351	1-0-1	.000	0	—	-8	15	-0.5
KONETCHY, ED	Edward Joseph "Big Ed"; B9.3.1885 LaCrosse WI; D5.27.1947 Ft.Worth TX; BR/TR/6´2.5˝/195; d6.29.1907; ▲																									
1910	StL N	0	0	ø	1	0	0	0	4	4	2	0	0	1	0	4.50	66	.267	.313	520-3-11	.302	0*	—	0	—	0.0
1913	StL N	1	0	1.000	1	0	0	0	4.2	1	0	0	0	4	3	0.00	ø	.071	.278	504-8-19	.276	0*	—	2	—	0.4
1918	Bos N	0	1	.000	1	1	1	0	8	14	8	0	0	2	3	6.75	40	.378	.410	437-2-16	.236	0*	0	-4	—	-0.4
Total	3	1	1	.500	3	1	1	0	16.2	19	10	0	0	7	6	4.32	67	.288	.356	1461-13-46	.273	1	0	-2	—	0.0
KONIECZNY, DOUG	Douglas James; B9.27.1951 Detroit MI; BR/TR/6´4˝/(220–225); [HouN71*A1/4]; d9.11; Col Wayne State (MI)																									
1973	Hou N	0	1	.000	2	2	0	0-0	13	12	8	0	0	4-0	6	5.54	66	.279	.333	4	.000	-0	85	-2	0	-0.2
1974	Hou N	0	3	.000	6	3	0	0-0	16	18	15	0	2	12-1	8	7.88	44	.290	.421	4	.000	-1	50	-8	0	-1.3
1975	Hou N	6	13	.316	32	29	4-1	0-0	171	184	93	15	1	87-1	89	4.47	76	.280	.361	50-0-5	.160	1	104	-22	0	-2.2
1977	Hou N	1	1	.500	4	4	0	0-0	21	26	15	1	1	8-0	7	6.00	60	.302	.361	7-0-1	.143	-0	98	-6	118	-0.5
Total	4	7	18	.280	44	38	4-1	0-0	221	240	131	16	4	111-2	110	4.93	70	.283	.364	65-0-6	.138	-0	98	-38	118	-4.2
KONIKOWSKI, ALEX	Alexander James "Whitey"; B6.8.1928 Throop PA; D9.28.1997 Seymour CT; BR/TR/6´1˝/187; d6.16; Mil 1952–53																									
1948	NY N	2	3	.400	22	1	0	1	33.1	46	34	7	0	17	9	7.56	52	.346	.420	2-0-1	.000	0	23	-14	0	-1.8
1951	†NY N	0	0	ø	3	0	0	0	4	2	0	0	0	0	5	0.00	ø	.154	.154	0	ø	0	—	2	0	0.1
1954	NY N	0	0	ø	10	0	0	0	12	10	10	1	0	12	6	7.50	54	.244	.415	1	.000	-0	—	-4	0	-0.2
Total	3	2	3	.400	35	1	0	1	49.1	58	44	8	0	29	20	6.93	57	.310	.403	3-0-1	.000	0	23	-16	0	-1.9
KONSTANTY, JIM	Casimir James; B3.2.1917 Strykersville NY; D6.11.1976 Oneonta NY; BR/TR/6´1.5˝/(195–202); d6.18; Mil 1945; Col Syracuse																									
1944	Cin N	6	4	.600	20	12	5-1	0	112.2	113	46	11	1	33	19	2.80	125	.266	.320	34-0-3	.294	2	108	7	0	0.8
1946	Bos N	0	1	.000	10	1	0	0	15.1	17	9	2	0	7	9	5.28	65	.283	.358	2	.000	0	175	-3	0	-0.1
1948	Phi N	1	0	1.000	6	0	0	2	9.2	7	1	0	0	2	7	0.93	424	.233	.281	3	.000	-0	—	3	0	0.4
1949	Phi N	9	5	.643	53	0	0	7	97	98	38	9	1	29	43	3.25	121	.280	.337	17-0-1	.176	-0	—	**8**	0	1.2
1950	†Phi N★	16	7	.696	**74**	0	0	**22**	152	108	51	11	0	50	56	2.66	152	.205	.274	37-0-2	.108	-2	—	**24**	0	**3.8**
1951	Phi N	4	11	.267	58	1	0	9	115.2	127	58	9	0	31	27	4.05	95	.282	.328	19-0-3	.158	-0	46	-3	0	-0.4
1952	Phi N	5	3	.625	42	2	2-1	6	80	87	44	9	0	21	16	3.94	93	.274	.319	14-0-1	.071	-0	97	-4	0	-0.5
1953	Phi N	14	10	.583	48	19	7	5	170.2	198	90	18	3	42	45	4.43	95	.290	.334	50-0-3	.220	-0	115	-1	0	-0.2
1954	Phi N	2	3	.400	33	1	0	3	50.1	62	27	7	0	12	11	3.75	108	.316	.352	13	.000	-2	88	0	0	-0.2
	NY A	1	1	.500	9	0	0	2	18.1	11	2	0	0	6	3	0.98	350	.183	.254	3	.000	-0	—	6	0	0.7

YEAR	TM LG	W	L	PCT	G	GS	CG-SHO	SV-BS	IP	H	R	HR	HB	BB-IB	SO	ERA	AERA	OAV	OOB	AB-HR-SH	AVG	PB	SUP	APR	DL	PW
1955	NY A	7	2	.778	45	0	0	11	73.2	68	28	5	0	24-2	19	2.32	161	.247	.305	8-0-3	.125	-0	—	10	0	1.4
1956	NY A	0	0	ø	8	0	0	2	11	15	6	3	0	6-0	6	4.91	79	.319	.396	2	.000	-0	—	-1	0	-0.1
	StL N	1	1	.500	27	0	0	5	39.1	46	20	4	0	6-1	7	4.58	83	.301	.325	0	ø	0	—	-2	0	-0.2
Total	11	66	48	.579	433	36	14-2	74	945.2	957	420	88	5	269-3	268	3.46	112	.268	.319	202-0-16	.163	-5	112	44	0	6.6
KONUSZEWSKI, DENNIS Dennis John; B2.4.1971 Bridgeport MI; BR/TR/6´3˝/210; [PitN92 7/203]; d8.4; Col Michigan																										
1995	Pit N	0	0	ø	1	0	0	0-0	0.1	3	2	0	0	1-0	0	54.00	8	1.000	1.000	0	ø	0	—	-2	0	-0.1
KOO, DAE-SUNG Dae-Sung; B8.2.1968 Daejeon, South Korea; BL/TL/6´1˝/185; d4.4; Col Hanyang																										
2005	NY N	0	0	ø	33	0	0	0-2	23	22	12	2	2	13-1	23	3.91	106	.250	.349	2	.500	1	—	0	43	0.1
KOOB, ERNIE Ernest Gerald; B9.11.1892 Keeler MI; D11.12.1941 Lemay MO; BL/TL/5´10˝/160; d6.23; Mil 1918; Col Western Michigan																										
1915	StL A	4	5	.444	28	13	6	1	133.2	119	50	2	10	50	37	2.36	122	.254	.339	37-0-2	.135	-1	86	8	—	0.3
1916	StL A	11	8	.579	33	20	10-2	2	166.2	153	54	1	6	56	26	2.54	108	.252	.321	41-0-1	.000	-1	85	7	—	0.6
1917	StL A	6	14	.300	39	18	3-1	1	133.2	139	81	1	6	57	47	3.91	67	.280	.361	35-0-3	.114	-1	95	-20	—	-3.0
1919	StL A	2	4	.333	25	4	0	0	66	77	37	3	2	23	11	4.64	72	.296	.358	15-0-1	.000	-2	83	-7	—	-0.8
Total	4	23	31	.426	125	55	19-3	4	500	488	222	7	24	186	121	3.13	90	.266	.342	128-0-7	.070	-5	87	-12	—	-2.9
KOONCE, CAL Calvin Lee; B11.18.1940 Fayetteville NC; D10.28.1993 Winston–Salem NC; BR/TR/6´1˝/(185–195); d4.14; Col Campbell																										
1962	Chi N	10	10	.500	35	30	3-1	0	190.2	200	93	17	7	86-3	84	3.97	105	.271	.350	64-0-3	.094	-4	88	5	0	0.1
1963	Chi N	2	6	.250	21	13	0	0	72.2	75	43	9	2	32-2	44	4.58	77	.273	.353	19-0-3	.105	-0	57	-8	0	-0.8
1964	Chi N	3	0	1.000	6	2	0	0	31	30	8	1	0	7-1	17	2.03	183	.254	.294	10	.000	-1	95	5	0	0.5
1965	Chi N	7	9	.438	38	23	3-1	0	173	181	83	17	6	52-8	88	3.69	100	.271	.327	49-0-3	.102	-0	94	0	0	0.0
1966	Chi N	5	5	.500	45	5	0	2	108.2	113	57	13	1	35-9	65	3.81	97	.268	.321	23-0-3	.130	0	153	-3	0	-0.2
1967	Chi N	2	2	.500	34	0	0	2	51	52	27	2	1	21-6	28	4.59	77	.268	.341	7	.000	-1	—	-5	0	-0.5
	NY N	3	3	.500	11	6	2-1	0	45	45	16	2	0	7-1	24	2.80	121	.259	.287	13-0-1	.154	-0*	73	3	0	0.4
	Year	5	5	.500	45	6	2-1	2	96	97	43	4	1	28-7	52	3.75	93	.264	.317	20-0-1	.100	-1	72	-2	0	-0.1
1968	NY N	6	4	.600	55	2	0	11	96.2	80	27	4	1	32-11	50	2.42	125	.235	.301	14	.000	-1	115	7	0	0.9
1969	NY N	6	3	.667	40	0	0	7-4	83	85	53	8	3	42-8	48	4.99	73	.269	.358	17	.235	0	—	-13	0	-1.4
1970	NY N	0	2	.000	13	0	0	0-0	22	25	9	2	1	14-5	10	3.27	124	.301	.408	1	.000	-0	—	2	0	0.2
	Bos A	3	4	.429	23	8	1	2-2	76.1	64	32	7	3	29-3	37	3.54	113	.231	.309	21-0-1	.095	-0	106	5	0	0.5
1971	Bos A	0	1	.000	13	1	0	0-1	21	22	16	3	0	11-0	9	5.57	67	.278	.367	1	.000	0	241	-5	0	-0.2
Total	10	47	49	.490	334	90	9-3	24-7	971	972	464	85	25	368-57	504	3.78	98	.264	.333	239-0-14	.100	-6	95	-7	0	-0.5
KOOSMAN, JERRY Jerome Martin; B12.23.1942 Appleton MN; BR/TL/6´2˝/(205–225); d4.14																										
1967	NY N	0	2	.000	9	3	0	0	22.1	22	17	3	0	19-4	11	6.04	56	.259	.390	2	.000	0	52	-7	0	-0.5
1968	NY N★	19	12	.613	35	34	17-7	0	263.2	221	72	16	8	69-7	178	2.08	145	.228	.283	91-1-3	.077	-3	101	25	0	2.8
1969	†NY N★	17	9	.654	32	32	16-6	0-0	241	187	66	14	4	68-11	180	2.28	161	.216	.275	84-0-4	.048	-7	82	37	0	3.2
1970	NY N	12	7	.632	30	29	5-1	0-0	212	189	87	22	2	71-14	118	3.14	129	.237	.299	70-0-8	.086	-2	107	20	0	1.3
1971	NY N	6	11	.353	26	24	4	0-0	165.2	160	66	12	1	51-4	96	3.04	113	.256	.309	50-0-6	.160	0	87	6	33	0.6
1972	NY N	11	12	.478	34	24	4-1	1-0	163	155	81	14	6	52-7	147	4.14	82	.250	.310	47-0-9	.085	-3	85	-12	0	-1.9
1973	†NY N	14	15	.483	35	35	12-3	0-0	263	234	93	18	4	76-6	156	2.84	128	.242	.298	78-0-15	.103	-3	77	23	0	2.1
1974	NY N	15	11	.577	35	35	13	0-0	265	258	113	16	7	85-7	188	3.36	107	.257	.316	86-0-10	.186	2	95	8	0	1.0
1975	NY N	14	13	.519	36	34	11-4	2-0	239.2	234	106	19	4	98-6	173	3.42	103	.261	.335	78-0-7	.179	1	99	1	0	0.3
1976	NY N	21	10	.677	34	32	17-3	0-1	247.1	205	81	19	1	66-7	200	2.69	124	.226	.278	79-0-13	.215	3	108	20	0	2.9
1977	NY N	8	20	.286	32	32	6-1	0-0	226.2	195	102	17	4	81-8	192	3.49	109	.232	.301	72-1-5	.111	-3	75	5	0	0.2
1978	NY N	3	15	.167	38	32	3	2-1	235.1	221	110	17	8	84-11	160	3.75	95	.255	.323	70-0-5	.086	-3	83	-6	0	-0.7
1979	Min A	20	13	.606	37	36	10-2	0-0	263.2	268	108	19	3	83-4	157	3.38	130	.268	.325	0	ø	0	94	29	0	3.4
1980	Min A	16	13	.552	38	34	8	2-0	243.1	252	119	24	5	69-5	149	4.03	108	.272	.324	0	ø	0	87	11	0	1.2
1981	Min A	3	9	.250	19	13	2-1	5-0	94.1	98	49	8	0	34-7	55	4.20	94	.272	.331	0	ø	0	61	-2	0	-0.3
	Chi A	1	4	.200	8	3	1	0-1	27	27	10	2	0	7-0	21	3.33	109	.260	.306	0	ø	0	132	2	0	0.3
	Year	4	13	.235	27	16	3-1	5-1	121.1	125	59	10	0	41-7	76	4.01	97	.269	.325	0	ø	0	74	-1	0	0.0
1982	Chi A	11	7	.611	42	19	3-1	3-1	173.1	194	81	9	2	38-3	88	3.84	106	.287	.325	0	ø	0	126	6	0	0.6
1983	†Chi A	11	7	.611	37	24	2-1	2-0	169.2	176	96	19	6	53-2	90	4.77	88	.266	.324	0	ø	0	107	-9	0	-0.8
1984	Phi N	14	15	.483	36	34	3-1	0-0	224	232	95	8	3	60-5	137	3.25	112	.267	.315	74-0-14	.108	-3	109	10	0	0.9
1985	Phi N	6	4	.600	19	18	3-1	0-0	99.1	107	56	14	3	34-3	60	4.62	80	.276	.336	34-0-1	.088	-2	122	-9	81	-1.0
Total	19	222	209	.515	612	527	140-33	17-4	3839.1	3635	1608	290	71	1198-121	2556	3.36	111	.252	.310	915-2-100	.119	-22	94	158	114	15.6
KOPLITZ, HOWIE Howard Dean; B5.4.1938 Oshkosh WI; BR/TR/5´11˝/(190–195); d9.8																										
1961	Det A	2	0	1.000	4	1	1	0	12	16	6	0	0	8-1	9	2.25	182	.327	.414	4	.000	-1	129	1	0	0.1
1962	Det A	3	0	1.000	10	6	1	0	37.2	54	24	5	0	10-1	10	5.26	77	.342	.379	13	.231	1*	183	-4	0	-0.2
1964	Was A	0	0	ø	6	1	0	0	17	20	9	3	0	13-1	9	4.76	78	.290	.402	4	.000	-0	144	-1	0	-0.1
1965	Was A	4	7	.364	33	11	0	1	106.2	97	51	11	3	48-4	59	4.05	86	.249	.333	30-0-1	.100	-1	108	-5	0	-0.6
1966	Was A	0	0	ø	1	0	0	0	2	0	0	0	0	1-0	0	0.00	ø	.000	.200	0	ø	0	—	1	22	0.0
Total	5	9	7	.563	54	19	2	1	175.1	187	90	19	3	80-7	87	4.21	87	.280	.356	51-0-1	.118	-1	138	-8	22	-0.8
KOPLOVE, MIKE Michael Paul; B8.30.1976 Philadelphia PA; BR/TR/6´0˝/(160–180); [AriN98 29/883]; d9.6; Col Delaware																										
2001	Ari N	0	1	.000	9	0	0	0-0	10	8	7	1	2	9-1	14	3.60	129	.211	.388	1	.000	-0	—	0	0	0.0
2002	†Ari N	6	1	.857	55	0	0	0-0	61.2	47	24	2	0	23-4	46	3.36	134	.213	.286	1	.000	-0	—	7	0	0.8
2003	Ari N	3	0	1.000	31	0	0	0-1	37.2	31	11	3	5	10-1	27	2.15	215	.225	.297	0	ø	0	—	9	118	0.7
2004	Ari N	4	4	.500	76	0	0	2-6	86.2	86	42	7	5	37-10	55	4.05	113	.269	.353	0	ø	0	—	6	0	0.6
2005	Ari N	2	1	.667	44	0	0	0-2	49.2	48	31	6	6	20-3	28	5.07	87	.257	.343	2	.000	-0	—	-4	0	-0.2
2006	Ari N	0	0	ø	2	0	0	0-0	3	5	1	0	0	2-0	1	3.00	156	.417	.500	1	.000	-0	—	1	0	0.0
Total	6	15	7	.682	217	0	0	2-9	248.2	225	116	19	18	101-19	171	3.76	120	.246	.330	5	.000	-1	—	19	118	1.9
KORINCE, GEORGE George Eugene "Moose"; B1.10.1946 Ottawa ON, Can.; BR/TR/6´3˝/200; d9.10																										
1966	Det A	0	0	ø	2	0	0	0	3	1	0	0	1	3-0	2	0.00	ø	.091	.333	0	ø	0	—	1	0	0.1
1967	Det A	1	0	1.000	9	0	0	0	14	10	8	1	0	11-1	11	5.14	63	.204	.339	1	.000	-0	—	-3	0	-0.2
Total	2	1	0	1.000	11	0	0	0	17	11	8	1	1	14-1	13	4.24	78	.183	.338	1	.000	-0	—	-2	0	-0.1
KORONKA, JOHN John Vincent; B7.3.1980 Clearwater FL; BL/TL/6´1˝/180; [CinN98 12/350]; d6.1																										
2005	Chi N	1	2	.333	4	3	0	0-0	15.2	19	13	2	0	8-0	10	7.47	59	.284	.360	4	.000	-0	79	-5	0	-0.8
2006	Tex A	7	7	.500	23	23	0	0-0	125	145	80	17	5	47-2	61	5.69	82	.294	.356	6	.000	-1	109	-12	0	-1.2
Total	2	8	9	.471	27	26	0	0-0	140.2	164	93	19	5	55-2	71	5.89	79	.292	.357	10	.000	-1	106	-17	0	-2.0
KORWAN, JIM James "Long Jim"; B3.4.1874 Brooklyn NY; D7.24.1899 Brooklyn NY; BR/TL/6´1˝/181; d4.24																										
1894	Bro N	0	0	ø	1	0	0	0	5	9	14	1	0	5	2	14.40	34	.391	.500	2	.000	-0	—	-7	—	-0.2
1897	Chi N	1	2	.333	5	4	3	0	34	47	36	1	1	28	12	5.82	77	.324	.437	12	.000	-2	92	-6	—	-0.5
Total	2	1	2	.333	6	4	3	0	39	56	50	2	1	33	14	6.92	66	.333	.446	14	.000	-2	92	-13	—	-0.7
KOSKI, BILL William John "T-Bone"; B2.6.1932 Madera CA; BR/TR/6´4˝/185; d4.28; Mil 1952–54																										
1951	Pit N	0	1	.000	13	1	0	0	27	26	23	2	0	28	6	6.67	63	.257	.419	4	.000	-1	63	-7	0	-0.4
KOSLO, DAVE George Bernard (b George Bernard Koslowski); B3.31.1920 Menasha WI; D12.1.1975 Menasha WI; BL/TL/5´11˝/(180–185); d9.12; Mil 1943–45																										
1941	NY N	1	2	.333	4	3	2	0	23.2	17	6	0	0	10	12	1.90	194	.202	.287	9	.111	-1	46	5	0	0.5
1942	NY N	3	6	.333	19	11	3-1	0	78	79	49	7	1	32	42	5.08	66	.261	.333	25	.120	-0	89	-13	0	-1.5
1946	NY N	14	19	.424	40	**35**	17-3	1	265.1	251	119	15	5	101	121	3.63	95	.249	.320	88-0-1	.125	-3*	86	-3	0	-0.6
1947	NY N	15	10	.600	39	31	10-3	0	217.1	223	118	23	3	82	86	4.39	93	.259	.326	78-0-1	.128	-1	132	-7	0	-0.8
1948	NY N	8	10	.444	35	18	5-3	3	149	168	69	7	1	62	58	3.87	102	.290	.359	44-0-3	.114	-1	85	4	0	0.3
1949	NY N	11	14	.440	38	23	15	4	212	193	72	13	0	43	64	**2.50**	**159**	.239	**.278**	69-2-6	.145	1*	76	34	0	4.1
1950	NY N	13	15	.464	40	22	7-1	3	186.2	190	89	18	5	68	56	3.91	105	.268	.337	65-1-1	.123	-1	107	5	0	0.6
1951	†NY N	10	9	.526	39	16	5-2	3	149.2	153	68	18	2	45	54	3.31	118	.258	.313	50	.100	-1	130	9	0	1.0
1952	NY N	10	7	.588	41	17	8-2	5	166.1	154	66	10	2	47	67	3.19	116	.242	.296	54-0-3	.037	-4	117	11	0	0.8
1953	NY N	6	12	.333	37	12	2	2	111.2	135	70	8	1	36	36	4.76	90	.296	.349	30-0-3	.033	-3	87	-6	0	-1.2
1954	Bal A	0	1	.000	3	1	0	0	14.1	20	7	1	0	3	3	3.14	114	.333	.365	3	.000	-0	0	0	0	-0.1
	Mil N	1	1	.500	12	0	0	1	17.1	13	6	0	0	9	7	3.12	120	.228	.324	1	.000	-0	—	2	0	0.1

YEAR	TM LG	W	L	PCT	G	GS	CG-SHO	SV-BS	IP	H	R	HR	HB	BB-IB	SO	ERA	AERA	OAV	OOB	AB-HR-SH	AVG	PB	SUP	APR	DL	PW
1955	Mil N	0	1	.000	1	0	0	0	0	1	1	1	0	0-0	0	(1)	ø	1.000	1.000	0	ø	0	—	-1	0	-0.1
Total	12	92	107	.462	348	189	74-15	22	1591.1	1597	740	121	20	538-0	606	3.68	105	.260	.321	516-3-18	.109	-15	101	40	0	3.1
KOSTAL, JOE	Joseph William "Cudgey"; B6.1.1876 Chicago IL; D10.17.1933 Guelph ON, Can.; BR/TR/5´6˝/130; d7.14																									
1896	Lou N	0	0	ø	2	0	0	0	2	4	4	0	0	0	0	0.00	ø	.400	.400	0	ø	0	—	0	—	0.0
KOUFAX, SANDY	Sanford (b Sanford Braun); B12.30.1935 Brooklyn NY; BR/TL/6´2˝/(198–210); d6.24; HF1972; Col Cincinnati																									
1955	Bro N	2	2	.500	12	5	2-2	0	41.2	33	15	2	1	28-1	30	3.02	134	.216	.341	12	.000	-2	75	5	30	0.3
1956	Bro N	2	4	.333	16	10	0	0	58.2	66	37	10	0	29-0	30	4.91	81	.286	.365	17	.118	-0	80	-7	0	-0.7
1957	Bro N	5	4	.556	34	13	2	0	104.1	83	49	14	2	51-1	122	3.88	107	.216	.309	26-0-1	.000	-3	91	4	0	-0.1
1958	LA N	11	11	.500	40	26	5	1	158.2	132	89	19	1	105-6	131	4.48	91	**.220**	.335	49-0-5	.122	-2	96	-7	0	-1.1
1959	†LA N	8	6	.571	35	23	6-1	2	153.1	136	74	23	0	92-4	173	4.05	104	.235	.338	54-0-2	.111	-1	117	4	0	0.2
1960	LA N	8	13	.381	37	26	7-2	1	175	133	83	20	1	100-6	197	3.91	102	**.207**	.314	57-0-4	.123	-2	91	2	0	0.0
1961	LA N★	18	13	.581	42	35	15-2	1	255.2	212	117	27	3	96-6	**269**	3.52	123	**.222**	.295	77-0-8	.065	-5	100	20	0	1.5
1962	LA N☆	14	7	.667	28	26	11-2	1	184.1	134	61	13	2	57-4	216	**2.54**	143	**.197**	**.261**	69-1-2	.087	-3	119	24	0	2.2
1963	†LA N☆	**25**	5	.833	40	40	20-**11**	0	311	214	68	18	3	58-7	**306**	**1.88**	161	**.189**	**.230**	110-1-7	.064	-4	123	**47**	0	4.1
1964	LA N☆	19	5	**.792**	29	28	15-**7**	1	223	154	49	13	0	53-5	223	**1.74**	**187**	**.191**	**.240**	74-0-3	.095	-2	97	41	0	4.3
1965	†LA N★	**26**	8	**.765**	43	41	**27**-8	2	**335.2**	216	90	26	5	71-4	**382**	**2.04**	160	**.179**	**.227**	113-0-3	.177	5	108	48	0	5.5
1966	†LA N★	**27**	9	.750	41	**41**	**27-5**	0	**323**	241	74	19	0	77-4	**317**	**1.73**	**191**	.205	.252	118	.076	-5	113	**60**	0	**6.1**
Total	12	165	87	.655	397	314	137-40	9	2324.1	1754	806	204	18	817-48	2396	2.76	131	.205	.275	776-2-35	.097	-25	106	241	30	22.3
KOUKALIK, JOE	Joseph; B3.3.1880 , Austria–Hungary; D1.2.1947 Chicago IL; BR/TR/5´8˝/160; d9.1																									
1904	Bro N	0	1	.000	1	1	1	0	8	10	3	0	0	4	1	1.13	244	.333	.412	3	.000	-0	0	1	—	0.0
KOUPAL, LOU	Louis Laddie; B12.19.1898 Tabor SD; D12.8.1961 San Gabriel CA; BR/TR/5´11˝/175; d4.17																									
1925	Pit N	0	0	ø	6	0	0	0	9	14	10	1	0	7	0	9.00	50	.378	.477	1	.000	-0*	—	-4	—	-0.2
1926	Pit N	0	2	.000	6	2	1	0	19.2	22	9	0	1	8	7	3.20	123	.289	.365	4	.250	0	32	1	—	0.1
1928	Bro N	1	0	1.000	17	1	1	1	37.1	43	22	0	1	15	10	2.41	165	.303	.373	9	.111	-1	170	3	—	0.1
1929	Bro N	0	1	.000	18	3	0	4	40.1	49	36	3	0	25	17	5.36	86	.308	.402	14	.071	-2	57	-7	—	-0.5
	Phi N	5	5	.500	15	11	3	2	86.2	106	56	5	2	29	18	4.78	109	.305	.362	32-0-2	.125	-2	95	2	—	-0.1
	Year	5	6	.455	33	14	3	6	127	155	92	8	2	54	35	4.96	101	.306	.375	46-0-2	.109	-4	88	-5	—	-0.6
1930	Phi N	0	4	.000	13	4	1	0	36.2	52	35	4	1	17	11	8.59	64	.344	.414	12	.083	-1	92	-9	—	-0.9
1937	StL A	4	9	.308	26	13	6	0	105.2	150	87	10	0	55	24	6.56	74	.339	.412	32-0-2	.094	-3	90	-20	—	-2.2
Total	6	10	21	.323	101	34	12	7	335.1	436	255	23	5	156	87	5.58	86	.322	.394	104-0-4	.106	-9	90	-34	—	-3.7
KOWALIK, FABIAN	Fabian Lorenz; B4.22.1908 Falls City TX; D8.14.1954 Karnes City TX; BR/TR (BB 1932, 35)/5´11˝/185; d9.4																									
1932	Chi A	0	1	.000	2	1	0	0	10.1	16	11	2	1	4	2	6.97	62	.340	.404	13	.385	1*	98	-4	—	-0.2
1935	†Chi N	2	2	.500	20	2	1	1	55	60	31	2	0	19	20	4.42	89	.280	.339	15	.200	-0	184	-3	—	-0.2
1936	Chi N	0	2	.000	6	0	0	1	16	24	12	1	0	7	1	6.75	59	.358	.419	5	.000	-1	—	-4	—	-0.6
	Phi N	1	5	.167	22	8	2	0	77	100	57	5	2	31	19	5.38	84	.308	.372	57-0-1	.228	-0*	103	-6	—	-0.5
	Bos N	0	1	.000	1	1	1	0	9	18	8	0	0	2	0	8.00	48	.419	.444	5	.400	1*	133	-4	—	-0.3
	Year	1	8	.111	29	9	3	1	102	142	77	6	2	40	20	5.82	75	.326	.386	67-0-1	.224	-0	107	-13	—	-1.4
Total	3	3	11	.214	51	12	4	2	167.1	218	119	10	3	63	42	5.43	78	.313	.373	95-0-1	.242	-0	120	-21	—	-1.8
KOZLOWSKI, BEN	Benjamin Anthony; B8.16.1980 St.Petersburg FL; BL/TL/6´6˝/220; [AtlN99 12/384]; d9.19; Col Santa Fe (FL) CC																									
2002	Tex A	0	0	ø	2	2	0	0-0	10	11	7	3	1	11-0	6	6.30	76	.289	.460	0	ø	0	193	-1	0	-0.1
KRAEMER, JOE	Joseph Wayne; B9.10.1964 Olympia WA; BL/TL/6´2˝/185; [ChiN85 16/416]; d8.22; Col Portland St.																									
1989	Chi N	0	1	.000	1	1	0	0-0	3.2	7	6	0	0	2-1	5	4.91	77	.368	.429	1	.000	-0	47	-2	0	-0.4
1990	Chi N	0	0	ø	18	0	0	0-1	25	31	25	2	2	14-2	16	7.20	57	.310	.398	0	ø	0	—	-9	0	-0.5
Total	2	0	1	.000	19	1	0	0-1	28.2	38	31	2	2	16-3	21	6.91	59	.319	.403	1	.000	-0	47	-11	0	-0.9
KRAKAUSKAS, JOE	Joseph Victor Lawrence; B3.28.1915 Montreal QC, Can.; D7.8.1960 Hamilton ON, Can.; BL/TL/6´1˝/203; d9.9; Mil 1943–45																									
1937	Was A	4	1	.800	5	4	3	0	40	33	14	0	0	22	18	2.70	164	.226	.327	16	.125	-0	103	8	—	0.8
1938	Was A	7	5	.583	29	10	5-1	0	121.1	99	61	4	3	88	104	3.12	145	.220	.352	33-0-3	.182	1	100	15	—	1.3
1939	Was A	11	17	.393	39	29	12	1	217.1	230	125	13	1	114	110	4.60	95	.276	.364	77-0-3	.208	3	101	-5	—	-0.4
1940	Was A	1	6	.143	32	10	2	2	109	137	90	7	0	73	68	6.44	65	.309	.406	32	.250	1	110	-28	—	-1.4
1941	Cle A	1	2	.333	12	5	0	0	41.2	39	25	3	0	29	25	4.10	96	.245	.362	13	.077	-1	123	-3	0	-0.2
1942	Cle A	0	0	ø	3	0	0	0	7	7	3	1	0	4	2	3.86	89	.259	.355	2	.000	-0	—	0	0	0.0
1946	Cle A	2	5	.286	29	5	0	1	47.1	60	31	2	0	25	20	5.51	60	.314	.394	10	.000	-1	83	-11	0	-1.7
Total	7	26	36	.419	149	63	22-1	4	583.2	605	349	30	4	355	347	4.53	93	.269	.369	183-0-6	.180	2	103	-24	0	-1.6
KRALICK, JACK	John Francis; B6.1.1935 Youngstown OH; BL/TL/6´2˝/(166–180); d4.15; Col Michigan St.																									
1959	Was A	0	0	ø	6	0	0	0	12.1	13	9	5	0	6-0	7	6.57	60	.289	.373	2	.000	-0	—	-3	0	-0.1
1960	Was A	8	6	.571	35	18	7-2	1	151	139	54	12	4	45-4	71	3.04	128	.245	.304	41-0-3	.122	-1	92	17	0	1.4
1961	Min A	13	11	.542	33	33	11-2	0	242	257	101	21	3	64-1	137	3.61	118	.274	.321	86-1-6	.151	-2	90	20	0	1.7
1962	Min A	12	11	.522	39	37	7-1	0	242.2	239	121	31	3	61-2	139	3.86	106	.258	.302	89-2-3	.202	3	96	4	0	0.7
1963	Min A	1	4	.200	5	5	1-1	0	25.2	28	16	2	1	8-0	13	3.86	94	.280	.339	6-0-1	.167	1*	39	-2	0	-0.3
	Cle A	13	9	.591	28	27	10-3	0	197.1	187	70	19	0	41-2	116	2.92	124	.249	.286	60-1-9	.183	1	106	17	0	1.9
	Year	14	13	.519	33	32	11-4	0	223	215	86	21	1	49-2	129	3.03	120	.253	.292	66-1-10	.182	2	95	15	0	1.6
1964	Cle A☆	12	7	.632	30	29	8-3	0	190.2	196	79	17	9	51-8	119	3.21	112	.267	.320	64-0-3	.156	-1	101	7	0	0.6
1965	Cle A	5	11	.313	30	16	1	0	86	106	58	9	2	21-3	34	4.92	71	.298	.338	21-0-3	.143	-1	93	-15	0	-2.7
1966	Cle A	3	4	.429	27	4	0	0	68.1	69	30	9	1	20-8	31	3.82	90	.268	.319	13-0-1	.077	-1	70	-2	0	-0.2
1967	Cle A	0	2	.000	2	0	0	0	2	4	3	0	0	1-0	1	9.00	36	.444	.500	0	ø	0	—	-2	0	-0.3
Total	9	67	65	.508	235	169	45-12	1	1218	1238	541	125	23	318-28	668	3.56	108	.264	.312	382-4-29	.162	0	94	41	0	2.7
KRALY, STEVE	Steve Charles "Lefty"; B4.18.1929 Whiting IN; BL/TL/5´10˝/152; d8.9																									
1953	NY A	0	2	.000	5	3	0	1	25	19	10	2	2	16	8	3.24	114	.209	.339	7	.000	-1	40	1	0	0.0
KRAMER, JACK	John Henry; B1.5.1918 New Orleans LA; D5.18.1995 Metairie LA; BR/TR/6´2˝/190; d4.25; Def 1942																									
1939	StL A	9	16	.360	40	31	10-2	0	211.2	269	150	18	3	127	68	5.83	84	.318	.409	66-1-7	.136	-1	103	-19	—	-2.0
1940	StL A	3	7	.300	16	9	1	0	64.2	86	48	4	0	26	12	6.26	73	.327	.388	20-0-1	.050	-1	89	-10	—	-1.4
1941	StL A	4	3	.571	29	3	0	2	59.1	69	48	5	0	40	20	5.16	83	.289	.391	8-0-1	.000	1	101	-10	0	-0.9
1943	StL A	0	0	ø	3	0	0	0	9	11	8	0	1	8	4	8.00	42	.297	.435	2	.500	1	—	-4	0	-0.1
1944	†StL A	17	13	.567	33	31	18-1	0	257	233	94	3	1	75	124	2.49	145	.241	.297	85-2-1	.165	1	90	27	0	3.4
1945	StL A★	10	15	.400	29	25	15-3	2	193	190	85	13	0	73	99	3.36	105	.254	.320	61-0-7	.148	-0	80	2	0	0.3
1946	StL A★	13	11	.542	31	28	13-3	0	194.2	190	84	6	0	68	69	3.19	117	.257	.319	59-0-8	.136	1	96	10	0	1.0
1947	StL A☆	11	16	.407	33	28	9-1	1	199.1	206	123	16	2	89	77	4.97	78	.270	.348	62-0-5	.113	-2	101	-22	0	-2.8
1948	Bos A	18	5	**.783**	29	29	14-2	0	205	233	104	12	0	64	72	4.35	101	.284	.336	73-1-7	.151	-1	152	3	0	0.1
1949	Bos A	6	8	.429	21	18	7-2	1	111.2	126	70	8	1	49	24	5.16	85	.286	.358	35-0-2	.257	3	117	-9	0	-0.8
1950	NY N	3	6	.333	35	9	1	1	86.2	91	46	6	2	39	27	3.53	116	.268	.346	20-1-1	.100	1	98	2	0	0.3
1951	NY N	0	0	ø	4	1	0	0	4.2	11	8	0	0	3	2	15.43	25	.524	.583	0	ø	0	271	-5	0	-0.3
	NY A	1	3	.250	19	3	0	0	40.2	46	27	1	0	21	15	4.65	82	.280	.362	10	.100	-0	162	-5	0	-0.6
Total	12	95	103	.480	322	215	88-14	7	1637.1	1761	895	92	10	682	613	4.24	96	.276	.347	501-5-40	.144	0	107	-40	0	-3.8
KRAMER, RANDY	Randall John; B9.20.1960 Palo Alto CA; BR/TR/6´2˝/180; [TexA82 S1/10]; d9.11; Col San Jose (CA) City																									
1988	Pit N	1	2	.333	5	1	0	0-0	10	12	6	1	1	1-0	7	5.40	64	.316	.341	2	.000	-0	180	-2	0	-0.4
1989	Pit N	5	9	.357	35	15	1-1	2-4	111.1	90	53	10	7	61-4	52	3.96	86	.224	.334	33-0-2	.152	-0*	99	-6	0	-0.8
1990	Pit N	0	1	.000	12	2	0	0-0	25.2	27	15	3	2	9-4	15	4.91	74	.273	.345	5	.000	-1	87	-3	0	-0.2
	Chi N	0	2	.000	10	2	0	0-0	20.1	20	10	3	1	12-2	12	3.98	103	.253	.359	1-0-1	.000	-0	88	0	0	0.0
	Year	0	3	.000	22	4	0	0-0	46	47	25	6	3	21-6	27	4.50	85	.264	.351	6-0-1	.000	-1	88	-3	0	-0.2
1992	Sea A	0	1	.000	4	4	0	0-0	16.1	30	14	2	1	7-0	6	7.71	52	.400	.458	0	ø	0	125	-6	0	-0.3
Total	4	6	15	.286	66	24	1-1	2-4	183.2	179	98	19	12	90-10	92	4.51	79	.259	.352	41-0-3	.122	-1	105	-17	0	-1.7
KRAMER, TOMMY	Thomas Joseph; B1.9.1968 Cincinnati OH; BB/TR/6´0˝/(185–205); [CleA87 5/125]; d9.12; Col John A. Logan (IL) CC																									
1991	Cle A	0	0	ø	4	0	0	0-0	4.2	10	9	1	0	6-0	4	17.36	24	.476	.533	0	ø	0	—	-6	0	-0.3

YEAR	TM LG	W	L	PCT	G	GS	CG-SHO	SV-BS	IP	H	R	HR	HB	BB-IB	SO	ERA	AERA	OAV	OOB	AB-HR-SH	AVG	PB	SUP	APR	DL	PW
1993	Cle A	7	3	.700	39	16	1	0-2	121	126	60	19	2	59-7	71	4.02	109	.269	.352	0	ø	0	121	5	18	0.3
Total	2	7	3	.700	43	16	1	0-2	125.2	136	69	20	2	65-7	75	4.51	97	.278	.361	0	ø	0	121	-1	18	0.0

KRAPP, GENE Eugene Hamlet "Rubber Arm"; B5.12.1887 Rochester NY; D4.13.1923 Detroit MI; BR/TR/5´5˝/165; d4.14

YEAR	TM LG	W	L	PCT	G	GS	CG-SHO	SV-BS	IP	H	R	HR	HB	BB-IB	SO	ERA	AERA	OAV	OOB	AB-HR-SH	AVG	PB	SUP	APR	DL	PW
1911	Cle A	13	9	.591	35	26	14-1	1	222	188	115	1	13	138	132	3.41	100	.232	.353	74-0-3	.230	4*	109	0	—	0.6
1912	Cle A	2	5	.286	9	7	4	0	58.2	57	39	0	4	42	22	4.60	74	.273	.404	22-0-1	.318	1*	96	-7	—	-0.5
1914	Buf F	16	14	.533	36	29	18-1	0	252.2	198	83	4	12	115	106	2.49	119	.210	.304	77-0-2	.143	-1*	89	14	—	1.7
1915	Buf F	9	19	.321	38	30	14-1	0	231	188	106	6	4	123	93	3.51	80	.230	.333	70-0-2	.129	-3*	77	-15	—	-1.7
Total	4	40	47	.460	118	92	50-3	1	764.1	631	343	11	33	418	353	3.23	95	.227	.335	243-0-8	.181	1	92	-8	—	0.1

KRAUS, JACK John William "Tex","Texas Jack"; B4.26.1918 San Antonio TX; D1.2.1976 San Antonio TX; BR/TL/6´4˝/190; d4.25; Mil 1944

YEAR	TM LG	W	L	PCT	G	GS	CG-SHO	SV-BS	IP	H	R	HR	HB	BB-IB	SO	ERA	AERA	OAV	OOB	AB-HR-SH	AVG	PB	SUP	APR	DL	PW
1943	Phi N	9	15	.375	34	25	10-1	2	199.2	197	83	7	0	78	48	3.16	107	.259	.328	60-0-9	.067	-5*	67	4	0	0.0
1945	Phi N	4	9	.308	19	13	0	0	81.2	96	55	3	4	40	28	5.40	71	.293	.376	25-0-2	.120	-1	71	-12	0	-1.7
1946	NY N	2	1	.667	17	1	0	0	25	25	17	4	1	15	7	6.12	56	.260	.366	3	.000	-0	100	-6	0	-0.7
Total	3	15	25	.375	70	39	10-1	2	306.1	318	155	14	5	133	83	4.00	88	.268	.345	88-0-11	.080	-6	70	-14	0	-2.4

KRAUSE, HARRY Harry William "Hal"; B7.12.1888 San Francisco CA; D10.23.1940 San Francisco CA; BB/TL/5´10˝/165; d4.20; Col St. Marys (CA)

YEAR	TM LG	W	L	PCT	G	GS	CG-SHO	SV-BS	IP	H	R	HR	HB	BB-IB	SO	ERA	AERA	OAV	OOB	AB-HR-SH	AVG	PB	SUP	APR	DL	PW
1908	Phi A	1	1	.500	4	2	2	0	21	20	11	0	3	4	10	2.57	100	.247	.307	7	.000	-1	80	-1	—	-0.2
1909	Phi A	18	8	.692	32	21	16-7	0	213	151	49	2	13	49	139	**1.39**	**173**	.204	.266	77-0-2	.156	-1	112	23	—	2.7
1910	Phi A	6	6	.500	16	11	9-2	0	112.1	99	46	4	8	42	60	2.88	82	.254	.339	38-0-4	.211	1	103	-3	—	-0.4
1911	Phi A	11	8	.579	27	19	12-1	2	169	155	65	2	9	47	85	3.04	104	.251	.313	59-0-4	.254	2	107	6	—	0.7
1912	Phi A	0	2	.000	4	2	0	0	5.1	10	8	0	1	2	3	13.50	23	.435	.500	4	.250	0	36	-6	—	-1.0
	Cle A	0	1	.000	2	2	0	0	4.2	11	6	0	0	2	1	11.57	29	.500	.542	0	ø	0	98	-3	—	-0.6
	Year	0	3	.000	6	4	0	0	10	21	14	0	1	4	4	12.60	26	.467	.520	4	.250	0	69	-9	—	-1.6
Total	5	36	26	.581	85	57	39-10	2	525.1	446	185	8	34	146	298	2.50	107	.238	.305	185-0-10	.195	1	105	16	—	1.2

KRAUSSE, LEW Lewis Bernard Jr.; B4.25.1943 Media PA; BR/TR/5´11˝/(185–186); d6.16; f–Lew

YEAR	TM LG	W	L	PCT	G	GS	CG-SHO	SV-BS	IP	H	R	HR	HB	BB-IB	SO	ERA	AERA	OAV	OOB	AB-HR-SH	AVG	PB	SUP	APR	DL	PW
1961	KC A	2	5	.286	12	8	2-1	0	55.2	49	33	3	1	46-0	32	4.85	86	.243	.382	17-0-1	.118	-1*	90	-3	0	-0.5
1964	KC A	0	2	.000	5	4	0	0	14.2	22	14	1	2	9-0	9	7.36	52	.349	.434	2	.000	0*	93	-6	0	-0.7
1965	KC A	2	4	.333	7	5	0	0	25	29	14	1	0	8-0	22	5.04	69	.284	.336	7-0-1	.000	-1*	55	-4	0	-0.8
1966	KC A	14	9	.609	36	22	4-1	3	177.2	144	69	8	6	63-8	87	2.99	114	.222	.294	52-0-6	.154	0*	91	7	0	0.9
1967	KC A	7	17	.292	48	19	0	6	160	140	85	17	4	67-6	96	4.27	75	.236	.314	41-1-1	.146	1*	58	-19	0	-2.8
1968	Oak A	10	11	.476	36	25	2	4	185	147	68	16	3	62-9	105	3.11	91	.217	.283	56-0-2	.161	3	91	-4	0	-0.2
1969	Oak A	7	7	.500	43	16	4-2	7-1	140	134	75	23	5	48-8	85	4.44	78	.256	.322	48-4-1	.167	4	127	-16	0	-1.3
1970	Mil A	13	18	.419	37	35	8-1	0-0	216	235	130	33	4	67-15	130	4.75	80	.275	.328	65-0-7	.138	1*	103	-24	0	-3.1
1971	Mil A	8	12	.400	43	22	1	0-0	180.1	164	67	23	5	62-10	92	2.94	119	.239	.306	44-0-5	.023	-3	76	11	0	0.8
1972	Bos A	1	3	.250	24	7	0	1-0	60.2	74	48	9	3	28-2	35	6.38	51	.308	.387	16	.125	-0	94	-19	0	-1.4
1973	StL N	0	0	ø	1	0	0	0-0	2	2	0	0	0	1-0	1	0.00	ø	.250	.333	0	ø	0	—	1	0	0.1
1974	Atl N	4	3	.571	29	4	0	0-0	66.2	65	32	3	2	32-4	27	4.18	91	.258	.345	6-1-2	.333	2	81	-2	0	0.0
Total	12	68	91	.428	321	167	21-5	21-1	1283.2	1205	635	137	35	493-62	721	4.00	85	.248	.320	354-6-26	.133	6	91	-78	0	-9.0

KRAUSSE, LEW Lewis Bernard Sr.; B6.8.1912 Media PA; D9.6.1988 Sarasota FL; BR/TR/6´0.5˝/167; d6.11; s–Lew

YEAR	TM LG	W	L	PCT	G	GS	CG-SHO	SV-BS	IP	H	R	HR	HB	BB-IB	SO	ERA	AERA	OAV	OOB	AB-HR-SH	AVG	PB	SUP	APR	DL	PW
1931	Phi A	1	0	1.000	3	1	1	0	11	6	6	2	0	6	1	4.09	110	.150	.261	2	.000	0	132	0	—	0.1
1932	Phi A	4	1	.800	20	3	2-1	0	57	64	31	3	0	24	16	4.58	99	.281	.349	15-0-2	.133	-0	239	0	—	0.0
Total	2	5	1	.833	23	4	3-1	0	68	70	37	5	0	30	17	4.50	100	.261	.336	17-0-2	.118	0	212	0	—	0.1

KRAVEC, KEN Kenneth Peter; B7.29.1951 Cleveland OH; BL/TL/6´2˝/(180–185); [ChiA73 3/69]; d9.4; Col Ashland

YEAR	TM LG	W	L	PCT	G	GS	CG-SHO	SV-BS	IP	H	R	HR	HB	BB-IB	SO	ERA	AERA	OAV	OOB	AB-HR-SH	AVG	PB	SUP	APR	DL	PW
1975	Chi A	0	1	.000	2	1	0	0-0	4.1	1	3	0	0	8-0	1	6.23	62	.071	.409	0	ø	0	0	-1	0	-0.2
1976	Chi A	1	5	.167	9	8	1	0-0	49.2	49	28	3	1	32-0	38	4.89	73	.257	.366	0	ø	0	74	-7	0	-0.7
1977	Chi A	11	8	.579	26	25	6-1	0-0	166.2	161	87	12	6	57-0	125	4.10	100	.250	.317	0	ø	0	113	-1	0	-0.1
1978	Chi A	11	16	.407	30	30	7-2	0-0	203	188	104	22	10	95-1	154	4.08	93	.245	.334	0	ø	0	77	-7	0	-0.9
1979	Chi A	15	13	.536	36	35	10-3	1-0	250	208	115	20	14	111-3	132	3.74	114	.233	.323	0	ø	0	94	16	0	1.6
1980	Chi A	3	6	.333	20	15	0	0-0	81.2	100	71	13	5	44-3	37	6.94	58	.298	.382	0	ø	0	90	-25	0	-2.3
1981	Chi N	1	6	.143	24	12	0	0-0	78.1	80	48	5	4	39-6	50	5.06	74	.268	.355	15-0-4	.000	-1*	59	-10	0	-0.9
1982	Chi N	1	1	.500	13	2	0	0-0	25	27	20	3	0	18-2	20	6.12	62	.267	.375	3	.000	-0	128	-7	0	-0.5
Total	8	43	56	.434	160	128	24-6	1-0	858.2	814	476	78	40	404-15	557	4.47	90	.251	.339	18-0-4	.000	-1	89	-42	0	-4.0

KRAWCZYK, RAY Raymond Allen; B10.9.1959 Pittsburgh PA; BR/TR/6´1˝/(184–190); [PitN81 S1/4]; d6.29; Col Oral Roberts

YEAR	TM LG	W	L	PCT	G	GS	CG-SHO	SV-BS	IP	H	R	HR	HB	BB-IB	SO	ERA	AERA	OAV	OOB	AB-HR-SH	AVG	PB	SUP	APR	DL	PW
1984	Pit N	0	0	ø	4	0	0	0-0	5.1	7	2	0	0	4-2	3	3.38	108	.350	.440	0	ø	0	—	0	0	0.0
1985	Pit N	0	2	.000	8	0	0	0-2	8.1	20	13	1	1	6-3	9	14.04	26	.455	.529	0	ø	0	—	-9	0	-1.7
1986	Pit N	0	1	.000	12	0	0	0-0	12.1	17	13	3	0	10-0	7	7.30	53	.321	.422	0	ø	0	—	-5	56	-0.4
1988	Cal A	0	1	.000	14	1	0	1-0	24.1	29	13	2	2	8-1	17	4.81	81	.299	.361	0	ø	0	94	-2	0	-0.1
1989	Mil A	0	0	ø	1	0	0	0-0	2	4	3	0	0	1-0	6	13.50	29	.400	.455	0	ø	0	—	-2	0	-0.1
Total	5	0	4	.000	39	1	0	1-2	52.1	77	44	6	3	29-6	42	7.05	54	.344	.421	0	ø	0	94	-18	56	-2.3

KREEGER, FRANK Frank; D7.14.1899 Shelby Co. IL; d7.28

YEAR	TM LG	W	L	PCT	G	GS	CG-SHO	SV-BS	IP	H	R	HR	HB	BB-IB	SO	ERA	AERA	OAV	OOB	AB-HR-SH	AVG	PB	SUP	APR	DL	PW
1884	KC U	0	1	.000	1	1	0	0	7	9	8	0	—	5	3	0.00	ø	.290	.389	3	.000	-1	38	0	—	-0.1

KREMER, RAY Remy Peter "Wiz"; B3.23.1893 Oakland CA; D2.8.1965 Pinole CA; BR/TR/6´1˝/190; d4.18

YEAR	TM LG	W	L	PCT	G	GS	CG-SHO	SV-BS	IP	H	R	HR	HB	BB-IB	SO	ERA	AERA	OAV	OOB	AB-HR-SH	AVG	PB	SUP	APR	DL	PW
1924	Pit N	18	10	.643	**41**	30	17-**4**	1	259.1	262	102	7	4	51	64	3.19	120	.265	.304	86-0-5	.151	-4*	109	21	—	1.6
1925	†Pit N	17	8	.680	40	27	14	2	214.2	232	106	19	9	47	62	3.69	121	.278	.323	71-0-5	.197	1	117	18	—	1.8
1926	Pit N	**20**	6	**.769**	37	26	18-3	5	231.1	221	79	9	4	51	74	**2.61**	**151**	.252	.296	83-1-6	.253	2	106	**34**	—	**3.9**
1927	†Pit N	19	8	.704	35	28	18-3	2	226	205	73	9	0	53	63	**2.47**	**166**	.244	.289	83-2-3	.169	-1	104	39	—	4.2
1928	Pit N	15	13	.536	34	31	17-1	0	219	253	124	16	4	68	61	4.64	87	.297	.352	78-0-3	.179	0	114	-10	—	-1.3
1929	Pit N	18	10	.643	34	27	14	0	221.2	226	114	21	1	60	66	4.26	112	.271	.320	86-1-1	.128	-2	103	16	—	1.3
1930	Pit N	**20**	12	.625	39	**38**	18-1	0	**276**	366	181	29	1	63	58	5.02	99	.322	.359	102-1-8	.157	-4	112	-2	—	-0.7
1931	Pit N	11	15	.423	30	30	15-1	0	230	246	110	6	5	65	58	3.33	116	.271	.323	75-0-3	.227	4	80	11	—	1.3
1932	Pit N	4	3	.571	11	10	3-1	0	56.2	61	35	5	1	16	6	4.29	89	.270	.321	19-0-2	.105	-1	106	-4	—	-0.6
1933	Pit N	1	0	1.000	7	0	0	0	20	36	26	2	0	9	4	10.35	32	.387	.441	4	.000	-1	—	-15	—	-0.8
Total	10	143	85	.627	308	247	134-14	10	1954.2	2108	950	123	29	483	516	3.76	113	.278	.323	687-5-36	.178	-7	107	108	—	10.7

KREMMEL, JIM James Louis; B2.28.1948 Belleville IL; BL/TL/6´0˝/175; [TexA71*A1/9]; d7.4; Col New Mexico

YEAR	TM LG	W	L	PCT	G	GS	CG-SHO	SV-BS	IP	H	R	HR	HB	BB-IB	SO	ERA	AERA	OAV	OOB	AB-HR-SH	AVG	PB	SUP	APR	DL	PW
1973	Tex A	0	2	.000	4	2	0	0-0	9	15	10	1	2	6-1	6	9.00	42	.366	.460	0	ø	0	59	-5	0	-0.9
1974	Chi N	0	2	.000	23	2	0	0-1	31	37	21	3	1	18-0	22	5.23	73	.303	.386	3	.000	-0	68	-4	0	-0.3
Total	2	0	4	.000	27	4	0	0-1	40	52	31	4	3	24-1	28	6.07	63	.319	.405	3	.000	-0	63	-9	0	-1.2

KRESS, RED Ralph; B1.2.1905 Columbia CA; D11.29.1962 Los Angeles CA; BR/TR/5´11.5˝/165; d9.24.1927; C15; ▲

YEAR	TM LG	W	L	PCT	G	GS	CG-SHO	SV-BS	IP	H	R	HR	HB	BB-IB	SO	ERA	AERA	OAV	OOB	AB-HR-SH	AVG	PB	SUP	APR	DL	PW
1935	Was A	0	0	ø	3	0	0	0	5.2	8	9	0	0	5	5	12.71	34	.333	.448	252-2-2	.298	1*	—	-5	—	-0.2
1946	NY N	0	0	ø	1	0	0	0	3.2	5	5	1	1	1	1	12.27	28	.333	.412	1	.000	0	—	-3	0	-0.1
Total	2	0	0	ø	4	0	0	0	9.1	13	14	1	1	6	6	12.54	32	.333	.435	253-2-2	.296	1	—	-8	0	-0.3

KRETLOW, LOU Louis Henry "Lena"; B6.27.1921 Apache OK; BR/TR/6´2˝/(185–190); d9.26

YEAR	TM LG	W	L	PCT	G	GS	CG-SHO	SV-BS	IP	H	R	HR	HB	BB-IB	SO	ERA	AERA	OAV	OOB	AB-HR-SH	AVG	PB	SUP	APR	DL	PW
1946	Det A	1	0	1.000	1	1	1	0	9	7	3	2	0	2	4	3.00	122	.206	.250	4	.500	1	141	1	0	0.2
1948	Det A	2	1	.667	5	2	1	0	23.1	21	14	1	0	11	9	4.63	94	.233	.317	8-0-1	.500	1	41	-1	0	0.0
1949	Det A	3	2	.600	25	10	1	0	76	85	58	5	1	69	40	6.16	68	.290	.427	26-0-1	.000	-4	153	-17	0	-1.2
1950	StL A	0	2	.000	9	2	0	0	14.1	25	19	2	2	18	10	11.93	41	.403	.549	3	.000	-0*	100	-9	0	-1.1
	Chi A	0	0	ø	11	1	0	0	21.1	17	13	1	0	27	14	3.80	118	.221	.423	4	.000	-1	141	0	0	-0.1
	Year	0	2	.000	20	3	0	0	35.2	42	32	3	2	45	24	7.07	66	.302	.478	7	.000	-1	116	-9	0	-1.2
1951	Chi A	6	9	.400	26	18	7-1	0	137	129	77	7	3	74	89	4.20	96	.250	.347	48-0-1	.083	-5	82	-4	0	-0.9
1952	Chi A	4	4	.500	19	11	4-2	1	79	52	31	5	1	56	63	2.96	123	.186	.323	20-0-2	.050	-1	83	5	0	0.4
1953	Chi A	0	0	ø	9	3	0	0	20.2	12	11	2	1	30	15	3.48	116	.171	.426	4	.000	-0	133	0	0	0.0
	StL A	1	5	.167	22	11	0	0	81	93	56	5	0	52	37	5.11	82	.286	.385	25-0-2	.200	-1	83	-9	0	-0.8
	Year	1	5	.167	31	14	0	0	101.2	105	67	7	1	82	52	4.78	87	.266	.393	29-0-2	.172	-1	93	-10	0	-0.8
1954	Bal A	6	11	.353	32	20	5	0	166.2	169	83	12	1	82	82	4.37	82	.269	.349	51-0-4	.157	-0	81	-11	0	-1.0
1955	Bal A	0	4	.000	15	5	0	0	38.1	50	39	3	1	27-0	26	8.22	46	.316	.411	11-0-1	.091	-1	98	-19	0	-1.7

YEAR	TM LG	W	L	PCT	G	GS	CG-SHO	SV-BS	IP	H	R	HR	HB	BB-IB	SO	ERA	AERA	OAV	OOB	AB-HR-SH	AVG	PB	SUP	APR	DL	PW
1956	KC A	4	9	.308	25	20	3	0	118.2	121	75	17	0	74-4	61	5.31	82	.262	.362	33-0-4	.061	-3	78	-11	0	-1.3
Total	10	27	47	.365	199	104	22-3	1	785.1	781	479	62	10	522-4	450	4.87	82	.261	.370	237-0-16	.114	-13	91	-75	0	-7.5
KREUGER, RICK	Richard Allen; B11.3.1948 Grand Rapids MI; BR/TL/6´2˝/185; d9.6; Col Michigan St.																									
1975	Bos A	0	0	ø	2	0	0	0-0	4	3	2	0	0	1-0	1	4.50	90	.200	.250	0	ø	0	—	0	0	0.0
1976	Bos A	2	1	.667	8	4	1	0-0	31	31	14	3	0	16-0	12	4.06	96	.272	.359	0	ø	0	130	0	0	0.1
1977	Bos A	0	1	.000	1	0	0	0-0	0	2	2	0	0	0-0	0	(2)	ø	1.000	1.000	0	ø	0	—	-2	0	-0.2
1978	Cle A	0	0	ø	6	0	0	0-0	9.1	6	4	1	0	3-0	7	3.86	98	.194	.243	0	ø	0	—	0	0	0.0
Total	4	2	2	.500	17	4	1	0-0	44.1	42	22	4	0	20-0	20	4.47	87	.259	.333	0	ø	0	130	-2	0	-0.1
KREUTZER, FRANK	Franklin James; B2.7.1939 Buffalo NY; BR/TL/6´1˝/(175–190); d9.20; Col Villanova																									
1962	Chi A	0	0	ø	1	0	0	0	1.1	0	0	0	0	1-0	1	0.00	ø	.000	.200	0	ø	0	—	1	0	0.0
1963	Chi A	1	0	1.000	1	1	0	0	5	3	1	1	0	1-0	0	1.80	195	.188	.235	2	.000	-0	177	1	0	0.2
1964	Chi A	3	1	.750	17	2	0	1	40.1	37	15	1	0	18-3	32	3.35	103	.239	.316	8-0-2	.125	-0	64	1	0	0.2
	Was A	2	6	.250	13	9	0	0	45.1	48	26	6	1	23-0	27	4.76	78	.267	.351	11-0-2	.000	-1	77	-5	0	-0.9
	Year	5	7	.417	30	11	0	1	85.2	85	41	7	1	41-3	59	4.10	87	.254	.335	19-0-4	.053	-1	77	-3	0	-0.7
1965	Was A	2	6	.250	33	14	2-1	0	85.1	73	48	7	2	54-1	65	4.32	80	.232	.344	22-1-0	.045	-1	108	-8	0	-0.9
1966	Was A	0	5	.000	9	6	0	0	31.1	30	24	9	1	10-1	24	6.03	57	.236	.297	8	.250	0	64	-9	0	-1.2
1969	Was A	0	0	ø	4	0	0	0-0	2	3	1	0	0	2-0	2	4.50	78	.333	.455	0	ø	0	—	0	0	0.0
Total	6	8	18	.308	78	32	2-1	1-0	210.2	194	115	24	4	109-5	151	4.40	80	.241	.332	51-1-4	.078	-2	91	-19	0	-2.6
KRIEGER, KURT	Kurt Ferdinand "Dutch"; B9.16.1926 Traisen, Austria; D8.16.1970 St.Louis MO; BR/TR/6´3˝/212; d4.21; Col Washington–St. Louis																									
1949	StL N	0	0	ø	1	0	0	0	1	0	0	0	0	1	0	0.00	ø	.000	.250	0	ø	0	—	0	0	0.0
1951	StL N	0	0	ø	2	0	0	0	4	6	7	1	0	5	3	15.75	25	.353	.500	0	ø	0	—	-5	0	-0.2
Total	2	0	0	ø	3	0	0	0	5	6	7	1	0	6	3	12.60	32	.300	.462	0	ø	0	—	-5	0	-0.2
KRIST, HOWIE	Howard Wilbur "Spud"; B2.28.1916 W.Henrietta NY; D4.23.1989 Buffalo NY; BL/TR/6´1˝/175; d9.12; Mil 1944–45																									
1937	StL N	3	1	.750	6	4	1	0	27.2	34	13	0	0	10	6	4.23	94	.304	.361	9-0-1	.000	-1	135	0	—	-0.1
1938	StL N	0	0	ø	2	0	0	0	1.1	1	0	0	0	0	1	0.00	ø	.250	.250	0	ø	0	—	1	—	0.0
1941	StL N	10	0	1.000	37	8	2	2	114	107	57	10	1	35	36	4.03	93	.246	.304	38-0-2	.237	1	163	-2	0	-0.1
1942	StL N	13	3	.813	34	8	3	1	118.1	103	34	2	2	43	47	2.51	136	.233	.304	42-0-1	.143	-1*	144	14	0	1.6
1943	†StL N	11	5	.688	34	17	9-2	3	164.1	141	57	5	4	62	57	2.90	116	.233	.309	60-0-4	.167	-2	114	11	0	0.6
1946	StL N	0	2	.000	15	0	0	0	18.2	22	15	3	1	8	3	6.75	51	.306	.383	0	ø	0	—	-6	0	-0.6
Total	6	37	11	.771	128	37	15-2	6	444.1	408	176	20	8	158	150	3.32	106	.244	.313	149-0-8	.168	-3	134	18	0	1.4
KRIVDA, RICK	Rick Michael; B1.19.1970 McKeesport PA; BR/TL/6´1˝/180; [BalA91 23/602]; d7.7; Col California (PA)																									
1995	Bal A	2	7	.222	13	13	1	0-0	75.1	76	40	9	4	25-1	53	4.54	105	.266	.329	0	ø	0	73	2	0	0.2
1996	Bal A	3	5	.375	22	11	0	0-0	81.2	89	48	14	1	39-2	54	4.96	100	.283	.361	0	ø	0	87	0	0	0.0
1997	Bal A	4	2	.667	10	10	0	0-0	50	67	36	7	0	18-1	29	6.30	70	.328	.379	0	ø	0	127	-10	0	-1.0
1998	Cle A	2	0	1.000	11	1	0	0-0	25	24	10	2	0	16-1	10	3.24	148	.250	.357	0	ø	0	156	4	0	0.3
	Cin N	0	2	.000	16	1	0	0-1	26.1	41	34	7	3	19-1	19	11.28	38	.366	.467	4	.000	-0	64	-20	0	-1.3
Total	4	11	16	.407	72	36	1	0-1	258.1	297	168	39	8	117-6	165	5.57	85	.293	.368	4	.000	-0	94	-24	0	-1.8
KROCK, GUS	August H.; B5.9.1866 Milwaukee WI; D3.22.1905 Pasadena CA; BR/TR/6´0˝/196; d4.24																									
1888	Chi N	25	14	.641	39	39	39-4	0	339.2	295	143	20	9	45	161	2.44	124	.227	.258	134-1	.164	-3	102	24	—	2.0
1889	Chi N	3	3	.500	7	7	5	0	60.2	86	43	10	2	14	16	4.90	85	.325	.363	24	.167	-1	113	-2	—	-0.3
	Ind N	2	2	.500	4	4	3	0	32	48	38	2	0	14	10	7.31	57	.336	.395	14	.357	1	117	-11	—	-0.9
	Was N	2	4	.333	6	6	6	0	48	65	50	1	1	22	17	5.25	75	.314	.383	23	.087	-2	128	-9	—	-1.0
	Year	7	9	.438	17	17	14	0	140.2	199	131	13	3	50	43	5.57	73	.324	.377	61	.180	-2	119	-23	—	-2.2
1890	Buf P	0	3	.000	4	3	3	0	25	43	37	1	0	15	5	6.12	67	.364	.436	12	.083	-1	84	-9	—	-0.8
Total	3	32	26	.552	60	59	56-4	0	505.1	537	311	34	12	110	209	3.49	97	.265	.306	207-1	.164	-7	106	-7	—	-1.0
KROH, RUBE	Floyd Myron; B8.25.1886 Friendship NY; D3.17.1944 New Orleans LA; BL/TL/6´2˝/186; d9.30																									
1906	Bos A	1	0	1.000	1	1	1-1	0	9	2	0	0	0	4	5	0.00	ø	.074	.194	3	.000	-0	52	3	—	0.3
1907	Bos A	1	4	.200	7	5	1	0	34.1	33	13	0	2	8	8	2.62	98	.256	.309	11	.273	0	52	0	—	0.1
1908	Chi N	0	0	ø	2	1	0	0	12	9	3	0	0	4	11	1.50	157	.200	.265	4	.000	-0	90	1	—	0.1
1909	Chi N	9	4	.692	17	13	10-2	0	120.1	97	26	2	1	30	51	1.65	154	.224	.276	40-0-1	.150	-0	108	14	—	1.6
1910	Chi N	3	1	.750	6	4	1	0	34.1	33	19	1	2	15	16	4.46	65	.254	.340	12-0-1	.250	0	110	-5	—	-0.5
1912	Bos N	0	0	ø	3	1	0	0	6.1	8	4	0	0	6	1	5.68	63	.364	.500	2	.500	0	102	-1	—	0.0
Total	6	14	9	.609	36	25	13-3	0	216.1	182	65	3	5	67	92	2.29	115	.232	.296	72-0-2	.181	-0	94	12	—	1.6
KROLL, GARY	Gary Melvin; B7.8.1941 Culver City CA; BR/TR/6´6˝/220; d7.26																									
1964	Phi N	0	0	ø	2	0	0	0	3	3	1	0	0	2-0	2	3.00	116	.250	.357	0	ø	0	—	0	0	0.0
	NY N	0	1	.000	8	2	0	0	21.2	19	11	1	1	15-0	24	4.15	86	.241	.365	3	.333	0	86	-1	0	0.0
	Year	0	1	.000	10	2	0	0	24.2	22	12	1	1	17-0	26	4.01	89	.242	.364	3	.333	0	86	-1	0	0.0
1965	NY N	6	6	.500	32	11	1	1	87	83	48	12	6	41-0	62	4.45	79	.249	.340	26-0-3	.115	-1	119	-8	0	-1.2
1966	Hou N	0	0	ø	10	0	0	0	23.2	26	10	2	0	11-0	22	3.80	90	.280	.356	3	.000	-0	—	0	0	-0.1
1969	Cle A	0	0	ø	19	0	0	0-0	24	16	14	3	0	22-0	28	4.13	92	.188	.352	0	ø	0	—	-1	0	-0.1
Total	4	6	7	.462	71	13	1	1-0	159.1	147	84	18	7	91-0	138	4.24	84	.244	.348	32-0-3	.125	-1	114	-10	0	-1.4
KROON, MARC	Marc Jason; B4.2.1973 Bronx NY; BB/TR/6´2˝/(190–195); [NYN91 2/72]; d7.7																									
1995	SD N	0	1	.000	2	0	0	0-0	1.2	1	2	0	0	2-0	2	10.80	38	.200	.429	0	ø	0	—	-1	0	-0.2
1997	SD N	0	1	.000	12	0	0	0-0	11.1	14	9	2	1	5-0	12	6.35	62	.280	.357	0	ø	0	—	-3	0	-0.3
1998	SD N	0	0	ø	2	0	0	0-0	2.1	0	0	0	0	1-0	2	0.00	ø	.000	.125	0	ø	0	—	1	0	0.1
	Cin N	0	0	ø	4	0	0	0-0	5.1	7	8	0	1	8-0	4	13.50	32	.333	.533	0	ø	0	—	-5	36	-0.2
	Year	0	0	ø	6	0	0	0-0	7.2	7	8	0	1	9-0	6	9.39	45	.250	.447	0	ø	0	—	-4	0	-0.1
2004	Col N	0	0	ø	6	0	0	0-0	6	7	4	1	0	10-0	3	6.00	79	.350	.548	0	ø	0	—	-1	0	0.0
Total	4	0	2	.000	26	0	0	0-0	26.2	29	23	3	2	26-0	23	7.43	57	.282	.432	0	ø	0	—	-9	36	-0.6
KRUEGER, BILL	William Culp; B4.24.1958 Waukegan IL; BL/TL/6´5˝/(205–215); d4.10; Col Portland																									
1983	Oak A	7	6	.538	17	16	2	0-0	109.2	104	54	7	2	53-1	58	3.61	108	.252	.336	0	ø	0	114	1	59	0.0
1984	Oak A	10	10	.500	26	24	1	0-0	142	156	95	9	2	85-2	61	4.75	79	.285	.378	0	ø	0	118	-22	0	-2.7
1985	Oak A	9	10	.474	32	23	2	0-0	151.1	165	95	13	2	69-1	56	4.52	86	.276	.351	0	ø	0	129	-17	0	-1.9
1986	Oak A	1	2	.333	11	3	0	1-0	34.1	40	25	4	0	13-0	10	6.03	65	.301	.358	0	ø	0	155	-9	94	-0.7
1987	Oak A	0	3	.000	9	0	0	0-0	5.2	9	7	0	0	8-3	2	9.53	44	.360	.515	0	ø	0	—	-4	0	-0.7
	LA N	0	0	ø	2	0	0	0-0	2.1	3	2	0	0	1-0	2	0.00	ø	.250	.308	0	ø	0	—	0	0	0.0
1988	LA N	0	0	ø	1	1	0	0-0	2.1	4	3	0	1	2-1	1	11.57	29	.364	.500	0	ø	0	133	-2	0	-0.1
1989	Mil A	3	2	.600	34	5	0	3-0	93.2	96	43	9	0	33-3	72	3.84	100	.264	.324	0	ø	0	108	1	0	0.0
1990	Mil A	6	8	.429	30	17	0	0-0	129	137	70	10	3	54-6	64	3.98	98	.276	.345	0	ø	0	121	-3	21	-0.3
1991	Sea A	11	8	.579	35	25	1	0-0	175	194	82	15	4	60-4	91	3.60	115	.289	.346	0	ø	0	88	8	0	0.8
1992	Min A	10	6	.625	27	27	2-2	0-0	161.1	166	82	18	3	46-2	86	4.30	95	.263	.316	0	ø	0	126	-3	0	-0.4
	Mon N	0	2	.000	9	2	0	0-0	17.1	23	13	0	1	7-0	13	6.75	52	.315	.383	3-0-1	.000	-0	169	-6	0	-0.7
1993	Det A	6	4	.600	32	7	0	0-3	82	90	43	6	4	30-5	60	3.40	128	.285	.351	0	ø	0	157	5	49	0.5
1994	Det A	0	2	.000	16	2	0	0-2	19.2	26	24	3	1	17-1	17	9.61	51	.321	.431	0	ø	0	131	-10	0	-0.8
	SD N	3	2	.600	8	7	1	0-0	41	42	24	5	1	7-1	30	4.83	86	.259	.292	12-0-2	.500	3	110	-3	0	0.0
1995	SD N	0	0	ø	6	0	0	0-0	7.2	13	6	1	0	4-1	6	7.04	58	.371	.436	0	ø	0	—	-2	0	-0.1
	Sea A	2	1	.667	6	5	0	0-0	20	37	17	4	0	4-1	10	5.85	82	.407	.432	0	ø	0	152	-4	0	-0.5
Total	13	68	66	.507	301	164	9-2	4-5	1194.1	1305	685	104	24	493-32	639	4.35	92	.280	.349	15-0-3	.400	2	120	-70	223	-7.6
KRUGER, ABE	Abraham; B2.14.1885 Morris Run PA; D7.4.1962 Elmira NY; BR/TR/6´2˝/190; d10.6																									
1908	Bro N	0	1	.000	2	1	0	0	6.1	5	5	0	3	3	2	4.26	55	.238	.407	2	.000	-0	60	-2	—	-0.2
KRUKOW, MIKE	Michael Edward; B1.21.1952 Long Beach CA; BR/TR/6´5˝/(195–205); [ChiN73 8/184]; d9.6; Col Cal Poly–San Luis Obispo																									
1976	Chi N	0	0	ø	2	0	0	0-0	4.1	6	4	0	0	2-0	1	8.31	47	.333	.400	1	.000	-0	—	-2	0	-0.1
1977	Chi N	8	14	.364	34	33	1-1	0-0	172	195	96	16	3	61-8	106	4.40	100	.281	.340	55-0-7	.200	-0	85	0	0	-0.1
1978	Chi N	9	3	.750	27	20	3-1	0-0	138.1	125	62	11	5	53-4	81	3.90	104	.243	.318	45-0-3	.244	2	99	4	0	0.6

YEAR	TM LG	W	L	PCT	G	GS	CG-SHO	SV-BS	IP	H	R	HR	HB	BB-IB	SO	ERA	AERA	OAV	OOB	AB-HR-SH	AVG	PB	SUP	APR	DL	PW
1979	Chi N	9	9	.500	28	28	0	0-0	164.2	172	84	13	3	81-12	119	4.21	99	.275	.359	51-1-7	.314	5	84	0	0	0.4
1980	Chi N	10	15	.400	34	34	3	0-0	205	200	117	13	8	80-5	130	4.39	90	.258	.329	65-1-7	.246	2	101	-10	0	-1.1
1981	Chi N	9	9	.500	25	**25**	2-1	0-0	144.1	146	68	11	2	55-6	101	3.68	102	.264	.330	50-0-6	.180	-0	103	0	0	0.1
1982	Phi N	13	11	.542	33	33	7-2	0-0	208	211	87	8	3	82-10	138	3.12	119	.268	.336	72-0-5	.181	-0	98	10	0	1.2
1983	SF N	11	11	.500	31	31	2-1	0-0	184.1	189	95	17	3	76-8	136	3.95	90	.261	.332	63-1-4	.254	5	118	-9	27	-0.6
1984	SF N	11	12	.478	35	33	3-1	1-0	199.1	234	117	22	5	78-5	141	4.56	78	.290	.353	72-0-2	.139	-1*	129	-24	0	-2.8
1985	SF N	8	11	.421	28	28	6-1	0-0	194.2	176	80	19	3	49-10	150	3.38	103	.238	.287	55-1-8	.218	5	74	4	0	0.9
1986	SF N★	20	9	.690	34	34	10-2	0-0	245	204	90	24	4	55-4	178	3.05	116	.223	.269	82-0-12	.146	0*	128	16	15	1.8
1987	†SF N	5	6	.455	30	28	3	0-0	163	182	98	24	2	46-6	104	4.80	80	.288	.334	54-0-5	.167	1	133	-19	19	-1.0
1988	SF N	7	4	.636	20	20	1	0-0	124.2	111	51	13	5	31-3	75	3.54	92	.236	.289	41-1-4	.073	-0	109	-2	48	-0.2
1989	SF N	4	3	.571	8	8	0	0-0	43	37	20	5	1	18-3	18	3.98	85	.236	.316	16	.063	-1	108	-2	144	-0.5
Total	14	124	117	.515	369	355	41-10	1-0	2190.2	2188	1069	196	47	767-84	1478	3.90	96	.260	.323	722-5-70	.193	16	105	-34	253	-1.4
Krumm, Al	Albert; B1.13.1865 Pittsburgh PA; D6.15.1937 San Diego CA; TR; d5.17																									
1889	Pit N	0	1	.000	1	1	1	0	9	8	11	0	0	10	4	10.00	37	.229	.400	4	.000	-1	125	-6	—	-0.4
Kubenka, Jeff	Jeffrey Scot; B8.24.1974 Weimar TX; BR/TL/6´2˝/191; [LAN96 38/1138]; d9.6; Col St. Marys (TX)																									
1998	LA N	1	0	1.000	6	0	0	0-1	9.1	4	1	0	0	8-0	10	0.96	418	.138	.316	0	ø	0	—	3	0	0.3
1999	LA N	0	1	.000	6	0	0	0-0	7.2	13	12	1	0	4-0	2	11.74	37	.371	.425	1	1.000	0	—	-7	0	-0.7
Total	2	1	1	.500	12	0	0	0-1	17	17	13	1	0	12-0	12	5.82	72	.266	.372	1	1.000	0	—	-4	0	-0.4
Kubinski, Tim	Timothy Mark; B1.20.1972 Pullman WA; BL/TL/6´4˝/205; [OakA93 7/209]; d7.16; Col UCLA																									
1997	Oak A	0	0	ø	11	0	0	0-0	12.2	12	9	2	1	6-1	10	5.68	81	.255	.339	0	ø	0	—	-2	0	-0.1
1999	Oak A	0	0	ø	14	0	0	0-1	12.1	14	8	3	1	5-1	7	5.84	81	.280	.351	0	ø	0	—	-1	0	0.0
Total	2	0	0	ø	25	0	0	0-1	25	26	17	5	2	11-2	17	5.76	81	.268	.345	0	ø	0	—	-3	0	-0.1
Kucab, Johnny	John Albert; B12.17.1919 Olyphant PA; D5.26.1977 Youngstown OH; BR/TR/6´2˝/185; d9.14																									
1950	Phi A	1	1	.500	4	2	2	0	26	29	10	4	0	8	8	3.46	131	.282	.333	9	.111	-0	59	4	0	0.2
1951	Phi A	4	3	.571	30	1	0	4	74.2	76	37	9	1	23	23	4.22	101	.265	.322	16	.000	-2	21	1	0	-0.1
1952	Phi A	0	1	.000	25	0	0	2	51.1	64	37	5	1	20	17	5.26	75	.312	.376	10	.200	-0*	—	-8	0	-0.5
Total	3	5	5	.500	59	3	2	6	152	169	84	18	2	51	48	4.44	95	.284	.343	35	.086	-2	49	-3	0	-0.4
Kucek, Jack	John Andrew Charles; B6.8.1953 Warren OH; BR/TR/6´2˝/(190–200); [ChiA74 2/32]; d8.8; Col Miami–Ohio																									
1974	Chi A	1	4	.200	9	7	0	0-0	37.2	48	25	3	1	21-0	25	5.26	71	.320	.402	0	ø	0	71	-6	0	-0.7
1975	Chi A	0	0	ø	2	0	0	0-0	3.2	9	2	0	0	4-0	2	4.91	79	.500	.591	0	ø	0	—	0	0	0.0
1976	Chi A	0	0	ø	2	0	0	0-0	4.2	9	5	2	0	4-0	2	9.64	37	.429	.500	0	ø	0	—	-3	0	-0.2
1977	Chi A	0	1	.000	8	3	0	0-0	34.2	35	20	4	2	10-0	25	3.63	112	.267	.324	0	ø	0	183	0	21	0.0
1978	Chi A	2	3	.400	10	5	3	1-0	52	42	23	5	0	27-2	30	3.29	116	.220	.315	0	ø	0	61	2	0	0.2
1979	Chi A	0	0	ø	1	0	0	0-0	0.2	0	4	0	0	3-0	0	0.00	ø	.000	.500	0	ø	0	—	-1	0	-0.1
	Phi N	1	0	1.000	4	0	0	0-0	4.1	6	4	2	0	1-1	2	8.31	47	.333	.368	0	ø	0	—	-2	0	-0.4
1980	Tor A	3	8	.273	23	12	0	1-0	68	83	56	9	1	41-1	35	6.75	64	.300	.391	0	ø	0	83	-17	0	-2.4
Total	7	7	16	.304	59	27	3	2-0	205.2	232	139	25	4	111-4	121	5.12	78	.287	.373	0	ø	0	88	-27	21	-3.6
Kucks, Johnny	John Charles; B7.27.1933 Hoboken NJ; BR/TR/6´3˝/(170–190); d4.17																									
1955	†NY A	8	7	.533	29	13	3-1	0	126.2	122	54	8	2	44-6	49	3.41	110	.252	.315	40-0-2	.050	-4	111	6	0	0.2
1956	†NY A☆	18	9	.667	34	31	12-3	0	224.1	223	113	19	10	72-0	67	3.85	100	.261	.323	77-0-6	.143	-2	127	-2	0	-0.3
1957	†NY A	8	10	.444	37	23	4-1	2	179.1	169	82	13	8	59-2	78	3.56	101	.251	.316	55-0-11	.109	-2	123	0	0	0.0
1958	†NY A	8	8	.500	34	15	4-1	4	126	132	67	14	6	39-2	46	3.93	90	.269	.328	40-0-6	.125	-1	122	-7	0	-0.9
1959	NY A	0	1	.000	9	1	0	0	16.2	21	16	5	0	9-0	9	8.64	42	.323	.405	2	.000	-0	97	-9	0	-0.5
	KC A	8	11	.421	33	23	6-1	1	151.1	163	76	10	12	42-0	51	3.87	104	.278	.336	47-0-3	.085	-3	75	2	0	0.0
	Year	8	12	.400	42	24	6-1	1	168	184	92	15	12	51-0	60	4.34	91	.282	.343	49-0-3	.082	-3	76	-7	0	-0.5
1960	KC A	4	10	.286	31	17	1	0	114	140	85	22	1	43-2	38	6.00	66	.306	.361	30-0-3	.133	-1	79	-24	0	-2.7
Total	6	54	56	.491	207	123	30-7	7	938.1	970	493	91	39	308-12	338	4.10	92	.269	.330	291-0-31	.110	-12	107	-34	0	-4.2
Kuczynski, Bert	Bernard Carl; B1.8.1920 Philadelphia PA; D1.19.1997 Allentown PA; BR/TR/6´0˝/195; d6.2; Mil 1943–45; Col Penn																									
1943	Phi A	0	1	.000	6	1	0	0	24.2	36	15	2	2	9	8	4.01	85	.336	.398	6	.000	-0	50	-3	0	-0.2
Kuhaulua, Fred	Fred Mahele; B2.23.1953 Honolulu HI; BL/TL/5´11˝/175; d8.2																									
1977	Cal A	0	0	ø	3	1	0	0-0	6.1	15	11	1	0	7-0	3	15.63	25	.455	.550	0	ø	0	69	-8	0	-0.4
1981	SD N	1	0	1.000	5	4	0	0-0	29.1	28	10	1	0	9-1	16	2.45	132	.257	.314	9-0-1	.111	-0	89	2	0	0.0
Total	2	1	0	1.000	8	5	0	0-0	35.2	43	21	2	0	16-1	19	4.79	70	.303	.373	9-0-1	.111	-0	85	-6	0	-0.4
Kuhn, Bub	Bernard Daniel; B10.12.1899 Vicksburg MI; D11.20.1956 Detroit MI; BL/TR/6´1.5˝/182; d9.1; Col Michigan St.																									
1924	Cle A	0	1	.000	1	0	0	0	1	4	3	1	0	0	0	27.00	16	.667	.667	0	ø	0	—	-2	—	-0.3
Kull, John	John A. (b John A Kolonauski); B6.24.1882 Shenandoah PA; D3.30.1936 Schuylkill Haven PA; BL/TL/6´2˝/190; d10.2																									
1909	Phi A	1	0	1.000	1	0	0	0	3	3	1	0	1	5	4	3.00	80	.250	.500	1	1.000	0	—	0	—	0.0
Kume, Mike	John Michael; B5.19.1926 Premier WV; BR/TR/6´1˝/195; d8.26																									
1955	KC A	0	2	.000	6	4	0	0	23.2	35	23	1	3	15-0	7	7.99	52	.354	.445	8	.125	-0	64	-9	0	-0.7
Kunkel, Bill	William Gustave James; B7.7.1936 Hoboken NJ; D5.4.1985 Red Bank NJ; BR/TR/6´1˝/(165–187); d4.15; U17; s–Jeff																									
1961	KC A	3	4	.429	58	2	0	4	88.2	103	58	11	0	32-2	46	5.18	81	.289	.345	8-0-1	.125	-0	0	-9	0	-0.7
1962	KC A	0	0	ø	9	0	0	0	7.2	8	7	3	0	4-0	6	3.52	120	.258	.333	0	ø	0	—	-1	0	-0.1
1963	NY A	3	2	.600	22	0	0	0	46.1	42	15	3	0	13-3	31	2.72	129	.239	.289	6	.333	1	—	4	0	0.5
Total	3	6	6	.500	89	2	0	4	142.2	153	80	17	0	49-5	83	4.29	92	.272	.327	14-0-1	.214	1	0	-6	0	-0.3
Kunz, Earl	Earl Dewey "Pinches"; B12.25.1898 Sacramento CA; D4.14.1963 Sacramento CA; BR/TR/5´10˝/170; d4.19; Col Santa Clara																									
1923	Pit N	1	2	.333	21	2	1	1	45.2	48	33	2	0	24	12	5.52	73	.293	.383	12	.083	-1	72	-8	—	-0.6
Kuo, Hong-Chih	Hong-Chih; B7.23.1981 Tainan City, Taiwan; BL/TL/6´0˝/200; d9.2																									
2005	LA N	0	1	.000	9	0	0	0-1	5.1	5	4	1	0	5-1	10	6.75	62	.238	.385	0	ø	0	—	-1	0	-0.2
2006	†LA N	1	5	.167	28	5	0	0-0	59.2	54	30	3	1	33-5	71	4.22	104	.244	.344	8-0-3	.125	0	105	1	0	0.1
Total	2	1	6	.143	37	5	0	0-1	65	59	34	4	1	38-6	81	4.43	99	.244	.348	8-0-3	.125	0	105	0	0	-0.1
Kurosaki, Ryan	Ryan Yoshitomo; B7.3.1952 Honolulu HI; BR/TR/5´10˝/160; d5.20; Col Nebraska																									
1975	StL N	0	0	ø	7	0	0	0-0	13	15	11	3	0	7-1	6	7.62	50	.283	.361	1	.000	-0	—	-4	0	-0.3
Kurtz, Hal	Harold James "Bud"; B8.20.1943 Washington DC; BR/TR/6´3˝/205; d4.18																									
1968	Cle A	1	0	1.000	28	0	0	1	38	37	24	2	5	15-6	16	5.21	57	.255	.343	4	.000	-0*	—	-9	0	-0.6
Kusel, Ed	Edward Daniel; B2.15.1886 Cleveland OH; D10.20.1948 Cleveland OH; TR/6´0˝/165; d9.18																									
1909	StL A	0	3	.000	3	3	3	0	24	43	28	1	0	1	2	7.13	34	.384	.389	10	.300	1	126	-14	—	-1.3
Kush, Emil	Emil Bènedict; B11.4.1916 Chicago IL; D11.26.1969 River Grove IL; BR/TR/5´11˝/185; d9.21; Mil 1943–45																									
1941	Chi N	0	0	ø	2	0	0	0	4	2	1	0	0	0	2	2.25	156	.143	.143	1	.000	-0	—	1	0	0.0
1942	Chi N	0	0	ø	1	0	0	0	2	1	0	0	0	1	1	0.00	ø	.167	.286	1	.000	-0	—	1	0	0.0
1946	Chi N	9	2	.818	40	6	1-1	2	129.2	120	47	4	3	43	50	3.05	109	.253	.319	38	.211	0	120	6	0	0.6
1947	Chi N	8	3	.727	47	1	1	5	91	80	38	8	3	53	44	3.36	117	.247	.358	20	.250	1	112	7	0	1.0
1948	Chi N	1	4	.200	34	1	0	3	72	70	39	5	2	37	31	4.38	89	.253	.345	13	.154	0	68	-3	0	-0.2
1949	Chi N	3	3	.500	26	0	0	2	47.2	51	21	7	2	24	22	3.78	107	.283	.374	9	.333	1	—	2	0	0.4
Total	6	21	12	.636	150	8	2-1	12	346.1	324	146	24	10	158	150	3.48	106	.254	.341	82	.220	2	106	14	0	1.8
Kutyna, Marty	Marion John; B11.14.1932 Philadelphia PA; BR/TR/6´0˝/(190–195); d9.19																									
1959	KC A	0	0	ø	4	0	0	1	7.1	7	0	0	0	1-0	1	0.00	ø	.250	.276	0	ø	0	—	3	0	0.2
1960	KC A	3	2	.600	51	0	0	4	61.2	64	33	7	0	32-3	20	3.94	101	.274	.358	5-0-1	.200	-0	—	-1	0	-0.1
1961	Was A	6	8	.429	50	6	0	3	143	147	79	12	2	48-2	64	3.97	101	.271	.330	34-0-4	.206	-0	92	-2	0	0.0

YEAR	TM LG	W	L	PCT	G	GS	CG-SHO	SV-BS	IP	H	R	HR	HB	BB-IB	SO	ERA	AERA	OAV	OOB	AB-HR-SH	AVG	PB	SUP	APR	DL	PW
1962	Was A	5	6	.455	54	0	0	0	78	83	42	9	0	27-2	25	4.04	100	.275	.329	8	.125	-0	—	-2	0	-0.2
Total	4	14	16	.467	159	6	0	8	290	301	154	28	2	108-7	110	3.88	103	.272	.335	47-0-5	.191	-0	92	-2	0	-0.1
Kutzler, Jerry	Jerry Scott; B3.25.1965 Waukegan IL; BL/TR/6´1˝/175; [ChiA87 6/141]; d4.28; Col William Penn																									
1990	Chi A	2	1	.667	7	7	0	0-0	31.1	38	23	2	0	14-1	21	6.03	64	.304	.371	0	ø	0	118	-8	0	-0.7
Kuzava, Bob	Robert Leroy "Sarge"; B5.28.1923 Wyandotte MI; BB/TL/6´2˝/204; d9.21																									
1946	Cle A	1	0	1.000	2	2	0	0	12	9	7	0	1	11	4	3.00	110	.191	.356	5	.200	-0	155	-1	0	0.0
1947	Cle A	1	1	.500	4	4	1-1	0	21.2	22	10	1	1	9	9	4.15	84	.265	.344	9	.111	-1	108	-1	0	-0.1
1949	Chi A	10	6	.625	29	18	9-1	0	156.2	139	76	6	1	91	83	4.02	104	.240	.344	56-0-5	.036	-6	101	4	0	-0.4
1950	Chi A	1	3	.250	10	7	1	0	44.1	43	28	5	0	27	21	5.68	79	.257	.361	12-0-2	.083	-0	112	-4	0	-0.4
	Was A	8	7	.533	22	22	8-1	0	155	156	80	8	1	75	84	3.95	114	.263	.346	50-1-3	.100	-2	86	9	0	0.5
	Year	9	10	.474	32	29	9-1	0	199.1	199	108	13	1	102	105	4.33	104	.261	.350	62-1-5	.097	-2	92	4	0	0.1
1951	Was A	3	3	.500	8	8	3	0	52.1	57	34	5	2	28	22	5.50	74	.284	.377	17	.176	-0	100	-7	0	-0.7
	†NY A	8	4	.667	23	8	4-1	5	82.1	76	27	5	1	27	50	2.40	159	.241	.303	22	.136	0*	113	13	0	1.9
	Year	11	7	.611	31	16	7-1	5	134.2	133	61	10	3	55	72	3.61	109	.258	.333	39	.154	0	107	5	0	1.2
1952	†NY A	8	8	.500	28	12	6-1	3	133	115	53	7	1	63	67	3.45	96	.240	.329	43	.093	-1	112	1	0	-0.1
1953	†NY A	6	5	.545	33	6	2-2	4	92.1	92	35	9	0	34	48	3.31	111	.264	.330	21-0-1	.048	-1	80	6	0	0.5
1954	NY A	1	3	.250	20	3	0	1	39.2	46	30	3	0	18	22	5.45	63	.297	.366	6	.000	-0	103	-11	0	-1.1
	Bal A	1	3	.250	4	4	0	0	23.2	30	11	0	0	11	15	4.18	86	.323	.387	7-0-1	.000	-1	62	-1	0	-0.3
	Year	2	6	.250	24	7	0	1	63.1	76	41	3	0	29	37	4.97	70	.306	.374	13-0-1	.000	-1	79	-12	0	-1.4
1955	Bal A	0	1	.000	6	1	0	0	12.1	10	7	0	0	4-1	5	3.65	105	.222	.280	1	.000	-0	0	0	0	-0.1
	Phi N	1	0	1.000	17	4	0	0	32.1	47	26	5	0	12-1	13	7.24	55	.333	.386	7	.143	-0	118	-10	0	-0.5
1957	Pit N	0	0	ø	4	0	0	0	2	3	2	0	0	3-0	1	9.00	42	.333	.500	0	ø	0	—	-1	0	-0.1
	StL N	0	0	ø	3	0	0	0	2.1	4	1	0	0	2-0	2	3.86	103	.364	.462	0	ø	0	—	0	0	0.0
	Year	0	0	ø	7	0	0	0	4.1	7	3	0	0	5-0	3	6.23	62	.350	.480	0	ø	0	—	-1	0	-0.1
Total	10	49	44	.527	213	99	34-7	13	862	849	427	54	8	415-2	446	4.05	97	.260	.344	256-1-12	.086	-14	100	-3	0	-0.9
Labine, Clem	Clement Walter; B8.6.1926 Lincoln RI; BR/TR/6´0˝/(180–195); d4.18																									
1950	Bro N	0	0	ø	1	0	0	0	2	2	1	0	0	1	0	4.50	91	.286	.375	0	ø	0	—	0	0	0.0
1951	Bro N	5	1	.833	14	6	5-2	0	65.1	52	17	4	0	20	39	2.20	178	.223	.285	21	.143	-1	146	13	0	1.0
1952	Bro N	8	4	.667	25	9	0	0	77	76	44	3	1	47	43	5.14	71	.259	.364	22-0-3	.045	-2*	125	-11	0	-1.7
1953	†Bro N	11	6	.647	37	7	0	7	110.1	92	39	9	0	30	44	2.77	154	.225	.278	28-0-3	.071	-1	81	18	0	2.5
1954	Bro N	7	6	.538	47	2	0	5	108.1	101	60	7	1	56	43	4.15	98	.247	.337	30	.033	-2	87	-3	0	-0.5
1955	†Bro N	13	5	.722	**60**	8	1	11	144.1	121	61	12	0	55-4	67	3.24	125	.229	.300	31-3-3	.097	1	82	13	0	1.8
1956	†Bro N☆	10	6	.625	62	3	1	**19**	115.2	111	48	11	3	39-8	75	3.35	119	.253	.317	23	.087	-1	96	7	0	1.1
1957	Bro N★	5	7	.417	58	0	0	**17**	104.2	104	50	8	1	27-6	67	3.44	121	.259	.301	20	.100	-1	—	6	0	0.8
1958	LA N	6	6	.500	52	2	0	14	104	112	55	8	1	33-8	43	4.15	99	.283	.336	18-0-1	.056	-1	110	-1	0	-0.3
1959	†LA N	5	10	.333	56	0	0	9	84.2	91	39	11	1	25-10	37	3.93	108	.282	.332	16-0-1	.000	-2	—	4	0	0.6
1960	LA N	0	1	.000	13	0	0	1	17	26	12	1	0	8-3	15	5.82	68	.356	.420	2	.500	1	—	-3	0	-0.2
	Det A	0	3	.000	14	0	0	2	19.1	19	12	2	0	12-4	6	5.12	77	.257	.360	2	.000	-0	—	-2	0	-0.4
	†Pit N	3	0	1.000	15	0	0	3	30.1	29	5	0	1	11-3	21	1.48	253	.254	.323	4-0-2	.000	-0	—	8	0	0.9
1961	Pit N	4	1	.800	56	1	0	8	92.2	102	43	4	2	31-8	49	3.69	108	.284	.343	10	.100	-0	111	3	0	0.1
1962	NY N	0	0	ø	3	0	0	0	4	5	6	1	0	1-0	2	11.25	37	.278	.316	0	ø	0	—	-3	0	-0.1
Total	13	77	56	.579	513	38	7-2	96	1079.2	1043	492	81	11	396-54	551	3.63	112	.256	.322	227-3-13	.075	-11	103	49	0	5.6
Lacey, Bob	Robert Joseph; B8.25.1953 Fredericksburg VA; BR/TL/6´5˝/(180–210); [OakA72*10/140]; d5.13; Col Central Arizona JC																									
1977	Oak A	6	8	.429	64	0	0	7-3	121.2	100	46	13	0	43-11	69	3.03	133	.234	.301	0	ø	0	—	14	0	1.9
1978	Oak A	8	9	.471	**74**	0	0	5-6	119.2	126	52	10	1	35-13	60	3.01	122	.270	.320	0	ø	0	—	7	0	1.1
1979	Oak A	1	5	.167	42	0	0	4-5	47.2	66	34	7	1	24-8	33	5.85	69	.327	.397	0	ø	0	—	-9	66	-1.2
1980	Oak A	3	2	.600	47	1	1-1	6-6	79.2	68	29	7	1	21-5	45	2.94	130	.234	.284	0	ø	0	94	8	0	0.6
1981	Cle A	0	0	ø	14	0	0	0-0	21.1	36	20	5	0	3-0	11	7.59	49	.371	.379	0	ø	0	—	-9	0	-0.5
	Tex A	0	0	ø	1	0	0	0-0	1	1	1	1	0	0-0	0	9.00	39	.250	.250	0	ø	0	—	-1	0	0.0
	Year	0	0	ø	15	0	0	0-0	22.1	37	21	6	0	3-0	11	7.66	48	.366	.374	0	ø	0	—	-10	0	-0.5
1983	Cal A	1	2	.333	8	0	0	0-2	8.2	12	5	1	0	0-0	7	5.19	78	.343	.343	0	ø	0	—	-1	0	-0.2
1984	SF N	1	3	.250	34	1	0	0-1	51	55	26	5	0	13-4	26	3.88	91	.276	.318	6	.333	1	75	-2	0	-0.1
Total	7	20	29	.408	284	2	1-1	22-23	450.2	464	213	49	3	139-41	251	3.67	104	.269	.322	6	.333	1	82	7	66	1.6
Lachemann, Marcel	Marcel Ernest; B6.13.1941 Los Angeles CA; BR/TR/6´0˝/(180–185); d6.4; M3/C15; b–Rene; Col USC																									
1969	Oak A	4	1	.800	28	0	0	2-1	43.1	43	24	1	2	19-2	16	3.95	87	.261	.340	2-0-1	.000	-0	—	-4	0	-0.5
1970	Oak A	3	3	.500	41	0	0	3-1	58.1	58	20	6	2	18-6	39	2.78	127	.266	.326	8	.000	-1	—	5	0	0.5
1971	Oak A	0	0	ø	1	0	0	0-0	0.1	2	2	0	0	1-0	0	54.00	6	1.000	1.000	0	ø	0	—	-2	0	-0.1
Total	3	7	4	.636	70	0	0	5-2	102	103	46	7	4	38-8	55	3.44	101	.268	.337	10-0-1	.000	-1	—	-1	0	-0.1
Lachowicz, Al	Allen Robert; B9.6.1960 Pittsburgh PA; BR/TR/6´3˝/185; [TexA81 1/24]; d9.13; Col Pittsburgh																									
1983	Tex A	0	1	.000	2	1	0	0-0	8	9	2	0	0	2-0	8	2.25	180	.281	.324	0	ø	0	0	2	0	0.2
Lackey, John	John Derran; B10.23.1978 Abilene TX; BR/TR/6´6˝/(200–235); [AnaA99 2/68]; d6.24; Col Texas–Arlington																									
2002	†Ana A	9	4	.692	18	18	1	0-0	108.1	113	52	10	4	33-0	69	3.66	123	.267	.323	0	ø	0	119	8	0	0.9
2003	Ana A	10	16	.385	33	33	2-**2**	0-0	204	223	117	31	10	66-4	151	4.63	94	.278	.339	3	.000	-0	90	-7	0	-0.8
2004	Ana A	14	13	.519	33	32	1-1	0-0	198.1	215	108	22	8	60-4	144	4.67	96	.278	.335	2	.000	-0	87	-4	0	-0.5
2005	†LA A	14	5	.737	33	33	1	0-0	209	208	85	13	11	71-3	199	3.44	124	.258	.325	6	.000	-1	103	20	0	1.5
2006	LA A	13	11	.542	33	33	3-**2**	0-0	217.2	203	98	14	9	72-4	190	3.56	125	.245	.311	3	.000	-0	103	22	0	2.1
Total	5	60	49	.550	150	149	8-5	0-0	937.1	962	460	90	42	302-15	753	4.01	110	.265	.327	14	.000	-1	99	39	0	3.2
Lackey, Bill	William D.; B12.8.1870 St.Albans WV; D5.15.1941 Columbus OH; d10.2																									
1890	Phi AA	0	0	ø	1	0	0	0	2	1	4	0	0	3	1	9.00	43	.143	.400	1	.000	-0	—	-2	—	-0.1
LaCorte, Frank	Frank Joseph; B10.13.1951 San Jose CA; BR/TR/6´1˝/180; d9.8; Col Gavilan (CA) JC; [DL 1985 Cal A 182]																									
1975	Atl N	0	3	.000	3	2	0	0-0	13.2	13	10	1	0	6-0	10	5.27	72	.245	.322	5	.000	-1	70	-2	0	-0.5
1976	Atl N	3	12	.200	19	17	1	0-0	105.1	97	58	6	6	53-2	79	4.70	81	.249	.344	33-0-3	.091	-2*	52	-8	0	-1.3
1977	Atl N	1	8	.111	14	7	0	0-0	37	67	51	10	2	29-1	28	11.68	38	.394	.485	10-0-2	.200	-0	71	-25	0	-4.2
1978	Atl N	0	1	.000	2	2	0	0-0	14.2	9	6	0	0	4-1	7	3.68	109	.180	.236	4-0-1	.000	-0	33	1	0	0.0
1979	Atl N	0	0	ø	6	0	0	0-0	8.1	9	7	2	0	5-1	6	7.56	53	.273	.368	1	.000	-0	—	-3	0	-0.2
	Hou N	1	2	.333	12	3	0	0-0	27	21	16	3	0	10-1	24	5.00	70	.208	.277	3	.000	-0	67	-4	0	-0.5
	Year	1	2	.333	18	3	0	0-0	35.1	30	23	5	0	15-2	30	5.60	65	.224	.300	4	.000	-0	65	-7	0	-0.7
1980	†Hou N	8	5	.615	55	0	0	11-3	83	61	29	4	0	43-5	66	2.82	116	.210	.307	6-0-2	.167	0	—	5	0	0.8
1981	†Hou N	4	2	.667	37	0	0	5-3	42	41	18	1	0	21-3	40	3.64	90	.258	.339	3	.333	0	—	-1	0	-0.2
1982	Hou N	1	5	.167	55	0	0	7-4	76.1	71	44	5	0	46-5	51	4.48	74	.247	.344	7-0-1	.000	-1	—	-11	0	-1.2
1983	Hou N	4	4	.500	37	0	0	3-2	53.1	35	32	8	2	28-3	48	5.06	68	.190	.302	5-0-1	.200	0	—	-9	38	-1.3
1984	Cal A	1	2	.333	13	1	0	0-0	29.1	33	26	9	0	13-4	13	7.06	57	.282	.351	0	ø	0	136	-10	80	-0.9
Total	10	23	44	.343	253	32	1	26-12	490	457	297	49	10	258-26	372	5.01	72	.249	.341	77-0-10	.104	-4	66	-67	300	-9.5
LaCoss, Mike	Michael James; B5.30.1956 Glendale CA; BR/TR/6´4˝/(186–200); [CinN74 3/71]; d7.18																									
1978	Cin N	4	8	.333	16	15	2-1	0-0	96	104	56	5	1	46-9	31	4.50	79	.288	.365	30-0-6	.067	-2*	88	-11	0	-1.5
1979	†Cin N★	14	8	.636	35	32	6-1	0-0	205.2	202	92	13	2	79-8	73	3.50	106	.263	.331	70-0-5	.129	-1	99	4	0	0.2
1980	Cin N	10	12	.455	34	29	4-2	0-1	169.1	207	101	9	1	68-8	59	4.62	76	.303	.366	55-0-6	.091	-3	104	-25	0	-3.1
1981	Cin N	4	7	.364	20	13	1-1	1-0	78	102	55	7	1	30-4	22	6.12	57	.325	.380	19-0-7	.000	-2	88	-21	0	-2.9
1982	Hou N	6	6	.500	41	8	0	0-2	115	107	41	3	4	54-6	51	2.90	115	.252	.342	24-0-3	.250	2	100	6	0	0.8
1983	Hou N	5	7	.417	38	17	2	1-1	138	142	81	10	2	56-11	53	4.43	77	.273	.342	35-0-4	.086	-2	105	-18	21	-1.6
1984	Hou N	7	5	.583	39	18	2-1	3-0	132	132	64	3	0	55-5	86	4.02	83	.261	.333	31-0-6	.129	-1	100	-8	0	-0.8
1985	KC A	1	1	.500	21	0	0	1-0	40.2	49	25	2	0	29-6	26	5.09	82	.304	.411	0	ø	0	—	-4	0	-0.2
1986	SF N	10	13	.435	37	31	4-1	0-0	204.1	179	99	14	6	70-8	86	3.57	99	.240	.309	61-2-5	.230	6	130	-4	0	0.2
1987	†SF N	13	10	.565	39	26	2-1	0-2	171	184	78	16	2	63-12	79	3.68	104	.283	.346	50-0-4	.060	-2	102	3	0	0.3
1988	SF N	7	7	.500	19	19	1-1	0-0	114.1	99	55	5	1	47-3	70	3.62	90	.234	.311	33-0-4	.242	3	90	-6	53	-0.3
1989	†SF N	10	10	.500	45	18	1	6-3	150.1	143	62	3	7	65-4	78	3.17	107	.255	.336	41-0-3	.073	-1	132	2	0	0.2

YEAR	TM LG	W	L	PCT	G	GS	CG-SHO	SV-BS	IP	H	R	HR	HB	BB-IB	SO	ERA	AERA	OAV	OOB	AB-HR-SH	AVG	PB	SUP	APR	DL	PW
1990	SF N	6	4	.600	13	12	1	0-0	77.2	75	37	5	0	39-2	39	3.94	93	.259	.342	23-0-8	.043	-1	136	-3	98	-0.5
1991	SF N	1	5	.167	18	5	0	0-1	47.1	61	39	4	2	24-0	30	7.23	50	.314	.392	9	.222	1	105	-19	0	-2.0
Total	14	98	103	.488	415	243	26-9	12-10	1739.2	1786	885	99	29	725-86	783	4.02	88	.270	.343	481-2-61	.125	-4	107	-104	172	-11.2
LACY, KERRY	Kerry Ardeen; B8.7.1972 Chattanooga TN; BR/TR/6´2˝/215; [TexA91 15/404]; d8.16; Col Chattanooga St. (TN) CC; [DL 1998 Bos A 181]																									
1996	Bos A	2	0	1.000	11	0	0	0-2	10.2	15	5	2	1	8-0	9	3.38	151	.333	.444	0	ø	0	—	2	0	0.3
1997	Bos A	1	1	.500	33	0	0	3-0	45.2	60	34	7	0	22-4	18	6.11	76	.314	.381	0	ø	0	—	-7	0	-0.4
Total	2	3	1	.750	44	0	0	3-2	56.1	75	39	9	1	30-4	27	5.59	85	.318	.394	0	ø	0	—	-5	181	-0.1
LADD, PETE	Peter Linwood; B7.17.1956 Portland ME; BR/TR/6´3˝/(235–240); [BosA77 25/620]; d8.17; Col U. of Mississippi																									
1979	Hou N	1	1	.500	10	0	0	0-0	12.1	8	5	1	2	8-0	6	2.92	120	.178	.327	1	.000	-0	—	1	0	0.1
1982	†Mil A	1	3	.250	16	0	0	3-2	18	16	8	5	0	6-3	12	4.00	96	.239	.297	0	ø	0	—	0	0	0.0
1983	Mil A	3	4	.429	44	0	0	25-6	49.1	30	17	3	1	16-2	41	2.55	148	.172	.242	0	ø	0	—	6	0	1.3
1984	Mil A	4	9	.308	54	1	0	3-7	91	94	58	16	1	38-6	75	5.24	74	.266	.336	0	ø	0	46	-13	0	-1.8
1985	Mil A	0	0	ø	29	0	0	2-1	45.2	58	26	5	2	10-0	22	4.53	93	.315	.347	0	ø	0	—	-2	0	-0.1
1986	Sea A	8	6	.571	52	0	0	6-3	70.2	69	33	10	3	18-3	53	3.82	112	.258	.306	0	ø	0	—	4	0	0.7
Total	6	17	23	.425	205	1	0	39-19	287	275	147	40	9	96-14	209	4.14	97	.252	.313	1	.000	-0	46	-4	0	0.2
LADE, DOYLE	Doyle Marion "Porky"; B2.17.1921 Fairbury NE; D5.18.2000 Lincoln NE; BR/TR (BB 1946–47)/5´10˝/183; d9.18																									
1946	Chi N	0	2	.000	3	2	0	0	15.1	15	8	0	1	3	8	4.11	81	.238	.284	5-0-1	.200	-0	52	-1	0	-0.2
1947	Chi N	11	10	.524	34	25	7-1	0	187.1	202	105	15	1	79	62	3.94	100	.276	.347	60-0-3	.217	2*	89	-3	0	0.0
1948	Chi N	5	6	.455	19	12	6	0	87.1	99	44	4	1	31	29	4.02	97	.283	.343	32	.156	-1	110	0	0	-0.1
1949	Chi N	4	5	.444	36	13	5-1	1	129.2	141	73	13	2	58	43	5.00	81	.274	.350	32-0-4	.219	2	103	-10	0	-0.5
1950	Chi N	5	6	.455	34	12	2	2	117.2	126	68	14	2	50	36	4.74	89	.275	.349	35-0-2	.286	3	121	-5	0	0.1
Total	5	25	29	.463	126	64	20-2	3	537.1	583	298	46	7	221	178	4.39	91	.275	.346	164-0-10	.220	6	101	-19	0	-0.7
LAFFERTY, FLIP	Frank Bernard; B5.4.1854 Scranton PA; D2.8.1910 Wilmington DE; TR; d9.15; ▲																									
1876	Phi N	0	1	.000	1	1	1	0	9	5	3	0	—	0	0	0.00	ø	.152	.152	3	.000	-1	0	2	—	0.1
LAFITTE, ED	Edward Francis "Doc"; B4.7.1886 New Orleans LA; D4.12.1971 Jenkintown PA; BR/TR/6´2˝/188; d4.16; Col Georgia Tech																									
1909	Det A	0	1	.000	3	1	1	1	14	22	14	2	1	2	11	3.86	65	.344	.373	4	.250	0	56	-4	—	-0.3
1911	Det A	11	8	.579	29	20	15	1	172.1	205	113	2	5	52	63	3.92	88	.302	.356	70-1-2	.157	-2*	102	-13	—	-1.6
1912	Det A	0	0	ø	1	0	0	0	1.2	2	4	0	0	2	0	16.20	20	.333	.500	0	ø	0	—	-2	—	-0.1
1914	Bro F	18	15	.545	42	33	23	2	290.2	260	110	7	16	127	137	2.63	109	.248	.338	101-1-4	.257	4	92	9	—	1.4
1915	Bro F	6	9	.400	17	15	7	1	117.2	126	66	6	1	57	34	3.90	70	.288	.371	53	.264	2	90	-15	—	-1.7
	Buf F	2	2	.500	14	5	1-1	1	50.1	53	25	1	2	22	17	3.40	82	.286	.368	17	.118	-1	110	-4	—	-0.4
	Year	8	11	.421	31	20	8-1	2	168	179	91	7	3	79	51	3.75	73	.287	.370	70	.229	1	95	-18	—	-2.1
Total	5	37	35	.514	106	74	47-1	6	646.2	668	332	18	25	262	262	3.33	90	.276	.353	245-2-6	.220	3	95	-29	—	-2.7
LAGGER, ED	Edwin Joseph; B7.14.1912 Joliet IL; D11.10.1981 Joliet IL; BR/TR/6´3˝/200; d6.15; Col Northwestern																									
1934	Phi A	0	0	ø	8	0	0	0	18	27	23	1	1	14	2	11.00	40	.342	.447	6	.000	-1	—	-13	—	-0.6
LAGROW, LERRIN	Lerrin Harris; B7.8.1948 Phoenix AZ; BR/TR/6´5˝/(210–230); [DetA69 6/137]; d7.28; Col Arizona St.																									
1970	Det A	0	1	.000	10	0	0	0-1	12.1	16	11	2	0	6-0	7	7.30	52	.308	.373	1	.000	-0	—	-5	0	-0.4
1972	†Det A	0	1	.000	16	0	0	2-0	27.1	22	4	0	0	6-2	9	1.32	241	.222	.264	0	ø	0	—	6	0	0.3
1973	Det A	1	5	.167	21	3	0	3-0	54	54	26	8	1	23-2	33	4.33	95	.263	.335	0	ø	0	87	0	25	0.0
1974	Det A	8	19	.296	37	34	11	0-0	216.1	245	132	21	3	80-8	85	4.66	82	.287	.349	0	ø	0	81	-21	0	-2.2
1975	Det A	7	14	.333	32	26	7-2	0-0	164.1	183	105	15	2	66-5	75	4.38	92	.280	.344	0	ø	0	83	-10	0	-1.3
1976	StL N	0	1	.000	8	2	1	0-0	24.1	21	4	0	1	7-2	10	1.48	242	.241	.302	5	.000	-1	25	6	0	0.3
1977	Chi A	7	3	.700	66	0	0	25-3	98.2	81	32	10	1	35-3	63	2.46	166	.230	.299	0	ø	0	—	17	0	2.6
1978	Chi A	6	5	.545	52	0	0	16-6	88	85	47	9	3	38-0	41	4.40	86	.260	.340	0	ø	0	—	-6	0	-0.8
1979	Chi A	0	3	.000	11	2	0	1-3	17.2	27	21	2	1	16-1	9	9.17	46	.346	.463	0	ø	0	85	-10	0	-1.5
	LA N	5	1	.833	31	0	0	4-3	37	38	16	2	0	18-2	22	3.41	106	.270	.350	3	.333	0	—	1	26	0.2
1980	Phi N	0	2	.000	25	0	0	3-1	39	42	22	5	0	17-2	21	4.15	92	.276	.343	4	.250	0	—	-2	0	-0.1
Total	10	34	55	.382	309	67	19-2	54-17	779	814	420	74	12	312-27	375	4.11	95	.271	.339	13	.154	-0	82	-24	51	-2.9
LAHTI, JEFF	Jeffrey Allen; B10.8.1956 Oregon City OR; BR/TR/6´0˝/180; [CinN78 5/121]; d6.27; Col Portland St.; [DL 1987 StL N 182]																									
1982	†StL N	5	4	.556	33	1	0	0-1	56.2	53	27	3	2	21-8	22	3.81	97	.245	.314	13	.077	-1	96	-1	0	-0.2
1983	StL N	3	3	.500	53	0	0	0-3	74	64	31	2	1	29-12	26	3.16	116	.240	.314	10	.000	-1	—	3	21	0.2
1984	StL N	4	2	.667	63	0	0	1-2	84.2	69	36	6	2	34-12	45	3.72	94	.225	.303	6-0-1	.167	-0	—	-1	0	0.0
1985	†StL N	5	2	.714	52	0	0	19-1	68.1	63	15	3	0	26-10	41	1.84	194	.251	.321	9	.000	-1	—	14	13	2.0
1986	StL N	0	0	ø	4	0	0	0-0	2.1	3	0	0	0	1-0	3	0.00	ø	.333	.400	0	ø	0	—	1	162	0.0
Total	5	17	11	.607	205	1	0	20-7	286	252	109	14	5	111-42	137	3.12	115	.240	.313	38-0-1	.053	-3	96	16	378	2.0
LAKE, EDDIE	Edward Erving "Sparky"; B3.18.1916 Antioch CA; D6.7.1995 Castro Valley CA; BR/TR/5´7˝/160; d9.26.1939; ▲																									
1944	Bos A	0	0	ø	6	0	0	0	19.1	20	13	2	3	11	7	4.19	81	.278	.395	126-0-4	.206	1*	—	-3	0	-0.1
LAKE, JOE	Joseph Henry; B1.6.1881 Brooklyn NY; D6.30.1950 Brooklyn NY; BR/TR/6´0˝/185; d4.21																									
1908	NY A	9	22	.290	38	27	19-2	0	269.1	252	157	6	6	77	118	3.17	78	.242	.298	112-1-1	.188	0*	79	-25	—	-3.0
1909	NY A	14	11	.560	31	26	17-3	1	215.1	180	81	2	5	59	117	1.88	135	.225	.283	81	.173	1	107	10	—	1.7
1910	StL A	11	17	.393	35	29	24-1	2	261.1	243	116	2	1	77	141	2.20	112	.248	.304	91	.231	2*	78	2	—	0.6
1911	StL A	10	15	.400	30	25	14-2	0	215.1	245	115	3	4	40	69	3.30	102	.282	.316	80-0-1	.262	2	83	1	—	0.6
1912	StL A	1	7	.125	11	6	4	0	57	70	41	0	1	16	28	4.42	75	.314	.363	20	.150	-1	74	-8	—	-1.0
	Det A	9	11	.450	26	14	11	1	162.2	190	94	3	3	39	86	3.10	105	.296	.340	62-1-2	.145	-3	76	-3	—	-0.7
	Year	10	18	.357	37	20	15	1	219.2	260	135	3	4	55	114	3.44	95	.301	.346	82-1-2	.146	-5	76	-11	—	-1.7
1913	Det A	8	7	.533	28	12	6	1	137	149	67	3	0	24	35	3.28	89	.279	.310	45-1-1	.267	4	104	-5	—	0.1
Total	6	62	90	.408	199	139	95-8	5	1318	1329	671	19	20	332	594	2.85	99	.261	.309	491-3-5	.206	4	86	-28	—	-1.7
LAMABE, JACK	John Alexander; B10.3.1936 Farmingdale NY; BR/TR/6´1˝/(193–205); d4.17; Col Vermont																									
1962	Pit N	3	1	.750	46	0	0	2	78	70	35	4	0	40-8	56	2.88	136	.238	.329	9	.000	-1	—	7	0	0.3
1963	Bos A	7	4	.636	65	2	0	6	151.1	139	63	8	4	46-11	93	3.15	120	.247	.306	32-1-1	.094	-1	82	8	0	0.6
1964	Bos A	9	13	.409	39	25	3	1	177.1	235	123	25	2	57-5	109	5.89	65	.318	.367	52-0-1	.115	-1	106	-35	0	-4.0
1965	Bos A	0	3	.000	14	0	0	0	25.1	34	24	5	3	14-2	17	8.17	46	.340	.432	4-0-1	.000	-0	—	-10	0	-1.2
	Hou N	0	2	.000	3	2	0	0	12.2	17	9	3	0	3-1	6	4.26	79	.315	.351	4	.250	0	52	-2	0	-0.3
1966	Chi A	7	9	.438	34	17	3-2	0	121.1	116	55	9	1	35-1	67	3.93	81	.251	.304	35-0-4	.057	-2	116	-8	0	-1.2
1967	Chi A	1	0	1.000	3	0	0	0	5	7	2	0	0	1-1	3	1.80	172	.318	.348	0	ø	0	—	0	0	0.1
	NY N	0	3	.000	16	2	0	1	31.2	24	15	4	0	8-1	23	3.98	85	.200	.248	5	.000	-0	52	-2	0	-0.2
	†StL N	3	4	.429	23	1	1-1	4	47.2	43	16	2	0	10-3	30	2.83	116	.244	.282	10-0-1	.200	0	160	3	0	0.5
	Year	3	7	.300	39	3	1-1	5	79.1	67	31	6	0	18-4	53	3.29	101	.226	.268	15-0-1	.133	-0	88	1	0	0.3
1968	Chi N	3	2	.600	42	0	0	1	60.2	68	33	7	1	24-7	30	4.30	73	.289	.350	5-0-1	.200	0	—	-8	0	-0.6
Total	7	33	41	.446	285	49	7-3	15	711	753	375	67	11	238-40	434	4.24	85	.272	.330	156-1-9	.096	-6	104	-47	0	-6.0
LAMACCHIA, AL	Alfred Anthony; B7.22.1921 St.Louis MO; BR/TR/5´10.5˝/190; d9.27																									
1943	StL A	0	1	.000	1	1	0	0	4	9	6	0	0	2	2	11.25	30	.450	.500	2	.000	-0	101	-4	0	-0.6
1945	StL A	2	0	1.000	5	0	0	0	9	6	2	0	0	3	2	2.00	176	.207	.281	1	.000	-0	—	2	0	0.3
1946	StL A	0	0	ø	8	0	0	0	15	17	10	2	0	7	3	6.00	62	.279	.353	3	.000	-0	—	-3	0	-0.2
	Was A	0	1	.000	2	0	0	0	2.2	6	5	1	0	2	0	16.88	20	.462	.533	0	ø	-0	—	-4	0	-0.7
	Year	0	1	.000	10	0	0	0	17.2	23	15	3	0	9	3	7.64	48	.311	.386	3	.000	-0	—	-7	0	-0.9
Total	3	2	2	.500	16	1	0	0	30.2	38	23	3	0	14	7	6.46	55	.309	.380	6	.000	-1	101	-9	0	-1.2
LAMANNA, FRANK	Frank "Hank"; B8.22.1919 Waterton PA; D9.1.1980 Syracuse NY; BR/TR/6´2.5˝/195; d4.16; Mil 1943–45																									
1940	Bos N	1	0	1.000	5	1	1	0	13.1	13	8	1	0	8	3	4.73	79	.271	.375	5	.200	0	117	-2	—	-0.1
1941	Bos N	5	4	.556	35	4	0	1	72.2	77	52	5	1	56	23	5.33	67	.285	.410	32	.281	1*	119	-15	0	-1.5
1942	Bos N	0	1	.000	5	0	0	0	6.2	5	4	1	0	3	2	5.40	62	.208	.296	2	.000	-0*	—	-1	0	-0.2
Total	3	6	5	.545	45	5	1	1	92.2	95	64	7	1	67	28	5.24	68	.278	.398	39	.256	1	119	-18	0	-1.8

YEAR	TM LG	W	L	PCT	G	GS	CG-SHO	SV-BS	IP	H	R	HR	HB	BB-IB	SO	ERA	AERA	OAV	OOB	AB-HR-SH	AVG	PB	SUP	APR	DL	PW
LAMANSKE, FRANK	Frank James "Lefty"; B9.30.1906 Oglesby IL; D8.4.1971 Olney IL; BL/TL/5´11˝/170; d4.27																									
1935	Bro N	0	0	ø	2	0	0	0	3.2	5	3	0	0	1	1	7.36	54	.313	.353	1	.000	-0	—	-1	—	-0.1
LAMASTER, WAYNE	Noble Wayne; B2.13.1907 Speed IN; D8.4.1989 New Albany IN; BL/TL/5´8˝/170; d4.19																									
1937	Phi N	15	19	.441	50	30	10-1	4	220.1	255	139	24	2	82	135	5.31	82	.290	.352	79-0-2	.190	-2*	95	-19	—	-3.0
1938	Phi N	4	7	.364	18	12	1-1	0	63.2	80	58	8	3	31	35	7.77	50	.301	.380	22-0-3	.409	4	120	-25	—	-3.1
	Bro N	0	1	.000	3	0	0	0	11.1	17	6	0	0	3	3	4.76	82	.340	.377	6	.167	-0*	—	-1	—	-0.1
	Year	4	8	.333	21	12	1-1	0	75	97	64	8	3	34	38	7.32	53	.307	.380	28-0-3	.357	4	120	-24	—	-3.2
Total	2	19	27	.413	71	42	11-2	4	295.1	352	203	32	5	116	173	5.82	72	.295	.360	107-0-5	.234	1	101	-45	—	-6.2
LAMB, JOHN	John Andrew; B7.20.1946 Sharon CT; BR/TR/6´3˝/(180–195); d8.12																									
1970	Pit N	0	1	.000	23	0	0	3-2	32.1	23	10	2	2	13-1	24	2.78	142	.209	.304	3	.000	-0	—	5	0	0.2
1971	Pit N	0	0	ø	2	0	0	0-0	4.1	3	0	0	0	1-0	1	0.00	ø	.188	.235	1	.000	-0	—	2	63	0.1
1973	Pit N	0	1	.000	22	0	0	2-0	29.2	37	24	3	0	10-3	11	6.07	58	.308	.359	3	.000	-0	—	-9	0	-0.5
Total	3	0	2	.000	47	0	0	5-2	66.1	63	34	5	2	24-4	36	4.07	92	.256	.326	7	.000	-1	—	-2	63	-0.2
LAMB, RAY	Raymond Richard; B12.28.1944 Glendale CA; BR/TR/6´1˝/(170–190); [LAN66 40/732]; d8.1; Col USC																									
1969	LA N	0	1	.000	10	0	0	1-0	15	12	3	2	0	7-0	11	1.80	186	.235	.328	1	.000	-0	—	3	0	0.2
1970	LA N	6	1	.857	35	0	0	0-0	57	59	27	4	4	27-9	32	3.79	102	.277	.366	4	.000	-0	—	0	0	-0.1
1971	Cle A	6	12	.333	43	21	3-1	1-0	158.1	147	67	11	1	69-7	91	3.35	116	.247	.323	43-0-4	.093	-2	92	7	0	0.5
1972	Cle A	5	6	.455	34	9	0	0-0	107.2	101	42	5	1	29-5	64	3.09	105	.248	.299	21-0-1	.000	-1	88	2	0	0.0
1973	Cle A	3	3	.500	32	1	0	2-1	86	98	44	7	2	42-6	60	4.60	86	.291	.369	0	ø	0	203	-4	0	-0.3
Total	5	20	23	.465	154	31	3-1	4-1	424	417	183	29	8	174-27	258	3.54	105	.260	.333	69-0-5	.058	-4	94	8	0	0.3
LAMBERT, CLAYTON	Clayton Patrick; B3.26.1917 Summit IL; D4.3.1981 Ogden UT; BR/TR/6´2˝/185; d4.22; Col Illinois College																									
1946	Cin N	2	2	.500	23	4	2	1	52.2	48	27	3	1	20	20	4.27	78	.251	.325	13	.154	-1	109	-4	0	-0.5
1947	Cin N	0	0	ø	3	0	0	0	5.2	12	10	3	0	6	1	15.88	26	.444	.545	1	.000	-0	—	-7	0	-0.3
Total	2	2	2	.500	26	4	2	1	58.1	60	37	6	1	26	21	5.40	63	.275	.355	14	.143	-1	109	-11	0	-0.8
LAMBERT, GENE	Eugene Marion; B4.26.1921 Crenshaw MS; D2.10.2000 Germantown TN; BR/TR/5´11˝/175; d9.14; Mil 1943–45																									
1941	Phi N	0	1	.000	2	1	0	0	9	11	2	0	0	2	3	2.00	185	.297	.333	2	.000	-0	0	2	0	0.2
1942	Phi N	0	0	ø	1	0	0	0	1	3	1	0	0	0	1	9.00	37	.500	.500	0	ø	0	—	-1	0	0.0
Total	2	0	1	.000	3	1	0	0	10	14	3	0	0	2	4	2.70	136	.326	.356	2	.000	-0	0	1	0	0.2
LAMBETH, OTIS	Otis Samuel; B5.13.1890 Berlin KS; D6.5.1976 Moran KS; BR/TR/6´0˝/175; d7.16; Mil 1918																									
1916	Cle A	4	4	.500	15	9	3	1	74	69	33	1	3	38	28	2.92	103	.256	.354	27-0-1	.111	-1*	92	0	—	-0.2
1917	Cle A	7	6	.538	26	10	2	2	97.1	97	48	2	11	30	27	3.14	90	.274	.349	32-0-3	.188	-0	112	-4	—	-0.6
1918	Cle A	0	0	ø	2	0	0	0	7	10	5	0	0	6	3	6.43	47	.370	.485	1	1.000	0	—	-2	—	-0.1
Total	3	11	10	.524	43	19	5	3	178.1	176	86	3	14	74	58	3.18	92	.270	.357	60-0-4	.167	-1	102	-6	—	-0.9
LAMLEIN, FRED	Frederick Arthur "Dutch"; B8.14.1887 Port Huron MI; D9.20.1970 Port Huron MI; BR/TR/5´11˝/171; d9.18																									
1912	Chi A	0	0	ø	1	0	0	0	2	7	7	0	0	2	1	31.50	10	.583	.643	0	ø	0	—	-6	—	-0.2
1915	StL N	0	0	ø	4	0	0	0	19	21	4	0	2	3	11	1.42	196	.300	.347	8	.125	-0	—	3	—	0.1
Total	2	0	0	ø	5	0	0	0	21	28	11	0	2	5	12	4.29	66	.341	.393	8	.125	-0	—	-3	—	-0.1
LAMP, DENNIS	Dennis Patrick; B9.23.1952 Los Angeles CA; BR/TR/6´3˝/(180–215); [ChiN71 3/62]; d8.21																									
1977	Chi N	0	2	.000	11	3	0	0-0	30	43	21	3	2	8-4	12	6.30	70	.344	.390	8	.375	1	67	-5	0	-0.2
1978	Chi N	7	15	.318	37	36	6-3	0-0	223.2	221	96	16	4	56-8	73	3.30	123	.258	.306	73-0-3	.205	0	82	14	0	1.5
1979	Chi N	11	10	.524	38	32	6-1	0-0	200.1	223	96	14	5	46-9	86	3.50	119	.287	.329	58-0-7	.155	-1	95	10	0	1.0
1980	Chi N	10	14	.417	41	37	2-1	0-1	202.2	259	123	16	1	82-7	83	5.20	76	.317	.378	61-0-7	.098	-3	94	-21	0	-2.5
1981	Chi A	7	6	.538	27	10	3	0-0	127	103	41	4	1	43-1	71	2.41	150	.222	.289	0	ø	0	74	17	0	1.7
1982	Chi A	11	8	.579	44	27	3-2	5-2	189.2	206	96	9	6	59-3	78	3.99	102	.279	.337	0	ø	0	116	2	0	0.3
1983	†Chi A	7	7	.500	49	5	1	15-5	116.1	123	52	6	4	29-7	44	3.71	114	.275	.324	0	ø	0	77	7	0	0.9
1984	Tor A	8	8	.500	56	4	0	9-5	85	97	53	9	1	38-7	45	4.55	91	.285	.358	0	ø	0	153	-6	0	-1.1
1985	†Tor A	11	0	1.000	53	1	0	2-5	105.2	96	42	7	0	27-3	68	3.32	128	.247	.292	0	ø	0	43	11	0	1.2
1986	Tor A	2	6	.250	40	2	0	2-1	73	93	50	5	0	23-6	30	5.05	84	.309	.357	0	ø	0	85	-9	0	-0.9
1987	Oak A	1	3	.250	36	5	0	0-0	56.2	76	38	5	1	22-3	36	5.08	82	.326	.382	0	ø	0	114	-7	0	-0.4
1988	Bos A	7	6	.538	46	0	0	0-1	82.2	92	39	3	2	19-3	49	3.48	119	.284	.326	0	ø	0	—	4	18	0.6
1989	Bos A	4	2	.667	42	0	0	2-1	112.1	96	37	4	0	27-6	61	2.32	177	.235	.280	0	ø	0	—	19	0	1.1
1990	†Bos A	3	5	.375	47	1	0	0-2	105.2	114	61	10	3	30-8	49	4.68	87	.279	.330	0	ø	0	44	-6	0	-0.4
1991	Bos A	6	3	.667	51	0	0	0-0	92	100	54	8	3	31-7	57	4.70	92	.275	.335	0	ø	0	—	-4	0	-0.4
1992	Pit N	1	1	.500	21	0	0	0-1	28	33	16	3	2	9-4	15	5.14	67	.292	.355	1	.000	-0	—	-5	0	-0.3
Total	16	96	96	.500	639	163	21-7	35-24	1830.2	1975	915	122	35	549-86	857	3.93	104	.278	.331	201-0-17	.164	-3	94	21	18	2.1
LAMPE, HENRY	Henry Joseph; B9.19.1872 Boston MA; D9.16.1936 Dorchester MA; BR/TL/5´11.5˝/175; d5.14																									
1894	Bos N	0	1	.000	2	1	0	0	5.1	17	19	5	0	7	1	11.81	48	.531	.615	2	.000	-0	337	-6	—	-0.7
1895	Phi N	0	2	.000	7	3	2	0	44	68	54	3	1	33	18	7.57	63	.347	.443	16	.125	-1	94	-15	—	-0.7
Total	2	0	3	.000	9	4	2	0	49.1	85	73	8	1	40	19	8.03	61	.373	.468	18	.111	-1	168	-21	—	-1.4
LANAHAN, DICK	Richard Anthony; B9.27.1911 Washington DC; D3.12.1975 Rochester MN; BL/TL/6´0˝/186; d9.15																									
1935	Was A	0	3	.000	3	3	0	0	20.2	27	13	2	2	17	10	5.66	76	.314	.438	6-0-1	.167	-0	40	-2	—	-0.3
1937	Was A	0	1	.000	6	2	0	0	11.1	16	16	2	1	13	2	12.71	35	.320	.469	1	.000	0	177	-10	—	-0.6
1940	Pit N	6	8	.429	40	8	4	2	108	121	63	8	1	42	45	4.25	90	.279	.345	34-0-1	.118	-2	103	-7	—	-1.0
1941	Pit N	0	1	.000	7	0	0	0	12	13	9	1	2	3	5	5.25	69	.283	.353	1	.000	-0	—	-2	0	-0.2
Total	4	6	13	.316	56	13	4	2	152	177	101	13	6	75	62	5.15	76	.288	.371	42-0-2	.119	-2	102	-21	0	-2.1
LANCASTER, LES	Lester Wayne; B4.21.1962 Dallas TX; BR/TR/6´2˝/(200–205); d4.7; Col Dallas Baptist																									
1987	Chi N	8	3	.727	27	18	0	0-0	132.1	138	76	14	1	51-5	78	4.90	88	.268	.332	49-0-1	.082	-2	100	-7	0	-0.8
1988	Chi N	4	6	.400	44	3	1	5-3	85.2	89	42	4	1	34-7	36	3.78	96	.273	.337	20-0-3	.050	-1	146	-2	36	-0.4
1989	†Chi N	4	2	.667	42	0	0	8-3	72.2	60	12	2	0	15-1	56	1.36	277	.226	.263	11	.182	0	—	**18**	0	1.9
1990	Chi N	9	5	.643	55	6	1-1	6-4	109	121	57	11	1	40-8	65	4.62	88	.283	.342	20-0-1	.050	-1	85	-4	0	-0.5
1991	Chi N	9	7	.563	64	11	1	3-3	156	150	68	13	4	49-7	102	3.52	111	.256	.315	28-0-6	.179	0	113	6	0	0.6
1992	Det A	3	4	.429	41	1	0	0-3	86.2	101	66	11	3	51-12	35	6.33	63	.294	.386	0	ø	0	0	-22	0	-1.6
1993	StL N	4	1	.800	50	0	0	0-0	61.1	56	24	5	1	21-5	36	2.93	137	.242	.307	4	.000	-0	—	7	58	0.5
Total	7	41	28	.594	323	39	3-1	22-16	703.2	715	345	60	11	261-45	408	4.05	98	.265	.329	132-0-11	.098	-4	105	-4	94	-0.3
LANCE, GARY	Gary Dean; B9.21.1948 Greenville SC; BB/TR/6´3˝/202; d9.28; Col South Carolina																									
1977	KC A	0	1	.000	1	0	0	0-0	2	2	1	0	0	2-0	0	4.50	90	.286	.444	0	ø	0	—	0	0	0.0
LANDIS, DOC	Samuel H.; B8.16.1854 Philadelphia PA; BR/5´11˝/172; d5.2																									
1882	Phi AA	1	1	.500	2	2	2	0	17	16	12	1	—	1	13	3.18	88	.232	.243	12	.167	-0*	101	-1	—	-0.1
	Bal AA	11	28	.282	42	40	35	0	343	416	257	7	—	46	62	3.38	81	.281	.302	175	.166	-6*	79	-29	—	-3.1
	Year	12	29	.293	44	42	37	0	360	432	269	8	—	47	75	3.38	82	.278	.300	187	.166	-7	80	-26	—	-3.2
LANDIS, BILL	William Henry; B10.8.1942 Hanford CA; BL/TL/6´2˝/(175–180); d9.28; Mil 1968; Col West Hills (CA) JC																									
1963	KC A	0	0	ø	1	0	0	0	1.2	0	0	0	0	1-0	3	0.00	ø	.000	.167	0	ø	0	—	1	0	0.0
1967	Bos A	1	0	1.000	18	1	0	0	25.2	24	16	6	0	11-3	23	5.26	66	.253	.330	2	.000	-0*	125	-4	0	-0.3
1968	Bos A	3	3	.500	38	1	0	3	60	48	22	4	2	30-2	59	3.15	100	.223	.320	6	.000	-1	55	1	0	0.0
1969	Bos A	5	5	.500	45	5	0	1-1	82.1	82	53	7	3	49-3	50	5.25	73	.269	.370	11	.000	-0*	51	-11	0	-1.3
Total	4	9	8	.529	102	7	0	4-1	169.2	154	91	17	5	91-8	135	4.46	79	.248	.345	19	.000	-1	64	-13	0	-1.6
LANDRETH, LARRY	Larry Robert; B3.11.1955 Stratford ON, Can.; BR/TR/6´1˝/175; d9.16																									
1976	Mon N	1	2	.333	3	3	0	0-0	11	13	8	1	0	10-0	7	4.09	92	.310	.434	3	.000	-0	70	-1	0	-0.3
1977	Mon N	0	2	.000	4	1	0	0-0	9.1	16	11	0	0	8-1	5	9.64	40	.381	.471	2	.000	-0	69	-6	0	-1.0
Total	2	1	4	.200	7	4	0	0-0	20.1	29	19	1	0	18-1	12	6.64	57	.345	.452	5	.000	-1	70	-7	0	-1.3

YEAR	TM LG	W	L	PCT	G	GS	CG-SHO	SV-BS	IP	H	R	HR	HB	BB-IB	SO	ERA	AERA	OAV	OOB	AB-HR-SH	AVG	PB	SUP	APR	DL	PW
LANDRUM, JOE	Joseph Butler; B12.13.1928 Columbia SC; BR/TR/5´11˝/(170–180); d7.13; s–Bill; Col Clemson																									
1950	Bro N	0	0	ø	7	0	0	1	6.2	12	8	2	1	1	5	8.10	51	.414	.452	0-0-1	ø	0	—	-4	0	-0.2
1952	Bro N	1	3	.250	9	5	2	0	38	46	24	3	1	10	17	5.21	70	.301	.348	8-0-3	.125	-0	113	-7	0	-0.7
Total	2	1	3	.250	16	5	2	1	44.2	58	32	5	2	11	22	5.64	66	.319	.364	8-0-4	.125	-0	113	-11	0	-0.9
LANDRUM, BILL	Thomas William; B8.17.1957 Columbia SC; BR/TR/6´2˝/(185–205); d8.31; f–Joe; Col South Carolina																									
1986	Cin N	0	0	ø	10	0	0	0-0	13.1	23	11	0	0	4-0	14	6.75	57	.390	.422	2	.000	-0	—	-4	0	-0.2
1987	Cin N	3	2	.600	44	2	0	2-1	65	68	35	3	0	34-6	42	4.71	90	.292	.379	5-0-1	.200	0	128	-2	0	-0.1
1988	Chi N	1	0	1.000	7	0	0	0-0	12.1	19	8	1	0	3-0	6	5.84	62	.365	.400	2	.000	-0	—	-3	0	-0.2
1989	Pit N	2	3	.400	56	0	0	26-3	81	60	18	2	0	28-8	51	1.67	204	.205	.273	3	.000	-0	—	16	0	1.9
1990	†Pit N	7	3	.700	54	0	0	13-3	71.2	69	22	4	0	21-5	39	2.13	171	.262	.314	9	.111	-0	—	11	0	1.9
1991	†Pit N	4	4	.500	61	0	0	17-5	76.1	76	32	4	0	19-5	45	3.18	113	.252	.296	4-0-1	.000	-0	—	3	0	0.3
1992	Mon N	1	1	.500	18	0	0	0-0	20	27	16	3	2	9-2	7	7.20	48	.325	.404	0	ø	0	—	-8	61	-0.7
1993	Cin N	0	2	.000	18	0	0	0-0	21.2	18	9	1	0	6-1	14	3.74	108	.231	.286	0-0-1	ø	0	—	1	122	0.1
Total	8	18	15	.545	268	2	0	58-12	361.1	360	151	18	2	124-27	218	3.39	109	.265	.325	25-0-3	.080	-1	128	14	183	3.0
LANE, JERRY	Gerald Hal; B2.7.1926 Ashland NY; D7.24.1988 Chattanooga TN; BR/TR/6´0.5˝/(185–205); d7.7; Col Ithaca																									
1953	Was A	1	4	.200	20	2	0	0	56.2	64	33	3	1	16	26	4.92	79	.288	.339	9-0-1	.111	0	46	-6	0	-0.4
1954	Cin N	1	0	1.000	3	0	0	0	10.2	9	2	0	0	3	2	1.69	248	.237	.293	4	.000	-0	—	3	0	0.2
1955	Cin N	0	2	.000	8	0	0	1	11	11	6	2	0	6-2	5	4.91	86	.289	.386	0	ø	0	—	0	0	-0.1
Total	3	2	6	.250	31	2	0	1	78.1	84	41	5	1	25-2	33	4.48	89	.282	.340	13-0-1	.077	0	46	-3	0	-0.3
LANFORD, SAM	Lewis Grover; B1.8.1886 Woodruff SC; D9.14.1970 Woodruff SC; BL/TR/5´7˝/155; d8.19																									
1907	Was A	0	1	.000	2	1	0	0	7	10	10	0	3	5	2	5.14	47	.333	.474	3	.333	0	56	-4	—	-0.4
LANFRANCONI, WALT	Walter Oswald; B11.9.1916 Barre VT; D8.18.1986 Barre VT; BR/TR/5´7.5˝/155; d9.12; Mil 1942–45																									
1941	Chi N	0	1	.000	2	1	0	0	6	7	3	0	0	2	1	3.00	117	.280	.333	1	.000	-0	0	0	0	0.0
1947	Bos N	4	4	.500	36	4	1	1	64	65	23	2	0	27	18	2.95	132	.272	.346	10-0-1	.000	-1*	57	**7**	0	0.8
Total	2	4	5	.444	38	5	1	1	70	72	26	2	0	29	19	2.96	131	.273	.345	11-0-1	.000	-1	46	7	0	0.8
LANG, MARTY	Martin John; B9.27.1905 Hooper NE; D1.13.1968 Lakewood CO; BR/TL/5´11˝/160; d7.4; Col Concordia (TX)																									
1930	Pit N	0	0	ø	2	0	0	0	1.2	9	10	2	0	3	2	54.00	9	.692	.750	0	ø	0	—	-8	—	-0.3
LANG, CHIP	Robert David; B8.21.1952 Pittsburgh PA; BR/TR/6´4˝/195; [MonN70 2/27]; d9.8																									
1975	Mon N	0	0	ø	1	1	0	0-0	1.2	2	2	0	0	3-0	2	10.80	36	.333	.556	0	ø	0	136	-1	0	-0.1
1976	Mon N	1	3	.250	29	2	0	0-0	62.1	56	32	3	3	34-2	30	4.19	90	.242	.346	6-0-2	.167	-0	35	-2	0	-0.1
Total	2	1	3	.250	30	3	0	0-0	64	58	34	3	3	37-2	32	4.36	86	.245	.353	6-0-2	.167	-0	70	-3	0	-0.2
LANGE, ERV	Erwin Henry; B8.12.1887 Forest Park IL; D4.24.1971 Maywood IL; BR/TR/5´10˝/170; d4.19																									
1914	Chi F	12	11	.522	36	22	10-2	2	190	162	69	3	3	55	87	2.23	119	.224	.282	51-0-1	.176	2	107	7	—	0.9
LANGE, FRANK	Frank Herman "Seagan"; B10.28.1883 Columbus WI; D12.26.1945 Madison WI; BR/TR/5´11˝/180; d5.16																									
1910	Chi A	9	4	.692	23	15	6-1	0	130.2	93	48	2	9	54	98	1.65	145	.204	.301	51	.255	3	121	7	—	1.0
1911	Chi A	8	8	.500	29	22	8-1	0	161.2	151	77	3	3	77	104	3.23	100	.251	.339	76-0-2	.289	8*	105	1	—	0.9
1912	Chi A	10	10	.500	31	20	11-2	3	165.1	165	85	4	4	68	96	3.27	98	.270	.347	65-0-3	.215	2*	112	-2	—	-0.1
1913	Chi A	1	3	.250	12	3	0	0	40.2	46	24	0	1	20	20	4.87	60	.299	.383	18-0-1	.167	1*	76	-6	—	-0.4
Total	4	28	25	.528	95	60	25-4	3	498.1	455	234	9	17	219	318	2.96	100	.250	.336	210-0-6	.248	14	110	0	—	1.4
LANGE, DICK	Richard Otto; B9.1.1948 Harbor Beach MI; BR/TR/5´10˝/185; [AnaA70 7/158]; d9.9; Col Central Michigan																									
1972	Cal A	0	0	ø	2	1	0	0-0	7.2	7	4	0	0	2-0	8	4.70	63	.233	.281	3	.000	-0	60	-1	0	-0.1
1973	Cal A	2	1	.667	17	4	1	0-1	52.2	61	30	9	1	21-2	27	4.44	81	.292	.356	0	ø	0	119	-6	0	-0.3
1974	Cal A	3	8	.273	21	18	1	0-0	113.2	111	63	10	4	47-0	57	3.80	91	.248	.323	0	ø	0*	97	-7	0	-0.7
1975	Cal A	4	6	.400	30	8	1	1-0	102	119	70	12	1	53-3	45	5.21	69	.292	.371	0	ø	0	86	-20	0	-1.8
Total	4	9	15	.375	70	31	3	1-1	276	298	167	31	6	123-5	137	4.47	79	.272	.346	3	.000	-0	96	-34	0	-2.9
LANGFORD, RICK	James Rick; B3.20.1952 Farmville VA; BR/TR/6´0˝/180; d6.13; C1; Col Florida St.																									
1976	Pit N	0	1	.000	12	1	0	0-1	23	27	17	2	0	14-0	17	6.26	56	.307	.398	5	.200	0	75	-6	0	-0.3
1977	Oak A	8	19	.296	37	31	6-1	0-0	208.1	223	107	18	2	73-3	141	4.02	100	.273	.332	0	ø	0	76	1	0	0.1
1978	Oak A	7	13	.350	37	24	4-2	0-1	175.2	169	77	15	3	56-8	92	3.43	107	.253	.311	0	ø	0*	61	6	0	0.7
1979	Oak A	12	16	.429	34	29	14-1	0-1	218.2	233	114	22	4	57-6	101	4.28	95	.273	.319	0	ø	0	81	-4	0	-0.3
1980	Oak A	19	12	.613	35	33	**28**-2	0-0	**290**	276	119	29	1	64-6	102	3.26	117	.255	.294	0	ø	0	105	18	0	1.9
1981	†Oak A	12	10	.545	24	24	**18**-2	0-0	195.1	190	81	14	3	58-2	84	2.99	118	.255	.308	0	ø	0	102	8	0	0.7
1982	Oak A	11	16	.407	32	31	15-2	0-0	237.1	265	121	33	2	49-1	79	4.21	94	.281	.316	1	.000	-0*	98	-6	0	-0.6
1983	Oak A	0	4	.000	7	7	0	0-0	20	43	28	4	2	10-1	2	12.15	32	.448	.495	0	ø	0	113	-18	149	-2.7
1984	Oak A	0	0	ø	3	2	0	0-0	8.2	15	8	2	0	2-0	2	8.31	45	.366	.395	0	ø	0	108	-4	152	-0.2
1985	Oak A	3	5	.375	23	3	0	0-0	59	60	24	8	0	15-2	21	3.51	111	.261	.306	0	ø	0	63	3	65	0.4
1986	Oak A	1	10	.091	16	11	0	0-0	55	69	49	13	1	18-0	30	7.36	53	.300	.351	0	ø	0*	51	-22	15	-3.6
Total	11	73	106	.408	260	196	85-10	0-3	1491	1570	745	160	18	416-29	671	4.01	96	.271	.319	6	.167	0	87	-24	381	-3.9
LANGSTON, MARK	Mark Edward; B8.20.1960 San Diego CA; BR/TL/6´2˝/(177–190); [SeaA81 2/35]; d4.7; Col San Jose St.																									
1984	Sea A	17	10	.630	35	33	5-2	0-1	225	188	99	16	8	118-5	**204**	3.40	118	.230	.330	0	ø	0	86	14	0	1.6
1985	Sea A	7	14	.333	24	24	2	0-0	126.2	122	85	22	2	91-2	72	5.47	77	.255	.375	0	ø	0	85	-17	45	-2.3
1986	Sea A	12	14	.462	37	36	9	0-0	239.1	234	142	30	4	123-1	**245**	4.85	88	.255	.343	0	ø	0	89	-14	0	-1.4
1987	Sea A★	19	13	.594	35	35	14-3	0-0	272	242	132	30	5	114-0	**262**	3.84	124	.238	.317	0	ø	0	88	25	0	2.7
1988	Sea A	15	11	.577	35	35	9-3	0-0	261.1	222	108	32	3	110-2	235	3.34	125	.233	.313	0	ø	0	91	24	0	2.4
1989	Sea A	4	5	.444	10	10	2-1	0-0	73.1	60	30	3	4	19-0	60	3.56	113	.221	.279	0	ø	0	87	5	0	0.6
	Mon N	12	9	.571	24	24	6-4	0-0	176.2	138	57	13	0	93-6	175	2.39	**149**	.218	.316	64-0-1	.172	-0	89	20	0	2.5
1990	Cal A	10	17	.370	33	33	5-1	0-0	223	215	120	13	5	104-1	195	4.40	87	.259	.343	0	ø	0	93	-12	0	-1.2
1991	Cal A☆	19	8	.704	34	34	7	0-0	246.1	190	89	30	2	96-3	183	3.00	138	.215	.291	0	ø	0	95	31	0	3.3
1992	Cal A★	13	14	.481	32	32	9-2	0-0	229	206	103	14	6	74-2	174	3.66	110	.242	.305	2	.000	-0*	80	8	0	1.0
1993	Cal A★	16	11	.593	35	35	7	0-0	256.1	220	100	22	1	85-2	196	3.20	142	.234	.295	0	ø	0	72	37	0	3.8
1994	Cal A	7	8	.467	18	18	2-1	0-0	119.1	121	67	19	0	54-1	109	4.68	105	.268	.340	0	ø	0	81	3	31	0.4
1995	Cal A	15	7	.682	31	31	2-1	0-0	200.1	212	109	21	3	64-1	142	4.63	102	.272	.329	0	ø	0	126	3	0	0.4
1996	Cal A	6	5	.545	18	18	2	0-0	123.1	116	68	18	2	45-0	83	4.82	105	.247	.315	0	ø	0	96	6	92	0.5
1997	Ana A	2	4	.333	9	9	0	0-0	47.2	61	34	8	0	29-1	30	5.85	79	.316	.402	0	ø	0	102	-7	128	-0.6
1998	†SD N	4	6	.400	22	16	0	0-1	81.1	107	55	11	1	41-1	56	5.86	68	.325	.397	24-0-4	.083	-0*	130	-17	54	-1.8
1999	Cle A	1	2	.333	25	5	0	0-1	61.2	69	40	9	0	29-6	43	5.25	97	.287	.362	2	.500	0	66	-2	46	0.0
Total	16	179	158	.531	457	428	81-18	0-3	2962.2	2723	1438	311	46	1289-34	2464	3.97	108	.246	.325	92-0-5	.152	-0	91	107	396	11.9
LANIER, MAX	Hubert Max; B8.18.1915 Denton NC; BR/TL/5´10˝/(187–195); d4.20; Mil 1945; s–Hal																									
1938	StL N	0	3	.000	18	3	1	0	45	57	30	1	2	28	14	4.20	94	.317	.414	10	.100	-0	93	-3	—	-0.2
1939	StL N	2	1	.667	7	6	2	0	37.2	29	11	0	1	13	14	2.39	172	.220	.295	14-0-1	.286	1	110	7	—	0.6
1940	StL N	9	6	.600	35	11	4-2	3	105	113	50	1	1	38	49	3.34	119	.276	.339	30-0-1	.200	-0	91	6	—	0.8
1941	StL N	10	8	.556	35	18	8-2	3	153	126	59	4	1	59	93	2.82	133	.225	.300	52-0-2	.192	-1	115	14	0	1.7
1942	†StL N	13	8	.619	34	20	8-2	2	161	137	55	4	2	60	93	2.96	116	.234	.308	47-0-4	.255	2	98	11	0	1.8
1943	†StL N☆	15	7	.682	32	25	14-2	3	213.1	195	62	3	2	75	123	1.90	**177**	.246	.312	73-0-11	.164	-2	112	31	0	3.1
1944	†StL N✳	17	12	.586	33	30	16-5	0	224.1	192	82	5	3	71	141	2.65	133	.234	.297	77-0-6	.182	-0	105	20	0	2.4
1945	StL N	2	2	.500	4	3	3	0	26	22	10	0	0	8	16	1.73	216	.222	.280	11	.182	-0	83	4	0	0.6
1946	StL N	6	0	1.000	6	6	6-2	0	56	45	13	1	1	19	36	1.93	179	.228	.300	25	.200	-0	153	10	0	1.1
1949	StL N	5	4	.556	15	15	4-1	0	92	92	42	5	0	35	37	3.82	109	.261	.328	27-0-4	.074	-2	95	5	0	0.2
1950	StL N	11	9	.550	27	27	10-2	0	181.1	173	70	13	1	68	89	3.13	137	.249	.317	68-0-4	.162	-1	99	23	0	2.2
1951	StL N	11	9	.550	31	23	9-2	1	160	149	60	14	1	50	59	3.26	122	.248	.306	53-0-3	.151	-2	66	14	0	1.5
1952	NY N	7	12	.368	37	16	6-1	5	137	124	64	11	3	65	47	3.94	94	.244	.333	41-0-5	.268	3*	71	-1	0	0.3
1953	NY N	0	0	ø	3	0	0	0	5.1	8	4	1	0	3	2	6.75	64	.381	.458	1	.000	-0	—	-1	0	-0.1
	StL A	0	1	.000	10	1	0	0	22.1	28	18	2	0	19	8	7.25	58	.322	.443	6	.167	-0	42	-6	0	-0.3
Total	14	108	82	.568	327	204	91-21	17	1619.1	1490	630	65	18	611	821	3.01	125	.247	.318	535-0-41	.185	-3	97	134	0	15.7

YEAR	TM LG	W	L	PCT	G	GS	CG-SHO	SV-BS	IP	H	R	HR	HB	BB-IB	SO	ERA	AERA	OAV	OOB	AB-HR-SH	AVG	PB	SUP	APR	DL	PW
Lankford, Frank	Frank Greenfield; B3.26.1971 Atlanta GA; BR/TR/6´2˝/190; [NYA93 17/477]; d3.31; Col Virginia																									
1998	LA N	0	2	.000	12	0	0	1-0	19.2	23	13	2	2	7-0	7	5.95	68	.287	.360	2	.000	-0	—	-4	0	-0.3
Lanning, Johnny	John Young "Tobacco Chewin' Johnny"; B9.6.1910 Asheville NC; D11.8.1989 Asheville NC; BR/TR/6´1˝/185; d4.17; Mil 1943–45; b–Tom; Col North Carolina St.																									
1936	Bos N	7	11	.389	28	20	3-1	0	153	154	75	9	0	55	33	3.65	105	.263	.326	52-1-2	.135	-2	81	2	—	-0.1
1937	Bos N	5	7	.417	32	11	4-1	2	116.2	107	59	10	1	40	37	3.93	91	.236	.300	33-0-2	.121	-1	57	-5	—	-0.6
1938	Bos N	8	7	.533	32	18	4-1	0	138	146	74	5	1	52	39	3.72	92	.267	.332	48-0-2	.188	-1	103	-8	—	-0.9
1939	Bos N	5	6	.455	37	6	3	4	129	120	53	6	2	53	45	3.42	108	.252	.329	42-0-2	.143	-1	43	6	—	0.4
1940	Pit N	8	4	.667	38	7	2	2	115.2	119	59	8	0	39	42	4.05	94	.268	.327	35-0-3	.200	1	150	-2	—	-0.1
1941	Pit N	11	11	.500	34	23	9	1	175.2	175	72	6	0	47	41	3.13	116	.256	.304	56-0-6	.107	-2	88	10	0	1.1
1942	Pit N	6	8	.429	34	8	2-1	1	119.1	125	52	7	1	26	31	3.32	102	.274	.314	29-0-2	.138	-0	59	1	0	0.1
1943	Pit N	4	1	.800	12	2	0	2	27	23	10	0	0	9	11	2.33	149	.223	.286	6	.167	-0	61	3	0	0.5
1945	Pit N	0	0	ø	1	0	0	0	2	8	8	1	0	0	0	36.00	11	.571	.571	0	ø	0	—	-6	0	-0.3
1946	Pit N	4	5	.444	27	9	3	1	91	97	36	3	1	31	16	3.07	115	.269	.329	21-0-3	.143	-0	70	5	0	0.4
1947	Bos N	0	0	ø	3	0	0	0	3.2	4	5	0	0	6	0	9.82	40	.400	.625	0	ø	0	—	-3	0	-0.1
Total	11	58	60	.492	278	104	30-4	13	1071	1078	503	55	6	358	295	3.58	101	.261	.321	322-1-22	.146	-7	83	3	0	0.4
Lanning, Red	Lester Alfred; B5.13.1895 Harvard IL; D6.13.1962 Bristol CT; BL/TL/5´9˝/165; d6.20; Col Wesleyan; ▲																									
1916	Phi A	0	3	.000	6	3	1	0	24.1	38	27	1	2	17	9	8.14	35	.362	.460	33-0-1	.182	1*	53	-13	—	-1.3
Lanning, Tom	Thomas Newton; B4.22.1907 Asheville NC; D11.4.1967 Marietta GA; BL/TL/6´1˝/165; d9.14; b–Johnny; Col Wake Forest																									
1938	Phi N	0	1	.000	3	1	0	0	7	9	7	0	0	2	2	6.43	60	.300	.344	1	1.000	0	22	-2	—	-0.3
Lansing, Gene	Eugene Hewitt "Jigger"; B1.11.1898 Albany NY; D1.18.1945 Rensselaer NY; BR/TR/6´1˝/185; d4.27																									
1922	Bos N	0	1	.000	15	1	0	0	40.2	46	28	1	0	22	14	5.98	67	.301	.389	11	.000	-1	61	-7	—	-0.4
LaPalme, Paul	Paul Edmore "Lefty"; B12.14.1923 Springfield MA; BL/TL/5´10˝/(175–184); d5.28																									
1951	Pit N	1	5	.167	22	8	1-1	0	54.1	79	48	6	1	31	24	6.29	67	.333	.413	10	.100	-0	104	-13	0	-1.3
1952	Pit N	1	2	.333	31	2	0	0	59.2	56	33	6	1	37	25	3.92	102	.253	.363	10-0-1	.100	-0	123	-1	0	-0.1
1953	Pit N	8	16	.333	35	24	7-1	2	176.1	191	107	20	0	64	86	4.59	97	.272	.333	59-0-3	.085	-5	76	-5	0	-1.1
1954	Pit N	4	10	.286	33	15	2	0	120.2	147	79	15	0	54	57	5.52	76	.302	.368	35-0-3	.143	-0	97	-15	0	-1.5
1955	StL N	4	3	.571	56	0	0	3	91.2	76	36	10	1	34-9	39	2.75	148	.228	.297	19	.211	0	—	11	0	0.9
1956	StL N	0	0	ø	1	0	0	0	0.2	4	6	0	0	2-0	0	81.00	5	.667	.750	0	ø	0	—	-5	0	-0.2
	Cin N	2	4	.333	11	2	0	0	27	26	14	7	0	4-0	4	4.67	85	.257	.283	4-0-2	.500	1	100	-1	0	-0.2
	Year	2	4	.333	12	2	0	0	27.2	30	20	7	0	6-0	4	6.51	61	.280	.316	4-0-2	.500	1	100	-6	0	-0.4
	Chi A	3	1	.750	29	0	0	2	45.2	31	14	2	0	27-2	23	2.36	173	.195	.310	6-0-1	.000	-1	—	9	0	0.7
1957	Chi A	1	4	.200	35	0	0	7	40.1	35	16	5	1	19-1	19	3.35	112	.235	.325	4-0-1	.500	1*	—	2	0	0.5
Total	7	24	45	.348	253	51	10-2	14	616.1	645	353	71	4	272-12	277	4.42	95	.269	.343	147-0-11	.136	-4	92	-18	0	-2.3
Lapihuska, Andy	Andrew "Apples"; B11.1.1922 Delmont NJ; D2.17.1996 Millville NJ; BL/TR/5´10.5˝/175; d9.12; Mil 1944–45																									
1942	Phi N	0	2	.000	3	2	0	0	20.2	17	13	0	2	13	8	5.23	63	.221	.348	7	.286	0	13	-4	0	-0.3
1943	Phi N	0	0	ø	1	0	0	0	2.1	5	6	1	0	3	0	23.14	15	.417	.533	2	.000	-0	—	-5	0	-0.2
Total	2	0	2	.000	4	2	0	0	23	22	19	1	2	16	8	7.04	47	.247	.374	9	.222	0	13	-9	0	-0.5
LaPoint, Dave	David Jeffrey; B7.29.1959 Glens Falls NY; BL/TL/6´3˝/(205–231); [MilA77 10/237]; d9.10																									
1980	Mil A	1	0	1.000	5	3	0	1-0	15	17	14	2	0	13-1	5	6.00	65	.293	.411	0	ø	0	213	-5	0	-0.4
1981	StL N	1	0	1.000	3	2	0	0-0	10.2	12	5	1	1	2-0	4	4.22	86	.293	.341	5	.000	-1	172	0	0	-0.1
1982	†StL N	9	3	.750	42	21	0	0-0	152.2	170	63	8	3	52-8	81	3.42	108	.290	.348	38-0-8	.053	-3	114	5	0	-0.1
1983	StL N	12	9	.571	37	29	1	0-0	191.1	191	92	12	4	84-7	113	3.95	93	.267	.342	59-0-5	.153	1	110	-4	0	-0.4
1984	StL N	12	10	.545	33	33	2-1	0-0	193	205	94	9	1	77-8	130	3.96	88	.278	.346	59-0-9	.068	-3	99	-10	15	-1.4
1985	SF N	7	17	.292	31	31	2-1	0-0	206.2	215	99	18	0	74-6	122	3.57	97	.269	.329	60-0-5	.167	2	78	-4	0	-0.4
1986	Det A	3	6	.333	16	8	0	0-1	67.2	85	49	11	0	32-3	36	5.72	73	.307	.377	0	ø	0	101	-12	0	-1.4
	SD N	1	4	.200	24	4	0	0-0	61.1	67	37	8	1	24-4	41	4.26	86	.276	.342	8-0-4	.000	-1	91	-6	0	-0.6
1987	StL N	1	1	.500	6	2	0	0-0	16	26	12	4	0	5-0	8	6.75	62	.351	.392	4	.000	-0	129	-4	0	-0.5
	Chi A	6	3	.667	14	12	2-1	0-0	82.2	69	29	7	1	31-0	43	2.94	157	.224	.297	0	ø	0	105	15	0	1.6
1988	Chi A	10	11	.476	25	25	1-1	0-0	161.1	151	69	10	2	47-1	79	3.40	118	.245	.299	0	ø	0	88	11	0	1.3
	Pit N	4	2	.667	8	8	1	0-0	52	54	18	4	0	10-2	19	2.77	125	.271	.305	16-0-1	.063	-1	103	4	0	0.3
1989	NY A	6	9	.400	20	20	0	0-0	113.2	146	73	12	2	45-4	51	5.62	69	.310	.370	0	ø	0	100	-19	77	-2.3
1990	NY A	7	10	.412	28	27	2	0-0	157.2	180	84	11	1	57-3	67	4.11	97	.292	.347	0	ø	0	88	-4	0	-0.4
1991	Phi N	0	1	.000	2	2	0	0-0	5	10	10	0	1	6-0	3	16.20	23	.435	.548	2	.000	-0	158	-7	0	-1.0
Total	12	80	86	.482	294	227	11-4	1-1	1486.2	1598	748	117	17	559-47	802	4.02	94	.277	.340	251-0-32	.104	-6	100	-40	92	-5.8
Lara, Juan	Juan Manuel; B1.26.1981 Azua, D.R.; BR/TL/6´2˝/190; d9.8																									
2006	Cle A	0	0	ø	9	0	0	0-1	5	4	2	0	0	1-0	2	1.80	240	.222	.263	0	ø	0	—	1	0	0.0
Lara, Yovanny	Yovanny B.; B9.20.1975 San Cristobal, D.R.; BR/TR/6´4˝/180; d6.28																									
2000	Mon N	0	0	ø	6	0	0	0-0	5.2	5	4	0	0	8-0	3	6.35	74	.250	.448	0	ø	0	—	-1	78	0.0
Larkin, Andy	Andrew Dane; B6.27.1974 Chelan WA; BR/TR/6´4˝/(175–190); [FlaN92 25/712]; d9.29																									
1996	Fla N	0	0	ø	1	1	0	0-0	5	3	1	0	1	4-0	2	1.80	229	.176	.364	2	.000	-0	87	1	67	0.0
1998	Fla N	3	8	.273	17	14	0	0-0	74.2	101	87	12	4	55-3	43	9.64	42	.329	.435	29-0-2	.138	-1	120	-48	0	-5.3
2000	Cin N	0	0	ø	3	0	0	0-0	6.2	6	4	1	0	5-0	7	5.40	88	.240	.367	1	.000	-0	—	0	0	0.0
	KC A	0	3	.000	18	0	0	1-2	19.1	29	20	5	0	11-2	17	8.84	59	.349	.421	0	ø	0	—	-7	0	-1.0
Total	3	3	11	.214	39	15	0	1-2	105.2	139	112	18	5	75-5	69	8.86	49	.322	.425	32-0-2	.125	-1	111	-54	67	-6.3
Larkin, Terry	Frank S.; D9.16.1894 Brooklyn NY; BR/TR; d5.20; ▲																									
1876	NY N	0	1	.000	1	1	1	0	9	9	7	0	—	0	0	3.00	71	.231	.231	4	.000	-1	72	-1	—	-0.1
1877	Har N	29	25	.537	56	56	55-4	0	501	510	285	2	—	53	96	2.14	114	**.245**	.264	228-1	.228	6*	111	14	—	1.6
1878	Chi N	29	26	.527	56	56	56-1	0	506	511	288	4	—	31	163	2.24	108	.246	.257	226	.288	13*	107	10	—	1.9
1879	Chi N	31	23	.574	58	58	57-4	0	513.1	514	277	5	—	30	142	2.44	105	.240	**.250**	228	.219	1*	96	8	—	0.5
1880	Tro N	0	5	.000	5	5	3	0	38	83	65	1	—	10	5	8.76	29	.421	.449	20	.150	-0*	90	-23	—	-2.1
Total	5	89	80	.527	176	176	172-9	0	1567.1	1627	922	12	—	124	406	2.43	102	.249	.263	706-1	.241	19	103	8	—	1.8
Larkin, Pat	Patrick Clibborn; B6.14.1960 Arcadia CA; BL/TL/6´0˝/180; d7.16; Col Santa Clara																									
1983	SF N	0	0	ø	5	0	0	0-0	10.1	13	6	1	2	3-1	6	4.35	81	.317	.383	1	.000	-0	—	-1	0	-0.1
Larkin, Steve	Stephen Patrick; B12.9.1910 Cincinnati OH; D5.2.1969 Norristown PA; BR/TR/6´1˝/195; d5.6																									
1934	Det A	0	0	ø	2	1	0	0	6	8	7	0	0	5	8	1.50	293	.296	.406	3	.333	1	79	-1	—	0.1
LaRoche, Dave	David Eugene; B5.14.1948 Colorado Springs CO; BL/TL/6´2˝/(185–200); [AnaA67*S5/86]; d5.11; C5; s–Adam; Col Nevada–Las Vegas																									
1970	Cal A	4	1	.800	38	0	0	4-2	49.2	41	20	6	4	21-6	44	3.44	105	.224	.316	8	.250	1	—	2	0	0.3
1971	Cal A	5	1	.833	56	0	0	9-3	72	55	21	3	1	27-10	63	2.50	130	.212	.285	11-0-1	.091	-0	—	7	0	0.7
1972	Min A	5	7	.417	62	0	0	10-3	95.1	72	33	9	6	39-6	79	2.83	113	.209	.300	11-0-1	.091	0	—	5	0	0.8
1973	Chi N	4	1	.800	45	0	0	4-1	54.1	55	37	7	1	29-3	34	5.80	68	.274	.362	4	.500	1	—	-9	12	-0.8
1974	Chi N	5	6	.455	49	4	0	5-6	92	103	54	9	3	47-7	49	4.79	80	.286	.371	27	.333	3*	80	-8	0	-0.7
1975	Cle A	5	3	.625	61	0	0	17-3	82.1	61	26	5	2	57-8	94	2.19	174	.210	.344	0	ø	0	—	13	0	1.9
1976	Cle A☆	1	4	.200	61	0	0	21-3	96.1	57	25	2	1	49-11	104	2.24	157	.175	.282	0	ø	0	—	14	0	1.4
1977	Cle A	2	2	.500	13	0	0	4-1	18.2	15	13	3	0	7-1	18	5.30	75	.234	.301	0	ø	0	—	-3	0	-0.6
	Cal A★	6	5	.545	46	0	0	13-2	81.1	64	31	8	2	37-8	61	3.10	127	.218	.306	0	ø	0	—	8	0	1.3
	Year	8	7	.533	59	0	0	17-3	100	79	44	11	2	44-9	79	3.51	112	.221	.305	0	ø	0	—	5	0	0.7
1978	Cal A	10	9	.526	59	0	0	25-6	95.2	73	35	7	2	48-11	70	2.82	129	.215	.315	0	ø	0	—	8	0	1.7
1979	†Cal A	7	11	.389	53	1	0	10-5	85.2	107	54	13	2	32-4	59	5.57	73	.314	.372	0	ø	0	0	-12	0	-2.3
1980	Cal A	3	5	.375	52	9	1	4-4	128	122	62	14	3	39-3	89	4.08	97	.256	.314	0	ø	0*	111	-1	0	-0.1
1981	†NY A	4	1	.800	26	1	0	0-2	47	38	16	3	1	16-1	24	2.49	145	.229	.291	0	ø	0	124	5	0	0.5
1982	NY A	4	2	.667	25	0	0	0-0	50	54	19	4	1	11-2	31	3.42	118	.273	.313	0	ø	0	—	4	0	0.4

YEAR	TM LG	W	L	PCT	G	GS	CG-SHO	SV-BS	IP	H	R	HR	HB	BB-IB	SO	ERA	AERA	OAV	OOB	AB-HR-SH	AVG	PB	SUP	APR	DL	PW
1983	NY A	0	0	ø	1	0	0	0-0	1	2	2	1	0	0-0	0	18.00	22	.400	.400	0	ø	0	—	-2	0	-0.1
Total	14	65	58	.528	647	15	1	126-41	1049.1	919	448	94	29	459-81	819	3.53	106	.239	.322	61-0-2	.246	4	100	31	12	4.4
LaRose, John	Henry John; B10.25.1951 Pawtucket RI; BL/TL/6´1˝/185; [BosA70 S1/14]; d9.20																									
1978	Bos A	0	0	ø	1	0	0	0-0	2	3	5	1	0	3-1	0	22.50	18	.375	.545	0	ø	0	—	-3	0	-0.2
Larsen, Don	Don James; B8.7.1929 Michigan City IN; BR/TR/6´4˝/(215–227); d4.18																									
1953	StL A	7	12	.368	38	22	7-2	2	192.2	201	99	11	4	64	96	4.16	101	.267	.328	81-3-0	.284	5*	95	2	0	0.9
1954	Bal A	3	21	.125	29	28	12-1	0	201.2	213	106	18	1	89	80	4.37	82	.274	.346	88-1-2	.250	8*	64	-16	0	-0.9
1955	†NY A	9	2	.818	19	13	5-1	2	97	81	38	8	2	51-3	44	3.06	122	.229	.328	41-2-0	.146	2*	139	8	0	1.0
1956	†NY A	11	5	.688	38	20	6-1	1	179.2	133	72	19	7	96-0	107	3.26	119	.204	.312	79-2-1	.241	6*	131	14	0	1.7
1957	†NY A	10	4	.714	27	20	4-1	0	139.2	113	68	12	0	87-0	81	3.74	96	.220	.332	56	.250	5*	133	-3	0	0.2
1958	†NY A	9	6	.600	19	19	5-3	0	114.1	100	43	4	4	52-3	55	3.07	115	.233	.320	49-4-2	.306	9*	134	7	0	1.8
1959	NY A	6	7	.462	25	18	3-1	0	124.2	122	65	14	2	76-2	69	4.33	84	.260	.361	47-0-1	.255	4*	147	-8	0	-0.4
1960	KC A	1	10	.091	22	15	0	0	83.2	97	55	11	0	42-1	43	5.38	74	.293	.370	29	.207	0*	69	-12	0	-1.4
1961	KC A	1	0	1.000	8	1	0	0	15	21	9	2	1	11-0	13	4.20	100	.344	.452	20-1-1	.300	1*	127	0	0	0.1
	Chi A	7	2	.778	25	3	0	2	74.1	64	36	5	1	29-2	53	4.12	95	.231	.306	25-1-1	.320	3	128	-1	0	0.2
	Year	8	2	.800	33	4	0	2	89.1	85	45	7	2	40-2	66	4.13	96	.251	.334	45-2-2	.311	4	128	-1	0	0.3
1962	†SF N	5	4	.556	49	0	0	11	86.1	83	44	9	2	47-7	58	4.38	87	.256	.352	25-0-1	.200	1*	—	-4	0	-0.5
1963	SF N	7	7	.500	46	0	0	3	62	46	23	8	0	30-9	44	3.05	105	.203	.296	11-0-1	.182	0	—	2	0	0.4
1964	SF N	0	1	.000	6	0	0	0	10.1	10	5	0	0	6-1	6	4.35	82	.256	.356	1	.000	-0	—	-1	0	-0.1
	Hou N	4	8	.333	30	10	2-1	1	103.1	92	36	4	1	20-4	58	2.26	151	.233	.270	31-0-1	.097	0*	67	11	0	1.3
	Year	4	9	.308	36	10	2-1	1	113.2	102	41	4	1	26-5	64	2.45	140	.235	.279	32-0-1	.094	0	67	10	0	1.2
1965	Hou N	0	0	ø	1	1	0	0	5.1	8	3	0	0	3-1	1	5.06	66	.348	.423	2	.000	-0	104	-1	0	0.0
	Bal A	1	2	.333	27	1	0	1	54	53	22	4	1	20-2	40	2.67	130	.255	.322	11	.273	1	101	3	0	0.3
1967	Chi N	0	0	ø	3	0	0	0	4	5	4	1	0	2-0	1	9.00	39	.333	.412	0	ø	0	—	-2	0	-0.1
Total	14	81	91	.471	412	171	44-11	23	1548	1442	728	130	26	725-35	849	3.78	99	.247	.331	596-14-11	.242	46	109	-1	0	4.5
Larson, Dan	Daniel James; B7.4.1954 Los Angeles CA; BR/TR/6´0˝/(170–180); [StLN72 1/21]; d7.18																									
1976	Hou N	5	8	.385	13	13	5	0-0	92.1	81	40	3	1	28-1	42	3.02	107	.236	.291	31-0-2	.290	4*	111	0	0	0.4
1977	Hou N	1	7	.125	32	10	1	1-1	97.2	108	72	13	2	45-2	44	5.81	62	.280	.355	28	.214	1*	111	-26	0	-1.9
1978	Phi N	0	0	ø	1	0	0	0-0	1	1	1	1	0	1-0	2	9.00	40	.250	.400	0	ø	0	—	-1	0	0.0
1979	Phi N	1	1	.500	3	3	0	0-0	19	17	9	1	1	9-0	9	4.26	91	.250	.342	5-0-1	.000	-1	114	0	0	-0.1
1980	Phi N	0	5	.000	12	7	0	0-0	45.2	46	24	4	0	24-6	17	3.15	121	.271	.359	13	.154	0	67	1	0	0.1
1981	Phi N	3	0	1.000	5	4	1	0-0	28	27	13	4	0	15-1	15	4.18	88	.260	.350	9-0-1	.111	0	212	-1	0	-0.1
1982	Chi N	0	4	.000	12	6	0	0-0	39.2	51	30	4	2	18-0	22	5.67	67	.327	.397	11	.273	0	89	-9	0	-0.7
Total	7	10	25	.286	78	43	7	1-1	323.1	331	189	30	6	140-10	151	4.40	81	.269	.342	97-0-4	.216	4	110	-36	0	-2.3
Lary, Al	Alfred Allen; B9.26.1928 Northport AL; D7.10.2001 Northport AL; BR/TR/6´3˝/185; d9.6; b–Frank; Col Alabama																									
1954	Chi N	0	0	ø	1	1	0	0	6	3	2	0	0	7	4	3.00	140	.150	.370	2	.500	0*	85	1	0	0.1
1962	Chi N	0	1	.000	15	3	0	0	34	42	27	5	0	15-0	18	7.15	58	.311	.370	6-0-2	.167	0*	56	-9	0	-0.4
Total	2	0	1	.000	16	4	0	0	40	45	29	5	0	22-0	22	6.52	64	.290	.370	8-0-2	.250	1	63	-8	0	-0.3
Lary, Frank	Frank Strong "Mule","The Yankee Killer"; B4.10.1930 Northport AL; BR/TR/5´11˝/(175–185); d9.14; b–Al; Col Alabama																									
1954	Det A	0	0	ø	3	0	0	0	3.2	4	1	0	0	3	5	2.45	150	.286	.412	0	ø	0	—	1	0	0.0
1955	Det A	14	15	.483	36	31	16-2	1	235	232	100	10	6	89-3	98	3.10	124	.262	.331	82-0-5	.195	1	100	16	0	2.0
1956	Det A	**21**	13	.618	41	**38**	20-3	1	**294**	289	116	20	12	116-4	165	3.15	131	.257	.331	103-1-6	.184	0	115	32	0	3.4
1957	Det A	11	16	.407	40	35	12-2	3	237.2	250	111	23	12	72-9	107	3.98	97	.276	.336	73-0-9	.123	-3	103	-1	0	-0.5
1958	Det A	16	15	.516	39	34	**19**-3	1	**260.1**	249	91	20	12	68-4	131	2.90	139	.251	.305	88-1-9	.170	-1	94	32	0	3.5
1959	Det A	17	10	.630	32	32	11-3	0	223	225	109	23	11	46-4	137	3.55	114	.261	.305	80-1-8	.125	-2	98	9	0	0.7
1960	Det A★	15	15	.500	38	**36**	**15**-2	1	**274.1**	262	125	25	19	62-3	149	3.51	113	.249	.301	93-2-8	.183	4*	104	12	0	1.5
1961	Det A★	23	9	.719	36	36	**22**-4	0	275.1	252	117	24	6	66-2	146	3.24	127	.243	.290	108-1-3	.231	4*	119	25	0	3.3
1962	Det A	2	6	.250	17	14	2-1	0	80	98	59	17	4	21-1	41	5.74	71	.297	.345	24	.167	1*	100	-15	32	-1.3
1963	Det A	4	9	.308	16	14	6	0	107.1	90	40	15	5	26-0	46	3.27	114	.226	.280	35-0-2	.229	1	107	7	0	1.0
1964	Det A	0	2	.000	6	4	0	0	18	24	15	3	3	10-1	6	7.00	52	.316	.416	7	.000	-1	103	-6	0	-0.7
	NY N	2	3	.400	13	8	3-1	1	57.1	62	33	7	4	14-2	27	4.55	79	.279	.332	17-0-1	.118	1	89	-6	0	-0.5
	Mil N	1	0	1.000	5	2	0	0	12.1	15	7	4	0	0-0	4	4.38	80	.306	.306	3	.000	-0	187	-1	0	-0.1
	Year	3	3	.500	18	10	3-1	1	69.2	77	40	11	4	14-2	31	4.52	79	.284	.328	20-0-1	.100	0	108	-7	0	-0.6
1965	NY N	1	3	.250	14	7	0	1	57.1	48	24	2	1	16-0	23	2.98	118	.233	.288	19	.211	0	85	3	0	0.2
	Chi A	1	0	1.000	14	1	0	2	26.2	23	12	4	2	7-2	14	4.05	79	.230	.294	2-0-1	.500	0	110	-2	0	-0.1
Total	12	128	116	.525	350	292	126-21	11	2162.1	2123	960	197	97	616-35	1099	3.49	113	.257	.314	734-6-52	.177	5	105	106	32	12.4
Lasher, Fred	Frederick Walter; B8.19.1941 Poughkeepsie NY; BR/TR/6´4˝/(186–210); d4.12																									
1963	Min A	0	0	ø	11	0	0	0	11.1	12	10	1	0	11-1	10	4.76	76	.286	.426	1	.000	-0	—	-3	0	-0.1
1967	Det A	2	1	.667	17	0	0	9	30	25	14	1	1	11-1	28	3.90	84	.221	.296	9-0-1	.111	-0	—	-2	0	-0.4
1968	†Det A	5	1	.833	34	0	0	5	48.2	37	19	5	0	22-7	32	3.33	90	.215	.303	9	.111	-0	—	-1	0	-0.2
1969	Det A	2	1	.667	32	0	0	0-1	44	34	16	5	2	22-1	26	3.07	123	.224	.326	4-0-1	.000	-0	—	4	0	0.2
1970	Det A	1	3	.250	12	0	0	3-1	9	10	6	0	1	12-1	8	5.00	75	.278	.460	1	.000	-0	—	-1	0	-0.3
	Cle A	1	7	.125	43	1	0	5-4	57.2	57	34	6	3	30-1	44	4.06	99	.264	.354	8-0-1	.000	-1	44	-3	0	-0.6
	Year	2	10	.167	55	1	0	8-5	66.2	67	40	6	4	42-2	52	4.18	95	.266	.372	9-0-1	.000	-1	45	-3	0	-0.9
1971	Cal A	0	0	ø	2	0	0	0-0	1.1	4	4	0	0	2-0	0	27.00	12	.667	.667	0	ø	0	—	-4	0	-0.2
Total	6	11	13	.458	151	1	0	22-6	202	179	103	18	7	110-12	148	3.88	92	.243	.342	32-0-3	.063	-2	50	-10	0	-1.6
Laskey, Bill	William Alan; B12.20.1957 Toledo OH; BR/TR/6´5˝/(190–200); [KCA78 S2/27]; d4.23; Col Kent St.																									
1982	SF N	13	12	.520	32	31	7-1	0-0	189.1	186	74	14	2	43-2	88	3.14	114	.261	.302	62-0-4	.129	-2	106	10	0	1.1
1983	SF N	13	10	.565	25	25	1	0-0	148.1	151	75	18	3	45-4	81	4.19	85	.266	.321	47-0-1	.106	0*	109	-8	0	-1.2
1984	SF N	9	14	.391	35	34	2	0-0	207.2	222	112	20	6	50-6	71	4.33	82	.273	.317	63-0-4	.063	-3	94	-18	0	-2.3
1985	SF N	5	11	.313	19	19	0	0-0	114	110	55	10	0	39-0	42	3.55	98	.255	.314	30-0-5	.133	0	72	-2	0	-0.3
	Mon N	0	5	.000	11	7	0	0-0	34.1	55	36	9	2	14-1	18	9.44	37	.362	.420	7-0-3	.143	-0	103	-22	0	-2.6
	Year	5	16	.238	30	26	0	0-0	148.1	165	91	19	2	53-1	60	4.91	70	.283	.342	37-0-8	.135	0	81	-24	0	-2.9
1986	SF N	1	1	.500	20	0	0	1-0	27.1	28	14	5	0	13-1	8	4.28	83	.275	.353	1	.000	-0	—	-2	0	-0.1
1988	Cle A	1	0	1.000	17	0	0	1-0	24.1	32	16	0	0	6-0	17	5.18	80	.320	.349	0	ø	0	—	-3	0	-0.1
Total	6	42	53	.442	159	116	10-1	2-0	745.1	784	382	76	13	210-14	325	4.14	86	.272	.322	210-0-17	.105	-4	97	-45	0	-5.5
Lasley, Bill	Willard Almond; B7.13.1902 Gallipolis OH; D8.21.1990 Seattle WA; BB/TR/6´0˝/175; d9.19																									
1924	StL A	0	0	ø	2	0	0	0	4	7	3	0	0	2	0	6.75	67	.412	.474	1	.000	-0	—	-1	—	-0.1
Lasorda, Tom	Thomas Charles; B9.22.1927 Norristown PA; BL/TL/5´10˝/175; d8.5; M21/C4; HF1997																									
1954	Bro N	0	0	ø	4	0	0	0	9	8	5	2	0	5	5	5.00	82	.242	.333	1	.000	-0	—	-1	0	-0.1
1955	Bro N	0	0	ø	4	1	0	0	4	5	6	1	1	6-0	4	13.50	30	.313	.500	0	ø	0	88	-4	0	-0.2
1956	KC A	0	4	.000	18	5	0	1	45.1	40	38	6	3	45-3	28	6.15	70	.240	.406	13	.077	-1*	86	-10	0	-0.9
Total	3	0	4	.000	26	6	0	1	58.1	53	49	9	4	56-3	37	6.48	66	.245	.404	14	.071	-2	87	-15	0	-1.2
Latham, Bill	William Carol; B8.29.1960 Birmingham AL; BL/TL/6´2˝/190; d4.15; Col Auburn																									
1985	NY N	1	3	.250	7	3	0	0-0	22.2	21	10	1	0	7-1	10	3.97	88	.250	.304	3-0-1	.333	1	76	-1	0	0.0
1986	Min A	0	1	.000	7	2	0	0-1	16	24	14	1	1	6-0	8	7.31	59	.358	.408	0	ø	0	94	-5	0	-0.3
Total	2	1	4	.200	14	5	0	0-1	38.2	45	24	2	1	13-1	18	5.35	72	.298	.351	3-0-1	.333	1	84	-6	0	-0.3
Lathrop, Bill	William George; B8.12.1891 Hanover WI; D11.20.1958 Janesville WI; BR/TR/6´2.5˝/184; d7.29; Col Notre Dame																									
1913	Chi A	0	1	.000	6	0	0	0	17	16	11	0	1	12	9	4.24	69	.267	.397	4	.000	-1	—	-2	—	-0.2
1914	Chi A	1	2	.333	19	1	0	0	47.2	41	20	0	2	19	7	2.64	102	.241	.325	12-0-1	.000	-1	54	0	—	-0.1
Total	2	1	3	.250	25	1	0	0	64.2	57	31	0	3	31	16	3.06	90	.248	.345	16-0-1	.000	-2	54	-2	—	-0.3

YEAR	TM LG	W	L	PCT	G	GS	CG-SHO	SV-BS	IP	H	R	HR	HB	BB-IB	SO	ERA	AERA	OAV	OOB	AB-HR-SH	AVG	PB	SUP	APR	DL	PW
Latman, Barry	Arnold Barry; B5.21.1936 Los Angeles CA; BR/TR/6´3˝/(208–215); d9.10; Col USC																									
1957	Chi A	1	2	.333	7	2	0	1	12.1	12	11	2	1	13-0	9	8.03	47	.267	.441	1	.000	-0	120	-6	0	-1.1
1958	Chi A	3	0	1.000	13	3	1-1	0	47.2	27	7	1	1	17-0	28	0.76	481	.162	.242	12-0-1	.083	-0	66	15	0	0.8
1959	Chi A	8	5	.615	37	21	5-2	0	156	138	71	15	4	72-3	97	3.75	100	.235	.321	47-0-2	.128	-1	136	1	0	-0.2
1960	Cle A	7	7	.500	31	20	4	0	147.1	146	78	19	6	72-2	94	4.03	93	.258	.345	41-0-7	.220	1	120	-6	0	-0.5
1961	Cle A☆	13	5	.722	45	18	4-2	5	176.2	163	84	23	5	54-3	108	4.02	98	.244	.303	55-0-1	.073	-3	104	1	0	-0.4
1962	Cle A	8	13	.381	45	21	7-1	5	179.1	179	96	23	5	72-9	117	4.17	93	.261	.334	53-1-3	.189	2	82	-7	0	-0.6
1963	Cle A	7	12	.368	38	21	4-2	2	149.1	146	90	23	6	52-3	133	4.94	73	.257	.323	44-1-3	.182	2	83	-21	0	-2.1
1964	LA A	6	10	.375	40	18	2-1	2	138	128	72	15	7	52-6	81	3.85	85	.244	.319	40-0-2	.125	-1	101	-11	0	-1.3
1965	Cal A	1	1	.500	18	0	0	0	31.2	30	12	3	0	16-3	18	2.84	120	.254	.343	2	.000	-0	—	2	0	0.0
1966	Hou N	2	7	.222	31	9	1-1	1	103	88	42	5	7	35-4	74	2.71	126	.233	.310	26	.154	0	57	6	18	0.5
1967	Hou N	3	6	.333	39	1	0	0	77.2	73	42	13	6	34-2	70	4.52	73	.252	.338	11-0-1	.091	-1	53	-9	0	-1.1
Total	11	59	68	.465	344	134	28-10	16	1219	1130	605	142	48	489-35	829	3.91	94	.246	.323	332-2-20	.145	-1	101	-35	18	-6.0
Lattimore, Bill	William Hershel "Slothful Bill"; B5.25.1884 Roxton TX; D10.30.1919 Colorado Springs CO; BL/TL/5´9˝/165; d4.17																									
1908	Cle A	1	2	.333	4	4	1-1	0	24	24	16	0	0	7	5	4.50	53	.247	.298	9-0-2	.444	1	150	-5	—	-0.5
Lauer, Chuck	John Charles; B4.5.1865 Pittsburgh PA; D5.14.1915 Buffalo NY; TR; d7.17; ▲																									
1884	Pit AA	0	2	.000	3	3	2	0	19	23	25	0	3	9	8	7.58	44	.277	.368	44	.114	-1*	85	-9	—	-0.8
Lauzerique, George	George Albert; B7.22.1947 Havana, Cuba; BR/TR/6´1˝/(170–180); [OakA65 8/186]; d9.17																									
1967	KC A	0	2	.000	3	2	0	0	16	11	4	2	1	6-0	10	2.25	142	.193	.281	3	.000	-0	27	2	0	0.3
1968	Oak A	0	0	ø	1	0	0	0	1	0	0	0	0	1-0	0	0.00	ø	.000	.333	0	ø	0	—	0	0	0.0
1969	Oak A	3	4	.429	19	8	1	0-1	61.1	58	32	14	2	27-0	39	4.70	73	.250	.331	20	.100	-1	100	-7	0	-0.8
1970	Mil A	1	2	.333	11	4	1	0-1	35	41	27	7	1	14-1	24	6.94	54	.295	.357	10-1-3	.200	1	177	-11	0	-0.8
Total	4	4	8	.333	34	14	2	0-2	113.1	110	63	23	4	48-1	73	5.00	70	.256	.333	33-1-3	.121	-0	114	-16	0	-1.3
Lavelle, Gary	Gary Robert; B1.3.1949 Scranton PA; BB/TL (BL 1981, BR 1982–83)/6´1˝/(180–210); [SFN67 20/397]; d9.10; [DL 1986 Tor A 182]																									
1974	SF N	0	3	.000	10	0	0	0-0	16.2	14	7	1	0	10-2	12	2.16	177	.222	.329	2-0-2	.000	-0	—	2	0	0.3
1975	SF N	6	3	.667	65	0	0	8-5	82.1	80	30	3	3	48-12	51	2.95	129	.260	.364	9	.111	-0	—	8	0	1.0
1976	SF N	10	6	.625	65	0	0	12-8	110.1	102	37	6	2	52-10	71	2.69	135	.246	.331	13-0-2	.077	-1	—	12	0	1.9
1977	SF N★	7	7	.500	73	0	0	20-8	118.1	106	35	4	0	37-18	93	2.05	192	.239	.295	14	.000	-2	—	23	0	3.3
1978	SF N	13	10	.565	67	0	0	14-10	97.2	96	41	3	2	44-11	63	3.32	105	.263	.341	15-0-1	.067	-1	—	1	0	0.2
1979	SF N	7	9	.438	70	0	0	20-9	96.2	86	31	5	2	42-15	80	2.51	139	.247	.327	4-0-2	.250	0	—	11	0	2.2
1980	SF N	6	8	.429	62	0	0	9-7	100	106	43	4	0	36-11	66	3.42	103	.275	.333	11-0-3	.000	-1	—	1	0	0.1
1981	SF N	2	6	.250	34	3	0	4-3	65.2	58	33	3	2	23-4	45	3.84	89	.244	.316	11-0-2	.273	1	96	-4	0	-0.3
1982	SF N	10	7	.588	68	0	0	8-5	104.2	97	35	6	1	29-12	76	2.67	134	.247	.298	13-0-2	.154	0	—	11	0	2.0
1983	SF N☆	7	4	.636	56	0	0	20-9	87	73	33	4	0	19-8	68	2.59	137	.229	.270	14	.000	-2	—	8	21	1.2
1984	SF N	5	4	.556	77	0	0	12-7	101	92	34	5	1	42-14	71	2.76	128	.246	.321	5	.000	-0	—	9	0	0.9
1985	†Tor A	5	7	.417	69	0	0	8-8	72.2	54	30	5	0	36-5	50	3.10	137	.214	.310	0	ø	0	—	8	0	1.4
1987	Tor A	2	3	.400	23	0	0	1-0	27.2	36	20	2	0	19-4	17	5.53	82	.313	.407	0	ø	0	—	-4	56	-0.6
	Oak A	0	0	ø	6	0	0	0-1	4.1	4	4	0	0	3-0	6	8.31	50	.267	.368	0	ø	0	—	-2	0	-0.1
	Year	2	3	.400	29	0	0	1-1	32	40	24	2	0	22-4	23	5.91	76	.308	.403	0	ø	0	—	-6	0	-0.7
Total	13	80	77	.510	745	3	0	136-80	1085	1004	413	51	13	440-126	769	2.93	126	.249	.322	111-0-14	.081	-6	96	84	259	13.5
Lavender, Jimmy	James Sanford; B5.26.1884 Barnesville GA; D1.12.1960 Cartersville GA; BR/TR/5´11˝/165; d4.23																									
1912	Chi N	16	13	.552	42	31	15-3	3	251.2	240	116	8	10	89	109	3.04	109	.257	.328	87-0-3	.149	-3	105	5	—	0.3
1913	Chi N	10	14	.417	40	20	10	2	204	206	111	6	13	98	91	3.66	87	.267	.359	68-0-3	.118	-4	116	-12	—	-1.9
1914	Chi N	11	11	.500	37	28	11-2	0	214.1	191	106	11	11	87	87	3.07	91	.247	.331	63-0-3	.175	2	103	-5	—	-0.1
1915	Chi N	10	16	.385	41	24	13-1	4	220	178	77	5	10	67	117	2.58	108	.228	.298	67-0-2	.134	-2	89	6	—	0.7
1916	Chi N	10	14	.417	36	25	9-4	2	188	163	76	3	9	62	91	2.82	103	.240	.312	53-0-3	.151	-2	78	2	—	0.0
1917	Phi N	6	8	.429	28	14	7	1	129.1	119	61	5	3	44	52	3.55	79	.250	.317	36-0-2	.139	-1	100	-8	—	-1.1
Total	6	63	76	.453	224	142	65-10	12	1207.1	1097	547	38	56	447	547	3.09	97	.249	.325	374-0-16	.144	-9	98	-12	—	-2.1
Law, Ron	Ronald David; B3.14.1946 Hamilton ON, Can.; BR/TR/6´2˝/165; d6.29																									
1969	Cle A	3	4	.429	35	1	0	1-2	52.1	68	34	2	2	34-5	29	4.99	76	.325	.419	7	.143	-0	140	-7	0	-0.9
Law, Vern	Vernon Sanders "Deacon"; B3.12.1930 Meridian ID; BR/TR/6´2˝/(195–200); d6.11; Mil 1952–53; C2; s–Vance																									
1950	Pit N	7	9	.438	27	17	5-1	0	128	137	83	11	4	49	57	4.92	89	.272	.341	41	.073	-2	104	-9	0	-1.2
1951	Pit N	6	9	.400	28	14	2-1	2	114	109	66	9	6	51	41	4.50	94	.253	.341	32-1-3	.344	5	85	-3	0	0.1
1954	Pit N	9	13	.409	39	18	7	3	161.2	201	109	20	3	56	57	5.51	76	.311	.362	52-1-6	.231	3*	70	-21	0	-2.1
1955	Pit N	10	10	.500	43	24	8-1	1	200.2	221	98	19	1	61-7	82	3.81	108	.280	.331	63-1-2	.254	3*	88	7	0	1.0
1956	Pit N	8	16	.333	39	32	6	2	195.2	218	110	24	6	49-10	60	4.32	87	.281	.326	57-1-3	.175	1	98	-13	0	-1.4
1957	Pit N	10	8	.556	31	25	9-3	1	172.2	172	72	18	2	32-8	55	2.87	132	.256	.290	63-0-4	.190	1*	110	14	0	1.5
1958	Pit N	14	12	.538	35	29	6-1	3	202.1	235	103	16	1	39-5	56	3.96	98	.297	.326	62-2-7	.194	6*	119	-4	0	0.1
1959	Pit N	18	9	.667	34	33	20-2	1	266	245	91	25	2	53-11	110	2.98	130	.243	.281	96-1-7	.167	1*	106	**31**	0	3.1
1960	†Pit N★	20	9	.690	35	35	**18**-3	0	271.2	266	104	25	4	40-8	120	3.08	122	.257	.286	94-1-7	.181	3	120	19	0	2.4
1961	Pit N	3	4	.429	11	10	1	0	59.1	72	33	10	1	18-3	20	4.70	85	.305	.355	19-0-2	.263	1	120	-4	87	-0.2
1962	Pit N	10	7	.588	23	20	7-2	0	139.1	156	67	21	1	27-4	78	3.94	100	.276	.310	45-0-7	.311	5	128	2	0	0.7
1963	Pit N	4	5	.444	18	12	1-1	0	76.2	91	45	11	0	13-0	31	4.93	67	.296	.321	23-0-1	.217	1*	118	-12	0	-1.2
1964	Pit N	12	13	.480	35	29	7-5	0	192	203	85	18	1	32-6	93	3.61	97	.270	.299	61-1-5	.311	8*	110	-1	0	0.7
1965	Pit N	17	9	.654	29	28	13-4	0	217.1	182	66	17	3	35-2	101	2.15	163	.229	.261	82-1-4	.244	4*	120	31	0	4.3
1966	Pit N	12	8	.600	31	28	8-4	0	177.2	203	85	19	4	24-1	88	4.05	88	.292	.318	66-1-4	.242	5*	136	-8	22	-0.2
1967	Pit N	2	6	.250	25	10	1	0	97	122	57	5	1	18-9	43	4.18	81	.308	.335	27-0-1	.111	-0*	107	-11	35	-0.9
Total	16	162	147	.524	483	364	119-28	13	2672	2833	1274	268	40	597-74	1092	3.77	101	.272	.312	883-11-63	.216	45	109	18	144	6.7
Lawrence, Brian	Brian Michael; B5.14.1976 Fort Collins CO; BR/TR/6´0˝/195; [SDN98 17/502]; d4.15; Col Northwestern Louisiana; [DL 2006 Was N 182]																									
2001	SD N	5	5	.500	27	15	1	0-0	114.2	107	53	10	5	34-5	84	3.45	120	.244	.304	26-0-2	.115	-0	85	8	0	0.6
2002	SD N	12	12	.500	35	31	2-2	0-0	210	230	97	16	11	52-6	149	3.69	105	.281	.331	63-0-3	.095	-1	100	4	0	0.4
2003	SD N	10	15	.400	33	33	1	0-0	210.2	206	106	27	11	57-8	116	4.19	96	.258	.314	67-1-2	.224	5	99	-5	0	0.1
2004	SD N	15	14	.517	34	34	2-1	0-0	203	226	101	26	7	55-7	121	4.12	96	.287	.335	62-0-8	.097	-2*	109	-4	0	-0.6
2005	†SD N	7	15	.318	33	33	1	0-0	195.2	211	106	18	11	57-7	109	4.83	81	.273	.329	59-0-7	.085	-3	92	-17	0	-2.0
Total	5	49	61	.445	162	146	7-3	0-0	934	980	463	97	45	255-33	579	4.10	97	.271	.324	277-1-22	.126	-1	98	-14	182	-1.5
Lawrence, Brooks	Brooks Ulysses "Bull"; B1.30.1925 Springfield OH; D4.27.2000 Springfield OH; BR/TR/6´0˝/(200–209); d6.24; Col Miami–Ohio																									
1954	StL N	15	6	.714	35	18	8	1	158.2	141	71	17	8	72	72	3.74	110	.243	.333	53-0-1	.189	0	125	8	0	1.0
1955	StL N	3	8	.273	46	10	2-1	1	96	102	73	11	7	58-7	52	6.56	62	.278	.384	21-0-2	.095	-2	99	-25	0	-2.7
1956	Cin N☆	19	10	.655	49	30	11-1	0	218.2	210	109	26	2	71-4	96	3.99	100	.256	.315	70-0-6	.157	-1	131	-1	0	0.0
1957	Cin N	16	13	.552	49	32	12-1	4	250.1	234	111	26	8	76-5	121	3.52	117	.247	.306	82-0-6	.171	-0	90	14	0	1.5
1958	Cin N	8	13	.381	46	23	6-2	5	181	194	89	12	4	55-7	74	4.13	100	.275	.330	53-0-1	.113	-2	98	1	0	-0.1
1959	Cin N	7	12	.368	43	14	3	10	128.1	144	74	17	4	45-9	64	4.77	85	.281	.343	40-0-2	.150	-1	99	-9	0	-1.4
1960	Cin N	1	0	1.000	7	0	0	1	7.2	9	12	1	0	8-1	2	10.57	36	.310	.447	0	ø	0	—	-6	0	-0.9
Total	7	69	62	.527	275	127	42-5	22	1040.2	1034	539	110	33	385-33	481	4.25	96	.261	.330	319-0-18	.154	-5	108	-18	0	-2.6
Lawrence, Bob	Robert Andrew "Larry"; B12.14.1899 Brooklyn NY; D11.6.1983 Jamaica NY; BR/TR/5´11˝/180; d7.19																									
1924	Chi A	0	0	ø	1	0	0	0	1	1	1	0	0	1	1	9.00	46	.250	.400	0	ø	0	—	0	—	0.0
Lawrence, Sean	Sean Christopher; B9.2.1970 Oak Park IL; BL/TL/6´4˝/215; [PitN92 6/175]; d8.25; Col St. Francis (IL)																									
1998	Pit N	2	1	.667	7	3	0	0-0	19.2	25	16	4	0	10-0	12	7.32	58	.313	.380	6	.000	-1	122	-6	0	-0.8
Lawson, Roxie	Alfred Voyle; B4.13.1906 Donnellson IA; D4.9.1977 Stockport IA; BR/TR/6´0˝/170; d8.3; Col Iowa Wesleyan																									
1930	Cle A	1	2	.333	7	4	2	0	33.2	46	27	1	0	23	10	6.15	79	.324	.418	11-0-1	.091	-1	129	-4	—	-0.4
1931	Cle A	0	2	.000	17	3	0	0	55.2	72	50	5	0	36	20	7.60	61	.304	.396	14	.143	-0	85	-15	—	-0.7
1933	Det A	0	1	.000	4	2	0	0	16	17	16	2	0	17	6	7.31	59	.270	.425	5	.000	-1	118	-5	—	-0.3
1935	Det A	3	1	.750	7	4	4-2	2	40	34	11	3	0	24	16	1.57	265	.233	.341	13-0-1	.308	1	109	11	—	1.2
1936	Det A	8	6	.571	41	8	3	3	128	139	87	13	4	71	34	5.48	90	.281	.376	45	.222	1	140	-6	—	-0.5

YEAR	TM LG	W	L	PCT	G	GS	CG-SHO	SV-BS	IP	H	R	HR	HB	BB-IB	SO	ERA	AERA	OAV	OOB	AB-HR-SH	AVG	PB	SUP	APR	DL	PW
1937	Det A	18	7	.720	37	29	15	1	217.1	236	141	17	1	115	68	5.26	89	.271	.357	81-0-5	.259	3	118	-13	—	-1.0
1938	Det A	8	9	.471	27	16	5	1	127	154	85	13	0	82	39	5.46	92	.299	.395	45-0-1	.044	-5	81	-6	—	-1.1
1939	Det A	1	1	.500	2	1	0	0	11.1	7	7	1	0	7	4	4.76	103	.167	.286	4-0-1	.000	-1	108	0	—	0.0
	StL A	3	7	.300	36	14	5	0	150.2	181	93	10	2	83	43	5.32	92	.307	.394	43-0-5	.186	-1*	80	-4	—	-0.3
	Year	4	8	.333	38	15	5	0	162	188	100	11	2	90	47	5.28	92	.297	.387	47-0-6	.170	-2	82	-4	—	-0.3
1940	StL A	5	3	.625	30	2	0	4	72	77	45	5	0	54	18	5.13	89	.278	.396	22	.045	-3	96	-4	—	-0.6
Total	9	47	39	.547	208	83	34-2	11	851.2	963	562	70	7	512	258	5.37	89	.285	.380	283-0-14	.173	-6	105	-46	—	-3.7
Lawson, Al	Alfred William; B3.24.1869 London, England; D11.29.1954 San Antonio TX; BR/TR/5´11˝/161; d5.13																									
1890	Bos N	0	1	.000	1	1	1	0	9	12	7	0	0	4	1	4.00	94	.308	.372	2	.000	-0	34	-1	—	-0.1
	Pit N	0	2	.000	2	2	1	0	10	15	20	0	0	10	2	9.00	37	.333	.455	4	.000	-1	105	-8	—	-1.1
	Year	0	3	.000	3	3	2	0	19	27	27	0	0	14	3	6.63	53	.321	.418	6	.000	-1	78	-9	—	-1.2
Lawson, Bob	Robert Baker; B8.23.1875 Lynchburg VA; D10.28.1952 Durham NC; BR/TR/5´10˝/170; d5.7; Col North Carolina																									
1901	Bos N	2	2	.500	6	4	4	0	46	45	28	0	3	28	12	3.33	109	.254	.365	27-1-2	.148	-0*	103	0	—	0.0
1902	Bal A	0	2	.000	3	2	1	0	13	21	11	0	2	3	5	4.85	78	.362	.413	6	.167	-0	76	-2	—	-0.2
Total	2	2	4	.333	9	6	5	0	59	66	39	0	5	31	17	3.66	100	.281	.376	33-1-2	.152	-1	94	-2	—	-0.2
Lawson, Steve	Steven George; B12.28.1950 Oakland CA; BR/TL/6´1˝/180; d8.3																									
1972	Tex A	0	0	ø	13	0	0	1-1	16	13	6	1	0	10-0	13	2.81	108	.213	.324	1	1.000	0	—	0	0	0.1
Laxton, Brett	Brett William; B10.5.1973 Stratford NJ; BL/TR/6´2˝/210; [OakA96 24/705]; d6.21; f–Bill; Col Louisiana St.																									
1999	Oak A	0	1	.000	3	2	0	0-0	9.2	12	12	1	2	7-1	9	7.45	64	.316	.420	0	ø	0	108	-4	0	-0.4
2000	KC A	0	1	.000	6	1	0	0-0	16.2	23	15	0	2	10-1	14	8.10	64	.348	.449	0	ø	0	0	-5	0	-0.2
Total	2	0	2	.000	9	3	0	0-0	26.1	35	27	1	4	17-2	23	7.86	64	.337	.438	0	ø	0	68	-9	0	-0.6
Laxton, Bill	William Harry; B1.5.1948 Camden NJ; BL/TL/6´1˝/(185–190); [PitN66 7/135]; d9.15; s–Brett																									
1970	Phi N	0	0	ø	2	0	0	0-0	2	2	3	2	1	2-0	2	13.50	30	.250	.455	0	ø	0	—	-2	0	-0.1
1971	SD N	0	2	.000	18	0	0	0-0	27.2	32	25	4	1	26-0	23	6.83	49	.305	.444	0	ø	0	—	-11	0	-0.8
1974	SD N	0	1	.000	30	1	0	0-0	44.2	37	22	5	3	38-8	40	4.03	89	.226	.375	5	.200	0	49	-2	0	-0.1
1976	Det A	0	5	.000	26	3	0	2-1	94.2	77	49	13	6	51-1	74	4.09	91	.221	.329	0	ø	0	24	-3	0	-0.3
1977	Sea A	3	2	.600	43	0	0	3-1	72.2	62	44	10	4	39-5	49	4.95	84	.233	.335	0	ø	0	—	-6	24	-0.5
	Cle A	0	0	ø	2	0	0	0-0	1.2	2	1	0	0	2-0	1	5.40	74	.286	.444	0	ø	0	—	0	0	0.0
	Year	3	2	.600	45	0	0	3-1	74.1	64	45	10	4	41-5	50	4.96	83	.234	.339	0	ø	0	—	-6	0	-0.5
Total	5	3	10	.231	121	4	0	5-2	243.1	212	144	34	15	158-14	189	4.73	80	.236	.356	5	.200	0	29	-24	24	-1.8
Layana, Tim	Timothy Joseph; B3.2.1964 Inglewood CA; D6.26.1999 Bakersfield CA; BR/TR/6´2˝/(190–195); [NYA86 3/80]; d4.9; Col Loyola Marymount																									
1990	Cin N	5	3	.625	55	0	0	2-0	80	71	33	7	2	44-5	53	3.49	113	.244	.344	5	.000	-1	—	4	0	0.4
1991	Cin N	0	2	.000	22	0	0	0-1	20.2	23	18	1	0	11-0	14	6.97	55	.277	.362	1	.000	-0*	—	-7	0	-0.6
1993	SF N	0	0	ø	1	0	0	0-0	2	7	5	1	0	1-1	1	22.50	17	.538	.571	0-0-1	ø	0	—	-4	0	-0.2
Total	3	5	5	.500	78	0	0	2-1	102.2	101	56	9	2	56-6	68	4.56	86	.261	.355	6-0-1	.000	-1	—	-7	0	-0.4
Lazar, Danny	John Daniel; B11.14.1943 East Chicago IN; BL/TL/6´1˝/190; [ChiA65 15/590]; d6.21; Col Indiana St.																									
1968	Chi A	0	1	.000	8	1	0	0	13.1	14	6	1	0	4-0	11	4.05	75	.269	.316	2	.000	0	29	-1	0	-0.1
1969	Chi A	0	0	ø	9	3	0	0-0	20.2	21	15	5	1	11-2	9	6.53	59	.280	.371	4-0-1	.000	-0	107	-5	0	-0.3
Total	2	0	1	.000	17	4	0	0-0	34	35	21	6	1	15-2	20	5.56	63	.276	.349	6-0-1	.000	-0	94	-6	0	-0.4
Lazorko, Jack	Jack Thomas; B3.30.1956 Hoboken NJ; BR/TR/5´11˝/(200–213); [HouN78 11/271]; d6.4; Col Mississippi St.																									
1984	Mil A	0	1	.000	15	1	0	1-0	39.2	37	19	7	1	22-2	24	4.31	90	.245	.343	0	ø	0	70	-1	0	0.0
1985	Sea A	0	0	ø	15	0	0	1-0	20.1	23	10	1	3	8-1	7	3.54	119	.291	.378	0	ø	0	—	1	0	0.1
1986	Det A	0	0	ø	3	0	0	0-0	6.2	8	3	0	0	4-1	3	4.05	103	.296	.387	0	ø	0	—	0	0	0.0
1987	Cal A	5	6	.455	26	11	2	0-0	117.2	108	68	20	2	44-5	55	4.59	94	.248	.318	0	ø	0	100	-4	0	-0.2
1988	Cal A	0	1	.000	10	3	0	0-0	37.2	37	15	5	1	16-0	19	3.35	116	.255	.331	0	ø	0	117	3	0	0.1
Total	5	5	8	.385	69	15	2	2-0	222	213	115	33	7	94-9	108	4.22	99	.254	.333	0	ø	0	102	-1	0	0.0
Lea, Charlie	Charles William; B12.25.1956 Orleans, France; BR/TR/6´4˝/(194–200); [MonN78 9/217]; d6.12; Col Memphis; [DL 1986 Mon N 182]																									
1980	Mon N	7	5	.583	21	19	0	0-0	104	103	51	5	2	55-4	56	3.72	98	.262	.353	37	.081	-2	113	-2	0	-0.5
1981	Mon N	5	4	.556	16	11	2-2	0-0	64.1	63	34	4	1	26-0	31	4.62	77	.268	.341	15-0-4	.133	-0	93	-6	0	-0.9
1982	Mon N	12	10	.545	27	27	4-2	0-0	177.2	145	70	16	0	56-6	115	3.24	114	.222	.283	65-0-1	.123	-1	106	10	0	1.0
1983	Mon N	16	11	.593	33	33	8-4	0-0	222	195	87	15	1	84-4	137	3.12	116	.238	.307	70-0-12	.114	-2	106	12	0	1.1
1984	Mon N★	15	10	.600	30	30	8	0-0	224.1	198	82	19	3	68-3	123	2.89	120	.239	.296	72-0-12	.111	-3	99	14	0	1.2
1987	Mon N	0	1	.000	1	1	0	0-0	1	4	4	1	0	2-0	1	36.00	12	.571	.667	0	ø	0	0	-3	0	-0.5
1988	Min A	7	7	.500	24	23	0	0-0	130	156	79	19	5	50-2	72	4.85	84	.301	.364	0	ø	0	123	-12	21	-1.2
Total	7	62	48	.564	152	144	22-8	0-0	923.1	864	407	79	12	341-19	535	3.54	103	.250	.317	259-0-29	.112	-8	107	13	203	0.2
Leach, Terry	Terry Hester; B3.13.1954 Selma AL; BR/TR/6´0˝/(185–215); d8.12; Col Auburn																									
1981	NY N	1	1	.500	21	1	0	0-1	35.1	26	11	2	0	12-1	16	2.55	139	.205	.273	1	.000	0	75	4	0	0.3
1982	NY N	2	1	.667	21	1	1-1	3-1	45.1	46	22	2	0	18-5	30	4.17	88	.271	.339	8-0-1	.125	-0	24	-1	0	-0.2
1985	NY N	3	4	.429	22	4	1-1	1-0	55.2	48	19	3	1	14-3	30	2.91	120	.235	.285	12-0-1	.167	1	202	4	0	0.6
1986	NY N	0	0	ø	6	0	0	0-0	6.2	6	3	0	0	3-0	4	2.70	133	.222	.300	0	ø	0	—	0	0	0.0
1987	NY N	11	1	.917	44	12	1-1	0-2	131.1	132	54	14	1	29-5	61	3.22	119	.262	.303	33-0-4	.061	-2	151	9	15	0.6
1988	†NY N	7	2	.778	52	0	0	3-1	92	95	32	5	3	24-4	51	2.54	128	.268	.318	14	.143	0	—	7	0	0.8
1989	NY N	0	0	ø	10	0	0	0-0	21.1	19	11	1	1	4-0	2	4.22	78	.244	.282	4	.000	-0	—	-2	0	-0.1
	KC A	5	6	.455	30	3	0	0-0	73.2	78	46	4	1	36-9	34	4.15	93	.278	.357	0	ø	0	62	-6	0	-0.8
1990	Min A	2	5	.286	55	0	0	2-4	81.2	84	31	2	1	21-10	46	3.20	130	.268	.315	0	ø	0	—	9	0	0.7
1991	†Min A	1	2	.333	50	0	0	0-2	67.1	82	28	3	0	14-5	32	3.61	119	.299	.332	0	ø	0	—	6	0	0.3
1992	Chi A	6	5	.545	51	0	0	0-0	73.2	57	17	2	4	20-5	22	1.95	199	.215	.279	0	ø	0	—	16	0	2.3
1993	Chi A	0	0	ø	14	0	0	1-0	16	15	5	0	1	2-1	3	2.81	150	.250	.281	0	ø	0	—	3	133	0.1
Total	11	38	27	.585	376	21	3-3	10-11	700	688	279	38	13	197-48	331	3.15	120	.259	.311	72-0-6	.097	-1	137	49	148	4.6
League, Brandon	Brandon Paul; B3.16.1983 Sacramento CA; BR/TR/6´3˝/(190–195); [TorA01 2/59]; d9.21																									
2004	Tor A	1	0	1.000	3	0	0	0-0	4.2	3	0	0	0	1-0	2	0.00	ø	.176	.222	0	ø	0	—	2	0	0.5
2005	Tor A	1	0	1.000	20	0	0	0-0	35.2	42	27	8	2	20-1	17	6.56	70	.302	.395	0	ø	0	—	-7	0	-0.3
2006	Tor A	1	2	.333	33	0	0	1-3	42.2	34	17	3	3	9-2	29	2.53	187	.214	.269	0	ø	0	—	8	0	0.6
Total	3	3	2	.600	56	0	0	1-3	83	79	44	11	5	30-3	48	4.12	114	.251	.325	0	ø	0	—	3	0	0.8
Leal, Luis	Luis Enrique (Alvarado); B3.21.1957 Barquisimeto, Lara, Venez.; BR/TR/6´3˝/(205–220); d5.25																									
1980	Tor A	3	4	.429	13	10	1	0-0	59.2	72	35	6	1	31-2	26	4.53	95	.314	.394	0	ø	0	114	-2	0	-0.2
1981	Tor A	7	13	.350	29	19	3	1-0	129.2	127	63	8	5	44-5	71	3.68	108	.254	.317	0	ø	0	69	3	0	0.4
1982	Tor A	12	15	.444	38	38	10	0-0	249.2	250	113	24	3	79-3	111	3.93	115	.262	.317	0	ø	0	86	18	0	1.7
1983	Tor A	13	12	.520	35	35	7-1	0-0	217.1	216	113	23	6	65-5	116	4.31	101	.257	.314	0	ø	0	107	1	0	0.1
1984	Tor A	13	8	.619	35	35	6-2	0-0	222.1	221	106	27	4	77-6	134	3.89	106	.258	.320	0	ø	0	114	6	0	0.5
1985	Tor A	3	6	.333	15	14	0	0-0	67.1	82	46	13	3	24-3	33	5.75	74	.303	.361	0	ø	0	86	-10	0	-1.2
Total	6	51	58	.468	165	151	27-3	1-0	946	968	476	101	22	320-24	491	4.14	103	.265	.325	0	ø	0	97	16	0	1.3
Lear, King	Charles Bernard; B1.23.1891 Greencastle PA; D10.31.1976 Waynesboro PA; BR/TR/6´0˝/175; d5.2; Col Princeton																									
1914	Cin N	1	2	.333	17	4	3-1	1	55.2	55	23	3	2	19	20	3.07	95	.271	.339	16	.188	1	79	1	—	0.1
1915	Cin N	6	10	.375	40	15	9	0	167.2	169	73	7	6	45	46	3.01	95	.270	.324	47-0-7	.170	-1	92	-3	—	-0.6
Total	2	7	12	.368	57	19	12-1	1	223.1	224	96	10	8	64	66	3.02	95	.270	.328	63-0-7	.175	-0	89	-2	—	-0.5
Leary, Frank	Francis Patrick; B2.26.1881 Wayland MA; D10.4.1907 Natick MA; TR/5´10˝/190; d4.30; Col Penn																									
1907	Cin N	0	1	.000	2	1	0	0	8	7	2	0	0	6	4	1.13	231	.269	.406	2	.000	-0	302	1	—	0.1
Leary, Jack	John J.; B7.1857 New Haven CT; TL/5´11˝/186; d8.21; ▲																									
1880	Bos N	0	1	.000	1	1	0	0	3	8	5	0	—	0	1	15.00	15	.727	.727	3	.000	-0	43	-3	—	-0.5
1881	Det N	0	2	.000	2	2	1	0	13	13	6	0	—	2	2	4.15	70	.255	.283	11	.273	1*	9	0	—	0.0
1882	Pit AA	1	0	1.000	3	2	1	0	18.2	28	22	0	—	3	5	6.75	39	.326	.348	257-1	.292	1*	197	-7	—	-0.3

YEAR	TM LG	W	L	PCT	G	GS	CG-SHO	SV-BS	IP	H	R	HR	HB	BB-IB	SO	ERA	AERA	OAV	OOB	AB-HR-SH	AVG	PB	SUP	APR	DL	PW
	Bal AA	2	1	.667	3	3	3	0	26	29	22	1	—	8	2	1.04	265	.264	.314	18	.222	0*	137	0	—	0.1
	Year	3	1	.750	6	5	4	0	44.2	57	44	1	—	11	7	3.43	79	.291	.329	275-1	.287	1	160	-7	—	-0.2
1884	Alt U	0	3	.000	3	3	2	0	24	31	30	0	—	2	7	5.25	51	.292	.306	33	.091	-2*	43	-7	—	-0.8
	CP U	0	2	.000	2	1	1	0	10	14	14	0	—	5	6	5.40	45	.311	.380	40	.175	-1*	53	-4	—	-0.6
	Year	0	5	.000	5	4	3	0	34	45	44	0	—	7	13	5.29	49	.298	.329	73	.137	-2	45	-11	—	-1.4
Total	4	3	9	.250	14	12	8	0	94.2	123	99	1	—	20	23	4.56	59	.301	.333	362-1	.254	-1	84	-21	—	-2.1
LEARY, TIM	Timothy James; B12.23.1958 Santa Monica CA; BR/TR/6´3˝/(190–220); [NYN79 1/2]; d4.12; Col UCLA																									
1981	NY N	0	0	ø	1	1	0	0-0	2	0	0	0	0	1-0	3	0.00	ø	.000	.143	1	.000	-0	50	1	107	0.0
1983	NY N	1	1	.500	2	2	1	0-0	10.2	15	10	0	0	4-0	9	3.38	109	.319	.365	3	.333	0	144	-2	0	-0.3
1984	NY N	3	3	.500	20	7	0	0-0	53.2	61	28	2	2	18-3	29	4.02	89	.285	.343	10-1-3	.300	2	81	-3	0	-0.2
1985	Mil A	1	4	.200	5	5	0	0-0	33.1	40	18	5	1	8-0	29	4.05	104	.296	.340	0	ø	0	43	0	0	0.0
1986	Mil A	12	12	.500	33	30	3-2	0-0	188.1	216	97	20	7	53-4	110	4.21	104	.289	.339	0	ø	0	92	5	0	0.6
1987	LA N	3	11	.214	39	12	0	1-1	107.2	121	62	15	2	36-5	61	4.76	84	.285	.343	23-0-3	.304	2	79	-9	0	-0.8
1988	†LA N	17	11	.607	35	34	9-6	0-0	228.2	201	87	13	6	56-4	180	2.91	115	.234	.284	67-0-13	.269	6*	93	10	0	1.9
1989	LA N	6	7	.462	19	17	2	0-0	117.1	107	45	9	2	37-7	59	3.38	102	.247	.306	33-0-6	.061	-2	74	3	0	0.1
	Cin N	2	7	.222	14	14	0	0-0	89.2	98	39	8	3	31-8	64	3.71	97	.278	.338	26-0-3	.192	2	67	0	0	0.2
	Year	8	14	.364	33	31	2	0-0	207	205	84	17	5	68-15	123	3.52	100	.261	.321	59-0-9	.119	-1	71	2	0	0.3
1990	NY A	9	19	.321	31	31	6-1	0-0	208	202	105	18	7	78-1	138	4.11	97	.257	.328	0	ø	0	70	-3	0	-0.2
1991	NY A	4	10	.286	28	18	1	0-0	120.2	150	89	20	4	57-1	83	6.49	64	.312	.388	0	ø	0	105	-28	0	-2.8
1992	NY A	5	6	.455	18	15	2	0-0	97	84	62	9	4	57-2	34	5.57	71	.245	.354	0	ø	0	97	-16	0	-1.6
	Sea A	3	4	.429	8	8	1	0-0	44	47	27	3	5	30-3	12	4.91	82	.280	.394	0	ø	0	105	-5	0	-0.6
	Year	8	10	.444	26	23	3	0-0	141	131	89	12	9	87-5	46	5.36	74	.256	.367	0	ø	0	100	-19	0	-2.2
1993	Sea A	11	9	.550	33	27	0	0-1	169.1	202	104	21	8	58-5	68	5.05	89	.300	.362	0	ø	0	102	-11	0	-1.1
1994	Tex A	1	1	.500	6	3	0	0-0	21	26	19	4	1	11-2	9	8.14	59	.306	.380	0	ø	0	95	-7	15	-0.5
Total	13	78	105	.426	292	224	25-9	1-2	1491.1	1570	792	147	52	535-45	888	4.36	90	.273	.338	163-1-28	.221	9	88	-65	122	-5.3
LECLAIR, GEORGE	George Lewis "Frenchy"; B10.18.1886 Milton VT; D10.10.1918 Farnham QC, Can.; BR/TR/5´9˝/170; d6.5																									
1914	Pit F	5	2	.714	22	7	5-1	0	103.1	99	52	0	1	25	49	4.01	72	.262	.309	34-0-1	.147	-2	109	-10	—	-0.9
1915	Pit F	1	2	.333	14	3	1	1	45.2	43	20	1	0	13	10	3.35	81	.253	.306	13	.154	-1	232	-3	—	-0.3
	Buf F	0	0	ø	1	0	0	0	3	4	2	0	0	1	2	6.00	47	.333	.385	0	ø	0	—	-1	—	-0.1
	Bal F	1	8	.111	18	9	6-1	1	84	76	43	2	0	22	30	2.46	116	.246	.296	24-0-2	.083	-2	68	-2	—	-0.4
	Year	2	10	.167	33	12	7-1	2	132.2	123	65	3	0	36	42	2.85	99	.251	.302	37-0-2	.108	-3	108	-4	—	-0.8
Total	2	7	12	.368	55	19	12-2	2	236	222	117	3	1	61	91	3.36	85	.255	.305	71-0-3	.127	-4	108	-16	—	-1.7
LEDBETTER, RAZOR	Ralph Overton; B12.8.1894 Rutherford College NC; D2.1.1969 W.Palm Beach FL; BR/TR/6´3˝/190; d4.16																									
1915	Det A	0	0	ø	1	0	0	0	1	1	0	0	0	0	0	0.00	ø	.333	.333	0	ø	0	—	0	—	0.0
LEDEZMA, WILFREDO	Wilfredo Jose; B1.21.1981 Guarico, Venezuela; BL/TL/6´3˝/(150–210); d4.2																									
2003	Det A	3	7	.300	34	8	0	0-1	84	99	55	12	3	35-3	49	5.79	76	.297	.365	0	ø	0	58	-12	0	-1.2
2004	Det A	4	3	.571	15	8	0	0-1	53.1	55	28	3	2	18-0	29	4.39	102	.272	.333	0	ø	0	109	0	0	0.0
2005	Det A	2	4	.333	10	10	0	0-0	49.2	61	46	10	2	24-0	30	7.07	61	.303	.377	0	ø	0	108	-17	0	-1.7
2006	†Det A	3	3	.500	24	7	0	0-1	60.1	60	28	5	2	23-0	39	3.58	125	.254	.324	0	ø	0	102	5	0	0.4
Total	4	12	17	.414	83	33	0	0-3	247.1	275	157	30	9	100-3	147	5.20	85	.283	.351	0	ø	0	94	-24	0	-2.5
LEE, CLIFF	Clifton Phifer; B8.30.1978 Benton AR; BL/TL/6´3˝/190; [MonN00 4/105]; d9.15; Col Arkansas																									
2002	Cle A	0	1	.000	2	2	0	0-0	10.1	6	2	0	0	8-1	6	1.74	255	.171	.326	0	ø	0	21	3	0	0.3
2003	Cle A	3	3	.500	9	9	0	0-0	52.1	41	28	7	2	20-1	44	3.61	123	.220	.301	0	ø	0	99	3	61	0.3
2004	Cle A	14	8	.636	33	33	0	0-0	179	188	113	30	11	81-1	161	5.43	80	.268	.350	3	.333	0	116	-21	0	-2.2
2005	Cle A	18	5	**.783**	32	32	1	0-0	202	194	91	22	0	52-1	143	3.79	110	.251	.295	8	.000	-1	138	10	0	0.8
2006	Cle A	14	11	.560	33	33	1	0-0	200.2	224	114	29	8	58-3	129	4.40	98	.278	.330	6	.167	0	127	-4	0	-0.5
Total	5	49	28	.636	109	109	2	0-0	644.1	653	348	88	21	219-7	483	4.39	98	.261	.323	17	.118	-0	123	-9	61	-1.3
LEE, COREY	Corey Wayne; B12.26.1974 Raleigh NC; BB/TL/6´2˝/180; [TexA96 1/32]; d8.24; Col North Carolina St.																									
1999	Tex A	0	1	.000	1	0	0	0-0	1	2	3	1	0	1-0	0	27.00	19	.400	.500	0	ø	0	—	-2	0	-0.3
LEE, DAVID	David Emmer; B3.12.1973 Pittsburgh PA; BR/TR/6´1˝/(200–202); [ColN95 23/627]; d5.22; Col Mercyhurst																									
1999	Col N	3	2	.600	36	0	0	0-0	49	43	21	4	4	29-1	38	3.67	158	.247	.364	5	.200	-0	—	9	0	0.8
2000	Col N	0	0	ø	7	0	0	1-0	5.2	10	9	3	1	6-0	6	11.12	52	.357	.486	0	ø	0	—	-3	0	-0.2
2001	SD N	1	0	1.000	41	0	0	0-0	48.2	52	20	6	6	27-1	42	3.70	112	.278	.385	1	.000	-0	—	4	37	0.1
2003	Cle A	1	0	1.000	8	0	0	0-0	7.2	4	4	1	0	6-1	7	4.70	94	.143	.294	0	ø	0	—	0	0	0.0
2004	Cle A	0	0	ø	4	0	0	0-0	4.1	8	7	0	0	4-0	4	10.38	42	.348	.444	0	ø	0	—	-4	0	-0.2
Total	5	5	2	.714	96	0	0	1-0	115.1	117	61	14	11	72-3	97	4.37	113	.266	.380	6	.167	-0	—	6	37	-0.5
LEE, DON	Donald Edward; B2.26.1934 Globe AZ; BR/TR/6´4˝/(200–210); d4.23; Mil 1970; f–Thornton; Col Arizona																									
1957	Det A	1	3	.250	11	6	0	0	38.2	48	22	6	1	18-0	19	4.66	83	.308	.379	12-0-1	.167	-0	116	-3	0	-0.4
1958	Det A	0	0	ø	1	0	0	0	2	1	2	1	1	1-0	0	9.00	45	.143	.333	0	ø	0	—	-1	0	-0.1
1960	Was A	8	7	.533	44	20	1	3	165	160	72	16	3	64-3	88	3.44	113	.258	.328	43-1-1	.116	-0	110	9	0	0.8
1961	Min A	3	6	.333	37	10	4	3	115	93	49	12	4	35-1	65	3.52	120	.221	.286	30-0-3	.067	-3	77	10	0	0.6
1962	Min A	3	3	.500	9	9	1	0	52	51	27	8	7	24-0	28	4.50	91	.256	.355	19	.211	0	102	-1	0	-0.1
	LA A	8	8	.500	27	22	4-2	2	153.1	153	64	12	3	39-1	74	3.11	124	.256	.304	49-0-2	.184	-0	105	12	0	1.1
	Year	11	11	.500	36	31	5-2	2	205.1	204	91	20	10	63-1	102	3.46	113	.256	.317	68-0-2	.191	0	104	9	0	1.0
1963	LA A	8	11	.421	40	22	3-2	1	154	148	74	12	9	51-4	89	3.68	93	.251	.317	45-0-7	.156	-1	104	-5	0	-0.7
1964	LA A	5	4	.556	33	8	0	2	89.1	99	39	6	1	25-1	73	2.72	121	.279	.326	23	.261	2	91	3	0	0.5
1965	Cal A	0	1	.000	10	0	0	0	14	21	11	4	1	5-2	12	6.43	53	.350	.409	3	.333	1	—	-5	0	-0.3
	Hou N	0	0	ø	7	0	0	0	8	8	3	0	1	3-0	3	3.38	99	.267	.353	1	.000	-0	—	0	0	0.0
1966	Hou N	2	0	1.000	9	0	0	0	18	17	5	1	0	4-1	9	2.50	137	.250	.292	1	1.000	1	—	2	0	0.3
	Chi N	2	1	.667	16	0	0	0	19	28	19	3	0	12-1	7	7.11	52	.346	.421	0	ø	0	—	-8	15	-1.1
	Year	4	1	.800	25	0	0	0	37	45	24	4	0	16-2	16	4.86	73	.302	.365	1	1.000	1	—	-7	0	-0.8
Total	9	40	44	.476	244	97	13-4	11	828.1	827	387	81	31	281-14	467	3.61	104	.260	.324	226-1-14	.164	-1	102	13	15	0.6
LEE, MARK	Mark Linden; B6.14.1953 Inglewood CA; BR/TR/6´4˝/225; [SDN76 13/293]; d4.23; Col Pepperdine																									
1978	SD N	5	1	.833	56	0	0	2-0	85	74	34	2	2	36-13	31	3.28	102	.240	.321	5-0-1	.000	-1	—	1	0	0.1
1979	SD N	2	4	.333	46	1	0	5-3	65	88	34	3	2	25-5	25	4.29	82	.332	.392	6-0-1	.333	1	176	-5	0	-0.4
1980	Pit N	0	1	.000	4	0	0	0-0	5.2	5	3	0	0	3-0	2	4.76	77	.227	.320	0	ø	0	—	-1	0	0.0
1981	Pit N	0	2	.000	12	0	0	2-1	19.2	17	6	1	0	5-1	5	2.75	133	.233	.282	2	.500	0	—	2	0	0.4
Total	4	7	8	.467	118	1	0	9-4	175.1	184	77	6	4	69-19	63	3.64	95	.275	.345	13-0-2	.231	1	176	-3	0	0.1
LEE, MARK	Mark Owen; B7.20.1964 Williston ND; BL/TL/6´3˝/(198–200); [DetA85 15/392]; d9.8; Col Florida International																									
1988	KC A	0	0	ø	4	0	0	0-0	5	6	2	0	0	1-0	0	3.60	111	.300	.333	0	ø	0	—	0	0	0.0
1990	Mil A	1	0	1.000	11	0	0	0-0	21.1	20	5	1	0	4-0	14	2.11	184	.256	.286	0	ø	0	—	5	0	0.2
1991	Mil A	2	5	.286	62	0	0	1-6	67.2	72	33	10	1	31-7	43	3.86	104	.283	.362	0	ø	0	—	0	0	0.1
1995	Bal A	2	0	1.000	39	0	0	1-1	33.1	31	18	5	1	18-3	27	4.86	98	.246	.340	0	ø	0	—	0	0	0.0
Total	4	5	5	.500	116	0	0	2-7	127.1	129	58	16	2	54-10	84	3.82	109	.270	.343	0	ø	0	—	5	0	0.3
LEE, MIKE	Michael Randall; B5.19.1941 Bell CA; BL/TL/6´5˝/(217–220); d5.6; Col East Los Angeles (CA) JC																									
1960	Cle A	0	0	ø	7	0	0	0	9	6	2	1	1	11-0	6	2.00	187	.207	.439	0	ø	0	—	2	0	0.1
1963	LA A	1	1	.500	6	4	0	0	26	30	11	3	1	14-0	11	3.81	90	.300	.391	7	.000	-1	78	0	0	-0.1
Total	2	1	1	.500	13	4	0	0	35	36	13	4	2	25-0	17	3.34	105	.279	.404	7	.000	-1	78	2	0	-0.0
LEE, BOB	Robert Dean "Moose","Horse"; B11.26.1937 Ottumwa IA; BR/TR/6´3˝/(215–230); d4.15																									
1964	LA A	6	5	.545	64	5	0	19	137	87	31	6	1	58-8	111	1.51	217	.182	.270	22	.000	-2	70	**28**	0	2.7
1965	Cal A☆	9	7	.563	69	0	0	23	131.1	95	35	11	1	42-8	89	1.92	177	.205	.269	21-1-4	.143	1	—	20	0	3.2
1966	Cal A	5	4	.556	61	0	0	16	101.2	90	39	8	1	31-2	46	2.74	122	.237	.294	11-0-3	.000	-0	—	5	0	0.5
1967	LA N	0	0	ø	4	0	0	0	6.2	6	8	2	1	3-0	2	5.40	57	.222	.313	0	ø	0	—	-4	0	-0.2
	Cin N	3	3	.500	27	1	0	2	50.2	51	26	0	0	25-7	33	4.44	84	.262	.338	8	.375	1	351	-3	0	-0.3

THE PITCHER REGISTER

YEAR	TM LG	W	L	PCT	G	GS	CG-SHO	SV-BS	IP	H	R	HR	HB	BB-IB	SO	ERA	AERA	OAV	OOB	AB-HR-SH	AVG	PB	SUP	APR	DL	PW
	Year	3	3	.500	31	1	0	2	57.1	57	34	2	1	28-7	35	4.55	81	.257	.335	8	.375	1	359	-5	0	-0.5
1968	Cin N	2	4	.333	44	1	0	3	64.2	73	38	4	1	37-10	34	5.15	61	.302	.387	5	.200	0	192	-12	0	-1.3
Total	5	25	23	.521	269	7	0	63	492	402	177	31	5	196-35	315	2.71	124	.225	.300	67-1-7	.104	-1	131	34	0	4.6

Lee, Roy Roy Edwin; B9.28.1917 Elmira NY; D11.11.1985 St.Louis MO; BL/TL/5´11.5˝/175; d9.23; Col Bowling Green

YEAR	TM LG	W	L	PCT	G	GS	CG-SHO	SV-BS	IP	H	R	HR	HB	BB-IB	SO	ERA	AERA	OAV	OOB	AB-HR-SH	AVG	PB	SUP	APR	DL	PW
1945	NY N	0	2	.000	3	1	0	0	7	8	9	3	0	3	0	11.57	34	.267	.333	1	.000	-0	87	-5	0	-0.9

Lee, Sang-Hoon Sang-Hoon; B3.11.1971 Seoul, South Korea; BL/TL/6´1˝/190; d6.29

YEAR	TM LG	W	L	PCT	G	GS	CG-SHO	SV-BS	IP	H	R	HR	HB	BB-IB	SO	ERA	AERA	OAV	OOB	AB-HR-SH	AVG	PB	SUP	APR	DL	PW
2000	Bos A	0	0	ø	9	0	0	0-0	11.2	11	4	2	2	4-0	6	3.09	163	.262	.347	0	ø	0	—	3	0	0.1

Lee, Tom Thomas Frank; B6.8.1862 Philadelphia PA; D3.4.1886 Milwaukee WI; d6.14

YEAR	TM LG	W	L	PCT	G	GS	CG-SHO	SV-BS	IP	H	R	HR	HB	BB-IB	SO	ERA	AERA	OAV	OOB	AB-HR-SH	AVG	PB	SUP	APR	DL	PW
1884	Chi N	1	4	.200	5	5	5	0	45.1	55	43	12	—	15	14	3.77	83	.272	.323	24	.125	-2*	95	-5	—	-0.5
	Bal U	5	8	.385	15	14	12	0	122	121	88	1	—	29	81	3.39	79	.242	.283	82	.280	-1*	89	-8	—	-0.8
Total	1	6	12	.333	20	19	17	0	167.1	176	131	13	—	44	95	3.50	80	.250	.295	106	.245	-2	90	-13	—	-1.3

Lee, Thornton Thornton Starr "Lefty"; B9.13.1906 Sonoma CA; D6.9.1997 Tucson AZ; BL/TL/6´3˝/205; d9.19; s–Don; Col Cal Poly–San Luis Obispo

YEAR	TM LG	W	L	PCT	G	GS	CG-SHO	SV-BS	IP	H	R	HR	HB	BB-IB	SO	ERA	AERA	OAV	OOB	AB-HR-SH	AVG	PB	SUP	APR	DL	PW
1933	Cle A	1	1	.500	3	2	2	0	17.1	13	9	1	0	11	7	4.15	107	.203	.320	8	.375	1	115	1	—	0.2
1934	Cle A	1	1	.500	24	6	0	0	85.2	105	57	8	3	44	41	5.04	90	.308	.392	21	.095	-1	124	-5	—	-0.3
1935	Cle A	7	10	.412	32	20	8-1	1	180.2	179	90	6	4	71	81	4.04	112	.259	.331	61-0-3	.197	-1	85	11	—	0.9
1936	Cle A	3	5	.375	43	8	2	3	127	138	86	2	2	67	49	4.89	103	.271	.358	41	.122	-2	107	-1	—	-0.2
1937	Chi A	12	10	.545	30	25	13-2	0	204.2	209	91	17	1	60	80	3.52	131	.260	.312	71-0-5	.211	1	77	26	—	2.4
1938	Chi A	13	12	.520	33	30	18-1	1	245.1	252	123	12	3	94	77	3.49	140	.263	.331	97-4-4	.258	6*	91	33	—	3.4
1939	Chi A	15	11	.577	33	29	15-2	3	235	260	121	14	3	70	81	4.21	112	.285	.338	91	.165	-3	95	14	—	1.1
1940	Chi A	12	13	.480	28	27	24-1	0	228	223	100	13	2	56	87	3.47	127	.254	.300	84-0-5	.274	4	98	25	—	2.7
1941	Chi A★	22	11	.667	35	34	**30**-3	1	300.1	258	98	18	4	92	130	**2.37**	**173**	.232	**.293**	114-0-1	.254	5	83	**56**	0	**6.5**
1942	Chi A	2	6	.250	11	8	6-1	0	76	82	38	4	2	31	25	3.32	109	.278	.351	30	.200	0	45	0	0	0.0
1943	Chi A	5	9	.357	19	19	7-1	0	127	129	66	8	4	50	35	4.18	80	.266	.340	42-0-1	.071	-4	84	-10	0	-1.6
1944	Chi A	3	9	.250	15	14	6	0	113.1	105	51	3	1	25	39	3.02	114	.246	.290	42-0-1	.095	-3	68	3	0	0.0
1945	Chi A✱	15	12	.556	29	28	19-1	0	228.1	208	81	6	10	76	108	2.44	136	.245	.314	78-0-2	.179	-1	92	18	0	2.0
1946	Chi A	2	4	.333	7	7	2	0	43.1	39	24	1	1	23	23	3.53	97	.244	.342	15	.267	1	72	-2	0	-0.2
1947	Chi A	3	7	.300	21	11	2-1	1	86.2	86	50	5	2	56	57	4.47	82	.261	.372	29	.207	0	79	-8	0	-0.8
1948	NY N	1	3	.250	11	4	1	0	32.2	41	20	3	1	12	17	4.41	89	.304	.365	11	.091	-1	96	-2	0	-0.3
Total	16	117	124	.485	374	272	155-14	10	2331.1	2327	1105	121	43	838	937	3.56	119	.260	.326	835-4-22	.200	1	87	159	0	15.8

Lee, Bill William Crutcher "Big Bill"; B10.21.1909 Plaquemine LA; D6.15.1977 Plaquemine LA; BR/TR/6´3˝/195; d4.29

YEAR	TM LG	W	L	PCT	G	GS	CG-SHO	SV-BS	IP	H	R	HR	HB	BB-IB	SO	ERA	AERA	OAV	OOB	AB-HR-SH	AVG	PB	SUP	APR	DL	PW
1934	Chi N	13	14	.481	35	29	16-4	1	214.1	218	91	9	2	74	104	3.40	114	.263	.325	76-0-3	.132	-2*	97	12	—	1.2
1935	†Chi N	20	6	**.769**	39	32	18-3	1	252	241	106	11	5	84	100	2.96	133	.251	.314	102-0-3	.235	2	133	24	—	2.4
1936	Chi N	18	11	.621	43	33	20-**4**	1	258.2	238	106	14	3	93	102	3.31	121	.246	.314	87-1-9	.138	-3	94	19	—	1.7
1937	Chi N	14	15	.483	42	**34**	17-2	3	272.1	289	122	14	0	73	108	3.54	113	.273	.320	87-1-12	.172	-1	93	12	—	1.2
1938	†Chi N★	**22**	9	**.710**	44	**37**	19-**9**	2	291	281	95	18	2	74	121	**2.66**	**144**	.252	.299	101-0-7	.198	1	102	**39**	—	**4.1**
1939	Chi N★	19	15	.559	37	**36**	20-1	0	282.1	295	125	18	1	85	105	3.44	114	.272	.325	103-1-8	.126	-4	101	15	—	1.4
1940	Chi N	9	17	.346	37	30	9-1	0	211.1	246	129	12	2	70	70	5.03	75	.294	.350	76-0-2	.132	-2	107	-27	—	-3.2
1941	Chi N	8	14	.364	28	22	12	1	167.1	179	87	6	2	43	62	3.76	93	.270	.316	59-2-9	.186	1	120	-7	—	-0.6
1942	Chi N	13	13	.500	32	30	18-1	0	219.2	221	99	4	1	67	75	3.85	83	.258	.312	69-0-5	.159	1	90	-11	0	-1.1
1943	Chi N	3	7	.300	13	12	4	0	78.1	83	37	4	0	27	18	3.56	94	.273	.332	26-0-2	.269	1	76	-2	0	-0.2
	Phi N	1	5	.167	13	7	2	3	60.2	70	35	4	1	21	17	4.60	73	.298	.358	17	.059	-2	65	-8	0	-1.0
	Year	4	12	.250	26	19	6	3	139	153	72	8	1	48	35	4.01	84	.284	.344	43-0-2	.186	-0	72	-10	0	-1.2
1944	Phi N	10	11	.476	31	28	11-3	1	208.1	199	88	9	3	57	50	3.15	115	.248	.300	72-0-3	.194	-0	84	9	0	1.0
1945	Phi N	3	6	.333	13	13	2	0	77.1	107	52	0	0	30	13	4.66	82	.318	.374	24-0-3	.167	-1	100	-8	0	-0.8
	Bos N	6	3	.667	16	13	6-1	0	106.1	112	43	6	0	36	12	2.79	137	.279	.338	31-0-5	.129	-1	90	10	0	0.8
	Year	9	9	.500	29	26	8-1	0	183.2	219	95	6	0	66	25	3.58	107	.297	.354	55-0-8	.145	-1	95	0	0	0.0
1946	Bos N	10	9	.526	25	21	8	0	140	148	73	7	1	45	32	4.18	82	.273	.330	47-0-3	.170	-1	90	-11	0	-1.4
1947	Chi N	0	2	.000	14	2	0	0	24	26	16	2	1	14	9	4.50	88	.268	.366	3	.333	0	101	-2	0	-0.1
Total	14	169	157	.518	462	379	182-29	13	2864	2953	1304	138	24	893	998	3.54	106	.266	.322	980-5-74	.168	-10	99	64	0	5.4

Lee, Bill William Francis "Spaceman"; B12.28.1946 Burbank CA; BL/TL/6´3˝/(190–206); [BosA68 22/507]; d6.25; Mil 1970; Col USC

YEAR	TM LG	W	L	PCT	G	GS	CG-SHO	SV-BS	IP	H	R	HR	HB	BB-IB	SO	ERA	AERA	OAV	OOB	AB-HR-SH	AVG	PB	SUP	APR	DL	PW
1969	Bos A	1	3	.250	20	1	0	0-1	52	56	27	9	2	28-0	45	4.50	85	.281	.372	10	.000	-1	46	-3	0	-0.3
1970	Bos A	2	2	.500	11	5	0	1-0	37	48	20	3	0	14-1	19	4.62	86	.320	.378	11	.000	-1	89	-2	0	-0.3
1971	Bos A	9	2	.818	47	3	0	2-2	102	102	35	7	1	46-7	74	2.74	136	.256	.333	23-0-3	.217	0	112	10	0	1.2
1972	Bos A	7	4	.636	47	0	0	5-2	84.1	75	31	5	1	32-8	43	3.20	101	.248	.320	16-1-0	.188	1	—	2	0	0.6
1973	Bos A☆	17	11	.607	38	33	18-1	1-0	284.2	275	100	20	5	76-2	120	2.75	146	.257	.307	0	ø	0	87	37	0	3.6
1974	Bos A	17	15	.531	38	37	16-1	0-0	282.1	320	123	25	4	67-0	95	3.51	110	.290	.331	0	ø	0	97	9	0	1.2
1975	†Bos A	17	9	.654	41	34	17-4	0-0	260	274	123	20	3	69-1	78	3.95	103	.273	.319	0	ø	0	105	5	0	0.6
1976	Bos A	5	7	.417	24	14	1	3-0	96	124	68	13	3	28-1	29	5.63	69	.307	.354	0	ø	0*	102	-16	52	-1.9
1977	Bos A	9	5	.643	27	16	4	1-0	128	155	67	14	0	29-1	31	4.43	101	.306	.341	0	ø	0	101	1	0	0.2
1978	Bos A	10	10	.500	28	24	8-1	0-0	177	198	89	20	2	59-2	44	3.46	119	.285	.340	0	ø	2	98	7	0	0.8
1979	Mon N	16	10	.615	33	33	6-3	0-0	222	230	91	20	1	46-1	59	3.04	122	.265	.302	74-0-7	.216	2	100	15	0	1.9
1980	Mon N	4	6	.400	24	18	2	0-0	118	156	71	13	3	22-1	34	4.96	73	.319	.349	41	.220	1*	120	-17	59	-1.2
1981	†Mon N	5	6	.455	31	7	0	6-0	88.2	90	33	6	2	14-2	34	2.94	121	.265	.297	22-1-0	.364	3	86	5	0	1.3
1982	Mon N	0	0	ø	7	0	0	0-0	12.1	19	7	1	0	1-0	8	4.38	84	.352	.357	0	ø	0	—	-1	0	0.0
Total	14	119	90	.569	416	225	72-10	19-5	1944.1	2122	885	176	27	531-27	713	3.62	108	.280	.327	197-2-10	.208	5	100	52	111	7.7

Lee, Watty Wyatt Arnold; B8.12.1879 Lynch Station VA; D3.6.1936 Washington DC; BL/TL/5´10.5˝/171; d4.30; ▲

YEAR	TM LG	W	L	PCT	G	GS	CG-SHO	SV-BS	IP	H	R	HR	HB	BB-IB	SO	ERA	AERA	OAV	OOB	AB-HR-SH	AVG	PB	SUP	APR	DL	PW
1901	Was A	16	16	.500	36	33	25-2	0	262	328	184	14	11	45	63	4.40	83	.303	.337	129-0-1	.256	4*	95	-22	—	-1.6
1902	Was A	5	6	.455	13	10	10	0	98	118	66	5	8	20	24	5.05	73	.298	.344	391-4-7	.256	3*	116	-11	—	-0.8
1903	Was A	8	12	.400	22	20	15-2	0	166.2	169	86	5	7	40	70	3.08	102	.262	.313	231-0-4	.208	1*	87	-3	—	0.0
1904	Pit N	1	2	.333	5	3	1	0	22.2	34	25	0	3	9	5	8.74	31	.337	.407	12	.333	1*	92	-13	—	-1.3
Total	4	30	36	.455	76	66	51-4	0	549.1	649	361	24	29	114	162	4.29	81	.292	.334	763-4-12	.242	10	96	-49	—	-3.7

Leever, Sam Samuel "Deacon","The Goshen Schoolmaster"; B12.23.1871 Goshen OH; D5.19.1953 Goshen OH; BR/TR/5´10.5˝/175; d5.26

YEAR	TM LG	W	L	PCT	G	GS	CG-SHO	SV-BS	IP	H	R	HR	HB	BB-IB	SO	ERA	AERA	OAV	OOB	AB-HR-SH	AVG	PB	SUP	APR	DL	PW
1898	Pit N	1	0	1.000	5	3	2	0	33	26	10	0	1	5	15	2.45	145	.215	.252	12	.250	0	113	5	—	0.3
1899	Pit N	21	23	.477	**51**	39	35-4	**3**	**379**	353	191	7	11	122	121	3.18	120	.247	.311	146-0-6	.226	3	97	25	—	2.8
1900	†Pit N	15	13	.536	30	29	25-3	0	232.2	236	101	2	8	48	84	2.71	134	.263	.306	88-1-0	.205	0	88	25	—	2.5
1901	Pit N	14	5	.737	21	20	18-2	0	176	182	82	2	7	39	82	2.86	114	.265	.311	71-0-2	.183	-0	141	9	—	0.8
1902	Pit N	15	7	.682	28	26	23-4	2	222	203	73	2	8	31	86	2.39	115	.243	.277	90	.178	-0*	116	11	—	0.8
1903	†Pit N	25	7	**.781**	36	34	30-**7**	1	284.1	255	98	2	5	60	90	**2.06**	**157**	.238	.282	115-0-4	.165	-4	115	37	—	3.4
1904	Pit N	18	11	.621	34	32	26-1	0	253.1	224	85	2	5	54	63	2.17	127	.237	.282	99-1-2	.263	7	116	15	—	2.3
1905	Pit N	20	5	**.800**	33	29	20-3	1	229.2	199	94	3	12	54	81	2.70	111	.231	.286	88-0-2	.102	-4	143	6	—	0.2
1906	Pit N	22	7	.759	36	31	25-6	0	260.1	232	84	3	7	48	76	2.32	115	.243	.284	95-0-1	.211	2	128	14	—	1.4
1907	Pit N	14	9	.609	31	24	17-5	0	216.2	182	70	3	8	46	65	1.66	147	.229	.278	73-0-4	.151	-1	109	15	—	1.2
1908	Pit N	15	7	.682	38	20	14-4	2	192.2	179	60	1	6	41	28	2.10	110	.249	.295	61-0-2	.148	0	106	5	—	0.4
1909	Pit N	8	1	.889	19	4	2	2	70	74	30	0	4	14	23	2.83	96	.276	.322	24	.167	0	96	-1	—	-0.1
1910	Pit N	6	5	.545	26	8	4	2	111	104	45	2	6	25	33	2.76	112	.259	.313	31-0-2	.065	-3	117	4	—	0.1
Total	13	194	100	.660	388	299	241-39	13	2660.2	2449	1023	29	88	587	847	2.47	123	.245	.293	993-2-25	.184	1	114	170	—	16.1

Lefebvre, Bill Wilfred Henry "Lefty"; B11.11.1915 Natick RI; BL/TL/5´11.5˝/180; d6.10; Mil 1945; Col Holy Cross; ▲

YEAR	TM LG	W	L	PCT	G	GS	CG-SHO	SV-BS	IP	H	R	HR	HB	BB-IB	SO	ERA	AERA	OAV	OOB	AB-HR-SH	AVG	PB	SUP	APR	DL	PW
1938	Bos A	0	0	ø	1	0	0	0	4	8	6	2	1	0	0	13.50	37	.400	.429	1-1-0	1.000	1	—	-3	—	0.0
1939	Bos A	1	1	.500	5	3	0	0	26.1	35	17	2	0	14	8	5.81	81	.333	.412	10	.300	1*	118	-2	—	-0.1
1943	Was A	2	0	1.000	6	3	1	0	32.1	33	18	3	0	16	10	4.45	72	.268	.353	14	.286	2*	123	-4	0	0.0
1944	Was A	2	4	.333	24	4	2	3	69.2	86	48	3	1	21	18	4.52	72	.305	.355	62	.258	3*	109	-12	0	-0.5
Total	4	5	5	.500	36	10	3	3	132.1	162	89	10	2	51	36	5.03	71	.306	.369	87-1-0	.276	7	119	-21	0	-0.6

Lefferts, Craig Craig Lindsay; B9.29.1957 Munich, West Germany; BL/TL/6´1˝/(180–230); [ChiN80 9/219]; d4.7; Col Arizona

YEAR	TM LG	W	L	PCT	G	GS	CG-SHO	SV-BS	IP	H	R	HR	HB	BB-IB	SO	ERA	AERA	OAV	OOB	AB-HR-SH	AVG	PB	SUP	APR	DL	PW
1983	Chi N	3	4	.429	56	5	0	1-0	89	80	35	13	2	29-3	60	3.13	122	.243	.308	18-0-1	.111	-1	65	6	0	0.4
1984	†SD N	3	4	.429	62	0	0	10-2	105.2	88	29	4	1	24-1	56	2.13	169	.229	.272	17-0-1	.294	1	—	17	0	1.5
1985	SD N	7	6	.538	60	0	0	2-3	83.1	75	34	7	0	30-4	48	3.35	106	.244	.311	4	.250	0	—	2	0	0.4

THE PITCHER REGISTER

YEAR	TM LG	W	L	PCT	G	GS	CG-SHO	SV-BS	IP	H	R	HR	HB	BB-IB	SO	ERA	AERA	OAV	OOB	AB-HR-SH	AVG	PB	SUP	APR	DL	PW
1986	SD N	9	8	.529	**83**	0	0	4-3	107.2	98	41	7	1	44-11	72	3.09	118	.253	.327	8-1-1	.125	1*	—	7	0	1.3
1987	SD N	2	2	.500	33	0	0	2-2	51.1	56	29	9	2	15-5	39	4.38	91	.272	.327	3	.333	0	—	-3	0	-0.2
	†SF N	3	3	.500	44	0	0	4-5	47.1	36	18	4	0	18-6	18	3.23	119	.216	.289	4	.250	1	—	4	0	0.5
	Year	5	5	.500	77	0	0	6-7	98.2	92	47	13	2	33-11	57	3.83	102	.247	.310	7	.286	1	—	1	0	0.3
1988	SF N	3	8	.273	64	0	0	11-3	92.1	74	33	7	1	23-5	58	2.92	112	.225	.275	9	.000	-1	—	4	0	0.4
1989	†SF N	2	4	.333	70	0	0	20-4	107	93	38	11	1	22-5	71	2.69	126	.233	.272	7	.000	-1	—	8	0	0.5
1990	SD N	7	5	.583	56	0	0	23-8	78.2	68	26	10	1	22-4	60	2.52	153	.228	.283	4-0-2	.250	0	—	11	0	2.2
1991	SD N	1	6	.143	54	0	0	23-7	69	74	35	5	1	14-3	48	3.91	97	.285	.318	6	.000	-1	—	-1	0	-0.3
1992	SD N	13	9	.591	27	27	0	0-0	163.1	180	76	16	0	35-2	81	3.69	97	.285	.320	52-0-9	.077	-3	108	-3	0	-0.7
	Bal A	1	3	.250	5	5	1	0-0	33	34	19	3	0	6-0	23	4.09	99	.268	.299	0	ø	0	54	-1	0	-0.2
1993	Tex A	3	9	.250	52	8	0	0-0	83.1	102	57	17	1	28-3	58	6.05	69	.304	.357	0	ø	0	113	-16	15	-1.9
1994	Cal A	1	1	.500	30	0	0	1-0	34.2	50	20	7	0	12-3	27	4.67	105	.350	.392	0	ø	0	—	1	0	0.0
Total	12	58	72	.446	696	45	1	101-37	1145.2	1108	490	120	11	322-55	719	3.43	109	.257	.308	132-1-14	.121	-3	98	36	15	3.9
LEFTWICH, PHIL	Philip Dale; B5.19.1969 Lynchburg VA; BR/TR/6´5˝/205; [CalA90 2/64]; d7.29; Col Radford; [DL 1995 Cal A 124]																									
1993	Cal A	4	6	.400	12	12	1	0-0	80.2	81	35	5	3	27-1	31	3.79	120	.262	.326	0	ø	0	101	8	0	0.8
1994	Cal A	5	10	.333	20	20	1	0-0	114	127	75	16	3	42-2	67	5.68	86	.283	.346	0	ø	0	73	-9	21	-1.0
1996	Cal A	0	1	.000	2	2	0	0-0	7.1	12	9	1	0	3-0	4	7.36	69	.375	.429	0	ø	0	92	-3	0	-0.3
Total	3	9	17	.346	34	34	2	0-0	202	220	119	22	6	72-3	102	4.99	96	.279	.342	0	ø	0	84	-4	145	-0.5
LEHENY, REGIS	Regis Francis; B1.5.1908 Pittsburgh PA; D11.2.1976 Pittsburgh PA; BL/TL/6´0.5˝/180; d5.21																									
1932	Bos A	0	0	ø	2	0	0	0	2.2	5	5	0	0	3	1	16.88	27	.417	.533	1	.000	-0	—	-3	—	-0.1
LEHEW, JIM	James Anthony; B8.19.1937 Baltimore MD; BR/TR/6´0˝/(175–185); d9.13																									
1961	Bal A	0	0	ø	2	0	0	0	2	1	0	0	0	0-0	0	0.00	ø	.167	.167	0	ø	0	—	1	0	0.0
1962	Bal A	0	0	ø	6	0	0	0	9.2	10	3	0	0	3-0	2	1.86	199	.303	.351	1	.000	-0	—	2	0	0.1
Total	2	0	0	ø	8	0	0	0	11.2	11	3	0	0	3-0	2	1.54	241	.282	.326	1	.000	-0	—	3	0	0.1
LEHMAN, KEN	Kenneth Karl; B6.10.1928 Seattle WA; BL/TL/6´0˝/(160–186); d9.5																									
1952	†Bro N	1	2	.333	4	3	0	0	15.1	19	11	1	0	6	7	5.28	69	.297	.357	4	.000	0	106	-3	0	-0.5
1956	Bro N	2	3	.400	25	4	0	0	49.1	65	35	11	0	23-2	29	5.66	70	.325	.389	10	.300	1	61	-9	0	-0.7
1957	Bro N	0	0	ø	3	0	0	0	7	7	0	0	0	1-0	3	0.00	ø	.259	.286	2	.500	0	—	3	0	0.2
	Bal A	8	3	.727	30	3	1	6	68	57	21	1	0	22-2	32	2.78	129	.232	.294	20	.200	1*	50	7	0	1.4
1958	Bal A	2	1	.667	31	1	1	0	62	64	26	5	2	18-4	36	3.48	103	.276	.326	14	.071	-1	0	1	0	-0.1
1961	Phi N	1	1	.500	41	2	0	1	63.1	61	32	6	1	25-8	27	4.26	96	.260	.331	6	.000	-1*	76	-1	0	-0.1
Total	5	14	10	.583	134	13	2	7	265	273	125	24	3	95-16	134	3.91	97	.272	.333	56	.161	1	67	-2	0	0.2
LEHR, JUSTIN	Charles Larry; B8.3.1977 Orange CA; BR/TR/6´1˝/(200–215); [OakA99 8/243]; d6.20; Col California–Santa Barbara/USC																									
2004	Oak A	1	1	.500	27	0	0	0-1	32.2	35	19	3	2	14-2	16	5.23	88	.280	.357	0	ø	0	—	-1	0	-0.1
2005	Mil N	1	1	.500	23	0	0	0-1	34.2	32	19	4	1	18-2	23	3.89	109	.242	.336	3	.000	-0	—	0	0	0.0
2006	Mil N	2	1	.667	16	0	0	0-0	15.2	24	16	2	1	7-1	12	8.62	52	.369	.432	0	ø	0	—	-7	0	-1.1
Total	3	4	3	.571	66	0	0	0-2	83	91	54	9	4	39-5	51	5.31	84	.283	.363	3	.000	-0	—	-8	0	-1.2
LEHR, NORM	Norman Carl Michael "King"; B5.28.1901 Rochester NY; D7.17.1968 Livonia NY; BR/TR/6´0˝/168; d5.20																									
1926	Cle A	0	0	ø	4	0	0	0	14.2	11	5	0	0	4	4	3.07	132	.216	.273	4	.000	-1	—	2	—	0.1
LEIBER, HANK	Henry Edward; B1.17.1911 Phoenix AZ; D11.8.1993 Tucson AZ; BR/TR/6´1.5˝/205; d4.16.1933; Col Arizona; ▲																									
1942	NY N	0	1	.000	1	1	1	0	9	9	9	0	1	5	5	6.00	56	.290	.405	147-4-1	.218	0*	25	-3	0	-0.3
LEIBRANDT, CHARLIE	Charles Louis; B10.4.1956 Chicago IL; BR/TL/6´3˝/(195–200); [CinN78 9/225]; d9.17; Col Miami–Ohio																									
1979	†Cin N	0	0	ø	3	0	0	0-0	4.1	2	2	0	0	2-0	1	0.00	ø	.154	.250	0	ø	0	—	1	0	0.0
1980	Cin N	10	9	.526	36	27	5-2	0-0	173.2	200	84	15	2	54-4	62	4.25	83	.292	.345	56-0-4	.196	2	106	-12	0	-1.0
1981	Cin N	1	1	.500	7	4	1-1	0-0	30	28	12	0	0	15-2	9	3.60	97	.262	.347	8	.000	-0	82	0	0	0.0
1982	Cin N	5	7	.417	36	11	0	2-0	107.2	130	68	4	2	48-9	34	5.10	72	.308	.380	25-0-4	.080	-1	98	-17	0	-1.9
1984	†KC A	11	7	.611	23	23	0	0-0	143.2	158	65	11	3	38-2	53	3.63	111	.277	.322	0	ø	0	92	6	0	0.6
1985	†KC A	17	9	.654	33	33	8-3	0-0	237.2	223	86	17	2	68-3	108	2.69	155	.248	.301	0	ø	0	100	36	0	4.0
1986	KC A	14	11	.560	35	34	8-1	0-0	231.1	238	112	18	4	63-0	108	4.09	105	.268	.317	0	ø	0	94	6	0	0.7
1987	KC A	16	11	.593	35	35	8-3	0-0	240.1	235	104	23	1	74-2	151	3.41	135	.253	.307	0	ø	0	92	30	0	3.3
1988	KC A	13	12	.520	35	35	7-2	0-0	243	244	98	20	4	62-3	125	3.19	126	.264	.311	0	ø	0	92	21	0	2.2
1989	KC A	5	11	.313	33	27	3-1	0-0	161	196	98	13	2	54-4	73	5.14	75	.304	.358	0	ø	0	113	-21	0	-1.8
1990	Atl N	9	11	.450	24	24	5-2	0-0	162.1	164	72	9	4	35-3	76	3.16	128	.261	.302	50-0-5	.180	1	93	12	55	1.5
1991	†Atl N	15	13	.536	36	36	1-1	0-0	229.2	212	105	18	4	56-3	128	3.49	111	.245	.292	70-0-12	.043	-4	93	8	0	0.8
1992	†Atl N	15	7	.682	32	31	5-2	0-0	193	191	78	9	5	42-4	104	3.36	109	.258	.301	58-0-8	.121	-1	103	7	0	0.8
1993	Tex A	9	10	.474	26	26	1	0-0	150.1	169	84	15	4	45-5	89	4.55	92	.284	.336	0	ø	0	119	-6	36	-0.4
Total	14	140	119	.541	394	346	52-18	2-0	2308	2390	1068	172	37	656-44	1121	3.71	108	.268	.319	267-0-33	.120	-5	99	71	91	8.8
LEICESTER, JON	Jonathan David; B2.7.1979 Mariposa CA; BR/TR/6´3˝/230; [ChiN00 11/313]; d6.9; Col Memphis																									
2004	Chi N	5	1	.833	32	0	0	0-2	41.2	40	20	7	0	15-0	35	3.89	114	.256	.318	1	.000	-0	—	2	0	0.2
2005	Chi N	0	2	.000	6	1	0	0-0	9	11	10	2	2	9-0	7	9.00	49	.324	.489	0-0-1	ø	0	86	-5	0	-0.9
Total	2	5	3	.625	38	1	0	0-2	50.2	51	30	9	2	24-0	42	4.80	92	.268	.353	1-0-1	.000	-0	86	-3	0	-0.7
LEIFIELD, LEFTY	Albert Peter; B9.5.1883 Trenton IL; D10.10.1970 Alexandria VA; BL/TL/6´1˝/165; d9.3; C9																									
1905	Pit N	5	2	.714	8	7	6-1	0	56	52	24	0	4	14	10	2.89	104	.248	.307	20	.350	3	106	0	—	0.4
1906	Pit N	18	13	.581	37	31	24-8	1	255.2	214	90	3	14	68	111	1.87	143	.231	.294	88-0-4	.125	-3	106	17	—	1.8
1907	Pit N	20	16	.556	40	33	24-6	1	286	270	107	1	12	100	112	2.33	105	.256	.328	102-0-2	.147	0	112	4	—	0.6
1908	Pit N	15	14	.517	34	26	18-5	2	218.2	168	69	1	12	86	87	2.10	110	.212	.299	75-0-3	.227	3	96	6	—	1.2
1909	†Pit N	19	8	.704	32	26	13-3	0	201.2	172	76	4	6	54	43	2.37	115	.229	.286	73-0-2	.192	2	131	7	—	0.9
1910	Pit N	15	13	.536	40	30	13-3	2	218.1	197	84	6	10	67	64	2.64	117	.253	.320	60-0-9	.183	0	76	11	—	1.6
1911	Pit N	16	16	.500	42	37	26-2	1	318	301	114	7	16	82	111	2.63	131	.260	.318	102-0-3	.235	6*	90	30	—	3.4
1912	Pit N	1	2	.333	6	1	1	0	23.2	29	15	0	2	10	8	4.18	78	.302	.380	7	.143	0	0	-3	—	-0.2
	Chi N	7	2	.778	13	9	4-1	0	70.2	68	26	0	3	21	23	2.42	137	.258	.319	26-0-3	.115	-1	115	7	—	0.7
	Year	8	4	.667	19	10	5-1	0	94.1	97	41	0	5	31	31	2.86	116	.269	.336	33-0-3	.121	-1	104	4	—	0.5
1913	Chi N	0	1	.000	6	1	0	0	21.1	28	14	0	0	5	4	5.48	58	.329	.367	7	.000	-1*	189	-4	—	-0.3
1918	StL A	2	6	.250	15	6	3-1	0	67	61	23	1	2	19	22	2.55	107	.252	.312	19	.053	-2	46	2	—	0.1
1919	StL A	6	4	.600	19	9	6-2	0	92	96	40	4	4	25	18	2.93	113	.270	.325	30	.100	-2	108	3	—	0.1
1920	StL A	0	0	ø	4	0	0	0	9	17	12	0	0	3	3	7.00	56	.405	.444	2	.000	-0	—	-4	—	-0.2
Total	12	124	97	.561	296	216	138-32	7	1838	1673	694	27	85	554	616	2.47	116	.248	.313	611-0-26	.175	6	100	76	—	10.1
LEIPER, DAVE	David Paul; B6.18.1962 Whittier CA; BL/TL/6´1˝/(160–175); [OakA82*S1/22]; d9.2; Col Fullerton (CA) JC																									
1984	Oak A	1	0	1.000	8	0	0	0-1	7	12	7	2	0	5-0	3	9.00	42	.353	.436	0	ø	0	—	-4	0	-0.5
1986	Oak A	2	2	.500	33	0	0	1-2	31.2	28	17	3	2	18-4	15	4.83	81	.252	.358	0	ø	0	—	-3	0	-0.3
1987	Oak A	2	1	.667	45	0	0	1-3	52.1	49	28	6	1	18-0	33	3.78	110	.246	.306	0	ø	0	—	1	0	0.1
	SD N	1	0	1.000	12	0	0	1-0	16	16	8	2	0	5-0	10	4.50	88	.267	.323	0	ø	0	—	-1	0	0.0
1988	SD N	3	0	1.000	35	0	0	1-0	54	45	19	1	0	14-5	33	2.17	157	.231	.276	2	.500	0	—	5	34	0.4
1989	SD N	0	1	.000	22	0	0	0-0	28.2	40	19	2	2	20-4	7	5.02	70	.333	.437	1	.000	-0	—	-5	31	-0.3
1994	Oak A	0	0	ø	26	0	0	1-0	18.2	13	4	0	1	6-1	14	1.93	233	.206	.278	0	ø	0	—	6	0	0.3
1995	Oak A	1	1	.500	24	0	0	0-0	22.2	23	10	3	1	13-1	10	3.57	127	.258	.359	0	ø	0	—	2	0	0.2
	Mon N	0	2	.000	26	0	0	2-1	22	16	8	2	0	6-0	12	2.86	150	.200	.256	1	.000	-0	—	3	0	0.3
1996	Phi N	2	0	1.000	26	0	0	0-0	21	31	16	4	0	7-2	10	6.43	67	.348	.396	0	ø	0	—	-5	0	-0.4
	Mon N	0	1	.000	7	0	0.	0-0	4	9	5	0	0	2-0	3	11.25	39	.474	.524	0	ø	0	—	-3	0	-0.5
	Year	2	1	.667	33	0	0	0-0	25	40	21	4	0	9-2	13	7.20	60	.370	.419	0	ø	0	—	-7	0	-0.9
Total	8	12	8	.600	264	0	0	7-7	278	282	141	25	7	114-17	150	3.98	100	.266	.338	4	.250	0	—	-4	65	-0.7
LEIPER, JACK	John Henry Thomas; B12.23.1867 Chester PA; D8.23.1960 West Goshen PA; BL/TL/5´11˝/?; d9.4																									
1891	Col AA	2	2	.500	6	5	4	0	45	41	43	3	4	39	19	5.40	64	.234	.385	21	.143	-2	101	-11	—	-0.9

YEAR	TM LG	W	L	PCT	G	GS	CG-SHO	SV-BS	IP	H	R	HR	HB	BB-IB	SO	ERA	AERA	OAV	OOB	AB-HR-SH	AVG	PB	SUP	APR	DL	PW
LEISTER, JOHN	John William; B1.3.1961 San Antonio TX; BR/TR/6´2˝/(200–215); [BosA84*S3/52]; d5.28; Col Michigan St.																									
1987	Bos A	0	2	.000	8	6	0	0-0	30.1	49	31	9	0	12-1	16	9.20	50	.368	.418	0	ø	0	140	-14	0	-0.8
1990	Bos A	0	0	ø	2	1	0	0-0	5.2	7	5	0	0	4-0	3	4.76	86	.304	.393	0	ø	0	111	-1	0	-0.1
Total	2	0	2	.000	10	7	0	0-0	36	56	36	9	0	16-1	19	8.50	53	.359	.414	0	ø	0	136	-15	0	-0.9
LEITER, AL	Alois Terry; B10.23.1965 Toms River NJ; BL/TL/6´3˝/(200–220); [NYA84 2/50]; d9.15; b–Mark																									
1987	NY A	2	2	.500	4	4	0	0-0	22.2	24	16	2	0	15-0	28	6.35	70	.273	.379	0	ø	0	72	-4	0	-0.6
1988	NY A	4	4	.500	14	14	0	0-0	57.1	49	27	7	5	33-0	60	3.92	101	.231	.348	0	ø	0	102	0	34	0.1
1989	NY A	1	2	.333	4	4	0	0-0	26.2	23	20	1	2	21-0	22	6.08	64	.235	.377	0	ø	0	99	-6	0	-0.6
	Tor A	0	0	ø	1	1	0	0-0	6.2	9	3	1	0	2-0	4	4.05	94	.310	.355	0	ø	0	96	0	144	0.0
	Year	1	2	.333	5	5	0	0-0	33.1	32	23	2	2	23-0	26	5.67	68	.252	.373	0	ø	0	98	-7	0	-0.6
1990	Tor A	0	0	ø	4	0	0	0-0	6.1	1	0	0	0	2-0	5	0.00	ø	.050	.136	0	ø	0	—	3	0	0.1
1991	Tor A	0	0	ø	3	0	0	0-0	1.2	3	5	0	0	5-0	1	27.00	16	.429	.667	0	ø	0	—	-4	168	-0.2
1992	Tor A	0	0	ø	1	0	0	0-0	1	1	1	0	0	2-0	0	9.00	46	.200	.429	0	ø	0	—	0	0	0.0
1993	†Tor A	9	6	.600	34	12	1-1	2-1	105	93	52	8	4	56-2	66	4.11	107	.240	.339	0	ø	0	91	3	16	0.4
1994	Tor A	6	7	.462	20	20	1	0-0	111.2	125	68	6	2	65-3	100	5.08	96	.285	.374	0	ø	0	83	-2	15	-0.2
1995	Tor A	11	11	.500	28	28	2-1	0-0	183	162	80	15	6	108-1	153	3.64	131	.238	.345	0	ø	0	71	23	0	2.4
1996	Fla N★	16	12	.571	33	33	2-1	0-0	215.1	153	74	14	11	119-3	200	2.93	141	**.202**	.318	70-0-7	.100	-2	101	31	0	3.4
1997	†Fla N	11	9	.550	27	27	0	0-0	151.1	133	78	13	12	91-4	132	4.34	93	.241	.359	48-0-2	.104	-1	95	-4	35	-0.7
1998	NY N	17	6	.739	28	28	4-2	0-0	193	151	55	8	11	71-2	174	2.47	167	.216	.298	57-0-5	.105	0	105	37	21	4.2
1999	†NY N	13	12	.520	32	32	1-1	0-0	213	209	107	19	9	93-8	162	4.23	103	.262	.342	57-0-11	.105	-2	100	1	0	-0.2
2000	†NY N★	16	8	.667	31	31	2-1	0-0	208	176	84	19	11	76-1	200	3.20	136	.228	.304	58-0-9	.052	-3	94	27	0	2.5
2001	NY N	11	11	.500	29	29	0	0-0	187.1	178	81	18	4	46-3	142	3.31	122	.252	.299	62	.065	-3	87	13	26	1.1
2002	NY N	13	13	.500	33	33	2-2	0-0	204.1	194	99	23	8	69-5	172	3.48	114	.250	.317	53-0-3	.151	2	97	6	0	1.0
2003	NY N	15	9	.625	30	30	1-1	0-0	180.2	176	83	15	9	94-11	139	3.99	105	.260	.355	53-0-5	.019	-5	98	5	20	0.2
2004	NY N	10	8	.556	30	30	0	0-0	173.2	138	65	16	11	97-8	117	3.21	134	.218	.332	54-0-2	.093	-2	78	23	20	2.0
2005	Fla N	3	7	.300	17	16	0	0-0	80	88	61	9	6	60-2	52	6.64	60	.292	.416	18-0-4	.000	-2	97	-23	0	-2.6
	†NY A	4	5	.444	16	10	0	0-0	62.1	66	42	4	6	38-0	45	5.49	78	.268	.375	0	ø	0	105	-9	0	-1.1
Total	19	162	132	.551	419	382	16-10	2-1	2391	2152	1101	198	117	1163-53	1974	3.80	112	.242	.336	530-0-48	.085	-18	92	120	499	11.2
LEITER, MARK	Mark Edward; B4.13.1963 Joliet IL; BR/TR/6´3˝/(210–220); [BalA83*4/103]; d7.24; b–Al; Col Ramapo																									
1990	NY A	1	1	.500	8	3	0	0-0	26.1	33	20	5	2	9-0	21	6.84	58	.314	.376	0	ø	0	129	-7	0	-0.4
1991	Det A	9	7	.563	38	15	1	1-1	134.2	125	66	16	6	50-4	103	4.21	99	.245	.316	0	ø	0	108	1	18	0.0
1992	Det A	8	5	.615	35	14	1	0-0	112	116	57	9	3	43-5	75	4.18	96	.277	.342	0	ø	0	149	-3	31	-0.3
1993	Det A	6	6	.500	27	13	1	0-1	106.2	111	61	17	3	44-5	70	4.73	92	.267	.338	0	ø	0	96	-4	28	-0.4
1994	Cal A	4	7	.364	40	7	0	2-1	95.1	99	56	13	9	35-6	71	4.72	104	.265	.340	0	ø	0	88	1	0	0.1
1995	SF N	10	12	.455	30	29	7-1	0-0	195.2	185	91	19	17	55-4	129	3.82	108	.254	.318	61-0-9	.098	-2	86	7	0	0.4
1996	SF N	4	10	.286	23	22	1	0-0	135.1	151	93	25	9	50-7	118	5.19	80	.283	.353	42-0-7	.143	-1	111	-18	0	-1.7
	Mon N	4	2	.667	12	12	1	0-0	69.2	68	35	12	7	19-1	46	4.39	99	.254	.316	25-0-2	.080	-1	116	1	0	0.0
	Year	8	12	.400	35	34	2	0-0	205	219	128	37	16	69-8	164	4.92	86	.273	.341	67-0-9	.119	-2	113	-18	0	-1.7
1997	Phi N	10	17	.370	31	31	3	0-0	182.2	216	132	25	9	64-4	148	5.67	74	.292	.352	51-0-10	.118	-1	104	-32	15	-4.0
1998	Phi N	7	5	.583	69	0	0	23-12	88.2	67	36	8	8	47-5	84	3.55	122	.216	.331	2	.000	-0	—	8	0	1.3
1999	Sea A	0	0	ø	2	0	0	0-0	1.1	2	1	0	0	0-0	1	6.75	71	.333	.333	0	ø	0	—	0	178	0.0
2001	Mil N	2	1	.667	20	3	0	0-0	36	32	16	6	2	8-2	26	3.75	114	.232	.284	7	.143	-0	143	2	113	0.2
Total	11	65	73	.471	335	149	15-1	26-15	1184.1	1205	664	155	75	424-43	892	4.57	93	.265	.334	188-0-28	.112	-6	106	-44	383	-4.8
LEITH, BILL	William "Shady Bill"; B5.31.1873 Matteawan NY; D7.16.1940 Beacon NY; TR/6´1˝/208; d9.25																									
1899	Was N	0	0	ø	1	0	0	0	2	4	5	0	1	2	1	18.00	22	.400	.538	1	.000	-0	—	-3	—	-0.1
LEITNER, DOC	George Aloysius; B9.14.1865 Piermont NY; D5.18.1937 New York NY; BR/TR/5´11.5˝/185; d8.10; Col Fordham																									
1887	Ind N	2	6	.250	8	8	8	0	65	69	66	6	0	41	27	5.68	73	.259	.358	27	.148	-3	90	-12	—	-1.3
LEITNER, DUMMY	George Michael; B6.19.1872 Parkton MD; D2.20.1960 Baltimore MD; BL/TR/5´7˝/120; d6.29																									
1901	Phi A	0	0	ø	1	0	0	0	2	1	0	0	0	1	1	0.00	ø	.143	.250	1	.000	-0	—	1	—	0.0
	NY N	0	2	.000	2	2	2	0	18	27	9	0	1	4	3	4.50	73	.342	.381	7	.143	-0	32	-1	—	-0.2
1902	Cle A	0	0	ø	1	1	0	0	8	11	4	0	0	1	0	4.50	77	.324	.343	4	.250	0	84	0	—	0.0
	Chi A	0	0	ø	1	0	0	0	4	9	7	0	2	2	0	13.50	25	.450	.542	3	.000	-0	—	-4	—	-0.2
	Year	0	0	ø	2	1	0	0	12	20	11	0	2	3	0	7.50	46	.370	.424	7	.143	-0	84	-4	—	-0.2
Total	2	0	2	.000	5	3	2	0	32	48	20	0	3	8	4	5.34	63	.343	.391	15	.133	-1	49	-4	—	-0.4
LELIVELT, BILL	William John; B10.21.1884 Chicago IL; D2.14.1968 Chicago IL; BR/TR/5´10˝/168; d7.19; b–Jack																									
1909	Det A	0	1	.000	4	2	1	1	20	27	12	0	0	2	4	4.50	56	.325	.341	6	.333	1	84	-4	—	-0.1
1910	Det A	0	1	.000	1	1	1	0	9	6	4	0	0	3	2	1.00	263	.207	.281	2	.500	1	0	1	—	0.1
Total	2	0	2	.000	5	3	2	1	29	33	16	0	0	5	6	3.41	75	.295	.325	8	.375	2	54	-3	—	0.0
LEMANCZYK, DAVE	David Lawrence; B8.17.1950 Syracuse NY; BR/TR/6´4˝/(225–230); [DetA72 16/380]; d4.15; Col Hartwick																									
1973	Det A	0	0	ø	1	0	0	0-0	2.1	4	3	0	0	0-0	0	11.57	35	.364	.364	0	ø	0	—	-2	0	-0.1
1974	Det A	2	1	.667	22	3	0	0-0	78.2	79	43	12	2	44-6	52	4.00	96	.261	.357	0	ø	0	84	-3	0	-0.1
1975	Det A	2	7	.222	26	6	4	0-1	109	120	62	8	3	46-5	67	4.46	91	.281	.352	0	ø	0	33	-4	24	-0.3
1976	Det A	4	6	.400	20	10	1	0-0	81.1	86	47	7	0	34-0	51	5.09	73	.271	.341	0	ø	0	83	-9	0	-1.0
1977	Tor A	13	16	.448	34	34	11	0-0	252	278	143	20	4	87-6	105	4.25	100	.282	.340	0	ø	0	84	-4	0	-0.4
1978	Tor A	4	14	.222	29	20	3	0-0	136.2	170	97	16	3	65-1	62	6.26	63	.313	.388	0	ø	0	74	-31	20	-3.6
1979	Tor A☆	8	10	.444	22	20	11-3	0-0	143	137	65	12	6	45-2	63	3.71	118	.258	.321	0	ø	0	63	11	23	1.3
1980	Tor A	2	5	.286	10	8	0	0-0	43.1	57	29	4	0	15-0	10	5.40	80	.322	.371	0	ø	0	65	-5	0	-0.6
	Cal A	2	4	.333	21	2	0	0-0	66.2	81	40	8	2	27-2	19	4.32	92	.301	.367	0	ø	0	124	-5	0	-0.5
	Year	4	9	.308	31	10	0	0-0	110	138	69	12	2	42-2	29	4.75	86	.309	.368	0	ø	0	79	-9	0	-1.1
Total	8	37	63	.370	185	103	30-3	0-1	913	1012	529	87	20	363-22	429	4.62	89	.284	.351	0	ø	0	74	-52	67	-5.3
LEMASTER, DENNY	Denver Clayton; B2.25.1939 Corona CA; BR/TL/6´1˝/(183–185); d7.15																									
1962	Mil N	3	4	.429	17	12	4-1	0	86.2	75	36	11	3	32-1	69	3.01	126	.233	.308	33-0-2	.121	-1	116	6	0	0.3
1963	Mil N	11	14	.440	46	31	10-1	1	237	199	87	30	1	85-14	190	3.04	106	.227	.295	74-2-6	.189	3	78	6	0	0.9
1964	Mil N	17	11	.607	39	35	9-3	1	221	216	112	27	4	75-4	185	4.15	85	.252	.313	67-0-7	.134	0	115	-14	0	-1.6
1965	Mil N	7	13	.350	32	23	4-1	0	146.1	140	75	12	3	58-7	111	4.43	80	.251	.324	45-0-2	.089	-1	95	-12	0	-1.7
1966	Atl N	11	8	.579	27	27	10-3	0	171	170	78	25	1	41-5	139	3.74	97	.258	.301	59-0-4	.119	-1	124	-1	0	-0.3
1967	Atl N✱	9	9	.500	31	31	8-2	0	215.1	184	86	20	3	72-7	148	3.34	99	.229	.293	67-0-7	.104	-2	82	2	0	0.0
1968	Hou N	10	15	.400	33	32	7-2	0	224	231	79	11	4	72-11	146	2.81	105	.262	.319	65-0-9	.031	-3	86	3	0	-0.1
1969	Hou N	13	17	.433	38	37	11-1	1-0	244.2	232	97	20	1	72-8	173	3.16	112	.246	.298	88-1-6	.170	3	87	12	0	1.8
1970	Hou N	7	12	.368	39	21	3	3-2	162	169	88	22	2	65-9	103	4.56	85	.268	.335	45-1-3	.178	2	86	-11	0	-1.0
1971	Hou N	0	2	.000	42	0	0	2-1	60	59	23	4	1	22-6	28	3.45	98	.262	.331	6-0-1	.167	-0	—	1	0	0.0
1972	Mon N	2	0	1.000	13	0	0	0-0	19.2	28	17	2	1	6-1	13	7.78	46	.329	.376	3	.333	1	—	-8	0	-0.8
Total	11	90	105	.462	357	249	66-14	8-3	1787.2	1703	778	184	24	600-73	1305	3.58	96	.249	.310	552-4-47	.130	0	96	-16	0	-2.5
LEMAY, DICK	Richard Paul; B8.28.1938 Cincinnati OH; BL/TL/6´3˝/(190–197); d6.13; Col Michigan																									
1961	SF N	3	6	.333	27	5	1	3	83.1	65	35	11	4	36-7	54	3.56	107	.217	.307	26-0-1	.077	-2	140	3	0	0.2
1962	SF N	0	1	.000	9	0	0	1	9.1	9	8	2	0	9-1	5	7.71	49	.265	.419	0	ø	0	—	-4	0	-0.4
1963	Chi N	0	1	.000	9	1	0	0	15.1	26	9	1	0	4-2	10	5.28	66	.394	.429	2	.000	-1	123	-2	0	-0.2
Total	3	3	8	.273	45	6	1	4	108	100	52	14	4	49-10	69	4.17	91	.250	.336	28-0-1	.071	-1	136	-3	0	-0.4
LEMON, BOB	Robert Granville; B9.22.1920 San Bernardino CA; D1.11.2000 Long Beach CA; BL/TR/6´0˝/185; d9.9.1941; Mil 1943–45; M8/C6; HF1976; ▲																									
1946	Cle A	4	5	.444	32	5	1	1	94	77	40	1	0	68	39	2.49	133	.229	.359	89-1-3	.180	2*	83	4	0	0.7
1947	Cle A	11	5	.688	37	15	6-1	3	167.1	150	68	7	4	97	65	3.44	101	.242	.348	56-2-2	.321	9*	119	2	0	1.5
1948	†Cle A☆	20	14	.588	43	37	**20-10**	2	**293.2**	231	104	12	3	129	147	2.82	144	.216	.302	119-5-2	.286	14*	122	42	0	**6.6**
1949	Cle A☆	22	10	.688	37	33	22-2	1	279.2	211	101	19	6	137	138	2.99	133	.211	.309	108-7-5	.269	16*	115	34	0	**5.6**
1950	Cle A★	**23**	11	.676	44	**37**	**22-3**	3	**288**	281	144	28	2	146	**170**	3.84	113	.257	.345	136-6-3	.272	17*	114	15	0	3.4
1951	Cle A★	17	14	.548	42	**34**	17-1	2	263.1	244	119	18	2	124	132	3.52	108	.244	.328	102-3-1	.206	5*	92	8	0	1.4

YEAR	TM LG	W	L	PCT	G	GS	CG-SHO	SV-BS	IP	H	R	HR	HB	BB-IB	SO	ERA	AERA	OAV	OOB	AB-HR-SH	AVG	PB	SUP	APR	DL	PW
1952	Cle A★	22	11	.667	42	**36**	**28**-5	4	**309.2**	236	104	15	6	105	131	2.50	134	**.208**	.279	124-2-6	.226	7*	134	30	0	4.4
1953	Cle A☆	21	15	.583	41	36	23-5	1	**286.2**	283	119	16	11	110	98	3.36	112	.262	.336	112-2-6	.232	8*	114	14	0	3.0
1954	†Cle A★	**23**	7	.767	36	33	**21**-2	0	258.1	228	95	12	4	92	110	2.72	135	.237	.303	98-2-8	.214	6*	134	25	0	3.7
1955	Cle A	**18**	10	.643	35	31	5	2	211.1	218	103	17	5	74-3	100	3.88	103	.266	.329	78-1-6	.244	6*	115	3	0	1.1
1956	Cle A	20	14	.588	39	35	**21**-2	3	255.1	230	103	23	6	89-2	94	3.03	139	.239	.305	93-5-7	.194	5*	95	31	0	4.6
1957	Cle A	6	11	.353	21	17	2	0	117.1	129	70	9	7	64-6	45	4.60	81	.287	.379	46-1-0	.065	-3*	98	-12	0	-1.7
1958	Cle A	0	1	.000	11	1	0	0	25.1	41	15	3	1	16-2	8	5.33	68	.376	.457	13	.231	0*	148	-4	31	-0.1
Total	13	207	128	.618	460	350	188-31	22	2850	2559	1185	180	57	1251-13	1277	3.23	119	.241	.323	1174-37-49	.233	90	114	192	31	34.2
LEMONDS, DAVE	David Lee; B7.5.1948 Charlotte NC; BL/TL/6´1.5˝/180; [ChiN68 S1/1]; d6.30; Col North Carolina; [DL 1973 Chi A 55]																									
1969	Chi N	0	1	.000	2	1	0	0-0	4.2	5	2	0	0	5-0	0	3.86	104	.313	.476	1	.000	-0	44	0	0	0.0
1972	Chi A	4	7	.364	31	18	0	0-0	94.2	87	39	6	1	38-3	69	2.95	106	.247	.319	25-0-2	.120	-1*	93	0	0	-0.1
Total	2	4	8	.333	33	19	0	0-0	99.1	92	41	6	1	43-3	69	2.99	106	.250	.327	26-0-2	.115	-1	90	0	55	-0.1
LEMONGELLO, MARK	Mark; B7.21.1955 Jersey City NJ; BR/TR/6´1˝/(180–185); d9.14																									
1976	Hou N	3	1	.750	4	4	1	0-0	29	26	12	2	0	7-2	9	2.79	116	.236	.282	8-0-1	.000	-1	89	1	0	0.1
1977	Hou N	9	14	.391	34	30	5	0-0	214.2	237	88	20	3	52-4	83	3.48	104	.281	.323	69-0-5	.087	-4*	71	6	0	0.2
1978	Hou N	9	14	.391	33	30	9-1	1-0	210.1	204	100	20	9	66-5	77	3.94	85	.259	.318	64-0-6	.172	1	106	-15	0	-1.4
1979	Tor A	1	9	.100	18	10	2	0-0	83	97	64	14	3	34-8	40	6.29	70	.299	.365	0	ø	0	74	-16	0	-1.6
Total	4	22	38	.367	89	74	17-1	1-0	537	564	264	56	15	159-19	209	4.06	89	.273	.326	141-0-12	.121	-3	85	-24	0	-2.7
LENNON, ED	Edward Francis; B8.17.1897 Philadelphia PA; D9.13.1947 Philadelphia PA; BR/TR/5´11˝/170; d6.30; Col Niagara																									
1928	Phi N	0	0	ø	5	0	0	0	12.1	19	14	0	0	10	6	8.76	49	.373	.475	4	.000	-1	—	-6	—	-0.4
LEON, DANNY	Danilo Enrique (Lineco); B4.3.1967 LaConcepcion, Venezuela; BR/TR/6´1˝/170; d6.6																									
1992	Tex A	1	1	.500	15	0	0	0-0	18.1	18	14	5	3	10-0	15	5.89	65	.254	.369	0	ø	0	—	-5	78	-0.4
LEON, IZZY	Isidoro (Becerra); B1.4.1911 Cruces, Cuba; D7.25.2002 Miami FL; BR/TR/5´10˝/160; d6.21; Negro Lg 1944–48																									
1945	Phi N	0	4	.000	14	4	0	0	38.2	49	25	3	0	19	11	5.35	72	.312	.386	9	.111	-0	44	-5	0	-0.5
LEON, MAX	Maximino (Molino); B2.4.1950 Acula, Veracruz, Mexico; BR/TR/6´0˝/170; d7.18																									
1973	Atl N	2	2	.500	12	1	1	0-2	27	30	18	6	3	9-1	18	5.33	74	.278	.344	7-0-1	.286	0*	156	-4	0	-0.5
1974	Atl N	4	7	.364	34	2	1-1	3-1	75	68	22	5	1	14-3	38	2.64	144	.242	.280	15-0-1	.133	-1	81	10	0	1.5
1975	Atl N	2	1	.667	50	1	0	6-3	85	90	52	5	7	33-8	53	4.13	92	.274	.349	9-0-1	.333	1	186	-5	0	-0.1
1976	Atl N	2	4	.333	30	0	0	3-3	36	32	15	2	2	15-3	16	2.75	138	.234	.314	2	.000	-0	—	3	35	0.5
1977	Atl N	4	4	.500	31	9	0	1-1	81.2	89	42	9	9	25-2	44	3.97	112	.280	.347	19-0-3	.316	1*	102	4	0	0.4
1978	Atl N	0	0	ø	5	0	0	0-0	5.2	6	4	1	1	4-0	1	6.35	63	.273	.393	0	ø	0*	—	-1	47	-0.1
Total	6	14	18	.438	162	13	2-1	13-10	310.1	315	153	28	23	100-17	170	3.71	107	.264	.330	52-0-6	.250	1	116	7	82	1.7
LEONARD, DENNIS	Dennis Patrick; B5.8.1951 Brooklyn NY; BR/TR/6´1˝/(190–200); [KCA72 2/42]; d9.4; Col Iona; [DL 1984 KC A 182]																									
1974	KC A	0	4	.000	5	4	0	0-0	22	28	15	0	3	12-0	8	5.32	72	.329	.430	0	ø	0	40	-3	0	-0.5
1975	KC A	15	7	.682	32	30	8	0-1	212.1	212	98	18	9	90-4	146	3.77	102	.263	.342	0	ø	0	110	4	0	0.4
1976	†KC A	17	10	.630	35	34	16-2	0-0	259	247	113	16	11	70-5	150	3.51	100	.255	.309	0	ø	0	135	2	0	0.0
1977	†KC A	**20**	12	.625	38	37	21-5	1-0	292.2	246	117	18	8	79-0	244	3.04	132	.227	.283	0	ø	0*	99	30	0	3.0
1978	†KC A	21	17	.553	40	**40**	20-4	0-0	294.2	283	125	27	9	78-7	183	3.33	115	.254	.307	0	ø	0	107	16	0	2.0
1979	KC A	14	12	.538	32	32	12-**5**	0-0	236	226	117	33	2	56-3	126	4.08	105	.253	.297	0	ø	0	110	7	0	0.7
1980	†KC A	20	11	.645	38	**38**	9-3	0-0	280.1	271	127	30	1	80-5	155	3.79	107	.253	.304	0	ø	0	117	10	0	1.0
1981	†KC A	13	11	.542	26	**26**	9-2	0-0	**201.2**	202	79	15	3	41-5	107	2.99	121	.258	.296	0	ø	0	84	12	0	1.4
1982	KC A	10	6	.625	21	21	2	0-0	130.2	145	82	20	2	46-3	58	5.10	80	.279	.337	0	ø	0	132	-15	78	-1.5
1983	KC A	6	3	.667	10	10	1	0-0	63	69	29	3	0	19-1	31	3.71	111	.277	.326	0	ø	0	73	3	127	0.4
1985	KC A	0	0	ø	2	0	0	0-0	2	1	0	0	0	0-0	1	0.00	ø	.143	.143	0	ø	0	—	1	148	0.0
1986	KC A	8	13	.381	33	30	5-2	0-0	192.2	207	106	22	4	51-6	114	4.44	96	.275	.321	0	ø	0	80	-4	0	-0.4
Total	12	144	106	.576	312	302	103-23	1-1	2187	2137	1008	202	52	622-39	1323	3.70	107	.257	.310	0	ø	0	106	63	535	6.5
LEONARD, ELMER	Elmer Ellsworth "Tiny"; B11.12.1888 Napa CA; D5.27.1981 Napa CA; BR/TR/6´3.5˝/210; d6.22; Col St. Marys (CA)																									
1911	Phi A	2	2	.500	5	1	1	0	19	26	11	0	2	10	10	2.84	111	.329	.418	7-0-1	.286	1	274	-1	—	-0.1
LEONARD, DUTCH	Emil John; B3.25.1909 Auburn IL; D4.17.1983 Springfield IL; BR/TR/6´0˝/(175–198); d8.31; C3																									
1933	Bro N	2	3	.400	10	3	2	0	40	42	17	0	0	10	6	2.93	110	.261	.304	11-0-2	.000	-1	95	1	—	-0.1
1934	Bro N	14	11	.560	44	21	11-2	5	183.2	210	90	12	4	33	58	3.28	119	.286	.320	67-0-5	.179	-1	128	8	—	1.1
1935	Bro N	2	9	.182	43	11	4	**8**	137.2	152	67	11	1	29	41	3.92	101	.280	.318	39-0-1	.026	-4	83	3	—	-0.2
1936	Bro N	0	0	ø	16	0	0	1	32	34	18	2	0	5	8	3.66	113	.262	.289	5-0-1	.400	0	—	1	—	0.1
1938	Was A	12	15	.444	33	31	15-3	0	223.1	221	109	11	7	53	68	3.43	132	.256	**.305**	82-0-2	.232	3	97	24	—	2.8
1939	Was A	20	8	.714	34	34	21-2	0	269.1	273	124	16	5	59	88	3.54	123	.262	.305	95-0-13	.221	0	94	25	—	2.3
1940	Was A☆	14	19	.424	35	35	23-2	0	289	328	136	19	2	78	124	3.49	120	.286	.332	101-0-8	.158	-5	84	21	—	1.9
1941	Was A	18	13	.581	34	33	19-4	0	256	271	117	6	3	54	91	3.45	117	.270	.309	88-0-11	.102	-5	108	17	0	1.3
1942	Was A	2	2	.500	6	5	1-1	0	35	28	16	1	0	5	15	4.11	89	.214	.243	10-0-1	.100	-0	89	-1	0	-0.1
1943	Was A★	11	13	.458	31	30	15-2	1	219.2	218	96	9	4	46	51	3.28	98	.257	.298	67-0-11	.104	-4	102	-1	0	-0.5
1944	Was A☆	14	14	.500	32	31	17-3	0	229.1	222	97	8	3	37	62	3.06	106	.252	.284	79-0-5	.228	2	108	5	0	0.9
1945	Was A✳	17	7	.708	31	29	12-4	1	216	208	72	5	2	35	96	2.13	146	.248	.279	78-0-8	.231	1	125	21	0	2.5
1946	Was A	10	10	.500	26	23	7-2	0	161.2	182	85	9	4	36	62	3.56	94	.281	.323	53-0-5	.170	-1	106	-7	0	-0.7
1947	Phi N	17	12	.586	32	29	19-3	0	235	224	86	14	2	57	103	2.68	149	.258	.306	80-0-6	.175	-1	87	33	0	3.9
1948	Phi N	12	17	.414	34	30	16-1	0	225.2	226	85	9	4	54	92	2.51	157	.265	.312	83-0-2	.145	-3	80	31	0	3.7
1949	Chi N	7	16	.304	33	28	10-1	0	180	198	94	4	7	43	83	4.15	97	.272	.319	59-0-2	.203	0	73	-2	0	-0.1
1950	Chi N	5	1	.833	35	1	0	6	74	70	41	7	2	27	28	3.77	111	.248	.318	16-0-1	.063	-2	147	2	0	0.0
1951	Chi N☆	10	6	.625	41	1	0	3	81.2	69	30	3	2	28	30	2.64	155	.234	.305	21-0-1	.000	-3	129	11	0	2.0
1952	Chi N	2	2	.500	45	0	0	11	66.2	56	18	3	3	24	37	2.16	178	.235	.313	10	.200	-0	—	12	0	1.3
1953	Chi N	2	3	.400	45	0	0	8	62.2	72	34	9	1	24	27	4.60	97	.289	.354	10	.300	1	—	0	0	0.1
Total	20	191	181	.513	640	375	192-30	44	3218.1	3304	1432	158	56	737	1170	3.25	119	.265	.309	1054-0-85	.168	-21	97	204	0	22.2
LEONARD, DUTCH	Hubert Benjamin; B4.16.1892 Birmingham OH; D7.11.1952 Fresno CA; BL/TL/5´10.5˝/185; d4.12; Mil 1918; Col St. Marys (CA)																									
1913	Bos A	14	17	.452	42	28	14-3	1	259.1	245	108	0	4	94	144	2.39	123	.255	.324	83-0-3	.181	1	120	11	—	1.2
1914	Bos A	19	5	.792	36	25	17-7	3	224.2	139	34	3	8	60	176	**0.96**	**280**	**.180**	**.246**	68-0-9	.147	-1	115	43	—	4.8
1915	†Bos A	15	7	.682	32	21	10-2	0	183.1	130	57	3	14	67	116	2.36	118	**.208**	.299	53-0-3	.264	5	105	12	—	1.7
1916	†Bos A	18	12	.600	48	34	17-6	6	274	244	87	6	8	66	144	2.36	117	.247	.300	85-0-4	.200	2	90	13	—	1.4
1917	Bos A	16	17	.485	37	36	26-4	1	294.1	257	88	4	5	72	144	2.17	119	.236	.286	104-0-2	.087	-6	83	16	—	0.8
1918	Bos A	8	6	.571	16	16	12-3	0	125.2	119	51	0	2	53	47	2.72	99	.254	.332	43-0-2	.186	0	133	-1	—	-0.2
1919	Det A	14	13	.519	29	28	18-4	0	217.1	212	89	7	7	65	102	2.77	115	.254	.313	71-0-6	.155	-3	94	8	—	0.4
1920	Det A	10	17	.370	28	27	10-3	0	191.1	192	107	8	8	63	76	4.33	86	.271	.338	57-0-3	.211	2	64	-7	—	-0.7
1921	Det A	11	13	.458	36	32	16-1	1	245	273	125	15	10	63	120	3.75	114	.286	.336	82-0-5	.171	-4	101	16	—	0.8
1924	Det A	3	2	.600	9	7	3	1	51.1	68	32	1	1	18	26	4.56	90	.327	.383	19-0-1	.211	-0	108	-3	—	-0.3
1925	Det A	11	4	.733	18	18	9	0	125.2	143	73	7	1	43	65	4.51	95	.289	.347	50-0-1	.200	-1	135	-3	—	-0.4
Total	11	139	113	.552	331	272	152-33	13	2192	2022	851	54	68	664	1160	2.76	115	.249	.312	715-0-39	.173	-5	102	105	—	9.5
LEONHARD, DAVE	David Paul; B1.22.1941 Arlington VA; BR/TR/5´11˝/(160–170); d9.21; Col Johns Hopkins																									
1967	Bal A	0	0	ø	3	2	0	1	14.1	11	5	1	1	6-0	9	3.14	100	.200	.290	5	.000	-1	83	0	0	0.0
1968	Bal A	7	7	.500	28	18	5-2	1	126.1	95	46	10	2	57-3	61	3.13	93	.216	.307	31-0-6	.129	-1*	129	-1	0	-0.1
1969	†Bal A	7	4	.636	37	3	1-1	1-0	94	78	28	8	0	38-8	37	2.49	144	.228	.304	21-0-4	.095	-0*	82	12	0	1.3
1970	Bal A	0	0	ø	23	0	0	1-0	28.1	32	18	5	0	18-3	14	5.08	72	.294	.385	1	.000	0*	—	-5	0	-0.2
1971	†Bal A	2	3	.400	12	6	1-1	1-1	54	51	18	5	1	19-0	18	2.83	120	.252	.318	18-0-1	.278	1*	79	4	0	0.5
1972	Bal A	0	0	ø	14	0	0	0-0	20	20	10	3	0	12-0	7	4.50	69	.260	.356	1	1.000	1*	—	-3	0	0.0
Total	6	16	14	.533	117	29	7-4	5-1	337	287	125	32	4	150-14	146	3.15	104	.234	.318	77-0-11	.156	1	104	7	0	1.5
LEOPOLD, RUDY	Rudolph Matas; B7.27.1905 Grand Cane LA; D9.3.1965 Baton Rouge LA; BL/TL/6´0˝/160; d7.4																									
1928	Chi A	0	0	ø	2	0	0	0	2.1	3	3	0	0	0	0	3.86	105	.273	.273	1	.000	-0	—	-1	—	-0.1

LERCH, RANDY Randy Louis; B10.9.1954 Sacramento CA; BL/TL/6´5˝/(170–195); [PhiN73 8/170]; d9.14

YEAR	TM LG	W	L	PCT	G	GS	CG-SHO	SV-BS	IP	H	R	HR	HB	BB-IB	SO	ERA	AERA	OAV	OOB	AB-HR-SH	AVG	PB	SUP	APR	DL	PW
1975	Phi N	0	0	ø	3	0	0	0-0	7	6	5	1	0	1-0	8	6.43	59	.231	.259	0	ø	0	—	-2	0	-0.1
1976	Phi N	0	0	ø	1	0	0	1-0	3	3	1	0	0	0-0	0	3.00	119	.250	.250	1	1.000	1	—	0	0	0.1
1977	Phi N	10	6	.625	32	28	3	0-0	168.2	207	102	20	1	75-3	81	5.07	79	.312	.379	54-0-2	.167	-0*	110	-17	0	-1.4
1978	†Phi N	11	8	.579	33	28	5	0-0	184	183	89	15	1	70-3	96	3.96	91	.263	.329	60-3-2	.250	7*	133	-7	0	0.1
1979	Phi N	10	13	.435	37	35	6-1	0-0	214	228	98	20	3	60-4	92	3.74	104	.281	.328	72-1-3	.153	1*	98	2	0	0.4
1980	Phi N	4	14	.222	30	22	2	0-1	150	178	98	15	0	55-5	57	5.16	74	.302	.356	45-0-4	.267	3*	88	-22	0	-2.0
1981	†Mil A	7	9	.438	23	18	1	0-0	110.2	134	63	8	0	43-2	53	4.31	80	.303	.361	0	ø	0	93	-14	0	-1.8
1982	Mil A	8	7	.533	21	20	1-1	0-0	108.2	123	68	12	3	51-1	33	4.97	77	.286	.361	0	ø	0	138	-15	0	-1.9
	Mon N	2	0	1.000	6	4	0	0-0	23.2	26	11	0	0	8-1	4	3.42	108	.289	.343	8	.250	0	131	0	0	0.0
1983	Mon N	1	3	.250	19	5	0	0-0	38.2	45	29	6	1	18-2	24	6.75	54	.292	.368	9-0-1	.222	1	112	-12	0	-1.1
	SF N	1	0	1.000	7	0	0	0-0	10.2	9	4	1	0	8-1	6	3.38	105	.231	.354	0	ø	0	—	1	0	0.1
	Year	2	3	.400	26	5	0	0-0	49.1	54	33	7	1	26-3	30	6.02	60	.280	.365	9-0-1	.222	1	113	-12	0	-1.0
1984	SF N	5	3	.625	37	4	0	2-1	72.1	80	36	3	1	36-3	48	4.23	84	.287	.362	15	.133	0	88	-5	56	-0.4
1986	Phi N	1	1	.500	4	0	0	0-0	8	10	8	0	0	7-1	5	7.88	50	.286	.405	3	.333	1	—	-3	0	-0.6
Total	11	60	64	.484	253	164	18-2	3-2	1099.1	1232	612	101	10	432-26	507	4.53	83	.289	.351	267-4-12	.206	14	110	-94	56	-8.6

LEREW, ANTHONY Anthony Allen; B10.28.1982 Carlisle PA; BL/TR/6´3˝/220; [AtlN01 11/345]; d9.4

YEAR	TM LG	W	L	PCT	G	GS	CG-SHO	SV-BS	IP	H	R	HR	HB	BB-IB	SO	ERA	AERA	OAV	OOB	AB-HR-SH	AVG	PB	SUP	APR	DL	PW
2005	Atl N	0	0	ø	7	0	0	0-1	8	9	5	1	0	5-2	5	5.63	75	.290	.389	0	ø	0	—	-1	0	0.0
2006	Atl N	0	0	ø	1	0	0	0-0	2	5	5	0	1	3-0	1	22.50	20	.455	.600	0	ø	0	—	-4	0	-0.2
Total	2	0	0	ø	8	0	0	0-1	10	14	10	1	1	8-2	6	9.00	48	.333	.451	0	ø	0	—	-5	0	-0.2

LEROY, JOHN John Michael; B4.19.1975 Bellevue WA; D6.25.2001 Sioux City IA; BR/TR/6´3˝/175; [AtlN93 15/432]; d9.26

YEAR	TM LG	W	L	PCT	G	GS	CG-SHO	SV-BS	IP	H	R	HR	HB	BB-IB	SO	ERA	AERA	OAV	OOB	AB-HR-SH	AVG	PB	SUP	APR	DL	PW
1997	Atl N	1	0	1.000	1	0	0	0-0	2	1	0	0	0	3-1	3	0.00	ø	.143	.400	0	ø	0	—	1	0	0.2

LEROY, LOUIS Louis Paul "Chief"; B2.18.1879 Omro WI; D10.10.1944 Shawano WI; BR/TR/5´10˝/180; d9.22

YEAR	TM LG	W	L	PCT	G	GS	CG-SHO	SV-BS	IP	H	R	HR	HB	BB-IB	SO	ERA	AERA	OAV	OOB	AB-HR-SH	AVG	PB	SUP	APR	DL	PW
1905	NY A	1	1	.500	3	3	2	0	24	26	14	2	1	1	8	3.75	78	.277	.292	8-0-1	.125	-0	113	-2	—	-0.2
1906	NY A	2	0	1.000	11	2	1	1	44.2	33	19	0	2	12	28	2.22	134	.209	.273	14-0-1	.143	-1	170	2	—	0.1
1910	Bos A	0	0	ø	1	0	0	0	4	7	9	1	0	2	3	11.25	23	.389	.450	1	.000	-0	—	-4	—	-0.2
Total	3	3	1	.750	15	5	3	1	72.2	66	42	3	3	15	39	3.22	91	.244	.292	23-0-2	.130	-1	136	-4	—	-0.3

LERSCH, BARRY Barry Lee; B9.7.1944 Denver CO; BB/TR (BL 1973–74)/6´0˝/(175–180); d4.8; Col Mesa St.

YEAR	TM LG	W	L	PCT	G	GS	CG-SHO	SV-BS	IP	H	R	HR	HB	BB-IB	SO	ERA	AERA	OAV	OOB	AB-HR-SH	AVG	PB	SUP	APR	DL	PW
1969	Phi N	0	3	.000	10	0	0	2-1	17.2	20	14	6	1	10-2	13	7.13	50	.286	.383	3	.000	-0	—	-6	0	-1.1
1970	Phi N	6	3	.667	42	11	3	3-0	138	119	52	17	1	47-5	92	3.26	123	.232	.295	31-0-5	.065	-2	91	13	0	0.6
1971	Phi N	5	14	.263	38	30	3	0-0	214.1	203	97	28	3	50-2	113	3.78	94	.252	.297	59-0-6	.169	2*	85	-3	0	-0.1
1972	Phi N	4	6	.400	36	8	3-1	0-0	100.2	86	37	8	3	33-7	48	3.04	119	.231	.297	23	.000	-2*	77	6	28	0.4
1973	Phi N	3	6	.333	42	4	0	1-0	98.1	105	49	10	2	27-4	51	4.39	87	.279	.324	17	.176	0*	75	-4	0	-0.4
1974	StL N	0	0	ø	1	0	0	0-0	1.1	3	6	1	0	5-0	0	40.50	9	.429	.667	0	ø	0	—	-5	0	-0.2
Total	6	18	32	.360	169	53	9-1	6-1	570.1	536	255	70	10	172-20	317	3.82	98	.250	.306	133-0-11	.113	-3	83	1	28	-0.8

LESHNOCK, DON Donald Lee; B11.25.1946 Youngstown OH; BR/TL/6´3˝/195; d6.7; Col Youngstown St.

YEAR	TM LG	W	L	PCT	G	GS	CG-SHO	SV-BS	IP	H	R	HR	HB	BB-IB	SO	ERA	AERA	OAV	OOB	AB-HR-SH	AVG	PB	SUP	APR	DL	PW
1972	Det A	0	0	ø	1	0	0	0-0	1	2	0	0	0	0-0	2	0.00	ø	.400	.400	0	ø	0	—	0	0	0.0

LESKANIC, CURTIS Curtis John; B4.2.1968 Homestead PA; BR/TR/6´0˝/(180–196); [CleA89 8/203]; d6.27; Col Louisiana St.; [DL 2002 Mil N 183]

YEAR	TM LG	W	L	PCT	G	GS	CG-SHO	SV-BS	IP	H	R	HR	HB	BB-IB	SO	ERA	AERA	OAV	OOB	AB-HR-SH	AVG	PB	SUP	APR	DL	PW
1993	Col N	1	5	.167	18	8	0	0-0	57	59	40	7	2	27-1	30	5.37	89	.266	.345	13-0-1	.154	-0	71	-4	0	-0.4
1994	Col N	1	1	.500	8	3	0	0-0	22.1	27	14	2	0	10-0	17	5.64	88	.314	.385	6	.167	0	110	-1	0	-0.1
1995	†Col N	6	3	.667	**76**	0	0	10-6	98	83	38	7	0	33-1	107	3.40	158	.226	.288	7-0-2	.143	-0	—	18	0	1.8
1996	Col N	7	5	.583	70	0	0	6-4	73.2	82	51	12	2	38-1	76	6.23	84	.285	.369	3-0-1	.333	0	—	-5	29	-0.8
1997	Col N	4	0	1.000	55	0	0	2-2	58.1	59	36	8	0	24-0	53	5.55	93	.271	.337	1	.000	-0	—	-1	11	-0.1
1998	Col N	6	4	.600	66	0	0	2-3	75.2	75	37	9	1	40-2	55	4.40	118	.258	.349	2-0-1	.000	-0	—	6	0	0.7
1999	Col N	6	2	.750	63	0	0	0-3	85	87	54	7	5	49-4	77	5.08	114	.272	.374	4-1-0	.500	1	—	4	0	0.5
2000	Mil N	9	3	.750	73	0	0	12-1	77.1	58	23	7	3	51-5	75	2.56	180	.212	.337	2	.000	-0	—	18	18	3.0
2001	Mil N	2	6	.250	70	0	0	17-7	69.1	63	30	11	2	31-5	64	3.63	118	.241	.327	1	.000	-0	—	6	0	0.7
2003	Mil N	4	0	1.000	26	0	0	0-0	26.2	22	8	1	1	18-0	28	2.70	160	.227	.353	0	ø	0	—	5	0	0.7
	KC A	1	0	1.000	27	0	0	2-1	26	16	7	1	0	11-1	22	1.73	278	.180	.267	0	ø	0	—	8	0	0.4
2004	KC A	0	3	.000	19	0	0	2-3	15.2	23	16	5	0	14-0	15	8.04	58	.324	.435	0	ø	0	—	-6	0	-1.1
	†Bos A	3	2	.600	32	0	0	2-1	27.2	24	11	3	1	16-3	22	3.58	136	.247	.353	0	ø	-0	—	4	23	0.7
	Year	3	5	.375	51	0	0	4-4	43.1	47	27	8	1	30-3	37	5.19	93	.280	.388	0	ø	0	—	-2	0	-0.4
Total	11	50	34	.595	603	11	0	55-31	712.2	678	365	80	17	362-23	641	4.36	116	.253	.343	39-1-5	.179	0	79	51	264	6.0

LESLEY, BRAD Bradley Jay; B9.11.1958 Turlock CA; BR/TR/6´6˝/(220–230); [CinN78 S1/9]; d7.31; Col Merced (CA) JC

YEAR	TM LG	W	L	PCT	G	GS	CG-SHO	SV-BS	IP	H	R	HR	HB	BB-IB	SO	ERA	AERA	OAV	OOB	AB-HR-SH	AVG	PB	SUP	APR	DL	PW
1982	Cin N	0	2	.000	28	0	0	4-2	38.1	27	13	1	0	13-4	29	2.58	142	.197	.267	1	.000	-0	—	4	0	0.3
1983	Cin N	0	0	ø	5	0	0	0-0	8.1	9	2	1	0	0-0	5	2.16	177	.290	.281	0-0-1	ø	0	—	2	0	0.1
1984	Cin N	0	1	.000	16	0	0	2-1	19.1	17	11	3	0	14-1	7	5.12	74	.246	.369	2	.500	0	—	-2	0	-0.1
1985	Mil A	1	0	1.000	5	0	0	0-1	6.1	8	7	2	0	2-0	5	9.95	42	.296	.345	0	ø	0	—	-4	0	-0.5
Total	4	1	3	.250	54	0	0	6-4	72.1	61	33	7	0	29-5	46	3.86	98	.231	.305	3-0-1	.333	0	—	0	0	-0.2

LESTER, JON Jonathan Tyler; B1.7.1984 Tacoma WA; BL/TL/6´2˝/190; [BosA02 2/57]; d6.10

YEAR	TM LG	W	L	PCT	G	GS	CG-SHO	SV-BS	IP	H	R	HR	HB	BB-IB	SO	ERA	AERA	OAV	OOB	AB-HR-SH	AVG	PB	SUP	APR	DL	PW
2006	Bos A	7	2	.778	15	15	0	0-0	81.1	91	43	7	5	43-1	60	4.76	98	.294	.381	4	.000	-0	121	1	39	0.0

LEVERENZ, WALT Walter Fred "Tiny"; B7.21.1888 Chicago IL; D3.19.1973 Atascadero CA; BL/TL/5´10˝/175; d4.18

YEAR	TM LG	W	L	PCT	G	GS	CG-SHO	SV-BS	IP	H	R	HR	HB	BB-IB	SO	ERA	AERA	OAV	OOB	AB-HR-SH	AVG	PB	SUP	APR	DL	PW
1913	StL A	6	17	.261	30	27	13-2	1	202.2	159	80	3	12	89	87	2.58	114	.225	.322	68-0-2	.176	-1*	72	8	—	0.7
1914	StL A	1	12	.077	27	16	5	0	111.1	107	67	5	4	63	41	3.80	71	.264	.368	33	.182	-0*	67	-15	—	-1.7
1915	StL A	1	2	.333	5	1	0	0	9	11	9	0	1	8	3	8.00	36	.333	.476	1	.000	-0	51	-4	—	-0.9
Total	3	8	31	.205	62	44	18-2	1	323	277	156	8	17	160	131	3.15	91	.242	.343	102-0-2	.176	-1	70	-11	—	-1.9

LEVERETT, DIXIE Gorham Vance; B3.29.1894 Georgetown TX; D2.20.1957 Beaverton OR; BR/TR/5´11˝/190; d5.6

YEAR	TM LG	W	L	PCT	G	GS	CG-SHO	SV-BS	IP	H	R	HR	HB	BB-IB	SO	ERA	AERA	OAV	OOB	AB-HR-SH	AVG	PB	SUP	APR	DL	PW
1922	Chi A	13	10	.565	33	27	16-4	2	223.2	224	95	11	3	79	60	3.34	122	.264	.329	83-0-1	.253	3	102	17	—	1.9
1923	Chi A	10	13	.435	38	24	9	3	192.2	212	108	6	6	64	64	4.06	97	.280	.341	60-0-6	.267	4	99	-5	—	-0.1
1924	Chi A	2	3	.400	21	11	4	0	99	123	72	2	3	41	29	5.82	71	.314	.383	32-0-2	.188	-1	110	-17	—	-0.9
1926	Chi A	1	1	.500	6	3	1	0	24	31	18	1	0	7	12	6.00	64	.316	.362	7-0-1	.143	-0	160	-6	—	-0.4
1929	Bos N	3	7	.300	24	12	3	1	97.2	135	81	5	5	30	28	6.36	74	.339	.393	32	.188	-0	93	-20	—	-1.6
Total	5	29	34	.460	122	77	33-4	6	637	725	374	25	17	221	193	4.51	92	.291	.353	214-0-10	.234	6	103	-31	—	-1.1

LEVERETTE, HOD Horace Wilbur "Levy"; B2.4.1889 Shreveport LA; D4.10.1958 St.Petersburg FL; BR/TR/6´0˝/180; d4.22

YEAR	TM LG	W	L	PCT	G	GS	CG-SHO	SV-BS	IP	H	R	HR	HB	BB-IB	SO	ERA	AERA	OAV	OOB	AB-HR-SH	AVG	PB	SUP	APR	DL	PW
1920	StL A	0	2	.000	3	2	0	0	10.1	9	6	1	0	12	0	5.23	75	.250	.438	3	.000	-1	71	-1	—	-0.2

LEVINE, AL Alan Brian; B5.22.1968 Park Ridge IL; BL/TR/6´4˝/(180–200); [ChiA91 11/306]; d6.22; Col Southern Illinois

YEAR	TM LG	W	L	PCT	G	GS	CG-SHO	SV-BS	IP	H	R	HR	HB	BB-IB	SO	ERA	AERA	OAV	OOB	AB-HR-SH	AVG	PB	SUP	APR	DL	PW
1996	Chi A	0	1	.000	16	0	0	0-1	18.1	22	14	1	1	7-1	12	5.40	88	.289	.353	0	ø	0	—	-2	0	-0.1
1997	Chi A	2	2	.500	25	0	0	0-1	27.1	35	22	4	2	16-1	22	6.91	64	.313	.402	0	ø	0	—	-7	0	-0.9
1998	Tex A	0	1	.000	30	0	0	0-0	58	68	30	6	0	16-1	19	4.50	109	.294	.336	0	ø	0	—	3	0	0.1
1999	Ana A	1	1	.500	50	1	0	0-1	85	76	40	13	3	29-2	37	3.39	144	.247	.311	0	ø	0	286	12	0	0.5
2000	Ana A	3	4	.429	51	5	0	2-0	95.1	98	44	10	2	49-5	42	3.87	133	.266	.352	0	ø	0	149	13	18	0.8
2001	Ana A	8	10	.444	64	1	0	2-4	75.2	71	25	7	2	28-4	40	2.38	196	.257	.325	0	ø	0	139	17	0	3.3
2002	Ana A	4	4	.500	52	0	0	5-2	63.2	61	35	8	2	34-3	40	4.24	106	.253	.342	0	ø	0	—	1	23	0.1
2003	TB A	3	5	.375	36	0	0	0-2	49.2	45	23	7	2	18-0	25	2.90	158	.243	.317	0	ø	0	—	7	0	0.9
	KC A	0	1	.000	18	0	0	1-1	21.1	22	6	2	1	11-1	5	2.53	190	.268	.362	0	ø	0	—	5	0	0.3
	Year	3	6	.333	54	0	0	1-3	71	67	29	9	3	29-1	30	2.79	167	.251	.331	0	ø	0	—	12	0	1.2
2004	Det A	3	4	.429	65	0	0	0-1	70.2	83	37	10	1	24-1	32	4.58	98	.295	.351	0	ø	0	—	0	0	0.0
2005	SF N	0	0	ø	9	0	0	0-0	10.1	16	11	2	0	4-1	4	9.58	44	.340	.392	2	.000	-0	—	-6	23	-0.3
Total	10	24	33	.421	416	7	0	10-13	575.1	597	287	70	16	236-20	278	3.96	120	.270	.341	2	.000	-0	176	43	64	4.7

YEAR	TM LG	W	L	PCT	G	GS	CG-SHO	SV-BS	IP	H	R	HR	HB	BB-IB	SO	ERA	AERA	OAV	OOB	AB-HR-SH	AVG	PB	SUP	APR	DL	PW
Levrault, Allen	Allen Harry; B8.15.1977 Fall River MA; BR/TR/6´3″/(230–250); [MilA96 13/373]; d6.13; Col CC of Rhode Island																									
2000	Mil N	0	1	.000	5	1	0	0-0	12	10	7	0	0	7-0	9	4.50	103	.238	.340	3	.000	-0	80	0	0	-0.1
2001	Mil N	6	10	.375	32	20	1	0-0	130.2	146	93	27	7	59-7	80	6.06	71	.281	.359	33-0-6	.061	-2	88	-25	0	-2.8
2003	Fla N	1	0	1.000	19	0	0	0-0	28	38	12	3	1	15-2	21	3.86	106	.333	.409	2	.000	-0	—	1	0	0.0
Total	3	7	11	.389	56	21	1	0-0	170.2	194	112	30	8	81-9	110	5.59	77	.287	.367	38-0-6	.053	-3	88	-24	0	-2.9
Levsen, Dutch	Emil Henry; B4.29.1898 Wyoming IA; D3.12.1972 St.Louis Park MN; BR/TR/6´0″/180; d9.28; Col Iowa St.																									
1923	Cle A	0	0	ø	3	0	0	0	4.1	4	0	0	0	0	1	0.00	ø	.267	.267	1	.000	-0	—	2	—	0.1
1924	Cle A	1	1	.500	4	1	1	0	16.1	22	8	0	0	4	3	4.41	97	.333	.371	5	.000	-1	237	1	—	0.0
1925	Cle A	1	2	.333	4	3	2	0	24.1	30	16	1	1	16	9	5.55	80	.313	.416	8-0-1	.250	0	70	-2	—	-0.2
1926	Cle A	16	13	.552	33	31	18-2	0	237.1	235	110	11	8	85	53	3.41	119	.261	.330	83-0-6	.205	-0	105	15	—	1.6
1927	Cle A	3	7	.300	25	13	2-1	0	80.1	96	54	1	2	37	15	5.49	77	.303	.379	25	.200	-1	84	-10	—	-1.0
1928	Cle A	0	3	.000	11	3	0	0	41.1	39	30	4	2	31	7	5.44	76	.258	.391	13	.000	-2	54	-6	—	-0.6
Total	6	21	26	.447	80	51	23-3	0	404	426	218	17	13	173	88	4.17	99	.276	.354	135-0-7	.178	-4	97	0	—	-0.1
Lewallyn, Dennis	Dennis Dale; B8.11.1953 Pensacola FL; BR/TR/6´4″/(175–200); [LAN72*S1/8]; d9.21; C1; Col Chipola (FL) JC																									
1975	LA N	0	0	ø	2	0	0	0-0	3	1	0	0	0	0-0	0	0.00	ø	.100	.100	0	ø	0	—	1	0	0.1
1976	LA N	1	1	.500	4	2	0	0-0	16.2	12	5	1	0	6-0	4	2.16	158	.207	.281	5	.000	-1	129	2	0	0.2
1977	LA N	3	1	.750	5	1	0	1-1	17	22	8	1	0	4-1	8	4.24	91	.306	.342	6-0-1	.000	-1	415	0	0	-0.2
1978	LA N	0	0	ø	1	0	0	0-0	2	2	0	0	0	0-0	0	0.00	ø	.250	.250	0	ø	0	—	1	0	0.0
1979	LA N	0	1	.000	7	0	0	0-0	12.1	19	8	0	1	5-3	1	5.11	71	.358	.417	2	.500	0	—	-2	0	-0.1
1980	Tex A	0	0	ø	4	0	0	0-1	5.2	7	5	0	0	4-1	1	7.94	49	.304	.407	0	ø	0	—	-2	0	-0.1
1981	Cle A	0	0	ø	7	0	0	0-0	13.1	16	8	1	0	2-0	11	5.40	68	.296	.316	0	ø	0	—	-2	0	-0.1
1982	Cle A	0	1	.000	4	0	0	0-0	10.1	13	8	3	0	1-0	3	6.97	60	.310	.311	0	ø	0	—	-3	0	-0.2
Total	8	4	4	.500	34	3	0	1-2	80.1	92	42	6	1	22-5	28	4.48	83	.287	.331	13-0-1	.077	-1	224	-5	0	-0.4
Lewandowski, Dan	Daniel William; B1.6.1928 Buffalo NY; D7.19.1996 Hamilton ON, Can.; BR/TR/6´0″/180; d9.22																									
1951	StL N	0	1	.000	2	0	0	0	1	3	1	0	0	1	1	9.00	44	.500	.571	0	ø	0	—	-1	0	-0.1
Lewis	B Brooklyn NY; d7.12																									
1890	Buf P	0	1	.000	1	1	0	0	3	13	20	3	0	7	1	60.00	7	.591	.690	5	.200	-0	238	-16	—	-1.4
Lewis, Colby	Colby Preston; B8.2.1979 Bakersfield CA; BR/TR/6´4″/(215–230); [TexA99 1/38]; d4.1; Col Bakersfield (CA) JC; [DL 2005 Det A 183]																									
2002	Tex A	1	3	.250	15	4	0	0-2	34.1	42	26	4	2	26-2	28	6.29	76	.304	.422	0	ø	0	82	-6	0	-0.5
2003	Tex A	10	9	.526	26	26	0	0-0	127	163	104	23	5	70-1	88	7.30	68	.317	.402	1	.000	-0	111	-27	0	-3.3
2004	Tex A	1	1	.500	3	3	0	0-0	15.1	13	7	1	1	13-0	11	4.11	120	.228	.380	0	ø	0	63	2	169	0.2
2006	Det A	0	0	ø	2	0	0	0-0	3	8	1	1	0	1-0	5	3.00	150	.471	.500	0	ø	0	—	1	0	0.0
Total	4	12	13	.480	46	33	0	0-2	179.2	226	138	29	8	110-3	132	6.76	73	.311	.406	1	.000	-0	104	-30	352	-3.6
Lewis, Ted	Edward Morgan "Parson"; B12.25.1872 Machynlleth, Wales; D5.23.1936 Durham NH; BR/TR/5´10.5″/158; d7.6; Col Williams																									
1896	Bos N	1	4	.200	6	5	4	0	41.2	37	32	2	0	27	12	3.24	140	.236	.348	18	.111	-2	91	3	—	0.1
1897	†Bos N	21	12	.636	38	34	30-2	1	290	316	177	11	10	125	65	3.85	116	.275	.351	113-0-7	.248	-2	112	17	—	1.1
1898	Bos N	26	8	**.765**	41	33	29-1	2	313.1	267	131	9	9	109	72	2.90	127	.229	.300	131-0-5	.282	4*	130	30	—	3.2
1899	Bos N	17	11	.607	29	25	23-2	0	234.2	245	119	10	8	73	60	3.49	119	.269	.328	96-0-2	.260	0	93	16	—	1.4
1900	Bos N	13	12	.520	30	22	19-1	0	209	215	122	11	4	86	66	4.13	100	.265	.339	73-0-2	.137	-4	81	5	—	0.0
1901	Bos A	16	17	.485	39	34	31-1	1	316.1	299	172	14	8	91	103	3.53	100	.247	.304	121-0-1	.174	-2	105	4	—	0.0
Total	6	94	64	.595	183	153	136-7	4	1405	1379	753	57	39	511	378	3.53	113	.255	.324	552-0-17	.223	-5	106	75	—	5.8
Lewis, Jim	James Martin; B10.12.1955 Miami FL; BR/TR/6´3″/190; d9.12; Col South Carolina																									
1979	Sea A	0	0	ø	2	0	0	0-0	2.1	10	7	1	0	1-0	0	15.43	28	.625	.647	0	ø	0	—	-4	0	-0.2
1982	NY A	0	0	ø	1	0	0	0-0	0.2	3	7	0	0	3-0	0	54.00	7	.500	.667	0	ø	0	—	-5	0	-0.2
1983	Min A	0	0	ø	6	0	0	0-0	18	24	13	5	1	7-0	8	6.50	66	.324	.390	0	ø	0	—	-4	0	-0.2
1985	Sea A	0	1	.000	2	1	0	0-0	4.2	8	4	1	2	1-0	1	7.71	55	.421	.500	0	ø	0	65	-2	0	-0.3
Total	4	0	1	.000	11	1	0	0-0	25.2	45	31	7	3	12-0	9	8.77	49	.391	.462	0	ø	0	65	-15	0	-0.9
Lewis, Jim	James Steven; B7.20.1964 Jackson MI; BR/TR/6´2″/200; [SDN85*5/125]; d8.9; Col Citrus (CA) JC																									
1991	SD N	0	0	ø	12	0	0	0-0	13	14	7	2	0	11-2	10	4.15	92	.275	.403	2	.000	-0	—	-1	0	0.0
Lewis, Richie	Richie Todd; B1.25.1966 Muncie IN; BR/TR/5´10″/175; [MonN87 2/44]; d7.31; Col Florida St.																									
1992	Bal A	1	1	.500	2	2	0	0-0	6.2	13	8	1	0	7-0	4	10.80	38	.406	.500	0	ø	0	79	-5	0	-0.8
1993	Fla N	6	3	.667	57	0	0	0-2	77.1	68	37	7	1	43-6	65	3.26	134	.239	.336	2-0-1	.500	0	—	6	0	0.7
1994	Fla N	1	4	.200	45	0	0	0-0	54	62	44	7	1	38-9	45	5.67	79	.284	.391	5	.000	-0	—	-9	0	-0.8
1995	Fla N	0	1	.000	21	1	0	0-0	36	30	15	9	1	15-5	32	3.75	115	.224	.307	1	.000	0	63	3	0	0.1
1996	Det A	4	6	.400	72	0	0	2-4	90.1	78	45	9	4	65-9	78	4.18	122	.238	.361	1	.000	-0	—	9	20	0.8
1997	Oak A	2	0	1.000	14	0	0	0-0	18.2	24	21	7	1	15-0	12	9.64	48	.316	.430	0	ø	0	—	-10	0	-0.9
	Cin N	0	0	ø	4	0	0	0-0	5.2	4	5	3	0	3-0	4	6.35	67	.200	.304	1	1.000	0	—	-2	0	0.0
1998	Bal A	0	0	ø	2	1	0	0-0	4.2	8	8	2	0	5-0	4	15.43	30	.421	.520	0	ø	0	204	-6	0	-0.3
Total	7	14	15	.483	217	4	0	2-6	293.1	287	183	45	8	191-29	244	4.88	95	.258	.366	10-0-1	.200	1	99	-14	20	-1.2
Lewis, Scott	Scott Allen; B12.5.1965 Grants Pass OR; BR/TR/6´3″/(178–190); [CalA88 11/273]; d9.25; Col Nevada–Las Vegas																									
1990	Cal A	1	1	.500	2	2	1	0-0	16.1	10	4	2	0	2-0	9	2.20	174	.172	.200	0	ø	0	107	3	0	0.4
1991	Cal A	3	5	.375	16	11	0	0-0	60.1	81	43	9	2	21-0	37	6.27	66	.316	.373	0	ø	0	121	-13	0	-1.5
1992	Cal A	4	0	1.000	21	2	0	0-0	38.1	36	18	3	2	14-1	18	3.99	101	.255	.325	0	ø	0	136	0	0	0.1
1993	Cal A	1	2	.333	15	4	0	0-0	32	37	16	3	2	12-1	10	4.22	108	.311	.364	0	ø	0	117	1	19	0.1
1994	Cal A	0	1	.000	20	0	0	0-0	31	46	23	5	2	10-2	10	6.10	81	.359	.414	0	ø	0	—	-4	53	-0.2
Total	5	9	9	.500	74	19	1	0-0	178	210	104	22	8	59-4	84	5.01	86	.299	.356	0	ø	0	117	-13	72	-1.1
Lewis, Bert	William Burton; B10.3.1895 Tonawanda NY; D3.24.1950 Tonawanda NY; BR/TR/6´2″/176; d4.19																									
1924	Phi N	0	0	ø	12	0	0	0	18	23	12	1	1	7	3	6.00	74	.315	.383	5	.000	-1	—	-2	—	-0.2
Ley, Terry	Terrence Richard; B2.21.1947 Portland OR; BL/TL/6´0″/180; [NYA67*S3/60]; d8.20; Col Oregon																									
1971	NY A	0	0	ø	6	0	0	0-0	9	9	9	1	2	9-2	7	5.00	66	.257	.426	0	ø	0	—	-3	0	-0.2
Libke, Al	Albert Walter; B9.12.1918 Tacoma WA; D3.7.2003 Wenatchee WA; BL/TR/6´4″/215; d4.19; ▲																									
1945	Cin N	0	0	ø	4	0	0	0	4.1	3	0	0	0	3	2	0.00	ø	.200	.333	449-4-4	.283	1*	—	2	0	0.1
1946	Cin N	0	0	ø	1	1	0	0	5	4	2	0	0	3	2	3.60	93	.235	.350	431-5-4	.253	0*	77	0	0	0.0
Total	2	0	0	ø	5	1	0	0	9.1	7	2	0	0	6	4	1.93	183	.219	.342	880-9-8	.268	2	77	2	0	0.1
Liddle, Don	Donald Eugene; B5.25.1925 Mt.Carmel IL; D6.5.2000 Mt.Carmel IL; BL/TL/5´10″/(165–170); d4.17																									
1953	Mil N	7	6	.538	31	15	4	2	128.2	119	54	6	2	55	63	3.08	127	.248	.328	34-0-4	.088	-2	90	12	0	0.9
1954	†NY N	9	4	.692	28	19	4-3	0	126.2	100	48	5	3	55	44	3.06	132	.223	.308	37-0-2	.189	2*	100	15	0	1.5
1955	NY N	10	4	.714	33	13	4	1	106.1	97	54	18	4	61-7	56	4.23	95	.246	.351	27-0-2	.185	1	131	-1	0	0.0
1956	NY N	1	2	.333	11	5	1	1	41.1	45	22	5	1	14-3	21	3.92	97	.278	.333	12-0-3	.167	-0	112	-1	0	-0.1
	StL N	1	2	.333	14	2	0	0	24.2	36	25	8	0	18-5	14	8.39	45	.353	.446	2	.000	-0*	47	-12	0	-1.3
	Year	2	4	.333	25	7	1	1	66	81	47	13	1	32-8	35	5.59	68	.307	.379	14-0-3	.143	-0	93	-14	0	-1.4
Total	4	28	18	.609	117	54	13-3	4	427.2	397	203	42	10	203-15	198	3.75	106	.250	.337	112-0-11	.152	1	104	13	0	1.0
Lidge, Brad	Bradley Thomas; B12.23.1976 Sacramento CA; BR/TR/6´5″/(200–210); [HouN98 1/17]; d4.26; Col Notre Dame																									
2002	Hou N	1	0	1.000	6	1	0	0-0	8.2	12	6	0	2	9-1	12	6.23	69	.333	.489	2	1.000	1	64	-2	0	0.0
2003	Hou N	6	3	.667	78	0	0	1-5	85	60	36	6	5	42-7	97	3.60	123	.202	.308	4	.000	-0	—	8	0	0.6
2004	†Hou N	6	5	.545	80	0	0	29-4	94.2	57	21	8	6	30-5	157	1.90	230	.174	.254	1	.000	-0	—	**26**	0	4.0
2005	†Hou N★	4	4	.500	70	0	0	42-4	70.2	58	21	5	3	23-1	103	2.29	184	.223	.293	0	ø	0	—	14	0	2.9
2006	Hou N	1	5	.167	78	0	0	32-6	75	69	47	10	6	36-4	104	5.28	85	.238	.332	0	ø	0	—	-6	0	-0.9
Total	5	18	17	.514	312	1	0	104-19	334	256	131	29	22	140-18	473	3.29	133	.211	.303	7	.286	1	64	40	0	6.6

YEAR	TM LG	W	L	PCT	G	GS	CG-SHO	SV-BS	IP	H	R	HR	HB	BB-IB	SO	ERA	AERA	OAV	OOB	AB-HR-SH	AVG	PB	SUP	APR	DL	PW
LIDLE, CORY Cory Fulton; B3.22.1972 Hollywood CA; D10.11.2006 New York NY; BR/TR/5´11˝/(180–190); d5.8; [DL 1998 Ari N 181]																										
1997	NY N	7	2	.778	54	2	0	2-1	81.2	86	38	7	3	20-4	54	3.53	114	.274	.320	5	.000	-0	196	3	0	0.3
1999	TB A	1	0	1.000	5	1	0	0-0	5	8	4	0	0	2-0	4	7.20	69	.364	.417	0	ø	0	113	-1	166	-0.2
2000	TB A	4	6	.400	31	11	0	0-0	96.2	114	61	13	3	29-3	62	5.03	97	.294	.347	2	.000	-0	84	-2	0	-0.2
2001	†Oak A	13	6	.684	29	29	1	0-0	188	170	84	23	10	47-7	118	3.59	127	.242	.299	2	.000	-0	107	19	0	1.7
2002	†Oak A	8	10	.444	31	30	2-2	0-0	192	191	90	17	6	39-3	111	3.89	115	.258	.298	1-0-1	.000	-0	103	13	17	1.3
2003	Tor A	12	15	.444	31	31	2	0-0	192.2	216	133	24	5	60-3	112	5.75	83	.282	.337	6	.333	0	96	-19	20	-2.1
2004	Cin N	7	10	.412	24	24	3-1	0-0	149	170	95	24	5	44-4	93	5.32	81	.288	.340	42-0-4	.143	1	85	-17	0	-1.4
	Phi N	5	2	.714	10	10	2-2	0-0	62.1	54	28	3	5	17-1	33	3.90	114	.236	.300	20-1-4	.150	1	120	4	0	0.5
	Year	12	12	.500	34	34	5-**3**	0-0	211.1	224	123	27	10	61-5	126	4.90	89	.273	.329	62-1-8	.145	2	96	-10	0	-0.9
2005	Phi N	13	11	.542	31	31	1	0-0	184.2	210	105	18	6	40-5	121	4.53	96	.289	.328	58-0-8	.138	-2	111	-6	15	-0.8
2006	Phi N	8	7	.533	21	21	0	0-0	125.1	132	74	19	8	39-3	98	4.74	99	.271	.333	34-0-4	.088	-1	103	-2	0	-0.2
	†NY A	4	3	.571	10	9	0	0-0	45.1	49	26	11	3	19-1	32	5.16	88	.272	.351	0	ø	0	111	-2	0	-0.2
Total	9	82	72	.532	277	199	11-5	2-1	1322.2	1400	738	159	54	356-34	838	4.57	99	.272	.324	170-1-21	.129	-1	103	-10	399	-1.3
LIEBER, DUTCH Charles Edwin; B2.1.1910 Alameda CA; D12.31.1961 Los Angeles CA; BR/TR/6´0.5˝/180; d4.18																										
1935	Phi A	1	1	.500	18	1	0	2	46.2	45	18	1	1	19	14	3.09	147	.263	.340	14	.143	-1*	134	8	—	0.3
1936	Phi A	0	1	.000	3	0	0	0	11.2	17	11	0	0	6	1	7.71	66	.362	.434	3	.000	-0	—	-3	—	-0.2
Total	2	1	2	.333	21	1	0	2	58.1	62	29	1	1	25	15	4.01	116	.284	.361	17	.118	-2	134	5	—	0.1
LIEBER, JON Jonathan Ray; B4.2.1970 Council Bluffs IA; BL/TR/6´2˝/(220–230); [KCA92 2/44]; d5.15; Col South Alabama; [DL 2003 NY A 183]																										
1994	Pit N	6	7	.462	17	17	1	0-0	108.2	116	62	12	1	25-3	71	3.73	117	.271	.311	39-0-2	.103	-2	96	2	0	0.0
1995	Pit N	4	7	.364	21	12	0	0-1	72.2	103	56	7	4	14-0	45	6.32	69	.346	.376	21	.048	-2	95	-15	0	-2.1
1996	Pit N	9	5	.643	51	15	0	1-3	142	156	70	19	3	28-2	94	3.99	110	.279	.315	36-0-3	.194	2	122	6	0	0.8
1997	Pit N	11	14	.440	33	32	1	0-0	188.1	193	102	23	1	51-8	160	4.49	95	.263	.309	58-0-2	.121	-0	97	-3	0	-0.4
1998	Pit N	8	14	.364	29	28	2	1-0	171	182	93	23	3	40-4	138	4.11	104	.269	.311	48-0-7	.167	0	85	1	24	0.2
1999	Chi N	10	11	.476	31	31	3-1	0-0	203.1	226	107	28	1	46-6	186	4.07	112	.279	.315	58-0-7	.121	-1	101	9	17	0.7
2000	Chi N	12	11	.522	35	**35**	6-1	0-0	**251**	248	130	36	10	54-3	192	4.41	104	.256	.301	82-0-10	.220	3*	96	5	0	0.8
2001	Chi N★	20	6	.769	34	34	5-1	0-0	232.1	226	104	25	7	41-4	148	3.80	110	.255	.290	76-0-9	.158	0*	120	12	0	1.3
2002	Chi N	6	8	.429	21	21	3	0-0	141	153	64	15	1	12-2	87	3.70	110	.277	.290	43-0-4	.163	-0	85	5	59	0.4
2004	†NY A	14	8	.636	27	27	0	0-0	176.2	216	95	20	2	18-2	102	4.33	106	.300	.316	3	.333	0	124	4	32	0.3
2005	Phi N	17	13	.567	35	**35**	1	0-0	218.1	223	107	33	5	41-6	149	4.20	103	.263	.299	73-0-3	.096	-3*	96	5	0	0.2
2006	Phi N	9	11	.450	27	27	2-1	0-0	168	196	100	27	6	24-3	100	4.93	95	.291	.319	53-0-6	.094	-2*	98	-4	38	-0.7
Total	12	126	115	.523	361	314	24-4	2-4	2073.1	2238	1090	268	44	394-43	1472	4.26	103	.274	.309	590-0-53	.142	-4	101	27	353	1.5
LIEBHARDT, GLENN Glenn Ignatius "Sandy"; B7.31.1910 Cleveland OH; D3.14.1992 Winston–Salem NC; BR/TR/5´10.5˝/170; d4.22; f–Glenn																										
1930	Phi A	0	1	.000	5	0	0	0	9	14	12	2	0	8	2	11.00	42	.359	.468	2	.000	-0	—	-6	—	-0.6
1936	StL A	0	0	ø	24	0	0	0	55.1	98	58	4	2	27	20	8.78	61	.375	.438	11	.000	-2	—	-18	—	-1.0
1938	StL A	0	0	ø	2	0	0	0	3	4	2	1	0	0	1	6.00	83	.308	.308	0	ø	0	—	0	—	0.0
Total	3	0	1	.000	31	0	0	0	67.1	116	72	7	2	35	23	8.96	59	.371	.437	13	.000	-2	—	-24	—	-1.6
LIEBHARDT, GLENN Glenn John; B3.10.1883 Milton IN; D7.13.1956 Cleveland OH; BR/TR/5´10˝/175; d10.2; s–Glenn																										
1906	Cle A	2	0	1.000	2	2	2	0	18	13	4	0	0	1	9	1.50	175	.206	.219	8	.000	-1	192	2	—	0.2
1907	Cle A	18	14	.563	38	34	27-4	1	280.1	254	100	1	10	85	110	2.05	122	.244	.307	87-0-2	.161	-1	90	13	—	1.4
1908	Cle A	15	16	.484	38	26	19-3	0	262	222	93	2	3	81	146	2.20	109	.235	.297	80-0-10	.175	0	75	5	—	0.7
1909	Cle A	1	5	.167	12	4	1	1	52.1	54	28	0	1	16	15	2.92	87	.314	.376	15-0-1	.000	-2	76	-3	—	-0.6
Total	4	36	35	.507	90	66	49-7	2	612.2	543	225	3	14	183	280	2.17	113	.244	.306	190-0-13	.147	-4	86	17	—	1.7
LIGTENBERG, KERRY Kerry Dale; B5.11.1971 Rapid City SD; BR/TR/6´2˝/(205–220); d8.12; Col Minnesota; [DL 1999 Atl N 182]																										
1997	†Atl N	1	0	1.000	15	0	0	1-0	15	12	5	4	0	4-2	19	3.00	140	.211	.262	0	ø	0	—	2	0	0.1
1998	†Atl N	3	2	.600	75	0	0	30-4	73	51	24	6	0	24-1	79	2.71	154	.193	.260	0	ø	0	—	12	0	1.5
2000	†Atl N	2	3	.400	59	0	0	12-2	52.1	43	21	7	0	24-5	51	3.61	125	.226	.312	0	ø	0	—	6	0	0.7
2001	†Atl N	3	3	.500	53	0	0	1-1	59.2	50	22	4	0	30-8	56	3.02	143	.226	.316	0	ø	0	—	9	0	0.7
2002	†Atl N	3	4	.429	52	0	0	0-0	66.2	52	23	6	0	33-3	51	2.97	136	.213	.306	0	ø	0	—	9	0	0.8
2003	Bal A	4	2	.667	68	0	0	1-3	59.1	60	23	9	2	14-3	47	3.34	138	.263	.310	0	ø	0	—	8	0	0.7
2004	Tor A	1	6	.143	57	0	0	3-2	55	73	40	6	2	25-7	49	6.38	77	.313	.385	0	ø	0	—	-8	15	-1.0
2005	Ari N	0	0	ø	7	0	0	0-0	9.2	16	15	4	0	4-0	5	13.97	32	.364	.417	1	.000	-0	—	-9	0	-0.5
Total	8	17	20	.459	386	0	0	48-12	390.2	357	173	46	4	158-29	357	3.82	115	.241	.315	1	.000	-0	—	29	197	3.0
LILLARD, GENE Robert Eugene; B11.12.1913 Santa Barbara CA; D4.12.1991 Goleta CA; BR/TR/5´10.5˝/178; d5.8.1936; b–Bill; ▲																										
1939	Chi N	3	5	.375	20	7	2	0	55	68	48	2	3	36	31	6.55	60	.309	.413	10	.100	1*	92	-17	—	-2.0
1940	StL N	0	1	.000	2	1	0	0	4.2	8	7	1	1	4	2	13.50	30	.364	.481	0	ø	0	65	-4	—	-0.7
Total	2	3	6	.333	22	8	2	0	59.2	76	55	3	4	40	33	7.09	56	.314	.420	10	.100	1	89	-21	—	-2.7
LILLIE, JIM James J. "Grasshopper" (b James J. Lilly); B7.27.1861 New Haven CT; D11.9.1890 Kansas City MO; BR; d5.17; ▲																										
1883	Buf N	0	1	.000	3	0	0	0	12	16	12	0	—	2	4	3.00	106	.302	.327	201-1	.234	0*	—	-1	—	-0.1
1884	Buf N	0	1	.000	2	1	0	0	13	22	24	0	—	5	4	6.23	51	.324	.370	471-3	.223	-0*	84	-6	—	-0.3
1886	KC N	0	0	ø	1	0	0	0	6	8	5	0	—	1	0	4.50	84	.348	.375	416	.175	-0*	—	-1	—	0.0
Total	3	0	2	.000	6	1	0	0	31	46	41	0	—	8	8	4.65	71	.319	.355	1088-4	.207	-0	84	-8	—	-0.4
LILLIQUIST, DEREK Derek Jansen; B2.20.1966 Winter Park FL; BL/TL/6´0˝/(195–214); [AtlN87 1/6]; d4.13; Col Georgia																										
1989	Atl N	8	10	.444	32	30	0	0-1	165.2	202	87	16	2	34-5	79	3.97	92	.301	.335	63-0-3	.190	0*	85	-7	0	-0.7
1990	Atl N	2	8	.200	12	11	0	0-0	61.2	75	45	10	1	19-4	34	6.28	64	.301	.348	23-2-0	.348	4*	71	-13	0	-1.5
	SD N	3	3	.500	16	7	1-1	0-0	60.1	61	29	6	2	23-1	29	4.33	89	.266	.337	20-0-2	.150	-0	101	-2	0	-0.2
	Year	5	11	.313	28	18	1-1	0-0	122	136	74	16	3	42-5	63	5.31	74	.285	.343	43-2-2	.256	4	83	-15	0	-1.7
1991	SD N	0	2	.000	6	2	0	0-0	14.1	25	14	3	0	4-1	7	8.79	43	.379	.414	2	.000	-0	106	-7	0	-0.8
1992	Cle A	5	3	.625	71	0	0	6-5	61.2	39	13	5	2	18-6	47	1.75	225	.186	.252	0	ø	0	—	15	0	2.1
1993	Cle A	4	4	.500	56	2	0	10-3	64	64	20	5	1	19-5	40	2.25	195	.263	.317	0	ø	0	126	14	0	1.9
1994	Cle A	1	3	.250	36	0	0	1-2	29.1	34	17	6	1	8-1	15	4.91	97	.304	.347	0	ø	0	—	0	0	0.0
1995	Bos A	2	1	.667	28	0	0	0-3	23	27	17	7	0	9-2	9	6.26	78	.303	.356	0	ø	0	—	-3	0	-0.4
1996	Cin N	0	0	ø	5	0	0	0-1	3.2	5	3	1	0	0-0	1	7.36	58	.357	.357	0	ø	0	—	-1	0	0.0
Total	8	25	34	.424	262	52	1-1	17-15	483.2	532	245	59	9	134-25	261	4.13	97	.283	.330	108-2-5	.213	4	83	-4	0	0.4
LILLY, TED Theodore Roosevelt; B1.4.1976 Lomita CA; BL/TL/6´0˝/(180–190); [LAN96 23/688]; d5.14; Col Fresno (CA) City																										
1999	Mon N	0	1	.000	9	3	0	0-0	23.2	30	20	7	3	9-0	28	7.61	59	.309	.382	5-0-1	.200	0	62	-7	0	-0.3
2000	NY A	0	0	ø	7	0	0	0-0	8	8	6	1	0	5-0	11	5.63	85	.235	.333	0	ø	0	—	-1	49	0.0
2001	NY A	5	6	.455	26	21	0	0-0	120.2	126	81	20	7	51-1	112	5.37	83	.267	.344	1-0-2	.000	-0	106	-14	0	-1.0
2002	NY A	3	6	.333	16	11	2-1	0-0	76.2	57	31	10	5	24-3	59	3.40	127	.202	.274	3	.000	-0	54	9	0	0.9
	†Oak A	2	1	.667	6	5	0	0-0	23.1	23	12	5	1	7-0	18	4.63	97	.253	.313	0	ø	0	79	0	49	0.0
	Year	5	7	.417	22	16	2-1	0-0	100	80	43	15	6	31-3	77	3.69	118	.214	.283	3	.000	-0	62	9	0	0.9
2003	†Oak A	12	10	.545	32	31	0	0-0	178.1	179	92	24	5	58-3	147	4.34	106	.255	.314	5	.000	-1	87	6	0	0.6
2004	Tor A★	12	10	.545	32	32	2-1	0-0	197.1	171	92	26	6	89-2	168	4.06	121	.230	.316	3-0-1	.000	-0	83	18	0	1.6
2005	Tor A	10	11	.476	25	25	0	0-0	126.1	135	79	23	3	58-1	96	5.56	83	.272	.348	3	.000	-0	104	-11	50	-1.5
2006	Tor A	15	13	.536	32	32	0	0-0	181.2	179	98	28	4	81-6	160	4.31	110	.254	.333	3	.000	-0	99	7	0	0.9
Total	8	59	58	.504	185	160	4-2	0-0	936	908	511	144	34	382-16	799	4.60	101	.250	.326	23-0-4	.043	-2	91	7	148	1.2
LIMA, JOSE Jose Desiderio Rodriguez (b Jose Desiderio Rodriguez (Lima)); B9.30.1972 Santiago, D.R.; BR/TR/6´2˝/(170–210); d4.20																										
1994	Det A	0	1	.000	3	1	0	0-0	6.2	11	10	2	0	3-1	7	13.50	36	.355	.412	0	ø	0	112	-6	0	-0.6
1995	Det A	3	9	.250	15	15	0	0-0	73.2	85	52	10	4	18-4	37	6.11	79	.288	.336	0	ø	0	70	-9	0	-1.3
1996	Det A	5	6	.455	39	4	0	3-4	72.2	87	48	13	5	22-4	59	5.70	89	.296	.352	0	ø	0	46	-4	0	-0.4
1997	†Hou N	1	6	.143	52	1	0	2-0	75	79	45	9	5	16-2	63	5.28	76	.271	.317	3-0-2	.000	-0	92	-9	0	-0.9
1998	Hou N	16	8	.667	33	33	3-1	0-0	233.1	229	100	34	7	32-1	169	3.70	109	.256	.285	79-0-9	.139	-1	127	11	0	1.0
1999	†Hou N★	21	10	.677	35	**35**	3	0-0	246.1	256	108	30	2	44-2	187	3.58	124	.265	.296	75-0-13	.080	-4*	101	23	0	2.0
2000	Hou N	7	16	.304	33	33	0	0-0	196.1	251	152	48	2	68-3	124	6.65	74	.313	.364	60-0-8	.167	-1	98	-33	0	-3.2
2001	Hou N	1	2	.333	14	9	0	0-0	53	77	48	12	5	16-1	41	7.30	63	.350	.400	16-0-1	.000	-2	107	-16	0	-0.9

YEAR	TM LG	W	L	PCT	G	GS	CG-SHO	SV-BS	IP	H	R	HR	HB	BB-IB	SO	ERA	AERA	OAV	OOB	AB-HR-SH	AVG	PB	SUP	APR	DL	PW
	Det A	5	10	.333	18	18	2	0-0	112.2	120	66	23	4	22-2	43	4.71	94	.274	.311	1	.000	-0	80	-4	0	-0.6
2002	Det A	4	6	.400	20	12	0	0-0	68.1	86	60	12	2	21-0	33	7.77	56	.314	.360	0	ø	0	93	-24	0	-2.8
2003	KC A	8	3	.727	14	14	0	0-0	73.1	80	40	7	5	26-0	32	4.91	98	.280	.347	2-0-1	.500	0	104	1	41	0.1
2004	†LA N	13	5	.722	36	24	0	0-0	170.1	178	81	33	1	34-6	93	4.07	102	.271	.307	48-0-8	.188	0*	98	2	0	0.2
2005	KC A	5	16	.238	32	32	1	0-0	168.2	219	140	31	9	61-1	80	6.99	63	.314	.373	3-0-1	.333	0	88	-49	0	-4.9
2006	NY N	0	4	.000	4	4	0	0-0	17.1	25	22	3	2	10-0	12	9.87	45	.329	.416	5-0-1	.000	-1	79	-11	0	-1.8
Total	13	89	102	.466	348	235	9-1	5-4	1567.2	1783	972	267	53	393-27	980	5.26	84	.287	.331	292-0-44	.130	-7	97	-128	41	-14.1
LINCOLN, EZRA	Ezra Perry; B11.17.1868 Raynham MA; D5.7.1951 Taunton MA; BL/TL/5´11˝/160; d5.2																									
1890	Cle N	3	11	.214	15	15	13	0	118	157	102	1	1	53	22	4.42	81	.310	.376	51	.157	-3	73	-15	—	-1.6
	Syr AA	0	3	.000	3	3	2	0	20	33	27	1	1	4	6	10.35	34	.359	.392	8	.000	-1	32	-15	—	-1.5
Total	1	3	14	.176	18	18	15	0	138	190	129	2	2	57	28	5.28	68	.317	.378	59	.136	-4	66	-30	—	-3.1
LINCOLN, MIKE	Michael George; B4.10.1975 Carmichael CA; BR/TR/6´2˝/(210–215); [MinA96 13/367]; d4.7; Col Tennessee; [DL 2005 StL N 183]																									
1999	Min A	3	10	.231	18	15	0	0-0	76.1	102	59	11	1	26-0	27	6.84	76	.321	.368	1	.000	-0	82	-12	0	-1.6
2000	Min A	0	3	.000	8	4	0	0-0	20.2	36	25	10	2	13-0	15	10.89	48	.383	.468	0	ø	0	107	-11	70	-1.3
2001	Pit N	2	1	.667	31	0	0	0-2	40.1	34	16	3	4	11-0	24	2.68	167	.225	.293	4-0-1	.250	0	—	6	15	0.5
2002	Pit N	2	4	.333	55	0	0	0-3	72.1	80	28	7	0	27-8	50	3.11	135	.290	.349	5	.000	-1	—	8	0	0.6
2003	Pit N	3	4	.429	36	0	0	5-3	36.1	38	22	5	1	13-0	28	5.20	83	.277	.342	0	ø	0	—	-3	93	-0.7
2004	StL N	3	2	.600	13	0	0	0-2	17.1	10	12	1	1	6-0	14	5.19	82	.164	.243	0	ø	0	—	-2	153	-0.5
Total	6	13	24	.351	161	19	0	5-10	263.1	300	162	37	9	96-8	158	5.16	90	.289	.350	10-0-1	.100	-1	98	-14	514	-3.0
LINDAMAN, VIVE	Vivan Alexander; B10.28.1877 Charles City IA; D2.13.1927 Charles City IA; BR/TR/6´1˝/200; d4.14																									
1906	Bos N	12	23	.343	39	36	32-2	0	307.1	303	132	4	11	90	115	2.43	111	.264	.324	106-0-3	.132	-2	73	3	—	0.1
1907	Bos N	11	15	.423	34	28	24-2	1	260	252	130	10	15	108	90	3.63	70	.265	.349	90-0-2	.122	-2	102	-28	—	-3.0
1908	Bos N	12	16	.429	43	30	21-2	1	270.2	246	112	7	10	70	68	2.36	102	.249	.306	85-0-4	.176	0	96	-3	—	-0.4
1909	Bos N	1	6	.143	15	6	6-1	0	66	75	44	1	1	28	13	4.64	61	.299	.371	22	.273	1	29	-11	—	-1.1
Total	4	36	60	.375	131	100	83-7	2	904	876	418	22	37	296	286	2.92	88	.263	.329	303-0-9	.152	-3	85	-39	—	-4.4
LINDBLAD, PAUL	Paul Aaron; B8.9.1941 Chanute KS; D1.1.2006 Arlington TX; BL/TL/6´1˝/(185–195); d9.15																									
1965	KC A	0	1	.000	4	0	0	0	7.1	12	9	3	1	0-0	12	11.05	32	.353	.371	1	.000	-0	—	-6	0	-0.7
1966	KC A	5	10	.333	38	14	0	1	121	138	63	14	3	37-10	69	4.17	82	.292	.347	34-0-1	.147	0	89	-10	0	-1.1
1967	KC A	5	8	.385	46	10	1-1	6	115.2	106	59	15	6	35-9	83	3.58	89	.241	.304	34-1-1	.206	2*	118	-8	0	-0.8
1968	Oak A	4	3	.571	47	1	0	2	56.1	51	19	6	0	14-4	42	2.40	118	.237	.281	8-0-1	.375	1	0	2	0	0.5
1969	Oak A	9	6	.600	60	0	0	9-2	78.1	72	37	8	2	33-8	64	4.14	83	.240	.319	12	.333	1	—	-5	0	-0.9
1970	Oak A	8	2	.800	62	0	0	3-0	63.1	52	23	7	0	28-7	42	2.70	131	.222	.305	6	.000	-1	—	5	0	0.8
1971	Oak A	1	0	1.000	8	0	0	0-2	16	18	7	1	1	2-1	4	3.94	84	.295	.328	3	.333	0	—	-1	0	0.0
	Was A	6	4	.600	43	0	0	8-5	83.2	58	25	6	2	29-6	50	2.58	131	.196	.272	19	.158	0	—	9	0	1.3
	Year	7	4	.636	51	0	0	8-7	99.2	76	32	7	3	31-7	54	2.80	120	.213	.281	22	.182	1	—	7	0	1.3
1972	Tex A	5	8	.385	**66**	0	0	9-5	99.2	95	31	7	0	29-6	51	2.62	116	.257	.309	15-0-2	.200	0	—	6	0	0.9
1973	†Oak A	1	5	.167	36	3	0	2-0	78	89	38	8	3	28-2	33	3.69	96	.292	.354	0	ø	0	25	-2	0	-0.2
1974	Oak A	4	4	.500	45	2	0	6-3	100.2	85	30	4	2	30-11	46	2.06	163	.231	.288	0	ø	0	92	14	0	1.3
1975	†Oak A	9	1	.900	68	0	0	7-1	122.1	105	44	6	0	43-10	58	2.72	134	.237	.300	1	.000	-0	—	12	0	1.2
1976	Oak A	6	5	.545	65	0	0	5-5	114.2	111	50	5	3	24-5	37	3.06	110	.253	.292	0	ø	0	—	1	0	0.2
1977	Tex A	4	5	.444	42	1	0	4-1	98.2	103	50	16	1	29-2	46	4.20	97	.270	.322	0	ø	0	44	0	0	0.0
1978	Tex A	1	1	.500	18	0	0	2-2	39.2	41	16	2	2	15-7	25	3.63	103	.279	.349	0	ø	0	—	2	19	0.1
	†NY A	0	0	ø	7	1	0	0-0	18.1	21	9	4	0	8-0	9	4.42	83	.284	.354	0	ø	0	98	-1	0	0.0
	Year	1	1	.500	25	1	0	2-2	58	62	25	6	2	23-7	34	3.88	96	.281	.351	0	ø	0	97	1	0	0.1
Total	14	68	63	.519	655	32	1-1	64-26	1213.2	1157	510	112	26	384-88	671	3.29	104	.253	.312	133-1-5	.195	4	86	18	19	2.6
LINDE, LYMAN	Lyman Gilbert; B9.30.1920 Rolling Prairie WI; D10.24.1995 Beaver Dam WI; BR/TR/5´11˝/185; d9.11; Col Wisconsin–Madison																									
1947	Cle A	0	0	ø	1	0	0	0	0.2	3	2	0	0	1	0	27.00	13	.600	.667	0	ø	0	—	-2	0	-0.1
1948	Cle A	0	0	ø	3	0	0	0	10	9	6	1	0	4	0	5.40	75	.243	.317	2	.000	-0	—	-1	0	-0.1
Total	2	0	0	ø	4	0	0	0	10.2	12	8	1	0	5	0	6.75	60	.286	.362	2	.000	-0	—	-3	0	-0.2
LINDELL, JOHNNY	John Harlan; B8.30.1916 Greeley CO; D8.27.1985 Newport Beach CA; BR/TR/6´4.5˝/(217–220); d4.18.1941; Mil 1945; ▲																									
1942	NY A	2	1	.667	23	2	0	1	52.2	52	25	3	1	22	28	3.76	92	.254	.329	24	.250	1*	99	-2	0	0.0
1953	Pit N	5	16	.238	27	23	13-1	0	175.2	173	106	17	6	116	102	4.71	95	.262	.377	91-4-0	.286	6*	76	-6	0	1.0
	Phi N	1	1	.500	5	3	2	0	23.1	22	16	0	0	23	16	4.24	99	.259	.417	18	.389	2*	85	-2	0	0.1
	Year	6	17	.261	32	26	15-1	0	199	195	122	17	6	139	118	4.66	95	.261	.382	109-4-0	.303	8	77	-9	0	1.1
Total	2	8	18	.308	55	28	15-1	1	251.2	247	147	20	7	161	146	4.47	95	.260	.371	133-4-0	.293	9	81	-10	0	1.1
LINDEMANN, ERNIE	Ernest Theodore; B6.10.1878 New York NY; D12.27.1951 Brooklyn NY; BR/TR/5´10.5˝/182; d6.28																									
1907	Bos N	0	0	ø	1	1	0	0	6.1	6	5	0	0	4	3	5.68	45	.286	.400	2-0-1	.500	0	167	-2	—	-0.1
LINDQUIST, CARL	Carl Emil; B5.9.1919 Morris Run PA; D9.3.2001 Blossburg PA; BR/TR/6´2˝/185; d9.27; Col Mansfield																									
1943	Bos N	0	2	.000	2	2	0	0	13	17	10	3	0	4	1	6.23	55	.315	.362	4	.000	-1	37	-4	0	-0.5
1944	Bos N	0	0	ø	5	0	0	0	8.2	8	5	1	0	2	4	3.12	123	.222	.263	1	.000	-0	—	0	0	0.0
Total	2	0	2	.000	7	2	0	0	21.2	25	15	4	0	6	5	4.98	72	.278	.323	5	.000	-1	37	-4	0	-0.5
LINDSEY, JIM	James Kendrick; B1.24.1898 Greensburg LA; D10.25.1963 Jackson LA; BR/TR/6´1˝/175; d5.1																									
1922	Cle A	4	5	.444	29	5	0	1	83.2	105	60	4	3	24	29	6.02	67	.324	.376	24	.167	-1	76	-17	—	-1.7
1924	Cle A	0	0	ø	3	0	0	0	3	8	7	0	0	3	0	21.00	20	.500	.579	3	.000	-1	—	-5	—	-0.3
1929	StL N	1	1	.500	2	2	1	0	16.1	20	11	1	1	2	8	5.51	85	.290	.319	5	.200	-0	75	-1	—	-0.2
1930	†StL N	7	5	.583	39	6	3	5	105.2	131	59	6	4	46	50	4.43	113	.312	.385	28-0-3	.286	1	84	7	—	0.7
1931	†StL N	6	4	.600	35	2	1-1	7	74.2	77	32	2	0	45	32	2.77	142	.270	.370	9-0-4	.111	-0	76	**7**	—	1.0
1932	StL N	3	3	.500	33	5	0	3	89.1	96	53	6	2	38	31	4.94	80	.279	.354	21-0-3	.143	-1	154	-8	—	-0.7
1933	StL N	0	0	ø	1	0	0	0	2	2	1	0	0	1	1	4.50	77	.286	.375	0	ø	0	—	0	—	0.0
1934	Cin N	0	0	ø	4	0	0	0	4	4	3	0	1	2	2	4.50	91	.286	.412	0	ø	0	—	0	—	0.0
	StL N	0	1	.000	11	0	0	1	14	21	13	2	0	3	7	6.43	66	.328	.358	1	.000	-0	—	-4	—	-0.3
	Year	0	1	.000	15	0	0	1	18	25	16	2	1	5	9	6.00	70	.321	.369	1	.000	-0	—	-4	—	-0.3
1937	Bro N	0	1	.000	20	0	0	2	38.1	43	22	4	1	12	15	3.52	115	.295	.352	6	.167	-0	—	1	—	0.0
Total	9	21	20	.512	177	20	5-1	19	431	507	261	25	12	176	175	4.70	91	.300	.370	97-0-10	.186	-3	99	-20	—	-1.5
LINDSTROM, AXEL	Axel Olaf; B8.26.1895 Gustavsberg, Sweden; D6.24.1940 Asheville NC; BR/TR/5´10˝/180; d10.3																									
1916	Phi A	0	0	ø	1	0	0	1	4	2	2	0	1	0	1	4.50	63	.182	.250	2	.500	0	—	0	—	0.0
LINEBRINK, SCOTT	Scott Cameron; B8.4.1976 Austin TX; BR/TR/6´3˝/(185–210); [SFN97 2/56]; d4.15; Col Southwest Texas																									
2000	SF N	0	0	ø	3	0	0	0-0	2.1	7	3	1	0	2-0	0	11.57	38	.500	.563	0	ø	0	—	-2	0	-0.1
	Hou N	0	0	ø	8	0	0	0-0	9.2	11	5	3	3	6-0	6	4.66	105	.289	.426	1	1.000	0	—	0	0	0.0
	Year	0	0	ø	11	0	0	0-0	12	18	8	4	3	8-0	6	6.00	80	.346	.460	1	1.000	0	—	-1	0	-0.1
2001	Hou N	0	0	ø	9	0	0	0-0	10.1	6	4	0	2	6-0	9	2.61	176	.176	.326	0	ø	0	—	2	0	0.1
2002	Hou N	0	0	ø	22	0	0	0-0	24.1	31	21	2	1	13-4	24	7.03	62	.298	.375	0	ø	0	—	-7	28	-0.4
2003	Hou N	1	1	.500	9	6	0	0-0	31.2	38	15	4	3	14-1	17	4.26	104	.317	.399	8-0-1	.000	-1	138	1	0	-0.1
	SD N	2	1	.667	43	0	0	0-0	60.2	55	22	5	3	22-3	51	2.82	142	.244	.314	4	.500	1	—	8	0	0.4
	Year	3	2	.600	52	6	0	0-0	92.1	93	37	9	6	36-4	68	3.31	125	.270	.344	12-0-1	.167	0	147	9	0	0.3
2004	SD N	7	3	.700	73	0	0	0-5	84	61	22	8	3	26-2	83	2.14	184	.209	.278	2-0-1	.000	-0	—	18	0	1.9
2005	†SD N	8	1	.889	73	0	0	1-5	73.2	55	17	4	0	23-4	70	1.83	214	.209	.273	1	.000	-0	—	18	0	2.0
2006	†SD N	7	4	.636	73	0	0	2-9	75.2	70	31	9	1	22-3	68	3.57	116	.243	.297	1	1.000	1	—	6	0	0.8
Total	7	25	10	.714	313	6	0	3-19	372.1	334	140	36	16	134-17	328	3.12	132	.242	.314	17-0-2	.235	1	148	44	28	4.6
LINES, DICK	Richard George; B8.17.1938 Montreal QC, Can.; BR/TL/6´1˝/(175–185); d4.16																									
1966	Was A	5	2	.714	53	0	0	2	83	63	23	4	1	24-7	49	2.28	152	.213	.273	10-0-2	.000	-1	—	11	0	1.0
1967	Was A	2	5	.286	54	0	0	4	85.2	83	43	6	0	24-6	54	3.36	94	.245	.292	9	.111	1	—	-5	0	-0.3
Total	2	7	7	.500	107	0	0	6	168.2	146	66	10	1	48-13	103	2.83	117	.230	.283	19-0-2	.053	-1	—	6	0	0.7

THE PITCHER REGISTER

LINK, FRED Edward Theodore "Laddie"; B3.11.1886 Columbus OH; D5.22.1939 Houston TX; BL/TL/6´0˝/170; d4.15

YEAR	TM LG	W	L	PCT	G	GS	CG-SHO	SV-BS	IP	H	R	HR	HB	BB-IB	SO	ERA	AERA	OAV	OOB	AB-HR-SH	AVG	PB	SUP	APR	DL	PW
1910	Cle A	5	6	.455	22	13	6-1	1	127.2	121	53	0	7	50	55	3.17	82	.259	.340	42-0-3	.167	-1	90	-5	—	-0.6
	StL A	0	1	.000	3	3	0	0	17	24	10	0	1	13	5	4.24	58	.375	.487	6	.167	-0	181	-3	—	-0.2
	Year	5	7	.417	25	16	6-1	1	144.2	145	63	0	8	63	60	3.30	78	.273	.359	48-0-3	.167	-1	106	-6	—	-0.8

LINKE, ED Edward Karl "Babe"; B11.9.1911 Chicago IL; D6.21.1988 Chicago IL; BR/TR/5´11˝/180; d4.27

YEAR	TM LG	W	L	PCT	G	GS	CG-SHO	SV-BS	IP	H	R	HR	HB	BB-IB	SO	ERA	AERA	OAV	OOB	AB-HR-SH	AVG	PB	SUP	APR	DL	PW
1933	Was A	1	0	1.000	3	2	0	0	16	15	10	0	0	11	6	5.06	83	.250	.366	6-0-1	.167	0	102	-2	—	-0.1
1934	Was A	2	2	.500	7	4	2	0	34.2	38	20	1	0	9	9	4.15	104	.277	.322	11-0-1	.182	0*	71	0	—	0.0
1935	Was A	11	7	.611	40	22	10-1	3	178	211	111	6	1	80	51	5.01	86	.296	.367	68-1-1	.294	6	131	-14	—	-0.7
1936	Was A	1	5	.167	13	6	1	0	52	73	46	4	0	14	11	7.10	67	.330	.370	15-1-0	.400	5	52	-13	—	-0.7
1937	Was A	6	1	.857	36	7	0	3	128.2	158	89	11	4	59	61	5.60	79	.304	.379	46-0-1	.217	1*	141	-15	—	-0.7
1938	StL A	1	7	.125	21	2	0	0	39.2	60	37	6	0	33	18	7.94	63	.357	.463	10	.200	0	124	-12	—	-1.8
Total	6	22	22	.500	120	43	13-1	6	449	555	313	28	5	206	156	5.61	79	.305	.377	156-2-4	.263	12	113	-56	—	-4.0

LINT, ROYCE Royce James; B1.1.1921 Birmingham AL; D4.3.2006 Greensboro NC; BL/TL/6´1˝/165; d4.13

YEAR	TM LG	W	L	PCT	G	GS	CG-SHO	SV-BS	IP	H	R	HR	HB	BB-IB	SO	ERA	AERA	OAV	OOB	AB-HR-SH	AVG	PB	SUP	APR	DL	PW
1954	StL N	2	3	.400	30	4	1-1	0	70.1	75	46	9	0	30	36	4.86	85	.273	.342	10-0-1	.100	1*	152	-7	0	-0.2

LINTON, DOUG Douglas Warren; B2.9.1965 Santa Ana CA; BR/TR/6´1˝/(185–190); [TorA86 43/878]; d8.3; Col California–Irvine

YEAR	TM LG	W	L	PCT	G	GS	CG-SHO	SV-BS	IP	H	R	HR	HB	BB-IB	SO	ERA	AERA	OAV	OOB	AB-HR-SH	AVG	PB	SUP	APR	DL	PW
1992	Tor A	1	3	.250	8	3	0	0-0	24	31	23	5	0	17-0	16	8.63	48	.323	.417	0	ø	0	96	-11	0	-1.5
1993	Tor A	0	1	.000	4	1	0	0-0	11	11	8	0	1	9-0	4	6.55	67	.256	.382	0	ø	0	63	-2	0	-0.2
	Cal A	2	0	1.000	19	0	0	0-1	25.2	35	22	8	0	14-1	19	7.71	59	.324	.398	0	ø	0	—	-8	0	-0.5
	Year	2	1	.667	23	1	0	0-1	36.2	46	30	8	1	23-1	23	7.36	61	.305	.393	0	ø	0	62	-10	0	-0.7
1994	NY N	6	2	.750	32	3	0	0-0	50.1	74	27	4	0	20-3	29	4.47	93	.341	.395	7-0-2	.000	-1	131	-1	0	-0.3
1995	KC A	0	1	.000	7	2	0	0-0	22.1	22	21	4	2	10-1	13	7.25	66	.256	.347	0	ø	0	29	-7	0	-0.3
1996	KC A	7	9	.438	21	18	0	0-0	104	111	65	13	8	26-1	87	5.02	100	.271	.325	0	ø	0	90	-1	0	-0.2
1999	Bal A	1	4	.200	14	8	0	0-0	59	69	41	14	2	25-1	31	5.95	79	.296	.369	0	ø	0	72	-8	0	-0.6
2003	Tor A	0	0	ø	7	0	0	0-0	9	7	3	2	0	4-0	7	3.00	158	.226	.314	0	ø	0	—	2	0	0.1
Total	7	17	20	.459	112	35	0	0-1	305.1	360	210	50	13	125-7	206	5.78	81	.294	.364	7-0-2	.000	-1	87	-36	0	-3.5

LINZY, FRANK Frank Alfred; B9.15.1940 Ft.Gibson OK; BR/TR/6´1˝/190; d8.14; Col Oklahoma St.

YEAR	TM LG	W	L	PCT	G	GS	CG-SHO	SV-BS	IP	H	R	HR	HB	BB-IB	SO	ERA	AERA	OAV	OOB	AB-HR-SH	AVG	PB	SUP	APR	DL	PW
1963	SF N	0	0	ø	8	1	0	0	16.2	22	9	0	1	10-0	14	4.86	66	.324	.418	3	.000	-0	189	-2	0	-0.1
1965	SF N	9	3	.750	57	0	0	21	81.2	76	19	2	3	23-8	35	1.43	251	.250	.309	18-1-0	.222	1	—	**18**	0	4.1
1966	SF N	7	11	.389	51	0	0	16	100.1	107	40	4	2	34-9	57	2.96	124	.273	.333	20-0-3	.150	0	—	7	0	1.6
1967	SF N	7	7	.500	57	0	0	17	95.2	67	21	4	0	34-7	38	1.51	218	.203	.274	15-0-3	.000	-2	—	18	0	3.5
1968	SF N	9	8	.529	57	0	0	12	95.1	76	30	1	1	27-14	36	2.08	142	.218	.274	11-0-4	.000	-1	—	8	0	1.8
1969	SF N	14	9	.609	58	0	0	11-10	116.1	129	57	5	3	38-15	62	3.64	97	.283	.341	30-0-3	.267	3	—	-2	0	0.0
1970	SF N	2	1	.667	20	0	0	1-0	25.2	33	20	2	1	11-4	16	7.01	57	.327	.391	4	.000	-0	—	-8	0	-0.9
	StL N	3	5	.375	47	0	0	2-2	61.1	66	26	3	0	23-10	19	3.67	113	.282	.344	7	.000	-1	—	4	0	0.5
	Year	5	6	.455	67	0	0	3-2	87	99	46	5	1	34-14	35	4.66	88	.296	.358	11	.000	-1	—	-3	0	-0.4
1971	StL N	4	3	.571	50	0	0	6-2	59.1	49	18	2	0	27-11	24	2.12	171	.226	.311	4	.500	1	—	8	22	1.3
1972	Mil A	2	2	.500	47	0	0	12-2	77.1	70	30	4	2	27-12	24	3.03	101	.248	.313	9-0-1	.111	-0	—	0	0	0.0
1973	Mil A	2	6	.250	42	1	0	13-4	63	68	34	7	1	21-6	21	3.57	107	.282	.338	0	ø	0	141	-1	0	-0.1
1974	Phi N	3	2	.600	22	0	0	0-1	24.2	27	11	1	0	7-1	12	3.28	116	.284	.333	0	ø	0	—	1	0	0.2
Total	11	62	57	.521	516	2	0	111-21	817.1	790	315	35	14	282-97	358	2.85	123	.257	.321	121-1-14	.149	0	164	51	22	11.9

LIPETRI, ANGELO Michael Angelo; B7.6.1929 Brooklyn NY; BR/TR/6´1.5˝/180; d4.25

YEAR	TM LG	W	L	PCT	G	GS	CG-SHO	SV-BS	IP	H	R	HR	HB	BB-IB	SO	ERA	AERA	OAV	OOB	AB-HR-SH	AVG	PB	SUP	APR	DL	PW
1956	Phi N	0	0	ø	6	0	0	0	11	7	5	2	1	3-0	8	3.27	114	.175	.250	1	.000	-0	—	0	0	0.0
1958	Phi N	0	0	ø	4	0	0	0	4	6	5	1	1	0-0	1	11.25	35	.353	.389	0	ø	0	—	-3	0	-0.1
Total	2	0	0	ø	10	0	0	0	15	13	10	3	2	3-0	9	5.40	70	.228	.290	1	.000	-0	—	-3	0	-0.1

LIPP, TOM Thomas Charles (b Thomas Charles Lieb); B6.4.1870 Baltimore MD; D5.30.1932 Baltimore MD; 5´11.5˝/170; d9.18

YEAR	TM LG	W	L	PCT	G	GS	CG-SHO	SV-BS	IP	H	R	HR	HB	BB-IB	SO	ERA	AERA	OAV	OOB	AB-HR-SH	AVG	PB	SUP	APR	DL	PW
1897	Phi N	0	1	.000	1	1	0	0	3	8	5	0	0	2	1	15.00	28	.471	.526	1	1.000	0	51	-3	—	-0.4

LIPSCOMB, NIG Gerard; B2.24.1911 Rutherfordton NC; D2.27.1978 Huntersville NC; BR/TR/6´0˝/175; d4.23; ▲

YEAR	TM LG	W	L	PCT	G	GS	CG-SHO	SV-BS	IP	H	R	HR	HB	BB-IB	SO	ERA	AERA	OAV	OOB	AB-HR-SH	AVG	PB	SUP	APR	DL	PW
1937	StL A	0	0	ø	3	0	0	0	9.2	13	9	3	0	5	1	6.52	74	.333	.409	96-0-1	.323	1*	—	-2	—	-0.1

LIRA, FELIPE Antonio Felipe; B4.26.1972 Santa Teresa, Miranda, Venez.; BR/TR/6´1˝/(170–215); d4.27

YEAR	TM LG	W	L	PCT	G	GS	CG-SHO	SV-BS	IP	H	R	HR	HB	BB-IB	SO	ERA	AERA	OAV	OOB	AB-HR-SH	AVG	PB	SUP	APR	DL	PW
1995	Det A	9	13	.409	37	22	0	1-2	146.1	151	74	17	8	56-7	89	4.31	112	.271	.341	0	ø	0	75	9	0	1.1
1996	Det A	6	14	.300	32	32	3-2	0-0	194.2	204	123	30	10	66-2	113	5.22	97	.269	.331	0	ø	0	80	-3	0	-0.2
1997	Det A	5	7	.417	20	15	1-1	0-0	92	101	61	15	2	45-2	64	5.77	80	.277	.358	0	ø	0	105	-10	0	-1.1
	Sea A	0	4	.000	8	3	0	0-0	18.2	31	21	3	4	10-0	9	9.16	50	.365	.446	0	ø	0	61	-10	0	-1.6
	Year	5	11	.313	28	18	1-1	0-0	110.2	132	82	18	6	55-2	73	6.34	73	.294	.375	0	ø	0	98	-20	0	-2.7
1998	Sea A	1	0	1.000	7	0	0	0-0	15.2	22	10	5	0	5-0	16	4.60	102	.319	.360	0	ø	0	—	0	0	0.0
1999	Det A	0	0	ø	2	0	0	0-0	3.1	7	5	2	0	2-0	3	10.80	46	.389	.450	0	ø	0	—	-2	0	-0.1
2000	Mon N	5	8	.385	53	7	0	0-0	101.2	129	71	11	4	36-6	51	5.40	87	.310	.363	19-2-1	.211	2*	47	-9	0	-0.8
2001	Mon N	0	0	ø	4	0	0	0-0	5	11	7	1	0	2-0	3	12.60	34	.440	.481	0	ø	0	—	-4	0	-0.2
Total	7	26	46	.361	163	79	4-3	1-2	577.1	656	372	84	28	222-17	348	5.32	91	.286	.352	19-2-1	.211	2	80	-29	0	-2.9

LIRIANO, FRANCISCO Francisco Casillas; B10.26.1983 San Cristobal, D.R.; BL/TL/6´2˝/(185–200); d9.5

YEAR	TM LG	W	L	PCT	G	GS	CG-SHO	SV-BS	IP	H	R	HR	HB	BB-IB	SO	ERA	AERA	OAV	OOB	AB-HR-SH	AVG	PB	SUP	APR	DL	PW
2005	Min A	1	2	.333	6	4	0	0-0	23.2	19	15	4	0	7-0	33	5.70	77	.221	.280	0	ø	0	69	-3	0	-0.3
2006	Min A☆	12	3	.800	28	16	0	1-0	121	89	31	9	1	32-0	144	2.16	212	.205	.260	5-0-1	.200	0	93	33	34	3.7
Total	2	13	5	.722	34	20	0	1-0	144.2	108	46	13	1	39-0	177	2.74	166	.208	.263	5-0-1	.200	0	88	30	34	3.4

LIRIANO, PEDRO Pedro Antonio; B10.23.1980 Fantino, D.R.; BR/TR/6´2˝/170; d8.27

YEAR	TM LG	W	L	PCT	G	GS	CG-SHO	SV-BS	IP	H	R	HR	HB	BB-IB	SO	ERA	AERA	OAV	OOB	AB-HR-SH	AVG	PB	SUP	APR	DL	PW
2004	Mil N	0	0	ø	11	0	0	0-0	15.2	15	10	3	1	3-0	10	4.02	109	.238	.284	1	.000	-0	—	0	0	0.0
2005	Phi N	0	0	ø	5	0	0	0-0	7.2	10	11	3	1	6-0	6	10.57	41	.313	.436	0-0-1	ø	0	—	-6	0	-0.3
Total	2	0	0	ø	16	0	0	0-0	23.1	25	21	6	2	9-0	16	6.17	71	.263	.340	1-0-1	.000	-0	—	-6	0	-0.3

LISENBEE, HOD Horace Milton; B9.23.1898 Clarksville TN; D11.14.1987 Clarksville TN; BR/TR/5´11˝/170; d4.23; Col Rhodes

YEAR	TM LG	W	L	PCT	G	GS	CG-SHO	SV-BS	IP	H	R	HR	HB	BB-IB	SO	ERA	AERA	OAV	OOB	AB-HR-SH	AVG	PB	SUP	APR	DL	PW
1927	Was A	18	9	.667	39	34	17-**4**	0	242	221	114	6	3	78	105	3.57	114	.245	.307	83-0-8	.133	-5	105	13	—	0.7
1928	Was A	2	6	.250	16	9	3	0	77	102	58	4	5	32	13	6.08	66	.326	.397	23-0-2	.174	-0	91	-16	—	-1.5
1929	Bos A	0	0	ø	5	0	0	0	8.2	10	5	1	0	4	2	5.19	82	.294	.368	2	.000	-0	—	0	—	0.0
1930	Bos A	10	17	.370	37	31	15	0	237.1	254	130	20	5	86	47	4.40	105	.280	.346	75-0-8	.267	1	75	7	—	0.6
1931	Bos A	5	12	.294	41	17	6	0	164.2	190	108	13	3	49	42	5.19	83	.281	.332	53	.226	0	89	-16	—	-1.4
1932	Bos A	0	4	.000	19	6	3	0	73.1	87	55	9	1	25	13	5.65	80	.296	.353	21-0-3	.048	-2	60	-9	—	-0.6
1936	Phi A	1	7	.125	19	7	4	0	85.2	115	69	9	0	24	17	6.20	82	.322	.365	25-0-2	.120	-1	62	-11	—	-0.9
1945	Cin N	1	3	.250	31	3	0	1	80.1	97	56	12	2	16	14	5.49	68	.294	.330	19	.000	-3	158	-16	0	-1.1
Total	8	37	58	.389	207	107	48-4	1	969	1076	595	74	19	314	253	4.81	90	.282	.340	301-0-23	.169	-10	88	-48	0	-4.2

LISKA, AD Adolph James; B7.10.1906 Dwight NE; D11.30.1998 Portland OR; BR/TR/5´11.5˝/160; d4.17; Col Nebraska

YEAR	TM LG	W	L	PCT	G	GS	CG-SHO	SV-BS	IP	H	R	HR	HB	BB-IB	SO	ERA	AERA	OAV	OOB	AB-HR-SH	AVG	PB	SUP	APR	DL	PW
1929	Was A	3	9	.250	24	10	4	0	94.1	87	53	1	3	42	33	4.77	89	.249	.335	29	.172	-1	72	-3	—	-0.2
1930	Was A	9	7	.563	32	16	7-1	1	150.2	140	69	6	5	71	40	3.29	140	.250	.340	52-0-4	.096	-4	98	19	—	1.7
1931	Was A	0	1	.000	2	1	0	0	4	9	3	0	0	1	2	6.75	64	.450	.476	1	.000	-0	39	-1	—	-0.2
1932	Phi N	2	0	1.000	8	0	0	1	26.2	22	5	0	1	10	6	1.69	261	.239	.320	7	.000	-1	—	7	—	0.5
1933	Phi N	3	1	.750	45	1	0	1	75.2	96	46	5	0	26	23	4.52	84	.310	.363	14	.071	-1*	240	-6	—	-0.3
Total	5	17	18	.486	111	28	11-1	3	351.1	354	176	12	9	150	104	3.87	112	.266	.344	103-0-4	.107	-7	93	16	—	1.5

LITTELL, MARK Mark Alan; B1.17.1953 Cape Girardeau MO; BL/TR/6´3˝/(195–210); [KCA71 12/274]; d6.14

YEAR	TM LG	W	L	PCT	G	GS	CG-SHO	SV-BS	IP	H	R	HR	HB	BB-IB	SO	ERA	AERA	OAV	OOB	AB-HR-SH	AVG	PB	SUP	APR	DL	PW
1973	KC A	1	3	.250	8	7	1	0-0	38	44	25	5	0	23-1	16	5.68	72	.288	.376	0	ø	0	109	-5	0	-0.5
1975	KC A	1	2	.333	7	3	1	0-0	24.1	19	11	1	0	15-0	19	3.70	104	.229	.347	0	ø	0	61	1	0	0.1
1976	†KC A	8	4	.667	60	1	0	16-5	104	68	26	1	0	60-4	92	2.08	169	.188	.301	1	.000	-0	201	**17**	0	2.6
1977	†KC A	8	4	.667	48	5	0	12-3	104.2	73	49	6	1	55-6	106	3.61	112	.198	.299	1	.000	-0	107	4	0	0.5
1978	StL N	4	8	.333	72	2	0	11-4	106.1	80	38	8	4	59-16	130	2.79	128	.213	.324	7	.000	-0	38	9	0	1.1
1979	StL N	9	4	.692	63	0	0	13-6	82.1	60	22	2	0	39-5	67	2.19	174	.203	.294	14-0-1	.000	-1	—	15	0	2.6
1980	StL N	0	2	.000	14	0	0	2-3	10.2	14	11	2	0	7-2	7	9.28	40	.318	.412	1	.000	-0	—	-6	115	-1.2
1981	StL N	1	3	.250	28	1	0	2-0	41	36	21	2	0	31-7	22	4.39	82	.237	.366	8	.250	0	74	-3	43	-0.3

YEAR	TM LG	W	L	PCT	G	GS	CG-SHO	SV-BS	IP	H	R	HR	HB	BB-IB	SO	ERA	AERA	OAV	OOB	AB-HR-SH	AVG	PB	SUP	APR	DL	PW
1982	StL N	0	1	.000	16	0	0	0-0	20.2	22	14	1	0	15-5	7	5.23	70	.272	.385	2	.000	-0	—	-4	0	-0.3
Total	9	32	31	.508	316	19	2	56-21	532	416	217	28	5	304-46	466	3.32	113	.217	.324	34-0-1	.059	-2	101	28	158	4.6
Little, Jeff	Donald Jeffrey; B12.25.1954 Fremont OH; BR/TL/6´6˝/220; [SFN73 3/54]; d9.6																									
1980	StL N	1	1	.500	7	2	0	0-0	18.2	18	9	0	0	9-0	17	3.86	97	.250	.333	6	.167	-0	71	0	0	-0.1
1982	Min A	2	0	1.000	33	0	0	0-2	36.1	33	20	6	0	27-3	26	4.21	101	.244	.368	0	ø	0	—	-1	0	0.0
Total	2	3	1	.750	40	2	0	0-2	55	51	29	6	0	36-3	43	4.09	100	.246	.357	6	.167	-0	71	-1	0	-0.1
Littlefield, John	John Andrew; B1.5.1954 Covina CA; BR/TR/6´2˝/200; [StLN76 30/655]; d6.8; Col Azusa Pacific																									
1980	StL N	5	5	.500	52	0	0	9-5	66	71	31	2	1	20-9	22	3.14	120	.282	.330	11-0-1	.000	-1	—	2	0	0.2
1981	SD N	2	3	.400	42	0	0	2-3	64	53	28	5	1	28-5	21	3.66	89	.235	.322	1-0-1	.000	-0	—	-3	0	-0.3
Total	2	7	8	.467	94	0	0	11-8	130	124	59	7	2	48-14	43	3.39	103	.259	.326	12-0-2	.000	-1	—	-1	0	-0.1
Littlefield, Dick	Richard Bernard; B3.18.1926 Detroit MI; D11.20.1997 Detroit MI; BL/TL/6´0˝/180; d7.7																									
1950	Bos A	2	2	.500	15	2	0	1	23.1	27	25	7	1	24	13	9.26	53	.297	.448	4	.000	-1	46	-10	0	-1.5
1951	Chi A	1	1	.500	4	2	0	0	9.2	9	12	1	0	17	7	8.38	48	.243	.481	1	.000	0	88	-5	0	-0.8
1952	Det A	0	3	.000	28	1	0	1	47.2	46	24	4	0	25	32	4.34	88	.257	.348	7	.143	-0	229	-2	0	-0.2
	StL A	2	3	.400	7	5	3	0	46.1	35	18	4	0	17	34	2.72	144	.205	.277	16	.063	-2	76	5	0	0.3
	Year	2	6	.250	35	6	3	1	94	81	42	8	0	42	66	3.54	109	.231	.314	23	.087	-2	102	4	0	0.1
1953	StL A	7	12	.368	36	22	2	0	152.1	153	93	17	4	84	104	5.08	83	.264	.361	42-0-5	.190	-1*	80	-12	0	-1.5
1954	Bal A	0	0	ø	3	0	0	0	6	8	7	0	1	6	5	10.50	34	.333	.484	1	.000	-0	—	-4	0	-0.2
	Pit N	10	11	.476	23	21	7-1	0	155	140	78	10	2	85	92	3.60	116	.239	.334	49-0-4	.163	0	77	7	0	0.8
1955	Pit N	5	12	.294	35	17	4-1	0	130	148	91	15	2	68-8	70	5.12	80	.290	.372	34-0-1	.176	0	71	-17	0	-2.0
1956	Pit N	0	0	ø	6	2	0	0	12.2	14	8	2	0	6-0	10	4.26	88	.286	.364	2	.000	-0	93	-1	0	-0.1
	StL N	0	2	.000	3	2	0	0	9.2	9	9	2	0	4-1	5	7.45	51	.237	.310	2	.000	-0	58	-4	0	-0.7
	NY N	4	4	.500	31	7	0	2	97	78	45	16	0	39-5	65	4.08	93	.231	.306	24-0-1	.083	-2	70	-1	0	-0.3
	Year	4	6	.400	40	11	0	2	119.1	101	62	20	0	49-6	80	4.37	86	.238	.313	28-0-1	.071	-2	72	-7	0	-1.1
1957	Chi N	2	3	.400	48	2	0	4	65.2	76	46	12	1	37-4	51	5.35	72	.295	.380	11	.182	0	23	-12	0	-1.0
1958	Mil N	0	1	.000	4	0	0	1	6.1	7	5	2	1	1-0	7	4.26	83	.280	.333	0	ø	0	—	-1	0	-0.3
Total	9	33	54	.379	243	83	16-2	9	761.2	750	461	92	12	413-18	495	4.71	86	.260	.353	193-0-11	.145	-5	77	-57	0	-7.5
Littlejohn, Carlisle	Charles Carlisle; B10.6.1901 Irene TX; D10.27.1977 Kansas City MO; BR/TR/5´10˝/175; d5.11; Col Austin																									
1927	StL N	3	1	.750	14	2	1	0	42	47	21	4	0	14	16	4.50	88	.292	.349	12	.417	2*	119	-1	—	0.1
1928	StL N	2	1	.667	12	2	1	0	32	36	16	2	0	14	6	3.66	109	.286	.357	11	.000	-2	116	1	—	-0.1
Total	2	5	2	.714	26	4	2	0	74	83	37	6	0	28	22	4.14	96	.289	.352	23	.217	-0	118	0	—	0.0
Littleton, Wes	Wes Avi; B9.2.1982 Hayward CA; BR/TR/6´2˝/210; [TexA03 4/106]; d7.4; Col Cal St.–Fullerton																									
2006	Tex A	2	1	.667	33	0	0	1-0	36.1	23	7	2	2	13-0	17	1.73	270	.189	.275	0	ø	0	—	12	0	0.9
Lively, Buddy	Everett Adrian "Red"; B2.14.1925 Birmingham AL; BR/TR/6´0.5˝/200; d4.17; f–Jack; [DL 1950 Cin N 64]																									
1947	Cin N	4	7	.364	38	17	3-1	0	123	126	75	16	0	63	52	4.68	88	.265	.351	32-0-3	.188	2	107	-9	0	-0.6
1948	Cin N	0	0	ø	10	0	0	0	22.2	13	7	0	1	11	12	2.38	164	.165	.275	2	.000	-0	—	4	0	0.1
1949	Cin N	4	6	.400	31	10	3-1	1	103.1	91	47	11	0	53	30	3.92	107	.245	.339	26-0-1	.154	0	67	5	0	0.4
Total	3	8	13	.381	79	27	6-2	1	249	230	129	27	1	127	94	4.16	99	.248	.339	60-0-4	.167	1	93	0	64	-0.1
Lively, Jack	Henry Everett; B5.29.1885 Joppa AL; D12.5.1967 Arab AL; BR/TR/5´9˝/185; d4.16; s–Buddy																									
1911	Det A	7	5	.583	18	14	10	0	113.2	143	73	1	7	34	45	4.59	75	.313	.369	43	.256	3*	110	-12	—	-0.9
Livengood, Wes	Wesley Amos; B7.18.1910 Salisbury NC; D9.2.1996 Winston–Salem NC; BR/TR/6´2˝/172; d5.30																									
1939	Cin N	0	0	ø	5	0	0	0	5.2	9	6	3	0	3	4	9.53	40	.360	.429	0	ø	0	—	-3	—	-0.2
Livingston, Bobby	Robert James; B9.3.1982 St.Louis MO; BL/TL/6´3˝/195; [SeaA01 4/129]; d4.25																									
2006	Sea A	0	0	ø	3	0	0	0-0	5	9	10	2	2	6-1	3	18.00	24	.375	.531	0	ø	0	—	-7	0	-0.3
Livingstone, Jake	Jacob M.; B1.1.1880 St.Petersburg, Russia; D3.22.1949 Wassaic NY; d9.6																									
1901	NY N	0	0	ø	2	0	0	0	12	26	13	0	3	7	6	9.00	37	.433	.514	6	.167	0	—	-6	—	-0.3
Llewellyn, Clem	Clement Manly "Lew"; B8.1.1895 Dobson NC; D11.27.1969 Concord NC; BL/TR/6´3.5˝/195; d6.18; Col North Carolina																									
1922	NY A	0	0	ø	1	0	0	0	1	1	0	0	0	0	0	0.00	ø	.250	.250	0	ø	0	—	0	—	0.0
Lloyd, Graeme	Graeme John; B4.9.1967 Victoria, Victoria, Australia; BL/TL/6´7˝/(215–234); d4.11; [DL 2000 Mon N 181]																									
1993	Mil A	3	4	.429	55	0	0	0-4	63.2	64	24	5	3	13-3	31	2.83	153	.256	.299	0	ø	0	—	10	15	1.0
1994	Mil A	2	3	.400	43	0	0	3-3	47	49	28	4	3	15-6	31	5.17	98	.269	.332	0	ø	0	—	0	0	0.0
1995	Mil A	0	5	.000	33	0	0	4-2	32	28	16	4	0	8-2	13	4.50	111	.246	.286	0	ø	0	—	2	47	0.4
1996	Mil A	2	4	.333	52	0	0	0-3	51	49	19	3	1	17-3	24	2.82	184	.254	.316	0	ø	0	—	12	0	1.2
	†NY A	0	2	.000	13	0	0	0-2	5.2	12	11	1	0	5-1	6	17.47	28	.429	.486	0	ø	0	—	-8	0	-1.3
	Year	2	6	.250	65	0	0	0-5	56.2	61	30	4	1	22-4	30	4.29	121	.276	.340	0	ø	0	—	5	0	-0.1
1997	†NY A	1	1	.500	46	0	0	1-0	49	55	24	6	1	20-7	26	3.31	135	.293	.355	0	ø	0	—	4	0	0.2
1998	†NY A	3	0	1.000	50	0	0	0-2	37.2	26	10	3	2	6-2	20	1.67	262	.191	.234	0	ø	0	—	11	15	0.7
1999	Tor A	5	3	.625	74	0	0	3-6	72	68	36	11	4	23-4	47	3.63	136	.250	.317	0	ø	0	—	8	0	0.8
2001	Mon N	9	5	.643	84	0	0	1-2	70.1	74	38	6	6	21-2	44	4.35	99	.272	.336	2	.000	0	—	-1	0	-0.1
2002	Mon N	2	3	.400	41	0	0	5-2	30.2	41	21	5	1	8-3	17	5.87	75	.325	.368	4	.000	-0	—	-4	0	-0.8
	Fla N	2	2	.500	25	0	0	0-1	26.1	26	13	1	1	11-1	20	4.44	88	.263	.336	0	ø	0	—	-1	0	-0.2
	Year	4	5	.444	66	0	0	5-3	57	67	34	6	2	19-4	37	5.21	80	.298	.353	4	.000	-0	—	-6	0	-1.0
2003	NY N	1	2	.333	36	0	0	0-0	35.1	39	16	2	0	7-2	17	3.31	127	.281	.311	0	ø	0	—	3	0	0.2
	KC A	0	2	.000	16	0	0	0-1	12.1	29	18	0	1	7-0	8	10.95	44	.453	.500	0	ø	0	—	-9	0	-1.2
Total	10	30	36	.455	568	0	0	17-28	533	560	274	51	23	161-36	304	4.04	114	.271	.327	6	.000	-0	—	27	258	0.9
Loaiza, Esteban	Esteban Antonio (Veyna); B12.31.1971 Tijuana, Baja California, Mexico; BR/TR/6´3˝/(190–215); d4.29																									
1995	Pit N	8	9	.471	32	**31**	1	0-0	172.2	205	115	21	5	55-3	85	5.16	84	.300	.352	52-0-7	.192	1*	101	-17	0	-1.4
1996	Pit N	2	3	.400	10	10	1-1	0-0	52.2	65	32	11	2	19-2	32	4.96	89	.308	.369	17-0-5	.118	-1*	111	-3	0	-0.3
1997	Pit N	11	11	.500	33	32	1	0-0	196.1	214	99	17	12	56-9	122	4.13	104	.279	.335	60-0-8	.167	-0	105	4	0	0.3
1998	Pit N	6	5	.545	21	14	0	0-1	91.2	96	50	13	3	30-1	53	4.52	95	.275	.332	29-0-3	.241	1	88	-1	0	0.0
	Tex A	3	6	.333	14	14	1	0-0	79.1	103	57	15	2	22-3	55	5.90	83	.316	.358	0	ø	0	91	-8	0	-0.8
1999	†Tex A	9	5	.643	30	15	0	0-0	120.1	128	65	10	0	40-2	77	4.56	113	.275	.329	0	ø	0	102	8	54	0.8
2000	Tex A	5	6	.455	20	17	0	1-0	107.1	133	67	21	3	31-1	75	5.37	95	.302	.349	3	.000	-0	86	-1	0	-0.1
	Tor A	5	7	.417	14	14	1-1	0-0	92	95	45	8	10	26-0	62	3.62	139	.270	.337	0	ø	0	76	12	0	1.4
	Year	10	13	.435	34	31	1-1	1-0	199.1	228	112	29	13	57-1	137	4.56	111	.288	.344	3	.000	-0	81	11	0	1.3
2001	Tor A	11	11	.500	36	30	1-1	0-0	190	239	113	27	9	40-1	110	5.02	91	.307	.347	2	.000	-0	106	-8	0	-0.9
2002	Tor A	9	10	.474	25	25	3-1	0-0	151.1	192	102	18	4	38-3	87	5.71	81	.309	.350	6	.167	-0	119	-17	44	-1.8
2003	Chi A★	21	9	.700	34	34	1	0-0	226.1	196	75	17	10	56-2	**207**	2.90	158	.233	.286	5-0-1	.200	0	92	44	0	**5.5**
2004	Chi A★	9	5	.643	21	21	2-1	0-0	140.2	156	81	23	1	45-3	83	4.86	97	.283	.335	5	.000	-1	106	-3	0	-0.2
	†NY A	1	2	.333	10	6	0	0-0	42.1	61	43	9	2	26-2	34	8.50	54	.337	.416	0	ø	0	107	-19	0	-1.0
	Year	10	7	.588	31	27	2-1	0-0	183	217	124	32	3	71-5	117	5.70	82	.296	.356	5	.000	-1	106	-20	0	-1.2
2005	Was N	12	10	.545	34	34	0	0-0	217	227	93	18	5	55-3	173	3.77	109	.270	.318	74-0-6	.162	-0	92	11	0	0.9
2006	†Oak A	11	9	.550	26	26	2-1	0-0	154.2	179	92	17	5	40-3	97	4.89	93	.288	.332	5-0-1	.000	-0	101	-7	40	-0.9
Total	12	123	108	.532	360	323	14-6	1-1	2034.2	2289	1129	245	73	579-38	1352	4.62	99	.285	.336	258-0-31	.167	-1	99	-5	138	1.5
Locke, Chuck	Charles Edward; B5.5.1932 Malden MO; BR/TR/5´11˝/185; d9.16																									
1955	Bal A	0	0	ø	2	0	0	0	3	0	0	0	0	1-0	1	0.00	ø	.000	.100	0	ø	0	—	1	0	0.1
Locke, Bobby	Lawrence Donald; B3.3.1934 Rowes Run PA; BR/TR/5´11˝/(180–185); d6.18																									
1959	Cle A	3	2	.600	24	7	0	2	77.2	66	33	6	3	41-2	40	3.13	118	.233	.333	24-1-2	.333	3	127	4	0	0.6
1960	Cle A	3	5	.375	32	11	2-2	2	123	121	51	10	2	37-3	53	3.37	111	.255	.311	38-0-3	.237	3*	109	6	0	0.8
1961	Cle A	4	4	.500	37	4	0	2	95.1	112	50	12	2	40-4	37	4.53	87	.300	.368	19	.211	0	129	-5	0	-0.3
1962	StL N	0	0	ø	1	0	0	0	2	1	0	0	0	2-0	1	0.00	ø	.143	.333	0	ø	0	—	1	0	0.1
	Phi N	1	0	1.000	5	0	0	0	15.2	16	12	4	0	10-0	9	5.74	67	.262	.366	7	.286	0	—	-4	0	-0.1

YEAR	TM LG	W	L	PCT	G	GS	CG-SHO	SV-BS	IP	H	R	HR	HB	BB-IB	SO	ERA	AERA	OAV	OOB	AB-HR-SH	AVG	PB	SUP	APR	DL	PW
	Year	1	0	1.000	6	0	0	0	17.2	17	12	4	0	12-0	10	5.09	77	.250	.363	7	.286	0	—	-3	0	0.0
1963	Phi N	0	0	ø	9	0	0	0	10.2	10	7	0	0	5-1	7	5.91	55	.244	.326	1	.000	-0	—	-3	0	-0.2
1964	Phi N	0	0	ø	8	0	0	0	19.1	21	6	2	0	6-3	11	2.79	124	.276	.329	2-0-1	.000	-0	—	2	0	0.1
1965	Cin N	0	1	.000	11	0	0	0	17.1	20	15	2	0	8-5	8	5.71	66	.299	.368	1	.000	0	—	-5	0	-0.2
1967	Cal A	3	0	1.000	9	1	0	2	19.1	14	6	1	1	3-0	7	2.33	135	.203	.243	3	.667	1	305	2	0	0.4
1968	Cal A	2	3	.400	29	0	0	2	36.1	51	29	3	1	13-3	21	6.44	45	.331	.385	3	.000	-0	—	-14	0	-2.2
Total	9	16	15	.516	165	23	2-2	10	416.2	432	209	40	9	165-21	194	4.02	91	.269	.339	98-1-6	.255	8	128	-16	0	-1.0
Locke, Ron Ronald Thomas; B4.4.1942 Wakefield RI; BR/TL/5´11˝/168; d4.23																										
1964	NY N	1	2	.333	25	3	0	0	41.1	46	23	3	1	22-0	17	3.48	103	.289	.377	5-0-3	.000	-0	57	-2	0	-0.2
Locker, Bob Robert Awtry; B3.15.1938 George IA; BB/TR (BR 1965–67)/6´3˝/(185–200); d4.14; Col Iowa St.; [DL 1974 Oak A 182]																										
1965	Chi A	5	2	.714	51	0	0	2	91.1	71	36	6	2	30-10	69	3.15	101	.216	.281	14	.000	-2	—	0	0	0.0
1966	Chi A	9	8	.529	56	0	0	12	95	73	32	2	5	23-13	70	2.46	129	.206	.264	16	.250	1	—	7	0	1.8
1967	Chi A	7	5	.583	**77**	0	0	20	124.2	102	34	5	10	23-5	80	2.09	148	.222	.273	10-0-1	.000	-1	—	15	0	2.2
1968	Chi A	5	4	.556	70	0	0	10	90.1	78	27	4	1	27-13	62	2.29	132	.234	.290	8	.000	-1	—	7	0	1.0
1969	Chi A	2	3	.400	17	0	0	4-3	22	26	18	6	0	6-1	15	6.55	59	.292	.333	1	.000	-0	—	-7	0	-1.3
	Sea A	3	3	.500	51	0	0	6-4	78.1	69	29	3	3	26-8	46	2.18	167	.234	.301	12	.083	-0	—	9	0	0.9
	Year	5	6	.455	68	0	0	10-7	100.1	95	47	9	3	32-9	61	3.14	117	.247	.308	13	.077	-1	—	3	0	-0.4
1970	Mil A	0	1	.000	28	0	0	3-1	31.2	37	18	1	5	10-1	19	3.41	111	.306	.380	1	.000	-0	—	-1	0	-0.1
	Oak A	3	3	.500	38	0	0	4-3	56.1	49	21	1	1	19-3	33	2.88	123	.232	.299	6	.167	-0	—	4	0	0.5
	Year	3	4	.429	66	0	0	7-4	88	86	39	2	6	29-4	52	3.07	118	.259	.329	7	.143	-0	—	4	0	0.4
1971	†Oak A	7	2	.778	47	0	0	6-5	72.1	68	28	2	1	19-9	46	2.86	116	.249	.298	6	.000	-0	—	3	0	0.4
1972	†Oak A	6	1	.857	56	0	0	10-3	78	69	25	1	2	16-5	47	2.65	107	.235	.277	6	.000	0	—	2	0	0.3
1973	Chi N	10	6	.625	63	0	0	18-6	106.1	96	40	6	4	42-10	76	2.54	155	.244	.321	15-0-1	.067	-1	—	13	0	2.3
1975	Chi N	0	1	.000	22	0	0	0-0	32.2	38	21	3	2	16-2	14	4.96	78	.306	.392	0	ø	0	—	-4	0	-0.2
Total	10	57	39	.594	576	0	0	95-25	879	776	329	40	36	257-80	577	2.75	122	.237	.297	95-0-2	.074	-4	—	48	182	7.8
Lockwood, Skip Claude Edward; B8.17.1946 Boston MA; BR/TR/6´0˝/(180–200); d4.23.1965; ▲																										
1969	Sea A	0	1	.000	6	3	0	0-0	23	24	9	3	0	6-0	10	3.52	103	.279	.323	7	.000	-1	49	1	0	0.0
1970	Mil A	5	12	.294	27	26	3-1	0-0	173.2	173	91	22	6	79-2	93	4.30	88	.266	.347	53-1-12	.226	2	89	-9	0	-0.7
1971	Mil A	10	15	.400	33	32	5-1	0-0	208	191	93	13	5	91-6	115	3.33	105	.246	.326	62-1-10	.081	-1*	79	2	0	-0.1
1972	Mil A	8	15	.348	29	27	5-3	0-0	170	148	75	11	4	71-6	106	3.60	85	.232	.311	53-0-3	.132	-1*	78	-10	0	-1.6
1973	Mil A	5	12	.294	37	15	3	0-0	154.2	164	75	10	6	59-6	87	3.90	98	.280	.349	0	ø	0	67	-1	0	-0.1
1974	Cal A	2	5	.286	37	2	0	1-4	81.1	81	42	8	5	32-4	39	4.32	80	.264	.339	0	ø	0	140	-6	0	-0.5
1975	NY N	1	3	.250	24	0	0	2-1	48.1	28	9	3	1	25-6	61	1.49	236	.174	.287	6-0-1	.167	-0	—	11	0	1.0
1976	NY N	10	7	.588	56	0	0	19-5	94.1	62	31	6	2	34-8	108	2.67	125	.186	.265	18-0-3	.333	3	—	8	0	1.9
1977	NY N	4	8	.333	63	0	0	20-4	104	87	40	5	4	31-11	84	3.38	113	.227	.288	15-0-3	.200	-0	—	6	0	0.8
1978	NY N	7	13	.350	57	0	0	15-8	90.2	78	36	10	0	31-5	73	3.57	99	.236	.298	11-1-2	.182	1	—	1	0	0.3
1979	NY N	2	5	.286	27	0	0	9-0	42.1	33	7	3	0	14-5	42	1.49	250	.224	.292	2-0-1	.000	-0*	—	11	103	2.2
1980	Bos A	3	1	.750	24	1	0	2-1	45.2	61	31	4	0	17-3	11	5.32	80	.321	.371	0	ø	0	84	-6	0	-0.5
Total	12	57	97	.370	420	106	16-5	68-23	1236	1130	539	98	33	490-62	829	3.55	100	.246	.320	227-3-35	.159	3	78	8	103	2.7
Lockwood, Milo Milo Hathaway; B4.7.1858 Solon OH; D10.9.1897 Economy PA; 5´10˝/160; d4.17; ▲																										
1884	Was U	1	9	.100	11	10	6	0	67.2	99	95	4	—	15	48	7.32	33	.319	.351	67	.209	-1*	76	-35	—	-3.6
Loe, Kameron Kameron David; B9.10.1981 Simi Valley CA; BR/TR/6´8˝/(225–240); [TexA02 20/592]; d9.26; Col Cal St.–Northridge																										
2004	Tex A	0	0	ø	2	1	0	0-0	6.2	6	5	0	1	6-0	3	5.40	91	.273	.448	0	ø	0	131	-1	0	0.0
2005	Tex A	9	6	.600	48	8	0	1-3	92	89	43	7	2	31-6	45	3.42	133	.252	.315	0	ø	0	107	9	0	1.3
2006	Tex A	3	6	.333	15	15	1-1	0-0	78.1	105	54	10	1	22-0	34	5.86	80	.317	.359	0	ø	0	97	-10	45	-0.9
Total	3	12	12	.500	65	24	1-1	1-3	177	200	102	17	4	59-6	82	4.58	101	.283	.340	0	ø	0	102	-2	45	0.4
Loes, Billy William; B12.13.1929 Long Island City NY; BR/TR/6´1˝/(165–190); d5.18; Mil 1951																										
1950	Bro N	0	0	ø	10	0	0	0	12.2	16	11	5	0	5	2	7.82	52	.314	.375	1	.000	0	—	-5	0	-0.2
1952	†Bro N	13	8	.619	39	21	8-4	1	187.1	154	62	12	3	71	115	2.69	135	.224	.299	54-0-10	.093	-3*	133	20	0	1.8
1953	†Bro N	14	8	.636	32	25	9-1	0	162.2	165	92	21	3	53	75	4.54	94	.261	.322	56-0-2	.125	-2	132	-6	0	-0.8
1954	Bro N	13	5	.722	28	21	6	0	147.2	154	73	14	1	60	97	4.14	99	.269	.336	51-0-4	.118	-2	127	0	0	-0.3
1955	†Bro N	10	4	.714	22	19	6	0	128	116	59	16	2	46-1	85	3.59	113	.240	.308	44-0-3	.091	-3	104	7	0	0.3
1956	Bro N	0	1	.000	1	1	0	0	1.1	5	6	1	0	1-0	2	40.50	10	.556	.600	0	ø	0	67	-5	0	-0.7
	Bal A	2	7	.222	21	6	1	3	56.2	65	33	4	2	23-1	22	4.76	82	.291	.360	17-0-1	.176	-1	64	-5	0	-0.8
1957	Bal A★	12	7	.632	31	18	8-3	4	155.1	142	59	8	4	37-4	86	3.24	111	.245	.292	50-0-7	.080	-3	138	7	0	0.6
1958	Bal A	3	9	.250	32	10	1	5	114	106	51	10	8	44-5	44	3.63	99	.252	.328	30-0-3	.067	-2	57	0	0	-0.3
1959	Bal A	4	7	.364	37	0	0	14	64.1	58	31	5	3	25-3	34	4.06	93	.239	.315	8	.125	-0	—	-1	0	-0.3
1960	SF N	3	2	.600	37	0	0	5	45.2	40	26	9	4	17-2	28	4.93	71	.247	.330	4-0-1	.250	0	—	-6	0	-0.7
1961	SF N	6	5	.545	26	18	3-1	0	114.2	114	62	13	5	39-4	55	4.24	90	.258	.324	32-0-4	.156	-0	103	-6	0	-0.6
Total	11	80	63	.559	316	139	42-9	32	1190.1	1135	565	118	35	421-20	645	3.89	99	.252	.319	347-0-35	.110	-17	118	0	0	-2.0
Loewen, Adam Adam A.; B4.9.1984 Surrey BC, Can.; BL/TL/6´5˝/235; [BalA02 1/4]; d5.23; Col Chipola (FL) JC																										
2006	Bal A	6	6	.500	22	19	0	0-0	112.1	111	72	8	8	62-0	98	5.37	84	.259	.360	2	.000	-0	89	-11	0	-1.0
Loewer, Carlton Carlton Ernest; B9.24.1973 Lafayette LA; BR/TR/6´6˝/(200–220); [PhiN94 1/23]; d6.14; Col Mississippi St.; [DL 2000 SD N 181]																										
1998	Phi N	7	8	.467	21	21	1	0-0	122.2	154	86	18	3	39-1	58	6.09	71	.312	.360	35-0-5	.086	-1	99	-22	0	-2.5
1999	Phi N	2	6	.250	20	13	2-1	0-0	89.2	100	54	9	0	26-0	48	5.12	91	.287	.332	22-0-2	.227	1	85	-4	92	-0.3
2001	SD N	0	2	.000	2	2	0	0-0	4.1	13	12	2	0	3-0	1	24.92	17	.520	.571	0	ø	0	33	-10	60	-1.3
2003	SD N	1	2	.333	5	5	0	0-0	21.2	35	17	3	1	8-1	11	6.65	60	.368	.419	5-0-1	.000	-0	89	-7	0	-0.8
Total	4	10	18	.357	48	41	3-1	0-0	238.1	302	169	32	4	76-2	118	6.12	72	.314	.361	62-0-8	.129	-1	89	-43	333	-4.9
Loftus, Frank Francis Patrick; B3.10.1898 Scranton PA; D10.27.1980 Belchertown MA; BR/TR/5´9˝/190; d9.26; Col St. Bonaventure																										
1926	Was A	0	0	ø	1	0	0	0	1	3	2	0	0	2	0	9.00	43	.600	.714	0	ø	0	—	-1	—	0.0
Logan, Boone Boone; B8.13.1984 San Antonio TX; BR/TL/6´5˝/200; [ChiA02 20/600]; d4.4; Col Temple (TX) JC																										
2006	Chi A	0	0	ø	21	0	0	1-1	17.1	21	18	2	3	15-2	15	8.31	56	.288	.424	0	ø	0	—	-7	0	-0.3
Logan, Bob Robert Dean "Lefty"; B2.10.1910 Thompson NE; D5.20.1978 Indianapolis IN; BR/TL/5´10˝/170; d4.18																										
1935	Bro N	0	1	.000	2	0	0	0	2.2	2	1	0	0	1	1	3.38	118	.182	.250	0	ø	0	—	0	—	0.1
1937	Det A	0	0	ø	1	0	0	0	0.2	1	0	0	0	1	1	0.00	ø	.333	.500	0	ø	0	—	0	—	0.0
	Chi N	0	0	ø	4	0	0	1	6.1	6	1	0	0	4	2	1.42	280	.261	.370	1	.000	-0	—	2	—	0.1
1938	Chi N	0	2	.000	14	0	0	2	22.2	18	9	0	1	17	10	2.78	138	.222	.364	3	.000	-0	—	2	—	0.2
1941	Cin N	0	1	.000	2	0	0	0	3.1	5	5	0	0	5	0	8.10	44	.333	.500	0	ø	0	—	-2	0	-0.4
1945	Bos N	7	11	.389	34	25	5-1	1	187	213	84	9	1	53	53	3.18	121	.283	.331	61-0-6	.213	1	95	10	0	1.1
Total	5	7	15	.318	57	25	5-1	4	222.2	245	100	9	2	81	67	3.15	122	.277	.339	65-0-6	.200	1	95	12	0	1.1
Lohrman, Bill William Le Roy; B5.22.1913 Brooklyn NY; D9.13.1999 Poughkeepsie NY; BR/TR/6´1˝/185; d6.19																										
1934	Phi N	0	1	.000	4	0	0	1	6	5	5	0	0	1	2	4.50	105	.217	.250	2	.500	0	—	0	—	0.0
1937	NY N	1	0	1.000	2	1	1	1	10	5	1	0	0	2	3	0.90	432	.152	.200	2-0-1	.000	-0	67	3	—	0.4
1938	NY N	9	6	.600	31	14	3	0	152	152	72	9	2	33	52	3.32	114	.253	.294	49-0-3	.082	-4	117	5	—	0.1
1939	NY N	12	13	.480	38	24	9-1	1	185.2	200	91	15	3	45	70	4.07	96	.282	.327	60-2-0	.233	4	100	-1	—	0.3
1940	NY N	10	15	.400	31	27	11-4	1	195	200	98	19	3	43	73	3.78	103	.264	.306	65-0-4	.123	-2	87	1	—	-0.1
1941	NY N	9	10	.474	33	20	6-2	3	159	184	87	7	0	40	61	4.02	92	.286	.327	48-0-3	.229	4	94	-8	0	-0.5
1942	StL N	1	1	.500	5	0	0	0	12.2	11	3	0	0	2	6	1.42	241	.244	.277	3	.667	1	—	2	0	0.5
	NY N	13	4	.765	26	19	12-2	0	158	143	52	11	2	33	41	2.56	131	.240	.282	58-0-3	.121	-3	118	14	0	1.2
	Year	14	5	.737	31	19	12-2	0	170.2	154	55	11	2	35	47	2.48	136	.240	.281	61-0-3	.148	-2	118	17	0	1.7
1943	NY N	5	6	.455	17	12	3	1	80.1	110	51	7	2	25	16	5.15	67	.324	.374	27-0-2	.037	-3*	107	-15	0	-2.2
	Bro N	0	2	.000	6	2	2	0	27.2	29	14	2	1	10	5	3.58	94	.274	.342	7	.143	0	88	-1	0	-0.1
	Year	5	8	.385	23	14	5	1	108	139	65	9	3	35	21	4.75	72	.312	.366	34-0-2	.059	-3	104	-15	0	-2.3
1944	Bro N	0	0	ø	3	0	0	0	2.2	4	0	0	0	4	1	0.00	ø	.500	.667	0	ø	0	—	1	0	0.0

YEAR	TM LG	W	L	PCT	G	GS	CG-SHO	SV-BS	IP	H	R	HR	HB	BB-IB	SO	ERA	AERA	OAV	OOB	AB-HR-SH	AVG	PB	SUP	APR	DL	PW
	Cin N	0	1	.000	2	1	0	0	1.2	5	5	0	0	2	0	27.00	13	.500	.583	0	ø	0	0	-4	0	-0.7
	Year	0	1	.000	5	1	0	0	4.1	9	5	0	0	6	1	10.38	34	.500	.625	0	ø	0	0	-3	0	-0.7
Total	9	60	59	.504	198	120	47-9	8	990.2	1048	479	70	13	240	330	3.69	101	.271	.315	321-2-16	.153	-3	100	-3	0	-1.1
Lohse, Kyle	Kyle Matthew; B10.4.1978 Chico CA; BR/TR/6´2˝/(190–200); [ChiN96 29/862]; d6.22; Col Butte (CA) CC																									
2001	Min A	4	7	.364	19	16	0	0-0	90.1	102	60	16	8	29-0	64	5.68	82	.284	.347	5	.400	1	92	-10	0	-0.9
2002	†Min A	13	8	.619	32	31	1-1	0-1	180.2	181	92	26	9	70-2	124	4.23	105	.259	.333	4	.250	0	108	4	0	0.4
2003	†Min A	14	11	.560	33	33	2-1	0-0	201	211	107	28	5	45-1	130	4.61	98	.268	.310	3-0-3	.333	0	101	-2	0	-0.2
2004	†Min A	9	13	.409	35	34	1-1	0-0	194	240	128	28	7	76-5	111	5.34	87	.305	.368	3-0-1	.000	-0	97	-17	0	-1.7
2005	Min A	9	13	.409	31	30	0	0-0	178.2	211	85	22	9	44-5	86	4.18	105	.299	.345	5	.000	-1	70	7	0	0.7
2006	Min A	2	5	.286	22	8	0	0-0	63.2	80	50	8	6	25-2	46	7.07	65	.308	.378	0	ø	0	108	-16	0	-1.4
	Cin N	3	5	.375	12	11	0	0-0	63	70	33	7	0	19-2	51	4.57	103	.287	.336	23-0-1	.174	0	82	2	0	0.3
Total	6	54	62	.466	184	163	4-3	0-1	971.1	1095	555	135	44	308-17	612	4.86	93	.285	.342	43-0-5	.186	1	94	-32	0	-2.8
Loiselle, Rich	Richard Frank; B1.12.1972 Neenah WI; BR/TR/6´5˝/(225–253); [SDN91 38/991]; d9.7; Col Odessa (TX) JC																									
1996	Pit N	1	0	1.000	5	3	0	0-0	20.2	22	8	3	0	8-1	9	3.05	144	.268	.333	8	.250	1	178	3	0	0.2
1997	Pit N	1	5	.167	72	0	0	29-5	72.2	76	29	7	1	24-3	66	3.10	138	.269	.326	1	.000	-0	—	9	0	1.2
1998	Pit N	2	7	.222	54	0	0	19-8	55	56	26	2	2	36-9	48	3.44	124	.262	.372	0-0-1	ø	0	—	4	28	0.9
1999	Pit N	3	2	.600	13	0	0	0-1	15.1	16	9	2	2	9-2	14	5.28	87	.281	.397	0-0-1	ø	0	—	-1	149	-0.1
2000	Pit N	2	3	.400	40	0	0	0-6	42.1	43	27	5	3	30-5	32	5.10	91	.262	.380	0	ø	0	—	-2	86	-0.2
2001	Pit N	0	1	.000	18	0	0	1-0	18	28	24	3	4	17-4	9	11.50	39	.359	.495	0	ø	0	—	-13	72	-0.8
Total	6	9	18	.333	202	3	0	49-20	224	241	123	22	12	124-24	178	4.38	100	.274	.370	9-0-2	.222	0	178	0	335	1.2
Lolich, Mickey	Michael Stephen; B9.12.1940 Portland OR; BB/TL (BR 1976, 78–79)/6´0˝/(185–225); d5.12; [DL 1978 Det A 80]																									
1963	Det A	5	9	.357	33	18	4	0	144.1	145	64	13	5	56-1	103	3.55	105	.265	.336	36-0-2	.056	-1	92	3	0	0.2
1964	Det A	18	9	.667	44	33	12-6	2	232	196	88	26	5	64-0	192	3.26	112	.225	.282	64-0-9	.109	1	113	12	0	1.3
1965	Det A	15	9	.625	43	37	7-3	3	243.2	216	103	23	12	72-2	226	3.44	101	.236	.298	86-0-3	.058	-6	114	1	0	-0.6
1966	Det A	14	14	.500	40	33	5-1	3	203.2	204	119	24	6	83-8	173	4.77	73	.257	.329	64-0-2	.141	1	124	-28	0	-3.7
1967	Det A	14	13	.519	31	30	11-**6**	0	204	165	71	14	7	56-2	174	3.04	107	.221	.281	61-0-7	.197	3*	98	7	0	1.2
1968	†Det A	17	9	.654	39	32	8-4	1	220	178	84	23	11	65-4	197	3.19	94	.219	.285	70-0-4	.114	0*	109	-4	0	-0.5
1969	Det A☆	19	11	.633	37	36	15-1	1-0	280.2	214	111	22	14	122-10	271	3.14	120	.210	.302	91-0-12	.088	-3*	110	18	0	1.6
1970	Det A	14	19	.424	40	39	13-3	0-0	272.2	272	125	27	5	109-3	230	3.80	99	.260	.330	82-0-7	.134	1*	79	0	0	0.2
1971	Det A★	**25**	14	.641	45	**45**	**29**-4	0-0	**376**	336	133	36	7	92-2	**308**	2.92	124	.237	.285	115-0-16	.130	1	117	28	0	2.9
1972	†Det A★	22	14	.611	41	41	23-4	0-0	327.1	282	100	29	11	74-5	250	2.50	127	.234	.283	89-0-11	.067	-0	92	25	0	2.7
1973	Det A	16	15	.516	42	42	17-3	0-0	308.2	315	143	35	5	79-7	214	3.82	107	.266	.314	0	ø	0	87	8	0	0.7
1974	Det A	16	21	.432	41	41	27-3	0-0	308	310	155	38	3	78-11	202	4.15	92	.268	.314	0	ø	0	83	-8	0	-1.0
1975	Det A	12	18	.400	32	32	19-1	0-0	240.2	260	119	19	0	64-5	139	3.78	107	.279	.322	0	ø	0	72	7	0	0.7
1976	NY N	8	13	.381	31	30	5-2	0-0	192.2	184	83	14	0	52-1	120	3.22	104	.252	.300	54-0-11	.130	0	85	1	0	0.1
1978	SD N	2	1	.667	20	2	0	1-0	34.2	30	6	0	1	11-3	13	1.56	215	.240	.307	3	.000	-0	54	8	0	0.7
1979	SD N	0	2	.000	27	5	0	0-0	49.1	59	33	4	0	22-3	20	4.74	74	.304	.372	6-0-1	.000	-0	140	-9	0	-0.5
Total	16	217	191	.532	586	496	195-41	11-0	3638.1	3366	1537	347	92	1099-67	2832	3.44	105	.246	.304	821-0-85	.110	-4	98	69	80	6.0
Lollar, Tim	William Timothy; B3.17.1956 Poplar Bluff MO; BL/TL/6´3˝/(195–204); [NYA78 4/104]; d6.28; Col Arkansas																									
1980	NY A	1	0	1.000	14	1	0	2-0	32.1	33	14	3	0	20-2	13	3.34	119	.280	.379	0	ø	0	45	2	0	0.1
1981	SD N	2	8	.200	24	11	0	1-0	76.2	87	56	4	3	51-8	38	6.10	53	.293	.399	18-1-0	.167	1	104	-26	0	-2.8
1982	SD N	16	9	.640	34	34	4-2	0-0	232.2	192	82	20	4	87-4	150	3.13	109	.224	.297	85-3-2	.247	9*	108	13	0	2.4
1983	SD N	7	12	.368	30	30	1	0-0	175.2	170	98	22	4	85-1	135	4.61	76	.258	.346	58-1-0	.241	6*	95	-22	0	-1.6
1984	†SD N	11	13	.458	31	31	3-2	0-0	195.2	168	89	18	1	105-2	131	3.91	92	.234	.331	68-3-1	.221	7	94	-4	0	0.1
1985	Chi A	3	5	.375	18	13	0	0-0	83	83	48	10	1	58-1	61	4.66	93	.266	.379	0	ø	0	95	-3	0	-0.3
	Bos A	5	5	.500	16	10	1	1-0	67	57	37	9	1	40-0	44	4.57	94	.230	.338	1	.000	-0*	103	-2	0	-0.3
	Year	8	10	.444	34	23	1	1-0	150	140	85	19	2	98-1	105	4.62	94	.250	.361	1	.000	-0	99	-4	0	-0.6
1986	Bos A	2	0	1.000	32	1	0	0-1	43	51	35	7	3	34-3	28	6.91	61	.304	.421	1	1.000	0*	259	-12	0	-0.5
Total	7	47	52	.475	199	131	9-4	4-1	906	841	459	93	17	480-21	600	4.27	86	.249	.343	231-8-3	.234	23	100	-54	0	-2.9
Lombardi, Vic	Victor Alvin; B9.20.1922 Reedley CA; D12.7.1997 Fresno CA; BL/TL/5´7˝/158; d4.18																									
1945	Bro N	10	11	.476	38	24	9	4	203.2	195	106	11	5	86	64	3.31	113	.252	.331	71-0-3	.183	-1*	97	6	0	0.4
1946	Bro N	13	10	.565	41	25	13-2	3	193	170	76	10	2	84	60	2.89	117	.235	.316	61-0-10	.230	2*	111	10	0	1.3
1947	†Bro N	12	11	.522	33	20	7-3	3	174.2	156	73	12	2	65	72	2.99	138	.241	.312	66-0-1	.242	2*	78	19	0	2.6
1948	Pit N	10	9	.526	38	17	9	4	163	156	72	9	2	67	54	3.70	110	.255	.330	48-0-1	.208	1*	90	8	0	1.0
1949	Pit N	5	5	.500	34	12	4	1	134	149	74	12	3	68	64	4.57	92	.286	.372	49	.347	5*	114	-5	0	0.3
1950	Pit N	0	5	.000	39	2	0	1	76.1	93	61	14	2	48	26	6.60	66	.310	.409	16-0-1	.250	1*	91	-17	0	-0.9
Total	6	50	51	.495	223	100	42-5	16	944.2	919	462	68	16	418	340	3.68	106	.257	.337	311-0-16	.238	10	96	21	0	4.7
Lombardo, Lou	Louis; B11.18.1928 Carlstadt NJ; D6.11.2001 Rock Hill SC; BL/TL/6´2˝/210; d9.22																									
1948	NY N	0	0	ø	2	0	0	0	5.1	5	4	1	1	5	0	6.75	58	.250	.423	2	.000	-0	—	-1	0	-0.1
Lomon, Kevin	Kevin Dale; B11.20.1971 Fort Smith AR; BR/TR/6´1˝/195; [AtlN91 14/361]; d4.27; Col Arkansas–Fort Smith [JC]																									
1995	NY N	0	1	.000	6	0	0	0-0	9.1	17	8	0	0	5-1	6	6.75	60	.405	.468	0-0-1	ø	0	—	-3	0	-0.3
1996	Atl N	0	0	ø	6	0	0	0-0	7.1	7	4	0	1	3-0	1	4.91	91	.259	.355	0	ø	0	—	0	0	0.0
Total	2	0	1	.000	12	0	0	0-0	16.2	24	12	0	1	8-1	7	5.94	71	.348	.423	0-0-1	ø	0	—	-3	0	-0.3
Lonborg, Jim	James Reynold; B4.16.1942 Santa Maria CA; BR/TR/6´5˝/(195–210); d4.23; Col Stanford																									
1965	Bos A	9	17	.346	32	31	7-1	0	185.1	193	112	20	3	65-3	113	4.47	83	.262	.323	59-0-5	.136	0	112	-16	0	-2.1
1966	Bos A	10	10	.500	45	23	3-1	2	181.2	173	86	18	7	55-5	131	3.86	98	.249	.308	54-0-6	.093	-2*	117	0	0	-0.2
1967	†Bos A☆	**22**	9	.710	39	**39**	15-2	0	273.1	228	102	23	19	83-5	**246**	3.16	110	.225	.294	99-0-6	.141	-1	110	12	0	1.0
1968	Bos A	6	10	.375	23	17	4-1	0	113.1	89	57	11	11	59-3	73	4.29	74	.216	.327	39-1-5	.282	3	104	-12	46	-1.4
1969	Bos A	7	11	.389	29	23	4	0-1	143.2	148	78	15	7	65-3	100	4.51	85	.270	.354	41-0-5	.098	-1	86	-8	0	-1.1
1970	Bos A	4	1	.800	9	4	0	0-0	34	33	12	3	0	9-0	21	3.18	125	.260	.304	9-1-0	.444	2	89	4	55	0.8
1971	Bos A	10	7	.588	27	26	5-1	0-0	167.2	167	86	15	14	67-6	100	4.13	90	.259	.341	53-0-2	.170	0	129	-8	0	-0.7
1972	Mil A	14	12	.538	33	30	11-2	1-0	223	197	75	17	11	76-11	143	2.83	108	.238	.309	69-0-9	.145	-1	108	7	0	0.7
1973	Phi N	13	16	.448	38	30	6	0-1	199.1	218	124	25	9	80-7	106	4.88	78	.279	.350	59-0-4	.136	0	99	-24	0	-3.2
1974	Phi N	17	13	.567	39	39	16-3	0-0	283	280	113	22	6	70-11	121	3.21	118	.261	.308	94-1-11	.096	-4	99	17	0	1.1
1975	Phi N	8	6	.571	27	26	6-2	0-0	159.1	161	84	12	5	45-7	72	4.12	91	.257	.310	44-0-6	.023	-3	111	-7	0	-0.9
1976	†Phi N	18	10	.643	33	32	8-1	1-0	222	210	85	18	5	50-4	118	3.08	116	.249	.292	67-0-6	.164	1	106	12	0	1.4
1977	†Phi N	11	4	.733	25	25	4-1	0-0	157.2	157	77	15	5	50-5	76	4.11	98	.261	.321	48-0-9	.104	-2	121	0	49	-0.3
1978	Phi N	8	10	.444	22	22	1	0-0	113.2	132	69	16	2	45-1	48	5.23	69	.293	.359	34-0-4	.176	1	105	-19	0	-2.6
1979	Phi N	0	1	.000	4	1	0	0-0	7.1	14	10	3	1	4-0	7	11.05	35	.389	.463	1	.000	-0	46	-6	0	-0.7
Total	15	157	137	.534	425	368	90-15	4-2	2464.1	2400	1170	233	105	823-71	1475	3.86	95	.255	.320	770-3-78	.136	-5	108	-48	150	-8.2
Long, Joey	Joey J.; B7.15.1970 Sidney OH; BR/TL/6´2˝/220; [SDN91 5/133]; d4.25; Col Kent St.																									
1997	SD N	0	0	ø	10	0	0	0-0	11	17	11	1	1	8-1	8	8.18	48	.340	.441	0	ø	0	—	-6	0	-0.3
Long, Lep	Lester; B7.12.1888 Summit NJ; D10.21.1958 Birmingham AL; BR/TR/5´10˝/153; d6.29; Col Lafayette																									
1911	Phi A	0	0	ø	4	0	0	0	8	15	6	0	0	5	4	4.50	70	.405	.476	3	.000	-0	—	-2	—	-0.1
Long, Red	Nelson; B9.28.1876 Burlington ON, Can.; D8.11.1929 Hamilton ON, Can.; BR/TR/6´1˝/190; d9.11																									
1902	Bos N	0	0	ø	1	1	1	0	8	4	2	0	1	3	5	1.13	251	.148	.258	1	.000	-0	48	1	—	0.0
Long, Bob	Robert Earl; B11.11.1954 Jasper TN; BR/TR/6´3˝/(178–185); [PitN76 24/565]; d9.2; Col Shorter																									
1981	Pit N	1	2	.333	5	3	0	0-0	19.2	23	14	2	0	10-0	8	5.95	61	.299	.375	4-0-1	.000	-0	65	-4	0	-0.7
1985	Sea A	0	0	ø	28	0	0	0-0	38.1	30	17	7	2	17-1	29	3.76	113	.210	.302	0	ø	0	—	2	0	0.1
Total	2	1	2	.333	33	3	0	0-0	58	53	31	9	2	27-1	37	4.50	90	.241	.328	4-0-1	.000	-0	65	-2	0	-0.6
Long, Tom	Thomas Francis "Little Hawk"; B4.22.1898 Memphis TN; D9.16.1973 Louisville KY; BL/TL/5´9˝/154; d4.26																									
1924	Bro N	0	0	ø	1	0	0	0	2	2	2	0	0	2	0	9.00	42	.333	.500	0	ø	0	—	-1	—	-0.1

YEAR	TM LG	W	L	PCT	G	GS	CG-SHO	SV-BS	IP	H	R	HR	HB	BB-IB	SO	ERA	AERA	OAV	OOB	AB-HR-SH	AVG	PB	SUP	APR	DL	PW
LONG, BILL	William Douglas; B2.29.1960 Cincinnati OH; BR/TR/6´0˝/185; [SDN81 2/32]; d7.21; Col Miami–Ohio																									
1985	Chi A	0	1	.000	4	3	0	0-0	14	25	17	4	0	5-2	13	10.29	42	.391	.429	0	ø	0	112	-9	0	-0.5
1987	Chi A	8	8	.500	29	23	5-2	1-0	169	179	85	20	3	28-1	72	4.37	106	.272	.303	0	ø	0	112	6	0	0.5
1988	Chi A	8	11	.421	47	18	3	2-1	174	187	89	21	4	43-4	77	4.03	99	.280	.323	0	ø	0	80	0	0	-0.1
1989	Chi A	5	5	.500	30	8	0	1-0	98.2	101	49	8	4	37-0	51	3.92	98	.265	.332	0	ø	0	80	-1	0	-0.1
1990	Chi A	0	1	.000	4	0	0	0-0	5.2	6	5	2	0	2-0	2	6.35	61	.261	.320	0	ø	0	—	-2	0	-0.3
	Chi N	6	1	.857	42	0	0	5-2	55.2	66	29	8	1	21-4	32	4.37	94	.301	.365	5	.000	-0	—	-1	21	-0.2
1991	Mon N	0	0	ø	3	0	0	0-0	1.2	4	2	0	0	4-0	0	10.80	34	.500	.667	0	ø	0	—	-1	0	-0.1
Total	6	27	27	.500	159	52	8-2	9-3	518.2	568	276	63	12	140-11	247	4.37	96	.281	.328	5	.000	-0	99	-8	21	-0.8
LOONEY, BRIAN	Brian James; B9.26.1969 New Haven CT; BL/TL/5´10˝/(175–185); [MonN91 10/269]; d9.26; Col Boston College																									
1993	Mon N	0	0	ø	3	1	0	0-0	6	8	2	0	0	2-0	7	3.00	139	.308	.357	1	.000	-0	108	1	0	0.0
1994	Mon N	0	0	ø	1	0	0	0-0	2	4	5	1	1	0-0	2	22.50	19	.400	.455	0	ø	0	—	-4	0	-0.2
1995	Bos A	0	1	.000	3	1	0	0-0	4.2	12	9	1	0	4-1	2	17.36	28	.545	.571	0	ø	0	57	-6	0	-0.9
Total	3	0	1	.000	7	2	0	0-0	12.2	24	16	2	1	6-1	11	11.37	39	.414	.463	1	.000	-0	82	-9	0	-1.1
LOOPER, AARON	Aaron Joseph; B9.7.1976 Ada OK; BR/TR/6´2˝/180; [SeaA97 30/913]; d8.2; Col Indian Hills (IA) CC																									
2003	Sea A	0	0	ø	6	0	0	0-0	7	7	4	1	1	2-0	6	5.14	84	.269	.345	0	ø	0	—	-1	0	0.0
LOOPER, BRADEN	Braden La Vern; B10.28.1974 Weatherford OK; BR/TR/6´5˝/(210–225); [StLN96 1/3]; d3.31; Col Wichita St.																									
1998	StL N	0	1	.000	4	0	0	0-2	3.1	5	4	1	0	1-0	4	5.40	78	.357	.375	0	ø	0	—	-1	0	-0.2
1999	Fla N	3	3	.500	72	0	0	0-4	83	96	43	7	1	31-6	50	3.80	115	.293	.351	0	ø	0	—	3	0	0.2
2000	Fla N	5	1	.833	73	0	0	2-3	67.1	71	41	3	5	36-6	29	4.41	99	.268	.364	2	.000	-0	—	-3	0	-0.2
2001	Fla N	3	3	.500	71	0	0	3-3	71	63	28	8	2	30-3	52	3.55	117	.242	.322	2	.000	-0	—	6	0	0.5
2002	Fla N	2	5	.286	78	0	0	13-3	86	73	31	8	1	28-3	55	3.14	125	.230	.295	1	.000	-0	—	9	0	0.9
2003	†Fla N	6	4	.600	74	0	0	28-6	80.2	82	34	4	1	29-1	56	3.68	111	.264	.326	1-0-1	1.000	0	—	5	0	0.8
2004	NY N	2	5	.286	71	0	0	29-5	83.1	86	28	5	3	16-3	60	2.70	159	.266	.305	2	.000	-0	—	15	0	1.9
2005	NY N	4	7	.364	60	0	0	28-8	59.1	65	31	7	5	22-3	27	3.94	105	.271	.345	0	ø	0	—	0	0	-0.1
2006	†StL N	9	3	.750	69	0	0	0-2	73.1	76	30	3	2	20-5	41	3.56	122	.277	.326	2	.500	1	—	7	0	1.1
Total	9	34	32	.515	572	0	0	103-36	607.1	617	270	46	20	213-30	374	3.57	118	.265	.329	10-0-1	.200	0	—	41	0	4.9
LOOS, PETE	Ivan; B3.23.1878 Philadelphia PA; D2.23.1956 Darby PA; TR/5´9˝/178; d5.2; Col Ursinus																									
1901	Phi A	0	1	.000	1	1	0	0	1	2	5	0	0	4	0	27.00	14	.400	.667	0	ø	0	215	-3	—	-0.4
LOPAT, ED	Edmund Walter (b Edmund Walter Lopatynski); B6.21.1918 New York NY; D6.15.1992 Darien CT; BL/TL/5´10˝/(182–185); d4.30; M2/C3																									
1944	Chi A	11	10	.524	27	25	13-1	0	210	217	96	12	2	59	75	3.26	105	.265	.316	81-0-1	.309	6*	98	2	0	1.0
1945	Chi A	10	13	.435	26	24	17-1	1	199.1	226	101	8	6	56	74	4.11	81	.285	.336	82-1-1	.293	5*	109	-16	0	-1.2
1946	Chi A	13	13	.500	29	29	20-2	0	231	216	80	18	1	48	89	2.73	125	.248	.288	87-0-2	.253	6*	109	21	0	3.2
1947	Chi A	16	13	.552	31	31	22-3	0	252.2	241	88	17	2	73	109	2.81	130	.253	.307	96-0-4	.198	0*	91	26	0	2.9
1948	NY A	17	11	.607	33	31	13-3	0	226.2	246	106	16	2	66	83	3.65	112	.284	.336	81-0-4	.173	-1*	110	10	0	1.0
1949	†NY A	15	10	.600	31	30	14-4	1	215.1	222	93	19	5	69	70	3.26	124	.269	.330	76-1-1	.263	7	98	17	0	2.6
1950	†NY A	18	8	.692	35	32	15-3	1	236.1	244	110	19	4	65	72	3.47	124	.266	.317	82-0-5	.232	8*	124	18	0	2.5
1951	†NY A★	21	9	.700	31	31	20-4	0	234.2	209	86	12	3	71	93	2.91	131	.239	**.298**	84-3-4	.179	1	99	26	0	3.3
1952	†NY A	10	5	.667	20	19	10-2	0	149.1	127	47	11	4	53	56	2.53	131	.234	.307	52-0-2	.173	1	119	15	0	1.6
1953	†NY A	16	4	**.800**	25	24	9-3	0	178.1	169	58	13	4	32	50	**2.42**	**152**	.250	.288	63-0-5	.190	1*	126	25	0	2.9
1954	NY A	12	4	.750	26	23	7	0	170	189	74	14	6	33	54	3.55	97	.288	.326	57-0-4	.018	-5	117	-2	0	-0.7
1955	NY A	4	8	.333	16	12	3-1	0	86.2	101	45	12	1	16-3	24	3.74	100	.294	.327	29	.138	-1	83	-2	0	-0.4
	Bal A	3	4	.429	10	7	1	0	49	57	24	8	3	9-2	10	4.22	90	.294	.332	17-0-1	.176	0	73	-1	0	-0.1
	Year	7	12	.368	26	19	4-1	0	135.2	158	69	20	4	25-5	34	3.91	96	.294	.329	46-0-1	.152	-1	79	-3	0	-0.5
Total	12	166	112	.597	340	318	164-27	3	2439.1	2464	1008	179	43	650-5	859	3.21	116	.264	.315	887-5-34	.211	29	107	139	0	18.6
LOPATKA, ART	Arthur Joseph; B5.28.1919 Chicago IL; BB/TL/5´10˝/170; d9.12; Col Chicago																									
1945	StL N	1	0	1.000	4	1	1	0	11.2	7	4	0	1	3	5	1.54	243	.159	.229	4	.250	0	68	2	0	0.2
1946	Phi N	0	1	.000	4	1	0	0	5.1	13	11	1	0	4	4	16.88	20	.448	.515	0	ø	0	150	-8	0	-1.2
Total	2	1	1	.500	8	2	1	0	17	20	15	1	1	7	9	6.35	57	.274	.346	4	.250	0	105	-6	0	-1.0
LOPEZ, ALBIE	Albert Anthony; B8.18.1971 Mesa AZ; BR/TR/6´2˝/(185–240); [CleA91 20/528]; d7.6; Col Mesa (AZ) CC																									
1993	Cle A	3	1	.750	9	9	0	0-0	49.2	49	34	7	1	32-1	25	5.98	73	.262	.371	0	ø	0	145	-8	0	-0.5
1994	Cle A	1	2	.333	4	4	1-1	0-0	17	20	11	3	1	6-0	18	4.24	112	.290	.355	0	ø	0	92	0	0	0.0
1995	Cle A	0	0	ø	6	2	0	0-0	23	17	8	4	1	7-1	22	3.13	151	.205	.272	0	ø	0	99	4	0	0.2
1996	Cle A	5	4	.556	13	10	0	0-0	62	80	47	14	2	22-1	45	6.39	77	.311	.369	0	ø	0	121	-10	0	-1.2
1997	Cle A	3	7	.300	37	6	0	0-1	76.2	101	61	11	4	40-9	63	6.93	68	.321	.402	1	.000	-0	124	-17	45	-1.8
1998	TB A	7	4	.636	54	0	0	1-4	79.2	73	31	7	3	32-4	62	2.60	185	.249	.326	1	.000	-0	—	16	25	2.0
1999	TB A	3	2	.600	51	0	0	1-2	64	66	40	8	1	24-2	37	4.64	107	.263	.325	0	ø	0	—	1	39	0.1
2000	TB A	11	13	.458	45	24	4-1	2-2	185.1	199	95	24	1	70-3	96	4.13	119	.277	.341	6-0-1	.000	-1	75	15	0	1.5
2001	TB A	5	12	.294	20	20	1-1	0-0	124.2	152	87	16	4	51-1	67	5.34	84	.302	.368	5	.000	-1	69	-13	0	-1.5
	†Ari N	4	7	.364	13	13	2-2	0-0	81	74	36	10	0	24-2	69	4.00	116	.247	.301	24-0-2	.042	-1	81	7	0	0.7
2002	Atl N	1	4	.200	30	4	0	0-0	55.2	66	29	1	0	18-3	39	4.37	93	.300	.349	9	.111	-0	57	-2	39	-0.2
2003	KC A	4	2	.667	15	0	0	0-3	22.2	41	32	7	0	17-1	15	12.71	38	.383	.468	0	ø	0	—	-18	30	-3.0
Total	11	47	58	.448	297	92	8-5	4-12	841.1	938	511	112	18	343-28	558	4.94	95	.284	.352	46-0-3	.043	-3	90	-25	178	-3.7
LOPEZ, AQUILINO	Aquilino (Roa); B4.21.1975 Villa Altagracia, D.R.; BR/TR/6´3˝/(160–165); d4.2																									
2003	Tor A	1	3	.250	72	0	0	14-2	73.2	58	31	5	5	34-5	64	3.42	139	.212	.309	0	ø	0	—	10	0	0.8
2004	Tor A	1	1	.500	18	0	0	0-0	21	21	15	5	2	13-3	13	6.00	82	.266	.379	0	ø	0	—	-3	0	-0.2
2005	Col N	0	0	ø	1	0	0	0-0	4	3	1	0	0	0-0	6	2.25	207	.200	.200	1	.000	-0	—	1	0	0.0
	Phi N	0	1	.000	10	0	0	0-0	12.2	13	4	2	0	7-1	16	2.13	204	.265	.357	0	ø	0	—	3	0	0.2
	Year	0	1	.000	11	0	0	0-0	16.2	16	5	2	0	7-1	22	2.16	204	.250	.324	1	.000	-0	—	4	0	0.2
Total	3	2	5	.286	101	0	0	14-2	111.1	95	51	12	7	54-9	99	3.72	127	.228	.325	1	.000	-0	—	11	0	0.8
LOPEZ, AURELIO	Aurelio Alejandro (Rios); B9.21.1948 Tecamachalco, Puebla, Mexico; D9.22.1992 Matehuala, San Luis Potosi, Mexico; BR/TR/6´0˝/(200–230); d9.1																									
1974	KC A	0	0	ø	8	1	0	0-0	16	21	12	0	0	10-0	5	5.63	68	.344	.425	0	ø	0	92	-3	0	-0.2
1978	StL N	4	2	.667	25	4	0	0-0	65	52	35	4	1	32-2	46	4.29	83	.218	.308	14-0-2	.214	0	157	-5	0	-0.5
1979	Det A	10	5	.667	61	0	0	21-5	127	95	37	12	3	51-3	106	2.41	181	.210	.292	0	ø	0	—	27	0	3.9
1980	Det A	13	6	.684	67	1	0	21-5	124	125	56	15	3	45-5	97	3.77	109	.263	.328	0	ø	0	87	5	0	0.8
1981	Det A	5	2	.714	29	3	0	3-2	81.2	70	34	8	2	31-2	53	3.64	104	.233	.306	0	ø	0	103	2	0	0.1
1982	Det A	3	1	.750	19	0	0	3-0	41	41	27	8	0	19-4	26	5.27	78	.268	.345	0	ø	0	—	-5	38	-0.6
1983	Det A☆	9	8	.529	57	0	0	18-8	115.1	87	36	12	1	49-7	90	2.81	141	.210	.292	0	ø	0	—	17	0	2.8
1984	†Det A	10	1	.909	71	0	0	14-2	137.2	109	51	16	2	52-6	94	2.94	135	.221	.295	0	ø	0	—	16	0	1.4
1985	Det A	3	7	.300	51	0	0	5-2	86.1	82	50	15	1	41-9	53	4.80	86	.250	.330	0	ø	0	—	-6	0	-0.7
1986	†Hou N	3	3	.500	45	0	0	7-1	78	64	32	6	0	25-1	44	3.46	104	.221	.280	9-0-1	.000	-1	—	2	0	0.0
1987	Hou N	2	1	.667	26	0	0	1-1	38	39	22	6	2	12-0	21	4.50	87	.273	.333	1-0-1	.000	-0	—	-3	0	-0.2
Total	11	62	36	.633	459	9	0	93-26	910	785	392	102	15	367-39	635	3.56	112	.234	.309	24-0-4	.125	-1	116	47	38	6.8
LOPEZ, JAVIER	Javier Alfonso; B6.11.1977 San Juan, PR; BL/TL/6´4˝/(200–220); [AriN98 4/133]; d4.1; Col Virginia																									
2003	Col N	4	1	.800	75	0	0	1-1	58.1	58	25	5	4	12-2	40	3.70	132	.258	.307	5	.200	-0	—	7	0	0.6
2004	Col N	1	2	.333	64	0	0	0-1	40.2	45	34	1	3	26-4	20	7.52	63	.287	.398	2-0-1	.000	-0	—	-11	0	-0.6
2005	Ari N	1	1	.500	29	0	0	2-1	14.1	19	15	2	1	11-3	11	9.42	47	.311	.425	0	ø	0	—	-7	0	-1.0
	Col N	0	0	ø	3	0	0	0-1	2	7	5	0	0	0-0	1	22.50	21	.538	.538	0	ø	0	—	-3	0	-0.2
	Year	1	1	.500	32	0	0	2-2	16.1	26	20	2	1	11-3	12	11.02	40	.351	.442	0	ø	0	—	-11	0	-1.2
2006	Bos A	1	0	1.000	27	0	0	1-0	16.2	13	10	1	2	10-1	11	2.70	173	.232	.362	0	ø	0	—	1	0	0.1
Total	4	7	4	.636	198	0	0	4-4	132	142	89	9	10	59-10	83	5.66	84	.277	.363	7-0-1	.143	-0	—	-13	0	-1.1
LOPEZ, RAMON	Jose Ramon (Hevia); B5.26.1933 Las Villas, Cuba; D9.4.1982 Miami FL; BR/TR/6´0˝/175; d8.21																									
1966	Cal A	0	1	.000	4	1	0	0	7	4	5	1	0	4-0	2	5.14	65	.154	.267	0	ø	0*	105	-2	0	-0.2

YEAR	TM LG	W	L	PCT	G	GS	CG-SHO	SV-BS	IP	H	R	HR	HB	BB-IB	SO	ERA	AERA	OAV	OOB	AB-HR-SH	AVG	PB	SUP	APR	DL	PW
LOPEZ, MARCELINO	Marcelino Pons; B9.23.1943 Havana, Cuba; D11.29.2001 Hialeah FL; BR/TL/6´3˝/(195–222); d4.14																									
1963	Phi N	1	0	1.000	4	2	0	0	6	8	5	0	0	7-1	2	6.00	54	.333	.469	2	.000	-0*	147	-2	0	-0.3
1965	Cal A	14	13	.519	35	32	8-1	1	215.1	185	79	12	4	82-6	122	2.93	116	.230	.304	69-1-7	.203	3*	83	11	0	2.0
1966	Cal A	7	14	.333	37	32	6-2	1	199	188	95	20	9	68-2	132	3.93	85	.251	.319	58-0-3	.190	2*	85	-12	0	-0.9
1967	Cal A	0	2	.000	4	3	0	0	9	11	10	1	0	9-0	6	9.00	35	.324	.455	2	.500	0*	120	-6	31	-1.1
	Bal A	1	0	1.000	4	4	0	0	17.2	15	5	1	0	10-0	15	2.55	124	.227	.329	5	.000	-0*	131	1	51	0.0
	Year	1	2	.333	8	7	0	0	26.2	26	15	2	0	19-0	21	4.73	67	.260	.375	7	.143	0	126	-4	0	-1.1
1969	†Bal A	5	3	.625	27	4	0	0-3	69.1	65	34	3	2	34-4	57	4.41	81	.252	.340	14-0-2	.214	1	105	-5	0	-0.4
1970	†Bal A	1	1	.500	25	3	0	0-0	60.2	47	19	2	0	37-3	49	2.08	177	.217	.327	13	.077	0	178	9	0	0.4
1971	Mil A	2	7	.222	31	11	0	0-1	67.2	64	48	5	0	60-1	42	4.66	75	.251	.390	17-0-1	.059	-1*	84	-12	0	-1.6
1972	Cle A	0	0	ø	4	2	0	0-0	8.1	8	5	0	0	10-0	1	5.40	60	.276	.462	1	.000	-0	41	-2	0	-0.1
Total	8	31	40	.437	171	93	14-3	2-4	653	591	300	44	15	317-17	426	3.62	95	.243	.331	181-1-13	.171	4	91	-18	82	-2.0
LOPEZ, RODRIGO	Rodrigo (Munoz); B12.14.1975 Tlalnepantla, Estado de Mexico, Mexico; BR/TR/6´1˝/(180–190); d4.29																									
2000	SD N	0	3	.000	6	6	0	0-0	24.2	40	24	5	0	13-0	17	8.76	51	.377	.442	9	.111	-0	117	-11	0	-1.1
2002	Bal A	15	9	.625	33	28	1	0-0	196.2	172	83	23	5	62-4	136	3.57	122	.234	.296	3	.000	-0	102	18	0	1.9
2003	Bal A	7	10	.412	26	26	3-1	0-0	147	188	101	24	10	43-6	103	5.82	79	.313	.365	2	.000	-0	96	-19	44	-1.9
2004	Bal A	14	9	.609	37	23	1-1	0-1	170.2	164	71	21	2	54-2	121	3.59	130	.252	.310	0	ø	0	98	22	0	2.6
2005	Bal A	15	12	.556	35	**35**	0	0-0	209.1	232	126	28	7	63-1	118	4.90	90	.276	.330	4	.000	-0	92	-11	0	-1.2
2006	Bal A	9	18	.333	36	29	0	0-0	189	234	129	32	4	59-2	136	5.90	77	.302	.353	2-0-1	.000	-0	96	-28	0	-3.3
Total	6	60	61	.496	173	147	5-2	0-1	937.1	1030	534	133	28	294-15	631	4.83	93	.278	.334	20-0-1	.050	-2	97	-29	44	-3.0
LORENZEN, LEFTY	Adolph Andreas; B1.12.1893 Davenport IA; D3.5.1963 Davenport IA; BL/TL/5´10˝/164; d9.12																									
1913	Det A	0	0	ø	1	0	0	0	2	4	4	0	0	3	0	18.00	16	.667	.778	2	.500	0	—	-3	—	-0.1
LORRAINE, ANDREW	Andrew Jason; B8.11.1972 Los Angeles CA; BL/TL/6´3˝/(195–205); [CalA93 4/103]; d7.17; Col Stanford																									
1994	Cal A	0	2	.000	4	3	0	0-0	18.2	30	23	7	0	11-0	10	10.61	46	.366	.436	0	ø	0	81	-11	0	-0.9
1995	Chi A	0	0	ø	5	0	0	0-0	8	3	3	0	1	2-0	5	3.38	133	.111	.200	0	ø	0	—	1	0	0.0
1997	Oak A	3	1	.750	12	6	0	0-0	29.2	45	22	2	1	15-0	18	6.37	72	.354	.418	0	ø	0	147	-6	0	-0.6
1998	Sea A	0	0	ø	4	0	0	0-0	3.2	3	1	0	0	4-0	0	2.45	191	.250	.438	0	ø	0	—	1	0	0.0
1999	Chi N	2	5	.286	11	11	2-1	0-0	61.2	71	42	9	0	22-3	40	5.55	82	.293	.350	15-0-4	.133	0*	86	-7	0	-0.6
2000	Chi N	1	2	.333	8	5	0	0-1	32	36	25	5	0	18-1	25	6.47	71	.286	.370	8-0-2	.125	-0	120	-7	0	-0.6
	Cle A	0	0	ø	10	0	0	0-0	9.1	8	4	1	0	5-0	5	3.86	130	.222	.317	0	ø	0	—	1	0	0.1
2002	Mil N	0	1	.000	5	1	0	0-0	12	22	18	7	0	6-0	10	11.25	37	.379	.438	1-0-1	.000	-0	225	-10	0	-0.7
Total	7	6	11	.353	59	26	2-1	0-1	175	218	138	31	2	83-4	113	6.53	70	.307	.377	24-0-7	.125	-0	111	-38	0	-3.3
LOTZ, JOE	Joseph Peter "Smokey"; B1.2.1891 Remsen IA; D1.1.1971 Castro Valley CA; BR/TR/5´8.5˝/175; d7.15; Col Creighton																									
1916	StL N	0	3	.000	12	3	1	0	40	31	20	1	1	17	18	4.27	62	.225	.314	12	.333	1	85	-5	—	-0.3
LOUDELL, ART	Arthur (b Arthur Laudel); B4.10.1882 Latham MO; D2.19.1961 Kansas City MO; BR/TR/5´11˝/173; d8.13																									
1910	Det A	1	1	.500	5	2	1	0	21.1	23	13	0	0	14	12	3.38	78	.284	.389	7-0-1	.143	-0	140	-2	—	-0.3
LOUGHLIN, LARRY	Larry John; B8.16.1941 Tacoma WA; D1.26.1999 Denver CO; BL/TL/6´1˝/190; d5.27; Col Santa Clara																									
1967	Phi N	0	0	ø	3	0	0	0	5.1	9	9	1	0	4-1	5	15.19	22	.375	.464	1	1.000	1	—	-6	0	-0.3
LOUN, DON	Donald Nelson; B11.9.1940 Frederick MD; BR/TL/6´2˝/185; d9.23																									
1964	Was A	1	1	.500	2	2	1-1	0	13	13	4	0	0	3-0	3	2.08	178	.250	.291	4	.000	-0	12	2	0	0.3
LOUX, SHANE	Shane A.; B8.13.1979 Rapid City SD; BR/TR/6´2˝/205; [DetA97 2/53]; d9.10																									
2002	Det A	0	3	.000	3	3	0	0-0	14	19	16	4	1	3-0	7	9.00	49	.317	.359	0	ø	0	71	-8	0	-1.1
2003	Det A	1	1	.500	11	4	0	0-0	30.1	37	24	4	4	12-1	8	7.12	62	.303	.381	0	ø	0	95	-9	0	-0.5
Total	2	1	4	.200	14	7	0	0-0	44.1	56	40	8	5	15-1	15	7.71	57	.308	.374	0	ø	0	84	-17	0	-1.6
LOVE, SLIM	Edward Haughton; B8.1.1890 Love MS; D11.30.1942 Memphis TN; BL/TL/6´7˝/195; d9.8																									
1913	Was A	1	0	1.000	5	1	0	1	16.2	14	5	0	0	6	5	1.62	182	.233	.303	5	.200	0	50	2	—	0.1
1916	NY A	2	0	1.000	20	1	0	0	47.2	46	29	2	0	23	21	4.91	59	.274	.361	14-0-1	.000	-2	79	-9	—	-0.7
1917	NY A	6	5	.545	33	9	2	1	130.1	115	50	0	1	57	82	2.35	114	.251	.335	36-0-2	.167	-1	71	3	—	0.0
1918	NY A	13	12	.520	38	29	13-1	1	228.2	207	92	3	10	116	95	3.07	92	.253	.353	74-0-1	.230	2	91	-5	—	-0.5
1919	Det A	6	4	.600	22	8	4	1	89.2	92	40	3	6	40	46	3.01	106	.275	.363	27-0-1	.222	0	86	1	—	0.0
1920	Det A	0	0	ø	1	0	0	0	4.1	6	4	0	0	4	2	8.31	45	.375	.500	0	ø	0	—	-2	—	-0.1
Total	6	28	21	.571	119	48	19-1	4	517.1	480	220	8	17	246	251	3.04	94	.259	.351	156-0-5	.192	-0	85	-10	—	-1.2
LOVELACE, VANCE	Vance Odell; B8.9.1963 Tampa FL; BL/TL/6´5˝/(205–235); [ChiN81 1/16]; d9.10																									
1988	Cal A	0	0	ø	3	0	0	0-0	1.1	2	2	1	0	3-0	0	13.50	29	.400	.625	0	ø	0	—	-1	0	-0.1
1989	Cal A	0	0	ø	1	0	0	0-0	1	0	0	0	0	1-1	1	0.00	ø	.000	.250	0	ø	0	—	0	0	0.0
1990	Sea A	0	0	ø	5	0	0	0-0	2.1	3	1	0	1	6-0	1	3.86	103	.300	.588	0	ø	0	—	0	0	0.0
Total	3	0	0	ø	9	0	0	0-0	4.2	5	3	1	1	10-1	2	5.79	68	.278	.552	0	ø	0	—	-1	0	-0.1
LOVENGUTH, LYNN	Lynn Richard; B11.29.1922 Camden NY; D9.29.2000 Beaverton OR; BL/TR/5´10.5˝/170; d4.18																									
1955	Phi N	0	1	.000	14	0	0	0	18	17	9	1	2	10-0	14	4.50	88	.258	.358	2	.000	-0	—	-1	0	-0.1
1957	StL N	0	1	.000	2	1	0	0	9	6	3	0	0	6-0	6	2.00	198	.182	.308	2	.000	-0*	44	2	0	0.1
Total	2	0	2	.000	16	1	0	0	27	23	12	1	2	16-0	20	3.67	108	.232	.342	4	.000	-1	44	1	0	0.0
LOVETT, JOHN	John; B5.6.1877 Monday OH; D12.5.1937 Murray City OH; d5.22																									
1903	StL N	0	0	ø	3	1	0	0	5	6	5	0	1	5	3	5.40	60	.300	.462	3	.333	0	21	-1	—	0.0
LOVETT, LEN	Leonard Walker; B7.17.1852 Lancaster Co. PA; D11.18.1922 Newark DE; BR/TR; d8.4; ▲																									
1873	Res NA	0	1	.000	1	1	1	0	9	22	16	0	—	1	1	7.00	50	.400	.411	5	.400	0	85	-2	—	-0.1
LOVETT, TOM	Thomas Joseph; B12.7.1863 Providence RI; D3.19.1928 Providence RI; BR/5´8˝/162; d6.4																									
1885	Phi AA	7	8	.467	16	16	15-1	0	138.2	130	96	3	5	38	56	3.70	93	.236	.291	58	.224	-0	113	-1	—	-0.1
1889	†Bro AA	17	10	.630	29	28	23-1	0	229	234	132	3	8	65	92	4.32	86	.256	.311	100-2	.190	-1	125	-6	—	-0.7
1890	†Bro N	30	11	**.732**	44	41	39-4	0	372	327	195	14	17	141	124	2.78	124	.229	.305	164-1	.201	-1	130	24	—	2.0
1891	Bro N	23	19	.548	44	43	39-3	0	365.2	361	229	14	20	129	129	3.69	90	.248	.318	153	.163	-5	108	-13	—	-1.7
1893	Bro N	3	5	.375	14	8	6	1	96	134	92	2	6	35	15	6.56	67	.321	.381	50	.180	-2*	101	-21	—	-1.4
1894	Bos N	8	6	.571	15	13	10	0	104	155	96	12	3	36	23	5.97	95	.341	.394	49-1-0	.143	-5	100	-2	—	-0.6
Total	6	88	59	.599	162	149	132-9	1	1305.1	1341	840	48	59	444	439	3.94	94	.257	.322	574-4-0	.185	-13	116	-19	—	-2.5
LOVRICH, PETE	Peter; B10.16.1942 Blue Island IL; BR/TR/6´4˝/200; d4.26; Mil 1964–65; Col Arizona St.																									
1963	KC A	1	1	.500	20	1	0	0	20.2	25	23	5	1	10-1	16	7.84	50	.291	.367	0-0-1	ø	0	46	-10	0	-0.9
LOWDERMILK, GROVER	Grover Cleveland "Slim"; B1.15.1885 Sandborn IN; D3.31.1968 Odin IL; BR/TR/6´4˝/190; d7.3; b–Lou																									
1909	StL N	0	2	.000	7	3	1	0	29	28	24	0	3	30	14	6.21	41	.292	.473	10	.100	-1	83	-11	—	-0.8
1911	StL N	0	1	.000	11	2	1-1	0	33.1	37	30	1	2	33	15	7.29	46	.301	.456	9	.111	-1	33	-13	—	-0.7
1912	Chi N	0	1	.000	2	1	1	0	13	17	18	1	0	14	8	9.69	34	.304	.443	4	.000	-1	22	-9	—	-0.6
1915	StL A	9	17	.346	38	29	14-1	0	222.1	183	110	1	16	133	130	3.12	92	.234	.357	72	.125	-3	79	-6	—	-1.0
	Det A	4	1	.800	7	5	0	0	28	17	16	0	1	24	18	4.18	73	.185	.359	8-0-1	.125	-0	120	-3	—	-0.5
	Year	13	18	.419	45	34	14-1	0	250.1	200	126	1	17	157	148	3.24	89	.229	.357	80-0-1	.125	-3	86	-13	—	-1.5
1916	Det A	0	0	ø	1	0	0	0	0.1	0	0	0	0	3	0	0.00	ø	.000	.750	0	ø	0	—	0	—	0.0
	Cle A	1	5	.167	10	9	2	0	51.1	52	33	0	3	45	28	3.16	95	.277	.424	18-0-1	.167	-0	89	-4	—	-0.5
	Year	1	5	.167	11	9	2	0	51.2	52	33	0	3	48	28	3.14	96	.275	.429	18-0-1	.167	-0	89	-4	—	-0.5
1917	StL A	2	1	.667	3	2	2-1	0	19	16	5	0	0	4	9	1.42	183	.225	.267	7	.000	-1	97	2	—	0.2
1918	StL A	2	6	.250	13	11	4	0	80	74	44	1	3	38	25	3.15	87	.255	.347	28	.250	1	97	-6	—	-0.3
1919	StL A	0	0	ø	7	0	0	0	12	6	2	0	5	4	6	0.75	442	.176	.349	1	.000	-0	—	3	—	0.1
	†Chi A	5	5	.500	20	11	5	0	96.2	95	44	0	4	43	43	2.79	114	.268	.353	34	.088	-3	128	2	—	-0.1
	Year	5	5	.500	27	11	5	0	108.2	101	46	0	9	47	49	2.57	125	.260	.353	35	.086	-4	127	5	—	0.0

YEAR	TM LG	W	L	PCT	G	GS	CG-SHO	SV-BS	IP	H	R	HR	HB	BB-IB	SO	ERA	AERA	OAV	OOB	AB-HR-SH	AVG	PB	SUP	APR	DL	PW
1920	Chi A	0	0	ø	3	0	0	0	5.1	9	4	0	0	5	0	6.75	56	.409	.519	0	ø	0	—	-1	—	0.0
Total	9	23	39	.371	122	73	30-3	0	590.1	534	330	4	37	376	296	3.58	82	.253	.375	191-0-2	.131	-8	91	-46	—	-4.2
LOWDERMILK, LOU	Louis Bailey; B2.23.1887 Sandborn IN; D12.27.1975 Centralia IL; BR/TL/6´1˝/180; d4.20; b–Grover																									
1911	StL N	3	4	.429	16	3	3	0	65	72	39	0	5	29	20	3.46	98	.304	.391	18	.111	-1	44	-3	—	-0.5
1912	StL N	1	1	.500	4	1	1	1	15	14	8	0	0	9	2	3.00	114	.246	.348	4-0-1	.250	0	107	0	—	0.1
Total	2	4	5	.444	20	4	4	1	80	86	47	0	5	38	22	3.37	100	.293	.383	22-0-1	.136	-1	61	-3	—	-0.4
LOWE, DEREK	Derek Christopher; B6.1.1973 Dearborn MI; BR/TR/6´6˝/(170–210); [SeaA91 8/214]; d4.26																									
1997	Sea A	2	4	.333	12	9	0	0-0	53	59	43	11	2	20-2	39	6.96	65	.282	.349	2	.000	-0	115	-14	0	-1.3
	Bos A	0	2	.000	8	0	0	0-2	16	15	6	0	2	3-1	13	3.38	138	.268	.323	1	.000	-0	—	2	0	0.3
	Year	2	6	.250	20	9	0	0-2	69	74	49	11	4	23-3	52	6.13	74	.279	.344	3	.000	-0	114	-11	0	-1.0
1998	†Bos A	3	9	.250	63	10	0	4-5	123	126	65	5	4	42-5	77	4.02	117	.267	.329	4	.000	-0	65	7	0	0.7
1999	†Bos A	6	3	.667	74	0	0	15-5	109.1	84	35	7	4	25-1	80	2.63	189	.208	.260	0	ø	0	—	28	0	2.6
2000	Bos A★	4	4	.500	74	0	0	**42**-5	91.1	90	27	6	2	22-5	79	2.56	196	.257	.304	1	.000	-0	—	**25**	0	3.9
2001	Bos A	5	10	.333	67	3	0	24-6	91.2	103	39	7	5	29-9	82	3.53	126	.283	.343	1	.000	-0	104	10	0	1.9
2002	Bos A★	21	8	.724	32	32	1-1	0-0	219.2	166	65	12	12	48-0	127	2.58	173	.211	.266	3-0-1	.333	1	123	**48**	0	**6.2**
2003	†Bos A	17	7	.708	33	33	1	0-0	203.1	216	113	17	11	72-4	110	4.47	104	.272	.339	4-0-1	.000	-0	128	4	0	0.5
2004	†Bos A	14	12	.538	33	33	0	0-0	182.2	224	138	15	8	71-2	105	5.42	90	.299	.365	4-0-1	.250	0	117	-16	0	-1.6
2005	LA N	12	15	.444	35	**35**	2-2	0-0	222	223	113	28	5	55-1	146	3.61	115	.260	.307	65-0-9	.154	-0	101	6	0	0.9
2006	†LA N	**16**	8	.667	35	34	1	0-0	218	221	97	14	5	55-2	123	3.63	121	.262	.310	64-0-10	.094	-1	100	18	0	1.9
Total	10	100	82	.549	466	189	5-3	85-23	1530	1527	741	122	60	442-32	981	3.81	120	.259	.316	149-0-22	.121	-1	110	118	0	16.0
LOWE, GEORGE	George Wesley "Doc"; B4.25.1895 Ridgefield Park NJ; D9.2.1981 Somers Point NJ; BR/TR/6´2˝/180; d7.28																									
1920	Cin N	0	0	ø	1	0	0	0	2	1	0	0	0	1	0	0.00	ø	.167	.286	0	ø	0	—	1	—	0.0
LOWE, SEAN	Jonathan Sean; B3.29.1971 Dallas TX; BR/TR/6´2˝/(205–215); [StLN92 1/15]; d8.29; Col Arizona St.																									
1997	StL N	0	2	.000	6	4	0	0-0	17.1	27	21	2	1	10-0	8	9.35	45	.360	.432	3	.333	0	116	-10	0	-1.0
1998	StL N	0	3	.000	4	1	0	0-0	5.1	11	9	1	0	5-0	2	15.19	28	.440	.533	2	.000	-0	66	-6	0	-1.1
1999	Chi A	4	1	.800	64	0	0	0-3	95.2	90	39	10	4	46-1	62	3.67	135	.262	.347	0	ø	0	—	15	0	0.7
2000	Chi A	4	1	.800	50	5	0	0-0	70.2	78	47	10	6	39-3	53	5.48	92	.284	.383	0	ø	0	111	-3	24	-0.2
2001	Chi A	9	4	.692	45	11	0	3-0	127	123	55	12	7	32-2	71	3.61	129	.256	.308	3	.333	0	83	15	0	1.4
2002	Pit N	4	2	.667	43	1	0	0-2	69	85	45	8	7	34-6	57	5.35	78	.307	.393	13-0-2	.077	-1	110	-9	0	-0.7
	Col N	1	1	.500	8	0	0	0-0	10.1	16	13	1	0	7-0	7	8.71	54	.348	.434	1	.000	-0	—	-5	0	-0.8
	Year	5	3	.625	51	1	0	0-2	79.1	101	58	9	7	41-6	64	5.79	74	.313	.398	14-0-2	.071	-1	109	-14	0	-1.5
2003	KC A	1	1	.500	28	0	0	0-1	44.2	55	32	7	2	21-5	28	6.25	77	.301	.377	0	ø	0	—	-6	0	-0.3
Total	7	23	15	.605	248	22	0	3-6	440	485	261	51	27	194-17	288	4.95	95	.284	.362	22-0-2	.136	-1	94	-9	24	-2.0
LOWE, MARK	Mark Christopher; B6.7.1983 Houston TX; BR/TR/6´3˝/190; [SeaA04 5/153]; d7.7; Col Texas–Arlington																									
2006	Sea A	1	0	1.000	15	0	0	0-0	18.2	12	4	1	2	9-1	20	1.93	228	.190	.311	0	ø	0	—	5	43	0.2
LOWN, TURK	Omar Joseph; B5.30.1924 Brooklyn NY; BR/TR/6´1˝/(180–185); d4.24																									
1951	Chi N	4	9	.308	31	18	3-1	0	127	125	80	14	1	90	39	5.46	75	.260	.378	39-0-2	.205	1	78	-16	0	-1.3
1952	Chi N	4	11	.267	33	19	5	0	156.2	154	87	13	3	93	73	4.37	88	.257	.359	50-0-5	.140	-0	86	-9	0	-0.7
1953	Chi N	8	7	.533	49	12	2	3	148.1	166	93	20	2	84	76	5.16	86	.282	.373	48-0-2	.125	-2	89	-9	0	-0.9
1954	Chi N	0	2	.000	15	0	0	0	22	23	18	1	0	15	16	6.14	68	.261	.365	0	ø	0*	—	-5	0	-0.4
1956	Chi N	9	8	.529	61	0	0	13	110.2	95	49	10	1	78-12	74	3.58	105	.240	.363	23-1-1	.217	2	—	3	0	0.7
1957	Chi N	5	7	.417	**67**	0	0	12	93	74	45	10	0	51-4	51	3.77	103	.221	.321	10	.200	0	—	0	0	0.2
1958	Chi N	0	0	ø	4	0	0	0	4	2	2	0	0	3-0	4	4.50	87	.154	.313	0	ø	0	—	0	0	0.0
	Cin N	0	2	.000	11	0	0	0	11.2	12	8	2	0	12-2	9	5.40	77	.273	.421	1	.000	-0	—	-2	0	-0.3
	Year	0	2	.000	15	0	0	0	15.2	14	10	2	0	15-2	13	5.17	79	.246	.397	1	.000	-0	—	-2	0	-0.3
	Chi A	3	3	.500	27	0	0	8	40.2	49	22	1	0	28-4	40	3.98	91	.308	.405	9-0-1	.333	1	—	-3	0	-0.4
1959	†Chi A	9	2	.818	60	0	0	**15**	93.1	73	32	12	2	42-4	63	2.89	130	.215	.303	12	.250	1	—	10	0	1.6
1960	Chi A	2	3	.400	45	0	0	5	67.1	60	31	6	0	34-6	39	3.88	98	.239	.326	5-0-2	.200	1	—	0	0	0.1
1961	Chi A	7	5	.583	59	0	0	11	101	87	37	13	0	35-3	50	2.76	142	.238	.300	14-0-1	.000	-2*	—	12	0	1.4
1962	Chi A	4	2	.667	42	0	0	6	56.1	58	21	3	1	25-5	40	3.04	129	.269	.346	3	.000	-0	—	5	0	0.7
Total	11	55	61	.474	504	49	10-1	73	1032	978	525	105	10	590-40	574	4.12	96	.252	.351	214-1-14	.164	1	86	-14	0	0.7
LOWRY, NOAH	Noah Ryan; B10.10.1980 Ventura CA; BR/TL/6´2˝/(190–210); [SFN01 1/30]; d9.5; Col Pepperdine																									
2003	SF N	0	0	ø	4	0	0	0-0	6.1	1	0	0	1	2-0	5	0.00	ø	.048	.167	2	.500	0	—	3	0	0.2
2004	SF N	6	0	1.000	16	14	2-1	0-0	92	91	41	10	0	28-1	72	3.82	114	.259	.312	33-0-3	.182	0	122	6	0	0.4
2005	SF N	13	13	.500	33	33	0	0-0	204.2	193	92	21	7	76-1	172	3.78	112	.249	.320	59-0-12	.271	5*	98	10	0	1.8
2006	SF N	7	10	.412	27	27	1-1	0-0	159.1	166	89	21	6	56-2	84	4.74	93	.273	.336	46-1-8	.152	1*	112	-5	31	-0.4
Total	4	26	23	.531	80	74	3-2	0-0	462.1	451	222	52	14	162-4	333	4.07	106	.257	.322	140-1-23	.214	7	108	14	31	2.0
LOWRY, SAM	Samuel Joseph; B3.25.1920 Philadelphia PA; D12.1.1992 Philadelphia PA; BR/TR/5´11˝/170; d9.19; Mil 1944–46																									
1942	Phi A	0	0	ø	1	0	0	0	3	3	2	0	0	1	0	6.00	63	.250	.308	1	.000	-0	—	-1	0	0.0
1943	Phi A	0	0	ø	5	0	0	0	18	18	10	1	0	9	3	5.00	68	.269	.355	6	.167	-0	—	-3	0	-0.1
Total	2	0	0	ø	6	0	0	0	21	21	12	1	0	10	3	5.14	67	.266	.348	7	.143	-0	—	-4	0	-0.1
LOYND, MIKE	Michael Wallace; B3.26.1964 St.Louis MO; BR/TR/6´4˝/210; [TexA86 7/163]; d7.24; Col Florida St.																									
1986	Tex A	2	2	.500	9	8	0	1-0	42	49	30	4	2	19-1	33	5.36	81	.290	.365	0	ø	0	118	-5	0	-0.5
1987	Tex A	1	5	.167	26	8	0	1-0	69.1	82	53	14	1	38-0	48	6.10	74	.287	.370	0	ø	0	93	-12	0	-0.9
Total	2	3	7	.300	35	16	0	2-0	111.1	131	83	18	3	57-1	81	5.82	76	.288	.368	0	ø	0	105	-17	0	-1.4
LUBY, PAT	John Perkins; B6.1869 Charleston SC; D4.24.1899 Charleston SC; TR/6´0˝/185; d6.16																									
1890	Chi N	20	9	.690	34	31	26	1	267.2	226	129	6	15	95	85	3.19	115	.222	.297	116-3	.267	8*	104	19	—	2.3
1891	Chi N	8	11	.421	30	24	18	1	206	221	148	11	19	94	52	4.76	70	.264	.352	98-2	.245	7*	113	-26	—	-1.3
1892	Chi N	11	16	.407	31	27	24-1	0	252.1	248	157	10	10	103	66	3.07	108	.247	.323	163-2	.190	1*	73	1	—	0.2
1895	Lou N	1	5	.167	11	6	5	0	71.1	115	90	5	7	19	12	6.81	68	.357	.405	53	.283	3*	72	-21	—	-1.0
Total	4	40	41	.494	106	88	73-1	2	797.1	810	524	32	51	311	215	3.88	92	.254	.331	430-7	.235	18	95	-27	—	0.2
LUCAS, RED	Charles Fred "The Nashville Narcissus"; B4.28.1902 Columbia TN; D7.9.1986 Nashville TN; BL/TR/5´9.5˝/170; d4.19; ▲																									
1923	NY N	0	0	ø	3	0	0	1	5.1	9	5	0	0	4	3	0.00	ø	.346	.433	2	.000	-0	—	0	—	0.0
1924	Bos N	1	4	.200	27	4	1	0	83.2	112	60	5	6	18	30	5.16	74	.332	.377	33	.333	2*	67	-14	—	-0.5
1926	Cin N	8	5	.615	39	11	7-1	2	154	161	68	6	2	30	34	3.68	100	.277	.314	76-0-5	.303	6*	98	4	—	1.2
1927	Cin N	18	11	.621	37	23	19-4	2	239.2	231	96	6	0	39	51	3.38	112	.256	.287	150-0-6	.313	7*	97	17	—	3.1
1928	Cin N	13	9	.591	27	19	13-**4**	1	167.1	164	73	9	0	42	35	3.39	117	.258	.304	73-0-1	.315	6*	72	10	—	1.9
1929	Cin N	19	12	.613	32	32	**28**-2	0	270	267	119	14	1	58	72	3.60	127	**.257**	**.297**	140-0-2	.293	11*	101	31	—	**4.3**
1930	Cin N	14	16	.467	33	28	18-1	1	210.2	270	135	15	1	44	53	5.38	90	.315	.349	113-2-7	.336	15*	97	-10	—	0.2
1931	Cin N	14	13	.519	29	29	**24**-3	0	238	261	110	10	0	39	56	3.59	104	.280	.309	153-0-6	.281	11*	117	5	—	1.7
1932	Cin N	13	17	.433	31	31	**28**	0	269.1	261	110	10	1	35	63	2.94	131	.249	.274	150-0-3	.287	13*	82	26	—	4.4
1933	Cin N	10	16	.385	29	29	21-3	0	219.2	248	106	13	2	18	40	3.40	100	.289	.305	122-1-2	.287	12*	92	-1	—	1.3
1934	Pit N	10	9	.526	29	22	12-1	0	172.2	198	89	14	2	40	44	4.38	94	.283	.324	105-0-1	.219	3*	125	-2	—	0.0
1935	Pit N	8	6	.571	20	19	8-2	0	125.2	136	60	10	2	23	29	3.44	119	.272	.307	66-0-2	.318	8*	100	9	—	1.7
1936	Pit N	15	4	.789	27	22	12	0	175.2	178	70	7	3	26	53	3.18	128	.257	.287	108-0-3	.241	4*	121	19	—	2.2
1937	Pit N	8	10	.444	20	20	9-1	0	126.1	150	69	12	1	23	20	4.27	90	.290	.322	82	.268	5*	107	-5	—	-0.2
1938	Pit N	6	3	.667	13	13	4	0	84	90	33	5	1	16	19	3.54	107	.283	.319	46-0-2	.109	-2*	105	5	—	0.2
Total	15	157	135	.538	396	302	204-22	7	2542	2736	1203	136	22	455	602	3.72	107	.275	.308	1419-3-40	.283	98	101	94	—	21.5
LUCAS, GARY	Gary Paul; B11.8.1954 Riverside CA; BL/TL/6´5˝/200; [SDN76 19/437]; d4.16; Col Chapman																									
1980	SD N	5	8	.385	46	18	0	3-1	150	138	59	8	1	43-14	85	3.24	106	.250	.302	35-0-7	.171	-0	87	3	0	0.3
1981	SD N	7	7	.500	**57**	0	0	13-4	90	78	26	1	3	36-15	53	2.00	162	.247	.325	10-0-2	.100	-1	—	11	0	2.1
1982	SD N	1	10	.091	65	0	0	16-9	97.1	89	42	5	1	29-7	64	3.24	106	.245	.298	14-0-3	.000	-1	—	1	0	0.1
1983	SD N	5	8	.385	62	0	0	17-6	91	85	38	9	0	34-11	60	2.87	122	.245	.310	12	.000	-1	—	4	0	0.5
1984	Mon N	0	3	.000	55	0	0	8-2	53	54	20	4	0	20-5	42	2.72	127	.267	.330	4	.000	-0	—	4	0	0.3

YEAR	TM LG	W	L	PCT	G	GS	CG-SHO	SV-BS	IP	H	R	HR	HB	BB-IB	SO	ERA	AERA	OAV	OOB	AB-HR-SH	AVG	PB	SUP	APR	DL	PW
1985	Mon N	6	2	.750	49	0	0	1-3	67.2	63	29	6	0	24-8	31	3.19	108	.251	.314	5	.000	-1	—	1	41	0.0
1986	†Cal A	4	1	.800	27	0	0	2-2	45.2	45	19	1	0	6-0	31	3.15	131	.253	.276	0	ø	0	—	4	101	0.5
1987	Cal A	1	5	.167	48	0	0	3-3	74.1	66	41	7	2	35-5	44	3.63	119	.241	.329	0	ø	0	—	3	0	0.3
Total	8	29	44	.397	409	18	0	63-30	669	618	274	41	7	227-65	410	3.01	118	.249	.310	80-0-12	.087	-4	87	31	142	4.1
Lucas, Ray	Ray Wesley "Luke"; B10.2.1908 Springfield OH; D10.9.1969 Harrison MI; BR/TR/6´2˝/175; d9.28																									
1929	NY N	0	0	ø	3	0	0	1	8	3	0	0	0	3	1	0.00	ø	.111	.200	2	.500	0	—	4	—	0.2
1930	NY N	0	0	ø	6	0	0	0	10.1	9	8	2	1	10	1	6.97	68	.265	.444	1	.000	-0	—	-2	—	-0.1
1931	NY N	0	0	ø	1	0	0	0	2	1	1	1	0	1	0	4.50	82	.143	.250	0	ø	0	—	0	—	0.0
1933	Bro N	0	0	ø	2	0	0	0	5	6	4	0	1	4	0	7.20	45	.316	.458	0	ø	0	—	-2	—	-0.1
1934	Bro N	1	1	.500	10	2	0	0	30.2	39	24	2	3	14	3	6.75	58	.328	.412	6-0-1	.333	1	122	-9	—	-0.3
Total	5	1	1	.500	22	2	0	1	56	58	37	5	5	32	5	5.79	71	.282	.391	9-0-1	.333	1	122	-9	—	-0.3
Lucey, Joe	Joseph Earl "Scootch"; B3.27.1897 Holyoke MA; D7.30.1980 Holyoke MA; BR/TR/6´0˝/168; d7.6.1920; Col Catholic America																									
1925	Bos A	0	1	.000	7	2	0	0	11	18	20	0	0	14	2	9.00	50	.360	.500	15	.133	-1*	102	-8	—	-0.6
Lucid, Con	Cornelius Cecil; B2.24.1874 Dublin, Ireland; D6.25.1931 Houston TX; 5´7˝/170; d5.1																									
1893	Lou N	0	1	.000	2	1	0	0	6	10	14	0	1	10	0	15.00	29	.357	.538	3	.333	0	16	-8	—	-0.8
1894	Bro N	5	3	.625	10	9	7	0	71.1	87	68	6	9	44	15	6.56	76	.298	.406	33	.212	-2	114	-12	—	-1.1
1895	Bro N	10	7	.588	21	19	12-2	0	137	164	113	4	7	72	24	5.52	80	.292	.380	53-0-2	.245	2	114	-20	—	-1.6
	Phi N	6	3	.667	10	10	7-1	0	69.2	80	56	3	9	35	19	5.94	80	.284	.380	29-0-1	.345	4	128	-7	—	-0.4
	Year	16	10	.615	31	29	19-3	0	206.2	244	169	7	16	107	43	5.66	80	.289	.380	82-0-3	.280	6	119	-21	—	-2.0
1896	Phi N	1	4	.200	5	5	5	0	42	75	43	2	2	17	3	8.36	52	.383	.437	16-0-1	.125	-2	69	-15	—	-1.4
1897	StL N	1	5	.167	6	6	5	0	49	66	46	0	0	26	4	3.67	120	.319	.395	17	.176	-0	49	-3	—	-0.2
Total	5	23	23	.500	54	50	36-3	0	375	482	340	15	28	204	65	6.02	76	.308	.397	151-0-4	.238	2	103	-65	—	-5.5
Lucier, Lou	Louis Joseph; B3.23.1918 Northbridge MA; BR/TR/5´8˝/160; d4.23																									
1943	Bos A	3	4	.429	16	9	3	0	74	94	35	1	2	33	23	3.89	85	.322	.394	20	.200	-0	99	-5	0	-0.2
1944	Bos A	0	0	ø	3	0	0	0	5.1	7	3	0	0	7	2	5.06	67	.292	.452	1	.000	-0	—	-1	0	-0.1
	Phi N	0	0	ø	1	0	0	0	2	3	3	0	0	2	1	13.50	27	.333	.455	0	ø	0	—	-2	0	-0.1
1945	Phi N	0	1	.000	13	0	0	1	20.1	14	9	1	0	5	5	2.21	173	.194	.247	4	.250	0	—	3	0	0.2
Total	3	3	5	.375	33	9	3	1	101.2	118	50	2	2	47	31	3.81	90	.297	.374	25	.200	-0	99	-5	0	-0.2
Ludolph, Willie	William Francis "Wee Willie"; B1.21.1900 San Francisco CA; D4.8.1952 Oakland CA; BR/TR/6´1.5˝/170; d5.28; Col St. Marys (CA)																									
1924	Det A	0	0	ø	3	0	0	0	5.2	5	3	0	1	2	1	4.76	86	.250	.348	1	.000	-0	—	0	—	0.0
Ludwick, Eric	Eric David; B12.14.1971 Whiteman Afb MO; BR/TR/6´5˝/(210–220); [NYN93 2/50]; d9.1; b–Ryan; Col Nevada–Las Vegas																									
1996	StL N	0	1	.000	6	1	0	0-0	10	11	11	4	1	3-0	12	9.00	47	.275	.333	2	.000	-0	64	-5	0	-0.5
1997	StL N	0	1	.000	5	0	0	0-0	6.2	12	7	1	0	6-0	7	9.45	44	.400	.500	0	ø	0	—	-4	0	-0.5
	Oak A	1	4	.200	6	5	0	0-0	24	32	24	7	1	16-1	14	8.25	56	.330	.430	2	.000	-0	72	-10	0	-1.5
1998	Fla N	1	4	.200	13	6	0	0-1	32.2	46	31	7	0	17-1	27	7.44	55	.333	.401	7	.000	-1	147	-13	123	-1.8
1999	Tor A	0	0	ø	1	0	0	0-0	1	3	3	0	0	2-0	0	27.00	18	.500	.625	0	ø	0	—	-2	0	-0.1
Total	4	2	10	.167	31	12	0	0-1	74.1	104	76	19	2	44-2	60	8.35	51	.334	.417	11	.000	-1	107	-34	123	-4.4
Luebber, Steve	Stephen Lee; B7.9.1949 Clinton MO; BR/TR/6´3˝/(175–210); [MinA67 13/257]; d6.27																									
1971	Min A	2	5	.286	18	12	0	1-0	68	73	42	7	4	37-3	35	5.03	70	.278	.373	19-0-2	.053	-2*	120	-11	0	-1.2
1972	Min A	0	0	ø	2	0	0	0-0	2.1	3	0	0	0	2-1	1	0.00	ø	.333	.417	0	ø	0	—	1	0	0.1
1976	Min A	4	5	.444	38	12	2-1	2-0	119.1	109	57	9	1	62-3	45	4.00	89	.248	.341	0	ø	0	129	-4	0	-0.3
1979	Tor A	0	0	ø	1	0	0	0-0	0	2	1	0	0	1-0	0	(1)	ø	1.000	1.000	0	ø	0	—	-1	0	-0.1
1981	Bal A	0	0	ø	7	0	0	0-0	16.2	26	14	3	1	4-1	12	7.56	48	.366	.403	0	ø	0	—	-6	0	-0.3
Total	5	6	10	.375	66	24	2-1	3-0	206.1	213	114	19	6	106-8	93	4.62	77	.271	.360	19-0-2	.053	-2	124	-21	0	-1.8
Luebbers, Larry	Larry Christopher; B10.11.1969 Cincinnati OH; BR/TR/6´6˝/(190–210); [CinN90 8/216]; d7.3; Col Kentucky																									
1993	Cin N	2	5	.286	14	14	0	0-0	77.1	74	49	7	1	38-3	38	4.54	89	.261	.345	24-0-1	.250	1	89	-7	0	-0.5
1999	StL N	3	3	.500	8	8	1	0-0	45.2	46	27	8	3	16-0	16	5.12	90	.261	.333	16-0-1	.125	-0	120	-2	0	-0.2
2000	Cin N	0	2	.000	14	1	0	1-0	20.1	27	15	1	0	12-2	9	6.20	77	.333	.419	0	ø	0	19	-3	0	-0.2
Total	3	5	10	.333	36	23	1	1-0	143.1	147	91	16	4	66-5	63	4.96	87	.272	.352	40-0-2	.200	1	96	-12	0	-0.9
Luebke, Dick	Richard Raymond; B4.8.1935 Chicago IL; D12.4.1974 San Diego CA; BR/TL/6´4˝/200; d8.11																									
1962	Bal A	0	1	.000	10	0	0	0	13.1	12	4	0	0	6-0	7	2.70	137	.250	.327	0	ø	0	—	2	0	0.1
Luecken, Rick	Richard Fred; B11.15.1960 McAllen TX; BR/TR/6´6˝/210; [SeaA83 27/667]; d6.6; Col Texas A&M																									
1989	KC A	2	1	.667	19	0	0	1-0	23.2	23	9	3	0	13-4	16	3.42	113	.258	.353	0	ø	0	—	2	0	0.2
1990	Atl N	1	4	.200	36	0	0	1-2	53	73	36	5	3	30-7	35	5.77	70	.336	.422	3	.333	1	—	-9	0	-0.7
	Tor A	0	0	ø	1	0	0	0-0	1	2	1	1	0	1-0	0	9.00	44	.500	.600	0	ø	0	—	-1	0	0.0
Total	2	3	5	.375	56	0	0	2-2	77.2	98	46	9	3	44-11	51	5.10	78	.316	.405	3	.333	1	—	-8	0	-0.5
Luff, Henry	Henry T.; B9.14.1856 Philadelphia PA; D10.11.1916 Philadelphia PA; 5´11˝/175; d4.19; ▲																									
1875	NH NA	1	6	.143	10	7	5	0	68.2	98	91	2	—	3	5	3.28	63	.295	.301	166-2	.271	3*	90	-12	—	-0.7
Lugo, Urbano	Rafael Urbano (Colina); B8.12.1962 Punto Fijo, Falcon, Venez.; BR/TR/6´0˝/(185–200); d4.28																									
1985	Cal A	3	4	.429	20	10	1	0-0	83	86	36	10	4	29-1	42	3.69	112	.274	.341	0	ø	0	95	5	15	0.4
1986	Cal A	1	1	.500	6	3	0	0-0	21.1	21	9	4	0	6-0	9	3.80	109	.266	.318	0	ø	0	110	1	59	0.1
1987	Cal A	0	2	.000	7	5	0	0-0	28	42	34	8	0	18-0	24	9.32	46	.339	.420	0	ø	0	101	-17	0	-1.0
1988	Cal A	0	0	ø	1	0	0	0-0	2	2	2	1	0	1-0	1	9.00	43	.250	.333	0	ø	0	—	-1	0	-0.1
1989	Mon N	0	0	ø	3	0	0	0-0	4	4	3	1	0	0-0	3	6.75	53	.250	.250	0	ø	0	—	-1	0	-0.1
1990	Det A	2	0	1.000	13	1	0	0-1	24.1	30	19	9	3	13-1	12	7.03	57	.313	.411	0	ø	0	114	-7	0	-0.5
Total	6	6	7	.462	50	19	1	0-1	162.2	185	103	33	7	67-2	91	5.31	78	.290	.363	0	ø	0	101	-20	74	-1.2
Lugo, Ruddy	Ruddy Joraider; B5.22.1980 Barahona, D.R.; BR/TR/5´10˝/205; [MilN99 3/94]; d4.3; b–Julio																									
2006	TB A	2	4	.333	64	0	0	0-0	85	75	39	4	5	37-0	48	3.81	122	.240	.323	0	ø	0	—	8	23	0.5
Luhrsen, Wild Bill	William Ferdinand; B4.14.1884 Buckley IL; D8.15.1973 Little Rock AR; BR/TR/5´9˝/165; d8.23																									
1913	Pit N	3	1	.750	5	3	2	0	29	25	10	3	2	16	11	2.48	122	.248	.361	10-0-1	.000	-1	91	2	—	0.2
Lukasiewicz, Mark	Mark Francis; B3.8.1973 Jersey City NJ; BL/TL/6´5˝/240; [TorA93 1/41]; d5.11; Col Oklahoma St.																									
2001	Ana A	0	2	.000	24	0	0	0-0	22.1	21	17	6	2	9-2	25	6.04	77	.247	.330	0	ø	0	—	-4	0	-0.3
2002	Ana A	2	0	1.000	17	0	0	0-0	14	17	6	0	0	9-0	15	3.86	116	.298	.388	0	ø	0	—	1	0	0.1
Total	2	2	2	.500	41	0	0	0-0	36.1	38	23	6	2	18-2	40	5.20	88	.268	.354	0	ø	0	—	-3	0	-0.2
Lukens, Al	Albert P.; B11.1868 PA; TR/5´9˝/168; d6.23																									
1894	Phi N	0	1	.000	3	2	1	0	15	26	22	0	3	10	0	10.20	50	.377	.476	8	.000	-2	117	-8	—	-0.5
Lumenti, Ralph	Raphael Anthony; B12.21.1936 Milford MA; BL/TL/6´3˝/(185–190); d9.7; Col Massachusetts																									
1957	Was A	0	1	.000	3	2	0	0	9.1	9	7	1	1	5-0	8	6.75	58	.250	.357	2	.000	-0	80	-3	0	-0.3
1958	Was A	1	2	.333	8	4	0	0	21	21	20	2	1	36-0	20	8.57	44	.266	.500	8	.250	0	71	-10	0	-1.2
1959	Was A	0	0	ø	2	0	0	0	3	2	0	0	0	1-0	2	0.00	ø	.200	.273	0	ø	0	—	1	0	0.1
Total	3	1	3	.250	13	6	0	0	33.1	32	27	3	2	42-0	30	7.29	53	.256	.450	10	.200	-0	74	-12	0	-1.4
Luna, Memo	Guillermo Romero; B6.25.1930 Mexico City, Distrito Federal, Mexico; BL/TL/6´0˝/168; d4.20																									
1954	StL N	0	1	.000	1	1	0	0	0.2	2	2	0	0	2	0	27.00	15	.667	.667	0	ø	0	130	-2	0	-0.3
Lundbom, Jack	John Frederick; B3.10.1877 Manistee MI; D10.31.1949 Manistee MI; BR/TR/6´0.5˝/187; d5.9																									
1902	Cle A	1	1	.500	8	3	1	0	34	48	35	1	1	16	7	6.62	52	.333	.404	15	.267	1	104	-11	—	-0.5

Lundgren, Carl Carl Leonard; B2.16.1880 Marengo IL; D8.21.1934 Marengo IL; BR/TR/5´11˝/175; d6.19; Col Illinois

YEAR	TM LG	W	L	PCT	G	GS	CG-SHO	SV-BS	IP	H	R	HR	HB	BB-IB	SO	ERA	AERA	OAV	OOB	AB-HR-SH	AVG	PB	SUP	APR	DL	PW
1902	Chi N	9	9	.500	18	18	17-1	0	160	158	59	2	6	45	68	1.97	137	.258	.315	66-0-2	.106	-4*	92	12	—	0.7
1903	Chi N	11	9	.550	27	20	16	**3**	193	191	103	1	6	60	67	2.94	107	.262	.323	61-0-3	.115	-1	97	3	—	0.0
1904	Chi N	17	9	.654	31	27	25-2	1	242	203	97	2	4	77	106	2.60	102	.226	.290	90-0-2	.222	4	99	3	—	0.6
1905	Chi N	13	5	.722	23	19	16-3	0	169.1	132	58	3	9	53	69	2.23	134	.220	.293	61-0-2	.180	1*	126	14	—	1.6
1906	Chi N	17	6	.739	27	24	21-5	2	207.2	160	63	3	8	89	103	2.21	119	.221	.313	67-0-6	.179	2*	107	13	—	1.7
1907	Chi N	18	7	.720	28	25	21-7	0	207	130	42	0	2	92	84	1.17	212	**.185**	.282	66-0-7	.106	-3	88	**29**	—	3.5
1908	Chi N	6	9	.400	23	15	9-1	0	138.2	149	72	5	0	56	38	4.22	56	.284	.353	47-0-5	.149	-1	112	-23	—	-2.7
1909	Chi N	0	1	.000	2	1	0	0	4.1	6	2	0	0	4	0	4.15	61	.353	.476	2	.500	0	83	0	—	-0.1
Total	8	91	55	.623	179	149	125-19	6	1322	1129	496	16	35	476	535	2.42	113	.235	.308	460-0-27	.157	-2	102	51	—	5.3

Lundgren, Del Ebin Delmar; B9.21.1899 Lindsborg KS; D10.19.1984 Lindsborg KS; BR/TR/5´8˝/160; d4.27

YEAR	TM LG	W	L	PCT	G	GS	CG-SHO	SV-BS	IP	H	R	HR	HB	BB-IB	SO	ERA	AERA	OAV	OOB	AB-HR-SH	AVG	PB	SUP	APR	DL	PW
1924	Pit N	0	1	.000	8	1	0	0	16.2	25	13	0	1	3	4	6.48	59	.403	.439	3	.000	-1	44	-4	—	-0.3
1926	Bos A	0	2	.000	18	2	0	0	31	35	28	2	3	28	11	7.55	54	.307	.455	4	.000	-0	62	-11	—	-0.6
1927	Bos A	5	12	.294	30	17	5-2	0	136.1	160	100	7	4	87	39	6.27	67	.302	.405	44-0-3	.159	-2	91	-25	—	-2.8
Total	3	5	15	.250	56	20	5-2	0	184	220	141	9	8	118	54	6.51	64	.312	.416	51-0-3	.137	-3	86	-40	—	-3.7

Lundquist, David David Bruce; B6.4.1973 Beverly MA; BR/TR/6´2˝/200; [ChiA93 5/145]; d4.6; Col Nevada–Las Vegas

YEAR	TM LG	W	L	PCT	G	GS	CG-SHO	SV-BS	IP	H	R	HR	HB	BB-IB	SO	ERA	AERA	OAV	OOB	AB-HR-SH	AVG	PB	SUP	APR	DL	PW
1999	Chi A	1	1	.500	17	0	0	0-0	22	28	21	3	1	12-0	18	8.59	58	.315	.394	0	ø	0	—	-8	0	-0.6
2001	SD N	0	1	.000	17	0	0	0-1	19.2	20	13	1	1	7-1	19	5.95	70	.260	.326	0	ø	0	—	-3	0	-0.2
2002	SD N	0	0	ø	3	0	0	0-1	2.2	8	5	0	1	5-2	0	16.88	23	.615	.737	0	ø	0	—	-4	93	-0.2
Total	3	1	2	.333	37	0	0	0-2	44.1	56	39	4	3	24-3	37	7.92	57	.313	.397	0	ø	0	—	-15	93	-1.0

Luque, Dolf Adolfo Domingo De Guzman "The Pride of Havana"; B8.4.1890 Havana, Cuba; D7.3.1957 Havana, Cuba; BR/TR/5´7˝/160; d5.20; C9

YEAR	TM LG	W	L	PCT	G	GS	CG-SHO	SV-BS	IP	H	R	HR	HB	BB-IB	SO	ERA	AERA	OAV	OOB	AB-HR-SH	AVG	PB	SUP	APR	DL	PW
1914	Bos N	0	1	.000	2	1	1	0	8.2	5	5	0	0	4	1	4.15	66	.167	.265	2-0-1	.000	-0	26	-1	—	-0.2
1915	Bos N	0	0	ø	2	1	0	0	5	6	3	0	0	4	3	3.60	72	.286	.400	2	.000	-0*	115	-1	—	-0.1
1918	Cin N	6	3	.667	12	10	9-1	0	83	84	44	1	1	32	26	3.80	70	.277	.348	28-0-1	.321	5*	147	-10	—	-0.6
1919	†Cin N	10	3	.769	30	9	6-2	3	106	89	35	2	2	36	40	2.63	105	.237	.308	32-0-2	.125	-0*	118	3	—	0.5
1920	Cin N	13	9	.591	37	23	10-1	1	207.2	168	65	5	4	60	72	2.51	121	**.225**	.286	64-0-5	.266	4	114	16	—	2.1
1921	Cin N	17	19	.472	41	36	25-**3**	3	304	318	132	13	1	64	102	3.38	106	.273	.312	111-0-5	.270	6*	91	11	—	1.8
1922	Cin N	13	23	.361	39	33	18	0	261	266	123	7	1	72	79	3.31	121	.268	.318	86-0-3	.209	2	71	19	—	2.4
1923	Cin N	**27**	8	**.771**	41	37	28-**6**	2	322	279	90	2	5	88	151	**1.93**	**200**	**.235**	.291	104-1-10	.202	2*	95	**70**	—	**7.6**
1924	Cin N	10	15	.400	31	28	13-2	0	219.1	229	99	5	2	53	86	3.16	119	.271	.316	73-1-3	.178	-1*	88	13	—	1.3
1925	Cin N	16	18	.471	36	36	22-**4**	0	291	263	109	7	2	78	140	**2.63**	**156**	**.239**	**.291**	102-2-4	.255	5*	76	**48**	—	**5.9**
1926	Cin N	13	16	.448	34	31	16-1	0	233.2	231	123	7	2	77	83	3.43	108	.260	.321	78-0-7	.346	8	87	1	—	1.0
1927	Cin N	13	12	.520	29	27	17-2	0	230.2	225	103	10	0	56	76	3.20	118	.260	.305	83-0-7	.217	2	86	14	—	1.8
1928	Cin N	11	10	.524	33	29	11-1	1	234.1	254	112	12	2	84	72	3.57	111	.284	.347	67-0-5	.119	-1	90	8	—	0.4
1929	Cin N	5	16	.238	32	22	8-1	0	176	213	103	7	2	56	43	4.50	101	.310	.364	54-1-4	.278	4	73	0	—	0.3
1930	Bro N	14	8	.636	31	24	16-2	2	199	221	107	18	0	58	62	4.30	114	.287	.337	75-0-4	.240	1	128	17	—	1.7
1931	Bro N	7	6	.538	19	15	5	0	102.2	122	59	6	1	27	25	4.56	84	.297	.342	30-0-2	.133	0	106	-8	—	-0.9
1932	NY N	6	7	.462	38	5	1	5	110	128	53	4	0	32	32	4.01	93	.290	.338	25	.040	-2	50	-1	—	-0.3
1933	†NY N	8	2	.800	35	0	0	4	80.1	75	27	4	0	19	23	2.69	119	.251	.296	19	.263	1	—	6	—	0.8
1934	NY N	4	3	.571	26	0	0	7	42.1	54	20	3	1	17	12	3.83	101	.316	.381	7-0-1	.286	1	—	1	—	0.3
1935	NY N	1	0	1.000	2	0	0	0	3.2	1	0	0	0	1	2	0.00	ø	.077	.143	1-0-1	1.000	0	—	2	—	0.4
Total	20	194	179	.520	550	367	206-26	28	3220.1	3231	1412	113	26	918	1130	3.24	117	.265	.318	1043-5-65	.227	37	92	208	—	26.2

Lush, Johnny John Charles; B10.8.1885 Williamsport PA; D11.18.1946 Beverly Hills CA; BL/TL/5´9.5˝/165; d4.22; ▲

YEAR	TM LG	W	L	PCT	G	GS	CG-SHO	SV-BS	IP	H	R	HR	HB	BB-IB	SO	ERA	AERA	OAV	OOB	AB-HR-SH	AVG	PB	SUP	APR	DL	PW
1904	Phi N	0	6	.000	7	6	3	0	42.2	52	40	0	7	27	27	3.59	75	.301	.415	369-2-6	.276	2*	81	-9	—	-0.9
1905	Phi N	2	0	1.000	2	2	1	0	17	12	4	0	1	8	8	1.59	184	.194	.296	16-0-1	.313	1*	235	3	—	0.4
1906	Phi N	18	15	.545	37	35	24-5	0	281	254	128	2	16	119	151	2.37	110	.236	.321	212	.264	7*	123	0	—	1.0
1907	Phi N	3	5	.375	8	8	5-2	0	57.1	48	22	0	3	21	20	2.98	81	.227	.306	40	.200	1*	74	-2	—	-0.2
	StL N	7	10	.412	20	19	15-3	0	144	132	63	2	8	42	71	2.50	100	.246	.311	82-0-1	.280	5*	87	-1	—	0.7
	Year	10	15	.400	28	27	20-5	0	201.1	180	85	2	11	63	91	2.64	94	.241	.309	122-0-1	.254	6	83	-3	—	0.5
1908	StL N	11	18	.379	38	32	23-3	1	250.2	221	102	6	11	57	93	2.12	111	.231	.283	89-0-4	.169	1*	80	3	—	0.6
1909	StL N	11	18	.379	34	28	21-2	0	221.1	215	96	1	10	69	66	3.13	81	.260	.324	92-0-1	.239	4*	116	-11	—	-0.8
1910	StL N	14	13	.519	36	25	13-1	1	225.1	235	116	6	7	70	54	3.20	93	.276	.336	93	.226	4*	124	-11	—	-0.9
Total	7	66	85	.437	182	155	105-16	2	1239.1	1169	571	17	63	413	490	2.68	97	.249	.318	993-2-13	.254	24	106	-28	—	-0.1

Lyle, Sparky Albert Walter; B7.22.1944 DuBois PA; BL/TL/6´1˝/(182–198); d7.4

YEAR	TM LG	W	L	PCT	G	GS	CG-SHO	SV-BS	IP	H	R	HR	HB	BB-IB	SO	ERA	AERA	OAV	OOB	AB-HR-SH	AVG	PB	SUP	APR	DL	PW
1967	Bos A	1	2	.333	27	0	0	5	43.1	33	13	3	2	14-1	42	2.28	153	.213	.283	8	.250	1	—	5	0	0.5
1968	Bos A	6	1	.857	49	0	0	11	65.2	67	25	6	0	14-2	52	2.74	115	.261	.298	8-0-1	.125	-0	—	2	0	0.2
1969	Bos A	8	3	.727	71	0	0	17-9	102.2	91	33	8	1	48-4	93	2.54	150	.240	.323	17	.118	-1	—	14	0	2.0
1970	Bos A	1	7	.125	63	0	0	20-10	67.1	62	37	5	1	34-5	51	3.88	103	.244	.334	13	.000	-1	—	-1	0	-0.3
1971	Bos A	6	4	.600	50	0	0	16-4	52.1	41	16	5	0	23-2	37	2.75	135	.228	.311	3-0-1	1.000	1	—	6	0	1.5
1972	NY A	9	5	.643	59	0	0	**35**-7	107.2	84	25	3	0	29-7	75	1.92	156	.216	.268	21-0-2	.190	1	—	**14**	0	3.1
1973	NY A★	5	9	.357	51	0	0	27-6	82.1	66	30	4	0	18-2	63	2.51	148	.216	.258	0	ø	0	—	10	0	2.0
1974	NY A	9	3	.750	66	0	0	15-7	114	93	30	6	1	43-7	89	1.66	214	.226	.297	1	.000	-0	—	22	0	2.9
1975	NY A	5	7	.417	49	0	0	6-6	89.1	94	34	1	2	36-5	65	3.12	119	.275	.345	0	ø	0	—	6	0	0.9
1976	†NY A☆	7	8	.467	64	0	0	**23**-8	103.2	82	33	5	0	42-7	61	2.26	151	.225	.302	0	ø	0	—	12	0	2.3
1977	†NY A★	13	5	.722	**72**	0	0	26-8	137	131	41	7	2	33-6	68	2.17	183	.257	.302	0	ø	0	—	**26**	0	4.3
1978	†NY A	9	3	.750	59	0	0	9-2	111.2	116	46	6	4	33-8	33	3.47	105	.278	.332	0	ø	0	—	4	0	0.5
1979	Tex A	5	8	.385	67	0	0	13-7	95	78	37	9	0	28-6	48	3.13	133	.226	.283	0	ø	0	—	11	0	1.6
1980	Tex A	3	2	.600	49	0	0	8-4	80.2	97	47	9	0	28-6	43	4.69	83	.306	.359	0	ø	0	—	-7	0	-0.5
	Phi N	0	0	ø	10	0	0	2-1	14	11	5	0	0	6-1	6	1.93	198	.220	.293	0	ø	0	—	2	0	0.1
1981	†Phi N	9	6	.600	48	0	0	2-2	75	85	40	4	1	33-9	29	4.44	82	.301	.372	5-0-1	.400	1	—	-6	0	-1.0
1982	Phi N	3	3	.500	34	0	0	2-5	36.2	50	23	3	0	12-3	12	5.15	72	.327	.373	2	.500	1	—	-6	0	-0.8
	Chi A	0	0	ø	11	0	0	1-0	12	11	4	0	0	7-0	6	3.00	136	.262	.360	0	ø	0	—	2	0	0.1
Total	16	99	76	.566	899	0	0	238-86	1390.1	1292	519	84	14	481-81	873	2.88	128	.251	.313	78-0-5	.192	2	—	116	0	19.4

Lyle, Jim James Charles; B7.24.1900 Lake MS; D10.10.1977 Williamsport PA; BR/TR/6´1˝/180; d10.2; Col Mississippi St.

YEAR	TM LG	W	L	PCT	G	GS	CG-SHO	SV-BS	IP	H	R	HR	HB	BB-IB	SO	ERA	AERA	OAV	OOB	AB-HR-SH	AVG	PB	SUP	APR	DL	PW
1925	Was A	0	0	ø	1	0	0	0	3	5	2	0	0	1	3	6.00	70	.333	.375	0	ø	0	—	0	—	0.0

Lynch, Adrian Adrian Ryan; B2.9.1897 Laurens IA; D3.16.1934 Davenport IA; BB/TR/6´1.5˝/185; d8.4; Col Notre Dame

YEAR	TM LG	W	L	PCT	G	GS	CG-SHO	SV-BS	IP	H	R	HR	HB	BB-IB	SO	ERA	AERA	OAV	OOB	AB-HR-SH	AVG	PB	SUP	APR	DL	PW
1920	StL A	2	0	1.000	5	3	1	0	22.1	23	15	1	1	17	8	5.24	75	.277	.406	9	.222	0	216	-3	—	-0.2

Lynch, Ed Edward Francis; B2.25.1956 Brooklyn NY; BR/TR/6´6˝/(207–210); [TexA77 22/547]; d8.31; Col South Carolina

YEAR	TM LG	W	L	PCT	G	GS	CG-SHO	SV-BS	IP	H	R	HR	HB	BB-IB	SO	ERA	AERA	OAV	OOB	AB-HR-SH	AVG	PB	SUP	APR	DL	PW
1980	NY N	1	1	.500	5	4	0	0-0	19.1	24	12	0	1	5-0	9	5.12	70	.304	.349	6	.333	0	74	-3	0	-0.2
1981	NY N	4	5	.444	17	13	0	0-0	80.1	79	32	6	1	21-2	27	2.91	121	.254	.302	21-0-2	.143	1	85	5	0	0.6
1982	NY N	4	8	.333	43	12	0	2-1	139.1	145	57	6	1	40-4	51	3.55	103	.273	.323	33-0-3	.000	-3	86	5	0	0.0
1983	NY N	10	10	.500	30	27	1	0-0	174.2	208	94	17	3	41-10	44	4.28	86	.302	.341	52-0-11	.154	-1	106	-11	0	-1.3
1984	NY N	9	8	.529	40	13	0	2-1	124	169	77	14	4	24-3	62	4.50	79	.324	.356	27-0-3	.222	1	88	-15	0	-1.9
1985	NY N	10	8	.556	31	29	6-1	0-0	191	188	76	19	1	27-1	65	3.44	102	.256	.281	52-0-9	.077	-2	103	3	0	-0.1
1986	NY N	0	0	ø	1	0	0	0-0	1.2	2	0	0	0	0-0	1	0.00	ø	.286	.286	0	ø	0	—	1	78	0.0
	Chi N	7	5	.583	23	13	1-1	0-0	99.2	105	48	10	1	23-6	57	3.79	107	.279	.319	30-0-1	.033	-2	98	2	0	-0.1
	Year	7	5	.583	24	13	1-1	0-0	101.1	107	48	10	1	23-6	58	3.73	109	.279	.319	30-0-1	.033	-2	98	3	0	-0.1
1987	Chi N	2	9	.182	58	8	0	4-2	110.1	130	74	17	2	48-7	80	5.38	80	.295	.366	16-0-2	.188	-0	71	-13	0	-1.2
Total	8	47	54	.465	248	119	8-2	8-4	940.1	1050	470	89	14	229-33	396	4.00	93	.284	.326	237-0-31	.114	-6	94	-26	78	-4.2

Lynch, Jack John H.; B2.5.1857 New York NY; D4.20.1923 Bronx NY; BR/TR/5´8˝/185; d5.2; Col Fordham

YEAR	TM LG	W	L	PCT	G	GS	CG-SHO	SV-BS	IP	H	R	HR	HB	BB-IB	SO	ERA	AERA	OAV	OOB	AB-HR-SH	AVG	PB	SUP	APR	DL	PW
1881	Buf N	10	9	.526	20	19	17	0	165.2	203	112	2	—	29	32	3.59	77	.297	.325	78	.167	-3*	98	-11	—	-1.2
1883	NY AA	13	15	.464	29	29	29-1	0	255	263	161	6	—	25	119	4.09	82	.250	.267	107	.187	-3	89	-19	—	-1.9
1884	NY AA	37	15	.712	55	53	53-5	0	496	420	225	10	10	42	292	2.67	117	.215	.236	198	.152	-7	114	28	—	1.5
1885	NY AA	23	21	.523	44	43	43-1	0	379	410	243	17	3	42	177	3.61	86	.263	.283	153	.196	1	100	-22	—	-2.1
1886	NY AA	20	30	.400	51	50	50-1	0	432.2	485	307	10	12	116	193	3.95	83	.271	.320	169	.160	-5	94	-33	—	-3.4
1887	NY AA	7	14	.333	21	21	21	0	187	245	158	8	4	36	45	5.10	83	.305	.338	83	.169	-4*	75	-15	—	-1.4

YEAR	TM LG	W	L	PCT	G	GS	CG-SHO	SV-BS	IP	H	R	HR	HB	BB-IB	SO	ERA	AERA	OAV	OOB	AB-HR-SH	AVG	PB	SUP	APR	DL	PW
1890	Bro AA	0	1	.000	1	1	1	0	9	22	18	1	0	5	1	12.00	32	.449	.500	4	.750	2	207	-8	—	-0.4
Total	7	110	105	.512	221	216	214-8	0	1924.1	2048	1224	54	29	295	859	3.69	89	.260	.289	792	.173	-18	98	-80	—	-8.9
LYNCH, MIKE	Michael Joseph; B6.28.1880 Holyoke MA; D4.2.1927 Garrison NY; BR/TR/6´2˝/170; d6.21; Col Brown																									
1904	Pit N	15	11	.577	27	24	24-1	0	222.2	200	90	1	15	91	95	2.71	101	.243	.330	87-0-1	.230	4*	114	1	—	0.4
1905	Pit N	17	8	.680	33	22	13	2	206.1	191	102	3	5	107	106	3.79	79	.254	.351	81-0-3	.136	-1	113	-14	—	-1.8
1906	Pit N	6	5	.545	18	12	7	0	119	101	48	2	8	31	48	2.42	110	.232	.295	39-0-4	.205	-0	100	2	—	0.1
1907	Pit N	2	2	.500	7	4	2	0	36	37	21	0	1	22	9	2.25	108	.282	.390	12-0-1	.250	1	139	-2	—	-0.1
	NY N	3	6	.333	12	10	7	1	72	68	35	3	0	30	34	3.38	73	.249	.323	27	.296	2	112	-7	—	-0.6
	Year	5	8	.385	19	14	9	1	108	105	56	3	1	52	43	3.00	82	.260	.346	39-0-1	.282	3	120	-7	—	-0.7
Total	4	43	32	.573	97	72	53-1	3	656	597	296	9	29	281	292	3.05	91	.248	.333	246-0-9	.203	5	112	-20	—	-2.0
LYNCH, TOM	Thomas S.; B1863 Peru IL; D5.13.1903 Peru IL; BL/5´11˝/175; d8.5																									
1884	Chi N	0	0	ø	1	1	0	0	7	7	4	1	—	3	2	2.57	122	.241	.313	4	.000	-1	85	0	—	0.0
LYNN, RED	Japhet Monroe; B12.27.1913 Kenney TX; D10.27.1977 Bellville TX; BR/TR/6´0˝/162; d4.25; Mil 1945																									
1939	Det A	0	1	.000	4	0	0	0	8.1	11	8	2	1	3	3	8.64	57	.324	.395	2	.000	-0	—	-3	—	-0.3
	NY N	1	0	1.000	26	0	0	1	49.2	44	21	3	2	21	22	3.08	127	.240	.325	6	.000	-1	—	4	—	0.1
1940	NY N	4	3	.571	33	0	0	3	42.1	40	21	3	1	24	25	3.83	101	.247	.348	4	.000	-1	—	0	—	-0.1
1944	Chi N	5	4	.556	22	7	4-1	1	84.1	80	41	4	1	37	35	4.06	87	.251	.331	29	.207	0	143	-3	0	-0.2
Total	3	10	8	.556	85	7	4-1	5	184.2	175	91	12	5	85	85	3.95	96	.251	.336	41	.146	-1	143	-2	0	-0.5
LYON, BRANDON	Brandon James; B8.10.1979 Salt Lake City UT; BR/TR/6´1˝/(175–190); [TorA99 14/433]; d8.4; Col Dixie (UT) JC; [DL 2003 Pit N 7, 2004 Ari N 183]																									
2001	Tor A	5	4	.556	11	11	0	0-0	63	63	31	6	1	15-0	35	4.29	107	.266	.305	0	ø	0	73	3	0	0.3
2002	Tor A	1	4	.200	15	10	0	0-1	62	78	47	14	2	19-2	30	6.53	71	.308	.359	0	ø	0	88	-12	0	-0.8
2003	Bos A	4	6	.400	49	0	0	9-3	59	73	33	6	2	19-5	50	4.12	113	.296	.346	0	ø	0	—	2	32	0.4
2005	Ari N	0	2	.000	32	0	0	14-1	29.1	44	25	6	2	10-2	17	6.44	69	.341	.394	0	ø	0	—	-7	92	-1.0
2006	Ari N	2	4	.333	68	0	0	0-7	69.1	68	32	7	0	22-7	46	3.89	120	.258	.310	0	ø	0	—	6	0	0.5
Total	5	12	20	.375	175	21	0	23-12	282.2	326	168	39	7	85-16	178	4.87	95	.288	.337	0	ø	0	80	-8	314	-0.6
LYONS, AL	Albert Harold; B7.18.1918 St.Joseph MO; D12.20.1965 Inglewood CA; BR/TR/6´2˝/195; d4.19; Mil 1944–45																									
1944	NY A	0	0	ø	11	0	0	0	39.2	43	22	2	2	24	14	4.54	77	.291	.397	26	.346	2*	—	-4	0	0.0
1946	NY A	0	1	.000	2	1	0	0	8.1	11	5	0	1	6	4	5.40	64	.314	.429	4	.000	-1	99	-1	0	-0.2
1947	NY A	1	0	1.000	6	0	0	0	11	18	11	2	0	9	7	9.00	39	.367	.466	6	.667	2*	—	-6	0	-0.3
	Pit N	1	2	.333	13	0	0	0	28.1	36	24	4	1	12	16	7.31	58	.300	.368	10-1-0	.200	1*	—	-8	0	-0.6
1948	Bos N	1	0	1.000	7	0	0	0	12.2	17	11	1	0	8	5	7.82	49	.309	.397	12	.167	0*	—	-5	0	-0.3
Total	4	3	3	.500	39	1	0	0	100	125	73	9	4	59	46	6.30	59	.307	.400	58-1-0	.293	5	99	-24	0	-1.4
LYONS, CURT	Curt Russell; B10.17.1974 Greencastle IN; BR/TR/6´5˝/240; [CinN92 6/157]; d9.19																									
1996	Cin N	2	0	1.000	3	3	0	0-0	16	17	8	1	1	7-0	14	4.50	95	.274	.357	5-0-1	.000	-1	112	0	0	-0.1
LYONS, GEORGE	George Tony "Smooth"; B1.25.1891 Bible Grove IL; D8.12.1981 Nevada MO; BR/TR/5´11˝/180; d9.6																									
1920	StL N	2	1	.667	7	2	1	0	23.1	21	8	2	1	9	5	3.09	97	.262	.344	7	.143	-0	105	1	—	0.1
1924	StL A	3	2	.600	26	6	2	0	77.2	97	52	2	5	45	25	5.21	87	.323	.420	20-0-2	.250	-0	131	-5	—	-0.2
Total	2	5	3	.625	33	8	3	0	101	118	60	4	6	54	30	4.72	88	.311	.405	27-0-2	.222	-0	126	-4	—	-0.1
LYONS, HERSH	Herschel Englebert; B7.23.1915 Fresno CA; BR/TR/5´11˝/195; d4.17; Col Occidental																									
1941	StL N	0	0	ø	1	0	0	0	1.1	1	0	0	0	3	1	0.00	ø	.200	.500	0	ø	0	—	1	0	0.1
LYONS, TED	Theodore Amar; B12.28.1900 Lake Charles LA; D7.25.1986 Sulphur LA; BB/TR/5´11˝/200; d7.2; Mil 1943–45; M3/C6; HF1955; Col Baylor																									
1923	Chi A	2	1	.667	9	1	0	0	22.2	30	21	2	1	15	6	6.35	62	.323	.422	5	.200	0	104	-7	—	-0.7
1924	Chi A	12	11	.522	41	22	12	3	216.1	279	143	10	2	72	52	4.87	85	.322	.375	77-0-4	.221	0	114	-20	—	-2.0
1925	Chi A	**21**	11	.656	43	32	19-**5**	3	262.2	274	111	7	2	83	45	3.26	128	.278	.335	97-0-9	.186	-3	104	28	—	2.8
1926	Chi A	18	16	.529	39	31	24-3	2	283.2	268	108	6	1	106	51	3.01	128	.252	.320	104-0-8	.212	-0*	86	29	—	3.3
1927	Chi A	**22**	14	.611	39	34	**30**-2	2	**307.2**	291	125	7	0	67	71	2.84	143	.251	.292	110-1-7	.255	5*	102	38	—	**4.7**
1928	Chi A	15	14	.517	39	27	21	6	240	276	133	11	2	68	60	3.98	102	.295	.344	91-0-5	.253	1*	100	-1	—	0.0
1929	Chi A	14	20	.412	37	31	21-1	2	259.1	276	136	11	2	76	57	4.10	105	.278	.331	91-0-4	.220	1*	88	7	—	1.1
1930	Chi A	22	15	.595	42	36	**29**-1	1	**297.2**	331	160	12	2	57	69	3.78	122	.285	.319	122-1-6	.311	8*	98	26	—	3.7
1931	Chi A	4	6	.400	22	12	7	0	101	117	50	6	0	33	16	4.01	106	.296	.350	33-0-3	.152	-1*	83	5	—	0.2
1932	Chi A	10	15	.400	33	26	19-1	2	230.2	243	104	10	3	71	58	3.28	132	.272	.327	73-1-6	.260	5*	74	28	—	3.1
1933	Chi A	10	21	.323	36	27	14-2	1	228	260	142	10	0	74	74	4.38	97	.280	.333	91-1-1	.286	6*	82	-7	—	-0.3
1934	Chi A	11	13	.458	30	24	21	1	205.1	249	138	15	2	66	53	4.87	97	.293	.345	97-1-4	.206	1*	95	-7	—	-0.4
1935	Chi A	15	8	.652	23	22	19-3	0	190.2	194	79	15	3	56	54	3.02	153	.262	.317	82-0-3	.220	-0*	84	30	—	3.2
1936	Chi A	10	13	.435	26	24	15-1	0	182	227	115	21	3	45	48	5.14	101	.305	.347	70-0-1	.157	-3	91	2	—	0.1
1937	Chi A	12	7	.632	22	22	11	0	169.1	182	86	21	1	45	45	4.15	111	.278	.326	57-0-6	.211	1*	89	11	—	1.2
1938	Chi A	9	11	.450	23	23	17-1	0	194.2	238	93	13	0	52	54	3.70	132	.299	.342	72-0-3	.194	-1*	86	26	—	2.2
1939	Chi A☆	14	6	.700	21	21	16	0	172.2	162	71	7	1	26	65	2.76	171	.247	**.276**	61-0-6	.295	4	90	32	—	3.7
1940	Chi A	12	8	.600	22	22	17-**4**	0	186.1	188	85	17	0	37	72	3.24	137	.252	.287	75-0-2	.240	2	112	21	—	2.1
1941	Chi A	12	10	.545	22	22	19-2	0	187.1	199	87	9	4	37	63	3.70	111	.269	.308	74-0-2	.270	4	114	10	0	1.4
1942	Chi A	14	6	.700	20	20	20-1	0	180.1	167	52	11	2	26	50	**2.10**	**172**	.245	.275	67-0-2	.239	4	109	29	0	**3.8**
1946	Chi A	1	4	.200	5	5	5	0	42.2	38	17	2	0	9	10	2.32	147	.235	.275	14-0-1	.000	-1	55	4	0	0.3
Total	21	260	230	.531	594	484	356-27	23	4161	4489	2056	223	31	1121	1073	3.67	118	.276	.324	1563-5-83	.233	32	95	284	0	33.5
LYONS, TOBY	Thomas Arthur; B3.27.1869 Cambridge MA; D8.27.1920 Boston MA; d4.18																									
1890	Syr AA	0	2	.000	3	3	2	0	22.1	40	36	1	1	21	6	10.48	34	.377	.484	12	.333	1	254	-19	—	-1.1
LYSANDER, RICK	Richard Eugene; B2.21.1953 Huntington Park CA; BR/TR/6´2˝/(188–195); [OakA74 19/445]; d4.12; Col Cal St.–Los Angeles																									
1980	Oak A	0	0	ø	5	0	0	0-0	13.2	24	13	3	0	4-0	5	7.90	48	.381	.418	0	ø	0	—	-6	0	-0.3
1983	Min A	5	12	.294	61	4	1-1	3-5	125	132	63	8	2	43-12	58	3.38	127	.275	.332	0	ø	0	80	7	0	0.9
1984	Min A	4	3	.571	36	0	0	5-2	56.2	62	23	2	0	27-7	22	3.49	121	.283	.357	0	ø	0	—	5	0	0.6
1985	Min A	0	2	.000	35	1	0	3-2	61	72	43	3	0	22-2	26	6.05	73	.305	.362	0	ø	0	41	-9	0	-0.5
Total	4	9	17	.346	137	5	1-1	11-9	256.1	290	142	16	2	96-21	111	4.28	100	.291	.350	0	ø	0	72	-3	0	0.7
LYSTON, JOHN	John Michael; B5.28.1867 Baltimore MD; D10.29.1909 Baltimore MD; BR/TR/5´11˝/185; d8.29																									
1891	Col AA	0	1	.000	1	1	1	0	6	10	8	0	1	6	1	10.50	33	.357	.486	2	.000	-0	36	-4	—	-0.4
1894	Cle N	0	0	ø	1	1	0	0	3.2	5	6	1	0	4	0	9.82	56	.313	.450	2	.000	-0	103	-2	—	-0.1
Total	2	0	1	.000	2	2	1	0	9.2	15	14	1	1	10	1	10.24	41	.341	.473	4	.000	-0	79	-6	—	-0.5
MAAS, DUKE	Duane Fredrick; B1.31.1929 Utica MI; D12.7.1976 Mt.Clemens MI; BR/TR/5´10˝/(165–176); d4.21																									
1955	Det A	5	6	.455	18	16	5-2	0	86.2	91	52	7	2	50-3	42	4.88	79	.271	.366	30-0-2	.167	0	117	-10	0	-1.1
1956	Det A	0	7	.000	26	7	0	0	63.1	81	51	9	6	32-3	34	6.54	63	.313	.398	16	.188	0	86	-17	0	-1.6
1957	Det A	10	14	.417	45	26	8-2	6	219.1	210	92	23	4	65-7	116	3.28	118	.252	.307	71-1-5	.085	-4	85	12	0	0.9
1958	KC A	4	5	.444	10	7	3-1	1	55.1	49	25	3	1	13-0	19	3.90	100	.241	.290	17-0-1	.176	0	62	1	0	0.2
	†NY A	7	3	.700	22	13	2-1	0	101.1	93	51	9	2	36-0	50	3.82	92	.242	.308	34-0-1	.088	-2	145	-4	0	-0.6
	Year	11	8	.579	32	20	5-2	1	156.2	142	76	12	3	49-0	69	3.85	95	.242	.302	51-0-2	.118	-1	114	-4	0	-0.4
1959	NY A	14	8	.636	38	21	3-1	4	138	149	82	14	2	53-1	67	4.43	82	.278	.342	40-0-5	.125	-1	114	-14	0	-2.2
1960	†NY A	5	1	.833	35	1	0	4	70.1	70	44	6	1	35-2	28	4.09	87	.265	.346	6	.000	-1	25	-8	0	-0.7
1961	NY A	0	0	ø	1	0	0	0	0.1	2	2	0	0	0-0	0	54.00	7	1.000	1.000	0	ø	0	—	-2	0	-0.1
Total	7	45	44	.506	195	91	21-7	15	734.2	745	399	71	18	284-16	356	4.19	90	.264	.333	214-1-14	.117	-7	103	-42	0	-5.2
MABE, BOB	Robert Lee; B10.8.1929 Danville VA; D1.9.2005 Danville VA; BR/TR/5´11˝/(160–170); d4.18																									
1958	StL N	3	9	.250	31	13	4	0	111.2	113	66	11	4	41-6	74	4.51	91	.260	.327	24-0-3	.042	-2*	69	-6	0	-0.8
1959	Cin N	4	2	.667	18	1	0	3	29.2	29	28	6	0	19-2	8	5.46	74	.254	.358	7-0-1	.000	-1	199	-8	0	-1.6
1960	Bal A	0	0	ø	2	0	0	0	0.2	4	6	0	0	1-0	0	27.00	14	.571	.625	0	ø	0	—	-3	0	-0.2
Total	3	7	11	.389	51	14	4	3	142	146	100	17	4	61-8	82	4.82	85	.263	.338	31-0-4	.032	-3	78	-17	0	-2.6

YEAR	TM LG	W	L	PCT	G	GS	CG-SHO	SV-BS	IP	H	R	HR	HB	BB-IB	SO	ERA	AERA	OAV	OOB	AB-HR-SH	AVG	PB	SUP	APR	DL	PW
Mabeus, Chris	Christopher Eugene; B2.11.1979 Peoria IL; BR/TR/6´3˝/235; [OakA01 13/401]; d5.29; Col Lewis–Clark St.																									
2006	Mil N	0	0	ø	1	0	0	0-0	1.2	4	4	1	0	3-0	2	21.60	21	.444	.583	0	ø	0	—	-3	0	-0.1
MacArthur, Mac	Malcolm; B1.19.1862 Glasgow, Scotland; D10.18.1932 Detroit MI; TR/5´9.5˝/164; d5.2																									
1884	Ind AA	1	5	.167	6	6	6	0	52	57	49	1	2	21	19	5.02	66	.263	.333	21	.095	-2	67	-10	—	-1.0
MacCormack, Frank	Frank Louis; B9.21.1954 Jersey City NJ; BR/TR/6´4˝/210; d6.14; Col Rutgers																									
1976	Det A	0	5	.000	9	8	0	0-0	32.2	35	24	1	1	34-0	14	5.79	64	.294	.449	3	.000	-0	80	-7	0	-1.0
1977	Sea A	0	0	ø	3	3	0	0-0	7	4	3	0	3	12-0	4	3.86	108	.174	.500	0	ø	0	130	0	16	0.0
Total	2	0	5	.000	12	11	0	0-0	39.2	39	27	1	4	46-0	18	5.45	70	.275	.459	3	.000	-0	95	-7	16	-1.0
MacDonald, Rob	Robert Joseph; B4.27.1965 East Orange NJ; BL/TL/6´3˝/(200–208); [TorA87 19/491]; d8.14; Col Rutgers																									
1990	Tor A	0	0	ø	4	0	0	0-0	2.1	0	0	0	0	2-0	0	0.00	ø	.000	.250	0	ø	0	—	1	0	0.0
1991	†Tor A	3	3	.500	45	0	0	0-4	53.2	51	19	5	0	25-4	24	2.85	148	.252	.332	0	ø	0	—	8	0	0.8
1992	Tor A	1	0	1.000	27	0	0	0-0	47.1	50	24	4	1	16-3	26	4.37	94	.270	.330	0	ø	0	—	-1	0	-0.1
1993	Det A	3	3	.500	68	0	0	3-3	65.2	67	42	8	1	33-5	39	5.35	82	.268	.349	0	ø	0	—	-7	0	-0.5
1995	NY A	1	1	.500	33	0	0	0-1	46.1	50	25	7	1	22-0	41	4.86	95	.282	.365	0	ø	0	—	0	0	0.0
1996	NY N	0	2	.000	20	0	0	0-0	19	16	10	2	0	9-0	12	4.26	94	.235	.321	0	ø	0	—	0	0	0.0
Total	6	8	9	.471	197	0	0	3-8	234.1	234	120	26	3	107-12	142	4.34	99	.264	.342	0	ø	0	—	1	0	0.2
MacDonald, Bill	William Paul; B3.28.1929 Alameda CA; D5.4.1991 Shasta Lake CA; BR/TR/5´10˝/170; d5.6; Mil 1951–52																									
1950	Pit N	8	10	.444	32	20	6-2	1	153	138	88	17	1	88	60	4.29	102	.243	.346	49-0-1	.122	-2	75	-1	0	-0.4
1953	Pit N	0	1	.000	4	1	0	0	7.1	12	10	0	1	8	4	12.27	36	.400	.538	0-0-1	ø	0	20	-6	0	-0.6
Total	2	8	11	.421	36	21	6-2	1	160.1	150	98	17	2	96	64	4.66	94	.251	.356	49-0-2	.122	-2	72	-7	0	-1.0
MacDougal, Mike	Robert Meiklejohn; B3.5.1977 Las Vegas NV; BR/TR/6´4˝/(185–195); [KCA99 1/25]; d9.22; Col Wake Forest																									
2001	KC A	1	1	.500	3	3	0	0-0	15.1	18	10	2	1	4-0	7	4.70	106	.290	.343	0	ø	0	81	0	0	0.0
2002	KC A	0	1	.000	6	0	0	0-0	9	5	5	0	0	7-1	10	5.00	100	.161	.316	0	ø	0	—	0	0	0.0
2003	KC A☆	3	5	.375	68	0	0	27-8	64	64	36	4	8	32-0	57	4.08	118	.267	.369	0	ø	0	—	3	0	0.5
2004	KC A	1	1	.500	13	0	0	1-2	11.1	16	8	2	1	9-0	14	5.56	84	.314	.426	0	ø	0	—	-1	20	-0.2
2005	KC A	5	6	.455	68	0	0	21-4	70.1	69	32	6	3	24-2	72	3.33	132	.257	.323	0	ø	0	—	6	0	1.2
2006	KC A	0	0	ø	4	0	0	1-0	4	2	0	0	0	0-0	2	0.00	ø	.154	.154	0	ø	0	—	2	101	0.1
	Chi A	1	1	.500	25	0	0	0-1	25	19	5	1	1	6-0	19	1.80	260	.213	.271	0	ø	0	—	8	0	0.5
	Year	1	1	.500	29	0	0	1-1	29	21	5	1	1	6-0	21	1.55	301	.206	.257	0	ø	0	—	10	0	0.6
Total	6	11	15	.423	187	3	0	50-15	199	193	96	15	14	82-3	181	3.62	129	.256	.338	0	ø	0	81	18	121	2.1
Mace, Jimmy	Harry F.; B Washington DC; D4.26.1930 Norfolk VA; 5´11˝/185; d5.5																									
1891	Was AA	0	1	.000	3	1	1	0	16	18	14	0	1	8	3	7.31	51	.273	.360	6	.000	-1	67	-4	—	-0.3
MacFayden, Danny	Daniel Knowles "Deacon Danny"; B6.10.1905 N.Truro MA; D8.26.1972 Brunswick ME; BR/TR/5´11˝/170; d8.25																									
1926	Bos A	0	1	.000	3	1	1	0	13	10	7	0	0	7	1	4.85	84	.217	.321	3	.333	0	21	-1	—	0.0
1927	Bos A	5	8	.385	34	16	6-1	2	160.1	176	88	9	6	59	42	4.27	99	.294	.363	46-1-5	.283	4*	79	0	—	0.4
1928	Bos A	9	15	.375	33	28	9	0	195	215	123	12	7	78	61	4.75	87	.289	.361	63-0-1	.143	-1*	87	-15	—	-1.7
1929	Bos A	10	18	.357	32	27	14-4	0	221	225	108	8	5	81	61	3.62	118	.271	.340	74-0-4	.176	-3	74	15	—	1.5
1930	Bos A	11	14	.440	36	33	18-1	2	269.1	293	141	9	6	93	76	4.21	109	.281	.343	92-0-8	.141	-4	86	14	—	0.8
1931	Bos A	16	12	.571	35	32	17-2	0	230.2	263	121	4	7	79	74	4.02	107	.281	.341	81-0-6	.123	-5	96	6	—	0.3
1932	Bos A	1	10	.091	12	11	6	0	77.2	91	55	3	1	33	29	5.10	88	.289	.358	25-0-2	.120	-2	48	-6	—	-0.8
	NY A	7	5	.583	17	15	9	1	121.1	137	69	11	2	37	33	3.93	104	.281	.334	49-0-2	.102	-3	138	-1	—	-0.4
	Year	8	15	.348	29	26	15	1	199	228	124	14	3	70	62	4.39	97	.284	.344	74-0-4	.108	-4	98	-6	—	-1.2
1933	NY A	3	2	.600	25	6	2	0	90.1	120	62	8	2	37	28	5.88	66	.319	.383	34-0-1	.029	-4	131	-19	—	-1.3
1934	NY A	4	3	.571	22	11	4	0	96	110	57	5	2	31	41	4.50	90	.288	.345	39-0-1	.103	-2	148	-6	—	-0.6
1935	Cin N	1	2	.333	7	4	1	0	36	39	22	1	0	13	13	4.75	84	.281	.342	11	.091	-1	75	-3	—	-0.2
	Bos N	5	13	.278	28	20	7-1	0	151.2	200	96	8	5	34	46	5.10	74	.314	.354	51-0-1	.157	-1	91	-22	—	-2.1
	Year	6	15	.286	35	24	8-1	0	187.2	239	118	9	5	47	59	5.04	76	.308	.352	62-0-1	.145	-2	88	-23	—	-2.3
1936	Bos N	17	13	.567	37	31	21-2	0	266.2	268	97	5	5	66	86	2.87	134	.259	.307	83-0-8	.096	-5	75	30	—	2.8
1937	Bos N	14	14	.500	32	32	16-2	0	246	250	96	5	2	60	70	2.93	123	.268	.313	83-0-8	.157	-2	92	17	—	1.7
1938	Bos N	14	9	.609	29	29	19-5	0	219.2	208	82	6	5	64	58	2.95	116	.247	.304	77-0-2	.117	-4	83	14	—	0.9
1939	Bos N	8	14	.364	33	28	8	2	191.2	221	100	11	4	59	46	3.90	95	.291	.345	67-0-5	.179	-1	96	-6	—	-0.6
1940	Pit N	5	4	.556	35	8	0	2	91.1	112	47	5	4	27	24	3.55	107	.302	.356	28-0-1	.179	-0	108	0	—	0.0
1941	Was A	0	1	.000	5	0	0	0	7	12	9	1	0	5	3	10.29	39	.375	.459	0	ø	0	—	-5	0	-0.5
1943	Bos N	2	1	.667	10	1	0	0	21.1	31	14	1	1	9	5	5.91	58	.344	.410	4	.250	0	75	-5	0	-0.6
Total	17	132	159	.454	465	333	158-18	9	2706	2981	1394	112	64	872	797	3.96	101	.281	.340	910-1-55	.142	-34	90	7	0	-0.4
Machado, Julio	Julio Segundo (Rondon); B12.1.1965 San Carlos de Zulia, Zulia, Venezuela; BR/TR/5´9˝/(160–165); d9.7																									
1989	NY N	0	1	.000	10	0	0	0-1	11	9	4	0	0	3-0	14	3.27	101	.214	.267	0	ø	0	—	0	0	0.0
1990	NY N	4	1	.800	27	0	0	0-1	34.1	32	13	4	2	17-4	27	3.15	120	.248	.340	0	ø	0	—	3	0	0.3
	Mil A	0	0	ø	10	0	0	3-0	13	9	1	0	0	8-2	12	0.69	561	.191	.304	0	ø	0	—	5	0	0.2
1991	Mil A	3	3	.500	54	0	0	3-3	88.2	65	36	12	3	55-1	98	3.45	116	.211	.334	0	ø	0	—	6	0	0.4
Total	3	7	5	.583	101	0	0	6-5	147	115	54	16	5	83-7	151	3.12	124	.219	.328	0	ø	0	—	14	0	0.9
Machemehl, Chuck	Charles Walter; B4.20.1946 Brenham TX; BR/TR/6´4˝/215; [CleA68 12/258]; d4.6; Col TCU																									
1971	Cle A	0	2	.000	14	0	0	3-2	18.1	16	16	2	0	15-3	9	6.38	61	.246	.373	2	.500	0	—	-5	0	-0.7
Mack, Denny	Dennis Joseph (b Dennis Joseph McGee); B1851 Easton PA; D4.10.1888 Wilkes–Barre PA; BR/TR/5´7˝/164; d5.6; M1/U2; Col Villanova; ▲																									
1871	Rok NA	0	1	.000	3	1	1	0	13	20	30	0	—	3	1	3.46	118	.299	.329	122	.246	-0*	97	-2	—	-0.1
Mack, Frank	Frank George "Stubby"; B2.2.1900 Oklahoma City OK; D7.2.1971 Clearwater FL; BR/TR/6´1.5˝/180; d8.16; Col St. Marys (CA)																									
1922	Chi A	2	2	.500	8	4	1-1	0	34.1	36	16	2	0	16	11	3.67	111	.281	.361	12	.250	1	73	1	—	0.2
1923	Chi A	0	1	.000	11	0	0	0	23.1	23	13	0	0	11	6	4.24	93	.284	.370	6	.000	-1	—	-1	—	-0.1
1925	Chi A	0	0	ø	8	0	0	0	13.1	24	14	1	0	13	6	9.45	44	.444	.552	3	.333	0	—	-7	—	-0.3
Total	3	2	3	.400	27	4	1-1	0	71	83	43	3	0	40	23	4.94	82	.316	.406	21	.190	0	73	-7	—	-0.2
Mack, Tony	Tony Lynn; B4.30.1961 Lexington KY; BR/TR/5´10˝/177; [AnaA82 3/62]; d7.27; Col Lamar																									
1985	Cal A	0	1	.000	1	1	0	0-0	2.1	8	4	0	0	0-0	0	15.43	27	.571	.571	0	ø	0	66	-3	0	-0.4
Mack, Bill	William Francis; B2.12.1885 Elmira NY; D9.30.1971 Elmira NY; BL/TL/6´1˝/155; d7.14; Col Syracuse																									
1908	Chi N	0	0	ø	2	0	0	0	6	5	3	1	1	1	2	3.00	78	.263	.333	3	.667	1	—	-1	—	0.1
MacKenzie, Ken	Kenneth Purvis; B3.10.1934 Gore Bay ON, Can.; BR/TL/6´0˝/(180–185); d5.2; Col Yale																									
1960	Mil N	0	1	.000	9	0	0	0	8.1	9	7	2	0	3-2	9	6.48	53	.281	.333	1	.000	-0	—	-3	0	-0.4
1961	Mil N	0	1	.000	5	0	0	0	7	8	5	1	1	2-0	5	5.14	73	.296	.367	2	.000	-0	—	-1	0	-0.2
1962	NY N	5	4	.556	42	1	0	1	80	87	47	10	3	34-3	51	4.95	84	.280	.353	12-0-1	.083	-1	0	-4	0	-0.5
1963	NY N	3	1	.750	34	0	0	3	58	63	35	11	2	12-2	41	4.97	70	.267	.307	10	.000	-1	—	-8	0	-0.8
	StL N	0	0	ø	8	0	0	0	9	9	6	1	0	3-1	7	4.00	89	.250	.308	0	ø	0	—	-1	0	-0.1
	Year	3	1	.750	42	0	0	3	67	72	41	12	2	15-3	48	4.84	72	.265	.307	10	.000	-1	—	-9	0	-0.9
1964	SF N	0	0	ø	10	0	0	1	9	9	7	1	0	3-0	3	5.00	71	.265	.308	0	ø	0	—	-2	0	-0.1
1965	Hou N	0	3	.000	21	0	0	0	37	46	22	7	0	6-0	26	3.89	86	.299	.325	11	.273	1	—	-4	0	-0.2
Total	6	8	10	.444	129	1	0	5	208.1	231	129	33	6	63-8	142	4.80	78	.278	.331	36-0-1	.111	-2	0	-23	0	-2.3
Mackinson, John	John Joseph; B10.29.1923 Orange NJ; D10.17.1989 Reseda CA; BR/TR/5´10.5˝/160; d4.16																									
1953	Phi A	0	0	ø	1	0	0	0	1.1	1	0	0	0	2	0	0.00	ø	.200	.429	0	ø	0	—	1	0	0.0
1955	StL N	0	1	.000	8	1	0	0	20.2	24	18	3	1	10-2	8	7.84	52	.296	.372	4	.000	-0*	197	-8	0	-0.4
Total	2	0	1	.000	9	1	0	0	22	25	18	3	1	12-2	8	7.36	55	.291	.376	4	.000	-0	197	-7	0	-0.4
Macon, Max	Max Cullen; B10.14.1915 Pensacola FL; D8.5.1989 Jupiter FL; BL/TL/6´3˝/175; d4.21; Mil 1945–46; ▲																									
[illegible]	[illegible]	[illegible]	11	[illegible]	[illegible]	[illegible]	[illegible]	[illegible]	[illegible]	[illegible]	83	[illegible]	[illegible]	61-0	[illegible]	[illegible]	[illegible]	[illegible]	[illegible]	[illegible]	[illegible]	[illegible]	95	[illegible]	[illegible]	[illegible]

YEAR	TM LG	W	L	PCT	G	GS	CG-SHO	SV-BS	IP	H	R	HR	HB	BB-IB	SO	ERA	AERA	OAV	OOB	AB-HR-SH	AVG	PB	SUP	APR	DL	PW
1940	Bro N	1	0	1.000	2	0	0	0	2	5	5	2	0	0	1	22.50	18	.455	.455	1	1.000	0	—	-4	—	-0.6
1942	Bro N	5	3	.625	14	8	4-1	1	84	67	22	3	2	33	27	1.93	169	.220	.300	43-0-3	.279	4*	100	12	0	1.6
1943	Bro N	7	5	.583	25	9	0	0	77	91	54	4	4	32	21	5.96	56	.291	.364	55	.164	-1*	185	-21	0	-3.0
1944	Bos N	0	0	ø	1	0	0	0	3	10	7	2	0	1	1	21.00	18	.556	.579	366-3-2	.273	0*	—	-5	0	-0.2
1947	Bos N	0	0	ø	1	0	0	0	2	1	0	0	0	1	1	0.00	ø	.167	.286	1	.000	-0	—	1	0	0.0
Total	6	17	19	.472	81	29	9-2	3	297.1	307	171	20	10	128	90	4.24	85	.267	.345	502-3-6	.265	5	122	-23	0	-2.7
MacPherson, Harry	Harry William; B7.10.1926 N.Andover MA; BR/TR/5´10˝/150; d8.14																									
1944	Bos N	0	0	ø	1	0	0	0	1	0	0	0	0	1	1	0.00	ø	.000	.250	0	ø	0	—	0	0	0.0
MacRae, Scott	Scott Patrick; B8.13.1974 Dearborn MI; BR/TR/6´3˝/205; [CinN95 32/895]; d7.24; Col Valdosta St.																									
2001	Cin N	0	1	.000	24	0	0	0-0	31.1	33	15	0	2	8-0	18	4.02	114	.266	.316	3	.000	-0	—	2	0	0.0
MacWhorter, Keith	Keith; B12.30.1955 Worcester MA; BR/TR/6´4˝/185; [LAN76 15/355]; d5.10; Col Bryant																									
1980	Bos A	0	3	.000	14	2	0	0-0	42.1	46	27	3	2	18-3	21	5.53	77	.280	.357	0	ø	0	42	-5	0	-0.3
Madden, Len	Leonard Joseph "Lefty"; B7.2.1890 Toledo OH; D9.9.1949 Toledo OH; BL/TL/6´2˝/165; d8.31																									
1912	Chi N	0	1	.000	6	2	0	0	12.1	16	10	1	1	9	5	2.92	114	.302	.413	4	.250	0	154	-1	—	-0.1
Madden, Mike	Michael Anthony; B1.13.1958 Denver CO; BL/TL/6´1˝/(185–190); d4.5; Col Northern Colorado																									
1983	Hou N	9	5	.643	28	13	0	0-0	94.2	76	37	4	1	45-3	44	3.14	109	.231	.323	22-0-6	.045	-1	85	4	21	0.4
1984	Hou N	2	3	.400	17	7	0	0-0	40.2	46	27	1	0	35-3	29	5.53	60	.297	.422	6	.333	1	72	-10	0	-1.0
1985	Hou N	0	0	ø	13	0	0	0-0	19	29	15	1	0	11-0	16	4.26	82	.363	.435	0	ø	0	—	-4	81	-0.2
1986	Hou N	1	2	.333	13	6	0	0-0	39.2	47	20	3	0	22-3	30	4.08	88	.297	.381	9-0-4	.000	-1	95	-2	0	-0.2
Total	4	12	10	.545	71	26	0	0-0	194	198	99	9	1	113-9	119	3.94	88	.274	.370	37-0-10	.081	-1	84	-12	102	-1.0
Madden, Kid	Michael Joseph; B10.22.1866 Portland ME; D3.16.1896 Portland ME; BL/TL/5´7.5˝/130; d5.6																									
1887	Bos N	21	14	.600	37	37	36-3	0	321	317	203	20	20	122	81	3.79	108	.251	.327	132-1	.242	3	106	8	—	0.9
1888	Bos N	7	11	.389	20	18	17-1	0	165	142	76	6	15	24	53	2.95	98	.228	.273	67	.164	-2	82	4	—	0.2
1889	Bos N	10	10	.500	22	19	18-1	1	178	194	131	7	16	71	64	4.40	95	.269	.348	86	.291	2*	105	-6	—	-0.4
1890	Bos P	3	2	.600	10	7	5-1	1	62	85	55	2	8	25	24	4.79	92	.313	.387	38	.184	-1*	109	-3	—	-0.3
1891	Bos AA	0	1	.000	1	1	1	0	8	10	12	2	3	6	6	6.75	52	.294	.442	3	.667	1	107	-4	—	-0.2
	Bal AA	13	12	.520	32	27	20-1	1	224	239	168	4	24	88	56	4.10	91	.264	.345	107-1	.271	5*	102	-7	—	-0.1
	Year	13	13	.500	33	28	21-1	1	232	249	180	6	27	94	62	4.19	89	.265	.349	110-1	.282	6	102	-11	—	-0.3
Total	5	54	50	.519	122	109	97-7	3	958	987	645	41	86	336	284	3.92	98	.259	.332	433-2	.245	9	102	-8	—	0.1
Madden, Morris	Morris De Wayne; B8.31.1960 Laurens SC; BL/TL/6´0˝/(155–165); [LAN79 24/617]; d6.11; Col Spartanburg Methodist (SC) JC																									
1987	Det A	0	0	ø	2	0	0	0-0	1.2	4	3	0	0	3-1	0	16.20	26	.444	.583	0	ø	0	—	-2	0	-0.1
1988	Pit N	0	0	ø	5	0	0	0-1	5.2	5	0	0	0	7-1	3	0.00	ø	.294	.500	0	ø	0*	—	2	0	0.1
1989	Pit N	2	2	.500	9	3	0	0-0	14	17	14	0	0	13-0	6	7.07	48	.327	.455	1-0-3	.000	-0*	139	-7	0	-1.3
Total	3	2	2	.500	16	3	0	0-1	21.1	26	17	0	0	23-2	9	5.91	59	.333	.480	1-0-3	.000	-0	139	-7	0	-1.3
Maddox, Nick	Nicholas; B11.9.1886 Govanstown MD; D11.27.1954 Pittsburgh PA; BL/TR/6´0˝/175; d9.13																									
1907	Pit N	5	1	.833	6	6	6-1	0	54	32	8	0	4	13	38	0.83	292	.178	.249	20	.250	2	137	9	—	1.5
1908	Pit N	23	8	.742	36	32	22-4	1	260.2	209	89	5	11	90	70	2.28	101	.223	.298	94-0-4	.266	8	147	2	—	1.1
1909	†Pit N	13	8	.619	31	27	17-4	0	203.1	173	72	2	15	39	56	2.21	123	.232	.283	67-0-4	.224	4	117	10	—	1.4
1910	Pit N	2	3	.400	20	7	2	0	87.1	73	40	0	5	28	29	3.40	91	.246	.321	28	.214	1*	137	-2	—	0.0
Total	4	43	20	.683	93	72	47-9	1	605.1	487	209	7	35	170	193	2.29	112	.225	.292	209-0-8	.244	15	133	19	—	4.0
Maddux, Greg	Gregory Alan; B4.14.1966 San Angelo TX; BR/TR/6´0˝/(150–185); [ChiN84 2/31]; d9.3; b–Mike																									
1986	Chi N	2	4	.333	6	5	1	0-0	31	44	20	3	1	11-2	20	5.52	74	.336	.392	12-0-1	.333	1	114	-4	0	-0.7
1987	Chi N	6	14	.300	30	27	1-1	0-0	155.2	181	111	17	4	74-13	101	5.61	77	.294	.373	42-0-7	.119	-2*	84	-23	0	-2.4
1988	Chi N☆	18	8	.692	34	34	9-3	0-0	249	230	97	13	9	81-16	140	3.18	115	.244	.309	96-0-1	.198	2*	102	12	0	1.6
1989	†Chi N	19	12	.613	35	35	7-1	0-0	238.1	222	90	13	6	82-13	135	2.95	128	.249	.315	81-0-8	.210	2	104	19	0	2.9
1990	Chi N	15	15	.500	35	**35**	8-2	0-0	237	242	116	11	4	71-10	144	3.46	118	.265	.319	83-0-4	.145	-2	85	9	0	1.3
1991	Chi N	15	11	.577	37	**37**	7-2	0-0	**263**	232	113	18	6	66-9	198	3.35	116	.237	.288	88-1-11	.205	3*	97	14	0	1.9
1992	Chi N★	**20**	11	.645	35	**35**	9-4	0-0	**268**	201	68	7	14	70-7	199	2.18	**166**	.210	.272	88-1-13	.170	2	94	**44**	0	**6.0**
1993	†Atl N	20	10	.667	36	**36**	**8**-1	0-0	**267**	228	85	14	6	52-7	197	**2.36**	**172**	.232	**.273**	91-0-10	.165	-1	90	**47**	0	**5.3**
1994	Atl N★	**16**	6	.727	25	25	**10-3**	0-0	**202**	150	44	4	6	31-3	156	**1.56**	**277**	**.207**	**.243**	63-0-9	.222	2	84	**58**	0	**6.8**
1995	†Atl N☆	**19**	2	**.905**	28	28	**10-3**	0-0	**209.2**	147	39	8	4	23-3	181	**1.63**	**265**	.197	**.224**	72-0-6	.153	-1	90	**62**	0	**6.5**
1996	†Atl N☆	15	11	.577	35	35	5-1	0-0	245	225	85	11	3	28-11	172	2.72	164	.241	.264	68-0-11	.147	-1	82	44	0	4.8
1997	†Atl N★	19	4	**.826**	33	33	5-2	0-0	232.2	200	58	9	6	20-6	177	2.20	191	.236	.256	67-0-6	.104	-1	102	54	0	5.3
1998	†Atl N★	18	9	.667	34	34	9-**5**	0-0	251	201	75	13	7	45-10	204	**2.22**	**187**	.220	**.260**	75-0-6	.240	4	98	**52**	0	**6.4**
1999	†Atl N	19	9	.679	33	33	4	0-0	219.1	258	103	16	4	37-8	136	3.57	125	.294	.323	64-2-13	.172	3	125	19	0	2.8
2000	†Atl N✳	19	9	.679	35	**35**	6-**3**	0-0	249.1	225	91	19	10	42-12	190	3.00	151	.238	.276	80-0-7	.188	2	89	43	0	**5.0**
2001	†Atl N	17	11	.607	34	34	3-**3**	0-0	233	220	86	20	7	27-10	173	3.05	141	.253	.278	64-0-13	.188	1*	82	34	0	4.2
2002	†Atl N	16	6	.727	34	34	0	0-0	199.1	194	67	14	4	45-7	118	2.62	155	.257	.301	59-0-9	.186	1*	94	31	12	3.6
2003	†Atl N	16	11	.593	36	**36**	1	0-0	218.1	225	112	24	8	33-7	124	3.96	106	.268	.299	68-0-8	.147	-0*	102	4	0	0.6
2004	Chi N	16	11	.593	33	33	2-1	0-0	212.2	218	103	35	9	33-4	151	4.02	110	.269	.302	69-0-9	.159	-1*	100	9	0	1.2
2005	Chi N	13	15	.464	35	**35**	3	0-0	225	239	112	29	7	36-4	136	4.24	103	.275	.308	76-1-7	.171	-0	98	3	0	0.6
2006	Chi N	9	11	.450	22	22	0	0-0	136.1	153	78	14	0	23-3	81	4.69	98	.284	.312	43-0-3	.093	-1	79	-1	0	-0.1
	†LA N	6	3	.667	12	12	0	0-0	73.2	66	31	6	0	14-4	36	3.30	133	.244	.280	25-0-3	.200	1	110	8	0	1.1
	Year	15	14	.517	34	34	0	0-0	210	219	109	20	0	37-7	117	4.20	108	.271	.301	68-0-6	.132	-1	90	6	0	1.0
Total	21	333	203	.621	677	673	108-35	0-0	4616.1	4301	1784	318	125	944-169	3169	3.07	136	.248	.290	1474-5-165	.174	12	95	538	12	64.7
Maddux, Mike	Michael Ausley; B8.27.1961 Dayton OH; BL/TR/6´2˝/(180–190); [PhiN82 5/119]; d6.3; C3; b–Greg; Col Texas–El Paso																									
1986	Phi N	3	7	.300	16	16	0	0-0	78	88	56	6	3	34-4	44	5.42	72	.286	.359	22-0-4	.045	-1	96	-14	0	-1.7
1987	Phi N	2	0	1.000	7	2	0	0-0	17	17	5	0	0	5-0	15	2.65	162	.254	.306	3-0-1	.000	-0	95	3	0	0.3
1988	Phi N	4	3	.571	25	11	0	0-0	88.2	91	41	6	5	34-4	59	3.76	96	.275	.349	23-0-2	.130	-0*	107	-1	41	-0.1
1989	Phi N	1	3	.250	16	4	2-1	1-0	43.2	52	29	3	2	14-3	26	5.15	70	.304	.362	10-0-1	.000	-1	99	-8	0	-0.7
1990	LA N	0	1	.000	11	2	0	0-0	20.2	24	15	3	1	4-0	11	6.53	56	.293	.330	2	.000	-0	135	-6	0	-0.3
1991	SD N	7	2	.778	64	1	0	5-2	98.2	78	30	4	1	27-3	57	2.46	155	.221	.277	13-0-3	.077	-0	260	14	0	1.4
1992	SD N	2	2	.500	50	1	0	5-4	79.2	71	25	2	0	24-4	60	2.37	152	.236	.290	9-0-3	.111	-0	0	10	20	0.7
1993	NY N	3	8	.273	58	0	0	5-6	75	67	34	3	4	27-7	57	3.60	112	.243	.313	3	.000	-0	—	4	0	0.6
1994	NY N	2	1	.667	27	0	0	2-2	44	45	25	7	0	13-4	32	5.11	82	.263	.312	3	.000	-0	—	-3	16	-0.2
1995	Pit N	1	0	1.000	8	0	0	0-0	9	14	9	0	0	3-1	4	9.00	48	.359	.405	0	ø	0	—	-4	0	-0.4
	†Bos A	4	1	.800	36	4	0	1-0	89.2	86	40	5	2	15-3	65	3.61	135	.247	.281	0	ø	0	139	12	0	0.6
1996	Bos A	3	2	.600	23	7	0	0-0	64.1	76	37	12	5	27-2	32	4.48	114	.295	.370	0	ø	0	99	4	88	0.3
1997	Sea A	1	0	1.000	6	0	0	0-0	10.2	20	12	1	1	8-2	7	10.13	45	.400	.492	0	ø	0	—	-6	21	-0.5
1998	Mon N	3	4	.429	51	0	0	1-1	55.2	50	24	3	1	15-1	33	3.72	113	.243	.293	2	.000	-0	—	4	56	0.4
1999	Mon N	0	0	ø	4	0	0	0-0	5	9	5	1	1	3-0	4	9.00	50	.409	.500	0	ø	0	—	-2	0	-0.1
	LA N	1	1	.500	49	0	0	0-0	54.2	54	21	5	4	19-2	41	3.29	132	.261	.332	0	ø	0	—	7	0	0.3
	Year	1	1	.500	53	0	0	0-0	59.2	63	26	6	5	22-2	45	3.77	116	.275	.349	0	ø	0	—	5	0	0.2
2000	Hou N	2	2	.500	21	0	0	0-0	27.1	31	20	6	2	12-0	17	6.26	78	.282	.360	2	.000	-0	—	-4	31	-0.4
Total	15	39	37	.513	472	48	2-1	20-15	861.2	873	428	67	32	284-40	564	4.05	102	.265	.326	92-0-14	.065	-4	105	10	273	0.2
Madigan, Tony	William J. "Tice"; B7.18.1868 Washington DC; D12.4.1954 Washington DC; TR/5´5.5˝/126; d7.10																									
1886	Was N	1	13	.071	14	13	13	0	114.2	154	110	3	—	44	29	4.87	66	.310	.366	48	.083	-4	50	-25	—	-2.6
Madison, Dave	David Pledger; B2.1.1921 Brooksville MS; D12.8.1985 Macon MS; BR/TR/6´3˝/(188–190); d9.26; Mil 1951; Col Louisiana St.																									
1950	NY A	0	0	ø	1	0	0	0	3	3	2	1	0	1	1	6.00	72	.273	.333	0	ø	0	—	-1	0	0.0
1952	StL A	4	2	.667	31	4	0	0	78	78	46	7	4	48	35	4.38	89	.264	.374	17-0-2	.118	-1	134	-5	0	-0.5
	Det A	1	1	.500	10	1	0	0	15	16	14	1	1	10	7	7.80	49	.291	.409	2	.000	0	0	-6	0	-0.7
	Year	5	3	.625	41	5	0	0	93	94	60	8	5	58	42	4.94	79	.268	.379	19-0-2	.105	-1	107	-10	0	-1.2
1953	Det A	3	4	.429	32	1	0	0	62	76	55	7	3	44	27	6.82	60	.303	.413	11	.091	-1	109	-20	0	-2.0
Total	3	8	7	.533	74	6	0	0	158	173	117	16	8	103	70	5.70	70	.282	.392	30-0-2	.100	-2	107	-32	0	-3.2

YEAR	TM LG	W	L	PCT	G	GS	CG-SHO	SV-BS	IP	H	R	HR	HB	BB-IB	SO	ERA	AERA	OAV	OOB	AB-HR-SH	AVG	PB	SUP	APR	DL	PW
MADRID, ALEX	Alexander; B4.18.1963 Springerville AZ; BR/TR/6´3´´/198; [MilA83 S2/44]; d7.20; Col Yavapai (AZ) JC																									
1987	Mil A	0	0	ø	3	0	0	0-0	5.1	11	9	1	0	1-0	1	15.19	30	.440	.429	0	ø	0	—	-6	0	-0.3
1988	Phi N	1	1	.500	5	2	1	0-0	16.1	15	5	0	0	6-2	2	2.76	131	.246	.304	3	.000	-0	25	2	0	0.2
1989	Phi N	1	2	.333	6	3	0	0-0	24.2	32	16	3	1	14-4	13	5.47	66	.314	.402	6	.000	-0	58	-5	0	-0.6
Total	3	2	3	.400	14	5	1	0-0	46.1	58	30	4	1	21-6	16	5.63	66	.309	.374	9	.000	-1	43	-9	0	-0.7
MADRITSCH, BOBBY	Robert Allen; B2.28.1976 Oak Lawn IL; BL/TL/6´2´´/190; [CinN98 6/170]; d7.21; Col Point Park; [DL 2006 KC A 151]																									
2004	Sea A	6	3	.667	15	11	1	0-0	88	74	33	3	4	33-2	60	3.27	137	.232	.312	0	ø	0	107	13	0	1.2
2005	Sea A	0	1	.000	1	1	0	0-0	4.1	4	3	1	0	1-0	1	6.23	67	.235	.278	0	ø	0	22	-1	179	-0.2
Total	2	6	4	.600	16	12	1	0-0	92.1	78	36	4	4	34-2	61	3.41	131	.232	.310	0	ø	0	100	12	330	1.0
MADSON, RYAN	Ryan Michael; B8.28.1980 Long Beach CA; BL/TR/6´6´´/(180–195); [PhiN98 9/254]; d9.27																									
2003	Phi N	0	0	ø	1	0	0	0-0	2	0	0	0	0	0-0	0	0.00	ø	.000	.000	0	ø	0	—	1	0	0.0
2004	Phi N	9	3	.750	52	1	0	1-1	77	68	23	6	5	19-4	55	2.34	190	.238	.296	3-0-1	.000	-0	231	17	39	2.3
2005	Phi N	6	5	.545	78	0	0	0-7	87	84	44	11	6	25-6	79	4.14	105	.259	.319	6-0-1	.000	-0	—	2	0	0.1
2006	Phi N	11	9	.550	50	17	0	2-2	134.1	176	92	20	10	50-4	99	5.69	82	.321	.386	33-0-4	.182	0	123	-14	0	-1.8
Total	4	26	17	.605	181	18	0	3-10	300.1	328	159	37	21	94-14	233	4.35	104	.282	.344	42-0-6	.143	-0	134	6	39	0.6
MADURO, CALVIN	Calvin Gregory; B9.5.1974 Santa Cruz, Aruba; BR/TR/6´0´´/(175–188); d9.8																									
1996	Phi N	0	1	.000	4	2	0	0-0	15.1	13	6	1	2	3-0	11	3.52	122	.232	.295	4	.000	-0	63	2	0	0.0
1997	Phi N	3	7	.300	15	13	0	0-0	71	83	59	12	3	41-5	31	7.23	58	.294	.385	20-0-1	.050	-2*	87	-22	0	-2.7
2000	Bal A	0	0	ø	15	2	0	0-0	23.1	29	25	8	2	16-1	18	9.64	49	.315	.420	0	ø	0	200	-13	138	-0.6
2001	Bal A	5	6	.455	22	12	0	0-0	93.2	83	44	10	4	36-0	51	4.23	102	.240	.319	0	ø	0	98	3	0	0.2
2002	Bal A	2	5	.286	12	10	0	0-0	56.2	64	37	12	1	22-1	29	5.56	78	.279	.344	0	ø	0	77	-8	122	-0.8
Total	5	10	19	.345	68	39	0	0-0	260	272	171	43	12	118-7	140	5.78	75	.271	.352	24-0-1	.042	-2	93	-38	260	-3.9
MAESTRI, HECTOR	Hector Anibal (Garcia); B4.19.1935 Havana, Cuba; BR/TR/5´10´´/158; d9.24																									
1960	Was A	0	0	ø	1	0	0	0	2	1	0	0	0	1-0	1	0.00	ø	.167	.286	0	ø	0	—	1	0	0.0
1961	Was A	0	1	.000	1	1	0	0	6	6	3	1	0	2-0	2	1.50	268	.250	.308	1	.000	-0	44	1	0	0.1
Total	2	0	1	.000	2	1	0	0	8	7	3	1	0	3-0	3	1.13	354	.233	.303	1	.000	-0	44	2	0	0.1
MAGEE, BILL	William J.; B7.6.1875 New Brunswick, Can; BR/TR/5´10´´/154; d5.18																									
1897	Lou N	4	12	.250	23	17	13-1	0	156.1	187	137	6	10	101	44	5.41	79	.294	.399	62-0-1	.210	-2	75	-18	—	-1.5
1898	Lou N	16	15	.516	38	33	29-3	0	295.1	294	163	8	19	129	55	4.05	88	.258	.343	111-0-1	.126	-9	83	-11	—	-1.8
1899	Lou N	3	7	.300	12	10	6-1	0	71	91	58	1	9	28	13	5.20	74	.311	.388	27-0-2	.111	-2	108	-9	—	-1.2
	Phi N	3	5	.375	9	9	7	0	70	82	50	0	7	32	4	5.66	65	.292	.378	31-0-1	.161	-2	95	-11	—	-1.2
	Was N	1	4	.200	8	7	4	0	42	54	45	3	7	28	11	8.57	46	.312	.428	15-0-1	.333	1	74	-18	—	-1.4
	Year	7	16	.304	29	26	17-1	0	183	227	153	4	23	88	28	6.15	62	.304	.394	73-0-4	.178	-2	95	-37	—	-3.8
1901	StL N	0	0	ø	1	1	0	0	8	8	4	0	0	4	3	4.50	71	.258	.343	4	.500	1	111	-1	—	0.1
	NY N	0	4	.000	6	5	4	0	42.1	56	36	4	4	11	14	5.95	56	.316	.370	14	.143	-1	90	-11	—	-0.9
	Year	0	4	.000	7	6	4	0	50.1	64	40	4	4	15	17	5.72	57	.308	.366	18	.222	1	94	-11	—	-0.8
1902	NY N	0	0	ø	2	1	0	0	5	5	2	0	0	1	2	3.60	78	.263	.300	1	.000	-0	121	0	—	0.0
	Phi N	2	4	.333	8	7	6	0	53.2	61	28	1	3	18	15	3.69	76	.285	.349	19	.211	-0	64	-4	—	-0.5
	Year	2	4	.333	10	8	6	0	58.2	66	30	1	3	19	17	3.68	76	.283	.345	20	.200	-1	72	-5	—	-0.5
Total	5	29	51	.363	107	90	69-5	0	743.2	838	523	23	59	352	161	4.94	75	.283	.370	284-0-6	.169	-13	84	-83	—	-8.4
MAGLIE, SAL	Salvatore Anthony "The Barber"; B4.26.1917 Niagara Falls NY; D12.28.1992 Niagara Falls NY; BR/TR/6´2´´/(180–190); d8.9; C6; Col Niagara																									
1945	NY N	5	4	.556	13	10	7-3	0	84.1	72	22	2	2	22	32	2.35	167	.231	.286	30-0-1	.167	-1*	84	15	0	1.5
1950	NY N	18	4	**.818**	47	16	12-**5**	1	206	169	71	14	10	86	96	2.71	**151**	.226	.314	66-0-3	.121	-1	110	32	0	3.1
1951	†NY N★	**23**	6	.793	42	37	22-3	4	298	254	110	27	6	86	146	2.93	**134**	**.230**	.289	112-1-9	.152	-3	117	**35**	0	3.0
1952	NY N☆	18	8	.692	35	31	12-5	1	216	199	80	16	6	75	112	2.92	127	.244	.312	69-0-12	.072	-3	113	20	0	2.0
1953	NY N	8	9	.471	27	24	9-3	0	145.1	158	79	19	1	47	80	4.15	103	.278	.334	48-0-6	.271	2	126	2	0	0.3
1954	†NY N	14	6	.700	34	32	9-1	2	218.1	222	83	21	3	70	117	3.26	124	.262	.319	63-0-13	.127	-2	99	23	0	1.7
1955	NY N	9	5	.643	23	21	6	0	129.2	142	67	18	3	48-2	71	3.75	107	.278	.340	40-0-6	.125	-2	106	2	0	-0.1
	Cle A	0	2	.000	10	2	0	2	25.2	26	14	0	1	7-0	11	3.86	103	.252	.306	5	.000	-0	67	0	0	-0.1
1956	Cle A	0	0	ø	2	0	0	0	5	6	2	1	0	2-0	2	3.60	117	.300	.364	0	ø	0	—	0	0	0.0
	†Bro N	13	5	.722	28	26	9-3	0	191	154	65	21	5	52-1	108	2.87	**138**	.222	.281	70-0-2	.129	-3	102	23	0	1.6
1957	Bro N	6	6	.500	19	17	4-1	1	101.1	94	42	12	4	26-1	50	2.93	142	.245	.298	29-0-4	.034	-3	82	11	0	0.9
	NY A	2	0	1.000	6	3	1-1	3	26	22	6	1	1	7-0	9	1.73	207	.227	.283	8	.250	0	100	6	0	0.6
1958	NY A	1	1	.500	7	3	0	0	23.1	27	12	3	0	9-2	7	4.63	76	.300	.364	7-1-0	.143	1	93	-2	0	-0.1
	StL N	2	6	.250	10	10	2	0	53	46	31	14	2	25-2	21	4.75	87	.232	.323	16-0-1	.125	-1	63	-3	0	-0.6
Total	10	119	62	.657	303	232	93-25	14	1723	1591	684	169	44	562-8	862	3.15	127	.245	.309	563-2-57	.135	-16	104	164	0	13.8
MAGNANTE, MIKE	Michael Anthony; B6.17.1965 Glendale CA; BL/TL/6´1´´/(180–220); [KCA88 11/283]; d4.22; Col UCLA																									
1991	KC A	0	1	.000	38	0	0	0-0	55	55	19	3	0	23-3	42	2.45	169	.262	.333	0	ø	0	—	9	0	0.5
1992	KC A	4	9	.308	44	12	0	0-3	89.1	115	53	5	2	35-5	31	4.94	83	.325	.382	0	ø	0	95	-8	18	-0.9
1993	KC A	1	2	.333	7	6	0	0-0	35.1	37	16	3	1	11-1	16	4.08	113	.282	.340	0	ø	0	57	2	0	0.2
1994	KC A	2	3	.400	36	1	0	0-0	47	55	27	5	0	16-1	21	4.60	109	.289	.340	0	ø	0	73	2	15	0.2
1995	KC A	1	1	.500	28	0	0	0-1	44.2	45	23	6	2	16-1	28	4.23	113	.268	.335	0	ø	0	—	3	0	0.2
1996	KC A	2	2	.500	38	0	0	0-1	54	58	38	5	4	24-1	32	5.67	89	.282	.361	0	ø	0	—	-5	25	-0.2
1997	†Hou N	3	1	.750	40	0	0	1-4	47.2	39	16	2	0	11-2	43	2.27	177	.223	.266	3	.000	-0	—	8	0	0.6
1998	Hou N	4	7	.364	48	0	0	2-2	51.2	56	28	2	4	26-4	39	4.88	83	.276	.368	2	1.000	1	—	-4	15	-0.5
1999	Ana A	5	2	.714	53	0	0	0-3	69.1	68	30	2	3	29-4	44	3.38	145	.262	.334	0	ø	0	—	11	0	1.0
2000	†Oak A	1	1	.500	55	0	0	0-3	39.2	50	22	3	2	19-7	17	4.31	113	.309	.388	1	.000	-0	—	2	30	0.2
2001	†Oak A	3	1	.750	65	0	0	0-1	55.1	50	23	7	1	13-3	23	2.77	165	.244	.287	0	ø	0	—	9	0	0.5
2002	Oak A	0	2	.000	32	0	0	0-1	28.2	38	22	2	1	11-1	11	5.97	75	.317	.373	0	ø	0	—	-5	0	-0.3
Total	12	26	32	.448	484	19	0	3-19	617.2	666	317	45	20	234-33	347	4.08	111	.279	.344	6	.333	1	77	24	103	1.5
MAGNUSON, JIM	James Robert; B8.18.1946 Marinette WI; D5.30.1991 Green Bay WI; BR/TL/6´2´´/190; [ChiA66 3/58]; d6.28; Col Wisconsin–Oshkosh																									
1970	Chi A	1	5	.167	13	6	0	0-0	44.2	45	28	7	1	16-1	20	4.84	80	.263	.328	11-0-1	.000	-1	80	-5	0	-0.7
1971	Chi A	1	1	.500	15	4	0	0-0	30	30	18	0	2	16-0	11	4.50	79	.265	.366	4	.000	-0	101	-3	0	-0.3
1973	NY A	0	1	.000	8	0	0	0-0	27.1	38	17	2	0	9-1	9	4.28	87	.342	.382	0	ø	0	—	-3	0	-0.1
Total	3	2	7	.222	36	10	0	0-0	102	113	63	9	3	41-2	40	4.59	82	.286	.354	15-0-1	.000	-2	88	-11	0	-1.1
MAGRANE, JOE	Joseph David; B7.2.1964 Des Moines IA; BR/TL/6´6´´/230; [StLN85 1/18]; d4.25; Col Arizona; [DL 1991 StL N 182]																									
1987	†StL N	9	7	.563	27	26	4-2	0-0	170.1	157	75	9	10	60-6	101	3.54	119	.245	.318	52-1-6	.135	1*	89	11	19	1.1
1988	StL N	5	9	.357	24	24	4-3	0-0	165.1	133	57	6	2	51-4	100	**2.18**	**162**	.217	.278	48-1-8	.167	1*	69	19	55	1.9
1989	StL N	18	9	.667	34	33	9-3	0-0	234.2	219	81	5	6	72-7	127	2.91	126	.251	.310	80-1-8	.138	0*	109	20	15	2.4
1990	StL N	10	17	.370	31	31	3-2	0-0	203.1	204	86	10	8	59-7	100	3.59	107	.264	.320	55-0-9	.127	-0	73	8	0	1.1
1992	StL N	1	2	.333	5	5	0	0-0	31.1	34	15	2	2	15-0	20	4.02	85	.279	.364	10-1-1	.200	1	127	-2	148	-0.1
1993	StL N	8	10	.444	22	20	0	0-0	116	127	68	15	5	37-3	38	4.97	81	.286	.343	35-0-4	.114	-1	83	-10	0	-1.5
	Cal A	3	2	.600	8	8	0	0-0	48	48	27	4	0	21-0	24	3.94	115	.265	.337	0	ø	0	101	1	0	0.3
1994	Cal A	2	6	.250	20	11	1	0-0	74	89	63	18	6	51-0	33	7.30	67	.300	.409	0	ø	0	99	-19	31	-1.6
1996	Chi A	1	5	.167	19	8	0	0-0	53.2	70	45	10	3	25-1	21	6.88	69	.318	.390	0	ø	0	85	-14	0	-1.2
Total	8	57	67	.460	190	166	21-10	0-0	1096.2	1081	517	79	42	391-28	564	3.81	104	.260	.327	280-4-36	.139	3	89	14	450	2.4
MAGRINI, PETE	Peter Alexander; B6.8.1942 San Francisco CA; BR/TR/6´0´´/195; d4.13; Col Santa Clara																									
1966	Bos A	0	1	.000	3	1	0	0	7.1	8	9	0	1	8-0	3	9.82	39	.308	.459	3	.000	-0	23	-4	0	-0.6
MAHAFFEY, ART	Arthur; B6.4.1938 Cincinnati OH; BR/TR/6´2´´/(195–200); d7.30																									
1960	Phi N	7	3	.700	14	12	5-1	0	93.1	78	29	9	1	34-1	56	2.31	168	.229	.298	30-0-5	.100	-2	81	15	0	1.3
1961	Phi N★	11	19	.367	36	32	12-3	0	219.1	205	110	27	7	70-6	158	4.10	99	.249	.311	63-0-12	.127	-2	79	0	0	-0.2
1962	Phi N★	19	14	.576	41	39	20-2	0	274	253	131	36	12	81-4	177	3.94	98	.246	.306	92-2-10	.141	1*	110	-1	0	-0.2
1963	Phi N	7	10	.412	26	22	6-1	0	149	143	73	18	5	48-1	97	3.99	81	.255	.314	50-0-3	.200	2	86	-11	45	-1.0
1964	Phi N	12	9	.571	34	29	2-2	0	157.1	161	84	17	6	82-5	80	4.52	77	.269	.361	50-1-5	.120	0	113	-15	0	-2.0

YEAR	TM LG	W	L	PCT	G	GS	CG-SHO	SV-BS	IP	H	R	HR	HB	BB-IB	SO	ERA	AERA	OAV	OOB	AB-HR-SH	AVG	PB	SUP	APR	DL	PW
1965	Phi N	2	5	.286	22	9	1	0	71	82	53	11	7	32-2	52	6.21	56	.294	.373	21-0-1	.095	-1	118	-21	0	-2.0
1966	StL N	1	4	.200	12	5	0	1	35	37	27	7	1	21-4	19	6.43	56	.276	.373	7	.000	-1	74	-10	0	-1.5
Total	7	59	64	.480	185	148	46-9	1	999	959	507	125	39	368-23	639	4.17	89	.255	.324	313-3-36	.134	-2	97	-43	45	-5.6
Mahaffey, Roy	Lee Roy "Popeye"; B2.9.1904 Belton SC; D7.23.1969 Anderson SC; BR/TR/6´0˝/180; d8.31																									
1926	Pit N	0	0	ø	4	0	0	0	4.2	5	4	0	1	1	3	0.00	ø	.294	.368	2	.000	-0	—	0	—	0.0
1927	Pit N	1	0	1.000	2	1	0	0	9.1	9	8	0	3	9	4	7.71	53	.300	.500	5	.400	0	207	-3	—	-0.2
1930	Phi A	9	5	.643	33	17	6	0	152.2	186	108	16	4	53	38	5.01	93	.298	.357	59-1-0	.119	-5	136	-10	—	-1.3
1931	†Phi A	15	4	.789	30	20	8	2	162.1	161	87	9	3	82	59	4.21	107	.258	.347	63-2-3	.190	1	107	6	—	0.6
1932	Phi A	13	13	.500	37	28	13	0	222.2	245	136	27	5	96	106	5.09	89	.274	.348	87-1-2	.172	-1	114	-13	—	-1.5
1933	Phi A	13	10	.565	33	23	9	0	179.1	198	114	5	4	74	66	5.17	83	.275	.346	65-0-2	.215	-0	130	-14	—	-1.6
1934	Phi A	6	7	.462	37	14	3	2	129	142	88	10	1	55	37	5.37	82	.276	.347	48	.271	2	101	-15	—	-1.1
1935	Phi A	8	4	.667	27	17	5	0	136	153	66	11	5	42	39	3.90	116	.283	.341	51-0-1	.176	-2	105	10	—	0.5
1936	StL A	2	6	.250	21	9	1	1	60	82	62	6	1	40	13	8.10	66	.315	.409	16	.063	-1	76	-17	—	-2.0
Total	9	67	49	.578	224	129	45	5	1056	1181	673	84	27	452	365	5.01	90	.280	.353	396-4-8	.184	-7	114	-56	—	-6.6
Mahaffey, Lou	Louis Wood; B1.3.1874 KY; D10.26.1949 Torrance CA; BR/5´9˝/170; d4.26																									
1898	Lou N	0	1	.000	1	1	1	0	9	10	9	0	0	5	1	3.00	119	.278	.366	4	.000	-0	158	-1	—	-0.2
Mahay, Ron	Ronald Matthew; B6.28.1971 Crestwood IL; BL/TL/6´2˝/(185–190); [BosA91 18/486]; d5.21.1995; Col South Suburban (IL) JC																									
1997	Bos A	3	0	1.000	28	0	0	0-2	25	19	7	3	0	11-0	22	2.52	185	.204	.288	0	ø	0	—	6	0	0.6
1998	Bos A	1	1	.500	29	0	0	1-1	26	26	16	2	2	15-1	14	3.46	137	.263	.358	0	ø	0	—	1	0	0.1
1999	Oak A	2	0	1.000	6	1	0	1-0	19.1	8	4	2	0	3-0	15	1.86	254	.123	.162	0	ø	0	59	7	0	0.6
2000	Oak A	0	1	.000	5	2	0	0-0	16	26	18	4	0	9-0	5	9.00	54	.366	.432	0	ø	0*	97	-8	0	-0.4
	Fla N	1	0	1.000	18	0	0	0-0	25.1	31	17	6	0	16-1	27	6.04	73	.310	.402	4	.500	1	—	-4	0	-0.1
2001	Chi N	0	0	ø	17	0	0	0-0	20.2	14	6	4	0	15-1	24	2.61	160	.197	.337	2	.000	-0	—	4	0	0.2
2002	Chi N	2	0	1.000	11	0	0	0-0	14.2	13	14	6	0	8-0	14	8.59	47	.228	.323	0	ø	0	—	-7	20	-0.8
2003	Tex A	3	3	.500	35	0	0	0-3	45.1	33	19	3	0	20-7	38	3.18	156	.195	.280	0	ø	0	—	7	0	0.9
2004	Tex A	3	0	1.000	60	0	0	0-2	67	60	23	5	2	29-5	54	2.55	193	.235	.318	1	.000	-0	—	16	0	0.8
2005	Tex A	0	2	.000	30	0	0	1-0	35.2	47	28	8	0	16-1	30	6.81	67	.313	.377	0	ø	0	—	-8	16	-0.4
2006	Tex A	1	3	.250	62	0	0	0-1	57	54	30	7	0	28-2	56	3.95	119	.250	.335	0	ø	0	—	3	0	0.1
Total	10	16	10	.615	301	3	0	3-9	352	331	182	50	4	170-18	299	4.12	114	.246	.330	7	.286	1	86	17	36	1.6
Mahler, Mickey	Michael James; B7.30.1952 Montgomery AL; BB/TL/6´3˝/(189–190); [AtlN74 10/221]; d9.13; b–Rick; Col Trinity (TX); [DL 1983 Cal A 180]																									
1977	Atl N	1	2	.333	5	5	0	0-0	23	31	19	4	1	9-0	14	6.26	71	.326	.380	6-0-1	.500	2	112	-4	0	-0.3
1978	Atl N	4	11	.267	34	21	1	0-1	134.2	130	82	16	7	66-6	92	4.68	86	.255	.345	41-0-5	.098	-2	97	-9	0	-1.3
1979	Atl N	5	11	.313	26	18	1	0-0	100	123	72	11	3	47-7	71	5.85	69	.304	.374	27-0-1	.111	-1	78	-17	0	-2.5
1980	Pit N	0	0	ø	2	0	0	0-0	1	4	7	1	0	3-0	1	63.00	6	.571	.700	0	ø	0	—	-6	0	-0.3
1981	Cal A	0	0	ø	6	0	0	0-0	6.1	1	0	0	0	2-0	5	0.00	ø	.056	.150	0	ø	0	—	3	0	0.1
1982	Cal A	2	0	1.000	6	0	0	0-0	8	9	1	0	0	6-1	5	1.13	364	.300	.417	0	ø	0	—	3	0	0.6
1985	Mon N	1	4	.200	9	7	1-1	1-0	48.1	40	22	3	1	24-1	32	3.54	97	.229	.323	16-0-1	.188	1	95	-1	0	-0.1
	Det A	1	2	.333	3	2	0	0-0	20.2	19	8	2	0	4-2	14	1.74	236	.241	.277	0	ø	0	78	4	0	0.5
1986	Tex A	0	2	.000	29	5	0	3-0	63	71	31	3	3	29-2	28	4.14	104	.295	.372	0	ø	0	105	2	0	0.1
	Tor A	0	0	ø	2	0	0	0-0	1	1	0	0	1	0-0	0	0.00	ø	.200	.333	0	ø	0	—	0	0	0.0
	Year	0	2	.000	31	5	0	3-0	64	72	31	3	4	29-2	28	4.08	106	.293	.371	0	ø	0	105	2	0	0.1
Total	8	14	32	.304	122	58	3-1	4-1	406	429	242	40	16	190-19	262	4.68	86	.274	.354	90-0-8	.144	-1	92	-25	180	-3.2
Mahler, Rick	Richard Keith; B8.5.1953 Austin TX; D3.2.2005 Jupiter FL; BR/TR/6´1˝/(190–205); d4.20; b–Mickey; Col Trinity (TX)																									
1979	Atl N	0	0	ø	15	0	0	0-0	22	28	16	4	0	11-2	12	6.14	65	.311	.386	2	.500	0	—	-4	0	-0.2
1980	Atl N	0	0	ø	2	0	0	0-0	3.2	2	1	0	0	0-0	1	2.45	150	.154	.154	0	ø	0	—	1	0	0.0
1981	Atl N	8	6	.571	34	14	1	2-0	112.1	109	41	5	1	43-5	54	2.80	126	.258	.326	27-0-2	.148	-0	58	8	0	1.0
1982	†Atl N	9	10	.474	39	33	5-2	0-1	205.1	213	105	18	1	62-5	105	4.21	88	.272	.324	58-1-11	.190	2	110	-10	0	-0.6
1983	Atl N	0	0	ø	10	0	0	0-2	14.1	16	8	0	0	9-1	7	5.02	77	.296	.385	2	.000	-0	—	-1	0	-0.1
1984	Atl N	13	10	.565	38	29	9-1	0-0	222	209	86	13	3	62-7	106	3.12	124	.251	.303	71-0-3	.296	5	81	18	0	2.5
1985	Atl N	17	15	.531	39	**39**	6-1	0-0	266.2	272	116	24	2	79-8	107	3.48	111	.268	.321	90-0-11	.156	-1	108	11	0	1.2
1986	Atl N	14	18	.438	39	**39**	7-1	0-0	237.2	283	139	25	3	95-10	137	4.88	81	.301	.364	83-0-9	.193	2*	91	-20	0	-2.1
1987	Atl N	8	13	.381	39	28	3-1	0-0	197	212	118	24	2	85-8	95	4.98	87	.283	.356	65-0-7	.169	1*	93	-11	0	-0.9
1988	Atl N	9	16	.360	39	34	5	0-1	249	279	125	17	8	42-6	131	3.69	99	.282	.315	72-0-11	.125	-2	100	-5	0	-0.6
1989	Cin N	9	13	.409	40	31	5-2	0-0	220.2	242	113	15	10	51-13	102	3.83	94	.282	.328	62-0-3	.177	2	98	-8	0	-0.6
1990	†Cin N	7	6	.538	35	16	2-1	4-0	134.2	134	67	16	3	39-4	68	4.28	92	.261	.314	35-0-5	.114	-1	124	-4	15	-0.4
1991	Mon N	1	3	.250	10	6	0	0-1	37.1	37	17	2	0	15-0	17	3.62	101	.268	.338	9-0-3	.111	-0	70	0	0	0.0
	Atl N	1	1	.500	13	2	0	0-1	28.2	33	20	2	2	13-1	10	5.65	69	.282	.364	5-0-1	.200	0	174	-5	0	-0.3
	Year	2	4	.333	23	8	0	0-2	66	70	37	4	2	28-1	27	4.50	83	.275	.350	14-0-4	.143	-0	96	-6	0	-0.3
Total	13	96	111	.464	392	271	43-9	6-6	1951.1	2069	972	165	35	606-70	952	3.99	96	.275	.330	581-1-66	.179	7	97	-30	15	-1.1
Maholm, Paul	Paul Gurner; B6.25.1982 Greenwood MS; BL/TL/6´2˝/(225–230); [PitN03 1/8]; d8.30; Col Mississippi St.																									
2005	Pit N	3	1	.750	6	6	0	0-0	41.1	31	10	2	3	17-0	26	2.18	195	.209	.304	15-0-1	.133	-0	78	10	0	0.9
2006	Pit N	8	10	.444	30	30	0	0-0	176	202	98	19	12	81-6	117	4.76	96	.295	.378	55-0-1	.109	-1	97	-1	0	-0.1
Total	2	11	11	.500	36	36	0	0-0	217.1	233	108	21	15	98-6	143	4.27	106	.280	.365	70-0-2	.114	-2	94	9	0	0.8
Mahomes, Pat	Patrick Lavon; B8.9.1970 Bryan TX; BR/TR/6´4˝/(175–212); [MinA88 6/155]; d4.12																									
1992	Min A	3	4	.429	14	13	0	0-0	69.2	73	41	5	0	37-0	44	5.04	81	.279	.364	0	ø	0	119	-6	0	-0.6
1993	Min A	1	5	.167	12	5	0	0-0	37.1	47	34	8	1	16-0	23	7.71	57	.309	.372	0	ø	0	29	-13	0	-1.7
1994	Min A	9	5	.643	21	21	0	0-0	120	121	68	22	1	62-1	53	4.72	104	.269	.357	0	ø	0*	119	3	17	0.2
1995	Min A	4	10	.286	47	7	0	3-4	94.2	100	74	22	2	47-1	67	6.37	76	.271	.355	0	ø	0	124	-16	0	-2.1
1996	Min A	1	4	.200	20	5	0	0-0	45	63	38	10	0	27-0	30	7.20	71	.330	.409	0	ø	0	83	-10	0	-0.9
	Bos A	2	0	1.000	11	0	0	2-0	12.1	9	8	3	0	6-0	6	5.84	87	.209	.306	0	ø	0	—	-1	0	-0.1
	Year	3	4	.429	31	5	0	2-0	57.1	72	46	13	0	33-0	36	6.91	74	.308	.390	0	ø	0	83	-10	0	-1.0
1997	Bos A	1	0	1.000	10	0	0	0-0	10	15	10	2	2	10-1	5	8.10	57	.366	.500	0	ø	0	—	-4	0	-0.3
1999	†NY N	8	0	1.000	39	0	0	0-1	63.2	44	26	7	2	37-5	51	3.68	118	.197	.314	16	.313	2*	—	5	0	0.8
2000	NY N	5	3	.625	53	5	0	0-1	94	96	63	15	2	66-4	76	5.46	80	.263	.376	17-0-2	.235	1	84	-12	0	-0.7
2001	Tex A	7	6	.538	56	4	0	0-1	107.1	115	71	17	0	55-9	61	5.70	84	.280	.359	1	1.000	0	82	-10	0	-0.9
2002	Chi N	1	1	.500	16	2	0	0-1	32.2	36	15	3	1	17-3	23	3.86	105	.286	.375	5	.000	-1*	80	1	0	0.0
2003	Pit N	0	1	.000	9	1	0	0-0	22.1	19	13	2	0	12-1	13	4.84	89	.241	.326	4	.250	0	87	-1	0	0.0
Total	11	42	39	.519	308	63	0	5-8	709	738	461	116	11	392-25	452	5.47	84	.272	.363	43-0-2	.256	3	104	-64	17	-6.3
Mahon, Al	Alfred Gwinn "Lefty"; B9.23.1909 Albion NE; D12.26.1977 New Haven CT; BL/TL/5´11˝/160; d4.22																									
1930	Phi A	0	0	ø	3	0	0	0	4.1	11	11	0	0	7	0	22.85	20	.579	.692	1	.000	0	—	-8	—	-0.3
Mahoney, Chris	Christopher John; B6.11.1885 Milton MA; D7.15.1954 Visalia CA; BR/TR/5´9˝/160; d7.12; Col Fordham																									
1910	Bos A	0	1	.000	2	1	0	1	11	16	11	1	0	5	6	3.27	78	.327	.389	7	.143	-0*	131	-3	—	-0.3
Mahoney, Bob	Robert Paul; B6.20.1928 LeRoy MN; D8.27.2000 Lincoln NE; BR/TR/6´1˝/(185–195); d5.3																									
1951	Chi A	0	0	ø	3	0	0	0	6.2	5	4	1	0	5	3	5.40	75	.208	.345	0	ø	0	—	-1	0	0.0
	StL A	2	5	.286	30	4	0	0	81	86	47	7	0	41	30	4.44	99	.274	.358	18-0-1	.222	-0	71	-1	0	-0.1
	Year	2	5	.286	33	4	0	0	87.2	91	51	8	0	46	33	4.52	97	.269	.357	18-0-1	.222	-0	71	-2	0	-0.1
1952	StL A	0	0	ø	3	0	0	0	3	8	6	0	0	4	1	18.00	22	.500	.600	0	ø	0	—	-4	0	-0.2
Total	2	2	5	.286	36	4	0	0	90.2	99	57	8	0	50	34	4.96	88	.280	.369	18-0-1	.222	-0	71	-6	0	-0.3
Mails, Duster	John Walter "Walter","The Great"; B10.1.1894 San Quentin CA; D7.5.1974 San Francisco CA; BL/TL/6´0˝/195; d9.28; Mil 1917–18; Col St. Marys (CA)																									
1915	Bro N	0	1	.000	2	0	0	0	5	6	5	2	0	5	3	3.60	77	.333	.478	1	.000	-0	—	-1	—	-0.2
1916	Bro N	0	1	.000	11	0	0	0	17.1	15	9	1	0	9	13	3.63	74	.242	.338	4	.250	0	—	-2	—	-0.1
1920	†Cle A	7	0	1.000	9	8	6-2	0	63.1	54	18	1	0	18	25	1.85	206	.230	.285	20-0-3	.200	0	115	13	—	1.3
1921	Cle A	14	8	.636	34	24	10-2	2	194.1	210	103	4	2	89	87	3.94	108	.283	.361	64-0-8	.094	-4	130	6	—	0.1
1922	Cle A	4	7	.364	26	13	4-1	0	104	122	69	8	4	40	54	5.28	76	.291	.359	31-0-1	.161	-0	99	-14	—	-1.3
1925	StL N	7	7	.500	21	16	9	0	131	145	78	11	7	58	49	4.60	94	.279	.360	45-0-2	.133	-2	101	-4	—	-0.6

YEAR	TM LG	W	L	PCT	G	GS	CG-SHO	SV-BS	IP	H	R	HR	HB	BB-IB	SO	ERA	AERA	OAV	OOB	AB-HR-SH	AVG	PB	SUP	APR	DL	PW
1926	StL N	0	1	.000	1	0	0	0	1	2	1	0	0	1	1	0.00	ø	.400	.500	0	ø	0	—	0	—	0.0
Total	7	32	25	.561	104	61	29-5	2	516	554	283	27	13	220	232	4.10	100	.277	.352	165-0-14	.133	-7	115	-2	—	-0.8
MAIN, WOODY	Forrest Harry; B2.12.1922 Delano CA; D6.27.1992 Whittier CA; BR/TR/6´3.5˝/(195–200); d4.21																									
1948	Pit N	1	1	.500	17	0	0	0	27	35	27	4	0	19	12	8.33	49	.324	.425	2	.000	-0	—	-12	0	-0.8
1950	Pit N	1	0	1.000	12	0	0	1	20.1	21	12	2	1	11	12	4.87	90	.256	.351	5	.400	0	—	-1	0	0.0
1952	Pit N	2	12	.143	48	11	2	2	153.1	149	78	14	0	52	79	4.46	90	.253	.314	37-0-3	.054	-3	59	-4	0	-0.9
1953	Pit N	0	0	ø	2	0	0	0	4	5	5	1	0	2	4	11.25	40	.294	.368	0	ø	0	—	-3	0	-0.1
Total	4	4	13	.235	79	11	2	3	204.2	210	122	21	1	84	107	5.14	79	.264	.335	44-0-3	.091	-3	59	-20	0	-1.8
MAIN, ALEX	Miles Grant; B5.13.1884 Montrose MI; D12.29.1965 Royal Oak MI; BL/TR/6´5˝/195; d4.18																									
1914	Det A	6	6	.500	32	12	5-1	3	138.1	131	51	2	3	59	55	2.67	105	.259	.340	40	.100	-2	93	4	—	0.4
1915	KC F	13	14	.481	35	28	18-2	3	230	181	88	4	5	75	91	2.54	103	.222	.291	76-0-3	.197	0*	82	1	—	0.2
1918	Phi N	2	2	.500	8	4	1-1	0	35	30	20	1	5	16	14	4.63	65	.240	.349	11-0-1	.091	-1*	82	-5	—	-0.6
Total	3	21	22	.488	75	44	24-4	6	403.1	342	159	7	13	150	160	2.77	98	.236	.313	127-0-4	.157	-2	85	0	—	0.0
MAINE, JOHN	John K.; B5.8.1981 Fredericksburg VA; BR/TR/6´4˝/(195–205); [BalA02 6/166]; d7.23; Col North Carolina–Charlotte																									
2004	Bal A	0	1	.000	1	1	0	0-0	3.2	7	4	1	0	3-0	1	9.82	48	.438	.526	0	ø	0	60	-2	0	-0.3
2005	Bal A	2	3	.400	10	8	0	0-0	40	39	30	8	1	24-0	24	6.30	70	.248	.348	0	ø	0	100	-8	0	-0.8
2006	†NY N	6	5	.545	16	15	1-1	0-0	90	69	40	15	2	33-1	71	3.60	122	.212	.287	28-0-3	.036	-2	98	8	40	0.7
Total	3	8	9	.471	27	24	1-1	0-0	133.2	115	74	24	3	60-1	96	4.58	96	.230	.315	28-0-3	.036	-2	97	-2	40	-0.4
MAINS, JIM	James Royal; B6.12.1922 Bridgton ME; D3.17.1969 Portland ME; BR/TR/6´2˝/190; d8.22; f–Willard; Col Harvard																									
1943	Phi A	0	1	.000	1	1	1	0	8	9	5	0	0	3	4	5.63	60	.281	.343	2	.000	0	50	-2	0	-0.2
MAINS, WILLARD	Willard Eben "Grasshopper"; B7.7.1868 N.Windham ME; D5.23.1923 Bridgton ME; TR/6´2˝/190; d8.3; s–Jim																									
1888	Chi N	1	1	.500	2	2	1	0	11	8	10	0	1	6	5	4.91	62	.211	.333	7	.143	-0	101	-2	—	-0.3
1891	Cin AA	12	12	.500	30	23	19	0	204	196	127	3	12	107	76	2.69	152	.244	.342	90-1	.244	1*	83	26	—	2.7
	Mil AA	0	2	.000	2	2	1	0	10	14	19	1	0	10	2	10.80	41	.318	.444	5	.600	1	64	-5	—	-0.7
	Year	12	14	.462	32	25	20	0	214	210	146	4	12	117	78	3.07	134	.248	.347	95-1	.263	2	82	16	—	2.0
1896	Bos N	3	2	.600	8	5	3	1	42.2	43	35	1	2	31	13	5.48	83	.261	.384	22	.273	-0*	119	-3	—	-0.3
Total	3	16	17	.485	42	32	24	1	267.2	261	191	5	15	154	96	3.53	117	.249	.353	124-1	.258	2	88	16	—	1.4
MAIRENA, OSWALDO	Oswaldo Antonio; B7.30.1975 Chinandega, Nicaragua; BL/TL/5´11˝/165; d9.5																									
2000	Chi N	0	0	ø	2	0	0	0-0	2	7	4	1	0	2-0	0	18.00	25	.583	.643	0	ø	0	—	-3	0	-0.1
2002	Fla N	2	3	.400	31	0	0	0-0	33.2	38	21	7	0	12-0	21	5.35	74	.288	.345	0	ø	0	—	-5	15	-0.7
Total	2	2	3	.400	33	0	0	0-0	35.2	45	25	8	0	14-0	21	6.06	65	.313	.371	0	ø	0	—	-8	15	-0.8
MAJEWSKI, GARY	Gary Wayne; B2.26.1980 Houston TX; BR/TR/6´1˝/215; [ChiA98 2/59]; d8.26																									
2004	Mon N	0	1	.000	16	0	0	1-1	21	28	15	2	2	5-1	12	3.86	119	.326	.372	2	.000	-0	—	-1	0	-0.1
2005	Was N	4	4	.500	79	0	0	1-4	86	80	32	2	7	37-6	50	2.93	140	.248	.334	6-0-1	.000	-1	—	11	0	0.8
2006	Was N	3	2	.600	46	0	0	0-5	55.1	49	24	4	1	25-1	34	3.58	122	.233	.318	3-0-1	.000	-0	—	5	0	0.3
	Cin N	1	2	.333	19	0	0	0-2	15	30	14	1	3	4-2	9	8.40	56	.435	.468	0	ø	0	—	-5	25	-0.9
	Year	4	4	.500	65	0	0	0-7	70.1	79	38	5	4	29-3	43	4.61	96	.283	.356	3-0-1	.000	-0	—	-1	0	-0.6
Total	3	8	9	.471	160	0	0	2-12	177.1	187	85	9	13	71-10	105	3.70	116	.272	.347	11-0-2	.000	-1	—	10	25	0.1
MAKOSKY, FRANK	Frank; B1.20.1910 Boonton NJ; D1.10.1987 Stroudsburg PA; BR/TR/6´1˝/185; d4.30																									
1937	NY A	5	2	.714	26	1	1	3	58	64	42	6	0	24	27	4.97	90	.277	.345	16-0-1	.313	1	59	-5	—	-0.4
MAKOWSKI, TOM	Thomas Anthony; B12.22.1950 Buffalo NY; BR/TL/5´11˝/185; d5.1; Col Buffalo																									
1975	Det A	0	0	ø	3	0	0	0-0	9.1	10	11	2	0	9-0	3	4.82	84	.278	.404	0	ø	0	—	-3	0	-0.1
MALARKEY, JOHN	John S. "Liz"; B5.4.1872 Springfield OH; D10.29.1949 Cincinnati OH; TR/5´11˝/155; d9.21																									
1894	Was N	2	1	.667	3	3	3	0	26	42	22	1	0	5	3	4.15	127	.359	.385	14	.071	-2*	54	3	—	0.0
1895	Was N	0	8	.000	22	8	5	2	100.2	135	113	3	8	60	32	5.99	80	.316	.410	37	.135	-4	85	-15	—	-1.3
1896	Was N	0	1	.000	1	1	0	0	7	9	7	1	0	3	0	1.29	343	.310	.375	2	.500	1	97	1	—	0.1
1899	Chi N	0	1	.000	1	1	1	0	9	19	13	0	1	5	7	13.00	29	.422	.490	5	.200	0	38	-7	—	-0.5
1902	Bos N	8	10	.444	21	19	17-1	1	170.1	158	82	0	0	58	39	2.59	109	.246	.309	62-1-1	.210	2*	106	0	—	0.4
1903	Bos N	11	16	.407	32	27	25-2	0	253	266	150	5	11	96	98	3.09	104	.272	.344	87-0-1	.161	1	93	-3	—	-0.1
Total	6	21	37	.362	80	59	51-3	3	566	629	387	10	20	227	179	3.64	96	.281	.353	207-1-2	.169	-2	90	-21	—	-1.4
MALARKEY, BILL	William John; B11.26.1878 Port Byron IL; D12.12.1956 Phoenix AZ; BR/TR/5´10˝/185; d4.16																									
1908	NY N	0	2	.000	15	0	0	2	35	31	16	1	1	10	12	2.57	94	.242	.302	6	.000	-1	—	-2	—	-0.2
MALASKA, MARK	Dennis Mark; B1.17.1978 Youngstown OH; BL/TL/6´3˝/(190–210); [TBA00 8/226]; d7.17; Col Akron																									
2003	TB A	2	1	.667	22	0	0	0-3	16	13	7	0	1	12-3	17	2.81	163	.232	.377	0	ø	0	—	2	0	0.4
2004	Bos A	1	1	.500	19	0	0	0-0	20	21	11	2	1	12-1	12	4.50	109	.266	.370	0	ø	0	—	1	0	0.1
Total	2	3	2	.600	41	0	0	0-3	36	34	18	2	2	24-4	29	3.75	127	.252	.373	0	ø	0	—	3	0	0.5
MALDONADO, CARLOS	Carlos Cesar (Delgado); B10.18.1966 Chepo, Pan; BB/TR/6´2˝/(210–215); d9.16																									
1990	KC A	0	0	ø	4	0	0	0-0	6	9	6	0	0	4-0	9	9.00	43	.346	.419	0	ø	0	—	-3	0	-0.2
1991	KC A	0	0	ø	5	0	0	0-0	7.2	11	9	0	0	9-1	1	8.22	50	.333	.476	0	ø	0	—	-4	0	-0.2
1993	Mil A	2	2	.500	29	0	0	1-0	37.1	40	20	2	0	17-5	18	4.58	94	.282	.350	0	ø	0	—	-1	0	-0.1
Total	3	2	2	.500	38	0	0	1-0	51	60	35	2	0	30-6	28	5.65	75	.299	.381	0	ø	0	—	-8	0	-0.5
MALIS, CY	Cyrus Sol; B2.26.1907 Philadelphia PA; D1.12.1971 N.Hollywood CA; BR/TR/5´11˝/175; d8.17																									
1934	Phi N	0	0	ø	1	0	0	0	3.2	4	2	0	0	2	1	4.91	96	.267	.353	0	ø	0	—	0	—	0.0
MALLETTE, BRIAN	Brian Drew; B1.19.1975 Dublin GA; BR/TR/6´0˝/185; [MilA97 27/817]; d4.12; Col Kennesaw St.																									
2002	Mil N	0	0	ø	5	0	0	0-0	5	7	6	3	1	3-1	5	10.80	38	.350	.458	0	ø	0	—	-3	0	-0.2
MALLETTE, MAL	Malcolm Francis; B1.30.1922 Syracuse NY; D11.25.2005 Durham NC; BL/TL/6´2˝/200; d9.25; Col Syracuse																									
1950	Bro N	0	0	ø	2	0	0	0	1.1	2	0	0	0	1	2	0.00	ø	.333	.429	0	ø	0	—	1	85	0.0
MALLICOAT, ROB	Robbin Dale; B11.16.1964 St.Helens OR; BL/TL/6´3˝/180; [HouN84*S1/16]; d9.11; Col Taft (CA) JC; [DL 1993 Hou N 182]																									
1987	Hou N	0	0	ø	4	1	0	0-0	6.2	8	5	0	0	6-0	4	6.75	58	.320	.452	0	ø	0	161	-2	0	-0.1
1991	Hou N	0	2	.000	24	0	0	1-0	23.1	22	10	2	2	13-1	18	3.86	92	.259	.363	1	.000	-0	—	0	0	-0.1
1992	Hou N	0	0	ø	23	0	0	0-0	23.2	26	19	2	5	19-2	20	7.23	47	.283	.427	1	.000	-0*	—	-10	0	-0.5
Total	3	0	2	.000	51	1	0	1-0	53.2	56	34	4	7	38-3	42	5.70	62	.277	.404	2	.000	-0	161	-12	182	-0.7
MALLOY, ALEX	Archibald Alexander "Lick"; B10.31.1886 Laurinburg NC; D3.1.1961 Ferris TX; BR/TR/6´2˝/180; d9.10																									
1910	StL A	0	6	.000	7	6	4	0	52.2	47	26	0	2	17	27	2.56	97	.261	.332	16	.063	-1	18	-1	—	-0.3
MALLOY, HERM	John Herman "Tug"; B6.1.1885 Massillon OH; D5.9.1942 Louisville OH; BR/TR/6´0˝/?; d10.6																									
1907	Det A	0	1	.000	1	1	1	0	8	13	10	1	0	5	6	5.63	46	.371	.450	4	.250	0	78	-3	—	-0.3
1908	Det A	0	2	.000	3	2	2	0	17	20	11	1	2	4	8	3.71	65	.278	.333	9	.333	1	42	-3	—	-0.2
Total	2	0	3	.000	4	3	3	0	25	33	21	2	2	9	14	4.32	57	.308	.373	13	.308	1	55	-6	—	-0.5
MALLOY, BOB	Robert Paul; B5.28.1918 Canonsburg PA; BR/TR/5´11˝/185; d5.4; Mil 1944–46; Col Pittsburgh																									
1943	Cin N	0	0	ø	6	0	0	0	10	14	8	1	0	8	4	6.30	53	.778	.846	3	.667	1	—	-3	0	-0.1
1944	Cin N	1	1	.500	9	0	0	0	23.1	22	10	0	0	11	4	3.09	113	.265	.351	7	.000	-1	—	1	0	0.0
1946	Cin N	2	5	.286	27	3	1	2	72	71	29	2	2	26	24	2.75	122	.265	.334	18	.278	1	94	4	0	0.4
1947	Cin N	0	0	ø	1	0	0	0	1	3	2	1	0	0	1	18.00	23	.600	.600	0	ø	0	—	-1	0	-0.1
1949	StL A	1	1	.500	5	0	0	0	9.2	6	3	0	0	7	2	2.79	162	.200	.351	3	.000	-0	—	2	0	0.3
Total	5	4	7	.364	48	3	1	2	116	116	52	4	2	52	35	3.26	106	.287	.371	31	.226	1	94	3	0	0.5

YEAR	TM LG	W	L	PCT	G	GS	CG-SHO	SV-BS	IP	H	R	HR	HB	BB-IB	SO	ERA	AERA	OAV	OOB	AB-HR-SH	AVG	PB	SUP	APR	DL	PW
MALLOY, BOB	Robert William; B11.24.1964 Arlington VA; BR/TR/6´5˝/200; [TexA86 19/475]; d5.26; Col Virginia																									
1987	Tex A	0	0	ø	2	2	0	0-0	11	13	11	6	0	3-0	8	6.55	69	.271	.314	0	ø	0	182	-3	0	-0.2
1990	Mon N	0	0	ø	1	0	0	0-0	2	1	0	0	0	1-0	1	0.00	ø	.143	.250	0	ø	0	—	1	0	0.0
Total	2	0	0	ø	3	2	0	0-0	13	14	11	6	0	4-0	9	5.54	79	.255	.305	0	ø	0	182	-2	0	-0.2
MALONE, CHUCK	Charles Ray; B7.8.1965 Harrisburg AR; BR/TR/6´7˝/250; [PhiN86*5/112]; d9.6; Col Arkansas St.																									
1990	Phi N	1	0	1.000	7	0	0	0-0	7.1	3	4	1	0	11-0	7	3.68	105	.130	.412	0	ø	0	—	0	0	0.0
MALONE, MARTIN	Martin; d6.20; ▲																									
1872	Eck NA	0	2	.000	2	2	2	0	18	51	50	1	—	4	0	10.50	32	.443	.462	16	.375	1*	90	-14	—	-0.8
MALONE, PAT	Perce Leigh; B9.25.1902 Altoona PA; D5.13.1943 Altoona PA; BL/TR (BB 1935–37)/6´0˝/200; d4.12; Col Juniata																									
1928	Chi N	18	13	.581	42	25	16-2	2	250.2	218	99	15	6	99	155	2.84	136	.236	.314	95-1-3	.189	1	118	27	—	3.1
1929	†Chi N	**22**	10	.688	40	30	19-**5**	2	267	283	120	12	6	102	**166**	3.57	129	.276	.345	105-2-0	.210	2	111	33	—	3.5
1930	Chi N	**20**	9	.690	45	35	**22**-1	4	271.2	290	145	14	6	96	142	3.94	124	.271	.334	105-4-4	.248	5	117	26	—	2.6
1931	Chi N	16	9	.640	36	30	12-2	0	228.1	229	115	9	4	88	112	3.90	99	.258	.328	79-1-9	.215	2	132	-1	—	0.0
1932	†Chi N	15	17	.469	37	32	17-2	0	237	222	111	13	6	78	120	3.38	111	.244	.308	78-1-8	.179	0	93	8	—	0.8
1933	Chi N	10	14	.417	31	26	13-2	0	186.1	186	91	10	5	59	72	3.91	84	.258	.318	63-0-3	.159	-2	105	-11	—	-1.6
1934	Chi N	14	7	.667	34	21	8-1	0	191	200	85	14	3	55	111	3.53	110	.270	.322	64-0-8	.172	-2	100	7	—	0.5
1935	NY A	3	5	.375	29	2	0	3	56.1	53	45	7	1	33	25	5.43	75	.252	.357	15-0-1	.000	-3	193	-12	—	-1.7
1936	†NY A	12	4	.750	35	9	5	**9**	134.2	144	60	4	4	60	72	3.81	122	.273	.352	51-0-2	.196	-1	160	16	—	1.6
1937	NY A	4	4	.500	28	9	3	6	92	109	65	5	4	35	49	5.48	81	.291	.357	33-0-2	.030	-5	146	-10	—	-1.4
Total	10	134	92	.593	357	219	115-15	26	1915	1934	936	103	45	705	1024	3.74	111	.262	.330	688-9-40	.188	-2	115	83	—	7.4
MALONEY, CHARLIE	Charles Michael; B5.22.1886 Cambridge MA; D1.17.1967 Arlington MA; BR/TR/5´8˝/155; d8.10; Col Boston College																									
1908	Bos N	0	0	ø	1	0	0	0	2	3	1	0	0	1	0	4.50	54	.429	.500	0	ø	0	—	0	—	0.0
MALONEY, JIM	James William; B6.2.1940 Fresno CA; BL/TR/6´2˝/(190–214); d7.27; Col Fresno (CA) City																									
1960	Cin N	2	6	.250	11	10	2-1	0	63.2	61	35	5	2	37-2	48	4.66	82	.255	.360	18-0-1	.111	-0	90	-5	0	-0.6
1961	†Cin N	6	7	.462	27	11	1	2	94.2	86	54	16	1	59-4	57	4.37	93	.242	.349	29-1-1	.379	4*	117	-4	0	-0.1
1962	Cin N	9	7	.563	22	17	3	1	115.1	90	52	11	2	66-3	105	3.51	115	.214	.320	43	.186	0*	96	6	0	0.7
1963	Cin N	23	7	.767	33	33	13-6	0	250.1	183	84	17	6	88-1	265	2.77	121	.202	.275	89-0-5	.169	1*	131	17	0	2.0
1964	Cin N	15	10	.600	31	31	11-2	0	216	175	72	16	1	83-5	214	2.71	133	.222	.296	73-1-1	.151	1	96	22	0	2.5
1965	Cin N★	20	9	.690	33	33	14-5	0	255.1	189	77	13	5	110-3	244	2.54	148	.206	.294	89-0-8	.225	7*	111	34	0	4.6
1966	Cin N	16	8	.667	32	32	10-**5**	0	224.2	174	75	18	10	90-4	216	2.80	139	.214	.299	81-0-3	.222	3*	92	26	0	3.0
1967	Cin N	15	11	.577	30	29	6-3	0	196.1	181	76	8	3	72-5	153	3.25	115	.247	.315	69-0-2	.159	-0*	85	11	0	1.5
1968	Cin N	16	10	.615	33	32	8-5	0	207	183	100	17	2	80-6	181	3.61	88	.239	.310	74-2-4	.243	6*	125	-12	0	-0.9
1969	Cin N	12	5	.706	30	27	6-3	0-0	178.2	135	64	11	1	86-4	102	2.77	136	.208	.301	55-3-6	.200	6	112	18	0	2.3
1970	Cin N	0	1	.000	7	3	0	1-0	16.2	26	22	3	2	15-0	7	11.34	36	.366	.478	3	.000	-0	148	-13	141	-0.8
1971	Cal A	0	3	.000	13	4	0	0-0	30.1	35	18	3	1	24-2	13	5.04	64	.294	.414	5	.200	0	62	-6	33	-0.6
Total	12	134	84	.615	302	262	74-30	4-0	1849	1518	729	138	36	810-39	1605	3.19	115	.224	.308	628-7-31	.201	26	106	94	174	13.6
MALONEY, SEAN	Sean Patrick; B5.25.1971 South Kingstown RI; BR/TR/6´7˝/(210–230); [MilA93 19/543]; d4.28; Col Georgetown																									
1997	Mil A	0	0	ø	3	0	0	0-0	7	7	4	1	2	2-0	5	5.14	90	.304	.379	0	ø	0	—	0	0	0.0
1998	LA N	0	1	.000	11	0	0	0-0	12.2	13	7	2	2	5-0	11	4.97	81	.265	.357	1	.000	-0	—	-1	0	-0.1
Total	2	0	1	.000	14	0	0	0-0	19.2	20	11	3	4	7-0	16	5.03	84	.278	.365	1	.000	-0	—	-1	0	-0.1
MALOY, PAUL	Paul Augustus "Biff"; B6.4.1892 Bascom OH; D3.18.1976 Sandusky OH; BR/TR/5´11˝/185; d7.11																									
1913	Bos A	0	0	ø	2	0	0	0	2	2	2	0	2	1	0	9.00	33	.286	.500	0	ø	0	—	-1	—	-0.1
MALTZBERGER, GORDON	Gordon Ralph "Maltzy"; B9.4.1912 Utopia TX; D12.11.1974 Rialto CA; BR/TR/6´0˝/170; d4.27; Mil 1945–46; C3																									
1943	Chi A	7	4	.636	37	0	0	**14**	98.2	86	29	8	2	24	48	2.46	136	.236	.287	25-0-2	.120	0	—	11	0	1.6
1944	Chi A	10	5	.667	46	0	0	**12**	91.1	81	31	2	1	19	49	2.96	116	.235	.277	22-0-2	.136	-1	—	7	0	1.2
1946	Chi A	2	0	1.000	19	0	0	2	39.2	30	7	3	1	6	17	1.59	215	.205	.242	6	.000	-0	—	9	0	0.5
1947	Chi A	1	4	.200	33	0	0	5	63.2	61	26	4	1	25	22	3.39	108	.257	.331	7-0-1	.143	1	—	3	0	0.4
Total	4	20	13	.606	135	0	0	33	293.1	258	93	17	5	74	136	2.70	128	.236	.288	60-0-5	.117	0	—	30	0	3.7
MAMAUX, AL	Albert Leon; B5.30.1894 Pittsburgh PA; D12.31.1962 Santa Monica CA; BR/TR/6´0.5˝/168; d9.23; Mil 1918; Col Duquesne																									
1913	Pit N	0	0	ø	1	0	0	0	3	2	1	0	0	2	2	3.00	101	.167	.286	1	.000	-0	—	0	—	0.0
1914	Pit N	5	2	.714	13	6	4-2	0	63	41	19	1	2	24	30	1.71	155	.186	.272	20	.250	1	117	5	—	0.8
1915	Pit N	21	8	.724	38	30	17-8	0	251.2	182	70	3	9	96	152	2.04	134	.208	.293	92-0-5	.163	-2	116	21	—	2.0
1916	Pit N	21	15	.583	45	37	26-1	2	310	264	123	3	9	136	163	2.53	106	.239	.327	110-0-2	.191	1	101	3	—	0.5
1917	Pit N	2	11	.154	16	13	5	0	85.2	92	59	1	3	50	22	5.25	54	.278	.378	31-0-1	.226	0	98	-21	—	-2.9
1918	Bro N	0	1	.000	2	1	0	0	8	14	6	0	0	2	2	6.75	41	.438	.471	2	.000	-0	54	-3	—	-0.3
1919	Bro N	10	12	.455	30	22	16-2	0	199.1	174	89	2	4	66	80	2.66	112	.245	.312	63-0-2	.175	0	88	2	—	0.3
1920	†Bro N	12	8	.600	41	17	9-2	4	190.2	172	70	2	4	63	101	2.69	119	.255	.322	60-0-2	.167	-0	98	11	—	1.2
1921	Bro N	3	3	.500	12	1	0	1	43	36	17	1	1	13	21	3.14	124	.240	.305	11-0-1	.182	-0	63	4	—	0.5
1922	Bro N	1	4	.200	37	7	1	3	87.2	97	46	7	2	33	35	3.70	110	.290	.358	17-1-2	.235	3	92	3	—	0.5
1923	Bro N	0	2	.000	5	1	0	0	13	20	13	0	0	6	5	8.31	47	.385	.448	2	.500	0	0	-6	—	-0.7
1924	NY A	1	1	.500	14	2	0	0	38	44	28	2	1	20	12	5.68	73	.308	.396	13	.077	-1	223	-7	—	-0.5
Total	12	76	67	.531	254	137	78-15	10	1293	1138	541	22	35	511	625	2.90	104	.245	.325	422-1-15	.182	2	100	12	—	1.4
MANDERS, HAL	Harold Carl; B6.14.1917 Waukee IA; BR/TR/6´0˝/187; d8.12; Col Iowa																									
1941	Det A	1	0	1.000	8	0	0	0	15.1	13	5	0	1	8	7	2.35	194	.236	.344	4	.000	-1	—	3	0	0.1
1942	Det A	2	0	1.000	18	0	0	0	33	39	19	4	1	15	14	4.09	97	.307	.385	4	.250	0	—	-1	0	0.0
1946	Det A	0	0	ø	2	0	0	0	6	8	7	1	1	2	3	10.50	35	.364	.440	2	.500	0	—	-4	0	-0.2
	Chi N	0	1	.000	2	1	0	0	6	11	6	1	1	3	4	9.00	37	.423	.500	2	.000	-0	26	-3	0	-0.5
Total	3	3	1	.750	30	1	0	0	60.1	71	37	6	4	28	28	4.77	84	.309	.393	12	.167	-0	26	-5	0	-0.6
MANGUM, LEO	Leo Allan "Blackie"; B5.24.1896 Durham NC; D7.9.1974 Lima OH; BR/TR/6´1˝/187; d7.11																									
1924	Chi A	1	4	.200	13	7	1	0	47	69	43	3	1	25	12	7.09	58	.359	.436	14	.071	-1	117	-15	—	-1.4
1925	Chi A	1	0	1.000	7	0	0	0	15	25	15	0	0	6	6	7.80	53	.373	.425	4	.500	1	—	-6	—	-0.3
1928	NY N	0	0	ø	1	1	0	0	3	6	5	0	0	5	1	15.00	26	.500	.647	1	1.000	0	260	-3	—	-0.1
1932	Bos N	0	0	ø	7	0	0	0	10.1	17	8	1	0	0	3	5.23	72	.333	.333	2	.000	-0	—	-2	—	-0.1
1933	Bos N	4	3	.571	25	5	2-1	0	84	93	33	2	0	11	28	3.32	92	.280	.303	22-0-2	.091	-2	92	-1	—	-0.2
1934	Bos N	5	3	.625	29	3	1	1	94.1	127	67	9	0	23	28	5.72	67	.315	.352	32	.281	2	38	-20	—	-1.3
1935	Bos N	0	0	ø	3	0	0	0	4.2	6	3	0	0	2	0	3.86	98	.300	.364	0	ø	0	—	0	—	0.0
Total	7	11	10	.524	85	16	4-1	1	258.1	343	174	15	1	72	78	5.37	68	.318	.362	75-0-2	.200	0	108	-47	—	-3.4
MANN, JIM	James Joseph; B11.17.1974 Brockton MA; BR/TR/6´3˝/225; [TorA93 54/1468]; d5.29; Col Massasoit (MA) CC																									
2000	NY N	0	0	ø	2	0	0	0-0	2.2	6	3	1	0	1-0	0	10.13	43	.429	.467	0	ø	0	—	-2	0	-0.1
2001	Hou N	0	0	ø	4	0	0	0-0	5.1	3	2	0	2	4-0	5	3.38	136	.176	.391	0	ø	0	—	1	0	0.0
2002	Hou N	0	1	.000	17	0	0	0-0	22	19	10	3	5	7-1	19	4.09	106	.235	.333	1	.000	-0	—	1	0	0.0
2003	Pit N	0	0	ø	2	0	0	0-0	1.2	5	4	1	0	1-0	1	10.80	40	.455	.500	0	ø	0	—	-2	0	-0.1
Total	4	0	1	.000	25	0	0	0-0	31.2	33	19	5	7	13-1	25	4.83	91	.268	.371	1	.000	-0	—	-2	0	-0.2
MANNING, DAVID	David Anthony; B8.14.1972 Buffalo NY; BR/TR/6´3˝/210; [TexA92 3/90]; d8.2; Col Palm Beach (FL) CC																									
2003	Mil N	0	2	.000	2	2	0	0-0	6.2	11	13	1	0	8-0	2	16.20	27	.393	.514	1	.000	-0	22	-9	0	-1.2
MANNING, ERNIE	Ernest Devon "Ed"; B10.9.1890 Florala AL; D4.28.1973 Pensacola FL; BL/TR/6´0˝/175; d5.3; Col Auburn																									
1914	StL A	0	0	ø	4	0	0	0	10	11	6	0	0	3	3	3.60	75	.297	.350	4-0-1	.000	-0*	—	-1	—	-0.1
MANNING, JIM	James Benjamin; B7.21.1943 L'Anse MI; BR/TR/6´1˝/185; d4.15																									
1962	Min A	0	0	ø	5	1	0	0	7	14	10	0	1	1-0	3	5.14	79	.389	.410	1	.000	-0	153	-3	0	-0.2

YEAR	TM LG	W	L	PCT	G	GS	CG-SHO	SV-BS	IP	H	R	HR	HB	BB-IB	SO	ERA	AERA	OAV	OOB	AB-HR-SH	AVG	PB	SUP	APR	DL	PW
Manning, Jack	John E.; B12.20.1853 Braintree MA; D8.15.1929 Boston MA; BR/TR/5´8.5˝/158; d4.23.1873; M1; ▲																									
1874	Bal NA	4	16	.200	22	20	17	0	176.2	222	168	2	—	12	12	2.09	107	.266	.277	174	.351	7*	50	-1	—	0.5
1875	Bos NA	16	2	.889	27	18	8-1	6	144	152	86	1	—	14	34	2.38	90	.247	.263	348-1	.270	4*	173	-4	—	-0.3
1876	Bos N	18	5	.783	34	20	13	**5**	197.1	213	139	1	—	32	24	2.14	105	.252	.279	288-2	.264	3*	153	-1	—	0.0
1877	Cin N	0	4	.000	10	4	2	1	44	83	65	1	—	7	6	6.95	38	.379	.398	252	.317	4*	55	-21	—	-1.3
1878	Bos N	1	0	1.000	3	1	1	0	11.1	24	19	1	—	5	2	14.29	17	.393	.439	248	.254	0*	111	-11	—	-0.7
Total	2NA	20	18	.526	49	38	25-1	6	320.2	374	254	3	—	26	46	2.22	99	.258	.271	522-1	.297	11	101	-5	—	0.2
Total	3	19	9	.679	47	25	16	6	252.2	320	223	3	—	44	32	3.53	66	.284	.311	788-2	.278	7	137	-33	—	-2.0
Manning, Rube	Walter S.; B4.29.1883 Chambersburg PA; D4.23.1930 Williamsport PA; BR/TR/6´0˝/180; d9.25																									
1907	NY A	0	1	.000	1	1	1	0	9	8	3	0	1	3	3	3.00	93	.242	.324	3	.000	-0	24	0	—	0.0
1908	NY A	13	16	.448	41	26	19-2	1	245	228	114	4	18	86	113	2.94	84	.256	.334	91-0-1	.187	0*	77	-11	—	-1.3
1909	NY A	7	11	.389	26	21	11-2	1	173	167	76	2	9	48	71	3.17	80	.265	.326	60-0-3	.183	-0	102	-8	—	-0.8
1910	NY A	2	4	.333	16	9	4	0	75	80	43	4	4	25	25	3.72	71	.283	.349	26	.192	0	123	-9	—	-0.7
Total	4	22	32	.407	84	57	35-4	2	502	483	236	10	32	162	212	3.14	81	.263	.333	180-0-4	.183	-0	93	-28	—	-2.8
Manon, Julio	Julio Alberto; B6.10.1973 Guerra, D.R.; BL/TR/6´0˝/200; d6.5																									
2003	Mon N	1	2	.333	23	0	0	1-0	28.1	26	13	3	1	17-1	15	4.13	107	.252	.358	1	.000	-0	—	2	0	0.1
2006	Bal A	0	1	.000	22	0	0	0-1	20	23	13	5	2	16-1	22	5.40	84	.274	.402	0	ø	0	—	-2	0	-0.1
Total	2	1	3	.250	45	0	0	1-1	48.1	49	26	8	3	33-2	37	4.66	96	.262	.378	1	.000	-0	—	0	0	0.0
Manon, Ramon	Ramon (Reyes); B1.20.1968 Santo Domingo, D.R.; BR/TR/6´0˝/170; d4.19																									
1990	Tex A	0	0	ø	1	0	0	0-0	2	3	3	0	0	3-1	0	13.50	29	.333	.500	0	ø	0	—	-2	0	-0.1
Manske, Lou	Louis Hugo; B7.4.1884 Milwaukee WI; D4.27.1963 Milwaukee WI; BL/TL/6´0˝/?; d8.31																									
1906	Pit N	0	0	ø	2	1	0	0	8	12	6	0	0	5	6	5.63	48	.387	.472	4	.000	-1	191	-2	—	-0.2
Mantei, Matt	Matthew Bruce; B7.7.1973 Tampa FL; BR/TR/6´1˝/(181–200); [SeaA91 25/656]; d6.18; [DL 1997 Fla N 181]																									
1995	Fla N	0	1	.000	12	0	0	0-0	13.1	12	8	1	0	13-0	15	4.73	91	.245	.397	0	ø	0	—	-1	88	0.0
1996	Fla N	1	0	1.000	14	0	0	0-1	18.1	13	13	2	1	21-1	25	6.38	65	.197	.398	1	.000	-0	—	-4	103	-0.2
1998	Fla N	3	4	.429	42	0	0	9-3	54.2	38	19	1	7	23-3	63	2.96	137	.203	.308	3	.333	0	—	7	16	1.1
1999	Fla N	1	2	.333	35	0	0	10-2	36.1	24	11	4	2	25-1	50	2.72	161	.186	.325	1	.000	-0	—	7	0	0.9
	†Ari N	0	1	.000	30	0	0	22-3	29	20	10	1	3	19-0	49	2.79	165	.192	.333	0	ø	0	—	6	0	1.0
	Year	1	3	.250	65	0	0	32-5	65.1	44	21	5	5	44-1	99	2.76	163	.189	.329	1	.000	-0	—	13	0	1.9
2000	Ari N	1	1	.500	47	0	0	17-3	45.1	31	24	4	2	35-1	53	4.57	105	.193	.343	0	ø	0	—	1	32	0.1
2001	Ari N	0	0	ø	8	0	0	2-0	7	6	2	2	0	4-0	12	2.57	180	.222	.323	0	ø	0	—	2	166	0.1
2002	†Ari N	2	2	.500	31	0	0	0-1	26.2	28	15	3	1	12-0	26	4.73	95	.257	.336	0	ø	0	—	-1	88	-0.1
2003	Ari N	5	4	.556	50	0	0	29-3	55	37	17	6	2	18-1	68	2.62	177	.191	.264	0	ø	0	—	12	33	2.3
2004	Ari N	0	3	.000	12	0	0	4-3	10.2	17	15	5	0	6-1	13	11.81	39	.354	.418	0	ø	0	—	-8	148	-1.4
2005	Bos A	1	0	1.000	34	0	0	0-0	26.1	23	20	1	5	24-1	22	6.49	70	.240	.416	0	ø	0	—	-5	93	-0.3
Total	10	14	18	.438	315	0	0	93-19	322.2	249	154	30	23	200-9	396	4.07	110	.213	.337	5	.200	0	—	16	948	3.5
Manuel, Barry	Barry Paul; B8.12.1965 Mamou LA; BR/TR/5´11˝/(180–185); [TexA87 2/51]; d9.6; Col Louisiana St.; [DL 1993 Tex A 76]																									
1991	Tex A	1	0	1.000	8	0	0	0-0	16	7	2	0	0	6-0	5	1.13	360	.143	.224	0	ø	0	—	5	0	0.3
1992	Tex A	1	0	1.000	3	0	0	0-0	5.2	6	3	2	1	1-0	9	4.76	80	.261	.320	0	ø	0	—	0	0	-0.1
1996	Mon N	4	1	.800	53	0	0	0-0	86	70	34	10	7	26-4	62	3.24	134	.219	.291	7-0-1	.000	-0	—	10	0	0.4
1997	NY N	0	1	.000	19	0	0	0-0	25.2	35	18	6	1	13-1	21	5.26	76	.324	.402	2	.000	-0	—	-4	0	-0.3
1998	Ari N	1	0	1.000	13	0	0	0-0	15.2	17	14	5	1	14-3	12	7.47	57	.266	.405	0	ø	0	—	-5	0	-0.3
Total	5	7	2	.778	96	0	0	0-0	149	135	71	23	10	60-8	109	3.87	109	.240	.321	9-0-1	.000	-1	—	6	76	0.0
Manuel, Moxie	Mark Garfield; B10.16.1881 Metropolis IL; D4.26.1924 Memphis TN; BR/TR/5´11˝/170; d9.25																									
1905	Was A	0	0	ø	3	1	1	0	10	9	9	0	1	3	3	5.40	49	.243	.317	4	.250	0	80	-3	—	-0.2
1908	Chi A	3	4	.429	18	6	3	1	60.1	52	25	0	2	25	25	3.28	71	.243	.328	16-0-1	.063	-1	98	-5	—	-0.7
Total	2	3	4	.429	21	7	4	1	70.1	61	34	0	3	28	28	3.58	66	.243	.326	20-0-1	.100	-1	96	-8	—	-0.9
Manville, Dick	Richard Wesley; B12.25.1926 Des Moines IA; BR/TR/6´4˝/192; d4.30; Col Yale																									
1950	Bos N	0	0	ø	1	0	0	0	2	0	0	0	0	3	2	0.00	ø	.000	.300	0	ø	0	—	1	0	0.0
1952	Chi N	0	0	ø	11	0	0	0	17	25	17	2	0	12	6	7.94	48	.362	.457	2	.500	0	—	-7	0	-0.3
Total	2	0	0	ø	12	0	0	0	19	25	17	2	0	15	8	7.11	54	.329	.440	2	.500	0	—	-6	0	-0.3
Manzanillo, Josias	Josias (Adams); B10.16.1967 San Pedro de Macoris, D.R.; BR/TR/6´0˝/(190–205); d10.5; b–Ravelo																									
1991	Bos A	0	0	ø	1	0	0	0-0	1	2	2	0	0	3-0	1	18.00	24	.400	.625	0	ø	0	—	-1	0	-0.1
1993	Mil A	1	1	.500	10	1	0	1-1	17	22	20	1	2	10-3	10	9.53	45	.314	.405	0	ø	0	85	-10	0	-1.0
	NY N	0	0	ø	6	0	0	0-0	12	8	7	1	0	9-0	11	3.00	134	.186	.321	1	.000	-0	—	0	0	0.0
1994	NY N	3	2	.600	37	0	0	2-3	47.1	34	15	4	3	13-2	48	2.66	157	.200	.269	4-0-1	.000	-0	—	8	16	0.8
1995	NY N	1	2	.333	12	0	0	0-0	16	18	15	3	0	6-2	14	7.88	51	.273	.329	0	ø	0	—	-7	0	-1.1
	NY A	0	0	ø	11	0	0	0-0	17.1	19	4	1	2	9-2	11	2.08	223	.279	.380	0	ø	0	—	5	88	0.3
1997	Sea A	0	1	.000	16	0	0	0-1	18.1	19	13	3	0	17-1	18	5.40	84	.275	.409	1	.000	-0	—	-2	64	-0.1
1999	NY N	0	0	ø	12	0	0	0-0	18.2	19	12	5	2	4-1	25	5.79	75	.264	.316	1	1.000	0*	—	-3	0	-0.1
2000	Pit N	2	2	.500	43	0	0	0-2	58.2	50	23	6	0	32-4	39	3.38	138	.240	.339	3-0-1	.000	-0	—	9	0	0.4
2001	Pit N	3	2	.600	71	0	0	2-5	79.2	60	32	4	5	26-3	80	3.39	132	.211	.281	1	.000	-0	—	10	0	0.5
2002	Pit N	0	0	ø	13	0	0	0-1	13	20	11	5	1	5-0	4	7.62	55	.364	.426	0	ø	0	—	-4	72	-0.2
2003	Cin N	0	2	.000	9	0	0	0-1	10.2	21	20	7	0	4-0	12	12.66	33	.389	.431	0	ø	0	—	-12	0	-1.8
2004	Fla N	3	3	.500	26	0	0	1-3	32.1	38	24	6	3	15-2	27	6.12	67	.292	.376	1	.000	-0	—	-8	0	-1.3
Total	11	13	15	.464	267	1	0	6-17	342	330	198	46	18	153-20	300	4.71	93	.255	.338	12-0-2	.083	-1	85	-15	240	-3.7
Manzanillo, Ravelo	Ravelo (Adams); B10.17.1963 San Pedro de Macoris, D.R.; BL/TL/5´10˝/(190–195); d9.25; b–Josias																									
1988	Chi A	0	1	.000	2	2	0	0-0	9.1	7	6	1	1	12-0	10	5.79	69	.212	.435	0	ø	0	91	-1	0	-0.1
1994	Pit N	4	2	.667	46	0	0	1-2	50	45	30	4	3	42-5	39	4.14	106	.245	.385	3	.667	1	—	-1	0	0.1
1995	Pit N	0	0	ø	5	0	0	0-0	3.2	3	3	0	1	2-0	1	4.91	89	.231	.375	1	.000	-0	—	-1	0	0.0
Total	3	4	3	.571	53	2	0	1-2	63	55	39	5	5	56-5	50	4.43	97	.239	.392	4	.500	1	91	-3	0	0.0
Mapel, Rolla	Rolla Hamilton "Lefty"; B3.9.1890 Lees Summit MO; D4.6.1966 San Diego CA; BL/TL/5´11.5˝/165; d8.31																									
1919	StL A	0	3	.000	4	3	2	0	20	17	12	0	3	17	2	4.50	74	.262	.435	6	.167	-0	8	-2	—	-0.3
Marak, Paul	Paul Patrick; B8.2.1965 Lakenheath, England; BR/TR/6´2˝/175; [AtlN85*11/256]; d9.1; Col Trinidad St. (CO) JC																									
1990	Atl N	1	2	.333	7	7	1-1	0-0	39	39	16	2	3	19-3	15	3.69	109	.267	.361	11-0-1	.091	-0	83	2	0	0.2
Maranda, Georges	Georges Henri; B1.15.1932 Levis QC, Can.; D7.14.2000 Levis QC, Can.; BR/TR/6´2˝/195; d4.26																									
1960	SF N	1	4	.200	17	4	0	0	50.2	50	32	6	0	30-7	28	4.62	75	.254	.351	12	.167	-0	51	-8	0	-0.6
1962	Min A	1	3	.250	32	4	0	0	72.2	69	43	10	4	35-3	36	4.46	92	.252	.343	16	.250	1	87	-4	0	0.0
Total	2	2	7	.222	49	8	0	0	123.1	119	75	16	4	65-10	64	4.52	85	.253	.346	28	.214	1	70	-12	0	-0.6
Marberry, Firpo	Fredrick; B11.30.1898 Streetman TX; D6.30.1976 Mexia TX; BR/TR/6´1˝/190; d8.11; U1																									
1923	Was A	4	0	1.000	11	4	2	0	44.2	42	16	1	3	17	18	2.82	133	.258	.339	14-0-1	.143	-1	148	5	—	0.3
1924	†Was A	11	12	.478	**50**	14	6	**15**	195.1	190	88	3	9	70	68	3.09	131	.262	.335	59-0-8	.136	-4	97	18	—	1.7
1925	†Was A	9	5	.643	**55**	0	0	**15**	93.1	84	50	4	4	45	53	3.47	122	.246	.341	19-0-2	.263	1	—	**5**	—	1.0
1926	Was A	12	7	.632	**64**	5	3	**22**	138	120	55	4	3	66	43	3.00	129	.243	.336	34-0-2	.176	-1	105	13	—	2.0
1927	Was A	10	7	.588	56	10	2	9	155.1	177	92	4	3	68	74	4.64	88	.296	.371	41-0-1	.122	-3	113	-9	—	-1.4
1928	Was A	13	13	.500	**48**	11	7-1	3	161.1	160	79	4	3	42	76	3.85	104	.268	.319	46-0-3	.109	-4	90	4	—	0.1
1929	Was A	19	12	.613	**49**	26	16	**11**	250.1	233	100	6	6	69	121	3.06	139	.252	**.308**	81-0-5	.235	2	99	33	—	**4.0**
1930	Was A	15	5	.750	33	22	9-2	1	185	190	92	15	0	53	56	4.09	113	.270	.321	73-0-4	.329	5	132	12	—	1.5
1931	Was A	16	4	.800	45	25	11-1	7	219	211	92	13	3	63	88	3.45	124	.252	.307	82-1-3	.232	1	125	24	—	2.1
1932	Was A	8	4	.667	**54**	15	8-1	**13**	197.2	202	98	13	2	72	66	4.01	108	.268	.333	66	.167	-2	105	7	—	0.3
1933	Det A	16	11	.593	37	32	15-1	2	238.1	232	98	13	1	61	84	3.29	131	.254	**.302**	90-0-3	.122	-5	100	29	—	2.3
1934	†Det A	15	5	.750	38	19	6-1	3	155.2	174	92	12	0	48	64	4.57	96	.276	.327	55-0-1	.218	2	151	-4	—	-0.3

YEAR	TM LG	W	L	PCT	G	GS	CG-SHO	SV-BS	IP	H	R	HR	HB	BB-IB	SO	ERA	AERA	OAV	OOB	AB-HR-SH	AVG	PB	SUP	APR	DL	PW
1935	Det A	0	1	.000	5	2	1	0	19	22	11	2	0	9	7	4.26	98	.289	.365	5	.200	0	62	-1	—	0.0
1936	NY N	0	0	ø	1	0	0	0	0.1	1	1	0	0	0	0	0.00	ø	.500	.500	1	.000	-0	—	0	—	0.0
	Was A	0	2	.000	5	1	0	0	14	11	7	2	1	3	4	3.86	124	.208	.263	2-0-1	.000	-0	37	2	—	0.1
Total	14	148	88	.627	551	186	86-7	101	2067.1	2049	971	96	38	686	822	3.63	116	.262	.325	668-1-34	.192	-8	114	138	—	13.7
Marbet, Walt	Walter William; B9.13.1890 Plymouth Co. IA; D9.24.1956 Hohenwald TN; BR/TR/6´1˝/175; d6.17																									
1913	StL N	0	1	.000	3	1	0	0	3.1	9	7	0	0	4	1	16.20	20	.500	.591	0	ø	0	116	-5	—	-0.8
Marchildon, Phil	Philip Joseph "Babe"; B10.25.1913 Penetanguishene ON, Can.; D1.10.1997 Toronto ON, Can.; BR/TR/5´11˝/175; d9.22; Mil 1943–45																									
1940	Phi A	0	2	.000	2	2	1	0	10	12	9	1	0	8	4	7.20	62	.286	.400	2-0-1	.000	-0	30	-3	—	-0.4
1941	Phi A	10	15	.400	30	27	14-1	0	204.1	188	94	15	3	118	74	3.57	117	.245	.348	66-0-8	.167	1	92	13	0	1.4
1942	Phi A	17	14	.548	38	31	18-1	1	244	215	126	14	4	140	110	4.20	90	.235	.339	84-0-5	.238	3	91	-8	0	-0.7
1945	Phi A	0	1	.000	3	2	0	0	9	5	5	0	0	11	2	4.00	86	.179	.410	2	.500	1	112	-1	0	0.0
1946	Phi A	13	16	.448	36	29	16-1	1	226.2	197	104	14	4	114	95	3.49	101	.237	.332	75-0-7	.067	-6	92	1	0	-0.6
1947	Phi A	19	9	.679	35	35	21-2	0	276.2	228	110	15	7	141	128	3.22	118	.224	.323	98-1-12	.153	-2	120	19	0	1.5
1948	Phi A	9	15	.375	33	30	12-1	0	226.1	214	133	19	4	131	66	4.53	95	.251	.353	72-0-3	.069	-5	92	-10	0	-1.5
1949	Phi A	0	3	.000	7	6	0	0	16	24	23	3	1	19	2	11.81	35	.358	.506	6	.167	-0	105	-14	0	-2.0
1950	Bos A	0	0	ø	1	0	0	0	1.1	1	1	0	0	2	0	6.75	73	.200	.429	0	ø	0	—	0	0	0.0
Total	9	68	75	.476	185	162	82-6	2	1214.1	1084	605	81	23	684	481	3.93	100	.240	.342	405-1-36	.143	-10	97	-3	0	-2.3
Marcum, Johnny	John Alfred "Footsie"; B9.9.1909 Campbellsburg KY; D9.10.1984 Louisville KY; BL/TR/5´11˝/197; d9.7																									
1933	Phi A	3	2	.600	5	5	4-2	0	37	28	12	0	0	20	14	1.95	220	.200	.300	12	.167	0	115	9	—	1.1
1934	Phi A	14	11	.560	37	31	17-2	0	232	257	131	13	4	88	92	4.50	97	.280	.346	112-1-2	.268	6*	116	-3	—	0.2
1935	Phi A	17	12	.586	39	27	19-2	3	242.2	256	125	9	2	83	99	4.08	111	.268	.328	119-2-4	.311	9*	116	13	—	2.1
1936	Bos A	8	13	.381	31	23	9-1	1	174	194	100	14	0	52	57	4.81	110	.281	.332	88-2-3	.205	1*	78	12	—	1.2
1937	Bos A	13	11	.542	37	23	9-1	3	183.2	230	104	17	2	47	59	4.85	98	.306	.348	86-0-2	.267	5*	95	2	—	0.7
1938	Bos A	5	6	.455	15	11	7	0	92.1	113	49	11	0	25	25	4.09	120	.298	.342	37	.135	-1*	86	8	—	0.7
1939	StL A	2	5	.286	12	6	2	0	47.2	66	43	12	1	10	14	7.74	63	.332	.367	22	.455	3*	66	-13	—	-1.2
	Chi A	3	3	.500	19	6	2	0	90	125	66	15	0	19	32	6.00	79	.326	.357	57	.281	2*	140	-12	—	-0.5
	Year	5	8	.385	31	12	4	0	137.2	191	109	27	1	29	46	6.60	72	.328	.361	79	.329	6	103	-25	—	-1.7
Total	7	65	63	.508	195	132	69-8	7	1099.1	1269	630	91	9	344	392	4.66	101	.287	.340	533-5-11	.265	25	101	16	—	4.3
Marcum, Shaun	Shaun Michal; B12.14.1981 Kansas City MO; BR/TR/6´0˝/(180–190); [TorA03 3/80]; d9.6; Col Missouri St.																									
2005	Tor A	0	0	ø	5	0	0	0-0	8	6	0	0	0	4-0	4	0.00	ø	.214	.313	0	ø	0	—	4	0	0.2
2006	Tor A	3	4	.429	21	14	0	0-0	78.1	87	44	14	4	38-3	65	5.06	94	.279	.362	0	ø	0	74	-1	0	-0.1
Total	2	3	4	.429	26	14	0	0-0	86.1	93	44	14	4	42-3	69	4.59	103	.274	.358	0	ø	0	74	3	0	0.1
Marentette, Leo	Leo John; B2.18.1941 Detroit MI; BR/TR/6´2˝/(200–220); d9.26																									
1965	Det A	0	0	ø	2	0	0	0	3	1	0	0	0	1-0	3	0.00	ø	.111	.200	0	ø	0	—	1	0	0.1
1969	Mon N	0	0	ø	3	0	0	0-1	5.1	9	4	1	0	1-1	4	6.75	55	.391	.400	1	.000	-0	—	-2	0	-0.1
Total	2	0	0	ø	5	0	0	0-1	8.1	10	4	1	0	2-1	7	4.32	84	.313	.343	1	.000	-0	—	-1	0	0.0
Margoneri, Joe	Joseph Emanuel; B1.13.1930 Somerset PA; BL/TL/6´0˝/(180–185); d4.25																									
1956	NY N	6	6	.500	23	13	2	0	91.2	88	45	12	0	49-3	49	3.93	96	.254	.343	29-1-3	.103	-1	91	-1	0	-0.3
1957	NY N	1	1	.500	13	2	1	0	34.1	44	23	1	1	21-2	18	5.24	75	.314	.402	8-0-1	.000	-1	101	-5	0	-0.4
Total	2	7	7	.500	36	15	3	0	126	132	68	13	1	70-5	67	4.29	89	.271	.361	37-1-4	.081	-2	92	-6	0	-0.7
Marichal, Juan	Juan Antonio (Sanchez) "Manito"; B10.20.1937 Laguna Verde, D.R.; BR/TR/6´0˝/185; d7.19; HF1983																									
1960	SF N	6	2	.750	11	11	6-1	0	81.1	59	29	5	0	28-1	58	2.66	131	.200	.269	31-0-1	.129	0	131	8	0	0.7
1961	SF N	13	10	.565	29	27	9-3	0	185	183	88	24	2	48-5	124	3.89	98	.257	.305	59-0-5	.119	-2*	117	-1	0	-0.4
1962	†SF N★	18	11	.621	37	36	18-3	1	262.2	233	112	34	3	90-5	153	3.36	113	.234	.299	89-0-7	.236	4*	108	12	0	1.6
1963	SF N☆	**25**	8	.758	41	40	18-5	0	**321.1**	259	102	27	2	61-6	248	2.41	133	.216	.255	112-1-4	.179	3*	116	29	0	3.1
1964	SF N★	21	8	.724	33	33	**22**-4	0	269	241	89	18	1	52-8	206	2.48	144	.236	.272	97-0-6	.144	-1	132	30	0	3.1
1965	SF N★	22	13	.629	39	37	24-**10**	1	295.1	224	78	27	4	46-4	240	2.13	**169**	.205	.239	98-0-9	.173	1	92	**48**	0	**6.0**
1966	SF N★	25	6	**.806**	37	36	25-4	0	307.1	228	88	32	5	36-3	222	2.23	165	**.202**	**.230**	112-1-5	.250	6	111	49	0	5.8
1967	SF N★	14	10	.583	26	26	18-2	0	202.1	195	79	20	1	42-9	166	2.76	119	.249	.287	79-0-2	.177	3	138	9	0	1.3
1968	SF N★	**26**	9	.743	38	38	**30**-5	0	**325.2**	295	106	21	6	46-9	218	2.43	121	.238	.268	123-0-9	.163	1	144	18	0	2.5
1969	SF N☆	21	11	.656	37	36	27-**8**	0-0	299.2	244	90	15	6	54-7	205	**2.10**	**167**	.222	.261	109-0-3	.138	-1*	92	45	0	5.0
1970	SF N	12	10	.545	34	33	14-1	0-0	242.2	269	128	28	1	48-3	123	4.12	97	.277	.309	85-0-5	.059	-6	129	-5	0	-0.9
1971	†SF N★	18	11	.621	37	37	18-4	0-0	279	244	113	27	3	56-6	159	2.94	116	.233	.273	105-2-7	.133	0	131	13	0	1.5
1972	SF N	6	16	.273	25	24	6	0-0	165	176	82	15	3	46-7	72	3.71	94	.277	.327	51-0-1	.196	1	84	-6	0	-0.6
1973	SF N	11	15	.423	34	32	9-2	0-0	207.1	231	104	22	1	37-7	87	3.82	101	.277	.307	69-0-7	.188	1	100	-1	0	0.3
1974	Bos A	5	1	.833	11	9	0	0-0	57.1	61	32	3	2	14-1	21	4.87	79	.270	.317	0	ø	0	138	-5	58	-0.5
1975	LA N	0	1	.000	2	2	0	0-0	6	11	9	2	0	5-1	1	13.50	25	.407	.500	2	.000	-0	154	-7	0	-0.8
Total	16	243	142	.631	471	457	244-52	2-0	3507	3153	1329	320	40	709-82	2303	2.89	122	.237	.277	1221-4-71	.165	10	116	236	58	27.7
Marion, Dan	Donald George "Rube"; B7.31.1889 Bowling Green OH; D1.18.1933 Milwaukee WI; BR/TR/6´1˝/187; d4.23																									
1914	Bro F	3	2	.600	17	9	4	0	89.1	97	52	1	6	38	41	3.93	73	.281	.362	36	.194	-1	125	-11	—	-0.8
1915	Bro F	12	9	.571	35	25	15-2	0	208.1	193	92	1	3	64	46	3.20	85	.248	.308	74-0-2	.176	-1	147	-9	—	-1.1
Total	2	15	11	.577	52	34	19-2	0	297.2	290	144	2	9	102	87	3.42	81	.258	.325	110-0-2	.182	-2	140	-20	—	-1.9
Markell, Duke	Harry Duquesne (b Harry Duquesne Makowsky); B8.17.1923 Paris, France; D6.14.1984 Ft.Lauderdale FL; BR/TR/6´1.5˝/209; d9.6																									
1951	StL A	1	1	.500	5	2	1	0	21.1	25	16	3	0	20	10	6.33	69	.298	.433	6	.167	-0	81	-4	0	-0.3
Markle, Cliff	Clifford Monroe; B5.3.1894 Dravosburg PA; D5.24.1974 Temple City CA; BR/TR/5´9˝/163; d9.18																									
1915	NY A	2	0	1.000	3	2	2	0	23	15	3	1	0	6	12	0.39	750	.185	.241	4-0-1	.000	0	124	6	—	0.5
1916	NY A	4	3	.571	11	7	3-1	0	45.2	41	26	0	4	31	14	4.53	64	.256	.390	13-0-1	.000	-1	138	-7	—	-1.2
1921	Cin N	2	6	.250	10	6	5	0	67	75	36	0	0	20	23	3.76	95	.291	.342	24	.125	-2	69	-2	—	-0.4
1922	Cin N	4	5	.444	25	3	2-1	0	75.2	75	41	3	0	33	34	3.81	105	.268	.345	20	.150	-0	95	1	—	0.1
1924	NY A	0	3	.000	7	3	0	0	23.1	29	26	5	0	20	7	8.87	47	.333	.458	8	.000	-1	95	-12	—	-1.4
Total	5	12	17	.414	56	21	12-2	0	234.2	235	132	9	4	110	90	4.10	87	.271	.356	69-0-2	.087	-5	99	-14	—	-2.4
Marlowe, Dick	Richard Burton; B6.27.1929 Hickory NC; D12.30.1968 Toledo OH; BR/TR/6´2˝/170; d9.19; Col Davidson																									
1951	Det A	0	1	.000	2	1	0	0	1.2	5	6	0	0	2	1	32.40	13	.500	.583	0	ø	0	21	-5	0	-0.8
1952	Det A	0	2	.000	4	1	0	0	11	21	10	1	0	3	3	7.36	52	.420	.453	2	.000	-0	23	-4	0	-0.7
1953	Det A	6	7	.462	42	11	2	0	119.2	152	74	13	2	42	52	5.26	77	.319	.377	32-0-1	.219	-0	77	-14	0	-1.4
1954	Det A	5	4	.556	38	2	0	2	84	76	45	11	0	40	39	4.18	88	.244	.326	18	.167	0	60	-5	0	-0.5
1955	Det A	1	0	1.000	4	1	1	1	15	12	4	1	0	4-1	9	1.80	213	.218	.271	4	.000	-0	231	3	0	0.2
1956	Det A	1	1	.500	7	1	0	0	11	12	8	1	0	9-0	4	5.73	72	.279	.404	1	.000	-0	43	-2	0	-0.3
	Chi A	0	0	ø	1	0	0	0	1	2	1	1	0	1-0	0	9.00	46	.500	.600	0	ø	0	—	-1	0	0.0
	Year	1	1	.500	8	1	0	0	12	14	9	2	0	10-0	4	6.00	69	.298	.421	1	.000	-0	43	-3	0	-0.3
Total	6	13	15	.464	98	17	3	3	243.1	280	148	28	2	101-1	108	4.99	78	.295	.362	57-0-1	.175	-1	77	-28	0	-3.5
Marmol, Carlos	Carlos Agustin; B10.14.1982 Bonao, D.R.; BR/TR/6´2˝/180; d6.4																									
2006	Chi N	5	7	.417	19	13	0	0-0	77	71	54	14	5	59-2	59	6.08	75	.250	.386	23-1-1	.261	2*	85	-11	16	-1.3
Marone, Lou	Louis Stephen; B12.3.1945 San Diego CA; BR/TL/5´11˝/185; d5.30; Col San Diego Mesa (CA) JC																									
1969	Pit N	1	1	.500	29	0	0	0-1	35.1	24	10	2	2	13-2	25	2.55	137	.195	.281	0	ø	0	—	4	0	0.2
1970	Pit N	0	0	ø	1	0	0	0-0	2.1	2	1	1	0	0-0	0	3.86	103	.222	.222	0	ø	0	—	0	0	0.0
Total	2	1	1	.500	30	0	0	0-1	37.2	26	11	3	2	13-2	25	2.63	134	.197	.277	0	ø	0	—	4	0	0.2
Maroth, Mike	Michael Warren; B8.17.1977 Orlando FL; BL/TL/6´0˝/(180–190); [BosA98 3/85]; d6.8; Col Central Florida																									
2002	Det A	6	10	.375	21	21	0	0-0	128.2	136	68	7	2	36-1	58	4.48	98	.276	.326	6	.167	-0	70	0	0	0.0
2003	Det A	9	21	.300	33	33	1	0-0	193.1	231	131	34	8	50-2	87	5.73	77	.299	.344	2-0-1	.500	1	99	-28	0	-3.4
2004	Det A	11	13	.458	33	33	2-1	0-0	217	244	112	25	7	59-1	108	4.31	104	.288	.338	4-0-1	.000	-0	98	4	0	0.4
2005	Det A	14	14	.500	34	34	0	0-0	209	235	123	30	9	51-1	115	4.74	90	.288	.333	4-0-1	.500	1*	97	-12	0	-1.3

YEAR	TM LG	W	L	PCT	G	GS	CG-SHO	SV-BS	IP	H	R	HR	HB	BB-IB	SO	ERA	AERA	OAV	OOB	AB-HR-SH	AVG	PB	SUP	APR	DL	PW
2006	Det A	5	2	.714	13	9	0	0-0	53.2	64	26	11	1	16-1	24	4.19	107	.295	.346	0	ø	0	86	2	103	0.3
Total	5	45	60	.429	134	130	3-1	0-0	801.2	910	460	107	27	212-6	392	4.78	92	.289	.337	16-0-3	.250	1	93	-34	103	-4.0
Marquard, Rube	Richard William; B10.9.1886 Cleveland OH; D6.1.1980 Baltimore MD; BB/TL/6´3˝/180; d9.25; HF1971																									
1908	NY N	0	1	.000	1	1	0	0	5	6	5	0	1	2	2	3.60	67	.316	.409	1	.000	-0	29	-1	—	-0.3
1909	NY N	5	13	.278	29	21	8	1	173	155	81	2	9	73	109	2.60	98	.248	.335	54-0-3	.148	-1	76	-3	—	-0.5
1910	NY N	4	4	.500	13	8	2	0	70.2	65	35	2	4	40	52	4.46	67	.254	.363	27-0-2	.111	-2	122	-7	—	-0.9
1911	†NY N	24	7	**.774**	45	33	22-5	3	277.2	221	98	9	4	106	**237**	2.50	135	.219	.296	104-1-3	.163	-1	110	28	—	2.7
1912	†NY N	**26**	11	.703	43	38	22-1	1	294.2	286	112	9	3	80	175	2.57	132	.255	.306	96-0-9	.219	2	119	30	—	3.5
1913	†NY N	23	10	.697	42	33	20-4	3	288	248	100	10	3	49	151	2.50	125	.237	.273	105-0-2	.219	2	106	23	—	2.4
1914	NY N	12	22	.353	39	33	15-4	2	268	261	117	9	2	47	92	3.06	87	.262	.297	84-0-5	.179	-1	79	-14	—	-1.8
1915	NY N	9	8	.529	27	21	10-2	2	169	178	85	8	1	33	79	3.73	69	.272	.308	55-0-2	.109	-3	130	-21	—	-2.4
	Bro N	2	2	.500	6	3	0	1	24.2	29	17	0	0	5	13	6.20	45	.276	.309	8-0-1	.125	-0	80	-7	—	-1.1
	Year	11	10	.524	33	24	10-2	3	193.2	207	102	8	1	38	92	4.04	64	.273	.308	63-0-3	.111	-3	123	-27	—	-3.5
1916	†Bro N	13	6	.684	36	21	15-2	5	205	169	54	2	0	38	107	1.58	170	.229	.267	63-0-2	.143	-1	102	23	—	2.1
1917	Bro N	19	12	.613	37	29	14-2	0	232.2	200	84	5	0	60	117	2.55	110	.232	.282	75-0-3	.200	0	83	6	—	0.6
1918	Bro N	9	18	.333	34	29	19-4	0	239	231	97	7	1	59	89	2.64	106	.260	.307	76-0-1	.171	-2	80	2	—	-0.1
1919	Bro N	3	3	.500	8	7	3	0	59	54	17	1	0	10	29	2.29	130	.244	.277	23-0-1	.261	1	88	5	—	0.6
1920	†Bro N	10	7	.588	28	26	10-1	0	189.2	181	83	5	1	35	89	3.23	99	.251	.287	59-0-3	.169	-1	110	1	—	-0.3
1921	Cin N	17	14	.548	39	36	18-2	0	265.2	291	123	8	7	50	88	3.39	106	.285	.323	95-0-3	.200	-1	105	6	—	0.4
1922	Bos N	11	15	.423	39	25	7	1	198	255	131	12	0	66	57	5.09	79	.322	.374	63-0-3	.222	-1	71	-21	—	-2.3
1923	Bos N	11	14	.440	38	29	11-3	0	239	265	127	10	2	65	78	3.73	107	.288	.337	86-0-5	.140	-6	102	4	—	-0.2
1924	Bos N	1	2	.333	6	6	1	0	36	33	17	3	1	13	10	3.00	127	.254	.326	11	.273	0	70	2	—	0.2
1925	Bos N	2	8	.200	26	8	0	0	72	105	60	5	0	27	19	5.75	70	.341	.394	22	.136	-1	108	-17	—	-2.1
Total	18	201	177	.532	536	407	197-30	19	3306.2	3233	1443	107	39	858	1593	3.08	103	.260	.310	1107-1-48	.179	-17	99	39	—	0.5
Marquez, Isidro	Isidro (Espinoza); B5.15.1965 Navojoa, Sonora, Mexico; BR/TR/6´3˝/190; d4.26																									
1995	Chi A	0	1	.000	7	0	0	0-0	6.2	9	5	3	0	2-0	8	6.75	66	.321	.367	0	ø	0	—	-2	0	-0.2
Marquis, Jim	James Milburn; B11.18.1900 Yoakum TX; D8.5.1992 Jackson CA; BR/TR/5´11˝/174; d8.8																									
1925	NY A	0	0	ø	2	0	0	0	7.1	12	8	1	0	6	0	9.82	43	.414	.514	2	.000	-0	—	-4	—	-0.2
Marquis, Jason	Jason Scott; B8.21.1978 Manhasset NY; BL/TR/6´1˝/(185–210); [AtlN96 S1/35]; d6.6																									
2000	Atl N	1	0	1.000	15	0	0	0-1	23.1	23	16	4	1	12-1	17	5.01	90	.261	.353	2	.000	-0	—	-2	0	-0.1
2001	†Atl N	5	6	.455	38	16	0	0-2	129.1	113	62	14	4	59-4	98	3.48	124	.234	.320	31-0-2	.032	-2*	67	9	0	0.5
2002	Atl N	8	9	.471	22	22	0	0-0	114.1	127	66	19	3	49-3	84	5.04	80	.283	.356	38-1-3	.132	-0*	102	-11	26	-1.4
2003	Atl N	0	0	ø	21	2	0	1-0	40.2	43	27	3	2	18-2	19	5.53	76	.270	.346	2-0-2	.500	1	167	-6	0	-0.2
2004	†StL N	15	7	.682	32	32	0	0-0	201.1	215	90	26	10	70-1	138	3.71	115	.275	.339	72-0-2	.292	7*	119	13	0	2.0
2005	†StL N	13	14	.481	33	32	3-1	0-0	207	206	110	29	5	69-2	100	4.13	102	.262	.324	87-1-2	.310	11*	93	0	0	1.1
2006	StL N	14	16	.467	33	33	0	0-0	194.1	221	136	35	16	75-2	96	6.02	72	.289	.364	78-0-4	.179	3*	100	-37	0	-4.3
Total	7	56	52	.519	194	137	3-1	1-3	910.1	948	507	130	41	352-15	552	4.55	93	.270	.341	310-2-15	.223	18	100	-34	26	-2.4
Marrero, Connie	Conrado Eugenio (Ramos); B8.11.1911 Sagua La Grande, Cuba; BR/TR/5´5˝/(158–170); d4.21																									
1950	Was A	6	10	.375	27	19	8-1	1	152	159	84	17	4	55	63	4.50	100	.269	.335	49-0-5	.122	-1	85	1	0	-0.1
1951	Was A☆	11	9	.550	25	25	16-2	0	187	198	87	8	3	71	66	3.90	105	.268	.335	61-0-3	.164	-2	100	6	0	0.3
1952	Was A	11	8	.579	22	22	16-2	0	184.1	175	68	9	4	53	77	2.88	123	.249	.305	63-0-5	.079	-5	85	14	0	0.7
1953	Was A	8	7	.533	22	20	10-2	2	145.2	130	56	14	5	48	65	3.03	129	.241	.309	48-0-1	.125	-2	100	14	0	1.1
1954	Was A	3	6	.333	22	8	1	0	66.1	74	37	12	0	22	26	4.75	75	.287	.340	15	.000	-1	102	-8	0	-1.1
Total	5	39	40	.494	118	94	51-7	3	735.1	736	332	60	16	249	297	3.67	108	.260	.323	236-0-14	.114	-11	94	27	0	0.9
Marrow, Buck	Charles Kennon; B8.29.1909 Tarboro NC; D11.21.1982 Newport News VA; BR/TR/6´4˝/200; d7.3; Col Davidson																									
1932	Det A	2	5	.286	18	7	2	1	63.2	70	40	6	6	29	31	4.81	98	.278	.366	19-0-1	.158	-0	67	0	—	0.0
1937	Bro N	1	2	.333	6	3	1	0	16.1	19	13	2	0	9	2	6.61	61	.284	.368	5	.000	-1	107	-4	—	-0.7
1938	Bro N	0	1	.000	15	0	0	0	19.2	23	10	1	3	11	6	4.58	85	.291	.398	1	.000	-0	—	-1	—	0.0
Total	3	3	8	.273	39	10	3	1	99.2	112	63	9	9	49	39	5.06	88	.281	.373	25-0-1	.120	-1	79	-5	—	-0.7
Mars, Ed	Edward M.; B12.4.1866 Chicago IL; D12.9.1941 Chicago IL; 5´9˝/166; d8.12																									
1890	Syr AA	9	5	.643	16	14	14	0	121.1	132	80	2	5	49	59	4.67	76	.269	.341	51	.275	4	151	-14	—	-0.9
Marshall, Cuddles	Clarence Westly; B4.28.1925 Bellingham WA; BR/TR/6´3˝/200; d4.24; Col Western Washington																									
1946	NY A	3	4	.429	23	11	1	0	81	96	49	4	0	56	32	5.33	65	.308	.413	28-0-1	.143	-1	138	-14	0	-1.2
1948	NY A	0	0	ø	1	0	0	0	1	0	0	0	0	3	0	0.00	ø	.000	.500	0	ø	0	—	0	0	0.0
1949	NY A	3	0	1.000	21	2	0	3	49.1	48	31	3	2	48	13	5.11	79	.259	.417	9-0-1	.111	-0	100	-6	0	-0.4
1950	StL A	1	3	.250	28	2	0	1	53.2	72	52	1	1	51	24	7.88	63	.321	.449	12	.333	0	118	-15	0	-1.0
Total	4	7	7	.500	73	15	1	4	185	216	132	8	3	158	69	5.98	67	.298	.426	49-0-2	.184	-1	121	-35	0	-2.6
Marshall, Mike	Michael Grant; B1.15.1943 Adrian MI; BR/TR/5´10˝/(180–185); d5.31																									
1967	Det A	1	3	.250	37	0	0	10	59	51	15	6	2	20-1	41	1.98	165	.233	.303	9-0-2	.222	0	—	8	0	0.9
1969	Sea A	3	10	.231	20	14	3-1	0-0	87.2	99	54	8	2	35-2	47	5.13	71	.281	.347	27-1-1	.259	3*	87	-13	0	-1.3
1970	Hou N	0	1	.000	4	0	0	0-0	5.1	8	5	0	1	4-0	5	8.44	46	.400	.520	0	ø	0	—	-3	0	-0.4
	Mon N	3	7	.300	24	5	0	3-0	64.2	56	34	4	0	29-4	38	3.48	119	.225	.305	11-0-2	.091	0	86	2	0	0.4
	Year	3	8	.273	28	5	0	3-0	70	64	39	4	1	33-4	43	3.86	107	.238	.322	11-0-2	.091	0	87	0	0	0.0
1971	Mon N	5	8	.385	66	0	0	23-7	111.1	100	56	9	4	50-13	85	4.28	83	.247	.333	16-0-2	.188	0	—	-7	0	-1.0
1972	Mon N	14	8	.636	**65**	0	0	18-7	116	82	26	3	2	47-7	95	1.78	199	.202	.286	22	.136	0	—	**22**	0	4.9
1973	Mon N	14	11	.560	**92**	0	0	**31**-12	179	163	62	10	4	75-12	124	2.66	143	.252	.331	33-0-4	.242	1	—	**22**	0	4.1
1974	†LA N★	15	12	.556	**106**	0	0	**21**-12	208.1	191	66	9	1	56-1	143	2.42	142	.247	.297	34-0-2	.235	1	—	**24**	0	3.7
1975	LA N☆	9	14	.391	57	0	0	13-8	109.1	98	46	8	4	39-4	64	3.29	104	.242	.311	15-0-4	.067	-1*	—	1	27	0.2
1976	LA N	4	3	.571	30	0	0	8-5	62.2	64	33	2	1	25-2	39	4.45	76	.270	.340	5	.000	0	—	-7	0	-0.8
	Atl N	2	1	.667	24	0	0	6-2	36.2	35	15	4	1	14-0	17	3.19	119	.259	.329	6-0-1	.167	0	—	2	34	0.3
	Year	6	4	.600	54	0	0	14-7	99.1	99	48	6	2	39-2	56	3.99	89	.266	.336	11-0-1	.091	1	—	-4	0	-0.5
1977	Atl N	1	0	1.000	4	0	0	0-0	6	12	6	1	0	2-0	6	9.00	49	.400	.438	1	1.000	0	—	-2	0	-0.3
	Tex A	2	2	.500	12	4	0	1-3	35.2	42	19	0	2	13-1	18	4.04	101	.304	.373	0	ø	0	171	0	97	0.0
1978	Min A	10	12	.455	54	0	0	21-6	99	80	31	3	1	37-1	56	2.45	156	.225	.299	0	ø	0	—	15	0	3.2
1979	Min A	10	15	.400	**90**	1	0	**32**-10	142.2	132	47	8	4	48-2	81	2.65	166	.254	.319	0	ø	0	62	26	0	5.4
1980	Min A	1	3	.250	18	0	0	1-2	32.1	42	23	2	2	12-1	13	6.12	71	.323	.381	0	ø	0	—	-5	0	-0.5
1981	NY N	3	2	.600	20	0	0	0-0	31	26	10	2	0	8-1	8	2.61	135	.224	.272	0	ø	0	—	3	0	0.6
Total	14	97	112	.464	723	24	3-1	188-74	1386.2	1281	548	79	31	514-52	880	3.14	119	.249	.319	179-1-18	.196	6	103	88	158	19.4
Marshall, Rube	Roy De Verne "Cy"; B7.19.1890 Salineville OH; D6.11.1980 Dover OH; BR/TR/5´11˝/170; d9.28																									
1912	Phi N	0	1	.000	2	1	0	0	3	12	11	0	0	1	2	21.00	17	.632	.650	0	ø	0	40	-6	—	-0.9
1913	Phi N	0	1	.000	14	1	0	1	45.1	54	29	2	1	22	18	4.57	73	.297	.376	11	.091	-1	45	-6	—	-0.4
1914	Phi N	6	7	.462	27	17	7	1	134.1	144	77	2	5	50	49	3.75	78	.279	.349	43-0-3	.140	-2	123	-10	—	-1.1
1915	Buf F	2	1	.667	21	4	2	0	59.1	62	34	1	2	33	21	3.94	71	.281	.379	17-0-1	.294	1*	100	-8	—	-0.4
Total	4	8	10	.444	64	23	9	2	242	272	151	5	8	106	90	4.17	72	.290	.367	71-0-4	.169	-2	112	-30	—	-2.8
Marshall, Sean	Sean Christopher; B8.30.1982 Richmond VA; BL/TL/6´7˝/205; [ChiN03 6/163]; d4.9; Col Virginia Commonwealth																									
2006	Chi N	6	9	.400	24	24	0	0-0	125.2	132	85	20	7	59-3	77	5.59	82	.270	.356	40-1-3	.125	-0	96	-13	40	-1.4
Marsonek, Sam	Samuel R.; B7.10.1978 Tampa FL; BR/TR/6´6˝/225; [TexA96 1/24]; d7.11																									
2004	NY A	0	0	ø	1	0	0	0-0	1.1	2	0	0	0	0-0	0	0.00	ø	.333	.333	0	ø	0	—	1	81	0.0
Marte, Damaso	Damaso (Sabinon); B2.14.1975 Santo Domingo, D.R.; BL/TL/6´0˝/(170–210); d6.30																									
1999	Sea A	0	1	.000	5	0	0	0-0	8.2	16	9	3	0	6-0	3	9.35	51	.390	.468	0	ø	0	—	-4	0	-0.4
2001	Pit N	0	1	.000	23	0	0	0-0	36.1	34	21	5	3	12-3	39	4.71	95	.250	.320	4	.000	-0	—	-1	0	-0.1
2002	Chi A	1	1	.500	68	0	0	10-2	60.1	44	19	5	4	18-2	72	2.83	159	.204	.276	1	.000	-0	—	12	0	0.7
2003	Chi A	4	2	.667	71	0	0	11-7	79.2	50	16	3	3	34-6	87	1.58	290	.185	.280	0	ø	0	—	**26**	0	2.4

YEAR	TM LG	W	L	PCT	G	GS	CG-SHO	SV-BS	IP	H	R	HR	HB	BB-IB	SO	ERA	AERA	OAV	OOB	AB-HR-SH	AVG	PB	SUP	APR	DL	PW
2004	Chi A	6	5	.545	74	0	0	6-6	73.2	56	28	10	3	34-4	68	3.42	137	.217	.309	0	ø	0	—	11	0	1.6
2005	†Chi A	3	4	.429	66	0	0	4-4	45.1	45	21	5	3	33-4	54	3.77	120	.256	.382	0	ø	0	—	3	17	0.5
2006	Pit N	1	7	.125	75	0	0	0-4	58.1	51	30	5	4	31-6	63	3.70	124	.244	.348	2	.000	-0	—	4	0	0.5
Total	7	15	21	.417	382	0	0	31-23	362.1	296	144	36	20	168-25	386	3.28	140	.226	.321	7	.000	-1	—	51	17	5.2
MARTIN, PHONNEY	Alphonse Case; B8.4.1845 New York NY; D5.24.1933 Hollis NY; 5´7˝/148; d4.26; M1; ▲																									
1872	Tro NA	1	2	.333	8	3	0	0	37.1	70	59	0	—	2	2	4.82	76	.350	.356	119	.303	1*	95	-5	—	-0.2
	Eck NA	2	7	.222	10	9	9	0	85	143	106	1	—	9	3	3.92	87	.326	.339	78	.192	-1*	59	-7	—	-0.5
	Year	3	9	.250	18	12	9	0	122.1	213	165	1	—	11	5	4.19	83	.333	.345	197	.259	-1	68	-14	—	-0.7
1873	Mut NA	0	1	.000	6	1	1	0	34	50	37	0	—	6	1	3.44	96	.292	.316	140	.221	-0*	113	-1	—	-0.1
Total	2NA	3	10	.231	24	13	10	0	156.1	263	202	1	—	17	6	4.03	85	.325	.339	337	.243	-1	72	-13	—	-0.8
MARTIN, BARNEY	Barnes Robertson; B3.3.1923 Columbia SC; D10.30.1997 Columbia SC; BR/TR/5´11˝/170; d4.22; s–Jerry																									
1953	Cin N	0	0	ø	1	0	0	0	2	3	2	0	0	1	1	9.00	48	.333	.400	0	ø	0	—	-1	0	0.0
MARTIN, RENIE	Donald Renie; B8.30.1955 Dover DE; BR/TR/6´4˝/(184–190); [KCA77 19/486]; d5.9; Col Richmond																									
1979	KC A	0	3	.000	25	0	0	5-2	34.2	32	20	1	1	14-3	25	5.19	82	.248	.322	0	ø	0	—	-2	0	-0.2
1980	†KC A	10	10	.500	32	20	2	2-0	137.1	133	84	18	1	70-2	68	4.39	92	.255	.342	0	ø	0	116	-9	0	-1.2
1981	†KC A	4	5	.444	29	0	0	4-1	61.2	55	25	2	0	29-7	25	2.77	130	.244	.322	0	ø	0	—	4	0	0.7
1982	SF N	7	10	.412	29	25	1	0-0	141.1	148	91	14	0	64-9	63	4.65	77	.274	.347	49-0-6	.265	3*	119	-20	0	-1.8
1983	SF N	2	4	.333	37	6	0	1-0	94.1	95	50	11	3	51-9	43	4.20	85	.268	.363	26-0-1	.346	4	108	-6	0	0.1
1984	SF N	1	1	.500	12	0	0	0-1	23.1	29	13	2	0	16-0	8	3.86	92	.305	.405	6	.500	1	—	-2	0	0.0
	Phi N	0	2	.000	9	0	0	0-1	15.2	17	12	2	0	12-4	5	4.60	80	.274	.392	2	.000	-0	—	-3	0	-0.3
	Year	1	3	.250	21	0	0	0-2	39	46	25	4	0	28-4	13	4.15	86	.293	.400	8	.375	1	—	-4	0	-0.3
Total	6	24	35	.407	173	51	3	12-5	508.1	509	295	50	5	256-34	237	4.27	88	.264	.348	83-0-7	.301	8	117	-38	0	-2.7
MARTIN, SPEED	Elwood Good; B9.15.1893 Wawawai WA; D6.14.1983 Lemon Grove CA; BR/TR/6´0˝/165; d7.5																									
1917	StL A	0	2	.000	9	2	0	0	15.2	20	13	0	0	5	5	5.74	45	.339	.391	2	.000	-0*	125	-5	—	-0.6
1918	Chi N	5	2	.714	9	5	4-1	1	53.2	47	19	0	1	14	16	1.84	151	.246	.301	16-0-1	.188	-0	54	4	—	0.6
1919	Chi N	8	8	.500	35	14	7-2	2	163.2	158	58	2	4	52	54	2.47	117	.259	.321	44-0-5	.182	-1	95	8	—	0.8
1920	Chi N	4	15	.211	35	13	6	2	136	165	96	2	1	50	44	4.83	66	.305	.365	44-1-1	.159	-0	102	-26	—	-3.3
1921	Chi N	11	15	.423	37	28	13-1	1	217.1	245	115	12	2	68	86	4.35	88	.298	.353	73-0-2	.233	1	91	-10	—	-0.8
1922	Chi N	1	0	1.000	1	1	0	0	6	10	5	0	0	2	2	7.50	56	.385	.429	1	.000	0	136	-2	—	-0.2
Total	6	29	42	.408	126	63	30-4	6	592.1	645	306	16	8	191	207	3.78	87	.287	.344	180-1-9	.194	-0	95	-31	—	-3.5
MARTIN, FRED	Fred Turner; B6.27.1915 Williams OK; D6.11.1979 Chicago IL; BR/TR/6´1˝/185; d4.21; C6																									
1946	StL N	2	1	.667	6	3	2	0	28.2	29	13	0	0	8	19	4.08	85	.254	.303	11	.273	0	149	-1	0	-0.1
1949	StL N	6	0	1.000	21	5	3	0	70	65	24	3	0	20	30	2.44	170	.243	.295	20-0-1	.300	1	144	12	0	1.0
1950	StL N	4	2	.667	30	2	0	0	63.1	87	43	4	1	30	19	5.12	84	.331	.401	15-0-1	.267	1*	31	-7	0	-0.4
Total	3	12	3	.800	57	10	5	0	162	181	80	7	1	58	68	3.78	108	.281	.341	46-0-2	.283	2	118	4	0	0.5
MARTIN, DOC	Harold Winthrop; B9.23.1887 Roxbury MA; D4.14.1935 Milton MA; BR/TR/5´11˝/165; d10.7; Col Tufts																									
1908	Phi A	0	1	.000	1	1	0	0	2	2	4	0	1	3	2	13.50	19	.286	.545	1	.000	-0	27	-2	—	-0.4
1911	Phi A	1	1	.500	11	3	1	0	38	40	26	1	5	17	21	4.50	70	.272	.367	14	.214	0	145	-7	—	-0.3
1912	Phi A	0	0	ø	2	0	0	0	4.1	5	5	0	1	5	4	10.38	30	.333	.524	3	.000	-1	—	-3	—	-0.2
Total	3	1	2	.333	14	4	1	0	44.1	47	35	1	7	25	27	5.48	57	.278	.393	18	.167	-0	115	-12	—	-0.9
MARTIN, JOHN	John Robert; B4.11.1956 Wyandotte MI; BB/TL/6´0˝/190; [DetA78 27/637]; d8.27; Col Eastern Michigan																									
1980	StL N	2	3	.400	9	5	1	0-0	42	39	20	1	0	9-1	23	4.29	88	.247	.284	11	.273	1	76	-1	0	-0.1
1981	StL N	8	5	.615	17	15	4	0-0	102.2	85	43	10	2	26-0	36	3.42	106	.228	.281	33-0-7	.212	2*	118	2	0	0.5
1982	StL N	4	5	.444	24	7	0	0-1	66	56	33	6	0	30-3	21	4.23	87	.230	.314	11-0-2	.091	-0	103	-3	0	-0.5
1983	StL N	3	1	.750	26	5	0	0-0	66.1	60	31	6	2	26-4	29	3.53	104	.242	.315	18-0-2	.222	1	145	0	0	0.1
	Det A	0	0	ø	15	0	0	1-0	13.1	15	11	2	0	4-1	11	7.43	53	.294	.339	0	ø	0	—	-5	0	-0.2
Total	4	17	14	.548	91	32	5	1-1	290.1	255	138	25	4	95-9	120	3.94	93	.238	.300	73-0-11	.205	3	112	-7	0	-0.2
MARTIN, MORRIE	Morris Webster "Lefty"; B9.3.1922 Dixon MO; BL/TL/6´0˝/(175–180); d4.25																									
1949	Bro N	1	3	.250	10	4	0	0	30.2	39	25	5	2	15	15	7.04	58	.320	.403	10	.200	-0	43	-9	0	-1.0
1951	Phi A	11	4	.733	35	13	3-1	0	138	139	70	13	5	63	35	3.78	113	.259	.343	50-0-4	.220	-1	136	5	0	0.5
1952	Phi A	0	2	.000	5	5	0	0	25.1	32	19	1	2	15	13	6.39	62	.302	.398	9	.111	-1	97	-6	30	-0.5
1953	Phi A	10	12	.455	58	11	2	7	156.1	158	85	12	8	59	64	4.43	97	.262	.336	42-0-2	.095	-4	85	-3	0	-0.8
1954	Phi A	2	4	.333	13	6	2	0	52.2	57	32	9	2	19	24	5.47	71	.278	.339	17-0-1	.235	0	49	-7	0	-0.7
	Chi A	5	4	.556	35	2	1	5	70	52	18	5	1	24	31	2.06	182	.210	.281	15-0-2	.133	-0	106	13	0	1.7
	Year	7	8	.467	48	8	3	5	122.2	109	50	14	3	43	55	3.52	108	.241	.308	32-0-3	.188	-0	64	6	0	1.0
1955	Chi A	2	3	.400	37	0	0	2	52	50	27	4	2	20-2	22	3.63	109	.259	.332	10	.300	0	—	0	0	0.1
1956	Chi A	1	0	1.000	10	0	0	0	18.1	21	10	1	0	7-0	9	4.91	84	.292	.350	5	.200	0	—	-1	0	0.0
	Bal A	1	1	.500	9	0	0	0	5	10	6	1	1	2-0	3	10.80	36	.400	.464	0	ø	0	—	-4	0	-0.7
	Year	2	1	.667	19	0	0	0	23.1	31	16	2	1	9-0	12	6.17	66	.320	.380	5	.200	0	—	-5	0	-0.7
1957	StL N	0	0	ø	4	1	0	0	10.2	5	3	0	1	4-0	7	2.53	157	.143	.244	2	.000	-0	89	2	0	0.1
1958	StL N	3	1	.750	17	0	0	0	24.2	19	13	3	2	12-0	16	4.74	87	.211	.317	5	.000	-1	—	-1	0	-0.2
	Cle A	2	0	1.000	14	0	0	1	18.2	20	7	0	0	8-0	5	2.41	151	.294	.364	0	ø	0	—	2	0	0.2
1959	Chi N	0	0	ø	3	0	0	0	2.1	5	5	2	1	1-0	1	19.29	20	.455	.538	0	ø	0	—	-4	0	-0.2
Total	10	38	34	.528	250	42	8-1	15	604.2	607	320	56	27	249-2	245	4.29	95	.262	.340	165-0-9	.170	-6	96	-13	30	-1.5
MARTIN, PAT	Patrick Francis; B4.13.1892 Brooklyn NY; D2.4.1949 Brooklyn NY; BL/TL/5´11.5˝/170; d9.20																									
1919	Phi A	0	2	.000	2	2	1	0	11	11	8	0	0	8	6	4.09	84	.256	.373	3	.000	-0	23	-1	—	-0.3
1920	Phi A	1	4	.200	8	5	2	0	32.1	48	36	2	4	25	14	6.12	66	.364	.478	10-0-2	.400	1	71	-9	—	-1.1
Total	2	1	6	.143	10	7	3	0	43.1	59	44	2	4	33	20	5.61	69	.337	.453	13-0-2	.308	1	58	-10	—	-1.4
MARTIN, PAUL	Paul Charles; B3.10.1932 Brownstown PA; BR/TR/6´6˝/235; d7.2																									
1955	Pit N	0	1	.000	7	1	0	0	7	13	12	0	1	17-0	3	14.14	29	.464	.633	0	ø	0	22	-7	0	-0.9
MARTIN, RAY	Raymond Joseph; B3.13.1925 Norwood MA; BR/TR/6´2˝/177; d8.15; Mil 1943–46																									
1943	Bos N	0	0	ø	2	0	0	0	3.1	3	3	0	0	1	1	8.10	42	.231	.286	1	.000	-0	—	-1	0	-0.1
1947	Bos N	1	0	1.000	1	1	1	0	9	7	1	0	0	4	2	1.00	389	.212	.297	3	.000	-0	45	3	0	0.4
1948	Bos N	0	0	ø	2	0	0	0	2.1	0	0	0	0	1	0	0.00	ø	.000	.125	0	ø	0	—	1	0	0.0
Total	3	1	0	1.000	5	1	1	0	14.2	10	4	0	0	6	3	2.45	154	.189	.271	4	.000	-0	45	3	0	0.3
MARTIN, TOM	Thomas Edgar; B5.21.1970 Charleston SC; BL/TL/6´1˝/(200–205); [BalA88 6/139]; d4.2																									
1997	†Hou N	5	3	.625	55	0	0	2-1	56	52	13	2	1	23-2	36	2.09	192	.254	.330	3	.000	-0	—	13	16	1.7
1998	Cle A	1	1	.500	14	0	0	0-0	14.2	29	21	3	0	12-0	9	12.89	37	.408	.488	0	ø	0	—	-12	38	-1.3
1999	Cle A	0	1	.000	6	0	0	0-0	9.1	13	9	2	0	3-1	8	8.68	59	.325	.364	0	ø	0	—	-3	126	-0.3
2000	Cle A	1	0	1.000	31	0	0	0-0	33.1	32	16	3	1	15-2	21	4.05	124	.254	.336	0	ø	0	—	3	51	0.2
2001	NY N	1	0	1.000	14	0	0	0-0	17	23	22	4	1	10-2	12	10.06	40	.319	.405	3	.000	-0	—	-13	95	-0.7
2002	TB A	0	0	ø	2	0	0	0-0	1.2	5	3	0	0	1-0	1	16.20	28	.500	.545	0	ø	0	—	-2	160	-0.1
2003	LA N	1	2	.333	80	0	0	0-1	51	36	21	6	2	24-4	51	3.53	117	.198	.295	1	.000	-0	—	4	0	0.2
2004	LA N	0	1	.000	47	0	0	1-0	28.1	32	13	3	3	14-1	18	4.13	100	.291	.380	0	ø	0	—	0	0	0.0
	†Atl N	0	1	.000	29	0	0	0-3	17	17	7	4	0	5-2	12	3.71	116	.270	.314	0	ø	0	—	1	0	0.1
	Year	0	2	.000	76	0	0	1-3	45.1	49	20	7	3	19-3	30	3.97	106	.283	.357	0	ø	0	—	2	0	0.1
2005	Atl N	0	0	ø	4	0	0	0-0	2.1	6	5	1	0	2-0	0	19.29	22	.500	.571	0	ø	0	—	-4	0	-0.2
2006	Col N	2	0	1.000	68	0	0	0-1	60.1	62	37	4	4	25-5	46	5.07	95	.264	.343	4	.000	-0	—	-2	0	-0.1
Total	10	11	9	.550	350	0	0	3-6	291	307	167	32	12	134-19	214	4.92	90	.273	.353	11	.000	-1	—	-15	486	-0.5
MARTINA, JOE	Joseph John "Oyster Joe"; B7.8.1889 New Orleans LA; D3.22.1962 New Orleans LA; BR/TR/6´0˝/183; d4.19																									
1924	†Was A	6	8	.429	24	14	8	0	125.1	129	69	7	6	56	57	4.67	86	.271	.355	43-0-1	.326	3*	94	-5	—	-0.3

YEAR	TM LG	W	L	PCT	G	GS	CG-SHO	SV-BS	IP	H	R	HR	HB	BB-IB	SO	ERA	AERA	OAV	OOB	AB-HR-SH	AVG	PB	SUP	APR	DL	PW
Martinez, Alfredo	Alfredo; B3.15.1957 Los Angeles CA; BR/TR/6´3˝/190; [NYN77 5/120]; d4.20; Col Cal St.–Los Angeles																									
1980	Cal A	7	9	.438	30	23	4-1	0-0	149.1	150	81	14	1	59-2	57	4.52	88	.259	.326	0	ø	0	96	-8	0	-0.9
1981	Cal A	0	0	ø	2	0	0	0-0	6	5	2	1	0	3-0	4	3.00	122	.227	.320	0	ø	0	—	1	0	0.0
Total	2	7	9	.438	32	23	4-1	0-0	155.1	155	83	15	1	62-2	61	4.46	88	.257	.326	0	ø	0	96	-7	0	-0.9
Martinez, Anastacio	Anastacio Euclides; B11.3.1978 Santa Cruz de Villomello, D.R.; BR/TR/6´2˝/180; d5.22																									
2004	Bos A	2	1	.667	11	0	0	0-0	10.2	13	10	2	1	6-0	5	8.44	58	.289	.385	0	ø	0	—	-3	0	-0.6
Martinez, Carlos	Carlos M.; B2.21.1986 Caracas, Venezuela; BR/TR/6´2˝/170; d4.3																									
2006	Fla N	0	1	.000	12	0	0	0-0	10.1	9	2	0	0	6-0	11	1.74	246	.250	.341	0	ø	0	—	3	147	0.3
Martinez, Tippy	Felix Anthony; B5.31.1950 LaJunta CO; BL/TL/5´10˝/(170–180); d8.9; Col Colorado St.; [DL 1987 Bal A 59]																									
1974	NY A	0	0	ø	10	0	0	0-0	12.2	14	7	0	1	9-2	10	4.26	83	.286	.400	0	ø	0	—	-1	0	-0.1
1975	NY A	1	2	.333	23	2	0	8-0	37	27	15	2	1	32-3	20	2.68	139	.208	.364	0	ø	0	36	3	0	0.4
1976	NY A	2	0	1.000	11	0	0	2-0	28	18	6	1	0	14-0	14	1.93	177	.191	.296	0	ø	0	—	5	0	0.5
	Bal A	3	1	.750	28	0	0	8-0	41.2	32	13	0	1	28-3	31	2.59	127	.222	.349	0	ø	0	—	4	0	0.6
	Year	5	1	.833	39	0	0	10-0	69.2	50	19	1	1	42-3	45	2.33	144	.210	.329	0	ø	0	—	9	0	1.1
1977	Bal A	5	1	.833	**41**	0	0	9-2	50	47	17	2	0	27-2	29	2.70	142	.266	.359	0	ø	0	—	6	0	1.0
1978	Bal A	3	3	.500	42	0	0	5-3	69	77	41	4	1	40-2	57	4.83	73	.281	.373	0	ø	0*	—	-10	0	-0.9
1979	†Bal A	10	3	.769	39	0	0	3-4	78	59	29	0	1	31-4	61	2.88	140	.210	.288	0	ø	0	—	10	0	1.6
1980	Bal A	4	4	.500	53	0	0	10-1	80.2	69	30	5	1	34-5	68	3.01	132	.240	.320	0	ø	0*	—	8	0	1.1
1981	Bal A	3	3	.500	37	0	0	11-3	59	48	21	4	0	32-6	50	2.90	126	.231	.329	0	ø	0	—	5	0	0.8
1982	Bal A	8	8	.500	76	0	0	16-7	95	81	39	6	1	37-5	78	3.41	119	.240	.312	0	ø	0	—	7	0	1.2
1983	†Bal A☆	9	3	.750	65	0	0	21-6	103.1	76	30	10	0	37-3	81	2.35	170	.211	.280	0	ø	0	—	19	22	3.0
1984	Bal A	4	9	.308	55	0	0	17-6	89.2	88	42	9	0	51-13	72	3.91	100	.260	.352	0	ø	0	—	1	0	0.2
1985	Bal A	3	3	.500	49	0	0	4-8	70	70	48	8	0	37-8	47	5.40	75	.261	.346	0	ø	0	—	-11	0	-0.9
1986	Bal A	0	2	.000	14	0	0	1-0	16	18	10	1	0	12-1	11	5.63	74	.295	.405	0	ø	0	—	-2	138	-0.3
1988	Min A	0	0	ø	3	0	0	0-0	4	8	9	1	1	4-0	3	18.00	23	.471	.542	0	ø	0	—	-6	0	-0.3
Total	14	55	42	.567	546	2	0	115-40	834	732	357	53	8	425-57	632	3.45	112	.242	.333	0	ø	0	36	38	219	7.9
Martinez, Javier	Javier Antonio; B2.5.1977 Bayamon, PR; BR/TR/6´2˝/210; [ChiN94 3/78]; d4.2; [DL 1999 Pit N 111]																									
1998	Pit N	0	1	.000	37	0	0	0-0	41	39	32	5	4	34-1	42	4.83	89	.248	.389	1	.000	-0	—	-5	0	-0.3
Martinez, Dennis	Jose Dennis (Emilia) "El Presidente"; B5.14.1955 Granada, Nicaragua; BR/TR/6´1˝/(168–185); d9.14																									
1976	Bal A	1	2	.333	4	2	1	0-0	27.2	23	8	1	0	8-0	18	2.60	127	.237	.295	0	ø	0	40	3	0	0.3
1977	Bal A	14	7	.667	42	13	5	4-1	166.2	157	86	10	8	64-5	107	4.10	94	.253	.327	0	ø	0	139	-7	0	-0.8
1978	Bal A	16	11	.593	40	38	15-2	0-0	276.1	257	121	20	3	93-4	142	3.52	100	.250	.312	0	ø	0	116	0	0	0.2
1979	†Bal A	15	16	.484	40	**39**	**18**-3	0-0	**292.1**	279	129	28	1	78-1	132	3.66	110	.253	.300	0	ø	0	88	15	0	1.6
1980	Bal A	6	4	.600	25	12	2	1-0	99.2	103	44	12	2	44-6	42	3.97	100	.272	.349	0	ø	0*	100	2	37	0.2
1981	Bal A	**14**	5	.737	25	24	9-2	0-0	179	173	84	10	2	62-1	88	3.32	110	.254	.316	0	ø	0	108	2	0	0.5
1982	Bal A	16	12	.571	40	39	10-2	0-0	252	262	123	30	7	87-2	111	4.21	96	.267	.329	0	ø	0	106	-3	0	-0.3
1983	Bal A	7	16	.304	32	25	4	0-1	153	209	108	21	2	45-0	71	5.53	72	.330	.374	0	ø	0	94	-28	0	-3.3
1984	Bal A	6	9	.400	34	20	2	0-0	141.2	145	81	26	5	37-2	77	5.02	78	.263	.312	0	ø	0	90	-14	0	-1.3
1985	Bal A	13	11	.542	33	31	3-1	0-0	180	203	110	29	9	63-3	68	5.15	79	.288	.349	0	ø	0	138	-21	0	-2.3
1986	Bal A	0	0	ø	4	0	0	0-0	6.2	11	5	0	0	2-0	2	6.75	62	.367	.394	0	ø	0	—	-2	49	-0.1
	Mon N	3	6	.333	19	15	1-1	0-0	98	103	52	11	3	28-4	63	4.59	82	.274	.328	30	.100	-1	71	-7	0	-0.6
1987	Mon N	11	4	.733	22	22	2-1	0-0	144.2	133	59	9	6	40-2	84	3.30	129	.244	.301	46-0-4	.065	-2	112	15	0	1.3
1988	Mon N	15	13	.536	34	34	9-2	0-0	235.1	215	94	21	6	55-3	120	2.72	134	.239	.286	78-0-10	.192	2	106	18	0	2.4
1989	Mon N	16	7	.696	34	33	5-2	0-0	232	227	88	21	7	49-4	142	3.18	112	.257	.300	72-0-9	.125	-1	111	11	0	1.1
1990	Mon N★	10	11	.476	32	32	7-2	0-0	226	191	80	16	6	49-9	156	2.95	125	.228	.274	68-0-12	.103	-2	106	19	0	1.5
1991	Mon N★	14	11	.560	31	31	**9-5**	0-0	222	187	70	9	4	62-3	123	**2.39**	**152**	.226	.282	72-0-10	.153	0*	86	30	0	3.6
1992	Mon N★	16	11	.593	32	32	6	0-0	226.1	172	75	12	9	60-3	147	2.47	141	.211	.271	74-0-10	.189	1	101	23	0	3.0
1993	Mon N	15	9	.625	35	34	2	1-0	224.2	211	110	27	11	64-7	138	3.85	109	.246	.306	69-0-9	.159	-0*	96	10	0	1.1
1994	Cle A	11	6	.647	24	24	7-3	0-0	176.2	166	75	14	7	44-2	92	3.52	135	.247	.298	0	ø	0	102	26	0	2.3
1995	†Cle A★	12	5	.706	28	28	3-2	0-0	187	174	71	17	12	46-2	99	3.08	153	.247	.302	0	ø	0	105	34	0	2.9
1996	Cle A	9	6	.600	20	20	1-1	0-0	112	122	63	12	2	37-2	48	4.50	109	.278	.335	0	ø	0	120	4	52	0.6
1997	Sea A	1	5	.167	9	9	0	0-0	49	65	46	8	7	29-1	17	7.71	59	.327	.424	0	ø	0	119	-18	0	-1.7
1998	†Atl N	4	6	.400	53	5	1-1	2-2	91	109	53	8	3	19-5	62	4.45	94	.295	.332	11-0-1	.091	-0	128	-4	0	-0.4
Total	23	245	193	.559	692	562	122-30	8-4	3999.2	3897	1835	372	122	1165-71	2149	3.70	107	.256	.312	520-0-65	.142	-3	105	108	138	11.8
Martinez, Jose	Jose Miguel (Martinez); B4.1.1971 Guayubin, D.R.; BR/TR/6´2˝/180; d5.10																									
1994	SD N	0	2	.000	4	1	0	0-0	12	18	9	2	0	5-2	7	6.75	61	.375	.434	2	.000	-0	0	-3	0	-0.4
Martinez, Luis	Luis; B1.20.1980 Santo Domingo, D.R.; BL/TL/6´6˝/200; d9.3																									
2003	Mil N	0	3	.000	4	4	0	0-0	16.1	25	18	3	0	15-2	10	9.92	44	.373	.488	4	.000	-0	109	-9	0	-1.3
Martinez, Pedro	Pedro (Aquino); B11.29.1968 Villa Mella, D.R.; BL/TL/6´2˝/(155–185); d6.29																									
1993	SD N	3	1	.750	32	0	0	0-1	37	23	11	4	1	13-1	32	2.43	170	.172	.250	4-0-2	.000	-0	—	7	0	0.6
1994	SD N	3	2	.600	48	1	0	3-2	68.1	52	31	4	1	49-9	52	2.90	143	.210	.341	5	.000	-1	176	7	0	0.5
1995	Hou N	0	0	ø	25	0	0	0-0	20.2	29	18	3	2	16-1	17	7.40	52	.330	.439	0	ø	0	—	-8	0	-0.4
1996	NY N	0	0	ø	5	0	0	0-0	7	8	7	1	0	7-4	6	6.43	63	.296	.429	0	ø	0	—	-3	0	-0.1
	Cin N	0	0	ø	4	0	0	0-0	3	5	2	1	0	1-0	3	6.00	71	.357	.400	0	ø	0	—	0	0	0.0
	Year	0	0	ø	9	0	0	0-0	10	13	9	2	0	8-4	9	6.30	65	.317	.420	0	ø	0	—	-3	0	-0.1
1997	Cin N	1	1	.500	8	0	0	0-0	6.2	8	9	1	1	7-0	4	9.45	45	.286	.432	0	ø	0	—	-4	0	-0.8
Total	5	7	4	.636	122	1	0	3-3	142.2	125	78	14	5	93-15	114	3.97	103	.232	.348	9-0-2	.000	-1	176	-1	0	-0.2
Martinez, Pedro	Pedro Jaime (b Pedro Jaime (Martinez)); B10.25.1971 Manoguayabo, D.R.; BR/TR/5´11˝/(150–180); d9.24; b–Ramon																									
1992	LA N	0	1	.000	2	1	0	0-0	8	6	2	0	0	1-0	8	2.25	154	.200	.226	2	.000	-0	26	1	0	0.1
1993	LA N	10	5	.667	65	2	0	2-1	107	76	34	5	4	57-4	119	2.61	148	.201	.309	4-0-2	.000	-0*	105	16	0	2.0
1994	Mon N	11	5	.688	24	23	1-1	1-0	144.2	115	58	11	11	45-3	142	3.42	124	.220	.294	44-0-5	.091	-1	99	14	0	1.3
1995	Mon N	14	10	.583	30	30	2-2	0-0	194.2	158	79	21	11	66-1	174	3.51	122	.227	.302	63-0-5	.111	-3	96	18	0	1.7
1996	Mon N★	13	10	.565	33	33	4-1	0-0	216.2	189	100	19	3	70-3	222	3.70	117	.232	.294	64-0-16	.094	-2	105	14	0	1.0
1997	Mon N★	17	8	.680	31	31	**13**-4	0-0	241.1	158	65	16	9	67-5	305	**1.90**	**220**	**.184**	**.249**	69-0-9	.116	-1	79	**58**	0	**5.8**
1998	†Bos A☆	19	7	.731	33	33	3-2	0-0	233.2	188	82	26	8	67-3	251	2.89	164	.217	.278	7	.000	-1	100	47	0	4.6
1999	†Bos A★	**23**	4	**.852**	31	29	5-1	0-0	213.1	160	56	9	9	37-1	**313**	**2.07**	**241**	**.205**	**.248**	2	.000	-0	103	**67**	15	**8.1**
2000	Bos A✷	18	6	.750	29	29	7-**4**	0-0	217	128	44	17	14	32-0	**284**	**1.74**	**288**	**.167**	**.213**	0	ø	0	84	**78**	16	**8.4**
2001	Bos A	7	3	.700	18	18	1	0-0	116.2	84	33	5	6	25-0	163	2.39	186	.199	.253	0	ø	0	85	27	90	2.1
2002	Bos A☆	20	4	**.833**	30	30	2	0-0	199.1	144	62	13	15	40-1	**239**	**2.26**	**198**	**.198**	**.254**	5-0-1	.000	-0	121	46	0	5.2
2003	†Bos A	14	4	.778	29	29	3	0-0	186.2	147	52	7	9	47-0	206	**2.22**	**210**	**.215**	**.272**	3	.000	-0	102	**49**	26	4.4
2004	†Bos A	16	9	.640	33	33	1-1	0-0	217	193	99	26	16	61-0	227	3.90	125	.238	.301	2	.000	-0	91	26	0	2.6
2005	NY N✷	15	8	.652	31	31	4-1	0-0	217	159	69	19	4	47-3	208	2.82	147	.204	**.252**	69-0-6	.087	-4	99	34	0	2.9
2006	NY N✷	9	8	.529	23	23	0	0-0	132.2	108	72	19	10	39-2	137	4.48	98	.220	.289	38-0-9	.105	-1	88	-1	60	-0.3
Total	15	206	92	.691	442	375	46-17	3-1	2645.2	2013	907	213	129	701-26	2998	2.81	160	.209	.270	372-0-53	.094	-13	97	494	207	49.9
Martinez, Ramon	Ramon Jaime (b Ramon Jaime (Martinez)); B3.22.1968 Santo Domingo, D.R.; BR/TR/6´4˝/(166–186); d8.13; b–Pedro																									
1988	LA N	1	3	.250	9	6	0	0-0	35.2	27	17	0	0	22-1	23	3.79	88	.216	.333	7-0-1	.000	-1	53	-2	0	-0.3
1989	LA N	6	4	.600	15	15	2-2	0-0	98.2	79	39	11	5	41-1	89	3.19	108	.219	.308	37-0-2	.162	0*	127	3	0	0.3
1990	LA N★	20	6	.769	33	33	**12**-3	0-0	234.1	191	89	22	4	67-5	223	2.92	126	.220	.278	80-0-9	.125	-2	121	20	0	1.9
1991	LA N	17	13	.567	33	33	6-4	0-0	220.1	190	89	18	7	69-4	150	3.27	110	.229	.293	77-1-8	.117	-1	111	9	0	1.0
1992	LA N	8	11	.421	25	25	1-1	0-0	150.2	141	82	11	5	69-4	101	4.00	87	.245	.331	50-0-5	.120	-2*	94	-11	0	-1.5
1993	LA N	10	12	.455	32	32	4-3	0-0	211.2	202	88	15	4	104-9	127	3.44	112	.255	.342	70-0-7	.129	-2	92	13	0	1.1
1994	LA N	12	7	.632	24	24	4-**3**	0-0	170	160	83	18	6	56-2	119	3.97	100	.249	.312	66-0-5	.273	5	123	-1	0	0.3
1995	†LA N	17	7	.708	30	30	4-2	0-0	206.1	176	95	19	5	81-5	138	3.66	106	.231	.308	64-0-13	.172	1	113	6	0	0.7
1996	†LA N	15	6	.714	28	27	2-2	0-0	168.2	153	76	12	8	86-5	133	3.42	115	.245	.341	59-0-8	.119	-2*	112	9	37	0.9
1997	LA N	10	5	.667	22	22	1	0-0	133.2	123	64	14	6	68-1	120	3.64	107	.243	.337	42-0-5	.190	1	123	2	66	0.3

YEAR	TM LG	W	L	PCT	G	GS	CG-SHO	SV-BS	IP	H	R	HR	HB	BB-IB	SO	ERA	AERA	OAV	OOB	AB-HR-SH	AVG	PB	SUP	APR	DL	PW
1998	LA N	7	3	.700	15	15	1	0-0	101.2	76	41	8	3	41-1	91	2.83	142	.206	.288	34-0-5	.176	1	90	12	105	1.2
1999	†Bos A	2	1	.667	4	4	0	0-0	20.2	14	8	2	2	8-0	15	3.05	163	.192	.286	0	ø	0	122	4	150	0.6
2000	Bos A	10	8	.556	27	27	0	0-0	127.2	143	94	16	9	67-3	89	6.13	82	.283	.372	5	.200	0	109	-15	31	-1.7
2001	Pit N	0	2	.000	4	4	0	0-0	15.2	16	15	4	2	16-0	9	8.62	52	.276	.442	5	.000	-1	98	-6	0	-0.7
Total	14	135	88	.605	301	297	37-20	0-0	1895.2	1691	880	170	66	795-41	1427	3.67	106	.239	.319	596-1-68	.153	-1	110	43	389	4.1

Martinez, Rogelio Rogelio (Ulloa) "Limonar"; B11.5.1918 Cidra, Cuba; BR/TR/6´0˝/180; d7.13

YEAR	TM LG	W	L	PCT	G	GS	CG-SHO	SV-BS	IP	H	R	HR	HB	BB-IB	SO	ERA	AERA	OAV	OOB	AB-HR-SH	AVG	PB	SUP	APR	DL	PW
1950	Was A	0	1	.000	2	1	0	0	1.1	4	4	0	0	2	0	27.00	17	.500	.600	0	ø	0	161	-3	0	-0.5

Martinez, Silvio Silvio Ramon (Cabrera); B8.19.1955 Santiago, D.R.; BR/TR/5´10˝/(154–160); d4.9

YEAR	TM LG	W	L	PCT	G	GS	CG-SHO	SV-BS	IP	H	R	HR	HB	BB-IB	SO	ERA	AERA	OAV	OOB	AB-HR-SH	AVG	PB	SUP	APR	DL	PW
1977	Chi A	0	1	.000	10	0	0	1-0	21	28	14	4	0	12-2	10	5.57	73	.337	.408	0	ø	0	—	-3	0	-0.2
1978	StL N	9	8	.529	22	22	5-2	0-0	138.1	114	65	11	2	71-7	45	3.64	98	.228	.322	47-0-6	.170	0	122	-2	0	-0.3
1979	StL N	15	8	.652	32	29	7-2	0-1	206.2	204	92	14	0	67-2	102	3.27	117	.259	.314	62-0-10	.129	-2*	102	9	0	0.6
1980	StL N	5	10	.333	25	20	2	0-0	119.2	127	75	8	2	48-3	39	4.81	78	.273	.340	35-0-3	.086	-2	95	-15	33	-2.0
1981	StL N	2	5	.286	18	16	0	0-0	97	95	48	4	1	39-3	34	3.99	91	.260	.329	35-0-1	.200	1	94	-4	0	-0.3
Total	5	31	32	.492	107	87	14-4	1-1	582.2	568	294	41	5	237-17	230	3.88	96	.258	.328	179-0-20	.145	-3	103	-15	33	-2.2

Martinez, Willie William Jose; B1.4.1978 Barquisimeto, Lara, Venez.; BR/TR/6´2˝/185; d6.14; [DL 1999 Cle A 64]

YEAR	TM LG	W	L	PCT	G	GS	CG-SHO	SV-BS	IP	H	R	HR	HB	BB-IB	SO	ERA	AERA	OAV	OOB	AB-HR-SH	AVG	PB	SUP	APR	DL	PW
2000	Cle A	0	0	ø	1	0	0	0-0	3	1	1	0	0	1-0	1	3.00	167	.111	.182	0	ø	0	—	1	0	0.0

Martini, Wedo Guido Joe "Southern"; B7.1.1913 Birmingham AL; D10.28.1970 Philadelphia PA; BR/TR/5´10˝/165; d7.28

YEAR	TM LG	W	L	PCT	G	GS	CG-SHO	SV-BS	IP	H	R	HR	HB	BB-IB	SO	ERA	AERA	OAV	OOB	AB-HR-SH	AVG	PB	SUP	APR	DL	PW
1935	Phi A	0	2	.000	3	2	0	0	6.1	8	13	0	0	11	1	17.05	27	.333	.543	2	.000	-0	29	-8	—	-1.3

Martz, Randy Randy Carl; B5.28.1956 Harrisburg PA; BL/TR/6´4˝/210; [ChiN77 1/12]; d9.6; Col South Carolina

YEAR	TM LG	W	L	PCT	G	GS	CG-SHO	SV-BS	IP	H	R	HR	HB	BB-IB	SO	ERA	AERA	OAV	OOB	AB-HR-SH	AVG	PB	SUP	APR	DL	PW
1980	Chi N	1	2	.333	6	6	0	0-0	30.1	28	14	1	0	11-1	5	2.08	191	.241	.302	9	.111	-1	71	3	0	0.3
1981	Chi N	5	7	.417	33	14	1	6-1	107.2	103	49	6	1	49-1	32	3.68	102	.256	.336	28-0-2	.214	1*	69	1	0	0.2
1982	Chi N	11	10	.524	28	24	1	1-1	147.2	157	80	17	3	36-4	40	4.21	90	.272	.317	42-0-7	.143	1	102	-8	25	-0.9
1983	Chi A	0	0	ø	1	1	0	0-0	5	4	2	0	0	4-0	1	3.60	117	.211	.348	0	ø	0	86	0	0	0.0
Total	4	17	19	.472	68	45	2	7-2	290.2	292	145	24	4	100-6	78	3.78	101	.262	.323	79-0-9	.165	1	88	-4	25	-0.4

Masaoka, Onan Onan Kainoa Satoshi; B10.27.1977 Hilo HI; BR/TL/6´0˝/188; [LAN95 3/79]; d4.5

YEAR	TM LG	W	L	PCT	G	GS	CG-SHO	SV-BS	IP	H	R	HR	HB	BB-IB	SO	ERA	AERA	OAV	OOB	AB-HR-SH	AVG	PB	SUP	APR	DL	PW
1999	LA N	2	4	.333	54	0	0	1-1	66.2	55	33	8	2	47-3	61	4.32	101	.222	.348	4-0-1	.000	-0	—	1	0	0.0
2000	LA N	1	1	.500	29	0	0	0-0	27	23	12	2	1	15-1	27	4.00	111	.230	.336	0	ø	0	—	2	0	0.1
Total	2	3	5	.375	83	0	0	1-1	93.2	78	45	10	3	62-4	88	4.23	104	.224	.345	4-0-1	.000	-0	—	3	0	0.1

Mason, Del Adelbert William; B10.29.1883 Newfane NY; D12.31.1962 Winter Park FL; BR/TR/6´0˝/160; d4.23; Col Rollins

YEAR	TM LG	W	L	PCT	G	GS	CG-SHO	SV-BS	IP	H	R	HR	HB	BB-IB	SO	ERA	AERA	OAV	OOB	AB-HR-SH	AVG	PB	SUP	APR	DL	PW
1904	Was A	0	3	.000	5	3	2	0	33	45	30	1	2	13	16	6.00	44	.326	.392	15	.000	-2	107	-12	—	-1.2
1906	Cin N	0	1	.000	2	1	1	0	12	10	6	1	1	6	4	4.50	61	.250	.362	5	.000	-1	79	-1	—	-0.2
1907	Cin N	5	12	.294	25	17	13-1	0	146	144	68	2	6	55	45	3.14	83	.277	.353	44-0-5	.182	-0	57	-7	—	-0.8
Total	3	5	16	.238	32	21	16-1	0	191	199	104	4	9	74	65	3.72	70	.286	.362	64-0-5	.125	-3	65	-20	—	-2.2

Mason, Ernie Ernest; B New Orleans LA; D7.30.1904 Covington LA; 6´0˝/150; d7.17

YEAR	TM LG	W	L	PCT	G	GS	CG-SHO	SV-BS	IP	H	R	HR	HB	BB-IB	SO	ERA	AERA	OAV	OOB	AB-HR-SH	AVG	PB	SUP	APR	DL	PW
1894	StL N	0	3	.000	4	2	2	0	22.2	34	29	1	0	10	3	7.15	76	.343	.404	12	.250	-0	59	-6	—	-0.5

Mason, Hank Henry; B6.19.1931 Marshall MO; BR/TR/6´0˝/185; d9.12

YEAR	TM LG	W	L	PCT	G	GS	CG-SHO	SV-BS	IP	H	R	HR	HB	BB-IB	SO	ERA	AERA	OAV	OOB	AB-HR-SH	AVG	PB	SUP	APR	DL	PW
1958	Phi N	0	0	ø	1	0	0	0	5	7	7	0	1	2-0	3	10.80	37	.368	.417	2	.000	-0	—	-4	0	-0.2
1960	Phi N	0	0	ø	3	0	0	0	5.2	9	6	1	0	5-1	3	9.53	41	.375	.467	1	.000	-0	—	-3	0	-0.2
Total	2	0	0	ø	4	0	0	0	10.2	16	13	1	1	7-1	6	10.13	39	.372	.444	3	.000	-0	—	-7	0	-0.4

Mason, Mike Michael Paul; B11.21.1958 Faribault MN; BL/TL/6´2˝/(195–205); [TexA80 S1/12]; d9.13; C1; Col Oral Roberts

YEAR	TM LG	W	L	PCT	G	GS	CG-SHO	SV-BS	IP	H	R	HR	HB	BB-IB	SO	ERA	AERA	OAV	OOB	AB-HR-SH	AVG	PB	SUP	APR	DL	PW
1982	Tex A	1	2	.333	4	4	0	0-0	23	21	13	3	0	9-1	8	5.09	76	.244	.316	0	ø	0	111	-3	0	-0.3
1983	Tex A	0	2	.000	5	0	0	0-1	10.2	10	7	0	1	6-0	9	5.91	69	.244	.354	0	ø	0	—	-2	0	-0.3
1984	Tex A	9	13	.409	36	24	4	0-0	184.1	159	78	18	2	51-4	113	3.61	116	.233	.285	0	ø	0	74	14	0	1.5
1985	Tex A	8	15	.348	38	30	1-1	0-1	179	212	113	22	3	73-4	92	4.83	88	.299	.362	0	ø	0	86	-14	0	-1.6
1986	Tex A	7	3	.700	27	22	2-1	0-0	135	135	71	11	0	56-3	85	4.33	100	.257	.327	0	ø	0	128	1	35	0.1
1987	Tex A	0	2	.000	8	6	0	0-0	29	37	20	6	4	22-2	21	5.59	81	.322	.444	0	ø	0	125	-3	0	-0.2
	Chi N	4	1	.800	17	4	0	0-0	38	43	25	4	1	23-0	28	5.68	76	.303	.396	9-0-3	.222	0*	178	-5	17	-0.5
1988	Min A	0	1	.000	5	0	0	0-0	6.2	8	8	1	0	9-0	7	10.80	38	.286	.459	0	ø	0	—	-5	0	-0.6
Total	7	29	39	.426	140	90	7-2	0-2	605.2	625	335	65	11	249-14	363	4.53	94	.268	.338	9-0-3	.222	0	101	-17	52	-1.9

Mason, Roger Roger Le Roy; B9.18.1958 Bellaire MI; BR/TR/6´6˝/(215–226); d9.4; Col Saginaw Valley St.

YEAR	TM LG	W	L	PCT	G	GS	CG-SHO	SV-BS	IP	H	R	HR	HB	BB-IB	SO	ERA	AERA	OAV	OOB	AB-HR-SH	AVG	PB	SUP	APR	DL	PW
1984	Det A	1	1	.500	5	2	0	1-0	22	23	11	1	0	10-0	15	4.50	88	.271	.340	0	ø	0	91	-1	0	-0.1
1985	SF N	1	3	.250	5	5	1-1	0-0	29.2	28	13	1	0	11-1	26	2.12	163	.243	.310	11	.091	-0	66	2	0	0.3
1986	SF N	3	4	.429	11	11	1	0-0	60	56	35	5	3	30-3	43	4.80	74	.250	.342	21-0-1	.048	-2	99	-8	123	-1.1
1987	SF N	1	1	.500	5	5	0	0-0	26	30	15	4	0	10-0	18	4.50	86	.303	.367	8	.125	0	132	-2	0	-0.1
1989	Hou N	0	0	ø	2	0	0	0-0	1.1	2	3	0	0	2-0	3	20.25	17	.333	.500	0	ø	0	—	-2	0	-0.1
1991	†Pit N	3	2	.600	24	0	0	3-0	29.2	21	11	2	1	6-1	21	3.03	119	.200	.248	0-0-1	ø	0	—	2	0	0.4
1992	†Pit N	5	7	.417	65	0	0	8-2	88	80	41	11	4	33-8	56	4.09	85	.246	.320	10	.000	-1	—	-5	0	-0.9
1993	SD N	0	7	.000	34	0	0	0-0	50	43	20	1	2	18-4	39	3.24	128	.242	.313	3	.000	-0	—	5	0	0.6
	†Phi N	5	5	.500	34	0	0	0-3	49.2	47	28	9	0	16-1	32	4.89	81	.246	.301	3	.333	0	—	-4	0	-0.7
	Year	5	12	.294	68	0	0	0-3	99.2	90	48	10	2	34-5	71	4.06	100	.244	.307	6	.167	-0	—	1	0	-0.1
1994	Phi N	1	1	.500	6	0	0	0-0	8.2	11	6	2	0	5-1	7	5.19	82	.306	.390	0	ø	0	—	-1	0	-0.2
	NY N	2	4	.333	41	0	0	1-1	51.1	44	23	6	2	20-4	26	3.51	119	.232	.310	0	ø	0	—	4	0	0.3
	Year	3	5	.375	47	0	0	1-1	60	55	29	8	2	25-5	33	3.75	112	.243	.323	0	ø	0	—	2	0	0.1
Total	9	22	35	.386	232	23	2-1	13-6	416.1	385	206	42	12	161-23	286	4.02	94	.248	.320	56-0-2	.071	-2	95	-10	123	-1.6

Masset, Nick Nicholas Allen; B5.17.1982 St.Petersburg FL; BR/TR/6´4˝/190; [TexA00 8/244]; d6.27; Col St.Petersburg (FL) JC

YEAR	TM LG	W	L	PCT	G	GS	CG-SHO	SV-BS	IP	H	R	HR	HB	BB-IB	SO	ERA	AERA	OAV	OOB	AB-HR-SH	AVG	PB	SUP	APR	DL	PW
2006	Tex A	0	0	ø	8	0	0	0-0	8.2	9	4	0	2	2-0	4	4.15	113	.300	.361	0	ø	0	—	1	0	0.0

Masters, Walt Walter Thomas; B3.28.1907 Pen Argyl PA; D7.10.1992 Ottawa ON, Can.; BR/TR/5´10.5˝/180; d7.9; Col Penn

YEAR	TM LG	W	L	PCT	G	GS	CG-SHO	SV-BS	IP	H	R	HR	HB	BB-IB	SO	ERA	AERA	OAV	OOB	AB-HR-SH	AVG	PB	SUP	APR	DL	PW
1931	Was A	0	0	ø	3	0	0	1	9	7	2	0	0	4	1	2.00	215	.226	.314	2	.000	-0	—	2	—	0.1
1937	Phi N	0	0	ø	1	0	0	0	1	5	4	0	0	1	0	36.00	12	.714	.750	0	ø	0	—	-3	—	-0.1
1939	Phi A	0	0	ø	4	0	0	0	11	15	9	0	0	8	2	6.55	72	.306	.404	2	.000	-0	—	-2	—	-0.1
Total	3	0	0	ø	8	0	0	1	21	27	15	0	0	13	3	6.00	75	.310	.400	4	.000	-1	—	-3	—	-0.1

Masterson, Paul Paul Nicholas "Lefty" (b Paul Nicholas Nastasowski); B10.16.1915 Chicago IL; D11.27.1997 Chicago IL; BL/TL/5´11˝/165; d9.15

YEAR	TM LG	W	L	PCT	G	GS	CG-SHO	SV-BS	IP	H	R	HR	HB	BB-IB	SO	ERA	AERA	OAV	OOB	AB-HR-SH	AVG	PB	SUP	APR	DL	PW
1940	Phi N	0	0	ø	2	0	0	0	5	5	4	0	0	2	3	7.20	54	.263	.333	1	.000	-0	—	-2	—	-0.1
1941	Phi N	1	0	1.000	2	1	1	0	11.1	11	6	0	0	6	8	4.76	78	.250	.340	4-0-1	.000	-1	183	-1	0	-0.1
1942	Phi N	0	0	ø	4	0	0	0	8.1	10	6	1	0	5	3	6.48	51	.303	.395	0	ø	0	—	-3	0	-0.1
Total	3	1	0	1.000	8	1	1	0	24.2	26	16	1	0	13	14	5.84	62	.271	.358	5-0-1	.000	-1	183	-6	0	-0.3

Masterson, Walt Walter Edward; B6.22.1920 Philadelphia PA; BR/TR/6´2˝/(180–189); d5.8; Mil 1943–45

YEAR	TM LG	W	L	PCT	G	GS	CG-SHO	SV-BS	IP	H	R	HR	HB	BB-IB	SO	ERA	AERA	OAV	OOB	AB-HR-SH	AVG	PB	SUP	APR	DL	PW
1939	Was A	2	2	.500	24	5	1	0	58.1	66	44	2	2	48	12	5.55	78	.293	.422	13	.154	-0	122	-10	—	-0.6
1940	Was A	3	13	.188	31	19	3	2	130.1	128	92	6	3	88	68	4.90	85	.257	.371	38-0-3	.184	0	79	-15	—	-1.6
1941	Was A	4	3	.571	34	6	1	3	78.1	101	56	3	1	53	40	5.97	68	.321	.420	19-0-2	.105	-1	128	-15	0	-1.3
1942	Was A	5	9	.357	25	15	8-4	2	142.2	138	75	6	2	54	63	3.34	109	.251	.321	45-0-3	.156	-0*	105	0	0	-0.1
1945	Was A	1	2	.333	4	2	1-1	0	25	21	8	1	0	10	14	1.08	287	.228	.304	9	.111	-1	220	4	0	0.4
1946	Was A	5	6	.455	29	9	2	1	91.1	105	70	8	3	67	61	6.01	56	.295	.411	25-0-1	.080	-1	137	-26	0	-3.0
1947	Was A★	12	16	.429	35	31	14-4	1	253	215	98	11	2	97	135	3.13	119	.234	.309	83-0-3	.133	-3*	67	17	0	1.7
1948	Was A★	8	15	.348	33	27	9-2	2	188	171	88	12	4	122	72	3.83	113	.247	.363	57-0-9	.193	-0	72	12	0	1.2
1949	Was A	3	2	.600	10	7	3	0	53	42	22	4	3	21	17	3.23	132	.216	.303	18-0-1	.056	-1*	87	6	0	0.4
	Bos A	3	4	.429	18	5	1	4	55	58	30	2	0	35	19	4.25	102	.283	.387	17	.118	-0	148	0	0	-0.1
	Year	6	6	.500	28	12	4	4	108	100	52	6	3	56	36	3.75	115	.251	.347	35-0-1	.086	-2	113	6	0	0.3
1950	Bos A	8	6	.571	33	15	6	1	129.1	145	91	15	1	82	60	5.64	87	.287	.387	44	.136	-3	118	-11	0	-1.2
1951	Bos A	3	0	1.000	30	1	0	2	59.1	53	24	1	0	32	39	3.34	134	.228	.322	11-0-1	.182	-1	100	7	0	0.3
1952	Bos A	1	1	.500	5	1	0	0	9.1	18	12	1	0	11	3	11.57	34	.400	.518	2	.000	0	22	-7	0	-1.2
	Was A	9	8	.529	24	21	11	2	160.2	153	71	11	3	72	89	3.70	96	.253	.336	50-0-8	.120	-1	99	-1	0	-0.2

THE PITCHER REGISTER

YEAR	TM LG	W	L	PCT	G	GS	CG-SHO	SV-BS	IP	H	R	HR	HB	BB-IB	SO	ERA	AERA	OAV	OOB	AB-HR-SH	AVG	PB	SUP	APR	DL	PW
	Year	10	9	.526	29	22	11	2	170	171	83	12	3	83	92	4.13	87	.263	.350	52-0-8	.115	-1	95	-7	0	-1.4
1953	Was A	10	12	.455	29	20	10-4	0	166.1	145	79	16	3	62	95	3.63	107	.232	.304	51-0-3	.137	-1	78	3	0	0.3
1956	Det A	1	1	.500	35	0	0	0	49.2	54	28	2	1	32-1	28	4.17	99	.289	.390	4	.250	0	—	-1	0	-0.1
Total	14	78	100	.438	399	184	70-15	20	1649.2	1613	888	101	28	886-1	815	4.15	96	.258	.353	486-0-34	.140	-14	92	-37	0	-5.1
Mastny, Tom	Thomas Raymond; B2.4.1981 East Bontang, Indonesia; BR/TR/6´6˝/220; [TorA03 11/320]; d7.30; Col Furman																									
2006	Cle A	0	1	.000	15	0	0	5-2	16.1	17	10	1	1	8-1	14	5.51	79	.279	.361	0	ø	0	—	-2	0	-0.2
Matarazzo, Len	Leonard; B9.12.1928 New Castle PA; BR/TR/6´4˝/195; d9.6																									
1952	Phi A	0	0	ø	1	0	0	0	1	1	0	0	0	1	0	0.00	ø	.250	.400	0	ø	0	—	0	0	0.0
Mateo, Juan	Juan Manuel; B12.17.1982 Bani, D.R.; BR/TR/6´2˝/180; d8.3																									
2006	Chi N	1	3	.250	11	10	0	0-0	45.2	51	31	6	3	23-1	35	5.32	86	.288	.376	12-0-2	.000	-1*	89	-4	0	-0.5
Mateo, Julio	Julio Cesar; B8.2.1977 Bani, D.R.; BR/TR/6´0˝/(175–220); d5.7																									
2002	Sea A	0	0	ø	12	0	0	0-0	21	20	10	2	1	12-0	15	4.29	100	.247	.351	0	ø	0	—	0	0	0.0
2003	Sea A	4	0	1.000	50	0	0	1-0	85.2	69	32	14	5	13-1	71	3.15	137	.220	.259	0	ø	0	—	12	0	0.5
2004	Sea A	1	2	.333	45	0	0	1-3	57.2	56	30	11	5	16-3	43	4.68	95	.251	.310	0	ø	0	—	0	49	-0.1
2005	Sea A	3	6	.333	55	1	0	0-2	88.1	79	32	12	7	17-6	52	3.06	137	.237	.287	0	ø	0	0	11	0	1.0
2006	Sea A	9	4	.692	48	0	0	0-3	53.2	62	27	6	3	22-8	31	4.19	105	.297	.364	0	ø	0	—	1	56	0.2
Total	5	17	12	.586	210	1	0	2-8	306.1	286	131	45	21	80-18	212	3.67	118	.247	.303	0	ø	0	0	24	105	1.6
Mathews, Greg	Gregory Inman; B5.17.1962 Harbor City CA; BR/TL (BB 1986)/6´2˝/180; [StLN84 10/243]; d6.3; Col Cal St.–Fullerton; [DL 1989 StL N 182]																									
1986	StL N	11	8	.579	23	22	1	0-0	145.1	139	61	15	2	44-3	67	3.65	101	.259	.317	43-0-7	.047	-3	83	3	0	-0.1
1987	†StL N	11	11	.500	32	32	2-1	0-0	197.2	184	87	17	0	71-5	108	3.73	113	.249	.314	68-0-7	.191	1	88	11	0	1.2
1988	StL N	4	6	.400	13	13	1	0-0	68	61	34	4	2	33-5	31	4.24	83	.247	.337	23-0-1	.174	0	83	-5	94	-0.6
1990	StL N	0	5	.000	11	10	0	0-0	50.2	53	34	2	2	30-1	18	5.33	72	.277	.378	14-0-1	.214	1*	84	-8	0	-0.5
1992	Phi N	2	3	.400	14	7	0	0-0	52.1	54	31	7	1	24-2	27	5.16	68	.270	.350	14-0-2	.000	-1	74	-9	0	-0.9
Total	5	28	33	.459	93	84	4-1	0-0	514	491	247	45	7	202-16	251	4.08	95	.256	.328	162-0-18	.136	-1	85	-8	276	-0.9
Mathews, Bobby	Robert T.; B11.21.1851 Baltimore MD; D4.17.1898 Baltimore MD; BR/TR/5´5.5˝/140; d5.4; U3; ▲																									
1871	Kek NA	6	11	.353	19	19	19-**1**	0	169	261	243	5	—	21	17	5.17	88	.305	.322	89	.270	-3	63	-10	—	-0.7
1872	Bal NA	25	18	.581	49	47	39	0	406	480	356	3	—	52	**57**	3.19	115	.257	.277	222	.225	-8*	96	26	—	1.0
1873	Mut NA	29	23	.558	52	52	47-2	0	443	489	348	5	—	62	**79**	2.58	128	.251	.274	223	.193	-2	90	**37**	—	2.5
1874	Mut NA	42	22	.656	65	65	62-**4**	0	578	652	371	3	—	41	**101**	1.90	118	.261	.273	298	.242	-2	100	22	—	1.5
1875	Mut NA	29	38	.433	70	**70**	**69**-3	0	**625.2**	711	421	4	—	20	75	2.49	94	.260	.265	264	.182	-10	69	-10	—	-2.0
1876	NY N	21	34	.382	56	56	55-2	0	516	693	395	8	—	24	37	2.86	75	.301	.308	218	.183	-10	83	-46	—	-4.5
1877	Cin N	3	12	.200	15	15	13	0	129.1	208	132	0	—	17	9	4.04	66	.339	.357	59	.169	-3	101	-25	—	-2.4
1879	Pro N	12	6	.667	27	25	15-1	**1**	189	194	85	4	—	26	90	2.29	103	.258	.282	173-1	.202	-0*	135	3	—	0.2
1881	Pro N	4	8	.333	14	14	10-1	0	102.1	121	81	2	—	21	28	3.17	84	.268	.300	57	.193	-2*	106	-7	—	-0.8
	Bos N	1	0	1.000	5	1	1	2	23	22	11	0	—	11	5	2.35	113	.239	.320	71	.169	-1*	204	1	—	0.0
	Year	5	8	.385	19	15	11-1	**2**	125.1	143	92	2	—	32	33	3.02	88	.263	.304	128	.180	-3	113	-6	—	-0.8
1882	Bos N	19	15	.559	34	32	31	0	285	278	151	5	—	22	153	2.87	100	.232	.246	169	.225	-2*	91	2	—	-0.1
1883	Phi AA	30	13	.698	44	44	41-1	0	381	396	224	11	—	31	203	2.46	144	.251	.265	167	.186	-7*	101	38	—	2.8
1884	Phi AA	30	18	.625	49	49	48-3	0	430.2	401	238	10	12	49	286	3.32	102	.232	.258	184	.185	-5	114	4	—	-0.3
1885	Phi AA	30	17	.638	48	48	46-2	0	422.1	394	229	3	20	57	286	2.43	142	.233	.267	179	.168	-7	104	42	—	3.3
1886	Phi AA	13	9	.591	24	24	22	0	197.2	226	148	3	13	53	93	3.96	88	.267	.320	88	.239	-0	119	-9	—	-0.8
1887	Phi AA	3	4	.429	7	7	7	0	58	75	64	4	3	25	9	6.67	64	.298	.368	25	.200	-0	121	-16	—	-1.3
Total	5NA	131	112	.539	255	253	236-10	0	2221.2	2593	1739	20	0	196	329	2.69	109	.262	.276	1096	.216	-25	86	65	—	2.3
Total	10	166	136	.550	323	315	289-10	3	2734.1	3008	1758	50	48	336	1199	3.00	100	.261	.285	1390-1	.192	-38	104	-13	—	-3.9
Mathews, Terry	Terry Alan; B10.5.1964 Alexandria LA; BL/TR/6´2˝/(200–225); [TexA87 5/129]; d6.21; Col Louisiana–Monroe																									
1991	Tex A	4	0	1.000	34	2	0	1-2	57.1	54	24	5	1	18-3	51	3.61	112	.251	.312	0	ø	0	226	4	0	0.2
1992	Tex A	2	4	.333	40	0	0	0-4	42.1	48	29	4	1	31-3	26	5.95	64	.294	.404	0	ø	0	—	-9	45	-1.2
1994	Fla N	2	1	.667	24	2	0	0-1	43	45	16	4	1	9-1	21	3.35	133	.268	.309	6	.500	1	133	6	0	0.5
1995	Fla N	4	4	.500	57	0	0	3-4	82.2	70	32	9	1	27-4	72	3.38	127	.235	.300	13	.462	3	—	9	15	1.1
1996	Fla N	2	4	.333	57	0	0	4-1	55	59	33	7	1	27-5	49	4.91	84	.273	.355	4	.000	-0	—	-5	15	-0.6
	†Bal A	2	2	.500	14	0	0	0-1	18.2	20	7	3	0	7-0	13	3.38	147	.282	.346	0	ø	0	—	4	0	0.6
1997	†Bal A	4	4	.500	57	0	0	1-1	63.1	63	35	8	0	36-2	39	4.41	100	.267	.359	0	ø	0	—	-1	0	-0.1
1998	Bal A	0	1	.000	17	0	0	0-1	20.1	26	15	6	0	8-3	10	6.20	73	.342	.400	0	ø	0	—	-4	41	-0.2
1999	KC A	2	1	.667	24	1	0	1-2	39	44	21	4	2	17-1	19	4.38	116	.289	.360	1	.000	-0	312	3	40	0.2
Total	8	22	21	.512	324	5	0	10-17	421.2	429	212	50	7	180-22	300	4.25	102	.269	.343	24	.375	3	211	7	156	0.5
Mathews, T. J.	Timothy Jay; B1.9.1970 Belleville IL; BR/TR/6´2˝/(200–225); [StLN92 36/1007]; d7.28; f–Nelson; Col Nevada–Las Vegas																									
1995	StL N	1	1	.500	23	0	0	2-0	29.2	21	7	1	0	11-1	28	1.52	282	.200	.276	2	.000	-0	—	8	0	0.6
1996	†StL N	2	6	.250	67	0	0	6-5	83.2	62	32	8	2	32-4	80	3.01	141	.203	.282	4	.000	-0	—	11	0	0.9
1997	StL N	4	4	.500	40	0	0	0-3	46	41	14	4	1	18-3	46	2.15	195	.238	.314	1	.000	-0	—	10	0	1.5
	Oak A	6	2	.750	24	0	0	3-3	28.2	34	18	5	1	12-1	24	4.40	105	.293	.362	0	ø	0	—	-1	0	-0.1
1998	Oak A	7	4	.636	66	0	0	1-3	72.2	71	44	6	4	29-3	53	4.58	101	.258	.328	0	ø	0	—	-1	0	-0.1
1999	Oak A	9	5	.643	50	0	0	3-2	59	46	28	9	2	20-4	42	3.81	124	.215	.287	0	ø	0	—	6	23	1.2
2000	Oak A	2	3	.400	50	0	0	0-1	59.2	73	40	10	2	25-5	42	6.03	80	.303	.368	0	ø	0	—	-6	19	-0.3
2001	Oak A	0	1	.000	20	0	0	1-0	23	28	14	2	0	11-3	19	5.09	90	.295	.368	0	ø	0	—	-1	0	-0.1
	StL N	1	0	1.000	10	0	0	0-0	14.2	11	6	2	0	1-0	10	3.07	141	.204	.214	3	.000	-0	—	2	0	0.1
2002	Hou N	0	0	ø	12	0	0	0-0	18.1	19	7	2	0	5-3	13	3.44	126	.271	.320	1	.000	-0	—	2	75	0.1
Total	8	32	26	.552	362	0	0	16-17	435.1	406	210	49	12	164-27	357	3.82	118	.246	.316	11	.000	-1	—	30	117	3.8
Mathewson, Christy	Christopher "Matty","Big Six"; B8.12.1880 Factoryville PA; D10.7.1925 Saranac Lake NY; BR/TR/6´1.5˝/195; d7.17; M3/C2; HF1936; b–Henry; Col Bucknell																									
1900	NY N	0	3	.000	6	1	1	0	33.2	37	32	1	4	20	15	5.08	71	.278	.389	11	.182	0	96	-6	—	-0.4
1901	NY N	20	17	.541	40	38	36-5	0	336	288	131	3	13	97	221	2.41	137	.230	.292	130-0-4	.215	-1*	81	32	—	3.6
1902	NY N	14	17	.452	35	33	30-**8**	0	284.2	246	118	3	10	77	164	2.12	132	.233	.292	130-2-2	.200	1*	73	16	—	2.1
1903	NY N	30	13	.698	45	42	37-3	2	366.1	321	136	4	10	100	**267**	2.26	148	.231	.287	124-1-16	.226	3	105	39	—	**4.6**
1904	NY N	33	12	.733	48	**46**	33-4	1	367.2	306	120	7	4	78	**212**	2.03	134	.226	.270	133-0-9	.226	6	135	27	—	4.2
1905	†NY N	**31**	9	.775	43	37	32-**8**	3	338.2	252	85	4	1	64	**206**	**1.28**	**230**	.205	**.245**	127-2-1	.236	10*	127	**57**	—	**8.5**
1906	NY N	22	12	.647	38	35	22-6	1	266.2	262	100	3	3	77	128	2.97	88	.259	.313	91-0-3	.264	7	124	-3	—	0.6
1907	NY N	**24**	12	.667	41	36	31-**8**	2	315	250	88	5	2	53	**178**	2.00	124	.212	**.247**	107-0-3	.187	3	89	19	—	2.7
1908	NY N	**37**	11	.771	**56**	**44**	**34-11**	**5**	**390.2**	281	85	5	3	42	**259**	**1.43**	**169**	.197	**.222**	129-0-7	.155	1	107	**41**	—	**6.5**
1909	NY N	25	6	**.806**	37	33	26-8	2	275.1	192	57	2	0	36	149	**1.14**	**223**	.200	**.228**	95-1-1	.263	7	100	42	—	**6.6**
1910	NY N	**27**	9	.750	38	35	**27**-2	0	318.1	292	100	5	3	60	184	1.89	157	.248	.286	107-1-4	.234	7	125	**35**	—	**5.3**
1911	†NY N	26	13	.667	45	37	29-5	3	307	303	102	5	1	38	141	**1.99**	**169**	.259	.283	112-0-3	.196	0	112	**42**	—	**5.7**
1912	†NY N	23	12	.657	43	34	27	5	310	311	107	5	2	34	134	2.12	159	.260	**.281**	110-0-3	.264	5	117	**43**	—	**5.3**
1913	†NY N	25	11	.694	40	35	25-4	2	306	291	94	8	0	21	93	**2.06**	**152**	.252	**.266**	103-0-4	.184	-0	107	**37**	—	**4.6**
1914	NY N	24	13	.649	41	35	29-5	2	312	314	133	16	2	23	80	3.00	88	.263	.278	105-0-4	.219	6	124	-13	—	-0.8
1915	NY N	8	14	.364	27	24	11-1	0	186	199	97	9	1	20	57	3.58	72	.277	.298	51-0-3	.157	3	81	-23	—	-2.3
1916	NY N	3	4	.429	12	6	4-1	2	65.2	59	27	3	0	7	16	2.33	104	.243	.264	17-0-2	.000	-1	102	-2	—	-0.2
	Cin N	1	0	1.000	1	1	1	0	9	15	8	1	0	1	3	8.00	32	.366	.381	5	.600	1	288	-5	—	-0.3
	Year	4	4	.500	13	7	5-1	2	74.2	74	35	4	0	8	19	3.01	81	.261	.281	22-0-2	.136	1	131	-6	—	-0.5
Total	17	373	188	.665	636	552	435-79	30	4788.2	4219	1620	89	59	848	2507	2.13	136	.236	.273	1687-7-69	.215	59	108	378	—	56.3
Mathewson, Henry	Henry; B12.24.1886 Factoryville PA; D7.1.1917 Factoryville PA; BR/TR/6´3˝/175; d9.28; b–Christy; Col Bucknell																									
1906	NY N	0	1	.000	2	1	1	1	10	7	7	0	1	14	2	5.40	48	.194	.431	2-0-1	.000	-0	28	-3	—	-0.3
1907	NY N	0	0	ø	1	0	0	1	1	1	0	0	0	0	0	0.00	ø	.250	.250	0	ø	0	—	0	—	0.1
Total	2	0	1	.000	3	1	1	2	11	8	7	0	1	14	2	4.91	53	.200	.418	2-0-1	.000	-0	28	-3	—	-0.2

YEAR	TM LG	W	L	PCT	G	GS	CG-SHO	SV-BS	IP	H	R	HR	HB	BB-IB	SO	ERA	AERA	OAV	OOB	AB-HR-SH	AVG	PB	SUP	APR	DL	PW
Mathias, Carl	Carl Lynwood "Stubby"; B6.13.1936 Bechtelsville PA; BB/TL/5´11˝/195; d7.31																									
1960	Cle A	0	1	.000	7	0	0	0	15.1	14	7	2	0	8-0	13	3.52	106	.233	.324	1	.000	-0	—	0	0	0.0
1961	Was A	0	1	.000	4	3	0	0	13.2	22	19	3	1	4-0	7	11.20	36	.361	.403	5	.200	-0	176	-11	0	-0.6
Total	2	0	2	.000	11	3	0	0	29	36	26	5	1	12-0	20	7.14	54	.298	.363	6	.167	-0	176	-11	0	-0.6
Mathieson, Scott	Scott William; B2.27.1984 Vancouver BC, Can; BR/TR/6´3˝/190; [PhiN02 17/509]; d6.17																									
2006	Phi N	1	4	.200	9	8	0	0-0	37.1	48	36	8	1	16-1	28	7.47	63	.312	.378	7-0-2	.143	-0	101	-12	29	-1.3
Mathis, Ron	Ronald Vance; B9.25.1958 Kansas City MO; BR/TR/6´0˝/(175–180); [DetA80 30/724]; d4.13; Col Missouri																									
1985	Hou N	3	5	.375	23	8	0	1-0	70	83	54	7	1	27-1	34	6.04	58	.293	.352	14-0-2	.071	-1	114	-20	0	-2.2
1987	Hou N	0	1	.000	8	0	0	0-0	12	10	8	2	0	11-0	8	5.25	75	.233	.389	2	.000	-0	—	-2	0	-0.2
Total	2	3	6	.333	31	8	0	1-0	82	93	62	9	1	38-1	42	5.93	60	.285	.358	16-0-2	.063	-1	114	-22	0	-2.4
Matlack, Jon	Jonathan Trumpbour; B1.19.1950 West Chester PA; BL/TL/6´3˝/(190–210); [NYN67 1/4]; d7.11; C1																									
1971	NY N	0	3	.000	7	6	0	0-0	37	31	18	2	0	15-0	24	4.14	83	.228	.303	11	.273	1	103	-2	0	-0.1
1972	NY N	15	10	.600	34	32	8-4	0-0	244	215	79	14	2	71-14	169	2.32	146	.234	.289	78-0-5	.128	1	92	26	0	2.8
1973	†NY N	14	16	.467	34	34	14-3	0-0	242	210	93	16	2	99-14	205	3.20	114	.236	.312	65-0-12	.138	2*	75	13	0	1.8
1974	NY N★	13	15	.464	34	34	14-**7**	0-0	265.1	221	82	8	5	76-11	195	2.41	150	.226	.283	79-0-11	.101	-4	78	36	0	3.3
1975	NY N★	16	12	.571	33	32	8-3	0-0	228.2	224	105	15	1	58-6	154	3.38	104	.254	.299	70-0-5	.100	0	105	0	0	-0.1
1976	NY N☆	17	10	.630	35	35	16-**6**	0-0	262	236	94	18	3	57-5	153	2.95	113	.242	.284	88-0-7	.193	4	120	14	0	1.8
1977	NY N	7	15	.318	26	26	5-3	0-0	169	175	86	19	2	43-7	123	4.21	90	.273	.317	50-0-1	.060	-2	77	-7	0	-1.0
1978	Tex A	15	13	.536	35	33	18-2	1-0	270	252	93	14	4	51-4	157	2.27	165	.245	.283	0	ø	0	72	38	0	4.0
1979	Tex A	5	4	.556	13	13	2	0-0	85	98	43	9	1	15-1	35	4.13	100	.293	.323	0	ø	0	97	1	87	0.1
1980	Tex A	10	10	.500	35	34	8-1	1-0	234.2	265	111	17	0	48-1	142	3.68	106	.287	.321	0	ø	0	98	5	0	0.3
1981	Tex A	4	7	.364	17	16	1-1	0-0	104.1	101	59	8	1	41-1	43	4.14	84	.258	.326	0	ø	0	111	-11	0	-1.1
1982	Tex A	7	7	.500	33	14	1	1-1	147.2	158	64	14	2	37-4	78	3.53	110	.275	.319	0	ø	0	80	6	0	0.5
1983	Tex A	2	4	.333	25	9	2	0-0	73.1	90	43	7	3	27-1	38	4.66	87	.307	.366	0	ø	0	87	-5	0	-0.3
Total	13	125	126	.498	361	318	97-30	3-1	2363	2276	970	161	26	638-69	1516	3.18	115	.254	.303	441-0-41	.129	2	91	114	87	12.0
Mattern, Al	Alonzo Albert; B6.16.1883 W.Rush NY; D11.6.1958 West Rush NY; BL/TL/5´10˝/165; d9.16																									
1908	Bos N	1	2	.333	5	3	1-1	0	30.1	30	10	0	0	6	8	2.08	116	.265	.303	8-0-2	.125	-0	68	1	—	0.1
1909	Bos N	15	21	.417	47	32	24-2	3	316.1	322	142	4	3	108	98	2.85	99	.268	.330	101-0-7	.168	-1	83	-2	—	-0.1
1910	Bos N	16	19	.457	**51**	37	17-**6**	1	305	288	145	5	6	121	94	2.98	112	.257	.332	98-0-10	.163	-4	62	10	—	0.6
1911	Bos N	4	15	.211	33	21	11	0	186.1	228	129	13	1	63	51	4.97	77	.320	.376	63-0-5	.175	-2	89	-19	—	-1.8
1912	Bos N	0	1	.000	2	1	0	0	6.1	10	9	0	0	1	3	7.11	50	.313	.333	2	.000	-0	102	-3	—	-0.4
Total	5	36	58	.383	138	94	53-9	4	844.1	878	435	22	10	299	254	3.37	95	.276	.340	272-0-24	.165	-8	77	-13	—	-1.6
Mattes, Troy	Troy Walter; B8.26.1975 Champaign IL; BR/TR/6´8˝/230; [MonN93 16/454]; d6.19; Col Miami–Dade Wolfson (FL) CC; [DL 2002 Mon N 183]																									
2001	Mon N	3	3	.500	8	8	0	0-0	45	51	33	9	4	21-2	26	6.00	72	.285	.371	15-0-1	.467	3	131	-9	0	-0.7
Matteson, C. V.	Clifford Virgil; B11.24.1861 Seville OH; D12.18.1931 Seville OH; d6.13																									
1884	StL U	1	0	1.000	1	1	0	0	6	9	11	1	—	3	3	9.00	27	.321	.387	4	.000	-1	286	-4	—	-0.5
Matteson, Eddie	Henry Edson "Matty"; B9.7.1884 Guys Mills PA; D9.1.1943 Westfield NY; BR/TR/5´10.5˝/160; d5.30																									
1914	Phi N	3	2	.600	15	3	2	0	58	58	29	1	1	23	28	3.10	95	.278	.352	22	.182	-0	105	-1	—	-0.2
1918	Was A	5	3	.625	14	6	2	0	67.2	57	20	2	1	15	17	1.73	158	.238	.286	19	.105	-2	69	7	—	0.6
Total	2	8	5	.615	29	9	4	0	125.2	115	49	3	2	38	45	2.36	120	.257	.318	41	.146	-2	81	6	—	0.4
Matthews, Joe	John Joseph "Lefty"; B9.29.1898 Baltimore MD; D2.8.1968 Hagerstown MD; BB/TL/6´0˝/170; d9.18																									
1922	Bos N	0	1	.000	3	1	0	0	10	5	6	1	1	6	0	3.60	111	.143	.286	2	.000	-0	0	0	—	0.0
Matthews, Mike	Michael Scott; B10.24.1973 Fredericksburg VA; BL/TL/6´2˝/(175–205); [CleA92 2/40]; d5.31; Col Montgomery (MD) CC																									
2000	StL N	0	0	ø	14	0	0	0-0	9.1	15	12	2	1	10-2	8	11.57	40	.349	.481	0	ø	0	—	-7	77	-0.3
2001	†StL N	3	4	.429	51	10	0	1-2	89	74	32	11	4	33-4	72	3.24	134	.227	.305	17-1-1	.118	0*	88	12	0	0.8
2002	StL N	2	1	.667	43	0	0	0-2	41.2	40	21	5	2	22-2	32	3.89	104	.260	.352	6	.167	-0	—	0	21	0.0
	Mil N	0	0	ø	4	0	0	0-0	4	3	2	0	0	7-1	2	4.50	91	.214	.476	0-0-1	ø	0	—	0	0	0.0
	Year	2	1	.667	47	0	0	0-2	45.2	43	23	5	2	29-3	34	3.94	103	.256	.365	6-0-1	.167	-0	—	0	0	0.0
2003	SD N	6	4	.600	77	0	0	0-3	64.2	65	34	4	4	29-5	44	4.45	90	.271	.353	2-0-1	.000	-0	—	-3	0	-0.4
2004	Cin N	2	1	.667	35	0	0	0-0	30	31	22	7	2	16-1	15	6.30	68	.265	.360	0	ø	0	—	-6	62	-0.6
2005	NY N	1	0	1.000	6	0	0	0-0	5	9	6	0	0	4-1	2	10.80	38	.429	.481	0	ø	0	—	-4	0	-0.6
Total	6	14	10	.583	230	10	0	1-7	243.2	237	129	29	13	121-16	175	4.54	92	.259	.349	25-1-3	.120	-0	88	-8	160	-1.1
Matthews, William	William Calvin; B1.12.1878 Mahanoy City PA; D1.23.1946 Mt.Carbon PA; TR; d8.28																									
1909	Bos A	0	0	ø	5	1	0	0	16.2	16	8	1	0	10	6	3.24	77	.271	.377	8	.000	-1	113	-1	—	-0.2
Matthewson, Dale	Dale Wesley; B5.15.1923 Catasauqua PA; D2.20.1984 Blairsville GA; BR/TR/5´11.5˝/145; d7.3																									
1943	Phi N	0	3	.000	11	1	0	0	26	26	14	1	0	8	8	4.85	70	.271	.327	2-0-1	.000	-0*	0	-3	0	-0.4
1944	Phi N	0	0	ø	17	0	0	0	32	27	14	1	0	16	8	3.94	92	.237	.331	3	.333	0	—	0	0	0.0
Total	2	0	3	.000	28	1	0	0	58	53	28	2	0	24	16	4.34	81	.252	.329	5-0-1	.200	-0	0	-3	0	-0.4
Mattimore, Mike	Michael Joseph; B8.1858 North Bend PA; D4.28.1931 Butte MT; BL/TL/5´8.5˝/160; d5.3; ▲																									
1887	NY N	3	3	.500	7	7	6-1	0	57.1	47	39	2	4	28	12	2.35	160	.218	.319	32	.250	-0*	135	5	—	0.3
1888	Phi AA	15	10	.600	26	24	24-4	0	221	221	146	6	13	65	80	3.38	88	.251	.312	142	.268	7*	142	-8	—	-0.1
1889	Phi AA	2	1	.667	5	1	1	1	31	42	27	0	1	13	6	5.81	65	.313	.378	73-1	.233	1*	131	-5	—	-0.3
	KC AA	0	0	ø	1	0	0	0	3	3	3	1	0	2	1	3.00	142	.250	.357	75	.160	-0*	—	0	—	0.0
	Year	2	1	.667	6	1	1	1	34	45	30	1	1	15	7	5.56	69	.308	.377	148-1	.196	1	130	-5	—	-0.3
1890	Bro AA	6	13	.316	19	19	19	0	178.1	201	149	3	13	76	33	4.54	86	.276	.355	129	.132	-3*	93	-15	—	-1.4
Total	4	26	27	.491	58	51	50-5	1	490.2	514	364	12	31	184	132	3.83	90	.261	.333	451-1	.204	5	121	-23	—	-1.5
Mattingly, Earl	Laurence Earl; B11.4.1904 Newport MD; D9.8.1993 Brookeville MD; BR/TR/5´10.5˝/164; d4.15																									
1931	Bro N	0	1	.000	8	0	0	0	14.1	15	4	0	2	10	6	2.51	152	.268	.397	3	.000	-0	—	2	—	0.1
Matula, Rick	Richard Carlton; B11.22.1953 Wharton TX; BR/TR/6´0˝/(190–195); [AtlN76 14/315]; d4.8; Col Sam Houston St.																									
1979	Atl N	8	10	.444	28	28	1	0-0	171.1	193	90	14	3	64-9	67	4.15	97	.286	.348	53-0-6	.094	-3	91	-1	0	-0.4
1980	Atl N	11	13	.458	33	30	3-1	0-0	176.2	195	100	17	0	60-9	62	4.58	80	.286	.339	57-0-5	.105	-3	81	-18	0	-2.4
1981	Atl N	0	0	ø	5	0	0	0-0	7	8	5	1	0	2-0	0	6.43	55	.286	.333	1	.000	-0	—	-2	0	-0.1
Total	3	19	23	.452	66	58	4-1	0-0	355	396	195	32	3	126-18	129	4.41	87	.286	.343	111-0-11	.099	-6	86	-21	0	-2.9
Matuzak, Harry	Harry George "Matty"; B1.27.1910 Omer MI; D11.16.1978 Fairhope AL; BR/TR/5´11.5˝/185; d4.19																									
1934	Phi A	0	3	.000	11	0	0	0	24	28	16	2	1	10	9	4.88	90	.292	.364	6-0-1	.167	0	—	-2	—	-0.2
1936	Phi A	0	1	.000	6	1	0	0	15	21	14	0	0	4	8	7.20	71	.318	.357	3-0-1	.000	-0	207	-4	—	-0.2
Total	2	0	4	.000	17	1	0	0	39	49	30	2	1	14	17	5.77	81	.302	.362	9-0-2	.111	-0	207	-6	—	-0.4
Mauck, Hal	Alfred Maris; B3.6.1869 Princeton IN; D4.27.1921 Princeton IN; BR/TR/5´11˝/185; d4.29																									
1893	Chi N	8	10	.444	23	18	12-1	0	143	168	112	2	9	60	23	4.41	105	.284	.359	61	.148	-5	84	0	—	-0.4
Maul, Al	Albert Joseph "Smiling Al"; B10.9.1865 Philadelphia PA; D5.3.1958 Philadelphia PA; BR/TR/6´0˝/175; d6.20; ▲																									
1884	Phi U	0	1	.000	1	1	1	0	8	10	7	0	—	1	7	4.50	51	.286	.306	4	.000	-1	55	-2	—	-0.3
1887	Phi N	4	2	.667	7	5	4	0	50.1	72	50	2	2	15	18	5.54	77	.326	.374	56-1	.304	3*	174	-7	—	-0.4
1888	Pit N	0	2	.000	3	1	1	0	17	26	20	0	0	5	12	6.35	42	.342	.383	259	.208	1*	23	-8	—	-0.7
1889	Pit N	1	4	.200	6	4	4	0	42	64	53	3	1	28	11	9.86	38	.340	.429	257-4	.276	2*	148	-26	—	-1.9
1890	Pit P	16	12	.571	30	28	26-2	0	246.2	258	189	13	12	104	81	3.79	103	.257	.335	162	.259	7*	124	0	—	0.7
1891	Pit N	1	2	.333	8	3	3	1	39	44	22	0	3	16	13	2.31	142	.273	.350	149	.188	1*	97	4	—	0.3
1893	Was N	12	21	.364	37	33	29-1	0	297	355	254	17	18	144	72	5.30	87	.288	.370	134	.254	10*	92	-22	—	-0.9
1894	Was N	11	15	.423	28	26	21	0	201.2	272	200	12	10	73	34	5.98	88	.319	.379	124-2-1	.242	3*	99	-9	—	-0.5
1895	Was N	10	5	.667	16	16	14	0	135.2	136	67	5	3	37	34	**2.45**	**196**	.257	.309	72-0-2	.250	1*	98	33	—	3.0

YEAR	TM LG	W	L	PCT	G	GS	CG-SHO	SV-BS	IP	H	R	HR	HB	BB-IB	SO	ERA	AERA	OAV	OOB	AB-HR-SH	AVG	PB	SUP	APR	DL	PW
1896	Was N	5	2	.714	8	8	7	0	62	75	50	0	4	20	18	3.63	122	.296	.357	28	.286	2	149	2	—	0.3
1897	Was N	0	1	.000	1	1	0	0	2	4	2	0	0	1	0	9.00	48	.400	.455	1	.000	-0	66	-1	—	-0.1
	Bal N	0	0	ø	2	2	0	0	7.2	9	8	0	4	8	2	7.04	59	.290	.488	3	.333	0	162	-2	—	-0.1
	Year	0	1	.000	3	3	0	0	9.2	13	10	0	4	9	2	7.45	56	.317	.481	4	.250	-0	130	-3	—	-0.2
1898	Bal N	20	7	.741	28	28	26-1	0	239.2	207	74	3	4	49	31	2.10	170	.231	.274	93-0-1	.204	4*	127	42	—	4.4
1899	Bro N	2	0	1.000	4	4	2	0	26	35	19	1	2	6	2	4.50	87	.321	.368	11	.273	0	161	-2	—	-0.1
1900	Phi N	2	3	.400	5	4	3	0	38	53	31	2	2	3	6	6.16	59	.329	.349	15	.200	0	72	-9	—	-0.9
1901	NY N	0	3	.000	3	3	2	0	19	39	27	1	2	8	5	11.37	29	.419	.476	8	.375	1	57	-15	—	-1.5
Total	15	84	80	.512	187	167	143-4	1	1431.2	1659	1073	59	67	518	346	4.43	96	.284	.349	1376-7-4	.241	32	112	-22	—	1.3
Maun, Ernie	Ernest Gerald; B2.3.1901 Clearwater KS; D1.1.1987 Corpus Christi TX; BR/TR/6´0˝/165; d5.16																									
1924	NY N	2	1	.667	22	0	0	1	35	46	24	2	1	10	5	5.91	62	.326	.375	3	.667	1	—	-8	—	-0.6
1926	Phi N	1	4	.200	14	5	0	0	37.2	57	36	4	1	18	9	6.45	64	.339	.406	12	.250	-0	101	-10	—	-1.2
Total	2	3	5	.375	36	5	0	1	72.2	103	60	6	2	28	14	6.19	63	.333	.392	15	.333	1	101	-18	—	-1.8
Mauney, Dick	Richard; B1.26.1920 Concord NC; D2.6.1970 Albemarle NC; BR/TR/5´11.5˝/164; d6.13																									
1945	Phi N	6	10	.375	20	16	6-2	1	122.2	127	54	7	2	27	35	3.08	124	.268	.310	41-0-1	.146	-0*	79	9	0	1.2
1946	Phi N	6	4	.600	24	7	3-1	2	90	98	36	4	3	18	31	2.70	127	.279	.320	24-0-3	.167	-1*	125	5	0	0.6
1947	Phi N	0	0	ø	9	1	0	1	16.1	15	8	1	1	7	6	3.86	104	.288	.383	2	.000	-0*	66	0	0	0.0
Total	3	12	14	.462	53	24	9-3	4	229	240	98	12	6	52	72	2.99	123	.274	.319	67-0-4	.149	-1	92	14	0	1.8
Maupin, Harry	Harry Carr; B7.11.1872 Wellsville MO; D8.25.1952 Parsons KS; TR/5´7˝/150; d10.5																									
1898	StL N	0	2	.000	2	2	2	0	18	22	11	0	3	3	3	5.50	69	.297	.350	7-0-1	.429	1	94	-2	—	-0.1
1899	Cle N	0	3	.000	5	3	2	0	25	55	36	0	1	7	3	12.60	29	.437	.470	10	.000	-2	91	-21	—	-1.9
Total	2	0	5	.000	7	5	4	0	43	77	47	0	4	10	6	9.63	39	.385	.425	17-0-1	.176	-1	92	-23	—	-2.0
Maurer, Dave	David Charles; B2.23.1975 Minneapolis MN; BR/TL/6´2˝/205; [SDN97 11/350]; d7.22; Col Oklahoma St.																									
2000	SD N	1	0	1.000	14	0	0	0-1	14.2	15	8	2	2	5-1	13	3.68	121	.263	.344	0	ø	0	—	1	0	0.0
2001	SD N	0	0	ø	3	0	0	0-0	5	8	6	1	0	4-0	4	10.80	38	.348	.444	1	.000	-0	—	-4	0	-0.2
2002	Cle A	0	1	.000	2	0	0	0-0	1.1	3	2	1	0	0-0	0	13.50	33	.429	.429	0	ø	0	—	-1	0	-0.2
2004	Tor A	0	0	ø	3	0	0	0-0	1.1	6	8	1	0	5-0	1	54.00	9	.600	.733	0	ø	0	—	-7	0	-0.3
Total	4	1	1	.500	22	0	0	0-1	22.1	32	24	5	2	14-1	18	8.87	50	.330	.425	1	.000	-0	—	-11	0	-0.7
Mauriello, Ralph	Ralph "Tami"; B8.25.1934 Brooklyn NY; BR/TR/6´3˝/195; d9.13																									
1958	LA N	1	1	.500	3	2	0	0	11.2	10	6	1	0	8-0	11	4.63	89	.238	.360	4	.000	-1	99	0	0	-0.1
Mauser, Tim	Timothy Edward; B10.4.1966 Fort Worth TX; BR/TR/6´0˝/(185–200); [PhiN88 3/68]; d7.7; Col TCU																									
1991	Phi N	0	0	ø	3	0	0	0-0	10.2	18	10	3	0	3-0	6	7.59	49	.367	.404	3	.000	-0	—	-5	0	-0.3
1993	Phi N	0	0	ø	8	0	0	0-0	16.1	15	9	1	1	7-0	14	4.96	80	.238	.324	4	.000	-0	—	-1	0	0.0
	SD N	0	1	.000	28	0	0	0-0	37.2	36	19	5	0	17-5	32	3.58	115	.248	.325	2	.000	-0	—	1	0	0.1
	Year	0	1	.000	36	0	0	0-0	54	51	28	6	1	24-5	46	4.00	102	.245	.325	6	.000	-0	—	0	0	0.1
1994	SD N	2	4	.333	35	0	0	2-0	49	50	21	3	1	19-3	32	3.49	118	.269	.335	4-0-1	.250	0	—	4	16	0.5
1995	SD N	0	1	.000	5	0	0	0-0	5.2	4	6	0	0	9-0	9	9.53	43	.190	.433	1	.000	-0	—	-3	0	-0.5
Total	4	2	6	.250	79	0	0	2-0	119.1	123	65	12	2	55-8	93	4.37	93	.265	.343	14-0-1	.071	-0	—	-4	16	-0.2
Maxcy, Brian	David Brian; B5.4.1971 Amory MS; BR/TR/6´1˝/170; [DetA92 20/560]; d5.26; Col U. of Mississippi																									
1995	Det A	4	5	.444	41	0	0	0-2	52.1	61	48	6	2	31-7	20	6.88	70	.293	.385	0	ø	0	—	-14	0	-1.9
1996	Det A	0	0	ø	2	0	0	0-0	3.1	8	5	2	0	2-0	1	13.50	38	.471	.526	0	ø	0	—	-3	0	-0.1
Total	2	4	5	.444	43	0	0	0-2	55.2	69	53	8	2	33-7	21	7.28	66	.307	.395	0	ø	0	—	-17	0	-2.0
Maxie, Larry	Larry Hans; B10.10.1940 Upland CA; BR/TR/6´4˝/220; d8.30; Col Chaffey (CA) JC																									
1969	Atl N	0	0	ø	2	0	0	0-0	3	1	1	0	1	1-1	1	3.00	121	.111	.250	0	ø	0	—	0	0	0.0
Maxwell, Bert	James Albert; B10.17.1886 Texarkana AR; D12.10.1961 Brady TX; BB/TR/6´0˝/180; d9.12																									
1906	Pit N	0	1	.000	1	1	0	0	8	8	6	0	0	2	1	5.63	48	.286	.333	3	.000	-0	136	-2	—	-0.3
1908	Phi A	0	0	ø	4	0	0	0	13	23	21	0	2	9	7	11.08	23	.348	.442	5	.000	-1	—	-11	—	-0.6
1911	NY N	1	2	.333	4	3	3	0	31	37	15	0	2	7	8	2.90	116	.311	.359	9-0-1	.111	-0	104	1	—	0.1
1914	Bro F	3	4	.429	12	8	6-1	1	71.1	76	31	0	1	24	19	3.28	88	.276	.337	23-0-1	.087	-2	92	-2	—	-0.4
Total	4	4	7	.364	21	12	9-1	1	123.1	144	73	0	5	42	35	4.16	71	.295	.357	40-0-2	.075	-3	99	-14	—	-1.2
May, Darrell	Darrell Kevin; B6.13.1972 San Bernardino CA; BL/TL/6´2˝/(170–185); [AtlN92 46/1293]; d9.10; Col Sacramento (CA) City																									
1995	Atl N	0	0	ø	2	0	0	0-0	4	10	5	0	0	0-0	1	11.25	38	.500	.476	0	ø	0	—	-3	0	-0.1
1996	Pit N	0	1	.000	5	2	0	0-0	8.2	15	10	5	1	4-0	5	9.35	47	.357	.426	3	.333	0	82	-5	0	-0.4
	Cal A	0	0	ø	5	0	0	0-0	2.2	3	3	1	0	2-0	1	10.13	50	.333	.385	0	ø	0	—	-1	0	-0.1
1997	Ana A	2	1	.667	29	2	0	0-1	51.2	56	31	6	0	25-2	42	5.23	88	.277	.351	2	.000	-0	169	-3	0	-0.2
2002	KC A	4	10	.286	30	21	2-1	0-1	131.1	144	83	28	1	50-3	95	5.35	93	.277	.339	4	.000	-0	80	-5	47	-0.4
2003	KC A	10	8	.556	35	32	2-1	0-1	210	197	98	31	2	53-1	115	3.77	128	.246	.292	4-0-1	.000	-0	97	21	0	1.5
2004	KC A	9	19	.321	31	31	3-1	0-0	186	234	130	38	2	55-4	120	5.61	83	.306	.350	4	.000	-0	88	-20	0	-2.6
2005	SD N	1	3	.250	22	8	0	0-0	59.1	73	38	10	0	20-1	32	5.61	70	.303	.354	9-0-1	.111	-0	117	-11	0	-0.7
	NY A	0	1	.000	2	1	0	0-0	7	14	13	4	0	3-0	3	16.71	26	.400	.447	0	ø	0	151	-9	0	-0.9
Total	7	26	43	.377	161	97	7-3	0-3	660.2	746	411	123	6	212-11	414	5.16	91	.283	.334	26-0-2	.077	-1	94	-36	47	-3.9
May, Jakie	Frank Spruiell; B11.25.1895 Youngsville NC; D6.3.1970 Wendell NC; BR/TL/5´8˝/178; d6.26; Mil 1918																									
1917	StL N	0	0	ø	15	1	0	0	29.1	29	13	0	3	11	18	3.38	80	.302	.391	4	.000	-1	56	-2	—	-0.1
1918	StL N	5	6	.455	29	15	6	0	152.2	149	83	2	13	69	61	3.83	71	.264	.358	45-1-4	.067	-1	113	-18	—	-1.5
1919	StL N	3	12	.200	28	19	8-1	0	125.2	99	64	1	14	87	58	3.22	87	.230	.377	37-0-3	.162	-1	82	-9	—	-1.3
1920	StL N	1	4	.200	16	5	3	0	70.2	65	38	0	7	37	33	3.06	98	.251	.360	22	.227	1	74	-4	—	-0.2
1921	StL N	1	3	.250	5	5	1	0	21	29	14	0	0	12	5	4.71	78	.333	.414	6	.333	1	90	-3	—	-0.4
1924	Cin N	3	3	.500	38	3	2	**6**	99	104	39	2	6	29	59	3.00	126	.276	.337	27-1-1	.111	-2	68	9	—	0.4
1925	Cin N	8	9	.471	36	12	7-1	2	137.1	146	74	3	7	45	74	3.87	106	.272	.337	43	.186	0	104	4	—	0.4
1926	Cin N	13	9	.591	45	15	9-1	3	167.2	175	66	4	7	44	103	3.22	115	.276	.329	48-0-6	.146	-1	99	12	—	1.3
1927	Cin N	15	12	.556	44	28	17-2	1	235.2	242	110	4	14	70	121	3.51	108	.274	.337	76-0-7	.184	0	103	8	—	0.9
1928	Cin N	3	5	.375	21	11	1-1	1	79.1	99	44	1	1	35	39	4.42	89	.315	.386	27-0-3	.296	1	101	-4	—	-0.3
1929	Cin N	10	14	.417	41	24	10	3	199	219	111	7	5	75	92	4.61	99	.285	.352	64-0-3	.203	-1	76	1	—	0.0
1930	Cin N	3	11	.214	26	18	5-1	0	112.1	147	83	6	6	41	44	5.77	84	.320	.383	39-0-1	.128	-1	84	-13	—	-1.3
1931	Chi N	5	5	.500	31	4	1	2	79	81	35	2	3	43	38	3.87	100	.275	.372	22-0-1	.227	1	122	2	—	0.3
1932	†Chi N	2	2	.500	35	0	0	1	53.2	61	34	3	2	19	20	4.36	86	.281	.345	8	.125	-0	—	-5	—	-0.4
Total	14	72	95	.431	410	160	70-7	19	1562.1	1645	808	35	88	617	765	3.88	97	.278	.355	468-2-29	.171	-4	93	-22	—	-2.2
May, Rudy	Rudolph; B7.18.1944 Coffeyville KS; BL/TL/6´3˝/(195–205); d4.18; [DL 1984 NY A 182]																									
1965	Cal A	4	9	.308	30	19	2-1	0	124	111	59	7	4	78-1	76	3.92	87	.245	.359	30-0-2	.200	3	71	-7	0	-0.4
1969	Cal A	10	13	.435	43	25	4	2-0	180.1	142	81	20	3	66-5	133	3.44	102	.220	.295	49-0-1	.082	-2*	76	0	0	-0.2
1970	Cal A	7	13	.350	38	34	2-2	0-0	208.2	190	102	20	3	81-7	164	4.01	90	.245	.318	69-0-2	.087	-2	71	-8	0	-1.0
1971	Cal A	11	12	.478	32	31	7-2	0-1	208.1	160	74	12	2	87-6	156	3.02	107	.213	.296	68-0-2	.147	0	77	8	23	0.9
1972	Cal A	12	11	.522	35	30	10-3	1-0	205.1	162	79	15	0	82-6	169	2.94	100	.215	.292	62-0-2	.113	-1	81	-1	0	-0.4
1973	Cal A	7	17	.292	34	28	10-4	0-2	185	177	101	20	3	80-9	134	4.38	82	.254	.330	0	ø	0	107	-17	0	-1.8
1974	Cal A	0	1	.000	18	3	0	2-0	27	29	24	2	1	10-0	12	7.00	50	.274	.331	0	ø	0	135	-11	0	-0.5
	NY A	8	4	.667	17	15	8-2	0-0	114.1	75	36	5	4	48-0	90	2.28	155	.188	.280	0	ø	0	129	15	21	1.5
	Year	8	5	.615	35	18	8-2	2-0	141.1	104	60	7	5	58-0	102	3.18	111	.206	.290	0	ø	0	130	3	0	1.0
1975	NY A	14	12	.538	32	31	13-1	0-0	212	179	87	9	2	99-2	145	3.06	121	.231	.317	0	ø	0	107	13	0	1.5
1976	NY A	4	3	.571	11	11	2-1	0-0	68	49	32	5	1	28-2	38	3.57	96	.206	.291	0	ø	0	140	-2	0	-0.2
	Bal A	11	7	.611	24	21	5-1	0-1	152.1	156	73	11	0	42-3	71	3.78	87	.267	.314	0	ø	0	123	-10	0	-1.1
	Year	15	10	.600	35	32	7-2	0-1	220.1	205	105	16	1	70-5	109	3.72	90	.249	.307	0	ø	0	129	-11	0	-1.3
1977	Bal A	18	14	.563	37	37	11-4	0-0	251.2	243	114	25	5	78-2	105	3.61	106	.255	.313	0	ø	0	105	4	0	0.4
1978	Mon N	8	10	.444	27	23	4-1	0-0	144	141	73	15	6	42-1	87	3.88	92	.255	.313	42-0-7	.143	0	125	-7	43	-0.8
1979	Mon N	10	3	.769	33	7	2-1	0-1	93.2	88	30	4	4	31-4	67	2.31	161	.255	.320	21-0-1	.143	-0	88	14	0	1.8

YEAR	TM LG	W	L	PCT	G	GS	CG-SHO	SV-BS	IP	H	R	HR	HB	BB-IB	SO	ERA	AERA	OAV	OOB	AB-HR-SH	AVG	PB	SUP	APR	DL	PW
1980	†NY A	15	5	.750	41	17	3-1	3-2	175.1	144	56	14	0	39-2	133	**2.46**	**161**	.224	**.268**	0	ø	0	94	29	13	3.2
1981	†NY A	6	11	.353	27	22	4	1-0	147.2	137	71	10	2	41-0	79	4.14	87	.246	.298	0	ø	0	95	-6	0	-0.6
1982	NY A	6	6	.500	41	6	0	3-3	106	109	43	4	1	14-5	85	2.89	140	.267	.289	0	ø	0	87	11	23	1.3
1983	NY A	1	5	.167	15	0	0	0-2	18.1	22	15	1	1	12-1	16	6.87	57	.293	.398	0	ø	0	—	-6	76	-1.1
Total	16	152	156	.494	535	360	87-24	12-12	2622	2314	1150	199	42	958-56	1760	3.46	103	.238	.308	341-0-17	.123	-3	96	19	381	2.5
May, Scott	Scott Francis; B11.11.1961 West Bend WI; BR/TR/6´1˝/185; [LAN83 6/150]; d9.2; Col Wisconsin–Stevens Point																									
1988	Tex A	0	0	ø	3	1	0	0-0	7.1	8	7	3	0	4-1	4	8.59	48	.296	.364	0	ø	0	133	-3	0	-0.2
1991	Chi N	0	0	ø	2	0	0	0-0	2	6	4	0	0	1-0	1	18.00	22	.545	.583	0	ø	0	—	-3	0	-0.1
Total	2	0	0	ø	5	1	0	0-0	9.1	14	11	3	0	5-1	5	10.61	38	.368	.422	0	ø	0	133	-6	0	-0.3
May, Buckshot	William Herbert; B12.13.1899 Bakersfield CA; D3.15.1984 Bakersfield CA; BR/TR/6´2˝/169; d5.9																									
1924	Pit N	0	0	ø	1	0	0	0	1	2	0	0	0	0	1	0.00	ø	.500	.500	0	ø	0	—	0	—	0.0
Mayer, Ed	Edwin David; B11.30.1931 San Francisco CA; BL/TL/6´2˝/185; d9.15; Col California																									
1957	Chi N	0	0	ø	3	1	0	0	7.2	8	5	2	1	2-0	3	5.87	66	.258	.324	2	.500	0	159	-1	0	0.0
1958	Chi N	2	2	.500	19	0	0	1	23.2	15	12	0	3	16-1	14	3.80	103	.190	.343	5	.200	-0	—	0	0	0.0
Total	2	2	2	.500	22	1	0	1	31.1	23	17	2	4	18-1	17	4.31	91	.209	.338	7	.286	0	159	-1	0	0.0
Mayer, Erskine	Erskine John (b Jacob Erskine); B1.16.1890 Atlanta GA; D3.10.1957 Los Angeles CA; BR/TR/6´0˝/168; d9.4; b–Sam; Col Georgia Tech																									
1912	Phi N	0	1	.000	7	1	0	0	21.1	27	15	1	1	7	5	6.33	57	.318	.376	3	.000	-0	20	-4	—	-0.2
1913	Phi N	9	9	.500	39	19	7-2	1	170.2	172	77	6	9	46	51	3.11	107	.272	.330	50	.120	-2	86	3	—	0.1
1914	Phi N	21	19	.525	48	38	24-4	2	321	308	135	8	13	91	116	2.58	114	.256	.315	108-1-3	.194	2	95	12	—	2.0
1915	†Phi N	21	15	.583	43	33	20-2	2	274.2	240	94	9	14	59	114	2.36	116	.243	.295	88-1-5	.239	5	90	14	—	2.5
1916	Phi N	7	7	.500	28	16	7-2	0	140	148	58	7	4	33	62	3.15	84	.281	.328	38-0-2	.132	-1	92	-5	—	-0.4
1917	Phi N	11	6	.647	28	18	11-1	0	160	160	62	6	4	33	64	2.76	102	.268	.310	51-0-5	.196	-0	144	2	—	0.2
1918	Phi N	7	4	.636	13	13	7	0	104	108	46	2	4	26	16	3.12	96	.276	.328	37-0-3	.216	1	113	-1	—	-0.1
	Pit N	9	3	.750	15	14	11-1	0	123.1	122	40	1	4	27	25	2.26	127	.268	.314	42-0-1	.167	2	139	8	—	0.9
	Year	16	7	.696	28	27	18-1	0	227.1	230	86	3	8	53	41	2.65	110	.272	.320	79-0-4	.190	2	126	6	—	0.8
1919	Pit N	5	3	.625	18	10	6	1	88.1	100	50	2	2	12	20	4.48	67	.267	.294	29-0-1	.207	0	156	-13	—	-1.2
	†Chi A	1	3	.250	6	2	0	0	23.2	30	23	1	0	11	9	8.37	38	.316	.387	7	.000	-1	123	-12	—	-1.7
Total	8	91	70	.565	245	164	93-12	6	1427	1415	600	43	55	345	482	2.96	99	.264	.316	453-2-20	.185	5	106	4	—	2.1
Mays, Al	Albert C.; B5.17.1865 Canal Dover (now Dover) OH; D5.7.1905 Parkersburg WV; BR; d5.10																									
1885	Lou AA	6	11	.353	17	17	17	0	150	129	102	3	8	43	61	2.76	117	.219	.282	61	.213	0	78	5	—	0.5
1886	NY AA	11	27	.289	41	40	39-1	0	350	330	231	7	14	140	163	3.39	96	.240	.317	135-1	.119	-9	80	-10	—	-1.6
1887	NY AA	17	34	.333	52	52	50	0	441.1	551	359	11	20	136	124	4.73	90	.298	.353	221-2	.204	-1*	77	-22	—	-1.6
1888	Bro AA	9	9	.500	18	18	17-1	0	160.2	150	81	1	11	32	67	2.80	107	.238	.287	63	.079	-4	95	5	—	0.2
1889	Col AA	10	7	.588	21	19	13-1	0	140	167	119	4	4	56	52	4.82	75	.287	.354	54	.130	-1	103	-20	—	-1.8
1890	Col AA	0	1	.000	1	1	1	0	9	14	13	0	1	8	2	8.00	45	.341	.460	3	.000	-0	56	-5	—	-0.4
Total	6	53	89	.373	150	147	137-3	0	1251	1341	905	26	58	415	469	3.91	92	.265	.328	537-3	.160	-15	83	-47	—	-4.7
Mays, Carl	Carl William "Sub"; B11.12.1891 Liberty KY; D4.4.1971 ElCajon CA; BL/TR/5´11.5˝/195; d4.15																									
1915	Bos A	6	5	.545	38	6	2	**7**	131.2	119	54	0	5	21	65	2.60	107	.244	.282	38-0-2	.237	2	118	2	—	0.4
1916	†Bos A	18	13	.581	44	24	14-2	3	245	208	79	3	9	74	76	2.39	116	.234	.299	77-0-3	.234	7*	97	11	—	2.8
1917	Bos A	22	9	.710	35	33	27-2	0	289	230	81	1	14	74	91	1.74	148	.221	.282	107-0-2	.252	6	108	25	—	4.0
1918	†Bos A	21	13	.618	35	33	**30-8**	0	293.1	230	94	2	11	81	114	2.21	121	.221	.284	104-0-4	.288	10*	119	16	—	3.7
1919	Bos A	5	11	.313	21	16	14-2	2	146	131	57	2	5	40	53	2.47	123	.247	.306	53-0-2	.151	-2*	78	6	—	0.6
	NY A	9	3	.750	13	13	12-1	0	120	96	34	3	5	37	54	1.65	193	.216	.283	45-0-1	.311	3	128	18	—	2.3
	Year	14	14	.500	34	29	26-3	2	266	227	91	5	10	77	107	2.10	148	.233	.295	98-0-3	.224	1	101	25	—	2.9
1920	NY A	26	11	.703	45	37	26-**6**	2	312	310	127	13	7	84	92	3.06	125	.263	.316	109-0-8	.239	2	133	28	—	3.5
1921	†NY A	**27**	9	**.750**	**49**	38	30-1	**7**	**336.2**	332	145	11	9	76	70	3.05	139	.257	.303	143-2-8	.343	12*	152	43	—	5.4
1922	†NY A	13	14	.481	34	29	21-1	2	240	257	111	12	7	50	41	3.60	111	.285	.327	92-0-3	.250	1*	110	11	—	1.5
1923	NY A	5	2	.714	23	7	2	0	81.1	119	59	8	4	32	16	6.20	64	.357	.420	27-1-1	.148	1	138	-19	—	-1.2
1924	Cin N	20	9	.690	37	27	15-2	0	226	238	97	3	4	36	63	3.15	120	.270	.302	83-1-0	.289	7*	107	15	—	3.0
1925	Cin N	3	5	.375	12	5	3	2	51.2	60	22	0	2	13	10	3.31	124	.294	.342	16	.250	1	66	5	—	0.9
1926	Cin N	19	12	.613	39	33	**24**-3	1	281	286	112	3	4	53	58	3.14	118	.269	.306	98-0-7	.224	2	114	21	—	2.9
1927	Cin N	3	7	.300	14	9	6	0	82	89	39	1	1	10	17	3.51	108	.276	.300	32-1-1	.406	5	52	2	—	1.0
1928	Cin N	4	1	.800	14	6	4-1	1	62.2	67	33	3	0	22	10	3.88	102	.275	.335	27	.296	1	119	0	—	0.1
1929	NY N	7	2	.778	37	8	1	4	123	140	67	8	2	31	32	4.32	106	.287	.333	34-0-2	.353	4	119	5	—	0.8
Total	15	208	126	.623	490	324	231-29	31	3021.1	2912	1211	73	89	734	862	2.92	119	.257	.307	1085-5-44	.268	64	117	189	—	31.7
Mays, Joe	Joseph Emerson; B12.10.1975 Flint MI; BB/TR/6´1˝/(185–200); [SeaA94 6/161]; d4.7; Col Manatee (FL) CC; [DL 2004 Min A 183]																									
1999	Min A	6	11	.353	49	20	2-1	0-0	171	179	92	24	2	67-2	115	4.37	119	.270	.336	3	.000	0	55	13	0	1.1
2000	Min A	7	15	.318	31	28	2-1	0-0	160.1	193	105	20	2	67-1	102	5.56	95	.299	.364	5-0-1	.400	1	69	-4	0	-0.4
2001	Min A★	17	13	.567	34	34	4-2	0-0	233.2	205	87	25	5	64-2	123	3.16	**148**	.235	.289	1-0-1	.000	-0	87	**38**	0	**4.4**
2002	†Min A	4	8	.333	17	17	1-1	0-0	95.1	113	60	14	2	25-0	38	5.38	83	.292	.337	0	ø	0	93	-9	96	-1.0
2003	Min A	8	8	.500	31	21	0	0-1	130	159	92	21	4	39-2	50	6.30	71	.302	.353	3-0-1	.333	1	115	-24	0	-2.4
2005	Min A	6	10	.375	31	26	1-1	0-0	156	203	109	23	3	41-1	59	5.65	78	.318	.361	3	.333	0	90	-23	0	-2.0
2006	KC A	0	4	.000	6	6	0	0-0	23.2	38	33	7	0	14-0	9	10.27	46	.369	.437	0	ø	0	84	-16	0	-2.0
	Cin N	0	1	.000	7	4	0	0-0	27	40	23	4	0	12-2	16	7.33	64	.342	.403	9-0-1	.222	0	137	-7	0	-0.3
Total	7	48	70	.407	206	156	10-6	0-1	997	1130	601	138	18	329-10	512	5.05	94	.286	.341	24-0-4	.250	2	85	-32	279	-2.6
Maysey, Matt	Matthew Samuel; B1.8.1967 Hamilton ON, Can.; BR/TR/6´4˝/225; [SDN85 7/180]; d7.8																									
1992	Mon N	0	0	ø	2	0	0	0-0	2.1	4	1	1	1	0-0	1	3.86	90	.364	.417	0	ø	0	—	0	0	0.0
1993	Mil A	1	2	.333	23	0	0	1-1	22	28	14	4	1	13-1	10	5.73	75	.322	.408	1	1.000	0	—	-3	0	-0.3
Total	2	1	2	.333	25	0	0	1-1	24.1	32	15	5	2	13-1	11	5.55	76	.327	.409	1	1.000	0	—	-3	0	-0.3
McAdams, Jack	George Decalve; B12.17.1886 Bryant AR; D5.21.1937 San Francisco CA; BR/TR/6´1.5˝/170; d7.22																									
1911	StL N	0	0	ø	6	0	0	0	9.2	7	5	0	2	5	4	3.72	91	.226	.368	1	.000	-0	—	0	—	0.0
McAfee, Bill	William Fort; B9.7.1907 Smithville GA; D7.8.1958 Culpeper VA; BR/TR/6´2˝/186; d5.12; Col Michigan																									
1930	Chi N	0	0	ø	2	0	0	0	1	3	5	0	0	2	0	0.00	ø	.375	.500	0	ø	0	—	-2	—	-0.1
1931	Bos N	0	1	.000	18	1	0	0	29.2	39	22	2	0	10	9	6.37	59	.333	.386	3	.000	-0	45	-8	—	-0.4
1932	Was A	6	1	.857	8	5	2	0	41.1	47	22	3	0	22	10	3.92	110	.287	.371	18-0-2	.111	-2	130	1	—	0.0
1933	Was A	3	2	.600	27	1	0	5	53	64	40	3	1	21	14	6.62	63	.296	.361	15-1-2	.267	2	102	-13	—	-1.1
1934	StL A	1	0	1.000	28	0	0	0	61.2	84	48	4	3	26	11	5.84	86	.332	.401	16	.188	-0	—	-5	—	-0.3
Total	5	10	4	.714	83	7	2	5	186.2	237	137	12	4	81	44	5.69	78	.313	.382	52-1-4	.173	0	111	-27	—	-1.9
McAllister, Sport	Lewis William; B7.23.1874 Austin MS; D7.17.1962 Wyandotte MI; BB/TR/5´11˝/180; d8.7; ▲																									
1896	Cle N	0	0	ø	1	0	0	0	4	9	3	0	0	2	0	6.75	67	.450	.500	27-0-1	.222	-0*	—	-1	—	0.0
1897	Cle N	1	2	.333	4	3	3	0	28	29	20	3	0	9	10	4.50	100	.266	.322	137-0-4	.219	-0*	106	0	—	0.0
1898	Cle N	3	4	.429	9	7	6	0	65.1	73	43	2	3	23	9	4.55	80	.281	.346	57-0-1	.228	1*	95	-5	—	-0.4
1899	Cle N	0	1	.000	3	1	1	0	16	29	22	0	4	10	2	9.56	39	.387	.483	418-1-12	.237	0*	20	-10	—	-0.5
Total	4	4	7	.364	17	11	10	0	113.1	140	88	5	7	44	21	5.32	73	.302	.371	639-1-18	.232	1	92	-16	—	-0.9
McAnally, Ernie	Ernest Lee; B8.15.1946 Pittsburg TX; BR/TR/6´1˝/190; [NYN66 20/381]; d4.11; Col Paris (TX) JC																									
1971	Mon N	11	12	.478	31	25	8-2	0-0	177.2	150	85	9	8	87-2	98	3.90	92	.228	.324	60-1-3	.117	-2	86	-6	0	-1.0
1972	Mon N	6	15	.286	29	27	4-2	0-0	170	165	79	13	4	71-6	102	3.81	93	.259	.332	53-0-5	.113	-2	74	-5	0	-0.6
1973	Mon N	7	9	.438	27	24	4	0-0	147	158	84	13	3	54-6	72	4.04	94	.274	.337	49-0-4	.184	-1	113	-6	0	-0.8
1974	Mon N	6	13	.316	25	21	5-2	0-0	128.2	126	73	10	4	56-5	79	4.48	86	.256	.336	42-0-2	.119	-2	80	-8	30	-1.3
Total	4	30	49	.380	112	97	21-6	0-0	623.1	599	321	45	19	268-19	351	4.03	91	.253	.332	204-1-14	.132	-6	88	-25	30	-3.7

YEAR	TM LG	W	L	PCT	G	GS	CG-SHO	SV-BS	IP	H	R	HR	HB	BB-IB	SO	ERA	AERA	OAV	OOB	AB-HR-SH	AVG	PB	SUP	APR	DL	PW
McAndrew, Jamie James Brian; B9.2.1967 Williamsport PA; BR/TR/6´2˝/190; [LAN89 1/28]; d7.17; f–Jim; Col Florida; [DL 1996 Mil A 182]																										
1995	Mil A	2	3	.400	10	4	0	0-0	36.1	37	21	2	1	12-2	19	4.71	107	.266	.329	0	ø	0	102	1	30	0.1
1997	Mil A	1	1	.500	5	4	0	0-0	19.1	24	19	1	2	23-0	8	8.38	55	.304	.471	0	ø	0	94	-8	0	-0.6
Total	2	3	4	.429	15	8	0	0-0	55.2	61	40	3	3	35-2	27	5.98	82	.280	.387	0	ø	0	97	-7	212	-0.5
McAndrew, Jim James Clement; B1.11.1944 Lost Nation IA; BR/TR/6´2˝/(175–190); [NYN65 9/245]; d7.21; s–Jamie; Col Iowa																										
1968	NY N	4	7	.364	12	12	2-1	0	79	66	20	5	4	17-4	46	2.28	133	.230	.281	22-0-2	.045	-1	38	7	0	0.9
1969	NY N	6	7	.462	27	21	4-2	0-0	135	112	57	12	2	44-6	90	3.47	106	.225	.288	37-0-5	.135	0	94	3	0	0.2
1970	NY N	10	14	.417	32	27	9-3	2-0	184.1	166	77	18	2	38-6	111	3.56	114	.239	.279	54-0-8	.148	1	84	12	0	1.5
1971	NY N	2	5	.286	24	10	0	0-1	90.1	78	50	10	1	32-5	42	4.38	78	.227	.292	23-0-1	.043	-1	95	-10	0	-0.8
1972	NY N	11	8	.579	28	23	4	1-0	160.2	133	54	12	5	38-5	81	2.80	121	.225	.276	43-0-10	.047	-2	91	12	0	1.1
1973	NY N	3	8	.273	23	12	0	1-0	80.1	109	60	9	3	31-8	38	5.38	68	.330	.386	15-0-2	.133	2*	105	-19	0	-2.2
1974	SD N	1	4	.200	15	5	1	0-0	41.2	48	30	7	0	13-2	16	5.62	64	.284	.332	7-0-2	.143	0	102	-10	0	-1.1
Total	7	37	53	.411	161	110	20-6	4-1	771.1	712	348	73	17	213-36	424	3.65	99	.245	.297	201-0-30	.100	-3	87	-5	0	-0.4
McArthur, Dixie Oland Alexander; B2.1.1892 Vernon AL; D5.31.1986 West Point MS; BR/TR/6´1˝/185; d7.10; Col Bethel																										
1914	Pit N	0	0	ø	1	0	0	0	1	1	1	0	0	0	1	0.00	ø	.250	.250	0	ø	0	—	0	—	0.0
McAvoy, Tom Thomas John; B8.12.1936 Brooklyn NY; BL/TL/6´3˝/195; d9.27; [DL 1960 Was A 168]																										
1959	Was A	0	0	ø	1	0	0	0	2.2	1	0	0	0	2-0	0	0.00	ø	.125	.300	1	.000	-0	—	1	0	0.0
McBean, Al Alvin O'Neal; B5.15.1938 Charlotte Amalie, V.I.; BR/TR/6´0˝/(165–180); d7.2																										
1961	Pit N	3	2	.600	27	2	0	0	74.1	72	35	4	4	42-5	49	3.75	106	.263	.365	15-1-1	.267	1*	33	2	0	0.4
1962	Pit N	15	10	.600	33	29	6-2	0	189.2	212	93	11	7	65-2	119	3.70	106	.285	.346	67-0-4	.209	2*	96	4	0	0.6
1963	Pit N	13	3	.813	55	7	2-1	11	122.1	100	42	5	2	39-9	74	2.57	128	.222	.287	31-1-1	.194	2*	131	10	0	1.7
1964	Pit N	8	3	.727	58	0	0	22	89.2	76	23	4	4	17-8	41	1.91	184	.234	.279	12-0-2	.083	-1	—	**15**	0	2.9
1965	Pit N	6	6	.500	62	1	0	18	114	111	33	5	3	42-11	54	2.29	153	.260	.327	27-0-2	.222	1	199	16	0	2.4
1966	Pit N	4	3	.571	47	0	0	3	86.2	95	38	9	2	24-6	54	3.22	111	.280	.330	10	.100	-1*	—	2	0	0.1
1967	Pit N	7	4	.636	51	8	5	4	131	118	41	6	1	43-6	54	2.54	132	.248	.310	29-0-1	.207	2	98	13	0	1.4
1968	Pit N	9	12	.429	36	28	9-2	0	198.1	204	88	10	5	63-5	100	3.58	82	.269	.327	67-1-2	.194	2*	119	-13	0	-0.9
1969	SD N	0	1	.000	1	1	0	0-0	7	10	4	1	0	2-0	1	5.14	70	.345	.387	2	.500	0	25	-1	0	-0.1
	LA N	2	6	.250	31	0	0	4-0	48.1	46	22	6	2	21-4	26	3.91	86	.258	.340	3	.000	0	—	-2	0	-0.5
	Year	2	7	.222	32	1	0	4-0	55.1	56	26	7	2	23-4	27	4.07	83	.271	.346	5	.200	0	26	-3	0	-0.6
1970	LA N	0	0	ø	1	0	0	0-0	1	1	0	0	0	0-0	0	0.00	ø	.333	.333	0	ø	0	—	0	0	0.0
	Pit N	0	0	ø	7	0	0	1-0	10	13	11	2	0	7-0	3	8.10	49	.317	.417	1	.000	-0	—	-5	0	-0.3
	Year	0	0	ø	8	0	0	1-0	11	14	11	2	0	7-0	3	7.36	54	.318	.412	1	.000	-0	—	-5	0	-0.3
Total	10	67	50	.573	409	76	22-5	63-0	1072.1	1058	430	63	30	365-56	575	3.13	111	.262	.325	264-3-13	.197	9	104	41	0	7.7
McBee, Pryor Pryor Edward "Lefty"; B6.20.1901 Blanco OK; D4.19.1963 Roseville CA; BR/TL/6´1˝/190; d5.22																										
1926	Chi A	0	0	ø	1	0	0	0	1.1	1	2	0	0	3	1	6.75	57	.250	.571	0	ø	0	—	-1	—	0.0
McBride, Dick James Dickson; B1845 Philadelphia PA; D10.10.1916 Philadelphia PA; TR/5´9˝/150; d5.20; M5																										
1871	Ath NA	18	5	**.783**	25	25	25	0	222	285	223	3	—	40	15	4.58	88	.280	.307	132	.235	-4	137	-15	—	-1.2
1872	Ath NA	30	14	.682	47	47	47-1	0	419.1	508	349	3	—	26	44	2.85	125	.265	.275	258	.287	5	124	34	—	2.6
1873	Ath NA	24	19	.558	46	46	38-**3**	0	382.2	453	325	3	—	47	25	3.34	107	.262	.281	253	.281	3*	96	15	—	1.2
1874	Ath NA	33	22	.600	55	55	55	0	487	514	344	6	—	32	37	**1.64**	**141**	**.240**	**.251**	263	.217	-7	101	**34**	—	1.9
1875	Ath NA	44	14	.759	60	60	59-6	0	538	607	297	4	—	24	27	2.33	103	.267	.275	270	.270	3	142	5	—	0.3
1876	Bos N	0	4	.000	4	4	3	0	33	53	35	1	—	5	2	2.73	83	.353	.374	16	.188	-1	56	-4	—	-0.4
Total	5NA	149	74	.668	233	233	224-10	0	2049	2367	1538	19	—	169	148	2.71	112	.261	.274	1176	.260	-0	117	73	—	4.8
McBride, Macay Joseph Macay; B10.24.1982 Augusta GA; BL/TL/5´11˝/210; [AtlN01 1/24]; d7.22																										
2005	†Atl N	1	0	1.000	23	0	0	1-0	14	18	11	0	0	7-0	22	5.79	73	.305	.373	0	ø	0	—	-3	0	-0.2
2006	Atl N	4	1	.800	71	0	0	1-1	56.2	53	28	2	1	32-4	46	3.65	124	.248	.348	0	ø	0	—	4	27	0.4
Total	2	5	1	.833	94	0	0	2-1	70.2	71	39	2	1	39-4	68	4.08	110	.260	.354	0	ø	0	—	1	27	0.2
McBride, Ken Kenneth Faye; B8.12.1935 Huntsville AL; BR/TR/6´0˝/(190–195); d8.4; C1																										
1959	Chi A	0	1	.000	11	2	0	1	22.2	20	11	1	0	17-0	12	3.18	118	.230	.356	6	.167	-0	70	1	0	0.0
1960	Chi A	0	1	.000	5	0	0	0	4.2	6	2	0	1	3-0	4	3.86	98	.333	.435	0	ø	0	—	0	0	0.0
1961	LA A☆	12	15	.444	38	36	11-1	1	241.2	229	114	28	7	102-4	180	3.65	124	.252	.331	83-0-6	.084	-5*	82	20	0	1.7
1962	LA A✱	11	5	.688	24	23	6-4	0	149.1	136	66	9	9	70-3	83	3.50	110	.249	.341	55-1-0	.164	0	110	7	0	1.0
1963	LA A★	13	12	.520	36	36	11-2	0	251	198	101	22	14	82-1	147	3.26	105	.218	.291	87-0-5	.172	2*	116	7	0	1.0
1964	LA A	4	13	.235	29	21	0	1	116.1	104	77	14	16	75-0	66	5.26	62	.239	.369	28-0-2	.214	3	101	-27	0	-3.1
1965	Cal A	0	3	.000	8	4	0	0	22	24	17	1	2	14-0	11	6.14	55	.270	.377	5	.000	-0	77	-7	36	-0.9
Total	7	40	50	.444	151	122	28-7	3	807.2	717	388	75	49	363-8	503	3.79	101	.240	.330	264-1-13	.144	-0	99	1	36	-0.3
McBride, Pete Peter William; B7.9.1875 Adams MA; D7.3.1944 N.Adams MA; BR/TR/5´10˝/170; d9.20; Col Manhattan																										
1898	Cle N	0	1	.000	1	1	1	0	7	9	6	0	1	4	6	6.43	56	.310	.412	2	1.000	2	98	-2	—	-0.1
1899	StL N	2	4	.333	11	6	4	0	64	65	46	4	4	40	26	4.08	98	.263	.375	27-1-0	.185	0*	93	-2	—	-0.1
Total	2	2	5	.286	12	7	5	0	71	74	52	4	5	44	32	4.31	92	.268	.378	29-1-0	.241	2	94	-4	—	-0.2
McCabe, Ralph Ralph Herbert "Mack"; B10.21.1918 Napanee ON, Can.; D5.3.1974 Windsor ON, Can.; BR/TR/6´4˝/195; d9.18																										
1946	Cle A	0	1	.000	1	1	0	0	4	5	5	3	1	2	3	11.25	29	.313	.421	1	.000	-0	26	-3	0	-0.5
McCabe, Dick Richard James; B2.21.1896 Mamaroneck NY; D4.11.1950 Buffalo NY; BR/TR/5´10.5˝/159; d5.30																										
1918	Bos A	0	1	.000	3	1	0	0	9.2	13	4	0	0	2	3	2.79	96	.351	.385	2	.000	-0	0	0	—	0.0
1922	Chi A	1	0	1.000	3	0	0	0	3.1	4	2	0	0	0	1	5.40	75	.308	.308	0	ø	0	—	0	—	-0.1
Total	2	1	1	.500	6	1	0	0	13	17	6	0	0	2	4	3.46	88	.340	.365	2	.000	-0	0	0	—	-0.1
McCabe, Tim Timothy J.; B10.19.1894 Graniteville MO; D4.12.1977 Ironton MO; BR/TR/6´0˝/190; d8.16																										
1915	StL A	3	1	.750	7	4	4-1	0	41.2	25	11	1	1	9	17	1.30	221	.177	.232	15	.067	-1	115	7	—	0.5
1916	StL A	2	0	1.000	13	0	0	0	25.2	29	20	0	2	7	7	3.16	87	.282	.339	4	.000	-0	—	-4	—	-0.3
1917	StL A	0	0	ø	1	0	0	0	2.1	4	6	1	0	4	2	23.14	11	.400	.571	0	ø	0	—	-5	—	-0.2
1918	StL A	0	0	ø	1	0	0	0	1.1	2	2	0	0	1	0	13.50	20	.333	.429	0	ø	0	—	-1	—	-0.1
Total	4	5	1	.833	22	4	4-1	0	71	60	39	2	3	21	26	2.92	96	.231	.296	19	.053	-1	115	-3	—	-0.1
McCaffrey, Bill William T.; B Baltimore MD; d6.15																										
1885	Cin AA	1	0	1.000	1	1	1	0	9	13	9	1	2	2	2	6.00	54	.342	.405	5	.000	-1	199	-3	—	-0.3
McCahan, Bill William Glenn; B6.7.1921 Philadelphia PA; D7.3.1986 Fort Worth TX; BR/TR/5´11˝/200; d9.15; Col Duke																										
1946	Phi A	1	1	.500	4	2	2-1	0	18	16	2	0	0	9	6	1.00	355	.246	.338	5	.400	1	36	5	0	0.7
1947	Phi A	10	5	.667	29	19	10-1	0	165.1	160	73	7	0	62	47	3.32	115	.252	.318	55-0-3	.164	-1	99	7	0	0.6
1948	Phi A	4	7	.364	17	15	5	0	86.2	98	58	8	0	65	20	5.71	75	.284	.398	31	.258	1	91	-13	0	-1.3
1949	Phi A	1	1	.500	7	4	0	0	20.2	23	9	0	0	9	3	2.61	157	.291	.364	5	.200	-0	93	3	0	0.2
Total	4	16	14	.533	57	40	17-2	0	290.2	297	142	15	0	145	76	3.84	103	.264	.348	96-0-3	.208	1	93	2	0	0.2
McCall, Windy John William; B7.18.1925 San Francisco CA; BL/TL/6´0˝/180; d4.25; Col San Francisco																										
1948	Bos A	0	1	.000	1	1	0	0	1.1	6	3	1	0	1	0	20.25	22	.600	.636	0	ø	0	82	-2	0	-0.3
1949	Bos A	0	0	ø	5	0	0	0	9.1	13	12	2	0	10	8	11.57	38	.333	.469	3-0-1	.667	1	—	-7	0	-0.3
1950	Pit N	0	0	ø	2	0	0	0	6.2	12	7	2	0	4	5	9.45	46	.387	.457	2	.000	0	—	-3	0	-0.1
1954	NY N	2	5	.286	33	4	0	2	61	50	26	5	3	29	38	3.25	124	.219	.314	11	.000	-1	83	5	0	0.4
1955	NY N	6	5	.545	42	6	4	3	95	86	45	8	6	37-6	50	3.69	109	.244	.325	17-0-3	.118	-1	100	4	0	0.4
1956	NY N	3	4	.429	46	4	0	7	77.1	74	36	7	1	20-5	41	3.61	105	.252	.301	15	.200	-0	76	1	0	0.0
1957	NY N	0	0	ø	5	0	0	0	3	8	5	1	1	2-0	2	15.00	26	.533	.579	0	ø	0	—	-3	0	-0.2
Total	7	11	15	.423	134	15	4	12	253.2	249	134	26	11	103-11	144	4.22	94	.257	.334	48-0-4	.146	-1	88	-5	0	-0.1

YEAR	TM LG	W	L	PCT	G	GS	CG-SHO	SV-BS	IP	H	R	HR	HB	BB-IB	SO	ERA	AERA	OAV	OOB	AB-HR-SH	AVG	PB	SUP	APR	DL	PW
McCall, Larry	Larry Stephen; B9.8.1952 Asheville NC; BL/TR/6´2˝/182; d9.10; C1																									
1977	†NY A	0	1	.000	2	0	0	0-0	6	12	7	1	0	1-0	0	7.50	53	.375	.394	0	ø	0*	—	-3	0	-0.4
1978	†NY A	1	1	.500	5	1	0	0-0	16	20	10	2	1	6-0	7	5.63	65	.323	.391	0	ø	0	49	-3	0	-0.3
1979	†Tex A	1	0	1.000	2	1	0	0-0	8.1	7	2	0	0	3-0	3	2.16	192	.226	.286	0	ø	0	87	2	0	0.2
Total	†3	2	2	.500	9	2	0	0-0	30.1	39	19	3	1	10-0	10	5.04	76	.312	.365	0	ø	0	70	-4	0	-0.5
McCall, Dutch	Robert Leonard; B12.27.1920 Columbia TN; D1.8.1996 Little Rock AR; BL/TL/6´1˝/184; d4.27																									
1948	Chi N	4	13	.235	30	20	5	0	151.1	158	93	14	1	85	89	4.82	81	.268	.361	53-0-2	.170	1	97	-15	0	-1.3
McCament, Randy	Larry Randall; B7.29.1962 Albuquerque NM; BR/TR/6´3˝/(180–195); [SFN85 15/368]; d6.28; Col Grand Canyon																									
1989	SF N	1	1	.500	25	0	0	0-0	36.2	32	22	4	1	23-2	12	3.93	86	.241	.354	3	.333	0	—	-4	0	-0.2
1990	SF N	0	0	ø	3	0	0	0-0	6	8	2	0	0	5-0	5	3.00	122	.333	.433	1	.000	-0	—	1	0	0.0
Total	2	1	1	.500	28	0	0	0-0	42.2	40	24	4	1	28-2	17	3.80	90	.255	.367	4	.250	0	—	-3	0	-0.2
McCann, Gene	Henry Eugene "Mike"; B6.13.1876 Baltimore MD; D4.26.1943 New York NY; TR/5´10˝/185; d4.19																									
1901	Bro N	2	3	.400	6	5	3	0	34	34	25	1	4	16	9	3.44	97	.260	.358	10-0-1	.000	-1	127	-3	—	-0.4
1902	Bro N	1	2	.333	3	3	3	0	30	32	18	0	0	12	9	2.40	115	.274	.341	12	.083	-1	82	-1	—	-0.2
Total	2	3	5	.375	9	8	6	0	64	66	43	1	4	28	18	2.95	104	.266	.350	22-0-1	.045	-2	113	-4	—	-0.6
McCarthy, Arch	Archibald Joseph; B Ypsilanti MI; TR/6´0˝/160; d8.14																									
1902	Det A	2	7	.222	10	8	8	0	72	90	57	2	4	31	10	6.13	60	.306	.380	28	.071	-3	72	-15	—	-1.8
McCarthy, Brandon	Brandon Patrick; B7.7.1983 Glendale CA; BR/TR/6´7˝/(190–195); [ChiA02 17/510]; d5.22; Col Lamar (CO) CC																									
2005	Chi A	3	2	.600	12	10	0	0-0	67	62	30	13	2	17-0	48	4.03	112	.242	.293	2	.000	-0	100	5	0	0.2
2006	Chi A	4	7	.364	53	2	0	0-1	84.2	77	44	17	0	33-9	69	4.68	100	.243	.313	1	.000	-0	91	1	0	0.2
Total	2	7	9	.438	65	12	0	0-1	151.2	139	74	30	2	50-9	117	4.39	105	.243	.305	3	.000	-0	98	6	0	0.4
McCarthy, Greg	Gregory O'Neil; B10.30.1968 Norwalk CT; BL/TL/6´2˝/215; [PhiN87 36/929]; d8.28; [DL 1991 Mon N 182]																									
1996	Sea A	0	0	ø	10	0	0	0-0	9.2	8	2	0	4	4-0	7	1.86	267	.229	.364	0	ø	0	—	3	0	0.2
1997	Sea A	1	1	.500	37	0	0	0-0	29.2	26	21	4	1	16-0	34	5.46	83	.230	.331	0	ø	0	—	-4	0	-0.2
1998	Sea A	1	2	.333	29	0	0	0-1	23.1	18	13	6	3	17-2	25	5.01	93	.214	.365	0	ø	0	—	0	0	0.0
Total	3	2	3	.400	76	0	0	0-1	62.2	52	36	10	8	37-2	66	4.74	98	.224	.349	0	ø	0	—	-1	182	0.0
McCarthy, Tommy	Thomas Francis Michael; B7.24.1863 Boston MA; D8.5.1922 Boston MA; BR/TR/5´7˝/170; d7.10; M1; HF1957; ▲																									
1884	Bos U	0	7	.000	7	6	5	0	56	73	53	2	—	14	18	4.82	49	.296	.333	209	.215	-1*	69	-14	—	-1.4
1886	Phi N	0	0	ø	1	0	0	0	1	0	0	0	—	1	1	0.00	ø	.000	.250	27	.185	0*	—	0	—	0.0
1888	†StL AA	0	1	.000	2	1	0	0	5.1	5	5	1	0	2	1	5.06	64	.238	.304	511-1	.274	0*	53	-1	—	-0.1
1889	StL AA	0	0	ø	1	0	0	0	5	4	4	0	0	6	1	7.20	59	.211	.400	604-2	.291	0*	—	-1	—	0.0
1891	StL AA	0	0	ø	1	0	0	0	1	2	2	0	0	0	0	9.00	47	.400	.400	570-8	.309	0*	—	-1	—	0.0
1894	Bos N	0	0	ø	1	0	0	0	2	1	1	0	0	3	0	4.50	126	.143	.400	539-13-9	.349	0*	—	0	—	0.0
Total	6	0	8	.000	13	7	5	0	70.1	85	65	3	0	26	21	4.99	54	.281	.338	2460-24-9	.297	-0	65	-17	—	-1.5
McCarthy, Tom	Thomas Michael; B6.18.1961 Lundstahl, West Germany; BR/TR/6´0˝/180; [BosA79 7/182]; d7.5																									
1985	Bos A	0	0	ø	3	0	0	0-0	5	7	6	1	0	4-0	2	10.80	40	.350	.440	0	ø	0	—	-3	0	-0.2
1988	Chi A	2	0	1.000	6	0	0	1-0	13	9	2	0	2	2-0	5	1.38	289	.191	.255	0	ø	0	—	4	0	0.6
1989	Chi A	1	2	.333	31	0	0	0-0	66.2	72	32	8	2	20-0	27	3.51	109	.280	.333	0	ø	0	—	1	0	0.1
Total	3	3	2	.600	40	0	0	1-0	84.2	88	40	9	4	26-0	34	3.61	108	.272	.330	0	ø	0	—	2	0	0.5
McCarthy, Tom	Thomas Patrick; B5.22.1884 Ft.Wayne IN; D3.28.1933 Mishawaka IN; TR/5´7˝/170; d5.10																									
1908	Cin N	0	1	.000	1	1	0	0	3.2	6	5	0	0	3	3	9.82	23	.300	.391	2	.000	-0	214	-3	—	-0.5
	Pit N	0	0	ø	2	1	0	0	6	3	1	0	0	6	1	0.00	ø	.176	.391	4	.000	-0*	398	1	—	0.0
	Bos N	7	3	.700	14	11	7-2	0	94	77	24	0	1	28	27	1.63	148	.235	.298	35-0-4	.171	0	135	8	—	1.0
	Year	7	4	.636	17	13	7-2	0	103.2	86	30	0	1	37	31	1.82	132	.236	.308	41-0-4	.146	-1	160	6	—	0.5
1909	Bos N	0	5	.000	8	7	3	0	46.1	47	28	3	2	28	11	3.50	81	.272	.379	16-0-1	.125	-0*	78	-4	—	-0.5
Total	2	7	9	.438	25	20	10-2	0	150	133	58	3	3	65	42	2.34	108	.248	.332	57-0-5	.140	-1	129	2	—	0.0
McCarthy, Bill	William Thomas; B4.11.1882 Ashland MA; D5.29.1939 Boston MA; BR/TR/5´11˝/180; d4.21																									
1906	Bos N	0	0	ø	1	0	0	0	2	2	6	0	0	3	0	9.00	30	.182	.357	1	.000	-0	—	-3	—	-0.1
McCarty, John	John A.; B St.Louis MO; TR; d4.18																									
1889	KC AA	8	6	.571	15	14	13	0	119.2	147	108	4	6	61	36	3.91	109	.293	.376	79	.228	-2*	120	0	—	-0.2
McCaskill, Kirk	Kirk Edward; B4.9.1961 Kapuskasing ON, Can.; BR/TR/6´1˝/(190–205); [CalA82 4/88]; d5.1; Col Vermont																									
1985	Cal A	12	12	.500	30	29	6-1	0-0	189.2	189	105	23	4	64-1	102	4.70	88	.258	.319	0	ø	0	107	-10	0	-1.1
1986	†Cal A	17	10	.630	34	33	10-2	0-0	246.1	207	98	19	5	92-1	202	3.36	123	.229	.302	0	ø	0	100	23	0	2.3
1987	Cal A	4	6	.400	14	13	1-1	0-0	74.2	84	52	14	2	34-0	56	5.67	76	.286	.363	0	ø	0*	78	-11	75	-1.2
1988	Cal A	8	6	.571	23	23	4-2	0-0	146.1	155	78	9	1	61-3	98	4.31	90	.274	.342	0	ø	0	130	-7	55	-0.6
1989	Cal A	15	10	.600	32	32	6-4	0-0	212	202	73	16	3	59-1	107	2.93	131	.254	.307	0	ø	0	88	23	0	2.7
1990	Cal A	12	11	.522	29	29	2-1	0-0	174.1	161	77	9	2	72-1	78	3.25	118	.244	.320	0	ø	0	93	10	0	1.2
1991	Cal A	10	19	.345	30	30	1	0-0	177.2	193	93	19	3	66-1	71	4.26	97	.283	.347	0	ø	0	65	-3	0	-0.4
1992	Chi A	12	13	.480	34	34	0	0-0	209	193	116	11	6	95-5	109	4.18	93	.242	.325	0	ø	0	104	-11	0	-1.1
1993	†Chi A	4	8	.333	30	14	0	2-0	113.2	144	71	12	1	36-6	65	5.23	81	.313	.362	0	ø	0	101	-12	15	-1.1
1994	Chi A	1	4	.200	40	0	0	3-3	52.2	51	22	6	0	22-4	37	3.42	137	.252	.322	0	ø	0	—	8	0	0.7
1995	Chi A	6	4	.600	55	1	0	2-3	81	97	50	10	5	33-4	50	4.89	92	.302	.373	0	ø	0	125	-5	0	-0.5
1996	Chi A	5	5	.500	29	4	0	0-1	51.2	72	41	6	2	31-8	28	6.97	68	.344	.432	0	ø	0	151	-12	0	-1.8
Total	12	106	108	.495	380	242	30-11	7-7	1729	1748	876	154	34	665-35	1003	4.12	99	.264	.332	0	ø	0	96	-7	145	-0.9
McCatty, Steve	Steven Earl; B3.20.1954 Detroit MI; BR/TR/6´3˝/(195–210); d9.17; C1; Col Macomb (MI) CC																									
1977	Oak A	0	0	ø	4	2	0	0-0	14.1	16	9	1	1	7-0	9	5.02	80	.276	.364	0	ø	0	89	-1	0	-0.1
1978	Oak A	0	0	ø	9	0	0	0-0	20	26	14	1	0	9-1	10	4.50	81	.310	.361	0	ø	0	—	-3	0	-0.2
1979	Oak A	11	12	.478	31	23	8	0-0	185.2	207	106	17	10	80-8	87	4.22	96	.284	.359	0	ø	0	91	-7	0	-0.8
1980	Oak A	14	14	.500	33	31	11-1	0-1	221.2	202	104	27	8	99-2	114	3.86	99	.240	.323	0	ø	0	120	0	0	-0.1
1981	†Oak A	**14**	7	.667	22	22	16-**4**	0-0	185.2	140	50	12	2	61-1	91	**2.33**	151	**.211**	.277	0	ø	0	110	**27**	0	3.1
1982	Oak A	6	3	.667	21	20	2	0-0	128.2	124	62	16	4	70-0	66	3.99	99	.255	.351	0	ø	0	130	0	21	0.0
1983	Oak A	6	9	.400	38	24	3-2	5-1	167	156	79	16	1	82-4	65	3.99	98	.247	.331	0	ø	0*	87	0	0	-0.1
1984	Oak A	8	14	.364	33	30	4	0-0	179.2	206	101	24	1	71-0	63	4.76	79	.289	.353	0	ø	0	116	-18	0	-2.1
1985	Oak A	4	4	.500	30	9	1	0-0	85.2	95	56	10	4	41-4	36	5.57	70	.286	.368	0	ø	0	143	-16	0	-1.3
Total	9	63	63	.500	221	161	45-7	5-2	1188.1	1172	581	124	31	520-20	541	3.99	96	.258	.336	0	ø	0	111	-18	21	-1.6
McCauley, Al	Allen A.; B3.4.1863 Indianapolis IN; D8.24.1917 Wayne Twnshp. IN; BL/TL/6´0˝/180; d6.21; ▲																									
1884	Ind AA	2	7	.222	10	9	9	0	76	87	74	2	0	25	34	5.09	65	.261	.313	53	.189	2*	90	-15	—	-1.1
McClain, Joe	Joseph Fred; B5.5.1933 Johnson City TN; BR/TR/6´0˝/183; d4.14; Col Tennessee																									
1961	Was A	8	18	.308	33	29	7-2	1	212	221	105	22	4	48-7	76	3.86	104	.270	.309	68-0-2	.206	1	71	4	0	0.4
1962	Was A	0	4	.000	10	4	0	0	24	33	25	8	2	11-1	6	9.38	43	.327	.397	7	.143	-0	72	-13	0	-1.8
Total	2	8	22	.267	43	33	7-2	1	236	254	130	30	6	59-8	82	4.42	91	.276	.319	75-0-2	.200	1	71	-9	0	-1.4
McClellan, Paul	Paul William; B2.3.1966 San Mateo CA; BR/TR/6´2˝/180; [SFN86*S1/6]; d9.2; Col San Mateo (CA) [JC]																									
1990	SF N	0	1	.000	4	1	0	0-0	7.2	14	10	3	1	6-0	2	11.74	31	.389	.488	2	.500	0	148	-7	0	-0.7
1991	SF N	3	6	.333	13	12	1	0-0	71	68	41	12	1	25-1	44	4.56	79	.252	.316	21-0-2	.143	-0	123	-9	0	-1.1
Total	2	3	7	.300	17	13	1	0-0	78.2	82	51	15	2	31-1	46	5.26	68	.268	.338	23-0-2	.174	0	125	-16	0	-1.8
McCloskey, Jim	James Ellwood "Irish"; B5.26.1910 Danville PA; D8.18.1971 Jersey City NJ; BL/TL/5´9.5˝/180; d4.21; Col St. Bonaventure																									
1936	Bos N	0	0	ø	4	1	0	0	8	14	10	1	1	3	2	11.25	34	.378	.439	1	.000	-0	133	-6	—	-0.3

YEAR	TM LG	W	L	PCT	G	GS	CG-SHO	SV-BS	IP	H	R	HR	HB	BB-IB	SO	ERA	AERA	OAV	OOB	AB-HR-SH	AVG	PB	SUP	APR	DL	PW
McCloskey, John	James John; B8.20.1882 Wyoming PA; D6.5.1919 Wilkes–Barre PA; d5.3																									
1906	Phi N	3	2	.600	9	4	3	0	41	46	21	2	1	9	6	2.85	92	.280	.322	15	.200	0	146	-2	—	-0.2
1907	Phi N	0	0	ø	3	0	0	0	9	15	9	0	1	6	3	7.00	35	.417	.512	4	.000	-0	—	-4	—	-0.3
Total	2	3	2	.600	12	4	3	0	50	61	30	2	2	15	9	3.60	72	.305	.359	19	.158	-0	146	-6	—	-0.5
McClung, Seth	Michael Seth; B2.7.1981 Lewisburg WV; BR/TR/6´6˝/(230–235); [TBA99 5/145]; d3.31; [DL 2004 TB A 126]																									
2003	TB A	4	1	.800	12	5	0	0-0	38.2	33	23	6	3	25-1	25	5.35	86	.241	.367	0	ø	0	93	-2	129	-0.3
2005	TB A	7	11	.389	34	17	0	0-1	109.1	106	85	20	7	62-1	92	6.59	67	.249	.350	0	ø	0	91	-25	0	-3.4
2006	TB A	6	12	.333	39	15	0	6-1	103	120	77	14	3	68-5	59	6.29	74	.294	.391	1-0-1	.000	-0	73	-18	0	-2.8
Total	3	17	24	.415	85	37	0	6-2	251	259	185	40	13	155-7	176	6.27	72	.267	.370	1-0-1	.000	-0	84	-45	255	-6.5
McClure, Bob	Robert Craig; B4.29.1952 Oakland CA; BR/TL/5´11˝/(170–188); [KCA73 S3/30]; d8.13; C2; Col San Mateo (CA) [JC]																									
1975	KC A	1	0	1.000	12	0	0	1-0	15.1	4	0	0	0	14-2	15	0.00	ø	.077	.273	0	ø	0	—	6	0	0.5
1976	KC A	0	0	ø	8	0	0	0-0	4	3	4	0	0	8-0	3	9.00	39	.214	.500	0	ø	0*	—	-2	0	-0.1
1977	Mil A	2	1	.667	68	0	0	6-1	71.1	64	25	2	1	34-5	57	2.52	163	.249	.333	0	ø	0	—	11	0	0.7
1978	Mil A	2	6	.250	44	0	0	9-4	65	53	30	8	6	30-4	47	3.74	102	.223	.322	0	ø	0	—	0	0	0.0
1979	Mil A	5	2	.714	36	0	0	5-1	51	53	29	6	3	24-0	37	3.88	108	.269	.352	0	ø	0	—	0	0	0.0
1980	Mil A	5	8	.385	52	5	2-1	10-5	90.2	83	34	6	2	37-2	47	3.08	127	.241	.314	0	ø	0	87	9	0	1.4
1981	†Mil A	0	0	ø	4	0	0	0-0	7.2	7	3	1	0	4-1	6	3.52	98	.233	.324	0	ø	0	—	0	146	0.0
1982	†Mil A	12	7	.632	34	26	5	0-0	172.2	160	90	21	4	74-4	99	4.22	91	.248	.327	0	ø	0	141	-8	0	-0.8
1983	Mil A	9	9	.500	24	23	4	0-0	142	152	75	11	5	68-1	68	4.50	84	.277	.360	0	ø	0	114	-11	21	-1.2
1984	Mil A	4	8	.333	39	18	1	1-0	139.2	154	76	9	2	52-4	68	4.38	89	.282	.342	0	ø	0	122	-7	0	-0.6
1985	Mil A	4	1	.800	38	1	0	3-1	85.2	91	43	10	3	30-2	57	4.31	97	.274	.338	0	ø	0	87	1	0	0.0
1986	Mil A	2	1	.667	13	0	0	0-0	16.1	18	7	2	0	10-1	11	3.86	113	.286	.378	0	ø	0	—	1	0	0.2
	Mon N	2	5	.286	52	0	0	6-2	62.2	53	22	2	1	23-2	42	3.02	124	.232	.303	4	.250	0	—	6	0	0.7
1987	Mon N	6	1	.857	52	0	0	5-1	52.1	47	30	8	0	20-3	33	3.44	124	.241	.309	2	.000	-0	—	2	0	0.2
1988	Mon N	1	3	.250	19	0	0	2-0	19	23	13	3	1	6-0	12	6.16	59	.307	.357	2	.000	-0	—	-4	0	-0.9
	NY N	1	0	1.000	14	0	0	1-0	11	12	5	1	1	2-0	7	4.09	80	.279	.326	0	ø	0	—	-1	0	-0.1
	Year	2	3	.400	33	0	0	3-0	30	35	18	4	2	8-0	19	5.40	65	.297	.346	2	.000	-0	—	-5	0	-1.0
1989	Cal A	6	1	.857	48	0	0	3-0	52.1	39	14	2	1	15-1	36	1.55	247	.212	.270	0	ø	0	—	12	0	1.5
1990	Cal A	2	0	1.000	11	0	0	0-1	7	7	6	0	0	3-0	6	6.43	60	.269	.345	0	ø	0	—	-2	127	-0.4
1991	Cal A	0	0	ø	13	0	0	0-0	9.2	13	11	3	1	5-0	5	9.31	44	.317	.396	0	ø	0	—	-6	11	-0.3
	StL N	1	1	.500	32	0	0	0-4	23	24	8	1	1	8-2	15	3.13	120	.282	.340	1	1.000	0	—	2	0	0.2
1992	StL N	2	2	.500	71	0	0	0-0	54	52	21	6	2	25-5	24	3.17	108	.261	.345	0	ø	0	—	1	0	0.1
1993	Fla N	1	1	.500	14	0	0	0-2	6.1	13	5	2	0	5-0	6	7.11	61	.419	.500	0	ø	0	—	-2	0	-0.3
Total	19	68	57	.544	698	73	12-1	52-22	1158.2	1125	551	104	34	497-39	701	3.81	102	.257	.334	9	.222	0	121	8	305	0.8
McCluskey, Harry	Harry Robert; B3.29.1892 Clay Center OH; D6.7.1962 Toledo OH; BL/TL/5´11.5˝/173; d7.29																									
1915	Cin N	0	0	ø	3	0	0	0	5	4	3	0	0	0	2	5.40	53	.182	.182	2	.000	-0	—	-1	—	-0.1
McColl, Alex	Alexander Boyd "Red"; B3.29.1894 Eagleville OH; D2.6.1991 Kingsville OH; BB/TR/6´1˝/178; d8.27																									
1933	†Was A	1	0	1.000	4	1	1	0	17	13	5	0	0	7	5	2.65	158	.210	.290	6	.333	1	61	3	—	0.2
1934	Was A	3	4	.429	42	2	1	1	112	129	56	6	1	36	29	3.86	112	.291	.345	31	.097	-2	40	5	—	0.2
Total	2	4	4	.500	46	3	2	1	129	142	61	6	1	43	34	3.70	116	.281	.338	37	.135	-1	47	8	—	0.4
McConnaughey, Ralph	Ralph Jennison; B8.5.1889 Homer City PA; D6.4.1966 Detroit MI; BR/TR/5´8.5˝/166; d7.8																									
1914	Ind F	0	2	.000	7	2	1	0	26	23	15	3	1	16	7	4.85	64	.245	.360	8	.125	-0	55	-3	—	-0.3
McConnell, George	George Neely "Slats"; B9.16.1877 Shelbyville TN; D5.10.1964 Chattanooga TN; BR/TR/6´3˝/190; d4.13; ▲																									
1909	NY A	0	1	.000	2	1	0	0	4	3	2	0	0	3	4	2.25	112	.231	.375	43-0-1	.209	0*	28	0	—	0.0
1912	NY A	8	12	.400	23	20	19	0	176.2	172	96	3	4	52	91	2.75	131	.269	.328	91-0-1	.297	3*	65	8	—	1.6
1913	NY A	4	15	.211	35	20	8	3	180	162	90	2	7	60	72	3.20	94	.247	.317	67-0-3	.179	-1*	83	-5	—	-0.4
1914	Chi N	0	1	.000	1	1	0	0	7	3	1	0	0	3	3	1.29	216	.125	.222	2	.000	-0	0	1	—	0.2
1915	Chi F	**25**	10	**.714**	44	35	23-4	1	303	262	103	8	8	89	151	2.20	114	.232	.292	125-1-3	.248	6*	124	9	—	1.7
1916	Chi N	4	12	.250	28	21	8-1	0	171.1	137	66	8	5	35	82	2.57	113	.223	.271	57-0-2	.158	-2	65	5	—	0.4
Total	6	41	51	.446	133	98	58-5	4	842	739	358	21	24	242	403	2.60	112	.240	.301	385-1-10	.229	5	86	18	—	3.5
McConnell, Sam	John Samuel; B12.31.1975 Middletown OH; BL/TL/6´5˝/230; [PitN97 11/332]; d6.25; Col Ball St.																									
2004	Atl N	1	0	1.000	10	0	0	0-0	9.1	11	4	0	1	4-1	4	3.86	112	.289	.372	1	.000	-0	—	1	0	0.0
McCool, Billy	William John; B7.14.1944 Batesville IN; BR/TL/6´2˝/(200–208); d4.24																									
1964	Cin N	6	5	.545	40	3	0	7	89.1	66	27	3	1	29-5	87	2.42	150	.206	.272	17-0-1	.000	-2	49	12	0	1.4
1965	Cin N	9	10	.474	62	2	0	21	105.1	93	53	9	4	47-7	120	4.27	88	.237	.324	27	.037	-2	70	-5	0	-1.2
1966	Cin N☆	8	8	.500	57	0	0	18	105.1	76	32	5	3	41-7	104	2.48	157	.205	.288	18	.167	-0	—	15	0	3.0
1967	Cin N	3	7	.300	31	11	0	2	97.1	92	45	8	5	56-7	83	3.42	110	.246	.351	26-0-1	.077	-1	83	2	21	0.1
1968	Cin N	3	4	.429	30	4	0	2	50.2	59	35	4	0	41-4	30	4.97	64	.294	.408	8-0-1	.125	-0	130	-11	0	-1.7
1969	SD N	3	5	.375	54	0	0	7-2	58.2	59	32	2	6	42-8	35	4.30	83	.266	.393	1	.000	-0	—	-5	21	-0.8
1970	StL N	0	3	.000	18	0	0	1-1	21.2	20	15	0	0	16-0	12	6.23	67	.250	.367	4-0-1	.000	-0	—	-4	0	-0.6
Total	7	32	42	.432	292	20	0	58-3	528.1	465	239	31	19	272-38	471	3.59	103	.237	.334	101-0-4	.069	-6	83	4	42	0.2
McCormick, Jim	James; B11.3.1856 Glasgow, Scotland; D3.10.1918 Paterson NJ; BR/TR/5´10.5˝/215; d5.20; M3																									
1878	Ind N	5	8	.385	14	14	12-1	0	117	128	47	0	—	15	36	1.69	120	.269	.292	56	.143	-3*	106	5	—	0.4
1879	Cle N	20	40	.333	62	60	59-3	0	546.1	582	308	3	—	74	197	2.42	103	.259	.282	282	.220	-1*	68	6	—	0.6
1880	Cle N	**45**	28	.616	**74**	**74**	**72**-7	0	**657.2**	585	274	2	—	75	260	1.85	127	.226	.247	289	.246	1*	101	**39**	—	**4.2**
1881	Cle N	26	30	.464	59	58	**57**-2	0	526	484	267	4	—	84	178	2.45	107	.235	.265	309	.256	6*	104	9	—	1.2
1882	Cle N	**36**	30	.545	**68**	**67**	**65**-4	0	**595.2**	550	274	14	—	103	200	2.37	118	.238	.271	262-2	.218	-4*	92	30	—	2.3
1883	Cle N	28	12	**.700**	43	41	36-1	1	342	316	151	1	—	65	145	**1.84**	**171**	.233	.268	157	.236	-1	102	47	—	4.8
1884	Cle N	19	22	.463	42	41	39-3	0	359	357	206	16	—	75	182	2.86	110	.247	.285	190	.263	2*	76	13	—	1.4
	Cin U	21	3	**.875**	24	24	24-**7**	0	210	151	57	3	—	14	161	**1.54**	**166**	**.188**	**.202**	110	.245	-3*	114	**26**	—	1.9
1885	Pro N	1	3	.250	4	4	4	0	37	34	26	1	—	20	8	2.43	110	.234	.327	14	.214	0	68	-1	—	0.1
	†Chi N	20	4	.833	24	24	24-3	0	215	187	103	8	—	40	88	2.43	124	.224	.260	103	.223	0*	158	14	—	1.4
	Year	21	7	.750	28	28	28-3	0	252	221	129	9	—	60	96	2.43	122	.226	.271	117	.222	1	146	10	—	1.5
1886	†Chi N	31	11	.738	42	42	38-2	0	347.2	341	165	18	—	100	172	2.82	128	.253	.304	174-2	.236	2	134	35	—	3.8
1887	Pit N	13	23	.361	36	36	36	0	322.1	377	217	12	12	84	77	4.30	89	.285	.334	136	.243	-0	75	-15	—	-1.0
Total	10	265	214	.553	492	485	466-33	1	4275.2	4092	2095	82	12	749	1704	2.43	117	.242	.274	2082-4	.236	-1	98	208	—	21.1
McCormick, Mike	Michael Francis; B9.29.1938 Pasadena CA; BL/TL/6´2˝/(185–200); d9.3																									
1956	NY N	0	1	.000	3	2	0	0	6.2	7	7	1	0	10-0	4	9.45	40	.269	.472	1	.000	-0	105	-4	0	-0.5
1957	NY N	3	1	.750	24	5	1	0	74.2	79	37	7	3	32-2	50	4.10	96	.280	.357	22-0-1	.273	1	99	-1	0	0.0
1958	SF N	11	8	.579	42	28	8-2	1	178.1	192	103	20	3	60-6	82	4.59	83	.276	.332	54-0-3	.222	1	98	-16	0	-1.3
1959	SF N	12	16	.429	47	31	7-3	4	225.2	213	117	24	1	86-13	151	3.99	96	.248	.314	66-0-11	.106	-2	104	-5	0	-0.7
1960	SF N★	15	12	.556	40	34	15-4	3	253	228	87	15	1	65-12	154	**2.70**	129	.241	.290	88-0-5	.182	1	111	25	0	3.0
1961	SF N★	13	16	.448	40	35	13-3	0	250	235	99	33	2	75-3	163	3.20	119	.249	.305	80-0-5	.188	1	108	18	0	2.0
1962	SF N	5	5	.500	28	15	1	0	98.2	112	64	18	1	45-2	42	5.38	71	.286	.356	28-1-0	.107	0*	122	-17	0	-1.5
1963	Bal A	6	8	.429	25	21	2	0	136	132	70	18	0	66-4	75	4.30	81	.256	.340	46-1-3	.174	1	106	-12	0	-1.1
1964	Bal A	0	2	.000	4	2	0	0	17.1	21	10	1	0	8-0	13	5.19	69	.288	.358	6	.167	-0	112	-3	0	-0.3
1965	Was A	8	8	.500	44	21	3-1	1	158	158	64	17	0	36-4	88	3.36	103	.260	.300	41-0-4	.073	-1*	91	4	0	0.2
1966	Was A	11	14	.440	41	32	8-3	0	216	193	98	23	2	51-8	101	3.46	100	.236	.281	66-2-5	.212	3	87	-2	0	0.1
1967	SF N	**22**	10	.688	40	35	14-5	0	262.1	220	88	25	5	81-18	150	2.85	115	.226	.289	84-1-6	.119	0*	115	17	0	1.9
1968	SF N	12	14	.462	38	28	9-2	1	198.1	196	92	17	2	49-13	121	3.58	82	.254	.298	58-1-5	.103	1	102	-13	0	-1.7
1969	SF N	11	9	.550	32	28	9	0-1	196.2	175	81	20	1	77-8	76	3.34	105	.237	.308	66-1-5	.136	1	110	6	0	0.6
1970	SF N	3	4	.429	23	11	1	2-1	78.1	80	58	15	3	36-7	37	6.20	64	.262	.343	25-0-2	.160	0	152	-18	0	-1.5
	NY A	2	0	1.000	9	4	0	0-0	20.2	26	15	2	0	13-1	12	6.10	59	.295	.386	5	.200	0	125	-6	0	-0.5
1971	KC A	0	0	ø	4	1	0	0-0	9.2	14	10	0	0	5-0	2	9.31	37	.350	.422	2	.000	-0	260	-6	0	-0.3
Total	16	134	128	.511	484	333	91-23	12-2	2380.1	2281	1100	256	24	795-101	1321	3.73	95	.251	.312	738-7-55	.156	9	107	-33	0	-1.6

YEAR	TM LG	W	L	PCT	G	GS	CG-SHO	SV-BS	IP	H	R	HR	HB	BB-IB	SO	ERA	AERA	OAV	OOB	AB-HR-SH	AVG	PB	SUP	APR	DL	PW
McCormick, Harry	Patrick Henry; B10.25.1855 Syracuse NY; D8.8.1889 Syracuse NY; BR/TR/5´9˝/155; d5.1																									
1879	Syr N	18	33	.353	54	54	49-5	0	457.1	517	291	3	—	31	96	2.99	79	.266	.277	230-1	.222	-0*	79	-30	—	-2.8
1881	Wor N	1	8	.111	9	9	9-1	0	78.1	89	50	1	—	15	7	3.56	85	.275	.307	45	.133	-2*	62	-4	—	-0.6
1882	Cin AA	14	11	.560	25	25	24-3	0	219.2	177	87	4	—	42	33	1.52	174	.206	.243	93	.129	-5*	88	25	—	1.8
1883	Cin AA	8	6	.571	15	15	14-1	0	128.2	139	70	1	—	27	21	2.87	113	.258	.294	55	.309	4	121	7	—	1.0
Total	4	41	58	.414	103	103	96-10	0	884	922	498	9	—	115	157	2.66	98	.252	.274	423-1	.203	-4	86	-2	—	-0.6
McCorry, Bill	William Charles; B7.9.1887 Saranac Lake NY; D3.22.1973 Augusta GA; BL/TR/5´9˝/157; d9.17																									
1909	StL A	0	2	.000	2	2	2	0	15	29	21	1	0	6	10	9.00	27	.397	.443	5	.000	-0	15	-12	—	-1.2
McCrabb, Les	Lester William "Buster"; B11.4.1914 Wakefield PA; BR/TR/5´11˝/175; d9.7; C5																									
1939	Phi A	1	2	.333	5	4	2	0	35.2	42	20	4	1	10	11	4.04	117	.290	.340	13-0-2	.000	-2	103	2	—	0.0
1940	Phi A	0	0	ø	4	0	0	0	11.2	19	13	2	1	2	4	6.94	64	.365	.400	4	.250	0	—	-4	—	-0.2
1941	Phi A	9	13	.409	26	23	11-1	2	157.1	188	105	16	3	49	40	5.49	76	.293	.346	56-0-1	.143	-2	77	-20	0	-2.7
1942	Phi A	0	0	ø	1	0	0	0	4	14	14	2	1	2	0	31.50	12	.560	.607	1	.000	-0	—	-11	0	-0.4
1950	Phi A	0	0	ø	2	0	0	0	1.1	7	4	0	0	0	2	27.00	17	.636	.636	0	ø	0	—	-3	0	-0.1
Total	5	10	15	.400	38	27	13-1	2	210	270	156	24	6	63	57	5.96	72	.309	.359	74-0-3	.122	-4	81	-36	0	-3.4
McCreery, Ed	Esley Porterfield "Big Ed"; B12.24.1889 Florence CO; D10.19.1960 Sacramento CA; BR/TR/6´0˝/190; d8.16																									
1914	Det A	1	0	1.000	3	1	0	0	4	6	5	0	0	3	4	11.25	25	.316	.409	1	.000	-0	337	-3	—	-0.6
McCreery, Tom	Thomas Livingston; B10.19.1874 Beaver PA; D7.3.1941 Beaver PA; BB/TR/5´11˝/180; d6.8; Col Georgetown; ▲																									
1895	Lou N	3	1	.750	8	4	3-1	1	48.2	51	40	0	5	38	14	5.36	86	.266	.400	108-0-2	.324	1*	108	-3	—	0.0
1896	Lou N	0	1	.000	1	1	0	0	1	4	10	1	0	5	0	36.00	12	.571	.750	441-7-9	.351	0*	49	-5	—	-0.6
1900	Pit N	0	0	ø	1	0	0	0	3	3	4	2	0	1	0	12.00	30	.250	.308	132-1-6	.220	0*	—	-2	—	-0.1
Total	3	3	2	.600	10	5	3-1	1	52.2	58	54	3	5	44	14	6.32	72	.275	.412	681-8-17	.322	2	97	-10	—	-0.7
McCullers, Lance	Lance Graye; B3.8.1964 Tampa FL; BB/TR/6´1˝/(185–218); [PhiN82 2/41]; d8.12																									
1985	SD N	0	2	.000	21	0	0	5-2	35	23	15	3	1	16-3	27	2.31	154	.195	.296	4-0-2	.000	-0	—	3	0	0.2
1986	SD N	10	10	.500	70	7	0	5-5	136	103	46	12	4	58-9	92	2.78	132	.216	.304	22-0-3	.091	0*	73	14	0	2.1
1987	SD N	8	10	.444	78	0	0	16-11	123.1	115	60	11	2	59-11	126	3.72	107	.244	.330	14-0-1	.071	-1	—	2	0	0.3
1988	SD N	3	6	.333	60	0	0	10-5	97.2	70	29	8	0	55-12	81	2.49	137	.205	.313	8	.250	1	—	10	0	1.2
1989	NY A	4	3	.571	52	1	0	3-3	84.2	83	46	9	3	37-4	82	4.57	85	.255	.332	0	ø	0	47	-6	0	-0.5
1990	NY A	1	0	1.000	11	0	0	0-1	15	14	8	2	0	6-2	11	3.60	111	.241	.308	0	ø	0	—	0	15	0.0
	Det A	1	0	1.000	9	1	0	0-0	29.2	18	11	2	0	13-1	20	2.73	146	.170	.256	0	ø	0	229	3	77	0.1
	Year	2	0	1.000	20	1	0	0-1	44.2	32	19	4	0	19-3	31	3.02	132	.195	.274	0	ø	0	229	4	0	0.1
1992	Tex A	1	0	1.000	5	0	0	0-0	5	1	4	0	0	8-0	3	5.40	71	.067	.391	0	ø	0	—	-1	0	-0.2
Total	7	28	31	.475	306	9	0	39-27	526.1	427	219	47	10	252-42	442	3.25	115	.223	.315	48-0-6	.104	0	88	25	92	3.2
McCullough, Charlie	Charles F.; B1866 Dublin, Ireland; D4.13.1898 Brooklyn NY; TR/6´1˝/185; d4.23																									
1890	Bro AA	4	21	.160	26	25	24	0	215.2	247	174	5	16	102	61	4.59	85	.279	.364	86	.023	-12	61	-16	—	-2.6
	Syr AA	1	2	.333	3	3	3	0	26	29	25	1	0	14	8	7.27	49	.274	.358	9	.111	0	108	-10	—	-0.8
	Year	5	23	.179	29	28	27	0	241.2	276	199	6	16	116	69	4.88	79	.278	.363	95	.032	-12	66	-34	—	-3.4
McCullough, Paul	Paul Willard; B7.28.1898 New Castle PA; D11.7.1970 New Castle PA; BR/TR/5´9.5˝/190; d7.2																									
1929	Was A	0	0	ø	3	0	0	0	7.1	7	7	1	0	2	3	8.59	49	.250	.300	1	.000	-0	—	-3	—	-0.2
McCullough, Phil	Pinson Lamar; B7.22.1917 Stockbridge GA; D1.16.2003 Decatur GA; BR/TR/6´4˝/204; d4.22; Mil 1943–45; Col Oglethorpe																									
1942	Was A	0	0	ø	1	0	0	0	3	5	4	0	0	2	2	6.00	61	.333	.412	1	.000	-0	—	-1	0	-0.1
McCurry, Jeff	Jeffrey Dee; B1.21.1970 Tokyo, Japan; BR/TR/6´6˝/(210–225); [PitN90 14/376]; d5.6; Col San Jacinto North (TX) JC																									
1995	Pit N	1	4	.200	55	0	0	1-1	61	82	38	9	5	30-4	27	5.02	87	.337	.421	3	.000	-0	—	-5	0	-0.4
1996	Det A	0	0	ø	2	0	0	0-0	3.1	9	9	3	0	2-0	0	24.30	21	.474	.524	0	ø	0	—	-7	0	-0.3
1997	Col N	1	4	.200	33	0	0	0-2	40.2	43	22	7	0	20-0	19	4.43	117	.277	.358	1	.000	-0	—	3	0	0.3
1998	Pit N	1	3	.250	16	0	0	0-0	19.1	24	14	4	1	9-0	11	6.52	66	.324	.400	0	ø	0	—	-4	0	-0.7
1999	Hou N	0	1	.000	5	0	0	0-0	4	11	8	1	0	2-0	3	15.75	28	.478	.520	0	ø	0	—	-5	0	-0.9
Total	5	3	12	.200	111	0	0	1-3	128.1	169	91	24	6	63-4	60	5.89	78	.329	.407	4	.000	-0	—	-18	0	-2.0
McDaniel, Lindy	Lyndall Dale; B12.13.1935 Hollis OK; BR/TR/6´3˝/(182–196); d9.2; b–Von; Col Oklahoma																									
1955	StL N	0	0	ø	4	2	0	0	19	22	10	4	0	7-1	7	4.74	86	.293	.349	5	.200	-0	110	-1	0	-0.1
1956	StL N	7	6	.538	39	7	1	0	116.1	121	60	7	0	42-7	59	3.40	111	.273	.333	32	.219	2	123	1	0	0.3
1957	StL N	15	9	.625	30	26	10-1	0	191	196	87	13	3	53-4	75	3.49	114	.266	.316	74-1-3	.257	4*	109	8	0	1.4
1958	StL N	5	7	.417	26	17	2-1	0	108.2	139	76	17	2	31-2	47	5.80	71	.305	.351	30-0-2	.067	-3	118	-18	0	-2.0
1959	StL N	14	12	.538	62	7	1	**15**	132	144	61	11	1	41-8	86	3.82	111	.283	.335	29-0-3	.034	-2	66	6	0	1.1
1960	StL N★	12	4	.750	65	2	1	**26**	116.1	85	28	8	1	24-3	105	2.09	196	.207	.249	26	.231	1	86	**25**	0	**4.7**
1961	StL N	10	6	.625	55	0	0	9	94.1	117	57	11	2	31-11	65	4.87	90	.305	.359	17-0-3	.235	-0	—	-3	0	-0.5
1962	StL N	3	10	.231	55	2	0	14	107	96	53	12	1	29-8	79	4.12	104	.239	.288	21-0-1	.095	-1	164	3	0	0.4
1963	Chi N	13	7	.650	57	0	0	**22**	88	82	32	9	0	27-5	75	2.86	123	.251	.304	22-1-1	.091	-0	—	6	0	1.3
1964	Chi N	1	7	.125	63	0	0	15	95	104	43	4	1	23-4	71	3.88	96	.276	.318	16-0-1	.125	-1	—	-1	0	-0.1
1965	Chi N	5	6	.455	71	0	0	2	128.2	115	45	12	0	47-20	92	2.59	142	.241	.307	8	.000	-1	—	14	0	1.3
1966	SF N	10	5	.667	64	0	0	6	121.2	103	48	5	0	35-9	93	2.66	138	.228	.282	22-0-4	.091	-1	—	11	0	1.3
1967	SF N	2	6	.250	41	3	0	3	72.2	69	34	5	2	24-10	48	3.72	88	.248	.310	11	.091	-1	53	-3	0	-0.4
1968	SF N	0	0	ø	12	0	0	0	19.1	30	16	2	0	5-0	9	7.45	40	.357	.393	2	.000	-0	—	-8	0	-0.5
	NY A	4	1	.800	24	0	0	10	51.1	30	10	5	1	12-3	43	1.75	166	.166	.221	13-0-2	.000	-1	—	7	0	1.1
1969	NY A	5	6	.455	51	0	0	5-4	83.2	84	37	4	0	23-6	60	3.55	99	.261	.305	8-0-2	.000	-1	—	0	0	0.0
1970	NY A	9	5	.643	62	0	0	29-6	111.2	88	29	7	0	23-5	81	2.01	177	.217	.258	24-0-1	.167	-0	—	20	0	**3.5**
1971	NY A	5	10	.333	44	0	0	4-7	69.2	82	41	12	0	24-6	39	5.04	65	.296	.350	9-0-1	.111	-0	—	-12	0	-2.6
1972	NY A	3	1	.750	37	0	0	0-0	68	54	23	4	0	25-5	47	2.25	133	.217	.287	7-1-1	.286	1	—	4	0	0.5
1973	NY A	12	6	.667	47	3	1	10-4	160.1	148	54	11	1	49-9	93	2.86	130	.250	.304	2	.000	-0	48	18	0	2.3
1974	KC A	1	4	.200	38	5	2	1-2	106.2	109	50	6	0	24-5	47	3.46	111	.265	.303	0	ø	0	65	3	0	0.2
1975	KC A	5	1	.833	40	0	0	1-2	78	81	40	3	0	24-5	40	4.15	93	.273	.323	0	ø	0	—	-2	29	-0.2
Total	21	141	119	.542	987	74	18-2	172-25	2139.1	2099	934	172	15	623-136	1361	3.45	109	.258	.309	378-3-25	.148	-4	107	78	29	13.0
McDaniel, Von	Max Von; B4.18.1939 Hollis OK; D8.20.1995 Lawton OK; BR/TR/6´2.5˝/(180–190); d6.13; b–Lindy																									
1957	StL N	7	5	.583	17	13	4-2	0	86.2	71	37	7	1	31-3	45	3.22	123	.225	.293	26-0-1	.000	-3	68	6	0	0.4
1958	StL N	0	0	ø	2	1	0	0	2	5	3	0	0	5-0	0	13.50	31	.500	.667	0-0-1	ø	0	174	-2	0	-0.1
Total	2	7	5	.583	19	14	4-2	0	88.2	76	40	7	1	36-3	45	3.45	115	.233	.309	26-0-2	.000	-3	76	4	0	0.3
McDermott, Joe	Joseph; d5.4.1871																									
1872	Eck NA	0	7	.000	7	7	7	0	63	143	144	3	—	14	1	8.14	42	.376	.398	32	.281	2	66	-35	—	-2.0
McDermott, Mickey	Maurice Joseph "Maury"; B8.29.1929 Poughkeepsie NY; D8.7.2003 Phoenix AZ; BL/TL/6´2˝/(170–190); d4.24; C1; ▲																									
1948	Bos A	0	0	ø	7	0	0	0	23.1	16	18	2	1	35	17	6.17	71	.208	.460	8	.375	1	—	-5	0	-0.1
1949	Bos A	5	4	.556	12	12	6-2	0	80	63	37	5	3	52	50	4.05	108	.220	.345	33	.212	1	120	4	0	0.5
1950	Bos A	7	3	.700	38	15	4	5	130	119	80	8	2	124	96	5.19	94	.249	.406	44	.364	6*	135	-3	0	0.4
1951	Bos A	8	8	.500	34	19	9-1	3	172	141	72	9	5	92	127	3.35	133	.226	.330	66-1-1	.273	2*	95	20	0	2.0
1952	Bos A	10	9	.526	30	21	7-2	0	162	139	70	14	3	92	117	3.72	106	.234	.340	62-1-3	.226	3*	95	6	0	0.9
1953	Bos A	18	10	.643	32	30	8-4	0	206.1	169	82	9	2	109	92	3.01	140	.224	.323	93-1-0	.301	7*	92	25	0	4.1
1954	Was A	7	15	.318	30	26	11-1	1	196.1	172	95	8	3	110	95	3.44	103	.239	.339	95-0-2	.200	3*	93	-1	0	0.2
1955	Was A	10	10	.500	31	20	8-1	1	156	140	75	9	9	100-2	78	3.75	102	.243	.361	95-1-1	.263	7*	96	1	0	1.0
1956	†NY A	2	6	.250	23	9	1	0	87	85	46	10	0	47-2	38	4.24	91	.261	.350	52-1-1	.212	3*	92	-4	0	-0.1
1957	KC A	1	4	.200	29	4	0	0	69	68	47	9	0	50-2	29	5.48	72	.266	.382	49-4-0	.245	3*	141	-11	0	0.0
1958	Det A	0	0	ø	2	0	0	0	2	6	4	0	0	2-0	0	9.00	45	.500	.571	3	.333	0*	—	-2	0	-0.1
1961	StL N	1	0	1.000	19	0	0	4	27	29	17	3	0	15-2	15	3.67	120	.271	.358	14	.071	-1*	—	0	0	-0.1
	KC A	0	0	ø	4	0	0	0	5.2	14	12	0	0	10-0	3	14.29	29	.452	.585	5	.200	1*	—	-7	0	-0.3
Total	12	69	69	.500	291	156	54-11	14	1316.2	1161	655	86	28	838-8	757	3.91	105	.240	.354	619-9-8	.252	36	102	23	0	8.4

YEAR	TM LG	W	L	PCT	G	GS	CG-SHO	SV-BS	IP	H	R	HR	HB	BB-IB	SO	ERA	AERA	OAV	OOB	AB-HR-SH	AVG	PB	SUP	APR	DL	PW
McDermott, Mike	Michael H.; B5.6.1864 Fall River MA; D5.7.1947 Fall River MA; TR/5´10˝/152; d9.2																									
1889	Lou AA	1	8	.111	9	9	9	0	84.1	108	65	4	2	34	22	4.16	92	.302	.365	33	.182	-1	68	-3	—	-0.3
McDermott, Mike	Michael Joseph; B9.7.1862 St.Louis MO; D6.30.1943 St.Louis MO; TR/5´8˝/145; d4.20																									
1895	Lou N	4	19	.174	33	26	18	0	207.1	258	203	8	11	103	42	5.99	77	.300	.382	82	.159	-2	106	-32	—	-2.6
1896	Lou N	2	7	.222	12	10	4-1	0	65	87	77	4	6	44	12	7.34	59	.318	.423	27-0-1	.296	1	82	-21	—	-1.9
1897	Cle N	4	5	.444	9	7	4	0	62	75	44	2	3	25	12	4.50	100	.296	.367	25	.320	1	68	0	—	0.0
	StL N	1	2	.333	4	4	1	0	21.1	23	23	2	0	19	3	9.28	47	.274	.408	9	.222	-0	73	-9	—	-0.8
	Year	5	7	.417	13	11	5	0	83.1	98	67	4	3	44	15	5.72	78	.291	.378	34	.294	1	70	-9	—	-0.8
Total	3	11	33	.250	58	47	27-1	0	355.2	443	347	16	20	191	69	6.17	74	.301	.389	143-0-1	.217	0	92	-62	—	-5.3
McDevitt, Danny	Daniel Eugene; B11.18.1932 New York NY; BL/TL/5´10˝/(164–175); d6.17; Col St. Bonaventure																									
1957	Bro N	7	4	.636	22	17	5-2	0	119	105	55	5	6	72-1	90	3.25	128	.238	.351	39-0-4	.154	-0	97	9	0	0.8
1958	LA N	2	6	.250	13	10	2	0	48.1	71	43	6	0	31-1	26	7.45	55	.355	.438	15	.133	-0	118	-17	0	-2.3
1959	LA N	10	8	.556	39	22	6-2	4	145	149	83	16	14	51-5	106	3.97	106	.263	.335	46-0-2	.109	-2	92	-1	0	-0.3
1960	LA N	0	4	.000	24	7	0	0	53	51	26	7	6	42-3	30	4.25	93	.260	.406	10-0-2	.200	0	89	-1	0	0.0
1961	NY A	1	2	.333	8	2	0	1	13	18	11	2	1	8-0	8	7.62	49	.353	.443	1	.000	0	83	-6	0	-1.0
	Min A	1	0	1.000	16	1	0	0	26.2	20	11	1	4	19-0	15	2.36	179	.213	.368	3	.000	-0	125	4	0	0.2
	Year	2	2	.500	24	3	0	1	39.2	38	22	3	5	27-0	23	4.08	100	.262	.393	4	.000	-0	94	-1	0	-0.8
1962	KC A	0	3	.000	33	1	0	2	51	47	37	5	1	41-2	28	5.82	73	.250	.385	9	.222	0	63	-9	0	-0.5
Total	6	21	27	.438	155	60	13-4	7	456	461	266	42	32	264-12	303	4.40	94	.265	.370	123-0-8	.138	-3	97	-21	0	-3.1
McDill, Allen	Allen Gabriel; B8.23.1971 Greenville MS; BL/TL/6´0˝/(155–170); [NYN92 20/553]; d5.15; Col Arkansas Tech																									
1997	KC A	0	0	ø	3	0	0	0-0	4	3	6	1	1	8-0	2	13.50	35	.214	.522	0	ø	0	—	-4	0	-0.2
1998	KC A	0	0	ø	7	0	0	0-0	6	9	7	3	0	2-0	3	10.50	46	.333	.379	0	ø	0	—	-3	0	-0.2
2000	Det A	0	0	ø	13	0	0	0-0	10	13	9	2	1	1-0	7	7.20	68	.317	.349	0	ø	0	—	-3	0	-0.1
2001	Bos A	0	0	ø	15	0	0	0-1	14.2	13	9	2	1	7-1	16	5.52	80	.236	.328	0	ø	0	—	-1	0	-0.1
Total	4	0	0	ø	38	0	0	0-1	34.2	38	31	8	3	18-1	28	7.79	60	.277	.371	0	ø	0	—	-11	0	-0.6
McDonald, Hank	Henry Monroe; B1.16.1911 Santa Monica CA; D10.17.1982 Hemet CA; BR/TR/6´3˝/200; d4.16																									
1931	Phi A	2	4	.333	19	10	1-1	0	70.1	62	43	3	1	41	23	3.71	121	.239	.346	21	.095	-1	111	2	—	0.0
1933	Phi A	1	1	.500	4	1	0	0	12.1	14	12	0	0	4	1	5.11	84	.264	.316	4	.000	-0	60	-3	—	-0.4
	StL A	0	4	.000	25	5	0	0	58.1	83	59	6	3	34	22	8.64	54	.332	.418	14	.143	-1	66	-22	—	-1.4
	Year	1	5	.167	29	6	0	0	70.2	97	71	6	3	38	23	8.02	57	.320	.401	18	.111	-1	65	-24	—	-1.8
Total	2	3	9	.250	48	16	1-1	0	141	159	114	9	4	79	46	5.87	77	.283	.375	39	.103	-2	93	-23	—	-1.8
McDonald, Jim	Jimmie Le Roy "Hot Rod"; B5.17.1927 Grants Pass OR; BR/TR (BB 1950–51)/5´10.5˝/(185–192); d7.27																									
1950	Bos A	1	0	1.000	9	0	0	0	19	23	9	1	1	10	5	3.79	129	.329	.420	3	.333	1	—	2	0	0.2
1951	StL A	4	7	.364	16	11	5	1	84	84	48	5	2	46	28	4.07	108	.260	.356	29-0-1	.207	-0*	81	1	0	0.1
1952	NY A	3	4	.429	26	5	1	0	69.1	71	31	1	2	40	20	3.50	95	.268	.368	19	.316	3	131	-1	0	0.4
1953	†NY A	9	7	.563	27	18	6-2	0	129.2	128	64	4	1	39	43	3.82	97	.260	.316	41-0-3	.098	-3*	122	-3	0	-0.5
1954	NY A	4	1	.800	16	10	3-1	0	71	54	28	3	1	45	20	3.17	108	.213	.332	19-0-2	.211	2	159	2	60	0.4
1955	Bal A	3	5	.375	21	8	0	0	51.2	76	48	5	0	30-1	20	7.14	53	.345	.421	11-0-1	.182	1	84	-20	0	-2.5
1956	Chi A	0	2	.000	8	3	0	0	18.2	29	18	2	1	7-0	10	8.68	47	.377	.425	5	.000	-0	36	-9	0	-0.8
1957	Chi A	0	1	.000	10	0	0	0	22.1	18	8	2	0	10-1	12	2.01	185	.234	.315	1	.000	0	—	3	0	0.2
1958	Chi A	0	0	ø	3	0	0	0	2.1	6	8	1	0	4-0	0	19.29	19	.429	.556	0	ø	0	—	-5	0	-0.3
Total	9	24	27	.471	136	55	15-3	1	468	489	262	24	8	231-2	158	4.27	89	.273	.357	128-0-7	.180	4	109	-30	60	-2.8
McDonald, John	John Joseph (b John Joseph McDonnell); B1.27.1883 Throop PA; D4.9.1950 Roselle NJ; BR/TR/6´1˝/170; d9.3																									
1907	Was A	0	0	ø	1	0	0	0	6	12	11	0	0	2	3	9.00	27	.414	.452	3	.333	1	—	-5	—	-0.2
McDonald, Ben	Larry Benard; B11.24.1967 Baton Rouge LA; BR/TR/6´7˝/(212–214); [BalA89 1/1]; d9.6; Col Louisiana St.																									
1989	Bal A	1	0	1.000	6	0	0	0-0	7.1	8	7	2	0	4-0	3	8.59	44	.286	.364	0	ø	0	—	-4	0	-0.4
1990	Bal A	8	5	.615	21	15	3-2	0-0	118.2	88	36	9	0	35-0	65	2.43	157	.205	.262	0	ø	0	76	18	43	1.9
1991	Bal A	6	8	.429	21	21	1	0-0	126.1	126	71	16	1	43-2	85	4.84	82	.261	.321	0	ø	0	107	-12	50	-1.2
1992	Bal A	13	13	.500	35	35	4-2	0-0	227	213	113	32	9	74-5	158	4.24	96	.247	.311	0	ø	0	113	-4	0	-0.3
1993	Bal A	13	14	.481	34	34	7-1	0-0	220.1	185	92	17	5	86-4	171	3.39	133	.228	.304	0	ø	0	84	25	0	3.0
1994	Bal A	14	7	.667	24	24	5-1	0-0	157.1	151	75	14	2	54-2	94	4.06	124	.255	.319	0	ø	0	97	16	0	1.9
1995	Bal A	3	6	.333	14	13	1	0-0	80	67	40	10	3	38-3	62	4.16	115	.224	.316	0	ø	0	79	5	80	0.5
1996	Mil A	12	10	.545	35	35	2	0-0	221.1	228	104	25	6	67-0	146	3.90	133	.264	.319	0	ø	0	97	31	0	2.6
1997	Mil A	8	7	.533	21	21	1	0-0	133	120	68	13	5	36-2	110	4.06	114	.237	.294	1	.000	-0	84	8	74	0.7
Total	9	78	70	.527	211	198	24-6	0-0	1291.1	1186	606	138	31	437-18	894	3.91	116	.243	.308	1	.000	-0	95	83	247	8.7
McDoolan	; d4.14																									
1873	Mar NA	0	1	.000	1	1	1	0	9	18	24	0	—	0	0	3.00	113	.305	.305	4	.000	-1	33	-2	—	-0.2
McDougal, Dewey	James H.; B9.19.1871 Aledo IL; D4.28.1935 Galesburg IL; TR/5´10˝/188; d4.24																									
1895	StL N	3	10	.231	18	14	10	0	114.2	187	146	11	10	46	23	8.32	58	.360	.423	41	.146	-2	90	-43	—	-3.5
1896	StL N	0	1	.000	3	1	0	0	10	13	11	2	1	4	0	8.10	54	.310	.383	3	.000	-1	65	-4	—	-0.3
Total	2	3	11	.214	21	15	10	0	124.2	200	157	13	11	50	23	8.30	58	.357	.420	44	.136	-3	89	-47	—	-3.8
McDougal, Sandy	John Auchanbolt; B5.21.1874 Buffalo NY; D10.2.1910 Buffalo NY; BR/TR/5´10˝/155; d6.12																									
1895	Bro N	0	0	ø	1	0	0	1	3	3	4	0	0	5	2	12.00	37	.250	.471	1	.000	-0	—	-2	—	-0.1
1905	StL N	1	4	.200	5	5	5	0	44.2	50	24	0	0	12	10	3.43	87	.301	.348	15-0-1	.133	-1	58	-3	—	-0.2
Total	2	1	4	.200	6	5	5	1	47.2	53	28	0	0	17	12	3.97	78	.298	.359	16-0-1	.125	-1	58	-5	—	-0.3
McDowell, Jack	Jack Burns; B1.16.1966 Van Nuys CA; BR/TR/6´5˝/(179–190); [ChiA87 1/5]; d9.15; Col Stanford																									
1987	Chi A	3	0	1.000	4	4	0	0-0	28	16	6	1	2	6-0	15	1.93	240	.168	.233	0	ø	0	94	8	0	0.9
1988	Chi A	5	10	.333	26	26	1	0-0	158.2	147	85	12	7	68-5	84	3.97	101	.245	.326	0	ø	0	82	-2	0	-0.2
1990	Chi A	14	9	.609	33	33	4	0-0	205	189	93	20	7	77-0	165	3.82	101	.244	.316	0	ø	0	104	1	0	0.1
1991	Chi A★	17	10	.630	35	**35**	**15**-3	0-0	253.2	212	97	19	4	82-2	191	3.41	117	.228	.292	0	ø	0	116	21	0	2.1
1992	Chi A★	20	10	.667	34	34	**13**-1	0-0	260.2	247	95	21	7	75-9	178	3.18	122	.251	.307	0	ø	0	114	24	0	2.6
1993	†Chi A★	**22**	10	.688	34	34	10-**4**	0-0	256.2	261	104	20	3	69-6	158	3.37	125	.266	.314	0	ø	0	107	26	0	3.1
1994	Chi A	10	9	.526	25	**25**	6-2	0-0	181	186	82	12	5	42-2	127	3.73	126	.266	.310	0	ø	0	89	21	0	1.9
1995	†NY A	15	10	.600	30	30	**8**-2	0-0	217.2	211	106	25	5	78-1	157	3.93	118	.254	.320	0	ø	0	99	15	0	1.4
1996	†Cle A	13	9	.591	30	30	5-1	0-0	192	214	119	22	4	67-2	141	5.11	96	.282	.341	0	ø	0	102	-5	18	-0.4
1997	Cle A	3	3	.500	8	6	0	0-0	40.2	44	25	6	1	18-1	38	5.09	92	.282	.356	0	ø	0	101	-2	139	-0.2
1998	Ana A	5	3	.625	14	14	0	0-0	76	96	45	11	1	19-1	45	5.09	93	.311	.350	0	ø	0	92	-2	99	-0.2
1999	Ana A	0	4	.000	4	4	0	0-0	19	31	17	4	2	5-0	12	8.05	61	.369	.413	0	ø	0	38	-6	109	-0.9
Total	12	127	87	.593	277	275	62-13	0-0	1889	1854	874	173	48	606-29	1311	3.85	111	.257	.317	0	ø	0	101	99	365	10.2
McDowell, Roger	Roger Alan; B12.21.1960 Cincinnati OH; BR/TR/6´1˝/(175–197); [NYN82 3/59]; d4.11; C1; Col Bowling Green																									
1985	NY N	6	5	.545	62	2	0	17-6	127.1	108	43	9	1	37-8	70	2.83	124	.230	.286	19-0-2	.158	0	88	10	0	1.3
1986	†NY N	14	9	.609	75	0	0	22-6	128	107	48	4	3	42-5	65	3.02	119	.228	.294	18-0-1	.278	1	—	9	0	2.0
1987	NY N	7	5	.583	56	0	0	25-7	88.2	95	41	7	2	28-4	32	4.16	92	.276	.330	13	.231	1	—	-1	38	0.0
1988	†NY N	5	5	.500	62	0	0	16-4	89	80	31	1	3	31-7	46	2.63	124	.238	.304	9	.333	2*	—	6	0	1.2
1989	NY N	1	5	.167	25	0	0	4-1	35.1	34	21	1	2	16-3	15	3.31	100	.254	.340	2	.500	0	—	-3	0	-0.4
	Phi N	3	3	.500	44	0	0	19-4	56.2	45	15	2	1	22-5	32	1.11	323	.220	.298	1	.000	-0	—	12	0	2.1
	Year	4	8	.333	69	0	0	23-5	92	79	36	3	3	38-8	47	1.96	178	.233	.315	3	.333	0	—	9	0	1.7
1990	Phi N	6	8	.429	72	0	0	22-6	86.1	92	41	2	2	35-9	39	3.86	100	.286	.355	2-0-1	.000	-0	—	0	0	0.0
1991	Phi N	3	6	.333	38	0	0	3-3	59	61	28	1	2	32-12	28	3.20	115	.266	.360	2	.000	-0	—	1	15	0.2
	LA N	6	3	.667	33	0	0	7-2	42.1	39	12	3	0	16-8	22	2.55	141	.257	.324	0	ø	0*	—	6	0	1.3
	Year	9	9	.500	71	0	0	10-5	101.1	100	40	4	2	48-20	50	2.93	125	.262	.346	2	.000	-0	—	7	0	1.5
1992	LA N	6	10	.375	65	0	0	14-8	83.2	103	46	3	1	42-13	50	4.09	85	.306	.381	3-0-1	.000	1	—	-7	0	-1.2
1993	LA N	5	3	.625	54	0	0	2-1	68	76	32	2	2	30-10	27	2.25	172	.288	.364	2	.500	0	—	7	0	1.0
1994	LA N	0	3	.000	32	0	0	0-1	41.1	50	25	3	1	22-6	29	5.23	76	.303	.388	1	.000	-0	—	-6	0	-0.4

YEAR	TM LG	W	L	PCT	G	GS	CG-SHO	SV-BS	IP	H	R	HR	HB	BB-IB	SO	ERA	AERA	OAV	OOB	AB-HR-SH	AVG	PB	SUP	APR	DL	PW
1995	Tex A	7	4	.636	64	0	0	4-4	85	86	39	5	6	34-7	49	4.02	120	.277	.354	0	ø	0	—	8	0	1.1
1996	Bal A	1	1	.500	41	0	0	4-2	59.1	69	32	7	2	23-1	20	4.25	117	.296	.363	0	ø	0	—	4	67	0.2
Total	12	70	70	.500	723	2	0	159-55	1050	1045	454	50	28	410-98	524	3.30	115	.263	.334	72-0-5	.222	6	88	46	120	8.4
McDowell, Sam	Samuel Edward Thomas "Sudden Sam"; B9.21.1942 Pittsburgh PA; BL/TL/6´5˝/(190–220); d9.15																									
1961	Cle A	0	0	ø	1	1	0	0	6.1	3	0	0	0	5-0	5	0.00	ø	.136	.296	2	.000	-0	45	3	0	0.1
1962	Cle A	3	7	.300	25	13	0	1	87.2	81	64	9	4	70-1	70	6.06	64	.243	.379	26-0-1	.154	-1	99	-21	0	-2.2
1963	Cle A	3	5	.375	14	12	3-1	0	65	63	37	6	0	44-0	63	4.85	75	.256	.368	19-0-4	.211	0*	100	-8	0	-0.8
1964	Cle A	11	6	.647	31	24	6-2	1	173.1	148	60	8	3	100-6	177	2.70	133	.229	.334	56-0-3	.143	0	97	17	0	1.6
1965	Cle A★	17	11	.607	42	35	14-3	4	273	178	80	9	6	132-7	**325**	**2.18**	**160**	**.185**	.286	95-0-5	.126	-3*	88	**37**	0	3.8
1966	Cle A✳	9	8	.529	35	28	8-**5**	3	194.1	130	66	12	6	102-3	**225**	2.87	120	**.188**	.297	60-0-3	.200	1*	93	14	0	1.4
1967	Cle A	13	15	.464	37	37	10-1	0	236.1	201	112	21	7	123-3	236	3.85	85	.233	.331	82-1-4	.183	1	98	-13	0	-1.4
1968	Cle A★	15	14	.517	38	37	11-3	0	269	181	78	13	10	110-9	**283**	1.81	164	.189	.278	85-0-6	.153	0	83	28	0	3.3
1969	Cle A★	18	14	.563	39	38	18-4	1-0	285	222	111	13	7	102-9	**279**	2.94	129	.213	.286	92-0-11	.174	-1	83	24	0	2.6
1970	Cle A★	20	12	.625	39	39	19-1	0-0	**305**	236	108	25	7	131-10	**304**	2.92	137	.213	.299	105-1-8	.124	-4*	91	33	0	2.9
1971	Cle A✳	13	17	.433	35	31	8-2	1-1	214.2	160	89	22	3	153-13	192	3.40	114	.207	.338	73-0-6	.178	-1	70	10	0	1.2
1972	SF N	10	8	.556	28	25	4	0-1	164.1	155	86	12	6	86-6	122	4.33	81	.253	.348	59-0-4	.119	-1	127	-13	21	-1.5
1973	SF N	1	2	.333	18	3	0	3-0	40	45	23	4	0	29-0	35	4.50	86	.285	.392	12-0-1	.167	-0	84	-3	0	-0.3
	NY A	5	8	.385	16	15	2-1	0-0	95.2	73	47	4	0	64-2	75	3.95	94	.212	.332	0	ø	0	82	-2	0	-0.2
1974	NY A	1	6	.143	13	7	0	0-0	48	42	27	6	0	41-2	33	4.69	76	.236	.379	0	ø	0	64	-5	68	-0.8
1975	Pit N	2	1	.667	14	1	0	0-0	34.2	30	11	0	0	20-3	29	2.86	126	.242	.345	8	.000	-1	221	4	0	0.2
Total	15	141	134	.513	425	346	103-23	14-2	2492.1	1948	999	164	59	1312-74	2453	3.17	113	.215	.317	774-2-56	.154	-9	91	105	89	9.9
McElroy, Chuck	Charles Dwayne; B10.1.1967 Port Arthur TX; BL/TL/6´0˝/(160–205); [PhiN86 8/192]; d9.4																									
1989	Phi N	0	0	ø	11	0	0	0-0	10.1	12	2	1	0	4-1	8	1.74	206	.286	.348	0	ø	0	—	2	0	0.1
1990	Phi N	0	1	.000	16	0	0	0-0	14	24	13	0	0	10-2	16	7.71	50	.369	.447	0	ø	0	—	-6	0	-0.4
1991	Chi N	6	2	.750	71	0	0	3-3	101.1	73	33	7	0	57-7	92	1.95	200	.210	.317	10	.300	1	—	**17**	0	1.5
1992	Chi N	4	7	.364	72	0	0	6-5	83.2	73	40	5	0	51-10	83	3.55	102	.237	.341	6	.667	3	—	-1	0	0.2
1993	Chi N	2	2	.500	49	0	0	0-0	47.1	51	30	4	1	25-5	31	4.56	88	.280	.368	6	.000	-1	—	-4	0	-0.4
1994	Cin N	1	2	.333	52	0	0	5-6	57.2	52	15	3	0	15-2	38	2.34	179	.244	.294	6	.167	-0	—	13	0	0.7
1995	Cin N	3	4	.429	44	0	0	0-3	40.1	46	29	5	1	15-3	27	6.02	69	.291	.350	3	.000	-0	—	-8	16	-1.3
1996	Cin N	2	0	1.000	12	0	0	0-0	12.1	13	10	2	0	10-1	13	6.57	65	.265	.390	2	.000	-0	—	-3	27	-0.5
	Cal A	5	1	.833	40	0	0	0-2	36.2	32	12	2	2	13-2	32	2.95	172	.239	.313	0	ø	0	—	9	17	1.3
1997	Ana A	0	0	ø	13	0	0	0-2	15.2	17	7	2	0	3-0	18	3.45	134	.270	.303	0	ø	0	—	2	0	0.1
	Chi A	1	3	.250	48	0	0	1-3	59.1	56	29	3	2	19-1	44	3.94	112	.247	.307	0	ø	0*	—	3	0	0.2
	Year	1	3	.250	61	0	0	1-5	75	73	36	5	2	22-1	62	3.84	116	.252	.306	0	ø	0	—	4	0	0.3
1998	Col N	6	4	.600	78	0	0	2-4	68.1	68	23	3	0	24-0	61	2.90	179	.268	.327	5-0-1	.200	-0	—	14	0	1.9
1999	Col N	3	1	.750	41	0	0	0-3	40.2	48	29	9	0	28-3	37	6.20	93	.296	.396	1-0-1	.000	-0	—	-1	0	-0.1
	NY N	0	0	ø	15	0	0	0-0	13.1	12	5	0	1	8-1	7	3.38	129	.250	.362	0	ø	0	—	2	0	0.1
	Year	3	1	.750	56	0	0	0-3	54	60	34	9	1	36-4	44	5.50	99	.286	.388	1-0-1	.000	-0	—	0	0	0.0
2000	Bal A	3	0	1.000	43	2	0	0-1	63.1	60	36	6	2	34-2	50	4.69	100	.247	.340	0	ø	0	150	0	0	0.0
2001	Bal A	1	2	.333	18	5	0	0-0	45.1	49	29	8	2	28-2	22	5.36	80	.269	.371	0	ø	0	103	-5	0	-0.2
	SD N	1	1	.500	31	0	0	0-3	29.2	38	24	6	0	18-4	25	5.16	80	.306	.392	3	.000	-0	—	-6	0	-0.3
Total	13	38	30	.559	654	7	0	17-35	739.1	724	366	66	11	362-46	604	3.90	112	.258	.342	42-0-2	.214	2	117	28	60	2.9
McElroy, Jim	James D.; B11.5.1862 Napa Co. CA; D7.24.1889 Needles CA; 5´10˝/170; d5.26; Col St. Marys (CA)																									
1884	Phi N	1	12	.077	13	13	13	0	111	115	112	1	—	54	45	4.86	61	.254	.333	48	.146	-3*	49	-22	—	-2.2
	Wil U	0	1	.000	1	1	0	0	5	10	6	0	—	0	3	10.80	25	.385	.385	2	.000	-0	16	-3	—	-0.3
Total	1	1	13	.071	14	14	13	0	116	125	118	1	—	54	48	5.12	58	.261	.336	50	.140	-4	47	-25	—	-2.5
McEnaney, Will	William Henry; B2.14.1952 Springfield OH; BL/TL/6´0˝/(175–180); [CinN70 8/188]; d7.3																									
1974	Cin N	2	1	.667	24	0	0	2-1	27	24	16	4	0	9-1	13	4.33	81	.250	.311	0	ø	0	—	-3	0	-0.4
1975	†Cin N	5	2	.714	70	0	0	15-4	91	92	29	6	2	23-7	48	2.47	145	.264	.310	14	.000	-2	—	10	0	0.9
1976	†Cin N	2	6	.250	55	0	0	7-2	72.1	97	44	3	1	23-8	28	4.85	72	.323	.370	6-0-1	.167	1	—	-11	0	-1.4
1977	Mon N	3	5	.375	69	0	0	3-5	86.2	92	39	6	2	22-4	38	3.95	98	.271	.314	8	.000	-1	—	1	0	0.0
1978	Pit N	0	0	ø	6	0	0	0-0	8.2	15	11	3	1	2-0	6	10.38	36	.395	.429	0	ø	0	—	-6	0	-0.3
1979	StL N	0	3	.000	45	0	0	2-2	64	60	26	3	2	16-8	15	2.95	129	.251	.299	3	.000	-0	—	5	0	0.3
Total	6	12	17	.414	269	0	0	29-14	349.2	380	165	25	8	95-28	148	3.76	98	.279	.326	31-0-1	.032	-2	—	-4	0	-0.9
McEvoy, Lou	Louis Anthony; B5.30.1902 Williamsburg KS; D12.17.1953 Webster Groves MO; BR/TR/6´2.5˝/203; d4.28																									
1930	NY A	1	3	.250	28	1	0	3	52.1	64	51	4	2	29	14	6.71	64	.288	.375	16	.125	-1	20	-17	—	-1.4
1931	NY A	0	0	ø	6	0	0	1	12.1	19	17	1	1	12	3	12.41	32	.358	.485	4	.000	-1	—	-12	—	-0.6
Total	2	1	3	.250	34	1	0	4	64.2	83	68	5	3	41	17	7.79	54	.302	.398	20	.100	-2	20	-29	—	-2.0
McFadden, Barney	Bernard Joseph; B3.20.1877 Eckley PA; D4.28.1924 Mauch Chunk PA; BR/TR/6´1˝/195; d4.24; Col Villanova																									
1901	Cin N	3	4	.429	8	5	4	0	46	54	39	2	6	40	11	6.07	53	.290	.431	20	.150	-1	111	-14	—	-1.7
1902	Phi N	0	1	.000	1	1	1	0	9	14	13	0	0	7	3	8.00	35	.350	.447	3	.000	-0	72	-6	—	-0.5
Total	2	3	5	.375	9	6	5	0	55	68	52	2	6	47	14	6.38	49	.301	.434	23	.130	-2	105	-20	—	-2.2
McFarlan, Dan	Anderson Daniel; B11.1.1873 Gainesville TX; D9.23.1924 Louisville KY; ?/178; d9.2; b–Alex; Col Washington and Lee																									
1895	Lou N	0	7	.000	7	7	6	0	46	80	56	4	5	15	10	6.65	70	.376	.429	21	.238	-1	77	-13	—	-1.3
1899	Bro N	0	0	ø	1	0	0	0	6	6	1	1	0	3	0	1.50	261	.261	.346	2	.000	-0	—	2	—	0.1
	Was N	8	18	.308	32	28	22-1	0	211.2	268	166	5	11	64	41	4.76	82	.308	.363	86-0-1	.186	-0	72	-24	—	-2.4
	Year	8	18	.308	33	28	22-1	0	217.2	274	167	6	11	67	41	4.67	84	.307	.363	88-0-1	.182	-1	72	-17	—	-2.3
Total	2	8	25	.242	40	35	28-1	0	263.2	354	223	10	16	82	51	5.02	81	.320	.375	109-0-1	.193	-1	74	-35	—	-3.6
McFarland, Chappie	Charles Amos; B3.13.1875 White Hall IL; D12.14.1924 Houston TX; TR/6´1˝/?; d9.15; b–Monte																									
1902	StL N	0	1	.000	2	1	1	0	11	11	7	1	0	3	3	5.73	48	.262	.311	4	.000	-1	99	-3	—	-0.2
1903	StL N	9	19	.321	28	26	25-1	0	229	253	133	2	6	48	76	3.07	106	.284	.325	74-0-3	.108	-4	73	2	—	0.0
1904	StL N	14	18	.438	32	31	28-1	0	269.1	266	149	7	4	56	111	3.21	84	.248	.288	99-0-2	.131	-2	123	-18	—	-1.9
1905	StL N	8	18	.308	31	28	22-3	1	250.1	281	145	3	6	65	85	3.81	78	.284	.332	85-0-1	.165	1	88	-24	—	-2.1
1906	StL N	2	1	.667	6	4	2	1	37.1	33	18	1	0	8	16	1.93	136	.219	.258	15	.133	-1	104	0	—	0.0
	Pit N	1	3	.250	6	5	2-1	0	35.1	39	14	0	2	7	11	2.55	105	.298	.343	13	.385	1	109	0	—	0.2
	Bro N	0	1	.000	1	1	1	0	9	10	8	1	0	5	5	8.00	32	.286	.375	3	.000	-0	29	-5	—	-0.4
	Year	3	5	.375	13	10	5-1	1	81.2	82	40	2	2	20	32	2.87	92	.259	.307	31	.226	0	100	-4	—	-0.2
Total	5	34	61	.358	106	96	81-6	2	841.1	893	474	15	18	192	307	3.35	87	.270	.313	293-0-6	.143	-6	95	-48	—	-4.4
McFarland, Monte	Lamont Amos; B11.7.1872 White Hall IL; D11.15.1913 Peoria IL; BR/5´10˝/175; d9.14; b–Chappie																									
1895	Chi N	2	0	1.000	2	2	2	0	14	21	11	0	0	5	5	5.14	99	.339	.388	7-0-1	.143	-1	182	0	—	-0.1
1896	Chi N	0	4	.000	4	3	2	0	25	32	25	0	2	21	3	7.20	63	.308	.433	12-0-1	.000	-2	37	-6	—	-0.8
Total	2	2	4	.333	6	5	4	0	39	53	36	0	2	26	8	6.46	73	.319	.418	19-0-2	.053	-3	99	-6	—	-0.9
McFetridge, Jack	John Reed; B8.25.1869 Philadelphia PA; D1.10.1917 Philadelphia PA; 6´0˝/175; d6.7; Col Penn																									
1890	Phi N	1	0	1.000	1	1	1	0	9	5	1	0	0	2	4	1.00	366	.156	.206	4	.750	1	69	3	—	0.4
1903	Phi N	1	11	.083	14	13	11	0	103	120	71	2	3	49	31	4.89	67	.299	.379	34-0-3	.176	0	92	-16	—	-1.5
Total	2	2	11	.154	15	14	12	0	112	125	72	2	3	51	35	4.58	72	.288	.367	38-0-3	.237	2	90	-13	—	-1.1
McGaffigan, Andy	Andrew Joseph; B10.25.1956 W.Palm Beach FL; BR/TR/6´3˝/(190–200); [NYA78 6/156]; d9.22; Col Florida Southern																									
1981	NY A	0	0	ø	2	0	0	0-0	7	5	3	1	0	3-0	2	2.57	141	.200	.267	0	ø	0	—	0	0	0.0
1982	SF N	1	0	1.000	4	0	0	0-0	8	5	1	0	1	1-0	4	0.00	ø	.179	.233	1	.000	-0	—	3	0	0.3
1983	SF N	3	9	.250	43	16	0	2-0	134.1	131	67	17	1	39-5	93	4.29	83	.255	.308	30-0-2	.067	-1	75	-8	0	-1.0
1984	Mon N	3	4	.429	21	3	0	1-1	46	37	14	2	0	15-2	39	2.54	136	.220	.283	8-0-1	.000	-1	136	5	0	0.7
	Cin N	0	2	.000	9	3	0	0-1	23	23	14	2	0	8-0	18	5.48	69	.261	.323	2-0-2	.000	-0	85	-3	0	-0.3
	Year	3	6	.333	30	6	0	1-2	69	60	28	4	0	23-2	57	3.52	101	.234	.296	10-0-3	.000	-1	111	2	0	0.4
1985	Cin N	3	3	.500	15	15	2	0-0	94.1	88	40	4	2	30-4	83	3.72	102	.247	.309	29-0-1	.034	-2	87	2	0	-0.1
1986	Mon N	10	5	.667	48	14	1-1	2-1	142.2	114	49	9	2	55-8	104	2.65	141	.223	.298	33-0-4	.061	-2*	119	16	0	1.4

YEAR	TM LG	W	L	PCT	G	GS	CG-SHO	SV-BS	IP	H	R	HR	HB	BB-IB	SO	ERA	AERA	OAV	OOB	AB-HR-SH	AVG	PB	SUP	APR	DL	PW
1987	Mon N	5	2	.714	69	0	0	12-1	120.1	105	38	5	3	42-7	100	2.39	178	.235	.303	17-0-2	.000	-1	—	23	0	1.5
1988	Mon N	6	0	1.000	63	0	0	4-5	91.1	81	31	4	2	37-7	71	2.76	132	.233	.309	5	.000	-0	—	9	17	0.6
1989	Mon N	3	5	.375	57	0	0	2-3	75	85	40	3	3	30-4	40	4.68	76	.293	.361	1	1.000	0	—	-8	15	-0.8
1990	SF N	0	0	ø	4	0	0	0-0	4.2	10	9	2	0	4-0	4	17.36	21	.455	.538	0	ø	0	—	-7	0	-0.4
	KC A	4	3	.571	24	11	0	1-0	78.2	75	40	6	2	28-1	49	3.09	125	.248	.313	0	ø	0	116	3	0	0.2
1991	KC A	0	0	ø	4	0	0	0-0	8	14	5	0	0	2-0	3	4.50	92	.389	.410	0	ø	0	—	-1	0	0.0
Total	11	38	33	.535	363	62	3-1	24-12	833.1	773	351	55	16	294-38	610	3.38	111	.247	.312	126-0-12	.048	-7	98	34	32	2.1

McGeachy, Jack John Charles; B5.23.1864 Clinton MA; D4.5.1930 Cambridge MA; BR/TR/5´8˝/165; d6.17.1886; ▲

YEAR	TM LG	W	L	PCT	G	GS	CG-SHO	SV-BS	IP	H	R	HR	HB	BB-IB	SO	ERA	AERA	OAV	OOB	AB-HR-SH	AVG	PB	SUP	APR	DL	PW
1887	Ind N	0	1	.000	1	0	0	0	6.1	13	17	2	0	4	3	11.37	37	.351	.415	405-1	.269	0*	—	-7	—	-0.6
1888	Ind N	0	0	ø	1	0	0	0	5	5	5	1	0	3	0	7.20	41	.238	.333	452	.219	0*	—	-2	—	-0.1
1889	Ind N	0	0	ø	3	0	0	0	4.2	7	9	2	0	6	3	11.57	36	.333	.481	532-2	.267	0*	—	-4	—	-0.2
Total	3	0	1	.000	5	0	0	0	16	25	31	5	0	13	6	10.13	37	.316	.413	1389-3	.252	0	—	-13	—	-0.9

McGee, Bill William Henry "Fiddler Bill"; B11.16.1909 Batchtown IL; D2.11.1987 St.Louis MO; BR/TR/6´1˝/215; d9.29

YEAR	TM LG	W	L	PCT	G	GS	CG-SHO	SV-BS	IP	H	R	HR	HB	BB-IB	SO	ERA	AERA	OAV	OOB	AB-HR-SH	AVG	PB	SUP	APR	DL	PW
1935	StL N	1	0	1.000	1	1	1	0	9	3	1	0	0	1	2	1.00	410	.103	.133	3	.333	0	41	3	—	0.4
1936	StL N	1	1	.500	7	2	0	0	16	23	14	3	0	4	8	7.88	50	.359	.397	4	.250	0	118	-6	—	-0.6
1937	StL N	1	0	1.000	4	1	1	0	14	13	4	1	1	4	9	2.57	155	.255	.321	5	.200	-0	325	2	—	0.2
1938	StL N	7	12	.368	47	25	10-1	5	216	216	101	4	1	78	104	3.21	123	.257	.321	67-0-4	.209	1	83	14	—	1.3
1939	StL N	12	5	.706	43	17	5-4	0	156	155	68	14	0	59	56	3.81	108	.261	.328	55-0-2	.145	-2	109	8	—	0.6
1940	StL N	16	10	.615	38	31	11-3	0	218	222	108	13	2	96	78	3.80	105	.263	.340	73-0-10	.178	-1	108	5	—	0.3
1941	StL N	0	1	.000	4	3	0	0	14	17	9	1	1	13	2	5.14	73	.298	.437	4-0-1	.000	-1	105	-2	0	-0.2
	NY N	2	9	.182	22	14	1	0	106	117	68	9	0	54	41	4.92	75	.285	.368	31-0-1	.161	-1	98	-15	0	-1.6
	Year	2	10	.167	26	17	1	0	120	134	77	10	1	67	43	4.95	75	.286	.377	35-0-2	.143	-2	100	-17	0	-1.8
1942	NY N	6	3	.667	31	8	2-1	1	104	95	50	8	1	46	40	2.94	114	.244	.326	29-0-2	.103	-2	100	1	0	-0.2
Total	8	46	41	.529	197	102	31-9	6	853	861	423	53	6	355	340	3.74	104	.263	.336	271-0-20	.170	-6	102	10	0	0.2

McGeehan, Conny Cornelius Bernard; B8.25.1882 Drifton PA; D7.4.1907 Hazleton PA; TR; d7.15; b–Dan; Col Holy Cross

YEAR	TM LG	W	L	PCT	G	GS	CG-SHO	SV-BS	IP	H	R	HR	HB	BB-IB	SO	ERA	AERA	OAV	OOB	AB-HR-SH	AVG	PB	SUP	APR	DL	PW
1903	Phi A	1	0	1.000	3	0	0	0	10	9	5	0	1	1	4	4.50	68	.237	.275	6	.000	-1*	—	-1	—	-0.1

McGehee, Kevin George Kevin; B1.18.1969 Alexandria LA; BR/TR/6´0˝/190; [SFN90 8/230]; d8.23; Col Louisiana Tech

YEAR	TM LG	W	L	PCT	G	GS	CG-SHO	SV-BS	IP	H	R	HR	HB	BB-IB	SO	ERA	AERA	OAV	OOB	AB-HR-SH	AVG	PB	SUP	APR	DL	PW
1993	Bal A	0	0	ø	5	0	0	0-0	16.2	18	11	5	2	7-2	7	5.94	76	.281	.365	0	ø	0	—	-2	0	-0.1

McGehee, Pat Patrick Henry; B7.2.1888 Meadville MS; D12.30.1946 Paducah KY; BL/TR/6´2.5˝/180; d8.23; Col Tulane

YEAR	TM LG	W	L	PCT	G	GS	CG-SHO	SV-BS	IP	H	R	HR	HB	BB-IB	SO	ERA	AERA	OAV	OOB	AB-HR-SH	AVG	PB	SUP	APR	DL	PW
1912	Det A	0	0	ø	1	1	0	0	0	1	0	0	0	1	0	(0)	ø	1.000	1.000	0	ø	0	91	0	—	0.0

McGilberry, Randy Randall Kent; B10.29.1953 Mobile AL; BB/TR/6´1˝/(195–198); [KCA75 14/321]; d9.6; Col Louisiana Tech

YEAR	TM LG	W	L	PCT	G	GS	CG-SHO	SV-BS	IP	H	R	HR	HB	BB-IB	SO	ERA	AERA	OAV	OOB	AB-HR-SH	AVG	PB	SUP	APR	DL	PW
1977	KC A	0	1	.000	3	0	0	0-0	7	7	4	1	0	1-0	1	5.14	78	.280	.308	0	ø	0	—	-1	0	-0.1
1978	KC A	0	1	.000	18	0	0	0-1	25.2	27	16	2	0	18-1	12	4.21	91	.276	.388	0	ø	0	—	-2	0	-0.1
Total	2	0	2	.000	21	0	0	0-1	32.2	34	20	3	0	19-1	13	4.41	88	.276	.373	0	ø	0	—	-3	0	-0.2

McGill, Bill William Jacob "Parson"; B6.29.1880 Galva KS; D8.7.1959 Alva OK; BR/TR/6´2˝/185; d9.16; Col Friends

YEAR	TM LG	W	L	PCT	G	GS	CG-SHO	SV-BS	IP	H	R	HR	HB	BB-IB	SO	ERA	AERA	OAV	OOB	AB-HR-SH	AVG	PB	SUP	APR	DL	PW
1907	StL A	1	0	1.000	2	2	1	0	18.1	22	8	0	0	2	8	3.44	73	.301	.320	9	.000	-1	121	-1	—	-0.2

McGill, Willie William Vaness "Kid"; B11.10.1873 Atlanta GA; D8.29.1944 Indianapolis IN; TL/5´6.5˝/170; d5.8

YEAR	TM LG	W	L	PCT	G	GS	CG-SHO	SV-BS	IP	H	R	HR	HB	BB-IB	SO	ERA	AERA	OAV	OOB	AB-HR-SH	AVG	PB	SUP	APR	DL	PW
1890	Cle P	11	9	.550	24	20	19	0	183.2	222	146	5	12	96	82	4.12	97	.286	.373	68	.147	2	114	1	—	0.4
1891	Cin AA	2	5	.286	8	8	6	0	65	69	56	1	3	37	19	4.98	82	.263	.361	20	.100	0	72	-3	—	-0.3
	StL AA	18	9	.667	33	29	20-1	1	233	207	140	10	12	126	146	2.70	155	.230	.332	83	.157	-0	109	29	—	2.5
	Year	20	14	.588	41	37	26-1	1	298	276	196	11	15	163	165	3.20	130	.238	.339	103	.146	-0	101	24	—	2.2
1892	Cin N	1	1	.500	3	3	1	0	17	18	14	0	0	5	7	5.29	62	.261	.311	7	.286	0	129	-3	—	-0.3
1893	Chi N	17	18	.486	39	34	26-1	0	302.2	311	206	6	14	181	91	4.61	101	.258	.361	124	.234	2*	103	8	—	0.7
1894	Chi N	7	19	.269	27	23	22	0	208	272	195	2	10	117	58	5.84	97	.312	.400	82-0-1	.244	0	81	-4	—	-0.4
1895	Phi N	10	8	.556	20	20	13	0	146	177	122	2	4	81	70	5.55	86	.295	.382	63-0-1	.222	-0	104	-12	—	-1.1
1896	Phi N	5	4	.556	12	11	7	0	79.2	87	62	0	4	53	29	5.31	81	.275	.386	29-0-2	.207	-0	141	-8	—	-0.7
Total	7	71	73	.493	166	148	114-2	1	1235	1363	941	26	59	696	502	4.57	100	.273	.368	476-0-4	.202	4	102	8	—	0.8

McGillen, John John Joseph; B8.6.1917 Eddystone PA; D8.11.1987 Upland PA; BL/TL/6´1˝/175; d4.20

YEAR	TM LG	W	L	PCT	G	GS	CG-SHO	SV-BS	IP	H	R	HR	HB	BB-IB	SO	ERA	AERA	OAV	OOB	AB-HR-SH	AVG	PB	SUP	APR	DL	PW
1944	Phi A	0	0	ø	2	0	0	0	1	1	2	0	0	2	0	18.00	19	.333	.600	0	ø	0	—	-1	0	-0.1

McGinley, Jim James William; B10.2.1878 Groveland MA; D9.20.1961 Haverhill MA; BR/TR/5´9.5˝/165; d9.22

YEAR	TM LG	W	L	PCT	G	GS	CG-SHO	SV-BS	IP	H	R	HR	HB	BB-IB	SO	ERA	AERA	OAV	OOB	AB-HR-SH	AVG	PB	SUP	APR	DL	PW
1904	StL N	2	1	.667	3	3	3	0	27	28	8	0	3	6	6	2.00	135	.267	.325	11	.091	-1	94	2	—	0.1
1905	StL N	0	1	.000	1	1	0	0	3	5	6	1	0	2	0	15.00	20	.333	.412	1	1.000	0	145	-4	—	-0.5
Total	2	2	2	.500	4	4	3	0	30	33	14	1	3	8	6	3.30	83	.275	.336	12	.167	-0	108	-2	—	-0.4

McGinn, Dan Daniel Michael; B11.29.1943 Omaha NE; BL/TL/6´0˝/(185–202); d9.3; Col Notre Dame

YEAR	TM LG	W	L	PCT	G	GS	CG-SHO	SV-BS	IP	H	R	HR	HB	BB-IB	SO	ERA	AERA	OAV	OOB	AB-HR-SH	AVG	PB	SUP	APR	DL	PW
1968	Cin N	0	1	.000	14	0	0	0	12	13	7	1	1	11-2	16	5.25	60	.271	.417	2	.000	-0	—	-2	0	-0.2
1969	Mon N	7	10	.412	74	1	0	6-3	132.1	123	67	8	5	65-8	112	3.94	94	.245	.337	29-1-0	.172	1	48	-4	0	-0.3
1970	Mon N	7	10	.412	52	19	3-2	0-0	130.2	154	88	13	7	78-4	83	5.44	76	.296	.394	35-0-3	.114	-2	82	-18	0	-2.1
1971	Mon N	1	4	.200	28	6	1	0-0	71	74	51	7	1	42-4	40	5.96	60	.274	.374	17	.235	0	91	-18	0	-1.1
1972	Chi N	0	5	.000	42	2	0	4-2	62.2	78	46	5	4	29-6	42	5.89	65	.301	.379	8	.250	1*	12	-13	0	-1.1
Total	5	15	30	.333	210	28	4-2	10-5	408.2	442	259	34	18	225-24	293	5.11	75	.276	.371	91-1-3	.165	-0	81	-55	0	-4.8

McGinnis, Jumbo George Washington; B2.22.1854 Alton MO; D5.18.1934 St.Louis MO; 5´10˝/197; d5.2

YEAR	TM LG	W	L	PCT	G	GS	CG-SHO	SV-BS	IP	H	R	HR	HB	BB-IB	SO	ERA	AERA	OAV	OOB	AB-HR-SH	AVG	PB	SUP	APR	DL	PW
1882	StL AA	25	18	.581	45	45	43-3	0	388.1	391	241	2	—	53	134	2.60	108	.245	.269	203	.217	1*	112	10	—	0.8
1883	StL AA	28	16	.636	45	45	41-**6**	0	382.2	325	174	3	—	69	128	2.33	150	.215	.249	180	.200	-6	89	49	—	4.2
1884	StL AA	24	16	.600	40	40	39-5	0	354.1	331	196	4	12	35	141	2.84	115	.233	.258	146	.233	3	108	19	—	1.9
1885	StL AA	6	6	.500	13	13	12-3	0	112	98	65	1	6	19	41	3.38	97	.225	.267	50-1	.220	0	99	0	—	0.0
1886	StL AA	5	5	.500	10	10	10-1	0	87.2	107	75	2	7	27	30	3.80	91	.288	.347	37	.189	-1	133	-7	—	-0.6
	Bal AA	11	13	.458	26	25	24	0	209.1	235	141	6	14	48	70	3.48	98	.280	.329	85-1	.188	-1	70	-5	—	-0.5
	Year	16	18	.471	36	35	34-1	0	297	342	216	8	21	75	100	3.58	96	.282	.335	122-1	.189	-2	88	-11	—	-1.1
1887	Cin AA	3	5	.375	8	8	8	0	69.1	85	66	3	8	43	18	5.45	80	.296	.402	31	.194	-0	126	-8	—	-0.7
Total	6	102	79	.564	187	186	177-18	0	1603.2	1572	958	21	47	294	562	2.95	112	.243	.281	732-2	.210	-5	101	58	—	5.1

McGinnis, Gus Gus; B8.1870 Barnesville OH; D4.20.1904 Barnesville OH; TL/5´11˝/168; d4.27

YEAR	TM LG	W	L	PCT	G	GS	CG-SHO	SV-BS	IP	H	R	HR	HB	BB-IB	SO	ERA	AERA	OAV	OOB	AB-HR-SH	AVG	PB	SUP	APR	DL	PW
1893	Chi N	2	5	.286	13	5	3	0	67.1	85	67	2	3	31	13	5.35	87	.299	.374	25	.240	2	106	-8	—	-0.5
	Phi N	1	3	.250	5	4	4-1	0	37.1	39	20	0	2	17	12	4.34	106	.262	.345	15	.200	-1	72	3	—	0.2
	Year	3	8	.273	18	9	7-1	0	104.2	124	87	2	5	48	25	4.99	93	.286	.364	40	.225	1	91	-3	—	-0.3

McGinnity, Joe Joseph Jerome "Iron Man" (b Joseph Jerome McGinty); B3.20.1871 Rock Island IL; D11.14.1929 Brooklyn NY; BR/TR/5´11˝/206; d4.18; C1; HF1946

YEAR	TM LG	W	L	PCT	G	GS	CG-SHO	SV-BS	IP	H	R	HR	HB	BB-IB	SO	ERA	AERA	OAV	OOB	AB-HR-SH	AVG	PB	SUP	APR	DL	PW
1899	Bal N	**28**	16	.636	48	41	38-4	2	366.1	358	164	3	26	93	74	2.68	148	.256	.314	145-0-5	.193	-5*	102	48	—	4.5
1900	†Bro N	**28**	8	**.778**	44	37	32-1	0	**343**	350	179	5	40	113	93	2.94	131	.264	.340	145-0-5	.193	-5*	105	23	—	1.4
1901	Bal A	26	20	.565	**48**	**43**	**39**-1	1	**382**	412	219	7	21	96	75	3.56	109	.272	.324	148-0-8	.209	-4	91	17	—	1.3
1902	Bal A	13	10	.565	25	23	19	0	198.2	219	100	3	8	46	39	3.44	110	.280	.327	87-0-4	.287	4*	104	10	—	1.4
	NY N	8	8	.500	19	16	16-1	0	153	122	52	1	9	32	67	2.06	136	.219	.273	66-0-8	.121	-4*	92	13	—	0.9
1903	NY N	**31**	20	.608	**55**	**48**	**44**-3	2	**434**	391	162	4	19	109	171	2.43	138	.236	.291	165-0-13	.206	-2	96	**42**	—	4.0
1904	NY N	**35**	8	**.814**	**51**	44	38-**9**	**5**	**408**	307	103	8	13	86	144	**1.61**	**169**	.206	.256	142-0-12	.176	-1	113	**50**	—	**5.4**
1905	†NY N	21	15	.583	**46**	38	26-2	3	320.1	289	131	6	14	71	125	2.87	102	.240	.290	120-0-1	.233	6	115	6	—	1.3
1906	NY N	**27**	12	.692	**45**	37	32-3	2	339.2	316	127	1	7	71	105	2.25	116	.246	.289	115-0-12	.130	-3	114	10	—	0.7
1907	NY N	18	18	.500	**47**	34	23-3	**4**	310.1	320	126	6	15	58	120	3.16	78	.266	.308	103-0-8	.175	0	121	-15	—	-1.8
1908	NY N	11	7	.611	37	20	7-5	**5**	186	192	73	8	7	37	55	2.27	106	.267	.310	61-0-5	.180	-0	120	-1	—	-0.2
Total	10	246	142	.634	465	381	314-32	24	3441.1	3276	1436	52	179	812	1068	2.66	120	.249	.302	1297-0-81	.194	-14	105	203	—	18.9

McGlinchy, Kevin Kevin Michael; B6.28.1977 Malden MA; BR/TR/6´5˝/220; [AtlN95 5/141]; d4.5; Col Central Florida CC; [DL 2001 Atl N 190, 2002 TB A 183]

YEAR	TM LG	W	L	PCT	G	GS	CG-SHO	SV-BS	IP	H	R	HR	HB	BB-IB	SO	ERA	AERA	OAV	OOB	AB-HR-SH	AVG	PB	SUP	APR	DL	PW
1999	†Atl N	7	3	.700	64	0	0	0-2	70.1	66	25	6	1	30-7	67	2.82	159	.255	.330	2	.000	-0	—	13	0	1.5
2000	Atl N	0	0	ø	10	0	0	0-0	8.1	11	4	1	0	6-1	9	2.16	209	.314	.415	0	ø	0	—	1	132	0.1
Total	2	7	3	.700	74	0	0	0-2	78.2	77	29	7	1	36-8	76	2.75	163	.262	.340	2	.000	-0	—	14	505	1.6

YEAR	TM LG	W	L	PCT	G	GS	CG-SHO	SV-BS	IP	H	R	HR	HB	BB-IB	SO	ERA	AERA	OAV	OOB	AB-HR-SH	AVG	PB	SUP	APR	DL	PW
McGlothen, Lynn	Lynn Everatt; B3.27.1950 Monroe LA; D8.14.1984 Dubach LA; BL/TR/6´2˝/(182–215); [BosA68 3/60]; d6.25																									
1972	Bos A	8	7	.533	22	22	4-1	0-0	145	135	66	9	7	59-1	112	3.41	95	.247	.326	53-0-3	.189	1	106	-4	0	-0.1
1973	Bos A	1	2	.333	6	3	0	0-1	23	39	23	6	1	8-0	16	8.22	49	.386	.429	0	ø	0	133	-10	0	-1.1
1974	StL N★	16	12	.571	31	31	8-3	0-0	237.1	212	80	12	2	89-14	142	2.69	134	.241	.312	83-0-3	.181	-1	92	24	0	2.8
1975	StL N	15	13	.536	35	34	9-2	0-0	239	231	110	21	4	97-11	146	3.92	97	.254	.326	80-0-10	.087	-5	96	3	0	-0.4
1976	StL N	13	15	.464	33	32	10-4	0-0	205	209	96	10	4	68-6	106	3.91	92	.268	.328	71-0-7	.211	2	92	-4	0	-0.5
1977	SF N	2	9	.182	21	15	2	0-0	80	94	62	9	1	52-4	42	5.62	70	.299	.397	19-0-1	.105	-1	83	-16	21	-2.1
1978	SF N	0	0	ø	5	1	0	0-0	12.2	15	9	0	0	4-0	9	4.97	70	.313	.358	3	.000	-0	181	-3	0	-0.2
	Chi N	5	3	.625	49	1	0	0-5	80	77	33	7	0	39-5	60	3.04	133	.257	.341	13	.231	1	67	7	0	0.6
	Year	5	3	.625	54	2	0	0-5	92.2	92	42	7	0	43-5	69	3.30	120	.264	.344	16	.188	0	113	4	0	0.4
1979	Chi N	13	14	.481	42	29	6-1	2-0	212	236	103	27	3	55-8	147	4.12	101	.283	.327	71-0-4	.225	1	93	3	0	0.4
1980	Chi N	12	14	.462	39	27	2-2	0-0	182.1	211	105	24	1	64-7	119	4.79	83	.293	.348	51-0-8	.196	2*	90	-13	0	-1.6
1981	Chi N	1	4	.200	20	6	0	0-0	54.2	71	32	1	1	28-4	26	4.77	78	.317	.394	12	.083	-1	71	-5	0	-0.5
	Chi A	0	0	ø	11	0	0	0-0	21.2	14	10	0	1	7-3	12	4.15	87	.189	.268	0	ø	0	—	-1	0	-0.1
1982	NY A	0	0	ø	4	0	0	0-0	5	9	6	1	0	2-0	2	10.80	37	.375	.423	0	ø	0	—	-4	21	-0.2
Total	11	86	93	.480	318	201	41-13	2-6	1497.2	1553	735	127	25	572-63	939	3.98	95	.270	.336	456-0-36	.173	-1	93	-23	42	-3.0
McGlothin, Pat	Ezra Mac; B10.20.1920 Coalfield TN; BL/TR/6´3.5˝/180; d4.25; Col Tennessee																									
1949	Bro N	1	1	.500	7	0	0	0	15.2	13	8	2	0	5	11	4.60	89	.224	.286	3	.000	-0	—	-1	0	-0.1
1950	Bro N	0	0	ø	1	0	0	0	2	5	3	0	0	1	2	13.50	30	.455	.500	0	ø	0	—	-2	0	-0.1
Total	2	1	1	.500	8	0	0	0	17.2	18	11	2	0	6	13	5.60	73	.261	.320	3	.000	-0	—	-3	0	-0.2
McGlothlin, Jim	James Milton "Red"; B10.6.1943 Los Angeles CA; D12.23.1975 Union KY; BR/TR/6´1˝/185; d9.20																									
1965	Cal A	0	3	.000	3	3	1	0	18	18	9	1	0	7-1	9	3.50	97	.261	.329	6	.000	-1	34	-1	0	-0.2
1966	Cal A	3	1	.750	19	11	0	0	67.2	79	37	9	1	19-0	41	4.52	74	.292	.338	17-0-1	.059	-0	134	-9	0	-0.5
1967	Cal A★	12	8	.600	32	29	9-**6**	0	197.1	163	74	13	4	56-2	137	2.96	106	.226	.284	57-0-7	.140	-0	105	5	0	0.5
1968	Cal A	10	15	.400	40	32	8	3	208.1	187	87	19	8	60-5	135	3.54	82	.244	.304	63-0-6	.111	-1	99	-13	0	-1.6
1969	Cal A	8	16	.333	37	35	4-1	0-0	201	188	86	19	5	58-1	96	3.18	110	.249	.306	58-0-5	.121	-1	72	5	0	0.6
1970	†Cin N	14	10	.583	35	34	5-3	0-0	210.2	192	91	19	3	86-8	97	3.59	113	.245	.319	66-1-4	.121	1	95	13	0	1.7
1971	Cin N	8	12	.400	30	26	6	0-0	170.2	151	65	15	4	47-4	93	3.22	105	.243	.300	51-1-3	.137	0	87	4	0	0.5
1972	†Cin N	9	8	.529	31	21	3-1	0-1	145	165	71	15	0	49-6	69	3.91	83	.287	.341	46-1-1	.174	3	142	-12	0	-1.1
1973	Cin N	3	3	.500	24	9	0	0-0	63.1	91	52	13	0	23-3	18	6.68	52	.340	.390	16-0-1	.125	0	142	-24	0	-2.0
	Chi A	0	1	.000	5	1	0	0-0	18.1	13	8	2	0	13-0	14	3.93	101	.203	.333	0	ø	0	23	0	0	0.0
Total	9	67	77	.465	256	201	36-11	3-1	1300.1	1247	580	125	25	418-30	709	3.61	94	.255	.315	380-3-28	.126	2	99	-32	0	-2.1
McGlynn, Stoney	Ulysses Simpson Grant; B5.26.1872 Lancaster PA; D8.26.1941 Manitowoc WI; BR/TR/5´11˝/185; d9.20																									
1906	StL N	2	2	.500	6	6	6	0	48	43	16	0	1	15	25	2.44	108	.249	.312	17	.059	-1	97	1	—	0.1
1907	StL N	14	25	.359	45	**39**	**33**-3	1	**352.1**	329	159	6	4	112	109	2.91	86	.251	.312	125-0-6	.200	3*	85	-12	—	-1.1
1908	StL N	1	6	.143	16	6	4	1	75.2	76	40	0	2	17	23	3.45	68	.256	.301	26-0-1	.077	-1	75	-8	—	-0.8
Total	3	17	33	.340	67	51	43-3	2	476	448	215	6	7	144	157	2.95	85	.252	.310	168-0-7	.167	0	86	-19	—	-1.8
McGowan, Dustin	Dustin Michael; B3.24.1982 Savannah GA; BR/TR/6´3˝/(215–220); [TorA00 1/33]; d7.30																									
2005	Tor A	1	3	.250	13	7	0	0-0	45.1	49	34	7	7	17-0	34	6.35	72	.277	.356	0	ø	0	89	-8	0	-0.6
2006	Tor A	1	2	.333	16	3	0	0-1	27.1	35	27	2	2	25-2	22	7.24	65	.304	.434	0	ø	0	93	-9	0	-0.8
Total	2	2	5	.286	29	10	0	0-1	72.2	84	61	9	9	42-2	56	6.69	69	.288	.388	0	ø	0	90	-17	0	-1.4
McGowan, Mickey	Tullis Earl; B11.26.1921 Dothan AL; D3.8.2003 Waycross GA; BL/TL/6´2˝/200; d4.22																									
1948	NY N	0	0	ø	3	0	0	0	3.2	3	3	1	0	4	2	7.36	53	.231	.412	1	.000	-0	—	-1	0	-0.1
McGraner, Howard	Howard "Muck"; B9.11.1889 Luhrig OH; D10.22.1952 Zaleski OH; BL/TL/5´7˝/155; d9.12																									
1912	Cin N	1	0	1.000	4	0	0	0	19	22	17	2	1	7	5	7.11	47	.293	.361	8	.250	1	—	-7	—	-0.2
McGraw, Tug	Frank Edwin; B8.30.1944 Martinez CA; D1.5.2004 Brentwood TN; BR/TL/6´0˝/(170–186); d4.18; Col Solano (CA) CC																									
1965	NY N	2	7	.222	37	9	2	1	97.2	88	47	8	3	48-2	57	3.32	106	.249	.341	23	.130	-1*	66	0	0	-0.1
1966	NY N	2	9	.182	15	12	1	0	62.1	72	38	11	0	25-2	34	5.34	68	.294	.355	17-0-2	.235	1	75	-10	24	-1.5
1967	NY N	0	3	.000	4	4	0	0	17.1	13	16	3	0	13-2	18	7.79	44	.206	.338	4-0-1	.250	0	84	-8	0	-1.1
1969	†NY N	9	3	.750	42	4	1	12-0	100.1	89	31	6	0	47-7	92	2.24	163	.243	.329	24	.167	0*	163	**14**	0	2.1
1970	NY N	4	6	.400	57	0	0	10-2	90.2	77	40	6	1	49-17	81	3.28	124	.231	.328	13	.308	1	—	7	0	1.0
1971	NY N	11	4	.733	51	1	0	8-2	111	73	22	4	3	41-11	109	1.70	202	.189	.271	18-1-2	.222	2	52	**22**	0	3.6
1972	NY N★	8	6	.571	54	0	0	27-5	106	71	26	3	3	40-11	92	1.70	199	.197	.279	20-0-2	.100	-0	—	19	0	3.7
1973	†NY N	5	6	.455	60	2	0	25-7	118.2	106	53	11	3	55-9	81	3.87	94	.243	.329	24-0-3	.167	1	121	-1	0	-0.1
1974	NY N	6	11	.353	41	4	1-1	3-6	88.2	96	43	12	0	32-6	54	4.16	87	.279	.338	14-0-1	.071	-0	85	-4	25	-0.7
1975	Phi N☆	9	6	.600	56	0	0	14-3	102.2	84	38	6	3	36-6	55	2.98	126	.226	.299	13-0-1	.154	-0	—	9	18	1.5
1976	†Phi N	7	6	.538	58	0	0	11-6	97.1	81	34	4	0	42-10	76	2.50	143	.226	.304	7	.143	0	—	10	0	1.5
1977	†Phi N	7	3	.700	45	0	0	9-3	79	62	25	6	1	24-5	58	2.62	154	.221	.282	10	.400	2	—	12	59	1.9
1978	†Phi N	8	7	.533	55	1	0	9-2	89.2	82	39	6	0	23-7	63	3.21	112	.245	.292	4-0-2	.000	-0	0	2	0	0.4
1979	Phi N	4	3	.571	65	1	0	16-2	83.2	83	56	9	2	29-7	57	5.16	75	.259	.321	6-0-1	.167	-0	137	-13	0	-1.6
1980	†Phi N	5	4	.556	57	0	0	20-5	92.1	62	16	3	2	23-9	75	1.46	261	.194	.250	8-0-3	.250	0	—	**23**	21	3.3
1981	†Phi N	2	4	.333	34	0	0	10-1	44	35	13	2	0	14-3	26	2.66	138	.219	.278	1-0-1	.000	-0	—	5	0	0.9
1982	Phi N	3	3	.500	34	0	0	5-6	39.2	50	19	3	1	12-6	25	4.31	86	.305	.356	2	.000	-0	—	-2	77	-0.3
1983	Phi N	2	1	.667	34	1	0	0-0	55.2	58	24	4	0	19-4	30	3.56	101	.271	.326	3-0-2	.333	0	123	1	0	0.1
1984	Phi N	2	0	1.000	25	0	0	0-0	38	36	17	1	0	10-4	26	3.79	97	.245	.289	3	.333	0	—	0	55	0.0
Total	19	96	92	.511	824	39	5-1	180-50	1514.2	1318	597	108	22	582-128	1109	3.14	117	.237	.309	214-1-21	.182	5	85	86	279	14.6
McGraw, John	John (b Roy Elmer Hoar); B12.8.1890 Intercourse PA; D4.27.1967 Torrance CA; BR/TR/5´9˝/160; d7.29; Col Carnegie Mellon																									
1914	Bro F	0	0	ø	1	0	0	0	2	0	0	0	1	0	2	0.00	ø	.000	.143	0	ø	0	—	1	—	0.0
McGraw, Bob	Robert Emmett; B4.10.1895 LaVeta CO; D6.2.1978 Boise ID; BR/TR/6´2˝/160; d9.25; Mil 1918–19; Col Georgetown																									
1917	NY A	0	1	.000	2	2	1	0	11	9	5	0	0	3	3	0.82	328	.257	.316	3	.000	-0	67	1	—	0.0
1918	NY A	0	1	.000	1	1	0	0	0	0	4	0	0	4	0	(4)	ø	ø	1.000	0	ø	0	107	-4	—	-0.3
1919	NY A	1	0	1.000	6	0	0	0	16.1	11	6	1	1	10	3	3.31	97	.216	.355	3	.000	-0	—	0	—	0.0
	Bos A	0	2	.000	10	1	0	0	26.2	33	23	0	3	17	6	6.75	45	.347	.461	10-0-1	.100	-1	182	-11	—	-0.9
	Year	1	2	.333	16	1	0	0	43	44	29	1	4	27	9	5.44	57	.301	.424	13-0-1	.077	-1	178	-10	—	-0.9
1920	NY A	0	0	ø	15	0	0	0	27	24	18	1	1	20	11	4.67	82	.240	.372	7	.000	-1	—	-3	—	-0.3
1925	Bro N	0	2	.000	2	2	2	0	19.2	14	9	0	0	13	3	3.20	130	.222	.355	6-0-1	.167	-0	61	2	—	0.1
1926	Bro N	9	13	.409	33	21	10	1	174.1	197	104	12	2	67	49	4.59	83	.292	.358	55-0-6	.145	-2	95	-13	—	-1.7
1927	Bro N	0	1	.000	1	1	0	0	4	5	5	1	0	2	2	9.00	44	.313	.389	1	.000	-0	64	-2	—	-0.4
	StL N	4	5	.444	18	12	4-1	0	94	121	65	3	0	30	37	5.07	78	.323	.373	33-1-4	.182	1	120	-12	—	-0.9
	Year	4	6	.400	19	13	4-1	0	98	126	70	4	0	32	39	5.23	75	.322	.374	34-1-4	.176	1	116	-14	—	-1.3
1928	Phi N	7	8	.467	39	3	0	1	120	148	86	7	2	56	28	5.18	83	.317	.392	36-0-3	.111	-2	106	-14	—	-1.8
1929	Phi N	5	5	.500	41	4	0	4	86.1	113	68	6	2	43	22	5.73	91	.324	.401	20-0-1	.200	0	126	-7	—	-0.7
Total	9	26	38	.406	168	47	17-1	6	579.1	675	393	31	11	265	164	5.00	81	.303	.380	174-1-16	.138	-6	101	-63	—	-6.9
McGraw, Tom	Thomas Virgil; B12.8.1967 Portland OR; BL/TL/6´2˝/195; [MilA90 6/169]; d5.7; Col Washington St.																									
1997	StL N	0	0	ø	2	0	0	0-0	1.2	2	0	0	0	1-0	0	0.00	ø	.333	.375	0	ø	0	—	1	0	0.0
McGregor, Scott	Scott Houston; B1.18.1954 Inglewood CA; BB/TL/6´1˝/(186–192); [NYA72 1/14]; d9.19																									
1976	Bal A	0	1	.000	3	2	0	0-0	14.2	17	7	0	0	5-0	6	3.68	90	.293	.349	0	ø	0	67	-1	0	0.0
1977	Bal A	3	5	.375	29	5	1	4-0	114	119	57	8	7	30-2	55	4.42	87	.275	.328	0	ø	0	103	-6	0	-0.5
1978	Bal A	15	13	.536	35	32	13-4	1-1	233	217	98	19	1	47-3	94	3.32	106	.248	.286	0	ø	0	91	5	0	0.6
1979	†Bal A	13	6	.684	27	23	7-2	0-0	174.2	165	70	19	2	23-0	81	3.35	121	.248	**.273**	0	ø	0	109	15	0	1.5
1980	Bal A	20	8	.714	36	36	12-4	0-0	252	254	101	16	2	58-3	119	3.32	120	.265	.306	0	ø	0*	121	18	0	1.8
1981	Bal A☆	13	5	.722	24	22	8-3	0-0	160	167	63	13	0	40-5	82	3.26	112	.273	.315	0	ø	0	108	8	0	0.9
1982	Bal A	14	12	.538	37	37	7-1	0-0	226.1	238	126	31	1	52-6	84	4.61	88	.267	.306	0	ø	0	106	-15	0	-1.6
1983	†Bal A	18	7	.720	36	36	12-2	0-0	260	271	101	24	1	45-2	86	3.18	126	.269	.298	0	ø	0	123	25	0	2.2

YEAR	TM LG	W	L	PCT	G	GS	CG-SHO	SV-BS	IP	H	R	HR	HB	BB-IB	SO	ERA	AERA	OAV	OOB	AB-HR-SH	AVG	PB	SUP	APR	DL	PW
1984	Bal A	15	12	.556	30	30	10-3	0-0	196.1	216	93	18	5	54-2	67	3.94	99	.280	.329	0	ø	0	98	1	33	0.2
1985	Bal A	14	14	.500	35	34	8-1	0-0	204	226	118	34	1	65-2	86	4.81	85	.283	.334	0	ø	0	110	-16	0	-1.9
1986	Bal A	11	15	.423	34	33	4-2	0-0	203	216	110	35	3	57-0	95	4.52	92	.270	.319	0	ø	0	102	-7	0	-0.8
1987	Bal A	2	7	.222	26	15	1-1	0-0	85.1	112	69	15	3	35-1	39	6.64	67	.326	.388	0	ø	0	90	-21	31	-1.7
1988	Bal A	0	3	.000	4	4	0	0-0	17.1	27	18	3	0	7-0	10	8.83	45	.370	.415	0	ø	0	70	-9	0	-1.2
Total	13	138	108	.561	356	309	83-23	5-1	2140.2	2245	1031	235	26	518-26	904	3.99	99	.271	.313	0	ø	0	107	-3	64	-0.5
McGrew, Slim	Walter Howard; B8.5.1899 Yoakum TX; D8.21.1967 Houston TX; BR/TR/6´7.5˝/235; d4.18																									
1922	Was A	0	0	ø	1	0	0	0	1.2	4	6	0	0	2	1	10.80	36	.500	.600	1	.000	-0	—	-3	—	-0.1
1923	Was A	0	0	ø	3	0	0	0	5	11	9	0	0	3	1	12.60	30	.440	.500	1	.000	-0	—	-5	—	-0.3
1924	Was A	0	1	.000	6	2	0	0	23.1	25	15	1	0	12	8	5.01	80	.281	.366	8	.000	-1	84	-2	—	-0.3
Total	3	0	1	.000	10	2	0	0	30	40	30	1	0	17	10	6.60	60	.328	.410	10	.000	-2	84	-10	—	-0.7
McGuire	; d6.16																									
1894	Cin N	0	0	ø	1	0	0	0	6	15	9	0	0	5	1	10.50	53	.469	.541	4	.250	-0	—	-3	—	-0.1
McGuire, Tom	Thomas Patrick "Elmer"; B2.1.1892 Chicago IL; D12.7.1959 Phoenix AZ; BR/TR/6´0˝/175; d4.18; Mil 1918																									
1914	Chi F	5	6	.455	24	12	7	0	131.1	143	76	7	4	57	37	3.70	72	.288	.366	70-1-0	.271	4*	131	-18	—	-0.8
1919	Chi A	0	0	ø	1	0	0	0	3	5	4	0	0	3	0	9.00	35	.500	.615	1	.000	-0	—	-2	—	-0.1
Total	2	5	6	.455	25	12	7	0	134.1	148	80	7	4	60	37	3.82	70	.292	.371	71-1-0	.268	4	131	-20	—	-0.9
McGunnigle, Bill	William Henry "Gunner"; B1.1.1855 Boston MA; D3.9.1899 Brockton MA; BR/TR/5´9˝/155; d5.2; M5; ▲																									
1879	Buf N	9	5	.643	14	13	13-2	0	120	113	66	0	—	16	62	2.63	99	**.235**	.260	171	.175	-2*	99	1	—	-0.1
1880	Buf N	2	3	.400	5	5	4-1	0	37	43	19	0	—	8	3	3.41	72	.279	.315	22	.182	-1*	48	-2	—	-0.3
Total	2	11	8	.579	19	18	17-3	0	157	156	85	0	—	24	65	2.81	92	.246	.274	193	.176	-3	86	-1	—	-0.4
McHale, Marty	Martin Joseph; B10.30.1886 Stoneham MA; D5.7.1979 Hempstead NY; BR/TR/5´11.5˝/174; d9.28; Col Maine																									
1910	Bos A	0	2	.000	2	2	1	0	13.2	15	8	0	1	6	14	4.61	55	.259	.338	6	.000	-1	105	-2	—	-0.4
1911	Bos A	0	0	ø	4	1	0	0	9.1	19	12	1	1	3	3	9.64	34	.475	.523	3	.000	-0	198	-6	—	-0.3
1913	NY A	2	4	.333	7	6	4-1	0	48.2	49	21	1	1	10	11	2.96	101	.268	.309	15	.000	-1	54	0	—	-0.1
1914	NY A	6	16	.273	31	23	12	1	191	195	82	3	4	33	75	2.97	93	.268	.303	60-0-2	.200	2*	73	-6	—	-0.6
1915	NY A	3	7	.300	13	11	6	0	78.1	86	45	1	0	19	25	4.25	69	.277	.318	21-0-2	.143	1	102	-11	—	-1.2
1916	Bos A	0	1	.000	2	1	0	0	6	7	7	0	1	4	1	3.00	92	.280	.400	0	ø	0	0	-2	—	-0.3
	Cle A	0	0	ø	5	0	0	0	11.1	10	7	1	0	6	2	5.56	54	.270	.372	2	.000	-0	—	-2	—	-0.2
	Year	0	1	.000	7	1	0	0	17.1	17	14	1	1	10	3	4.67	63	.274	.384	2	.000	0	0	-4	—	-0.5
Total	6	11	30	.268	64	44	23-1	1	358.1	381	182	7	8	81	131	3.57	80	.276	.320	107-0-4	.140	-0	81	-29	—	-3.1
McIlree, Vance	Vance Elmer; B10.14.1897 Riverside IA; D5.6.1959 Kansas City MO; BR/TR/6´0˝/160; d9.13; Col Iowa																									
1921	Was A	0	0	ø	1	0	0	0	1	1	1	0	0	0	0	9.00	46	.200	.200	0	ø	0	—	0	—	0.0
McIlwain, Stover	Stover William "Smokey" (b William Stover McIlwain); B9.22.1939 Savannah GA; D1.15.1966 Buffalo NY; BR/TR/6´4˝/(195–200); d9.25; Col Rollins																									
1957	Chi A	0	0	ø	1	0	0	0	1	2	0	0	0	1-0	0	0.00	ø	.500	.600	0	ø	0	—	0	0	0.0
1958	Chi A	0	0	ø	1	1	0	0	4	4	1	1	0	0-0	4	2.25	162	.250	.250	1	.000	-0	272	1	0	0.0
Total	2	0	0	ø	2	1	0	0	5	6	1	1	0	1-0	4	1.80	203	.300	.333	1	.000	-0	272	1	0	0.0
McIntire, Harry	John Reid; B1.11.1879 Dayton OH; D1.9.1949 Daytona Beach FL; BR/TR/5´11˝/180; d4.14																									
1905	Bro N	8	25	.242	40	35	29-1	1	308.2	340	188	6	20	101	135	3.70	78	.285	.351	138-1-3	.246	7*	69	-31	—	-2.4
1906	Bro N	13	21	.382	39	31	25-4	3	276	254	123	2	14	89	121	2.97	85	.247	.316	103-0-1	.175	1*	74	-15	—	-1.8
1907	Bro N	7	15	.318	28	22	19-3	0	199.2	178	82	6	7	79	49	2.39	98	.248	.329	69-0-2	.217	5*	58	-3	—	0.2
1908	Bro N	11	20	.355	40	35	26-4	2	288	259	106	5	20	90	108	2.69	87	.252	.324	100-0-1	.200	2	89	-7	—	-0.7
1909	Bro N	7	17	.292	32	26	20-2	1	228	200	114	5	21	91	84	3.63	71	.246	.337	76-0-3	.171	1	84	-24	—	-2.3
1910	†Chi N	13	9	.591	28	19	10-2	0	176	152	70	5	10	50	65	3.07	94	.240	.305	66-1-3	.258	3*	106	-1	—	0.3
1911	Chi N	11	7	.611	25	17	9-1	0	149	147	81	5	4	33	56	4.11	81	.257	.302	53-0-3	.264	4*	128	-10	—	-0.6
1912	Chi N	1	2	.333	4	3	2	0	23.2	22	11	0	0	6	8	3.80	87	.256	.304	10-0-1	.300	1*	51	-1	—	0.1
1913	Cin N	0	1	.000	1	0	0	0	1	3	3	0	0	0	0	27.00	12	.600	.600	0	ø	0	—	-2	—	-0.4
Total	9	71	117	.378	237	188	140-17	7	1650	1555	778	34	96	539	626	3.22	83	.256	.326	615-2-17	.218	24	84	-94	—	-7.6
McIntosh, Joe	Joseph Anthony; B8.4.1951 Billings MT; BB/TR/6´2˝/185; [SDN73 13/292]; d4.5; Col Washington St.; [DL 1976 Hou N 179]																									
1974	SD N	0	4	.000	10	5	0	0-0	37.1	36	19	3	1	17-2	22	3.62	99	.250	.329	10-0-1	.000	-1	49	-1	0	-0.3
1975	SD N	8	15	.348	37	28	4-1	0-1	183	195	88	14	2	60-9	71	3.69	95	.273	.330	48-0-5	.188	2*	87	-3	0	-0.2
Total	2	8	19	.296	47	33	4-1	0-1	220.1	231	107	17	3	77-11	93	3.68	96	.270	.330	58-0-6	.155	1	81	-4	179	-0.5
McIntyre, Frank	Frank W.; B7.12.1859 Walled Lake MI; D7.8.1887 Detroit MI; d5.16																									
1883	Det N	1	0	1.000	1	1	1	0	11	11	10	0	—	1	0	0.82	379	.234	.250	4	.000	-0	190	1	—	0.0
	Col AA	1	1	.500	2	2	2	0	19	20	19	0	—	7	6	5.21	59	.253	.314	7	.000	-0	178	-5	—	-0.4
Total	1	2	1	.667	3	3	3	0	30	31	29	0	—	8	6	3.60	86	.246	.291	11	.000	-1	181	-4	—	-0.4
McJames, Doc	James McCutchen (b James Mc Cutchen James); B8.27.1874 Williamsburg Co. SC; D9.23.1901 Charleston SC; TR; d9.24; Col South Carolina																									
1895	Was N	1	1	.500	2	2	2	0	17	17	11	0	0	16	9	1.59	302	.258	.402	7	.143	-1	96	4	—	0.3
1896	Was N	12	20	.375	37	33	29	1	280.1	310	208	2	6	135	103	4.27	103	.278	.359	111-0-3	.162	-9	93	5	—	-0.3
1897	Was N	15	23	.395	44	39	33-**3**	2	323.2	361	212	7	21	137	**156**	3.61	120	.280	.358	124	.169	-7	72	22	—	1.4
1898	Bal N	27	15	.643	45	42	40-2	0	374	327	148	5	12	113	178	2.36	152	.234	.296	149-0-1	.181	-4	114	49	—	4.3
1899	Bro N	19	15	.559	37	34	27-1	1	275.1	295	166	4	10	122	105	3.50	112	.274	.353	112	.170	-5	96	8	—	0.5
1901	Bro N	5	6	.455	13	12	6	0	91	104	71	1	7	40	42	4.75	71	.285	.367	34	.029	-4	125	-15	—	-1.9
Total	6	79	80	.497	178	162	137-6	4	1361.1	1414	816	19	56	563	593	3.43	116	.266	.343	537-0-4	.162	-30	95	73	—	4.3
McKain, Archie	Archie Richard "Happy"; B5.12.1911 Delphos KS; D5.21.1985 Salina KS; BB/TL (BL 1941, 43)/5´10˝/175; d4.25																									
1937	Bos A	8	8	.500	36	18	3	2	137	152	84	7	0	64	66	4.66	102	.273	.348	49-0-1	.265	3*	97	0	—	0.2
1938	Bos A	5	4	.556	37	5	1	6	99.2	119	60	6	2	44	27	4.52	109	.297	.369	31-0-2	.065	-2	96	3	—	0.2
1939	Det A	5	6	.455	32	11	4-1	4	129.2	120	66	6	0	54	49	3.68	133	.247	.322	41-2-0	.220	4	90	15	—	1.5
1940	†Det A	5	0	1.000	27	0	0	3	51	48	18	2	0	25	24	2.82	168	.247	.333	7-0-1	.143	0	—	10	—	1.1
1941	Det A	2	1	.667	15	0	0	0	43	58	24	3	0	11	14	5.02	90	.330	.369	11	.000	-1	—	-1	0	0.0
	StL A	0	1	.000	8	0	0	1	10	16	9	2	1	4	2	8.10	53	.364	.429	2	.000	-0	—	-4	0	-0.4
	Year	2	2	.500	23	0	0	1	53	74	33	5	1	15	16	5.60	80	.336	.381	13	.000	-1	—	-4	0	-0.4
1943	StL A	1	1	.500	10	0	0	0	16	16	9	0	0	6	6	3.94	84	.242	.306	1	.000	-0	—	-1	0	-0.2
Total	6	26	21	.553	165	34	8-1	16	486.1	529	270	26	3	208	188	4.26	112	.275	.347	142-2-4	.176	3	96	22	0	2.4
McKain, Hal	Harold Le Roy; B7.10.1906 Logan IA; D1.24.1970 Sacramento CA; BL/TR/5´11˝/185; d9.22																									
1927	Cle A	0	1	.000	2	1	0	0	11	18	6	0	0	4	5	4.09	103	.391	.440	4	.000	-1	40	0	—	0.0
1929	Chi A	6	9	.400	34	10	4-1	1	158	158	84	10	10	85	33	3.65	117	.275	.378	44-0-1	.227	2	71	8	—	1.1
1930	Chi A	6	4	.600	32	5	0	5	89	108	67	0	3	42	52	5.56	83	.299	.377	31-0-2	.419	7*	138	-9	—	-0.2
1931	Chi A	6	9	.400	27	8	3	0	112	134	82	10	3	57	39	5.71	75	.295	.377	42-0-1	.119	-1*	74	-17	—	-1.8
1932	Chi A	0	0	ø	8	0	0	0	11.1	17	15	1	0	5	7	11.12	39	.340	.400	1	.000	-0	—	-8	—	-0.4
Total	5	18	23	.439	103	24	7-1	6	381.1	435	254	21	16	193	136	4.93	88	.293	.380	122-0-4	.230	8	85	-26	—	-1.3
McKay, Reeve	Reeve Stewart "Rip"; B11.16.1881 Morgan TX; D1.18.1946 Dallas TX; TR/6´1.5˝/168; d10.2																									
1915	StL A	0	0	ø	1	0	0	0	1	1	1	0	0	0	0	9.00	32	.500	.500	0	ø	0	—	-1	—	0.0
McKee, Jim	James Marion; B2.1.1947 Columbus OH; D9.14.2002 Pickaway Co. OH; BR/TR/6´7˝/215; [PitN69 4/80]; d9.15; Col Otterbein																									
1972	Pit N	1	0	1.000	2	0	0	0-0	5	2	0	0	0	1-0	4	0.00	ø	.125	.176	0	ø	0	—	2	0	0.4
1973	Pit N	0	1	.000	15	1	0	0-0	27	31	21	2	1	17-0	13	5.67	62	.287	.389	4	.000	-0	326	-7	0	-0.4
Total	2	1	1	.500	17	1	0	0-0	32	33	21	2	1	18-0	17	4.78	73	.266	.364	4	.000	-0	326	-5	0	0.0
McKee, Rogers	Rogers Hornsby; B9.16.1926 Shelby NC; BL/TL/6´1˝/160; d8.18; Mil 1945–46																									
1943	Phi N	1	0	1.000	4	1	1	0	13.1	12	9	0	0	5	1	6.08	56	.226	.293	5	.200	0	277	-3	0	-0.2
1944	Phi N	0	0	ø	1	0	0	0	2	2	1	1	0	1	0	4.50	80	.250	.333	0	ø	0	—	0	0	0.0
Total	2	1	0	1.000	5	1	1	0	15.1	14	10	1	0	6	1	5.87	58	.230	.299	5	.200	0	277	-3	0	-0.2

YEAR	TM LG	W	L	PCT	G	GS	CG-SHO	SV-BS	IP	H	R	HR	HB	BB-IB	SO	ERA	AERA	OAV	OOB	AB-HR-SH	AVG	PB	SUP	APR	DL	PW
McKeithan, Tim	Emmett James; B11.2.1906 Shelby NC; D8.30.1969 Forest City NC; BR/TR/6´2˝/182; d7.21; Col Duke																									
1932	Phi A	0	1	.000	4	2	0	0	12.2	18	11	0	0	5	0	7.11	64	.340	.397	3	.000	0	85	-4	—	-0.2
1933	Phi A	1	0	1.000	3	1	0	0	9	10	4	0	0	4	3	4.00	107	.278	.350	3	.333	0	218	1	—	0.1
1934	Phi A	0	0	ø	3	0	0	0	4	7	7	2	0	5	0	15.75	28	.389	.522	1	.000	-0	—	-5	—	-0.2
Total	3	1	1	.500	10	3	0	0	25.2	35	22	2	0	14	3	7.36	60	.327	.405	7	.143	0	129	-8	—	-0.3
McKelvy, Russ	Russell Errett; B9.8.1854 Swissvale PA; D10.19.1915 Omaha NE; BR/TR; d5.1; Col Allegheny; ▲																									
1878	Ind N	0	2	.000	4	1	1	0	25	38	23	1	—	3	3	2.16	94	.322	.339	253-2	.225	0*	107	-3	—	-0.1
McKenna, Kit	James William; B2.10.1873 Lynchburg VA; D3.31.1941 Lynchburg VA; TR/5´9˝/180; d7.7																									
1898	Bro N	2	6	.250	14	9	7	0	100.2	118	75	4	17	57	27	5.63	64	.290	.399	40-0-1	.225	0	66	-18	—	-1.1
1899	Bal N	2	3	.400	8	4	4	1	45	66	38	1	3	19	7	4.60	86	.340	.407	17	.059	-1*	118	-5	—	-0.5
Total	2	4	9	.308	22	13	11	1	145.2	184	113	5	20	76	34	5.31	70	.306	.402	57-0-1	.175	-0	83	-23	—	-1.6
McKenry, Limb	Frank Gordon "Big Pete"; B8.13.1888 Piney Flats TN; D11.1.1956 Fresno CA; BR/TR/6´4˝/205; d7.24																									
1915	Cin N	5	5	.500	21	11	5	0	110.1	94	43	2	3	39	37	2.94	97	.238	.311	33-0-3	.152	0	83	0	—	0.1
1916	Cin N	1	1	.500	6	1	0	0	14.2	14	8	0	2	8	2	4.30	60	.259	.375	5	.400	2	115	-2	—	-0.2
Total	2	6	6	.500	27	12	5	0	125	108	51	2	5	47	39	3.10	91	.241	.319	38-0-3	.184	2	85	-2	—	-0.1
McKeon, Joel	Joel Jacob; B2.25.1963 Covington KY; BL/TL/6´0˝/185; [ChiA82 S1/16]; d5.6; Col Miami–Dade North (FL) CC																									
1986	Chi A	3	1	.750	30	0	0	1-2	33	18	10	2	0	17-2	18	2.45	177	.165	.273	0	ø	0	—	7	75	0.7
1987	Chi A	1	2	.333	13	0	0	0-0	21	27	22	8	0	15-0	14	9.43	49	.318	.416	0	ø	0	—	-10	0	-1.2
Total	2	4	3	.571	43	0	0	1-2	54	45	32	10	0	32-2	32	5.17	86	.232	.336	0	ø	0	—	-3	75	-0.5
McKeon, Larry	Lawrence G.; B3.25.1866 NY; D7.18.1915 Indianapolis IN; 5´10˝/168; d5.1																									
1884	Ind AA	18	41	.305	61	60	59-2	0	512	488	350	20	18	94	308	3.50	94	.235	.275	250	.212	-3*	74	-14	—	-1.2
1885	Cin AA	20	13	.606	33	33	32-2	0	290	273	143	5	13	50	117	2.86	114	.241	.281	121	.165	-5	94	14	—	0.8
1886	Cin AA	8	8	.500	19	19	16	0	156	174	118	6	3	54	46	5.08	69	.276	.336	75	.253	1	132	-22	—	-1.6
	KC N	0	2	.000	3	3	3	0	21	44	32	0	—	8	3	10.71	35	.411	.452	9	.000	-1	54	-13	—	-0.9
Total	3	46	64	.418	116	115	110-4	0	979	979	643	31	34	206	474	3.71	90	.248	.291	455	.202	-9	90	-35	—	-2.9
McKnight, Tony	Tony Mark; B6.29.1977 Texarkana AR; BL/TR/6´5˝/205; [HouN95 1/22]; d8.10																									
2000	Hou N	4	1	.800	6	6	1	0-0	35	35	19	4	2	9-0	23	3.86	127	.245	.297	13-0-1	.000	-2	162	3	0	0.2
2001	Hou N	1	0	1.000	3	3	0	0-0	18	21	8	4	2	3-0	10	4.00	115	.288	.329	7	.000	-1	141	1	0	0.0
	Pit N	2	6	.250	12	12	0	0-0	69.1	88	44	15	3	21-4	36	5.19	86	.307	.358	17-0-4	.000	-1	81	-6	0	-0.7
	Year	3	6	.333	15	15	0	0-0	87.1	109	52	19	5	24-4	46	4.95	91	.303	.352	24-0-4	.000	-2	93	-4	0	-0.7
Total	2	7	7	.500	21	21	1	0-0	122.1	144	71	23	7	33-4	69	4.63	100	.286	.336	37-0-5	.000	-4	114	-2	0	-0.5
McLain, Denny	Dennis Dale; B3.29.1944 Chicago IL; BR/TR/6´1˝/(180–185); d9.21																									
1963	Det A	2	1	.667	3	3	2	0	21	20	12	2	0	16-0	22	4.29	87	.253	.375	5-1-1	.200	1	103	-2	0	-0.1
1964	Det A	4	5	.444	19	16	3	0	100	84	48	16	1	37-0	70	4.05	90	.225	.296	37-0-4	.135	-1*	126	-4	0	-0.6
1965	Det A	16	6	.727	33	29	13-4	1	220.1	174	73	25	2	62-1	192	2.61	133	.216	.273	74-0-4	.054	-4	117	20	0	1.6
1966	Det A★	20	14	.588	38	38	14-4	0	264.1	205	120	42	3	104-3	192	3.92	89	.214	.292	93-0-5	.183	2	110	-9	0	-1.0
1967	Det A	17	16	.515	37	37	10-3	0	235	209	110	35	3	73-3	161	3.79	86	.237	.295	85-0-5	.118	-3*	96	-14	0	-2.3
1968	†Det A★	**31**	6	**.838**	41	**41**	**28-6**	0	**336**	241	86	31	6	63-2	280	1.96	154	.200	.243	111-0-16	.162	0*	146	36	0	4.4
1969	Det A★	**24**	9	.727	42	**41**	23-**9**	0-0	**325**	288	105	25	4	67-7	181	2.80	135	.237	.278	106-0-13	.160	-1	99	**37**	0	3.3
1970	Det A	3	5	.375	14	14	1	0-0	91.1	100	51	19	3	28-0	52	4.63	81	.273	.327	31-0-3	.065	-2	111	-8	0	-0.8
1971	Was A	10	22	.313	33	32	9-3	0-0	216.2	233	115	31	3	72-8	103	4.28	79	.281	.337	58-0-9	.103	-1	73	-22	23	-3.0
1972	Oak A	1	2	.333	5	5	0	0-0	22.1	32	17	4	0	8-0	8	6.04	47	.323	.374	4-0-2	.000	-0	118	-9	0	-1.1
	Atl N	3	5	.375	15	8	2	1-0	54	60	41	12	1	18-0	21	6.50	58	.279	.335	12-0-2	.167	0	99	-14	0	-1.9
Total	10	131	91	.590	280	264	105-29	2-0	1886	1646	778	242	26	548-24	1282	3.39	101	.234	.290	616-1-64	.133	-9	109	11	23	-1.5
McLaughlin, Barney	Bernard; B1857 , Ireland; D2.13.1921 Lowell MA; BR/TR; d8.2; b–Frank; ▲																									
1884	KC U	1	3	.250	7	4	4	0	48.2	62	44	2	—	15	14	5.36	42	.291	.338	162	.228	0*	43	-15	—	-0.9
McLaughlin, Byron	Byron Scott; B9.29.1955 Van Nuys CA; BR/TR/6´1˝/(175–192); d9.18																									
1977	Sea A	0	0	ø	1	0	0	0-0	1.1	5	4	1	0	0-0	1	27.00	15	.625	.625	0	ø	0	—	-3	0	-0.1
1978	Sea A	4	8	.333	20	17	4	0-0	107	97	58	15	6	39-0	87	4.37	88	.238	.312	0	ø	0	78	-6	0	-0.7
1979	Sea A	7	7	.500	47	7	1	14-3	123.2	114	58	13	2	60-8	74	4.22	104	.251	.337	0	ø	0	145	5	0	0.5
1980	Sea A	3	6	.333	45	4	0	2-3	90.2	124	74	15	2	50-14	41	6.85	61	.331	.410	0	ø	0	38	-25	0	-2.4
1983	Cal A	2	4	.333	16	7	0	0-2	55.2	63	32	3	2	22-3	45	5.17	78	.286	.351	0	ø	0	119	-6	0	-0.5
Total	5	16	25	.390	129	35	5	16-8	378.1	403	226	47	12	171-25	248	5.11	81	.275	.353	0	ø	0	94	-35	0	-3.2
McLaughlin, Frank	Francis Edward; B6.19.1856 Lowell MA; D4.5.1917 Lowell MA; BR/TR/5´9˝/160; d8.9.1882; b–Barney; ▲																									
1883	Pit AA	0	0	ø	2	0	0	0	9	14	21	0	—	3	1	13.00	25	.333	.378	114-1	.219	0*	—	-10	—	-0.4
1884	KC U	0	0	ø	2	1	0	0	10	15	12	0	—	2	3	5.40	41	.326	.354	123-1	.228	0*	229	-4	—	-0.2
Total	2	0	0	ø	4	1	0	0	19	29	33	0	—	5	4	9.00	30	.330	.366	237-2	.224	0	229	-14	—	-0.6
McLaughlin, Jim	James Thomas; B11.18.1860 Cleveland OH; D11.16.1895 Cleveland OH; BL/TL/?/157; d5.30																									
1884	Bal AA	1	2	.333	3	2	2	0	22	27	22	2	0	11	8	3.68	94	.300	.376	22	.227	0*	104	-2	—	-0.2
McLaughlin, Joey	Joey Richard; B7.11.1956 Tulsa OK; BR/TR/6´2˝/(192–215); [AtlN74 2/29]; d6.11																									
1977	Atl N	0	0	ø	3	2	0	0-0	6	10	10	3	0	3-0	0	15.00	30	.385	.448	1	.000	-0	150	-6	0	-0.3
1979	Atl N	5	3	.625	37	0	0	5-0	69	54	23	3	1	34-4	40	2.48	162	.224	.319	11	.182	0	—	11	0	1.3
1980	Tor A	6	9	.400	55	10	0	4-3	135.2	159	79	16	4	53-11	70	4.51	96	.302	.366	0	ø	0	91	-4	0	-0.5
1981	Tor A	1	5	.167	40	0	0	10-1	60	55	24	2	0	21-2	38	2.85	139	.249	.313	0	ø	0	—	6	0	0.8
1982	Tor A	8	6	.571	44	0	0	8-6	70	54	27	7	1	30-3	49	3.21	140	.212	.296	0	ø	0	—	9	0	2.0
1983	Tor A	7	4	.636	50	0	0	9-11	64.2	63	33	11	0	37-7	47	4.45	98	.259	.353	0	ø	0	—	0	0	0.0
1984	Tor A	0	0	ø	6	0	0	0-0	10.2	12	6	0	0	7-1	3	2.53	163	.286	.380	0	ø	0	—	1	0	0.1
	Tex A	2	1	.667	15	0	0	0-2	32.2	33	17	4	0	13-1	21	4.41	95	.260	.326	0	ø	0	—	0	0	0.0
	Year	2	1	.667	21	0	0	0-2	43.1	45	23	4	0	20-2	24	3.95	106	.266	.340	0	ø	0	—	0	0	0.1
Total	7	29	28	.509	250	12	0	36-23	448.2	440	219	46	6	198-29	268	3.85	110	.262	.339	12	.167	0	104	17	0	3.4
McLaughlin, Jud	Justin Theodore; B3.24.1912 Brighton MA; D9.27.1964 Cambridge MA; BL/TL/5´11˝/155; d6.23; Col Boston College																									
1931	Bos A	0	0	ø	9	0	0	0	12	23	16	1	0	8	3	12.00	36	.397	.470	0	ø	0	—	-9	—	-0.4
1932	Bos A	0	0	ø	1	0	0	0	3	5	5	0	0	4	0	15.00	30	.385	.529	1	.000	-0	—	-3	—	-0.1
1933	Bos A	0	0	ø	6	0	0	0	8.2	14	7	1	0	5	1	6.23	70	.359	.432	0	ø	0	—	-2	—	-0.1
Total	3	0	0	ø	16	0	0	0	23.2	42	28	2	0	17	4	10.27	42	.382	.465	1	.000	-0	—	-14	—	-0.6
McLaughlin, Bo	Michael Duane; B10.23.1953 Oakland CA; BR/TR/6´5˝/(175–210); [HouN75 1/14]; d7.20; Col Lipscomb; [DL 1983 Cal A 25]																									
1976	Hou N	4	5	.444	17	11	4-2	1-0	79	71	31	6	2	17-1	32	2.85	113	.244	.288	19-0-2	.000	-1	67	3	0	0.1
1977	Hou N	4	7	.364	46	6	0	5-2	84.2	81	44	6	6	34-6	59	4.25	85	.260	.341	9-0-2	.000	-1	82	-6	19	-0.8
1978	Hou N	0	1	.000	12	1	0	2-0	23.1	30	17	2	2	16-2	10	5.01	67	.313	.417	3	.000	-0	108	-6	0	-0.4
1979	Hou N	1	2	.333	12	0	0	0-1	16.1	22	15	2	0	4-0	12	5.51	64	.314	.347	1	.000	-0	—	-6	0	-0.9
	Atl N	1	1	.500	37	1	0	0-0	49.2	63	33	2	2	16-6	45	4.89	82	.303	.357	5-0-1	.000	-1	44	-5	0	-0.4
	Year	2	3	.400	49	1	0	0-1	66	85	48	4	2	20-6	57	5.05	77	.306	.354	6-0-1	.000	-1	46	-11	0	-1.3
1981	Oak A	0	0	ø	11	0	0	1-0	11.2	17	15	1	1	9-0	3	11.57	30	.333	.443	0	ø	0	—	-10	99	-0.5
1982	Oak A	0	4	.000	21	2	1	0-0	48.1	51	31	3	1	27-1	27	4.84	82	.267	.359	0	ø	0	69	-6	0	-0.4
Total	6	10	20	.333	156	21	5-2	9-3	313	335	186	22	14	123-16	188	4.49	80	.275	.346	37-0-5	.000	-3	70	-36	143	-3.3
McLaughlin, Pat	Patrick Elmer; B8.17.1910 Taylor TX; D11.1.1999 Houston TX; BR/TR/6´2˝/175; d4.25; Col St. Edwards																									
1937	Det A	0	2	.000	10	3	0	0	32.2	39	23	3	0	16	8	6.34	74	.291	.367	10	.100	-1*	124	-5	—	-0.3
1940	Phi A	0	0	ø	1	0	0	0	1.2	4	3	1	0	1	0	16.20	27	.444	.500	0	ø	0	—	-2	—	-0.1
1945	Det A	0	0	ø	1	0	0	0	1	2	2	0	0	0	0	9.00	39	.400	.400	0	ø	0	—	-1	0	-0.1
Total	3	0	2	.000	12	3	0	0	35.1	45	28	4	0	17	8	6.88	67	.304	.376	10	.100	-1	124	-8	0	-0.5

YEAR	TM LG	W	L	PCT	G	GS	CG-SHO	SV-BS	IP	H	R	HR	HB	BB-IB	SO	ERA	AERA	OAV	OOB	AB-HR-SH	AVG	PB	SUP	APR	DL	PW
McLaughlin, Warren	Warren A.; B1.22.1876 N.Plainfield NJ; D10.22.1923 Plainfield NJ; TL; d7.7																									
1900	Phi N	0	0	ø	1	0	0	0	6	4	4	0	0	6	1	4.50	80	.190	.370	2	.500	1	—	-1	—	0.0
1902	Pit N	3	0	1.000	3	3	3	0	26	27	13	0	1	9	13	2.77	99	.267	.333	11	.364	1	199	-1	—	0.0
1903	Phi N	0	3	.000	3	2	2	0	23	38	24	0	1	11	3	7.04	46	.376	.442	10	.200	0	41	-9	—	-0.9
Total	3	3	3	.500	7	5	5	0	55	69	41	0	2	26	17	4.75	64	.309	.386	23	.304	2	124	-11	—	-0.9
McLean, Al	Albert Eldon "Elrod"; B9.20.1912 Chicago IL; D9.29.1990 Asheboro NC; BR/TR/6´0˝/175; d7.16																									
1935	Was A	0	0	ø	4	0	0	0	8.2	12	8	0	0	5	3	7.27	59	.324	.405	2	.000	-0	—	-3	—	-0.2
McLeary, Marty	Marty Lee; B10.26.1974 Kettering OH; BR/TR/6´5˝/(225–230); [BosA97 10/311]; d8.22; Col Mount Vernon Nazarene																									
2004	SD N	0	0	ø	3	0	0	0-0	3.2	7	6	2	0	2-0	4	14.73	27	.438	.474	0	ø	0	—	-5	0	-0.2
2006	Pit N	2	0	1.000	5	2	0	0-0	17.2	17	5	1	0	6-1	8	2.04	225	.258	.315	5	.000	-1	40	5	0	0.4
Total	2	2	0	1.000	8	2	0	0-0	21.1	24	11	3	0	8-1	12	4.22	106	.293	.348	5	.000	-1	40	0	0	0.2
McLeland, Wayne	Wayne Gaffney "Nubbin"; B8.29.1924 Stockport IA; D5.9.2004 Houston TX; BR/TR/6´0˝/180; d4.20																									
1951	Det A	0	1	.000	6	1	0	0	11	20	10	1	1	4	0	8.18	51	.400	.455	1-0-1	.000	-0	64	-4	0	-0.3
1952	Det A	0	0	ø	4	0	0	0	2.2	4	3	0	0	6	0	10.13	38	.444	.667	0	ø	0	—	-2	0	-0.1
Total	2	0	1	.000	10	1	0	0	13.2	24	13	1	1	10	0	8.56	48	.407	.500	1-0-1	.000	-0	64	-6	0	-0.4
McLish, Cal	Calvin Coolidge Julius Caesar Tuskahoma "Buster"; B12.1.1925 Anadarko OK; BB/TR/6´1˝/(200–210); d5.13; Mil 1945–46; C16																									
1944	Bro N	3	10	.231	23	13	3	0	84	110	81	10	1	48	24	7.82	45	.321	.406	32-0-1	.219	0*	118	-39	0	-4.9
1946	Bro N	0	0	ø	1	0	0	0	0	1	2	0	0	0	0	(2)	ø	1.000	1.000	0	ø	0	—	-2	0	-0.2
1947	Pit N	0	0	ø	1	0	0	0	1	2	2	0	1	0	0	18.00	23	.400	.500	0	ø	0	—	-1	0	-0.1
1948	Pit N	0	0	ø	2	1	0	0	5	8	5	0	0	2	1	9.00	45	.400	.455	1	.000	-0*	174	-2	0	-0.1
1949	Chi N	1	1	.500	8	2	0	0	23	31	21	6	0	12	6	5.87	69	.341	.417	9-1-0	.333	2*	153	-6	0	-0.3
1951	Chi N	4	10	.286	30	17	5-1	0	145.2	159	76	16	3	52	46	4.45	92	.283	.347	42	.119	-1*	72	-3	0	-0.4
1956	Cle A	2	4	.333	37	2	0	1	61.2	67	36	5	0	32-5	27	4.96	85	.282	.364	9	.111	1*	64	-4	0	-0.2
1957	Cle A	9	7	.563	42	7	2	1	144.1	118	55	11	2	67-10	88	2.74	135	.220	.308	43-2-4	.186	3*	130	14	0	1.9
1958	Cle A	16	8	.667	39	30	13	1	225.2	214	92	25	1	70-4	97	2.99	122	.251	.307	64-0-4	.094	-1	137	13	0	1.3
1959	Cle A★	19	8	.704	35	32	13	1	235.1	253	110	26	5	72-6	113	3.63	101	.270	.325	74-0-9	.189	1	118	0	0	0.3
1960	Cin N	4	14	.222	37	21	2-1	0	151.1	170	85	16	7	48-8	56	4.16	92	.287	.345	41-0-1	.049	-3	78	-9	0	-1.2
1961	Chi A	10	13	.435	31	27	4	1	162.1	178	87	21	1	47-1	80	4.38	89	.280	.328	54-0-3	.167	-1	86	-8	0	-1.0
1962	Phi N	11	5	.688	32	24	5-1	1	154.2	184	84	15	2	45-6	71	4.25	91	.293	.341	51-0-1	.078	-2	107	-8	0	-0.9
1963	Phi N	13	11	.542	32	32	10-2	0	209.2	184	85	14	4	56-3	98	3.26	99	.239	.292	69-0-4	.203	4*	110	1	0	0.6
1964	Phi N	0	1	.000	2	1	0	0	5.1	6	3	0	0	1-1	6	3.38	103	.261	.292	1	.000	-0	76	0	77	0.0
Total	15	92	92	.500	352	209	57-5	6	1609	1685	824	165	27	552-44	713	4.01	93	.270	.331	490-3-27	.149	4	106	-54	77	-5.2
McMackin, Sam	Samuel; B1872 Cleveland OH; D2.11.1903 Columbus OH; BR/TL; d9.4																									
1902	Chi A	0	0	ø	1	0	0	0	3	1	1	0	0	0	2	0.00	ø	.100	.100	1	.000	-0	—	1	—	0.0
	Det A	0	1	.000	1	1	1	0	8.1	9	5	0	1	4	2	3.24	113	.273	.368	4	.500	1	79	0	—	0.1
	Year	0	1	.000	2	1	1	0	11.1	10	6	0	1	4	4	2.38	150	.233	.313	5	.400	0	80	1	—	0.1
McMahan, Jack	Jack Wally; B7.22.1932 Hot Springs AR; BR/TL/6´0˝/175; d4.18; Col Arkansas–Little Rock																									
1956	Pit N	0	0	ø	11	0	0	0	13.1	18	9	1	0	9-0	9	6.08	62	.340	.435	1	.000	-0	—	-3	0	-0.1
	KC A	0	5	.000	23	9	0	0	61.2	69	40	7	2	31-0	13	4.82	90	.290	.374	14	.000	-2	69	-4	0	-0.5
Total	1	0	5	.000	34	9	0	0	75	87	49	8	2	40-0	22	5.04	84	.299	.385	15	.000	-2	69	-7	0	-0.6
McMahon, Don	Donald John; B1.4.1930 Brooklyn NY; D7.22.1987 Los Angeles CA; BR/TR/6´2˝/(213–225); d6.30; C11																									
1957	†Mil N	2	3	.400	32	0	0	9	46.2	33	13	0	0	29-4	46	1.54	227	.196	.312	8	.250	1	—	9	0	1.5
1958	†Mil N☆	7	2	.778	38	0	0	8	58.2	50	25	4	2	29-5	37	3.68	96	.235	.328	9-0-1	.111	0	—	0	0	-0.1
1959	Mil N	5	3	.625	60	0	0	**15**	80.2	81	26	5	1	37-5	55	2.57	138	.259	.335	9	.222	1	—	10	0	1.3
1960	Mil N	3	6	.333	48	0	0	10	63.2	66	48	9	2	32-4	50	5.94	58	.263	.350	11	.000	-1	—	-20	0	-3.3
1961	Mil N	6	4	.600	53	0	0	8	92	84	35	4	2	51-6	55	2.84	132	.249	.349	16-0-1	.188	0	—	8	0	1.0
1962	Mil N	0	1	.000	2	0	0	0	3	3	2	1	0	0-0	3	6.00	63	.250	.250	0	ø	0	—	-1	0	-0.1
	Hou N	5	5	.500	51	0	0	8	76.2	53	14	4	1	33-1	69	1.53	245	.201	.288	12	.083	-1	—	20	0	2.9
	Year	5	6	.455	53	0	0	8	79.2	56	16	5	1	33-1	72	1.69	221	.203	.287	12	.083	-1	—	19	0	2.8
1963	Hou N	1	5	.167	49	2	0	5	80	83	38	10	0	26-2	51	4.05	78	.270	.323	12	.083	0	68	-7	0	-0.5
1964	Cle A	6	4	.600	70	0	0	16	101	67	31	7	2	52-5	92	2.41	150	.189	.293	14	.143	-0	—	13	0	1.6
1965	Cle A	3	3	.500	58	0	0	11	85	79	36	8	1	37-7	60	3.28	106	.248	.328	9-0-1	.222	0	—	2	0	0.2
1966	Cle A	1	1	.500	12	0	0	1	12.1	8	4	1	0	6-0	5	2.92	118	.190	.286	2	.000	-0	—	1	0	0.1
	Bos A	8	7	.533	49	0	0	9	78	65	29	7	3	38-8	57	2.65	143	.232	.326	11	.091	-0	—	8	0	1.7
	Year	9	8	.529	61	0	0	10	90.1	73	33	8	3	44-8	62	2.69	140	.227	.321	13	.077	-0	—	9	0	1.8
1967	Bos A	1	2	.333	11	0	0	2	17.2	14	8	3	0	13-0	10	3.57	98	.215	.346	2	.000	-0	—	0	0	-0.1
	Chi A	5	0	1.000	52	0	0	3	91.2	54	21	5	6	27-4	74	1.67	186	.173	.251	11	.182	0	—	15	0	0.9
	Year	6	2	.750	63	0	0	5	109.1	68	29	8	6	40-4	84	1.98	160	.180	.269	13	.154	-0	—	14	0	0.8
1968	Chi A	2	1	.667	25	0	0	0	46	31	10	2	3	20-6	32	1.96	155	.190	.287	3	.333	0	—	6	0	0.4
	†Det A	3	1	.750	20	0	0	1	35.2	22	8	2	0	10-1	33	2.02	149	.180	.241	4	.000	-0	—	4	0	0.5
	Year	5	2	.714	45	0	0	1	81.2	53	18	4	3	30-7	65	1.98	152	.186	.268	7	.143	-0	—	11	0	0.9
1969	Det A	3	5	.375	34	0	0	11-2	37	25	17	2	1	18-1	38	3.89	97	.192	.293	6	.000	-1	—	0	0	-0.1
	SF N	3	1	.750	13	0	0	2-3	23.2	13	9	1	0	9-0	21	3.04	116	.157	.239	3-0-1	.333	0	—	2	0	0.3
1970	SF N	9	5	.643	61	0	0	19-5	94.1	70	32	9	2	45-13	74	2.96	134	.202	.297	14-0-1	.143	0	—	12	23	2.2
1971	†SF N	10	6	.625	61	0	0	4-5	82	73	40	9	7	37-6	71	4.06	84	.242	.335	7-0-1	.000	-1	—	-4	0	-0.9
1972	SF N	3	3	.500	44	0	0	5-2	63	46	26	8	1	21-3	45	3.71	94	.206	.274	4-0-1	.250	0	—	0	0	0.0
1973	SF N	4	0	1.000	22	0	0	6-0	30.1	21	5	1	0	7-3	20	1.48	260	.189	.237	1	1.000	0	—	8	0	1.4
1974	SF N	0	0	ø	9	0	0	0-0	11.2	13	5	2	0	2-0	5	3.09	124	.283	.306	0	ø	0	—	1	0	0.0
Total	18	90	68	.570	874	2	0	153-17	1310.2	1054	482	104	34	579-84	1003	2.96	119	.221	.308	168-0-7	.137	-1	68	87	23	10.9
McMahon, Doc	Henry John; B12.19.1886 Woburn MA; D12.11.1929 Woburn MA; TR; d10.6; Col Holy Cross																									
1908	Bos A	1	0	1.000	1	1	1	0	9	14	3	0	0	0	3	3.00	82	.350	.350	5	.400	1	306	0	—	0.0
McMahon, Sadie	John Joseph; B9.19.1867 Wilmington DE; D2.20.1954 Wilmington DE; BR/TR/5´9.5˝/165; d7.5																									
1889	Phi AA	14	12	.538	28	27	27-2	0	242	230	160	5	14	102	117	3.53	107	.243	.325	104	.154	-6*	109	6	—	0.1
1890	Phi AA	29	18	.617	48	46	44	1	410	414	238	5	20	133	225	3.34	116	.254	.318	175-2	.229	3*	109	18	—	2.3
	Bal AA	7	3	.700	12	11	11-1	0	99	84	49	1	6	33	66	3.00	135	.223	.296	39	.103	-4	86	10	—	0.5
	Year	**36**	21	.632	**60**	**57**	**55**-1	1	**509**	498	287	6	26	166	**291**	3.27	120	.248	.314	214-2	.206	-1	104	24	—	2.8
1891	Bal AA	**35**	24	.593	61	**58**	**53-5**	1	**503**	493	259	13	17	149	219	2.81	133	.248	.306	210-1	.205	-3	92	54	—	4.9
1892	Bal N	19	25	.432	48	46	44-2	1	397	430	260	9	9	145	118	3.24	106	.265	.329	177	.141	-9*	109	1	—	-0.8
1893	Bal N	23	18	.561	43	40	35	1	346.1	378	232	6	9	156	79	4.37	109	.269	.346	148	.243	-3	101	17	—	1.3
1894	Bal N	25	8	.758	35	33	26	0	275.2	317	175	7	9	111	60	4.21	130	.285	.355	126-0-8	.286	0	135	36	—	3.1
1895	†Bal N	10	4	.714	15	15	15-**4**	0	122.1	110	54	1	4	32	37	2.94	162	.237	.291	51-0-1	.314	1	97	25	—	2.3
1896	Bal N	11	9	.550	22	22	19	0	175.2	195	109	4	3	55	33	3.48	123	.279	.334	73	.123	-7	118	10	—	0.3
1897	Bro N	0	6	.000	9	7	5	0	63	75	56	1	3	29	13	5.86	70	.293	.372	25	.200	-1	77	-13	—	-1.0
Total	9	173	127	.577	321	305	279-14	4	2634	2726	1592	52	94	945	967	3.51	118	.260	.326	1128-3-9	.204	-29	107	164	—	13.0
McMakin, John	John Weaver "Spartanburg John"; B3.6.1878 Spartanburg SC; D9.25.1956 Lyman SC; BR/TL/5´11˝/165; d4.19; Col Clemson																									
1902	Bro N	2	2	.500	4	4	4	0	32	34	18	0	2	11	6	3.09	89	.272	.341	11	.182	1	129	-2	—	-0.2
McManus, Joe	Joab Logan; B9.7.1887 Palmyra IL; D12.23.1955 Beckley WV; BR/TR/5´11˝/180; d4.12																									
1913	Cin N	0	0	ø	1	0	0	0	2	3	4	0	0	4	1	18.00	18	.375	.583	0	ø	0	—	-3	—	-0.1
McManus, Pat	Patrick A.; B10.1859 , Ireland; D5.19.1917 Mount Hope NY; d5.22																									
1879	Tro N	0	2	.000	2	2	2	0	21	24	21	1	—	1	6	3.00	83	.258	.266	8	.125	-1	102	-2	—	-0.2

YEAR	TM LG	W	L	PCT	G	GS	CG-SHO	SV-BS	IP	H	R	HR	HB	BB-IB	SO	ERA	AERA	OAV	OOB	AB-HR-SH	AVG	PB	SUP	APR	DL	PW
McMichael, Greg	Gregory Winston; B12.1.1966 Knoxville TN; BR/TR/6´3˝/(215–222); [CleA88 7/163]; d4.12; Col Tennessee																									
1993	†Atl N	2	3	.400	74	0	0	19-2	91.2	68	22	3	0	29-4	89	2.06	196	.206	.269	4	.000	-0	—	21	0	1.8
1994	Atl N	4	6	.400	51	0	0	21-10	58.2	66	29	1	0	19-6	47	3.84	113	.280	.332	1	.000	-0	—	2	0	0.4
1995	†Atl N	7	2	.778	67	0	0	2-2	80.2	64	27	8	0	32-9	74	2.79	155	.213	.289	6	.000	-0	—	13	0	1.3
1996	†Atl N	5	3	.625	73	0	0	2-6	86.2	84	37	4	1	27-7	78	3.22	138	.253	.309	0	ø	0	—	10	0	0.9
1997	NY N	7	10	.412	73	0	0	7-11	87.2	73	34	8	2	27-6	81	2.98	134	.233	.295	3	.667	1	—	10	0	1.9
1998	NY N	1	2	.333	22	0	0	0-0	22.2	23	12	1	1	14-2	22	3.97	104	.271	.380	0	ø	0	—	0	0	0.0
	LA N	0	1	.000	12	0	0	1-2	14.1	17	8	1	1	6-3	11	4.40	92	.309	.381	0	ø	0	—	-1	0	0.0
	NY N	4	1	.800	30	0	0	1-3	31	41	19	7	2	15-5	22	4.06	101	.318	.392	1	.000	-0	—	-2	0	-0.3
	Year	5	4	.556	64	0	0	2-5	68	81	39	9	4	35-10	55	4.10	100	.301	.386	1	.000	-0	—	-3	0	-0.3
1999	NY N	1	1	.500	19	0	0	0-1	18.2	20	10	3	0	8-3	18	4.82	90	.270	.337	0	ø	0	—	-1	67	-0.1
	Oak A	0	0	ø	17	0	0	0-0	15	15	9	3	2	12-2	3	5.40	88	.283	.426	0	ø	0	—	-1	0	0.0
2000	Atl N	0	0	ø	15	0	0	0-0	16.1	12	8	3	0	4-1	14	4.41	102	.214	.262	0	ø	0	—	1	126	0.0
Total	8	31	29	.517	453	0	0	53-37	523.1	483	215	42	9	193-48	459	3.25	130	.246	.314	15	.133	-0	—	52	193	5.9
McMullen, George	George; B CA; d7.2																									
1887	NY AA	2	1	.667	3	3	2	0	21	25	25	2	0	19	2	7.71	55	.269	.393	12	.083	-2	130	-7	—	-0.7
McMullin, John	John F. "Lefty"; B1848 Philadelphia PA; D4.11.1881 Philadelphia PA; BR/TL/5´9˝/160; d5.9; ▲																									
1871	Tro NA	12	15	.444	29	29	28	0	249	430	362	4	—	75	12	5.53	76	.342	.379	136	.279	1	114	-37	—	-2.1
1872	Mut NA	1	0	1.000	3	1	1	1	15	18	15	0	—	2	1	3.60	94	.247	.267	236	.254	0*	125	-1	—	0.0
1873	Ath NA	1	0	1.000	1	1	1	0	8	10	5	0	—	1	2	2.25	158	.303	.324	227	.273	0*	178	1	—	0.1
1875	Phi NA	0	0	ø	4	0	0	0	11.1	32	23	0	—	1	0	7.94	29	.464	.471	222-2	.257	1*	—	-7	—	-0.3
Total	4NA	14	15	.483	37	31	30	1	283.1	490	405	4	—	79	15	5.43	75	.342	.376	821-2	.264	2	118	-44	—	-2.3
McMurtry, Craig	Joe Craig; B11.5.1959 Troy TX; BR/TR/6´5˝/(192–195); [AtlN80*1/4]; d4.10; Col McLennan (TX) CC; [DL 1987 Tor A 73]																									
1983	Atl N	15	9	.625	36	35	6-3	0-0	224.2	204	86	13	1	88-1	105	3.08	125	.243	.314	70-0-12	.086	-3	109	17	0	1.6
1984	Atl N	9	17	.346	37	30	0	0-0	183.1	184	100	16	1	102-4	99	4.32	89	.268	.359	52-0-8	.115	-1*	72	-9	0	-1.1
1985	Atl N	0	3	.000	17	6	0	1-0	45	56	36	6	1	27-1	28	6.60	58	.306	.394	14-0-1	.071	-1	61	-12	0	-0.9
1986	Atl N	1	6	.143	37	5	0	0-1	79.2	82	46	7	2	43-5	50	4.74	83	.265	.357	16-0-1	.125	-0*	90	-6	36	-0.5
1988	Tex A	3	3	.500	32	0	0	3-4	60	37	16	5	1	24-4	35	2.25	182	.180	.266	0	ø	0	—	12	0	1.3
1989	Tex A	0	0	ø	19	0	0	0-1	23	29	21	3	2	13-1	14	7.43	54	.312	.400	0	ø	0	—	-8	104	-0.4
1990	Tex A	0	3	.000	23	3	0	0-0	41.2	43	25	4	1	30-0	14	4.32	91	.281	.398	0	ø	0	54	-3	0	-0.2
1995	Hou N	0	1	.000	11	0	0	0-1	10.1	15	11	0	1	9-1	4	7.84	49	.357	.463	1	.000	-0	—	-5	0	-0.4
Total	8	28	42	.400	212	79	6-3	4-7	667.2	650	341	54	10	336-17	349	4.08	96	.259	.345	153-0-22	.098	-6	88	-14	213	-0.6
McNabb, Edgar	Edgar J. "Texas"; B10.24.1865 Coshocton OH; D2.28.1894 Pittsburgh PA; BR/TR/5´11.5˝/170; d5.12																									
1893	Bal N	8	7	.533	21	14	12	0	142	167	109	5	8	53	18	4.12	115	.284	.352	67	.194	-2	100	4	—	0.2
McNally, Dave	David Arthur; B10.31.1942 Billings MT; D12.1.2002 Billings MT; BR/TL/5´11˝/(188–191); d9.26																									
1962	Bal A	1	0	1.000	1	1	1-1	0	9	2	0	0	0	3-0	4	0.00	ø	.071	.161	3	.000	-0	72	4	0	0.5
1963	Bal A	7	8	.467	29	20	2	1	125.2	133	67	9	5	55-4	78	4.58	76	.276	.352	38-0-3	.053	-2	104	-14	0	-1.8
1964	Bal A	9	11	.450	30	23	5-3	0	159.1	157	72	15	9	51-1	88	3.67	97	.260	.325	51-0-2	.137	0	84	-2	0	-0.2
1965	Bal A	11	6	.647	35	29	6-2	0	198.2	163	69	15	6	73-6	116	2.85	122	.222	.297	65-0-3	.092	-3	100	16	0	1.0
1966	†Bal A	13	6	.684	34	33	5-1	0	213	212	91	22	4	64-1	158	3.17	105	.256	.311	77-0-4	.195	3	136	0	0	0.4
1967	Bal A	7	7	.500	24	22	3-1	0	119	134	65	13	2	39-1	70	4.54	69	.295	.353	38-0-7	.158	0	122	-18	22	-2.1
1968	Bal A	22	10	.688	35	35	18-5	0	273	175	67	24	10	55-1	202	1.95	150	.182	**.232**	86-3-8	.128	4	110	31	0	4.3
1969	†Bal A★	20	7	.741	41	40	11-4	0-0	268.2	232	103	21	5	84-6	166	3.22	112	.234	.296	94-1-8	.085	-2	126	13	0	0.9
1970	†Bal A☆	**24**	9	.727	40	**40**	16-1	0-0	296	277	114	29	7	78-3	185	3.22	114	.250	.301	105-1-6	.133	4*	124	17	0	2.1
1971	†Bal A	21	5	**.808**	30	30	11-1	0-0	224.1	188	75	24	5	58-2	91	2.89	118	.229	.282	74-2-14	.162	3	151	16	27	2.1
1972	Bal A★	13	17	.433	36	36	12-6	0-0	241	220	85	15	2	68-15	120	2.95	106	.247	.301	79-2-2	.152	1	82	6	0	0.9
1973	†Bal A	17	17	.500	38	38	17-4	0-0	266	247	100	16	5	81-6	87	3.21	117	.251	.310	0	ø	0	90	20	0	2.5
1974	†Bal A	16	10	.615	39	37	13-4	1-0	259	260	112	19	8	81-6	111	3.58	97	.270	.330	0	ø	0	109	0	0	0.1
1975	Mon N	3	6	.333	12	12	0	0-0	77.1	88	50	8	4	36-4	36	5.24	74	.280	.362	21-0-1	.190	2	89	-11	0	-1.0
Total	14	184	119	.607	424	396	120-33	2-0	2730	2488	1070	230	72	826-56	1512	3.24	106	.245	.305	731-9-58	.133	9	111	78	49	9.7
McNamara, Tim	Timothy Augustine; B11.20.1898 Millville MA; D11.5.1994 N.Smithfield RI; BR/TR/5´11˝/170; d6.27; Col Fordham																									
1922	Bos N	3	4	.429	24	5	4-2	0	70.2	55	26	2	1	26	16	2.42	165	.225	.303	17-0-1	.118	-1	110	**12**	—	0.9
1923	Bos N	3	13	.188	32	16	3	0	139.1	185	95	8	5	29	32	4.91	81	.320	.357	39	.179	1	101	-15	—	-1.5
1924	Bos N	8	12	.400	35	21	6-2	0	179	242	119	9	3	31	35	5.18	74	.334	.364	43-0-6	.140	-1	82	-27	—	-2.6
1925	Bos N	0	0	ø	1	0	0	0	0.2	6	6	0	0	2	1	81.00	5	.857	.889	0	ø	0	—	-6	—	-0.2
1926	NY N	0	0	ø	6	0	0	0	6	7	6	0	0	4	4	9.00	42	.304	.407	0	ø	0	—	-3	—	-0.1
Total	5	14	29	.326	98	42	13-4	0	395.2	495	252	19	9	92	88	4.78	82	.314	.355	99-0-7	.152	-1	93	-39	—	-3.5
McNaughton, Gordon	Gordon Joseph; B7.31.1910 Chicago IL; D8.6.1942 Chicago IL; BR/TR/6´1˝/190; d8.13; Col Loyola–Chicago																									
1932	Bos A	0	1	.000	6	2	0	0	21	21	15	1	3	22	6	6.43	70	.259	.434	8	.250	0	133	-3	—	-0.1
McNeal, Harry	John Harley; B8.13.1878 Iberia OH; D1.11.1945 Cleveland OH; BL/TR/6´2˝/175; d8.5																									
1901	Cle A	5	5	.500	12	10	9	0	85.1	120	68	4	8	30	15	4.43	80	.328	.391	37-0-1	.162	-2	108	-10	—	-1.1
McNichol, Brian	Brian David; B5.20.1974 Fairfax VA; BL/TL/6´5˝/225; [ChiN95 2/34]; d9.7; Col James Madison																									
1999	Chi N	0	2	.000	4	2	0	0-0	10.2	15	8	4	1	7-0	12	6.75	68	.333	.426	2-0-1	.000	-0	40	-2	0	-0.4
McNichol, Ed	Edwin Briggs; B1.10.1879 Martins Ferry OH; D11.1.1952 Salineville OH; BR/TR/5´5˝/170; d7.9																									
1904	Bos N	2	12	.143	17	15	12-1	0	122	120	70	3	5	74	39	4.28	64	.262	.371	43	.093	-4	65	-16	—	-2.0
McPartlin, Frank	Frank; B2.16.1872 Hoosick Falls NY; D11.13.1943 New York NY; TR/6´0˝/180; d8.22																									
1899	NY N	0	0	ø	1	0	0	0	4	4	4	0	2	3	2	4.50	83	.267	.450	1	.000	-0	—	-1	—	0.0
McPherson, John	John Jacob; B3.9.1869 Easton PA; D9.30.1941 Easton PA; TR; d7.12																									
1901	Phi A	0	1	.000	1	1	0	0	4	7	5	0	1	4	0	11.25	34	.368	.500	1	.000	-0	54	-3	—	-0.4
1904	Phi N	1	12	.077	15	12	11-1	0	128	130	82	1	6	46	32	3.66	73	.264	.334	47-0-1	.064	-4	49	-15	—	-1.7
Total	2	1	13	.071	16	13	11-1	0	132	137	87	1	7	50	32	3.89	70	.268	.341	48-0-1	.063	-4	51	-18	—	-2.1
McQuaid, Herb	Herbert George; B3.29.1899 San Francisco CA; D4.4.1966 Richmond CA; BR/TR/6´2˝/185; d6.22																									
1923	Cin N	1	0	1.000	12	1	0	0	34.1	31	11	0	3	10	9	2.36	164	.238	.308	7	.000	-1	106	6	—	0.2
1926	NY A	1	0	1.000	17	1	0	0	38.1	48	34	5	2	13	6	6.10	63	.329	.391	7-0-1	.000	-1	87	-11	—	-0.6
Total	2	2	0	1.000	29	2	0	0	72.2	79	45	5	5	23	15	4.33	89	.286	.352	14-0-1	.000	-2	97	-5	—	-0.4
McQueen, Mike	Michael Robert; B8.30.1950 Oklahoma City OK; BL/TL/5´11˝/(170–190); d10.2																									
1969	Atl N	0	0	ø	1	1	0	0-0	3	2	1	0	0	3-0	3	3.00	121	.182	.357	0	ø	0	73	0	0	0.0
1970	Atl N	1	5	.167	22	8	1	1-0	66	67	48	10	1	31-2	54	5.59	77	.266	.345	20	.300	2	68	-10	0	-0.7
1971	Atl N	4	1	.800	17	3	0	1-0	56	47	24	7	2	23-4	38	3.54	105	.228	.309	19-0-2	.211	0	182	2	50	0.1
1972	Atl N	0	5	.000	23	7	1	1-0	78.1	79	45	11	1	44-3	40	4.60	83	.260	.352	23	.087	-2	56	-6	22	-0.6
1974	Cin N	0	0	ø	10	0	0	0-0	15	17	10	4	0	11-0	5	5.40	65	.288	.394	1	1.000	0	—	-3	0	-0.1
Total	5	5	11	.313	73	19	2	3-0	218.1	212	128	32	4	112-9	140	4.66	84	.255	.343	63-0-2	.206	1	82	-17	72	-1.3
McQuillan, Hugh	Alvin Hugh "Handsome Hugh"; B9.15.1895 New York NY; D8.26.1947 New York NY; BR/TR/6´0˝/170; d7.26																									
1918	Bos N	1	0	1.000	1	1	1	0	9	7	3	0	0	5	1	3.00	90	.219	.324	4	.250	0	338	0	—	0.0
1919	Bos N	2	3	.400	16	7	2	1	60	66	34	3	1	14	13	3.45	83	.288	.332	18-0-1	.222	0*	155	-6	—	-0.5
1920	Bos N	11	15	.423	38	26	17-1	5	225.2	230	110	3	2	70	53	3.55	86	.273	.330	74-1-6	.257	6	96	-13	—	-0.8
1921	Bos N	13	17	.433	45	31	13-2	5	250	284	137	9	2	90	94	4.00	91	.291	.352	88-1-5	.205	1	113	-14	—	-1.3
1922	Bos N	5	10	.333	28	17	7	0	136	154	70	3	1	56	33	4.24	94	.299	.369	42-0-5	.167	-1*	77	1	—	0.0
	†NY N	6	5	.545	15	13	5	1	94.1	111	48	7	0	34	24	3.82	105	.301	.360	37	.189	-1	95	2	—	0.1
	Year	11	15	.423	43	30	12	1	230.1	265	118	10	1	90	57	4.06	98	.300	.365	79-0-5	.177	-2	85	1	—	0.1
1923	†NY N	15	14	.517	38	32	15-5	0	229.2	224	96	12	5	66	75	3.41	112	.259	.315	82-0-3	.171	-2*	85	12	—	1.1

YEAR	TM LG	W	L	PCT	G	GS	CG-SHO	SV-BS	IP	H	R	HR	HB	BB-IB	SO	ERA	AERA	OAV	OOB	AB-HR-SH	AVG	PB	SUP	APR	DL	PW
1924	†NY N	14	8	.636	27	23	14-1	3	184	179	68	8	2	43	49	2.69	136	.259	.304	67-0-4	.209	-1*	124	19	—	2.0
1925	NY N	2	3	.400	14	11	2	1	70	95	49	9	1	23	23	6.04	67	.343	.395	21-0-1	.143	-1*	99	-14	—	-0.9
1926	NY N	11	10	.524	33	22	12-1	0	167	171	72	7	1	42	47	3.72	101	.271	.318	53-0-1	.132	-3*	95	5	—	0.4
1927	NY N	5	4	.556	11	9	5	0	58	73	32	4	1	22	17	4.50	86	.309	.371	19	.211	1	147	-3	—	-0.4
	Bos N	3	5	.375	13	12	2	0	78	109	65	2	2	24	17	5.54	67	.332	.381	22-0-5	.227	0	113	-20	—	-1.7
	Year	8	9	.471	24	21	7	0	136	182	97	6	3	46	34	5.10	74	.323	.377	41-0-5	.220	1	128	-22	—	-2.1
Total	10	88	94	.484	279	204	95-10	16	1561.2	1703	784	67	18	489	446	3.83	95	.284	.340	527-2-31	.195	0	104	-31	—	-2.0
McQuillan, George	George Watt; B5.1.1885 Brooklyn NY; D3.30.1940 Columbus OH; BR/TR/5´11.5˝/175; d5.8																									
1907	Phi N	4	0	1.000	6	5	5-3	0	41	21	3	0	1	11	28	0.66	368	.158	.228	11-0-1	.364	3	82	9	—	1.3
1908	Phi N	23	17	.575	48	42	32-7	2	359.2	263	88	1	6	91	114	1.53	159	.207	.263	119-0-6	.151	-1	99	33	—	3.8
1909	Phi N	13	16	.448	41	28	16-4	2	247.2	202	87	5	1	54	96	2.14	121	.226	.271	76-0-7	.118	-3	103	10	—	0.7
1910	Phi N	9	6	.600	24	17	13-3	1	152.1	109	42	2	3	50	71	**1.60**	196	.204	.276	47-0-5	.149	-1	113	23	—	2.2
1911	Cin N	2	6	.250	19	5	2	0	77	92	60	2	4	31	28	4.68	71	.308	.380	22-0-1	.091	-1	77	-14	—	-1.4
1913	Pit N	8	6	.571	25	16	7	1	141.2	144	60	1	1	35	59	3.43	88	.273	.319	39-0-3	.103	-1	108	-3	—	-0.4
1914	Pit N	13	17	.433	45	28	15	4	259.1	248	100	8	8	60	96	2.98	89	.261	.310	73-0-8	.068	-4	87	-6	—	-1.1
1915	Pit N	8	10	.444	30	20	9	1	149	160	64	1	2	39	56	2.84	96	.284	.332	44-0-3	.091	-3	79	-3	—	-0.6
	Phi N	4	3	.571	9	8	5	0	63.2	60	31	1	1	11	13	2.12	129	.247	.282	23-0-1	.043	-2	149	1	—	-0.2
	Year	12	13	.480	39	28	14	1	212.2	220	95	2	3	50	69	2.62	104	.273	.317	67-0-4	.075	-5	99	-1	—	-0.8
1916	Phi N	1	7	.125	21	3	1	2	62	58	33	2	3	15	22	2.76	96	.251	.305	11-0-4	.091	-1	19	-3	—	-0.6
1918	Cle A	0	1	.000	5	1	0	1	23	25	10	0	0	4	7	2.35	128	.284	.315	4	.000	-0	0	1	—	0.0
Total	10	85	89	.489	273	173	105-17	14	1576.1	1382	578	23	30	401	590	2.38	114	.241	.294	469-0-39	.117	-14	96	48	—	3.7
McRae, Norm	Norman; B9.26.1947 Elizabeth NJ; D7.25.2003 Garland TX; BR/TR/6´1˝/195; d9.13																									
1969	Det A	0	0	ø	3	0	0	0-0	3	2	2	0	0	1-0	3	6.00	63	.200	.250	0	ø	0	—	-1	0	0.0
1970	Det A	0	0	ø	19	0	0	0-0	31.1	26	13	1	1	25-0	16	2.87	131	.226	.366	1-0-1	.000	-0	—	2	0	0.1
Total	2	0	0	ø	22	0	0	0-0	34.1	28	15	1	1	26-0	19	3.15	120	.224	.357	1-0-1	.000	-0	—	1	0	0.1
McTigue, Bill	William Patrick "Rebel"; B1.3.1891 Nashville TN; D5.8.1920 Nashville TN; BL/TL/6´1.5˝/175; d5.2																									
1911	Bos N	0	5	.000	14	8	0	0	37	37	32	3	2	49	23	7.05	54	.280	.481	12	.083	-1	74	-10	—	-1.2
1912	Bos N	2	0	1.000	10	1	1	0	34.2	39	26	0	0	18	17	5.45	66	.289	.373	13	.077	-1	225	-6	—	-0.4
1916	Det A	0	0	ø	3	0	0	0	5.1	5	6	0	0	5	1	5.06	57	.278	.435	1	.000	-0	—	-2	—	-0.1
Total	3	2	5	.286	27	9	1	0	77	81	64	3	2	72	41	6.19	59	.284	.432	26	.077	-2	93	-18	—	-1.7
McVey, Cal	Calvin Alexander; B8.30.1849 Montrose IA; D8.20.1926 San Francisco CA; BR/TR/5´9˝/170; d5.5.1871; M3; ▲																									
1875	Bos NA	1	0	1.000	3	2	0	1	11	15	9	0	—	1	1	4.91	44	.294	.308	389-3	.355	2*	148	-2	—	-0.2
1876	Chi N	5	2	.714	11	6	5	2	59.1	57	22	0	—	2	9	1.52	161	.235	.241	308-1	.347	3*	119	6	—	0.7
1877	Chi N	4	8	.333	17	10	6	**2**	92	129	87	2	—	11	20	4.50	66	.301	.319	266	.368	6*	93	-15	—	-1.3
1879	Cin N	0	2	.000	3	1	1	0	14	34	23	1	—	2	7	8.36	28	.453	.468	354	.297	1*	119	-8	—	-0.8
Total	3	9	12	.429	31	17	12	4	165.1	220	132	3	—	15	36	3.76	73	.295	.309	928-1	.334	10	104	-17	—	-1.4
McWeeny, Doug	Douglas Lawrence "Buzz"; B8.17.1896 Chicago IL; D1.1.1953 Melrose Park IL; BR/TR/6´2˝/190; d4.24																									
1921	Chi A	3	6	.333	27	8	3	2	97.2	127	76	7	0	45	46	6.08	70	.325	.394	31-0-1	.032	-4	86	-20	—	-2.0
1922	Chi A	0	1	.000	4	1	0	0	10.2	13	8	0	0	7	5	5.91	69	.325	.426	1	.000	0	0	-2	—	-0.2
1924	Chi A	1	3	.250	13	5	2	0	43.1	47	25	2	2	17	18	4.57	90	.294	.369	9-0-1	.000	-0	78	-2	—	0.0
1926	Bro N	11	13	.458	42	24	10-1	1	216.1	213	97	6	8	84	96	3.04	126	.258	.333	64-0-4	.109	-4	77	16	—	1.1
1927	Bro N	4	8	.333	34	22	6	1	164.1	167	80	13	8	70	73	3.56	111	.266	.347	47-0-6	.043	-4	88	7	—	0.1
1928	Bro N	14	14	.500	42	32	12-**4**	1	244	218	108	11	5	114	79	3.17	125	.235	.322	81-0-3	.173	-1	85	22	—	2.4
1929	Bro N	4	10	.286	36	22	4	1	146	167	119	17	3	93	59	6.10	76	.288	.390	48-0-3	.104	-2	127	-25	—	-2.2
1930	Cin N	0	2	.000	8	2	0	0	25.2	28	23	0	0	20	10	7.36	66	.283	.403	7	.143	-0	72	-7	—	-0.4
Total	8	37	57	.394	206	116	37-5	6	948	980	536	56	26	450	386	4.17	98	.269	.353	288-0-18	.104	-16	92	-11	—	-1.2
McWilliams, Larry	Larry Dean; B2.10.1954 Wichita KS; BL/TL/6´5˝/(175–185); [AtlN74*1/6]; d7.17; Col Paris (TX) JC																									
1978	Atl N	9	3	.750	15	15	3-1	0-0	99.1	84	38	11	2	35-4	42	2.81	143	.224	.294	32-0-4	.063	-2	120	11	0	1.2
1979	Atl N	3	2	.600	13	13	1	0-0	66.1	69	41	4	4	22-2	32	5.56	72	.272	.338	24-0-2	.208	1	119	-8	84	-0.4
1980	Atl N	9	14	.391	30	30	4-1	0-0	163.2	188	97	27	7	39-2	77	4.95	74	.285	.331	51-0-4	.157	0	93	-21	0	-2.7
1981	Atl N	2	1	.667	6	5	2-1	0-0	37.2	31	13	2	0	8-0	23	3.11	114	.230	.269	10-0-1	.100	-0	111	2	0	0.2
1982	Atl N	2	3	.400	27	2	0	0-1	37.2	52	30	3	2	20-5	24	6.21	59	.327	.407	6-0-1	.167	0	96	-11	0	-1.2
	Pit N	6	5	.545	19	18	2-2	1-0	121.2	106	49	9	4	24-1	94	3.11	121	.232	.275	32-0-9	.188	-0*	89	7	0	0.7
	Year	8	8	.500	46	20	2-2	1-1	159.1	158	79	12	6	44-6	118	3.84	97	.256	.311	38-0-10	.184	-0	90	-3	0	-0.5
1983	Pit N	15	8	.652	35	35	8-4	0-0	238	205	99	19	3	87-7	199	3.25	115	.230	.298	79-0-10	.114	-3	99	12	0	0.8
1984	Pit N	12	11	.522	34	32	7-2	1-1	227.1	226	86	18	2	78-7	149	2.93	124	.263	.324	74-0-12	.122	-3*	107	16	0	1.3
1985	Pit N	7	9	.438	30	19	2	0-0	126.1	139	70	9	7	62-11	52	4.70	77	.283	.369	40-0-4	.125	-1*	112	-14	38	-1.6
1986	Pit N	3	11	.214	49	15	0	0-1	122.1	129	75	16	7	49-5	80	5.15	76	.268	.345	29-0-3	.138	0*	107	-15	0	-1.6
1987	Atl N	0	1	.000	9	2	0	0-0	20.1	25	15	2	2	7-1	13	5.75	75	.301	.366	5	.200	0	94	-3	0	-0.1
1988	StL N	6	9	.400	42	17	2-1	1-1	136	130	64	10	4	45-7	70	3.90	90	.253	.317	37-0-1	.162	1*	92	-5	0	-0.4
1989	Phi N	2	11	.154	40	16	2-1	0-1	120.2	123	67	3	4	49-4	54	4.10	87	.265	.337	27-0-3	.111	-1*	94	-9	0	-0.9
	KC A	2	2	.500	8	5	1	0-0	32.2	31	15	2	3	8-1	24	4.13	94	.254	.313	0	ø	0	61	0	0	0.0
1990	KC A	0	0	ø	13	0	0	0-0	8.1	10	9	2	1	9-1	7	9.72	40	.313	.476	0	ø	0	—	-5	0	-0.2
Total	13	78	90	.464	370	224	34-13	3-5	1558.1	1548	768	137	52	542-58	940	3.99	94	.259	.324	446-0-54	.135	-8	101	-43	122	-4.9
Meacham, Rusty	Russell Loren; B1.27.1968 Stuart FL; BR/TR/6´2˝/(155–180); [DetA87 33/858]; d6.29; Col Indian River (FL) CC																									
1991	Det A	2	1	.667	10	4	0	0-0	27.2	35	17	4	0	11-0	14	5.20	80	.315	.368	0	ø	0	148	-3	0	-0.3
1992	KC A	10	4	.714	64	0	0	2-4	101.2	88	39	5	1	21-5	64	2.74	149	.233	.269	0	ø	0	—	12	0	1.7
1993	KC A	2	2	.500	15	0	0	0-0	21	31	15	2	3	5-1	13	5.57	83	.326	.375	0	ø	0	—	-3	145	-0.4
1994	KC A	3	3	.500	36	0	0	4-1	50.2	51	23	7	2	12-1	36	3.73	135	.263	.307	0	ø	0	—	7	0	0.8
1995	KC A	4	3	.571	49	0	0	2-1	59.2	72	36	6	1	19-5	30	4.98	96	.304	.352	0	ø	0	—	-1	0	-0.1
1996	Sea A	1	1	.500	15	5	0	1-0	42.1	57	28	9	4	13-1	25	5.74	87	.328	.385	0	ø	0	134	-3	0	-0.2
2000	Hou N	0	0	ø	5	0	0	0-0	4.2	8	6	3	0	2-0	3	11.57	42	.381	.435	0	ø	0	—	-3	0	-0.1
2001	TB A	1	3	.250	24	0	0	0-0	35.1	39	24	3	2	10-0	13	5.60	80	.277	.325	0	ø	0	—	-4	0	-0.4
Total	8	23	17	.575	218	9	0	9-6	343	381	188	39	13	93-13	198	4.43	103	.282	.328	0	ø	0	142	2	145	1.0
Meador, Johnny	John Davis; B12.4.1892 Madison NC; D4.11.1970 Winston–Salem NC; BR/TR/5´10.5˝/165; d4.24																									
1920	Pit N	0	2	.000	12	2	0	0	36.1	48	18	1	0	7	5	4.21	76	.340	.372	6	.167	-0	61	-3	—	-0.1
Meadows, Lee	Henry Lee "Specs"; B7.12.1894 Oxford NC; D1.29.1963 Daytona Beach FL; BL/TR (BB 1920–21, 26, 28)/6´0˝/190; d4.19																									
1915	StL N	13	11	.542	39	26	14-1	0	244	232	112	5	5	88	104	2.99	93	.259	.329	83-0-1	.096	-4	104	-7	—	-1.2
1916	StL N	12	23	.343	**51**	36	11-1	2	289	261	117	3	14	119	120	2.58	102	.247	.332	95-0-3	.158	-1	84	-1	—	-0.2
1917	StL N	15	9	.625	43	37	18-4	2	265.2	253	99	5	4	90	100	3.08	87	.262	.328	89-0-7	.101	-6	109	-7	—	-1.5
1918	StL N	8	14	.364	30	23	12	1	165.1	176	91	1	10	56	49	3.59	75	.280	.348	55-0-2	.127	-2*	95	-17	—	-2.5
1919	StL N	4	10	.286	22	12	3-1	0	92	100	44	3	2	30	28	3.03	92	.292	.352	29-0-1	.103	-2	81	-5	—	-0.7
	Phi N	8	10	.444	18	17	15-3	0	158.1	128	55	3	7	49	88	2.33	138	.229	.300	51-0-4	.118	-3*	65	12	—	1.0
	Year	12	20	.375	40	29	18-4	0	250.1	228	99	6	9	79	116	2.59	118	.253	.320	80-0-5	.112	-5	71	10	—	0.3
1920	Phi N	16	14	.533	35	33	19-3	0	247	249	104	5	8	90	95	2.84	120	.270	.341	82-0-2	.171	-3*	89	13	—	1.3
1921	Phi N	11	16	.407	28	27	15-2	0	194.1	226	118	10	4	62	52	4.31	98	.288	.343	62-3-4	.210	2	81	1	—	0.6
1922	Phi N	12	18	.400	33	33	19-2	0	237	264	127	8	11	71	62	4.03	116	.288	.346	86-0-5	.314	3	77	18	—	2.6
1923	Phi N	1	3	.250	8	5	0	1	19.2	40	32	0	0	15	10	13.27	35	.430	.509	10-1-0	.400	2	129	-15	—	-2.3
	Pit N	16	10	.615	31	25	17-1	0	227	250	97	3	1	44	66	3.01	133	.284	.319	88-0-3	.250	3	112	22	—	2.6
	Year	17	13	.567	39	30	17-1	1	246.2	290	129	3	1	59	76	3.83	106	.298	.339	98-1-3	.265	5	117	2	—	0.3
1924	Pit N	13	12	.520	36	30	15-3	0	229.1	240	99	7	4	51	61	3.26	118	.278	.322	82-0-2	.195	-1	88	14	—	1.1
1925	†Pit N	19	10	.655	35	31	20-1	1	255.1	272	128	11	8	67	87	3.67	122	.273	.323	97-1-5	.175	-1	124	21	—	2.0
1926	Pit N	**20**	9	.690	36	31	15-1	0	226.2	254	125	10	4	52	54	3.97	99	.287	.329	88-0-1	.227	-1	130	-2	—	-0.2
1927	†Pit N	19	10	.655	40	**38**	**25**-2	0	299.1	315	131	11	8	66	84	3.40	121	.273	.317	115-0-3	.157	-5	118	23	—	1.4
1928	Pit N	1	1	.500	4	2	1	0	10	18	11	0	0	5	3	8.10	50	.383	.442	4	.500	1	156	-5	—	-0.7
1929	Pit N	0	0	ø	1	0	0	0	0.2	2	1	0	0	1	0	13.50	35	.500	.600	1	.000	-0	—	-1	—	0.0
Total	15	188	180	.511	490	406	219-25	7	3160.2	3280	1491	85	90	956	1063	3.37	106	.274	.332	1117-5-43	.180	-19	101	64	—	3.3

YEAR	TM LG	W	L	PCT	G	GS	CG-SHO	SV-BS	IP	H	R	HR	HB	BB-IB	SO	ERA	AERA	OAV	OOB	AB-HR-SH	AVG	PB	SUP	APR	DL	PW
Meadows, Brian	Matthew Brian; B11.21.1975 Montgomery AL; BR/TR/6´4˝/(200–230); [FlaN94 3/70]; d4.4																									
1998	Fla N	11	13	.458	31	31	1	0-0	174.1	222	106	20	3	46-3	88	5.21	78	.315	.358	54-0-2	.130	-1	77	-21	16	-2.5
1999	Fla N	11	15	.423	31	31	0	0-0	178.1	214	117	31	5	57-5	72	5.60	78	.302	.354	50-0-7	.140	0	87	-23	0	-2.8
2000	SD N	7	8	.467	22	22	0	0-0	124.2	150	80	24	8	50-6	53	5.34	83	.301	.373	40-0-4	.150	-1	116	-12	0	-1.3
	KC A	6	2	.750	11	10	2	0-0	71.2	84	39	8	0	14-0	26	4.77	109	.293	.322	0	ø	0	102	4	0	0.3
2001	KC A	1	6	.143	10	10	0	0-0	50.1	73	41	12	1	12-2	21	6.97	71	.351	.386	0	ø	0	86	-9	0	-1.1
2002	Pit N	1	6	.143	11	11	0	0-0	62.2	62	29	7	1	14-8	31	3.88	108	.256	.300	18-0-3	.000	-2	54	2	0	0.0
2003	Pit N	2	1	.667	34	7	0	1-0	76.1	91	45	8	1	11-2	38	4.72	92	.290	.315	14-0-3	.071	-1	124	-4	0	-0.3
2004	Pit N	2	4	.333	68	0	0	1-1	78	76	40	7	0	19-7	46	3.58	121	.259	.300	3	.000	-0	—	4	0	0.3
2005	Pit N	3	1	.750	65	0	0	0-2	74.2	84	42	8	0	21-7	44	4.58	93	.287	.325	1	.000	-0	—	-3	0	-0.2
2006	TB A	3	6	.333	53	0	0	8-2	69.2	90	43	14	0	15-4	35	5.17	90	.311	.339	0	ø	0	—	-4	0	-0.5
Total	9	47	62	.431	336	122	3	10-5	960.2	1146	582	139	19	259-44	454	5.05	87	.299	.343	180-0-19	.117	-4	91	-66	16	-8.1
Meadows, Rufus	Rufus Rivers; B8.25.1907 Chase City VA; D5.10.1970 Wichita KS; BL/TL/5´11˝/175; d4.23																									
1926	Cin N	0	0	ø	1	0	0	0	0.1	0	0	0	0	0	0	0.00	ø	.000	.000	1	.000	-0	—	0	—	0.0
Meads, Dave	David Donald; B1.7.1964 Montclair NJ; BL/TL/6´0˝/175; [HouN84*6/148]; d4.13; Col Middlesex Co. (NJ) JC; [DL 1989 Hou N 182]																									
1987	Hou N	5	3	.625	45	0	0	0-1	48.2	60	31	8	1	16-2	32	5.55	71	.321	.372	3	.333	1	—	-8	0	-1.2
1988	Hou N	3	1	.750	22	2	0	0-0	39.2	37	20	4	0	14-0	27	3.18	105	.240	.302	4	.250	1	27	-1	0	0.0
Total	2	8	4	.667	67	2	0	0-1	88.1	97	51	12	1	30-2	59	4.48	82	.284	.340	7	.286	1	27	-9	182	-1.2
Meakim, George	George Clinton; B7.11.1865 Brooklyn NY; D2.17.1923 Queens NY; BR/TR/5´7.5˝/154; d5.2																									
1890	†Lou AA	12	7	.632	28	21	16-3	1	192	173	100	4	5	63	123	2.91	133	.233	.298	72	.153	-2*	73	22	—	1.6
1891	Phi AA	1	4	.200	6	6	4	0	35	51	45	1	1	22	13	6.94	55	.329	.416	15	.200	0	109	-14	—	-1.3
1892	Chi N	0	1	.000	1	1	1	0	9	18	14	0	0	2	0	11.00	30	.400	.426	5	.400	0	190	-6	—	-0.5
	Cin N	1	1	.500	3	3	1	0	13.2	19	18	1	2	9	4	8.56	38	.317	.423	5	.000	-1	142	-8	—	-0.9
	Year	1	2	.333	4	4	2	0	22.2	37	32	1	2	11	4	9.53	35	.352	.424	10	.200	-0	154	-13	—	-1.4
1895	Lou N	1	0	1.000	1	1	1	0	7	7	2	0	0	4	2	2.57	180	.259	.355	3	.333	0	77	2	—	0.2
Total	4	15	13	.536	39	32	23-3	1	256.2	268	179	6	8	100	142	4.03	95	.260	.331	100	.170	-2	90	-4	—	-0.9
Mears, Chris	Christopher Peter; B1.20.1978 Ottawa ON, Can.; BR/TR/6´4˝/190; [SeaA96 5/147]; d6.29																									
2003	Det A	1	3	.250	29	3	0	5-0	41.1	50	28	5	3	11-0	21	5.44	80	.307	.360	0	ø	0	28	-5	0	-0.6
Meche, Gil	Gilbert Allen; B9.8.1978 Lafayette LA; BR/TR/6´3˝/(180–220); [SeaA96 1/22]; d7.6; [DL 2001 Sea A 190]																									
1999	Sea A	8	4	.667	16	15	0	0-0	85.2	73	48	9	2	57-1	47	4.73	101	.237	.357	0	ø	0	78	1	0	0.1
2000	Sea A	4	4	.500	15	15	1-1	0-0	85.2	75	37	7	1	40-0	60	3.78	127	.240	.324	0	ø	0	87	11	76	0.8
2003	Sea A	15	13	.536	32	32	1	0-0	186.1	187	97	30	3	63-2	130	4.59	94	.263	.324	5	.200	0	101	-4	0	-0.5
2004	Sea A	7	7	.500	23	23	1-1	0-0	127.2	139	73	21	5	47-0	99	5.01	89	.273	.339	0	ø	0	93	-7	0	-0.7
2005	Sea A	10	8	.556	29	26	0	0-0	143.1	153	92	18	2	72-1	83	5.09	82	.274	.356	4	.250	0	109	-18	27	-1.9
2006	Sea A	11	8	.579	32	32	1	0-0	186.2	183	106	24	8	84-2	156	4.48	98	.256	.340	4	.000	-0	112	-5	0	-0.5
Total	6	55	44	.556	147	143	4-2	0-0	815.1	810	453	109	21	363-6	575	4.65	96	.260	.339	13	.154	-0	99	-22	293	-2.7
Mecir, Jim	James Jason; B5.16.1970 Bayside NY; BB/TR/6´1˝/(195–230); [SeaA91 3/84]; d9.4; Col Eckerd																									
1995	Sea A	0	0	ø	2	0	0	0-0	4.2	5	1	0	0	2-0	3	0.00	ø	.263	.333	0	ø	0	—	2	0	0.1
1996	NY A	1	1	.500	26	0	0	0-0	40.1	42	24	6	0	23-4	38	5.13	97	.275	.361	0	ø	0	—	-1	0	0.0
1997	NY A	0	4	.000	25	0	0	0-1	33.2	36	23	5	2	10-1	25	5.88	76	.279	.338	0	ø	0	—	-5	0	-0.5
1998	TB A	7	2	.778	68	0	0	0-3	84	68	30	6	3	33-5	77	3.11	154	.225	.306	1	.000	-0	—	16	0	1.5
1999	TB A	0	1	.000	17	0	0	0-2	20.2	15	7	0	1	14-0	15	2.61	190	.203	.330	0	ø	0	—	5	145	0.3
2000	TB A	7	2	.778	38	0	0	1-3	49.2	35	17	2	1	22-0	33	3.08	159	.201	.293	0	ø	0	—	11	25	1.7
	†Oak A	3	1	.750	25	0	0	4-5	35.1	35	14	2	1	14-2	37	2.80	173	.255	.327	0	ø	0	—	7	0	0.8
	Year	10	3	.769	63	0	0	5-8	85	70	31	4	2	36-2	70	2.96	165	.225	.308	0	ø	0	—	18	0	2.5
2001	†Oak A	2	8	.200	54	0	0	3-5	63	54	25	4	1	26-7	61	3.43	133	.231	.310	0	ø	0	—	8	34	1.3
2002	†Oak A	6	4	.600	61	0	0	1-5	67.2	68	36	5	4	29-4	53	4.26	105	.259	.337	0	ø	0	—	1	0	0.2
2003	†Oak A	2	3	.400	41	0	0	1-1	37	40	25	4	1	16-1	25	5.59	82	.280	.352	0	ø	0	—	-4	44	-0.4
2004	Oak A	0	5	.000	65	0	0	2-5	47.2	45	21	5	4	19-2	49	3.59	129	.239	.322	0	ø	0	—	5	0	0.5
2005	Fla N	1	4	.200	52	0	0	0-4	43.1	39	17	2	5	17-2	34	3.12	129	.248	.337	0	ø	0	—	4	27	0.4
Total	11	29	35	.453	474	0	0	12-34	527	482	240	41	23	225-28	450	3.77	123	.244	.326	1	.000	-0	—	49	275	5.9
Medders, Brandon	Brandon Edward; B1.26.1980 Tuscaloosa AL; BR/TR/6´2˝/195; [AriN01 8/248]; d6.20; Col Mississippi St.																									
2005	Ari N	4	1	.800	27	0	0	0-0	30.1	21	6	2	1	11-0	31	1.78	249	.194	.270	1	.000	-0	—	9	0	1.3
2006	Ari N	5	3	.625	60	0	0	0-1	71.2	76	37	5	2	28-3	47	3.64	128	.270	.339	2	.000	-0	—	5	16	0.5
Total	2	9	4	.692	87	0	0	0-1	102	97	43	7	3	39-3	78	3.09	149	.249	.320	3	.000	-0	—	14	16	1.8
Medich, Doc	George Francis; B12.9.1948 Aliquippa PA; BR/TR/6´5˝/(225–227); [NYA70 30/700]; d9.5; Col Pittsburgh																									
1972	NY A	0	0	ø	1	1	0	0-0	0	2	2	0	0	2-0	0	(2)	ø	1.000	1.000	0	ø	0	207	-2	0	-0.2
1973	NY A	14	9	.609	34	32	11-3	0-0	235	217	84	20	3	74-6	145	2.95	126	.241	.299	0	ø	0	105	23	0	2.0
1974	NY A	19	15	.559	38	38	17-4	0-0	279.2	275	122	24	8	91-8	154	3.60	98	.259	.321	0	ø	0*	107	2	0	0.1
1975	NY A	16	16	.500	38	37	15-2	0-0	272.1	271	115	25	1	72-5	132	3.50	106	.264	.309	0	ø	0	105	9	0	0.8
1976	Pit N	8	11	.421	29	26	3	0-0	179	193	80	10	2	48-9	86	3.52	100	.281	.326	52-0-8	.096	-2	82	0	0	-0.1
1977	Oak A	10	6	.625	26	25	1	0-0	147.2	155	89	19	3	49-3	74	4.69	86	.265	.322	0	ø	0	118	-11	0	-1.1
	Sea A	2	0	1.000	3	3	1	0-0	22.1	26	9	1	2	4-0	3	3.63	114	.286	.327	0	ø	0	145	2	0	0.1
	Year	12	6	.667	29	28	2	0-0	170	181	98	20	5	53-3	77	4.55	89	.268	.323	0	ø	0	120	-10	0	-1.0
	NY N	0	1	.000	1	1	0	0-0	7	6	3	0	0	1-0	3	3.86	98	.261	.280	2	.000	-0	47	0	0	0.0
1978	Tex A	9	8	.529	28	22	6-2	2-0	171	166	78	10	3	52-2	71	3.74	100	.255	.311	0	ø	0	102	2	0	0.2
1979	Tex A	10	7	.588	29	19	4-1	0-1	149	156	78	9	4	49-3	58	4.17	100	.269	.328	0	ø	0	112	0	0	0.0
1980	Tex A	14	11	.560	34	32	6	0-0	204.1	230	104	13	3	56-1	91	3.92	99	.285	.333	0	ø	0*	120	-1	0	-0.2
1981	Tex A	10	6	.625	20	20	4-4	0-0	143.1	136	51	8	2	33-5	65	3.08	113	.252	.296	0	ø	0	119	8	0	0.9
1982	Tex A	7	11	.389	21	21	2	0-0	122.2	146	73	8	3	61-5	37	5.06	77	.307	.383	0	ø	0	83	-16	0	-2.0
	†Mil A	5	4	.556	10	10	1	0-0	63	57	37	4	1	32-1	36	5.00	77	.242	.332	0	ø	0	107	-8	0	-1.0
	Year	12	15	.444	31	31	3	0-0	185.2	203	110	12	4	93-6	73	5.04	77	.286	.366	0	ø	0	90	-23	0	-3.0
Total	11	124	105	.541	312	287	71-16	2-1	1996.1	2036	925	151	35	624-48	955	3.78	99	.266	.321	54-0-8	.093	-2	106	8	0	-0.5
Medina, Rafael	Rafael Eduardo; B2.15.1975 Panama City, Pan; BR/TR/6´3˝/(195–240); d4.2																									
1998	Fla N	2	6	.250	12	12	0	0-0	67.1	76	50	8	3	52-3	49	6.01	67	.289	.407	19-0-6	.053	-2	91	-15	90	-1.7
1999	Fla N	1	1	.500	20	0	0	0-0	23.1	20	15	3	1	20-2	16	5.79	76	.227	.376	0	ø	0	—	-3	0	-0.3
Total	2	3	7	.300	32	12	0	0-0	90.2	96	65	11	4	72-5	65	5.96	70	.274	.399	19-0-6	.053	-2	91	-18	90	-2.0
Medlinger, Irv	Irving John; B6.18.1927 Chicago IL; D9.3.1975 Wheeling IL; BL/TL/5´11˝/185; d4.20																									
1949	StL A	0	0	ø	3	0	0	0	4	11	13	1	0	3	4	27.00	17	.478	.538	0	ø	0	—	-9	0	-0.4
1951	StL A	0	0	ø	6	0	0	0	9.2	10	10	1	0	12	5	8.38	52	.270	.449	0	ø	0	—	-4	0	-0.2
Total	2	0	0	ø	9	0	0	0	13.2	21	23	2	0	15	9	13.83	32	.350	.480	0	ø	0	—	-13	0	-0.6
Medvin, Scott	Scott Howard; B9.16.1961 North Olmsted OH; BR/TR/6´1˝/190; d5.9; Col Baldwin–Wallace																									
1988	Pit N	3	0	1.000	17	0	0	0-0	27.2	23	16	1	1	9-2	16	4.88	71	.230	.297	3-0-1	.000	-0	—	-4	0	-0.5
1989	Pit N	0	1	.000	6	0	0	0-0	6.1	6	5	0	0	5-2	4	5.68	60	.240	.367	0	ø	0	—	-2	0	-0.3
1990	Sea A	0	1	.000	5	0	0	0-1	4.1	7	4	0	1	2-0	1	6.23	64	.368	.455	0	ø	0	—	-1	0	-0.2
Total	3	3	2	.600	28	0	0	0-1	38.1	36	25	1	2	16-4	21	5.17	68	.250	.331	3-0-1	.000	-0	—	-7	0	-1.0
Meegan, Pete	Peter James "Steady Pete"; B11.13.1863 San Francisco CA; D3.15.1905 San Francisco CA; ?/160; d8.12																									
1884	Ric AA	7	12	.368	22	22	22-1	0	179	177	130	7	14	29	106	4.32	77	.246	.288	75	.160	-2*	77	-18	—	-1.6
1885	Pit AA	7	8	.467	18	16	14-1	0	146	146	90	1	10	38	58	3.39	95	.247	.303	67	.194	-1*	95	-3	—	-0.4
Total	2	14	20	.412	40	38	36-2	0	325	323	220	8	24	67	164	3.90	84	.246	.295	142	.176	-3	85	-21	—	-2.0
Meehan, Bill	William Thomas; B9.4.1889 Osceola Mills PA; D10.8.1982 Douglas WY; BR/TR/5´9˝/155; d9.17																									
1915	Phi A	0	1	.000	1	1	0	0	4	7	5	0	0	3	4	11.25	26	.389	.476	1	1.000	0	150	-3	—	-0.4

MEEKER, ROY Charles Roy; B9.15.1900 Lead Mine MO; D3.25.1929 Orlando FL; BL/TL/5´9˝/175; d9.22

YEAR	TM LG	W	L	PCT	G	GS	CG-SHO	SV-BS	IP	H	R	HR	HB	BB-IB	SO	ERA	AERA	OAV	OOB	AB-HR-SH	AVG	PB	SUP	APR	DL	PW
1923	Phi A	3	0	1.000	5	2	2	0	25	24	10	0	0	13	12	3.60	114	.253	.343	9	.111	-1	171	2	—	0.2
1924	Phi A	5	12	.294	30	14	5-1	0	146	166	86	7	5	81	37	4.68	91	.288	.381	48-0-5	.229	-0	76	-5	—	-0.5
1926	Cin N	0	2	.000	7	1	1	0	21	24	18	1	0	9	5	6.43	57	.324	.398	6	.000	-1	23	-7	—	-0.6
Total	3	8	14	.364	42	17	8-1	0	192	214	114	8	5	103	54	4.73	89	.287	.377	63-0-5	.190	-2	85	-10	—	-0.9

MEEKIN, JOUETT George Jouett; B2.21.1867 New Albany IN; D12.14.1944 New Albany IN; BR/TR/6´1˝/180; d6.13

YEAR	TM LG	W	L	PCT	G	GS	CG-SHO	SV-BS	IP	H	R	HR	HB	BB-IB	SO	ERA	AERA	OAV	OOB	AB-HR-SH	AVG	PB	SUP	APR	DL	PW
1891	Lou AA	9	16	.360	28	25	24-2	0	221	223	154	2	6	106	141	4.28	85	.253	.338	94-1	.223	4*	88	-13	—	-0.9
1892	Lou N	7	10	.412	19	18	17	0	156.1	168	108	3	6	78	67	4.03	76	.264	.350	64	.078	-5*	101	-16	—	-1.8
	Was N	3	10	.231	14	14	13-1	0	112	112	91	2	4	48	58	3.46	94	.250	.328	45-2	.133	-1	97	-8	—	-0.8
	Year	10	20	.333	33	32	30-1	0	268.1	280	199	5	10	126	125	3.79	83	.258	.341	109-2	.101	-5	99	-22	—	-2.6
1893	Was N	10	15	.400	31	28	24-1	0	245	289	201	6	7	140	91	4.96	93	.285	.376	113-3	.257	3*	85	-10	—	-0.5
1894	†NY N	33	9	**.786**	53	49	41-1	2	418	414	240	13	11	176	137	3.70	142	.256	.333	174-5-1	.276	6	90	81	—	6.2
1895	NY N	16	11	.593	29	29	24-1	0	225.2	296	170	10	9	73	76	5.30	88	.312	.366	96-1-0	.292	4*	99	-9	—	-0.5
1896	NY N	26	14	.650	42	41	34	0	334.1	378	205	8	15	127	110	3.82	110	.283	.351	144-2-0	.299	12*	119	14	—	2.2
1897	NY N	20	11	.645	37	34	30-2	0	303.2	328	176	9	8	99	83	3.76	110	.273	.333	137	.299	6*	105	19	—	1.9
1898	NY N	16	18	.471	38	37	34-1	0	320	329	185	9	12	108	82	3.77	92	.264	.328	129	.209	1	102	-3	—	-0.5
1899	NY N	5	11	.313	18	18	16	0	148.1	169	103	4	8	70	30	4.37	86	.286	.369	58-1-0	.207	1	92	-11	—	-1.0
	Bos N	7	6	.538	13	13	12	0	108	111	52	0	2	23	23	2.83	147	.266	.307	41	.171	-1	67	12	—	1.0
	Year	12	17	.414	31	31	28	0	256.1	280	155	4	10	93	53	3.72	105	.278	.344	99-1-0	.192	-1	80	7	—	0.0
1900	Pit N	0	2	.000	2	2	1	0	13	20	21	1	1	8	3	6.92	53	.351	.439	4	.000	-1	38	-7	—	-0.8
Total	10	152	133	.533	324	308	270-9	2	2605.1	2837	1706	67	89	1056	901	4.07	103	.273	.345	1099-15-1	.243	29	97	49	—	4.5

MEELER, PHIL Charles Phillip; B7.3.1948 South Boston VA; BR/TR/6´5˝/215; d5.10

YEAR	TM LG	W	L	PCT	G	GS	CG-SHO	SV-BS	IP	H	R	HR	HB	BB-IB	SO	ERA	AERA	OAV	OOB	AB-HR-SH	AVG	PB	SUP	APR	DL	PW
1972	Det A	0	1	.000	7	0	0	0-0	8.1	10	6	0	0	7-1	5	4.32	73	.303	.405	2	.000	-0	—	-2	0	-0.2

MEERS, RUSS Russell Harlan "Babe"; B11.28.1918 Tilton IL; D11.16.1994 Lancaster PA; BL/TL/5´10˝/170; d9.28; Mil 1942–45

YEAR	TM LG	W	L	PCT	G	GS	CG-SHO	SV-BS	IP	H	R	HR	HB	BB-IB	SO	ERA	AERA	OAV	OOB	AB-HR-SH	AVG	PB	SUP	APR	DL	PW
1941	Chi N	0	1	.000	1	1	0	0	8	5	2	0	1	0	5	1.13	312	.172	.200	2	.000	-0	24	2	0	0.2
1946	Chi N	1	2	.333	7	2	0	0	11.1	10	6	0	0	10	2	3.18	104	.238	.385	1-0-1	1.000	0	155	0	0	0.0
1947	Chi N	2	0	1.000	35	1	0	0	64.1	61	34	5	2	38	28	4.48	88	.263	.371	14	.143	-1	179	-2	0	-0.2
Total	3	3	3	.500	43	4	0	0	83.2	76	42	5	3	48	35	3.98	96	.251	.359	17-0-1	.176	-0	120	0	0	0.0

MEINE, HEINIE Henry William "The Count of Luxemburg"; B5.1.1896 St.Louis MO; D3.18.1968 St.Louis MO; BR/TR/5´11˝/180; d8.16

YEAR	TM LG	W	L	PCT	G	GS	CG-SHO	SV-BS	IP	H	R	HR	HB	BB-IB	SO	ERA	AERA	OAV	OOB	AB-HR-SH	AVG	PB	SUP	APR	DL	PW
1922	StL A	0	0	ø	1	0	0	0	4	5	3	1	0	2	0	4.50	92	.313	.389	1	.000	-0	—	0	—	0.0
1929	Pit N	7	6	.538	22	13	7-1	1	108	120	62	4	7	34	19	4.50	106	.291	.355	39-0-3	.103	-2	107	4	—	0.1
1930	Pit N	6	8	.429	20	16	4	1	117.1	168	89	6	5	44	18	6.14	81	.346	.406	41-0-2	.122	-3	84	-13	—	-1.3
1931	Pit N	**19**	13	.594	36	**35**	22-3	0	**284**	278	121	8	7	87	58	2.98	129	.254	.313	96-0-7	.146	-2	90	25	—	2.4
1932	Pit N	12	9	.571	28	25	13-1	1	172.1	193	92	6	3	45	32	3.86	99	.278	.324	61-0-5	.164	-2	110	-1	—	-0.4
1933	Pit N	15	8	.652	32	29	12-2	0	207.1	227	99	10	2	50	50	3.65	91	.278	.321	75-0-6	.173	-1	117	-6	—	-0.9
1934	Pit N	7	6	.538	26	14	2	0	106.1	134	60	12	1	25	22	4.32	95	.306	.345	28-0-2	.107	-1	79	-3	—	-0.5
Total	7	66	50	.569	165	132	60-7	3	999.1	1125	526	47	25	287	199	3.95	101	.284	.337	341-0-25	.144	-12	98	6	—	-0.6

MEINKE, FRANK Frank Louis; B10.18.1863 Chicago IL; D11.8.1931 Chicago IL; BR/5´10.5˝/172; d5.1; s–Bob; ▲

YEAR	TM LG	W	L	PCT	G	GS	CG-SHO	SV-BS	IP	H	R	HR	HB	BB-IB	SO	ERA	AERA	OAV	OOB	AB-HR-SH	AVG	PB	SUP	APR	DL	PW
1884	Det N	8	23	.258	35	31	31-1	0	289	341	217	10	—	63	124	3.18	91	.275	.310	341-6	.164	-3*	72	-13	—	-1.4
1885	Det N	0	1	.000	1	1	0	0	5	13	12	0	—	4	0	3.60	79	.433	.500	3	.000	-0	20	-3	—	-0.4
Total	2	8	24	.250	36	32	31-1	0	294	354	229	10	—	67	124	3.18	91	.279	.315	344-6	.163	-3	70	-16	—	-1.8

MELENDEZ, JOSE Jose Luis (Garcia); B9.2.1965 Naguabo, PR; BR/TR/6´2˝/(175–190); d9.11

YEAR	TM LG	W	L	PCT	G	GS	CG-SHO	SV-BS	IP	H	R	HR	HB	BB-IB	SO	ERA	AERA	OAV	OOB	AB-HR-SH	AVG	PB	SUP	APR	DL	PW
1990	Sea A	0	0	ø	3	0	0	0-0	5.1	8	8	2	1	3-0	7	11.81	34	.333	.429	0	ø	0	—	-5	0	-0.2
1991	SD N	8	5	.615	31	9	0	3-1	93.2	77	35	11	1	24-3	60	3.27	117	.221	.269	20	.100	-0	84	7	0	0.8
1992	SD N	6	7	.462	56	3	0	0-2	89.1	82	32	9	3	20-7	82	2.92	123	.249	.295	5-0-1	.000	-0	59	6	0	0.8
1993	Bos A	2	1	.667	9	0	0	0-1	16	10	4	2	0	5-3	14	2.25	206	.179	.238	0	ø	0	—	4	147	0.7
1994	Bos A	0	1	.000	10	0	0	0-0	16.1	20	11	3	2	8-2	9	6.06	83	.323	.417	0	ø	0	—	-1	0	-0.1
Total	5	16	14	.533	109	12	0	3-4	220.2	197	90	27	7	60-15	172	3.47	112	.241	.294	25-0-1	.080	-1	76	11	147	2.0

MELTER, STEVE Stephen Blasius; B1.2.1886 Cherokee IA; D1.28.1962 Mishawaka IN; BR/TR/6´2˝/180; d6.27

YEAR	TM LG	W	L	PCT	G	GS	CG-SHO	SV-BS	IP	H	R	HR	HB	BB-IB	SO	ERA	AERA	OAV	OOB	AB-HR-SH	AVG	PB	SUP	APR	DL	PW
1909	StL N	0	1	.000	23	1	0	3	64.1	79	49	1	2	20	24	3.50	72	.322	.378	15	.133	-0	166	-12	—	-0.6

MELTON, CLIFF Clifford George "Mickey Mouse","Mountain Music"; B1.3.1912 Brevard NC; D7.28.1986 Baltimore MD; BL/TL/6´5.5˝/203; d4.25

YEAR	TM LG	W	L	PCT	G	GS	CG-SHO	SV-BS	IP	H	R	HR	HB	BB-IB	SO	ERA	AERA	OAV	OOB	AB-HR-SH	AVG	PB	SUP	APR	DL	PW
1937	†NY N	20	9	.690	46	27	14-2	**7**	248	216	90	9	6	55	142	2.61	149	.233	.280	82-0-10	.122	-5	105	33	—	3.4
1938	NY N	14	14	.500	36	31	10-1	0	243	266	126	19	1	61	101	3.89	97	.276	.319	80-0-13	.175	-1	110	-5	—	-0.5
1939	NY N	12	15	.444	41	23	9-2	5	207.1	214	94	7	4	65	95	3.56	110	.269	.327	66-0-8	.182	-1	101	8	—	1.0
1940	NY N	10	11	.476	37	21	4-1	2	166.2	185	103	9	3	68	91	4.91	79	.285	.355	54-0-6	.222	2	113	-18	—	-1.8
1941	NY N	8	11	.421	42	22	9-3	1	194.1	181	83	14	2	61	100	3.01	123	.246	.305	61-0-8	.115	-3	95	11	0	0.9
1942	NY N✱	11	5	.688	23	17	12-2	1	143.2	122	51	9	2	33	61	2.63	128	.229	.276	47-0-2	.234	2	112	11	0	1.6
1943	NY N	9	13	.409	34	28	6-2	0	186.1	184	85	7	3	69	55	3.19	108	.257	.325	54-0-3	.148	0	97	1	0	0.3
1944	NY N	2	2	.500	13	10	1	0	64.1	78	40	5	1	19	15	4.06	90	.294	.344	25-0-1	.120	-2	133	-5	0	-0.4
Total	8	86	80	.518	272	179	65-13	16	1453.2	1446	672	79	22	431	660	3.42	109	.259	.314	469-0-51	.164	-9	106	36	0	4.5

MELTON, RUBE Reuben Franklin; B2.27.1917 Cramerton NC; D9.11.1971 Greer SC; BR/TR/6´5˝/205; d4.17; Mil 1945–46; Col Campbell

YEAR	TM LG	W	L	PCT	G	GS	CG-SHO	SV-BS	IP	H	R	HR	HB	BB-IB	SO	ERA	AERA	OAV	OOB	AB-HR-SH	AVG	PB	SUP	APR	DL	PW
1941	Phi N	1	5	.167	25	5	2	0	83.2	81	48	7	0	47	57	4.73	78	.258	.355	19-0-2	.105	-1	55	-8	0	-0.7
1942	Phi N	9	20	.310	42	29	10-1	4	209.1	180	95	7	3	114	107	3.70	89	.234	.335	65-1-0	.123	-1	61	-7	0	-1.2
1943	Bro N	5	8	.385	30	17	4-2	0	119.1	106	62	3	5	79	63	3.92	86	.243	.365	38-0-5	.105	-2	126	-9	0	-1.2
1944	Bro N	9	13	.409	37	23	6-1	0	187.1	178	92	1	2	96	91	3.46	103	.254	.345	57-0-9	.123	-3	83	-1	0	-0.4
1946	Bro N	6	3	.667	24	12	3-2	1	99.2	72	27	3	3	52	44	1.99	170	.206	.314	28-0-3	.107	-2	101	15	0	1.2
1947	Bro N	0	1	.000	4	1	0	0	4.2	7	7	1	0	7	1	13.50	31	.350	.519	1	1.000	0	0	-4	0	-0.7
Total	6	30	50	.375	162	87	25-6	5	704	624	331	22	13	395	363	3.62	95	.241	.344	208-1-19	.120	-9	83	-14	0	-3.0

MENDOZA, MIKE Michael Joseph; B11.26.1955 Inglewood CA; BR/TR/6´5˝/215; [HouN73 5/116]; d9.7

YEAR	TM LG	W	L	PCT	G	GS	CG-SHO	SV-BS	IP	H	R	HR	HB	BB-IB	SO	ERA	AERA	OAV	OOB	AB-HR-SH	AVG	PB	SUP	APR	DL	PW
1979	Hou N	0	0	ø	1	0	0	0-0	1	0	0	0	0	0-0	0	0.00	ø	.000	.000	0	ø	0*	—	0	0	0.0

MENDOZA, RAMIRO Ramiro; B6.15.1972 Los Santos, Pan; BR/TR/6´2˝/(154–195); d5.25

YEAR	TM LG	W	L	PCT	G	GS	CG-SHO	SV-BS	IP	H	R	HR	HB	BB-IB	SO	ERA	AERA	OAV	OOB	AB-HR-SH	AVG	PB	SUP	APR	DL	PW
1996	NY A	4	5	.444	12	11	0	0-0	53	80	43	5	4	10-1	34	6.79	73	.343	.379	0	ø	0	75	-11	0	-1.4
1997	†NY A	8	6	.571	39	15	0	2-2	133.2	157	67	15	5	28-2	82	4.24	105	.292	.330	0	ø	0	128	4	0	0.5
1998	†NY A	10	2	.833	41	14	1-1	1-3	130.1	131	50	9	9	30-6	56	3.25	135	.264	.314	0-0-1	ø	0	141	17	0	1.5
1999	†NY A	9	9	.500	53	6	0	3-3	123.2	141	68	13	3	27-3	80	4.29	110	.284	.323	0	ø	0	82	5	0	0.7
2000	NY A	7	4	.636	14	9	1-1	0-1	65.2	66	32	9	4	20-1	30	4.25	112	.260	.321	0	ø	0	140	5	95	0.6
2001	†NY A	8	4	.667	56	2	0	6-2	100.2	89	44	9	2	23-3	70	3.75	118	.241	.287	2	.000	-0	136	9	9	1.0
2002	†NY A	8	4	.667	62	0	0	4-4	91.2	102	43	8	2	16-2	61	3.44	126	.275	.305	1	.000	-0	—	8	8	1.0
2003	Bos A	3	5	.375	37	5	0	0-1	66.2	98	51	10	5	20-4	36	6.75	69	.349	.397	0	ø	0	131	-13	53	-1.3
2004	†Bos A	2	1	.667	27	0	0	0-0	30.2	25	12	3	1	7-1	13	3.52	139	.225	.277	0	ø	0	—	5	98	0.4
2005	NY A	0	0	ø	1	0	0	0-0	1	2	2	1	0	0-0	1	18.00	24	.400	.400	0	ø	0	—	-1	0	-0.1
Total	10	59	40	.596	342	62	2-2	16-16	797	891	412	82	35	181-23	463	4.30	106	.283	.326	3-0-1	.000	-0	120	28	263	2.9

MENEFEE, JOCK John; B1.15.1868 Rowlesburg WV; D3.11.1953 Belle Vernon PA; BR/TR/6´0˝/165; d8.17; ▲

YEAR	TM LG	W	L	PCT	G	GS	CG-SHO	SV-BS	IP	H	R	HR	HB	BB-IB	SO	ERA	AERA	OAV	OOB	AB-HR-SH	AVG	PB	SUP	APR	DL	PW
1892	Pit N	0	0	ø	1	0	0	0	4	10	6	0	0	2	0	11.25	29	.455	.500	3	.000	-0*	—	-3	—	-0.1
1893	Lou N	8	7	.533	15	15	14-1	0	129.1	150	95	3	3	40	30	4.24	103	.281	.335	73	.274	4*	102	-3	—	0.1
1894	Lou N	8	17	.320	28	24	20-1	0	211.2	258	153	4	9	50	43	4.29	119	.297	.342	79-0-8	.165	-6*	77	19	—	1.3
	Pit N	5	8	.385	13	13	13	0	111.2	159	95	3	2	39	33	5.40	97	.331	.383	47-0-2	.255	0	92	-4	—	-0.2
	Year	13	25	.342	41	37	33-1	0	323.1	417	248	7	11	89	76	4.68	110	.309	.357	126-0-10	.198	-5	83	15	—	1.1
1895	Pit N	0	1	.000	2	1	0	0	1.2	2	8	0	1	7	0	16.20	28	.286	.667	0	ø	0	0	-4	—	-0.5
1898	NY N	0	1	.000	1	1	1	0	9.1	11	8	0	2	2	3	4.82	72	.289	.357	5	.000	-1	163	-2	—	-0.2
1900	Chi N	9	4	.692	16	13	11	0	117	140	74	1	10	35	30	3.85	94	.296	.357	46-0-2	.109	-3*	109	-1	—	-0.4
1901	Chi N	8	12	.400	21	20	19	0	182.1	201	102	4	6	34	55	3.80	85	.278	.315	152-0-7	.257	4*	92	-7	—	-0.2
1902	Chi N	12	10	.545	22	21	20-3	0	197.1	201	81	1	6	26	60	2.42	112	.264	.293	216-0-14	.231	3*	122	8	—	1.1

THE PITCHER REGISTER

YEAR	TM LG	W	L	PCT	G	GS	CG-SHO	SV-BS	IP	H	R	HR	HB	BB-IB	SO	ERA	AERA	OAV	OOB	AB-HR-SH	AVG	PB	SUP	APR	DL	PW
1903	Chi N	8	10	.444	20	17	13-1	0	147	157	85	3	6	38	39	3.00	105	.275	.327	64-0-2	.203	1*	99	-1	—	0.1
Total	9	58	70	.453	139	125	111-6	0	1111.1	1289	707	19	45	273	293	3.81	101	.288	.335	685-0-35	.222	2	96	2	—	1.0
Menendez, Tony	Antonio Gustavo (Remon); B2.20.1965 Havana, Cuba; BR/TR/6´2˝/(190–195); [ChiA84 1/20]; d6.22																									
1992	Cin N	1	0	1.000	3	0	0	0-0	4.2	1	1	1	0	0-0	5	1.93	187	.067	.067	0	ø	0	—	1	0	0.2
1993	Pit N	2	0	1.000	14	0	0	0-0	21	20	8	4	1	4-0	13	3.00	136	.256	.298	1	.000	-0	—	2	0	0.2
1994	SF N	0	1	.000	6	0	0	0-1	3.1	8	8	2	0	2-0	2	21.60	19	.471	.526	0	ø	0	—	-6	0	-1.1
Total	3	3	1	.750	23	0	0	0-1	29	29	17	7	1	6-0	20	4.97	81	.264	.305	1	.000	-0	—	-3	0	-0.7
Menhart, Paul	Paul Gerard; B3.25.1969 St.Louis MO; BR/TR/6´2˝/190; [TorA90 8/231]; d4.27; Col Western Carolina; [DL 1994 Tor A 131]																									
1995	Tor A	1	4	.200	21	9	1	0-0	78.2	72	49	9	6	47-4	50	4.92	97	.248	.360	0	ø	0	85	-2	0	-0.1
1996	Sea A	2	2	.500	11	6	0	0-0	42	55	36	9	2	25-0	18	7.29	68	.327	.421	0	ø	0	121	-11	47	-0.8
1997	SD N	2	3	.400	9	8	0	0-0	44	42	23	6	0	13-0	22	4.70	84	.256	.309	12-0-2	.000	-1	138	-3	0	-0.4
Total	3	5	9	.357	41	23	1	0-0	164.2	169	108	24	8	85-4	90	5.47	84	.272	.364	12-0-2	.000	-1	110	-16	178	-1.3
Meola, Mike	Emile Michael; B10.19.1905 New York NY; D9.1.1976 Fair Lawn NJ; BR/TR/5´11˝/175; d4.24																									
1933	Bos A	0	0	ø	3	0	0	0	2.1	5	6	0	0	2	1	23.14	19	.417	.500	0	ø	0	—	-4	—	-0.2
1936	StL A	0	1	.000	9	0	0	0	19.1	29	20	0	1	13	6	9.31	58	.358	.453	2	.500	1	—	-7	—	-0.2
	Bos A	0	2	.000	6	3	1	1	21.1	29	17	0	1	10	8	5.48	97	.326	.400	7	.143	-0	50	-1	—	-0.1
	Year	0	3	.000	15	3	1	1	40.2	58	37	0	2	23	14	7.30	73	.341	.426	9	.222	0	49	-8	—	-0.3
Total	2	0	3	.000	18	3	1	1	43	63	43	0	2	25	15	8.16	65	.346	.431	9	.222	0	50	-12	—	-0.5
Mercado, Hector	Hector Luis; B4.29.1974 Catano, PR; BL/TL/6´3˝/235; [HouN92 13/349]; d4.4; [DL 1998 NY N 181]																									
2000	Cin N	0	0	ø	12	0	0	0-0	14	12	7	2	0	8-0	13	4.50	106	.240	.339	1	.000	-0	—	1	0	0.0
2001	Cin N	3	2	.600	56	0	0	0-2	53	55	27	6	0	30-1	59	4.08	113	.266	.356	2	.000	-0	—	3	0	0.2
2002	Phi N	2	2	.500	31	3	0	0-0	39	32	21	2	3	25-2	40	4.62	83	.224	.349	4	.250	0	97	-3	0	-0.3
2003	Phi N	0	0	ø	13	0	0	1-1	18.2	18	12	5	1	12-0	15	5.79	69	.254	.360	2	.000	-0	—	-4	38	-0.2
Total	4	5	4	.556	112	3	0	1-3	124.2	117	67	15	4	75-3	127	4.55	94	.248	.353	9	.111	-0	97	-3	219	-0.3
Mercedes, Jose	Jose Miguel (Santana); B3.5.1971 Santa Cruz de El Seibo, D.R.; BR/TR/6´1˝/(180–208); d5.31																									
1994	Mil A	2	0	1.000	19	0	0	0-1	31	22	9	4	2	16-1	11	2.32	219	.216	.333	0	ø	0	—	9	57	0.5
1995	Mil A	0	1	.000	5	0	0	0-2	7.1	12	9	1	0	8-0	6	9.82	51	.375	.476	0	ø	0	—	-4	141	-0.4
1996	Mil A	0	2	.000	11	0	0	0-1	16.2	20	18	6	0	5-0	6	9.18	57	.294	.338	0	ø	0	—	-7	0	-0.7
1997	Mil A	7	10	.412	29	23	2-1	0-0	159	146	76	24	5	53-2	80	3.79	122	.248	.314	2	.000	-0	79	14	0	1.2
1998	Mil N	2	2	.500	7	5	0	0-0	32	42	25	5	1	9-1	11	6.75	64	.316	.359	11	.091	-0	93	-8	146	-0.9
2000	Bal A	14	7	.667	36	20	1	0-0	145.2	150	71	15	3	64-1	70	4.02	117	.270	.345	1	.000	-0	109	11	0	1.2
2001	Bal A	8	17	.320	33	31	2	0-0	184	219	125	20	10	63-3	123	5.82	74	.294	.354	5	.000	-0	89	-29	0	-3.4
2003	Mon N	0	0	ø	5	0	0	0-0	7.1	6	3	0	0	5-0	3	0.00	ø	.231	.355	0	ø	0	—	2	0	0.1
Total	8	33	39	.458	145	79	5-1	0-4	583	617	336	75	21	223-8	310	4.75	96	.274	.342	19	.053	-1	90	-12	344	-2.4
Mercer, Win	George Barclay; B6.20.1874 Chester WV; D1.12.1903 San Francisco CA; BR/TR/5´7˝/140; d4.21; ▲																									
1894	Was N	17	23	.425	50	39	30	3	339.1	445	285	9	14	126	72	3.85	137	.313	.375	165-2-1	.291	3*	95	41	—	3.8
1895	Was N	13	23	.361	44	38	32	2	313.1	432	281	17	18	96	85	4.42	109	.322	.376	201-1-5	.254	-0*	90	3	—	0.3
1896	Was N	25	18	.581	46	45	38-2	0	366.1	456	266	10	20	117	94	4.13	107	.302	.360	156-1-2	.244	0*	100	11	—	1.1
1897	Was N	21	20	.512	**47**	**43**	35-**3**	**3**	342	403	219	5	28	104	91	3.18	136	.291	.353	139-0-4	.317	8*	89	33	—	3.9
1898	Was N	12	18	.400	33	30	24	0	233.2	309	181	3	18	71	52	4.81	76	.316	.373	249-2-9	.321	8*	90	-30	—	-2.5
1899	Was N	7	14	.333	23	21	21	0	186	234	128	2	6	53	28	4.60	85	.307	.356	375-1-6	.299	5*	98	-13	—	-0.5
1900	NY N	13	17	.433	33	29	26-1	0	242.2	303	138	5	20	58	39	3.86	94	.305	.355	248-0-3	.294	7*	89	1	—	0.8
1901	Was A	9	13	.409	24	22	19-1	1	179.2	217	126	8	10	50	31	4.56	80	.295	.348	140-0-3	.300	6*	86	-16	—	-0.9
1902	Det A	15	18	.455	35	33	28-4	1	281.2	282	129	5	10	80	40	3.04	120	.261	.318	100-0-3	.180	-2	65	20	—	2.0
Total	9	132	164	.446	335	300	253-11	10	2484.2	3081	1753	64	144	755	532	3.98	107	.302	.358	1773-7-36	.285	35	90	50	—	8.0
Mercer, Jack	Harry Vernon; B3.10.1889 Zanesville OH; D6.25.1945 Dayton OH; d8.2																									
1910	Pit N	0	0	ø	1	0	0	0	1	0	0	0	0	2	1	0.00	ø	.000	.500	0	ø	0	—	0	—	0.0
Mercer, Mark	Mark Kenneth; B5.22.1954 Fort Bragg NC; BL/TL/6´5˝/220; [PitN73 S1/2]; d9.1; Col Hill (TX) JC																									
1981	Tex A	0	1	.000	7	0	0	2-1	7.2	7	4	1	0	7-0	8	4.70	74	.241	.389	0	ø	0	—	-1	0	-0.2
Mercker, Kent	Kent Franklin; B2.1.1968 Indianapolis IN; BL/TL/6´2˝/(175–205); [AtlN86 1/5]; d9.22																									
1989	Atl N	0	0	ø	2	1	0	0-0	4.1	8	6	0	0	6-0	4	12.46	29	.400	.538	1	.000	-0	121	-4	0	-0.2
1990	Atl N	4	7	.364	36	0	0	7-3	48.1	43	22	6	2	24-3	39	3.17	127	.236	.329	3	.000	-0	—	3	27	0.6
1991	†Atl N	5	3	.625	50	4	0	6-2	73.1	56	23	5	1	35-3	62	2.58	150	.211	.303	10	.100	-0	87	10	15	1.2
1992	†Atl N	3	2	.600	53	0	0	6-3	68.1	51	27	4	3	35-1	49	3.42	107	.207	.312	5	.000	-0	—	3	0	0.1
1993	†Atl N	3	1	.750	43	6	0	0-3	66	52	24	2	2	36-3	59	2.86	141	.212	.318	13	.000	-1	74	8	0	0.2
1994	Atl N	9	4	.692	20	17	2-1	0-0	112.1	90	46	16	0	45-3	111	3.45	125	.220	.295	37-0-3	.054	-2	96	11	0	0.9
1995	†Atl N	7	8	.467	29	26	0	0-0	143	140	73	16	3	61-2	102	4.15	104	.258	.332	48-0-6	.104	-2	109	2	0	0.1
1996	Bal A	3	6	.333	14	12	0	0-0	58	73	56	12	3	35-1	22	7.76	64	.307	.396	0	ø	0	98	-19	0	-2.3
	Cle A	1	0	1.000	10	0	0	0-0	11.2	10	4	1	0	3-1	7	3.09	158	.244	.283	0	ø	0	—	3	0	0.2
	Year	4	6	.400	24	12	0	0-0	69.2	83	60	13	3	38-2	29	6.98	71	.297	.380	0	ø	0	99	-17	0	-2.1
1997	Cin N	8	11	.421	28	25	0	0-0	144.2	135	65	16	2	62-6	75	3.92	109	.250	.327	45-0-4	.156	1*	67	7	15	1.0
1998	StL N	11	11	.500	30	29	0	0-0	161.2	199	99	11	3	53-4	72	5.07	83	.310	.361	54-1-5	.148	1*	121	-15	17	-1.7
1999	StL N	6	5	.545	25	18	0	0-0	103.2	125	73	16	2	51-3	64	5.12	90	.303	.380	28-0-4	.179	1*	117	-10	0	-0.8
	†Bos A	2	0	1.000	5	5	0	0-0	25.2	23	12	0	1	13-0	17	3.51	142	.235	.327	0	ø	0	82	4	16	0.3
2000	Ana A	1	3	.250	21	7	0	0-0	48.1	57	35	12	2	29-3	30	6.52	79	.300	.396	0	ø	0	104	-6	89	-0.4
2002	Col N	3	1	.750	58	0	0	0-3	44	55	33	12	2	22-2	37	6.14	77	.299	.380	1	.000	-0	—	-6	54	-0.5
2003	Cin N	0	2	.000	49	0	0	0-3	38.1	31	13	5	0	25-2	41	2.35	177	.225	.344	0	ø	0	—	7	15	0.4
	†Atl N	0	0	ø	18	0	0	1-1	17	15	3	1	0	7-2	7	1.06	397	.231	.301	1	.000	-0	—	6	0	0.2
	Year	0	2	.000	67	0	0	1-4	55.1	46	16	6	0	32-4	48	1.95	214	.227	.331	1	.000	-0	—	13	0	0.6
2004	Chi N	3	1	.750	71	0	0	0-3	53	39	15	4	3	27-2	51	2.55	174	.205	.309	2	.000	-0	—	11	19	0.7
2005	Cin N	3	1	.750	78	0	0	4-3	61.2	64	27	8	3	19-4	45	3.65	117	.270	.330	0	ø	0	—	4	0	0.3
2006	Cin N	1	1	.500	37	0	0	1-2	28.1	28	15	6	0	11-1	17	4.13	114	.259	.325	0	ø	0	—	1	83	0.1
Total	17	73	67	.521	677	150	2-1	25-26	1311.2	1294	671	153	32	599-46	911	4.16	104	.259	.340	248-1-22	.113	-5	102	20	350	-0.4
Meredith, Cla	Olise Cla; B6.4.1983 Richmond VA; BR/TR/6´0˝/180; [BosA04 6/185]; d5.8; Col Virginia Commonwealth																									
2005	Bos A	0	0	ø	3	0	0	0-0	2.1	6	7	1	1	4-0	0	27.00	17	.462	.611	0	ø	0	—	-5	0	-0.2
2006	†SD N	5	1	.833	45	0	0	0-2	50.2	30	6	3	2	6-3	37	1.07	389	.170	.207	0-0-1	ø	0	—	19	0	2.0
Total	2	5	1	.833	48	0	0	0-2	53	36	13	4	3	10-3	37	2.21	189	.190	.243	0-0-1	ø	0	—	14	0	1.8
Merena, Spike	John Joseph; B11.18.1909 Paterson NJ; D3.9.1977 Bridgeport CT; BL/TL/6´0˝/185; d9.16																									
1934	Bos A	1	2	.333	4	3	2-1	0	24.2	20	8	2	1	16	7	2.92	165	.222	.346	7-0-2	.143	-0	60	5	—	0.5
Meridith, Ron	Ronald Knox; B11.26.1956 San Pedro CA; BL/TL/6´0˝/(174–175); [HouN78 4/89]; d9.16; Col Oral Roberts																									
1984	Chi N	0	0	ø	3	0	0	0-0	5.1	6	5	1	0	2-1	4	3.38	116	.273	.320	0	ø	0	—	-1	0	0.0
1985	Chi N	3	2	.600	32	0	0	1-3	46.1	53	24	3	1	24-6	23	4.47	90	.301	.382	4	.250	0	—	-2	0	-0.1
1986	Tex A	1	0	1.000	5	0	0	0-0	3	2	1	0	0	1-1	2	3.00	144	.286	.333	0	ø	0	—	0	0	0.1
1987	Tex A	1	0	1.000	11	0	0	0-1	20.2	25	18	7	0	12-2	17	6.10	74	.298	.385	0	ø	0	—	-4	0	-0.2
Total	4	5	2	.714	51	0	0	1-4	75.1	86	48	11	1	39-10	46	4.78	87	.298	.377	4	.250	0	—	-7	0	-0.2
Merriman, Brett	Brett Alan; B7.15.1966 Jacksonville IL; BR/TR/6´2˝/(180–216); [CleA88 9/215]; d4.8; Col Grand Canyon																									
1993	Min A	1	1	.500	19	0	0	0-0	27	36	29	3	3	23-2	14	9.67	46	.343	.466	0	ø	0	—	-14	0	-0.9
1994	Min A	0	1	.000	15	0	0	0-1	17	18	13	0	4	14-0	10	6.35	78	.269	.414	0	ø	0	—	-3	0	-0.1
Total	2	1	2	.333	34	0	0	0-1	44	54	42	3	7	37-2	24	8.39	55	.314	.445	0	ø	0	—	-17	0	-1.0

YEAR	TM LG	W	L	PCT	G	GS	CG-SHO	SV-BS	IP	H	R	HR	HB	BB-IB	SO	ERA	AERA	OAV	OOB	AB-HR-SH	AVG	PB	SUP	APR	DL	PW
Merritt, George	George Washington; B4.14.1880 Paterson NJ; D2.21.1938 Memphis TN; TR/6´0˝/160; d9.6; ▲																									
1901	Pit N	3	0	1.000	3	3	3	0	24	28	18	0	2	5	5	4.88	67	.289	.337	11	.273	1*	260	-4	—	-0.3
1903	Pit N	0	0	ø	1	0	0	0	4	4	3	0	0	1	2	2.25	144	.267	.313	27-0-1	.148	0*	—	0	—	0.0
Total	2	3	0	1.000	4	3	3	0	28	32	21	0	2	6	7	4.50	73	.286	.333	38-0-1	.184	1	260	-4	—	-0.3
Merritt, Jim	James Joseph; B12.9.1943 Altadena CA; BL/TL/6´2˝/(175–180); d8.2																									
1965	†Min A	5	4	.556	16	9	1	2	76.2	68	29	11	0	20-1	61	3.17	112	.239	.287	22-0-1	.136	0	121	4	0	0.6
1966	Min A	7	14	.333	31	18	5-1	3	144	112	57	17	0	33-3	124	3.38	107	.212	.257	39-0-2	.103	-1	64	6	0	0.8
1967	Min A	13	7	.650	37	28	11-4	0	227.2	196	72	21	7	30-6	161	2.53	137	.230	.260	74-0-3	.135	0	100	23	0	2.0
1968	Min A	12	16	.429	38	34	11-1	1	238.1	207	102	21	7	52-1	181	3.25	95	.232	.277	71-0-4	.141	0	99	-4	0	-0.5
1969	Cin N	17	9	.654	42	36	8-1	0-0	251	269	127	33	5	61-8	144	4.37	86	.273	.316	77-1-15	.143	0	116	-11	0	-1.2
1970	†Cin N★	20	12	.625	35	35	12-1	0-0	234	248	114	21	1	53-12	136	4.08	99	.270	.310	83-3-6	.169	3	108	2	0	0.4
1971	Cin N	1	11	.083	28	11	0	0-0	107	115	55	14	3	31-8	38	4.37	77	.279	.332	29-0-2	.138	0*	62	-12	0	-1.3
1972	Cin N	1	0	1.000	4	1	0	0-0	8	13	4	1	0	2-1	4	4.50	72	.361	.395	2	.000	-0	55	-1	0	-0.1
1973	Tex A	5	13	.278	35	19	8-1	1-0	160	191	79	18	1	34-3	65	4.05	93	.296	.327	0	ø	0	91	-4	0	-0.4
1974	Tex A	0	0	ø	26	1	0	0-0	32.2	46	17	3	0	6-2	18	4.13	87	.329	.349	0	ø	0	74	-2	21	-0.1
1975	Tex A	0	0	ø	5	0	0	0-0	3.2	3	1	0	1	0-0	0	0.00	ø	.214	.267	0	ø	0	—	1	31	0.0
Total	11	81	86	.485	297	192	56-9	7-0	1483	1468	657	160	25	322-45	932	3.65	98	.257	.297	397-4-33	.141	3	99	2	52	0.2
Merritt, Lloyd	Lloyd Wesley; B4.8.1933 St.Louis MO; BR/TR/6´0˝/184; d4.22; Col Washington–St. Louis																									
1957	StL N	1	2	.333	44	0	0	7	65.1	60	29	7	4	28-5	35	3.31	120	.251	.337	7	.000	-0	—	4	0	0.2
Mertz, Jim	James Verlin; B8.10.1916 Lima OH; D2.4.2003 Waycross GA; BR/TR/5´10.5˝/170; d5.1; Mil 1944–46																									
1943	Was A	5	7	.417	33	10	2	3	116.2	109	65	7	0	58	53	4.63	69	.251	.339	38-0-3	.184	0	166	-16	0	-1.6
Mesa, Jose	Jose Ramon Nova (b Jose Ramon Nova (Mesa)); B5.22.1966 Pueblo Viejo, D.R.; BR/TR/6´3˝/(170–235); d9.10																									
1987	Bal A	1	3	.250	6	5	0	0-0	31.1	38	23	7	0	15-0	17	6.03	74	.297	.371	0	ø	0	74	-6	0	-0.6
1990	Bal A	3	2	.600	7	7	0	0-0	46.2	37	20	2	1	27-2	24	3.86	99	.218	.325	0	ø	0	106	1	0	0.0
1991	Bal A	6	11	.353	23	23	2-1	0-0	123.2	151	86	11	3	62-2	64	5.97	67	.307	.385	0	ø	0*	112	-27	15	-3.1
1992	Bal A	3	8	.273	13	12	0	0-0	67.2	77	41	9	2	27-1	22	5.19	78	.287	.353	0	ø	0	82	-8	0	-1.1
	Cle A	4	4	.500	15	15	1-1	0-0	93	92	45	5	2	43-0	40	4.16	95	.262	.344	0	ø	0	117	-1	0	-0.1
	Year	7	12	.368	28	27	1-1	0-0	160.2	169	86	14	4	70-1	62	4.59	87	.273	.348	0	ø	0	102	-7	0	-1.2
1993	Cle A	10	12	.455	34	33	3	0-0	208.2	232	122	21	7	62-2	118	4.92	89	.286	.339	0	ø	0	102	-10	0	-1.0
1994	Cle A	7	5	.583	51	0	0	2-4	73	71	33	3	3	26-7	63	3.82	124	.254	.321	0	ø	0	—	9	0	1.2
1995	†Cle A★	3	0	1.000	62	0	0	**46**-2	64	49	9	3	0	17-2	58	1.13	420	.216	.268	0	ø	0	—	**25**	0	4.3
1996	†Cle A☆	2	7	.222	69	0	0	39-5	72.1	69	32	6	3	28-4	64	3.73	131	.257	.331	0	ø	0	—	10	0	1.8
1997	†Cle A	4	4	.500	66	0	0	16-5	82.1	83	28	7	3	28-3	69	2.40	196	.259	.322	0	ø	0	—	19	0	2.2
1998	Cle A	3	4	.429	44	0	0	1-2	54	61	36	7	4	20-3	35	5.17	93	.282	.351	0	ø	0	—	-3	0	-0.4
	SF N	5	3	.625	32	0	0	0-1	30.2	30	14	1	0	18-2	28	3.52	114	.256	.356	0	ø	0	—	1	0	0.2
1999	Sea A	3	6	.333	68	0	0	33-5	68.2	84	42	11	4	40-4	42	4.98	96	.305	.396	0	ø	0	—	-2	0	-0.3
2000	†Sea A	4	6	.400	66	0	0	1-2	80.2	89	48	11	5	41-0	84	5.36	90	.280	.365	0	ø	0	—	-3	0	-0.3
2001	Phi N	3	3	.500	71	0	0	42-4	69.1	65	26	4	2	20-2	59	2.34	176	.246	.301	0	ø	0	—	11	0	2.1
2002	Phi N	4	6	.400	74	0	0	45-9	75.2	65	26	5	4	39-7	64	2.97	129	.231	.332	0	ø	0	—	8	0	1.7
2003	Phi N	5	7	.417	61	0	0	24-4	58	71	44	7	1	31-2	45	6.52	61	.296	.379	0	ø	0	—	-17	0	-3.3
2004	Pit N	5	2	.714	70	0	0	43-5	69.1	78	26	6	1	20-3	37	3.25	133	.291	.340	0	ø	0	—	9	0	1.7
2005	Pit N	2	8	.200	55	0	0	27-7	56.2	61	30	7	3	26-3	37	4.76	89	.285	.361	1-0-1	.000	-0	—	-2	0	-0.4
2006	Col N	1	5	.167	79	0	0	1-7	72.1	74	32	9	5	36-6	39	3.86	124	.273	.366	1	.000	-0	—	8	0	0.6
Total	18	78	106	.424	966	95	6-2	320-62	1498	1577	763	142	53	626-55	1009	4.27	102	.273	.346	2-0-1	.000	0	98	22	15	5.2
Messenger, Bud	Andrew Warren; B2.1.1898 Grand Blanc MI; D11.4.1971 Lansing MI; BR/TR/6´0˝/175; d7.31																									
1924	Cle A	2	0	1.000	5	2	1	0	25	28	13	4	0	14	4	4.32	99	.283	.372	8-0-2	.125	-0	237	1	—	0.0
Messenger, Randy	Randall Jerome; B8.13.1981 Reno NV; BR/TR/6´6˝/245; [FlaN99 11/326]; d6.22																									
2005	Fla N	0	0	ø	29	0	0	0-0	37	39	22	5	0	30-7	29	5.35	75	.273	.392	3	.333	1	—	-5	0	-0.2
2006	Fla N	2	7	.222	59	0	0	0-1	60.1	72	42	8	1	24-2	45	5.67	76	.296	.359	2	.000	-0	—	-10	0	-1.3
Total	2	2	7	.222	88	0	0	0-1	97.1	111	64	13	1	54-9	74	5.55	75	.288	.372	5	.200	0	—	-15	0	-1.5
Messersmith, Andy	John Alexander; B8.6.1945 Toms River NJ; BR/TR/6´1˝/(195–200); [AnaA66 S1/12]; d7.4; Col California																									
1968	Cal A	4	2	.667	28	5	2-1	4	81.1	44	21	3	1	35-4	74	2.21	132	.157	.252	20-0-4	.100	-1*	78	7	0	0.6
1969	Cal A	16	11	.593	40	33	10-2	2-0	250	169	81	17	5	100-7	211	2.52	139	**.190**	.274	77-0-6	.156	2*	101	28	0	3.2
1970	Cal A	11	10	.524	37	26	6-1	5-0	194.2	144	75	21	6	78-6	162	3.01	121	**.205**	.289	70-1-5	.157	0*	91	13	0	1.4
1971	Cal A☆	20	13	.606	38	38	14-4	0-0	276.2	224	112	16	7	121-6	179	2.99	109	.218	.303	93-2-6	.172	4*	103	5	0	1.0
1972	Cal A	8	11	.421	25	21	10-3	2-0	169.2	125	56	5	2	68-8	142	2.81	104	.207	.288	53-0-2	.189	2*	75	4	49	0.8
1973	LA N	14	10	.583	33	33	10-3	0-0	249.2	196	90	24	6	77-3	177	2.70	129	.214	.278	89-0-5	.169	2*	116	21	0	2.1
1974	†LA N★	**20**	6	**.769**	39	39	13-3	0-0	292.1	227	93	24	3	94-0	221	2.59	133	.212	**.277**	96-1-4	.240	9	118	31	0	3.8
1975	LA N☆	19	14	.576	42	**40**	**19-7**	1-0	**321.2**	244	92	22	5	96-2	213	2.29	149	**.213**	.275	108-0-5	.157	2*	93	**43**	0	4.5
1976	Atl N✳	11	11	.500	29	28	12-3	1-0	207.1	166	83	14	2	74-1	135	3.04	125	.219	.287	67-0-6	.179	0	85	15	0	1.6
1977	Atl N	5	4	.556	16	16	1	0-0	102.1	101	54	12	2	39-5	69	4.40	101	.256	.323	34-1-2	.118	-0	96	2	59	0.2
1978	NY A	0	3	.000	6	5	0	0-0	22.1	24	21	7	1	15-0	16	5.64	65	.267	.377	0	ø	0	93	-7	119	-0.9
1979	LA N	2	4	.333	11	11	1	0-0	62.1	55	34	9	0	34-2	26	4.91	74	.244	.342	22-0-1	.091	-1	125	-7	86	-0.7
Total	12	130	99	.568	344	295	98-27	15-0	2230.1	1719	812	174	40	831-44	1625	2.86	121	.212	.287	729-5-46	.170	20	101	155	313	17.6
Metcalf, Tom	Thomas John; B7.16.1940 Amherst WI; BR/TR/6´2.5˝/175; d8.4; Col Northwestern																									
1963	NY A	1	0	1.000	8	0	0	0	13	12	4	1	0	3-1	3	2.77	127	.250	.294	0	ø	0	—	1	0	0.1
Metivier, Dewey	George Dewey; B5.6.1898 Cambridge MA; D3.2.1947 Cambridge MA; BL/TR/5´11˝/175; d9.15																									
1922	Cle A	2	0	1.000	2	2	2	0	18	18	9	1	1	3	1	4.50	89	.265	.306	6	.167	-0	138	0	—	0.0
1923	Cle A	4	2	.667	26	5	1	1	73.1	111	66	1	6	38	9	6.50	61	.368	.448	20	.150	-0	159	-21	—	-1.5
1924	Cle A	1	5	.167	26	6	1	3	76.1	110	50	3	0	34	14	5.31	81	.358	.422	24	.125	-2	89	-6	—	-0.7
Total	3	7	7	.500	54	13	4	4	167.2	239	125	5	7	75	24	5.74	72	.353	.423	50	.140	-2	122	-27	—	-2.2
Metzger, Butch	Clarence Edward; B5.23.1952 Lafayette IN; BR/TR/6´1˝/185; [SFN70 2/41]; d9.8																									
1974	SF N	1	0	1.000	10	0	0	0-0	12.2	11	5	0	0	12-7	5	3.55	107	.239	.397	0	ø	0	—	1	0	0.0
1975	SD N	1	0	1.000	4	0	0	0-0	4.2	6	4	1	0	4-1	6	7.71	45	.316	.417	0	ø	0	—	-2	0	-0.4
1976	SD N	11	4	.733	77	0	0	16-8	123.1	119	44	5	3	52-14	89	2.92	113	.258	.335	8-0-2	.000	-0	—	6	0	0.9
1977	SD N	0	0	ø	17	1	0	0-1	22.2	27	16	5	1	12-4	6	5.56	64	.307	.388	3	.000	-0	273	-5	0	-0.3
	StL N	4	2	.667	58	0	0	7-3	92.2	78	36	8	1	38-2	48	3.11	126	.228	.305	4-0-2	.000	-0	—	8	0	0.5
	Year	4	2	.667	75	1	0	7-4	115.1	105	52	13	2	50-6	54	3.59	107	.244	.323	7-0-2	.000	-1	255	3	0	0.2
1978	NY N	1	3	.250	25	0	0	0-0	37.1	48	28	4	1	22-7	21	6.51	54	.324	.406	0	ø	0	—	-12	0	-1.2
Total	5	18	9	.667	191	1	0	23-12	293.1	289	133	23	6	140-35	175	3.74	95	.262	.344	15-0-4	.000	-1	274	-4	0	-0.5
Meyer, Brian	Brian Scott; B1.29.1963 Camden NJ; BR/TR/6´0˝/190; [HouN86 16/406]; d9.3; Col Rollins																									
1988	Hou N	0	0	ø	8	0	0	0-0	12.1	9	2	2	0	4-0	10	1.46	228	.225	.295	0	ø	0	—	3	0	0.2
1989	Hou N	0	1	.000	12	0	0	1-0	18	16	13	0	1	13-3	13	4.50	76	.239	.366	0-0-1	ø	0	—	-4	0	-0.2
1990	Hou N	0	4	.000	14	0	0	1-0	20.1	16	7	3	0	6-0	6	2.21	169	.211	.268	1	.000	-0	—	3	0	0.6
Total	3	0	5	.000	34	0	0	2-0	50.2	41	22	5	1	23-3	29	2.84	124	.224	.313	1-0-1	.000	-0	—	2	0	0.6
Meyer, Dan	Daniel Livingston; B7.3.1981 Woodbury NJ; BR/TL/6´3˝/210; [AtlN02 1/34]; d9.14; Col James Madison																									
2004	Atl N	0	0	ø	2	0	0	0-0	2	2	0	0	0	1-1	1	0.00	ø	.286	.375	0	ø	0	—	1	0	0.0
Meyer, Jack	John Robert; B3.23.1932 Philadelphia PA; D3.9.1967 Philadelphia PA; BR/TR/6´1˝/(175–185); d4.16; Col Wake Forest																									
1955	Phi N	6	11	.353	50	5	0	**16**	110.1	75	50	14	3	66-6	97	3.43	116	.190	.310	20-0-1	.100	0	67	6	0	0.9
1956	Phi N	7	11	.389	41	7	2	2	96	86	49	8	4	51-11	66	4.41	84	.242	.343	20-1-2	.200	1	51	-5	0	-0.8
1957	Phi N	0	2	.000	19	2	0	0	37.2	44	30	6	1	28-2	34	5.73	66	.297	.408	6-0-1	.167	0	139	-10	0	-0.4
1958	Phi N	3	6	.333	37	5	1	2	90.1	77	38	8	1	33-3	87	3.59	110	.232	.301	18-0-1	.278	1	136	5	0	0.5
1959	Phi N	5	3	.625	47	1	1	1	93.2	76	43	9	1	53-2	71	3.36	122	.222	.326	14	.071	-1	0	6	0	0.4

YEAR	TM LG	W	L	PCT	G	GS	CG-SHO	SV-BS	IP	H	R	HR	HB	BB-IB	SO	ERA	AERA	OAV	OOB	AB-HR-SH	AVG	PB	SUP	APR	DL	PW
1960	Phi N	3	1	.750	7	4	0	0	25	25	13	2	0	11-0	18	4.32	90	.272	.336	8-0-1	.125	-0	97	-1	93	-0.1
1961	Phi N	0	0	ø	1	0	0	0	2	2	2	1	0	2-0	2	9.00	45	.286	.444	0	ø	0	—	-1	0	-0.1
Total	7	24	34	.414	202	24	4	21	455	385	225	48	10	244-24	375	3.92	100	.230	.330	86-1-6	.163	1	84	0	93	0.4

MEYER, BOB Robert Bernard; B8.4.1939 Toledo OH; BR/TL/6´2˝/(185–195); d4.20; Col Toledo

YEAR	TM LG	W	L	PCT	G	GS	CG-SHO	SV-BS	IP	H	R	HR	HB	BB-IB	SO	ERA	AERA	OAV	OOB	AB-HR-SH	AVG	PB	SUP	APR	DL	PW
1964	NY A	0	3	.000	7	1	0	0	18.1	16	12	1	0	12-0	12	4.91	74	.235	.350	4	.000	-0	0	-3	0	-0.5
	LA A	1	1	.500	6	5	0	0	18	25	10	2	1	13-0	13	5.00	66	.333	.438	5-0-2	.000	-1	162	-3	0	-0.4
	KC A	1	4	.200	9	7	2	0	42	37	23	2	0	33-0	30	3.86	99	.248	.378	12-0-1	.000	-1*	77	-2	0	-0.3
	Year	2	8	.200	22	13	2	0	78.1	78	45	5	1	58-0	55	4.37	84	.267	.387	21-0-3	.000	-2	99	-7	0	-1.2
1969	Sea A	0	3	.000	6	5	1	0-0	32.2	30	14	4	2	10-0	17	3.31	110	.252	.316	11	.091	-1	73	1	0	0.0
1970	Mil A	0	1	.000	10	0	0	0-0	18.1	24	13	2	0	12-0	20	6.38	59	.329	.424	3-0-2	.333	0	—	-5	108	-0.2
Total	3	2	12	.143	38	18	3	0-0	129.1	132	72	11	3	80-0	92	4.38	84	.273	.376	35-0-5	.057	-3	92	-12	108	-1.4

MEYER, RUSS Russell Charles “Rowdy”,“The Mad Monk”; B10.25.1923 Peru IL; D11.16.1998 Oglesby IL; BB/TR/6´1˝/(175–185); d9.13; C1

YEAR	TM LG	W	L	PCT	G	GS	CG-SHO	SV-BS	IP	H	R	HR	HB	BB-IB	SO	ERA	AERA	OAV	OOB	AB-HR-SH	AVG	PB	SUP	APR	DL	PW
1946	Chi N	0	0	ø	4	1	0	1	17	21	7	2	0	10	10	3.18	104	.309	.397	5	.200	0	129	0	0	0.0
1947	Chi N	3	2	.600	23	2	1	0	45	43	17	4	1	14	22	3.40	116	.257	.319	12	.250	0	67	4	62	0.4
1948	Chi N	10	10	.500	29	26	8-3	0	164.2	157	75	8	1	77	89	3.66	107	.254	.338	56-0-7	.107	-3	107	6	0	0.3
1949	Phi N	17	8	.680	37	28	14-2	1	213	199	84	14	1	70	78	3.08	128	.250	.311	70-0-6	.143	-1	93	19	0	1.9
1950	†Phi N	9	11	.450	32	25	3	1	159.2	193	108	21	2	67	74	5.30	76	.304	.373	50-0-7	.140	-1	99	-23	0	-2.5
1951	Phi N	8	9	.471	28	24	7-2	0	168	172	69	13	2	55	65	3.48	111	.263	.322	48-0-13	.104	-2	112	8	0	0.4
1952	Phi N	13	14	.481	37	32	14-1	1	232.1	235	99	10	2	65	92	3.14	116	.260	.311	79-1-5	.089	-2	110	12	0	0.9
1953	†Bro N	15	5	.750	34	32	10-2	0	191.1	201	109	25	1	63	106	4.56	93	.269	.327	75-0-6	.147	-2	143	-8	0	-1.0
1954	Bro N	11	6	.647	36	28	6-2	0	180.1	193	89	17	2	49	70	3.99	102	.275	.322	47-0-14	.043	-3	122	2	0	-0.3
1955	†Bro N	6	2	.750	18	11	2-1	0	73	86	46	8	0	31-6	26	5.42	75	.300	.364	27-0-2	.037	-3	171	-9	30	-1.1
1956	Chi N	1	6	.143	20	9	0	0	57	71	41	11	2	26-4	28	6.32	60	.313	.384	12-0-2	.083	-1	96	-14	0	-1.5
	Cin N	0	0	ø	1	0	0	0	1	1	0	0	0	0-0	1	0.00	ø	.250	.250	0	ø	0	—	0	0	0.0
	Year	1	6	.143	21	9	0	0	58	72	41	11	2	26-4	29	6.21	61	.312	.382	12-0-2	.083	-1	96	-14	0	-1.5
1957	Bos A	0	0	ø	2	1	0	0	5	10	5	0	0	3-0	1	5.40	74	.417	.464	1	1.000	0	90	-1	0	0.0
1959	KC A	1	0	1.000	18	0	0	1	24	24	12	3	1	11-0	10	4.50	89	.261	.340	2	.000	-0	—	0	0	-0.1
Total	13	94	73	.563	319	219	65-13	5	1531.1	1606	761	136	15	541-10	672	3.99	99	.271	.333	484-1-62	.114	-18	116	-4	92	-2.6

MEYERLE, LEVI Levi Samuel “Long Levi”; B7.1845 Philadelphia PA; D11.4.1921 Philadelphia PA; BR/TR/6´1˝/177; d5.20; ▲

YEAR	TM LG	W	L	PCT	G	GS	CG-SHO	SV-BS	IP	H	R	HR	HB	BB-IB	SO	ERA	AERA	OAV	OOB	AB-HR-SH	AVG	PB	SUP	APR	DL	PW
1871	Ath NA	0	0	ø	1	0	0	0	1	1	1	0	—	2	0	9.00	45	.250	.500	130-4	.492	1*	—	0	—	0.0
1876	Phi N	0	2	.000	2	2	2	0	18	28	23	0	—	1	0	5.00	48	.337	.345	256	.340	1*	64	-4	—	-0.3

MIADICH, BART John Barton; B2.3.1976 Torrance CA; BR/TR/6´4˝/205; d9.2

YEAR	TM LG	W	L	PCT	G	GS	CG-SHO	SV-BS	IP	H	R	HR	HB	BB-IB	SO	ERA	AERA	OAV	OOB	AB-HR-SH	AVG	PB	SUP	APR	DL	PW
2001	Ana A	0	0	ø	11	0	0	0-0	10	6	5	2	0	8-0	11	4.50	103	.182	.341	0	ø	0	—	0	0	0.0
2003	Ana A	0	0	ø	1	0	0	0-0	2	5	4	0	1	1-0	3	18.00	24	.500	.583	0	ø	0	—	-3	0	-0.1
Total	2	0	0	ø	12	0	0	0-0	12	11	9	2	1	9-0	14	6.75	68	.256	.396	0	ø	0	—	-3	0	-0.1

MICELI, DAN Daniel; B9.9.1970 Newark NJ; BR/TR/6´0˝/(205–225); d9.9

YEAR	TM LG	W	L	PCT	G	GS	CG-SHO	SV-BS	IP	H	R	HR	HB	BB-IB	SO	ERA	AERA	OAV	OOB	AB-HR-SH	AVG	PB	SUP	APR	DL	PW
1993	Pit N	0	0	ø	9	0	0	0-0	5.1	6	3	0	0	3-0	4	5.06	81	.273	.360	0	ø	0	—	0	0	0.0
1994	Pit N	2	1	.667	28	0	0	2-1	27.1	28	19	5	2	11-2	27	5.93	74	.267	.342	3	.000	-0	—	-4	0	-0.5
1995	Pit N	4	4	.500	58	0	0	21-6	58	61	30	7	4	28-5	56	4.66	93	.270	.355	1	.000	-0	—	-1	0	-0.1
1996	Pit N	2	10	.167	44	9	0	1-0	85.2	99	65	15	3	45-5	66	5.78	76	.291	.372	13	.000	-1	87	-14	0	-2.0
1997	Det A	3	2	.600	71	0	0	3-5	82.2	77	49	13	1	38-4	79	5.01	92	.248	.330	0	ø	0	—	-3	0	-0.2
1998	†SD N	10	5	.667	67	0	0	2-6	72.2	64	28	6	1	27-4	70	3.22	123	.238	.308	1	1.000	1	—	7	0	1.2
1999	SD N	4	5	.444	66	0	0	2-2	68.2	67	39	7	2	36-5	59	4.46	96	.266	.360	1	.000	-0	—	-2	0	-0.3
2000	Fla N	6	4	.600	45	0	0	0-3	48.2	45	23	4	1	18-2	40	4.25	103	.242	.311	0	ø	0	—	2	49	0.3
2001	Fla N	0	5	.000	29	0	0	0-3	24.2	29	21	5	0	11-2	31	6.93	60	.287	.354	0	ø	0	—	-8	0	-1.4
	Col N	2	0	1.000	22	0	0	1-0	20.1	18	8	2	0	5-0	17	2.21	241	.231	.274	0	ø	0	—	5	0	0.4
	Year	2	5	.286	51	0	0	1-3	45	47	29	7	0	16-2	48	4.80	98	.263	.320	0	ø	0	—	-2	0	-1.0
2002	Tex A	0	2	.000	9	0	0	0-1	8.1	13	8	1	0	3-0	5	8.64	55	.333	.381	0	ø	0	—	-3	0	-0.6
2003	Col N	0	2	.000	14	0	0	0-0	20.2	24	13	7	1	9-1	18	5.66	86	.286	.362	0	ø	0	—	-1	0	-0.1
	Cle A	1	1	.500	13	0	0	0-1	15	9	4	1	0	6-1	19	1.20	369	.164	.246	0	ø	0	—	5	0	0.6
	NY A	0	0	ø	7	0	0	1-0	4.2	4	3	2	0	3-0	1	5.79	76	.211	.318	0	ø	0	—	-1	0	0.0
	Year	1	1	.500	20	0	0	1-1	19.2	13	7	3	0	9-1	20	2.29	193	.176	.265	0	ø	0	—	4	0	0.6
	Hou N	1	1	.500	23	0	0	0-0	30	22	7	3	1	7-1	20	2.10	210	.208	.263	1	.000	-0	—	8	0	0.4
2004	†Hou N	6	6	.500	74	0	0	2-6	77.2	74	34	10	2	27-12	83	3.59	122	.247	.311	2	.500	0	—	6	18	0.9
2005	Col N	1	2	.333	19	0	0	0-2	18.1	19	12	1	1	13-0	19	5.89	79	.271	.393	0	ø	0	—	-2	59	-0.3
2006	TB A	1	2	.333	33	0	0	4-3	32	25	17	4	1	20-3	18	3.94	118	.217	.331	0	ø	0	—	2	94	0.2
Total	14	43	52	.453	631	9	0	39-39	700.2	684	383	93	20	310-47	632	4.48	99	.256	.334	22	.091	-1	87	-4	220	-1.5

MICHAELS, JOHN John Joseph; B7.10.1907 Bridgeport CT; D11.18.1996 Sebring FL; BL/TL/5´10.5˝/154; d4.16; gs–Jason

YEAR	TM LG	W	L	PCT	G	GS	CG-SHO	SV-BS	IP	H	R	HR	HB	BB-IB	SO	ERA	AERA	OAV	OOB	AB-HR-SH	AVG	PB	SUP	APR	DL	PW
1932	Bos A	1	6	.143	28	8	2	0	80.2	101	59	4	3	27	16	5.13	88	.304	.362	21	.143	-1*	71	-7	—	-0.6

MICHAELSON, JOHN John August “Mike”; B8.12.1893 Tivalkoski, Finland; D4.16.1968 Woodruff WI; BR/TR/5´9˝/165; d8.28

YEAR	TM LG	W	L	PCT	G	GS	CG-SHO	SV-BS	IP	H	R	HR	HB	BB-IB	SO	ERA	AERA	OAV	OOB	AB-HR-SH	AVG	PB	SUP	APR	DL	PW
1921	Chi A	0	0	ø	2	0	0	0	2.2	4	3	0	0	1	1	10.13	42	.400	.455	0	ø	0	—	-2	—	-0.1

MICHALAK, CHRIS Christian Matthew; B1.4.1971 Joliet IL; BL/TL/6´2˝/195; [OakA93 12/349]; d8.22; Col Notre Dame

YEAR	TM LG	W	L	PCT	G	GS	CG-SHO	SV-BS	IP	H	R	HR	HB	BB-IB	SO	ERA	AERA	OAV	OOB	AB-HR-SH	AVG	PB	SUP	APR	DL	PW
1998	Ari N	0	0	ø	5	0	0	0-0	5.1	9	7	1	0	4-0	5	11.81	36	.375	.448	0	ø	0	—	-4	0	-0.2
2001	Tor A	6	7	.462	24	18	0	0-0	115	133	66	14	12	49-5	57	4.62	99	.296	.377	3-0-2	.333	1	84	-1	0	0.1
	Tex A	2	2	.500	11	0	0	1-1	21.2	24	8	5	1	6-0	10	3.32	144	.279	.333	0	ø	0	—	3	0	0.6
	Year	8	9	.471	35	18	0	1-1	136.2	157	74	19	13	55-5	67	4.41	105	.293	.371	3-0-2	.333	1	84	3	0	0.7
2002	Tex A	0	2	.000	13	0	0	0-0	14.1	20	7	1	1	10-2	5	4.40	109	.339	.437	0	ø	0	—	1	0	0.1
2006	Cin N	2	4	.333	8	6	0	0-0	35	42	21	6	3	16-2	10	4.89	97	.304	.389	8-0-2	.250	1	55	-1	0	0.0
Total	4	10	15	.400	61	24	0	1-1	191.1	228	109	27	17	85-9	87	4.70	99	.302	.382	11-0-4	.273	2	76	-2	0	0.6

MICKENS, GLENN Glenn Roger; B7.26.1930 Wilmar CA; BR/TR/6´0˝/175; d7.19; Col UCLA

YEAR	TM LG	W	L	PCT	G	GS	CG-SHO	SV-BS	IP	H	R	HR	HB	BB-IB	SO	ERA	AERA	OAV	OOB	AB-HR-SH	AVG	PB	SUP	APR	DL	PW
1953	Bro N	0	1	.000	4	2	0	0	6.1	11	9	2	0	4	5	11.37	37	.393	.469	2	.000	-0	178	-5	0	-0.7

MIDDLEBROOK, JASON Jason Douglas; B6.26.1975 Jackson MI; BR/TR/6´3˝/215; [SDN96 9/260]; d9.17; Col Stanford

YEAR	TM LG	W	L	PCT	G	GS	CG-SHO	SV-BS	IP	H	R	HR	HB	BB-IB	SO	ERA	AERA	OAV	OOB	AB-HR-SH	AVG	PB	SUP	APR	DL	PW
2001	SD N	2	1	.667	4	3	0	0-0	19.1	18	11	6	1	10-1	10	5.12	81	.247	.345	7	.143	-0	126	-2	0	-0.2
2002	SD N	1	3	.250	12	2	0	0-0	35.1	31	20	1	1	15-2	28	5.09	76	.244	.322	6-0-1	.333	1	83	-4	30	-0.4
	NY N	1	0	1.000	3	3	0	0-0	16	13	7	1	0	7-0	14	3.94	100	.220	.303	5	.000	-0	109	0	17	0.0
	Year	2	3	.400	15	5	0	0-0	51.1	44	27	2	1	22-2	42	4.73	83	.237	.316	11-0-1	.182	0	100	-4	0	-0.4
2003	NY N	0	0	ø	5	0	0	0-0	7	13	8	0	0	4-0	3	10.29	41	.433	.486	0	ø	0	—	-5	0	-0.2
Total	3	4	4	.500	24	8	0	0-0	77.2	75	46	8	2	36-3	55	5.33	75	.260	.341	18-0-1	.167	0	110	-11	47	-0.8

MIDDLETON, JIM James Blaine “Rifle Jim”; B5.28.1889 Argos IN; D1.12.1974 Argos IN; BR/TR/5´11.5˝/165; d4.18

YEAR	TM LG	W	L	PCT	G	GS	CG-SHO	SV-BS	IP	H	R	HR	HB	BB-IB	SO	ERA	AERA	OAV	OOB	AB-HR-SH	AVG	PB	SUP	APR	DL	PW
1917	NY N	1	1	.500	13	0	0	1	36	35	18	1	1	8	9	2.75	93	.255	.301	8	.000	-1	—	-3	—	-0.3
1921	Det A	6	11	.353	38	10	2	**7**	121.2	149	83	5	2	44	31	5.03	85	.302	.361	34-0-4	.147	-2	117	-9	—	-1.3
Total	2	7	12	.368	51	10	2	8	157.2	184	101	6	3	52	40	4.51	86	.292	.348	42-0-4	.119	-3	117	-12	—	-1.6

MIDDLETON, JOHN John Wayne “Lefty”; B4.11.1900 Mt.Calm TX; D11.3.1986 Amarillo TX; BL/TL/6´1˝/185; d9.6; Col Hardin–Simmons

YEAR	TM LG	W	L	PCT	G	GS	CG-SHO	SV-BS	IP	H	R	HR	HB	BB-IB	SO	ERA	AERA	OAV	OOB	AB-HR-SH	AVG	PB	SUP	APR	DL	PW
1922	Cle A	0	1	.000	2	1	0	0	7.1	8	7	1	0	6	2	7.36	54	.286	.412	3	.333	0	106	-3	—	-0.3

MIDKIFF, DICK Richard; B9.28.1914 Gonzales TX; D10.30.1956 Temple TX; BR/TR/6´2˝/185; d4.24; Col Texas

YEAR	TM LG	W	L	PCT	G	GS	CG-SHO	SV-BS	IP	H	R	HR	HB	BB-IB	SO	ERA	AERA	OAV	OOB	AB-HR-SH	AVG	PB	SUP	APR	DL	PW
1938	Bos A	1	1	.500	13	2	0	0	35.1	43	30	5	0	21	10	5.09	97	.305	.395	10	.200	0	107	-4	—	-0.2

MIELKE, GARY Gary Roger; B1.28.1963 St.James MN; BR/TR/6´3˝/(180–199); [TexA85 26/655]; d8.19; Col Mankato St.

YEAR	TM LG	W	L	PCT	G	GS	CG-SHO	SV-BS	IP	H	R	HR	HB	BB-IB	SO	ERA	AERA	OAV	OOB	AB-HR-SH	AVG	PB	SUP	APR	DL	PW
1987	Tex A	0	0	ø	3	0	0	0-0	3	3	2	2	0	1-0	3	6.00	75	.250	.308	0	ø	0	—	0	0	0.0
1989	Tex A	1	0	1.000	43	0	0	1-1	49.2	52	18	4	2	25-3	26	3.26	122	.280	.369	0	ø	0	—	5	0	0.2
1990	Tex A	0	3	.000	33	0	0	0-1	41	42	17	4	2	15-5	13	3.73	106	.271	.343	0	ø	0	—	2	57	0.1
Total	3	1	3	.250	79	0	0	1-2	93.2	97	37	10	4	41-8	42	3.56	112	.275	.356	0	ø	0	—	7	57	0.3

YEAR	TM LG	W	L	PCT	G	GS	CG-SHO	SV-BS	IP	H	R	HR	HB	BB-IB	SO	ERA	AERA	OAV	OOB	AB-HR-SH	AVG	PB	SUP	APR	DL	PW
Mikkelsen, Pete	Peter James; B10.25.1939 Staten Island NY; D11.29.2006 Mabton WA; BR/TR/6´2˝/(210–220); d4.17																									
1964	†NY A	7	4	.636	50	0	0	12	86	79	35	3	4	41-5	63	3.56	102	.247	.338	16-0-4	.063	-1	—	2	0	0.2
1965	NY A	4	9	.308	41	3	0	1	82.1	78	40	10	3	36-9	69	3.28	104	.249	.332	10-0-1	.100	-0	9	-2	0	-0.2
1966	Pit N	9	8	.529	71	0	0	14	126	106	45	8	5	51-9	76	3.07	116	.234	.318	20-0-2	.150	-0	—	8	0	1.3
1967	Pit N	1	2	.333	32	0	0	2	56.1	50	29	7	3	19-5	30	4.31	78	.237	.308	4-0-2	.000	-0	—	-5	0	-0.4
	Chi N	0	0	ø	7	0	0	0	7	9	6	1	1	5-0	0	6.43	55	.333	.455	0	ø	0	—	-2	0	-0.1
	Year	1	2	.333	39	0	0	2	63.1	59	35	8	4	24-5	30	4.55	74	.248	.326	4-0-2	.000	-0	—	-7	0	-0.5
1968	Chi N	0	0	ø	3	0	0	0	4.2	7	4	3	0	1-0	5	7.71	41	.350	.381	1	1.000	0	—	-2	0	-0.1
	StL N	0	0	ø	5	0	0	0	16	10	5	0	0	7-3	8	1.13	257	.179	.270	3	.000	-0	—	2	0	0.1
	Year	0	0	ø	8	0	0	0	20.2	17	9	3	0	8-3	13	2.61	113	.224	.298	4	.250	0	—	0	0	0.0
1969	LA N	7	5	.583	48	0	0	4-0	81.1	57	34	9	4	30-8	51	2.77	121	.193	.277	6-0-1	.167	-0	—	3	0	0.5
1970	LA N	4	2	.667	33	0	0	6-3	62	48	20	5	4	20-4	47	2.76	140	.211	.286	6-0-1	.333	1	—	8	49	1.0
1971	LA N	8	5	.615	41	0	0	5-6	74	67	38	10	1	17-5	46	3.65	89	.242	.286	10	.200	0	—	-5	0	-0.9
1972	LA N	5	5	.500	33	0	0	5-1	57.2	65	32	3	5	23-4	41	4.06	83	.283	.360	7	.000	-0	—	-5	0	-0.9
Total	9	45	40	.529	364	3	0	49-10	653.1	576	288	59	30	250-52	436	3.38	103	.237	.315	83-0-11	.133	-2	9	2	49	0.5
Miklos, Hank	John Joseph; B11.27.1910 Chicago IL; D3.29.2000 Adrian MI; BL/TL/5´11˝/175; d4.23																									
1944	Chi N	0	0	ø	2	0	0	0	7	9	6	1	0	3	0	7.71	46	.333	.400	2	.000	-0	—	-3	0	-0.1
Milacki, Bob	Robert; B7.28.1964 Trenton NJ; BR/TR/6´4˝/(220–234); [BalA83 S2/29]; d9.18; Col Yavapai (AZ) JC																									
1988	Bal A	2	0	1.000	3	3	1-1	0-0	25	9	2	1	0	9-0	18	0.72	547	.110	.198	0	ø	0	70	9	0	0.8
1989	Bal A	14	12	.538	37	**36**	3-2	0-0	243	233	105	21	2	88-4	113	3.74	102	.254	.318	0	ø	0	94	3	0	0.3
1990	Bal A	5	8	.385	27	24	1-1	0-0	135.1	143	73	18	0	61-2	60	4.46	86	.273	.346	0	ø	0	92	-10	32	-0.9
1991	Bal A	10	9	.526	31	26	3-1	0-0	184	175	86	17	1	53-3	108	4.01	99	.253	.305	0	ø	0	93	0	0	0.0
1992	Bal A	6	8	.429	23	20	0	1-0	115.2	140	78	16	2	44-2	51	5.84	70	.296	.356	0	ø	0	101	-21	0	-2.3
1993	Cle A	1	1	.500	5	2	0	0-0	16	19	8	3	0	11-0	7	3.38	130	.302	.405	0	ø	0	42	1	0	0.1
1994	KC A	0	5	.000	10	10	0	0-0	55.2	68	43	6	1	20-3	17	6.14	82	.298	.352	0	ø	0	90	-7	0	-0.5
1996	Sea A	1	4	.200	7	4	0	0-0	21	30	20	3	0	15-3	13	6.86	73	.330	.425	0	ø	0	112	-6	0	-1.0
Total	8	39	47	.453	143	125	8-5	1-0	795.2	817	415	85	6	301-17	387	4.38	92	.266	.330	0	ø	0	94	-31	32	-3.5
Milchin, Mike	Michael Wayne; B2.28.1968 Knoxville TN; BL/TL/6´3˝/190; [StLN89 2/36]; d5.14; Col Clemson																									
1996	Min A	2	1	.667	26	0	0	0-1	21.2	31	21	6	0	12-1	19	8.31	62	.341	.417	0	ø	0	—	-7	0	-0.8
	Bal A	1	0	1.000	13	0	0	0-0	11	13	7	0	0	5-1	10	5.73	86	.325	.375	0	ø	0	—	-1	0	0.0
	Year	3	1	.750	39	0	0	0-1	32.2	44	28	6	0	17-2	29	7.44	68	.336	.404	0	ø	0	—	-8	0	-0.8
Miles, Carl	Carl Thomas; B3.22.1918 Trenton MO; BB/TL/5´11˝/178; d6.8; Col Missouri																									
1940	Phi A	0	0	ø	2	0	0	0	8	9	12	2	0	8	6	13.50	33	.281	.425	4	.750	2	—	-7	—	-0.2
Miles, Jim	James Charlie; B8.8.1943 Grenada MS; BR/TR/6´2˝/210; d9.7; Col Delta St.																									
1968	Was A	0	0	ø	3	0	0	0	4.1	8	6	0	0	2-0	5	12.46	23	.421	.455	0	ø	0	—	-4	0	-0.2
1969	Was A	0	1	.000	10	1	0	0-0	20.1	19	15	2	4	15-1	15	6.20	57	.257	.400	3	.333	0*	76	-6	0	-0.2
Total	2	0	1	.000	13	1	0	0-0	24.2	27	21	2	4	17-1	20	7.30	47	.290	.410	3	.333	0	76	-10	0	-0.4
Militello, Sam	Sam Salvatore; B11.26.1969 Tampa FL; BR/TR/6´3˝/(195–200); [NYA90 6/165]; d8.9; Col Tampa																									
1992	NY A	3	3	.500	9	9	0	0-0	60	43	24	6	2	32-1	42	3.45	115	.195	.302	0	ø	0	100	4	0	0.3
1993	NY A	1	1	.500	3	2	0	0-0	9.1	10	8	1	2	7-1	5	6.75	62	.270	.413	0	ø	0	110	-3	0	-0.5
Total	2	4	4	.500	12	11	0	0-0	69.1	53	32	7	4	39-2	47	3.89	102	.205	.319	0	ø	0	102	1	0	-0.2
Miljus, Johnny	John Kenneth "Jovo","Big Serb"; B6.30.1895 Pittsburgh PA; D2.11.1976 Fort Harrison MT; BR/TR/6´1˝/178; d10.2; Mil 1918; Col Duquesne																									
1915	Pit F	0	0	ø	1	0	0	0	1	1	0	0	0	0	0	0.00	ø	.250	.250	0	ø	0	—	0	—	0.0
1917	Bro N	0	1	.000	4	1	1	0	15	14	3	0	3	8	9	0.60	466	.250	.373	5	.000	-1	27	3	—	0.1
1920	Bro N	1	0	1.000	9	0	0	0	23.1	24	10	2	0	4	9	3.09	104	.267	.298	6	.333	1*	—	0	—	0.2
1921	Bro N	6	3	.667	28	9	3	1	93.2	115	49	1	2	27	37	4.23	92	.312	.362	30	.167	-2	106	-2	—	-0.3
1927	†Pit N	8	3	.727	19	6	3-2	0	75.2	62	21	0	0	17	24	1.90	216	.228	.273	28-0-1	.179	-1	79	17	—	2.3
1928	Pit N	5	7	.417	21	10	3	1	69.2	90	48	2	3	33	26	5.30	77	.313	.389	26	.308	1	94	-9	—	-1.3
	Cle A	1	4	.200	11	4	1	1	50.2	46	25	1	0	20	19	2.66	156	.243	.316	15	.200	-0	51	5	—	0.5
1929	Cle A	8	8	.500	34	15	4	2	128.1	174	93	10	3	64	42	5.19	86	.331	.406	43-0-2	.256	1	96	-12	—	-1.1
Total	7	29	26	.527	127	45	15-2	5	457.1	526	249	16	11	173	166	3.92	104	.293	.359	153-0-3	.222	0	92	2	—	0.4
Miller, Andrew	Andrew Mark; B5.21.1985 Gainesville FL; BR/TL/6´6˝/210; [DetA06 1/6]; d8.30; Col North Carolina																									
2006	Det A	0	1	.000	8	0	0	0-0	10.1	8	9	0	2	10-0	6	6.10	74	.205	.392	0	ø	0	—	-3	0	-0.2
Miller, Dyar	Dyar K; B5.29.1946 Batesville IN; BR/TR/6´1˝/(200–215); d6.9; C2; Col Utah St.																									
1975	Bal A	6	3	.667	30	0	0	8-4	46.1	32	14	3	0	16-4	33	2.72	130	.199	.267	0	ø	0	—	5	0	1.1
1976	Bal A	2	4	.333	49	0	0	7-3	88.2	79	31	5	1	36-5	37	2.94	112	.246	.321	0	ø	0	—	4	0	0.3
1977	Bal A	2	2	.500	12	0	0	1-1	22.1	25	14	6	0	10-1	9	5.64	68	.278	.350	0	ø	0	—	-4	0	-0.7
	Cal A	4	4	.500	41	0	0	4-3	92.1	81	35	10	0	30-7	49	3.02	130	.242	.300	0	ø	0	—	10	0	0.8
	Year	6	6	.500	53	0	0	5-4	114.2	106	49	16	0	40-8	58	3.53	111	.249	.311	0	ø	0	—	6	0	0.1
1978	Cal A	6	2	.750	41	0	0	1-0	84.2	85	29	3	5	41-3	34	2.66	137	.264	.352	0	ø	0	—	9	24	0.7
1979	Cal A	1	0	1.000	14	1	0	0-0	35.1	44	14	2	2	13-0	16	3.31	123	.319	.376	0	ø	0	111	3	0	0.1
	Tor A	0	0	ø	10	0	0	0-0	15.1	27	18	3	0	5-0	7	10.57	42	.391	.427	0	ø	0	—	-9	0	-0.4
	Year	1	0	1.000	24	1	0	0-0	50.2	71	32	5	2	18-0	23	5.51	76	.343	.392	0	ø	0	109	-6	0	-0.3
1980	NY N	1	2	.333	31	0	0	1-1	42	37	9	1	0	11-3	28	1.93	187	.242	.289	1-0-1	.000	-0	—	8	0	0.6
1981	NY N	1	0	1.000	23	0	0	0-1	38.1	49	20	2	1	15-2	22	3.29	108	.327	.387	3	.333	0	—	0	0	0.0
Total	7	23	17	.575	251	1	0	22-13	465.1	459	184	35	9	177-25	235	3.23	114	.264	.331	4-0-1	.250	0	121	26	24	2.5
Miller, Elmer	Elmer Joseph "Lefty"; B4.17.1903 Detroit MI; D1.8.1987 Corona CA; BL/TL/5´11˝/189; d6.21; ▲																									
1929	Phi N	0	1	.000	8	2	0	0	11.1	12	18	1	3	21	5	11.12	47	.279	.537	38-1-0	.237	0*	118	-8	—	-0.5
Miller, Frank	Frank Lee "Bullet"; B5.13.1886 Allegan MI; D2.19.1974 Allegan MI; BR/TR/6´0˝/188; d7.12																									
1913	Chi A	0	1	.000	1	1	0	0	1.2	4	5	0	0	3	2	27.00	11	.571	.700	0	ø	0	0	-4	—	-0.6
1916	Pit N	7	10	.412	30	20	10-2	1	173	135	55	4	7	49	88	2.29	117	.226	.292	51-0-7	.137	-1	97	9	—	0.8
1917	Pit N	10	19	.345	38	28	14-5	1	224	216	98	1	5	60	92	3.13	91	.251	.304	76-0-5	.118	-4*	76	-7	—	-1.4
1918	Pit N	11	8	.579	23	23	14-2	0	170.1	152	60	1	7	37	47	2.38	121	.250	.301	57-0-7	.105	-3	109	9	—	0.6
1919	Pit N	13	12	.520	32	26	16-3	0	201.2	170	79	6	5	34	59	3.03	99	.234	.272	66-0-6	.106	-5	106	0	—	-0.5
1922	Bos N	11	13	.458	31	23	14-2	1	200	213	100	7	2	60	65	3.51	114	.279	.333	68-0-5	.118	-5	85	10	—	0.6
1923	Bos N	0	3	.000	8	6	0	1	39.1	54	26	2	3	11	6	4.58	87	.335	.389	7-0-1	.143	-0	93	-3	—	-0.3
Total	7	52	66	.441	163	127	68-14	4	1010	944	423	21	29	254	359	3.01	104	.253	.306	325-0-31	.117	-18	92	14	—	-0.8
Miller, Fred	Frederick Holman "Speedy"; B6.28.1886 Fairfield IN; D5.2.1953 Brookville IN; BL/TL/6´2˝/190; d7.8																									
1910	Bro N	1	1	.500	6	2	0	0	21	25	19	1	3	13	2	4.71	64	.309	.423	8	.250	0	86	-6	—	-0.4
Miller, Bert	Herbert Alexander; B10.26.1875 Riley MI; D6.14.1937 Flint MI; d7.15																									
1897	Lou N	0	1	.000	4	1	1	0	17	32	23	0	0	3	3	7.94	54	.395	.417	6	.167	-1	0	-7	—	-0.3
Miller, Ox	John Anthony; B5.4.1915 Gause TX; BR/TR/6´1˝/190; d8.7																									
1943	Was A	0	0	ø	3	0	0	0	6	10	7	1	0	5	1	10.50	31	.370	.469	1	.000	-0	—	-4	0	-0.2
	StL A	0	0	ø	2	0	0	0	6	7	8	2	2	3	3	12.00	28	.304	.429	1	.000	-0	—	-5	0	-0.2
	Year	0	0	ø	5	0	0	0	12	17	15	3	2	8	4	11.25	29	.340	.450	2	.000	-0	—	-10	0	-0.4
1945	StL A	2	1	.667	4	3	3	0	28.1	23	5	2	0	5	4	1.59	222	.219	.255	11-0-1	.182	-0*	65	6	0	0.6
1946	StL A	1	3	.250	11	3	0	1	35.1	52	28	5	0	15	12	6.88	54	.338	.396	7-0-1	.286	1	100	-10	0	-1.0
1947	Chi N	1	2	.333	4	4	1	0	16	31	18	2	0	5	7	10.13	39	.397	.434	7-1-0	.429	2	101	-10	0	-1.2
Total	4	4	6	.400	24	10	4	1	91.2	123	66	12	2	33	27	6.38	57	.318	.374	27-1-2	.259	2	92	-23	0	-2.0

YEAR	TM LG	W	L	PCT	G	GS	CG-SHO	SV-BS	IP	H	R	HR	HB	BB-IB	SO	ERA	AERA	OAV	OOB	AB-HR-SH	AVG	PB	SUP	APR	DL	PW
MILLER, JOHN	John Ernest; B5.30.1941 Baltimore MD; BR/TR/6´2˝/(200–210); d9.22																									
1962	Bal A	1	1	.500	2	1	0	0	10	2	1	0	0	5-0	4	0.90	411	.065	.194	3	.000	-0	0	3	0	0.7
1963	Bal A	1	1	.500	3	2	0	0	17	12	6	0	0	14-0	16	3.18	109	.194	.342	6	.000	-1	90	1	0	0.0
1965	Bal A	6	4	.600	16	16	1	0	93.1	75	38	4	1	58-0	71	3.18	109	.223	.336	30-0-1	.100	-1	120	3	0	0.3
1966	Bal A	4	8	.333	23	16	0	0	100.2	92	59	15	0	58-3	81	4.74	70	.241	.340	34-0-4	.118	-1	104	-16	0	-1.9
1967	Bal A	0	0	ø	2	0	0	0	6	7	5	1	2	3-0	6	7.50	42	.304	.429	0	ø	0	—	-3	0	-0.1
Total	5	12	14	.462	46	35	1	0	227	188	109	20	3	138-3	178	3.89	88	.225	.336	73-0-5	.096	-3	108	-12	0	-1.0
MILLER, CYCLONE	Joseph H.; B9.24.1859 Springfield MA; D10.13.1916 New London CT; TL/5´9.5˝/165; d7.11																									
1884	CP U	1	0	1.000	1	1	1	0	9	4	2	0	—	0	13	1.00	243	.125	.125	4	.250	-0	176	1	—	0.1
	Pro N	3	2	.600	6	5	2	0	34.2	36	24	0	—	11	12	2.08	137	.259	.313	23	.043	-3	149	1	—	-0.1
	Phi N	0	1	.000	1	1	1	0	9	17	19	5	—	6	1	10.00	30	.386	.460	4	.000	-1	124	-7	—	-0.5
	Year	3	3	.500	7	6	3	0	43.2	53	43	5	—	17	13	3.71	78	.290	.350	27	.037	-4	144	-6	—	-0.6
1886	Phi AA	10	8	.556	19	19	19-1	0	169.2	158	109	6	4	59	99	2.97	118	.239	.305	66	.136	-1*	84	7	—	0.6
Total	2	14	11	.560	27	26	23-1	0	222.1	215	154	11	4	76	125	3.04	110	.245	.308	97	.113	-5	100	2	—	0.1
MILLER, JUSTIN	Justin Mark; B8.27.1977 Torrance CA; BR/TR/6´2˝/(209–210); [ColN97 5/162]; d4.12; Col Los Angeles Harbor (CA) JC																									
2002	Tor A	9	5	.643	25	18	0	0-0	102.1	103	70	12	11	66-2	68	5.54	83	.268	.385	2	.000	-0	95	-11	0	-1.3
2004	Tor A	3	4	.429	19	15	0	0-0	81.2	101	58	14	5	42-3	47	6.06	81	.316	.397	0	ø	0	86	-10	65	-0.7
2005	Tor A	0	0	ø	1	0	0	0-0	2.1	5	4	3	0	0-0	2	15.43	30	.417	.417	0	ø	0	—	-3	0	-0.1
Total	3	12	9	.571	45	33	0	0-0	186.1	209	132	29	16	108-5	117	5.89	80	.291	.390	2	.000	-0	91	-24	65	-2.1
MILLER, WHITEY	Kenneth Albert; B5.2.1915 St.Louis MO; D4.3.1991 St.Louis MO; BR/TR/6´1˝/195; d9.15																									
1944	NY N	0	1	.000	4	0	0	0	5	1	2	0	0	4	2	0.00	ø	.059	.238	1	.000	-0*	—	1	0	0.2
MILLER, KURT	Kurt Everett; B8.24.1972 Tucson AZ; BR/TR/6´5˝/(205–225); [PitN90 1/5]; d6.11																									
1994	Fla N	1	3	.250	4	4	0	0-0	20	26	18	3	2	7-0	11	8.10	55	.317	.380	6-0-1	.167	-0	56	-7	0	-1.0
1996	Fla N	1	3	.250	26	5	0	0-2	46.1	57	41	5	2	33-8	30	6.80	61	.313	.422	8-0-1	.375	1	171	-15	0	-1.0
1997	Fla N	0	1	.000	7	0	0	0-0	7.1	12	8	2	1	7-0	7	9.82	41	.364	.488	0	ø	0	—	-5	153	-0.5
1998	Chi N	0	0	ø	3	0	0	0-0	4	3	0	0	0	0-0	6	0.00	ø	.200	.200	0	ø	0	—	2	0	0.1
1999	Chi N	0	0	ø	4	0	0	0-0	3	6	6	1	0	3-0	1	18.00	25	.462	.563	0	ø	0	—	-4	45	-0.2
Total	5	2	7	.222	44	9	0	0-2	80.2	104	73	11	5	50-8	55	7.48	57	.320	.416	14-0-2	.286	1	119	-29	198	-2.6
MILLER, LARRY	Larry Don; B6.19.1937 Topeka KS; BL/TL/6´0˝/(185–195); d6.21; Col Kansas																									
1964	LA N	4	8	.333	16	14	1	0	79.2	87	44	1	2	28-4	50	4.18	78	.275	.334	26-0-2	.269	2	107	-9	0	-1.1
1965	NY N	1	4	.200	28	5	0	0	57.1	66	32	6	1	25-0	36	5.02	70	.289	.357	11	.182	0	40	-8	0	-0.6
1966	NY N	0	2	.000	4	1	0	0	8.1	9	7	3	0	4-0	7	7.56	48	.273	.351	2	.500	0	0	-3	0	-0.6
Total	3	5	14	.263	48	20	1	0	145.1	162	83	10	3	57-4	93	4.71	72	.281	.344	39-0-2	.256	2	82	-20	0	-2.3
MILLER, RED	Leo Alphonso; B2.11.1897 Philadelphia PA; D10.20.1973 Orlando FL; BR/TR/5´11˝/195; d7.13																									
1923	Phi N	0	0	ø	1	0	0	0	1.2	6	6	0	0	1	0	32.40	14	.545	.583	1	.000	-0	—	-4	—	-0.2
MILLER, MATT	Matt Jacob; B11.23.1971 Greenwood MS; BR/TR/6´3˝/(210–215); d6.27; Col Delta State																									
2003	Col N	0	0	ø	4	0	0	0-0	4.1	5	1	0	0	2-0	5	2.08	236	.313	.389	0	ø	0	—	1	0	0.1
2004	Cle A	4	1	.800	57	0	0	1-1	55.1	42	22	1	6	23-8	55	3.09	141	.216	.317	0	ø	0	—	8	0	0.6
2005	Cle A	1	0	1.000	23	0	0	1-1	29.2	22	6	1	3	10-3	23	1.82	229	.212	.297	0	ø	0	—	8	79	0.4
2006	Cle A	1	0	1.000	14	0	0	0-0	15.2	11	6	2	2	9-0	12	3.45	125	.212	.338	0	ø	0	—	2	138	0.1
Total	4	6	1	.857	98	0	0	2-2	105	80	35	4	11	44-11	95	2.74	157	.219	.318	0	ø	0	—	19	217	1.2
MILLER, MATT	Matthew Lincoln; B8.2.1974 Lubbock TX; BL/TL/6´3˝/175; [DetA96 2/41]; d5.8; Col Texas Tech																									
2001	Det A	0	0	ø	13	0	0	0-0	9.2	16	8	0	1	4-0	6	7.45	59	.372	.438	0	ø	0	—	-3	0	-0.1
2002	Det A	0	0	ø	2	0	0	0-1	0.2	4	2	1	0	1-0	1	13.50	32	.571	.625	0	ø	0	—	-1	178	-0.1
Total	2	0	0	ø	15	0	0	0-1	10.1	20	10	1	1	5-0	7	7.84	56	.400	.464	0	ø	0	—	-4	178	-0.2
MILLER, PAUL	Paul Robert; B4.27.1965 Burlington WI; BR/TR/6´5˝/(215–220); [PitN87 53/1199]; d7.30; Col Carthage																									
1991	Pit N	0	0	ø	1	1	0	0-0	5	4	3	0	0	3-0	2	5.40	67	.222	.333	3	.000	-0	75	-1	0	-0.1
1992	Pit N	1	0	1.000	6	0	0	0-0	11.1	11	3	0	0	1-0	5	2.38	146	.256	.267	3	.000	-0	—	1	48	0.1
1993	Pit N	0	0	ø	3	2	0	0-0	10	15	6	2	0	2-0	2	5.40	76	.349	.378	2	.000	-0	99	-1	0	-0.1
Total	3	1	0	1.000	10	3	0	0-0	26.1	30	12	2	0	6-0	9	4.10	91	.288	.324	8	.000	-1	97	-1	48	-0.1
MILLER, RALPH	Ralph Darwin; B3.15.1873 Cincinnati OH; D5.8.1973 Cincinnati OH; BR/TR/5´11˝/170; d5.4																									
1898	Bro N	4	14	.222	23	21	16	0	151.2	161	119	4	13	86	43	5.34	67	.270	.374	62-0-1	.194	-1*	85	-27	—	-2.6
1899	Bal N	1	3	.250	6	4	3	1	37	44	28	0	4	14	3	4.38	91	.295	.371	11	.182	1	86	-2	—	-0.1
Total	2	5	17	.227	29	25	19	1	188.2	205	147	4	17	100	46	5.15	71	.275	.374	73-0-1	.192	1	85	-29	—	-2.7
MILLER, RALPH	Ralph Henry "Moose","Lefty"; B1.14.1899 Vinton IA; D2.18.1967 White Bear Lake MN; BR/TL/6´1.5˝/190; d9.16; b–Bing																									
1921	Was A	0	0	ø	1	0	0	0	1	0	0	0	0	0	0	0.00	ø	.000	.000	0	ø	0	—	0	—	0.0
MILLER, RANDY	Randall Scott; B3.18.1953 Oxnard CA; BR/TR/6´1˝/180; [BalA74 5/120]; d9.7; Col California–San Diego																									
1977	Bal A	0	0	ø	1	0	0	0-0	0.2	4	3	0	0	0-0	0	40.50	9	.800	.667	0	ø	0	—	-3	0	-0.1
1978	Mon N	0	1	.000	5	0	0	0-0	7	11	9	1	0	3-1	6	10.29	35	.393	.424	1	.000	-0	—	-5	0	-0.7
Total	2	0	1	.000	6	0	0	0-0	7.2	15	12	1	0	3-1	6	12.91	28	.455	.462	1	.000	-0	—	-8	0	-0.8
MILLER, BOB	Robert Gerald; B7.15.1935 Berwyn IL; BR/TL/6´1˝/(175–185); d6.25																									
1953	Det A	1	2	.333	13	1	0	0	36.1	43	25	2	1	21	9	5.94	68	.289	.380	8	.125	-1	66	-7	0	-0.5
1954	Det A	1	1	.500	32	1	0	1	69.2	62	25	1	0	26	27	2.45	150	.244	.312	15	.133	-0*	72	8	0	0.3
1955	Det A	2	1	.667	7	3	1	0	25.1	26	12	4	0	12-1	11	2.49	154	.263	.339	9	.222	0*	123	2	0	0.2
1956	Det A	0	2	.000	11	3	0	0	31.2	37	23	5	0	22-2	16	5.68	72	.308	.413	7	.143	0	108	-6	0	-0.3
1962	Cin N	0	0	ø	6	0	0	0	5.1	14	13	1	2	3-0	4	21.94	18	.538	.576	1	.000	-0	—	-10	0	-0.5
	NY N	2	2	.500	17	0	0	1	20.1	24	16	2	1	8-0	8	7.08	59	.312	.379	1	.000	-0	—	-5	0	-0.9
	Year	2	2	.500	23	0	0	1	25.2	38	29	3	3	11-0	12	10.17	41	.369	.433	2	.000	-0	—	-15	0	-1.4
Total	5	6	8	.429	86	8	1	2	188.2	206	114	15	4	92-3	75	4.72	83	.284	.365	41	.146	-1	104	-18	0	-1.7
MILLER, BOB	Robert John; B6.16.1926 Detroit MI; BR/TR/6´3˝/(190–195); d9.16; Col Detroit Mercy																									
1949	Phi N	0	0	ø	3	0	0	0	2.2	2	0	0	0	2	0	0.00	ø	.200	.333	0	ø	0	—	1	0	0.1
1950	†Phi N	11	6	.647	35	22	7-2	1	174	190	78	9	5	57	44	3.57	113	.277	.337	61-0-2	.180	-1	98	10	0	0.9
1951	Phi N	2	1	.667	17	3	0	0	34.1	47	33	2	1	18	10	6.82	56	.331	.410	7	.429	1	168	-14	0	-1.0
1952	Phi N	0	1	.000	3	1	0	0	9	13	6	2	0	1	2	6.00	61	.351	.368	1	.000	-0	0	-2	0	-0.2
1953	Phi N	8	9	.471	35	20	8-3	2	157.1	169	76	14	2	42	63	4.00	105	.271	.319	55-0-1	.182	-1	89	6	0	0.4
1954	Phi N	7	9	.438	30	16	5	0	150	176	84	14	3	39	42	4.56	89	.300	.340	50-1-3	.160	0	116	-8	0	-0.7
1955	Phi N	8	4	.667	40	0	0	1	89.2	80	26	6	1	28-6	28	2.41	165	.242	.300	18-0-1	.278	1	—	16	0	2.1
1956	Phi N	3	6	.333	49	6	3-1	5	122.1	115	55	14	3	34-11	53	3.24	115	.248	.301	22-0-2	.091	-1	79	5	0	0.2
1957	Phi N	2	5	.286	32	1	0	6	60.1	61	18	4	1	17-5	12	2.69	142	.265	.315	8-1-0	.250	2	116	9	0	1.3
1958	Phi N	1	1	.500	17	0	0	0	22.1	36	30	7	0	9-2	9	11.69	34	.360	.402	1-0-1	.000	-0	—	-18	0	-1.4
Total	10	42	42	.500	261	69	23-6	15	822	889	406	72	16	247-24	263	3.96	101	.277	.329	223-2-10	.184	1	101	5	0	1.7
MILLER, BOB	Robert Lane (b Robert Lane Gemeinweiser); B2.18.1939 St.Louis MO; D8.6.1993 Rancho Bernardo CA; BR/TR/6´1˝/(175–195); d6.26; C4																									
1957	StL N	0	0	ø	5	0	0	0	9	13	9	2	0	5-0	7	7.00	57	.325	.391	0	ø	0*	—	-3	0	-0.2
1959	StL N	4	3	.571	11	10	3	0	70.2	66	31	2	1	21-2	43	3.31	128	.248	.303	24-0-1	.208	0	91	6	0	0.6
1960	StL N	4	3	.571	15	7	0	0	52.2	53	21	2	1	17-2	33	3.42	120	.262	.320	14-0-1	.143	-1*	102	4	49	0.5
1961	StL N	1	3	.250	34	5	0	3	74.1	82	41	6	0	46-7	39	4.24	104	.290	.388	14-0-2	.357	2*	52	1	0	0.3
1962	NY N	1	12	.077	33	21	1	0	143.2	146	98	20	6	62-2	91	4.89	86	.259	.335	41-0-2	.122	-1*	57	-13	0	-1.0
1963	LA N	10	8	.556	42	23	2	1	187	171	71	7	3	65-9	125	2.89	105	.244	.310	57-0-5	.070	-3	119	3	0	0.3
1964	LA N	7	7	.500	**74**	2	0	9	137.2	115	49	1	2	63-16	94	2.62	124	.226	.312	19-0-2	.158	1	122	9	0	1.3
1965	†LA N	6	7	.462	61	1	0	9	103	82	37	9	3	26-3	77	2.97	110	.225	.277	16-0-1	.000	-1	54	4	0	0.6
1966	†LA N	4	2	.667	46	0	0	5	84.1	70	31	5	1	29-7	58	2.77	119	.230	.297	13-0-2	.077	-1	—	5	0	0.2

YEAR	TM LG	W	L	PCT	G	GS	CG-SHO	SV-BS	IP	H	R	HR	HB	BB-IB	SO	ERA	AERA	OAV	OOB	AB-HR-SH	AVG	PB	SUP	APR	DL	PW
1967	LA N	2	9	.182	52	4	0	0	85.2	88	46	9	3	27-9	32	4.31	72	.273	.332	8-0-1	.125	-0	21	-12	0	-1.5
1968	Min A	0	3	.000	45	0	0	2	72.1	65	26	1	5	24-7	41	2.74	113	.239	.311	7	.143	-0	—	3	0	0.2
1969	†Min A	5	5	.500	48	11	1	3-3	119.1	118	42	9	0	32-7	57	3.02	121	.264	.311	31-0-2	.000	-3	130	10	23	0.6
1970	Cle A	2	2	.500	15	2	0	1-0	28	35	14	1	0	15-2	15	4.18	96	.310	.388	5	.200	0	133	-1	0	-0.1
	Chi A	4	6	.400	15	12	0	0-0	70	88	42	11	4	33-3	36	5.01	77	.315	.391	23-0-2	.174	0*	90	-7	0	-0.8
	Year	6	8	.429	30	14	0	1-0	98	123	56	12	4	48-5	51	4.78	82	.314	.390	28-0-2	.179	1	96	-7	0	-0.9
	Chi N	0	0	ø	7	1	0	2-0	9	6	5	3	0	6-1	4	5.00	90	.194	.316	0	ø	0	100	0	0	0.0
1971	Chi N	0	0	ø	2	0	0	0-0	7	10	4	0	0	1-0	2	5.14	77	.357	.367	1	.000	-0	—	-1	0	0.0
	SD N	7	3	.700	38	0	0	7-2	63.2	53	12	0	1	26-7	36	1.41	235	.227	.308	10-0-2	.000	-1	—	14	0	2.5
	†Pit N	1	2	.333	16	0	0	3-4	28	20	8	1	0	13-4	13	1.29	265	.200	.292	1	.000	0	—	5	0	0.7
	Year	8	5	.615	56	0	0	10-6	98.2	83	24	1	1	40-11	51	1.64	206	.230	.308	12-0-2	.000	-1	—	18	0	3.2
1972	†Pit N	5	2	.714	36	0	0	3-1	54.1	54	19	3	1	24-7	18	2.65	125	.263	.343	4-0-1	.000	-0	—	4	21	0.5
1973	SD N	0	0	ø	18	0	0	0-0	30.2	29	18	4	0	12-1	15	4.11	86	.244	.311	2	.000	-0	—	-3	0	-0.2
	NY N	0	0	ø	1	0	0	0-0	1	0	0	0	0	0-0	1	0.00	ø	.000	.000	0	ø	0	—	0	0	0.0
	Year	0	0	ø	19	0	0	0-0	31.2	29	18	4	0	12-1	16	3.98	88	.238	.304	2	.000	-0	—	-3	0	-0.2
	Det A	4	2	.667	22	0	0	1-1	42	34	16	3	0	22-2	23	3.43	120	.230	.324	0	ø	0	—	3	0	0.5
1974	NY N	2	2	.500	58	0	0	2-2	78	89	39	2	1	39-13	35	3.58	101	.296	.375	9	.111	-0	—	-1	0	-0.1
Total	17	69	81	.460	694	99	7	51-13	1551.1	1487	679	101	32	608-111	895	3.37	105	.255	.326	299-0-24	.110	-8	95	30	93	4.9

MILLER, BOB Robert W.; B1862; D5.23.1931 Newark NJ; d8.30

YEAR	TM LG	W	L	PCT	G	GS	CG-SHO	SV-BS	IP	H	R	HR	HB	BB-IB	SO	ERA	AERA	OAV	OOB	AB-HR-SH	AVG	PB	SUP	APR	DL	PW
1890	Roc AA	3	7	.300	13	12	11	1	92.1	89	58	2	3	26	20	4.29	83	.246	.302	40	.150	-1*	53	-5	—	-0.5
1891	Was AA	2	5	.286	7	7	3	0	42	53	51	3	6	24	13	4.29	87	.298	.399	18	.111	-2	69	-8	—	-1.1
Total	2	5	12	.294	20	19	14	1	134.1	142	109	5	9	50	33	4.29	84	.263	.336	58	.138	-3	60	-13	—	-1.6

MILLER, ROGER Roger Wesley; B8.1.1954 Connellsville PA; D4.26.1993 Mill Run PA; BR/TR/6´3˝/200; d9.8

YEAR	TM LG	W	L	PCT	G	GS	CG-SHO	SV-BS	IP	H	R	HR	HB	BB-IB	SO	ERA	AERA	OAV	OOB	AB-HR-SH	AVG	PB	SUP	APR	DL	PW
1974	Mil A	0	0	ø	2	0	0	0-0	2.1	3	3	1	1	0-0	2	11.57	31	.300	.364	0	ø	0	—	-2	0	-0.1

MILLER, RONNIE Roland Arthur; B8.28.1918 Mason City IA; D1.6.1998 Ferguson MO; BB/TR/5´11˝/167; d9.10; Mil 1942–45; Col Upper Iowa

YEAR	TM LG	W	L	PCT	G	GS	CG-SHO	SV-BS	IP	H	R	HR	HB	BB-IB	SO	ERA	AERA	OAV	OOB	AB-HR-SH	AVG	PB	SUP	APR	DL	PW
1941	Was A	0	0	ø	1	0	0	0	2	2	1	0	0	1	0	4.50	90	.333	.429	0	ø	0	—	0	0	0.0

MILLER, ROSCOE Roscoe Clyde "Roxy","Rubberlegs"; B12.2.1876 Greenville IN; D4.18.1913 Corydon IN; BR/TR/6´2˝/190; d4.25

YEAR	TM LG	W	L	PCT	G	GS	CG-SHO	SV-BS	IP	H	R	HR	HB	BB-IB	SO	ERA	AERA	OAV	OOB	AB-HR-SH	AVG	PB	SUP	APR	DL	PW
1901	Det A	23	13	.639	38	36	35-3	1	332	339	168	1	13	98	79	2.95	130	.261	.320	130-0-2	.208	0	106	33	—	3.3
1902	Det A	6	12	.333	20	18	15-1	1	148.2	158	85	3	9	57	39	3.69	99	.273	.347	60	.183	-2	65	-1	—	-0.2
	NY N	1	8	.111	10	9	7	0	72.2	77	40	1	5	11	15	4.58	61	.271	.310	21-0-2	.048	-2	51	-9	—	-1.3
1903	NY N	2	5	.286	15	8	6	**3**	85	101	53	1	1	24	30	4.13	81	.302	.351	31	.161	-1	70	-7	—	-0.7
1904	Pit N	7	7	.500	19	17	11-2	0	134.1	133	67	4	4	39	35	3.35	82	.256	.313	46	.043	-4	103	-9	—	-1.3
Total	4	39	45	.464	102	88	74-6	5	772.2	808	413	10	32	229	198	3.45	100	.268	.326	288-0-4	.160	-8	89	7	—	-0.2

MILLER, RUSS Russell Lewis; B3.25.1900 Etna OH; D4.30.1962 Bucyrus OH; BR/TR/5´11˝/165; d9.24; b–Jake; Col Ohio St.

YEAR	TM LG	W	L	PCT	G	GS	CG-SHO	SV-BS	IP	H	R	HR	HB	BB-IB	SO	ERA	AERA	OAV	OOB	AB-HR-SH	AVG	PB	SUP	APR	DL	PW
1927	Phi N	1	1	.500	2	2	1	0	15.1	21	9	2	1	3	4	5.28	78	.339	.379	3-0-3	.333	0	93	-1	—	-0.1
1928	Phi N	0	12	.000	33	12	1	1	108	137	79	14	0	34	19	5.42	79	.315	.365	27-0-1	.148	-1*	89	-15	—	-1.6
Total	2	1	13	.071	35	14	2	1	123.1	158	88	16	1	37	23	5.40	79	.318	.366	30-0-4	.167	-1	90	-16	—	-1.7

MILLER, STU Stuart Leonard; B12.26.1927 Northampton MA; BR/TR/5´11.5˝/(155–165); d8.12

YEAR	TM LG	W	L	PCT	G	GS	CG-SHO	SV-BS	IP	H	R	HR	HB	BB-IB	SO	ERA	AERA	OAV	OOB	AB-HR-SH	AVG	PB	SUP	APR	DL	PW
1952	StL N	6	3	.667	12	11	6-2	0	88	63	25	3	2	26	64	2.05	182	.197	.262	25-0-6	.120	-1	74	15	0	1.6
1953	StL N	7	8	.467	40	18	8-2	4	137.2	161	86	19	2	47	79	5.56	77	.293	.351	43-0-4	.186	1*	99	-17	0	-1.4
1954	StL N	2	3	.400	19	4	0	2	46.2	55	36	5	3	29	22	5.79	71	.307	.405	13	.308	1*	157	-9	0	-0.8
1956	StL N	0	1	.000	3	0	0	1	7.1	12	6	3	0	5-0	5	4.91	77	.387	.459	1	.000	-0*	—	-2	0	-0.2
	Phi N	5	8	.385	24	15	2	0	106.2	109	65	16	4	51-12	55	4.47	83	.263	.347	25-0-1	.160	2*	87	-11	0	-1.0
	Year	5	9	.357	27	15	2	1	114	121	71	19	4	56-12	60	4.50	83	.271	.356	26-0-1	.154	2	87	-14	0	-1.2
1957	NY N	7	9	.438	38	13	0	1	124	110	53	15	3	45-6	60	3.63	108	.242	.313	35-0-1	.057	-3	91	6	0	0.4
1958	SF N	6	9	.400	41	20	4-1	0	182	160	60	16	2	49-3	119	**2.47**	**154**	.233	**.286**	50-0-5	.120	-0*	105	27	0	2.1
1959	SF N	8	7	.533	59	9	2	8	167.2	164	66	15	5	57-13	95	2.84	134	.260	.322	45-0-4	.044	-3	117	17	0	1.4
1960	SF N	7	6	.538	47	3	2	2	101.2	100	49	9	3	31-5	65	3.90	89	.256	.312	25-0-3	.200	1	93	-4	0	-0.3
1961	SF N★	14	5	.737	63	0	0	**17**	122	95	41	4	1	37-11	89	2.66	143	.215	.277	20-0-1	.200	2*	—	**16**	0	3.1
1962	†SF N	5	8	.385	59	0	0	19	107	107	55	8	2	42-7	78	4.12	92	.268	.337	16-0-1	.125	-0*	—	-4	0	-0.6
1963	Bal A	5	8	.385	**71**	0	0	**27**	112.1	93	36	5	3	53-13	114	2.24	155	.232	.323	16-0-2	.313	2	—	14	0	2.6
1964	Bal A	7	7	.500	66	0	0	23	97	77	37	7	3	34-14	87	3.06	117	.222	.295	9-0-2	.111	-0	—	5	0	1.0
1965	Bal A	14	7	.667	67	0	0	24	119.1	87	26	5	1	32-10	104	1.89	184	.207	.265	16-0-4	.063	-1	—	22	0	**4.9**
1966	Bal A	9	4	.692	51	0	0	18	92	65	24	5	4	22-6	67	2.25	148	.201	.259	19-0-2	.105	-1	—	12	0	2.1
1967	Bal A	3	10	.231	42	0	0	8	81.1	63	28	5	1	36-12	60	2.55	124	.220	.307	11	.000	-1	—	4	0	0.6
1968	Atl N	0	0	ø	2	0	0	0	0.2	1	4	0	0	4-2	1	54.00	6	.500	.833	0	ø	0	—	-4	0	-0.2
Total	16	105	103	.505	704	93	24-5	154	1693.1	1522	697	140	39	600-114	1164	3.24	115	.242	.311	369-0-36	.133	-2	103	87	0	15.3

MILLER, TRAVIS Travis Eugene; B11.2.1972 Dayton OH; BR/TL/6´3˝/(200–215); [MinA94 1/34]; d8.25; Col Kent St.

YEAR	TM LG	W	L	PCT	G	GS	CG-SHO	SV-BS	IP	H	R	HR	HB	BB-IB	SO	ERA	AERA	OAV	OOB	AB-HR-SH	AVG	PB	SUP	APR	DL	PW
1996	Min A	1	2	.333	7	7	0	0-0	26.1	45	29	7	0	9-0	15	9.23	56	.388	.432	0	ø	0	103	-12	0	-1.0
1997	Min A	1	5	.167	13	7	0	0-0	48.1	64	49	8	1	23-2	26	7.63	61	.320	.389	0	ø	0	93	-18	0	-1.7
1998	Min A	0	2	.000	14	0	0	0-0	23.1	25	10	0	0	11-1	23	3.86	124	.272	.346	0	ø	0	—	3	0	0.2
1999	Min A	2	2	.500	52	0	0	0-2	49.2	55	19	3	0	16-3	40	2.72	191	.284	.335	0	ø	0	—	11	0	0.8
2000	Min A	2	3	.400	67	0	0	1-3	67	83	35	4	1	32-2	62	3.90	135	.297	.368	0	ø	0	—	8	0	0.5
2001	Min A	1	4	.200	45	0	0	0-0	48.2	54	30	5	1	20-1	30	4.81	97	.283	.347	0	ø	0	—	-2	0	-0.2
2002	Min A	0	0	ø	5	0	0	0-0	4	5	2	0	0	2-2	3	4.50	99	.294	.368	0	ø	0	—	0	0	0.0
Total	7	7	18	.280	203	14	0	1-5	267.1	331	174	27	3	113-11	199	5.05	98	.304	.367	0	ø	0	98	-10	0	-1.4

MILLER, TREVER Trever Douglas; B5.29.1973 Louisville KY; BR/TL/6´4˝/(175–200); [DetA91 1/41]; d9.4

YEAR	TM LG	W	L	PCT	G	GS	CG-SHO	SV-BS	IP	H	R	HR	HB	BB-IB	SO	ERA	AERA	OAV	OOB	AB-HR-SH	AVG	PB	SUP	APR	DL	PW
1996	Det A	0	4	.000	5	4	0	0-0	16.2	28	17	3	2	9-0	8	9.18	55	.384	.453	0	ø	0	46	-7	0	-1.1
1998	†Hou N	2	0	1.000	37	1	0	1-1	53.1	57	21	4	1	20-1	30	3.04	133	.266	.332	3	.333	1	91	6	15	0.3
1999	†Hou N	3	2	.600	47	0	0	1-0	49.2	58	29	6	5	29-1	37	5.07	87	.299	.400	3-0-2	.000	-0	—	-3	0	-0.3
2000	Phi N	0	0	ø	14	0	0	0-0	14	19	16	3	1	9-1	10	8.36	55	.317	.408	0	ø	0	—	-7	0	-0.3
	LA N	0	0	ø	2	0	0	0-0	2.1	8	6	0	1	3-0	1	23.14	19	.571	.667	0	ø	0	—	-5	0	-0.2
	Year	0	0	ø	16	0	0	0-0	16.1	27	22	3	2	12-1	11	10.47	44	.365	.461	0	ø	0	—	-12	0	-0.5
2003	Tor A	2	2	.500	**79**	0	0	3-1	52.2	46	30	7	5	28-3	44	4.61	103	.231	.341	0	ø	0	—	1	0	0.0
2004	TB A	1	1	.500	60	0	0	1-2	49	48	21	3	3	15-4	43	3.12	150	.257	.322	0	ø	0	—	7	0	0.4
2005	TB A	2	2	.500	61	0	0	0-3	44.1	45	23	4	7	29-6	35	4.06	108	.278	.399	0	ø	0	—	1	15	0.1
2006	Hou N	2	3	.400	70	0	0	1-2	50.2	42	17	7	4	13-2	56	3.02	149	.225	.286	0	ø	0	—	9	23	0.8
Total	8	12	14	.462	375	5	0	7-9	332.2	351	180	37	29	155-18	264	4.41	102	.272	.360	6-0-2	.167	0	57	2	53	-0.3

MILLER, WADE Wade T.; B9.13.1976 Reading PA; BR/TR/6´2˝/(185–220); [HouN96 20/594]; d7.7; Col Alvernia

YEAR	TM LG	W	L	PCT	G	GS	CG-SHO	SV-BS	IP	H	R	HR	HB	BB-IB	SO	ERA	AERA	OAV	OOB	AB-HR-SH	AVG	PB	SUP	APR	DL	PW
1999	Hou N	0	1	.000	5	1	0	0-0	10.1	17	11	4	0	5-0	8	9.58	46	.362	.423	1	.000	-0	145	-6	0	-0.5
2000	Hou N	6	6	.500	16	16	2	0-0	105	104	66	14	3	42-1	89	5.14	95	.257	.331	40-0-1	.100	-2	110	-3	0	-0.5
2001	†Hou N	16	8	.667	32	32	1	0-0	212	183	91	31	4	76-3	183	3.40	135	.234	.304	66-0-10	.167	-0	96	25	0	2.7
2002	Hou N	15	4	.789	26	26	1-1	0-0	164.2	151	63	14	6	62-9	144	3.28	132	.249	.322	62-0-6	.177	-0	117	19	46	2.1
2003	Hou N	14	13	.519	33	33	1	0-0	187.1	168	96	17	10	77-1	161	4.13	107	.242	.323	63-0-5	.159	0*	102	5	0	0.6
2004	Hou N	7	7	.500	15	15	0	0-0	88.2	76	35	11	0	44-0	74	3.35	131	.228	.317	27-0-8	.259	1*	98	10	100	1.6
2005	Bos A	4	4	.500	16	16	0	0-0	91	96	53	8	3	47-0	64	4.95	92	.267	.354	3	.667	1	102	-4	90	-0.2
2006	Chi N	0	2	.000	5	5	0	0-0	21.2	19	12	4	1	18-1	20	4.57	100	.232	.376	7	.143	-0	89	0	151	0.0
Total	8	62	45	.579	148	144	5-1	0-0	880.2	814	427	103	27	371-15	743	4.00	113	.246	.325	269-0-30	.171	-1	103	46	387	5.8

MILLER, JAKE Walter; B2.28.1898 Wagram OH; D8.20.1975 Venice FL; BL/TL/6´2˝/170; d9.11; b–Russ

YEAR	TM LG	W	L	PCT	G	GS	CG-SHO	SV-BS	IP	H	R	HR	HB	BB-IB	SO	ERA	AERA	OAV	OOB	AB-HR-SH	AVG	PB	SUP	APR	DL	PW
1924	Cle A	0	1	.000	2	2	1	0	12	13	6	0	0	5	4	3.00	142	.265	.333	5	.000	-1	99	1	—	0.0
1925	Cle A	10	13	.435	32	22	13	2	190.1	207	85	4	7	62	51	3.31	133	.279	.340	71-0-3	.183	-3	80	23	—	2.1
1926	Cle A	7	4	.636	18	11	5-3	1	82.2	99	34	1	2	18	24	3.27	124	.307	.348	24	.083	-2	70	8	—	0.7
1927	Cle A	10	8	.556	34	23	11	0	185.1	189	80	4	6	48	53	3.21	131	.271	.324	58-0-3	.138	-4	86	20	—	1.3
1928	Cle A	8	9	.471	25	24	8	0	158	203	89	6	5	43	37	4.44	93	.332	.381	52-0-6	.135	-4	75	-3	—	-0.7
1929	Cle A	14	12	.538	29	29	14-2	0	206	227	98	7	7	60	58	3.58	124	.279	.334	75-0-7	.200	-3	81	19	—	1.9
1930	Cle A	4	4	.500	24	9	1	0	88.1	147	89	6	4	38	31	7.13	68	.373	.433	33-0-5	.303	1	105	-23	—	-1.5

YEAR	TM LG	W	L	PCT	G	GS	CG-SHO	SV-BS	IP	H	R	HR	HB	BB-IB	SO	ERA	AERA	OAV	OOB	AB-HR-SH	AVG	PB	SUP	APR	DL	PW
1931	Cle A	2	1	.667	10	5	1-1	0	41.1	45	26	2	0	19	17	4.35	106	.273	.348	13	.077	-1	143	0	—	-0.1
1933	Chi A	5	6	.455	26	14	4-2	0	105.2	130	75	3	6	47	30	5.62	75	.297	.373	37-0-3	.189	-1*	102	-15	—	-1.3
Total	9	60	58	.508	200	139	58-8	3	1069.2	1260	582	33	37	340	305	4.09	106	.298	.355	368-0-27	.171	-19	86	30	—	2.4
MILLER, WALT	Walter W.; B10.19.1883 Spiceland IN; D3.1.1956 Marion IN; BR/TR/5´11.5˝/180; d9.20																									
1911	Bro N	0	1	.000	3	2	0	0	11	16	14	0	1	6	0	6.55	51	.356	.442	4	.000	-1	56	-6	—	-0.5
MILLER, BILL	William Francis "Wild Bill"; B4.12.1910 Hannibal MO; D2.26.1982 Hannibal MO; BR/TR/6´0˝/180; d10.2																									
1937	StL A	0	1	.000	1	1	0	0	4	7	6	1	1	4	1	13.50	36	.389	.522	1	.000	-0	36	-3	—	-0.5
MILLER, BILL	William Paul "Lefty","Hooks"; B7.26.1927 Minersville PA; D7.1.2003 Lititz PA; BL/TL/6´0˝/175; d4.20																									
1952	NY A	4	6	.400	21	13	5-2	0	88	78	43	5	2	49	45	3.48	96	.241	.345	28-0-2	.214	1	125	-3	0	-0.3
1953	NY A	2	1	.667	13	3	0	1	34	46	19	3	1	19	17	4.76	77	.324	.407	10-0-1	.200	0	112	-4	0	-0.3
1954	NY A	0	1	.000	2	1	0	0	5.2	9	4	0	0	1	6	6.35	54	.375	.385	1	.000	-0	51	-2	0	-0.3
1955	Bal A	0	1	.000	5	1	0	0	4	3	6	0	0	10-1	4	13.50	28	.200	.520	1	1.000	0	163	-4	0	-0.7
Total	4	6	9	.400	41	18	5-2	1	131.2	136	72	8	3	79-1	72	4.24	81	.270	.371	40-0-3	.225	1	121	-13	0	-1.6
MILLIGAN, JOHN	John Alexander; B1.22.1904 Schuylerville NY; D5.15.1972 Fort Pierce FL; BR/TL/5´10˝/172; d8.11; Col Cornell																									
1928	Phi N	2	5	.286	13	7	3	0	68	69	39	2	1	32	22	4.37	98	.274	.358	20-0-4	.050	-2	96	-1	—	-0.3
1929	Phi N	0	1	.000	8	3	0	0	9.2	29	19	0	2	10	2	16.76	31	.527	.612	3	.333	0	140	-11	—	-0.8
1930	Phi N	1	2	.333	9	2	1	0	28.1	26	16	0	2	21	7	3.18	172	.255	.392	9	.111	-1	88	5	—	0.4
1931	Phi N	0	0	ø	3	0	0	0	8	11	5	0	1	4	6	3.38	126	.324	.410	2	.000	-0	—	0	—	0.0
1934	Was A	0	0	ø	2	0	0	0	2.2	6	3	0	0	0	1	10.13	43	.500	.500	0	ø	0	—	-2	—	-0.1
Total	5	3	8	.273	35	12	4	0	116.2	141	82	2	6	67	38	5.17	90	.310	.405	34-0-4	.088	-3	108	-9	—	-0.8
MILLIGAN, BILLY	William Joseph; B8.19.1878 Buffalo NY; D10.14.1928 Buffalo NY; BR/TL/5´7˝/?; d4.30																									
1901	Phi A	0	3	.000	6	3	2	0	33	43	24	1	2	14	5	4.36	86	.312	.383	15-1-1	.333	2*	137	-3	—	0.0
1904	NY N	0	1	.000	5	1	1	2	25	36	22	2	1	4	6	5.40	51	.310	.339	9	.111	0	0	-8	—	-0.4
Total	2	0	4	.000	11	4	3	2	58	79	46	3	3	18	11	4.81	69	.311	.364	24-1-1	.250	2	118	-11	—	-0.4
MILLIKEN, BOB	Robert Fogle "Bobo"; B8.25.1926 Majorsville WV; BR/TR/6´0˝/(190–195); d4.22; C7																									
1953	†Bro N	8	4	.667	37	10	3	2	117.2	94	52	13	0	42	65	3.37	127	.214	.283	34-0-2	.118	-1	107	10	0	0.7
1954	Bro N	5	2	.714	24	3	0	2	62.2	58	31	12	2	18	25	4.02	102	.246	.304	17	.176	-0	80	0	0	-0.1
Total	2	13	6	.684	61	13	3	4	180.1	152	83	25	2	60	90	3.59	117	.225	.290	51-0-2	.137	-2	101	10	0	0.6
MILLS, ALAN	Alan Bernard; B10.18.1966 Lakeland FL; BR/TR/6´1˝/(190–195); [CalA86 S1/8]; d4.14; Col Tuskegee																									
1990	NY A	1	5	.167	36	0	0	0-2	41.2	48	21	4	1	33-6	24	4.10	97	.298	.418	0	ø	0	—	-1	0	0.0
1991	NY A	1	1	.500	6	2	0	0-0	16.1	16	9	1	0	8-0	11	4.41	95	.254	.333	0	ø	0	44	-1	0	0.0
1992	Bal A	10	4	.714	35	3	0	2-1	103.1	78	33	5	1	54-10	60	2.61	156	.215	.315	0	ø	0	105	16	0	2.1
1993	Bal A	5	4	.556	45	0	0	4-3	100.1	80	39	14	4	51-5	68	3.23	140	.225	.324	0	ø	0	—	14	0	1.2
1994	Bal A	3	3	.500	47	0	0	2-2	45.1	43	26	7	2	24-2	44	5.16	98	.251	.348	0	ø	0	—	0	0	0.0
1995	Bal A	3	0	1.000	21	0	0	0-1	23	30	20	4	2	18-4	16	7.43	64	.309	.424	0	ø	0	—	-7	0	-0.7
1996	†Bal A	3	2	.600	49	0	0	3-5	54.2	40	26	10	1	35-2	50	4.28	116	.208	.330	0	ø	0	—	5	40	0.4
1997	†Bal A	2	3	.400	39	0	0	0-0	38.2	41	23	5	1	33-1	32	4.89	90	.268	.399	0	ø	0	—	-2	66	-0.3
1998	Bal A	3	4	.429	72	0	0	2-3	77	55	32	8	1	50-8	57	3.74	122	.203	.326	0	ø	0	—	8	0	0.6
1999	LA N	3	4	.429	68	0	0	0-5	72.1	70	33	10	4	43-4	49	3.73	117	.261	.367	2	.000	-0	—	5	0	0.4
2000	LA N	2	1	.667	18	0	0	1-0	25.2	31	12	3	1	16-0	18	4.21	106	.304	.403	3	.000	-0	—	1	0	0.1
	Bal A	2	0	1.000	23	0	0	1-0	23.2	25	17	6	1	19-1	18	6.46	73	.263	.391	0	ø	0	—	-4	25	-0.3
2001	Bal A	1	1	.500	15	0	0	0-0	14	20	15	6	2	11-3	9	9.64	45	.333	.452	0	ø	0	—	-8	102	-1.0
Total	12	39	32	.549	474	5	0	15-22	636	577	306	83	21	395-46	456	4.12	109	.245	.356	5	.000	-0	74	26	233	2.5
MILLS, ART	Arthur Grant; B3.2.1903 Utica NY; D7.23.1975 Utica NY; BR/TR/5´10˝/155; d4.16; C5; f–Willie																									
1927	Bos N	0	1	.000	15	1	0	0	37.2	41	19	1	3	18	7	3.82	97	.287	.378	7	.000	-1	229	-1	—	-0.1
1928	Bos N	0	0	ø	4	0	0	0	7.2	17	11	3	2	8	0	12.91	30	.472	.587	1	.000	-0	—	-7	—	-0.3
Total	2	0	1	.000	19	1	0	0	45.1	58	30	4	5	26	7	5.36	70	.324	.424	8	.000	-1	229	-8	—	-0.4
MILLS, LEFTY	Howard Robinson; B5.12.1910 Dedham MA; D9.23.1982 Riverside CA; BL/TL/6´1˝/187; d6.10																									
1934	StL A	0	0	ø	4	0	0	0	8.2	10	4	0	0	11	2	4.15	120	.303	.477	3	.333	0	—	1	—	0.0
1937	StL A	1	1	.500	2	2	1	0	12.2	16	13	1	0	10	10	6.39	75	.286	.394	5	.000	-1	81	-3	—	-0.5
1938	StL A	10	12	.455	30	27	15-1	0	210.1	216	139	16	8	116	134	5.31	94	.262	.358	66-0-5	.091	-3	90	-8	—	-1.0
1939	StL A	4	11	.267	34	14	4	2	144.1	147	114	16	8	113	103	6.55	74	.264	.395	47-1-2	.234	1	69	-24	—	-2.0
1940	StL A	0	6	.000	26	5	1	0	59	64	55	7	3	52	18	7.78	59	.275	.413	13	.154	-0	31	-19	—	-1.6
Total	5	15	30	.333	96	48	21-1	2	435	453	325	40	19	302	267	6.06	81	.266	.382	134-1-7	.149	-3	78	-53	—	-5.1
MILLS, DICK	Richard Alan; B1.29.1945 Boston MA; BR/TR/6´3˝/199; [BosA66 S3/54]; d9.7																									
1970	Bos A	0	0	ø	2	0	0	0-0	3.2	6	4	0	1	3-0	3	2.45	162	.353	.476	0	ø	0	—	-1	0	0.0
MILLS, WILLIE	William Grant "Wee Willie"; B8.15.1877 Schenevus NY; D7.5.1914 Norwood NY; BR/TR/5´7˝/150; d7.13; s–Art																									
1901	NY N	0	2	.000	2	2	2	0	16	21	15	2	1	4	3	8.44	39	.313	.361	6	.167	0	64	-7	—	-0.7
MILLWOOD, KEVIN	Kevin Austin; B12.24.1974 Gastonia NC; BR/TR/6´4˝/(205–235); [AtlN93 11/320]; d7.14																									
1997	Atl N	5	3	.625	12	8	0	0-0	51.1	55	26	1	2	21-1	42	4.03	104	.281	.348	12-0-1	.000	-1	132	1	0	0.0
1998	Atl N	17	8	.680	31	29	3-1	0-0	174.1	175	86	18	3	56-3	163	4.08	102	.258	.316	50-0-6	.080	-1	112	3	0	0.2
1999	†Atl N★	18	7	.720	33	33	2	0-0	228	168	80	24	4	59-2	205	2.68	167	**.202**	**.258**	78-1-6	.154	0	100	44	0	4.3
2000	†Atl N	10	13	.435	36	**35**	0	0-0	212.2	213	115	26	3	62-2	168	4.66	97	.258	.311	59-0-14	.119	-1	98	-1	0	-0.3
2001	†Atl N	7	7	.500	21	21	0	0-0	121	121	66	20	1	40-6	84	4.31	100	.260	.319	43-0-1	.093	-2	121	-1	74	-0.3
2002	†Atl N	18	8	.692	35	34	1-1	0-0	217	186	83	16	8	65-7	178	3.24	125	.230	.292	70-1-11	.200	3	102	21	0	2.6
2003	Phi N	14	12	.538	35	35	5-**3**	0-0	222	210	103	19	4	68-6	169	4.01	99	.250	.307	68-0-6	.059	-3	101	0	0	-0.3
2004	Phi N	9	6	.600	25	25	0	0-0	141	155	81	14	7	51-5	125	4.85	91	.278	.345	46-0-5	.174	1	99	-6	37	-0.5
2005	Cle A	9	11	.450	30	30	1	0-0	192	182	72	20	4	52-0	146	**2.86**	146	.248	.300	2	.000	-0	81	27	21	2.4
2006	Tex A	16	12	.571	34	**34**	2	0-0	215	228	114	23	4	53-4	157	4.52	104	.272	.317	5-0-1	.000	-1	99	4	0	0.5
Total	10	123	87	.586	292	284	14-5	0-0	1774.1	1693	826	181	40	527-36	1437	3.85	112	.250	.306	433-2-51	.122	-5	102	92	132	8.6
MILNAR, AL	Albert Joseph "Happy" (b Albert Joseph Mlinar); B12.26.1913 Cleveland OH; D6.30.2005 Cleveland OH; BL/TL/6´2˝/195; d4.30; Mil 1944–45																									
1936	Cle A	1	2	.333	4	3	1	0	22	26	20	0	0	18	9	7.36	68	.286	.404	10	.300	0	70	-5	—	-0.5
1938	Cle A	3	1	.750	23	5	2	1	68.1	90	48	5	0	26	29	5.00	93	.320	.378	26-1-0	.154	-0*	121	-5	—	-0.3
1939	Cle A	14	12	.538	37	26	12-2	3	209	212	96	11	0	99	76	3.79	116	.264	.345	79	.253	4*	109	17	—	2.2
1940	Cle A☆	18	10	.643	37	33	15-**4**	3	242.1	242	120	14	1	99	99	3.27	129	.257	.328	94-0-3	.181	-1	112	18	—	1.5
1941	Cle A	12	19	.387	35	30	9-1	0	229.1	236	128	9	1	116	82	4.36	90	.266	.352	82-2-1	.171	2	89	-13	0	-1.4
1942	Cle A	6	8	.429	28	19	8-2	0	157	146	82	3	4	85	35	4.13	84	.251	.350	70-1-1	.171	2*	120	-11	0	-0.7
1943	Cle A	1	3	.250	16	6	0	0	39	51	38	0	1	35	12	6.08	38	.329	.455	19	.211	0*	99	-21	0	-2.0
	StL A	1	2	.333	3	2	1	0	14.2	23	11	0	0	9	7	5.52	60	.354	.432	6-0-1	.333	1	190	-4	0	-0.6
	Year	2	5	.286	19	8	1	0	53.2	74	49	0	1	44	19	7.38	43	.336	.449	25-0-1	.240	1	123	-25	0	-2.6
1946	StL A	1	1	.500	4	2	1-1	0	14.2	15	4	1	0	6	1	2.45	152	.278	.350	4	.750	1	57	2	0	0.4
	Phi N	0	0	ø	1	1	0	0	0	2	4	0	0	2	0	(4)	ø	1.000	1.000	0	ø	0	225	-4	0	-0.3
Total	8	57	58	.496	188	127	49-10	7	996.1	1043	551	43	7	495	350	4.22	96	.270	.354	390-4-6	.203	9	106	-26	0	-1.7
MILSTEAD, GEORGE	George Earl "Cowboy"; B6.26.1903 Cleburne TX; D8.9.1977 Cleburne TX; BL/TL/5´10˝/144; d6.27																									
1924	Chi N	1	1	.500	13	2	1	0	29.2	41	25	3	1	13	6	6.07	64	.328	.396	6	.167	0	76	-8	—	-0.4
1925	Chi N	1	1	.500	5	3	1	0	21	26	12	0	0	8	7	3.00	144	.310	.370	7	.000	-1	98	1	—	0.0
1926	Chi N	1	5	.167	18	4	0	2	55.1	63	30	0	1	24	14	3.58	107	.309	.384	19	.053	-2	65	0	—	-0.1
Total	3	3	7	.300	36	9	2	2	106	130	67	3	2	45	27	4.16	95	.315	.385	32	.063	-3	80	-7	—	-0.5
MILTON, ERIC	Eric Robert; B8.4.1975 State College PA; BL/TL/6´3˝/(200–220); [NYA96 1/20]; d4.5; Col Maryland																									
1998	Min A	8	14	.364	32	32	1	0-0	172.1	195	113	25	2	70-0	107	5.64	85	.282	.347	9	.444	1	89	-15	0	-1.5
1999	Min A	7	11	.389	34	34	5-2	0-0	206.1	190	111	28	3	63-2	163	4.49	115	.243	.299	2	.000	0	87	14	0	1.0
2000	Min A	13	10	.565	33	33	0	0-0	200	205	123	35	7	44-0	160	4.86	108	.260	.303	2	.000	-0	92	5	0	0.4

YEAR	TM LG	W	L	PCT	G	GS	CG-SHO	SV-BS	IP	H	R	HR	HB	BB-IB	SO	ERA	AERA	OAV	OOB	AB-HR-SH	AVG	PB	SUP	APR	DL	PW
2001	Min A☆	15	7	.682	35	34	2-1	0-0	220.2	222	109	35	5	61-0	157	4.32	108	.257	.308	2	.000	-0	102	10	0	0.7
2002	†Min A	13	9	.591	29	29	2-1	0-0	171	173	96	24	3	30-0	121	4.84	92	.258	.291	5	.400	1*	86	-6	26	-0.7
2003	†Min A	1	0	1.000	3	3	0	0-0	17	15	5	2	0	1-0	7	2.65	170	.234	.242	0	ø	0	109	4	168	0.2
2004	Phi N	14	6	.700	34	34	0	0-0	201	196	110	43	1	75-6	161	4.75	93	.255	.320	65-0-5	.154	-0	123	-5	0	-0.5
2005	Cin N	8	15	.348	34	34	0	0-0	186.1	237	141	40	7	52-2	123	6.47	66	.302	.349	56-2-5	.143	1	111	-44	0	-4.5
2006	Cin N	8	8	.500	26	26	0	0-0	152.2	163	94	29	5	42-4	90	5.19	91	.269	.320	49-0-6	.224	3*	103	-6	31	-0.3
Total	9	87	80	.521	260	259	10-4	0-0	1527.1	1596	902	261	33	438-14	1089	5.01	94	.265	.316	190-2-16	.184	6	99	-43	225	-5.2
MILTON, LARRY	Samuel Lawrence "Tug"; B5.4.1879 Owensboro KY; D5.15.1942 Hannibal MO; TR; d5.7																									
1903	StL N	0	0	ø	1	0	0	0	4	3	1	0	0	1	0	2.25	145	.200	.250	2	.500	0	—	1	—	0.1
MIMBS, MIKE	Michael Randall; B2.13.1969 Macon GA; BL/TL/6´2˝/(182–190); [LAN90 24/645]; d5.6; Col Mercer																									
1995	Phi N	9	7	.563	35	19	2-1	1-0	136.2	127	70	10	6	75-2	93	4.15	102	.250	.348	35-0-8	.143	-1	86	0	0	0.0
1996	Phi N	3	9	.250	21	17	0	0-0	99.1	116	66	13	2	41-1	56	5.53	78	.294	.361	33-0-2	.121	-1	79	-12	26	-1.4
1997	Phi N	0	3	.000	17	1	0	0-0	28.2	31	27	6	3	27-1	29	7.53	56	.272	.424	2	.000	-0	22	-11	0	-1.0
Total	3	12	19	.387	73	37	2-1	1-0	264.2	274	163	29	11	143-4	178	5.03	85	.270	.362	70-0-10	.129	-2	81	-23	26	-2.4
MINAHAN, COTTON	Edmund Joseph; B12.10.1882 Springfield OH; D5.20.1958 E.Orange NJ; BR/TR/6´0˝/190; d4.21; Col Manhattan																									
1907	Cin N	0	2	.000	2	2	1	0	14	12	8	0	1	13	4	1.29	202	.261	.433	5	.000	-1	82	0	—	-0.1
MINARCIN, RUDY	Rudolph Anthony "Buster"; B3.25.1930 N.Vandergrift PA; BR/TR/6´0˝/195; d4.11																									
1955	Cin N	5	9	.357	41	12	3-1	1	115.2	116	73	17	3	51-7	45	4.90	86	.261	.339	28	.179	-1	100	-9	0	-0.9
1956	Bos A	1	0	1.000	3	1	0	0	9.2	9	4	2	1	8-0	5	2.79	165	.250	.400	2	.500	1	96	2	0	0.2
1957	Bos A	0	0	ø	26	0	0	2	44.2	44	30	5	1	30-4	20	4.43	90	.267	.375	2	.000	0	—	-4	0	-0.2
Total	3	6	9	.400	70	13	3-1	3	170	169	107	24	5	89-11	70	4.66	90	.262	.352	32	.188	0	101	-11	0	-0.9
MINCHEY, NATE	Nathan Derek; B8.31.1969 Austin TX; BR/TR/6´8˝/225; [MonN87 2/36]; d9.12																									
1993	Bos A	1	2	.333	5	5	1	0-0	33	35	16	5	0	8-2	18	3.55	131	.265	.307	0	ø	0	103	3	0	0.2
1994	Bos A	2	3	.400	6	5	0	0-0	23	44	26	1	0	14-2	15	8.61	59	.427	.483	0	ø	0	58	-9	0	-1.5
1996	Bos A	0	2	.000	2	2	0	0-0	6	16	11	1	0	5-0	4	15.00	34	.533	.583	0	ø	0	91	-6	94	-0.9
1997	Col N	0	0	ø	2	0	0	0-0	2	5	3	0	0	1-0	1	13.50	38	.556	.600	0	ø	0	—	-1	0	-0.1
Total	4	3	7	.300	15	12	1	0-0	64	100	56	7	0	28-4	38	6.75	72	.365	.418	0	ø	0	82	-13	94	-2.3
MINER, RAY	Raymond Theadore "Lefty"; B4.4.1897 Glens Falls NY; D9.15.1963 Glenridge NY; BR/TL/5´11˝/160; d9.15																									
1921	Phi A	0	0	ø	1	0	0	0	1	2	4	0	0	3	0	36.00	12	.400	.625	0	ø	0	—	-3	—	-0.1
MINER, ZACH	Zachary Charles; B3.12.1982 St.Louis MO; BR/TR/6´3˝/200; [AtlN00 4/106]; d6.4																									
2006	†Det A	7	6	.538	27	16	1	0-0	93	100	53	11	0	32-1	59	4.84	93	.276	.333	6	.167	0	119	-3	0	-0.4
MINETTO, CRAIG	Craig Stephen; B4.25.1954 Stockton CA; BL/TL/6´0˝/185; d7.4; Col San Joaquin Delta (CA) JC																									
1978	Oak A	0	0	ø	4	1	0	0-0	12	13	10	1	2	7-0	3	3.75	98	.283	.393	0	ø	0	221	-2	0	-0.1
1979	Oak A	1	5	.167	36	13	0	0-1	118.1	131	85	16	3	58-3	64	5.55	73	.282	.360	0	ø	0	91	-22	0	-1.1
1980	Oak A	0	2	.000	7	1	0	1-0	8	11	7	2	0	3-1	5	7.88	48	.324	.368	0	ø	0	47	-3	25	-0.7
1981	Oak A	0	0	ø	8	0	0	0-0	6.2	7	2	0	1	4-0	4	2.70	130	.280	.387	0	ø	0	—	1	0	0.0
Total	4	1	7	.125	55	15	0	1-1	145	162	104	19	6	72-4	76	5.40	74	.284	.364	0	ø	0	97	-26	25	-1.9
MINGORI, STEVE	Stephen Bernard; B2.29.1944 Kansas City MO; BL/TL/5´10˝/(165–170); d8.5; Col Pittsburg St. (KS)																									
1970	Cle A	1	0	1.000	21	0	0	1-0	20.1	17	8	2	1	12-5	16	2.66	151	.227	.341	1	.000	-0	—	2	0	0.1
1971	Cle A	1	2	.333	54	0	0	4-2	56.2	31	10	2	1	24-6	45	1.43	271	.166	.259	2	.500	0	—	14	23	1.0
1972	Cle A	0	6	.000	41	0	0	10-3	57	67	28	4	2	36-8	47	3.95	83	.293	.392	8	.125	-0*	—	-4	0	-0.6
1973	Cle A	0	0	ø	5	0	0	0-1	11.2	10	8	3	0	10-1	4	6.17	64	.233	.377	0	ø	0	—	-2	0	-0.1
	KC A	3	3	.500	19	1	0	1-0	56.1	59	21	6	3	23-6	46	3.04	135	.267	.344	0	ø	0	0	6	0	0.6
	Year	3	3	.500	24	1	0	1-1	68	69	29	9	3	33-7	50	3.57	114	.261	.350	0	ø	0	0	4	0	0.5
1974	KC A	2	3	.400	36	0	0	2-4	67.1	53	31	4	2	23-5	43	2.81	136	.212	.282	0	ø	0	—	4	0	0.4
1975	KC A	0	3	.000	36	0	0	2-2	50.1	42	21	2	1	20-4	25	2.50	154	.226	.300	1	.000	-0	—	5	21	0.4
1976	†KC A	5	5	.500	55	0	0	10-2	85.1	73	23	3	3	25-8	38	2.32	151	.238	.301	0	ø	0	—	12	0	1.9
1977	†KC A	2	4	.333	43	0	0	4-2	64	59	26	4	1	19-4	19	3.09	130	.254	.307	0	ø	0	—	6	0	0.6
1978	†KC A	1	4	.200	45	0	0	7-1	69	64	25	5	3	16-4	28	2.74	140	.242	.290	0	ø	0	—	8	0	0.7
1979	KC A	3	3	.500	30	1	0	1-0	46.2	69	36	10	1	17-2	18	5.79	74	.348	.401	0	ø	0	85	-9	23	-1.0
Total	10	18	33	.353	385	2	0	42-17	584.2	544	237	45	18	225-53	329	3.03	126	.248	.321	12	.167	-0	47	42	67	4.0
MINNER, PAUL	Paul Edison "Lefty"; B7.30.1923 New Wilmington PA; D3.28.2006 Lemoyne PA; BL/TL/6´5˝/(200–210); d9.12																									
1946	Bro N	0	1	.000	3	0	0	0	4	6	4	1	0	3	3	6.75	50	.333	.429	0	ø	0	—	-2	0	-0.3
1948	Bro N	4	3	.571	28	2	0	1	62.2	61	23	5	0	26	23	2.44	164	.257	.331	21	.190	1*	155	9	0	1.1
1949	†Bro N	3	1	.750	27	1	0	2	47.1	49	22	7	1	18	17	3.80	108	.272	.342	14	.214	-0	172	1	0	0.1
1950	Chi N	8	13	.381	39	24	9-1	4	190.1	217	105	18	1	72	99	4.11	102	.287	.350	65-1-1	.215	2*	89	1	0	0.5
1951	Chi N	6	17	.261	33	28	14-3	1	201.2	219	97	20	0	64	68	3.79	108	.277	.331	71-1-2	.254	5*	85	6	0	1.4
1952	Chi N	14	9	.609	28	27	12-2	0	180.2	180	84	13	1	54	61	3.74	103	.258	.312	64-1-3	.234	6*	117	3	0	1.1
1953	Chi N	12	15	.444	31	27	9-2	1	201	227	109	15	3	40	64	4.21	106	.283	.320	68-1-3	.221	2	71	5	0	1.0
1954	Chi N	11	11	.500	32	29	12	1	218	236	107	19	1	50	79	3.96	106	.280	.317	76-2-1	.171	3*	109	6	0	0.9
1955	Chi N	9	9	.500	22	22	7-1	0	157.2	173	67	15	1	47-10	53	3.48	117	.283	.333	56-0-1	.232	2	102	11	0	1.5
1956	Chi N	2	5	.286	10	9	1	0	47	60	38	9	2	19-2	14	6.89	55	.324	.389	12	.250	2	101	-15	97	-1.7
Total	10	69	84	.451	253	169	64-9	10	1310.1	1428	656	122	10	393-12	481	3.94	105	.279	.331	447-6-11	.219	22	96	25	97	5.6
MINNICK, DON	Donald Athey; B4.14.1931 Lynchburg VA; BR/TR/6´3˝/195; d9.23																									
1957	Was A	0	1	.000	2	1	0	0	9.1	14	8	1	0	2-0	7	4.82	81	.341	.372	2	.000	-0	23	-2	0	-0.2
MINOR, BLAS	Blas; B3.20.1966 Merced CA; BR/TR/6´3˝/(195–203); [PitN88 6/148]; d7.28; Col Arizona St.																									
1992	Pit N	0	0	ø	1	0	0	0-0	2	3	2	0	0	0-0	0	4.50	77	.333	.333	0	ø	0	—	-1	0	0.0
1993	Pit N	8	6	.571	65	0	0	2-1	94.1	94	43	8	4	26-3	84	4.10	100	.263	.316	10	.200	1	—	1	0	0.2
1994	Pit N	0	1	.000	17	0	0	1-0	19	27	17	4	1	9-2	17	8.05	54	.351	.420	0-0-1	ø	0	—	-7	0	-0.4
1995	NY N	4	2	.667	35	0	0	1-0	46.2	44	21	6	1	13-1	43	3.66	110	.253	.309	2	.000	-0	—	2	31	0.2
1996	NY N	0	0	ø	17	0	0	0-1	25.2	23	11	4	0	6-2	20	3.51	115	.237	.279	1	.000	-0	—	2	0	0.1
	Sea A	0	1	.000	11	0	0	0-0	25.1	27	14	6	0	11-0	14	4.97	100	.276	.349	0	ø	0	—	1	0	0.0
1997	Hou N	1	0	1.000	11	0	0	1-2	12	13	7	1	1	5-0	6	4.50	89	.277	.352	0	ø	0	—	-1	0	-0.1
Total	6	13	10	.565	157	0	0	5-4	225	231	115	29	7	70-8	184	4.40	95	.269	.326	13-0-1	.154	0	—	-3	31	0.0
MINSHALL, JIM	James Edward; B7.4.1947 Covington KY; BR/TR/6´6˝/205; [PitN66 2/35]; d9.14																									
1974	Pit N	0	1	.000	5	0	0	0-1	4.1	1	1	0	0	2-1	3	0.00	ø	.083	.200	0	ø	0	—	1	0	0.3
1975	Pit N	0	0	ø	1	0	0	0-0	1	0	0	0	0	2-0	2	0.00	ø	.000	.400	0	ø	0	—	0	0	0.0
Total	2	0	1	.000	6	0	0	0-1	5.1	1	1	0	0	4-1	5	0.00	ø	.067	.250	0	ø	0	—	1	0	0.3
MINTON, GREG	Gregory Brian; B7.29.1951 Lubbock TX; BB/TR/6´2˝/(180–207); [KCA70*3/55]; d9.7; Col San Diego Mesa (CA) JC																									
1975	SF N	1	1	.500	4	2	0	0-0	17	19	14	1	1	11-3	6	6.88	55	.288	.397	6-0-1	.000	-1	92	-5	0	-0.6
1976	SF N	0	3	.000	10	2	0	0-0	25.2	32	18	0	1	12-1	7	4.91	74	.317	.388	5	.200	-0*	109	-4	0	-0.4
1977	SF N	1	1	.500	2	2	0	0-0	14	14	8	0	0	4-0	5	4.50	88	.264	.316	3-0-1	.333	1*	90	-1	0	0.0
1978	SF N	0	1	.000	11	0	0	0-1	15.2	22	14	3	1	8-1	6	8.04	43	.338	.413	1	.000	-0	—	-7	0	-0.5
1979	SF N	4	3	.571	46	0	0	4-3	79.2	59	25	0	2	27-7	33	1.81	193	.215	.289	4-0-1	.000	-0	—	13	57	1.3
1980	SF N	4	6	.400	68	0	0	19-6	91.1	81	28	0	0	34-6	42	2.46	143	.243	.312	8-0-2	.125	-0	—	11	0	1.8
1981	SF N	4	5	.444	55	0	0	21-4	84.1	84	28	0	0	36-8	29	2.88	118	.267	.340	12-0-1	.000	-1	—	6	0	0.9
1982	SF N★	10	4	.714	78	0	0	30-7	123	108	29	5	2	42-17	58	1.83	196	.244	.310	17-0-1	.176	0	—	**24**	0	**3.9**
1983	SF N	7	11	.389	73	0	0	22-6	106.2	117	51	6	0	47-13	38	3.54	100	.283	.352	11-1-0	.545	4	—	-1	0	0.3
1984	SF N	4	9	.308	74	1	0	19-5	124.1	130	60	6	0	57-20	48	3.76	94	.267	.341	21-0-1	.048	-1	50	-4	0	-0.5
1985	SF N	5	4	.556	68	0	0	4-3	96.2	98	42	6	0	54-18	37	3.54	98	.272	.364	8	.000	-1	—	0	0	0.1
1986	SF N	4	4	.500	48	0	0	5-4	68.2	63	35	4	1	34-15	34	3.93	90	.251	.339	5	.400	2	—	-4	23	-0.2
1987	SF N	1	0	1.000	15	0	0	1-0	23.1	30	9	2	1	10-3	9	3.47	111	.323	.394	2-0-1	.000	-0	—	2	0	0.1

YEAR	TM LG	W	L	PCT	G	GS	CG-SHO	SV-BS	IP	H	R	HR	HB	BB-IB	SO	ERA	AERA	OAV	OOB	AB-HR-SH	AVG	PB	SUP	APR	DL	PW
	Cal A	5	4	.556	41	0	0	10-2	76	71	28	4	1	29-4	35	3.08	141	.257	.328	0	ø	0	—	12	0	1.6
1988	Cal A	4	5	.444	44	0	0	7-10	79	67	37	1	3	34-10	46	2.85	136	.233	.317	0	ø	0	—	5	37	0.7
1989	Cal A	4	3	.571	62	0	0	8-3	90	76	22	4	2	37-4	42	2.20	174	.230	.310	0	ø	0	—	17	15	1.6
1990	Cal A	1	1	.500	11	0	0	0-0	15.1	11	4	1	1	7-1	4	2.35	164	.212	.317	0	ø	0	—	3	133	0.3
Total	16	59	65	.476	710	7	0	150-54	1130.2	1082	452	43	16	483-131	479	3.10	118	.257	.334	103-1-9	.146	2	94	67	265	10.4

MINTZ, STEVE Stephen Wayne; B11.24.1968 Wilmington NC; BL/TR/5´11˝/190; [LAN90 17/461]; d5.18; Col Mount Olive

YEAR	TM LG	W	L	PCT	G	GS	CG-SHO	SV-BS	IP	H	R	HR	HB	BB-IB	SO	ERA	AERA	OAV	OOB	AB-HR-SH	AVG	PB	SUP	APR	DL	PW
1995	SF N	1	2	.333	14	0	0	0-1	19.1	26	16	4	2	12-3	7	7.45	55	.329	.426	3	.000	-0	—	-6	0	-0.9
1999	Ana A	0	0	ø	3	0	0	0-0	5	8	2	1	0	2-0	2	3.60	136	.381	.435	0	ø	0	—	1	0	0.0
Total	2	1	2	.333	17	0	0	0-1	24.1	34	18	5	2	14-3	9	6.66	64	.340	.427	3	.000	-0	—	-5	0	-0.9

MINUTELLI, GINO Gino Michael; B5.23.1964 Wilmington DE; BL/TL/6´0˝/(180–190); d9.18; Col Southwestern (CA) CC

YEAR	TM LG	W	L	PCT	G	GS	CG-SHO	SV-BS	IP	H	R	HR	HB	BB-IB	SO	ERA	AERA	OAV	OOB	AB-HR-SH	AVG	PB	SUP	APR	DL	PW
1990	Cin N	0	0	ø	2	0	0	0-0	1	0	1	0	1	2-0	0	9.00	44	.000	.500	0	ø	0	—	-1	0	0.0
1991	Cin N	0	2	.000	16	3	0	0-0	25.1	30	17	5	0	18-1	21	6.04	63	.288	.387	3	.000	-0	95	-5	15	-0.4
1993	SF N	0	1	.000	9	0	0	0-1	14.1	7	9	2	0	15-0	10	3.77	104	.152	.349	4	.000	-0	—	-1	0	-0.1
Total	3	0	3	.000	27	3	0	0-1	40.2	37	27	7	1	35-1	31	5.31	73	.242	.378	7	.000	-1	95	-7	15	-0.5

MIRABELLA, PAUL Paul Thomas; B3.20.1954 Belleville NJ; BL/TL/6´2˝/(185–196); [TexA76*S1/21]; d7.28; Col Montclair St.

YEAR	TM LG	W	L	PCT	G	GS	CG-SHO	SV-BS	IP	H	R	HR	HB	BB-IB	SO	ERA	AERA	OAV	OOB	AB-HR-SH	AVG	PB	SUP	APR	DL	PW
1978	Tex A	3	2	.600	10	4	0	1-0	28	30	18	2	0	17-0	23	5.79	65	.286	.379	0	ø	0	156	-5	0	-0.9
1979	NY A	0	4	.000	10	1	0	0-0	14.1	16	15	3	1	10-1	4	8.79	47	.276	.391	0	ø	0	66	-7	0	-1.4
1980	Tor A	5	12	.294	33	22	3-1	0-1	130.2	151	73	11	3	66-3	53	4.34	100	.294	.375	0	ø	0	81	-1	0	-0.2
1981	Tor A	0	0	ø	8	1	0	0-0	14.2	20	16	2	1	7-0	9	7.36	54	.313	.384	0	ø	0	136	-6	0	-0.3
1982	Tex A	1	1	.500	40	0	0	3-3	50.2	46	28	4	2	22-5	29	4.80	81	.241	.324	0	ø	0	—	-5	0	-0.2
1983	Bal A	0	0	ø	3	2	0	0-0	9.2	9	6	1	0	7-0	4	5.59	72	.243	.364	0	ø	0	136	-1	0	-0.1
1984	Sea A	2	5	.286	52	1	0	3-3	68	74	39	6	1	32-6	41	4.37	92	.282	.359	0	ø	0	22	-4	0	-0.3
1985	Sea A	0	0	ø	10	0	0	0-0	13.2	9	4	0	2	4-1	8	1.32	321	.188	.268	0	ø	0	—	4	0	0.2
1986	Sea A	0	0	ø	8	0	0	0-0	6.1	13	7	1	0	3-0	6	8.53	50	.419	.471	0	ø	0	—	-3	0	-0.1
1987	Mil A	2	1	.667	29	0	0	2-2	29.1	30	20	0	0	16-3	14	4.91	94	.268	.351	0	ø	0	—	-2	0	-0.2
1988	Mil A	2	2	.500	38	0	0	4-0	60	44	12	3	0	21-5	33	1.65	243	.204	.272	0	ø	0	—	16	15	1.2
1989	Mil A	0	0	ø	13	0	0	0-0	15.1	18	14	1	1	7-3	6	7.63	51	.290	.356	0	ø	0	—	-6	117	-0.3
1990	Mil A	4	2	.667	44	2	0	0-1	59	66	32	9	2	27-2	28	3.97	98	.281	.357	0	ø	0	82	-1	0	-0.1
Total	13	19	29	.396	298	33	3-1	13-10	499.2	526	284	43	13	239-29	258	4.45	92	.272	.352	0	ø	0	94	-21	132	-2.7

MIRANDA, ANGEL Angel Luis (Andujar); B11.9.1969 Arecibo, PR; BL/TL/6´1˝/(160–195); d6.5

YEAR	TM LG	W	L	PCT	G	GS	CG-SHO	SV-BS	IP	H	R	HR	HB	BB-IB	SO	ERA	AERA	OAV	OOB	AB-HR-SH	AVG	PB	SUP	APR	DL	PW
1993	Mil A	4	5	.444	22	17	2	0-0	120	100	53	12	2	52-4	88	3.30	131	.226	.309	0	ø	0	93	12	57	0.7
1994	Mil A	2	5	.286	8	8	1	0-0	46	39	28	8	0	27-0	24	5.28	96	.234	.338	0	ø	0	82	0	86	-0.1
1995	Mil A	4	5	.444	30	10	0	1-2	74	83	47	8	0	49-2	45	5.23	96	.291	.391	0	ø	0	87	-2	32	-0.2
1996	Mil A	7	6	.538	46	12	0	1-1	109.1	116	68	12	2	69-4	78	4.94	105	.277	.376	0	ø	0	97	2	0	0.1
1997	Mil A	0	0	ø	10	0	0	0-0	14	17	6	1	3	9-2	8	3.86	120	.309	.433	0	ø	0	—	1	19	0.1
Total	5	17	21	.447	116	47	3	2-3	363.1	355	202	41	7	206-12	243	4.46	108	.260	.356	0	ø	0	91	13	194	0.6

MISCH, PATRICK Patrick Theodore Joseph; B8.18.1981 Northbrook IL; BR/TL/6´2˝/195; [SFN03 7/213]; d9.21; Col Western Michigan

YEAR	TM LG	W	L	PCT	G	GS	CG-SHO	SV-BS	IP	H	R	HR	HB	BB-IB	SO	ERA	AERA	OAV	OOB	AB-HR-SH	AVG	PB	SUP	APR	DL	PW
2006	SF N	0	0	ø	1	0	0	0-0	1	2	0	0	0	0-0	1	0.00	ø	.400	.400	0	ø	0	—	0	0	0.0

MISURACA, MIKE Michael William; B8.21.1968 Long Beach CA; BR/TR/6´0˝/190; d7.27

YEAR	TM LG	W	L	PCT	G	GS	CG-SHO	SV-BS	IP	H	R	HR	HB	BB-IB	SO	ERA	AERA	OAV	OOB	AB-HR-SH	AVG	PB	SUP	APR	DL	PW
1997	Mil A	0	0	ø	5	0	0	0-0	10.1	15	13	5	0	7-1	10	11.32	41	.333	.423	0	ø	0	—	-7	0	-0.3

MITCHELL, ROY Albert Roy; B4.19.1885 Belton TX; D9.8.1959 Temple TX; BR/TR/5´9.5˝/170; d9.10

YEAR	TM LG	W	L	PCT	G	GS	CG-SHO	SV-BS	IP	H	R	HR	HB	BB-IB	SO	ERA	AERA	OAV	OOB	AB-HR-SH	AVG	PB	SUP	APR	DL	PW
1910	StL A	4	2	.667	6	6	6	0	52	43	24	0	2	12	23	2.60	95	.244	.300	19	.211	0	113	-1	—	-0.1
1911	StL A	4	8	.333	28	12	8-1	0	133.1	134	79	4	6	45	40	3.85	88	.273	.341	49-0-1	.224	1*	82	-6	—	-0.3
1912	StL A	3	4	.429	13	7	5	0	62	81	36	2	4	17	22	4.65	71	.323	.375	19	.316	3	95	-6	—	-0.3
1913	StL A	13	16	.448	33	27	21-4	1	245.1	265	111	6	5	47	59	3.01	97	.282	.320	88-0-2	.148	-1*	99	-2	—	-0.4
1914	StL A	4	5	.444	28	9	4	**4**	103.1	134	77	1	6	38	38	4.35	62	.320	.384	34	.206	1	84	-22	—	-1.9
1918	Chi A	0	1	.000	2	2	0	0	12	18	14	1	0	4	3	7.50	36	.346	.393	2-0-1	.000	-0	124	-7	—	-0.5
	Cin N	4	0	1.000	5	3	3-2	0	36.1	27	3	0	0	5	9	0.74	359	.208	.237	14	.214	0	189	8	—	1.1
1919	Cin N	0	1	.000	7	1	0	0	31	32	16	0	0	9	10	2.32	119	.276	.328	10	.000	-2	0	-1	—	-0.2
Total	7	32	37	.464	122	67	47-7	5	675.1	734	360	14	23	177	204	3.42	86	.285	.337	235-0-4	.187	3	98	-37	—	-2.6

MITCHELL, CHARLIE Charles Ross; B6.24.1962 Dickson TN; BR/TR/6´3˝/170; [BosA82*4/95]; d8.9; b–John; Col Columbia St. (TN) CC

YEAR	TM LG	W	L	PCT	G	GS	CG-SHO	SV-BS	IP	H	R	HR	HB	BB-IB	SO	ERA	AERA	OAV	OOB	AB-HR-SH	AVG	PB	SUP	APR	DL	PW
1984	Bos A	0	0	ø	10	0	0	0-0	16.1	14	7	1	2	6-3	7	2.76	153	.226	.314	0	ø	0	—	2	0	0.1
1985	Bos A	0	0	ø	2	0	0	0-1	1.2	5	3	1	0	0-0	2	16.20	27	.500	.500	0	ø	0	—	-2	0	-0.1
Total	2	0	0	ø	12	0	0	0-1	18	19	10	2	2	6-3	9	4.00	105	.264	.338	0	ø	0	—	0	0	0.0

MITCHELL, CLARENCE Clarence Elmer; B2.22.1891 Franklin NE; D11.6.1963 Grand Island NE; BL/TL/5´11.5˝/190; d6.2; Mil 1918; C2; ▲

YEAR	TM LG	W	L	PCT	G	GS	CG-SHO	SV-BS	IP	H	R	HR	HB	BB-IB	SO	ERA	AERA	OAV	OOB	AB-HR-SH	AVG	PB	SUP	APR	DL	PW
1911	Det A	1	0	1.000	5	1	0	0	14.1	20	13	1	0	7	4	8.16	42	.351	.422	4	.500	1	125	-6	—	-0.3
1916	Cin N	11	10	.524	29	24	17-1	0	194.2	211	87	4	10	45	52	3.14	83	.285	.334	117-0-1	.239	2*	132	-12	—	-0.9
1917	Cin N	9	15	.375	32	20	10-2	1	159.1	166	73	4	2	34	37	3.22	81	.268	.308	90-0-2	.278	4*	91	-8	—	-0.7
1918	Bro N	0	1	.000	1	1	0	0	0.1	4	4	0	0	0	0	108.00	3	1.000	1.000	24-0-1	.250	0*	136	-3	—	-0.5
1919	Bro N	7	5	.583	23	11	9	0	108.2	123	49	0	0	23	43	3.06	97	.297	.334	49-1-0	.367	6*	129	-1	—	0.6
1920	†Bro N	5	2	.714	19	7	3-1	1	78.2	85	35	1	0	23	18	3.09	104	.288	.340	107-0-1	.234	1*	102	1	—	0.2
1921	Bro N	11	9	.550	37	18	13-**3**	2	190	206	91	7	5	46	39	2.89	135	.280	.327	91	.264	3*	102	14	—	1.9
1922	Bro N	0	3	.000	5	3	0	0	12.2	28	24	0	1	7	1	14.21	29	.467	.529	155-3-3	.290	2*	153	-14	—	-2.1
1923	Phi N	9	10	.474	29	19	8-1	0	139.1	170	93	8	4	46	41	4.72	98	.299	.355	78-1-0	.269	3*	93	-3	—	-0.1
1924	Phi N	6	13	.316	30	26	9-1	1	165	223	113	10	6	58	36	5.62	79	.321	.379	102-0-2	.255	-1*	84	-16	—	-1.5
1925	Phi N	10	17	.370	32	26	12-1	1	199.1	245	130	23	5	51	46	5.28	90	.302	.347	92-0-4	.196	-2*	85	-5	—	-0.5
1926	Phi N	9	14	.391	28	25	12	1	178.2	232	111	7	4	55	52	4.58	90	.318	.369	78-0-1	.244	1*	94	-9	—	-0.6
1927	Phi N	6	3	.667	13	12	8-1	0	94.2	99	44	7	2	28	17	4.09	101	.271	.327	42-1-2	.238	2*	115	2	—	0.4
1928	Phi N	0	0	ø	3	0	0	0	5.2	13	6	0	0	2	0	9.53	45	.542	.577	4	.250	0*	—	-3	—	-0.1
	†StL N	8	9	.471	19	18	9-1	0	150	149	59	8	3	38	31	3.30	121	.265	.315	56-0-5	.125	-3	81	15	—	1.3
	Year	8	9	.471	22	18	9-1	0	155.2	162	65	8	3	40	31	3.53	114	.276	.326	60-0-5	.133	-3	81	10	—	1.2
1929	StL N	8	11	.421	25	22	16	0	173	221	89	13	5	60	39	4.27	109	.320	.379	66-0-6	.273	4*	99	10	—	1.2
1930	StL N	1	0	1.000	1	1	0	0	3	5	2	0	0	2	1	6.00	84	.357	.438	2	.500	0	139	0	—	0.0
	NY N	10	3	.769	24	16	5	0	129	151	68	10	1	36	40	3.98	119	.298	.346	47-0-2	.255	0	138	11	—	1.0
	Year	11	3	.786	25	17	5	0	132	156	70	10	1	38	41	4.02	118	.300	.349	49-0-2	.265	1	139	9	—	1.0
1931	NY N	13	11	.542	27	25	13	0	190.1	221	103	12	3	52	39	4.07	91	.285	.332	73-1-0	.219	2	128	-8	—	-0.8
1932	NY N	1	3	.250	8	3	1	2	30.1	41	21	1	1	11	7	4.15	89	.325	.384	10	.200	0	174	-3	—	-0.4
Total	18	125	139	.473	390	278	145-12	9	2217	2613	1215	116	52	624	543	4.12	95	.297	.347	1287-7-30	.252	26	105	-38	—	-1.9

MITCHELL, CRAIG Craig Seton; B4.14.1954 Santa Rosa CA; BR/TR/6´3˝/190; [OakA73 S1/1]; d9.25; Col Spokane Falls (WA) CC

YEAR	TM LG	W	L	PCT	G	GS	CG-SHO	SV-BS	IP	H	R	HR	HB	BB-IB	SO	ERA	AERA	OAV	OOB	AB-HR-SH	AVG	PB	SUP	APR	DL	PW
1975	Oak A	0	1	.000	1	1	0	0-0	3.2	6	5	0	0	2-0	2	12.27	30	.375	.444	0	ø	0	48	-3	0	-0.5
1976	Oak A	0	0	ø	1	0	0	0-0	3.1	3	1	0	0	0-0	0	2.70	125	.231	.231	0	ø	0	—	0	0	0.0
1977	Oak A	0	1	.000	3	1	0	0-0	5.2	9	6	1	0	2-0	1	7.94	51	.346	.393	0	ø	0	22	-3	0	-0.4
Total	3	0	2	.000	5	2	0	0-0	12.2	18	12	1	0	4-0	3	7.82	48	.327	.373	0	ø	0	36	-6	0	-0.9

MITCHELL, FRED Frederick Francis (b Frederick Francis Yapp); B6.5.1878 Cambridge MA; D10.13.1970 Newton MA; BR/TR/5´9.5˝/185; d4.27; M7/C3; ▲

YEAR	TM LG	W	L	PCT	G	GS	CG-SHO	SV-BS	IP	H	R	HR	HB	BB-IB	SO	ERA	AERA	OAV	OOB	AB-HR-SH	AVG	PB	SUP	APR	DL	PW
1901	Bos A	6	6	.500	17	13	10	0	108.2	115	67	2	11	51	34	3.81	93	.268	.360	44	.159	-1*	96	-3	—	-0.4
1902	Bos A	0	1	.000	1	0	0	0	4	8	5	1	0	5	2	11.25	32	.421	.542	1	.000	-0	—	-3	—	-0.4
	Phi A	5	8	.385	18	14	9	1	107.2	120	71	4	8	59	22	3.59	102	.282	.380	48-0-3	.188	-1*	98	-2	—	-0.2
	Year	5	9	.357	19	14	9	1	111.2	128	76	5	8	64	24	3.87	95	.288	.388	49-0-3	.184	-1	98	-5	—	-0.6
1903	Phi N	11	16	.407	28	28	24-1	0	227	250	155	4	19	102	69	4.48	73	.284	.370	95-0-2	.200	-1*	111	-30	—	-3.1
1904	Phi N	4	7	.364	13	13	11	0	108.2	133	62	3	7	25	29	3.40	79	.306	.353	82-0-3	.207	1*	117	-8	—	-0.5
	Bro N	2	5	.286	8	8	8-1	0	66	73	37	0	3	23	16	3.82	72	.291	.357	24-0-1	.292	2	91	-6	—	-0.3
	Year	6	12	.333	21	21	19-1	0	174.2	206	99	3	10	48	45	3.56	76	.300	.355	106-0-4	.226	4	107	-16	—	-0.8
1905	Bro N	3	7	.300	12	10	9	0	96.1	107	73	2	5	38	44	4.76	61	.285	.358	79-0-1	.190	0*	90	-21	—	-1.8
Total	5	31	50	.383	97	86	71-2	1	718.1	806	470	16	53	303	216	4.10	78	.286	.366	373-0-10	.198	1	103	-73	—	-6.7

YEAR	TM LG	W	L	PCT	G	GS	CG-SHO	SV-BS	IP	H	R	HR	HB	BB-IB	SO	ERA	AERA	OAV	OOB	AB-HR-SH	AVG	PB	SUP	APR	DL	PW
MITCHELL, JOHN	John Kyle; B8.11.1965 Dickson TN; BR/TR/6´2˝/(165–195); [BosA83 7/177]; d9.8; b–Charlie																									
1986	NY N	0	1	.000	4	1	0	0-0	10	10	4	1	0	4-0	2	3.60	100	.278	.350	2	.000	-0	25	0	0	0.0
1987	NY N	3	6	.333	20	19	1	0-0	111.2	124	64	6	2	36-3	57	4.11	93	.279	.333	35-0-5	.114	-1	113	-7	0	-0.5
1988	NY N	0	0	ø	1	0	0	0-0	1	2	0	0	0	1-0	1	0.00	ø	.500	.600	1	.000	-0	—	0	0	0.0
1989	NY N	0	1	.000	2	0	0	0-0	3	3	7	0	0	4-1	4	6.00	55	.231	.412	0	ø	0	—	-3	0	-0.6
1990	Bal A	6	6	.500	24	17	0	0-0	114.1	133	63	7	3	48-3	43	4.64	82	.300	.366	0	ø	0	111	-11	0	-1.0
Total	5	9	14	.391	51	37	1	0-0	240	272	138	14	5	93-7	107	4.35	88	.289	.352	38-0-5	.105	-1	110	-21	0	-2.1
MITCHELL, LARRY	Larry Paul; B10.16.1971 Flint MI; BR/TR/6´1˝/219; [PhiN92 5/137]; d8.11; Col James Madison																									
1996	Phi N	0	0	ø	7	0	0	0-0	12	14	6	1	0	5-1	7	4.50	96	.311	.373	2	.000	-0	—	0	0	0.0
MITCHELL, MONROE	Monroe Barr; B9.11.1901 Starkville MS; D9.4.1976 Valdosta GA; BR/TR/6´1.5˝/170; d7.11; Col Mississippi St.																									
1923	Was A	2	4	.333	10	6	3-1	2	41.2	57	35	0	1	22	8	6.48	58	.350	.430	12	.250	1	84	-13	—	-1.5
MITCHELL, PAUL	Paul Michael; B8.19.1949 Worcester MA; BR/TR/6´1˝/(195–200); [BalA71 D1/7]; d7.1; Col Old Dominion																									
1975	Bal A	3	0	1.000	11	4	1	0-1	57	41	23	8	0	19-4	31	3.63	98	.204	.271	0	ø	0	224	0	0	0.0
1976	Oak A	9	7	.563	26	26	4-1	0-0	142	169	74	15	1	30-0	67	4.25	79	.294	.328	0	ø	0	123	-14	0	-1.5
1977	Oak A	0	3	.000	5	3	0	0-0	13.2	21	16	3	0	7-0	5	10.54	38	.339	.406	0	ø	0	45	-9	0	-1.5
	Sea A	3	3	.500	9	9	0	0-0	39.2	50	26	7	1	16-1	20	4.99	83	.311	.370	0	ø	0	80	-4	0	-0.6
	Year	3	6	.333	14	12	0	0-0	53.1	71	42	10	1	23-1	25	6.41	64	.318	.380	0	ø	0	71	-13	0	-2.1
1978	Sea A	8	14	.364	29	29	4-2	0-0	168	173	86	21	2	79-1	75	4.18	92	.270	.350	0	ø	0	80	-5	0	-0.7
1979	Sea A	1	4	.200	10	6	1	0-0	36.2	46	26	4	0	15-0	18	4.42	99	.309	.370	0	ø	0	69	-3	0	-0.3
	Mil A	3	3	.500	18	8	0	0-0	75	81	50	11	3	10-0	32	5.76	73	.276	.301	0	ø	0	121	-11	0	-0.8
	Year	4	7	.364	28	14	1	0-0	111.2	127	76	15	3	25-0	50	5.32	80	.287	.325	0	ø	0	99	-14	0	-1.1
1980	Mil A	5	5	.500	17	11	1-1	1-0	89.1	92	40	7	1	15-3	29	3.53	111	.267	.298	0	ø	0	96	4	0	0.4
Total	6	32	39	.451	125	96	11-4	1-1	621.1	673	341	76	8	191-9	277	4.45	86	.278	.330	0	ø	0	100	-42	0	-5.0
MITCHELL, BOBBY	Robert McKasha; B2.6.1856 Cincinnati OH; D5.1.1933 Springfield OH; BL/TL/5´5˝/135; d9.6																									
1877	Cin N	6	5	.545	12	12	11-1	0	100	123	69	0	—	11	41	3.51	75	.281	.299	49	.204	-0*	86	-8	—	-0.6
1878	Cin N	7	2	.778	9	9	9-1	0	80	69	32	1	—	18	51	2.14	100	**.223**	.265	49	.245	1*	116	3	—	0.4
1879	Cle N	7	15	.318	23	22	20	0	194.2	236	153	1	—	42	90	3.28	76	.283	.317	109	.147	-4*	84	-17	—	-2.1
1882	StL AA	0	1	.000	1	1	0	0	7	12	13	0	—	2	2	7.71	36	.353	.389	4	.000	-1	110	-4	—	-0.4
Total	4	20	23	.465	45	44	40-2	0	381.2	440	267	2	—	73	184	3.18	77	.272	.304	211	.180	-5	91	-26	—	-2.7
MITCHELL, WILLIE	William; B12.1.1889 Pleasant Grove MS; D11.23.1973 Sardis MS; BR/TL/6´0˝/176; d9.22; Mil 1918; Col Mississippi St.																									
1909	Cle A	1	2	.333	3	3	3	0	23	18	6	0	4	10	8	1.57	163	.225	.340	7	.286	1	46	2	—	0.4
1910	Cle A	12	8	.600	35	18	11-1	0	183.2	155	77	2	15	55	102	2.60	100	.236	.310	63-0-3	.159	-3	120	-1	—	-0.6
1911	Cle A	7	14	.333	30	22	9	0	177.1	190	102	1	13	60	78	3.76	91	.284	.354	64-0-2	.109	-5*	84	-7	—	-1.3
1912	Cle A	5	8	.385	29	15	8	1	163.2	149	88	0	7	56	94	2.80	121	.240	.309	53-0-1	.113	-4	105	5	—	-0.2
1913	Cle A	14	8	.636	35	22	14-4	0	217	153	62	1	8	88	141	1.91	159	.202	.292	70-0-6	.143	-2	108	27	—	2.3
1914	Cle A	11	17	.393	39	32	16-3	1	257	228	127	3	7	124	179	3.19	91	.238	.330	81-0-8	.086	-3	103	-7	—	-1.4
1915	Cle A	11	14	.440	36	30	12-1	1	236	210	103	1	2	84	149	2.82	108	.241	.309	79-0-6	.127	-5	96	6	—	-0.1
1916	Cle A	2	5	.286	12	6	1	1	43.2	55	35	1	0	19	24	5.15	58	.309	.376	11-0-1	.000	-1	101	-11	—	-1.7
	Det A	7	5	.583	23	17	7-2	0	127.2	119	53	1	5	48	60	3.31	86	.253	.329	36-0-1	.250	2	121	-4	—	-0.3
	Year	9	10	.474	35	23	8-2	1	171.1	174	88	2	5	67	84	3.78	77	.269	.342	47-0-2	.191	1	116	-15	—	-2.0
1917	Det A	12	8	.600	30	22	12-5	0	185.1	172	66	2	13	46	80	2.19	121	.250	.309	59-0-4	.119	-3*	106	9	—	0.5
1918	Det A	0	1	.000	1	1	0	0	4	3	4	0	0	5	2	9.00	30	.200	.400	2	.000	-0	85	-3	—	-0.4
1919	Det A	1	2	.333	3	2	0	0	13.2	12	8	2	1	10	4	5.27	61	.255	.397	5	.200	0	110	-2	—	-0.4
Total	11	83	92	.474	276	190	93-16	4	1632	1464	731	14	75	605	921	2.88	103	.244	.320	530-0-32	.130	-24	102	14	—	-3.2
MITRE, SERGIO	Sergio Armando; B2.16.1981 Los Angeles CA; BR/TR/6´4˝/210; [ChiN01 7/198]; d7.22; Col San Diego (CA) City																									
2003	Chi N	0	1	.000	3	2	0	0-0	8.2	15	8	1	0	4-1	3	8.31	52	.395	.442	2	.500	0	65	-3	0	-0.3
2004	Chi N	2	4	.333	12	9	0	0-0	51.2	71	38	6	4	20-1	37	6.62	67	.327	.394	15-0-3	.067	-1*	126	-11	0	-1.1
2005	Chi N	2	5	.286	21	7	1-1	0-0	60.1	62	37	11	3	23-2	37	5.37	81	.261	.330	11-0-1	.364	1	117	-6	0	-0.4
2006	Fla N	1	5	.167	15	7	0	0-1	41	44	28	7	6	20-3	31	5.71	75	.275	.374	12-0-2	.167	0*	101	-6	88	-0.8
Total	4	5	15	.250	51	25	1-1	0-1	161.2	192	111	25	13	67-7	108	6.01	73	.294	.369	40-0-6	.200	1	112	-26	88	-2.6
MIZELL, VINEGAR BEND	Wilmer David; B8.13.1930 Leakesville MS; D2.21.1999 Kerrville TX; BR/TL/6´3.5˝/205; d4.22; Mil 1954–55																									
1952	StL N	10	8	.556	30	30	7-2	0	190	171	89	12	1	103	146	3.65	102	.237	.333	68-0-4	.044	-5	103	1	0	-0.6
1953	StL N	13	11	.542	33	33	10-1	0	224.1	193	93	12	4	114	173	3.49	122	.227	.321	83-1-3	.084	-4	89	20	0	1.5
1956	StL N	14	14	.500	33	33	11-3	0	208.2	172	93	20	7	92-5	153	3.62	104	.222	.310	75-0-5	.107	-3	94	5	0	0.4
1957	StL N	8	10	.444	33	21	7-2	0	149.1	136	69	18	1	51-4	87	3.74	106	.241	.303	45-0-1	.089	-2	89	4	0	0.3
1958	StL N	10	14	.417	30	29	8-2	0	189.2	178	81	17	2	91-9	80	3.42	121	.252	.335	61-0-5	.115	-3	59	14	0	1.3
1959	StL N✱	13	10	.565	31	30	8-1	0	201.1	196	104	21	8	89-7	108	4.20	101	.252	.333	75-0-5	.187	1	109	1	0	0.0
1960	StL N	1	3	.250	9	9	0	0	55.1	64	31	7	0	28-4	42	4.55	90	.291	.369	18-0-1	.111	-1	84	-3	0	-0.2
	†Pit N	13	5	.722	23	23	8-3	0	155.2	141	59	7	3	46-6	71	3.12	120	.247	.305	51-0-4	.137	-1	107	11	0	1.0
	Year	14	8	.636	32	32	8-3	0	211	205	90	14	3	74-10	113	3.50	110	.259	.323	69-0-5	.130	-1	101	10	0	0.8
1961	Pit N	7	10	.412	25	17	2-1	0	100	120	61	16	0	31-8	37	5.04	79	.299	.348	23-0-5	.130	-1	75	-11	0	-1.7
1962	Pit N	1	1	.500	4	3	0	0	16.1	15	10	3	1	10-0	6	4.96	79	.254	.366	6	.000	-0	82	-2	0	-0.2
	NY N	0	2	.000	17	2	0	0	38	48	35	10	1	25-0	15	7.34	57	.324	.416	8	.250	0	105	-12	0	-0.6
	Year	1	3	.250	21	5	0	0	54.1	63	45	13	2	35-0	21	6.63	62	.304	.402	14	.143	-0	90	-15	0	-0.8
Total	9	90	88	.506	268	230	61-15	0	1528.2	1434	725	143	28	680-43	918	3.85	104	.247	.328	513-1-33	.111	-19	91	28	0	1.2
MLICKI, DAVE	David John; B6.8.1968 Cleveland OH; BR/TR/6´4˝/(185–205); [CleA90 17/460]; d9.12; Col Oklahoma St.																									
1992	Cle A	0	2	.000	4	4	0	0-0	21.2	23	14	3	1	16-0	16	4.98	79	.280	.404	0	ø	0	110	-3	0	-0.2
1993	Cle A	0	0	ø	3	3	0	0-0	13.1	11	6	2	2	6-0	7	3.38	130	.220	.328	0	ø	0	98	1	121	0.1
1995	NY N	9	7	.563	29	25	0	0-0	160.2	160	82	23	4	54-2	123	4.26	95	.256	.317	39-0-12	.051	-1	111	-3	0	-0.4
1996	NY N	6	7	.462	51	2	0	1-2	90	95	46	9	6	33-8	83	3.30	122	.277	.348	10	.100	-0	90	4	0	0.4
1997	NY N	8	12	.400	32	32	1-1	0-0	193.2	194	89	21	5	76-7	157	4.00	100	.259	.329	48-0-3	.188	2*	105	3	0	0.4
1998	NY N	1	4	.200	10	10	1	0-0	57	68	38	8	5	25-4	39	5.68	73	.297	.374	16-0-3	.188	1	120	-10	0	-0.7
	LA N	7	3	.700	20	20	2-1	0-0	124.1	120	64	15	2	38-1	78	4.05	99	.253	.308	34-0-7	.059	-2	112	-1	0	-0.3
	Year	8	7	.533	30	30	3-1	0-0	181.1	188	102	23	7	63-5	117	4.57	89	.267	.330	50-0-10	.100	-1	115	-12	0	-1.0
1999	LA N	0	1	.000	2	0	0	0-0	7.1	10	4	1	0	2-0	1	4.91	89	.323	.364	1-0-2	1.000	0	—	0	0	0.0
	Det A	14	12	.538	31	31	2	0-0	191.2	209	108	24	12	70-1	119	4.60	109	.276	.344	4	.000	0	81	7	0	0.7
2000	Det A	6	11	.353	24	21	0	0-0	119.1	143	79	17	3	44-1	57	5.58	88	.291	.349	2	.000	-0	81	-8	43	-0.9
2001	Det A	4	8	.333	15	15	0	0-0	81	118	69	19	6	41-2	48	7.33	60	.348	.424	1	.000	-0	84	-25	0	-2.9
	†Hou N	7	3	.700	19	14	0	0-0	86.2	85	53	18	9	33-1	49	5.09	90	.260	.339	26-0-4	.115	-1	113	-4	0	-0.6
2002	Hou N	4	10	.286	22	16	0	0-0	86	101	57	11	3	34-5	57	5.34	81	.290	.356	27	.185	0	71	-10	61	-1.5
Total	10	66	80	.452	262	193	6-2	1-2	1232.2	1337	709	171	58	472-32	834	4.72	92	.276	.344	208-0-31	.125	-0	96	-49	225	-5.9
MMAHAT, KEVIN	Kevin Paul; B11.9.1964 Memphis TN; BL/TL/6´5˝/220; [TexA87 31/805]; d9.9; Col Tulane																									
1989	NY A	0	2	.000	4	2	0	0-0	7.2	13	12	2	1	8-0	3	12.91	30	.406	.500	0	ø	0	81	-8	0	-1.3
MODAK, MIKE	Michael; B5.18.1922 Campbell OH; D12.12.1995 Lakeland FL; BR/TR/5´10.5˝/195; d7.4; Mil 1946; Col Indiana																									
1945	Cin N	1	2	.333	20	3	1-1	1	42.1	52	27	0	0	23	7	5.74	65	.308	.391	10	.100	-1	68	-8	0	-0.7
MOEHLER, BRIAN	Brian Merritt; B12.31.1971 Rockingham NC; BR/TR/6´3˝/(195–235); [DetA93 6/165]; d9.22; Col North Carolina–Greensboro																									
1996	Det A	0	1	.000	2	2	0	0-0	10.1	11	10	1	0	8-1	2	4.35	117	.262	.380	0	ø	0	82	-1	0	-0.1
1997	Det A	11	12	.478	31	31	2-1	0-0	175.1	198	97	22	5	61-1	97	4.67	99	.285	.343	3	.000	-0	106	-1	15	-0.1
1998	Det A	14	13	.519	33	33	4-3	0-0	221.1	220	103	30	2	56-1	123	3.90	122	.259	.306	4	.000	-0	85	21	0	2.2
1999	Det A	10	16	.385	32	32	2-2	0-0	196.1	229	116	22	7	59-5	106	5.04	99	.294	.347	1	.000	0	85	0	0	0.1
2000	Det A	12	9	.571	29	29	2	0-0	178	222	99	20	2	40-0	103	4.50	109	.305	.342	4	.000	-0	109	7	31	0.8
2001	Det A	0	0	ø	1	1	0	0-0	8	6	3	0	0	1-0	2	3.38	131	.207	.233	0	ø	0	105	1	185	0.1
2002	Det A	1	1	.500	3	3	0	0-0	19.2	17	5	3	0	2-0	13	2.29	191	.233	.250	0	ø	0	78	5	94	0.4
	Cin N	2	4	.333	10	9	0	0-0	43.1	61	34	8	1	11-0	18	6.02	71	.330	.369	14-0-1	.000	-1	121	-9	16	-1.1

YEAR	TM LG	W	L	PCT	G	GS	CG-SHO	SV-BS	IP	H	R	HR	HB	BB-IB	SO	ERA	AERA	OAV	OOB	AB-HR-SH	AVG	PB	SUP	APR	DL	PW
2003	Hou N	0	0	ø	3	3	0	0-0	13.2	22	12	4	0	6-0	5	7.90	56	.379	.431	4	.000	-0	120	-5	165	-0.2
2005	Fla N	6	12	.333	37	25	0	0-0	158.1	198	82	16	5	42-9	95	4.55	88	.313	.359	40-0-5	.075	-2	95	-8	0	-0.8
2006	Fla N	7	11	.389	29	21	0	0-1	122	164	95	19	5	38-3	58	6.57	65	.325	.377	31-0-7	.065	-1*	95	-31	28	-3.8
Total	10	63	79	.444	210	189	10-6	0-1	1146.1	1348	656	145	27	324-20	622	4.78	97	.295	.343	101-0-13	.050	-6	97	-21	534	-2.5

MOELLER, DENNIS Dennis Michael; B9.15.1967 Tarzana CA; BR/TL/6´2˝/195; [KCA86 17/443]; d7.28; Col Los Angeles Valley (CA) JC

YEAR	TM LG	W	L	PCT	G	GS	CG-SHO	SV-BS	IP	H	R	HR	HB	BB-IB	SO	ERA	AERA	OAV	OOB	AB-HR-SH	AVG	PB	SUP	APR	DL	PW
1992	KC A	0	3	.000	5	4	0	0-0	18	24	17	5	0	11-2	6	7.00	58	.333	.407	0	ø	0	95	-6	0	-0.9
1993	Pit N	1	0	1.000	10	0	0	0-0	16.1	26	20	2	1	7-1	13	9.92	41	.356	.420	0	ø	0	—	-11	0	-0.6
Total	2	1	3	.250	15	4	0	0-0	34.1	50	37	7	1	18-3	19	8.39	49	.345	.413	0	ø	0	95	-17	0	-1.5

MOELLER, JOE Joseph Douglas; B2.15.1943 Blue Island IL; BR/TR/6´5˝/(192–225); d4.12; Mil 1962

YEAR	TM LG	W	L	PCT	G	GS	CG-SHO	SV-BS	IP	H	R	HR	HB	BB-IB	SO	ERA	AERA	OAV	OOB	AB-HR-SH	AVG	PB	SUP	APR	DL	PW
1962	LA N	6	5	.545	19	15	1	1	85.2	87	55	10	0	58-1	46	5.25	69	.266	.375	33-0-1	.212	1	145	-15	0	-1.6
1964	LA N	7	13	.350	27	24	1	0	145.1	153	89	14	4	31-4	97	4.21	77	.265	.305	45-0-4	.067	-2	78	-21	0	-2.9
1966	†LA N	2	4	.333	29	8	0	0	78.2	73	31	4	3	14-8	31	2.52	131	.244	.283	12-0-3	.167	1	83	5	0	0.5
1967	LA N	0	0	ø	6	0	0	0	5	9	5	1	0	3-1	2	9.00	34	.409	.462	0	ø	0	—	-3	0	-0.2
1968	LA N	1	1	.500	3	3	0	0	16	17	10	1	1	2-0	11	5.06	55	.270	.299	7	.000	-1	94	-4	0	-0.5
1969	LA N	1	0	1.000	23	4	0	1-0	51.1	54	23	4	0	13-0	25	3.33	101	.278	.322	10	.200	0	145	-1	0	0.0
1970	LA N	7	9	.438	31	19	2-1	4-0	135.1	131	63	16	1	43-3	63	3.92	98	.248	.305	39-0-3	.154	0	77	0	0	-0.1
1971	LA N	2	4	.333	28	1	0	1-1	66.1	72	32	5	0	12-2	32	3.80	86	.279	.307	9	.000	-0	55	-5	0	-0.4
Total	8	26	36	.419	166	74	4-1	7-1	583.2	596	308	55	9	176-19	307	4.01	86	.263	.316	155-0-11	.129	-2	97	-44	0	-5.2

MOELLER, RON Ronald Ralph "The Kid"; B10.13.1938 Cincinnati OH; BL/TL/6´0˝/180; d9.8; Mil 1962

YEAR	TM LG	W	L	PCT	G	GS	CG-SHO	SV-BS	IP	H	R	HR	HB	BB-IB	SO	ERA	AERA	OAV	OOB	AB-HR-SH	AVG	PB	SUP	APR	DL	PW
1956	Bal A	0	1	.000	4	1	0	0	8.2	10	5	0	0	3-0	2	4.15	94	.286	.333	1	.000	-0	23	-1	0	-0.1
1958	Bal A	0	0	ø	4	0	0	0	4.1	6	2	0	0	3-0	3	4.15	87	.333	.429	0	ø	0	—	0	0	0.0
1961	LA A	4	8	.333	33	18	1-1	0	112.2	122	80	15	2	83-0	87	5.83	77	.275	.391	29-0-1	.207	2*	103	-14	0	-1.0
1963	LA A	0	0	ø	3	0	0	0	2.2	5	2	1	0	1-0	2	6.75	51	.385	.429	0	ø	0	—	-1	0	0.0
	Was A	2	0	1.000	8	3	0	0	24.1	31	17	4	1	10-0	10	6.29	59	.316	.385	9	.222	0	128	-6	0	-0.5
	Year	2	0	1.000	11	3	0	0	27	36	19	5	1	11-0	12	6.33	58	.324	.390	9	.222	0	129	-7	0	-0.5
Total	4	6	9	.400	52	22	1-1	0	152.2	174	106	20	3	100-0	104	5.78	74	.287	.389	39-0-1	.205	2	105	-22	0	-1.6

MOFFETT, SAM Samuel R.; B3.14.1857 Wheeling VA (now West Virginia); D5.5.1907 Butte MT; BR/TR/6´0˝/175; d5.15; b–Joe; ▲

YEAR	TM LG	W	L	PCT	G	GS	CG-SHO	SV-BS	IP	H	R	HR	HB	BB-IB	SO	ERA	AERA	OAV	OOB	AB-HR-SH	AVG	PB	SUP	APR	DL	PW
1884	Cle N	3	19	.136	24	22	21	0	197.2	236	165	9	—	58	84	3.87	81	.284	.330	256	.184	-3*	60	-16	—	-1.5
1887	Ind N	1	5	.167	6	6	6	0	50	47	45	1	4	23	3	3.78	110	.242	.335	41	.122	-2*	65	-2	—	-0.4
1888	Ind N	2	5	.286	7	7	6-1	0	56	62	40	3	2	17	7	4.66	64	.278	.335	35	.114	-1*	151	-10	—	-1.1
Total	3	6	29	.171	37	35	33-1	0	303.2	345	250	13	6	98	94	4.00	82	.276	.332	332	.169	-6	76	-28	—	-3.0

MOFFITT, RANDY Randall James; B10.13.1948 Long Beach CA; BR/TR/6´3˝/(190–195); [SFN70*1/18]; d6.11; Col Cal St.–Long Beach

YEAR	TM LG	W	L	PCT	G	GS	CG-SHO	SV-BS	IP	H	R	HR	HB	BB-IB	SO	ERA	AERA	OAV	OOB	AB-HR-SH	AVG	PB	SUP	APR	DL	PW
1972	SF N	1	5	.167	40	0	0	4-2	70.2	72	31	5	2	30-6	37	3.69	95	.266	.341	8-0-2	.000	-1	—	-1	0	-0.1
1973	SF N	4	4	.500	60	0	0	14-4	100.1	86	30	9	1	31-4	65	2.42	159	.225	.284	17-0-1	.059	-1	—	16	0	1.4
1974	SF N	5	7	.417	61	1	0	15-4	102	99	52	9	2	29-4	49	4.50	85	.256	.308	16-0-2	.313	2	69	-4	0	-0.4
1975	SF N	4	5	.444	55	0	0	11-6	74	73	35	6	3	32-6	39	3.89	98	.257	.336	14	.214	1	—	0	0	0.0
1976	SF N	6	6	.500	58	0	0	14-2	103	92	36	6	1	35-9	50	2.27	160	.238	.300	14	.143	-0	—	13	0	1.8
1977	SF N	4	9	.308	64	0	0	11-7	87.2	91	41	4	3	39-13	68	3.59	110	.273	.348	3-0-1	.000	-0	—	3	0	0.5
1978	SF N	8	4	.667	70	0	0	12-9	81.2	79	35	5	3	33-13	52	3.31	105	.258	.331	7-0-1	.143	0	—	1	0	0.1
1979	SF N	2	5	.286	28	0	0	2-1	35	53	33	5	2	14-6	16	7.71	45	.356	.416	4	.000	-0*	—	-17	67	-3.2
1980	SF N	1	1	.500	13	0	0	0-1	16.2	18	10	2	1	4-2	10	4.86	72	.281	.333	1	.000	-0	—	-2	94	-0.3
1981	SF N	0	0	ø	10	0	0	0-0	11.1	15	10	2	0	2-1	11	7.94	43	.313	.333	0	ø	0	—	-5	0	-0.3
1982	Hou N	2	4	.333	30	0	0	3-3	41.2	36	15	3	5	13-3	20	3.02	110	.228	.305	2-0-1	.000	-0	—	2	0	0.2
1983	Tor A	6	2	.750	45	0	0	10-3	57.1	52	27	5	1	24-6	38	3.77	116	.243	.318	0	ø	0	—	3	0	0.5
Total	12	43	52	.453	534	1	0	96-42	781.1	766	355	61	24	286-73	455	3.65	102	.257	.324	86-0-8	.140	-1	69	9	161	0.2

MOFORD, HERB Herbert; B8.6.1928 Brooksville KY; D12.3.2005 Cincinnati OH; BR/TR/6´1˝/(170–175); d4.12

YEAR	TM LG	W	L	PCT	G	GS	CG-SHO	SV-BS	IP	H	R	HR	HB	BB-IB	SO	ERA	AERA	OAV	OOB	AB-HR-SH	AVG	PB	SUP	APR	DL	PW
1955	StL N	1	1	.500	14	1	0	2	24	29	23	5	1	15-3	8	7.88	52	.299	.395	2	.000	-0	66	-10	0	-0.9
1958	Det A	4	9	.308	25	11	6	1	109.2	83	45	10	9	42-6	58	3.61	112	.214	.304	37-0-3	.027	-4	73	7	0	0.4
1959	Bos A	0	2	.000	4	2	0	0	8.2	10	11	3	0	6-0	7	11.42	36	.286	.390	1	.000	-0	98	-6	0	-1.1
1962	NY N	0	1	.000	7	0	0	0	15	21	15	3	0	1-0	5	7.20	58	.318	.324	4	.250	0	—	-5	0	-0.3
Total	4	5	13	.278	50	14	6	3	157.1	143	94	21	10	64-9	78	5.03	81	.244	.327	44-0-3	.045	-4	76	-14	0	-1.9

MOGRIDGE, GEORGE George Anthony; B2.18.1889 Rochester NY; D3.4.1962 Rochester NY; BL/TL/6´2˝/165; d8.17

YEAR	TM LG	W	L	PCT	G	GS	CG-SHO	SV-BS	IP	H	R	HR	HB	BB-IB	SO	ERA	AERA	OAV	OOB	AB-HR-SH	AVG	PB	SUP	APR	DL	PW
1911	Chi A	0	2	.000	4	1	0	0	12.2	12	10	1	0	1	5	4.97	65	.255	.271	5	.400	0	179	-3	—	-0.3
1912	Chi A	3	4	.429	17	8	2	3	64.2	69	32	2	1	15	31	4.04	79	.264	.307	16	.125	-0	78	-3	—	-0.4
1915	NY A	2	3	.400	6	5	3-1	0	41	33	11	0	3	11	11	1.76	167	.219	.285	12	.083	-1	89	5	—	0.5
1916	NY A	6	12	.333	30	21	10-2	0	194.2	174	71	3	7	45	66	2.31	125	.252	.305	66-0-2	.212	1	72	9	—	1.0
1917	NY A	9	11	.450	29	25	15-1	0	196.1	185	82	5	9	39	46	2.98	90	.255	.301	69-0-4	.159	-1	94	-5	—	-0.6
1918	NY A	16	13	.552	**45**	19	13-1	**7**	239.1	232	78	6	8	43	62	2.18	130	.263	.304	79-0-6	.190	-0*	125	14	—	2.0
1919	NY A	10	9	.526	35	18	13-3	0	169	159	68	6	7	46	58	2.77	115	.250	.307	48-0-2	.125	-1	100	7	—	0.7
1920	NY A	5	9	.357	26	15	7	1	125.1	146	83	4	3	36	35	4.31	89	.287	.338	42-0-1	.167	-1	103	-10	—	-1.0
1921	Was A	18	14	.563	38	36	21-4	0	288	301	119	12	7	66	101	3.00	137	.269	.313	98-0-3	.153	-5	75	36	—	3.0
1922	Was A	18	13	.581	34	32	18-3	0	251.2	300	120	12	11	72	61	3.58	108	.304	.358	86-1-9	.244	4	97	9	—	1.4
1923	Was A	13	13	.500	33	30	17-3	1	211	228	90	10	3	56	62	3.11	121	.285	.334	75-0-6	.227	1	105	16	—	2.0
1924	†Was A	16	11	.593	30	30	13-2	0	213	217	97	2	7	61	48	3.76	107	.270	.327	74-0-4	.176	-2	86	11	—	1.0
1925	Was A	3	4	.429	10	8	3	0	53	58	27	2	4	18	12	4.08	104	.291	.362	19-0-1	.105	-2	97	2	—	0.0
	StL A	1	1	.500	2	2	1	0	15.1	17	10	2	1	5	8	5.87	80	.279	.343	4	.000	-0	99	-1	—	-0.1
	Year	4	5	.444	12	10	4	0	68.1	75	37	4	5	23	20	4.48	97	.288	.358	23-0-1	.087	-2	97	1	—	-0.1
1926	Bos N	6	10	.375	39	10	2	3	142	173	82	6	3	36	46	4.50	79	.311	.356	46-0-5	.174	-1*	120	-15	—	-1.6
1927	Bos N	6	4	.600	20	1	0	5	48.2	48	23	4	2	15	26	3.70	100	.257	.319	15	.200	-0	23	0	—	0.1
Total	15	132	133	.498	398	261	138-20	20	2265.2	2352	1003	77	76	565	678	3.23	109	.273	.323	754-1-43	.182	-8	95	72	—	7.7

MOHART, GEORGE George Benjamin; B3.6.1892 Buffalo NY; D10.2.1970 Silver Creek NY; BR/TR/5´9˝/165; d4.15

YEAR	TM LG	W	L	PCT	G	GS	CG-SHO	SV-BS	IP	H	R	HR	HB	BB-IB	SO	ERA	AERA	OAV	OOB	AB-HR-SH	AVG	PB	SUP	APR	DL	PW
1920	Bro N	0	1	.000	13	1	0	0	35.2	33	17	0	3	7	13	1.77	181	.250	.303	8	.125	-0	123	2	—	0.2
1921	Bro N	0	0	ø	2	0	0	0	7	8	5	0	1	1	1	3.86	101	.296	.345	2	.500	0	—	-1	—	0.0
Total	2	0	1	.000	15	1	0	0	42.2	41	22	0	4	8	14	2.11	157	.258	.310	10	.200	0	123	1	—	0.2

MOHLER, MIKE Michael Ross; B7.26.1968 Dayton OH; BR/TL/6´2˝/(195–209); [OakA89 42/1101]; d4.7; Col Nicholls St.

YEAR	TM LG	W	L	PCT	G	GS	CG-SHO	SV-BS	IP	H	R	HR	HB	BB-IB	SO	ERA	AERA	OAV	OOB	AB-HR-SH	AVG	PB	SUP	APR	DL	PW
1993	Oak A	1	6	.143	42	9	0	0-1	64.1	57	45	10	2	44-4	42	5.60	74	.241	.361	0	ø	0	79	-12	0	-1.1
1994	Oak A	0	1	.000	1	1	0	0-0	2.1	2	3	1	0	2-0	4	7.71	58	.167	.286	0	ø	0	82	-1	0	-0.2
1995	Oak A	1	1	.500	28	0	0	1-1	23.2	16	8	0	0	18-1	15	3.04	149	.198	.343	0	ø	0	—	4	0	0.3
1996	Oak A	6	3	.667	72	0	0	7-6	81	79	36	9	1	41-6	64	3.67	136	.263	.350	0	ø	0	—	11	0	1.3
1997	Oak A	1	10	.091	62	10	0	1-3	101.2	116	65	11	7	54-8	66	5.13	90	.301	.391	0	ø	0*	72	-7	0	-0.6
1998	Oak A	3	3	.500	57	0	0	0-1	61	70	38	6	4	26-3	42	5.16	90	.289	.365	0	ø	0	—	-3	0	-0.3
1999	StL N	1	1	.500	48	0	0	1-1	49.1	47	26	3	1	23-2	31	4.38	105	.254	.338	3	.000	-0	—	1	0	0.0
2000	StL N	1	1	.500	22	0	0	0-2	19	26	20	1	2	15-1	8	9.00	52	.321	.439	1	1.000	0	—	-9	0	-0.8
	Cle A	0	1	.000	2	0	0	0-1	1	1	1	1	0	0-0	2	9.00	56	.250	.250	0	ø	0	—	0	0	-0.1
2001	Ari N	0	0	ø	13	0	0	0-2	13.2	14	11	3	0	9-0	7	7.24	64	.286	.390	0	ø	0	—	-3	0	-0.2
Total	9	14	27	.341	347	20	0	10-18	417	428	253	45	17	232-25	281	4.99	92	.272	.368	4	.250	0	72	-19	0	-1.7

MOHORCIC, DALE Dale Robert; B1.25.1956 Cleveland OH; BR/TR/6´3˝/220; d5.31; Col Cleveland St.

YEAR	TM LG	W	L	PCT	G	GS	CG-SHO	SV-BS	IP	H	R	HR	HB	BB-IB	SO	ERA	AERA	OAV	OOB	AB-HR-SH	AVG	PB	SUP	APR	DL	PW
1986	Tex A	2	4	.333	58	0	0	7-5	79	86	25	5	1	15-6	29	2.51	173	.279	.315	0	ø	0	—	15	0	1.3
1987	Tex A	7	6	.538	74	0	0	16-7	99.1	88	34	11	2	19-6	48	2.99	151	.244	.285	0	ø	0	—	18	15	2.8
1988	Tex A	2	6	.250	43	0	0	5-3	52	62	35	6	5	20-5	25	4.85	85	.295	.363	0	ø	0	—	-6	23	-0.9
	NY A	2	2	.500	13	0	0	1-2	22.2	21	7	1	3	9-2	19	2.78	143	.239	.327	0	ø	0	—	3	0	0.5
	Year	4	8	.333	56	0	0	6-5	74.2	83	42	7	8	29-7	44	4.22	96	.279	.352	0	ø	0	—	-3	0	-0.4
1989	NY A	2	1	.667	32	0	0	2-3	57.2	65	41	8	6	18-3	24	4.99	78	.286	.352	0	ø	0	—	-10	0	-0.5
1990	Mon N	1	2	.333	34	0	0	2-2	53	56	21	6	4	18-3	29	3.23	114	.286	.350	8-0-1	.125	-0	—	3	0	0.1
Total	5	16	21	.432	254	0	0	33-22	363.2	378	163	37	21	99-25	174	3.49	119	.272	.327	8-0-1	.125	-0	—	23	38	3.3

YEAR	TM LG	W	L	PCT	G	GS	CG-SHO	SV-BS	IP	H	R	HR	HB	BB-IB	SO	ERA	AERA	OAV	OOB	AB-HR-SH	AVG	PB	SUP	APR	DL	PW
Moisan, Bill	William Joseph; B7.30.1925 Bradford MA; BL/TR/6´1˝/170; d9.17																									
1953	Chi N	0	0	ø	3	0	0	0	5	5	3	0	1	2	1	5.40	82	.278	.381	0	ø	0	—	0	0	0.0
Molesworth, Carlton	Carlton; B2.15.1876 Frederick MD; D7.25.1961 Frederick MD; BL/TL/5´7.5˝/162; d9.14																									
1895	Was N	0	2	.000	4	3	1	0	16	33	34	1	4	15	7	14.63	33	.418	.531	7	.143	-1	124	-15	—	-1.3
Molina, Gabe	Cruz Gabriel; B5.3.1975 Denver CO; BR/TR/5´11˝/(202–220); [BalA96 21/621]; d5.1; Col Arizona St.																									
1999	Bal A	1	2	.333	20	0	0	0-1	23	22	19	4	0	16-1	14	6.65	71	.256	.373	0	ø	0	—	-6	0	-0.6
2000	Bal A	0	0	ø	9	0	0	0-0	13	25	14	2	0	9-0	8	9.00	52	.397	.459	0	ø	0	—	-7	0	-0.3
	Atl N	0	0	ø	2	0	0	0-0	2	3	4	1	1	1-0	1	9.00	50	.375	.455	0	ø	0	—	-2	0	-0.1
2002	StL N	1	0	1.000	12	0	0	0-0	11.1	6	2	1	0	6-0	4	1.59	254	.162	.279	0	ø	0	—	3	0	0.3
2003	StL N	0	0	ø	3	0	0	0-0	2.2	5	4	1	0	1-0	1	13.50	31	.385	.429	0	ø	0	—	-3	0	-0.1
Total	4	2	2	.500	46	0	0	0-1	52	61	43	9	1	33-1	28	6.58	69	.295	.389	0	ø	0	—	-15	0	-0.8
Moloney, Richie	Richard Henry; B6.7.1950 Brookline MA; BR/TR/6´3˝/185; [ChiA68 14/314]; d9.20																									
1970	Chi A	0	0	ø	1	0	0	0-0	1	2	0	0	0	0-0	1	0.00	ø	.400	.400	0	ø	0	—	0	0	0.0
Molyneaux, Vince	Vincent Leo; B8.17.1888 Lewiston NY; D5.4.1950 Stamford CT; BR/TR/6´0˝/180; d7.5; Col Villanova																									
1917	StL A	0	0	ø	7	0	0	0	22	18	15	0	0	20	4	4.91	53	.237	.396	4	.000	-1	—	-5	—	-0.3
1918	Bos A	1	0	1.000	6	0	0	0	10.2	3	4	0	0	8	1	3.38	80	.086	.256	2	.000	-0	—	0	—	-0.1
Total	2	1	0	1.000	13	0	0	0	32.2	21	19	0	0	28	5	4.41	60	.189	.353	6	.000	-1	—	-5	—	-0.4
Monahan, Rinty	Edward Francis; B4.28.1928 Brooklyn NY; BR/TR/6´1.5˝/195; d8.9; Col Niagara																									
1953	Phi A	0	0	ø	4	0	0	0	10.2	11	5	0	0	7	2	4.22	102	.275	.383	2	.000	-0	—	0	101	0.0
Monbouquette, Bill	William Charles; B8.11.1936 Medford MA; BR/TR/5´11˝/(190–195); d7.18; C3																									
1958	Bos A	3	4	.429	10	8	3	0	54.1	52	25	4	0	20-4	30	3.31	121	.251	.313	17-0-2	.176	-1	98	3	0	0.3
1959	Bos A	7	7	.500	34	17	4	0	151.2	165	86	15	3	33-1	87	4.15	98	.285	.323	46-0-3	.065	-4*	96	-5	0	-0.9
1960	Bos A★	14	11	.560	35	30	12-3	0	215	217	91	18	2	68-9	134	3.64	111	.263	.319	65-0-8	.092	-3*	91	12	0	0.9
1961	Bos A	14	14	.500	32	32	12-1	0	236.1	233	106	24	0	100-1	161	3.39	123	.254	.326	69-0-14	.130	-1*	88	18	0	1.9
1962	Bos A☆	15	13	.536	35	35	11-4	0	235.1	227	100	22	3	65-1	153	3.33	124	.251	.302	73-0-8	.096	-3	91	19	0	1.6
1963	Bos A☆	20	10	.667	37	36	13-1	0	266.2	258	119	31	0	42-6	174	3.81	99	.250	.279	88-0-10	.114	-3	119	2	0	-0.2
1964	Bos A	13	14	.481	36	35	7-5	1	234	258	114	34	1	40-4	120	4.04	95	.277	.306	72-0-5	.083	-2*	95	-3	0	-0.6
1965	Bos A	10	18	.357	35	35	10-2	0	228.2	239	114	32	1	40-5	110	3.70	101	.269	.299	68-0-10	.059	-3*	92	-1	0	-0.4
1966	Det A	7	8	.467	30	14	2-1	0	102.2	120	60	14	3	22-4	61	4.73	74	.293	.330	26-0-4	.154	-0	107	-14	0	-1.9
1967	Det A	0	0	ø	2	0	0	0	2	1	0	0	0	0-0	2	0.00	ø	.143	.143	0	ø	0	—	1	0	0.0
	NY A	6	5	.545	33	10	2-1	1	133.1	122	39	6	4	17-7	53	2.36	132	.246	.274	32-0-3	.156	-0	86	12	0	1.0
	Year	6	5	.545	35	10	2-1	1	135.1	123	39	6	4	17-7	55	2.33	134	.245	.273	32-0-3	.156	-0	86	13	0	1.0
1968	NY A	5	7	.417	17	11	2	0	89.1	92	47	7	3	13-2	32	4.43	66	.264	.293	26-0-2	.115	0	98	-14	0	-1.7
	SF N	0	1	.000	7	0	0	1	12	11	9	4	0	2-0	5	3.75	78	.239	.265	0	ø	0	—	-2	0	-0.3
Total	11	114	112	.504	343	263	78-18	3	1961.1	1995	910	211	20	462-44	1122	3.68	104	.263	.305	582-0-69	.103	-20	97	28	0	-0.3
Monge, Sid	Isidro Pedroza; B4.11.1951 Agua Prieta, Sonora, Mexico; BB/TL/6´2˝/(165–202); [AnaA70 24/569]; d9.12																									
1975	Cal A	0	2	.000	4	2	2	0-0	23.2	22	12	3	1	10-0	17	4.18	86	.242	.324	0	ø	0	62	-1	0	-0.1
1976	Cal A	6	7	.462	32	13	2	0-0	117.2	108	50	10	1	49-0	53	3.37	100	.248	.324	0	ø	0	89	0	0	0.0
1977	Cal A	0	1	.000	4	0	0	1-0	12.1	14	6	2	0	6-0	4	2.92	135	.304	.377	0	ø	0	—	1	0	0.1
	Cle A	1	2	.333	33	0	0	3-1	39	47	31	6	0	27-4	25	6.23	64	.309	.407	0	ø	0	—	-10	0	-0.9
	Year	1	3	.250	37	0	0	4-1	51.1	61	37	8	0	33-4	29	5.44	73	.308	.400	0	ø	0	—	-9	0	-0.8
1978	Cle A	4	3	.571	48	2	0	6-4	84.2	71	36	4	0	51-6	54	2.76	137	.225	.330	0	ø	0	107	6	0	0.6
1979	Cle A☆	12	10	.545	76	0	0	19-7	131	96	37	9	1	64-8	108	2.40	179	.209	.300	0	ø	0	—	28	0	5.2
1980	Cle A	3	5	.375	67	0	0	14-7	94.1	80	39	12	3	40-6	61	3.53	117	.227	.310	0	ø	0	—	7	0	0.7
1981	Cle A	3	5	.375	31	0	0	4-2	58	58	31	9	0	21-2	41	4.34	85	.266	.326	0	ø	0	—	-4	0	-0.7
1982	Phi N	7	1	.875	47	0	0	2-3	72	70	35	8	2	22-3	43	3.75	99	.256	.312	9-0-2	.111	-0	—	-1	0	-0.1
1983	Phi N	3	0	1.000	14	0	0	0-0	11.2	20	10	4	0	6-1	7	6.94	52	.377	.433	1	.000	-0	—	-4	0	-0.9
	SD N	7	3	.700	47	0	0	7-1	68.2	65	24	4	1	31-6	32	3.15	112	.257	.338	10-0-1	.100	-0	—	4	0	0.6
	Year	10	3	.769	61	0	0	7-1	80.1	85	34	8	1	37-7	39	3.70	95	.278	.354	11-0-1	.091	-1	—	-1	0	-0.3
1984	SD N	2	1	.667	13	0	0	0-1	15	17	10	3	0	17-3	7	4.80	75	.293	.447	1	.000	-0	—	-2	0	-0.5
	Det A	1	0	1.000	19	0	0	0-0	36	40	21	5	2	12-0	19	4.25	93	.282	.340	0	ø	0	—	-2	0	-0.1
Total	10	49	40	.551	435	17	4	56-26	764	708	342	79	11	356-39	471	3.53	108	.248	.331	21-0-3	.095	-1	80	22	0	3.9
Monroe, Ed	Edward Oliver "Peck"; B2.22.1895 Louisville KY; D4.29.1969 Louisville KY; BR/TR/6´5˝/187; d5.29; Mil 1918																									
1917	NY A	1	0	1.000	9	1	1	1	28.2	35	15	1	2	6	12	3.45	78	.310	.355	12	.167	-0	134	-3	—	-0.2
1918	NY A	0	0	ø	1	0	0	0	2	1	2	0	0	2	1	4.50	63	.143	.333	0	ø	0	—	-1	—	0.0
Total	2	1	0	1.000	10	1	1	1	30.2	36	17	1	2	8	13	3.52	77	.300	.354	12	.167	-0	134	-4	—	-0.2
Monroe, Larry	Lawrence James; B6.20.1956 Detroit MI; BR/TR/6´4˝/200; [ChiA74 1/8]; d8.23																									
1976	Chi A	0	1	.000	8	2	0	0-0	21.2	23	11	0	0	13-0	9	4.15	86	.284	.379	0	ø	0	49	-1	0	-0.1
Monroe, Zach	Zachary Charles; B7.8.1931 Peoria IL; BR/TR/6´0˝/198; d6.27; Col Bradley																									
1958	†NY A	4	2	.667	21	6	1	1	58	57	29	8	0	27-1	18	3.26	108	.263	.344	17	.118	-1	199	0	0	-0.1
1959	NY A	0	0	ø	3	0	0	0	3.1	3	2	2	0	2-0	1	5.40	67	.231	.333	0	ø	0	—	-1	0	0.0
Total	2	4	2	.667	24	6	1	1	61.1	60	31	10	0	29-1	19	3.38	105	.261	.344	17	.118	-1	199	-1	0	-0.1
Montague, John	John Evans; B9.12.1947 Newport News VA; BR/TR/6´2˝/(195–205); [BalA67*S3/50]; d9.9; Col Old Dominion																									
1973	Mon N	0	0	ø	4	0	0	0-0	7.2	8	3	0	1	2-2	7	3.52	108	.286	.344	1	.000	-0	—	0	0	0.0
1974	Mon N	3	4	.429	46	1	0	3-2	82.2	73	37	5	4	38-5	43	3.16	122	.241	.329	10	.100	-0	23	4	0	0.3
1975	Mon N	0	1	.000	12	0	0	2-0	17.2	23	11	4	2	6-1	9	5.60	69	.324	.383	1	.000	-0*	—	-3	0	-0.2
	Phi N	0	0	ø	3	0	0	0-0	5	8	5	1	0	4-1	1	9.00	42	.400	.500	0	ø	0	—	-3	0	-0.1
	Year	0	1	.000	15	0	0	2-0	22.2	31	16	5	2	10-2	10	6.35	61	.341	.410	1	.000	-0	—	-5	0	-0.3
1977	Sea A	8	12	.400	47	15	2	4-1	182.1	193	95	20	4	75-5	98	4.29	97	.272	.343	0	ø	0	80	-2	0	-0.2
1978	Sea A	1	3	.250	19	0	0	2-1	43.2	52	31	2	0	24-4	14	6.18	62	.308	.386	0	ø	0	—	-10	104	-1.0
1979	Sea A	6	4	.600	41	1	0	1-3	116.1	125	73	14	2	47-13	60	5.57	79	.284	.349	0	ø	0	21	-12	0	-0.9
	†Cal A	2	0	1.000	14	0	0	6-2	17.2	16	12	3	0	9-0	6	5.09	80	.242	.333	0	ø	0	—	-2	0	-0.5
	Year	8	4	.667	55	1	0	7-5	134	141	85	17	2	56-13	66	5.51	79	.279	.347	0	ø	0	21	-14	0	-1.4
1980	Cal A	4	2	.667	37	0	0	3-1	73.2	97	47	8	1	21-1	22	5.13	77	.324	.365	0	ø	0	—	-10	0	-0.8
Total	7	24	26	.480	223	17	2	21-10	546.2	595	314	57	14	226-32	260	4.76	86	.283	.351	12	.083	-0	74	-38	104	-3.4
Montalvo, Rafael	Rafael Edgardo (Torres); B3.31.1964 Rio Piedras, PR; BR/TR/6´0˝/185; d4.13																									
1986	Hou N	0	0	ø	1	0	0	0-0	1	1	1	0	0	2-0	0	9.00	40	.250	.500	0	ø	0	—	-1	0	0.0
Monteagudo, Aurelio	Aurelio Faustino (Cintra); B11.19.1943 Caibarien, Cuba; D11.10.1990 Ramos Arizpe, Coahuila, Mexico; BR/TR/5´11˝/(170–185); d9.1; f–Rene																									
1963	KC A	0	0	ø	4	0	0	0	7	4	2	0	0	3-0	3	2.57	152	.182	.269	0	ø	0	—	1	0	0.1
1964	KC A	0	4	.000	11	6	0	0	31.1	40	32	11	1	10-0	14	8.90	43	.317	.370	7	.286	1	70	-16	0	-1.7
1965	KC A	0	0	ø	4	0	0	0	7	5	4	1	0	4-1	5	3.86	90	.185	.290	0	ø	0*	—	-1	0	0.0
1966	KC A	0	0	ø	6	0	0	0	12.2	12	4	0	0	7-0	3	2.84	120	.261	.352	0	ø	0	—	1	0	0.1
	Hou N	0	0	ø	10	0	0	1	15.1	14	8	1	0	11-1	7	4.70	73	.241	.362	1	.000	-0	—	-2	0	-0.1
1967	Chi A	0	1	.000	1	1	0	0	1.1	4	3	1	0	2-0	0	20.25	15	.500	.600	0	ø	0	0	-2	0	-0.4
1970	KC A	1	1	.500	21	0	0	0-0	27.1	20	11	2	1	9-0	18	2.96	126	.200	.273	2	.000	-0	—	2	0	0.1
1973	Cal A	2	1	.667	15	0	0	3-2	30	23	18	2	4	16-3	8	4.20	85	.215	.336	0	ø	0	—	-3	0	-0.4
Total	7	3	7	.300	72	7	0	4-2	132	122	82	18	6	62-5	58	5.05	72	.247	.336	10	.200	1	63	-20	0	-2.3
Monteagudo, Rene	Rene (Miranda); B3.12.1916 Havana, Cuba; D9.14.1973 Hialeah FL; BL/TL/5´7˝/165; d9.6; s–Aurelio; ▲																									
1938	Was A	1	1	.500	5	3	2	0	22	26	15	3	0	15	13	5.73	79	.286	.387	6-0-1	.500	1	143	-3	—	-0.1
1940	Was A	2	6	.250	27	8	3	2	100.2	128	70	7	3	52	64	6.08	69	.316	.398	33	.182	0	97	-18	—	-1.3
1945	Phi N	0	0	ø	14	0	0	0	45.2	67	42	1	2	28	16	7.49	51	.347	.435	193-0-4	.301	2*	—	-16	0	-0.6
Total	3	3	7	.300	46	11	5	2	168.1	221	127	11	5	95	93	6.42	64	.321	.407	232-0-5	.289	4	113	-37	0	-2.0

YEAR	TM LG	W	L	PCT	G	GS	CG-SHO	SV-BS	IP	H	R	HR	HB	BB-IB	SO	ERA	AERA	OAV	OOB	AB-HR-SH	AVG	PB	SUP	APR	DL	PW
MONTEFUSCO, JOHN John Joseph "Count"; B5.25.1950 Long Branch NJ; BR/TR/6´1˝/(180–192); d9.3; Col Brookdale (NJ) CC																										
1974	SF N	3	2	.600	7	5	1-1	0-1	39.1	41	22	3	0	19-0	34	4.81	79	.256	.335	14-2-0	.286	3	101	-3	0	-0.1
1975	SF N	15	9	.625	35	34	10-4	0-0	243.2	210	85	11	8	86-12	215	2.88	132	.233	.303	80-1-9	.087	-2	93	25	0	2.1
1976	SF N★	16	14	.533	37	36	11-**6**	0-0	253.1	224	90	11	4	74-8	172	2.84	128	.238	.294	78-0-6	.103	-2*	81	24	0	2.4
1977	SF N	7	12	.368	26	25	4	0-0	157.1	170	82	10	3	46-6	110	3.49	113	.273	.321	49-1-4	.122	-1	81	3	40	0.2
1978	SF N	11	9	.550	36	36	3	0-0	238.2	233	110	25	4	68-6	177	3.81	91	.255	.308	70-0-9	.057	-3*	108	-8	0	-1.1
1979	SF N	3	8	.273	22	22	0	0-0	137	145	64	15	2	51-7	76	3.94	89	.279	.343	42-0-2	.167	2*	83	-6	48	-0.3
1980	SF N	4	8	.333	22	17	1	0-0	113.1	120	61	15	2	39-6	85	4.37	80	.265	.325	30-0-3	.033	-2	94	-10	38	-1.3
1981	Atl N	2	3	.400	26	9	0	1-0	77.1	75	32	9	0	27-2	34	3.49	101	.260	.321	15	.067	-1	109	1	0	0.0
1982	SD N	10	11	.476	32	32	1	0-0	184.1	177	93	17	3	41-2	83	4.00	86	.251	.290	58-0-6	.086	-2	101	-12	0	-1.5
1983	SD N	9	4	.692	31	10	1	4-1	95.1	94	38	6	1	32-6	52	3.30	106	.265	.326	19-0-4	.053	-1	113	3	0	0.2
	NY A	5	0	1.000	6	6	0	0-0	38	39	14	3	1	10-0	15	3.32	119	.271	.318	0	ø	0	107	3	0	0.4
1984	NY A	5	3	.625	11	11	0	0-0	55.1	55	26	5	1	13-2	23	3.58	107	.253	.295	0	ø	0	103	1	109	0.1
1985	NY A	0	0	ø	3	1	0	0-0	7	12	8	3	0	2-0	2	10.29	39	.387	.412	0	ø	0	225	-5	166	-0.2
1986	NY A	0	0	ø	4	0	0	0-1	12.1	9	3	2	0	5-0	3	2.19	189	.200	.280	0	ø	0	—	3	157	0.2
Total	13	90	83	.520	298	244	32-11	5-3	1652.1	1604	728	135	29	513-57	1081	3.54	103	.255	.311	455-4-43	.097	-10	95	19	558	1.1
MONTEJO, MANNY Manuel (Bofill); B10.16.1935 Caibarien, Cuba; BR/TR/5´11˝/150; d7.25																										
1961	Det A	0	0	ø	12	0	0	0	16.1	13	7	2	2	6-1	15	3.86	106	.217	.309	0	ø	0	—	1	0	0.0
MONTELEONE, RICH Richard; B3.22.1963 Tampa FL; BR/TR/6´2˝/(205–236); [DetA82 1/20]; d4.15; C4																										
1987	Sea A	0	0	ø	3	0	0	0-0	7	10	5	2	1	4-0	2	6.43	74	.345	.441	0	ø	0	—	-1	0	0.0
1988	Cal A	0	0	ø	3	0	0	0-0	4.1	4	0	0	1	1-1	3	0.00	ø	.222	.300	0	ø	0	—	2	0	0.1
1989	Cal A	2	2	.500	24	0	0	0-2	39.2	39	15	3	1	13-1	27	3.18	121	.255	.314	0	ø	0	—	3	0	0.3
1990	NY A	0	1	.000	5	0	0	0-0	7.1	8	5	0	0	2-0	8	6.14	65	.276	.323	0	ø	0	—	-1	0	-0.2
1991	NY A	3	1	.750	26	0	0	0-0	47	42	27	5	0	19-3	34	3.64	115	.236	.307	0	ø	0	—	0	0	0.0
1992	NY A	7	3	.700	47	0	0	0-2	92.2	82	35	7	0	27-3	62	3.30	120	.235	.289	0	ø	0	—	8	0	0.7
1993	NY A	7	4	.636	42	0	0	0-1	85.2	85	52	14	0	35-10	50	4.94	85	.262	.329	0	ø	0	—	-8	0	-0.9
1994	SF N	4	3	.571	39	0	0	0-1	45.1	43	18	6	0	13-2	16	3.18	128	.253	.299	3	.000	-0	—	4	32	0.5
1995	Cal A	1	0	1.000	9	0	0	0-1	9	8	2	1	0	3-0	5	2.00	236	.267	.314	0	ø	0	—	3	0	0.3
1996	Cal A	0	3	.000	12	0	0	0-0	15.1	23	11	5	1	2-0	5	5.87	86	.348	.377	0	ø	0	—	-1	52	-0.2
Total	10	24	17	.585	210	0	0	0-7	353.1	344	170	43	4	119-20	212	3.87	106	.255	.314	3	.000	-0	—	9	84	0.6
MONTERO, AGUSTIN Agustin (Alcantara); B8.26.1977 San Pedro de Macoris, D.R.; BR/TR/6´3˝/210; d5.12																										
2006	Chi A	1	0	1.000	11	0	0	0-0	14	15	10	3	0	2-0	7	5.14	91	.278	.288	0	ø	0	—	-1	0	-0.1
MONTGOMERY, JEFF Jeffrey Thomas; B1.7.1962 Wellston OH; BR/TR/5´11˝/(175–180); [CinN83 9/212]; d8.1; Col Marshall																										
1987	Cin N	2	2	.500	14	1	0	0-0	19.1	25	15	2	0	9-1	13	6.52	65	.313	.382	2	.000	-0	43	-5	0	-0.8
1988	KC A	7	2	.778	45	0	0	1-2	62.2	54	25	6	2	30-1	47	3.45	116	.231	.321	0	ø	0	—	5	0	0.6
1989	KC A	7	3	.700	63	0	0	18-6	92	66	16	3	2	25-4	94	1.37	283	.198	.257	0	ø	0	—	**26**	0	3.5
1990	KC A	6	5	.545	73	0	0	24-10	94.1	81	36	6	5	34-8	94	2.39	162	.227	.302	0	ø	0	—	12	0	1.9
1991	KC A	4	4	.500	67	0	0	33-6	90	83	32	6	2	28-2	77	2.90	143	.246	.305	0	ø	0	—	13	0	1.8
1992	KC A★	1	6	.143	65	0	0	39-7	82.2	61	23	5	3	27-2	69	2.18	188	.205	.277	0	ø	0	—	16	0	2.7
1993	KC A★	7	5	.583	69	0	0	**45**-6	87.1	65	22	3	2	23-4	66	2.27	204	.206	.263	0	ø	0	—	**22**	0	4.5
1994	KC A	2	3	.400	42	0	0	27-5	44.2	48	21	5	1	15-1	50	4.03	125	.276	.335	0	ø	0	—	5	0	0.9
1995	KC A	2	3	.400	54	0	0	31-7	65.2	60	27	7	2	25-4	49	3.43	140	.252	.322	0	ø	0	—	10	0	1.4
1996	KC A☆	4	6	.400	48	0	0	24-10	63.1	59	31	14	3	19-3	45	4.26	118	.251	.314	0	ø	0	—	6	0	1.1
1997	KC A	1	4	.200	55	0	0	14-3	59.1	53	24	9	0	18-5	48	3.49	136	.240	.295	0	ø	0	—	8	15	1.0
1998	KC A	2	5	.286	56	0	0	36-5	56	58	35	8	2	22-2	54	4.98	98	.264	.335	0	ø	0	—	-1	0	-0.2
1999	KC A	1	4	.200	49	0	0	12-7	51.1	72	40	7	2	21-3	27	6.84	74	.343	.404	0	ø	0	—	-8	31	-1.0
Total	13	46	52	.469	700	1	0	304-74	868.2	785	347	81	26	296-40	733	3.27	135	.241	.308	2	.000	-0	43	109	46	17.4
MONTGOMERY, MONTY Monty Bryson; B9.1.1946 Albemarle NC; BR/TR/6´3˝/(200–205); [KCA68 9/204]; d9.14; Col Pfeiffer																										
1971	KC A	3	0	1.000	3	2	0	0-0	21.1	16	5	0	0	3-0	12	2.11	163	.205	.235	7-0-1	.000	-0	130	3	0	0.5
1972	KC A	3	3	.500	9	8	1-1	0-0	56.1	55	21	2	0	17-2	24	3.04	100	.263	.316	17-0-3	.176	0	106	0	0	0.0
Total	2	6	3	.667	12	10	1-1	0-0	77.2	71	26	2	0	20-2	36	2.78	113	.247	.294	24-0-4	.125	0	110	3	0	0.5
MONTGOMERY, STEVE Steven Lewis; B12.25.1970 Westminster CA; BR/TR/6´4˝/(200–212); [StLN92 3/83]; d4.3; Col Pepperdine																										
1996	Oak A	1	0	1.000	8	0	0	0-0	13.2	18	14	5	0	13-2	8	9.22	54	.310	.437	0	ø	0	—	-6	0	-0.4
1997	Oak A	0	1	.000	4	0	0	0-0	6.1	10	7	2	0	8-2	1	9.95	46	.385	.514	0	ø	0	—	-4	0	-0.5
1999	Phi N	1	5	.167	53	0	0	3-0	64.2	54	25	10	0	31-3	55	3.34	140	.229	.318	1	1.000	0	—	10	16	0.9
2000	SD N	0	2	.000	7	0	0	0-0	5.2	6	6	3	0	4-0	3	7.94	56	.273	.385	0	ø	0	—	-2	159	-0.5
Total	4	2	8	.200	72	0	0	3-0	90.1	88	52	20	0	56-7	67	4.98	94	.257	.361	1	1.000	0	—	-2	175	-0.5
MONZANT, RAMON Ramon Segundo (Espina); B1.4.1933 Maracaibo, Zulia, Venez.; D8.10.2001 Maracaibo, Zulia, Venez.; BR/TR/6´0˝/(160–165); d7.2																										
1954	NY N	0	0	ø	6	1	0	0	7.2	8	5	0	0	11	5	4.70	86	.276	.463	2	.000	-0	199	-1	0	-0.1
1955	NY N	4	8	.333	28	12	3	0	94.2	98	47	11	3	43-5	54	3.99	101	.278	.357	24-0-2	.125	-1*	76	1	0	0.0
1956	NY N	1	0	1.000	4	1	1	0	13	8	7	4	0	7-0	11	4.15	91	.170	.278	4	.000	-1*	186	-1	0	-0.1
1957	NY N	3	2	.600	24	2	0	0	49.2	55	27	6	2	16-1	37	3.99	99	.286	.340	10	.300	1	11	-1	0	-0.1
1958	SF N	8	11	.421	43	16	4-1	1	150.2	160	89	20	6	57-5	93	4.72	81	.273	.339	49-0-1	.163	-1*	119	-15	0	-1.8
1960	SF N	0	0	ø	1	0	0	0	1	1	1	1	0	0-0	1	9.00	39	.250	.250	0	ø	0	—	-1	0	0.0
Total	6	16	21	.432	106	32	8-1	1	316.2	330	176	42	11	134-11	201	4.38	89	.273	.346	89-0-3	.157	-2	100	-18	0	-2.1
MOODY, ERIC Eric Lane; B1.6.1971 Greenville SC; BR/TR/6´6˝/185; [TexA93 24/675]; d8.3; Col Erskine; [DL 1998 Tex A 10]																										
1997	Tex A	0	1	.000	10	1	0	0-1	19	26	10	4	0	2-0	12	4.26	114	.329	.341	0	ø	0	38	1	0	0.0
MOON, LEO Leo "Lefty"; B6.22.1899 Bellemont NC; D8.25.1970 New Orleans LA; BR/TL/5´11˝/165; d7.9																										
1932	Cle A	0	0	ø	1	0	0	0	5.2	11	8	0	0	7	1	11.12	43	.379	.500	2	.500	0	—	-4	—	-0.1
MOONEY, JIM Jim Irving; B9.4.1906 Mooresburg TN; D4.27.1979 Johnson City TN; BR/TL/5´11˝/168; d8.14; Col East Tennessee																										
1931	NY N	7	1	.875	10	8	6-2	0	71.2	71	19	1	1	16	38	2.01	184	.262	.306	25-0-1	.160	-1	119	14	—	1.4
1932	NY N	6	10	.375	29	18	4-1	0	124.2	154	79	18	0	42	37	5.05	73	.299	.352	41	.122	-2	103	-17	—	-2.1
1933	StL N	2	5	.286	21	8	2	1	77.1	87	36	1	0	26	14	3.72	93	.296	.353	20-0-2	.050	-2	87	-1	—	-0.3
1934	†StL N	2	4	.333	32	7	1	1	82.1	114	59	3	4	49	27	5.47	77	.326	.414	19-0-1	.053	-2	99	-11	—	-1.0
Total	4	17	20	.459	92	41	13-3	2	356	426	193	23	5	133	116	4.25	89	.298	.360	105-0-4	.105	-7	102	-15	—	-2.0
MOONEYHAM, BILL William Craig; B8.16.1960 Livermore CA; BR/TR/6´0˝/175; [AnaA80 S1/10]; d4.19; Col Merced (CA) JC																										
1986	Oak A	4	5	.444	45	6	0	2-3	99.2	103	53	4	3	67-4	75	4.52	86	.270	.382	0	ø	0	124	-6	0	-0.5
MOORE, BALOR Balor Lilbon; B1.25.1951 Smithville TX; BL/TL/6´2˝/(184–194); [MonN69 1/22]; d5.21																										
1970	Mon N	0	2	.000	6	2	0	0-0	9.2	14	9	0	0	8-0	6	7.45	56	.368	.458	3	.333	0	43	-3	0	-0.6
1972	Mon N	9	9	.500	22	22	6-3	0-0	147.2	122	61	15	5	59-5	161	3.47	102	.226	.305	55-0-1	.145	-0	112	2	0	0.2
1973	Mon N	7	16	.304	35	32	3-1	0-0	176.1	151	98	18	3	109-2	151	4.49	85	.233	.343	53-0-2	.057	-3	79	-11	0	-1.6
1974	Mon N	0	2	.000	8	2	0	0-0	13.2	13	8	1	0	15-0	16	3.95	97	.245	.412	2	.000	-0	45	-1	0	-0.1
1977	Cal A	0	2	.000	7	3	0	0-0	22.2	28	19	7	3	10-1	14	3.97	99	.298	.376	0	ø	0	137	-3	0	-0.3
1978	Tor A	6	9	.400	37	18	2	0-3	144.1	165	85	16	7	54-1	75	4.93	80	.294	.360	0	ø	0	83	-15	0	-1.3
1979	Tor A	5	7	.417	34	16	5	0-1	139.1	135	85	17	8	79-4	51	4.84	91	.262	.366	0	ø	0	97	-7	0	-0.5
1980	Tor A	1	1	.500	31	3	0	1-0	64.2	76	43	6	4	31-3	22	5.29	82	.309	.391	0	ø	0	104	-7	0	-0.4
Total	8	28	48	.368	180	98	16-4	1-4	718.1	704	408	80	30	365-16	496	4.52	87	.261	.352	113-0-3	.106	-3	90	-45	0	-4.6
MOORE, BRAD Bradley Alan; B6.21.1964 Loveland CO; BR/TR/6´1˝/185; d6.14; Col Grand Canyon																										
1988	Phi N	0	0	ø	5	0	0	0-0	5.2	4	0	0	0	4-1	2	0.00	ø	.267	.421	0	ø	0	—	2	0	0.1
1990	Phi N	0	0	ø	3	0	0	0-0	2.2	4	1	0	0	2-1	1	3.38	114	.400	.462	0	ø	0	—	0	0	0.0
Total	2	0	0	ø	8	0	0	0-0	8.1	8	1	0	0	6-2	3	1.08	342	.320	.438	0	ø	0	—	2	0	0.1

YEAR	TM LG	W	L	PCT	G	GS	CG-SHO	SV-BS	IP	H	R	HR	HB	BB-IB	SO	ERA	AERA	OAV	OOB	AB-HR-SH	AVG	PB	SUP	APR	DL	PW
Moore, Carlos	Carlos Whitman; B8.13.1906 Clinton TN; D7.2.1958 New Orleans LA; BR/TR/6´1.5˝/180; d5.4																									
1930	Was A	0	0	ø	4	0	0	0	11.2	9	3	0	0	4	2	2.31	199	.225	.295	4	.000	-1	—	3	—	0.1
Moore, Donnie	Donnie Ray; B2.13.1954 Lubbock TX; D7.18.1989 Anaheim CA; BL/TR/6´0˝/(170–192); [ChiN73*S1/3]; d9.14; Col Ranger (TX) JC																									
1975	Chi N	0	0	ø	4	1	0	0-0	8.2	12	4	1	0	4-0	8	4.15	93	.316	.381	3	.000	-0	113	0	0	0.0
1977	Chi N	4	2	.667	27	1	0	0-1	48.2	51	27	1	0	18-7	34	4.07	108	.285	.345	10	.300	1	182	1	0	0.2
1978	Chi N	9	7	.563	71	1	0	4-5	102.2	117	55	7	2	31-11	50	4.12	98	.287	.337	15-0-1	.267	1	178	-2	0	-0.2
1979	Chi N	1	4	.200	39	1	0	1-0	73	95	46	8	2	25-7	43	5.18	80	.321	.375	13	.154	0	64	-7	0	-0.4
1980	StL N	1	1	.500	11	0	0	0-0	21.2	25	15	1	1	5-1	10	6.23	60	.298	.341	4-0-2	.750	2	—	-5	0	-0.3
1981	Mil A	0	0	ø	3	0	0	0-0	4	4	3	0	0	4-0	2	6.75	51	.286	.421	0	ø	0	—	-1	0	-0.1
1982	†Atl N	3	1	.750	16	0	0	1-2	27.2	32	13	1	2	7-3	17	4.23	87	.294	.345	1	.000	-0	—	-1	0	-0.1
1983	Atl N	2	3	.400	43	0	0	6-1	68.2	72	30	6	0	10-3	41	3.67	105	.279	.300	8-0-1	.500	1	—	2	21	0.2
1984	Atl N	4	5	.444	47	0	0	16-3	64.1	63	27	3	1	18-6	47	2.94	131	.258	.309	3	.000	-0	—	5	35	0.9
1985	Cal A★	8	8	.500	65	0	0	31-8	103	91	28	9	0	21-3	72	1.92	215	.237	.275	0	ø	0	—	24	0	4.8
1986	†Cal A	4	5	.444	49	0	0	21-8	72.2	60	28	10	0	22-4	53	2.97	139	.228	.285	0	ø	0	—	9	36	1.4
1987	Cal A	2	2	.500	14	0	0	5-2	26.2	28	12	2	0	13-2	17	2.70	160	.259	.339	0	ø	0	—	4	101	0.6
1988	Cal A	5	2	.714	27	0	0	4-3	33	48	20	4	0	8-2	22	4.91	79	.343	.373	0	ø	0	—	-4	59	-0.8
Total	13	43	40	.518	416	4	0	89-33	654.2	698	308	53	8	186-49	416	3.67	110	.276	.325	57-0-4	.281	4	138	25	252	6.2
Moore, Earl	Earl Alonzo "Big Ebbie","Crossfire"; B7.29.1879 Pickerington OH; D11.28.1961 Columbus OH; BR/TR/6´0˝/195; d4.25																									
1901	Cle A	16	14	.533	31	30	28-4	0	251.1	234	129	4	8	107	99	2.90	122	.244	.325	99-0-3	.162	-5	109	17	—	1.0
1902	Cle A	17	18	.486	36	34	29-4	1	293	304	158	8	7	101	84	2.95	117	.268	.331	113-0-3	.212	-0	93	12	—	1.2
1903	Cle A	20	8	.714	29	27	27-3	0	247.2	196	88	0	5	62	148	**1.74**	**164**	**.217**	.271	87-0-5	.092	-5	127	27	—	2.2
1904	Cle A	12	11	.522	26	24	22-1	0	227.2	186	83	2	10	61	139	2.25	113	.224	.285	86-0-2	.140	-2	130	7	—	0.1
1905	Cle A	15	15	.500	31	30	28-3	0	269	232	111	6	18	92	131	2.64	99	.234	.311	96-0-1	.104	-4	118	-2	—	-0.8
1906	Cle A	1	1	.500	5	4	2	0	29.2	27	15	1	2	18	8	3.94	66	.245	.362	10	.000	-1	117	-3	—	-0.4
1907	Cle A	1	1	.500	3	2	1	0	19.1	18	14	0	1	8	7	4.66	54	.250	.333	7	.000	-1	108	-4	—	-0.5
	NY A	2	6	.250	12	9	3	1	64	72	49	1	4	30	28	3.94	71	.286	.371	22	.273	1	97	-10	—	-1.1
	Year	3	7	.300	15	11	4	1	83.1	90	63	1	5	38	35	4.10	66	.278	.362	29	.207	0	99	-14	—	-1.6
1908	Phi N	2	1	.667	3	3	3-1	0	26	20	4	0	2	8	16	0.00	ø	.217	.294	9-0-1	.222	0	97	5	—	0.8
1909	Phi N	18	12	.600	38	34	24-4	0	299.2	238	93	7	9	108	173	2.10	124	.210	.283	96-0-5	.094	-4	82	17	—	1.0
1910	Phi N	22	15	.595	46	35	18-**6**	0	283	228	98	5	10	121	**185**	2.58	121	.228	.318	87-0-8	.230	2	103	20	—	2.6
1911	Phi N	15	19	.441	42	36	21-5	1	308.1	265	123	11	12	164	174	2.63	131	.240	.345	101-0-3	.109	-6	84	26	—	1.9
1912	Phi N	9	14	.391	31	24	10-1	0	182.1	186	101	3	7	77	79	3.31	110	.275	.355	56-0-3	.107	-4	70	4	—	-0.1
1913	Phi N	1	3	.250	12	5	0	1	52	50	37	3	1	40	24	5.02	66	.254	.382	16-0-1	.000	-2	113	-10	—	-0.9
	Chi N	1	1	.500	7	2	0	0	28.1	34	19	3	0	12	12	4.45	71	.321	.390	8	.125	-0	71	-4	—	-0.3
	Year	2	4	.333	19	7	0	1	80.1	84	56	6	1	52	36	4.82	68	.277	.385	24-0-1	.042	-2	102	-12	—	-1.2
1914	Buf F	11	15	.423	36	27	14-2	2	194.2	184	109	3	10	99	96	4.30	69	.263	.362	56-0-3	.161	-2	91	-26	—	-3.5
Total	14	163	154	.514	388	326	230-34	6	2776	2474	1231	57	106	1108	1403	2.78	110	.241	.321	949-0-38	.141	-34	100	76	—	3.2
Moore, Euel	Euel Walton "Chief"; B5.27.1908 Reagan OK; D2.12.1989 Tishomingo OK; BR/TR/6´2˝/185; d7.8																									
1934	Phi N	5	7	.417	20	16	3	1	122.1	145	60	9	0	41	38	4.05	117	.288	.342	46	.109	-4	63	9	—	0.4
1935	Phi N	1	6	.143	15	8	1	1	40.1	63	40	5	2	20	15	7.81	58	.354	.425	15-0-1	.400	1	89	-12	—	-1.7
	NY N	1	0	1.000	6	0	0	0	8	9	5	0	0	4	3	5.63	69	.281	.361	2	.000	-0	—	-1	—	-0.2
	Year	2	6	.250	21	8	1	1	48.1	72	45	5	2	24	18	7.45	59	.343	.415	17-0-1	.353	1	91	-14	—	-1.9
1936	Phi N	2	3	.400	20	5	1	1	54.1	76	50	4	1	12	19	6.96	65	.311	.346	18	.222	-0	101	-12	—	-1.1
Total	3	9	16	.360	61	29	5	3	225	293	155	18	3	77	75	5.48	84	.306	.360	81-0-1	.185	-3	77	-16	—	-2.6
Moore, Gene	Eugene Sr. "Blue Goose"; B11.9.1885 Lancaster TX; D8.31.1938 Dallas TX; BL/TL/6´2˝/185; d9.28; s–Gene																									
1909	Pit N	0	0	ø	1	0	0	0	2	4	4	0	0	3	2	18.00	15	.364	.500	1	.000	-0	—	-3	—	-0.2
1910	Pit N	2	1	.667	4	1	0	0	17.1	19	7	1	0	7	9	3.12	99	.268	.333	6	.000	-1	72	0	—	0.0
1912	Cin N	0	1	.000	5	2	0	1	14.2	17	11	0	2	11	6	4.91	68	.304	.435	4	.000	-1	44	-3	—	-0.3
Total	3	2	2	.500	10	3	0	1	34	40	22	1	2	21	17	4.76	67	.290	.391	11	.000	-2	54	-6	—	-0.5
Moore, Frank	Frank J.; B9.12.1877 Dover OH; D5.20.1964 Portsmouth OH; BR/TR/6´4˝/200; d6.14																									
1905	Pit N	0	0	ø	1	0	0	0	3	2	0	0	0	0	1	0.00	ø	.200	.200	1	.000	-0	—	1	—	0.0
Moore, Jim	James Stanford; B12.14.1903 Prescott AR; D5.19.1973 Seattle WA; BR/TR/6´0˝/165; d9.21; Col Hendrix																									
1928	Cle A	0	1	.000	1	1	1	0	9	5	2	0	0	5	1	2.00	207	.161	.278	3	.000	-0	20	2	—	0.2
1929	Cle A	0	0	ø	2	0	0	0	5.2	6	6	1	0	4	0	9.53	47	.273	.385	2	.000	-0	—	-3	—	-0.1
1930	Chi A	2	1	.667	9	5	2	1	40	42	18	0	0	12	11	3.60	128	.268	.320	13-0-2	.231	-0	104	5	—	0.3
1931	Chi A	0	2	.000	33	4	0	0	83.2	93	52	3	1	27	15	4.95	86	.282	.338	16	.063	-1	65	-5	—	-0.3
1932	Chi A	0	0	ø	1	0	0	0	1	1	0	0	0	1	2	0.00	ø	.250	.400	1	.000	-0	—	0	—	0.0
Total	5	2	4	.333	46	10	3	1	139.1	147	78	4	1	49	29	4.52	97	.270	.332	35-0-2	.114	-2	82	-1	—	0.1
Moore, Whitey	Lloyd Albert; B6.10.1912 Tuscarawas OH; D12.10.1987 Uhrichsville OH; BR/TR/6´1˝/195; d9.27; Mil 1943–45																									
1936	Cin N	1	0	1.000	1	0	0	0	5	3	3	0	0	3	4	5.40	71	.167	.286	2-0-1	.000	-0	—	-1	—	-0.1
1937	Cin N	0	3	.000	13	6	0	0	38.2	32	22	1	4	39	27	4.89	76	.239	.424	8	.000	-1	58	-4	—	-0.4
1938	Cin N	6	4	.600	19	11	3-1	0	90.1	66	41	4	3	42	38	3.49	105	.205	.302	26-0-1	.077	-2	91	1	—	-0.1
1939	†Cin N	13	12	.520	42	24	9-2	3	187.2	177	88	10	6	95	81	3.45	111	.254	.348	61-0-7	.098	-4	100	6	—	0.3
1940	†Cin N	8	8	.500	25	15	5-1	1	116.2	100	48	8	7	56	60	3.63	104	.231	.329	39-0-4	.128	-1	104	4	—	0.2
1941	Cin N	2	1	.667	23	4	1	0	61.2	62	35	2	3	45	17	4.38	82	.256	.379	18	.167	-1	165	-6	0	-0.4
1942	Cin N	0	0	ø	1	0	0	0	1	0	0	0	0	1	0	0.00	ø	.000	.250	0	ø	0	—	0	0	0.0
	StL N	0	1	.000	9	0	0	0	12.1	10	6	0	1	11	1	4.38	78	.217	.379	2	.000	-0	—	-1	0	-0.1
	Year	0	1	.000	10	0	0	0	13.1	10	6	0	1	12	1	4.05	84	.204	.371	2	.000	-0	—	0	0	-0.1
Total	7	30	29	.508	133	60	18-4	4	513.1	450	243	25	24	292	228	3.75	100	.237	.346	156-0-13	.103	-10	100	-1	0	-0.6
Moore, Marcus	Marcus Braymont; B11.2.1970 Oakland CA; BB/TR/6´5˝/(195–204); [CalA88 17/429]; d7.9; Col Sacramento (CA) City																									
1993	Col N	3	1	.750	27	0	0	0-2	26.1	30	25	4	1	20-0	13	6.84	70	.291	.398	1	.000	-0	—	-6	0	-0.9
1994	Col N	1	1	.500	29	0	0	0-0	33.2	33	26	4	5	21-2	33	6.15	81	.252	.376	1	.000	-0	—	-4	0	-0.2
1996	Cin N	3	3	.500	23	0	0	2-0	26.1	26	21	3	2	22-1	27	5.81	74	.263	.397	3	.333	1	—	-5	0	-1.0
Total	3	7	5	.583	79	0	0	2-2	86.1	89	72	11	8	63-3	73	6.25	75	.267	.389	5	.200	0	—	-15	0	-2.1
Moore, Mike	Michael Wayne; B11.26.1959 Eakly OK; BR/TR/6´4˝/205; [SeaA81 1/1]; d4.11; Col Oral Roberts																									
1982	Sea A	7	14	.333	28	27	1-1	0-0	144.1	159	91	21	2	79-0	73	5.36	80	.285	.373	0	ø	0	75	-15	0	-1.8
1983	Sea A	6	8	.429	22	21	3-2	0-0	128	130	75	10	3	60-4	108	4.71	91	.267	.348	0	ø	0	83	-6	0	-0.5
1984	Sea A	7	17	.292	34	33	6	0-0	212	236	127	16	5	85-10	158	4.97	81	.282	.350	0	ø	0	87	-21	0	-1.9
1985	Sea A	17	10	.630	35	34	14-2	0-0	247	230	100	18	4	70-2	155	3.46	122	.247	.300	0	ø	0	94	23	16	2.4
1986	Sea A	11	13	.458	38	**37**	11-1	1-0	266	279	141	28	12	94-6	146	4.30	99	.273	.339	0	ø	0	103	0	0	-0.1
1987	Sea A	9	19	.321	33	33	12	0-0	231	268	145	29	0	84-3	115	4.71	101	.292	.348	1	.000	-0	78	-4	0	-0.4
1988	Sea A	9	15	.375	37	32	9-3	1-1	228.2	196	104	24	3	63-6	182	3.78	111	.232	.286	0	ø	0	80	11	0	1.2
1989	†Oak A★	19	11	.633	35	35	6-3	0-0	241.2	193	82	14	2	83-1	172	2.61	142	.219	.286	0	ø	0	97	30	0	3.7
1990	†Oak A	13	15	.464	33	33	3	0-0	199.1	204	113	14	3	84-2	73	4.65	80	.267	.339	0	ø	0	92	-21	0	-2.5
1991	Oak A	17	8	.680	33	33	3-1	0-0	210	176	75	11	5	105-1	153	2.96	130	.229	.324	0	ø	0*	94	21	17	2.5
1992	†Oak A	17	12	.586	36	**36**	2	0-0	223	229	113	20	8	103-5	117	4.12	92	.268	.349	0	ø	0	120	-8	0	-1.0
1993	Det A	13	9	.591	36	**36**	4-3	0-0	213.2	227	135	35	3	89-10	89	5.22	83	.271	.340	0	ø	0	127	-19	0	-1.5
1994	Det A	11	10	.524	25	**25**	4	0-0	154.1	152	97	27	3	89-8	62	5.42	91	.263	.361	0	ø	0	96	-6	0	-0.5
1995	Det A	5	15	.250	25	25	1	0-0	132.2	179	118	24	2	68-3	64	7.53	64	.323	.396	0	ø	0	93	-38	0	-4.4
Total	14	161	176	.478	450	440	79-16	2-1	2831.2	2858	1516	291	55	1156-61	1667	4.39	95	.264	.335	1	.000	-0	95	-53	33	-4.8
Moore, Ray	Raymond Leroy "Farmer"; B6.1.1926 Meadows MD; D3.2.1995 Clinton MD; BR/TR/6´1˝/(195–210); d8.1																									
1952	Bro N	1	2	.333	14	2	0	0	28.1	29	17	3	2	26	11	4.76	76	.274	.425	3	.000	-0	49	-4	0	-0.4
1953	Bro N	0	1	.000	1	1	1	0	8	6	3	1	0	4	4	3.38	126	.214	.313	3	.000	-0	21	1	0	0.0
1955	Bal A	10	10	.500	46	14	3-1	6	151.2	128	75	14	4	80-1	80	3.92	97	.229	.327	44-0-2	.136	-2	100	-1	0	-0.4
1956	Bal A	12	7	.632	32	27	9-1	0	185	161	90	12	1	99-1	105	4.18	94	.238	.332	70-2-4	.271	6	89	-3	0	0.2

YEAR	TM LG	W	L	PCT	G	GS	CG-SHO	SV-BS	IP	H	R	HR	HB	BB-IB	SO	ERA	AERA	OAV	OOB	AB-HR-SH	AVG	PB	SUP	APR	DL	PW
1957	Bal A	11	13	.458	34	32	7-1	0	227.1	196	99	17	2	112-5	117	3.72	97	.236	.326	84-3-3	.214	4	86	-2	0	0.1
1958	Chi A	9	7	.563	32	20	4-2	2	136.2	107	63	10	0	70-2	73	3.82	95	.220	.315	44-1-5	.205	2	99	-2	0	-0.1
1959	†Chi A	3	6	.333	29	8	0	0	89.2	86	46	10	1	46-3	49	4.12	91	.261	.348	23-0-1	.087	-1	59	-4	0	-0.5
1960	Chi A	1	1	.500	14	0	0	0	20.2	19	13	5	0	11-0	3	5.66	67	.253	.345	2	.000	-0	—	-4	0	-0.4
	Was A	3	2	.600	37	0	0	13	65.2	49	24	5	1	27-3	29	2.88	135	.213	.296	14	.071	-1	—	8	0	0.7
	Year	4	3	.571	51	0	0	13	86.1	68	37	10	1	38-3	32	3.54	109	.223	.308	16	.063	-1	—	4	0	0.3
1961	Min A	4	4	.500	46	0	0	14	56.1	49	23	8	1	38-3	45	3.67	115	.233	.351	4-0-1	.000	0	—	5	0	0.9
1962	Min A	8	3	.727	49	0	0	9	64.2	55	35	8	2	30-4	58	4.73	86	.231	.319	5-0-1	.000	-1	—	-3	0	-0.7
1963	Min A	1	3	.250	31	1	0	2	38.2	50	34	8	1	17-2	38	6.98	52	.309	.378	3	.333	0	73	-14	0	-1.5
Total	11	63	59	.516	365	105	24-5	46	1072.2	935	522	101	15	560-24	612	4.06	93	.238	.332	299-6-17	.187	6	86	-23	0	-2.1
Moore, Barry	Robert Barry; B4.3.1943 Statesville NC; BL/TL/6´1˝/(175–190); d5.29; Col Pfeiffer																									
1965	Was A	0	0	ø	1	0	0	0	1	1	1	0	0	1-0	0	0.00	ø	.333	.500	0	ø	0	—	0	0	0.0
1966	Was A	3	3	.500	12	11	1	0	62.1	55	26	3	1	39-2	28	3.75	92	.240	.352	19-0-1	.105	-1	93	-1	0	-0.1
1967	Was A	7	11	.389	27	26	3-1	0	143.2	127	67	15	3	71-6	74	3.76	84	.240	.332	46-0-4	.130	-0	86	-9	21	-1.0
1968	Was A	4	6	.400	32	18	0	3	117.2	116	55	8	2	42-2	56	3.37	87	.261	.326	31-0-3	.097	-1*	108	-8	0	-0.8
1969	Was A	9	8	.529	31	25	4	0-0	134	123	70	12	2	67-1	51	4.30	82	.246	.334	43-0-2	.209	1*	112	-11	0	-1.2
1970	Cle A	3	5	.375	13	12	0	0-0	70.1	70	34	8	1	46-3	35	4.22	95	.262	.370	21-0-1	.095	-1	87	-1	0	-0.2
	Chi A	0	4	.000	24	7	0	0-0	70.2	85	56	12	8	34-0	34	6.37	61	.302	.386	19-0-1	.263	1	95	-18	0	-0.8
	Year	3	9	.250	37	19	0	0-0	141	155	90	20	9	80-3	69	5.30	74	.283	.378	40-0-2	.175	-0	90	-17	0	-1.0
Total	6	26	37	.413	140	99	8-1	3-0	599.2	577	309	58	17	300-14	278	4.16	82	.256	.345	179-0-12	.151	-1	98	-48	21	-4.1
Moore, Bobby	Robert Devell; B11.8.1958 Sweetwater LA; BR/TR/6´4˝/200; [OakA76 11/264]; d9.11																									
1985	SF N	0	0	ø	11	0	0	0-0	16.2	18	6	1	0	10-2	10	3.24	107	.269	.364	2	.000	-0	—	1	0	0.0
Moore, Roy	Roy Daniel; B10.26.1898 Austin TX; D4.5.1951 Seattle WA; BB/TL/6´0˝/185; d4.15																									
1920	Phi A	1	13	.071	24	14	5	0	132.2	161	89	6	3	64	45	4.68	86	.314	.393	50-1-1	.200	-1*	52	-7	—	-0.7
1921	Phi A	10	10	.500	29	26	12	0	191.2	206	110	4	4	122	64	4.51	99	.280	.385	74-3-0	.257	3*	82	3	—	0.7
1922	Phi A	0	3	.000	15	6	0	0	50.2	65	43	1	3	32	29	7.64	56	.319	.418	19-0-1	.263	1	116	-15	—	-0.6
	Det A	0	0	ø	9	0	0	2	19.2	29	14	0	5	10	9	5.95	65	.367	.468	7	.429	1	—	-4	—	-0.1
	Year	0	3	.000	24	6	0	2	70.1	94	57	1	8	42	38	7.17	58	.332	.432	26-0-1	.308	2	119	-18	—	-0.7
1923	Det A	0	0	ø	3	0	0	1	12	15	4	0	0	11	7	3.00	129	.288	.413	5	.000	-0*	—	2	—	0.1
Total	4	11	26	.297	80	46	17	3	406.2	476	260	11	15	239	154	4.98	85	.300	.397	155-4-2	.239	4	78	-21	—	-0.6
Moore, Tommy	Tommy Joe; B7.7.1948 Lynwood CA; BR/TR/5´11˝/175; [NYN67*S10/152]; d9.15; Col Cerritos (CA) JC																									
1972	NY N	0	0	ø	3	1	0	0-0	12.1	12	4	1	0	1-0	5	2.92	116	.273	.283	3	.333	0	52	1	0	0.1
1973	NY N	0	1	.000	3	1	0	0-0	3.1	6	5	1	0	3-0	1	10.80	34	.400	.500	0	ø	0*	121	-3	0	-0.6
1975	StL N	0	0	ø	10	0	0	0-0	18.2	15	10	2	0	12-1	6	3.86	99	.203	.314	2	.500	0	—	0	0	0.0
	Tex A	0	2	.000	12	0	0	0-1	21	31	21	1	1	12-4	15	8.14	46	.352	.436	0	ø	0*	—	-10	0	-0.8
1977	Sea A	2	1	.667	14	1	0	0-1	33	36	22	1	3	21-2	13	4.91	84	.281	.390	0	ø	0	65	-4	0	-0.3
Total	4	2	4	.333	42	3	0	0-2	88.1	100	62	6	4	49-7	40	5.40	71	.287	.378	5	.400	1	77	-16	0	-1.6
Moore, Trey	Warren Neal; B10.2.1972 Houston TX; BL/TL/6´1˝/(190–200); [SeaA94 2/48]; d4.5; Col Texas A&M; [DL 1999 Mon N 182]																									
1998	Mon N	2	5	.286	13	11	0	0-0	61	78	37	5	1	17-3	35	5.02	84	.306	.348	17-0-1	.235	1*	68	-5	113	-0.4
2000	Mon N	1	5	.167	8	8	0	0-0	35.1	55	31	7	4	21-1	24	6.62	71	.364	.455	8-0-2	.125	-0	78	-8	0	-1.1
2001	Atl N	0	0	ø	2	0	0	0-0	4	7	5	0	0	2-0	1	11.25	38	.368	.429	1	1.000	1	—	-3	0	-0.1
Total	3	3	10	.231	23	19	0	0-0	100.1	140	73	12	5	40-4	60	5.83	75	.329	.391	26-0-3	.231	2	73	-16	295	-1.6
Moore, Cy	William Austin; B2.7.1905 Elberton GA; D3.28.1972 Augusta GA; BR/TR/6´1˝/178; d6.7																									
1929	Bro N	3	3	.500	32	3	0	2	68	87	45	3	0	31	17	5.56	83	.320	.389	16-0-1	.188	-0	63	-5	—	-0.5
1930	Bro N	0	0	ø	1	0	0	0	0	2	1	0	0	0	0	(0)	ø	1.000	1.000	0	ø	0	—	0	—	0.0
1931	Bro N	1	2	.333	23	1	1	0	61.2	62	31	5	4	13	35	3.79	100	.262	.311	13-0-1	.154	-1	22	0	—	-0.1
1932	Bro N	0	3	.000	20	2	0	0	48.2	56	32	3	1	17	21	4.81	79	.293	.354	14	.214	0*	99	-6	—	-0.3
1933	Phi N	8	9	.471	36	18	9-3	1	161.1	177	74	7	3	42	53	3.74	102	.279	.326	48-0-1	.063	-4	81	3	—	-0.1
1934	Phi N	4	9	.308	35	15	3	0	126.2	163	98	11	2	65	55	6.47	73	.309	.387	42-0-1	.143	-3	91	-18	—	-1.9
Total	6	16	26	.381	147	39	13-3	3	466.1	547	281	29	10	168	181	4.86	86	.293	.355	133-0-4	.128	-8	84	-26	—	-2.9
Moore, Bill	William Christopher; B9.3.1902 Corning NY; D1.24.1984 Corning NY; BR/TR/6´3˝/195; d4.15																									
1925	Det A	0	0	ø	1	0	0	0	0	0	2	0	0	3	0	(2)	ø	ø	1.000	0	ø	0	—	-2	—	-0.2
Moore, Wilcy	William Wilcy "Cy"; B5.20.1897 Bonita TX; D3.29.1963 Hollis OK; BR/TR/6´0˝/195; d4.14																									
1927	†NY A	19	7	.731	50	12	6-1	**13**	213	185	68	3	1	59	75	**2.28**	**169**	**.234**	**.289**	75-1-7	.080	-7	119	39	—	4.5
1928	NY A	4	4	.500	35	2	0	2	60.1	71	44	4	0	31	18	4.18	90	.286	.366	14-0-2	.143	-1	203	-8	—	-0.9
1929	NY A	6	4	.600	41	0	0	8	61	64	36	4	0	19	21	4.13	93	.268	.322	15-0-1	.067	-2	—	-3	—	-0.6
1931	Bos A	11	13	.458	53	15	8-1	**10**	185.1	195	88	7	1	55	37	3.88	111	.269	.322	56-0-2	.161	-3	64	10	—	1.3
1932	Bos A	4	10	.286	37	2	0	4	84.1	98	59	5	1	42	28	5.23	86	.284	.363	22	.045	-2	28	-7	—	-1.1
	†NY A	2	0	1.000	10	1	0	4	25	27	8	1	0	6	8	2.52	162	.273	.314	8	.000	-1	84	5	—	0.4
	Year	6	10	.375	47	3	0	8	109.1	125	67	6	1	48	36	4.61	95	.282	.353	30	.033	-4	45	-2	—	-0.7
1933	NY A	5	6	.455	35	0	0	8	62	92	53	1	0	20	17	5.52	70	.333	.378	15-0-2	.133	-1	—	-16	—	-2.9
Total	6	51	44	.537	261	32	14-2	49	691	732	356	25	3	232	204	3.70	110	.269	.327	205-1-14	.102	-17	91	20	—	0.7
Moorhead, Bob	Charles Robert; B1.23.1938 Chambersburg PA; D12.3.1986 Lemoyne PA; BR/TR/6´1˝/208; d4.11																									
1962	NY N	0	2	.000	38	7	0	0	105.1	118	69	13	4	42-4	63	4.53	92	.289	.358	22-0-1	.045	-1	126	-6	0	-0.3
1965	NY N	0	1	.000	9	0	0	0	14.1	16	7	0	0	5-0	5	4.40	80	.271	.328	0	ø	0	—	-1	0	0.0
Total	2	0	3	.000	47	7	0	0	119.2	134	76	13	4	47-4	68	4.51	91	.287	.354	22-0-1	.045	-1	126	-7	0	-0.3
Moose, Bob	Robert Ralph; B10.9.1947 Export PA; D10.9.1976 Martins Ferry OH; BR/TR/6´0˝/(170–200); [PitN65 11/348]; d9.19																									
1967	Pit N	1	0	1.000	2	2	1	0	14.2	14	6	1	1	4-0	7	3.68	91	.259	.322	6	.333	1	196	0	0	0.1
1968	Pit N	8	12	.400	38	22	3-3	3	170.2	136	61	5	3	41-7	126	2.74	107	.218	.268	54-0-2	.093	-2	78	4	0	0.3
1969	Pit N	14	3	.824	44	19	6-1	4-1	170	149	64	9	5	62-3	165	2.91	120	.231	.302	53-0-4	.075	-1	166	10	0	0.9
1970	†Pit N	11	10	.524	28	27	9-2	0-0	189.2	186	88	14	3	64-5	119	3.99	99	.262	.325	66-0-4	.182	3*	92	2	0	0.3
1971	†Pit N	11	7	.611	30	18	3-1	1-0	140	169	73	12	2	35-11	68	4.11	83	.301	.340	39-0-5	.103	-1	138	-12	0	-1.6
1972	†Pit N	13	10	.565	31	30	6-3	1-0	226	213	84	11	4	47-9	144	2.91	114	.248	.288	71-0-6	.169	3*	121	11	0	1.5
1973	Pit N	12	13	.480	33	29	6-3	0-0	201.1	219	86	11	4	70-11	111	3.53	100	.280	.340	67-0-4	.134	-0*	99	2	0	0.3
1974	Pit N	1	5	.167	7	6	0	0-0	35.2	59	30	4	2	7-3	15	7.57	46	.386	.410	11	.182	0	84	-15	126	-1.9
1975	Pit N	2	2	.500	23	5	1	0-0	67.2	63	30	4	2	25-3	34	3.72	96	.246	.318	18-0-2	.167	0	103	0	23	0.1
1976	Pit N	3	9	.250	53	2	0	10-3	88	100	44	4	4	32-7	38	3.68	96	.294	.356	12-1-0	.250	2	25	-3	0	-0.3
Total	10	76	71	.517	289	160	35-13	19-4	1303.2	1308	566	75	30	387-59	827	3.50	99	.262	.317	397-1-27	.141	4	111	-1	149	-0.3
Mooty, Jake	Jake T.; B4.13.1912 Millsap TX; D4.20.1970 Fort Worth TX; BR/TR/5´10.5˝/170; d9.9; Col Texas A&M																									
1936	Cin N	0	0	ø	8	0	0	1	13.2	10	6	0	0	4	11	3.95	97	.204	.264	1	.000	-0	—	0	—	0.0
1937	Cin N	0	3	.000	14	2	0	1	39	54	39	2	0	22	11	8.31	45	.327	.406	8-0-1	.000	-1*	46	-19	—	-1.5
1940	Chi N	6	6	.500	20	12	6	1	114	101	45	11	1	49	42	2.92	128	.243	.325	38-0-3	.263	2*	77	10	—	1.1
1941	Chi N	8	9	.471	33	14	7-1	4	153.1	143	69	9	2	56	45	3.35	105	.251	.320	50-0-3	.200	1	85	2	0	0.4
1942	Chi N	2	5	.286	19	10	1	1	84.1	89	48	11	0	44	28	4.70	68	.265	.350	28-0-1	.214	0	137	-13	0	-1.0
1943	Chi N	0	0	ø	2	0	0	0	1	2	0	0	0	1	1	0.00	ø	.400	.500	0	ø	0	—	0	0	0.0
1944	Det A	0	0	ø	15	0	0	0	28.1	35	20	0	1	18	7	4.45	80	.310	.409	7	.143	-0	—	-4	0	-0.3
Total	7	16	23	.410	111	38	14-1	8	433.2	434	227	33	4	194	145	4.03	88	.263	.341	132-0-8	.205	1	92	-24	0	-1.3
Moraga, David	David Michael; B7.8.1975 Torrance CA; BL/TL/6´0˝/185; [MonN93 30/846]; d6.11; Col Sacramento (CA) City																									
2000	Mon N	0	0	ø	3	0	0	0-0	1.2	6	7	0	0	2-0	2	37.80	12	.600	.615	0	ø	0	—	-6	0	-0.3
	Col N	0	0	ø	1	0	0	0-0	1	4	5	1	1	0-0	0	45.00	13	.667	.625	0	ø	0	—	-3	0	-0.1
	Year	0	0	ø	4	0	0	0-0	2.2	10	12	1	1	2-0	2	40.50	13	.625	.619	0	ø	0	—	-9	0	-0.4

THE PITCHER REGISTER

YEAR	TM LG	W	L	PCT	G	GS	CG-SHO	SV-BS	IP	H	R	HR	HB	BB-IB	SO	ERA	AERA	OAV	OOB	AB-HR-SH	AVG	PB	SUP	APR	DL	PW
MORAN, HIKER Albert Thomas; B1.1.1912 Rochester NY; D1.7.1998 Saratoga Springs NY; BR/TR/6´4.5˝/185; d9.29																										
1938	Bos N	0	0	ø	1	0	0	0	3	1	0	0	0	1	0	0.00	ø	.111	.200	1	.000	-0	—	1	—	0.0
1939	Bos N	1	1	.500	6	2	1	0	20	21	10	3	0	11	4	4.50	82	.276	.368	5-0-1	.200	1	142	-1	—	-0.1
Total	2	1	1	.500	7	2	1	0	23	22	10	3	0	12	4	3.91	94	.259	.351	6-0-1	.167	0	142	0	—	-0.1
MORAN, BILL Carl William "Bugs"; B9.26.1950 Portsmouth VA; BR/TR/6´4˝/210; d4.12; Col Louisburg (NC) JC																										
1974	Chi A	1	3	.250	15	5	0	0-0	46.1	57	27	5	6	23-2	17	4.66	80	.302	.393	0	ø	0	113	-5	0	-0.4
MORAN, CHARLIE Charles Barthell "Uncle Charlie"; B2.22.1878 Nashville TN; D6.14.1949 Horse Cave KY; BR/TR/5´8˝/180; d9.9; U22; Col Vanderbilt; ▲																										
1903	StL N	0	1	.000	3	2	2	0	24	30	29	0	1	19	7	5.25	62	.297	.413	14	.429	1*	124	-7	—	-0.2
MORAN, HARRY Harry Edwin; B4.2.1889 Slater (now Thayer) WV; D11.28.1962 Beckley WV; BL/TL/6´1˝/165; d6.23; Col Washington and Lee																										
1912	Det A	0	1	.000	5	2	1	0	14.2	19	14	1	2	12	3	4.91	66	.339	.471	5	.200	-0	125	-4	—	-0.3
1914	Buf F	10	7	.588	34	16	7-2	2	154	159	87	7	11	53	73	4.27	69	.276	.348	51-0-3	.196	0	114	-21	—	-2.2
1915	New F	13	9	.591	34	23	13-2	0	205.2	193	80	2	18	66	87	2.54	101	.262	.337	61-0-9	.180	0*	96	1	—	0.1
Total	3	23	17	.575	73	41	21-4	2	374.1	371	181	10	31	131	163	3.34	82	.271	.348	117-0-12	.188	0	105	-24	—	-2.4
MORAN, SAM Samuel; B9.16.1870 Rochester NY; D8.27.1897 Rochester NY; TL/?/160; d8.28																										
1895	Pit N	2	4	.333	10	6	6	0	62.2	78	63	2	3	51	19	7.47	60	.300	.420	26-1-0	.154	-1*	103	-17	—	-1.2
MORE, FORREST Forrest Thedore; B9.30.1881 Hayden IN; D8.17.1968 Columbus IN; BR/TR/6´0˝/180; d4.15																										
1909	StL N	1	5	.167	15	2	1	0	50	48	33	0	3	20	17	5.04	50	.258	.340	13-0-1	.154	1	111	-12	—	-1.3
	Bos N	1	5	.167	10	4	3	0	48.2	47	47	0	4	20	10	4.44	64	.270	.359	15	.067	-1	50	-12	—	-1.5
	Year	2	10	.167	25	6	4	0	98.2	95	80	0	7	40	27	4.74	56	.264	.349	28-0-1	.107	-1	70	-24	—	-2.8
MOREHEAD, DAVE David Michael "Moe"; B9.5.1942 San Diego CA; BR/TR/6´1˝/(180–200); d4.13																										
1963	Bos A	10	13	.435	29	29	6-1	0	174.2	137	82	20	0	99-2	136	3.81	99	.211	.316	57-0-3	.105	-3	89	-1	0	-0.4
1964	Bos A	8	15	.348	32	30	3-1	0	166.2	156	101	14	4	112-2	139	4.97	78	.248	.358	54-0-2	.093	-2	86	-19	0	-2.6
1965	Bos A	10	18	.357	34	33	5-2	0	192.2	157	103	18	3	113-1	163	4.06	92	.217	.325	61-0-4	.131	0	80	-7	0	-1.1
1966	Bos A	1	2	.333	12	5	0	0	28	31	17	7	0	7-0	20	5.46	70	.274	.317	6	.500	1	120	-4	16	-0.3
1967	†Bos A	5	4	.556	10	9	1-1	0	47.2	48	24	0	2	22-0	40	4.34	80	.264	.348	12-0-3	.083	-0	111	-3	0	-0.7
1968	Bos A	1	4	.200	11	9	3-1	0	55	52	17	3	2	20-0	28	2.45	129	.249	.320	16-0-1	.125	-0	98	4	0	0.3
1969	KC A	2	3	.400	21	2	0	0-0	33	28	22	7	0	28-1	32	5.73	65	.239	.384	2	.000	0	24	-6	36	-0.9
1970	KC A	3	5	.375	28	17	1	1-0	121.2	121	64	9	1	62-3	69	3.62	103	.261	.347	36-0-3	.167	-0	100	-2	0	-0.2
Total	8	40	64	.385	177	134	19-6	1-0	819.1	730	430	78	12	463-9	627	4.15	90	.237	.336	244-0-16	.127	-5	90	-38	52	-5.9
MOREHEAD, SETH Seth Marvin "Moe"; B8.15.1934 Houston TX; D1.17.2006 Shreveport LA; BL/TL/6´0.5˝/195; d4.27; Col Baylor																										
1957	Phi N	1	1	.500	34	1	1	1	58.2	57	27	1	2	20-4	36	3.68	103	.254	.315	6	.000	-1	46	1	0	-0.1
1958	Phi N	1	6	.143	27	11	0	0	92.1	121	67	8	1	26-3	54	5.85	68	.319	.359	22-0-3	.182	0	87	-19	0	-1.3
1959	Phi N	0	2	.000	3	3	0	0	10	15	11	3	1	3-0	8	9.90	41	.333	.388	3	.000	-0	138	-6	0	-0.9
	Chi N	0	1	.000	11	2	0	0	18.2	25	13	1	0	8-2	9	4.82	82	.313	.375	2	.500	1	136	-3	0	-0.1
	Year	0	3	.000	14	5	0	0	28.2	40	24	4	1	11-2	17	6.59	61	.320	.380	5	.200	0	138	-8	0	-1.0
1960	Chi N	2	9	.182	45	7	2	4	123.1	123	61	17	2	46-6	64	3.94	96	.258	.324	29-0-1	.138	-1	80	-2	0	-0.2
1961	Mil N	1	0	1.000	12	0	0	0	15.1	16	11	4	1	7-0	13	6.46	58	.271	.358	0	ø	0	—	-4	0	-0.3
Total	5	5	19	.208	132	24	3	5	318.1	357	190	34	7	110-15	184	4.81	80	.282	.340	62-0-4	.145	-1	95	-33	0	-2.9
MOREL, RAMON Ramon Rafael; B8.15.1974 Villa Gonzalez, D.R.; BR/TR/6´2˝/(175–200); d7.6																										
1995	Pit N	0	1	.000	5	0	0	0-1	6.1	6	2	0	0	2-1	3	2.84	153	.300	.364	0	ø	0	—	1	0	0.2
1996	Pit N	2	1	.667	29	0	0	0-0	42	57	27	4	1	19-5	22	5.36	82	.324	.391	4-0-1	.000	-0	—	-4	0	-0.3
1997	Pit N	0	0	ø	5	0	0	0-0	7.2	11	4	2	0	4-1	4	4.70	91	.344	.417	0	ø	0	—	0	0	0.0
	Chi N	0	0	ø	3	0	0	0-0	3.2	3	2	1	0	3-0	3	4.91	88	.214	.353	0	ø	0	—	0	0	0.0
	Year	0	0	ø	8	0	0	0-0	11.1	14	6	3	0	7-1	7	4.76	90	.304	.396	0	ø	0	—	0	0	0.0
Total	3	2	2	.500	42	0	0	0-1	59.2	77	35	7	1	28-7	32	4.98	88	.318	.390	4-0-1	.000	-0	—	-3	0	-0.1
MOREN, LEW Lewis Howard "Hicks"; B8.4.1883 Pittsburgh PA; D11.2.1966 Pittsburgh PA; BR/TR/5´11˝/150; d9.21; Col Duquesne																										
1903	Pit N	0	1	.000	1	1	1	0	6	9	7	0	1	2	2	9.00	36	.346	.414	2	.000	-0	62	-3	—	-0.4
1904	Pit N	0	0	ø	1	0	0	0	4	7	6	1	1	4	0	9.00	30	.412	.545	2	.000	-0	—	-3	—	-0.2
1907	Phi N	11	18	.379	37	31	21-3	1	255	202	106	3	9	101	98	2.54	95	.226	.311	74-0-3	.081	-2	89	-7	—	-1.1
1908	Phi N	8	9	.471	28	16	9-4	0	154	146	68	1	2	49	72	2.92	83	.258	.320	49-0-2	.245	2	67	-8	—	-0.8
1909	Phi N	16	15	.516	40	31	19-2	1	257.2	226	103	6	4	93	110	2.65	98	.239	.309	90-0-2	.111	-3	109	-1	—	-0.7
1910	Phi N	13	14	.481	34	26	12-1	1	205.1	207	104	6	9	82	74	3.55	88	.269	.347	74	.149	-1	103	-8	—	-1.2
Total	6	48	57	.457	141	105	62-10	3	882	797	394	17	26	331	356	2.95	90	.248	.323	291-0-7	.134	-5	96	-30	—	-4.4
MORENO, ANGEL Angel (Veneroso); B6.6.1955 Soledad de Doblado, Veracruz, Mexico; BL/TL/5´9˝/165; d8.15																										
1981	Cal A	1	3	.250	8	4	1	0-0	31.1	27	10	2	0	14-0	12	2.87	128	.233	.313	0	ø	0	37	3	0	0.4
1982	Cal A	3	7	.300	13	8	2	1-1	49.1	55	31	7	1	23-0	22	4.74	86	.288	.364	0	ø	0	67	-5	0	-0.9
Total	2	4	10	.286	21	12	3	1-1	80.2	82	41	9	1	37-0	34	4.02	98	.267	.345	0	ø	0	58	-2	0	-0.5
MORENO, JUAN Juan Carlos (Vegas); B2.28.1975 Maiquetia, Vargas, Venez.; BL/TL/6´1˝/205; d5.17																										
2001	Tex A	3	3	.500	45	0	0	0-2	41.1	22	21	6	0	28-2	36	3.92	122	.153	.291	0	ø	0	—	3	0	0.3
2002	SD N	0	0	ø	4	0	0	0-0	6	6	6	1	0	10-1	3	7.50	52	.261	.471	0	ø	0	—	-3	0	-0.1
Total	2	3	3	.500	49	0	0	0-2	47.1	28	27	7	0	38-3	39	4.37	107	.168	.320	0	ø	0	—	0	0	0.2
MORENO, JULIO Julio (Gonzalez); B1.28.1921 Guines, Cuba; D1.2.1987 Miami FL; BR/TR/5´8˝/(158–170); d9.8																										
1950	Was A	1	1	.500	4	3	1	0	21.1	22	13	1	1	12	7	4.64	97	.268	.368	8-0-1	.125	-1	114	-1	0	-0.1
1951	Was A	5	11	.313	31	18	5	2	132.2	132	82	18	1	80	37	4.88	84	.256	.357	40-0-3	.175	-1	95	-12	0	-1.4
1952	Was A	9	9	.500	26	22	7	0	147.1	154	75	10	5	52	62	3.97	90	.270	.337	49-0-1	.122	-2	96	-8	0	-1.1
1953	Was A	3	1	.750	12	2	1	0	35.1	41	11	2	0	13	13	2.80	139	.291	.351	9	.000	-1	125	5	0	0.4
Total	4	18	22	.450	73	45	14	2	336.2	349	181	31	7	157	119	4.25	91	.267	.349	106-0-5	.132	-5	98	-16	0	-2.2
MORENO, ORBER Orber (Aquiles); B4.27.1977 Caracas, Distrito Capital, Venez.; BR/TR/6´2˝/(190–200); d5.25; [DL 2001 KC A 57]																										
1999	KC A	0	0	ø	7	0	0	0-1	8	4	5	1	0	6-0	7	5.63	90	.143	.294	0	ø	0	—	0	116	0.0
2003	NY N	0	0	ø	7	0	0	0-0	8	10	7	1	0	3-0	5	7.88	53	.313	.371	1	.000	-0	—	-3	0	-0.2
2004	NY N	3	1	.750	33	0	0	1-2	34.2	29	17	0	3	11-0	29	3.38	127	.221	.297	1	.000	-0	—	2	92	0.2
Total	3	3	1	.750	47	0	0	1-3	50.2	43	29	2	3	20-0	41	4.44	99	.225	.308	2	.000	-0	—	-1	265	0.0
MORET, ROGER Rogelio (Torres); B9.16.1949 Guayama, PR; BB/TL/6´4˝/(160–175); d9.13																										
1970	Bos A	1	0	1.000	3	1	0	0-0	8.1	7	3	0	0	4-0	2	3.24	123	.226	.314	3	.000	-0	89	1	0	0.1
1971	Bos A	4	3	.571	13	7	4-1	0-0	71	50	24	5	2	40-4	47	2.92	128	.205	.321	23	.087	-1	103	6	0	0.5
1972	Bos A	0	0	ø	3	0	0	0-0	5	5	3	0	0	6-0	4	3.60	90	.263	.440	1	.000	-0	—	0	0	0.0
1973	Bos A	13	2	.867	30	15	5-2	3-1	156.1	138	60	19	3	67-2	90	3.17	127	.238	.318	0	ø	0	120	15	21	1.4
1974	Bos A	9	10	.474	31	21	10-1	2-0	173.1	158	79	15	2	79-4	111	3.74	103	.243	.323	0	ø	0	87	2	0	0.1
1975	†Bos A	14	3	.824	36	16	4-1	1-0	145	132	60	8	2	76-6	80	3.60	113	.248	.341	0	ø	0*	129	9	0	0.9
1976	Atl N	3	5	.375	27	12	1	1-2	77.1	84	44	7	1	27-2	30	5.00	76	.280	.339	23-0-2	.130	-1	118	-8	57	-0.9
1977	Tex A	3	3	.500	18	8	0	4-0	72.1	59	41	6	0	38-2	39	3.73	109	.220	.313	0	ø	0	99	0	81	-0.1
1978	Tex A	0	1	.000	7	2	0	1-0	14.2	23	8	1	1	2-0	5	4.91	76	.390	.413	0	ø	0	36	-1	126	-0.1
Total	9	47	27	.635	168	82	24-5	12-3	723.1	656	322	61	11	339-20	408	3.66	108	.245	.329	50-0-2	.100	-2	107	24	285	1.9
MOREY, DAVE David Beale; B2.25.1889 Malden MA; D1.4.1986 Oak Bluffs MA; BL/TR/6´0˝/185; d7.4; Col Dartmouth																										
1913	Phi A	0	0	ø	2	0	0	0	4	2	2	0	1	2	1	4.50	61	.222	.417	1	.000	-0	—	-1	—	0.0
MORGAN, CY Cyril Arlon; B11.11.1895 Lakeville MA; D9.11.1946 Lakeville MA; BR/TR/6´0˝/170; d6.8																										
1921	Bos N	1	1	.500	17	0	0	1	30.1	37	24	0	1	17	8	6.53	56	.314	.404	5	.000	-1	—	-9	—	-0.6
1922	Bos N	0	0	ø	2	0	0	0	1.1	8	8	0	0	2	0	27.00	15	.667	.714	0	ø	0	—	-5	—	-0.2
Total	2	1	1	.500	19	0	0	1	31.2	45	32	0	1	19	8	7.39	50	.346	.433	5	.000	-1	—	-14	—	-0.8

YEAR	TM LG	W	L	PCT	G	GS	CG-SHO	SV-BS	IP	H	R	HR	HB	BB-IB	SO	ERA	AERA	OAV	OOB	AB-HR-SH	AVG	PB	SUP	APR	DL	PW
Morgan, Dan	Daniel; B5.1853 MO; D1.30.1910 St.Louis MO; d5.4; ▲																									
1875	RS NA	1	3	.250	7	4	4-1	0	42	40	40	0	—	1	7	1.29	170	.212	.216	69	.261	1*	64	1	—	0.2
Morgan, Cy	Harry Richard; B11.10.1878 Pomeroy OH; D6.28.1962 Wheeling WV; BR/TR/6´0˝/175; d9.18																									
1903	StL A	0	2	.000	2	1	1	0	13	12	12	0	2	6	6	4.15	70	.245	.351	4	.250	0	49	-3	—	-0.4
1904	StL A	0	2	.000	8	3	2	0	51	51	23	3	2	10	24	3.71	67	.262	.304	18	.056	-2	57	-5	—	-0.4
1905	StL A	2	5	.286	13	8	5-1	0	77.1	82	59	1	9	37	44	3.61	71	.273	.370	31	.258	2	153	-15	—	-1.0
1907	StL A	2	5	.286	10	6	4	0	55	77	43	3	2	17	14	6.05	42	.333	.384	20	.100	-1	103	-19	—	-2.2
	Bos A	6	6	.500	16	13	9-2	0	114.1	77	35	1	3	34	50	1.97	131	.193	.262	35-0-1	.057	-4	61	8	—	0.4
	Year	8	11	.421	26	19	13-2	0	169.1	154	78	4	5	51	64	3.30	78	.245	.307	55-0-1	.073	-5	74	-10	—	-1.8
1908	Bos A	14	13	.519	30	26	17-2	1	205	166	78	7	10	90	99	2.46	100	.226	.319	63-0-5	.127	-3	94	1	—	-0.1
1909	Bos A	2	6	.250	12	10	5	1	64.2	52	19	0	6	31	30	2.37	106	.240	.350	20-0-1	.050	-2	68	3	—	0.3
	Phi A	16	11	.593	28	26	21-5	0	228.2	152	56	3	16	71	81	1.65	146	.191	.271	74-0-8	.108	-3	103	20	—	2.1
	Year	18	17	.514	40	36	26-5	1	293.1	204	75	3	22	102	111	1.81	134	**.202**	.289	94-0-9	.096	-4	93	24	—	2.4
1910	Phi A	18	12	.600	36	34	23-3	0	290.2	214	92	0	18	117	134	1.55	153	.216	.310	99-0-12	.141	-4	125	24	—	2.1
1911	Phi A	15	7	.682	38	30	15-2	1	249.2	217	109	0	21	113	136	2.70	117	.243	.341	94-0-2	.160	-5	130	9	—	0.3
1912	Phi A	3	8	.273	16	14	5	0	93.2	75	56	0	5	51	47	3.75	82	.226	.338	30-0-2	.033	-3	84	-9	—	-1.1
1913	Cin N	0	1	.000	1	1	0	0	2.1	5	4	0	1	1	2	15.43	21	.500	.583	1	.000	-0	23	-3	—	-0.4
Total	10	78	78	.500	210	172	107-15	3	1445.1	1180	586	18	95	578	667	2.51	105	.229	.318	489-0-31	.125	-25	105	11	—	-0.4
Morgan, Mike	Michael Thomas; B10.8.1959 Tulare CA; BR/TR/6´2˝/(185–226); [OakA78 1/4]; d6.11																									
1978	Oak A	0	3	.000	3	3	1	0-0	12.1	19	12	1	0	8-0	0	7.30	50	.373	.458	0	ø	0	49	-5	0	-0.9
1979	Oak A	2	10	.167	13	13	2	0-0	77.1	102	57	7	3	50-0	17	5.94	68	.332	.426	0	ø	0	60	-16	0	-2.0
1982	NY A	7	11	.389	30	23	2	0-0	150.1	167	77	15	2	67-5	71	4.37	92	.285	.358	0	ø	0	89	-4	0	-0.4
1983	Tor A	0	3	.000	16	4	0	0-0	45.1	48	26	6	0	21-0	22	5.16	84	.273	.348	0	ø	0	73	-3	52	-0.1
1985	Sea A	1	1	.500	2	2	0	0-0	6	11	8	2	0	5-0	2	12.00	35	.393	.485	0	ø	0	226	-5	173	-0.8
1986	Sea A	11	17	.393	37	33	9-1	1-0	216.1	243	122	24	4	86-3	116	4.53	94	.286	.353	0	ø	0	101	-6	0	-0.8
1987	Sea A	12	17	.414	34	31	8-2	0-0	207	245	117	25	5	53-3	85	4.65	102	.296	.340	0	ø	0	92	3	0	0.4
1988	Bal A	1	6	.143	22	10	2	1-0	71.1	70	45	6	1	23-1	29	5.43	73	.255	.315	0	ø	.0	79	-11	92	-1.0
1989	LA N	8	11	.421	40	19	0	0-1	152.2	130	51	6	2	33-8	72	2.53	135	.234	.277	36-0-3	.083	-2	65	14	0	1.8
1990	LA N	11	15	.423	33	33	6-**4**	0-0	211	216	100	19	5	60-5	106	3.75	98	.266	.319	71-0-5	.113	-2	97	-1	0	-0.2
1991	LA N★	14	10	.583	34	33	5-1	1-0	236.1	197	85	12	3	61-10	140	2.78	130	.226	.278	76-0-8	.092	-3	90	21	0	1.8
1992	Chi N	16	8	.667	34	34	6-1	0-0	240	203	80	14	3	79-10	123	2.55	142	.234	.298	74-0-11	.108	-2	101	26	0	2.5
1993	Chi N	10	15	.400	32	32	1-1	0-0	207.2	206	100	15	7	74-8	111	4.03	100	.262	.329	66-0-5	.061	-4	74	1	15	-0.2
1994	Chi N	2	10	.167	15	15	1	0-0	80.2	111	65	12	4	35-2	57	6.69	63	.338	.402	24-0-1	.125	-1	101	-22	53	-2.8
1995	Chi N	2	1	.667	4	4	0	0-0	24.2	19	8	2	1	9-1	15	2.19	191	.216	.296	7-0-1	.143	-0	76	5	30	0.6
	StL N	5	6	.455	17	17	1	0-0	106.2	114	48	10	5	25-1	46	3.88	110	.283	.329	31-0-3	.032	-2	88	7	20	0.5
	Year	7	7	.500	21	21	1	0-0	131.1	133	56	12	6	34-2	61	3.56	120	.271	.323	38-0-4	.053	-2	86	11	0	1.1
1996	StL N	4	8	.333	18	18	0	0-0	103	118	63	14	0	40-0	55	5.24	81	.294	.353	33-0-9	.061	-3	95	-10	47	-1.3
	Cin N	2	3	.400	5	5	0	0-0	27.1	28	9	2	1	7-0	19	2.30	186	.267	.316	7-0-2	.000	-1	101	5	0	0.9
	Year	6	11	.353	23	23	0	0-0	130.1	146	72	16	1	47-0	74	4.63	92	.289	.346	40-0-11	.050	-3	96	-4	0	-0.4
1997	Cin N	9	12	.429	31	30	1	0-0	162	165	91	13	8	49-6	103	4.78	90	.266	.327	44-0-9	.091	-2	82	-8	16	-1.1
1998	Min A	4	2	.667	18	17	0	0-0	98	108	41	13	7	24-1	50	3.49	137	.286	.337	2	.500	0	102	14	48	0.8
	†Chi N	0	1	.000	5	5	0	0-0	22.2	30	21	8	1	15-1	10	7.15	62	.323	.422	6-0-1	.667	2	159	-7	0	-0.1
1999	Tex A	13	10	.565	34	25	1	0-1	140	184	108	25	7	48-2	61	6.24	83	.323	.380	4	.250	0	107	-18	15	-2.3
2000	Ari N	5	5	.500	60	4	0	5-1	101.2	123	55	10	1	40-5	56	4.87	98	.311	.372	16-0-1	.438	2	62	1	0	0.3
2001	†Ari N	1	0	1.000	31	1	0	0-1	38	45	20	2	0	17-4	24	4.26	109	.306	.373	0	ø	0	159	1	99	0.0
2002	Ari N	1	1	.500	29	0	0	0-1	34	41	22	7	3	9-1	13	5.29	85	.289	.344	0	ø	0	—	-3	69	-0.2
Total	22	141	186	.431	597	411	46-10	8-5	2772.1	2943	1431	270	73	938-77	1403	4.23	98	.276	.337	497-0-59	.109	-16	92	-21	729	-4.6
Morgan, Tom	Tom Stephen "Plowboy"; B5.20.1930 ElMonte CA; D1.13.1987 Anaheim CA; BR/TR/6´2˝/(190–200); d4.20; Mil 1952–53; C8																									
1951	†NY A	9	3	.750	27	16	4-2	2	124.2	119	56	11	3	36	57	3.68	104	.253	.310	44-1-1	.273	2	101	3	0	0.6
1952	NY A	5	4	.556	16	12	2-1	2	93.2	86	34	8	4	33	35	3.07	108	.252	.325	33-1-0	.182	1	155	4	0	0.6
1954	NY A	11	5	.688	32	17	7-4	1	143	149	58	8	5	40	34	3.34	103	.274	.327	49-1-1	.143	0	133	3	0	0.4
1955	†NY A	7	3	.700	40	1	0	10	72	72	29	3	5	24-4	17	3.25	115	.267	.337	18-0-1	.222	0	119	5	0	0.9
1956	†NY A	6	7	.462	41	0	0	11	71.1	74	41	2	3	27-4	20	4.16	93	.284	.347	13-0-3	.154	-0	—	-4	0	-0.8
1957	KC A	9	7	.563	46	13	5	7	143.2	160	76	19	3	61-9	32	4.64	85	.299	.370	33-0-4	.091	-2	90	-8	0	-0.9
1958	Det A	2	5	.286	39	1	0	1	62.2	70	28	7	1	4-0	32	3.16	128	.286	.299	10-0-1	.200	-0	111	4	0	0.4
1959	Det A	1	4	.200	46	1	0	9	92.2	94	48	11	6	18-3	39	3.98	102	.265	.308	23-2-0	.391	4	87	0	0	0.4
1960	Det A	3	2	.600	22	0	0	1	29	33	17	6	0	10-1	12	4.66	85	.295	.347	0-0-1	ø	0	—	-2	0	-0.3
	Was A	1	3	.250	14	0	0	0	24	36	15	6	1	5-3	11	3.75	104	.343	.375	5	.000	-1	—	-1	0	-0.2
	Year	4	5	.444	36	0	0	1	53	69	32	12	1	15-4	23	4.25	92	.318	.360	5-0-1	.000	-1	—	-3	0	-0.5
1961	LA A	8	2	.800	59	0	0	10	91.2	74	31	7	5	17-3	39	2.36	191	.224	.269	12	.083	-1	—	18	0	2.2
1962	LA A	5	2	.714	48	0	0	9	58.2	53	23	6	1	19-6	29	2.91	132	.247	.304	6-0-2	.000	-1	—	6	0	0.7
1963	LA A	0	0	ø	13	0	0	1	16.1	20	11	1	3	6-1	7	5.51	62	.313	.392	1	.000	-0	—	-4	0	-0.2
Total	12	67	47	.588	443	61	18-7	64	1023.1	1040	467	95	40	300-34	364	3.61	106	.270	.326	247-5-14	.186	3	112	24	0	3.8
Moriarity, Gene	Eugene John; B7.5.1855 Holyoke MA; BL/TL/5´8˝/130; d6.18; ▲																									
1884	Ind AA	0	2	.000	2	2	2	0	13.2	16	13	0	1	7	4	5.27	62	.267	.353	37	.216	0*	46	-3	—	-0.3
1885	Det N	0	0	ø	1	0	0	0	2	3	3	0	—	1	1	9.00	32	.300	.364	39	.026	-0*	—	-1	—	-0.1
Total	2	0	2	.000	3	2	2	0	15.2	19	16	0	1	8	5	5.74	56	.271	.354	76	.118	-0	46	-4	—	-0.4
Morillo, Juan	Juan Bautista; B11.5.1983 San Pedro de Macoris, D.R.; BR/TR/6´3˝/190; d9.24																									
2006	Col N	0	0	ø	1	1	0	0-0	4	8	7	3	1	3-0	4	15.75	30	.421	.522	1	.000	-0	173	-4	0	-0.2
Morlan, John	John Glen; B11.22.1947 Columbus OH; BR/TR/6´0˝/185; d7.20; Col Ohio U.																									
1973	Pit N	2	2	.500	10	7	1	0-0	41	42	18	4	0	23-3	23	3.95	89	.276	.369	11	.182	1	107	-1	0	0.0
1974	Pit N	0	3	.000	39	0	0	0-0	65	54	37	2	3	48-5	38	4.29	81	.227	.357	7	.000	-1	—	-7	0	-0.5
Total	2	2	5	.286	49	7	1	0-0	106	96	55	6	3	71-8	61	4.16	84	.246	.362	18	.111	0	107	-8	0	-0.5
Morman, Alvin	Alvin; B1.6.1969 Rockingham NC; BL/TL/6´3˝/210; [HouN91 39/1015]; d4.2; Col Wingate																									
1996	Hou N	4	1	.800	53	0	0	0-2	42	43	24	8	0	24-6	31	4.93	79	.261	.353	0	ø	0	—	-4	0	-0.4
1997	†Cle A	0	0	ø	34	0	0	2-0	18.1	19	13	2	1	14-3	13	5.89	80	.268	.395	1	.000	-0	—	-2	34	-0.1
1998	Cle A	0	1	.000	31	0	0	0-1	22	25	13	1	0	11-1	16	5.32	90	.298	.375	0	ø	0	—	-1	15	0.0
	SF N	0	1	.000	9	0	0	0-1	7	8	4	4	0	3-0	7	5.14	78	.276	.344	0	ø	0	—	-1	25	-0.1
1999	KC A	2	4	.333	49	0	0	1-2	53.1	66	27	6	4	23-0	31	4.05	126	.307	.378	0	ø	0	—	6	0	0.6
Total	4	6	7	.462	176	0	0	3-6	142.2	161	81	21	5	75-10	98	4.79	95	.285	.371	1	.000	-0	—	-2	74	0.0
Morogiello, Dan	Daniel Joseph; B3.26.1955 Brooklyn NY; BL/TL/6´1˝/200; [AtlN76 3/51]; d5.20; Col Seton Hall																									
1983	Bal A	0	1	.000	22	0	0	1-0	37.2	39	10	1	1	10-3	15	2.39	168	.265	.314	0	ø	0	—	7	0	0.3
Moroney, Jim	James Francis; B12.4.1883 Boston MA; D2.26.1929 Philadelphia PA; BL/TL/6´1˝/175; d4.24																									
1906	Bos N	0	3	.000	3	3	3	0	27	28	20	1	6	12	11	5.33	50	.259	.365	10	.100	-1	72	-7	—	-0.7
1910	Phi N	1	2	.333	12	2	1	1	42	43	20	1	4	11	13	2.14	146	.295	.360	10	.000	-1	48	2	—	0.0
1912	Chi N	1	1	.500	10	3	1	1	23.2	25	13	0	4	17	5	4.56	73	.316	.460	6	.500	1	95	-2	—	-0.1
Total	3	2	6	.250	25	8	5	2	92.2	96	53	2	14	40	29	3.69	83	.288	.388	26	.154	-1	75	-7	—	-0.8
Morrell, Bill	Willard Blackmer; B4.9.1893 Hyde Park MA; D8.5.1975 Birmingham AL; BR/TR/6´0˝/172; d4.20; Col Tufts																									
1926	Was A	3	3	.500	26	2	1	1	69.2	83	48	5	2	29	16	5.30	73	.311	.383	17	.235	1	109	-12	—	-0.9
1930	NY N	0	0	ø	2	0	0	0	8	6	1	0	0	1	3	1.13	421	.214	.241	2	.000	-0	—	3	—	0.1
1931	NY N	5	3	.625	20	7	2	1	66	83	34	4	0	27	16	4.36	85	.306	.369	18-0-2	.111	-0	116	-3	—	-0.4
Total	3	8	6	.571	48	9	3	2	143.2	172	83	9	2	57	35	4.64	83	.304	.370	37-0-2	.162	-0	111	-12	—	-1.2

YEAR	TM LG	W	L	PCT	G	GS	CG-SHO	SV-BS	IP	H	R	HR	HB	BB-IB	SO	ERA	AERA	OAV	OOB	AB-HR-SH	AVG	PB	SUP	APR	DL	PW
MORRILL, JOHN	John Francis "Honest John"; B2.19.1855 Boston MA; D4.2.1932 Brookline MA; BR/TR/5´10.5˝/155; d4.24.1876; M8; ▲																									
1880	Bos N	0	0	ø	3	0	0	0	10.2	9	3	0	—	1	0	0.84	269	.273	.294	342-2	.237	0*	—	1	—	0.1
1881	Bos N	0	1	.000	3	0	0	1	5.2	9	8	0	—	1	0	6.35	42	.333	.357	311-1	.289	1*	—	-3	—	-0.4
1882	Bos N	0	0	ø	1	0	0	0	2	3	0	0	—	0	2	0.00	ø	.375	.375	349-2	.289	0*	—	1	—	0.0
1883	Bos N	1	0	1.000	2	1	1	0	13	15	11	0	—	4	5	2.77	112	.268	.317	404-6	.319	1*	86	0	—	0.0
1884	Bos N	0	1	.000	7	1	1	**2**	23	34	23	0	—	6	13	7.43	39	.315	.351	438-3	.260	1*	37	-9	—	-0.4
1886	Bos N	0	0	ø	1	0	0	0	4	5	1	0	—	0	2	0.00	ø	.313	.313	430-7	.247	0*	—	1	—	0.1
1889	Was N	0	0	ø	1	0	0	0	0.1	0	0	0	0	0	0	0.00	ø	.000	.000	146-2	.185	0*	—	0	—	0.0
Total	7	1	2	.333	18	2	2	3	58.2	75	46	0	0	12	22	4.30	66	.301	.333	2420-23	.268	4	66	-9	—	-0.6
MORRIS, DANNY	Danny Walker; B6.11.1946 Greenville KY; BR/TR/6´1˝/(200–203); d9.10																									
1968	Min A	0	1	.000	3	2	0	0	10.2	11	5	0	0	4-0	6	1.69	183	.262	.326	3	.000	-0	113	1	0	0.0
1969	Min A	0	1	.000	3	1	0	0-0	5.1	5	4	1	0	4-1	1	5.06	72	.238	.360	0	ø	0	24	-1	0	-0.2
Total	2	0	2	.000	6	3	0	0-0	16	16	9	1	0	8-1	7	2.81	116	.254	.338	3	.000	-0	80	0	0	-0.2
MORRIS, ED	Edward "Cannonball"; B9.29.1862 Brooklyn NY; D4.12.1937 Pittsburgh PA; BB/TL/5´7˝/165; d5.1; Col St. Marys (CA)																									
1884	Col AA	34	13	**.723**	52	52	47-3	0	429.2	335	159	3	13	51	302	2.18	139	.204	.234	199	.186	2*	105	46	—	4.5
1885	Pit AA	39	24	.619	**63**	**63**	**63-7**	0	**581**	459	245	5	14	101	**298**	2.35	137	**.208**	**.247**	237	.186	-5*	88	58	—	4.7
1886	Pit AA	**41**	20	.672	64	63	63-**12**	**1**	555.1	455	244	5	7	118	326	2.45	138	.214	**.258**	227-1	.167	-7	95	62	—	4.8
1887	Pit N	14	22	.389	38	38	37-1	0	317.2	375	225	13	8	71	91	4.31	89	.286	.326	126	.198	-4	78	-19	—	-2.0
1888	Pit N	29	23	.558	**55**	**55**	**54**-5	0	480	470	216	7	8	74	135	2.31	115	.245	.276	189	.101	-11	85	13	—	0.1
1889	Pit N	6	13	.316	21	21	18	0	170	196	107	4	6	48	40	4.13	91	.281	.332	72	.097	-5	78	-6	—	-1.1
1890	Pit P	8	7	.533	18	15	15-1	0	144.1	178	116	5	3	35	25	4.86	80	.290	.332	63	.143	-4	93	-11	—	-1.2
Total	7	171	122	.584	311	307	297-29	1	2678	2468	1312	42	59	498	1217	2.82	116	.235	.273	1113-1	.161	-34	90	143	—	9.8
MORRIS, JIM	James Samuel; B1.19.1964 Brownwood TX; BL/TL/6´3˝/215; [MilA83*S1/4]; d9.18; Col Ranger (TX) JC																									
1999	TB A	0	0	ø	5	0	0	0-0	4.2	3	3	1	1	2-0	3	5.79	86	.167	.286	0	ø	0	—	0	0	0.0
2000	TB A	0	0	ø	16	0	0	0-0	10.1	10	9	1	0	7-1	10	4.35	112	.250	.362	0	ø	0	—	-1	0	-0.1
Total	2	0	0	ø	21	0	0	0-0	15	13	12	2	1	9-1	13	4.80	103	.224	.338	0	ø	0	—	-1	0	-0.1
MORRIS, JACK	John Scott; B5.16.1955 St.Paul MN; BR/TR/6´3˝/(190–210); [DetA76 5/98]; d7.26; Col Brigham Young																									
1977	Det A	1	1	.500	7	6	1	0-0	45.2	38	20	4	0	23-0	28	3.74	115	.235	.328	0	ø	0	73	3	0	0.2
1978	Det A	3	5	.375	28	7	0	0-0	106	107	57	8	3	49-5	48	4.33	90	.268	.345	0	ø	0	115	-5	0	-0.4
1979	Det A	17	7	.708	27	27	9-1	0-0	197.2	179	76	19	4	59-4	113	3.28	133	.244	.301	0	ø	0*	106	24	0	2.7
1980	Det A	16	15	.516	36	36	11-2	0-0	250	252	125	20	4	87-5	112	4.18	99	.262	.322	0	ø	-0*	97	-1	0	0.0
1981	Det A★	**14**	7	.667	25	25	15-1	0-0	198	153	69	14	2	78-11	97	3.05	124	.218	.295	0	ø	0	126	17	0	1.7
1982	Det A	17	16	.515	37	37	17-3	0-0	266.1	247	131	37	0	96-7	135	4.06	101	.247	.311	0	ø	0	91	2	0	0.2
1983	Det A	20	13	.606	37	37	20-1	0-0	**293.2**	257	117	30	3	83-5	**232**	3.34	118	.233	.287	0	ø	0*	108	22	0	2.2
1984	†Det A★	19	11	.633	35	35	9-1	0-0	240.1	221	108	20	2	87-7	148	3.60	110	.241	.307	0	ø	0	114	10	0	1.2
1985	Det A★	16	11	.593	35	35	13-4	0-0	257	212	102	21	5	110-7	191	3.33	123	.225	.307	0	ø	0*	103	25	0	2.3
1986	Det A	21	8	.724	35	35	15-**6**	0-0	267	229	105	40	0	82-7	223	3.27	127	.229	.287	0	ø	0	118	28	0	2.8
1987	†Det A★	18	11	.621	34	34	13	0-0	266	227	111	39	1	93-7	208	3.38	126	.228	.293	1	.000	-0*	111	28	0	2.6
1988	Det A	15	13	.536	34	34	10-2	0-0	235	225	115	20	4	83-7	168	3.94	97	.251	.317	0	ø	0	103	-3	0	-0.4
1989	Det A	6	14	.300	24	24	10	0-0	170.1	189	102	23	2	59-3	115	4.86	79	.283	.339	0	ø	0	83	-19	60	-1.9
1990	Det A	15	18	.455	36	**36**	**11**-3	0-0	249.2	231	144	26	6	97-13	162	4.51	88	.242	.313	0	ø	0	110	-18	0	-2.2
1991	†Min A★	18	12	.600	35	**35**	10-2	0-0	246.2	226	107	18	5	92-5	163	3.43	125	.245	.315	0	ø	0	103	21	0	2.3
1992	†Tor A	**21**	6	.778	34	34	6-1	0-0	240.2	222	114	18	10	80-2	132	4.04	102	.246	.312	0	ø	0	121	3	0	0.3
1993	Tor A	7	12	.368	27	27	4-1	0-0	152.2	189	116	18	3	65-2	103	6.19	71	.302	.368	0	ø	0	89	-31	19	-3.2
1994	Cle A	10	6	.625	23	23	1	0-0	141.1	163	96	14	4	67-2	100	5.60	85	.292	.369	0	ø	0	126	-12	0	-1.1
Total	18	254	186	.577	549	527	175-28	0-0	3824	3567	1815	389	58	1390-99	2478	3.90	105	.247	.313	1	.000	-0	107	94	79	9.3
MORRIS, JOHN	John Wallace; B8.23.1941 Lewes DE; BR/TL/6´1˝/(196–198); d7.19																									
1966	Phi N	1	1	.500	13	0	0	0	13.2	15	8	2	1	3-1	8	5.27	68	.278	.328	0	ø	0	—	-2	0	-0.3
1968	Bal A	2	0	1.000	19	0	0	0	31.2	19	11	4	4	17-2	22	2.56	114	.173	.303	6	.000	-1	—	1	0	0.0
1969	Sea A	0	0	ø	6	0	0	0-0	12.2	16	10	2	0	8-1	8	6.39	57	.308	.400	1	1.000	1	—	-4	0	-0.1
1970	Mil A	4	3	.571	20	9	2	0-0	73.1	70	33	4	2	22-3	40	3.93	96	.253	.312	17-0-1	.176	0	89	0	95	0.1
1971	Mil A	2	2	.500	43	1	0	1-0	67.2	69	34	4	1	27-9	42	3.72	94	.270	.334	5-0-1	.200	0	128	-3	36	-0.1
1972	SF N	0	0	ø	7	0	0	0-0	6.1	9	6	2	0	2-0	5	4.26	82	.310	.355	0	ø	0	—	-2	0	-0.1
1973	SF N	1	0	1.000	7	0	0	0-1	6.1	12	8	0	0	3-0	3	8.53	45	.429	.469	1	.000	-0	—	-4	59	-0.5
1974	SF N	1	1	.500	17	0	0	1-0	20.2	17	7	1	0	4-1	9	3.05	125	.215	.253	1	1.000	0	—	2	0	0.2
Total	8	11	7	.611	132	10	2	2-1	232.1	227	117	19	8	86-17	137	3.95	90	.256	.325	31-0-2	.194	1	97	-12	190	-0.8
MORRIS, BUGS	Joseph Harley (aka Joseph Harley Bennett in 1918); B4.19.1892 Weir City KS; D11.21.1957 Noel MO; BR/TR/5´9.5˝/163; d7.20																									
1918	StL A	0	2	.000	4	2	0	0	10.1	12	7	1	0	7	0	3.48	79	.308	.413	4	.250	0	96	-2	—	-0.3
1921	Chi A	0	3	.000	3	2	1	0	17.2	19	14	1	0	16	2	6.11	69	.297	.438	6	.333	0	10	-4	—	-0.5
	StL A	0	0	ø	3	1	0	0	5.2	11	10	1	2	6	3	14.29	31	.407	.543	1	1.000	0	93	-6	—	-0.2
	Year	0	3	.000	6	3	1	0	23.1	30	24	2	2	22	5	8.10	53	.330	.470	7	.429	1	39	-9	—	-0.7
Total	2	0	5	.000	10	5	1	0	33.2	42	31	3	2	29	5	6.68	57	.323	.453	11	.364	1	56	-12	—	-1.0
MORRIS, MATT	Matthew Christian; B8.9.1974 Middletown NY; BR/TR/6´5˝/(210–220); [StLN95 1/12]; d4.4; Col Seton Hall; [DL 1999 StL N 182]																									
1997	StL N	12	9	.571	33	33	3	0-0	217	208	88	12	7	69-2	149	3.19	131	.258	.319	73-0-2	.205	3*	95	24	0	2.3
1998	StL N	7	5	.583	17	17	2-1	0-0	113.2	101	37	8	3	42-6	79	2.53	166	.243	.316	29-0-7	.069	-0	103	21	100	2.0
2000	†StL N	3	3	.500	31	0	0	4-3	53	53	22	3	2	17-1	34	3.57	130	.261	.323	3-0-3	.333	0*	—	7	54	0.7
2001	†StL N★	**22**	8	.733	34	34	2-1	0-0	216.1	218	86	13	13	54-3	185	3.16	137	.265	.318	72-0-11	.139	-1	122	27	0	3.3
2002	†StL N☆	17	9	.654	32	32	1-1	0-0	210.1	210	86	16	6	64-3	171	3.42	118	.261	.317	71-0-5	.169	1	113	15	17	1.7
2003	StL N	11	8	.579	27	27	5-**3**	0-0	172.1	164	76	20	4	39-1	120	3.76	110	.252	.297	52-1-12	.192	3	125	7	32	0.9
2004	†StL N	15	10	.600	32	32	3-2	0-0	202	205	116	35	6	56-3	131	4.72	90	.266	.319	62-0-8	.161	1	128	-11	0	-1.1
2005	†StL N	14	10	.583	31	31	2	0-0	192.2	209	101	22	8	37-3	117	4.11	102	.276	.314	57-0-8	.088	-2	125	1	16	-0.1
2006	SF N	10	15	.400	33	33	2	0-0	207.2	218	123	22	14	63-9	117	4.98	89	.268	.330	60-0-14	.200	2	86	-13	0	-1.1
Total	9	111	77	.590	270	239	20-8	4-3	1585	1586	735	151	63	441-31	1103	3.79	112	.262	.317	479-1-70	.161	7	112	78	401	8.6
MORRIS, ED	Walter Edward "Big Ed"; B12.7.1899 Foshee AL; D3.3.1932 Century FL; BR/TR/6´2˝/185; d8.5																									
1922	Chi N	0	0	ø	5	0	0	0	12	22	17	1	0	6	5	8.25	51	.386	.444	4	.250	-0	—	-7	—	-0.3
1928	Bos A	19	15	.559	47	29	20	5	257.2	255	118	7	5	80	104	3.53	117	.264	.323	91-0-2	.154	-4	95	16	—	1.5
1929	Bos A	14	14	.500	33	26	17-2	1	208.1	227	118	7	2	95	73	4.45	96	.282	.360	69-1-7	.232	2	81	-2	—	-0.1
1930	Bos A	4	9	.308	18	9	3	0	65.1	67	42	1	0	38	28	4.13	112	.260	.355	19-0-1	.316	2	35	0	—	0.2
1931	Bos A	5	7	.417	37	14	3	0	130.2	131	80	4	5	74	46	4.75	91	.260	.361	38-0-2	.158	-2	83	-7	—	-0.7
Total	5	42	45	.483	140	78	43-2	6	674	702	375	20	12	293	256	4.19	101	.271	.348	221-1-12	.195	-1	81	0	—	0.6
MORRISETTE, BILL	William Lee; B11.21.1894 Portsmouth VA; D3.25.1966 Virginia Beach VA; BR/TR/6´0˝/176; d9.19																									
1915	Phi A	2	0	1.000	4	1	1	0	20	15	6	0	0	5	11	1.35	217	.195	.244	7	.286	0	174	3	—	0.3
1916	Phi A	0	0	ø	1	0	0	0	4	6	3	0	0	5	2	6.75	42	.429	.579	1	.000	0	—	-1	—	0.0
1920	Det A	1	1	.500	8	3	1	0	27	25	21	0	3	19	15	4.33	86	.245	.379	8	.000	-1	92	-3	—	-0.4
Total	3	3	1	.750	13	4	2	0	51	46	30	0	3	29	28	3.35	100	.238	.347	16	.125	-1	115	-1	—	-0.1
MORRISON, JOHNNY	John Dewey "Jughandle Johnny"; B10.22.1895 Pellville KY; D3.20.1966 Louisville KY; BR/TR/5´11˝/188; d9.28; b–Phil																									
1920	Pit N	1	0	1.000	2	1	1-1	0	7	4	0	0	0	1	3	0.00	ø	.167	.200	3	.000	-0	147	2	—	0.3
1921	Pit N	9	7	.563	21	17	11-**3**	0	144	131	49	3	1	33	52	2.88	133	.258	.305	42-0-4	.119	-1	76	18	—	1.7
1922	Pit N	17	11	.607	45	33	20-**5**	1	286.1	315	130	10	6	87	104	3.43	119	.286	.341	101-0-10	.198	-2	113	21	—	1.5
1923	Pit N	25	13	.658	42	37	27-2	2	301.2	287	136	6	5	110	114	3.49	115	.253	.321	115-0-6	.183	-3	103	18	—	1.6
1924	Pit N	11	16	.407	**41**	25	10	2	237.2	213	114	7	4	73	85	3.75	102	.245	.307	77-0-11	.169	-2	80	3	—	0.0
1925	†Pit N	17	14	.548	**44**	26	10	**4**	211	245	113	12	7	60	60	3.88	115	.291	.343	73-0-6	.178	-2	104	12	—	1.2
1926	Pit N	6	8	.429	26	13	6-2	2	122.1	119	52	2	2	44	39	3.38	116	.267	.335	39	.077	-4	67	9	—	0.5
1927	Pit N	3	2	.600	21	2	1	3	53.2	63	27	2	0	21	21	4.19	98	.304	.368	13-0-1	.154	-0	166	0	—	-0.1
1929	Bro N	13	7	.650	39	10	4	**8**	136.2	150	87	11	3	61	57	4.48	103	.279	.355	43-0-1	.163	-2	104	0	—	-0.4

YEAR	TM LG	W	L	PCT	G	GS	CG-SHO	SV-BS	IP	H	R	HR	HB	BB-IB	SO	ERA	AERA	OAV	OOB	AB-HR-SH	AVG	PB	SUP	APR	DL	PW
1930	Bro N	1	2	.333	16	0	0	1	34.2	47	29	4	0	16	11	5.45	90	.346	.414	5	.000	-1	—	-4	—	-0.3
Total	10	103	80	.563	297	164	90-13	23	1535	1574	737	57	28	506	546	3.65	113	.271	.332	511-0-39	.164	-18	97	79	—	6.0
Morrison, Mike	Michael; B2.6.1867 Erie PA; D6.16.1955 Erie PA; BR/TR/5´8.5˝/156; d4.19																									
1887	Cle AA	12	25	.324	40	40	35	0	316.2	385	341	13	22	205	158	4.92	88	.294	.398	141	.191	-4*	93	-30	—	-2.4
1888	Cle AA	1	3	.250	4	4	4	0	35	40	35	3	1	19	14	5.40	57	.278	.366	17	.235	-0	89	-8	—	-0.8
1890	Syr AA	6	9	.400	17	14	13-1	0	127	131	112	4	13	81	69	5.88	60	.258	.374	120-1	.242	3*	97	-35	—	-2.7
	Bal AA	1	2	.333	4	4	3	0	26	15	20	0	2	20	13	3.81	107	.163	.325	9	.111	-1	104	-1	—	-0.1
	Year	7	11	.389	21	18	16-1	0	153	146	132	4	15	101	82	5.53	66	.244	.366	129-1	.233	3	99	-36	—	-2.8
Total	3	20	39	.339	65	62	55-1	0	504.2	571	508	20	38	325	254	5.14	78	.278	.387	287-1	.213	-2	95	-74	—	-6.0
Morrison, Phil	Philip Melvin; B10.18.1894 Rockport IN; D1.18.1955 Lexington KY; BB/TR/6´2˝/190; d9.30; b–Johnny																									
1921	Pit N	0	0	ø	1	0	0	0	0.2	1	0	0	0	0	1	0.00	ø	.333	.333	0	ø	0	—	0	—	0.0
Morrison, Hank	Stephen Henry; B5.22.1866 Olneyville RI; D9.30.1927 Attleboro MA; BR/TR/5´10˝/180; d5.28																									
1887	Ind N	3	4	.429	7	7	5	0	57	79	73	2	1	27	13	7.58	55	.307	.375	26	.115	-2	96	-21	—	-2.0
Morrison, Guy	Walter Guy; B8.29.1895 Hinton WV; D8.14.1934 Grand Rapids MI; BR/TR/5´11˝/185; d8.31																									
1927	Bos N	1	2	.333	11	3	1	0	34.1	40	22	1	0	15	6	4.46	83	.296	.367	8-1-0	.125	1	138	-4	—	-0.2
1928	Bos N	0	0	ø	1	0	0	0	3	4	4	1	0	3	0	12.00	33	.308	.438	0	ø	0	—	-2	—	-0.1
Total	2	1	2	.333	12	3	1	0	37.1	44	26	2	0	18	6	5.06	74	.297	.373	8-1-0	.125	1	138	-6	—	-0.3
Morrissey, Frank	Michael Joseph "Deacon"; B5.5.1876 Baltimore MD; D2.22.1939 Baltimore MD; TR/5´4˝/140; d7.13																									
1901	Bos A	0	0	ø	1	0	0	0	4.1	5	1	0	2	2	1	2.08	170	.278	.409	3	.000	-1	—	1	—	0.0
1902	Chi N	1	3	.250	5	5	5	0	40	40	16	0	2	8	13	2.25	120	.260	.305	22	.091	-1*	65	2	—	0.1
Total	2	1	3	.250	6	5	5	0	44.1	45	17	0	4	10	14	2.23	125	.262	.317	25	.080	-1	65	3	—	0.1
Morton, Carl	Carl Wendle; B1.18.1944 Kansas City MO; D4.12.1983 Tulsa OK; BR/TR/6´0˝/(180–200); d4.11; Col Oklahoma																									
1969	Mon N	0	3	.000	8	5	0	0-0	29.1	29	15	2	2	18-3	16	4.60	80	.264	.368	7	.000	-0	48	-2	0	-0.2
1970	Mon N	18	11	.621	43	37	10-4	0-1	284.2	281	123	27	4	125-17	154	3.60	115	.262	.339	93-2-11	.161	2	100	19	0	2.0
1971	Mon N	10	18	.357	36	35	9	1-0	213.2	252	129	22	4	83-13	84	4.80	74	.295	.358	77-2-2	.182	2	94	-30	0	-3.3
1972	Mon N	7	13	.350	27	27	3-1	0-0	172	170	84	16	3	53-6	51	3.92	91	.258	.314	52-0-4	.135	1*	66	-8	0	-0.7
1973	Atl N	15	10	.600	38	37	10-4	0-0	256.1	254	114	18	4	70-7	112	3.41	116	.259	.309	94-3-2	.181	3*	117	13	0	1.6
1974	Atl N	16	12	.571	38	38	7-1	0-0	274.2	293	110	10	2	89-12	113	3.15	121	.277	.331	89-0-12	.112	-4	99	18	0	1.3
1975	Atl N	17	16	.515	39	39	11-2	0-0	277.2	302	122	19	3	82-3	78	3.50	108	.278	.328	94-0-5	.160	-1	81	11	0	1.2
1976	Atl N	4	9	.308	26	24	1-1	0-0	140.1	172	79	6	5	45-4	42	4.17	91	.306	.359	45-0-5	.178	-0*	93	-8	0	-0.6
Total	8	87	92	.486	255	242	51-13	1-1	1648.2	1753	776	120	27	565-65	650	3.73	103	.275	.334	551-7-41	.156	3	93	13	0	1.3
Morton, Charlie	Charles Hazen; B10.12.1854 Kingsville OH; D12.9.1921 Massillon OH; BR/TR/?/150; d5.2.1882; M3/U1; ▲																									
1884	Tol AA	0	1	.000	3	1	1	0	23.1	18	14	0	1	5	7	3.09	111	.209	.261	111	.162	-0*	35	1	—	0.0
Morton, Guy	Guy Sr. "The Alabama Blossom"; B6.1.1893 Vernon AL; D10.18.1934 Sheffield AL; BR/TR/6´1˝/175; d6.20; Mil 1918; s–Guy																									
1914	Cle A	1	13	.071	25	13	5	1	128	116	62	1	3	55	80	3.02	95	.257	.341	35-0-2	.029	-4	56	-2	—	-0.7
1915	Cle A	16	15	.516	34	27	15-6	1	240	189	75	5	2	60	134	2.14	143	.216	.268	82-0-3	.146	-4	74	25	—	2.7
1916	Cle A	12	6	.667	27	18	9	0	149.2	139	63	1	3	42	88	2.89	104	.246	.302	57-0-2	.211	-1	116	2	—	0.1
1917	Cle A	10	10	.500	35	18	6-1	2	161	158	74	3	2	59	62	2.74	103	.266	.335	47-0-3	.085	-4	86	-1	—	-0.7
1918	Cle A	14	8	.636	30	28	13-1	0	214.2	189	87	1	3	77	123	2.64	114	.240	.310	77	.156	-1	101	6	—	0.5
1919	Cle A	9	9	.500	26	20	9-3	0	147.1	128	65	3	0	47	64	2.81	119	.233	.293	56-0-1	.161	-2	98	7	—	0.5
1920	Cle A	8	6	.571	29	17	6-1	1	137	140	80	2	1	57	72	4.47	85	.270	.344	46-0-1	.217	-1	93	-9	—	-1.0
1921	Cle A	8	3	.727	30	7	3-2	0	107.2	98	45	1	2	32	45	2.76	155	.244	.303	35-0-3	.171	-2	53	16	—	1.1
1922	Cle A	14	9	.609	38	23	13-3	0	202.2	218	117	7	4	85	102	4.00	100	.277	.351	68-0-6	.191	-2	112	-6	—	-0.6
1923	Cle A	6	6	.500	33	14	3-2	1	129.1	133	67	3	2	56	54	4.24	93	.276	.354	44-0-1	.159	-2	115	0	—	-0.3
1924	Cle A	0	1	.000	10	0	0	0	12.1	12	12	0	0	13	6	6.57	65	.250	.410	1	.000	-0	—	-3	—	-0.3
Total	11	98	86	.533	317	185	82-19	6	1629.2	1520	747	27	22	583	830	3.13	108	.251	.319	548-0-22	.157	-24	93	35	—	1.3
Morton, Kevin	Kevin Joseph; B8.3.1968 Norwalk CT; BR/TL/6´2˝/185; [BosA89 1/29]; d7.5; Col Seton Hall																									
1991	Bos A	6	5	.545	16	15	1	0-0	86.1	93	49	9	1	40-2	45	4.59	94	.284	.356	0	ø	0	127	-2	0	-0.2
Morton, Sparrow	William P.; TL; d7.15																									
1884	Phi N	0	2	.000	2	2	2	0	17	16	20	0	—	11	5	5.29	56	.222	.325	8	.375	1	53	-5	—	-0.3
Moseley, Dustin	Dustin Aaron; B12.26.1981 Texarkana TX; BR/TR/6´4˝/190; [CinN00 1/34]; d7.17																									
2006	LA A	1	0	1.000	3	2	0	0-0	11	22	11	3	0	2-0	3	9.00	49	.431	.444	0	ø	0	212	-5	0	-0.4
Moseley, Earl	Earl Victor "Vic"; B9.7.1887 Middleburg OH; D7.1.1963 Alliance OH; BR/TR/5´9.5˝/168; d6,17																									
1913	Bos A	8	5	.615	24	15	7-3	0	120.2	105	56	1	0	49	62	3.13	94	.248	.326	37-0-1	.081	-2	89	-2	—	-0.4
1914	Ind F	19	18	.514	43	38	29-4	1	316.2	303	149	5	4	123	205	3.47	90	.258	.330	109-0-7	.110	-7	98	-8	—	-1.7
1915	New F	15	15	.500	38	32	22-5	1	268	222	87	2	2	99	142	**1.91**	134	.229	.302	88-0-7	.148	-3*	94	17	—	1.3
1916	Cin N	7	10	.412	31	15	7	1	150.1	145	75	5	0	69	60	3.89	67	.257	.338	46-0-2	.087	-2	123	-19	—	-2.5
Total	4	49	48	.505	136	100	65-12	3	855.2	775	367	13	6	340	469	3.01	94	.247	.322	280-0-17	.114	-15	99	-12	—	-3.3
Moser, Walter	Walter Fredrick; B2.27.1881 Concord NC; D12.10.1946 Philadelphia PA; BR/TR/5´9˝/170; d9.3																									
1906	Phi N	0	4	.000	6	4	4	0	42.2	49	35	0	1	15	17	3.59	73	.295	.357	14	.000	-2	14	-8	—	-0.9
1911	Bos A	0	1	.000	6	3	1	0	24.2	37	28	0	1	11	11	4.01	82	.366	.434	7	.000	-1	132	-6	—	-0.4
	StL A	0	2	.000	2	2	0	0	3.1	11	12	0	0	4	2	21.60	16	.478	.556	1	1.000	0	53	-7	—	-1.0
	Year	0	3	.000	8	5	1	0	28	48	40	0	1	15	13	6.11	54	.387	.457	8	.125	-1	101	-14	—	-1.4
Total	2	0	7	.000	14	9	5	0	70.2	97	75	0	2	30	30	4.58	63	.334	.401	22	.045	-2	70	-21	—	-2.3
Moskau, Paul	Paul Richard; B12.20.1953 St.Joseph MO; BR/TR/6´2˝/(205–210); [CinN75 3/70]; d6.21; Col Azusa Pacific																									
1977	Cin N	6	6	.500	20	19	2-2	0-0	108	116	51	10	1	40-3	71	4.00	98	.278	.338	38-1-1	.184	2*	106	0	0	0.2
1978	Cin N	6	4	.600	26	25	2-1	1-0	145	139	65	17	3	57-4	88	3.97	89	.255	.327	49-1-2	.204	4*	138	-4	0	0.0
1979	Cin N	5	4	.556	21	15	1	0-0	106.1	107	53	9	0	51-3	58	3.89	95	.263	.341	37-0-6	.081	-2	104	-3	0	-0.4
1980	Cin N	9	7	.563	33	19	2-1	2-1	152.2	147	69	13	1	41-2	94	4.01	88	.257	.305	44-0-8	.159	-0	109	-6	0	-0.7
1981	Cin N	2	1	.667	27	1	0	2-1	54.2	54	31	4	1	32-5	32	4.94	71	.258	.355	6-0-2	.000	-0	152	-8	0	-0.5
1982	Pit N	1	3	.250	13	5	0	0-1	35	43	21	7	0	8-0	15	4.37	86	.303	.338	11-0-1	.091	-1	118	-3	66	-0.4
1983	Chi N	3	2	.600	8	8	0	0-0	32	44	25	7	0	14-1	16	6.75	57	.331	.395	11-0-2	.182	0	116	-9	0	-1.2
Total	7	32	27	.542	148	92	7-4	5-3	633.2	650	315	67	6	243-18	374	4.22	87	.268	.333	196-2-22	.153	2	117	-33	66	-3.0
Moss, Mal	Charles Malcolm; B4.18.1905 Sullivan IN; D2.5.1983 Savannah GA; BR/TL/6´0˝/175; d4.29; Col Vanderbilt																									
1930	Chi N	0	0	ø	12	1	0	1	18.2	18	13	0	0	14	4	6.27	78	.254	.376	11	.273	0	214	-2	—	-0.1
Moss, Damian	Damian Joseph; B11.24.1976 Darlinghurst, New South Wales, Australia; BR/TL/6´0˝/(185–187); d4.26; [DL 1999 Atl N 57]																									
2001	Atl N	0	0	ø	5	1	0	0-0	9	3	3	1	0	9-0	8	3.00	144	.097	.300	1	.000	0	43	1	42	0.1
2002	†Atl N	12	6	.667	33	29	0	0-0	179	140	80	20	6	89-5	111	3.42	118	.221	.321	50-0-6	.100	-1	114	10	0	0.9
2003	SF N	9	7	.563	21	20	0	0-0	115	121	62	12	5	63-3	57	4.70	91	.273	.367	29-0-7	.241	1	94	-5	0	-0.5
	Bal A	1	5	.167	10	9	0	0-0	50.2	63	40	12	6	29-2	22	6.22	74	.307	.405	0	ø	0	76	-10	0	-1.0
2004	TB A	0	1	.000	5	2	0	0-0	8	13	15	2	1	5-0	6	16.88	28	.351	.442	0	ø	0	89	-10	0	-1.0
Total	4	22	19	.537	74	61	0	0-0	361.2	340	200	47	18	195-10	204	4.50	93	.252	.352	80-0-13	.150	0	99	-14	99	-1.5
Moss, Ray	Raymond Earl; B12.5.1901 Chattanooga TN; D8.9.1998 Chattanooga TN; BR/TR/6´1˝/185; d4.17																									
1926	Bro N	0	0	ø	1	0	0	0	1	3	1	0	0	0	0	9.00	42	.600	.600	1	.000	-0	—	0	—	0.0
1927	Bro N	1	0	1.000	1	1	0	0	8.1	11	3	0	0	1	1	3.24	122	.333	.353	3-0-1	.333	1	86	1	—	0.2
1928	Bro N	0	3	.000	22	5	1-1	1	60.1	62	43	5	0	35	5	4.92	81	.279	.377	25	.320	2*	98	-7	—	-0.1
1929	Bro N	11	6	.647	39	20	7-2	0	182	214	115	9	7	81	59	5.04	92	.296	.373	66-0-2	.076	-5*	96	-6	—	-1.0
1930	Bro N	9	6	.600	36	11	5	1	118.1	127	78	13	4	55	30	5.10	96	.270	.352	39-0-2	.154	-2	100	-1	—	-0.4
1931	Bro N	0	0	ø	1	0	0	0	1	1	0	0	0	1	0	0.00	ø	.333	.500	0	ø	0	—	0	—	0.0
	Bos N	1	3	.250	12	5	0	0	45	56	32	2	0	16	14	4.60	82	.306	.362	15	.133	-1	63	-7	—	-0.6

THE PITCHER REGISTER

YEAR	TM LG	W	L	PCT	G	GS	CG-SHO	SV-BS	IP	H	R	HR	HB	BB-IB	SO	ERA	AERA	OAV	OOB	AB-HR-SH	AVG	PB	SUP	APR	DL	PW
	Year	1	3	.250	13	5	0	0	46	57	32	2	0	17	14	4.50	84	.306	.365	15	.133	-1	63	-6	—	-0.6
Total	6	22	18	.550	112	42	13-3	2	416	474	272	29	11	189	109	4.95	91	.289	.367	149-0-5	.148	-5	94	-20	—	-1.9
Mossi, Don	Donald Louis "The Sphinx"; B1.11.1929 St.Helena CA; BL/TL/6´1˝/195; d4.17																									
1954	†Cle A	6	1	.857	40	5	2	7	93	56	22	5	1	39	55	1.94	190	.176	.267	19-0-1	.158	0	67	**19**	0	1.7
1955	Cle A	4	3	.571	57	1	0	9	81.2	81	28	4	1	18-2	69	2.42	164	.253	.292	9	.111	0	156	13	0	1.4
1956	Cle A	6	5	.545	48	3	0	11	87.2	79	38	6	1	33-5	59	3.59	117	.240	.311	20	.150	0	85	7	0	1.0
1957	Cle A★	11	10	.524	36	22	6-1	2	159	165	82	16	2	57-5	97	4.13	90	.265	.327	55	.218	2	107	-6	0	-0.7
1958	Cle A	7	8	.467	43	5	0	3	101.2	106	49	6	4	30-6	55	3.90	94	.269	.324	26	.115	-2	64	-3	0	-0.6
1959	Det A	17	9	.654	34	30	15-3	0	228	210	92	20	3	49-0	125	3.36	121	.243	.284	77-1-5	.169	0*	94	19	0	2.1
1960	Det A	9	8	.529	23	22	9-2	0	158.1	158	68	17	1	32-4	69	3.47	114	.258	.293	43-0-3	.116	-0	86	9	0	0.9
1961	Det A	15	7	.682	35	34	12-1	1	240.1	237	97	29	0	47-3	137	2.96	139	.258	.292	79-1-6	.165	1	121	28	0	2.5
1962	Det A	11	13	.458	35	27	8-1	1	180.1	195	92	24	1	36-1	121	4.19	97	.270	.303	55-0-1	.164	1*	103	-1	0	-0.1
1963	Det A	7	7	.500	24	16	3	2	122.2	110	58	20	4	17-0	68	3.74	100	.236	.268	39-0-2	.205	2	108	-1	0	0.2
1964	Chi A	3	1	.750	34	0	0	7	40	37	16	9	1	7-2	36	2.93	118	.240	.278	6	.167	-0	—	2	0	0.2
1965	KC A	5	8	.385	51	0	0	7	55.1	59	30	0	0	20-6	41	3.74	93	.278	.333	8	.000	-1	—	-3	0	-0.8
Total	12	101	80	.558	460	165	55-8	50	1548	1493	672	156	19	385-34	932	3.43	114	.252	.297	436-2-18	.163	4	103	83	0	7.8
Mossor, Earl	Earl Dalton; B7.21.1925 Forbus TN; D12.29.1988 Batavia OH; BL/TR/6´1˝/175; d4.30																									
1951	Bro N	0	0	ø	3	0	0	0	1.2	2	6	1	0	7	1	32.40	12	.333	.692	1	1.000	0	—	-5	0	-0.2
Mota, Danny	Daniel (Avila); B10.9.1975 Seybo, D.R.; BR/TR/6´0˝/180; d9.15																									
2000	Min A	0	0	ø	4	0	0	0-0	5.1	10	5	1	0	1-0	3	8.44	62	.370	.393	0	ø	0	—	-2	0	-0.1
Mota, Guillermo	Guillermo; B7.25.1973 San Pedro de Macoris, D.R.; BR/TR/6´4˝/(185–210); d5.2																									
1999	Mon N	2	4	.333	51	0	0	0-1	55.1	54	24	5	2	25-3	27	2.93	152	.257	.338	1-1-0	1.000	1	—	8	0	0.9
2000	Mon N	1	1	.500	29	0	0	0-0	30	27	21	3	2	12-0	24	6.00	79	.245	.328	1	.000	-0	—	-4	0	-0.2
2001	Mon N	1	3	.250	53	0	0	0-3	49.2	51	30	9	1	18-1	31	5.26	82	.271	.335	3	.333	0	—	-4	50	-0.3
2002	LA N	1	3	.250	43	0	0	0-1	60.2	45	30	4	2	27-6	49	4.15	94	.202	.292	4	.250	0	—	-2	0	-0.1
2003	LA N	6	3	.667	76	0	0	1-2	105	78	23	7	1	26-4	99	1.97	209	.206	.258	9-1-0	.222	1	—	27	0	2.2
2004	LA N	8	4	.667	52	0	0	1-0	63	51	15	4	2	27-5	52	2.14	193	.228	.314	6	.000	-1	—	15	0	2.5
	Fla N	1	4	.200	26	0	0	3-4	33.2	24	18	4	2	10-1	33	4.81	85	.200	.271	6	.333	1	—	-2	0	-0.2
	Year	9	8	.529	78	0	0	4-4	96.2	75	33	8	4	37-6	85	3.07	134	.218	.299	12	.167	0	—	14	0	2.3
2005	Fla N	2	2	.500	56	0	0	2-2	67	65	38	5	1	32-7	60	4.70	85	.254	.336	3	.000	-0	—	-5	26	-0.4
2006	Cle A	1	3	.250	34	0	0	0-0	37.2	45	27	9	0	19-3	27	6.21	70	.298	.370	0	ø	0	—	-7	0	-0.7
	†NY N	3	0	1.000	18	0	0	0-0	18	10	2	2	0	5-1	19	1.00	440	.159	.221	0	ø	0	—	7	0	1.0
Total	8	26	27	.491	438	0	0	7-13	520	450	228	52	13	201-31	421	3.70	113	.234	.308	33-2-0	.212	3	—	33	76	4.7
Moulder, Glen	Glen Hubert; B9.28.1917 Cleveland OK; D11.27.1994 Decatur GA; BR/TR/6´0˝/180; d4.28																									
1946	Bro N	0	0	ø	1	0	0	0	2	2	1	1	0	1	1	4.50	75	.286	.375	0	ø	0	—	0	0	0.0
1947	StL A	4	2	.667	32	2	0	2	73	78	37	4	0	43	23	3.82	101	.283	.379	17-0-1	.235	-0	114	0	0	0.0
1948	Chi A	3	6	.333	33	9	0	2	85.2	108	67	8	1	54	26	6.41	66	.316	.411	20-0-4	.300	2	78	-20	0	-1.8
Total	3	7	8	.467	66	11	0	4	160.2	188	105	13	1	98	50	5.21	78	.301	.396	37-0-5	.270	1	86	-20	0	-1.8
Mounce, Tony	Anthony David; B2.8.1975 Sacramento CA; BL/TL/6´2˝/170; [HouN94 7/192]; d6.13																									
2003	Tex A	1	5	.167	11	11	0	0-0	50.2	65	42	9	5	25-0	30	7.11	70	.317	.403	2	.000	-0	62	-11	0	-1.0
Mountain, Frank	Frank Henry; B5.17.1860 Ft.Edward NY; D11.19.1939 Schenectady NY; BR/TR/5´11˝/185; d7.19; Col Union (NY); ▲																									
1880	Tro N	1	1	.500	2	2	2	0	17	23	17	0	—	6	2	5.29	48	.307	.358	9	.222	-0	157	-4	—	-0.4
1881	Det N	3	4	.429	7	7	7	0	60	80	63	2	—	18	13	5.25	56	.292	.336	25	.160	-0	114	-13	—	-1.3
1882	Wor N	0	5	.000	5	5	5	0	42	47	30	0	—	11	5	3.00	104	.255	.297	16	.063	-2	27	0	—	-0.2
	Phi AA	2	6	.250	8	8	8	0	69	72	49	1	—	11	15	3.91	72	.251	.279	36	.333	3*	89	-7	—	-0.3
	Wor N	2	11	.154	13	13	11	0	102	138	93	4	—	24	24	3.97	78	.299	.334	70-2	.271	2*	45	-9	—	-0.7
1883	Col AA	26	33	.441	59	59	57-4	0	503	546	345	8	—	123	159	3.60	86	.259	.300	276-3	.217	7*	88	-27	—	-1.8
1884	Col AA	23	17	.575	42	41	40-5	**1**	360.2	289	163	7	11	78	156	2.45	124	.209	.257	210-4	.238	9*	94	23	—	3.3
1885	Pit AA	1	4	.200	5	5	5	0	46	56	31	1	2	24	7	4.30	75	.320	.408	20	.100	-1	88	-4	—	-0.4
1886	Pit AA	0	2	.000	2	2	2	0	16	22	21	0	5	14	2	7.88	43	.319	.466	55	.145	0*	105	-7	—	-0.6
Total	7	58	83	.411	143	142	137-9	1	1215.2	1273	812	23	18	309	383	3.47	88	.254	.299	717-9	.220	17	86	-48	—	-2.4
Mountjoy, Bill	William Henry "Medicine Bill"; B12.11.1858 London ON, Can.; D5.19.1894 London ON, Can.; BL/TR/5´6˝/150; d9.29																									
1883	Cin AA	0	1	.000	1	1	1	0	8	9	4	0	—	2	3	2.25	144	.265	.306	3	.000	-1	18	1	—	0.0
1884	Cin AA	19	12	.613	33	33	32-3	0	289	274	148	5	16	43	96	2.93	114	.238	.275	119	.151	-3*	118	7	—	0.3
1885	Cin AA	10	7	.588	17	17	17-1	0	153.2	149	89	5	7	52	50	3.16	103	.247	.314	60	.167	0	123	1	—	0.0
	Bal AA	2	4	.333	6	6	6-1	0	53	72	47	1	4	13	15	5.43	60	.316	.363	18	.056	-0*	85	-11	—	-0.9
	Year	12	11	.522	23	23	23-2	0	206.2	221	136	6	11	65	65	3.75	87	.266	.327	78	.141	0	113	-10	—	-0.9
Total	3	31	24	.564	57	57	56-5	0	503.2	504	288	11	27	110	164	3.25	102	.250	.297	200	.145	-4	114	-2	—	-0.6
Moyer, Ed	Charles Edward; B8.15.1885 Andover OH; D11.18.1962 Jacksonville FL; d7.20																									
1910	Was A	0	3	.000	6	3	2	0	25	22	15	1	3	13	3	3.24	77	.253	.369	8	.125	-1	90	-3	—	-0.3
Moyer, Jamie	Jamie; B11.18.1962 Sellersville PA; BL/TL/6´0˝/(170–180); [ChiN84 6/135]; d6.16; Col St. Josephs (PA)																									
1986	Chi N	7	4	.636	16	16	1-1	0-0	87.1	107	52	10	3	42-1	45	5.05	81	.311	.388	22-0-4	.091	-0	105	-8	0	-0.9
1987	Chi N	12	15	.444	35	33	1	0-0	201	210	127	28	5	97-9	147	5.10	85	.271	.353	61-0-7	.230	3*	79	-17	0	-1.6
1988	Chi N	9	15	.375	34	30	3-1	0-2	202	212	84	20	4	55-7	121	3.48	105	.272	.322	60-0-8	.083	-2	80	4	0	0.5
1989	Tex A	4	9	.308	15	15	1	0-0	76	84	51	10	2	33-0	44	4.86	82	.283	.354	0	ø	0	80	-9	93	-1.3
1990	Tex A	2	6	.250	33	10	1	0-0	102.1	115	59	6	4	39-4	58	4.66	84	.290	.354	0	ø	0	95	-8	0	-0.5
1991	StL N	0	5	.000	8	7	0	0-0	31.1	38	21	5	1	16-0	20	5.74	65	.319	.399	8	.000	-1	62	-6	0	-0.9
1993	Bal A	12	9	.571	25	25	3-1	0-0	152	154	63	11	6	38-2	90	3.43	132	.265	.316	0	ø	0	106	17	0	2.3
1994	Bal A	5	7	.417	23	23	0	0-0	149	158	81	23	2	38-3	87	4.77	106	.271	.316	0	ø	0	85	5	0	0.3
1995	Bal A	8	6	.571	27	18	0	0-0	115.2	117	70	18	3	30-0	65	5.21	92	.265	.314	0	ø	0	103	-5	0	-0.5
1996	Bos A	7	1	.875	23	10	0	0-0	90	111	50	14	1	27-2	50	4.50	113	.300	.347	0	ø	0	129	6	0	0.5
	Sea A	6	2	.750	11	11	0	0-0	70.2	66	36	9	1	19-3	29	3.31	150	.243	.292	0	ø	0	122	9	0	0.9
	Year	13	3	.813	34	21	0	0-0	160.2	177	86	23	2	46-5	79	3.98	127	.276	.323	0	ø	0	125	14	0	1.4
1997	†Sea A	17	5	.773	30	30	2	0-0	188.2	187	82	21	7	43-2	113	3.86	117	.256	.303	3	.333	0	149	17	28	1.9
1998	Sea A	15	9	.625	34	34	4-3	0-0	234.1	234	99	23	10	42-2	158	3.53	133	.256	.295	2	.000	-0	95	30	0	2.8
1999	Sea A	14	8	.636	32	32	4	0-0	228	235	108	23	9	48-1	137	3.87	124	.267	.311	2-0-1	.500	1	88	23	0	2.2
2000	Sea A	13	10	.565	26	26	0	0-0	154	173	103	22	3	53-2	98	5.49	88	.281	.339	2	.000	-0	111	-13	47	-1.5
2001	†Sea A	20	6	.769	33	33	1	0-0	209.2	187	84	24	10	44-4	119	3.43	124	.239	.285	1-0-1	.000	-0	118	22	0	2.4
2002	Sea A	13	8	.619	34	34	4-2	0-0	230.2	198	89	28	9	50-4	147	3.32	130	.230	.278	5	.200	0	108	27	0	2.4
2003	Sea A★	21	7	.750	33	33	1	0-0	215	199	83	19	8	66-3	129	3.27	133	.246	.307	5-0-1	.400	1	116	26	0	3.3
2004	Sea A	7	13	.350	34	33	1	0-0	202	217	127	44	11	63-3	125	5.21	86	.272	.331	2	.500	0	95	-18	0	-1.5
2005	Sea A	13	7	.650	32	32	1	0-0	200	225	99	23	8	52-2	102	4.28	98	.283	.331	1-0-1	.000	-0	114	-2	0	-0.1
2006	Sea A	6	12	.333	25	25	2-1	0-0	160	179	85	25	3	44-3	82	4.39	100	.285	.331	3	.333	0	83	0	0	0.0
	Phi N	5	2	.714	8	8	0	0-0	51.1	49	25	8	2	7-2	26	4.03	116	.250	.280	18-0-3	.056	-1	121	4	0	0.4
Total	20	216	166	.565	571	518	30-9	0-2	3351	3455	1678	414	112	946-59	1992	4.17	107	.266	.320	195-0-26	.149	1	102	104	168	11.1
Moylan, Peter	Peter Michael; B12.2.1978 Attadale, Western Australia, Australia; BR/TR/6´2˝/200; d4.12																									
2006	Atl N	0	0	ø	15	0	0	0-0	15	18	8	1	0	5-1	14	4.80	94	.290	.343	0	ø	0	—	0	0	0.0
Mrozinski, Ron	Ronald Frank; B9.16.1930 White Haven PA; D10.19.2005 Washington NJ; BR/TL/5´11˝/160; d6.20																									
1954	Phi N	1	1	.500	15	4	1	0	48	49	26	10	0	25	26	4.50	90	.261	.347	12-0-2	.083	-1	83	-2	0	-0.2
1955	Phi N	0	2	.000	22	1	0	1	34.1	38	26	2	4	19-2	18	6.55	61	.299	.396	4	.000	-1	67	-9	0	-0.6
Total	2	1	3	.250	37	5	1	1	82.1	87	52	12	4	44-2	44	5.36	75	.276	.368	16-0-2	.063	-2	80	-11	0	-0.8
Mudrock, Phil	Philip Ray; B6.12.1937 Louisville CO; BR/TR/6´1˝/190; d4.19																									
1963	Chi N	0	0	ø	1	0	0	0	1	2	1	0	0	0-0	0	9.00	39	.400	.400	0	ø	0	—	-1	0	0.0

YEAR	TM LG	W	L	PCT	G	GS	CG-SHO	SV-BS	IP	H	R	HR	HB	BB-IB	SO	ERA	AERA	OAV	OOB	AB-HR-SH	AVG	PB	SUP	APR	DL	PW
MUELLER, GORDIE	Joseph Gordon; B12.10.1922 Baltimore MD; D9.7.2006 Baltimore MD; BR/TR/6´4˝/200; d4.19; Col Loyola–Maryland																									
1950	Bos A	0	0	ø	8	0	0	0	7	11	8	1	0	13	1	10.29	48	.344	.533	1	.000	-0	—	-4	0	-0.2
MUELLER, LES	Leslie Clyde; B3.4.1919 Belleville IL; BR/TR/6´3˝/190; d8.15; Mil 1942–44																									
1941	Det A	0	0	ø	4	0	0	0	13	9	9	1	0	10	8	4.85	94	.205	.352	3	.000	-0	—	-1	0	-0.1
1945	†Det A	6	8	.429	26	18	6-2	1	134.2	117	63	8	2	58	42	3.68	96	.234	.316	44-1-1	.182	0	79	-1	0	-0.1
Total	2	6	8	.429	30	18	6-2	1	147.2	126	72	9	2	68	50	3.78	95	.231	.319	47-1-1	.170	0	79	-2	0	-0.2
MUELLER, WILLIE	Willard Lawrence; B8.30.1956 West Bend WI; BR/TR/6´4˝/220; d8.12																									
1978	Mil A	1	0	1.000	5	0	0	0-0	12.2	16	11	1	0	6-0	6	6.39	59	.291	.361	0	ø	0	—	-4	0	-0.3
1981	Mil A	0	0	ø	1	0	0	0-0	2	4	1	0	0	0-0	1	4.50	77	.400	.400	0	ø	0	—	0	0	0.0
Total	2	1	0	1.000	6	0	0	0-0	14.2	20	12	1	0	6-0	7	6.14	61	.308	.366	0	ø	0	—	-4	0	-0.3
MUFFETT, BILLY	Billy Arnold "Muff"; B9.21.1930 Hammond IN; BR/TR/6´1˝/(186–198); d8.3; C18																									
1957	StL N	3	2	.600	23	0	0	8	44	35	11	1	0	13-4	21	2.25	176	.222	.279	7-0-1	.000	-1	—	9	0	1.2
1958	StL N	4	6	.400	35	6	1	5	84	107	52	11	5	42-9	41	4.93	84	.316	.397	20-0-1	.200	0	91	-7	0	-0.9
1959	SF N	0	0	ø	5	0	0	0	6.2	11	6	2	0	3-1	3	5.40	71	.407	.467	0	ø	0	—	-2	0	-0.1
1960	Bos A	6	4	.600	23	14	4-1	0	125	116	53	6	5	36-2	75	3.24	125	.242	.299	41-0-1	.268	2	67	9	0	0.9
1961	Bos A	3	11	.214	38	11	2	2	112.2	130	87	18	2	36-2	47	5.67	73	.291	.344	23-1-1	.217	2	62	-20	0	-2.1
1962	Bos A	0	0	ø	1	1	0	0	4	8	4	0	0	2-0	1	9.00	46	.471	.500	1	.000	-0	130	-2	0	-0.1
Total	6	16	23	.410	125	32	7-1	15	376.1	407	213	38	12	132-18	188	4.33	94	.277	.339	92-1-4	.217	3	72	-13	0	-1.1
MUICH, JOE	Ignatius Andrew; B11.23.1903 St.Louis MO; D7.2.1993 St.Louis MO; BR/TR/6´2˝/175; d9.4																									
1924	Bos N	0	0	ø	3	0	0	0	9	19	12	1	0	5	1	11.00	35	.432	.490	3	.000	-1	—	-7	—	-0.4
MUIR, JOE	Joseph Allen; B11.26.1922 Oriole MD; D6.25.1980 Baltimore MD; BL/TL/6´1˝/172; d4.21																									
1951	Pit N	0	2	.000	9	1	0	0	16.1	11	6	2	0	7	5	2.76	153	.180	.265	1	.000	-0	21	2	0	0.3
1952	Pit N	2	3	.400	12	5	1	0	35.2	42	28	3	0	18	17	6.31	63	.288	.366	9	.111	-0	94	-9	0	-1.1
Total	2	2	5	.286	21	6	1	0	52	53	34	5	0	25	22	5.19	78	.256	.336	10	.100	-0	80	-7	0	-0.8
MUJICA, EDWARD	Edward Jose; B5.10.1984 Valencia, Venezuela; BR/TR/6´2˝/220; d6.21																									
2006	Cle A	0	1	.000	10	0	0	0-0	18.1	25	6	1	1	0-0	12	2.95	147	.333	.333	0	ø	0	—	3	0	0.1
MULCAHY, HUGH	Hugh Noyes "Losing Pitcher"; B9.9.1913 Brighton MA; D10.19.2001 Aliquippa PA; BR/TR/6´2˝/190; d7.24; Mil 1941–45; C1; Col Dean (MA) JC																									
1935	Phi N	1	5	.167	18	5	0	1	52.2	62	35	2	5	25	11	4.78	95	.295	.383	17	.000	-2*	45	-2	—	-0.4
1936	Phi N	1	1	.500	3	2	2	0	22.2	20	8	0	2	12	2	3.18	143	.238	.347	8-0-1	.250	0	84	4	—	0.3
1937	Phi N	8	18	.308	**56**	26	9-1	3	215.2	256	147	17	7	97	54	5.13	84	.296	.372	73-0-3	.151	-3	107	-21	—	-2.3
1938	Phi N	10	20	.333	46	34	15	1	267.1	294	162	14	6	120	90	4.61	84	.278	.354	94-0-7	.170	-2*	80	-23	—	-2.4
1939	Phi N	9	16	.360	38	32	14-1	4	225.2	246	144	19	11	93	59	4.99	80	.282	.359	76-0-5	.158	-3	82	-26	—	-2.8
1940	Phi N☆	13	22	.371	36	36	21-3	0	280	283	141	12	3	91	82	3.60	108	.261	.320	94-0-6	.202	1*	78	3	—	0.6
1945	Phi N	1	3	.250	5	4	1	0	28.1	33	17	1	0	9	2	3.81	101	.295	.347	7-0-1	.000	-1	55	-1	0	-0.1
1946	Phi N	2	4	.333	16	5	1	0	62.2	69	34	3	5	33	12	4.45	77	.295	.393	16-0-1	.188	1	80	-6	0	-0.4
1947	Pit N	0	0	ø	2	1	0	0	6.2	8	7	1	0	7	2	4.05	104	.333	.484	3	.333	0	230	-1	0	0.0
Total	9	45	89	.336	220	145	63-5	9	1161.2	1271	695	69	39	487	314	4.49	89	.280	.355	388-0-24	.165	-9	84	-73	0	-7.5
MULDER, MARK	Mark Alan; B8.5.1977 South Holland IL; BL/TL/6´6˝/(200–215); [OakA98 1/2]; d4.18; Col Michigan St.																									
2000	Oak A	9	10	.474	27	27	0	0-0	154	191	106	22	4	69-3	88	5.44	89	.308	.376	4	.000	-0	100	-11	0	-1.1
2001	†Oak A	**21**	8	.724	34	34	6-**4**	0-0	229.1	214	92	16	5	51-4	153	3.45	132	.249	.294	5	.200	0	107	30	0	3.6
2002	†Oak A	19	7	.731	30	30	2-1	0-0	207.1	182	88	21	11	55-3	159	3.47	129	.232	.290	5	.000	-1	101	23	28	2.7
2003	Oak A★	15	9	.625	26	26	**9-2**	0-0	186.2	180	66	15	2	40-2	128	3.13	146	.269	.300	4-0-1	.000	-0	94	32	40	4.0
2004	Oak A★	17	8	.680	33	33	**5**-1	0-0	225.2	223	119	25	12	83-1	140	4.43	104	.264	.337	4	.000	0	120	6	0	0.8
2005	†StL N	16	8	.667	32	32	3-2	0-0	205	212	90	19	9	70-1	111	3.64	115	.273	.339	62-0-1	.145	-1	118	14	0	1.7
2006	StL N	6	7	.462	17	17	0	0-0	93.1	124	77	19	5	35-1	50	7.14	61	.327	.390	25-1-6	.280	5	114	-29	96	-2.7
Total	7	103	57	.644	199	199	25-10	0-0	1301.1	1326	638	137	48	403-15	829	4.11	110	.267	.327	109-1-8	.156	3	108	65	164	9.0
MULHOLLAND, TERRY	Terence John; B3.9.1963 Uniontown PA; BR/TL/6´3˝/(200–225); [SFN84 1/24]; d6.8; Col Marietta																									
1986	SF N	1	7	.125	15	10	0	0-0	54.2	51	33	3	1	35-2	27	4.94	72	.251	.363	19-0-1	.053	-1	63	-9	0	-1.3
1988	SF N	2	1	.667	9	6	2-1	0-0	46	50	20	3	1	7-0	18	3.72	88	.281	.312	14	.000	-1	118	-2	63	-0.2
1989	SF N	0	0	ø	5	1	0	0-0	11	15	5	0	0	4-0	6	4.09	83	.319	.373	2-0-1	.000	-0	79	-1	0	0.0
	Phi N	4	7	.364	20	17	2-1	0-0	104.1	122	61	8	4	32-3	60	5.00	72	.292	.347	34-0-2	.059	-2	81	-14	0	-1.5
	Year	4	7	.364	25	18	2-1	0-0	115.1	137	66	8	4	36-3	66	4.92	73	.295	.350	36-0-3	.056	-2	81	-15	0	-1.5
1990	Phi N	9	10	.474	33	26	6-1	0-1	180.2	172	78	15	2	42-7	75	3.34	115	.252	.292	62-0-4	.097	-2	86	8	16	0.4
1991	Phi N	16	13	.552	34	34	8-3	0-0	232	231	100	15	3	49-2	142	3.61	103	.260	.299	80-0-5	.087	-4*	91	3	0	-0.1
1992	Phi N	13	11	.542	32	32	**12**-2	0-0	229	227	101	14	3	46-3	125	3.81	92	.261	.298	83-0-6	.096	-2	119	-5	0	-0.7
1993	†Phi N★	12	9	.571	29	28	7-2	0-0	191	177	80	20	3	40-2	116	3.25	122	.241	.282	62-0-8	.065	-4	113	15	0	1.0
1994	NY A	6	7	.462	24	19	2	0-0	120.2	150	94	24	3	37-1	72	6.49	71	.303	.353	0	ø	0	135	-26	0	-2.3
1995	SF N	5	13	.278	29	24	2	0-0	149	190	112	25	4	38-1	65	5.80	71	.313	.354	49-1-3	.102	-0*	107	-31	28	-3.2
1996	Phi N	8	7	.533	21	21	3	0-0	133.1	157	74	17	3	21-1	52	4.66	93	.293	.320	45-1-4	.178	1	91	-4	0	-0.4
	Sea A	5	4	.556	12	12	0	0-0	69.1	75	38	5	2	28-3	34	4.67	106	.286	.356	0	ø	0	113	3	0	0.3
1997	Chi N	6	12	.333	25	25	1	0-0	157	162	79	20	9	45-2	74	4.07	106	.271	.330	49-0-3	.163	-0	63	3	0	0.4
	SF N	0	1	.000	15	2	0	0-0	29.2	28	21	4	2	6-1	25	5.16	80	.248	.295	6-0-1	.167	0	101	-4	0	-0.2
	Year	6	13	.316	40	27	1	0-0	186.2	190	100	24	11	51-3	99	4.24	101	.267	.324	55-0-4	.164	0	66	-1	0	0.2
1998	†Chi N	6	5	.545	70	6	0	3-2	112	100	49	7	4	39-7	72	2.89	152	.235	.304	17-0-1	.294	2	94	13	0	1.4
1999	Chi N	6	6	.500	26	16	0	0-0	110	137	71	16	1	32-4	44	5.15	89	.309	.355	32-0-3	.094	-2	83	-8	0	-0.9
	†Atl N	4	2	.667	16	8	0	1-0	60.1	64	24	5	0	13-2	39	2.98	150	.274	.310	16-0-2	.125	0	98	9	0	0.9
	Year	10	8	.556	42	24	0	1-0	170.1	201	95	21	1	45-6	83	4.39	103	.297	.340	48-0-5	.104	-2	88	1	0	0.0
2000	†Atl N	9	9	.500	54	20	1	1-2	156.2	198	96	24	4	41-7	78	5.11	88	.308	.351	36-0-9	.250	2	104	-10	0	-0.8
2001	Pit N	0	0	ø	22	1	0	0-0	36.1	38	15	5	1	10-1	17	3.72	120	.277	.329	3	.000	-0	124	4	67	0.2
	LA N	1	1	.500	19	3	0	0-0	29.1	40	20	7	1	7-0	25	5.83	71	.315	.356	6	.000	-1	67	-6	1	-0.4
	Year	1	1	.500	41	4	0	0-0	65.2	78	35	12	2	17-1	42	4.66	93	.295	.342	9	.000	-1	80	-2	0	-0.2
2002	LA N	0	0	ø	21	0	0	0-0	32	45	29	10	2	7-0	17	7.31	53	.331	.367	1	.000	-0	—	-13	31	-0.6
	Cle A	3	2	.600	16	3	0	0-0	47	56	27	5	4	14-3	21	4.60	97	.301	.356	0	ø	0	125	-1	0	-0.1
2003	Cle A	3	4	.429	45	3	0	0-2	99	117	60	17	6	37-6	42	4.91	90	.295	.360	1	.000	-0	180	-5	0	-0.3
2004	†Min A	5	9	.357	39	15	0	0-0	123.1	163	76	17	5	33-3	60	5.18	89	.327	.371	2	.000	-0	88	-7	0	-0.8
2005	Min A	0	2	.000	49	0	0	0-1	59	61	30	6	2	17-4	18	4.27	103	.276	.332	0	ø	0	—	1	0	0.1
2006	Ari N	0	0	ø	5	0	0	0-1	3	7	3	1	0	1-0	1	9.00	52	.500	.533	0	ø	0	—	-1	67	-0.1
Total	20	124	142	.466	685	332	46-10	5-9	2575.2	2833	1396	293	70	681-65	1325	4.41	94	.281	.328	619-2-53	.111	-16	98	-88	273	-9.2
MULLANE, TONY	Anthony John "Count","The Apollo of the Box"; B1.20.1859 Cork, Ireland; D4.25.1944 Chicago IL; BB/TR (BL 1882, TB 1882p, 1893p)/5´10.5˝/165; d8.27; ▲																									
1881	Det N	1	4	.200	5	5	5	0	44	55	42	2	—	17	7	4.91	59	.302	.362	19	.263	-0	100	-8	—	-0.7
1882	Lou AA	30	24	.556	**55**	**55**	51-5	0	460.1	418	212	3	—	78	**170**	1.88	132	.226	.257	303	.257	11*	107	34	—	5.0
1883	StL AA	35	15	**.700**	53	49	49-3	**1**	460.2	372	222	3	—	74	191	2.19	**159**	.207	.238	307	.225	1*	83	60	—	5.5
1884	Tol AA	36	26	.581	67	65	64-**7**	0	567	481	276	5	32	89	325	2.52	135	.214	.255	352-3	.276	15*	77	55	—	7.1
1886	Cin AA	33	27	.550	63	56	55-1	0	529.2	501	315	11	18	166	250	3.70	95	.242	.303	324	.225	2*	103	-8	—	-0.4
1887	Cin AA	31	17	.646	48	48	47-**6**	0	416.1	414	234	11	32	121	97	3.24	134	.257	.322	199-3	.221	2*	100	51	—	4.6
1888	Cin AA	26	16	.619	44	42	41-4	**1**	380.1	341	194	9	29	75	186	2.84	112	.231	.282	175-1	.251	5*	110	15	—	1.9
1889	Cin AA	11	9	.550	33	24	17	**5**	220	218	133	4	13	89	112	2.99	131	.251	.329	196	.296	9*	87	17	—	1.9
1890	Cin N	12	10	.545	25	21	21	1	209	175	101	7	8	96	91	2.24	159	.220	.310	286	.276	7*	94	27	—	3.0
1891	Cin N	23	26	.469	51	47	42-1	0	426.1	390	250	15	18	187	124	3.23	104	.234	.318	209	.148	-5*	83	7	—	0.2
1892	Cin N	21	13	.618	37	34	30-3	1	295	222	131	12	12	127	109	2.59	126	**.201**	.290	118	.169	-1*	93	21	—	2.3
1893	Cin N	6	6	.500	15	13	11	1	122.1	130	84	4	9	65	24	4.41	108	.264	.360	52-1	.288	3*	81	4	—	0.5
	Bal N	12	16	.429	34	26	23	1	244.2	277	177	4	7	124	71	4.45	107	.277	.360	114	.228	-3*	93	7	—	0.4
	Year	18	22	.450	49	39	34	**2**	367	407	261	8	16	189	95	4.44	107	.273	.360	166-1	.247	-0	89	20	—	0.9
1894	Bal N	6	9	.400	21	15	9	4	122.2	155	117	4	7	90	43	6.31	87	.305	.417	53	.396	5	111	-13	—	-0.7
	Cle N	1	2	.333	4	4	3	0	33	46	35	3	0	10	3	7.64	72	.326	.371	13-0-1	.077	-1	120	-6	—	-0.4

YEAR	TM LG	W	L	PCT	G	GS	CG-SHO	SV-BS	IP	H	R	HR	HB	BB-IB	SO	ERA	AERA	OAV	OOB	AB-HR-SH	AVG	PB	SUP	APR	DL	PW
	Year	7	11	.389	25	19	12	**4**	155.2	201	152	7	7	100	46	6.59	83	.310	.407	66-0-1	.333	4	113	-15	—	-1.1
Total	13	284	220	.563	555	504	468-30	15	4531.1	4195	2523	97	185	1408	1803	3.05	118	.235	.298	2720-8-1	.243	50	94	263	—	30.2
MULLEN, SCOTT	Kenneth Scott; B1.17.1975 San Benito TX; BR/TL/6´2˝/(190–195); [KCA96 7/199]; d8.31; Col Dallas Baptist																									
2000	KC A	0	0	ø	11	0	0	0-0	10.1	10	5	2	0	3-0	7	4.35	120	.244	.295	0	ø	0	—	1	0	0.0
2001	KC A	0	0	ø	17	0	0	0-0	10	13	6	0	0	9-0	3	4.50	110	.310	.423	0	ø	0	—	0	33	0.0
2002	KC A	4	5	.444	44	0	0	0-2	40	40	16	5	2	13-2	21	3.15	158	.267	.329	0	ø	0	—	7	0	1.3
2003	KC A	0	0	ø	2	0	0	0-0	4.1	11	8	2	0	5-0	3	16.62	29	.458	.552	0	ø	0	—	-5	0	-0.2
	LA N	0	0	ø	1	1	0	0-0	3	2	3	0	1	5-0	1	9.00	46	.200	.471	1	.000	-0	182	-2	0	-0.1
Total	4	4	5	.444	75	1	0	0-2	67.2	76	38	9	3	35-2	35	4.66	107	.285	.369	1	.000	-0	182	1	33	1.0
MULLIGAN, JOE	Joseph Ignatius "Big Joe"; B7.31.1913 Weymouth MA; D6.5.1986 W.Roxbury MA; BR/TR/6´4˝/210; d6.28; Col Holy Cross																									
1934	Bos A	1	0	1.000	14	2	1	0	44.2	46	21	1	2	27	13	3.63	132	.279	.387	12-0-1	.000	-1	190	6	—	0.1
MULLIGAN, DICK	Richard Charles; B3.18.1918 Swoyersville PA; D12.15.1992 Victoria TX; BL/TL/6´0˝/167; d9.24; Mil 1942–45																									
1941	Was A	0	1	.000	1	1	1	0	9	11	5	0	0	2	2	5.00	81	.306	.342	3	.000	-0	86	-1	0	-0.1
1946	Phi N	2	2	.500	19	5	1	1	54.2	61	32	0	4	27	16	4.77	72	.289	.380	11-0-1	.000	-1	90	-7	0	-0.6
	Bos N	1	0	1.000	4	0	0	0	15.1	6	4	1	0	9	4	2.35	146	.122	.259	4	.000	0	—	2	0	0.1
	Year	3	2	.600	23	5	1	1	70	67	36	1	4	36	20	4.24	81	.258	.357	15-0-1	.000	-1	90	-5	0	-0.5
1947	Bos N	0	0	ø	1	0	0	0	2	4	2	0	0	1	1	9.00	43	.400	.455	0	ø	0	—	-1	0	-0.1
Total	3	3	3	.500	25	6	2	1	81	82	43	1	4	39	23	4.44	79	.268	.358	18-0-1	.000	-1	90	-7	0	-0.7
MULLIN, GEORGE	George Joseph "Wabash George"; B7.4.1880 Toledo OH; D1.7.1944 Wabash IN; BR/TR/5´11˝/188; d5.4																									
1902	Det A	13	16	.448	35	30	25	0	260	282	155	4	7	95	78	3.67	99	.277	.343	120-0-1	.325	9*	106	-3	—	0.7
1903	Det A	19	15	.559	41	36	31-6	**2**	320.2	284	128	4	8	106	170	2.25	130	.237	.303	126-1-4	.278	8*	110	21	—	3.5
1904	Det A	17	23	.425	45	44	42-7	0	382.1	345	154	1	10	131	161	2.40	106	.242	.310	155-0-3	.290	11*	74	3	—	2.4
1905	Det A	21	21	.500	44	**41**	**35**-1	0	**347.2**	303	149	4	8	138	168	2.51	109	.236	.314	135-0-3	.259	6*	79	4	—	1.7
1906	Det A	21	18	.538	40	40	35-2	0	330	315	139	3	15	108	123	2.78	99	.254	.322	142-0-1	.225	3*	88	-2	—	0.3
1907	†Det A	20	20	.500	46	42	35-5	3	357.1	346	153	1	15	106	146	2.59	100	.256	.318	157	.217	3*	120	1	—	0.8
1908	†Det A	17	13	.567	39	30	26-1	0	290.2	301	142	1	7	71	121	3.10	78	.271	.319	125-1-3	.256	8*	139	-20	—	-1.1
1909	†Det A	**29**	8	**.784**	40	35	29-3	1	303.2	258	96	1	8	78	124	2.22	113	.234	.289	126-0-2	.214	5*	129	12	—	2.3
1910	Det A	21	12	.636	38	32	27-5	0	289	260	125	7	14	102	98	2.87	92	.254	.330	129-1-0	.256	6*	126	-8	—	-0.1
1911	Det A	18	10	.643	30	29	25-2	0	234.1	245	99	7	12	61	87	3.07	113	.276	.331	98-0-1	.286	8*	100	13	—	2.1
1912	Det A	12	17	.414	30	29	22-2	0	226	214	112	3	9	92	88	3.54	92	.255	.335	90-0-2	.278	9*	97	-4	—	0.6
1913	Det A	1	6	.143	7	7	4	0	52.1	53	28	1	2	18	16	2.75	106	.270	.338	20	.350	3*	40	-1	—	0.2
	Was A	3	5	.375	11	9	3	0	57.1	69	34	1	5	25	14	5.02	59	.294	.374	21	.190	0*	103	-10	—	-1.2
	Year	4	11	.267	18	16	7	0	109.2	122	62	2	7	43	30	3.94	75	.283	.358	41	.268	3	76	-11	—	-1.0
1914	Ind F	14	10	.583	36	20	11-1	2	203	202	100	4	10	91	74	2.70	115	.261	.346	77-0-4	.312	8*	90	2	—	0.8
1915	New F	2	2	.500	5	4	3	0	32.1	41	22	0	0	16	14	5.85	44	.318	.393	10-0-1	.100	-0*	96	-10	—	-1.1
Total	14	228	196	.538	487	428	353-35	8	3686.2	3518	1636	42	130	1238	1482	2.82	101	.255	.322	1531-3-25	.262	88	103	-2	—	11.9
MULLINS, GREG	Gregory Eugene; B12.13.1971 Palatka FL; BL/TL/5´10˝/160; d9.18; Col North Florida																									
1998	Mil N	0	0	ø	2	0	0	0-0	1	1	0	0	1	0-0	1	0.00	ø	.250	.400	0	ø	0	—	0	0	0.0
MULRENAN, DOMINIC	Dominic Joseph; B12.18.1893 Woburn MA; D7.27.1964 Melrose MA; BR/TR/5´11˝/170; d4.24																									
1921	Chi A	2	8	.200	12	10	3	0	56	84	52	2	2	36	10	7.23	59	.359	.449	20-0-1	.150	-1	77	-19	—	-2.7
MULRONEY, FRANK	Francis Joseph; B4.8.1903 Mallard IA; D11.11.1985 Aberdeen WA; BR/TR/6´0˝/170; d4.15; Col Iowa																									
1930	Bos A	0	1	.000	2	0	0	0	3	3	2	0	0	0	2	3.00	154	.273	.273	0	ø	0	—	0	—	0.0
MUNCRIEF, BOB	Robert Cleveland; B1.28.1916 Madill OK; D2.6.1996 Duncanville TX; BR/TR/6´2˝/190; d9.30																									
1937	StL A	0	0	ø	1	1	0	0	2	3	2	1	0	2	0	4.50	107	.300	.417	0	ø	0	180	0	—	0.0
1939	StL A	0	0	ø	2	0	0	0	3	7	5	1	0	3	1	15.00	32	.500	.588	0	ø	0	—	-3	—	-0.1
1941	StL A	13	9	.591	36	24	12-2	1	214.1	221	95	18	5	53	67	3.65	118	.266	.314	76-0-5	.237	2	102	16	0	1.6
1942	StL A	6	8	.429	24	18	7-1	0	134.1	149	61	11	0	31	39	3.89	95	.280	.319	45-0-1	.111	-1	91	0	0	-0.1
1943	StL A	13	12	.520	35	27	12-3	1	205	211	80	13	2	48	80	2.81	118	.264	.307	66-0-8	.152	-2	100	9	0	0.7
1944	†StL A★	13	8	.619	33	27	12-3	1	219.1	216	83	11	3	50	88	3.08	117	.258	.302	78-0-5	.231	1	108	15	0	1.5
1945	StL A	13	4	.765	27	15	10	1	145.2	132	51	8	2	44	54	2.72	130	.239	.297	45-0-8	.067	-4*	132	12	0	0.9
1946	StL A	3	12	.200	29	14	4-1	0	115.1	149	75	6	0	31	49	4.99	75	.314	.356	32-0-2	.031	-3	79	-15	0	-2.2
1947	StL A	8	14	.364	31	23	7	0	176.1	210	108	14	2	51	74	4.90	79	.299	.348	57-0-4	.105	-3	83	-19	0	-2.4
1948	†Cle A	5	4	.556	21	9	1-1	0	72.1	76	37	8	0	31	24	3.98	102	.279	.353	18-0-2	.111	-1	89	0	0	-0.1
1949	Pit N	1	5	.167	13	4	1	3	35.2	44	27	8	0	13	11	6.31	67	.310	.368	7-0-3	.143	-0	73	-8	0	-1.2
	Chi N	5	6	.455	34	3	1	2	75	80	42	7	1	31	36	4.56	88	.276	.348	14-0-1	.286	1	102	-4	0	-0.4
	Year	6	11	.353	47	7	2	5	110.2	124	69	15	1	44	47	5.12	80	.287	.354	21-0-4	.238	1	86	-10	0	-1.6
1951	NY A	0	0	ø	2	0	0	0	3	5	3	0	0	4	2	9.00	43	.417	.563	0	ø	0	—	-2	0	-0.1
Total	12	80	82	.494	288	165	67-11	9	1401.1	1503	669	106	15	392	525	3.80	100	.275	.325	438-0-39	.155	-10	98	1	0	-1.9
MUNGER, RED	George David; B10.4.1918 Houston TX; D7.23.1996 Houston TX; BR/TR/6´2˝/(200–210); d5.1; Mil 1944–46																									
1943	StL N	9	5	.643	32	9	5	2	93.1	101	47	2	0	42	45	3.95	85	.281	.357	28	.214	1	146	-6	0	-0.7
1944	StL N✳	11	3	.786	21	12	7-2	2	121	92	23	2	2	41	55	1.34	263	.212	.284	44	.114	-3	65	29	0	3.4
1946	†StL N	2	2	.500	10	7	2	1	48.2	47	19	0	0	12	28	3.33	104	.255	.301	16	.250	1	117	2	0	0.3
1947	StL N☆	16	5	.762	40	31	13-6	3	224.1	218	94	12	2	76	123	3.37	123	.255	.318	81-0-3	.185	1	120	20	0	1.9
1948	StL N	10	11	.476	39	25	7-2	0	166	179	91	13	1	74	72	4.50	91	.272	.347	50-0-2	.160	0	101	-8	0	-0.8
1949	StL N★	15	8	.652	35	28	12-2	2	188.1	179	86	13	2	87	82	3.87	108	.255	.339	66-1-5	.258	4	122	9	0	1.4
1950	StL N	7	8	.467	32	20	5-1	0	154.2	158	73	15	3	70	61	3.90	110	.262	.342	51-0-3	.137	-2	93	7	0	0.5
1951	StL N	4	6	.400	23	11	3	0	94.2	106	58	13	0	46	44	5.32	74	.286	.365	29-0-1	.172	-0	81	-13	0	-1.1
1952	StL N	0	1	.000	1	1	0	0	4.1	7	6	2	1	1	1	12.46	30	.389	.450	2	.000	-0	24	-4	0	-0.6
	Pit N	0	3	.000	5	4	0	0	26.1	30	21	5	0	10	8	7.18	56	.283	.345	7-0-1	.000	-1	50	-8	0	-0.8
	Year	0	4	.000	6	5	0	0	30.2	37	27	7	1	11	9	7.92	50	.298	.360	9-0-1	.000	-1	45	-11	0	-1.4
1956	Pit N	3	4	.429	35	13	0	2	107	126	56	8	0	41-6	45	4.04	93	.299	.359	28-0-2	.107	-0	86	-4	0	-0.3
Total	10	77	56	.579	273	161	54-13	12	1228.2	1243	574	85	11	500-6	564	3.83	103	.264	.336	402-1-17	.174	0	104	24	0	3.2
MUNGO, VAN	Van Lingle; B6.8.1911 Pageland SC; D2.12.1985 Pageland SC; BR/TR/6´2˝/185; d9.7; C1																									
1931	Bro N	3	1	.750	5	4	2-1	0	31	27	9	0	1	13	12	2.32	164	.241	.325	12	.250	1	67	5	—	0.7
1932	Bro N	13	11	.542	39	33	11-1	2	223.1	224	120	9	6	115	107	4.43	86	.260	.351	79-0-4	.203	0	103	-13	—	-1.2
1933	Bro N	16	15	.516	41	28	18-3	0	248	223	89	7	0	84	110	2.72	118	.236	.298	84-0-4	.179	-0	91	15	—	1.8
1934	Bro N★	18	16	.529	45	**38**	22-3	3	**315.1**	300	137	15	3	104	184	3.37	116	.249	.310	121-0-1	.248	4*	100	20	—	2.6
1935	Bro N	16	10	.615	37	26	18-**4**	2	214.1	205	100	13	2	90	143	3.65	109	.252	.328	90-0-1	.289	5*	106	10	—	1.6
1936	Bro N☆	18	19	.486	45	**37**	22-2	3	311.2	275	137	8	3	118	**238**	3.35	123	**.234**	.305	123-0-4	.179	-4*	92	28	—	2.7
1937	Bro N★	9	11	.450	25	21	14	3	161	136	65	3	3	56	122	2.91	139	**.229**	.298	64	.250	2*	87	19	—	2.8
1938	Bro N	4	11	.267	24	18	6-2	0	133.1	133	78	11	2	72	72	3.92	100	.259	.353	47-0-4	.191	1*	94	-4	—	-0.2
1939	Bro N	4	5	.444	14	10	1	0	77.1	70	36	7	3	33	34	3.26	124	.239	.322	29-0-1	.345	2*	95	5	—	0.8
1940	Bro N	1	0	1.000	7	0	0	1	22	24	6	1	0	10	9	2.45	163	.282	.358	7	.000	-1*	—	4	—	0.1
1941	Bro N	0	0	ø	2	0	0	0	2	1	1	0	0	2	0	4.50	81	.143	.333	0	ø	0	—	0	0	0.0
1942	NY N	1	2	.333	9	5	0	0	36.1	38	32	4	0	21	27	5.94	57	.273	.369	14	.214	-0	115	-12	0	-0.9
1943	NY N	3	7	.300	45	13	2-2	2	154.1	140	68	7	6	79	83	3.91	88	.243	.341	44-0-2	.159	-1*	100	-4	0	-0.4
1945	NY N✳	14	7	.667	26	26	7-2	0	183	161	77	4	4	71	101	3.20	122	.238	.314	73	.233	4*	106	13	0	1.7
Total	14	120	115	.511	364	259	123-20	16	2113	1957	955	89	33	868	1242	3.47	110	.245	.321	787-0-21	.221	13	98	86	0	12.1
MUNIZ, MANNY	Manuel (Rodriguez); B12.31.1947 Caguas, PR; BR/TR/5´11˝/175; d9.3																									
1971	Phi N	0	1	.000	5	0	0	0-0	10.1	9	8	2	0	8-1	6	6.97	51	.225	.354	1	.000	-0	—	-3	0	-0.3
MUNNINGHOFF, SCOTT	Scott Andrew; B12.5.1958 Cincinnati OH; BR/TR/6´0˝/180; [PhiN77 1/22]; d4.13																									
1980	Phi N	0	0	ø	4	0	0	0-0	6	8	3	0	0	5-0	2	4.50	85	.320	.419	1	1.000	1	—	0	0	0.1

YEAR	TM LG	W	L	PCT	G	GS	CG-SHO	SV-BS	IP	H	R	HR	HB	BB-IB	SO	ERA	AERA	OAV	OOB	AB-HR-SH	AVG	PB	SUP	APR	DL	PW
MUNNS, LES	Leslie Ernest "Big Ed","Nemo"; B12.1.1908 Fort Bragg CA; D2.28.1997 Cedar Rapids IA; BR/TR/6´5˝/212; d4.22																									
1934	Bro N	3	7	.300	33	9	4	0	99.1	106	67	7	0	60	41	4.71	83	.280	.378	29	.241	2*	76	-12	—	-0.8
1935	Bro N	1	3	.250	21	5	0	1	58.1	74	47	5	4	33	13	5.55	72	.319	.413	16	.188	-0*	115	-12	—	-0.9
1936	StL N	0	3	.000	7	1	0	1	24	23	18	2	0	12	4	3.00	131	.240	.324	9	.111	-1*	129	-1	—	-0.2
Total	3	4	13	.235	61	15	4	2	181.2	203	132	14	4	105	58	4.76	83	.287	.382	54	.204	1	93	-25	—	-1.9
MUNOZ, ARNIE	Arnaldo Rafel; B6.21.1982 Mao, D.R.; BL/TL/5´9˝/170; d6.19																									
2004	Chi A	0	1	.000	11	1	0	0-0	14.1	20	16	4	1	12-1	11	10.05	47	.339	.446	1	.000	-0	276	-8	0	-0.5
MUNOZ, OSCAR	Juan Oscar; B9.25.1969 Hialeah FL; BR/TR/6´3˝/222; [CleA90 5/136]; d8.6; Col Miami																									
1995	Min A	2	1	.667	10	3	0	0-0	35.1	40	28	6	1	17-0	25	5.60	86	.276	.354	0	ø	0	122	-5	0	-0.4
MUNOZ, MIKE	Michael Anthony; B7.12.1965 Baldwin Park CA; BL/TL/6´2˝/(190–200); [LAN86 3/74]; d9.6; Col Cal Poly–Pomona																									
1989	LA N	0	0	ø	3	0	0	0-0	2.2	5	5	1	0	2-0	3	16.88	20	.417	.500	0	ø	0	—	-4	0	-0.2
1990	LA N	0	1	.000	8	0	0	0-1	5.2	6	2	0	0	3-0	2	3.18	116	.300	.391	1	.000	-0	—	0	0	0.1
1991	Det A	0	0	ø	6	0	0	0-0	9.1	14	10	0	0	5-0	3	9.64	43	.350	.413	0	ø	0	—	-5	0	-0.2
1992	Det A	1	2	.333	65	0	0	2-1	48	44	16	3	0	25-6	23	3.00	133	.246	.335	0	ø	0	—	6	0	0.5
1993	Det A	0	1	.000	8	0	0	0-0	3	4	2	1	0	6-1	1	6.00	73	.308	.526	0	ø	0	—	0	0	-0.1
	Col N	2	1	.667	21	0	0	0-2	18	21	12	1	0	9-3	16	4.50	106	.309	.380	0	ø	0	—	0	0	0.0
1994	Col N	4	2	.667	57	0	0	1-1	45.2	37	22	3	0	31-5	32	3.74	133	.223	.343	0	ø	0	—	5	0	0.7
1995	†Col N	2	4	.333	64	0	0	2-2	43.2	54	38	9	1	27-0	37	7.42	72	.307	.398	2	.500	1	—	-7	0	-0.8
1996	Col N	2	2	.500	54	0	0	0-3	44.2	55	33	4	1	16-2	45	6.65	78	.302	.360	1	.000	-0	—	-5	19	-0.3
1997	Col N	3	3	.500	64	0	0	2-0	45.2	52	25	4	0	13-0	26	4.53	114	.294	.339	1	.000	0	—	3	0	0.3
1998	Col N	2	2	.500	40	0	0	3-1	41.1	53	32	2	1	16-2	24	5.66	91	.312	.372	2-0-1	.000	-0	—	-3	0	-0.3
1999	Tex A	2	1	.667	56	0	0	1-2	52.2	52	24	5	1	18-2	27	3.93	132	.263	.323	0	ø	0	—	7	0	0.4
2000	Tex A	0	1	.000	7	0	0	0-1	4	11	6	1	0	3-1	1	13.50	38	.524	.583	0	ø	0	—	-3	157	-0.6
Total	12	18	20	.474	453	0	0	11-14	364.1	408	227	34	4	174-22	240	5.19	95	.287	.363	7-0-1	.143	1	—	-6	176	-0.5
MUNOZ, BOBBY	Roberto (Sbert); B3.3.1968 Rio Piedras, PR; BR/TR/6´7˝/(237–259); [NYA88 15/391]; d5.29; Col Palm Beach (FL) CC																									
1993	NY A	3	3	.500	38	0	0	0-2	45.2	48	27	1	0	26-5	33	5.32	79	.270	.357	0	ø	0	—	-5	0	-0.6
1994	Phi N	7	5	.583	21	14	1	1-1	104.1	101	40	8	1	35-0	59	2.67	160	.252	.310	34-1-2	.206	1	90	16	0	1.9
1995	Phi N	0	2	.000	3	3	0	0-0	15.2	15	13	2	3	9-0	6	5.74	73	.268	.386	5	.000	-1	57	-4	148	-0.4
1996	Phi N	0	3	.000	6	6	0	0-0	25.1	42	28	5	1	7-1	8	7.82	55	.375	.413	7-0-1	.143	0	70	-11	159	-1.1
1997	Phi N	1	5	.167	8	7	0	0-0	33.1	47	35	4	2	15-1	20	8.91	47	.338	.403	10-0-1	.300	1	75	-17	0	-2.2
1998	Bal A	0	0	ø	9	1	0	0-0	12	18	13	4	1	6-0	6	9.75	47	.383	.439	0	ø	0	163	-7	0	-0.3
2001	Mon N	0	4	.000	15	7	0	0-0	42	53	25	6	2	21-1	21	5.14	84	.321	.404	11	.000	-1	46	-3	0	-0.4
Total	7	11	22	.333	100	38	1	1-3	278.1	324	181	30	10	119-8	153	5.17	83	.295	.364	67-1-4	.164	1	76	-31	307	-3.1
MUNRO, PETE	Peter Daniel; B6.14.1975 Flushing NY; BR/TR/6´2˝/(200–210); [BosA93 6/163]; d4.6; Col Okaloosa–Walton (FL) CC																									
1999	Tor A	0	2	.000	31	2	0	0-1	55.1	70	38	6	2	23-0	38	6.02	82	.318	.382	0	ø	0	114	-6	0	-0.2
2000	Tor A	1	1	.500	9	3	0	0-0	25.2	38	22	1	3	16-0	16	5.96	84	.355	.452	1	.000	-0	106	-4	29	-0.3
2002	Hou N	5	5	.500	19	14	0	0-0	80.2	89	37	5	3	23-3	45	3.57	121	.283	.338	22-0-1	.136	-1	90	5	0	0.6
2003	Hou N	3	4	.429	40	2	0	0-1	54	63	30	7	5	26-2	27	4.67	95	.294	.382	1-0-2	.000	0	95	-1	0	-0.1
2004	†Hou N	4	7	.364	21	19	0	0-0	99.2	120	59	12	10	26-2	63	5.15	85	.302	.357	29-0-3	.069	-1*	96	-7	0	-0.8
Total	5	13	19	.406	120	40	0	0-2	315.1	380	186	31	23	114-7	189	4.88	93	.304	.370	53-0-6	.094	-2	94	-13	29	-0.8
MUNTER, SCOTT	Scott Michael; B3.7.1980 Norfolk NE; BR/TR/6´6˝/(235–240); [SFN01 47/1411]; d5.11; Col Butler Co.(KS) CC																									
2005	SF N	2	0	1.000	45	0	0	0-3	38.2	40	15	1	1	12-1	11	2.56	166	.280	.338	0-0-1	ø	0	—	6	21	0.4
2006	SF N	0	1	.000	27	0	0	0-0	22.2	30	22	1	2	18-2	7	8.74	51	.366	.485	1	1.000	1	—	-10	0	-0.4
Total	2	2	1	.667	72	0	0	0-3	61.1	70	37	2	3	30-3	18	4.84	89	.311	.396	1-0-1	1.000	1	—	-4	21	0.0
MURA, STEVE	Stephen Andrew; B2.12.1955 New Orleans LA; BR/TR/6´2˝/(188–190); [SDN76 2/29]; d9.5; Col Tulane																									
1978	SD N	0	2	.000	5	2	0	0-0	7.2	15	10	1	0	5-0	5	11.74	29	.441	.500	1	.000	-0	54	-7	0	-1.3
1979	SD N	4	4	.500	38	5	0	2-3	73	57	30	6	1	37-2	59	3.08	115	.217	.314	10-0-3	.000	-1	80	3	36	0.2
1980	SD N	8	7	.533	37	23	3-1	2-1	168.2	149	74	9	3	86-4	109	3.68	93	.246	.338	51	.137	-0*	106	-4	0	-0.4
1981	SD N	5	14	.263	23	22	2	0-0	138.2	156	72	10	0	50-2	70	4.28	76	.285	.344	44-0-2	.136	-0*	87	-17	0	-2.1
1982	StL N	12	11	.522	35	30	7-1	0-0	184.1	196	89	16	0	80-4	84	4.05	91	.278	.348	53-0-10	.057	-4	117	-6	0	-1.2
1983	Chi A	0	0	ø	6	0	0	0-0	12.1	13	11	1	0	6-0	4	4.38	96	.260	.333	0	ø	0	—	-2	0	-0.1
1985	Oak A	1	1	.500	23	1	0	1-0	48	41	25	3	0	25-4	29	4.13	94	.225	.317	0	ø	0	70	-2	0	-0.1
Total	7	30	39	.435	167	83	12-2	5-4	632.2	627	311	46	4	289-16	360	4.00	88	.263	.340	159-0-15	.101	-5	101	-35	36	-5.0
MURAKAMI, MASANORI	Masanori; B5.6.1944 Otsuki, Japan; BL/TL/6´0˝/180; d9.1																									
1964	SF N	1	0	1.000	9	0	0	1	15	8	3	1	0	1-0	15	1.80	198	.163	.176	3	.000	-0	—	3	0	0.2
1965	SF N	4	1	.800	45	1	0	8	74.1	57	31	9	3	22-5	85	3.75	96	.205	.271	13	.154	-0	364	1	0	0.0
Total	2	5	1	.833	54	1	0	9	89.1	65	34	10	3	23-5	100	3.43	105	.199	.257	16	.125	-1	364	4	0	0.2
MURCHISON, TIM	Thomas Malcolm; B10.8.1896 Liberty NC; D10.20.1962 Liberty NC; BR/TL/6´0˝/185; d6.21; Col Guilford																									
1917	StL N	0	0	ø	1	0	0	0	1	0	0	0	0	2	2	0.00	ø	.000	.400	0	ø	0	—	0	—	0.0
1920	Cle A	0	0	ø	2	0	0	0	5	3	1	0	0	4	0	0.00	ø	.200	.368	1	.000	-0	—	2	—	0.1
Total	2	0	0	ø	3	0	0	0	6	3	1	0	0	6	2	0.00	ø	.167	.375	1	.000	-0	—	2	—	0.1
MURFF, RED	John Robert; B4.1.1921 Burlington TX; BR/TR/6´3˝/195; d4.21; Col Gettysburg																									
1956	Mil N	0	0	ø	14	1	0	1	24.1	25	14	3	0	7-0	18	4.44	78	.272	.320	5	.200	0	127	-3	66	-0.1
1957	Mil N	2	2	.500	12	1	0	2	26	31	14	3	0	11-1	13	4.85	72	.301	.368	6-0-1	.000	-1	252	-3	0	-0.6
Total	2	2	2	.500	26	2	0	3	50.1	56	28	6	0	18-1	31	4.65	75	.287	.346	11-0-1	.091	-1	190	-6	66	-0.7
MURPHY, CON	Cornelius B. "Monk","Razzle Dazzle"; B10.15.1863 Worcester MA; D8.1.1914 Worcester MA; TR/5´9˝/130; d9.11																									
1884	Phi N	0	3	.000	3	3	3	0	26	37	34	1	—	6	10	6.58	45	.319	.352	10	.000	-1	36	-10	—	-0.9
1890	Bro P	4	10	.286	20	14	11	2	139	168	134	2	6	82	29	4.79	93	.286	.379	69	.217	-1*	85	-7	—	-0.6
Total	2	4	13	.235	23	17	14	2	165	205	168	3	6	88	39	5.07	83	.292	.375	79	.190	-3	78	-17	—	-1.5
MURPHY, DANNY	Daniel Francis; B8.23.1942 Beverly MA; BL/TR/5´11˝/(180–185); d6.18.1960; ▲																									
1969	Chi A	2	1	.667	17	0	0	4-1	31.1	28	8	2	2	10-0	16	2.01	191	.252	.323	1	.000	0	—	6	0	0.8
1970	Chi A	2	3	.400	51	0	0	5-3	80.2	82	55	11	4	49-8	42	5.69	68	.273	.378	6-1-0	.333	2	—	-14	0	-0.8
Total	2	4	4	.500	68	0	0	9-4	112	110	63	13	6	59-8	58	4.66	83	.268	.364	7-1-0	.286	2	—	-8	0	0.0
MURPHY, DAN	Daniel Lee; B9.18.1964 Artesia CA; BR/TR/6´2˝/195; d8.10																									
1989	SD N	0	0	ø	7	0	0	0-0	6.1	6	6	1	0	4-1	1	5.68	62	.231	.333	0	ø	0	—	-2	0	-0.1
MURPHY, ED	Edward J.; B1.22.1877 Auburn NY; D1.29.1935 Weedsport NY; TR/6´1˝/186; d4.23																									
1898	Phi N	1	2	.333	7	3	2	0	30	41	23	3	1	10	8	5.10	67	.323	.377	14-0-1	.357	1	96	-5	—	-0.3
1901	StL N	10	9	.526	23	21	16	0	165	201	105	5	1	32	42	4.20	76	.298	.331	64-1-1	.250	3	141	-21	—	-1.6
1902	StL N	10	6	.625	23	17	12-1	1	164	187	86	7	2	31	37	3.02	91	.286	.321	61	.262	1	123	-7	—	-0.4
1903	StL N	4	8	.333	15	12	9	0	106	108	62	2	6	38	16	3.31	99	.262	.333	64-0-2	.203	-1*	69	0	—	-0.1
Total	4	25	25	.500	68	53	39-1	1	465	537	276	17	10	111	103	3.64	84	.288	.331	203-1-4	.246	5	115	-33	—	-2.4
MURPHY, JOHN	John Henry; 5´11˝/165; d4.17																									
1884	Alt U	5	6	.455	14	10	10	0	111.2	141	90	3	—	9	46	3.87	69	.289	.302	94	.149	-5*	59	-14	—	-1.4
	Wil U	0	6	.000	7	6	5	0	48	52	36	3	—	2	27	3.00	89	.259	.266	31	.065	-3*	32	-1	—	-0.4
	Year	5	12	.294	21	16	15	0	159.2	193	126	6	—	11	73	3.61	74	.280	.291	125	.128	-8	49	-17	—	-1.8
MURPHY, JOHNNY	John Joseph "Grandma" "Fireman","Fordham Johnny"; B7.14.1908 New York NY; D1.14.1970 New York NY; BR/TR/6´2˝/190; d5.19; Def 1944–45; Col Fordham																									
1932	NY A	0	0	ø	2	0	0	0	3.1	7	6	0	0	3	2	16.20	25	.438	.526	1	1.000	1	—	-4	—	-0.2
1934	NY A	14	10	.583	40	20	10	4	207.2	193	79	11	0	76	70	3.12	130	.250	.317	71-0-5	.099	-3	94	26	—	2.5
1935	NY A	10	5	.667	40	8	4	5	117	110	67	7	0	55	28	4.08	99	.243	.325	32-0-2	.156	2	123	-2	—	-0.1
1936	†NY A	9	3	.750	27	5	2	5	88	90	38	5	1	36	34	3.38	138	.262	.334	36	.361	4	189	13	—	2.0

YEAR	TM LG	W	L	PCT	G	GS	CG-SHO	SV-BS	IP	H	R	HR	HB	BB-IB	SO	ERA	AERA	OAV	OOB	AB-HR-SH	AVG	PB	SUP	APR	DL	PW
1937	†NY A☆	13	4	.765	39	4	0	10	110	121	59	7	1	50	36	4.17	107	.277	.352	35-0-3	.229	2	157	4	—	0.9
1938	†NY A☆	8	2	.800	32	2	1	**11**	91.1	90	47	5	1	41	43	4.24	107	.256	.336	32-0-2	.063	-3	87	**5**	—	0.4
1939	†NY A☆	3	6	.333	38	0	0	**19**	61.1	57	33	2	0	28	30	4.40	99	.252	.335	11-0-1	.182	1	—	0	—	0.1
1940	NY A	8	4	.667	35	1	0	9	63.1	58	27	5	0	15	23	3.69	109	.247	.292	13-0-2	.077	0	109	4	—	0.7
1941	†NY A	8	3	.727	35	0	0	**15**	77.1	68	20	1	0	40	29	1.98	199	.237	.330	18-0-3	.056	-1	—	**18**	0	2.9
1942	NY A	4	10	.286	31	0	0	**11**	58	66	27	2	2	23	24	3.41	101	.293	.364	13-0-2	.154	0	—	-1	0	-0.1
1943	†NY A	12	4	.750	37	0	0	8	68	44	22	2	0	30	31	2.51	128	.183	.273	19-0-1	.053	-2	—	6	0	1.0
1946	NY A	4	2	.667	27	0	0	7	45	40	22	4	0	19	19	3.40	102	.240	.317	6-0-1	.000	-0	—	-1	0	-0.1
1947	Bos A	0	0	ø	32	0	0	3	54.2	41	17	1	0	28	9	2.80	139	.206	.304	11	.273	1	—	7	0	0.5
Total	13	93	53	.637	415	40	17	107	1045	985	464	52	5	444	378	3.50	117	.249	.326	298-0-22	.154	-0	123	75	0	10.5
Murphy, Joe	Joseph Akin; B9.7.1866 St.Louis MO; D3.28.1951 Coral Gables FL; 5´11˝/160; d4.28; Col St. Louis																									
1886	Cin AA	2	3	.400	5	5	5	0	46	50	34	0	1	21	11	4.89	72	.256	.332	18	.000	-3	54	-6	—	-0.8
	StL N	0	4	.000	4	4	3	0	33	45	41	3	—	16	11	8.18	39	.319	.389	14	.214	0	62	-15	—	-1.3
	StL AA	1	0	1.000	1	1	1	0	7	5	4	0	0	3	3	3.86	89	.179	.258	3	.000	-1	155	0	—	-0.1
1887	StL AA	1	0	1.000	1	1	1	0	9	13	8	0	0	4	5	5.00	91	.317	.378	6	.167	-1	309	-1	—	-0.1
Total	2	4	7	.364	11	11	10	0	95	113	87	3	1	44	30	5.97	59	.279	.351	41	.098	-4	94	-22	—	-2.3
Murphy, Rob	Robert Albert; B5.26.1960 Miami FL; BL/TL/6´2˝/(200–215); [CinN81*S1/3]; d9.13; Col Florida																									
1985	Cin N	0	0	ø	2	0	0	0-0	3	2	2	1	0	2-0	1	6.00	63	.200	.333	0	ø	0	—	-1	0	0.0
1986	Cin N	6	0	1.000	34	0	0	1-2	50.1	26	4	0	0	21-2	36	0.72	539	.155	.245	3	.000	-0	—	17	0	2.0
1987	Cin N	8	5	.615	87	0	0	3-4	100.2	91	37	7	0	32-5	99	3.04	139	.239	.297	5-0-1	.200	0	—	13	0	1.6
1988	Cin N	0	6	.000	**76**	0	0	3-3	84.2	69	31	3	1	38-6	74	3.08	116	.229	.317	0	ø	0	—	5	0	0.4
1989	Bos A	5	7	.417	74	0	0	9-7	105	97	38	7	1	41-8	107	2.74	150	.251	.323	0	ø	0	—	14	0	1.8
1990	†Bos A	0	6	.000	68	0	0	7-3	57	85	46	10	1	32-3	54	6.32	65	.348	.420	0	ø	0	—	-14	0	-1.6
1991	Sea A	0	1	.000	57	0	0	4-0	48	47	17	4	1	19-4	34	3.00	138	.250	.322	0	ø	0	—	6	0	0.3
1992	Hou N	3	1	.750	59	0	0	0-2	55.2	56	28	2	0	21-4	42	4.04	84	.260	.322	1-0-1	.000	-0	—	-4	19	-0.3
1993	StL N	5	7	.417	73	0	0	1-3	64.2	73	37	8	1	20-6	41	4.87	83	.290	.342	2-0-1	.500	0	—	-5	0	-0.8
1994	StL N	4	3	.571	50	0	0	2-1	40.1	35	18	7	0	13-2	25	3.79	112	.230	.291	0	ø	0	—	2	0	0.3
	NY A	0	0	ø	3	0	0	0-0	1.2	3	3	2	0	0-0	0	16.20	28	.375	.375	0	ø	0	—	-2	0	-0.1
1995	LA N	0	1	.000	6	0	0	0-0	5	6	7	2	0	3-0	2	12.60	31	.300	.391	1	1.000	1	—	-5	0	-0.7
	Fla N	1	1	.500	8	0	0	0-0	7.1	8	9	1	0	5-1	5	9.82	44	.286	.394	0	ø	0	—	-4	0	-0.8
	Year	1	2	.333	14	0	0	0-0	12.1	14	16	3	0	8-1	7	10.95	38	.292	.393	1	1.000	1	—	-9	0	-1.5
Total	11	32	38	.457	597	0	0	30-25	623.1	598	277	54	5	247-41	520	3.64	109	.254	.324	12-0-3	.250	0	—	22	19	2.1
Murphy, Bob	Robert J.; B12.26.1866 Dutchess Co. NY; 6´0˝/173; d5,27																									
1890	NY N	1	0	1.000	3	2	1	0	18	23	17	0	0	10	8	5.50	64	.303	.384	9	.111	-1	90	-3	—	-0.2
	Bro AA	3	9	.250	12	12	10	0	96	121	95	6	5	46	26	5.72	68	.299	.377	50-1	.180	0*	81	-19	—	-1.6
Total	1	4	9	.308	15	14	11	0	114	144	112	6	5	56	34	5.68	67	.299	.378	59-1	.169	-1	82	-22	—	-1.8
Murphy, Tom	Thomas Andrew; B12.30.1945 Cleveland OH; BR/TR/6´3˝/(185–205); [AnaA67*S1/6]; d6.13; Col Ohio U.																									
1968	Cal A	5	6	.455	15	15	3	0	99.1	67	30	5	5	28-0	56	2.17	134	.191	.258	28-0-5	.000	-3	100	7	0	0.4
1969	Cal A	10	16	.385	36	35	4	0-0	215.2	213	110	12	21	69-3	100	4.21	83	.260	.332	71-0-5	.141	-0	81	-15	0	-1.7
1970	Cal A	16	13	.552	39	38	5-2	0-0	227	223	114	32	7	81-10	99	4.24	85	.261	.329	76-1-8	.184	3	100	-14	0	-1.4
1971	Cal A	6	17	.261	37	36	7	0-0	243.1	228	108	24	9	82-9	89	3.77	86	.256	.323	75-0-6	.173	1	86	-12	0	-0.9
1972	Cal A	0	0	ø	6	0	0	0-0	10	13	6	0	0	8-1	2	5.40	54	.342	.447	1	.000	-0	—	-2	0	-0.1
	KC A	4	4	.500	18	9	1-1	1-0	70.1	77	26	3	6	16-0	34	3.07	99	.287	.341	13-0-5	.000	-1*	142	0	0	-0.1
	Year	4	4	.500	24	9	1-1	1-0	80.1	90	32	3	6	24-1	36	3.36	90	.294	.356	14-0-5	.000	-1	143	-2	0	-0.2
1973	StL N	3	7	.300	19	13	2	0-0	88.2	89	38	5	3	22-0	42	3.76	98	.269	.317	23-0-3	.174	0	80	1	0	0.2
1974	Mil A	10	10	.500	70	0	0	20-7	123	97	27	6	2	51-18	47	1.90	191	.224	.306	2	.500	0	—	**24**	0	**5.0**
1975	Mil A	1	9	.100	52	0	0	20-9	72.1	85	43	5	5	27-5	32	4.60	84	.295	.362	0	ø	0*	—	-6	20	-1.2
1976	Mil A	0	1	.000	15	0	0	1-2	18.1	25	18	2	2	9-3	7	7.36	48	.313	.396	0	ø	0	—	-8	0	-0.5
	Bos A	4	5	.444	37	0	0	8-5	81	91	43	5	2	25-11	32	3.44	113	.290	.343	0	ø	0	—	1	0	0.1
	Year	4	6	.400	52	0	0	9-7	99.1	116	61	7	4	34-14	39	4.17	92	.294	.354	0	ø	0	—	-7	0	-0.4
1977	Bos A	0	1	.000	16	0	0	0-0	30.2	44	25	6	0	12-0	13	6.75	67	.338	.392	0	ø	0	—	-7	0	-0.3
	Tor A	2	1	.667	19	1	0	2-0	52	63	22	6	1	18-3	26	3.63	117	.304	.358	0	ø	0	127	4	0	0.2
	Year	2	2	.500	35	1	0	2-0	82.2	107	47	12	1	30-3	39	4.79	91	.318	.371	0	ø	0	124	-3	0	-0.1
1978	Tor A	6	9	.400	50	0	0	7-4	94	87	43	11	0	37-10	36	3.93	101	.256	.322	0	ø	0	—	1	0	0.2
1979	Tor A	1	2	.333	10	0	0	0-2	18.1	23	11	1	0	8-0	6	5.40	81	.311	.378	0	ø	0	—	-1	0	-0.2
Total	12	68	101	.402	439	147	22-3	59-29	1444	1425	664	123	63	493-73	621	3.78	94	.263	.329	289-1-32	.145	0	89	-27	20	-0.3
Murphy, Walter	Walter Joseph; B9.27.1907 New York NY; D3.23.1976 Houston TX; BR/TR/6´1.5˝/180; d4.19																									
1931	Bos A	0	0	ø	2	0	0	0	2	4	2	0	0	1	0	9.00	48	.444	.500	0	ø	0	—	-1	—	0.0
Murray, Amby	Ambrose Joseph; B6.4.1913 Fall River MA; D2.6.1997 Port Salerno FL; BL/TL/5´7˝/150; d7.5; Col Brown																									
1936	Bos N	0	0	ø	4	1	0	0	11	15	5	1	0	3	2	4.09	94	.319	.360	4	.250	0	199	0	—	0.0
Murray, Dale	Dale Albert; B2.2.1950 Cuero TX; BR/TR/6´4˝/(200–205); [MonN70 18/418]; d7.7; Col Blinn (TX) JC																									
1974	Mon N	1	1	.500	32	0	0	10-0	69.2	46	12	1	0	23-2	31	1.03	372	.187	.256	10	.000	-1	—	19	0	1.1
1975	Mon N	15	8	.652	63	0	0	9-10	111.1	134	59	0	3	39-10	43	3.96	98	.305	.361	14	.214	1	—	-3	36	-0.4
1976	Mon N	4	9	.308	**81**	0	0	13-8	113.1	117	47	1	0	37-12	35	3.26	115	.277	.331	8-0-3	.000	-1	—	6	0	0.9
1977	Cin N	7	2	.778	61	1	0	4-4	102	125	60	13	2	46-6	42	4.94	80	.314	.382	12-0-2	.167	-0	339	-11	0	-1.0
1978	Cin N	1	1	.500	15	0	0	2-0	32.2	34	20	1	1	17-4	25	4.13	86	.272	.356	3-0-2	.000	-0	—	-4	0	-0.3
	NY N	8	5	.615	53	0	0	5-2	86.1	85	39	4	2	36-19	37	3.65	97	.266	.340	7	.000	-0	—	-1	0	-0.2
	Year	9	6	.600	68	0	0	7-2	119	119	59	5	3	53-23	62	3.78	94	.268	.344	10-0-2	.000	-1	—	-5	0	-0.5
1979	NY N	4	8	.333	58	0	0	4-7	97	105	58	6	0	52-14	37	4.82	77	.287	.373	6-0-2	.000	-0	—	-12	0	-1.5
	Mon N	1	2	.333	9	0	0	1-1	13.1	14	4	1	0	3-2	4	2.70	138	.292	.327	2	.000	-0	—	2	0	0.3
	Year	5	10	.333	67	0	0	5-8	110.1	119	62	7	0	55-16	41	4.57	81	.287	.368	8-0-2	.000	-1	—	-10	0	-1.2
1980	Mon N	0	1	.000	16	0	0	0-0	29.1	39	23	3	0	12-2	16	6.14	59	.315	.372	3	.000	-0	—	-8	0	-0.5
1981	Tor A	1	0	1.000	11	0	0	0-0	15.1	12	2	0	0	5-0	12	1.17	338	.211	.274	0	ø	0	—	5	0	0.3
1982	Tor A	8	7	.533	56	0	0	11-7	111	115	48	3	3	32-5	60	3.16	143	.268	.323	0	ø	0	—	13	0	2.1
1983	NY A	2	4	.333	40	0	0	1-2	94.1	113	56	5	1	22-4	45	4.48	88	.297	.333	0	ø	0	—	-7	0	-0.4
1984	NY A	1	2	.333	19	0	0	0-1	23.2	30	15	2	2	5-0	13	4.94	78	.306	.352	0	ø	0	—	-3	96	-0.4
1985	NY A	0	0	ø	3	0	0	0-0	2	4	3	0	0	0-0	0	13.50	30	.400	.400	0	ø	0	—	-2	0	-0.1
	Tex A	0	0	ø	1	0	0	0-0	1	3	2	0	0	0-0	0	18.00	24	.750	.750	0	ø	0	—	-1	0	-0.1
	Year	0	0	ø	4	0	0	0-0	3	7	5	0	0	0-0	0	15.00	27	.500	.500	0	ø	0	—	-3	0	-0.2
Total	12	53	50	.515	518	1	0	60-42	902.1	976	448	40	14	329-80	400	3.85	101	.282	.343	65-0-9	.077	-3	339	-7	132	-0.2
Murray, Dan	Daniel Saffle; B11.21.1973 Los Alamitos CA; BR/TR/6´1˝/(193–195); [NYN95 10/273]; d8.9; Col San Diego St.																									
1999	NY N	0	0	ø	1	0	0	0-0	2	4	3	0	0	2-0	1	13.50	32	.444	.500	0	ø	0	—	-2	0	-0.1
	KC A	0	0	ø	4	0	0	0-0	8.1	9	8	4	1	4-0	8	6.48	78	.265	.359	0	ø	0	—	-2	0	-0.1
2000	KC A	0	0	ø	10	0	0	0-0	19.1	20	10	7	1	10-0	16	4.66	112	.278	.369	0	ø	0	—	1	0	0.1
Total	2	0	0	ø	15	0	0	0-0	29.2	33	21	11	2	16-0	25	5.76	89	.287	.378	0	ø	0	—	-3	0	-0.1
Murray, George	George King "Smiler"; B9.23.1898 Charlotte NC; D10.18.1955 Memphis TN; BR/TR/6´2˝/200; d5.8; Col North Carolina St.																									
1922	NY A	3	2	.600	22	2	0	0	56.2	53	27	0	1	26	14	3.97	101	.255	.340	18-1-0	.278	2	85	**1**	—	0.2
1923	Bos A	7	11	.389	39	18	5	0	177.2	190	111	9	7	87	40	4.91	84	.291	.380	55-0-6	.164	-3	69	-11	—	-1.3
1924	Bos A	2	9	.182	28	7	0	0	80.1	97	68	6	7	32	27	6.72	65	.307	.383	22-0-1	.182	-1	55	-19	—	-2.2
1926	Was A	6	3	.667	12	12	5	0	81.1	89	56	1	6	37	28	5.64	69	.287	.374	36-0-3	.139	-2	140	-15	—	-1.6
1927	Was A	1	1	.500	7	3	0	0	18	18	18	1	2	15	5	7.00	58	.265	.412	6-0-1	.167	-0	130	-7	—	-0.6
1933	Chi A	0	0	ø	2	0	0	0	2.1	3	2	0	0	2	0	7.71	55	.375	.500	0	ø	0	—	-1	—	0.0
Total	6	19	26	.422	110	42	10	0	416.1	450	282	17	23	199	114	5.38	76	.288	.376	137-1-11	.175	-4	90	-52	—	-5.5

YEAR	TM LG	W	L	PCT	G	GS	CG-SHO	SV-BS	IP	H	R	HR	HB	BB-IB	SO	ERA	AERA	OAV	OOB	AB-HR-SH	AVG	PB	SUP	APR	DL	PW
Murray, Heath	Heath Robertson; B4.19.1973 Troy OH; BL/TL/6´4˝/(205–210); [SDN94 3/66]; d5.24; Col Michigan; [DL 1998 SD N 9]																									
1997	SD N	1	2	.333	17	3	0	0-0	33.1	50	25	3	4	21-3	16	6.75	58	.376	.472	6	.000	-1	109	-10	20	-0.9
1999	SD N	0	4	.000	22	8	0	0-0	50	60	33	7	1	26-4	25	5.76	74	.297	.377	13-0-1	.154	0	108	-8	0	-0.5
2001	Det A	1	7	.125	40	4	0	0-2	63.1	82	48	11	3	40-5	42	6.54	68	.322	.418	0	ø	0	63	-14	0	-1.5
2002	Cle A	0	2	.000	9	0	0	0-0	12	12	10	3	2	7-0	11	7.50	59	.267	.389	0	ø	0	—	-4	70	-0.5
Total	4	2	15	.118	88	15	0	0-2	158.2	204	116	24	10	94-12	94	6.41	67	.321	.415	19-0-1	.105	-1	95	-36	99	-3.4
Murray, Jim	James Francis "Big Jim"; B12.31.1900 Scranton PA; D7.15.1973 Queens NY; BB/TL/6´2˝/210; d7.3; Col Syracuse																									
1922	Bro N	0	0	ø	4	0	0	1	6	8	3	0	0	3	3	4.50	90	.320	.393	2	.500	0	—	0	—	0.0
Murray, Joe	Joseph Ambrose; B11.11.1920 Wilkes–Barre PA; D10.19.2001 San Clemente CA; BL/TL/6´0˝/165; d8.17																									
1950	Phi A	0	3	.000	8	2	0	0	30	34	20	1	0	21	8	5.70	80	.283	.390	11	.000	-2	99	-3	0	-0.4
Murray, Matt	Matthew Michael; B9.26.1970 Boston MA; BL/TR/6´6˝/235; [AtlN88 2/41]; d8.12; [DL 1993 Atl N 97]																									
1995	Atl N	0	2	.000	4	1	0	0-0	10.2	10	8	3	1	5-0	3	6.75	64	.256	.356	2	.500	0	84	-2	0	-0.3
	Bos A	0	1	.000	2	1	0	0-0	3.1	11	10	1	0	3-0	1	18.90	26	.524	.583	0	ø	0	77	-6	0	-0.9
Total	1	0	3	.000	6	2	0	0-0	14	21	18	4	1	8-0	4	9.64	46	.350	.435	2	.500	0	82	-8	97	-1.2
Murray, Pat	Patrick Joseph; B7.18.1897 Scottsville NY; D11.5.1983 Rochester NY; BR/TL/6´0˝/175; d7.1; Col Notre Dame																									
1919	Phi N	0	2	.000	8	2	1	0	34.1	50	28	0	4	12	11	6.29	51	.347	.412	12	.000	-1	37	-10	—	-0.7
Musgraves, Dennis	Dennis Eugene; B12.25.1943 Indianapolis IN; BR/TR/6´4˝/190; d7.9; Col Missouri																									
1965	NY N	0	0	ø	5	1	0	0	16	11	2	0	2	7-0	11	0.56	627	.200	.313	2	.000	-0	25	5	44	0.2
Musselman, Jeff	Jeffrey Joseph; B6.21.1963 Doylestown PA; BL/TL/6´0˝/(180–185); [TorA85 6/157]; d9.2; Col Harvard																									
1986	Tor A	0	0	ø	6	0	0	0-0	5.1	8	7	1	0	5-1	4	10.13	42	.333	.448	0	ø	0	—	-4	0	-0.2
1987	Tor A	12	5	.706	68	1	0	3-5	89	75	43	7	3	54-12	54	4.15	109	.237	.353	0	ø	0	101	4	0	0.8
1988	Tor A	8	5	.615	15	15	0	0-0	85	80	34	4	3	30-2	39	3.18	125	.252	.320	0	ø	0	126	7	72	1.0
1989	Tor A	0	1	.000	5	3	0	0-0	11	19	15	2	0	9-0	3	10.64	36	.404	.491	0	ø	0	103	-9	69	-0.7
	NY N	3	2	.600	20	0	0	0-0	26.1	27	11	1	0	14-3	11	3.08	107	.267	.357	0	ø	0	—	0	0	0.2
1990	NY N	0	2	.000	28	0	0	0-1	32	40	22	3	1	11-1	14	5.63	67	.310	.364	1	.000	-0	—	-6	0	-0.4
Total	5	23	15	.605	142	19	0	3-6	248.2	249	132	18	7	123-19	125	4.31	94	.266	.354	1	.000	0	118	-8	141	0.7
Musselman, Ron	Ralph Ronald; B11.11.1954 Wilmington NC; BR/TR/6´2˝/(185–195); [SeaA77 5/130]; d8.18; Col Clemson																									
1982	Sea A	1	0	1.000	12	0	0	0-0	15.2	18	7	2	1	6-1	9	3.45	124	.300	.362	0	ø	0	—	1	0	0.1
1984	Tor A	0	2	.000	11	0	0	1-0	21.1	18	7	2	0	10-2	9	2.11	196	.225	.304	0	ø	0	—	4	0	0.4
1985	Tor A	3	0	1.000	25	4	0	0-0	52.1	59	28	2	0	24-2	29	4.47	95	.284	.352	0	ø	0	123	-1	0	-0.1
Total	3	4	2	.667	48	4	0	1-0	89.1	95	42	6	1	40-5	47	3.73	113	.273	.343	0	ø	0	123	4	0	0.4
Musser, Paul	Paul; B6.24.1889 Millheim PA; D7.7.1973 State College PA; BR/TR/6´0˝/175; d6.6; Mil 1918–19; Col Susquehanna																									
1912	Was A	0	0	ø	7	2	0	2	20.2	16	7	0	2	16	10	2.61	128	.225	.382	7	.000	-1	144	2	—	0.0
1919	Bos A	0	2	.000	5	4	1	0	19.2	26	16	0	0	8	14	4.12	73	.342	.405	8	.000	-1	123	-5	—	-0.6
Total	2	0	2	.000	12	6	1	2	40.1	42	23	0	2	24	24	3.35	95	.286	.393	15	.000	-2	127	-3	—	-0.6
Mussill, Barney	Bernard James; B10.1.1919 Bower Hill PA; BR/TL/6´1˝/200; d4.20; Col Bowling Green																									
1944	Phi N	0	1	.000	16	0	0	0	19.1	20	16	1	0	13	5	6.05	60	.267	.375	1	.000	-0	—	-6	0	-0.3
Mussina, Mike	Michael Cole; B12.8.1968 Williamsport PA; BR/TR/6´1˝/(180–190); [BalA90 1/20]; d8.4; Col Stanford																									
1991	Bal A	4	5	.444	12	12	2	0-0	87.2	77	31	7	1	21-0	52	2.87	138	.239	.286	0	ø	0	96	11	0	1.0
1992	Bal A★	18	5	**.783**	32	32	8-4	0-0	241	212	70	16	2	48-2	130	2.54	160	.239	**.278**	0	ø	0	100	41	0	3.8
1993	Bal A☆	14	6	.700	25	25	3-2	0-0	167.2	163	84	20	3	44-2	117	4.46	101	.256	.306	0	ø	0	119	4	29	0.3
1994	Bal A★	16	5	.762	24	24	3	0-0	176.1	163	63	19	1	42-1	99	3.06	165	.248	.291	0	ø	0	95	37	0	4.0
1995	Bal A	**19**	9	.679	32	32	7-**4**	0-0	221.2	187	86	24	1	50-4	158	3.29	145	.226	.270	0	ø	0	91	36	0	4.1
1996	†Bal A	19	11	.633	36	**36**	4-1	0-0	243.1	264	137	31	3	69-0	204	4.81	103	.275	.325	0	ø	0	124	5	0	0.5
1997	†Bal A☆	15	8	.652	33	33	4-1	0-0	224.2	197	87	27	3	54-3	218	3.20	138	.234	.282	4	.250	0	109	31	0	2.8
1998	Bal A	13	10	.565	29	29	4-2	0-0	206.1	189	85	22	4	41-3	175	3.49	130	.242	.282	2	.000	-0	101	24	38	2.5
1999	Bal A★	18	7	.720	31	31	4	0-0	203.1	207	88	16	1	52-0	172	3.50	134	.268	.312	11	.273	1	129	27	0	3.2
2000	Bal A	11	15	.423	34	34	6-1	0-0	**237.2**	236	105	28	3	46-0	210	3.79	124	.255	.291	6	.000	-1	66	26	0	2.4
2001	†NY A	17	11	.607	34	34	4-3	0-0	228.2	202	87	20	4	42-2	214	3.15	141	.237	**.274**	7	.143	-0	86	33	0	3.7
2002	†NY A	18	10	.643	33	33	2-2	0-0	215.2	208	103	27	5	48-1	182	4.05	107	.253	.296	5-0-1	.600	1	125	9	0	1.3
2003	†NY A	17	8	.680	31	31	2-1	0-0	214.2	192	86	21	3	40-4	195	3.40	129	.238	.275	2	.000	-0	93	26	0	2.8
2004	†NY A	12	9	.571	27	27	1	0-0	164.2	178	91	22	2	40-1	132	4.59	100	.276	.318	1	.000	-0	110	0	42	0.0
2005	†NY A	13	8	.619	30	30	2-2	0-0	179.2	199	93	23	7	47-0	142	4.41	98	.283	.333	3	.000	-0	117	-1	0	-0.1
2006	†NY A	15	7	.682	32	32	1	0-0	197.1	184	88	22	5	35-1	172	3.51	129	.241	.279	4	.000	-0	117	20	13	1.9
Total	16	239	134	.641	475	475	57-23	0-0	3210.1	3058	1384	345	48	719-24	2572	3.63	125	.251	.293	45-0-1	.178	1	105	329	122	34.2
Mustaikis, Alex	Alexander Dominick; B3.26.1909 Chelsea MA; D1.17.1970 Scranton PA; BR/TR/6´3˝/180; d7.7																									
1940	Bos A	0	1	.000	6	1	0	0	15	15	18	1	0	15	6	9.00	50	.254	.405	6	.333	1	78	-8	—	-0.3
Mutis, Jeff	Jeffrey Thomas; B12.20.1966 Allentown PA; BL/TL/6´2˝/(185–195); [CleA88 1/27]; d6.15; Col Lafayette																									
1991	Cle A	0	3	.000	3	3	0	0-0	12.1	23	16	1	0	7-1	6	11.68	36	.397	.455	0	ø	0	66	-9	0	-1.4
1992	Cle A	0	2	.000	3	2	0	0-0	11.1	24	14	4	0	6-0	8	9.53	41	.429	.469	0	ø	0	58	-7	0	-1.0
1993	Cle A	3	6	.333	17	13	1-1	0-0	81	93	56	14	7	33-2	29	5.78	76	.289	.365	0	ø	0	86	-12	0	-1.1
1994	Fla N	1	0	1.000	35	0	0	0-0	38.1	51	25	6	1	15-3	30	5.40	82	.331	.390	3	.000	-0	—	-3	0	-0.2
Total	4	4	11	.267	58	18	1-1	0-0	143	191	111	25	8	61-6	73	6.48	67	.324	.390	3	.000	-0	79	-31	0	-3.7
Myers, Brett	Brett Allen; B8.17.1980 Jacksonville FL; BR/TR/6´4˝/(215–225); [PhiN99 1/12]; d7.24																									
2002	Phi N	4	5	.444	12	12	1	0-0	72	73	38	11	6	29-1	34	4.25	90	.277	.359	23-0-3	.130	-0	107	-4	0	-0.5
2003	Phi N	14	9	.609	32	32	1-1	0-0	193	205	99	20	9	76-8	143	4.43	90	.272	.344	62-0-5	.145	-0*	128	-9	0	-1.0
2004	Phi N	11	11	.500	32	31	1-1	0-0	176	196	113	31	6	62-4	116	5.52	80	.281	.343	51-0-8	.196	2	117	-19	0	-1.9
2005	Phi N	13	8	.619	34	34	2	0-0	215.1	193	94	31	11	68-2	208	3.72	117	.237	.304	65-0-11	.154	-0	121	15	0	1.4
2006	Phi N	12	7	.632	31	31	1	0-0	198	194	93	29	3	63-3	189	3.91	120	.257	.315	63-0-7	.032	-4	85	17	0	1.0
Total	5	54	40	.574	141	140	6-2	0-0	854.1	861	437	122	35	298-18	690	4.34	99	.262	.329	264-0-34	.129	-3	112	0	0	-1.0
Myers, Elmer	Elmer Glenn; B3.2.1894 York Springs PA; D7.29.1976 Collingswood NJ; BR/TR/6´2˝/185; d10.6; Mil 1918																									
1915	Phi A	1	0	1.000	1	1	1-1	0	9	2	0	0	0	5	12	0.00	ø	.074	.219	3-0-1	.000	-0	100	3	—	0.2
1916	Phi A	14	23	.378	44	35	31-2	1	315	280	169	7	14	168	182	3.66	78	.248	.353	126-0-4	.214	2*	85	-28	—	-2.5
1917	Phi A	9	16	.360	38	23	13-2	3	201.2	221	122	2	5	79	88	4.42	62	.283	.353	73-0-2	.247	2	97	-31	—	-3.4
1918	Phi A	4	8	.333	18	15	5-1	1	95.1	101	66	4	4	42	17	4.63	63	.283	.365	35	.143	-2	89	-18	—	-2.3
1919	Cle A	8	7	.533	23	15	6-1	1	134.2	134	68	3	10	43	38	3.74	89	.264	.334	46-0-1	.239	2	87	-4	—	-0.1
1920	Cle A	2	4	.333	16	7	2	1	71.2	93	52	1	4	23	16	4.77	80	.316	.374	25-0-2	.240	0	96	-10	—	-0.7
	Bos A	9	1	.900	12	10	9-1	0	97	90	30	1	2	24	34	2.13	171	.249	.299	38	.316	3	142	16	—	1.8
	Year	11	5	.688	28	17	11-1	1	168.2	183	82	2	6	47	50	3.25	114	.279	.333	63-0-2	.286	3	122	7	—	1.1
1921	Bos A	8	12	.400	30	20	11	0	172	217	107	11	10	53	40	4.87	87	.315	.373	65-0-1	.215	-2	94	-12	—	-1.4
1922	Bos A	0	1	.000	3	1	0	0	5.2	10	11	1	2	3	1	17.47	24	.370	.469	1	.000	-0	41	-7	—	-1.0
Total	8	55	72	.433	185	127	78-8	7	1102	1148	625	30	51	440	428	4.06	80	.275	.352	412-0-11	.226	4	94	-91	—	-9.4
Myers, Henry	Henry C.; B5.1858 Philadelphia PA; D4.18.1895 Philadelphia PA; BR/TR/5´9˝/159; d8.20.1881; M1; ▲																									
1882	Bal AA	0	2	.000	6	2	1	0	26	30	28	2	—	4	7	6.58	42	.270	.296	294	.180	-1*	84	-9	—	-0.6
Myers, Jimmy	James Xavier; B4.28.1969 Oklahoma City OK; BR/TR/6´1˝/190; [SFN87 35/902]; d4.6																									
1996	Bal A	0	0	ø	11	0	0	0-0	14	18	13	4	0	3-1	6	7.07	70	.305	.328	0	ø	0	—	-4	0	-0.2
Myers, Joseph	Joseph William; B3.18.1882 Wilmington DE; D2.11.1956 Delaware City DE; BR/TR/5´10.5˝/205; d10.7																									
1905	Phi A	0	0	ø	1	1	1	0	5	3	3	0	1	3	5	3.60	74	.176	.333	2	.000	-0	80	-1	—	-0.1

YEAR	TM LG	W	L	PCT	G	GS	CG-SHO	SV-BS	IP	H	R	HR	HB	BB-IB	SO	ERA	AERA	OAV	OOB	AB-HR-SH	AVG	PB	SUP	APR	DL	PW
MYERS, MIKE	Michael Stanley; B6.26.1969 Cook Co. IL; BL/TL/6´4˝/(197–220); [SFN90 4/122]; d4.25; Col Iowa St.; [DL 1994 Fla N 60]																									
1995	Fla N	0	0	ø	2	0	0	0-0	2	1	0	0	0	3-0	0	0.00	ø	.167	.444	0	ø	0	—	1	0	0.0
	Det A	1	0	1.000	11	0	0	0-1	6.1	10	7	1	2	4-0	4	9.95	48	.385	.485	0	ø	0	—	-3	0	-0.4
1996	Det A	1	5	.167	**83**	0	0	6-2	64.2	70	41	6	4	34-8	69	5.01	102	.272	.365	0	ø	0	—	0	0	0.0
1997	Det A	0	4	.000	**88**	0	0	2-3	53.2	58	36	12	2	25-2	50	5.70	81	.274	.351	0	ø	0	—	-6	0	-0.4
1998	Mil N	2	2	.500	70	0	0	1-2	50	44	19	5	6	22-1	40	2.70	161	.249	.348	0	ø	0	—	8	0	0.6
1999	Mil N	2	1	.667	71	0	0	0-3	41.1	46	24	7	3	13-1	35	5.23	88	.291	.356	1	.000	-0	—	-2	0	-0.1
2000	Col N	0	1	.000	78	0	0	1-1	45.1	24	10	2	2	24-3	41	1.99	292	.160	.284	0	ø	0	—	16	0	0.8
2001	Col N	2	3	.400	73	0	0	0-2	40	32	17	2	1	24-7	36	3.60	148	.225	.339	0	ø	0	—	6	0	0.8
2002	†Ari N	4	3	.571	69	0	0	4-5	37	39	18	2	8	17-0	31	4.38	102	.275	.381	0	ø	0	—	1	0	0.2
2003	Ari N	0	1	.000	64	0	0	0-3	36.1	38	23	4	5	21-1	21	5.70	81	.262	.374	0	ø	0	—	-3	0	-0.1
2004	Sea A	4	1	.800	50	0	0	0-0	27.2	29	15	3	2	17-4	23	4.88	92	.279	.387	0	ø	0	—	-1	0	-0.1
	†Bos A	1	0	1.000	25	0	0	0-0	15	16	7	2	0	6-1	9	4.20	116	.267	.333	0	ø	0	—	1	0	0.1
	Year	5	1	.833	75	0	0	0-0	42.2	45	22	5	2	23-5	32	4.64	99	.274	.368	0	ø	0	—	1	0	0.0
2005	†Bos A	3	1	.750	65	0	0	0-1	37.1	30	14	3	2	13-2	21	3.13	145	.224	.300	0	ø	0	—	6	0	0.6
2006	†NY A	1	2	.333	62	0	0	0-1	30.2	29	14	3	3	10-1	22	3.23	140	.244	.318	0	ø	0	—	3	0	0.3
Total	12	21	24	.467	811	0	0	14-24	487.1	466	245	52	40	233-31	402	4.23	114	.254	.349	1	.000	-0	—	27	60	2.3
MYERS, RANDY	Randall Kirk; B9.19.1962 Vancouver WA; BL/TL/6´1˝/(190–230); [NYN82 S1/9]; d10.6; Col Clark (WA) CC; [DL 1999 SD N 181, 2000 SD N 181]																									
1985	NY N	0	0	ø	1	0	0	0-0	2	0	0	0	0	1-0	2	0.00	ø	.000	.143	0	ø	0	—	1	0	0.1
1986	NY N	0	0	ø	10	0	0	0-0	10.2	11	5	1	1	9-1	13	4.22	85	.256	.396	0	ø	0	—	0	0	0.0
1987	NY N	3	6	.333	54	0	0	6-3	75	61	36	6	0	30-5	92	3.96	97	.225	.296	7	.286	0	—	-1	0	0.0
1988	†NY N	7	3	.700	55	0	0	26-3	68	45	15	5	2	17-2	69	1.72	190	.190	.248	4	.250	1	—	12	0	2.7
1989	NY N	7	4	.636	65	0	0	24-5	84.1	62	23	4	0	40-4	88	2.35	140	.206	.297	5	.000	-1	—	10	0	1.8
1990	†Cin N★	4	6	.400	66	0	0	31-6	86.2	59	24	6	3	38-8	98	2.08	190	.193	.287	4	.250	0	—	16	0	3.0
1991	Cin N	6	13	.316	58	12	1	6-4	132	116	61	8	1	80-5	108	3.55	107	.242	.347	29-0-3	.172	0	79	3	0	0.4
1992	SD N	3	6	.333	66	0	0	38-8	79.2	84	38	7	1	34-3	66	4.29	84	.279	.349	7-0-1	.143	-0	—	-4	0	-0.9
1993	Chi N	2	4	.333	73	0	0	**53**-6	75.1	65	26	7	1	26-2	86	3.11	130	.230	.295	2-0-1	.500	1*	—	9	0	1.8
1994	Chi N★	1	5	.167	38	0	0	21-5	40.1	40	18	3	0	16-1	32	3.79	111	.260	.327	1	.000	-0	—	2	0	0.4
1995	Chi N★	1	2	.333	57	0	0	**38**-6	55.2	49	25	7	0	28-1	59	3.88	108	.237	.324	0	ø	0	—	3	0	0.5
1996	†Bal A	4	4	.500	62	0	0	31-7	58.2	60	24	7	1	29-4	74	3.53	140	.265	.347	0	ø	0	—	10	0	1.8
1997	†Bal A★	2	3	.400	61	0	0	**45**-1	59.2	47	12	2	0	22-2	56	1.51	293	.217	.289	0	ø	0	—	19	0	3.8
1998	Tor A	3	4	.429	41	0	0	28-5	42.1	44	21	4	2	19-4	32	4.46	104	.265	.346	1	.000	-0	—	2	0	0.3
	†SD N	1	3	.250	21	0	0	0-1	14.1	15	10	2	0	7-1	9	6.28	63	.273	.355	0	ø	0	—	-4	0	-0.7
Total	14	44	63	.411	728	12	1	347-60	884.2	758	338	69	12	396-43	884	3.19	123	.233	.316	60-0-5	.183	2	79	78	362	15.0
MYERS, RODNEY	Rodney Luther; B6.26.1969 Rockford IL; BR/TR/6´1˝/(200–215); [KCA90 12/342]; d4.3; Col Wisconsin–Madison																									
1996	Chi N	2	1	.667	45	0	0	0-0	67.1	61	38	6	3	38-3	50	4.68	93	.243	.343	5	.000	-1	—	-2	0	-0.2
1997	Chi N	0	0	ø	5	1	0	0-0	9	12	6	1	1	7-1	6	6.00	72	.333	.455	0	ø	0	85	-1	0	-0.1
1998	Chi N	0	0	ø	12	0	0	0-1	18	26	14	3	0	6-0	15	7.00	63	.342	.390	1	.000	-0	—	-5	0	-0.2
1999	Chi N	3	1	.750	46	0	0	0-1	63.2	71	34	10	1	25-2	41	4.38	104	.289	.354	7	.429	1	—	1	0	0.1
2000	SD N	0	0	ø	3	0	0	0-0	2	2	1	0	0	0-0	3	4.50	99	.250	.250	0	ø	0	—	0	173	0.0
2001	SD N	1	2	.333	37	0	0	1-1	47.1	53	31	6	4	20-0	29	5.32	78	.291	.367	2	.000	-0	—	-6	29	-0.4
2002	SD N	1	1	.500	14	0	0	0-0	21.1	29	20	1	3	10-0	11	5.91	66	.333	.420	1	.000	-0	—	-7	0	-0.6
2003	LA N	0	0	ø	4	0	0	0-0	9	10	7	1	1	4-0	5	6.00	69	.270	.357	2	.000	-0	—	-2	0	-0.1
2004	LA N	0	0	ø	1	0	0	0-0	2	1	0	0	0	0-0	1	0.00	ø	.167	.167	0	ø	0	—	1	0	0.0
Total	9	7	5	.583	167	1	0	1-3	239.2	265	151	28	13	110-6	161	5.07	85	.285	.365	18	.167	0	85	-21	202	-1.5
MYETTE, AARON	Aaron Kenneth; B9.26.1977 New Westminster BC, Can.; BR/TR/6´4˝/(195–210); [ChiA97 1/43]; d9.7; Col Washington																									
1999	Chi A	0	2	.000	4	3	0	0-0	15.2	17	11	2	2	14-1	11	6.32	78	.266	.412	0	ø	0	38	-2	0	-0.2
2000	Chi A	0	0	ø	2	0	0	0-0	2.2	0	0	0	0	4-0	1	0.00	ø	.000	.333	0	ø	0	—	1	35	0.1
2001	Tex A	4	5	.444	19	15	0	0-0	80.2	94	65	12	11	37-0	67	7.14	67	.293	.381	0	ø	0	109	-19	0	-1.7
2002	Tex A	2	5	.286	15	12	0	0-0	48.1	64	57	11	6	41-0	48	10.06	48	.325	.448	0	ø	0	114	-26	0	-3.0
2003	Cle A	0	0	ø	2	0	0	0-0	2.2	7	7	1	1	2-0	1	23.63	19	.467	.556	0	ø	0	—	-5	20	-0.2
2004	Cin N	0	0	ø	5	0	0	0-0	4.1	3	4	0	2	8-0	6	8.31	52	.188	.500	0	ø	0	—	-2	0	-0.1
Total	6	6	12	.333	47	30	0	0-0	154.1	185	144	26	22	106-1	134	8.16	59	.298	.413	0	ø	0	104	-53	55	-5.1
MYRICK, BOB	Robert Howard; B10.1.1952 Hattiesburg MS; BR/TL/6´1˝/200; [NYN74 20/461]; d5.28; Col Mississippi St.; [DL 1979 NY N 33]																									
1976	NY N	1	1	.500	21	1	0	0-0	27.2	34	13	2	0	13-1	11	3.25	103	.306	.376	3	.000	-0	53	0	0	0.0
1977	NY N	2	2	.500	44	4	0	2-0	87.1	86	39	5	1	33-5	49	3.61	105	.265	.331	11	.182	-0	82	2	24	0.1
1978	NY N	0	3	.000	17	0	0	0-2	24.2	18	10	3	0	13-2	13	3.28	108	.207	.310	2	.000	-0	—	1	0	0.1
Total	3	3	6	.333	82	5	0	2-2	139.2	138	62	10	1	59-8	73	3.48	105	.264	.337	16	.125	-1	78	3	57	0.2
NABHOLZ, CHRIS	Christopher William; B1.5.1967 Harrisburg PA; BL/TL/6´5˝/(210–215); [MonN88 2/49]; d6.11; Col Towson																									
1990	Mon N	6	2	.750	11	11	1-1	0-0	70	43	23	6	2	32-1	53	2.83	130	.176	.274	21-0-2	.000	-2	87	7	0	0.6
1991	Mon N	8	7	.533	24	24	1	0-0	153.2	134	66	5	2	57-4	99	3.63	100	.237	.307	52-0-3	.115	-1	103	2	48	0.1
1992	Mon N	11	12	.478	32	32	1-1	0-0	195	176	80	11	5	74-2	130	3.32	105	.244	.317	65-0-7	.123	-1	107	3	0	0.5
1993	Mon N	9	8	.529	26	21	1	0-0	116.2	100	57	9	8	63-4	74	4.09	102	.236	.343	39-0-3	.128	-1	104	4	31	0.3
1994	Cle A	0	1	.000	6	4	0	0-0	11	23	16	1	1	9-0	5	11.45	42	.418	.500	0	ø	0	126	-8	40	-0.6
	Bos A	3	4	.429	8	8	0	0-0	42	44	32	5	2	29-1	23	6.64	76	.282	.399	0	ø	0	71	-6	0	-0.8
	Year	3	5	.375	14	12	0	0-0	53	67	48	6	3	38-1	28	7.64	65	.318	.425	0	ø	0	88	-14	0	-1.4
1995	Chi N	0	1	.000	34	0	0	0-0	23.1	22	15	4	0	14-3	21	5.40	77	.253	.350	1	.000	-0	—	-3	35	-0.1
Total	6	37	35	.514	141	100	4-2	0-0	611.2	542	289	41	20	278-15	405	3.94	97	.240	.327	178-0-15	.107	-5	101	-1	154	-0.0
NABORS, JACK	Herman John; B11.19.1887 Montevallo AL; D10.29.1923 Wilton AL; BR/TR/6´3˝/185; d8.9																									
1915	Phi A	0	5	.000	10	7	2	0	54	58	46	1	5	35	18	5.50	53	.304	.424	16-0-1	.125	-1	93	-16	—	-1.4
1916	Phi A	1	20	.048	40	30	11	1	212.2	206	110	2	3	95	74	3.47	82	.266	.349	69	.101	-4	68	-15	—	-2.0
1917	Phi A	0	0	ø	2	0	0	0	3	2	1	0	0	1	2	3.00	92	.200	.273	0	ø	0	—	0	—	0.0
Total	3	1	25	.038	52	37	13	1	269.2	266	157	3	8	131	94	3.87	74	.273	.364	85-0-1	.106	-6	73	-31	—	-3.4
NAGEOTTE, CLINT	Clinton Scott; B10.25.1980 Parma OH; BR/TR/6´3˝/(200–225); [SeaA99 5/155]; d6.1																									
2004	Sea A	1	6	.143	12	5	0	0-0	36.2	48	31	3	4	27-1	24	7.36	61	.324	.436	2	.000	-0	95	-12	37	-1.7
2005	Sea A	0	0	ø	3	0	0	0-0	4	6	3	0	1	1-0	1	6.75	62	.353	.421	0	ø	0	—	-1	0	0.0
2006	Sea A	0	0	ø	1	0	0	0-0	1	2	3	1	0	2-1	1	27.00	16	.400	.571	0	ø	0	—	-2	0	-0.1
Total	3	1	6	.143	16	5	0	0-0	41.2	56	37	4	5	30-2	26	7.78	57	.329	.440	2	.000	-0	95	-15	37	-1.8
NAGLE, JUDGE	Walter Harold "Lucky"; B3.10.1880 Santa Rosa CA; D5.26.1971 Santa Rosa CA; BR/TR/6´0˝/176; d4.26																									
1911	Pit N	4	2	.667	8	3	1	1	27.1	33	16	3	1	6	11	3.62	95	.324	.367	7	.143	-0	73	-1	—	-0.3
	Bos A	1	1	.500	5	1	0	0	27	27	12	2	0	6	12	3.33	98	.262	.303	10-0-1	.100	-1	110	1	—	-0.1
Total	1	5	3	.625	13	4	1	1	54.1	60	28	5	1	12	23	3.48	97	.293	.335	17-0-1	.118	-1	82	0	—	-0.4
NAGY, CHARLES	Charles Harrison; B5.5.1967 Bridgeport CT; BL/TR/6´3˝/200; [CleA88 1/17]; d6.29; Col Connecticut																									
1990	Cle A	2	4	.333	9	8	0	0-0	45.2	58	31	7	1	21-1	26	5.91	67	.315	.386	0	ø	0	87	-9	0	-1.0
1991	Cle A	10	15	.400	33	33	6-1	0-0	211.1	228	103	15	6	66-7	109	4.13	101	.275	.330	0	ø	0	71	3	0	0.3
1992	Cle A★	17	10	.630	33	33	10-3	0-0	252	245	91	11	2	57-1	169	2.96	133	.260	.300	0	ø	0	95	28	0	3.1
1993	Cle A	2	6	.250	9	9	1	0-0	48.2	66	38	6	2	13-1	30	6.29	70	.322	.367	0	ø	0	112	-10	138	-1.3
1994	Cle A	10	8	.556	23	23	3	0-0	169.1	175	76	15	5	48-1	108	3.45	138	.265	.319	0	ø	0	117	24	0	2.2
1995	†Cle A	16	6	.727	29	29	2-1	0-0	178	194	95	20	6	61-0	139	4.55	104	.278	.339	0	ø	0	135	5	0	0.7
1996	†Cle A★	17	5	**.773**	32	32	5	0-0	222	217	89	21	3	61-2	167	3.41	144	.255	.306	0	ø	0	105	39	0	3.5
1997	†Cle A	15	11	.577	34	34	1-1	0-0	227	253	115	27	7	77-4	149	4.28	110	.282	.342	5	.200	0	106	11	0	1.3
1998	†Cle A	15	10	.600	33	33	2	0-0	210.1	250	139	34	9	66-12	120	5.22	92	.297	.352	5	.000	-1	109	-13	0	-1.2
1999	†Cle A☆	17	11	.607	33	32	1	0-0	202	238	120	26	6	59-4	126	4.95	103	.293	.344	6	.000	-1*	115	3	0	0.4
2000	Cle A	2	7	.222	11	11	0	0-0	57	71	53	15	2	21-2	41	8.21	61	.300	.359	0	ø	0	95	-19	125	-2.2
2001	Cle A	5	6	.455	15	13	0	0-0	70.1	102	53	10	0	20-1	29	6,40	72	.342	.379	1-0-1	1.000	0	126	-13	106	-1.6
2002	Cle A	1	4	.200	19	7	0	0-0	48.2	76	51	10	2	13-1	22	8.88	50	.360	.399	0	ø	0*	74	-24	45	-2.0

YEAR	TM LG	W	L	PCT	G	GS	CG-SHO	SV-BS	IP	H	R	HR	HB	BB-IB	SO	ERA	AERA	OAV	OOB	AB-HR-SH	AVG	PB	SUP	APR	DL	PW
2003	SD N	0	2	.000	5	0	0	0-0	12.1	15	7	0	0	3-0	7	4.38	92	.313	.353	2	.000	-0	—	-1	0	-0.1
Total	14	129	105	.551	318	297	31-6	0-0	1954.2	2188	1061	217	51	586-37	1242	4.51	102	.284	.336	19-0-1	.105	-1	106	24	414	2.1
Nagy, Mike	Michael Timothy; B3.25.1948 Bronx NY; BR/TR/6´3˝/(195–200); d4.21																									
1969	Bos A	12	2	.857	33	28	7-1	0-0	196.2	183	84	10	11	106-3	84	3.11	123	.245	.347	65-0-4	.077	-2*	128	12	0	0.6
1970	Bos A	6	5	.545	23	20	4	0-0	128.2	138	71	16	2	64-2	56	4.48	89	.275	.358	44-0-2	.250	2	114	-5	0	-0.3
1971	Bos A	1	3	.250	12	7	0	0-1	38	46	29	4	0	20-1	9	6.63	56	.315	.395	12	.083	-1	89	-11	0	-1.1
1972	Bos A	0	0	ø	1	0	0	0-0	2	3	2	0	1	0-0	2	9.00	36	.375	.400	0	ø	0	—	-1	0	-0.1
1973	StL N	0	2	.000	9	7	0	0-0	40.2	44	21	4	1	15-2	14	4.20	87	.282	.345	11	.091	-1	86	-2	0	-0.2
1974	Hou N	1	1	.500	9	0	0	0-0	12.2	17	13	3	1	5-0	5	8.53	41	.309	.371	1	.000	-0	—	-7	0	-1.0
Total	6	20	13	.606	87	62	11-1	0-1	418.2	431	220	37	16	210-8	170	4.15	92	.267	.356	133-0-6	.135	-2	115	-14	0	-2.1
Nagy, Steve	Stephen; B5.28.1919 Franklin NJ; BL/TL/5´10˝/170; d4.20; Col Seton Hall																									
1947	Pit N	1	3	.250	6	1	0	0	14	18	10	1	0	9	4	5.79	73	.310	.403	4	.250	0	21	-2	0	-0.4
1950	Was A	2	5	.286	9	9	2	0	53.1	69	50	5	0	29	17	6.58	68	.307	.386	22-1-1	.227	2*	85	-15	0	-1.3
Total	2	3	8	.273	15	10	2	0	67.1	87	60	6	0	38	21	6.42	69	.307	.389	26-1-1	.231	2	79	-17	0	-1.7
Nahem, Sam	Samuel Ralph "Subway Sam"; B10.19.1915 New York NY; D4.19.2004 Berkeley CA; BR/TR/6´1.5˝/190; d10.2; Mil 1943–45																									
1938	Bro N	1	0	1.000	1	1	1	0	9	6	3	0	0	4	2	3.00	130	.194	.286	5	.400	0	152	1	—	0.2
1941	StL N	5	2	.714	26	8	2	1	81.2	76	35	2	2	38	31	2.98	126	.243	.329	23-0-6	.174	-1	135	6	0	0.4
1942	Phi N	1	3	.250	35	2	0	0	74.2	72	48	2	2	40	38	4.94	67	.254	.350	20	.100	-1	102	-14	0	-0.8
1948	Phi N	3	3	.500	28	1	0	0	59	68	52	4	3	45	30	7.02	56	.288	.408	13	.154	-0	90	-19	0	-1.8
Total	4	10	8	.556	90	12	3	1	224.1	222	138	8	7	127	101	4.69	78	.257	.357	61-0-6	.164	-2	130	-26	0	-2.0
Nakamura, Micheal	Micheal Yoshihide; B9.6.1976 Nara, Japan; BR/TR/5´10˝/170; d6.7; Col South Alabama																									
2003	Min A	0	0	ø	12	0	0	1-0	12.2	20	11	4	1	2-0	14	7.82	58	.339	.371	0	ø	0	—	-4	0	-0.2
2004	Tor A	0	3	.000	19	0	0	0-0	25.2	27	23	7	2	7-0	24	7.36	67	.262	.319	0	ø	0	—	-7	0	-0.7
Total	2	0	3	.000	31	0	0	1-0	38.1	47	34	11	3	9-0	38	7.51	63	.290	.337	0	ø	0	—	-11	0	-0.9
Naktenis, Pete	Peter Ernest; B6.12.1914 Aberdeen WA; BL/TL/6´1˝/185; d6.13; Col Duke																									
1936	Phi A	0	1	.000	7	1	0	0	18.2	24	26	2	2	27	18	12.54	41	.324	.515	5	.200	-0	34	-14	—	-0.6
1939	Cin N	0	0	ø	3	0	0	0	4	2	1	0	2	0	1	2.25	170	.154	.267	0	ø	0	—	1	—	0.1
Total	2	0	1	.000	10	1	0	0	22.2	26	27	2	4	27	19	10.72	45	.299	.483	5	.200	-0	34	-13	—	-0.5
Nance, Shane	Joseph Shane; B9.7.1977 Houston TX; BL/TL/5´8˝/(180–190); [LAN00 11/327]; d8.24; Col Houston																									
2002	Mil N	0	0	ø	4	0	0	0-0	6.1	4	3	1	0	4-0	5	4.26	97	.174	.296	3	.333	0	—	0	29	0.0
2003	Mil N	0	2	.000	26	0	0	0-1	24.1	34	16	5	1	10-1	25	4.81	90	.327	.385	0	ø	0	—	-2	0	-0.1
2004	Ari N	1	1	.500	19	0	0	0-1	12.1	19	11	2	3	12-4	9	5.84	78	.352	.493	0	ø	0	—	-2	33	-0.4
Total	3	1	3	.250	49	0	0	0-2	43	57	30	8	4	26-5	39	5.02	87	.315	.408	3	.333	0	—	-4	62	-0.5
Napier, Buddy	Skelton Le Roy; B12.18.1889 Byromville GA; D3.29.1968 Hutchins TX; BR/TR/5´11˝/165; d8.14																									
1912	StL A	1	2	.333	7	2	0	0	25.1	33	21	0	3	5	10	4.97	67	.317	.366	7	.000	-1	22	-5	—	-0.7
1918	Chi N	0	0	ø	1	0	0	0	6.2	10	4	0	0	4	2	5.40	52	.357	.438	3	.333	0	—	-1	—	-0.1
1920	Cin N	4	2	.667	9	5	5-1	0	49	47	12	0	1	7	17	1.29	236	.254	.285	14	.214	1	119	9	—	1.2
1921	Cin N	0	2	.000	22	6	1	1	56.2	72	38	2	0	13	14	5.56	64	.329	.366	14	.143	1	100	-11	—	-0.4
Total	4	5	6	.455	39	13	6-1	1	137.2	162	75	2	4	29	43	3.92	84	.302	.343	38	.158	1	94	-8	—	0.0
Naranjo, Cholly	Lazaro Ramon Gonzalo "Gonzalo"; B11.25.1934 Havana, Cuba; BL/TR/5´11.5˝/165; d7.8																									
1956	Pit N	1	2	.333	17	3	0	0	34.1	37	22	7	1	17-1	26	4.46	85	.282	.364	7	.143	0	62	-4	0	-0.2
Narleski, Ray	Raymond Edmond; B11.25.1928 Camden NJ; BR/TR/6´1˝/(175–185); d4.17; f–Bill; [DL 1960 Det A 156]																									
1954	†Cle A	3	3	.500	42	2	1	13	89	59	25	8	2	44	52	2.22	165	.189	.293	16-0-2	.000	-2	60	15	0	1.2
1955	Cle A	9	1	.900	**60**	1	1	**19**	111.2	91	47	11	0	52-3	94	3.71	108	.220	.306	24-0-3	.292	1	67	6	0	0.7
1956	Cle A✳	3	2	.600	32	0	0	4	59.1	36	11	5	1	19-0	42	1.52	277	.170	.240	8	.250	0	—	**18**	0	1.6
1957	Cle A	11	5	.688	46	15	7-1	16	154.1	136	65	15	4	70-6	93	3.09	120	.235	.320	43-1-4	.093	-2	112	9	0	0.7
1958	Cle A★	13	10	.565	44	24	7	1	183.1	179	87	21	3	91-10	102	4.07	90	.255	.341	54-0-4	.204	1	126	-6	0	-0.8
1959	Det A	4	12	.250	42	10	1	5	104.1	105	83	21	1	59-3	71	5.78	70	.254	.343	21-0-4	.095	-1	100	-21	0	-3.3
Total	6	43	33	.566	266	52	17-1	58	702	606	318	81	11	335-22	454	3.60	106	.230	.318	166-1-17	.157	-2	110	21	156	0.1
Narron, Sam	Samuel Franklin; B7.12.1981 Goldsboro NC; BL/TL/6´7˝/210; [TexA02 15/442]; d7.30; gf–Sam; Col East Carolina																									
2004	Tex A	0	0	ø	1	1	0	0-0	2.2	5	4	3	0	4-0	1	13.50	37	.385	.529	0	ø	0	131	-2	0	-0.1
Narum, Buster	Leslie Ferdinand; B11.16.1940 Philadelphia PA; D5.17.2004 Clearwater FL; BR/TR/6´1˝/200; d4.14																									
1963	Bal A	0	0	ø	7	0	0	0	9	8	3	0	0	5-2	5	3.00	116	.242	.342	1-1-0	1.000	1	—	1	0	0.2
1964	Was A	9	15	.375	38	32	7-2	0	199	195	104	31	5	73-4	121	4.30	86	.259	.325	66-1-5	.061	-5	89	-10	0	-1.8
1965	Was A	4	12	.250	46	24	2	0	173.2	176	98	16	7	91-11	86	4.46	78	.267	.360	46-1-6	.043	-2	93	-18	0	-1.7
1966	Was A	0	0	ø	3	0	0	0	3.1	11	9	2	0	4-0	0	21.60	16	.579	.652	0	ø	0	—	-7	0	-0.3
1967	Was A	1	0	1.000	2	2	0	0	11.2	8	4	1	0	4-0	8	3.09	103	.195	.267	5	.000	-1	96	0	0	0.0
Total	5	14	27	.341	96	58	9-2	0	396.2	398	218	50	12	177-17	220	4.45	80	.264	.344	118-3-11	.059	-6	91	-34	0	-3.6
Narveson, Chris	Christopher Gregg; B12.20.1981 Englewood CO; BL/TL/6´3˝/205; [StLN00 2/53]; d9.8																									
2006	StL N	0	0	ø	5	1	0	0-0	9.1	6	5	1	1	5-0	12	4.82	90	.176	.300	1	.000	-0	106	0	0	0.0
Nash, Jim	James Edwin; B2.9.1945 Hawthorne NV; BR/TR/6´5˝/(215–220); d7.3																									
1966	KC A	12	1	.923	18	17	5	1	127	95	32	6	0	47-3	98	2.06	165	.204	.276	49-0-3	.102	-2	140	20	0	1.8
1967	KC A	12	17	.414	37	34	8-2	0	222.1	200	103	21	4	87-5	186	3.76	85	.242	.314	70-0-3	.100	-2	93	-14	0	-2.0
1968	Oak A	13	13	.500	34	33	12-6	0	228.2	185	63	18	3	55-12	169	2.28	124	.219	.269	74-2-6	.068	-2	100	16	0	1.5
1969	Oak A	8	8	.500	26	19	3-1	0-0	115.1	112	53	17	2	30-3	75	3.67	94	.247	.296	36-0-3	.111	-1	122	-4	24	-0.6
1970	Atl N	13	9	.591	34	33	6-2	0-0	212.1	211	105	22	5	90-7	153	4.07	105	.257	.332	80-2-3	.087	-3	107	6	0	0.2
1971	Atl N	9	7	.563	32	19	2	2-0	133	166	81	17	0	50-3	65	4.94	75	.314	.370	47	.149	-1*	120	-16	0	-2.0
1972	Atl N	1	1	.500	11	4	0	1-0	31.1	35	20	2	0	25-1	10	5.46	70	.307	.420	9	.222	0	99	-5	0	-0.3
	Phi N	0	8	.000	9	8	0	0-0	37.1	46	33	5	3	17-2	15	6.27	58	.311	.384	10	.100	-0	61	-12	36	-2.2
	Year	1	9	.100	20	12	0	1-0	68.2	81	53	7	3	42-3	25	5.90	63	.309	.400	19	.158	-0	74	-16	0	-2.5
Total	7	68	64	.515	201	167	36-11	4-0	1107.1	1050	490	108	17	401-36	771	3.58	96	.250	.316	375-4-18	.101	-11	108	-9	60	-3.6
Nastu, Philip	Philip; B3.8.1955 Bridgeport CT; BL/TL/6´2˝/180; d9.15; Col Bridgeport																									
1978	SF N	0	1	.000	3	1	0	0-0	8	8	5	1	0	2-0	5	5.63	62	.258	.303	1	.000	-0	0	-2	0	-0.2
1979	SF N	3	4	.429	25	14	1	0-0	100	105	51	14	2	41-5	47	4.32	81	.272	.344	24-0-4	.042	-1	110	-8	0	-0.6
1980	SF N	0	0	ø	6	0	0	0-0	6	10	9	1	0	5-1	1	6.00	59	.357	.455	0	ø	0	—	-4	0	-0.2
Total	3	3	5	.375	34	15	1	0-0	114	123	65	16	2	48-6	53	4.50	78	.276	.349	25-0-4	.040	-1	103	-14	0	-1.0
Nathan, Joe	Joseph Michael; B11.22.1974 Houston TX; BR/TR/6´4˝/(195–220); [SFN95 6/159]; d4.21; Col Stony Brook																									
1999	SF N	7	4	.636	19	14	0	1-0	90.1	84	45	17	1	46-0	54	4.18	102	.243	.333	28-0-5	.179	1	112	1	0	0.2
2000	SF N	5	2	.714	20	15	0	0-1	93.1	89	63	12	4	63-4	61	5.21	84	.255	.371	32-2-4	.156	2	139	-11	58	-0.5
2002	SF N	0	0	ø	4	0	0	0-0	3.2	1	0	0	0	0-0	2	0.00	ø	.083	.083	0	ø	0	—	2	0	0.1
2003	†SF N	12	4	.750	78	0	0	0-3	79	51	26	7	3	33-3	83	2.96	144	.186	.277	1-0-1	.000	-0	—	12	0	2.2
2004	†Min A★	1	2	.333	73	0	0	44-3	72.1	48	14	3	2	23-3	89	1.62	286	.187	.259	1	.000	-0	—	24	0	3.6
2005	Min A★	7	4	.636	69	0	0	43-5	70	46	22	5	0	22-1	94	2.70	162	.183	.247	0	ø	0	—	13	0	2.6
2006	†Min A	7	0	1.000	64	0	0	36-2	68.1	38	12	3	1	16-4	95	1.58	289	.158	.212	1	.000	-0	—	23	0	4.2
Total	7	39	16	.709	327	29	0	124-14	477	357	182	47	11	203-15	478	3.17	139	.206	.292	63-2-10	.159	3	125	64	58	12.4
Nation, Joey	Joseph Paul; B9.28.1978 Oklahoma City OK; BL/TL/6´2˝/205; [AtlN97 2/80]; d9.23																									
2000	Chi N	0	2	.000	2	2	0	0-0	11.2	12	9	2	2	8-0	8	6.94	66	.279	.407	4	.500	1	70	-3	0	-0.3

NAULTY, DAN Daniel Donovan; B1.6.1970 Los Angeles CA; BR/TR/6´6˝/(211–224); [MinA92 14/402]; d4.2; Col Cal St.–Fullerton

YEAR	TM LG	W	L	PCT	G	GS	CG-SHO	SV-BS	IP	H	R	HR	HB	BB-IB	SO	ERA	AERA	OAV	OOB	AB-HR-SH	AVG	PB	SUP	APR	DL	PW
1996	Min A	3	2	.600	49	0	0	4-5	57	43	26	5	0	35-3	56	3.79	135	.207	.321	0	ø	0	—	8	56	0.7
1997	Min A	1	1	.500	29	0	0	1-2	30.2	29	20	8	0	10-0	23	5.87	80	.254	.305	0	ø	0	—	-3	98	-0.2
1998	Min A	0	2	.000	19	0	0	0-1	23.2	25	16	3	0	10-1	15	4.94	97	.269	.337	0	ø	0	—	-1	78	-0.1
1999	NY A	1	0	1.000	33	0	0	0-0	49.1	40	24	8	4	22-0	25	4.38	108	.225	.322	0	ø	0	—	3	0	0.2
Total	4	5	5	.500	130	0	0	5-8	160.2	137	86	24	4	77-4	119	4.54	107	.231	.321	0	ø	0	—	7	232	0.6

NAVARRO, JAIME Jaime (Cintron); B3.27.1967 Bayamon, PR; BR/TR/6´4˝/(210–250); [MilA87 3/71]; d6.20; f–Julio; Col Miami–Dade Wolfson (FL) CC

YEAR	TM LG	W	L	PCT	G	GS	CG-SHO	SV-BS	IP	H	R	HR	HB	BB-IB	SO	ERA	AERA	OAV	OOB	AB-HR-SH	AVG	PB	SUP	APR	DL	PW
1989	Mil A	7	8	.467	19	17	1	0-0	109.2	119	47	6	1	32-3	56	3.12	124	.277	.327	0	ø	0	77	7	0	0.9
1990	Mil A	8	7	.533	32	22	3	1-1	149.1	176	83	11	4	41-3	75	4.46	87	.293	.340	0	ø	0	124	-9	0	-0.8
1991	Mil A	15	12	.556	34	34	10-2	0-0	234	237	117	18	6	73-3	114	3.92	102	.261	.318	0	ø	0	105	-1	0	-0.1
1992	Mil A	17	11	.607	34	34	5-3	0-0	246	224	98	14	6	64-4	100	3.33	116	.246	.295	0	ø	0	106	16	0	1.5
1993	Mil A	11	12	.478	35	34	5-1	0-0	214.1	254	135	21	11	73-4	114	5.33	81	.300	.356	0	ø	0	101	-22	0	-2.1
1994	Mil A	4	9	.308	29	10	0	0-0	89.2	115	71	10	4	35-4	65	6.62	77	.314	.377	0	ø	0	78	-14	0	-1.7
1995	Chi N	14	6	.700	29	29	1-1	0-0	200.1	194	79	19	3	56-7	128	3.28	127	.251	.303	65-0-8	.185	1	108	21	0	1.9
1996	Chi N	15	12	.556	35	35	4-1	0-0	236.2	244	116	25	10	72-5	158	3.92	112	.269	.327	77-0-8	.130	-2	98	10	0	0.6
1997	Chi A	9	14	.391	33	33	2	0-0	209.2	267	155	22	3	73-6	142	5.79	76	.309	.359	1-0-1	.000	-0	109	-36	0	-3.3
1998	Chi A	8	16	.333	37	27	1	1-0	172.2	223	135	30	7	77-1	71	6.36	72	.315	.384	1	.000	-0	102	-34	0	-4.0
1999	Chi A	8	13	.381	32	27	0	0-0	159.2	206	126	29	11	71-1	74	6.09	81	.313	.387	3-0-1	.000	-0	94	-23	0	-2.5
2000	Mil N	0	5	.000	5	5	0	0-0	18.2	34	31	6	0	18-3	7	12.54	37	.410	.505	5	.000	-1	64	-18	0	-2.6
	Cle A	0	1	.000	7	2	0	0-0	14.2	20	13	3	1	5-0	9	7.98	63	.328	.377	0	ø	0	140	-4	0	-0.3
Total	12	116	126	.479	361	309	32-8	2-1	2055.1	2313	1206	214	67	690-44	1113	4.72	91	.285	.342	152-0-18	.145	-2	102	-107	0	-12.5

NAVARRO, JULIO Julio (Ventura) "Whiplash"; B1.9.1936 Vieques, PR; BR/TR/5´11˝/(180–190); d9.3; s–Jaime

YEAR	TM LG	W	L	PCT	G	GS	CG-SHO	SV-BS	IP	H	R	HR	HB	BB-IB	SO	ERA	AERA	OAV	OOB	AB-HR-SH	AVG	PB	SUP	APR	DL	PW
1962	LA A	1	1	.500	9	0	0	0	15.1	20	9	2	0	4-2	11	4.70	82	.317	.353	2	.500	0	—	-1	0	-0.1
1963	LA A	4	5	.444	57	0	0	12	90.1	75	36	7	2	32-6	53	2.89	119	.228	.296	15-0-1	.200	1	—	5	0	0.7
1964	LA A	0	0	ø	5	0	0	1	9.1	5	2	0	2	5-0	8	1.93	170	.167	.324	2	.000	-0	—	2	0	0.1
	Det A	2	1	.667	26	0	0	2	41	40	19	9	2	16-1	36	3.95	93	.250	.324	5	.000	-1	—	-1	0	-0.2
	Year	2	1	.667	31	0	0	3	50.1	45	21	9	4	21-1	44	3.58	100	.237	.324	7	.000	-1	—	1	0	-0.1
1965	Det A	0	2	.000	15	1	0	1	30	25	16	5	0	12-1	22	4.20	83	.238	.308	4-0-1	.000	-0	126	-3	0	-0.2
1966	Det A	0	0	ø	1	0	0	0	0	2	3	2	1	0-0	0	(3)	ø	1.000	1.000	0	ø	0	—	-3	0	-0.3
1970	Atl N	0	0	ø	17	0	0	1-1	26.1	24	12	7	1	1-0	21	4.10	105	.233	.248	6	.167	-0	—	1	0	0.0
Total	6	7	9	.438	130	1	0	17-1	212.1	191	97	32	8	70-10	151	3.65	99	.241	.306	34-0-2	.147	-0	126	0	0	0.0

NAYLOR, EARL Earl Eugene; B5.19.1919 Kansas City MO; D1.16.1990 Winter Haven FL; BR/TR/6´0˝/190; d4.15; Mil 1944–45; ▲

YEAR	TM LG	W	L	PCT	G	GS	CG-SHO	SV-BS	IP	H	R	HR	HB	BB-IB	SO	ERA	AERA	OAV	OOB	AB-HR-SH	AVG	PB	SUP	APR	DL	PW
1942	Phi N	0	5	.000	20	4	1	0	60.1	68	43	5	0	29	19	6.12	54	.286	.363	168-0-3	.196	1*	38	-17	0	-1.2

NAYLOR, ROLLIE Roleine Cecil; B2.4.1892 Krum TX; D6.18.1966 Fort Worth TX; BR/TR/6´1.5˝/180; d9.14; Mil 1918

YEAR	TM LG	W	L	PCT	G	GS	CG-SHO	SV-BS	IP	H	R	HR	HB	BB-IB	SO	ERA	AERA	OAV	OOB	AB-HR-SH	AVG	PB	SUP	APR	DL	PW
1917	Phi A	2	2	.500	5	5	3	0	33	30	10	1	1	11	11	1.64	168	.265	.336	11	.091	-1	94	3	—	0.4
1919	Phi A	5	18	.217	31	23	17	0	204.2	210	109	2	4	64	68	3.34	103	.280	.339	71-0-4	.169	-2	51	-3	—	-0.6
1920	Phi A	10	23	.303	42	36	20	0	251.1	306	147	7	6	86	90	3.47	116	.312	.371	86-0-2	.163	-6	69	10	—	0.7
1921	Phi A	3	13	.188	32	19	6	0	169.1	214	106	10	3	55	39	4.84	92	.315	.369	52-0-1	.115	-4*	93	-4	—	-0.7
1922	Phi A	10	15	.400	35	26	11	0	171.1	212	115	7	3	51	37	4.73	90	.309	.359	55-1-2	.200	1*	98	-12	—	-1.3
1923	Phi A	12	7	.632	26	20	9-2	0	143	149	68	5	0	59	27	3.46	119	.273	.344	45	.244	1	104	10	—	1.2
1924	Phi A	0	5	.000	10	7	1	0	38.1	53	29	2	0	20	10	6.34	68	.333	.408	8	.375	1	43	-7	—	-0.7
Total	7	42	83	.336	181	136	67-2	0	1011	1174	584	34	17	346	282	3.93	102	.300	.359	328-1-9	.177	-11	80	-3	—	-1.0

NAYMICK, MIKE Michael John; B8.26.1917 Berlin PA; D10.12.2005 Stockton CA; BR/TR/6´8˝/225; d9.24

YEAR	TM LG	W	L	PCT	G	GS	CG-SHO	SV-BS	IP	H	R	HR	HB	BB-IB	SO	ERA	AERA	OAV	OOB	AB-HR-SH	AVG	PB	SUP	APR	DL	PW
1939	Cle A	0	1	.000	2	1	1	0	4.2	3	1	0	0	5	3	1.93	228	.188	.381	3	.000	-0	0	1	—	0.2
1940	Cle A	1	2	.333	13	4	0	0	30	36	17	1	3	17	15	5.10	83	.290	.389	6	.167	0	78	-2	—	-0.1
1943	Cle A	4	4	.500	29	4	0	2	62.2	32	23	3	3	47	41	2.30	135	.160	.328	16-0-2	.188	-0	61	4	0	0.5
1944	Cle A	0	0	ø	7	0	0	0	13	16	15	1	0	10	4	9.69	34	.314	.426	1	.000	-0	—	-9	0	-0.5
	StL N	0	0	ø	1	0	0	0	2	2	1	0	0	1	1	4.50	78	.333	.429	0	ø	0	—	0	0	0.0
Total	4	5	7	.417	52	9	1	2	112.1	89	57	5	6	80	64	3.93	89	.224	.362	26-0-2	.154	-1	65	-6	0	0.1

NEAGLE, DENNY Dennis Edward; B9.13.1968 Gambrills MD; BL/TL/6´2˝/(200–225); [MinA89 3/85]; d7.27; Col Minnesota; [DL 2004 Col N 183]

YEAR	TM LG	W	L	PCT	G	GS	CG-SHO	SV-BS	IP	H	R	HR	HB	BB-IB	SO	ERA	AERA	OAV	OOB	AB-HR-SH	AVG	PB	SUP	APR	DL	PW
1991	Min A	0	1	.000	7	3	0	0-0	20	28	9	3	0	7-2	14	4.05	106	.329	.380	0	ø	0	100	1	15	0.0
1992	†Pit N	4	6	.400	55	6	0	2-2	86.1	81	46	9	2	43-8	77	4.48	77	.247	.335	11-0-2	.000	-1*	100	-10	0	-1.3
1993	Pit N	3	5	.375	50	7	0	1-0	81.1	82	49	10	3	37-3	73	5.31	77	.258	.340	14-0-2	.000	-2	88	-10	0	-1.1
1994	Pit N	9	10	.474	24	24	2	0-0	137	135	80	18	3	49-3	122	5.12	85	.259	.322	42-1-5	.190	1	82	-8	0	-0.9
1995	Pit N★	13	8	.619	31	**31**	5-1	0-0	**209.2**	221	91	20	3	45-3	150	3.43	127	.273	.312	74-1-5	.122	-1*	103	19	0	1.8
1996	Pit N	14	6	.700	27	27	1	0-0	182.2	186	67	21	3	34-2	131	3.05	144	.267	.303	55-0-16	.182	-0*	93	27	0	2.7
	†Atl N	2	3	.400	6	6	1	0-0	38.2	40	26	5	0	14-0	18	5.59	80	.268	.329	14	.143	-0	81	-4	0	-0.5
	Year	16	9	.640	33	33	2	0-0	221.1	226	93	26	3	48-2	149	3.50	126	.267	.308	69-0-16	.174	-0	91	23	0	2.2
1997	†Atl N☆	**20**	5	.800	34	34	4-4	0-0	233.1	204	87	18	6	49-5	172	2.97	141	.233	.277	72-1-9	.153	1	113	32	0	3.3
1998	†Atl N	16	11	.593	32	31	5-2	0-0	210.1	196	91	25	6	60-3	165	3.55	117	.250	.307	63-0-9	.175	1	113	15	0	1.8
1999	Cin N	9	5	.643	20	19	0	0-0	111.2	95	54	23	4	40-3	76	4.27	110	.229	.300	37-0-5	.162	-0	120	7	87	0.6
2000	Cin N	8	2	.800	18	18	0	0-0	117.2	111	48	15	3	50-3	88	3.52	136	.247	.325	37-0-7	.189	1*	116	17	0	1.3
	†NY A	7	7	.500	16	15	1	0-0	91.1	99	61	16	2	31-1	58	5.81	82	.278	.335	0	ø	0	114	-10	0	-1.2
2001	Col N	9	8	.529	30	30	0	0-0	170.2	192	107	29	7	60-3	139	5.38	99	.284	.344	56-2-8	.196	2	104	0	15	0.2
2002	Col N	8	11	.421	35	28	1	0-0	164.1	170	101	26	10	63-5	111	5.26	90	.266	.338	45-0-5	.267	2	85	-7	0	-0.5
2003	Col N	2	4	.333	7	7	0	0-0	35.1	47	31	12	1	12-0	21	7.90	62	.320	.375	11-0-2	.000	-1	74	-9	149	-1.4
Total	13	124	92	.574	392	286	20-7	3-2	1890.1	1887	948	250	53	594-44	1415	4.24	105	.260	.319	531-5-75	.164	3	103	60	449	4.8

NEAGLE, JACK John Henry; B1.2.1858 Syracuse NY; D9.20.1904 Syracuse NY; BR/TR/5´6˝/155; d7.8; ▲

YEAR	TM LG	W	L	PCT	G	GS	CG-SHO	SV-BS	IP	H	R	HR	HB	BB-IB	SO	ERA	AERA	OAV	OOB	AB-HR-SH	AVG	PB	SUP	APR	DL	PW
1879	Cin N	0	1	.000	2	2	1	0	13	13	12	0	—	5	4	3.46	67	.241	.305	12	.167	-0*	99	-2	—	-0.2
1883	Phi N	1	7	.125	8	7	6	0	61.1	88	77	1	—	21	13	6.90	45	.315	.363	73	.164	-2*	74	-25	—	-2.4
	Bal AA	1	4	.200	6	5	4	0	46	48	48	1	—	20	9	4.89	71	.251	.322	35	.286	1*	76	-7	—	-0.4
	Pit AA	3	12	.200	16	16	12	0	114	156	123	9	—	25	41	5.84	56	.306	.338	101	.188	-1*	73	-34	—	-3.3
	Year	4	16	.200	22	21	16	0	160	204	171	10	—	45	50	5.57	60	.291	.334	136	.213	-0	73	-42	—	-3.7
1884	Pit AA	11	26	.297	38	38	37-2	0	326	354	219	6	18	70	85	3.73	89	.255	.300	148	.149	-5*	61	-17	—	-2.1
Total	3	16	50	.242	70	68	60-2	0	560.1	659	479	17	18	141	152	4.59	71	.272	.317	369	.176	-8	67	-85	—	-8.4

NEAL, BLAINE Blaine; B4.6.1978 Marlton NJ; BL/TR/6´5˝/(205–250); [FlaN96 4/104]; d9.3

YEAR	TM LG	W	L	PCT	G	GS	CG-SHO	SV-BS	IP	H	R	HR	HB	BB-IB	SO	ERA	AERA	OAV	OOB	AB-HR-SH	AVG	PB	SUP	APR	DL	PW
2001	Fla N	0	0	ø	4	0	0	0-0	5.1	7	4	0	0	5-0	3	6.75	62	.304	.429	0	ø	0	—	-1	0	-0.1
2002	Fla N	3	0	1.000	32	0	0	0-0	33	32	12	1	0	14-2	33	2.73	144	.248	.322	0	ø	0	—	4	0	0.3
2003	Fla N	0	0	ø	18	0	0	0-0	21	38	20	2	1	9-1	10	8.14	50	.413	.449	0	ø	0	—	-10	0	-0.5
2004	SD N	1	1	.500	40	0	0	0-2	42	49	19	6	2	11-3	36	4.07	97	.295	.343	0	ø	0	—	0	0	0.1
2005	Bos A	0	1	.000	8	0	0	0-0	8	15	9	2	0	3-0	3	9.00	50	.429	.462	0	ø	0	—	-4	0	-0.4
	Col N	1	2	.333	11	0	0	0-2	14.2	20	10	2	0	9-2	8	6.14	76	.339	.414	1	.000	-0	—	-2	84	-0.4
Total	5	5	4	.556	113	0	0	0-4	124	161	74	13	3	51-8	93	5.08	81	.319	.379	1	.000	-0	—	-13	84	-1.0

NEALE, JOE Joseph Hunt; B5.7.1866 Wadsworth OH; D12.30.1913 Akron OH; BR/TR/5´8˝/153; d6.21

YEAR	TM LG	W	L	PCT	G	GS	CG-SHO	SV-BS	IP	H	R	HR	HB	BB-IB	SO	ERA	AERA	OAV	OOB	AB-HR-SH	AVG	PB	SUP	APR	DL	PW
1886	Lou AA	0	1	.000	1	1	0	0	7	11	12	0	1	7	0	7.71	47	.393	.528	5	.000	-0*	82	-3	—	-0.3
1887	Lou AA	1	4	.200	5	4	4	0	41.1	60	50	4	2	15	11	6.97	63	.326	.383	19	.053	-2	80	-11	—	-1.0
1890	StL AA	5	3	.625	10	9	8	0	69	53	37	4	4	15	23	3.39	127	.206	.261	30	.067	-3*	104	7	—	0.3
1891	StL AA	6	4	.600	15	11	9-1	**3**	110.1	109	73	4	7	36	24	4.24	99	.249	.317	51-1	.118	-3	114	3	—	0.0
Total	4	12	12	.500	31	25	21-1	3	227.2	233	172	12	14	73	58	4.59	93	.257	.322	105-1	.086	-9	103	-4	—	-1.0

NECCIAI, RON Ronald Andrew; B6.18.1932 Gallatin PA; BR/TR/6´5˝/185; d8.10; Mil 1953; [DL 1953 Pit N 77]

YEAR	TM LG	W	L	PCT	G	GS	CG-SHO	SV-BS	IP	H	R	HR	HB	BB-IB	SO	ERA	AERA	OAV	OOB	AB-HR-SH	AVG	PB	SUP	APR	DL	PW
1952	Pit N	1	6	.143	12	9	0	0	54.2	63	45	5	1	32	31	7.08	56	.296	.390	17	.059	-1	62	-16	0	-1.9

YEAR	TM LG	W	L	PCT	G	GS	CG-SHO	SV-BS	IP	H	R	HR	HB	BB-IB	SO	ERA	AERA	OAV	OOB	AB-HR-SH	AVG	PB	SUP	APR	DL	PW
NEGRAY, RON	Ronald Alvin; B2.26.1930 Akron OH; BR/TR/6´1˝/(180–185); d9.14																									
1952	Bro N	0	0	ø	4	1	0	0	13	15	5	0	0	5	5	3.46	105	.294	.357	2	.000	-0	122	0	0	0.0
1955	Phi N	4	3	.571	19	10	2	0	71.2	71	31	13	0	21-2	30	3.52	113	.257	.308	24-0-2	.000	-3	92	4	0	0.0
1956	Phi N	2	3	.400	39	4	0	3	66.2	72	36	6	1	24-9	44	4.18	89	.280	.340	7-0-1	.429	1	89	-4	0	-0.2
1958	LA N	0	0	ø	4	0	0	0	11.1	12	9	4	0	7-0	2	7.15	57	.279	.373	2	.000	-0	—	-3	0	-0.2
Total	4	6	6	.500	66	15	2	3	162.2	170	81	23	1	57-11	81	4.04	95	.271	.330	35-0-3	.086	-3	94	-3	0	-0.4
NEHER, JIM	James Gilmore; B2.5.1889 Rochester NY; D11.11.1951 Buffalo NY; BR/TR/5´11˝/185; d9.10																									
1912	Cle A	0	0	ø	1	0	0	0	1	0	0	0	0	0	0	0.00	ø	.000	.000	0	ø	0	—	0	—	0.0
NEHF, ART	Arthur Neukom; B7.31.1892 Terre Haute IN; D12.18.1960 Phoenix AZ; BL/TL/5´9.5˝/176; d8.13; Col Rose–Hulman Tech																									
1915	Bos N	5	4	.556	12	10	6-4	0	78.1	60	29	0	3	21	39	2.53	103	.214	.276	28-0-1	.143	-1	98	1	—	0.0
1916	Bos N	7	5	.583	22	13	6-1	0	121	110	40	1	3	20	36	2.01	124	.244	.281	40	.125	-0*	113	5	—	0.4
1917	Bos N	17	8	.680	38	23	16-4	0	233.1	197	78	4	4	39	101	2.16	118	.231	.268	70-0-3	.171	5	109	7	—	1.4
1918	Bos N	15	15	.500	32	31	**28**-2	0	284.1	274	107	2	6	76	96	2.69	100	.259	.312	95-0-6	.168	1*	104	1	—	0.6
1919	Bos N	8	9	.471	22	19	13-1	0	168.2	151	66	6	6	40	53	3.09	92	.242	.294	63-0-1	.206	2*	97	-2	—	0.1
	NY N	9	2	.818	13	12	9-2	0	102	70	23	2	2	19	24	1.50	187	.196	.240	35-1-1	.229	3	130	15	—	2.1
	Year	17	11	.607	35	31	22-3	0	270.2	221	89	8	8	59	77	2.49	114	.225	.275	98-1-2	.214	5	109	13	—	2.2
1920	NY N	21	12	.636	40	33	22-4	0	280.2	273	113	8	1	45	79	3.08	97	.260	.291	97-0-4	.268	5	139	0	—	0.6
1921	†NY N	20	10	.667	41	34	18-2	1	260.2	266	116	18	2	55	67	3.63	101	.271	.311	89-0-8	.202	0*	121	4	—	0.6
1922	†NY N	19	13	.594	37	35	20-2	1	268.1	286	122	15	4	64	60	3.29	122	.276	.321	98-1-4	.255	4	107	21	—	2.5
1923	†NY N	13	10	.565	34	27	7-1	2	196	219	112	14	2	49	50	4.50	85	.281	.326	63-0-1	.190	1	141	-16	—	-1.5
1924	†NY N	14	4	.778	30	20	11	2	171.2	167	75	14	2	42	72	3.62	101	.254	.301	57-5-4	.228	6*	157	3	—	1.0
1925	NY N	11	9	.550	29	20	8-1	1	155	193	86	7	1	50	63	3.77	107	.308	.360	51-0-1	.216	1*	102	1	—	0.3
1926	NY N	0	0	ø	2	0	0	0	1.2	2	2	0	0	1	0	10.80	35	.286	.375	1	.000	-0	—	-1	—	-0.1
	Cin N	0	1	.000	7	1	0	0	17	25	10	0	1	5	4	3.71	100	.379	.431	5	.200	-0	68	-1	—	0.0
	Year	0	1	.000	9	1	0	0	18.2	27	12	0	1	6	4	4.34	85	.370	.425	6	.167	-0	68	-2	—	-0.1
1927	Cin N	3	5	.375	21	5	1	4	45.1	59	33	2	0	14	21	5.56	68	.319	.367	13-0-1	.077	-1	90	-9	—	-1.5
	Chi N	1	1	.500	8	2	2-1	1	26.1	25	5	0	0	9	12	1.37	283	.260	.324	7	.429	1	66	7	—	0.7
	Year	4	6	.400	29	7	3-1	5	71.2	84	38	2	0	23	33	4.02	95	.299	.352	20-0-1	.200	0	83	-1	—	-0.8
1928	Chi N	13	7	.650	31	21	10-2	0	176.2	190	62	3	1	52	40	2.65	145	.281	.334	58-1-5	.190	2	102	24	—	2.8
1929	†Chi N	8	5	.615	32	14	4	1	120.2	148	85	11	2	39	27	5.59	83	.310	.365	45-0-1	.289	4	130	-12	—	-0.7
Total	15	184	120	.605	451	320	181-27	13	2707.2	2715	1164	107	40	640	844	3.20	105	.265	.310	915-8-41	.210	34	119	48	—	9.3
NEIBAUER, GARY	Gary Wayne; B10.29.1944 Billings MT; BR/TR/6´3˝/(195–200); [AtlN66 S2/27]; d4.12; Col Nebraska																									
1969	†Atl N	1	2	.333	29	0	0	0-0	57.2	42	28	9	1	31-2	42	3.90	93	.204	.310	10	.000	-1	—	-2	0	-0.2
1970	Atl N	0	3	.000	7	0	0	0-0	12.2	11	7	0	0	8-1	9	4.97	86	.239	.352	2	.000	-0	—	-1	0	-0.1
1971	Atl N	1	0	1.000	6	1	0	1-0	21	14	5	3	1	9-1	6	2.14	174	.187	.282	5-0-1	.000	-1	24	4	0	0.2
1972	Atl N	0	0	ø	8	0	0	0-0	17.1	27	15	6	1	6-0	8	7.27	52	.360	.410	4-0-1	.000	-0	—	-6	0	-0.4
	Phi N	0	2	.000	9	2	0	0-1	18.2	17	12	1	1	14-0	7	5.30	68	.239	.372	4	.250	0	61	-3	24	-0.3
	Year	0	2	.000	17	2	0	0-1	36	44	27	7	2	20-0	15	6.25	59	.301	.391	8-0-1	.125	-0	60	-9	0	-0.7
1973	Atl N	2	1	.667	16	1	0	0-2	21.1	24	19	3	2	19-1	9	7.17	55	.282	.421	4-1-1	.250	1	67	-7	0	-0.8
Total	5	4	8	.333	75	4	0	1-3	148.2	135	86	22	6	87-5	81	4.78	79	.242	.349	29-1-3	.069	-1	53	-15	24	-1.6
NEIDLINGER, JIM	James Llewellyn; B9.24.1964 Vallejo CA; BB/TR/6´4˝/180; d8.1; Col Marin (CA) CC																									
1990	LA N	5	3	.625	12	12	0	0-0	74	67	30	4	1	15-1	46	3.28	112	.241	.279	25	.120	-0	121	4	0	0.3
NEIGER, AL	Alvin Edward; B3.26.1939 Wilmington DE; BL/TL/6´0˝/190; d7.30; Col Delaware																									
1960	Phi N	0	0	ø	6	0	0	0	12.2	16	8	2	2	4-1	3	5.68	68	.340	.393	2	.500	0	—	-2	0	-0.1
NEKOLA, BOTS	Francis Joseph; B12.10.1906 New York NY; D3.11.1987 Rockville MD; BL/TL/5´11.5˝/175; d7.19; Col Holy Cross																									
1929	NY A	0	0	ø	9	1	0	0	18.2	21	10	0	0	15	2	4.34	89	.296	.419	4-0-1	.500	1	241	-1	—	0.1
1933	Det A	0	0	ø	2	0	0	0	1.1	4	4	1	0	1	0	27.00	16	.500	.556	0	ø	0	—	-3	—	-0.1
Total	2	0	0	ø	11	1	0	0	20	25	14	1	0	16	2	5.85	66	.316	.432	4-0-1	.500	1	241	-4	—	0.0
NELSON, RED	Albert Francis (b Albert W. Horazdovsky); B5.19.1886 Cleveland OH; D10.26.1956 St.Petersburg FL; BR/TR/5´11˝/190; d9.9																									
1910	StL A	5	1	.833	7	6	6-1	0	60	57	26	0	4	14	30	2.55	97	.261	.318	23-1-0	.261	2	117	0	—	0.4
1911	StL A	3	9	.250	16	13	6	0	81	103	68	1	7	44	24	5.22	65	.324	.417	27-0-1	.111	-2	85	-17	—	-2.3
1912	StL A	0	2	.000	8	3	0	1	18	21	14	0	0	13	9	7.00	47	.318	.430	3	.333	1	82	-5	—	-0.5
	Phi N	2	0	1.000	4	2	1	0	19.1	25	10	2	2	6	2	3.72	97	.305	.367	10	.100	-1	202	0	—	-0.1
1913	Phi N	0	0	ø	2	0	0	0	8.1	9	2	0	0	4	3	2.16	154	.290	.371	3	.333	0	—	1	—	0.1
	Cin N	0	0	ø	2	0	0	0	1.2	6	7	1	1	4	0	37.80	9	.667	.786	0	ø	0	—	-5	—	-0.3
	Year	0	0	ø	4	0	0	0	10	15	9	1	1	8	3	8.10	41	.375	.490	3	.333	0	—	-4	—	-0.2
Total	4	10	12	.455	39	24	13-1	1	188.1	221	127	4	14	85	68	4.54	68	.305	.389	66-1-1	.182	0	104	-26	—	-2.7
NELSON, ANDY	Andrew Anthony "Peaches"; B11.30.1884 St.Paul MN; TL; d5.26																									
1908	Chi A	0	0	ø	2	1	0	0	9	11	4	0	1	4	1	2.00	116	.282	.364	2	.000	0	148	0	—	0.0
NELSON, EMMETT	George Emmett "Ramrod"; B2.26.1905 Viborg SD; D8.25.1967 Sioux Falls SD; BR/TR/6´3˝/180; d6.24																									
1935	Cin N	4	4	.500	19	7	3-1	1	60.1	70	31	2	2	23	14	4.33	92	.295	.363	15-0-1	.133	-1	79	-1	—	-0.2
1936	Cin N	1	0	1.000	6	1	0	0	17	24	8	1	1	4	3	3.18	120	.333	.377	6	.167	-0	133	1	—	0.0
Total	2	5	4	.556	25	8	3-1	1	77.1	94	39	3	3	27	17	4.07	97	.304	.366	21-0-1	.143	-1	86	0	—	-0.2
NELSON, JIM	James Lorin; B7.4.1947 Birmingham AL; D8.22.2004 Sacramento CA; BR/TR/6´0˝/180; [PitN65 15/588]; d5.30																									
1970	Pit N	4	2	.667	15	10	1-1	0-0	68.1	64	32	5	3	38-5	42	3.42	116	.255	.355	20-0-1	.200	0	116	3	0	0.2
1971	Pit N	2	2	.500	17	2	0	0-0	34.2	27	9	0	5	26-4	11	2.34	146	.225	.382	6	.500	2	26	5	0	0.7
Total	2	6	4	.600	32	12	1-1	0-0	103	91	41	5	8	64-9	53	3.06	123	.245	.364	26-0-1	.269	2	105	8	0	0.9
NELSON, JEFF	Jeffrey Allan; B11.17.1966 Baltimore MD; BR/TR/6´8˝/(225–235); [LAN84 22/569]; d4.16; Col Catonsville (MD) CC																									
1992	Sea A	1	7	.125	66	0	0	6-8	81	71	34	7	6	44-12	46	3.44	116	.245	.353	0	ø	0	—	5	0	0.5
1993	Sea A	5	3	.625	71	0	0	1-10	60	57	30	5	8	34-10	61	4.35	103	.258	.371	0	ø	0	—	1	0	0.2
1994	Sea A	0	0	ø	28	0	0	0-0	42.1	35	18	3	8	20-4	44	2.76	178	.226	.342	0	ø	0	—	8	0	0.4
1995	†Sea A	7	3	.700	62	0	0	2-2	78.2	58	21	4	6	27-5	96	2.17	219	.209	.291	0	ø	0	—	22	0	2.6
1996	†NY A	4	4	.500	73	0	0	2-2	74.1	75	38	6	2	36-1	91	4.36	114	.262	.348	0	ø	0	—	5	0	0.5
1997	†NY A	3	7	.300	77	0	0	2-6	78.2	53	32	7	4	37-12	81	2.86	156	.191	.294	0	ø	0	—	12	0	1.5
1998	†NY A	5	3	.625	45	0	0	3-3	40.1	44	18	1	8	22-4	35	3.79	115	.278	.387	1-0-1	.000	-0	—	3	71	0.5
1999	†NY A	2	1	.667	39	0	0	1-1	30.1	27	14	2	3	22-2	35	4.15	114	.245	.380	0	ø	0	—	3	86	0.3
2000	†NY A	8	4	.667	73	0	0	0-4	69.2	44	24	2	2	45-1	71	2.45	195	.183	.314	1	.000	-0	—	17	0	2.4
2001	†Sea A★	4	3	.571	69	0	0	4-1	65.1	30	21	3	6	44-1	88	2.76	155	.136	.295	0	ø	0	—	12	0	1.2
2002	Sea A	3	2	.600	41	0	0	2-2	45.2	36	20	4	3	27-3	55	3.94	109	.221	.335	0	ø	0	—	3	52	0.3
2003	Sea A	3	2	.600	46	0	0	7-4	37.2	34	16	3	2	14-1	47	3.35	129	.248	.323	0	ø	0	—	4	0	0.5
	†NY A	1	0	1.000	24	0	0	1-2	17.2	17	9	1	2	10-2	21	4.58	96	.246	.358	0	ø	0	—	0	0	0.0
	Year	4	2	.667	70	0	0	8-6	55.1	51	25	4	4	24-3	68	3.74	116	.248	.335	0	ø	0	—	4	0	0.5
2004	Tex A	1	2	.333	29	0	0	1-0	23.2	17	16	3	0	19-0	22	5.32	93	.207	.353	0	ø	0	—	-1	105	-0.2
2005	Sea A	1	3	.250	49	0	0	1-3	36.2	32	17	3	4	22-0	34	3.93	106	.237	.358	0	ø	0	—	1	0	0.1
2006	Chi A	0	1	.000	6	0	0	0-1	2.2	3	1	1	0	5-1	2	3.38	139	.300	.533	0	ø	0	—	0	121	0.1
Total	15	48	45	.516	798	0	0	33-49	784.2	633	329	55	64	428-59	829	3.41	133	.224	.336	2-0-1	.000	-0	—	95	435	10.9
NELSON, JOE	Joseph George; B10.25.1974 Alameda CA; BR/TR/6´2˝/(185–210); [AtlN96 4/122]; d6.13; Col San Francisco																									
2001	Atl N	0	0	ø	2	0	0	0-0	2	7	9	1	1	2-0	0	36.00	12	.583	.625	0	ø	0	—	-7	110	-0.3
2004	Bos A	0	0	ø	3	0	0	0-0	2.2	4	5	0	2	3-0	5	16.88	29	.364	.563	0	ø	0	—	-3	0	-0.1
2006	KC A	1	1	.500	43	0	0	9-1	44.2	37	22	5	1	24-4	44	4.43	106	.226	.326	0	ø	0	—	2	0	0.2
Total	3	1	1	.500	48	0	0	9-1	49.1	48	36	6	4	29-4	49	6.39	73	.257	.365	0	ø	0	—	-8	110	-0.2
NELSON, LUKE	Luther Martin; B12.4.1893 Cable IL; D11.14.1985 Moline IL; BR/TR/6´0˝/180; d5.25																									
1919	NY A	3	0	1.000	9	1	0	0	24.1	22	9	1	1	11	11	2.96	108	.244	.333	7	.143	-0	246	1	—	0.1

YEAR	TM LG	W	L	PCT	G	GS	CG-SHO	SV-BS	IP	H	R	HR	HB	BB-IB	SO	ERA	AERA	OAV	OOB	AB-HR-SH	AVG	PB	SUP	APR	DL	PW
NELSON, LYNN	Lynn Bernard "Line Drive"; B2.24.1905 Sheldon ND; D2.15.1955 Kansas City MO; BL/TR/5´10.5˝/170; d4.18																									
1930	Chi N	3	2	.600	37	3	0	0	81.1	97	52	10	6	28	29	5.09	96	.300	.367	18	.222	0	149	-1	—	0.0
1933	Chi N	5	5	.500	24	3	3	1	75.2	65	34	2	0	30	20	3.21	102	.232	.306	21-0-2	.238	2*	85	0	—	0.2
1934	Chi N	0	1	.000	2	1	0	0	1	4	4	1	0	1	0	36.00	11	.667	.714	0	ø	0	134	-4	—	-0.6
1937	Phi A	4	9	.308	30	4	1	2	116	140	78	12	2	51	49	5.90	80	.300	.371	113-4-1	.354	6*	111	-10	—	0.0
1938	Phi A	10	11	.476	32	23	13	2	191	215	142	29	5	79	75	5.65	85	.277	.347	112	.277	4*	108	-17	—	-1.1
1939	Phi A	10	13	.435	35	24	12-2	1	197.2	233	117	27	3	64	75	4.78	98	.292	.347	80	.188	-2*	74	1	—	-0.1
1940	Det A	1	1	.500	6	2	0	0	14	23	19	5	0	9	7	10.93	44	.371	.451	23-1-0	.348	2*	83	-9	—	-0.8
Total	7	33	42	.440	166	60	29-2	6	676.2	777	446	86	16	262	255	5.25	88	.287	.353	367-5-3	.281	13	97	-40	—	-2.4
NELSON, MEL	Melvin Frederick; B5.30.1936 San Diego CA; BR/TL/6´0˝/(185–190); d9.27; Col San Bernardino Valley (CA) JC																									
1960	StL N	0	1	.000	2	1	0	0	8	7	3	1	0	2-1	7	3.38	121	.226	.273	2	.500	0	43	1	0	0.1
1963	LA A	2	3	.400	36	3	0	1	52.2	55	34	7	2	32-5	41	5.30	65	.263	.365	11	.091	-1*	43	-11	0	-1.0
1965	Min A	0	4	.000	28	3	0	3	54.2	57	29	7	2	23-3	31	4.12	86	.261	.337	9-0-1	.111	-0	107	-3	0	-0.3
1967	Min A	0	0	ø	1	0	0	0	0.1	3	2	1	0	0-0	0	54.00	6	.750	.750	0	ø	0	—	-2	0	-0.1
1968	†StL N	2	1	.667	18	4	1	1	52.2	49	20	3	0	9-3	16	2.91	100	.254	.284	12	.167	0	120	0	0	0.0
1969	StL N	0	1	.000	8	0	0	0-0	5.1	13	7	0	0	3-0	3	11.81	30	.520	.533	0	ø	0	—	-4	0	-0.8
Total	6	4	10	.286	93	11	1	5-0	173.2	184	95	19	4	69-12	98	4.40	76	.271	.339	34-0-1	.147	-1	86	-19	0	-2.1
NELSON, ROGER	Roger Eugene "Spider"; B6.7.1944 Altadena CA; BR/TR/6´3˝/(190–205); d9.9; Col Mt. San Antonio (CA) JC																									
1967	Chi A	0	1	.000	5	0	0	0	7	4	1	1	2	0-0	4	1.29	241	.182	.250	0	ø	0	—	2	0	0.2
1968	Bal A	4	3	.571	19	6	0	1	71	49	21	3	1	26-3	70	2.41	121	.192	.270	16-0-4	.063	-0	74	5	0	0.4
1969	KC A	7	13	.350	29	29	8-1	0-0	193.1	170	78	12	6	65-4	82	3.31	112	.243	.309	58-0-5	.138	-1	82	9	0	0.8
1970	KC A	0	2	.000	4	2	0	0-0	9	18	10	3	1	0-0	3	10.00	37	.419	.422	0	ø	0	119	-6	21	-1.0
1971	KC A	0	1	.000	13	1	0	0-0	34	35	20	1	0	5-0	29	5.29	65	.269	.294	6	.333	1	182	-6	0	-0.2
1972	KC A	11	6	.647	34	19	10-6	2-0	173.1	120	41	13	1	31-1	120	2.08	147	.196	**.234**	54-0-4	.093	-2	89	20	0	2.0
1973	†Cin N	3	2	.600	14	8	1	0-0	54.2	49	25	4	3	24-1	17	3.46	100	.246	.333	18-0-1	.111	-1	131	-1	60	-0.1
1974	Cin N	4	4	.500	14	12	1	1-0	85.1	67	36	7	1	35-1	42	3.38	104	.213	.293	28-0-2	.179	0	77	1	73	0.1
1976	KC A	0	0	ø	3	0	0	0-0	8.2	4	2	0	2	4-1	4	2.08	169	.138	.278	0	ø	0	—	2	0	0.1
Total	9	29	32	.475	135	77	20-7	4-0	636.1	516	234	44	17	190-11	371	3.06	110	.224	.286	180-0-16	.128	-3	91	26	154	2.3
NELSON, GENE	Wayland Eugene; B12.3.1960 Tampa FL; BR/TR/6´0˝/(174–180); [TexA78 30/690]; d5.4																									
1981	NY A	3	1	.750	8	7	0	0-0	39.1	40	24	5	1	23-1	16	4.81	75	.261	.358	0	ø	0	138	-5	24	-0.5
1982	Sea A	6	9	.400	22	19	2-1	0-0	122.2	133	70	16	2	60-1	71	4.62	93	.279	.360	0	ø	0	84	-4	0	-0.4
1983	Sea A	0	3	.000	10	5	1	0-0	32	38	29	6	1	21-2	11	7.88	54	.295	.397	0	ø	0	102	-11	0	-0.9
1984	Chi A	3	5	.375	20	9	2	1-0	74.2	72	38	9	1	17-0	36	4.46	94	.254	.297	0	ø	0	67	-1	0	-0.1
1985	Chi A	10	10	.500	46	18	1	2-2	145.2	144	74	23	7	67-4	101	4.26	102	.258	.344	1	.000	-0*	94	2	0	0.2
1986	Chi A	6	6	.500	54	1	0	6-5	114.2	118	52	7	3	41-5	70	3.85	113	.271	.337	0	ø	0	21	7	0	0.8
1987	Oak A	6	5	.545	54	6	0	3-3	123.2	120	58	12	5	35-0	94	3.93	106	.249	.304	0	ø	0*	70	5	0	0.3
1988	†Oak A	9	6	.600	54	1	0	3-3	111.2	93	42	9	3	38-4	67	3.06	124	.228	.296	0	ø	0*	96	9	0	1.2
1989	†Oak A	3	5	.375	50	0	0	3-1	80	60	33	5	2	30-3	70	3.26	113	.203	.277	0	ø	0*	—	4	15	0.3
1990	†Oak A	3	3	.500	51	0	0	5-3	74.2	55	14	5	3	17-1	38	1.57	239	.208	.259	0	ø	0	—	19	0	1.6
1991	Oak A	1	5	.167	44	0	0	0-5	48.2	60	38	12	3	23-1	23	6.84	56	.306	.381	0	ø	0	—	-17	40	-1.8
1992	Oak A	3	1	.750	28	2	0	0-1	51.2	68	37	5	0	22-5	23	6.45	59	.335	.391	0	ø	0*	109	-14	0	-1.0
1993	Cal A	0	5	.000	46	0	0	4-2	52.2	50	25	3	2	23-4	31	3.08	148	.251	.329	0	ø	0	—	6	0	0.6
	Tex A	0	0	ø	6	0	0	1-1	8	10	3	0	0	1-1	4	3.38	124	.303	.324	0	ø	0	—	1	0	0.0
	Year	0	5	.000	52	0	0	5-3	60.2	60	28	3	2	24-5	35	3.12	144	.259	.328	0	ø	0	—	7	0	0.6
Total	13	53	64	.453	493	68	6-1	28-26	1080	1061	537	117	33	418-32	655	4.13	99	.258	.328	1	.000	-0	92	1	79	0.3
NELSON, BILL	William F.; B9.28.1863 Terre Haute IN; D6.23.1941 Terre Haute IN; TR; d9.3																									
1884	Pit AA	1	2	.333	3	3	3	0	26	26	21	1	4	8	6	4.50	73	.252	.330	12	.167	-1	97	-4	—	-0.4
NEN, ROBB	Robert Allen; B11.28.1969 San Pedro CA; BR/TR/6´5˝/(200–222); [TexA87 32/831]; d4.10; f-Dick; [DL 2003 SF N 183, 2004 SF N 183]																									
1993	Tex A	1	1	.500	9	3	0	0-0	22.2	28	17	1	0	26-0	12	6.35	66	.326	.478	0	ø	0	183	-5	35	-0.4
	Fla N	1	0	1.000	15	1	0	0-0	33.1	35	28	5	0	20-0	27	7.02	62	.255	.348	4	.000	-0	144	-9	0	-0.5
1994	Fla N	5	5	.500	44	0	0	15-0	58	46	20	6	0	17-2	60	2.95	151	.222	.280	3	.000	-0	—	10	0	1.9
1995	Fla N	0	7	.000	62	0	0	23-6	65.2	62	26	6	1	23-3	68	3.29	131	.244	.308	0	ø	0	—	7	0	1.2
1996	Fla N	5	1	.833	75	0	0	35-7	83	67	21	2	1	21-6	92	1.95	211	.225	.277	2	.000	-0	—	**20**	0	2.7
1997	†Fla N	9	3	.750	73	0	0	35-7	74	72	35	7	0	40-7	81	3.89	104	.250	.338	0	ø	0	—	-1	0	0.3
1998	SF N★	7	7	.500	78	0	0	40-5	88.2	59	21	4	1	25-5	110	1.52	265	.180	.239	3	.000	-0	—	**24**	0	4.8
1999	SF N✱	3	8	.273	72	0	0	37-9	72.1	79	36	8	0	27-3	77	3.98	107	.275	.337	0	ø	0	—	2	0	0.4
2000	†SF N	4	3	.571	68	0	0	41-5	66	37	15	4	2	19-1	92	1.50	290	.162	.230	0	ø	0	—	21	0	4.1
2001	SF N	4	5	.444	79	0	0	**45**-7	77.2	58	28	6	1	22-6	93	3.01	136	.203	.260	1	.000	-0	—	10	0	1.9
2002	†SF N★	6	2	.750	68	0	0	43-8	73.2	64	19	2	1	20-8	81	2.20	180	.232	.286	2	.500	0	—	15	0	3.1
Total	10	45	42	.517	643	4	0	314-54	715	607	266	51	7	260-41	793	2.98	140	.227	.295	15	.067	-1	175	96	401	19.5
NESHEK, PAT	Patrick J.; B9.4.1980 Madison WI; BB/TR/6´3˝/205; [MinA02 6/182]; d7.7; Col Butler																									
2006	†Min A	4	2	.667	32	0	0	0-2	37	23	9	6	0	6-0	53	2.19	208	.176	.210	0	ø	0	—	10	0	1.4
NEU, MIKE	Michael David; B3.9.1978 Napa CA; BB/TR/5´10˝/(175–190); [CinN99 29/878]; d4.9; Col Miami																									
2003	Oak A	0	0	ø	32	0	0	1-0	42	43	18	2	2	26-2	20	3.64	126	.261	.368	0	ø	0	—	5	0	0.3
2004	Fla N	0	0	ø	1	0	0	0-0	4	5	2	1	0	2-0	2	4.50	91	.313	.389	0	ø	0	—	0	0	0.0
Total	2	0	0	ø	33	0	0	1-0	46	48	20	3	2	28-2	22	3.72	122	.265	.370	0	ø	0	—	5	0	0.3
NEUBAUER, HAL	Harold Charles; B5.13.1902 Hoboken NJ; D9.9.1949 Providence RI; BR/TR/6´0.5˝/185; d6.12; Col Brown																									
1925	Bos A	1	0	1.000	7	0	0	0	10.1	17	18	2	0	11	4	12.19	37	.378	.500	0	ø	0	—	-9	—	-0.7
NEUER, TEX	John S.; B6.8.1877 Fremont OH; D1.14.1966 Northumberland PA; TL; d8.28																									
1907	NY A	4	2	.667	7	6	6-3	0	54	40	21	1	0	19	22	2.17	129	.208	.280	21	.095	-2	133	3	—	0.1
NEUGEBAUER, NICK	Nickolas Donald; B7.15.1980 Riverside CA; BR/TR/6´3˝/235; [MilN98 2/56]; d8.19; [DL 2003 Mil N 183]																									
2001	Mil N	1	1	.500	2	2	0	0-0	6	6	5	1	0	6-0	11	7.50	57	.250	.400	3	.000	-0	129	-2	44	-0.4
2002	Mil N	1	7	.125	12	12	0	0-0	55.1	56	33	10	0	44-3	47	4.72	87	.264	.389	19-0-1	.105	-1	71	-4	113	-0.7
Total	2	2	8	.200	14	14	0	0-0	61.1	62	38	11	0	50-3	58	4.99	83	.263	.390	22-0-1	.091	-1	80	-6	340	-1.1
NEUMEIER, DAN	Daniel George; B3.9.1948 Shawano WI; BR/TR/6´5˝/205; [ChiA68 S3/42]; d9.8; Col Wisconsin–Oshkosh																									
1972	Chi A	0	0	ø	3	0	0	0-0	3	2	3	0	0	3-0	0	9.00	35	.200	.385	1	.000	-0	—	-2	0	-0.1
NEVEL, ERNIE	Ernie Wyre; B8.17.1918 Charleston MO; D7.10.1988 Springfield MO; BR/TR/6´1˝/(190–200); d9.26																									
1950	NY A	0	1	.000	3	1	0	0	6.1	10	7	0	0	6	3	9.95	43	.345	.457	1-0-1	.000	-0	63	-4	0	-0.5
1951	NY A	0	0	ø	1	0	0	1	4	1	0	0	0	1	1	0.00	ø	.083	.154	1	.000	-0	—	2	0	0.1
1953	Cin N	0	0	ø	10	0	0	0	10.1	16	7	0	0	1	5	6.10	71	.390	.405	0	ø	0	—	-2	0	-0.1
Total	3	0	1	.000	14	1	0	1	20.2	27	14	0	0	8	9	6.10	69	.329	.389	2-0-1	.000	-0	63	-4	0	-0.5
NEVERS, ERNIE	Ernest Alonzo; B6.11.1902 Willow River MN; D5.3.1976 San Rafael CA; BR/TR/6´0˝/205; d4.26; Col Stanford																									
1926	StL A	2	4	.333	11	7	4	0	74.2	82	41	4	1	24	16	4.46	96	.290	.347	27	.185	-1*	67	0	—	0.0
1927	StL A	3	8	.273	27	5	2	2	94.2	105	61	8	2	35	22	4.94	88	.311	.379	32-0-1	.219	-1	65	-5	—	-0.5
1928	StL A	1	0	1.000	6	0	0	0	9	9	4	1	0	2	1	3.00	140	.281	.324	1	.000	-0	—	1	—	0.1
Total	3	6	12	.333	44	12	6	2	178.1	196	106	13	3	61	39	4.64	93	.300	.363	60-0-1	.200	-2	66	-4	—	-0.4
NEWCOMBE, DON	Donald "Newk"; B6.14.1926 Madison NJ; BL/TR/6´4˝/(225–248); d5.20; Mil 1952–53; Negro Lg 1944–45																									
1949	†Bro N★	17	8	.680	38	31	19-**5**	1	244.1	223	89	17	3	73	149	3.17	129	.243	.301	96-0-1	.229	3*	119	27	0	2.9
1950	Bro N★	19	11	.633	40	35	20-4	3	267.1	258	120	22	2	75	130	3.70	111	.254	.306	97-1-3	.247	7	116	12	0	1.9
1951	Bro N★	20	9	.690	40	36	18-3	0	272	235	115	19	6	91	**164**	3.28	120	.230	.297	103-0-2	.223	5	138	17	0	2.2
1954	Bro N	9	8	.529	29	25	6	0	144.1	158	81	24	5	49	82	4.55	90	.274	.335	47-0-3	.319	4*	116	-7	0	-0.4
1955	†Bro N★	20	5	**.800**	34	31	17-1	0	233.2	222	103	35	1	38-1	143	3.20	127	.249	**.279**	117-7-1	.359	20*	156	19	0	**4.0**

YEAR	TM LG	W	L	PCT	G	GS	CG-SHO	SV-BS	IP	H	R	HR	HB	BB-IB	SO	ERA	AERA	OAV	OOB	AB-HR-SH	AVG	PB	SUP	APR	DL	PW
1956	†Bro N	**27**	7	**.794**	38	36	18-5	0	268	219	101	33	3	46-8	139	3.06	130	**.221**	**.257**	111-2-3	.234	8*	129	26	0	**4.1**
1957	Bro N	11	12	.478	28	28	12-4	0	198.2	199	86	28	1	33-4	90	3.49	119	.258	.288	74-1-1	.230	5*	106	14	0	2.1
1958	LA N	0	6	.000	11	8	1	0	34.1	53	37	11	0	8-1	16	7.86	52	.346	.377	12	.417	2	88	-15	0	-2.0
	Cin N	7	7	.500	20	18	7	1	133.1	159	61	20	1	28-4	53	3.85	108	.298	.333	60-1-0	.350	8*	107	4	0	1.2
	Year	7	13	.350	31	26	8	1	167.2	212	98	31	1	36-5	69	4.67	89	.309	.343	72-1-0	.361	10	101	-10	0	-0.8
1959	Cin N	13	8	.619	30	29	17-2	1	222	216	87	25	5	27-3	100	3.16	128	.253	.279	105-3-1	.305	15*	131	22	0	3.6
1960	Cin N	4	6	.400	16	15	1	0	82.2	99	48	12	3	14-0	36	4.57	84	.304	.333	36-0-2	.139	-0*	86	-7	0	-0.9
	Cle A	2	3	.400	20	2	0	1	54	61	28	6	0	8-0	27	4.33	86	.289	.315	20	.300	2*	83	-3	0	-0.1
Total	10	149	90	.623	344	294	136-24	7	2154.2	2102	956	252	30	490-21	1129	3.56	114	.254	.298	878-15-17	.271	79	122	109	0	18.6
NEWELL, TOM	Thomas Dean; B5.17.1963 Monrovia CA; BR/TR/6´1˝/185; [PhiN83 24/610]; d9.9; Col Lassen (CA) CC																									
1987	Phi N	0	0	ø	2	0	0	0-0	1	4	4	1	0	3-1	1	36.00	12	.571	.700	0	ø	0	—	-3	0	-0.2
NEWHAUSER, DON	Donald Louis; B11.7.1947 Miami FL; BR/TR/6´4˝/(195–200); [BosA67*2/24]; d6.15; Col Broward (FL) CC																									
1972	Bos A	4	2	.667	31	0	0	4-1	37	30	11	2	2	25-5	27	2.43	133	.226	.354	2	.000	-0	—	3	0	0.6
1973	Bos A	0	0	ø	9	0	0	1-0	12	9	2	0	1	13-2	8	0.00	ø	.205	.390	0	ø	0	—	4	49	0.2
1974	Bos A	0	1	.000	2	0	0	0-0	3.2	5	4	0	0	4-1	2	9.82	39	.357	.474	0	ø	0	—	-2	0	-0.4
Total	3	4	3	.571	42	0	0	5-1	52.2	44	17	2	3	42-8	37	2.39	145	.230	.372	2	.000	-0	—	5	49	0.4
NEWHOUSER, HAL	Harold "Prince Hal"; B5.20.1921 Detroit MI; D11.10.1998 Southfield MI; BL/TL/6´2˝/192; d9.29; HF1992																									
1939	Det A	0	1	.000	1	1	1	0	5	3	3	0	0	4	4	5.40	91	.188	.350	1	.000	-0	0	0	—	0.0
1940	Det A	9	9	.500	28	20	7	0	133.1	149	81	12	2	76	89	4.86	98	.282	.374	40-0-4	.200	-1	88	0	—	0.0
1941	Det A	9	11	.450	33	27	5-1	0	173	166	109	6	1	137	106	4.79	95	.249	.378	60-0-5	.150	-2	108	-5	0	-0.6
1942	Det A☆	8	14	.364	38	23	11-1	5	183.2	137	73	4	2	114	103	2.45	161	**.207**	.325	52-0-3	.154	-1*	64	23	0	2.9
1943	Det A★	8	17	.320	37	25	10-1	1	195.2	163	88	3	0	111	144	3.04	116	.224	.327	65-0-4	.185	-1	79	6	0	0.9
1944	Det A★	**29**	9	.763	47	34	25-6	2	312.1	264	94	6	1	102	**187**	2.22	161	.230	.293	120-0-6	.242	3	117	45	0	6.1
1945	†Det A✳	**25**	9	**.735**	40	**36**	**29-8**	2	**313.1**	239	73	5	0	110	**212**	**1.81**	**194**	**.211**	.281	109-0-8	.257	4	106	**58**	0	**7.6**
1946	Det A★	**26**	9	.743	37	34	29-6	1	292.2	215	77	10	1	98	275	**1.94**	**189**	**.201**	**.269**	103-2-8	.126	-1	104	**51**	0	**6.4**
1947	Det A★	17	17	.500	40	36	**24**-3	2	285	268	105	9	2	110	176	2.87	131	.249	.320	96-0-3	.198	2	86	28	0	**3.7**
1948	Det A★	**21**	12	.636	39	35	19-2	1	272.1	249	109	10	1	99	143	3.01	145	.242	.309	92-0-6	.207	1	86	38	0	4.5
1949	Det A	18	11	.621	38	35	22-3	1	292	277	118	19	0	111	144	3.36	124	.251	.319	91-0-14	.198	2	106	28	0	2.9
1950	Det A	15	13	.536	35	30	15-1	3	213.2	232	110	23	4	81	87	4.34	108	.279	.346	74-0-5	.176	-2	85	10	0	0.9
1951	Det A	6	6	.500	15	14	7-1	0	96.1	98	47	9	3	19	37	3.92	106	.268	.310	29-0-4	.310	2*	102	3	0	0.6
1952	Det A	9	9	.500	25	19	8	0	154	148	72	13	0	47	57	3.74	102	.254	.310	46-0-1	.217	3*	99	1	0	0.5
1953	Det A	0	1	.000	7	4	0	1	21.2	31	22	4	2	8	6	7.06	58	.348	.414	8	.500	2	131	-8	0	-0.3
1954	†Cle A	7	2	.778	26	1	0	7	46.2	34	16	3	0	18	25	2.51	147	.209	.286	13-0-1	.154	-0	72	6	0	1.1
1955	Cle A	0	0	ø	2	0	0	0	2.1	1	0	0	0	4-1	1	0.00	ø	.125	.417	0	ø	0	—	1	0	0.0
Total	17	207	150	.580	488	374	212-33	26	2993	2674	1197	136	19	1249-1	1796	3.06	130	.239	.316	999-2-72	.201	12	96	285	0	37.2
NEWKIRK, FLOYD	Floyd Elmo "Three-Finger"; B7.16.1908 Norris City IL; D4.15.1976 Clayton MO; BR/TR/5´11˝/178; d8.21; b–Joel; Col Illinois College																									
1934	NY A	0	0	ø	1	0	0	0	1	1	0	0	0	1	0	0.00	ø	.333	.500	0	ø	0	—	0	—	0.0
NEWKIRK, JOEL	Joel Inez "Sailor"; B5.1.1896 Kyana IN; D1.22.1966 Eldorado IL; BR/TR/6´0˝/180; d8.20; b–Floyd																									
1919	Chi N	0	0	ø	1	0	0	0	2	2	3	0	1	3	1	13.50	21	.286	.545	1	.000	-0	—	-2	—	-0.1
1920	Chi N	0	1	.000	2	1	0	0	6.2	8	6	1	0	6	2	5.40	59	.333	.467	3	.000	-0	74	-2	—	-0.3
Total	2	0	1	.000	3	1	0	0	8.2	10	9	1	1	9	3	7.27	43	.323	.488	4	.000	-1	74	-4	—	-0.4
NEWLIN, MAURY	Maurice Milton; B6.22.1914 Bloomingdale IN; D8.14.1978 Houston TX; BR/TR/6´0˝/176; d9.20; Mil 1942–45																									
1940	StL A	1	0	1.000	1	1	0	0	6	4	4	1	0	2	3	6.00	76	.190	.261	2	.500	0	134	-1	—	-0.1
1941	StL A	0	2	.000	14	0	0	1	27.2	43	24	4	0	12	10	6.51	66	.361	.420	6	.000	-1	—	-7	0	-0.5
Total	2	1	2	.333	15	1	0	1	33.2	47	28	5	0	14	13	6.42	68	.336	.396	8	.125	-1	134	-8	0	-0.6
NEWMAN, AL	Alan Spencer; B10.2.1969 LaHabra CA; BL/TL/6´6˝/240; [MinA88 2/50]; d5.14; Col Fullerton (CA) JC																									
1999	TB A	2	2	.500	18	0	0	0-1	15.2	22	12	2	1	9-0	20	6.89	72	.333	.421	0	ø	0	—	-3	0	-0.5
2000	Cle A	0	0	ø	1	0	0	0-0	1.1	6	3	1	0	1-0	0	20.25	25	.667	.700	0	ø	0	—	-2	0	-0.1
Total	2	2	2	.500	19	0	0	0-1	17	28	15	3	1	10-0	20	7.94	63	.373	.453	0	ø	0	—	-5	0	-0.6
NEWMAN, FRED	Frederick William; B2.21.1942 Boston MA; D6.24.1987 Framingham MA; BR/TR/6´3˝/(180–190); d9.16																									
1962	LA A	0	1	.000	4	1	0	0	6.1	11	7	0	0	3-1	4	9.95	39	.393	.452	1	.000	-0	69	-4	0	-0.5
1963	LA A	1	5	.167	12	8	0	0	44	56	27	6	2	15-2	16	5.32	64	.316	.374	16	.250	1	101	-8	0	-1.0
1964	LA A	13	10	.565	32	28	7-2	0	190	177	68	9	7	39-8	83	2.75	120	.246	.291	61-1-5	.180	2*	83	13	0	2.0
1965	Cal A	14	16	.467	36	36	10-2	0	260.2	225	94	15	1	64-10	109	2.93	116	.234	.282	74-1-7	.095	-0	82	14	0	2.0
1966	Cal A	4	7	.364	21	19	1	0	102.2	112	54	7	6	31-2	42	4.73	71	.289	.349	30-0-3	.200	1	101	-13	41	-1.2
1967	Cal A	1	0	1.000	3	1	0	0	6.1	8	5	1	1	2-0	0	1.42	221	.320	.393	1	.000	-0	55	0	0	-0.1
Total	6	33	39	.458	108	93	18-4	0	610	589	255	38	17	154-23	254	3.41	99	.256	.307	183-2-15	.153	3	87	2	41	1.2
NEWMAN, RAY	Raymond Francis; B6.20.1945 Evansville IN; BL/TL/6´5˝/(201–205); d5.16; Col Muskegon (MI) CC																									
1971	Chi N	1	2	.333	30	0	0	2-0	38.1	30	15	4	0	17-0	35	3.52	112	.219	.305	6	.000	-1	—	2	0	0.1
1972	Mil A	0	0	ø	4	0	0	1-0	7	4	0	0	0	2-0	1	0.00	ø	.182	.250	1	1.000	0	—	2	0	0.2
1973	Mil A	2	1	.667	11	0	0	1-2	18.1	19	6	2	0	5-1	10	2.95	129	.260	.304	0	ø	0	—	2	0	0.4
Total	3	3	3	.500	45	0	0	4-2	63.2	53	21	6	0	24-1	46	2.97	128	.228	.300	7	.143	-0	—	6	0	0.7
NEWSOM, BOBO	Louis Norman "Buck"; B8.11.1907 Hartsville SC; D12.7.1962 Orlando FL; BR/TR/6´2˝/(195–220); d9.11																									
1929	Bro N	0	3	.000	3	2	0	0	9.1	15	12	0	0	5	6	10.61	44	.375	.444	2	.000	-0	57	-6	—	-0.9
1930	Bro N	0	0	ø	2	0	0	0	3	2	2	0	0	2	1	0.00	ø	.167	.286	0	ø	0	—	1	—	0.0
1932	Chi N	0	0	ø	1	0	0	0	1	1	0	0	0	0	0	0.00	ø	.333	.333	0	ø	0	—	0	—	0.0
1934	StL A	16	20	.444	47	32	15-2	5	262.1	259	138	15	1	149	135	4.01	124	.261	.358	93-0-3	.183	-3*	67	26	—	2.9
1935	StL A	0	6	.000	7	6	1	1	42.2	54	29	2	0	13	22	4.85	99	.303	.351	11-0-2	.091	-1	39	-1	—	-0.3
	Was A	11	12	.478	28	23	17-2	2	198.1	222	108	9	4	84	65	4.45	97	.288	.361	73-0-4	.301	4	94	-2	—	0.1
	Year	11	18	.379	35	29	18-2	3	241	276	137	11	4	97	87	4.52	97	.291	.359	84-0-6	.274	3	82	-3	—	-0.2
1936	Was A	17	15	.531	43	**38**	24-4	2	285.2	294	160	13	3	146	156	4.32	111	.268	.355	108-0-4	.213	0*	102	15	—	1.4
1937	Was A	3	4	.429	11	10	3	0	67.2	76	49	4	3	48	39	5.85	76	.287	.402	25-1-0	.120	-1*	110	-10	—	-0.9
	Bos A	13	10	.565	30	27	14-1	0	207.2	193	114	14	3	119	127	4.46	106	.243	.344	75-0-4	.253	2*	82	8	—	0.8
	Year	16	14	.533	41	**37**	17-1	0	275.1	269	163	18	6	167	166	4.81	97	.254	.359	100-1-4	.220	1	89	1	—	-0.1
1938	StL A☆	20	16	.556	44	**40**	**31**	1	**329.2**	334	205	30	5	192	226	5.08	98	.265	.364	124-0-14	.250	1*	96	-3	—	-0.2
1939	StL A	3	1	.750	6	6	3	0	45.2	50	26	5	1	22	28	4.73	103	.266	.346	18	.222	-0	112	1	—	0.1
	Det A☆	17	10	.630	35	31	21-3	2	246	222	100	14	2	104	164	3.37	145	.238	.316	97-0-4	.186	-4	91	42	—	3.7
	Year	20	11	.645	41	**37**	**24**-3	2	291.2	272	126	19	3	126	192	3.58	136	.243	.321	115-0-4	.191	-4	95	42	—	3.8
1940	†Det A★	21	5	.808	36	34	20-3	0	264	235	110	19	3	100	164	2.83	**168**	.238	.310	107-0-4	.215	-1	109	47	—	3.9
1941	Det A	12	20	.375	43	36	12-2	2	250.1	265	140	15	3	118	175	4.60	99	.264	.343	88-0-5	.102	-6	70	2	0	-0.5
1942	Was A	11	17	.393	30	29	15-2	0	213.2	236	135	5	3	92	**113**	4.93	74	.280	.353	75-0-4	.160	-2	81	-28	0	-3.5
	Bro N	2	2	.500	6	5	2-1	0	32	28	13	1	1	14	21	3.38	97	.235	.321	11-0-1	.000	-1	103	0	0	-0.2
1943	Bro N	9	4	.692	22	12	6-1	1	125	113	51	4	2	57	75	3.02	111	.244	.329	44-0-3	.250	1	124	3	0	0.4
	StL A	1	6	.143	10	9	0	0	52.1	69	45	7	1	35	37	7.39	45	.318	.415	15-0-1	.333	1	87	-22	0	-2.4
	Was A	3	3	.500	6	6	2	0	40	38	22	1	2	21	11	3.82	84	.247	.345	15	.133	-1	127	-3	0	-0.6
	Year	4	9	.308	16	15	2	0	92.1	107	67	8	3	56	48	5.85	56	.288	.386	30-0-1	.233	0	103	-25	0	-3.0
1944	Phi A★	13	15	.464	37	33	18-2	1	265	243	100	11	4	82	142	2.82	123	.244	.304	88-0-9	.114	-6	68	18	0	1.2
1945	Phi A	8	20	.286	36	34	16-3	0	257.1	255	111	12	3	103	127	3.29	104	.260	.332	86-0-7	.163	-4	76	3	0	-0.4
1946	Phi A	3	5	.375	10	9	3-1	0	58.2	61	27	2	5	30	32	3.38	105	.266	.364	19-0-4	.105	-1	86	1	0	-0.1
	Was A	11	8	.579	24	22	14-2	1	178	163	63	5	2	60	82	2.78	120	.242	.306	62-0-7	.161	-2	101	13	0	1.0
	Year	14	13	.519	34	31	17-3	1	236.2	224	90	7	7	90	114	2.93	116	.248	.321	81-0-11	.148	-3	97	11	0	0.9
1947	Was A	4	6	.400	14	13	1	0	83.2	99	44	2	1	37	40	4.09	91	.296	.368	29-0-2	.241	1	88	-4	0	-0.4
	†NY A	7	5	.583	17	15	6-2	0	115.2	109	38	8	2	30	42	2.80	126	.250	.301	42-0-1	.095	-3	127	11	0	0.6
	Year	11	11	.500	31	28	7-2	0	199.1	208	82	10	3	67	82	3.34	108	.270	.331	71-0-3	.155	-3	108	7	0	0.2
1948	NY N	0	4	.000	11	4	0	0	25.2	35	16	1	0	13	9	4.21	94	.330	.403	7-0-1	.429	1	79	-2	0	-0.2
1952	Was A	1	1	.500	10	0	0	2	12.2	16	7	2	0	9	5	4.97	72	.302	.403	2	.000	-0	—	-2	0	-0.3

YEAR	TM LG	W	L	PCT	G	GS	CG-SHO	SV-BS	IP	H	R	HR	HB	BB-IB	SO	ERA	AERA	OAV	OOB	AB-HR-SH	AVG	PB	SUP	APR	DL	PW
	Phi A	3	3	.500	14	5	1	1	47.2	38	19	2	2	23	22	3.59	110	.220	.318	15-0-1	.133	-1	93	3	0	0.3
	Year	4	4	.500	24	5	1	3	60.1	54	26	4	2	32	27	3.88	100	.239	.338	17-0-1	.118	-1	95	2	0	0.0
1953	Phi A	2	1	.667	17	2	1	0	38.2	44	24	3	5	24	16	4.89	88	.282	.395	6-0-1	.167	-0	124	-3	0	-0.2
Total	20	211	222	.487	600	483	246-31	21	3759.1	3769	1908	206	61	1732	2082	3.98	107	.261	.342	1337-1-86	.189	-26	89	108	0	5.3
NEWSOME, DICK	Heber Hampton; B12.13.1909 Ahoskie NC; D12.15.1965 Ahoskie NC; BR/TR/6´0˝/185; d4.25; Col Wake Forest																									
1941	Bos A	19	10	.655	36	29	17-2	0	213.2	235	115	13	7	79	58	4.13	101	.277	.344	78-0-6	.244	3	112	1	0	0.5
1942	Bos A	8	10	.444	24	23	11	0	158	174	98	11	0	67	40	5.01	74	.278	.348	55-0-6	.236	2	105	-21	0	-1.9
1943	Bos A	8	13	.381	25	22	8-2	0	154.1	166	83	8	5	68	40	4.49	74	.274	.352	48-0-2	.146	-1*	90	-19	0	-2.5
Total	3	35	33	.515	85	74	36-4	0	526	575	296	32	12	214	138	4.50	84	.276	.347	181-0-14	.215	3	104	-39	0	-3.9
NEWTON, DOC	Eustace James; B10.26.1877 Indianapolis IN; D5.14.1931 Memphis TN; BL/TL/6´0˝/185; d4.27																									
1900	Cin N	9	15	.375	36	27	22-1	0	235.2	255	146	4	12	100	89	4.12	89	.275	.354	86-0-4	.198	-1	74	-11	—	-1.2
1901	Cin N	4	13	.235	20	18	17	0	168.1	190	117	6	14	59	65	4.12	78	.282	.353	69-0-1	.130	-4	90	-21	—	-2.2
	Bro N	6	5	.545	13	12	9	0	105	110	42	1	7	30	45	2.83	119	.268	.328	41	.220	1	107	8	—	0.8
	Year	10	18	.357	33	30	26	0	273.1	300	159	7	21	89	110	3.62	90	.277	.343	110-0-1	.164	-4	97	-9	—	-1.4
1902	Bro N	15	14	.517	31	28	26-4	2	264.1	208	95	2	11	87	107	2.42	114	**.217**	.289	109-0-2	.174	-1*	97	11	—	1.0
1905	NY A	2	2	.500	11	7	2	0	59.2	61	23	1	2	24	15	2.11	139	.266	.341	22	.136	-1	107	4	—	0.1
1906	NY A	7	5	.583	21	15	6-2	0	125	118	53	3	7	33	52	3.17	94	.252	.311	41-0-1	.220	-0	94	-1	—	-0.1
1907	NY A	7	10	.412	19	15	10	0	133	132	66	0	7	31	70	3.18	88	.261	.313	37-0-5	.108	-1	95	-4	—	-0.6
1908	NY A	4	5	.444	23	13	6-1	1	88.1	78	52	0	7	41	49	2.95	84	.242	.341	25-0-1	.160	-0	134	-7	—	-0.8
1909	NY A	0	3	.000	4	4	1	0	22.1	27	17	0	3	11	11	2.82	90	.300	.394	6	.167	0	63	-3	—	-0.3
Total	8	54	72	.429	178	139	99-8	3	1201.2	1179	611	17	70	416	503	3.22	96	.257	.328	436-0-14	.172	-9	93	-24	—	-3.3
NICHOLS, KID	Charles Augustus; B9.14.1869 Madison WI; D4.11.1953 Kansas City MO; BB/TR/5´10.5˝/175; d4.23; M2; HF1949																									
1890	Bos N	27	19	.587	48	47	47-**7**	0	424	374	175	8	11	112	222	2.23	169	.229	.283	174	.247	1*	75	63	—	5.9
1891	Bos N	30	17	.638	52	48	45-5	**3**	425.1	413	219	15	17	103	240	2.39	**153**	.245	.295	183	.197	-3	96	**48**	—	**4.5**
1892	†Bos N	35	16	.686	53	51	49-5	0	453	404	211	15	10	121	192	2.84	124	.229	.283	197-2	.203	1*	85	34	—	3.3
1893	Bos N	34	14	.708	52	44	43-1	1	425	426	222	15	15	118	94	3.52	140	.253	.308	177-2	.220	-2*	93	66	—	5.5
1894	Bos N	32	13	.711	50	46	40-**3**	0	407	488	308	23	9	121	113	4.75	119	.294	.345	170-0-2	.294	3*	104	39	—	3.3
1895	Bos N	26	16	.619	48	43	43-1	**3**	390.2	434	222	15	5	90	148	3.41	149	.277	.318	161-0-1	.230	-5*	95	67	—	5.2
1896	Bos N	**30**	14	.682	49	43	37-3	1	372.1	387	211	14	7	101	102	2.83	161	.266	.316	147-1-9	.190	-3*	103	**59**	—	5.4
1897	†Bos N	**31**	11	.738	46	40	37-2	**3**	**368**	362	152	9	3	68	127	2.64	**169**	.255	**.291**	147-3-2	.265	4	106	**70**	—	**6.9**
1898	Bos N	**31**	12	.721	**50**	42	40-5	**4**	388	316	136	7	14	85	138	2.13	173	**.221**	**.272**	158-2-3	.241	3*	95	62	—	**6.4**
1899	Bos N	21	19	.525	42	37	37-4	1	343.1	326	155	11	6	82	108	2.99	139	.250	.298	136-1-2	.191	-5	86	40	—	3.4
1900	Bos N	13	16	.448	29	27	25-**4**	0	231.1	215	116	11	11	72	53	3.07	134	.246	.311	90-1-2	.200	-2	105	23	—	2.3
1901	Bos N	19	16	.543	38	34	33-4	0	321	306	146	8	10	90	143	3.22	112	.250	.306	163-4-4	.282	9*	81	16	—	2.6
1904	StL N	21	13	.618	36	35	35-3	1	317	268	97	3	5	50	134	2.02	134	.222	.256	109	.156	-1	78	27	—	2.8
1905	StL N	1	5	.167	7	7	5	0	51.2	64	47	1	0	18	16	5.40	55	.296	.350	22	.227	0*	83	-16	—	-1.6
	Phi N	10	6	.625	17	16	15-1	0	138.2	129	47	1	4	28	50	2.27	129	.250	.294	53	.189	0	88	11	—	1.0
	Year	11	11	.500	24	23	20-1	0	190.1	193	94	2	4	46	66	3.12	94	.264	.311	75	.200	0	87	-6	—	-0.6
1906	Phi N	0	1	.000	4	2	1	0	11	17	16	0	2	13	1	9.82	27	.386	.542	3	.000	-0	279	-8	—	-0.7
Total	15	361	208	.634	621	562	532-48	17	5067.1	4929	2480	156	129	1272	1881	2.96	139	.250	.300	2090-16-25	.226	-0	94	601	—	56.2
NICHOLS, CHET	Chester Raymond Jr.; B2.22.1931 Pawtucket RI; D3.27.1995 Lincoln RI; BB/TL/6´1.5˝/(170–195); d4.19; Mil 1952–53; f-Chet																									
1951	Bos N	11	8	.579	33	19	12-3	2	156	142	61	4	1	69	71	**2.88**	127	.246	.327	51-0-4	.137	-2	92	13	0	1.4
1954	Mil N	9	11	.450	35	20	5-1	1	122.1	132	68	5	4	65	55	4.41	84	.286	.376	35-0-4	.086	-3	109	-10	0	-1.7
1955	Mil N	9	8	.529	34	21	6	1	144	139	79	20	1	67-6	44	4.00	94	.253	.334	52-0-1	.154	-2	123	-7	0	-0.9
1956	Mil N	0	1	.000	2	0	0	0	4	9	3	1	0	3-1	2	6.75	51	.563	.632	1	.000	-0	—	-1	0	-0.3
1960	Bos A	0	2	.000	6	1	0	0	12.2	12	6	0	0	4-0	11	4.26	95	.240	.296	3	.000	-0	22	0	0	0.0
1961	Bos A	3	2	.600	26	2	0	3	51.2	40	12	3	0	26-1	20	2.09	199	.221	.317	9	.111	-0	42	12	31	1.4
1962	Bos A	1	1	.500	29	1	0	3	57	61	25	3	0	22-1	33	3.00	138	.276	.339	9-0-2	.000	-1	195	5	0	0.3
1963	Bos A	1	3	.250	21	7	0	1	52.2	61	30	8	0	24-0	27	4.78	79	.298	.365	13-0-1	.231	0	101	-5	0	-0.4
1964	Cin N	0	0	ø	3	0	0	0	3	4	2	1	0	0-0	3	6.00	60	.308	.308	0	ø	0	—	-1	0	0.0
Total	9	34	36	.486	189	71	23-4	10	603.1	600	286	45	6	280-9	266	3.64	105	.264	.344	173-0-12	.127	-8	104	6	31	-0.2
NICHOLS, CHET	Chester Raymond Sr. "Nick"; B7.3.1897 Woonsocket RI; D7.11.1982 Pawtucket RI; BR/TR/5´11˝/160; d7.30; s-Chet																									
1926	Pit N	0	0	ø	3	0	0	0	7.2	13	11	0	0	5	2	8.22	48	.342	.419	3	.333	0	—	-5	—	-0.2
1927	Pit N	0	3	.000	8	0	0	0	27.2	34	19	1	1	17	9	5.86	70	.309	.406	9	.111	-0	—	-4	—	-0.4
1928	NY N	0	0	ø	3	0	0	0	2.2	11	13	0	1	3	1	23.63	17	.611	.682	0	ø	0	—	-8	—	-0.4
1930	Phi N	1	2	.333	16	5	1	0	59.2	76	51	8	2	16	15	6.79	80	.306	.353	20	.300	0*	93	-7	—	-0.3
1931	Phi N	0	1	.000	3	0	0	0	5.2	10	6	0	0	1	1	9.53	45	.435	.458	2	.000	-0	—	-3	—	-0.4
1932	Phi N	0	2	.000	11	0	0	1	19.1	23	16	2	0	14	5	6.98	63	.299	.407	4	.000	-1	—	-4	—	-0.5
Total	6	1	8	.111	44	5	1	1	122.2	167	116	11	4	56	33	7.19	67	.325	.395	38	.211	-1	93	-31	—	-2.2
NICHOLS, DOLAN	Dolan Levon "Nick"; B2.28.1930 Tishomingo MS; D11.20.1989 Tupelo MS; BR/TR/6´0˝/195; d4.15																									
1958	Chi N	0	4	.000	24	0	0	1	41.1	46	27	1	1	16-2	9	5.01	78	.295	.362	5	.000	-1	—	-5	0	-0.5
NICHOLS, TRICKY	Frederick C.; B7.26.1850 Bridgeport CT; D8.22.1897 Bridgeport CT; BR/TR/5´7.5˝/150; d4.19																									
1875	NH NA	4	29	.121	34	33	30	0	288	321	245	2	—	9	48	2.38	87	.242	.248	119	.193	-2	56	-11	—	-0.7
1876	Bos N	1	0	1.000	1	1	1	0	9	7	5	0	—	0	0	1.00	226	.200	.200	4	.000	-1	103	1	—	0.0
1877	StL N	18	23	.439	42	39	35-1	0	350	376	195	2	—	53	80	2.60	100	.263	.289	186	.167	-6*	80	2	—	-0.4
1878	Pro N	4	7	.364	11	10	10	0	98	157	98	0	—	8	21	4.22	52	.344	.356	49	.184	-0	138	-21	—	-1.8
1880	Wor N	0	2	.000	2	2	2	0	17.2	29	16	0	—	4	4	4.08	64	.358	.388	7	.000	-1	57	-3	—	-0.4
1882	Bal AA	1	12	.077	16	13	12	0	118.1	155	113	2	—	17	21	5.02	55	.296	.319	95	.158	-2*	78	-27	—	-2.4
Total	5	24	44	.353	72	65	60-1	0	593	724	427	4	—	82	126	3.37	76	.287	.309	341	.161	-10	88	-48	—	-5.0
NICHOLS, ROD	Rodney Lea; B12.29.1964 Burlington IA; BR/TR/6´2˝/190; [CleA85 5/115]; d7.30; Col New Mexico																									
1988	Cle A	1	7	.125	11	10	3	0-0	69.1	73	41	5	2	23-1	31	5.06	82	.272	.332	0	ø	0	64	-6	38	-0.6
1989	Cle A	4	6	.400	15	11	0	0-0	71.2	81	42	9	2	24-0	42	4.40	91	.285	.343	0	ø	0	83	-5	70	-0.6
1990	Cle A	0	3	.000	4	2	0	0-0	16	24	14	5	2	6-0	3	7.88	50	.343	.410	0	ø	0	58	-6	0	-1.0
1991	Cle A	2	11	.154	31	16	3-1	1-1	137.1	145	63	6	6	30-3	76	3.54	118	.273	.316	0	ø	0	49	8	0	0.7
1992	Cle A	4	3	.571	30	9	0	0-0	105.1	114	58	13	2	31-1	56	4.53	87	.273	.323	0	ø	0	113	-7	0	-0.4
1993	LA N	0	1	.000	4	0	0	0-1	6.1	9	5	1	0	2-2	3	5.68	68	.360	.407	0	ø	0	—	-2	0	-0.2
1995	Atl N	0	0	ø	5	0	0	0-0	6.2	14	11	3	0	5-1	3	5.40	80	.424	.500	0	ø	0	—	-4	0	-0.2
Total	7	11	31	.262	100	48	6-1	1-2	412.2	460	234	42	14	121-8	214	4.43	92	.282	.335	0	ø	0	72	-22	108	-2.3
NICHOLSON, FRANK	Frank Collins; B8.29.1889 Berlin PA; D11.10.1972 Jersey Shore PA; BR/TR/6´2˝/175; d9.6																									
1912	Phi N	0	0	ø	2	0	0	0	4	8	3	1	0	2	1	6.75	54	.471	.526	0	ø	0	—	-1	—	0.0
NICHTING, CHRIS	Christopher Thomas; B5.13.1966 Cincinnati OH; BR/TR/6´1˝/(205–220); [LAN87 3/66]; d5.15; Col Northwestern; [DL 1996 Tex A 155]																									
1995	Tex A	0	0	ø	13	0	0	0-0	24.1	36	19	1	1	13-1	6	7.03	69	.343	.413	0	ø	0	—	-5	0	-0.2
2000	Cle A	0	0	ø	7	0	0	0-1	9	13	7	0	2	5-1	7	7.00	72	.342	.435	0	ø	0	—	-2	0	-0.1
2001	Cin N	0	3	.000	36	0	0	1-2	36.1	46	24	6	0	8-1	33	4.46	103	.307	.338	1	.000	-0	—	-1	0	-0.1
	Col N	0	0	ø	7	0	0	0-0	6	9	3	2	0	0-0	7	4.50	119	.346	.346	0-0-1	ø	0	—	1	0	0.1
	Year	0	3	.000	43	0	0	1-2	42.1	55	27	8	0	8-1	40	4.46	105	.313	.339	1-0-1	.000	-0	—	-1	0	0.0
2002	Col N	1	1	.500	29	0	0	0-0	36.1	40	18	7	1	5-0	25	4.46	106	.280	.307	3	.333	0	—	2	0	0.1
Total	4	1	4	.200	92	0	0	1-3	112	144	71	16	4	31-3	78	5.22	91	.312	.356	4-0-1	.250	0	—	-5	155	-0.2
NICKLE, DOUG	Douglas Alan; B10.2.1974 Sonoma CA; BR/TR/6´4˝/210; [AnaA97 13/387]; d9.18; Col California																									
2000	Phi N	0	0	ø	4	0	0	0-0	2.2	5	4	0	1	2-0	0	13.50	34	.417	.533	0	ø	0	—	-3	0	-0.1
2001	Phi N	0	0	ø	2	0	0	0-0	2	1	0	0	0	0-0	1	0.00	ø	.143	.143	0	ø	0	—	1	0	0.0
2002	Phi N	0	0	ø	4	0	0	0-0	4.1	6	3	2	0	4-0	2	6.23	62	.316	.435	1	.000	-0	—	-1	0	-0.1
	SD N	1	0	1.000	10	0	0	0-0	11.2	20	13	1	1	9-0	7	8.49	46	.357	.448	0	ø	-0	—	-7	0	-0.5
	Year	1	0	1.000	14	0	0	0-0	16	26	16	3	1	13-0	9	7.88	49	.347	.444	1	.000	-0	—	-8	0	-0.6
Total	3	1	0	1.000	20	0	0	0-0	20.2	32	20	3	2	15-0	10	7.84	51	.340	.438	1	.000	-0	—	-10	0	-0.7

YEAR	TM LG	W	L	PCT	G	GS	CG-SHO	SV-BS	IP	H	R	HR	HB	BB-IB	SO	ERA	AERA	OAV	OOB	AB-HR-SH	AVG	PB	SUP	APR	DL	PW
NICOL, GEORGE	George Edward; B10.17.1870 Barry IL; D8.4.1924 Milwaukee WI; BR/TL/5´7˝/155; d9.23; ▲																									
1890	StL AA	2	1	.667	3	3	2	0	17	11	13	1	2	19	16	4.76	91	.180	.390	7	.286	1	161	-1	—	0.0
1891	Chi N	0	1	.000	3	2	0	0	11	14	20	0	1	10	12	4.91	68	.298	.431	6	.333	1	233	-5	—	-0.3
1894	Pit N	3	4	.429	9	5	3	0	46.1	58	38	2	5	39	13	6.22	84	.304	.434	22-0-2	.409	2	62	-3	—	-0.3
	Lou N	0	1	.000	2	2	2	0	17	35	35	4	1	16	4	13.76	37	.417	.515	112-0-1	.339	1*	76	-16	—	-0.5
	Year	3	5	.375	11	7	5	0	63.1	93	73	6	6	55	17	8.24	63	.338	.458	134-0-3	.351	2	66	-18	—	-0.8
Total	3	5	7	.417	17	12	7	0	91.1	118	106	7	9	84	45	7.19	67	.308	.443	147-0-3	.347	4	108	-25	—	-1.1
NIED, DAVID	David Glen; B12.22.1968 Dallas TX; BR/TR/6´2˝/(175–188); [AtlN87 14/350]; d9.1																									
1992	Atl N	3	0	1.000	6	2	0	0-0	23	10	3	0	0	5-0	19	1.17	312	.130	.183	7	.286	0	74	6	0	0.9
1993	Col N	5	9	.357	16	16	1	0-0	87	99	53	8	1	42-4	46	5.17	92	.296	.369	23-0-3	.174	0	88	-2	99	-0.3
1994	Col N	9	7	.563	22	22	2-1	0-0	122	137	70	15	4	47-5	74	4.80	104	.287	.354	40-0-3	.100	-2	91	2	0	-0.1
1995	Col N	0	0	ø	2	0	0	0-0	4.1	11	10	2	0	3-0	3	20.77	26	.458	.519	0	ø	0	—	-5	102	-0.3
1996	Col N	0	2	.000	6	1	0	0-0	5.1	5	8	1	0	8-0	4	13.50	39	.250	.448	1	.000	-0	52	-4	0	-0.7
Total	5	17	18	.486	52	41	3-1	0-0	241.2	262	144	26	5	105-9	146	5.06	95	.281	.353	71-0-6	.141	-2	90	-3	201	-0.5
NIEDENFUER, TOM	Thomas Edward; B8.13.1959 St.Louis Park MN; BR/TR/6´5˝/(217–230); d8.15; Col Washington St.																									
1981	†LA N	3	1	.750	17	0	0	2-1	26	25	11	1	1	6-2	12	3.81	87	.258	.305	0	ø	0	—	-1	0	-0.2
1982	LA N	3	4	.429	55	0	0	9-5	69.2	71	22	3	2	25-8	60	2.71	128	.269	.333	3	.000	-0	—	7	0	0.8
1983	†LA N	8	3	.727	66	0	0	11-4	94.2	55	22	6	1	29-11	66	1.90	190	.170	.237	4	.000	-0	—	19	0	2.5
1984	LA N	2	5	.286	33	0	0	11-3	47.1	39	14	3	2	23-7	45	2.47	144	.227	.325	3-0-1	.000	-0	—	6	52	1.1
1985	†LA N	7	9	.438	64	0	0	19-6	106.1	86	32	6	1	24-5	102	2.71	129	.223	.268	9-0-1	.111	-0	—	12	0	2.1
1986	LA N	6	6	.500	60	0	0	11-6	80	86	35	11	1	29-15	55	3.71	93	.280	.341	4-0-1	.500	1	—	-1	15	-0.2
1987	LA N	1	0	1.000	15	0	0	1-1	16.1	13	5	1	1	9-1	10	2.76	145	.220	.329	0	ø	0	—	3	0	0.2
	Bal A	3	5	.375	45	0	0	13-3	52.1	55	32	11	1	22-3	37	4.99	89	.266	.335	0	ø	0	—	-3	0	-0.6
1988	Bal A	3	4	.429	52	0	0	18-5	59	59	23	8	2	19-3	40	3.51	112	.259	.320	0	ø	0	—	4	0	0.6
1989	Sea A	0	3	.000	25	0	0	0-3	36.1	46	29	7	1	15-5	15	6.69	60	.309	.371	0	ø	0	—	-10	48	-0.7
1990	StL N	0	6	.000	52	0	0	2-1	65	66	26	3	0	25-7	32	3.46	111	.269	.331	3	.000	-0	—	4	0	0.3
Total	10	36	46	.439	484	0	0	97-38	653	601	251	60	13	226-67	474	3.29	112	.247	.311	26-0-3	.115	-1	—	40	115	5.9
NIEHAUS, DICK	Richard J.; B10.24.1892 Covington KY; D3.12.1957 Atlanta GA; BL/TL/5´11˝/165; d9.9																									
1913	StL N	0	2	.000	3	3	2	0	24	20	17	1	0	13	4	4.13	78	.241	.344	7	.286	1	62	-4	—	-0.2
1914	StL N	1	0	1.000	8	1	1	0	17.1	18	11	1	0	8	6	3.12	90	.269	.347	4	.250	1	102	-1	—	0.0
1915	StL N	2	1	.667	15	2	0	0	45.1	48	35	2	1	22	21	3.97	70	.281	.366	14	.071	-1	147	-9	—	-0.6
1920	Cle A	1	2	.333	19	3	0	2	40	42	21	0	1	16	12	3.60	106	.269	.341	9	.444	2	70	0	—	0.1
Total	4	4	5	.444	45	9	3	2	126.2	128	84	4	2	59	43	3.77	85	.268	.351	34	.235	2	87	-14	—	-0.7
NIEKRO, JOE	Joseph Franklin; B11.7.1944 Martins Ferry OH; D10.27.2006 Tampa FL; BR/TR/6´1˝/(185–195); [ChiN66 S3/43]; d4.16; b–Phil s–Lance; Col West Liberty St.																									
1967	Chi N	10	7	.588	36	22	7-2	0	169.2	171	68	15	2	32-7	77	3.34	106	.257	.291	46-0-9	.196	1	114	4	0	0.5
1968	Chi N	14	10	.583	34	29	2-1	2	177.1	204	93	18	3	59-8	65	4.31	73	.294	.349	60-0-9	.100	-2	128	-21	0	-3.0
1969	Chi N	0	1	.000	4	3	0	0-0	19.1	24	9	3	0	6-0	7	3.72	108	.304	.349	5-0-1	.200	0	74	1	0	0.1
	SD N	8	17	.320	37	31	8-3	0-0	202	213	91	15	0	45-9	55	3.70	97	.273	.311	51-0-5	.118	0*	76	-2	0	-0.3
	Year	8	18	.308	41	34	8-3	0-0	221.1	237	100	18	0	51-9	62	3.70	98	.276	.314	56-0-6	.125	0	76	-1	0	-0.2
1970	Det A	12	13	.480	38	34	6-2	0-0	213	221	107	28	3	72-4	101	4.06	93	.266	.325	66-0-15	.197	4*	108	-7	0	-0.3
1971	Det A	6	7	.462	31	15	0	1-0	122.1	136	62	13	2	49-3	43	4.49	81	.283	.350	30-0-6	.133	-0*	111	-9	0	-1.0
1972	†Det A	3	2	.600	18	7	1	1-0	47	62	20	3	1	8-1	24	3.83	83	.330	.360	12-0-1	.250	1	108	-2	25	-0.2
1973	Atl N	2	4	.333	20	0	0	3-4	24	23	11	2	0	11-1	12	4.13	96	.277	.351	3	.333	0	—	0	0	0.1
1974	Atl N	3	2	.600	27	2	0	0-3	43	36	19	5	2	18-2	31	3.56	107	.237	.322	5-0-1	.000	-1	115	1	0	0.1
1975	Hou N	6	4	.600	40	4	1-1	4-0	88	79	32	3	2	39-4	54	3.07	111	.240	.320	14-0-2	.214	1	117	4	0	0.5
1976	Hou N	4	8	.333	36	13	0	0-1	118	107	60	8	1	56-1	77	3.36	96	.238	.322	27-1-4	.185	2	120	-6	0	-0.4
1977	Hou N	13	8	.619	44	14	9-2	5-3	180.2	155	66	14	1	64-3	101	3.04	119	.237	.304	50-0-3	.140	-1	111	14	0	1.5
1978	Hou N	14	14	.500	35	29	10-1	0-0	202.2	190	97	13	9	73-1	97	3.86	86	.248	.318	65-0-9	.138	-1*	99	-14	0	-1.9
1979	Hou N☆	**21**	11	.656	38	38	11-**5**	0-0	263.2	221	102	17	7	107-1	119	3.00	117	.228	.308	83-0-13	.120	-2	98	15	0	1.5
1980	†Hou N	20	12	.625	37	36	11-2	0-0	256	268	119	12	4	79-3	127	3.55	92	.270	.323	80-0-18	.275	8	132	-10	0	-0.4
1981	†Hou N	9	9	.500	24	24	5-2	0-0	166	150	60	8	0	47-4	77	2.82	116	.243	.294	51-0-11	.176	1	105	8	0	0.9
1982	Hou N	17	12	.586	35	35	16-5	0-0	270	224	79	12	5	64-1	130	2.47	135	.229	.278	89-0-7	.090	-4	90	30	0	2.8
1983	Hou N	15	14	.517	38	**38**	9-1	0-0	263.2	238	115	15	3	101-5	152	3.48	98	.241	.311	85-0-12	.094	-3	106	-1	0	-0.5
1984	Hou N	16	12	.571	38	**38**	6-1	0-0	248.1	223	104	16	4	89-4	127	3.04	110	.241	.308	83-0-11	.133	-2	127	7	0	0.6
1985	Hou N	9	12	.429	32	32	4-1	0-0	213	197	100	21	5	99-6	117	3.72	94	.247	.329	68-0-10	.250	4	99	-5	0	-0.1
	NY A	2	1	.667	3	3	0	0-0	12.1	14	8	3	0	8-0	4	5.84	69	.280	.379	0	ø	0	142	-2	0	-0.4
1986	NY A	9	10	.474	25	25	0	0-0	125.2	139	84	15	1	63-3	59	4.87	85	.275	.356	0	ø	0	109	-14	18	-1.8
1987	NY A	3	4	.429	8	8	1	0-0	50.2	40	25	4	4	19-0	30	3.55	125	.215	.300	0	ø	0	69	3	0	0.4
	†Min A	4	9	.308	19	18	0	0-0	96.1	115	76	11	6	45-0	54	6.26	74	.296	.375	0	ø	0	81	-18	0	-2.0
	Year	7	13	.350	27	26	1	0-0	147	155	101	15	10	64-0	84	5.33	86	.270	.351	0	ø	0	78	-15	0	-1.6
1988	Min A	1	1	.500	5	2	0	0-0	11.2	16	13	2	0	9-0	7	10.03	41	.320	.424	0	ø	0	123	-7	0	-1.0
Total	22	221	204	.520	702	500	107-29	16-11	3584.1	3466	1620	276	65	1262-71	1747	3.59	98	.255	.319	973-1-147	.156	6	106	-31	43	-4.3
NIEKRO, PHIL	Philip Henry; B4.1.1939 Blaine OH; BR/TR/6´1˝/(180–195); d4.15; HF1997; b–Joe																									
1964	Mil N	0	0	ø	10	0	0	0	15	15	10	1	1	7-0	8	4.80	73	.273	.365	0	ø	0	—	-3	0	-0.1
1965	Mil N	2	3	.400	41	1	0	6	74.2	73	32	5	3	26-3	49	2.89	122	.258	.323	10	.100	-0*	223	3	0	0.2
1966	Atl N	4	3	.571	28	0	0	2	50.1	48	32	4	2	23-5	17	4.11	88	.249	.335	8-0-3	.000	-1	—	-5	0	-0.7
1967	Atl N	11	9	.550	46	20	10-1	9	207	164	64	9	7	55-3	129	**1.87**	**178**	.218	.275	57-0-6	.123	-0	87	27	0	3.0
1968	Atl N	14	12	.538	37	34	15-5	2	256.2	228	83	16	5	45-3	140	2.59	115	.239	.276	77-2-18	.104	-1	89	12	0	1.4
1969	†Atl N★	23	13	.639	40	35	21-4	1-1	284.1	235	93	21	5	57-7	193	2.56	141	.221	.264	95-0-9	.211	3	101	32	0	4.6
1970	Atl N	12	18	.400	34	32	10-3	0-1	229.2	222	124	40	6	68-2	168	4.27	100	.248	.304	79-1-6	.152	-1	86	0	0	-0.1
1971	Atl N	15	14	.517	42	36	18-4	2-0	268.2	248	112	27	3	70-6	173	2.98	125	.245	.294	92-0-7	.152	-2	94	16	0	1.6
1972	Atl N	16	12	.571	38	36	17-1	0-1	282.1	254	112	22	5	53-3	164	3.06	124	.236	.274	93-1-11	.194	1	96	19	0	2.1
1973	Atl N	13	10	.565	42	30	9-1	4-1	245	214	103	21	5	89-4	131	3.31	120	.234	.305	82-1-7	.122	-2	109	16	0	1.4
1974	Atl N	**20**	13	.606	41	39	**18**-6	1-0	**302.1**	249	91	19	6	88-3	195	2.38	159	.225	.284	104-0-9	.192	-0	102	**45**	0	**5.0**
1975	Atl N☆	15	15	.500	39	37	13-1	0-1	275.2	285	115	29	11	72-3	144	3.20	118	.269	.321	99-0-4	.172	-0	80	18	0	1.8
1976	Atl N	17	11	.607	38	37	10-2	0-0	270.2	249	116	18	8	101-7	173	3.29	115	.242	.313	94-1-9	.191	1	103	12	0	1.4
1977	Atl N	16	20	.444	44	**43**	**20**-2	0-0	**330.1**	315	166	26	8	164-12	**262**	4.03	110	.255	.344	109-0-12	.174	-3	81	15	0	1.3
1978	Atl N★	19	18	.514	44	**42**	**22**-4	1-0	**334.1**	295	129	16	13	102-5	248	2.88	140	.235	.298	120-0-4	.225	3*	81	**35**	0	**4.5**
1979	Atl N	**21**	20	.512	44	**44**	**23**-1	0-0	**342**	311	160	41	11	113-8	208	3.39	118	.241	.306	123-0-7	.195	2	100	18	0	2.5
1980	Atl N	15	18	.455	40	**38**	11-3	1-0	275	256	119	30	3	85-3	176	3.63	101	.249	.306	90-0-5	.133	-2	84	3	0	0.2
1981	Atl N	7	7	.500	22	22	3-3	0-0	139.1	120	56	6	1	56-2	62	3.10	114	.233	.309	52-0-3	.077	-4	100	6	0	0.1
1982	†Atl N☆	17	4	**.810**	35	35	4-2	0-0	234.1	225	106	23	3	73-1	144	3.61	102	.255	.313	87-1-3	.195	2	129	2	16	0.5
1983	Atl N	11	10	.524	34	33	2	0-0	201.2	212	94	18	2	105-3	128	3.97	97	.276	.362	65-0-6	.185	0	100	-1	0	-0.1
1984	NY A☆	16	8	.667	32	31	5-1	0-0	215.2	219	85	15	3	76-0	136	3.09	124	.267	.327	0	ø	0	124	17	0	1.8
1985	NY A	16	12	.571	33	33	7-1	0-0	220	203	110	29	2	120-1	149	4.09	99	.245	.341	0	ø	0	106	0	0	-0.1
1986	Cle A	11	11	.500	34	32	5	0-0	210.1	241	126	24	6	95-1	81	4.32	97	.287	.362	0	ø	0	108	-8	0	-0.8
1987	Tor A	0	2	.000	3	3	0	0-0	12	15	11	4	0	7-0	7	8.25	55	.306	.393	0	ø	0	60	-4	0	-0.6
	Cle A	7	11	.389	22	22	2	0-0	123.2	142	83	18	4	53-1	57	5.89	77	.286	.356	0	ø	0	85	-14	0	-1.6
	Year	7	13	.350	25	25	2	0-0	135.2	157	94	22	4	60-1	64	6.10	75	.288	.359	0	ø	0	82	-21	0	-2.2
	Atl N	0	0	ø	1	1	0	0-0	3	6	5	0	0	6-0	0	15.00	29	.429	.600	1	.000	-0	125	-3	0	-0.2
Total	24	318	274	.537	864	716	245-45	29-5	5404	5044	2337	482	123	1809-86	3342	3.35	115	.247	.311	1537-7-129	.169	-5	97	258	16	29.1
NIELSEN, JERRY	Gerald Arthur; B8.5.1966 Sacramento CA; BL/TL/6´3˝/185; [NYA88 18/469]; d7.12; Col Florida St.																									
1992	NY A	1	0	1.000	20	0	0	0-0	19.2	17	10	1	0	18-2	12	4.58	86	.243	.393	0	ø	0	—	-1	0	0.0
1993	Cal A	0	0	ø	10	0	0	0-0	12.1	18	13	1	1	4-0	8	8.03	57	.340	.377	0	ø	0	—	-5	0	-0.2
Total	2	1	0	1.000	30	0	0	0-0	32	35	23	2	1	22-2	20	5.91	71	.285	.387	0	ø	0	—	-6	0	-0.2

YEAR	TM LG	W	L	PCT	G	GS	CG-SHO	SV-BS	IP	H	R	HR	HB	BB-IB	SO	ERA	AERA	OAV	OOB	AB-HR-SH	AVG	PB	SUP	APR	DL	PW
NIELSEN, SCOTT	Jeffrey Scott; B12.18.1958 Salt Lake City UT; BR/TR/6´1″/190; [SeaA83 6/139]; d7.7; Col Brigham Young																									
1986	NY A	4	4	.500	10	9	2-2	0-0	56	66	29	12	2	12-0	20	4.02	103	.299	.340	0	ø	0	129	0	0	0.0
1987	Chi A	3	5	.375	19	7	1-1	2-0	66.1	83	48	9	1	25-1	23	6.24	74	.307	.366	0	ø	0	127	-11	0	-1.2
1988	NY A	1	2	.333	7	2	0	0-0	19.2	27	16	5	0	13-2	4	6.86	58	.333	.426	0	ø	0	126	-6	0	-0.8
1989	NY A	1	0	1.000	2	0	0	0-0	0.2	2	1	0	0	1-0	0	13.50	29	.500	.600	0	ø	0	—	-1	0	-0.1
Total	4	9	11	.450	38	18	3-3	2-0	142.2	178	94	26	3	51-3	47	5.49	79	.309	.367	0	ø	0	127	-18	0	-2.1
NIEMANN, RANDY	Randal Harold; B11.15.1955 Scotia CA; BL/TL/6´4″/(200–215); [NYA75 S2/30]; d5.20; C5; Col Redwoods (CA) [JC]; [DL 1981 Hou N 33]																									
1979	Hou N	3	2	.600	26	7	3-2	1-0	67	68	32	1	1	22-3	24	3.76	93	.272	.326	15-0-1	.133	-0	108	-2	0	-0.2
1980	Hou N	0	1	.000	22	1	0	1-0	33	40	21	2	0	12-1	18	5.45	60	.299	.354	6	.333	1	109	-8	0	-0.3
1982	Pit N	1	1	.500	20	0	0	1-0	35.1	34	22	1	2	17-4	26	5.09	74	.254	.344	2	1.000	1	—	-5	0	-0.2
1983	Pit N	0	1	.000	8	1	0	0-0	13.2	20	14	2	1	7-1	8	9.22	41	.357	.431	1	.000	-0	95	-7	0	-0.5
1984	Chi A	0	0	ø	5	0	0	0-0	5.1	5	1	0	0	5-1	5	1.69	248	.263	.417	0	ø	0	—	1	0	0.1
1985	NY N	0	0	ø	4	0	0	0-0	4.2	5	0	0	0	0-0	2	0.00	ø	.278	.278	0	ø	0	—	2	0	0.1
1986	NY N	2	3	.400	31	1	0	0-0	35.2	44	17	2	0	12-2	18	3.79	95	.308	.359	6	.333	1	224	-1	0	0.0
1987	Min A	1	0	1.000	6	0	0	0-0	5.1	3	5	0	2	7-0	1	8.44	55	.158	.429	0	ø	0	—	-2	0	-0.3
Total	8	7	8	.467	122	10	3-2	3-0	200	219	112	8	6	82-12	102	4.64	77	.283	.352	30-0-1	.267	2	116	-22	33	-1.3
NIEMES, JACK	Jacob Leland; B10.19.1919 Cincinnati OH; D3.4.1966 Hamilton OH; BR/TL/6´1″/180; d5.30; Mil 1944–46; Col Cincinnati																									
1943	Cin N	0	0	ø	3	0	0	0	3	5	3	0	0	2	1	6.00	55	.385	.467	0	ø	0	—	-1	0	-0.1
NIESON, CHUCK	Charles Bassett; B9.24.1942 Hanford CA; BR/TR/6´2″/185; d9.18; Col Cal St.–Fresno																									
1964	Min A	0	0	ø	2	0	0	0	2	1	1	1	0	1-0	5	4.50	79	.143	.250	0	ø	0	—	0	0	0.0
NIEVE, FERNANDO	Fernando Alexis; B7.15.1982 Puerto Cabello, Venezuela; BR/TR/6´0″/195; d4.4																									
2006	Hou N	3	3	.500	40	11	0	0-0	96.1	87	46	18	2	41-5	70	4.20	107	.242	.320	16-0-5	.125	0	104	4	14	0.2
NIEVES, JUAN	Juan Manuel (Cruz); B1.5.1965 Las Lomas, PR; BL/TL/6´3″/(175–190); d4.10; [DL 1989 Mil A 182, 1990 Mil A 58]																									
1986	Mil A	11	12	.478	35	33	4-3	0-0	184.2	224	124	17	1	77-0	116	4.92	89	.299	.363	0	ø	0	102	-15	0	-1.7
1987	Mil A	14	8	.636	34	33	3-1	0-0	195.2	199	112	24	2	100-5	163	4.88	95	.264	.348	0	ø	0	114	-4	0	-0.4
1988	Mil A	7	5	.583	25	15	1-1	1-0	110.1	84	53	13	1	50-4	73	4.08	98	.208	.295	0	ø	0	112	0	63	0.0
Total	3	32	25	.561	94	81	8-5	1-0	490.2	507	289	54	4	227-9	352	4.71	93	.266	.343	0	ø	0	109	-19	303	-2.1
NIGGELING, JOHNNY	John Arnold; B7.10.1903 Remsen IA; D9.16.1963 LeMars IA; BR/TR/6´0″/170; d4.30																									
1938	Bos N	1	0	1.000	2	0	0	0	2	4	2	0	0	1	1	9.00	38	.400	.455	0	ø	0	—	-1	—	-0.2
1939	Cin N	2	1	.667	10	5	2-1	0	40.1	51	28	2	2	13	20	5.80	66	.309	.367	13-0-2	.154	-0	132	-8	—	-0.6
1940	StL A	7	11	.389	28	20	10	0	153.2	148	88	9	5	69	82	4.45	103	.250	.333	51-0-1	.176	-1	81	1	—	0.0
1941	StL A	7	9	.438	24	20	13-1	0	168.1	168	83	17	1	63	68	3.80	113	.255	.320	60-0-4	.167	-1	83	8	0	0.5
1942	StL A	15	11	.577	28	27	16-3	0	206.1	173	76	10	11	93	107	2.66	139	.226	.319	72-0-5	.139	-2	86	22	0	2.3
1943	StL A	6	8	.429	20	20	7	0	150.1	122	61	7	6	57	73	3.17	105	.220	.299	49-0-5	.061	-4	92	3	0	-0.3
	Was A	4	2	.667	6	6	5-3	0	51	27	6	0	0	17	24	0.88	363	.153	.227	18	.278	1	79	14	0	2.1
	Year	10	10	.500	26	26	12-3	0	201.1	149	67	7	6	74	97	2.59	127	.204	.282	67-0-5	.119	-3	90	16	0	1.8
1944	Was A	10	8	.556	24	24	14-2	0	206	164	65	5	4	88	121	2.32	141	.221	.307	69-0-4	.130	-2	92	23	0	1.7
1945	Was A	7	12	.368	26	25	8-2	0	176.2	161	80	7	3	73	90	3.16	98	.240	.318	59	.119	-4	96	-3	0	-0.8
1946	Was A	3	2	.600	8	6	3	0	38	39	22	1	1	21	10	4.03	83	.265	.361	11-0-2	.182	0	128	-4	0	-0.4
	Bos N	2	5	.286	8	8	3	0	58	54	23	2	1	21	24	3.26	105	.243	.311	18-0-2	.111	-1	59	2	0	0.1
Total	9	64	69	.481	184	161	81-12	0	1250.2	1111	534	60	34	516	620	3.22	113	.236	.316	420-0-25	.140	-14	89	57	0	4.4
NIPPER, AL	Albert Samuel; B4.2.1959 San Diego CA; BR/TR/6´0″/(188–195); [BosA80 8/206]; d9.6; C5; Col Truman St.																									
1983	Bos A	1	1	.500	3	2	1	0-0	16	17	4	0	1	7-0	5	2.25	195	.293	.373	0	ø	0	41	4	0	0.4
1984	Bos A	11	6	.647	29	24	6	0-0	182.2	183	86	18	7	52-1	84	3.89	108	.257	.313	0	ø	0	112	8	0	0.8
1985	Bos A	9	12	.429	25	25	5	0-0	162	157	83	14	9	82-3	85	4.06	106	.256	.350	0	ø	0	86	3	7	0.5
1986	†Bos A	10	12	.455	26	26	3	0-0	159	186	108	24	4	47-2	79	5.38	78	.290	.340	0	ø	0	105	-22	37	-2.4
1987	Bos A	11	12	.478	30	30	6	0-0	174	196	115	30	7	62-1	89	5.43	84	.284	.345	0	ø	0	111	-17	24	-1.8
1988	Chi N	2	4	.333	22	12	0	1-0	80	72	37	9	3	34-2	27	3.04	120	.238	.321	23-0-2	.087	-1	102	2	47	0.0
1990	Cle A	2	3	.400	9	5	0	0-0	24	35	19	2	2	19-0	12	6.75	58	.354	.448	0	ø	0	92	-7	0	-1.3
Total	7	46	50	.479	144	124	21	1-0	797.2	846	452	97	33	303-9	381	4.52	94	.271	.339	23-0-2	.087	-1	102	-29	115	-3.8
NIPPERT, DUSTIN	Dustin David; B5.6.1981 Wheeling WV; BR/TR/6´7″/(215–225); [AriN02 15/459]; d9.8; Col West Virginia																									
2005	Ari N	1	0	1.000	3	3	0	0-0	14.2	10	9	1	1	13-0	11	5.52	80	.185	.353	4	.250	0	106	-1	0	0.0
2006	Ari N	0	2	.000	2	2	0	0-0	10	15	13	5	0	7-0	9	11.70	40	.349	.440	2	.000	-0	59	-7	0	-1.0
Total	2	1	2	.333	5	5	0	0-0	24.2	25	22	6	1	20-0	20	8.03	56	.258	.390	6	.167	0	87	-8	0	-1.0
NIPPERT, MERLIN	Merlin Lee; B9.1.1938 Mangum OK; BR/TR/6´1″/175; d9.12; Col Oklahoma St.																									
1962	Bos A	0	0	ø	4	0	0	0	6	4	3	1	0	4-1	3	4.50	92	.200	.320	0	ø	0	—	0	0	0.0
NISCHWITZ, RON	Ronald Lee; B7.1.1937 Dayton OH; BB/TL/6´3″/205; d9.4; Col Ohio St.																									
1961	Det A	0	1	.000	6	1	0	0	11.1	13	12	2	0	8-1	8	5.56	74	.295	.382	2	.000	-0	108	-3	0	-0.3
1962	Det A	4	5	.444	48	0	0	4	64.2	73	30	5	1	26-1	28	3.90	104	.285	.351	12	.417	2	—	2	0	0.5
1963	Cle A	0	2	.000	14	0	0	1	16.2	17	13	3	0	8-2	10	6.48	56	.262	.342	1	.000	-0	—	-5	0	-0.6
1965	Det A	1	0	1.000	20	0	0	1	22.2	21	10	2	0	6-1	12	2.78	125	.259	.307	3	.000	-0	—	1	0	0.0
Total	4	5	8	.385	88	1	0	6	115.1	124	65	12	1	48-5	58	4.21	92	.278	.345	18	.278	1	108	-5	0	-0.4
NITCHOLAS, OTHO	Otho James; B9.13.1908 McKinney TX; D9.11.1986 McKinney TX; BR/TR/6´0″/190; d4.18																									
1945	Bro N	1	0	1.000	7	0	0	0	18.2	19	14	4	0	1	4	5.30	71	.257	.267	4	.250	0	—	-3	0	-0.2
NITKOWSKI, C. J.	Christopher John; B3.9.1973 Suffern NY; BL/TL/6´3″/(190–210); [CinN94 1/9]; d6.3; Col St. Johns																									
1995	Cin N	1	3	.250	9	7	0	0-1	32.1	41	25	4	2	15-1	18	6.12	68	.306	.382	10	.200	0	71	-8	0	-0.8
	Det A	1	4	.200	11	11	0	0-0	39.1	53	32	7	3	20-2	13	7.09	68	.335	.413	0	ø	0	70	-9	0	-0.9
1996	Det A	2	3	.400	11	8	0	0-0	45.2	62	44	7	7	38-1	36	8.08	63	.332	.457	0	ø	0	141	-15	18	-1.2
1998	Hou N	3	3	.500	43	0	0	3-2	59.2	49	27	4	6	23-2	44	3.77	108	.228	.317	4-0-1	.000	-0	—	2	0	0.2
1999	Det A	4	5	.444	68	7	0	0-0	81.2	63	44	11	3	45-3	66	4.30	116	.213	.319	1	.000	-0*	104	5	0	0.5
2000	Det A	4	9	.308	67	11	0	0-2	109.2	124	79	13	4	49-3	81	5.25	93	.286	.358	0	ø	0	96	-8	0	-0.7
2001	Det A	0	3	.000	56	0	0	0-6	45.1	51	30	7	5	31-7	38	5.56	80	.283	.401	0	ø	0	—	-5	0	-0.3
	NY N	1	0	1.000	5	0	0	0-0	5.2	3	0	0	0	3-1	4	0.00	ø	.167	.286	0	ø	0	—	3	0	0.4
2002	Tex A	0	1	.000	12	0	0	0-0	13.2	11	4	0	0	13-0	14	2.63	182	.224	.387	0	ø	0	—	3	0	0.2
2003	Tex A	0	0	ø	6	0	0	0-0	9.2	17	8	0	0	8-1	5	7.45	67	.415	.490	0	ø	0	—	-2	0	-0.1
2004	Atl N	1	0	1.000	22	0	0	0-0	20	22	11	3	2	10-0	16	4.50	96	.275	.362	0	ø	0	—	0	0	0.0
	NY A	1	1	.500	19	0	0	0-0	13	18	11	1	4	6-0	10	7.62	60	.327	.431	0	ø	0	—	-4	0	-0.5
2005	Was N	0	0	ø	7	0	0	0-0	3.1	5	3	0	0	2-0	2	8.10	51	.357	.438	0	ø	0	—	-1	0	-0.1
Total	10	18	32	.360	336	44	0	3-11	479	519	318	57	36	263-21	347	5.37	87	.279	.375	15-0-1	.133	-1	99	-39	18	-3.3
NIXON, WILLARD	Willard Lee; B6.17.1928 Taylorsville GA; D12.10.2000 Rome GA; BL/TR/6´2″/195; d7.7; Col Auburn																									
1950	Bos A	8	6	.571	22	15	2	2	101.1	126	75	7	2	58	57	6.04	81	.310	.398	36-0-3	.139	-1	103	-12	0	-1.6
1951	Bos A	7	4	.636	33	14	2-1	1	125	136	79	12	7	56	70	4.90	91	.285	.368	45-1-1	.289	3*	129	-7	0	-0.3
1952	Bos A	5	4	.556	23	13	5	0	103.2	115	64	12	4	61	50	4.86	81	.290	.390	53	.208	1*	128	-10	0	-0.7
1953	Bos A	4	8	.333	23	15	5-1	0	116.2	114	57	6	1	59	57	3.93	107	.254	.343	42-0-1	.190	0	99	4	0	0.4
1954	Bos A	11	12	.478	31	30	8-2	0	199.2	182	102	16	9	87	102	4.06	101	.248	.333	68-1-2	.265	5	88	2	0	0.8
1955	Bos A	12	10	.545	31	31	7-3	0	208	207	102	10	3	85-2	95	4.07	105	.259	.330	69-0-4	.261	5	84	7	0	1.3
1956	Bos A	9	8	.529	23	22	9-1	0	145.1	142	79	9	8	57-2	74	4.21	110	.255	.331	54-0-2	.204	-1	106	6	0	0.6
1957	Bos A	12	13	.480	29	29	11-1	0	191	207	86	10	7	56-3	96	3.68	108	.280	.335	75	.293	5*	114	7	0	1.3
1958	Bos A	1	7	.125	10	8	2	0	43.1	48	30	7	0	11-0	15	6.02	67	.281	.324	17	.294	1	73	-8	77	-1.2
Total	9	69	72	.489	225	177	51-9	3	1234	1277	674	89	41	530-7	616	4.39	97	.270	.348	459-2-13	.242	17	101	-11	77	0.6

YEAR	TM LG	W	L	PCT	G	GS	CG-SHO	SV-BS	IP	H	R	HR	HB	BB-IB	SO	ERA	AERA	OAV	OOB	AB-HR-SH	AVG	PB	SUP	APR	DL	PW
Nolan, The Only	Edward Sylvester; B11.7.1857 Paterson NJ; D5.18.1913 Paterson NJ; BL/TR/5´8˝/171; d5.1																									
1878	Ind N	13	22	.371	38	38	37-1	0	347	357	208	1	—	56	125	2.57	79	.253	.281	152	.243	6	99	-21	—	-1.0
1881	Cle N	8	14	.364	22	21	20	0	180	183	111	3	—	38	54	3.05	86	.251	.288	168	.244	1*	79	-9	—	-0.9
1883	Pit AA	0	7	.000	7	7	6	0	55	81	44	0	—	10	23	4.25	76	.321	.347	26	.308	1	73	-7	—	-0.5
1884	Wil U	1	4	.200	5	5	5	0	40	44	28	1	—	7	52	2.93	91	.262	.291	33	.273	0*	32	0	—	0.0
1885	Phi N	1	5	.167	7	7	6	0	54	55	43	1	—	24	20	4.17	67	.256	.331	26	.077	-2	49	-7	—	-0.7
Total	5	23	52	.307	79	78	74-1	0	676	720	434	6	—	135	274	2.98	80	.259	.294	405	.240	7	82	-44	—	-3.1
Nolan, Gary	Gary Lynn; B5.27.1948 Herlong CA; BR/TR/6´2.5˝/(190–197); [CinN66 1/13]; d4.15																									
1967	Cin N	14	8	.636	33	32	8-5	0	226.2	193	73	18	5	62-7	206	2.58	145	.228	.282	67-0-8	.104	-1	69	27	0	2.4
1968	Cin N	9	4	.692	23	22	4-2	0	150	105	48	10	3	49-1	111	2.40	132	.196	.266	46-1-7	.130	2	122	11	0	1.1
1969	Cin N	8	8	.500	16	15	2-1	0-0	108.2	102	45	11	0	40-3	83	3.56	106	.247	.312	35-0-8	.229	3*	107	4	0	0.8
1970	†Cin N	18	7	.720	37	37	4-2	0-0	250.2	226	102	25	1	96-9	181	3.27	124	.240	.309	82-0-9	.159	1	100	23	0	2.1
1971	Cin N	12	15	.444	35	35	9	0-0	244.2	208	91	12	2	59-11	146	3.16	107	.227	.275	75-0-6	.147	-1	92	7	0	0.7
1972	†Cin N✳	15	5	**.750**	25	25	6-2	0-0	176	147	48	13	1	30-5	90	1.99	163	.227	.259	60-0-4	.117	-1	130	24	0	2.6
1973	Cin N	0	1	.000	2	2	0	0-0	10.1	6	4	1	0	7-1	3	3.48	99	.167	.295	2	.000	0	13	0	166	0.0
1975	†Cin N	15	9	.625	32	32	5-1	0-0	210.2	202	75	18	1	29-5	74	3.16	113	.251	.275	68-0-6	.176	2	124	12	0	1.4
1976	†Cin N	15	9	.625	34	34	7-1	0-0	239.1	232	96	28	1	27-3	113	3.46	101	.254	.275	79-0-6	.101	-3	119	4	0	-0.2
1977	Cin N	4	1	.800	8	8	0	0-0	39.1	53	22	5	0	12-1	28	4.81	82	.321	.367	15-0-2	.067	-1	141	-3	0	-0.5
	Cal A	0	3	.000	5	5	0	0-0	18.1	31	19	5	0	2-0	4	8.84	44	.365	.371	0	ø	0*	87	-10	43	-1.2
Total	10	110	70	.611	250	247	45-14	0-0	1674.2	1505	623	146	14	413-46	1039	3.08	116	.239	.285	529-1-56	.138	0	106	99	209	9.2
Nolasco, Ricky	Carlos Enrique; B12.13.1982 Corona CA; BR/TR/6´2˝/220; [ChiN01 4/108]; d4.5																									
2006	Fla N	11	11	.500	35	22	0	0-0	140	157	86	20	10	41-5	99	4.82	89	.286	.344	41-1-6	.171	2	97	-10	0	-1.3
Nold, Dick	Richard Louis; B5.4.1943 San Francisco CA; BR/TR/6´2˝/180; d8.19; Col San Francisco (CA) City																									
1967	Was A	0	2	.000	7	3	0	0	20.1	19	13	1	0	13-0	10	4.87	65	.241	.348	3	.000	-0	92	-4	0	-0.4
Noles, Dickie	Dickie Ray; B11.19.1956 Charlotte NC; BR/TR/6´2˝/(178–190); [PhiN75 4/84]; d7.5																									
1979	Phi N	3	4	.429	14	14	0	0-0	90	80	40	6	2	38-2	42	3.80	102	.246	.325	30-0-1	.100	-1	87	1	0	0.0
1980	†Phi N	1	4	.200	48	3	0	6-1	81	80	42	5	1	42-11	57	3.89	98	.254	.342	13-0-2	.308	1	148	-2	0	-0.1
1981	†Phi N	2	2	.500	13	8	0	0-0	58.1	57	30	2	3	23-2	34	4.17	88	.260	.336	19-0-2	.105	-1	112	-3	0	-0.4
1982	Chi N	10	13	.435	31	30	2-2	0-0	171	180	99	11	5	61-2	85	4.42	86	.274	.336	56-0-4	.107	-2	96	-14	21	-1.9
1983	Chi N	5	10	.333	24	18	1-1	0-0	116.1	133	69	9	1	37-3	59	4.72	81	.287	.339	38-0-3	.237	1	89	-12	53	-1.3
1984	Chi N	2	2	.500	21	1	0	0-3	50.2	60	29	4	1	16-1	14	5.15	76	.305	.356	10	.000	-1	0	-5	0	-0.5
	Tex A	2	3	.400	18	6	0	0-0	57.2	60	38	6	5	30-0	39	5.15	81	.262	.360	0	ø	0	130	-6	0	-0.5
1985	Tex A	4	8	.333	28	13	0	1-0	110.1	129	67	11	6	33-1	59	5.06	84	.289	.346	0	ø	0	82	-9	20	-0.9
1986	Cle A	3	2	.600	32	0	0	0-0	54.2	56	33	9	5	30-4	32	5.10	82	.269	.367	0	ø	0	—	-5	61	-0.4
1987	Chi N	4	2	.667	41	1	0	2-2	64.1	59	31	1	5	27-1	33	3.50	124	.239	.325	11	.000	-1	0	4	50	0.3
	Det A	0	0	ø	4	0	0	2-1	2	2	1	0	0	1-0	0	4.50	95	.250	.333	0	ø	0	—	0	0	0.0
1988	Bal A	0	2	.000	2	2	0	0-0	3.1	11	10	2	1	0-0	1	24.30	16	.500	.522	0	ø	0	116	-8	0	-1.1
1990	Phi N	0	1	.000	1	0	0	0-0	0.1	2	1	0	0	0-0	0	27.00	14	.667	.667	0	ø	0	—	-1	82	-0.2
Total	11	36	53	.404	277	96	3-3	11-7	860	909	490	66	35	338-27	455	4.56	87	.272	.343	177-0-12	.136	-4	93	-60	287	-7.0
Nolte, Eric	Eric Carl; B4.28.1964 Canoga Park CA; BL/TL/6´3˝/200; [SDN85 6/154]; d8.1; Col UCLA																									
1987	SD N	2	6	.250	12	12	1	0-0	67.1	57	28	6	2	36-2	44	3.21	124	.226	.326	21-0-3	.095	-1	78	5	0	0.5
1988	SD N	0	0	ø	2	0	0	0-0	3	3	2	1	0	2-0	1	6.00	57	.273	.385	0	ø	0	—	-1	0	0.0
1989	SD N	0	0	ø	3	1	0	0-0	9	15	12	1	0	7-1	8	11.00	32	.375	.458	2	.000	-0	278	-7	35	-0.4
1991	SD N	3	2	.600	6	6	0	0-0	22	37	27	6	0	10-0	15	11.05	34	.378	.423	9-0-2	.111	-0	126	-16	0	-2.6
	Tex A	0	0	ø	3	0	0	0-0	2.2	3	1	0	0	3-0	1	3.38	120	.273	.429	0	ø	0	—	0	0	0.0
Total	4	5	8	.385	26	19	1	0-0	104	115	70	14	2	58-3	69	5.63	69	.279	.367	32-0-5	.094	-1	103	-19	35	-2.5
Nomo, Hideo	Hideo; B8.31.1968 Osaka, Japan; BR/TR/6´2˝/(200–235); d5.2																									
1995	†LA N★	13	6	.684	28	28	4-**3**	0-0	191.1	124	63	14	5	78-2	**236**	2.54	152	**.182**	.269	66-0-5	.091	-4	104	30	0	2.2
1996	†LA N	16	11	.593	33	33	3-2	0-0	228.1	180	93	23	2	85-6	234	3.19	123	.218	.290	75-0-10	.133	-0	97	20	0	2.1
1997	LA N	14	12	.538	33	33	1	0-0	207.1	193	104	23	9	92-2	233	4.25	92	.243	.328	69-0-5	.159	2	119	-7	0	-0.7
1998	LA N	2	7	.222	12	12	2	0-0	67.2	57	39	8	3	38-0	73	5.05	80	.228	.334	20-1-2	.050	-1	51	-7	0	-0.9
	NY N	4	5	.444	17	16	1	0-0	89.2	73	49	11	1	56-2	94	4.82	86	.224	.337	30-0-2	.267	2	110	-6	0	-0.4
	Year	6	12	.333	29	28	3	0-0	157.1	130	88	19	4	94-2	167	4.92	83	.226	.336	50-1-4	.180	1	85	-13	0	-1.3
1999	Mil N	12	8	.600	28	28	0	0-0	176.1	173	96	27	3	78-2	161	4.54	101	.256	.333	56-0-7	.214	2*	110	2	0	0.3
2000	Det A	8	12	.400	32	31	1	0-0	190	191	102	31	3	89-1	181	4.74	104	.263	.344	6	.000	-1	88	7	18	0.5
2001	Bos A	13	10	.565	33	33	2-2	0-0	198	171	105	26	3	96-2	**220**	4.50	99	.231	.320	5	.200	0	108	1	0	0.1
2002	LA N	16	6	.727	34	34	0	0-0	220.1	189	92	26	2	101-5	193	3.39	115	.236	.321	63-1-6	.063	-1	115	12	0	0.8
2003	LA N	16	13	.552	33	33	2-2	0-0	218.1	175	82	24	1	98-6	177	3.09	133	.223	.309	65-1-6	.138	0	75	26	0	3.2
2004	LA N	4	11	.267	18	18	0	0-0	84	105	77	19	4	42-1	54	8.25	50	.312	.391	26-1-1	.115	-0	95	-38	81	-5.1
2005	TB A	5	8	.385	19	19	0	0-0	100.2	127	82	16	2	51-2	59	7.24	61	.314	.386	4	.000	-0	105	-28	0	-3.0
Total	11	123	109	.530	320	318	16-9	0-0	1972	1758	984	248	38	904-31	1915	4.21	99	.239	.324	485-4-44	.134	-1	101	12	99	-0.9
Nomura, Takahito	Takahito; B1.10.1969 Kouchi Prefecture, Japan; BL/TL/5´7˝/175; d4.3																									
2002	Mil N	0	0	ø	21	0	0	0-1	13.2	11	14	2	2	18-4	9	8.56	48	.224	.437	0	ø	0	—	-7	0	-0.3
Nops, Jerry	Jeremiah Henry; B6.23.1875 Toledo OH; D3.26.1937 Camden NJ; BL/TL/5´8.5˝/168; d9.7																									
1896	Phi N	1	0	1.000	1	1	1	0	7	11	5	0	0	1	1	5.14	84	.355	.375	4	.000	-1	165	0	—	-0.1
	Bal N	2	1	.667	3	3	3	0	22	29	15	0	0	2	8	6.14	70	.315	.330	9	.111	-1	105	-2	—	-0.3
	Year	3	1	.750	4	4	4	0	29	40	20	0	0	3	9	5.90	73	.325	.341	13	.077	-2	120	-3	—	-0.4
1897	†Bal N	20	6	.769	30	25	23-1	0	220.2	235	107	5	9	52	69	2.81	148	.270	.318	92-0-2	.196	-3	97	31	—	2.5
1898	Bal N	16	9	.640	33	29	23-2	0	235	241	130	5	16	78	91	3.56	100	.263	.332	91-0-1	.220	2	99	2	—	0.1
1899	Bal N	17	11	.607	33	33	26-2	0	259	296	156	1	11	71	60	4.03	98	.287	.339	105	.276	1*	93	2	—	0.1
1900	Bro N	4	4	.500	9	8	6-1	0	68	79	45	1	2	18	22	3.84	100	.289	.338	25	.160	-1	104	-2	—	-0.3
1901	Bal A	12	10	.545	27	23	17-1	1	176.2	192	123	5	13	59	43	4.08	95	.274	.341	59-0-4	.220	-0	96	-3	—	-0.6
Total	6	72	41	.637	136	122	99-7	1	988.1	1083	581	17	51	281	294	3.70	106	.277	.333	385-0-7	.221	-2	97	28	—	1.4
Noriega, John	John Alan; B12.20.1943 Ogden UT; D9.29.2001 Bountiful UT; BR/TR/6´4˝/180; [CinN66*S4/62]; d5.1; Col Utah																									
1969	Cin N	0	0	ø	5	0	0	0-0	7.2	12	6	1	0	3-0	4	5.87	64	.400	.429	0	ø	0	—	-2	0	-0.1
1970	Cin N	0	0	ø	8	0	0	0-0	18	25	17	0	2	10-1	6	8.00	51	.333	.420	4	.250	0	—	-7	0	-0.3
Total	2	0	0	ø	13	0	0	0-0	25.2	37	23	1	2	13-1	10	7.36	54	.352	.423	4	.250	0	—	-9	0	-0.4
Norman, Fred	Fredie Hubert; B8.20.1942 San Antonio TX; BB/TL (BL 1962–64, 66–67, 70)/5´8˝/(158–170); d9.21																									
1962	KC A	0	0	ø	2	0	0	0	4	4	1	0	0	1-0	2	2.25	188	.250	.294	0	ø	0	—	1	0	0.0
1963	KC A	0	1	.000	2	2	0	0	6.1	9	9	1	0	7-0	6	11.37	34	.346	.471	1	.000	-0	80	-5	0	-0.6
1964	Chi N	0	4	.000	8	5	0	0	31.2	34	25	9	1	21-5	20	6.54	57	.279	.389	11	.091	-1	62	-9	0	-1.1
1966	Chi N	0	0	ø	2	0	0	0	4	5	2	0	0	2-1	6	4.50	82	.313	.389	0	ø	0	—	0	0	0.0
1967	Chi N	0	0	ø	1	0	0	0	1	0	0	0	0	0-0	3	0.00	ø	.000	.000	0	ø	0	—	0	0	0.0
1970	LA N	2	0	1.000	30	0	0	1-1	62	65	40	8	2	33-1	47	5.23	74	.273	.364	7-0-2	.143	0	—	-10	0	-0.5
	StL N	0	0	ø	1	0	0	0-0	1	1	0	0	0	0-0	0	0.00	ø	.333	.250	0	ø	0	—	0	0	0.0
	Year	2	0	1.000	31	0	0	1-1	63	66	40	8	2	33-1	47	5.14	75	.274	.362	7-0-2	.143	0	—	-9	0	-0.5
1971	StL N	0	0	ø	4	0	0	0-0	3.2	7	5	1	0	7-0	4	12.27	30	.438	.583	0	ø	0	—	-3	0	-0.2
	SD N	3	12	.200	20	18	5	0-1	127.1	114	48	7	2	56-7	77	3.32	100	.240	.321	38-0-3	.237	2*	50	3	0	0.6
	Year	3	12	.200	24	18	5	0-1	131	121	53	8	2	63-7	81	3.57	93	.246	.332	38-0-3	.237	2	50	-1	0	0.4
1972	SD N	9	11	.450	42	28	10-6	2-0	211.2	195	88	18	2	88-12	167	3.44	96	.244	.318	64-0-5	.125	1*	103	-2	0	-0.1
1973	SD N	1	7	.125	12	11	1	0-0	74	72	35	9	1	29-2	49	4.26	83	.262	.332	22-0-1	.136	-0	57	-4	0	-0.4
	†Cin N	12	6	.667	24	24	7-3	0-0	166.1	136	67	18	1	72-9	112	3.30	104	.224	.304	58-0-6	.052	-4	132	3	0	-0.1
	Year	13	13	.500	36	35	8-3	0-0	240.1	208	102	27	2	101-11	161	3.60	97	.236	.313	80-0-7	.075	-4	108	0	0	-0.5
1974	Cin N	13	12	.520	35	26	8-2	0-1	186.1	170	69	15	2	68-9	141	3.14	111	.241	.307	61-0-7	.131	-2	124	10	0	0.9
1975	†Cin N	12	4	.750	34	26	2	0-0	188	163	85	23	0	84-5	119	3.73	96	.235	.316	60-0-9	.117	-2	131	-4	0	-0.6

YEAR	TM LG	W	L	PCT	G	GS	CG-SHO	SV-BS	IP	H	R	HR	HB	BB-IB	SO	ERA	AERA	OAV	OOB	AB-HR-SH	AVG	PB	SUP	APR	DL	PW
1976	†Cin N	12	7	.632	33	24	8-3	0-0	180.1	153	71	10	3	70-5	126	3.09	113	.231	.305	50-0-7	.140	-1	119	7	0	0.4
1977	Cin N	14	13	.519	35	34	8-1	0-1	221.1	200	97	28	3	98-9	160	3.38	117	.241	.322	73-0-6	.110	-2	100	10	0	0.9
1978	Cin N	11	9	.550	36	31	0	1-0	177.1	173	86	19	3	82-6	111	3.70	96	.255	.336	50-0-8	.140	-1	102	-5	0	-0.6
1979	†Cin N	11	13	.458	34	31	5	0-0	195.1	193	86	14	0	57-4	95	3.64	102	.258	.309	59-0-6	.153	1	106	3	0	0.3
1980	Mon N	4	4	.500	48	8	2	4-0	98	96	50	8	3	40-4	58	4.13	88	.259	.333	20-0-2	.050	-2	89	-5	0	-0.7
Total	16	104	103	.502	403	268	56-15	8-4	1939.2	1790	864	188	23	815-79	1303	3.64	98	.246	.321	574-0-62	.125	-11	105	-10	0	-1.8
Norris, Mike	Michael Kelvin; B3.19.1955 San Francisco CA; BR/TR/6´2˝/(160–190); [OakA73*1/24]; d4.10; [DL 1985 Oak A 182]																									
1975	Oak A	1	0	1.000	4	3	1-1	0-0	16.2	6	2	0	0	8-0	5	0.00	ø	.107	.215	0	ø	0	137	6	144	0.4
1976	Oak A	4	5	.444	24	19	1-1	0-0	96	91	53	10	2	56-2	44	4.78	70	.250	.350	0	ø	0	117	-14	0	-1.0
1977	Oak A	2	7	.222	16	12	1-1	0-0	77.1	77	45	14	4	31-1	35	4.77	85	.260	.336	1	.000	-0*	78	-5	0	-0.5
1978	Oak A	0	5	.000	14	5	1	0-0	49	46	35	2	3	35-1	36	5.51	66	.249	.373	0	ø	0*	64	-10	0	-0.9
1979	Oak A	5	8	.385	29	18	3	0-0	146.1	146	87	11	9	94-9	96	4.80	85	.265	.376	0	ø	0	83	-12	26	-1.0
1980	Oak A	22	9	.710	33	33	24-1	0-0	284.1	215	88	18	6	83-2	180	2.53	151	**.209**	.270	0	ø	0	110	**44**	0	4.8
1981	†Oak A★	12	9	.571	23	23	12-2	0-0	172.2	145	77	17	10	63-0	78	3.75	94	.228	.305	0	ø	0	105	-3	0	-0.4
1982	Oak A	7	11	.389	28	28	7-1	0-0	166.1	154	103	25	6	84-1	83	4.76	83	.242	.335	0	ø	0*	91	-18	21	-1.6
1983	Oak A	4	5	.444	16	16	2	0-0	88.2	68	42	11	3	36-0	63	3.76	104	.213	.297	0	ø	0	98	1	91	0.0
1990	Oak A	1	0	1.000	14	0	0	0-0	27	24	10	0	2	9-0	16	3.00	125	.242	.315	0	ø	0	—	2	0	0.1
Total	10	58	59	.496	201	157	52-7	0-0	1124.1	972	542	108	45	499-16	636	3.89	98	.233	.319	1	.000	-0	99	-9	464	-0.1
North, Lou	Louis Alexander; B6.15.1891 Elgin IL; D5.15.1974 Shelton CT; BR/TR/5´11˝/175; d8.22; Mil 1918																									
1913	Det A	0	1	.000	1	1	0	0	6	10	11	1	0	9	3	15.00	19	.370	.528	2	.000	-0	178	-7	—	-0.8
1917	StL N	0	0	ø	5	0	0	0	11.1	14	5	1	0	4	4	3.97	68	.350	.409	3	.000	-0	—	-1	—	-0.1
1920	StL N	3	2	.600	24	6	3	1	88	90	42	3	2	32	37	3.27	91	.278	.346	31-0-1	.226	0*	145	-4	—	-0.3
1921	StL N	4	4	.500	40	0	0	**7**	86.1	81	39	5	1	32	28	3.54	103	.256	.327	19	.158	-1	—	**2**	—	0.1
1922	StL N	10	3	.769	**53**	10	4	4	149.2	164	90	4	6	64	84	4.45	87	.283	.361	47-1-2	.234	2	131	-10	—	-0.5
1923	StL N	3	4	.429	34	3	0	1	71.2	90	50	8	3	31	24	5.15	76	.308	.380	22	.182	-1	211	-10	—	-0.9
1924	StL N	0	0	ø	6	1	0	0	14.2	15	12	1	0	9	8	6.75	56	.273	.375	4	.250	-0	135	-4	—	-0.2
	Bos N	1	2	.333	9	4	1	0	35.1	45	25	1	0	19	11	5.35	71	.321	.403	9	.111	-1	89	-6	—	-0.6
	Year	1	2	.333	15	5	1	0	50	60	37	2	0	28	19	5.76	66	.308	.395	13	.154	-1	98	-11	—	-0.8
Total	7	21	16	.568	172	25	8	13	463	509	274	24	12	200	199	4.43	82	.287	.363	137-1-3	.197	-1	139	-40	—	-3.3
Northrop, Jake	George Howard "Jerky"; B3.5.1888 Monroeton PA; D11.16.1945 Monroeton PA; BL/TR/5´11˝/170; d7.29; Col Bucknell																									
1918	Bos N	5	1	.833	7	4	4-1	0	40	26	9	0	0	3	4	1.35	199	.183	.200	13-0-2	.154	-1	106	6	—	0.8
1919	Bos N	1	5	.167	11	3	2	0	37.1	43	22	2	1	10	9	4.58	62	.301	.351	8-0-1	.500	3	74	-7	—	-0.6
Total	2	6	6	.500	18	7	6-1	0	77.1	69	31	2	1	13	13	2.91	95	.242	.278	21-0-3	.286	2	92	-1	—	0.2
Norton, Effie	Elisha Strong "Leiter"; B8.17.1873 Conneaut OH; D3.5.1950 Aspinwall PA; BR/TR/5´10.5˝/170; d8.8; Col Ohio St.																									
1896	Was N	3	1	.750	8	5	2	0	44	49	25	2	6	14	13	3.07	144	.280	.354	19	.211	-0	87	6	—	0.4
1897	Was N	2	1	.667	4	2	1	0	17	31	18	0	0	11	3	6.88	63	.387	.462	18	.278	1*	90	-4	—	-0.5
Total	2	5	2	.714	12	7	3	0	61	80	43	2	6	25	16	4.13	106	.314	.388	37	.243	0	88	2	—	-0.1
Norton, Phil	Phillip Douglas; B2.1.1976 Texarkana TX; BR/TL/6´1˝/(190–215); [ChiN96 10/292]; d8.3; Col Texarkana (TX) JC																									
2000	Chi N	0	1	.000	2	2	0	0-0	8.2	14	10	5	0	7-0	6	9.35	49	.350	.447	3-0-1	.667	1	100	-5	0	-0.4
2003	Chi N	0	0	ø	4	0	0	0-0	3.1	2	2	0	0	3-0	0	5.40	80	.182	.357	0	ø	0	—	0	0	0.0
	Cin N	0	0	ø	17	0	0	0-0	14.2	7	4	0	0	6-0	7	2.45	170	.149	.245	1	.000	-0	—	3	0	0.1
	Year	0	0	ø	21	0	0	0-0	18	9	6	0	0	9-0	7	3.00	140	.155	.269	1	.000	-0	—	3	0	0.1
2004	Cin N	2	5	.286	69	0	0	0-2	65.2	71	41	5	2	38-7	48	5.07	85	.284	.380	0	ø	0	—	-6	0	-0.5
Total	3	2	6	.250	92	2	0	0-2	92.1	94	57	10	2	54-7	61	5.07	85	.270	.369	4-0-1	.500	1	100	-8	0	-0.8
Norton, Tom	Thomas John; B4.26.1950 Elyria OH; BR/TR/6´1˝/193; d4.18; Col St. Clair Co. (MI) CC																									
1972	Min A	0	1	.000	21	0	0	0-0	32.1	31	14	1	1	14-0	22	2.78	115	.252	.333	0	ø	0	—	1	63	0.1
Nosek, Randy	Randall William; B1.8.1967 Omaha NE; BR/TR/6´4˝/216; [DetA85 1/26]; d5.27																									
1989	Det A	0	2	.000	2	2	0	0-0	5.1	7	8	2	0	10-0	4	13.50	28	.333	.548	0	ø	0	47	-5	0	-0.9
1990	Det A	1	1	.500	3	2	0	0-0	7	7	7	1	0	9-1	3	7.71	52	.280	.457	0	ø	0	103	-3	0	-0.6
Total	2	1	3	.250	5	4	0	0-0	12.1	14	15	3	0	19-1	7	10.22	38	.304	.500	0	ø	0	75	-8	0	-1.5
Nottebart, Don	Donald Edward; B1.23.1936 West Newton MA; BR/TR/6´1˝/(190–208); d7.1																									
1960	Mil N	1	0	1.000	5	1	0	1	15.1	14	10	0	0	15-2	8	4.11	83	.233	.387	5	.000	-1	180	-2	0	-0.2
1961	Mil N	6	7	.462	38	11	2	3	126.1	117	61	11	2	48-2	66	4.06	92	.251	.321	38-0-1	.184	0	103	-4	0	-0.3
1962	Mil N	2	2	.500	39	0	0	2	64	64	30	4	4	20-3	36	3.23	117	.258	.321	6	.333	1	—	2	0	0.3
1963	Hou N	11	8	.579	31	27	9-2	0	193	170	80	10	1	39-1	118	3.17	99	.234	.272	66-0-3	.167	0	101	-1	0	-0.1
1964	Hou N	6	11	.353	28	24	2	0	157	165	76	12	1	37-1	90	3.90	88	.275	.314	47-0-5	.064	-2	89	-7	0	-0.8
1965	Hou N	4	15	.211	29	25	3	0	158	166	99	14	5	55-11	77	4.67	72	.273	.337	48-0-4	.104	-1	104	-27	0	-2.9
1966	Cin N	5	4	.556	59	1	0	11	111.1	97	45	11	2	43-5	69	3.07	127	.235	.309	24-0-1	.167	-0	45	8	0	0.8
1967	Cin N	0	3	.000	47	0	0	4	79.1	75	25	4	2	19-4	48	1.93	194	.253	.299	3-0-2	.000	-0	—	12	0	0.7
1969	NY A	0	0	ø	4	0	0	0-0	6	6	3	1	1	0-0	5	4.50	78	.261	.292	0	ø	0	—	0	0	0.0
	Chi N	1	1	.500	16	0	0	0-0	18	28	14	2	0	7-0	8	7.00	57	.350	.398	1	.000	0	—	-5	0	-0.5
Total	9	36	51	.414	296	89	16-2	21-0	928.1	902	443	69	18	283-29	525	3.65	96	.256	.312	238-0-16	.134	-3	95	-24	0	-3.0
Nourse, Chet	Chester Linwood; B8.7.1887 Ipswich MA; D4.20.1958 Clearwater FL; BR/TR/6´3˝/185; d7.27; Col Brown																									
1909	Bos A	0	0	ø	3	0	0	0	5	5	5	0	0	5	3	7.20	35	.263	.417	2	.000	-0	—	-2	—	-0.2
Novoa, Rafael	Rafael Angel; B10.26.1967 New York NY; BL/TL/6´0˝/180; [SFN89 9/232]; d7.31; Col Villanova																									
1990	SF N	0	1	.000	7	2	0	1-0	18.2	21	14	3	0	13-1	14	6.75	54	.284	.386	5	.200	0	111	-6	0	-0.3
1993	Mil A	0	3	.000	15	7	2	0-0	56	58	32	7	4	22-2	17	4.50	96	.267	.343	0	ø	0	67	-2	15	-0.1
Total	2	0	4	.000	22	9	2	1-0	74.2	79	46	10	4	35-3	31	5.06	82	.271	.354	5	.200	0	76	-8	15	-0.4
Novoa, Roberto	Roberto; B8.15.1979 Las Matas de Farfan, D.R.; BR/TR/6´5˝/200; d7.29																									
2004	Det A	1	1	.500	16	0	0	0-1	21	25	15	4	2	6-0	15	5.57	80	.309	.355	0	ø	0	—	-3	0	-0.2
2005	Chi N	4	5	.444	49	0	0	0-5	44.2	47	22	4	0	25-6	47	4.43	99	.264	.355	1	.000	-0	—	0	0	0.0
2006	Chi N	2	1	.667	66	0	0	0-0	76	77	47	15	6	32-5	53	4.26	108	.262	.344	5	.200	0	—	-1	0	-0.1
Total	3	7	7	.500	131	0	0	0-6	141.2	149	84	23	8	63-11	115	4.51	100	.269	.349	6	.167	0	—	-4	0	-0.3
Noyes, Win	Winfield Charles; B6.16.1889 Pleasanton NE; D4.8.1969 Cashmere WA; BR/TR/6´0˝/180; d5.19; Mil 1918; Col Nebraska Wesleyan																									
1913	Bos N	0	0	ø	11	0	0	0	20.2	22	18	1	4	6	5	4.79	69	.289	.372	4	.250	0	—	-4	—	-0.2
1917	Phi A	10	10	.500	27	22	11-1	1	171	156	74	5	4	77	64	2.95	93	.258	.345	52-0-2	.115	-2	95	-2	—	-0.5
1919	Phi A	1	5	.167	10	6	3	0	49	66	34	1	1	15	20	5.69	60	.332	.381	16	.125	-1	88	-10	—	-1.1
	Chi A	0	0	ø	1	1	0	0	6	10	5	0	0	0	4	7.50	42	.385	.385	2	.500	0	123	-2	—	-0.1
	Year	1	5	.167	11	7	3	0	55	76	39	1	1	15	24	5.89	58	.338	.382	18	.167	-1	92	-12	—	-1.2
Total	3	11	15	.423	49	29	14-1	1	246.2	254	131	7	9	98	93	3.76	78	.280	.356	74-0-2	.135	-3	93	-18	—	-1.9
Nunez, Edwin	Edwin (Martinez); B5.27.1963 Humacao, PR; BR/TR/6´5˝/(220–240); d4.7																									
1982	Sea A	1	2	.333	8	5	0	0-0	35.1	36	18	7	0	16-0	27	4.58	93	.269	.347	0	ø	0	106	0	22	0.0
1983	Sea A	0	4	.000	14	5	0	0-0	37	40	21	3	3	22-1	35	4.38	98	.278	.385	0	ø	0	51	-1	0	-0.1
1984	Sea A	2	2	.500	37	0	0	7-2	67.2	55	26	8	3	21-2	57	3.19	126	.218	.283	0	ø	0	—	7	0	0.5
1985	Sea A	7	3	.700	70	0	0	16-5	90.1	79	36	13	0	34-5	58	3.09	137	.234	.302	0	ø	0	—	10	0	1.4
1986	Sea A	1	2	.333	14	1	0	0-2	21.2	25	15	5	0	5-1	17	5.82	73	.284	.323	0	ø	0	64	-3	37	-0.4
1987	Sea A	3	4	.429	48	0	0	12-5	47.1	45	20	7	1	18-3	34	3.80	125	.262	.328	0	ø	0	—	6	15	1.0
1988	Sea A	1	4	.200	14	3	0	0-0	29.1	45	33	4	2	14-3	19	7.98	52	.366	.427	0	ø	0	65	-13	0	-1.9
	NY N	1	0	1.000	10	0	0	0-0	14	21	7	1	0	3-0	8	4.50	73	.339	.369	0	ø	0	—	-2	0	-0.1
1989	Det A	3	4	.429	27	0	0	1-2	54	49	33	6	0	36-13	41	4.17	92	.254	.366	0	ø	0	—	-4	0	-0.5
1990	Det A	3	1	.750	42	0	0	6-1	80.1	65	26	4	2	37-6	66	2.24	178	.218	.308	0	ø	0	—	13	38	0.7
1991	Mil A	2	1	.667	23	0	0	8-1	25.1	28	20	6	0	13-2	24	6.04	66	.277	.353	0	ø	0	—	-7	86	-1.0
1992	Mil A	1	1	.500	10	0	0	0-0	13.2	12	5	1	0	6-0	10	2.63	147	.231	.310	0	ø	0	—	2	0	0.2

YEAR	TM LG	W	L	PCT	G	GS	CG-SHO	SV-BS	IP	H	R	HR	HB	BB-IB	SO	ERA	AERA	OAV	OOB	AB-HR-SH	AVG	PB	SUP	APR	DL	PW
	Tex A	0	2	.000	39	0	0	3-1	45.2	51	29	5	2	16-0	39	5.52	69	.279	.337	0	ø	0	—	-8	0	-0.4
	Year	1	3	.250	49	0	0	3-1	59.1	63	34	6	2	22-0	49	4.85	79	.268	.331	0	ø	0	—	-6	0	-0.2
1993	Oak A	3	6	.333	56	0	0	1-3	75.2	89	36	2	6	29-2	58	3.81	109	.298	.369	0	ø	0	—	2	0	0.2
1994	Oak A	0	0	ø	15	0	0	0-0	15	26	20	2	0	10-0	15	12.00	37	.382	.456	0	ø	0	—	-12	0	-0.5
Total	13	28	36	.438	427	14	0	54-22	652.1	666	345	74	19	280-38	508	4.19	98	.266	.341	0	ø	0	77	-10	198	-0.9
Nunez, Franklin	Franklin; B1.18.1977 Nagua, D.R.; BR/TR/6´0˝/175; d8.14																									
2004	TB A	0	3	.000	8	0	0	0-1	10.2	11	8	1	3	7-0	14	5.91	79	.268	.396	0	ø	0	—	-2	0	-0.3
2005	TB A	1	0	1.000	5	0	0	0-0	5	5	6	0	0	4-0	2	10.80	41	.278	.409	0	ø	0	—	-3	55	-0.5
Total	2	1	3	.250	13	0	0	0-1	15.2	16	14	1	3	11-0	16	7.47	61	.271	.400	0	ø	0	—	-5	55	-0.8
Nunez, Jose	Jose (Jimenez); B1.13.1964 Jarabacoa, D.R.; BR/TR/6´3˝/(175–190); d4.9																									
1987	Tor A	5	2	.714	37	9	0	0-0	97	91	57	12	0	58-8	99	5.01	91	.256	.356	0	ø	0*	130	-4	0	-0.3
1988	Tor A	0	1	.000	13	2	0	0-1	29.1	28	11	3	1	17-3	18	3.07	129	.259	.365	0	ø	0	81	3	15	0.1
1989	Tor A	0	0	ø	6	1	0	0-0	10.2	8	3	0	0	2-0	14	2.53	150	.200	.238	0	ø	0	119	2	0	0.1
1990	Chi N	4	7	.364	21	10	0	0-0	60.2	61	47	5	0	34-4	40	6.53	63	.270	.361	11-0-3	.000	-1	113	-14	0	-2.4
Total	4	9	10	.474	77	22	0	0-1	197.2	188	118	20	1	111-15	171	5.05	85	.258	.353	11-0-3	.000	-1	117	-13	15	-2.5
Nunez, Jose	Jose Antonio; B3.14.1979 Monte Cristi, D.R.; BL/TL/6´2˝/173; d4.3																									
2001	LA N	0	1	.000	6	0	0	0-1	7.1	14	15	4	0	5-0	11	13.50	31	.389	.463	0	ø	0	—	-10	0	-1.1
	SD N	4	1	.800	56	0	0	0-1	51.2	48	20	3	4	20-3	49	3.31	125	.245	.324	3	.000	-0	—	6	0	0.4
	Year	4	2	.667	62	0	0	0-2	59	62	35	7	4	25-3	60	4.58	91	.267	.346	3	.000	-0	—	-4	0	-0.7
2002	SD N	0	0	ø	1	0	0	0-0	1	0	0	0	0	1-0	0	0.00	ø	.000	.250	0	ø	0	—	0	181	0.0
Total	2	4	2	.667	63	0	0	0-2	60	62	35	7	4	26-3	60	4.50	92	.264	.345	3	.000	-0	—	-4	181	-0.7
Nunez, Leo	Leonel (Morales); B8.14.1983 Jamao Norte, D.R.; BR/TR/6´1˝/(160–165); d5.9																									
2005	KC A	3	2	.600	41	0	0	0-1	53.2	73	45	9	3	18-2	32	7.55	58	.329	.384	0	ø	0	—	-17	0	-1.4
2006	KC A	0	0	ø	7	0	0	0-0	13.1	15	7	2	2	5-0	7	4.73	99	.300	.379	0	ø	0	—	0	0	0.0
Total	2	3	2	.600	48	0	0	0-1	67	88	52	11	5	23-2	39	6.99	64	.324	.383	0	ø	0	—	-17	0	-1.4
Nunez, Vladimir	Vladimir (Zarabaza); B3.15.1975 Havana, Cuba; BR/TR/6´4˝/(224–240); d9.11																									
1998	Ari N	0	0	ø	4	0	0	0-0	5.1	7	6	0	0	2-0	2	10.13	42	.318	.360	0	ø	0	—	-3	0	-0.2
1999	Ari N	3	2	.600	27	0	0	1-1	34	29	15	2	1	20-5	28	2.91	159	.242	.347	3	.000	-0	—	5	0	0.6
	Fla N	4	8	.333	17	12	0	0-1	74.2	66	48	9	3	34-1	58	4.58	96	.243	.330	25-0-2	.160	-0	80	-5	0	-0.7
	Year	7	10	.412	44	12	0	1-2	108.2	95	63	11	4	54-6	86	4.06	110	.242	.336	28-0-2	.143	-1	79	0	0	-0.1
2000	Fla N	0	6	.000	17	12	0	0-0	68.1	88	63	12	2	34-2	45	7.90	55	.319	.391	17-1-4	.118	0	89	-27	0	-1.9
2001	Fla N	4	5	.444	52	3	0	0-1	92	79	33	9	5	30-5	64	2.74	152	.234	.302	9-0-2	.111	-0	81	14	15	1.2
2002	Fla N	6	5	.545	77	0	0	20-8	97.2	80	38	8	0	37-1	73	3.41	115	.224	.294	5	.200	0	—	7	0	0.9
2003	Fla N	0	3	.000	14	0	0	0-3	10.2	21	21	7	0	7-0	10	16.03	26	.396	.452	0	ø	0	—	-15	0	-2.7
2004	Col N	3	3	.500	22	0	0	0-3	25.2	26	22	6	1	14-0	22	7.01	68	.280	.363	0	ø	0	—	-6	0	-1.2
Total	7	20	32	.385	230	27	0	21-17	408.1	396	246	53	12	178-14	302	4.83	88	.259	.335	59-1-8	.136	-0	87	-30	15	-4.0
Nunn, Howie	Howard Ralph; B10.18.1935 Westfield NC; BR/TR/6´0˝/(170–175); d4.11																									
1959	StL N	2	2	.500	16	0	0	0	21.1	23	18	3	0	15-5	20	7.59	56	.291	.404	1-0-1	.000	-0	—	-7	0	-1.1
1961	Cin N	2	1	.667	24	0	0	0	37.2	35	17	0	1	24-4	26	3.58	113	.252	.357	8	.250	0	—	2	44	0.1
1962	Cin N	0	0	ø	6	0	0	0	9.2	15	6	0	0	3-1	4	5.59	72	.375	.400	1	.000	-0	—	-1	0	-0.1
Total	3	4	3	.571	46	0	0	0	68.2	73	41	3	1	42-10	50	5.11	80	.283	.378	10-0-1	.200	-0	—	-6	44	-1.1
Nuxhall, Joe	Joseph Henry; B7.30.1928 Hamilton OH; BL/TL/6´3˝/(219–234); d6.10																									
1944	Cin N	0	0	ø	1	0	0	0	0.2	2	5	0	0	5	0	67.50	5	.500	.778	0	ø	0	—	-5	0	-0.2
1952	Cin N	1	4	.200	37	5	2	1	92.1	83	33	4	3	42	52	3.22	117	.246	.334	23	.087	-1	71	7	0	0.3
1953	Cin N	9	11	.450	30	17	5-1	2	141.2	136	77	13	8	69	52	4.32	101	.252	.345	49-3-2	.327	7	83	0	0	0.7
1954	Cin N	12	5	.706	35	14	5-1	0	166.2	188	77	11	6	59	85	3.89	108	.292	.353	52-3-4	.173	4*	125	7	0	1.0
1955	Cin N★	17	12	.586	50	33	14-**5**	3	257	240	108	25	5	78-6	98	3.47	122	.249	.307	86-3-4	.198	4*	116	23	0	2.8
1956	Cin N☆	13	11	.542	44	32	10-2	3	200.2	196	96	18	6	87-6	120	3.72	107	.257	.336	59-2-4	.186	3	92	4	0	0.7
1957	Cin N	10	10	.500	39	28	6-2	1	174.1	192	104	24	7	53-3	99	4.75	87	.275	.331	59-0-5	.237	3*	111	-13	0	-1.2
1958	Cin N	12	11	.522	36	26	5	0	175.2	169	78	15	1	63-5	111	3.79	109	.257	.322	62-0-2	.210	0	95	7	0	0.9
1959	Cin N	9	9	.500	28	21	6-1	1	131.2	155	76	10	1	35-1	75	4.24	96	.292	.335	44-0-2	.250	3	119	-5	0	-0.4
1960	Cin N	1	8	.111	38	6	0	0	112	130	58	8	4	27-6	72	4.42	86	.297	.340	26	.077	-1*	50	-6	0	-0.5
1961	KC A	5	8	.385	37	13	1	1	128	135	81	12	3	65-2	81	5.34	78	.268	.352	65-2-5	.292	7*	85	-13	0	-0.5
1962	LA A	0	0	ø	5	0	0	0	5.1	7	6	0	1	5-0	2	10.13	38	.304	.448	0	ø	0	—	-3	0	-0.2
	Cin N	5	0	1.000	12	9	1	1	66	59	20	4	1	25-1	57	2.45	164	.240	.311	26-1-3	.269	3	160	11	0	1.1
1963	Cin N	15	8	.652	35	29	14-2	2	217.1	194	73	14	6	39-2	169	2.61	128	.237	.275	76-0-4	.158	0	110	17	0	1.7
1964	Cin N	9	8	.529	32	22	7-4	2	154.2	146	73	19	6	51-3	111	4.07	89	.250	.316	54-1-1	.130	-1*	99	-5	0	-0.7
1965	Cin N	11	4	.733	32	16	5-1	2	148.2	142	57	18	3	31-2	117	3.45	109	.252	.294	45-0-6	.178	1	112	8	0	0.7
1966	Cin N	6	8	.429	35	16	2-1	0	130	136	71	14	9	42-7	71	4.50	87	.270	.336	40-0-1	.100	-2	96	-8	15	-1.1
Total	16	135	117	.536	526	287	83-20	19	2302.2	2310	1093	209	70	776-44	1372	3.90	102	.262	.325	766-15-43	.198	28	104	26	15	5.1
Nye, Rich	Richard Raymond; B8.4.1944 Oakland CA; BL/TL/6´4˝/(185–190); [ChiN66 14/265]; d9.16; Col California																									
1966	Chi N	0	2	.000	3	2	0	0	17	16	4	1	0	7-2	9	2.12	174	.254	.329	4	.250	0	0	3	0	0.4
1967	Chi N	13	10	.565	35	30	7	0	205	179	82	15	2	52-4	119	3.20	111	.234	.282	75-0-3	.213	3	92	7	0	1.1
1968	Chi N	7	12	.368	27	20	6-1	1	132.2	145	65	16	1	34-4	74	3.80	83	.276	.319	44-0-1	.182	-0	85	-10	0	-1.5
1969	Chi N	3	5	.375	34	5	1	3-1	68.2	72	43	13	1	21-4	39	5.11	79	.271	.324	16	.063	-1*	75	-7	0	-1.0
1970	StL N	0	0	ø	6	0	0	0-0	8	13	5	2	0	6-1	5	4.50	92	.371	.452	2	.500	1	—	-1	0	0.0
	Mon N	3	2	.600	8	6	2	0-0	46.1	47	23	3	0	20-3	21	4.08	102	.260	.330	17-0-1	.176	0*	112	1	0	0.0
	Year	3	2	.600	14	6	2	0-0	54.1	60	28	5	0	26-4	26	4.14	100	.278	.351	19-0-1	.211	1	112	0	0	0.0
Total	5	26	31	.456	113	63	16-1	4-1	477.2	472	222	50	4	140-18	267	3.71	96	.257	.309	158-0-5	.190	2	86	-7	0	-1.0
Nye, Ryan	Ryan Craig; B6.24.1973 Biloxi MS; BR/TR/6´2˝/195; [PhiN94 2/57]; d6.7; Col Texas Tech																									
1997	Phi N	0	2	.000	4	2	0	0-0	12	20	11	2	2	9-0	7	8.25	51	.392	.484	2-0-1	.000	-0	44	-5	25	-0.7
1998	Phi N	0	0	ø	1	0	0	0-0	1	3	3	1	0	0-0	3	27.00	16	.500	.500	0	ø	0	—	-2	0	-0.1
Total	2	0	2	.000	5	2	0	0-0	13	23	14	3	2	9-0	10	9.69	44	.404	.486	2-0-1	.000	-0	44	-7	25	-0.8
Nyman, Jerry	Gerald Smith; B11.23.1942 Logan UT; BL/TL/5´10˝/170; d8.24; Col Brigham Young																									
1968	Chi A	2	1	.667	8	7	1-1	0	40.1	38	13	1	0	16-1	27	2.01	151	.247	.314	13-0-1	.154	-0	74	3	0	0.2
1969	Chi A	4	4	.500	20	10	2-1	0-0	64.2	58	40	7	0	39-1	40	5.29	73	.244	.346	20-0-1	.050	-1*	110	-9	0	-1.2
1970	SD N	0	2	.000	2	2	0	0-0	5.1	8	9	1	0	2-0	2	15.19	26	.364	.400	0	ø	0*	101	-6	0	-0.9
Total	3	6	7	.462	30	19	3-2	0-0	110.1	104	62	9	0	57-2	69	4.57	78	.251	.338	33-0-2	.091	-1	98	-12	0	-1.9
Oana, Prince	Henry Kawaihoa; B1.22.1908 Waipahu HI; D6.19.1976 Austin TX; BR/TR/6´2˝/193; d4.22.1934; ▲																									
1943	Det A	3	2	.600	10	0	0	0	34	34	21	4	2	19	15	4.50	78	.262	.364	26-1-0	.385	4*	—	-4	0	-0.1
1945	Det A	0	0	ø	3	1	0	1	11.1	3	2	0	0	7	3	1.59	221	.086	.238	5	.200	-0*	48	2	0	0.1
Total	2	3	2	.600	13	1	0	1	45.1	37	23	4	2	26	18	3.77	93	.224	.337	31-1-0	.355	4	48	-2	0	0.0
Oberbeck, Henry	Henry A.; B5.17.1858 MO; D8.26.1921 St.Louis MO; d5.7.1883; ▲																									
1884	Bal U	0	0	ø	2	1	0	0	6	9	3	0	—	2	1	3.00	89	.321	.367	125	.184	-1*	80	0	—	0.0
	KC U	0	5	.000	6	4	3	0	29.2	47	35	0	—	3	6	5.76	39	.338	.352	90	.189	-1*	19	-12	—	-1.5
	Year	0	5	.000	8	5	3	0	35.2	56	38	0	—	5	7	5.30	44	.335	.355	215	.186	-1	33	-12	—	-1.5
Oberlander, Doc	Hartman Louis; B5.12.1864 Waukegan IL; D11.14.1922 Pryor MT; TL/5´10.5˝/165; d5.16; Col Syracuse																									
1888	Cle AA	1	2	.333	3	3	3	0	25.2	27	33	2	1	18	23	5.26	59	.260	.374	14	.214	0	200	-8	—	-0.7
Oberlin, Frank	Frank Rufus "Flossie"; B3.29.1876 Elsie MI; D1.6.1952 Ashley IN; BR/TR/6´1˝/165; d9.20																									
1906	Bos A	1	3	.250	4	4	4	0	34	38	20	0	2	13	13	3.18	87	.286	.358	13	.154	-0	79	-3	—	-0.3
1907	Bos A	1	5	.167	12	4	2	0	46	48	31	2	2	24	18	4.30	60	.271	.365	13	.154	-0	20	-8	—	-1.1
	Was A	2	6	.250	11	8	3	0	48.2	57	38	0	2	12	18	4.62	52	.294	.341	18	.056	-2*	87	-13	—	-2.1
	Year	3	11	.214	23	12	5	0	94.2	105	69	2	4	36	36	4.47	56	.283	.353	31	.097	-2	63	-22	—	-3.2

YEAR	TM LG	W	L	PCT	G	GS	CG-SHO	SV-BS	IP	H	R	HR	HB	BB-IB	SO	ERA	AERA	OAV	OOB	AB-HR-SH	AVG	PB	SUP	APR	DL	PW
1909	Was A	1	4	.200	9	4	1	0	41	41	22	1	6	16	13	3.73	65	.266	.358	14	.143	-1*	65	-5	—	-0.7
1910	Was A	0	6	.000	8	6	6	0	57.1	52	32	0	2	23	18	2.98	84	.259	.341	19	.053	-2	45	-5	—	-0.7
Total	4	5	24	.172	44	26	16	0	227	236	143	3	14	88	80	3.77	67	.275	.352	77	.104	-4	62	-34	—	-4.9
Obermueller, Wes	Wesley Mitchell; B12.22.1976 Cedar Rapids IA; BR/TR/6´2˝/(195–210); [KCA99 2/58]; d9.20; Col Iowa																									
2002	KC A	0	2	.000	2	2	0	0-0	7.2	14	10	3	0	2-0	5	11.74	43	.378	.410	0	ø	0	46	-5	0	-0.8
2003	Mil N	2	5	.286	12	11	0	0-0	65.2	81	40	10	6	25-2	34	5.07	85	.301	.371	23-0-2	.130	-1	81	-6	0	-0.5
2004	Mil N	6	8	.429	25	20	1-1	0-0	118	138	80	15	3	42-0	59	5.80	76	.291	.349	39-0-2	.385	5*	97	-16	0	-1.2
2005	Mil N	1	4	.200	23	8	0	0-0	65	74	41	7	5	36-2	33	5.26	81	.289	.382	15-0-1	.200	1*	97	-7	0	-0.4
Total	4	9	19	.321	62	41	1-1	0-0	256.1	307	171	35	14	105-4	131	5.65	77	.296	.365	77-0-5	.273	6	91	-34	0	-2.9
O'Brien, Dan	Daniel Jogues; B4.22.1954 St.Petersburg FL; BR/TR/6´4˝/215; [StLN76*S3/61]; d9.4; Col Florida St.																									
1978	StL N	0	2	.000	7	2	0	0-0	18	22	12	1	2	8-2	12	4.50	79	.301	.381	3-0-1	.000	-0	88	-3	0	-0.3
1979	StL N	1	1	.500	6	0	0	0-0	11	21	10	0	0	3-0	5	8.18	47	.420	.436	2	.000	-0	—	-5	0	-0.8
Total	2	1	3	.250	13	2	0	0-0	29	43	22	1	2	11-2	17	5.90	62	.350	.403	5-0-1	.000	-1	88	-8	0	-1.1
O'Brien, Eddie	Edward Joseph; B12.11.1930 S.Amboy NJ; BR/TR/5´9˝/(165–170); d4.25.1953; Mil 1954–55; C1; twb–Johnny; Col Seattle; ▲																									
1956	Pit N	0	0	ø	1	0	0	0	2	1	0	0	1	0-0	0	0.00	ø	.167	.286	53-0-3	.264	0*	—	1	0	0.0
1957	Pit N	1	0	1.000	3	1	1	0	12.1	11	3	2	0	3-0	10	2.19	173	.229	.275	4	.000	-1	70	2	0	0.1
1958	Pit N	0	0	ø	1	0	0	0	2	4	3	1	0	1-0	1	13.50	29	.444	.500	0	ø	0	—	-2	0	-0.1
Total	3	1	0	1.000	5	1	1	0	16.1	16	6	3	1	4-0	11	3.31	115	.254	.309	57-0-3	.246	-0	70	1	0	0.0
O'Brien, Darby	John F.; B4.15.1867 Troy NY; D3.11.1892 W.Troy NY; BR/TR/5´10˝/165; d6.23																									
1888	Cle AA	11	19	.367	30	30	30-1	0	259	245	162	5	12	99	135	3.30	94	.241	.315	109	.183	-3*	88	-5	—	-0.7
1889	Cle N	22	17	.564	41	41	39-1	0	346.2	345	216	9	24	167	122	4.15	97	.252	.344	140	.250	4	95	3	—	0.7
1890	Cle P	8	16	.333	25	25	22	0	206.1	229	171	9	19	93	54	3.40	117	.269	.354	96	.156	-6*	91	8	—	0.1
1891	Bos AA	18	13	.581	40	30	22	2	268.2	300	197	13	20	127	87	3.65	95	.273	.359	128	.234	1*	153	-11	—	-1.2
Total	4	59	65	.476	136	126	113-2	2	1080.2	1119	746	36	75	486	398	3.68	100	.258	.343	473	.211	-4	106	-5	—	-1.1
O'Brien, Johnny	John Thomas; B12.11.1930 S.Amboy NJ; BR/TR/5´9˝/(170–175); d4.19.1953; Mil 1954–55; twb–Eddie; Col Seattle; ▲																									
1956	Pit N	1	0	1.000	8	0	0	0	19	8	6	2	2	9-0	9	2.84	133	.133	.260	104-0-4	.173	-0*	—	2	0	0.1
1957	Pit N	0	3	.000	16	1	0	0	40	46	32	7	1	24-2	19	6.07	62	.293	.384	35-0-1	.314	2*	70	-11	0	-0.6
1958	StL N	0	0	ø	1	0	0	0	2	7	5	0	0	2-0	2	22.50	18	.538	.600	2	.000	0*	—	-4	0	-0.2
Total	3	1	3	.250	25	1	0	0	61	61	43	9	3	35-2	30	5.61	68	.265	.363	141-0-5	.206	2	70	-13	0	-0.7
O'Brien, Bob	Robert Allen; B4.23.1949 Pittsburgh PA; BL/TL/5´10˝/170; [LAN69*4/74]; d4.11; Col Arizona																									
1971	LA N	2	2	.500	14	4	1-1	0-0	42	42	18	4	1	13-1	15	3.00	108	.262	.320	9-0-2	.111	-0	75	0	0	-0.1
O'Brien, Buck	Thomas Joseph; B5.9.1882 Brockton MA; D7.25.1959 Boston MA; BR/TR/5´10˝/188; d9.9																									
1911	Bos A	5	1	.833	6	5	5-2	0	47.2	30	9	0	1	21	31	0.38	868	.180	.275	16	.125	-1	66	14	—	1.7
1912	†Bos A	20	13	.606	37	34	25-2	0	275.2	237	107	3	10	90	115	2.58	132	.237	.306	94-0-4	.138	-5	91	24	—	2.1
1913	Bos A	4	9	.308	15	12	6	0	90.1	103	42	0	0	35	54	3.69	80	.307	.373	30-0-1	.167	0	99	-4	—	-0.5
	Chi A	0	2	.000	6	3	0	0	18.1	21	14	0	0	13	4	3.93	74	.323	.436	3	.000	-0	76	-3	—	-0.4
	Year	4	11	.267	21	15	6	0	108.2	124	56	0	0	48	58	3.73	79	.310	.384	33-0-1	.152	-0	94	-8	—	-0.9
Total	3	29	25	.537	64	54	36-4	0	432	391	172	3	11	159	204	2.63	125	.250	.323	143-0-5	.140	-6	89	31	—	2.9
O'Brien, Billy	William Smith; B3.14.1860 Albany NY; D5.26.1911 Kansas City MO; BR/TR/6´0˝/185; d9.27; ▲																									
1884	StP U	1	0	1.000	2	0	0	0	10	8	5	0	—	3	7	1.80	74	.205	.262	30	.233	0*	—	-1	—	-0.1
Ockey, Walter	Walter Andrew "Footie" (b Walter Andrew Okpych); B1.4.1920 New York NY; D12.4.1971 Staten Island NY; BR/TR/6´0˝/175; d5.3																									
1944	NY N	0	0	ø	2	0	0	0	2.2	2	1	1	0	2	1	3.38	109	.200	.333	0	ø	0	—	0	0	0.0
O'Connor, Andy	Andrew James; B9.14.1884 Roxbury MA; D9.26.1980 Norwood MA; BR/TR/6´0˝/160; d10.6																									
1908	NY A	0	1	.000	1	1	1	0	8	15	11	0	3	7	5	10.13	24	.429	.556	3	.000	-0	83	-6	—	-0.6
O'Connor, Brian	Brian Michael; B1.4.1977 Cincinnati OH; BL/TL/6´2˝/190; [PitN95 11/293]; d5.13																									
2000	Pit N	0	0	ø	6	1	0	0-0	12.1	12	11	2	1	11-0	7	5.11	91	.250	.393	2	.500	0	218	-2	0	-0.1
O'Connor, Frank	Frank Henry; B9.15.1870 Keeseville NY; D12.26.1913 Brattleboro VT; BL/TL/6´0˝/185; d8.3; Col Dartmouth																									
1893	Phi N	0	0	ø	3	1	0	1	4	2	5	0	0	9	0	11.25	41	.143	.478	2-1	1.000	2	335	-2	—	0.0
O'Connor, Jack	Jack William; B6.2.1958 Twentynine Palms CA; BL/TL/6´3˝/(200–215); [MonN76 9/201]; d4.9																									
1981	Min A	3	2	.600	28	0	0	0-3	35.1	46	27	3	2	30-6	16	5.86	67	.336	.462	0	ø	0	—	-7	0	-0.9
1982	Min A	8	9	.471	23	19	6-1	0-0	126	122	63	13	2	57-4	56	4.29	100	.255	.336	0	ø	0	89	1	0	-0.1
1983	Min A	2	3	.400	27	8	0	0-0	83	107	59	13	0	36-1	56	5.86	73	.315	.376	0	ø	0	114	-14	0	-0.8
1984	Min A	0	0	ø	2	0	0	0-0	4.2	1	1	1	0	4-0	0	1.93	220	.067	.263	0	ø	0	—	1	0	0.0
1985	Mon N	0	2	.000	20	1	0	0-1	23.2	21	14	1	0	13-7	16	4.94	70	.239	.330	0	ø	0	51	-4	0	-0.3
1987	Bal A	1	1	.500	29	0	0	2-1	46	46	23	5	0	23-4	33	4.30	103	.263	.343	0	ø	0	—	1	45	0.0
Total	6	14	17	.452	129	28	6-1	2-5	318.2	343	187	36	4	163-22	177	4.89	86	.278	.361	0	ø	0	96	-22	45	-2.1
O'Connor, Michael	Michael Patrick; B8.17.1980 Dallas TX; BL/TL/6´3˝/170; [MonN02 7/197]; d4.27; Col George Washington																									
2006	Was N	3	8	.273	21	20	0	0-0	105	96	61	15	7	45-5	59	4.80	91	.244	.330	31-0-1	.065	-2	91	-5	0	-0.7
O'Day, Hank	Henry Francis; B7.8.1862 Chicago IL; D7.2.1935 Chicago IL; TR/6´0˝/180; d5.2; M2/U30; Col St. Marys (CA)																									
1884	Tol AA	9	28	.243	41	40	35-2	**1**	326.2	335	241	6	18	66	163	3.75	91	.252	.297	242	.211	-1*	73	-12	—	-1.0
1885	Pit AA	5	7	.417	12	12	10	0	103	110	77	4	7	16	36	3.67	88	.258	.296	49	.245	1*	115	-8	—	-0.6
1886	Was N	2	2	.500	6	6	6	0	49	41	17	1	—	17	47	1.65	195	.219	.284	19	.053	-2	44	8	—	0.4
1887	Was N	8	20	.286	30	30	29	0	254.2	255	197	15	9	109	86	4.17	96	.254	.332	116	.198	-3*	87	-7	—	-0.7
1888	Was N	16	29	.356	46	46	46-2	0	403	359	208	19	16	117	186	3.10	89	.232	.293	166	.139	-6*	66	-12	—	-1.9
1889	Was N	2	10	.167	13	13	11	0	108	117	88	7	6	57	23	4.33	91	.268	.361	44	.182	-1	51	-7	—	-0.6
	†NY N	9	1	.900	10	10	8	0	78	83	51	2	7	35	28	4.27	92	.265	.352	31	.097	-1	135	0	—	-0.2
	Year	11	11	.500	23	23	19	0	186	200	139	9	13	92	51	4.31	92	.267	.357	75	.147	-2	87	-10	—	-0.8
1890	NY P	22	13	.629	43	35	32-1	**3**	329	355	249	11	18	161	94	4.21	108	.264	.350	150-1	.227	-3	110	11	—	0.4
Total	7	73	110	.399	201	192	177-5	4	1651.1	1655	1128	65	81	578	663	3.74	96	.251	.319	817-1	.190	-16	86	-27	—	-4.2
O'Dell, Billy	William Oliver; B2.10.1932 Whitmire SC; BB/TL/5´11˝/(170–180); d6.20; Mil 1955–56; Col Clemson																									
1954	Bal A	1	1	.500	7	2	1	0	16.1	15	7	0	0	5	6	2.76	130	.242	.299	3	.000	-0	25	1	0	0.1
1956	Bal A	0	0	ø	4	1	0	0	8	6	1	0	0	6-1	6	1.13	349	.222	.353	1	.000	-0	91	3	0	0.1
1957	Bal A	4	10	.286	35	15	2-1	4	140.1	107	48	12	5	39-2	97	2.69	133	.212	.275	34-0-5	.147	-1*	58	14	0	1.2
1958	Bal A★	14	11	.560	41	25	12-3	8	221.1	201	83	13	4	51-6	137	2.97	121	.241	.284	72-1-4	.111	-1*	108	15	0	1.7
1959	Bal A★	10	12	.455	38	24	6-2	1	199.1	163	74	18	1	67-7	88	2.93	129	.220	.284	60-1-2	.083	-3*	77	19	0	1.7
1960	SF N	8	13	.381	43	24	6-1	2	202.2	198	80	16	2	72-8	145	3.20	109	.252	.314	56-0-3	.107	1*	99	9	0	0.9
1961	SF N	7	5	.583	46	14	4-1	2	130.1	132	63	10	1	33-6	110	3.59	106	.260	.305	39-0-4	.103	-2*	126	1	0	-0.2
1962	†SF N	19	14	.576	43	39	20-2	0	280.2	282	126	18	7	66-1	195	3.53	108	.258	.303	90-0-10	.133	-1*	116	7	0	0.6
1963	SF N	14	10	.583	36	33	10-3	1	222.1	218	90	14	7	70-12	116	3.16	101	.253	.313	78-0-5	.205	4*	131	2	0	0.3
1964	SF N	8	7	.533	36	8	1	2	85	82	55	10	4	35-6	54	5.40	66	.252	.329	22	.000	-2*	74	-16	0	-2.9
1965	Mil N	10	6	.625	62	1	0	18	111.1	87	35	10	2	30-8	78	2.18	161	.215	.269	23-0-2	.174	1	50	14	0	2.7
1966	Atl N	2	3	.400	24	0	0	6	41.1	44	14	3	2	18-1	20	2.40	152	.272	.352	8	.250	0*	—	5	0	0.8
	Pit N	3	2	.600	37	2	0	4	71.1	74	24	3	4	23-1	47	2.78	129	.275	.339	16	.063	-1	86	7	0	0.4
	Year	5	5	.500	61	2	0	10	112.2	118	38	6	6	41-2	67	2.64	136	.274	.344	24	.125	-1	86	11	0	1.2
1967	Pit N	5	6	.455	27	11	1	0	86.2	88	58	10	3	41-7	34	5.82	58	.265	.347	26-0-1	.115	-0*	138	-21	0	-2.5
Total	13	105	100	.512	479	199	63-13	48	1817	1697	758	137	42	556-66	1133	3.29	109	.246	.304	528-2-36	.125	-7	104	60	0	4.9
Odenwald, Ted	Theodore Joseph "Lefty"; B1.4.1902 Hudson WI; D10.23.1965 Shakopee MN; BR/TL/5´10˝/147; d4.13																									
1921	Cle A	1	0	1.000	10	0	0	0	17.1	16	5	0	1	6	4	1.56	274	.262	.338	3	.000	-1	—	5	—	0.2
1922	Cle A	0	0	ø	1	0	0	0	1.1	6	6	0	0	2	2	40.50	10	.600	.667	0	ø	0	—	-5	—	-0.2
Total	2	1	0	1.000	11	0	0	0	18.2	22	11	0	1	8	6	4.34	98	.310	.387	3	.000	-1	—	0	—	0.0

Odom, Dave David Everett "Blimp","Porky"; B6.5.1918 Dinuba CA; D11.19.1987 Myrtle Beach SC; BR/TR/6´1˝/220; d5.31

YEAR	TM LG	W	L	PCT	G	GS	CG-SHO	SV-BS	IP	H	R	HR	HB	BB-IB	SO	ERA	AERA	OAV	OOB	AB-HR-SH	AVG	PB	SUP	APR	DL	PW
1943	Bos N	0	3	.000	22	3	1	2	54.2	54	32	3	4	30	17	5.27	65	.269	.374	12	.000	-2	58	-8	0	-0.8

Odom, Blue Moon Johnny Lee; B5.29.1945 Macon GA; BR/TR/6´0˝/(175–185); d9.5

YEAR	TM LG	W	L	PCT	G	GS	CG-SHO	SV-BS	IP	H	R	HR	HB	BB-IB	SO	ERA	AERA	OAV	OOB	AB-HR-SH	AVG	PB	SUP	APR	DL	PW
1964	KC A	1	2	.333	5	5	1-1	0	17	29	21	5	0	11-0	10	10.06	38	.363	.440	5	.000	-0	135	-11	0	-1.6
1965	KC A	0	0	ø	1	0	0	0	1	2	1	0	0	2-0	0	9.00	39	.400	.571	0	ø	0	—	-1	0	0.0
1966	KC A	5	5	.500	14	14	4-2	0	90.1	70	31	1	2	53-2	47	2.49	136	.215	.326	31-0-1	.097	-1*	87	8	0	0.9
1967	KC A	3	8	.273	29	17	0	0	103.2	94	67	9	3	68-7	67	5.04	63	.243	.359	28	.286	2*	109	-22	0	-2.0
1968	Oak A★	16	10	.615	32	31	9-4	0	231.1	179	74	9	7	98-9	143	2.45	115	.216	.302	78-1-4	.218	6*	121	9	0	1.9
1969	Oak A★	15	6	.714	32	32	10-3	0-0	231.1	179	87	15	6	112-5	150	2.92	118	.215	.310	79-5-8	.266	11*	133	12	0	2.3
1970	Oak A	9	8	.529	29	29	4-1	0-0	156.1	128	77	14	8	100-1	88	3.80	93	.227	.348	54-3-1	.241	6*	98	-6	45	0.1
1971	Oak A	10	12	.455	25	25	3-1	0-0	140.2	147	78	13	0	71-7	69	4.29	78	.271	.352	50-1-1	.160	1*	93	-17	33	-2.3
1972	†Oak A	15	6	.714	31	30	4-2	0-0	194.1	164	62	10	3	87-2	86	2.50	114	.234	.319	66-2-5	.121	0*	125	8	0	0.9
1973	†Oak A	5	12	.294	30	24	3	0-0	150.1	153	86	14	2	67-3	83	4.49	79	.263	.339	1	.000	-0*	101	-16	0	-1.7
1974	†Oak A	1	5	.167	34	5	1	1-2	87.1	85	39	4	3	52-3	52	3.81	88	.267	.373	0	ø	0*	47	-3	0	-0.2
1975	Oak A	0	2	.000	7	2	0	0-0	11	19	15	1	1	11-1	4	12.27	30	.422	.534	0	ø	0*	145	-10	0	-1.5
	Cle A	1	0	1.000	3	1	1-1	0-1	10.1	4	3	1	0	8-0	10	2.61	146	.118	.286	0	ø	0	92	2	0	0.1
	Year	1	2	.333	10	3	1-1	0-1	21.1	23	18	2	1	19-1	14	7.59	49	.291	.430	0	ø	0	126	-8	0	-1.4
	Atl N	1	7	.125	15	10	0	0-0	56	78	46	5	0	28-0	30	7.07	54	.342	.411	13-0-1	.077	-1	81	-17	0	-2.2
1976	Chi A	2	2	.500	8	4	0	0-0	28	31	21	2	1	20-0	18	5.79	62	.282	.394	0	ø	0	129	-7	21	-1.0
Total	13	84	85	.497	295	229	40-15	1-3	1509	1362	708	103	36	788-40	857	3.70	89	.244	.339	405-12-21	.195	26	109	-71	99	-6.3

O'Donnell, George George Dana; B5.27.1929 Winchester IL; BR/TR/6´3˝/175; d4.18

YEAR	TM LG	W	L	PCT	G	GS	CG-SHO	SV-BS	IP	H	R	HR	HB	BB-IB	SO	ERA	AERA	OAV	OOB	AB-HR-SH	AVG	PB	SUP	APR	DL	PW
1954	Pit N	3	9	.250	21	10	3	1	87.1	105	50	4	2	21	8	4.53	92	.315	.348	23-1-0	.087	-1	45	-3	0	-0.4

O'Donoghue, John John Eugene; B10.7.1939 Kansas City MO; BR/TL/6´3˝/(197–210); d9.29; s–John; Col Missouri

YEAR	TM LG	W	L	PCT	G	GS	CG-SHO	SV-BS	IP	H	R	HR	HB	BB-IB	SO	ERA	AERA	OAV	OOB	AB-HR-SH	AVG	PB	SUP	APR	DL	PW
1963	KC A	0	1	.000	1	1	0	0	6	6	2	0	0	2-0	1	1.50	260	.286	.348	2	.000	-0	23	1	0	0.1
1964	KC A	10	14	.417	39	32	2-1	0	173.2	202	104	24	3	65-4	79	4.92	78	.286	.347	55-1-7	.236	2*	90	-20	0	-2.4
1965	KC A☆	9	18	.333	34	30	4-1	0	177.2	183	92	15	1	66-8	82	3.95	88	.267	.331	55-1-6	.218	3*	76	-11	0	-1.3
1966	Cle A	6	8	.429	32	13	2	0	108	109	50	13	2	23-2	49	3.83	90	.264	.303	33	.152	-0	108	-4	0	-0.5
1967	Cle A	8	9	.471	33	17	5-2	2	130.2	120	52	10	2	33-3	81	3.24	101	.247	.296	40-1-1	.100	-0	89	1	0	0.4
1968	Bal A	0	0	ø	16	0	0	2	22	34	15	2	0	7-3	11	6.14	48	.374	.414	2	.000	-0	—	-7	0	-0.4
1969	Sea A	2	2	.500	55	0	0	6-2	70	58	28	5	3	37-4	48	2.96	123	.230	.331	13-0-3	.077	-1	—	4	0	0.3
1970	Mil A	2	0	1.000	25	0	0	0-3	23.1	29	15	4	0	9-1	13	5.01	75	.299	.358	2	.000	-0	—	-3	0	-0.3
	Mon N	2	3	.400	9	3	0	0-1	22.1	20	14	2	2	11-1	6	5.24	79	.263	.359	4	.000	-0	86	-2	0	-0.5
1971	Mon N	0	0	ø	13	0	0	0-0	17.1	19	10	3	0	7-1	7	4.67	76	.271	.333	0	ø	0	—	-2	0	-0.1
Total	9	39	55	.415	257	96	13-4	10-6	751	780	382	78	13	260-27	377	4.07	87	.269	.330	206-3-17	.170	2	88	-43	0	-4.7

O'Donoghue, John John Preston; B5.26.1969 Wilmington DE; BL/TL/6´6˝/198; d6.27; f–John; Col Louisiana St.

YEAR	TM LG	W	L	PCT	G	GS	CG-SHO	SV-BS	IP	H	R	HR	HB	BB-IB	SO	ERA	AERA	OAV	OOB	AB-HR-SH	AVG	PB	SUP	APR	DL	PW
1993	Bal A	0	1	.000	11	1	0	0-0	19.2	22	12	4	1	10-1	16	4.58	99	.278	.367	0	ø	0	102	-1	0	-0.1

O'Doul, Lefty Francis Joseph; B3.4.1897 San Francisco CA; D12.7.1969 San Francisco CA; BL/TL/6´0˝/180; d4.29; ▲

YEAR	TM LG	W	L	PCT	G	GS	CG-SHO	SV-BS	IP	H	R	HR	HB	BB-IB	SO	ERA	AERA	OAV	OOB	AB-HR-SH	AVG	PB	SUP	APR	DL	PW
1919	NY A	0	0	ø	3	0	0	0	5	7	6	0	0	4	2	3.60	89	.304	.407	16	.250	0*	—	-2	—	-0.1
1920	NY A	0	0	ø	2	0	0	0	3.2	4	2	0	1	2	2	4.91	78	.286	.412	12	.167	-0*	—	0	—	0.0
1922	NY A	0	0	ø	6	0	0	0	16	24	13	0	0	12	5	3.38	119	.353	.450	9	.333	1*	—	-1	—	0.0
1923	Bos A	1	1	.500	23	1	0	0	53	69	50	2	4	31	10	5.43	76	.337	.433	35-0-2	.143	-1*	121	-11	—	-0.7
Total	4	1	1	.500	34	1	0	0	77.2	104	71	2	5	49	19	4.87	83	.335	.434	72-0-2	.194	1	121	-14	—	-0.8

Oelkers, Bryan Bryan Alois; B3.11.1961 Zaragoza, Spain; BL/TL/6´3˝/(192–195); [MinA82 1/4]; d4.9; Col Wichita St.

YEAR	TM LG	W	L	PCT	G	GS	CG-SHO	SV-BS	IP	H	R	HR	HB	BB-IB	SO	ERA	AERA	OAV	OOB	AB-HR-SH	AVG	PB	SUP	APR	DL	PW
1983	Min A	0	5	.000	10	8	0	0-0	34.1	56	34	7	0	17-0	13	8.65	50	.376	.437	0	ø	0	87	-15	0	-1.8
1986	Cle A	3	3	.500	35	4	0	1-1	69	70	38	13	6	40-2	33	4.70	89	.262	.368	0	ø	0	103	-3	0	-0.3
Total	2	3	8	.273	45	12	0	1-1	103.1	126	72	20	6	57-2	46	6.01	70	.303	.392	0	ø	0	93	-18	0	-2.1

Oeschger, Joe Joseph Carl; B5.24.1892 Chicago IL; D7.28.1986 Rohnert Park CA; BR/TR/6´0˝/190; d4.21; Col St. Marys (CA)

YEAR	TM LG	W	L	PCT	G	GS	CG-SHO	SV-BS	IP	H	R	HR	HB	BB-IB	SO	ERA	AERA	OAV	OOB	AB-HR-SH	AVG	PB	SUP	APR	DL	PW
1914	Phi N	4	8	.333	32	12	5	1	124	129	74	5	10	54	47	3.77	78	.279	.366	40-0-1	.075	-4	102	-10	—	-1.4
1915	Phi N	1	0	1.000	6	1	1	0	23.2	21	13	1	0	9	8	3.42	80	.247	.319	7	.000	-1	81	-2	—	-0.2
1916	Phi N	1	0	1.000	14	0	0	0	30.1	18	8	2	1	14	17	2.37	112	.184	.292	5-0-1	.000	-1	—	2	—	0.1
1917	Phi N	15	14	.517	42	30	18-5	1	262	241	108	7	6	72	123	2.75	102	.249	.305	88-0-2	.114	-4*	95	1	—	-0.6
1918	Phi N	6	18	.250	30	23	13-2	**3**	184	159	87	3	7	83	60	3.03	99	.238	.328	60-0-1	.083	-4	78	-4	—	-1.0
1919	Phi N	0	1	.000	5	4	2	0	38	52	29	1	2	16	5	5.92	54	.340	.409	15	.000	-2	179	-10	—	-0.7
	NY N	0	1	.000	5	1	0	0	8	12	4	0	0	2	3	4.50	62	.400	.438	1	.000	-0	57	-1	—	-0.2
	Bos N	4	2	.667	7	7	4-1	0	56.2	63	19	0	1	21	16	2.54	112	.300	.366	22	.091	-1	88	2	—	0.0
	Year	4	4	.500	17	12	6-1	0	102.2	127	52	1	3	39	24	3.94	76	.323	.389	38	.053	-4	118	-9	—	-0.9
1920	Bos N	15	13	.536	38	30	20-5	0	299	294	124	10	8	99	80	3.46	88	.265	.329	101-0-5	.178	-3	86	-7	—	-1.0
1921	Bos N	20	14	.588	46	36	19-**3**	0	299	303	128	11	15	97	68	3.52	104	.274	.341	110-0-2	.255	2	93	8	—	1.1
1922	Bos N	6	21	.222	46	23	10-1	1	195.2	234	137	8	8	81	51	5.06	79	.303	.375	63-0-1	.190	-0	73	-23	—	-2.6
1923	Bos N	5	15	.250	44	19	6-1	2	166.1	227	117	4	5	54	33	5.68	70	.330	.383	52-0-2	.231	-0	78	-27	—	-2.8
1924	NY N	2	0	1.000	10	2	0	0	29	35	17	1	0	14	10	3.10	118	.287	.360	7	.429	1	208	-1	—	0.0
	Phi N	2	7	.222	19	8	0	0	65.1	88	44	6	3	16	8	4.41	101	.333	.378	20	.250	-1	62	-2	—	-0.3
	Year	4	7	.364	29	10	0	0	94.1	123	61	7	3	30	18	4.01	105	.319	.372	27	.296	0	89	-3	—	-0.3
1925	Bro N	1	2	.333	21	3	1	0	37	60	38	2	1	19	6	6.08	69	.382	.452	8-0-1	.125	-0	101	-11	—	-0.8
Total	12	82	116	.414	365	199	99-18	8	1818	1936	947	61	67	651	535	3.81	88	.281	.349	599-0-16	.165	-18	88	-85	—	-10.4

O'Flaherty, Eric Eric George; B2.5.1985 Walla Walla WA; BL/TL/6´2˝/195; [SeaA03 6/176]; d8.16

YEAR	TM LG	W	L	PCT	G	GS	CG-SHO	SV-BS	IP	H	R	HR	HB	BB-IB	SO	ERA	AERA	OAV	OOB	AB-HR-SH	AVG	PB	SUP	APR	DL	PW
2006	Sea A	0	0	ø	15	0	0	0-0	11	18	9	2	0	6-3	6	4.09	108	.360	.429	0	ø	0	—	-1	0	-0.1

Ogden, Jack John Mahlon; B11.5.1897 Ogden PA; D11.9.1977 Philadelphia PA; BR/TR/6´0˝/190; d6.22; b–Curly; Col Swarthmore

YEAR	TM LG	W	L	PCT	G	GS	CG-SHO	SV-BS	IP	H	R	HR	HB	BB-IB	SO	ERA	AERA	OAV	OOB	AB-HR-SH	AVG	PB	SUP	APR	DL	PW
1918	NY N	0	0	ø	5	0	0	0	8.2	8	4	0	2	3	1	3.12	84	.296	.406	1	.000	-0	—	-1	—	-0.1
1928	StL A	15	16	.484	38	31	18-1	2	242.2	257	121	23	1	80	67	4.15	101	.274	.331	85-0-2	.200	-1	93	5	—	0.3
1929	StL A	4	8	.333	34	14	7	0	131.1	154	83	8	0	44	32	4.93	90	.301	.357	45-0-2	.244	0	95	-7	—	-0.5
1931	Cin N	4	8	.333	22	9	3-1	1	89	79	42	3	0	32	24	2.93	127	.242	.310	27-0-1	.148	-1*	61	5	—	0.4
1932	Cin N	2	2	.500	24	3	1	0	57	72	40	5	0	22	20	5.21	74	.310	.370	12	.167	0*	58	-9	—	-0.5
Total	5	25	34	.424	123	57	29-2	3	528.2	570	290	39	3	181	144	4.24	97	.280	.340	170-0-5	.200	-1	88	-7	—	-0.4

Ogden, Curly Warren Harvey; B1.24.1901 Ogden PA; D8.6.1964 Upland PA; BR/TR/6´1.5˝/180; d7.18; b–Jack; Col Swarthmore

YEAR	TM LG	W	L	PCT	G	GS	CG-SHO	SV-BS	IP	H	R	HR	HB	BB-IB	SO	ERA	AERA	OAV	OOB	AB-HR-SH	AVG	PB	SUP	APR	DL	PW
1922	Phi A	1	4	.200	15	6	4	0	72.1	59	29	4	5	33	20	3.11	137	.237	.338	29	.241	-0*	50	9	—	0.5
1923	Phi A	1	2	.333	18	2	0	0	46.1	63	39	2	3	32	14	5.63	73	.330	.434	17	.294	1*	50	-9	—	-0.4
1924	Phi A	0	3	.000	5	1	0	0	12.2	14	9	1	1	7	4	4.97	86	.275	.373	3	.000	-1	118	-1	—	-0.3
	†Was A	9	5	.643	16	16	9-3	0	108	83	36	3	2	51	23	2.58	156	.221	.317	47-0-1	.277	2*	114	19	—	2.4
	Year	9	8	.529	21	17	9-3	0	120.2	97	45	4	3	58	27	2.83	143	.227	.324	50-0-1	.260	1	114	17	—	2.1
1925	Was A	3	1	.750	17	4	2-1	0	42	45	24	1	2	18	6	4.50	94	.288	.369	12	.250	-0	124	-1	—	-0.1
1926	Was A	4	4	.500	22	9	4	0	96.1	114	55	2	5	45	21	4.30	90	.305	.387	27-0-1	.185	-1	123	-5	—	-0.5
Total	5	18	19	.486	93	38	19-4	0	377.2	378	192	13	18	186	88	3.79	108	.271	.364	135-0-2	.244	1	103	12	—	1.6

Ogea, Chad Chad Wayne; B11.9.1970 Lake Charles LA; BR/TR/6´2˝/(200–220); [CleA91 3/86]; d5.3; Col Louisiana St.

YEAR	TM LG	W	L	PCT	G	GS	CG-SHO	SV-BS	IP	H	R	HR	HB	BB-IB	SO	ERA	AERA	OAV	OOB	AB-HR-SH	AVG	PB	SUP	APR	DL	PW
1994	Cle A	0	1	.000	4	1	0	0-0	16.1	21	11	2	1	10-2	11	6.06	78	.304	.400	0	ø	0	19	-2	0	-0.1
1995	†Cle A	8	3	.727	20	14	1	0-0	106.1	95	38	11	1	29-0	57	3.05	155	.233	.283	0	ø	0	114	20	0	1.8
1996	†Cle A	10	6	.625	29	21	1-1	0-0	146.2	151	82	22	5	42-3	101	4.79	102	.266	.321	0	ø	0	106	3	30	0.2
1997	†Cle A	8	9	.471	21	21	1	0-0	126.1	139	79	13	5	47-4	80	4.99	94	.283	.348	2-0-2	.000	-0	106	-5	69	-0.6
1998	†Cle A	5	4	.556	19	9	0	0-1	69	74	44	9	7	25-1	43	5.61	85	.273	.346	0	ø	0	104	-5	108	-0.6
1999	Phi N	6	12	.333	36	28	0	0-0	168	192	110	36	4	61-1	77	5.63	83	.288	.349	44-0-7	.091	-2	93	-16	0	-1.7
Total	6	37	35	.514	129	94	3-1	0-1	632.2	672	364	93	23	214-11	369	4.88	97	.272	.333	46-0-9	.087	-2	102	-5	207	-1.0

Ogrodowski, Joe Joseph Anthony; B11.20.1906 Hoytville PA; D6.24.1959 Elmira NY; BR/TR/5´11˝/165; d4.27

YEAR	TM LG	W	L	PCT	G	GS	CG-SHO	SV-BS	IP	H	R	HR	HB	BB-IB	SO	ERA	AERA	OAV	OOB	AB-HR-SH	AVG	PB	SUP	APR	DL	PW
1925	Bos N	0	0	ø	1	0	0	0	1	6	8	0	0	3	0	54.00	7	.600	.692	0	ø	0	—	-6	—	-0.3

OHKA, TOMO Tomokazu; B3.18.1976 Kyoto, Japan; BR/TR (BB 2005p)/6´1˝/(179–200); d7.19

YEAR	TM LG	W	L	PCT	G	GS	CG-SHO	SV-BS	IP	H	R	HR	HB	BB-IB	SO	ERA	AERA	OAV	OOB	AB-HR-SH	AVG	PB	SUP	APR	DL	PW
1999	Bos A	1	2	.333	8	2	0	0-0	13	21	12	2	0	6-0	8	6.23	80	.362	.415	0	ø	0	112	-3	0	-0.5
2000	Bos A	3	6	.333	13	12	0	0-0	69.1	70	25	7	2	26-0	40	3.12	161	.263	.331	0	ø	-0	50	15	0	1.7
2001	Bos A	2	5	.286	12	11	0	0-0	52.1	69	40	7	2	19-0	37	6.19	72	.317	.375	3	.000	-0	93	-10	0	-1.2
	Mon N	1	4	.200	10	10	0	0-0	54.2	65	30	8	1	10-0	31	4.77	90	.302	.335	15-0-3	.200	0	83	-2	0	-0.2
2002	Mon N	13	8	.619	32	31	2	0-0	192.2	194	83	19	7	45-7	118	3.18	138	.264	.310	55-0-8	.127	-1	97	21	0	2.1
2003	Mon N	10	12	.455	34	34	2	0-0	199	233	106	24	9	45-11	118	4.16	107	.292	.335	55-0-8	.182	0*	94	4	0	0.5
2004	Mon N	3	7	.300	15	15	0	0-0	84.2	98	40	11	1	20-1	38	3.40	135	.288	.328	25	.080	-1	58	9	95	0.8
2005	Was N	4	3	.571	10	9	0	0-0	54	44	23	6	1	27-1	17	3.33	123	.224	.320	16-0-1	.250	1*	135	4	0	0.5
	Mil N	7	6	.538	22	20	1-1	0-0	126.1	145	65	16	2	28-4	81	4.35	98	.285	.323	38-0-2	.053	-2	123	0	0	-0.3
	Year	11	9	.550	32	29	1-1	0-0	180.1	189	88	22	3	55-5	98	4.04	104	.268	.322	54-0-3	.111	-2	127	3	0	0.2
2006	Mil N	4	5	.444	18	18	0	0-0	97	98	58	12	5	35-1	50	4.82	93	.266	.334	31-0-3	.161	0	91	-4	77	-0.3
Total	8	48	58	.453	174	162	5-1	0-0	943	1037	482	112	30	261-25	538	4.04	110	.280	.330	238-0-25	.139	-4	92	34	172	3.1

OHL, JOE Joseph Earl (b Joseph Earl Von Ohl); B1.10.1888 Jobstown NJ; D12.18.1951 Camden NJ; BL/TL/6´1˝/175; d7.29

YEAR	TM LG	W	L	PCT	G	GS	CG-SHO	SV-BS	IP	H	R	HR	HB	BB-IB	SO	ERA	AERA	OAV	OOB	AB-HR-SH	AVG	PB	SUP	APR	DL	PW
1909	Was A	0	0	ø	4	0	0	0	8.2	7	4	0	1	1	2	2.08	117	.194	.237	2	.000	-0	—	0	—	0.0

OHMAN, WILL William McDaniel; B8.13.1977 Frankfurt, West Germany; BL/TL/6´2˝/(190–200); [ChiN98 8/226]; d9.19; Col Pepperdine; [DL 2002 Chi N 183, 2003 Chi N 183]

YEAR	TM LG	W	L	PCT	G	GS	CG-SHO	SV-BS	IP	H	R	HR	HB	BB-IB	SO	ERA	AERA	OAV	OOB	AB-HR-SH	AVG	PB	SUP	APR	DL	PW
2000	Chi N	1	0	1.000	6	0	0	0-0	3.1	4	3	0	0	4-1	2	8.10	57	.308	.471	0	ø	0	—	-1	0	-0.2
2001	Chi N	0	1	.000	11	0	0	0-0	11.2	14	10	2	0	6-0	12	7.71	54	.292	.370	2	.000	-0	—	-4	0	-0.4
2005	Chi N	2	2	.500	69	0	0	0-3	43.1	32	14	6	3	24-3	45	2.91	150	.201	.317	0	ø	0	—	7	0	0.6
2006	Chi N	1	1	.500	78	0	0	0-0	65.1	51	30	6	5	34-2	74	4.13	111	.208	.315	1	1.000	0	—	5	0	0.2
Total	4	4	4	.500	164	0	0	0-3	123.2	101	57	14	8	68-6	133	4.15	108	.217	.326	3	.333	0	—	7	366	0.2

OHME, KEVIN Kevin Arthur; B4.13.1971 Palm Beach FL; BL/TL/6´1˝/180; [MinA93 9/261]; d4.14; Col North Florida

YEAR	TM LG	W	L	PCT	G	GS	CG-SHO	SV-BS	IP	H	R	HR	HB	BB-IB	SO	ERA	AERA	OAV	OOB	AB-HR-SH	AVG	PB	SUP	APR	DL	PW
2003	StL N	0	0	ø	2	0	0	0-0	4.1	3	0	0	0	1-1	2	0.00	ø	.200	.235	1	1.000	0	—	2	0	0.2

OJALA, KIRT Kirt Stanley; B12.24.1968 Kalamazoo MI; BL/TL/6´2˝/(210–215); [NYA90 4/111]; d8.18; Col Michigan

YEAR	TM LG	W	L	PCT	G	GS	CG-SHO	SV-BS	IP	H	R	HR	HB	BB-IB	SO	ERA	AERA	OAV	OOB	AB-HR-SH	AVG	PB	SUP	APR	DL	PW
1997	Fla N	1	2	.333	7	5	0	0-0	28.2	28	10	4	0	18-0	19	3.14	129	.252	.354	7-0-1	.000	-1	100	3	0	0.3
1998	Fla N	2	7	.222	41	13	1	0-0	125	128	71	14	4	59-4	75	4.25	96	.267	.351	26-0-2	.154	1	77	-6	0	-0.2
1999	Fla N	0	1	.000	8	1	0	0-0	10.2	21	17	1	0	6-0	5	14.34	31	.438	.482	0	ø	0	42	-12	0	-0.9
Total	3	3	10	.231	56	19	1	0-0	164.1	177	98	19	4	83-4	99	4.71	87	.277	.362	33-0-3	.121	0	81	-15	0	-0.8

OJEDA, BOB Robert Michael; B12.17.1957 Los Angeles CA; BL/TL/6´1˝/(185–195); d7.13; Col Sequoias (CA) [JC]

YEAR	TM LG	W	L	PCT	G	GS	CG-SHO	SV-BS	IP	H	R	HR	HB	BB-IB	SO	ERA	AERA	OAV	OOB	AB-HR-SH	AVG	PB	SUP	APR	DL	PW
1980	Bos A	1	1	.500	7	7	0	0-0	26	39	20	2	0	14-1	12	6.92	62	.361	.434	0	ø	0	105	-6	0	-0.4
1981	Bos A	6	2	.750	10	10	2	0-0	66.1	50	25	6	2	25-2	28	3.12	126	.212	.292	0	ø	0	119	6	0	0.7
1982	Bos A	4	6	.400	22	14	0	0-0	78.1	95	53	13	1	29-0	52	5.63	77	.296	.355	0	ø	0	97	-10	21	-1.2
1983	Bos A	12	7	.632	29	28	5	0-0	173.2	173	85	15	3	73-2	94	4.04	109	.265	.336	0	ø	0	104	7	0	0.7
1984	Bos A	12	12	.500	33	32	8-**5**	0-0	216.2	211	106	17	2	96-2	137	3.99	105	.259	.336	0	ø	0	100	6	16	0.7
1985	Bos A	9	11	.450	39	22	5	1-0	157.2	166	74	11	2	48-9	102	4.00	108	.273	.327	0	ø	0	80	6	0	0.8
1986	†NY N	18	5	**.783**	32	30	7-2	0-0	217.1	185	72	15	2	52-3	148	2.57	140	.230	.278	71-0-8	.113	-2	120	25	0	2.3
1987	NY N	3	5	.375	10	7	0	0-0	46.1	45	23	5	0	10-1	21	3.88	99	.253	.291	14	.071	-0	118	-1	113	-0.1
1988	NY N	10	13	.435	29	29	5-5	0-0	190.1	158	74	6	4	33-2	133	2.88	113	.225	.261	61-0-4	.164	1*	81	7	0	1.0
1989	NY N	13	11	.542	31	31	5-2	0-0	192	179	83	16	2	78-5	95	3.47	95	.245	.317	66-0-6	.106	-2*	112	-4	0	-0.6
1990	NY N	7	6	.538	38	12	0	0-2	118	123	53	10	2	40-4	62	3.66	103	.272	.332	30-0-1	.133	-0	108	2	0	0.3
1991	LA N	12	9	.571	31	31	2-1	0-0	189.1	181	78	15	3	70-9	120	3.18	113	.257	.323	56-1-6	.161	1	95	8	0	1.1
1992	LA N	6	9	.400	29	29	2-1	0-0	166.1	169	80	8	1	81-8	94	3.63	96	.268	.349	49-0-5	.102	-1	97	-4	0	-0.4
1993	Cle A	2	1	.667	9	7	0	0-0	43	48	22	5	0	21-0	27	4.40	100	.289	.363	0	ø	0	105	0	124	0.1
1994	NY A	0	0	ø	2	2	0	0-0	3	11	8	1	0	6-0	3	24.00	19	.611	.680	0	ø	0	120	-6	0	-0.3
Total	15	115	98	.540	351	291	41-16	1-2	1884.1	1833	856	145	24	676-48	1128	3.65	104	.257	.321	347-1-30	.127	-4	101	36	274	4.7

OKRIE, FRANK Frank Anthony "Lefty"; B10.27.1896 Detroit MI; D10.16.1959 Detroit MI; BL/TL/5´11˝/175; d4.20; s–Len

YEAR	TM LG	W	L	PCT	G	GS	CG-SHO	SV-BS	IP	H	R	HR	HB	BB-IB	SO	ERA	AERA	OAV	OOB	AB-HR-SH	AVG	PB	SUP	APR	DL	PW
1920	Det A	1	2	.333	21	1	1	0	41	44	29	2	5	18	9	5.27	71	.295	.390	5-0-1	.200	-0	107	-6	—	-0.1

OLDHAM, RED John Cyrus; B7.15.1893 Zion MD; D1.28.1961 Costa Mesa CA; BB/TL (BL 1922, 25–26)/6´0˝/176; d8.19

YEAR	TM LG	W	L	PCT	G	GS	CG-SHO	SV-BS	IP	H	R	HR	HB	BB-IB	SO	ERA	AERA	OAV	OOB	AB-HR-SH	AVG	PB	SUP	APR	DL	PW
1914	Det A	2	4	.333	9	7	3	0	45.1	42	22	1	3	8	23	3.38	83	.243	.288	15-0-1	.267	1	78	-2	—	-0.2
1915	Det A	3	0	1.000	17	2	1	4	57.2	52	22	1	4	17	17	2.81	108	.243	.311	14	.143	-0	84	2	—	0.1
1920	Det A	8	13	.381	39	22	10-1	1	215.1	248	132	5	6	91	62	3.85	97	.302	.376	69-0-4	.174	-1	93	-6	—	-0.5
1921	Det A	11	14	.440	40	28	12-1	1	229.1	258	129	11	6	81	67	4.24	101	.288	.351	85-2-2	.224	2*	117	3	—	0.6
1922	Det A	10	13	.435	43	28	9	3	212	256	130	14	11	59	72	4.67	83	.305	.358	73-0-1	.260	4	123	-19	—	-1.3
1925	†Pit N	3	2	.600	11	4	3	1	53	66	27	2	2	18	10	3.91	114	.313	.372	18	.333	2	80	4	—	0.5
1926	Pit N	2	2	.500	17	2	0	2	41.2	56	27	1	1	18	16	5.62	70	.359	.429	9-0-1	.222	0	85	-6	—	-0.5
Total	7	39	48	.448	176	93	38-2	12	854.1	978	489	35	33	292	267	4.15	93	.295	.358	283-2-9	.226	9	108	-24	—	-1.3

OLIN, STEVE Steven Robert; B10.4.1965 Portland OR; D3.22.1993 Little Lake Nellie FL; BR/TR/6´3˝/(185–190); [CleA87 16/411]; d7.29; Col Portland St.

YEAR	TM LG	W	L	PCT	G	GS	CG-SHO	SV-BS	IP	H	R	HR	HB	BB-IB	SO	ERA	AERA	OAV	OOB	AB-HR-SH	AVG	PB	SUP	APR	DL	PW
1989	Cle A	1	4	.200	25	0	0	1-0	36	35	16	1	0	14-2	24	3.75	106	.255	.325	0	ø	0	—	1	0	0.2
1990	Cle A	4	4	.500	50	1	0	1-2	92.1	96	41	3	6	26-2	64	3.41	116	.270	.329	0	ø	0	92	4	0	0.4
1991	Cle A	3	6	.333	48	0	0	17-5	56.1	61	26	2	1	23-7	38	3.36	124	.274	.344	0	ø	0	—	4	0	0.8
1992	Cle A	8	5	.615	72	0	0	29-7	88.1	80	25	8	4	27-6	47	2.34	168	.248	.313	0	ø	0	—	16	0	3.2
Total	4	16	19	.457	195	1	0	48-14	273	272	108	14	11	90-17	173	3.10	129	.262	.327	0	ø	0	92	25	0	4.6

OLIVARES, OMAR Omar (Palqu); B7.6.1967 Mayaguez, PR; BR/TR/6´1˝/(185–210); d8.18; f–Ed; Col Miami–Dade Wolfson (FL) CC

YEAR	TM LG	W	L	PCT	G	GS	CG-SHO	SV-BS	IP	H	R	HR	HB	BB-IB	SO	ERA	AERA	OAV	OOB	AB-HR-SH	AVG	PB	SUP	APR	DL	PW
1990	StL N	1	1	.500	9	6	0	0-0	49.1	45	17	2	2	17-0	20	2.92	132	.249	.320	17-1-0	.176	1	82	5	0	0.4
1991	StL N	11	7	.611	28	24	0	1-0	167.1	148	72	13	5	61-1	91	3.71	101	.243	.316	53-0-4	.226	3	101	3	0	0.7
1992	StL N	9	9	.500	32	30	1	0-0	197	189	84	20	4	63-5	124	3.84	89	.257	.316	68-1-3	.235	4*	101	-6	17	0.0
1993	StL N	5	3	.625	58	9	0	1-4	118.2	134	60	10	9	54-7	63	4.17	97	.288	.370	26-0-3	.269	2*	112	-1	16	0.3
1994	StL N	3	4	.429	14	12	1	1-0	73.2	84	53	10	4	37-0	26	5.74	74	.294	.379	28-1-2	.214	2*	120	-14	0	-1.0
1995	Col N	1	3	.250	11	6	0	0-0	31.2	44	28	4	2	21-0	15	7.39	73	.349	.447	7-0-1	.143	0*	79	-5	0	-0.6
	Phi N	0	1	.000	5	0	0	0-0	10	11	6	1	1	2-0	7	5.40	78	.282	.326	2-1-0	.500	1	—	-1	0	0.0
	Year	1	4	.200	16	6	0	0-0	41.2	55	34	5	3	23-0	22	6.91	74	.333	.420	9-1-1	.222	1	83	-6	0	-0.6
1996	Det A	7	11	.389	25	25	4	0-0	160	169	90	16	9	75-4	81	4.89	104	.275	.359	0	ø	0	88	6	44	0.5
1997	Det A	5	6	.455	19	19	3-2	0-0	115	110	68	8	9	53-1	74	4.70	98	.253	.344	3	.667	1*	107	-3	0	0.0
	Sea A	1	4	.200	13	12	0	0-0	62.1	81	41	10	4	28-3	29	5.49	83	.315	.387	2	.500	0	100	-7	0	-0.4
	Year	6	10	.375	32	31	3-2	0-0	177.1	191	109	18	13	81-4	103	4.97	92	.276	.360	5	.600	2	104	-9	0	-0.4
1998	Ana A	9	9	.500	37	26	1	0-0	183	189	92	19	5	91-1	112	4.03	118	.270	.357	2	.000	0*	91	13	0	1.3
1999	Ana A	8	9	.471	20	20	3	0-0	131	135	62	11	6	49-0	49	4.05	121	.273	.342	6-0-1	.333	1	73	13	0	1.6
	Oak A	7	2	.778	12	12	1	0-0	74.2	82	43	8	3	32-0	36	4.34	109	.283	.358	0	ø	0	123	2	0	0.2
	Year	15	11	.577	32	32	4	0-0	205.2	217	105	19	9	81-0	85	4.16	116	.276	.348	6-0-1	.333	1	92	15	0	1.8
2000	Oak A	4	8	.333	21	16	1	0-0	108	134	86	10	7	60-0	57	6.75	72	.309	.396	1	1.000	0	99	-21	55	-1.8
2001	Pit N	6	9	.400	45	12	1	1-1	110	123	87	17	10	42-8	69	6.55	68	.283	.356	27-1-0	.222	2*	108	-25	0	-2.7
Total	12	77	86	.472	349	229	16-2	4-5	1591.2	1678	889	159	80	685-30	853	4.67	94	.275	.353	242-5-14	.240	18	98	-41	132	-1.5

OLIVER, DARREN Darren Christopher; B10.6.1970 Rio Linda CA; BR/TL/6´2˝/(170–220); [TexA88 3/63]; d9.1; f–Bob

YEAR	TM LG	W	L	PCT	G	GS	CG-SHO	SV-BS	IP	H	R	HR	HB	BB-IB	SO	ERA	AERA	OAV	OOB	AB-HR-SH	AVG	PB	SUP	APR	DL	PW
1993	Tex A	0	0	ø	2	0	0	0-0	3.1	2	1	1	0	1-1	4	2.70	155	.154	.214	0	ø	0	—	1	0	0.0
1994	Tex A	4	0	1.000	43	0	0	2-1	50	40	24	4	6	35-4	50	3.42	142	.223	.368	0	ø	0	—	7	0	0.6
1995	Tex A	4	2	.667	17	7	0	0-0	49	47	25	3	1	32-1	39	4.22	115	.257	.369	0	ø	0	88	3	97	0.4
1996	†Tex A	14	6	.700	30	30	1-1	0-0	173.2	190	97	20	10	76-3	112	4.66	113	.279	.356	0	ø	0	104	11	0	1.0
1997	Tex A	13	12	.520	32	32	3-1	0-0	201.1	213	111	29	11	82-3	104	4.20	116	.271	.346	2	.500	1	105	11	0	1.1
1998	Tex A	6	7	.462	19	19	2	0-0	103.1	140	84	11	10	43-1	58	6.53	75	.325	.394	6	.167	0	116	-19	15	-1.9
	StL N	4	4	.500	10	10	0	0-0	57	64	31	7	0	23-1	29	4.26	99	.283	.347	23	.087	-1*	90	-1	0	-0.2
1999	StL N	9	9	.500	30	30	2-1	0-0	196.1	197	96	16	11	74-4	119	4.26	108	.265	.339	73-0-8	.274	5*	96	10	0	1.4
2000	Tex A	2	9	.182	21	21	0	0-0	108	151	95	16	4	42-3	49	7.42	69	.339	.397	2	.000	0	111	-25	63	-2.0
2001	Tex A	11	11	.500	28	28	1	0-0	154	189	109	23	6	65-0	104	6.02	79	.305	.374	6-0-2	.333	1	115	-20	29	-2.2
2002	Bos A	4	5	.444	14	9	1-1	0-0	58	70	30	7	6	27-0	32	4.66	96	.317	.401	1	.000	-0	85	0	0	0.0
2003	Col N	13	11	.542	33	32	1	0-0	180.1	201	108	21	8	61-3	88	5.04	97	.284	.345	67-1-2	.254	4*	108	-2	0	0.1

YEAR	TM LG	W	L	PCT	G	GS	CG-SHO	SV-BS	IP	H	R	HR	HB	BB-IB	SO	ERA	AERA	OAV	OOB	AB-HR-SH	AVG	PB	SUP	APR	DL	PW
2004	Fla N	2	3	.400	18	8	0	0-0	58.2	75	44	13	1	17-1	33	6.44	64	.319	.363	19-0-2	.158	-0	127	-16	0	-1.1
	Hou N	1	0	1.000	9	2	0	0-0	14	12	6	1	0	4-0	13	3.86	113	.240	.296	3-0-1	.000	-0*	138	1	31	0.0
	Year	3	3	.500	27	10	0	0-0	72.2	87	50	14	1	21-1	46	5.94	70	.305	.352	22-0-3	.136	-1	129	-13	0	-1.1
2006	†NY N	4	1	.800	45	0	0	0-0	81	70	33	13	3	21-2	60	3.44	128	.231	.284	15	.133	0	—	9	0	0.5
Total	13	91	80	.532	351	228	11-4	2-1	1488	1661	894	185	77	603-27	894	4.98	96	.285	.357	217-1-15	.221	9	107	-30	235	-2.3
OLIVERAS, FRANCISCO	Francisco Javier (Noa); B1.31.1963 Santurce, PR; BR/TR/5´10˝/(170–180); d5.3																									
1989	Min A	3	4	.429	12	8	1	0-0	55.2	64	28	8	1	15-0	24	4.53	92	.288	.335	0	ø	0	115	-1	0	-0.2
1990	SF N	2	2	.500	33	2	0	2-0	55.1	47	22	5	2	21-6	41	2.77	132	.230	.304	5	.000	-1	111	4	24	0.2
1991	SF N	6	6	.500	55	1	0	3-1	79.1	69	36	12	1	22-4	48	3.86	93	.242	.296	10	.200	0	75	-2	0	-0.3
1992	SF N	0	3	.000	16	7	0	0-0	44.2	41	19	11	1	10-2	17	3.63	92	.250	.294	7	.143	0	58	-1	17	-0.1
Total	4	11	15	.423	116	18	1	5-1	235	221	105	36	5	68-12	130	3.71	99	.253	.307	22	.136	-0	94	0	41	-0.4
OLIVO, DIOMEDES	Diomedes Antonio (Maldonado); B1.22.1919 Guayubin, D.R.; D2.15.1977 Santo Domingo, D.R.; BL/TL/6´1˝/195; d9.5; b–Chi–Chi s–Gilberto																									
1960	Pit N	0	0	ø	4	0	0	0	9.2	8	3	1	0	5-1	10	2.79	134	.216	.310	1	.000	-0	—	1	0	0.0
1962	Pit N	5	1	.833	62	1	0	7	84.1	88	30	5	0	25-7	66	2.77	142	.277	.325	16-0-2	.188	1	89	11	0	1.0
1963	StL N	0	5	.000	19	0	0	0	13.1	16	9	1	1	9-1	9	5.40	66	.296	.400	0	ø	0	—	-2	0	-0.5
Total	3	5	6	.455	85	1	0	7	107.1	112	42	7	1	39-9	85	3.10	125	.274	.334	17-0-2	.176	0	89	10	0	0.5
OLIVO, CHI-CHI	Federico Emilio (Maldonado); B3.18.1928 Guayubin, D.R.; D2.3.1977 Guayubin, D.R.; BR/TR/6´2˝/215; d6.5; b–Diomedes																									
1961	Mil N	0	0	ø	3	0	0	0	2	3	4	1	0	5-1	1	18.00	21	.500	.727	0	ø	0	—	-3	0	-0.2
1964	Mil N	2	1	.667	38	0	0	5	60	55	25	7	0	21-5	45	3.75	94	.247	.309	4	.250	0	—	0	0	0.0
1965	Mil N	0	1	.000	8	0	0	0	13	12	2	1	0	5-2	11	1.38	254	.267	.327	0	ø	0	—	3	0	0.2
1966	Atl N	5	4	.556	47	0	0	7	66	59	34	4	1	19-5	41	4.23	86	.240	.293	9	.111	-0	—	-4	0	-0.7
Total	4	7	6	.538	96	0	0	12	141	129	65	13	1	50-13	98	3.96	90	.248	.311	13	.154	-0	—	-4	0	-0.7
OLLOM, JIM	James Donald; B7.8.1945 Snohomish WA; BR/TL (BR 1966)/6´4˝/(204–210); d9.3																									
1966	Min A	0	0	ø	3	1	0	0	10	6	4	1	1	1-0	11	3.60	100	.167	.211	2	.000	-0	123	0	0	0.0
1967	Min A	0	1	.000	21	2	0	0	35	33	24	4	4	11-1	17	5.40	64	.258	.331	5	.200	0	76	-7	0	-0.4
Total	2	0	1	.000	24	3	0	0	45	39	28	5	5	12-1	28	5.00	70	.238	.306	7	.143	-0	92	-7	0	-0.4
OLMSTEAD, FRED	Frederic William; B7.3.1881 Grand Rapids MI; D10.22.1936 Muskogee OK; BR/TR/5´11˝/170; d7.2																									
1908	Chi A	0	0	ø	1	0	0	0	2	6	3	0	0	1	1	13.50	17	.600	.636	1	.000	1	—	-2	—	-0.1
1909	Chi A	3	2	.600	8	6	5	0	54.2	52	17	1	1	12	21	1.81	129	.277	.323	21	.095	-1	105	3	—	0.1
1910	Chi A	10	12	.455	32	20	14-4	0	184.1	174	64	1	4	50	68	1.95	123	.260	.316	65-0-2	.154	-2	64	8	—	0.8
1911	Chi A	6	6	.500	25	11	7-1	2	117.2	146	78	3	6	30	45	4.21	77	.309	.358	37-0-1	.189	-0	124	-15	—	-1.4
Total	4	19	20	.487	66	37	26-5	2	358.2	378	162	5	11	93	135	2.74	97	.283	.334	124-0-3	.153	-3	90	-6	—	-0.6
OLMSTED, AL	Alan Ray; B3.18.1957 St.Louis MO; BR/TL/6´2˝/195; [StLN75 13/304]; d9.12																									
1980	StL N	1	1	.500	5	5	0	0-0	34.2	32	13	2	1	14-1	14	2.86	131	.244	.322	11-0-2	.182	-0	100	3	0	0.2
OLMSTED, HANK	Henry Theodore; B1.12.1879 Sac Bay MI; D1.6.1969 Bradenton FL; BR/TR/5´8.5˝/147; d7.15; Col Notre Dame																									
1905	Bos A	1	2	.333	3	3	3	0	25	18	10	0	0	12	6	3.24	83	.205	.300	8	.125	-0	26	-1	—	-0.1
OLSEN, OLE	Arthur Ole; B9.12.1894 S.Norwalk CT; D9.12.1980 Norwalk CT; BR/TR/5´10˝/163; d4.12; Col Cornell																									
1922	Det A	7	6	.538	37	15	5	3	137	147	84	8	14	40	52	4.53	86	.281	.348	39-0-3	.179	-1*	112	-11	—	-1.0
1923	Det A	1	1	.500	17	2	1	0	41.1	42	30	1	5	17	12	6.31	61	.290	.383	8-0-1	.125	-1	193	-10	—	-0.6
Total	2	8	7	.533	54	17	6	3	178.1	189	114	9	19	57	64	4.95	78	.283	.356	47-0-4	.170	-2	122	-21	—	-1.6
OLSEN, KEVIN	Kevin Gary; B7.26.1976 Covina CA; BR/TR/6´2˝/200; [FlaN98 26/790]; d9.7; Col Oklahoma																									
2001	Fla N	0	0	ø	4	2	0	0-0	15	11	2	0	0	2-1	13	1.20	347	.204	.232	3-0-1	.000	-0	22	5	0	0.2
2002	Fla N	0	5	.000	17	8	0	0-0	55.2	57	31	5	1	31-1	38	4.53	87	.270	.363	12	.083	-1	97	-4	0	-0.4
2003	Fla N	0	0	ø	7	0	0	0-0	12	25	18	2	0	4-1	12	12.75	32	.431	.468	0	ø	0	—	-12	72	-0.6
Total	3	0	5	.000	28	10	0	0-0	82.2	93	51	7	1	37-3	63	5.12	78	.288	.361	15-0-1	.067	-1	81	-11	72	-0.8
OLSEN, SCOTT	Scott Matthew; B1.12.1984 Kalamazoo MI; BL/TL/6´4˝/200; [FlaN02 6/173]; d6.25																									
2005	Fla N	1	1	.500	5	4	0	0-0	20.1	21	13	5	0	10-0	21	3.98	101	.259	.341	3-0-1	.000	-0	88	-1	0	-0.2
2006	Fla N	12	10	.545	31	31	0	0-0	180.2	160	94	23	7	75-1	166	4.04	106	.239	.321	58-0-6	.190	1*	97	3	0	0.5
Total	2	13	11	.542	36	35	0	0-0	201	181	107	28	7	85-1	187	4.03	106	.241	.323	61-0-7	.180	1	96	2	0	0.3
OLSEN, VERN	Vern Jarl; B3.16.1918 Hillsboro OR; D7.13.1989 Maywood IL; BR/TL/6´0.5˝/175; d9.8; Mil 1943–45																									
1939	Chi N	1	0	1.000	4	0	0	0	7.2	2	0	0	0	7	3	0.00	ø	.087	.300	1	.000	0	—	3	—	0.5
1940	Chi N	13	9	.591	34	20	9-4	0	172.2	172	64	5	2	62	71	2.97	126	.260	.325	57-0-3	.263	3*	95	16	—	2.5
1941	Chi N	10	8	.556	37	23	10-2	1	185.2	202	84	7	1	59	73	3.15	111	.276	.331	63-1-2	.238	3	108	5	0	0.9
1942	Chi N	6	9	.400	32	17	4-1	1	140.1	161	75	6	1	55	46	4.49	71	.283	.347	48-0-1	.188	1	103	-17	0	-1.5
1946	Chi N	0	0	ø	5	0	0	0	9.2	10	3	0	0	9	8	2.79	119	.294	.442	0	ø	0	—	1	0	0.0
Total	5	30	26	.536	112	60	23-7	2	516	547	226	18	4	192	201	3.40	103	.271	.335	169-1-6	.231	8	102	8	0	2.4
OLSON, GREGG	Greggory William; B10.11.1966 Scribner NE; BR/TR/6´4˝/(206–212); [BalA88 1/4]; d9.2; Col Auburn																									
1988	Bal A	1	1	.500	10	0	0	0-1	11	10	4	1	0	10-1	9	3.27	120	.244	.392	0	ø	0	—	1	0	0.2
1989	Bal A	5	2	.714	64	0	0	27-6	85	57	17	1	1	46-10	90	1.69	226	.188	.295	0	ø	0	—	20	0	2.8
1990	Bal A☆	6	5	.545	64	0	0	37-5	74.1	57	20	3	3	31-3	74	2.42	158	.213	.299	0	ø	0	—	13	0	2.6
1991	Bal A	4	6	.400	72	0	0	31-8	73.2	74	28	1	1	29-5	72	3.18	125	.261	.331	0	ø	0	—	7	0	1.3
1992	Bal A	1	5	.167	60	0	0	36-8	61.1	46	14	3	0	24-0	58	2.05	198	.211	.287	0	ø	0	—	14	0	2.7
1993	Bal A	0	2	.000	50	0	0	29-6	45	37	9	1	0	18-3	44	1.60	283	.223	.296	1	.000	-0	—	14	42	2.1
1994	Atl N	0	2	.000	16	0	0	1-0	14.2	19	15	1	1	13-3	10	9.20	47	.317	.440	1	.000	-0	—	-7	57	-0.9
1995	Cle A	0	0	ø	3	0	0	0-0	2.2	5	4	1	0	2-0	0	13.50	35	.417	.500	0	ø	0	—	-2	0	-0.1
	KC A	3	3	.500	20	0	0	3-2	30.1	23	11	3	0	17-2	21	3.26	147	.215	.317	0	ø	0	—	5	0	1.0
	Year	3	3	.500	23	0	0	3-2	33	28	15	4	0	19-2	21	4.09	117	.235	.336	0	ø	0	—	3	0	0.9
1996	Det A	3	0	1.000	43	0	0	8-2	43	43	25	6	1	28-4	29	5.02	101	.259	.369	0	ø	0	—	1	0	0.0
	Hou N	1	0	1.000	9	0	0	0-0	9.1	12	5	1	0	7-2	8	4.82	80	.308	.404	0	ø	0	—	-1	0	-0.1
1997	Min A	0	0	ø	11	0	0	0-0	8.1	19	17	0	0	11-1	6	18.36	25	.432	.545	0	ø	0	—	-12	0	-0.5
	KC A	4	3	.571	34	0	0	1-3	41.2	39	18	3	1	17-3	28	3.02	157	.260	.337	0	ø	0	—	6	0	1.0
	Year	4	3	.571	45	0	0	1-3	50	58	35	3	1	28-4	34	5.58	85	.299	.388	0	ø	0	—	-5	0	0.5
1998	Ari N	3	4	.429	64	0	0	30-4	68.2	56	25	4	1	25-1	55	3.01	142	.223	.295	2-1-0	.500	1	—	10	0	1.7
1999	†Ari N	9	4	.692	61	0	0	14-9	60.2	54	28	9	2	25-2	45	3.71	124	.238	.316	0	ø	0	—	6	15	1.1
2000	LA N	0	1	.000	13	0	0	0-1	17.2	21	11	4	1	7-0	15	5.09	87	.296	.363	0	ø	0	—	-1	108	-0.1
2001	LA N	0	1	.000	28	0	0	0-1	24.2	26	24	4	0	20-1	24	8.03	51	.268	.383	0	ø	0	—	-11	0	-0.6
Total	14	40	39	.506	622	0	0	217-56	672	598	275	46	12	330-41	588	3.46	123	.239	.328	4-1-0	.250	1	—	63	222	14.2
OLSON, TED	Theodore Otto; B8.27.1912 Quincy MA; D12.9.1980 Weymouth MA; BR/TR/6´2.5˝/185; d6.21; Col Dartmouth																									
1936	Bos A	1	1	.500	5	3	1	0	18.1	24	16	3	0	8	5	7.36	72	.324	.390	7	.143	-0	66	-3	—	-0.3
1937	Bos A	0	0	ø	11	0	0	0	32.1	42	28	4	0	15	11	7.24	66	.318	.388	10	.300	1	—	-8	—	-0.3
1938	Bos A	0	0	ø	2	0	0	0	7	9	5	0	0	2	2	6.43	77	.310	.355	1	.000	-0	—	-1	—	-0.1
Total	3	1	1	.500	18	3	1	0	57.2	75	49	7	0	25	18	7.18	69	.319	.385	18	.222	1	66	-12	—	-0.7
OLWINE, ED	Edward R.; B5.28.1958 Greenville OH; BR/TL/6´2˝/(165–170); d6.2; Col Morehead St.																									
1986	Atl N	0	0	ø	37	0	0	1-0	47.2	35	20	5	1	17-7	37	3.40	117	.207	.282	3	.333	1	—	3	0	0.2
1987	Atl N	0	1	.000	27	0	0	1-1	23.1	25	16	4	1	8-1	12	5.01	86	.269	.330	0-0-1	ø	0	—	-2	0	-0.1
1988	Atl N	0	0	ø	16	0	0	1-0	18.2	22	15	4	1	4-1	5	6.75	54	.286	.329	0	ø	0	—	-6	86	-0.3
Total	3	0	1	.000	80	0	0	3-1	89.2	82	51	13	3	29-9	54	4.52	88	.242	.306	3-0-1	.333	1	—	-5	86	-0.2
O'MALLEY, RYAN	Ryan Joseph; B4.9.1980 Springfield IL; BR/TL/6´1˝/205; d8.16; Col Memphis																									
2006	Chi N	1	1	.500	2	2	0	0-0	12.2	10	3	0	1	7-0	4	2.13	215	.213	.327	4	.000	-0	40	4	15	0.5

YEAR	TM LG	W	L	PCT	G	GS	CG-SHO	SV-BS	IP	H	R	HR	HB	BB-IB	SO	ERA	AERA	OAV	OOB	AB-HR-SH	AVG	PB	SUP	APR	DL	PW
O'NEAL, SKINNY	Oran Herbert; B5.2.1899 Gatewood MO; D6.2.1981 Springfield MO; BR/TR/5´11˝/160; d4.18; Col East Central																									
1925	Phi N	0	0	ø	11	1	0	0	20.1	35	23	2	0	12	6	9.30	51	.407	.480	6	.167	-0	106	-8	—	-0.4
1927	Phi N	0	0	ø	2	0	0	0	5	9	5	0	0	2	2	9.00	46	.409	.458	1	.000	-0	—	-2	—	-0.1
Total	2	0	0	ø	13	1	0	0	25.1	44	28	2	0	14	8	9.24	50	.407	.475	7	.143	-0	106	-10	—	-0.5
O'NEAL, RANDY	Randall Jeffrey; B8.30.1960 Ashland KY; BR/TR/6´2˝/195; [DetA81 S1/15]; d9.12; Col Florida																									
1984	Det A	2	1	.667	4	3	0	0-0	18.2	16	7	0	0	6-0	12	3.38	117	.222	.282	0	ø	0	107	2	0	0.2
1985	Det A	5	5	.500	28	12	1	1-0	94.1	82	42	8	2	36-3	52	3.24	127	.240	.310	0	ø	0	92	7	0	0.8
1986	Det A	3	7	.300	37	11	1	2-1	122.2	121	69	13	3	44-9	68	4.33	96	.260	.324	0	ø	0	103	-4	0	-0.3
1987	Atl N	4	2	.667	16	10	0	0-0	61	79	41	12	2	24-3	33	5.61	77	.316	.378	19-0-1	.105	-1*	125	-7	0	-0.6
	StL N	0	0	ø	1	1	0	0-0	5	2	1	0	0	2-0	4	1.80	234	.111	.200	1	1.000	0	21	1	0	0.1
	Year	4	2	.667	17	11	0	0-0	66	81	42	12	2	26-3	37	5.32	81	.302	.366	20-0-1	.150	-0	116	-6	0	-0.5
1988	StL N	2	3	.400	10	8	0	0-0	53	57	29	7	2	10-1	20	4.58	77	.274	.314	19-0-1	.000	-2	120	-6	62	-0.6
1989	Phi N	0	1	.000	20	1	0	0-1	39	46	28	5	0	9-2	29	6.23	58	.301	.333	5	.000	-1	395	-10	0	-0.6
1990	SF N	1	0	1.000	26	0	0	0-0	47	58	23	3	0	18-4	30	3.83	96	.314	.371	6-0-1	.167	-0	—	-2	23	-0.1
Total	7	17	19	.472	142	46	2	3-2	440.2	461	240	48	9	149-22	248	4.35	92	.272	.331	50-0-3	.080	-3	114	-19	85	-1.1
O'NEIL, ED	Edward J.; B3.11.1859 Fall River MA; D9.30.1892 Fall River MA; TR/5´11˝/180; d6.20																									
1890	Tol AA	0	2	.000	2	2	2	0	16	27	18	0	0	13	2	7.88	50	.365	.460	9	.000	-2	145	-6	—	-0.6
	Phi AA	0	6	.000	6	6	6	0	52	84	77	0	7	32	17	9.69	40	.353	.444	31	.161	-1*	58	-32	—	-2.5
	Year	0	8	.000	8	8	8	0	68	111	95	0	7	45	19	9.26	42	.356	.448	40	.125	-2	80	-40	—	-3.1
O'NEILL, J.	J.; B Brooklyn NY; d8,20																									
1875	Atl NA	0	4	.000	5	4	3	0	34	59	45	3	—	0	0	5.03	41	.343	.343	26	.077	-2*	68	-9	—	-0.9
O'NEILL, TIP	James Edward; B5.25.1858 Springfield ON, Can.; D12.31.1915 Montreal QC, Can.; BR/TR/6´1.5˝/167; d5.5; ▲																									
1883	NY N	5	12	.294	19	19	15	0	148	182	129	5	—	64	55	4.07	76	.289	.354	76	.197	-1*	83	-14	—	-1.4
1884	StL AA	11	4	.733	17	14	14	0	141	125	95	3	4	51	36	2.68	122	.219	.288	297-3	.276	5*	112	4	—	0.7
Total	2	16	16	.500	36	33	29	0	289	307	224	8	4	115	91	3.39	94	.256	.323	373-3	.260	3	95	-10	—	-0.7
O'NEILL, HARRY	Joseph Henry; B11.20.1892 Lindsay ON, Can.; D9.5.1969 Ridgetown ON, Can.; BR/TR/6´0˝/180; d9.15																									
1922	Phi A	0	0	ø	1	0	0	0	3	2	1	0	1	1	0	3.00	142	.200	.333	1	.000	-0	—	0	—	0.0
1923	Phi A	0	0	ø	3	0	0	0	2	1	0	0	0	3	2	0.00	ø	.167	.444	0	ø	0	—	1	—	0.0
Total	2	0	0	ø	4	0	0	0	5	3	1	0	1	4	2	1.80	233	.188	.381	1	.000	-0	—	1	—	0.0
O'NEILL, MIKE	Michael Joyce (aka Michael Joyce in 1901); B9.7.1877 Maam, Ireland; D8.12.1959 Scranton PA; BL/TL/5´11˝/185; d9.20; b–Jim b–Jack b–Steve; Col Villanova																									
1901	StL N	2	2	.500	5	4	4-1	0	41	29	12	2	5	10	16	1.32	242	.197	.272	15	.400	3*	139	7	—	1.0
1902	StL N	16	15	.516	36	32	29-2	2	288.1	297	136	3	12	66	105	2.90	94	.266	.314	135-2-1	.319	9*	92	-5	—	0.8
1903	StL N	4	13	.235	19	17	12	0	145	184	124	2	6	43	39	3.79	86	.304	.356	110	.227	2*	66	-17	—	-1.4
1904	StL N	10	14	.417	25	24	23-1	0	220	229	86	1	3	50	68	2.09	129	.262	.304	91-0-5	.231	5*	94	11	—	2.0
Total	4	32	44	.421	85	77	68-4	2	694.1	739	358	8	26	169	228	2.73	105	.269	.318	351-2-6	.271	19	89	-4	—	2.4
O'NEILL, EMMETT	Robert Emmett "Pinky"; B1.13.1918 San Mateo CA; D10.11.1993 Sparks NV; BR/TR/6´2.5˝/180; d8.3; Col St. Marys (CA)																									
1943	Bos A	1	4	.200	11	5	1	0	57.2	56	31	3	1	46	20	4.53	73	.256	.387	16	.188	1	51	-7	0	-0.5
1944	Bos A	6	11	.353	28	22	8-1	0	151.2	154	88	6	2	89	68	4.63	73	.265	.365	55	.182	-0	109	-20	0	-2.2
1945	Bos A	8	11	.421	24	22	10-1	0	141.2	134	87	5	5	117	55	5.15	66	.258	.399	50-1-1	.180	2	107	-24	0	-2.7
1946	Chi N	0	0	ø	1	0	0	0	1	0	0	0	0	3	1	0.00	ø	.000	.500	0	ø	0	—	0	0	0.0
	Chi A	0	0	ø	2	0	0	0	3.2	4	2	0	0	5	0	0.00	ø	.333	.529	1	.000	-0	—	1	0	0.0
Total	4	15	26	.366	66	49	19-2	0	355.2	348	208	14	8	260	144	4.76	71	.261	.385	122-1-1	.180	2	103	-50	0	-5.4
ONTIVEROS, STEVE	Steven; B3.5.1961 Tularosa NM; BR/TR/6´0˝/(180–190); [OakA82 2/54]; d6.14; Col Michigan; [DL 1991 Phi N 182, 1997 Ana A 181]																									
1985	Oak A	1	3	.250	39	0	0	8-1	74.2	45	17	4	2	19-2	36	1.93	201	.174	.234	0	ø	0	—	18	0	1.3
1986	Oak A	2	2	.500	46	0	0	10-3	72.2	72	40	10	1	25-3	54	4.71	83	.265	.322	0	ø	0*	—	-6	52	-0.5
1987	Oak A	10	8	.556	35	22	2-1	1-3	150.2	141	78	19	4	50-3	97	4.00	104	.242	.305	0	ø	0	119	1	18	0.2
1988	Oak A	3	4	.429	10	10	0	0-0	54.2	57	32	4	0	21-1	30	4.61	83	.265	.331	0	ø	0*	161	-6	112	-0.6
1989	Phi N	2	1	.667	6	5	0	0-0	30.2	34	15	2	0	15-1	12	3.82	94	.288	.368	12	.083	-0	113	-1	150	0.0
1990	Phi N	0	0	ø	5	0	0	0-0	10	9	3	1	0	3-0	6	2.70	143	.225	.279	0	ø	0	—	1	152	0.1
1993	Sea A	0	2	.000	14	0	0	0-0	18	18	3	0	0	6-2	13	1.00	447	.277	.338	0	ø	0	—	6	0	0.6
1994	Oak A	6	4	.600	27	13	2	0-0	115.1	93	39	7	6	26-1	56	**2.65**	169	.217	**.271**	0	ø	0	85	24	0	1.9
1995	Oak A★	9	6	.600	22	22	2-1	0-0	129.2	144	75	12	4	38-0	77	4.37	104	.283	.335	0	ø	0	103	-1	39	0.0
2000	Bos A	1	1	.500	3	1	0	0-0	5.1	9	6	1	0	4-0	1	10.13	50	.375	.464	0	ø	0	37	-3	0	-0.5
Total	10	34	31	.523	207	73	6-2	19-7	661.2	622	308	60	17	207-13	382	3.67	114	.248	.307	12	.083	-0	112	33	886	2.5
OQUIST, MIKE	Michael Lee; B5.30.1968 LaJunta CO; BR/TR/6´2˝/(170–190); [BalA89 13/323]; d8.14; Col Arkansas																									
1993	Bal A	0	0	ø	5	0	0	0-0	11.2	12	5	0	0	4-1	8	3.86	117	.261	.320	0	ø	0	—	1	0	0.0
1994	Bal A	3	3	.500	15	9	0	0-0	58.1	75	41	7	6	30-4	39	6.17	82	.319	.404	0	ø	0	91	-7	0	-0.5
1995	Bal A	2	1	.667	27	0	0	0-1	54	51	27	6	2	41-3	27	4.17	115	.246	.370	0	ø	0	—	3	0	0.1
1996	SD N	0	0	ø	8	0	0	0-0	7.2	6	2	0	0	4-2	4	2.35	171	.231	.333	0	ø	0	—	2	0	0.1
1997	Oak A	4	6	.400	19	17	1	0-0	107.2	111	62	15	6	43-3	72	5.02	92	.266	.340	4-0-1	.250	0*	106	-4	37	-0.3
1998	Oak A	7	11	.389	31	29	0	0-0	175	210	125	27	5	57-1	112	6.22	74	.298	.352	1-0-1	.000	-0	100	-26	0	-2.3
1999	Oak A	9	10	.474	28	24	0	0-0	140.2	158	86	18	2	64-5	89	5.37	88	.283	.358	2	.000	-0	102	-7	0	-0.8
Total	7	25	31	.446	133	79	1	0-1	555	623	348	73	21	243-19	351	5.46	86	.284	.358	7-0-2	.143	-0	101	-38	37	-3.7
O'RILEY, DON	Donald Lee; B3.12.1945 Topeka KS; D5.2.1997 Kansas City MO; BR/TR/6´3˝/(180–200); d6.20																									
1969	KC A	1	1	.500	18	0	0	1-0	23.1	32	23	0	0	15-2	10	6.94	53	.311	.395	3	.000	-0*	—	-9	0	-0.9
1970	KC A	0	0	ø	9	2	0	0-0	23.1	26	15	5	1	9-0	13	5.40	69	.277	.343	3-0-2	.000	-0	155	-4	0	-0.3
Total	2	1	1	.500	27	2	0	1-0	46.2	58	38	5	1	24-2	23	6.17	60	.294	.371	6-0-2	.000	-1	155	-13	0	-1.2
OROPESA, EDDIE	Edilberto; B11.23.1971 Colon, Cuba; BL/TL/6´3˝/(205–215); [LAN94 14/384]; d4.2																									
2001	Phi N	1	0	1.000	30	0	0	0-1	19	16	10	1	0	17-6	15	4.74	87	.232	.384	0	ø	0	—	-1	22	-0.1
2002	Ari N	2	0	1.000	32	0	0	0-1	25.1	39	30	6	2	15-0	18	10.30	44	.348	.431	0	ø	0	—	-15	0	-1.0
2003	Ari N	3	3	.500	47	0	0	0-0	38.2	38	27	3	2	27-2	39	5.82	79	.257	.379	0	ø	0	—	-5	0	-0.6
2004	SD N	2	1	.667	16	0	0	0-0	9	6	12	1	0	13-3	6	11.00	36	.188	.422	0	ø	0	—	-8	0	-1.4
Total	4	8	4	.667	125	0	0	0-2	92	99	79	11	4	72-11	78	7.34	60	.274	.400	0	ø	0	—	-29	22	-3.1
OROSCO, JESSE	Jesse Russell; B4.21.1957 Santa Barbara CA; BR/TL/6´2˝/(174–205); [MinA78*2/41]; d4.5; Col Santa Barbara (CA) City																									
1979	NY N	1	2	.333	18	2	0	0-0	35	33	20	4	2	22-0	22	4.89	76	.260	.377	6-0-1	.000	-1	95	-4	0	-0.3
1981	NY N	0	1	.000	8	0	0	1-0	17.1	13	4	2	0	6-2	18	1.56	227	.213	.284	2	.000	-0	—	4	0	0.2
1982	NY N	4	10	.286	54	2	0	4-1	109.1	92	37	7	2	40-2	89	2.72	135	.230	.300	14	.143	-0	108	12	0	1.5
1983	NY N★	13	7	.650	62	0	0	17-5	110	76	27	3	1	38-7	84	1.47	249	.197	.269	12-0-2	.333	1	—	**24**	0	**5.2**
1984	NY N☆	10	6	.625	60	0	0	31-8	87	58	29	7	2	34-6	85	2.59	138	.185	.267	4-0-1	.250	1	—	10	0	2.2
1985	NY N	8	6	.571	54	0	0	17-8	79	66	26	6	0	34-7	68	2.73	128	.224	.303	7-0-2	.429	1	—	7	0	1.6
1986	†NY N	8	6	.571	58	0	0	21-8	81	64	23	6	3	35-3	62	2.33	154	.217	.304	3	.000	0	—	12	0	2.6
1987	NY N	3	9	.250	58	0	0	16-6	77	78	41	5	2	31-9	78	4.44	86	.266	.336	8-0-1	.000	-1	—	-5	0	-0.9
1988	†LA N	3	2	.600	55	0	0	9-6	53	41	18	4	2	30-3	43	2.72	123	.215	.323	2	.000	-0	—	4	0	0.5
1989	Cle A	3	4	.429	69	0	0	3-4	78	54	20	7	2	26-4	79	2.08	192	.198	.270	0	ø	0	—	16	0	1.5
1990	Cle A	5	4	.556	55	0	0	2-1	64.2	58	35	9	0	38-7	55	3.90	101	.239	.338	0	ø	0	—	-2	0	-0.2
1991	Cle A	2	0	1.000	47	0	0	0-0	45.2	52	20	4	1	15-8	36	3.74	111	.286	.338	0	ø	0	—	3	0	0.1
1992	Mil A	3	1	.750	59	0	0	1-1	39	33	15	5	1	13-1	40	3.23	120	.232	.297	0	ø	0	—	3	0	0.3
1993	Mil A	3	5	.375	57	0	0	8-5	56.2	47	25	2	3	17-3	67	3.18	136	.224	.289	1	.000	-0	—	6	0	1.0
1994	Mil A	3	1	.750	40	0	0	0-4	39	32	26	4	2	26-2	36	5.08	100	.222	.345	0	ø	0	—	-1	0	-0.1
1995	Bal A	2	4	.333	**65**	0	0	3-3	49.2	28	19	4	1	27-7	58	3.26	147	.169	.283	0	ø	0	—	8	0	1.0
1996	†Bal A	3	1	.750	66	0	0	0-3	55.2	42	22	5	2	28-4	52	3.40	146	.207	.308	0	ø	0	—	10	0	0.6
1997	†Bal A	6	3	.667	71	0	0	0-4	50.1	29	13	6	0	30-0	46	2.32	190	.169	.289	0	ø	0	—	13	0	2.0
1998	Bal A	4	1	.800	69	0	0	7-2	56.2	46	20	6	1	28-1	50	3.18	143	.221	.314	0	ø	0	—	9	0	0.9
1999	Bal A	0	2	.000	65	0	0	1-3	32	28	21	5	2	20-3	35	5.34	88	.239	.352	0	ø	0	—	-3	0	-0.1

YEAR	TM LG	W	L	PCT	G	GS	CG-SHO	SV-BS	IP	H	R	HR	HB	BB-IB	SO	ERA	AERA	OAV	OOB	AB-HR-SH	AVG	PB	SUP	APR	DL	PW
2000	StL N	0	0	ø	6	0	0	0-0	2.1	3	3	1	2	3-2	4	3.86	120	.273	.500	0	ø	0	—	-1	161	0.0
2001	LA N	0	1	.000	35	0	0	0-2	16	17	7	3	0	7-1	21	3.94	105	.279	.348	0	ø	0	—	1	19	0.0
2002	LA N	1	2	.333	56	0	0	1-0	27	24	10	4	0	12-1	22	3.00	130	.229	.305	0	ø	0	—	3	15	0.3
2003	SD N	1	1	.500	42	0	0	2-1	25	33	22	4	2	10-0	22	7.56	53	.317	.381	0	ø	0	—	-10	0	-0.8
	NY A	0	0	ø	15	0	0	0-1	4.1	4	6	0	0	6-3	4	10.38	42	.250	.435	0	ø	0	—	-3	0	-0.1
	Min A	1	1	.500	8	0	0	0-0	4.2	4	3	0	1	5-0	3	5.79	78	.235	.417	0	ø	0	—	-1	0	-0.1
	Year	1	1	.500	23	0	0	0-1	9	8	9	0	1	11-3	7	8.00	56	.242	.426	0	ø	0	—	-4	0	-0.2
Total	24	87	80	.521	1252	4	0	144-76	1295.1	1055	512	113	34	581-86	1179	3.16	126	.223	.309	59-0-7	.169	2	97	115	195	18.9
O'Rourke	; d7.9																									
1872	Eck NA	0	1	.000	1	1	1	0	9	16	15	0	—	2	0	8.00	43	.327	.353	4	.000	-1	34	-4	—	-0.3
O'Rourke, Jim	James Henry "Orator Jim"; B9.1.1850 Bridgeport CT; D1.8.1919 Bridgeport CT; BR/TR/5´8˝/185; d4.26.1872; M5/U1; HF1945; b–John s–Queenie; ▲																									
1883	Buf N	0	0	ø	2	0	0	1	7	10	9	0	—	1	1	6.43	49	.357	.379	436-1	.328	1*	—	-2	—	-0.1
1884	Buf N	0	1	.000	4	0	0	1	12.2	7	5	0	—	1	3	2.84	111	.175	.195	467-5	.347	2*	—	1	—	0.1
Total	2	0	1	.000	6	0	0	2	19.2	17	14	0	—	2	4	4.12	77	.250	.271	903-6	.338	2	—	-1	—	0.0
O'Rourke, Mike	Michael Joseph; B9.1.1868; D3.3.1934 Richmond VA; 5´10˝/195; d9.1																									
1890	Bal AA	1	2	.333	5	5	5	0	41	45	19	0	3	10	8	3.95	103	.271	.324	26	.115	-1*	60	2	—	0.1
Orr, Dave	David L.; B9.29.1859 New York NY; D6.2.1915 Richmond Hill NY; BR/TR/5´11˝/250; d5.17.1883; M1; ▲																									
1885	NY AA	0	0	ø	3	0	0	0	10	11	13	2	0	5	1	7.20	43	.250	.327	444-6	.342	2*	—	-5	—	-0.2
Orrell, Joe	Forrest Gordon; B3.6.1917 National City CA; D1.12.1993 Chula Vista CA; BR/TR/6´4˝/210; d8.12																									
1943	Det A	0	0	ø	10	0	0	1	19.1	18	9	0	2	11	2	3.72	95	.257	.373	4	.250	0	—	0	0	0.0
1944	Det A	2	1	.667	10	2	0	0	22.1	26	13	0	1	11	10	2.42	147	.286	.369	4	.250	0	105	0	0	0.1
1945	Det A	2	3	.400	12	5	1	0	48	46	18	1	2	24	14	3.00	117	.260	.355	15	.133	-1	53	3	0	0.2
Total	3	4	4	.500	32	7	1	1	89.2	90	40	1	5	46	26	3.01	117	.266	.362	23	.174	-1	68	3	0	0.3
Ortega, Phil	Filomeno Coronado "Kemo"; B10.7.1939 Gilbert AZ; BR/TR/6´2˝/(175–195); d9.10																									
1960	LA N	0	0	ø	3	1	0	0	6.1	12	12	1	0	5-0	4	17.05	23	.400	.486	1	.000	-0	178	-8	0	-0.4
1961	LA N	0	2	.000	4	2	1	0	13	10	9	6	0	2-0	15	5.54	78	.208	.240	4	.250	0	41	-2	0	-0.2
1962	LA N	0	2	.000	24	3	0	1	53.2	60	43	8	3	39-2	30	6.88	53	.276	.392	7	.000	-1	40	-19	0	-1.0
1963	LA N	0	0	ø	1	0	0	0	1	2	2	1	0	0-0	1	18.00	17	.400	.400	0	ø	0	—	-2	0	-0.1
1964	LA N	7	9	.438	34	25	4-3	1	157.1	149	74	22	6	56-2	107	4.00	81	.249	.317	44-0-7	.136	-0*	104	-11	0	-1.2
1965	Was A	12	15	.444	35	29	4-2	0	179.2	176	107	33	5	97-7	88	5.11	68	.262	.356	53-0-3	.208	4	97	-28	0	-3.4
1966	Was A	12	12	.500	33	31	5-1	0	197.1	158	91	29	5	53-5	121	3.92	88	.218	.274	54-0-8	.056	-2	96	-7	0	-1.2
1967	Was A	10	10	.500	34	34	5-2	0	219.2	189	77	16	6	57-3	122	3.03	104	.231	.286	66-0-7	.061	-3	97	7	0	0.3
1968	Was A	5	12	.294	31	16	1-1	0	115.2	115	70	12	5	62-8	57	4.98	59	.263	.356	24-0-5	.167	1	104	-26	0	-3.5
1969	Cal A	0	0	ø	5	0	0	0-0	8	13	13	3	0	7-1	4	10.13	35	.333	.435	0	ø	0	—	-7	59	-0.4
Total	10	46	62	.426	204	141	20-9	2-0	951.2	884	498	131	30	378-28	549	4.43	75	.246	.321	253-0-30	.115	-1	97	-103	59	-11.1
Orth, Al	Albert Lewis "Smiling Al","The Curveless Wonder"; B9.5.1872 Tipton IN; D10.8.1948 Lynchburg VA; BL/TR/6´0˝/200; d8.15; U6; Col DePauw; ▲																									
1895	Phi N	8	1	.889	11	10	9	1	88	103	50	0	2	22	25	3.89	123	.288	.332	45-1-2	.356	4	159	9	—	1.0
1896	Phi N	15	10	.600	25	23	19	0	196	244	128	10	3	46	23	4.41	98	.302	.342	82-1-0	.256	3	103	-1	—	0.2
1897	Phi N	14	19	.424	36	34	29-2	0	282.1	349	194	12	6	82	64	4.62	91	.301	.350	152-1-2	.329	7*	104	-14	—	-0.4
1898	Phi N	15	13	.536	32	28	25-1	0	250	290	131	2	8	53	52	3.02	114	.288	.329	123-1-7	.293	8*	122	9	—	1.7
1899	Phi N	14	3	.824	21	15	13-3	1	144.2	149	67	0	3	19	35	**2.49**	148	.266	.294	62-1-1	.210	1*	105	17	—	1.6
1900	Phi N	14	14	.500	33	30	24-2	1	262	302	145	4	13	60	68	3.78	96	.288	.335	129-1-0	.310	7*	105	-2	—	0.5
1901	Phi N	20	12	.625	35	33	30-**6**	1	281.2	250	101	3	8	32	92	2.27	150	.237	**.264**	128-1-0	.281	5*	95	33	—	**4.4**
1902	Was A	19	18	.514	38	37	36-1	0	324	367	181	18	9	40	76	3.97	93	.286	.312	175-2-3	.217	1*	101	-5	—	-0.3
1903	Was A	10	22	.313	36	32	30-2	**2**	279.2	326	174	8	7	62	88	4.34	72	.290	.331	162-0-1	.302	9*	75	-34	—	-2.4
1904	Was A	3	4	.429	10	7	7	0	73.2	88	49	2	3	15	23	4.76	56	.297	.338	102	.216	0*	134	-15	—	-1.3
	NY A	11	6	.647	20	18	11-2	0	137.2	122	47	0	3	19	47	2.68	101	.238	.270	64-0-1	.297	3*	98	3	—	0.8
	Year	14	10	.583	30	25	18-2	0	211.1	210	96	2	6	34	70	3.41	79	.260	.295	166-0-1	.247	3	108	-10	—	-0.5
1905	NY A	18	16	.529	40	37	26-6	0	305.1	273	122	8	7	61	121	2.86	103	.241	.284	131-1-3	.183	-1*	99	7	—	0.6
1906	NY A	**27**	17	.614	45	39	**36**-3	0	**338.2**	317	115	2	1	66	133	2.34	127	.251	.289	135-1-3	.274	6*	90	21	—	3.4
1907	NY A	14	21	.400	36	33	21-2	0	248.2	244	134	2	6	53	78	2.61	107	.259	.303	105-1-2	.324	7*	98	-4	—	0.5
1908	NY A	2	13	.133	21	17	8-1	0	139.1	134	62	4	4	30	22	3.42	72	.255	.300	69-0-2	.290	5*	93	-9	—	-0.5
1909	NY A	0	0	ø	1	1	0	0	3	6	4	0	0	1	1	12.00	21	.429	.467	34-0-1	.265	0*	251	-2	—	-0.1
Total	15	204	189	.519	440	394	324-31	6	3354.2	3564	1704	75	83	661	948	3.37	101	.272	.311	1698-12-28	.273	63	101	13	—	9.7
Ortiz, Ramon	Diogenes Ramon (Ortiz); B3.23.1973 Cotui, D.R.; BR/TR/6´0˝/(165–175); d8.19																									
1999	Ana A	2	3	.400	9	9	0	0-0	48.1	50	35	7	2	25-0	44	6.52	75	.265	.353	0	ø	0	80	-7	0	-0.6
2000	Ana A	8	6	.571	18	18	2	0-0	111.1	96	69	18	2	55-0	73	5.09	101	.236	.327	0	ø	0	102	0	7	0.0
2001	Ana A	13	11	.542	32	32	2	0-0	208.2	223	114	25	12	76-6	135	4.36	107	.274	.343	7	.000	-1	91	5	0	0.3
2002	†Ana A	15	9	.625	32	32	4-1	0-0	217.1	188	97	40	5	68-0	162	3.77	119	.230	.292	7	.000	-1	126	18	0	1.6
2003	Ana A	16	13	.552	32	32	1	0-0	180	209	121	28	12	63-0	94	5.20	84	.287	.350	5-0-1	.000	-0	113	-21	0	-2.9
2004	†Ana A	5	7	.417	34	14	0	0-0	128	139	64	18	4	38-4	82	4.43	101	.280	.335	3	.000	-0	118	2	0	0.1
2005	Cin N	9	11	.450	30	30	1	0-0	171.1	206	110	34	7	51-1	96	5.36	80	.302	.353	54-0-6	.074	-3	116	-21	22	-2.3
2006	Was N	11	16	.407	33	33	0	0-0	190.2	230	127	31	18	64-14	104	5.57	78	.297	.362	56-1-7	.107	-0*	87	-26	0	-3.1
Total	8	79	76	.510	220	200	10-1	0-0	1255.2	1341	737	201	62	440-25	790	4.85	93	.273	.338	132-1-14	.076	-5	105	-50	29	-6.9
Ortiz, Baby	Oliverio (Nunez); B12.5.1919 Camaguey, Cuba; D3.27.1984 Central Senado, Cuba; BR/TR/6´0˝/190; d9.23; b–Roberto																									
1944	Was A	0	2	.000	2	2	1	0	13	13	11	0	0	6	4	6.23	52	.255	.333	6	.167	-0	103	-4	0	-0.6
Ortiz, Russ	Russell Reid; B6.5.1974 Van Nuys CA; BR/TR/6´1˝/(190–220); [SFN95 4/103]; d4.2; Col Oklahoma																									
1998	SF N	4	4	.500	22	13	0	0-0	88.1	90	51	11	4	46-1	75	4.99	81	.269	.360	25-1-5	.280	3	144	-9	0	-0.4
1999	SF N	18	9	.667	33	33	3	0-0	207.2	189	109	24	6	125-5	164	3.81	112	.244	.351	71-1-7	.197	3	115	5	0	0.9
2000	†SF N	14	12	.538	33	32	0	0-0	195.2	192	117	28	7	112-1	167	5.01	87	.261	.361	61-0-6	.197	4	116	-14	0	-1.1
2001	SF N	17	9	.654	33	33	1-1	0-0	218.2	187	90	13	0	91-3	169	3.29	124	.232	.309	67-0-8	.194	4	124	20	0	2.7
2002	†SF N	14	10	.583	33	33	2	0-0	214.1	191	89	15	4	94-5	137	3.61	109	.241	.323	69-2-7	.246	8	121	11	0	2.1
2003	†Atl N★	**21**	7	.750	34	34	1-1	0-0	212.1	177	101	17	4	102-7	149	3.81	110	.223	.312	70-2-6	.257	8*	127	9	0	1.8
2004	†Atl N	15	9	.625	34	34	2-1	0-0	204.2	197	98	23	3	112-7	143	4.13	104	.258	.352	59-0-10	.102	-2	102	7	0	0.6
2005	Ari N	5	11	.313	22	22	0	0-0	115	147	92	18	4	65-3	46	6.89	64	.313	.396	34-0-6	.206	1*	100	-28	58	-3.2
2006	Ari N	0	5	.000	6	6	0	0-0	22.2	27	21	3	1	22-1	21	7.54	62	.303	.446	4-0-1	.000	-0	59	-7	43	-1.2
	Bal A	0	3	.000	20	5	0	0-0	40.1	59	39	15	2	18-0	23	8.48	53	.349	.416	2	1.000	1	113	-17	0	-1.0
Total	9	108	79	.578	270	245	9-3	0-0	1519.2	1456	807	167	35	787-33	1094	4.39	96	.254	.345	462-6-56	.208	31	116	-23	101	1.2
Orvella, Chad	Chad Robert; B10.1.1980 Renton WA; BR/TR/5´11˝/190; [TBA03 13/368]; d5.31; Col North Carolina St.																									
2005	TB A	3	3	.500	37	0	0	1-1	50	47	26	4	1	23-2	43	3.60	122	.246	.324	0	ø	0	—	3	0	0.3
2006	TB A	1	5	.167	22	0	0	0-3	24.1	36	23	6	3	20-0	17	7.40	63	.346	.461	0	ø	0	—	-8	0	-1.4
Total	2	4	8	.333	59	0	0	1-4	74.1	83	49	10	4	43-2	60	4.84	93	.281	.375	0	ø	0	—	-5	0	-1.1
Orwoll, Ossie	Oswald Christian; B11.17.1900 Portland OR; D5.8.1967 Decorah IA; BL/TL/6´0˝/174; d4.13; Col Luther; ▲																									
1928	Phi A	6	5	.545	27	8	3	2	106	110	59	7	2	50	53	4.58	87	.274	.358	170-0-5	.306	7*	84	-4	—	0.0
1929	Phi A	0	2	.000	12	0	0	1	30	32	23	6	0	6	12	4.80	88	.278	.314	51	.255	1*	—	-4	—	-0.2
Total	2	6	7	.462	39	8	3	3	136	142	82	13	2	56	65	4.63	88	.275	.348	221-0-5	.294	7	84	-8	—	-0.2
Osborn, Ozzie	Danny Leon; B6.19.1946 Springfield MO; BR/TR/6´2˝/195; d4.26; Col Mesa St.																									
1975	Chi A	3	0	1.000	24	0	0	0-0	58	57	29	2	2	37-1	38	4.50	86	.265	.375	0	ø	0	—	-2	0	-0.2
Osborn, Bob	John Bode; B4.17.1903 San Diego TX; D4.19.1960 Paris AR; BR/TR/6´1˝/175; d9.16																									
1925	Chi N	0	0	ø	1	0	0	0	2	6	2	0	0	0	0	0.00	ø	.600	.600	0	ø	0	—	0	—	0.0
1926	Chi N	6	5	.545	31	15	6	1	136.1	157	64	3	0	58	43	3.63	106	.301	.371	41-0-4	.146	-3	91	4	—	0.1
1927	Chi N	5	5	.500	24	12	2	0	107.2	125	54	2	1	48	45	4.18	92	.294	.367	39-0-1	.205	-0	112	-2	—	-0.2

YEAR	TM LG	W	L	PCT	G	GS	CG-SHO	SV-BS	IP	H	R	HR	HB	BB-IB	SO	ERA	AERA	OAV	OOB	AB-HR-SH	AVG	PB	SUP	APR	DL	PW
1929	Chi N	0	0	ø	3	1	0	0	9	8	3	0	0	2	1	3.00	154	.242	.286	4	.250	0	113	2	—	0.1
1930	Chi N	10	6	.625	35	13	3	1	126.2	147	74	9	1	53	42	4.97	98	.300	.369	42-0-3	.095	-5	136	2	—	-0.1
1931	Pit N	6	1	.857	27	2	0	0	64.2	85	43	3	1	20	9	5.01	77	.316	.366	18	.167	-0	189	-8	—	-0.8
Total	6	27	17	.614	121	43	11	2	446.1	528	240	17	3	181	140	4.32	97	.302	.368	144-0-8	.153	-8	117	-2	—	-0.9
OSBORNE, DONOVAN	Donovan Alan; B6.21.1969 Roseville CA; BB/TL/6´2˝/(195–210); [StLN90 1/13]; d4.9; Col Nevada–Las Vegas; [DL 1994 StL N 131]																									
1992	StL N	11	9	.550	34	29	0	0-0	179	193	91	14	2	38-2	104	3.77	91	.275	.312	58-0-2	.121	-1	93	-12	0	-1.5
1993	StL N	10	7	.588	26	26	1	0-0	155.2	153	73	18	7	47-4	83	3.76	107	.257	.318	49-0-7	.204	2*	102	5	0	0.7
1995	StL N	4	6	.400	19	19	0	0-0	113.1	112	58	17	2	34-2	82	3.81	112	.260	.316	31-0-3	.161	1	66	4	60	0.5
1996	†StL N	13	9	.591	30	30	2-1	0-0	198.2	191	87	22	1	57-5	134	3.53	120	.254	.306	59-1-10	.220	4	85	15	16	1.8
1997	StL N	3	7	.300	14	14	0	0-0	80.1	84	46	10	1	23-2	51	4.93	85	.274	.323	24-0-1	.208	1	82	-5	87	-0.5
1998	StL N	5	4	.556	14	14	1-1	0-0	83.2	84	42	11	1	22-2	60	4.09	103	.256	.301	25-0-4	.040	-1	116	1	108	-0.1
1999	StL N	1	3	.250	6	6	0	0-0	29.1	34	18	4	2	10-0	21	5.52	83	.298	.362	10-0-1	.100	-0	113	-2	150	-0.2
2002	Chi N	0	1	.000	11	0	0	0-0	16	19	11	1	0	10-2	13	6.19	66	.297	.387	3	.000	-0	—	-3	116	-0.2
2004	NY A	2	0	1.000	9	2	0	0-0	17.2	25	16	3	2	5-0	10	7.13	64	.347	.405	0	ø	0	141	-5	0	-0.5
Total	9	49	46	.516	163	140	4-2	0-0	873.2	895	442	100	18	246-19	558	4.03	100	.266	.317	259-1-28	.162	5	92	-2	668	0.0
OSBORNE, TINY	Earnest Preston; B4.9.1893 Porterdale GA; D1.5.1969 Atlanta GA; BL/TR/6´4.5˝/215; d4.15; s–Bobo																									
1922	Chi N	9	5	.643	41	14	7-1	3	184	183	113	7	12	95	81	4.50	93	.271	.370	67-0-2	.134	-4	112	-7	—	-1.0
1923	Chi N	8	15	.348	37	25	8-1	1	179.2	174	117	14	2	89	69	4.56	88	.255	.342	60	.200	-1	85	-14	—	-1.7
1924	Chi N	0	0	ø	2	0	0	1	3	3	1	0	0	2	2	3.00	130	.300	.417	0	ø	0	—	0	—	0.0
	Bro N	6	5	.545	21	13	6	0	104.1	123	67	1	4	54	52	5.09	74	.298	.384	36-0-1	.250	1	104	-14	—	-1.2
	Year	6	5	.545	23	13	6	1	107.1	126	68	1	4	56	54	5.03	75	.298	.385	36-0-1	.250	1	104	-15	—	-1.2
1925	Bro N	8	15	.348	41	22	10	1	175	210	111	9	4	75	59	4.94	85	.304	.375	57-0-1	.246	1	91	-13	—	-1.4
Total	4	31	40	.437	142	74	31-2	6	646	693	409	31	22	315	263	4.72	86	.280	.367	220-0-4	.200	-3	95	-48	—	-5.3
OSBORNE, FRED	Frederick W.; B Alberta, Can; BL/TL; d7.14; ▲																									
1890	Pit N	0	5	.000	8	5	5	0	58	82	87	6	7	45	14	8.38	39	.323	.438	168-1	.238	1*	100	-36	—	-2.1
OSBORNE, WAYNE	Wayne Harold "Ossie","Fish Hook"; B10.11.1912 Watsonville CA; D3.13.1987 Vancouver WA; BL/TR/6´2.5˝/172; d4.18																									
1935	Pit N	0	0	ø	2	0	0	0	1.1	1	1	0	0	0	1	6.75	61	.250	.250	0	ø	0*	—	0	—	0.0
1936	Bos N	1	1	.500	5	3	0	0	20	31	13	1	0	9	8	5.85	66	.352	.412	8	.250	0	133	-4	—	-0.3
Total	2	1	1	.500	7	3	0	0	21.1	32	14	1	0	9	9	5.91	65	.348	.406	8	.250	0	133	-4	—	-0.3
OSBURN, PAT	Larry Patrick; B5.4.1949 Murray KY; BL/TL/6´4˝/(190–195); [CinN70 S1/9]; d4.13; Col Florida St.																									
1974	Cin N	0	0	ø	6	0	0	0-0	9	11	9	2	0	4-0	4	8.00	44	.297	.357	2	.000	-0	—	-5	0	-0.2
1975	Mil A	0	1	.000	6	1	0	0-0	11.2	19	9	2	2	9-0	1	5.40	71	.404	.492	0	ø	0	46	-2	0	-0.2
Total	2	0	1	.000	12	1	0	0-0	20.2	30	18	4	2	13-0	5	6.53	57	.357	.437	2	.000	-0	46	-7	0	-0.4
OSGOOD, CHARLIE	Charles Benjamin; B11.23.1926 Somerville MA; BR/TR/5´10˝/180; d6.18																									
1944	Bro N	0	0	ø	1	0	0	0	3	2	1	0	1	3	0	3.00	118	.222	.462	0	ø	0	—	0	0	0.0
OSINSKI, DAN	Daniel; B11.17.1933 Chicago IL; BR/TR/6´2˝/(190–200); d4.11																									
1962	KC A	0	0	ø	4	0	0	0	4.2	8	9	1	0	8-0	4	17.36	24	.381	.533	0	ø	0	—	-6	0	-0.3
	LA A	6	4	.600	33	0	0	4	54.1	45	22	3	0	30-3	44	2.82	137	.223	.323	11-0-1	.000	-1	—	6	0	1.0
	Year	6	4	.600	37	0	0	4	59	53	31	4	0	38-3	48	3.97	98	.238	.347	11-0-1	.000	-1	—	-2	0	0.7
1963	LA A	8	8	.500	47	16	4-1	0	159.1	145	66	15	2	80-6	100	3.28	105	.242	.331	45-0-2	.111	-2	102	3	0	0.0
1964	LA A	3	3	.500	47	4	1-1	2	93	87	47	8	2	39-7	88	3.48	94	.244	.321	18-0-2	.056	-1	108	-4	0	-0.3
1965	Mil N	0	3	.000	61	0	0	6	83	81	28	4	1	40-9	54	2.82	125	.261	.347	6	.167	-0	—	7	0	0.3
1966	Bos A	4	3	.571	44	1	0	2	67.1	68	33	8	1	28-6	44	3.61	105	.274	.349	6	.333	0	46	1	0	0.1
1967	†Bos A	3	1	.750	34	0	0	2	63.2	61	19	5	0	14-2	38	2.54	137	.243	.283	9	.333	1	—	7	0	0.6
1969	Chi A	5	5	.500	51	0	0	2-2	60.2	56	28	3	0	23-5	27	3.56	108	.251	.320	3	.000	-0	—	1	0	0.2
1970	Hou N	0	1	.000	3	0	0	0-1	3.2	5	4	0	0	2-1	1	9.82	40	.357	.412	0	ø	0	—	-2	0	-0.4
Total	8	29	28	.509	324	21	5-2	18-3	589.2	556	256	47	6	264-39	400	3.34	107	.250	.330	98-0-5	.122	-3	96	13	0	1.2
OSORIA, FRANQUELIS	Franquelis Antonio; B9.12.1981 Santiago, D.R.; BR/TR/6´0˝/165; d6.7																									
2005	LA N	0	2	.000	24	0	0	0-2	29.2	28	14	3	3	8-0	15	3.94	105	.259	.328	3	.000	-0	—	1	0	0.0
2006	LA N	0	2	.000	12	0	0	0-0	17.2	27	14	4	1	9-1	13	7.13	61	.360	.435	2	.000	-0	—	-5	0	-0.5
Total	2	0	4	.000	36	0	0	0-2	47.1	55	28	7	4	17-1	28	5.13	83	.301	.373	5	.000	-1	—	-4	0	-0.5
OSTEEN, CLAUDE	Claude Wilson; B8.9.1939 Caney Spring TN; BL/TL/5´11˝/(165–173); d7.6; Mil 1970; C15																									
1957	Cin N	0	0	ø	3	0	0	0	4	4	1	0	0	3-0	3	2.25	183	.250	.368	1	.000	-0	—	1	0	0.0
1959	Cin N	0	0	ø	2	0	0	0	7.2	11	10	2	0	9-1	3	7.04	58	.333	.465	2	.000	-0	—	-4	0	-0.2
1960	Cin N	0	1	.000	20	3	0	0	48.1	53	29	4	1	30-4	15	5.03	76	.293	.393	12	.083	-1*	108	-6	0	-0.4
1961	Cin N	0	0	ø	1	0	0	0	0.1	0	0	0	0	0-0	0	0.00	ø	.000	.000	0	ø	0*	—	0	0	0.0
	Was A	1	1	.500	3	3	0	0	18.1	14	11	3	1	9-0	14	4.91	82	.219	.320	7-0-1	.143	-0	103	-2	0	-0.2
1962	Was A	8	13	.381	28	22	7-2	1	150.1	140	62	12	4	47-6	59	3.65	111	.246	.308	48-0-1	.208	1*	69	9	0	1.3
1963	Was A	9	14	.391	40	29	8-2	0	212.1	222	101	23	1	60-4	109	3.35	111	.270	.318	70-1-5	.171	1*	78	4	0	0.4
1964	Was A	15	13	.536	37	36	13	0	257	256	107	20	3	64-8	133	3.33	111	.259	.304	90-1-7	.156	1*	99	12	0	1.5
1965	†LA N	15	15	.500	40	40	9-1	0	287	253	95	19	3	78-10	162	2.79	117	.236	.290	99-0-6	.121	-1*	92	19	0	2.2
1966	†LA N	17	14	.548	39	38	8-3	0	240.1	238	92	6	2	65-13	137	2.85	116	.261	.309	76-1-2	.211	6	96	11	0	2.1
1967	LA N☆	17	17	.500	39	39	14-5	0	288.1	298	116	19	2	52-10	152	3.22	96	.270	.301	101-2-5	.178	6*	105	-4	0	0.2
1968	LA N	12	18	.400	39	36	5-3	0	254	267	109	14	5	54-10	119	3.08	90	.275	.314	84-0-9	.179	2*	84	-13	0	-1.2
1969	LA N	20	15	.571	41	41	16-7	0-0	321	293	103	17	6	74-8	183	2.66	126	.245	.291	111-1-8	.216	6*	105	28	0	3.9
1970	LA N★	16	14	.533	37	37	11-4	0-0	258.2	280	121	24	4	52-3	114	3.83	101	.276	.312	93-1-1	.204	5*	120	1	0	0.6
1971	LA N	14	11	.560	38	38	11-4	0-0	259	262	108	25	3	63-2	109	3.51	93	.266	.311	86-0-8	.186	2*	131	-5	0	0.1
1972	LA N	20	11	.645	33	33	14-4	0-0	252	232	82	16	4	69-4	100	2.64	127	.245	.299	88-1-6	.273	10*	95	24	0	4.2
1973	LA N★	16	11	.593	33	33	12-3	0-0	236.2	227	97	20	2	61-2	86	3.31	105	.258	.306	78-0-8	.154	-1	102	6	0	0.7
1974	Hou N	9	9	.500	23	21	7-2	0-0	138.1	158	67	8	2	47-1	45	3.71	94	.292	.348	46-0-2	.283	3	104	-5	0	-0.2
	StL N	0	2	.000	8	2	0	0-0	22.2	26	14	1	0	11-5	6	4.37	83	.286	.363	7	.000	-1	121	-3	0	-0.3
	Year	9	11	.450	31	23	7-2	0-0	161	184	81	9	2	58-6	51	3.80	92	.291	.350	53-0-2	.245	3	105	-7	0	-0.5
1975	Chi A	7	16	.304	37	37	5	0-0	204.1	237	110	16	2	92-2	63	4.36	89	.294	.365	0	ø	0	81	-11	0	-1.0
Total	18	196	195	.501	541	488	140-40	1-0	3460.2	3471	1435	249	45	940-93	1612	3.30	104	.263	.313	1099-8-69	.188	38	98	62	0	13.7
OSTEEN, DARRELL	Milton Darrell; B2.14.1943 Oklahoma City OK; BR/TR/6´1˝/(162–170); d9.2; Mil 1970																									
1965	Cin N	0	0	ø	3	0	0	0	3	2	0	0	0	4-0	1	0.00	ø	.200	.429	0	ø	0	—	1	0	0.1
1966	Cin N	0	2	.000	13	0	0	1	15	26	21	3	0	9-2	17	12.00	33	.371	.443	2	.500	0*	—	-12	0	-1.6
1967	Cin N	0	2	.000	10	0	0	2	14.1	10	10	1	3	13-1	13	6.28	60	.196	.388	1-0-1	.000	-0*	—	-3	0	-0.5
1970	Oak A	1	0	1.000	3	1	0	0-0	5.2	9	4	0	0	3-0	3	6.35	56	.346	.414	2	.000	-0	126	-2	0	-0.3
Total	4	1	4	.200	29	1	0	3-0	38	47	35	4	3	29-3	34	8.05	47	.299	.418	5-0-1	.200	-0	126	-16	0	-2.3
OSTENDORF, FRED	Frederick K.; B8.5.1892 Baltimore MD; D3.2.1965 Kecoughtan (now part of Hampton) VA; BL/TL/6´0.5˝/169; d7.16																									
1914	Ind F	0	0	ø	1	0	0	0	2	5	5	0	1	2	0	22.50	14	.500	.615	1	.000	-0	—	-3	—	-0.2
OSTER, BILL	William Charles; B1.2.1933 New York NY; BL/TL/6´3˝/198; d8.23; Col NYU																									
1954	Phi A	0	1	.000	8	1	0	0	15.2	19	15	2	0	12	5	6.32	62	.311	.425	3	.333	0	45	-5	0	-0.3
OSTERMUELLER, FRITZ	Frederick Raymond; B9.15.1907 Quincy IL; D12.17.1957 Quincy IL; BL/TL/5´11˝/175; d4.21; Mil 1945																									
1934	Bos A	10	13	.435	33	23	10	3	198.2	200	93	7	1	99	75	3.49	138	.262	.348	78	.167	-2	72	27	—	2.7
1935	Bos A	7	8	.467	22	19	10	1	137.2	135	67	0	3	78	41	3.92	121	.257	.356	49-0-2	.286	1	80	13	—	1.4
1936	Bos A	10	16	.385	43	23	7-1	2	180.2	210	115	8	3	84	90	4.88	109	.288	.364	64-0-4	.234	0	91	7	—	0.9
1937	Bos A	3	7	.300	25	7	2	1	86.2	101	64	2	1	44	29	4.98	95	.286	.367	33-0-3	.333	3	108	-6	—	-0.3
1938	Bos A	13	5	.722	31	18	10-1	2	176.2	199	98	15	3	58	46	4.58	108	.275	.331	74-0-3	.216	2*	127	9	—	0.9
1939	Bos A	11	7	.611	34	20	8	4	159.1	173	86	6	2	58	61	4.24	112	.277	.341	56-0-5	.161	-2	122	9	—	0.7
1940	Bos A	5	9	.357	31	16	5	0	143.2	166	86	7	0	70	80	4.95	91	.284	.361	54	.315	4*	100	-7	—	-0.2
1941	StL A	0	3	.000	15	2	0	0	46	45	26	3	0	23	20	4.50	96	.257	.343	14-0-2	.214	0*	121	-1	0	0.0

YEAR	TM LG	W	L	PCT	G	GS	CG-SHO	SV-BS	IP	H	R	HR	HB	BB-IB	SO	ERA	AERA	OAV	OOB	AB-HR-SH	AVG	PB	SUP	APR	DL	PW
1942	StL A	3	1	.750	10	4	2	0	43.2	46	22	4	0	17	21	3.71	100	.266	.332	16	.188	-0	144	0	0	-0.1
1943	StL A	0	2	.000	11	3	0	0	28.2	36	16	1	0	13	4	5.02	66	.321	.392	7	.286	0	59	-4	0	-0.3
	Bro N	1	1	.500	7	1	0	0	27.1	21	11	0	0	12	15	3.29	102	.212	.297	11-0-1	.000	-1*	51	0	0	-0.1
1944	Bro N	2	1	.667	10	4	3	1	41.2	46	17	3	0	12	17	3.24	110	.267	.315	13-0-1	.154	-0*	94	2	0	0.1
	Pit N	11	7	.611	28	24	14-1	1	204.2	201	79	7	1	65	80	2.73	136	.260	.318	80-0-1	.250	2*	102	21	0	1.9
	Year	13	8	.619	38	28	17-1	2	246.1	247	96	10	1	77	97	2.81	131	.261	.317	93-0-2	.237	2	101	23	0	2.0
1945	Pit N	5	4	.556	14	11	4-1	0	80.2	74	45	6	2	37	29	4.57	86	.236	.321	28-0-1	.321	2	111	-4	0	-0.2
1946	Pit N	13	10	.565	27	25	16-2	0	193.1	193	70	5	3	56	57	2.84	124	.263	.318	64-0-5	.328	6*	94	15	0	2.5
1947	Pit N	12	10	.545	26	24	12-3	0	183	181	94	18	1	68	66	3.84	110	.254	.320	64-0-6	.188	0	124	6	0	0.5
1948	Pit N	8	11	.421	23	22	10-2	0	134.1	143	73	13	1	41	43	4.42	92	.262	.315	44-0-3	.182	-0	80	-5	0	-0.7
Total	15	114	115	.498	390	246	113-11	15	2066.2	2170	1062	105	21	835	774	3.99	109	.268	.337	749-0-37	.234	16	100	82	0	9.7
Osting, Jimmy	James Michael; B4.7.1977 Louisville KY; BR/TL/6´5˝/190; [AtlN95 4/113]; d5.2																									
2001	SD N	0	0	ø	3	0	0	0-0	2	1	0	0	0	2-1	3	0.00	ø	.143	.333	0	ø	0	—	1	0	0.0
2002	Mil N	0	2	.000	3	3	0	0-0	12	18	11	3	0	10-0	7	7.50	55	.340	.444	3-0-1	.000	-0	15	-5	33	-0.6
Total	2	0	2	.000	6	3	0	0-0	14	19	11	3	0	12-1	10	6.43	64	.317	.431	3-0-1	.000	-0	15	-4	33	-0.6
Ostrowski, Joe	Joseph Paul "Professor","Specs"; B11.15.1916 W.Wyoming PA; D1.3.2003 Wilkes-Barre PA; BL/TL/6´0˝/180; d7.18; Col Scranton																									
1948	StL A	4	6	.400	26	9	3	3	78.1	108	54	6	0	17	20	5.97	76	.333	.367	18-0-3	.222	1	70	-10	0	-1.0
1949	StL A	8	8	.500	40	13	4	2	141	185	94	16	0	27	34	4.79	95	.307	.337	37	.189	2	103	-6	0	-0.4
1950	StL A	2	4	.333	9	7	2	0	57.1	57	22	2	0	7	15	2.51	197	.251	.274	18	.222	1	68	13	0	1.4
	NY A	1	1	.500	21	4	1	3	43.2	50	26	11	0	15	15	5.15	83	.294	.351	9-0-1	.111	-0	147	-4	0	-0.2
	Year	3	5	.375	30	11	3	3	101	107	48	13	0	22	30	3.65	128	.270	.308	27-0-1	.185	1	95	11	0	1.2
1951	†NY A	6	4	.600	34	3	2	5	95.1	103	44	4	1	18	30	3.49	110	.279	.314	28	.107	-2	209	3	0	0.1
1952	NY A	2	2	.500	20	1	0	2	40	56	31	5	1	14	17	5.62	59	.327	.382	8-0-2	.000	-1	105	-12	0	-1.4
Total	5	23	25	.479	150	37	12	15	455.2	559	271	44	2	98	131	4.54	95	.300	.336	118-0-6	.161	1	104	-16	0	-1.5
Osuna, Al	Alfonso; B8.10.1965 Inglewood CA; BR/TL/6´3˝/200; [HouN87 16/418]; d9.2; Col Stanford																									
1990	Hou N	2	0	1.000	12	0	0	0-1	11.1	10	6	1	3	6-1	6	4.76	78	.270	.396	0	ø	0	—	-1	0	-0.2
1991	Hou N	7	6	.538	71	0	0	12-9	81.2	59	39	5	3	46-5	68	3.42	103	.201	.311	2-0-1	.000	-0	—	-1	0	-0.2
1992	Hou N	6	3	.667	66	0	0	0-2	61.2	52	29	8	1	38-5	37	4.23	80	.236	.343	0	ø	0	—	-5	0	-0.6
1993	Hou N	1	1	.500	44	0	0	2-0	25.1	17	10	3	1	13-2	21	3.20	121	.200	.301	0	ø	0	—	2	0	0.2
1994	LA N	2	0	1.000	15	0	0	0-1	8.2	13	6	0	0	4-0	7	6.23	64	.333	.395	0	ø	0	—	-2	0	-0.4
1996	SD N	0	0	ø	10	0	0	0-1	4	5	1	0	1	2-1	4	2.25	179	.313	.400	1	.000	-0	—	1	0	0.0
Total	6	18	10	.643	218	0	0	14-14	192.2	156	91	17	9	109-14	143	3.83	93	.226	.332	3-0-1	.000	-0	—	-6	0	-1.2
Osuna, Antonio	Antonio Pedro; B4.12.1973 Guasave, Sinaloa, Mexico; BR/TR/5´11˝/(160–225); d4.25																									
1995	†LA N	2	4	.333	39	0	0	0-2	44.2	39	22	5	1	20-2	46	4.43	87	.241	.326	2	.000	-0	—	-1	28	-0.2
1996	†LA N	9	6	.600	73	0	0	4-5	84	65	33	6	2	32-12	85	3.00	131	.220	.296	1	.000	0	—	9	0	1.5
1997	LA N	3	4	.429	48	0	0	0-0	61.2	46	15	6	1	19-2	68	2.19	178	.209	.274	2	.500	0	—	13	0	1.5
1998	LA N	7	1	.875	54	0	0	6-5	64.2	50	26	8	2	32-0	72	3.06	132	.214	.311	2	.000	-0	—	7	19	0.8
1999	LA N	0	0	ø	5	0	0	0-0	4.2	4	5	0	1	3-0	5	7.71	56	.222	.364	0	ø	0	—	-2	166	-0.1
2000	LA N	3	6	.333	46	0	0	0-3	67.1	57	30	7	2	35-2	70	3.74	119	.229	.325	2	.000	-0	—	6	32	0.6
2001	Chi A	0	0	ø	4	0	0	0-1	4.1	8	10	3	1	2-1	6	20.77	22	.421	.478	0	ø	0	—	-7	179	-0.3
2002	Chi A	8	2	.800	59	0	0	11-3	67.2	64	32	1	4	28-4	66	3.86	117	.250	.330	0	ø	0	—	5	0	0.8
2003	NY A	2	5	.286	48	0	0	0-1	50.2	58	22	3	2	20-3	47	3.73	118	.282	.348	0	ø	0	—	4	49	0.5
2004	SD N	2	1	.667	31	0	0	0-2	36.2	32	11	3	1	11-0	36	2.45	161	.232	.291	0	ø	0	—	7	101	0.5
2005	Was N	0	0	ø	4	0	0	0-0	2.1	9	11	2	0	7-1	0	42.43	10	.600	.696	0	ø	0	—	-10	175	-0.5
Total	11	36	29	.554	411	0	0	21-22	488.2	432	217	44	17	209-27	501	3.68	112	.238	.320	9	.111	-0	—	31	749	5.1
Oswalt, Roy	Roy Edward; B8.29.1977 Kosciusko MS; BR/TR/6´0˝/(170–185); [HouN96 23/684]; d5.6; Col Holmes (MS) CC																									
2001	Hou N	14	3	.824	28	20	3-1	0-0	141.2	126	48	13	6	24-2	144	2.73	168	.235	.273	47-0-3	.191	0	126	27	0	3.1
2002	Hou N	19	9	.679	35	34	0	0-0	233	215	86	17	5	62-4	208	3.01	144	.247	.299	77-0-7	.130	-1	102	32	0	3.5
2003	Hou N	10	5	.667	21	21	0	0-0	127.1	116	48	15	5	29-0	108	2.97	149	.246	.296	39-0-7	.179	0	107	19	73	2.1
2004	†Hou N	**20**	10	.667	36	**35**	2-2	0-0	237	233	100	17	11	62-5	206	3.49	125	.260	.315	71-0-13	.141	-1	109	22	0	2.5
2005	†Hou N★	20	12	.625	35	**35**	4-1	0-0	241.2	243	85	18	8	48-3	184	2.94	143	.262	.302	73-0-7	.178	0	87	35	0	4.4
2006	Hou N★	15	8	.652	33	32	2	0-0	220.2	220	76	18	6	38-4	166	**2.98**	**151**	.263	.299	66-1-20	.152	1*	105	**39**	15	**3.8**
Total	6	98	47	.676	188	177	11-4	0-0	1201.1	1153	443	98	41	263-18	1016	3.05	144	.254	.299	373-1-57	.158	1	105	174	88	19.4
Otey, Bill	William Tilford "Steamboat Bill"; B12.16.1886 Dayton OH; D4.23.1931 Dayton OH; BL/TL/6´2˝/181; d9.27																									
1907	Pit N	0	1	.000	3	2	1	0	16.1	23	11	1	1	4	5	4.41	55	.319	.364	4	.250	0	88	-3	—	-0.2
1910	Was A	0	1	.000	9	1	1	0	34.2	40	17	1	1	6	12	3.38	74	.301	.336	13	.385	2	27	-3	—	0.0
1911	Was A	1	3	.250	12	2	0	0	49.2	68	44	2	3	15	16	6.34	52	.333	.387	17-0-1	.059	-2	66	-15	—	-1.1
Total	3	1	5	.167	24	5	2	0	100.2	131	72	4	5	25	33	5.01	57	.320	.367	34-0-1	.206	0	64	-21	—	-1.3
Otis, Harry	Harry George "Cannonball"; B10.5.1886 W.New York NJ; D1.29.1976 Teaneck NJ; BR/TL/6´0˝/180; d9.5																									
1909	Cle A	2	2	.500	5	3	0	0	26.1	26	11	0	3	18	6	1.37	187	.283	.416	9-0-1	.111	-0	83	2	—	0.2
O'Toole, Dennis	Dennis Joseph; B3.13.1949 Chicago IL; BR/TR/6´3˝/(194–195); [ChiA67 6/113]; d9.8; b–Jim																									
1969	Chi A	0	0	ø	2	0	0	0-0	4	5	3	0	0	2-0	4	6.75	57	.333	.389	0	ø	0	—	-1	0	-0.1
1970	Chi A	0	0	ø	3	0	0	0-0	3.1	5	1	0	0	2-0	3	2.70	144	.357	.412	0	ø	0	—	0	0	0.0
1971	Chi A	0	0	ø	1	0	0	0-0	2	0	0	0	0	1-0	2	0.00	ø	.000	.143	0	ø	0	—	1	0	0.0
1972	Chi A	0	0	ø	3	0	0	0-0	5	10	3	0	0	2-0	5	5.40	58	.417	.462	0	ø	0	—	-1	0	-0.1
1973	Chi A	0	0	ø	6	0	0	0-0	16	23	11	3	0	3-0	8	5.63	70	.329	.356	0	ø	0	—	-3	0	-0.1
Total	5	0	0	ø	15	0	0	0-0	30.1	43	18	3	0	10-0	22	5.04	75	.333	.376	0	ø	0	—	-4	0	-0.3
O'Toole, Jim	James Jerome; B1.10.1937 Chicago IL; BB/TL/6´0˝/(190–205); d9.26; b–Dennis; Col Wisconsin–Madison																									
1958	Cin N	0	1	.000	1	1	0	0	7	4	2	0	0	5-0	4	1.29	322	.154	.290	2	.000	-0	22	2	0	0.2
1959	Cin N	5	8	.385	28	19	3-1	0	129.1	144	78	14	4	73-2	68	5.15	79	.287	.380	37-0-3	.135	-0*	127	-13	0	-1.1
1960	Cin N	12	12	.500	34	31	7-2	1	196.1	198	94	14	4	66-4	124	3.80	100	.263	.323	66-0-7	.106	-3	86	0	0	-0.5
1961	†Cin N	19	9	.679	39	35	11-3	2	252.2	229	101	16	3	93-7	178	3.10	131	.240	.309	93-0-4	.172	-1	109	**26**	0	2.6
1962	Cin N	16	13	.552	36	34	11-3	0	251.2	222	115	20	5	87-4	170	3.50	115	.238	.305	91-0-3	.110	-5	116	12	0	0.7
1963	Cin N★	17	14	.548	33	32	12-5	0	234.1	208	85	13	3	57-4	146	2.88	116	.239	.285	74-0-6	.149	-1	104	12	0	1.3
1964	Cin N	17	7	.708	30	30	9-3	0	220	194	71	8	0	51-7	145	2.66	136	.235	.277	70-0-7	.100	-1	91	24	0	2.4
1965	Cin N	3	10	.231	29	22	2	1	127.2	154	98	14	3	47-4	71	5.92	63	.294	.352	45-0-3	.089	-2	126	-31	0	-3.1
1966	Cin N	5	7	.417	25	24	2	0	142	139	65	16	3	49-6	96	3.55	110	.254	.317	47-0-1	.128	-2	98	3	0	0.0
1967	Chi A	4	3	.571	15	10	1-1	0	54.1	53	21	4	1	18-2	37	2.82	110	.251	.313	13-0-1	.077	-1	70	2	63	0.1
Total	10	98	84	.538	270	238	58-18	4	1615.1	1545	730	119	26	546-40	1039	3.57	106	.251	.313	538-0-35	.125	-15	104	37	63	2.6
O'Toole, Marty	Martin James; B11.27.1888 Wm.Penn PA; D2.18.1949 Aberdeen WA; BR/TR/5´11˝/175; d9.21																									
1908	Cin N	1	0	1.000	3	2	1	0	15	15	8	0	0	7	5	2.40	96	.273	.355	5	.200	-0	214	-1	—	-0.1
1911	Pit N	3	2	.600	5	5	3	0	38	28	17	1	0	20	34	2.37	145	.215	.320	14	.357	2	105	3	—	0.5
1912	Pit N	15	17	.469	37	36	17-**6**	0	275.1	237	110	4	2	159	150	2.71	120	.241	.348	99-0-2	.222	2	96	16	—	1.9
1913	Pit N	6	8	.429	26	16	7	1	144.2	148	69	3	3	55	58	3.30	92	.271	.341	53-0-1	.132	-2	136	-5	—	-0.7
1914	Pit N	1	8	.111	19	9	1	1	92.1	92	56	2	0	47	36	4.68	57	.270	.358	30	.167	0	60	-20	—	-1.8
	NY N	1	1	.500	10	5	2	0	34	34	17	0	0	12	13	4.24	63	.262	.324	10-0-1	.300	1	92	-5	—	-0.2
	Year	2	9	.182	29	14	3	1	126.1	126	73	2	0	59	49	4.56	58	.268	.349	40-0-1	.200	1	71	-20	—	-2.0
Total	5	27	36	.429	100	73	31-6	2	599.1	554	277	10	5	300	296	3.21	95	.254	.345	211-0-4	.204	2	104	-12	—	-0.4
Otsuka, Akinori	Akinori; B1.13.1972 Chiba, Japan; BR/TR/6´0˝/(200–210); d4.6																									
2004	SD N	7	2	.778	73	0	0	2-5	77.1	56	16	6	0	26-6	87	1.75	226	.199	.266	1	.000	-0	—	21	0	2.3
2005	†SD N	2	8	.200	66	0	0	1-6	62.2	55	28	3	2	34-8	60	3.59	109	.234	.336	1	.000	-0	—	2	0	0.3
2006	Tex A	2	4	.333	63	0	0	32-4	59.2	53	17	3	0	11-0	47	2.11	222	.241	.276	0	ø	0	—	16	0	2.9
Total	3	11	14	.440	202	0	0	35-15	199.2	164	61	12	2	71-14	194	2.43	171	.223	.292	2	.000	-0	—	39	0	5.5

YEAR	TM LG	W	L	PCT	G	GS	CG-SHO	SV-BS	IP	H	R	HR	HB	BB-IB	SO	ERA	AERA	OAV	OOB	AB-HR-SH	AVG	PB	SUP	APR	DL	PW
OTTEN, JIM	James Edward; B7.1.1951 Lewistown MT; BR/TR/6´2˝/(185–195); [ChiA73 2/45]; d7.31; Col Arizona St.																									
1974	Chi A	0	1	.000	5	1	0	0-0	16.1	22	11	0	1	12-2	11	5.51	68	.324	.432	0	ø	0	47	-3	0	-0.2
1975	Chi A	0	0	ø	2	0	0	0-0	5.1	4	5	1	0	7-0	3	6.75	58	.235	.440	0	ø	0	—	-2	0	-0.1
1976	Chi A	0	0	ø	2	0	0	0-0	6	9	6	0	0	2-0	3	4.50	79	.333	.379	0	ø	0	—	-2	0	-0.1
1980	StL N	0	5	.000	31	4	0	0-0	55.1	71	38	3	2	26-7	38	5.53	68	.323	.393	5	.200	-0	65	-10	0	-0.9
1981	StL N	1	0	1.000	24	0	0	0-0	35.2	44	23	3	0	20-5	20	5.30	68	.321	.405	2-0-1	.000	-0	—	-6	22	-0.4
Total	5	1	6	.143	64	5	0	0-0	118.2	150	83	7	3	67-14	75	5.46	68	.320	.404	7-0-1	.143	-0	62	-23	22	-1.7
OTTO, DAVE	David Alan; B11.12.1964 Chicago IL; BL/TL/6´7˝/210; [OakA85 2/39]; d9.8; Col Missouri																									
1987	Oak A	0	0	ø	3	0	0	0-0	6	7	6	1	0	1-0	3	9.00	46	.304	.333	0	ø	0	—	-3	0	-0.2
1988	Oak A	0	0	ø	3	2	0	0-0	10	9	2	0	0	6-0	7	1.80	211	.243	.349	0	ø	0	108	2	0	0.1
1989	Oak A	0	0	ø	1	1	0	0-0	6.2	6	2	0	0	2-0	4	2.70	137	.261	.320	0	ø	0	98	1	0	0.0
1990	Oak A	0	0	ø	2	0	0	0-0	2.1	3	3	0	0	3-0	2	7.71	48	.300	.462	0	ø	0	—	-1	158	-0.1
1991	Cle A	2	8	.200	18	14	1	0-0	100	108	52	7	4	27-6	47	4.23	99	.283	.333	0	ø	0	77	0	0	0.0
1992	Cle A	5	9	.357	18	16	0	0-0	80.1	110	64	12	1	33-0	32	7.06	56	.333	.395	0	ø	0	71	-25	16	-3.6
1993	Pit N	3	4	.429	28	8	0	0-0	68	85	40	9	3	28-1	30	5.03	81	.317	.387	18-0-1	.222	1	91	-7	0	-0.5
1994	Chi N	0	1	.000	36	0	0	0-1	45	49	20	4	1	22-4	19	3.80	111	.283	.367	2	.000	-0	—	2	0	0.1
Total	8	10	22	.313	109	41	1	0-1	318.1	377	189	33	9	122-11	144	5.06	81	.303	.367	20-0-1	.200	1	78	-31	174	-4.2
OVERALL, ORVAL	Orval; B2.2.1881 Farmersville CA; D7.14.1947 Fresno CA; BB/TR/6´2˝/214; d4.16; Col California																									
1905	Cin N	18	23	.439	42	39	32-2	0	318	290	146	4	14	147	173	2.86	116	.252	.343	117-0-5	.145	-2	85	16	—	1.7
1906	Cin N	4	5	.444	13	10	6	0	82.1	77	52	1	4	46	33	4.26	65	.253	.359	31	.194	0	130	-12	—	-1.3
	†Chi N	12	3	.800	18	14	13-2	1	144	116	43	1	4	51	94	1.88	141	.217	.290	53-0-3	.170	-1	118	12	—	1.2
	Year	16	8	.667	31	24	19-2	1	226.1	193	95	2	8	97	127	2.74	98	.230	.316	84-0-3	.179	-1	123	-3	—	-0.1
1907	†Chi N	23	7	.767	36	30	26-**8**	3	268.1	201	62	3	11	69	141	1.68	149	.208	.268	94-0-8	.213	3	112	28	—	**3.9**
1908	†Chi N	15	11	.577	37	27	16-4	4	225	165	74	3	2	78	167	1.92	123	.208	.280	70-0-8	.129	-0*	101	7	—	0.8
1909	Chi N	20	11	.645	38	32	23-**9**	3	285	204	66	1	8	80	**205**	1.42	179	**.198**	.262	96-2-4	.229	8	100	35	—	5.2
1910	†Chi N	12	6	.667	23	21	11-4	1	144.2	106	44	2	1	54	92	2.68	108	.212	.291	41-0-6	.122	-1*	103	8	—	1.0
1913	Chi N	4	5	.444	11	9	6-1	0	68	73	33	1	1	26	30	3.31	96	.284	.352	24-0-1	.250	2	83	-1	—	0.1
Total	7	108	71	.603	218	182	133-30	12	1535.1	1232	520	16	45	551	935	2.23	123	.223	.298	526-2-35	.179	9	101	93	—	12.6
OVERMIRE, STUBBY	Frank W.; B5.16.1919 Moline MI; D3.3.1977 Lakeland FL; BR/TL/5´7˝/170; d4.25; C4; Col Western Michigan																									
1943	Det A	7	6	.538	29	18	8-3	1	147	135	56	5	1	38	48	3.18	111	.243	.293	42-0-5	.167	0	89	7	0	0.6
1944	Det A	11	11	.500	32	28	11-3	1	199.2	214	84	2	2	41	57	3.07	116	.271	.309	63-0-5	.175	1	101	10	0	1.3
1945	†Det A	9	9	.500	31	22	9	4	162.1	189	81	6	3	42	36	3.88	91	.294	.341	53-0-6	.189	0	102	-5	0	-0.5
1946	Det A	5	7	.417	24	13	3	1	97.1	106	54	6	0	29	34	4.62	79	.274	.325	33-0-4	.152	-1	128	-9	0	-1.1
1947	Det A	11	5	.688	28	17	7-3	0	140.2	142	62	9	1	44	33	3.77	100	.259	.315	47-0-2	.149	-1	108	3	0	0.2
1948	Det A	3	4	.429	37	4	0	3	66.1	89	48	5	0	31	14	5.97	73	.326	.395	14	.071	-1	150	-11	0	-1.1
1949	Det A	1	3	.250	14	1	0	0	17.1	29	21	2	1	9	3	9.87	42	.377	.448	3	.333	0	22	-11	0	-1.9
1950	StL A	9	12	.429	31	19	8-2	0	161	200	89	11	1	45	39	4.19	118	.298	.343	48-0-2	.167	1	69	12	0	1.3
1951	StL A	1	6	.143	8	7	3	0	53.1	61	26	5	0	21	13	3.54	124	.281	.345	14-0-3	.071	-1	40	4	0	0.3
	NY A	1	1	.500	15	4	1	0	44.2	50	27	2	2	18	14	4.63	83	.287	.361	7	.143	0	133	-5	0	-0.2
	Year	2	7	.222	23	11	4	0	98	111	53	7	2	39	27	4.04	102	.284	.352	21-0-3	.095	-0	72	0	0	0.1
1952	StL A	0	3	.000	17	4	0	0	41	44	21	3	0	7	10	3.73	105	.270	.300	11	.182	-0	50	0	0	0.0
Total	10	58	67	.464	266	137	50-11	10	1130.2	1259	569	56	11	325	301	3.96	98	.280	.330	335-0-27	.161	-1	94	-5	0	-1.1
OVERY, MIKE	Harry Michael; B1.27.1951 Clinton IL; BR/TR/6´2˝/190; [AnaA73*S2/28]; d8.14; Col Olivet Nazarene																									
1976	Cal A	0	2	.000	5	0	0	0-2	7.1	6	5	1	1	3-1	8	6.14	55	.214	.313	0	ø	0	—	-2	0	-0.4
OVITZ, ERNIE	Ernest Gayhart; B10.7.1885 Mineral Point WI; D9.11.1980 Green Bay WI; BR/TR/5´8.5˝/156; d6.22; Col Illinois																									
1911	Chi N	0	0	ø	1	0	0	0	2	3	2	0	0	3	0	4.50	74	.375	.545	0	ø	0	—	-1	—	0.0
OWCHINKO, BOB	Robert Dennis; B1.1.1955 Detroit MI; BL/TL/6´2˝/(185–195); [SDN76 1/5]; d9.25; Col Eastern Michigan																									
1976	SD N	0	2	.000	2	2	0	0-0	4.1	11	8	0	0	3-1	4	16.62	20	.478	.538	1-0-1	.000	-0	120	-6	0	-1.0
1977	SD N	9	12	.429	30	28	3-2	0-0	170	191	93	20	0	67-5	101	4.45	80	.287	.351	49-0-11	.082	-2	113	-16	0	-2.0
1978	SD N	10	13	.435	36	33	4-1	0-1	202.1	198	87	14	1	78-12	94	3.56	94	.263	.330	63-0-6	.175	1	79	-3	0	-0.2
1979	SD N	6	12	.333	42	20	2	0-1	149.1	144	73	16	2	55-6	66	3.74	95	.259	.327	33-0-7	.121	-0	90	-5	0	-0.6
1980	Cle A	2	9	.182	29	14	1-1	0-0	114.1	138	71	13	2	47-2	66	5.27	78	.301	.365	0	ø	0	63	-13	0	-1.1
1981	†Oak A	4	3	.571	29	0	0	2-4	39.1	34	15	2	1	19-2	26	3.20	110	.245	.335	0	ø	0	—	2	0	0.3
1982	Oak A	2	4	.333	54	0	0	3-3	102	111	60	11	0	52-5	67	5.21	76	.275	.356	0	ø	0	—	-12	0	-0.8
1983	Pit N	0	0	ø	1	0	0	0-1	0	2	1	1	0	0-0	0	(1)	ø	1.000	1.000	0	ø	0	—	-1	0	-0.1
1984	Cin N	3	5	.375	49	4	0	2-1	94	91	47	10	0	39-2	60	4.12	92	.253	.325	12-0-1	.167	1	99	-3	16	-0.2
1986	Mon N	1	0	1.000	3	3	0	0-0	15	17	6	1	0	3-0	6	3.60	104	.288	.323	5	.200	0	119	1	0	0.1
Total	10	37	60	.381	275	104	10-4	7-11	890.2	937	461	88	6	363-35	490	4.28	85	.274	.343	163-0-26	.135	-0	89	-56	16	-5.6
OWEN, FRANK	Frank Malcolm "Yip"; B12.23.1879 Ypsilanti MI; D11.24.1942 Dearborn MI; BB/TR/5´11˝/160; d4.26																									
1901	Det A	1	3	.250	8	5	3	0	56	70	43	1	4	30	17	4.34	89	.302	.391	20-0-2	.050	-2*	74	-3	—	-0.3
1903	Chi A	8	12	.400	26	20	15-1	1	167.1	167	85	1	7	44	66	3.50	80	.259	.314	57-0-2	.123	-1	94	-9	—	-1.0
1904	Chi A	21	15	.583	37	36	34-4	1	315	243	95	2	11	61	103	1.94	126	.214	.261	107-2-3	.215	5	114	18	—	3.2
1905	Chi A	21	13	.618	42	38	32-3	0	334	276	110	6	9	56	125	2.10	117	.227	.266	124-0-8	.145	-4	109	15	—	1.3
1906	†Chi A	22	13	.629	42	36	27-7	0	293	289	114	4	4	54	66	2.33	109	.261	.298	103-0-5	.136	-2	116	5	—	0.6
1907	Chi A	2	3	.400	11	4	2	0	47	43	22	1	0	13	15	2.49	96	.246	.298	16	.250	0	92	-2	—	-0.2
1908	Chi A	6	7	.462	25	14	5-1	0	140	142	79	2	3	37	48	3.41	68	.260	.310	50-0-1	.180	1	93	-21	—	-1.7
1909	Chi A	1	1	.500	3	2	1	0	16	19	8	0	1	3	3	4.50	52	.279	.319	6	.167	-0	120	-3	—	-0.4
Total	8	82	67	.550	194	155	119-16	2	1368.1	1249	556	17	39	298	443	2.55	100	.244	.290	483-2-21	.159	-3	106	0	—	1.5
OWENS, HENRY	Henry Jay; B4.23.1979 Miami FL; BR/TR/6´3˝/230; d7.7; Col Barry																									
2006	NY N	0	0	ø	3	0	0	0-0	4	4	4	0	0	4-0	2	9.00	49	.286	.421	0	ø	0	—	-2	0	-0.1
OWENS, JIM	James Philip "Bear"; B1.16.1934 Gifford PA; BR/TR/5´11˝/(180–200); d4.19; Mil 1957–58; C6																									
1955	Phi N	0	2	.000	3	2	0	0	8.2	13	8	2	0	7-0	6	8.31	48	.382	.488	1-0-1	.000	-0	79	-4	0	-0.7
1956	Phi N	0	4	.000	10	5	0	0	29.2	35	26	3	2	22-1	22	7.28	51	.313	.431	6-0-1	.167	0	90	-11	0	-1.3
1958	Phi N	1	0	1.000	1	1	0	0	7	4	4	1	0	5-0	3	2.57	154	.154	.290	2	.000	0	136	0	0	0.0
1959	Phi N	12	12	.500	31	30	11-1	1	221.1	203	97	14	4	73-11	135	3.21	128	.244	.306	75-0-3	.120	-1	73	18	0	1.7
1960	Phi N	4	14	.222	31	22	6	0	150	182	95	21	1	64-7	83	5.04	77	.299	.365	44-0-3	.068	-3	78	-19	0	-2.4
1961	Phi N	5	10	.333	20	17	3	0	106.2	119	62	8	0	32-2	38	4.47	91	.287	.335	27-0-5	.074	-1*	65	-6	0	-0.9
1962	Phi N	2	4	.333	23	12	1	0	69.2	90	53	12	0	33-1	21	6.33	61	.318	.388	14-0-3	.143	0	113	-19	0	-1.4
1963	Cin N	0	2	.000	19	3	0	4	42.1	42	28	6	0	24-2	29	5.31	63	.259	.353	8	.125	0	137	-9	0	-0.6
1964	Hou N	8	7	.533	48	11	0	6	118	115	48	7	0	32-6	88	3.28	104	.262	.309	29-0-1	.103	-1	89	3	0	0.2
1965	Hou N	6	5	.545	50	0	0	8	71.1	64	28	4	0	29-8	53	3.28	102	.238	.310	8-0-1	.125	-0	—	1	0	0.2
1966	Hou N	4	7	.364	40	0	0	2	50	53	29	5	1	17-7	32	4.68	73	.273	.332	4	.000	-0	—	-7	0	-1.4
1967	Hou N	0	1	.000	10	0	0	0	10.2	12	5	1	0	2-1	6	4.22	78	.308	.341	0	ø	0	—	-1	0	-0.1
Total	12	42	68	.382	286	103	21-1	21	885.1	932	483	84	8	340-46	516	4.31	88	.273	.338	218-0-18	.101	-7	84	-54	0	-6.7
OWNBEY, RICK	Richard Wayne; B10.20.1957 Corona CA; BR/TR/6´3˝/(170–185); [NYN80 13/313]; d8.17; Col Santa Ana (CA) JC; [DL 1985 StL N 42]																									
1982	NY N	1	2	.333	8	8	2	0-0	50.1	44	23	3	0	43-1	28	3.75	98	.242	.382	15-0-1	.200	1*	108	0	0	0.0
1983	NY N	1	3	.250	10	4	0	0-0	34.2	31	19	4	1	21-0	19	4.67	79	.240	.351	9-0-1	.111	-0*	66	-3	0	-0.4
1984	StL N	0	3	.000	4	4	0	0-0	19	23	13	1	0	8-0	11	4.74	74	.303	.360	4-0-2	.000	-0*	50	-4	0	-0.5
1986	StL N	1	3	.250	17	3	0	0-0	42.2	47	20	4	2	19-0	25	3.80	97	.294	.372	7-0-3	.000	-1	72	-1	0	-0.2
Total	4	3	11	.214	39	19	2	0-0	146.2	145	75	12	3	91-1	83	4.11	89	.265	.369	35-0-7	.114	-1	82	-8	42	-1.1
OXSPRING, CHRIS	Chris Andrew; B5.13.1977 Ipswich, Queensland, Australia; BL/TR/6´0˝/185; d9.2																									
2005	SD N	0	0	ø	5	0	0	0-0	12	9	8	2	0	6-0	11	3.75	105	.225	.313	2	.000	-0	—	-1	0	-0.1
OZMER, DOC	Horace Robert; B5.25.1901 Atlanta GA; D12.28.1970 Atlanta GA; BR/TR/5´10.5˝/185; d5.11; Col Milligan																									
1923	Phi A	0	0	ø	1	0	0	0	2	1	1	0	0	1	1	4.50	91	.167	.286	0	ø	0	—	0	—	0.0

YEAR	TM LG	W	L	PCT	G	GS	CG-SHO	SV-BS	IP	H	R	HR	HB	BB-IB	SO	ERA	AERA	OAV	OOB	AB-HR-SH	AVG	PB	SUP	APR	DL	PW
PABOR, CHARLIE	Charles Henry; B9.24.1846 New York NY; D4.23.1913 New Haven CT; BL/TL/5´8˝/155; d5.4; M2; ▲																									
1871	Cle NA	0	2	.000	7	1	1	0	29.1	50	53	4	—	6	0	6.75	61	.325	.350	142	.296	0*	77	-7	—	-0.2
1872	Cle NA	1	1	.500	2	2	2	0	18	20	15	0	—	3	0	4.00	89	.247	.274	92	.207	-0*	145	-1	—	-0.1
1875	Atl NA	0	1	.000	1	1	0	0	4	11	12	0	—	1	0	9.00	23	.407	.429	153	.235	0*	102	-3	—	-0.4
Total	3NA	1	4	.200	10	4	3	0	51.1	81	80	4	—	10	0	5.96	63	.309	.335	387	.251	-0	106	-11	—	-0.7
PACELLA, JOHN	John Lewis; B9.15.1956 Brooklyn NY; BR/TR/6´3˝/(180–195); [NYN74 4/89]; d9.15																									
1977	NY N	0	0	ø	3	0	0	0-0	4	2	2	0	0	2-0	1	0.00	ø	.133	.235	0	ø	0	—	1	0	0.0
1979	NY N	0	2	.000	4	3	0	0-0	16.1	16	8	0	0	4-0	12	4.41	84	.246	.290	4	.000	-0	56	-1	0	-0.1
1980	NY N	3	4	.429	32	15	0	0-0	84	89	51	5	2	59-2	68	5.14	70	.280	.396	20-0-2	.100	-1	119	-13	0	-1.1
1982	NY A	0	1	.000	3	1	0	0-0	10	13	8	0	1	9-1	2	7.20	56	.342	.451	0	ø	0	23	-3	0	-0.3
	Min A	1	2	.333	21	1	0	2-1	51.2	61	48	14	0	37-0	20	7.32	58	.299	.402	0	ø	0	43	-18	24	-1.1
	Year	1	3	.250	24	2	0	2-1	61.2	74	56	14	1	46-1	22	7.30	58	.306	.410	0	ø	0	32	-20	0	-1.4
1984	Bal A	0	1	.000	6	1	0	0-0	14.2	15	13	2	0	9-1	8	6.75	58	.268	.369	0	ø	0	115	-5	0	-0.3
1986	Det A	0	0	ø	5	0	0	1-0	11	10	5	0	0	13-1	5	4.09	102	.294	.469	0	ø	0	—	0	0	0.1
Total	6	4	10	.286	74	21	0	3-1	191.2	206	135	21	3	133-5	116	5.73	68	.282	.391	24-0-2	.083	-1	96	-39	24	-2.8
PACHECO, ALEX	Alexander Melchor (Lara); B7.19.1973 Caracas, Distrito Capital, Venez.; BR/TR/6´3˝/200; d4.17																									
1996	Mon N	0	0	ø	5	0	0	0-0	5.2	8	7	2	0	1-0	7	11.12	39	.320	.346	0	ø	0	—	-4	0	-0.2
PACILLO, PAT	Patrick Michael; B7.23.1963 Jersey City NJ; BR/TR/6´2˝/(205–210); [CinN84 1/5]; d5.23; Col Seton Hall																									
1987	Cin N	3	3	.500	12	7	0	0-0	39.2	41	30	7	1	19-0	23	6.13	69	.270	.351	11-0-1	.091	-0*	110	-8	0	-1.1
1988	Cin N	1	0	1.000	6	0	0	0-0	10.2	14	7	2	0	4-0	11	5.06	71	.318	.375	1	.000	-0	—	-2	21	-0.2
Total	2	4	3	.571	18	7	0	0-0	50.1	55	37	9	1	23-0	34	5.90	69	.281	.356	12-0-1	.083	-0	110	-10	21	-1.3
PACKARD, GENE	Eugene Milo; B7.13.1887 Colorado Springs CO; D5.18.1959 Riverside CA; BL/TL/5´10˝/155; d9.27																									
1912	Cin N	1	0	1.000	1	1	1	0	9	7	3	0	0	4	2	3.00	112	.206	.289	4	.250	1	218	1	—	0.1
1913	Cin N	7	11	.389	39	21	9-2	0	190.2	208	97	2	8	64	73	2.97	109	.286	.350	61-0-4	.180	-0*	114	1	—	0.1
1914	KC F	20	14	.588	42	34	24-4	5	302	282	127	5	3	88	154	2.89	96	.246	.301	116-1-5	.241	3*	122	-3	—	0.3
1915	KC F	20	12	.625	42	31	21-5	2	281.2	250	111	3	9	74	108	2.68	98	.242	.298	95-1-8	.232	2*	99	-3	—	0.2
1916	Chi N	10	6	.625	37	16	5-2	5	155.1	154	60	4	3	38	36	2.78	105	.256	.304	54-0-2	.130	-1*	108	3	—	0.5
1917	Chi N	0	0	ø	2	0	0	0	1.2	3	2	1	0	0	1	10.80	27	.375	.375	0	ø	0	—	-1	—	-0.1
	StL N	9	6	.600	34	11	6	2	153.1	138	48	4	3	25	44	2.47	109	.246	.281	52	.288	3*	89	5	—	0.9
	Year	9	6	.600	36	11	6	2	155	141	50	5	3	25	45	2.55	105	.247	.283	52	.288	3	89	5	—	0.8
1918	StL N	12	12	.500	30	23	10-1	2	182.1	184	84	6	5	33	46	3.50	77	.266	.304	69-0-4	.174	-1*	119	-12	—	-1.7
1919	Phi N	6	8	.429	21	16	10-1	1	134.1	167	70	3	4	30	24	4.15	78	.321	.363	51	.137	-2*	123	-11	—	-1.3
Total	8	85	69	.552	248	153	86-15	17	1410.1	1393	602	28	35	356	488	3.01	95	.262	.312	502-2-23	.205	6	113	-20	—	-1.0
PACTWA, JOE	Joseph Martin; B6.2.1948 Hammond IN; BL/TL/5´11˝/185; [NYA66 18/350]; d9.15																									
1975	Cal A	1	0	1.000	4	3	0	0-0	16.1	23	7	0	0	10-0	3	3.86	93	.343	.423	0	ø	0	90	0	0	0.0
PADILLA, JUAN	Juan Miguel; B2.17.1977 Rio Piedras, PR; BR/TR/6´0˝/200; [MinA98 24/709]; d7.16; Col Jacksonville; [DL 2006 NY N 182]																									
2004	NY A	0	0	ø	6	0	0	0-0	11.1	16	5	1	0	4-0	5	3.97	116	.348	.400	0	ø	0	—	1	0	0.1
	Cin N	1	0	1.000	12	0	0	0-0	14.1	23	17	6	1	8-0	12	10.67	40	.359	.438	0	ø	0	—	-10	0	-0.6
2005	NY N	3	1	.750	24	0	0	1-1	36.1	24	7	0	2	13-2	17	1.49	278	.180	.264	2	.500	0	—	11	0	1.2
Total	2	4	1	.800	42	0	0	1-1	62	63	29	7	3	25-2	34	4.06	105	.259	.336	2	.500	0	—	2	182	0.7
PADILLA, VICENTE	Vicente De La Cruz; B9.27.1977 Chinandega, Nicaragua; BR/TR/6´2˝/(200–220); d6.29																									
1999	Ari N	0	1	.000	5	0	0	0-1	2.2	7	5	1	0	3-0	0	16.88	27	.467	.556	0	ø	0	—	-3	0	-0.6
2000	Ari N	2	1	.667	27	0	0	0-1	35	32	10	0	0	10-2	30	2.31	207	.242	.294	1	1.000	0	—	9	0	0.7
	Phi N	2	6	.250	28	0	0	2-4	30.1	40	23	3	1	18-5	21	5.34	86	.328	.413	0	ø	0	—	-4	0	-0.8
	Year	4	7	.364	55	0	0	2-5	65.1	72	33	3	1	28-7	51	3.72	126	.283	.353	1	1.000	0	—	5	0	-0.1
2001	Phi N	3	1	.750	23	0	0	0-3	34	36	18	1	0	12-0	29	4.24	97	.273	.333	3-0-1	.333	1	—	-1	26	0.0
2002	Phi N★	14	11	.560	32	32	1-1	0-0	206	198	83	16	15	53-5	128	3.28	117	.254	.312	58-0-7	.052	-4	113	13	0	1.0
2003	Phi N	14	12	.538	32	32	1-1	0-0	208.2	196	94	22	16	62-4	133	3.62	110	.251	.317	67-0-3	.060	-3	118	7	0	0.5
2004	Phi N	7	7	.500	20	20	0	0-0	115.1	119	63	16	10	36-6	82	4.53	98	.267	.333	35-0-3	.114	-1	94	-1	72	-0.3
2005	Phi N	9	12	.429	27	27	0	0-0	147	146	79	22	8	74-9	103	4.71	92	.260	.352	41-0-5	.146	1	111	-4	16	-0.4
2006	Tex A	15	10	.600	33	33	0	0-0	200	206	108	21	17	70-2	156	4.50	104	.266	.338	1-0-1	.000	-0	110	3	0	0.4
Total	8	66	61	.520	227	144	2-2	2-9	979	980	483	102	67	338-33	682	4.06	105	.262	.332	206-0-20	.092	-5	110	19	114	0.5
PAGAN, DAVE	David Percy; B9.15.1949 Nipawin SK, Can.; BR/TR/6´2˝/175; d7.1																									
1973	NY A	0	0	ø	4	1	0	0-0	12.2	16	4	1	0	1-0	9	2.84	131	.320	.333	0	ø	0	265	2	0	0.1
1974	NY A	1	3	.250	16	6	1	0-0	49.1	49	29	1	0	28-0	39	5.11	69	.265	.362	0	ø	0	112	-7	0	-0.6
1975	NY A	0	0	ø	13	0	0	1-0	31	30	16	2	2	13-5	18	4.06	91	.256	.336	0	ø	0	—	-1	0	-0.1
1976	NY A	1	1	.500	7	2	1	0-0	23.2	18	7	0	0	4-0	13	2.28	150	.222	.253	0	ø	0	77	3	0	0.2
	Bal A	1	4	.200	20	5	0	1-1	46.2	54	33	2	1	23-1	34	5.98	55	.298	.370	0	ø	0	107	-14	0	-1.5
	Year	2	5	.286	27	7	1	1-1	70.1	72	40	2	1	27-1	47	4.73	70	.275	.336	0	ø	0	98	-11	0	-1.3
1977	Sea A	1	1	.500	24	4	1-1	2-1	66	86	52	3	2	26-2	30	6.14	68	.323	.383	0	ø	0	108	-15	0	-0.8
	Pit N	0	0	ø	1	0	0	0-0	3	1	0	0	0	0-0	4	0.00	ø	.100	.100	0	ø	0	—	1	0	0.1
Total	5	4	9	.308	85	18	3-1	4-2	232.1	254	141	9	5	95-8	147	4.96	74	.285	.353	0	ø	0	112	-31	0	-2.6
PAGE, JOE	Joseph Francis "Fireman"; B10.28.1917 Cherry Valley PA; D4.21.1980 Latrobe PA; BL/TL/6´2˝/205; d4.19																									
1944	NY A☆	5	7	.417	19	16	4	0	102.2	100	65	3	3	52	63	4.56	76	.258	.351	32-0-2	.156	-0	97	-14	0	-1.5
1945	NY A	6	3	.667	20	9	4	0	102	95	43	1	0	46	50	2.82	123	.246	.326	36	.250	1	139	5	0	0.4
1946	NY A	9	8	.529	31	17	6-1	3	136	126	66	7	4	72	77	3.57	97	.252	.351	43-1-6	.163	-0*	142	-4	0	-0.5
1947	†NY A★	14	8	.636	56	2	0	**17**	141.1	105	41	5	1	72	116	2.48	142	.208	.308	46-1-2	.217	1	163	**18**	0	3.3
1948	NY A☆	7	8	.467	**55**	1	0	16	107.2	116	59	6	1	66	77	4.26	96	.275	.374	24-0-1	.292	3	243	-3	0	-0.2
1949	†NY A	13	8	.619	**60**	0	0	**27**	135.1	103	44	8	5	75	99	2.59	156	.215	.328	40	.175	-1	—	**23**	0	4.0
1950	NY A	3	7	.300	37	0	0	13	55.1	66	34	8	0	31	33	5.04	85	.295	.380	8	.250	1	—	-5	0	-0.9
1954	Pit N	0	0	ø	7	0	0	0	9.2	16	17	4	1	7	4	11.17	37	.364	.462	0	ø	0	—	-9	0	-0.4
Total	8	57	49	.538	285	45	14-1	76	790	727	369	42	15	421	519	3.53	106	.247	.344	229-2-11	.205	5	124	11	0	4.2
PAGE, PHIL	Philippe Rausac; B8.23.1905 Springfield MA; D7.27.1958 Springfield MA; BR/TL/6´2˝/175; d9.18; C6; Col Penn St.																									
1928	Det A	2	0	1.000	3	2	2	0	22	21	9	1	0	10	3	2.45	167	.256	.337	9	.222	-0	124	3	—	0.3
1929	Det A	0	2	.000	10	4	1	0	25.1	29	24	1	1	19	6	8.17	53	.296	.415	8	.125	-1	147	-9	—	-0.7
1930	Det A	0	1	.000	12	0	0	0	12	23	16	1	0	9	2	9.75	49	.434	.516	0	ø	0	—	-7	—	-0.4
1934	Bro N	1	0	1.000	6	0	0	0	10	13	7	1	0	6	4	5.40	72	.342	.432	1	.000	-0	—	-2	—	-0.1
Total	4	3	3	.500	31	6	3	0	69.1	86	56	4	1	44	15	6.23	68	.317	.415	18	.167	-1	140	-15	—	-0.9
PAGE, SAM	Samuel Walter; B2.11.1916 Woodruff SC; D5.29.2002 Greenville SC; BL/TR/6´0˝/172; d9.11																									
1939	Phi A	0	3	.000	4	3	1	0	22	34	27	1	0	15	11	6.95	68	.343	.430	7-0-1	.429	1	106	-8	—	-0.7
PAGE, VANCE	Vance Linwood; B9.15.1905 Elm City NC; D7.14.1951 Wilson NC; BR/TR/6´0˝/180; d8.6																									
1938	†Chi N	5	4	.556	13	9	3	1	68	90	33	4	0	13	18	3.84	100	.323	.353	26-0-1	.154	-1	93	0	—	0.0
1939	Chi N	7	7	.500	27	17	8-1	1	139.1	169	77	8	1	37	43	3.88	102	.298	.342	47-0-2	.255	3	102	-2	—	0.1
1940	Chi N	1	3	.250	30	1	0	2	59	65	38	1	0	26	22	4.42	85	.271	.342	13	.308	2*	278	-6	—	-0.2
1941	Chi N	2	2	.500	25	3	1	1	48.1	48	24	2	2	30	17	4.28	82	.254	.362	7-0-1	.286	1	64	-3	0	-0.1
Total	4	15	16	.484	95	30	12-1	5	314.2	372	172	15	3	106	100	4.03	95	.292	.348	93-0-4	.237	4	103	-11	0	-0.2
PAIGE, PAT	George Lynn "Piggy"; B5.5.1882 Paw Paw MI; D6.8.1939 Berlin WI; BL/TR/5´10˝/175; d5.20																									
1911	Cle A	1	0	1.000	2	1	1	0	16	21	12	0	0	7	6	4.50	76	.339	.406	7	.143	-0	169	-2	—	-0.1
PAIGE, SATCHEL	Leroy Robert; B7.7.1906 Mobile AL; D6.8.1982 Kansas City MO; BR/TR/6´3.5˝/180; d7.9; C2; HF1971; Negro Lg 1926–67																									
1948	†Cle A	6	1	.857	21	7	3-2	1	72.2	61	21	2	1	22	43	2.48	164	.228	.290	23-0-2	.087	-2	121	14	0	1.0
1949	Cle A	4	7	.364	31	5	1	5	83	70	29	4	1	33	54	3.04	131	.230	.308	16	.063	-1	63	10	0	1.2
1951	StL A	3	4	.429	23	3	0	5	62	67	39	6	1	29	48	4.79	92	.276	.355	16-0-1	.125	-2	61	-3	0	-0.6

YEAR	TM LG	W	L	PCT	G	GS	CG-SHO	SV-BS	IP	H	R	HR	HB	BB-IB	SO	ERA	AERA	OAV	OOB	AB-HR-SH	AVG	PB	SUP	APR	DL	PW
1952	StL A☆	12	10	.545	46	6	3-2	10	138	116	51	5	3	57	91	3.07	128	.226	.307	39-0-4	.128	-2	56	13	0	2.1
1953	StL A★	3	9	.250	57	4	0	11	117.1	114	51	12	1	39	51	3.53	119	.257	.319	29-0-1	.069	-3	95	9	0	0.6
1965	KC A	0	0	ø	1	1	0	0	3	1	0	0	0	0-0	0	0.00	ø	.100	.100	1	.000	0	50	1	0	0.0
Total	6	28	31	.475	179	26	7-4	32	476	429	191	29	7	180-0	288	3.29	124	.241	.313	124-0-8	.097	-10	80	44	0	4.3

PAINE, PHIL Phillips Steere "Flip"; B6.8.1930 Chepachet RI; D2.19.1978 Lebanon PA; BR/TR/6´2˝/181; d7.14; Mil 1952–53

YEAR	TM LG	W	L	PCT	G	GS	CG-SHO	SV-BS	IP	H	R	HR	HB	BB-IB	SO	ERA	AERA	OAV	OOB	AB-HR-SH	AVG	PB	SUP	APR	DL	PW
1951	Bos N	2	0	1.000	21	0	0	0	35.1	36	15	2	4	20	17	3.06	120	.271	.382	4	.000	-1	—	2	0	0.0
1954	Mil N	1	0	1.000	11	0	0	0	14	14	9	1	1	12	11	3.86	97	.292	.443	0	ø	0	—	-1	0	-0.1
1955	Mil N	2	0	1.000	15	0	0	0	25.1	20	8	2	0	14-3	26	2.49	151	.225	.324	3	.333	0	—	4	0	0.3
1956	Mil N	0	0	ø	1	0	0	0	0	3	2	0	0	0-0	0	(2)	ø	1.000	1.000	0	ø	0	—	-2	0	-0.2
1957	Mil N	0	0	ø	1	0	0	0	2	1	0	0	0	3-0	2	0.00	ø	.143	.400	0	ø	0	—	1	0	0.1
1958	StL N	5	1	.833	46	0	0	1	73.1	70	33	7	5	31-4	45	3.56	116	.256	.342	7-0-1	.286	0	—	4	0	0.4
Total	6	10	1	.909	95	0	0	1	150	144	67	12	10	80-7	101	3.36	116	.260	.362	14-0-1	.214	-0	—	8	0	0.5

PAINTER, LANCE Lance Telford; B7.21.1967 Bedford, England; BL/TL/6´1˝/(194–200); [SDN90 25/681]; d5.19; Col Wisconsin–Madison

YEAR	TM LG	W	L	PCT	G	GS	CG-SHO	SV-BS	IP	H	R	HR	HB	BB-IB	SO	ERA	AERA	OAV	OOB	AB-HR-SH	AVG	PB	SUP	APR	DL	PW
1993	Col N	2	2	.500	10	6	1	0-0	39	52	26	5	0	9-0	16	6.00	80	.333	.370	10-0-3	.300	1	116	-3	0	-0.2
1994	Col N	4	6	.400	15	14	0	0-0	73.2	91	51	9	1	26-2	41	6.11	82	.302	.354	21-0-3	.143	-1	114	-7	0	-0.8
1995	†Col N	3	0	1.000	33	1	0	1-0	45.1	55	23	9	2	10-0	36	4.37	123	.296	.338	9-0-1	.111	-0	202	4	11	0.3
1996	Col N	4	2	.667	34	1	0	0-1	50.2	56	37	12	3	25-3	48	5.86	89	.280	.364	15	.133	-1*	17	-3	55	-0.4
1997	StL N	1	1	.500	14	0	0	0-0	17	13	9	1	0	8-2	11	4.76	88	.213	.304	1	.000	-0	—	-1	141	0.0
1998	StL N	4	0	1.000	65	0	0	1-1	47.1	42	24	5	4	28-3	39	3.99	105	.249	.365	1-0-1	1.000	0	—	1	0	0.2
1999	StL N	4	5	.444	56	4	0	1-2	63.1	63	37	6	2	25-1	56	4.83	95	.265	.336	7	.000	-1	65	-1	15	-0.2
2000	Tor A	2	0	1.000	42	2	0	0-1	66.2	69	37	9	2	22-1	53	4.72	107	.271	.332	0	ø	0	130	3	19	0.2
2001	Tor A	0	1	.000	10	0	0	0-0	18.1	27	17	4	1	11-0	14	7.85	58	.342	.429	0	ø	0	—	-6	31	-0.3
	Mil N	1	0	1.000	13	0	0	0-0	10.2	11	5	3	0	7-2	6	4.22	102	.268	.375	0	ø	0	—	0	46	0.0
2003	StL N	0	1	.000	22	0	0	0-1	18	17	12	3	0	7-1	11	5.50	75	.246	.316	1	.000	-0	—	-3	111	-0.1
Total	10	25	18	.581	314	28	1	3-6	450	496	278	66	15	178-15	331	5.24	92	.283	.351	65-0-8	.154	-1	111	-16	429	-1.3

PALACIOS, VICENTE Vicente (Diaz); B7.19.1963 Manlio Fabio Altamirano, Veracruz, Mexico; BR/TR/6´3˝/(175–208); d9.4

YEAR	TM LG	W	L	PCT	G	GS	CG-SHO	SV-BS	IP	H	R	HR	HB	BB-IB	SO	ERA	AERA	OAV	OOB	AB-HR-SH	AVG	PB	SUP	APR	DL	PW
1987	Pit N	2	1	.667	6	4	0	0-0	29.1	27	14	1	1	9-1	13	4.30	97	.250	.314	9	.111	-0	119	0	0	-0.1
1988	Pit N	1	2	.333	7	3	0	0-0	24.1	28	18	3	0	15-1	15	6.66	52	.295	.387	8	.000	-0	197	-8	0	-0.9
1990	Pit N	0	0	ø	7	0	0	3-0	15	4	0	0	0	2-0	8	0.00	ø	.083	.120	4	.000	-0	—	6	0	0.3
1991	Pit N	6	3	.667	36	7	1-1	3-2	81.2	69	34	12	1	38-2	64	3.75	96	.228	.315	14-0-5	.071	-1	114	1	29	0.0
1992	Pit N	3	2	.600	20	8	0	0-0	53	56	25	1	0	27-1	33	4.25	82	.280	.364	14-0-2	.071	-1	111	-4	108	-0.4
1994	StL N	3	8	.273	31	17	1-1	1-0	117.2	104	60	16	3	43-2	95	4.44	96	.245	.314	33-0-3	.000	-4	67	-2	0	-0.5
1995	StL N	2	3	.400	20	5	0	0-0	40.1	48	29	7	2	19-1	34	5.80	74	.300	.379	6-0-1	.167	-0	93	-6	102	-0.7
2000	SD N	0	1	.000	7	0	0	0-0	10.2	12	10	4	0	5-1	8	6.75	66	.308	.378	0	ø	0	—	-3	0	-0.2
Total	8	17	20	.459	134	44	2-2	7-2	372	348	190	44	7	158-9	270	4.43	89	.253	.330	88-0-11	.045	-6	98	-16	239	-2.5

PALAGYI, MIKE Michael Raymond; B7.4.1917 Conneaut OH; BR/TR/6´2˝/185; d8.18

YEAR	TM LG	W	L	PCT	G	GS	CG-SHO	SV-BS	IP	H	R	HR	HB	BB-IB	SO	ERA	AERA	OAV	OOB	AB-HR-SH	AVG	PB	SUP	APR	DL	PW
1939	Was A	0	0	ø	1	0	0	0	0	0	3	0	1	3	0	(3)	ø	ø	1.000	0	ø	0	—	-3	—	-0.2

PALICA, ERV Ervin Martin (b Ervin Martin Pavliecivich); B2.9.1928 Lomita CA; D5.29.1982 Huntington Beach CA; BR/TR/6´1.5˝/(180–190); d4.21.1945; Mil 1952–53

YEAR	TM LG	W	L	PCT	G	GS	CG-SHO	SV-BS	IP	H	R	HR	HB	BB-IB	SO	ERA	AERA	OAV	OOB	AB-HR-SH	AVG	PB	SUP	APR	DL	PW
1947	Bro N	0	1	.000	3	0	0	0	3	2	1	0	1	2	1	3.00	138	.182	.357	0	ø	0	—	0	0	0.1
1948	Bro N	6	6	.500	41	10	3	3	125.1	111	63	13	3	58	74	4.45	90	.239	.327	39-0-1	.128	0*	109	-3	0	-0.3
1949	†Bro N	8	9	.471	49	1	0	6	97	93	43	6	1	49	44	3.62	113	.261	.352	19-0-4	.158	0	86	5	0	0.9
1950	Bro N	13	8	.619	43	19	10-2	1	201.1	176	89	13	2	98	131	3.58	115	.237	.327	68-1-3	.221	2*	117	11	0	1.1
1951	Bro N	2	6	.250	19	8	0	0	53	55	28	10	0	20	15	4.75	83	.259	.323	13-0-1	.154	0*	98	-4	0	-0.5
1953	Bro N	0	0	ø	4	0	0	0	6	10	8	1	0	8	3	12.00	36	.370	.514	1	1.000	0	—	-5	0	-0.2
1954	Bro N	3	3	.500	25	3	0	0	67.2	77	45	9	1	31	25	5.32	77	.285	.357	16	.250	1*	102	-10	0	-0.7
1955	Bal A	5	11	.313	33	25	5-1	2	169.2	165	91	10	2	83-4	68	4.14	92	.260	.342	55-0-2	.236	2	86	-7	0	-0.3
1956	Bal A	4	11	.267	29	14	2	0	116.1	117	64	10	1	50-3	62	4.49	87	.264	.336	32	.156	-2*	66	-8	0	-1.0
Total	9	41	55	.427	246	80	20-3	12	839.1	806	432	72	11	399-7	423	4.22	94	.255	.338	243-1-11	.198	5	94	-21	0	-0.9

PALL, DONN Donn Steven; B1.11.1962 Chicago IL; BR/TR/6´1˝/(179–185); [ChiA85 23/579]; d8.1; Col Illinois

YEAR	TM LG	W	L	PCT	G	GS	CG-SHO	SV-BS	IP	H	R	HR	HB	BB-IB	SO	ERA	AERA	OAV	OOB	AB-HR-SH	AVG	PB	SUP	APR	DL	PW
1988	Chi A	0	2	.000	17	0	0	0-0	28.2	39	11	1	0	8-1	16	3.45	116	.328	.367	0	ø	0	—	2	0	0.2
1989	Chi A	4	5	.444	53	0	0	6-4	87	90	35	9	8	19-3	58	3.31	116	.270	.323	0	ø	0	—	6	14	0.5
1990	Chi A	3	5	.375	56	0	0	2-1	76	63	33	7	4	24-8	39	3.32	116	.232	.301	0	ø	0	—	3	0	0.3
1991	Chi A	7	2	.778	51	0	0	0-1	71	59	22	7	3	20-3	40	2.41	166	.231	.295	0	ø	0	—	12	0	1.4
1992	Chi A	5	2	.714	39	0	0	1-1	73	79	43	9	2	27-8	27	4.93	79	.272	.335	0	ø	0	—	-8	0	-0.8
1993	Chi A	2	3	.400	39	0	0	1-1	58.2	62	25	5	2	11-3	29	3.22	131	.268	.306	0	ø	0	—	6	0	0.5
	Phi N	1	0	1.000	8	0	0	0-0	17.2	15	7	1	0	3-0	11	2.55	156	.231	.265	0	ø	0	—	2	0	0.1
1994	NY A	1	2	.333	26	0	0	0-0	35	43	18	3	1	9-0	21	3.60	128	.295	.338	0	ø	0	—	3	0	0.2
	Chi N	0	0	ø	2	0	0	0-0	4	8	2	1	0	1-0	2	4.50	94	.444	.474	0	ø	0	—	0	0	0.0
1996	Fla N	1	1	.500	12	0	0	0-0	18.2	16	15	3	0	9-1	9	5.79	71	.232	.316	2	.000	0	—	-4	0	-0.4
1997	Fla N	0	0	ø	2	0	0	0-1	2.1	3	1	1	0	1-0	0	3.86	105	.300	.364	1	.000	-0	—	0	0	0.0
1998	Fla N	0	1	.000	23	0	0	0-0	33.1	42	19	5	1	7-2	26	5.13	79	.326	.362	2	.000	-0	—	-3	0	-0.2
Total	10	24	23	.511	328	0	0	10-9	505.1	519	231	52	21	139-29	278	3.63	110	.268	.322	5	.000	-0	—	19	14	1.8

PALM, MIKE Richard Paul; B2.13.1925 Boston MA; BR/TR/6´3.5˝/190; d7.11

YEAR	TM LG	W	L	PCT	G	GS	CG-SHO	SV-BS	IP	H	R	HR	HB	BB-IB	SO	ERA	AERA	OAV	OOB	AB-HR-SH	AVG	PB	SUP	APR	DL	PW
1948	Bos A	0	0	ø	3	0	0	0	3	6	2	0	0	5	1	6.00	73	.400	.550	3	.000	-0	—	0	0	-0.1

PALMER, BILLY Billy; B St.Louis MO; d5.28

YEAR	TM LG	W	L	PCT	G	GS	CG-SHO	SV-BS	IP	H	R	HR	HB	BB-IB	SO	ERA	AERA	OAV	OOB	AB-HR-SH	AVG	PB	SUP	APR	DL	PW
1885	StL N	0	4	.000	4	4	4	0	34	46	33	2	—	20	9	3.44	80	.311	.393	11	.091	-0	67	-6	—	-0.6

PALMER, DAVID David William; B10.19.1957 Glens Falls NY; BR/TR/6´1˝/(195–205); [MonN76 21/489]; d9.9; [DL 1981 Mon N 123, 1983 Mon N 169]

YEAR	TM LG	W	L	PCT	G	GS	CG-SHO	SV-BS	IP	H	R	HR	HB	BB-IB	SO	ERA	AERA	OAV	OOB	AB-HR-SH	AVG	PB	SUP	APR	DL	PW
1978	Mon N	0	1	.000	5	1	0	0-0	9.2	9	4	1	0	2-0	7	2.79	128	.243	.282	1	.000	-0	76	1	0	0.1
1979	Mon N	10	2	.833	36	11	2-1	2-1	122.2	110	41	10	2	30-7	72	2.64	141	.237	.285	31-0-4	.032	-3	123	15	0	1.1
1980	Mon N	8	6	.571	24	19	3-1	0-0	129.2	124	53	11	2	30-1	73	2.98	122	.255	.299	45-0-2	.200	1*	109	7	37	0.9
1982	Mon N	6	4	.600	13	13	1	0-0	73.2	60	34	3	2	36-2	46	3.18	116	.224	.315	24-0-3	.042	-2	112	2	44	0.1
1984	Mon N	7	3	.700	20	19	1-1	0-0	105.1	101	45	5	0	44-4	66	3.84	90	.256	.330	33-1-6	.152	1	98	-2	27	-0.1
1985	Mon N	7	10	.412	24	23	0	0-0	135.2	128	60	5	3	67-5	106	3.71	93	.250	.340	36-0-5	.111	-1	86	-3	23	-0.4
1986	Atl N	11	10	.524	35	35	2	0-0	209.2	181	98	17	5	102-8	170	3.65	109	.234	.325	66-1-10	.182	2	84	6	0	0.9
1987	Atl N	8	11	.421	28	28	0	0-0	152.1	169	94	17	7	64-4	111	4.90	88	.281	.354	48-1-8	.125	-0	104	-9	36	-1.0
1988	Phi N	7	9	.438	22	22	1-1	0-0	129	129	67	8	0	48-5	85	4.47	81	.261	.324	39-2-9	.256	5	84	-10	15	-0.7
1989	Det A	0	3	.000	5	5	0	0-0	17.1	25	19	1	0	11-0	12	7.79	49	.342	.424	0	ø	0	137	-9	0	-1.2
Total	10	64	59	.520	212	176	10-4	2-1	1085	1036	515	78	21	434-36	748	3.78	100	.252	.325	323-5-47	.149	2	98	-2	474	-0.3

PALMER, JIM James Alvin; B10.15.1945 New York NY; BR/TR/6´3˝/(190–196); d4.17; HF1990; [DL 1968 Bal A 38]

YEAR	TM LG	W	L	PCT	G	GS	CG-SHO	SV-BS	IP	H	R	HR	HB	BB-IB	SO	ERA	AERA	OAV	OOB	AB-HR-SH	AVG	PB	SUP	APR	DL	PW
1965	Bal A	5	4	.556	27	6	0	1	92	75	49	6	2	56-1	75	3.72	93	.229	.342	26-1-0	.192	1*	72	-4	0	-0.3
1966	†Bal A	15	10	.600	30	30	6	0	208.1	176	83	21	0	91-1	147	3.46	96	.231	.311	73-1-2	.096	-2*	132	0	0	-0.3
1967	Bal A	3	1	.750	9	9	2-1	0	49	34	18	6	0	20-0	23	2.94	107	.199	.281	13-0-3	.077	0	154	1	0	0.1
1969	†Bal A	16	4	**.800**	26	23	11-6	0-0	181	131	48	11	1	64-1	123	2.34	154	.200	.272	64-0-2	.203	2*	134	27	41	3.1
1970	†Bal A★	20	10	.667	39	39	17-**5**	0-0	**305**	263	98	21	1	100-4	199	2.71	136	.231	.293	113-1-7	.150	-1*	108	**35**	0	3.1
1971	†Bal A★	20	9	.690	37	37	20-3	0-0	282	231	94	19	4	106-6	184	2.68	127	.221	.294	102-0-11	.196	2*	121	23	0	2.6
1972	Bal A★	21	10	.677	36	36	18-3	0-0	274.1	219	73	21	1	70-1	184	2.07	151	.217	.268	98-0-6	.224	4	117	30	0	4.1
1973	†Bal A	22	9	.710	38	37	19-6	1-0	296.1	225	86	16	3	113-5	158	**2.40**	157	.211	.288	0	ø	0	111	47	0	4.8
1974	†Bal A	7	12	.368	26	26	5-2	0-0	178.2	176	78	12	3	69-4	84	3.27	106	.257	.326	0	ø	0	86	2	54	0.3
1975	Bal A☆	**23**	11	.676	39	38	25-**10**	1-0	323	253	87	20	2	80-4	193	**2.09**	**170**	.216	.266	0	ø	0	101	**53**	0	**5.7**
1976	Bal A	**22**	13	.629	40	**40**	23-6	0-0	**315**	255	101	20	8	84-5	159	2.51	131	.224	.278	0	ø	0	90	27	0	3.1
1977	Bal A★	**20**	11	.645	39	**39**	**22**-3	0-0	**319**	263	106	24	3	99-1	193	2.91	132	.229	.290	0	ø	0	99	38	0	3.4
1978	Bal A★	21	12	.636	38	38	19-6	0-0	**296**	246	94	19	1	97-1	138	2.46	143	.227	.290	0	ø	0	94	36	0	4.0
1979	†Bal A	10	6	.625	23	22	7	0-0	155.2	144	66	12	0	43-0	67	3.30	123	.246	.295	0	ø	0	126	12	26	1.1
1980	Bal A	16	10	.615	34	33	4	0-0	224	238	108	26	3	74-0	109	3.98	100	.275	.332	0	ø	0*	114	-1	0	0.0
1981	Bal A	7	8	.467	22	22	5	0-0	127.1	117	60	14	2	46-1	35	3.75	97	.247	.313	0	ø	0	102	-1	0	-0.1
1982	Bal A	15	5	**.750**	36	32	8-2	1-0	227	195	85	22	4	63-1	103	3.13	130	.231	**.286**	0	ø	0	105	23	0	1.9

YEAR	TM LG	W	L	PCT	G	GS	CG-SHO	SV-BS	IP	H	R	HR	HB	BB-IB	SO	ERA	AERA	OAV	OOB	AB-HR-SH	AVG	PB	SUP	APR	DL	PW
1983	†Bal A	5	4	.556	14	11	0	0-0	76.2	86	42	11	0	19-0	34	4.23	95	.281	.320	0	ø	0	101	-3	98	-0.3
1984	Bal A	0	3	.000	5	3	0	0-0	17.2	22	19	2	0	17-1	4	9.17	43	.319	.443	0	ø	0	77	-10	0	-1.3
Total	19	268	152	.638	558	521	211-53	4-0	3948	3349	1395	303	38	1311-37	2212	2.86	126	.230	.294	489-3-31	.174	6	108	335	257	35.0

PALMER, LOWELL Lowell Raymond; B8.18.1947 Sacramento CA; BR/TR/6´1˝/190; [PhiN66*S1/6]; d6.21; Col American River (CA) CC

YEAR	TM LG	W	L	PCT	G	GS	CG-SHO	SV-BS	IP	H	R	HR	HB	BB-IB	SO	ERA	AERA	OAV	OOB	AB-HR-SH	AVG	PB	SUP	APR	DL	PW
1969	Phi N	2	8	.200	26	9	1-1	0-0	90	91	54	12	6	47-7	68	5.20	69	.264	.356	22-1-2	.136	1	86	-15	0	-1.4
1970	Phi N	1	2	.333	38	5	0	0-0	102	98	66	15	5	55-4	85	5.47	74	.255	.353	27-0-1	.148	1	125	-16	0	-0.7
1971	Phi N	0	0	ø	3	1	0	0-0	15	13	11	3	4	13-0	6	6.00	59	.236	.411	5	.200	-0	125	-4	68	-0.2
1972	StL N	0	3	.000	16	2	0	0-0	34.2	30	16	2	1	26-1	25	3.89	88	.244	.375	5	.000	-1*	26	-1	0	-0.2
	Cle A	0	0	ø	1	0	0	0-0	2	2	1	0	0	2-0	3	4.50	72	.222	.364	0	ø	0	—	0	0	0.0
1974	SD N	2	5	.286	22	8	1	0-0	73	68	48	9	7	59-6	52	5.67	63	.256	.398	23	.087	-1*	97	-15	0	-1.5
Total	5	5	18	.217	106	25	2-1	0-0	316.2	302	196	41	23	202-18	239	5.29	70	.255	.370	82-1-3	.122	-0	94	-51	68	-4.0

PALMERO, EMILIO Emilio Antonio "Pal"; B6.13.1895 Guanabacoa, Cuba; D7.15.1970 Toledo OH; BL/TL (BB 1915–16)/5´11˝/157; d9.21

YEAR	TM LG	W	L	PCT	G	GS	CG-SHO	SV-BS	IP	H	R	HR	HB	BB-IB	SO	ERA	AERA	OAV	OOB	AB-HR-SH	AVG	PB	SUP	APR	DL	PW
1915	NY N	0	2	.000	3	2	1	0	11.2	10	4	0	3	9	8	3.09	83	.233	.400	4	.250	0	44	0	—	0.0
1916	NY N	0	3	.000	4	2	0	0	15.2	17	14	2	1	8	8	8.04	30	.288	.382	3	.000	-0*	107	-9	—	-1.4
1921	StL A	4	7	.364	24	9	4	0	90	109	63	1	6	49	26	5.00	90	.319	.413	37	.216	1*	85	-6	—	-0.5
1926	Was A	2	2	.500	7	3	0	0	17	22	15	1	1	15	6	4.76	81	.344	.475	3	.333	0	58	-4	—	-0.7
1928	Bos N	0	1	.000	3	1	0	0	6.2	14	8	0	0	2	0	5.40	72	.452	.485	1-0-1	.000	-0	65	-2	—	-0.3
Total	5	6	15	.286	41	17	5	0	141	172	104	4	11	83	48	5.17	77	.319	.420	48-0-1	.208	1	76	-21	—	-2.9

PALMQUIST, ED Edwin Lee; B6.10.1933 Los Angeles CA; BR/TR/6´3˝/(190–195); d6.10

YEAR	TM LG	W	L	PCT	G	GS	CG-SHO	SV-BS	IP	H	R	HR	HB	BB-IB	SO	ERA	AERA	OAV	OOB	AB-HR-SH	AVG	PB	SUP	APR	DL	PW
1960	LA N	0	1	.000	22	0	0	0	39	34	16	6	1	16-5	23	2.54	156	.243	.317	7	.000	-1	—	4	0	0.1
1961	LA N	0	1	.000	5	0	0	1	8.2	10	8	0	2	7-0	5	6.23	70	.333	.463	0	ø	0	—	-2	0	-0.3
	Min A	1	1	.500	9	2	0	0	21	33	23	7	3	13-3	13	9.43	45	.359	.450	3-0-2	.000	-0	94	-11	0	-0.9
Total	2	1	3	.250	36	2	0	1	68.2	77	47	13	6	36-8	41	5.11	80	.294	.383	10-0-2	.000	-1	94	-9	0	-1.1

PANIAGUA, JOSE Jose Luis (Sanchez); B8.20.1973 San Jose de Ocoa, D.R.; BR/TR/6´2˝/(185–195); d4.4

YEAR	TM LG	W	L	PCT	G	GS	CG-SHO	SV-BS	IP	H	R	HR	HB	BB-IB	SO	ERA	AERA	OAV	OOB	AB-HR-SH	AVG	PB	SUP	APR	DL	PW
1996	Mon N	2	4	.333	13	11	0	0-0	51	55	24	7	3	23-0	27	3.53	123	.282	.365	11-0-1	.000	-1	81	4	21	0.3
1997	Mon N	1	2	.333	9	3	0	0-0	18	29	24	2	4	16-1	8	12.00	35	.372	.495	5	.000	-1	147	-15	0	-2.0
1998	Sea A	2	0	1.000	18	0	0	1-1	22	15	5	3	3	5-0	16	2.05	229	.200	.277	0	ø	0	—	7	0	0.6
1999	Sea A	6	11	.353	59	0	0	3-9	77.2	75	37	5	7	52-4	74	4.06	118	.264	.387	0	ø	0	—	7	0	1.3
2000	†Sea A	3	0	1.000	69	0	0	5-3	80.1	68	31	6	7	38-3	71	3.47	139	.234	.331	1	.000	-0	—	13	0	0.6
2001	†Sea A	4	3	.571	60	0	0	3-1	66	59	35	7	4	38-2	46	4.36	98	.233	.341	1	.000	-0	—	-1	0	-0.2
2002	Det A	0	1	.000	41	0	0	1-1	41.2	50	30	10	3	15-1	34	5.83	75	.294	.356	0	ø	0	—	-7	0	-0.3
2003	Chi A	0	0	ø	1	0	0	0-0	0.1	3	4	0	0	1-0	0	108.00	4	.750	.800	0	ø	0	—	-4	0	-0.2
Total	8	18	21	.462	270	14	0	13-15	357	354	190	40	31	188-11	276	4.49	101	.262	.362	18-0-1	.000	-1	92	4	21	0.1

PANTHER, JIM James Edward; B3.1.1945 Burlington IA; BR/TR/6´1˝/190; [OakA67*S5/92]; d4.5; Col Southern Illinois

YEAR	TM LG	W	L	PCT	G	GS	CG-SHO	SV-BS	IP	H	R	HR	HB	BB-IB	SO	ERA	AERA	OAV	OOB	AB-HR-SH	AVG	PB	SUP	APR	DL	PW
1971	Oak A	0	1	.000	4	0	0	0-0	5.2	10	9	1	0	5-2	4	11.12	30	.385	.484	1	.000	-0	—	-6	0	-0.9
1972	Tex A	5	9	.357	58	4	0	0-1	93.2	101	55	8	5	46-8	44	4.13	74	.277	.365	8-0-3	.125	0	36	-14	0	-2.0
1973	Atl N	2	3	.400	23	0	0	0-2	30.2	45	26	3	0	9-1	8	7.63	52	.363	.391	0	ø	0	—	-10	0	-1.6
Total	3	7	13	.350	85	4	0	0-3	130	156	90	12	5	60-11	56	5.26	62	.303	.377	9-0-3	.111	-0	36	-30	0	-4.5

PAPA, JOHN John Paul; B12.5.1940 Bridgeport CT; BR/TR/5´11˝/(182–190); d4.11; Col Bridgeport

YEAR	TM LG	W	L	PCT	G	GS	CG-SHO	SV-BS	IP	H	R	HR	HB	BB-IB	SO	ERA	AERA	OAV	OOB	AB-HR-SH	AVG	PB	SUP	APR	DL	PW
1961	Bal A	0	0	ø	2	0	0	0	1	2	2	1	0	3-0	3	18.00	21	.400	.625	0	ø	0	—	-2	0	-0.1
1962	Bal A	0	0	ø	1	0	0	0	1	3	3	0	0	1-0	0	27.00	14	.600	.571	0	ø	0	—	-3	0	-0.1
Total	2	0	0	ø	3	0	0	0	2	5	5	1	0	4-0	3	22.50	17	.500	.600	0	ø	0	—	-5	0	-0.2

PAPAI, AL Alfred Thomas; B5.7.1917 Divernon IL; D9.7.1995 Springfield IL; BR/TR/6´3˝/185; d4.24

YEAR	TM LG	W	L	PCT	G	GS	CG-SHO	SV-BS	IP	H	R	HR	HB	BB-IB	SO	ERA	AERA	OAV	OOB	AB-HR-SH	AVG	PB	SUP	APR	DL	PW
1948	StL N	0	1	.000	10	0	0	0	16	14	10	3	0	7	8	5.06	81	.241	.323	2	.000	-0*	—	-2	0	-0.1
1949	StL A	4	11	.267	42	15	6	2	142.1	175	103	8	1	81	31	5.06	90	.298	.384	38-0-1	.079	-2	84	-11	0	-1.1
1950	Bos A	4	2	.667	16	3	2	2	50.2	61	41	5	0	28	19	6.75	73	.293	.377	17-0-1	.176	-0	68	-10	0	-1.0
	StL N	1	0	1.000	13	0	0	0	19	21	12	0	0	14	7	5.21	82	.300	.417	3	.000	-0	—	-2	0	-0.1
1955	Chi A	0	0	ø	7	0	0	0	11.2	10	5	1	0	8-2	5	3.86	102	.244	.360	2	.000	-0	—	0	0	0.0
Total	4	9	14	.391	88	18	8	4	239.2	281	171	17	1	138-2	70	5.37	84	.291	.380	62-0-2	.097	-3	82	-25	0	-2.3

PAPE, LARRY Laurence Albert; B7.21.1883 Norwood OH; D7.21.1918 Swissvale PA; BR/TR/5´11˝/175; d7.6

YEAR	TM LG	W	L	PCT	G	GS	CG-SHO	SV-BS	IP	H	R	HR	HB	BB-IB	SO	ERA	AERA	OAV	OOB	AB-HR-SH	AVG	PB	SUP	APR	DL	PW
1909	Bos A	2	0	1.000	11	3	2-1	2	57.1	46	17	0	5	12	18	2.04	123	.221	.280	21	.143	-1	103	3	—	0.0
1911	Bos A	10	8	.556	27	19	10-1	0	176.1	167	68	3	4	63	49	2.45	134	.264	.335	64-0-3	.203	-1	74	19	—	1.8
1912	Bos A	1	1	.500	13	2	1	1	48.2	74	36	0	2	16	17	4.99	68	.366	.418	17	.235	1	98	-9	—	-0.3
Total	3	13	9	.591	51	24	13-2	3	282.1	287	121	3	11	91	84	2.81	112	.275	.340	102-0-3	.196	-1	80	13	—	1.5

PAPELBON, JONATHAN Jonathan Robert; B11.23.1980 Baton Rouge LA; BR/TR/6´4˝/230; [BosA03 4/114]; d7.31; Col Mississippi St.

YEAR	TM LG	W	L	PCT	G	GS	CG-SHO	SV-BS	IP	H	R	HR	HB	BB-IB	SO	ERA	AERA	OAV	OOB	AB-HR-SH	AVG	PB	SUP	APR	DL	PW
2005	†Bos A	3	1	.750	17	3	0	0-1	34	33	11	4	3	17-2	34	2.65	172	.260	.361	0	ø	0	129	7	0	0.7
2006	Bos A☆	4	2	.667	59	0	0	35-6	68.1	40	8	3	1	13-2	75	0.92	507	.167	.211	0	ø	0	—	**28**	0	4.6
Total	2	7	3	.700	76	3	0	35-7	102.1	73	19	7	4	30-4	109	1.50	310	.199	.266	0	ø	0	129	35	0	5.3

PAPISH, FRANK Frank Richard "Pap"; B10.21.1917 Pueblo CO; D8.30.1965 Pueblo CO; BR/TL/6´2˝/192; d5.8

YEAR	TM LG	W	L	PCT	G	GS	CG-SHO	SV-BS	IP	H	R	HR	HB	BB-IB	SO	ERA	AERA	OAV	OOB	AB-HR-SH	AVG	PB	SUP	APR	DL	PW
1945	Chi A	4	4	.500	19	5	3	1	84.1	75	36	3	0	40	45	3.74	89	.241	.328	26-0-3	.231	1	123	-2	0	0.0
1946	Chi A	7	5	.583	31	15	6-2	0	138	122	52	7	1	63	66	2.74	125	.243	.328	43-0-3	.186	-0	107	11	0	0.9
1947	Chi A	12	12	.500	38	26	6-1	3	199	185	82	6	2	98	79	3.26	112	.245	.333	58-0-6	.086	-5	78	10	0	0.6
1948	Chi A	2	8	.200	32	14	2	4	95.1	97	65	7	3	75	41	5.00	85	.265	.394	27-0-1	.185	-1	109	-11	0	-1.1
1949	Cle A	1	0	1.000	25	3	1	1	62	54	24	2	0	39	23	3.19	125	.240	.352	8-0-3	.125	0	120	6	0	0.3
1950	Pit N	0	0	ø	4	1	0	0	2.1	8	7	1	0	4	1	27.00	16	.533	.632	0	ø	0	121	-5	0	-0.2
Total	6	26	29	.473	149	64	18-3	9	581	541	266	26	6	319	255	3.58	103	.249	.346	162-0-16	.154	-5	99	9	0	0.5

PAPPALAU, JOHN John Joseph; B4.3.1875 Albany NY; D5.12.1944 Albany NY; BR/TR/6´0˝/175; d6.9; Col Holy Cross

YEAR	TM LG	W	L	PCT	G	GS	CG-SHO	SV-BS	IP	H	R	HR	HB	BB-IB	SO	ERA	AERA	OAV	OOB	AB-HR-SH	AVG	PB	SUP	APR	DL	PW
1897	Cle N	0	1	.000	2	1	1	0	12	22	16	0	2	6	3	10.50	43	.393	.469	5	.000	-0	95	-7	—	-0.4

PAPPAS, MILT Milton Stephen "Gimpy" (b Miltiades Stergios Pappastediodis); B5.11.1939 Detroit MI; BR/TR/6´3˝/(190–214); d8.10

YEAR	TM LG	W	L	PCT	G	GS	CG-SHO	SV-BS	IP	H	R	HR	HB	BB-IB	SO	ERA	AERA	OAV	OOB	AB-HR-SH	AVG	PB	SUP	APR	DL	PW
1957	Bal A	0	0	ø	4	0	0	0	9	6	1	0	0	3-0	3	1.00	359	.200	.273	1	.000	-0	—	3	17	0.1
1958	Bal A	10	10	.500	31	21	3	0	135.1	135	67	8	2	48-1	72	4.06	89	.262	.326	42-1-3	.143	-0*	90	-7	0	-0.9
1959	Bal A	15	9	.625	33	27	15-4	3	209.1	175	82	8	4	75-2	120	3.27	116	.226	.297	79-0-1	.139	-3	98	14	0	1.1
1960	Bal A	15	11	.577	30	27	11-3	0	205.2	184	81	15	6	83-4	126	3.37	113	.243	.320	70-1-5	.043	-5	92	13	0	1.0
1961	Bal A	13	9	.591	26	23	11-4	1	177.2	134	67	16	7	78-5	89	3.04	127	.208	.300	66-3-3	.136	1	92	17	0	2.1
1962	Bal A★	12	10	.545	35	32	9-1	0	205.1	200	105	31	2	75-3	130	4.03	92	.257	.322	69-4-3	.087	-0	97	-8	0	-0.7
1963	Bal A	16	9	.640	34	32	11-4	0	216.2	186	80	21	5	69-6	120	3.03	115	.233	.296	71-2-7	.127	-0*	111	12	0	1.4
1964	Bal A	16	7	.696	37	36	13-7	0	251.2	225	89	21	7	48-10	157	2.97	120	.239	.280	93-0-2	.129	-2	120	18	0	1.4
1965	Bal A★	13	9	.591	34	34	9-3	0	221.1	192	81	22	3	52-3	127	2.60	133	.233	.279	70-0-7	.071	-3	89	19	0	1.3
1966	Cin N	12	11	.522	33	32	6-2	0	209.2	224	106	23	3	39-4	133	4.29	91	.275	.308	75-1-3	.107	-2*	101	-8	0	-1.0
1967	Cin N	16	13	.552	34	32	5-3	0	217.2	218	88	19	5	38-5	129	3.35	112	.259	.293	72-1-2	.097	-2	95	10	0	1.1
1968	Cin N	2	5	.286	15	11	0	0	62.2	70	41	9	2	10-3	43	5.60	56	.275	.306	16-0-4	.063	-1*	105	-15	0	-1.7
	Atl N	10	8	.556	22	19	3-1	0	121.1	111	36	8	3	22-6	75	2.37	126	.246	.283	37-1-2	.162	2	76	9	0	1.6
	Year	12	13	.480	37	30	3-1	0	184	181	77	17	5	32-9	118	3.47	88	.256	.291	53-1-6	.132	1	87	-7	0	-0.1
1969	†Atl N	6	10	.375	26	24	1	0-0	144	149	66	14	4	44-9	72	3.63	100	.267	.323	45-2-1	.156	3	89	-1	0	0.2
1970	Atl N	2	2	.500	11	3	1	0-0	35.2	44	25	6	2	7-1	25	6.06	71	.293	.331	10	.000	-1	84	-6	0	-0.7
	Chi N	10	8	.556	21	20	6-2	0-0	144.2	135	53	14	0	36-9	80	2.68	168	.248	.292	50-2-1	.240	4	94	25	0	3.4
	Year	12	10	.545	32	23	7-2	0-0	180.1	179	78	20	2	43-10	105	3.34	134	.258	.300	60-2-1	.200	3	93	19	0	2.7
1971	Chi N	17	14	.548	35	35	14-5	0-0	261.1	279	109	25	5	62-6	99	3.51	112	.274	.317	91-0-2	.154	-1	91	13	0	1.3
1972	Chi N	17	7	.708	29	28	10-3	0-0	195	187	72	18	8	29-3	80	2.77	138	.251	.286	68-1-4	.191	1	112	19	0	2.6
1973	Chi N	7	12	.368	30	29	1-1	0-0	162	192	82	20	4	40-9	48	4.28	92	.299	.342	48-1-2	.063	-2	79	-4	0	-0.7
Total	17	209	164	.560	520	465	129-43	4-0	3186	3046	1331	298	72	858-89	1728	3.40	110	.252	.304	1073-20-52	.123	-14	96	123	17	12.9

THE PITCHER REGISTER

YEAR	TM LG	W	L	PCT	G	GS	CG-SHO	SV-BS	IP	H	R	HR	HB	BB-IB	SO	ERA	AERA	OAV	OOB	AB-HR-SH	AVG	PB	SUP	APR	DL	PW
PARK, CHAN HO	Chan Ho; B6.30.1973 Kongju, South Korea; BR/TR/6´2˝/(185–210); d4.8																									
1994	LA N	0	0	ø	2	0	0	0-0	4	5	5	1	1	5-0	6	11.25	35	.294	.478	0	ø	0	—	-3	0	-0.2
1995	LA N	0	0	ø	2	1	0	0-0	4	2	2	1	0	2-0	7	4.50	86	.143	.250	1	.000	-0	93	0	0	0.0
1996	LA N	5	5	.500	48	10	0	0-0	108.2	82	48	7	4	71-3	119	3.64	107	.209	.335	19-0-3	.053	-1	90	5	0	0.4
1997	LA N	14	8	.636	32	29	2	0-0	192	149	80	24	8	70-1	166	3.38	116	.213	.290	51-0-11	.176	3	111	12	0	1.5
1998	LA N	15	9	.625	34	34	2	0-0	220.2	199	101	16	11	97-1	191	3.71	109	.244	.328	72-0-6	.194	2	115	8	0	1.1
1999	LA N	13	11	.542	33	33	0	0-0	194.1	208	120	31	14	100-4	174	5.23	83	.276	.369	59-0-6	.153	0	112	-18	0	-1.7
2000	LA N	18	10	.643	34	34	3-1	0-0	226	173	92	21	12	124-4	217	3.27	136	.214	.325	70-2-6	.214	5	97	30	0	4.1
2001	LA N★	15	11	.577	36	**35**	2-1	0-0	234	183	98	23	20	91-1	218	3.50	118	.216	.305	69-0-7	.145	1	96	18	0	2.0
2002	Tex A	9	8	.529	25	25	0	0-0	145.2	154	95	20	17	78-2	121	5.75	83	.273	.376	4	.000	-0	124	-13	56	-1.3
2003	Tex A	1	3	.250	7	7	0	0-0	29.2	34	26	5	6	25-0	16	7.58	66	.306	.448	0	ø	0	85	-8	153	-0.8
2004	Tex A	4	7	.364	16	16	0	0-0	95.2	105	63	22	13	33-0	63	5.46	90	.281	.356	0	ø	0	87	-5	98	-0.5
2005	Tex A	8	5	.615	20	20	0	0-0	109.2	130	70	8	6	54-1	80	5.66	80	.299	.382	5	.400	1	130	-11	0	-0.9
	SD N	4	3	.571	10	9	0	0-0	45.2	50	33	3	4	26-0	33	5.91	66	.278	.379	14-0-4	.214	0	150	-11	0	-1.4
2006	†SD N	7	7	.500	24	21	1-1	0-0	136.2	146	81	20	10	44-7	96	4.81	86	.271	.336	41-0-7	.268	3*	115	-12	48	-0.8
Total	13	113	87	.565	323	274	10-3	0-0	1746.2	1620	914	202	126	820-24	1507	4.37	98	.247	.340	405-2-50	.183	14	110	-8	355	1.5
PARK, JIM	James; B11.10.1892 Richmond KY; D12.17.1970 Lexington KY; BR/TR/6´2˝/175; d9.7; Col Kentucky																									
1915	StL A	2	0	1.000	3	3	1	0	22.2	18	8	1	0	9	5	1.19	240	.214	.290	10	.400	1	204	3	—	0.4
1916	StL A	1	4	.200	26	6	1	0	79	69	28	2	1	25	26	2.62	105	.244	.307	20	.100	-2	55	2	—	-0.1
1917	StL A	1	1	.500	13	0	0	0	20.1	27	20	1	0	12	9	6.64	39	.333	.419	2	.000	-0	—	-9	—	-0.9
Total	3	4	5	.444	42	9	2	0	122	114	56	4	1	46	40	3.02	91	.254	.325	32	.188	-0	109	-4	—	-0.6
PARKER, CHRISTIAN	Christian Michael; B7.3.1975 Albuquerque NM; BR/TR/6´1˝/200; [MonN96 4/100]; d4.6; Col Notre Dame; [DL 2002 NY A 183]																									
2001	NY A	0	1	.000	1	1	0	0-0	3	8	7	2	0	1-0	1	21.00	21	.471	.500	0	ø	0	83	-5	184	-0.7
PARKER, DOC	Harley Park; B6.14.1872 Theresa NY; D3.3.1941 Chicago IL; BR/TR/6´2˝/200; d7.11; b–Jay																									
1893	Chi N	0	0	ø	1	0	0	1	2	5	3	0	0	1	0	13.50	34	.455	.500	1	.000	-0	—	-2	—	-0.1
1895	Chi N	4	2	.667	7	6	5-1	0	51.1	65	30	1	3	9	9	3.68	138	.304	.341	22	.318	1	98	8	—	0.7
1896	Chi N	1	5	.167	9	7	7	0	73	100	71	3	3	27	15	6.16	74	.323	.382	36	.278	0*	74	-13	—	-0.8
1901	Cin N	0	1	.000	1	1	1	0	8	26	21	1	0	2	0	15.75	20	.531	.549	3	.000	-0	66	-12	—	-0.9
Total	4	5	8	.385	18	14	13-1	1	134.1	196	125	5	6	39	24	5.90	79	.336	.383	62	.274	0	85	-19	—	-1.1
PARKER, HARRY	Harry William; B9.14.1947 Highland IL; BR/TR/6´3˝/190; [StLN65 4/73]; d8.8																									
1970	StL N	1	1	.500	7	4	0	0-0	22.1	24	13	0	0	15-0	9	3.22	129	.276	.382	8	.250	0	97	0	0	0.1
1971	StL N	0	0	ø	4	0	0	0-0	5	6	4	2	0	2-0	2	7.20	50	.286	.348	0	ø	0	—	-2	0	-0.1
1973	†NY N	8	4	.667	38	9	0	5-1	96.2	79	40	7	3	36-3	63	3.35	109	.217	.291	23-0-5	.174	-0	105	3	0	0.3
1974	NY N	4	12	.250	40	16	1	4-3	131	145	64	10	3	46-5	58	3.92	92	.281	.342	36-0-3	.000	-4	56	-4	0	-0.9
1975	NY N	2	3	.400	18	1	0	2-0	34.2	37	17	2	0	19-5	22	4.41	80	.272	.361	2-0-1	.000	1	100	-3	25	-0.3
	StL N	0	1	.000	14	0	0	1-0	18.2	21	13	3	0	10-2	13	6.27	61	.288	.365	1-0-1	.000	0	—	-4	0	-0.2
	Year	2	4	.333	32	1	0	3-0	53.1	58	30	5	0	29-7	35	5.06	71	.278	.363	3-0-2	.000	1	97	-6	0	-0.5
1976	Cle A	0	0	ø	3	0	0	0-0	7	3	0	0	0	0-0	5	0.00	ø	.136	.136	0	ø	0	—	3	0	0.2
Total	6	15	21	.417	124	30	1	12-4	315.1	315	151	24	6	128-15	172	3.85	95	.258	.330	70-0-10	.086	-3	79	-7	25	-0.9
PARKER, CLAY	James Clayton; B12.19.1962 Columbia LA; BR/TR/6´1˝/(175–185); [SeaA85 15/373]; d9.14; Col Louisiana St.																									
1987	Sea A	0	0	ø	3	1	0	0-0	7.2	15	10	2	1	4-0	8	10.57	45	.405	.465	0	ø	0	96	-5	0	-0.2
1989	NY A	4	5	.444	22	17	2	0-0	120	123	53	12	2	31-3	53	3.68	106	.264	.311	0	ø	0	93	4	21	0.3
1990	NY A	1	1	.500	5	2	0	0-0	22	19	11	5	0	7-1	20	4.50	89	.229	.286	0	ø	0	125	-1	0	-0.1
	Det A	2	2	.500	24	1	0	0-0	51	45	18	6	1	25-5	20	3.18	125	.242	.332	0	ø	0	69	5	0	0.4
	Year	3	3	.500	29	3	0	0-0	73	64	29	11	1	32-6	40	3.58	111	.238	.318	0	ø	0	107	5	0	0.3
1992	Sea A	0	2	.000	8	6	0	0-0	33.1	47	28	6	2	11-0	20	7.56	53	.338	.390	0	ø	0	118	-12	118	-0.6
Total	4	7	10	.412	62	27	2	0-0	234	249	120	31	6	78-9	121	4.42	90	.273	.332	0	ø	0	100	-9	139	-0.2
PARKER, JAY	Jay; B7.8.1874 Theresa NY; D6.8.1935 Hartford MI; BL/TR/5´11˝/185; d9.27; b–Harley																									
1899	Pit N	0	0	ø	1	1	0	0	0	0	2	0	1	2	0	(2)	ø	ø	1.000	0	ø	0	132	-2	—	-0.1
PARKER, ROY	Roy William; B2.29.1896 Union MO; D5.17.1954 Tulsa OK; BR/TR/6´3˝/200; d9.10																									
1919	StL N	0	0	ø	2	0	0	0	2	6	7	0	1	1	0	31.50	9	.333	.400	0	ø	0	—	-6	—	-0.3
PARKS, SLICKER	Vernon Henry; B11.10.1895 Dallas (now Fowler) MI; D2.21.1978 Royal Oak MI; BR/TR/5´10˝/158; d7.11; Col Michigan																									
1921	Det A	3	2	.600	10	1	0	0	25.1	33	17	2	1	16	10	5.68	75	.306	.400	9-0-1	.111	-1	98	-3	—	-0.5
PARKS, BILL	William Robert; B6.4.1849 Easton PA; D10.10.1911 Easton PA; BR/TR/5´8˝/150; d4.26; M1; ▲																									
1875	Was NA	4	8	.333	14	11	9	0	106.2	144	120	3	—	5	3	3.29	72	.280	.287	111	.180	-3*	66	-9	—	-1.0
	Phi NA	0	0	ø	2	0	0	0	5.1	13	11	0	—	1	0	8.44	27	.419	.438	6	.167	-0	—	-3	—	-0.2
	Year	4	8	.333	16	11	9	0	112	157	131	3	—	6	3	3.54	67	.288	.295	117	.179	-3	66	-17	—	-1.2
PARMELEE, ROY	Le Roy Earl "Tarzan"; B4.25.1907 Lambertville MI; D8.31.1981 Monroe MI; BR/TR/6´1˝/190; d9.28; Col Eastern Michigan																									
1929	NY N	1	0	1.000	2	1	0	0	7	13	7	1	1	3	1	9.00	51	.481	.548	2	.500	0	171	-3	—	-0.3
1930	NY N	0	1	.000	11	1	0	0	21	18	26	3	0	26	19	9.43	50	.228	.419	4	.250	1	147	-12	—	-0.5
1931	NY N	2	2	.500	13	5	4	0	58.2	47	25	1	3	33	30	3.68	100	.223	.336	20-0-1	.200	-0	74	2	—	0.1
1932	NY N	0	3	.000	8	3	0	0	25.1	25	18	0	2	14	23	3.91	95	.250	.353	5	.400	1	60	-3	—	-0.2
1933	NY N	13	8	.619	32	32	14-3	0	218.1	191	94	9	14	77	132	3.17	101	.232	.309	81-1-1	.235	4*	122	1	—	0.5
1934	NY N	10	6	.625	22	21	7-2	0	152.2	134	59	6	6	60	83	3.42	113	**.238**	.318	55-2-2	.200	2	96	13	—	1.4
1935	NY N	14	10	.583	34	31	13	0	226	214	117	20	9	97	79	4.22	91	.249	.332	86	.209	3	115	-8	—	-0.4
1936	StL N	11	11	.500	37	28	9	2	221	226	125	13	10	107	79	4.56	86	.270	.360	76-0-2	.197	-0	101	-14	—	-1.3
1937	Chi N	7	8	.467	33	18	8	0	145.2	165	93	13	7	79	55	5.13	78	.286	.379	52-2-1	.173	0*	153	-18	—	-1.6
1939	Phi A	1	6	.143	14	5	0	1	44.2	42	41	2	3	35	13	6.45	73	.235	.369	15	.133	-1*	82	-10	—	-1.3
Total	10	59	55	.518	206	145	55-5	3	1120.1	1075	605	68	55	531	514	4.27	89	.253	.343	396-5-7	.207	9	112	-52	—	-3.6
PARNELL, MEL	Melvin Lloyd "Dusty"; B6.13.1922 New Orleans LA; BL/TL/6´0˝/180; d4.20; [DL 1957 Bos A 86]																									
1947	Bos A	2	3	.400	15	5	1	0	50.2	60	41	1	1	27	23	6.39	61	.296	.381	18	.056	-2	105	-14	0	-1.4
1948	Bos A	15	8	.652	35	27	16-1	0	212	205	87	7	4	90	77	3.14	140	.252	.330	80-0-2	.162	-4	106	26	0	2.2
1949	Bos A★	**25**	7	.781	39	33	**27**-4	2	**295.1**	258	102	8	5	134	122	2.77	157	.237	.324	114-0-10	.254	2	123	**49**	0	5.2
1950	Bos A	18	10	.643	40	31	21-2	3	249	244	116	17	7	106	93	3.61	136	.259	.338	98-0-3	.194	-1	119	30	0	3.1
1951	Bos A★	18	11	.621	36	29	11-3	2	221	229	99	11	0	77	77	3.26	137	.272	.333	81-0-4	.309	4*	99	24	0	**3.3**
1952	Bos A	12	12	.500	33	29	15-3	2	214	207	94	13	5	89	107	3.62	109	.255	.332	84-1-0	.095	-3*	95	9	0	0.6
1953	Bos A	21	8	.724	38	34	12-5	0	241	217	98	15	4	116	136	3.06	137	.239	.328	94-0-6	.223	1	93	28	0	3.2
1954	Bos A	3	7	.300	19	15	4-1	0	92.1	104	45	7	1	35	38	3.70	111	.287	.349	34-0-1	.088	-2	93	3	47	0.2
1955	Bos A	2	3	.400	13	9	0	1	46	62	44	12	1	25-1	18	7.83	55	.318	.395	19	.316	1*	140	-16	0	-1.4
1956	Bos A	7	6	.538	21	20	6-1	0	131.1	129	71	13	0	59-2	41	3.77	123	.256	.333	46-0-4	.152	-2	95	8	30	0.5
Total	10	123	75	.621	289	232	113-20	10	1752.2	1715	797	104	28	758-3	732	3.50	125	.257	.335	668-1-30	.198	-7	106	147	163	15.5
PARNHAM, RUBE	James Arthur; B2.1.1894 Heidelberg PA; D11.25.1963 McKeesport PA; BR/TR/6´3˝/185; d9.20																									
1916	Phi A	2	1	.667	4	3	2	0	24.2	27	14	0	0	13	8	4.01	71	.300	.388	11	.273	1	150	-3	—	-0.2
1917	Phi A	0	1	.000	2	2	0	0	11	12	6	1	0	9	4	4.09	67	.316	.447	3	.000	-0	105	-1	—	-0.2
Total	2	2	2	.500	6	5	2	0	35.2	39	20	1	0	22	12	4.04	70	.305	.407	14	.214	0	132	-4	—	-0.4
PARONTO, CHAD	Chad Michael; B7.28.1975 Woodsville NH; BR/TR/6´5˝/(250–255); [BalA96 8/231]; d4.18; Col Massachusetts																									
2001	Bal A	1	3	.250	24	0	0	0-1	27	33	24	5	1	11-0	16	5.00	86	.289	.354	0	ø	0	—	-6	0	-0.7
2002	Cle A	0	2	.000	29	0	0	0-0	35.2	34	19	3	2	11-1	23	4.04	110	.248	.305	0	ø	0	—	1	63	0.0
2003	Cle A	0	2	.000	6	0	0	0-0	6.2	7	8	1	0	3-0	6	9.45	47	.292	.357	0	ø	0	—	-4	0	-0.7
2006	Atl N	2	3	.400	65	0	0	0-2	56.2	53	23	5	3	19-3	41	3.18	143	.252	.322	1	.000	-0	—	8	0	0.6
Total	4	3	10	.231	124	0	0	0-3	126	127	74	14	6	44-4	86	4.14	107	.262	.327	1	.000	-0	—	-1	63	-0.8

YEAR	TM LG	W	L	PCT	G	GS	CG-SHO	SV-BS	IP	H	R	HR	HB	BB-IB	SO	ERA	AERA	OAV	OOB	AB-HR-SH	AVG	PB	SUP	APR	DL	PW
PARQUE, JIM Jim Vo; B2.8.1975 Norwalk CA; BL/TL/5´11˝/(165–170); [ChiA97 1/46]; d5.26; Col UCLA																										
1998	Chi A	7	5	.583	21	21	0	0-0	113	135	72	14	6	49-0	77	5.10	90	.299	.375	1-0-2	.000	-0	107	-7	0	-0.6
1999	Chi A	9	15	.375	31	30	1	0-0	173.2	210	111	23	10	79-2	111	5.13	96	.299	.374	5-0-1	.400	1	89	-4	0	-0.5
2000	†Chi A	13	6	.684	33	32	0	0-0	187	208	105	21	11	71-1	111	4.28	118	.283	.352	4	.000	-0	126	13	0	1.1
2001	Chi A	0	3	.000	5	5	1	0-0	28	36	26	7	2	10-1	15	8.04	58	.308	.369	0	ø	0	107	-9	164	-0.8
2002	Chi A	1	4	.200	8	4	0	0-0	25.1	34	29	11	1	16-0	13	9.95	45	.318	.405	0	ø	0	67	-14	0	-2.1
2003	TB A	1	1	.500	5	5	0	0-0	17.1	27	23	2	1	16-0	8	11.94	38	.351	.468	0	ø	0	125	-13	30	-1.2
Total	6	31	34	.477	103	97	2	0-0	544.1	650	366	78	31	241-4	335	5.42	90	.297	.372	10-0-3	.200	0	107	-34	194	-4.1
PARRA, JOSE Jose Miguel; B11.28.1972 Jacagua, D.R.; BR/TR/5´11˝/(165–175); d5.7																										
1995	LA N	0	0	ø	8	0	0	0-0	10.1	10	8	2	1	6-1	7	4.35	89	.256	.362	0-0-2	ø	0	—	-2	0	-0.1
	Min A	1	5	.167	12	12	0	0-0	61.2	83	59	11	2	22-0	29	7.59	63	.313	.366	0	ø	0	87	-20	0	-1.5
1996	Min A	5	5	.500	27	5	0	0-1	70	88	48	15	3	27-0	50	6.04	85	.308	.370	0	ø	0	79	-6	0	-0.7
2000	Pit N	0	1	.000	6	2	0	0-0	11.2	17	9	3	1	7-0	9	6.94	67	.354	.446	0	ø	1	59	-3	0	-0.1
2002	Ari N	0	1	.000	16	0	0	0-0	14	13	5	0	1	11-2	8	3.21	140	.255	.397	0	ø	0	—	2	0	0.1
2004	NY N	1	0	1.000	13	0	0	0-0	14	14	6	2	0	6-1	14	3.21	134	.255	.328	0	ø	0	—	1	78	0.1
Total	5	7	12	.368	82	19	0	0-1	181.2	225	135	33	8	79-4	117	6.09	79	.302	.372	0-0-2	ø	1	83	-28	78	-2.2
PARRETT, JEFF Jeffrey Dale; B8.26.1961 Indianapolis IN; BR/TR/6´3˝/(185–205); [MilA83 9/236]; d4.11; Col Kentucky																										
1986	Mon N	0	1	.000	12	0	0	0-0	20.1	19	11	3	0	13-0	21	4.87	77	.247	.352	2	.500	0	—	-2	0	-0.1
1987	Mon N	7	6	.538	45	0	0	6-5	62	53	33	8	0	30-4	56	4.21	101	.229	.317	5	.000	-1	—	0	0	0.0
1988	Mon N	12	4	.750	61	0	0	6-4	91.2	66	29	8	1	45-9	62	2.65	137	.214	.311	0	ø	0	—	11	29	1.9
1989	Phi N	12	6	.667	72	0	0	6-6	105.2	90	43	6	0	44-13	98	2.98	120	.232	.307	5	.000	-1	—	6	23	0.9
1990	Phi N	4	9	.308	47	5	0	1-3	81.2	92	51	10	1	36-8	69	5.18	74	.293	.366	10-0-2	.000	-1	94	-11	0	-1.8
	Atl N	1	1	.500	20	0	0	1-3	27	27	11	1	1	19-2	17	3.00	134	.281	.392	1	1.000	0	—	3	0	0.2
	Year	5	10	.333	67	5	0	2-6	108.2	119	62	11	2	55-10	86	4.64	84	.290	.373	11-0-2	.091	-1	93	-8	0	-1.6
1991	Atl N	1	2	.333	18	0	0	1-0	21.1	31	18	2	0	12-2	14	6.33	61	.326	.402	0	ø	0	—	-6	0	-0.7
1992	†Oak A	9	1	.900	66	0	0	0-1	98.1	81	35	7	2	42-3	78	3.02	125	.226	.308	0	ø	0	—	10	0	0.9
1993	Col N	3	3	.500	40	6	0	1-3	73.2	78	47	6	2	45-9	66	5.38	89	.274	.371	11	.091	-1	119	-3	67	-0.3
1995	StL N	4	7	.364	59	0	0	0-2	76.2	71	33	8	1	28-5	71	3.64	118	.243	.310	2	.500	0	—	6	0	0.8
1996	StL N	2	2	.500	33	0	0	0-2	42.1	40	20	2	1	20-2	42	4.25	100	.245	.330	2	.000	0	—	1	0	0.1
	Phi N	1	1	.500	18	0	0	0-0	24	24	5	0	0	11-2	22	1.88	230	.270	.347	0	ø	0	—	7	0	0.5
	Year	3	3	.500	51	0	0	0-2	66.1	64	25	2	1	31-4	64	3.39	126	.254	.336	2	.000	0	—	8	0	0.6
Total	10	56	43	.566	491	11	0	22-29	724.2	672	336	61	9	345-59	616	3.80	105	.249	.333	38-0-2	.105	-1	119	22	119	2.4
PARRIS, STEVE Steven Michael; B12.17.1967 Joliet IL; BR/TR/6´0˝/(190–195); [PhiN89 5/118]; d6.21; Col St. Francis (IL)																										
1995	Pit N	6	6	.500	15	15	1-1	0-0	82	89	49	12	7	33-1	61	5.38	81	.283	.361	28-0-1	.250	1	84	-7	0	-0.7
1996	Pit N	0	3	.000	8	4	0	0-0	26.1	35	22	4	1	11-0	27	7.18	61	.321	.385	6-0-2	.167	0	103	-7	124	-0.7
1998	Cin N	6	5	.545	18	16	1-1	0-0	99	89	44	9	4	32-3	77	3.73	115	.236	.302	29-0-3	.138	-1	99	6	0	0.6
1999	Cin N	11	4	.733	22	21	2-1	0-0	128.2	124	59	16	6	52-4	86	3.50	134	.260	.338	38-0-5	.158	-1	91	15	37	1.4
2000	Cin N	12	17	.414	33	33	0	0-0	192.2	227	109	30	4	71-5	117	4.81	99	.294	.355	55-0-4	.127	-1*	83	1	0	-0.1
2001	Tor A	4	6	.400	19	19	1	0-0	105.2	126	60	18	2	41-4	49	4.60	100	.299	.362	1-0-1	.000	-0	89	-1	76	-0.1
2002	Tor A	5	5	.500	14	14	0	0-0	75.1	96	50	13	3	35-5	48	5.97	77	.314	.387	4	.000	-0	107	-9	76	-1.1
2003	TB A	0	3	.000	10	7	0	0-0	43.2	60	32	12	0	13-0	14	6.18	74	.328	.369	1	.000	-0	78	-7	27	-0.5
Total	8	44	49	.473	139	129	5-3	0-0	753.1	846	425	114	27	288-22	479	4.75	96	.286	.353	162-0-16	.154	-2	90	-9	340	-1.2
PARRISH, JOHN John Henry; B11.26.1977 Lancaster PA; BL/TL/5´11˝/(170–200); [BalA96 25/741]; d7.24; [DL 2002 Bal A 183, 2006 Bal A 182]																										
2000	Bal A	2	4	.333	8	8	0	0-0	36.1	40	32	6	1	35-0	28	7.18	65	.288	.425	0	ø	0	102	-11	0	-1.4
2001	Bal A	1	2	.333	16	1	0	0-0	22	22	17	5	3	17-1	20	6.14	70	.256	.396	0	ø	0	107	-5	0	-0.6
2003	Bal A	0	1	.000	14	0	0	0-2	23.2	17	7	2	1	8-2	15	1.90	242	.205	.280	0	ø	0	—	6	0	0.3
2004	Bal A	6	3	.667	56	1	0	1-0	78	68	39	4	3	55-6	71	3.46	135	.238	.360	1	.000	-0	60	8	0	0.8
2005	Bal A	1	0	1.000	14	0	0	0-0	17.1	19	6	1	0	17-1	25	3.12	141	.279	.424	0	ø	0*	—	3	27	0.2
Total	5	10	10	.500	108	10	0	1-2	177.1	166	101	18	8	132-10	159	4.31	107	.251	.376	1	.000	-0	99	1	392	-0.7
PARROTT, MIKE Michael Everett Arch; B12.6.1954 Oxnard CA; BR/TR/6´4˝/(205–210); [BalA73 1/15]; d9.5																										
1977	Bal A	0	0	ø	3	0	0	0-0	4.1	4	1	0	0	2-0	2	2.08	185	.250	.333	0	ø	0	—	1	0	0.0
1978	Sea A	1	5	.167	27	10	0	1-1	82.1	108	59	8	3	32-5	41	5.14	75	.316	.373	0	ø	0	110	-14	59	-1.0
1979	Sea A	14	12	.538	38	30	13-2	0-0	229.1	231	104	17	6	86-16	127	3.77	116	.267	.336	0	ø	0	100	16	0	1.8
1980	Sea A	1	16	.059	27	16	1	3-1	94	136	83	16	1	42-9	53	7.28	57	.348	.411	0	ø	0	64	-31	21	-4.6
1981	Sea A	3	6	.333	24	12	0	1-0	85	102	51	3	1	28-1	43	5.08	76	.299	.350	0	ø	0	98	-10	0	-1.0
Total	5	19	39	.328	119	68	14-2	5-2	495	581	298	44	11	190-31	266	4.87	85	.297	.360	0	ø	0	93	-38	80	-4.8
PARROTT, TOM Thomas William "Tacky Tom"; B4.10.1868 Portland OR; D1.1.1932 Dundee OR; BR/TR/5´10.5˝/170; d6.18; b–Jiggs; ▲																										
1893	Chi N	0	3	.000	4	3	2	0	27	35	30	1	0	17	7	6.67	69	.304	.394	27	.259	-0*	141	-6	—	-0.5
	Cin N	10	7	.588	22	17	11-1	0	154	174	95	1	9	70	33	4.09	117	.276	.357	68-1	.191	-3*	85	12	—	0.8
	Year	10	10	.500	26	20	13-1	0	181	209	125	2	9	87	40	4.48	106	.281	.363	95-1	.211	-3	93	11	—	0.3
1894	Cin N	17	19	.472	41	36	31-1	1	308.2	402	268	19	11	126	61	5.60	99	.311	.377	229-4-1	.323	8*	83	0	—	0.7
1895	Cin N	11	18	.379	41	31	23	**3**	263.1	382	228	8	5	76	57	5.47	91	.334	.378	201-3-6	.343	10*	90	-16	—	-0.5
1896	StL N	1	1	.500	7	2	2	0	42	62	39	4	3	18	8	6.21	70	.339	.407	474-7-14	.291	1*	82	-8	—	-0.3
Total	4	39	48	.448	115	89	69-2	4	795	1055	660	33	28	307	166	5.33	96	.314	.376	999-15-21	.301	17	88	-18	—	0.2
PARSON, JIGGS William Edwin; B12.27.1885 Parker SD; D5.19.1967 Los Angeles CA; BR/TR/6´2˝/180; d5.16; Col Bucknell																										
1910	Bos N	0	2	.000	10	4	0	0	35.1	35	23	2	2	26	7	3.82	87	.278	.409	12	.083	-1	162	-2	—	-0.3
1911	Bos N	0	1	.000	7	0	0	0	25	36	30	2	4	15	7	6.48	59	.375	.478	10	.200	-0	—	-9	—	-0.5
Total	2	0	3	.000	17	4	0	0	60.1	71	53	4	6	41	14	4.92	72	.320	.439	22	.136	-2	162	-11	—	-0.8
PARSONS, CHARLIE Charles James; B7.18.1863 Cherry Flats PA; D3.24.1936 Mansfield PA; BL/TL/5´10˝/160; d5.29																										
1886	Bos N	0	2	.000	2	2	2	0	16	20	13	0	—	4	5	3.94	82	.308	.348	8	.375	1	48	-1	—	-0.1
1887	NY AA	1	1	.500	4	4	4	0	34	51	36	0	1	6	5	4.50	94	.319	.347	15	.200	-1	116	-4	—	-0.2
1890	Cle N	0	1	.000	2	1	0	0	9	12	11	0	4	6	2	6.00	60	.308	.449	4	.750	1	194	-3	—	-0.2
Total	3	1	4	.200	8	7	6	0	59	83	60	0	5	16	12	4.58	84	.314	.365	27	.333	2	109	-8	—	-0.5
PARSONS, TOM Thomas Anthony; B9.13.1939 Lakeville CT; BR/TR/6´7˝/(200–210); d9.5																										
1963	Pit N	0	1	.000	1	1	0	0	4.1	7	6	1	0	2-0	2	8.31	40	.368	.429	2	.000	-0	0	-3	0	-0.5
1964	NY N	1	2	.333	4	2	1	0	19.1	20	9	1	0	6-0	10	4.19	85	.274	.321	7	.000	-1	74	-1	0	-0.2
1965	NY N	1	10	.091	35	11	1-1	1	90.2	108	53	17	0	17-2	58	4.67	76	.290	.321	18-0-1	.056	-1	61	-11	0	-1.3
Total	3	2	13	.133	40	14	2-1	1	114.1	135	68	19	0	25-2	70	4.72	75	.291	.325	27-0-1	.037	-2	58	-15	0	-2.0
PARSONS, BILL William Raymond; B8.17.1948 Riverside CA; BR/TR/6´6˝/195; d4.13; Col Utah																										
1971	Mil A	13	17	.433	36	35	12-4	0-0	244.2	219	95	19	4	93-10	139	3.20	109	.241	.312	72-1-8	.167	3	85	10	0	1.6
1972	Mil A	13	13	.500	33	30	10-2	0-0	214	194	102	27	3	68-8	111	3.91	78	.240	.299	67-0-6	.164	0	99	-20	0	-2.4
1973	Mil A	3	6	.333	20	17	0	0-0	59.2	59	50	6	0	67-1	30	6.79	56	.257	.423	0	ø	0	95	-19	0	-2.5
1974	Oak A	0	0	ø	4	0	0	0-0	2	1	0	0	0	3-0	2	0.00	ø	.143	.400	0	ø	0	—	1	0	0.0
Total	4	29	36	.446	93	82	22-6	0-0	520.1	473	247	52	7	231-19	282	3.89	86	.242	.322	139-1-14	.165	3	94	-28	0	-3.3
PARTENHEIMER, STAN Stanwood Wendell "Party"; B10.21.1922 Chicopee Falls MA; D1.28.1989 Wilson NC; BR/TL/5´11˝/175; d5.27; f–Steve; Col Wooster																										
1944	Bos A	0	0	ø	1	1	0	0	1	3	2	0	0	2	0	18.00	19	.500	.625	1	.000	-0	49	-2	0	-0.1
1945	StL N	0	0	ø	8	2	0	0	13.1	12	9	2	0	16	6	6.08	62	.250	.438	3	.000	-0	170	-3	0	-0.2
Total	2	0	0	ø	9	3	0	0	14.1	15	11	2	0	18	6	6.91	54	.278	.458	4	.000	-1	129	-5	0	-0.3
PASCHALL, BILL William Herbert; B4.22.1954 Norfolk VA; BR/TR/6´0˝/175; [KCA76*S3/53]; d9.20; Col North Carolina																										
1978	KC A	0	1	.000	2	0	0	1-0	8	6	3	0	1	0-0	5	3.38	113	.207	.226	0	ø	0	—	1	0	0.1
1979	KC A	0	1	.000	7	0	0	0-1	13.2	18	11	2	2	5-3	3	6.59	65	.300	.368	0	ø	0	—	-3	0	-0.2
1981	KC A	0	0	ø	2	0	0	0-0	2	2	1	0	0	0-0	1	4.50	80	.286	.286	0	ø	0	—	0	0	0.0
Total	3	0	2	.000	11	0	0	1-1	23.2	26	15	2	3	5-3	9	5.32	76	.271	.321	0	ø	0	—	-2	0	-0.1

THE PITCHER REGISTER

Pascual, Camilo Camilo Alberto (Lus); B1.20.1934 Havana, Cuba; BR/TR/5´11˝/(150–185); d4.15; C3; b–Carlos

YEAR	TM LG	W	L	PCT	G	GS	CG-SHO	SV-BS	IP	H	R	HR	HB	BB-IB	SO	ERA	AERA	OAV	OOB	AB-HR-SH	AVG	PB	SUP	APR	DL	PW
1954	Was A	4	7	.364	48	4	1	3	119.1	126	65	7	6	61	60	4.22	84	.276	.368	30-0-1	.133	-0	81	-9	0	-0.8
1955	Was A	2	12	.143	43	16	1	3	129	158	94	5	6	70-6	82	6.14	62	.311	.395	32-0-2	.219	0	93	-32	0	-3.0
1956	Was A	6	18	.250	39	27	6	2	188.2	194	131	33	6	89-4	162	5.87	74	.261	.342	58-0-6	.138	-2*	81	-27	0	-3.1
1957	Was A	8	17	.320	29	26	8-2	0	175.2	168	85	11	3	76-5	113	4.10	95	.258	.333	50-0-5	.140	-2*	80	-3	0	-0.5
1958	Was A	8	12	.400	31	27	6-2	0	177.1	166	66	14	3	60-2	146	3.15	121	.248	.311	57-0-4	.158	-1	75	13	0	1.4
1959	Was A✻	17	10	.630	32	30	**17-6**	0	238.2	202	80	10	3	69-7	185	2.64	148	.226	.282	86-0-5	.302	6	105	34	0	**4.7**
1960	Was A✻	12	8	.600	26	22	8-3	2	151.2	139	65	11	2	53-2	143	3.03	128	.240	.305	51-1-4	.176	3*	120	12	0	1.9
1961	Min A★	15	16	.484	35	33	15-**8**	0	252.1	205	114	26	3	100-1	**221**	3.46	123	.217	.293	85-0-5	.165	-0	102	19	0	2.2
1962	Min A★	20	11	.645	34	33	**18-5**	0	257.2	236	100	25	2	59-5	**206**	3.32	123	.241	.285	97-2-0	.268	8	107	24	0	3.7
1963	Min A	21	9	.700	31	31	**18**-3	0	248.1	205	76	21	3	81-4	**202**	2.46	148	.224	.288	92-0-5	.250	6*	129	33	0	4.7
1964	Min A★	15	12	.556	36	36	14-1	0	267.1	245	121	30	3	98-6	213	3.30	108	.241	.308	94-0-4	.181	4	112	5	0	0.9
1965	†Min A	9	3	.750	27	27	5-1	0	156	126	67	12	5	63-0	96	3.35	106	.217	.298	60-2-2	.200	3	122	4	34	0.7
1966	Min A	8	6	.571	21	19	2	0	103	113	63	9	2	30-0	56	4.89	73	.278	.328	37-0-1	.216	1	103	-13	37	-1.5
1967	Was A	12	10	.545	28	27	5-1	0	164.2	147	73	15	3	43-3	106	3.28	96	.237	.288	51-0-6	.176	1	108	-4	0	-0.4
1968	Was A	13	12	.520	31	31	8-4	0	201	181	72	11	4	59-4	111	2.69	109	.239	.297	65-0-4	.185	1	98	4	0	0.6
1969	Was A	2	5	.286	14	13	0	0-0	55.1	49	42	12	5	38-1	34	6.83	51	.239	.371	17	.235	0*	117	-18	0	-2.0
	Cin N	0	0	ø	5	1	0	0-0	7.1	14	7	2	0	4-0	3	8.59	44	.424	.486	0	ø	0	448	-3	21	-0.2
1970	LA N	0	0	ø	10	0	0	0-0	14	12	4	2	1	5-1	8	2.57	150	.231	.310	0	ø	0	—	2	21	0.1
1971	Cle A	2	2	.500	9	1	0	0-0	23.1	17	9	0	1	11-0	20	3.09	126	.205	.302	5-0-1	.600	1	23	2	0	0.5
Total	18	174	170	.506	529	404	132-36	10-0	2930.2	2703	1334	256	61	1069-51	2167	3.63	103	.244	.312	967-5-55	.205	29	103	43	113	9.9

Pascual, Carlos Carlos Alberto (Lus) "Little Potato"; B3.13.1931 Havana, Cuba; BR/TR/5´6˝/165; d9.24; b–Camilo

YEAR	TM LG	W	L	PCT	G	GS	CG-SHO	SV-BS	IP	H	R	HR	HB	BB-IB	SO	ERA	AERA	OAV	OOB	AB-HR-SH	AVG	PB	SUP	APR	DL	PW
1950	Was A	1	1	.500	2	2	2	0	17	12	5	0	1	8	3	2.12	212	.194	.296	4-0-1	.250	0	60	4	0	0.5

Pashnick, Larry Larry John; B4.25.1956 Lincoln Park MI; BR/TR/6´3˝/(195–200); d4.10; Col Michigan St.

YEAR	TM LG	W	L	PCT	G	GS	CG-SHO	SV-BS	IP	H	R	HR	HB	BB-IB	SO	ERA	AERA	OAV	OOB	AB-HR-SH	AVG	PB	SUP	APR	DL	PW
1982	Det A	4	4	.500	28	13	1	0-0	94.1	110	46	17	1	25-2	19	4.01	102	.297	.342	0	ø	0	91	1	0	0.1
1983	Det A	1	3	.250	12	6	0	0-1	37.2	48	27	5	3	18-1	17	5.26	75	.308	.383	0	ø	0	80	-7	0	-0.6
1984	Min A	2	1	.667	13	1	0	0-0	38.1	38	19	3	2	11-1	10	3.52	120	.260	.321	0	ø	0	64	2	0	0.1
Total	3	7	8	.467	53	20	1	0-1	170.1	196	92	25	6	54-4	46	4.17	98	.292	.347	0	ø	0	85	-4	0	-0.4

Passeau, Claude Claude William; B4.9.1909 Waynesboro MS; D8.30.2003 Lucedale MS; BR/TR/6´3˝/198; d9.29; Col Millsaps

YEAR	TM LG	W	L	PCT	G	GS	CG-SHO	SV-BS	IP	H	R	HR	HB	BB-IB	SO	ERA	AERA	OAV	OOB	AB-HR-SH	AVG	PB	SUP	APR	DL	PW
1935	Pit N	0	1	.000	1	1	0	0	3	7	4	0	0	2	1	12.00	34	.500	.563	1	.000	-0	124	-2	—	-0.3
1936	Phi N	11	15	.423	49	21	8-2	3	217.1	247	118	7	4	55	85	3.48	130	.280	.325	78-2-2	.282	3*	93	18	—	2.4
1937	Phi N	14	18	.438	50	**34**	18-1	2	**292.1**	348	158	16	5	79	135	4.34	100	.296	.343	107-1-1	.196	-0	93	0	—	0.0
1938	Phi N	11	18	.379	44	33	15	1	239	281	147	8	8	93	100	4.52	86	.287	.354	80-0-4	.162	-2*	85	-20	—	-2.2
1939	Phi N	2	4	.333	8	8	4-1	0	53.1	54	26	1	1	25	29	4.22	95	.263	.346	20	.200	-0	95	0	—	-0.1
	Chi N	13	9	.591	34	27	13-1	3	221	215	86	8	4	48	108	3.05	129	.254	.297	77-1-2	.156	-1*	109	22	—	2.0
	Year	15	13	.536	42	35	17-2	3	274.1	269	112	9	5	73	**137**	3.28	120	.256	.307	97-1-2	.165	-2	106	22	—	1.9
1940	Chi N	20	13	.606	46	31	20-4	5	280.2	259	97	8	4	59	124	2.50	150	.237	.278	98-1-3	.204	6	116	37	—	**5.1**
1941	Chi N★	14	14	.500	34	30	20-3	0	231	262	99	10	1	52	80	3.35	105	.281	.320	86-3-4	.221	5	115	6	0	1.1
1942	Chi N★	19	14	.576	35	34	24-3	0	278.1	284	116	13	3	74	89	2.68	119	.260	.309	105-2-5	.181	1	110	9	0	1.1
1943	Chi N☆	15	12	.556	35	31	18-1	1	257	245	96	10	4	66	93	2.91	115	.249	.299	96-0-6	.198	1	110	13	0	1.5
1944	Chi N	15	9	.625	34	27	18-2	3	227	234	80	8	1	50	89	2.89	122	.266	.306	80-0-7	.162	-1	85	20	0	2.0
1945	†Chi N✻	17	9	.654	34	27	19-**5**	1	227	205	70	4	2	59	98	2.46	149	.238	.289	91-2-3	.187	2	119	**33**	0	**3.9**
1946	Chi N★	9	8	.529	21	21	10-2	0	129.1	118	53	5	1	42	47	3.13	106	.237	.298	49-3-3	.204	3	108	2	0	0.6
1947	Chi N	2	6	.250	19	6	1-1	2	63.1	97	54	7	1	24	26	6.25	63	.353	.407	14-0-1	.000	-2	52	-18	0	-2.2
Total	13	162	150	.519	444	331	188-26	21	2719.2	2856	1204	105	39	728	1104	3.32	113	.267	.316	982-15-41	.192	13	102	120	0	14.9

Pastore, Frank Frank Enrico; B8.21.1957 Alhambra CA; BR/TR/6´3˝/(205–215); [CinN75 2/46]; d4.4

YEAR	TM LG	W	L	PCT	G	GS	CG-SHO	SV-BS	IP	H	R	HR	HB	BB-IB	SO	ERA	AERA	OAV	OOB	AB-HR-SH	AVG	PB	SUP	APR	DL	PW
1979	†Cin N	6	7	.462	30	9	2-1	4-2	95.1	102	47	8	1	23-5	63	4.25	87	.271	.313	25-0-2	.160	-0	106	-4	0	-0.6
1980	Cin N	13	7	.650	27	27	9-2	0-0	184.2	161	72	13	0	42-3	110	3.27	108	.233	.275	64-0-6	.156	-1	112	5	26	0.4
1981	Cin N	4	9	.308	22	22	2-1	0-0	132	125	73	11	3	35-1	81	4.02	87	.247	.297	44-0-6	.114	-2	106	-11	0	-1.3
1982	Cin N	8	13	.381	31	29	3-2	0-0	188.1	210	86	13	4	57-8	94	3.97	93	.286	.338	58-1-5	.172	1	94	-3	25	-0.3
1983	Cin N	9	12	.429	36	29	4-1	0-0	184.1	207	104	20	1	64-3	93	4.88	78	.290	.346	59-1-3	.186	2	103	-18	0	-1.8
1984	Cin N	3	8	.273	24	16	1	0-0	98.1	110	74	10	3	40-3	53	6.50	58	.285	.353	28-0-2	.071	-2	98	-26	22	-2.7
1985	Cin N	2	1	.667	17	6	1	0-0	54	60	23	1	1	16-1	29	3.83	99	.287	.336	14-0-2	.143	-0	97	1	79	0.0
1986	Min A	3	1	.750	33	1	0	2-3	49.1	54	28	4	0	24-6	18	4.01	108	.283	.356	0	ø	0	105	0	21	0.0
Total	8	48	58	.453	220	139	22-7	6-5	986.1	1029	507	80	13	301-30	541	4.29	86	.270	.323	292-2-26	.151	-2	102	-56	173	-6.3

Pastorius, Jim James Washington "Sunny Jim"; B7.12.1881 Pittsburgh PA; D5.10.1941 Pittsburgh PA; BL/TL/5´9˝/165; d4.15

YEAR	TM LG	W	L	PCT	G	GS	CG-SHO	SV-BS	IP	H	R	HR	HB	BB-IB	SO	ERA	AERA	OAV	OOB	AB-HR-SH	AVG	PB	SUP	APR	DL	PW
1906	Bro N	10	14	.417	29	24	16-3	0	211.2	225	111	4	3	69	58	3.61	70	.274	.333	71-0-5	.141	-0	103	-26	—	-2.9
1907	Bro N	16	12	.571	28	26	20-4	0	222	218	74	2	6	77	70	2.35	100	.264	.331	73-0-4	.205	3*	92	3	—	0.8
1908	Bro N	4	20	.167	28	25	16-2	0	213.2	171	88	5	7	74	54	2.44	96	.216	.288	62-0-3	.129	-0	58	-6	—	-0.7
1909	Bro N	1	9	.100	12	9	5-1	0	79.2	91	65	4	1	58	23	5.76	45	.313	.429	25	.080	-1	57	-27	—	-3.0
Total	4	31	55	.360	97	84	57-10	0	727	705	338	15	17	278	205	3.12	78	.258	.330	231-0-12	.152	1	81	-56	—	-5.8

Pate, Joe Joseph William; B6.6.1892 Alice TX; D12.26.1948 Fort Worth TX; BL/TL/5´10˝/184; d4.15; Col Tulane

YEAR	TM LG	W	L	PCT	G	GS	CG-SHO	SV-BS	IP	H	R	HR	HB	BB-IB	SO	ERA	AERA	OAV	OOB	AB-HR-SH	AVG	PB	SUP	APR	DL	PW
1926	Phi A	9	0	1.000	47	2	0	6	113	109	38	3	2	51	24	2.71	154	.262	.345	27-0-2	.148	-0	81	**20**	—	1.8
1927	Phi A	0	3	.000	32	0	0	6	53.2	67	36	3	1	21	14	5.20	82	.318	.382	10	.300	1	—	-5	—	-0.3
Total	2	9	3	.750	79	2	0	12	166.2	176	74	6	3	72	38	3.51	120	.281	.358	37-0-2	.189	1	81	15	—	1.5

Patrick, Bronswell Bronswell Dante; B9.16.1970 Greenville NC; BR/TR/6´1˝/(205–237); [OakA88 23/593]; d5.18

YEAR	TM LG	W	L	PCT	G	GS	CG-SHO	SV-BS	IP	H	R	HR	HB	BB-IB	SO	ERA	AERA	OAV	OOB	AB-HR-SH	AVG	PB	SUP	APR	DL	PW
1998	Mil N	4	1	.800	32	3	0	0-0	78.2	83	43	9	0	29-1	49	4.69	92	.279	.339	15-1-1	.200	2	92	-2	0	0.0
1999	SF N	1	0	1.000	6	0	0	1-0	5.1	9	7	1	0	3-0	6	10.13	42	.375	.429	1	.000	-0	—	-4	0	-0.7
Total	2	5	1	.833	38	3	0	1-0	84	92	50	10	0	32-1	55	5.04	86	.286	.346	16-1-1	.188	1	92	-6	0	-0.7

Patten, Case Case Lyman "Casey"; B5.7.1874 Westport NY; D5.31.1935 Rochester NY; BB/TL/6´0˝/175; d5.4

YEAR	TM LG	W	L	PCT	G	GS	CG-SHO	SV-BS	IP	H	R	HR	HB	BB-IB	SO	ERA	AERA	OAV	OOB	AB-HR-SH	AVG	PB	SUP	APR	DL	PW
1901	Was A	18	10	.643	32	30	26-4	0	254.1	285	163	8	17	74	109	3.93	93	.280	.339	96-1-6	.135	-5	115	-9	—	-1.2
1902	Was A	18	17	.514	36	34	33-1	0	299.2	331	186	11	11	89	92	4.05	91	.281	.337	125-0-3	.096	-10*	94	-13	—	-2.2
1903	Was A	11	22	.333	36	34	32	1	300	313	163	11	4	80	133	3.60	87	.268	.317	106-0-5	.132	-6	68	-16	—	-2.2
1904	Was A	14	23	.378	45	39	37-2	**3**	357.2	367	162	2	20	79	150	3.07	87	.266	.315	126-0-4	.127	-5	77	-15	—	-2.1
1905	Was A	14	21	.400	42	36	29-2	0	309.2	300	145	3	10	86	113	3.14	84	.256	.312	103-0-4	.155	-2	94	-14	—	-1.8
1906	Was A	19	16	.543	38	32	28-7	0	282.2	253	106	2	6	79	96	2.17	122	.242	.299	94-1-1	.117	-4	72	11	—	0.8
1907	Was A	12	16	.429	36	29	20-1	0	237.1	272	135	3	6	63	58	3.56	68	.290	.339	87-0-3	.126	-3	96	-30	—	-3.9
1908	Was A	0	2	.000	4	3	1	0	18	25	14	0	0	6	6	3.50	65	.333	.383	5	.200	-0	179	-4	—	-0.4
	Bos A	0	1	.000	1	1	0	0	3	8	5	0	0	1	0	15.00	16	.533	.563	1	.000	-0	139	-3	—	-0.5
	Year	0	3	.000	5	4	1	0	21	33	19	0	0	7	6	5.14	45	.367	.412	6	.167	-0	170	-7	—	-0.9
Total	8	106	128	.453	270	238	206-17	4	2062.1	2154	1079	40	74	557	757	3.36	88	.270	.323	743-2-26	.127	-35	90	-93	—	-13.5

Patterson, Danny Danny Shane; B2.17.1971 San Gabriel CA; BR/TR/6´0˝/(185–225); [TexA89 47/1199]; d7.26; Col Cerritos (CA) JC

YEAR	TM LG	W	L	PCT	G	GS	CG-SHO	SV-BS	IP	H	R	HR	HB	BB-IB	SO	ERA	AERA	OAV	OOB	AB-HR-SH	AVG	PB	SUP	APR	DL	PW
1996	†Tex A	0	0	ø	7	0	0	0-0	8.2	10	4	0	0	3-1	5	0.00	ø	.286	.342	0	ø	0	—	3	0	0.1
1997	Tex A	10	6	.625	54	0	0	1-7	71	70	29	3	0	23-4	69	3.42	142	.263	.318	0	ø	0	—	11	28	2.1
1998	Tex A	2	5	.286	56	0	0	2-0	60.2	64	31	11	2	19-2	33	4.45	110	.274	.332	0	ø	0	—	4	17	0.4
1999	†Tex A	2	0	1.000	53	0	0	0-1	60.1	77	38	5	1	19-3	43	5.67	91	.304	.353	1	.000	-0	—	-2	0	-0.1
2000	Det A	5	1	.833	58	0	0	0-2	56.2	69	26	4	2	14-2	29	3.97	124	.309	.353	0	ø	0	—	6	15	0.6
2001	Det A	5	4	.556	60	0	0	1-4	64.2	64	24	4	4	12-5	27	3.06	144	.274	.316	0	ø	0	—	10	0	1.2
2002	Det A	0	2	.000	6	0	0	0-1	3	5	5	0	1	2-0	1	15.00	29	.357	.471	0	ø	0	—	-3	170	-0.6
2003	Det A	0	0	ø	19	0	0	3-0	17.2	15	8	1	1	4-0	19	4.08	107	.227	.282	0	ø	0	—	1	109	0.1
2004	Det A	0	4	.000	37	0	0	2-2	41.2	44	24	7	5	16-2	24	4.75	94	.282	.367	0	ø	0	—	-2	24	-0.2
Total	9	24	22	.522	350	0	0	9-17	384.1	418	189	35	16	112-19	250	4.14	116	.282	.337	1	.000	-0	—	28	363	3.6

YEAR	TM LG	W	L	PCT	G	GS	CG-SHO	SV-BS	IP	H	R	HR	HB	BB-IB	SO	ERA	AERA	OAV	OOB	AB-HR-SH	AVG	PB	SUP	APR	DL	PW
Patterson, Daryl	Daryl Alan; B11.21.1943 Coalinga CA; BL/TR/6´4˝/(195–205); d4.10; Mil 1969; Col Sequoias (CA) [JC]																									
1968	†Det A	2	3	.400	38	1	0	7	68	53	19	3	4	27-1	49	2.12	142	.213	.299	13	.000	-1	116	6	0	0.5
1969	Det A	0	2	.000	18	0	0	0-2	22.1	15	8	2	0	19-3	12	2.82	133	.205	.358	1	.000	-0	—	2	0	0.1
1970	Det A	7	1	.875	43	0	0	2-2	78	81	47	9	5	39-1	55	4.85	78	.269	.361	11	.000	-1	—	-9	0	-1.1
1971	Det A	0	1	.000	12	0	0	0-0	9.1	14	7	1	1	6-1	5	4.82	75	.359	.457	0	ø	0	—	-2	0	-0.2
	Oak A	0	0	ø	4	0	0	0-0	5.2	5	5	3	1	4-0	2	7.94	42	.238	.385	1	.000	-0	—	-3	0	-0.2
	Year	0	1	.000	16	0	0	0-0	15	19	12	4	2	10-1	7	6.00	59	.317	.431	1	.000	-0	—	-5	0	-0.4
	StL N	0	1	.000	13	2	0	1-0	26.2	20	14	3	0	15-1	11	4.39	83	.211	.313	5	.000	-0	98	-2	0	-0.2
1974	Pit N	2	1	.667	14	0	0	1-1	21	35	19	3	0	9-1	8	7.29	48	.376	.427	4	.000	-1	—	-9	0	-1.3
Total	5	11	9	.550	142	3	0	11-5	231	223	119	24	11	119-8	142	4.09	85	.256	.350	35	.000	-3	101	-17	0	-2.4
Patterson, Dave	David Glenn; B7.25.1956 Springfield MO; BR/TR/6´0˝/170; [LAN76*2/44]; d6.9; Col Cerritos (CA) JC																									
1979	LA N	4	1	.800	36	0	0	6-1	53	62	35	5	0	22-6	34	5.26	69	.292	.356	7-0-2	.143	-0*	—	-10	0	-1.1
Patterson, Gil	Gilbert Thomas; B9.5.1955 Philadelphia PA; BR/TR/6´1˝/185; [NYA75 S1/7]; d4.19; C4; Col Miami–Dade Kendall (FL) CC																									
1977	NY A	1	2	.333	10	6	0	1-0	33.1	38	20	3	3	20-1	29	5.40	73	.290	.396	0	ø	0	110	-4	0	-0.4
Patterson, Jeff	Jeffrey Simmons; B10.1.1968 Anaheim CA; BR/TR/6´2˝/200; [PhiN88 58/1353]; d4.30; Col Cypress (CA) JC																									
1995	NY A	0	0	ø	3	0	0	0-0	3.1	3	1	1	0	3-0	3	2.70	171	.231	.375	0	ø	0	—	1	0	0.0
Patterson, John	John Hollis; B1.30.1978 Orange TX; BR/TR/6´6˝/(200–210); d7.20																									
2002	Ari N	2	0	1.000	7	5	0	0-0	30.2	27	11	7	1	7-0	31	3.23	139	.235	.285	10-0-1	.100	-0	173	4	0	0.2
2003	Ari N	1	4	.200	16	8	0	1-0	55	61	39	7	2	30-5	43	6.05	76	.281	.371	13	.077	-1	96	-7	0	-0.8
2004	Mon N	4	7	.364	19	19	0	0-0	98.1	100	58	18	8	46-4	99	5.03	91	.260	.349	33-0-5	.121	-1	83	-3	78	-0.5
2005	Was N	9	7	.563	31	31	2-1	0-0	198.1	172	71	19	5	65-11	185	3.13	131	.233	.298	59-0-8	.102	-2	87	24	15	1.5
2006	Was N	1	2	.333	8	8	0	0-0	40.2	36	21	4	3	9-1	42	4.43	99	.237	.286	8-0-2	.250	0	111	0	146	0.0
Total	5	17	20	.459	81	71	2-1	1-0	423	396	200	55	19	157-21	400	4.09	106	.246	.319	123-0-16	.114	-4	96	18	239	0.4
Patterson, Ken	Kenneth Brian; B7.8.1964 Costa Mesa CA; BL/TL/6´4˝/(210–230); [NYA85 3/77]; d7.8; Col Baylor																									
1988	Chi A	0	2	.000	9	2	0	1-0	20.2	25	11	2	0	7-0	8	4.79	84	.294	.348	0	ø	0	91	-1	0	-0.1
1989	Chi A	6	1	.857	50	1	0	0-1	65.2	64	37	11	2	28-3	43	4.52	85	.257	.332	0	ø	0	165	-5	0	-0.5
1990	Chi A	2	1	.667	43	0	0	2-0	66.1	58	27	6	2	34-1	40	3.39	113	.242	.335	0	ø	0	—	3	0	0.2
1991	Chi A	3	0	1.000	43	0	0	1-1	63.2	48	22	5	1	35-1	32	2.83	141	.214	.321	0	ø	0	—	8	0	0.4
1992	Chi N	2	3	.400	32	1	0	0-2	41.2	41	25	7	1	27-6	23	3.89	93	.268	.373	1-0-1	.000	-0	249	-3	42	-0.4
1993	Cal A	1	1	.500	46	0	0	1-1	59	54	30	7	0	35-5	36	4.58	99	.249	.352	0	ø	0	—	1	0	0.0
1994	Cal A	0	0	ø	1	0	0	0-0	0.2	0	0	0	0	0-0	1	0.00	ø	.000	.000	0	ø	0	—	0	110	0.0
Total	7	14	8	.636	224	4	0	5-5	317.2	290	152	38	6	166-16	183	3.88	103	.248	.340	1-0-1	.000	-0	143	3	152	-0.4
Patterson, Reggie	Reginald Allen; B11.7.1958 Birmingham AL; BR/TR/6´4˝/(180–185); d8.13																									
1981	Chi A	0	1	.000	6	1	0	0-0	7.1	14	11	1	0	6-0	2	13.50	27	.412	.500	0	ø	0	149	-7	0	-0.9
1983	Chi N	1	2	.333	5	2	0	0-0	18.2	17	12	3	2	6-0	10	4.82	79	.246	.321	6-0-2	.000	-1	151	-2	0	-0.4
1984	Chi N	0	1	.000	3	1	0	0-0	6	10	7	1	0	2-0	5	10.50	37	.357	.400	2	.000	-0	23	-4	0	-0.5
1985	Chi N	3	0	1.000	8	5	1	0-0	39	36	13	2	0	10-1	17	3.00	133	.250	.297	10-0-2	.100	-0	110	4	0	0.3
Total	4	4	4	.500	22	9	1	0-0	71	77	43	7	2	24-1	34	5.20	75	.280	.340	18-0-4	.056	-1	113	-9	0	-1.5
Patterson, Bob	Robert Chandler; B5.16.1959 Jacksonville FL; BR/TL/6´2˝/(185–195); [SDN82 21/524]; d9.2; Col East Carolina																									
1985	SD N	0	0	ø	3	0	0	0-0	4	13	11	2	0	3-0	1	24.75	14	.565	.615	0	ø	0	—	-9	0	-0.4
1986	Pit N	2	3	.400	11	5	0	0-0	36.1	49	20	0	0	5-2	20	4.95	79	.322	.342	8-0-2	.125	-0	78	-3	0	-0.4
1987	Pit N	1	4	.200	15	7	0	0-0	43	49	34	5	1	22-4	27	6.70	62	.290	.369	12-0-1	.083	-1	90	-11	0	-1.2
1989	Pit N	4	3	.571	12	3	0	1-0	26.2	23	13	3	0	8-2	20	4.05	84	.232	.287	3-0-2	.000	0	104	-2	0	-0.4
1990	†Pit N	8	5	.615	55	5	0	5-3	94.2	88	33	9	3	21-7	70	2.95	124	.249	.294	19-0-1	.053	-1	104	9	0	1.1
1991	†Pit N	4	3	.571	54	1	0	2-1	65.2	67	32	7	0	15-1	57	4.11	88	.267	.306	4	.250	0	100	-3	0	-0.3
1992	†Pit N	6	3	.667	60	0	0	9-4	64.2	59	22	7	0	23-6	43	2.92	119	.246	.309	6	.333	1	—	4	0	0.8
1993	Tex A	2	4	.333	52	0	0	1-1	52.2	59	28	8	1	11-0	46	4.78	88	.282	.318	0	ø	0	—	-2	0	-0.2
1994	Cal A	2	3	.400	47	0	0	1-0	42	35	21	6	2	15-2	30	4.07	121	.229	.306	0	ø	0	—	3	0	0.3
1995	Cal A	5	2	.714	62	0	0	0-1	53.1	48	18	6	1	13-3	41	3.04	155	.246	.295	0	ø	0	—	11	0	1.1
1996	Chi N	3	3	.500	79	0	0	8-2	54.2	46	19	6	1	22-7	53	3.13	140	.229	.303	3	.333	0	—	8	0	1.0
1997	Chi N	1	6	.143	76	0	0	0-3	59.1	47	23	9	0	10-1	58	3.34	130	.222	.252	1	.000	-0	—	7	0	0.7
1998	Chi N	1	1	.500	33	0	0	1-1	20.1	36	20	2	0	12-3	17	7.52	59	.391	.453	0-0-1	ø	0	—	-8	17	-0.7
Total	13	39	40	.494	559	21	0	28-16	617.1	619	294	70	9	180-38	483	4.08	99	.263	.315	56-0-7	.125	-1	89	4	17	1.4
Patterson, Roy	Roy Lewis "Boy Wonder"; B12.17.1876 Stoddard WI; D4.14.1953 St.Croix Falls WI; BR/TR/6´0˝/185; d4.24																									
1901	Chi A	20	15	.571	41	35	30-4	0	312.1	345	164	11	11	62	127	3.37	103	.277	.317	117-1-6	.222	1	109	10	—	1.0
1902	Chi A	19	14	.576	34	30	26-2	0	268	262	111	5	3	67	61	3.06	111	.256	.304	105-0-5	.190	-2	99	13	—	1.2
1903	Chi A	15	15	.500	34	30	26-2	1	293	275	119	5	11	69	89	2.70	104	.248	.298	105-0-3	.105	-6	96	8	—	0.2
1904	Chi A	9	9	.500	22	17	14-4	0	165	148	52	1	7	24	64	2.29	107	.241	.277	58-0-3	.103	-4	96	5	—	0.1
1905	Chi A	4	6	.400	13	9	7	0	88.2	73	34	0	0	16	29	1.83	135	.226	.263	30-0-1	.267	2	83	4	—	0.7
1906	Chi A	10	7	.588	21	18	12-3	1	142	119	46	1	4	17	45	2.09	121	.231	.261	49-0-4	.061	-5	88	8	—	0.5
1907	Chi A	4	6	.400	19	13	4-1	0	96	105	42	0	2	18	27	2.63	91	.280	.316	31	.097	-3	121	-4	—	-0.7
Total	7	81	72	.529	184	152	119-16	2	1365	1327	568	23	38	273	442	2.75	107	.255	.297	495-1-22	.156	-16	101	44	—	3.0
Pattin, Marty	Martin William; B4.6.1943 Charleston IL; BR/TR/5´11˝/180; [AnaA65 7/127]; d5.14; C1; Col Eastern Illinois																									
1968	Cal A	4	4	.500	52	4	0	3	84	67	27	7	2	37-4	66	2.79	105	.221	.307	12-0-1	.083	-1	127	2	0	0.1
1969	Sea A	7	12	.368	34	27	2-1	0-0	158.2	166	104	29	2	71-5	126	5.62	65	.268	.345	58-0-2	.155	-1*	110	-31	0	-3.5
1970	Mil A	14	12	.538	37	29	11	0-0	233.1	204	91	20	6	71-9	161	3.39	111	.235	.296	70-0-7	.129	-2*	84	13	0	1.2
1971	Mil A☆	14	14	.500	36	36	9-5	0-0	264.2	225	100	29	4	73-11	169	3.13	112	.235	.289	83-0-11	.084	-3	85	13	0	1.0
1972	Bos A	17	13	.567	38	35	13-4	0-1	253	232	102	19	9	65-3	168	3.24	100	.243	.295	86-2-7	.140	0	106	1	0	0.2
1973	Bos A	15	15	.500	34	30	11-2	1-0	219.1	238	112	31	8	69-7	119	4.31	93	.277	.335	0	ø	0	123	-5	0	-0.6
1974	KC A	3	7	.300	25	11	2	0-1	117.1	121	55	10	2	28-3	50	3.99	96	.264	.306	0	ø	0	84	0	0	-0.1
1975	KC A	10	10	.500	44	15	5-1	5-1	177	173	77	13	3	45-6	89	3.25	119	.253	.300	0	ø	0*	117	10	0	1.1
1976	†KC A	8	14	.364	44	15	4-1	5-3	141	114	51	9	3	38-9	65	2.49	141	.216	.271	0	ø	0	105	14	0	2.2
1977	†KC A	10	3	.769	31	10	4	0-0	128.1	115	56	16	2	37-2	55	3.58	113	.242	.297	0	ø	0	100	7	0	0.6
1978	†KC A	3	3	.500	32	5	2	4-1	78.2	72	41	8	2	25-7	30	3.32	115	.248	.307	0	ø	0	61	1	0	0.0
1979	KC A	5	2	.714	31	7	1	3-0	94.1	109	50	11	1	21-2	41	4.58	93	.293	.329	0	ø	0	103	-1	20	-0.1
1980	†KC A	4	0	1.000	37	0	0	4-0	89	97	39	7	1	23-7	40	3.64	111	.277	.321	0	ø	0	—	5	0	0.2
Total	13	114	109	.511	475	224	64-14	25-7	2038.2	1933	905	209	45	603-75	1179	3.62	102	.250	.306	309-2-28	.123	-7	101	29	20	2.3
Pattison, Jimmy	James Wells; B12.18.1908 Bronx NY; D2.22.1991 Melbourne FL; BL/TL/6´0˝/185; d4.18																									
1929	Bro N	0	1	.000	6	0	0	0	11.2	9	6	1	0	4	5	4.63	100	.231	.302	2	.500	0	—	0	—	0.1
Patton, Harry	Harry Claude; B6.29.1884 Gillespie IL; D6.9.1930 St.Louis MO; d8.22																									
1910	StL N	0	0	ø	1	0	0	0	4	4	2	0	0	2	2	2.25	132	.267	.353	0	ø	0	—	0	—	0.0
Paul, Mike	Michael George; B4.18.1945 Detroit MI; BL/TL/6´0˝/(180–190); d5.27; C6; Col Arizona																									
1968	Cle A	5	8	.385	36	7	0	3	91.2	72	42	11	5	35-5	87	3.93	76	.213	.295	24-0-1	.167	0	117	-8	0	-1.2
1969	Cle A	5	10	.333	47	12	0	2-0	117.1	104	48	12	2	54-11	98	3.61	105	.241	.325	27-0-1	.000	-3	45	5	0	0.3
1970	Cle A	2	8	.200	30	15	1	0-2	88	91	51	13	0	45-0	70	4.81	83	.271	.351	26-0-1	.154	-1	67	-8	0	-0.9
1971	Cle A	2	7	.222	17	12	1	0-0	62	78	42	8	5	14-3	33	5.95	65	.318	.365	19-0-1	.053	-1	64	-12	0	-1.7
1972	Tex A	8	9	.471	49	20	2-1	1-2	161.2	149	50	4	2	52-12	108	2.17	141	.246	.306	48-0-3	.167	1	73	14	0	1.6
1973	Tex A	5	4	.556	36	10	1	2-2	87.1	104	55	9	5	36-2	49	4.95	76	.295	.364	0	ø	0*	83	-12	0	-1.1
	Chi N	0	1	.000	11	1	0	0-0	18.1	17	7	2	0	9-2	6	3.44	115	.258	.342	4	.000	-0	45	1	0	0.0
1974	Chi N	0	1	.000	2	0	0	0-0	1.1	4	4	1	0	1-1	1	27.00	14	.500	.556	0	ø	0	—	-3	0	-0.5
Total	7	27	48	.360	228	77	5-1	8-6	627.2	619	299	60	19	246-36	452	3.91	90	.260	.331	148-0-7	.115	-4	71	-23	0	-3.5
Pauley, David	David Wayne; B6.17.1983 Longmont CO; BR/TR/6´2˝/185; [SDN01 8/240]; d5.31																									
2006	Bos A	0	2	.000	3	3	0	0-0	16	31	14	1	2	6-1	10	7.88	59	.419	.476	0	ø	0	101	-5	34	-0.5

YEAR	TM LG	W	L	PCT	G	GS	CG-SHO	SV-BS	IP	H	R	HR	HB	BB-IB	SO	ERA	AERA	OAV	OOB	AB-HR-SH	AVG	PB	SUP	APR	DL	PW
PAULSEN, GIL	Guilford Paul Hans; B11.14.1902 Graettinger IA; D4.2.1994 Harlan IA; BR/TR/6´2.5˝/190; d10.3; Col Cornell																									
1925	StL N	0	0	ø	1	0	0	0	2	1	0	0	0	0	1	0.00	ø	.125	.125	0	ø	0	—	1	—	0.1
PAVANO, CARL	Carl Anthony; B1.8.1976 New Britain CT; BR/TR/6´5˝/(225–240); [BosA94 13/355]; d5.23; [DL 2006 NY A 182]																									
1998	Mon N	6	9	.400	24	23	0	0-0	134.2	130	70	18	8	43-1	83	4.21	100	.251	.315	38-0-6	.158	-0	82	0	0	-0.1
1999	Mon N	6	8	.429	19	18	1-1	0-0	104	117	66	8	4	35-1	70	5.63	79	.285	.345	33-0-5	.061	-2	82	-10	61	-1.2
2000	Mon N	8	4	.667	15	15	0	0-0	97	89	40	8	8	34-1	64	3.06	154	.248	.324	35-0-3	.143	-1	101	16	98	1.7
2001	Mon N	1	6	.143	8	8	0	0-0	42.2	59	33	7	2	16-1	36	6.33	68	.331	.391	13-0-1	.077	-1	35	-10	136	-1.4
2002	Mon N	3	8	.273	15	14	0	0-0	74.1	98	55	14	7	31-5	51	6.30	70	.318	.391	24-0-3	.208	0	94	-14	0	-1.7
	Fla N	3	2	.600	22	8	0	0-0	61.2	76	33	5	3	14-3	41	3.79	104	.306	.348	16-0-2	.188	1	150	-1	0	-0.1
	Year	6	10	.375	37	22	0	0-0	136	174	88	19	10	45-8	92	5.16	81	.313	.372	40-0-5	.200	1	114	-16	0	-1.8
2003	†Fla N	12	13	.480	33	32	2	0-0	201	204	99	19	7	49-10	133	4.30	95	.265	.311	61-0-5	.098	-1	91	-3	0	-0.5
2004	Fla N★	18	8	.692	31	31	2-2	0-0	222.1	212	80	16	11	49-13	139	3.00	137	.253	.302	68-2-9	.191	4	112	28	0	3.5
2005	NY A	4	6	.400	17	17	1-1	0-0	100	129	66	17	8	18-1	56	4.77	90	.315	.354	7	.000	-1	111	-9	97	-0.9
Total	8	61	64	.488	184	166	6-4	0-0	1037.2	1114	542	112	58	289-36	673	4.27	100	.276	.331	295-2-34	.139	-1	96	-3	574	-0.7
PAVLAS, DAVE	David Lee; B8.12.1962 Frankfurt, West Germany; BR/TR/6´7˝/(180–205); d8.21; Col Rice																									
1990	Chi N	2	0	1.000	13	0	0	0-0	21.1	23	7	2	0	6-2	12	2.11	194	.271	.312	1	.000	0	—	4	0	0.3
1991	Chi N	0	0	ø	1	0	0	0-0	1	3	2	1	0	0-0	0	18.00	22	.750	.750	0	ø	0	—	-1	0	-0.1
1995	NY A	0	0	ø	4	0	0	0-0	5.2	8	2	0	0	0-0	3	3.18	146	.333	.333	0	ø	0	—	1	0	0.0
1996	NY A	0	0	ø	16	0	0	1-0	23	23	7	0	1	7-2	18	2.35	211	.264	.326	0	ø	0	—	6	0	0.3
Total	4	2	0	1.000	34	0	0	1-0	51	57	18	3	1	13-4	33	2.65	172	.285	.329	1	.000	0	—	10	0	0.5
PAVLIK, ROGER	Roger Allen; B10.4.1967 Houston TX; BR/TR/6´2˝/220; [TexA86 2/32]; d5.2																									
1992	Tex A	4	4	.500	13	12	1	0-0	62	66	32	3	3	34-0	45	4.21	91	.280	.375	0	ø	0	111	-2	0	-0.3
1993	Tex A	12	6	.667	26	26	2	0-0	166.1	151	67	18	5	80-3	131	3.41	123	.245	.334	0	ø	0	112	16	0	1.6
1994	Tex A	2	5	.286	11	11	0	0-0	50.1	61	45	8	4	30-1	31	7.69	63	.300	.394	0	ø	0	85	-14	83	-1.5
1995	Tex A	10	10	.500	31	31	2-1	0-0	191.2	174	96	19	4	90-5	149	4.37	111	.243	.329	0	ø	0	84	12	0	1.2
1996	†Tex A★	15	8	.652	34	34	7	0-0	201	216	120	28	5	81-5	127	5.19	101	.276	.346	0	ø	0	108	3	0	0.1
1997	Tex A	3	5	.375	11	11	0	0-0	57.2	59	29	7	1	31-1	35	4.37	111	.267	.358	0	ø	0	74	4	118	0.4
1998	Tex A	1	1	.500	5	0	0	1-0	14	16	8	2	1	5-1	8	3.86	127	.286	.349	0	ø	0	—	1	157	0.1
Total	7	47	39	.547	131	125	12-1	1-0	743	743	397	85	23	351-16	526	4.58	103	.262	.346	0	ø	0	98	20	358	1.6
PAWLOWSKI, JOHN	John; B9.6.1963 Johnson City NY; BR/TR/6´2˝/175; [ChiA85 6/137]; d9.19; Col Clemson																									
1987	Chi A	0	0	ø	2	0	0	0-0	3.2	7	2	0	0	3-0	2	4.91	94	.438	.500	0	ø	0	—	0	0	0.0
1988	Chi A	1	0	1.000	6	0	0	0-0	14	20	14	2	0	3-0	10	8.36	48	.328	.354	0	ø	0	—	-6	0	-0.4
Total	2	1	0	1.000	8	0	0	0-0	17.2	27	16	2	0	6-0	12	7.64	54	.351	.388	0	ø	0	—	-6	0	-0.4
PAXTON, MIKE	Michael De Wayne; B9.3.1953 Memphis TN; BR/TR/5´11˝/190; [BosA75 23/538]; d5.25; Col Memphis																									
1977	Bos A	10	5	.667	29	12	2-1	0-1	108	134	53	7	3	25-2	58	3.83	117	.311	.350	0	ø	0	127	6	0	0.7
1978	Cle A	12	11	.522	33	27	5-2	1-2	191	179	89	13	8	63-5	96	3.86	98	.247	.313	0	ø	0	105	-1	0	-0.1
1979	Cle A	8	8	.500	33	24	3	0-0	159.2	210	118	14	2	52-1	70	5.92	73	.315	.363	0	ø	0	122	-29	0	-2.5
1980	Cle A	0	0	ø	4	0	0	0-1	7.2	13	11	4	0	6-1	6	12.91	32	.394	.475	0	ø	0	—	-7	0	-0.3
Total	4	30	24	.556	99	63	10-3	1-4	466.1	536	271	38	13	146-9	230	4.71	88	.289	.342	0	ø	0	116	-31	0	-2.2
PAYNE, GEORGE	George Washington; B5.23.1889 Mt.Vernon KY; D1.24.1959 Bellflower CA; BR/TR/5´11˝/172; d5.8																									
1920	Chi A	1	1	.500	12	0	0	0	29.2	39	24	2	0	9	7	5.46	69	.312	.358	8	.125	-0	—	-7	—	-0.5
PAYNE, HARLEY	Harley Fenwick "Lady"; B1.9.1868 Windsor OH; D12.29.1935 Orwell OH; BB/TL/6´0˝/160; d4.18																									
1896	Bro N	14	16	.467	34	28	24-2	0	241.2	284	129	4	8	58	52	3.39	122	.290	.335	98-0-4	.214	0*	72	21	—	2.2
1897	Bro N	14	17	.452	40	38	30-1	0	280	350	215	8	17	71	86	4.63	88	.303	.353	110-0-3	.236	-0*	90	-24	—	-2.0
1898	Bro N	1	0	1.000	1	1	1	0	9	11	8	0	0	3	2	4.00	90	.297	.350	4	.750	1	178	-1	—	0.0
1899	Pit N	1	3	.250	5	5	2	0	26.1	33	19	2	2	4	8	3.76	101	.306	.342	10	.100	-1	79	-1	—	-0.1
Total	4	30	36	.455	80	72	57-3	0	557	678	371	14	27	136	148	4.04	101	.298	.345	222-0-7	.230	0	83	-5	—	0.1
PAYNE, MIKE	Michael Earl; B11.15.1961 Woonsocket RI; D8.4.2002 Dunnellon FL; BR/TR/5´11˝/167; [AtlN79 6/134]; d8.22																									
1984	Atl N	0	1	.000	3	1	0	0-0	5.2	7	4	0	0	3-0	3	6.35	61	.333	.417	1	.000	-0	46	-1	0	-0.2
PAZIK, MIKE	Michael Joseph; B1.26.1950 Lynn MA; BL/TL/6´2˝/200; [NYA71 D1/13]; d5.11; C4; Col Holy Cross																									
1975	Min A	0	4	.000	5	3	0	0-0	19.2	28	20	5	0	10-0	8	8.24	47	.329	.400	0	ø	0	54	-9	0	-1.5
1976	Min A	0	0	ø	5	0	0	0-0	9	13	9	0	1	4-0	6	7.00	51	.342	.419	0	ø	0	—	-4	0	-0.2
1977	Min A	1	0	1.000	3	3	0	0-0	18	18	5	1	0	6-0	6	2.50	160	.265	.320	0	ø	0	128	3	161	0.2
Total	3	1	4	.200	13	6	0	0-0	46.2	59	34	6	1	20-0	20	5.79	66	.309	.376	0	ø	0	92	-10	161	-1.5
PEARCE, FRANK	Franklin Johnson; B3.30.1860 Jefferson Co. KY; D11.13.1926 Louisville KY; d10.4																									
1876	Lou N	0	0	ø	1	0	0	0	4	5	4	0	—	1	1	4.50	60	.263	.300	2	.000	-0	—	0	—	-0.1
PEARCE, FRANK	Franklin Thomas; B8.31.1905 Middletown KY; D9.3.1950 Van Buren NY; BR/TR/6´0˝/170; d4.20																									
1933	Phi N	5	4	.556	20	7	3-1	0	82	78	41	5	0	29	18	3.62	105	.251	.315	26-0-4	.192	-1	106	1	—	0.0
1934	Phi N	0	2	.000	7	1	0	0	20	25	16	4	0	5	4	7.20	66	.301	.341	3	.667	1	73	-4	—	-0.3
1935	Phi N	0	0	ø	5	0	0	0	13	22	15	0	0	6	7	8.31	55	.361	.418	4	.500	1	—	-5	—	-0.2
Total	3	5	6	.455	32	8	3-1	0	115	125	72	9	0	40	29	4.77	85	.275	.333	33-0-4	.273	1	98	-8	—	-0.5
PEARCE, JIM	James Madison; B6.9.1925 Zebulon NC; D7.17.2005 Raleigh NC; BR/TR/6´6˝/180; d9.8																									
1949	Was A	0	1	.000	2	1	0	0	5.1	9	10	1	0	5	1	8.44	50	.375	.483	2	.000	-0	21	-4	0	-0.6
1950	Was A	2	1	.667	20	3	1	0	56.2	58	40	2	1	37	18	6.04	74	.270	.379	13	.154	-1	141	-8	0	-0.5
1953	Was A	0	1	.000	4	1	0	0	9.1	15	10	3	0	6	0	7.71	51	.405	.488	1	.000	-0	91	-5	0	-0.4
1954	Cin N	1	0	1.000	2	1	1	0	11	7	1	0	1	5	3	0.00	ø	.194	.310	3-0-1	.000	-0	64	5	0	0.4
1955	Cin N	0	1	.000	2	1	0	0	3.1	8	5	0	0	0-0	0	10.80	39	.471	.444	0	ø	0	105	-2	0	-0.4
Total	5	3	4	.429	30	7	2	0	85.2	97	66	6	2	53-0	22	5.78	76	.295	.395	19-0-1	.105	-2	100	-14	0	-1.5
PEARCE, JOSH	Joshua Ray; B8.20.1977 Yakima WA; BR/TR/6´3˝/(215–220); [StLN99 2/82]; d4.20; Col Arizona																									
2002	StL N	0	0	ø	3	3	0	0-0	13	20	13	1	1	8-0	1	7.62	53	.377	.460	4-0-2	.250	0	115	-6	31	-0.3
2003	StL N	0	0	ø	7	0	0	0-0	9	11	3	0	1	2-0	4	3.00	137	.306	.359	0	ø	0	—	1	0	0.1
2004	StL N	0	0	ø	3	0	0	0-0	2.1	3	1	0	0	0-0	0	3.86	111	.375	.375	0	ø	0	—	0	0	0.0
Total	3	0	0	ø	13	3	0	0-0	24.1	34	17	1	2	10-0	5	5.55	74	.351	.418	4-0-2	.250	0	115	-5	31	-0.2
PEARS, FRANK	Frank H.; B8.30.1866 Louisville KY; D11.29.1923 St.Louis MO; TR/5´9˝/145; d10.6; U2																									
1889	KC AA	0	2	.000	3	2	2	0	22	21	16	2	1	9	5	4.91	87	.244	.323	11	.091	-1	51	0	—	-0.1
1893	StL N	0	0	ø	1	0	0	0	4	9	7	0	1	2	0	13.50	35	.429	.500	2	.000	-0	—	-3	—	-0.2
Total	2	0	2	.000	4	2	2	0	26	30	23	2	2	11	5	6.23	70	.280	.358	13	.077	-2	51	-3	—	-0.3
PEARSON, ALEX	Alexander Franklin; B3.9.1877 Greensboro PA; D10.30.1966 Rochester PA; BR/TR/5´10.5˝/160; d8.1																									
1902	StL N	2	6	.250	11	10	8	0	82	90	47	0	3	22	24	3.95	69	.279	.330	34	.265	0	79	-9	—	-0.8
1903	Cle A	1	2	.333	4	3	2	0	30.1	34	15	1	1	3	12	3.56	80	.281	.304	12	.083	-1	109	-1	—	-0.2
Total	2	3	8	.273	15	13	10	0	112.1	124	62	1	4	25	36	3.85	72	.279	.323	46	.217	-0	86	-10	—	-1.0
PEARSON, IKE	Issac Overton; B3.1.1917 Grenada MS; D3.17.1985 Sarasota FL; BR/TR/6´1˝/180; d6.6; Mil 1943–45; Col U. of Mississippi																									
1939	Phi N	2	13	.133	26	13	4	0	125	144	84	15	5	56	29	5.76	70	.296	.374	37-0-4	.054	-3*	55	-21	—	-2.5
1940	Phi N	3	14	.176	29	20	5-1	1	145.1	160	91	13	3	57	43	5.45	72	.275	.343	44-0-4	.205	1	75	-21	—	-2.0
1941	Phi N	4	14	.222	46	10	0	6	136	139	75	8	8	70	38	3.57	104	.266	.361	40	.125	-2	41	-3	0	-0.7
1942	Phi N	1	6	.143	35	7	0	0	85.1	87	48	4	4	50	21	4.54	73	.271	.376	23	.043	-2	65	-11	0	-1.1
1946	Phi N	1	0	1.000	5	2	1-1	0	14.1	16	8	1	1	8	6	3.77	91	.271	.368	5-1-0	.200	1	237	-1	0	0.0
1948	Chi A	2	3	.400	23	2	0	1	53	62	32	8	2	27	12	4.92	87	.292	.378	10-0-2	.200	-0	106	-4	0	-0.3
Total	6	13	50	.206	164	54	10-2	8	559	608	338	49	23	268	149	4.83	79	.279	.363	159-1-10	.126	-6	69	-61	0	-6.6

YEAR	TM LG	W	L	PCT	G	GS	CG-SHO	SV-BS	IP	H	R	HR	HB	BB-IB	SO	ERA	AERA	OAV	OOB	AB-HR-SH	AVG	PB	SUP	APR	DL	PW
Pearson, Jason	Jason John; B12.29.1975 Freeport IL; BL/TL/6´0˝/195; d6.4; Col Illinois St.																									
2002	SD N	0	0	ø	2	0	0	0-0	1.2	1	0	0	0	0-0	3	0.00	ø	.167	.167	0	ø	0	—	1	0	0.0
2003	StL N	0	0	ø	2	0	0	0-0	1	4	7	1	0	3-0	1	63.00	7	.571	.700	0	ø	0	—	-7	0	-0.3
Total	2	0	0	ø	4	0	0	0-0	2.2	5	7	1	0	3-0	4	23.63	17	.385	.500	0	ø	0	—	-6	0	-0.3
Pearson, Monte	Montgomery Marcellus "Hoot"; B9.2.1909 Oakland CA; D1.27.1978 Fresno CA; BR/TR/6´0˝/175; d4.22; Col California; [DL 1942 Cin N 140]																									
1932	Cle A	0	0	ø	8	0	0	0	8	10	9	1	0	11	5	10.13	47	.323	.500	0	ø	0	—	-4	—	-0.1
1933	Cle A	10	5	.667	19	16	10	0	135.1	111	45	5	0	55	54	**2.33**	191	.221	.297	50-0-2	.260	1	98	30	—	3.1
1934	Cle A	18	13	.581	39	33	19	2	254.2	257	144	16	1	130	140	4.52	101	.260	.346	92-1-6	.272	6	106	3	—	0.9
1935	Cle A	8	13	.381	30	24	10-1	0	181.2	199	117	9	0	103	90	4.90	92	.279	.371	62-0-1	.177	-0	91	-9	—	-0.8
1936	†NY A☆	19	7	**.731**	33	31	15-1	1	223	191	99	13	3	135	118	3.71	125	**.233**	.343	91-1-6	.253	6	152	27	—	3.3
1937	†NY A	9	3	.750	22	20	7-1	1	144.2	145	60	6	1	64	71	3.17	140	.261	.339	51-0-4	.216	1	121	21	—	1.6
1938	†NY A	16	7	.696	28	27	17-1	0	202	198	107	12	0	113	98	3.97	114	.258	.354	76-0-3	.171	1	133	13	—	1.3
1939	†NY A	12	5	.706	22	20	8	0	146.1	151	77	9	1	70	76	4.49	97	.272	.354	53-0-5	.321	6	158	0	—	0.6
1940	NY A☆	7	5	.583	16	16	7-1	0	109.2	108	48	8	0	44	43	3.69	109	.262	.333	33-0-7	.121	-1	108	6	—	0.6
1941	Cin N	1	3	.250	7	4	1	0	24.1	22	15	3	0	15	8	5.18	69	.242	.349	5-0-1	.000	-1*	71	-4	0	-0.6
Total	10	100	61	.621	224	191	94-5	4	1429.2	1392	721	82	6	740	703	4.00	112	.256	.346	513-2-35	.228	19	121	83	140	9.9
Pearson, Terry	Terry Bobby Gene; B11.10.1971 Tuscaloosa AL; BR/TR/6´0˝/200; d4.4; Col West Alabama																									
2002	Det A	0	0	ø	4	0	0	0-0	6	8	7	2	0	2-1	4	10.50	42	.320	.370	0	ø	0	—	-4	0	-0.2
Peasley, Marv	Marvin Warren; B7.16.1889 Jonesport ME; D12.27.1948 San Francisco CA; BL/TL/6´1˝/175; d9.27																									
1910	Det A	0	1	.000	2	1	0	0	10	13	14	0	1	11	4	8.10	32	.295	.446	3	.000	0	127	-6	—	-0.5
Peavy, Jake	Jacob Edward; B5.3.1981 Mobile AL; BR/TR/6´1˝/180; [SDN99 15/472]; d6.22																									
2002	SD N	6	7	.462	17	17	0	0-0	97.2	106	54	11	3	33-4	90	4.52	86	.274	.334	33-0-2	.212	2	102	-7	0	-0.6
2003	SD N	12	11	.522	32	32	0	0-0	194.2	173	94	33	6	82-3	156	4.11	97	.238	.318	55-0-8	.073	-2	96	-2	0	-0.4
2004	SD N	15	6	.714	27	27	0	0-0	166.1	146	49	13	11	53-4	173	**2.27**	174	.236	.305	59-0-5	.169	1	125	32	43	4.1
2005	†SD N★	13	7	.650	30	30	3-3	0-0	203	162	70	18	7	50-3	**216**	2.88	136	.217	.271	53-0-5	.189	2	97	26	0	2.6
2006	†SD N	11	14	.440	32	32	2	0-0	202.1	187	93	23	6	62-11	215	4.09	101	.242	.303	60-2-8	.167	3	97	4	0	0.8
Total	5	57	45	.559	138	138	5-3	0-0	864	774	360	98	33	280-25	850	3.51	114	.238	.303	260-2-28	.158	7	103	53	43	6.5
Pechiney, George	George Adolphe "Pisch"; B9.20.1861 Cincinnati OH; D7.14.1943 Cincinnati OH; BR/TR/5´9˝/184; d8.4																									
1885	Cin AA	7	4	.636	11	11	11-1	0	98	95	45	1	6	30	49	2.02	161	.247	.311	40	.150	-2	91	10	—	0.8
1886	Cin AA	15	21	.417	40	40	35-2	0	330.1	355	230	4	14	133	110	4.14	85	.266	.339	144-1	.208	-1*	104	-24	—	-2.3
1887	Cle AA	1	9	.100	10	10	10	0	86	118	124	8	3	44	24	7.12	61	.303	.378	36	.250	-0	88	-27	—	-2.1
Total	3	23	34	.404	61	61	56-3	0	514.1	568	399	13	23	207	183	4.23	85	.269	.341	220-1	.205	-3	99	-41	—	-3.6
Peek, Steve	Stephen George; B7.30.1914 Springfield MA; D9.20.1991 Syracuse NY; BB/TR/6´2˝/195; d4.16; Mil 1942–45; Col St. Lawrence																									
1941	NY A	4	2	.667	17	8	2	0	80	85	48	6	0	39	18	5.06	78	.276	.357	28-0-1	.036	-3	121	-9	0	-0.8
Peery, Red	George Allan; B8.15.1906 Payson UT; D5.6.1985 Salt Lake City UT; BL/TL/5´11˝/160; d9.22																									
1927	Pit N	0	0	ø	1	0	0	0	1	0	1	0	0	1	0	0.00	ø	.000	.333	0	ø	0	—	0	—	0.0
1929	Bos N	0	1	.000	9	1	0	0	44	53	28	1	0	9	3	5.11	91	.305	.339	14	.214	1*	56	-2	—	0.0
Total	2	0	1	.000	10	1	0	0	45	53	29	1	0	10	3	5.00	93	.301	.339	14	.214	1	56	-2	—	0.0
Peitz, Heinie	Henry Clement; B11.28.1870 St.Louis MO; D10.23.1943 Cincinnati OH; BR/TR/5´11˝/165; d10.15.1892; C3; b–Joe; ▲																									
1894	StL N	0	0	ø	1	0	0	0	3	7	7	0	1	2	0	9.00	60	.438	.526	338-3-7	.263	0*	—	-2	—	-0.1
1897	Cin N	0	1	.000	2	1	1	0	8	9	8	0	2	4	0	7.88	58	.281	.395	266-1-7	.293	0*	125	-2	—	-0.2
1899	Cin N	0	0	ø	1	0	0	0	5	6	3	0	0	1	3	5.40	73	.300	.333	293-1-10	.270	0*	—	0	—	0.0
Total	3	0	1	.000	4	1	1	0	16	22	18	0	3	7	3	7.31	62	.324	.410	897-5-24	.274	1	125	-4	—	-0.3
Pelfrey, Mike	Michael Alan; B1.14.1984 Wright–Patterson Afb OH; BR/TR/6´7˝/210; [NYN05 1/9]; d7.8; Col Wichita St.																									
2006	NY N	2	1	.667	4	4	0	0-0	21.1	25	14	1	3	12-0	13	5.48	80	.305	.408	9	.000	-1	179	-3	0	-0.4
Pelty, Barney	Barney; B9.10.1880 Farmington MO; D5.24.1939 Farmington MO; BR/TR/5´9˝/175; d8.20																									
1903	StL A	3	3	.500	7	6	5	1	48.2	49	25	1	2	15	20	2.40	121	.261	.322	20	.150	-0	90	0	—	0.0
1904	StL A	15	18	.455	39	35	31-2	0	301	270	121	7	20	77	126	2.84	87	.241	.301	118-0-2	.127	-6*	89	-9	—	-1.8
1905	StL A	14	14	.500	31	28	27-1	0	258.2	222	106	3	12	68	114	2.75	93	.233	.293	98-0-4	.153	-3	119	-3	—	-0.6
1906	StL A	16	11	.593	34	30	25-4	2	260.2	189	77	1	18	59	92	1.59	163	**.206**	.267	91-0-3	.165	-3	110	27	—	2.9
1907	StL A	12	21	.364	36	31	29-5	1	273	234	101	1	18	64	85	2.57	98	.234	.292	95-0-3	.168	-2	79	1	—	0.0
1908	StL A	7	4	.636	20	13	7-1	0	122	104	44	0	10	32	36	1.99	120	.241	.309	42-0-4	.119	-3*	138	4	—	0.1
1909	StL A	11	11	.500	27	23	17-5	0	199.1	158	63	2	5	53	88	2.30	105	.222	.281	91-0-4	.165	0*	100	4	—	0.8
1910	StL A	5	11	.313	27	19	13-3	0	165.1	157	81	3	8	70	48	3.48	71	.263	.348	56-0-4	.089	-4*	67	-13	—	-1.4
1911	StL A	7	15	.318	28	22	18-1	0	197	197	87	4	4	69	59	2.97	114	.265	.331	65-0-2	.138	-3*	55	11	—	0.8
1912	StL A	1	5	.167	6	6	2	0	38.2	43	27	0	3	15	10	5.59	59	.297	.374	12	.000	-2	70	-8	—	-1.1
	Was A	1	4	.200	11	4	1	0	43.2	40	18	0	4	10	15	3.30	101	.250	.310	9	.222	0	55	2	—	0.2
	Year	2	9	.182	17	10	3	0	82.1	83	45	0	7	25	25	4.37	76	.272	.341	21	.095	-2	64	-6	—	-0.9
Total	10	92	117	.440	266	217	175-22	4	1908	1663	750	22	104	532	693	2.63	100	.239	.302	697-0-26	.143	-25	90	16	—	-0.1
Pember, Dave	David Joseph; B5.24.1978 Cincinnati OH; BR/TR/6´5˝/225; [MilN99 8/244]; d9.3; Col Western Carolina																									
2002	Mil N	0	1	.000	4	1	0	0-0	8.2	7	6	1	0	6-0	5	5.19	79	.219	.333	1	.000	-0	23	-1	0	-0.2
Pena, Alejandro	Alejandro (Vasquez); B6.25.1959 Cambiaso, D.R.; BR/TR/6´1˝/(190–228); d8.13; [DL 1993 Pit N 182]																									
1981	†LA N	1	1	.500	14	0	0	2-2	25.1	18	8	2	0	11-1	14	2.84	116	.194	.279	6	.000	-1	—	2	0	0.1
1982	LA N	0	2	.000	29	0	0	0-0	35.2	37	24	2	1	21-7	20	4.79	72	.272	.373	0	ø	0	—	-7	0	-0.3
1983	†LA N	12	9	.571	34	26	4-3	1-1	177	152	67	7	1	51-7	120	2.75	131	.229	.283	60-1-1	.100	-2	89	16	0	1.7
1984	LA N	12	6	.667	28	28	8-**4**	0-0	199.1	186	67	7	3	46-7	135	**2.48**	**143**	.246	.291	66-0-4	.121	-1	94	23	0	1.8
1985	LA N	0	1	.000	2	1	0	0-0	4.1	7	5	1	0	3-1	2	8.31	42	.350	.435	1	.000	-0	126	-2	150	-0.5
1986	LA N	1	2	.333	24	10	0	1-0	70	74	40	6	1	30-5	46	4.89	71	.270	.343	17-0-3	.176	0	124	-11	49	-0.6
1987	LA N	2	7	.222	37	7	0	11-0	87.1	82	41	9	2	37-5	76	3.50	114	.251	.325	13-0-1	.077	-1	58	3	21	0.2
1988	†LA N	6	7	.462	60	0	0	12-2	94.1	75	29	4	1	27-6	83	1.91	175	.218	.275	6	.000	-1	—	13	0	2.0
1989	LA N	4	3	.571	53	0	0	5-4	76	62	20	6	2	18-4	75	2.13	161	.220	.271	1	1.000	0	—	11	15	1.1
1990	NY N	3	3	.500	52	0	0	5-0	76	71	31	4	1	22-5	76	3.20	118	.245	.295	6	.167	0	—	4	0	0.4
1991	NY N	6	1	.857	44	0	0	4-5	63	63	20	5	0	19-4	49	2.71	135	.267	.317	0	ø	0	—	7	0	0.9
	†Atl N	2	0	1.000	15	0	0	11-0	19.1	11	3	1	0	3-0	13	1.40	278	.167	.203	1	.000	-0	—	5	0	1.1
	Year	8	1	.889	59	0	0	15-5	82.1	74	23	6	0	22-4	62	2.40	155	.245	.293	1	.000	-0	—	12	0	2.0
1992	Atl N	1	6	.143	41	0	0	15-3	42	40	19	7	0	13-5	34	4.07	90	.255	.310	2	.000	-0	—	-1	33	-0.3
1994	Pit N	3	2	.600	22	0	0	7-1	28.2	22	16	4	1	10-2	27	5.02	87	.206	.280	1	.000	-0	—	-1	28	-0.3
1995	Bos A	1	1	.500	17	0	0	0-0	24.1	33	23	5	0	12-2	25	7.40	66	.314	.385	0	ø	0	—	-7	0	-0.5
	Fla N	2	0	1.000	13	0	0	0-1	18	11	3	2	0	3-1	21	1.50	286	.169	.206	1	.000	-0	—	6	0	0.5
	†Atl N	0	0	ø	14	0	0	0-0	13	11	6	1	0	4-0	18	4.15	104	.224	.283	0	ø	0	—	0	0	0.0
	Year	2	0	1.000	27	0	0	0-1	31	22	9	3	0	7-1	39	2.61	165	.193	.240	1	.000	-0	—	6	0	0.5
1996	Fla N	0	1	.000	4	0	0	0-0	4	4	5	2	0	1-0	5	4.50	92	.235	.278	0	ø	0	—	-1	169	-0.3
Total	15	56	52	.519	503	72	12-7	74-19	1057.2	959	427	75	13	331-62	839	3.11	118	.240	.299	181-1-9	.110	-5	92	60	647	7.0
Pena, Hipolito	Hipolito (Concepcion); B1.30.1964 Fantino, D.R.; BL/TL/6´3˝/165; d9.1																									
1986	Pit N	0	3	.000	10	1	0	1-0	8.1	7	10	3	1	3-1	6	8.64	45	.206	.289	0	ø	0	0	-5	0	-0.9
1987	Pit N	0	3	.000	16	1	0	1-0	25.2	16	14	2	0	26-3	16	4.56	91	.184	.372	6	.167	-0	22	-1	0	-0.1
1988	NY A	1	1	.500	16	0	0	0-0	14.1	10	8	1	0	9-1	10	3.14	126	.192	.306	0	ø	0	—	0	0	0.0
Total	3	1	7	.125	42	2	0	2-0	48.1	33	32	6	1	38-5	32	4.84	84	.191	.338	6	.167	-0	11	-6	0	-1.0
Pena, Jim	James Patrick; B9.17.1964 Los Angeles CA; BL/TL/6´0˝/175; [SFN86 16/396]; d7.7; Col Cal St.–Dominguez Hills																									
1992	SF N	1	1	.500	25	2	0	0-0	44	49	19	4	1	20-5	32	3.48	96	.282	.357	5-0-3	.200	0	204	-1	0	0.0

PENA, JESUS Jesus; B3.8.1975 Santo Domingo, D.R.; BL/TL/6´0˝/170; d8.7

YEAR	TM LG	W	L	PCT	G	GS	CG-SHO	SV-BS	IP	H	R	HR	HB	BB-IB	SO	ERA	AERA	OAV	OOB	AB-HR-SH	AVG	PB	SUP	APR	DL	PW
1999	Chi A	0	0	ø	26	0	0	0-1	20.1	21	15	3	1	23-5	20	5.31	93	.259	.429	0	ø	0	—	-2	0	-0.1
2000	Chi A	2	1	.667	20	0	0	1-0	23.1	25	18	6	1	16-0	19	5.40	94	.278	.385	0	ø	0	—	-2	0	-0.2
	Bos A	0	0	ø	2	0	0	0-0	3	3	1	1	0	3-0	1	3.00	167	.273	.429	0	ø	0	—	1	0	0.0
	Year	2	1	.667	22	0	0	1-0	26.1	28	19	7	1	19-0	20	5.13	99	.277	.390	0	ø	0	—	-1	0	-0.2
Total	2	2	1	.667	48	0	0	1-1	46.2	49	34	10	2	42-5	40	5.21	96	.269	.408	0	ø	0	—	-3	0	-0.3

PEÑA, JOSE Jose (Gutierrez); B12.3.1942 Ciudad Juarez, Chihuahua, Mexico; BR/TR/6´2˝/(189–190); d6.1

YEAR	TM LG	W	L	PCT	G	GS	CG-SHO	SV-BS	IP	H	R	HR	HB	BB-IB	SO	ERA	AERA	OAV	OOB	AB-HR-SH	AVG	PB	SUP	APR	DL	PW
1969	Cin N	1	1	.500	6	0	0	0-0	5	10	10	0	0	5-1	3	18.00	21	.400	.500	0	ø	0	—	-7	0	-1.3
1970	LA N	4	3	.571	29	0	0	4-2	57	51	32	8	3	29-5	31	4.42	87	.241	.336	8	.125	0	—	-4	0	-0.5
1971	LA N	2	0	1.000	21	0	0	1-0	43	32	18	7	1	18-1	44	3.56	91	.211	.295	3	.667	1	—	-1	0	0.0
1972	LA N	0	0	ø	5	0	0	0-0	7.1	13	8	1	0	6-1	4	8.59	39	.371	.452	0	ø	0	—	-4	0	-0.2
Total	4	7	4	.636	61	0	0	5-2	112.1	106	68	16	4	58-8	82	4.97	72	.250	.341	11	.273	1	—	-16	0	-2.0

PENA, JUAN Juan Francisco; B6.27.1977 Santo Domingo, D.R.; BR/TR/6´5˝/215; [BosA95 27/746]; d5.8; Col Miami–Dade Wolfson (FL) CC; [DL 2000 Bos A 181, 2001 Bos A 57]

YEAR	TM LG	W	L	PCT	G	GS	CG-SHO	SV-BS	IP	H	R	HR	HB	BB-IB	SO	ERA	AERA	OAV	OOB	AB-HR-SH	AVG	PB	SUP	APR	DL	PW
1999	Bos A	2	0	1.000	2	2	0	0-0	13	9	1	0	0	3-0	15	0.69	720	.196	.245	0	ø	0	103	6	63	1.0

PENA, ORLANDO Orlando Gregorio (Quevara); B11.17.1933 Victoria de las Tunas, Cuba; BR/TR/5´11˝/(150–165); d8.24

YEAR	TM LG	W	L	PCT	G	GS	CG-SHO	SV-BS	IP	H	R	HR	HB	BB-IB	SO	ERA	AERA	OAV	OOB	AB-HR-SH	AVG	PB	SUP	APR	DL	PW
1958	Cin N	1	0	1.000	9	0	0	3	15	10	1	0	0	4-1	11	0.60	691	.185	.241	0	ø	0	—	6	0	0.6
1959	Cin N	5	9	.357	46	8	1	5	136	150	80	26	0	39-5	76	4.76	85	.280	.325	34-0-5	.088	-0	85	-10	0	-1.1
1960	Cin N	0	1	.000	4	0	0	0	9.1	8	3	0	0	3-2	9	2.89	132	.222	.282	1	.000	-0	—	1	0	0.1
1962	KC A	6	4	.600	13	12	6-1	0	89.2	71	31	9	1	27-2	56	3.01	140	.213	.272	31	.161	-0	109	12	0	1.2
1963	KC A	12	20	.375	35	33	9-3	0	217	218	93	24	5	53-2	128	3.69	106	.260	.306	62-1-10	.145	0	70	7	0	0.9
1964	KC A	12	14	.462	40	32	5	0	219.1	231	126	40	8	73-2	184	4.43	86	.268	.329	75-1-3	.160	0*	90	-17	0	-2.0
1965	KC A	0	6	.000	12	5	0	0	35.1	42	30	4	2	13-0	24	6.88	51	.302	.368	9	.111	-0	65	-13	0	-2.0
	Det A	4	6	.400	30	0	0	4	57.1	54	18	5	1	20-5	55	2.51	138	.252	.318	8-0-1	.250	1	—	6	0	1.1
	Year	4	12	.250	42	5	0	4	92.2	96	48	9	3	33-5	79	4.18	83	.272	.338	17-0-1	.176	1	66	-6	0	-0.9
1966	Det A	4	2	.667	54	0	0	7	108	105	47	16	5	35-6	79	3.08	113	.252	.315	18-0-2	.111	-1	—	2	0	0.2
1967	Det A	0	1	.000	2	0	0	0	2	5	3	0	1	0-0	2	13.50	24	.500	.500	0	ø	0	—	-2	0	-0.4
	Cle A	0	3	.000	48	1	0	8	88.1	67	34	8	1	22-5	72	3.36	97	.208	.259	8-0-1	.000	-1	27	1	0	-0.1
	Year	0	4	.000	50	1	0	8	90.1	72	37	8	2	22-5	74	3.59	91	.217	.267	8-0-1	.000	-1	27	-1	0	-0.5
1970	Pit N	2	1	.667	23	0	0	2-1	37.2	38	21	6	1	7-2	25	4.78	83	.268	.305	6-0-1	.000	-1	—	-3	0	-0.3
1971	Bal A	0	1	.000	5	0	0	0-0	14.2	16	7	0	0	5-1	4	3.07	111	.281	.339	3	.000	-0	—	0	0	0.0
1973	Bal A	1	1	.500	11	2	0	1-1	44.2	36	20	10	2	8-1	23	4.03	94	.218	.260	0	ø	0	59	0	0	0.0
	StL N	4	4	.500	42	0	0	6-1	62	60	17	3	0	14-4	38	2.18	169	.251	.290	7-0-1	.143	-0	—	10	0	1.5
1974	StL N	5	2	.714	42	0	0	1-2	45	45	15	0	1	20-3	23	2.60	139	.269	.342	2	.500	0	—	5	0	0.8
	Cal A	0	0	ø	4	0	0	3-0	8	6	0	0	0	1-0	5	0.00	ø	.214	.241	0	ø	0	—	3	0	0.3
1975	Cal A	0	2	.000	7	0	0	0-0	12.2	13	3	0	0	8-1	4	2.13	168	.283	.382	0	ø	0	—	2	0	0.3
Total	14	56	77	.421	427	93	21-4	40-5	1202	1175	549	151	28	352-42	818	3.71	102	.255	.309	264-2-24	.136	-3	85	10	0	1.1

PENA, TONY Ramon Antonio; B1.9.1982 Santo Domingo, D.R.; BR/TR/6´1˝/220; d7.18

YEAR	TM LG	W	L	PCT	G	GS	CG-SHO	SV-BS	IP	H	R	HR	HB	BB-IB	SO	ERA	AERA	OAV	OOB	AB-HR-SH	AVG	PB	SUP	APR	DL	PW
2006	Ari N	3	4	.429	25	0	0	1-0	30.2	36	21	6	0	8-0	21	5.58	84	.290	.331	2	.000	-0	—	-3	0	-0.6

PENA, RAMON Ramon Arturo (Padilla); B5.5.1962 Santiago, D.R.; BR/TR/5´10˝/155; d4.27; b–Tony

YEAR	TM LG	W	L	PCT	G	GS	CG-SHO	SV-BS	IP	H	R	HR	HB	BB-IB	SO	ERA	AERA	OAV	OOB	AB-HR-SH	AVG	PB	SUP	APR	DL	PW
1989	Det A	0	0	ø	8	0	0	0-0	18	26	13	0	2	8-3	12	6.00	64	.338	.409	0	ø	0	—	-4	21	-0.2

PENCE, RUSTY Russell William; B3.11.1900 Marine IL; D8.11.1971 Hot Springs AR; BR/TR/6´0˝/185; d5.13

YEAR	TM LG	W	L	PCT	G	GS	CG-SHO	SV-BS	IP	H	R	HR	HB	BB-IB	SO	ERA	AERA	OAV	OOB	AB-HR-SH	AVG	PB	SUP	APR	DL	PW
1921	Chi A	0	0	ø	4	0	0	0	5.1	6	5	0	1	7	2	8.44	50	.286	.483	1	.000	-0	—	-2	—	-0.1

PENN, HAYDEN Hayden Andrew; B10.13.1984 LaJolla CA; BR/TR/6´3˝/195; [BalA02 5/136]; d5.28

YEAR	TM LG	W	L	PCT	G	GS	CG-SHO	SV-BS	IP	H	R	HR	HB	BB-IB	SO	ERA	AERA	OAV	OOB	AB-HR-SH	AVG	PB	SUP	APR	DL	PW
2005	Bal A	3	2	.600	8	8	0	0-0	38.1	46	30	6	0	21-3	18	6.34	69	.295	.379	1-0-1	.000	0	97	-8	0	-0.8
2006	Bal A	0	4	.000	6	6	0	0-0	19.2	38	33	8	2	13-0	8	15.10	30	.392	.473	0	ø	0	45	-22	58	-3.0
Total	2	3	6	.333	14	14	0	0-0	58	84	63	14	2	34-3	26	9.31	48	.332	.415	1-0-1	.000	0	75	-30	58	-3.8

PENNER, KEN Kenneth William; B4.24.1896 Boonville IN; D5.28.1959 Sacramento CA; BL/TR/5´11.5˝/170; d9.11

YEAR	TM LG	W	L	PCT	G	GS	CG-SHO	SV-BS	IP	H	R	HR	HB	BB-IB	SO	ERA	AERA	OAV	OOB	AB-HR-SH	AVG	PB	SUP	APR	DL	PW
1916	Cle A	1	1	.500	4	2	0	0	12.2	14	6	0	0	4	5	4.26	71	.304	.360	2	.000	-0	88	-1	—	-0.1
1929	Chi N	0	1	.000	5	0	0	0	12.2	14	11	1	0	6	3	2.84	162	.280	.357	4	.250	0	—	0	—	0.0
Total	2	1	2	.333	9	2	0	0	25.1	28	17	1	0	10	8	3.55	108	.292	.358	6	.167	-0	88	-1	—	-0.1

PENNINGTON, BRAD Brad Lee; B4.14.1969 Salem IN; BL/TL/6´5˝/(205–215); [BalA89 12/297]; d4.17; Col Vincennes (IN) JC

YEAR	TM LG	W	L	PCT	G	GS	CG-SHO	SV-BS	IP	H	R	HR	HB	BB-IB	SO	ERA	AERA	OAV	OOB	AB-HR-SH	AVG	PB	SUP	APR	DL	PW
1993	Bal A	3	2	.600	34	0	0	4-3	33	34	25	7	2	25-0	39	6.55	69	.266	.391	0	ø	0	—	-7	0	-1.0
1994	Bal A	0	1	.000	8	0	0	0-1	6	9	8	2	0	8-0	7	12.00	42	.346	.500	0	ø	0	—	-4	0	-0.6
1995	Bal A	0	1	.000	8	0	0	0-1	6.2	3	7	1	0	11-1	10	8.10	59	.136	.424	0	ø	0	—	-3	0	-0.3
	Cin N	0	0	ø	6	0	0	0-0	9.2	9	8	0	1	11-0	7	5.59	75	.273	.447	2	.000	-0	—	-2	0	-0.1
1996	Bos A	0	2	.000	14	0	0	0-0	13	6	5	1	0	15-1	13	2.77	184	.140	.356	0	ø	0	—	3	0	0.4
	Cal A	0	0	ø	8	0	0	0-0	7.1	5	10	1	0	16-0	7	12.27	41	.185	.488	0	ø	0	—	-5	25	-0.2
	Year	0	2	.000	22	0	0	0-0	20.1	11	15	2	0	31-1	20	6.20	82	.157	.412	0	ø	0	—	-2	0	0.2
1998	TB A	0	0	ø	1	0	0	0-0	0	1	1	0	0	3-0	0	(1)	ø	1.000	1.000	0	ø	0	—	-1	0	-0.1
Total	5	3	6	.333	79	0	0	4-5	75.2	67	64	12	3	89-2	83	7.02	67	.239	.423	2	.000	-0	—	-19	25	-1.9

PENNINGTON, KEWPIE George Louis; B9.24.1896 New York NY; D5.3.1953 Newark NJ; BR/TR/5´8.5˝/168; d4.14

YEAR	TM LG	W	L	PCT	G	GS	CG-SHO	SV-BS	IP	H	R	HR	HB	BB-IB	SO	ERA	AERA	OAV	OOB	AB-HR-SH	AVG	PB	SUP	APR	DL	PW
1917	StL A	0	0	ø	1	0	0	0	1	1	0	0	0	0	0	0.00	ø	.250	.250	0	ø	0	—	0	—	0.0

PENNOCK, HERB Herbert Jefferis "The Knight of Kennett Square"; B2.10.1894 Kennett Square PA; D1.30.1948 New York NY; BB/TL/6´0˝/160; d5.14; Mil 1918; C4; HF1948

YEAR	TM LG	W	L	PCT	G	GS	CG-SHO	SV-BS	IP	H	R	HR	HB	BB-IB	SO	ERA	AERA	OAV	OOB	AB-HR-SH	AVG	PB	SUP	APR	DL	PW
1912	Phi A	1	2	.333	17	2	1	2	50	48	31	1	3	30	38	4.50	68	.262	.375	15-0-1	.133	-1	120	-8	—	-0.5
1913	Phi A	2	1	.667	14	3	1	0	33.1	30	24	4	0	22	17	5.13	54	.242	.356	9	.111	-0	223	-10	—	-0.8
1914	†Phi A	11	4	.733	28	14	8-3	3	151.2	136	56	1	2	65	90	2.79	94	.248	.330	56-0-1	.214	2	140	-3	—	-0.1
1915	Phi A	3	6	.333	11	8	3-1	1	44	46	34	2	2	29	24	5.32	55	.266	.377	18	.278	1	81	-11	—	-1.9
	Bos A	0	0	ø	5	1	0	0	14	23	16	0	0	10	7	9.64	29	.390	.478	6	.167	0	262	-10	—	-0.5
	Year	3	6	.333	16	9	3-1	1	58	69	50	2	2	39	31	6.36	45	.297	.403	24	.250	1	101	-21	—	-2.4
1916	Bos A	0	2	.000	9	2	0	1	26.2	23	11	0	1	8	12	3.04	91	.245	.311	8	.125	-0*	27	-1	—	-0.1
1917	Bos A	5	5	.500	24	5	4-1	1	100.2	90	49	2	3	23	35	3.31	78	.243	.292	24-0-1	.167	2	117	-9	—	-0.7
1919	Bos A	16	8	.667	32	26	16-5	0	219	223	78	2	3	48	70	2.71	111	.274	.316	75-0-6	.173	1	120	9	—	1.0
1920	Bos A	16	13	.552	37	31	19-4	2	242.1	244	108	9	4	61	68	3.68	99	.264	.312	77-0-7	.260	4*	97	3	—	0.6
1921	Bos A	13	14	.481	32	31	15-1	0	222.2	268	121	7	2	59	91	4.04	105	.307	.352	85-1-4	.212	2	79	2	—	0.5
1922	Bos A	10	17	.370	32	26	15-1	1	202	230	108	7	1	74	59	4.32	95	.297	.359	65-0-2	.138	-3	72	-3	—	-0.5
1923	†NY A	19	6	**.760**	35	27	21-1	3	238.1	235	86	11	2	68	93	3.13	126	.261	.314	83-0-8	.193	0	121	25	—	2.4
1924	NY A	21	9	.700	40	34	25-4	3	286.1	302	104	13	1	64	101	2.83	147	.273	.314	101-2-10	.158	-2	107	43	—	3.8
1925	NY A	16	17	.485	47	31	21-2	2	**277**	267	117	11	2	71	88	2.96	144	.254	**.303**	99-0-9	.202	-3	84	36	—	3.3
1926	†NY A	23	11	.676	40	33	19-1	2	266.1	294	133	11	4	43	78	3.62	107	.282	**.313**	85-0-16	.212	3	119	6	—	1.0
1927	†NY A	19	8	.704	34	26	18-1	2	209.2	225	89	5	2	48	51	3.00	128	.283	.325	69-0-13	.217	-0	134	19	—	2.1
1928	NY A	17	6	.739	28	24	18-**5**	3	211	215	71	2	0	40	53	2.56	147	.267	.302	74-0-7	.203	-1	114	31	—	3.1
1929	NY A	9	11	.450	27	23	8-1	2	157.1	205	101	11	3	28	49	4.92	78	.318	.349	51-0-6	.176	-1	108	-19	—	-2.1
1930	NY A	11	7	.611	25	19	11-1	0	156.1	194	95	8	0	20	46	4.32	100	.301	.322	60-0-1	.183	-2	137	-2	—	-0.5
1931	NY A	11	6	.647	25	25	12-1	0	189.1	247	96	7	1	30	65	4.28	93	.315	.342	66-1-7	.152	1	147	-3	—	-0.2
1932	†NY A	9	5	.643	22	21	9-1	0	146.2	191	94	8	0	38	54	4.60	89	.310	.350	53-0-5	.151	0	143	-13	—	-1.0
1933	NY A	7	4	.636	23	5	2-1	4	65	96	46	4	0	21	22	5.54	70	.342	.387	21-0-6	.238	0	180	-13	—	-1.9
1934	Bos A	2	0	1.000	30	2	1	1	62	68	31	2	0	16	16	3.05	158	.276	.321	14-0-1	.214	-0	163	**9**	—	0.3
Total	22	241	162	.598	617	419	247-35	33	3571.2	3900	1699	128	36	916	1227	3.60	106	.282	.328	1214-4-111	.191	3	113	78	—	7.3

PENNY, BRAD Bradley Wayne; B5.24.1978 Broken Arrow OK; BR/TR/6´4˝/(200–250); [AriN96 5/155]; d4.7

YEAR	TM LG	W	L	PCT	G	GS	CG-SHO	SV-BS	IP	H	R	HR	HB	BB-IB	SO	ERA	AERA	OAV	OOB	AB-HR-SH	AVG	PB	SUP	APR	DL	PW
2000	Fla N	8	7	.533	23	22	0	0-0	119.2	120	70	13	5	60-4	80	4.81	91	.263	.354	45-0-1	.111	-2*	116	-6	43	-0.8
2001	Fla N	10	10	.500	31	31	1-1	0-0	205	183	92	15	7	54-3	154	3.69	113	.240	.296	62-0-3	.161	1	86	11	0	0.9
2002	Fla N	8	7	.533	24	24	1-1	0-0	129.1	148	76	18	1	50-7	93	4.66	84	.288	.350	48-0-1	.167	0	109	-13	44	-1.3
2003	†Fla N	14	10	.583	32	32	0	0-0	196.1	195	96	21	3	56-6	138	4.13	99	.264	.316	68-2-5	.132	1*	116	-1	0	-0.1
2004	Fla N	8	8	.500	21	21	0	0-0	131.1	124	50	10	3	39-6	105	3.15	130	.249	.306	47-0-1	.064	-3	81	14	0	1.2

YEAR	TM LG	W	L	PCT	G	GS	CG-SHO	SV-BS	IP	H	R	HR	HB	BB-IB	SO	ERA	AERA	OAV	OOB	AB-HR-SH	AVG	PB	SUP	APR	DL	PW
	LA N	1	2	.333	3	3	0	0-0	11.2	6	5	2	0	6-0	6	3.09	134	.154	.267	4	.000	-0	30	1	44	0.1
	Year	9	10	.474	24	24	0	0-0	143	130	55	12	3	45-6	111	3.15	131	.243	.303	51-0-1	.059	-4	74	17	0	1.3
2005	LA N	7	9	.438	29	29	1	0-0	175.1	185	78	17	3	41-2	122	3.90	106	.270	.313	50-0-9	.160	1	101	7	21	0.7
2006	†LA N★	**16**	9	.640	34	33	0	0-0	189	206	94	19	9	54-4	148	4.33	101	.279	.334	65-0-5	.185	1	114	4	0	0.5
Total	7	72	62	.537	197	195	3-2	0-0	1157.2	1167	561	115	31	360-32	846	4.06	103	.263	.322	389-2-25	.141	-2	103	17	152	1.2
PENSON, PAUL	Paul Eugene; B7.12.1931 Kansas City KS; BR/TR/6´1˝/185; d4.21																									
1954	Phi N	1	1	.500	5	3	0	0	16	14	11	1	0	14	3	4.50	90	.237	.368	7	.000	-1	132	-2	0	-0.3
PENTZ, GENE	Eugene David; B6.21.1953 Johnstown PA; BR/TR/6´1˝/(192–215); [DetA71 7/157]; d7.29																									
1975	Det A	0	4	.000	13	0	0	0-1	25.1	27	14	0	0	20-4	21	3.20	126	.293	.412	0	ø	0	—	1	0	0.1
1976	Hou N	3	3	.500	40	0	0	5-2	63.2	62	26	5	1	31-2	36	2.97	109	.259	.343	5	.200	0	—	1	43	0.2
1977	Hou N	5	2	.714	41	4	0	2-2	87	76	41	8	1	44-5	51	3.83	94	.236	.324	13	.000	-2	117	-2	0	-0.3
1978	Hou N	0	0	ø	10	0	0	0-0	15	12	13	1	1	13-3	8	6.00	56	.214	.366	1	.000	-0	—	-6	115	-0.3
Total	4	8	9	.471	104	4	0	7-5	191	177	94	14	3	108-14	116	3.63	97	.250	.346	19	.053	-1	117	-6	158	-0.3
PEOPLES, JIMMY	James Elsworth; B10.8.1863 Big Beaver MI; D8.29.1920 Detroit MI; TR/5´8˝/200; d5.29.1884; U1; ▲																									
1885	Cin AA	0	2	.000	2	2	1	0	15	30	28	0	3	2	4	12.00	27	.390	.427	22	.182	-0*	118	-13	—	-1.1
PEPPER, LAURIN	Hugh McLaurin; B1.18.1931 Vaughan MS; BR/TR/5´11˝/190; d7.4; Col Southern Mississippi																									
1954	Pit N	1	5	.167	14	8	0	0	50.2	63	53	4	0	43	17	7.99	52	.315	.429	17	.235	0	75	-21	0	-2.0
1955	Pit N	0	1	.000	14	1	0	0	20	30	24	5	2	25-0	7	10.35	40	.370	.523	2	.000	-0	43	-13	0	-0.6
1956	Pit N	1	1	.500	11	7	0	0	30	30	17	1	0	25-1	12	3.00	126	.256	.385	6	.000	-0	67	0	0	-0.1
1957	Pit N	0	1	.000	5	1	0	0	9	11	8	1	0	5-2	4	8.00	47	.297	.381	0	ø	0*	70	-4	0	-0.4
Total	4	2	8	.200	44	17	0	0	109.2	134	102	11	2	98-3	40	7.06	57	.308	.433	25	.160	-0	69	-38	0	-3.1
PEPPER, BOB	Robert Ernest; B5.3.1895 Rosston PA; D4.8.1968 Ford Cliff PA; BR/TR/6´2˝/178; d7.23																									
1915	Phi A	0	0	ø	1	0	0	0	5	6	5	0	1	4	0	1.80	163	.333	.478	2	.000	-0	—	-1	—	-0.1
PEPPERS, HARRISON	William Harrison (b William Harrison Pepper); B9.1866 KY; D11.5.1903 Webb City MO; BL; d6.30																									
1894	Lou N	0	1	.000	2	1	0	0	8	10	7	0	0	4	0	6.75	76	.303	.378	4	.000	-1	83	-1	—	-0.1
PERALTA, JOEL	Joel (Gutierrez); B3.23.1976 Bonao, D.R.; BR/TR/5´11˝/(170–180); d5.25																									
2005	LA A	1	0	1.000	28	0	0	0-0	34.2	28	15	6	0	14-2	30	3.89	110	.219	.294	0	ø	0	—	2	0	0.1
2006	KC A	1	3	.250	64	0	0	1-2	73.2	74	37	10	2	17-2	57	4.40	107	.263	.307	0	ø	0	—	3	0	0.1
Total	2	2	3	.400	92	0	0	1-2	108.1	102	52	16	2	31-4	87	4.24	107	.249	.303	0	ø	0	—	5	0	0.2
PERAZA, LUIS	Luis (Rios); B6.17.1942 Rio Piedras, PR; BR/TR/5´11˝/185; d4.9																									
1969	Phi N	0	0	ø	8	0	0	0-0	9	12	6	1	0	2-0	7	6.00	59	.364	.378	1	.000	-0	—	-2	0	-0.1
PERAZA, OSWALDO	Oswald Jose; B10.19.1962 Puerto Cabello, Carabobo, Venez.; BR/TR/6´4˝/172; d4.4; [DL 1989 Bal A 182]																									
1988	Bal A	5	7	.417	19	15	1	0-0	86	98	62	10	2	37-2	61	5.55	71	.282	.352	0	ø	0	96	-17	0	-2.1
PERCIVAL, TROY	Troy Eugene; B8.9.1969 Fontana CA; BR/TR/6´3˝/(200–236); [CalA90 6/179]; d4.26; Col California–Riverside; [DL 2006 Det A 182]																									
1995	Cal A	3	2	.600	62	0	0	3-3	74	37	19	6	1	26-2	94	1.95	242	.147	.229	0	ø	0	—	22	0	1.4
1996	Cal A★	0	2	.000	62	0	0	36-3	74	38	20	8	2	31-4	100	2.31	219	.149	.246	1	.000	-0	—	23	0	2.4
1997	Ana A	5	5	.500	55	0	0	27-4	52	40	20	6	4	22-2	72	3.46	133	.205	.296	0	ø	0	—	7	39	1.4
1998	Ana A★	2	7	.222	67	0	0	42-6	66.2	45	31	5	3	37-4	87	3.65	130	.186	.299	0	ø	0	—	7	0	1.3
1999	Ana A☆	4	6	.400	60	0	0	31-8	57	38	24	9	3	22-0	58	3.79	129	.186	.274	0	ø	0	—	8	0	1.4
2000	Ana A	5	5	.500	54	0	0	32-10	50	42	27	7	2	30-4	49	4.50	115	.228	.339	0	ø	0	—	3	20	0.6
2001	Ana A★	4	2	.667	57	0	0	39-3	57.2	39	19	3	2	18-1	71	2.65	175	.187	.258	0	ø	0	—	12	0	2.3
2002	†Ana A	4	1	.800	58	0	0	40-4	56.1	38	12	5	0	25-1	68	1.92	234	.188	.276	0	ø	0	—	16	30	3.2
2003	Ana A	0	5	.000	52	0	0	33-4	49.1	33	22	7	3	23-1	48	3.47	126	.184	.286	0	ø	0	—	5	15	0.8
2004	Ana A	2	3	.400	52	0	0	33-5	49.2	43	19	7	3	19-3	33	2.90	154	.230	.308	0	ø	0	—	8	25	1.5
2005	Det A	1	3	.250	26	0	0	8-3	25	19	16	7	2	11-3	20	5.76	74	.207	.302	0	ø	0	—	-4	113	-0.7
Total	11	30	41	.423	605	0	0	324-53	611.2	412	229	70	25	264-25	700	3.10	152	.187	.280	1	.000	-0	—	107	424	15.6
PERDUE, HUB	Herbert Rodney "The Gallatin Squash"; B6.7.1882 Bethpage TN; D10.31.1968 Gallatin TX; BR/TR/5´10.5˝/192; d4.19																									
1911	Bos N	6	10	.375	24	19	9	1	137.1	180	100	10	4	41	40	4.98	77	.321	.372	48-0-4	.208	-1	117	-16	—	-1.7
1912	Bos N	13	16	.448	37	30	20-1	3	249	295	135	11	2	54	101	3.80	94	.303	.341	87-0-6	.138	-5	83	-4	—	-1.1
1913	Bos N	16	13	.552	38	32	16-3	1	212.1	201	107	7	4	39	91	3.26	101	.249	.287	67-0-4	.104	-5	95	1	—	-0.7
1914	Bos N	2	5	.286	9	9	2	0	51	60	35	5	3	11	13	5.82	47	.311	.357	14-0-1	.071	-0	92	-15	—	-1.8
	StL N	8	8	.500	22	19	12	1	153.1	160	60	3	5	35	43	2.82	99	.290	.338	48-0-5	.167	-1	92	3	—	-0.1
	Year	10	13	.435	31	28	14	1	204.1	220	95	8	8	46	56	3.57	78	.296	.343	62-0-6	.145	-1	92	-9	—	-1.9
1915	StL N	6	12	.333	31	13	5-1	1	115.1	141	66	7	2	19	29	4.21	66	.311	.341	36-0-1	.111	-1	96	-16	—	-2.5
Total	5	51	64	.443	161	122	64-5	7	918.1	1037	503	43	20	199	317	3.85	85	.293	.334	300-0-21	.140	-13	95	-47	—	-7.9
PEREZ, BELTRAN	Beltran Ogilbio; B10.24.1981 San Francisco de Macoris, D.R.; BR/TR/6´2˝/180; d9.2																									
2006	Was N	2	1	.667	8	3	0	0-0	21	16	9	3	0	13-2	9	3.86	113	.222	.341	6	.500	1*	113	2	0	0.4
PEREZ, CARLOS	Carlos Gross (b Carlos Gross (Perez)); B4.14.1971 Nigua, D.R.; BL/TL/6´3˝/(195–210); d4.27; b–Pascual b–Melido; [DL 1996 Mon N 182, 2001 LA N 34]																									
1995	Mon N★	10	8	.556	28	23	2-1	0-0	141.1	142	61	18	5	28-2	106	3.69	116	.257	.299	45-1-4	.133	1	90	10	0	1.3
1997	Mon N	12	13	.480	33	32	8-**5**	0-0	206.2	206	109	21	4	48-1	110	3.88	108	.260	.303	64-1-5	.172	2	99	3	0	0.6
1998	Mon N	7	10	.412	23	23	3	0-0	163.1	177	79	12	3	33-3	82	3.75	112	.277	.314	47-1-11	.191	2	70	7	0	0.9
	LA N	4	4	.500	11	11	4-2	0-0	77.2	67	30	9	0	30-1	46	3.24	124	.234	.307	24-0-3	.083	-0	75	8	0	0.7
	Year	11	14	.440	34	34	7-2	0-0	241	244	109	21	3	63-4	128	3.59	116	.263	.312	71-1-14	.155	1	72	13	0	1.6
1999	LA N	2	10	.167	17	16	0	0-0	89.2	116	77	23	6	39-1	40	7.43	59	.317	.389	27-1-3	.296	4	82	-30	27	-2.8
2000	LA N	5	8	.385	30	22	0	0-1	144	192	95	25	8	33-1	64	5.56	80	.324	.367	43-0-7	.047	-3*	100	-17	0	-1.5
Total	5	40	53	.430	142	127	17-8	0-1	822.2	900	451	108	26	211-9	448	4.44	96	.279	.327	250-4-33	.152	6	88	-19	243	-0.8
PEREZ, GEORGE	George Thomas; B12.29.1937 San Fernando CA; BR/TR/6´2.5˝/200; d4.17																									
1958	Pit N	0	1	.000	4	0	0	1	8.1	9	5	1	0	4-0	2	5.40	72	.300	.371	2	.000	-0	—	-1	0	-0.2
PEREZ, JUAN	Juan P.; B9.3.1978 Villa Rivas, D.R.; BR/TL/6´0˝/170; d9.7																									
2006	Pit N	0	1	.000	7	0	0	0-0	3.1	5	3	1	2	1-0	3	8.10	57	.385	.471	0	ø	0	—	-1	0	-0.2
PEREZ, MELIDO	Melido Turpen Gross (b Melido Turpen Gross (Perez)); B2.15.1966 San Cristobal, D.R.; BR/TR/6´4˝/(180–210); d9.4; b–Pascual b–Carlos; [DL 1996 NY A 182]																									
1987	KC A	1	1	.500	3	3	0	0-0	10.1	18	12	2	0	5-0	5	7.84	59	.375	.434	0	ø	0	126	-4	0	-0.7
1988	Chi A	12	10	.545	32	32	3-1	0-0	197	186	105	26	2	72-0	138	3.79	106	.248	.313	0	ø	0	99	0	0	-0.1
1989	Chi A	11	14	.440	31	31	2	0-0	183.1	187	106	23	3	90-3	141	5.01	77	.264	.348	0	ø	0	96	-20	0	-2.5
1990	Chi A	13	14	.481	35	35	3-3	0-0	197	177	111	14	2	86-1	161	4.61	83	.241	.320	0	ø	0	102	-18	0	-2.2
1991	Chi A	8	7	.533	49	8	0	1-4	135.2	111	49	15	1	52-0	128	3.12	128	.224	.299	0	ø	0	86	15	0	1.5
1992	NY A	13	16	.448	33	33	10-1	0-0	247.2	212	94	16	5	93-5	218	2.87	138	.235	.308	0	ø	0	89	26	0	2.9
1993	NY A	6	14	.300	25	25	0	0-0	163	173	103	22	1	64-5	148	5.19	81	.267	.333	0	ø	0	74	-19	13	-2.0
1994	NY A	9	4	.692	22	22	1	0-0	151.1	134	74	16	3	58-5	109	4.10	112	.238	.311	0	ø	0	100	9	0	0.6
1995	NY A	5	5	.500	13	12	1	0-0	69.1	70	46	10	1	31-2	44	5.58	83	.261	.337	0	ø	0	129	-8	69	-1.0
Total	9	78	85	.479	243	201	20-5	1-4	1354.2	1268	700	144	18	551-21	1092	4.17	98	.248	.321	0	ø	0	96	-19	264	-3.5
PEREZ, MIKE	Michael Irvin (Ortega); B10.19.1964 Yauco, PR; BR/TR/6´0˝/(187–200); [StLN86 12/312]; d9.5; Col Troy St.																									
1990	StL N	1	0	1.000	13	0	0	1-1	13.2	12	6	0	0	3-0	5	3.95	97	.240	.273	1	.000	-0	—	0	0	0.0
1991	StL N	0	2	.000	14	0	0	0-0	17	19	11	1	1	7-2	7	5.82	64	.288	.365	0	ø	0	—	-3	0	-0.4
1992	StL N	9	3	.750	77	0	0	0-3	93	70	23	4	1	32-9	46	1.84	186	.210	.278	4-0-2	.000	-0	—	16	0	2.0
1993	StL N	7	2	.778	65	0	0	7-3	72.2	65	24	4	1	20-1	58	2.48	163	.243	.294	1	.000	0	—	12	40	1.6
1994	StL N	2	3	.400	36	0	0	12-2	31	52	32	5	3	10-1	20	8.71	49	.391	.430	0	ø	0	—	-15	44	-2.9
1995	Chi N	2	6	.250	68	0	0	2-1	71.1	72	30	8	4	27-8	49	3.66	114	.268	.340	4-0-1	.000	0	—	5	0	0.5
1996	Chi N	1	0	1.000	24	0	0	0-0	27	29	14	2	3	13-1	22	4.67	94	.264	.357	1	.000	-0	—	0	0	0.0

YEAR	TM LG	W	L	PCT	G	GS	CG-SHO	SV-BS	IP	H	R	HR	HB	BB-IB	SO	ERA	AERA	OAV	OOB	AB-HR-SH	AVG	PB	SUP	APR	DL	PW
1997	KC A	2	0	1.000	16	0	0	0-0	20.1	15	8	2	1	8-0	17	3.54	134	.214	.304	0	ø	0	—	3	0	0.3
Total	8	24	16	.600	313	0	0	22-10	346	334	148	26	14	120-22	224	3.56	111	.257	.323	11-0-3	.000	-0	—	18	84	1.1
PEREZ, ODALIS	Odalis Amadol; B6.11.1977 Las Matas de Farfan, D.R.; BL/TL/6´0˝/(150–220); d9.1; [DL 2000 Atl N 181]																									
1998	†Atl N	0	1	.000	10	0	0	0-1	10.2	10	5	1	0	4-0	5	4.22	99	.244	.311	0	ø	0	—	0	0	0.0
1999	Atl N	4	6	.400	18	17	0	0-0	93	100	65	12	1	53-2	82	6.00	75	.275	.366	30-0-4	.133	-1	110	-14	73	-1.3
2001	Atl N	7	8	.467	24	16	0	0-0	95.1	108	55	7	1	39-0	71	4.91	88	.290	.357	26-0-2	.192	1	94	-5	41	-0.6
2002	LA N★	15	10	.600	32	32	4-2	0-0	222.1	182	76	21	4	38-5	155	3.00	130	.226	.262	64-1-10	.156	2	108	25	0	3.2
2003	LA N	12	12	.500	30	30	0	0-0	185.1	191	98	28	3	46-4	141	4.52	91	.267	.313	52-0-10	.096	-2	91	-7	0	-0.9
2004	†LA N	7	6	.538	31	31	0	0-0	196.1	180	76	26	3	44-4	128	3.25	127	.250	.294	62-0-6	.113	-1	93	20	20	1.1
2005	LA N	7	8	.467	19	19	0	0-0	108.2	109	59	13	0	28-2	74	4.56	91	.262	.308	33-0-8	.121	-1	93	-5	88	-0.7
2006	LA N	4	4	.500	20	8	0	0-1	59.1	89	49	9	2	13-1	33	6.83	64	.346	.380	15-0-1	.067	-1*	126	-16	0	-1.8
	KC A	2	4	.333	12	12	0	0-0	67	80	44	9	1	18-1	48	5.64	83	.295	.336	0	ø	0	107	-6	0	-0.5
Total	8	58	59	.496	196	165	4-2	0-2	1038	1049	527	126	15	283-19	737	4.33	97	.265	.314	282-1-41	.128	-4	101	-8	403	-1.5
PEREZ, OLIVER	Oliver (Martinez); B8.15.1981 Culiacan, Sinaloa, Mexico; BL/TL/6´3˝/(160–210); d6.16																									
2002	SD N	4	5	.444	16	15	0	0-0	90	71	37	13	5	48-1	94	3.50	111	.218	.325	30-0-3	.133	-1	89	5	26	0.3
2003	SD N	4	7	.364	19	19	0	0-0	103.2	103	65	20	3	65-2	117	5.38	74	.258	.365	33-0-3	.212	1	92	-16	0	-1.4
	Pit N	0	3	.000	5	5	0	0-0	23	26	15	2	1	12-1	24	5.87	74	.283	.371	6	.000	-1	69	-3	0	-0.4
	Year	4	10	.286	24	24	0	0-0	126.2	129	80	22	4	77-3	141	5.47	74	.263	.366	39-0-3	.179	0	87	-19	0	-1.8
2004	Pit N	12	10	.545	30	30	2-1	0-0	196	145	71	22	9	81-2	239	2.98	145	.207	.295	58-0-10	.190	1*	84	29	0	3.2
2005	Pit N	7	5	.583	20	20	0	0-0	103	102	68	23	6	70-1	97	5.85	72	.264	.382	33-0-7	.182	0	136	-16	68	-1.6
2006	Pit N	2	10	.167	15	15	0	0-0	76	88	64	13	3	51-0	61	6.63	69	.296	.396	25-0-1	.120	-1*	82	-18	0	-2.4
	†NY N	1	3	.250	7	7	1-1	0-0	36.2	41	26	7	3	17-0	41	6.38	69	.287	.370	13	.077	-0	114	-7	0	-0.7
	Year	3	13	.188	22	22	1-1	0-0	112.2	129	90	20	6	68-0	102	6.55	69	.293	.387	38-0-1	.105	-1	92	-26	0	-3.1
Total	5	30	43	.411	112	111	3-2	0-0	628.1	576	346	100	30	344-7	673	4.67	91	.246	.346	198-0-24	.162	-0	96	-26	94	-3.0
PEREZ, PASCUAL	Pascual Gross (b Pascual Gross (Perez)); B5.17.1957 San Cristobal, D.R.; BR/TR/6´2˝/(162–183); d5.7; b–Melido b–Carlos																									
1980	Pit N	0	1	.000	2	2	0	0-0	12	15	6	0	2	2-0	7	3.75	98	.341	.380	4	.250	0	85	0	0	0.0
1981	Pit N	2	7	.222	17	13	2	0-0	86.1	92	50	5	3	34-9	46	3.96	92	.273	.345	22-0-2	.136	-0*	82	-6	0	-0.6
1982	†Atl N	4	4	.500	16	11	0	0-0	79.1	85	35	4	0	17-3	29	3.06	120	.276	.311	18-0-5	.167	1	96	3	0	0.5
1983	Atl N★	15	8	.652	33	33	7-1	0-0	215.1	213	88	20	4	51-5	144	3.43	113	.260	.306	75-0-7	.160	-1	103	10	0	1.0
1984	Atl N	14	8	.636	30	30	4-1	0-0	211.2	208	96	26	3	51-5	145	3.74	103	.260	.305	66-0-6	.076	-2*	99	4	28	0.4
1985	Atl N	1	13	.071	22	22	0	0-0	95.1	115	72	10	1	57-10	57	6.14	63	.297	.386	25-0-4	.120	-0	88	-22	62	-2.9
1987	Mon N	7	0	1.000	10	10	2	0-0	70.1	52	21	5	1	16-1	58	2.30	185	.206	.256	24-0-1	.042	-2*	119	14	0	1.2
1988	Mon N	12	8	.600	27	27	4-2	0-0	188	133	59	15	7	44-6	131	2.44	149	.196	**.252**	54-0-6	.037	-3*	89	24	44	2.3
1989	Mon N	9	13	.409	33	28	2	0-1	198.1	178	85	15	4	45-13	152	3.31	108	.237	.282	54-0-9	.204	2*	93	4	0	0.6
1990	NY A	1	2	.333	3	3	0	0-0	14	8	3	0	0	3-0	12	1.29	311	.163	.212	0	ø	0	38	4	161	0.8
1991	NY A	2	4	.333	14	14	0	0-0	73.2	68	26	7	0	24-1	41	3.18	131	.250	.311	0	ø	0	83	9	112	0.7
Total	11	67	68	.496	207	193	21-4	0-1	1244.1	1167	541	107	25	344-53	822	3.44	111	.249	.302	342-0-40	.120	-5	94	44	407	4.0
PEREZ, RAFAEL	Rafael Jerome; B5.15.1982 Santo Domingo, D.R.; BL/TL/6´3˝/185; d4.20																									
2006	Cle A	0	0	ø	18	0	0	0-1	12.1	10	6	2	0	6-1	15	4.38	99	.204	.291	0	ø	0	—	0	0	0.0
PEREZ, YORKIS	Yorkis Miguel Vargas (b Yorkis Miguel Vargas (Perez)); B9.30.1967 Bajos de Haina, D.R.; BL/TL/6´0˝/(160–213); d9.30																									
1991	Chi N	1	0	1.000	3	0	0	0-1	4.1	2	1	0	0	2-0	3	2.08	188	.167	.250	0	ø	0	—	1	0	0.2
1994	Fla N	3	0	1.000	44	0	0	0-2	40.2	33	18	4	1	14-3	41	3.54	126	.220	.291	2	.000	-0	—	4	20	0.2
1995	Fla N	2	6	.250	69	0	0	1-3	46.2	35	29	6	2	28-4	47	5.21	82	.203	.320	2	.000	-0	—	-4	0	-0.7
1996	Fla N	3	4	.429	64	0	0	0-2	47.2	51	28	2	1	31-4	47	5.29	78	.274	.377	1	.000	-0	—	-5	0	-0.6
1997	NY N	0	1	.000	9	0	0	0-1	8.2	15	8	2	0	4-0	7	8.31	48	.375	.422	1	.000	-0	—	-4	63	-0.4
1998	Phi N	0	2	.000	57	0	0	0-0	52	40	23	3	0	25-0	42	3.81	113	.209	.297	2	.000	-0	—	3	23	0.1
1999	Phi N	3	1	.750	35	0	0	0-1	32	29	15	4	0	15-1	26	3.94	119	.244	.326	2	.000	-0	—	3	94	0.2
2000	Hou N	2	1	.667	33	0	0	0-2	22.2	25	18	4	0	14-2	21	5.16	95	.266	.355	1	.000	-0	—	-2	0	-0.3
2002	Bal A	0	0	ø	23	0	0	1-0	27.1	21	12	4	0	14-1	25	3.29	132	.198	.292	0	ø	0	—	3	14	0.1
Total	9	14	15	.483	337	0	0	2-12	282	251	152	29	4	147-15	259	4.44	99	.235	.326	11	.000	-1	—	-1	214	-1.2
PERISHO, MATT	Matthew Alan; B6.8.1975 Burlington IA; BL/TL/6´0˝/(175–205); [AnaA93 3/75]; d5.27																									
1997	Ana A	0	2	.000	11	8	0	0-0	45	59	34	6	3	28-0	35	6.00	77	.324	.419	1	.000	-0	95	-7	0	-0.3
1998	Tex A	0	2	.000	2	2	0	0-0	5	15	17	2	2	8-0	2	27.00	18	.500	.625	0	ø	0	133	-12	0	-1.5
1999	Tex A	0	0	ø	4	1	0	0-0	10.1	8	3	0	0	2-1	17	2.61	198	.211	.250	0	ø	0	0	3	0	0.1
2000	Tex A	2	7	.222	34	13	0	0-1	105	136	99	20	6	67-3	74	7.37	69	.316	.411	4	.000	-0	84	-27	0	-1.9
2001	Det A	2	3	.400	30	4	0	0-2	39.1	54	29	5	4	14-1	19	5.72	77	.327	.391	0	ø	0	73	-6	20	-0.7
2002	Det A	0	0	ø	5	0	0	0-0	10.1	16	11	2	0	6-0	3	8.71	50	.372	.440	0	ø	0	—	-5	0	-0.2
2004	Fla N	5	3	.625	66	0	0	0-2	47	45	23	6	2	26-2	42	4.40	93	.247	.346	0	ø	0	—	-1	0	-0.2
2005	Fla N	2	0	1.000	24	0	0	0-0	14	12	4	1	1	11-0	10	1.93	208	.245	.387	0	ø	0	—	3	0	0.4
	Bos A	0	0	ø	1	0	0	0-0	0	1	1	0	0	0-0	0	(1)	ø	1.000	1.000	0	ø	0	—	-1	0	-0.1
Total	8	11	17	.393	177	28	0	0-5	276	346	221	42	18	162-7	202	6.39	73	.309	.401	5	.000	-1	89	-53	20	-4.4
PERKINS, CECIL	Cecil Boyce; B12.1.1940 Baltimore MD; BR/TR/6´0˝/175; d7.5; Col Shepherd																									
1967	NY A	0	1	.000	2	1	0	0	5	6	5	1	0	2-0	1	9.00	35	.316	.381	1	.000	-0	111	-3	0	-0.5
PERKINS, CHARLIE	Charles Sullivan "Lefty"; B9.9.1905 Ensley AL; D5.25.1988 Salem OR; BR/TL/6´1˝/175; d6.27; Col Williams																									
1930	Phi A	0	0	ø	8	1	0	0	23.2	25	20	0	0	15	15	6.46	72	.313	.421	8	.125	-1	129	-5	—	-0.3
1934	Bro N	0	3	.000	11	2	0	0	24.1	37	25	3	2	14	5	8.51	46	.336	.421	7	.286	0	88	-12	—	-1.2
Total	2	0	3	.000	19	3	0	0	48	62	45	3	2	29	20	7.50	57	.326	.421	15	.200	-1	101	-17	—	-1.5
PERKINS, DAN	Daniel Lee; B3.15.1975 Miami FL; BR/TR/6´2˝/193; [MinA93 2/63]; d4.7																									
1999	Min A	1	7	.125	29	12	0	0-0	86.2	117	69	14	5	43-0	44	6.54	79	.326	.401	2	.500	0	75	-13	0	-1.0
PERKINS, GLEN	Glen Weston; B3.2.1983 St.Paul MN; BL/TL/5´11˝/200; [MinA04 1/22]; d9.21; Col Minnesota																									
2006	†Min A	0	0	ø	4	0	0	0-0	5.2	3	1	0	0	0-0	6	1.59	287	.150	.150	0	ø	0	—	2	0	0.1
PERKOVICH, JOHN	John Joseph "Perky"; B3.10.1924 Chicago IL; D9.16.2000 Little Rock AR; BR/TR/5´11˝/170; d5.6																									
1950	Chi A	0	0	ø	1	0	0	0	5	7	4	3	0	1	3	7.20	62	.318	.348	1	.000	-0	—	-1	0	-0.1
PERKOWSKI, HARRY	Harry Walter; B9.6.1922 Dante VA; BL/TL/6´2.5˝/(190–196); d9.13																									
1947	Cin N	0	0	ø	3	1	0	0	7.1	12	3	1	0	3	2	3.68	111	.375	.429	1	.000	0	150	1	0	0.0
1949	Cin N	1	1	.500	5	3	2	0	23.2	21	14	2	0	14	3	4.56	92	.236	.340	9	.333	1	91	-1	0	-0.1
1950	Cin N	0	0	ø	22	0	0	0	34.1	36	21	6	1	23	19	5.24	81	.286	.400	22	.318	2*	—	-3	0	0.1
1951	Cin N	3	6	.333	35	7	1	1	102	96	42	2	1	46	56	2.82	144	.251	.333	25-0-3	.040	-3*	53	12	0	0.7
1952	Cin N	12	10	.545	33	24	11-1	0	194	197	91	9	3	89	86	3.80	99	.265	.347	75-0-1	.160	-0	119	-2	0	-0.1
1953	Cin N	12	11	.522	33	25	7-2	2	193	204	107	26	1	62	70	4.52	96	.271	.327	69	.203	1	94	-3	0	-0.1
1954	Cin N	2	8	.200	28	12	3-1	0	95.2	100	71	16	1	62	32	6.11	69	.276	.379	25-1-2	.160	0	83	-19	0	-1.7
1955	Chi N	3	4	.429	25	4	0	2	47.2	53	32	3	0	25-4	28	5.29	77	.283	.366	13	.154	-0*	71	-7	0	-0.9
Total	8	33	40	.452	184	76	24-4	5	697.2	719	381	65	7	324-4	296	4.37	94	.269	.349	239-1-6	.180	1	95	-22	0	-2.1
PERLMAN, JON	Jonathan Samuel; B12.13.1956 Dallas TX; BL/TR/6´3˝/(175–185); [ChiN79 1/12]; d9.6; Col Baylor																									
1985	Chi N	1	0	1.000	6	0	0	0-0	8.2	10	11	3	0	8-2	4	11.42	35	.313	.439	1	.000	-0	—	-6	0	-0.6
1987	SF N	0	0	ø	10	0	0	0-0	11.1	11	7	1	1	4-0	3	3.97	97	.256	.320	0	ø	0	—	-1	0	-0.1
1988	Cle A	0	2	.000	10	0	0	0-1	19.2	25	12	0	0	11-3	10	5.49	75	.309	.391	0	ø	0	—	-2	86	-0.2
Total	3	1	2	.333	26	0	0	0-1	39.2	46	30	4	1	23-5	17	6.35	64	.295	.383	1	.000	-0	—	-9	86	-0.9
PERME, LEN	Leonard John; B11.25.1917 Cleveland OH; BL/TL/6´0˝/170; d9.8; Mil 1943–45																									
1942	Chi A	0	1	.000	4	1	1	0	13	5	2	0	1	4	4	1.38	260	.119	.213	3	.333	0	0	3	0	0.3
1946	Chi A	0	0	ø	4	0	0	0	4.1	6	4	0	0	7	2	8.31	41	.316	.500	0	ø	0	—	-2	0	-0.1
Total	2	0	1	.000	8	1	1	0	17.1	11	6	0	1	11	6	3.12	114	.180	.315	3	.333	0	0	1	0	0.2

YEAR	TM LG	W	L	PCT	G	GS	CG-SHO	SV-BS	IP	H	R	HR	HB	BB-IB	SO	ERA	AERA	OAV	OOB	AB-HR-SH	AVG	PB	SUP	APR	DL	PW
PERNOLL, HUB	Henry Huston; B3.14.1888 Applegate OR; D2.18.1944 Grants Pass OR; BR/TL/5´8˝/175; d4.25																									
1910	Det A	4	3	.571	11	5	4	0	54.2	54	20	1	5	14	25	2.96	89	.270	.333	16-0-1	.063	-2	122	0	—	-0.1
1912	Det A	0	0	ø	3	0	0	0	9	9	6	0	0	4	3	6.00	54	.265	.342	3	.000	-0	—	-2	—	-0.1
Total	2	4	3	.571	14	5	4	0	63.2	63	26	1	5	18	28	3.39	80	.269	.335	19-0-1	.053	-2	122	-2	—	-0.2
PERRANOSKI, RON	Ronald Peter (b Ronald Peter Perzanowski); B4.1.1936 Paterson NJ; BL/TL/6´0˝/(180–192); d4.14; C17; Col Michigan St.																									
1961	LA N	7	5	.583	53	1	0	6	91.2	82	31	5	4	41-7	56	2.65	164	.244	.330	12	.083	-0	245	16	0	2.1
1962	LA N	6	6	.500	**70**	0	0	20	107.1	103	40	1	0	36-9	68	2.85	127	.255	.314	14-0-1	.071	-1	—	10	0	1.3
1963	†LA N	16	3	**.842**	**69**	0	0	21	129	112	30	7	4	43-14	75	1.67	180	.231	.298	24-0-2	.125	0	—	**20**	0	3.9
1964	LA N	5	7	.417	72	0	0	14	125.1	128	62	5	1	46-19	79	3.09	105	.263	.325	19-0-3	.105	-0	—	-3	0	-0.3
1965	†LA N	6	6	.500	59	0	0	17	104.2	85	28	2	3	40-7	53	2.24	146	.226	.303	19	.158	1	—	14	0	2.1
1966	†LA N	6	7	.462	55	0	0	7	82	82	32	4	1	31-11	50	3.18	104	.269	.337	8-0-1	.250	1	—	2	0	0.6
1967	LA N	6	7	.462	**70**	0	0	16	110	97	36	4	3	45-13	75	2.45	126	.240	.318	10	.100	-0	—	8	0	1.2
1968	Min A	8	7	.533	66	0	0	6	87	86	36	5	0	38-12	65	3.10	99	.252	.325	7	.000	-1	—	0	0	-0.1
1969	†Min A	9	10	.474	75	0	0	**31**-11	119.2	85	32	4	1	52-16	62	2.11	173	.205	.292	24-0-4	.083	-1	—	20	0	**4.3**
1970	†Min A	7	8	.467	67	0	0	**34**-11	111	108	38	7	1	42-7	55	2.43	152	.259	.325	24-0-1	.042	-2	—	14	0	2.4
1971	Min A	1	4	.200	36	0	0	5-6	42.2	60	39	2	3	28-4	21	6.75	52	.337	.431	3-0-1	.000	-0	—	-16	0	-2.3
	Det A	0	1	.000	11	0	0	2-1	18	16	9	2	1	3-1	8	2.50	145	.254	.290	2	.000	-0	—	1	0	0.0
	Year	1	5	.167	47	0	0	7-7	60.2	76	48	4	4	31-5	29	5.49	65	.315	.396	5-0-1	.000	-1	—	-16	0	-2.3
1972	Det A	0	1	.000	17	0	0	0-0	18.2	23	16	2	1	8-1	10	7.71	41	.307	.381	1	.000	-0	—	-8	0	-0.5
	LA N	2	0	1.000	9	0	0	0-0	16.2	19	8	0	0	8-0	5	2.70	124	.292	.365	0	ø	0	—	0	0	0.0
1973	Cal A	0	2	.000	8	0	0	0-0	11	11	5	0	1	7-0	5	4.09	88	.282	.404	0	ø	0	—	0	74	0.0
Total	13	79	74	.516	737	1	0	179-29	1174.2	1097	442	50	24	468-121	687	2.79	123	.250	.323	167-0-13	.096	-4	245	78	74	14.7
PERRIN, BILL	William Joseph "Lefty"; B6.23.1910 New Orleans LA; D6.30.1974 New Orleans LA; BR/TL/5´11˝/172; d9.30																									
1934	Cle A	0	1	.000	1	1	0	0	5	13	9	0	1	2	3	14.40	32	.520	.571	2	.000	-0	96	-5	—	-0.6
PERRITT, POL	William Dayton; B8.30.1891 Arcadia LA; D10.15.1947 Shreveport LA; BR/TR/6´2˝/168; d9.7																									
1912	StL N	1	1	.500	6	3	1	0	31	25	16	0	0	10	13	3.19	107	.243	.310	9	.222	-0	71	1	—	0.0
1913	StL N	6	14	.300	36	21	8	0	175	205	123	9	8	64	64	5.25	62	.300	.367	59-0-1	.203	-1	82	-40	—	-4.0
1914	StL N	16	13	.552	41	32	18-3	2	286	248	106	7	15	93	115	2.36	118	.245	.318	92-0-7	.141	-2	100	14	—	1.0
1915	NY N	12	18	.400	35	29	16-4	0	220	226	95	6	12	59	91	2.66	96	.266	.323	68-0-2	.162	-1	86	-7	—	-1.3
1916	NY N	18	11	.621	40	29	17-5	2	251	243	82	11	7	56	115	2.62	93	.257	.304	83-0-5	.084	-4	133	-2	—	-0.8
1917	†NY N	17	7	.708	35	26	14-5	1	215	186	61	3	7	45	72	1.88	135	.237	.284	70-0-2	.157	-2	131	15	—	1.5
1918	NY N	18	13	.581	35	31	19-6	0	233	212	82	5	1	38	60	2.74	96	.246	.278	80-0-5	.175	-1*	92	0	—	-0.3
1919	NY N	1	1	.500	11	3	0	1	19	27	18	0	2	12	2	7.11	39	.386	.488	4	.000	-1	113	-9	—	-1.1
1920	NY N	0	0	ø	8	0	0	2	15	9	3	0	0	4	3	1.80	167	.167	.224	4	.000	-1	—	2	—	0.1
1921	NY N	2	0	1.000	5	1	0	0	11.2	17	9	0	0	2	5	3.86	95	.321	.345	3	.000	-0	112	-2	—	-0.3
	Det A	1	0	1.000	4	2	0	0	13	18	9	0	1	7	3	4.85	88	.383	.473	5	.400	0	137	-1	—	0.0
Total	10	92	78	.541	256	177	93-23	8	1469.2	1416	604	41	53	390	543	2.89	94	.259	.315	477-0-22	.151	-13	103	-29	—	-5.2
PERRY, GAYLORD	Gaylord Jackson; B9.15.1938 Williamston NC; BR/TR/6´4˝/(205–220); d4.14; HF1991; b–Jim																									
1962	SF N	3	1	.750	13	7	1	0	43	54	29	3	0	14-2	20	5.23	73	.310	.354	13-0-2	.231	0	158	-8	0	-0.6
1963	SF N	1	6	.143	31	4	0	2	76	84	41	10	2	29-7	52	4.03	79	.279	.345	18	.222	1*	121	-8	0	-0.7
1964	SF N	12	11	.522	44	19	5-2	5	206.1	179	65	16	5	43-6	155	2.75	130	.232	.275	56-0-7	.054	-3*	82	21	0	2.0
1965	SF N	8	12	.400	47	26	6	1	195.2	194	105	21	6	70-16	170	4.19	86	.256	.322	64-0-5	.156	-0*	96	-13	0	-1.1
1966	SF N★	21	8	.724	36	35	13-3	0	255.2	242	92	15	5	40-3	201	2.99	123	.247	.279	86-0-6	.186	-0	105	22	15	2.5
1967	SF N	15	17	.469	39	37	18-3	1	293	231	98	20	4	84-17	230	2.61	126	.214	.273	91-0-15	.143	-1*	90	23	0	2.6
1968	SF N	16	15	.516	39	38	19-3	1	290.2	240	93	10	4	59-12	173	2.45	120	.222	.264	97-0-8	.113	-3	92	17	0	1.8
1969	SF N	19	14	.576	40	39	26-3	0-1	**325.1**	290	115	23	11	91-14	233	2.49	141	.237	.295	117-1-7	.120	-2	102	35	0	3.5
1970	SF N★	**23**	13	.639	41	**41**	23-**5**	0-0	**328.2**	292	138	27	8	84-8	214	3.20	124	.237	.289	120-1-10	.117	-4	111	26	0	2.5
1971	†SF N	16	12	.571	37	37	14-2	0-0	280	255	116	20	5	67-4	158	2.76	123	.242	.287	98-1-10	.102	-3*	110	15	0	1.1
1972	Cle A★	**24**	16	.600	41	40	**29**-5	1-0	342.2	253	79	17	12	82-16	234	1.92	**170**	.205	.261	110-1-14	.155	0	79	**49**	0	**6.8**
1973	Cle A	19	19	.500	41	41	**29**-7	0-0	344	315	143	34	5	115-9	238	3.38	117	.246	.310	0	ø	0	90	21	0	2.3
1974	Cle A★	21	13	.618	37	37	28-4	0-0	322.1	230	98	25	6	99-7	216	2.51	**145**	.204	.270	0	ø	0	101	**42**	0	4.5
1975	Cle A	6	9	.400	15	15	10-1	0-0	121.2	120	57	16	1	34-5	85	3.55	107	.256	.308	0	ø	0	68	3	0	0.4
	Tex A	12	8	.600	22	22	15-4	0-0	184	157	70	12	3	36-1	148	3.03	124	.227	.267	0	ø	0	107	16	0	1.6
	Year	18	17	.514	37	37	25-5	0-0	305.2	277	127	28	4	70-6	233	3.24	117	.239	.284	0	ø	0	91	18	0	2.0
1976	Tex A	15	14	.517	32	32	21-2	0-0	250.1	232	93	14	0	52-3	143	3.24	111	.247	.285	0	ø	0	94	14	0	1.4
1977	Tex A	15	12	.556	34	34	13-4	0-0	238	239	108	21	5	56-4	177	3.37	121	.262	.307	0	ø	0	86	15	0	1.5
1978	SD N	**21**	6	**.778**	37	37	5-2	0-0	260.2	241	96	9	2	66-8	154	2.73	123	.248	.295	87-0-13	.092	-3	119	17	0	1.3
1979	SD N★	12	11	.522	32	32	10	0-0	232.2	225	90	12	4	67-10	140	3.06	116	.257	.312	71-1-11	.085	-2	82	13	0	1.1
1980	Tex A	6	9	.400	24	24	6-2	0-0	155	159	74	12	7	46-3	107	3.43	114	.268	.327	0	ø	0	100	6	0	0.5
	NY A	4	4	.500	10	8	0	0-0	50.2	65	33	2	1	18-0	28	4.44	89	.320	.372	0	ø	0	90	-5	0	-0.7
	Year	10	13	.435	34	32	6-2	0-0	205.2	224	107	14	8	64-3	135	3.68	106	.281	.338	0	ø	0	97	1	0	-0.2
1981	Atl N	8	9	.471	23	23	3	0-0	150.2	182	70	9	4	24-1	60	3.94	89	.304	.332	48-1-5	.250	3*	108	-5	0	-0.3
1982	Sea A	10	12	.455	32	32	6	0-0	216.2	245	117	27	4	54-4	116	4.40	97	.287	.331	0	ø	0	85	-2	0	-0.2
1983	Sea A	3	10	.231	16	16	2	0-0	102	116	60	18	3	23-3	42	4.94	87	.286	.327	0	ø	0	60	-6	0	-0.7
	KC A	4	4	.500	14	14	1-1	0-0	84.1	98	48	6	1	26-1	40	4.27	96	.292	.342	0	ø	0	81	-3	0	-0.2
	Year	7	14	.333	30	30	3-1	0-0	186.1	214	108	24	4	49-4	82	4.64	91	.289	.334	0	ø	0	69	-9	0	-0.9
Total	22	314	265	.542	777	690	303-53	11-1	5350	4938	2128	399	108	1379-164	3534	3.11	117	.245	.296	1076-6-113	.131	-16	96	305	15	32.9
PERRY, SCOTT	Herbert Scott; B4.17.1891 Denison TX; D10.27.1959 Kansas City MO; BL/TR/6´0˝/175; d5.13																									
1915	StL A	0	0	ø	1	1	0	0	2	5	3	0	1	1	0	13.50	21	.455	.538	0	ø	0	153	-2	—	-0.1
1916	Chi N	2	1	.667	4	3	2-1	0	28.1	30	9	0	0	3	10	2.54	115	.291	.311	11	.273	1	68	2	—	0.3
1917	Cin N	0	0	ø	4	1	0	0	13.1	17	15	0	1	8	4	6.75	39	.321	.419	5	.000	-1	288	-7	—	-0.4
1918	Phi A	20	19	.513	44	**36**	**30**-3	2	**332.1**	295	97	1	2	111	81	1.98	148	.247	.312	112-0-6	.134	-6	73	32	—	3.5
1919	Phi A	4	17	.190	25	21	12	1	183.2	193	92	4	2	72	38	3.58	96	.282	.352	59-0-5	.136	-3	78	-3	—	-0.2
1920	Phi A	11	25	.306	42	34	20-1	1	263.2	310	151	14	7	65	79	3.62	111	.300	.345	83-1-5	.157	-4	67	10	—	0.8
1921	Phi A	3	6	.333	12	8	5	1	70	77	36	4	1	24	19	4.11	108	.288	.349	26	.038	-4	75	4	—	0.1
Total	7	40	68	.370	132	104	69-5	5	893.1	927	403	23	14	284	231	3.07	113	.277	.336	296-1-16	.135	-17	75	36	—	4.0
PERRY, JIM	James Evan; B10.30.1935 Williamston NC; BB/TR/6´4˝/(185–205); d4.23; b–Gaylord; Col Campbell																									
1959	Cle A	12	10	.545	44	13	8-2	4	153	122	54	10	2	55-7	79	2.65	139	.225	.295	50-0-1	.300	3	109	17	0	2.7
1960	Cle A	**18**	10	**.643**	41	**36**	10-**4**	1	261.1	257	118	35	4	91-3	120	3.62	103	.260	.321	91-0-5	.242	3*	97	4	0	0.7
1961	Cle A☆	10	17	.370	35	35	6-1	0	223.2	238	132	28	6	87-5	90	4.71	84	.273	.341	73-0-5	.164	-1	87	-19	0	-2.1
1962	Cle A	12	12	.500	35	27	7-3	0	193.2	213	94	21	2	59-1	74	4.14	94	.285	.337	60-0-7	.183	0	100	-3	0	-0.3
1963	Cle A	0	0	ø	5	0	0	0	10.1	12	6	0	0	2-0	7	5.23	69	.293	.326	2	.000	-0	—	-1	0	-0.1
	Min A	9	9	.500	35	25	5-1	1	168.1	167	77	17	2	57-4	65	3.74	97	.256	.315	51-0-1	.216	3	101	-1	0	0.2
	Year	9	9	.500	40	25	5-1	1	178.2	179	83	17	2	59-4	72	3.83	95	.258	.316	53-0-1	.208	3	101	-2	0	0.1
1964	Min A	6	3	.667	42	1	0	2	65.1	61	26	7	1	23-4	55	3.44	104	.245	.309	13	.154	-0	174	2	0	0.3
1965	†Min A	12	7	.632	36	19	4-2	0	167.2	142	57	18	3	47-2	88	2.63	135	.232	.286	53-0-4	.170	1	96	17	0	1.9
1966	Min A	11	7	.611	33	25	8-1	0	184.1	149	61	17	5	53-4	122	2.54	142	.222	.281	59-1-2	.220	4	106	20	0	2.4
1967	Min A	8	7	.533	37	11	3-2	0	130.2	123	51	8	3	50-5	94	3.03	114	.255	.325	42-1-0	.190	1*	98	6	0	0.7
1968	Min A	8	6	.571	32	18	3-2	1	139	113	37	8	5	26-2	69	2.27	136	.219	.262	42-2-4	.143	2	96	14	0	1.8
1969	†Min A	20	6	.769	46	36	12-3	0-0	261.2	244	87	18	9	66-10	153	2.82	129	.247	.298	93-0-3	.172	1*	128	27	0	2.6
1970	†Min A★	**24**	12	.667	40	**40**	13-4	0-0	278.2	258	112	20	9	57-10	168	3.04	122	.243	.286	97-1-10	.247	5*	107	20	0	3.1
1971	Min A☆	17	17	.500	40	39	8	1-0	270	263	135	39	5	102-10	126	4.23	84	.259	.326	92-0-4	.185	1	110	-17	0	-2.0
1972	Min A	13	16	.448	35	35	5-2	0-0	217.2	191	93	14	8	60-5	85	3.35	96	.236	.292	71-0-5	.155	-1	88	-1	0	-0.3
1973	Det A	14	13	.519	35	34	7-1	0-0	203	225	96	22	4	55-5	66	4.03	102	.282	.329	0	ø	0	88	2	0	0.2
1974	Cle A	17	12	.586	36	36	8-3	0-0	252	242	94	11	5	64-10	71	2.96	123	.254	.303	0	ø	0	95	19	0	2.1
1975	Cle A	1	6	.143	8	6	0	0-0	37.2	46	34	8	0	18-5	11	6.69	57	.309	.383	0	ø	0	69	-13	0	-1.9
	Oak A	3	4	.429	15	11	2-1	0-1	67.2	61	43	7	7	26-1	33	4.66	78	.237	.319	0	ø	0	90	-9	0	-0.9
	Year	4	10	.286	23	17	2-1	0-1	105.1	107	77	15	7	44-6	44	5.38	69	.264	.342	0	ø	0	82	-22	0	-2.8
Total	17	215	174	.553	630	447	109-32	10-1	3285.2	3127	1407	308	80	998-93	1576	3.45	106	.252	.309	889-5-51	.199	24	100	84	0	11.1

YEAR	TM LG	W	L	PCT	G	GS	CG-SHO	SV-BS	IP	H	R	HR	HB	BB-IB	SO	ERA	AERA	OAV	OOB	AB-HR-SH	AVG	PB	SUP	APR	DL	PW
PERRY, PAT	William Patrick; B2.4.1959 Taylorville IL; BL/TL/6´1˝/(170–190); [HouN78*2/38]; d9.12; Col Lincoln Land (IL) CC																									
1985	StL N	1	0	1.000	6	0	0	0-0	12.1	3	0	0	0	3-1	6	0.00	ø	.077	.143	2	.500	0	—	5	0	0.4
1986	StL N	2	3	.400	46	0	0	2-0	68.2	59	31	5	0	34-9	29	3.80	97	.239	.323	8	.000	-1	—	0	0	-0.1
1987	StL N	4	2	.667	45	0	0	1-1	65.2	54	34	7	2	21-3	33	4.39	96	.222	.288	7	.143	-0	—	-1	0	-0.1
	Cin N	1	0	1.000	12	0	0	1-1	15.1	6	0	0	1	4-1	6	0.00	ø	.122	.204	0	ø	0	—	7	0	0.5
	Year	5	2	.714	57	0	0	2-2	81	60	34	7	3	25-4	39	3.56	118	.205	.274	7	.143	-0	—	7	0	0.4
1988	Cin N	2	2	.500	12	0	0	0-0	20.2	21	17	4	0	9-4	11	5.66	63	.262	.326	2	.000	-0	—	-6	0	-1.1
	Chi N	2	2	.500	35	0	0	1-3	38	40	15	5	1	7-0	24	3.32	110	.270	.304	1-1-0	1.000	1	—	1	21	0.3
	Year	4	4	.500	47	0	0	1-3	58.2	61	32	9	1	16-4	35	4.14	87	.268	.312	3-1-0	.333	1	—	-4	0	-0.8
1989	Chi N	0	1	.000	19	0	0	1-0	35.2	23	8	2	0	16-3	20	1.77	214	.187	.279	6	.167	-0	—	7	93	0.4
1990	LA N	0	0	ø	7	0	0	0-0	6.2	9	7	0	1	5-1	2	8.10	45	.310	.417	1	.000	-0	—	-3	125	-0.2
Total	6	12	10	.545	182	0	0	6-5	263	215	112	23	5	99-22	131	3.46	111	.224	.296	27-1-0	.148	0	—	10	239	0.1
PERRYMAN, PARSON	Emmett Key; B10.24.1888 Everett Springs GA; D9.12.1966 Starke FL; BR/TR/6´4.5˝/193; d4.14; Col Emory																									
1915	StL A	2	4	.333	24	3	0	0	50.1	52	27	2	1	16	19	3.93	73	.281	.342	6	.000	-1	102	-5	—	-0.6
PERSON, ROBERT	Robert Alan; B10.6.1969 Lowell MA; BR/TR/6´0˝/(180–195); [CleA89 25/645]; d9.18; Col Seminole St. (OK) JC																									
1995	NY N	1	0	1.000	3	1	0	0-0	12	5	1	1	0	2-0	10	0.75	538	.119	.159	3	.667	1	112	5	0	0.4
1996	NY N	4	5	.444	27	13	0	0-0	89.2	86	50	16	2	35-3	76	4.52	89	.247	.316	21-0-5	.143	-0*	102	-4	0	-0.5
1997	Tor A	5	10	.333	23	22	0	0-0	128.1	125	86	19	5	60-2	99	5.61	82	.255	.338	4	.000	-0	72	-14	39	-1.4
1998	Tor A	3	1	.750	27	0	0	6-2	38.1	45	31	9	2	22-1	31	7.04	66	.294	.379	0	ø	0	—	-9	0	-1.1
1999	Tor A	0	2	.000	11	0	0	2-0	11	9	12	1	4	15-1	12	9.82	50	.231	.467	0	ø	0	—	-5	7	-1.0
	Phi N	10	5	.667	31	22	0	0-0	137	130	72	23	2	70-1	127	4.27	109	.252	.341	41-0-4	.073	-2	119	5	0	0.2
2000	Phi N	9	7	.563	28	28	1-1	0-0	173.1	144	73	13	6	95-1	164	3.63	126	.229	.332	53-0-8	.132	-0	91	20	32	1.5
2001	Phi N	15	7	.682	33	33	3-1	0-0	208.1	179	103	34	8	80-3	183	4.19	98	.234	.311	67-2-5	.119	1	102	-1	0	-0.1
2002	Phi N	4	5	.444	16	16	0	0-0	87.2	79	58	13	5	51-0	61	5.44	70	.241	.350	24-2-3	.083	1*	124	-17	102	-1.5
2003	Bos A	0	0	ø	7	0	0	1-0	11.2	11	10	0	1	8-0	10	7.71	60	.250	.364	1	.000	-0	—	-3	157	-0.2
Total	9	51	42	.548	206	135	4-2	9-2	897.1	813	496	129	35	438-12	773	4.64	94	.242	.332	214-4-25	.117	0	99	-23	337	-3.7
PERTICA, BILL	William Andrew; B8.17.1898 Santa Barbara CA; D12.28.1967 Los Angeles CA; BR/TR/5´9˝/165; d8.7																									
1918	Bos A	0	0	ø	1	0	0	0	3	3	1	0	0	0	1	3.00	89	.273	.273	1	.000	-0	—	0	—	0.0
1921	StL N	14	10	.583	38	31	15-2	2	208.1	212	104	9	10	70	67	3.37	109	.267	.334	70-0-5	.143	-3	110	4	—	-0.1
1922	StL N	8	8	.500	34	15	2	0	117.1	153	94	5	3	65	30	5.91	65	.333	.419	33	.182	-0*	121	-28	—	-3.1
1923	StL N	0	0	ø	1	1	0	0	2.1	2	2	0	1	3	0	3.86	101	.250	.500	1	.000	-0	42	0	—	0.0
Total	4	22	18	.550	74	47	17-2	2	331	370	201	14	14	138	98	4.27	87	.291	.367	105-0-5	.152	-4	112	-24	—	-3.2
PERZANOWSKI, STAN	Stanley; B8.25.1950 East Chicago IN; BB/TR/6´2˝/(170–175); [ChiA68 16/362]; d6.20																									
1971	Chi A	0	1	.000	5	0	0	1-0	6	14	10	1	0	3-0	5	12.00	30	.412	.447	2	.000	-0	—	-6	0	-1.0
1974	Chi A	0	0	ø	2	1	0	0-0	2.1	8	7	1	0	2-0	2	19.29	19	.533	.588	0	ø	0	94	-4	0	-0.2
1975	Tex A	3	3	.500	12	8	1	0-0	66	59	25	1	5	25-2	26	3.00	126	.246	.327	0	ø	0	70	6	0	0.6
1976	Tex A	0	0	ø	5	0	0	0-0	11.2	20	15	3	2	4-0	6	10.03	36	.385	.448	0	ø	0	—	-8	0	-0.4
1978	Min A	2	7	.222	13	7	1	1-0	56.2	59	37	1	4	26-0	31	5.24	73	.276	.362	0	ø	0	114	-9	0	-1.2
Total	5	5	11	.313	37	16	2	2-0	142.2	160	94	7	11	60-2	70	5.11	74	.288	.366	2	.000	-0	91	-21	0	-2.2
PETEREK, JEFF	Jeffrey Allen; B9.22.1963 Michigan City IN; BR/TR/6´2˝/195; d8.14; Col Mary Hardin–Baylor																									
1989	Mil A	0	2	.000	7	4	0	0-0	31.1	31	14	3	0	14-1	16	4.02	96	.252	.328	0	ø	0	59	0	0	0.0
PETERS, CHRIS	Christopher Michael; B1.28.1972 Fort Thomas KY; BL/TL/6´1˝/(162–175); [PitN93 37/1046]; d7.19; Col Indiana																									
1996	Pit N	2	4	.333	16	10	0	0-0	64	72	43	9	1	25-0	28	5.63	78	.287	.350	19-0-1	.211	0	70	-8	0	-0.6
1997	Pit N	2	2	.500	31	1	0	0-1	37.1	38	23	6	3	21-4	17	4.58	93	.277	.383	4	.250	0	86	-2	0	-0.2
1998	Pit N	8	10	.444	39	21	1	1-0	148	142	63	13	3	55-4	103	3.47	123	.252	.319	39-0-4	.231	1	106	14	0	1.6
1999	Pit N	5	4	.556	19	11	0	0-0	71	98	59	17	4	27-0	46	6.59	70	.322	.381	22-0-1	.273	2	116	-16	89	-1.4
2000	Pit N	0	1	.000	18	0	0	1-0	28.1	23	9	2	1	14-2	16	2.86	162	.221	.319	6	.167	-0	—	6	55	0.3
2001	Mon N	2	4	.333	13	6	0	0-1	31	47	26	7	2	15-1	14	7.55	57	.367	.435	11	.091	-1	93	-10	0	-1.7
Total	6	19	25	.432	136	49	1	2-2	379.2	420	223	54	14	157-11	224	4.81	91	.282	.353	101-0-6	.218	2	99	-16	144	-2.0
PETERS, GARY	Gary Charles; B4.21.1937 Grove City PA; BL/TL/6´2˝/(190–200); d9.10; Col Grove City																									
1959	Chi A	0	0	ø	2	0	0	0	1	2	0	0	0	2-0	1	0.00	ø	.400	.571	0	ø	0	—	0	0	0.0
1960	Chi A	0	0	ø	2	0	0	0	3.1	4	1	0	0	1-0	4	2.70	140	.286	.333	0	ø	0	—	0	0	0.0
1961	Chi A	0	0	ø	3	0	0	1	10.1	10	2	0	0	2-0	6	1.74	225	.270	.308	3	.333	0	—	3	0	0.2
1962	Chi A	0	1	.000	5	0	0	0	6.1	8	5	0	1	1-0	4	5.68	69	.308	.345	0	ø	0	—	-2	0	-0.2
1963	Chi A	19	8	.704	41	30	13-4	1	243	192	69	9	8	68-2	189	**2.33**	**150**	.216	.277	81-3-2	.259	9*	96	**34**	0	4.8
1964	Chi A☆	**20**	8	.714	37	36	11-3	0	273.2	217	89	20	7	104-9	205	2.50	138	.219	.296	120-4-3	.208	8*	109	29	0	3.9
1965	Chi A	10	12	.455	33	30	1	0	176.1	181	76	19	4	63-8	95	3.62	88	.265	.329	72-1-0	.181	2*	98	-7	0	-0.6
1966	Chi A	12	10	.545	30	27	11-4	0	204.2	156	54	11	3	45-6	129	**1.98**	**160**	.212	**.260**	81-1-3	.235	6*	102	**29**	0	**4.0**
1967	Chi A★	16	11	.593	38	36	11-3	0	260	187	81	15	11	91-8	215	2.28	136	**.199**	.276	99-2-4	.212	7*	109	24	0	3.6
1968	Chi A	4	13	.235	31	25	6-1	1	162.2	146	79	7	7	60-6	110	3.76	80	.242	.315	72-2-0	.208	7*	93	-13	0	-0.6
1969	Chi A	10	15	.400	36	32	7-3	0-0	218.2	238	118	21	5	78-1	140	4.53	85	.283	.344	71-2-6	.169	2*	106	-15	0	-1.4
1970	Bos A	16	11	.593	34	34	10-4	0-0	221.2	221	114	20	7	83-2	155	4.06	98	.257	.325	82-1-2	.244	6*	122	-1	0	0.5
1971	Bos A	14	11	.560	34	32	9-1	1-0	214	241	111	25	6	70-3	100	4.37	85	.288	.346	96-3-5	.271	8*	112	-14	0	-0.8
1972	Bos A	3	3	.500	33	4	0	1-1	85.1	91	48	10	3	38-8	67	4.32	75	.279	.356	30	.200	1	130	-10	0	-0.7
Total	14	124	103	.546	359	286	79-23	5-1	2081	1894	847	157	62	706-53	1420	3.25	106	.243	.309	807-19-25	.222	57	107	57	0	12.7
PETERS, RUBE	Oscar Casper; B3.15.1885 Grantfork IL; D2.7.1965 Pequannock NJ; BR/TR/6´1˝/195; d4.13																									
1912	Chi A	5	6	.455	28	11	4	0	108.2	134	73	2	6	33	39	4.14	77	.309	.366	31-0-2	.194	-1	86	-14	—	-1.1
1914	Bro F	2	2	.500	11	3	1	0	37.2	52	27	1	0	16	13	3.82	75	.335	.398	11-0-1	.091	-1	151	-6	—	-0.7
Total	2	7	8	.467	39	14	5	0	146.1	186	100	3	6	49	52	4.06	77	.316	.374	42-0-3	.167	-1	100	-20	—	-1.8
PETERS, RAY	Raymond James; B8.27.1946 Buffalo NY; BR/TR/6´5.5˝/220; [MilA69*S1/22]; d6.4; Col Harvard																									
1970	Mil A	0	2	.000	2	2	0	0-0	2	7	7	0	0	5-0	1	31.50	12	.583	.667	0	ø	0	83	-6	0	-0.9
PETERS, STEVE	Steven Bradley; B11.14.1962 Oklahoma City OK; BL/TL/5´10˝/(170–175); [StLN85 5/124]; d8.11; Col Oklahoma																									
1987	StL N	0	0	ø	12	0	0	1-0	15	17	3	1	0	6-1	11	1.80	234	.298	.365	2	.000	-0	—	4	0	0.2
1988	StL N	3	3	.500	44	0	0	0-1	45	57	34	8	0	22-7	30	6.40	55	.313	.382	3	.000	-0	—	-13	0	-1.7
Total	2	3	3	.500	56	0	0	1-1	60	74	37	9	0	28-8	41	5.25	70	.310	.378	5	.000	-1	—	-9	0	-1.5
PETERSON, ADAM	Adam Charles; B12.11.1965 Long Beach CA; BR/TR/6´3˝/190; [ChiA84 5/132]; d9.19																									
1987	Chi A	0	0	ø	1	1	0	0-0	4	8	6	1	0	3-0	1	13.50	34	.444	.500							
1988	Chi A	0	1	.000	2	2	0	0-0	6	6	9	0	0	6-1	5	13.50	30	.240	.387	0	ø	0	197	-4	0	-0.2
1989	Chi A	0	1	.000	3	2	0	0-0	5.1	13	9	1	0	2-0	3	15.19	25	.464	.500	0	ø	0	91	-6	0	-0.7
1990	Chi A	2	5	.286	20	11	2	0-0	85	90	46	12	2	26-0	29	4.55	85	.278	.332	0	ø	0	165	-6	0	-0.9
1991	SD N	3	4	.429	13	11	0	0-0	54.2	50	33	10	0	28-2	37	4.45	86	.242	.329	0	ø	0	108	-6	0	-0.6
Total	5	5	11	.313	39	27	2	0-0	155	167	103	24	2	65-3	75	5.46	71	.277	.347	13-0-1	.000	-1	90	-5	0	-0.7
																				13-0-1	.000	-1	108	-27	0	-3.1
PETERSON, ADAM	Adam L.; B5.18.1979 Savannah GA; BR/TR/6´3˝/220; [TorA02 4/116]; d6.24; Col Wichita St.																									
2004	Tor A	0	0	ø	3	0	0	0-0	2.2	7	5	1	0	3-0	2	16.88	29	.467	.556	0	ø	0	—	-3	0	-0.2
PETERSON, FRITZ	Fritz Fred (b Fred Ingels Peterson); B2.8.1942 Chicago IL; BB/TL/6´0˝/(185–207); d4.15; Col Northern Illinois																									
1966	NY A	12	11	.522	34	32	11-2	0	215	196	89	15	3	40-6	96	3.31	101	.241	.277	67-0-8	.224	4	110	1	0	0.6
1967	NY A	8	14	.364	36	30	6-1	0	181.1	179	88	11	3	43-9	102	3.47	90	.256	.301	48-0-3	.146	1	78	-10	0	-1.0
1968	NY A	12	11	.522	36	27	6-2	0	212.1	187	72	13	4	29-9	115	2.63	111	.241	.270	63-0-5	.079	-2	100	7	0	0.8
1969	NY A	17	16	.515	37	37	16-4	0-0	272	228	95	15	3	43-11	150	2.55	138	.229	.261	80-0-7	.112	-0	74	27	0	3.4
1970	NY A★	20	11	.645	39	37	8-2	0-0	260.1	247	102	24	3	40-6	127	2.90	123	.248	**.279**	90-2-7	.222	5	111	18	0	2.8
1971	NY A	15	13	.536	37	35	16-4	1-0	274	269	106	25	4	42-7	139	3.05	108	.258	.287	85-0-14	.082	-3	101	8	0	0.6
1972	NY A	17	15	.531	35	35	12-3	0-0	250.1	270	98	17	5	44-5	100	3.24	92	.276	.309	82-0-15	.232	3	121	-5	0	-0.2
1973	NY A	8	15	.348	31	31	6	0-0	184.1	207	93	18	7	49-10	59	3.95	94	.286	.336	0	ø	0	73	-5	0	-0.6

YEAR	TM LG	W	L	PCT	G	GS	CG-SHO	SV-BS	IP	H	R	HR	HB	BB-IB	SO	ERA	AERA	OAV	OOB	AB-HR-SH	AVG	PB	SUP	APR	DL	PW
1974	NY A	0	0	ø	3	1	0	0-0	7.2	13	4	1	0	2-1	5	4.70	76	.361	.395	0	ø	0	149	-1	0	0.0
	Cle A	9	14	.391	29	29	3	0-0	152.2	187	89	16	4	37-7	52	4.36	83	.305	.346	0	ø	0	97	-14	0	-1.9
	Year	9	14	.391	32	30	3	0-0	160.1	200	93	17	4	39-8	57	4.38	83	.308	.349	0	ø	0	99	-17	0	-1.9
1975	Cle A	14	8	.636	25	25	6-2	0-0	146.1	154	73	15	6	40-4	47	3.94	97	.275	.330	0	ø	0	123	-2	28	-0.2
1976	Cle A	0	3	.000	9	9	0	0-0	47	59	31	3	0	10-0	19	5.55	63	.309	.342	0	ø	0	128	-10	0	-0.6
	Tex A	1	0	1.000	4	2	0	0-1	15	21	7	0	0	7-0	4	3.60	100	.344	.412	0	ø	0	122	0	68	0.0
	Year	1	3	.250	13	11	0	0-1	62	80	38	3	0	17-0	23	5.08	70	.317	.359	0	ø	0	127	-10	0	-0.6
Total	11	133	131	.504	355	330	90-20	1-1	2218.1	2217	947	173	42	426-75	1015	3.30	102	.261	.298	515-2-59	.159	8	100	14	96	3.7

PETERSON, JIM James Niels; B8.18.1908 Philadelphia PA; D4.8.1975 Palm Beach FL; BR/TR/6´0.5˝/200; d7.9; Col Penn

YEAR	TM LG	W	L	PCT	G	GS	CG-SHO	SV-BS	IP	H	R	HR	HB	BB-IB	SO	ERA	AERA	OAV	OOB	AB-HR-SH	AVG	PB	SUP	APR	DL	PW
1931	Phi A	0	1	.000	6	1	1	0	13	18	10	0	0	4	7	6.23	72	.321	.367	2	.500	1	94	-2	—	-0.1
1933	Phi A	2	5	.286	32	5	0	0	90.2	114	64	6	0	36	18	4.96	86	.305	.366	27	.148	-1	115	-9	—	-0.5
1937	Bro N	0	0	ø	3	0	0	0	5.2	8	5	3	0	2	4	7.94	51	.333	.385	0	ø	0	—	-2	—	-0.1
Total	3	2	6	.250	41	6	1	0	109.1	140	79	9	0	42	29	5.27	82	.308	.367	29	.172	0	112	-13	—	-0.7

PETERSON, KENT Kent Franklin "Pete"; B12.21.1925 Goshen UT; D4.27.1995 Highland UT; BR/TL/5´10˝/175; d7.15; Mil 1945–46

YEAR	TM LG	W	L	PCT	G	GS	CG-SHO	SV-BS	IP	H	R	HR	HB	BB-IB	SO	ERA	AERA	OAV	OOB	AB-HR-SH	AVG	PB	SUP	APR	DL	PW
1944	Cin N	0	0	ø	1	0	0	0	1	0	0	0	0	0	0	0.00	ø	.000	.000	0	ø	0	—	0	0	0.0
1947	Cin N	6	13	.316	37	17	3-1	2	152.1	156	74	8	3	62	78	4.25	96	.265	.338	44-0-4	.068	-3	62	1	0	-0.4
1948	Cin N	2	15	.118	43	17	2	1	137	146	82	10	6	59	64	4.60	85	.271	.350	36-0-2	.139	-2	67	-12	0	-1.5
1949	Cin N	4	5	.444	30	7	2	0	66.1	66	54	8	4	46	28	6.24	67	.261	.383	18-0-2	.056	-2	78	-15	0	-2.0
1950	Cin N	0	3	.000	9	2	0	0	20	25	20	4	0	17	6	7.20	59	.305	.424	3-0-1	.333	0	42	-7	0	-0.9
1951	Cin N	1	1	.500	9	0	0	0	9.2	13	8	0	1	8	5	6.52	63	.317	.440	1	.000	-0	—	-2	0	-0.5
1952	Phi N	0	0	ø	3	0	0	2	7	2	0	0	0	2	7	0.00	ø	.091	.167	1	.000	-0	—	3	0	0.2
1953	Phi N	0	1	.000	15	0	0	0	27	26	20	3	1	21	20	6.67	63	.252	.384	7	.000	-1	—	-6	0	-0.4
Total	8	13	38	.255	147	43	7-1	5	420.1	434	258	33	15	215	208	4.95	82	.266	.357	110-0-9	.091	-8	65	-38	0	-5.5

PETERSON, KYLE Kyle Johnathan; B4.9.1976 Elkhorn NE; BL/TR/6´3˝/(215–220); [MilA97 1/13]; d7.19; Col Stanford; [DL 2000 Mil N 181]

YEAR	TM LG	W	L	PCT	G	GS	CG-SHO	SV-BS	IP	H	R	HR	HB	BB-IB	SO	ERA	AERA	OAV	OOB	AB-HR-SH	AVG	PB	SUP	APR	DL	PW
1999	Mil N	4	7	.364	17	12	0	0-1	77	87	46	3	4	25-2	34	4.56	101	.285	.344	22-0-2	.136	-0	90	-1	0	-0.3
2001	Mil N	1	2	.333	3	2	0	0-0	14.2	19	10	3	0	4-2	12	5.52	78	.302	.343	5	.200	0	86	-2	0	-0.3
Total	2	5	9	.357	20	14	0	0-1	91.2	106	56	6	4	29-4	46	4.71	97	.288	.344	27-0-2	.148	-0	89	-3	181	-0.6

PETERSON, SID Sidney Herbert; B1.31.1918 Havelock ND; D8.29.2001 Wichita Falls TX; BR/TR/6´3˝/220; d5.4

YEAR	TM LG	W	L	PCT	G	GS	CG-SHO	SV-BS	IP	H	R	HR	HB	BB-IB	SO	ERA	AERA	OAV	OOB	AB-HR-SH	AVG	PB	SUP	APR	DL	PW
1943	StL A	2	0	1.000	3	0	0	0	10	15	3	0	1	3	0	2.70	123	.341	.396	2	.000	-0	—	1	0	0.1

PETIT, YUSMEIRO Yusmeiro Alberto; B11.22.1984 Maracaibo, Venezuela; BR/TR/6´0˝/230; d5.14

YEAR	TM LG	W	L	PCT	G	GS	CG-SHO	SV-BS	IP	H	R	HR	HB	BB-IB	SO	ERA	AERA	OAV	OOB	AB-HR-SH	AVG	PB	SUP	APR	DL	PW
2006	Fla N	1	1	.500	15	1	0	0-0	26.1	46	28	7	0	9-1	20	9.57	45	.390	.430	5	.200	0	388	-15	0	-1.0

PETKOVSEK, MARK Mark Joseph; B11.18.1965 Beaumont TX; BR/TR/6´0˝/(185–198); [TexA87 1/29]; d6.8; Col Texas

YEAR	TM LG	W	L	PCT	G	GS	CG-SHO	SV-BS	IP	H	R	HR	HB	BB-IB	SO	ERA	AERA	OAV	OOB	AB-HR-SH	AVG	PB	SUP	APR	DL	PW
1991	Tex A	0	1	.000	4	1	0	0-0	9.1	21	16	4	0	4-0	6	14.46	28	.438	.472	0	ø	0	158	-11	0	-0.9
1993	Pit N	3	0	1.000	26	0	0	0-0	32.1	43	25	7	0	9-2	14	6.96	59	.328	.369	0	ø	0	—	-10	0	-0.7
1995	StL N	6	6	.500	26	21	1-1	0-0	137.1	136	71	11	6	35-3	71	4.00	107	.262	.313	37-0-3	.081	-1	88	4	0	0.1
1996	†StL N	11	2	.846	48	6	0	0-3	88.2	83	37	9	5	35-2	45	3.55	119	.251	.331	16	.188	0	74	7	18	1.0
1997	StL N	4	7	.364	55	2	0	2-0	96	109	61	14	6	31-4	51	5.06	83	.292	.354	11-0-1	.091	-0	99	-9	0	-0.9
1998	StL N	7	4	.636	48	10	0	0-5	105.2	131	63	9	8	36-3	55	4.77	88	.312	.375	22-0-2	.318	2	109	-7	0	-0.5
1999	Ana A	10	4	.714	64	0	0	1-3	83	85	37	6	2	21-2	43	3.47	141	.269	.314	0	ø	0	—	12	0	1.8
2000	Ana A	4	2	.667	64	1	0	2-2	81	86	40	8	3	23-6	31	4.33	119	.277	.332	0	ø	0	36	8	25	0.5
2001	Tex A	1	2	.333	55	0	0	0-4	76.2	103	61	14	5	28-4	42	6.69	71	.323	.379	1	.000	-0	—	-16	0	-0.8
Total	9	46	28	.622	390	41	1-1	5-17	710	797	411	82	35	222-26	358	4.74	94	.288	.346	87-0-6	.161	1	89	-22	43	-0.4

PETRY, DAN Daniel Joseph; B11.13.1958 Palo Alto CA; BR/TR/6´4˝/(180–215); [DetA76 4/74]; d7.8

YEAR	TM LG	W	L	PCT	G	GS	CG-SHO	SV-BS	IP	H	R	HR	HB	BB-IB	SO	ERA	AERA	OAV	OOB	AB-HR-SH	AVG	PB	SUP	APR	DL	PW
1979	Det A	6	5	.545	15	15	2	0-0	98	90	46	11	4	33-5	43	3.95	110	.254	.321	0	ø	0	86	5	0	0.4
1980	Det A	10	9	.526	27	25	4-3	0-0	164.2	156	82	9	1	83-14	88	3.94	105	.253	.340	0	ø	0	105	2	0	0.3
1981	Det A	10	9	.526	23	22	7-2	0-0	141	115	53	10	1	57-4	79	3.00	126	.224	.301	0	ø	0	78	10	0	1.5
1982	Det A	15	9	.625	35	35	8-1	0-0	246	220	98	15	4	100-5	132	3.22	127	.241	.317	0	ø	0	112	24	0	2.4
1983	Det A	19	11	.633	38	**38**	9-2	0-0	266.1	256	126	37	6	99-7	122	3.92	101	.256	.325	0	ø	0	121	2	0	0.3
1984	†Det A	18	8	.692	35	35	7-2	0-0	233.1	231	94	21	3	66-4	144	3.24	122	.259	.312	0	ø	0	120	19	0	2.2
1985	Det A★	15	13	.536	34	34	8	0-0	238.2	190	98	24	3	81-9	109	3.36	122	.217	.285	0	ø	0	89	21	0	2.3
1986	Det A	5	10	.333	20	20	2	0-0	116	122	78	15	5	53-3	56	4.66	89	.268	.348	0	ø	0	90	-12	74	-1.2
1987	†Det A	9	7	.563	30	21	0	0-0	134.2	148	101	22	10	76-5	93	5.61	76	.279	.375	0	ø	0	149	-24	0	-2.3
1988	Cal A	3	9	.250	22	22	4-1	0-0	139.2	139	70	18	6	59-5	64	4.38	89	.263	.341	0	ø	0	94	-6	65	-0.3
1989	Cal A	3	2	.600	19	4	0	0-0	51	53	32	8	1	23-0	21	5.47	70	.275	.347	0	ø	0	89	-9	0	-0.8
1990	Det A	10	9	.526	32	23	1	0-0	149.2	148	78	14	1	77-7	73	4.45	89	.263	.349	0	ø	0	96	-7	0	-0.7
1991	Det A	2	3	.400	17	6	0	0-0	54.2	66	35	9	0	19-3	18	4.94	85	.300	.356	0	ø	0	109	-6	0	-0.4
	Atl N	0	0	ø	10	0	0	0-0	24.1	29	17	2	1	14-1	9	5.55	70	.296	.389	5	.200	0	—	-4	0	-0.2
	Bos A	0	0	ø	13	0	0	1-0	22.1	21	17	3	1	12-2	12	4.43	98	.250	.347	0	ø	0	—	-2	0	-0.1
Total	13	125	104	.546	370	300	52-11	1-0	2080.1	1984	1025	218	47	852-74	1063	3.95	103	.253	.328	5	.200	0	105	13	139	3.4

PETTIBONE, JAY Harry Jonathan; B6.21.1957 Mt.Clemens MI; BR/TR/6´4˝/182; [TexA79 30/743]; d9.11; Col Chapman

YEAR	TM LG	W	L	PCT	G	GS	CG-SHO	SV-BS	IP	H	R	HR	HB	BB-IB	SO	ERA	AERA	OAV	OOB	AB-HR-SH	AVG	PB	SUP	APR	DL	PW
1983	Min A	0	4	.000	4	4	1	0-0	27	28	16	8	2	8-0	10	5.33	80	.280	.345	0	ø	0	48	-2	0	-0.3

PETTIT, PAUL George William Paul "Lefty"; B11.29.1931 Los Angeles CA; BL/TL/6´2˝/195; d5.4

YEAR	TM LG	W	L	PCT	G	GS	CG-SHO	SV-BS	IP	H	R	HR	HB	BB-IB	SO	ERA	AERA	OAV	OOB	AB-HR-SH	AVG	PB	SUP	APR	DL	PW
1951	Pit N	0	0	ø	2	0	0	0	2.2	2	1	1	0	1	0	3.38	125	.200	.273	1	.000	-0	—	0	0	0.0
1953	Pit N	1	2	.333	10	5	0	0	28	33	27	1	0	20	14	7.71	58	.297	.405	8-0-1	.250	1*	112	-10	0	-0.8
Total	2	1	2	.333	12	5	0	0	30.2	35	28	2	0	21	14	7.34	61	.289	.394	9-0-1	.222	1	112	-10	0	-0.8

PETTIT, LEON Leon Arthur "Lefty"; B6.23.1902 Waynesburg PA; D11.21.1974 Columbia TN; BL/TL/5´10.5˝/165; d4.18

YEAR	TM LG	W	L	PCT	G	GS	CG-SHO	SV-BS	IP	H	R	HR	HB	BB-IB	SO	ERA	AERA	OAV	OOB	AB-HR-SH	AVG	PB	SUP	APR	DL	PW
1935	Was A	8	5	.615	41	7	1	3	109	129	65	6	4	58	45	4.95	87	.301	.390	25-0-1	.080	0	126	-7	—	-0.7
1937	Phi N	0	1	.000	3	1	0	0	4	6	5	1	0	4	0	11.25	39	.353	.476	0	ø	0	80	-3	—	-0.5
Total	2	8	6	.571	44	8	1	3	113	135	70	7	4	62	45	5.18	84	.303	.393	25-0-1	.080	0	120	-10	—	-1.2

PETTITTE, ANDY Andrew Eugene; B6.15.1972 Baton Rouge LA; BL/TL/6´5˝/(225–235); d4.29; Col San Jacinto North (TX) JC

YEAR	TM LG	W	L	PCT	G	GS	CG-SHO	SV-BS	IP	H	R	HR	HB	BB-IB	SO	ERA	AERA	OAV	OOB	AB-HR-SH	AVG	PB	SUP	APR	DL	PW
1995	†NY A	12	9	.571	31	26	3	0-0	175	183	86	15	1	63-3	114	4.17	111	.272	.333	0	ø	0	91	9	0	0.9
1996	†NY A☆	**21**	8	.724	35	34	2	0-0	221	229	105	23	3	72-2	162	3.87	128	.271	.330	0	ø	0	102	25	0	2.8
1997	†NY A	18	7	.720	35	**35**	4-1	0-0	240.1	233	86	7	3	65-0	166	2.88	154	.256	.307	0	ø	0	128	42	0	4.1
1998	†NY A	16	11	.593	33	32	5	0-0	216.1	226	110	20	6	87-1	146	4.24	103	.274	.344	4-0-2	.000	-0	102	3	0	0.3
1999	†NY A	14	11	.560	31	31	0	0-0	191.2	216	105	20	3	89-3	121	4.70	101	.289	.364	5	.200	0	109	3	12	0.5
2000	†NY A	19	9	.679	32	32	3-1	0-0	204.2	219	111	17	4	80-4	125	4.35	110	.271	.338	5	.000	-0	130	8	17	1.0
2001	†NY A★	15	10	.600	31	31	2	0-0	200.2	224	103	14	6	41-3	164	3.99	111	.281	.319	4-0-1	.000	-0	109	8	15	0.9
2002	†NY A	13	5	.722	22	22	3-1	0-0	134.2	144	58	6	4	32-2	97	3.27	132	.272	.317	3	.333	1	117	15	59	2.0
2003	†NY A	21	8	.724	33	33	1	0-0	208.1	227	109	21	1	50-3	180	4.02	109	.272	.312	7	.143	-0	139	6	0	0.7
2004	Hou N	6	4	.600	15	15	0	0-0	83	71	37	8	0	31-2	79	3.90	112	.226	.296	23-0-3	.174	1	75	5	102	0.7
2005	†Hou N	17	9	.654	33	33	0	0-0	222.1	188	66	17	3	41-0	171	2.39	177	.230	.268	62-0-15	.081	-4	100	44	0	4.8
2006	Hou N	14	13	.519	36	**35**	2-1	0-0	214.1	238	114	27	2	70-9	178	4.20	107	.284	.339	62-1-10	.194	3*	91	4	0	0.7
Total	12	186	104	.641	367	359	25-4	0-0	2312.1	2398	1090	195	36	721-32	1703	3.81	119	.268	.324	175-1-31	.137	-0	109	172	205	19.4

PETTY, CHARLIE Charles E.; B6.28.1866 Nashville TN; TR/?/175; d7.30

YEAR	TM LG	W	L	PCT	G	GS	CG-SHO	SV-BS	IP	H	R	HR	HB	BB-IB	SO	ERA	AERA	OAV	OOB	AB-HR-SH	AVG	PB	SUP	APR	DL	PW
1889	Cin AA	2	3	.400	5	5	5	0	44	44	29	3	6	20	10	5.52	71	.253	.350	20	.300	1	98	-3	—	-0.2
1893	NY N	5	2	.714	9	6	4	0	54	66	36	0	1	28	12	3.33	140	.292	.373	22-1	.318	3	168	6	—	0.8
1894	Was N	3	8	.273	16	12	8	0	103	156	114	4	9	32	14	5.59	95	.344	.399	41-0-5	.195	-2	85	-6	—	-0.6
	Cle N	0	2	.000	4	3	2	0	27	42	37	4	3	14	4	8.67	63	.350	.431	12	.083	-2	103	-9	—	-0.6
	Year	3	10	.231	20	15	10	0	130	198	151	8	12	46	18	6.23	85	.346	.406	53-0-5	.170	-4	89	-21	—	-1.2
Total	3	10	15	.400	34	26	19	0	228	308	216	11	19	94	40	5.41	91	.317	.388	95-1-5	.232	-0	107	-12	—	-0.6

PETTY, JESSE Jesse Lee "The Silver Fox"; B11.23.1894 Orr OK; D10.23.1971 St.Paul MN; BR/TL/6´0˝/195; d4.14

YEAR	TM LG	W	L	PCT	G	GS	CG-SHO	SV-BS	IP	H	R	HR	HB	BB-IB	SO	ERA	AERA	OAV	OOB	AB-HR-SH	AVG	PB	SUP	APR	DL	PW
1921	Cle A	0	0	ø	4	0	0	0	9	10	2	0	0	0	0	2.00	213	.345	.345	2	.000	-0	—	2	—	0.1
1925	Bro N	9	9	.500	28	21	7	0	153	188	97	15	2	47	39	4.88	86	.304	.355	50-0-3	.140	-3	95	-11	—	-1.4
1926	Bro N	17	17	.500	38	33	23-1	1	275.2	246	118	9	3	79	101	2.84	135	**.240**	.296	97-0-3	.175	-3	71	25	—	2.4
1927	Bro N	13	18	.419	42	33	19-2	1	271.2	263	108	13	4	53	101	2.98	133	.254	.293	91-0-1	.099	-7	53	29	—	2.2
1928	Bro N	15	15	.500	40	31	15-2	1	234	264	119	18	5	56	74	4.04	98	.289	.334	81-0-4	.111	-5	93	4	—	-0.3
1929	Pit N	11	10	.524	36	25	12-1	0	184.1	197	100	12	0	42	58	3.71	129	.277	.317	67-0-1	.104	-5	95	17	—	1.0
1930	Pit N	1	6	.143	10	7	0	1	41.1	67	43	8	2	13	16	8.27	60	.362	.410	12-0-1	.083	-1	88	-14	—	-2.0
	Chi N	1	3	.250	9	3	0	0	39.1	51	18	2	0	6	18	2.97	164	.317	.341	13-0-1	.231	0	30	7	—	0.6
	Year	2	9	.182	19	10	0	1	80.2	118	61	10	2	19	34	5.69	87	.341	.379	25-0-2	.160	-1	71	-8	—	-1.4
Total	7	67	78	.462	207	153	76-6	4	1208.1	1286	605	77	16	296	407	3.68	113	.275	.320	413-0-14	.128	-25	80	59	—	2.6

PETTYJOHN, ADAM Adam Christopher; B6.11.1977 Phoenix AZ; BR/TL/6´3˝/190; [DetA98 2/73]; d7.16; Col Cal St.–Fresno; [DL 2002 Det A 183]

YEAR	TM LG	W	L	PCT	G	GS	CG-SHO	SV-BS	IP	H	R	HR	HB	BB-IB	SO	ERA	AERA	OAV	OOB	AB-HR-SH	AVG	PB	SUP	APR	DL	PW
2001	Det A	1	6	.143	16	9	0	0-0	65	81	48	10	4	21-2	40	5.82	76	.309	.366	2	.000	-0	67	-11	0	-1.0

PEZZULLO, PRETZEL John; B12.10.1910 Bridgeport CT; D5.16.1990 Dallas TX; BL/TL/5´11.5˝/180; d4.18

YEAR	TM LG	W	L	PCT	G	GS	CG-SHO	SV-BS	IP	H	R	HR	HB	BB-IB	SO	ERA	AERA	OAV	OOB	AB-HR-SH	AVG	PB	SUP	APR	DL	PW
1935	Phi N	3	5	.375	41	7	2	1	84.1	115	74	5	7	45	24	6.40	71	.321	.407	24	.250	0	78	-16	—	-1.4
1936	Phi N	0	0	ø	1	0	0	0	2	1	1	0	0	6	0	4.50	101	.167	.583	0	ø	0	—	0	—	0.0
Total	2	3	5	.375	42	7	2	1	86.1	116	75	5	7	51	24	6.36	71	.319	.412	24	.250	0	78	-16	—	-1.4

PFANN, BILL William F.; B6.1863 Hamilton ON, Can.; D6.3.1904 Hamilton ON, Can.; TR/6´0˝/205; d6.16

YEAR	TM LG	W	L	PCT	G	GS	CG-SHO	SV-BS	IP	H	R	HR	HB	BB-IB	SO	ERA	AERA	OAV	OOB	AB-HR-SH	AVG	PB	SUP	APR	DL	PW
1894	Cin N	0	1	.000	1	1	0	0	3	10	10	1	0	4	0	27.00	21	.526	.609	1	.000	-0	115	-6	—	-0.7

PFEFFER, JEFF Edward Joseph; B3.4.1888 Seymour IL; D8.15.1972 Chicago IL; BR/TR/6´3˝/210; d4.16; Mil 1918; b–Big Jeff

YEAR	TM LG	W	L	PCT	G	GS	CG-SHO	SV-BS	IP	H	R	HR	HB	BB-IB	SO	ERA	AERA	OAV	OOB	AB-HR-SH	AVG	PB	SUP	APR	DL	PW
1911	StL A	0	0	ø	2	0	0	0	10	11	11	0	0	4	4	7.20	47	.297	.366	4	.000	-1	—	-4	—	-0.3
1913	Bro N	0	1	.000	5	2	1	0	24.1	28	16	0	4	13	13	3.33	99	.311	.421	7-0-1	.000	-1	103	-2	—	-0.2
1914	Bro N	23	12	.657	43	34	27-3	4	315	264	99	9	7	91	135	1.97	145	.232	.293	116-0-1	.198	-1*	104	30	—	3.2
1915	Bro N	19	14	.576	40	34	26-6	3	291.2	243	93	8	17	76	84	2.10	132	.231	.293	106-0-1	.255	5	114	22	—	2.9
1916	†Bro N	25	11	.694	41	36	30-6	1	328.2	274	91	5	17	63	128	1.92	140	.230	.278	122-0-3	.279	7*	110	30	—	4.1
1917	Bro N	11	15	.423	30	30	24-3	0	266	225	84	4	16	66	115	2.23	125	.234	.294	100-0-5	.130	-4*	92	16	—	1.0
1918	Bro N	1	0	1.000	1	1	1-1	0	9	2	0	0	0	3	1	0.00	ø	.071	.161	4	.250	0	54	3	—	0.4
1919	Bro N	17	13	.567	30	30	26-4	0	267	270	95	7	12	49	92	2.66	112	.267	.308	97-0-3	.206	1	101	12	—	1.5
1920	†Bro N	16	9	.640	30	28	20-2	0	215	225	81	5	5	45	80	3.01	106	.273	.314	74-0-6	.243	1	110	8	—	0.8
1921	Bro N	1	5	.167	6	5	2	0	31.2	36	19	0	1	9	8	4.55	86	.310	.365	11	.000	-2	51	-2	—	-0.5
	StL N	9	3	.750	18	13	7-1	0	98.2	115	51	3	5	28	22	4.29	86	.305	.361	29-0-4	.138	-1	128	-4	—	-0.6
	Year	10	8	.556	24	18	9-1	0	130.1	151	70	3	6	37	30	4.35	86	.306	.362	40-0-4	.100	-2	106	-7	—	-1.1
1922	StL N	19	12	.613	44	32	19-1	2	261.1	286	126	12	11	58	83	3.58	108	.279	.324	98-0-2	.245	4*	111	9	—	1.4
1923	StL N	8	9	.471	26	18	7-1	0	152.1	171	80	8	9	40	32	4.02	97	.287	.341	55-0-1	.127	-4	98	-1	—	-0.5
1924	StL N	4	5	.444	16	12	3	0	78	102	52	3	1	30	20	5.31	71	.318	.378	26-0-1	.115	-2	82	-12	—	-1.5
	Pit N	5	3	.625	15	4	1	0	58.2	68	23	3	0	17	19	3.07	125	.293	.341	25-0-1	.240	-0	116	5	—	0.5
	Year	9	8	.529	31	16	4	0	136.2	170	75	6	1	47	39	4.35	88	.307	.363	51-0-2	.176	-3	90	-8	—	-1.0
Total	13	158	112	.585	347	279	194-28	10	2407.1	2320	921	67	105	592	836	2.77	114	.258	.311	874-0-29	.206	2	104	110	—	12.2

PFEFFER, BIG JEFF Francis Xavier; B3.31.1882 Champaign IL; D12.19.1954 Kankakee IL; BR/TR/6´1˝/185; d4.15; b–Jeff; Col Illinois

YEAR	TM LG	W	L	PCT	G	GS	CG-SHO	SV-BS	IP	H	R	HR	HB	BB-IB	SO	ERA	AERA	OAV	OOB	AB-HR-SH	AVG	PB	SUP	APR	DL	PW
1905	Chi N	4	4	.500	15	11	9	0	101	84	36	2	4	36	56	2.50	120	.240	.318	40-0-1	.200	1	77	6	—	0.5
1906	Bos N	13	22	.371	36	36	33-4	0	302.1	270	138	4	16	114	158	2.95	91	.246	.325	158-1-2	.196	3*	78	-9	—	-0.4
1907	Bos N	6	8	.429	19	16	12-1	0	144	129	62	3	7	61	65	3.00	85	.253	.341	60-0-1	.250	3*	99	-7	—	-0.3
1908	Bos N	0	0	ø	4	0	0	0	10	18	16	1	0	8	3	12.60	19	.383	.473	2	.000	-0	—	-10	—	-0.6
1910	Chi N	1	0	1.000	13	1	1	0	41.1	43	31	1	1	16	11	3.27	88	.281	.353	17-0-1	.176	1*	77	-7	—	-0.3
1911	Bos N	7	5	.583	26	6	4-1	2	97	116	74	3	0	57	24	4.73	81	.301	.391	46-1-0	.196	1*	95	-11	—	-1.1
Total	6	31	39	.443	113	70	59-6	2	695.2	660	357	14	28	292	317	3.30	87	.260	.342	323-2-5	.204	8	83	-38	—	-2.2

PFEFFER, FRED Nathaniel Frederick "Fritz","Dandelion"; B3.17.1860 Louisville KY; D4.10.1932 Chicago IL; BR/TR/5´10.5˝/184; d5.1.1882; M1; ▲

YEAR	TM LG	W	L	PCT	G	GS	CG-SHO	SV-BS	IP	H	R	HR	HB	BB-IB	SO	ERA	AERA	OAV	OOB	AB-HR-SH	AVG	PB	SUP	APR	DL	PW
1884	Chi N	0	0	ø	1	0	0	0	1	3	2	0	—	1	0	9.00	35	.333	.400	467-25	.289	0*	—	-1	—	0.0
1885	†Chi N	2	1	.667	5	2	2	**2**	31.2	26	15	1	—	8	13	2.56	118	.222	.272	469-5	.241	1*	94	2	—	0.2
1892	Lou N	0	0	ø	1	0	0	0	5	4	3	0	0	5	0	1.80	170	.211	.375	470-2	.257	0*	—	0	—	0.0
1894	Lou N	0	0	ø	1	0	0	0	7	8	6	0	1	6	0	2.57	198	.286	.429	414-5-15	.309	0*	—	1	—	0.0
Total	4	2	1	.667	8	2	2	2	44.2	41	26	1	1	20	13	2.62	129	.237	.320	1820-37-15	.273	1	94	2	—	0.2

PFIESTER, JACK John Albert "Jack the Giant Killer" (b John Albert Hagenbush); B5.24.1878 Cincinnati OH; D9.3.1953 Loveland OH; BR/TL/5´11˝/180; d9.8

YEAR	TM LG	W	L	PCT	G	GS	CG-SHO	SV-BS	IP	H	R	HR	HB	BB-IB	SO	ERA	AERA	OAV	OOB	AB-HR-SH	AVG	PB	SUP	APR	DL	PW
1903	Pit N	0	3	.000	3	3	2	0	19	26	21	0	2	10	15	6.16	53	.321	.409	6	.000	-1	69	-7	—	-0.9
1904	Pit N	1	1	.500	3	2	1	0	20	28	18	0	0	9	6	7.20	38	.318	.381	7	.286	1	125	-8	—	-0.6
1906	†Chi N	20	8	.714	31	29	20-4	0	250.2	173	63	3	13	63	153	1.51	175	.194	.258	84-0-2	.048	-7	129	30	—	2.6
1907	†Chi N	14	9	.609	30	22	13-3	0	195	143	61	1	5	48	90	**1.15**	**216**	.207	.263	64-0-8	.094	-3	126	21	—	2.1
1908	†Chi N	12	10	.545	33	29	18-3	0	252	204	82	1	11	70	117	2.00	118	.223	.287	79-0-4	.101	-4	113	7	—	0.1
1909	Chi N	17	6	.739	29	25	13-5	0	196.2	179	67	1	5	49	73	2.43	105	.240	.291	65-0-3	.169	0	131	6	—	0.8
1910	†Chi N	6	3	.667	14	13	5-2	0	100.1	82	28	0	1	26	34	1.79	161	.225	.279	33-0-1	.091	-2	83	12	—	0.7
1911	Chi N	1	4	.200	6	5	3	0	33.2	34	25	0	2	18	15	4.01	83	.262	.360	11-0-1	.182	0	77	-5	—	-0.6
Total	8	71	44	.617	149	128	75-17	0	1067.1	869	365	6	39	293	503	2.02	128	.223	.284	349-0-19	.103	-15	117	56	—	4.2

PFISTER, DAN Daniel Albin; B12.20.1936 Plainfield NJ; BR/TR/6´0˝/(182–187); d9.9

YEAR	TM LG	W	L	PCT	G	GS	CG-SHO	SV-BS	IP	H	R	HR	HB	BB-IB	SO	ERA	AERA	OAV	OOB	AB-HR-SH	AVG	PB	SUP	APR	DL	PW
1961	KC A	0	0	ø	2	0	0	0	2.1	5	4	2	0	4-0	3	15.43	27	.417	.563	0	ø	0	—	-3	0	-0.1
1962	KC A	4	14	.222	41	25	2	1	196.1	175	112	27	9	106-2	123	4.54	93	.238	.340	65-0-2	.185	-1*	85	-8	0	-0.8
1963	KC A	1	0	1.000	3	1	0	0	9.1	8	2	1	1	3-0	9	1.93	202	.229	.308	3	.000	-0*	159	2	123	0.2
1964	KC A	1	5	.167	19	3	0	0	41.1	50	32	10	6	29-4	21	6.53	58	.311	.431	6	.000	-0*	93	-11	0	-1.6
Total	4	6	19	.240	65	29	2	1	249.1	238	150	40	16	142-6	156	4.87	85	.252	.358	74-0-2	.162	-2	89	-20	123	-2.3

PFUND, LEE Le Roy Herbert; B10.10.1919 Oak Park IL; BR/TR/6´1˝/185; d4.21

YEAR	TM LG	W	L	PCT	G	GS	CG-SHO	SV-BS	IP	H	R	HR	HB	BB-IB	SO	ERA	AERA	OAV	OOB	AB-HR-SH	AVG	PB	SUP	APR	DL	PW
1945	Bro N	3	2	.600	15	10	2	0	62.1	69	51	4	5	35	27	5.20	72	.274	.373	22-0-1	.182	0	203	-12	62	-0.8

PHEBUS, BILL Raymond William; B8.2.1909 Cherryvale KS; D10.11.1989 Bartow FL; BR/TR/5´9˝/170; d9.6

YEAR	TM LG	W	L	PCT	G	GS	CG-SHO	SV-BS	IP	H	R	HR	HB	BB-IB	SO	ERA	AERA	OAV	OOB	AB-HR-SH	AVG	PB	SUP	APR	DL	PW
1936	Was A	0	0	ø	2	1	0	0	7.1	4	6	1	1	4	4	2.45	195	.114	.225	1	.000	0	129	0	—	0.0
1937	Was A	3	2	.600	6	5	4-1	1	40.2	33	13	2	2	24	12	2.21	200	.232	.351	8-0-1	.000	1	67	10	—	1.2
1938	Was A	0	0	ø	5	0	0	1	6.1	9	9	1	0	7	2	11.37	40	.346	.485	1	.000	-0	—	-5	—	-0.2
Total	3	3	2	.600	13	6	4-1	2	54.1	46	28	4	3	35	18	3.31	135	.227	.349	10-0-1	.000	1	78	5	—	1.0

PHELPS, RAY Raymond Clifford; B12.11.1903 Dunlap TN; D7.7.1971 Fort Pierce FL; BR/TR/6´2˝/200; d4.23

YEAR	TM LG	W	L	PCT	G	GS	CG-SHO	SV-BS	IP	H	R	HR	HB	BB-IB	SO	ERA	AERA	OAV	OOB	AB-HR-SH	AVG	PB	SUP	APR	DL	PW
1930	Bro N	14	7	.667	36	24	11-2	0	179.2	198	98	21	3	52	64	4.11	120	.280	.332	68-1-1	.147	-2	113	16	—	1.4
1931	Bro N	7	9	.438	28	26	3-1	0	149.1	184	88	3	4	44	50	5.00	76	.306	.357	51	.157	-1	108	-16	—	-1.6
1932	Bro N	4	5	.444	20	9	4-1	0	79.1	101	58	5	3	27	21	5.90	65	.323	.382	23-0-2	.087	-1	122	-18	—	-1.8
1935	Chi A	4	8	.333	27	17	4	1	125	126	77	10	3	55	38	4.82	96	.262	.341	41-0-1	.122	-4	90	-3	—	-0.5
1936	Chi A	4	6	.400	15	4	2	0	68.2	91	54	9	2	42	17	6.03	86	.331	.423	26	.231	1	68	-7	—	-0.7
Total	5	33	35	.485	126	80	24-4	1	602	700	375	48	15	220	190	4.93	90	.294	.358	209-1-4	.148	-8	103	-28	—	-3.2

PHELPS, TOMMY Thomas Allen; B3.4.1974 Seoul, South Korea; BL/TL/6´3˝/(190–215); [MonN92 8/211]; d3.31

YEAR	TM LG	W	L	PCT	G	GS	CG-SHO	SV-BS	IP	H	R	HR	HB	BB-IB	SO	ERA	AERA	OAV	OOB	AB-HR-SH	AVG	PB	SUP	APR	DL	PW
2003	Fla N	3	2	.600	27	7	0	0-0	63	70	32	3	2	23-1	43	4.00	103	.282	.345	11-0-1	.091	0	121	0	30	0.0
2004	Fla N	1	1	.500	19	4	0	0-0	34	34	20	6	0	12-0	28	4.76	86	.268	.326	6	.000	-1	119	-3	0	-0.2
2005	Mil N	0	2	.000	29	0	0	1-1	23.1	25	12	2	2	12-4	14	4.63	92	.272	.368	0	ø	0	—	0	0	0.0
Total	3	4	5	.444	75	11	0	1-1	120.1	129	64	11	4	47-5	85	4.34	95	.276	.345	17-0-1	.059	-1	119	-3	30	-0.2

PHELPS, TRAVIS Travis Howard; B7.25.1977 Neosho MO; BR/TR/6´2˝/(170–195); [TBA96 89/1721]; d4.19; Col Crowder (MO) CC

YEAR	TM LG	W	L	PCT	G	GS	CG-SHO	SV-BS	IP	H	R	HR	HB	BB-IB	SO	ERA	AERA	OAV	OOB	AB-HR-SH	AVG	PB	SUP	APR	DL	PW
2001	TB A	2	2	.500	49	0	0	5-1	62	53	30	6	3	24-1	54	3.48	129	.226	.301	0	ø	0	—	6	0	0.4
2002	TB A	1	2	.333	26	0	0	0-0	37.2	30	20	7	5	27-0	36	4.78	95	.222	.367	0	ø	0	—	0	0	0.0
2004	Mil N	0	1	.000	4	0	0	0-0	6	8	7	2	0	3-0	3	10.50	42	.286	.355	1	.000	-0	—	-4	0	-0.5
Total	3	3	5	.375	79	0	0	5-1	105.2	91	57	15	8	54-1	93	4.34	104	.229	.328	1	.000	-0	—	2	0	-0.1

YEAR	TM LG	W	L	PCT	G	GS	CG-SHO	SV-BS	IP	H	R	HR	HB	BB-IB	SO	ERA	AERA	OAV	OOB	AB-HR-SH	AVG	PB	SUP	APR	DL	PW
Phillippe, Deacon	Charles Louis; B5.23.1872 Rural Retreat VA; D3.30.1952 Avalon PA; BR/TR/6´0.5˝/180; d4.21																									
1899	Lou N	21	17	.553	42	38	33-2	1	321	331	178	10	7	64	68	3.17	122	.266	.306	128-0-5	.203	-1*	97	22	—	2.0
1900	†Pit N	20	13	.606	38	33	29-1	0	279	274	127	7	7	42	75	2.84	128	.257	**.289**	105-0-4	.181	-2	83	26	—	2.2
1901	Pit N	22	12	.647	37	32	30-1	2	296	274	115	7	10	38	103	2.22	147	.244	.275	113-1-2	.230	5*	120	33	—	4.1
1902	Pit N	20	9	.690	31	30	29-5	0	272	265	90	1	4	26	122	2.05	134	.255	.276	113-1-3	.221	3*	135	19	—	2.1
1903	†Pit N	25	9	.735	36	33	31-4	2	289.1	269	116	4	4	29	123	2.43	133	.241	**.263**	124	.210	2*	125	27	—	2.9
1904	Pit N	10	10	.500	21	19	17-3	1	166.2	183	82	1	3	26	82	3.24	85	.272	.302	65-0-1	.123	-4	77	-9	—	-1.4
1905	Pit N	20	13	.606	38	33	25-5	0	279	235	95	0	10	48	133	2.19	137	.233	.274	97-0-2	.093	-4	93	22	—	2.0
1906	Pit N	15	10	.600	33	24	19-3	0	218.2	216	78	3	2	26	90	2.47	108	.252	.276	82	.244	3	89	7	—	1.1
1907	Pit N	14	11	.560	35	26	17-1	2	214	214	83	2	5	36	61	2.61	93	.264	.300	65-0-5	.185	1	124	-2	—	-0.2
1908	Pit N	0	0	ø	5	0	0	0	12	20	15	0	0	3	1	11.25	20	.357	.390	4	.250	0	—	-10	—	-0.5
1909	†Pit N	8	3	.727	22	13	7-1	0	131.2	121	41	2	4	14	38	2.32	117	.253	.280	42-0-1	.071	-3	101	8	—	0.2
1910	Pit N	14	2	.875	31	8	5-1	4	121.2	111	46	4	3	9	30	2.29	135	.239	.258	41-1-1	.220	1	153	9	—	1.1
1911	Pit N	0	0	ø	3	0	0	0	6	5	5	0	0	2	3	7.50	46	.238	.304	1	1.000	1	—	-2	—	0.0
Total	13	189	109	.634	372	289	242-27	12	2607	2518	1071	41	59	363	929	2.59	120	.253	.283	980-3-24	.189	2	107	150	—	15.6
Phillips, Buz	Albert Abernathy; B5.25.1904 Newton NC; D11.6.1964 Baltimore MD; BR/TR/5´11.5˝/185; d8.5; Col Lenoir–Rhyne																									
1930	Phi N	0	0	ø	14	1	0	0	43.2	68	44	6	1	18	9	8.04	68	.354	.412	13-1-0	.462	2	80	-11	—	-0.3
Phillips, Red	Clarence Lemuel; B11.3.1908 Pauls Valley OK; D2.1.1988 Wichita KS; BR/TR/6´3.5˝/195; d7.24; Col East Central																									
1934	Det A	2	0	1.000	7	1	1	1	23.1	31	17	1	0	16	3	6.17	71	.316	.412	12	.250	1	317	-4	—	-0.3
1936	Det A	2	4	.333	22	6	3	0	87.1	124	67	12	0	22	15	6.49	76	.332	.370	33	.303	2	86	-13	—	-0.5
Total	2	4	4	.500	29	7	4	1	110.2	155	84	13	0	38	18	6.42	75	.329	.379	45	.289	3	117	-17	—	-0.8
Phillips, Jason	Jason Charles; B3.22.1974 Williamsport PA; BR/TR/6´6˝/225; [PitN92 14/399]; d4.5																									
1999	Pit N	0	0	ø	6	0	0	0-0	7	11	9	2	0	6-1	7	11.57	40	.393	.486	0	ø	0	—	-5	0	-0.2
2002	Cle A	1	3	.250	8	6	0	0-0	41.2	41	24	7	4	20-0	23	4.97	89	.259	.353	0	ø	0	111	-2	33	-0.2
2003	Cle A	0	1	.000	3	0	0	0-0	5	9	5	1	0	2-0	2	9.00	49	.409	.440	0	ø	0	—	-2	0	-0.4
Total	3	1	4	.200	17	6	0	0-0	53.2	61	38	10	4	28-1	32	6.20	72	.293	.381	0	ø	0	111	-9	33	-0.8
Phillips, Jack	John Stephen; B5.24.1919 St.Louis MO; D6.16.1958 St.Louis MO; BR/TR/6´1˝/185; d7.13																									
1945	NY N	0	0	ø	1	0	0	0	4.1	5	5	1	1	4	0	10.38	38	.294	.455	2	.500	0*	—	-3	0	-0.1
Phillips, Ed	Norman Edwin; B9.20.1944 Ardmore OK; BR/TR/6´1˝/190; [BosA66 16/304]; d4.9; Col Colby																									
1970	Bos A	0	2	.000	18	0	0	0-0	23.2	29	14	4	2	10-1	23	5.32	75	.312	.387	3	.000	-0	—	-2	0	-0.3
Phillips, Tom	Thomas Gerald; B4.5.1889 Philipsburg PA; D4.12.1929 Philipsburg PA; BR/TR/6´2˝/190; d9.13																									
1915	StL A	1	3	.250	5	4	1	0	27.1	28	13	0	2	12	5	2.96	97	.283	.372	9-0-1	.111	-1	57	0	—	-0.2
1919	Cle A	3	2	.600	22	3	1	0	55	55	27	2	3	34	18	2.95	114	.272	.385	11	.364	1	86	**1**	—	0.1
1921	Was A	1	0	1.000	1	1	1	0	9	9	2	0	0	3	2	2.00	206	.290	.353	3	.000	-1	61	2	—	0.2
1922	Was A	3	7	.300	17	7	2-1	0	70	72	43	2	4	22	19	4.89	79	.273	.338	20-0-1	.150	-1	78	-7	—	-0.9
Total	4	8	12	.400	45	15	5-1	0	161.1	164	85	4	9	71	44	3.74	95	.275	.361	43-0-2	.186	-1	73	-4	—	-0.8
Phillips, Bill	William Corcoran "Whoa Bill","Silver Bill"; B11.9.1868 Allenport PA; D10.25.1941 Charleroi PA; BR/TR/5´11˝/180; d8.11; M2																									
1890	Pit N	1	9	.100	10	10	9	0	82	123	97	8	1	29	25	7.57	44	.336	.386	46	.239	1*	69	-38	—	-3.1
1895	Cin N	6	7	.462	18	9	6	2	109	126	90	6	7	44	15	6.03	82	.285	.359	48	.313	2*	120	-9	—	-0.6
1899	Cin N	17	9	.654	33	27	18-1	1	227.2	234	121	3	14	71	43	3.32	118	.265	.330	92-0-4	.130	-5*	99	13	—	0.7
1900	Cin N	9	11	.450	29	24	16-3	0	207.1	229	140	5	13	67	50	4.30	85	.280	.344	79-0-1	.165	-4	115	-16	—	-1.3
1901	Cin N	14	18	.438	37	36	29-1	0	281.1	364	196	7	12	67	109	4.64	69	.311	.354	109-0-1	.202	2*	93	-45	—	-3.8
1902	Cin N	16	16	.500	33	33	30	0	269	267	121	3	9	55	85	2.51	119	.259	.302	114-0-2	.342	10*	116	12	—	2.6
1903	Cin N	7	6	.538	16	13	11-1	0	118.1	134	74	0	7	30	46	3.35	106	.279	.330	57	.175	-1*	118	1	—	0.0
Total	7	70	76	.479	176	152	119-6	3	1294.2	1477	839	32	63	363	373	4.09	87	.284	.339	545-0-8	.224	4	103	-82	—	-5.5
Phillips, Taylor	William Taylor "Tay"; B6.18.1933 Atlanta GA; BL/TL/5´11˝/(175–185); d6.8																									
1956	Mil N	5	3	.625	23	6	3	2	87.2	69	25	6	7	33-8	36	2.26	153	.223	.310	21-0-1	.000	-2	81	13	0	1.1
1957	Mil N	3	2	.600	27	6	0	2	73	82	46	3	1	40-3	36	5.55	63	.300	.388	20	.100	-4	130	-16	0	-1.2
1958	Chi N	7	10	.412	39	27	5-1	1	170.1	178	102	22	6	79-5	102	4.76	82	.266	.348	54-0-5	.056	-4	106	-16	0	-1.8
1959	Chi N	0	2	.000	7	2	0	0	16.2	22	14	3	2	11-2	5	7.56	52	.319	.422	4	.000	-0	57	-6	0	-0.7
	Phi N	1	4	.200	32	3	1	1	63	72	35	4	4	31-1	35	5.00	82	.303	.389	11	.091	-1	80	-4	0	-0.4
	Year	1	6	.143	39	5	1	1	79.2	94	49	7	6	42-3	40	5.54	74	.306	.397	15	.067	-1	70	-10	0	-1.1
1960	Phi N	0	1	.000	10	1	0	0	14	21	13	2	1	4-0	6	8.36	46	.356	.388	1	.000	-0	182	-6	0	-0.4
1963	Chi A	0	0	ø	9	0	0	0	14	16	16	2	1	13-5	13	10.29	34	.302	.441	2	.000	-0	—	-10	0	-0.5
Total	6	16	22	.421	147	45	9-1	6	438.2	460	251	42	22	211-24	233	4.82	78	.275	.362	113-0-6	.053	-9	104	-45	0	-3.9
Phoebus, Tom	Thomas Harold; B4.7.1942 Baltimore MD; BR/TR/5´8˝/(185–191); d9.15																									
1966	Bal A	2	1	.667	3	3	2-2	0	22	16	3	0	0	6-0	17	1.23	271	.213	.272	6-0-1	.167	0	62	5	0	0.9
1967	Bal A	14	9	.609	33	33	7-4	0	208	177	84	16	0	114-1	179	3.33	95	.227	.325	76-1-3	.145	1	142	-4	0	-0.5
1968	Bal A	15	15	.500	36	36	9-3	0	240.2	186	81	10	4	105-5	193	2.62	112	.212	.299	82-1-7	.183	3	98	8	0	1.4
1969	Bal A	14	7	.667	35	33	6-2	0-0	202	180	89	23	4	87-5	117	3.52	102	.241	.321	75-0-5	.200	2	119	1	0	0.2
1970	†Bal A	5	5	.500	27	21	3	0-1	135	106	58	11	6	62-2	72	3.07	120	.219	.312	43-0-3	.163	-0	119	6	0	0.4
1971	SD N	3	11	.214	29	21	2	0-0	133.1	144	67	14	3	64-6	80	4.45	75	.280	.361	36-0-2	.167	1	89	-13	0	-1.1
1972	SD N	0	1	.000	1	1	0	0-0	5.2	3	5	2	0	6-0	8	7.94	42	.150	.346	2	.000	-0	27	-3	0	-0.4
	Chi N	3	3	.500	37	1	0	6-3	83.1	76	40	9	2	45-4	59	3.78	101	.247	.343	15-0-1	.133	-1*	46	0	0	0.0
	Year	3	4	.429	38	2	0	6-3	89	79	45	11	2	51-4	67	4.04	93	.241	.343	17-0-1	.118	-1	35	-2	0	-0.4
Total	7	56	52	.519	201	149	29-11	6-4	1030	888	427	85	19	489-23	725	3.33	100	.233	.322	335-2-22	.170	5	112	0	0	0.9
Phoenix, Steve	Steven Robert; B1.31.1968 Phoenix AZ; BR/TR/6´2˝/(175–185); d7.30; Col Grand Canyon																									
1994	Oak A	0	0	ø	2	0	0	0-0	4.1	4	3	0	0	2-0	3	6.23	72	.235	.316	0	ø	0	—	-1	0	0.0
1995	Oak A	0	0	ø	1	0	0	0-0	1.2	3	6	1	0	3-0	3	32.40	14	.429	.600	0	ø	0	—	-5	0	-0.2
Total	2	0	0	ø	3	0	0	0-0	6	7	9	1	0	5-0	6	13.50	33	.292	.414	0	ø	0	—	-6	0	-0.2
Phyle, Bill	William Joseph; B6.25.1875 Duluth MN; D8.6.1953 Los Angeles CA; TR; d9.17; ▲																									
1898	Chi N	2	1	.667	3	3	3-2	0	23	24	15	0	2	6	4	0.78	458	.267	.327	9	.111	-0*	119	4	—	0.4
1899	Chi N	1	8	.111	10	9	9	1	83.2	92	58	2	4	29	10	4.20	89	.279	.344	34	.176	-2	77	-4	—	-0.5
1901	NY N	7	10	.412	24	19	16	1	168.2	208	121	2	6	54	62	4.27	77	.301	.356	66	.182	-1*	126	-21	—	-1.8
Total	3	10	19	.345	37	31	28-2	2	275.1	324	194	4	12	89	76	3.96	88	.291	.350	109	.174	-4	110	-21	—	-1.9
Piatt, Doug	Douglas William; B9.26.1965 Beaver PA; BL/TR/6´1˝/185; d6.11; Col Western Kentucky																									
1991	Mon N	0	0	ø	21	0	0	0-0	34.2	29	11	3	0	17-0	29	2.60	140	.230	.322	1	.000	-0	—	4	0	0.2
Piatt, Wiley	Wiley Harold "Iron Man"; B7.13.1874 Blue Creek OH; D9.20.1946 Cincinnati OH; BL/TL/5´10˝/175; d4.22; Col Ohio U.																									
1898	Phi N	24	14	.632	39	37	33-**6**	0	306	285	156	2	19	97	121	3.18	108	.245	.314	122-0-1	.262	4*	100	10	—	1.3
1899	Phi N	23	15	.605	39	38	31-2	0	305	323	173	6	23	86	89	3.45	107	.271	.332	122-0-3	.270	4*	115	7	—	0.8
1900	Phi N	9	10	.474	22	20	16-1	0	160.2	194	120	5	16	71	47	4.65	78	.298	.380	68-0-1	.250	2	111	-21	—	-2.0
1901	Phi A	5	12	.294	18	16	15	1	140	176	112	3	3	60	45	4.63	82	.303	.372	58-0-1	.224	0	115	-16	—	-1.7
	Chi A	4	2	.667	7	6	4-1	0	51.2	42	29	2	4	14	19	2.79	125	.220	.287	17	.118	-1	110	3	—	0.1
	Year	9	14	.391	25	22	19-1	1	191.2	218	141	5	7	74	64	4.13	89	.283	.351	75-0-1	.200	-1	114	-13	—	-1.6
1902	Chi A	12	12	.500	32	30	22-2	0	246	263	129	3	9	66	96	3.51	96	.274	.327	85-0-4	.200	2	115	-5	—	-0.4
1903	Bos N	9	14	.391	25	23	18	0	181	198	107	5	4	61	100	3.18	101	.280	.340	71-0-2	.225	2*	107	-3	—	-0.2
Total	6	86	79	.521	182	170	139-12	1	1390.1	1481	826	26	78	455	517	3.60	98	.272	.337	543-0-12	.239	13	110	-25	—	-2.1
Pichardo, Hipolito	Hipolito Antonio (Balbina); B8.22.1969 Jicome Esperanza, D.R.; BR/TR/6´1˝/(160–195); d4.21; [DL 1999 KC A 182]																									
1992	KC A	9	6	.600	31	24	1-1	0-0	143.2	148	71	9	3	49-1	59	3.95	104	.267	.327	0	ø	0	116	1	0	0.1
1993	KC A	7	8	.467	30	25	2	0-0	165	183	85	10	6	53-2	70	4.04	114	.282	.338	0	ø	0	85	7	18	0.7
1994	KC A	5	3	.625	45	0	0	3-2	67.2	82	42	4	7	24-5	36	4.92	102	.308	.378	0	ø	0	—	0	0	0.1
1995	KC A	8	4	.667	44	0	0	1-1	64	66	34	4	4	30-7	43	4.36	110	.265	.352	2	.000	-0	—	3	17	0.5

YEAR	TM LG	W	L	PCT	G	GS	CG-SHO	SV-BS	IP	H	R	HR	HB	BB-IB	SO	ERA	AERA	OAV	OOB	AB-HR-SH	AVG	PB	SUP	APR	DL	PW
1996	KC A	3	5	.375	57	0	0	3-2	68	74	41	5	2	26-5	43	5.43	93	.284	.351	0	ø	0	—	-2	0	-0.1
1997	KC A	3	5	.375	47	0	0	11-2	49	51	24	7	1	24-8	34	4.22	112	.271	.357	0	ø	0	—	3	52	0.7
1998	KC A	7	8	.467	27	18	0	1-0	112.1	126	73	11	4	43-2	55	5.13	95	.280	.346	2	.000	-0	91	-5	55	-0.5
2000	Bos A	6	3	.667	38	1	0	1-1	65	63	29	1	3	26-2	37	3.46	145	.260	.337	1	.000	-0	75	10	0	1.2
2001	Bos A	2	1	.667	30	0	0	0-3	34.2	42	23	3	5	10-3	17	4.93	90	.300	.363	0	ø	0	—	-3	58	-0.2
2002	Hou N	0	1	.000	1	0	0	0-0	0.1	3	3	0	0	2-1	0	81.00	5	.750	.833	0	ø	0	—	-3	28	-0.4
Total	10	50	44	.532	350	68	3-1	20-11	769.2	838	425	54	35	287-36	394	4.44	105	.279	.346	5	.000	-1	94	11	410	2.1
Piche, Ron	Ronald Jacques; B5.22.1935 Verdun QC, Can.; BR/TR/5´11˝/(160–165); d5.30; C1																									
1960	Mil N	3	5	.375	37	0	0	9	48	48	26	3	3	23-4	38	3.56	96	.258	.346	7	.000	-0	—	-3	0	-0.6
1961	Mil N	2	2	.500	12	1	1	1	23.1	20	12	1	0	16-2	16	3.47	108	.238	.353	5-0-1	.000	-1	71	0	0	-0.1
1962	Mil N	3	2	.600	14	8	2	0	52	54	32	6	3	29-3	28	4.85	78	.273	.369	18	.056	-1*	118	-6	0	-0.6
1963	Mil N	1	1	.500	37	1	0	0	53	53	32	4	0	25-6	40	3.40	95	.256	.333	7	.000	-1	80	-5	0	-0.3
1965	Cal A	0	3	.000	14	1	0	0	19.2	20	15	5	0	12-2	14	6.86	50	.267	.364	1	.000	-0	77	-7	0	-1.0
1966	StL N	1	3	.250	20	0	0	2	25.1	21	13	4	1	18-4	21	4.26	84	.214	.339	4-0-1	.000	-0	—	-2	0	-0.3
Total	6	10	16	.385	134	11	3	12	221.1	216	130	23	7	123-21	157	4.19	84	.255	.350	42-0-2	.024	-3	113	-23	0	-2.9
Pickett, Ricky	Cecil Lee; B1.19.1970 Fort Worth TX; BL/TL/6´1˝/200; [CinN92 28/773]; d4.28; Col NE Oklahoma A&M JC																									
1998	Ari N	0	0	ø	2	0	0	0-0	0.2	3	6	0	0	4-0	2	81.00	5	.600	.778	0	ø	0	—	-5	0	-0.2
Pickett, Charlie	Charles Albert; B3.1.1883 Delaware OH; D5.20.1969 Springfield OH; BR/TR/6´1˝/175; d6.21																									
1910	StL N	0	0	ø	2	0	0	0	6	7	2	0	0	2	2	1.50	199	.280	.333	0	ø	0	—	1	—	0.1
Pickford, Kevin	Kevin Patrick; B3.12.1975 Fresno CA; BL/TL/6´4˝/200; [PitN93 2/54]; d5.16																									
2002	SD N	0	2	.000	16	4	0	0-0	30	37	23	3	3	20-1	18	6.00	65	.314	.423	5	.000	-1	89	-8	0	-0.5
Pickrel, Clarence	Clarence Douglas; B3.28.1911 Gretna VA; D11.4.1983 Rocky Mount VA; BR/TR/6´1˝/180; d4.22																									
1933	Phi N	1	0	1.000	9	0	0	0	13.2	20	7	0	1	3	6	3.95	97	.357	.400	1	.000	-0	—	0	—	-0.1
1934	Bos N	0	0	ø	10	1	0	0	16	24	9	0	0	7	9	5.06	76	.333	.392	2	.000	-0	203	-2	—	-0.1
Total	2	1	0	1.000	19	1	0	0	29.2	44	16	0	1	10	15	4.55	85	.344	.396	3	.000	-0	203	-2	—	-0.2
Pico, Jeff	Jeffrey Mark; B2.12.1966 Antioch CA; BR/TR/6´1˝/170; [ChiN84 13/317]; d5.31																									
1988	Chi N	6	7	.462	29	13	3-2	1-1	112.2	108	57	6	0	37-6	57	4.15	88	.252	.309	34-0-2	.147	-0	103	-6	0	-0.7
1989	Chi N	3	1	.750	53	5	0	2-1	90.2	99	43	8	0	31-10	38	3.77	100	.278	.334	10-0-3	.100	-1	117	0	0	0.0
1990	Chi N	4	4	.500	31	8	0	2-1	92	120	53	7	1	37-10	37	4.79	85	.321	.382	22-0-1	.273	2	144	-6	0	-0.2
Total	3	13	12	.520	113	26	3-2	5-3	295.1	327	153	21	1	105-26	132	4.24	90	.282	.340	66-0-6	.182	1	119	-12	0	-0.9
Picone, Mario	Mario Peter "Babe"; B7.5.1926 Brooklyn NY; BR/TR/5´11˝/(180–190); d9.27																									
1947	NY N	0	0	ø	2	1	0	0	7	10	6	1	0	2	1	7.71	53	.345	.387	2	.500	1	152	-2	0	0.0
1952	NY N	0	1	.000	2	1	0	0	9	11	8	2	0	5	3	7.00	53	.306	.390	2-0-1	.000	-0	72	-3	0	-0.3
1954	NY N	0	0	ø	5	0	0	0	13.2	13	8	1	0	11	6	5.27	77	.283	.421	1	.000	0	—	-1	0	-0.1
	Cin N	0	1	.000	4	1	0	0	10.1	9	7	3	0	7	1	6.10	69	.243	.364	1	.000	0	43	-2	0	-0.1
	Year	0	1	.000	9	1	0	0	24	22	15	4	0	18	7	5.63	73	.265	.396	2	.000	0	43	-3	0	-0.2
Total	3	0	2	.000	13	3	0	0	40	43	29	7	0	25	11	6.30	64	.291	.393	6-0-1	.167	1	89	-8	0	-0.5
Piechota, Al	Aloysius Edward "Pie"; B1.19.1914 Chicago IL; D6.13.1996 Chicago IL; BR/TR/6´0˝/195; d5.7																									
1940	Bos N	2	5	.286	21	8	2	0	61	68	45	6	0	41	18	5.75	65	.278	.381	20-0-1	.200	1	93	-15	—	-1.4
1941	Bos N	0	0	ø	1	0	0	0	1	0	0	0	0	1	0	0.00	ø	.000	.250	0	ø	0	—	0	0	0.0
Total	2	2	5	.286	22	8	2	0	62	68	45	6	0	42	18	5.66	66	.274	.379	20-0-1	.200	1	93	-15	0	-1.4
Pieh, Cy	Edwin John; B9.29.1886 Waunakee WI; D9.12.1945 Jacksonville FL; BR/TR/6´2˝/190; d9.6																									
1913	NY A	1	0	1.000	4	0	0	0	10.1	10	8	0	0	7	6	4.35	69	.256	.370	4	.250	0	—	-2	—	-0.1
1914	NY A	3	4	.429	18	4	1	0	62.1	68	41	6	0	29	24	5.05	55	.289	.367	17-0-1	.118	-0*	86	-15	—	-1.6
1915	NY A	4	5	.444	21	8	3-2	0	94	78	40	2	5	39	46	2.87	102	.234	.324	30	.067	-3	75	0	—	-0.4
Total	3	8	9	.471	43	12	4-2	0	166.2	156	89	8	5	75	76	3.78	76	.257	.344	51-0-1	.098	-3	78	-17	—	-2.1
Pierce, Ed	Edward John; B10.6.1968 Arcadia CA; BL/TL/6´1˝/185; [KCA89 7/179]; d9.6; Col California–Santa Barbara																									
1992	KC A	0	0	ø	2	1	0	0-0	5.1	9	2	1	0	4-0	3	3.38	121	.429	.500	0	ø	0	67	0	0	0.0
Pierce, George	George Thomas "Filbert"; B1.10.1888 Shabbona Grove IL; D10.11.1935 Joliet IL; BL/TL/5´10.5˝/175; d4.16																									
1912	Chi N	0	0	ø	3	2	0	0	14.2	15	13	0	0	12	9	5.52	60	.185	.290	6	.167	0	77	-4	—	-0.2
1913	Chi N	13	5	.722	25	21	14-3	0	164	137	60	4	3	59	73	2.30	138	.234	.308	55-0-3	.073	-3	129	14	—	1.1
1914	Chi N	9	12	.429	30	17	4	1	141	122	82	3	2	65	78	3.51	79	.239	.327	45-0-2	.089	-3	109	-11	—	-1.8
1915	Chi N	13	9	.591	36	20	8-2	0	176	158	83	1	4	77	96	3.32	84	.244	.328	56-0-3	.196	1	92	-11	—	-1.2
1916	Chi N	0	0	ø	4	1	0	0	4.1	6	5	0	0	1	0	2.08	140	.300	.333	0	ø	0	103	-1	—	-0.1
1917	StL N	1	1	.500	5	0	0	0	10.1	7	7	0	1	3	4	3.48	77	.184	.262	4	.000	-1	—	-2	—	-0.4
Total	6	36	27	.571	103	61	26-5	1	510.1	445	250	8	10	217	260	3.10	94	.236	.318	166-0-8	.120	-6	110	-15	—	-2.6
Pierce, Jeff	Jeffrey Charles; B6.7.1969 Poughkeepsie NY; BR/TR/6´1˝/185; d4.26; Col North Carolina St.																									
1995	Bos A	0	3	.000	12	0	0	0-1	15	16	12	0	0	14-4	12	6.60	74	.286	.423	0	ø	0	—	-3	0	-0.5
Pierce, Ray	Raymond Lester "Lefty"; B6.6.1897 Emporia KS; D5.4.1963 Denver CO; BL/TL/5´7˝/156; d5.12; Col Kansas																									
1924	Chi N	0	0	ø	6	0	0	0	7.1	7	6	2	0	4	2	7.36	53	.269	.367	0	ø	0	—	-2	—	-0.1
1925	Phi N	5	4	.556	23	8	4	0	90	134	67	7	1	24	18	5.50	87	.356	.397	28-0-4	.179	-0	115	-6	—	-0.5
1926	Phi N	2	7	.222	37	7	1	0	84.2	128	71	3	1	35	18	5.63	74	.348	.406	24-0-2	.125	-2*	80	-16	—	-1.7
Total	3	7	11	.389	66	15	5	0	182	269	144	12	2	63	38	5.64	79	.349	.400	52-0-6	.154	-2	101	-24	—	-2.3
Pierce, Tony	Tony Michael; B1.29.1946 Brunswick GA; BR/TL/6´1˝/190; d4.14																									
1967	KC A	3	4	.429	49	6	0	7	97.2	79	42	6	5	30-6	61	3.04	105	.221	.290	20-0-1	.000	-2	77	-1	0	-0.3
1968	Oak A	1	2	.333	17	3	0	1	32.2	39	16	3	1	10-2	16	3.86	73	.295	.347	6-0-1	.000	-1	113	-4	0	-0.4
Total	2	4	6	.400	66	9	0	8	130.1	118	58	9	6	40-8	77	3.25	95	.241	.305	26-0-2	.000	-3	88	-5	0	-0.7
Pierce, Billy	Walter William; B4.2.1927 Detroit MI; BL/TL/5´10˝/(155–175); d6.1																									
1945	Det A	0	0	ø	5	0	0	0	10	6	2	1	1	10	10	1.80	195	.182	.386	2	.000	-0	—	2	0	0.1
1948	Det A	3	0	1.000	22	5	0	0	55.1	47	40	5	1	51	36	6.34	69	.234	.391	17	.294	2	145	-10	0	-0.3
1949	Chi A	7	15	.318	32	26	8	0	171.2	145	89	11	0	112	95	3.88	108	.228	.344	51-0-6	.176	-1*	88	3	0	0.4
1950	Chi A	12	16	.429	33	29	15-1	1	219.1	189	112	11	2	137	118	3.98	113	.228	.339	77-0-4	.260	4*	82	11	0	1.5
1951	Chi A	15	14	.517	37	28	18-1	2	240.1	237	93	14	1	73	113	3.03	133	.258	.313	79-0-5	.203	-0*	94	28	0	3.1
1952	Chi A	15	12	.556	33	32	14-4	1	255.1	214	76	12	3	79	144	2.57	142	.227	.289	91-0-5	.187	0*	102	33	0	3.5
1953	Chi A★	18	12	.600	40	33	19-7	3	271.1	216	94	20	3	102	**186**	2.72	148	**.218**	.292	87-0-10	.126	-4*	82	**38**	0	3.5
1954	Chi A	9	10	.474	36	26	12-4	3	188.2	179	86	15	3	86	148	3.48	107	.249	.330	57-0-6	.193	0*	96	3	0	0.2
1955	Chi A★	15	10	.600	33	26	16-6	1	205.2	162	50	16	3	64-5	157	**1.97**	**200**	.213	**.277**	70-0-8	.171	-1*	81	**45**	0	**5.3**
1956	Chi A★	20	9	.690	35	33	**21**-1	1	276.1	261	108	24	3	100-7	192	3.32	123	.249	.316	102-0-7	.157	-4*	124	26	0	1.9
1957	Chi A★	**20**	12	.625	37	34	**16**-4	2	257	228	98	18	1	71-9	171	3.26	115	.234	.287	99-0-3	.172	-2*	96	15	0	1.6
1958	Chi A☆	17	11	.607	35	32	**19**-3	2	245	204	83	33	1	66-2	144	2.68	136	.227	.279	83-0-6	.205	2	95	26	0	3.0
1959	†Chi A☆	14	15	.483	34	33	12-2	0	224	217	98	26	3	62-4	114	3.62	104	.253	.305	68-0-6	.191	3	79	5	0	0.9
1960	Chi A	14	7	.667	32	30	8-1	0	196.1	201	81	24	0	46-1	108	3.62	104	.266	.307	67-0-3	.179	1	115	7	0	0.7
1961	Chi A☆	10	9	.526	39	28	5-1	3	180	190	85	17	1	54-3	106	3.80	103	.275	.326	56-0-6	.143	-2	104	2	0	0.0
1962	†SF N	16	6	.727	30	23	7-2	1	162.1	147	67	19	3	35-2	76	3.49	109	.239	.283	56-0-7	.214	2	131	7	0	1.0
1963	SF N	3	11	.214	38	13	3-1	8	99	106	49	12	1	20-1	52	4.27	75	.272	.308	31-0-1	.129	-0	116	-9	0	-1.4
1964	SF N	3	0	1.000	34	1	0	4	49	40	14	6	0	10-1	29	2.20	162	.222	.260	9	.333	1	123	7	0	0.6
Total	18	211	169	.555	585	432	193-38	32	3306.2	2989	1325	284	30	1178-35	1999	3.27	119	.240	.307	1102-0-83	.184	0	98	239	0	25.6
Piercy, Bill	William Benton "Wild Bill"; B5.2.1896 ElMonte CA; D8.28.1951 Long Beach CA; BR/TR/6´1˝/185; d10.3																									
1917	NY A	0	1	.000	1	1	1	0	9	9	3	0	0	2	4	3.00	90	.257	.297	2	.000	0	27	0	—	0.0
1921	†NY A	5	4	.556	14	10	5-1	0	81.2	82	40	4	7	28	35	2.98	142	.263	.337	28	.214	0	97	9	—	0.9
1922	Bos A	3	9	.250	29	12	7-1	0	121.1	140	77	2	6	62	24	4.67	88	.304	.394	34-0-4	.147	-1	59	-9	—	-0.8

YEAR	TM LG	W	L	PCT	G	GS	CG-SHO	SV-BS	IP	H	R	HR	HB	BB-IB	SO	ERA	AERA	OAV	OOB	AB-HR-SH	AVG	PB	SUP	APR	DL	PW
1923	Bos A	8	17	.320	30	24	11	0	187.1	193	105	5	14	73	51	3.41	121	.277	.357	53-0-8	.132	-3	74	8	—	0.8
1924	Bos A	5	7	.417	23	18	3	0	121	156	87	4	10	66	20	5.95	73	.335	.429	39-0-5	.154	-2	108	-17	—	-1.5
1926	Chi N	6	5	.545	19	5	1	0	90.1	96	52	1	6	37	31	4.48	86	.280	.360	35	.257	1	126	-5	—	-0.5
Total	6	27	43	.386	116	70	28-2	0	610.2	676	364	16	43	268	165	4.26	97	.292	.376	191-0-17	.173	-5	88	-14	—	-1.1

Pieretti, Marino Marino Paul "Chick"; B9.23.1920 Lucca, Italy; D1.30.1981 San Francisco CA; BR/TR/5´7˝/158; d4.19

YEAR	TM LG	W	L	PCT	G	GS	CG-SHO	SV-BS	IP	H	R	HR	HB	BB-IB	SO	ERA	AERA	OAV	OOB	AB-HR-SH	AVG	PB	SUP	APR	DL	PW
1945	Was A	14	13	.519	44	27	14-3	2	233.1	235	114	3	1	91	66	3.32	94	.257	.325	81-0-4	.222	2	102	-10	0	-0.9
1946	Was A	2	2	.500	30	2	1	0	62	70	48	9	2	40	20	5.95	56	.292	.397	14-0-1	.214	0	102	-18	0	-1.0
1947	Was A	2	4	.333	23	10	2-1	0	83.1	97	50	3	2	47	32	4.21	88	.287	.377	26-0-2	.231	-0	126	-7	0	-0.5
1948	Was A	0	2	.000	8	1	0	0	11.2	18	14	1	0	7	6	10.80	40	.375	.455	2	.000	-0*	83	-7	0	-1.1
	Chi A	8	10	.444	21	18	4	1	120	117	70	6	0	52	28	4.95	86	.262	.339	39-0-1	.179	-1*	80	-8	0	-1.0
	Year	8	12	.400	29	19	4	1	131.2	135	84	7	0	59	34	5.47	78	.273	.351	41-0-1	.171	-1	80	-15	0	-2.1
1949	Chi A	4	6	.400	39	9	0	4	116	131	77	10	0	54	25	5.51	76	.289	.364	38-0-1	.237	1*	93	-16	0	-1.2
1950	Cle A	0	1	.000	29	1	0	1	47.1	45	24	2	0	30	11	4.18	104	.253	.361	7	.286	0*	146	1	0	0.1
Total	6	30	38	.441	194	68	21-4	8	673.2	713	397	34	5	321	188	4.53	81	.272	.353	207-0-9	.217	2	98	-65	0	-5.6

Pierotti, Al Albert Felix; B10.24.1895 Boston MA; D2.12.1964 Everett MA; BR/TR/5´10.5˝/195; d8.9; Col Washington and Lee

YEAR	TM LG	W	L	PCT	G	GS	CG-SHO	SV-BS	IP	H	R	HR	HB	BB-IB	SO	ERA	AERA	OAV	OOB	AB-HR-SH	AVG	PB	SUP	APR	DL	PW
1920	Bos N	1	1	.500	6	2	2	0	25	23	9	2	0	9	12	2.88	106	.250	.317	8-0-1	.250	0	90	1	—	0.1
1921	Bos N	0	1	.000	2	0	0	0	1.2	3	4	0	0	3	1	21.60	17	.375	.545	1	.000	-0	—	-3	—	-0.6
Total	2	1	2	.333	8	2	2	0	26.2	26	13	2	0	12	13	4.05	76	.260	.339	9-0-1	.222	-0	90	-2	—	-0.5

Pierro, Bill William Leonard "Wild Bill"; B4.15.1926 Brooklyn NY; D4.1.2006 Brooklyn NY; BR/TR/6´1˝/155; d7.17; [DL 1951 Pit N 94]

YEAR	TM LG	W	L	PCT	G	GS	CG-SHO	SV-BS	IP	H	R	HR	HB	BB-IB	SO	ERA	AERA	OAV	OOB	AB-HR-SH	AVG	PB	SUP	APR	DL	PW
1950	Pit N	0	2	.000	12	3	0	0	29	33	34	2	2	28	13	10.55	42	.289	.438	9	.222	-0*	74	-17	0	-1.0

Piersoll, Chris Christopher Earl; B9.25.1977 Van Nuys CA; BR/TR/6´4˝/195; [ChiN97 19/574]; d8.31; Col Fullerton (CA) JC

YEAR	TM LG	W	L	PCT	G	GS	CG-SHO	SV-BS	IP	H	R	HR	HB	BB-IB	SO	ERA	AERA	OAV	OOB	AB-HR-SH	AVG	PB	SUP	APR	DL	PW
2001	Cin N	0	0	ø	11	0	0	0-0	11.1	12	4	0	1	6-0	7	2.38	193	.267	.365	0	ø	0	—	2	0	0.1

Pierson, William William Morris; B6.14.1899 Atlantic City NJ; D2.20.1959 Atlantic City NJ; BL/TL/6´2˝/180; d7.4

YEAR	TM LG	W	L	PCT	G	GS	CG-SHO	SV-BS	IP	H	R	HR	HB	BB-IB	SO	ERA	AERA	OAV	OOB	AB-HR-SH	AVG	PB	SUP	APR	DL	PW
1918	Phi A	0	1	.000	8	1	0	0	21.2	20	10	0	2	20	6	3.32	88	.286	.457	4	.250	-0	26	-1	—	-0.1
1919	Phi A	0	0	ø	2	1	0	0	7.2	9	3	0	0	8	4	3.52	97	.333	.486	3	.333	0	160	0	—	0.0
1924	Phi A	0	0	ø	1	0	0	0	2.2	3	1	0	0	3	0	3.38	127	.300	.462	0	ø	0	—	0	—	0.0
Total	3	0	1	.000	11	2	0	0	32	32	14	0	2	31	10	3.38	94	.299	.464	7	.286	0	97	-1	—	-0.1

Piktuzis, George George Richard; B1.3.1932 Chicago IL; D11.28.1993 Long Beach CA; BR/TL/6´2˝/200; d4.25

YEAR	TM LG	W	L	PCT	G	GS	CG-SHO	SV-BS	IP	H	R	HR	HB	BB-IB	SO	ERA	AERA	OAV	OOB	AB-HR-SH	AVG	PB	SUP	APR	DL	PW
1956	Chi N	0	0	ø	2	0	0	0	5	6	4	1	0	2-0	3	7.20	52	.333	.400	0	ø	0	—	-2	0	-0.1

Pillette, Duane Duane Xavier "Dee"; B7.24.1922 Detroit MI; BR/TR/6´3˝/(195–205); d7.19; f–Herman; Col Santa Clara

YEAR	TM LG	W	L	PCT	G	GS	CG-SHO	SV-BS	IP	H	R	HR	HB	BB-IB	SO	ERA	AERA	OAV	OOB	AB-HR-SH	AVG	PB	SUP	APR	DL	PW
1949	NY A	2	4	.333	12	3	2	0	37.1	43	20	6	0	19	9	4.34	93	.299	.380	11-0-2	.000	-1	89	-1	0	-0.2
1950	NY A	0	0	ø	4	0	0	0	7	9	3	0	0	3	4	1.29	334	.321	.387	0	ø	0	—	2	0	0.1
	StL A	3	5	.375	24	7	1	2	73.2	104	62	6	2	44	18	7.09	70	.337	.423	22-0-1	.136	-1*	81	-14	0	-1.4
	Year	3	5	.375	28	7	1	2	80.2	113	65	6	2	47	22	6.58	74	.335	.420	22-0-1	.136	-1	82	-13	0	-1.3
1951	StL A	6	14	.300	35	24	6-1	0	191	205	113	14	5	115	65	4.99	88	.276	.376	59-0-6	.136	-3*	60	-10	0	-1.3
1952	StL A	10	13	.435	30	30	9-1	0	205.1	222	94	14	7	55	62	3.59	109	.274	.325	66-0-6	.182	0*	99	7	0	0.6
1953	StL A	7	13	.350	31	25	5-1	0	166.2	181	90	16	2	62	58	4.48	94	.277	.341	53-1-2	.132	-1	73	-3	0	-0.5
1954	Bal A	10	14	.417	25	25	11-1	0	179	158	79	9	1	67	66	3.12	115	.234	.303	53-0-6	.132	-1	81	5	0	0.8
1955	Bal A	0	3	.000	7	5	0	0	20.2	31	16	0	0	14-1	13	6.53	58	.344	.433	6	.167	0	65	-6	51	-0.7
1956	Phi N	0	0	ø	20	0	0	0	23.1	32	21	2	0	12-4	10	6.56	57	.330	.396	1	.000	-0	—	-8	0	-0.4
Total	8	38	66	.365	188	119	34-4	2	904	985	498	67	17	391-5	305	4.40	93	.277	.351	271-1-23	.140	-7	78	-28	51	-3.0

Pillette, Herman Herman Polycarp "Old Folks"; B12.26.1896 St.Paul OR; D4.30.1960 Sacramento CA; BR/TR/6´2˝/190; d7.30; s–Duane

YEAR	TM LG	W	L	PCT	G	GS	CG-SHO	SV-BS	IP	H	R	HR	HB	BB-IB	SO	ERA	AERA	OAV	OOB	AB-HR-SH	AVG	PB	SUP	APR	DL	PW
1917	Cin N	0	0	ø	1	0	0	0	1	4	2	0	0	0	0	18.00	15	.571	.571	0	ø	0	—	-1	—	-0.1
1922	Det A	19	12	.613	40	37	18-4	1	274.2	270	110	6	15	95	71	2.85	136	.258	.328	99-0-3	.172	-3	120	30	—	2.9
1923	Det A	14	19	.424	47	36	14	1	250.1	280	138	7	6	83	64	3.85	100	.288	.347	85-0-2	.247	4	106	-4	—	0.0
1924	Det A	1	1	.500	19	3	1	1	37.2	46	30	1	3	14	13	4.78	86	.297	.366	11	.364	1	150	-5	—	-0.2
Total	4	34	32	.515	107	76	33-4	3	563.2	600	280	14	24	192	148	3.45	113	.275	.340	195-0-5	.215	2	115	20	—	2.6

Pillion, Squiz Cecil Randolph; B4.13.1894 Hartford CT; D9.30.1962 Pittsburgh PA; BL/TL/6´0˝/178; d8.20

YEAR	TM LG	W	L	PCT	G	GS	CG-SHO	SV-BS	IP	H	R	HR	HB	BB-IB	SO	ERA	AERA	OAV	OOB	AB-HR-SH	AVG	PB	SUP	APR	DL	PW
1915	Phi A	0	0	ø	2	0	0	0	5.1	10	5	0	1	2	0	6.75	43	.400	.464	1	.000	-0	—	-2	—	-0.1

Pina, Horacio Horacio (Garcia); B3.12.1945 Matamoros, Coahuila, Mexico; BR/TR/6´2˝/177; d8.14

YEAR	TM LG	W	L	PCT	G	GS	CG-SHO	SV-BS	IP	H	R	HR	HB	BB-IB	SO	ERA	AERA	OAV	OOB	AB-HR-SH	AVG	PB	SUP	APR	DL	PW
1968	Cle A	1	1	.500	12	3	0	2	31.1	24	7	0	1	15-1	24	1.72	172	.218	.315	6-0-2	.000	-1	108	4	0	0.3
1969	Cle A	4	2	.667	31	4	0	1-2	46.2	44	29	6	5	27-2	32	5.21	73	.256	.371	6	.500	1	99	-6	0	-0.7
1970	Was A	5	3	.625	61	0	0	6-4	71	66	25	4	3	35-9	41	2.79	129	.250	.341	3	.000	-0	—	7	0	0.8
1971	Was A	1	1	.500	56	0	0	2-2	57.2	47	26	2	4	31-7	38	3.59	94	.227	.335	1	.000	-0	—	-1	0	0.0
1972	Tex A	2	7	.222	60	0	0	15-3	76	61	33	3	8	43-7	60	3.20	95	.228	.351	5-0-2	.200	0	—	-2	0	-0.1
1973	†Oak A	6	3	.667	47	0	0	8-2	88	58	31	8	8	34-5	41	2.76	129	.193	.290	0	ø	0	—	9	0	1.1
1974	Chi N	3	4	.429	34	0	0	4-3	47.1	49	22	4	2	28-4	32	3.99	96	.268	.367	5	.200	-0	—	0	0	0.1
	Cal A	1	2	.333	11	0	0	0-1	11.2	9	3	1	0	3-2	6	2.31	150	.209	.261	0	ø	0	—	2	0	0.4
1978	Phi N	0	0	ø	2	0	0	0-0	2.1	0	0	0	0	0-0	4	0.00	ø	.000	.000	1	.000	-0	—	1	0	0.0
Total	8	23	23	.500	314	7	0	38-17	432	358	176	28	31	216-37	278	3.25	107	.231	.334	27-0-4	.185	0	102	14	0	1.9

Pineda, Luis Luis A.; B10.17.1974 San Cristobal, D.R.; BR/TR/6´1˝/160; d8.4

YEAR	TM LG	W	L	PCT	G	GS	CG-SHO	SV-BS	IP	H	R	HR	HB	BB-IB	SO	ERA	AERA	OAV	OOB	AB-HR-SH	AVG	PB	SUP	APR	DL	PW
2001	Det A	0	1	.000	16	0	0	0-0	18.1	16	10	2	0	14-2	13	4.91	90	.239	.366	0	ø	0	—	-1	0	0.0
2002	Cin N	1	3	.250	26	2	0	0-0	32.1	25	16	4	2	24-1	31	4.18	102	.221	.362	3	.000	-0	184	1	91	0.0
Total	2	1	4	.200	42	2	0	0-0	50.2	41	26	6	2	38-3	44	4.44	97	.228	.363	3	.000	-0	184	0	91	0.0

Pineiro, Joel Joel Alberto; B9.25.1978 Rio Piedras, PR; BR/TR/6´1˝/(180–200); [SeaA97 12/373]; d8.8; Col Edison (FL) CC

YEAR	TM LG	W	L	PCT	G	GS	CG-SHO	SV-BS	IP	H	R	HR	HB	BB-IB	SO	ERA	AERA	OAV	OOB	AB-HR-SH	AVG	PB	SUP	APR	DL	PW
2000	Sea A	1	0	1.000	8	1	0	0-0	19.1	25	13	3	0	13-0	10	5.59	86	.316	.404	0	ø	0	234	-2	0	-0.1
2001	†Sea A	6	2	.750	17	11	0	0-0	75.1	50	24	2	3	21-0	56	2.03	210	.191	.257	0	ø	0	79	17	0	1.6
2002	Sea A	14	7	.667	37	28	2-1	0-0	194.1	189	75	24	7	54-1	136	3.24	133	.256	.310	7	.143	-0	111	24	0	2.4
2003	Sea A	16	11	.593	32	32	3-**2**	0-0	211.2	192	94	19	6	76-3	151	3.78	114	.241	.309	4-0-1	.000	-0	113	14	0	1.5
2004	Sea A	6	11	.353	21	21	1	0-0	140.2	144	77	21	4	43-1	111	4.67	96	.265	.321	5	.200	0	89	-3	70	-0.3
2005	Sea A	7	11	.389	30	30	2	0-0	189	224	118	23	6	56-4	107	5.62	74	.299	.350	4-0-1	.000	-0	108	-29	12	-2.3
2006	Sea A	8	13	.381	40	25	1	1-1	165.2	209	123	23	10	64-13	87	6.36	69	.311	.376	4-0-2	.000	-0	106	-36	0	-3.8
Total	7	58	55	.513	185	148	9-3	1-1	996	1033	524	115	36	327-22	658	4.48	97	.269	.329	24-0-4	.083	-1	105	-15	82	-1.0

Pinkham, Ed Edward; B1846 Brooklyn NY; D12.19.1906 Brooklyn NY; BL/TL/5´7˝/142; d5.8; ▲

YEAR	TM LG	W	L	PCT	G	GS	CG-SHO	SV-BS	IP	H	R	HR	HB	BB-IB	SO	ERA	AERA	OAV	OOB	AB-HR-SH	AVG	PB	SUP	APR	DL	PW
1871	Chi NA	1	0	1.000	3	0	0	1	10.1	10	8	0	—	3	0	3.48	132	.208	.255	95-1	.263	1*	—	**2**	—	0.1

Pinnance, Ed Elijah Edward "Peanuts"; B10.22.1879 Walpole Island ON, Can.; D12.12.1944 Walpole Island ON, Can.; BL/TR/6´1˝/180; d9.14; Col Michigan St.

YEAR	TM LG	W	L	PCT	G	GS	CG-SHO	SV-BS	IP	H	R	HR	HB	BB-IB	SO	ERA	AERA	OAV	OOB	AB-HR-SH	AVG	PB	SUP	APR	DL	PW
1903	Phi A	0	0	ø	2	1	0	1	7	5	2	0	0	2	2	2.57	119	.200	.259	3	.000	-0	117	1	—	0.0

Pinto, Renyel Renyel Eligio; B7.8.1982 Cupira, Miranda, Venezuela; BL/TL/6´4˝/195; d5.18

YEAR	TM LG	W	L	PCT	G	GS	CG-SHO	SV-BS	IP	H	R	HR	HB	BB-IB	SO	ERA	AERA	OAV	OOB	AB-HR-SH	AVG	PB	SUP	APR	DL	PW
2006	Fla N	0	0	ø	27	0	0	1-0	29.2	20	12	3	1	27-0	36	3.03	141	.189	.356	1	.000	-0	—	4	0	0.2

Pinto, Lerton William Lerton; B4.8.1899 Chillicothe OH; D5.13.1983 Oxnard CA; BL/TL/6´0˝/190; d5.23

YEAR	TM LG	W	L	PCT	G	GS	CG-SHO	SV-BS	IP	H	R	HR	HB	BB-IB	SO	ERA	AERA	OAV	OOB	AB-HR-SH	AVG	PB	SUP	APR	DL	PW
1922	Phi N	0	1	.000	9	0	0	0	24.2	31	20	1	0	14	4	5.11	91	.320	.405	9	.111	-1	—	-2	—	-0.2
1924	Phi N	0	0	ø	3	0	0	0	4	7	4	1	0	0	1	9.00	50	.467	.467	1	.000	-0	—	-2	—	-0.1
Total	2	0	1	.000	12	0	0	0	28.2	38	24	2	0	14	5	5.65	82	.339	.413	10	.100	-1	—	-4	—	-0.3

Pipgras, Ed Edward John; B6.15.1904 Schleswig IA; D4.13.1964 Currie MN; BR/TR/6´2.5˝/175; d8.25; b–George

YEAR	TM LG	W	L	PCT	G	GS	CG-SHO	SV-BS	IP	H	R	HR	HB	BB-IB	SO	ERA	AERA	OAV	OOB	AB-HR-SH	AVG	PB	SUP	APR	DL	PW
1932	Bro N	0	1	.000	5	1	0	0	10	16	11	2	0	6	5	5.40	71	.348	.423	2	.000	-0	154	-4	—	-0.3

Pipgras, George George William; B12.20.1899 Ida Grove IA; D10.19.1986 Gainesville FL; BR/TR/6´1.5˝/185; d6.9; U9; b–Ed

YEAR	TM LG	W	L	PCT	G	GS	CG-SHO	SV-BS	IP	H	R	HR	HB	BB-IB	SO	ERA	AERA	OAV	OOB	AB-HR-SH	AVG	PB	SUP	APR	DL	PW
1923	NY A	1	3	.250	8	2	2	0	33.1	34	22	2	1	25	12	5.94	66	.276	.403	9	.000	-1	84	-6	—	-0.7
1924	NY A	0	1	.000	9	1	0	1	15.1	20	18	0	4	18	4	9.98	42	.351	.532	3	.333	0	101	-9	—	-0.6
1927	†NY A	10	3	.769	29	21	9-1	0	166.1	148	81	2	1	77	81	4.11	94	.247	.334	67-1-2	.239	2	156	0	—	0.1

YEAR	TM LG	W	L	PCT	G	GS	CG-SHO	SV-BS	IP	H	R	HR	HB	BB-IB	SO	ERA	AERA	OAV	OOB	AB-HR-SH	AVG	PB	SUP	APR	DL	PW
1928	†NY A	**24**	13	.649	46	**38**	22-4	3	**300.2**	314	132	4	3	103	139	3.38	111	.272	.333	115-0-6	.157	-4	127	15	—	1.1
1929	NY A	18	12	.600	39	33	13-3	0	225.1	229	132	16	5	95	125	4.23	91	.264	.340	84-0-4	.143	-4	129	-12	—	-1.8
1930	NY A	15	15	.500	44	30	15-**3**	4	221	230	133	9	8	70	111	4.11	105	.263	.324	80-1-6	.150	-2	143	0	—	-0.3
1931	NY A	7	6	.538	36	14	6-1	3	137.2	134	73	8	2	58	59	3.79	105	.251	.327	41-0-1	.024	-6	99	0	—	-0.6
1932	†NY A	16	9	.640	32	27	14-2	0	219	235	120	15	6	87	111	4.19	97	.269	.340	82-0-5	.220	1	130	-4	—	-0.4
1933	NY A	2	2	.500	4	4	3	0	33	32	13	1	0	12	14	3.27	119	.252	.317	11	.091	-1	99	3	—	0.3
	Bos A	9	8	.529	22	17	9-2	1	128.1	140	65	5	2	45	56	4.07	108	.276	.337	46-0-2	.196	-1	102	6	—	0.5
	Year	11	10	.524	26	21	12-2	1	161.1	172	78	6	2	57	70	3.90	110	.271	.333	57-0-2	.175	-1	101	9	—	0.8
1934	Bos A	0	0	ø	2	1	0	0	3.1	4	3	1	0	3	0	8.10	59	.308	.438	1	.000	-0	109	-1	—	0.0
1935	Bos A	0	1	.000	5	1	0	0	5	9	9	3	1	5	2	14.40	33	.391	.517	0-0-1	ø	0	37	-5	—	-0.8
Total	11	102	73	.583	276	189	93-16	12	1488.1	1529	801	66	33	598	714	4.09	98	.266	.339	539-2-27	.163	-15	127	-13	—	-3.2
Pippen, Cotton Henry Harold; B4.2.1911 Cisco TX; D2.15.1981 Williams CA; BR/TR/6´2˝/180; d8.28; Col Texas A&M																										
1936	StL N	0	2	.000	6	3	0	0	21	37	18	5	2	8	8	7.71	51	.402	.461	6	.167	0	72	-8	—	-0.6
1939	Phi A	4	11	.267	25	17	5	1	118.2	169	97	13	1	40	33	5.99	79	.329	.378	35-0-3	.086	-2	77	-18	—	-2.0
	Det A	0	1	.000	3	2	0	0	14	18	13	1	0	6	5	7.07	69	.310	.375	5	.400	0	108	-3	—	-0.2
	Year	4	12	.250	28	19	5	1	132.2	187	110	14	1	46	38	6.11	77	.327	.378	40-0-3	.125	-2	80	-23	—	-2.2
1940	Det A	1	2	.333	4	3	0	0	21.1	29	16	3	1	10	9	6.75	70	.326	.400	8	.000	-1	49	-3	—	-0.5
Total	3	5	16	.238	38	25	5	1	175	253	144	22	4	64	55	6.38	73	.336	.391	54-0-3	.111	-3	76	-32	—	-3.3
Pirtle, Gerry Gerald Eugene; B12.3.1947 Tulsa OK; BR/TR/6´1˝/185; [NYA67 S7/128]; d7.2; Col Bacone																										
1978	Mon N	0	2	.000	19	0	0	0-1	25.2	33	24	5	2	23-6	14	5.96	60	.314	.446	0	ø	0	—	-9	0	-0.7
Pisciotta, Marc Marc George; B8.7.1970 Edison NJ; BR/TR/6´5˝/225; [PitN91 19/513]; d6.30; Col Georgia Tech																										
1997	Chi N	3	1	.750	24	0	0	0-1	28.1	20	10	1	1	16-0	21	3.18	136	.200	.314	1	.000	-0	—	4	0	0.5
1998	Chi N	1	2	.333	43	0	0	0-0	44	44	21	4	2	32-3	31	4.09	108	.259	.380	3	.333	0	—	2	0	0.1
1999	KC A	0	2	.000	8	0	0	0-0	8.1	9	8	1	0	10-0	3	8.64	59	.281	.452	0	ø	0	—	-3	0	-0.5
Total	3	4	5	.444	75	0	0	0-1	80.2	73	39	6	3	58-3	55	4.24	105	.242	.367	4	.250	0	—	3	0	0.1
Pitlock, Skip Lee Patrick Thomas; B11.6.1947 Hillside IL; BL/TL/6´2˝/(180–185); [SFN69 11/256]; d6.12; Col Southern Illinois																										
1970	SF N	5	5	.500	18	15	1	0-0	87	92	48	13	4	48-2	56	4.66	85	.274	.369	25-1-3	.080	-0	105	-5	0	-0.5
1974	Chi A	3	3	.500	40	5	0	1-1	105.2	103	58	7	7	55-4	68	4.43	85	.257	.353	0	ø	0	113	-7	0	-0.5
1975	Chi A	0	0	ø	1	0	0	0-0	0	1	0	0	0	0-0	0	(0)	ø	1.000	1.000	0	ø	0	—	0	0	0.0
Total	3	8	8	.500	59	20	1	1-1	192.2	196	106	20	11	103-6	124	4.53	85	.266	.361	25-1-3	.080	-0	108	-12	0	-1.0
Pittinger, Togie Charles Reno; B1.12.1872 Greencastle PA; D1.14.1909 Greencastle PA; BL/TR/6´2˝/175; d4.26																										
1900	Bos N	2	9	.182	18	13	8	0	114	135	97	7	8	54	27	5.13	80	.293	.377	46	.130	-4	88	-12	—	-1.4
1901	Bos N	13	16	.448	34	33	27-1	0	281.1	288	135	7	8	76	129	3.01	120	.263	.316	100-0-2	.110	-8	65	15	—	0.7
1902	Bos N	27	16	.628	46	40	36-7	0	389.1	360	139	4	16	128	174	2.52	112	.245	.313	147-0-4	.136	-8	100	18	—	0.9
1903	Bos N	18	22	.450	44	39	35-3	1	351.2	396	205	12	17	143	140	3.48	92	.294	.369	128-1-3	.109	-9	76	-10	—	-1.9
1904	Bos N	15	21	.417	38	37	35-5	0	335.1	298	149	1	14	144	146	2.66	104	.242	.329	121-0-3	.107	-9	74	2	—	-0.5
1905	Phi N	23	14	.622	**46**	37	29-4	2	337.1	311	155	3	16	104	136	3.09	94	.247	.313	122-0-12	.156	-3	126	-5	—	-1.0
1906	Phi N	8	10	.444	20	16	9-2	0	129.2	128	62	2	12	50	43	3.40	77	.252	.334	44-0-1	.091	-1	92	-8	—	-1.3
1907	Phi N	9	5	.643	16	12	8-1	0	102	101	43	3	5	35	37	3.00	81	.261	.330	36	.139	-1	105	-6	—	-0.9
Total	8	115	113	.504	262	227	187-23	3	2040.2	2017	985	39	96	734	832	3.10	98	.260	.332	744-1-25	.124	-43	89	-6	—	-5.4
Pittsley, Jim James Michael; B4.3.1974 DuBois PA; BR/TR/6´7˝/(215–230); [KCA92 1/17]; d5.23; [DL 1996 KC A 96]																										
1995	KC A	0	0	ø	1	1	0	0-0	3.1	7	5	3	0	1-0	0	13.50	36	.438	.471	0	ø	0	116	-3	46	-0.1
1997	KC A	5	8	.385	21	21	0	0-0	112	120	72	15	6	54-1	52	5.46	87	.277	.361	2	.500	1	92	-8	0	-0.8
1998	KC A	1	1	.500	39	2	0	0-0	68.1	88	56	13	2	37-1	44	6.59	74	.322	.401	2-0-1	.000	-0	38	-13	0	-0.6
1999	KC A	1	2	.333	5	5	0	0-0	23.1	33	22	2	1	15-0	7	6.94	73	.337	.426	0	ø	0	95	-6	0	-0.6
	Mil N	0	1	.000	15	0	0	0-1	18.2	20	12	3	1	10-0	13	4.82	95	.274	.365	1	.000	0	—	-1	0	0.0
Total	4	7	12	.368	81	29	0	0-1	225.2	268	167	36	10	117-2	116	6.02	80	.300	.382	5-0-1	.200	1	90	-31	142	-2.1
Pitula, Stan Stanley; B3.23.1931 Hackensack NJ; D8.15.1965 Hackensack NJ; BR/TR/5´10˝/170; d4.24																										
1957	Cle A	2	2	.500	23	5	1	0	59.2	67	37	8	2	32-4	17	4.98	75	.296	.384	15	.200	0*	130	-8	36	-0.5
Pizarro, Juan Juan Ramon (Cordova); B2.7.1937 Santurce, PR; BL/TL/5´11˝/(170–197); d5.4																										
1957	†Mil N	5	6	.455	24	10	3	0	99.1	99	58	16	1	51-2	68	4.62	76	.261	.348	36-1-0	.250	3*	101	-14	0	-1.1
1958	†Mil N	6	4	.600	16	10	7-1	1	96.2	75	36	12	4	47-0	84	2.70	130	.212	.311	32	.250	3	107	8	0	1.1
1959	Mil N	6	2	.750	29	14	6-2	0	133.2	117	61	13	8	70-3	126	3.77	94	.237	.340	41-0-2	.122	-0	133	-2	0	-0.1
1960	Mil N	6	7	.462	21	17	3	0	114.2	105	63	13	4	72-1	88	4.55	75	.244	.354	40-0-1	.275	3*	123	-14	0	-1.2
1961	Chi A	14	7	.667	39	25	12-1	2	194.2	164	73	17	4	89-1	188	3.05	128	.226	.312	69-0-1	.246	5*	110	19	0	2.5
1962	Chi A	12	14	.462	36	32	9-1	1	203.1	182	97	16	1	97-3	173	3.81	103	.236	.320	69-0-3	.159	-0*	94	1	0	0.0
1963	Chi A★	16	8	.667	32	28	10-3	1	214.2	177	69	14	3	63-1	163	2.39	147	.224	.282	73-2-3	.178	3	110	25	0	3.0
1964	Chi A☆	19	9	.679	33	33	11-4	0	239	193	78	23	3	55-5	162	2.56	135	.219	.267	90-3-2	.211	5	105	24	0	3.3
1965	Chi A	6	3	.667	18	18	2-1	0	97	96	42	9	1	37-3	65	3.43	93	.254	.321	34-1-1	.235	3*	119	-3	31	0.1
1966	Chi A	8	6	.571	34	9	1	3	88.2	91	49	9	1	39-7	42	3.76	84	.269	.346	26-0-3	.154	0	120	-9	0	-1.3
1967	Pit N	8	10	.444	50	9	1-1	9	107	99	55	10	2	52-15	96	3.95	85	.245	.332	27	.259	2	67	-8	0	-1.2
1968	Pit N	1	1	.500	12	0	0	0	11	14	7	2	1	10-2	6	3.27	89	.311	.439	2	.000	-0*	—	-1	0	-0.3
	Bos A	6	8	.429	19	12	6	2	107.2	97	46	15	0	44-4	84	3.59	88	.242	.315	31-0-4	.161	1*	97	-4	0	-0.3
1969	Bos A	0	1	.000	6	0	0	2-0	9	14	7	2	0	6-0	4	6.00	64	.359	.444	3	.333	0	—	-2	0	-0.3
	Cle A	3	3	.500	48	4	1	4-3	82.2	67	34	6	2	49-7	44	3.16	120	.229	.335	15-0-1	.200	0	122	5	0	0.5
	Oak A	1	1	.500	3	0	0	1-0	7.2	3	2	1	0	3-0	4	2.35	147	.125	.214	2	.500	0	—	1	0	0.3
	Year	4	5	.444	57	4	1	7-3	99.1	84	43	9	2	58-7	52	3.35	113	.236	.339	20-0-1	.250	1	123	4	0	0.5
1970	Chi N	0	0	ø	12	0	0	1-0	15.2	16	9	2	1	9-0	14	4.60	98	.262	.366	3	.000	-0	—	0	0	0.0
1971	Chi N	7	6	.538	16	14	6-3	0-0	101.1	78	43	10	2	40-3	67	3.46	114	.209	.288	34-1-2	.176	1	80	5	0	0.7
1972	Chi N	4	5	.444	16	7	1	1-0	59.1	66	28	7	1	32-5	24	3.94	97	.293	.384	21	.143	-0	63	0	21	0.0
1973	Chi N	0	1	.000	2	0	0	0-1	4	6	5	1	1	1-0	3	11.25	35	.353	.400	1	.000	-0	—	-3	0	-0.5
	Hou N	2	2	.500	15	1	0	0-0	23.1	28	17	1	1	11-3	10	6.56	56	.301	.381	3-0-1	.000	-0	73	-7	0	-1.0
	Year	2	3	.400	17	1	0	0-1	27.1	34	22	2	2	12-3	13	7.24	51	.309	.384	4-0-1	.000	-0	72	-9	0	-1.5
1974	†Pit N	1	1	.500	7	2	0	0-0	24	20	11	2	0	11-2	7	1.88	186	.220	.298	6	.333	0	163	2	0	0.2
Total	18	131	105	.555	488	245	79-17	28-4	2034.1	1807	890	201	41	888-67	1522	3.43	104	.237	.319	658-8-24	.202	29	105	23	52	4.4
Pladson, Gordie Gordon Cecil; B7.31.1956 New Westminster BC, Can.; BR/TR/6´4˝/210; d9.7																										
1979	Hou N	0	0	ø	4	0	0	0-0	4	9	2	1	0	2-0	2	4.50	78	.450	.500	0	ø	0	—	0	0	0.0
1980	Hou N	0	4	.000	12	6	0	0-0	41.1	38	23	3	0	16-0	13	4.35	75	.244	.312	10	.000	-1	86	-5	0	-0.6
1981	Hou N	0	0	ø	2	0	0	0-0	4	9	4	0	0	3-0	3	9.00	36	.429	.500	0	ø	0	—	-2	0	-0.1
1982	Hou N	0	0	ø	2	0	0	0-0	1.1	10	8	0	0	2-0	0	54.00	6	.769	.750	0	ø	0	—	-8	0	-0.4
Total	4	0	4	.000	20	6	0	0-0	50.2	66	37	4	0	23-0	18	6.04	55	.314	.379	10	.000	-1	86	-15	0	-1.1
Planeta, Emil Emil Joseph; B1.31.1909 Higganum CT; D2.2.1963 Rocky Hill CT; BR/TR/6´0˝/190; d9.20																										
1931	NY N	0	0	ø	2	0	0	0	5.1	7	7	0	0	4	0	10.13	36	.292	.393	1	.000	-0	—	-4	—	-0.2
Plank, Ed Edward Arthur; B4.9.1952 Chicago IL; BR/TR/6´1˝/195; [SFN73 10/222]; d9.6; Col Nevada–Reno																										
1978	SF N	0	0	ø	5	0	0	0-0	6.2	6	3	1	0	2-1	1	4.05	86	.273	.320	0	ø	0	—	0	0	0.0
1979	SF N	0	0	ø	4	0	0	0-0	3.2	9	5	0	0	2-1	1	7.36	47	.450	.500	0	ø	0	—	-2	0	-0.1
Total	2	0	0	ø	9	0	0	0-0	10.1	15	8	1	0	4-2	2	5.23	67	.357	.404	0	ø	0	—	-2	0	-0.1
Plank, Eddie Edward Stewart "Gettysburg Eddie"; B8.31.1875 Gettysburg PA; D2.24.1926 Gettysburg PA; BL/TL/5´11.5˝/175; d5.13; HF1946; Col Gettysburg																										
1901	Phi A	17	13	.567	33	32	28-1	0	260.2	254	133	3	7	68	90	3.31	114	.252	.304	99-0-2	.182	-3	96	14	—	0.9
1902	Phi A	20	15	.571	36	32	31-1	0	300	319	140	5	18	61	107	3.30	111	.273	.319	120-0-4	.292	6	107	18	—	2.3
1903	Phi A	23	16	.590	**43**	**40**	33-3	0	336	317	128	5	23	65	176	2.38	128	.249	.297	134-1-2	.187	-1*	100	20	—	2.0
1904	Phi A	26	17	.605	44	43	37-7	0	357.1	311	111	2	19	86	201	2.17	124	.235	.292	129-0-6	.240	3*	93	23	—	3.2
1905	†Phi A	24	12	.667	41	**41**	**35**-4	0	346.2	287	113	3	24	75	210	2.26	118	.227	.283	126-0-2	.230	3	108	20	—	2.2
1906	Phi A	19	6	**.760**	26	25	21-5	0	211.2	173	70	1	15	51	108	2.25	121	.226	.288	73-0-5	.233	2	126	13	—	1.6

YEAR	TM LG	W	L	PCT	G	GS	CG-SHO	SV-BS	IP	H	R	HR	HB	BB-IB	SO	ERA	AERA	OAV	OOB	AB-HR-SH	AVG	PB	SUP	APR	DL	PW
1907	Phi A	24	16	.600	43	40	33-**8**	0	343.2	282	115	5	17	85	183	2.20	118	.226	.285	123-1-8	.211	2	84	17	—	2.2
1908	Phi A	14	16	.467	34	28	21-4	1	244.2	202	71	1	9	46	135	2.17	118	.224	.269	89-0-1	.180	-1*	80	14	—	1.4
1909	Phi A	19	10	.655	34	33	24-3	0	265.1	215	74	1	8	62	132	1.76	136	.224	.277	96-1-2	.219	4*	111	19	—	2.6
1910	Phi A	16	10	.615	38	32	22-1	2	250.1	218	89	3	8	55	123	2.01	118	.237	.286	86-0-2	.128	-3	138	10	—	0.6
1911	†Phi A	23	8	.742	40	30	24-**6**	**4**	256.2	237	85	2	14	77	149	2.10	150	.255	.322	94-0-6	.191	-1	121	29	—	3.2
1912	Phi A	26	6	.813	37	30	23-5	2	259.2	234	90	1	6	83	110	2.22	139	.245	.309	90-0-11	.267	4	132	25	—	3.2
1913	†Phi A	18	10	.643	41	30	18-7	4	242.2	211	87	3	5	57	151	2.60	106	.243	.293	76-0-6	.105	-0	145	4	—	0.4
1914	†Phi A	15	7	.682	34	22	12-4	3	185.1	178	68	2	6	42	110	2.87	91	.266	.315	60-0-7	.150	0	142	-4	—	-0.6
1915	StL F	21	11	.656	42	31	23-6	3	268.1	212	75	1	3	54	147	2.08	**138**	.218	**.262**	93-0-4	.258	4	101	23	—	**3.0**
1916	StL A	16	15	.516	37	26	17-3	3	235.2	203	78	2	6	67	88	2.33	118	.237	.297	81-0-4	.185	-0	121	12	—	1.4
1917	StL A	5	6	.455	20	14	8-1	1	131	105	39	2	2	38	26	1.79	145	.225	.287	38-0-4	.105	-1	83	11	—	0.7
Total	17	326	194	.627	623	529	410-69	23	4495.2	3958	1566	42	190	1072	2246	2.35	122	.239	.293	1607-3-76	.206	17	109	268	—	30.3
Plantenberg, Erik	Erik John; B10.30.1968 Renton WA; BB/TL/6´1˝/180; [BosA90 16/443]; d7.31; Col San Diego St.																									
1993	Sea A	0	0	ø	20	0	0	1-0	9.2	11	7	0	1	12-1	3	6.52	69	.282	.462	0	ø	0	—	-2	0	-0.1
1994	Sea A	0	0	ø	6	0	0	0-0	7	4	0	0	1	7-0	1	0.00	ø	.174	.387	0	ø	0	—	4	0	0.2
1997	Phi N	0	0	ø	35	0	0	0-0	25.2	25	14	1	1	12-0	12	4.91	86	.255	.339	0	ø	0	—	-1	0	-0.1
Total	3	0	0	ø	61	0	0	1-0	42.1	40	21	1	3	31-1	16	4.46	98	.250	.379	0	ø	0	—	1	0	0.0
Pleis, Bill	William; B8.5.1937 St.Louis MO; BL/TL/5´10˝/175; d4.16																									
1961	Min A	4	2	.667	37	0	0	2	56.1	59	35	4	4	34-5	32	4.95	86	.266	.370	9	.111	-1	—	-4	0	-0.5
1962	Min A	2	5	.286	21	4	0	3	45	46	27	7	1	14-2	31	4.40	93	.264	.319	14	.286	1	66	-2	0	-0.3
1963	Min A	6	2	.750	36	4	1	0	68	67	37	10	0	16-2	37	4.37	83	.258	.297	16-0-1	.125	0	165	-5	0	-0.6
1964	Min A	4	1	.800	47	0	0	4	50.2	43	23	6	1	31-3	42	3.91	92	.232	.342	4-0-1	.250	0	—	-1	0	0.0
1965	†Min A	4	4	.500	41	2	0	4	51.1	49	20	3	0	27-5	33	2.98	119	.250	.336	7-0-1	.000	-1	25	3	0	0.4
1966	Min A	1	2	.333	8	0	0	0	9.1	5	6	1	0	4-0	9	1.93	186	.152	.243	0	ø	0	—	0	0	0.0
Total	6	21	16	.568	190	10	1	13	280.2	269	148	31	6	126-17	184	4.07	93	.251	.330	50-0-3	.160	0	96	-9	0	-1.0
Plesac, Dan	Daniel Thomas; B2.4.1962 Gary IN; BL/TL/6´5˝/(210–220); [MilA83 1/26]; d4.11; Col North Carolina St.																									
1986	Mil A	10	7	.588	51	0	0	14-4	91	81	34	5	0	29-1	75	2.97	147	.240	.296	0	ø	0	—	14	0	2.7
1987	Mil A★	5	6	.455	57	0	0	23-13	79.1	63	30	8	3	23-1	89	2.61	177	.213	.275	0	ø	0	—	15	0	2.7
1988	Mil A★	1	2	.333	50	0	0	30-5	52.1	46	14	2	0	12-2	52	2.41	166	.234	.278	0	ø	0	—	10	0	1.6
1989	Mil A★	3	4	.429	52	0	0	33-7	61.1	47	16	6	0	17-1	52	2.35	164	.213	.264	0	ø	0	—	11	0	2.3
1990	Mil A	3	7	.300	66	0	0	24-10	69	67	36	5	3	31-6	65	4.43	88	.257	.340	0	ø	0	—	-3	0	-0.6
1991	Mil A	2	7	.222	45	10	0	8-4	92.1	92	49	12	3	39-1	61	4.29	93	.263	.336	0	ø	0	121	-3	0	-0.4
1992	Mil A	5	4	.556	44	4	0	1-2	79	64	28	5	3	35-5	54	2.96	131	.229	.317	0	ø	0	124	8	0	0.9
1993	Chi N	2	1	.667	57	0	0	0-2	62.2	74	37	10	0	21-6	47	4.74	85	.298	.349	1	.000	-0	—	-5	0	-0.3
1994	Chi N	2	3	.400	54	0	0	1-2	54.2	61	30	9	1	13-0	53	4.61	92	.279	.321	4	.000	-0	—	-2	0	-0.3
1995	Pit N	4	4	.500	58	0	0	3-2	60.1	53	26	3	1	27-7	57	3.58	122	.237	.318	4	.250	0	—	5	0	0.7
1996	Pit N	6	5	.545	73	0	0	11-6	70.1	67	35	4	0	24-6	76	4.09	107	.247	.305	5	.000	-1	—	2	0	0.3
1997	Tor A	2	4	.333	73	0	0	1-4	50.1	47	22	8	0	19-4	61	3.58	128	.244	.310	0	ø	0	—	6	0	0.6
1998	Tor A	4	3	.571	78	0	0	4-1	50	41	23	4	1	16-1	55	3.78	123	.224	.286	0	ø	0	—	5	0	0.6
1999	Tor A	0	3	.000	30	0	0	0-2	22.2	28	21	4	0	9-1	26	8.34	59	.308	.366	0	ø	0	—	-8	0	-0.8
	†Ari N	2	1	.667	34	0	0	1-0	21.2	22	9	3	0	8-1	27	3.32	139	.259	.323	1	.000	-0	—	3	0	0.4
2000	Ari N	5	1	.833	62	0	0	0-4	40	34	21	4	0	26-2	45	3.15	152	.228	.341	0	ø	0	—	4	0	0.5
2001	Tor A	4	5	.444	62	0	0	1-1	45.1	34	18	4	1	24-5	68	3.57	128	.207	.311	0	ø	0	—	6	0	1.0
2002	Tor A	1	2	.333	19	0	0	0-1	13.1	11	5	1	0	6-0	14	3.38	137	.216	.293	0	ø	0	—	2	0	0.4
	Phi N	2	1	.667	41	0	0	1-2	23	16	12	5	0	12-3	27	4.70	82	.190	.292	0	ø	0	—	-2	0	-0.2
2003	Phi N	2	1	.667	58	0	0	2-2	33.1	29	12	3	1	11-1	37	2.70	147	.228	.295	0	ø	0	—	4	0	0.4
Total	18	65	71	.478	1064	14	0	158-74	1072	977	478	105	17	402-54	1041	3.64	117	.242	.311	15	.067	-1	114	72	0	12.5
Plitt, Norman	Norman William; B2.21.1893 York PA; D2.1.1954 New York NY; BR/TR/5´11˝/180; d4.26																									
1918	Bro N	0	0	ø	1	0	0	0	2	3	1	0	0	1	0	4.50	62	.429	.500	1	1.000	0	—	0	—	0.0
1927	Bro N	2	6	.250	19	8	1	0	62.1	73	40	3	1	36	9	4.91	81	.303	.396	18-0-2	.222	-0	75	-6	—	-0.7
	NY N	1	0	1.000	3	0	0	0	7.1	9	3	0	1	1	0	3.68	105	.310	.355	1	.000	-0	—	0	—	0.1
	Year	3	6	.333	22	8	1	0	69.2	82	43	3	2	37	9	4.78	83	.304	.392	19-0-2	.211	-0	75	-6	—	-0.6
Total	2	3	6	.333	23	8	1	0	71.2	85	44	3	2	38	9	4.77	82	.307	.394	20-0-2	.250	0	76	-6	—	-0.6
Plodinec, Tim	Timothy Alfred; B1.27.1947 Aliquippa PA; BR/TR/6´4˝/190; [StLN68 33/738]; d6.2; Col Arizona																									
1972	StL N	0	0	ø	1	0	0	0-0	0.1	3	1	0	0	0-0	0	27.00	13	.750	.750	0	ø	0	—	-1	0	0.0
Plunk, Eric	Eric Vaughn; B9.3.1963 Wilmington CA; BR/TR/6´5˝/(210–224); [NYA81 4/103]; d5.12																									
1986	Oak A	4	7	.364	26	15	0	0-0	120.1	91	75	14	5	102-2	98	5.31	73	.214	.370	0	ø	0	95	-19	0	-1.6
1987	Oak A	4	6	.400	32	11	0	2-3	95	91	53	8	2	62-3	90	4.74	88	.253	.361	0	ø	0	94	-5	0	-0.5
1988	†Oak A	7	2	.778	49	0	0	5-4	78	62	27	6	1	39-4	79	3.00	127	.217	.311	0	ø	0	—	8	15	0.9
1989	Oak A	1	1	.500	23	0	0	1-2	28.2	17	7	1	1	12-0	24	2.20	168	.172	.268	0	ø	0	—	5	0	0.4
	NY A	7	5	.583	27	7	0	0-0	75.2	65	36	9	0	52-2	61	3.69	106	.237	.355	0	ø	0	116	1	0	0.1
	Year	8	6	.571	50	7	0	1-2	104.1	82	43	10	1	64-2	85	3.28	117	.220	.333	0	ø	0	118	6	0	0.5
1990	NY A	6	3	.667	47	0	0	0-1	72.2	58	27	6	2	43-4	67	2.72	147	.225	.340	0	ø	0	—	9	0	1.1
1991	NY A	2	5	.286	43	8	0	0-0	111.2	128	69	18	1	62-1	103	4.76	88	.286	.371	0	ø	0	69	-9	0	-0.6
1992	Cle A	9	6	.600	58	0	0	4-4	71.2	61	31	5	0	38-2	50	3.64	108	.229	.324	0	ø	0	—	3	0	0.6
1993	Cle A	4	5	.444	70	0	0	15-3	71	61	29	5	0	30-4	77	2.79	157	.226	.301	0	ø	0	—	10	0	1.5
1994	Cle A	7	2	.778	41	0	0	3-4	71	61	25	3	2	37-5	73	2.54	188	.231	.329	0	ø	0	—	17	0	1.9
1995	†Cle A	6	2	.750	56	0	0	2-3	64	48	19	5	4	27-2	71	2.67	177	.211	.303	0	ø	0	—	15	0	1.7
1996	†Cle A	3	2	.600	56	0	0	2-1	77.2	56	21	6	3	34-2	85	2.43	201	.203	.293	0	ø	0	—	23	0	1.3
1997	†Cle A	4	5	.444	55	0	0	0-2	65.2	62	37	12	1	36-7	66	4.66	101	.245	.339	1	.000	-0*	—	0	0	0.0
1998	Cle A	3	1	.750	37	0	0	0-3	41	44	23	6	2	15-1	38	4.83	99	.282	.349	0	ø	0	—	0	0	0.0
	Mil N	1	2	.333	26	0	0	1-2	31.2	33	14	3	3	15-1	36	3.69	117	.270	.359	1	.000	0	—	2	0	0.2
1999	Mil N	4	4	.500	68	0	0	0-3	75.1	71	44	15	5	43-5	63	5.02	92	.251	.357	0	ø	0	—	-3	0	-0.3
Total	14	72	58	.554	714	41	0	35-35	1151	1009	537	122	32	647-45	1081	3.82	112	.236	.339	2	.000	0	88	57	15	6.7
Plympton, Jeff	Jeffrey Hunter; B11.24.1965 Framingham MA; BR/TR/6´2˝/205; [BosA87 10/266]; d6.15; Col Maine																									
1991	Bos A	0	0	ø	4	0	0	0-0	5.1	5	0	0	0	4-0	2	0.00	ø	.263	.375	0	ø	0	—	2	0	0.1
Poat, Ray	Raymond Willis; B12.19.1917 Chicago IL; D4.29.1990 Oak Lawn IL; BR/TR/6´2˝/200; d4.15; Def 1945; Col Illinois																									
1942	Cle A	1	3	.250	4	4	1-1	0	18.1	24	11	1	1	9	8	5.40	64	.296	.374	5	.000	-0	93	-3	0	-0.6
1943	Cle A	2	5	.286	17	4	1	0	45	44	22	3	0	20	31	4.40	71	.259	.337	13	.154	-1	108	-5	0	-0.8
1944	Cle A	4	8	.333	36	6	1	1	80.2	82	50	9	0	37	40	5.13	64	.265	.343	17-0-2	.000	-2	105	-15	0	-2.3
1947	NY N	4	3	.571	7	7	5	0	60	53	18	8	0	13	25	2.55	160	.238	.280	21-1-1	.190	2	99	11	0	1.4
1948	NY N	11	10	.524	39	24	7-3	0	157.2	162	95	21	3	67	57	4.34	91	.262	.337	56-0-1	.125	-1	146	-10	0	-1.3
1949	NY N	0	0	ø	2	0	0	0	2.1	8	6	0	0	1	0	19.29	21	.615	.643	0	ø	0	—	-4	0	-0.2
	Pit N	0	1	.000	11	2	0	0	36	52	29	6	0	15	17	6.25	67	.335	.394	10	.100	-1	52	-8	0	-0.5
	Year	0	1	.000	13	2	0	0	38.1	60	35	6	0	16	17	7.04	59	.357	.413	10	.100	-1	53	-11	0	-0.7
Total	6	22	30	.423	116	47	15-4	1	400	425	231	48	4	162	178	4.55	82	.271	.340	122-1-4	.115	-3	124	-34	0	-4.3
Podbielan, Bud	Clarence Anthony; B3.6.1924 Curlew WA; D10.26.1982 Syracuse NY; BR/TR/6´1.5˝/(170–180); d4.25																									
1949	Bro N	0	1	.000	7	1	0	0	12.1	9	9	1	1	9	5	3.65	112	.205	.352	3	.000	-0	107	-1	0	-0.1
1950	Bro N	5	4	.556	20	10	2	1	72.2	93	47	10	2	29	28	5.33	77	.307	.371	28-0-2	.107	-1	131	-10	0	-1.2
1951	Bro N	2	2	.500	27	5	1	0	79.2	67	32	9	2	36	26	3.50	112	.233	.322	23	.304	1	103	5	0	0.4
1952	Bro N	0	0	ø	3	0	0	0	2	4	5	1	0	3	1	18.00	20	.444	.583	0	ø	0*	—	-4	0	-0.2
	Cin N	4	5	.444	24	7	4-1	1	86.2	78	30	8	1	26	22	2.80	135	.245	.304	25	.160	0	64	9	0	0.9
	Year	4	5	.444	27	7	4-1	1	88.2	82	35	9	1	29	23	3.15	120	.251	.314	25	.160	0	64	7	0	0.7
1953	Cin N	6	16	.273	36	24	8-1	1	186.1	214	112	21	8	67	74	4.73	92	.290	.356	56-0-3	.125	-3	85	-9	0	-1.2
1954	Cin N	7	10	.412	27	24	4	0	131	157	92	20	2	58	42	5.36	78	.300	.370	42-0-3	.143	-1	105	-19	0	-2.2
1955	Cin N	1	2	.333	17	2	0	0	42	36	16	4	1	11-0	26	3.21	132	.234	.284	5-0-1	.400	1	42	5	34	0.4
1957	Cin N	0	1	.000	5	3	1	0	16	18	11	4	0	4-0	13	6.19	66	.290	.333	5	.000	-1	114	-3	0	-0.3

YEAR	TM LG	W	L	PCT	G	GS	CG-SHO	SV-BS	IP	H	R	HR	HB	BB-IB	SO	ERA	AERA	OAV	OOB	AB-HR-SH	AVG	PB	SUP	APR	DL	PW
1959	Cle A	0	1	.000	6	0	0	0	12.1	17	8	1	0	2-0	5	5.84	63	.354	.380	1	.000	-0	—	-3	0	-0.2
Total	9	25	42	.373	172	76	20-2	3	641	693	362	79	17	245-0	242	4.49	92	.279	.347	188-0-9	.154	-4	98	-30	34	-3.7
PODGAJNY, JOHNNY	John Sigmund "Specs"; B6.10.1920 Chester PA; D3.2.1971 Chester PA; BR/TR/6´2˝/173; d9.15																									
1940	Phi N	1	3	.250	4	4	3	0	35	33	14	0	1	1	12	2.83	138	.250	.261	12	.167	-0	45	3	—	0.4
1941	Phi N	9	12	.429	34	24	8	0	181.1	191	96	8	4	70	53	4.62	80	.270	.339	62-0-3	.129	-3*	88	-13	0	-1.6
1942	Phi N	6	14	.300	43	23	6	0	186.2	191	95	9	11	63	40	3.91	85	.268	.337	60-0-2	.183	-0*	84	-13	0	-1.4
1943	Phi N	4	4	.500	13	5	3	0	64	77	32	4	0	16	13	4.22	80	.310	.352	20-0-1	.250	1	116	-5	0	-0.4
	Pit N	0	4	.000	15	5	0	0	34.1	37	28	1	0	13	7	4.72	74	.266	.329	7	.143	-0*	73	-7	0	-0.7
	Year	4	8	.333	28	10	3	0	98.1	114	60	5	0	29	20	4.39	78	.295	.344	27-0-1	.222	0	95	-12	0	-1.1
1946	Cle A	0	0	ø	6	0	0	0	9	13	8	0	0	2	4	5.00	66	.302	.333	0	ø	0	—	-3	0	-0.1
Total	5	20	37	.351	115	61	20	0	510.1	542	273	22	16	165	129	4.20	84	.273	.334	161-0-6	.168	-3	85	-38	0	-3.8
PODRES, JOHNNY	John Joseph; B9.30.1932 Witherbee NY; BL/TL/5´11˝/(170–192); d4.17; Mil 1956; C13																									
1953	†Bro N	9	4	.692	33	18	3-1	0	115	126	62	12	1	64	82	4.23	101	.282	.373	36-0-1	.306	2*	120	-1	0	0.1
1954	Bro N	11	7	.611	29	21	6-2	0	151.2	147	77	13	1	53	79	4.27	96	.255	.317	60-0-3	.283	5*	116	-2	30	0.2
1955	†Bro N	9	10	.474	27	24	5-2	0	159.1	160	80	15	4	57-2	114	3.95	103	.259	.325	60-0-4	.183	-0*	126	2	0	0.1
1957	Bro N	12	9	.571	31	27	10-**6**	3	196	168	64	15	1	44-1	109	**2.66**	**156**	.230	**.273**	72-0-3	.208	1*	95	31	0	3.4
1958	LA N☆	13	15	.464	39	31	10-2	1	210.1	208	96	27	2	78-8	143	3.72	110	.261	.326	71-0-4	.127	-3*	95	9	0	0.7
1959	†LA N	14	9	.609	34	29	6-2	0	195	192	93	23	3	74-7	145	4.11	103	.261	.330	65-0-3	.246	3	98	5	0	1.0
1960	LA N★	14	12	.538	34	33	8-1	0	227.2	217	88	25	1	71-9	159	3.08	129	.250	.307	66-0-10	.136	-1	85	21	0	2.1
1961	LA N	18	5	**.783**	32	29	6-1	0	182.2	192	81	27	4	51-2	124	3.74	116	.271	.322	69-0-4	.232	1	111	13	0	1.5
1962	LA N★	15	13	.536	40	40	8	0	255	270	121	20	3	71-14	178	3.81	95	.272	.321	88-1-5	.159	1	110	-3	0	-0.4
1963	†LA N	14	12	.538	37	34	10-5	1	198.1	196	91	16	3	64-13	134	3.54	85	.257	.315	64-1-3	.141	1	115	-12	0	-1.4
1964	LA N	0	2	.000	2	2	0	0	2.2	5	5	1	0	3-1	0	16.88	19	.417	.533	0	ø	0	54	-4	96	-0.7
1965	LA N	7	6	.538	27	22	2-1	1	134	126	57	17	2	39-4	63	3.43	95	.247	.301	45-0-1	.178	1	83	-2	0	-0.3
1966	LA N	0	0	ø	1	0	0	0	1.2	2	0	0	0	1-1	1	0.00	ø	.400	.429	0	ø	0	—	1	0	0.0
	Det A	4	5	.444	36	13	2-1	4	107.2	106	48	12	1	34-3	53	3.43	102	.259	.313	30	.233	2	94	0	0	0.2
1967	Det A	3	1	.750	21	8	0	1	63.1	58	29	12	1	11-2	34	3.84	85	.244	.280	20	.100	-1	117	-4	22	-0.4
1969	SD N	5	6	.455	17	9	1	0-1	64.2	66	34	7	1	28-3	17	4.31	83	.264	.337	16-0-2	.063	-1	88	-5	0	-0.9
Total	15	148	116	.561	440	340	77-24	11-1	2265	2239	1026	242	28	743-70	1435	3.68	105	.259	.318	762-2-43	.190	11	103	49	148	5.2
POETZ, JOE	Joseph Frank "Bull Montana"; B6.22.1900 St.Louis MO; D2.7.1942 St.Louis MO; BR/TR/5´10.5˝/175; d9.14																									
1926	NY N	0	1	.000	2	1	0	0	8	5	3	2	1	8	0	3.38	111	.192	.400	1	.000	0	44	1	—	0.1
POFFENBERGER, BOOTS	Cletus Elwood; B7.1.1915 Williamsport MD; D9.1.1999 Williamsport MD; BR/TR/5´10˝/178; d6.11																									
1937	Det A	10	5	.667	29	16	5	3	137.1	147	83	8	4	79	35	4.65	100	.277	.375	51-0-2	.216	-0	144	-1	—	-0.1
1938	Det A	6	7	.462	25	15	8-1	1	125	147	74	8	2	66	28	4.82	104	.297	.382	44-0-1	.182	-1	80	2	—	0.0
1939	Bro N	0	0	ø	3	1	0	0	5	7	3	1	0	4	2	5.40	75	.318	.423	1	.000	-0	130	-1	—	0.0
Total	3	16	12	.571	57	32	13-1	4	267.1	301	160	17	6	149	65	4.75	101	.287	.379	96-0-3	.198	-2	113	0	—	-0.1
POHOLSKY, TOM	Thomas George; B8.26.1929 Detroit MI; D1.6.2001 Kirkwood MO; BR/TR/6´3˝/(190–205); d4.20; Mil 1952–53																									
1950	StL N	0	0	ø	5	1	0	0	14.2	16	6	2	0	3	2	3.68	117	.281	.317	2	.000	-0	41	1	0	0.0
1951	StL N	7	13	.350	38	26	10-1	1	195	204	106	15	0	68	70	4.43	89	.271	.331	67-0-6	.209	0	125	-10	0	-0.8
1954	StL N	5	7	.417	25	13	4	0	106	101	43	11	4	20	55	3.06	135	.254	.293	27-0-6	.148	-1	120	11	0	1.1
1955	StL N	9	11	.450	30	24	8-2	0	151	143	71	26	2	35-4	66	3.81	106	.244	.289	44-0-5	.182	-0	91	3	0	0.3
1956	StL N	9	14	.391	33	29	7-2	0	203	210	100	27	5	44-7	95	3.59	105	.268	.309	69-0-3	.159	-1	88	1	0	0.0
1957	Chi N	1	7	.125	28	11	1	0	84	117	55	9	2	22-4	28	4.93	79	.330	.366	19-0-1	.105	-1	103	-11	0	-1.0
Total	6	31	52	.373	159	104	30-5	1	753.2	791	381	90	13	192-15	316	3.93	101	.270	.316	228-0-21	.171	-3	103	-5	0	-0.4
POINDEXTER, JENNINGS	Chester Jennings "Jinx"; B9.30.1910 Pauls Valley OK; D3.3.1983 Norman OK; BL/TL/5´10˝/165; d9.15																									
1936	Bos A	0	2	.000	3	3	0	0	10.2	13	11	0	0	16	2	6.75	79	.302	.492	4	.000	-1	44	-2	—	-0.4
1939	Phi N	0	0	ø	11	1	0	0	30.1	29	19	0	0	15	12	4.15	96	.250	.336	10	.200	-0	153	-2	—	-0.1
Total	2	0	2	.000	14	4	0	0	41	42	30	0	0	31	14	4.83	90	.264	.384	14	.143	-1	76	-4	—	-0.5
POLCHOW, LOU	Louis William; B3.14.1880 Mankato MN; D8.15.1912 Good Thunder MN; 5´9˝/?; d9.14																									
1902	Cle A	0	1	.000	1	1	1	0	8	9	5	0	0	4	2	5.63	61	.281	.361	4	.000	-1	63	-1	—	-0.2
POLE, DICK	Richard Henry; B10.13.1950 Trout Creek MI; BR/TR/6´3˝/(195–200); d8.3; C18																									
1973	Bos A	3	2	.600	12	7	0	0-0	54.2	70	35	4	0	18-0	24	5.60	72	.318	.370	0	ø	0	155	-8	0	-0.7
1974	Bos A	1	1	.500	15	2	0	1-0	45	55	28	6	1	13-0	32	4.20	92	.304	.352	0	ø	0	160	-4	0	-0.2
1975	†Bos A	4	6	.400	18	11	2-1	0-0	89.2	102	46	11	2	32-4	42	4.42	92	.290	.349	0	ø	0	79	-2	62	-0.2
1976	Bos A	6	5	.545	31	15	1	0-0	120.2	131	62	8	2	48-3	49	4.33	90	.279	.346	1	.000	-0	83	-3	0	-0.4
1977	Sea A	7	12	.368	25	24	3	0-0	122.1	127	76	16	6	57-2	51	5.15	81	.270	.353	0	ø	0	80	-13	26	-1.8
1978	Sea A	4	11	.267	21	18	2	0-1	98.2	122	82	16	3	41-3	41	6.48	59	.306	.371	0	ø	0	103	-29	0	-3.8
Total	6	25	37	.403	122	77	8-1	1-1	531	607	329	61	14	209-12	239	5.05	79	.290	.356	1	.000	-0	94	-59	88	-7.1
POLITTE, CLIFF	Clifford Anthony; B2.27.1974 Kirkwood MO; BR/TR/5´11˝/(185–200); [StLN95 54/1439]; d4.2; Col Jefferson (MO) CC																									
1998	StL N	2	3	.400	8	8	0	0-0	37	45	32	6	1	18-0	22	6.32	67	.302	.379	14-0-1	.071	-1	117	-10	0	-1.2
1999	Phi N	1	0	1.000	13	0	0	0-0	17.2	19	14	2	0	15-0	15	7.13	65	.275	.405	0	ø	0	—	-4	0	-0.2
2000	Phi N	4	3	.571	12	8	0	0-0	59	55	24	8	0	27-1	50	3.66	125	.248	.328	15-0-2	.133	0	83	7	0	0.8
2001	Phi N	2	3	.400	23	0	0	0-0	26	24	8	2	1	8-3	23	2.42	170	.250	.306	2	.000	0	—	5	96	0.9
2002	Phi N	2	0	1.000	13	0	0	0-1	16.1	19	10	0	1	9-1	15	3.86	99	.288	.382	1	.000	-0	—	-1	0	-0.2
	Tor A	1	3	.250	55	0	0	1-2	57.1	38	23	5	1	19-1	57	3.61	128	.186	.258	0	ø	0	—	7	0	0.4
2003	Tor A	1	5	.167	54	0	0	12-6	49.1	52	32	11	1	17-4	40	5.66	84	.268	.326	0	ø	0	—	-4	26	-0.6
2004	Chi A	0	3	.000	54	0	0	1-0	51.1	52	26	6	2	22-5	48	4.38	107	.261	.338	0	ø	0	—	2	0	0.1
2005	†Chi A	7	1	.875	68	0	0	1-1	67.1	42	15	7	3	21-4	57	2.00	225	.181	.254	1	1.000	0	—	19	0	2.0
2006	Chi A	2	2	.500	30	0	0	0-2	30	47	30	9	1	15-7	15	8.70	54	.353	.417	0	ø	0	—	-13	24	-1.4
Total	9	22	23	.489	330	16	0	15-12	411.1	393	214	56	11	171-26	342	4.40	103	.251	.326	33-0-3	.121	-0	97	8	146	0.6
POLIVKA, KEN	Kenneth Lyle "Soup"; B1.21.1921 Chicago IL; D7.23.1988 Aurora IL; BL/TL/5´10.5˝/175; d4.18																									
1947	Cin N	0	0	ø	2	0	0	0	3	3	1	0	0	3	1	3.00	137	.250	.400	0	ø	0	—	0	0	0.0
POLLET, HOWIE	Howard Joseph; B6.26.1921 New Orleans LA; D8.8.1974 Houston TX; BL/TL/6´1.5˝/175; d8.20; Mil 1944–45; C7																									
1941	StL N	5	2	.714	9	8	6-2	0	70	55	18	1	1	27	37	1.93	195	.212	.289	28-0-1	.179	-0	107	14	0	1.4
1942	†StL N	7	5	.583	27	13	5-2	0	109.1	102	43	7	2	39	42	2.88	119	.242	.309	31-0-2	.226	3	123	6	0	0.9
1943	StL N✳	8	4	.667	16	14	12-5	0	118.1	83	26	2	2	32	61	**1.75**	192	.200	.261	43-0-1	.163	-1	83	22	0	2.1
1946	†StL N☆	**21**	10	.677	40	32	22-4	5	**266**	228	84	12	5	86	107	**2.10**	**165**	.234	.300	87-0-7	.161	-0	99	**35**	0	4.3
1947	StL N	9	11	.450	37	24	9	2	176.1	195	96	11	3	87	73	4.34	95	.286	.369	65	.231	2	103	-3	0	-0.1
1948	StL N	13	8	.619	36	26	11	0	186.1	216	102	10	2	67	80	4.54	90	.289	.349	68-0-5	.118	-3*	123	-9	0	-1.1
1949	StL N★	20	9	.690	39	28	17-**5**	1	230.2	228	80	9	2	59	108	2.77	150	.256	.304	82-0-3	.195	1	100	**35**	0	**4.2**
1950	StL N	14	13	.519	37	30	14-2	2	232.1	228	103	19	1	68	117	3.29	130	.256	.310	84-0-2	.143	-2*	96	22	0	2.1
1951	StL N	0	3	.000	6	2	0	1	12.1	10	10	1	0	8	10	4.38	91	.208	.321	1	.000	1	111	-2	0	-0.3
	Pit N	6	10	.375	21	21	4-1	0	128.2	149	81	24	1	51	47	5.04	84	.294	.360	36-0-4	.139	-0	86	-10	0	-1.1
	Year	6	13	.316	27	23	4-1	1	141	159	91	25	1	59	57	4.98	84	.287	.357	37-0-4	.135	0	88	-11	0	-1.4
1952	Pit N	7	16	.304	31	30	9-1	0	214	217	111	22	3	71	90	4.12	97	.266	.327	68-0-2	.191	2	70	-3	0	0.0
1953	Pit N	1	1	.500	5	2	0	0	12.2	27	15	2	0	6	8	10.66	42	.482	.532	3-0-1	.333	0	200	-8	0	-0.9
	Chi N	5	6	.455	25	17	2	1	111.1	120	62	6	1	44	45	4.12	108	.271	.338	31-0-3	.129	-1	78	3	0	0.1
	Year	6	7	.462	30	19	2	1	124	147	77	8	1	50	53	4.79	93	.295	.360	34-0-4	.147	-1	91	-7	0	-0.8
1954	Chi N	8	10	.444	20	20	4-2	0	128.1	131	60	4	0	54	58	3.58	117	.263	.332	47-0-3	.277	2	94	7	0	1.2
1955	Chi N	4	3	.571	24	7	1-1	5	61	62	41	11	0	27-3	27	5.61	73	.265	.337	15-0-1	.400	3	112	-10	0	-0.8
1956	Chi A	3	1	.750	11	4	0	0	26.1	27	15	2	0	11-0	14	4.10	100	.252	.322	8-0-1	.375	1*	174	-1	0	0.0
	Pit N	0	4	.000	19	0	0	3	23.1	18	10	3	0	8-1	10	3.09	122	.212	.277	1-0-1	.000	0	—	1	0	0.3
Total	14	131	116	.530	403	278	116-25	20	2107.1	2096	957	146	23	745-4	934	3.51	113	.260	.324	698-0-37	.185	7	99	99	0	12.3

YEAR	TM LG	W	L	PCT	G	GS	CG-SHO	SV-BS	IP	H	R	HR	HB	BB-IB	SO	ERA	AERA	OAV	OOB	AB-HR-SH	AVG	PB	SUP	APR	DL	PW
Polley, Dale	Ezra Dale; B8.9.1965 Georgetown KY; BR/TL/6´0˝/185; d6.23; Col Kentucky St.																									
1996	NY A	1	3	.250	32	0	0	0-0	21.2	23	20	5	3	11-1	14	7.89	63	.264	.363	0	ø	0	—	-7	0	-1.1
Polli, Lou	Louis Americo "Crip"; B7.9.1901 Baveno, Italy; D12.19.2000 Berlin VT; BR/TR/5´10.5˝/165; d4.18																									
1932	StL A	0	0	ø	5	0	0	0	6.2	13	8	0	0	3	5	5.40	90	.406	.457	2	.500	0	—	-2	—	-0.1
1944	NY N	0	2	.000	19	0	0	3	35.2	42	25	3	0	20	6	4.54	81	.294	.380	6	.000	-1	—	-5	0	-0.4
Total	2	0	2	.000	24	0	0	3	42.1	55	33	3	0	23	11	4.68	82	.314	.394	8	.125	-1	—	-7	0	-0.5
Poloni, John	John Paul; B2.28.1954 Dearborn MI; BL/TL/6´5˝/210; [TexA75 6/137]; d9.16; Col Arizona St.																									
1977	Tex A	1	0	1.000	2	1	0	0-0	7	8	5	1	0	1-0	5	6.43	63	.286	.310	0	ø	0	176	-2	0	-0.2
Pomorski, John	John Leon; B12.30.1905 Brooklyn NY; D12.6.1977 Brampton ON, Can.; BR/TR/6´0˝/178; d4.17																									
1934	Chi A	0	0	ø	3	0	0	0	1.2	1	2	0	0	2	0	5.40	88	.143	.333	0	ø	0	—	0	—	0.0
Pond, Arlie	Erasmus Arlington; B1.19.1873 Saugus MA; D9.19.1930 Cebu, Philippines; BR/TR/5´10˝/160; d7.4; Mil 1898; Col Vermont																									
1895	Bal N	0	1	.000	6	1	1	2	13.2	10	13	0	1	12	13	5.93	80	.200	.365	6	.333	1*	45	-2	—	-0.1
1896	Bal N	16	8	.667	28	26	21-2	0	214.1	232	133	4	6	57	80	3.49	123	.274	.324	81-0-5	.235	0	112	13	—	1.0
1897	Bal N	18	9	.667	32	28	23	0	248	267	131	4	15	72	59	3.52	118	.273	.332	90-0-3	.244	2*	122	21	—	1.9
1898	Bal N	1	1	.500	3	2	1-1	0	20	8	4	0	2	9	4	0.45	795	.123	.250	7	.286	1	178	6	—	0.6
Total	4	35	19	.648	69	57	46-3	2	496	517	281	8	24	150	156	3.45	122	.266	.327	184-0-8	.245	3	117	38	—	3.4
Ponder, Elmer	Charles Elmer; B6.26.1893 Reed OK; D4.20.1974 Albuquerque NM; BR/TR/6´0˝/178; d9.18; Mil 1918–19; Col Oklahoma																									
1917	Pit N	1	1	.500	3	2	1-1	0	21.1	12	5	0	1	6	11	1.69	168	.167	.241	7	.000	-1	13	3	—	0.1
1919	Pit N	0	5	.000	9	5	0	0	47.1	55	26	0	3	6	6	3.99	76	.297	.330	15	.133	-1	37	-6	—	-0.7
1920	Pit N	11	15	.423	33	23	13-2	0	196	182	76	3	2	40	62	2.62	123	.246	.286	59-0-3	.119	-4	71	10	—	0.9
1921	Pit N	2	0	1.000	8	1	1	0	24.2	29	8	1	0	3	3	2.19	175	.305	.327	10	.000	-2	150	4	—	0.1
	Chi N	3	6	.333	16	11	5	0	89.1	117	58	7	3	17	31	4.74	81	.321	.356	33-0-2	.121	-2	92	-10	—	-1.1
	Year	5	6	.455	24	12	6	0	114	146	66	8	3	20	34	4.18	91	.317	.350	43-0-2	.093	-4	97	-6	—	-1.0
Total	4	17	27	.386	69	42	20-3	0	378.2	395	173	11	9	72	113	3.21	105	.271	.309	124-0-5	.105	-10	73	1	—	-0.7
Ponson, Sidney	Sidney Alton; B11.2.1976 Noord, Aruba; BR/TR/6´2˝/(200–265); d4.19																									
1998	Bal A	8	9	.471	31	20	0	1-1	135	157	82	19	3	42-2	85	5.27	86	.293	.345	4	.500	1	100	-11	0	-1.2
1999	Bal A	12	12	.500	32	32	6	0-0	210	227	118	35	1	80-2	112	4.71	100	.282	.345	3-0-1	.000	-0	104	0	0	-0.1
2000	Bal A	9	13	.409	32	32	6-1	0-0	222	223	125	30	1	83-0	152	4.82	97	.258	.323	1-0-2	.000	-0	97	-2	0	-0.2
2001	Bal A	5	10	.333	23	23	3-1	0-0	138.1	161	83	21	6	37-0	84	4.94	87	.289	.339	3	.000	-0	90	-10	23	-0.9
2002	Bal A	7	9	.438	28	28	3	0-0	176	172	84	26	2	63-1	120	4.09	106	.258	.323	3	.333	1	106	6	25	0.6
2003	Bal A	14	6	.700	21	21	4	0-0	148	147	65	10	4	43-2	100	3.77	122	.258	.313	5	.000	-1	115	14	0	1.7
	†SF N	3	6	.333	10	10	0	0-0	68	64	29	6	1	18-3	34	3.71	115	.255	.305	22-0-3	.091	-1	75	5	0	0.5
2004	Bal A	11	15	.423	33	33	**5-2**	0-0	215.2	265	136	23	8	69-3	115	5.30	88	.305	.361	5	.000	-1	97	-14	0	-1.4
2005	Bal A	7	11	.389	23	23	1	0-0	130.1	177	97	16	3	48-1	68	6.21	71	.331	.384	4	.250	0	106	-25	24	-2.7
2006	StL N	4	4	.500	14	13	0	0-0	68.2	82	42	7	4	29-1	33	5.24	83	.308	.385	13-0-5	.231	1	103	-7	19	-0.6
	NY A	0	1	.000	5	3	0	0-0	16.1	26	20	3	0	7-0	15	10.47	43	.351	.407	0	ø	0	166	-11	0	-0.5
Total	9	80	96	.455	252	238	28-4	1-1	1528.1	1701	881	196	33	519-15	918	4.89	93	.284	.343	63-0-11	.143	1	101	-55	91	-4.8
Poole, Ed	Edward Isaih; B9.7.1874 Canton OH; D3.11.1919 Malvern OH; BR/TR/5´10˝/175; d10.6																									
1900	Pit N	1	0	1.000	1	0	0	0	7	4	1	0	0	0	3	1.29	283	.167	.167	4-1-0	.500	1*	—	2	—	0.4
1901	Pit N	5	4	.556	12	10	8-1	0	80	78	45	3	6	30	26	3.60	91	.254	.332	78-1-0	.205	1*	126	-2	—	-0.1
1902	Pit N	0	0	ø	1	0	0	0	8	7	4	0	0	3	2	1.13	244	.233	.303	4	.250	0	—	0	—	0.0
	Cin N	12	4	.750	16	16	16-2	0	138	129	47	2	8	54	55	2.15	139	.248	.328	61	.115	-4*	108	13	—	1.0
	Year	12	4	.750	17	16	16-2	0	146	136	51	2	8	57	57	2.10	142	.247	.326	65	.123	-4	108	12	—	1.0
1903	Cin N	7	13	.350	25	21	18-1	0	184	188	105	4	12	77	73	3.28	109	.270	.352	70-0-3	.243	0	104	5	—	0.6
1904	Bro N	8	14	.364	25	23	19-1	1	178	178	86	4	8	74	67	3.39	81	.268	.349	62-0-3	.129	-3	87	-7	—	-1.1
Total	5	33	35	.485	80	70	61-5	1	595	584	288	13	34	238	226	3.04	103	.260	.340	279-2-6	.183	-6	103	11	—	0.8
Poole, Jim	James Richard; B4.28.1966 Rochester NY; BL/TL/6´2˝/(190–203); [LAN88 9/218]; d6.15; Col Georgia Tech																									
1990	LA N	0	0	ø	16	0	0	0-0	10.2	7	5	1	0	8-4	6	4.22	87	.184	.326	0	ø	0	—	0	0	0.0
1991	Tex A	0	0	ø	5	0	0	1-0	6	10	4	0	0	3-0	4	4.50	90	.370	.419	0	ø	0	—	-1	0	0.0
	Bal A	3	2	.600	24	0	0	0-0	36	19	10	3	0	9-2	34	2.00	198	.157	.212	0	ø	0	—	7	0	1.0
	Year	3	2	.600	29	0	0	1-0	42	29	14	3	0	12-2	38	2.36	169	.196	.252	0	ø	0	—	7	0	1.0
1992	Bal A	0	0	ø	6	0	0	0-1	3.1	3	3	0	0	1-0	3	0.00	ø	.231	.286	0	ø	0	—	0	78	0.0
1993	Bal A	2	1	.667	55	0	0	2-1	50.1	30	18	2	0	21-5	29	2.15	211	.175	.263	0	ø	0	—	10	0	0.6
1994	Bal A	1	0	1.000	38	0	0	0-2	20.1	32	15	4	0	11-2	18	6.64	76	.372	.430	0	ø	0	—	-3	0	-0.1
1995	†Cle A	3	3	.500	42	0	0	0-0	50.1	40	22	7	2	17-0	41	3.75	126	.217	.288	0	ø	0	—	6	0	0.6
1996	Cle A	4	0	1.000	32	0	0	0-1	26.2	29	15	3	0	14-4	19	3.04	161	.274	.355	0	ø	0	—	3	0	0.4
	SF N	2	1	.667	35	0	0	0-3	23.2	15	7	2	1	13-3	19	2.66	156	.188	.309	2	.000	-0	—	4	0	0.5
1997	SF N	3	1	.750	63	0	0	0-0	49.1	73	44	6	4	25-4	26	7.11	58	.353	.429	0-0-1	ø	0	—	-17	0	-1.2
1998	SF N	1	3	.250	26	0	0	0-2	32.1	38	20	5	0	9-5	16	5.29	76	.302	.346	4-0-2	.250	0	—	-5	0	-0.4
	†Cle A	0	0	ø	12	0	0	0-1	7	9	4	0	1	3-1	11	5.14	93	.300	.382	0	ø	0	—	0	0	0.0
1999	Phi N	1	1	.500	51	0	0	1-1	35.1	48	20	3	3	15-1	22	4.33	108	.327	.400	2	.000	-0	—	1	0	0.0
	Cle A	1	0	1.000	3	0	0	0-0	1	2	2	0	0	3-1	0	18.00	28	.667	.714	0	ø	0	—	-1	0	-0.2
2000	Det A	1	0	1.000	18	0	0	0-1	8.2	13	8	4	1	1-0	5	7.27	68	.361	.375	0	ø	0	—	-2	0	-0.2
	Mon N	0	0	ø	5	0	0	0-0	2	8	6	1	0	3-1	3	27.00	17	.571	.647	0	ø	0	—	-5	0	-0.2
Total	11	22	12	.647	431	0	0	4-13	363	376	203	41	12	156-33	256	4.31	102	.271	.346	8-0-3	.125	0	—	-3	78	0.8
Poorman, Tom	Thomas Iverson; B10.14.1857 Lock Haven PA; D2.18.1905 Lock Haven PA; BL/TR/5´7˝/135; d5.5; ▲																									
1880	Buf N	1	8	.111	11	9	9	1	85	117	90	3	—	19	13	4.13	59	.307	.340	70	.157	-3*	51	-18	—	-1.8
	Chi N	2	0	1.000	2	1	0	0	15	12	5	0	—	8	0	2.40	101	.203	.299	25	.200	0*	102	1	—	0.1
	Year	3	8	.273	13	10	9	1	100	129	95	3	—	27	13	3.87	63	.293	.334	95	.168	-3	56	-17	—	-1.7
1884	Tol AA	0	1	.000	1	1	1	0	9	13	11	1	0	2	0	3.00	114	.310	.341	382	.233	0*	18	-1	—	-0.1
1887	Phi AA	0	0	ø	1	0	0	0	0.2	5	4	1	0	1	1	40.50	11	.714	.750	585-4	.265	0*	—	-3	—	-0.1
Total	3	3	9	.250	15	11	10	1	109.2	147	110	5	0	30	14	4.02	63	.301	.341	1062-4	.245	-2	52	-21	—	-1.9
Popp, Bill	William Peter; B6.7.1877 St.Louis MO; D9.5.1909 St.Louis MO; TR/5´10.5˝/170; d4.19																									
1902	StL N	2	6	.250	9	7	5	0	60.1	87	60	2	5	26	20	4.92	56	.337	.408	21-0-2	.048	-3	120	-19	—	-2.3
Porray, Ed	Edmund Joseph; B12.5.1888 , At Sea On Atlantic Ocean; D7.13.1954 Lackawaxen PA; BR/TR/5´11˝/170; d4.17																									
1914	Buf F	0	1	.000	3	3	0	0	10.1	18	9	2	0	7	0	4.35	68	.391	.472	4	.000	-1	147	-3	—	-0.3
Porter, Chuck	Charles William; B1.12.1956 Baltimore MD; BR/TR/6´3˝/188; [AnaA76 7/150]; d9.14; Col Clemson																									
1981	Mil A	0	0	ø	3	0	0	0-0	4.1	6	2	0	0	1-0	1	4.15	84	.316	.350	0	ø	0	—	0	0	0.0
1982	Mil A	0	0	ø	3	0	0	0-0	3.2	3	2	0	0	1-0	3	4.91	78	.250	.308	0	ø	0	—	0	0	0.0
1983	Mil A	7	9	.438	25	21	6-1	0-0	134	162	72	9	2	38-2	76	4.50	84	.298	.342	0	ø	0	118	-11	0	-1.1
1984	Mil A	6	4	.600	17	12	1	0-0	81.1	92	37	8	0	12-2	48	3.87	101	.284	.309	0	ø	0	110	1	90	0.2
1985	Mil A	0	0	ø	6	1	0	0-0	13.2	15	8	1	0	2-0	8	1.98	213	.273	.298	0	ø	0	195	1	0	0.0
Total	5	13	13	.500	54	34	7-1	0-0	237	278	121	18	2	54-4	136	4.14	93	.291	.328	0	ø	0	117	-9	90	-0.9
Porter, Ned	Ned Swindell; B5.6.1905 Apalachicola FL; D6.30.1968 Gainesville FL; BR/TR/6´0˝/173; d8.7; Col Florida																									
1926	NY N	0	0	ø	2	0	0	0	2	2	1	1	0	0	1	4.50	83	.250	.250	0	ø	0	—	0	—	0.0
1927	NY N	0	0	ø	1	0	0	0	2	3	1	0	0	1	0	0.00	ø	.333	.400	0	ø	0	—	0	—	0.0
Total	2	0	0	ø	3	0	0	0	4	5	2	1	0	1	1	2.25	169	.294	.333	0	ø	0	—	0	—	0.0
Porter, Odie	Odie Oscar; B5.24.1877 Borden IN; D5.2.1903 Borden IN; TL; d6.16; Col Indiana																									
1902	Phi A	0	1	.000	1	1	1	0	8	12	10	0	0	5	2	3.38	109	.343	.425	3	.000	-0	98	-2	—	-0.2

YEAR	TM LG	W	L	PCT	G	GS	CG-SHO	SV-BS	IP	H	R	HR	HB	BB-IB	SO	ERA	AERA	OAV	OOB	AB-HR-SH	AVG	PB	SUP	APR	DL	PW
PORTER, HENRY	Walter Henry; B6.1858 Vergennes VT; D12.30.1906 Brockton MA; BR/TR/?/142; d9.27																									
1884	Mil U	3	3	.500	6	6	6-1	0	51	32	25	1	—	9	71	3.00	44	.168	.205	40	.275	2*	144	-19	—	-1.4
1885	Bro AA	33	21	.611	54	54	53-2	0	481.2	427	261	11	16	107	197	2.78	118	.223	.270	195	.205	-2	102	25	—	2.2
1886	Bro AA	27	19	.587	48	48	48-1	0	424	439	277	8	5	120	163	3.42	102	.252	.303	184	.179	-9	113	5	—	-0.5
1887	Bro AA	15	24	.385	40	40	38-1	0	339.2	416	264	7	7	96	74	4.21	102	.297	.345	146-1	.199	-3	92	-2	—	-0.5
1888	KC AA	18	37	.327	55	54	53-4	0	474	527	336	16	23	120	145	4.16	81	.272	.321	195	.144	-13	66	-32	—	-3.9
1889	KC AA	0	3	.000	4	4	3	0	23	52	46	0	1	14	9	12.52	34	.433	.496	10	.100	-1	84	-16	—	-1.4
Total	6	96	107	.473	207	206	201-9	0	1793.1	1893	1209	43	52	466	659	3.70	95	.259	.308	770-1	.184	-26	93	-39	—	-5.5
PORTERFIELD, BOB	Erwin Coolidge; B8.10.1923 Newport VA; D4.28.1980 Sealy TX; BR/TR/6´0˝/(187–190); d8.8																									
1948	NY A	5	3	.625	16	12	2-1	0	78	85	42	5	0	34	30	4.50	91	.273	.345	24-0-7	.250	0	138	-3	0	-0.3
1949	NY A	2	5	.286	12	8	3	0	57.2	53	26	3	1	29	25	4.06	100	.251	.344	19	.053	-2	97	1	0	0.0
1950	NY A	1	1	.500	10	2	0	1	19.2	28	19	2	0	8	9	8.69	49	.341	.400	3	.333	1*	84	-9	42	-0.8
1951	NY A	0	0	ø	2	0	0	0	3	5	6	0	0	3	2	15.00	26	.385	.500	0	ø	0	—	-4	0	-0.2
	Was A	9	8	.529	19	19	10-3	0	133.1	109	51	8	0	54	53	3.24	126	.224	.302	46	.130	-3	78	14	0	1.3
	Year	9	8	.529	21	19	10-3	0	136.1	114	57	8	0	57	55	3.50	117	.228	.308	46	.130	-3	78	10	0	1.1
1952	Was A	13	14	.481	31	29	15-3	0	231.1	222	80	7	4	85	80	2.72	131	.254	.323	79-0-3	.190	0	68	22	0	2.4
1953	Was A	**22**	10	.688	34	32	**24-9**	0	255	243	99	19	1	73	77	3.35	116	.257	.310	98-3-4	.255	8*	119	19	0	3.3
1954	Was A★	13	15	.464	32	31	**21**-2	0	244	249	104	14	3	77	82	3.32	107	.266	.322	88-1-5	.102	-3	98	7	0	0.5
1955	Was A	10	17	.370	30	27	8-2	0	178	197	103	14	2	54-5	74	4.45	86	.282	.333	63-0-5	.190	1	100	-14	0	-1.8
1956	Bos A	3	12	.200	25	18	4-1	0	126	127	82	21	1	64-4	53	5.14	90	.260	.347	43-1-1	.326	3	83	-6	0	-0.4
1957	Bos A	4	4	.500	28	9	3-1	1	102.1	107	54	8	1	30-2	28	4.05	99	.272	.324	29	.172	-0	92	-2	0	-0.1
1958	Bos A	0	0	ø	2	0	0	0	4	3	2	1	0	0-0	1	4.50	89	.214	.214	0	ø	0	—	0	0	0.0
	Pit N	4	6	.400	37	6	2-1	5	87.2	78	33	7	1	19-3	39	3.29	118	.241	.281	20-1-0	.050	-1	93	7	0	0.8
1959	Pit N	0	0	ø	6	0	0	0	5.1	6	2	1	0	2-1	1	1.69	229	.286	.348	0	ø	0	—	1	0	0.0
	Chi N	0	0	ø	4	0	0	0	6.1	14	9	1	0	3-0	0	11.37	35	.424	.472	1	.000	-0	—	-5	0	-0.3
	Pit N	1	2	.333	30	0	0	1	36	45	20	2	0	17-5	18	4.75	81	.321	.395	3	.000	-0	—	-3	0	-0.2
	Year	1	2	.333	40	0	0	1	47.2	65	31	4	0	22-6	19	5.29	73	.335	.403	4	.000	-0	—	-7	0	-0.5
Total	12	87	97	.473	318	193	92-23	8	1567.2	1571	732	113	14	552-<u>20</u>	572	3.79	102	.263	.326	516-6-25	.184	4	96	25	42	4.2
PORTO, AL	Alfred "Lefty"; B6.27.1926 Heilwood PA; BL/TL/5´11˝/176; d4.22																									
1948	Phi N	0	0	ø	3	0	0	0	4	2	0	0	0	1	1	0.00	ø	.143	.200	0	ø	0	—	2	0	0.1
PORTOCARRERO, ARNIE	Arnold Mario; B7.5.1931 New York NY; D6.21.1986 Kansas City KS; BR/TR/6´3˝/(196–210); d4.18																									
1954	Phi A	9	18	.333	34	33	16-1	0	248	233	124	25	5	114	132	4.06	96	.249	.329	75-1-7	.107	-2	73	-4	0	-0.8
1955	KC A	5	9	.357	24	20	4-1	0	111.1	109	66	12	4	67-4	34	4.77	88	.259	.364	37-1-2	.108	-1	95	-7	31	-1.0
1956	KC A	0	1	.000	3	1	0	0	8	9	9	2	0	7-0	2	10.13	43	.300	.432	1	.000	-0	82	-4	0	-0.5
1957	KC A	4	9	.308	33	17	1	0	114.2	103	55	10	3	34-2	42	3.92	101	.240	.298	28-0-3	.107	-1	78	1	0	-0.1
1958	Bal A	15	11	.577	32	27	10-3	2	204.2	173	81	17	3	57-3	90	3.25	110	.229	.284	67-1-3	.164	0	93	9	0	0.9
1959	Bal A	2	7	.222	27	14	1	0	90	107	73	10	2	32-0	23	6.80	56	.294	.352	21-0-3	.000	-3	82	-29	0	-2.7
1960	Bal A	3	2	.600	13	5	1	0	40.2	44	23	6	0	9-0	15	4.43	86	.275	.312	11	.000	-1	116	-3	0	-0.5
Total	7	38	57	.400	166	117	33-5	2	817.1	778	431	82	17	320-<u>9</u>	338	4.32	89	.252	.322	240-3-18	.108	-9	85	-37	31	-4.7
PORTUGAL, MARK	Mark Steven; B10.30.1962 Los Angeles CA; BR/TR/6´0˝/(170–215); d8.14																									
1985	Min A	1	3	.250	6	4	0	0-0	24.1	24	16	3	0	14-0	12	5.55	80	.270	.362	0	ø	0	103	-3	0	-0.3
1986	Min A	6	10	.375	27	15	3	1-1	112.2	112	56	10	1	50-1	67	4.31	101	.265	.342	0	ø	0	110	2	0	0.2
1987	Min A	1	3	.250	13	7	0	0-1	44	58	40	13	1	24-1	28	7.77	60	.326	.407	0	ø	0	90	-14	0	-1.1
1988	Min A	3	3	.500	26	0	0	3-1	57.2	60	30	11	1	17-1	31	4.53	90	.274	.325	0	ø	0	—	-2	21	-0.3
1989	Hou N	7	1	.875	20	15	2-1	0-0	108	91	34	7	2	37-0	86	2.75	124	.232	.301	34-1-3	.206	3	111	9	0	1.0
1990	Hou N	11	10	.524	32	32	1	0-0	196.2	187	90	21	4	67-4	136	3.62	103	.250	.313	66-0-5	.136	-1	83	2	0	0.1
1991	Hou N	10	12	.455	32	27	1	1-1	168.1	163	91	19	2	59-5	120	4.49	79	.256	.318	46-0-6	.196	3*	120	-18	26	-1.9
1992	Hou N	6	3	.667	18	16	1-1	0-0	101.1	76	32	7	1	41-3	62	2.66	127	.213	.295	28-0-6	.107	-1	88	9	96	0.7
1993	Hou N	18	4	**.818**	33	33	1-1	0-0	208	194	75	10	4	77-3	131	2.77	140	.248	.318	65-1-10	.231	4	115	25	0	2.9
1994	SF N	10	8	.556	21	21	1	0-0	137.1	135	68	17	6	45-2	87	3.93	103	.260	.324	48-0-4	.354	7	110	1	22	0.8
1995	SF N	5	5	.500	17	17	1	0-0	104	106	56	10	2	34-2	63	4.15	99	.262	.323	29-0-7	.103	-0	112	-2	0	-0.2
	†Cin N	6	5	.545	14	14	0	0-0	77.2	79	35	7	2	22-0	33	3.82	109	.262	.316	29-0-1	.172	1	134	3	0	0.5
	Year	11	10	.524	31	**31**	1	0-0	181.2	185	91	17	4	56-2	96	4.01	103	.262	.320	58-0-8	.138	1	122	2	0	0.3
1996	Cin N	8	9	.471	27	26	1-1	0-0	156	146	77	20	2	42-2	93	3.98	108	.248	.297	48-0-7	.167	-0*	93	5	19	0.4
1997	Phi N	0	2	.000	3	3	0	0-0	13.2	17	8	0	0	5-0	2	4.61	91	.321	.373	4	.000	-0	51	-1	167	-0.1
1998	Phi N	10	5	.667	26	26	3	0-0	166.1	186	88	26	4	32-2	104	4.44	97	.283	.319	50-0-4	.260	4	106	-2	41	0.3
1999	Bos A	7	12	.368	31	27	1	0-0	150.1	179	100	28	4	41-1	79	5.51	90	.292	.337	3-0-1	.000	-0	92	-7	0	-0.7
Total	15	109	95	.534	346	283	16-4	5-4	1826.1	1813	896	209	36	607-27	1134	4.03	100	.261	.321	450-2-54	.198	19	104	7	392	2.3
PORZIO, MIKE	Lawrence Michael; B8.20.1972 Waterbury CT; BL/TL/6´3˝/(190–208); d7.9; Col Villanova																									
1999	Col N	0	0	ø	16	0	0	0-0	14.2	21	14	5	0	10-0	10	8.59	67	.328	.419	0	ø	0	—	-3	0	-0.1
2002	Chi A	2	2	.500	32	0	0	0-0	43	40	25	10	3	23-2	33	4.81	94	.248	.347	0	ø	0	—	-1	0	-0.1
2003	Chi A	1	1	.500	3	3	0	0-0	14	18	10	2	2	1-0	9	6.43	71	.321	.350	0	ø	0	80	-2	0	-0.3
Total	3	3	3	.500	51	3	0	0-0	71.2	79	49	17	5	34-2	52	5.90	81	.281	.364	0	ø	0	80	-6	0	-0.5
POSEDEL, BILL	William John "Sailor Bill","Barnacle Bill"; B8.2.1906 San Francisco CA; D11.28.1989 Livermore CA; BR/TR/5´11˝/175; d4.23; Mil 1942–45; C18																									
1938	Bro N	8	9	.471	33	17	6-1	1	140	178	96	14	2	46	49	5.66	69	.311	.365	44-0-4	.227	1	121	-23	—	-2.5
1939	Bos N	15	13	.536	33	29	18-5	0	220.2	221	103	8	0	78	73	3.92	94	.268	.331	73-0-5	.110	-4	94	-1	—	-0.6
1940	Bos N	12	17	.414	35	32	18	1	233	263	118	16	1	81	86	4.13	90	.288	.346	82-0-2	.171	1	89	-10	—	-1.0
1941	Bos N	4	4	.500	18	9	3	0	57.1	61	36	6	1	30	10	4.87	73	.279	.368	25-0-1	.320	2	116	-8	0	-0.8
1946	Bos N	2	0	1.000	19	0	0	4	28.1	34	24	4	0	13	9	6.99	49	.304	.376	3	.000	-0	—	-10	0	-1.1
Total	5	41	43	.488	138	87	45-6	6	679.1	757	377	48	4	248	227	4.56	82	.286	.349	227-0-12	.176	0	100	-52	0	-6.0
POSER, BOB	John Falk; B3.16.1910 Columbus WI; D5.21.2002 Columbus WI; BL/TR/6´0˝/173; d4.17; Col Wisconsin–Madison																									
1932	Chi A	0	0	ø	1	0	0	0	0.2	3	2	0	0	2	1	27.00	16	.600	.714	3	.000	-0*	—	-2	—	-0.1
1935	StL A	1	1	.500	4	1	0	0	13.2	26	15	0	0	4	1	9.22	52	.400	.435	4-0-1	.250	0	54	-6	—	-0.7
Total	2	1	1	.500	5	1	0	0	14.1	29	17	0	0	6	2	10.05	47	.414	.461	7-0-1	.143	0	54	-8	—	-0.8
POSSEHL, LOU	Louis Thomas; B4.12.1926 Chicago IL; D10.7.1997 Sarasota FL; BR/TR/6´2˝/180; d8.25; gf–George Rooks; Col Illinois																									
1946	Phi N	1	2	.333	4	4	0	0	13.2	19	9	0	1	10	4	5.93	58	.339	.448	3-0-1	.000	-0	62	-3	0	-0.6
1947	Phi N	0	0	ø	2	0	0	0	4.1	5	2	0	1	0	1	4.15	96	.385	.429	0	ø	0	—	0	0	0.1
1948	Phi N	1	1	.500	3	2	1	0	14.2	17	8	3	0	4	7	4.91	80	.304	.350	4	.250	0*	135	-1	0	-0.1
1951	Phi N	0	1	.000	2	1	0	0	6	9	5	0	0	3	6	6.00	64	.333	.400	1	.000	-0	92	-2	0	-0.3
1952	Phi N	0	1	.000	4	1	0	0	12.2	12	9	3	0	7	4	4.97	73	.235	.328	2	.000	-0	73	-2	0	-0.2
Total	5	2	5	.286	15	8	1	0	51.1	62	33	6	2	24	22	5.26	71	.305	.384	10-0-1	.100	-0	85	-8	0	-1.1
POTE, LOU	Louis William; B8.21.1971 Evergreen Park IL; BR/TR/6´3˝/(190–208); [SFN90 29/787]; d8.11; Col Kishwaukee (IL) CC																									
1999	Ana A	1	1	.500	20	0	0	3-0	29.1	23	9	1	0	12-1	20	2.15	228	.219	.299	0	ø	0	—	8	0	0.6
2000	Ana A	1	1	.500	32	1	0	1-0	50.1	52	23	4	0	17-1	44	3.40	152	.267	.324	0	ø	0	36	8	0	0.4
2001	Ana A	2	0	1.000	44	1	0	2-1	86.2	88	41	11	3	32-5	66	4.15	112	.258	.325	0	ø	0	60	6	0	0,3
2002	Ana A	0	2	.000	31	0	0	0-1	50.1	33	20	7	3	26-2	32	3.22	139	.194	.304	0	ø	0	—	7	0	0.4
2004	Cle A	0	0	ø	2	0	0	0-0	3	3	3	0	0	1-0	5	9.00	48	.250	.308	0	ø	0	—	-2	0	-0.1
Total	5	4	4	.500	129	2	0	6-2	219.2	199	96	23	6	88-9	167	3.56	133	.242	.316	0	ø	0	49	27	0	1.6
POTT, NELLIE	Nelson Adolph "Lefty"; B7.16.1899 Cincinnati OH; D12.3.1963 Cincinnati OH; BL/TL/6´0˝/185; d4.19																									
1922	Cle A	0	0	ø	2	0	0	0	2	7	7	1	0	2	0	31.50	13	.583	.643	0	ø	0	—	-6	—	-0.3
POTTER, DYKES	Maryland Dykes; B11.18.1910 Ashland KY; D2.27.2002 Greenup KY; BR/TR/6´0˝/185; d4.26; b–Squire																									
1938	Bro N	0	0	ø	2	0	0	0	2	4	1	1	0	0	1	4.50	87	.400	.400	0	ø	0	—	0	—	0.0

POTTER, NELS Nelson Thomas "Nellie"; B8.23.1911 Mt.Morris IL; D9.30.1990 Mt.Morris IL; BL/TR/5´11˝/180; d4.25; Col Manchester

YEAR	TM LG	W	L	PCT	G	GS	CG-SHO	SV-BS	IP	H	R	HR	HB	BB-IB	SO	ERA	AERA	OAV	OOB	AB-HR-SH	AVG	PB	SUP	APR	DL	PW
1936	StL N	0	0	ø	1	0	0	0	1	0	0	0	0	0	0	0.00	ø	.000	.000	0	ø	0	—	0	—	0.0
1938	Phi A	2	12	.143	35	9	4	5	111.1	139	95	15	2	49	43	6.47	75	.306	.376	39-0-1	.256	1*	75	-20	—	-2.1
1939	Phi A	8	12	.400	41	25	9	2	196.1	258	163	26	5	88	60	6.60	71	.321	.391	67-0-4	.179	-1	106	-37	—	-3.2
1940	Phi A	9	14	.391	31	25	13	0	200.2	213	115	18	1	71	73	4.44	100	.269	.330	71-0-6	.254	2	82	1	—	0.3
1941	Phi A	1	1	.500	10	3	1	2	23.1	35	26	3	0	16	7	9.26	45	.337	.425	6-0-1	.167	0	152	-12	0	-1.1
	Bos A	2	0	1.000	10	0	0	0	20	21	10	0	0	16	6	4.50	93	.284	.411	3	.000	-0	—	0	0	0.0
	Year	3	1	.750	20	3	1	2	43.1	56	36	3	0	32	13	7.06	59	.315	.419	9-0-1	.111	0	152	-12	0	-1.1
1943	StL A	10	5	.667	33	13	8	1	168.1	146	56	11	3	54	80	2.78	120	.235	.299	55-0-4	.145	-1	88	12	0	1.0
1944	†StL A	19	7	.731	32	29	16-3	0	232	211	79	6	1	70	91	2.83	127	.244	.301	82-0-5	.159	-2	137	22	0	2.3
1945	StL A	15	11	.577	32	32	21-3	0	255.1	212	75	10	1	68	129	2.47	143	.226	.279	92-0-5	.304	4	88	30	0	3.6
1946	StL A	8	9	.471	23	19	10	0	145	152	72	9	3	59	72	3.72	100	.268	.340	52	.231	2	80	-1	0	0.1
1947	StL A	4	10	.286	32	10	3	2	122.2	130	61	13	2	44	65	4.04	96	.277	.342	35	.257	3	73	-1	0	0.2
1948	StL A	1	1	.500	2	2	0	0	10.1	11	7	1	2	4	4	5.23	87	.262	.354	4	.500	1	79	-1	0	-0.1
	Phi A	2	2	.500	8	0	0	1	18	17	8	1	0	5	13	4.00	107	.250	.301	4	.250	0	—	1	0	0.2
	Year	3	3	.500	10	2	0	1	28.1	28	15	2	2	9	17	4.45	99	.255	.322	8	.375	1	82	0	0	0.1
	†Bos N	5	2	.714	18	7	3	2	85	77	27	4	0	8	47	2.33	165	.245	.264	29-0-2	.379	3	145	14	0	1.5
1949	Bos N	6	11	.353	41	3	1	7	96.2	99	49	6	1	30	57	4.19	90	.265	.321	23	.130	-0	93	-3	0	-0.5
Total	12	92	97	.487	349	177	89-6	22	1686	1721	843	123	21	582	747	3.99	99	.265	.328	562-0-28	.228	11	99	5	0	2.2

POTTER, SQUIRE Robert; B3.18.1902 Flatwoods KY; D1.27.1983 Ashland KY; BR/TR/6´1˝/185; d8.7; b–Dykes

YEAR	TM LG	W	L	PCT	G	GS	CG-SHO	SV-BS	IP	H	R	HR	HB	BB-IB	SO	ERA	AERA	OAV	OOB	AB-HR-SH	AVG	PB	SUP	APR	DL	PW
1923	Was A	0	0	ø	1	0	0	0	3	11	9	0	0	4	1	21.00	18	.688	.750	0	ø	0	—	-6	—	-0.3

POTTS, MIKE Michael Larry; B9.5.1970 Langdale AL; BL/TL/5´9˝/170; [AtlN90 18/480]; d4.6; Col Gordon (GA) JC

YEAR	TM LG	W	L	PCT	G	GS	CG-SHO	SV-BS	IP	H	R	HR	HB	BB-IB	SO	ERA	AERA	OAV	OOB	AB-HR-SH	AVG	PB	SUP	APR	DL	PW
1996	Mil A	1	2	.333	24	0	0	1-0	45.1	58	39	7	0	30-2	21	7.15	73	.319	.407	0	ø	0	—	-9	0	-0.6

POUNDS, BILL Jeared Wells; B3.11.1878 Paterson NJ; D7.7.1936 Paterson NJ; BR/TR/5´10.5˝/178; d5.2

YEAR	TM LG	W	L	PCT	G	GS	CG-SHO	SV-BS	IP	H	R	HR	HB	BB-IB	SO	ERA	AERA	OAV	OOB	AB-HR-SH	AVG	PB	SUP	APR	DL	PW
1903	Cle A	0	0	ø	1	0	0	0	5	8	7	0	0	0	2	10.80	26	.364	.364	2	.500	1	—	-4	—	-0.1
	Bro N	0	0	ø	1	0	0	0	6	8	5	1	0	2	2	6.00	53	.348	.400	3	.667	1	—	-2	—	0.0
Total	1	0	0	ø	2	0	0	0	11	16	12	1	0	2	4	8.18	37	.356	.383	5	.600	1	—	-6	—	-0.1

POWELL, ABNER Abner Charles "Ab"; B12.15.1860 Shenandoah PA; D8.7.1953 New Orleans LA; BL/TR/5´7˝/160; d8.4; ▲

YEAR	TM LG	W	L	PCT	G	GS	CG-SHO	SV-BS	IP	H	R	HR	HB	BB-IB	SO	ERA	AERA	OAV	OOB	AB-HR-SH	AVG	PB	SUP	APR	DL	PW
1884	Was U	6	12	.333	18	17	14-1	0	134	135	107	3	—	19	78	3.43	70	.245	.270	191	.283	2*	64	-19	—	-1.8
1886	Bal AA	2	5	.286	7	7	7	0	60	66	51	2	1	26	15	5.10	67	.264	.336	39	.179	-1*	77	-10	—	-0.9
	Cin AA	0	1	.000	4	1	1	0	15.1	16	13	0	0	9	4	4.70	75	.271	.368	74	.230	-0*	67	-2	—	-0.1
	Year	2	6	.250	11	8	8	0	75.1	82	64	2	1	35	19	5.02	69	.265	.342	113	.212	-1	75	-12	—	-1.0
Total	2	8	18	.308	29	25	22-1	0	209.1	217	171	5	1	54	97	4.00	69	.252	.297	304	.257	1	67	-31	—	-2.8

POWELL, DENNIS Dennis Clay; B8.13.1963 Moultrie GA; BR/TL/6´3˝/(200–227); d7.7

YEAR	TM LG	W	L	PCT	G	GS	CG-SHO	SV-BS	IP	H	R	HR	HB	BB-IB	SO	ERA	AERA	OAV	OOB	AB-HR-SH	AVG	PB	SUP	APR	DL	PW
1985	LA N	1	1	.500	16	2	0	1-0	29.1	30	19	7	1	13-3	19	5.22	67	.263	.341	3-0-2	.000	-0	88	-5	0	-0.4
1986	LA N	2	7	.222	27	6	0	0-0	65.1	65	32	5	1	25-7	31	4.27	81	.272	.341	14	.214	1	64	-5	37	-0.5
1987	Sea A	1	3	.250	16	3	0	0-1	34.1	32	13	3	0	15-0	17	3.15	151	.250	.324	0	ø	0	116	6	0	0.6
1988	Sea A	1	3	.250	12	2	0	0-0	18.2	29	20	2	2	11-2	15	8.68	48	.363	.442	0	ø	0	153	-9	0	-1.6
1989	Sea A	2	2	.500	43	1	0	2-0	45	49	25	6	2	21-0	27	5.00	81	.285	.364	0	ø	0	67	-3	0	-0.2
1990	Sea A	0	0	ø	2	0	0	0-0	3	5	3	0	1	2-0	0	9.00	44	.357	.471	0	ø	0	—	-1	0	-0.1
	Mil A	0	4	.000	9	7	0	0-0	39.1	59	37	0	1	19-0	23	6.86	57	.341	.405	0	ø	0	90	-14	0	-1.2
	Year	0	4	.000	11	7	0	0-0	42.1	64	40	0	2	21-0	23	7.02	55	.342	.410	0	ø	0	90	-16	0	-1.3
1992	Sea A	4	2	.667	49	0	0	0-0	57	49	30	5	3	29-2	35	4.58	88	.238	.340	0	ø	0	—	-3	0	-0.3
1993	Sea A	0	0	ø	33	2	0	0-0	47.2	42	22	7	1	24-2	32	4.15	108	.255	.349	0	ø	0	62	2	0	0.1
Total	8	11	22	.333	207	23	0	3-1	339.2	360	201	35	12	159-16	199	4.95	81	.279	.360	17-0-2	.176	1	89	-32	37	-3.6

POWELL, GROVER Grover David; B10.10.1940 Sayre PA; D5.21.1985 Raleigh NC; BL/TL/5´10˝/175; d7.13; Col Penn

YEAR	TM LG	W	L	PCT	G	GS	CG-SHO	SV-BS	IP	H	R	HR	HB	BB-IB	SO	ERA	AERA	OAV	OOB	AB-HR-SH	AVG	PB	SUP	APR	DL	PW
1963	NY N	1	1	.500	20	4	1-1	0	49.2	37	23	2	1	32-0	39	2.72	128	.202	.323	10	.200	1	68	2	0	0.2

POWELL, JAY James Willard; B1.9.1972 Meridian MS; BR/TR/6´4˝/(225–230); [BalA93 1/19]; d9.10; Col Mississippi St.

YEAR	TM LG	W	L	PCT	G	GS	CG-SHO	SV-BS	IP	H	R	HR	HB	BB-IB	SO	ERA	AERA	OAV	OOB	AB-HR-SH	AVG	PB	SUP	APR	DL	PW
1995	Fla N	0	0	ø	9	0	0	0-0	8.1	7	2	0	2	6-1	4	1.08	398	.241	.405	0	ø	0	—	3	0	0.1
1996	Fla N	4	3	.571	67	0	0	2-3	71.1	71	41	5	4	36-1	52	4.54	91	.255	.348	5-0-1	.000	-1	—	-4	20	-0.5
1997	†Fla N	7	2	.778	74	0	0	2-2	79.2	71	35	3	4	30-3	65	3.28	124	.242	.317	4	.500	1	—	6	0	0.7
1998	Fla N	4	4	.500	33	0	0	3-3	36.1	36	19	5	2	22-6	24	4.21	96	.263	.370	0	ø	0	—	-1	0	-0.1
	†Hou N	3	3	.500	29	0	0	4-1	34	22	9	1	1	15-3	38	2.38	170	.182	.277	1	.000	-0	—	7	0	1.2
	Year	7	7	.500	62	0	0	7-4	70.1	58	28	6	3	37-9	62	3.33	122	.225	.328	1	.000	-0	—	6	0	1.1
1999	†Hou N	5	4	.556	67	0	0	4-3	75	82	38	3	3	40-4	77	4.32	102	.282	.372	0	ø	0	—	1	0	0.1
2000	Hou N	1	1	.500	29	0	0	0-0	27	29	18	1	0	19-1	16	5.67	87	.271	.381	1	.000	-0*	—	-2	107	-0.1
2001	Hou N	2	2	.500	35	0	0	0-5	36.1	41	18	4	0	19-0	28	3.72	124	.275	.355	1	.000	-0	—	3	0	0.2
	Col N	3	1	.750	39	0	0	7-1	38.2	34	18	5	2	12-3	26	2.79	191	.245	.314	0	ø	0	—	7	0	0.9
	Year	5	3	.625	74	0	0	7-6	75	75	36	9	2	31-3	54	3.24	154	.260	.335	1	.000	-0	—	10	0	1.1
2002	Tex A	3	2	.600	51	0	0	0-4	49.2	50	28	5	1	24-4	35	3.44	139	.253	.336	0	ø	0	—	4	71	0.3
2003	Tex A	3	0	1.000	51	0	0	0-0	58.2	75	58	7	2	34-3	40	7.82	64	.318	.399	0	ø	0	—	-18	20	-0.9
2004	Tex A	1	1	.500	23	0	0	0-0	24	24	11	3	0	11-1	17	3.38	146	.267	.343	0	ø	0	—	3	121	0.2
2005	Atl N	0	0	ø	5	0	0	0-0	3.1	1	0	0	0	4-0	1	0.00	ø	.091	.333	0	ø	0	—	2	65	0.1
Total	11	36	23	.610	512	0	0	22-22	542.1	543	295	42	21	272-30	423	4.17	108	.261	.350	12-0-1	.167	-0	—	11	404	2.2

POWELL, JEREMY Jeremy Robert; B6.18.1976 Bellflower CA; BR/TR/6´5˝/(225–230); [MonN94 4/112]; d7.23

YEAR	TM LG	W	L	PCT	G	GS	CG-SHO	SV-BS	IP	H	R	HR	HB	BB-IB	SO	ERA	AERA	OAV	OOB	AB-HR-SH	AVG	PB	SUP	APR	DL	PW
1998	Mon N	1	5	.167	7	6	0	0-0	25	27	25	5	4	11-0	14	7.92	53	.290	.382	6	.000	-1	95	-10	0	-1.9
1999	Mon N	4	8	.333	17	17	0	0-0	97	113	60	14	8	44-2	44	4.73	94	.302	.385	30-0-1	.133	0	86	-4	0	-0.4
2000	Mon N	0	3	.000	11	4	0	0-0	26	35	27	6	0	9-0	19	7.96	59	.321	.370	5	.600	1	97	-10	0	-0.8
Total	3	5	16	.238	35	27	0	0-0	148	175	112	25	12	64-2	77	5.84	76	.304	.381	41-0-1	.171	1	89	-24	0	-3.1

POWELL, JACK John Joseph "Red"; B7.9.1874 Bloomington IL; D10.17.1944 Chicago IL; BR/TR/5´11˝/195; d6.23

YEAR	TM LG	W	L	PCT	G	GS	CG-SHO	SV-BS	IP	H	R	HR	HB	BB-IB	SO	ERA	AERA	OAV	OOB	AB-HR-SH	AVG	PB	SUP	APR	DL	PW
1897	Cle N	15	10	.600	27	26	24-2	0	225	245	117	2	9	62	61	3.16	142	.275	.328	97-0-4	.206	-4*	111	29	—	2.2
1898	Cle N	23	15	.605	42	41	36-**6**	0	342	328	154	8	16	112	93	3.00	121	.251	.317	136-0-2	.132	-7	100	27	—	1.8
1899	StL N	23	19	.548	48	**43**	**40**-2	0	373	433	197	15	15	85	87	3.52	113	.290	.334	134-1-4	.201	-1*	87	24	—	2.0
1900	StL N	17	16	.515	38	37	28-3	0	287.2	325	194	9	3	77	77	4.44	82	.284	.331	109-1-4	.284	10	107	-21	—	-1.1
1901	StL N	19	19	.500	**45**	37	33-2	**3**	338.1	351	168	14	12	50	133	3.54	90	.266	.299	119-2-9	.176	1	108	-11	—	-1.2
1902	StL A	22	17	.564	42	39	36-3	**2**	328.1	320	144	12	9	93	137	3.21	110	.256	.312	127-1-3	.205	4*	99	16	—	1.7
1903	StL A	15	19	.441	38	34	33-4	**2**	306.1	294	131	11	5	58	169	2.91	100	.252	.290	120-0-3	.208	2*	84	3	—	0.5
1904	NY A	23	19	.548	47	45	38-3	0	390.1	340	154	15	10	92	202	2.44	111	.235	.286	146-0-4	.178	-3	90	7	—	0.1
1905	NY A	8	13	.381	37	23	13-1	1	203	214	107	4	6	57	84	3.50	84	.272	.326	65-1-0	.185	-0	95	-10	—	-1.4
	StL A	2	1	.667	3	3	3	0	28	22	6	0	1	5	12	1.61	158	.218	.262	10	.100	-0	83	3	—	0.3
	Year	10	14	.417	40	26	16-1	1	231	236	113	4	7	62	96	3.27	88	.266	.319	75-1-0	.173	-1	94	-10	—	-1.1
1906	StL A	13	14	.481	28	26	25-3	1	244	196	77	2	8	55	132	1.77	146	.223	.275	91-1-2	.231	3	74	21	—	2.6
1907	StL A	13	16	.448	32	31	27-4	1	255.2	229	104	4	5	62	96	2.68	94	.242	.292	91-0-1	.132	-3	92	-4	—	-1.0
1908	StL A	16	13	.552	33	32	23-5	1	256	208	73	1	6	47	85	2.11	113	.231	.274	89-0-4	.236	3	92	13	—	1.4
1909	StL A	12	16	.429	34	27	18-4	3	239	221	83	1	4	42	82	2.11	115	.250	.287	78-0-4	.179	0	77	5	—	0.4
1910	StL A	7	11	.389	21	18	8-3	0	129.1	121	45	0	1	28	52	2.30	108	.250	.292	43-0-1	.163	-1	63	5	—	0.3
1911	StL A	8	19	.296	31	27	18-1	1	207.2	224	120	7	7	44	52	3.29	102	.262	.304	73-0-4	.164	-3*	94	-2	—	-0.8
1912	StL A	9	17	.346	32	27	19	0	235.1	248	117	5	3	52	67	3.10	107	.276	.318	82-1-1	.183	0	83	4	—	0.2
Total	16	245	254	.491	578	516	422-46	15	4389	4319	1991	110	120	1021	1621	2.97	106	.258	.305	1610-8-50	.192	-1	94	109	—	8.0

POWELL, JACK Reginald Bertrand; B8.17.1891 Holcomb MO; D3.12.1930 Memphis TN; TR/6´2˝/?; d6.14

YEAR	TM LG	W	L	PCT	G	GS	CG-SHO	SV-BS	IP	H	R	HR	HB	BB-IB	SO	ERA	AERA	OAV	OOB	AB-HR-SH	AVG	PB	SUP	APR	DL	PW
1913	StL A	0	0	ø	2	0	0	0	2	1	3	0	0	2	0	0.00	ø	.143	.333	0	ø	0	—	0	—	0.0

YEAR	TM LG	W	L	PCT	G	GS	CG-SHO	SV-BS	IP	H	R	HR	HB	BB-IB	SO	ERA	AERA	OAV	OOB	AB-HR-SH	AVG	PB	SUP	APR	DL	PW
Powell, Ross	Ross John; B1.24.1968 Grand Rapids MI; BL/TL/6´0˝/180; [CinN89 3/80]; d9.5; Col Michigan																									
1993	Cin N	0	3	.000	9	1	0	0-0	16.1	13	8	1	0	6-0	17	4.41	91	.224	.297	1	.000	-0	45	0	0	-0.1
1994	Hou N	0	0	ø	12	0	0	0-0	7.1	6	1	0	1	5-0	5	1.23	322	.240	.387	0	ø	0	—	2	0	0.1
1995	Hou N	0	0	ø	15	0	0	0-0	9	16	12	1	0	11-4	8	11.00	35	.381	.500	0	ø	0	—	-8	0	-0.4
	Pit N	0	2	.000	12	3	0	0-0	20.2	20	14	5	2	10-0	12	5.23	83	.253	.352	3-0-1	.000	-0	131	-2	0	-0.2
	Year	0	2	.000	27	3	0	0-0	29.2	36	26	6	2	21-4	20	6.98	60	.298	.407	3-0-1	.000	-0	136	-9	0	-0.6
Total	3	0	5	.000	48	4	0	0-0	53.1	55	35	7	3	32-4	42	5.40	76	.270	.375	4-0-1	.000	-0	115	-8	0	-0.6
Powell, Brian	William Brian; B10.10.1973 Bainbridge GA; BR/TR/6´2˝/(200–205); [DetA95 2/41]; d6.27; Col Georgia																									
1998	Det A	3	8	.273	18	16	0	0-0	83.2	101	67	17	2	36-2	46	6.35	75	.294	.364	1	.000	-0	79	-16	0	-1.7
2000	Hou N	2	1	.667	9	5	0	0-0	31.1	34	21	8	1	13-0	14	5.74	85	.279	.348	9	.222	1	142	-2	0	-0.2
2001	Hou N	0	1	.000	1	1	0	0-0	3	5	6	1	0	3-0	3	18.00	26	.357	.471	1	.000	-0	101	-4	0	-0.6
2002	Det A	1	5	.167	13	9	0	0-0	57.2	64	34	11	1	21-0	30	4.84	90	.278	.339	0	ø	0	63	-3	0	-0.3
2003	SF N	0	1	.000	1	1	0	0-0	4.2	8	7	3	0	1-0	3	13.50	32	.381	.409	2	.000	-0	66	-5	0	-0.6
2004	Phi N	1	2	.333	17	2	0	0-0	39.1	39	23	5	1	16-4	24	5.03	88	.275	.341	8-0-1	.125	-0	115	-2	45	-0.2
Total	6	7	18	.280	59	34	0	0-0	219.2	251	158	45	5	90-6	120	5.94	78	.288	.354	21-0-1	.143	-0	88	-32	45	-3.6
Powell, Bill	William Burris "Big Bill"; B5.8.1885 Taylor Co. WV; D9.28.1967 E.Liverpool OH; BR/TR/6´2.5˝/182; d4.16																									
1909	Pit N	0	1	.000	3	1	0	0	7.1	7	6	0	1	6	2	3.68	74	.292	.452	3	.333	0	77	-1	—	-0.2
1910	Pit N	4	6	.400	12	9	4-2	0	75	65	32	0	5	34	23	2.40	129	.242	.338	23-0-1	.261	1	61	4	—	0.6
1912	Chi N	0	0	ø	1	0	0	0	2	2	2	0	0	1	0	9.00	37	.250	.333	0	ø	0	—	-1	—	0.0
1913	Cin N	0	1	.000	1	1	0	0	0.1	2	2	0	0	2	0	54.00	6	1.000	1.000	0	ø	0	116	-2	—	-0.3
Total	4	4	8	.333	17	11	4-2	0	84.2	76	42	0	6	43	25	2.87	107	.251	.355	26-0-1	.269	1	68	0	—	0.1
Power, Ted	Ted Henry; B1.31.1955 Guthrie OK; BR/TR/6´4˝/(215–225); [LAN76 5/115]; d9.9; Col Kansas St.; [DL 1994 Sea A 131]																									
1981	LA N	1	3	.250	5	2	0	0-0	14.1	16	6	0	1	7-2	7	3.14	105	.286	.364	3	.000	-0	13	0	0	-0.1
1982	LA N	1	1	.500	12	4	0	0-0	33.2	38	27	4	0	23-1	15	6.68	52	.288	.391	6-0-1	.000	-1	127	-12	0	-0.7
1983	Cin N	5	6	.455	49	6	1	2-0	111	120	62	10	1	49-3	57	4.54	84	.286	.357	16-0-3	.000	-1	77	-8	0	-1.1
1984	Cin N	9	7	.563	**78**	0	0	11-4	108.2	93	37	4	0	46-8	81	2.82	135	.237	.311	5-0-1	.000	-0	—	11	0	1.8
1985	Cin N	8	6	.571	64	0	0	27-9	80	65	27	2	1	45-8	42	2.70	140	.227	.330	0	ø	0	—	9	0	1.9
1986	Cin N	10	6	.625	56	10	0	1-1	129	115	59	13	1	52-10	95	3.70	104	.245	.318	24-0-3	.125	0	137	2	0	0.3
1987	Cin N	10	13	.435	34	34	2-1	0-0	204	213	115	28	3	71-7	133	4.50	94	.267	.327	59-1-9	.119	0*	96	-7	0	-0.9
1988	KC A	5	6	.455	22	12	2-2	0-0	80.1	98	54	7	3	30-3	44	5.94	68	.305	.366	0	ø	0	121	-15	16	-1.8
	Det A	1	1	.500	4	2	0	0-0	18.2	23	13	1	0	8-4	13	5.79	66	.307	.373	0	ø	0	59	-4	0	-0.4
	Year	6	7	.462	26	14	2-2	0-0	99	121	67	8	3	38-7	57	5.91	67	.306	.367	0	ø	0	113	-19	0	-2.2
1989	StL N	7	7	.500	23	15	0	0-0	97	96	47	7	1	21-3	43	3.71	99	.255	.294	33-0-3	.091	-2	100	-2	33	-0.5
1990	†Pit N	1	3	.250	40	0	0	7-0	51.2	50	23	5	0	17-6	42	3.66	100	.255	.312	8	.125	0	—	0	54	0.0
1991	Cin N	5	3	.625	68	0	0	3-1	87	87	37	6	2	31-5	51	3.62	105	.265	.329	3	.000	-0	—	3	0	0.2
1992	Cle A	3	3	.500	64	0	0	6-5	99.1	88	33	7	4	35-9	51	2.54	155	.248	.316	0	ø	0	—	15	15	1.0
1993	Cle A	0	2	.000	20	0	0	0-1	20	30	17	2	0	8-3	11	7.20	61	.333	.384	0	ø	0	—	-6	55	-0.5
	Sea A	2	2	.500	25	0	0	13-2	25.1	27	11	1	0	9-1	16	3.91	114	.287	.346	0	ø	0	—	2	0	0.4
	Year	2	4	.333	45	0	0	13-3	45.1	57	28	3	0	17-4	27	5.36	83	.310	.365	0	ø	0	—	-3	0	-0.1
Total	13	68	69	.496	564	85	5-3	70-23	1160	1159	568	97	17	452-73	701	4.00	98	.264	.331	157-1-20	.089	-4	104	-12	304	-0.4
Powers, Jim	James T.; B1868 New York NY; 5´10˝/150; d4.18																									
1890	Bro AA	1	2	.333	4	2	2	0	30	38	29	1	1	16	3	5.70	68	.299	.382	13	.154	-0	43	-6	—	-0.5
Powers, Ike	John Lloyd; B3.13.1906 Hancock MD; D12.22.1968 Hancock MD; BR/TR/6´0.5˝/188; d7.26																									
1927	Phi A	1	1	.500	11	1	0	0	26	26	16	1	0	7	3	4.50	95	.271	.320	5	.400	1	98	-1	—	0.0
1928	Phi A	1	0	1.000	9	0	0	2	12	8	6	1	1	10	4	4.50	89	.222	.404	0	ø	0	—	0	—	0.0
Total	2	2	1	.667	20	1	0	2	38	34	22	2	1	17	7	4.50	93	.258	.347	5	.400	1	98	-1	—	0.0
Prall, Willie	Wilfred Anthony; B4.20.1950 Hackensack NJ; BL/TL/6´3˝/195; [SFN71 3/64]; d9.3																									
1975	Chi N	0	2	.000	3	3	0	0-0	14.2	21	15	1	0	8-0	7	8.59	45	.339	.408	4-0-2	.000	-0	98	-7	0	-0.8
Pratt, Al	Albert George "Uncle Al"; B11.19.1848 Allegheny (now part of Pittsburgh) PA; D11.21.1937 Pittsburgh PA; TR/5´7˝/140; d5.4; M2/U2																									
1871	Cle NA	10	17	.370	28	28	22	0	224.2	296	288	9	—	47	**34**	3.77	110	.277	.307	130	.262	2*	83	7	—	0.8
1872	Cle NA	2	9	.182	15	12	8	0	105.2	150	133	3	—	14	7	5.79	62	.286	.305	65	.277	0*	72	-26	—	-1.6
Total	2NA	12	26	.316	43	40	30	0	330.1	446	421	12	—	61	41	4.41	90	.280	.306	195	.267	2	80	-19	—	-0.8
Pratt, Andy	Andrew Elias; B8.27.1979 Mesa AZ; BL/TL/5´11˝/(160–185); [TexA98 9/263]; d9.28																									
2002	Atl N	0	0	ø	1	0	0	0-0	1.1	1	1	0	0	4-0	1	6.75	60	.200	.556	0	ø	0	—	0	0	0.0
2004	Chi N	0	1	.000	4	0	0	0-0	1.2	0	4	0	1	7-1	1	21.60	21	.000	.615	0	ø	0	—	-3	0	-0.5
Total	2	0	1	.000	5	0	0	0-0	3	1	5	0	1	11-1	2	15.00	28	.100	.591	0	ø	0	—	-3	0	-0.5
Pregenzer, John	John Arthur; B8.2.1932 Burlington WI; BR/TR/6´5˝/220; d4.20; Col Illinois Wesleyan																									
1963	SF N	0	0	ø	6	0	0	1	9.1	8	5	0	1	8-2	5	4.82	66	.242	.405	0	ø	0	—	-1	0	-0.1
1964	SF N	2	0	1.000	13	0	0	0	18.1	21	15	1	1	11-3	8	4.91	73	.296	.398	0	ø	0	—	-4	0	-0.5
Total	2	2	0	1.000	19	0	0	1	27.2	29	20	1	2	19-5	13	4.88	70	.279	.400	0	ø	0	—	-5	0	-0.6
Prendergast, Jim	James Bartholomew; B8.23.1917 Brooklyn NY; D8.23.1994 Amherst NY; BL/TL/6´1˝/208; d4.25																									
1948	Bos N	1	1	.500	10	2	0	1	16.2	30	20	1	0	5	3	10.26	37	.380	.417	5	.000	-1	116	-12	0	-1.4
Prendergast, Mike	Michael Thomas; B12.15.1888 Arlington IL; D11.18.1967 Omaha NE; BR/TR/5´9.5˝/165; d4.26																									
1914	Chi F	5	9	.357	30	19	7-1	0	136	131	53	5	3	40	71	2.38	111	.255	.313	37-0-4	.108	-2	73	3	—	-0.1
1915	Chi F	14	12	.538	42	30	16-3	0	253.2	220	93	6	4	67	95	2.48	101	.240	.295	80-0-4	.075	-8	88	0	—	-1.0
1916	Chi N	6	11	.353	35	10	4-2	2	152	127	53	5	1	23	56	2.31	126	.228	.260	46-0-1	.152	-2	62	8	—	0.7
1917	Chi N	3	6	.333	35	8	1	1	99.1	112	42	6	0	21	43	3.35	86	.302	.339	28	.250	1	114	-2	—	0.0
1918	Phi N	13	14	.481	33	30	20	1	252.1	257	102	6	1	46	41	2.89	104	.273	.308	85-0-2	.082	-8	80	3	—	-0.6
1919	Phi N	0	1	.000	5	1	0	0	15	20	15	0	1	10	5	8.40	38	.351	.456	3	.333	0	25	-7	—	-0.4
Total	6	41	53	.436	180	98	48-6	4	908.1	867	358	28	10	207	311	2.74	102	.258	.304	279-0-11	.115	-18	81	5	—	-1.4
Prentiss, George	George Pepper (aka George Pepper Wilson in 1901); B6.10.1876 Wilmington DE; D9.8.1902 Wilmington DE; BB/TR/5´11˝/175; d9.23																									
1901	Bos A	1	0	1.000	2	1	1	0	10	7	4	0	0	6	0	1.80	196	.194	.310	3	.333	1	134	2	—	0.2
1902	Bos A	2	2	.500	7	4	3	0	41	55	31	0	0	10	9	5.27	68	.322	.359	16	.313	1	136	-6	—	-0.5
	Bal A	0	1	.000	2	2	0	0	6.2	14	10	1	0	5	1	10.80	35	.424	.500	4	.000	-1	124	-4	—	-0.6
	Year	2	3	.400	9	6	3	0	47.2	69	41	1	0	15	10	6.04	60	.338	.384	20	.250	-0	133	-11	—	-1.1
Total	2	3	3	.500	11	7	4	0	57.2	76	45	1	0	21	10	5.31	68	.317	.372	23	.261	1	133	-8	—	-0.9
Presko, Joe	Joseph Edward "Baby Joe"; B10.7.1928 Kansas City MO; BR/TR/6´0˝/(165–170); d5.3																									
1951	StL N	7	4	.636	15	12	5	2	88.2	86	36	9	2	20	38	3.45	115	.251	.296	37	.162	-1	113	6	0	0.5
1952	StL N	7	10	.412	28	18	5-1	0	146.2	140	74	16	1	57	63	4.05	92	.247	.317	43-0-3	.093	-2	99	-5	0	-0.8
1953	StL N	6	13	.316	34	25	4	1	161.2	165	95	19	5	65	56	5.01	85	.261	.335	59-0-4	.220	1*	106	-12	0	-1.1
1954	StL N	4	9	.308	37	6	1-1	0	71.2	97	56	14	5	41	36	6.91	60	.327	.416	16	.250	0*	101	-19	0	-3.0
1957	Det A	1	1	.500	7	0	0	0	11	10	3	0	1	4-1	3	1.64	236	.278	.357	1	.000	-0	—	2	0	0.4
1958	Det A	0	0	ø	7	0	0	2	10.2	13	4	0	0	1-0	6	3.38	120	.317	.326	0	ø	0	—	1	0	0.1
Total	6	25	37	.403	128	61	15-2	5	490.1	511	268	58	14	188-1	202	4.61	87	.267	.336	156-0-7	.173	-1	105	-27	0	-3.9
Pressnell, Tot	Forest Charles; B8.8.1906 Findlay OH; D1.6.2001 Findlay OH; BR/TR/5´10˝/175; d4.21																									
1938	Bro N	11	14	.440	43	19	6-1	3	192	209	86	11	8	56	57	3.56	110	.276	.332	63-0-1	.143	-1	91	8	—	0.9
1939	Bro N	9	7	.563	31	18	10-2	2	156.2	171	76	8	1	33	43	4.02	100	.273	.311	51-0-3	.196	-1	111	1	—	0.0
1940	Bro N	6	5	.545	24	4	1-1	2	68.1	58	31	4	2	17	21	3.69	108	.221	.274	17-0-4	.000	-2	71	2	—	0.1
1941	Chi N	5	3	.625	29	1	0	1	70	69	26	2	4	23	27	3.09	114	.253	.320	15-0-1	.200	0	73	**5**	0	0.5
1942	Chi N	1	1	.500	27	0	0	4	39.1	40	28	5	5	5	9	5.49	58	.260	.305	3	.667	1	—	-10	0	-0.6
Total	5	32	30	.516	154	42	17-4	12	526.1	547	247	30	20	134	157	3.80	101	.264	.315	149-0-9	.161	-3	100	6	0	0.9

YEAR	TM LG	W	L	PCT	G	GS	CG-SHO	SV-BS	IP	H	R	HR	HB	BB-IB	SO	ERA	AERA	OAV	OOB	AB-HR-SH	AVG	PB	SUP	APR	DL	PW
Price, Joe	Joseph Walter; B11.29.1956 Inglewood CA; BR/TL/6´4˝/(210–220); [CinN77 4/102]; d6.14; Col Oklahoma																									
1980	Cin N	7	3	.700	24	13	2	0-0	111.1	95	45	10	1	37-0	44	3.56	99	.236	.302	39-0-3	.128	-2	107	1	0	-0.2
1981	Cin N	6	1	.857	41	0	0	4-2	53.2	42	19	3	0	18-2	41	2.52	139	.222	.286	3	.000	-0	—	5	0	0.7
1982	Cin N	3	4	.429	59	1	0	3-5	72.2	73	26	7	4	32-8	71	2.85	129	.263	.346	3-0-2	.333	0	96	6	0	0.6
1983	Cin N	10	6	.625	21	21	5	0-0	144	118	46	12	0	46-2	83	2.88	133	.225	.285	41-0-3	.098	-1	66	17	25	1.7
1984	Cin N	7	13	.350	30	30	3-1	0-0	171.2	176	91	19	2	61-5	129	4.19	90	.261	.322	48-0-9	.146	-1	92	-8	0	-1.1
1985	Cin N	2	2	.500	26	8	0	1-0	64.2	59	35	10	0	23-7	52	3.90	97	.242	.301	14-0-1	.000	-1	105	-2	31	-0.3
1986	Cin N	1	2	.333	25	2	0	0-1	41.2	49	30	5	0	22-2	30	5.40	71	.293	.366	7	.143	0	127	-8	46	-0.5
1987	†SF N	2	2	.500	20	0	0	1-0	35	19	10	5	1	13-2	42	2.57	150	.154	.241	6	.167	-0	—	6	0	0.6
1988	SF N	1	6	.143	38	3	0	4-1	61.2	59	33	5	1	27-6	49	3.94	83	.249	.328	8-0-2	.000	-0	127	-6	41	-0.8
1989	SF N	1	1	.500	7	1	0	0-1	14	16	9	3	0	4-2	10	5.79	58	.314	.357	2	.000	0	157	-3	0	-0.4
	Bos A	2	5	.286	31	5	0	0-1	70.1	71	35	8	0	30-3	52	4.35	95	.262	.332	0	ø	0	79	0	0	-0.1
1990	Bal A	3	4	.429	50	0	0	0-2	65.1	62	29	8	0	24-2	54	3.58	107	.253	.319	0	ø	0	—	1	18	0.1
Total	11	45	49	.479	372	84	10-1	13-13	906	839	408	95	9	337-41	657	3.65	102	.246	.313	171-0-20	.111	-5	92	9	161	0.3
Price, Bill	William; B Philadelphia PA; d4.27																									
1890	Phi AA	1	0	1.000	1	1	1	0	9	6	3	0	1	7	1	2.00	194	.182	.341	4	.250	-0	87	2	—	0.2
Priddy, Bob	Robert Simpson; B12.10.1939 Pittsburgh PA; BR/TR/6´1˝/(200–205); d9.20																									
1962	Pit N	1	0	1.000	2	0	0	0	3	4	1	0	0	1-0	1	3.00	131	.308	.357	0	ø	0	—	0	0	0.1
1964	Pit N	1	2	.333	19	0	0	1	34.1	35	16	2	1	15-1	23	3.93	89	.282	.354	3	.000	0	—	-1	0	-0.2
1965	SF N	1	0	1.000	8	0	0	0	10.1	6	2	1	0	2-0	7	1.74	207	.176	.216	1	.000	-0*	—	2	0	0.2
1966	SF N	6	3	.667	38	3	0	1	91	88	45	8	3	28-3	51	3.96	93	.259	.317	17	.176	0*	40	-2	0	-0.3
1967	Was A	3	7	.300	46	8	1	4	110	98	48	12	0	33-5	57	3.44	92	.240	.295	22-0-2	.182	1*	62	-3	0	-0.1
1968	Chi A	3	11	.214	35	18	2	0	114	106	50	14	4	41-1	66	3.63	83	.244	.314	24-1-3	.042	-1*	96	-6	0	-0.9
1969	Chi A	0	0	ø	4	0	0	0-0	8	10	5	2	0	2-0	5	4.50	86	.303	.343	0	ø	0	—	-1	0	0.0
	Cal A	0	1	.000	15	0	0	0-0	26.1	24	14	4	0	7-1	15	4.78	73	.242	.292	2-0-1	.000	0	—	-3	0	-0.1
	Year	0	1	.000	19	0	0	0-0	34.1	34	19	6	0	9-1	20	4.72	76	.258	.305	2-0-1	.000	0	—	-4	0	-0.1
	Atl N	0	0	ø	1	0	0	0-0	2	1	0	0	0	1-0	1	0.00	ø	.143	.250	0	ø	0	—	1	0	0.0
1970	Atl N	5	5	.500	41	0	0	8-2	73	75	46	9	3	24-2	32	5.42	79	.269	.331	15-0-2	.200	0	—	-7	0	-1.0
1971	Atl N	4	9	.308	40	0	0	4-3	64	71	36	8	1	44-5	36	4.22	88	.289	.396	11	.182	0	—	-4	0	-0.8
Total	9	24	38	.387	249	29	3	18-5	536	518	263	60	12	198-18	294	4.00	88	.257	.324	95-1-8	.137	1	72	-24	0	-3.1
Priest, Eddie	Eddie Lee; B4.8.1974 Boaz AL; BR/TL/6´1˝/200; [CinN94 9/240]; d5.27; Col Southern Union St. (AL) CC																									
1998	Cin N	0	1	.000	2	2	0	0-0	6	12	8	2	0	1-0	1	10.50	41	.444	.448	2	.000	-0	107	-4	0	-0.6
Prieto, Ariel	Ariel; B10.22.1969 Havana, Cuba; BR/TR/6´3˝/(225–247); [OakA95 1/5]; d7.2; [DL 1999 Oak A 182]																									
1995	Oak A	2	6	.250	14	9	1	0-0	58	57	35	4	5	32-1	37	4.97	91	.264	.369	0	ø	0	78	-3	15	-0.4
1996	Oak A	6	7	.462	21	21	2	0-0	125.2	130	66	9	7	54-2	75	4.15	120	.273	.352	0	ø	0	89	10	70	0.8
1997	Oak A	6	8	.429	22	22	0	0-0	125	155	84	16	5	70-3	90	5.04	91	.306	.393	0	ø	0	101	-10	72	-0.9
1998	Oak A	0	1	.000	2	2	0	0-0	8.1	17	11	2	1	5-1	8	11.88	39	.415	.489	0	ø	0	90	-6	0	-0.5
2000	Oak A	1	2	.333	8	6	0	0-0	31.2	42	21	3	1	13-0	19	5.12	95	.321	.384	2	.000	-0	122	-1	0	-0.1
2001	TB A	0	0	ø	3	0	0	0-0	3.2	6	1	0	1	2-0	2	2.45	184	.375	.474	0	ø	0	—	1	150	0.0
Total	6	15	24	.385	70	60	3	0-0	352.1	407	218	34	20	176-7	231	4.85	98	.294	.378	2	.000	-0	95	-9	489	-1.1
Prim, Ray	Raymond Lee "Pop"; B12.30.1906 Salitpa AL; D4.29.1995 Monte Rio CA; BR/TL/6´0˝/178; d9.24; Col Auburn																									
1933	Was A	0	1	.000	2	1	0	0	14.1	13	6	0	0	2	6	3.14	133	.232	.259	5-0-1	.000	-1*	0	2	—	0.1
1934	Was A	0	2	.000	8	1	0	0	14.2	19	11	1	0	8	3	6.75	64	.339	.422	3	.000	-0	60	-4	—	-0.4
1935	Phi N	3	4	.429	29	6	1	0	73.1	110	54	4	0	15	27	5.77	79	.340	.369	24	.083	-2	69	-8	—	-0.9
1943	Chi N	4	3	.571	29	5	0	1	60	67	24	2	0	14	27	2.55	131	.282	.321	12-0-2	.167	-0	122	4	0	0.5
1945	†Chi N	13	8	.619	34	19	9-2	2	165.1	142	58	9	1	23	88	2.40	**153**	**.228**	**.256**	51-0-5	.255	3	99	21	0	2.9
1946	Chi N	2	3	.400	14	2	0	1	23.1	28	17	5	0	10	10	5.79	57	.289	.355	5	.200	0	90	-6	60	-1.2
Total	6	22	21	.512	116	34	10-2	4	351	379	170	21	1	72	161	3.56	107	.272	.308	100-0-8	.180	-0	90	9	60	1.0
Prince, Don	Donald Mark; B4.5.1938 Clarkton NC; BR/TR/6´4˝/215; d9.21; Col Campbell																									
1962	Chi N	0	0	ø	1	0	0	0	1	0	0	0	1	1-0	0	0.00	ø	.000	.500	0	ø	0	—	0	0	0.0
Prinz, Bret	Bret Randolph; B6.15.1977 Chicago Heights IL; BR/TR/6´3˝/(185–215); [AriN98 18/553]; d4.22; Col Phoenix (AZ) JC																									
2001	Ari N	4	1	.800	46	0	0	9-3	41	33	13	4	1	19-1	27	2.63	176	.220	.310	0	ø	0	—	9	0	1.3
2002	Ari N	0	2	.000	20	0	0	0-2	13.1	23	14	1	1	10-1	10	9.45	47	.404	.493	0	ø	0	—	-6	0	-0.8
2003	Ari N	0	0	ø	1	0	0	0-0	1	1	0	0	0	1-1	1	0.00	ø	.250	.400	0	ø	0	—	0	114	0.0
	NY A	0	0	ø	2	0	0	0-0	2	6	4	1	0	3-1	2	18.00	24	.500	.600	0	ø	0	—	-3	0	-0.1
2004	NY A	1	0	1.000	26	0	0	0-0	28.1	28	17	5	1	14-0	22	5.08	90	.259	.347	0	ø	0	—	-1	0	-0.1
2005	LA A	0	1	.000	3	0	0	0-0	3	4	1	1	0	1-0	1	3.00	142	.308	.357	0	ø	0	—	0	143	0.1
Total	5	5	4	.556	98	0	0	9-5	88.2	95	49	12	3	48-4	63	4.77	96	.276	.367	0	ø	0	—	-1	257	0.4
Prior, Mark	Mark William; B9.7.1980 San Diego CA; BR/TR/6´5˝/(225–230); [ChiN01 1/2]; d5.22; Col USC																									
2002	Chi N	6	6	.500	19	19	1	0-0	116.2	98	45	14	7	38-0	147	3.32	122	.226	.296	35-0-2	.171	2	99	11	15	1.1
2003	†Chi N☆	18	6	.750	30	30	3-1	0-0	211.1	183	67	15	9	50-4	245	2.43	179	.231	.283	72-1-7	.250	5*	101	43	23	**5.1**
2004	Chi N	6	4	.600	21	21	0	0-0	118.2	112	53	14	3	48-2	139	4.02	110	.251	.325	36-0-6	.139	-1	106	7	61	0.5
2005	Chi N	11	7	.611	27	27	1	0-0	166.2	143	73	25	4	59-2	188	3.67	119	.227	.296	48-0-6	.229	2	98	12	38	1.3
2006	Chi N	1	6	.143	9	9	0	0-0	43.2	46	39	9	8	28-2	38	7.21	64	.269	.392	13-0-1	.077	-1	72	-13	144	-1.7
Total	5	42	29	.592	106	106	5-1	0-0	657	582	277	77	31	223-10	757	3.51	123	.235	.305	204-1-22	.201	7	98	60	281	6.3
Proctor, Jim	James Arthur; B9.9.1935 Brandywine MD; BR/TR/6´0˝/165; d9.14																									
1959	Det A	0	1	.000	2	1	0	0	2.2	8	5	0	0	3-0	0	16.88	24	.533	.611	0	ø	0	109	-3	0	-0.6
Proctor, Red	Noah Richard; B10.27.1900 Williamsburg VA; D12.17.1954 Richmond VA; BR/TR/6´1˝/165; d8.6																									
1923	Chi A	0	0	ø	2	0	0	0	4	11	8	0	0	2	0	13.50	29	.550	.591	0	ø	0	—	-5	—	-0.2
Proctor, Scott	Scott Christopher; B1.2.1977 Stuart FL; BR/TR/6´1˝/200; [LAN98 5/156]; d4.20; Col Florida St.																									
2004	NY A	2	1	.667	26	0	0	0-0	25	29	18	5	0	14-0	21	5.40	85	.284	.364	0	ø	0	—	-3	0	-0.3
2005	†NY A	1	0	1.000	29	1	0	0-0	44.2	46	32	10	2	17-4	36	6.04	71	.257	.327	0	ø	0	194	-8	0	-0.4
2006	†NY A	6	4	.600	**83**	0	0	1-7	102.1	89	41	12	2	33-6	89	3.52	129	.232	.292	0	ø	0	—	13	0	1.1
Total	3	9	5	.643	138	1	0	1-7	172	164	91	27	4	64-10	146	4.45	101	.247	.313	0	ø	0	194	2	0	0.4
Proeser, George	George "Yatz"; B5.30.1864 Cincinnati OH; D10.13.1941 New Burlington OH; BL/TL/5´10˝/190; d9.15; ▲																									
1888	Cle AA	3	4	.429	7	7	7-1	0	59	53	39	4	7	30	20	3.81	81	.231	.338	23	.304	2	83	-3	—	-0.2
Prokopec, Luke	Kenneth Luke; B2.23.1978 Blackwood, South Australia, Australia; BL/TR/5´11˝/166; d9.4; [DL 2003 Cin N 183]																									
2000	LA N	1	1	.500	5	3	0	0-0	21	19	10	2	2	9-0	12	3.00	148	.253	.345	5-0-1	.000	-1*	110	2	0	0.1
2001	LA N	8	7	.533	29	22	0	0-0	138.1	146	80	27	4	40-1	91	4.88	84	.268	.321	36-0-7	.194	1*	123	-12	16	-1.1
2002	Tor A	2	9	.182	22	12	0	0-0	71.2	90	57	19	7	25-2	41	6.78	68	.302	.364	0	ø	0	65	-16	81	-2.1
Total	3	11	17	.393	56	37	0	0-0	231	255	147	48	13	74-3	144	5.30	81	.278	.337	41-0-8	.171	0	102	-26	280	-3.1
Proly, Mike	Michael James; B12.15.1950 Jamaica NY; BR/TR/6´0˝/(184–185); [StLN72 9/213]; d4.10; Col St. Johns																									
1976	StL N	1	0	1.000	14	0	0	0-1	17	21	9	0	0	6-1	4	3.71	97	.328	.370	0-0-1	ø	0	—	-1	0	0.0
1978	Chi A	5	2	.714	14	6	2	1-0	65.2	63	24	4	0	12-0	19	2.74	139	.250	.282	0	ø	0	122	7	33	0.7
1979	Chi A	3	8	.273	38	6	0	9-2	88.1	89	43	6	1	40-7	32	3.87	110	.260	.337	0	ø	0	89	4	44	0.6
1980	Chi A	5	10	.333	62	3	0	8-6	146.2	136	67	7	3	58-9	56	3.07	132	.253	.323	0	ø	0	88	12	0	1.3
1981	Phi N	2	1	.667	35	2	0	2-0	63	66	29	6	1	19-5	19	3.86	95	.282	.335	7	.000	-1	85	-1	0	-0.1
1982	Chi N	5	3	.625	44	1	0	1-5	82	77	22	5	2	22-5	24	2.30	164	.257	.310	14-0-5	.286	1	93	14	0	1.4
1983	Chi N	1	5	.167	60	0	0	1-2	83	79	35	5	1	38-13	31	3.58	107	.259	.339	11-0-2	.091	-0	—	3	19	0.2
Total	7	22	29	.431	267	18	2	22-16	545.2	531	229	33	8	195-40	185	3.23	121	.261	.324	32-0-8	.156	-0	100	38	96	4.1

YEAR	TM LG	W	L	PCT	G	GS	CG-SHO	SV-BS	IP	H	R	HR	HB	BB-IB	SO	ERA	AERA	OAV	OOB	AB-HR-SH	AVG	PB	SUP	APR	DL	PW
Prough, Bill	Herschel Clinton "Clint"; B11.28.1887 Markle IN; D12.29.1936 Richmond IN; BR/TR/6´3˝/185; d4.27																									
1912	Cin N	0	0	ø	1	0	0	0	3	7	5	0	0	1	1	6.00	56	.538	.571	1	.000	-0	—	-2	—	-0.1
Prudhomme, Augie	John Olgus; B11.20.1902 Frierson LA; D10.4.1992 Shreveport LA; BR/TR/6´2˝/186; d4.19																									
1929	Det A	1	6	.143	34	6	2	1	94	119	78	7	2	53	26	6.22	69	.322	.410	21	.238	1	157	-20	—	-1.1
Pruett, Hub	Hubert Shelby "Shucks"; B9.1.1900 Malden MO; D1.28.1982 Ladue MO; BL/TL/5´10.5˝/165; d4.26; Col Missouri																									
1922	StL A	7	7	.500	39	8	4	7	119.2	99	48	2	5	59	70	2.33	178	.235	.336	34-0-3	.147	-1	82	19	—	2.3
1923	StL A	4	7	.364	32	8	3	2	104.1	109	57	3	3	64	59	4.31	97	.279	.385	23-0-4	.130	-1	79	0	—	0.0
1924	StL A	3	4	.429	33	1	0	0	65	64	42	1	4	42	27	4.57	99	.270	.389	15-0-1	.200	-1	37	-2	—	-0.2
1927	Phi N	7	17	.292	31	28	12-1	1	186	238	147	6	12	89	90	6.05	68	.314	.395	60-0-5	.217	1	86	-41	—	-4.1
1928	Phi N	2	4	.333	13	9	4	0	71.1	78	49	2	3	49	35	4.54	94	.291	.406	24-0-2	.208	-0	86	-5	—	-0.4
1930	NY N	5	4	.556	45	8	1	3	135.2	152	83	11	4	63	49	4.78	99	.287	.367	37-0-2	.135	-1	94	0	—	-0.1
1932	Bos N	1	5	.167	18	7	4	0	63	76	42	3	6	30	27	5.14	73	.308	.396	19	.105	-1	48	-10	—	-0.8
Total	7	29	48	.377	211	69	28-1	13	745	816	468	28	37	396	357	4.63	92	.286	.380	212-0-17	.170	-3	80	-39	—	-3.3
Pruiett, Tex	Charles Le Roy; B4.10.1883 Osgood IN; D3.6.1953 Ventura CA; BL/TR/5´8˝/176; d4.26																									
1907	Bos A	3	11	.214	35	17	6-2	3	173.2	166	77	1	8	59	54	3.11	83	.254	.323	51-0-1	.157	-1	59	-7	—	-0.6
1908	Bos A	1	7	.125	13	6	1-1	2	58.2	55	26	1	2	21	28	1.99	123	.275	.350	16	.063	-2	32	1	—	-0.1
Total	2	4	18	.182	48	23	7-3	5	232.1	221	103	2	10	80	82	2.83	90	.259	.329	67-0-1	.134	-2	52	-6	—	-0.7
Puckett, Troy	Troy Levi; B12.10.1889 Winchester IN; D4.13.1971 Winchester IN; BL/TR/6´2˝/186; d10.4; Col Wabash																									
1911	Phi N	0	0	ø	1	0	0	0	2	4	3	0	1	2	1	13.50	26	.444	.583	0	ø	0	—	-2	—	-0.1
Puente, Miguel	Miguel Antonio (Aguilar); B5.8.1948 San Luis Potosi, San Luis Potosi, Mexico; BR/TR/6´0˝/160; d5.3																									
1970	SF N	1	3	.250	6	4	1	0-0	18.2	25	18	5	0	11-1	14	8.20	49	.325	.409	7-0-1	.000	-1	130	-8	0	-1.5
Puffer, Brandon	Brandon Duane; B10.5.1975 Downey CA; BR/TR/6´3˝/(185–190); [MinA94 27/743]; d4.17																									
2002	Hou N	3	3	.500	55	0	0	0-0	69	67	37	3	5	38-8	48	4.43	98	.258	.361	6-0-1	.000	-0	—	-1	0	-0.1
2003	Hou N	0	0	ø	13	0	0	0-1	21	24	13	2	1	16-3	10	5.14	86	.300	.423	3	.000	-0	—	-2	0	-0.1
2004	SD N	0	1	.000	14	0	0	0-0	18	24	13	3	1	11-1	12	5.50	72	.320	.414	0	ø	0	—	-4	0	-0.2
2005	SF N	0	0	ø	3	0	0	0-0	7	9	8	2	0	2-0	1	10.29	41	.310	.355	0	ø	0	—	-4	0	-0.2
Total	4	3	4	.429	85	0	0	0-1	115	124	71	10	7	67-12	71	5.09	84	.279	.381	9-0-1	.000	-1	—	-11	0	-0.6
Pugh, Tim	Timothy Dean; B1.26.1967 S.Lake Tahoe CA; BR/TR/6´6˝/(225–230); [CinN89 6/160]; d9.1; Col Oklahoma St.																									
1992	Cin N	4	2	.667	7	7	0	0-0	45.1	47	15	2	1	13-3	18	2.58	140	.276	.330	13-0-1	.077	-0	75	5	0	0.5
1993	Cin N	10	15	.400	31	27	3-1	0-0	164.1	200	102	19	7	59-1	94	5.26	77	.303	.363	54-0-7	.222	2	99	-21	0	-2.6
1994	Cin N	3	3	.500	10	9	1	0-0	47.2	60	37	5	3	26-0	24	6.04	69	.314	.396	14-0-1	.357	2	111	-10	0	-0.9
1995	Cin N	6	5	.545	28	12	0	0-0	98.1	100	46	13	1	32-2	38	3.84	109	.266	.324	28-0-4	.143	0*	115	3	0	0.3
1996	Cin N	1	0	1.000	9	0	0	0-0	15.1	20	18	3	1	11-2	9	10.57	41	.317	.421	0-0-1	ø	0	—	-10	0	-0.5
	KC A	0	1	.000	19	1	0	0-0	36.1	42	24	9	2	12-1	27	5.45	92	.282	.341	0	ø	0	111	-2	0	-0.1
	Cin N	0	1	.000	1	0	0	0-0	0.1	4	2	0	0	0-0	0	54.00	8	.800	.800	0	ø	0	—	-2	0	-0.3
1997	Det A	1	1	.500	2	2	0	0-0	9	6	5	0	0	5-0	4	5.00	92	.188	.297	0	ø	0	129	0	0	0.0
Total	6	25	28	.472	107	58	4-1	0-0	416.2	479	249	51	15	158-9	214	4.97	83	.291	.355	109-0-14	.202	4	102	-37	0	-3.6
Puleo, Charlie	Charles Michael; B2.7.1955 Glen Ridge NJ; BR/TR/6´3˝/(190–200); d9.16; Col Seton Hall																									
1981	NY N	0	0	ø	4	1	0	0-0	13.1	8	1	0	0	8-2	8	0.00	ø	.182	.308	2	.000	-0	50	5	0	0.2
1982	NY N	9	9	.500	36	24	1-1	1-0	171	179	99	13	2	90-7	98	4.47	82	.275	.362	48-0-6	.125	-1	101	-15	0	-1.5
1983	Cin N	6	12	.333	27	24	0	0-0	143.2	145	86	18	5	91-9	71	4.89	78	.269	.375	50-0-2	.100	-2	91	-16	28	-2.0
1984	Cin N	1	2	.333	5	4	0	0-0	22	27	15	2	0	15-2	6	5.73	66	.297	.393	5-0-2	.200	0	93	-4	0	-0.5
1986	Atl N	1	2	.333	5	3	1	0-0	24.1	13	10	4	1	12-1	18	2.96	134	.160	.274	6-0-1	.333	0	90	2	0	0.3
1987	Atl N	6	8	.429	35	16	1	0-0	123.1	122	63	11	3	40-0	99	4.23	102	.262	.319	28-1-6	.179	1*	78	2	0	0.2
1988	Atl N	5	5	.500	53	3	0	1-1	106.1	101	46	9	3	47-7	70	3.47	106	.251	.330	13-0-4	.231	0	73	2	0	0.2
1989	Atl N	1	1	.500	15	1	0	0-0	29	26	15	2	0	16-1	17	4.66	79	.245	.333	1-0-1	.000	-0	24	-2	13	-0.2
Total	8	29	39	.426	180	76	3-1	2-1	633	621	335	59	14	319-29	387	4.25	90	.261	.348	153-1-22	.144	-1	90	-26	41	-3.3
Pulido, Alfonso	Alfonso (Manzo); B1.23.1957 Tierra Blanca, Veracruz, Mexico; BL/TL/5´11˝/(170–175); d9.5																									
1983	Pit N	0	0	ø	1	1	0	0-0	2	4	3	2	0	1-0	1	9.00	42	.400	.455	0-0-1	ø	0	142	-1	0	-0.1
1984	Pit N	0	0	ø	1	0	0	0-0	2	3	2	0	0	1-0	2	9.00	40	.333	.400	0	ø	0	—	-1	0	-0.1
1986	NY A	1	1	.500	10	3	0	1-0	30.2	38	17	8	0	9-0	13	4.70	88	.306	.351	0	ø	0	124	-2	0	-0.1
Total	3	1	1	.500	12	4	0	1-0	34.2	45	22	10	0	11-0	16	5.19	79	.315	.361	0-0-1	ø	0	127	-4	0	-0.3
Pulido, Carlos	Juan Carlos (Valera); B8.5.1971 Caracas, Distrito Capital, Venez.; BL/TL/6´0˝/(180–205); d4.9																									
1994	Min A	3	7	.300	19	14	0	0-0	84.1	87	57	17	1	40-1	32	5.98	83	.273	.352	0	ø	0	95	-8	0	-0.8
2003	Min A	0	1	.000	7	1	0	0-0	15.2	15	9	0	0	3-0	6	4.02	112	.254	.281	0	ø	0	123	0	0	0.0
2004	Min A	0	0	ø	6	0	0	0-0	11.1	16	13	2	1	4-1	9	8.74	53	.333	.382	0	ø	0	—	-6	0	-0.3
Total	3	3	8	.273	32	15	0	0-0	111.1	118	79	19	2	47-2	47	5.98	81	.277	.346	0	ø	0	98	-14	0	-1.1
Pulsipher, Bill	William Thomas; B10.9.1973 Fort Benning GA; BL/TL/6´3˝/(200–228); [NYN91 2/66]; d6.17; [DL 1997 NY N 32]																									
1995	NY N	5	7	.417	17	17	2	0-0	126.2	122	58	11	4	45-0	81	3.98	101	.255	.324	38-0-4	.105	0	88	3	0	0.3
1998	NY N	0	0	ø	15	1	0	0-1	14.1	23	11	2	0	5-1	13	6.91	60	.371	.418	1	.000	-0*	156	-4	0	-0.2
	Mil N	3	4	.429	11	10	0	0-0	58	63	30	6	1	26-3	38	4.66	93	.289	.361	19-0-1	.158	-0	85	-1	0	-0.2
	Year	3	4	.429	26	11	0	0-1	72.1	86	41	8	1	31-4	51	5.10	84	.307	.373	20-0-1	.150	-1	91	-5	0	-0.4
1999	Mil N	5	6	.455	19	16	0	0-0	87.1	100	65	19	2	36-2	42	5.98	77	.286	.352	21-0-8	.143	-1	110	-14	77	-1.5
2000	NY N	0	2	.000	2	2	0	0-0	6.2	12	9	1	1	6-0	7	12.15	36	.387	.500	2	.000	-0	42	-6	0	-0.9
2001	Bos A	0	0	ø	23	0	0	0-0	22	25	15	3	2	14-0	16	5.32	83	.294	.402	0	ø	0	—	-2	0	-0.1
	Chi A	0	0	ø	14	0	0	0-0	8	11	8	2	1	7-0	4	7.88	59	.314	.432	0	ø	0	—	-3	0	-0.1
	Year	0	0	ø	37	0	0	0-0	30	36	23	5	3	21-0	20	6.00	75	.300	.411	0	ø	0	—	-5	0	-0.2
2005	StL N	0	0	ø	5	0	0	0-0	4	5	3	0	0	2-1	1	6.75	62	.357	.412	0	ø	0	—	-1	24	0.0
Total	6	13	19	.406	106	46	2	0-1	327	361	199	44	11	141-7	202	5.15	83	.284	.357	81-0-13	.123	-1	95	-28	133	-2.7
Pumpelly, Spencer	Spencer Armstrong; B4.11.1893 Owego NY; D12.5.1973 Sayre PA; TR/5´11˝/175; d7.11; Col Yale																									
1925	Was A	0	0	ø	1	0	0	0	1	1	1	1	0	1	0	9.00	47	.333	.500	0	ø	0	—	0	—	0.0
Purcell, Blondie	William Aloysius; B Paterson NJ; BR/TR/5´9.5˝/159; d5.1; M1; ▲																									
1879	Syr N	4	15	.211	22	17	15	0	179.2	245	165	1	—	19	28	3.76	63	.303	.319	277	.260	3*	64	-33	—	-2.5
	Cin N	0	2	.000	2	2	2	0	18	27	15	0	—	2	3	4.00	58	.355	.372	50	.220	-0*	69	-2	—	-0.2
	Year	4	17	.190	24	19	17	0	197.2	272	180	1	—	21	31	3.78	63	.308	.324	327	.254	3	65	-39	—	-2.7
1880	Cin N	3	17	.150	25	21	21	0	196	235	149	1	—	32	47	3.21	77	.271	.297	325-1	.292	4*	56	-11	—	-0.5
1881	Buf N	4	1	.800	9	5	5	0	61.2	62	37	2	—	9	15	2.77	100	.248	.274	113	.292	2*	117	0	—	0.2
1882	Buf N	2	1	.667	6	3	2	0	31	44	30	1	—	4	9	4.94	59	.338	.358	380-2	.276	1*	138	-7	—	-0.5
1883	Phi N	2	6	.250	11	9	7	0	80	110	71	0	—	12	30	4.39	70	.306	.329	425-1	.268	2*	75	-13	—	-0.8
1884	Phi N	0	0	ø	1	0	0	0	4	3	1	0	—	0	1	2.25	133	.188	.188	428-1	.252	0*	—	1	—	0.0
1885	Phi AA	0	1	.000	1	0	0	0	6	11	9	0	0	2	3	6.00	57	.423	.464	304	.296	0*	—	-2	—	-0.2
1886	Bal AA	0	0	ø	1	0	0	0	1	1	1	0	0	0	0	9.00	38	.200	.200	85	.224	0*	—	0	—	0.0
1887	Bal AA	0	0	ø	1	0	0	0	4	8	8	0	1	4	2	15.75	26	.381	.500	567-4	.250	0*	—	-4	—	-0.2
Total	9	15	43	.259	79	57	52	0	581.1	746	486	5	1	84	138	3.73	70	.292	.314	2954-9	.267	12	72	-71	—	-4.7
Purdin, John	John Nolan; B7.16.1942 Lynx OH; BR/TR/6´2˝/(160–185); d9.16																									
1964	LA N	2	0	1.000	3	2	1-1	0	16	6	1	1	0	6-0	8	0.56	576	.115	.207	5	.200	0	176	5	0	0.7
1965	LA N	2	1	.667	11	2	0	0	22.2	26	19	8	0	13-3	16	6.75	48	.283	.368	3	.000	-0	120	-9	0	-1.2
1968	LA N	2	3	.400	35	1	0	2	55.2	42	22	2	0	21-7	38	3.07	90	.206	.276	6	.500	1*	251	-2	0	-0.1
1969	LA N	0	0	ø	9	0	0	0-0	16.1	19	11	7	0	12-1	6	6.06	55	.292	.403	2	.000	-0	—	-5	23	-0.3
Total	4	6	4	.600	58	5	1-1	2-0	110.2	93	53	18	0	52-11	68	3.90	77	.225	.309	16	.250	1	173	-11	23	-0.9

YEAR	TM LG	W	L	PCT	G	GS	CG-SHO	SV-BS	IP	H	R	HR	HB	BB-IB	SO	ERA	AERA	OAV	OOB	AB-HR-SH	AVG	PB	SUP	APR	DL	PW
PURKEY, BOB	Robert Thomas; B7.14.1929 Pittsburgh PA; BR/TR/6´2˝/(175–201); d4.14																									
1954	Pit N	3	8	.273	36	11	0	0	131.1	145	78	3	7	62	38	5.07	83	.293	.375	26-0-3	.077	-1	75	-10	0	-0.5
1955	Pit N	2	7	.222	14	10	2	1	67.2	77	47	5	2	25-1	24	5.32	77	.287	.353	19-1-3	.316	2	58	-9	0	-0.9
1956	Pit N	0	0	ø	2	0	0	0	4	2	1	1	0	0-0	1	2.25	168	.143	.143	0	ø	0	—	1	0	0.0
1957	Pit N	11	14	.440	48	21	6-1	2	179.2	194	84	10	7	38-9	51	3.86	98	.278	.317	45-0-2	.111	-0	69	1	0	0.1
1958	Cin N☆	17	11	.607	37	34	17-3	0	250	259	106	25	4	49-3	70	3.60	115	.268	.304	81-1-6	.111	-2	87	15	0	1.5
1959	Cin N	13	18	.419	38	33	9-1	1	218	241	118	25	6	43-2	78	4.25	95	.279	.316	66-1-4	.167	3	90	-5	0	-0.4
1960	Cin N	17	11	.607	41	33	11-1	0	252.2	259	114	23	9	59-5	97	3.60	106	.265	.311	83-0-6	.133	-2	113	6	0	0.5
1961	†Cin N★	16	12	.571	36	34	13-1	1	246.1	245	118	27	6	51-4	116	3.73	109	.255	.296	80-1-7	.100	-3	96	8	0	0.8
1962	Cin N★	23	5	**.821**	37	37	18-2	0	288.1	260	109	28	14	64-3	141	2.81	143	.240	.289	107-2-7	.103	-2	114	**35**	0	3.0
1963	Cin N	6	10	.375	21	21	4-1	0	137	143	60	12	2	33-6	55	3.55	94	.272	.317	41-0-3	.098	-1	87	-3	0	-0.3
1964	Cin N	11	9	.550	34	25	9-2	1	195.2	181	77	16	7	49-4	78	3.04	119	.246	.298	58-0-8	.052	-4	116	11	0	0.8
1965	StL N	10	9	.526	32	17	3-1	2	124.1	148	83	20	7	33-4	39	5.79	66	.294	.344	35-0-7	.029	-3	123	-23	0	-3.4
1966	Pit N	0	1	.000	10	0	0	1	19.2	16	3	0	0	4-0	5	1.37	260	.235	.278	4	.000	-0*	—	5	0	0.3
Total	13	129	115	.529	386	276	92-13	9	2114.2	2170	998	195	71	510-41	793	3.79	103	.266	.313	645-6-56	.110	-13	97	32	0	1.5
PURNER, OSCAR	Oscar E.; B12.9.1873 Washington DC; D12.4.1915 Douglas AZ; d9.2																									
1895	Was N	0	0	ø	1	0	0	0	2	4	2	1	0	3	0	9.00	53	.400	.538	1	.000	-0	—	-1	—	0.0
PUTTMANN, AMBROSE	Ambrose Nicholas "Putty","Brose"; B9.9.1880 Cincinnati OH; D6.21.1936 Jamaica NY; TL/6´4˝/185; d9.4																									
1903	NY A	2	0	1.000	3	2	1	0	19	16	9	0	1	4	8	0.95	330	.229	.280	7	.143	-0	206	2	—	0.3
1904	NY A	2	0	1.000	9	3	2-1	0	49.1	40	21	0	0	17	26	2.74	99	.222	.289	18	.278	2	105	0	—	0.2
1905	NY A	2	7	.222	17	9	5-1	1	86.1	79	50	2	5	37	39	4.27	69	.245	.332	32	.313	3*	96	-9	—	-0.7
1906	StL N	2	2	.500	4	4	0	0	18.2	23	13	2	2	9	12	5.30	50	.303	.391	6	.333	0	139	-5	—	-0.9
Total	4	8	9	.471	33	18	8-2	1	173.1	158	93	4	8	67	85	3.58	80	.244	.322	63	.286	4	119	-12	—	-1.1
PUTZ, J.J.	Joseph Jason; B2.2.1977 Trenton MI; BR/TR/6´5˝/(220–250); [SeaA99 6/185]; d8.11; Col Michigan																									
2003	Sea A	0	0	ø	3	0	0	0-0	3.2	4	2	0	0	3-0	3	4.91	88	.267	.389	0	ø	0	—	0	0	0.0
2004	Sea A	0	3	.000	54	0	0	9-4	63	66	35	10	5	24-4	47	4.71	95	.274	.349	0	ø	0	—	-2	0	-0.1
2005	Sea A	6	5	.545	64	0	0	1-3	60	58	27	8	2	23-2	45	3.60	116	.254	.324	0	ø	0	—	3	0	0.6
2006	Sea A	4	1	.800	72	0	0	36-7	78.1	59	20	4	2	13-1	104	2.30	192	.207	.245	0	ø	0	—	20	0	2.6
Total	4	10	9	.526	193	0	0	46-14	205	187	84	22	9	63-7	199	3.47	126	.243	.305	0	ø	0	—	21	0	3.1
PYECHA, JOHN	John Nicholas; B11.25.1931 Aliquippa PA; BR/TR/6´5˝/200; d4.24; Col Appalachian St.																									
1954	Chi N	0	1	.000	1	0	0	0	2.2	4	3	1	0	2	2	10.13	41	.333	.429	1	.000	-0	—	-2	0	-0.3
PYLE, EWALD	Ewald "Lefty"; B8.27.1910 St.Louis MO; D1.10.2004 DuQuoin IL; BL/TL/6´0.5˝/175; d4.23																									
1939	StL A	0	2	.000	6	1	0	0	8.1	17	15	3	0	11	5	12.96	38	.405	.528	2	.000	-0	145	-8	—	-1.3
1942	StL A	0	0	ø	2	0	0	0	5.1	6	4	0	0	4	1	6.75	55	.286	.400	3	.000	-0	—	-1	0	-0.1
1943	Was A	4	8	.333	18	11	2-1	1	72.2	70	38	0	1	45	25	4.09	78	.254	.360	20-0-1	.100	-1	60	-6	0	-1.2
1944	NY N	7	10	.412	31	21	3	0	164	152	89	12	6	68	79	4.34	85	.241	.321	51-0-1	.157	-0	95	-10	0	-1.0
1945	NY N	0	0	ø	6	1	0	0	6.1	16	12	0	0	4	2	17.05	23	.457	.513	2	.000	-0	108	-8	0	-0.4
	Bos N	0	1	.000	4	2	0	0	13.2	16	15	1	0	18	10	7.24	53	.302	.479	6	.333	1	155	-6	0	-0.3
	Year	0	1	.000	10	3	0	0	20	32	27	1	0	22	12	10.35	37	.364	.491	8	.250	0	139	-15	0	-0.7
Total	5	11	21	.344	67	36	5-1	1	270.1	277	173	16	7	150	122	5.03	71	.262	.357	84-0-2	.143	-2	91	-39	0	-4.3
PYLE, HARLAN	Harlan Albert "Firpo"; B11.29.1905 Burchard NE; D1.13.1993 Beatrice NE; BR/TR/6´2˝/180; d9.21																									
1928	Cin N	0	0	ø	2	1	0	0	1.1	1	3	0	0	4	1	20.25	20	.143	.455	1	.000	-0	128	-2	—	-0.1
PYLE, SHADOW	Harry Thomas; B11.29.1861 Reading PA; D12.26.1908 Reading PA; TL/5´8˝/136; d10.15																									
1884	Phi N	0	1	.000	1	1	1	0	9	9	8	0	—	6	4	4.00	75	.257	.366	4	.000	-1	0	-1	—	-0.2
1887	Chi N	1	3	.250	4	4	3	0	26.2	32	27	1	2	21	5	4.73	95	.291	.414	16-1	.188	-0	90	-2	—	-0.2
Total	2	1	4	.200	5	5	4	0	35.2	41	35	1	2	27	9	4.54	90	.283	.402	20-1	.150	-1	76	-3	—	-0.4
QUALLS, CHAD	Chad Michael; B8.17.1978 Lomita CA; BR/TR/6´5˝/220; [HouN00 2/67]; d7.22; Col Nevada–Reno																									
2004	†Hou N	4	0	1.000	25	0	0	1-1	33	34	13	3	4	8-1	24	3.55	123	.266	.326	1	.000	-0	—	3	0	0.4
2005	†Hou N	6	4	.600	77	0	0	0-0	79.2	73	33	7	6	23-2	60	3.28	129	.249	.314	1	.000	-0	—	8	0	0.9
2006	Hou N	7	3	.700	81	0	0	0-6	88.2	76	38	10	6	28-6	56	3.76	120	.242	.313	0	ø	0	—	8	0	0.8
Total	3	17	7	.708	183	0	0	1-7	201.1	183	84	20	16	59-9	140	3.53	124	.249	.315	2	.000	-0	—	19	0	2.1
QUALTERS, TOM	Thomas Francis "Money Bags"; B4.1.1935 McKeesport PA; BR/TR/6´0.5˝/190; d9.13																									
1953	Phi N	0	0	ø	1	0	0	0	0.1	4	6	1	1	1	0	162.00	3	.800	.857	0	ø	0	—	-6	0	-0.2
1957	Phi N	0	0	ø	6	0	0	0	7.1	12	6	0	0	4-1	6	7.36	52	.400	.471	0	ø	0	—	-3	0	-0.1
1958	Phi N	0	0	ø	1	0	0	0	2	2	1	0	0	1-0	0	4.50	88	.222	.300	0	ø	0	—	0	0	0.0
	Chi A	0	0	ø	26	0	0	0	43	45	22	1	0	20-4	14	4.19	87	.281	.359	2	.000	0	—	-3	0	-0.1
Total	3	0	0	ø	34	0	0	0	52.2	63	35	2	1	26-5	20	5.64	65	.309	.388	2	.000	0	—	-12	0	-0.4
QUANTRILL, PAUL	Paul John; B11.3.1968 London ON, Can.; BL/TR/6´1˝/(175–200); [BosA89 6/163]; d7.20; Col Wisconsin–Madison																									
1992	Bos A	2	3	.400	27	0	0	1-4	49.1	55	18	1	1	15-5	24	2.19	194	.288	.340	0	ø	0	—	9	0	0.8
1993	Bos A	6	12	.333	49	14	1-1	1-1	138	151	73	13	2	44-14	66	3.91	118	.279	.334	0	ø	0	68	8	0	0.9
1994	Bos A	1	1	.500	17	0	0	0-2	23	25	10	4	2	5-1	15	3.52	143	.278	.323	0	ø	0	—	4	0	0.3
	Phi N	2	2	.500	18	1	0	1-1	30	39	21	3	3	10-3	13	6.00	71	.331	.394	3	.000	-0	64	-5	0	-0.6
1995	Phi N	11	12	.478	33	29	0	0-0	179.1	212	102	20	6	44-3	103	4.67	90	.295	.338	57-0-7	.105	-2	89	-9	0	-1.2
1996	Tor A	5	14	.263	38	20	0	0-2	134.1	172	90	27	2	51-3	86	5.43	92	.316	.373	0	ø	0	82	-7	0	-0.7
1997	Tor A	6	7	.462	77	0	0	5-5	88	103	25	5	1	17-3	56	1.94	236	.297	.329	1	.000	-0	—	**24**	0	3.3
1998	Tor A	3	4	.429	82	0	0	7-7	80	88	26	5	3	22-6	59	2.59	180	.285	.334	0	ø	0	—	18	0	1.7
1999	Tor A	3	2	.600	41	0	0	0-4	48.2	53	19	5	4	17-1	28	3.33	148	.282	.351	0	ø	0	—	9	71	0.8
2000	Tor A	2	5	.286	68	0	0	1-2	83.2	100	45	7	2	25-1	47	4.52	111	.298	.347	0	ø	0	—	5	0	0.4
2001	Tor A★	11	2	.846	**80**	0	0	2-7	83	86	29	6	6	12-7	58	3.04	151	.274	.311	0	ø	0	—	15	0	2.0
2002	LA N	5	4	.556	**86**	0	0	1-2	76.2	80	27	1	3	25-7	53	2.70	144	.267	.328	3	.333	0	—	10	0	1.1
2003	LA N	2	5	.286	**89**	0	0	1-4	77.1	61	18	2	3	15-2	44	1.75	236	.227	.275	1	.000	-0	—	20	0	1.8
2004	†NY A	7	3	.700	**86**	0	0	1-4	95.1	124	54	5	4	20-9	37	4.72	97	.316	.352	1	.000	-0	—	-1	0	-0.2
2005	NY A	1	0	1.000	22	0	0	0-1	32	48	24	5	2	7-2	11	6.75	64	.361	.383	0	ø	0	—	-8	0	-0.4
	SD N	1	1	.500	22	0	0	0-0	31.2	37	13	2	1	2-1	24	3.41	115	.294	.303	1	.000	-0	—	2	0	0.1
	Fla N	0	1	.000	6	0	0	0-0	5.1	8	7	1	0	5-0	1	8.44	47	.348	.464	0	ø	0	—	-4	0	-0.6
	Year	1	2	.333	28	0	0	0-0	37	45	20	3	1	7-1	25	4.14	95	.302	.331	1	.000	-0	—	-2	0	-0.5
Total	14	68	78	.466	841	64	1-1	21-46	1255.2	1442	601	112	45	336-68	725	3.83	118	.292	.339	67-0-7	.104	-2	83	90	71	9.5
QUARLES, BILL	William H.; B1869 Petersburg VA; D3.25.1897 Petersburg VA; 6´3˝/?; d5.21																									
1891	Was AA	1	1	.500	3	2	2	0	22	32	27	1	2	12	10	8.18	46	.330	.414	11	.000	-2	100	-9	—	-0.7
1893	Bos N	2	1	.667	3	3	3	0	27	31	20	2	2	5	6	4.67	106	.279	.322	9	.222	0	127	1	—	0.0
Total	2	3	2	.600	6	5	5	0	49	63	47	3	4	17	16	6.24	70	.303	.367	20	.100	-2	119	-8	—	-0.7
QUEEN, MEL	Melvin Douglas; B3.26.1942 Johnson City NY; BL/TR/6´1˝/(190–197); d4.13.1964; M1/C5; s–Mel; ▲																									
1966	Cin N	0	0	ø	7	0	0	1	7	11	5	0	0	6-0	9	6.43	61	.367	.459	55-0-1	.127	0*	—	-2	28	-0.1
1967	Cin N	14	8	.636	31	24	6-2	0	195.2	155	69	17	6	52-5	154	2.76	136	.215	.271	81-0-3	.210	3*	80	19	0	2.4
1968	Cin N	0	1	.000	5	4	0	0	18.1	25	15	7	0	6-4	20	5.89	54	.333	.383	8	.125	0*	158	-6	84	-0.3
1969	Cin N	1	0	1.000	2	2	0	0-0	12	7	3	2	1	3-0	7	2.25	167	.163	.234	6	.167	-0	212	2	0	0.1
1970	Cal A	3	6	.333	34	3	0	9-3	60	58	28	5	5	28-6	44	4.20	86	.261	.354	16	.250	1*	49	-2	21	-0.4
1971	Cal A	2	2	.500	44	0	0	4-3	65.2	49	17	3	8	29-6	53	1.78	182	.212	.319	8-0-1	.000	-1*	—	10	0	0.7
1972	Cal A	0	0	ø	17	0	0	0-0	31	31	17	2	3	19-1	19	4.35	67	.265	.376	2	.000	0	—	-5	0	-0.3
Total	7	20	17	.541	140	33	6-2	14-6	389.2	336	154	36	23	143-22	306	3.14	113	.233	.310	176-0-5	.170	3	97	16	133	2.1

YEAR	TM LG	W	L	PCT	G	GS	CG-SHO	SV-BS	IP	H	R	HR	HB	BB-IB	SO	ERA	AERA	OAV	OOB	AB-HR-SH	AVG	PB	SUP	APR	DL	PW
QUEEN, MEL	Melvin Joseph; B3.4.1918 Maxwell PA; D4.4.1982 Fort Smith AR; BR/TR/6´0.5˝/(200–204); d4.18; Mil 1945; f–Mel																									
1942	NY A	1	0	1.000	4	0	0	0	5.2	6	0	0	2	3	0	0.00	ø	.300	.440	0	ø	0	—	2	0	0.4
1944	NY A	6	3	.667	10	10	4-1	0	81.2	68	32	7	1	34	30	3.31	105	.227	.308	31-0-3	.194	0	125	3	0	0.2
1946	NY A	1	1	.500	14	3	1	0	30.1	40	28	2	0	21	26	6.53	53	.315	.412	7	.143	-0	116	-12	0	-0.8
1947	NY A	0	0	ø	5	0	0	0	6.2	9	7	2	1	4	2	9.45	37	.321	.424	1	.000	-0	—	-4	0	-0.2
	Pit N	3	7	.300	14	12	2	0	74	70	39	8	1	51	34	4.01	105	.244	.360	26-0-1	.077	-2	106	1	0	-0.1
1948	Pit N	4	4	.500	25	8	0	1	66.1	82	51	8	3	40	34	6.65	61	.308	.405	17-0-2	.059	-2	76	-17	0	-2.0
1950	Pit N	5	14	.263	33	21	4-1	0	120.1	135	95	18	2	73	76	5.98	73	.284	.381	35-0-2	.057	-3	90	-22	0	-3.2
1951	Pit N	7	9	.438	39	21	4-1	0	168.1	149	90	21	1	99	123	4.44	95	.233	.337	47-0-6	.106	-3	100	-2	0	-0.6
1952	Pit N	0	2	.000	2	2	0	0	3.1	8	12	2	0	4	3	29.70	13	.381	.480	0	ø	0	89	-9	0	-1.3
Total	8	27	40	.403	146	77	15-3	1	556.2	567	354	68	11	329	328	5.09	80	.262	.362	164-0-14	.104	-10	100	-60	0	-7.6
QUEVEDO, RUBEN	Ruben Eduardo; B1.5.1979 Valencia, Carabobo, Venez.; BR/TR/6´1˝/(230–245); d4.14																									
2000	Chi N	3	10	.231	21	15	1	0-0	88	96	81	21	3	54-4	65	7.47	61	.271	.370	30-0-1	.133	-1	78	-30	0	-3.6
2001	Mil N	4	5	.444	10	10	0	0-0	56.2	56	30	9	0	30-4	60	4.61	93	.257	.344	16-0-4	.250	1	84	-1	0	-0.1
2002	Mil N	6	11	.353	26	25	1-1	0-0	139	159	100	28	4	68-3	93	5.76	71	.288	.368	42-0-3	.095	-2	106	-27	0	-3.1
2003	Mil N	1	4	.200	9	8	0	0-0	42.2	53	32	12	0	23-1	19	6.75	64	.314	.390	10-0-1	.300	1	84	-10	84	-1.0
Total	4	14	30	.318	66	58	2-1	0-0	326.1	364	243	70	7	175-12	237	6.15	70	.281	.367	98-0-9	.153	-2	91	-68	84	-7.8
QUICK, EDDIE	Edward; B12.1881 Baltimore MD; D6.19.1913 Rocky Ford CO; TR/5´11˝/?; d9.28																									
1903	NY A	0	0	ø	1	1	0	0	2	5	5	0	0	1	0	9.00	35	.455	.500	1	.000	-0	160	-2	—	-0.1
QUINN, TAD	Clarence Carr; B9.25.1881 Torrington CT; D8.6.1946 Waterbury CT; TR/6´1˝/210; d9.27																									
1902	Phi A	0	1	.000	1	1	1	0	8	12	9	1	0	1	3	4.50	82	.343	.361	3	.000	-0	78	-2	—	-0.2
1903	Phi A	0	0	ø	2	0	0	0	9	11	6	0	1	5	1	5.00	61	.297	.395	3	.667	1	—	-2	—	0.1
Total	2	0	1	.000	3	1	1	0	17	23	15	1	1	6	4	4.76	70	.319	.380	6	.333	1	78	-4	—	-0.1
QUINN, FRANK	Frank William; B11.27.1927 Springfield MA; D1.11.1993 Boynton Beach FL; BR/TR/6´2˝/180; d5.29; Col Yale																									
1949	Bos A	0	0	ø	8	0	0	0	22	18	7	2	1	9	4	2.86	152	.222	.308	6	.167	-0	—	4	0	0.1
1950	Bos A	0	0	ø	1	0	0	0	2	2	2	0	0	1	0	9.00	54	.250	.333	0	ø	0	—	-1	0	0.0
Total	2	0	0	ø	9	0	0	0	24	20	9	2	1	10	4	3.38	131	.225	.310	6	.167	-0	—	3	0	0.1
QUINN, JACK	John Picus (b John Quinn Picus); B7.5.1883 Janesville PA; D4.17.1946 Pottsville PA; BR/TR/6´0˝/196; d4.15																									
1909	NY A	9	5	.643	23	11	8	1	118.2	110	45	1	4	24	36	1.97	128	.252	.297	45-0-1	.156	0	119	5	—	0.8
1910	NY A	18	12	.600	35	31	20	0	235.2	214	88	2	6	58	82	2.37	112	.247	.299	82-0-4	.232	4	102	6	—	1.6
1911	NY A	8	10	.444	40	16	7	2	174.2	203	111	2	4	41	71	3.76	96	.297	.341	61-1-2	.164	-1	74	-7	—	-0.6
1912	NY A	5	7	.417	18	11	7	0	102.2	139	89	4	4	23	47	5.79	62	.325	.365	39-0-1	.205	-1	84	-22	—	-2.1
1913	Bos N	4	3	.571	8	7	6-1	0	56.1	55	22	1	1	7	33	2.40	137	.261	.288	20	.200	1*	72	5	—	0.9
1914	Bal F	26	14	.650	46	42	27-4	1	342.2	335	129	3	8	65	164	2.60	117	.266	.307	121-2-8	.273	7*	89	15	—	2.5
1915	Bal F	9	22	.290	44	31	21	1	273.2	289	137	9	8	63	118	3.45	83	.278	.325	110-0-3	.264	4*	83	-18	—	-1.4
1918	Chi A	5	1	.833	6	5	5	0	51	38	13	0	0	7	22	2.29	119	.216	.246	18	.222	1	143	4	—	0.7
1919	NY A	15	14	.517	38	31	18-4	0	266	242	96	8	6	65	97	2.61	123	.244	.295	91-0-4	.209	1	99	18	—	2.0
1920	NY A	18	10	.643	41	32	17-2	3	253.1	271	110	8	2	48	101	3.20	119	.273	.308	88-2-3	.091	-5	105	18	—	1.4
1921	†NY A	8	7	.533	33	13	6	0	119	158	61	2	5	32	44	3.78	112	.327	.375	41-1-2	.220	1	97	6	—	0.8
1922	Bos A	13	16	.448	40	32	16-4	0	256	263	119	9	3	59	67	3.48	118	.267	.311	91-1-3	.099	-5	99	16	—	1.4
1923	Bos A	13	17	.433	42	28	16-1	7	243	302	125	6	6	53	71	3.89	106	.316	.356	80-0-6	.225	0	75	9	—	1.0
1924	Bos A	12	13	.480	44	25	13-2	7	228.2	241	109	10	12	52	64	3.27	134	.273	.322	78-0-4	.179	-4	82	23	—	2.2
1925	Bos A	7	8	.467	19	15	8	0	105	140	68	3	3	26	24	4.37	104	.315	.357	32-0-2	.094	-2	89	1	—	0.0
	Phi A	6	3	.667	18	13	4	0	99.2	119	56	3	3	16	19	3.88	120	.296	.328	31-0-1	.097	-3	90	6	—	0.3
	Year	13	11	.542	37	28	12	0	204.2	259	124	6	6	42	43	4.13	111	.306	.343	63-0-3	.095	-5	89	8	—	0.3
1926	Phi A	10	11	.476	31	21	8-3	1	163.2	191	74	4	1	36	58	3.41	122	.296	.334	46-0-6	.174	-0	98	15	—	1.8
1927	Phi A	15	10	.600	34	26	11-3	1	201.1	211	82	8	4	37	43	3.26	131	.278	.315	66-0-7	.091	-7	82	24	—	1.9
1928	Phi A	18	7	.720	31	28	18-4	1	211.1	239	92	3	7	34	43	2.90	139	.286	.320	79-0-6	.165	-3	142	22	—	2.1
1929	†Phi A	11	9	.550	35	18	7	2	161	182	87	8	1	39	41	3.97	107	.290	.332	60-0-4	.133	-4	104	3	—	-0.1
1930	†Phi A	9	7	.563	35	6	0	6	89.2	109	51	6	1	22	28	4.42	106	.302	.344	34-1-0	.265	1	61	**2**	—	0.5
1931	Bro N	5	4	.556	39	1	0	**15**	64.1	65	28	1	1	24	25	2.66	143	.266	.335	15-0-1	.200	0	90	6	—	1.1
1932	Bro N	3	7	.300	42	0	0	**8**	87.1	102	36	1	1	24	28	3.30	116	.296	.343	20-0-3	.200	0	—	**5**	—	0.7
1933	Cin N	0	1	.000	14	0	0	1	15.2	20	9	0	0	5	3	4.02	84	.323	.373	1	.000	-0	—	-1	—	-0.1
Total	23	247	218	.531	756	443	243-28	57	3920.1	4238	1837	102	91	860	1329	3.29	113	.280	.323	1349-8-71	.184	-15	95	161	—	19.4
QUINN, WIMPY	Wellington Hunt; B5.14.1918 Birmingham AL; D9.1.1954 Santa Monica CA; BR/TR/6´2˝/187; d6.8; Col Oregon																									
1941	Chi N	0	0	ø	3	0	0	0	5	3	4	0	0	3	2	7.20	49	.158	.273	2	.500	0	—	-2	0	-0.1
QUINTANA, LUIS	Luis Joaquin (Santos); B12.25.1951 Vega Baja, PR; BL/TL/6´2˝/175; d7.9; [DL 1976 Atl N 56]																									
1974	Cal A	2	1	.667	18	0	0	0-2	12.2	17	6	0	0	14-1	11	4.26	81	.327	.463	0	ø	0	—	-1	0	-0.2
1975	Cal A	0	2	.000	4	0	0	0-0	7	13	6	2	0	6-1	5	6.43	56	.394	.487	0	ø	0	—	-2	0	-0.5
Total	2	2	3	.400	22	0	0	0-2	19.2	30	12	2	0	20-2	16	5.03	70	.353	.472	0	ø	0	—	-3	56	-0.7
QUIRICO, RAFAEL	Rafael Octavio (Dottin); B9.7.1969 Santo Domingo, D.R.; BL/TL/6´3˝/212; d6.25																									
1996	Phi N	0	1	.000	1	1	0	0-0	1.2	4	7	1	0	5-0	1	37.80	11	.444	.643	0	ø	0	21	-6	0	-0.8
QUIRK, ART	Arthur Lincoln; B4.11.1938 Providence RI; BR/TL/5´11˝/170; d4.17; Col Dartmouth																									
1962	Bal A	2	2	.500	7	5	0	0	27.1	36	20	3	0	18-0	18	5.93	62	.308	.400	7-0-1	.143	0	92	-7	0	-0.8
1963	Was A	1	0	1.000	7	3	0	0	21	23	13	3	0	8-1	12	4.29	87	.280	.341	4	.250	0	152	-2	0	-0.1
Total	2	3	2	.600	14	8	0	0	48.1	59	33	6	0	26-1	30	5.21	71	.296	.376	11-0-1	.182	0	114	-9	0	-0.9
QUISENBERRY, DAN	Daniel Raymond; B2.7.1953 Santa Monica CA; D9.30.1998 Leawood KS; BR/TR/6´2˝/(180–185); d7.8; Col La Verne																									
1979	KC A	3	2	.600	32	0	0	5-5	40	42	16	5	0	7-5	13	3.15	135	.278	.306	0	ø	0	—	5	0	0.7
1980	†KC A	12	7	.632	**75**	0	0	**33**-3	128.1	129	47	5	1	27-15	37	3.09	131	.265	.302	0	ø	0	—	15	0	3.0
1981	†KC A	1	4	.200	40	0	0	18-4	62.1	59	16	1	1	15-8	20	1.73	208	.258	.301	0	ø	0	—	12	0	1.9
1982	KC A★	9	7	.563	72	0	0	**35**-9	136.2	126	43	12	0	12-2	46	2.57	159	.252	.266	0	ø	0	—	23	0	4.2
1983	KC A★	5	3	.625	**69**	0	0	**45**-8	139	118	35	6	0	11-2	48	1.94	212	.229	.243	0	ø	0	—	**33**	0	**4.0**
1984	†KC A☆	6	3	.667	72	0	0	**44**-9	129.1	121	39	10	0	12-4	41	2.64	153	.247	.264	0	ø	0	—	21	0	2.9
1985	†KC A	8	9	.471	**84**	0	0	**37**-12	129	142	41	8	1	16-5	54	2.37	176	.280	.301	0	ø	0	—	25	0	4.4
1986	KC A	3	7	.300	62	0	0	12-4	81.1	92	30	2	3	24-12	36	2.77	154	.291	.342	0	ø	0	—	12	0	1.8
1987	KC A	4	1	.800	47	0	0	8-3	49	58	15	3	1	10-3	17	2.76	167	.287	.322	0	ø	0	—	11	0	1.4
1988	KC A	0	1	.000	20	0	0	1-0	25.1	32	11	0	0	5-2	9	3.55	113	.305	.336	0	ø	0	—	1	0	0.1
	StL N	2	0	1.000	33	0	0	0-1	38	54	26	4	0	6-1	19	6.16	57	.344	.364	1	.000	0	—	-10	0	-0.5
1989	StL N	3	1	.750	63	0	0	6-1	78.1	78	25	2	0	14-9	37	2.64	139	.261	.293	4	.250	0	—	9	0	0.7
1990	SF N	0	1	.000	5	0	0	0-1	6.2	13	12	1	0	3-2	2	13.50	27	.419	.432	1	.000	-0	—	-8	0	-1.0
Total	12	56	46	.549	674	0	0	244-60	1043.1	1064	356	59	7	162-70	379	2.76	147	.267	.294	6	.167	0	—	149	0	23.6
RABE, CHARLIE	Charles Henry; B5.6.1932 Boyce TX; BL/TL/6´1˝/(175–180); d9.21																									
1957	Cin N	0	1	.000	2	1	0	0	8.1	5	2	2	0	0-0	6	2.16	190	.167	.167	2	.000	-0	21	2	0	0.2
1958	Cin N	0	3	.000	9	1	0	0	18.2	25	10	3	0	9-0	10	4.34	96	.321	.391	4	.000	-1	43	0	0	-0.1
Total	2	0	4	.000	11	2	0	0	27	30	12	5	0	9-0	16	3.67	113	.278	.333	6	.000	-1	32	2	0	0.1
RACHUNOK, STEVE	Stephen Stepanovich "The Mad Russian"; B12.5.1916 Rittman OH; D5.11.2002 Corona CA; BR/TR/6´4.5˝/205; d9.17																									
1940	Bro N	0	1	.000	2	1	1	0	10	9	5	0	0	5	10	4.50	89	.243	.333	2	.000	0	87	0	—	0.0
RACZKA, MIKE	Michael; B11.16.1962 New Britain CT; BL/TL/6´0˝/200; [BalA84 5/131]; d8.15; Col New Haven																									
1992	Oak A	0	0	ø	8	0	0	0-0	6.1	8	7	0	0	5-0	2	8.53	44	.308	.394	0	ø	0	—	-4	0	-0.2

YEAR	TM LG	W	L	PCT	G	GS	CG-SHO	SV-BS	IP	H	R	HR	HB	BB-IB	SO	ERA	AERA	OAV	OOB	AB-HR-SH	AVG	PB	SUP	APR	DL	PW
RADATZ, DICK	Richard Raymond "The Monster"; B4.2.1937 Detroit MI; D3.16.2005 Easton MA; BR/TR/6´5˝/(230–235); d4.10; Col Michigan St.																									
1962	Bos A	9	6	.600	**62**	0	0	**24**	124.2	95	32	9	4	40-2	144	2.24	184	.211	.278	31-0-2	.097	-2	—	**26**	0	**3.9**
1963	Bos A★	15	6	.714	66	0	0	25	132.1	94	31	9	5	51-13	162	1.97	192	.201	.285	29-0-2	.069	-2	—	**26**	0	**5.0**
1964	Bos A★	16	9	.640	79	0	0	**29**	157	103	44	13	7	58-9	181	2.29	168	.186	.269	37-0-2	.162	-0	—	26	0	4.9
1965	Bos A	9	11	.450	63	0	0	22	124.1	104	57	11	5	53-11	121	3.91	95	.227	.312	27-1-2	.185	1	—	0	0	0.1
1966	Bos A	0	2	.000	16	0	0	4	19	24	10	3	0	11-2	19	4.74	80	.304	.389	2	.000	-0	—	-1	0	-0.2
	Cle A	0	3	.000	39	0	0	10	56.2	49	33	6	3	34-6	49	4.61	75	.233	.344	9	.111	-0	—	-8	0	-0.8
	Year	0	5	.000	55	0	0	14	75.2	73	43	9	3	45-8	68	4.64	76	.253	.356	11	.091	-1	—	-8	0	-1.0
1967	Cle A	0	0	ø	3	0	0	0	3	5	2	1	0	2-0	1	6.00	54	.357	.438	0	ø	0	—	-1	0	0.0
	Chi N	1	0	1.000	20	0	0	5	23.1	12	21	4	5	24-2	18	6.56	54	.154	.380	4	.250	0	—	-8	0	-0.8
1969	Det A	2	2	.500	11	0	0	0-1	18.2	14	8	3	0	5-0	18	3.38	112	.212	.268	2	.000	-0	—	1	0	0.1
	Mon N	0	4	.000	22	0	0	3-1	34.2	32	22	6	1	18-1	32	5.71	65	.244	.340	4	.250	0	—	-6	0	-0.8
Total	7	52	43	.547	381	0	0	122-2	693.2	532	260	65	30	296-46	745	3.13	122	.212	.300	145-1-8	.131	-3	—	55	0	11.4
RADBOURN, CHARLEY	Charles Gardner "Old Hoss"; B12.11.1854 Rochester NY; D2.5.1897 Bloomington IL; BR/TR (BB 1886p)/5´9˝/168; d5.5.1880; HF1939																									
1881	Pro N	25	11	**.694**	41	36	34-3	0	325.1	309	162	1	—	64	117	2.43	109	**.235**	.270	270	.219	-1*	122	14	—	1.4
1882	Pro N	33	19	.635	54	51	50-**6**	0	466	422	213	6	—	51	**201**	2.11	134	.226	.247	326-1	.239	-1*	109	**35**	—	**3.2**
1883	Pro N	**48**	25	.658	**76**	68	66-4	1	632.1	563	275	7	—	56	315	2.05	150	.227	**.244**	381-3	.283	14*	118	**74**	—	**8.3**
1884	†Pro N	**59**	12	**.831**	**75**	**73**	**73**-11	1	**678.2**	528	216	18	—	98	**441**	**1.38**	**206**	.205	.234	361-1	.230	5*	112	116	—	**10.7**
1885	Pro N	28	21	.571	49	49	49-2	0	445.2	423	209	4	—	83	154	2.20	122	.241	.275	249	.233	11*	97	22	—	3.4
1886	Bos N	27	31	.466	58	58	57-3	0	509.1	521	300	18	—	111	218	3.00	107	.254	.292	253-2	.237	7*	101	12	—	2.0
1887	Bos N	24	23	.511	50	50	48-1	0	425	505	305	20	14	133	87	4.55	90	.286	.340	175-1	.229	2*	103	-19	—	-1.6
1888	Bos N	7	16	.304	24	24	24-1	0	207	187	110	8	8	45	64	2.87	100	.234	.282	79	.215	1	74	1	—	0.1
1889	Bos N	20	11	.645	33	31	28-1	0	277	282	151	14	8	72	99	3.67	113	.256	.307	122-1	.189	-1*	114	19	—	1.6
1890	Bos P	27	12	.692	41	38	36-1	0	343	352	183	8	11	100	80	3.31	133	.254	.309	154	.253	0*	99	46	—	3.9
1891	Cin N	11	13	.458	26	24	23-2	0	218	236	149	13	13	62	54	4.25	79	.266	.323	96	.177	-1*	84	-15	—	-1.5
Total	11	309	194	.614	527	502	488-35	2	4527.1	4328	2273	117	54	875	1830	2.68	120	.241	.278	2466-9	.236	38	106	305	—	31.5
RADBOURN, GEORGE	George B. "Dordy"; B4.8.1856 Bloomington IL; D1.1.1904 Bloomington IL; ?/160; d5.30																									
1883	Det N	1	2	.333	3	3	2	0	22	38	28	1	—	7	2	6.55	47	.345	.385	12	.167	-1	92	-8	—	-0.8
RADEBAUGH, ROY	Roy; B2.22.1881 Champaign IL; D1.17.1945 Cedar Rapids IA; BR/TR/5´7˝/160; d9.22																									
1911	StL N	0	0	ø	2	1	0	0	10	6	3	0	0	4	1	2.70	125	.176	.263	3	.000	-0	67	1	—	0.0
RADER, DREW	Drew Leon "Lefty"; B5.14.1901 Elmira NY; D6.5.1975 Catskill NY; BR/TL/6´2˝/187; d7.18; Col Syracuse																									
1921	Pit N	0	0	ø	1	0	0	0	2	2	0	0	0	0	0	0.00	ø	.286	.286	1	.000	-0	—	1	—	0.0
RADFORD, PAUL	Paul Revere "Shorty"; B10.14.1861 Roxbury MA; D2.21.1945 Boston MA; BR/TR/5´6˝/148; d5.1.1883; ▲																									
1884	†Pro N	0	2	.000	2	2	1	0	13	27	19	0	—	3	2	7.62	37	.403	.429	355-1	.197	0*	74	-6	—	-0.7
1885	Pro N	0	2	.000	3	2	2	0	18.1	34	27	1	—	8	3	7.85	34	.378	.429	371	.243	1*	74	-10	—	-0.8
1887	NY AA	0	0	ø	2	0	0	0	5	15	16	1	0	3	4	18.00	24	.789	.818	486-4	.265	1*	—	-8	—	-0.3
1890	Cle P	0	0	ø	1	0	0	0	5	7	5	1	0	1	3	3.60	110	.318	.348	466-2	.292	0*	—	0	—	0.0
1891	Bos AA	0	0	ø	1	0	0	0	1	0	0	0	0	0	0	0.00	ø	.000	.000	456	.259	0*	—	0	—	0.0
1893	Was N	0	0	ø	1	0	0	0	1	2	2	2	0	2	1	18.00	26	.400	.571	464-2	.228	0*	—	-1	—	0.0
Total	6	0	4	.000	10	4	3	0	43.1	85	69	5	0	17	13	8.52	37	.413	.457	2598-9	.250	2	69	-25	—	-1.8
RADINSKY, SCOTT	Scott David; B3.3.1968 Glendale CA; BL/TL/6´3˝/(190–221); [ChiA86 3/75]; d4.9; [DL 1994 Chi A 131]																									
1990	Chi A	6	1	.857	62	0	0	4-1	52.1	47	29	1	2	36-1	46	4.82	80	.241	.362	0	ø	0	—	-5	0	-0.7
1991	Chi A	5	5	.500	67	0	0	8-7	71.1	53	18	4	1	23-2	49	2.02	198	.206	.270	0	ø	0	—	16	0	2.4
1992	Chi A	3	7	.300	68	0	0	15-8	59.1	54	21	3	2	34-5	48	2.73	142	.243	.347	0	ø	0	—	7	0	1.5
1993	†Chi A	8	2	.800	73	0	0	4-1	54.2	61	33	3	1	19-3	44	4.28	99	.268	.327	0	ø	0	—	-2	0	-0.4
1995	Chi A	2	1	.667	46	0	0	1-2	38	46	23	7	0	17-4	14	5.45	82	.309	.371	0	ø	0	—	-3	29	-0.2
1996	†LA N	5	1	.833	58	0	0	1-3	52.1	52	19	2	0	17-5	48	2.41	163	.264	.318	1	.000	-0	—	8	11	0.9
1997	LA N	5	1	.833	75	0	0	3-2	62.1	54	22	4	1	21-5	44	2.89	135	.236	.298	4	.000	-0	—	8	0	0.7
1998	LA N	6	6	.500	62	0	0	13-11	61.2	63	21	5	4	20-1	45	2.63	153	.272	.337	0	ø	0	—	10	0	1.9
1999	StL N	2	1	.667	43	0	0	3-0	27.2	27	16	2	1	18-3	17	4.88	94	.270	.371	0	ø	0	—	-1	69	-0.1
2000	StL N	0	0	ø	1	0	0	0-0	0	0	0	0	0	1-0	0	(0)	ø	ø	1.000	0	ø	0	—	0	174	0.0
2001	Cle A	0	0	ø	2	0	0	0-0	2	4	6	2	0	3-0	3	27.00	17	.400	.538	0	ø	0	—	-5	0	-0.2
Total	11	42	25	.627	557	0	0	52-35	481.2	461	208	33	12	209-29	358	3.44	118	.253	.330	5	.000	-1	—	33	414	5.8
RADKE, BRAD	Brad William; B10.27.1972 Eau Claire WI; BR/TR/6´2˝/(185–190); [MinA91 8/206]; d4.29																									
1995	Min A	11	14	.440	29	28	2-1	0-0	181	195	112	32	4	47-0	75	5.32	91	.275	.319	0	ø	0	93	-8	0	-0.9
1996	Min A	11	16	.407	35	35	3	0-0	232	231	125	40	4	57-2	148	4.46	115	.256	.302	0	ø	0	88	16	0	1.4
1997	Min A	20	10	.667	35	**35**	4-1	0-0	239.2	238	114	28	3	48-1	174	3.87	121	.257	.293	3-0-1	.000	-0	109	19	0	2.1
1998	Min A★	12	14	.462	32	32	5-1	0-0	213.2	238	109	23	9	43-1	146	4.30	112	.283	.324	2	.000	-0	86	12	0	1.2
1999	Min A	12	14	.462	33	33	4	0-0	218.2	239	97	28	1	44-0	121	3.75	138	.280	.314	5	.000	-1	70	33	0	3.5
2000	Min A	12	16	.429	34	34	4-1	0-0	226.2	261	119	27	5	51-1	141	4.45	118	.286	.326	2	.000	-0	67	20	0	2.1
2001	Min A	15	11	.577	33	33	6-2	0-0	226	235	105	24	10	26-0	137	3.94	118	.271	.298	4	.500	1	102	17	17	2.0
2002	†Min A	9	5	.643	21	21	2-1	0-0	118.1	124	64	12	7	20-0	62	4.72	95	.272	.309	0	ø	0	107	-2	80	-0.3
2003	†Min A	14	10	.583	33	33	3-1	0-0	212.1	242	111	32	5	28-2	120	4.49	100	.288	.314	5	.200	0	104	1	0	0.1
2004	†Min A	11	8	.579	34	34	1-1	0-0	219.2	229	92	23	6	26-1	143	3.48	133	.267	.291	2-0-1	.000	-0	92	28	0	2.0
2005	Min A	9	12	.429	31	31	3-1	0-0	200.2	214	98	33	7	23-1	117	4.04	109	.272	.295	5-0-2	.000	-1	103	8	0	0.7
2006	†Min A	12	9	.571	28	28	0	0-0	162.1	197	87	24	1	32-3	83	4.32	106	.307	.336	1-0-1	.000	-0	102	3	0	0.4
Total	12	148	139	.516	378	377	37-10	0-0	2451	2643	1233	326	62	445-12	1467	4.22	113	.276	.310	29-0-5	.103	-1	92	147	97	14.3
RADLOSKY, ROB	Robert Vincent; B1.7.1974 W.Palm Beach FL; BR/TR/6´2˝/204; [MinA93 22/625]; d5.25; Col Central Florida CC																									
1999	Min A	0	1	.000	7	0	0	0-1	8.2	15	12	7	1	4-0	3	12.46	42	.375	.444	0	ø	0	—	-6	0	-0.6
RAETHER, HAL	Harold Herman "Bud"; B10.10.1932 Lake Mills WI; BR/TR/6´1˝/185; d7.4; Col Wisconsin–Madison																									
1954	Phi A	0	0	ø	1	0	0	0	2	1	1	0	0	4	0	4.50	87	.200	.556	0	ø	0	—	0	0	0.0
1957	KC A	0	0	ø	1	0	0	0	2	2	2	1	0	0-0	0	9.00	44	.250	.250	0	ø	0	—	-1	0	-0.1
Total	2	0	0	ø	2	0	0	0	4	3	3	1	0	4-0	0	6.75	58	.231	.412	0	ø	0	—	-1	0	-0.1
RAFFENSBERGER, KEN	Kenneth David; B8.8.1917 York PA; D11.10.2002 York PA; BR/TL/6´2˝/(185–205); d4.25; Mil 1945																									
1939	StL N	0	0	ø	1	0	0	0	1	2	0	0	0	0	1	0.00	ø	.400	.400	0	ø	0	—	0	—	0.0
1940	Chi N	7	9	.438	43	10	3	3	114.2	120	54	10	2	29	55	3.38	111	.271	.319	30-0-2	.167	-1	70	3	—	0.3
1941	Chi N	0	1	.000	10	1	0	0	18	17	9	0	0	7	5	4.50	78	.262	.333	5-0-1	.000	-1	145	-1	0	-0.1
1943	Phi N	0	1	.000	1	1	1	0	8	7	3	0	0	2	3	1.13	300	.241	.290	3	.000	-0	0	1	0	0.1
1944	Phi N★	13	20	.394	37	31	18-3	0	258.2	257	101	9	2	45	136	3.06	118	.252	.285	80-0-13	.138	-3*	72	17	0	1.5
1945	Phi N	0	3	.000	5	4	1	0	24.1	28	19	3	0	14	6	4.44	86	.283	.372	8	.000	-1	88	-3	0	-0.4
1946	Phi N	8	15	.348	39	23	14-2	**6**	196	203	89	10	1	39	73	3.63	95	.265	.302	60-0-9	.167	-1	72	-3	0	-0.5
1947	Phi N	2	6	.250	10	7	3-1	0	41	50	30	4	1	8	16	5.49	73	.307	.343	15	.267	0	72	-7	0	-1.1
	Cin N	6	5	.545	19	15	7	1	106.2	132	54	11	0	29	38	4.13	99	.305	.348	37-0-2	.162	-1	86	0	0	-0.1
	Year	8	11	.421	29	22	10-1	1	147.2	182	84	15	1	37	54	4.51	90	.305	.347	52-0-2	.192	-0	82	-7	0	-1.2
1948	Cin N	11	12	.478	40	24	7-4	0	180.1	187	88	15	1	37	57	3.84	102	.259	.296	62-0-3	.113	-3	75	1	0	-0.3
1949	Cin N	18	17	.514	41	**38**	20-**5**	0	284	289	129	23	2	80	103	3.39	123	.264	.315	90-1-12	.178	0	90	21	0	2.3
1950	Cin N	14	19	.424	38	35	18-4	0	239	271	127	34	2	40	87	4.26	100	.279	.308	82-1-3	.134	-2	95	0	0	-0.3
1951	Cin N	16	17	.485	42	33	14-5	5	248.2	232	108	29	6	38	81	3.44	119	.246	.279	82-0-6	.122	-3	89	18	0	1.8
1952	Cin N	17	13	.567	38	33	18-**6**	1	247	247	85	18	2	45	93	2.81	134	.261	.295	75-1-11	.107	-2	85	26	0	2.7
1953	Cin N	7	14	.333	26	26	9-1	0	174	200	87	23	0	33	47	3.93	111	.289	.322	57-1-8	.140	-1	84	7	0	0.7
1954	Cin N	0	2	.000	6	1	0	0	10.1	15	10	2	0	3	5	7.84	53	.333	.367	2	.500	0	276	-4	0	-0.6
Total	15	119	154	.436	396	282	133-31	16	2151.2	2257	993	191	19	449	806	3.60	110	.267	.306	688-4-70	.141	-17	84	76	0	6.0
RAFFO, AL	Albert Martin; B11.27.1941 San Francisco CA; BR/TR/6´5˝/210; d4.29																									
1969	Phi N	1	3	.250	45	0	0	1-0	72.1	81	35	6	4	25-3	38	4.11	87	.286	.349	6-0-2	.167	0	—	-3	0	-0.1

YEAR	TM LG	W	L	PCT	G	GS	CG-SHO	SV-BS	IP	H	R	HR	HB	BB-IB	SO	ERA	AERA	OAV	OOB	AB-HR-SH	AVG	PB	SUP	APR	DL	PW
RAGAN, RIP	Arthur Edgar; B6.5.1878 Lincoln IL; D6.8.1953 Kansas City MO; BR/TR/5´11˝/170; d9.19																									
1903	Cin N	0	2	.000	3	2	2	0	18	40	30	0	1	7	7	6.00	59	.455	.500	8	.250	0	161	-8	—	-0.7
RAGAN, PAT	Don Carlos Patrick; B11.15.1885 Blanchard IA; D9.4.1956 Los Angeles CA; BR/TR/5´10.5˝/185; d4.21; C1; Col Cornell																									
1909	Cin N	0	1	.000	2	0	0	0	8	7	4	0	0	4	2	3.38	77	.259	.355	2	.500	0	—	-1	—	0.0
	Chi N	0	0	ø	2	0	0	0	3.2	4	2	0	0	1	2	2.45	104	.286	.333	2	.000	-0	—	0	—	0.0
	Year	0	1	.000	4	0	0	0	11.2	11	6	0	0	5	4	3.09	84	.268	.348	4	.250	0	—	-1	—	0.0
1911	Bro N	4	3	.571	22	7	5-1	1	93.2	81	32	0	2	31	39	2.11	158	.252	.321	29	.138	-1	74	11	—	0.6
1912	Bro N	7	18	.280	36	26	12-1	1	208	211	101	7	4	65	101	3.63	92	.270	.329	67-0-4	.060	-7	87	-2	—	-1.0
1913	Bro N	15	18	.455	44	32	14	0	264.2	284	145	10	4	64	109	3.77	87	.281	.327	91-0-3	.165	-2	119	-15	—	-1.8
1914	Bro N	10	15	.400	38	25	14-1	3	208.1	214	104	5	3	85	106	2.98	96	.270	.343	75-0-1	.133	-3	103	-4	—	-0.8
1915	Bro N	1	0	1.000	5	0	0	0	19.2	11	6	0	0	8	7	0.92	304	.164	.253	6	.167	-0	—	3	—	0.1
	Bos N	16	12	.571	33	26	13-3	0	227	208	71	2	7	59	81	2.46	105	.255	.311	80-0-1	.150	-0	105	9	—	0.8
	Year	17	12	.586	38	26	13-3	0	246.2	219	77	2	7	67	88	2.34	112	.248	.306	86-0-1	.151	-1	104	12	—	0.9
1916	Bos N	9	9	.500	28	23	14-3	0	182	143	53	3	0	47	94	2.08	120	.218	.270	60-0-2	.217	3*	93	9	—	1.4
1917	Bos N	6	9	.400	30	13	5-1	1	147.2	138	59	6	1	35	61	2.93	87	.250	.295	48-1-3	.125	-1	100	-6	—	-0.7
1918	Bos N	8	17	.320	30	25	15-2	0	206.1	212	95	4	4	54	68	3.23	83	.270	.320	71-0-4	.183	-2	121	-12	—	-1.6
1919	Bos N	0	2	.000	4	3	0	0	12.2	16	13	0	0	3	3	7.11	40	.281	.317	4	.250	0	56	-6	—	-0.9
	NY N	1	0	1.000	7	1	1	0	22.2	19	7	0	0	14	7	1.59	177	.247	.363	7	.429	1	199	2	—	0.3
	Year	1	2	.333	11	4	1	0	35.1	35	20	0	0	17	10	3.57	79	.261	.344	11	.364	1	92	-4	—	-0.6
	Chi A	0	0	ø	1	0	0	0	1	1	0	0	0	0	0	0.00	ø	.250	.250	0	ø	0	—	0	—	0.0
1923	Phi N	0	0	ø	1	0	0	0	3	6	2	1	0	0	0	6.00	77	.400	.400	2	.500	0	—	0	—	0.0
Total	11	77	104	.425	283	181	93-12	6	1608.1	1555	694	38	25	470	680	2.99	97	.260	.317	544-1-18	.154	-13	103	-12	—	-3.6
RAGGIO, BRADY	Brady John; B9.17.1972 Los Angeles CA; BR/TR/6´4˝/210; [StLN92 20/559]; d4.15; Col Chabot (CA) JC																									
1997	StL N	1	2	.333	15	4	0	0-0	31.1	44	24	1	1	16-0	21	6.89	61	.336	.407	3-0-1	.000	-0	171	-8	0	-0.7
1998	StL N	1	1	.500	4	1	0	0-0	7	22	12	1	1	3-0	3	15.43	27	.579	.605	1	.000	-0	153	-8	0	-1.4
2003	Ari N	0	0	ø	10	0	0	1-0	8.1	9	6	1	0	6-1	8	6.48	71	.290	.405	0	ø	0	—	-1	0	-0.1
Total	3	2	3	.400	29	5	0	1-0	46.2	75	42	3	2	25-1	32	8.10	53	.375	.443	4-0-1	.000	-0	165	-17	0	-2.2
RAGLAND, FRANK	Frank Roland; B5.26.1904 Water Valley MS; D7.28.1959 Paris MS; BR/TR/6´1˝/186; d4.17																									
1932	Was A	1	0	1.000	12	1	0	0	37.2	54	33	5	3	21	11	7.41	58	.346	.433	11	.273	1	99	-13	—	-0.5
1933	Phi N	0	4	.000	11	5	0	0	38.1	51	32	1	1	10	4	6.81	56	.317	.360	10	.200	-0	57	-10	—	-0.9
Total	2	1	4	.200	23	6	0	0	76	105	65	6	4	31	15	7.11	58	.331	.398	21	.238	1	62	-23	—	-1.4
RAICH, ERIC	Eric James; B11.1.1951 Detroit MI; BR/TR/6´4˝/230; [CleA72*1/1]; d5.24; Col USC																									
1975	Cle A	7	8	.467	18	17	2	0-0	92.2	118	61	12	1	31-6	34	5.54	69	.320	.368	0	ø	0	94	-16	0	-2.2
1976	Cle A	0	0	ø	1	0	0	0-0	2.2	7	5	1	0	0-0	1	16.88	21	.467	.467	0	ø	0	—	-4	0	-0.2
Total	2	7	8	.467	19	17	2	0-0	95.1	125	66	13	1	31-6	35	5.85	65	.326	.371	0	ø	0	94	-20	0	-2.4
RAIN, STEVE	Steven Nicholas; B6.2.1975 Los Angeles CA; BR/TR/6´6˝/(250–260); [ChiN93 11/306]; d7.17																									
1999	Chi N	0	1	.000	16	0	0	0-0	14.2	28	17	1	1	7-0	12	9.20	50	.418	.474	0	ø	0	—	-8	0	-0.4
2000	Chi N	3	4	.429	37	0	0	0-3	49.2	46	25	10	1	27-0	54	4.35	105	.250	.347	2	.000	0	—	2	0	0.2
Total	2	3	5	.375	53	0	0	0-3	64.1	74	42	11	2	34-0	66	5.46	84	.295	.381	2	.000	0	—	-6	0	-0.2
RAINEY, CHUCK	Charles David; B7.14.1954 San Diego CA; BR/TR/5´11˝/195; [BosA74*1/19]; d4.8; Col San Diego Mesa (CA) JC																									
1979	Bos A	8	5	.615	20	16	4-1	1-0	103.2	97	47	7	3	41-1	41	3.82	117	.250	.325	0	ø	0	97	8	22	0.9
1980	Bos A	8	3	.727	16	13	2-1	0-0	87	92	49	7	2	41-3	43	4.86	88	.273	.353	0	ø	0	113	-4	94	-0.5
1981	Bos A	0	1	.000	11	2	0	0-0	40	39	21	2	0	13-1	20	2.70	145	.252	.306	0	ø	0	103	2	0	0.1
1982	Bos A	7	5	.583	27	25	3-3	0-0	129	146	75	14	2	63-2	57	5.02	87	.294	.373	0	ø	0	103	-7	0	-0.6
1983	Chi N	14	13	.519	34	34	1-1	0-0	191	219	109	17	3	74-3	84	4.48	85	.295	.358	56-0-10	.161	1	104	-15	0	-1.7
1984	Chi N	5	7	.417	17	16	0	0-0	88.1	102	55	4	2	38-1	45	4.28	91	.290	.361	31-0-1	.097	-1	105	-7	0	-1.0
	Oak A	1	1	.500	16	0	0	1-1	30.2	43	27	2	0	17-4	10	6.75	56	.333	.403	0	ø	0	—	-11	0	-0.7
Total	6	43	35	.551	141	106	10-6	2-1	669.2	738	383	53	12	287-15	300	4.50	91	.284	.355	87-0-11	.138	-1	104	-34	116	-3.5
RAJSICH, DAVE	David Christopher; B9.28.1951 Youngstown OH; BL/TL/6´5˝/(175–180); d7.2; b-Gary; Col Arizona																									
1978	NY A	0	0	ø	4	2	0	0-0	13.1	16	6	0	0	6-0	9	4.05	90	.320	.379	0	ø	0	123	0	0	0.0
1979	Tex A	1	3	.250	27	3	0	0-0	53.2	56	25	7	0	18-0	32	3.52	118	.267	.325	0	ø	0	66	3	0	0.3
1980	Tex A	2	1	.667	24	1	0	2-0	48.1	56	34	7	3	22-0	35	5.96	65	.295	.370	0	ø	0	23	-10	0	-0.7
Total	3	3	4	.429	55	6	0	2-0	115.1	128	65	14	3	46-0	76	4.60	87	.284	.350	0	ø	0	75	-7	0	-0.4
RAKERS, AARON	Aaron James; B1.22.1977 Highland IL; BR/TR/6´3˝/(205–220); [BalA99 23/697]; d9.8; Col Southern Illinois–Edwardsville; [DL 2006 Bal A 182]																									
2004	Bal A	0	0	ø	3	0	0	0-0	4.1	5	2	0	0	1-0	3	4.15	112	.278	.316	0	ø	0	—	0	0	0.0
2005	Bal A	1	0	1.000	10	0	0	0-0	13.2	11	5	3	0	3-0	11	3.29	134	.220	.255	0	ø	0	—	2	0	0.1
Total	2	1	0	1.000	13	0	0	0-0	18	16	7	3	0	4-0	14	3.50	128	.235	.270	0	ø	0	—	2	182	0.1
RAKERS, JASON	Jason Paul; B6.29.1973 Pittsburgh PA; BR/TR/6´2˝/200; [CleA95 25/698]; d5.6; Col New Mexico St.																									
1998	Cle A	0	0	ø	1	0	0	0-0	1	0	1	0	0	3-0	0	9.00	53	.000	.500	0	ø	0	—	0	0	0.0
1999	Cle A	0	0	ø	1	0	0	0-0	2	2	1	1	0	1-0	0	4.50	113	.250	.333	0	ø	0	—	0	34	0.0
2000	KC A	2	0	1.000	11	0	0	0-0	21.2	33	22	5	0	7-0	16	9.14	57	.351	.392	0	ø	0	—	-8	0	-0.6
Total	3	2	0	1.000	13	0	0	0-0	24.2	35	24	6	0	11-0	16	8.76	59	.337	.393	0	ø	0	—	-8	34	-0.6
RAKOW, ED	Edward Charles "Rock"; B5.30.1935 Pittsburgh PA; D8.26.2000 West Palm Beach FL; BB/TR (BR 1960–61)/5´11˝/(175–178); d4.22																									
1960	LA N	0	1	.000	9	2	0	0	22	30	19	5	0	11-3	9	7.36	54	.323	.390	6	.333	0	67	-7	0	-0.3
1961	KC A	2	8	.200	45	11	1	1	124.2	131	80	14	8	49-1	81	4.76	88	.269	.341	29-0-3	.103	-2	98	-9	0	-0.8
1962	KC A	14	17	.452	42	35	11-2	1	235.1	232	126	31	4	98-5	159	4.25	99	.260	.334	82-0-5	.098	-5	92	-2	0	-0.7
1963	KC A	9	10	.474	34	26	7-1	0	174.1	173	85	18	5	61-4	104	3.92	99	.261	.326	57-0-2	.105	-2	91	-1	0	-0.2
1964	Det A	8	9	.471	42	13	1	3	152.1	155	70	14	6	59-1	96	3.72	98	.266	.337	39-0-4	.000	-4	95	-2	0	-0.5
1965	Det A	0	0	ø	6	0	0	0	13.1	14	11	2	0	11-0	10	6.08	57	.280	.403	3	.000	-0	—	-4	0	-0.3
1967	Atl N	3	2	.600	17	3	0	0	39.1	36	23	4	1	15-3	25	5.26	63	.240	.311	10	.000	-1	132	-7	0	-1.0
Total	7	36	47	.434	195	90	20-3	5	761.1	771	414	88	24	304-17	484	4.33	92	.264	.336	226-0-14	.084	-13	94	-32	0	-3.8
RALEIGH, JOHN	John Austin; B4.21.1887 Elkhorn WI; D8.24.1955 Escondido CA; BR/TL/5´9˝/165; d8.4																									
1909	StL N	1	10	.091	15	10	3	0	80.2	85	42	0	3	21	26	3.79	67	.285	.339	23-0-1	.087	-2	39	-10	—	-1.4
1910	StL N	0	0	ø	3	1	0	0	5	8	5	0	0	0	2	9.00	33	.364	.364	1	.000	-0	125	-3	—	-0.2
Total	2	1	10	.091	18	11	3	0	85.2	93	47	0	3	21	28	4.10	62	.291	.340	24-0-1	.083	-2	47	-13	—	-1.6
RAMBERT, PEP	Elmer Donald; B8.1.1916 Cleveland OH; D11.16.1974 W.Palm Beach FL; BR/TR/6´0˝/175; d9.23																									
1939	Pit N	0	0	ø	2	0	0	0	3.2	7	4	0	0	1	4	9.82	39	.389	.421	0	ø	0	—	-2	—	-0.1
1940	Pit N	0	1	.000	3	1	0	0	8.1	12	8	0	3	4	0	7.56	50	.333	.442	2	.000	0	68	-3	—	-0.3
Total	2	0	1	.000	5	1	0	0	12	19	12	0	3	5	4	8.25	46	.352	.435	2	.000	0	68	-5	—	-0.4
RAMBO, PETE	Warren Dawson; B11.1.1906 Thorofare NJ; D6.19.1991 Camden NJ; BR/TR/5´9˝/150; d9.16																									
1926	Phi N	0	0	ø	1	0	0	0	3.2	6	8	0	0	4	4	14.73	28	.353	.476	1	1.000	0	—	-4	—	-0.2
RAMIREZ, ALLAN	Daniel Allan; B5.1.1957 Victoria TX; BR/TR/5´10˝/190; [BalA79 5/123]; d6.8; Col Rice																									
1983	Bal A	4	4	.500	11	10	1	0-0	57	46	22	6	0	30-1	20	3.47	115	.229	.328	0	ø	0	113	5	0	0.6
RAMIREZ, ELIZARDO	Elizardo (De Palma); B1.28.1983 Villa Mella, D.R.; BL/TR/6´0˝/180; d5.25																									
2004	Phi N	0	0	ø	7	0	0	0-0	15	17	8	3	1	5-1	9	4.80	92	.283	.343	0	ø	0	—	0	0	0.0
2005	Cin N	0	3	.000	6	4	0	0-0	22.1	33	22	5	2	10-2	9	8.46	50	.344	.417	8	.000	-1	116	-10	0	-1.2
2006	Cin N	4	9	.308	21	19	0	0-0	104	123	70	14	8	29-2	69	5.37	88	.293	.348	26-0-2	.192	1	91	-8	28	-0.8
Total	3	4	12	.250	34	23	0	0-0	141.1	173	100	22	11	44-5	87	5.79	80	.300	.359	34-0-2	.147	0	95	-18	28	-2.0

YEAR	TM LG	W	L	PCT	G	GS	CG-SHO	SV-BS	IP	H	R	HR	HB	BB-IB	SO	ERA	AERA	OAV	OOB	AB-HR-SH	AVG	PB	SUP	APR	DL	PW
Ramirez, Erasmo	Erasmo; B4.29.1976 Santa Ana CA; BL/TL/6´0˝/(180–190); [SFN98 11/338]; d4.30; Col Cal St.–Fullerton/Cal St.–Northridge																									
2003	Tex A	3	1	.750	34	0	0	0-1	49	46	21	4	4	9-0	28	3.86	129	.251	.298	0	ø	0	—	6	0	0.4
2004	Tex A	5	3	.625	34	0	0	0-2	35.2	34	19	5	3	7-1	21	4.29	115	.252	.301	0	ø	0	—	2	15	0.4
2005	Tex A	0	0	ø	16	0	0	0-1	23	24	10	3	2	3-0	6	3.91	116	.273	.312	0	ø	0	—	2	88	0.1
Total	3	8	4	.667	84	0	0	0-4	107.2	104	50	12	9	19-1	55	4.01	121	.256	.302	0	ø	0	—	10	103	0.9
Ramirez, Hector	Hector Bienvenido; B12.15.1971 Santa Cruz de El Seibo, D.R.; BR/TR/6´3˝/218; d8.28																									
1999	Mil N	1	2	.333	15	0	0	0-3	21	19	8	1	0	11-2	9	3.43	134	.247	.341	3	.000	-0	—	3	0	0.3
2000	Mil N	0	1	.000	6	0	0	0-0	9	11	10	1	0	5-0	4	10.00	46	.289	.372	1	1.000	0	—	-5	0	-0.4
Total	2	1	3	.250	21	0	0	0-3	30	30	18	2	0	16-2	13	5.40	85	.261	.351	4	.250	0	—	-2	0	-0.1
Ramirez, Horacio	Horacio; B11.24.1979 Carson CA; BL/TL/6´1˝/(170–220); [AtlN97 5/172]; d4.2; [DL 2002 Atl N 76]																									
2003	Atl N	12	4	.750	29	29	1	0-0	182.1	181	91	21	6	72-10	100	4.00	105	.263	.337	61-0-6	.098	-3	142	4	0	0.1
2004	Atl N	2	4	.333	10	9	1	0-0	60.1	51	24	7	0	30-5	31	2.39	181	.226	.315	21-0-1	.095	-1*	69	10	122	0.9
2005	Atl N	11	9	.550	33	32	1-1	0-0	202.1	214	108	31	2	67-4	80	4.63	91	.282	.339	73-0-3	.219	2*	108	-8	0	-0.4
2006	Atl N	5	5	.500	14	14	0	0-0	76.1	85	42	6	4	31-2	37	4.48	101	.287	.359	24-0-3	.125	-0	111	0	105	0.1
Total	4	30	22	.577	86	84	3-1	0-0	521.1	531	265	65	12	200-21	248	4.13	104	.270	.339	179-0-13	.151	-2	116	6	303	0.7
Ramirez, Ramon	Ramon Santo; B8.31.1981 Santo Domingo, D.R.; BR/TR/5´11˝/190; d4.14																									
2006	Col N	4	3	.571	61	0	0	0-2	67.2	58	28	5	1	27-3	61	3.46	139	.230	.304	4-0-1	.500	1	—	10	0	0.9
Ramirez, Roberto	Roberto Sanchez; B8.17.1972 Vega de Alatorre, Veracruz, Mexico; BL/TL/6´0˝/(170–171); d6.12																									
1998	SD N	1	0	1.000	21	0	0	0-0	14.2	12	13	4	0	12-1	17	6.14	65	.211	.348	0	ø	0	—	-5	0	-0.3
1999	Col N	1	5	.167	32	4	0	1-0	40.1	68	42	8	0	22-2	32	8.26	70	.368	.435	7-0-1	.143	-0	115	-10	0	-1.2
Total	2	2	5	.286	53	4	0	1-0	55	80	55	12	0	34-3	49	7.69	69	.331	.413	7-0-1	.143	-0	115	-15	0	-1.5
Ramirez, Santiago	Santiago; B8.15.1978 Bonao, D.R.; BR/TR/5´11˝/210; d5.24																									
2006	Was N	0	0	ø	4	0	0	0-0	3.1	6	3	1	0	2-0	1	8.10	54	.375	.444	0	ø	0	—	-1	28	-0.1
Ramos, Edgar	Edgar Jose (Malave); B3.6.1975 Cumana, Sucre, Venezuela; BR/TR/6´4˝/210; d5.21																									
1997	Phi N	0	2	.000	4	2	0	0-0	14	15	9	3	1	6-0	4	5.14	82	.288	.373	3-0-1	.000	-0	33	-2	45	-0.2
Ramos, Mario	Mario Martin; B10.19.1977 Aurora IL; BL/TL/6´1˝/180; [OakA99 6/183]; d6.19; Col Rice																									
2003	Tex A	1	1	.500	3	3	0	0-0	13	11	9	3	2	13-0	8	6.23	80	.224	.406	1	.000	-0	105	-1	0	-0.2
Ramos, Pedro	Pedro (Guerra) "Pete"; B4.28.1935 Pinar Del Rio, Cuba; BB/TR (BR 1955–59)/6´0˝/(175–189); d4.11																									
1955	Was A	5	11	.313	45	9	3-1	5	130	121	62	13	11	39-3	34	3.88	99	.253	.319	38	.079	-3*	90	0	0	-0.3
1956	Was A	12	10	.545	37	18	4	0	152	178	95	23	3	76-0	54	5.27	82	.299	.377	44-0-4	.205	0*	106	-13	0	-1.6
1957	Was A	12	16	.429	43	30	7-1	0	231	251	131	43	7	69-4	91	4.79	81	.271	.325	76-1-3	.171	-1*	93	-21	0	-2.4
1958	Was A	14	18	.438	43	**37**	10-4	3	259.1	277	133	38	5	77-9	132	4.23	90	.273	.325	88-0-7	.239	1*	98	-13	0	-1.4
1959	Was A☆	13	19	.406	37	35	11	0	233.2	233	127	30	9	52-4	95	4.16	94	.257	.301	75-1-6	.147	-0*	90	-7	0	-0.9
1960	Was A	11	18	.379	43	**36**	14-1	2	274	254	126	24	7	99-8	160	3.45	113	.245	.313	86-2-7	.116	-2*	94	12	0	1.1
1961	Min A	11	20	.355	42	34	9-3	2	264.1	265	134	39	4	79-6	174	3.95	107	.258	.312	93-3-2	.172	1*	90	8	0	0.8
1962	Cle A	10	12	.455	37	27	7-2	1	201.1	189	104	28	5	85-5	96	3.71	104	.246	.323	68-3-2	.147	2*	86	-1	0	0.1
1963	Cle A	9	8	.529	36	22	5	0	184.2	156	74	29	4	41-6	169	3.12	116	.226	.272	55-3-4	.109	1*	107	10	0	0.8
1964	Cle A	7	10	.412	36	19	3-1	0	133	144	84	18	4	26-6	98	5.14	70	.273	.310	39-2-1	.179	2*	105	-23	0	-2.5
	NY A	1	0	1.000	13	0	0	8	21.2	13	3	1	0	0-0	21	1.25	291	.183	.176	5-0-1	.000	-1	—	6	0	0.6
	Year	8	10	.444	49	19	3-1	8	154.2	157	87	19	4	26-6	119	4.60	78	.263	.294	44-2-2	.159	1	105	-15	0	-1.9
1965	NY A	5	5	.500	65	0	0	19	92.1	80	34	7	1	27-9	68	2.92	116	.237	.294	12-0-2	.083	-1	—	5	0	0.6
1966	NY A	3	9	.250	52	1	0	13	89.2	98	43	10	1	18-4	58	3.61	92	.283	.317	13	.154	-0	53	-4	0	-0.7
1967	Phi N	0	0	ø	6	0	0	0	8	14	8	1	2	8-1	1	9.00	38	.412	.545	1	.000	-0	—	-4	0	-0.2
1969	Pit N	0	1	.000	5	0	0	0-0	6	8	4	2	0	0-0	4	6.00	58	.320	.320	1	.000	-0	—	-2	0	-0.2
	Cin N	4	3	.571	38	0	0	2-2	66.1	73	41	8	5	24-11	40	5.16	73	.284	.357	8-0-2	.000	-1	—	-9	0	-1.0
	Year	4	4	.500	43	0	0	2-2	72.1	81	45	10	5	24-11	44	5.23	72	.287	.354	9-0-2	.000	-1	—	-10	0	-1.2
1970	Was A	0	0	ø	4	0	0	0-0	8.1	10	7	2	0	4-0	10	7.56	48	.294	.368	1	.000	0*	—	-3	0	-0.1
Total	15	117	160	.422	582	268	73-13	55-2	2355.2	2364	1210	316	68	724-76	1305	4.08	95	.261	.318	703-15-41	.155	-0	96	-59	0	-7.3
Ramsay, Robert	Robert Arthur; B12.3.1973 Vancouver WA; BL/TL/6´5˝/(215–220); [BosA96 7/211]; d8.27; Col Washington St.; [DL 2002 SD N 183]																									
1999	Sea A	0	2	.000	6	3	0	0-0	18.1	23	13	3	0	9-1	11	6.38	75	.324	.395	0	ø	0	84	-3	0	-0.3
2000	†Sea A	1	1	.500	37	1	0	0-0	50.1	43	22	3	1	40-3	32	3.40	142	.234	.368	0	ø	0	58	7	14	0.4
Total	2	1	3	.250	43	4	0	0-0	68.2	66	35	6	1	49-4	43	4.19	115	.259	.375	0	ø	0	78	4	197	0.1
Ramsdell, Willie	James Willard "The Knuck"; B4.4.1916 Williamsburg KS; D10.8.1969 Wichita KS; BR/TR/5´10˝/180; d9.24																									
1947	Bro N	1	1	.500	2	0	0	0	2.2	4	6	0	1	3	3	6.75	61	.333	.500	1	1.000	0	—	-2	0	-0.4
1948	Bro N	4	4	.500	27	1	0	4	50.1	48	35	6	3	41	34	5.19	77	.251	.391	11	.091	-1	22	-7	0	-1.2
1950	Bro N	1	2	.333	5	0	0	1	6.1	7	3	0	1	2	2	2.84	144	.292	.370	3	.000	-0	—	1	0	0.1
	Cin N	7	12	.368	27	22	8-1	0	157.1	151	77	17	2	75	83	3.72	114	.255	.341	50-0-6	.200	1	90	7	0	0.8
	Year	8	14	.364	32	22	8-1	1	163.2	158	80	17	3	77	85	3.68	115	.257	.342	53-0-6	.189	0	90	8	0	0.9
1951	Cin N	9	17	.346	31	31	10-1	0	196	204	103	18	8	70	88	4.04	101	.266	.333	58-0-5	.155	-1	73	1	0	-0.1
1952	Chi N	2	3	.400	19	4	0	0	67	41	22	5	5	24	30	2.42	159	.173	.263	18	.056	-1	69	10	0	0.6
Total	5	24	39	.381	111	58	18-2	5	479.2	455	246	46	20	215	240	3.83	107	.250	.335	141-0-11	.156	-2	79	10	0	-0.2
Ramsey, Toad	Thomas H.; B8.8.1864 Indianapolis IN; D3.27.1906 Indianapolis IN; BR/TL; d9.5																									
1885	Lou AA	3	6	.333	9	9	9	0	79	44	38	1	1	28	83	1.94	167	.150	.227	31	.129	-2	87	10	—	0.8
1886	Lou AA	38	27	.585	67	67	**66**-3	0	**588.2**	447	297	3	12	207	499	2.45	149	**.198**	.269	241	.241	-3	87	**77**	—	6.7
1887	Lou AA	37	27	.578	65	64	61	0	561	544	358	9	16	167	**355**	3.43	128	.242	.299	225	.191	-10	96	58	—	3.7
1888	Lou AA	8	30	.211	40	40	37-1	0	342.1	362	278	10	11	86	228	3.42	90	.262	.310	142	.120	-7*	74	-19	—	-2.5
1889	Lou AA	1	16	.059	18	18	15	0	140	175	152	7	2	71	60	5.59	69	.297	.374	57	.263	0	62	-29	—	-2.6
	StL AA	3	1	.750	5	3	3	0	41	44	29	0	1	10	33	3.95	107	.265	.311	17	.294	0	108	1	—	0.1
	Year	4	17	.190	23	21	18	0	181	219	181	7	3	81	93	5.22	75	.290	.361	74	.270	1	68	-27	—	-2.5
1890	StL AA	23	17	.575	44	40	34-1	0	348.2	325	221	10	8	102	257	3.69	117	.239	.296	145	.228	-1	94	20	—	1.4
Total	6	113	124	.477	248	241	225-5	0	2100.2	1941	1373	40	51	671	1515	3.29	117	.234	.295	858	.204	-22	87	118	—	7.6
Randall, Scott	Scott Philip; B10.29.1975 Fullerton CA; BR/TR/6´3˝/200; [ColN95 11/291]; d8.26; Col California–Santa Barbara/Santa Barbara (CA) City																									
2003	Cin N	2	5	.286	15	2	0	0-1	27.2	34	20	1	2	11-3	25	6.51	64	.304	.376	4	.250	0	11	-7	0	-1.2
Randolph, Stephen	Stephen Le Charles; B5.1.1974 Okinawa, Japan; BL/TL/6´3˝/(180–200); [NYA95 18/506]; d3.31; Col Texas																									
2003	Ari N	8	1	.889	50	0	0	0-0	60	50	28	7	2	43-3	50	4.05	114	.226	.357	3-0-1	.000	-0	—	4	26	0.5
2004	Ari N	2	5	.286	45	6	0	0-0	81.2	73	56	11	1	76-2	62	5.51	83	.235	.384	12	.417	2*	85	-8	0	-0.4
Total	2	10	6	.625	95	6	0	0-0	141.2	123	84	18	3	119-5	112	4.89	94	.232	.373	15-0-1	.333	2	85	-4	26	0.1
Raney, Ribs	Frank Robert Donald (b Frank Robert Donald Raniszewski); B2.16.1923 Detroit MI; D7.7.2003 Warren MI; BR/TR/6´4˝/190; d9.18; Col Western Michigan																									
1949	StL A	1	2	.333	3	3	1	0	16.1	23	15	2	0	12	5	7.71	59	.333	.432	6	.000	-1	92	-5	0	-0.8
1950	StL A	0	1	.000	1	0	0	0	2	2	2	0	0	2	2	4.50	110	.250	.400	1	.000	-0	—	0	0	-0.1
Total	2	1	3	.250	4	3	1	0	18.1	25	17	2	0	14	7	7.36	62	.325	.429	7	.000	-1	92	-5	0	-0.9
Rapp, Pat	Patrick Leland; B7.13.1967 Jennings LA; BR/TR/6´3˝/(195–230); [SFN89 15/388]; d7.10; Col Southern Mississippi																									
1992	SF N	0	2	.000	3	2	0	0-0	10	8	8	0	1	6-1	3	7.20	46	.235	.366	2-0-1	.000	-0	41	-4	0	-0.7
1993	Fla N	4	6	.400	16	16	1	0-0	94	101	49	7	2	39-1	57	4.02	109	.281	.351	31-0-2	.194	0	80	2	0	0.2
1994	Fla N	7	8	.467	24	23	2-1	0-0	133.1	132	67	13	7	69-3	75	3.85	116	.266	.361	41-0-4	.122	-2*	88	7	0	0.5
1995	Fla N	14	7	.667	28	28	3-2	0-0	167.1	158	72	10	7	76-2	102	3.44	125	.253	.340	56-0-9	.107	-3	109	15	0	1.4
1996	Fla N	8	16	.333	30	29	0	0-0	162.1	184	95	12	3	91-6	86	5.10	81	.301	.390	58	.121	-2	102	-15	0	-2.1
1997	Fla N	4	6	.400	19	19	1-1	0-0	108.2	121	59	11	3	51-3	64	4.47	91	.286	.365	35-1-4	.143	0	111	-5	0	-0.4
	SF N	1	2	.333	8	6	0	0-0	33	37	24	5	2	21-1	28	6.00	69	.294	.395	12	.000	-1	112	-7	17	-0.7
	Year	5	8	.385	27	25	1-1	0-0	141.2	158	83	16	5	72-4	92	4.83	84	.288	.372	47-1-4	.106	-1	111	-12	0	-1.1
1998	KC A	12	13	.480	32	32	1-1	0-0	188.1	208	117	24	10	107-7	132	5.30	92	.285	.381	2-0-1	.000	-0	85	-7	0	-0.8

YEAR	TM LG	W	L	PCT	G	GS	CG-SHO	SV-BS	IP	H	R	HR	HB	BB-IB	SO	ERA	AERA	OAV	OOB	AB-HR-SH	AVG	PB	SUP	APR	DL	PW
1999	†Bos A	6	7	.462	37	26	0	0-0	146.1	147	78	13	7	69-1	90	4.12	121	.263	.351	2	.000	-0	105	13	0	0.9
2000	Bal A	9	12	.429	31	30	0	0-0	174	203	125	18	5	83-5	106	5.90	80	.289	.365	3	.000	-0	125	-26	0	-2.5
2001	Ana A	5	12	.294	31	28	1	0-0	170	169	96	20	2	71-2	82	4.76	98	.261	.332	5	.000	-1	86	-1	0	-0.1
Total	10	70	91	.435	259	239	9-5	0-0	1387.1	1468	790	133	49	683-32	825	4.68	96	.276	.361	247-1-21	.117	-8	99	-28	17	-4.3
RASCHI, VIC	Victor John Angelo; B3.28.1919 W.Springfield MA; D10.14.1988 Groveland NY; BR/TR/6´1˝/(185–210); d9.23; Col William and Mary																									
1946	NY A	2	0	1.000	2	2	2	0	16	14	7	0	0	5	11	3.94	88	.230	.288	4-0-3	.250	0	137	0	0	0.0
1947	†NY A	7	2	.778	15	14	6-1	0	104.2	89	47	11	1	38	51	3.87	91	.226	.296	40-0-1	.250	2	139	-3	0	-0.1
1948	NY A★	19	8	.704	36	31	18-6	1	222.2	208	103	15	3	74	124	3.84	106	.247	.310	81-0-4	.235	2	134	8	0	1.0
1949	†NY A★	21	10	.677	38	**37**	21-3	0	274.2	247	120	16	6	138	124	3.34	121	.241	.334	83-0-11	.157	1	123	20	0	2.1
1950	†NY A★	21	8	**.724**	33	32	17-2	1	256.2	232	120	19	3	116	155	4.00	107	.243	.327	86-1-10	.198	1	116	11	0	1.1
1951	†NY A	21	10	.677	35	**34**	15-4	0	258.1	233	110	20	5	103	**164**	3.27	117	.242	.319	85-0-13	.176	-2	123	16	0	1.4
1952	†NY A★	16	6	.727	31	31	13-4	0	223	174	78	12	6	91	127	2.78	119	.216	.300	69-0-10	.188	3	113	16	0	1.6
1953	†NY A	13	6	.684	28	26	7-4	1	181	150	74	11	1	55	76	3.33	111	.224	**.283**	63-0-5	.143	-2	135	9	0	0.5
1954	StL N	8	9	.471	30	29	6-2	0	179	182	99	24	0	71	73	4.73	87	.268	.335	64-0-3	.141	-2	105	-9	0	-0.9
1955	StL N	0	1	.000	1	1	0	0	1.2	5	4	0	0	1-1	1	21.60	19	.556	.545	0	ø	0	88	-3	0	-0.5
	KC A	4	6	.400	20	18	1	0	101.1	132	66	10	1	35-4	38	5.42	77	.312	.364	33-0-3	.182	-0	80	-13	0	-1.1
Total	10	132	66	.667	269	255	106-26	3	1819	1666	828	138	26	727-5	944	3.72	105	.244	.319	608-1-63	.184	3	119	52	0	5.1
RASMUSSEN, DENNIS	Dennis Lee; B4.18.1959 Los Angeles CA; BL/TL/6´7˝/(223–240); [CalA80 1/17]; d9.16; gf–Bill Brubaker; Col Creighton																									
1983	SD N	0	0	ø	4	1	0	0-0	13.2	10	5	1	0	8-0	13	1.98	178	.200	.310	3	.000	-0	101	2	0	0.1
1984	NY A	9	6	.600	24	24	1	0-0	147.2	127	79	16	4	60-0	110	4.57	84	.234	.312	0	ø	0	129	-11	0	-1.0
1985	NY A	3	5	.375	22	16	2	0-0	101.2	97	56	10	1	42-1	63	3.98	102	.255	.327	0	ø	0	104	-2	0	-0.1
1986	NY A	18	6	.750	31	31	3-1	0-0	202	160	91	28	2	74-0	131	3.88	107	.217	.289	0	ø	0	128	9	0	0.9
1987	NY A	9	7	.563	26	25	2	0-0	146	145	78	31	4	55-1	89	4.75	93	.260	.328	0	ø	0	120	-3	0	-0.3
	Cin N	4	1	.800	7	7	0	0-0	45.1	39	22	5	1	12-0	39	3.97	106	.229	.283	15	.067	-1	119	1	0	0.1
1988	Cin N	2	6	.250	11	11	1-1	0-0	56.1	68	36	8	2	22-4	27	5.75	62	.300	.364	22	.227	1	90	-12	0	-1.4
	SD N	14	4	.778	20	20	6	0-0	148.1	131	48	9	2	36-0	85	2.55	133	.238	.286	48-0-6	.188	2	129	14	0	2.1
	Year	16	10	.615	31	31	7-1	0-0	204.2	199	84	17	4	58-4	112	3.43	101	.256	.309	70-0-6	.200	3	115	2	0	0.7
1989	SD N	10	10	.500	33	33	1	0-0	183.2	190	100	18	3	72-6	87	4.26	82	.270	.335	65-0-3	.169	1	99	-16	0	-1.5
1990	SD N	11	15	.423	32	32	3-1	0-0	187.2	217	110	28	3	62-4	86	4.51	85	.292	.348	62-0-6	.290	5*	110	-16	0	-1.4
1991	SD N	6	13	.316	24	24	1-1	0-0	146.2	155	74	12	2	49-3	75	3.74	102	.271	.328	44-0-3	.136	1*	83	-1	47	0.0
1992	Chi N	0	0	ø	3	1	0	0-0	5	7	6	2	1	2-1	0	10.80	34	.350	.417	0-0-1	ø	0	100	-4	19	-0.2
	KC A	4	1	.800	5	5	1-1	0-0	37.2	25	7	0	0	6-0	12	1.43	285	.197	.233	0	ø	0	63	11	0	1.6
1993	KC A	1	2	.333	9	4	0	0-0	29	40	25	4	1	14-1	12	7.45	62	.328	.399	0	ø	0	125	-8	60	-0.7
1995	KC A	0	1	.000	5	1	0	0-0	10	13	10	3	0	8-2	6	9.00	53	.302	.412	0	ø	0	97	-4	0	-0.4
Total	12	91	77	.542	256	235	21-5	0-0	1460.2	1424	747	175	26	522-23	835	4.15	94	.257	.321	259-0-19	.193	8	111	-40	126	-2.2
RASMUSSEN, ERIC	Eric Ralph (Born Harold Ralph Rasmussen); B3.22.1952 Racine WI; BR/TR/6´3˝/205; [StLN73 32/676]; d7.21; Col New Orleans																									
1975	StL N	5	5	.500	14	13	2-1	0-0	81	86	44	8	0	20-2	59	3.78	101	.264	.306	26-0-1	.154	-0	89	-1	0	-0.2
1976	StL N	6	12	.333	43	17	2-1	0-2	150.1	139	67	10	2	54-6	76	3.53	101	.247	.313	38-0-4	.105	-1	91	1	0	0.2
1977	StL N	11	17	.393	34	34	11-3	0-0	233	223	103	24	5	63-7	120	3.48	112	.254	.305	72-0-6	.139	0	82	10	0	1.1
1978	StL N	2	5	.286	10	10	2-1	0-0	60.1	61	32	4	0	20-2	32	4.18	85	.270	.324	18-0-2	.111	-1	58	-4	0	-0.5
	SD N	12	10	.545	27	24	3-2	0-0	146.1	154	72	16	1	43-6	59	4.06	83	.277	.327	46-0-8	.152	-1	102	-11	0	-1.5
	Year	14	15	.483	37	34	5-3	0-0	206.2	215	104	20	1	63-8	91	4.09	83	.275	.326	64-0-10	.141	-2	88	-17	0	-2.0
1979	SD N	6	9	.400	45	20	5-3	3-2	156.2	142	59	9	0	42-6	54	3.27	108	.244	.292	36-0-6	.056	-2*	93	7	0	0.5
1980	SD N	4	11	.267	40	14	0	1-3	111.1	130	60	9	3	33-6	50	4.37	78	.295	.347	21-0-6	.095	-1	78	-13	0	-1.7
1982	StL N	1	2	.333	8	3	0	0-0	18.1	21	13	2	0	8-4	15	4.42	83	.288	.354	3-0-1	.000	-0	48	-3	0	-0.4
1983	StL N	0	0	ø	6	0	0	1-0	7.2	16	11	1	0	4-2	6	11.74	31	.444	.500	0	ø	0	—	-7	0	-0.3
	KC A	3	6	.333	11	9	2-1	0-0	52.2	61	28	4	0	22-0	18	4.78	86	.289	.355	0	ø	0	76	-2	0	-0.4
Total	8	50	77	.394	238	144	27-12	5-7	1017.2	1033	489	87	11	309-41	489	3.85	95	.266	.319	260-0-34	.119	-6	85	-23	0	-3.2
RASMUSSEN, HANS	Henry Florian; B4.18.1895 Chicago IL; D1.1.1949 Chicago IL; BR/TR/6´6˝/220; d8.11																									
1915	Chi F	0	0	ø	2	0	0	0	2	3	3	0	0	2	2	13.50	19	.600	.714	1	.000	-0	—	-2	—	-0.1
RASNER, DARRELL	Darrell Wayne; B1.13.1981 Carson City NV; BR/TR/6´3˝/210; [MonN02 2/46]; d9.6; Col Nevada–Reno																									
2005	Was N	0	1	.000	5	1	0	0-0	7.1	5	3	0	2	2-1	4	3.68	112	.192	.300	0	ø	0	46	0	0	0.0
2006	NY A	3	1	.750	6	3	0	0-0	20.1	18	10	2	1	5-0	11	4.43	102	.237	.293	0	ø	0	125	1	83	0.1
Total	2	3	2	.600	11	4	0	0-0	27.2	23	13	2	3	7-1	15	4.23	105	.225	.295	0	ø	0	107	1	83	0.1
RATH, GARY	Alfred Gary; B1.10.1973 Gulfport MS; BL/TL/6´2˝/186; [LAN94 2/47]; d6.2; Col Mississippi St.																									
1998	LA N	0	0	ø	3	0	0	0-0	3.1	3	4	1	0	2-0	4	10.80	37	.250	.357	0	ø	0	—	-2	0	-0.1
1999	Min A	0	1	.000	5	1	0	0-0	4.2	6	6	1	0	5-0	1	11.57	45	.300	.440	0	ø	0	90	-3	0	-0.5
Total	2	0	1	.000	8	1	0	0-0	8	9	10	2	0	7-0	5	11.25	42	.281	.410	0	ø	0	90	-5	0	-0.6
RATH, FRED	Frederick Helsher Jr.; B1.5.1973 Dallas TX; BR/TR/6´3˝/220; d7.29; f–Fred; Col South Florida																									
1998	Col N	0	0	ø	2	0	0	0-0	5.1	6	1	0	0	2-0	2	1.69	307	.300	.348	2	.000	-0	—	2	0	0.1
RATH, FRED	Frederick Helsher Sr.; B9.1.1943 Little Rock AR; BR/TR/6´3˝/190; [ChiA65 4/80]; d9.10; s–Fred; Col Baylor																									
1968	Chi A	0	0	ø	5	0	0	0	11.1	8	5	0	1	3-1	3	1.59	190	.182	.250	0	ø	0	—	1	0	0.0
1969	Chi A	0	2	.000	3	2	0	0	11.2	11	10	4	0	8-1	4	7.71	50	.256	.373	3	.000	-0	34	-4	0	-0.7
Total	2	0	2	.000	8	2	0	0-0	23	19	15	4	1	11-2	7	4.70	73	.218	.313	3	.000	-0	34	-3	0	-0.7
RATLIFF, JON	Jon Charles; B12.22.1971 Syracuse NY; BR/TR/6´4˝/195; [ChiN93 1/24]; d9.15; Col LeMoyne (NY)																									
2000	Oak A	0	0	ø	1	0	0	0-0	1	0	0	0	0	0-0	0	0.00	ø	.000	.000	0	ø	0	—	1	0	0.0
RATZER, STEVE	Steven Wayne; B9.9.1953 Paterson NJ; BR/TR/6´1˝/192; d10.5; Col St. Johns																									
1980	Mon N	0	0	ø	1	1	0	0-0	4	9	5	0	0	2-0	0	11.25	32	.450	.500	1	.000	-0	197	-3	0	-0.1
1981	Mon N	1	1	.500	12	0	0	0-0	17.1	23	14	2	0	7-1	4	6.23	57	.311	.370	2	.000	-0	—	-5	0	-0.6
Total	2	1	1	.500	13	1	0	0-0	21.1	32	19	2	0	9-1	4	7.17	50	.340	.398	3	.000	-0	197	-8	0	-0.7
RAU, DOUG	Douglas James; B12.15.1948 Columbus TX; BL/TL/6´2˝/(175–178); [LAN70 S1/7]; d9.2; Col Texas A&M; [DL 1980 LA N 180]																									
1972	LA N	2	2	.500	7	3	2	0-0	32.2	18	11	1	1	11-2	19	2.20	152	.159	.236	7-0-1	.143	1	61	4	0	0.6
1973	LA N	4	2	.667	31	3	0	3-1	63.2	64	28	5	1	28-2	51	3.96	88	.259	.336	11-0-2	.091	-1	34	-2	0	-0.3
1974	†LA N	13	11	.542	36	35	3-1	0-0	198.1	191	90	20	4	70-1	126	3.72	92	.251	.316	64-0-8	.141	-1	124	-5	0	-0.6
1975	LA N	15	9	.625	38	38	8-2	0-0	257.2	227	96	18	3	61-1	151	3.11	110	.236	.282	87-0-10	.195	2	116	11	0	1.2
1976	LA N	16	12	.571	34	32	8-3	0-0	231	221	71	18	7	69-1	98	2.57	132	.258	.317	60-0-8	.150	1	84	23	0	2.9
1977	†LA N	14	8	.636	32	32	4-2	0-0	212.1	232	87	15	6	49-2	126	3.43	112	.282	.325	71-0-3	.141	-1	99	11	0	1.0
1978	†LA N	15	9	.625	30	30	7-2	0-0	199	219	82	17	2	68-5	95	3.26	108	.284	.342	63-0-13	.143	-1	122	6	0	0.5
1979	LA N	1	5	.167	11	11	1-1	0-0	56	73	37	3	4	22-0	28	5.30	68	.320	.384	14-0-1	.143	1	89	-10	119	-0.9
1981	Cal A	1	2	.333	3	3	0	0-0	10.1	14	10	2	0	4-0	3	8.71	42	.341	.400	0	ø	0	90	-5	74	-0.9
Total	9	81	60	.574	222	187	33-11	3-1	1261	1259	512	99	28	382-14	697	3.35	105	.262	.318	377-0-46	.154	2	106	33	373	3.5
RAUCH, JON	Jon Erich; B9.27.1978 Louisville KY; BR/TR/6´11˝/(230–260); [ChiA99 3/99]; d4.2; Col Morehead St.																									
2002	Chi A	2	1	.667	8	6	0	0-0	28.2	28	26	7	2	14-2	19	6.59	68	.248	.338	0	ø	0	151	-8	0	-0.7
2004	Chi A	1	1	.500	2	2	0	0-0	8.2	16	6	0	0	4-0	4	6.23	75	.432	.476	0	ø	0	79	-1	0	-0.2
	Mon N	3	0	1.000	9	2	0	0-0	23.1	14	4	1	0	7-2	18	1.54	298	.175	.241	6-1-0	.167	1	142	8	31	1.0
2005	Was N	2	4	.333	15	1	0	0-0	30	24	12	3	1	11-2	23	3.60	114	.218	.293	7-0-1	.143	-0	253	2	103	0.4
2006	Was N	4	5	.444	85	0	0	2-3	91.1	78	37	13	2	36-6	86	3.35	130	.231	.304	4	.000	-0	—	11	0	0.8
Total	4	12	11	.522	119	11	0	2-3	182	160	85	24	5	72-12	150	3.81	115	.236	.310	17-1-1	.118	0	148	12	134	1.3
RAUCH, BOB	Robert John; B6.16.1949 Brookings SD; BR/TR/6´4˝/195; d6.29; Col San Bernardino Valley (CA) JC																									
1972	NY N	0	1	.000	19	0	0	1-0	27	27	16	3	0	21-2	23	5.00	68	.273	.393	3	.000	-0	—	-5	0	-0.3

YEAR	TM LG	W	L	PCT	G	GS	CG-SHO	SV-BS	IP	H	R	HR	HB	BB-IB	SO	ERA	AERA	OAV	OOB	AB-HR-SH	AVG	PB	SUP	APR	DL	PW
Rautzhan, Lance	Clarence George; B8.20.1952 Pottsville PA; BR/TL/6´1˝/(200–203); [LAN70 3/57]; d7.23																									
1977	†LA N	4	1	.800	25	0	0	2-4	20.2	25	10	0	0	7-1	13	4.35	89	.313	.364	1	.000	-0	—	-1	0	-0.1
1978	†LA N	2	1	.667	43	0	0	4-2	61.1	61	22	1	1	19-3	25	2.93	120	.263	.318	4-0-2	.000	-0	—	4	0	0.3
1979	LA N	0	2	.000	12	0	0	1-2	9.2	9	9	0	1	11-2	5	7.45	49	.273	.447	0	ø	0	—	-4	0	-0.8
	Mil A	0	0	ø	3	0	0	0-0	3	3	3	0	0	10-0	2	9.00	47	.300	.650	0	ø	0	—	-1	0	-0.1
Total	3	6	4	.600	83	0	0	7-8	94.2	98	44	1	2	47-6	45	3.90	93	.276	.359	5-0-2	.000	-1	—	-2	0	-0.7
Rawley, Shane	Shane William; B7.27.1955 Racine WI; BR/TL/6´0˝/(155–185); [MonN74 S2/29]; d4.6; Col Indian Hills (IA) CC																									
1978	Sea A	4	9	.308	52	2	0	4-1	111.1	114	57	7	5	51-3	66	4.12	93	.275	.356	0	ø	0*	70	-3	0	-0.3
1979	Sea A	5	9	.357	48	3	0	11-5	84.1	88	40	2	1	40-5	48	3.84	114	.278	.357	0	ø	0*	124	5	52	0.9
1980	Sea A	7	7	.500	59	0	0	13-9	113.2	103	44	3	3	63-16	68	3.33	125	.257	.360	0	ø	0	—	12	0	1.7
1981	Sea A	4	6	.400	46	0	0	8-7	68.1	64	31	1	1	38-6	35	3.95	98	.257	.354	0	ø	0	—	0	16	0.1
1982	NY A	11	10	.524	47	17	3	3-1	164	165	79	10	2	54-5	111	4.06	99	.267	.324	0	ø	0	97	1	0	0.2
1983	NY A	14	14	.500	34	33	13-2	1-0	238.1	246	111	19	3	79-1	124	3.78	105	.269	.327	0	ø	0	96	5	0	0.5
1984	NY A	2	3	.400	11	10	0	0-0	42	46	33	0	0	27-0	24	6.21	62	.272	.372	0	ø	0	78	-12	15	-1.2
	Phi N	10	6	.625	18	18	3	0-0	120.1	117	55	13	1	27-2	58	3.81	96	.257	.298	43	.116	-2*	102	0	0	-0.2
1985	Phi N	13	8	.619	36	31	6-2	0-0	198.2	188	82	16	2	81-6	106	3.31	112	.249	.321	58-0-7	.138	0	109	9	0	1.0
1986	Phi N☆	11	7	.611	23	23	7-1	0-0	157.2	166	67	13	1	50-4	73	3.54	110	.270	.325	52-0-10	.173	0	129	8	68	0.9
1987	Phi N	17	11	.607	36	**36**	4-1	0-0	229.2	250	118	23	5	86-8	123	4.39	98	.279	.343	79-0-12	.152	-1*	104	0	0	0.0
1988	Phi N	8	16	.333	32	32	4-1	0-0	198	220	111	27	4	78-7	87	4.18	86	.286	.351	57-0-11	.105	-1	95	-16	23	-1.9
1989	Min A	5	12	.294	27	25	1	0-0	145	167	89	19	0	60-1	68	5.21	80	.293	.359	0	ø	0	85	-15	0	-1.6
Total	12	111	118	.485	469	230	41-7	40-23	1871.1	1934	917	153	28	734-64	991	4.02	98	.271	.338	289-0-40	.138	-3	100	-6	174	0.1
Ray, Carl	Carl Grady; B1.31.1889 Danbury NC; D4.2.1970 Lexington NC; BL/TL/5´11˝/170; d9.25																									
1915	Phi A	0	1	.000	2	1	0	0	7.1	11	7	0	4	6	6	4.91	60	.333	.488	2	.000	0	25	-2	—	-0.3
1916	Phi A	0	1	.000	3	1	0	0	9.1	9	8	0	1	14	5	4.82	59	.257	.480	3	.000	-0	53	-3	—	-0.3
Total	2	0	2	.000	5	2	0	0	16.2	20	15	0	5	20	11	4.86	59	.294	.484	5	.000	-0	39	-5	—	-0.6
Ray, Chris	Christopher Thomas; B1.12.1982 Tampa FL; BR/TR/6´3˝/(200–225); [BalA03 3/74]; d6.14; Col William and Mary																									
2005	Bal A	1	3	.250	41	0	0	0-4	40.2	34	15	5	1	18-3	43	2.66	166	.222	.306	0	ø	0	—	7	0	0.6
2006	Bal A	4	4	.500	61	0	0	33-5	66	45	22	10	1	27-2	51	2.73	166	.193	.275	0	ø	0	—	13	0	2.5
Total	2	5	7	.417	102	0	0	33-9	106.2	79	37	15	2	45-5	94	2.70	166	.205	.288	0	ø	0	—	20	0	3.1
Ray, Jim	James Francis "Sting"; B12.1.1944 Rock Hill SC; BR/TR/6´1˝/(185–195); d9.16																									
1965	Hou N	0	2	.000	3	2	0	0	7.2	11	9	1	0	6-0	7	10.57	32	.355	.447	2	.000	-0	117	-6	0	-1.0
1966	Hou N	0	0	ø	1	0	0	0	0	0	1	0	0	1-0	0	(1)	ø	ø	1.000	0	ø	0	—	-1	0	-0.1
1968	Hou N	2	3	.400	41	2	1	1	81	65	26	5	1	25-8	71	2.67	111	.220	.278	15-0-1	.067	-1*	103	3	0	0.0
1969	Hou N	8	2	.800	40	13	0	0-0	115	105	55	11	2	48-4	115	3.91	91	.245	.322	26-0-3	.115	-1	92	-3	0	-0.4
1970	Hou N	6	3	.667	52	2	0	5-1	105	97	39	13	0	49-2	67	3.26	120	.251	.333	27	.185	-0	69	9	0	0.8
1971	Hou N	10	4	.714	47	1	0	3-1	97.2	72	27	3	2	31-5	46	2.12	159	.211	.277	18	.167	0	79	13	0	1.9
1972	Hou N	10	9	.526	54	0	0	8-9	90.1	77	50	10	3	44-6	50	4.28	78	.227	.319	16-0-1	.063	-1	—	-11	0	-2.5
1973	Hou N	6	4	.600	42	0	0	6-3	69	65	37	5	3	38-8	25	4.43	82	.253	.355	13-0-2	.231	0	—	-6	0	-0.9
1974	Det A	1	3	.250	28	0	0	2-1	52.1	49	27	4	1	29-4	26	4.47	86	.254	.350	0	ø	0	—	-2	0	-0.2
Total	9	43	30	.589	308	20	1	25-15	618	541	271	52	12	271-37	407	3.61	97	.238	.320	117-0-7	.137	-3	92	-4	0	-2.4
Ray, Ken	Kenneth Alan; B11.27.1974 Atlanta GA; BR/TR/6´2˝/200; [KCA93 18/497]; d7.10																									
1999	KC A	1	0	1.000	13	0	0	0-0	11.1	23	12	2	1	6-0	0	8.74	58	.460	.526	0	ø	0	—	-4	0	-0.3
2006	Atl N	1	1	.500	69	0	0	5-3	67.2	66	36	9	0	38-4	50	4.52	100	.259	.353	1	.000	-0	—	1	0	0.0
Total	2	2	1	.667	82	0	0	5-3	79	89	48	11	1	44-4	50	5.13	90	.292	.381	1	.000	-0	—	-3	0	-0.3
Ray, Farmer	Robert Henry; B9.17.1886 Ft.Lyon CO; D3.11.1963 Electra TX; BL/TR/5´11˝/160; d6.13																									
1910	StL A	4	10	.286	21	16	11	0	140.2	146	77	3	7	49	35	3.58	69	.285	.356	40-0-3	.175	0	73	-14	—	-1.5
Raydon, Curt	Curtis Lowell; B11.18.1933 Bloomington IL; BR/TR/6´4˝/185; d4.15																									
1958	Pit N	8	4	.667	31	20	2-1	1	134.1	118	64	18	5	61-4	85	3.62	107	.236	.323	38-0-4	.026	-2	120	2	0	-0.2
Raymond, Bugs	Arthur Lawrence; B2.24.1882 Chicago IL; D9.7.1912 Chicago IL; BR/TR/5´10˝/180; d9.23																									
1904	Det A	0	1	.000	5	2	1	0	14.2	14	9	0	2	6	7	3.07	83	.250	.344	5	.000	-1	14	-2	—	-0.1
1907	StL N	2	4	.333	8	6	6-1	0	64.2	56	34	3	1	21	34	1.67	150	.230	.294	22	.091	-0	81	1	—	0.0
1908	StL N	15	25	.375	48	37	23-5	2	324.1	236	116	2	14	95	145	2.03	116	.207	.277	90-0-3	.189	1	61	11	—	1.8
1909	NY N	18	12	.600	39	30	18-2	0	270	239	98	7	6	87	121	2.47	104	.245	.311	89-0-5	.146	0	90	7	—	0.9
1910	NY N	4	11	.267	19	11	6	0	99.1	106	63	2	8	40	55	3.81	78	.280	.362	32-0-1	.156	-1	78	-12	—	-1.5
1911	NY N	6	4	.600	17	9	4-1	0	81.2	73	40	1	2	33	39	3.31	102	.248	.328	25-0-3	.200	-0	104	0	—	0.0
Total	6	45	57	.441	136	95	58-9	2	854.2	724	360	15	33	282	401	2.49	105	.235	.306	263-0-12	.160	-0	78	5	—	1.1
Raymond, Harry	Harry H. "Jack"; B2.20.1862 Utica NY; D3.21.1925 San Diego CA; 5´9˝/179; d9.9.1888; ▲																									
1889	Lou AA	1	0	1.000	1	1	1	0	9	8	2	0	0	11	1	1.00	385	.229	.413	515	.239	0*	97	3	—	0.2
Raymond, Claude	Joseph Claude Marc "Frenchy"; B5.7.1937 St.Jean QC, Can.; BR/TR/5´10˝/(175–180); d4.15																									
1959	Chi A	0	0	ø	3	0	0	0	4	5	4	2	0	2-0	1	9.00	42	.333	.389	0	ø	0	—	-2	0	-0.1
1961	Mil N	1	0	1.000	13	0	0	2	20.1	22	9	2	1	9-1	13	3.98	94	.275	.356	3	.000	-0	—	0	0	0.0
1962	Mil N	5	5	.500	26	0	0	10	42.2	37	15	5	2	15-2	40	2.74	138	.236	.309	8-0-1	.000	-1	—	5	0	0.9
1963	Mil N	4	6	.400	45	0	0	5	53.1	57	36	12	4	27-4	44	5.40	60	.268	.361	4	.500	2	—	-13	0	-2.3
1964	Hou N	5	5	.500	38	0	0	0	79.2	64	28	3	3	22-1	56	2.82	121	.229	.289	14-0-2	.071	-0*	—	6	0	0.7
1965	Hou N	7	4	.636	33	7	2	5	96.1	87	35	6	5	16-2	79	2.90	116	.244	.285	26	.115	-1*	97	5	0	0.6
1966	Hou N☆	7	5	.583	62	0	0	16	92	85	39	10	4	25-6	73	3.13	109	.242	.298	9-0-1	.111	-0	—	2	0	0.2
1967	Hou N	0	4	.000	21	0	0	5	31	31	12	5	2	7-4	17	3.19	104	.256	.305	5	.200	0	—	1	0	0.1
	Atl N	4	1	.800	28	0	0	5	34.1	33	11	2	0	11-5	14	2.62	127	.260	.314	2	.000	-0	—	3	0	0.5
	Year	4	5	.444	49	0	0	10	65.1	64	23	7	2	18-9	31	2.89	115	.258	.310	7	.143	0	—	4	0	0.6
1968	Atl N	3	5	.375	36	0	0	10	60.1	56	21	4	1	18-9	37	2.83	106	.256	.313	7	.143	-0	—	1	0	0.3
1969	Atl N	2	2	.500	33	0	0	1-1	48	56	34	4	2	13-2	15	5.25	69	.298	.346	7-0-1	.286	0	—	-10	0	-0.8
	Mon N	1	2	.333	15	0	0	1-1	22	21	12	2	2	8-3	11	4.09	90	.256	.333	4	.000	-0	—	-1	0	-0.2
	Year	3	4	.429	48	0	0	2-2	70	77	46	6	4	21-5	26	4.89	75	.285	.342	11-0-1	.182	-0	—	-11	0	-1.0
1970	Mon N	6	7	.462	59	0	0	23-6	83.1	76	48	13	2	27-7	68	4.43	94	.240	.300	11-0-2	.000	-1	—	-3	0	-0.8
1971	Mon N	1	7	.125	37	0	0	0-1	53.2	81	34	5	0	25-8	29	4.70	76	.373	.433	1-0-1	.000	-0	—	-8	0	-1.1
Total	12	46	53	.465	449	7	2	83-9	721	711	338	75	28	225-54	497	3.66	96	.261	.321	101-0-8	.109	-2	97	-14	0	-2.0
Raziano, Barry	Barry John; B2.5.1947 New Orleans LA; BB/TR/5´10˝/175; [NYN65 27/815]; d8.18																									
1973	KC A	0	0	ø	2	0	0	0-0	5	6	3	1	1	1-1	0	5.40	76	.316	.381	0	ø	0	—	-1	0	0.0
1974	Cal A	1	2	.333	13	0	0	1-2	16.2	15	14	1	0	8-1	9	6.48	54	.246	.333	0	ø	0	—	-6	0	-1.0
Total	2	1	2	.333	15	0	0	1-2	21.2	21	17	2	1	9-2	9	6.23	58	.262	.344	0	ø	0	—	-7	0	-1.0
Reames, Britt	William Britt; B8.19.1973 Seneca SC; BR/TR/5´11˝/(175–180); [StLN95 17/463]; d8.20; Col The Citadel																									
2000	†StL N	2	1	.667	8	7	0	0-0	40.2	30	17	4	1	23-1	31	2.88	162	.207	.318	12-0-1	.167	-0*	76	7	0	0.4
2001	Mon N	4	8	.333	41	13	0	0-1	95	101	68	16	5	48-3	86	5.59	77	.273	.362	17-1-3	.118	2	74	-15	0	-1.4
2002	Mon N	1	4	.200	42	6	0	0-1	68	70	42	8	3	38-6	76	5.03	87	.266	.364	9-0-2	.111	-0	78	-4	0	-0.3
2003	Mon N	0	0	ø	2	0	0	0-0	1.1	4	4	0	0	2-0	1	27.00	16	.500	.600	1	.000	-0	—	-3	0	-0.2
2005	Oak A	0	0	ø	2	0	0	0-0	5.2	10	6	2	1	2-0	4	9.53	46	.400	.448	0	ø	0	—	-3	0	-0.1
2006	Pit N	0	0	ø	6	0	0	0-0	7.1	11	8	2	0	5-1	6	9.82	47	.355	.432	0	ø	0	—	-4	0	-0.2
Total	6	7	13	.350	101	26	0	0-2	218	226	145	32	10	118-11	204	5.28	84	.268	.363	39-1-6	.128	1	76	-22	0	-1.8
Reardon, Jeff	Jeffrey James; B10.1.1955 Dalton MA; BR/TR/6´1˝/(190–205); d8.25; Col Massachusetts																									
1979	NY N	1	2	.333	18	0	0	2-0	20.2	12	7	2	0	9-3	10	1.74	213	.174	.266	0	ø	0	—	3	0	0.5
1980	NY N	8	7	.533	61	0	0	6-4	110.1	96	36	10	0	47-15	101	2.61	138	.231	.306	8	.000	-1	—	12	0	1.5
1981	NY N	1	0	1.000	18	0	0	2-0	28.2	27	11	2	1	12-4	28	3.45	102	.245	.323	1	.000	-0	—	1	0	0.0
	†Mon N	2	0	1.000	25	0	0	6-1	41.2	21	6	3	1	9-0	21	1.30	275	.148	.204	4-0-2	.000	-0	—	11	0	0.7

YEAR	TM LG	W	L	PCT	G	GS	CG-SHO	SV-BS	IP	H	R	HR	HB	BB-IB	SO	ERA	AERA	OAV	OOB	AB-HR-SH	AVG	PB	SUP	APR	DL	PW
	Year	3	0	1.000	43	0	0	8-1	70.1	48	17	5	2	21-4	49	2.18	163	.190	.257	5-0-2	.000	-1	—	12	0	0.7
1982	Mon N	7	4	.636	75	0	0	26-8	109	87	28	6	2	36-4	86	2.06	179	.221	.287	10-0-1	.100	-0	—	20	0	2.7
1983	Mon N	7	9	.438	66	0	0	21-8	92	87	34	7	1	44-9	78	3.03	120	.250	.334	8	.125	-0	—	6	0	1.1
1984	Mon N	7	7	.500	68	0	0	23-3	87	70	31	5	3	37-7	79	2.90	119	.220	.306	9	.000	-1	—	6	0	1.0
1985	Mon N★	2	8	.200	63	0	0	**41**-9	87.2	68	31	7	1	26-4	67	3.18	108	.209	.269	7-0-2	.286	0	—	4	0	0.9
1986	Mon N☆	7	9	.438	62	0	0	35-13	89	83	42	12	1	26-2	67	3.94	95	.251	.306	8-0-1	.125	-0	—	-1	0	-0.3
1987	†Min A	8	8	.500	63	0	0	31-10	80.1	70	41	14	3	28-4	83	4.48	104	.232	.301	0	ø	0	—	3	0	0.4
1988	Min A☆	2	4	.333	63	0	0	42-8	73	68	21	6	2	15-2	56	2.47	166	.245	.288	0	ø	0	—	13	0	2.3
1989	Min A	5	4	.556	65	0	0	31-11	73	68	33	8	3	12-3	46	4.07	102	.246	.280	0	ø	0	—	2	0	0.2
1990	†Bos A	5	3	.625	47	0	0	21-7	51.1	39	19	5	1	19-4	33	3.16	130	.206	.282	0	ø	0	—	6	44	1.1
1991	Bos A★	1	4	.200	57	0	0	40-9	59.1	54	21	9	1	16-3	44	3.03	143	.236	.286	0	ø	0	—	9	0	1.6
1992	Bos A	2	2	.500	46	0	0	27-8	42.1	53	20	6	1	7-0	32	4.25	100	.308	.335	0	ø	0	—	1	0	0.2
	†Atl N	3	0	1.000	14	0	0	3-2	15.2	14	2	0	1	2-1	7	1.15	319	.241	.279	0	ø	0	—	4	0	0.9
1993	Cin N	4	6	.400	58	0	0	8-4	61.2	66	34	4	5	10-0	35	4.09	99	.270	.308	2-0-1	.000	-0	—	-2	0	-0.4
1994	NY A	1	0	1.000	11	0	0	2-1	9.2	17	9	3	0	3-0	4	8.38	55	.386	.426	0	ø	0	—	-4	0	-0.5
Total	16	73	77	.487	880	0	0	367-106	1132.1	1000	426	109	27	358-65	877	3.16	122	.236	.297	57-0-7	.088	-3	—	94	44	13.9

REARDON, JEREMIAH Jeremiah J.; B9.1868; D4.22.1907 St.Louis MO; d7.17

YEAR	TM LG	W	L	PCT	G	GS	CG-SHO	SV-BS	IP	H	R	HR	HB	BB-IB	SO	ERA	AERA	OAV	OOB	AB-HR-SH	AVG	PB	SUP	APR	DL	PW
1886	StL N	0	1	.000	1	1	1	0	8	10	8	1	—	5	0	6.75	48	.323	.417	4	.250	0	57	-2	—	-0.2
	Cin AA	0	1	.000	1	1	0	0	2	5	4	0	0	4	0	18.00	20	.500	.643	3	.000	-1	67	-3	—	-0.4
Total	1	0	2	.000	2	2	1	0	10	15	12	1	0	9	0	9.00	36	.366	.480	7	.143	-1	65	-5	—	-0.6

REBERGER, FRANK Frank Beall "Crane"; B6.7.1944 Caldwell ID; BL/TR/6´5˝/(200–210); d6.6; C3; Col Idaho

YEAR	TM LG	W	L	PCT	G	GS	CG-SHO	SV-BS	IP	H	R	HR	HB	BB-IB	SO	ERA	AERA	OAV	OOB	AB-HR-SH	AVG	PB	SUP	APR	DL	PW
1968	Chi N	0	1	.000	3	1	0	0	6	9	4	1	0	2-0	3	4.50	70	.346	.393	0	ø	0	220	-1	0	-0.1
1969	SD N	1	2	.333	67	0	0	6-2	87.2	83	38	6	2	41-8	65	3.59	100	.258	.342	5	.200	0	—	0	0	0.1
1970	SF N	7	8	.467	45	18	3	2-1	152	178	108	13	7	98-6	117	5.57	71	.293	.395	47-0-3	.234	1*	129	-28	0	-2.4
1971	SF N	3	0	1.000	13	7	0	0-0	43.2	37	20	5	2	19-0	21	3.92	87	.228	.315	13	.231	0*	152	-1	27	0.0
1972	SF N	3	4	.429	20	11	2	0-0	99.1	97	49	10	5	37-2	52	3.99	88	.257	.329	35	.229	2*	117	-5	0	-0.1
Total	5	14	15	.483	148	37	5	8-3	388.2	404	219	35	16	197-16	258	4.52	82	.270	.359	100-0-3	.230	4	132	-35	27	-2.5

RECCIUS, JOHN John; B10.29.1859 Louisville KY; D9.1.1930 Louisville KY; 5´6.5˝/168; d5.2; b–Phil; ▲

YEAR	TM LG	W	L	PCT	G	GS	CG-SHO	SV-BS	IP	H	R	HR	HB	BB-IB	SO	ERA	AERA	OAV	OOB	AB-HR-SH	AVG	PB	SUP	APR	DL	PW
1882	Lou AA	4	6	.400	13	10	9-1	0	95	106	70	3	—	22	31	3.03	82	.264	.303	266-1	.237	3*	133	-6	—	-0.3
1883	Lou AA	0	0	ø	1	0	0	0	4	10	3	0	—	0	0	2.25	133	.455	.455	63	.143	-0*	—	0	—	0.0
Total	2	4	6	.400	14	10	9-1	0	99	116	73	3	—	22	31	3.00	83	.274	.310	329-1	.219	3	133	-6	—	-0.3

RECCIUS, PHIL Phillip; B6.7.1862 Louisville KY; D2.15.1903 Louisville KY; 5´9˝/163; d9.25.1882; b–John; ▲

YEAR	TM LG	W	L	PCT	G	GS	CG-SHO	SV-BS	IP	H	R	HR	HB	BB-IB	SO	ERA	AERA	OAV	OOB	AB-HR-SH	AVG	PB	SUP	APR	DL	PW
1884	Lou AA	6	7	.462	18	11	11	0	129.1	118	80	2	4	19	46	2.71	114	.228	.261	263-3	.240	2*	64	2	—	0.4
1885	Lou AA	0	4	.000	7	5	4	1	40	46	35	0	1	11	10	3.82	84	.253	.299	402-1	.241	1*	88	-3	—	-0.2
1886	Lou AA	0	1	.000	1	1	0	0	3	7	6	0	0	3	0	9.00	40	.467	.556	13	.308	0*	82	-2	—	-0.3
1887	Cle AA	0	0	ø	1	0	0	0	7	8	7	0	0	5	0	7.71	56	.320	.433	229	.205	-0*	—	-2	—	-0.1
Total	4	6	12	.333	27	17	15	1	179.1	179	128	2	5	38	56	3.26	97	.242	.284	907-4	.233	4	73	-5	—	-0.2

REDDING, PHIL Philip Hayden; B1.28.1889 Crystal Springs MS; D3.31.1928 Greenwood MS; BL/TR/5´11.5˝/190; d9.14

YEAR	TM LG	W	L	PCT	G	GS	CG-SHO	SV-BS	IP	H	R	HR	HB	BB-IB	SO	ERA	AERA	OAV	OOB	AB-HR-SH	AVG	PB	SUP	APR	DL	PW
1912	StL N	2	1	.667	3	3	2	0	25.1	31	17	2	0	11	9	4.97	69	.313	.382	8-0-1	.000	-1	100	-3	—	-0.4
1913	StL N	0	0	ø	1	0	0	0	2.2	2	2	0	0	1	1	6.75	48	.286	.375	1	.000	-0	—	-1	—	-0.1
Total	2	2	1	.667	4	3	2	0	28	33	19	2	0	12	10	5.14	66	.311	.381	9-0-1	.000	-1	100	-4	—	-0.5

REDDING, TIM Timothy James; B2.12.1978 Rochester NY; BR/TR/6´0˝/(180–200); [HouN97 20/610]; d6.24; Col Monroe (NY) CC

YEAR	TM LG	W	L	PCT	G	GS	CG-SHO	SV-BS	IP	H	R	HR	HB	BB-IB	SO	ERA	AERA	OAV	OOB	AB-HR-SH	AVG	PB	SUP	APR	DL	PW
2001	Hou N	3	1	.750	13	9	0	0-0	55.2	62	38	11	3	24-0	55	5.50	84	.286	.360	14-0-2	.214	0	116	-6	0	-0.4
2002	Hou N	3	6	.333	18	14	0	0-0	73.1	78	49	10	0	35-3	63	5.40	80	.276	.352	20-0-1	.100	-1	112	-9	0	-1.0
2003	Hou N	10	14	.417	33	32	0	0-0	176	179	85	16	7	65-4	116	3.68	120	.261	.329	50-0-8	.200	2	80	11	0	1.5
2004	Hou N	5	7	.417	27	17	0	0-0	100.2	125	73	15	5	43-3	56	5.72	76	.309	.380	29-0-1	.138	-1	106	-17	0	-1.8
2005	SD N	0	5	.000	9	6	0	0-0	29.2	40	35	7	2	13-1	17	9.10	43	.328	.393	8-0-1	.000	-1	64	-20	44	-2.6
	NY A	0	1	.000	1	1	0	0-0	1	4	6	0	0	4-0	2	54.00	8	.571	.727	0	ø	0	22	-5	0	-0.7
Total	5	21	34	.382	101	79	0	0-0	436.1	488	286	59	17	184-11	309	5.16	85	.284	.356	121-0-13	.157	-1	93	-46	44	-5.0

REDFERN, PETE Peter Irvine; B8.25.1954 Glendale CA; BR/TR/6´2˝/(185–195); [MinA76*S1/1]; d5.15; Col USC

YEAR	TM LG	W	L	PCT	G	GS	CG-SHO	SV-BS	IP	H	R	HR	HB	BB-IB	SO	ERA	AERA	OAV	OOB	AB-HR-SH	AVG	PB	SUP	APR	DL	PW
1976	Min A	8	8	.500	23	23	1-1	0-0	118	105	61	6	3	63-1	74	3.51	102	.241	.339	0	ø	0	141	-2	0	-0.3
1977	Min A	6	9	.400	30	28	1	0-0	137.1	164	89	13	4	66-2	73	5.18	77	.304	.382	0	ø	0	122	-19	21	-1.8
1978	Min A	0	2	.000	3	2	0	0-0	9.2	10	12	2	0	6-0	4	6.52	59	.294	.381	0	ø	0	94	-5	0	-0.8
1979	Min A	7	3	.700	40	6	0	1-2	108.1	106	45	8	1	35-0	85	3.49	126	.258	.315	0	ø	0*	141	11	0	0.9
1980	Min A	7	7	.500	23	16	2	2-1	104.2	117	58	11	0	33-3	73	4.56	96	.283	.333	0	ø	0	82	-1	42	-0.2
1981	Min A	9	8	.529	24	23	3	0-1	141.2	140	70	12	2	52-1	77	4.07	97	.261	.326	0	ø	0	86	-1	0	-0.2
1982	Min A	5	11	.313	27	13	2	0-1	94.1	122	74	16	1	51-3	40	6.58	65	.322	.401	0	ø	0	80	-23	23	-3.3
Total	7	42	48	.467	170	111	9-1	3-5	714	764	409	68	11	306-10	426	4.54	90	.278	.350	0	ø	0	106	-40	86	-5.7

REDMAN, MARK Mark Allen; B1.5.1974 San Diego CA; BL/TL/6´5˝/(220–245); [MinA95 1/13]; d7.24; Col Oklahoma

YEAR	TM LG	W	L	PCT	G	GS	CG-SHO	SV-BS	IP	H	R	HR	HB	BB-IB	SO	ERA	AERA	OAV	OOB	AB-HR-SH	AVG	PB	SUP	APR	DL	PW
1999	Min A	1	0	1.000	5	1	0	0-0	12.2	17	13	3	1	7-0	11	8.53	61	.298	.385	0	ø	0	180	-5	16	-0.3
2000	Min A	12	9	.571	32	24	0	0-0	151.1	168	81	22	3	45-0	117	4.76	111	.281	.333	4-0-1	.000	-0	84	10	0	1.1
2001	Min A	2	4	.333	9	9	0	0-0	49	57	26	6	0	19-0	29	4.22	111	.286	.349	0	ø	0	79	2	68	0.2
	Det A	0	2	.000	2	2	0	0-0	9	11	6	1	1	4-0	4	6.00	74	.306	.390	0	ø	0	42	-1	25	-0.2
	Year	2	6	.250	11	11	0	0-0	58	68	32	7	1	23-0	33	4.50	103	.289	.355	0	ø	0	73	1	0	0.0
2002	Det A	8	15	.348	30	30	3	0-0	203	211	107	15	6	51-2	109	4.21	104	.268	.314	5	.200	0	67	3	0	0.3
2003	†Fla N	14	9	.609	29	29	3	0-0	190.2	172	82	16	5	61-3	151	3.59	114	.239	.301	61-0-4	.016	-6	112	11	30	0.5
2004	Oak A	11	12	.478	32	32	2	0-0	191	218	110	28	6	68-6	102	4.71	98	.292	.353	5	.000	-0	91	-2	0	-0.3
2005	Pit N	5	15	.250	30	30	2-1	0-0	178.1	188	100	18	2	56-3	101	4.90	87	.278	.332	53-0-4	.113	-2	74	-10	0	-1.1
2006	KC A☆	11	10	.524	29	29	2-1	0-0	167	202	110	19	8	63-1	76	5.71	82	.307	.372	1-0-1	.000	0	94	-16	13	-1.7
Total	8	64	76	.457	198	186	12-2	0-0	1152	1244	635	128	32	374-15	700	4.65	97	.278	.336	129-0-10	.062	-8	87	-8	152	-1.5

REED, HOWIE Howard Dean "Diz"; B12.21.1936 Dallas TX; D12.7.1984 Corpus Christi TX; BR/TR/6´1˝/(195–211); d9.13; Col Texas

YEAR	TM LG	W	L	PCT	G	GS	CG-SHO	SV-BS	IP	H	R	HR	HB	BB-IB	SO	ERA	AERA	OAV	OOB	AB-HR-SH	AVG	PB	SUP	APR	DL	PW
1958	KC A	1	0	1.000	3	1	1	0	10.1	5	1	0	0	4-0	5	0.87	449	.132	.214	2-0-1	.000	0	46	3	0	0.3
1959	KC A	0	3	.000	6	3	0	0	20.2	26	19	3	0	10-0	11	7.40	54	.313	.379	3	.000	-0	66	-7	0	-0.9
1960	KC A	0	0	ø	1	0	0	0	1.2	2	1	1	0	0-0	1	0.00	ø	.286	.286	0	ø	0	—	0	0	0.0
1964	LA N	3	4	.429	26	7	0	1	90	79	34	4	0	36-9	52	3.20	101	.236	.309	20	.100	-0	81	2	0	0.2
1965	†LA N	7	5	.583	38	5	0	1	78	73	31	6	3	27-6	47	3.12	105	.243	.311	12	.000	0	86	1	0	0.2
1966	LA N	0	0	ø	1	0	0	0	1.2	1	0	0	0	0-0	0	0.00	ø	.167	.167	1	.000	-0	—	1	0	0.0
	Cal A	0	1	.000	19	1	0	1	43	39	14	5	0	15-2	17	2.93	115	.247	.307	6	.000	-1	26	3	0	0.1
1967	Hou N	1	1	.500	4	2	0	0	18.1	19	8	0	0	2-0	9	3.44	96	.268	.288	4	.000	-0	80	0	0	-0.1
1969	Mon N	6	7	.462	31	15	2-1	1-0	106	119	59	7	2	50-7	59	4.84	76	.290	.365	32-1-3	.125	1	93	-10	0	-1.0
1970	Mon N	6	5	.545	57	1	0	5-1	89	81	34	7	2	40-5	42	3.13	133	.252	.336	10-0-1	.000	-0	151	10	0	1.2
1971	Mon N	2	3	.400	43	0	0	0-0	56.2	66	28	8	0	24-7	25	4.29	83	.296	.360	1	.000	-0	—	-4	0	-0.3
Total	10	26	29	.473	229	35	3-1	9-1	515.1	510	229	41	7	208-36	268	3.72	96	.261	.332	91-1-5	.066	-1	85	-1	0	-0.3

REED, JERRY Jerry Maxwell; B10.8.1955 Bryson City NC; BR/TR/6´1˝/190; [PhiN77 22/559]; d9.11; Col Western Carolina

YEAR	TM LG	W	L	PCT	G	GS	CG-SHO	SV-BS	IP	H	R	HR	HB	BB-IB	SO	ERA	AERA	OAV	OOB	AB-HR-SH	AVG	PB	SUP	APR	DL	PW
1981	Phi N	0	1	.000	4	0	0	0-0	4.2	7	4	0	0	6-0	5	7.71	47	.333	.481	0	ø	0	—	-2	0	-0.4
1982	Phi N	1	0	1.000	7	0	0	0-0	8.2	11	6	0	1	3-0	1	5.19	71	.324	.395	0	ø	0	—	-2	0	-0.2
	Cle A	1	1	.500	6	1	0	0-0	15.2	15	6	1	0	3-0	10	3.45	120	.250	.286	0	ø	0	22	2	0	0.2
1983	Cle A	0	0	ø	7	0	0	0-0	21.1	26	19	4	0	9-1	11	7.17	60	.310	.372	0	ø	0	—	-7	0	-0.3
1985	Cle A	3	5	.375	33	5	0	8-2	72.1	67	41	12	3	19-2	37	4.11	101	.245	.298	0	ø	0	79	-2	0	-0.2
1986	Sea A	4	0	1.000	11	4	0	0-0	34.2	38	13	3	0	13-0	16	3.12	137	.273	.336	0	ø	0	186	5	63	0.5
1987	Sea A	1	2	.333	39	1	0	7-1	81.2	79	32	7	3	24-3	51	3.42	139	.255	.314	0	ø	0	58	12	26	0.6
1988	Sea A	1	1	.500	46	0	0	1-2	86.1	82	42	8	2	33-7	48	3.96	106	.256	.325	0	ø	0*	—	2	0	0.1
1989	Sea A	7	7	.500	52	1	0	0-4	101.2	89	44	10	1	43-10	50	3.19	127	.235	.313	0	ø	0	0	8	0	1.0
1990	Sea A	0	1	.000	4	0	0	0-0	7.1	8	4	1	0	3-0	2	4.91	81	.286	.355	0	ø	0	—	-1	0	-0.1
	Bos A	2	1	.667	29	0	0	2-1	45	55	27	1	0	16-2	17	4.80	85	.302	.353	0	ø	0	—	-3	0	-0.2

YEAR	TM LG	W	L	PCT	G	GS	CG-SHO	SV-BS	IP	H	R	HR	HB	BB-IB	SO	ERA	AERA	OAV	OOB	AB-HR-SH	AVG	PB	SUP	APR	DL	PW
	Year	2	2	.500	33	0	0	2-1	52.1	63	31	2	0	19-2	19	4.82	85	.300	.353	0	ø	0	—	-4	0	-0.3
Total	9	20	19	.513	238	12	0	18-10	479.1	477	238	47	10	172-25	248	3.94	107	.261	.325	0	ø	0	102	12	89	1.0
Reed, Rick	Richard Allen; B8.16.1964 Huntington WV; BR/TR/6´0˝/(190–210); [PitN86 26/644]; d8.8; Col Marshall																									
1988	Pit N	1	0	1.000	2	2	0	0-0	12	10	4	1	0	2-0	6	3.00	115	.233	.267	4	.000	-0	142	1	0	0.0
1989	Pit N	1	4	.200	15	7	0	0-0	54.2	62	35	5	2	11-3	34	5.60	61	.290	.326	13	.077	-0	63	-12	0	-1.1
1990	Pit N	2	3	.400	13	8	1-1	1-0	53.2	62	32	6	1	12-6	27	4.36	84	.279	.318	16	.250	1	114	-6	0	-0.4
1991	Pit N	0	0	ø	1	1	0	0-0	4.1	8	6	1	0	1-0	2	10.38	35	.400	.429	2	.500	1	150	-3	0	-0.1
1992	KC A	3	7	.300	19	18	1-1	0-0	100.1	105	47	10	5	20-3	49	3.68	111	.271	.312	0	ø	0	81	3	0	0.3
1993	KC A	0	0	ø	1	0	0	0-0	3.2	6	4	0	1	1-0	3	9.82	47	.375	.444	0	ø	0	—	-2	0	-0.1
	Tex A	1	0	1.000	2	0	0	0-0	4	6	1	1	1	1-0	2	2.25	187	.375	.444	0	ø	0	—	1	0	0.2
	Year	1	0	1.000	3	0	0	0-0	7.2	12	5	1	2	2-0	5	5.87	75	.375	.444	0	ø	0	—	-1	0	0.1
1994	Tex A	1	1	.500	4	3	0	0-0	16.2	17	13	3	1	7-0	12	5.94	81	.254	.333	0	ø	0	139	-2	0	-0.2
1995	Cin N	0	0	ø	4	3	0	0-0	17	18	12	5	0	3-0	10	5.82	72	.273	.304	3-0-2	.000	-0	159	-3	0	-0.2
1997	NY N	13	9	.591	33	31	2	0-0	208.1	186	76	19	5	31-4	113	2.89	138	.239	.272	57-1-6	.175	4	100	26	0	2.9
1998	NY N☆	16	11	.593	31	31	2-1	0-0	212.1	208	84	30	6	29-2	153	3.48	119	.261	.290	64-1-12	.125	-1	91	17	0	2.0
1999	†NY N	11	5	.688	26	26	1-1	0-0	149.1	163	77	23	1	47-2	104	4.58	95	.281	.334	45-0-8	.244	2*	123	-3	47	0.0
2000	†NY N	11	5	.688	30	30	0	0-0	184	192	90	28	5	34-3	121	4.11	106	.266	.302	49-0-14	.204	1	120	7	16	0.5
2001	NY N✳	8	6	.571	20	20	3-1	0-0	134.2	119	53	16	1	17-3	99	3.48	116	.236	.262	40-0-4	.125	-1	94	11	0	1.1
	Min A	4	6	.400	12	12	0	0-0	67.2	92	45	12	4	14-0	43	5.19	90	.325	.363	0	ø	0	83	-5	0	-0.6
2002	†Min A	15	7	.682	33	32	2-1	0-0	188	192	89	32	6	26-0	121	3.78	118	.259	.288	4-0-1	.250	0	111	12	0	1.3
2003	†Min A	6	12	.333	27	21	2-1	0-1	135	155	80	21	5	29-2	71	5.07	89	.285	.325	0	ø	0	70	-8	37	-1.0
Total	15	93	76	.550	273	245	14-7	1-1	1545.2	1601	748	213	44	285-28	970	4.03	104	.267	.303	297-2-47	.172	8	102	34	100	4.6
Reed, Bob	Robert Edward; B1.12.1945 Boston MA; BR/TR/5´10˝/170; [DetA66 S2/22]; d9.5; Col Michigan																									
1969	Det A	0	0	ø	8	1	0	0-0	14.2	9	3	0	0	8-0	9	1.84	205	.184	.298	2	.500	0	71	3	0	0.2
1970	Det A	2	4	.333	16	4	0	2-0	46.1	54	25	5	0	14-0	26	4.86	78	.292	.342	12	.083	-0*	77	-4	0	-0.6
Total	2	2	4	.333	24	5	0	2-0	61	63	28	5	0	22-0	35	4.13	91	.269	.332	14	.143	-0	76	-1	0	-0.4
Reed, Ron	Ronald Lee; B11.2.1942 LaPorte IN; BR/TR/6´6˝/(215–225); d9.26; Col Notre Dame																									
1966	Atl N	1	1	.500	2	2	0	0	8.1	7	2	1	0	4-0	6	2.16	168	.226	.314	2	.000	-0	73	1	0	0.3
1967	Atl N	1	1	.500	3	3	0	0	21.1	21	8	1	2	3-0	11	2.95	112	.262	.299	8	.000	-1	88	1	0	0.0
1968	Atl N★	11	10	.524	35	28	6-1	0	201.2	189	87	10	6	49-11	111	3.35	89	.246	.294	62-0-9	.161	1	87	-8	0	-0.8
1969	†Atl N	18	10	.643	36	33	7-1	0-0	241.1	227	103	24	6	56-5	160	3.47	104	.246	.292	80-0-13	.125	-2*	114	4	0	0.2
1970	Atl N	7	10	.412	21	18	6	0-0	134.2	140	69	16	2	39-5	68	4.41	97	.266	.319	44-0-5	.091	-2*	91	0	58	-0.2
1971	Atl N	13	14	.481	32	32	8-1	0-0	222.1	221	105	26	2	54-10	129	3.72	100	.261	.304	74-0-6	.149	-3	78	0	0	-0.3
1972	Atl N	11	15	.423	31	30	11-1	0-0	213	222	109	18	6	60-7	111	3.93	97	.270	.321	73-0-5	.178	-1	89	-5	0	-0.6
1973	Atl N	4	11	.267	20	19	2	1-0	116.1	133	71	7	3	31-6	64	4.41	90	.287	.334	45-0-1	.200	-0*	89	-8	63	-0.9
1974	Atl N	10	11	.476	28	28	6-2	0-0	186	171	76	16	2	41-6	78	3.39	112	.243	.285	57-0-7	.105	-3	75	9	40	0.5
1975	Atl N	4	5	.444	10	10	1	0-0	74.2	93	39	1	0	16-2	40	4.22	90	.304	.335	26	.231	1	93	-2	0	-0.1
	StL N	9	8	.529	24	24	7-2	0-0	175.2	181	79	4	4	37-5	99	3.23	118	.263	.304	56-0-5	.161	-0	97	9	0	0.8
	Year	13	13	.500	34	34	8-2	0-0	250.1	274	118	5	4	53-7	139	3.52	108	.276	.313	82-0-5	.183	1	96	6	0	0.7
1976	†Phi N	8	7	.533	59	4	1	14-9	128	88	39	8	2	32-7	96	2.46	145	.193	.247	24-0-2	.167	-0	117	15	0	2.1
1977	†Phi N	7	5	.583	60	3	0	15-3	124.1	101	41	9	1	37-7	84	2.75	146	.223	.283	18-0-1	.111	-0	125	18	0	2.0
1978	†Phi N	3	4	.429	66	0	0	17-2	108.2	87	32	6	5	23-5	85	2.24	161	.223	.273	6	.000	-0	—	15	0	1.4
1979	Phi N	13	8	.619	61	0	0	5-5	102	110	52	9	2	32-9	58	4.15	93	.278	.332	10-0-2	.300	1	—	-4	0	-0.6
1980	†Phi N	7	5	.583	55	0	0	9-4	91.1	88	45	4	1	30-10	54	4.04	95	.253	.311	10	.300	1	—	-2	0	-0.1
1981	†Phi N	5	3	.625	39	0	0	8-2	61.1	54	26	6	1	17-8	40	3.08	119	.237	.290	6	.500	1	—	2	0	0.5
1982	Phi N	5	5	.500	57	2	0	14-2	98	85	30	4	3	24-5	57	2.66	139	.235	.286	12-0-1	.333	2	143	12	0	1.8
1983	†Phi N	9	1	.900	61	0	0	8-4	95.2	89	42	5	1	34-14	73	3.48	104	.248	.312	6-0-1	.167	-0	—	2	0	0.1
1984	Chi A	0	6	.000	51	0	0	12-5	73	67	29	7	1	14-2	57	3.08	136	.248	.286	1	.000	-0	—	8	15	0.9
Total	19	146	140	.510	751	236	55-8	103-36	2477.2	2374	1084	182	50	633-124	1481	3.46	108	.252	.301	620-0-58	.158	-6	91	67	176	7.0
Reed, Steve	Steven Vincent; B3.11.1965 Los Angeles CA; BR/TR/6´2˝/(200–212); d8.30; Col Lewis–Clark St.																									
1992	SF N	1	0	1.000	18	0	0	0-0	15.2	13	5	2	1	3-0	11	2.30	145	.220	.270	0	ø	0	—	2	0	0.1
1993	Col N	9	5	.643	64	0	0	3-3	84.1	80	47	13	3	30-5	51	4.48	107	.259	.328	9-0-2	.000	-1	—	2	0	0.3
1994	Col N	3	2	.600	**61**	0	0	3-7	64	79	33	9	6	26-3	51	3.94	127	.306	.374	2	.000	-0	—	5	0	0.3
1995	†Col N	5	2	.714	71	0	0	3-3	84	61	24	8	1	21-3	79	2.14	251	.203	.256	3	.333	0	—	**23**	0	1.9
1996	Col N	4	3	.571	70	0	0	0-6	75	66	38	11	6	19-0	51	3.96	132	.239	.298	3	.333	0	—	8	0	0.6
1997	Col N	4	6	.400	63	0	0	6-7	62.1	49	28	10	5	27-1	43	4.04	128	.219	.315	1	.000	-0	—	7	0	1.2
1998	SF N	2	1	.667	50	0	0	1-4	54.2	30	10	4	4	19-5	50	1.48	272	.160	.251	3	.333	0	—	16	0	0.8
	†Cle A	2	2	.500	20	0	0	0-1	25.2	26	19	4	1	8-0	23	6.66	72	.260	.321	0	ø	0	—	-5	0	-0.6
1999	†Cle A	3	2	.600	63	0	0	0-3	61.2	69	33	10	3	20-5	44	4.23	120	.285	.341	0	ø	0	—	5	0	0.3
2000	Cle A	2	0	1.000	57	0	0	0-1	56	58	30	7	1	21-4	39	4.34	115	.269	.335	0	ø	0	—	3	0	0.2
2001	Cle A	1	1	.500	31	0	0	0-1	27.1	22	11	3	2	10-2	21	3.62	127	.212	.293	0	ø	0*	—	3	0	0.2
	†Atl N	2	2	.500	39	0	0	1-0	31	30	14	3	1	13-3	25	3.48	124	.259	.336	0	ø	0	—	3	0	0.3
2002	SD N	2	4	.333	40	0	0	1-2	41	33	9	2	6	10-2	36	1.98	197	.228	.304	1	.000	-0*	—	10	0	1.4
	NY N	0	1	.000	24	0	0	0-1	26	23	6	0	2	4-1	14	2.08	190	.240	.284	1	.000	-0	—	6	0	0.3
	Year	2	5	.286	64	0	0	1-3	67	56	15	2	8	14-3	50	2.01	194	.232	.297	2	.000	-0	—	15	0	1.7
2003	Col N	5	3	.625	67	0	0	0-2	63.1	59	24	9	8	26-3	39	3.27	150	.254	.348	0	ø	0	—	10	0	1.2
2004	Col N	3	8	.273	65	0	0	0-4	66	72	29	7	7	17-7	38	3.68	129	.281	.342	2	.500	0	—	7	0	1.0
2005	Bal A	1	2	.333	30	0	0	0-0	32.2	41	24	5	4	11-2	15	6.61	67	.308	.376	0	ø	0	—	-7	0	-0.5
Total	14	49	44	.527	833	0	0	18-45	870.2	811	384	107	61	285-46	630	3.63	132	.249	.319	25-0-2	.160	-1	—	98	0	9.0
Reeder, Bill	William Edgar; B2.20.1922 Dike TX; D3.12.2001 Sulphur Springs TX; BR/TR/6´5˝/205; d4.23																									
1949	StL N	1	1	.500	21	1	0	0	33.2	33	22	2	1	30	21	5.08	82	.270	.418	3	.000	-0	85	-3	0	-0.2
Rees, Stan	Stanley Milton "Nellie"; B2.25.1899 Cynthiana KY; D8.30.1937 Lexington KY; BL/TL/6´3˝/190; d6.12																									
1918	Was A	1	0	1.000	2	0	0	0	2	3	0	0	0	4	1	0.00	ø	.500	.700	0	ø	0	—	1	—	0.1
Regan, Mike	Michael John; B11.19.1888 Phoenix NY; D5.22.1961 Albany NY; BR/TR/5´10˝/160; d5.13																									
1917	Cin N	11	10	.524	32	26	16-1	0	216	228	106	4	4	41	50	2.71	97	.273	.310	75	.200	1*	107	-6	—	-0.3
1918	Cin N	5	5	.500	22	6	4-3	2	80	77	38	0	0	29	15	3.26	82	.262	.328	27	.296	2*	104	-6	—	-0.5
1919	Cin N	0	0	ø	1	0	0	0	2.1	1	1	0	0	0	1	0.00	ø	.143	.143	1	.000	-0	—	0	—	0.0
Total	3	16	15	.516	55	32	20-4	2	298.1	306	145	4	4	70	66	2.84	93	.269	.314	103	.223	3	107	-12	—	-0.8
Regan, Phil	Philip Raymond "The Vulture"; B4.6.1937 Otsego MI; BR/TR/6´3˝/200; d7.19; M1/C7																									
1960	Det A	0	4	.000	17	7	0	1	68	70	39	11	2	25-1	38	4.50	88	.267	.333	17-0-1	.059	-1	89	-4	0	-0.4
1961	Det A	10	7	.588	32	16	6	2	120	134	70	19	1	41-1	46	5.25	78	.281	.337	40-0-3	.075	-2*	101	-10	0	-1.6
1962	Det A	11	9	.550	35	23	6	0	171.1	169	89	23	1	64-0	87	4.04	101	.254	.318	63-0-4	.206	1	115	0	0	0.0
1963	Det A	15	9	.625	38	27	5-1	1	189	179	95	33	7	59-5	115	3.86	97	.245	.305	63-1-3	.143	-1	123	-4	0	-0.7
1964	Det A	5	10	.333	32	21	2	1	146.2	162	87	21	5	49-4	91	5.03	73	.282	.341	41-0-4	.317	5*	117	-21	0	-1.5
1965	Det A	1	5	.167	16	7	1	0	51.2	57	31	6	0	20-1	37	5.05	69	.282	.341	12-0-2	.083	-0	87	-8	0	-1.0
1966	†LA N☆	14	1	.933	65	0	0	**21**	116.2	85	24	6	0	24-9	88	1.62	203	.207	.248	21-0-2	.143	0	—	**24**	0	4.1
1967	LA N	6	9	.400	55	3	0	6	96.1	108	38	2	2	32-17	53	2.99	104	.284	.339	10	.100	-0	28	0	0	0.1
1968	LA N	2	0	1.000	5	0	0	0	7.2	10	3	1	0	1-0	7	3.52	79	.313	.333	1	.000	-0	—	0	0	-0.1
	Chi N	10	5	.667	68	0	0	25	127	109	36	9	2	24-6	60	2.20	144	.232	.271	20-0-3	.150	0	—	12	0	2.2
	Year	12	5	.706	73	0	0	**25**	134.2	119	39	10	2	25-6	67	2.27	138	.237	.274	21-0-3	.143	0	—	12	0	2.1
1969	Chi N	12	6	.667	71	0	0	17-3	112	120	49	6	2	35-13	56	3.70	109	.282	.335	15	.067	-0	—	5	0	0.9
1970	Chi N	5	9	.357	54	0	0	12-9	75.2	81	43	8	1	32-7	31	4.76	95	.287	.356	9	.000	-1	—	-1	0	-0.2
1971	Chi N	5	5	.500	48	1	0	6-4	73.1	84	37	4	2	33-13	28	3.93	100	.301	.374	8-0-3	.000	-1	68	0	0	-0.1
1972	Chi N	0	1	.000	5	0	0	0-0	4	6	1	0	0	2-0	2	2.25	169	.400	.471	0	ø	0	—	1	0	0.1
	Chi A	0	1	.000	10	0	0	0-1	13.1	18	7	1	1	6-2	4	4.05	77	.346	.417	1	1.000	0	—	-1	0	0.0
Total	13	96	81	.542	551	105	20-1	92-17	1372.2	1392	649	150	26	447-79	743	3.84	97	.265	.322	321-1-25	.153	1	112	-7	0	1.8

YEAR	TM LG	W	L	PCT	G	GS	CG-SHO	SV-BS	IP	H	R	HR	HB	BB-IB	SO	ERA	AERA	OAV	OOB	AB-HR-SH	AVG	PB	SUP	APR	DL	PW
Regilio, Nick	Nicholas D.; B9.4.1978 Miami FL; BR/TR/6´2˝/205; [TexA99 2/72]; d7.9; Col Jacksonville																									
2004	Tex A	0	4	.000	6	4	0	0-0	19.1	20	16	3	2	15-1	12	6.05	81	.278	.411	0	ø	0	19	-3	0	-0.5
2005	Tex A	1	2	.333	18	0	0	0-2	17.2	22	10	2	1	7-1	14	4.58	99	.297	.361	0	ø	0	—	0	116	0.0
Total	2	1	6	.143	24	4	0	0-2	37	42	26	5	3	22-2	26	5.35	89	.288	.387	0	ø	0	19	-3	116	-0.5
Reichert, Dan	Daniel Robert; B7.12.1976 Monterey CA; BR/TR/6´3˝/175; [KCA97 1/7]; d7.16; Col Pacific (CA)																									
1999	KC A	2	2	.500	8	8	0	0-0	36.2	48	38	2	2	32-1	20	9.08	56	.327	.451	3-0-1	.333	0	144	-15	41	-1.2
2000	KC A	8	10	.444	44	18	1-1	2-4	153.1	157	92	15	7	91-1	94	4.70	111	.271	.372	1	.000	-0	91	5	0	0.5
2001	KC A	8	8	.500	27	19	0	0-0	123	131	83	14	8	67-2	77	5.63	88	.278	.374	5	.000	-1	94	-8	0	-0.9
2002	KC A	3	5	.375	30	6	0	0-0	66	77	48	10	4	25-2	36	5.32	94	.306	.373	0	ø	0	68	-5	0	-0.4
2003	Tor A	0	0	ø	15	0	0	0-1	16.1	28	12	2	2	8-3	13	6.06	78	.389	.463	0	ø	0	—	-2	0	-0.1
Total	5	21	25	.457	124	51	1-1	2-5	395.1	441	273	43	23	223-9	240	5.55	91	.290	.385	9-0-1	.111	-0	98	-25	41	-2.1
Reid, Earl	Earl Percy; B6.8.1913 Bangor AL; D5.11.1984 Cullman AL; BL/TR/6´3˝/190; d5.8																									
1946	Bos N	1	0	1.000	2	0	0	0	3	4	3	0	0	3	2	3.00	114	.308	.438	0	ø	0	—	-1	0	-0.1
Reidy, Bill	William Joseph; B10.9.1873 Cleveland OH; D10.14.1915 Cleveland OH; BR/TR/5´10˝/175; d7.21																									
1896	NY N	0	1	.000	2	1	1	0	13	24	11	0	3	2	1	7.62	55	.393	.439	5	.000	-1	34	-3	—	-0.3
1899	Bro N	1	0	1.000	2	1	1	1	7	9	2	0	0	2	2	2.57	152	.310	.355	3	.000	-1	129	1	—	0.2
1901	Mil A	16	20	.444	37	33	28-2	0	301.1	364	183	14	9	62	50	4.21	85	.295	.333	112-0-7	.143	-6	94	-11	—	-1.8
1902	StL A	3	5	.375	12	9	7	0	95	111	52	0	7	13	16	4.45	79	.292	.327	41	.195	-0*	82	-6	—	-0.4
1903	StL A	1	4	.200	5	5	5-1	0	43	53	31	1	3	7	8	3.98	73	.301	.339	15	.067	-2	59	-7	—	-0.9
	Bro N	6	7	.462	15	13	11	0	104	130	54	0	6	14	21	3.46	92	.315	.346	37-0-1	.243	1	107	-2	—	-0.2
1904	Bro N	0	4	.000	6	4	2	1	38.1	49	33	0	2	6	11	4.46	62	.293	.326	32	.156	-0*	63	-9	—	-0.9
Total	6	27	41	.397	79	66	55-3	2	601.2	740	366	15	30	106	109	4.17	82	.301	.337	245-0-8	.159	-9	90	-37	—	-4.3
Reinhart, Art	Arthur Conrad; B5.29.1899 Ackley IA; D11.11.1946 Houston TX; BL/TL/6´1˝/170; d4.26; Col Iowa																									
1919	StL N	0	0	ø	1	0	0	0	0	0	0	0	1	0	0	(0)	ø	ø	1.000	0	ø	0	—	0	—	0.0
1925	StL N	11	5	.688	20	16	15-1	0	144.2	149	61	7	4	47	26	3.05	142	.278	.341	67-0-2	.328	5*	115	19	—	2.3
1926	†StL N	10	5	.667	27	11	9	0	143	159	75	5	3	47	26	4.22	93	.295	.355	63-0-3	.317	4*	151	-3	—	0.2
1927	StL N	5	2	.714	21	9	4-2	1	81.2	82	47	5	0	36	15	4.19	94	.267	.344	32-0-1	.313	2*	108	-2	—	0.0
1928	StL N	4	6	.400	23	9	3-1	2	75.1	80	39	3	0	27	12	2.87	140	.272	.333	24	.167	-0*	73	5	—	0.6
Total	5	30	18	.625	92	45	31-4	3	444.2	470	222	20	8	157	79	3.60	113	.280	.345	186-0-6	.301	10	114	19	—	3.1
Reis, Jack	Harrie Crane; B6.14.1891 Carthage OH; D7.20.1939 Cincinnati OH; BR/TR/5´10.5˝/160; d9.9; Col Cincinnati																									
1911	StL N	0	0	ø	3	0	0	0	9.1	5	3	0	0	8	4	0.96	350	.156	.325	2	.000	-0	—	2	—	0.1
Reis, Laurie	Lawrence P.; B11.20.1858 IL; D1.24.1921 Chicago IL; BB/TR/?/160; d10.1																									
1877	Chi N	3	1	.750	4	4	4-1	0	36	29	8	1	—	6	11	0.75	396	.213	.246	16	.125	-2	111	8	—	0.6
1878	Chi N	1	3	.250	4	4	4	0	36	55	34	0	—	4	8	3.25	75	.335	.351	20	.150	-1*	148	-4	—	-0.5
Total	2	4	4	.500	8	8	8-1	0	72	84	42	1	—	10	19	2.00	135	.280	.303	36	.139	-2	129	4	—	0.1
Reis, Bobby	Robert Joseph Thomas; B1.2.1909 Woodside NY; D5.1.1973 St.Paul MN; BR/TR/6´1˝/175; d9.19.1931; ▲																									
1935	Bro N	3	2	.600	14	2	1	2	41.1	46	26	0	1	24	7	2.83	140	.277	.372	85	.247	1*	128	1	—	0.3
1936	Bos N	6	5	.545	35	5	3	0	138.2	152	77	7	5	74	25	4.48	86	.283	.375	60	.217	1*	75	-9	—	-0.4
1937	Bos N	0	0	ø	4	0	0	0	5	3	1	0	0	5	0	1.80	199	.158	.333	86	.244	1*	—	1	—	0.1
1938	Bos N	1	6	.143	16	2	1	0	57.2	61	35	5	6	41	20	4.99	69	.271	.397	49-0-2	.184	-0*	62	-10	—	-1.0
Total	4	10	13	.435	69	9	5	2	242.2	262	139	12	12	144	52	4.27	88	.277	.379	280-0-2	.229	3	85	-17	—	-1.0
Reis, Tommy	Thomas Edward; B8.6.1914 Newport KY; BR/TR/6´2˝/180; d4.27																									
1938	Phi N	0	1	.000	4	0	0	0	4.2	8	11	0	0	8	2	19.29	20	.364	.533	2	.000	-0	—	-8	—	-1.3
	Bos N	0	0	ø	4	0	0	0	6.1	8	5	1	0	1	4	7.11	48	.296	.321	0	ø	0	—	-2	—	-0.1
	Year	0	1	.000	8	0	0	0	11	16	16	1	0	9	6	12.27	30	.327	.431	2	.000	-0	—	-10	—	-1.4
Reisigl, Bugs	Jacob; B12.12.1887 Brooklyn NY; D2.24.1957 Amsterdam NY; BR/TR/5´10.5˝/175; d9.20																									
1911	Cle A	0	1	.000	2	1	1	0	13	13	9	1	0	3	6	6.23	55	.271	.314	5	.000	-1	85	-3	—	-0.3
Reisling, Doc	Frank Carl; B7.25.1874 Martins Ferry OH; D3.4.1955 Tulsa OK; BR/TR/5´10˝/180; d9.10; Col Ohio U.																									
1904	Bro N	3	4	.429	7	7	6-1	0	51	45	16	0	9	10	19	2.12	130	.238	.308	13	.154	0	43	4	—	0.6
1905	Bro N	0	1	.000	2	0	0	0	3	3	1	0	0	4	2	3.00	96	.273	.467	1	.000	0	—	0	—	0.1
1909	Was A	2	4	.333	10	6	6-1	0	66.2	70	29	0	0	17	22	2.43	100	.270	.315	24-0-2	.167	0*	145	-1	—	-0.1
1910	Was A	10	10	.500	30	20	13-2	1	191	185	77	3	5	44	57	2.54	98	.264	.312	60-0-5	.200	2*	96	0	—	0.2
Total	4	15	19	.441	49	33	25-4	1	311.2	303	123	3	14	75	100	2.45	103	.261	.314	98-0-7	.184	2	92	3	—	0.8
Reith, Brian	Brian Eric; B2.28.1978 Fort Wayne IN; BR/TR/6´5˝/(190–220); [NYA96 6/179]; d5.16																									
2001	Cin N	0	7	.000	9	8	0	0-0	40.1	56	37	13	2	16-0	22	7.81	59	.333	.394	12	.250	0	50	-13	0	-1.8
2003	Cin N	2	3	.400	42	1	0	1-0	61.1	61	32	8	1	36-6	39	4.11	101	.263	.358	7	.000	-1	90	0	0	-0.2
2004	Cin N	2	2	.500	22	0	0	0-1	26	30	21	5	3	19-1	24	7.27	59	.288	.413	0	ø	0	—	-8	0	-1.0
Total	3	4	12	.250	73	9	0	1-1	127.2	147	90	26	6	71-7	85	5.92	73	.292	.381	19	.158	-0	57	-21	0	-3.0
Reitsma, Chris	Christopher Michael; B12.31.1977 Minneapolis MN; BR/TR/6´5˝/(214–235); [BosA96 1/34]; d4.4																									
2001	Cin N	7	15	.318	36	29	0	0-0	182	209	121	23	5	49-6	96	5.29	87	.288	.334	48-0-7	.104	-1*	94	-14	0	-1.5
2002	Cin N	6	12	.333	32	21	1-1	0-0	138.1	144	73	17	5	45-5	84	3.64	117	.267	.327	30-0-7	.100	-1	80	5	0	0.4
2003	Cin N	9	5	.643	57	3	0	12-6	84	92	41	14	0	19-6	53	4.29	97	.281	.320	8	.125	-0	112	0	0	-0.1
2004	†Atl N	6	4	.600	84	0	0	2-7	79.2	89	38	9	3	20-3	60	4.07	106	.284	.327	0	ø	0	—	3	0	0.3
2005	†Atl N	3	6	.333	76	0	0	15-9	73.1	79	32	3	0	14-3	42	3.93	108	.272	.304	1	.000	-0	—	3	0	0.5
2006	Atl N	1	2	.333	27	0	0	8-4	28	46	27	7	3	8-3	13	8.68	52	.362	.410	0	ø	0	—	-12	110	-1.6
Total	6	32	44	.421	312	53	1-1	37-26	585.1	659	332	73	16	155-26	348	4.58	95	.284	,330	87-0-14	.103	-3	92	-15	110	-2.0
Rekar, Bryan	Bryan Robert; B6.3.1972 Oak Lawn IL; BR/TR/6´3˝/(208–220); [ColN93 2/70]; d7.19; Col Bradley																									
1995	Col N	4	6	.400	15	14	1	0-0	85	95	51	11	3	24-2	60	4.98	108	.282	.332	26-0-4	.038	-2	75	3	0	0.1
1996	Col N	2	4	.333	14	11	0	0-1	58.1	87	61	11	5	26-1	25	8.95	58	.345	.413	15-0-1	.267	1	112	-19	0	-1.6
1997	Col N	1	0	1.000	2	2	0	0-0	9.1	11	7	3	0	6-0	4	5.79	89	.282	.378	4	.250	0	143	-1	0	-0.1
1998	TB A	2	8	.200	16	15	1	0-0	86.2	95	56	16	2	21-0	55	4.98	96	.282	.321	0	ø	0	83	-4	97	-0.4
1999	TB A	6	6	.500	27	12	0	0-0	94.2	121	68	14	5	41-2	55	5.80	86	.313	.385	5	.200	0	127	-8	0	-0.8
2000	TB A	7	10	.412	30	27	2	0-0	173.1	200	92	22	4	39-0	95	4.41	111	.291	.328	3	.333	1	87	10	26	0.8
2001	TB A	3	13	.188	25	25	0	0-0	140.2	167	104	21	6	45-2	87	5.89	77	.294	.348	2	.000	-0	74	-21	37	-2.0
2002	KC A	0	2	.000	2	2	0	0-0	7	12	12	1	0	6-0	2	15.43	32	.387	.474	0	ø	0	65	-7	0	-1.0
Total	8	25	49	.338	131	108	4	0-1	655	788	451	99	25	208-7	383	5.62	88	.299	.351	55-0-5	.145	-1	89	-47	160	-5.0
Remlinger, Mike	Michael John; B3.23.1966 Middletown NY; BL/TL/6´1˝/(195–215); [SFN87 1/16]; d6.15; Col Dartmouth																									
1991	SF N	2	1	.667	8	6	1-1	0-0	35	36	17	5	0	20-1	19	4.37	82	.271	.364	7-0-4	.000	-0	183	-2	0	-0.2
1994	NY N	1	5	.167	10	9	0	0-0	54.2	55	30	9	1	35-4	33	4.61	91	.261	.364	16-0-3	.000	-1	70	-2	0	-0.4
1995	NY N	0	1	.000	5	0	0	0-1	5.2	7	5	1	0	2-0	6	6.35	64	.292	.346	1	.000	-0	—	-2	0	-0.3
	Cin N	0	0	ø	2	0	0	0-0	1	2	1	0	0	3-0	1	9.00	46	.500	.714	0	ø	0	—	-1	0	0.0
	Year	0	1	.000	7	0	0	0-1	6.2	9	6	1	0	5-0	7	6.75	60	.321	.424	1	.000	-0	—	-2	0	-0.3
1996	Cin N	0	1	.000	19	4	0	0-0	27.1	24	17	4	3	19-2	19	5.60	77	.242	.377	7	.143	0	111	-3	0	-0.1
1997	Cin N	8	8	.500	69	12	2	2-0	124	100	61	11	7	60-6	145	4.14	103	.223	.322	21-0-3	.095	0*	106	2	0	0.3
1998	Cin N	8	15	.348	35	28	1-1	0-0	164.1	164	96	23	5	87-1	144	4.82	89	.266	.358	47-0-7	.106	-2	88	-10	0	-1.5
1999	†Atl N	10	1	.909	73	0	0	1-2	83.2	66	24	9	1	35-5	81	2.37	189	.215	.297	2-0-2	.000	-0	—	20	13	2.3
2000	†Atl N	5	3	.625	71	0	0	12-4	72.2	55	29	6	3	37-1	72	3.47	130	.207	.308	3	.000	-0	—	10	19	1.2
2001	†Atl N	3	3	.500	74	0	0	1-4	75	67	25	9	2	23-4	93	2.76	156	.234	.296	2	.000	-0*	—	13	0	0.9
2002	†Atl N★	7	3	.700	73	0	0	0-5	68	48	17	3	1	28-3	69	1.99	204	.198	.284	2	.000	-0	—	16	16	2.1
2003	†Chi N	6	5	.545	73	0	0	0-1	69	54	30	11	2	39-4	83	3.65	119	.211	.318	1	.000	-0	—	6	0	0.8
2004	Chi N	1	2	.333	48	0	0	2-4	36.2	33	16	3	1	16-3	35	3.44	129	.246	.323	1	.000	-0	—	3	65	0.3
2005	Chi N	0	3	.000	35	0	0	0-1	33	31	19	5	2	12-2	30	4.91	89	.250	.326	0	ø	0	—	-2	15	-0.1

YEAR	TM LG	W	L	PCT	G	GS	CG-SHO	SV-BS	IP	H	R	HR	HB	BB-IB	SO	ERA	AERA	OAV	OOB	AB-HR-SH	AVG	PB	SUP	APR	DL	PW
	Bos A	0	0	ø	8	0	0	0-0	6.2	15	14	2	0	5-0	5	14.85	31	.417	.488	0	ø	0	—	-8	0	-0.4
2006	Atl N	2	4	.333	36	0	0	2-3	22.1	27	11	2	2	9-2	19	4.03	112	.293	.369	0	ø	0	—	1	0	0.3
Total	14	53	55	.491	639	59	4-2	20-25	879	784	412	103	30	430-38	854	3.90	110	.239	.331	110-0-19	.073	-4	98	41	128	5.2
REMMERSWAAL, WIN Wilhelmus Abraham; B3.8.1954 The Hague, Netherlands; BR/TR/6´2˝/160; d8.3																										
1979	Bos A	1	0	1.000	8	0	0	0-0	20.1	26	16	1	1	12-1	16	7.08	63	.317	.402	0	ø	0	—	-5	0	-0.3
1980	Bos A	2	1	.667	14	0	0	0-0	35.1	39	18	4	0	9-1	20	4.58	93	.295	.338	0	ø	0	—	0	0	-0.1
Total	2	3	1	.750	22	0	0	0-0	55.2	65	34	5	1	21-2	36	5.50	79	.304	.364	0	ø	0	—	-5	0	-0.4
REMNEAS, ALEX Alexander Norman; B2.21.1886 Minneapolis MN; D8.27.1975 Phoenix AZ; BR/TR/6´1˝/180; d4.15																										
1912	Det A	0	0	ø	1	0	0	0	1.2	5	5	0	0	0	0	27.00	12	.455	.455	0	ø	0	—	-4	—	-0.1
1915	StL A	0	0	ø	2	0	0	0	6	3	4	0	1	3	5	1.50	191	.136	.269	1	.000	-0	—	0	—	0.0
Total	2	0	0	ø	3	0	0	0	7.2	8	9	0	1	3	5	7.04	42	.242	.324	1	.000	0	—	-4	—	-0.1
RENFER, ERWIN Erwin Arthur; B12.11.1891 Elgin IL; D10.26.1957 Sycamore IL; BR/TR/6´0˝/180; d9.18; Col VPI																										
1913	Det A	0	1	.000	1	1	0	0	6	5	5	0	1	3	1	6.00	49	.227	.346	2	.000	-0	25	-2	—	-0.3
RENFROE, LADDIE Cohen Williams; B5.9.1962 Natchez MS; BB/TR/5´11˝/200; [ChiN84 25/622]; d7.3; Col U. of Mississippi																										
1991	Chi N	0	1	.000	4	0	0	0-1	4.2	11	7	1	0	2-1	4	13.50	29	.440	.481	1	.000	-0	—	-4	0	-0.8
RENFROE, MARSHALL Marshall Daniel; B5.25.1936 Century FL; D12.10.1970 Pensacola FL; BL/TL/6´0˝/180; d9.27																										
1959	SF N	0	0	ø	1	1	0	0	2	3	6	1	0	3-0	3	27.00	14	.333	.500	1	.000	-0	188	-5	0	-0.2
RENIFF, HAL Harold Eugene "Porky"; B7.2.1938 Warren OH; D9.7.2004 Ontario CA; BR/TR/6´0˝/(205–215); d6.8																										
1961	NY A	2	0	1.000	25	0	0	2	45.1	31	14	1	0	31-3	21	2.58	144	.197	.330	5	.000	-1	—	6	0	0.2
1962	NY A	0	0	ø	2	0	0	0	3.2	6	3	0	1	5-1	1	7.36	51	.400	.545	0	ø	0	—	-1	0	-0.1
1963	†NY A	4	3	.571	48	0	0	18	89.1	63	31	3	2	42-5	56	2.62	134	.202	.300	15-0-1	.000	-1	—	8	0	1.0
1964	†NY A	6	4	.600	41	0	0	9	69.1	47	26	3	0	30-4	38	3.12	116	.199	.287	10	.100	-1*	—	4	0	0.6
1965	NY A	3	4	.429	51	0	0	3	85.1	74	40	4	5	48-7	74	3.80	90	.232	.340	2-0-1	.000	-0	—	-3	0	-0.3
1966	NY A	3	7	.300	56	0	0	9	95.1	80	37	2	5	49-8	79	3.21	104	.229	.330	14-0-2	.286	1	—	2	0	0.3
1967	NY A	0	2	.000	24	0	0	0	40	40	22	0	3	14-2	24	4.27	73	.256	.328	2-0-1	.000	-0	—	-5	0	-0.3
	NY N	3	3	.500	29	0	0	4	43	42	20	1	1	23-4	21	3.35	101	.266	.361	4	.000	-0	—	-1	0	-0.2
Total	7	21	23	.477	276	0	0	45	471.1	383	193	14	17	242-34	314	3.27	106	.225	.326	52-0-5	.096	-2	—	10	0	1.2
RENINGER, JIM James David; B3.7.1915 Aurora IL; D8.23.1993 N.Fort Myers FL; BR/TR/6´3˝/210; d9.17																										
1938	Phi A	0	2	.000	4	4	1	0	22.2	28	18	3	0	14	9	7.15	68	.295	.385	7	.000	-0	73	-4	—	-0.3
1939	Phi A	0	2	.000	4	2	0	0	16.1	24	15	3	0	12	3	7.71	61	.369	.468	6	.167	-0	28	-5	—	-0.5
Total	2	0	4	.000	8	6	1	0	39	52	33	6	0	26	12	7.38	65	.325	.419	13	.077	-1	58	-9	—	-0.8
RENKO, STEVE Steven; B12.10.1944 Kansas City KS; BR/TR/6´5˝/(220–240); [NYN65 16/620]; d6.27; Col Kansas																										
1969	Mon N	6	7	.462	18	15	4	0-0	103.1	94	54	14	2	50-6	68	4.01	92	.243	.330	36-1-2	.167	1	117	-4	0	-0.4
1970	Mon N	13	11	.542	41	33	7-1	1-0	222.2	203	121	27	6	104-7	142	4.32	96	.241	.327	80-1-3	.200	2	115	-5	0	-0.2
1971	Mon N	15	14	.517	40	37	9-3	0-1	275.2	256	128	24	3	135-11	129	3.75	95	.247	.333	100-2-4	.210	4*	95	-6	0	-0.2
1972	Mon N	1	10	.091	30	12	0	0-0	97	96	60	11	0	67-10	66	5.20	69	.262	.375	24	.292	1*	64	-17	0	-1.6
1973	Mon N	15	11	.577	36	34	9	1-0	249.2	201	94	26	1	108-12	164	2.81	136	.218	.299	88-0-4	.273	7*	94	26	0	3.5
1974	Mon N	12	16	.429	37	35	8-1	0-0	227.2	222	115	17	0	81-8	138	4.03	95	.257	.318	81-1-2	.210	3	92	-3	0	0.1
1975	Mon N	6	12	.333	31	25	3-1	1-0	170.1	175	89	20	1	76-7	99	4.07	95	.265	.340	54-1-5	.278	5*	95	-5	0	0.0
1976	Mon N	0	1	.000	5	1	0	0-1	13	15	8	2	0	3-0	4	5.54	68	.288	.327	3	.333	0	0	-2	0	-0.1
	Chi N	8	11	.421	28	27	4-1	0-0	163.1	164	79	12	0	43-8	112	3.86	101	.258	.304	53-0-4	.094	-3*	73	0	0	-0.4
	Year	8	12	.400	33	28	4-1	0-1	176.1	179	87	14	0	46-8	116	3.98	97	.260	.306	56-0-4	.107	-3	71	-1	0	-0.5
1977	Chi N	2	2	.500	13	8	0	1-0	51.1	51	32	10	1	21-6	34	4.56	97	.258	.330	12	.167	0	91	-2	54	-0.2
	Chi A	5	0	1.000	8	8	0	0-0	53.1	55	23	3	1	17-0	36	3.54	115	.274	.330	0	ø	0	107	4	0	0.3
1978	Oak A	6	12	.333	27	25	3-1	0-0	151	152	77	10	2	67-4	89	4.29	85	.265	.342	0	ø	0	72	-7	0	-0.8
1979	Bos A	11	9	.550	27	27	4-1	0-0	171	174	86	22	2	53-1	99	4.11	108	.260	.315	0	ø	0	109	7	0	0.6
1980	Bos A	9	9	.500	32	23	1	0-0	165.1	180	86	17	1	56-4	90	4.19	102	.281	.337	0	ø	0	92	0	0	0.0
1981	Cal A	8	4	.667	22	15	0	1-0	102	93	40	7	1	42-1	50	3.44	107	.250	.323	0	ø	0	108	4	0	0.4
1982	Cal A	11	6	.647	31	23	4	0-1	156	163	78	17	1	51-0	81	4.44	92	.269	.325	0	ø	0	107	-4	0	-0.5
1983	KC A	6	11	.353	25	17	1	1-0	121.1	144	63	9	0	36-1	54	4.30	96	.293	.338	0	ø	0	107	-2	0	-0.2
Total	15	134	146	.479	451	365	57-9	6-3	2494	2438	1233	248	22	1010-86	1455	3.99	98	.256	.327	531-6-24	.215	20	96	-16	54	0.3
REPLOGLE, ANDY Andrew David; B10.7.1953 South Bend IN; BR/TR/6´5˝/205; [StLN75 9/208]; d4.11; Col Kansas St.																										
1978	Mil A	9	5	.643	32	18	3-2	0-1	149.1	177	75	14	1	47-3	41	3.92	97	.301	.350	0	ø	0	113	-3	0	-0.4
1979	Mil A	0	0	ø	3	0	0	0-0	8	13	5	0	0	2-0	2	5.63	75	.382	.417	0	ø	0	—	-1	0	0.0
Total	2	9	5	.643	35	18	3-2	0-1	157.1	190	80	14	1	49-3	43	4.00	95	.305	.353	0	ø	0	113	-4	0	-0.4
RESCIGNO, XAVIER Xavier Frederick "Mr. X"; B10.13.1912 New York NY; D12.24.2005 Sun City West AZ; BR/TR/5´10.5˝/175; d4.22; Col Manhattan																										
1943	Pit N	6	9	.400	37	14	5-1	2	132.2	125	52	6	2	45	41	2.98	117	.252	.317	35	.143	0	94	8	0	0.8
1944	Pit N	10	8	.556	48	6	2	5	124	146	69	9	1	34	45	4.35	85	.291	.337	22-0-1	.091	-1	90	-7	0	-1.0
1945	Pit N	3	5	.375	44	1	0	9	78.2	95	57	6	1	34	29	5.72	69	.303	.372	15-0-1	.133	-0	0	-14	0	-1.6
Total	3	19	22	.463	129	21	7-1	16	335.1	366	178	21	4	113	115	4.13	89	.279	.338	72-0-2	.125	-1	85	-13	0	-1.8
RESOP, CHRIS Christopher Paul; B11.4.1982 Naples FL; BR/TR/6´3˝/220; [FlaN01 4/122]; d6.28																										
2005	Fla N	2	0	1.000	15	0	0	0-0	17	22	16	1	1	9-0	15	8.47	47	.324	.400	1	.000	-0	—	-8	0	-0.9
2006	Fla N	1	2	.333	22	0	0	0-1	21.1	26	9	1	1	16-5	10	3.38	127	.310	.426	0	ø	0	—	2	0	0.2
Total	2	3	2	.600	37	0	0	0-1	38.1	48	25	2	2	25-5	25	5.63	74	.316	.414	1	.000	-0	—	-6	0	-0.7
RETTGER, GEORGE George Edward; B7.29.1868 Cleveland OH; D6.5.1921 Lakewood OH; BR/TR/5´11˝/175; d8.13																										
1891	StL AA	7	3	.700	14	12	10-1	1	92.2	85	63	4	8	51	49	3.40	123	.235	.343	42-1	.071	-3*	104	6	—	0.3
1892	Cle N	1	3	.250	6	5	3	0	38	32	27	2	1	31	12	4.26	80	.219	.360	15	.133	-0	93	-3	—	-0.3
	Cin N	1	0	1.000	1	1	1	0	9	8	5	0	1	10	1	4.00	82	.229	.413	8	.125	-0*	310	0	—	0.0
	Year	2	3	.400	7	6	4	0	47	40	32	2	2	41	13	4.21	80	.221	.371	23	.130	-0	128	-3	—	-0.3
Total	2	9	6	.600	21	18	14-1	1	139.2	125	95	6	10	92	62	3.67	106	.231	.352	65-1	.092	-3	111	3	—	0.0
RETTIG, OTTO Adolph John; B1.29.1894 New York NY; D6.16.1977 Stuart FL; BR/TR/5´11˝/165; d7.19; Col Seton Hall																										
1922	Phi A	1	2	.333	4	4	1	0	18.1	18	11	0	1	12	3	4.91	87	.265	.383	6	.000	-1	40	-1	—	-0.2
REULBACH, ED Edward Marvin "Big Ed"; B12.1.1882 Detroit MI; D7.17.1961 Glens Falls NY; BR/TR/6´1˝/190; d5.16; Col Vermont																										
1905	Chi N	18	14	.563	34	29	28-5	1	291.2	208	71	1	18	73	152	1.42	210	**.201**	.266	110-0-2	.127	-6*	81	48	—	4.6
1906	†Chi N	19	4	**.826**	33	24	20-6	3	218	129	51	2	13	92	94	1.65	160	**.175**	.278	83-0-6	.157	-2*	123	26	—	2.8
1907	†Chi N	17	4	**.810**	27	22	16-4	0	192	147	48	1	9	64	96	1.69	148	.217	.294	63-1-4	.175	0	99	19	—	2.2
1908	†Chi N	24	7	**.774**	46	35	25-7	1	297.2	227	81	4	12	106	133	2.03	116	.214	.292	99-0-9	.232	7	143	14	—	2.2
1909	Chi N	19	10	.655	35	32	23-6	0	262.2	194	69	1	11	82	105	1.78	143	.212	.285	86-0-7	.140	-1	90	24	—	2.9
1910	†Chi N	12	8	.600	24	23	14-1	0	173.1	161	76	1	9	49	55	3.12	92	.250	.312	56-0-6	.107	-3	126	-4	—	-0.8
1911	Chi N	16	9	.640	33	29	15-2	0	221.2	191	97	3	4	103	79	2.96	112	.236	.325	67-0-7	.090	-1	106	9	—	1.0
1912	Chi N	10	6	.625	39	19	8	4	169	161	86	7	8	60	75	3.78	88	.259	.332	55-0-1	.109	-3	131	-7	—	-0.7
1913	Chi N	1	3	.250	10	3	1	0	38.2	41	27	1	1	21	10	4.42	72	.281	.375	12	.250	0	126	-6	—	-0.6
	Bro N	7	6	.538	15	12	8-2	0	110	77	34	3	4	34	46	2.05	161	.202	.274	29-0-3	.103	0	65	14	—	1.6
	Year	8	9	.471	25	15	9-2	0	148.2	118	61	4	5	55	56	2.66	123	.223	.303	41-0-3	.146	0	77	10	—	1.0
1914	Bro N	11	18	.379	44	29	14-3	3	256	228	108	5	10	83	119	2.64	108	.242	.310	74-0-3	.122	-0	89	6	—	0.7
1915	New F	21	10	.677	33	30	23-4	1	270	233	88	3	3	69	117	2.23	115	.236	.287	92-0-8	.196	-1	117	12	—	1.2
1916	Bos N	7	6	.538	21	11	6	0	109.1	99	38	1	4	41	47	2.47	101	.251	.328	33-0-2	.091	-1	101	1	—	0.2
1917	Bos N	0	1	.000	5	2	0	0	22.1	21	13	0	1	15	9	2.82	90	.256	.378	3	.000	1	89	-2	—	0.0
Total	13	182	106	.632	399	300	201-40	13	2632.1	2117	887	33	107	892	1137	2.28	122	.224	.299	862-1-58	.147	-10	107	154	—	17.3

YEAR	TM LG	W	L	PCT	G	GS	CG-SHO	SV-BS	IP	H	R	HR	HB	BB-IB	SO	ERA	AERA	OAV	OOB	AB-HR-SH	AVG	PB	SUP	APR	DL	PW
REUSCHEL, PAUL	Paul Richard; B1.12.1947 Quincy IL; BR/TR/6´4˝/210; [ChiN68 S4/61]; d7.25; b–Rick; Col Western Illinois																									
1975	Chi N	1	3	.250	28	0	0	5-2	36	44	15	1	1	13-2	12	3.50	111	.312	.372	4	.000	-0	—	2	0	0.2
1976	Chi N	4	2	.667	50	2	0	3-0	87	94	46	12	1	33-4	55	4.55	85	.278	.341	13	.154	-0	113	-4	0	-0.3
1977	Chi N	5	6	.455	69	0	0	4-5	107	105	58	9	0	40-8	62	4.37	101	.262	.326	11-0-1	.000	-1	—	1	0	0.0
1978	Chi N	2	0	1.000	16	0	0	0-0	28	29	16	4	1	13-3	13	5.14	79	.269	.352	4	.000	-0	—	-2	28	-0.2
	Cle A	2	4	.333	18	6	1	0-0	89.2	95	33	5	2	22-1	24	3.11	122	.271	.316	0	ø	0	51	7	0	0.5
1979	Cle A	2	1	.667	17	1	0	1-0	45.1	73	43	7	0	11-0	22	7.94	54	.365	.398	0	ø	0	148	-18	75	-1.0
Total	5	16	16	.500	198	9	1	13-7	393	440	211	38	5	132-18	188	4.51	90	.286	.342	32-0-1	.063	-2	73	-14	103	-0.8
REUSCHEL, RICK	Rickey Eugene; B5.16.1949 Quincy IL; BR/TR/6´3˝/(210–250); [ChiN70 3/67]; d6.19; b–Paul; Col Western Illinois; [DL 1982 NY A 182, 1983 NY A 66]																									
1972	Chi N	10	8	.556	21	18	5-4	0-0	129	127	46	3	2	29-6	87	2.93	130	.259	.302	44-0-6	.136	-1	107	12	0	1.6
1973	Chi N	14	15	.483	36	36	7-3	0-0	237	244	95	15	5	62-6	168	3.00	131	.263	.312	73-0-9	.123	-3	73	21	0	2.3
1974	Chi N	13	12	.520	41	38	8-2	0-0	240.2	262	130	18	6	83-12	160	4.30	89	.276	.335	86-0-9	.221	2	101	-9	0	-0.5
1975	Chi N	11	17	.393	38	37	6	1-0	234	244	116	17	7	67-8	155	3.73	104	.268	.322	77-1-6	.208	2	88	1	0	0.5
1976	Chi N	14	12	.538	38	37	9-2	1-0	260	260	117	17	8	64-5	146	3.46	112	.265	.311	83-0-7	.229	4	96	9	0	1.5
1977	Chi N★	20	10	.667	39	37	8-4	1-0	252	233	84	13	5	74-11	166	2.79	158	.247	.304	87-1-6	.207	1*	71	42	0	5.3
1978	Chi N	14	15	.483	35	35	9-1	0-0	242.2	235	98	16	5	54-8	115	3.41	119	.254	.297	73-0-10	.137	-1	83	17	0	1.9
1979	Chi N	18	12	.600	36	36	5-1	0-0	239	251	104	16	10	75-8	125	3.62	115	.274	.333	79-0-5	.165	1*	105	15	0	2.1
1980	Chi N	11	13	.458	38	**38**	6	0-0	257	281	111	13	4	76-10	140	3.40	117	.286	.336	82-0-10	.159	-1*	82	15	0	1.5
1981	Chi N	4	7	.364	13	13	1	0-0	85.2	87	40	4	4	23-4	53	3.47	108	.267	.323	25-0-4	.080	-1*	78	1	0	0.1
	†NY A	4	4	.500	12	11	3	0-0	70.2	75	24	4	1	10-0	22	2.67	135	.280	.306	0	ø	0	104	7	0	0.8
1983	Chi N	1	1	.500	4	4	0	0-0	20.2	18	9	1	0	10-2	9	3.92	97	.234	.318	7	.143	-0	75	0	0	0.0
1984	Chi N	5	5	.500	19	14	1	0-0	92.1	123	57	7	3	23-0	43	5.17	76	.339	.374	29-0-4	.241	2*	108	-11	28	-0.9
1985	Pit N	14	8	.636	31	26	9-1	1-0	194	153	58	7	3	52-10	138	2.27	160	.215	.271	59-1-6	.169	2	90	27	0	3.6
1986	Pit N	9	16	.360	35	34	4-2	0-0	215.2	232	106	20	8	57-2	125	3.96	98	.274	.322	70-0-8	.157	0*	96	-2	0	0.0
1987	Pit N★	8	6	.571	25	25	9-3	0-0	177	163	63	12	6	35-1	80	2.75	152	.246	.287	60-1-6	.150	2	96	26	0	2.2
	†SF N	5	3	.625	9	8	3-1	0-0	50	44	28	1	2	7-2	27	4.32	89	.230	.264	19-0-1	.105	-0	138	-3	0	-0.5
	Year	13	9	.591	34	33	**12-4**	0-0	227	207	91	13	8	42-3	107	3.09	132	.242	.282	79-1-7	.139	1	106	24	0	1.7
1988	SF N	19	11	.633	36	**36**	7-2	0-0	245	242	88	11	6	42-8	92	3.12	105	.260	.293	73-0-19	.110	-1	121	8	0	0.6
1989	†SF N★	17	8	.680	32	32	2	0-0	208.1	195	75	18	2	54-4	111	2.94	115	.247	.294	61-0-16	.164	1	110	11	17	1.4
1990	SF N	3	6	.333	15	13	0	1-0	87	102	40	8	1	31-9	49	3.93	93	.297	.353	26-0-3	.154	0	103	-2	110	-0.2
1991	SF N	0	2	.000	4	1	0	0-1	10.2	17	5	0	0	7-1	4	4.22	85	.370	.453	2	.000	-0	50	-1	56	-0.1
Total	19	214	191	.528	557	529	102-26	5-1	3548.1	3588	1494	221	88	935-117	2015	3.37	115	.264	.313	1115-4-135	.168	7	94	184	459	23.2
REUSS, JERRY	Jerry; B6.19.1949 St.Louis MO; BL/TL/6´5˝/(195–227); [StLN67 2/30]; d9.27																									
1969	StL N	1	0	1.000	1	1	0	0-0	7	2	0	0	2	3-0	3	0.00	ø	.091	.259	3	.333	0	49	3	0	0.6
1970	StL N	7	8	.467	20	20	5-2	0-0	127.1	132	62	9	1	49-2	74	4.10	101	.271	.337	40-0-5	.050	-3	82	2	0	0.0
1971	StL N	14	14	.500	36	35	7-2	0-0	211	228	125	15	7	109-11	131	4.78	76	.279	.366	65-0-11	.123	0	119	-26	0	-3.2
1972	Hou N	9	13	.409	33	30	4-1	1-0	192	177	101	14	10	83-3	174	4.17	81	.246	.329	66-0-1	.106	-1	122	-19	0	-2.2
1973	Hou N	16	13	.552	41	**40**	12-3	0-0	279.1	271	123	17	3	117-6	177	3.74	98	.256	.330	95-0-9	.137	-1*	105	-1	0	-0.3
1974	†Pit N	16	11	.593	35	35	14-1	0-0	260	259	115	20	1	101-16	105	3.50	100	.261	.327	86-0-4	.151	-0	108	0	0	-0.1
1975	†Pit N★	18	11	.621	32	32	15-6	0-0	237.1	224	73	10	0	78-8	131	2.54	141	.253	.313	71-0-10	.197	2	92	30	0	4.1
1976	Pit N	14	9	.609	31	29	11-3	2-0	209.1	209	98	16	2	51-10	108	3.53	100	.256	.301	66-0-3	.242	6	116	-2	0	0.3
1977	Pit N	10	13	.435	33	33	8-2	0-0	208	225	109	11	4	71-2	116	4.11	98	.280	.339	70-0-4	.171	1*	100	-3	0	-0.2
1978	Pit N	3	2	.600	23	12	3-1	0-0	82.2	97	48	5	3	23-1	42	4.90	76	.297	.346	27	.185	0	126	-9	0	-0.5
1979	LA N	7	14	.333	39	21	4-1	3-3	160	178	88	4	3	60-7	83	3.54	102	.282	.347	42-0-3	.167	1	84	-5	0	-0.5
1980	LA N★	18	6	.750	37	29	10-**6**	3-2	229.1	193	74	12	0	40-9	111	2.51	138	.227	.260	68-1-4	.088	-1	112	24	0	2.5
1981	†LA N	10	4	.714	22	22	8-2	0-0	152.2	138	44	6	4	27-3	51	2.30	144	.243	.282	51-0-7	.196	0	127	17	0	1.7
1982	LA N	18	11	.621	39	37	8-4	0-0	254.2	232	98	11	2	50-10	138	3.11	112	.240	.277	77-0-16	.221	3	113	11	0	1.7
1983	†LA N	12	11	.522	32	31	7	0-0	223.1	233	94	12	2	50-5	143	2.94	123	.271	.311	71-0-10	.282	5	92	14	0	2.2
1984	LA N	5	7	.417	30	15	2	1-1	99	102	51	4	0	31-7	44	3.82	93	.266	.319	24-0-2	.167	1	93	-4	34	-0.3
1985	†LA N	14	10	.583	34	33	5-3	0-0	212.2	210	78	13	3	58-7	84	2.92	120	.260	.310	74-0-6	.135	-1	102	16	0	1.5
1986	LA N	2	6	.250	19	13	0	1-0	74	96	57	13	2	17-4	29	5.84	59	.313	.353	20	.250	2	113	-23	48	-2.0
1987	LA N	0	0	ø	1	0	0	0-0	2	2	1	0	0	0-0	2	4.50	89	.333	.286	0	ø	0	—	0	0	0.0
	Cin N	0	5	.000	7	7	0	0-0	34.2	52	31	2	1	12-2	10	7.79	54	.351	.404	8-0-2	.125	0	67	-12	0	-1.5
	Year	0	5	.000	8	7	0	0-0	36.2	54	32	2	1	12-2	12	7.61	55	.351	.399	8-0-2	.125	0	68	-12	0	-1.5
	Cal A	4	5	.444	17	16	1-1	0-0	82.1	112	60	16	2	17-1	37	5.25	83	.327	.361	0	ø	0	115	-11	15	-1.0
1988	Chi A	13	9	.591	32	29	2	0-0	183	183	79	15	3	43-1	73	3.44	116	.263	.307	0	ø	0	102	12	0	1.3
1989	Chi A	8	5	.615	23	19	1-1	0-1	106.2	135	65	12	3	21-1	27	5.06	76	.308	.340	0	ø	0	114	-14	0	-1.6
	Mil A	1	4	.200	7	7	0	0-0	33.2	36	23	7	1	13-1	13	5.35	72	.273	.342	0	ø	0	77	-6	15	-0.8
	Year	9	9	.500	30	26	1-1	0-1	140.1	171	88	19	4	34-2	40	5.13	75	.300	.340	0	ø	0	104	-20	0	-2.4
1990	Pit N	0	0	ø	4	1	0	0-0	7.2	8	3	1	0	3-1	1	3.52	104	.267	.333	0-0-2	ø	0	74	0	0	0.0
Total	22	220	191	.535	628	547	127-39	11-7	3669.2	3734	1700	245	59	1127-118	1907	3.64	100	.265	.320	1024-1-99	.167	14	106	-6	112	1.7
REVENIG, TODD	Todd Michael; B6.28.1969 Brainerd MN; BR/TR/6´1˝/185; [OakA90 37/999]; d8.24; Col Mankato St.; [DL 1993 Oak A 182]																									
1992	Oak A	0	0	ø	2	0	0	0-0	2	2	0	0	0	0-0	1	0.00	ø	.286	.286	0	ø	0	—	1	0	0.0
REYES, ANTHONY	Anthony Loza; B10.16.1981 Downey CA; BR/TR/6´2˝/215; [StLN03 15/455]; d8.9; Col Southern California																									
2005	StL N	1	1	.500	4	1	0	0-0	13.1	6	4	2	0	4-1	12	2.70	155	.133	.200	4	.000	-0	112	2	0	0.3
2006	†StL N	5	8	.385	17	17	1	0-0	85.1	84	48	17	7	34-0	72	5.06	86	.262	.342	25-0-2	.120	-1*	75	-6	0	-0.9
Total	2	6	9	.400	21	18	1	0-0	98.2	90	52	19	7	38-1	84	4.74	91	.246	.325	29-0-2	.103	-1	77	-4	0	-0.6
REYES, CARLOS	Carlos Alberto; B4.4.1969 Miami FL; BB/TR/6´1˝/190; d4.7; Col Florida Southern																									
1994	Oak A	0	3	.000	27	9	0	1-0	78	71	38	10	2	44-1	57	4.15	108	.242	.342	0	ø	0	75	4	17	0.1
1995	Oak A	4	6	.400	40	1	0	0-1	69	71	43	10	5	28-4	48	5.09	89	.264	.344	0	ø	0	82	-5	0	-0.6
1996	Oak A	7	10	.412	46	10	0	0-0	122.1	134	71	19	2	61-8	78	4.78	104	.281	.359	0	ø	0	62	2	0	0.1
1997	Oak A	3	4	.429	37	6	0	0-1	77.1	101	52	13	2	25-2	43	5.82	79	.316	.367	0	ø	0	67	-10	22	-0.7
1998	SD N	2	2	.500	22	0	0	1-1	27.2	23	11	4	2	6-0	24	3.58	111	.235	.290	0-0-1	ø	0	—	2	0	0.2
	Bos A	1	1	.500	24	0	0	0-0	38.1	35	15	2	1	14-2	23	3.52	134	.246	.316	0	ø	0	—	6	0	0.3
1999	SD N	2	4	.333	65	0	0	1-1	77.1	76	38	11	0	24-4	57	3.72	115	.254	.307	1	.000	-0	—	4	0	0.3
2000	Phi N	0	2	.000	10	0	0	0-0	10.1	10	6	2	0	5-0	4	5.23	88	.270	.357	0	ø	0	—	-1	9	-0.1
	SD N	1	1	.500	12	0	0	1-2	18	15	12	5	1	8-0	13	6.00	74	.221	.312	1	.000	-0	—	-3	0	-0.3
	Year	1	3	.250	22	0	0	1-2	28.1	25	18	7	1	13-0	17	5.72	79	.238	.328	1	.000	-0	—	-3	0	-0.4
2003	TB A	0	3	.000	10	3	0	0-0	39.2	40	23	10	2	5-0	13	5.22	88	.265	.294	1	.000	0	60	-2	0	-0.1
Total	8	20	36	.357	293	29	0	4-6	558	576	309	86	17	220-21	360	4.66	98	.267	.337	3-0-1	.000	-0	69	-3	48	-0.8
REYES, DENNYS	Dennys (Valarde); B4.19.1977 Higuera de Zaragoza, Sinaloa, Mexico; BL/TL/6´3˝/(245–246); d7.13																									
1997	LA N	2	3	.400	14	5	0	0-0	47	51	21	4	1	18-3	36	3.83	102	.280	.347	9-0-1	.000	-1	118	1	0	0.1
1998	LA N	0	4	.000	11	3	0	0-0	28.2	27	17	1	0	20-4	33	4.71	86	.255	.370	5-0-1	.000	-1	114	-2	0	-0.3
	Cin N	3	1	.750	8	7	0	0-0	38.2	35	19	2	1	27-1	44	4.42	97	.255	.380	12	.083	-0	126	0	0	0.0
	Year	3	5	.375	19	10	0	0-0	67.1	62	36	3	1	47-5	77	4.54	92	.255	.375	17-0-1	.059	-1	123	-3	0	-0.3
1999	Cin N	2	2	.500	65	1	0	2-1	61.2	53	30	5	3	39-1	72	3.79	124	.232	.348	4	.000	-0	20	5	0	0.3
2000	Cin N	2	1	.667	62	0	0	0-1	43.2	43	31	5	1	29-0	36	4.53	105	.262	.371	2	.000	0	—	-2	0	-0.1
2001	Cin N	2	6	.250	35	6	0	0-0	53	51	35	5	1	35-1	52	4.92	93	.248	.357	11	.182	-0*	54	-3	33	-0.4
2002	Col N	0	1	.000	43	0	0	0-0	40.1	43	19	1	0	24-3	30	4.24	112	.279	.372	0	ø	0	—	3	0	0.1
	Tex A	4	3	.571	15	5	0	0-0	42.1	55	33	9	0	21-1	29	6.38	75	.316	.390	0	ø	0	116	-7	0	-1.0
2003	Pit N	0	0	ø	12	0	0	0-0	10.1	10	13	1	0	9-1	11	10.45	41	.263	.388	0	ø	0	—	-7	0	-0.3
	Ari N	0	0	ø	3	0	0	0-0	2.1	5	3	1	0	1-0	5	11.57	40	.417	.462	0	ø	0	—	-2	0	-0.1
	Year	0	0	ø	15	0	0	0-0	12.2	15	16	2	0	10-1	16	10.66	41	.300	.403	0	ø	0	—	-9	0	-0.4
2004	KC A	4	8	.333	40	12	0	0-1	108	114	64	12	4	50-3	91	4.75	98	.273	.353	6	.000	-1	71	-1	0	-0.2
2005	SD N	3	2	.600	36	1	0	0-1	43.2	57	30	3	1	32-2	35	5.15	76	.315	.421	5	.200	0	48	-8	0	-0.8
2006	†Min A	5	0	1.000	66	0	0	0-1	50.2	35	8	3	0	15-2	49	0.89	514	.197	.259	0	ø	0	—	19	0	1.7
Total	10	27	31	.466	410	40	0	2-5	570.1	579	323	52	12	320-22	523	4.45	101	.266	.360	54-0-2	.074	-3	89	-4	33	-1.0

YEAR	TM LG	W	L	PCT	G	GS	CG-SHO	SV-BS	IP	H	R	HR	HB	BB-IB	SO	ERA	AERA	OAV	OOB	AB-HR-SH	AVG	PB	SUP	APR	DL	PW
REYES, AL	Rafael Alberto; B4.10.1971 San Cristobal, D.R.; BR/TR/6´1˝/(193–210); d4.27																									
1995	Mil A	1	1	.500	27	0	0	1-0	33.1	19	9	3	3	18-2	29	2.43	206	.167	.292	0	ø	0	—	9	75	0.5
1996	Mil A	1	0	1.000	5	0	0	0-0	5.2	8	5	1	0	2-0	2	7.94	65	.320	.370	0	ø	0	—	-1	0	-0.2
1997	Mil A	1	2	.333	19	0	0	1-0	29.2	32	19	4	3	9-0	28	5.46	85	.274	.341	0	ø	0	—	-2	0	-0.2
1998	Mil N	5	1	.833	50	0	0	0-1	57	55	26	9	2	31-1	58	3.95	110	.253	.351	5	.200	0	—	3	45	0.3
1999	Mil N	2	0	1.000	26	0	0	0-1	36	27	17	5	3	25-1	39	4.25	108	.206	.344	2	.000	-0	—	2	0	0.1
	Bal A	2	3	.400	27	0	0	0-3	29.2	23	16	4	3	16-2	28	4.85	97	.225	.341	0	ø	0	—	0	0	0.0
2000	Bal A	1	0	1.000	13	0	0	0-1	13	13	10	2	0	11-1	10	6.92	68	.271	.393	0	ø	0	—	-3	0	-0.2
	LA N	0	0	ø	6	0	0	0-0	6.2	2	0	0	0	1-0	8	0.00	ø	.087	.125	0	ø	0	—	3	0	0.2
2001	LA N	2	1	.667	19	0	0	1-1	25.2	28	13	3	1	13-1	23	3.86	107	.269	.350	3-0-1	.333	0	—	0	0	0.1
2002	Pit N	0	0	ø	15	0	0	0-1	17	9	5	1	2	7-0	21	2.65	158	.161	.273	0	ø	0	—	3	0	0.2
2003	NY A	0	0	ø	13	0	0	0-1	17	13	7	1	0	9-1	9	3.18	138	.203	.301	0	ø	0	—	2	0	0.1
2004	†StL N	0	0	ø	12	2	0	0-0	12	3	1	0	0	2-0	11	0.75	568	.081	.128	1	1.000	0	153	5	0	0.3
2005	StL N	4	2	.667	65	0	0	3-0	62.2	38	15	5	5	20-2	67	2.15	195	.177	.261	1-0-1	.000	0	—	15	0	1.5
Total	11	19	10	.655	297	2	0	6-9	345.1	270	143	38	22	164-11	333	3.60	124	.215	.314	12-0-2	.250	1	153	36	120	2.7
REYNOLDS, ALLIE	Allie Pierce "Superchief"; B2.10.1917 Bethany OK; D12.26.1994 Oklahoma City OK; BR/TR/6´0˝/195; d9.17; Col Oklahoma St.																									
1942	Cle A	0	0	ø	2	0	0	0	5	5	1	0	0	4	2	0.00	ø	.250	.375	2	.000	-0	—	2	0	0.0
1943	Cle A	11	12	.478	34	21	11-3	3	198.2	140	72	3	7	109	**151**	2.99	104	**.202**	.316	67-0-5	.149	-1*	112	5	0	0.5
1944	Cle A	11	8	.579	28	21	5-1	1	158	141	63	2	4	91	84	3.30	100	.240	.346	57-0-3	.123	-3*	102	2	0	-0.1
1945	Cle A✱	18	12	.600	44	30	16-2	4	247.1	227	102	7	5	130	112	3.20	101	.247	.343	85-0-7	.094	-7	108	1	0	-0.7
1946	Cle A	11	15	.423	31	28	9-3	0	183.1	180	93	10	1	108	107	3.88	85	.259	.359	63-0-6	.222	1*	96	-14	0	-1.7
1947	†NY A	19	8	**.704**	34	30	17-4	2	241.2	207	94	23	4	123	129	3.20	110	.227	.322	89-0-7	.146	-2*	153	9	0	0.7
1948	NY A	16	7	.696	39	31	11-1	3	236.1	240	108	17	4	111	101	3.77	108	.268	.351	83-1-5	.193	0*	129	10	0	0.7
1949	†NY A☆	17	6	.739	35	31	4-2	1	213.2	200	102	15	4	123	105	4.00	101	.250	.353	78-0-2	.218	6*	126	4	0	0.8
1950	†NY A★	16	12	.571	35	29	14-2	2	240.2	215	108	12	8	138	160	3.74	115	.242	.349	81-0-9	.185	1*	122	16	0	1.7
1951	†NY A	17	8	.680	40	26	16-**7**	7	221	171	84	12	5	100	126	3.05	125	**.213**	.304	76-0-5	.184	0*	140	21	0	2.2
1952	†NY A☆	20	8	.714	35	29	24-**6**	6	244.1	194	70	10	7	97	**160**	**2.06**	**161**	.218	.300	85-0-4	.153	-1*	118	35	0	4.1
1953	†NY A★	13	7	.650	41	15	5-1	13	145	140	64	9	5	61	86	3.41	108	.253	.333	41	.122	1*	106	4	0	0.5
1954	NY A✱	13	4	.765	36	18	5-4	7	157.1	133	65	13	3	66	100	3.32	104	.233	.314	50-0-5	.160	-0	185	2	0	0.2
Total	13	182	107	.630	434	309	137-36	49	2492.1	2193	1026	133	57	1261	1423	3.30	110	.238	.333	857-1-58	.163	-5	125	97	0	8.9
REYNOLDS, ARCHIE	Archie Edward; B1.3.1946 Glendale CA; BR/TR/6´2˝/205; [ChiN66 38/703]; d8.15; Col Paris (TX) JC																									
1968	Chi N	0	1	.000	7	1	0	0	13.1	14	10	1	1	7-0	6	6.75	47	.259	.355	2	.500	1	110	-5	0	-0.3
1969	Chi N	0	1	.000	2	2	0	0-0	7.1	11	5	1	0	7-1	4	2.45	164	.379	.500	1	.000	0	99	0	0	0.1
1970	Chi N	0	2	.000	7	1	0	0-0	15	17	11	2	1	9-0	9	6.60	68	.298	.403	2	.000	0	20	-3	0	-0.3
1971	Cal A	0	3	.000	15	1	0	0-0	27.1	32	15	2	0	18-5	15	4.61	70	.305	.407	2	.000	-0	0	-4	0	-0.4
1972	Mil A	0	1	.000	5	2	0	0-0	18.2	26	18	2	0	8-1	13	7.23	42	.338	.391	4	.500	1	101	-9	0	-0.4
Total	5	0	8	.000	36	7	0	0-0	81.2	100	59	8	2	49-7	47	5.73	61	.311	.403	11	.273	2	77	-21	0	-1.3
REYNOLDS, CHARLIE	Charles E.; B7.31.1857 Allegany NY; D5.1.1913 Buffalo NY; d5.18																									
1882	Phi AA	1	1	.500	2	2	1	0	12	18	11	0	—	3	4	5.25	53	.327	.362	8	.125	-1	110	-3	—	-0.4
REYNOLDS, KEN	Kenneth Lee; B1.4.1947 Trevose PA; BL/TL/6´0˝/(180–185); [PhiN66 4/69]; d9.5; Col New Mexico Highlands																									
1970	Phi N	0	0	ø	4	0	0	0-0	2.1	3	0	0	0	4-0	1	0.00	ø	.333	.538	0	ø	0	—	1	0	0.1
1971	Phi N	5	9	.357	35	25	2-1	0-0	162.1	163	89	11	6	82-1	81	4.49	79	.269	.358	50-0-1	.200	2*	97	-15	0	-1.1
1972	Phi N	2	15	.118	33	23	2	0-0	154.1	149	76	17	1	60-6	87	4.26	85	.258	.327	40-0-1	.200	1*	75	-8	0	-0.7
1973	Mil A	0	1	.000	2	1	0	0-0	7.1	5	7	1	1	10-0	3	7.36	52	.200	.444	0	ø	0	23	-3	0	-0.3
1975	StL N	0	1	.000	10	0	0	0-0	17	12	4	0	0	11-2	7	1.59	239	.214	.343	2	.000	-0	—	4	0	0.2
1976	SD N	0	3	.000	19	2	0	1-0	32.1	38	27	0	0	29-4	18	6.40	51	.309	.435	5	.000	-1	134	-12	0	-1.2
Total	6	7	29	.194	103	51	4-1	1-0	375.2	370	203	29	8	196-13	197	4.46	80	.265	.356	97-0-2	.186	2	86	-33	0	-3.0
REYNOLDS, SHANE	Richard Shane; B3.26.1968 Bastrop LA; BR/TR/6´3˝/(210–215); [HouN89 3/72]; d7.20; Col Texas																									
1992	Hou N	1	3	.250	8	5	0	0-0	25.1	42	22	2	0	6-1	10	7.11	48	.385	.414	4-0-2	.500	1	133	-11	0	-1.4
1993	Hou N	0	0	ø	5	1	0	0-0	11	11	4	0	0	6-1	10	0.82	474	.256	.347	2	.500	0	93	3	0	0.2
1994	Hou N	8	5	.615	33	14	1-1	0-0	124	128	46	10	6	21-3	110	3.05	130	.263	.302	33-0-7	.091	-2	107	14	0	1.1
1995	Hou N	10	11	.476	30	30	3-2	0-0	189.1	196	87	15	2	37-6	175	3.47	111	.263	.300	63-0-10	.127	-2*	118	7	0	0.7
1996	Hou N	16	10	.615	35	35	4-1	0-0	239	227	103	20	8	44-3	204	3.65	106	.249	.288	76-2-14	.184	4	98	9	0	1.3
1997	†Hou N	9	10	.474	30	30	2	0-0	181	189	92	19	3	47-5	152	4.23	95	.267	.313	53-0-7	.113	-0	112	-4	34	-0.3
1998	†Hou N	19	8	.704	35	**35**	3-1	0-0	233.1	257	99	25	2	53-2	209	3.51	115	.280	.318	82-0-7	.159	1	135	15	0	1.8
1999	†Hou N	16	14	.533	35	**35**	4-2	0-0	231.2	250	108	23	1	37-0	197	3.85	115	.275	.303	66-1-17	.167	1	94	15	0	2.0
2000	Hou N☆	7	8	.467	22	22	0	0-0	131	150	86	20	6	45-2	93	5.22	94	.287	.345	40-1-4	.225	2	101	-6	63	-0.3
2001	†Hou N	14	11	.560	28	28	3	0-0	182.2	208	95	24	4	36-2	102	4.34	106	.290	.327	52-1-10	.077	-2	98	5	35	0.4
2002	Hou N	3	6	.333	13	13	0	0-0	74	80	43	13	1	26-2	47	4.86	89	.274	.334	21-0-9	.048	-2	82	-4	108	-0.6
2003	Atl N	11	9	.550	30	29	0	0-0	167.1	191	104	20	8	59-6	94	5.43	77	.293	.358	54-0-10	.093	-3	142	-19	0	-2.3
2004	Ari N	0	1	.000	1	1	0	0-0	2	6	6	0	0	2-0	0	4.50	101	.500	.571	0	ø	0	102	-2	182	-0.3
Total	13	114	96	.543	305	278	20-7	0-0	1791.2	1935	895	191	41	419-33	1403	4.09	102	.275	.318	546-5-97	.141	-0	111	22	422	2.3
REYNOLDS, BOB	Robert Allen; B1.21.1947 Seattle WA; BR/TR/6´0˝/(192–205); [SFN66 1/17]; d9.19																									
1969	Mon N	0	0	ø	1	1	0	0-0	1.1	3	6	0	0	3-0	2	20.25	18	.429	.545	0	ø	0	240	-3	0	-0.2
1971	StL N	0	0	ø	4	0	0	0-0	7	15	8	2	1	6-1	4	10.29	35	.441	.537	1	.000	-0	—	-5	0	-0.3
	Mil A	0	1	.000	3	0	0	0-0	6	4	2	0	0	3-0	4	3.00	116	.222	.318	1	.000	-0	—	0	0	0.1
1972	Bal A	0	0	ø	3	0	0	0-0	9.2	8	2	0	0	7-2	5	1.86	167	.258	.395	2	.000	-0	—	1	0	0.0
1973	†Bal A	7	5	.583	42	1	0	9-3	111	88	27	3	0	31-6	77	1.95	194	.219	.272	0	ø	0	142	23	9	2.7
1974	†Bal A	7	5	.583	54	0	0	7-3	69.1	75	23	4	1	14-3	43	2.73	128	.278	.314	0	ø	0	—	6	0	1.2
1975	Bal A	0	1	.000	7	0	0	0-2	6	11	6	1	0	1-0	1	9.00	39	.423	.429	0	ø	0	—	-4	0	-0.5
	Det A	0	2	.000	21	0	0	3-1	34.2	40	20	8	1	14-1	26	4.67	86	.288	.355	0	ø	0	—	-2	0	-0.1
	Cle A	0	2	.000	5	0	0	2-0	9.2	11	7	0	0	3-1	5	4.66	82	.289	.341	0	ø	0	—	-1	0	-0.3
	Year	0	5	.000	33	0	0	5-3	50.1	62	33	9	1	18-2	32	5.19	76	.305	.362	0	ø	0	—	-7	0	-0.9
Total	6	14	16	.467	140	2	0	21-9	254.2	255	101	18	3	82-14	167	3.15	117	.264	.320	4	.000	-0	192	15	9	2.6
REYNOLDS, ROSS	Ross Ernest "Doc"; B8.20.1887 Barksdale TX; D6.23.1970 Ada OK; BR/TR/6´2˝/185; d5.2																									
1914	Det A	5	3	.625	26	7	3-1	0	78	62	26	0	6	39	31	2.08	135	.230	.340	21-0-1	.048	-2	67	6	—	0.3
1915	Det A	0	1	.000	4	2	0	0	11.1	17	9	0	1	5	2	6.35	48	.378	.451	3	.000	-0	60	-3	—	-0.3
Total	2	5	4	.556	30	9	3-1	0	89.1	79	35	0	7	44	33	2.62	108	.251	.355	24-0-1	.042	-2	66	3	—	0.0
REYNOSO, ARMANDO	Armando Martin (Gutierrez); B5.1.1966 San Luis Potosi, San Luis Potosi, Mexico; BR/TR/6´0˝/(186–210); d8.11																									
1991	Atl N	2	1	.667	6	5	0	0-0	23.1	26	18	4	3	10-1	10	6.17	63	.299	.390	7	.000	-0	139	-6	0	-0.6
1992	Atl N	1	0	1.000	3	1	0	1-0	7.2	11	4	2	1	2-1	2	4.70	78	.393	.452	2-0-1	.000	-0	198	-1	0	-0.1
1993	Col N	12	11	.522	30	30	4	0-0	189	206	101	22	9	63-7	117	4.00	120	.277	.337	63-2-6	.127	-1*	92	11	0	1.3
1994	Col N	3	4	.429	9	9	1	0-0	52.1	54	30	5	6	22-1	25	4.82	104	.278	.366	17-0-3	.176	-0	116	1	83	0.2
1995	†Col N	7	7	.500	20	18	0	0-0	93	116	61	12	5	36-3	40	5.32	101	.316	.383	30-0-2	.133	-2	82	0	54	0.0
1996	Col N	8	9	.471	30	30	0	0-0	168.2	195	97	27	9	49-0	88	4.96	105	.291	.347	52-0-7	.173	-1	95	5	0	0.5
1997	NY N	6	3	.667	16	16	1-1	0-0	91.1	95	47	7	6	29-4	47	4.53	88	.275	.338	29-1-0	.241	3	129	-4	88	0.0
1998	NY N	7	3	.700	11	11	0	0-0	68.1	64	31	4	5	32-3	40	3.82	108	.256	.351	30-0-1	.167	0	95	2	115	0.5
1999	Ari N	10	6	.625	31	27	0	0-0	167	178	90	20	6	67-7	79	4.37	106	.276	.347	49-0-8	.163	-0	119	4	0	0.4
2000	Ari N	11	12	.478	31	30	2	0-0	170.2	179	102	22	6	52-5	89	5.27	91	.273	.330	48-0-7	.104	-2	93	-6	0	-0.8
2001	Ari N	1	6	.143	9	9	0	0-0	46.2	58	32	13	4	13-2	15	5.98	78	.312	.366	10-0-3	.100	-0	89	-6	144	-0.7
2002	Ari N	0	0	ø	2	0	0	0-0	1.2	3	2	0	0	1-0	2	10.80	42	.375	.444	0	ø	0	—	-1	158	-0.1
Total	12	68	62	.523	198	186	8-1	1-0	1079.2	1185	615	138	60	376-34	554	4.74	100	.283	.349	337-3-38	.148	-4	101	-1	642	0.6
RHEINECKER, JOHN	John Philip; B5.29.1979 Belleville IL; BL/TL/6´2˝/230; [OakA01 1/37]; d4.22; Col Southwest Missouri St.																									
2006	Tex A	4	6	.400	21	13	0	0-0	70.2	104	46	6	3	19-0	28	5.86	80	.349	.393	0	ø	0	82	-8	0	-0.8

YEAR	TM LG	W	L	PCT	G	GS	CG-SHO	SV-BS	IP	H	R	HR	HB	BB-IB	SO	ERA	AERA	OAV	OOB	AB-HR-SH	AVG	PB	SUP	APR	DL	PW
RHEM, FLINT	Charles Flint "Shad"; B1.24.1901 Rhems SC; D7.30.1969 Columbia SC; BR/TR/6´2˝/180; d9.6; Col Clemson																									
1924	StL N	2	2	.500	6	3	3	1	32.1	31	18	1	0	17	20	4.45	85	.254	.345	12	.167	-0	135	-2	—	-0.3
1925	StL N	8	13	.381	30	24	8-1	1	170	204	114	16	4	58	66	4.92	88	.299	.357	59-1-5	.237	1	109	-13	—	-1.2
1926	†StL N	**20**	7	.741	34	34	20-1	0	258	241	121	12	1	75	72	3.21	122	.250	.305	96-1-5	.188	-2	143	15	—	1.2
1927	StL N	10	12	.455	27	26	9-2	0	169.1	189	102	6	4	54	51	4.41	90	.285	.342	59-0-3	.068	-5	97	-9	—	-1.6
1928	†StL N	11	8	.579	28	22	9	3	169.2	199	91	13	3	71	47	4.14	97	.296	.365	67-1-1	.164	-1	124	-2	—	-0.2
1930	†StL N	12	8	.600	26	19	9	0	139.2	173	90	11	3	37	47	4.45	113	.306	.352	52-0-4	.231	-1	144	5	—	0.3
1931	†StL N	11	10	.524	33	26	10-2	1	207.1	214	100	17	3	60	72	3.56	111	.268	.321	69-0-5	.130	-4	116	6	—	0.1
1932	StL N	4	2	.667	6	6	5-1	0	50	48	19	3	0	10	18	3.06	129	.257	.294	16-0-3	.188	0	128	5	—	0.6
	Phi N	11	7	.611	26	20	10	1	168.2	177	79	13	0	49	35	3.74	118	.269	.319	62-0-4	.113	-5	117	12	—	0.7
	Year	15	9	.625	32	26	15-1	1	218.2	225	98	16	0	59	53	3.58	120	.266	.314	78-0-7	.128	-5	120	18	—	1.3
1933	Phi N	5	14	.263	28	19	3	2	125	182	109	10	2	33	27	6.62	58	.340	.381	46-0-1	.087	-4	100	-34	—	-5.0
1934	StL N	1	0	1.000	5	1	0	1	15.2	26	12	0	0	7	6	4.60	92	.394	.452	2	.000	-0	163	-2	—	-0.2
	Bos N	8	8	.500	25	20	5-1	0	152.2	164	71	5	0	38	56	3.60	106	.273	.317	52-0-1	.058	-5	78	4	—	-0.1
	Year	9	8	.529	30	21	5-1	1	168.1	190	83	5	0	45	62	3.69	105	.285	.331	54-0-1	.056	-5	82	3	—	-0.3
1935	Bos N	0	5	.000	10	6	0	0	40.1	61	37	4	0	11	10	5.36	71	.341	.379	10-0-1	.000	-1	67	-12	—	-1.3
1936	StL N	2	1	.667	10	4	0	0	26.2	49	26	2	0	9	7	6.75	58	.405	.446	8	.125	-0	172	-10	—	-1.0
Total	12	105	97	.520	294	230	91-8	10	1725.1	1958	989	113	20	529	534	4.20	98	.287	.340	610-3-33	.144	-28	117	-37	—	-8.0
RHINES, BILLY	William Pearl "Bunker"; B3.14.1869 Ridgway PA; D1.30.1922 Ridgway PA; BR/TR/5´11˝/168; d4.22; Col Bucknell																									
1890	Cin N	28	17	.622	46	45	45-6	0	401.1	337	163	6	15	113	182	**1.95**	**183**	.221	**.281**	154	.188	-5	71	**68**	—	**6.0**
1891	Cin N	17	24	.415	48	43	40-1	1	372.2	364	224	4	22	124	138	2.87	117	.246	.314	148	.122	-9	84	12	—	0.4
1892	Cin N	3	7	.300	11	9	6	0	74.2	102	71	0	4	36	10	5.42	60	.313	.388	27-1	.185	1*	84	-19	—	-1.9
1893	Lou N	1	4	.200	5	5	3	0	31	49	37	3	3	19	0	8.71	50	.348	.436	11	.091	-2	86	-15	—	-1.6
1895	Cin N	19	10	.655	38	33	25	0	267.2	322	195	4	21	76	72	4.81	103	.293	.351	113-0-2	.221	-3	116	6	—	0.1
1896	Cin N	8	6	.571	19	17	11-3	0	143	128	52	1	9	48	32	**2.45**	**188**	**.238**	**.311**	52-0-1	.192	-3	71	33	—	2.4
1897	Cin N	21	15	.583	41	32	26-1	0	288.2	311	175	4	17	86	65	4.08	111	.273	.333	107-0-2	.159	-6	71	14	—	0.7
1898	Pit N	12	16	.429	31	29	27-2	0	258	289	143	0	13	61	48	3.52	101	.281	.329	100-0-1	.150	-4	80	0	—	-0.2
1899	Pit N	4	4	.500	9	9	4	0	54	59	42	3	4	13	6	6.00	64	.277	.330	23-0-1	.435	4*	113	-10	—	-0.9
Total	9	113	103	.523	248	222	187-13	1	1891	1961	1102	25	108	576	553	3.48	114	.262	.324	735-1-7	.177	-27	85	89	—	5.0
RHOADS, BOB	Robert Barton "Dusty" (b Barton Emory Rhoads); B10.4.1879 Wooster OH; D2.12.1967 San Bernardino CA; BR/TR/6´1˝/215; d4.19																									
1902	Chi N	4	8	.333	16	12	12-1	1	118	131	66	1	6	42	43	3.20	84	.281	.348	45	.222	0	61	-6	—	-0.6
1903	StL N	5	8	.385	17	13	12-1	0	129	154	88	3	3	47	52	4.60	71	.303	.366	50-1-2	.140	-2*	87	-14	—	-1.4
	Cle A	2	3	.400	5	5	5	0	41	55	34	2	2	3	21	5.27	54	.320	.339	17	.118	-1	90	-10	—	-1.2
1904	Cle A	10	9	.526	22	19	18	0	175.1	175	72	1	5	48	72	2.87	88	.261	.315	92	.196	0*	104	-4	—	-0.5
1905	Cle A	16	9	.640	28	26	24-4	0	235	219	96	4	10	55	61	2.83	93	.249	.300	95-1-3	.221	4*	111	-4	—	0.1
1906	Cle A	22	10	.688	38	34	31-7	0	315	259	95	5	5	92	89	1.80	145	.227	.288	118-0-6	.161	-3	114	**28**	—	2.5
1907	Cle A	15	14	.517	35	31	23-5	1	275	258	105	0	14	84	76	2.29	109	.250	.316	92-0-6	.185	-1	90	7	—	0.5
1908	Cle A	18	12	.600	37	30	20-1	0	270	229	82	2	7	73	62	1.77	135	.239	.298	90-0-5	.222	4	104	16	—	2.5
1909	Cle A	5	9	.357	20	15	9-2	0	133.1	124	63	1	6	50	46	2.90	88	.281	.361	43-0-4	.163	-0	118	-5	—	-0.6
Total	8	97	82	.542	218	185	154-21	2	1691.2	1604	701	19	58	494	522	2.61	100	.256	.316	642-2-26	.188	-0	100	8	—	1.3
RHODEN, RICK	Richard Alan; B5.16.1953 Boynton Beach FL; BR/TR/6´3˝/(190–203); [LAN71 1/20]; d7.5																									
1974	LA N	1	0	1.000	4	0	0	0-0	9	5	2	1	0	4-1	7	2.00	172	.161	.257	2	.500	0	—	2	0	0.2
1975	LA N	3	3	.500	26	11	1	0-1	99.1	94	40	8	1	32-1	40	3.08	111	.253	.310	28-0-1	.071	-2	100	3	0	0.0
1976	LA N★	12	3	.800	27	26	10-3	0-0	181	165	66	17	1	53-2	77	2.98	114	.242	.296	65-1-7	.308	7	120	9	0	1.3
1977	†LA N	16	10	.615	31	31	4-1	0-0	216.1	223	98	20	2	63-1	122	3.74	103	.270	.321	78-3-6	.231	5*	106	3	0	0.7
1978	†LA N	10	8	.556	30	23	6-3	0-0	164.2	160	77	13	3	51-0	79	3.66	96	.255	.311	52-0-6	.135	-0	128	-3	0	-0.4
1979	Pit N	0	1	.000	1	1	0	0-0	5	5	4	0	0	2-0	2	7.20	54	.263	.333	1	1.000	0	23	-2	142	-0.2
1980	Pit N	7	5	.583	20	19	2	0-0	126.2	133	58	9	3	40-4	70	3.84	96	.273	.330	40-1-4	.375	6	102	-1	0	0.6
1981	Pit N	9	4	.692	21	21	4-2	0-0	136.1	147	66	6	2	53-2	76	3.89	94	.283	.348	48-0-3	.188	0	107	-3	0	-0.2
1982	Pit N	11	14	.440	35	35	6-1	0-0	230.1	239	115	14	2	70-8	128	4.14	91	.267	.320	83-3-2	.265	8*	99	-8	0	0.2
1983	Pit N	13	13	.500	36	35	7-2	1-0	244.1	256	95	13	2	68-15	153	3.09	121	.276	.325	86-0-2	.151	-2	91	17	0	1.6
1984	Pit N	14	9	.609	33	33	6-3	0-0	238.1	216	81	13	1	62-0	136	2.72	134	.243	.292	84-0-5	.333	9*	91	24	0	3.5
1985	Pit N	10	15	.400	35	35	2	0-0	213.1	254	119	18	6	69-3	128	4.47	81	.296	.352	74-0-2	.189	2*	88	-20	0	-2.0
1986	Pit N☆	15	12	.556	34	34	12-1	0-0	253.2	211	82	17	2	76-8	159	2.84	137	.228	.286	90-1-7	.278	9*	102	31	0	4.4
1987	NY A	16	10	.615	30	29	4	0-0	181.2	184	84	22	3	61-5	107	3.86	115	.268	.327	0	ø	0	83	12	0	1.4
1988	NY A	12	12	.500	30	30	5-1	0-0	197	206	107	20	8	56-4	94	4.29	92	.269	.322	1	.000	-0*	100	-9	22	-1.1
1989	Hou N	2	6	.250	20	17	0	0-0	96.2	108	49	7	3	41-8	41	4.28	80	.289	.361	29-0-2	.207	1	86	-9	79	-0.6
Total	16	151	125	.547	413	380	69-17	1-1	2593.2	2606	1143	198	39	801-62	1419	3.59	104	.264	.319	761-9-47	.238	44	99	46	243	9.4
RHODES, ARTHUR	Arthur Lee; B10.24.1969 Waco TX; BL/TL/6´2˝/(190–210); [BalA88 2/34]; d8.21																									
1991	Bal A	0	3	.000	8	8	0	0-0	36	47	35	4	0	23-0	23	8.00	50	.320	.405	0	ø	0	89	-17	0	-1.2
1992	Bal A	7	5	.583	15	15	2-1	0-0	94.1	87	39	6	1	38-2	77	3.63	112	.249	.324	0	ø	0	102	5	0	0.6
1993	Bal A	5	6	.455	17	17	0	0-0	85.2	91	62	16	1	49-1	49	6.51	69	.274	.366	0	ø	0	93	-16	78	-1.8
1994	Bal A	3	5	.375	10	10	3-2	0-0	52.2	51	34	8	2	30-1	47	5.81	87	.254	.352	0	ø	0	102	-4	18	-0.5
1995	Bal A	2	5	.286	19	9	0	0-1	75.1	68	53	13	0	48-1	77	6.21	77	.239	.349	0	ø	0	104	-11	38	-0.9
1996	†Bal A	9	1	.900	28	2	0	1-0	53	48	28	6	0	23-3	62	4.08	121	.241	.318	0	ø	0	122	4	71	0.6
1997	†Bal A	10	3	.769	53	0	0	1-1	95.1	75	32	9	4	26-5	102	3.02	146	.218	.278	1	.000	-0*	—	16	0	2.0
1998	Bal A	4	4	.500	45	0	0	4-4	77	65	30	8	1	34-2	83	3.51	130	.233	.313	2	.500	0	—	10	43	0.9
1999	Bal A	3	4	.429	43	0	0	3-2	53	43	37	9	0	45-6	59	5.43	87	.221	.364	0	ø	0	—	-6	0	-0.7
2000	†Sea A	5	8	.385	72	0	0	0-7	69.1	51	34	6	0	29-3	77	4.28	112	.205	.286	0	ø	0	—	5	0	0.8
2001	†Sea A	8	0	1.000	71	0	0	3-4	68	46	14	5	1	12-0	83	1.72	247	.189	.230	1	.000	-0*	—	20	0	2.3
2002	Sea A	10	4	.714	66	0	0	2-5	69.2	45	18	4	0	13-1	81	2.33	185	.187	.227	0	ø	0	—	17	0	3.0
2003	Sea A	3	3	.500	67	0	0	3-3	54	53	25	4	1	18-2	48	4.17	104	.256	.319	0	ø	0	—	2	0	0.2
2004	Oak A	3	3	.500	37	0	0	9-5	38.2	46	23	9	0	21-4	34	5.12	90	.293	.374	0	ø	0	—	-2	51	-0.3
2005	Cle A	3	1	.750	47	0	0	0-3	43.1	33	13	2	1	12-2	43	2.08	200	.206	.263	0	ø	0	—	10	21	0.8
2006	Phi N	0	5	.000	55	0	0	4-3	45.2	47	27	2	2	30-7	48	5.32	88	.260	.371	0	ø	0	—	-2	0	-0.2
Total	16	75	60	.556	653	61	5-3	30-38	1011	896	504	111	14	451-40	993	4.31	105	.238	.319	4	.250	0	99	31	320	5.6
RHODES, CHARLIE	Charles Anderson "Dusty"; B4.7.1885 Caney KS; D10.26.1918 Caney KS; BR/TR/5´7˝/180; d7.26																									
1906	StL N	3	4	.429	9	6	3	0	45	37	21	0	6	20	32	3.40	77	.223	.328	16	.188	-0	97	-3	—	-0.5
1908	Cin N	0	0	ø	1	0	0	0	4	1	2	0	1	2	4	0.00	ø	.077	.250	1	.000	-0	—	0	—	0.0
	StL N	1	2	.333	4	4	3	0	33	23	14	2	1	12	15	3.00	79	.200	.281	12	.250	1	104	-1	—	0.0
	Year	1	2	.333	5	4	3	0	37	24	16	2	2	14	19	2.68	88	.188	.278	13	.231	1	105	-2	—	0.0
1909	StL N	3	5	.375	12	10	4	0	61	55	36	0	2	33	25	3.98	63	.256	.360	19	.211	1	113	-10	—	-0.9
Total	3	7	11	.389	26	20	10	0	143	116	73	2	10	67	76	3.46	73	.228	.329	48	.208	2	107	-14	—	-1.4
RHODES, GORDON	John Gordon "Dusty"; B8.11.1907 Winnemucca NV; D3.22.1960 Long Beach CA; BR/TR/6´0˝/187; d4.29																									
1929	NY A	0	4	.000	10	4	0	0	42.2	57	32	3	2	16	13	4.85	80	.333	.397	10-0-3	.300	1	82	-7	—	-0.5
1930	NY A	0	0	ø	3	0	0	0	2	3	3	0	0	4	1	9.00	48	.500	.700	0	ø	0	—	-1	—	-0.1
1931	NY A	6	3	.667	18	11	4	0	87	82	49	3	0	52	36	3.41	116	.235	.334	28-0-4	.214	1	147	1	—	0.1
1932	NY A	1	2	.333	10	2	1	0	24	25	22	0	0	21	15	7.88	52	.275	.411	7	.286	0	230	-10	—	-0.9
	Bos A	1	8	.111	12	11	4	0	79.1	79	46	5	0	31	22	5.11	88	.261	.329	27	.074	-2	45	-2	—	-0.4
	Year	2	10	.167	22	13	5	0	103.1	104	68	5	0	52	37	5.75	76	.264	.350	34	.118	-2	72	-11	—	-1.3
1933	Bos A	12	15	.444	34	29	14	0	232	242	126	13	1	93	85	4.03	109	.265	.334	86-1-4	.267	4*	114	7	—	1.2
1934	Bos A	12	12	.500	44	31	10	2	219	247	133	10	4	98	79	4.56	105	.285	.360	75-1-1	.133	-3	103	5	—	0.2
1935	Bos A	2	10	.167	34	19	1	2	146.1	195	103	14	1	60	44	5.41	88	.324	.387	48-0-1	.146	-4*	83	-10	—	-1.1
1936	Phi A	9	20	.310	35	28	13-1	1	216.1	266	162	26	2	102	61	5.74	89	.304	.378	75-0-2	.213	-2	68	-17	—	-2.0
Total	8	43	74	.368	200	135	47-1	5	1048.2	1196	676	74	10	477	356	4.85	95	.286	.361	356-2-15	.194	-5	95	-34	—	-3.5
RHODES, BILL	William Clarence; B Pottstown PA; d6.14																									
1893	Lou N	5	12	.294	20	19	17	0	151.2	244	173	10	10	66	22	7.60	58	.352	.416	70	.129	-4	127	-59	—	-4.7

YEAR	TM LG	W	L	PCT	G	GS	CG-SHO	SV-BS	IP	H	R	HR	HB	BB-IB	SO	ERA	AERA	OAV	OOB	AB-HR-SH	AVG	PB	SUP	APR	DL	PW
Ribant, Dennis	Dennis Joseph; B9.20.1941 Detroit MI; BR/TR/5´11˝/(165–175); d8.9																									
1964	NY N	1	5	.167	14	7	1-1	1	57.2	65	35	8	0	9-1	35	5.15	69	.281	.308	20	.100	-0*	105	-9	0	-0.9
1965	NY N	1	3	.250	19	1	0	3	35.1	29	16	5	0	6-0	13	3.82	92	.228	.261	6	.000	-1	25	-1	0	-0.2
1966	NY N	11	9	.550	39	26	10-1	3	188.1	184	78	20	1	40-5	84	3.20	114	.254	.291	61-0-4	.197	0*	99	9	0	1.0
1967	Pit N	9	8	.529	38	22	2	0	172	186	78	16	3	40-5	75	4.08	82	.280	.323	60-0-2	.267	5*	108	-9	0	-0.2
1968	Det A	2	2	.500	14	0	0	1	24.1	20	7	1	1	10-2	7	2.22	136	.217	.301	5	.200	0*	—	2	0	0.4
	Chi A	0	2	.000	17	0	0	1	31.1	42	24	3	2	17-4	20	6.03	50	.318	.399	7	.000	-1	—	-10	0	-0.8
	Year	2	4	.333	31	0	0	2	55.2	62	31	4	3	27-6	27	4.37	69	.277	.359	12	.083	-0	—	-8	0	-0.4
1969	StL N	0	0	ø	1	0	0	0-0	1.1	4	2	1	0	1-0	0	13.50	27	.571	.556	0	ø	0*	—	-1	0	-0.1
	Cin N	0	0	ø	7	0	0	0-1	8.1	6	5	1	0	3-0	7	1.08	348	.188	.257	0	ø	0	—	1	0	0.0
	Year	0	0	ø	8	0	0	0-1	9.2	10	7	2	0	4-0	7	2.79	134	.256	.318	0	ø	0	—	-1	0	-0.1
Total	6	24	29	.453	149	56	13-2	9-1	518.2	536	245	55	7	126-17	241	3.87	90	.267	.310	159-0-6	.195	4	103	-18	0	-0.8
Riccelli, Frank	Frank Joseph; B2.24.1953 Syracuse NY; BL/TL/6´3˝/(190–205); [SFN71 1/18]; d9.11																									
1976	SF N	1	1	.500	4	3	0	0-0	16	16	10	1	0	5-0	11	5.63	65	.258	.309	6	.167	-0	97	-3	0	-0.3
1978	Hou N	0	0	ø	2	0	0	0-0	3	1	0	0	0	0-0	1	0.00	ø	.100	.100	0	ø	0	—	1	0	0.1
1979	Hou N	2	2	.500	11	2	0	0-0	22	22	11	0	0	18-0	20	4.09	86	.262	.392	6	.333	1	139	-1	70	-0.1
Total	3	3	3	.500	17	5	0	0-0	41	39	21	1	0	23-0	32	4.39	81	.250	.344	12	.250	1	114	-3	70	-0.3
Ricci, Chuck	Charles Mark; B11.20.1968 Abington PA; BR/TR/6´2˝/180; [BalA87 4/91]; d9.8																									
1995	Phi N	1	0	1.000	7	0	0	0-0	10	9	2	0	1	3-0	9	1.80	234	.273	.333	0	ø	0	—	3	0	0.2
Rice, Sam	Edgar Charles; B2.20.1890 Morocco IN; D10.13.1974 Rossmoor MD; BL/TR/5´9˝/150; d8.7; Mil 1918; HF1963; ▲																									
1915	Was A	1	0	1.000	4	2	1	0	18	13	8	0	0	9	9	2.00	148	.213	.314	8	.375	1	147	1	—	0.1
1916	Was A	0	1	.000	5	1	0	0	21.1	18	10	0	0	10	3	2.95	95	.237	.326	197-1-1	.299	2*	54	-1	—	0.1
Total	2	1	1	.500	9	3	1	0	39.1	31	18	0	0	19	12	2.52	114	.226	.321	205-1-1	.302	2	121	0	—	0.2
Rice, Pat	Patrick Edward; B11.2.1963 Rapid City SD; BR/TR/6´2˝/200; d5.18; Col Arkansas																									
1991	Sea A	1	1	.500	7	2	0	0-0	21	18	10	3	1	10-1	12	3.00	138	.234	.319	0	ø	0	77	2	0	0.1
Rich, Woody	Woodrow Earl; B3.9.1916 Morganton NC; D4.18.1983 Morganton NC; BL/TR/6´2˝/185; d4.22; Mil 1945																									
1939	Bos A	4	3	.571	21	12	3	1	77	78	46	2	5	35	24	4.91	96	.264	.352	27-0-1	.259	0	138	0	—	0.1
1940	Bos A	1	0	1.000	3	1	1	0	11.2	9	3	2	0	1	8	0.77	583	.214	.233	4	.000	-1	78	4	—	0.2
1941	Bos A	0	0	ø	2	1	0	0	3.2	8	7	1	0	2	4	17.18	24	.421	.476	0	ø	0	166	-5	0	-0.2
1944	Bos N	1	1	.500	7	2	1	0	25	32	17	3	3	12	6	5.76	66	.327	.416	8-0-1	.125	-1	110	-4	0	-0.4
Total	4	6	4	.600	33	16	5	1	117.1	127	73	8	8	50	42	5.06	89	.280	.361	39-0-2	.205	-1	135	-5	0	-0.3
Richard, J.R.	James Rodney; B3.7.1950 Vienna LA; BR/TR/6´8˝/(222–237); [HouN69 1/2]; d9.5; [DL 1981 Hou N 146, 1982 Hou N 150, 1983 Hou N 182]																									
1971	Hou N	2	1	.667	4	4	1	0-0	21	17	9	1	0	16-0	29	3.43	98	.215	.344	7-0-2	.000	-1	92	0	0	-0.1
1972	Hou N	1	0	1.000	4	1	0	0-0	6	10	9	0	2	8-0	8	13.50	25	.385	.556	0	ø	0	184	-7	0	-0.9
1973	Hou N	6	2	.750	16	10	2-1	0-0	72	54	37	2	1	38-0	75	4.00	91	.210	.313	28-0-1	.179	-0	153	-4	0	-0.5
1974	Hou N	2	3	.400	15	9	0	0-0	64.2	58	31	3	1	36-0	42	4.18	84	.243	.343	21-1-1	.143	0	108	-4	0	-0.3
1975	Hou N	12	10	.545	33	31	7-1	0-0	203	178	107	8	4	138-0	176	4.39	77	.238	.358	74-1-5	.203	4	141	-24	0	-2.0
1976	Hou N	20	15	.571	39	39	14-3	0-0	291	221	105	14	4	151-4	214	2.75	117	**.212**	.312	100-2-1	.140	0	104	15	0	1.8
1977	Hou N	18	12	.600	36	36	13-3	0-0	267	212	94	18	0	104-1	214	2.97	122	.218	.292	87-2-11	.230	6	105	23	0	3.3
1978	Hou N	18	11	.621	36	36	16-3	0-0	275.1	192	104	12	2	141-4	**303**	3.11	107	**.196**	.298	101-1-5	.178	1*	124	7	0	1.0
1979	Hou N	18	13	.581	38	38	19-4	0-0	292.1	220	98	13	3	98-5	**313**	**2.71**	130	**.209**	.276	95-2-11	.126	-0	85	**29**	0	2.8
1980	Hou N★	10	4	.714	17	17	4-4	0-0	113.2	65	31	2	0	40-1	119	1.90	173	.166	.242	39-1-4	.154	1	93	18	82	2.3
Total	10	107	71	.601	238	221	76-19	0-0	1606	1227	625	73	17	770-15	1493	3.15	109	.212	.305	552-10-41	.168	11	111	53	560	7.4
Richards, Duane	Duane Lee; B12.16.1936 Spartanburg IN; BR/TR/6´3˝/200; d9.25																									
1960	Cin N	0	0	ø	2	0	0	0	3	5	4	0	0	2-0	2	9.00	42	.385	.438	0	ø	0	—	-2	0	-0.1
Richards, Rusty	Russell Earl; B1.27.1965 Houston TX; BL/TR/6´4˝/(200–210); d9.20; Col Texas																									
1989	Atl N	0	0	ø	2	2	0	0-0	9.1	10	5	2	1	6-0	4	4.82	76	.278	.395	3-0-1	.000	-0	133	-1	0	-0.1
1990	Atl N	0	0	ø	1	0	0	0-0	1	2	3	1	0	1-0	0	27.00	15	.400	.500	0	ø	0	—	-2	0	-0.1
Total	2	0	0	ø	3	2	0	0-0	10.1	12	8	3	1	7-0	4	6.97	53	.293	.408	3-0-1	.000	-0	133	-3	0	-0.2
Richardson, Hardy	Abram Harding "Old True Blue"; B4.21.1855 Clarksboro NJ; D1.14.1931 Utica NY; BR/TR/5´9.5˝/170; d5.1.1879; ▲																									
1885	Buf N	0	0	ø	1	0	0	0	4	5	2	0	—	3	1	2.25	133	.294	.400	426-6	.319	0*	—	0	—	0.0
1886	Det N	3	0	1.000	4	0	0	0	12	11	8	1	—	10	5	4.50	74	.208	.333	538-11	.351	2*	—	-1	—	-0.1
Total	2	3	0	1.000	5	0	0	0	16	16	10	1	—	13	6	3.94	82	.229	.349	964-17	.337	3	—	-1	—	-0.1
Richardson, Danny	Daniel; B1.25.1863 Elmira NY; D9.12.1926 New York NY; BR/TR/5´8˝/165; d5.22.1884; M1; ▲																									
1885	NY N	7	1	.875	9	8	7-1	0	75	58	30	0	—	18	21	2.40	111	.205	.252	198	.263	2*	175	5	—	0.5
1886	NY N	0	2	.000	5	1	1	0	25	33	24	1	—	11	17	5.76	56	.320	.386	237-1	.232	1*	19	-7	—	-0.3
1887	NY N	0	0	ø	1	0	0	0	0	0	0	0	0	1	0	(0)	ø	ø	1.000	450-3	.278	0*	—	0	—	0.0
Total	3	7	3	.700	15	9	8-1	0	100	91	54	1	0	30	38	3.24	86	.236	.291	885-4	.262	3	154	-2	—	0.2
Richardson, Gordie	Gordon Clark; B7.19.1938 Colquitt GA; BR/TL/6´0˝/(185–190); d7.26																									
1964	†StL N	4	2	.667	19	6	1	1	47	40	18	2	1	15-0	28	2.30	166	.231	.296	13	.077	-0	104	6	0	0.7
1965	NY N	2	2	.500	35	0	0	2	52.1	41	27	5	2	16-2	43	3.78	93	.224	.289	7-0-1	.000	-1	—	-2	0	-0.3
1966	NY N	0	2	.000	15	1	0	1	18.2	24	19	7	0	6-1	15	9.16	40	.312	.353	1	.000	-0	48	-10	0	-1.1
Total	3	6	6	.500	69	7	1	4	118	105	64	14	3	37-3	86	4.04	90	.242	.303	21-0-1	.048	-1	99	-6	0	-0.7
Richardson, Jeff	Jeffrey Scott; B8.29.1963 Wichita KS; BR/TR/6´3˝/185; [TorA84 S1/24]; d9.19; Col Connors St. (OK) JC; [DL 1991 Cal A 182]																									
1990	Cal A	0	0	ø	1	0	0	0-0	0.1	1	0	0	0	0-0	0	0.00	ø	.500	.500	0	ø	0	—	0	0	0.0
Richardson, Jack	John William; B10.3.1892 Central City IL; D1.18.1970 Marion IL; BB/TR/6´3˝/197; d9.17																									
1915	Phi A	0	1	.000	3	3	2	0	24	21	13	0	1	14	11	2.63	111	.253	.367	8	.000	-1	116	0	—	-0.2
1916	Phi A	0	0	ø	1	0	0	0	0.2	2	3	0	0	1	1	40.50	7	.667	.750	0	ø	0	—	-2	—	-0.1
Total	2	0	1	.000	4	3	2	0	24.2	23	16	0	1	15	12	3.65	80	.267	.382	8	.000	-1	116	-2	—	-0.3
Richert, Pete	Peter Gerard; B10.29.1939 Floral Park NY; BL/TL/6´0˝/(170–196); d4.12; Mil 1968																									
1962	LA N	5	4	.556	19	12	1	0	81.1	77	35	6	1	45-1	75	3.87	94	.249	.346	25-0-1	.080	-1	137	0	33	-0.1
1963	LA N	5	3	.625	20	12	1	0	78	80	40	7	1	28-3	54	4.50	67	.262	.326	22-0-2	.182	1	138	-11	0	-1.0
1964	LA N	2	3	.400	8	6	1-1	0	34.2	38	17	2	2	18-2	25	4.15	78	.271	.360	11	.091	-0	113	-3	0	-0.4
1965	Was A★	15	12	.556	34	29	6	0	194	146	64	18	2	84-7	161	2.60	134	.210	.296	64-0-3	.156	-0*	78	19	0	2.6
1966	Was A★	14	14	.500	36	34	7	0	245.2	196	106	36	1	69-6	195	3.37	103	.215	.270	86-1-5	.163	2*	94	1	0	0.3
1967	Was A	2	6	.250	11	10	1-1	0	54.1	49	29	5	1	15-0	41	4.64	68	.237	.288	17-0-1	.059	-1*	44	-8	0	-1.2
	Bal A	7	10	.412	26	19	5-1	2	132.1	107	53	11	1	41-1	90	2.99	105	.220	.279	37-0-5	.108	-1*	71	0	0	0.0
	Year	9	16	.360	37	29	6-2	2	186.2	156	82	16	2	56-1	131	3.47	91	.225	.282	54-0-6	.093	-2	62	-6	0	-1.2
1968	Bal A	6	3	.667	36	0	0	6	62.1	51	25	7	3	12-1	47	3.47	84	.225	.273	10-0-1	.200	0	—	-3	0	-0.3
1969	†Bal A	7	4	.636	44	0	0	12-3	57.1	42	17	7	0	14-2	54	2.20	163	.202	.249	8-0-2	.125	-0	—	8	0	1.8
1970	†Bal A	7	2	.778	50	0	0	13-4	54.2	36	14	5	1	24-3	66	1.98	186	.194	.284	4	.000	-0	—	10	0	2.1
1971	†Bal A	3	5	.375	35	0	0	4-1	36.1	26	15	3	1	22-6	35	3.47	98	.205	.325	2-0-1	.000	-0	—	0	0	0.0
1972	LA N	2	3	.400	37	0	0	6-3	52	42	17	3	1	18-5	38	2.25	149	.219	.286	6-0-1	.500	1	—	6	0	0.8
1973	LA N	3	3	.500	39	0	0	7-6	51	44	18	5	1	19-5	31	3.18	110	.234	.306	5-0-1	.200	0	—	3	0	0.5
1974	StL N	0	0	ø	13	0	0	1-0	11.1	10	7	1	0	11-1	4	2.38	152	.244	.389	0	ø	0	—	0	0	0.0
	Phi N	2	1	.667	21	0	0	0-0	20.1	15	6	0	0	4-3	9	2.21	172	.205	.244	0	ø	0	—	3	0	0.4
	Year	2	1	.667	34	0	0	1-0	31.2	25	13	1	0	15-4	13	2.27	164	.219	.303	0	ø	0	—	3	0	0.4
Total	13	80	73	.523	429	122	22-3	51-17	1165.2	959	463	116	16	424-46	925	3.19	106	.223	.294	297-1-23	.145	-1	92	25	33	5.5

RICHIE, LEW Elwood Lewis; B8.23.1883 Ambler PA; D8.15.1936 South Mountain PA; BR/TR/5´8˝/165; d5.8

YEAR	TM LG	W	L	PCT	G	GS	CG-SHO	SV-BS	IP	H	R	HR	HB	BB-IB	SO	ERA	AERA	OAV	OOB	AB-HR-SH	AVG	PB	SUP	APR	DL	PW
1906	Phi N	9	11	.450	33	22	14-3	0	205.2	170	86	3	6	79	65	2.41	109	.230	.309	60-0-1	.050	-3	82	2	—	-0.3
1907	Phi N	6	6	.500	25	12	9-2	0	117	88	37	0	5	38	40	1.77	137	.215	.290	43-0-2	.163	0	64	6	—	0.6
1908	Phi N	7	10	.412	25	15	13-2	1	157.2	125	50	1	6	49	58	1.83	133	.233	.304	52	.212	2	62	8	—	1.0
1909	Phi N	1	1	.500	11	1	0	1	45	40	14	0	2	18	11	2.00	130	.263	.349	16	.250	1	188	3	—	0.2
	Bos N	7	7	.500	22	13	9-2	2	131.2	118	58	2	1	44	42	2.32	121	.247	.312	44-0-1	.114	-2	82	3	—	-0.1
	Year	8	8	.500	33	14	9-2	3	176.2	158	72	2	3	62	53	2.24	123	.251	.321	60-0-1	.150	-1	90	7	—	0.1
1910	Bos N	0	3	.000	4	2	0	0	16.1	20	11	0	0	9	7	2.76	121	.317	.403	4	.000	-1	34	0	—	-0.1
	†Chi N	11	4	.733	30	11	8-3	4	130	117	45	1	3	51	53	2.70	107	.257	.336	40-0-2	.225	3	131	5	—	0.9
	Year	11	7	.611	34	13	8-3	4	146.1	137	56	1	3	60	60	2.71	108	.264	.344	44-0-2	.205	2	115	4	—	0.8
1911	Chi N	15	11	.577	36	29	18-4	1	253	213	88	6	2	103	78	2.31	143	.235	.315	91-0-2	.154	-3	100	28	—	2.4
1912	Chi N	16	8	.667	39	27	15-4	0	238	222	102	5	6	74	69	2.95	113	.261	.324	76-0-6	.132	-3	100	9	—	0.4
1913	Chi N	2	4	.333	16	5	1	0	65	77	53	3	1	30	15	5.82	55	.304	.380	17-0-1	.118	-0	109	-18	—	-1.6
Total	8	74	65	.532	241	137	87-20	9	1359.1	1190	544	21	32	495	438	2.54	115	.246	.320	443-0-15	.147	-7	92	46	—	3.4

RICHMOND, BERYL Beryl Justice; B8.24.1907 Glen Easton WV; D4.24.1980 Cameron WV; BB/TL (BR 1933)/6´1˝/185; d4.21

YEAR	TM LG	W	L	PCT	G	GS	CG-SHO	SV-BS	IP	H	R	HR	HB	BB-IB	SO	ERA	AERA	OAV	OOB	AB-HR-SH	AVG	PB	SUP	APR	DL	PW
1933	Chi N	0	0	ø	4	0	0	0	4.2	10	1	0	0	2	2	1.93	170	.455	.500	1	.000	-0*	—	1	—	0.0
1934	Cin N	1	2	.333	6	2	1	0	19.1	23	11	0	0	10	9	3.72	110	.303	.384	5	.000	-1	85	0	—	0.0
Total	2	1	2	.333	10	2	1	0	24	33	12	0	0	12	11	3.38	116	.337	.409	6	.000	-1	85	1	—	0.0

RICHMOND, LEE J Lee; B5.5.1857 Sheffield OH; D10.1.1929 Toledo OH; TL/5´10˝/155; d9.27; Col Brown; ▲

YEAR	TM LG	W	L	PCT	G	GS	CG-SHO	SV-BS	IP	H	R	HR	HB	BB-IB	SO	ERA	AERA	OAV	OOB	AB-HR-SH	AVG	PB	SUP	APR	DL	PW
1879	Bos N	1	0	1.000	1	1	1	0	9	4	6	0	—	1	11	2.00	124	.114	.139	6	.333	0	224	0	—	0.0
1880	Wor N	32	32	.500	**74**	66	57-5	**3**	590.2	541	278	7	—	74	243	2.15	121	.232	.255	309	.227	-4*	97	25	—	1.8
1881	Wor N	25	26	.490	53	52	50-3	0	462.1	547	302	7	—	68	156	3.39	89	.284	.309	252	.250	-1*	98	-19	—	-1.7
1882	Wor N	14	33	.298	48	46	44	0	411	525	343	11	—	88	123	3.74	83	.294	.327	228-2	.281	7*	90	-23	—	-1.3
1883	Pro N	3	7	.300	12	12	8	0	92	122	67	2	—	27	13	3.33	93	.314	.358	194-1	.284	3*	88	-3	—	0.0
1886	Cin AA	0	2	.000	3	2	1	0	18	24	22	0	2	11	6	8.00	44	.308	.407	29	.276	0*	126	-8	—	-0.6
Total	6	75	100	.429	191	179	161-8	3	1583	1763	1018	27	2	269	552	3.06	95	.269	.298	1018-3	.257	7	96	-28	—	-1.8

RICHMOND, RAY Raymond Sinclair; B6.15.1896 Fillmore IL; D10.21.1969 DeSoto MO; BR/TR/6´0˝/175; d9.25; Col Eastern Illinois

YEAR	TM LG	W	L	PCT	G	GS	CG-SHO	SV-BS	IP	H	R	HR	HB	BB-IB	SO	ERA	AERA	OAV	OOB	AB-HR-SH	AVG	PB	SUP	APR	DL	PW
1920	StL A	2	0	1.000	2	2	1	0	17	18	12	0	0	9	4	6.35	62	.273	.360	6-0-1	.167	-0	233	-3	—	-0.3
1921	StL A	0	1	.000	6	2	0	0	14.1	21	19	1	3	13	6	11.30	40	.362	.500	4	.000	-1	93	-9	—	-0.6
Total	2	2	1	.667	8	4	1	0	31.1	39	31	1	3	22	10	8.62	48	.315	.430	10-0-1	.100	-1	161	-12	—	-0.9

RICHTER, REGGIE Emil Henry; B9.14.1888 Dusseldorf, Germany; D8.2.1934 Winfield IL; BR/TR/6´2˝/180; d5.30

YEAR	TM LG	W	L	PCT	G	GS	CG-SHO	SV-BS	IP	H	R	HR	HB	BB-IB	SO	ERA	AERA	OAV	OOB	AB-HR-SH	AVG	PB	SUP	APR	DL	PW
1911	Chi N	1	3	.250	22	5	0	2	54.2	62	30	1	3	20	34	3.13	106	.307	.378	10	.100	-1	118	-1	—	-0.2

RICKETTS, DICK Richard James; B12.4.1933 Pottstown PA; D3.6.1988 Rochester NY; BL/TR/6´7˝/225; d6.14; b–Dave; Col Duquesne

YEAR	TM LG	W	L	PCT	G	GS	CG-SHO	SV-BS	IP	H	R	HR	HB	BB-IB	SO	ERA	AERA	OAV	OOB	AB-HR-SH	AVG	PB	SUP	APR	DL	PW
1959	StL N	1	6	.143	12	9	0	0	55.2	68	42	7	0	30-4	25	5.82	73	.301	.381	18-0-2	.056	-2	70	-10	0	-1.3

RIDDLE, ELMER Elmer Ray; B7.31.1914 Columbus GA; D5.14.1984 Columbus GA; BR/TR/5´11.5˝/170; d10.1; b–Johnny

YEAR	TM LG	W	L	PCT	G	GS	CG-SHO	SV-BS	IP	H	R	HR	HB	BB-IB	SO	ERA	AERA	OAV	OOB	AB-HR-SH	AVG	PB	SUP	APR	DL	PW
1939	Cin N	0	0	ø	1	0	0	0	2	1	0	0	0	0	0	0.00	ø	.143	.143	0	ø	0	—	1	—	0.0
1940	†Cin N	1	2	.333	15	1	1	2	33.2	30	12	0	0	17	9	1.87	202	.250	.343	7	.143	0	23	5	—	0.5
1941	Cin N	19	4	**.826**	33	22	15-4	1	216.2	180	68	8	5	59	80	**2.24**	**160**	.224	.282	71-0-9	.225	3	115	30	0	3.5
1942	Cin N	7	11	.389	29	19	7-1	0	158.1	157	74	7	4	79	78	3.69	89	.260	.349	58	.259	3	89	-5	0	-0.3
1943	Cin N	**21**	11	.656	36	33	19-5	3	260.1	235	87	6	2	107	69	2.63	126	.245	.322	93-0-6	.194	1	112	19	0	2.4
1944	Cin N	2	2	.500	4	4	2	0	26.2	25	12	0	0	12	6	4.05	86	.250	.330	8-0-1	.125	-0	84	-1	0	-0.1
1945	Cin N	1	4	.200	12	3	0	0	29.2	39	27	4	0	27	5	8.19	46	.333	.458	11	.273	1	90	-13	0	-1.8
1947	Cin N	1	0	1.000	16	3	0	0	30.1	42	30	5	1	31	8	8.31	49	.333	.468	5-0-1	.000	-0	143	-13	0	-0.7
1948	Pit N☆	12	10	.545	28	27	12-3	1	191	184	83	20	3	81	63	3.49	117	.250	.327	64-1-6	.188	1*	86	12	0	1.4
1949	Pit N	1	8	.111	16	12	1	1	74.1	81	45	9	4	45	24	5.33	79	.281	.386	22-0-1	.136	-1	82	-7	0	-1.0
Total	10	65	52	.556	190	124	57-13	8	1023	974	438	59	19	458	342	3.40	107	.252	.335	339-1-24	.204	7	99	28	0	3.9

RIDDLEBERGER, DENNY Dennis Michael; B11.22.1945 Clifton Forge VA; BR/TL/6´3˝/(195–197); d9.15; Col Old Dominion

YEAR	TM LG	W	L	PCT	G	GS	CG-SHO	SV-BS	IP	H	R	HR	HB	BB-IB	SO	ERA	AERA	OAV	OOB	AB-HR-SH	AVG	PB	SUP	APR	DL	PW
1970	Was A	0	0	ø	8	0	0	0-0	9.1	7	2	1	0	2-0	5	0.96	374	.219	.257	0	ø	0	—	2	0	0.1
1971	Was A	3	1	.750	57	0	0	1-0	69.2	67	27	9	1	32-7	56	3.23	105	.260	.341	4	.000	0	—	2	0	0.1
1972	Cle A	1	3	.250	38	0	0	0-1	54	45	23	5	2	22-3	34	2.50	130	.237	.319	4	.000	-0	—	2	0	0.1
Total	3	4	4	.500	103	0	0	1-1	133	119	52	15	3	56-10	95	2.77	121	.248	.327	8	.000	-0	—	6	0	0.3

RIDDLEMOSER, DORSEY Dorsey Lee; B3.25.1875 Frederick MD; D5.11.1954 Frederick MD; BR/TR; d8.22

YEAR	TM LG	W	L	PCT	G	GS	CG-SHO	SV-BS	IP	H	R	HR	HB	BB-IB	SO	ERA	AERA	OAV	OOB	AB-HR-SH	AVG	PB	SUP	APR	DL	PW
1899	Was N	0	0	ø	1	0	0	0	2	7	4	0	0	2	0	18.00	22	.538	.600	1	.000	-0	—	-3	—	-0.1

RIDGWAY, JACK Jacob A.; B7.23.1889 Philadelphia PA; D2.23.1928 Philadelphia PA; BL/TR/5´11˝/174; d5.20

YEAR	TM LG	W	L	PCT	G	GS	CG-SHO	SV-BS	IP	H	R	HR	HB	BB-IB	SO	ERA	AERA	OAV	OOB	AB-HR-SH	AVG	PB	SUP	APR	DL	PW
1914	Bal F	0	1	.000	4	1	0	0	9	20	11	1	1	3	2	11.00	28	.444	.490	1	.000	-0	136	-6	—	-0.6

RIDZIK, STEVE Stephen George; B4.29.1929 Yonkers NY; BR/TR/5´11˝/(170–195); d9.4

YEAR	TM LG	W	L	PCT	G	GS	CG-SHO	SV-BS	IP	H	R	HR	HB	BB-IB	SO	ERA	AERA	OAV	OOB	AB-HR-SH	AVG	PB	SUP	APR	DL	PW
1950	Phi N	0	0	ø	1	0	0	0	3	3	2	1	0	1	2	6.00	67	.300	.364	0	ø	0	—	-1	0	0.0
1952	Phi N	4	2	.667	24	9	2	0	92.2	74	37	11	1	37	43	3.01	121	.218	.297	22-0-2	.136	0	100	6	0	0.3
1953	Phi N	9	6	.600	42	12	1	0	124	119	61	15	5	48	53	3.77	112	.256	.332	36-1-2	.194	2	74	6	0	0.8
1954	Phi N	4	5	.444	35	6	0	0	80.2	72	42	7	0	44	45	4.13	98	.233	.326	22-0-1	.227	1	63	-1	0	0.0
1955	Phi N	0	1	.000	3	1	0	0	11	7	9	1	3	8-0	6	2.45	162	.179	.360	4	.000	-1	45	-1	0	-0.1
	Cin N	0	3	.000	13	2	0	0	30	35	16	4	1	14-1	6	4.50	94	.299	.376	6	.167	-0	53	0	0	-0.1
	Year	0	4	.000	16	3	0	0	41	42	25	5	4	22-1	12	3.95	105	.269	.372	10	.100	-1	50	-1	0	-0.2
1956	NY N	6	2	.750	41	5	1-1	0	92.1	80	42	7	5	65-5	53	3.80	99	.240	.369	28	.250	1*	98	1	0	0.1
1957	NY N	0	2	.000	15	0	0	0	26.2	19	14	3	2	19-1	13	4.73	83	.213	.360	5	.200	-0*	—	-2	0	-0.1
1958	Cle A	0	2	.000	6	0	0	0	8.2	9	7	1	0	5-2	6	2.08	176	.257	.341	1	.000	-0	—	-1	0	-0.1
1963	Was A	5	6	.455	20	10	0	1	89.2	82	53	16	5	35-0	47	4.82	77	.240	.316	29	.172	0	93	-10	0	-1.1
1964	Was A	5	5	.500	49	3	0	2	112	96	46	10	7	31-6	60	2.89	128	.236	.298	27-0-2	.222	1	64	8	0	0.8
1965	Was A	6	4	.600	63	0	0	8	109.2	108	61	18	7	43-4	72	4.02	86	.257	.333	18-0-2	.167	0	—	-9	0	-0.8
1966	Phi N	0	0	ø	2	0	0	0	2.1	5	2	0	0	1-0	0	7.71	47	.455	.462	0	ø	0	—	-1	0	-0.1
Total	12	39	38	.506	314	48	4-1	11	782.2	709	392	94	36	351-19	406	3.79	101	.243	.330	198-1-9	.192	4	83	-5	0	-0.4

RIEDLING, JOHN John Richard; B8.29.1975 Ft.Lauderdale FL; BR/TR/5´11˝/190; [CinN94 22/604]; d8.30

YEAR	TM LG	W	L	PCT	G	GS	CG-SHO	SV-BS	IP	H	R	HR	HB	BB-IB	SO	ERA	AERA	OAV	OOB	AB-HR-SH	AVG	PB	SUP	APR	DL	PW
2000	Cin N	3	1	.750	13	0	0	1-1	15.1	11	7	1	1	8-0	18	2.35	203	.208	.323	2	.000	-0	—	3	0	0.5
2001	Cin N	1	1	.500	29	0	0	1-2	33.2	22	9	1	2	14-0	23	2.41	191	.186	.284	1	.000	-0	—	8	115	0.5
2002	Cin N	2	4	.333	33	0	0	0-0	46.2	39	16	2	3	26-6	30	2.70	158	.234	.345	1	.000	-0	—	8	46	0.9
2003	Cin N	2	3	.400	55	8	0	1-3	101	107	61	7	3	47-0	65	4.90	85	.270	.347	18-0-1	.222	0	127	-9	15	-0.4
2004	Cin N	5	3	.625	70	0	0	0-7	77.2	90	54	10	4	40-5	46	5.10	84	.286	.370	3	.000	-0	—	-10	0	-0.9
2005	Fla N	4	1	.800	29	0	0	0-0	27.2	34	23	3	1	13-2	16	7.16	56	.298	.372	2	.000	-0	—	-10	47	-1.5
Total	6	17	13	.567	229	8	0	3-13	302	303	170	24	14	148-13	198	4.41	97	.260	.348	27-0-1	.148	-1	127	-10	223	-0.9

RIEGER, ELMER Elmer Jay; B2.25.1889 Perris CA; D10.21.1959 Los Angeles CA; BB/TR/6´0˝/175; d4.20

YEAR	TM LG	W	L	PCT	G	GS	CG-SHO	SV-BS	IP	H	R	HR	HB	BB-IB	SO	ERA	AERA	OAV	OOB	AB-HR-SH	AVG	PB	SUP	APR	DL	PW
1910	StL N	0	2	.000	13	1	0	0	21.1	26	16	1	1	7	9	5.48	54	.325	.386	3	.000	0	125	-6	—	-0.5

RIGBY, BRAD Bradley Kenneth; B5.14.1973 Milwaukee WI; BR/TR/6´6˝/(195–215); [OakA94 2/36]; d6.28; Col Georgia Tech; [DL 1998 Oak A 10]

YEAR	TM LG	W	L	PCT	G	GS	CG-SHO	SV-BS	IP	H	R	HR	HB	BB-IB	SO	ERA	AERA	OAV	OOB	AB-HR-SH	AVG	PB	SUP	APR	DL	PW
1997	Oak A	1	7	.125	14	14	0	0-0	77.2	92	44	14	2	22-2	34	4.87	95	.302	.344	3	.000	-0	81	-2	15	-0.2
1999	Oak A	3	4	.429	29	0	0	0-1	62.1	69	31	5	5	26-7	26	4.33	109	.284	.361	0	ø	0	—	4	0	0.3
	KC A	1	2	.333	20	0	0	0-1	21.1	33	20	6	2	5-0	10	7.17	71	.351	.388	0	ø	0	—	-5	0	-0.6
	Year	4	6	.400	49	0	0	0-2	83.2	102	51	11	7	31-7	36	5.06	95	.303	.368	0	ø	0	—	-2	0	-0.3
2000	KC A	0	0	ø	4	0	0	1-0	8.1	19	16	6	1	5-0	3	16.20	32	.422	.490	0	ø	0	—	-10	0	-0.4
	Mon N	0	0	ø	6	0	0	1-0	5.1	8	5	0	1	3-0	2	5.06	93	.348	.444	1	.000	-0	—	-1	0	-0.1
Total	3	5	13	.278	73	14	0	2-2	175	221	116	31	11	61-9	75	5.50	86	.311	.369	4	.000	-0	81	-14	25	-1.0

YEAR	TM LG	W	L	PCT	G	GS	CG-SHO	SV-BS	IP	H	R	HR	HB	BB-IB	SO	ERA	AERA	OAV	OOB	AB-HR-SH	AVG	PB	SUP	APR	DL	PW
RIGDON, PAUL	Paul David; B11.2.1975 Jacksonville FL; BR/TR/6´5˝/(210–242); [CleA96 6/183]; d5.21; Col Florida; [DL 2002 Mil N 183]																									
2000	Cle A	1	1	.500	5	4	0	0-0	17.2	21	15	4	0	9-1	15	7.64	66	.300	.380	0	ø	0	140	-5	15	-0.4
	Mil N	4	4	.500	12	12	0	0-0	69.2	68	37	14	1	26-4	48	4.52	102	.255	.318	16-1-7	.188	1	106	1	0	0.3
2001	Mil N	3	5	.375	15	15	0	0-0	79.1	86	52	13	3	46-6	49	5.79	74	.287	.385	20-0-5	.200	0	96	-12	115	-1.0
Total	2	8	10	.444	32	31	0	0-0	166.2	175	104	31	4	81-11	112	5.45	83	.275	.357	36-1-12	.194	2	106	-16	313	-1.1
RIGGAN, JERROD	Jerrod Ashley; B5.16.1974 Brewster WA; BR/TR/6´3˝/197; [CalA96 8/235]; d8.29; Col San Diego St.																									
2000	NY N	0	0	ø	1	0	0	0-0	2	3	2	0	0	0-0	1	0.00	ø	.300	.300	0	ø	0	—	0	0	0.0
2001	NY N	3	3	.500	35	0	0	0-1	47.2	42	19	5	0	24-7	41	3.40	119	.243	.330	2	.000	-0	—	4	0	0.4
2002	Cle A	2	1	.667	29	0	0	0-0	33	53	28	3	0	18-4	22	7.64	58	.373	.433	0	ø	0	—	-11	0	-0.8
2003	Cle A	0	0	ø	2	0	0	0-0	4	7	4	0	0	1-0	2	9.00	49	.412	.421	0	ø	0	—	-2	0	-0.1
Total	4	5	4	.556	67	0	0	0-1	86.2	105	53	8	0	43-11	66	5.19	81	.307	.377	2	.000	-0	—	-9	0	-0.5
RIGHETTI, DAVE	David Allan; B11.28.1958 San Jose CA; BL/TL/6´3˝/(175–220); [TexA77*1/9]; d9.16; C7; Col San Jose (CA) City																									
1979	NY A	0	1	.000	3	3	0	0-0	17.1	10	7	2	0	10-0	13	3.63	113	.182	.303	0	ø	0	73	1	0	0.1
1981	†NY A	8	4	.667	15	15	2	0-0	105.1	75	25	1	0	38-0	89	2.05	176	.196	.268	0	ø	0	96	19	0	2.2
1982	NY A	11	10	.524	33	27	4	1-0	183	155	88	11	6	108-4	163	3.79	107	.229	.338	0	ø	0	94	4	0	0.3
1983	NY A	14	8	.636	31	31	7-2	0-0	217	194	96	12	2	67-2	169	3.44	115	.237	.296	0	ø	0	119	11	0	1.0
1984	NY A	5	6	.455	64	0	0	31-9	96.1	79	29	5	0	37-7	90	2.34	164	.223	.293	0	ø	0	—	16	15	2.7
1985	NY A	12	7	.632	74	0	0	29-10	107	96	36	5	0	45-3	92	2.78	146	.241	.316	0	ø	0	—	16	0	3.2
1986	NY A★	8	8	.500	74	0	0	**46**-10	106.2	88	31	4	2	35-7	83	2.45	169	.226	.291	0	ø	0	—	21	0	4.2
1987	NY A★	8	6	.571	60	0	0	31-13	95	95	45	9	2	44-4	77	3.51	127	.262	.341	0	ø	0	—	7	0	1.4
1988	NY A	5	4	.556	60	0	0	25-9	87	86	35	5	1	37-2	70	3.52	113	.257	.332	0	ø	0	—	5	0	0.7
1989	NY A	2	6	.250	55	0	0	25-9	69	73	32	3	1	26-6	51	3.00	130	.277	.341	0	ø	0	—	4	0	0.7
1990	NY A	1	1	.500	53	0	0	36-3	53	48	24	8	2	26-2	43	3.57	112	.234	.325	0	ø	0	—	2	0	0.2
1991	SF N	2	7	.222	61	0	0	24-5	71.2	64	29	4	3	28-6	51	3.39	106	.240	.317	3-0-1	.000	-0	—	2	0	0.3
1992	SF N	2	7	.222	54	4	0	3-2	78.1	79	47	4	0	36-5	47	5.06	66	.269	.344	7-0-4	.143	-0	75	-15	0	-1.8
1993	SF N	1	1	.500	51	0	0	1-2	47.1	58	31	11	1	17-0	31	5.70	69	.305	.365	1	1.000	0	—	-9	0	-0.4
1994	Oak A	0	0	ø	7	0	0	0-1	7	13	13	3	1	9-0	4	16.71	27	.419	.548	0	ø	0	—	-10	0	-0.4
	Tor A	0	1	.000	13	0	0	0-1	13.1	9	10	2	0	10-0	10	6.75	72	.188	.322	0	ø	-0	—	-2	0	-0.1
	Year	0	1	.000	20	0	0	0-2	20.1	22	23	5	1	19-0	14	10.18	47	.278	.416	0	ø	0	—	-11	0	-0.5
1995	Chi A	3	2	.600	10	9	0	0-0	49.1	65	24	6	0	18-0	29	4.20	107	.325	.377	0	ø	0	113	2	0	0.2
Total	16	82	79	.509	718	89	13-2	252-74	1403.2	1287	602	95	21	591-48	1112	3.46	114	.244	.321	11-0-5	.182	0	103	74	15	14.5
RIGHTNOWAR, RON	Ronald Gene; B9.5.1964 Toledo OH; BR/TR/6´3˝/190; d5.20; Col Eastern Michigan																									
1995	Mil A	2	1	.667	34	0	0	1-3	36.2	35	23	3	5	18-3	22	5.40	93	.271	.374	0	ø	0	—	-1	0	-0.1
RIGNEY, JOHNNY	John Dungan; B10.28.1914 Oak Park IL; D10.21.1984 Lombard IL; BR/TR/6´2˝/190; d4.21; Mil 1942–45; Col St. Thomas (MN)																									
1937	Chi A	2	5	.286	22	4	0	1	90.2	107	65	10	3	46	38	4.96	93	.290	.373	30-0-2	.167	-0	80	-7	—	-0.5
1938	Chi A	9	9	.500	38	12	7-1	1	167	164	74	16	2	72	84	3.56	138	.256	.333	55-0-3	.145	-3	66	26	—	2.1
1939	Chi A	15	8	.652	35	29	11-2	0	218.2	208	103	10	2	84	119	3.70	128	.247	.316	80-0-5	.200	-1	98	23	—	1.9
1940	Chi A	14	18	.438	39	33	19-2	3	280.2	240	117	22	2	90	141	3.11	142	.230	.292	93-0-12	.215	1*	82	39	—	4.1
1941	Chi A	13	13	.500	30	29	18-3	0	237	224	116	21	2	92	119	3.84	107	.249	.320	84-0-2	.202	2	92	8	0	0.9
1942	Chi A	3	3	.500	7	7	6	0	59	40	23	2	1	16	34	3.20	112	.185	.245	19-0-2	.053	-1	92	3	0	0.2
1946	Chi A	5	5	.500	15	11	3-2	0	82.2	76	37	6	2	35	51	4.03	85	.240	.319	26-0-4	.154	-1	78	-2	0	-0.3
1947	Chi A	2	3	.400	11	7	2	0	50.2	42	15	3	0	15	19	1.95	187	.228	.286	14-0-1	.000	-2	62	9	0	0.7
Total	8	63	64	.496	197	132	66-10	5	1186.1	1101	550	90	14	450	605	3.59	121	.244	.314	401-0-31	.177	-6	85	99	0	9.1
RIJO, JOSE	Jose Antonio (Abreu); B5.13.1965 San Cristobal, D.R.; BR/TR/6´2˝/(160–215); d4.5; [DL 1997 Cin N 181]																									
1984	NY A	2	8	.200	24	5	0	2-1	62.1	74	40	5	1	33-1	47	4.76	80	.298	.382	0	ø	0	61	-8	0	-1.2
1985	Oak A	6	4	.600	12	9	0	0-1	63.2	57	26	6	1	28-2	65	3.53	110	.239	.322	0	ø	0	86	3	0	0.5
1986	Oak A	9	11	.450	39	26	4	1-2	193.2	172	116	24	4	108-7	176	4.65	84	.237	.336	0	ø	0	111	-20	0	-1.9
1987	Oak A	2	7	.222	21	14	1	0-0	82.1	106	67	10	2	41-1	67	5.90	70	.305	.378	0	ø	0	86	-20	0	-1.8
1988	Cin N	13	8	.619	49	19	0	0-2	162	120	47	7	3	63-7	160	2.39	149	.209	.288	37-1-4	.054	-2	94	21	21	2.5
1989	Cin N	7	6	.538	19	19	1-1	0-0	111	101	39	6	2	48-3	86	2.84	127	.249	.328	38-0-1	.211	1	87	9	46	1.2
1990	†Cin N	14	8	.636	29	29	7-1	0-0	197	151	65	10	2	78-1	152	2.70	147	.212	.291	62-0-11	.161	-0	100	26	22	2.9
1991	Cin N	15	6	**.714**	30	30	3-1	0-0	204.1	165	69	8	3	55-4	172	2.51	152	.219	**.272**	67-0-9	.209	1*	121	26	34	2.8
1992	Cin N	15	10	.600	33	33	2	0-0	211	185	67	15	3	44-1	171	2.56	141	.238	.281	72-0-6	.194	1	100	23	15	3.0
1993	Cin N	14	9	.609	36	**36**	2-1	0-0	257.1	218	76	19	2	62-2	**227**	2.48	162	.230	.278	82-1-12	.268	7	88	45	0	4.8
1994	Cin N✱	9	6	.600	26	**26**	2	0-0	172.1	177	73	16	4	52-1	171	3.08	136	.265	.321	49-0-10	.204	2	103	18	0	1.7
1995	Cin N	5	4	.556	14	14	0	0-0	69	76	33	6	0	22-1	62	4.17	100	.285	.336	22-0-2	.136	-0	105	1	90	0.0
2001	Cin N	0	0	ø	13	0	0	0-0	17	19	6	2	0	9-2	12	2.12	217	.271	.354	0	ø	0	—	4	0	0.2
2002	Cin N	5	4	.556	31	9	0	0-0	77	89	48	13	1	20-1	38	5.14	83	.283	.327	16-0-3	.125	-1	116	-7	41	-0.8
Total	14	116	91	.560	376	269	22-4	3-6	1880	1710	772	147	28	663-34	1606	3.24	121	.243	.308	445-2-58	.191	9	99	121	450	13.9
RILEY, GEORGE	George Michael; B10.6.1956 Philadelphia PA; BL/TL/6´4˝/200; [ChiN74 4/79]; d9.15																									
1979	Chi N	0	1	.000	4	1	0	0-0	13	16	9	1	2	6-1	5	5.54	75	.320	.414	2-0-1	.000	-0	21	-2	0	-0.1
1980	Chi N	0	4	.000	22	0	0	0-0	36	41	29	2	2	20-5	18	5.75	69	.293	.389	1-0-1	.000	-0	—	-8	0	-0.7
1984	SF N	1	0	1.000	5	4	0	0-0	29.1	39	14	1	2	7-0	12	3.99	89	.315	.358	10-0-1	.100	-0	94	-1	0	-0.1
1986	Mon N	0	0	ø	10	0	0	0-0	8.2	7	4	0	1	8-3	5	4.15	90	.212	.372	0	ø	0	—	0	0	0.0
Total	4	1	5	.167	41	5	0	0-0	87	103	56	4	7	41-9	40	4.97	77	.297	.380	13-0-3	.077	-1	74	-11	0	-0.9
RILEY, MATT	Matthew Paul; B8.2.1979 Antioch CA; BL/TL/6´1˝/(201–220); [BalA97 3/105]; d9.9; Col Sacramento (CA) City; [DL 2001 Bal A 190]																									
1999	Bal A	0	0	ø	3	3	0	0-0	11	17	9	4	0	13-0	6	7.36	64	.378	.508	0	ø	0	152	-3	0	-0.1
2003	Bal A	1	0	1.000	2	2	0	0-0	10	7	2	1	0	5-0	8	1.80	256	.194	.293	0	ø	0	70	3	0	0.3
2004	Bal A	3	4	.429	14	13	0	0-0	64	60	43	11	1	44-0	60	5.63	83	.244	.361	2	.000	-0	99	-7	15	-0.7
2005	Tex A	1	0	1.000	7	0	0	0-0	12.2	16	14	2	1	10-0	4	9.95	46	.320	.435	0	ø	0	—	-7	0	-0.5
Total	4	5	4	.556	26	18	0	0-0	97.2	100	68	18	2	72-0	78	5.99	78	.265	.384	2	.000	-0	105	-14	205	-1.0
RINCON, ANDY	Andrew John; B3.5.1959 Monterey Park CA; BR/TR/6´3˝/195; [StLN77 5/110]; d9.15																									
1980	StL N	3	1	.750	4	4	1	0-0	31	23	9	1	0	7-1	22	2.61	144	.215	.263	12-0-1	.250	0	83	4	0	0.6
1981	StL N	3	1	.750	5	5	1-1	0-0	35.2	27	8	0	2	5-1	13	1.77	205	.214	.256	13-0-2	.231	1	162	7	31	0.9
1982	StL N	2	3	.400	11	6	1	0-0	40	35	22	1	0	25-0	11	4.72	78	.241	.351	10-0-1	.100	-0	92	-4	0	-0.5
Total	3	8	5	.615	20	15	3-1	0-0	106.2	85	39	2	2	37-2	46	3.12	118	.225	.297	35-0-4	.200	1	113	7	31	1.0
RINCON, JUAN	Juan Manuel; B1.23.1979 Maracaibo, Zulia, Venez.; BR/TR/5´11˝/(187–215); d6.7																									
2001	Min A	0	0	ø	4	0	0	0-0	5.2	7	5	1	0	5-0	4	6.35	74	.318	.444	1	1.000	0	—	-1	0	0.0
2002	Min A	0	2	.000	10	3	0	0-1	28.2	44	23	5	0	9-0	21	6.28	71	.352	.393	0	ø	0	69	-6	0	-0.4
2003	†Min A	5	6	.455	58	0	0	0-1	85.2	74	38	5	4	38-7	63	3.68	122	.231	.315	0	ø	0	—	7	0	0.9
2004	†Min A	11	6	.647	77	0	0	2-4	82	52	27	5	2	32-1	106	2.63	176	.181	.265	1	.000	-0	—	18	0	3.2
2005	Min A	6	6	.500	75	0	0	0-5	77	63	26	2	3	30-3	84	2.45	179	.224	.305	0	ø	0	—	15	0	2.1
2006	†Min A	3	1	.750	75	0	0	1-2	74.1	76	30	2	3	24-3	65	2.91	157	.270	.332	0	ø	0	—	12	0	0.6
Total	6	25	21	.543	299	3	0	3-13	353.1	316	149	20	12	138-14	343	3.26	139	.240	.315	2	.500	0	69	45	0	6.4
RINCON, RICARDO	Ricardo (Espinoza); B4.13.1970 Cuitlahuac, Veracruz, Mexico; BL/TL/5´10˝/(187–190); d4.3																									
1997	Pit N	4	8	.333	62	0	0	4-2	60	51	26	5	2	24-6	71	3.45	124	.230	.309	1-0-1	.000	-0	—	5	15	1.0
1998	Pit N	0	2	.000	60	0	0	14-3	65	50	31	6	0	29-2	64	2.91	147	.208	.292	2	.000	-0	—	7	14	0.4
1999	†Cle A	2	3	.400	59	0	0	0-2	44.2	41	22	6	1	24-5	30	4.43	115	.248	.346	0	ø	0	—	4	33	0.4
2000	Cle A	2	0	1.000	35	0	0	0-0	20	17	7	1	1	13-1	20	2.70	186	.224	.344	0	ø	0	—	5	97	0.4
2001	†Cle A	2	1	.667	67	0	0	2-2	54	44	18	3	0	21-5	50	2.83	162	.223	.294	0	ø	0	—	11	0	0.6
2002	Cle A	1	4	.200	46	0	0	0-3	35.2	36	21	3	1	8-1	30	4.79	93	.263	.304	1	.000	-0	—	-2	0	-0.2
	†Oak A	0	0	ø	25	0	0	1-1	20.1	11	7	1	0	3-0	19	3.10	145	.164	.194	0	ø	0	—	3	0	0.2
	Year	1	4	.200	71	0	0	1-4	56	47	28	4	1	11-1	49	4.18	107	.230	.268	1	.000	-0	—	2	0	0.0
2003	†Oak A	8	4	.667	64	0	0	0-3	55.1	45	21	4	3	32-4	40	3.25	141	.230	.343	0	ø	0	—	9	0	1.6
2004	Oak A	1	1	.500	67	0	0	0-4	44	45	22	3	1	22-4	40	3.68	126	.256	.340	0	ø	0	—	4	0	0.1

YEAR	TM LG	W	L	PCT	G	GS	CG-SHO	SV-BS	IP	H	R	HR	HB	BB-IB	SO	ERA	AERA	OAV	OOB	AB-HR-SH	AVG	PB	SUP	APR	DL	PW
2005	Oak A	1	1	.500	67	0	0	0-2	37.1	34	19	7	1	20-4	27	4.34	101	.246	.344	0	ø	0	—	1	0	0.0
2006	StL N	0	0	ø	5	0	0	0-0	3.1	6	4	1	1	4-0	6	10.80	40	.375	.524	0	ø	0	—	-2	166	-0.1
Total	10	21	24	.467	557	0	0	21-22	439.2	380	198	40	11	200-32	397	3.58	127	.233	.318	4-0-1	.000	-0	—	45	325	4.4
Rineer, Jeff	Jeffrey Alan; B7.3.1955 Lancaster PA; BL/TL/6´4˝/210; [BalA75 S3/43]; d9.30; Col Franklin & Marshall																									
1979	Bal A	0	0	ø	1	0	0	0-0	1	0	0	0	0	0-0	0	0.00	ø	.000	.000	0	ø	0	—	0	0	0.0
Ring, Jimmy	James Joseph; B2.15.1895 Brooklyn NY; D7.6.1965 Queens NY; BR/TR/6´1˝/170; d4.13																									
1917	Cin N	3	7	.300	24	7	3	2	88	90	47	2	1	35	33	4.40	60	.272	.343	26	.077	-2	173	-13	—	-1.6
1918	Cin N	9	5	.643	21	18	13-4	0	142.1	130	57	5	3	48	26	2.85	94	.247	.314	50-0-4	.120	-3	161	-2	—	-0.7
1919	†Cin N	10	9	.526	32	18	12-2	3	183	150	53	2	3	51	61	2.26	123	.232	.291	62-0-2	.097	-5	86	13	—	1.0
1920	Cin N	17	16	.515	42	33	18-1	1	266.2	268	134	4	5	92	73	3.54	86	.264	.329	96-0-2	.198	-0	113	-16	—	-1.9
1921	Phi N	10	19	.345	34	30	21	1	246	258	161	8	5	88	88	4.24	100	.274	.340	83-0-5	.145	-4	86	-1	—	-0.4
1922	Phi N	12	18	.400	40	33	17	1	249.1	292	160	19	3	103	116	4.58	102	.297	.365	88-1-4	.148	-5	90	4	—	0.2
1923	Phi N	18	16	.529	39	36	23	0	304.1	336	151	13	1	115	112	3.87	119	.283	.347	113-1-9	.106	-9*	86	25	—	1.8
1924	Phi N	10	12	.455	32	31	16-1	0	215.1	236	123	9	4	108	72	3.97	112	.286	.371	74-0-5	.230	-1	95	5	—	0.6
1925	Phi N	14	16	.467	38	37	21-1	0	270	325	166	14	1	119	93	4.37	109	.297	.367	101-2-5	.109	-7	86	9	—	0.3
1926	NY N	11	10	.524	39	23	5	2	183.1	207	114	12	1	74	76	4.57	82	.290	.357	56-0-3	.143	-3	105	-18	—	-2.2
1927	StL N	0	4	.000	13	3	1	0	33	39	28	3	1	17	13	6.55	60	.300	.385	8	.375	1	93	-9	—	-0.8
1928	Phi N	4	17	.190	35	25	4	1	176	220	135	14	2	103	70	6.44	66	.320	.410	60-0-1	.183	-2	79	-36	—	-3.7
Total	12	118	149	.442	389	294	154-9	11	2357.1	2551	1329	105	30	953	833	4.13	95	.281	.351	817-4-40	.147	-40	97	-39	—	-7.4
Ring, Royce	Roger Royce; B12.21.1980 LaMesa CA; BL/TL/6´0˝/220; [ChiA02 1/18]; d4.29; Col San Diego St.																									
2005	NY N	0	2	.000	15	0	0	0-0	10.2	10	6	0	0	10-1	8	5.06	82	.250	.400	0	ø	0	—	-1	0	-0.1
2006	NY N	0	0	ø	11	0	0	0-0	12.2	7	3	2	0	3-0	8	2.13	206	.156	.208	0	ø	0	—	3	0	0.2
Total	2	0	2	.000	26	0	0	0-0	23.1	17	9	2	0	13-1	16	3.47	123	.200	.306	0	ø	0	—	2	0	0.1
Rios, Danny	Daniel; B11.11.1972 Madrid, Spain; BR/TR/6´2˝/192; d5.30; Col Miami																									
1997	NY A	0	0	ø	2	0	0	0-0	2.1	9	5	3	1	2-0	1	19.29	23	.563	.632	0	ø	0	—	-4	0	-0.2
1998	KC A	0	1	.000	5	0	0	0-0	7.1	9	9	1	1	6-0	6	6.14	79	.300	.421	0	ø	0	—	-3	0	-0.3
Total	2	0	1	.000	7	0	0	0-0	9.2	18	14	4	2	8-0	7	9.31	51	.391	.491	0	ø	0	—	-7	0	-0.5
Ripley, Allen	Allen Stevens; B10.18.1952 Norwood MA; BR/TR/6´3˝/(180–200); d4.10; f–Walt																									
1978	Bos A	2	5	.286	15	11	1	0-0	73	92	49	10	3	22-2	26	5.55	74	.311	.362	0	ø	0	83	-10	0	-0.9
1979	Bos A	3	1	.750	16	3	0	1-1	64.2	77	42	9	3	25-5	34	5.15	86	.295	.362	0	ø	0	109	-5	0	-0.4
1980	SF N	9	10	.474	23	20	2	0-1	112.2	119	59	10	4	36-6	65	4.15	85	.274	.331	40-0-3	.150	-0	94	-8	0	-1.3
1981	SF N	4	4	.500	19	14	1	0-0	90.2	103	45	5	3	27-2	47	4.07	84	.289	.342	30-0-2	.133	-1	108	-6	0	-0.6
1982	Chi N	5	7	.417	28	19	0	0-0	122.2	130	61	12	2	38-6	57	4.26	89	.285	.338	38-0-2	.132	-2	77	-4	20	-0.5
Total	5	23	27	.460	101	67	4	1-2	463.2	521	256	46	15	148-21	229	4.52	84	.289	.345	108-0-7	.139	-3	89	-33	20	-3.7
Ripley, Walt	Walter Franklin; B11.26.1916 Worcester MA; D10.7.1990 Attleboro MA; BR/TR/6´0˝/168; d8.17; s–Allen																									
1935	Bos A	0	0	ø	2	0	0	0	4	7	4	0	0	3	0	9.00	53	.412	.500	0	ø	0	—	-1	—	-0.1
Rippelmeyer, Ray	Raymond Roy; B7.9.1933 Valmeyer IL; BR/TR/6´3˝/200; d4.14; C9; Col Southern Illinois																									
1962	Was A	1	2	.333	18	1	0	0	39.1	47	24	7	0	17-2	17	5.49	74	.294	.358	6-1-0	.500	2	0	-5	0	0.0
Ripple, Charlie	Charles Dawson; B12.1.1920 Bolton NC; D5.6.1979 Wilmington NC; BL/TL/6´2˝/210; d9.25; Col Wake Forest																									
1944	Phi N	0	0	ø	1	1	0	0	2.1	6	4	0	0	4	2	15.43	23	.500	.625	1	1.000	0	139	-3	0	-0.1
1945	Phi N	0	1	.000	4	0	0	0	7.2	7	6	0	0	10	5	7.04	54	.241	.436	1	.000	-0	—	-2	0	-0.3
1946	Phi N	1	0	1.000	6	0	0	0	3.1	5	4	0	0	6	3	10.80	32	.385	.579	0	ø	0	—	-2	0	-0.5
Total	3	1	1	.500	11	1	0	0	13.1	18	14	0	0	20	10	9.45	39	.333	.514	2	.500	0	139	-7	0	-0.9
Riske, David	David Richard; B10.23.1976 Renton WA; BR/TR/6´2˝/(175–195); [CleA96 56/1560]; d8.14; Col Green River (WA) CC; [DL 2000 Cle A 17]																									
1999	Cle A	1	1	.500	12	0	0	0-1	14	20	15	2	0	6-0	16	8.36	61	.333	.388	0	ø	0	—	-5	16	-0.6
2001	†Cle A	2	0	1.000	26	0	0	1-0	27.1	20	7	3	2	18-3	29	1.98	232	.206	.339	0	ø	0	—	8	0	0.6
2002	Cle A	2	2	.500	51	0	0	1-0	51.1	49	32	8	4	35-4	65	5.26	84	.257	.378	0	ø	0	—	-5	28	-0.3
2003	Cle A	2	2	.500	68	0	0	8-5	74.2	52	21	9	3	20-3	82	2.29	193	.196	.260	0	ø	0	—	18	0	1.2
2004	Cle A	7	3	.700	72	0	0	5-7	77.1	69	32	11	2	41-4	78	3.72	117	.240	.336	0	ø	0	—	7	0	0.8
2005	Cle A	3	4	.429	58	0	0	1-0	72.2	55	28	11	4	15-0	48	3.10	134	.208	.260	0	ø	0	—	9	0	0.7
2006	Bos A	0	1	.000	8	0	0	0-0	9.2	8	4	2	2	3-0	5	3.72	125	.222	.317	0	ø	0	—	1	47	0.1
	Chi A	1	1	.500	33	0	0	0-1	34.1	32	16	4	1	14-1	23	3.93	119	.246	.320	0	ø	0	—	3	0	0.1
	Year	1	2	.333	41	0	0	0-1	44	40	20	6	3	17-1	28	3.89	120	.241	.319	0	ø	0	—	4	0	0.2
Total	7	18	14	.563	328	0	0	16-14	361.1	305	155	50	18	152-15	346	3.59	123	.229	.314	0	ø	0	—	36	108	2.6
Risley, Bill	William Charles; B5.29.1967 Chicago IL; BR/TR/6´2˝/(210–230); [CinN87 14/362]; d7.8; Col Truman (IL) JC; [DL 1999 Tor A 182]																									
1992	Mon N	1	0	1.000	1	1	0	0-0	5	4	1	0	0	1-0	2	1.80	194	.235	.278	2	.000	-0	104	1	0	0.2
1993	Mon N	0	0	ø	2	0	0	0-0	3	2	3	1	1	2-0	2	6.00	70	.200	.385	0	ø	0	—	-1	0	0.0
1994	Sea A	9	6	.600	37	0	0	0-2	52.1	31	20	7	0	19-4	61	3.44	143	.170	.246	0	ø	0	—	10	0	1.8
1995	†Sea A	2	1	.667	45	0	0	1-6	60.1	55	21	7	1	18-1	65	3.13	152	.244	.300	0	ø	0	—	12	15	0.5
1996	Tor A	0	1	.000	25	0	0	0-2	41.2	33	20	7	0	25-0	29	3.89	129	.221	.330	0	ø	0	—	5	67	0.2
1997	Tor A	0	1	.000	3	0	0	0-1	4.1	3	4	2	0	2-0	2	8.31	55	.188	.278	0	ø	0	—	-2	164	-0.3
1998	Tor A	3	4	.429	44	0	0	0-0	54.2	52	37	7	4	34-4	42	5.27	88	.259	.372	0	ø	0	—	-5	0	-0.5
Total	7	15	13	.536	157	1	0	1-11	221.1	180	106	31	6	101-9	203	3.98	120	.225	.313	2	.000	-0	104	20	428	1.9
Ritchie, Jay	Jay Seay; B11.20.1936 Salisbury NC; BR/TR/6´4˝/(175–190); d8.4																									
1964	Bos A	1	1	.500	21	0	0	0	46	43	21	4	0	14-2	35	2.74	141	.249	.303	9	.111	-1	—	3	0	0.1
1965	Bos A	1	2	.333	44	0	0	2	71	83	30	3	1	26-5	55	3.17	118	.302	.361	5	.200	0	—	4	0	0.2
1966	Atl N	0	1	.000	22	0	0	4	35.1	32	17	3	0	12-4	33	4.08	89	.241	.303	4-0-1	.500	1	—	-1	0	0.0
1967	Atl N	4	6	.400	52	0	0	2	82.1	75	32	6	4	29-11	57	3.17	105	.245	.317	10	.300	1	—	2	0	0.4
1968	Cin N	2	3	.400	28	2	0	0	56.2	68	32	7	1	13-2	32	4.61	69	.293	.332	7	.000	-1	55	-8	0	-0.9
Total	5	8	13	.381	167	2	0	8	291.1	301	132	23	6	94-24	212	3.49	101	.269	.327	35-0-1	.200	1	55	0	0	-0.2
Ritchie, Todd	Todd Everett; B11.7.1971 Portsmouth VA; BR/TR/6´3˝/(190–222); [MinA90 1/12]; d4.3																									
1997	Min A	2	3	.400	42	0	0	0-2	74.2	87	41	11	2	28-0	44	4.58	102	.290	.353	2	.000	-0	—	1	0	0.0
1998	Min A	0	0	ø	15	0	0	0-0	24	30	17	1	0	9-0	21	5.63	85	.288	.345	0	ø	0	—	-3	0	-0.2
1999	Pit N	15	9	.625	28	26	2	0-0	172.2	169	79	17	4	54-3	107	3.49	132	.259	.318	53-0-8	.151	-1*	113	20	15	2.3
2000	Pit N	9	8	.529	31	31	1-1	0-0	187	208	111	26	3	51-1	124	4.81	96	.282	.329	60-0-2	.217	2	103	-3	17	0.0
2001	Pit N	11	15	.423	33	33	4-2	0-0	207.1	211	118	23	7	52-7	124	4.47	100	.259	.308	59-0-8	.153	0*	66	-3	0	-0.3
2002	Chi A	5	15	.250	26	23	0	0-0	133.2	176	104	18	5	52-2	77	6.06	74	.318	.378	4	.250	0*	95	-25	37	-3.0
2003	Mil N	1	2	.333	5	5	0	0-0	28.1	36	17	4	4	10-0	15	5.08	85	.319	.388	9-0-2	.222	0	78	-2	157	-0.2
2004	TB A	0	2	.000	4	2	0	0-0	8	12	9	4	1	6-0	4	9.00	52	.343	.452	0	ø	0	50	-4	0	-0.7
Total	8	43	54	.443	184	120	7-3	0-2	835.2	929	496	104	26	262-13	516	4.71	97	.281	.336	187-0-20	.176	2	91	-19	226	-2.1
Ritchie, Wally	Wallace Reid; B7.12.1965 Glendale CA; BL/TL/6´2˝/180; [PhiN85 4/96]; d5.1; Col Brigham Young																									
1987	Phi N	3	2	.600	49	0	0	3-0	62.1	60	27	8	1	29-11	45	3.75	114	.254	.336	4	.250	0	—	4	0	0.4
1988	Phi N	0	0	ø	19	0	0	0-0	26	19	14	1	1	17-2	8	3.12	116	.207	.327	0	ø	0	—	0	0	0.0
1991	Phi N	1	2	.333	39	0	0	0-3	50.1	44	17	4	2	17-5	26	2.50	148	.234	.299	3	.000	-0	—	6	22	0.3
1992	Phi N	2	1	.667	40	0	0	1-1	39	44	17	3	0	17-3	19	3.00	117	.288	.359	1	.000	0	—	1	0	0.1
Total	4	6	5	.545	147	0	0	4-4	177.2	167	75	16	4	80-21	98	3.14	123	.250	.329	8	.125	0	—	11	22	0.8
Ritter, Reggie	Reggie Blake; B1.23.1960 Malvern AR; BL/TR/6´2˝/195; d5.17; Col Henderson St.																									
1986	Cle A	0	0	ø	5	0	0	0-0	10	14	10	1	1	4-0	6	6.30	66	.341	.396	0	ø	0	—	-3	0	-0.1
1987	Cle A	1	1	.500	14	0	0	0-1	26.2	33	21	5	0	16-1	11	6.08	75	.300	.386	0	ø	0	—	-5	34	-0.3
Total	2	1	1	.500	19	0	0	0-1	36.2	47	31	6	1	20-1	17	6.14	73	.311	.389	0	ø	0	—	-8	34	-0.4

Ritter, Hank William Herbert; B10.12.1893 McCoysville PA; D9.3.1964 Akron OH; BR/TR/6´0˝/180; d8.3; Col Albright

YEAR	TM LG	W	L	PCT	G	GS	CG-SHO	SV-BS	IP	H	R	HR	HB	BB-IB	SO	ERA	AERA	OAV	OOB	AB-HR-SH	AVG	PB	SUP	APR	DL	PW
1912	Phi N	0	0	ø	3	0	0	0	6	5	5	0	0	5	1	4.50	81	.192	.323	1	.000	-0	—	-1	—	-0.1
1914	NY N	1	0	1.000	1	0	0	0	8	4	1	0	0	4	4	1.13	236	.160	.276	3	.000	-0	—	2	—	0.1
1915	NY N	2	1	.667	22	1	0	2	58.1	66	38	4	5	15	35	4.63	55	.291	.348	16	.125	-1*	87	-14	—	-0.9
1916	NY N	1	0	1.000	3	0	0	0	5	3	0	0	1	0	3	0.00	ø	.200	.250	0	ø	0*	—	1	—	0.3
Total	4	4	1	.800	29	1	0	2	77.1	78	44	4	6	24	43	3.96	67	.266	.334	20	.100	-1	87	-12	—	-0.6

Rittwage, Jim James Michael; B10.23.1944 Cleveland OH; BR/TR/6´3˝/175; d9.7

YEAR	TM LG	W	L	PCT	G	GS	CG-SHO	SV-BS	IP	H	R	HR	HB	BB-IB	SO	ERA	AERA	OAV	OOB	AB-HR-SH	AVG	PB	SUP	APR	DL	PW
1970	Cle A	1	1	.500	8	3	1	0-0	26	18	12	0	0	21-0	16	4.15	96	.194	.342	8	.375	1	104	0	0	0.1

Ritz, Kevin Kevin D; B6.8.1965 Eatontown NJ; BR/TR/6´4˝/(195–226); [DetA85 S4/85]; d7.15; Col William Penn; [DL 1993 Col N 182, 1999 Col N 182]

YEAR	TM LG	W	L	PCT	G	GS	CG-SHO	SV-BS	IP	H	R	HR	HB	BB-IB	SO	ERA	AERA	OAV	OOB	AB-HR-SH	AVG	PB	SUP	APR	DL	PW
1989	Det A	4	6	.400	12	12	1	0-0	74	75	41	2	1	44-5	56	4.38	88	.265	.360	0	ø	0	91	-5	0	-0.6
1990	Det A	0	4	.000	4	4	0	0-0	7.1	14	12	0	0	14-2	3	11.05	36	.400	.571	0	ø	0	69	-7	0	-1.1
1991	Det A	0	3	.000	11	5	0	0-1	15.1	17	22	1	2	22-1	9	11.74	36	.288	.482	0	ø	0	118	-13	0	-2.0
1992	Det A	2	5	.286	23	11	0	0-0	80.1	88	52	4	3	44-4	57	5.60	71	.278	.368	0	ø	0	102	-13	62	-1.0
1994	Col N	5	6	.455	15	15	0	0-0	73.2	88	49	5	4	35-4	53	5.62	89	.303	.384	20-0-5	.000	-2	87	-4	0	-0.7
1995	†Col N	11	11	.500	31	28	0	2-0	173.1	171	91	16	6	65-3	120	4.21	128	.259	.329	48-0-11	.188	-1	77	17	0	2.1
1996	Col N	17	11	.607	35	35	2	0-0	213	236	135	24	12	105-3	105	5.28	99	.282	.368	65-1-11	.231	2	109	-1	0	0.3
1997	Col N	6	8	.429	18	18	1	0-0	107.1	142	72	16	1	46-3	56	5.87	88	.330	.392	35-0-2	.057	-2	98	-5	80	-0.8
1998	Col N	0	2	.000	2	2	0	0-0	9	17	11	1	1	2-0	3	11.00	47	.395	.435	3	.333	0	62	-4	170	-0.7
Total	9	45	56	.446	151	130	4	2-1	753.1	848	485	69	30	377-25	462	5.35	92	.287	.371	171-1-29	.158	-3	94	-35	676	-4.5

Rivera, Ben Bienvenido Santana; B1.11.1968 San Pedro de Macoris, D.R.; BR/TR/6´6˝/(210–250); d4.9

YEAR	TM LG	W	L	PCT	G	GS	CG-SHO	SV-BS	IP	H	R	HR	HB	BB-IB	SO	ERA	AERA	OAV	OOB	AB-HR-SH	AVG	PB	SUP	APR	DL	PW
1992	Atl N	0	1	.000	8	0	0	0-0	15.1	21	8	1	2	13-2	11	4.70	78	.339	.462	1	.000	-0	—	-1	0	-0.1
	Phi N	7	3	.700	20	14	4-1	0-0	102	78	32	8	2	32-2	66	2.82	124	.211	.277	32-0-2	.094	-1	151	9	21	0.8
	Year	7	4	.636	28	14	4-1	0-0	117.1	99	40	9	4	45-4	77	3.07	115	.230	.307	33-0-2	.091	-1	150	8	0	0.7
1993	†Phi N	13	9	.591	30	28	1-1	0-0	163	175	99	16	6	85-4	123	5.02	79	.273	.361	51-0-13	.098	-2	146	-17	0	-2.3
1994	Phi N	3	4	.429	9	7	0	0-0	38	40	29	7	1	22-0	19	6.87	62	.274	.371	9-0-3	.000	-1	91	-9	78	-1.4
Total	3	23	17	.575	67	49	5-2	0-0	318.1	314	168	32	11	152-8	219	4.52	85	.258	.343	93-0-18	.086	-3	140	-18	99	-3.0

Rivera, Luis Luis (Gutierrez); B6.21.1978 Chihuahua, Chihuahua, Mexico; BR/TR/6´3˝/163; d4.4; [DL 2001 Bal A 190, 2002 Bal A 183]

YEAR	TM LG	W	L	PCT	G	GS	CG-SHO	SV-BS	IP	H	R	HR	HB	BB-IB	SO	ERA	AERA	OAV	OOB	AB-HR-SH	AVG	PB	SUP	APR	DL	PW
2000	Atl N	1	0	1.000	5	0	0	0-0	6.2	4	1	0	0	5-1	5	1.35	334	.190	.346	0	ø	0	—	2	0	0.3
	Bal A	0	0	ø	1	0	0	0-0	0.2	1	0	0	0	1-0	0	0.00	ø	.333	.500	0	ø	0	—	0	0	0.0
Total	1	1	0	1.000	6	0	0	0-0	7.1	5	1	0	0	6-1	5	1.23	369	.208	.367	0	ø	0	—	2	373	0.3

Rivera, Mariano Mariano; B11.29.1969 Panama City, Pan; BR/TR/6´2˝/(168–185); d5.23

YEAR	TM LG	W	L	PCT	G	GS	CG-SHO	SV-BS	IP	H	R	HR	HB	BB-IB	SO	ERA	AERA	OAV	OOB	AB-HR-SH	AVG	PB	SUP	APR	DL	PW
1995	†NY A	5	3	.625	19	10	0	0-1	67	71	43	11	2	30-0	51	5.51	84	.266	.342	0	ø	0	105	-6	0	-0.6
1996	†NY A	8	3	.727	61	0	0	5-3	107.2	73	25	1	2	34-3	130	2.09	237	.189	.258	0	ø	0	—	**35**	0	3.3
1997	†NY A★	6	4	.600	66	0	0	43-9	71.2	65	17	5	0	20-6	68	1.88	236	.237	.285	0	ø	0	—	21	0	4.1
1998	†NY A	3	0	1.000	54	0	0	36-5	61.1	48	13	3	1	17-1	36	1.91	230	.215	.270	0	ø	0	—	18	18	2.6
1999	†NY A✳	4	3	.571	66	0	0	**45**-4	69	43	15	2	3	18-3	52	1.83	259	.176	.239	0	ø	0	—	23	0	4.5
2000	†NY A★	7	4	.636	66	0	0	36-5	75.2	58	26	4	0	25-3	58	2.85	167	.208	.271	0	ø	0	—	17	0	3.2
2001	†NY A✳	4	6	.400	71	0	0	**50**-7	80.2	61	24	5	1	12-2	83	2.34	190	.209	.242	0	ø	0	—	19	0	3.8
2002	†NY A★	1	4	.200	45	0	0	28-4	46	35	16	3	2	11-2	41	2.74	158	.203	.259	0	ø	0	—	8	67	1.6
2003	†NY A	5	2	.714	64	0	0	40-6	70.2	61	15	3	4	10-1	63	1.66	265	.235	.272	0	ø	0	—	22	30	4.3
2004	†NY A★	4	2	.667	74	0	0	**53**-4	78.2	65	17	3	5	20-3	66	1.94	236	.225	.287	0	ø	0	—	24	0	4.9
2005	†NY A★	7	4	.636	71	0	0	43-4	78.1	50	18	2	4	18-0	80	1.38	312	.177	.235	0	ø	0	—	**24**	0	**4.9**
2006	†NY A★	5	5	.500	63	0	0	34-3	75	61	16	3	5	11-4	55	1.80	252	.223	.264	1	.000	-0	—	23	0	**4.6**
Total	12	59	40	.596	720	10	0	413-55	881.2	691	245	45	29	226-28	783	2.29	200	.213	.269	1	.000	-0	105	228	115	41.2

Rivera, Saul Rabell Saul; B12.7.1977 San Juan, PR; BB/TR/5´11˝/150; [MinA98 9/259]; d5.25; Col Mobile

YEAR	TM LG	W	L	PCT	G	GS	CG-SHO	SV-BS	IP	H	R	HR	HB	BB-IB	SO	ERA	AERA	OAV	OOB	AB-HR-SH	AVG	PB	SUP	APR	DL	PW
2006	Was N	3	0	1.000	54	0	0	1-2	60.1	59	28	4	4	32-6	41	3.43	127	.250	.348	4	.000	-0	—	5	0	0.2

Rivera, Roberto Roberto (Diaz); B1.1.1969 Bayamon, PR; BL/TL/6´0˝/(175–200); d9.3

YEAR	TM LG	W	L	PCT	G	GS	CG-SHO	SV-BS	IP	H	R	HR	HB	BB-IB	SO	ERA	AERA	OAV	OOB	AB-HR-SH	AVG	PB	SUP	APR	DL	PW
1995	Chi N	0	0	ø	7	0	0	0-0	5	8	3	1	0	2-0	2	5.40	77	.381	.435	0	ø	0	—	-1	0	0.0
1999	SD N	1	2	.333	12	0	0	0-0	7	6	4	1	0	3-0	3	3.86	111	.240	.310	0	ø	0	—	0	0	0.0
Total	2	1	2	.333	19	0	0	0-0	12	14	7	2	0	5-0	5	4.50	94	.304	.365	0	ø	0	—	-1	0	0.0

Riviere, Tink Arthur Bernard; B8.2.1899 Liberty TX; D9.27.1965 Liberty TX; BR/TR/5´10˝/167; d4.15

YEAR	TM LG	W	L	PCT	G	GS	CG-SHO	SV-BS	IP	H	R	HR	HB	BB-IB	SO	ERA	AERA	OAV	OOB	AB-HR-SH	AVG	PB	SUP	APR	DL	PW
1921	StL N	1	0	1.000	18	2	0	0	38.1	45	30	2	2	20	15	6.10	60	.280	.366	8	.375	2	79	-10	—	-0.4
1925	Chi A	0	0	ø	3	0	0	0	4.2	6	7	0	1	7	1	13.50	31	.429	.636	1	.000	-0	—	-5	—	-0.2
Total	2	1	0	1.000	21	2	0	0	43	51	37	2	3	27	16	6.91	54	.291	.395	9	.333	2	79	-15	—	-0.6

Rixey, Eppa Eppa "Jeptha"; B5.3.1891 Culpeper VA; D2.28.1963 Cincinnati OH; BR/TL/6´5˝/210; d6.21; Mil 1918–19; HF1963; Col Virginia

YEAR	TM LG	W	L	PCT	G	GS	CG-SHO	SV-BS	IP	H	R	HR	HB	BB-IB	SO	ERA	AERA	OAV	OOB	AB-HR-SH	AVG	PB	SUP	APR	DL	PW
1912	Phi N	10	10	.500	23	20	10-3	0	162	147	57	2	2	54	59	2.50	145	.256	.322	53-0-2	.170	-2	64	21	—	2.2
1913	Phi N	9	5	.643	35	19	9-1	2	155.2	148	67	4	6	56	75	3.12	107	.258	.331	47-0-3	.191	-0	106	4	—	0.3
1914	Phi N	2	11	.154	24	15	2	0	103	124	73	0	3	45	41	4.37	67	.313	.387	26	.038	-1	105	-15	—	-1.9
1915	†Phi N	11	12	.478	29	22	10-2	1	176.2	163	67	2	2	64	88	2.39	115	.250	.319	55-0-5	.164	-0	95	6	—	0.8
1916	Phi N	22	10	.688	38	33	20-3	0	287	239	91	2	7	74	134	1.85	143	.229	.284	97-0-4	.155	-2	124	21	—	2.5
1917	Phi N	16	21	.432	39	36	23-4	1	281.1	249	102	1	5	67	121	2.27	124	.241	.290	94-0-6	.191	-1	75	13	—	1.8
1919	Phi N	6	12	.333	23	18	11-1	0	154	160	88	4	3	50	63	3.97	81	.278	.339	47-0-3	.149	-2	84	-14	—	-1.6
1920	Phi N	11	22	.333	41	34	25	2	284.1	288	137	5	4	69	109	3.48	98	.274	.321	101-1-3	.248	1*	68	0	—	0.3
1921	Cin N	19	18	.514	40	37	21-2	1	301	324	128	1	5	66	76	2.78	129	.282	.324	101-0-9	.129	-5	91	23	—	2.2
1922	Cin N	**25**	13	.658	40	**38**	26-2	0	**313.1**	337	146	13	4	45	80	3.53	113	.275	.303	109-0-11	.193	-1	102	19	—	1.9
1923	Cin N	20	15	.571	42	37	23-3	1	309	334	124	3	4	65	97	2.80	138	.280	.320	107-0-9	.159	-5	97	37	—	3.3
1924	Cin N	15	14	.517	35	29	15-**4**	1	238.1	219	86	3	2	47	57	2.76	137	.246	.285	84-1-6	.214	1	97	29	—	3.4
1925	Cin N	21	11	.656	39	36	22-2	1	287.1	302	109	8	7	47	69	2.88	143	.273	.307	103-0-5	.214	-1	102	43	—	4.1
1926	Cin N	14	8	.636	37	29	14-3	0	233	231	104	12	2	58	61	3.40	109	.265	.313	84-0-6	.226	0	128	9	—	0.7
1927	Cin N	12	10	.545	34	29	11-1	1	219.2	240	106	3	3	43	42	3.48	109	.287	.325	81-0-3	.247	4	115	6	—	0.9
1928	Cin N	19	18	.514	43	**37**	17-3	2	291.1	317	127	4	3	67	58	3.43	115	.288	.330	104-1-3	.173	-1	82	17	—	1.8
1929	Cin N	10	13	.435	35	24	11	1	201	235	102	6	3	60	37	4.16	110	.296	.348	65-0-5	.231	0	76	11	—	1.0
1930	Cin N	9	13	.409	32	21	5	0	164	207	103	11	7	47	37	5.10	95	.317	.370	55-0-3	.200	-1	88	-4	—	-0.5
1931	Cin N	4	7	.364	22	17	4	0	126.2	143	71	4	0	30	22	3.91	96	.291	.332	40-0-1	.150	-1	90	-5	—	-0.3
1932	Cin N	5	5	.500	25	11	6-2	0	111.2	108	50	3	4	16	14	2.66	145	.254	.288	34	.265	1	71	11	—	1.1
1933	Cin N	6	3	.667	16	12	5-1	0	94.1	118	48	1	0	12	10	3.15	108	.298	.319	35	.257	2	116	0	—	0.2
Total	21	266	251	.515	692	554	290-37	14	4494.2	4633	1986	92	76	1082	1350	3.15	116	.272	.318	1522-3-87	.191	-15	94	232	—	24.2

Rizzo, Todd Todd Michael; B5.24.1971 Media PA; BR/TL/6´3˝/220; d4.2; Col Delaware Co. (PA) CC

YEAR	TM LG	W	L	PCT	G	GS	CG-SHO	SV-BS	IP	H	R	HR	HB	BB-IB	SO	ERA	AERA	OAV	OOB	AB-HR-SH	AVG	PB	SUP	APR	DL	PW
1998	Chi A	0	0	ø	9	0	0	0-0	6.2	12	12	0	0	6-0	3	13.50	34	.387	.474	0	ø	0	—	-7	0	-0.3
1999	Chi A	0	2	.000	3	0	0	0-0	1.1	4	2	0	0	3-1	2	6.75	73	.500	.636	0	ø	0	—	-1	0	-0.1
Total	2	0	2	.000	12	0	0	0-0	8	16	14	0	0	9-1	5	12.38	37	.410	.510	0	ø	0	—	-8	0	-0.4

Rleal, Sendy Sendy; B6.21.1980 San Pedro de Macoris, D.R.; BR/TR/6´1˝/180; d4.5

YEAR	TM LG	W	L	PCT	G	GS	CG-SHO	SV-BS	IP	H	R	HR	HB	BB-IB	SO	ERA	AERA	OAV	OOB	AB-HR-SH	AVG	PB	SUP	APR	DL	PW
2006	Bal A	1	1	.500	42	0	0	0-1	46.2	48	25	10	0	23-1	19	4.44	102	.274	.353	0	ø	0	—	0	0	0.0

Roa, Joe Joseph Rodger; B10.11.1971 Southfield MI; BR/TR/6´1˝/(194–200); [AtlN89 18/454]; d9.20

YEAR	TM LG	W	L	PCT	G	GS	CG-SHO	SV-BS	IP	H	R	HR	HB	BB-IB	SO	ERA	AERA	OAV	OOB	AB-HR-SH	AVG	PB	SUP	APR	DL	PW
1995	Cle A	0	1	.000	1	1	0	0-0	6	9	4	1	0	2-0	0	6.00	79	.360	.407	0	ø	0	59	-1	0	-0.1
1996	Cle A	0	0	ø	1	0	0	0-0	1.2	4	2	0	0	3-0	0	10.80	45	.500	.636	0	ø	0	—	-1	0	0.0
1997	SF N	2	5	.286	28	3	0	0-0	65.2	86	40	8	2	20-5	34	5.21	79	.333	.380	15	.133	-0	127	-7	0	-0.6
2002	Phi N	4	4	.500	14	11	0	0-0	71.1	78	33	11	1	13-2	35	4.04	95	.279	.310	25-0-3	.240	2	108	-1	0	0.0
2003	Phi N	0	2	.000	6	3	0	0-0	19.1	28	13	3	1	4-0	16	6.05	66	.341	.379	4	.250	0	55	-4	0	-0.3
	Col N	0	0	ø	4	0	0	0-0	6.2	7	3	2	0	0-0	4	4.05	121	.269	.269	0	ø	0	—	1	0	0.0
	SD N	1	1	.500	18	1	0	0-0	25.1	34	20	5	1	6-0	18	6.75	59	.315	.353	3	.333	0	94	-8	0	-0.5
	Year	1	3	.250	28	4	0	0-0	51.1	69	36	10	2	10-0	38	6.14	67	.319	.354	7	.286	0	63	-11	0	-0.8
2004	Min A	2	3	.400	48	0	0	0-1	70	84	38	9	5	24-0	47	4.50	103	.297	.360	0	ø	0	—	1	0	0.1
Total	6	9	16	.360	120	19	0	0-1	266	330	153	39	10	72-7	154	4.94	85	.308	.355	47-0-3	.213	2	93	-20	0	-1.4

YEAR	TM LG	W	L	PCT	G	GS	CG-SHO	SV-BS	IP	H	R	HR	HB	BB-IB	SO	ERA	AERA	OAV	OOB	AB-HR-SH	AVG	PB	SUP	APR	DL	PW
Roach, Jason	Jason Glenn; B4.20.1976 Kinston NC; BR/TR/6´4˝/190; [NYN97 20/600]; d6.14; Col North Carolina–Wilmington																									
2003	NY N	0	2	.000	2	2	0	0-0	9	14	12	3	1	4-0	2	12.00	35	.350	.422	2	1.000	1	67	-8	0	-1.0
Roach, John	John F.; B11.19.1867 North Bend PA; D4.2.1934 Peoria IL; BR/TL/5´9˝/175; d5.14; b–Mike																									
1887	NY N	0	1	.000	1	1	1	0	8	18	17	0	1	4	3	11.25	33	.419	.479	4	.250	-0	34	-7	—	-0.6
Roach, Skel	Rudolph Charles (b Rudolph Charles Weichbrodt); B10.20.1871 Danzig, Germany; D3.9.1958 Oak Park IL; BR/TR/6´2˝/?; d8.9																									
1899	Chi N	1	0	1.000	1	1	1	0	9	13	3	0	0	1	0	3.00	125	.333	.350	4	.000	-1	115	1	—	0.0
Robbins, Bruce	Bruce Duane; B9.10.1959 Portland IN; BL/TL/6´1˝/190; [DetA77 14/343]; d7.28																									
1979	Det A	3	3	.500	10	8	0	0-0	46	45	21	3	0	21-0	22	3.91	111	.265	.342	0	ø	0	120	3	0	0.3
1980	Det A	4	2	.667	15	6	0	0-0	51.2	60	40	12	0	28-0	23	6.62	62	.287	.368	0	ø	0	130	-13	0	-1.3
Total	2	7	5	.583	25	14	0	0-0	97.2	105	61	15	0	49-0	45	5.34	79	.277	.356	0	ø	0	125	-10	0	-1.0
Robbins, Jake	Philip Jacob; B5.23.1976 Charlotte NC; BR/TR/6´5˝/190; [NYA94 11/311]; d9.20																									
2004	Cle A	0	0	ø	2	0	0	0-0	1.2	3	1	1	0	0-0	0	5.40	80	.375	.375	0	ø	0	—	0	0	0.0
Roberge, Bert	Bertrand Roland; B10.3.1954 Lewiston ME; BR/TR/6´4˝/190; [HouN76 17/385]; d5.28; Col Maine																									
1979	Hou N	3	0	1.000	26	0	0	4-1	32	20	6	0	0	17-0	13	1.69	208	.196	.308	2	.000	-0	—	7	21	0.8
1980	Hou N	2	0	1.000	14	0	0	0-0	24.1	24	16	2	2	10-1	9	5.92	55	.261	.343	3-0-1	.000	-0	—	-7	0	-0.5
1982	Hou N	1	2	.333	22	0	0	3-2	25.2	29	12	0	0	6-3	18	4.21	79	.284	.324	1	.000	-0	—	-2	0	-0.3
1984	Chi A	3	3	.500	21	0	0	0-2	40.2	36	18	2	3	15-1	25	3.76	111	.240	.320	0	ø	0	—	2	32	0.3
1985	Mon N	3	3	.500	42	0	0	2-5	68	58	28	5	2	22-5	34	3.44	100	.232	.299	1	.000	-0	—	0	39	0.0
1986	Mon N	0	4	.000	21	0	0	1-0	28.2	33	20	2	1	10-3	20	6.28	60	.295	.352	2	.000	-0	—	-7	0	-1.0
Total	6	12	12	.500	146	0	0	10-10	219.1	200	100	11	8	80-13	119	3.98	90	.248	.320	9-0-1	.000	-1	—	-7	92	-0.7
Roberson, Sid	Sidney Dean; B9.7.1971 Jacksonville FL; BL/TL/5´9˝/170; [MilA92 29/808]; d5.20; Col North Florida																									
1995	Mil A	6	4	.600	26	13	0	0-0	84.1	102	55	16	8	37-3	40	5.76	87	.307	.388	0	ø	0	99	-5	0	-0.6
Roberts, Dale	Dale "Mountain Man"; B4.12.1942 Owenton KY; BR/TL/6´4˝/180; d9.9																									
1967	NY A	0	0	ø	2	0	0	0	2	3	2	0	2	2-1	0	9.00	35	.429	.636	0	ø	0	—	-1	0	-0.1
Roberts, Dave	David Arthur; B9.11.1944 Gallipolis OH; BL/TL/6´2˝/(185–197); d7.6; [DL 1983 Phi N 39]																									
1969	SD N	0	3	.000	22	5	0	1-0	48.2	65	30	5	3	19-0	19	4.81	74	.322	.387	15	.267	1*	69	-7	0	-0.3
1970	SD N	8	14	.364	43	21	3-2	1-2	181.2	182	80	16	1	43-11	102	3.81	105	.261	.304	59-2-4	.153	1	73	7	0	0.9
1971	SD N	14	17	.452	37	34	14-2	0-0	269.2	238	79	9	5	61-9	135	2.10	158	.240	.285	86-0-8	.221	2*	62	36	0	4.7
1972	Hou N	12	7	.632	35	28	7-3	2-0	192	227	100	18	2	57-3	111	4.50	75	.296	.345	67-2-6	.239	6	144	-22	0	-1.6
1973	Hou N	17	11	.607	39	36	12-6	0-1	249.1	264	92	15	2	62-8	119	2.85	128	.271	.314	85-0-12	.129	-3*	102	20	0	1.8
1974	Hou N	10	12	.455	34	30	8-2	1-0	204	216	83	6	3	65-2	72	3.40	103	.276	.332	73-1-2	.219	5*	100	4	0	1.1
1975	Hou N	8	14	.364	32	27	7	1-1	198.1	182	98	16	2	73-4	101	4.27	80	.244	.310	63-0-10	.143	-0	90	-19	0	-1.8
1976	Det A	16	17	.485	36	36	18-4	0-0	252	254	122	16	4	63-4	79	4.00	93	.264	.309	0	ø	0	82	-4	0	-0.4
1977	Det A	4	10	.286	22	22	5	0-0	129.1	143	88	20	2	41-2	46	5.15	84	.274	.328	0	ø	0	91	-13	0	-1.3
	Chi N	1	1	.500	17	6	1	1-0	53	55	22	1	1	12-8	23	3.23	137	.275	.315	17	.059	-2	74	6	0	0.2
1978	Chi N	6	8	.429	35	20	2-1	1-0	142.1	159	87	17	3	56-15	54	5.25	77	.288	.353	52-2-3	.327	6*	109	-15	14	-0.7
1979	SF N	0	2	.000	26	1	0	3-5	42	42	15	3	1	18-3	23	2.57	136	.262	.339	5	.000	-1	177	4	0	0.2
	†Pit N	5	2	.714	21	3	0	1-0	38.2	47	18	1	1	12-4	15	3.26	120	.318	.366	5	.000	-1	136	2	0	0.3
	Year	5	4	.556	47	4	0	4-5	80.2	89	33	4	2	30-7	38	2.90	127	.289	.352	10	.000	-1	150	5	0	0.5
1980	Pit N	0	1	.000	2	0	0	0-0	2.1	2	1	0	0	1-0	1	3.86	96	.250	.333	0	ø	0	—	0	0	0.0
	Sea A	2	3	.400	37	4	0	3-1	80.1	86	46	7	1	27-7	47	4.37	95	.270	.324	0	ø	0	70	-3	0	-0.2
1981	NY N	0	3	.000	7	4	0	0-0	15.1	26	18	5	0	5-0	10	9.39	38	.366	.408	4	.250	0	50	-9	0	-1.6
Total	13	103	125	.452	445	277	77-20	15-10	2099	2188	979	155	31	615-80	957	3.78	97	.270	.321	531-7-45	.194	15	93	-13	53	1.3
Roberts, Grant	Grant William; B9.13.1977 ElCajon CA; BR/TR/6´3˝/205; [NYN95 11/301]; d7.27																									
2000	NY N	0	0	ø	4	1	0	0-0	7	11	10	0	0	4-1	6	11.57	38	.344	.395	0-0-1	ø	0	189	-6	0	-0.3
2001	NY N	1	0	1.000	16	0	0	0-1	26	24	11	2	0	8-1	29	3.81	106	.240	.294	3	.000	-0	—	1	0	0.0
2002	NY N	3	1	.750	34	0	0	0-0	45	43	12	3	1	16-7	31	2.20	180	.253	.317	1	1.000	0	—	9	80	0.8
2003	NY N	0	3	.000	18	0	0	1-0	19	19	9	0	1	3-1	10	3.79	111	.257	.295	0	ø	0	—	1	130	0.1
2004	NY N	0	0	ø	4	0	0	0-0	4.2	9	9	2	0	6-1	1	17.36	25	.429	.536	0	ø	0	—	-6	132	-0.3
Total	5	4	4	.500	76	1	0	1-1	101.2	106	51	7	2	37-11	77	4.25	96	.267	.328	4-0-1	.250	0	189	-1	342	0.3
Roberts, Jim	James Newson "Big Jim"; B10.13.1895 Artesia MS; D6.24.1984 Columbus MS; BR/TR/6´3˝/205; d7.27; Col Mississippi St.																									
1924	Bro N	0	3	.000	11	5	0	0	25.1	41	28	1	2	8	10	7.46	50	.360	.411	7	.143	-0	72	-12	—	-1.2
1925	Bro N	0	0	ø	1	0	0	0	1	1	1	0	0	0	0	0.00	ø	.500	.500	0	ø	0	—	0	—	0.0
Total	2	0	3	.000	12	5	0	0	26.1	42	29	1	2	8	10	7.18	52	.362	.413	7	.143	-0	72	-12	—	-1.2
Roberts, Ray	Raymond; B8.25.1895 Cruger MS; D1.30.1962 Cruger MS; BL/TR/5´11˝/180; d9.12; Col Mississippi St.																									
1919	Phi A	0	2	.000	3	2	0	0	14	21	14	0	0	3	2	7.71	44	.368	.400	4	.250	-0	114	-6	—	-0.7
Roberts, Robin	Robin Evan; B9.30.1926 Springfield IL; BB/TR (BL 1948–52)/6´0˝/(190–195); d6.18; HF1976; Col Michigan St.																									
1948	Phi N	7	9	.438	20	20	9	0	146.2	148	63	10	4	61	84	3.19	124	.278	.356	44-1-3	.250	4*	70	12	0	1.6
1949	Phi N	15	15	.500	43	31	11-3	4	226.2	229	101	15	5	75	95	3.69	107	.273	.337	67-0-5	.075	-3	99	7	0	0.4
1950	†Phi N★	20	11	.645	40	**39**	21-**5**	1	304.1	282	112	29	2	77	146	3.02	134	.248	.297	102-0-7	.118	-4	99	**38**	0	3.2
1951	Phi N★	21	15	.583	44	**39**	22-6	2	**315**	284	115	20	3	64	127	3.03	127	.237	**.278**	87-0-14	.172	5	99	30	0	**3.8**
1952	Phi N☆	**28**	7	.800	39	**37**	**30**-3	2	**330**	292	104	22	5	45	148	2.59	141	.234	.263	112-0-13	.125	2	122	**43**	0	**4.6**
1953	Phi N★	**23**	16	.590	44	**41**	**33**-5	2	**346.2**	324	119	30	2	61	**198**	2.75	153	.242	.276	123-1-9	.179	2	96	**59**	0	6.4
1954	Phi N★	**23**	15	.605	45	**38**	**29**-4	4	**336.2**	289	116	35	5	56	**185**	2.97	136	.231	**.266**	122-0-4	.123	-3	107	44	0	4.3
1955	Phi N★	**23**	14	.622	41	**38**	**26**-1	3	**305**	292	137	41	2	53-3	160	3.28	121	.246	.279	107-2-5	.252	14*	104	18	0	3.4
1956	Phi N☆	19	18	.514	43	37	**22**-1	3	297.1	328	155	46	2	40-3	157	4.45	84	.282	.305	100-1-3	.200	4	103	-18	0	-1.7
1957	Phi N	10	22	.313	39	32	14-2	2	249.2	246	122	40	1	43-16	128	4.07	93	.252	.283	80-0-4	.162	0	79	-6	0	-0.6
1958	Phi N	17	14	.548	35	34	21-1	0	269.2	270	112	30	2	51-5	130	3.24	122	.259	.292	99-0-3	.202	4*	95	21	0	2.6
1959	Phi N	15	17	.469	35	35	19-2	0	257.1	267	137	34	5	35-4	137	4.27	96	.263	.290	89-0-2	.191	3	77	-4	0	-0.1
1960	Phi N	12	16	.429	35	33	13-2	1	237.1	256	113	31	2	34-7	122	4.02	97	.275	.300	79-0-4	.152	-1	81	-1	0	-0.3
1961	Phi N	1	10	.091	26	18	2	0	117	154	85	19	2	23-6	54	5.85	70	.326	.354	33-0-1	.091	-2	89	-23	30	-2.1
1962	Bal A	10	9	.526	27	25	6	0	191.1	176	63	17	4	41-7	102	2.78	133	.244	.288	52-0-7	.192	2	84	23	0	2.4
1963	Bal A	14	13	.519	35	35	9-2	0	251.1	230	100	35	3	40-8	124	3.33	104	.240	.272	79-0-8	.203	2	104	6	0	0.8
1964	Bal A	13	7	.650	31	31	8-4	0	204	203	69	18	3	52-6	109	2.91	123	.261	.308	68-0-4	.132	-1	97	17	0	1.4
1965	Bal A	5	7	.417	20	15	5-1	0	114.2	110	51	17	1	20-3	63	3.38	103	.252	.282	35-0-3	.171	1	94	1	0	0.2
	Hou N	5	2	.714	10	10	3-2	0	76	61	22	1	0	10-1	34	1.89	177	.216	.243	21-0-3	.238	3	104	11	0	1.4
1966	Hou N	3	5	.375	13	12	1-1	1	63.2	79	31	7	1	10-0	26	3.82	90	.307	.331	16-0-3	.063	-1	88	-3	0	-0.4
	Chi N	2	3	.400	11	9	1	0	48.1	62	35	8	0	11-0	28	6.14	60	.313	.349	10-0-3	.200	1	88	-12	0	-1.0
	Year	5	8	.385	24	21	2-1	1	112	141	66	15	1	21-0	54	4.82	73	.310	.339	26-0-6	.115	-0	88	-17	0	-1.4
Total	19	286	245	.539	676	609	305-45	25	4688.2	4582	1962	505	54	902-69	2357	3.41	113	.255	.292	1525-5-108	.167	34	95	263	30	30.3
Roberts, Willis	Willis Augusto (De Leon); B6.19.1975 San Cristobal, D.R.; BR/TR/6´3˝/(175–240); d7.2																									
1999	Det A	0	0	ø	1	0	0	0-0	1.1	3	4	0	1	0-0	0	13.50	37	.500	.500	0	ø	0	—	-2	0	-0.1
2001	Bal A	9	10	.474	46	18	1	6-4	132	142	75	15	11	55-1	95	4.91	88	.274	.354	4-0-1	.250	0	97	-7	0	-0.9
2002	Bal A	5	4	.556	66	0	0	1-2	75	79	34	5	4	32-3	51	3.36	129	.270	.345	0	ø	0	—	7	0	0.7
2003	Bal A	3	1	.750	26	0	0	0-0	39.1	41	26	7	7	16-2	26	5.72	80	.273	.370	0	ø	0	—	-4	92	-0.4
2004	Pit N	0	0	ø	9	0	0	0-0	12	12	7	0	2	9-0	7	5.25	83	.279	.411	1	.000	-0	—	-1	0	0.0
Total	5	17	15	.531	148	18	1	7-6	259.2	277	146	27	25	112-6	179	4.64	94	.274	.358	5-0-1	.200	0	97	-7	92	-0.7
Robertson, Charlie	Charles Culbertson; B1.31.1896 Dexter TX; D8.23.1984 Fort Worth TX; BL/TR/6´0˝/175; d5.13; Col Austin																									
1919	Chi A	0	1	.000	1	1	0	0	2	5	2	0	0	0	1	9.00	35	.556	.556	0	ø	0	25	-1	—	-0.2
1922	Chi A	14	15	.483	37	34	21-3	0	272	294	124	9	4	89	83	3.64	112	.286	.345	87-0-8	.184	-2	95	13	—	0.8
1923	Chi A	13	18	.419	38	34	18-1	0	255	262	126	8	5	104	91	3.81	104	.272	.346	85-0-8	.247	0	88	5	—	0.4
1924	Chi A	4	10	.286	17	14	5	0	97.1	108	65	2	0	54	29	4.99	83	.293	.383	33-0-3	.182	-1	70	-10	—	-1.4

YEAR	TM LG	W	L	PCT	G	GS	CG-SHO	SV-BS	IP	H	R	HR	HB	BB-IB	SO	ERA	AERA	OAV	OOB	AB-HR-SH	AVG	PB	SUP	APR	DL	PW
1925	Chi A	8	12	.400	24	23	6-2	0	137	181	96	8	2	47	27	5.26	79	.327	.381	45-0-2	.222	0	91	-19	—	-2.3
1926	StL A	1	2	.333	8	7	1	0	28	38	27	4	2	21	13	8.36	51	.333	.445	10	.300	1	109	-10	—	-0.8
1927	Bos N	7	17	.292	28	21	6	0	154.1	188	90	2	4	46	49	4.72	79	.308	.360	50-0-3	.240	1	70	-16	—	-2.1
1928	Bos N	2	5	.286	13	7	3	1	59.1	73	40	5	0	16	17	5.31	74	.308	.352	17-0-2	.000	-1	114	-9	—	-1.0
Total	8	49	80	.380	166	141	60-6	1	1005	1149	570	38	17	377	310	4.44	90	.296	.361	327-0-26	.208	-2	88	-47	—	-6.6
Robertson, Jeriome	Jeriome Paul; B3.30.1977 San Jose CA; BL/TL/6´1˝/(190–200); d9.2																									
2002	Hou N	0	2	.000	11	1	0	0-0	9.2	13	8	4	0	5-3	6	6.52	66	.394	.439	0	ø	0	43	-2	0	-0.4
2003	Hou N	15	9	.625	32	31	0	0-0	160.2	180	98	23	6	64-8	99	5.10	87	.287	.356	52-0-5	.154	-0*	116	-11	0	-1.4
2004	Cle A	1	1	.500	8	0	0	0-1	14	22	22	5	2	9-2	6	12.21	36	.349	.440	0	ø	0	—	-14	0	-1.5
Total	3	16	12	.571	51	32	0	0-1	184.1	215	128	32	8	78-13	111	5.71	77	.297	.368	52-0-5	.154	-0	113	-27	0	-3.3
Robertson, Jerry	Jerry Lee; B10.13.1943 Winchester KS; D3.24.1996 Burlington KS; BB/TR (BR 1969p)/6´2˝/200; [StLN65 14/532]; d4.8; Col Washburn Topeka																									
1969	Mon N	5	16	.238	38	27	3	1-0	179.2	186	87	17	4	81-11	133	3.96	93	.272	.348	56-0-2	.089	-3	67	-3	0	-0.8
1970	Det A	0	0	ø	11	0	0	0-0	14.2	19	8	1	0	5-1	11	3.68	102	.306	.353	0	ø	0	—	0	0	0.0
Total	2	5	16	.238	49	27	3	1-0	194.1	205	95	18	4	86-12	144	3.94	94	.274	.348	56-0-2	.089	-3	67	-3	0	-0.8
Robertson, Nate	Nathan Daniel; B9.3.1977 Wichita KS; BR/TL/6´2˝/(215–225); [FlaN99 5/146]; d9.7; Col Wichita St.																									
2002	Fla N	0	1	.000	6	1	0	0-0	8.1	15	11	3	2	4-1	3	11.88	33	.375	.457	2	.000	-0	24	-7	0	-0.8
2003	Det A	1	2	.333	8	8	0	0-0	44.2	55	27	6	0	23-2	33	5.44	81	.306	.384	0	ø	0	95	-4	0	-0.2
2004	Det A	12	10	.545	34	32	1	1-0	196.2	210	116	30	4	66-1	155	4.90	91	.274	.333	3	.000	-0	123	-10	0	-1.0
2005	Det A	7	16	.304	32	32	2	0-0	196.2	202	113	28	7	65-2	122	4.48	95	.266	.325	3-0-1	.000	-0	82	-7	0	-0.8
2006	†Det A	13	13	.500	32	32	1	0-0	208.2	206	98	29	8	67-2	137	3.84	117	.259	.320	6	.167	-0	82	15	0	1.6
Total	5	33	42	.440	112	105	4	1-0	655	688	365	96	21	225-8	450	4.56	97	.271	.333	14-0-1	.071	-1	95	-13	0	-1.2
Robertson, Dick	Preston James; B9.16.1891 Rockville MD; D10.2.1944 New Orleans LA; BR/TR/5´9˝/160; d9.16																									
1913	Cin N	0	1	.000	2	1	1	0	10	13	9	0	0	9	1	7.20	45	.342	.468	3	.000	-0	0	-4	—	-0.4
1918	Bro N	3	6	.333	13	9	7-1	0	87	87	34	0	0	28	18	2.59	108	.272	.330	30	.300	2*	60	1	—	0.3
1919	Was A	0	1	.000	7	4	0	0	27.2	25	11	1	0	9	7	2.28	141	.253	.315	7	.000	-1	61	2	—	0.0
Total	3	3	8	.273	22	14	8-1	0	124.2	125	54	1	0	46	26	2.89	101	.274	.340	40	.225	0	56	-1	—	-0.1
Robertson, Rich	Richard Paul; B10.14.1944 Albany CA; BR/TR/6´2˝/(195–215); [SFN65 5/92]; d9.10; Col Santa Clara																									
1966	SF N	0	0	ø	1	0	0	0	2.1	3	3	0	0	2-0	2	7.71	48	.300	.417	0	ø	0	—	-1	0	-0.1
1967	SF N	0	0	ø	1	0	0	0	2	3	1	0	0	0-0	1	4.50	73	.333	.333	0	ø	0	—	0	0	0.0
1968	SF N	2	0	1.000	3	1	0	0	9	9	6	0	0	3-0	8	6.00	49	.265	.324	2-0-1	.500	0	324	-3	0	-0.5
1969	SF N	1	3	.250	17	7	1-1	0-0	44.1	53	32	4	1	21-1	20	5.48	64	.298	.368	10-0-1	.000	-1	130	-10	0	-0.9
1970	SF N	8	9	.471	41	26	6	1-1	183.2	199	113	22	1	96-3	121	4.85	82	.277	.359	59-2-7	.102	-0	109	-19	0	-1.6
1971	SF N	2	2	.500	23	6	1	1-0	61	66	40	5	2	31-3	32	4.57	75	.267	.351	15	.067	-1	113	-9	0	-0.8
Total	6	13	14	.481	86	40	8-1	2-1	302.1	333	195	31	4	153-7	184	4.94	76	.278	.358	86-2-9	.093	-2	118	-42	0	-3.9
Robertson, Rich	Richard Wayne; B9.15.1968 Nacogdoches TX; BL/TL/6´4˝/(175–182); [PitN90 9/241]; d4.30; Col Texas A&M																									
1993	Pit N	0	1	.000	9	0	0	0-1	9	15	6	0	0	4-0	5	6.00	68	.385	.442	0	ø	0	—	-2	0	-0.2
1994	Pit N	0	0	ø	8	0	0	0-0	15.2	20	12	2	0	10-4	8	6.89	63	.313	.400	4	.250	0	—	-4	0	-0.2
1995	Min A	2	0	1.000	25	4	1	0-0	51.2	48	28	4	0	31-4	38	3.83	126	.253	.354	0	ø	0	97	4	0	0.1
1996	Min A	7	17	.292	36	31	5-**3**	0-1	186.1	197	113	22	9	116-2	114	5.12	100	.273	.378	0	ø	0	79	0	0	0.1
1997	Min A	8	12	.400	31	26	0	0-0	147	169	105	19	6	70-3	69	5.69	82	.292	.370	5	.200	0	79	-19	0	-2.2
1998	Ana A	0	0	ø	5	0	0	0-0	5.2	11	11	3	0	2-0	3	15.88	30	.393	.419	0	ø	0	—	-7	0	-0.3
Total	6	17	30	.362	114	61	6-3	0-2	415.1	460	275	50	15	233-13	237	5.40	90	.284	.375	9	.222	0	81	-28	0	-2.7
Robinson, Dewey	Dewey Everett; B4.28.1955 Evanston IL; BR/TR/6´0˝/(180–195); [ChiA77 19/467]; d4.6; C2; Col Southern Illinois																									
1979	Chi A	0	1	.000	11	0	0	0-0	14.1	11	12	1	0	9-2	5	6.28	68	.212	.328	0	ø	0	—	-3	0	-0.2
1980	Chi A	1	1	.500	15	0	0	0-1	35	26	13	2	0	16-0	28	3.09	132	.215	.302	0	ø	0	—	4	0	0.2
1981	Chi A	1	0	1.000	4	0	0	0-0	4	5	2	1	0	3-1	2	4.50	80	.357	.471	0	ø	0	—	0	0	-0.1
Total	3	2	2	.500	30	0	0	0-1	53.1	42	27	4	0	28-3	35	4.05	101	.225	.323	0	ø	0	—	1	0	-0.1
Robinson, Don	Don Allen; B6.8.1957 Ashland KY; BR/TR/6´4˝/(225–240); [PitN75 3/68]; d4.10																									
1978	Pit N	14	6	.700	35	32	9-1	1-0	228.1	203	98	20	3	57-4	135	3.47	108	.236	.283	85-0-4	.235	2	111	8	0	0.9
1979	†Pit N	8	8	.500	29	25	4	0-0	160.2	171	74	12	4	52-5	96	3.87	101	.277	.335	49-0-4	.204	1	114	3	0	0.2
1980	Pit N	7	10	.412	29	24	3-2	1-0	160.1	157	74	14	5	45-5	103	3.99	93	.257	.312	57-1-0	.333	6*	90	-3	22	0.3
1981	Pit N	0	3	.000	16	2	0	2-1	38.1	47	27	4	0	23-4	17	5.87	62	.313	.400	12	.250	1*	122	-8	59	-0.6
1982	Pit N	15	13	.536	38	30	6	0-0	227	213	123	26	3	103-11	165	4.28	88	.250	.331	85-2-2	.282	8*	114	-14	0	-0.8
1983	Pit N	2	2	.500	9	6	0	0-1	36.1	43	21	5	0	21-3	28	4.46	84	.297	.386	13-1-0	.154	1*	110	-3	102	-0.3
1984	Pit N	5	6	.455	51	1	0	10-4	122	99	45	6	0	49-4	110	3.02	120	.226	.298	31-1-0	.290	4*	49	9	0	1.3
1985	Pit N	5	11	.313	44	6	0	3-5	95.1	95	49	6	2	42-11	65	3.87	94	.255	.334	21-1-0	.238	2	73	-4	0	-0.4
1986	Pit N	3	4	.429	50	0	0	14-1	69.1	61	27	5	2	27-3	53	3.38	115	.237	.310	6	.667	2	—	5	47	0.8
1987	Pit N	6	6	.500	42	0	0	12-7	65.1	66	29	6	0	22-3	53	3.86	108	.267	.326	7	.143	0*	—	3	0	0.6
	†SF N	5	1	.833	25	0	0	7-0	42.2	39	13	1	0	18-3	26	2.74	140	.239	.311	11-1-0	.273	2	—	6	0	1.2
	Year	11	7	.611	67	0	0	19-7	108	105	42	7	0	40-6	79	3.42	118	.256	.320	18-1-0	.222	2	—	9	0	1.8
1988	SF N	10	5	.667	51	19	3-2	6-3	176.2	152	63	11	3	49-12	122	2.45	133	.231	.284	52-1-2	.173	3*	103	13	0	1.4
1989	†SF N	12	11	.522	34	32	5-1	0-0	197	184	80	22	2	37-6	96	3.43	99	.248	.283	81-3-0	.185	4*	113	1	0	0.3
1990	SF N	10	7	.588	26	25	4	0-0	157.2	173	84	18	1	41-8	78	4.57	80	.280	.324	63-2-3	.143	1*	103	-15	44	-1.5
1991	SF N	5	9	.357	34	16	0	1-0	121.1	123	64	12	1	50-7	78	4.38	82	.265	.334	40	.150	0*	98	-11	16	-1.2
1992	Cal A	1	0	1.000	3	3	0	0-0	16.1	19	4	1	0	3-0	9	2.20	182	.292	.324	0	ø	0	76	3	22	0.2
	Phi N	1	4	.200	8	8	0	0-0	43.2	49	32	6	1	4-0	17	6.18	57	.290	.300	18	.389	3*	116	-13	15	-1.0
Total	15	109	106	.507	524	229	34-6	57-22	1958.1	1894	907	175	27	643-89	1251	3.79	97	.255	.314	631-13-15	.231	40	105	-20	327	1.4
Robinson, Humberto	Humberto Valentino; B6.25.1930 Colon, Pan; BR/TR/6´1˝/(150–155); d4.20																									
1955	Mil N	3	1	.750	13	2	1	2	38	31	13	1	4	25-2	19	3.08	122	.235	.368	13	.077	-1	119	4	0	0.3
1956	Mil N	0	0	ø	1	0	0	0	2	1	0	0	0	2-0	0	0.00	ø	.167	.375	0	ø	0	—	1	0	0.1
1958	Mil N	2	4	.333	19	0	0	1	41.2	30	15	4	2	13-2	26	3.02	116	.203	.276	6	.167	1	—	3	0	0.5
1959	Cle A	1	0	1.000	5	0	0	0	8.2	9	4	0	0	4-1	6	4.15	89	.281	.361	0	ø	0	—	0	0	0.0
	Phi N	2	4	.333	31	4	1	1	73	70	36	6	0	24-6	32	3.33	123	.251	.308	13-0-1	.231	1	60	4	0	0.4
1960	Phi N	0	4	.000	33	1	0	0	49.2	48	24	6	0	22-5	31	3.44	113	.255	.333	6	.167	-0	23	1	0	0.1
Total	5	8	13	.381	102	7	2	4	213	189	92	17	6	90-16	114	3.25	119	.241	.322	38-0-1	.158	0	73	13	0	1.4
Robinson, Jeff	Jeffrey Daniel; B12.13.1960 Santa Ana CA; BR/TR/6´4˝/200; [SFN83 2/44]; d4.7; Col Cal St.–Fullerton																									
1984	SF N	7	15	.318	34	33	1-1	0-0	171.2	195	99	12	7	52-4	102	4.56	78	.288	.341	61-0-1	.115	-2	87	-20	0	-2.5
1985	SF N	0	0	ø	8	0	0	0-0	12.1	16	11	2	0	10-1	8	5.11	68	.333	.441	0	ø	0	—	-4	0	-0.2
1986	SF N	6	3	.667	64	1	0	8-1	104.1	92	46	8	1	32-7	90	3.36	105	.234	.291	15-0-1	.067	-1*	177	1	0	0.0
1987	SF N	6	8	.429	63	0	0	10-6	96.2	69	34	10	1	48-10	82	2.79	138	.207	.306	18	.111	-1	—	12	0	1.7
	Pit N	2	1	.667	18	0	0	4-1	26.2	20	9	1	0	6-1	19	3.04	137	.215	.263	4-1-1	.250	1	—	4	0	0.6
	Year	8	9	.471	81	0	0	14-7	123.1	89	43	11	1	54-11	101	2.85	138	.209	.297	22-1-1	.136	0	—	16	0	2.3
1988	Pit N	11	5	.688	75	0	0	9-4	124.2	113	44	6	3	39-5	87	3.03	114	.244	.303	16-0-5	.188	0	—	7	0	1.0
1989	Pit N	7	13	.350	50	19	0	4-4	141.1	161	92	14	1	59-11	95	4.58	74	.283	.347	35-1-5	.229	2	119	-24	0	-3.0
1990	NY A	3	6	.333	54	4	1	0-2	88.2	82	35	8	1	34-3	43	3.45	116	.248	.319	0	ø	0	74	6	0	0.7
1991	Cal A	0	3	.000	39	0	0	3-2	57	56	34	9	2	29-4	57	5.37	77	.259	.349	0	ø	0	—	-6	0	-0.4
1992	Chi N	4	3	.571	49	5	0	1-3	78	76	29	5	2	40-7	46	3.00	121	.263	.354	12-0-2	.000	-1	70	5	0	0.4
Total	9	46	57	.447	454	62	2-1	39-23	901.1	880	433	75	18	349-53	629	3.79	96	.258	.327	161-2-15	.137	-1	94	-19	0	-1.7
Robinson, Jeff	Jeffrey Mark; B12.14.1961 Ventura CA; BR/TR/6´6˝/(210–240); [DetA83 3/69]; d4.12; Col Azusa Pacific																									
1987	†Det A	9	6	.600	29	21	2-1	0-0	127.1	132	86	16	7	54-3	98	5.37	79	.262	.340	0	ø	0	122	-17	0	-1.7
1988	Det A	13	6	.684	24	23	6-2	0-0	172	121	61	19	3	72-5	114	2.98	129	**.197**	.282	0	ø	0	105	18	40	1.9
1989	Det A	4	5	.444	16	16	1-1	0-0	78	76	47	10	1	46-1	40	4.73	81	.259	.358	0	ø	0	139	-8	61	-0.9
1990	Det A	10	9	.526	27	27	1-1	0-0	145	141	101	23	6	88-9	76	5.96	67	.255	.361	0	ø	0	123	-30	0	-3.4
1991	Bal A	4	9	.308	21	19	0	0-0	104.1	119	62	12	6	51-2	65	5.18	77	.289	.375	0	ø	0	82	-13	0	-1.5
1992	Tex A	4	4	.500	16	4	0	0-2	45.2	50	30	6	0	21-1	18	5.72	67	.281	.351	0	ø	0	119	-9	0	-1.3

YEAR	TM LG	W	L	PCT	G	GS	CG-SHO	SV-BS	IP	H	R	HR	HB	BB-IB	SO	ERA	AERA	OAV	OOB	AB-HR-SH	AVG	PB	SUP	APR	DL	PW
	Pit N	3	1	.750	8	7	0	0-0	36.1	33	18	2	1	15-0	14	4.46	78	.244	.322	11-0-2	.091	-1	164	-3	0	-0.4
Total	6	47	40	.540	141	117	10-5	0-2	708.2	672	405	88	24	347-21	425	4.79	82	.250	.339	11-0-2	.091	-1	117	-62	101	-7.3
Robinson, Jack	John Edward; B2.20.1921 Orange NJ; D3.2.2000 Ormond Beach FL; BR/TR/6´0˝/175; d5.4																									
1949	Bos A	0	0	ø	3	0	0	0	4	4	1	0	1	1	1	2.25	194	.267	.353	0	ø	0	—	1	0	0.1
Robinson, Hank	John Henry "Rube" (b John Henry Roberson); B8.16.1887 Floyd AR; D7.3.1965 N.Little Rock AR; BR/TL/5´11.5˝/160; d9.2																									
1911	Pit N	0	1	.000	5	0	0	0	13	13	7	0	1	5	8	2.77	124	.283	.365	3	.000	-0	—	0	—	0.0
1912	Pit N	12	7	.632	33	16	11	2	175	146	54	3	10	30	79	2.26	144	.237	.284	59	.254	3	91	21	—	2.4
1913	Pit N	14	9	.609	43	22	8-1	0	196.1	184	72	2	7	41	50	2.38	127	.255	.301	61-0-3	.180	-1	96	13	—	1.2
1914	StL N	7	8	.467	26	16	6-1	0	126	128	61	1	4	32	30	3.00	93	.274	.325	35-0-3	.171	-0	98	-3	—	-0.3
1915	StL N	7	8	.467	32	15	6-1	0	143	128	54	1	7	35	57	2.45	114	.245	.301	47	.106	-2	123	4	—	0.3
1918	NY A	2	4	.333	11	3	1	0	48	47	21	0	3	16	14	3.00	94	.269	.340	13	.000	-2	71	-1	—	-0.4
Total	6	42	37	.532	150	72	32-3	2	701.1	646	269	7	32	159	238	2.53	118	.253	.305	218-0-6	.170	-3	99	34	—	3.2
Robinson, Ken	Kenneth Neal; B11.3.1969 Barberton OH; D2.28.1999 Tucson AZ; BR/TR/5´7˝/170; [TorA91 10/276]; d7.20; Col Florida St.; [DL 1998 Ari N 181]																									
1995	Tor A	1	2	.333	21	0	0	0-0	39	25	21	7	2	22-1	31	3.69	129	.179	.295	0	ø	0	—	3	0	0.2
1996	KC A	1	0	1.000	5	0	0	0-0	6	9	4	0	0	3-1	5	6.00	84	.346	.400	0	ø	0	—	-1	0	-0.1
1997	Tor A	0	0	ø	3	0	0	0-1	3.1	1	1	1	0	1-0	4	2.70	170	.100	.182	0	ø	0	—	1	0	0.1
Total	3	2	2	.500	29	0	0	0-1	48.1	35	26	8	2	26-2	40	3.91	122	.199	.304	0	ø	0	—	3	181	0.2
Robinson, Ron	Ronald Dean; B3.24.1962 Exeter CA; BR/TR/6´4˝/(200–235); [CinN80 1/19]; d8.14																									
1984	Cin N	1	2	.333	12	5	1	0-0	39.2	35	18	3	0	13-3	24	2.72	139	.232	.291	8-0-1	.000	-1	107	2	0	0.1
1985	Cin N	7	7	.500	33	12	0	1-0	108.1	107	53	11	1	32-3	76	3.99	95	.259	.311	22-0-5	.091	-1	74	-2	0	-0.4
1986	Cin N	10	3	.769	70	0	0	14-6	116.2	110	44	10	2	43-8	117	3.24	119	.253	.321	14	.071	-1	—	9	0	1.1
1987	Cin N	7	5	.583	48	18	0	4-2	154	148	71	14	1	43-8	99	3.68	115	.256	.305	36-0-5	.194	0	131	8	0	0.5
1988	Cin N	3	7	.300	17	16	0	0-0	78.2	88	47	5	2	26-4	38	4.12	87	.285	.339	25-0-1	.200	1	81	-8	67	-0.9
1989	Cin N	5	3	.625	15	15	0	0-0	83.1	80	36	8	2	28-2	36	3.35	108	.252	.316	28-0-2	.214	1	126	2	105	0.3
1990	Cin N	2	2	.500	6	5	0	0-0	31.1	36	18	2	0	14-0	14	4.88	81	.295	.368	11-0-1	.091	-1	137	-3	0	-0.4
	Mil A	12	5	.706	22	22	7-2	0-0	148.1	158	60	5	6	37-1	57	2.91	133	.275	.322	0	ø	0	131	14	0	1.5
1991	Mil A	0	1	.000	1	1	0	0-0	4.1	6	3	0	1	3-1	0	6.23	64	.353	.476	0	ø	0	69	-1	178	-0.2
1992	Mil A	1	4	.200	8	8	0	0-0	35.1	51	26	3	2	14-0	12	5.86	66	.331	.392	0	ø	0	97	-8	114	-1.0
Total	9	48	39	.552	232	102	8-2	19-8	800	819	376	61	17	253-30	473	3.63	107	.267	.323	144-0-15	.153	-2	111	13	464	0.6
Robinson, Yank	William H.; B9.19.1859 Philadelphia PA; D8.25.1894 St.Louis MO; BR/TR/5´6.5˝/170; d8.24; ▲																									
1882	Det N	0	0	ø	1	0	0	0	2	0	0	0	—	1	0	0.00	ø	.000	.125	39	.179	-0*	—	1	—	0.0
1884	Bal U	3	3	.500	11	3	3	0	75	96	61	1	—	18	61	3.48	77	.292	.329	415-3	.267	1*	101	-7	—	-0.6
1886	†StL AA	0	1	.000	1	1	1	0	9	10	11	0	0	7	1	3.00	115	.286	.405	481-3	.274	0*	121	-1	—	-0.1
1887	†StL AA	0	0	ø	1	0	0	1	3	3	2	0	1	3	0	3.00	151	.333	.538	430-1	.305	0*	—	0	—	0.0
Total	4	3	4	.429	14	4	4	1	89	109	74	1	1	29	62	3.34	85	.287	.339	1365-7	.279	1	104	-7	—	-0.7
Robitaille, Chick	Joseph Anthony; B3.2.1879 Whitehall NY; D7.30.1947 Waterford NY; BR/TR/5´8˝/150; d9.2																									
1904	Pit N	4	3	.571	9	8	8	0	66	52	22	1	1	13	34	1.91	144	.208	.250	21	.095	-2	47	5	—	0.2
1905	Pit N	8	5	.615	17	12	10	0	120.1	126	54	1	3	28	32	2.92	103	.276	.322	45-0-1	.133	-2	80	0	—	-0.3
Total	2	12	8	.600	26	20	18	0	186.1	178	76	2	4	41	66	2.56	114	.252	.297	66-0-1	.121	-4	67	5	—	-0.1
Roche, Armando	Armando (Baez); B12.7.1926 Havana, Cuba; D6.26.1997 Chicago IL; BR/TR/6´0˝/190; d5.10																									
1945	Was A	0	0	ø	2	0	0	0	6	10	4	0	0	2	0	6.00	52	.400	.444	1	.000	-0	—	-2	0	-0.1
Rochford, Mike	Michael Joseph; B3.14.1963 Methuen MA; BL/TL/6´4˝/205; [BosA82*1/17]; d9.3; Col Santa Fe (FL) CC																									
1988	Bos A	0	0	ø	2	0	0	0-0	2.1	4	0	0	0	1-0	1	0.00	ø	.364	.417	0	ø	0	—	1	0	0.1
1989	Bos A	0	0	ø	4	0	0	0-0	4	4	7	1	0	4-1	1	6.75	61	.267	.400	0	ø	0	—	-3	0	-0.1
1990	Bos A	0	1	.000	2	1	0	0-0	4	10	10	1	0	4-0	0	18.00	23	.526	.583	0	ø	0	156	-6	0	-1.0
Total	3	0	1	.000	8	1	0	0-0	10.1	18	17	2	0	9-1	2	9.58	43	.400	.482	0	ø	0	156	-8	0	-1.0
Rocker, John	John Loy; B10.17.1974 Statesboro GA; BR/TL/6´4˝/(210–225); [AtlN93 18/516]; d5.5																									
1998	†Atl N	1	3	.250	47	0	0	2-2	38	22	10	4	3	22-4	42	2.13	195	.172	.307	0	ø	0	—	9	0	0.9
1999	†Atl N	4	5	.444	74	0	0	38-7	72.1	47	24	5	1	37-4	104	2.49	180	.180	.284	0	ø	0	—	15	0	3.0
2000	†Atl N	1	2	.333	59	0	0	24-3	53	42	25	5	2	48-4	77	2.89	156	.210	.368	0	ø	0	—	7	0	0.9
2001	Atl N	2	2	.500	30	0	0	19-4	32	25	13	2	2	16-1	36	3.09	139	.216	.319	0	ø	0	—	4	0	0.8
	†Cle A	3	7	.300	38	0	0	4-3	34.2	33	23	2	3	25-3	43	5.45	84	.250	.379	0	ø	0	—	-3	0	-0.6
2002	Tex A	2	3	.400	30	0	0	1-3	24.1	29	19	5	0	13-1	30	6.66	72	.299	.372	0	ø	0	—	-5	88	-0.8
2003	TB A	0	0	ø	2	0	0	0-0	1	2	1	0	1	3-0	0	9.00	51	.500	.750	0	ø	0	—	0	0	0.0
Total	6	13	22	.371	280	0	0	88-22	255.1	200	115	23	12	164-17	332	3.42	130	.213	.336	0	ø	0	—	27	88	4.2
Rodas, Rich	Richard Martin; B11.7.1959 Roseville CA; BL/TL/6´1˝/(170–180); d9.6; Col Sacramento (CA) City																									
1983	LA N	0	0	ø	7	0	0	0-0	4.2	4	1	0	0	3-1	5	1.93	187	.222	.333	0	ø	0	—	1	0	0.0
1984	LA N	0	0	ø	3	0	0	0-0	5	5	3	2	0	1-0	1	5.40	66	.250	.286	1	.000	-0	—	-1	103	0.0
Total	2	0	0	ø	10	0	0	0-0	9.2	9	4	2	0	4-1	6	3.72	96	.237	.310	1	.000	-0	—	0	103	0.0
Rodney, Fernando	Fernando; B3.18.1977 Samana, D.R.; BR/TR/5´11˝/(170–220); d5.4; [DL 2004 Det A 183]																									
2002	Det A	1	3	.250	20	0	0	0-4	18	25	15	2	0	10-2	10	6.00	73	.329	.402	0	ø	0	—	-4	0	-0.8
2003	Det A	1	3	.250	27	0	0	3-3	29.2	35	20	2	1	17-1	33	6.07	72	.294	.379	0	ø	0	—	-5	0	-0.7
2005	Det A	2	3	.400	39	0	0	9-6	44	39	14	5	2	17-3	42	2.86	149	.238	.317	0	ø	0	—	8	67	1.0
2006	†Det A	7	4	.636	63	0	0	7-4	71.2	51	36	6	8	34-4	65	3.52	128	.196	.308	1	.000	-0	—	5	0	0.8
Total	4	11	13	.458	149	0	0	19-17	163.1	150	85	15	11	78-10	150	4.08	108	.242	.336	1	.000	-0	—	4	250	0.3
Rodriguez, Eddy	Eddy; B8.8.1981 San Pedro de Macoris, D.R.; BR/TR/6´1˝/(195–215); d5.31																									
2004	Bal A	1	0	1.000	29	0	0	0-0	43.1	36	23	5	5	30-5	37	4.78	98	.231	.370	1	.000	-0	—	0	0	0.0
2006	Bal A	1	1	.500	9	0	0	0-0	15	17	14	5	0	10-0	11	7.20	63	.283	.375	0	ø	0	—	-5	0	-0.6
Total	2	2	1	.667	38	0	0	0-0	58.1	53	37	10	5	40-5	48	5.40	86	.245	.371	1	.000	-0	—	-5	0	-0.6
Rodriguez, Eduardo	Eduardo (Reyes); B3.6.1952 Barceloneta, PR; BR/TR/6´0˝/(180–185); d6.20																									
1973	Mil A	9	7	.563	30	6	2	5-5	76.1	71	33	6	2	47-7	49	3.30	115	.247	.354	1	1.000	1	156	4	0	0.9
1974	Mil A	7	4	.636	43	6	0	4-4	111.2	97	49	7	5	51-5	58	3.63	100	.241	.330	0	ø	0	73	0	0	0.0
1975	Mil A	7	0	1.000	43	1	0	7-0	87.2	77	37	9	5	44-9	65	3.49	111	.235	.332	0	ø	0	160	4	0	0.3
1976	Mil A	5	13	.278	45	12	3	8-3	136	124	68	10	3	65-6	77	3.64	97	.249	.334	0	ø	0	67	-5	0	-0.7
1977	Mil A	5	6	.455	42	5	1-1	4-2	142.2	126	70	15	3	56-6	104	4.35	94	.236	.310	0	ø	0	79	-1	0	-0.1
1978	Mil A	5	5	.500	32	8	0	2-2	105.1	107	49	9	2	26-3	51	3.93	97	.262	.306	0	ø	0	121	-1	0	-0.1
1979	KC A	4	1	.800	29	1	1	2-0	74.1	79	42	9	3	34-4	26	4.84	88	.276	.355	0	ø	0	297	-3	22	-0.3
Total	7	42	36	.538	264	39	7-1	32-16	734	681	348	65	23	323-40	430	3.89	99	.248	.329	1	1.000	1	101	-2	22	0.0
Rodriguez, Felix	Felix Antonio; B9.9.1972 Monte Cristi, D.R.; BR/TR/6´1˝/(180–210); d5.13																									
1995	LA N	1	1	.500	11	0	0	0-1	10.2	11	3	2	0	5-0	5	2.53	153	.275	.356	0	ø	0	—	2	0	0.3
1997	Cin N	0	0	ø	26	1	0	0-0	46	48	23	2	6	28-2	34	4.30	99	.271	.387	3-0-1	.000	-0	151	0	0	-0.1
1998	Ari N	0	2	.000	43	0	0	5-3	44	44	31	5	1	29-1	36	6.14	70	.259	.365	0	ø	0	—	-8	39	-0.4
1999	SF N	2	3	.400	47	0	0	0-1	66.1	67	32	6	2	29-2	55	3.80	112	.262	.338	6-1-1	.333	2	—	3	0	0.4
2000	†SF N	4	2	.667	76	0	0	3-5	81.2	65	29	5	3	42-2	95	2.64	164	.220	.320	4	.000	-0	—	15	0	0.9
2001	SF N	9	1	.900	80	0	0	0-3	80.1	53	16	5	1	27-2	91	1.68	243	.188	.259	0	ø	0	—	**23**	0	2.5
2002	†SF N	8	6	.571	71	0	0	0-6	69	53	33	5	4	29-1	58	4.17	95	.212	.301	1	1.000	0	—	-1	0	-0.2
2003	†SF N	8	2	.800	68	0	0	2-1	61	59	21	5	4	29-2	46	3.10	137	.259	.351	1	1.000	0	—	9	15	1.3
2004	SF N	3	5	.375	53	0	0	0-3	44.2	43	18	7	4	19-2	31	3.43	127	.250	.337	1	.000	-0	—	5	0	0.7
	Phi N	2	3	.400	23	0	0	1-0	21	18	7	1	1	10-2	28	3.00	148	.231	.326	0	ø	0	—	3	0	0.7
	Year	5	8	.385	76	0	0	1-3	65.2	61	25	8	5	29-4	59	3.29	133	.244	.333	1	.000	-0	—	9	0	1.4
2005	NY A	0	0	ø	34	0	0	0-0	32.1	33	18	2	2	20-0	18	5.01	86	.264	.374	0	ø	0	—	-2	73	-0.1

YEAR	TM LG	W	L	PCT	G	GS	CG-SHO	SV-BS	IP	H	R	HR	HB	BB-IB	SO	ERA	AERA	OAV	OOB	AB-HR-SH	AVG	PB	SUP	APR	DL	PW
2006	Was N	1	1	.500	31	0	0	0-0	29.1	32	25	5	4	16-3	15	7.67	57	.281	.380	1	.000	-0	—	-10	108	-0.6
Total	11	38	26	.594	563	1	0	11-23	586.1	526	256	50	32	283-19	512	3.71	114	.240	.333	17-1-2	.235	2	151	39	235	5.4
RODRIGUEZ, FREDDY	Fernando Pedro (Borrego); B4.29.1924 Havana, Cuba; BR/TR/6´0˝/185; d4.18																									
1958	Chi N	0	0	ø	7	0	0	2	7.1	8	6	2	1	5-0	5	7.36	53	.267	.389	1	.000	-0	—	-2	0	-0.2
1959	Phi N	0	0	ø	1	0	0	0	2	4	3	1	1	0-0	1	13.50	30	.400	.455	0	ø	0	—	-2	0	-0.1
Total	2	0	0	ø	8	0	0	2	9.1	12	9	3	2	5-0	6	8.68	46	.300	.404	1	.000	-0	—	-4	0	-0.3
RODRIGUEZ, FRANK	Francisco; B12.11.1972 Brooklyn NY; BR/TR/6´0˝/(195–210); [BosA90 2/41]; d4.26																									
1995	Bos A	0	2	.000	9	2	0	0-0	15.1	21	19	3	0	10-1	14	10.57	46	.323	.413	0	ø	0	201	-9	0	-0.9
	Min A	5	6	.455	16	16	0	0-0	90.1	93	64	8	5	47-0	45	5.38	90	.269	.361	0	ø	0	98	-8	0	-0.7
	Year	5	8	.385	25	18	0	0-0	105.2	114	83	11	5	57-1	59	6.13	79	.277	.369	0	ø	0	109	-18	0	-1.6
1996	Min A	13	14	.481	38	33	3	2-0	206.2	218	129	27	5	78-1	110	5.05	102	.272	.337	0	ø	0	98	-1	0	-0.1
1997	Min A	3	6	.333	43	15	0	0-2	142.1	147	82	12	4	60-9	65	4.62	101	.271	.346	1	.000	-0	104	-1	0	0.0
1998	Min A	4	6	.400	20	11	0	0-0	70	88	58	6	3	30-0	62	6.56	73	.303	.369	0	ø	0	93	-15	0	-1.7
1999	Sea A	2	4	.333	28	5	0	3-1	73.1	94	47	11	4	30-2	47	5.65	85	.314	.383	3	.333	0*	93	-6	0	-0.4
2000	Sea A	2	1	.667	23	0	0	0-0	47.1	60	33	8	0	22-2	19	6.27	77	.317	.383	1	.000	-0	—	-7	61	-0.3
2001	Cin N	0	0	ø	7	0	0	0-0	8.2	16	12	1	0	5-2	9	11.42	40	.400	.457	1	.000	-0	—	-6	0	-0.3
Total	7	29	39	.426	184	82	3	5-3	654	737	444	76	21	282-17	371	5.53	88	.286	.358	6	.167	-0	101	-53	61	-4.4
RODRIGUEZ, FRANCISCO	Francisco Jose; B1.7.1982 Caracas, Distrito Capital, Venezuela; BR/TR/6´0˝/(165–180); d9.18																									
2002	†Ana A	0	0	ø	5	0	0	0-0	5.2	3	0	0	1	2-1	13	0.00	ø	.167	.286	0	ø	0	—	3	0	0.1
2003	Ana A	8	3	.727	59	0	0	2-4	86	50	30	12	2	35-5	95	3.03	144	.172	.262	0	ø	0	—	14	0	1.6
2004	†Ana A★	4	1	.800	69	0	0	12-7	84	51	21	2	1	33-1	123	1.82	245	.171	.255	0	ø	0	—	24	0	1.9
2005	†LA A	2	5	.286	66	0	0	**45**-5	67.1	45	20	7	0	32-3	91	2.67	160	.184	.277	0	ø	0	—	13	17	2.5
2006	LA A	2	3	.400	69	0	0	**47**-4	73	52	16	6	1	28-5	98	1.73	258	.197	.276	0	ø	0	—	23	0	3.9
Total	5	16	12	.571	268	0	0	106-20	316	201	87	27	5	130-15	420	2.28	193	.180	.267	0	ø	0	—	77	17	10.0
RODRIGUEZ, JOSE	Jose Ilich (Jose); B12.18.1974 Cayey, PR; BL/TL/6´1˝/(205–215); [StLN97 24/734]; d5.18; Col Florida International																									
2000	StL N	0	0	ø	6	0	0	0-0	4	2	2	0	1	3-0	2	0.00	ø	.143	.316	1	.000	-0	—	1	0	0.0
2002	StL N	0	0	ø	2	0	0	0-0	0.1	4	2	0	0	2-0	0	54.00	7	.800	.857	0	ø	0	—	-2	0	-0.1
	Min A	0	1	.000	4	0	0	0-0	3.2	8	6	0	0	4-1	1	14.73	30	.421	.522	0	ø	0	—	-4	78	-0.7
Total	2	0	1	.000	12	0	0	0-0	8	14	10	0	1	9-1	3	9.00	50	.368	.490	1	.000	-0	—	-5	78	-0.8
RODRIGUEZ, NERIO	Nerio; B3.4.1971 San Pedro de Macoris, D.R.; BR/TR/6´0˝/(165–205); d8.16																									
1996	Bal A	0	1	.000	8	1	0	0-0	16.2	18	11	2	1	7-0	12	4.32	115	.265	.338	0	ø	0	19	0	0	0.0
1997	Bal A	2	1	.667	6	2	0	0-1	22	21	15	2	1	8-0	11	4.91	90	.250	.309	0	ø	0	52	-2	0	-0.2
1998	Bal A	1	3	.250	6	4	0	0-0	19	25	17	0	0	9-0	8	8.05	57	.321	.382	0	ø	0	87	-7	35	-1.2
	Tor A	1	0	1.000	7	0	0	0-0	8.1	10	9	1	1	8-0	3	9.72	48	.286	.432	0	ø	0	—	-4	0	-0.4
	Year	2	3	.400	13	4	0	0-0	27.1	35	26	1	1	17-0	11	8.56	54	.310	.398	0	ø	0	86	-11	0	-1.6
1999	Tor A	0	1	.000	2	0	0	0-0	2	2	3	2	0	2-0	2	13.50	36	.250	.400	0	ø	0	—	-2	0	-0.3
2002	Cle A	0	0	ø	1	0	0	0-0	0.1	0	0	0	0	0-0	0	0.00	ø	.000	.000	0	ø	0	—	0	0	0.0
	StL N	0	0	ø	2	0	0	0-0	4.1	4	3	1	0	1-0	2	4.15	97	.222	.263	1	.000	-0	—	0	0	0.0
Total	5	4	6	.400	32	7	0	0-1	72.2	80	58	8	3	35-0	38	6.32	73	.274	.350	1	.000	-0	66	-15	35	-2.1
RODRIGUEZ, RICK	Ricardo; B9.21.1960 Oakland CA; BR/TR/6´3˝/(190–200); [OakA81 2/41]; d9.17; Col California–Riverside																									
1986	Oak A	1	2	.333	3	3	0	0-0	16.1	17	12	4	0	7-0	2	6.61	59	.262	.333	0	ø	0	70	-5	0	-0.7
1987	Oak A	1	0	1.000	15	0	0	0-0	24.1	32	8	1	1	15-1	9	2.96	141	.337	.432	0	ø	0	—	4	0	0.2
1988	Cle A	1	2	.333	10	5	0	0-0	33	43	28	4	1	17-1	9	7.09	58	.323	.401	0	ø	0	97	-10	0	-0.8
1990	SF N	0	0	ø	3	0	0	0-0	3.1	5	3	0	0	2-0	2	8.10	45	.357	.438	0	ø	0	—	-2	0	-0.1
Total	4	3	4	.429	31	8	0	0-0	77	97	51	9	2	41-2	22	5.73	71	.316	.399	0	ø	0	86	-13	0	-1.4
RODRIGUEZ, RICARDO	Ricardo Antonio; B3.21.1978 Guayubin, D.R.; BL/TR/6´3˝/(190–195); d8.21; [DL 2003 Tex A 73]																									
2002	Cle A	2	2	.500	7	7	0	0-0	41.1	40	27	5	8	18-3	24	5.66	78	.255	.361	0	ø	0	104	-5	0	-0.4
2003	Cle A	3	9	.250	15	15	0	0-0	81.2	89	57	16	3	28-1	41	5.73	77	.275	.336	3	.000	-0	72	-11	33	-1.3
2004	Tex A	3	1	.750	5	4	1-1	0-0	26.2	28	10	1	0	12-0	15	2.03	243	.262	.336	2	.000	-0	108	7	73	0.9
2005	Tex A	2	3	.400	12	10	0	0-0	57	67	39	11	1	17-0	24	5.53	82	.289	.339	3	.333	0	112	-6	55	-0.5
Total	4	10	15	.400	39	36	1-1	0-0	206.2	224	133	33	12	75-4	104	5.18	87	.273	.342	8	.125	-0	93	-15	234	-1.3
RODRIGUEZ, RICH	Richard Anthony; B3.1.1963 Downey CA; BL/TL/6´0˝/(194–205); [NYN84 9/211]; d6.30; Col Tennessee																									
1990	SD N	1	1	.500	32	0	0	1-0	47.2	52	17	2	1	16-4	22	2.83	136	.287	.347	3	.000	-0	—	5	0	0.3
1991	SD N	3	1	.750	64	1	0	0-2	80	66	31	8	0	44-8	40	3.26	117	.234	.335	5	.000	-1*	24	5	0	0.2
1992	SD N	6	3	.667	61	1	0	0-1	91	77	28	4	0	29-4	64	2.37	151	.229	.289	6-0-2	.000	-0	0	11	0	1.1
1993	SD N	2	3	.400	34	0	0	2-3	30	34	15	2	1	9-3	22	3.30	125	.281	.336	0	ø	0	—	2	0	0.3
	Fla N	0	1	.000	36	0	0	1-1	46	39	23	8	1	24-5	21	4.11	106	.229	.328	2	.000	-0	—	1	0	0.1
	Year	2	4	.333	70	0	0	3-4	76	73	38	10	2	33-8	43	3.79	113	.251	.331	2	.000	-0	—	3	0	0.4
1994	StL N	3	5	.375	56	0	0	0-3	60.1	62	30	6	1	26-4	43	4.03	105	.270	.345	1	.000	-0	—	1	0	0.0
1995	StL N	0	0	ø	1	0	0	0-0	1.2	0	0	0	0	0-0	0	0.00	ø	.000	.000	0	ø	0	—	1	158	0.0
1997	†SF N	4	3	.571	71	0	0	1-4	65.1	65	24	7	1	21-4	32	3.17	130	.264	.325	3	.333	1	—	8	0	0.9
1998	SF N	4	0	1.000	68	0	0	2-4	65.2	69	28	7	0	20-5	44	3.70	109	.272	.322	6-0-1	.167	-0	—	3	0	0.2
1999	SF N	3	0	1.000	62	0	0	0-2	56.2	60	33	8	1	28-5	44	5.24	82	.274	.356	1-0-1	1.000	1	—	-5	0	-0.1
2000	NY N	0	1	.000	32	0	0	0-0	37	59	40	7	3	15-0	18	7.78	56	.364	.416	1	.000	-0	—	-17	0	-0.8
2001	Cle A	2	2	.500	53	0	0	0-2	39	41	24	2	2	17-3	31	4.15	110	.270	.349	0	ø	0	—	0	0	0.0
2002	Tex A	3	2	.600	36	0	0	1-2	16.2	14	10	1	1	11-1	12	5.40	89	.237	.366	0	ø	0	—	-1	98	-0.1
2003	Ana A	0	0	ø	3	0	0	0-0	3.2	4	1	0	0	1-0	3	2.45	178	.308	.333	0	ø	0	—	1	0	0.0
Total	13	31	22	.585	609	2	0	8-24	640.2	642	304	62	12	261-46	396	3.81	107	.264	.337	28-0-4	.107	-0	11	15	256	2.1
RODRIGUEZ, ROSARIO	Rosario Isabel (Echavarria); B7.8.1969 Los Mochis, Sinaloa, Mexico; BR/TL/6´0˝/(185–195); d9.1																									
1989	Cin N	1	1	.500	7	0	0	0-1	4.1	3	2	0	0	3-1	0	4.15	87	.188	.316	0	ø	0	—	0	0	0.0
1990	Cin N	0	0	ø	9	0	0	0-0	10.1	15	7	3	1	2-0	8	6.10	65	.357	.391	0	ø	0	—	-2	0	-0.1
1991	†Pit N	1	1	.500	18	0	0	6-0	15.1	14	7	1	1	8-0	10	4.11	88	.246	.348	1	.000	-0	—	0	0	-0.1
Total	3	2	2	.500	34	0	0	6-1	30	32	16	4	2	13-1	18	4.80	77	.278	.359	1	.000	-0	—	-2	0	-0.2
RODRIGUEZ, WANDY	Wandy E.; B1.18.1979 Santiago Rodriguez, D.R.; BB/TL/5´11˝/160; d5.23																									
2005	†Hou N	10	10	.500	25	22	0	0-0	128.2	135	82	19	8	53-2	80	5.53	76	.274	.352	40-0-1	.150	-0	111	-17	0	-2.3
2006	Hou N	9	10	.474	30	24	0	0-0	135.2	154	96	17	6	63-7	98	5.64	80	.290	.369	37-0-5	.081	-2	102	-19	0	-2.5
Total	2	19	20	.487	55	46	0	0-0	264.1	289	178	36	14	116-9	178	5.58	78	.282	.361	77-0-6	.117	-2	106	-36	0	-4.8
RODRIGUEZ, WILFREDO	Wilfredo Jose; B3.20.1979 Ciudad Bolivar, Bolivar, Venez.; BL/TL/6´3˝/180; d9.21																									
2001	Hou N	0	0	ø	2	0	0	0-0	3	6	5	2	0	1-0	3	15.00	31	.429	.438	0	ø	0	—	-3	0	-0.1
RODRIQUEZ, ROBERTO	Roberto (Munoz); B11.29.1941 Caracas, Distrito Capital, Venez.; BR/TR/6´3˝/(185–186); d5.13																									
1967	KC A	1	1	.500	15	5	0	2	40.1	42	17	4	1	14-1	29	3.57	89	.268	.331	9	.000	-1	93	-1	0	-0.2
1970	Oak A	0	0	ø	6	0	0	0-0	12.1	10	5	2	0	3-0	8	2.92	121	.227	.271	1	.000	-0	—	1	0	0.0
	SD N	0	0	ø	10	0	0	3-1	16.1	26	16	1	0	5-0	8	6.61	61	.366	.408	3	.000	-0	—	-6	0	-0.3
	Chi N	3	2	.600	26	0	0	2-1	43.1	50	33	6	0	15-2	46	5.82	78	.289	.340	8-1-0	.125	1	—	-6	0	-0.6
	Year	3	2	.600	36	0	0	5-2	59.2	76	49	7	0	20-2	54	6.03	72	.311	.360	11-1-0	.091	0	—	-12	0	-0.9
Total	2	4	3	.571	57	5	0	7-2	112.1	128	71	13	1	37-3	91	4.81	80	.288	.341	21-1-0	.048	-1	93	-12	0	-1.1
ROE, PREACHER	Elwin Charles; B2.26.1915 Ash Flat AR; BR/TL/6´2˝/(163–170); d8.22; Col Harding																									
1938	StL N	0	0	ø	1	0	0	0	2.2	6	4	0	0	2	1	13.50	29	.429	.500	1	.000	-0	—	-2	—	-0.1
1944	Pit N	13	11	.542	39	25	7-1	1	185.1	182	82	7	2	59	88	3.11	120	.253	.311	53-0-6	.132	-2	92	11	0	1.0
1945	Pit N✱	14	13	.519	33	31	15-3	1	235	228	77	11	1	46	**148**	2.87	137	.259	.296	75-0-8	.107	-3	87	32	0	3.2
1946	Pit N	3	8	.273	21	10	1	2	70	83	50	5	2	25	28	5.14	69	.294	.356	15	.067	-1	83	-13	0	-2.0
1947	Pit N	4	15	.211	38	22	4-1	2	144	156	93	19	0	63	59	5.25	80	.276	.348	40-0-4	.125	-2	66	-15	0	-1.9
1948	Bro N	12	8	.600	34	22	8-2	2	177.2	156	60	14	2	33	86	2.63	152	.233	.271	51-0-9	.098	-2	104	27	0	2.6

THE PITCHER REGISTER

YEAR	TM LG	W	L	PCT	G	GS	CG-SHO	SV-BS	IP	H	R	HR	HB	BB-IB	SO	ERA	AERA	OAV	OOB	AB-HR-SH	AVG	PB	SUP	APR	DL	PW
1949	†Bro N★	15	6	**.714**	30	27	13-3	1	212.2	201	69	25	2	44	109	2.79	147	.252	.293	70-0-7	.114	-2	105	32	0	2.6
1950	Bro N☆	19	11	.633	36	32	16-2	1	250.2	245	96	34	4	66	125	3.30	124	.257	.308	91-0-8	.154	-3	102	25	0	2.3
1951	Bro N☆	22	3	**.880**	34	33	19-2	0	257.2	247	91	30	0	64	113	3.04	129	.258	.304	89-0-9	.112	-5	112	28	0	1.9
1952	†Bro N✳	11	2	.846	27	25	8-2	0	158.2	163	59	16	3	39	83	3.12	117	.270	.317	57-0-5	.070	-3	131	10	0	0.4
1953	†Bro N	11	3	.786	25	24	9-1	0	157	171	78	27	1	40	85	4.36	98	.278	.323	57-1-5	.053	-4	134	1	0	-0.3
1954	Bro N	3	4	.429	15	10	1	0	63	69	40	11	0	23	31	5.00	82	.279	.339	21-0-2	.143	-0	103	-7	0	-0.7
Total	12	127	84	.602	333	261	101-17	10	1914.1	1907	799	199	17	504	956	3.43	116	.261	.310	620-1-63	.110	-27	103	129	0	9.0
Roe, Clay	James Clay "Shad"; B1.7.1904 Greenbrier TN; D4.4.1956 Cleveland MS; BL/TL/6´1˝/180; d10.3																									
1923	Was A	0	1	.000	1	1	0	0	1.2	0	4	0	0	6	2	0.00	ø	.000	.500	0	ø	0	176	-1	—	-0.2
Roebuck, Ed	Edward Jack; B7.3.1931 East Millsboro PA; BR/TR/6´2˝/(180–197); d4.18																									
1955	†Bro N	5	6	.455	47	0	0	12	84	96	51	14	3	24-5	33	4.71	86	.288	.341	18	.111	-1	—	-6	0	-1.0
1956	†Bro N	5	4	.556	43	0	0	1	89.1	83	49	15	2	29-2	60	3.93	101	.251	.314	18-0-1	.333	2	—	-2	0	0.0
1957	Bro N	8	2	.800	44	1	0	8	96.1	70	37	9	2	46-6	73	2.71	154	.205	.303	21-2-0	.238	2	0	**13**	0	1.9
1958	LA N	0	1	.000	32	0	0	5	44	45	22	9	2	15-3	26	3.48	118	.271	.335	4	.500	1	—	2	0	0.2
1960	LA N	8	3	.727	58	0	0	8	116.2	109	42	13	0	38-11	77	2.78	143	.256	.315	24-0-4	.167	-0	—	14	0	1.6
1961	LA N	2	0	1.000	5	0	0	0	9	12	5	1	0	2-0	9	5.00	87	.324	.359	2	.000	-0	—	0	144	-0.1
1962	LA N	10	2	.833	64	0	0	9	119.1	102	60	11	6	54-6	72	3.09	117	.232	.321	28	.214	1	—	2	0	0.3
1963	LA N	2	4	.333	29	0	0	0	40.1	54	25	4	2	21-5	26	4.24	71	.321	.399	4	.250	0	—	-7	0	-1.0
	Was A	2	1	.667	26	0	0	4	57.1	63	27	5	2	29-2	25	3.30	113	.284	.369	11-0-1	.182	0	—	1	0	0.1
1964	Was A	0	0	ø	2	0	0	0	1	0	1	0	0	2-0	0	9.00	41	.000	.333	0	ø	0	—	-1	0	0.0
	Phi N	5	3	.625	60	0	0	12	77.1	55	21	7	4	25-6	42	2.21	157	.196	.270	6-0-1	.000	-1	—	11	0	1.5
1965	Phi N	5	3	.625	44	0	0	3	50.1	55	27	2	5	15-5	29	3.40	102	.288	.349	1-0-1	.000	-0	—	-2	0	-0.4
1966	Phi N	0	2	.000	6	0	0	0	6	9	7	0	0	2-0	5	6.00	60	.333	.367	0	ø	0	—	-3	0	-0.6
Total	11	52	31	.627	460	1	0	62	791	753	374	90	28	302-51	477	3.35	114	.254	.326	137-2-8	.204	3	0	22	144	2.5
Roesler, Mike	Michael Joseph; B9.12.1963 Fort Wayne IN; BR/TR/6´5˝/(195–205); [CinN85 17/422]; d8.9; Col Ball St.																									
1989	Cin N	0	1	.000	17	0	0	0-0	25	22	11	4	0	9-1	14	3.96	91	.239	.307	0	ø	0	—	0	0	-0.1
1990	Pit N	1	0	1.000	5	0	0	0-0	6	5	2	1	0	2-0	4	3.00	122	.217	.280	1	.000	-0	—	1	0	0.1
Total	2	1	1	.500	22	0	0	0-0	31	27	13	5	0	11-1	18	3.77	96	.235	.302	1	.000	-0	—	1	0	0.0
Roettger, Oscar	Oscar Frederick Louis "Okkie"; B2.19.1900 St.Louis MO; D7.4.1986 St.Louis MO; BR/TR/6´0˝/170; d7.7; b–Wally; ▲																									
1923	NY A	0	0	ø	5	0	0	1	11.2	16	15	3	1	12	7	8.49	46	.340	.483	2	.000	-0	—	-7	—	-0.4
1924	NY A	0	0	ø	1	0	0	0	0	1	0	0	0	2	0	(0)	ø	1.000	1.000	0	ø	0	—	0	—	0.0
Total	2	0	0	ø	6	0	0	1	11.2	17	15	3	1	14	7	8.49	46	.354	.508	2	.000	-0	—	-7	—	-0.4
Rogalski, Joe	Joseph Anthony; B7.16.1915 Ashland WI; D11.20.1951 Ashland WI; BR/TR/6´2˝/187; d9.14																									
1938	Det A	0	0	ø	2	0	0	0	7	12	4	0	0	0	2	2.57	194	.400	.400	2	.000	-0	—	1	—	0.0
Rogers, Brian	Brian Alan; B7.17.1982 Dallas TX; BR/TR/6´4˝/190; [DetA03 11/310]; d9.1; Col Georgia Southern																									
2006	Pit N	0	0	ø	10	0	0	0-0	8.2	11	8	2	1	2-0	7	8.31	55	.324	.378	0	ø	0	—	-3	0	-0.2
Rogers, Kevin	Charles Kevin; B8.20.1968 Cleveland MS; BB/TL/6´2˝/(190–198); [SFN88 9/230]; d9.4; Col Mississippi Delta JC; [DL 1995 SF N 160]																									
1992	SF N	0	2	.000	6	6	0	0-0	34	37	17	4	1	13-1	26	4.24	79	.280	.349	9-0-3	.222	0	86	-3	0	-0.2
1993	SF N	2	2	.500	64	0	0	0-2	80.2	71	28	3	4	28-5	62	2.68	147	.236	.308	3	.000	-0	—	11	0	0.5
1994	SF N	0	0	ø	9	0	0	0-1	10.1	10	4	1	0	6-0	7	3.48	117	.250	.348	0	ø	0	—	1	102	0.0
Total	3	2	4	.333	79	6	0	0-3	125	118	49	8	5	47-6	95	3.17	119	.249	.323	12-0-3	.167	-0	86	9	262	0.3
Rogers, Jimmy	James Randall; B1.3.1967 Tulsa OK; BR/TR/6´2˝/200; [TorA86 16/419]; d7.30; Col Seminole St. (OK) JC																									
1995	Tor A	2	4	.333	19	0	0	0-0	23.2	21	15	4	0	18-4	13	5.70	83	.239	.364	0	ø	0	—	-2	0	-0.3
Rogers, Kenny	Kenneth Scott; B11.10.1964 Savannah GA; BL/TL/6´1˝/(190–217); [TexA82 39/816]; d4.6																									
1989	Tex A	3	4	.429	73	0	0	2-3	73.2	60	28	2	4	42-9	63	2.93	136	.232	.344	0	ø	0	—	8	0	0.9
1990	Tex A	10	6	.625	69	3	0	15-8	97.2	93	40	6	1	42-5	74	3.13	126	.249	.323	0	ø	0	62	8	0	1.5
1991	Tex A	10	10	.500	63	9	0	5-1	109.2	121	80	14	6	61-7	73	5.42	75	.281	.375	0	ø	0	120	-20	0	-3.3
1992	Tex A	3	6	.333	**81**	0	0	6-4	78.2	80	32	7	0	26-8	70	3.09	124	.261	.318	0	ø	0	—	6	0	0.8
1993	Tex A	16	10	.615	35	33	5	0-0	208.1	210	108	18	4	71-2	140	4.10	102	.263	.325	0	ø	0	124	0	0	0.3
1994	Tex A	11	8	.579	24	24	6-2	0-0	167.1	169	93	24	3	52-1	120	4.46	108	.260	.315	0	ø	0	107	7	0	0.8
1995	Tex A★	17	7	.708	31	31	3-1	0-0	208	192	87	26	2	76-1	140	3.38	143	.243	.309	0	ø	0	99	32	0	3.4
1996	†NY A	12	8	.600	30	30	2-1	0-0	179	179	97	16	8	83-2	92	4.68	106	.261	.346	0	ø	0	106	6	0	0.7
1997	NY A	6	7	.462	31	22	1	0-0	145	161	100	18	7	62-1	78	5.65	79	.280	.354	3	.000	-0	130	-20	0	-1.3
1998	Oak A	16	8	.667	34	34	7-1	0-0	238.2	215	96	19	7	67-0	138	3.17	146	.242	.299	4	.000	-0	98	38	0	3.8
1999	Oak A	5	3	.625	19	19	3	0-0	119.1	135	66	8	9	41-0	68	4.30	110	.288	.353	3	.000	-0	112	5	0	0.5
	†NY N	5	1	.833	12	12	2-1	0-0	76	71	35	8	4	28-1	58	4.03	108	.253	.328	25-0-3	.120	-0	129	3	0	0.3
2000	Tex A	13	13	.500	34	34	2	0-0	227.1	257	126	20	11	78-2	127	4.55	112	.285	.348	4-0-1	.500	1	90	14	0	1.6
2001	Tex A	5	7	.417	20	20	0	0-0	120.2	150	88	18	8	49-2	74	6.19	77	.307	.376	2	.000	-0	106	-18	76	-1.3
2002	Tex A	13	8	.619	33	33	2-1	0-0	210.2	212	101	21	6	70-1	107	3.84	125	.261	.324	3	.667	1*	87	18	0	2.0
2003	†Min A	13	8	.619	33	31	0	0-0	195	227	108	22	11	50-5	116	4.57	98	.292	.342	4	.000	-0	107	-3	0	-0.1
2004	Tex A☆	18	9	.667	35	**35**	2-1	0-0	211.2	248	117	24	9	66-0	126	4.76	104	.292	.348	5	.000	-1	108	6	0	0.8
2005	Tex A★	14	8	.636	30	30	1-1	0-0	195.1	205	86	15	8	53-1	87	3.46	132	.271	.323	3	.333	1	106	21	0	2.5
2006	†Det A★	17	8	.680	34	33	0	0-0	204	195	97	23	9	62-2	99	3.84	117	.253	.314	7	.143	0	124	14	0	1.6
Total	18	207	139	.598	721	433	36-9	28-16	3066	3180	1585	309	117	1079-50	1850	4.19	110	.268	.333	63-0-4	.143	1	108	125	76	15.5
Rogers, Lee	Lee Otis "Buck"; B10.8.1913 Tuscaloosa AL; D11.23.1995 Little Rock AR; BR/TL/5´11˝/170; d4.27; Col Alabama																									
1938	Bos A	1	1	.500	14	2	0	0	27.2	32	24	4	0	18	7	6.51	76	.302	.403	6	.000	-0	80	-5	—	-0.3
	Bro N	0	2	.000	12	2	0	0	23.2	23	16	0	1	10	11	5.70	68	.256	.337	1	.000	0*	54	-4	—	-0.2
Total	1	1	3	.250	26	4	0	0	51.1	55	40	4	1	28	18	6.14	73	.281	.373	7	.000	0	68	-9	—	-0.5
Rogers, Buck	Orlin Woodrow "Lefty"; B11.5.1912 Spring Garden VA; D2.20.1999 Winston–Salem NC; BR/TL/5´8.5˝/164; d9.15; Col Virginia																									
1935	Was A	0	1	.000	2	1	0	0	10	16	15	0	0	6	7	7.20	60	.340	.415	3	.000	-1	80	-6	—	-0.5
Rogers, Steve	Stephen Douglas; B10.26.1949 Jefferson City MO; BR/TR/6´1˝/(175–190); [MonN71 D1/4]; d7.18; Col Tulsa																									
1973	Mon N	10	5	.667	17	17	7-3	0-0	134	93	28	5	1	49-3	64	1.54	247	.199	.274	41-0-5	.098	-1	68	32	0	3.8
1974	Mon N☆	15	22	.405	38	38	11-1	0-0	253.2	255	139	19	5	80-7	154	4.47	86	.265	.322	79-0-7	.139	-1	75	-14	0	-1.9
1975	Mon N	11	12	.478	35	35	12-3	0-0	251.2	248	104	13	4	88-8	137	3.29	118	.260	.324	77-0-6	.169	1	87	15	0	1.4
1976	Mon N	7	17	.292	33	32	8-4	1-0	230	212	93	10	4	69-7	150	3.21	117	.250	.307	74-0-6	.149	-2*	67	14	33	1.4
1977	Mon N	17	16	.515	40	40	17-4	0-0	301.2	272	122	16	5	81-3	206	3.10	124	.242	.294	96-0-12	.104	-5	90	23	0	2.0
1978	Mon N★	13	10	.565	30	29	11-1	1-0	219	186	64	12	2	64-2	126	2.47	145	.235	.293	71-0-8	.113	-2	77	28	0	2.8
1979	Mon N★	13	12	.520	37	37	13-**5**	0-0	248.2	232	97	14	4	78-9	143	3.00	124	.251	.311	77-0-2	.156	1*	98	19	0	2.0
1980	Mon N	16	11	.593	37	37	**14**-4	0-0	281	247	101	16	3	85-7	147	2.98	122	.238	.296	81-0-15	.160	1*	106	22	0	2.1
1981	†Mon N	12	8	.600	22	22	7-3	0-0	160.2	149	64	7	2	41-4	87	3.42	104	.248	.296	55-0-4	.145	-1*	100	4	0	0.3
1982	Mon N★	19	8	.704	35	35	14-4	0-0	277	245	84	12	6	65-7	179	**2.40**	**154**	.237	.285	85-0-12	.129	0	102	**39**	0	3.8
1983	Mon N☆	17	12	.586	36	36	13-**5**	0-0	273	258	108	14	5	78-12	146	3.23	112	.252	.306	82-0-20	.146	-1	96	12	0	1.0
1984	Mon N	6	15	.286	31	28	1	0-0	169.1	171	93	12	2	78-5	64	4.31	80	.267	.346	49-0-4	.143	0	80	-18	17	-2.0
1985	Mon N	2	4	.333	8	7	1	0-0	38	51	25	1	0	20-1	18	5.68	61	.329	.401	14	.143	0	88	-9	0	-1.2
Total	13	158	152	.510	399	393	129-37	2-0	2837.2	2619	1122	151	43	876-75	1621	3.17	117	.248	.306	881-0-101	.138	-9	88	167	50	15.5
Rogers, Tom	Thomas Andrew "Shotgun"; B2.12.1892 Sparta TN; D3.7.1936 Nashville TN; BR/TR/6´0.5˝/180; d4.14																									
1917	StL A	3	6	.333	24	8	3	0	108.2	112	58	2	3	44	27	3.89	67	.277	.352	29-0-2	.172	-1	76	-13	—	-1.2
1918	StL A	8	10	.444	29	16	11	2	154	148	66	3	3	49	29	3.27	84	.267	.330	53-0-3	.245	2	95	-6	—	-0.5
1919	StL A	0	1	.000	2	0	0	0	1	7	6	0	0	0	1	27.00	12	.700	.700	0	ø	0	—	-3	—	-0.6
	Phi A	4	12	.250	23	18	7-1	0	140	152	82	9	3	60	37	4.31	80	.292	.369	49-1-1	.224	-0	83	-12	—	-1.0
	Year	4	13	.235	25	18	7-1	0	141	159	88	9	3	60	38	4.47	77	.300	.374	49-1-1	.224	-0	83	-15	—	-1.6
1921	†NY A	0	1	.000	5	0	0	1	11	12	9	1	1	9	0	7.36	58	.300	.440	3	.333	0*	—	-3	—	-0.2
Total	4	15	30	.333	83	42	21-1	3	414.2	431	221	15	10	162	94	3.95	75	.282	.354	134-1-6	.224	1	86	-37	—	-3.5

ROGGE, CLINT Francis Clinton; B7.19.1889 Memphis MI; D1.6.1969 Mt.Clemens MI; BL/TR/5´10˝/185; d4.11; Col Adrian

YEAR	TM LG	W	L	PCT	G	GS	CG-SHO	SV-BS	IP	H	R	HR	HB	BB-IB	SO	ERA	AERA	OAV	OOB	AB-HR-SH	AVG	PB	SUP	APR	DL	PW
1915	Pit F	17	11	.607	37	31	17-5	0	254.1	240	96	6	9	93	93	2.55	106	.257	.330	81-0-8	.173	-1	94	1	—	0.1
1921	Cin N	1	2	.333	6	2	0	0	35.1	43	19	2	0	9	12	4.08	88	.307	.349	10	.100	0	103	-2	—	-0.1
Total	2	18	13	.581	43	33	17-5	0	289.2	283	115	8	9	102	105	2.73	103	.264	.332	91-0-8	.165	-0	94	-1	—	0.0

ROGGENBURK, GARRY Garry Earl; B4.16.1940 Cleveland OH; BR/TL/6´6˝/(195–200); d4.20; Col Dayton; [DL 1964 Min A 161]

YEAR	TM LG	W	L	PCT	G	GS	CG-SHO	SV-BS	IP	H	R	HR	HB	BB-IB	SO	ERA	AERA	OAV	OOB	AB-HR-SH	AVG	PB	SUP	APR	DL	PW
1963	Min A	2	4	.333	36	2	0	4	50	47	26	3	5	22-3	24	2.16	169	.253	.344	7	.143	0	98	3	0	0.4
1965	Min A	1	0	1.000	12	0	0	2	21	21	10	1	0	12-2	6	3.43	104	.266	.359	3-0-2	.000	-0	—	0	0	0.0
1966	Min A	1	2	.333	12	0	0	1	12.1	14	8	4	0	10-0	3	5.84	62	.292	.414	0	ø	0	—	-2	0	-0.5
	Bos A	0	0	ø	1	0	0	0	0.1	1	0	0	0	1-0	0	0.00	ø	.500	.667	0	ø	0	—	0	0	0.0
	Year	1	2	.333	13	0	0	1	12.2	15	8	4	0	11-0	3	5.68	63	.300	.426	0	ø	0	—	-2	0	-0.5
1968	Bos A	0	0	ø	4	0	0	0	8.1	9	2	0	0	3-0	4	2.16	146	.257	.316	0	ø	0	—	1	65	0.0
1969	Bos A	0	1	.000	7	0	0	0-0	9.2	13	9	1	1	5-0	8	8.38	46	.342	.432	2	.000	-0	—	-4	0	-0.4
	Sea A	2	2	.500	7	4	1	0-1	24.1	27	12	6	1	11-0	11	4.44	82	.276	.351	8-0-1	.125	-0	85	-1	0	-0.3
	Year	2	3	.400	14	4	1	0-1	34	40	21	7	2	16-0	19	5.56	66	.294	.374	10-0-1	.100	-1	84	-6	0	-0.7
Total	5	6	9	.400	79	6	1	7-1	126	132	67	15	7	64-5	56	3.64	99	.272	.362	20-0-3	.100	-1	90	-3	226	-0.8

ROGOVIN, SAUL Saul Walter; B10.10.1923 Brooklyn NY; D1.23.1995 New York NY; BR/TR/6´2˝/205; d4.28

YEAR	TM LG	W	L	PCT	G	GS	CG-SHO	SV-BS	IP	H	R	HR	HB	BB-IB	SO	ERA	AERA	OAV	OOB	AB-HR-SH	AVG	PB	SUP	APR	DL	PW
1949	Det A	0	1	.000	5	0	0	0	5.2	13	9	1	0	7	2	14.29	29	.464	.571	0	ø	0	—	-6	0	-0.8
1950	Det A	2	1	.667	11	5	1	0	40	39	21	5	2	26	11	4.50	104	.258	.374	16-1-0	.188	0	119	1	0	0.1
1951	Det A	1	1	.500	5	4	0	0	24	23	15	4	0	7	5	5.25	80	.247	.300	7	.286	1	144	-3	0	-0.1
	Chi A	11	7	.611	22	22	17-3	0	192.2	166	64	11	1	67	77	2.48	163	.234	.301	74	.203	-0*	90	33	0	2.9
	Year	12	8	.600	27	26	17-3	0	216.2	189	79	15	1	74	82	**2.78**	**146**	.235	.301	81	.210	1	99	**30**	0	2.8
1952	Chi A	14	9	.609	33	30	12-3	1	231.2	224	104	14	3	79	121	3.85	95	.255	.318	84-1-4	.202	3	106	-2	0	0.0
1953	Chi A	7	12	.368	22	19	4-1	1	131	151	82	17	2	48	62	5.22	77	.289	.351	37-0-2	.135	-0	94	-16	36	-2.1
1955	Bal A	1	8	.111	14	12	1	0	71	79	42	5	2	27-1	35	4.56	84	.288	.355	22	.091	-1*	52	-6	0	-0.9
	Phi N	5	3	.625	12	11	5-2	0	73	60	25	3	0	17-2	27	3.08	129	.230	.274	24-1-2	.250	2*	94	9	0	1.1
1956	Phi N	7	6	.538	22	18	3	0	106.2	122	65	22	0	27-3	48	4.98	75	.282	.324	36-0-3	.111	-2	128	-14	0	-1.8
1957	Phi N	0	0	ø	4	0	0	0	8	11	8	1	0	3-1	0	9.00	42	.333	.378	0	ø	0	—	-4	0	-0.2
Total	8	48	48	.500	150	121	43-9	2	883.2	888	435	83	10	308-7	388	4.06	96	.262	.325	300-3-11	.180	2	100	-8	36	-1.8

ROHR, LES Leslie Norvin; B3.5.1946 Lowestoft, England; BL/TL/6´5˝/(205–210); [NYN65 1/2]; d9.19

YEAR	TM LG	W	L	PCT	G	GS	CG-SHO	SV-BS	IP	H	R	HR	HB	BB-IB	SO	ERA	AERA	OAV	OOB	AB-HR-SH	AVG	PB	SUP	APR	DL	PW
1967	NY N	2	1	.667	3	3	0	0	17	13	7	1	0	9-0	15	2.12	160	.224	.319	6	.000	-1	112	1	0	0.1
1968	NY N	0	2	.000	2	1	0	0	6	9	4	0	0	7-3	5	4.50	67	.333	.471	0	ø	0	57	-1	0	-0.2
1969	NY N	0	0	ø	1	0	0	0-0	1.1	5	4	0	0	1-0	0	20.25	18	.625	.667	0	ø	0	—	-3	0	-0.1
Total	3	2	3	.400	6	4	0	0-0	24.1	27	15	1	0	17-3	20	3.70	90	.290	.393	6	.000	-0	99	-3	0	-0.2

ROHR, BILLY William Joseph; B7.1.1945 San Diego CA; BL/TL/6´3˝/170; d4.14

YEAR	TM LG	W	L	PCT	G	GS	CG-SHO	SV-BS	IP	H	R	HR	HB	BB-IB	SO	ERA	AERA	OAV	OOB	AB-HR-SH	AVG	PB	SUP	APR	DL	PW
1967	Bos A	2	3	.400	10	8	2-1	0	42.1	43	27	4	2	22-2	16	5.10	68	.256	.349	10-0-3	.000	-1	103	-7	0	-0.9
1968	Cle A	1	0	1.000	17	0	0	1	18.1	18	16	5	0	10-2	5	6.87	43	.265	.354	1	.000	-0	—	-8	0	-0.5
Total	2	3	3	.500	27	8	2-1	1	60.2	61	43	9	2	32-4	21	5.64	59	.258	.351	11-0-3	.000	-1	103	-15	0	-1.4

ROJAS, MEL Melquiades (Medrano); B12.10.1966 Haina, D.R.; BR/TR/5´11˝/(175–212); d8.1

YEAR	TM LG	W	L	PCT	G	GS	CG-SHO	SV-BS	IP	H	R	HR	HB	BB-IB	SO	ERA	AERA	OAV	OOB	AB-HR-SH	AVG	PB	SUP	APR	DL	PW
1990	Mon N	3	1	.750	23	0	0	1-1	40	34	17	5	2	24-4	26	3.60	102	.234	.351	3-0-3	.000	-0	—	1	0	0.0
1991	Mon N	3	3	.500	37	0	0	6-3	48	42	21	4	1	13-1	37	3.75	97	.228	.280	4-0-1	.000	-0	—	0	0	-0.1
1992	Mon N	7	1	.875	68	0	0	10-1	100.2	71	17	2	2	34-8	70	1.43	244	.199	.271	15	.067	-1	—	**23**	0	2.2
1993	Mon N	5	8	.385	66	0	0	10-9	88.1	80	39	6	4	30-3	48	2.95	141	.242	.308	12	.083	-1	—	10	15	1.4
1994	Mon N	3	2	.600	58	0	0	16-2	84	71	35	11	4	21-0	84	3.32	127	.227	.283	10	.200	0	—	8	0	0.7
1995	Mon N	1	4	.200	59	0	0	30-9	67.2	69	32	2	7	29-4	61	4.12	104	.262	.350	6-0-2	.000	-1	—	2	0	0.2
1996	Mon N	7	4	.636	74	0	0	36-4	81	56	30	5	2	28-3	92	3.22	134	.193	.265	8	.375	1	—	11	0	2.3
1997	Chi N	0	4	.000	54	0	0	13-6	59	54	30	11	5	30-1	61	4.42	98	.244	.346	1	.000	-0	—	0	0	-0.1
	NY N	0	2	.000	23	0	0	2-1	26.1	24	17	4	2	6-1	32	5.13	78	.235	.288	0	ø	0	—	-4	0	-0.3
	Year	0	6	.000	77	0	0	15-7	85.1	78	47	15	7	36-2	93	4.64	91	.241	.329	1	.000	-0	—	-3	0	-0.4
1998	NY N	5	2	.714	50	0	0	2-4	58	68	39	9	3	30-5	41	6.05	68	.305	.391	0	ø	0	—	-12	0	-1.3
1999	LA N	0	0	ø	5	0	0	0-0	5	5	7	3	0	3-1	3	12.60	35	.250	.348	0	ø	0	—	-4	0	-0.2
	Det A	0	0	ø	5	0	0	0-0	6.1	12	16	3	3	4-0	6	22.74	22	.387	.487	0	ø	0	—	-12	0	-0.5
	Mon N	0	0	ø	3	0	0	0-0	2.2	5	5	0	2	2-0	1	16.88	26	.417	.529	0	ø	0	—	-3	0	-0.2
Total	10	34	31	.523	525	0	0	126-40	667	591	305	65	37	254-31	562	3.82	106	.237	.315	59-0-6	.119	-2	—	20	15	4.1

ROJAS, MINNIE Minervino Alejandro (Landin); B11.26.1933 Remidios, Cuba; D3.23.2002 Los Angeles CA; BR/TR/6´1˝/(182–185); d5.30

YEAR	TM LG	W	L	PCT	G	GS	CG-SHO	SV-BS	IP	H	R	HR	HB	BB-IB	SO	ERA	AERA	OAV	OOB	AB-HR-SH	AVG	PB	SUP	APR	DL	PW
1966	Cal A	7	4	.636	47	2	0	10	84.1	83	28	9	1	15-2	37	2.88	117	.262	.296	14-0-1	.071	-0	92	6	0	0.8
1967	Cal A	12	9	.571	72	0	0	**27**	121.2	106	45	7	3	38-17	83	2.52	125	.232	.292	17-0-3	.059	-1	—	6	0	1.2
1968	Cal A	4	3	.571	38	0	0	6	55	55	29	11	0	15-4	33	4.25	69	.252	.299	10	.100	-0	—	-8	56	-1.4
Total	3	23	16	.590	157	2	0	43	261	244	102	27	4	68-23	153	3.00	105	.246	.295	41-0-4	.073	-2	92	4	56	0.6

ROLAND, JIM James Ivan; B12.14.1942 Franklin NC; BR/TL/6´3˝/(185–200); d9.20

YEAR	TM LG	W	L	PCT	G	GS	CG-SHO	SV-BS	IP	H	R	HR	HB	BB-IB	SO	ERA	AERA	OAV	OOB	AB-HR-SH	AVG	PB	SUP	APR	DL	PW
1962	Min A	0	0	ø	1	0	0	0	2	1	0	0	0	0-0	1	0.00	ø	.143	.143	0	ø	0	—	1	0	0.0
1963	Min A	4	1	.800	10	7	2-1	0	49	32	17	4	0	27-1	34	2.57	142	.185	.292	15-0-3	.000	-2	129	5	68	0.4
1964	Min A	2	6	.250	30	13	1	3	94.1	76	48	12	4	55-2	63	4.10	87	.218	.329	27	.148	-1	88	-5	0	-0.6
1966	Min A	0	0	ø	1	0	0	0	2	0	0	0	0	0-0	1	0.00	ø	.000	.000	0	ø	0	—	1	0	0.0
1967	Min A	0	1	.000	25	0	0	2	35.2	33	12	3	0	17-5	16	3.03	114	.244	.325	3	.000	-0	—	2	0	0.1
1968	Min A	4	1	.800	28	4	1	0	61.2	55	33	3	2	24-2	36	3.50	88	.238	.314	8-0-2	.000	-1*	113	-5	0	-0.4
1969	Oak A	5	1	.833	39	3	2	1-0	86.1	59	24	2	6	46-6	48	2.19	157	.197	.314	21	.095	-1	154	12	0	0.8
1970	Oak A	3	3	.500	28	2	0	2-0	43.1	28	14	2	0	23-1	26	2.70	131	.181	.285	6	.000	-0	114	4	27	0.6
1971	Oak A	1	3	.250	31	0	0	1-0	45.1	34	18	4	5	19-3	30	3.18	105	.214	.310	3-0-1	.000	-0	—	1	0	0.0
1972	Oak A	0	0	ø	2	0	0	0-0	2.1	5	2	0	0	0-0	0	3.86	74	.455	.455	0	ø	0	—	-1	0	0.0
	NY A	0	1	.000	16	0	0	0-0	25	27	14	3	1	16-1	13	5.04	59	.287	.396	1	.000	-0	—	-5	0	-0.3
	Tex A	0	0	ø	5	0	0	0-0	3.1	7	3	1	1	2-1	4	8.10	38	.412	.500	0	ø	0	—	-2	0	-0.1
	Year	0	1	.000	23	0	0	0-0	30.2	39	19	4	2	18-2	17	5.28	57	.320	.415	1	.000	-0	—	-7	0	-0.4
Total	10	19	17	.528	216	29	6-1	9-0	450.1	357	185	34	19	229-22	272	3.22	106	.218	.319	84-0-6	.071	-5	112	8	95	0.5

ROMAN, JOSE Jose Rafael (Sarita); B5.21.1963 Santo Domingo, D.R.; BR/TR/6´0˝/175; d9.5

YEAR	TM LG	W	L	PCT	G	GS	CG-SHO	SV-BS	IP	H	R	HR	HB	BB-IB	SO	ERA	AERA	OAV	OOB	AB-HR-SH	AVG	PB	SUP	APR	DL	PW
1984	Cle A	0	2	.000	3	2	0	0-0	6	9	12	1	0	11-0	3	18.00	23	.391	.541	0	ø	0	77	-8	0	-1.3
1985	Cle A	0	4	.000	5	3	0	0-0	16.1	13	17	3	0	14-0	12	6.61	63	.200	.342	0	ø	0	29	-6	0	-1.1
1986	Cle A	1	2	.333	6	5	0	0-0	22	23	20	3	1	17-0	9	6.55	64	.280	.394	0	ø	0	91	-7	0	-0.8
Total	3	1	8	.111	14	10	0	0-0	44.1	45	49	7	1	42-0	24	8.12	51	.265	.400	0	ø	0	70	-21	0	-3.2

ROMANICK, RON Ronald James; B11.6.1960 Burley ID; BR/TR/6´4˝/(195–203); [AnaA81*S1/4]; d4.5; Col Arizona St.

YEAR	TM LG	W	L	PCT	G	GS	CG-SHO	SV-BS	IP	H	R	HR	HB	BB-IB	SO	ERA	AERA	OAV	OOB	AB-HR-SH	AVG	PB	SUP	APR	DL	PW
1984	Cal A	12	12	.500	33	33	8-2	0-0	229.2	240	107	23	4	61-3	87	3.76	106	.270	.316	0	ø	0	90	5	0	0.3
1985	Cal A	14	9	.609	31	31	6-1	0-0	195	210	101	29	4	62-1	64	4.11	100	.280	.334	0	ø	0	106	-1	0	-0.2
1986	Cal A	5	8	.385	18	18	1-1	0-0	106.1	124	68	13	0	44-0	38	5.50	75	.297	.360	0	ø	0	106	-15	0	-1.6
Total	3	31	29	.517	82	82	15-4	0-0	531	574	276	65	8	167-4	189	4.24	96	.279	.332	0	ø	0	100	-11	0	-1.5

ROMANO, JIM James King; B4.6.1927 Brooklyn NY; D9.12.1990 New York NY; BR/TR/6´4˝/190; d9.21

YEAR	TM LG	W	L	PCT	G	GS	CG-SHO	SV-BS	IP	H	R	HR	HB	BB-IB	SO	ERA	AERA	OAV	OOB	AB-HR-SH	AVG	PB	SUP	APR	DL	PW
1950	Bro N	0	0	ø	3	1	0	0	6.1	8	6	0	0	2	8	5.68	72	.296	.345	1	.000	-0	216	-2	0	-0.1

ROMANO, MIKE Michael Desport; B3.3.1972 New Orleans LA; BR/TR/6´2˝/195; [TorA93 3/85]; d9.5; Col Tulane

YEAR	TM LG	W	L	PCT	G	GS	CG-SHO	SV-BS	IP	H	R	HR	HB	BB-IB	SO	ERA	AERA	OAV	OOB	AB-HR-SH	AVG	PB	SUP	APR	DL	PW
1999	Tor A	0	0	ø	3	0	0	0-0	5.1	8	8	1	0	5-0	3	11.81	42	.364	.464	0	ø	0	—	-4	0	-0.2

ROMBERGER, DUTCH Allen Isaiah; B5.26.1927 Klingerstown PA; D5.26.1983 Weikert PA; BR/TR/6´0˝/185; d5.31

YEAR	TM LG	W	L	PCT	G	GS	CG-SHO	SV-BS	IP	H	R	HR	HB	BB-IB	SO	ERA	AERA	OAV	OOB	AB-HR-SH	AVG	PB	SUP	APR	DL	PW
1954	Phi A	1	1	.500	10	0	0	0	15.2	28	20	3	0	12	6	11.49	34	.406	.488	2	.000	0	—	-12	0	-1.3

ROMERO, DAVIS Davis Javier (Rodriguez); B3.30.1983 Aguadulce, Pan; BL/TL/5´10˝/170; d8.18

YEAR	TM LG	W	L	PCT	G	GS	CG-SHO	SV-BS	IP	H	R	HR	HB	BB-IB	SO	ERA	AERA	OAV	OOB	AB-HR-SH	AVG	PB	SUP	APR	DL	PW
2006	Tor A	1	0	1.000	7	0	0	0-0	16.1	19	7	1	1	6-1	10	3.86	123	.297	.366	0	ø	0	—	2	0	0.1

ROMERO, J.C. Juan Carlos; B6.4.1976 Rio Piedras, PR; BB/TL/5´11˝/(193–205); [MinA97 21/633]; d9.15; Col Mobile

YEAR	TM LG	W	L	PCT	G	GS	CG-SHO	SV-BS	IP	H	R	HR	HB	BB-IB	SO	ERA	AERA	OAV	OOB	AB-HR-SH	AVG	PB	SUP	APR	DL	PW
1999	Min A	0	0	ø	5	0	0	0-0	9.2	13	4	0	0	0-0	4	3.72	139	.333	.333	0	ø	0	—	2	0	0.1
2000	Min A	2	7	.222	12	11	0	0-0	57.2	72	51	8	1	30-0	50	7.02	75	.312	.390	0	ø	0	84	-12	36	-1.4
2001	Min A	1	4	.200	14	11	0	0-0	65	71	48	10	1	24-1	39	6.23	75	.277	.339	2	.500	1	97	-11	0	-0.6
2002	†Min A	9	2	.818	81	0	0	1-4	81	62	17	3	4	36-4	76	1.89	236	.213	.308	0	ø	0	—	**24**	0	2.9
2003	†Min A	2	0	1.000	73	0	0	0-4	63	66	37	7	6	42-7	50	5.00	90	.272	.392	1	.000	-0	—	-4	0	-0.1
2004	†Min A	7	4	.636	74	0	0	1-7	74.1	61	32	4	5	38-6	69	3.51	132	.224	.329	0	ø	0	—	9	0	1.2
2005	Min A	4	3	.571	68	0	0	0-1	57	50	26	6	6	39-8	48	3.47	126	.235	.367	0	ø	0	—	5	0	0.6
2006	LA A	1	2	.333	65	0	0	0-1	48.1	57	40	3	1	28-2	31	6.70	66	.298	.382	0	ø	0	—	-12	0	-0.6
Total	8	26	22	.542	392	22	0	2-17	456	452	255	41	24	237-28	367	4.60	101	.260	.355	3	.333	1	97	1	36	2.1

ROMERO, RAMON Ramon (De Los Santos); B1.8.1959 San Pedro de Macoris, D.R.; BL/TL/6´4˝/170; d9.18

YEAR	TM LG	W	L	PCT	G	GS	CG-SHO	SV-BS	IP	H	R	HR	HB	BB-IB	SO	ERA	AERA	OAV	OOB	AB-HR-SH	AVG	PB	SUP	APR	DL	PW
1984	Cle A	0	0	ø	1	0	0	0-0	3	0	0	0	1	0-0	3	0.00	ø	.000	.111	0	ø	0	—	1	0	0.1
1985	Cle A	2	3	.400	19	10	0	0-0	64.1	69	48	13	5	38-0	38	6.58	63	.276	.381	0	ø	0	85	-15	0	-1.1
Total	2	2	3	.400	20	10	0	0-0	67.1	69	48	13	6	38-0	41	6.28	66	.267	.373	0	ø	0	85	-14	0	-1.0

ROMMEL, EDDIE Edwin Americus; B9.13.1897 Baltimore MD; D8.26.1970 Baltimore MD; BR/TR/6´2˝/197; d4.19; C2/U22

YEAR	TM LG	W	L	PCT	G	GS	CG-SHO	SV-BS	IP	H	R	HR	HB	BB-IB	SO	ERA	AERA	OAV	OOB	AB-HR-SH	AVG	PB	SUP	APR	DL	PW
1920	Phi A	7	7	.500	33	12	8-2	1	173.2	165	68	5	4	43	43	2.85	141	.259	.309	51-0-8	.216	-0*	74	24	—	2.0
1921	Phi A	16	23	.410	46	32	20	3	285.1	312	155	21	1	87	71	3.94	113	.284	.337	94-0-10	.191	-2	77	16	—	1.8
1922	Phi A	**27**	13	.675	**51**	33	22-3	2	294	294	128	21	5	63	54	3.28	130	.267	.309	94-0-6	.181	-3	91	30	—	3.6
1923	Phi A	18	19	.486	**56**	31	19-3	5	297.2	306	141	14	3	108	76	3.27	126	.271	.336	101-0-4	.238	1	75	24	—	3.2
1924	Phi A	18	15	.545	43	34	21-3	1	278	302	139	8	3	94	72	3.95	108	.284	.344	95-0-6	.158	-6*	95	13	—	1.0
1925	Phi A	**21**	10	.677	52	28	14-1	3	261	285	127	10	7	95	67	3.69	126	.281	.346	81-1-11	.185	-1	99	27	—	2.9
1926	Phi A	11	11	.500	37	26	12-3	0	219	225	91	10	2	54	52	3.08	135	.268	.314	61-0-10	.098	-4	82	27	—	2.2
1927	Phi A	11	3	.786	30	17	8-2	1	146.2	166	83	6	3	48	33	4.36	98	.286	.343	51-0-4	.157	-2	125	-1	—	-0.2
1928	Phi A	13	5	.722	43	11	6	4	173.2	177	70	11	2	26	37	3.06	131	.266	.295	47-0-4	.255	3	100	19	—	2.2
1929	†Phi A	12	2	.857	32	6	4	4	113.2	135	52	10	1	34	25	2.85	148	.294	.344	39-0-4	.205	-0	156	14	—	1.5
1930	Phi A	9	4	.692	35	9	5	3	130.1	142	66	11	1	27	35	4.28	109	.277	.315	38-0-3	.263	3	102	8	—	1.0
1931	†Phi A	7	5	.583	25	10	8-1	0	118	136	50	5	1	27	18	2.97	151	.291	.331	54	.259	2*	113	18	—	1.8
1932	Phi A	1	2	.333	17	0	0	2	65.1	84	43	6	0	18	16	5.51	82	.315	.358	20	.300	2	—	-7	—	0.0
Total	13	171	119	.590	500	249	147-18	29	2556.1	2729	1213	138	33	724	599	3.54	122	.277	.329	826-1-70	.199	-7	92	212	—	23.0

ROMO, ENRIQUE Enrique (Navarro); B7.15.1947 Santa Rosalia, Baja California, Mexico; BR/TR/5´11˝/185; d4.7; b–Vicente

YEAR	TM LG	W	L	PCT	G	GS	CG-SHO	SV-BS	IP	H	R	HR	HB	BB-IB	SO	ERA	AERA	OAV	OOB	AB-HR-SH	AVG	PB	SUP	APR	DL	PW
1977	Sea A	8	10	.444	58	3	0	16-7	114.1	93	40	8	5	39-7	105	2.83	146	.227	.300	0	ø	0	94	16	21	2.9
1978	Sea A	11	7	.611	56	0	0	10-12	107.1	88	46	12	5	39-6	62	3.69	104	.227	.302	0	ø	0	—	3	0	0.5
1979	†Pit N	10	5	.667	84	0	0	5-8	129.1	122	50	11	3	43-9	106	2.99	131	.253	.317	12-0-4	.167	-0	—	12	0	1.5
1980	Pit N	5	5	.500	74	0	0	11-7	123.2	117	53	10	1	28-4	82	3.27	113	.252	.293	11-1-2	.455	3*	—	4	0	0.8
1981	Pit N	1	3	.250	33	0	0	9-1	41.2	47	27	5	0	18-7	23	4.54	80	.288	.353	4-0-2	.000	-0	—	-5	21	-0.8
1982	Pit N	9	3	.750	45	0	0	1-0	86.2	81	43	11	1	36-6	58	4.36	86	.245	.321	10-0-1	.300	1*	—	-4	0	-0.4
Total	6	44	33	.571	350	3	0	52-35	603	548	259	57	15	203-39	436	3.45	112	.245	.310	37-1-9	.270	4	94	26	42	4.5

ROMO, VICENTE Vicente (Navarro) "Huevo"; B4.12.1943 Santa Rosalia, Baja California, Mexico; BR/TR/6´1˝/(180–195); d4.11; b–Enrique

YEAR	TM LG	W	L	PCT	G	GS	CG-SHO	SV-BS	IP	H	R	HR	HB	BB-IB	SO	ERA	AERA	OAV	OOB	AB-HR-SH	AVG	PB	SUP	APR	DL	PW
1968	LA N	0	0	ø	1	0	0	0	1	1	1	0	0	0-0	0	0.00	ø	.250	.200	0	ø	0	—	0	0	0.0
	Cle A	5	3	.625	40	1	0	12	83.1	43	15	5	2	32-6	54	1.62	183	.154	.241	14-0-4	.143	-0	88	14	0	1.9
1969	Cle A	1	1	.500	3	0	0	0-0	8	7	3	0	0	3-1	7	2.25	169	.233	.294	2	.500	0	—	1	0	0.3
	Bos A	7	9	.438	52	11	4-1	11-2	127.1	116	51	14	1	50-6	89	3.18	120	.247	.319	31-0-3	.129	-1	90	9	0	1.2
	Year	8	10	.444	55	11	4-1	11-2	135.1	123	54	14	1	53-7	96	3.13	122	.246	.318	33-0-3	.152	-0	91	10	0	1.5
1970	Bos A	7	3	.700	48	10	0	6-1	108	115	51	14	0	43-6	71	4.08	98	.273	.338	27-1-2	.148	0	121	1	0	0.2
1971	Chi A	1	7	.125	45	2	0	5-0	72	52	27	5	0	37-6	48	3.38	106	.202	.300	11-0-1	.364	1	63	4	0	0.7
1972	Chi A	3	0	1.000	28	0	0	1-3	51.2	47	19	5	1	18-2	46	3.31	94	.246	.311	9	.000	-1	—	0	21	-0.1
1973	SD N	2	3	.400	49	1	0	7-3	87.2	85	43	11	0	46-8	51	3.70	95	.260	.347	16-0-2	.125	-0.	50	-2	0	-0.2
1974	SD N	5	5	.500	54	1	0	9-5	71	78	47	6	2	37-13	26	4.56	79	.290	.374	6-0-1	.000	-1	49	-11	0	-1.7
1982	LA N	1	2	.333	15	6	0	1-0	35.2	25	12	1	2	14-0	24	3.03	115	.195	.285	5-0-4	.200	0	102	3	35	0.2
Total	8	32	33	.492	335	32	4-1	52-14	645.2	569	269	61	8	280-48	416	3.36	106	.239	.318	121-1-17	.149	-1	103	19	56	2.5

ROMONOSKY, JOHN John; B7.7.1929 Harrisburg IL; BR/TR/6´2˝/(190–195); d9.6

YEAR	TM LG	W	L	PCT	G	GS	CG-SHO	SV-BS	IP	H	R	HR	HB	BB-IB	SO	ERA	AERA	OAV	OOB	AB-HR-SH	AVG	PB	SUP	APR	DL	PW
1953	StL N	0	0	ø	2	2	0	0	7.2	9	6	1	1	4	3	4.70	91	.281	.378	2	.000	-0	105	-1	0	-0.1
1958	Was A	2	4	.333	18	5	1	0	55.1	52	42	6	0	28-4	38	6.51	59	.243	.328	13-1-1	.308	2*	90	-16	0	-1.3
1959	Was A	1	0	1.000	12	2	0	0	38.1	36	15	4	3	19-0	22	3.29	119	.254	.352	11	.182	0*	158	3	0	0.2
Total	3	3	4	.429	32	9	1	0	101.1	97	63	11	4	51-4	63	5.15	75	.250	.341	26-1-1	.231	2	110	-14	0	-1.2

RONDON, GILBERTO Gilberto; B11.18.1953 Bronx NY; BR/TR/6´2˝/200; [BalA73*S3/59]; d4.10; f–Diomedes Olivo

YEAR	TM LG	W	L	PCT	G	GS	CG-SHO	SV-BS	IP	H	R	HR	HB	BB-IB	SO	ERA	AERA	OAV	OOB	AB-HR-SH	AVG	PB	SUP	APR	DL	PW
1976	Hou N	2	2	.500	19	7	0	0-0	53.2	70	37	6	0	39-0	21	5.70	57	.315	.416	14-0-2	.286	1	160	-15	27	-1.0
1979	Chi A	0	0	ø	4	0	0	0-0	9.2	11	5	2	0	6-0	3	3.72	114	.282	.370	0	ø	0	—	0	0	0.0
Total	2	2	2	.500	23	7	0	0-0	63.1	81	42	8	0	45-0	24	5.40	63	.310	.409	14-0-2	.286	1	160	-15	27	-1.0

RONEY, MATT Matthew Stephen; B1.10.1980 Tulsa OK; BR/TR/6´3˝/(230–245); [ColN98 1/28]; d4.2

YEAR	TM LG	W	L	PCT	G	GS	CG-SHO	SV-BS	IP	H	R	HR	HB	BB-IB	SO	ERA	AERA	OAV	OOB	AB-HR-SH	AVG	PB	SUP	APR	DL	PW
2003	Det A	1	9	.100	45	11	0	0-2	100.2	102	67	17	4	48-4	47	5.45	80	.262	.346	2	.500	0	77	-13	0	-1.1
2006	Oak A	0	1	.000	3	0	0	0-0	4	5	2	0	0	1-1	0	4.50	101	.333	.353	0	ø	0	—	0	0	0.0
Total	2	1	10	.091	48	11	0	0-2	104.2	107	69	17	4	49-5	47	5.42	81	.265	.346	2	.500	0	77	-13	0	-1.1

ROOKER, JIM James Phillip; B9.23.1942 Lakeview OR; BR/TL/6´0˝/(190–195); d6.30

YEAR	TM LG	W	L	PCT	G	GS	CG-SHO	SV-BS	IP	H	R	HR	HB	BB-IB	SO	ERA	AERA	OAV	OOB	AB-HR-SH	AVG	PB	SUP	APR	DL	PW
1968	Det A	0	0	ø	2	0	0	0	4.2	4	2	0	0	1-0	4	3.86	78	.235	.278	2	.000	-0	—	0	0	0.0
1969	KC A	4	16	.200	28	22	8-1	0-0	158.1	136	80	13	1	73-3	108	3.75	99	.229	.312	57-4-0	.281	8*	86	-3	0	0.5
1970	KC A	10	15	.400	38	29	6-3	1-0	203.2	190	99	11	1	102-4	117	3.54	106	.252	.339	70-1-2	.200	3*	86	1	0	0.5
1971	KC A	2	7	.222	20	7	1-1	0-1	54	59	35	2	1	24-1	31	5.33	65	.284	.354	10-0-1	.000	-1*	60	-11	0	-1.8
1972	KC A	5	6	.455	18	10	4-2	0-0	72	78	37	3	1	24-0	44	4.38	70	.280	.337	20	.100	-1	93	-10	0	-1.6
1973	Pit N	10	6	.625	41	18	6-3	5-0	170.1	143	59	12	2	52-10	122	2.85	123	.229	.288	49-0-5	.245	3*	129	15	0	1.7
1974	†Pit N	15	11	.577	33	33	15-1	0-0	262.2	228	93	11	4	83-6	139	2.78	125	.238	.299	95-0-5	.305	10	104	21	0	3.3
1975	†Pit N	13	11	.542	28	28	7-1	0-0	196.2	177	80	16	3	76-13	102	2.97	121	.238	.309	63-0-9	.095	-3	106	12	0	1.1
1976	Pit N	15	8	.652	30	29	10-1	1-0	198.2	201	83	12	2	72-5	92	3.35	105	.263	.325	74-1-5	.216	3*	128	5	0	0.8
1977	Pit N	14	9	.609	30	30	7-2	0-0	204.1	196	87	24	0	64-4	89	3.08	131	.253	.308	70-0-1	.186	0	107	17	0	1.8
1978	Pit N	9	11	.450	28	28	1	0-0	163.1	160	94	13	3	81-4	76	4.24	88	.259	.346	56-0-1	.161	-0*	102	-11	0	-1.2
1979	†Pit N	4	7	.364	19	17	1	0-0	103.2	106	58	11	0	39-5	44	4.60	85	.266	.329	33-0-2	.121	-1	93	-7	64	-0.8
1980	Pit N	2	2	.500	4	4	0	0-0	18	16	7	0	0	12-0	8	3.50	105	.262	.378	7-1-1	.143	1	79	1	156	0.2
Total	13	103	109	.486	319	255	66-15	7-1	1810.1	1694	814	128	18	703-55	976	3.46	105	.249	.319	606-7-32	.201	22	103	30	220	4.5

ROOT, CHARLIE Charles Henry "Chinski"; B3.17.1899 Middletown OH; D11.5.1970 Hollister CA; BR/TR/5´10.5˝/190; d4.18; C6

YEAR	TM LG	W	L	PCT	G	GS	CG-SHO	SV-BS	IP	H	R	HR	HB	BB-IB	SO	ERA	AERA	OAV	OOB	AB-HR-SH	AVG	PB	SUP	APR	DL	PW
1923	StL A	0	4	.000	27	2	0	0	60	68	45	4	6	18	27	5.70	73	.302	.369	13	.077	-1	50	-9	—	-0.7
1926	Chi N	18	17	.514	42	32	21-2	2	271.1	267	104	10	6	62	127	2.82	136	.264	.310	91-1-4	.143	-4	93	30	—	3.1
1927	Chi N	**26**	15	.634	**48**	36	21-4	2	**309**	296	148	16	9	117	145	3.76	103	.254	.326	122-0-5	.221	3	127	5	—	0.7
1928	Chi N	14	18	.438	40	30	13-1	2	237	214	109	15	7	73	122	3.57	108	.242	.305	73-0-8	.178	-0	67	8	—	0.9
1929	†Chi N	19	6	**.760**	43	31	19-4	5	272	286	120	12	3	83	124	3.47	133	.275	.330	96-1-5	.156	0	118	**37**	—	2.7
1930	Chi N	16	14	.533	37	30	15-**4**	3	220.1	247	122	17	7	63	124	4.33	113	.281	.334	80-1-2	.262	5	102	14	—	1.9
1931	Chi N	17	14	.548	39	31	19-3	2	251	240	109	7	7	71	131	3.48	111	.252	.309	90-0-1	.222	3	101	12	—	1.6
1932	†Chi N	15	10	.600	39	24	11	3	216.1	211	99	10	5	55	96	3.58	105	.253	.303	76-1-2	.171	-1	103	6	—	0.3
1933	Chi N	15	10	.600	35	30	20-2	0	242.1	232	85	14	10	61	86	2.60	126	.252	.306	85-0-4	.094	-4	102	18	—	1.2
1934	Chi N	4	7	.364	34	9	2	0	117.2	141	62	8	5	53	46	4.28	90	.298	.375	40-2-1	.175	2	94	-5	—	-0.3
1935	†Chi N	15	8	.652	38	18	11-1	2	201.1	193	85	15	3	47	94	3.08	127	.252	.298	69-1-12	.203	2	131	18	—	1.9
1936	Chi N	3	6	.333	33	4	0	1	73.2	81	34	3	2	20	32	4.15	96	.280	.331	15	.333	1	149	0	—	0.1
1937	Chi N	13	5	.722	43	15	5	5	178.2	173	71	18	4	32	74	3.38	118	.253	.290	67-1-2	.179	0	133	13	—	1.3
1938	†Chi N	8	7	.533	44	11	5	8	160.2	163	62	10	2	30	70	2.86	134	.258	.294	48-0-1	.167	-0	72	15	—	1.4
1939	Chi N	8	8	.500	35	16	8	4	167.1	189	83	11	2	34	65	4.03	98	.286	.323	57-2-3	.175	2	98	0	—	0.0
1940	Chi N	2	4	.333	36	8	1	1	112	118	61	9	1	33	50	3.86	97	.265	.317	31	.129	-1	125	-4	—	-0.3

YEAR	TM LG	W	L	PCT	G	GS	CG-SHO	SV-BS	IP	H	R	HR	HB	BB-IB	SO	ERA	AERA	OAV	OOB	AB-HR-SH	AVG	PB	SUP	APR	DL	PW
1941	Chi N	8	7	.533	19	15	6	0	106.2	133	68	8	0	37	46	5.40	65	.306	.360	33-1-4	.152	2	113	-20	0	-2.3
Total	17	201	160	.557	632	342	177-21	40	3197.1	3252	1467	187	79	889	1459	3.59	110	.264	.318	1086-11-54	.180	8	105	138	0	13.5
Roper, John	John Christopher; B11.21.1971 Southern Pines NC; BR/TR/6´0˝/175; [CinN90 12/324]; d5.16																									
1993	Cin N	2	5	.286	16	15	0	0-0	80	92	51	10	4	36-3	54	5.62	72	.295	.372	28-0-1	.179	-0	121	-13	30	-1.0
1994	Cin N	6	2	.750	16	15	0	0-0	92	90	49	16	4	30-0	51	4.50	93	.255	.318	33-0-2	.182	0	141	-2	0	-0.1
1995	Cin N	0	0	ø	2	2	0	0-0	7	13	9	3	0	4-0	6	10.29	41	.406	.472	1-0-1	.000	-0	162	-5	42	-0.2
	SF N	0	0	ø	1	0	0	0-0	1	2	3	0	0	2-0	0	27.00	15	.500	.571	0	ø	0	—	-2	0	-0.1
	Year	0	0	ø	3	2	0	0-0	8	15	12	3	0	6-0	6	12.38	34	.417	.488	1-0-1	.000	-0	162	-7	0	-0.3
Total	3	8	7	.533	35	32	0	0-0	180*	197	112	29	8	72-3	111	5.35	77	.281	.352	62-0-4	.177	0	133	-22	72	-1.4
Roque, Rafael	Rafael Antonio; B1.1.1972 Cotui, D.R.; BL/TL/6´4˝/(186–189); d8.1																									
1998	Mil N	4	2	.667	9	9	0	0-0	48	42	28	9	1	24-0	34	4.88	89	.237	.332	13-0-4	.077	-1	122	-3	0	-0.3
1999	Mil N	1	6	.143	43	9	0	1-1	84.1	96	52	16	4	42-1	66	5.34	86	.286	.369	17-0-1	.059	-1	82	-6	0	-0.5
2000	Mil N	0	0	ø	4	0	0	0-0	5.1	7	6	1	0	7-1	4	10.13	46	.333	.483	0	ø	0	—	-3	0	-0.1
Total	3	5	8	.385	56	18	0	1-1	137.2	145	86	26	5	73-2	104	5.36	84	.272	.362	30-0-5	.067	-2	101	-12	0	-0.9
Rosado, Jose	Jose Antonio; B11.9.1974 Newark NJ; BL/TL/6´0˝/(175–185); [KCA94 12/331]; d6.12; Col Galveston (TX) CC; [DL 2001 KC A 190]																									
1996	KC A	8	6	.571	16	16	2-1	0-0	106.2	101	39	7	4	26-1	64	3.21	157	.249	.298	0	ø	0	82	22	0	2.6
1997	KC A★	9	12	.429	33	33	2	0-0	203.1	208	117	26	4	73-3	129	4.69	101	.264	.326	2	.000	-0*	80	0	0	0.0
1998	KC A	8	11	.421	38	25	2-1	1-0	174.2	180	106	25	5	57-2	135	4.69	104	.260	.320	2	.500	0	88	0	0	0.1
1999	KC A★	10	14	.417	33	33	5	0-0	208	197	103	24	5	72-1	141	3.85	132	.248	.314	5	.000	-1	89	25	0	2.4
2000	KC A	2	2	.500	5	5	0	0-0	27.2	29	18	4	4	9-0	15	5.86	89	.271	.347	0	ø	0	86	-1	153	-0.2
Total	5	37	45	.451	125	112	11-2	1-0	720.1	715	383	86	22	237-7	484	4.27	115	.257	.318	9	.111	-0	85	46	343	4.9
Rosario, Francisco	Francisco Alberto (Divison); B9.28.1980 San Rafael Del Yuma, D.R.; BR/TR/6´0˝/195; d5.6																									
2006	Tor A	1	2	.333	17	1	0	0-0	23	24	17	4	1	16-2	21	6.65	71	.264	.380	1	.000	-0	20	-4	0	-0.5
Rosario, Rodrigo	Rodrigo; B12.14.1977 LaRomana, D.R.; BR/TR/6´2˝/160; d6.21																									
2003	Hou N	1	0	1.000	2	2	0	0-0	8	5	2	0	1	3-1	6	1.13	393	.172	.273	0	ø	0	170	2	93	0.3
Rose, Brian	Brian Leonard; B2.13.1976 New Bedford MA; BR/TR/6´3˝/(212–220); [BosA94 3/75]; d7.25																									
1997	Bos A	0	0	ø	1	1	0	0-0	3	5	4	0	0	2-0	3	12.00	39	.357	.438	0	ø	0	99	-2	0	-0.1
1998	Bos A	1	4	.200	8	8	0	0-0	37.2	43	32	9	2	14-0	18	6.93	68	.285	.351	0	ø	0	118	-9	138	-1.0
1999	Bos A	7	6	.538	22	18	0	0-0	98	112	59	19	2	29-2	51	4.87	102	.280	.332	2-0-1	.000	-0	83	2	0	0.2
2000	Bos A	3	5	.375	15	12	0	0-0	53	58	37	11	3	21-3	24	6.11	82	.274	.345	3	.000	-0	87	-5	0	-0.7
	Col N	4	5	.444	12	12	0	0-0	63.2	72	41	10	3	30-6	40	5.51	105	.281	.361	21-0-3	.048	-2	79	2	0	0.0
2001	NY N	0	1	.000	3	0	0	0-0	8.2	10	4	3	0	2-1	4	4.15	97	.286	.324	1	.000	-0	—	0	0	0.0
	TB A	0	2	.000	7	3	0	0-0	20.1	31	20	4	0	12-0	11	8.85	51	.356	.426	0	ø	0	82	-9	0	-0.7
Total	5	15	23	.395	68	54	0	0-0	284.1	331	197	56	10	110-12	151	5.86	87	.287	.352	27-0-4	.037	-2	88	-21	138	-2.3
Rose, Chuck	Charles Alfred; B9.1.1885 Macon MO; D8.4.1961 Salina KS; BL/TL/5´8.5˝/158; d9.13																									
1909	StL A	1	2	.333	3	3	3	0	25	32	17	1	3	7	6	5.40	45	.330	.393	7-0-1	.000	-1	68	-7	—	-0.9
Rose, Don	Donald Gary; B3.19.1947 Covina CA; BR/TR/6´3˝/195; d9.15; Col Stanford																									
1971	NY N	0	0	ø	1	0	0	0-0	2	2	0	0	0	0-0	1	0.00	ø	.286	.286	0	ø	0	—	1	0	0.0
1972	Cal A	1	4	.200	16	4	0	0-0	42.2	49	25	9	0	19-5	39	4.22	70	.283	.352	10-1-1	.200	1	151	-7	0	-0.7
1974	SF N	0	0	ø	2	0	0	0-1	1	4	1	0	0	1-0	0	9.00	42	.667	.714	0	ø	0	—	0	0	0.0
Total	3	1	4	.200	19	4	0	0-1	45.2	55	26	9	0	20-5	40	4.14	72	.296	.362	10-1-1	.200	1	151	-6	0	-0.7
Rosebraugh, Zeke	Eli Ethelbert; B9.8.1876 Charleston IL; D7.16.1930 Fresno CA; TL; d9.21																									
1898	Pit N	0	2	.000	4	2	2	0	21.2	23	14	0	3	9	6	3.32	107	.271	.361	8	.375	1	50	-1	—	0.0
1899	Pit N	0	1	.000	2	2	0	0	6	14	8	0	1	3	2	9.00	42	.452	.514	2	.000	-0	47	-3	—	-0.4
Total	2	0	3	.000	6	4	2	0	27.2	37	22	0	4	12	8	4.55	79	.319	.402	10	.300	1	49	-4	—	-0.4
Roseman, Chief	James John; B1856 New York NY; D7.4.1938 Brooklyn NY; BR/TR/5´7˝/167; d5.1.1882; M1; ▲																									
1885	NY AA	0	1	.000	1	1	0	0	1	3	5	0	0	2	0	27.00	12	.333	.455	410-4	.278	0*	246	-3	—	-0.4
1886	NY AA	0	0	ø	1	0	0	0	7	6	6	0	0	0	0	5.14	63	.240	.240	559-5	.227	0*	—	-1	—	0.0
1887	NY AA	0	0	ø	2	0	0	0	8	11	14	0	2	5	1	7.88	54	.407	.529	241-1	.228	-0*	—	-4	—	-0.2
Total	3	0	1	.000	4	1	0	0	16	20	25	0	2	7	1	7.88	47	.328	.414	1210-10	.245	0	246	-8	—	-0.6
Rosenberg, Steve	Steven Allen; B10.31.1964 Brooklyn NY; BL/TL/6´0˝/185; [NYA86 4/106]; d6.4; Col Florida; [DL 1992 NY N 182]																									
1988	Chi A	0	1	.000	33	0	0	1-0	46	53	22	5	0	19-0	28	4.30	93	.298	.360	0	ø	0	—	0	0	0.0
1989	Chi A	4	13	.235	38	21	2	0-0	142	148	92	14	1	58-1	77	4.94	78	.273	.339	0	ø	0	80	-20	0	-2.1
1990	Chi A	1	0	1.000	6	0	0	0-0	10	10	6	2	0	5-0	4	5.40	71	.256	.341	0	ø	0	—	-2	0	-0.1
1991	SD N	1	1	.500	10	0	0	0-1	11.2	11	9	3	0	5-1	6	6.94	55	.250	.327	1	.000	-0	—	-3	0	-0.6
Total	4	6	15	.286	87	21	2	1-1	209.2	222	129	24	1	87-2	115	4.94	78	.276	.343	1	.000	-0	80	-25	182	-2.8
Rosenthal, Wayne	Wayne Scott; B2.19.1965 Brooklyn NY; BR/TR/6´5˝/(220–240); [TexA86 24/601]; d6.26; C2; Col St. Johns																									
1991	Tex A	1	4	.200	36	0	0	1-1	70.1	72	43	9	1	36-1	61	5.25	77	.257	.341	0	ø	0	—	-8	0	-0.6
1992	Tex A	0	0	ø	6	0	0	0-0	4.2	7	4	1	0	2-0	1	7.71	50	.333	.391	0	ø	0	—	-2	0	-0.1
Total	2	1	4	.200	42	0	0	1-1	75	79	47	10	1	38-1	62	5.40	75	.262	.344	0	ø	0	—	-10	0	-0.7
Roser, Steve	Emerson Corey; B1.25.1918 Rome NY; D2.8.2002 Utica NY; BR/TR/6´4˝/220; d5.5; Col Clarkson																									
1944	NY A	4	3	.571	16	6	1	1	84	80	39	3	0	34	34	3.86	90	.256	.329	30-0-2	.100	-2	96	-2	0	-0.4
1945	NY A	0	0	ø	11	0	0	0	27	27	15	1	0	8	11	3.67	94	.262	.315	8	.125	-0	—	-2	0	-0.1
1946	NY A	1	1	.500	4	1	0	0	3.1	7	6	0	0	4	1	16.20	21	.438	.550	0	ø	0	124	-4	0	-0.8
	Bos N	1	1	.500	14	1	0	1	35	33	15	1	0	18	18	3.60	95	.250	.340	5	.000	-1	75	0	0	-0.1
Total	3	6	5	.545	45	8	1	2	149.1	147	75	5	0	64	64	4.04	86	.261	.336	43-0-2	.093	-3	97	-8	0	-1.4
Ross, Buster	Chester Franklin; B3.11.1903 Kuttawa KY; D4.24.1982 Mayfield KY; BL/TL/6´1˝/195; d6.15																									
1924	Bos A	4	3	.571	30	2	1-1	1	93.1	109	49	3	0	30	16	3.47	126	.307	.361	25	.200	-0	145	7	—	0.4
1925	Bos A	3	8	.273	33	8	0	0	94.1	119	86	9	5	40	15	6.20	73	.313	.386	24-0-2	.125	-1	90	-18	—	-1.9
1926	Bos A	0	1	.000	1	0	0	0	2.2	5	7	0	0	4	0	16.88	24	.385	.529	1	.000	-0	—	-4	—	-0.6
Total	3	7	12	.368	64	10	1-1	1	190.1	233	142	12	5	74	31	5.01	89	.311	.377	50-0-2	.160	-2	102	-15	—	-2.1
Ross, Cliff	Clifford David; B8.3.1928 Philadelphia PA; D4.12.1999 Philadelphia PA; BL/TL/6´4˝/190; d9.11																									
1954	Cin N	0	0	ø	4	0	0	1	2.2	0	0	0	0	0	1	0.00	ø	.000	.000	0	ø	0	—	1	0	0.1
Ross, Ernie	Ernest Bertram "Curly"; B3.31.1880 Toronto ON, Can.; D3.28.1950 Toronto ON, Can.; BL/TL/5´8˝/150; d9.17																									
1902	Bal A	1	1	.500	2	2	2	0	17	20	18	0	1	12	2	7.41	51	.294	.407	8	.000	-1	76	-6	—	-0.6
Ross, Bob	Floyd Robert; B11.2.1928 Fullerton CA; BR/TL/6´0˝/165; d6.16; Mil 1952–53; Col San Jose St.																									
1950	Was A	0	1	.000	6	2	0	0	12.2	15	12	1	0	15	2	8.53	53	.300	.462	3	.000	-0	70	-5	0	-0.4
1951	Was A	0	1	.000	11	1	0	0	31.2	36	25	3	0	21	23	6.54	63	.295	.399	9	.111	-0	43	-8	0	-0.5
1956	Phi N	0	0	ø	3	0	0	0	3.1	4	3	1	0	2-0	4	8.10	46	.333	.400	0	ø	0	—	-1	0	-0.1
Total	3	0	2	.000	20	3	0	0	47.2	55	40	5	0	38-0	29	7.17	58	.299	.417	12	.083	-1	64	-14	0	-1.0
Ross, Gary	Gary Douglas; B9.16.1947 McKeesport PA; BR/TR/6´1˝/(175–195); [ChiN67*S1/7]; d6.28; Col Grand View																									
1968	Chi N	1	1	.500	13	5	1	0	41	44	22	1	0	25-3	31	4.17	76	.288	.383	11	.091	-1	82	-5	0	-0.3
1969	Chi N	0	0	ø	2	1	0	0-0	2	1	3	0	0	2-0	2	13.50	30	.143	.333	0	ø	0	110	-2	0	-0.1
	SD N	3	12	.200	46	7	0	3-4	109.2	104	58	5	5	56-8	58	4.19	86	.252	.345	23-0-5	.000	-2	39	-8	0	-1.2
	Year	3	12	.200	48	8	0	3-4	111.2	105	61	5	5	58-8	60	4.35	82	.250	.345	23-0-5	.000	-2	49	-9	0	-1.3
1970	SD N	2	3	.400	33	2	0	1-1	62.1	72	37	8	3	36-10	39	5.20	77	.305	.402	8-0-2	.500	2	201	-7	0	-0.3
1971	SD N	1	3	.250	13	0	0	0-0	24.1	27	10	0	1	11-2	13	2.96	112	.300	.375	1-0-1	.000	-0	—	1	0	0.1
1972	SD N	4	3	.571	60	0	0	3-3	91.2	87	35	2	4	49-12	46	2.45	135	.261	.359	13-0-1	.154	-0	—	6	0	0.5
1973	SD N	4	4	.500	58	0	0	0-1	76.1	93	51	8	4	33-8	44	5.42	65	.304	.376	4-0-1	.000	-0	—	-16	0	-1.6

YEAR	TM LG	W	L	PCT	G	GS	CG-SHO	SV-BS	IP	H	R	HR	HB	BB-IB	SO	ERA	AERA	OAV	OOB	AB-HR-SH	AVG	PB	SUP	APR	DL	PW
1974	SD N	0	0	ø	9	0	0	0-0	18	23	10	1	0	6-4	11	4.50	80	.315	.363	1	.000	-0	—	-2	0	-0.1
1975	Cal A	0	1	.000	1	1	0	0-0	5	6	3	1	0	1-0	4	5.40	66	.273	.304	0	ø	0	0	-1	0	-0.2
1976	Cal A	8	16	.333	34	31	7-2	0-0	225	224	89	12	5	58-5	100	3.00	112	.258	.306	0	ø	0	83	8	0	1.1
1977	Cal A	2	4	.333	14	12	0	0-0	58.1	83	41	10	2	11-1	30	5.55	71	.337	.369	0	ø	0	86	-11	83	-0.9
Total	10	25	47	.347	283	59	8-2	7-9	713.2	764	359	48	24	288-53	378	3.92	89	.278	.349	61-0-10	.115	-2	82	-37	83	-3.0
Ross, George	George Sidney; B6.27.1892 San Rafael CA; D4.22.1935 Amityville NY; BL/TL/5´10.5˝/175; d6.27																									
1918	NY N	0	0	ø	1	0	0	1	2.1	2	0	0	0	3	2	0.00	ø	.222	.417	1	.000	-0	—	1	—	0.1
Ross, Buck	Lee Ravon; B2.3.1915 Norwood NC; D11.23.1978 Charlotte NC; BR/TR/6´2˝/170; d5.7																									
1936	Phi A	9	14	.391	30	27	12-1	0	200.2	253	146	17	0	83	47	5.83	88	.304	.367	71-0-4	.169	-1	91	-15	—	-1.5
1937	Phi A	5	10	.333	28	22	7-1	0	147.1	183	102	12	2	63	37	4.89	96	.306	.373	49	.102	-3	92	-6	—	-0.8
1938	Phi A	9	16	.360	29	28	10	0	184.1	218	132	23	0	80	54	5.32	91	.289	.357	63-1-5	.190	-0	79	-11	—	-1.2
1939	Phi A	6	14	.300	29	28	6-1	0	174	216	143	17	0	95	43	6.00	78	.302	.384	58-0-7	.207	-1	91	-27	—	-2.6
1940	Phi A	5	10	.333	24	19	10	1	156.1	160	91	15	0	60	43	4.38	102	.256	.322	53-1-2	.132	-2	89	1	—	-0.2
1941	Phi A	0	1	.000	1	1	0	0	4	10	9	2	0	2	0	18.00	23	.435	.480	1	.000	-0	83	-6	0	-0.8
	Chi A	3	8	.273	20	11	7	0	108.1	99	51	6	1	43	30	3.16	130	.239	.312	32-0-4	.219	1	67	9	0	0.8
	Year	3	9	.250	21	12	7	0	112.1	109	60	8	1	45	30	3.69	111	.249	.321	33-0-4	.212	1	69	3	0	0.0
1942	Chi A	5	7	.417	22	14	4-2	1	113.1	118	63	6	0	39	37	5.00	72	.264	.323	38-0-2	.158	0	95	-13	0	-1.4
1943	Chi A	11	7	.611	21	21	7-1	0	149.1	140	61	6	2	56	41	3.19	105	.253	.324	46-1-4	.087	-1	101	3	0	0.2
1944	Chi A	2	7	.222	20	9	2	0	90.1	97	56	7	2	35	20	5.18	66	.280	.350	26-0-2	.077	-2	106	-15	0	-1.7
1945	Chi A	1	1	.500	13	2	0	0	37.1	51	28	3	0	17	8	5.79	57	.327	.393	11	.182	-0	51	-10	0	-0.6
Total	10	56	95	.371	237	182	65-6	2	1365.1	1545	882	114	7	573	360	4.94	88	.283	.351	448-3-30	.154	-11	90	-90	0	-9.8
Ross, Mark	Mark Joseph; B8.8.1957 Galveston TX; BR/TR/6´0˝/(195–200); [HouN79 7/164]; d9.12; Col Texas A&M																									
1982	Hou N	0	0	ø	4	0	0	0-0	6	3	1	0	0	0-0	4	1.50	222	.143	.143	0	ø	0	—	1	0	0.1
1984	Hou N	1	0	1.000	2	0	0	0-0	2.1	1	0	0	0	0-0	1	0.00	ø	.125	.125	0	ø	0	—	1	0	0.2
1985	Hou N	0	2	.000	8	0	0	1-1	13	12	7	2	0	2-0	3	4.85	72	.240	.269	1	.000	-0	—	-2	0	-0.3
1987	Pit N	0	0	ø	1	0	0	0-0	1	1	1	1	0	0-0	0	9.00	46	.250	.250	0	ø	0	—	0	0	0.0
1988	Tor A	0	0	ø	3	0	0	0-0	7.1	5	6	0	0	4-1	4	4.91	81	.185	.281	0	ø	0	—	-1	0	-0.1
1990	Pit N	1	0	1.000	9	0	0	0-0	12.2	11	5	2	0	4-2	5	3.55	103	.244	.306	1	.000	-0	—	0	0	0.0
Total	6	2	2	.500	27	0	0	1-1	42.1	33	20	5	0	10-3	17	3.83	94	.213	.259	2	.000	-0	—	-1	0	-0.1
Rosselli, Joey	Joseph Donald; B5.28.1972 Burbank CA; BR/TL/6´1˝/170; [SFN90 2/70]; d4.30																									
1995	SF N	2	1	.667	9	5	0	0-0	30	39	29	5	0	20-2	7	8.70	47	.342	.428	10-0-1	.200	0	136	-14	49	-1.2
Rosso, Frank	Francis James; B3.1.1921 Agawam MA; D1.26.1980 Springfield MA; BR/TR/5´11˝/180; d9.15																									
1944	NY N	0	0	ø	2	0	0	0	4	11	5	0	0	3	1	9.00	41	.550	.609	0	ø	0*	—	-2	0	-0.1
Rotblatt, Marv	Marvin "Rotty"; B10.18.1927 Chicago IL; BB/TL/5´7˝/160; d7.4; Col Illinois																									
1948	Chi A	0	1	.000	7	2	0	0	18.1	19	16	0	1	23	4	7.85	54	.271	.457	4	.000	-0	74	-7	0	-0.4
1950	Chi A	0	0	ø	2	0	0	0	8.2	11	7	2	0	5	6	6.23	72	.344	.432	2	.000	-0	—	-2	0	-0.1
1951	Chi A	4	2	.667	26	2	0	2	47.2	44	21	4	1	23	20	3.40	119	.244	.333	9-0-2	.000	-2	242	3	0	0.3
Total	3	4	3	.571	35	4	0	2	74.2	74	44	6	2	51	30	4.82	86	.262	.379	15-0-2	.000	-2	156	-6	0	-0.2
Rothschild, Larry	Lawrence Lee; B3.12.1954 Chicago IL; BL/TR/6´2˝/(180–190); d9.11; M4/C12; Col Florida St.																									
1981	Det A	0	0	ø	5	0	0	1-0	5.2	4	1	0	0	6-1	1	1.59	238	.200	.370	0	ø	0	—	1	0	-0.1
1982	Det A	0	0	ø	2	0	0	0-0	2.2	4	4	1	0	2-0	0	13.50	30	.333	.429	0	ø	0	—	-3	0	-0.1
Total	2	0	0	ø	7	0	0	1-0	8.1	8	5	1	0	8-1	1	5.40	72	.250	.390	0	ø	0	—	-2	0	0.0
Rounsaville, Gene	Virle Gene; B9.27.1944 Konawa OK; BR/TR/6´3˝/205; d4.7; Col Diablo Valley (CA) JC																									
1970	Chi A	0	1	.000	8	0	0	0-0	6.1	10	8	1	0	2-0	3	9.95	39	.357	.400	0	ø	0	—	-4	0	-0.6
Rowan, Jack	John Albert; B6.16.1886 New Castle PA; D9.29.1966 Dayton OH; BR/TR/6´1˝/210; d9.6																									
1906	Det A	0	1	.000	1	1	1	0	9	15	13	0	0	6	0	11.00	25	.375	.457	4	.250	0	130	-7	—	-0.6
1908	Cin N	3	3	.500	8	7	4-1	0	49.1	46	17	0	0	16	24	1.82	126	.253	.313	14	.071	-0	105	2	—	0.2
1909	Cin N	11	12	.478	38	23	14	0	225.2	185	86	0	3	104	81	2.79	93	.233	.324	65-0-2	.092	-1	106	2	—	-0.2
1910	Cin N	14	13	.519	42	30	18-4	1	261	242	122	4	9	105	108	2.93	99	.254	.334	83-0-3	.229	3	100	-1	—	0.1
1911	Phi N	2	4	.333	12	6	2	0	45.2	59	35	3	1	20	17	4.73	73	.316	.385	13-0-1	.077	-1	80	-8	—	-0.9
	Chi N	0	0	ø	1	0	0	0	2	1	4	0	1	2	0	4.50	74	.143	.400	1	.000	-0	—	-1	—	-0.1
	Year	2	4	.333	13	6	2	0	47.2	60	39	3	2	22	17	4.72	73	.309	.385	14-0-1	.071	-1	80	-9	—	-1.0
1913	Cin N	0	4	.000	5	5	5	0	39	37	14	0	1	9	21	3.00	108	.264	.313	11	.182	1	32	2	—	0.3
1914	Cin N	1	3	.250	12	2	0	2	39	38	22	1	0	10	16	3.46	85	.262	.310	8	.000	-1	73	-2	—	-0.4
Total	7	31	40	.437	119	74	44-5	3	670.2	623	313	8	15	272	267	3.07	92	.255	.333	199-0-6	.151	1	95	-13	—	-1.6
Rowe, Dave	David Elwood; B10.9.1854 Harrisburg PA; D12.9.1930 Glendale CA; BR/TR/5´9˝/180; d5.30; M2; b–Jack; ▲																									
1877	Chi N	0	1	.000	1	1	0	0	1	3	2	0	—	2	0	18.00	17	.600	.714	7	.286	0*	16	-1	—	-0.2
1882	Cle N	0	1	.000	1	1	1	0	9	29	35	3	—	7	0	12.00	23	.492	.545	97-1	.258	0*	76	-13	—	-0.8
1883	Bal AA	0	0	ø	1	0	0	0	4	12	11	1	—	2	1	20.25	17	.500	.538	256	.313	0*	—	-5	—	-0.2
1884	StL U	1	0	1.000	1	1	1	0	9	10	3	0	—	0	2	2.00	119	.263	.263	485-4	.293	0*	107	1	—	0.1
Total	4	1	2	.333	4	3	2	0	23	54	51	4	—	11	3	9.78	28	.429	.474	845-5	.295	1	66	-18	—	-1.1
Rowe, Don	Donald Howard; B4.3.1936 Brawley CA; D10.15.2005 Newport Beach CA; BL/TL/6´0˝/180; d4.9; C8; Col Compton (CA) CC																									
1963	NY N	0	0	ø	26	1	0	0	54.2	59	27	6	1	21-0	27	4.28	81	.280	.346	13	.231	0	148	-3	0	-0.2
Rowe, Ken	Kenneth Darrell; B12.31.1933 Ferndale MI; BR/TR/6´2˝/185; d4.14; C2																									
1963	LA N	1	1	.500	14	0	0	1	27.2	28	16	2	1	11-3	12	2.93	103	.264	.336	5	.000	-1	—	-2	0	-0.2
1964	Bal A	1	0	1.000	6	0	0	0	4.1	10	10	1	0	1-0	4	8.31	43	.455	.478	0	ø	0	—	-5	0	-0.9
1965	Bal A	0	0	ø	6	0	0	0	13.1	17	5	0	0	2-1	3	3.38	103	.321	.333	1	1.000	0	—	1	0	0.0
Total	3	2	1	.667	26	0	0	1	45.1	55	31	3	1	14-4	19	3.57	90	.304	.352	6	.167	-0	—	-6	0	-1.1
Rowe, Schoolboy	Lynwood Thomas; B1.11.1910 Waco TX; D1.8.1961 ElDorado AR; BR/TR/6´4.5˝/210; d4.15; Mil 1944–45; C2																									
1933	Det A	7	4	.636	19	15	8-1	0	123.1	129	60	7	1	31	75	3.58	121	.269	.315	50-0-2	.220	-0*	100	9	—	0.8
1934	†Det A	24	8	.750	45	30	20-3	1	266	259	110	12	1	81	149	3.45	127	.256	.312	109-2-4	.303	12*	115	31	—	4.5
1935	†Det A☆	19	13	.594	42	34	21-**6**	3	275.2	272	121	11	2	68	140	3.69	113	.255	**.301**	109-3-3	.312	14*	141	20	—	3.2
1936	Det A★	19	10	.655	41	35	19-4	3	245.1	266	134	15	2	64	115	4.51	110	.275	.321	90-1-2	.256	7*	95	16	—	2.3
1937	Det A	1	4	.200	10	2	1	0	31.1	49	32	7	1	9	6	8.62	54	.350	.393	10-0-1	.200	-0	84	-13	—	-1.5
1938	Det A	0	2	.000	4	3	0	0	21	20	11	1	0	11	4	3.00	167	.256	.348	6-0-1	.167	-0	53	3	—	0.3
1939	Det A	10	12	.455	28	24	8-1	0	164	192	113	17	2	61	51	4.99	98	.291	.353	61-1-3	.246	2*	110	-5	—	-0.3
1940	†Det A	16	3	**.842**	27	23	11-1	0	169	170	68	15	1	43	61	3.46	137	.259	.305	67-1-1	.269	5	137	26	—	3.1
1941	Det A	8	6	.571	27	14	4	1	139	155	70	6	0	33	54	4.14	110	.278	.318	55-1-1	.273	5*	95	7	0	1.2
1942	Det A	1	0	1.000	2	1	0	0	10.1	9	2	0	0	2	7	0.00	ø	.220	.256	4-0-1	.000	-1	87	3	0	0.3
	Bro N	1	0	1.000	9	2	0	0	30.1	36	19	2	1	12	6	5.34	61	.288	.355	19	.211	0*	180	-6	0	-0.3
1943	Phi N	14	8	.636	27	25	11-3	1	199	196	73	7	3	29	52	2.94	115	.249	.279	120-4-1	.300	16*	112	10	0	3.3
1946	Phi N	11	4	.733	17	16	9-2	0	136	112	39	3	6	21	51	2.12	162	.224	.263	61-1-1	.180	2*	80	19	0	2.3
1947	Phi N★	14	10	.583	31	28	15-1	1	195.2	232	106	22	3	45	74	4.32	93	.292	.333	79-2-2	.278	10*	105	-6	0	0.3
1948	Phi N	10	10	.500	30	20	8	2	148	167	74	5	2	31	46	4.07	97	.281	.319	52-1-2	.192	2*	93	0	0	0.2
1949	Phi N	3	7	.300	23	6	2	0	65.1	68	43	2	2	17	22	4.82	82	.300	.354	17-1-0	.235	2	67	-8	0	-0.9
Total	15	158	101	.610	382	278	137-22	12	2219.1	2332	1075	132	27	558	913	3.87	110	.269	.315	909-18-25	.263	76	109	106	0	18.8
Rowland, Mike	Michael Evan; B1.31.1953 Chicago IL; BR/TR/6´3˝/(205–215); [SFN75 22/509]; d7.25; Col Millikin																									
1980	SF N	1	1	.500	19	0	0	0-0	27	20	8	2	1	8-2	8	2.33	150	.206	.271	0	ø	0	—	4	0	0.2
1981	SF N	0	1	.000	9	1	0	0-0	15.2	13	7	1	1	6-2	8	3.45	99	.232	.313	1	1.000	0	313	0	0	0.0
Total	2	1	2	.333	28	1	0	0-0	42.2	33	15	3	2	14-4	16	2.74	127	.216	.287	1	1.000	0	313	4	0	0.2
Roy, Emil	Emil Arthur; B5.26.1907 Brighton MA; D1.5.1997 Crystal River FL; BR/TR/5´11˝/180; d9.30; Col Boston College																									
1933	Phi A	0	1	.000	1	1	0	0	2.1	4	7	0	0	4	3	27.00	16	.364	.533	0	ø	0	20	-5	—	-0.7

YEAR	TM LG	W	L	PCT	G	GS	CG-SHO	SV-BS	IP	H	R	HR	HB	BB-IB	SO	ERA	AERA	OAV	OOB	AB-HR-SH	AVG	PB	SUP	APR	DL	PW
Roy, Jean-Pierre	Jean-Pierre; B6.26.1920 Montreal QC, Can.; BB/TR/5´10˝/160; d5.5																									
1946	Bro N	0	0	ø	3	1	0	0	6.1	5	7	2	0	5	6	9.95	34	.200	.333	2	.000	-0	177	-4	0	-0.2
Roy, Luther	Luther Franklin; B7.29.1902 Ooltewah TN; D7.24.1963 Grand Rapids MI; BR/TR/5´10.5˝/161; d6.12; b–Charlie																									
1924	Cle A	0	5	.000	16	5	2	0	48.2	62	48	3	0	31	14	7.77	55	.318	.412	15-0-1	.267	-0	63	-17	—	-1.4
1925	Cle A	0	0	ø	6	1	0	0	10	14	7	1	0	11	1	3.60	123	.368	.510	2	.000	-0	76	0	—	-0.1
1927	Chi N	3	1	.750	11	0	0	0	19.2	14	9	0	1	11	5	2.29	169	.209	.329	3	.333	0	—	2	—	0.4
1929	Phi N	3	6	.333	21	11	1	0	88.2	137	91	11	3	37	16	8.42	62	.350	.411	32	.281	2	108	-28	—	-2.0
	Bro N	0	0	ø	2	0	0	0	3.2	4	2	0	0	2	0	4.91	94	.286	.375	1	.000	-0	—	0	—	0.0
	Year	3	6	.333	23	11	1	0	92.1	141	93	11	3	39	16	8.29	62	.348	.409	33	.273	2	109	-28	—	-2.0
Total	4	6	12	.333	56	17	3	0	170.2	231	157	15	4	92	36	7.17	66	.328	.408	53-0-1	.264	2	98	-43	—	-3.1
Roy, Normie	Norman Brooks "Jumbo"; B11.15.1928 Newton MA; BR/TR/6´0˝/200; d4.23																									
1950	Bos N	4	3	.571	19	6	2	1	59.2	72	38	6	2	39	25	5.13	75	.305	.408	18-0-1	.167	0	126	-9	0	-0.9
Roy, Charlie	Robert Charles; B6.22.1884 Beaulieu MN; D2.10.1950 Blackfoot ID; BR/TR/5´10˝/190; d6.27; b–Luther																									
1906	Phi N	0	1	.000	7	1	0	0	18.1	24	12	0	1	5	6	4.91	53	.316	.366	7-0-1	.000	-1*	84	-4	—	-0.3
Rozek, Dick	Richard Louis; B3.27.1927 Cedar Rapids IA; D9.27.2001 LaQuinta CA; BL/TL/6´0.5˝/190; d4.29																									
1950	Cle A	0	0	ø	12	2	0	0	25.1	28	15	3	0	19	14	4.97	87	.283	.398	5-0-1	.000	-1	177	-1	0	-0.2
1951	Cle A	0	0	ø	7	1	0	0	15.1	18	12	1	1	11	5	2.93	129	.286	.400	3	.333	0	164	-1	0	-0.1
1952	Cle A	1	0	1.000	10	1	0	0	12.2	11	8	0	0	13	5	4.97	67	.224	.387	2	.000	-0	209	-2	0	-0.2
1953	Phi A	0	0	ø	2	0	0	0	10.2	8	6	3	0	9	2	5.06	85	.222	.378	2	.000	-0	—	-1	0	0.0
1954	Phi A	0	0	ø	2	0	0	0	1.1	0	1	0	1	3	0	6.75	58	.000	.500	0	ø	0	—	0	0	0.0
Total	5	1	0	1.000	33	4	0	0	65.1	65	42	7	2	55	26	4.55	88	.260	.396	12-0-1	.083	-1	178	-5	0	-0.5
Rozema, Dave	David Scott; B8.5.1956 Grand Rapids MI; BR/TR/6´4˝/(190–200); [DetA75*S4/71]; d4.11; Col Grand Rapids (MI) CC																									
1977	Det A	15	7	.682	28	28	16-1	0-0	218.1	222	87	25	7	34-4	92	3.09	140	.265	.298	0	ø	0	110	27	0	2.5
1978	Det A	9	12	.429	28	28	11-2	0-0	209.1	205	83	17	2	41-1	57	3.14	124	.260	.297	0	ø	0	86	16	0	1.5
1979	Det A	4	4	.500	16	16	4-1	0-0	97.1	101	52	12	6	30-2	33	3.51	124	.270	.329	0	ø	0	108	4	72	0.3
1980	Det A	6	9	.400	42	13	2-1	4-1	144.2	152	68	11	5	49-14	49	3.92	105	.277	.339	0	ø	0	117	4	0	0.4
1981	Det A	5	5	.500	28	9	2-2	3-2	104	99	42	12	3	25-8	46	3.63	104	.256	.305	0	ø	0	58	3	0	0.2
1982	Det A	3	0	1.000	8	2	0	1-0	27.2	17	5	2	1	7-1	15	1.63	252	.179	.243	0	ø	0	67	8	142	0.9
1983	Det A	8	3	.727	29	16	1	2-0	105	100	50	10	1	29-6	63	3.43	115	.248	.297	0	ø	0	139	4	0	0.4
1984	Det A	7	6	.538	29	16	0	0-0	101	110	49	13	2	18-3	48	3.74	106	.274	.307	0	ø	0	96	2	0	0.2
1985	Tex A	3	7	.300	34	4	0	7-4	88	100	45	10	2	22-3	42	4.19	102	.287	.332	0	ø	0	64	1	33	0.1
1986	Tex A	0	0	ø	6	0	0	0-0	10.2	19	9	1	0	3-0	3	5.91	73	.404	.423	0	ø	0	—	-2	0	-0.1
Total	10	60	53	.531	248	132	36-7	17-7	1106	1125	490	113	29	258-42	448	3.47	118	.266	.310	0	ø	0	102	67	247	6.4
Rubio, Jorge	Jorge Jesus (Chavez); B4.23.1945 Mexicali, Baja California, Mexico; BR/TR/6´3˝/200; d4.21																									
1966	Cal A	2	1	.667	7	4	1-1	0	27.1	22	10	2	1	16-1	27	2.96	113	.220	.333	8-0-1	.000	-1	52	1	0	0.0
1967	Cal A	0	2	.000	3	3	0	0	15	18	7	2	4	9-0	4	3.60	87	.316	.443	3	.333	1	18	-1	0	0.0
Total	2	2	3	.400	10	7	1-1	0	42.1	40	17	4	5	25-1	31	3.19	103	.255	.374	11-0-1	.091	-0	38	0	0	0.0
Rucker, Dave	David Michael; B9.1.1957 San Bernardino CA; BL/TL/6´1˝/(185–190); [DetA78 16/402]; d4.12; Col La Verne																									
1981	Det A	0	0	ø	2	0	0	0-0	4	3	4	0	1	1-0	2	6.75	56	.188	.278	0	ø	0	—	-2	0	-0.1
1982	Det A	5	6	.455	27	4	1	0-2	64	62	26	4	2	23-3	31	3.38	121	.251	.320	0	ø	0	78	5	0	0.9
1983	Det A	1	2	.333	4	3	0	0-0	9	18	17	2	1	8-0	6	17.00	23	.419	.519	0	ø	0	146	-13	0	-1.9
	StL N	5	3	.625	34	0	0	0-0	37	36	14	1	1	18-0	22	2.43	150	.263	.353	4	.000	-0	—	4	0	0.8
1984	StL N	2	3	.400	50	0	0	0-1	73	62	23	0	1	34-2	38	2.10	167	.237	.324	7	.143	-0	—	10	0	0.6
1985	Phi N	3	2	.600	39	3	0	1-1	79.1	83	42	6	2	40-6	41	4.31	86	.279	.361	12-0-1	.333	2*	119	-5	0	-0.1
1986	Phi N	0	2	.000	19	0	0	0-0	25	34	19	4	0	14-3	14	5.76	68	.340	.410	1	.000	-0	—	-5	0	-0.4
1988	Pit N	0	2	.000	31	0	0	0-0	28.1	39	19	2	0	9-1	16	4.76	72	.328	.369	2	.000	-0	—	-5	0	-0.4
Total	7	16	20	.444	206	10	1	1-4	319.2	337	164	19	8	147-15	170	3.94	95	.276	.354	26-0-1	.192	1	115	-11	0	-0.6
Rucker, Nap	George; B9.30.1884 Crabapple GA; D12.19.1970 Alpharetta GA; BR/TL/5´11˝/190; d4.15																									
1907	Bro N	15	13	.536	37	30	26-4	0	275.1	242	94	3	8	80	131	2.06	114	.242	.303	97-0-3	.155	-1	104	8	—	0.7
1908	Bro N	17	19	.472	42	37	30-6	1	333.1	265	107	1	19	125	199	2.08	113	.231	.317	117-0-1	.179	-1	75	9	—	1.2
1909	Bro N	13	19	.406	38	33	28-6	1	309.1	245	95	6	14	101	201	2.24	116	.228	.303	101-0-7	.119	-5	70	14	—	0.8
1910	Bro N	17	18	.486	41	**39**	**27-6**	0	**320.1**	293	112	5	9	84	147	2.58	117	.251	.306	110-0-4	.209	-1	77	18	—	1.7
1911	Bro N	22	18	.550	48	33	23-5	4	315.2	255	102	12	8	110	190	2.71	123	.226	.300	104-1-7	.202	2	61	30	—	3.9
1912	Bro N	18	21	.462	45	34	23-**6**	4	297.2	272	101	6	3	72	151	2.21	152	.250	.298	102-0-4	.245	2	91	37	—	5.1
1913	Bro N	14	15	.483	41	33	16-4	3	260	236	99	3	7	67	111	2.87	115	.249	.304	87-0-2	.241	2	72	14	—	1.6
1914	Bro N	7	6	.538	16	16	5	0	103.2	113	57	2	2	27	35	3.39	84	.275	.323	34-0-3	.265	2	102	-6	—	-0.5
1915	Bro N	9	4	.692	19	15	7-1	1	122.2	134	42	3	2	28	38	2.42	115	.279	.322	42	.214	1	95	6	—	0.9
1916	†Bro N	2	1	.667	9	4	1	0	37.1	34	14	0	1	7	14	1.69	159	.241	.282	11	.091	-1	118	3	—	0.1
Total	10	134	134	.500	336	274	186-38	14	2375.1	2089	823	41	73	701	1217	2.42	119	.243	.306	805-1-31	.195	1	81	133	—	15.5
Rudolph, Ernie	Ernest William; B2.13.1909 Black River Falls WI; D1.13.2003 Black River Falls WI; BL/TR/5´8˝/165; d6.16																									
1945	Bro N	1	0	1.000	7	0	0	0	8.2	12	10	1	0	7	3	5.19	72	.333	.442	0	ø	1	—	-3	0	-0.2
Rudolph, Don	Frederick Donald; B8.16.1931 Baltimore MD; D9.12.1968 Granada Hills CA; BL/TL/5´11˝/195; d9.21																									
1957	Chi A	1	0	1.000	5	0	0	0	12	6	3	2	0	2-0	2	2.25	166	.146	.186	2	.500	1	—	2	0	0.2
1958	Chi A	1	0	1.000	7	0	0	1	7	4	2	0	0	5-1	2	2.57	141	.190	.346	0	ø	0	—	1	0	0.2
1959	Chi A	0	0	ø	4	0	0	1	3	4	0	0	0	2-1	0	0.00	ø	.333	.429	0	ø	0	—	1	0	0.1
	Cin N	0	0	ø	5	0	0	0	7.1	13	4	1	0	3-1	8	4.91	83	.394	.444	1	.000	-0	—	0	0	0.0
1962	Cle A	0	0	ø	1	0	0	0	0.1	1	0	0	0	0-0	0	0.00	ø	1.000	1.000	0	ø	0	—	0	0	0.0
	Was A	8	10	.444	37	23	6-2	0	176.1	187	84	13	3	42-2	68	3.62	111	.274	.316	57-0-1	.175	1	92	5	0	0.6
	Year	8	10	.444	38	23	6-2	0	176.2	188	84	13	3	42-2	68	3.62	112	.275	.317	57-0-1	.175	1	92	6	0	0.6
1963	Was A	7	19	.269	37	26	4	1	174	189	98	28	6	36-3	70	4.55	82	.275	.314	45-1-5	.178	2	77	-15	0	-1.9
1964	Was A	1	3	.250	28	8	0	0	70.1	81	36	10	0	12-5	32	4.09	90	.290	.317	15	.067	-1	54	-3	0	-0.2
Total	6	18	32	.360	124	57	10-2	3	450.1	485	227	54	9	102-13	182	4.00	96	.276	.317	120-1-6	.167	3	81	-9	0	-1.0
Rudolph, Dick	Richard "Baldy"; B8.25.1887 New York NY; D10.20.1949 Bronx NY; BR/TR (BB 1919–27)/5´9.5˝/160; d9.30; M1/C7; Col Fordham																									
1910	NY N	0	1	.000	3	1	1	2	12	21	11	0	0	2	9	7.50	40	.350	.371	4	.250	0	50	-5	—	-0.6
1911	NY N	0	0	ø	1	0	0	0	2	2	2	0	0	0	0	9.00	37	.250	.250	1	1.000	0	—	-1	—	0.0
1913	Bos N	14	13	.519	33	22	17-2	0	249.1	258	101	4	2	59	109	2.92	112	.276	.320	88-0-4	.239	4*	92	14	—	2.2
1914	†Bos N	26	10	.722	42	36	31-6	0	336.1	288	105	9	4	61	138	2.35	117	.238	.276	120-0-5	.125	-1*	112	18	—	1.9
1915	Bos N	22	19	.537	44	**43**	30-3	1	341.1	304	125	4	6	64	147	2.37	109	.242	.282	116-1-4	.198	6*	109	7	—	1.6
1916	Bos N	19	12	.613	41	38	27-5	3	312	266	93	7	3	38	133	2.16	115	.235	**.261**	101-0-4	.158	1	93	14	—	1.9
1917	Bos N	13	14	.481	31	30	22-5	0	242.2	252	104	1	4	54	96	3.41	75	.272	.314	87-0-7	.230	3*	123	-20	—	-1.8
1918	Bos N	9	10	.474	21	20	15-3	0	154	144	63	2	0	30	48	2.57	104	.255	.292	54-0-3	.185	-1	66	0	—	-0.1
1919	Bos N	13	18	.419	37	32	24-2	2	273.2	282	95	2	3	54	76	2.17	132	.276	.314	88-1-1	.193	3	80	16	—	2.3
1920	Bos N	4	8	.333	18	11	3	0	89	104	57	4	4	24	24	4.04	75	.294	.346	27-0-2	.185	-0	96	-13	—	-1.7
1922	Bos N	0	2	.000	3	3	1	0	16	22	10	2	0	5	3	5.06	79	.328	.375	5	.400	1	88	-1	—	-0.1
1923	Bos N	1	2	.333	4	4	1-1	0	19.1	27	12	0	1	10	3	3.72	107	.333	.413	7	.000	-1	88	0	—	-0.1
1927	Bos N	0	0	ø	1	0	0	0	1.1	1	0	0	0	1	0	0.00	ø	.200	.333	0	ø	0	—	1	—	0.0
Total	13	121	109	.526	279	240	172-27	8	2049	1971	778	35	27	402	786	2.66	104	.258	.298	698-2-30	.188	14	97	30	—	5.5
Ruebel, Matt	Matthew Alexander; B10.16.1969 Cincinnati OH; BL/TL/6´2˝/180; [PitN91 3/97]; d5.21; Col Oklahoma																									
1996	Pit N	1	1	.500	26	7	0	1-0	58.2	64	38	7	6	25-0	22	4.60	95	.277	.358	13-0-2	.231	1	120	-3	0	-0.1
1997	Pit N	3	2	.600	44	0	0	0-1	62.2	77	50	8	5	27-3	50	6.32	68	.301	.372	7-0-1	.000	-1	—	-14	16	-1.1
1998	TB A	0	2	.000	7	1	0	0-0	8.2	11	7	3	0	4-0	6	6.23	77	.314	.385	0	ø	0	39	-2	0	-0.3
Total	3	4	5	.444	77	8	0	1-1	130	152	95	18	11	56-3	78	5.54	79	.291	.367	20-0-3	.150	-0	112	-19	16	-1.5

RUETER, KIRK Kirk Wesley; B12.1.1970 Hoyleton IL; BL/TL/6´3˝/(190–212); [MonN91 18/477]; d7.7; Col Murray St.

YEAR	TM LG	W	L	PCT	G	GS	CG-SHO	SV-BS	IP	H	R	HR	HB	BB-IB	SO	ERA	AERA	OAV	OOB	AB-HR-SH	AVG	PB	SUP	APR	DL	PW
1993	Mon N	8	0	1.000	14	14	1	0-0	85.2	85	33	5	0	18-1	31	2.73	153	.264	.303	26-0-8	.077	-1	111	12	0	1.1
1994	Mon N	7	3	.700	20	20	0	0-0	92.1	106	60	11	2	23-1	50	5.17	82	.294	.335	34-0-2	.118	-1	134	-10	0	-1.0
1995	Mon N	5	3	.625	9	9	1-1	0-0	47.1	38	17	3	1	9-0	28	3.23	133	.224	.267	16-0-2	.000	-2	96	6	0	0.8
1996	Mon N	5	6	.455	16	16	0	0-0	78.2	91	44	12	2	22-0	30	4.58	95	.294	.344	25-0-2	.120	-1	130	-2	16	-0.2
	SF N	1	2	.333	4	3	0	0-0	23.1	18	6	0	0	5-0	16	1.93	215	.207	.250	7	.143	0	51	6	0	0.7
	Year	6	8	.429	20	19	0	0-0	102	109	50	12	2	27-0	46	3.97	108	.275	.324	32-0-2	.125	-1	118	4	0	0.5
1997	†SF N	13	6	.684	32	32	0	0-0	190.2	194	83	17	1	51-8	115	3.45	120	.264	.311	65-0-7	.138	-1	117	14	0	1.4
1998	SF N	16	9	.640	33	33	1	0-0	187.2	193	100	27	7	57-3	102	4.36	92	.265	.321	67-0-9	.209	1*	139	-8	0	-0.8
1999	SF N	15	10	.600	33	33	1	0-0	184.2	219	118	28	2	55-2	94	5.41	79	.297	.346	58-0-8	.155	1	123	-23	0	-2.4
2000	†SF N	11	9	.550	32	31	0	0-0	184	205	92	23	2	62-5	71	3.96	110	.290	.345	60-0-10	.200	2*	116	7	0	1.1
2001	SF N	14	12	.538	34	34	0	0-0	195.1	213	105	25	4	66-4	83	4.42	93	.283	.341	58-0-10	.172	2*	117	-8	0	-0.5
2002	†SF N	14	8	.636	33	33	0	0-0	203.2	204	83	22	1	54-7	76	3.23	122	.262	.308	62-0-13	.177	0*	117	15	0	1.6
2003	†SF N	10	5	.667	27	27	0	0-0	147	170	77	14	1	47-2	41	4.53	94	.297	.350	53-0-6	.132	-1	123	-3	45	-0.3
2004	SF N	9	12	.429	33	33	0	0-0	190.1	225	108	21	1	66-5	56	4.73	92	.296	.351	61-0-3	.131	-1*	95	-8	0	-0.6
2005	SF N	2	7	.222	20	18	0	0-0	107.1	131	78	12	1	47-3	25	5.95	71	.305	.368	30-0-6	.167	0*	104	-21	7	-1.4
Total	13	130	92	.586	340	336	4-1	0-0	1918	2092	1004	220	25	582-41	818	4.27	98	.281	.333	622-0-86	.153	-1	117	-23	68	-0.5

RUETHER, DUTCH Walter Henry; B9.13.1893 Alameda CA; D5.16.1970 Phoenix AZ; BL/TL/6´1.5˝/180; d4.13; Mil 1918; ▲

YEAR	TM LG	W	L	PCT	G	GS	CG-SHO	SV-BS	IP	H	R	HR	HB	BB-IB	SO	ERA	AERA	OAV	OOB	AB-HR-SH	AVG	PB	SUP	APR	DL	PW
1917	Chi N	2	0	1.000	10	4	1	0	36.1	37	12	0	3	12	23	2.48	117	.285	.359	44-0-1	.273	2*	162	2	—	0.4
	Cin N	1	2	.333	7	4	1-1	0	35.2	43	17	0	2	14	12	3.53	74	.323	.396	24	.208	1*	101	-3	—	-0.1
	Year	3	2	.600	17	8	2-1	0	72	80	29	0	5	26	35	3.00	92	.304	.378	68-0-1	.250	3	133	-1	—	0.3
1918	Cin N	0	1	.000	2	2	1	0	10	10	9	0	1	3	10	2.70	99	.244	.311	3	.000	-0	28	-2	—	-0.2
1919	†Cin N	19	6	**.760**	33	29	20-3	0	242.2	195	69	1	7	83	78	1.82	153	.223	.295	92-0-3	.261	6*	117	24	—	3.1
1920	Cin N	16	12	.571	37	33	23-5	3	265.2	235	87	2	9	96	99	2.47	123	.247	.321	104-0-2	.192	-1*	93	19	—	2.0
1921	Bro N	10	13	.435	36	27	12-1	2	211.1	247	116	7	7	67	78	4.26	91	.299	.356	97-2-2	.351	11*	89	-6	—	0.5
1922	Bro N	21	12	.636	35	35	26-2	0	267.1	290	123	11	6	92	89	3.53	115	.282	.345	125-2-5	.208	6*	96	18	—	2.5
1923	Bro N	15	14	.517	34	34	20	0	275	308	157	11	6	86	87	4.22	92	.287	.343	117-0-2	.274	4*	116	-8	—	-0.2
1924	Bro N	8	13	.381	30	21	13-2	3	168	190	92	4	5	45	63	3.91	96	.282	.332	62-0-1	.242	2*	86	-4	—	-0.2
1925	†Was A	18	7	.720	30	29	16-1	0	223.1	241	105	5	8	105	68	3.87	109	.281	.365	108-1-3	.333	6*	120	14	—	2.2
1926	Was A	12	6	.667	23	23	9	0	169.1	214	100	5	4	66	48	4.84	80	.311	.375	92-1-3	.250	4*	134	-16	—	-1.1
	†NY A	2	3	.400	5	5	1	0	36	32	14	0	1	18	8	3.50	110	.248	.345	21	.095	-2*	79	3	—	0.1
	Year	14	9	.609	28	28	10	0	205.1	246	114	5	5	84	56	4.60	84	.301	.370	113-1-3	.221	3	125	-14	—	-1.0
1927	NY A	13	6	.684	27	26	12-3	0	184	202	88	8	7	52	45	3.38	114	.287	.343	80-1-0	.262	5*	132	9	—	1.2
Total	11	137	95	.591	309	272	155-18	8	2124.2	2244	989	54	66	739	708	3.50	104	.277	.342	969-7-22	.258	45	109	50	—	10.2

RUFFCORN, SCOTT Scott Patrick; B12.29.1969 Austin TX; BR/TR/6´4˝/210; [ChiA91 1/25]; d6.19; Col Baylor

YEAR	TM LG	W	L	PCT	G	GS	CG-SHO	SV-BS	IP	H	R	HR	HB	BB-IB	SO	ERA	AERA	OAV	OOB	AB-HR-SH	AVG	PB	SUP	APR	DL	PW
1993	Chi A	0	2	.000	3	2	0	0-0	10	9	11	2	0	10-0	2	8.10	52	.265	.422	0	ø	0	66	-5	0	-0.8
1994	Chi A	0	2	.000	2	2	0	0-0	6.1	15	11	1	0	5-0	3	12.79	37	.455	.513	0	ø	0	49	-6	0	-0.9
1995	Chi A	0	0	ø	4	0	0	0-0	8	10	7	0	2	13-0	5	7.88	57	.333	.556	0	ø	0	—	-3	0	-0.1
1996	Chi A	0	1	.000	3	1	0	0-0	6.1	10	8	1	0	6-0	3	11.37	42	.370	.485	0	ø	0	39	-5	0	-0.5
1997	Phi N	0	3	.000	18	4	0	0-0	39.2	42	40	4	7	36-1	33	7.71	55	.275	.423	6-0-1	.000	-0	82	-17	42	-1.1
Total	5	0	8	.000	30	9	0	0-0	70.1	86	77	8	9	70-1	46	8.57	51	.310	.455	6-0-1	.000	-0	66	-36	42	-3.4

RUFFIN, BRUCE Bruce Wayne; B10.4.1963 Lubbock TX; BB/TL (BR 1986–87)/6´2˝/(205–215); [PhiN85 2/34]; d6.28; Col Texas

YEAR	TM LG	W	L	PCT	G	GS	CG-SHO	SV-BS	IP	H	R	HR	HB	BB-IB	SO	ERA	AERA	OAV	OOB	AB-HR-SH	AVG	PB	SUP	APR	DL	PW
1986	Phi N	9	4	.692	21	21	6	0-0	146.1	138	53	6	1	44-6	70	2.46	159	.251	.306	55-0-1	.073	-3	110	19	0	1.3
1987	Phi N	11	14	.440	35	35	3-1	0-0	204.2	236	118	17	2	73-4	93	4.35	99	.298	.355	73-0-6	.055	-5	82	-5	0	-1.0
1988	Phi N	6	10	.375	55	15	3	3-2	144.1	151	86	7	3	80-6	82	4.43	82	.275	.368	33	.121	-0	72	-16	0	-1.7
1989	Phi N	6	10	.375	24	23	1	0-0	125.2	152	69	10	0	62-6	70	4.44	81	.301	.377	34-0-1	.176	2	103	-11	0	-1.0
1990	Phi N	6	13	.316	32	25	2-1	0-0	149	178	99	14	1	62-7	79	5.38	72	.297	.361	44-0-6	.068	-2	99	-25	0	-3.0
1991	Phi N	4	7	.364	31	15	1-1	0-0	119	125	52	6	1	38-3	85	3.78	98	.272	.327	24-0-6	.000	-1	83	0	0	-0.1
1992	Mil A	1	6	.143	25	6	1	0-2	58	66	43	7	0	41-3	45	6.67	58	.293	.398	0	ø	0	67	-17	0	-1.8
1993	Col N	6	5	.545	59	12	0	2-1	139.2	145	71	10	1	69-9	126	3.87	124	.269	.350	25-0-3	.080	-1	110	11	0	0.7
1994	Col N	4	5	.444	56	0	0	16-5	55.2	55	28	6	1	30-2	65	4.04	123	.253	.343	4	.250	0	—	5	0	0.9
1995	†Col N	0	1	.000	37	0	0	11-1	34	26	8	1	0	19-1	23	2.12	254	.222	.331	2	.000	-0	—	10	76	0.8
1996	Col N	7	5	.583	71	0	0	24-5	69.2	55	35	5	0	29-3	74	4.00	130	.212	.288	1	.000	0	—	7	0	1.4
1997	Col N	0	2	.000	23	0	0	7-2	22	18	15	3	0	18-0	31	5.32	97	.220	.360	0	ø	0	—	-1	123	-0.1
Total	12	60	82	.423	469	152	17-3	63-18	1268	1345	677	92	10	565-50	843	4.19	99	.275	.348	295-0-23	.081	-10	89	-23	199	-3.6

RUFFIN, JOHNNY Johnny Renando; B7.29.1971 Butler AL; BR/TR/6´3˝/(170–180); [ChiA88 4/93]; d8.8

YEAR	TM LG	W	L	PCT	G	GS	CG-SHO	SV-BS	IP	H	R	HR	HB	BB-IB	SO	ERA	AERA	OAV	OOB	AB-HR-SH	AVG	PB	SUP	APR	DL	PW
1993	Cin N	2	1	.667	21	0	0	2-1	37.2	36	16	4	1	11-1	30	3.58	112	.247	.304	3	.333	0	—	2	0	0.2
1994	Cin N	7	2	.778	51	0	0	1-2	70	57	26	7	0	27-3	44	3.09	135	.223	.295	8	.000	-1	—	9	0	0.9
1995	Cin N	0	0	ø	10	0	0	0-0	13.1	4	3	0	0	11-0	11	1.35	309	.093	.278	2	.000	-0	—	4	31	0.2
1996	Cin N	1	3	.250	49	0	0	0-1	62.1	71	42	10	2	37-5	69	5.49	78	.292	.386	4	.500	1	—	-8	0	-0.4
2000	Ari N	0	0	ø	5	0	0	0-0	9	14	9	4	0	3-1	5	9.00	53	.350	.395	0	ø	0	—	-4	49	-0.2
2001	Fla N	0	0	ø	3	0	0	0-0	3.2	5	4	0	1	4-1	4	4.91	85	.313	.476	0	ø	0	—	-1	0	-0.1
Total	6.	10	6	.625	139	0	0	3-4	196	187	100	25	4	93-11	163	4.13	102	.251	.336	17	.176	-0	—	2	80	0.6

RUFFING, RED Charles Herbert; B5.3.1905 Granville IL; D2.17.1986 Mayfield Hts. OH; BR/TR/6´1.5˝/205; d5.31; Mil 1943–44; C1; HF1967; ▲

YEAR	TM LG	W	L	PCT	G	GS	CG-SHO	SV-BS	IP	H	R	HR	HB	BB-IB	SO	ERA	AERA	OAV	OOB	AB-HR-SH	AVG	PB	SUP	APR	DL	PW
1924	Bos A	0	0	ø	8	2	0	0	23	29	17	0	3	9	10	6.65	66	.333	.414	7	.143	-0	135	-4	—	-0.2
1925	Bos A	9	18	.333	37	27	13-3	1	217.1	253	135	10	2	75	64	5.01	91	.299	.357	79-0-2	.215	-0	88	-4	—	-0.5
1926	Bos A	6	15	.286	37	22	6	2	166	169	96	4	5	68	58	4.39	93	.274	.351	51-1-2	.196	0	69	-6	—	-0.8
1927	Bos A	5	13	.278	26	18	10	2	158.1	160	94	7	4	87	77	4.66	91	.277	.375	55-0-6	.255	1*	72	-6	—	-0.4
1928	Bos A	10	25	.286	42	34	**25**-1	2	289.1	303	147	8	10	96	118	3.89	106	.275	.339	121-2-7	.314	11*	71	6	—	1.8
1929	Bos A	9	22	.290	35	32	18-1	1	244.1	280	162	17	2	118	109	4.86	88	.297	.376	114-2-3	.307	5*	76	-18	—	-1.1
1930	Bos A	0	3	.000	4	3	1	0	24	32	19	1	1	6	14	6.38	72	.323	.368	11	.273	1*	56	-5	—	-0.4
	NY A	15	5	.750	34	25	12-2	1	197.2	200	106	10	2	62	117	4.14	104	.260	.317	99-4-0	.374	17*	130	6	—	1.9
	Year	15	8	.652	38	28	13-2	1	221.2	232	125	11	3	68	131	4.38	99	.268	.323	110-4-0	.364	18	122	1	—	1.5
1931	NY A	16	14	.533	37	30	19-1	2	237	240	130	11	6	87	132	4.41	90	.256	.323	109-3-6	.330	11*	143	-11	—	-0.1
1932	†NY A	18	7	.720	35	29	22-3	2	259	219	102	16	3	115	**190**	3.09	132	**.226**	.311	124-3-2	.306	14*	129	32	—	4.0
1933	NY A	9	14	.391	35	28	18	3	235	230	118	7	4	93	122	3.91	99	.258	.330	115-2-2	.252	8*	111	0	—	0.7
1934	NY A★	19	11	.633	36	31	19-5	0	256.1	232	134	18	1	104	149	3.93	103	.236	.310	113-2-0	.248	7*	122	2	—	0.7
1935	NY A	16	11	.593	30	29	19-2	0	222	201	88	17	1	76	81	3.12	130	.239	.303	109-2-1	.339	14*	103	27	—	4.2
1936	†NY A	20	12	.625	33	33	25-3	0	271	274	133	22	3	90	102	3.85	121	.263	.323	127-5-2	.291	16*	119	25	—	3.9
1937	†NY A	20	7	.741	31	31	22-4	0	256.1	242	101	17	1	68	131	2.98	149	.247	.296	129-1-2	.202	3*	137	43	—	4.0
1938	†NY A☆	**21**	7	**.750**	31	31	22-3	0	247.1	246	104	16	0	82	127	3.31	137	.258	.317	107-3-1	.224	10*	127	**37**	—	**4.5**
1939	†NY A★	21	7	.750	28	28	22-**5**	0	233.1	211	88	15	2	75	95	2.93	149	.240	.301	114-1-3	.307	9*	152	38	—	4.8
1940	NY A★	15	12	.556	30	30	20-3	0	226	218	98	24	3	76	97	3.38	119	.252	.314	89-1-1	.124	-3*	99	17	—	1.3
1941	†NY A☆	15	6	.714	23	23	13-2	0	185.2	177	87	13	1	54	60	3.54	111	.252	.306	89-2-1	.303	12*	136	7	0	1.7
1942	†NY A☆	14	7	.667	24	24	16-4	0	193.2	183	72	10	3	41	80	3.21	107	.250	.292	80-1-2	.250	7*	142	9	0	1.5
1945	NY A	7	3	.700	11	11	8-1	0	87.1	85	32	2	1	20	24	2.89	120	.251	.294	46-1-0	.217	1*	132	6	0	0.6
1946	NY A	5	1	.833	8	8	4-2	0	61	37	13	2	0	23	19	1.77	195	.171	.251	25	.120	-1	102	12	73	1.0
1947	Chi A	3	5	.375	9	9	1	0	53	63	39	7	0	16	11	6.11	60	.290	.339	24	.208	-0*	118	-13	65	-1.7
Total	22	273	225	.548	624	538	335-45	16	4344	4284	2115	254	58	1541	1987	3.80	109	.258	.323	1937-36-43	.269	143	112	200	138	31.4

RUHLE, VERN Vernon Gerald; B1.25.1951 Coleman MI; BR/TR/6´1˝/(175–195); [DetA72 17/404]; d9.9; C8; Col Olivet

YEAR	TM LG	W	L	PCT	G	GS	CG-SHO	SV-BS	IP	H	R	HR	HB	BB-IB	SO	ERA	AERA	OAV	OOB	AB-HR-SH	AVG	PB	SUP	APR	DL	PW
1974	Det A	2	0	1.000	5	3	1	0-0	33	35	13	1	1	6-0	10	2.73	140	.273	.307	0	ø	0	107	3	0	0.1
1975	Det A	11	12	.478	32	31	8-3	0-0	190	199	104	17	7	65-6	67	4.03	100	.266	.328	0	ø	0	89	-1	0	-0.3
1976	Det A	9	12	.429	32	32	5-1	0-0	199.2	227	99	19	4	59-4	88	3.92	95	.288	.339	0	ø	0	99	-4	0	-0.4
1977	Det A	3	5	.375	14	10	0	0-0	66.1	83	44	9	3	15-0	27	5.70	76	.305	.346	0	ø	0	65	-8	26	-0.9
1978	Hou N	3	3	.500	13	10	2-2	0-0	68	57	17	0	1	20-1	27	2.12	157	.224	.282	18-0-1	.056	-1	94	10	0	0.7
1979	Hou N	2	6	.250	13	10	2-2	0-1	66.1	64	33	9	2	8-0	33	4.07	86	.249	.277	19-0-2	.053	-1	86	-4	110	-0.6
1980	†Hou N	12	4	.750	28	22	6-2	0-0	159.1	148	51	7	3	29-1	55	2.37	138	.251	.287	49-0-4	.245	4	98	16	0	2.0
1981	†Hou N	4	6	.400	20	15	1	1-1	102	97	36	6	1	20-1	39	2.91	113	.250	.288	24-0-4	.250	3	97	5	21	0.8
1982	Hou N	9	13	.409	31	21	3-2	1-1	149	169	81	12	4	24-4	56	3.93	85	.289	.319	41-0-5	.098	-0	80	-14	0	-2.1

YEAR	TM LG	W	L	PCT	G	GS	CG-SHO	SV-BS	IP	H	R	HR	HB	BB-IB	SO	ERA	AERA	OAV	OOB	AB-HR-SH	AVG	PB	SUP	APR	DL	PW
1983	Hou N	8	5	.615	41	9	0	3-0	114.2	107	49	13	3	36-7	43	3.69	93	.249	.308	19-0-4	.105	0	106	-1	0	-0.1
1984	Hou N	1	9	.100	40	6	0	2-0	90.1	112	58	5	3	29-7	60	4.58	73	.309	.363	12	.083	-0	106	-15	0	-1.6
1985	Cle A	2	10	.167	42	16	1	3-1	125	139	65	16	2	30-6	54	4.32	96	.283	.324	0	ø	0	71	-1	33	-0.2
1986	†Cal A	1	3	.250	16	3	0	1-0	47.2	46	25	5	1	7-0	23	4.15	100	.247	.276	0	ø	0	80	0	0	0.0
Total	13	67	88	.432	327	188	29-12	11-4	1411.1	1483	675	119	35	348-37	582	3.73	98	.270	.316	182-0-20	.148	6	90	-14	190	-2.6
Runyan, Sean	Sean David; B6.21.1974 Fort Smith AR; BL/TL/6´3˝/(200–210); [HouN92 5/125]; d3.31																									
1998	Det A	1	4	.200	**88**	0	0	1-2	50.1	47	23	7	2	28-3	39	3.58	133	.255	.348	0	ø	0	—	6	0	0.5
1999	Det A	0	1	.000	12	0	0	0-0	10.2	9	4	2	1	3-1	6	3.38	148	.237	.295	0	ø	0	—	2	150	0.2
2000	Det A	0	0	ø	3	0	0	0-0	3	2	2	0	0	2-0	1	6.00	82	.222	.333	0	ø	0	—	0	61	0.0
Total	3	1	5	.167	103	0	0	1-2	64	58	29	9	3	33-4	46	3.66	131	.251	.339	0	ø	0	—	8	211	0.7
Rupe, Josh	Joshua Matthew; B8.18.1982 Portsmouth VA; BR/TR/6´2˝/(200–210); [ChiA02 3/90]; d9.16; Col Louisburg (NC) JC																									
2005	Tex A	1	0	1.000	4	1	0	0-0	9.2	7	4	0	2	4-0	6	2.79	163	.219	.342	0	ø	0	102	1	0	0.1
2006	Tex A	0	1	.000	16	0	0	0-1	29	33	11	2	1	9-0	14	3.41	137	.287	.344	0	ø	0	—	4	87	0.2
Total	2	1	1	.500	20	1	0	0-1	38.2	40	15	2	3	13-0	20	3.26	143	.272	.344	0	ø	0	102	5	87	0.3
Rupe, Ryan	Ryan Kittman; B3.31.1975 Houston TX; BR/TR/6´5˝/230; [TBA98 6/192]; d5.5; Col Texas A&M																									
1999	TB A	8	9	.471	24	24	0	0-0	142.1	136	81	17	12	57-2	97	4.55	109	.253	.334	4	.000	-0	85	7	0	0.6
2000	TB A	5	6	.455	18	18	0	0-0	91	121	75	19	9	31-3	61	6.92	71	.321	.381	1	.000	-0	101	-20	20	-1.9
2001	TB A	5	12	.294	28	26	0	0-1	143.1	161	111	30	11	48-0	123	6.59	68	.283	.348	3	.333	1	89	-30	0	-2.9
2002	TB A	5	10	.333	15	15	2	0-0	90	83	60	11	10	25-0	67	5.60	81	.243	.311	1	.000	-0	75	-10	97	-1.5
2003	Bos A	1	1	.500	4	1	0	0-1	10	13	9	4	0	1-0	7	6.30	74	.302	.318	0	ø	0	79	-2	0	-0.4
Total	5	24	38	.387	89	84	2	0-2	476.2	514	336	81	42	162-5	355	5.85	81	.275	.343	9	.111	-0	88	-55	117	-6.1
Rusch, Glendon	Glendon James; B11.7.1974 Seattle WA; BL/TL/6´1˝/(195–225); [KCA93 17/469]; d4.6																									
1997	KC A	6	9	.400	30	27	1	0-0	170.1	206	111	28	7	52-0	116	5.50	86	.301	.353	3	.000	-0	90	-13	15	-1.1
1998	KC A	6	15	.286	29	24	1-1	1-0	154.2	191	104	22	4	50-0	94	5.88	83	.304	.358	3	.000	-0	74	-14	26	-1.6
1999	KC A	0	1	.000	3	0	0	0-0	4	7	7	1	1	3-0	4	15.75	32	.368	.478	0	ø	0	—	-4	0	-0.7
	NY N	0	0	ø	1	0	0	0-0	1	1	0	0	0	0-0	0	0.00	ø	.333	.333	0	ø	0	—	1	0	0.0
2000	†NY N	11	11	.500	31	30	2	0-0	190.2	196	91	18	6	44-2	157	4.01	109	.267	.311	50-0-4	.060	-3	80	9	0	0.6
2001	NY N	8	12	.400	33	33	1	0-0	179	216	101	23	7	43-2	156	4.63	87	.300	.344	54-0-6	.056	-4	73	-13	0	-1.7
2002	Mil N	10	16	.385	34	34	4-1	0-0	210.2	227	118	30	5	76-1	140	4.70	88	.279	.343	66-1-14	.288	5*	95	-13	0	-1.0
2003	Mil N	1	12	.077	32	19	1	1-0	123.1	171	93	11	4	45-3	93	6.42	67	.331	.387	34-0-4	.206	1*	67	-28	24	-2.4
2004	Chi N	6	2	.750	32	16	0	2-0	129.2	127	54	10	4	33-1	90	3.47	128	.255	.305	39-2-7	.154	1*	107	13	0	0.9
2005	Chi N	9	8	.529	46	19	1-1	0-1	145.1	175	79	14	1	53-8	111	4.52	97	.302	.357	41	.146	-0	78	-3	0	-0.3
2006	Chi N	3	8	.273	25	9	0	0-0	66.1	86	57	21	1	33-2	59	7.46	61	.320	.395	15-0-3	.200	0	92	-19	36	-2.6
Total	10	60	94	.390	296	211	11-3	4-1	1375	1603	815	178	40	432-19	1020	5.01	88	.293	.347	305-3-38	.154	0	83	-84	101	-9.9
Rush, Andy	Jesse Howard; B12.26.1889 Hartland KS; D3.16.1969 Fresno CA; BR/TR/6´3˝/180; d4.16																									
1925	Bro N	0	1	.000	4	2	0	0	9.2	16	14	3	0	5	4	9.31	45	.364	.429	3	.000	-0	91	-6	—	-0.6
Rush, Bob	Robert Ransom; B12.21.1925 Battle Creek MI; BR/TR/6´4˝/(200–205); d4.22																									
1948	Chi N	5	11	.313	36	16	4	0	133.1	153	70	8	1	37	72	3.92	100	.287	.335	39-0-2	.128	-2*	54	-1	0	-0.2
1949	Chi N	10	18	.357	35	27	9-1	4	201	197	104	9	0	79	80	4.07	99	.255	.324	63-0-5	.032	-7	66	-1	0	-0.8
1950	Chi N☆	13	20	.394	39	34	19-1	1	254.2	261	124	11	6	93	93	3.71	113	.265	.332	90-1-1	.167	-1*	66	14	0	1.7
1951	Chi N	11	12	.478	37	29	12-2	2	211.1	212	108	16	3	68	129	3.83	107	.254	.312	68-0-4	.191	-0	100	3	0	0.3
1952	Chi N★	17	13	.567	34	32	17-4	0	250.1	205	99	14	6	81	157	2.70	143	.216	.282	96-0-2	.292	7	102	26	0	4.0
1953	Chi N	9	14	.391	29	28	8-1	0	166.2	177	97	17	5	66	84	4.54	98	.270	.341	54-0-3	.111	-2	71	-2	0	-0.4
1954	Chi N	13	15	.464	33	32	11	0	236.1	213	102	12	5	103	124	3.77	111	.243	.323	83-2-1	.277	7	84	15	0	2.5
1955	Chi N	13	11	.542	33	33	14-3	0	234	204	95	19	2	73-4	130	3.50	117	.234	.293	82-1-3	.110	-3	95	18	0	1.4
1956	Chi N	13	10	.565	32	32	13-1	0	239.2	210	101	30	2	59-8	104	3.19	118	.233	.280	82-0-4	.098	-3	93	14	0	0.9
1957	Chi N	6	16	.273	31	29	5	0	205.1	211	111	16	2	66-6	103	4.38	88	.265	.318	69-0-3	.203	2	93	-11	0	-1.0
1958	†Mil N	10	6	.625	28	20	5-2	0	147.1	142	59	13	1	31-7	84	3.42	103	.253	.291	45-0-3	.200	2	122	3	0	0.4
1959	Mil N	5	6	.455	31	9	1-1	0	101.1	102	39	5	1	23-2	64	2.40	148	.257	.298	32-0-1	.188	0	95	10	0	1.0
1960	Mil N	2	0	1.000	10	0	0	1	15	24	9	2	0	5-2	8	4.20	82	.369	.403	3	.333	1	—	-2	0	-0.2
	Chi A	0	0	ø	9	0	0	0	14.1	16	10	4	0	5-2	12	5.65	67	.302	.362	1	1.000	0	—	-3	0	-0.1
Total	13	127	152	.455	417	321	118-16	8	2410.2	2327	1128	176	34	789-31	1244	3.65	109	.251	.311	807-4-32	.173	0	87	83	0	9.5
Rusie, Amos	Amos Wilson "The Hoosier Thunderbolt"; B5.30.1871 Mooresville IN; D12.6.1942 Seattle WA; BR/TR/6´1˝/200; d5.9; HF1977																									
1889	Ind N	12	10	.545	33	22	19-1	0	225	246	181	12	9	116	109	5.32	78	.270	.358	103	.175	-3	110	-25	—	-2.2
1890	NY N	29	34	.460	67	62	56-4	1	548.2	436	300	3	26	289	**341**	2.56	137	**.211**	.316	284	.278	10*	79	50	—	5.9
1891	NY N	33	20	.623	61	57	52-**6**	1	500.1	391	244	6	18	262	**337**	2.55	125	**.207**	.310	220	.245	4*	110	40	—	3.9
1892	NY N	32	31	.508	65	62	59-2	0	541	410	290	7	12	270	304	2.84	113	.202	.299	256-1	.215	0*	99	23	—	2.5
1893	NY N	33	21	.611	**56**	**52**	**50-4**	1	**482**	451	260	15	16	218	**208**	3.23	144	**.240**	.324	212-3	.269	3	103	**74**	—	**6.8**
1894	†NY N	**36**	13	.735	54	**50**	45-**3**	1	444	426	228	10	5	200	**195**	**2.78**	**189**	**.250**	**.330**	186-3-2	.280	2*	86	118	—	**10.2**
1895	NY N	23	23	.500	49	47	42-**4**	0	393.1	384	248	9	7	159	**201**	3.73	125	.252	.325	179-1-0	.246	-5*	100	37	—	2.8
1897	NY N	28	10	.737	38	37	35-2	0	322.1	314	143	6	10	87	135	**2.54**	163	.253	.308	144	.278	3*	126	58	—	5.9
1898	NY N	20	11	.645	37	36	33-4	1	300	288	149	6	9	103	114	3.03	115	.251	.317	138	.210	-1*	101	18	—	1.4
1901	Cin N	0	1	.000	3	2	2	0	22	43	25	1	0	3	6	8.59	37	.406	.422	8	.125	-0	44	-12	—	-0.5
Total	10	246	174	.586	463	427	393-30	5	3778.2	3389	2068	75	112	1707	1950	3.07	130	.234	.319	1730-8-2	.248	13	99	381	—	36.7
Ruskin, Scott	Scott Drew; B6.8.1963 Jacksonville FL; BR/TL/6´2˝/(185–195); [PitN86 S3/64]; d4.9; Col Florida																									
1990	Pit N	2	2	.500	44	0	0	2-3	47.2	50	21	2	2	28-3	34	3.02	121	.269	.367	6	.333	2	—	2	0	0.3
	Mon N	1	0	1.000	23	0	0	0-3	27.2	25	7	2	0	10-3	23	2.28	161	.243	.310	2	.000	-0	—	5	0	0.2
	Year	3	2	.600	67	0	0	2-6	75.1	75	28	4	2	38-6	57	2.75	133	.260	.347	8	.250	1	—	7	0	0.5
1991	Mon N	4	4	.500	64	0	0	6-5	63.2	57	31	4	3	30-2	46	4.24	86	.241	.333	2	.000	0	—	-3	0	-0.4
1992	Cin N	4	3	.571	57	0	0	0-3	53.2	56	31	6	1	20-4	43	5.03	72	.275	.339	3-0-2	.000	-0	—	-8	0	-0.9
1993	Cin N	0	0	ø	4	0	0	0-0	1	3	2	1	0	2-0	0	18.00	22	.500	.625	0	ø	0	—	-1	0	-0.1
Total	4	11	9	.550	192	0	0	8-14	193.2	191	92	15	6	90-12	146	3.95	92	.260	.343	13-0-2	.154	1	—	-5	0	-0.9
Russell, Allan	Allan "Rubberarm"; B7.31.1893 Baltimore MD; D10.20.1972 Baltimore MD; BB/TR/5´11˝/165; d9.13; b–Lefty																									
1915	NY A	1	2	.333	5	3	1	0	27	21	10	1	1	21	21	2.67	110	.228	.377	8-0-1	.250	0	50	1	—	0.1
1916	NY A	6	10	.375	34	19	8-1	6	171.1	138	83	8	7	75	104	3.20	90	.232	.324	45-0-6	.044	-3*	84	-8	—	-1.1
1917	NY A	7	8	.467	25	10	6	2	104.1	89	42	2	7	39	55	2.24	120	.236	.319	31-0-1	.323	3*	72	2	—	0.7
1918	NY A	7	11	.389	27	18	7-2	4	141	139	68	6	5	73	54	3.26	87	.267	.363	42-0-4	.167	-1*	90	-9	—	-1.3
1919	NY A	5	5	.500	23	9	4-1	1	90.2	89	48	5	2	32	50	3.47	92	.251	.317	30-0-1	.233	0	85	-5	—	-0.4
	Bos A	10	4	.714	21	11	9-1	4	121.1	105	38	1	1	39	63	2.52	120	.246	.310	41-0-2	.122	-1	132	9	—	0.8
	Year	15	9	.625	44	20	13-2	**5**	212	194	86	6	3	71	113	2.93	106	.248	.313	71-0-3	.169	-1	110	4	—	0.4
1920	Bos A	5	6	.455	16	10	7	1	107.2	100	44	3	3	38	53	3.01	121	.251	.321	41-0-2	.122	-2*	98	7	—	0.5
1921	Bos A	6	11	.353	39	14	7	3	173	204	92	10	9	77	60	4.11	103	.303	.382	57	.123	-5*	75	2	—	-0.3
1922	Bos A	6	7	.462	34	11	1	2	125.2	152	81	6	5	57	34	5.01	82	.314	.392	38	.079	-3	51	-12	—	-1.3
1923	Was A	10	7	.588	52	5	4	**9**	181.1	177	81	9	2	77	67	3.03	124	.270	.348	50-0-7	.200	2*	83	13	—	1.2
1924	†Was A	5	1	.833	37	0	0	8	82.1	83	49	1	1	45	17	4.37	92	.282	.379	18-0-1	.278	2	—	-4	—	-0.2
1925	Was A	2	4	.333	32	2	0	2	68.2	85	57	6	1	37	25	5.77	73	.315	.399	14-0-1	.143	-1	50	-14	—	-1.1
Total	11	70	76	.479	345	112	54-5	42	1394.1	1382	693	58	44	610	603	3.52	99	.269	.351	415-0-26	.157	-10	80	-18	—	-2.4
Russell, Lefty	Clarence Dickson; B7.8.1890 Baltimore MD; D1.22.1962 Baltimore MD; BL/TL/6´1˝/165; d10.1; b–Allan																									
1910	Phi A	1	0	1.000	1	1	1-1	0	9	8	0	0	0	2	5	0.00	ø	.258	.303	3	.000	-0	85	3	—	0.3
1911	Phi A	0	3	.000	7	2	0	0	31.2	45	32	1	5	18	7	7.67	41	.357	.456	13	.385	1	126	-16	—	-1.1
1912	Phi A	0	2	.000	5	2	1	0	17.1	18	18	1	3	14	9	7.27	42	.265	.412	4	.000	-0	72	-8	—	-0.8
Total	3	1	5	.167	13	5	2-1	0	58	71	50	2	8	34	21	6.36	47	.316	.423	20	.250	0	96	-21	—	-1.6

YEAR	TM LG	W	L	PCT	G	GS	CG-SHO	SV-BS	IP	H	R	HR	HB	BB-IB	SO	ERA	AERA	OAV	OOB	AB-HR-SH	AVG	PB	SUP	APR	DL	PW
RUSSELL, REB	Ewell Albert; B3.12.1889 Jackson MS; D9.30.1973 Indianapolis IN; BL/TL/5´11˝/185; d4.18; ▲																									
1913	Chi A	22	16	.579	**52**	36	26-8	4	316.2	250	89	2	7	79	122	1.90	154	.220	.275	106-1-4	.189	3*	69	38	—	4.7
1914	Chi A	7	12	.368	38	23	8-1	1	167.1	168	80	3	3	33	79	2.90	92	.268	.308	64	.266	4*	91	-5	—	-0.2
1915	Chi A	11	10	.524	41	25	10-3	2	229.1	215	90	0	6	47	90	2.59	115	.249	.292	86-0-2	.244	4*	101	9	—	1.1
1916	Chi A	18	11	.621	56	25	16-5	3	264.1	207	88	1	1	42	112	2.42	114	.220	**.254**	91-0-2	.143	-4	103	13	—	1.0
1917	†Chi A	15	5	**.750**	35	24	11-5	3	189.1	170	61	1	1	32	54	1.95	136	.245	.279	68-0-4	.279	5*	121	13	—	2.0
1918	Chi A	7	5	.583	19	15	10-2	0	124.2	117	45	0	0	33	38	2.60	105	.252	.302	50-0-4	.140	-1*	105	3	—	0.0
1919	Chi A	0	0	ø	1	0	0	0	0	1	0	0	0	1	0	(0)	ø	1.000	1.000	0	ø	0	—	0	—	0.0
Total	7	80	59	.576	242	148	81-24	13	1291.2	1128	453	7	18	267	495	2.33	120	.239	.282	465-1-16	.209	10	95	71	—	8.6
RUSSELL, JACK	Jack Erwin; B10.24.1905 Paris TX; D11.3.1990 Clearwater FL; BR/TR/6´1.5˝/178; d5.5																									
1926	Bos A	0	5	.000	36	5	1	0	98	94	40	2	1	24	17	3.58	114	.268	.316	21-0-1	.190	-0	87	8	—	0.6
1927	Bos A	4	9	.308	34	15	4-1	0	147	172	80	5	5	40	25	4.10	103	.298	.348	48-0-1	.125	-3*	94	2	—	-0.1
1928	Bos A	11	14	.440	32	26	10-2	0	201.1	233	102	6	4	41	27	3.84	107	.294	.332	62-0-7	.210	-0*	78	5	—	0.6
1929	Bos A	6	18	.250	35	32	13	0	227.1	263	132	12	3	40	37	3.92	109	.290	.322	70-0-5	.129	-4*	76	3	—	0.1
1930	Bos A	9	20	.310	35	30	15	0	229.2	302	162	11	3	53	35	5.45	85	.321	.359	79-1-2	.177	-3*	72	-23	—	-2.4
1931	Bos A	10	18	.357	36	31	13	0	232	298	145	7	2	65	45	5.16	83	.310	.355	82-0-4	.195	-0*	78	-19	—	-1.7
1932	Bos A	1	7	.125	11	6	1	0	39.2	61	35	2	0	15	7	6.81	66	.343	.394	11-0-1	.091	-1*	57	-10	—	-1.6
	Cle A	5	7	.417	18	11	6	1	113	146	67	5	1	27	27	4.70	101	.310	.349	40-0-1	.300	2	87	2	—	0.4
	Year	6	14	.300	29	17	7	1	152.2	207	102	7	1	42	34	5.25	89	.319	.361	51-0-2	.255	1	76	-7	—	-1.2
1933	†Was A	12	6	.667	50	3	2	**13**	124	119	45	3	1	32	28	2.69	156	.255	.305	34-0-2	.147	-1	122	**20**	—	3.1
1934	Was A☆	5	10	.333	**54**	9	3	**7**	157.2	179	86	6	2	56	38	4.17	104	.287	.348	44-0-2	.159	3	99	1	—	0.5
1935	Was A	4	9	.308	43	7	2	3	126	170	88	10	2	37	30	5.71	76	.324	.371	35	.200	1	121	-19	—	-1.6
1936	Was A	3	2	.600	18	5	1	3	49.2	66	46	3	0	25	6	6.34	75	.317	.391	15-0-1	.000	-2	181	-11	—	-1.2
	Bos A	0	3	.000	23	2	0	0	40	57	27	2	0	16	9	5.62	94	.345	.403	7	.286	0	8	-1	—	0.1
	Year	3	5	.375	41	7	1	3	89.2	123	73	5	0	41	15	6.02	83	.330	.396	22-0-1	.091	-2	125	-12	—	-1.1
1937	Det A	2	5	.286	25	0	0	4	40.1	63	35	4	1	20	10	7.59	62	.362	.431	7-0-1	.000	-0	—	-11	—	-1.8
1938	†Chi N	6	1	.857	42	0	0	3	102.1	100	43	1	1	30	29	3.34	115	.258	.313	32-0-1	.219	1	—	6	—	0.7
1939	Chi N	4	3	.571	39	0	0	3	68.2	78	32	3	0	24	32	3.67	107	.282	.339	17	.000	-2*	—	2	—	0.1
1940	StL N	3	4	.429	26	0	0	1	54	53	22	1	0	26	16	2.50	160	.252	.335	13	.000	-2	—	7	—	0.7
Total	15	85	141	.376	557	182	71-3	38	2050.2	2454	1187	83	26	571	418	4.46	97	.299	.346	617-1-29	.167	-11	85	-38	—	-3.5
RUSSELL, JEFF	Jeffrey Lee; B9.2.1961 Cincinnati OH; BR/TR/6´3˝/(195–210); [CinN79 5/126]; d8.13																									
1983	Cin N	4	5	.444	10	10	2	0-0	68.1	58	30	7	0	22-3	40	3.03	126	.233	.290	21-1-2	.143	1	86	4	0	0.6
1984	Cin N	6	18	.250	33	30	4-2	0-0	181.2	186	97	15	4	65-8	101	4.26	89	.263	.327	57-0-5	.140	-0*	72	-10	0	-1.2
1985	Tex A	3	6	.333	13	13	0	0-0	62	85	55	10	2	27-1	44	7.55	56	.324	.388	0	ø	0	95	-21	0	-2.4
1986	Tex A	5	2	.714	37	0	0	2-0	82	74	40	11	1	31-2	54	3.40	127	.244	.315	0	ø	0	—	6	0	0.5
1987	Tex A	5	4	.556	52	2	0	3-1	97.1	109	56	9	2	52-5	56	4.44	102	.285	.369	0	ø	0	61	0	39	0.1
1988	Tex A★	10	9	.526	34	24	5	0-0	188.2	183	86	15	7	66-3	88	3.82	107	.257	.324	1	.000	-0*	95	8	0	0.8
1989	Tex A★	6	4	.600	71	0	0	**38**-6	72.2	45	21	4	3	24-5	77	1.98	201	.182	.260	0	ø	0	—	15	0	3.1
1990	Tex A	1	5	.167	27	0	0	10-2	25.1	23	15	1	0	16-5	16	4.26	92	.253	.361	0	ø	0	—	-2	104	-0.3
1991	Tex A	6	4	.600	68	0	0	30-10	79.1	71	36	11	1	26-1	52	3.29	123	.235	.294	0	ø	0	—	5	0	1.0
1992	Tex A	2	3	.400	51	0	0	28-9	56.2	51	14	3	2	22-3	43	1.91	201	.238	.313	0	ø	0	—	12	0	2.1
	†Oak A	2	0	1.000	8	0	0	2-0	9.2	4	0	0	0	3-0	5	0.00	ø	.125	.200	0	ø	0	—	4	0	0.9
	Year	4	3	.571	59	0	0	30-9	66.1	55	14	3	2	25-3	48	1.63	235	.224	.298	0	ø	0	—	17	0	3.0
1993	Bos A	1	4	.200	51	0	0	33-4	46.2	39	16	1	1	14-1	45	2.70	172	.231	.287	0	ø	0	—	9	30	1.9
1994	Bos A	0	5	.000	29	0	0	12-3	28	30	17	3	1	13-2	18	5.14	98	.270	.346	0	ø	0	—	0	0	0.0
	Cle A	1	1	.500	13	0	0	5-3	12.2	13	8	2	0	3-0	10	4.97	96	.265	.308	0	ø	0	—	0	0	-0.1
	Year	1	6	.143	42	0	0	17-6	40.2	43	25	5	1	16-2	28	5.09	97	.269	.335	0	ø	0	—	0	0	-0.1
1995	Tex A	1	0	1.000	37	0	0	20-4	32.2	36	12	3	0	9-1	21	3.03	160	.277	.324	0	ø	0	—	6	31	0.8
1996	†Tex A	3	3	.500	55	0	0	3-3	56	58	22	5	4	22-3	23	3.38	156	.269	.341	0	ø	0	—	11	0	1.1
Total	14	56	73	.434	589	79	11-2	186-45	1099.2	1065	525	100	28	415-43	693	3.75	112	.255	.323	79-1-7	.139	1	81	47	204	8.9
RUSSELL, JOHN	John Albert; B10.20.1894 San Mateo CA; D11.19.1930 Ely NV; BL/TL/6´2˝/195; d7.4; Mil 1918																									
1917	Bro N	0	1	.000	5	1	1	0	16	12	8	1	0	6	1	4.50	62	.222	.300	4	.250	0	27	-2	—	-0.1
1918	Bro N	0	0	ø	1	0	0	0	1	2	2	0	0	1	0	18.00	15	.500	.600	0	ø	0	—	-1	—	-0.1
1921	Chi A	2	5	.286	11	9	4	0	66.1	82	42	3	1	35	15	5.29	80	.314	.397	25-0-1	.400	3	112	-7	—	-0.3
1922	Chi A	0	1	.000	4	1	0	1	6.2	7	5	0	0	4	3	6.75	60	.280	.379	1	.000	-0	125	-2	—	-0.3
Total	4	2	7	.222	21	11	5	1	90	103	57	4	1	46	19	5.40	73	.299	.384	30-0-1	.367	3	110	-12	—	-0.8
RUSSO, MARIUS	Marius Ugo "Lefty"; B7.19.1914 Brooklyn NY; D3.26.2005 Fort Myers FL; BR/TL/6´1˝/190; d6.6; Mil 1944–45; Col Long Island–Brooklyn																									
1939	NY A	8	3	.727	21	11	9-2	2	116	86	37	6	1	41	55	2.41	181	.210	.283	41-0-2	.244	1	131	26	—	2.4
1940	NY A	14	8	.636	30	24	15	1	189.1	181	79	17	1	55	87	3.28	123	.249	.303	64-0-6	.188	2	133	17	—	2.1
1941	†NY A☆	14	10	.583	28	27	17-3	1	209.2	195	85	8	1	87	105	3.09	127	.247	.322	78-0-5	.231	3	108	20	0	2.4
1942	NY A	4	1	.800	9	5	2	0	45.1	41	15	2	1	14	15	2.78	124	.244	.306	17-0-1	.235	1	154	4	0	0.5
1943	†NY A	5	10	.333	24	14	5-1	1	101.2	89	53	7	2	45	42	3.72	87	.235	.319	31-0-2	.194	1	92	-7	0	-0.9
1946	NY A	0	2	.000	8	3	0	0	18.2	26	9	1	0	11	7	4.34	80	.333	.416	4	.000	-1*	41	-1	0	-0.2
Total	6	45	34	.570	120	84	48-6	5	680.2	618	278	41	6	253	311	3.13	124	.242	.312	235-0-16	.213	8	116	59	0	6.3
RUSTECK, RICH	Richard Frank; B7.12.1941 Chicago IL; BR/TL/6´1˝/170; d6.10; Col Notre Dame																									
1966	NY N	1	2	.333	8	3	1-1	0	24	24	10	1	0	8-0	9	3.00	121	.276	.337	5	.000	-1	113	1	33	0.1
RUTH, BABE	George Herman "The Bambino","The Sultan of Swat"; B2.6.1895 Baltimore MD; D8.16.1948 New York NY; BL/TL/6´2˝/215; d7.11; C1; HF1936; ▲																									
1914	Bos A	2	1	.667	4	3	1	0	23	21	12	1	0	7	3	3.91	69	.236	.292	10	.200	0*	153	-3	—	-0.3
1915	†Bos A	18	8	.692	32	28	16-1	0	217.2	166	80	3	6	85	112	2.44	114	.212	.294	92-4-2	.315	16*	137	8	—	2.8
1916	†Bos A	23	12	.657	44	**41**	23-**9**	1	323.2	230	83	0	8	118	170	**1.75**	**158**	**.201**	.280	136-3-4	.272	14*	108	**35**	—	**5.7**
1917	Bos A	24	13	.649	41	38	**35**-6	2	326.1	244	93	2	11	108	128	2.01	128	.211	.284	123-2-7	.325	17*	103	22	—	4.9
1918	†Bos A	13	7	.650	20	19	18-1	0	166.1	125	51	1	2	49	40	2.22	121	.214	.277	317-11-3	.300	12*	112	10	—	2.9
1919	Bos A	9	5	.643	17	15	12	1	133.1	148	59	2	2	58	30	2.97	102	.290	.365	432-29-3	.322	14*	99	-1	—	1.4
1920	NY A	1	0	1.000	1	1	0	0	4	3	4	0	0	2	0	4.50	85	.200	.294	458-54-5	.376	1*	291	-1	—	-0.1
1921	†NY A	2	0	1.000	2	1	0	0	9	14	10	1	0	9	2	9.00	47	.350	.469	540-59-4	.378	2*	256	-4	—	-0.6
1930	NY A	1	0	1.000	1	1	1	0	9	11	3	0	0	2	3	3.00	143	.306	.342	518-49-21	.359	1*	180	2	—	0.3
1933	NY A★	1	0	1.000	1	1	1	0	9	12	5	0	0	3	0	5.00	78	.308	.357	459-34-0	.301	1*	131	-1	—	0.0
Total	10	94	46	.671	163	148	107-17	4	1221.1	974	400	10	29	441	488	2.28	122	.221	.297	3085-245-49	.338	78	117	67	—	17.0
RUTHERFORD, JOHNNY	John William "Doc"; B5.5.1925 Belleville ON, Can.; BL/TR/5´10.5˝/170; d4.30; Col Detroit Mercy																									
1952	†Bro N	7	7	.500	22	11	4	2	97.1	97	51	9	2	29	29	4.25	86	.262	.319	31-0-1	.290	2	98	-7	0	-0.7
RUTHVEN, DICK	Richard David; B3.27.1951 Sacramento CA; BR/TR/6´3˝/(187–200); [PhiN73*S1/1]; d4.17; Col Cal St.–Fresno																									
1973	Phi N	6	9	.400	25	23	3-1	1-0	128.1	125	69	10	3	75-9	98	4.21	91	.257	.358	38-0-6	.132	-1*	88	-6	29	-0.8
1974	Phi N	9	13	.409	35	35	6	0-0	212.2	182	106	11	3	116-7	153	4.02	95	.231	.329	68-0-5	.191	-1	83	-5	0	-0.7
1975	Phi N	2	2	.500	11	7	0	0-0	40.2	37	22	2	1	22-0	26	4.20	90	.243	.341	13-0-2	.154	-0*	100	-2	0	-0.3
1976	Atl N☆	14	17	.452	36	36	8-4	0-0	240.1	255	112	14	8	90-8	142	4.19	90	.275	.343	76-0-9	.171	-0*	85	-4	0	-0.4
1977	Atl N	7	13	.350	25	23	6-2	0-0	151	158	86	14	1	62-6	84	4.23	105	.267	.336	45-1-5	.267	3	76	1	63	0.4
1978	Atl N	2	6	.250	13	13	2-1	0-0	81	78	43	8	0	28-2	45	4.11	98	.257	.317	24-0-3	.083	-2	70	-1	0	-0.3
	†Phi N	13	5	.722	20	20	9-2	0-0	150.2	136	52	13	1	28-1	75	2.99	121	.248	.283	53-0-3	.283	4*	103	12	0	1.8
	Year	15	11	.577	33	33	11-3	0-0	231.2	214	95	21	1	56-3	120	3.38	111	.251	.295	77-0-6	.221	3	90	9	0	1.5
1979	Phi N	7	5	.583	20	20	3-2	0-0	122.1	121	59	10	2	37-6	58	4.27	91	.256	.311	41-0-2	.146	-0*	117	-4	68	-0.4
1980	†Phi N	17	10	.630	33	33	6-1	0-0	223.1	241	99	9	3	74-9	86	3.55	108	.283	.340	68-0-12	.235	3	109	6	0	1.1
1981	†Phi N★	12	7	.632	23	22	5	0-0	146.2	162	94	10	3	54-4	80	5.15	71	.281	.342	50-0-5	.140	-0	120	-24	0	-2.9
1982	Phi N	11	11	.500	33	31	8-2	0-0	204.1	189	99	18	6	59-10	115	3.79	98	.246	.301	64-0-12	.109	-2	94	-3	0	-0.7
1983	Phi N	1	3	.250	7	7	0	0-0	33.2	46	23	5	0	10-0	26	5.61	64	.333	.368	9-0-3	.111	-0	116	-7	0	-0.7
	Chi N	12	9	.571	25	25	5-2	0-0	149.1	156	78	17	3	28-3	73	4.10	93	.269	.304	53-0-4	.226	2	117	-6	0	-0.4
	Year	13	12	.520	32	32	5-2	0-0	183	202	101	22	3	38-3	99	4.38	86	.281	.317	62-0-7	.210	2	116	-14	0	-1.1
1984	Chi N	6	10	.375	23	22	0	0-0	126.2	154	75	14	4	41-4	55	5.04	78	.302	.357	44-0-5	.159	0*	88	-13	56	-1.5

YEAR	TM LG	W	L	PCT	G	GS	CG-SHO	SV-BS	IP	H	R	HR	HB	BB-IB	SO	ERA	AERA	OAV	OOB	AB-HR-SH	AVG	PB	SUP	APR	DL	PW
1985	Chi N	4	7	.364	20	15	0	0-0	87.1	103	49	6	0	37-3	26	4.53	88	.299	.362	24-0-6	.208	0	75	-5	51	-0.7
1986	Chi N	0	0	ø	6	0	0	0-0	10.2	12	9	4	0	6-0	3	5.06	81	.293	.383	1	.000	-0	—	-2	0	-0.1
Total	14	123	127	.492	355	332	61-17	1-0	2109	2155	1075	165	38	767-72	1145	4.14	93	.267	.331	671-1-82	.183	5	95	-63	267	-6.6
Ryan, Jack	Jack "Gulfport"; B9.19.1884 Lawrenceville IL; D10.16.1949 Handsboro MS; BR/TR/5´10˝/165; d7.2																									
1908	Cle A	1	1	.500	8	1	1	1	35.2	27	12	3	1	2	7	2.27	105	.220	.238	11	.091	0	143	1	—	0.1
1909	Bos A	3	3	.500	13	8	2	0	59.1	64	34	0	4	20	24	3.34	75	.288	.358	19-0-2	.211	0*	92	-7	—	-0.7
1911	Bro N	0	1	.000	3	1	0	0	6	9	7	1	1	4	1	3.00	111	.375	.483	1	.000	-0	68	-2	—	-0.2
Total	3	4	5	.444	24	10	3	1	101	100	53	4	6	26	32	2.94	85	.271	.329	31-0-2	.161	1	95	-8	—	-0.8
Ryan, Jimmy	James Edward "Pony"; B2.11.1863 Clinton MA; D10.26.1923 Chicago IL; BR/TL/5´9˝/162; d10.8.1885; Col Boston College; ▲																									
1886	†Chi N	0	0	ø	5	0	0	1	23.1	19	13	3	—	13	15	4.63	78	.257	.368	327-4	.306	1*	—	0	—	0.1
1887	Chi N	2	1	.667	8	3	2	0	45	53	36	3	6	17	14	4.20	107	.305	.386	508-11	.285	2*	115	1	—	0.2
1888	Chi N	4	0	1.000	8	2	1	0	38.1	47	29	2	0	12	11	3.05	99	.297	.347	549-16	.332	4*	101	-2	—	0.0
1891	Chi N	0	0	ø	2	0	0	1	5.2	11	7	0	0	2	2	1.59	210	.393	.433	505-9	.277	1*	—	-1	—	0.0
1893	Chi N	0	0	ø	1	0	0	0	4.2	3	0	0	0	0	1	0.00	ø	.176	.176	341-3	.299	0*	—	2	—	0.1
Total	5	6	1	.857	24	5	3	2	117	133	85	8	6	44	43	3.62	105	.295	.365	2230-43	.300	9	114	0	—	0.4
Ryan, Jason	Jason Paul; B1.21.1976 Long Branch NJ; BB/TR/6´3˝/(185–195); [ChiN94 9/246]; d8.24																									
1999	Min A	1	4	.200	8	8	1	0-0	40.2	46	23	9	3	17-0	15	4.87	106	.286	.363	0	ø	0	59	1	0	0.1
2000	Min A	0	1	.000	16	1	0	0-0	26	37	24	8	1	10-0	19	7.62	69	.330	.384	0	ø	0	53	-7	0	-0.3
Total	2	1	5	.167	24	9	1	0-0	66.2	83	47	17	4	27-0	34	5.94	88	.304	.371	0	ø	0	58	-6	0	-0.2
Ryan, John	John A.; B Birmingham MI; BL/TR; d4.19																									
1884	Bal U	3	2	.600	6	6	5	0	51	61	42	1	—	16	33	3.35	80	.277	.326	25	.080	-3*	130	-5	—	-0.7
Ryan, Johnny	John Joseph; B10.1853 Philadelphia PA; D3.22.1902 Philadelphia PA; 5´7.5˝/150; d8.19.1873; ▲																									
1874	Bal NA	0	0	ø	1	0	0	0	3.1	13	8	0	—	0	0	16.20	14	.565	.565	181	.193	-0*	—	-3	—	-0.1
1875	NH NA	1	5	.167	10	6	4	0	59.1	70	55	1	—	9	1	3.19	65	.255	.279	146	.158	-1*	45	-6	—	-0.5
1876	Lou N	0	0	ø	1	0	0	0	8	22	20	0	—	0	1	5.63	48	.449	.449	241-1	.253	-0*	—	-3	—	-0.1
Total	2NA	1	5	.167	11	6	4	0	62.2	83	63	1	—	9	1	3.88	54	.279	.301	327	.177	-1	45	-9	—	-0.6
Ryan, Ken	Kenneth Frederick; B10.24.1968 Pawtucket RI; BR/TR/6´3˝/(200–230); d8.31																									
1992	Bos A	0	0	ø	7	0	0	1-0	7	4	5	2	0	5-0	5	6.43	66	.174	.310	0	ø	0	—	-1	0	-0.1
1993	Bos A	7	2	.778	47	0	0	1-3	50	43	23	2	3	29-5	49	3.60	129	.235	.342	0	ø	0	—	5	0	0.9
1994	Bos A	2	3	.400	42	0	0	13-3	48	46	14	1	1	17-3	32	2.44	207	.256	.323	0	ø	0	—	13	0	1.8
1995	Bos A	0	4	.000	28	0	0	7-3	32.2	34	20	4	1	24-6	34	4.96	98	.268	.388	0	ø	0	—	0	0	-0.1
1996	Phi N	3	5	.375	62	0	0	8-5	89	71	32	4	1	45-8	70	2.43	178	.223	.321	7-0-1	.143	-0	—	16	0	1.5
1997	Phi N	1	0	1.000	22	0	0	0-0	20.2	31	23	5	2	13-1	10	9.58	44	.344	.430	0	ø	0	—	-12	123	-0.6
1998	Phi N	0	0	ø	17	1	0	0-0	22.2	21	12	1	1	20-1	16	4.37	99	.253	.396	1	.000	-0	192	0	122	0.0
1999	Phi N	1	2	.333	15	0	0	0-0	15.2	16	11	2	0	11-2	9	6.32	74	.267	.380	0	ø	0	—	-2	0	-0.4
Total	8	14	16	.467	240	1	0	30-14	285.2	266	140	21	9	164-26	225	3.91	117	.250	.352	8-0-1	.125	-0	192	19	245	3.0
Ryan, Nolan	Lynn Nolan; B1.31.1947 Refugio TX; BR/TR/6´2˝/(155–212); [NYN65 10/295]; d9.11; HF1999																									
1966	NY N	0	1	.000	2	1	0	0	3	5	5	1	0	3-1	6	15.00	24	.357	.471	0	ø	0	48	-3	0	-0.6
1968	NY N	6	9	.400	21	18	3	0	134	93	50	12	4	75-4	133	3.09	98	.200	.314	44-0-1	.114	-1	80	-1	33	-0.3
1969	†NY N	6	3	.667	25	10	2	1-0	89.1	60	38	3	1	53-3	92	3.53	104	.189	.306	29-0-3	.103	-1	111	2	27	-0.1
1970	NY N	7	11	.389	27	19	5-2	1-1	131.2	86	59	10	4	97-2	125	3.42	119	.188	.333	45-0-2	.178	-1	78	8	0	0.9
1971	NY N	10	14	.417	30	26	3	0-0	152	125	78	8	15	116-4	137	3.97	87	.219	.365	47-0-3	.128	-0	86	-10	0	-1.6
1972	Cal A☆	19	16	.543	39	39	20-**9**	0-0	284	166	80	14	10	157-4	**329**	2.28	129	**.171**	.291	96-0-1	.135	0	84	22	0	2.9
1973	Cal A★	21	16	.568	41	39	26-4	1-0	326	238	113	18	7	162-2	**383**	2.87	125	.203	.302	0	ø	0	88	30	0	3.2
1974	Cal A	22	16	.579	42	41	26-3	0-1	**332.2**	221	127	18	9	202-3	**367**	2.89	120	**.190**	.313	0	ø	0	104	21	0	2.4
1975	Cal A☆	14	12	.538	28	28	10-5	0-0	198	152	90	13	7	132-0	186	3.45	104	.213	.339	0	ø	0	93	2	0	0.1
1976	Cal A	17	18	.486	39	39	21-**7**	0-0	284.1	193	117	13	5	183-2	**327**	3.36	100	**.195**	.322	0	ø	0	72	2	0	0.2
1977	Cal A✳	19	16	.543	37	37	**22**-4	0-0	299	198	110	12	9	204-7	**341**	2.77	142	**.193**	.329	0	ø	0	91	38	0	4.3
1978	Cal A	10	13	.435	31	31	14-3	0-0	234.2	183	106	12	3	148-7	**260**	3.72	98	.220	.335	0	ø	0	100	-1	38	-0.1
1979	†Cal A★	16	14	.533	34	34	17-**5**	0-0	222.2	169	104	15	6	114-3	**223**	3.60	113	**.212**	.311	0	ø	0	109	10	0	1.2
1980	†Hou N	11	10	.524	35	35	4-2	0-0	233.2	205	100	10	3	98-1	200	3.35	98	.236	.314	70-1-5	.086	-1	109	-2	0	-0.4
1981	†Hou N★	11	5	.688	21	21	5-3	0-0	149	99	34	2	1	68-1	140	**1.69**	**194**	**.188**	.280	51-0-4	.216	3	97	**27**	0	**3.4**
1982	Hou N	16	12	.571	35	35	10-3	0-0	250.1	196	100	20	8	109-3	245	3.16	105	**.213**	.301	83-0-6	.120	-1	102	5	0	0.3
1983	Hou N	14	9	.609	29	29	5-2	0-0	196.1	134	74	9	4	101-3	183	2.98	115	**.195**	.300	69-0-4	.072	-4	96	11	46	0.8
1984	Hou N	12	11	.522	30	30	5-2	0-0	183.2	143	78	12	4	69-2	197	3.04	110	.211	.286	61-0-5	.098	-2	106	4	30	0.2
1985	Hou N★	10	12	.455	35	35	4	0-0	232	205	108	12	9	95-8	209	3.80	92	.239	.318	63-0-14	.111	-1	98	-6	0	-0.8
1986	†Hou N	12	8	.600	30	30	1	0-0	178	119	72	14	4	82-5	194	3.34	108	.188	.283	59-0-3	.102	-2	93	6	38	0.3
1987	Hou N	8	16	.333	34	34	0	0-0	211.2	154	75	14	4	87-2	**270**	**2.76**	**142**	**.199**	.284	65-1-7	.062	-3	77	**27**	0	2.5
1988	Hou N	12	11	.522	33	33	4-1	0-0	220	186	98	18	7	87-6	**228**	3.52	95	.227	.304	70-0-7	.057	-3	103	-5	0	-1.0
1989	Tex A★	16	10	.615	32	32	6-2	0-0	239.1	162	96	17	9	98-3	**301**	3.20	125	**.187**	.275	0	ø	0	99	21	0	2.1
1990	Tex A	13	9	.591	30	30	5-2	0-0	204	137	86	18	7	74-2	**232**	3.44	114	**.188**	**.267**	0	ø	0	99	12	19	1.1
1991	Tex A	12	6	.667	27	27	2-2	0-0	173	102	58	12	5	72-0	203	2.91	139	**.172**	**.263**	0	ø	0	106	24	36	2.3
1992	Tex A	5	9	.357	27	27	2	0-0	157.1	138	75	9	12	69-0	157	3.72	103	.238	.327	0	ø	0	91	1	23	0.1
1993	Tex A	5	5	.500	13	13	0	0-0	66.1	54	47	5	1	40-0	46	4.88	86	.220	.329	0	ø	0	88	-9	115	-1.2
Total	27	324	292	.526	807	773	222-61	3-2	5386	3923	2178	321	158	2795-78	5714	3.19	112	.204	.307	852-2-65	.110	-17	95	236	405	22.2
Ryan, B.J.	Robert Victor; B12.28.1975 Bossier City LA; BL/TL/6´6˝/(230–260); [CinN98 17/500]; d7.28; Col Louisiana–Lafayette																									
1999	Cin N	0	0	ø	1	0	0	0-0	2	4	1	0	0	1-0	1	4.50	104	.500	.556	0	ø	0	—	0	0	0.0
	Bal A	1	0	1.000	13	0	0	0-0	18.1	9	6	0	0	12-1	28	2.95	160	.150	.288	0	ø	0	—	4	0	0.2
2000	Bal A	2	3	.400	42	0	0	0-3	42.2	36	29	7	0	31-1	41	5.91	80	.225	.349	0	ø	0	—	-6	0	-0.5
2001	Bal A	2	4	.333	61	0	0	2-2	53	47	31	6	2	30-4	54	4.25	102	.233	.335	1	.000	-0	—	-1	0	-0.2
2002	Bal A	2	1	.667	67	0	0	1-1	57.2	51	31	7	4	33-4	56	4.68	93	.241	.353	1	.000	-0	—	-2	0	-0.1
2003	Bal A	4	1	.800	76	0	0	0-2	50.1	42	19	1	3	27-0	63	3.40	135	.227	.330	0	ø	0	—	7	0	0.6
2004	Bal A	4	6	.400	76	0	0	3-4	87	64	24	4	1	35-9	122	2.28	205	.200	.279	0	ø	0	—	23	0	2.4
2005	Bal A★	1	4	.200	69	0	0	36-5	70.1	54	20	4	2	26-2	100	2.43	181	.208	.284	0	ø	0	—	16	0	2.3
2006	Tor A★	2	2	.500	65	0	0	38-4	72.1	42	12	3	0	20-1	86	1.37	346	.169	.230	0	ø	0	—	26	0	3.7
Total	8	18	21	.462	470	0	0	80-21	453.2	349	173	32	12	215-22	551	3.19	143	.211	.304	2	.000	-0	—	67	0	8.4
Ryan, Rosy	Wilfred Patrick Dolan; B3.15.1898 Worcester MA; D12.10.1980 Scottsdale AZ; BL/TR/6´0˝/185; d9.7; Col Holy Cross																									
1919	NY N	1	2	.333	4	3	1	0	20.1	20	9	0	1	9	7	3.10	91	.260	.345	6	.000	-1	66	-1	—	-0.2
1920	NY N	0	1	.000	3	1	1	0	15.1	14	6	1	0	4	5	1.76	170	.259	.310	5	.000	-1	52	1	—	0.0
1921	NY N	7	10	.412	36	16	5	3	147.1	140	72	6	1	32	58	3.73	98	.255	.297	45-0-3	.200	1	112	-1	—	-0.1
1922	†NY N	17	12	.586	46	22	12-1	3	191.2	194	87	5	2	74	75	3.01	133	.269	.338	62-0-3	.194	1	94	18	—	2.5
1923	†NY N	16	5	.762	**45**	15	7	4	172.2	169	77	8	2	46	58	3.49	109	.257	.308	53-0-7	.208	0	176	6	—	0.7
1924	†NY N	8	6	.571	37	9	2	5	124.2	137	64	1	2	37	36	4.26	86	.285	.339	36-0-1	.139	-1	111	-7	—	-1.0
1925	Bos N	2	8	.200	37	7	1	2	122.2	152	103	7	0	52	48	6.31	64	.303	.368	39-1-0	.282	3*	150	-33	—	-2.1
1926	Bos N	0	2	.000	7	2	0	0	19	29	19	1	0	7	1	7.58	47	.392	.444	5	.200	-0	47	-9	—	-0.8
1928	NY A	0	0	ø	3	0	0	0	6	17	11	1	0	1	5	16.50	23	.486	.500	4	.000	-1	—	-8	—	-0.4
1933	Bro N	1	1	.500	30	0	0	2	61.1	69	38	3	3	16	22	4.55	71	.276	.327	13	.154	0	—	-10	—	-0.5
Total	10	52	47	.525	248	75	29-1	19	881	941	486	33	11	278	315	4.14	91	.277	.333	268-1-14	.190	1	121	-44	—	-1.9
Ryba, Mike	Dominic Joseph; B6.9.1903 DeLancey PA; D12.13.1971 Brookline Station MO; BR/TR/5´11.5˝/195; d9.22; C4; Col St. Francis (PA)																									
1935	StL N	1	1	.500	2	1	1	0	16	15	6	0	0	1	6	3.38	121	.242	.254	5-0-1	.400	1	62	2	—	0.3
1936	StL N	5	1	.833	14	0	0	0	45	55	33	3	2	16	25	5.40	73	.294	.356	18-0-1	.167	-0*	—	-8	—	-1.0
1937	StL N	9	6	.600	38	8	5	0	135	152	76	8	2	40	57	4.13	96	.284	.336	48-0-1	.313	4*	119	-3	—	0.1
1938	StL N	1	1	.500	3	0	0	0	5	8	3	0	0	1	0	5.40	73	.348	.375	0	ø	0	—	-1	—	-0.1
1941	Bos A	7	3	.700	40	3	0	6	121	143	72	14	0	42	54	4.46	93	.297	.353	37-0-4	.216	1	166	-5	0	-0.2
1942	Bos A	3	3	.500	18	0	0	3	44.1	49	25	5	1	13	16	3.86	97	.278	.332	17	.294	1*	—	-2	0	-0.2
1943	Bos A	7	5	.583	40	8	4-1	2	143.2	142	57	4	0	57	50	3.26	102	.262	.333	43-0-4	.186	0	130	1	0	0.1

YEAR	TM LG	W	L	PCT	G	GS	CG-SHO	SV-BS	IP	H	R	HR	HB	BB-IB	SO	ERA	AERA	OAV	OOB	AB-HR-SH	AVG	PB	SUP	APR	DL	PW
1944	Bos A	12	7	.632	42	7	2	2	138	119	57	7	0	39	50	3.33	102	.233	.287	41-0-5	.146	-0	116	2	0	0.3
1945	Bos A	7	6	.538	34	9	4-1	2	123	122	45	5	2	33	44	2.49	137	.259	.310	36-0-4	.250	2	106	10	0	1.2
1946	†Bos A	0	1	.000	9	0	0	1	12.2	12	7	1	0	5	5	3.55	103	.261	.333	2	1.000	1	—	0	0	0.0
Total	10	52	34	.605	240	36	16-2	16	783.2	817	381	47	7	247	307	3.66	100	.269	.326	247-0-20	.235	9	118	-4	0	0.5

RYERSON, GARY Gary Lawrence; B6.17.1948 Los Angeles CA; BR/TL/6´1˝/160; [SFN66 13/257]; d6.28

YEAR	TM LG	W	L	PCT	G	GS	CG-SHO	SV-BS	IP	H	R	HR	HB	BB-IB	SO	ERA	AERA	OAV	OOB	AB-HR-SH	AVG	PB	SUP	APR	DL	PW
1972	Mil A	3	8	.273	20	14	4-1	0-0	102	119	48	9	0	21-5	45	3.62	85	.290	.323	24-0-2	.042	-1	68	-7	0	-1.0
1973	Mil A	0	1	.000	9	4	0	0-0	23	32	23	0	0	7-1	10	7.83	49	.327	.364	0	ø	0	106	-10	0	-0.5
Total	2	3	9	.250	29	18	4-1	0-0	125	151	71	9	0	28-6	55	4.39	73	.297	.331	24-0-2	.042	-1	79	-17	0	-1.5

RYU, JAE KUK Jae Kuk; B5.30.1983 Choon Chung Do, South Korea; BR/TR/6´3˝/220; d5.14

YEAR	TM LG	W	L	PCT	G	GS	CG-SHO	SV-BS	IP	H	R	HR	HB	BB-IB	SO	ERA	AERA	OAV	OOB	AB-HR-SH	AVG	PB	SUP	APR	DL	PW
2006	Chi N	0	1	.000	10	1	0	0-0	15	23	14	7	2	6-1	17	8.40	55	.348	.419	1	.000	-0	241	-6	0	-0.3

SAARLOOS, KIRK Kirk Craig; B5.23.1979 Long Beach CA; BR/TR/6´0˝/(180–185); [HouN01 3/86]; d6.18; Col Cal St.–Fullerton

YEAR	TM LG	W	L	PCT	G	GS	CG-SHO	SV-BS	IP	H	R	HR	HB	BB-IB	SO	ERA	AERA	OAV	OOB	AB-HR-SH	AVG	PB	SUP	APR	DL	PW
2002	Hou N	6	7	.462	17	17	1-1	0-0	85.1	100	59	12	6	27-5	54	6.01	72	.301	.362	30-0-5	.067	-2	111	-14	0	-2.0
2003	Hou N	2	1	.667	36	4	0	0-0	49.1	55	31	4	3	17-3	43	4.93	90	.281	.346	5-0-3	.000	-0	164	-3	0	-0.2
2004	Oak A	2	1	.667	6	5	0	0-0	24.1	27	13	4	2	12-0	10	4.44	104	.284	.373	0	ø	0	108	1	58	0.1
2005	Oak A	10	9	.526	29	27	2-1	0-0	159.2	170	75	11	11	54-8	53	4.17	105	.278	.346	1	.000	-0	92	7	0	0.8
2006	Oak A	7	7	.500	35	16	0	2-1	121.1	149	70	19	3	53-3	52	4.75	96	.308	.375	0	ø	0	105	-4	0	-0.3
Total	5	27	25	.519	123	69	3-2	2-1	440	501	248	50	25	163-19	212	4.79	93	.292	.359	36-0-8	.056	-2	105	-13	58	-1.6

SABATHIA, C.C. Carsten Charles; B7.21.1980 Vallejo CA; BL/TL/6´7˝/(260–290); [CleA98 1/20]; d4.8

YEAR	TM LG	W	L	PCT	G	GS	CG-SHO	SV-BS	IP	H	R	HR	HB	BB-IB	SO	ERA	AERA	OAV	OOB	AB-HR-SH	AVG	PB	SUP	APR	DL	PW
2001	†Cle A	17	5	.773	33	33	0	0-0	180.1	149	93	19	7	95-1	171	4.39	105	.228	.330	4-0-1	.000	-0	107	5	0	0.5
2002	Cle A	13	11	.542	33	33	2	0-0	210	198	109	17	1	88-2	149	4.37	102	.252	.324	5	.200	0	100	2	0	0.1
2003	Cle A☆	13	9	.591	30	30	2-1	0-0	197.2	190	85	19	6	66-3	141	3.60	123	.255	.319	6	.500	1*	80	21	0	2.1
2004	Cle A★	11	10	.524	30	30	1-1	0-0	188	176	90	20	7	72-3	139	4.12	106	.252	.325	4	.250	0	105	7	0	0.6
2005	Cle A	15	10	.600	31	31	1	0-0	196.2	185	92	19	7	62-1	161	4.03	103	.248	.311	6-1-0	.333	2	112	5	14	0.7
2006	Cle A	12	11	.522	28	28	**6-2**	0-0	192.2	182	83	17	7	44-3	172	3.22	134	.247	.293	9	.222	0	92	22	29	2.3
Total	6	81	56	.591	185	185	12-4	0-0	1165.1	1080	552	111	35	427-13	933	3.95	111	.247	.317	34-1-1	.265	4	100	62	43	6.3

SABEL, ERIK Erik Douglas; B10.14.1974 Lafayette IN; BR/TR/6´3˝/(185–193); [AriN96 42/1262]; d7.9; Col Tennessee Tech

YEAR	TM LG	W	L	PCT	G	GS	CG-SHO	SV-BS	IP	H	R	HR	HB	BB-IB	SO	ERA	AERA	OAV	OOB	AB-HR-SH	AVG	PB	SUP	APR	DL	PW
1999	Ari N	0	0	ø	7	0	0	0-0	9.2	12	7	1	2	6-2	6	6.52	71	.300	.417	2	.000	-0	—	-2	0	-0.1
2001	Ari N	3	2	.600	42	0	0	0-0	51.1	57	26	8	3	12-3	25	4.38	106	.282	.332	0	ø	0	—	2	0	0.1
2002	Det A	0	0	ø	1	0	0	0-0	0	2	2	1	0	0-0	0	(2)	ø	1.000	1.000	0	ø	0	—	-2	0	-0.2
Total	3	3	2	.600	50	0	0	0-0	61	71	35	10	5	18-5	31	5.02	92	.291	.352	2	.000	-0	—	-2	0	-0.2

SABERHAGEN, BRET Bret William; B4.11.1964 Chicago Heights IL; BR/TR/6´1˝/(160–200); [KCA82 19/480]; d4.4; [DL 1996 Col N 182, 2000 Bos A 181]

YEAR	TM LG	W	L	PCT	G	GS	CG-SHO	SV-BS	IP	H	R	HR	HB	BB-IB	SO	ERA	AERA	OAV	OOB	AB-HR-SH	AVG	PB	SUP	APR	DL	PW
1984	†KC A	10	11	.476	38	18	2-1	1-0	157.2	138	71	13	2	36-4	73	3.48	116	.237	.281	0	ø	0*	77	8	0	1.0
1985	†KC A	20	6	.769	32	32	10-1	0-0	235.1	211	79	19	1	38-1	158	2.87	146	.241	**.271**	0	ø	0	98	37	0	3.9
1986	KC A	7	12	.368	30	25	4-2	0-0	156	165	77	15	2	29-1	112	4.15	103	.268	.302	0	ø	0	71	3	22	0.4
1987	KC A★	18	10	.643	33	33	15-4	0-0	257	246	99	27	6	53-2	163	3.36	137	.252	.293	0	ø	0	105	38	0	3.8
1988	KC A	14	16	.467	35	35	9	0-0	260.2	271	122	18	4	59-5	171	3.80	106	.269	.309	0	ø	0	86	7	0	0.7
1989	KC A	**23**	6	**.793**	36	35	**12**-4	0-0	**262.1**	209	74	13	2	43-6	193	**2.16**	**179**	.217	**.251**	0	ø	0*	107	**48**	0	**5.3**
1990	KC A★	5	9	.357	20	20	5	0-0	135	146	52	9	1	28-1	87	3.27	118	.279	.314	0	ø	0	108	11	56	1.2
1991	KC A	13	8	.619	28	28	7-2	0-0	196.1	165	76	12	9	45-5	136	3.07	135	.228	.280	0	ø	0	102	23	30	2.4
1992	NY N	3	5	.375	17	15	1-1	0-1	97.2	84	39	6	4	27-1	81	3.50	100	.233	.292	28-0-3	.107	-1	81	1	99	0.2
1993	NY N	7	7	.500	19	19	4-1	0-0	139.1	131	55	11	3	17-4	93	3.29	122	.250	.275	45-0-8	.111	-0	99	13	62	1.3
1994	NY N☆	14	4	**.778**	24	24	4	0-0	177.1	169	58	13	4	13-0	143	2.74	152	.254	.271	58-0-8	.172	1	112	30	0	3.1
1995	NY N	5	5	.500	16	16	3	0-0	110	105	45	13	5	20-2	71	3.35	120	.251	.291	35-0-5	.114	-1	109	9	0	0.7
	†Col N	2	1	.667	9	9	0	0-0	43	60	33	8	5	13-1	29	6.28	86	.323	.382	14	.071	-1	105	-3	0	-0.3
	Year	7	6	.538	25	25	3	0-0	153	165	78	21	10	33-3	100	4.18	106	.273	.320	49-0-5	.102	-2	110	4	0	0.4
1997	Bos A	0	1	.000	6	6	0	0-0	26	30	20	5	2	10-0	14	6.58	71	.288	.353	1	.000	-0	115	-5	143	-0.3
1998	†Bos A	15	8	.652	31	31	0	0-0	175	181	82	22	6	29-1	100	3.96	119	.264	.299	5	.000	-1	100	16	0	1.7
1999	†Bos A	10	6	.625	22	22	0	0-0	119	122	43	11	2	11-0	81	2.95	169	.265	.284	4	.000	-0	99	27	63	3.2
2001	Bos A	1	2	.333	3	3	0	0-0	15	19	11	3	1	0-0	10	6.00	74	.302	.313	0	ø	0	104	-3	178	-0.4
Total	16	167	117	.588	399	371	76-16	1-1	2562.2	2452	1036	218	59	471-34	1715	3.34	126	.252	.289	190-0-24	.121	-2	99	260	1016	27.9

SACKINSKY, BRIAN Brian Walter; B6.22.1971 Pittsburgh PA; BR/TR/6´4˝/220; [BalA92 2/42]; d4.20; Col Stanford

YEAR	TM LG	W	L	PCT	G	GS	CG-SHO	SV-BS	IP	H	R	HR	HB	BB-IB	SO	ERA	AERA	OAV	OOB	AB-HR-SH	AVG	PB	SUP	APR	DL	PW
1996	Bal A	0	0	ø	3	0	0	0-0	4.2	6	2	1	0	3-0	2	3.86	128	.316	.409	0	ø	0	—	1	0	0.0

SADECKI, RAY Raymond Michael; B12.26.1940 Kansas City KS; BL/TL/5´11˝/(180–185); d5.19

YEAR	TM LG	W	L	PCT	G	GS	CG-SHO	SV-BS	IP	H	R	HR	HB	BB-IB	SO	ERA	AERA	OAV	OOB	AB-HR-SH	AVG	PB	SUP	APR	DL	PW
1960	StL N	9	9	.500	26	26	7-1	0	157.1	148	76	15	1	86-1	95	3.78	109	.249	.342	57-0-2	.211	-0*	94	4	0	0.3
1961	StL N	14	10	.583	31	31	13	0	222.2	196	100	28	3	102-2	114	3.72	118	.238	.321	87-0-2	.253	2*	95	19	0	1.8
1962	StL N	6	8	.429	22	17	4-1	1	102.1	121	74	13	3	43-3	50	5.54	77	.296	.362	37-1-2	.081	-2*	100	-14	0	-1.9
1963	StL N	10	10	.500	36	28	4-1	1	193.1	198	100	25	4	78-3	136	4.10	87	.266	.338	64-0-7	.141	-1*	121	-10	0	-1.3
1964	†StL N	20	11	.645	37	32	9-2	1	220	232	104	16	1	60-4	119	3.68	103	.273	.319	75-0-9	.160	2*	105	4	0	0.6
1965	StL N	6	15	.286	36	28	4	1	172.2	192	107	26	0	64-4	122	5.21	74	.284	.344	55-0-3	.200	2	87	-23	0	-2.5
1966	StL N	2	1	.667	5	3	1	0	24.1	16	9	2	0	9-0	21	2.22	162	.188	.266	7-1-1	.429	2*	82	3	0	0.6
	SF N	3	7	.300	26	19	3-1	0	105	125	82	20	4	39-2	62	5.40	68	.293	.354	34-2-2	.324	5	110	-23	0	-1.5
	Year	5	8	.385	31	22	4-1	0	129.1	141	91	22	4	48-2	83	4.80	76	.276	.339	41-3-3	.341	7	106	-24	0	-0.9
1967	SF N	12	6	.667	35	24	10-2	0	188	165	65	8	4	58-4	145	2.78	118	.238	.298	73-0-1	.247	4*	100	12	0	1.6
1968	SF N	12	18	.400	38	36	13-6	0	253.2	225	94	14	3	70-17	206	2.91	101	.237	.290	85-0-4	.094	-1*	92	3	0	0.1
1969	SF N	5	8	.385	29	17	4-3	0-0	138.1	137	73	18	2	53-4	104	4.23	83	.259	.325	40-1-4	.125	2*	116	-9	0	-0.5
1970	NY N	8	4	.667	28	19	4	0-1	138.2	134	67	18	0	52-9	89	3.89	104	.255	.320	39-0-8	.205	1	117	3	0	0.2
1971	NY N	7	7	.500	34	20	5-2	0-0	163.1	139	56	10	4	44-5	120	2.92	118	.229	.283	50-0-5	.200	1	84	11	0	0.9
1972	NY N	2	1	.667	34	2	0	0-1	75.2	73	33	3	2	31-6	38	3.09	110	.257	.331	13-0-1	.154	-0	91	1	0	0.0
1973	†NY N	5	4	.556	31	11	1	1-0	116.2	109	47	11	1	41-3	87	3.39	107	.248	.312	31-0-2	.226	1	103	4	0	0.3
1974	NY N	8	8	.500	34	10	3-1	0-1	103	107	49	7	2	35-6	46	3.41	106	.274	.332	27	.259	1	68	1	0	0.2
1975	StL N	1	0	1.000	8	0	0	0-0	11	13	7	0	0	7-2	8	3.27	116	.289	.370	0	ø	0	—	0	0	0.0
	Atl N	2	3	.400	25	5	0	1-1	66.1	73	39	3	4	21-5	24	4.21	90	.286	.341	15-0-1	.200	0	93	-4	0	-0.3
	Year	3	3	.500	33	5	0	1-1	77.1	86	46	3	4	28-7	32	4.07	93	.287	.346	15-0-1	.200	0	93	-4	0	-0.3
	KC A	1	0	1.000	5	0	0	0-2	3	5	2	0	0	3-0	0	3.00	129	.333	.444	0	ø	0	—	0	0	0.0
1976	KC A	0	0	ø	3	0	0	0-1	4.2	7	0	0	0	3-0	1	0.00	ø	.368	.455	0	ø	0	—	2	0	0.1
	Mil A	2	0	1.000	36	0	0	1-0	37.1	38	20	2	3	20-2	27	4.34	81	.262	.363	0	ø	0	—	-3	0	-0.2
	Year	2	0	1.000	39	0	0	1-1	42	45	20	2	3	23-2	28	3.86	91	.274	.374	0	ø	0	—	-1	0	-0.1
1977	NY N	0	1	.000	4	0	0	0-1	3	3	2	1	0	3-0	0	6.00	63	.300	.462	0	ø	0	—	-1	0	-0.1
Total	18	135	131	.508	563	328	85-20	7-8	2500.1	2456	1206	240	41	922-82	1614	3.78	97	.258	.324	789-5-54	.191	19	101	-20	0	-1.6

SADLER, CARL William Carl; B10.11.1976 Gainesville FL; BL/TL/6´2˝/180; [MonN96 34/1000]; d7.31

YEAR	TM LG	W	L	PCT	G	GS	CG-SHO	SV-BS	IP	H	R	HR	HB	BB-IB	SO	ERA	AERA	OAV	OOB	AB-HR-SH	AVG	PB	SUP	APR	DL	PW
2002	Cle A	1	2	.333	24	0	0	0-1	20.1	15	10	2	0	11-0	23	4.43	100	.211	.317	0	ø	0	—	0	0	0.0
2003	Cle A	0	0	ø	18	0	0	0-0	9.2	11	2	0	2	5-0	10	1.86	238	.306	.409	0	ø	0	—	3	0	0.1
Total	2	1	2	.333	42	0	0	0-1	30	26	12	2	2	16-0	33	3.60	123	.243	.349	0	ø	0	—	3	0	0.1

SADLER, BILLY William Henry; B9.21.1981 Pensacola FL; BR/TR/6´0˝/190; [SFN03 6/183]; d9.15; Col Louisiana St.

YEAR	TM LG	W	L	PCT	G	GS	CG-SHO	SV-BS	IP	H	R	HR	HB	BB-IB	SO	ERA	AERA	OAV	OOB	AB-HR-SH	AVG	PB	SUP	APR	DL	PW
2006	SF N	0	0	ø	5	0	0	0-0	4	5	3	2	1	2-0	6	6.75	66	.294	.400	0	ø	0	—	-1	0	0.0

SADOWSKI, JIM James Michael; B8.7.1951 Pittsburgh PA; BR/TR/6´3˝/178; d4.27

YEAR	TM LG	W	L	PCT	G	GS	CG-SHO	SV-BS	IP	H	R	HR	HB	BB-IB	SO	ERA	AERA	OAV	OOB	AB-HR-SH	AVG	PB	SUP	APR	DL	PW
1974	Pit N	0	1	.000	4	0	0	0-0	9	7	6	1	0	9-0	1	6.00	58	.233	.400	1	.000	0	—	-2	0	-0.2

SADOWSKI, BOB Robert; B2.19.1938 Pittsburgh PA; BR/TR/6´2˝/(188–195); d6.19; b–Ed b–Ted

YEAR	TM LG	W	L	PCT	G	GS	CG-SHO	SV-BS	IP	H	R	HR	HB	BB-IB	SO	ERA	AERA	OAV	OOB	AB-HR-SH	AVG	PB	SUP	APR	DL	PW
1963	Mil N	5	7	.417	19	18	5-1	0	116.2	99	36	8	5	30-6	72	2.62	123	.231	.288	35-0-3	.057	-2	95	9	0	0.7
1964	Mil N	9	10	.474	51	18	5	5	166.2	159	85	18	7	56-5	96	4.10	86	.251	.317	52-0-6	.154	0	143	-10	0	-1.1
1965	Mil N	5	9	.357	34	13	3	3	123	117	62	11	3	35-5	78	4.32	82	.250	.305	35-0-2	.086	-2	78	-9	0	-1.2
1966	Bos A	1	1	.500	11	5	0	0	33.1	41	26	4	1	9-1	11	5.40	70	.311	.354	7-0-1	.000	-1	102	-7	0	-0.5
Total	4	20	27	.426	115	54	13-1	8	439.2	416	209	41	16	130-17	257	3.87	90	.250	.309	129-0-12	.101	-4	107	-17	0	-2.1

YEAR	TM LG	W	L	PCT	G	GS	CG-SHO	SV-BS	IP	H	R	HR	HB	BB-IB	SO	ERA	AERA	OAV	OOB	AB-HR-SH	AVG	PB	SUP	APR	DL	PW
SADOWSKI, TED	Theodore; B4.1.1936 Pittsburgh PA; D7.18.1993 Shaler Twp. PA; BR/TR/6´1.5˝/(190–200); d9.2; b–Ed b–Bob																									
1960	Was A	1	0	1.000	9	1	0	1	17.1	17	10	4	1	9-1	12	5.19	75	.258	.351	3	.000	-0	91	-2	0	-0.1
1961	Min A	0	2	.000	15	1	0	0	33	49	29	6	1	11-2	12	6.82	62	.348	.396	6	.000	-1	42	-9	0	-0.5
1962	Min A	1	1	.500	19	0	0	0	34	37	19	6	1	11-0	15	5.03	81	.301	.363	4	.500	1	—	-2	0	-0.1
Total	3	2	3	.400	43	2	0	1	84.1	103	58	16	3	31-3	39	5.76	71	.312	.374	13	.154	-0	65	-13	0	-0.7
SAENZ, CHRIS	Christopher Andrew; B8.14.1981 Tucson AZ; BR/TR/6´3˝/200; [MilN01 28/838]; d4.24; Col Pima (AZ) CC																									
2004	Mil N	1	0	1.000	1	1	0	0-0	6	2	0	0	1	3-0	7	0.00	ø	.100	.250	2	.000	-0	63	3	0	0.5
SAGER, A. J.	Anthony Joseph; B3.3.1965 Columbus OH; BR/TR/6´4˝/220; [SDN88 10/240]; d4.4; Col Toledo																									
1994	SD N	1	4	.200	22	3	0	0-0	46.2	62	34	4	2	16-5	26	5.98	69	.325	.379	10-0-1	.100	0	59	-9	0	-0.8
1995	Col N	0	0	ø	10	0	0	0-1	14.2	19	16	1	0	7-1	10	7.36	73	.311	.382	3	.000	-0	—	-4	0	-0.2
1996	Det A	4	5	.444	22	9	0	0-0	79	91	46	10	2	29-2	52	5.01	102	.294	.355	0	ø	0	97	2	0	0.1
1997	Det A	3	4	.429	38	1	0	3-1	84	81	43	10	1	24-6	53	4.18	111	.258	.307	0	ø	0	0	4	0	0.3
1998	Det A	4	2	.667	31	3	0	2-1	59.1	79	47	7	1	23-4	23	6.52	73	.325	.383	1	.000	-0	124	-12	0	-1.0
Total	5	12	15	.444	123	16	0	5-3	283.2	332	186	32	6	99-18	164	5.36	88	.297	.353	14-0-1	.071	-0	91	-19	0	-1.6
SAIN, JOHNNY	John Franklin; B9.25.1917 Havana AR; D11.7.2006 Downers Grove IL; BR/TR/6´2˝/(185–200); d4.24; Mil 1943–45; C17																									
1942	Bos N	4	7	.364	40	3	0	6	97	79	54	8	5	63	68	3.90	86	.228	.354	27-0-2	.074	-2	50	-8	0	-1.2
1946	Bos N	20	14	.588	37	34	**24**-3	2	265	225	80	8	2	87	129	2.21	155	.230	.294	94-0-10	.298	5*	98	34	0	**5.4**
1947	Bos N★	21	12	.636	38	35	22-3	1	266	265	117	19	4	79	132	3.52	111	.255	.310	107-0-8	.346	12*	126	12	0	2.7
1948	†Bos N★	**24**	15	.615	42	**39**	**28**-4	1	**314.2**	297	105	19	5	83	137	2.60	147	.245	.296	115-0-16	.217	3*	110	43	0	**5.3**
1949	Bos N	10	17	.370	37	36	16-1	0	243	285	150	15	4	75	73	4.81	78	.291	.344	97-0-3	.206	1*	99	-30	0	-2.8
1950	Bos N	20	13	.606	37	37	25-3	0	278.1	294	139	34	2	70	96	3.94	98	.269	.314	102-1-7	.206	4	112	-2	0	0.0
1951	Bos N	5	13	.278	26	22	6-1	1	160.1	195	88	16	3	45	63	4.21	87	.299	.347	52-1-4	.212	3	82	-11	0	-0.9
	†NY A	2	1	.667	7	4	1	1	37	41	17	5	0	8	21	4.14	93	.281	.318	14	.286	1	110	0	0	0.1
1952	†NY A	11	6	.647	35	16	8	7	148.1	149	70	15	2	38	57	3.46	96	.261	.310	71-1-1	.268	7*	144	-4	0	0.1
1953	†NY A☆	14	7	.667	40	19	10-1	9	189	189	68	16	3	45	84	3.00	123	.262	.308	68-0-4	.250	5*	136	17	0	2.4
1954	NY A	6	6	.500	45	0	0	**22**	77	66	27	11	0	15	33	3.16	109	.229	.266	17-0-1	.353	3	—	4	0	1.1
1955	NY A	0	0	ø	3	0	0	0	5.1	6	4	4	0	1-0	5	6.75	55	.300	.333	2	.000	-0	—	-2	0	-0.1
	KC A	2	5	.286	25	0	0	1	44.2	54	28	10	0	10-4	12	5.44	77	.297	.332	8	.000	-1	—	-5	0	-0.9
	Year	2	5	.286	28	0	0	1	50	60	32	14	0	11-4	17	5.58	74	.297	.332	10	.000	-1	—	-6	0	-1.0
Total	11	139	116	.545	412	245	140-16	51	2125.2	2145	947	180	30	619-4	910	3.49	106	.261	.315	774-3-56	.245	40	111	48	0	11.2
ST.CLAIRE, RANDY	Randy Anthony; B8.23.1960 Glens Falls NY; BR/TR/6´2˝/(180–195); d9.11; C4; f–Ebba																									
1984	Mon N	0	0	ø	4	0	0	0-0	8	11	4	0	1	2-1	4	4.50	77	.344	.378	0	ø	0	—	-1	0	0.0
1985	Mon N	5	3	.625	42	0	0	0-1	68.2	69	32	3	1	26-7	25	3.93	88	.265	.333	5-0-1	.200	1	—	-3	0	-0.3
1986	Mon N	2	0	1.000	11	0	0	1-0	19	13	5	2	0	6-1	21	2.37	158	.186	.250	1-0-1	.000	-0	—	3	0	0.4
1987	Mon N	3	3	.500	44	0	0	7-2	67	64	31	9	1	20-4	43	4.03	106	.249	.302	6-0-2	.333	0	—	3	0	0.3
1988	Mon N	0	0	ø	6	0	0	0-0	7.1	11	5	2	0	5-1	6	6.14	59	.344	.421	0	ø	0	—	-2	0	-0.1
	Cin N	1	0	1.000	10	0	0	0-0	13.2	13	8	3	0	5-2	8	2.63	136	.241	.300	1	.000	-0	—	0	0	0.0
	Year	1	0	1.000	16	0	0	0-0	21	24	13	5	0	10-3	14	3.86	93	.279	.347	1	.000	-0	—	-2	0	-0.1
1989	Min A	1	0	1.000	14	0	0	1-0	22.1	19	13	4	2	10-2	14	5.24	79	.226	.320	0	ø	0	—	-2	0	-0.1
1991	†Atl N	0	0	ø	19	0	0	0-0	28.2	31	17	4	0	9-3	30	4.08	95	.282	.333	2	.500	0	—	-2	0	0.0
1992	Atl N	0	0	ø	10	0	0	0-0	15.1	17	11	1	0	8-3	7	5.87	62	.283	.368	0	ø	0	—	-4	0	-0.2
1994	Tor A	0	0	ø	2	0	0	0-0	2	4	4	0	0	2-1	2	9.00	54	.444	.545	0	ø	0	—	-2	0	-0.1
Total	9	12	6	.667	162	0	0	9-3	252	252	130	28	5	93-25	160	4.14	92	.260	.325	15-0-4	.267	1	—	-10	0	-0.1
ST.VRAIN, JIM	James Marcellin; B6.6.1883 Ralls Co. MO; D6.12.1937 Butte MT; BR/TL/5´9˝/175; d4.20																									
1902	Chi N	4	6	.400	12	11	10-1	0	95	88	36	0	5	25	51	2.08	130	.246	.304	31	.097	-2	82	6	—	0.5
SAIPE, MIKE	Michael Eric; B9.10.1973 San Diego CA; BR/TR/6´1˝/188; [ColN94 12/322]; d6.25; Col San Diego																									
1998	Col N	0	1	.000	2	2	0	0-0	10	22	12	5	2	0-0	2	10.80	48	.431	.453	1	.000	0	98	-5	0	-0.4
SAITO, TAKASHI	Takashi; B2.14.1970 Miyagi, Japan; BL/TR/6´1˝/200; d4.9; Col Tottoku Fukushi																									
2006	†LA N	6	2	.750	72	0	0	24-2	78.1	48	19	3	2	23-3	107	2.07	212	.177	.243	0	ø	0	—	**21**	0	3.1
SALAS, JUAN	Juan; B11.7.1978 Santo Domingo, D.R.; BR/TR/6´2˝/210; d9.5																									
2006	TB A	0	0	ø	8	0	0	0-1	10	13	7	1	0	3-0	8	5.40	86	.295	.333	0	ø	0	—	-1	0	0.0
SALE, FREDDY	Frederick Link; B5.2.1902 Chester SC; D5.27.1956 Hermosa Beach CA; BR/TR/5´9˝/160; d6.30; Col Georgia																									
1924	Pit N	0	0	ø	1	0	0	0	1	2	0	0	0	0	0	0.00	ø	.500	.500	0	ø	0	—	0	—	0.0
SALISBURY, HARRY	Henry H.; B5.15.1855 Providence RI; D3.29.1933 Chicago IL; BL/5´8.5˝/162; d8.28; Col Brown																									
1879	Tro N	4	6	.400	10	10	9	0	89	103	72	0	—	11	31	2.22	112	.265	.285	36	.056	-4	76	-1	—	-0.3
1882	Pit AA	20	18	.526	38	38	38-1	0	335	315	188	1	—	37	135	2.63	99	.232	.253	145	.152	-6*	107	-1	—	-0.7
Total	2	24	24	.500	48	48	47-1	0	424	418	260	1	—	48	166	2.55	102	.239	.260	181	.133	-10	100	-2	—	-1.0
SALISBURY, BILL	William Ansil "Solly"; B11.12.1876 Algona IA; D1.17.1952 Rowena OR; BR/TR/6´0˝/180; d4.19																									
1902	Phi N	0	0	ø	2	1	0	0	6	15	10	1	1	2	0	13.50	21	.469	.514	1	.000	-0	145	-6	—	-0.3
SALKELD, ROGER	Roger William; B3.6.1971 Burbank CA; BR/TR/6´5˝/215; [SeaA89 1/3]; d9.8; gf–Bill																									
1993	Sea A	0	0	ø	3	2	0	0-0	14.1	13	4	0	1	4-0	13	2.51	178	.232	.295	0	ø	0	52	3	0	0.2
1994	Sea A	2	5	.286	13	13	0	0-0	59	76	47	7	1	45-1	46	7.17	69	.314	.419	0	ø	0	106	-12	0	-1.2
1996	Cin N	8	5	.615	29	19	1-1	0-0	116	114	69	18	6	54-2	82	5.20	82	.261	.349	32-0-4	.031	-3	117	-9	0	-1.2
Total	3	10	10	.500	45	34	1-1	0-0	189.1	203	120	25	8	103-3	141	5.61	80	.277	.369	32-0-4	.031	-3	110	-18	0	-2.2
SALLEE, SLIM	Harry Franklin "Scatter"; B2.3.1885 Higginsport OH; D3.23.1950 Higginsport OH; BR/TL/6´3˝/180; d4.16																									
1908	StL N	3	8	.273	25	12	7-1	0	128.2	144	65	1	3	36	39	3.15	75	.274	.324	41-0-1	.049	-3	55	-10	—	-1.1
1909	StL N	10	11	.476	32	27	12-1	0	219	223	107	3	5	59	55	2.42	104	.264	.315	71-0-6	.113	-2	129	-7	—	-0.8
1910	StL N	7	8	.467	18	13	9-1	2	115	112	44	4	1	24	46	2.97	100	.251	.290	37-0-2	.108	-2	90	2	—	0.0
1911	StL N	15	9	.625	36	30	18-1	3	245	234	102	6	5	64	74	2.76	123	.257	.309	89-0-4	.169	-2	96	15	—	1.0
1912	StL N	16	17	.485	48	32	20-3	**6**	294	289	122	6	6	72	108	2.60	132	.266	.315	103-0-2	.136	-4	84	26	—	2.3
1913	StL N	19	15	.559	50	29	18-3	5	276	257	98	11	5	60	106	2.71	119	.255	.301	95-2-6	.211	2	86	16	—	2.2
1914	StL N	18	17	.514	46	29	18-3	**6**	282.1	252	92	5	9	72	105	2.10	133	.246	.302	91-0-6	.231	2	87	22	—	3.1
1915	StL N	13	17	.433	46	33	17-2	3	275.1	245	121	6	3	57	91	2.84	98	.238	.280	92-0-4	.120	-3	86	-3	—	-0.8
1916	StL N	5	5	.500	16	7	4-2	1	70	75	28	2	2	23	28	3.47	76	.290	.352	18-0-2	.167	-0	56	-3	—	-0.6
	NY N	9	4	.692	15	11	7-2	0	111.2	96	24	2	0	10	35	1.37	178	.234	.252	35-0-1	.257	2	117	13	—	1.8
	Year	14	9	.609	31	18	11-4	1	181.2	171	52	4	2	33	63	2.18	115	.256	.293	53-0-3	.226	2	92	9	—	1.2
1917	†NY N	18	7	.720	34	24	18-1	**4**	215.2	199	70	4	1	34	54	2.17	118	.249	.280	77-0-6	.221	1	149	8	—	0.9
1918	NY N	8	8	.500	18	16	12-1	2	132	122	44	3	0	12	33	2.25	117	.241	**.259**	41-0-4	.122	-2	92	5	—	0.3
1919	†Cin N	21	7	.750	29	28	22-4	0	227.2	221	63	4	1	20	24	2.06	135	.258	.276	74-0-8	.189	2	116	20	—	2.5
1920	Cin N	5	6	.455	21	12	6	2	116	129	57	4	2	16	13	3.34	91	.293	.320	35-0-1	.171	-1	121	-5	—	-0.7
	NY N	1	0	1.000	5	2	1	0	17	16	7	0	0	0	2	1.59	189	.239	.239	3-0-1	.333	1	171	1	—	0.1
	Year	6	6	.500	26	14	7	2	133	145	64	4	2	16	15	3.11	97	.285	.310	38-0-2	.184	-0	128	-5	—	-0.6
1921	NY N	6	4	.600	37	0	0	2	96.1	115	48	7	0	14	23	3.64	101	.307	.332	22-0-4	.364	2	—	-1	—	0.0
Total	14	174	143	.549	476	305	189-25	36	2821.2	2729	1092	68	43	573	836	2.56	114	.258	.299	924-2-58	.171	-8	99	99	—	10.2
SALMON, ROGER	Roger Elliott; B5.11.1891 Newark NJ; D6.17.1974 Belfast ME; BL/TL/6´2˝/170; d5.3; Col Princeton																									
1912	Phi A	1	0	1.000	2	1	0	0	5	7	7	0	0	4	5	9.00	34	.318	.423	1-0-1	.000	-0	96	-4	—	-0.6
SALVE, GUS	Augustus William; B12.29.1885 Boston MA; D3.29.1971 Providence RI; BL/TL/6´0˝/190; d9.14																									
1908	Phi A	0	1	.000	2	1	1	0	15.1	17	7	1	1	9	6	4.11	62	.266	.365	5	.000	-1	27	-2	—	-0.2

THE PITCHER REGISTER

YEAR	TM LG	W	L	PCT	G	GS	CG-SHO	SV-BS	IP	H	R	HR	HB	BB-IB	SO	ERA	AERA	OAV	OOB	AB-HR-SH	AVG	PB	SUP	APR	DL	PW
Salveson, Jack	John Theodore; B1.5.1914 Fullerton CA; D12.28.1974 Norwalk CA; BR/TR/6´0.5˝/180; d6.3																									
1933	NY N	0	2	.000	8	2	2	0	30.2	30	17	4	0	14	8	3.82	84	.252	.331	9	.111	-1	26	-3	—	-0.2
1934	NY N	3	1	.750	12	4	0	0	38.1	43	16	2	0	13	18	3.52	110	.281	.337	10	.300	0*	134	2	—	0.3
1935	Pit N	0	1	.000	5	0	0	0	7	11	12	1	1	5	2	9.00	46	.306	.405	2	.000	-0	—	-5	—	-0.6
	Chi A	1	2	.333	20	2	2	1	66.2	79	39	6	0	23	22	4.86	95	.298	.354	20-1-0	.300	2	150	-1	—	0.1
1943	Cle A	5	3	.625	23	11	4-3	3	86	87	36	5	1	26	24	3.35	93	.266	.322	26-1-2	.231	2	94	-2	0	0.0
1945	Cle A	0	0	ø	19	0	0	0	44	52	23	3	1	6	11	3.68	88	.294	.321	10-1-0	.400	3	—	-3	0	0.2
Total	5	9	9	.500	87	19	8-3	4	272.2	302	143	21	3	87	85	3.99	91	.280	.336	77-3-2	.260	7	99	-12	0	-0.2
Salvo, Manny	Manuel "Gyp"; B6.30.1912 Sacramento CA; D2.7.1997 Vallejo CA; BR/TR/6´4˝/210; d4.22																									
1939	NY N	4	10	.286	32	18	4	1	136	150	84	11	5	75	69	4.63	85	.285	.380	41-1-0	.098	-2	101	-12	—	-1.3
1940	Bos N	10	9	.526	21	20	14-**5**	0	160.2	151	63	9	2	43	60	3.08	121	.248	.300	58	.103	-3	95	11	—	0.9
1941	Bos N	7	16	.304	35	27	11-2	0	195	192	103	9	4	93	67	4.06	88	.255	.340	62	.113	-0	89	-10	0	-1.2
1942	Bos N	7	8	.467	25	14	6-1	0	130.2	129	52	7	4	41	25	3.03	110	.260	.322	41-0-2	.122	-1	70	4	0	0.3
1943	Bos N	0	1	.000	1	1	0	0	5	5	4	0	0	6	1	7.20	47	.250	.423	2	1.000	2	75	-2	0	-0.2
	Phi N	0	0	ø	1	0	0	0	0.1	2	1	0	0	1	0	27.00	12	.667	.750	0	ø	0	—	-1	0	0.0
	Bos N	5	6	.455	20	13	5-1	0	93.2	94	45	6	1	25	25	3.27	105	.261	.311	28-0-2	.214	0	69	0	0	0.0
	Year	5	7	.417	22	14	5-1	0	99	101	50	6	1	32	26	3.55	96	.264	.322	30-0-2	.267	2	69	-3	0	-0.2
Total	5	33	50	.398	135	93	40-9	1	721.1	723	352	42	16	284	247	3.69	98	.261	.334	232-1-4	.129	-4	87	-10	0	-1.5
Sambito, Joe	Joseph Charles; B6.28.1952 Brooklyn NY; BL/TL/6´1˝/(185–190); [HouN73 17/404]; d7.20; Col Adelphi; [DL 1983 Hou N 182]																									
1976	Hou N	3	2	.600	20	4	1-1	1-0	53.1	45	21	4	0	14-1	26	3.54	91	.237	.286	9	.222	1	109	-1	0	0.1
1977	Hou N	5	5	.500	54	1	0	7-4	89	77	34	6	0	24-2	67	2.33	155	.235	.286	13	.154	-0	0	10	0	1.2
1978	Hou N	4	9	.308	62	0	0	11-4	88	85	32	5	0	32-7	96	3.07	109	.260	.322	6-0-1	.167	0	—	3	0	0.6
1979	Hou N★	8	7	.533	63	0	0	22-6	91.1	80	20	8	4	23-4	83	1.77	198	.235	.290	7	.286	2	—	19	0	**4.3**
1980	†Hou N	8	4	.667	64	0	0	17-5	90.1	65	26	3	2	22-3	75	2.19	150	.200	.254	9	.000	-1	—	12	0	1.9
1981	†Hou N	5	5	.500	49	0	0	10-3	63.2	43	17	4	2	22-5	41	1.84	178	.192	.269	5	.000	-1	—	10	0	1.8
1982	Hou N	0	0	ø	9	0	0	4-1	12.2	7	2	0	0	2-2	7	0.71	468	.159	.196	1	.000	-0*	—	4	137	0.2
1984	Hou N	0	0	ø	32	0	0	0-0	47.2	39	16	5	0	16-2	26	3.02	111	.228	.289	2	.000	-0	—	3	53	0.1
1985	NY N	0	0	ø	8	0	0	0-0	10.2	21	18	1	0	8-0	3	12.66	28	.420	.492	0	ø	0	—	-12	0	-0.6
1986	†Bos A	2	0	1.000	53	0	0	12-0	44.2	54	26	4	2	16-3	30	4.84	87	.298	.362	0	ø	0	—	-3	0	-0.2
1987	Bos A	2	6	.250	47	0	0	0-4	37.2	46	29	8	0	16-3	35	6.93	66	.301	.367	0	ø	0	—	-9	0	-1.5
Total	11	37	38	.493	461	5	1-1	84-27	629	562	241	48	10	195-32	489	3.03	116	.241	.300	52-0-1	.135	2	81	36	372	7.9
Sampen, Bill	William Albert; B1.18.1963 Lincoln IL; BR/TR/6´2˝/(180–200); [PitN85 12/294]; d4.10; Col MacMurray																									
1990	Mon N	12	7	.632	59	4	0	2-1	90.1	94	34	7	2	33-6	69	2.99	123	.268	.332	8-0-2	.000	-1	233	6	0	1.2
1991	Mon N	9	5	.643	43	8	0	0-1	92.1	96	49	13	3	46-7	52	4.00	91	.273	.358	13-0-2	.231	0	99	-5	0	-0.7
1992	Mon N	1	4	.200	44	1	0	0-1	63.1	62	22	4	1	29-6	23	3.13	111	.268	.351	6-0-1	.000	-1	0	4	0	0.2
	KC A	0	2	.000	8	1	0	0-0	19.2	21	10	0	3	3-1	14	3.66	112	.292	.338	0	ø	0	45	0	0	0.0
1993	KC A	2	2	.500	18	0	0	0-4	18.1	25	12	1	4	9-0	9	5.89	78	.338	.437	0	ø	0	—	-2	0	-0.4
1994	Cal A	1	1	.500	10	0	0	0-0	15.1	14	11	1	3	13-0	9	6.46	76	.241	.405	0	ø	0	—	-2	0	-0.2
Total	5	25	21	.543	182	14	0	2-6	299.1	312	138	26	16	133-20	176	3.73	101	.274	.355	27-0-5	.111	-1	124	1	0	0.1
Sampson, Benj	Benjamin Damon; B4.27.1975 Des Moines IA; BR/TL/6´2˝/210; [MinA93 6/177]; d9.9																									
1998	Min A	1	0	1.000	5	2	0	0-0	17.1	10	3	0	1	6-0	16	1.56	308	.172	.254	0	ø	0	78	6	0	0.3
1999	Min A	3	2	.600	30	4	0	0-0	71	107	65	17	0	34-3	56	8.11	64	.351	.410	3	.000	-0	126	-20	0	-1.2
Total	2	4	2	.667	35	6	0	0-0	88.1	117	68	17	1	40-3	72	6.83	75	.322	.384	3	.000	-0	110	-14	0	-0.9
Sampson, Chris	Christopher Keith; B5.23.1978 Pasadena TX; BR/TR/6´1˝/190; [HouN99 8/263]; d6.2; Col Texas Tech																									
2006	Hou N	2	1	.667	12	3	0	0-0	34	25	10	3	1	5-1	15	2.12	213	.205	.240	5-0-2	.000	-1	48	8	0	0.7
Samuels, Joe	Joseph Jonas "Skabotch"; B3.21.1905 Scranton PA; D10.28.1996 Bath NY; BR/TR/6´1.5˝/196; d4.23																									
1930	Det A	0	0	ø	2	0	0	0	6	10	11	1	0	6	1	16.50	29	.417	.533	1	.000	-0	—	-7	—	-0.3
Samuels, Roger	Roger Howard; B1.5.1961 San Jose CA; BL/TL/6´5˝/210; [HouN83 10/244]; d7.20; Col Santa Clara																									
1988	SF N	1	2	.333	15	0	0	0-0	23.1	17	10	4	1	7-0	22	3.47	94	.202	.272	3	.000	-0	—	0	0	-0.1
1989	Pit N	0	0	ø	5	0	0	0-0	3.2	9	4	1	0	4-0	2	9.82	35	.474	.565	0	ø	0	—	-2	0	-0.1
Total	2	1	2	.333	20	0	0	0-0	27	26	14	5	1	11-0	24	4.33	76	.252	.330	3	.000	-0	—	-2	0	-0.2
Sanches, Brian	Brian Lee; B8.8.1978 Beaumont TX; BR/TR/6´0˝/190; [KCA99 2/54]; d6.1; Col Lamar																									
2006	Phi N	0	0	ø	18	0	0	0-0	21.1	23	14	5	0	13-3	22	5.91	79	.271	.367	0	ø	0	—	-2	0	-0.1
Sanchez, Alex	Alex Anthony; B4.8.1966 Concord CA; BR/TR/6´2˝/185; [TorA87 1/17]; d5.23; Col UCLA																									
1989	Tor A	0	1	.000	4	3	0	0-0	11.2	16	13	1	0	14-0	4	10.03	38	.356	.492	0	ø	0	135	-8	0	-0.5
Sanchez, Anibal	Anibal Alejandro; B2.27.1984 Maracay, Venezuela; BR/TR/6´0˝/180; d6.25																									
2006	Fla N	10	3	.769	18	17	2-1	0-0	114.1	90	39	9	4	46-1	72	2.83	151	.217	.300	35-0-3	.114	-1	95	20	0	2.0
Sanchez, Duaner	Duaner; B10.14.1979 Cotui, D.R.; BR/TR/6´0˝/(160–190); d6.14																									
2002	Ari N	0	0	ø	6	0	0	0-1	3.2	3	2	1	0	5-0	4	4.91	91	.214	.421	0	ø	0	—	0	0	0.0
	Pit N	0	0	ø	3	0	0	0-0	2.1	3	4	1	0	2-0	2	15.43	27	.300	.417	0	ø	0	—	-3	0	-0.1
	Year	0	0	ø	9	0	0	0-1	6	6	6	2	0	7-0	6	9.00	49	.250	.419	0	ø	0	—	-3	0	-0.1
2003	Pit N	1	0	1.000	6	0	0	0-0	6	15	11	2	2	1-0	3	16.50	26	.500	.529	0	ø	0	—	-8	0	-1.0
2004	†LA N	3	1	.750	67	0	0	0-1	80	81	34	9	6	27-2	44	3.37	123	.266	.335	4-0-1	.250	0	—	6	0	0.3
2005	LA N	4	7	.364	79	0	0	8-4	82	75	36	8	3	36-6	71	3.73	111	.248	.332	4	.000	-0	—	4	0	0.5
2006	NY N	5	1	.833	49	0	0	0-1	55.1	43	19	3	4	24-6	44	2.60	169	.223	.316	1	.000	0	—	10	64	1.0
Total	5	13	9	.591	210	0	0	8-7	229.1	220	106	24	15	95-14	168	3.81	111	.258	.339	9-0-1	.111	0	—	9	64	0.7
Sanchez, Felix	Felix Antonio; B8.3.1981 Puerto Plata, D.R.; BL/TL/6´3˝/180; [BosA00 11/332]; d9.3																									
2003	Chi N	0	0	ø	3	0	0	0-0	1.2	2	2	1	0	3-0	2	10.80	40	.333	.556	0	ø	0	—	-1	0	-0.1
Sanchez, Israel	Israel (Matos); B8.20.1963 Falcon Lasvias, Cuba; BL/TL/5´9˝/(165–170); [KCA82 9/220]; d7.7; [DL 1989 KC A 182]																									
1988	KC A	3	2	.600	19	1	0	1-0	35.2	36	20	0	0	18-2	14	4.54	88	.265	.348	0	ø	0	182	-2	0	-0.3
1990	KC A	0	0	ø	11	0	0	0-0	9.2	16	9	1	1	3-0	5	8.38	46	.381	.426	0	ø	0	—	-4	0	-0.2
Total	2	3	2	.600	30	1	0	1-0	45.1	52	29	1	1	21-2	19	5.36	74	.292	.366	0	ø	0	182	-6	182	-0.5
Sanchez, Jesus	Jesus Paulino; B10.11.1974 Nizao Bani, D.R.; BL/TL/5´10˝/(153–170); d3.31																									
1998	Fla N	7	9	.438	35	29	0	0-1	173	178	98	18	4	91-2	137	4.47	91	.272	.363	52-0-4	.135	-1*	105	-10	0	-0.8
1999	Fla N	5	7	.417	59	10	0	0-2	76.1	84	53	16	4	60-11	62	6.01	73	.291	.411	12-0-2	.083	-0*	103	-13	0	-1.8
2000	Fla N	9	12	.429	32	32	2-2	0-0	182	197	118	32	4	76-4	123	5.34	82	.280	.348	56-0-3	.232	2*	107	-20	0	-1.8
2001	Fla N	2	4	.333	16	9	0	0-0	62.2	61	33	7	2	31-2	46	4.74	88	.256	.346	17-0-2	.235	1*	108	-3	0	-0.2
2002	Chi N	0	0	ø	8	0	0	0-0	8.1	15	12	4	1	10-1	6	12.96	31	.395	.510	1	.000	-0	—	-8	0	-0.4
2003	Col N	0	0	ø	9	0	0	0-0	8	11	8	1	0	4-2	2	9.00	54	.324	.395	0	ø	0	—	-3	0	-0.1
2004	Cin N	0	2	.000	3	3	0	0-0	14.1	18	12	4	0	9-0	8	7.53	57	.305	.397	4-0-1	.000	-0	43	-5	0	-0.6
Total	7	23	34	.404	162	83	2-2	0-3	524.2	564	334	82	15	281-22	384	5.32	80	.280	.368	142-0-12	.176	1	103	-62	0	-5.7
Sanchez, Jonathan	Jonathan O.; B11.19.1982 Mayaguez, PR; BL/TL/6´2˝/165; [SFN04 27/820]; d5.28; Col Ohio Dominican																									
2006	SF N	3	1	.750	27	4	0	0-0	40	39	26	2	4	23-0	33	4.95	90	.250	.357	7	.000	-0	146	-3	0	-0.4
Sanchez, Luis	Luis Mercedes (b Luis Mercedes Escoba (Sanchez)); B8.24.1953 Cariaco, Sucre, Venez.; D2.4.2005 LaGuaira, Vargas, Venez.; BR/TR/6´2˝/(170–215); d4.10																									
1981	Cal A	0	2	.000	17	0	0	2-2	33.2	39	16	4	1	11-0	13	2.94	125	.287	.342	0	ø	0	—	1	0	0.1
1982	†Cal A	7	4	.636	46	0	0	5-3	92.2	89	36	3	7	34-4	58	3.21	128	.259	.337	0	ø	0	—	9	0	1.1
1983	Cal A	10	8	.556	56	1	0	7-9	98.1	92	42	6	3	40-14	49	3.66	111	.254	.332	0	ø	0	67	5	0	1.0
1984	Cal A	9	7	.563	49	0	0	11-10	83.2	84	34	10	3	33-9	62	3.33	120	.268	.340	0	ø	0	—	6	0	1.2
1985	Cal A	2	0	1.000	26	0	0	2-0	61.1	67	41	9	1	27-3	34	5.72	72	.283	.354	0	ø	0	—	-10	50	-0.5
Total	5	28	21	.571	194	1	0	27-24	369.2	371	169	32	15	145-30	216	3.75	107	.267	.340	0	ø	0	67	11	50	2.9

YEAR	TM LG	W	L	PCT	G	GS	CG-SHO	SV-BS	IP	H	R	HR	HB	BB-IB	SO	ERA	AERA	OAV	OOB	AB-HR-SH	AVG	PB	SUP	APR	DL	PW
Sanchez, Raul	Raul Guadalupe (Rodriguez); B12.12.1930 Marianao, Cuba; BR/TR/6´0˝/150; d4.17																									
1952	Was A	1	1	.500	3	2	1-1	0	12.2	13	5	0	0	7	6	3.55	100	.260	.351	5	.000	-1	61	0	0	0.0
1957	Cin N	3	2	.600	38	0	0	5	62.1	61	37	7	4	25-3	37	4.76	86	.262	.341	7-0-1	.286	1	—	-5	0	-0.3
1960	Cin N	1	0	1.000	8	0	0	0	14.2	12	9	1	3	11-1	5	4.91	78	.226	.388	2	.500	0	—	-2	0	-0.1
Total	3	5	3	.625	49	2	1-1	5	89.2	86	51	8	7	43-4	48	4.62	86	.256	.351	14-0-1	.214	0	61	-7	0	-0.4
Sanders, Ben	Alexander Bennett; B2.16.1865 Catharpin VA; D8.29.1930 Memphis TN; BR/TR/6´0˝/210; d6.6; Col Roanoke; ▲																									
1888	Phi N	19	10	.655	31	29	28-**8**	0	275.1	240	100	3	3	33	121	1.90	157	.228	.253	236-1	.246	5*	94	30	—	3.7
1889	Phi N	19	18	.514	44	39	34-1	1	349.2	406	217	9	4	96	123	3.55	122	.282	.329	169	.278	6	83	24	—	2.4
1890	Phi P	19	18	.514	43	40	37-2	1	346.2	412	237	13	10	69	107	3.76	114	.283	.320	189	.312	9*	92	20	—	2.3
1891	Phi AA	11	5	.688	19	18	15	0	145	157	85	3	8	37	40	3.79	100	.267	.319	156-1	.250	2*	123	1	—	0.3
1892	Lou N	12	19	.387	31	31	30-3	0	268.1	281	150	6	2	62	77	3.22	95	.259	.300	198-3	.273	10*	84	-3	—	0.7
Total	5	80	70	.533	168	157	144-14	2	1385	1496	789	34	27	297	468	3.24	116	.266	.306	948-5	.271	33	93	72	—	9.4
Sanders, Dave	David Andrew; B8.29.1979 Oklahoma City OK; BL/TL/6´0˝/200; [ChiA99 6/189]; d4.23; Col Barton Co. (KS) CC																									
2003	Chi A	0	0	ø	20	0	0	0-0	22	25	16	5	1	11-0	14	6.14	75	.281	.363	0	ø	0	—	-4	0	-0.2
2005	Chi A	0	0	ø	2	0	0	0-0	2	3	3	1	0	1-0	1	13.50	33	.375	.400	0	ø	0	—	-2	0	-0.1
Total	2	0	0	ø	22	0	0	0-0	24	28	19	6	1	12-0	15	6.75	68	.289	.366	0	ø	0	—	-6	0	-0.3
Sanders, Dee	Dee Wilman; B4.8.1921 Quitman TX; BR/TR/6´3˝/195; d8.12; Col Oklahoma																									
1945	StL A	0	0	ø	2	0	0	0	1.1	7	7	0	0	1	1	40.50	9	.700	.727	0	ø	0	—	-5	0	-0.3
Sanders, Ken	Kenneth George "Daffy"; B7.8.1941 St.Louis MO; BR/TR/5´11˝/(170–185); d8.6																									
1964	KC A	0	2	.000	21	0	0	1	27	23	12	2	1	17-4	18	3.67	104	.232	.345	0	ø	0	—	0	0	0.1
1966	Bos A	3	6	.333	24	0	0	2	47.1	36	22	2	2	28-9	33	3.80	100	.214	.332	6-0-3	.000	-0	—	0	0	0.1
	KC A	3	4	.429	38	1	0	1	65.1	59	28	8	1	48-7	41	3.72	91	.250	.374	8-0-1	.250	0	130	-1	0	-0.1
	Year	6	10	.375	62	1	0	3	112.2	95	50	10	3	76-16	74	3.75	95	.235	.357	14-0-4	.143	0	123	0	0	0.0
1968	Oak A	0	1	.000	7	0	0	0	10.2	8	5	1	0	8-2	6	3.38	84	.229	.372	0	ø	0	—	-1	0	-0.1
1970	Mil A	5	2	.714	50	0	0	13-6	92.1	64	19	1	4	25-6	64	1.75	215	.201	.266	13-0-2	.231	1	—	21	0	2.3
1971	Mil A	7	12	.368	**83**	0	0	**31**-4	136.1	111	35	9	4	34-10	80	1.91	182	.227	.282	14-0-1	.000	-1	—	**23**	0	4.5
1972	Mil A	2	9	.182	62	0	0	17-4	92.1	88	38	10	2	31-13	51	3.12	98	.245	.308	7-0-1	.143	0	—	-2	0	-0.2
1973	Min A	2	4	.333	27	0	0	8-3	44.1	53	31	4	2	21-1	19	6.09	65	.299	.374	0	ø	0	—	-9	0	-1.4
	Cle A	5	1	.833	15	0	0	5-1	27.1	18	6	2	0	9-2	14	1.65	240	.188	.257	0	ø	0	—	7	0	1.4
	Year	7	5	.583	42	0	0	13-4	71.2	71	37	6	2	30-3	33	4.40	90	.260	.334	0	ø	0	—	-3	0	0.0
1974	Cle A	0	1	.000	9	0	0	1-0	11	21	12	5	0	5-2	4	9.82	37	.404	.456	0	ø	0	—	-7	0	-0.7
	Cal A	0	0	ø	9	0	0	1-1	9.2	10	5	0	0	3-0	4	2.79	124	.278	.317	0	ø	0	—	0	0	0.0
	Year	0	1	.000	18	0	0	2-1	20.2	31	17	5	0	8-2	8	6.53	55	.352	.398	0	ø	0	—	-7	0	-0.7
1975	NY N	1	1	.500	29	0	0	5-1	43	31	11	2	0	14-7	8	2.30	153	.205	.271	2	.000	-0*	—	7	22	0.4
1976	NY N	1	2	.333	31	0	0	1-0	47	39	16	4	1	12-4	16	2.87	117	.231	.281	2	.000	-0	—	3	0	0.2
	KC A	0	0	ø	3	0	0	0-0	3	3	0	0	0	3-0	2	0.00	ø	.273	.429	0	ø	0	—	1	0	0.1
Total	10	29	45	.392	408	1	0	86-20	656.2	564	240	50	17	258-67	360	2.97	119	.235	.312	52-0-8	.115	-0	126	42	22	6.6
Sanders, Roy	Roy Garvin "Butch","Pepe"; B8.1.1892 Stafford KS; D1.17.1950 Kansas City MO; BR/TR/6´0.5˝/195; d4.16; Col William Jewell																									
1917	Cin N	0	1	.000	2	2	1	0	14	12	7	0	1	16	3	4.50	58	.273	.475	6	.000	-1*	101	-2	—	-0.2
1918	Pit N	7	9	.438	28	14	6-1	1	156	135	59	1	2	52	55	2.60	111	.239	.305	53-0-2	.151	-1	81	5	—	0.5
Total	2	7	10	.412	30	16	7-1	1	170	147	66	1	3	68	58	2.75	104	.241	.321	59-0-2	.136	-2	83	3	—	0.3
Sanders, Roy	Roy Lee "Simon"; B6.10.1894 Pittsburg KS; D7.8.1963 Louisville KY; BR/TR/6´0˝/185; d8.6																									
1918	NY A	0	2	.000	6	2	0	0	25.2	28	15	0	2	16	8	4.21	67	.301	.414	7	.000	-1	27	-4	—	-0.5
1920	StL A	1	1	.500	8	1	0	0	17.1	20	10	1	1	17	2	5.19	75	.313	.463	4	.000	-1	243	-1	—	-0.2
Total	2	1	3	.250	14	3	0	0	43	48	25	1	3	33	10	4.60	71	.306	.435	11	.000	-2	110	-5	—	-0.7
Sanders, Scott	Scott Gerald; B3.25.1969 Hannibal MO; BR/TR/6´4˝/(215–220); [SDN90 1/32]; d8.6; Col Nicholls St.																									
1993	SD N	3	3	.500	9	9	0	0-0	52.1	54	32	4	1	23-1	37	4.13	100	.265	.339	16-0-4	.063	-1	77	-2	0	-0.4
1994	SD N	4	8	.333	23	20	0	1-0	111	103	63	10	5	48-4	109	4.78	86	.245	.326	32-0-6	.125	-0	101	-7	16	-0.6
1995	SD N	5	5	.500	17	15	1	0-0	90	79	46	14	2	31-4	88	4.30	95	.228	.294	27-0-3	.296	2	108	-1	69	0.1
1996	†SD N	9	5	.643	46	16	0	0-0	144	117	58	10	2	48-5	157	3.38	119	.221	.284	36-0-4	.194	2	126	12	0	1.1
1997	Sea A	3	6	.333	33	6	0	2-2	65.1	73	48	16	3	38-5	62	6.47	70	.280	.371	0	ø	0	84	-13	0	-1.6
	Det A	3	8	.273	14	14	1-1	0-0	74.1	79	44	14	1	24-1	58	5.33	87	.276	.329	0	ø	0	67	-4	0	-0.5
	Year	6	14	.300	47	20	1-1	2-2	139.2	152	92	30	4	62-6	120	5.86	78	.278	.350	0	ø	0	72	-17	0	-2.1
1998	Det A	0	2	.000	3	2	0	0-0	9.2	24	19	1	0	6-2	6	17.69	27	.471	.526	0	ø	0	39	-13	0	-1.7
	SD N	3	1	.750	23	0	0	0-0	30.2	33	20	5	0	5-1	26	4.11	97	.270	.299	0-0-1	ø	0	—	-3	0	-0.3
1999	Chi N	4	7	.364	67	6	0	2-3	104.1	112	69	19	0	53-8	89	5.52	83	.277	.358	18-0-2	.278	1	70	-10	0	-0.8
Total	7	34	45	.430	235	88	2-1	5-5	681.2	674	399	93	14	276-31	632	4.86	88	.257	.327	129-0-20	.194	4	93	-41	85	-4.7
Sanders, War	Warren Williams; B8.2.1877 Maynardville TN; D8.3.1962 Chattanooga TN; BR/TL/5´10˝/160; d4.18; Col Tennessee																									
1903	StL N	1	6	.143	8	6	3	0	40	48	37	0	2	21	9	6.07	54	.286	.372	15	.067	-2	69	-11	—	-1.6
1904	StL N	1	2	.333	4	3	1	0	19	25	15	1	1	1	11	4.74	57	.298	.314	6	.000	-1	60	-4	—	-0.7
Total	2	2	8	.200	12	9	4	0	59	73	52	1	3	22	20	5.64	55	.290	.354	21	.048	-2	66	-15	—	-2.3
Sanderson, Scott	Scott Douglas; B7.22.1956 Dearborn MI; BR/TR/6´5˝/(192–200); [MonN77 3/54]; d8.6; Col Vanderbilt																									
1978	Mon N	4	2	.667	10	9	1-1	0-0	61	52	20	3	1	21-0	50	2.51	142	.232	.298	19-0-2	.105	-1	87	7	0	0.5
1979	Mon N	9	8	.529	34	24	5-3	1-0	168	148	69	16	3	54-4	138	3.43	108	.236	.297	50-0-7	.160	-0	95	7	0	0.6
1980	Mon N	16	11	.593	33	33	7-3	0-0	211.1	206	76	18	3	56-3	125	3.11	117	.257	.307	64-0-8	.078	-3	93	15	0	1.4
1981	†Mon N	9	7	.563	22	22	4-1	0-0	137.1	122	50	10	1	31-2	77	2.95	121	.236	.278	35-0-5	.114	2	121	9	0	1.1
1982	Mon N	12	12	.500	32	32	7	0-0	224	212	98	24	3	58-5	158	3.46	107	.251	.299	57-1-16	.140	1	106	6	0	0.5
1983	Mon N	6	7	.462	18	16	0	1-0	81.1	98	50	12	0	20-0	55	4.65	78	.303	.343	28-0-1	.143	-0	93	-11	58	-1.7
1984	†Chi N	8	5	.615	24	24	3	0-0	140.2	140	54	5	2	24-3	76	3.14	125	.264	.294	42-0-4	.119	-1	105	11	34	0.9
1985	Chi N	5	6	.455	19	19	2	0-0	121	100	49	13	0	27-4	80	3.12	128	.228	.268	31-0-6	.065	-2	96	9	54	0.7
1986	Chi N	9	11	.450	37	28	1-1	1-0	169.2	165	85	21	2	37-2	124	4.19	97	.255	.295	51-0-6	.059	-3*	84	-2	0	-0.6
1987	Chi N	8	9	.471	32	22	0	2-2	144.2	156	72	23	3	50-5	106	4.29	101	.274	.333	40-1-4	.075	-1	89	2	33	0.1
1988	Chi N	1	2	.333	11	0	0	0-2	15.1	13	9	1	0	3-1	6	5.28	69	.232	.258	0	ø	0	—	-2	140	-0.4
1989	†Chi N	11	9	.550	37	23	2	0-0	146.1	155	69	16	2	31-6	86	3.94	96	.273	.312	43-0-6	.047	-2	95	-1	0	-0.5
1990	†Oak A	17	11	.607	34	34	2-1	0-0	206.1	205	99	27	4	66-2	128	3.88	96	.255	.312	0	ø	0	108	-4	0	-0.6
1991	NY A☆	16	10	.615	34	34	2-2	0-0	208	200	95	22	3	29-0	130	3.81	109	.252	.279	0	ø	0	101	9	0	0.8
1992	NY A	12	11	.522	33	33	2-1	0-0	193.1	220	116	28	4	64-5	104	4.93	80	.286	.340	0	ø	0	118	-21	0	-2.3
1993	Cal A	7	11	.389	21	21	4-1	0-0	135.1	153	77	15	5	27-5	66	4.46	102	.289	.325	0	ø	0	86	0	0	0.0
	SF N	4	2	.667	11	8	0	0-0	48.2	48	20	12	1	7-2	36	3.51	112	.255	.283	14-0-1	.000	-1	112	3	0	0.2
1994	Chi A	8	4	.667	18	14	1	0-0	92	110	57	20	2	12-1	36	5.09	92	.296	.321	0	ø	0	136	-4	0	-0.4
1995	Cal A	1	3	.250	7	7	0	0-0	39.1	48	23	6	2	4-1	23	4.12	114	.298	.320	0	ø	0	102	1	123	0.1
1996	Cal A	0	2	.000	5	4	0	0-0	18	39	21	5	2	4-0	7	7.50	67	.433	.464	0	ø	0	105	-7	28	-0.6
Total	19	163	143	.533	472	407	43-14	5-4	2561.2	2590	1209	297	43	625-51	1611	3.84	103	.263	.307	474-2-66	.097	-12	101	27	470	-0.2
Sanford, Fred	John Frederick; B8.9.1919 Garfield UT; BB/TR (BR 1948)/6´1˝/200; d5.5; Mil 1944–45																									
1943	StL A	0	0	ø	3	0	0	0	9.1	7	2	0	0	4	2	1.93	172	.219	.306	0-0-1	ø	0	—	2	0	0.1
1946	StL A	2	1	.667	3	3	2-2	0	22	19	7	0	0	9	8	2.05	182	.235	.311	7	.286	1	46	3	0	0.6
1947	StL A	7	16	.304	34	23	9	4	186.2	186	89	17	0	76	62	3.71	104	.261	.332	54-0-7	.204	-0	66	3	0	0.2
1948	StL A	12	21	.364	42	33	9-1	2	227	250	123	19	2	91	79	4.64	98	.279	.347	73-1-2	.151	-2*	73	1	0	0.0
1949	NY A	7	3	.700	29	11	3	0	95.1	100	53	9	0	57	51	3.87	105	.270	.367	34-0-2	.118	-2	115	-1	0	-0.4
1950	NY A	5	4	.556	26	12	2	0	112.2	103	60	9	1	79	54	4.55	94	.252	.374	35-0-1	.229	1	103	-2	0	0.0
1951	NY A	0	3	.000	11	2	0	0	26.2	15	11	2	0	25	10	3.71	103	.169	.351	5	.000	-1	58	1	0	0.1
	Was A	2	3	.400	7	7	0	0	37	51	27	5	0	27	12	6.57	62	.329	.429	14-0-1	.071	-1	115	-9	0	-1.1
	StL A	2	4	.333	9	7	1	0	27.1	37	33	6	0	23	7	10.21	43	.308	.420	7	.286	1	136	-16	0	-2.6
	Year	4	10	.286	27	16	1	0	91	103	71	13	0	75	29	6.82	60	.283	.405	26-0-1	.115	-1	120	-24	0	-3.6
Total	7	37	55	.402	164	98	26-3	6	744	768	405	67	3	391	285	4.45	94	.268	.357	229-1-14	.170	-4	87	-18	0	-3.1

SANFORD, JACK John Stanley; B5.18.1929 Wellesley Hills MA; D3.7.2000 Beckley WV; BR/TR/6´0˝/(175–196); d9.16; C2

YEAR	TM LG	W	L	PCT	G	GS	CG-SHO	SV-BS	IP	H	R	HR	HB	BB-IB	SO	ERA	AERA	OAV	OOB	AB-HR-SH	AVG	PB	SUP	APR	DL	PW
1956	Phi N	1	0	1.000	3	1	0	0	13	7	2	0	1	13-0	6	1.38	269	.184	.404	3	.333	0	95	4	0	0.3
1957	Phi N★	19	8	.704	33	33	15-3	0	236.2	194	94	22	3	94-2	**188**	3.08	124	**.221**	.297	89-0-4	.169	-1	112	18	0	1.8
1958	Phi N	10	13	.435	38	27	7-2	0	186.1	197	103	15	3	81-6	106	4.44	89	.274	.347	59-0-3	.169	1	94	-9	0	-1.0
1959	SF N	15	12	.556	36	31	10	1	222.1	198	90	22	7	70-4	132	3.16	121	.235	.298	72-0-5	.111	-1	111	17	0	1.8
1960	SF N	12	14	.462	37	34	11-**6**	0	219	199	111	11	2	99-6	125	3.82	91	.243	.325	74-0-5	.176	1	126	-9	0	-1.0
1961	SF N	13	9	.591	38	33	6	0	217.1	203	114	22	5	87-7	112	4.22	90	.249	.322	74-3-5	.216	6*	112	-10	0	-0.4
1962	†SF N	24	7	.774	39	38	13-2	0	265.1	233	110	23	3	92-4	147	3.43	111	.234	.300	98-0-4	.153	0	130	13	0	1.4
1963	SF N	16	13	.552	42	**42**	11	0	284.1	273	123	21	5	76-8	158	3.51	91	.251	.303	94-0-7	.138	3*	128	-7	0	-0.3
1964	SF N	5	7	.417	18	17	3-1	1	106.1	91	44	7	4	37-3	64	3.30	108	.228	.298	30-0-3	.133	1*	88	3	84	0.4
1965	SF N	4	5	.444	23	16	0	2	91	92	50	11	7	30-7	43	3.96	91	.256	.324	25-0-1	.120	-0	100	-5	0	-0.6
	Cal A	1	2	.333	9	5	0	1	29.1	35	16	2	0	10-1	13	4.60	74	.324	.381	7-0-1	.143	-0	114	-4	0	-0.4
1966	Cal A	13	7	.650	50	6	0	5	108	108	51	11	4	27-6	54	3.83	88	.271	.316	22-0-1	.136	1	96	-6	0	-0.9
1967	Cal A	3	2	.600	12	9	0	1	48.1	53	26	6	0	7-1	21	4.47	70	.288	.311	15-0-2	.200	1	142	-7	0	-0.5
	KC A	1	2	.333	10	1	0	0	22	24	18	1	2	14-4	13	6.55	49	.296	.408	3	.000	-0	82	-8	0	-1.0
	Year	4	4	.500	22	10	0	1	70.1	77	44	7	2	21-5	34	5.12	62	.291	.344	18-0-2	.167	1	135	-15	0	-1.5
Total	12	137	101	.576	388	293	76-14	11	2049.1	1907	952	174	46	737-59	1182	3.69	98	.247	.314	665-3-41	.158	12	115	-10	84	-0.4

SANFORD, MO Meredith Leroy; B12.24.1966 Americus GA; BR/TR/6´6˝/(220–233); [CinN88 32/826]; d8.9; Col Alabama

YEAR	TM LG	W	L	PCT	G	GS	CG-SHO	SV-BS	IP	H	R	HR	HB	BB-IB	SO	ERA	AERA	OAV	OOB	AB-HR-SH	AVG	PB	SUP	APR	DL	PW
1991	Cin N	1	2	.333	5	5	0	0-0	28	19	14	3	1	15-1	31	3.86	99	.186	.297	8-0-2	.000	-1	90	0	0	-0.1
1993	Col N	1	2	.333	11	6	0	0-0	35.2	37	25	4	0	27-0	36	5.30	90	.278	.395	8-0-1	.000	-1	82	-2	0	-0.3
1995	Min A	0	0	ø	11	0	0	0-0	18.2	16	11	7	2	16-0	17	5.30	91	.225	.382	0	ø	0	—	-1	0	-0.1
Total	3	2	4	.333	27	11	0	0-0	82.1	72	50	14	3	58-1	84	4.81	93	.235	.360	16-0-3	.000	-2	83	-3	0	-0.5

SANTANA, ERVIN Ervin Ramon; B1.10.1983 LaRomana, D.R.; BR/TR/6´2˝/160; d5.17

YEAR	TM LG	W	L	PCT	G	GS	CG-SHO	SV-BS	IP	H	R	HR	HB	BB-IB	SO	ERA	AERA	OAV	OOB	AB-HR-SH	AVG	PB	SUP	APR	DL	PW
2005	†LA A	12	8	.600	23	23	1-1	0-0	133.2	139	73	17	8	47-2	99	4.65	92	.266	.333	0	ø	0	91	-5	0	-0.7
2006	LA A	16	8	.667	33	33	0	0-0	204	181	106	21	11	70-2	141	4.28	104	.241	.311	4	.250	0	116	5	0	0.4
Total	2	28	16	.636	56	56	1-1	0-0	337.2	320	179	38	19	117-4	240	4.42	99	.251	.320	4	.250	0	106	0	0	-0.3

SANTANA, JOHAN Johan Alexander; B3.13.1979 Tovar, Merida, Venez.; BL/TL/6´0˝/(195–210); d4.3

YEAR	TM LG	W	L	PCT	G	GS	CG-SHO	SV-BS	IP	H	R	HR	HB	BB-IB	SO	ERA	AERA	OAV	OOB	AB-HR-SH	AVG	PB	SUP	APR	DL	PW
2000	Min A	2	3	.400	30	5	0	0-0	86	102	64	11	2	54-0	64	6.49	81	.302	.398	1	.000	-0	78	-10	0	-0.4
2001	Min A	1	0	1.000	15	4	0	0-0	43.2	50	25	6	3	16-0	28	4.74	99	.292	.358	0	ø	0	149	-1	76	0.0
2002	†Min A	8	6	.571	27	14	0	1-0	108.1	84	41	7	1	49-0	137	2.99	149	.212	.298	4	.250	0	105	17	0	2.0
2003	†Min A	12	3	.800	45	18	0	0-0	158.1	127	56	17	3	47-1	169	3.07	147	.216	.276	3	.333	0	105	26	0	2.1
2004	†Min A	20	6	.769	34	34	1-1	0-0	228	156	70	24	9	54-0	**265**	**2.61**	**178**	**.192**	**.249**	8	.375	1	103	**52**	0	**5.6**
2005	Min A★	16	7	.696	33	33	3-2	0-0	231.2	180	77	22	1	45-1	**238**	2.87	**152**	**.210**	**.250**	6	.167	-0	94	**40**	0	3.7
2006	†Min A★	**19**	6	.760	34	**34**	1	0-0	**233.2**	186	79	24	4	47-0	**245**	**2.77**	**165**	**.216**	**.258**	2	.000	-0	106	**46**	0	4.6
Total	7	78	31	.716	218	142	5-3	1-0	1089.2	885	412	111	23	312-2	1146	3.20	143	.220	.279	24	.250	1	102	170	76	17.6

SANTANA, JULIO Julio Franklin; B1.20.1973 San Pedro de Macoris, D.R.; BR/TR/6´0˝/(175–215); d4.6; [DL 1999 Bos A 74]

YEAR	TM LG	W	L	PCT	G	GS	CG-SHO	SV-BS	IP	H	R	HR	HB	BB-IB	SO	ERA	AERA	OAV	OOB	AB-HR-SH	AVG	PB	SUP	APR	DL	PW
1997	Tex A	4	6	.400	30	14	0	0-1	104	141	86	16	4	49-2	64	6.75	72	.323	.392	2	.500	0	101	-21	26	-1.6
1998	Tex A	0	0	ø	3	0	0	0-0	5.1	7	5	0	0	4-1	1	8.44	58	.304	.407	0	ø	0	—	-2	0	-0.1
	TB A	5	6	.455	32	19	1	0-0	140.1	144	72	18	5	58-2	60	4.23	113	.270	.344	4	.000	-0	92	8	0	0.4
	Year	5	6	.455	35	19	1	0-0	145.2	151	77	18	5	62-3	61	4.39	109	.272	.347	4	.000	-0	92	7	0	0.3
1999	TB A	1	4	.200	22	5	0	0-0	55.1	66	49	10	7	32-0	34	7.32	68	.300	.404	1	1.000	0	56	-13	21	-1.0
2000	Mon N	1	5	.167	36	4	0	0-2	66.2	69	45	11	2	33-2	58	5.67	83	.271	.356	7	.000	-1	97	-6	0	-0.5
2002	Det A	3	5	.375	38	0	0	0-1	57	49	19	8	2	28-2	38	2.84	154	.238	.335	0	ø	0	—	10	50	1.2
2005	Mil N	3	5	.375	41	0	0	1-3	42	34	21	6	0	19-4	49	4.50	94	.221	.301	1	.000	-0	—	0	43	-0.1
2006	Phi N	0	0	ø	7	0	0	0-0	8.1	8	9	1	1	9-1	4	7.56	62	.258	.419	1-0-1	.000	-0	—	-3	157	-0.2
Total	7	17	31	.354	209	42	1	1-7	479	518	306	70	21	232-14	308	5.30	89	.279	.362	16-0-1	.125	-1	94	-27	371	-1.9

SANTANA, MARINO Marino (Castro); B5.10.1972 San Jose de los Llanos, D.R.; BR/TR/6´1˝/175; d9.4

YEAR	TM LG	W	L	PCT	G	GS	CG-SHO	SV-BS	IP	H	R	HR	HB	BB-IB	SO	ERA	AERA	OAV	OOB	AB-HR-SH	AVG	PB	SUP	APR	DL	PW
1998	Det A	0	0	ø	7	0	0	0-0	7.1	9	3	1	1	8-2	10	3.68	129	.310	.474	0	ø	0	—	1	0	0.0
1999	Bos A	0	0	ø	3	0	0	0-0	4	8	7	3	0	3-0	4	15.75	32	.444	.500	0	ø	0	—	-4	69	-0.2
Total	2	0	0	ø	10	0	0	0-0	11.1	17	10	4	1	11-2	14	7.94	61	.362	.483	0	ø	0	—	-3	69	-0.2

SANTIAGO, JOSE Jose Guillermo (Guzman) "Pants"; B9.4.1928 Coamo, PR; BR/TR/5´10˝/175; d4.17; Negro Lg 1947–48

YEAR	TM LG	W	L	PCT	G	GS	CG-SHO	SV-BS	IP	H	R	HR	HB	BB-IB	SO	ERA	AERA	OAV	OOB	AB-HR-SH	AVG	PB	SUP	APR	DL	PW
1954	Cle A	0	0	ø	1	0	0	0	1.2	0	1	0	0	2	1	0.00	ø	.000	.286	0	ø	0	—	0	0	0.0
1955	Cle A	2	0	1.000	17	0	0	0	32.2	31	11	1	5	14-1	19	2.48	161	.256	.350	4-0-2	.500	1	—	5	0	0.4
1956	KC A	1	2	.333	9	5	0	0	21.2	36	26	8	5	17-0	9	8.31	52	.387	.500	5-0-1	.400	0	169	-11	0	-1.2
Total	3	3	2	.600	27	5	0	0	56	67	38	9	10	33-1	29	4.66	88	.306	.414	9-0-3	.444	2	169	-6	0	-0.8

SANTIAGO, JOSE Jose Rafael (Alfonso); B8.15.1940 Juana Diaz, PR; BR/TR/6´2˝/(185–192); d9.9

YEAR	TM LG	W	L	PCT	G	GS	CG-SHO	SV-BS	IP	H	R	HR	HB	BB-IB	SO	ERA	AERA	OAV	OOB	AB-HR-SH	AVG	PB	SUP	APR	DL	PW
1963	KC A	1	0	1.000	4	0	0	0	7	8	7	4	0	2-0	6	9.00	43	.276	.323	0	ø	0	—	-3	0	-0.4
1964	KC A	0	6	.000	34	8	0	0	83.2	84	53	9	4	35-1	64	4.73	81	.258	.336	18-0-2	.000	-2	102	-10	0	-0.9
1965	KC A	0	0	ø	4	0	0	0	5	8	5	1	0	4-2	8	9.00	39	.364	.462	0	ø	0	—	-3	0	-0.1
1966	Bos A	12	13	.480	35	28	7-1	2	172	155	87	17	2	58-0	119	3.66	104	.238	.300	56-0-4	.196	0*	94	0	0	0.0
1967	†Bos A	12	4	.750	50	11	2	5	145.1	138	61	15	2	47-3	109	3.59	97	.251	.312	42-1-1	.190	2	157	0	0	0.3
1968	Bos A✶	9	4	.692	18	18	7-2	0	124	96	34	9	3	42-0	86	2.25	140	.215	.286	43-0-3	.163	1*	100	12	70	1.5
1969	Bos A	0	0	ø	10	0	0	0-0	7.2	11	5	2	0	4-0	4	3.52	109	.324	.395	0	ø	0	—	0	134	0.0
1970	Bos A	0	2	.000	8	0	0	1-0	11.1	18	13	0	0	8-1	8	10.32	39	.353	.441	3	.667	1*	—	-7	22	-1.1
Total	8	34	29	.540	163	65	16-3	8-0	556	518	265	57	11	200-7	404	3.74	96	.246	.313	162-1-10	.173	2	107	-11	226	-0.7

SANTIAGO, JOSE Jose Rafael (Fuentes); B11.5.1974 Fajardo, PR; BR/TR/6´3˝/(215–225); [KCA94 70/1627]; d6.7

YEAR	TM LG	W	L	PCT	G	GS	CG-SHO	SV-BS	IP	H	R	HR	HB	BB-IB	SO	ERA	AERA	OAV	OOB	AB-HR-SH	AVG	PB	SUP	APR	DL	PW
1997	KC A	0	0	ø	4	0	0	0-0	4.2	7	2	0	1	2-1	1	1.93	246	.333	.417	0	ø	0	—	1	21	0.0
1998	KC A	0	0	ø	2	0	0	0-0	2	4	2	0	0	0-0	2	9.00	54	.444	.444	0	ø	0	—	-1	0	0.0
1999	KC A	3	4	.429	34	0	0	2-1	47.1	46	23	7	2	14-2	15	3.42	149	.251	.307	0	ø	0	—	7	85	0.9
2000	KC A	8	6	.571	45	0	0	2-6	69	70	33	7	3	26-3	44	3.91	133	.260	.329	0	ø	0	—	9	0	1.6
2001	KC A	2	2	.500	20	0	0	0-1	29.1	40	22	2	1	9-1	15	6.75	74	.333	.376	0	ø	0	—	-4	0	-0.5
	Phi N	2	4	.333	53	0	0	0-1	62.1	66	25	3	2	13-1	28	3.61	114	.272	.312	3	.000	0	—	5	0	0.3
2002	Phi N	1	3	.250	42	0	0	0-1	47	56	35	7	3	15-1	30	6.70	57	.290	.347	2	.000	0	—	-15	0	-1.1
2003	Cle A	1	3	.250	25	0	0	0-2	31.2	37	11	2	0	14-3	15	2.84	156	.298	.370	0	ø	0	—	6	0	0.6
2005	NY N	0	0	ø	4	0	0	0-0	5.2	10	2	0	1	2-0	3	3.18	130	.417	.481	0	ø	0	—	1	0	0.0
Total	8	17	22	.436	229	0	0	4-12	299	336	155	28	13	95-12	153	4.36	105	.283	.340	5	.000	0	—	9	106	1.8

SANTORINI, AL Alan Joel; B5.19.1948 Irvington NJ; BR/TR/6´0˝/(185–195); [AtlN66 1/11]; d9.10

YEAR	TM LG	W	L	PCT	G	GS	CG-SHO	SV-BS	IP	H	R	HR	HB	BB-IB	SO	ERA	AERA	OAV	OOB	AB-HR-SH	AVG	PB	SUP	APR	DL	PW
1968	Atl N	0	1	.000	1	1	0	0	3	4	4	1	0	0-0	0	0.00	ø	.286	.286	0	ø	0	58	-1	0	-0.2
1969	SD N	8	14	.364	32	30	2-1	0-0	184.2	194	95	11	7	73-10	111	3.95	91	.270	.341	63-1-3	.111	-1	71	-10	0	-1.2
1970	SD N	1	8	.111	21	12	0	1-0	75.2	91	56	11	3	43-6	41	6.07	66	.294	.382	18	.000	-2	78	-17	0	-2.0
1971	SD N	0	2	.000	18	3	0	0-1	38.1	43	19	4	0	11-1	21	3.76	89	.285	.329	5	.400	1	62	-2	0	-0.1
	StL N	0	2	.000	19	5	0	2-0	49.2	51	21	2	1	19-2	21	3.81	96	.270	.340	10	.300	1	98	0	0	0.0
	Year	0	4	.000	37	8	0	2-1	88	94	40	6	1	30-3	42	3.78	92	.276	.335	15	.333	1	86	-2	0	-0.1
1972	StL N	8	11	.421	30	19	3-3	0-1	133.2	136	63	6	1	46-7	72	4.11	83	.263	.323	40-0-3	.075	-2	92	-8	0	-1.3
1973	StL N	0	0	ø	6	0	0	0-0	8.1	14	5	1	1	2-0	2	5.40	68	.400	.436	1	.000	-0	—	-1	0	-0.1
Total	6	17	38	.309	127	70	5-4	3-2	493.1	533	263	36	13	194-26	268	4.29	84	.276	.344	137-1-6	.109	-4	79	-39	0	-4.9

SANTOS, VICTOR Victor Irving; B10.2.1976 San Pedro de Macoris, D.R.; BR/TR/6´3˝/(175–205); d4.9; Col St. Peters

YEAR	TM LG	W	L	PCT	G	GS	CG-SHO	SV-BS	IP	H	R	HR	HB	BB-IB	SO	ERA	AERA	OAV	OOB	AB-HR-SH	AVG	PB	SUP	APR	DL	PW
2001	Det A	2	2	.500	33	7	0	0-0	76.1	62	33	9	3	49-4	52	3.30	134	.222	.341	0	ø	0	144	9	0	0.4
2002	Col N	0	4	.000	24	2	0	0-0	26	41	30	3	0	22-3	25	10.38	46	.360	.460	2	.500	0	137	-13	0	-1.7
2003	Tex A	0	2	.000	8	4	0	0-0	25.2	29	21	5	1	16-1	15	7.01	71	.296	.397	2-0-1	.000	-0	74	-5	0	-0.4
2004	Mil N	11	12	.478	31	28	0	0-0	154	169	95	18	7	57-5	115	4.97	88	.278	.344	39-0-6	.051	-2	82	-10	0	-1.7
2005	Mil N	4	13	.235	29	24	1	0-0	141.2	153	87	20	5	60-8	89	4.57	93	.269	.343	40-0-3	.075	-3	77	-9	0	-1.2
2006	Pit N	5	9	.357	25	19	0	0-0	115.1	150	80	16	4	42-3	81	5.70	80	.321	.379	38-0-6	.158	-0	95	-14	25	-1.5
Total	6	22	42	.344	150	84	1	0-0	539	604	346	71	20	246-24	377	5.14	86	.283	.360	121-0-16	.099	-5	89	-42	25	-6.1

YEAR	TM LG	W	L	PCT	G	GS	CG-SHO	SV-BS	IP	H	R	HR	HB	BB-IB	SO	ERA	AERA	OAV	OOB	AB-HR-SH	AVG	PB	SUP	APR	DL	PW
Sarfate, Dennis	Dennis Scott; B4.9.1981 Queens NY; BR/TR/6´4˝/210; [MilN01 9/268]; d9.3; Col Chandler–Gilbert (AZ) CC																									
2006	Mil N	0	0	ø	8	0	0	0-0	8.1	9	4	0	0	4-1	11	4.32	104	.265	.342	0	ø	0	—	0	0	0.0
Sarmiento, Manny	Manuel Eduardo (Aponte); B2.2.1956 Cagua, Aragua, Venez.; BR/TR/6´0˝/(136–170); d7.30; [DL 1984 Pit N 182]																									
1976	†Cin N	5	1	.833	22	0	0	0-0	43.2	36	14	1	1	12-3	20	2.06	170	.222	.278	7	.000	-1	—	6	0	0.6
1977	Cin N	0	0	ø	24	0	0	1-0	40.1	28	13	6	0	11-2	23	2.45	160	.196	.247	1-0-1	.000	-0	—	6	0	0.2
1978	Cin N	9	7	.563	63	4	0	5-3	127.1	109	65	16	1	54-10	72	4.38	81	.234	.310	16-0-1	.000	-1*	70	-10	0	-1.4
1979	Cin N	0	4	.000	23	1	0	0-2	38.2	47	21	2	1	7-2	23	4.66	80	.311	.337	6-0-1	.000	-1	215	-3	0	-0.4
1980	Sea A	0	1	.000	9	0	0	1-1	14.2	14	7	2	0	6-1	15	3.68	113	.255	.317	0	ø	0	—	1	0	0.0
1982	Pit N	9	4	.692	35	17	4	1-0	164.2	153	69	7	0	46-4	81	3.39	111	.246	.295	47-0-7	.191	1	133	6	0	0.4
1983	Pit N	3	5	.375	52	0	0	4-1	84.1	74	35	8	0	36-8	49	2.99	125	.243	.318	10-0-2	.000	-1	—	5	0	0.4
Total	7	26	22	.542	228	22	4	12-7	513.2	461	224	42	3	172-30	283	3.49	106	.242	.301	87-0-12	.103	-3	126	11	182	-0.2
Sasaki, Kazuhiro	Kazuhiro; B2.22.1968 Tokyo, Japan; BR/TR/6´4˝/(209–220); d4.5																									
2000	†Sea A	2	5	.286	63	0	0	37-3	62.2	42	25	10	2	31-5	78	3.16	152	.184	.285	0	ø	0	—	11	0	2.0
2001	†Sea A★	0	4	.000	69	0	0	45-7	66.2	48	24	6	4	11-2	62	3.24	131	.195	.241	0	ø	0	—	9	0	1.4
2002	Sea A★	4	5	.444	61	0	0	37-8	60.2	44	24	6	2	20-4	73	2.52	171	.201	.268	0	ø	0	—	10	0	1.9
2003	Sea A	1	2	.333	35	0	0	10-4	33.1	31	17	2	1	15-2	29	4.05	107	.238	.318	0	ø	0	—	1	77	0.0
Total	4	7	16	.304	228	0	0	129-22	223.1	165	90	24	9	77-13	242	3.14	141	.200	.273	0	ø	0	—	31	77	5.3
Saucier, Kevin	Kevin Andrew; B8.9.1956 Pensacola FL; BR/TL/6´1˝/(190–196); [PhiN74 2/27]; d10.1																									
1978	Phi N	0	1	.000	1	0	0	0-0	2	4	4	0	1	1-0	2	18.00	20	.400	.500	0	ø	0	—	-3	0	-0.5
1979	Phi N	1	4	.200	29	2	0	1-1	62.1	68	31	4	3	33-3	21	4.19	93	.291	.381	10	.100	-1	34	-2	0	-0.2
1980	†Phi N	7	3	.700	40	0	0	0-2	50	50	21	2	4	20-8	25	3.42	112	.281	.359	8	.000	-1	—	2	18	0.3
1981	Det A	4	2	.667	38	0	0	13-2	49	26	11	1	5	21-3	23	1.65	229	.160	.277	0	ø	0	—	11	0	2.0
1982	Det A	3	1	.750	31	1	0	5-2	40.1	35	15	0	2	29-4	23	3.12	131	.254	.391	0	ø	0	111	5	0	0.6
Total	5	15	11	.577	139	3	0	19-7	203.2	183	82	7	15	104-18	94	3.31	117	.253	.356	18	.056	-2	62	13	18	2.2
Sauerbeck, Scott	Scott William; B11.9.1971 Cincinnati OH; BR/TL/6´3˝/(190–200); [NYN94 23/624]; d4.5; Col Miami–Ohio																									
1999	Pit N	4	1	.800	65	0	0	2-3	67.2	53	19	6	4	38-5	55	2.00	230	.220	.336	1-0-1	.000	-0	—	19	0	1.3
2000	Pit N	5	4	.556	75	0	0	1-3	75.2	76	36	4	1	61-8	83	4.04	115	.270	.399	1	.000	-0	—	6	17	0.6
2001	Pit N	2	2	.500	70	0	0	2-2	62.2	61	41	4	2	40-6	79	5.60	80	.257	.369	2	.000	-0	—	-7	0	-0.5
2002	Pit N	5	4	.556	78	0	0	0-0	62.2	50	18	4	1	27-4	70	2.30	183	.220	.306	2	.000	-0*	—	13	0	1.7
2003	Pit N	3	4	.429	53	0	0	0-4	40	30	20	5	1	25-2	32	4.05	107	.207	.327	1	.000	-0	—	1	0	0.2
	†Bos A	0	1	.000	26	0	0	0-1	16.2	17	14	1	4	18-3	18	6.48	72	.266	.448	0	ø	0	—	-4	0	-0.2
2005	Cle A	1	0	1.000	58	0	0	0-2	35.2	35	18	4	4	16-2	35	4.04	103	.259	.353	0	ø	0	—	0	0	0.0
2006	Cle A	0	1	.000	24	0	0	0-2	13	9	9	2	1	9-1	11	6.23	69	.196	.339	0	ø	0	—	-2	0	-0.1
	Oak A	0	0	ø	22	0	0	0-0	12.1	13	8	1	6	9-0	6	3.65	124	.271	.444	0	ø	0	—	0	14	0.0
	Year	0	1	.000	46	0	0	0-2	25.1	22	17	3	7	18-1	17	4.97	89	.234	.395	0	ø	0	—	-2	0	-0.1
Total	7	20	17	.541	471	0	0	5-17	386.1	344	183	31	24	243-31	389	3.82	116	.242	.360	7-0-1	.000	-1	—	26	31	3.0
Saunders, Tony	Anthony Scott; B4.29.1974 Baltimore MD; BL/TL/6´2˝/205; d4.5; [DL 2000 TB A 181]																									
1997	†Fla N	4	6	.400	22	21	0	0-0	111.1	99	62	12	2	64-1	102	4.61	88	.244	.347	37-1-1	.081	-1	116	-7	52	-0.7
1998	TB A	6	15	.286	31	31	2	0-0	192.1	191	95	15	7	111-1	172	4.12	116	.265	.364	2	1.000	1	65	14	0	1.4
1999	TB A	3	3	.500	9	9	0	0-0	42	53	39	6	4	29-0	30	6.43	77	.315	.424	0	ø	0	102	-9	130	-1.0
Total	3	13	24	.351	62	61	2	0-0	345.2	343	196	33	13	204-2	304	4.56	100	.265	.367	39-1-1	.128	0	87	-2	363	-0.3
Saunders, Dennis	Dennis James; B1.4.1949 Alhambra CA; BB/TR/6´3˝/195; [DetA67 6/115]; d5.21																									
1970	Det A	1	1	.500	8	0	0	1-2	14	16	5	1	1	5-1	8	3.21	117	.286	.355	5	.000	-1	—	1	0	0.1
Saunders, Joe	Joseph Francis; B6.16.1981 Falls Church VA; BL/TL/6´3˝/210; [AnaA02 1/12]; d8.16; Col Virginia Tech																									
2005	LA A	0	0	ø	2	2	0	0-0	9.1	10	8	3	0	4-0	4	7.71	55	.270	.341	0	ø	0	130	-3	0	-0.2
2006	LA A	7	3	.700	13	13	0	0-0	70.2	71	42	6	1	29-1	51	4.71	94	.264	.336	0	ø	0	117	-2	0	-0.3
Total	2	7	3	.700	15	15	0	0-0	80	81	50	9	1	33-1	55	5.06	87	.265	.336	0	ø	0	119	-5	0	-0.5
Sauveur, Rich	Richard Daniel; B11.23.1963 Arlington VA; BL/TL/6´4˝/(163–195); [PitN83 S5/81]; d7.1; Col Manatee (FL) CC																									
1986	Pit N	0	0	ø	3	3	0	0-0	12	17	8	3	2	6-0	6	6.00	65	.354	.446	3-0-1	.333	0	115	-2	0	-0.1
1988	Mon N	0	0	ø	4	0	0	0-0	3	3	2	1	0	2-0	3	6.00	61	.250	.357	0	ø	0	—	-1	0	0.0
1991	NY N	0	0	ø	6	0	0	0-2	3.1	7	4	1	0	2-0	4	10.80	34	.467	.529	0	ø	0	—	-2	0	-0.1
1992	KC A	0	1	.000	8	0	0	0-0	14.1	15	7	1	2	8-1	7	4.40	93	.273	.385	0	ø	0	—	0	0	0.0
1996	Chi A	0	0	ø	3	0	0	0-0	3	3	5	1	1	5-0	1	15.00	32	.333	.600	0	ø	0	—	-3	0	-0.1
2000	Oak A	0	0	ø	10	0	0	0-0	10.1	13	5	3	0	1-0	7	4.35	111	.310	.326	0	ø	0	—	1	0	0.0
Total	6	0	1	.000	34	3	0	0-2	46	58	31	10	5	24-1	28	6.07	69	.320	.414	3-0-1	.333	0	115	-7	0	-0.3
Savage, Jack	John Joseph; B4.22.1964 Louisville KY; BR/TR/6´3˝/185; [LAN85 8/194]; d9.14; Col Kentucky																									
1987	LA N	0	0	ø	3	0	0	0-0	3.1	4	1	0	0	0-0	0	2.70	148	.286	.286	0	ø	0	—	1	0	0.0
1990	Min A	0	2	.000	17	0	0	1-2	26	37	26	3	0	11-1	12	8.31	50	.339	.397	0	ø	0	—	-11	0	-0.8
Total	2	0	2	.000	20	0	0	1-2	29.1	41	27	3	0	11-1	12	7.67	54	.333	.385	0	ø	0	—	-10	0	-0.8
Savage, Bob	John Robert; B12.1.1921 Manchester NH; BR/TR/6´2˝/180; d6.24; Mil 1943–45; Col Staunton Mil. Academy (JC)																									
1942	Phi A	0	1	.000	8	3	0	0	30.2	24	16	0	0	31	10	3.23	117	.220	.393	9	.111	0	113	1	0	0.0
1946	Phi A	3	15	.167	40	19	7-1	2	164	164	80	5	2	93	78	4.06	87	.259	.355	41-0-1	.122	1	78	-7	0	-0.7
1947	Phi A	8	10	.444	44	8	2-1	2	146	135	71	8	0	55	56	3.76	101	.245	.314	40-0-2	.050	-4	90	0	0	-0.5
1948	Phi A	5	1	.833	33	1	1	5	75.1	98	55	9	0	33	26	6.21	69	.318	.384	13-0-2	.077	-1	21	-15	0	-1.3
1949	StL A	0	0	ø	4	0	0	0	7	12	5	1	0	3	1	6.43	70	.400	.455	1	.000	-0	—	-1	0	-0.1
Total	5	16	27	.372	129	31	10-2	9	423	433	227	23	2	215	171	4.32	88	.265	.352	104-0-5	.087	-3	80	-22	0	-2.6
Savidge, Don	Donald Snyder; B8.28.1908 Berwick PA; D3.22.1983 Santa Barbara CA; BR/TR/6´1˝/180; d8.6; f–Ralph; Col Albright																									
1929	Was A	0	0	ø	3	0	0	0	6	12	7	1	0	2	2	9.00	47	.414	.452	0	ø	0	—	-3	—	-0.1
Savidge, Ralph	Ralph Austin "The Human Whipcord"; B2.3.1879 Jerseytown PA; D7.22.1959 Berwick PA; BR/TR/6´2˝/210; d9.22; s–Don																									
1908	Cin N	0	1	.000	4	1	1	0	21	18	9	0	0	8	7	2.57	90	.247	.321	7	.000	-1	0	-1	—	-0.2
1909	Cin N	0	0	ø	1	0	0	0	4	10	12	1	1	3	2	22.50	12	.588	.667	1	.000	-0	—	-8	—	-0.4
Total	2	0	1	.000	5	1	1	0	25	28	21	1	1	11	9	5.76	41	.311	.392	8	.000	-1	0	-9	—	-0.6
Savransky, Moe	Morris; B1.13.1929 Cleveland OH; BL/TL/5´11˝/175; d4.23; Col Ohio St.																									
1954	Cin N	0	2	.000	16	0	0	0	24	23	13	6	2	8	7	4.88	86	.247	.320	2	.500	1	—	-1	0	0.0
Sawyer, Rick	Richard Clyde; B4.7.1948 Bakersfield CA; BR/TR/6´2˝/200; [CleA68*S3/45]; d4.28; Col Bakersfield (CA) JC																									
1974	NY A	0	0	ø	1	0	0	0-0	1.2	2	3	0	0	1-0	1	16.20	22	.500	.600	0	ø	0	—	-2	0	-0.1
1975	NY A	0	0	ø	4	0	0	0-0	6	7	4	0	0	2-0	3	3.00	124	.304	.360	0	ø	0	—	0	0	0.0
1976	SD N	5	3	.625	13	11	4-2	0-0	81.2	84	24	2	1	38-8	33	2.53	130	.272	.351	24-0-5	.208	1	109	8	0	0.9
1977	SD N	7	6	.538	56	9	0	0-0	111	136	77	15	7	55-11	45	5.84	61	.316	.399	20-0-2	.150	1	138	-28	0	-2.7
Total	4	12	9	.571	74	20	4-2	0-0	200.1	229	108	17	8	96-19	82	4.49	77	.299	.380	44-0-7	.182	2	121	-22	0	-1.9
Sawyer, Will	Willard Newton; B7.29.1864 Brimfield OH; D1.5.1936 Kent OH; BL/TL; d7.21; Col Case Western Reserve																									
1883	Cle N	4	10	.286	17	15	15	0	141	119	79	1	—	47	76	2.36	133	**.217**	.279	47	.021	-7	52	11	—	0.2
Sayles, Bill	William Nisbeth; B7.27.1917 Portland OR; D11.20.1996 Lincoln City OR; BR/TR/6´2˝/175; d7.17; Mil 1944–45; Col Oregon																									
1939	Bos A	0	0	ø	5	0	0	0	14	14	13	1	0	13	9	7.07	67	.264	.409	7	.143	-0	—	-4	—	-0.2
1943	NY N	1	3	.250	18	3	1	0	53	60	29	1	0	23	38	4.75	72	.284	.355	13	.308	1*	82	-6	0	-0.4
	Bro N	0	0	ø	5	0	0	0	11.2	13	14	0	0	10	5	7.71	44	.271	.397	2	.500	0*	—	-7	0	-0.3
	Year	1	3	.250	23	3	1	0	64.2	73	43	1	0	33	43	5.29	65	.282	.363	15	.333	1	82	-13	0	-0.7
Total	2	1	3	.250	28	3	1	0	78.2	87	56	2	0	46	52	5.61	65	.279	.372	22	.273	1	78	-17	0	-0.9

YEAR	TM LG	W	L	PCT	G	GS	CG-SHO	SV-BS	IP	H	R	HR	HB	BB-IB	SO	ERA	AERA	OAV	OOB	AB-HR-SH	AVG	PB	SUP	APR	DL	PW
SAYLOR, PHIL	Philip Andrew "Lefty"; B1.2.1871 Van Wert Co. OH; D7.23.1937 W.Alexandria OH; TL; d7.11; Col Ohio Wesleyan																									
1891	Phi N	0	0	ø	1	0	0	0	3	2	2	1	0	0	0	6.00	57	.182	.182	1	.000	-0	—	-1	—	0.0
SCANLAN, FRANK	Frank Aloysius; B4.28.1890 Syracuse NY; D4.9.1969 Brooklyn NY; BL/TL/6´1.5˝/175; d8.6; b–Doc; Col Notre Dame																									
1909	Phi N	0	0	ø	6	0	0	1	11	8	3	0	0	5	5	1.64	159	.211	.302	4	.000	-1	—	1	—	0.0
SCANLAN, BOB	Robert Guy; B8.9.1966 Los Angeles CA; BR/TR/6´8˝/(200–215); [PhiN84 25/636]; d5.7																									
1991	Chi N	7	8	.467	40	13	0	1-1	111	114	60	5	3	40-3	44	3.89	100	.268	.331	24-0-2	.042	-2	82	-3	0	-0.5
1992	Chi N	3	6	.333	69	0	0	14-4	87.1	76	32	4	1	30-6	42	2.89	126	.235	.301	4	.000	-0	—	7	0	0.9
1993	Chi N	4	5	.444	70	0	0	0-3	75.1	79	41	6	3	28-7	44	4.54	89	.278	.343	2-0-1	.500	0	—	-4	0	-0.4
1994	Mil A	2	6	.250	30	12	0	2-1	103	117	53	11	4	28-2	65	4.11	124	.288	.339	0	ø	0	63	10	0	0.7
1995	Mil A	4	7	.364	17	14	0	0-0	83.1	101	66	9	7	44-3	29	6.59	76	.304	.391	0	ø	0	102	-14	70	-1.4
1996	Det A	0	0	ø	8	0	0	0-0	11	16	15	1	1	9-1	3	10.64	48	.348	.464	0	ø	0	—	-7	0	-0.3
	KC A	0	1	.000	9	0	0	0-1	11.1	13	4	1	1	3-1	3	3.18	158	.295	.354	0	ø	0	—	2	0	0.2
	Year	0	1	.000	17	0	0	0-1	22.1	29	19	2	2	12-2	6	6.85	74	.322	.413	0	ø	0	—	-5	0	-0.1
1998	Hou N	0	1	.000	27	0	0	0-0	26.1	24	12	4	1	13-0	9	3.08	132	.245	.330	0	ø	0	—	2	0	0.1
2000	Mil N	0	0	ø	2	0	0	0-0	1.2	6	6	0	1	0-0	1	27.00	17	.600	.583	0	ø	0	—	-4	0	-0.2
2001	Mon N	0	0	ø	18	0	0	0-0	26.1	37	23	0	1	14-0	5	7.86	55	.339	.419	0	ø	0	—	-10	0	-0.5
Total	9	20	34	.370	290	39	0	17-10	536.2	583	312	41	23	209-23	245	4.63	94	.281	.349	30-0-3	.067	-2	89	-21	70	-1.4
SCANLAN, DOC	William Dennis; B3.7.1881 Syracuse NY; D5.29.1949 Brooklyn NY; BL/TR/5´8˝/165; d9.24; b–Frank; Col Syracuse																									
1903	Pit N	0	1	.000	1	1	1	0	9	5	7	0	0	6	0	4.00	81	.167	.306	2	.000	0	42	-1	—	-0.1
1904	Pit N	1	3	.250	4	3	1	0	22	21	18	0	2	20	10	4.91	56	.236	.387	6	.000	-1	109	-6	—	-1.0
	Bro N	6	6	.500	13	12	11-3	0	104	94	39	0	2	40	40	2.16	127	.242	.316	35-0-5	.143	-2	88	6	—	0.4
	Year	7	9	.438	17	15	12-3	0	126	115	57	0	4	60	50	2.64	104	.241	.331	41-0-5	.122	-2	92	1	—	-0.6
1905	Bro N	14	12	.538	33	28	22-2	0	249.2	220	119	4	8	104	135	2.92	99	.237	.319	96-0-3	.167	-2	103	-2	—	-0.5
1906	Bro N	18	13	.581	38	33	28-6	2	288	230	128	5	6	127	120	3.19	79	.214	.301	97-0-3	.186	3	109	-19	—	-2.1
1907	Bro N	6	8	.429	17	15	10-2	0	107	90	50	1	3	61	59	3.20	73	.239	.349	34	.265	5	93	-9	—	-0.7
1909	Bro N	8	7	.533	19	17	12-2	0	141.1	125	53	2	4	65	72	2.93	88	.252	.343	44-0-1	.273	5	87	-3	—	0.3
1910	Bro N	9	11	.450	34	25	14	2	217.1	175	76	1	5	116	103	2.61	116	.234	.341	69-0-2	.203	1	72	12	—	1.1
1911	Bro N	3	10	.231	22	15	3	1	113.2	101	67	2	6	69	45	3.64	92	.256	.374	33-0-2	.121	-2	66	-7	—	-1.0
Total	8	65	71	.478	181	149	102-15	5	1252	1061	557	15	36	608	584	3.00	93	.234	.330	416-0-16	.188	8	90	-29	—	-3.6
SCANTLEBURY, PAT	Patricio Athelstan; B11.11.1917 Gatun, Canal Zone; D5.24.1991 Glen Ridge NJ; BL/TL/6´1˝/180; d4.19; Negro Lg 1944–50																									
1956	Cin N	0	1	.000	6	2	0	0	19	24	14	5	0	5-0	10	6.63	60	.293	.333	3-0-1	.000	-0*	144	-5	0	-0.3
SCARBERY, RANDY	Randy James; B6.22.1952 Fresno CA; BB/TR/6´1˝/185; [OakA73 1/23]; d4.16; Col USC																									
1979	Chi A	2	8	.200	45	5	0	4-0	101.1	102	56	9	3	34-3	45	4.62	92	.262	.323	0	ø	0	43	-2	0	-0.2
1980	Chi A	1	2	.333	15	0	0	2-0	28.2	24	14	1	2	7-0	18	4.08	99	.238	.297	0	ø	0	—	0	0	0.0
Total	2	3	10	.231	60	5	0	6-0	130	126	70	10	5	41-3	63	4.50	94	.257	.318	0	ø	0	43	-2	0	-0.2
SCARBOROUGH, RAY	Ray Wilson (b Rae Wilson Scarborough); B7.23.1917 Mt.Gilead NC; D7.1.1982 Mount Olive NC; BR/TR/6´0˝/(178–185); d6.26; Mil 1943–45; C1; Col Wake Forest																									
1942	Was A	2	1	.667	17	5	1-1	0	63.1	68	32	2	0	32	16	4.12	89	.272	.355	21-0-1	.190	0	197	-2	0	-0.1
1943	Was A	4	4	.500	24	6	2	3	86	93	42	2	0	46	43	2.83	113	.273	.359	24-0-2	.333	2	171	0	0	0.2
1946	Was A	7	11	.389	32	20	6-1	1	155.2	176	85	8	1	74	46	4.05	83	.286	.364	50-0-4	.140	-2	83	-13	0	-1.4
1947	Was A	6	13	.316	33	18	8-2	0	161	165	74	5	1	67	63	3.41	109	.267	.339	50-0-3	.120	-3	58	3	0	0.0
1948	Was A	15	8	.652	31	26	9	1	185.1	166	71	10	3	72	76	2.82	154	.233	.307	64-0-6	.219	-0	98	29	0	3.4
1949	Was A	13	11	.542	34	27	11-1	0	199.2	204	115	10	7	88	81	4.60	93	.265	.346	67-0-7	.194	-0	94	-7	0	-0.7
1950	Was A	3	5	.375	8	8	4-2	0	58.1	62	30	2	2	22	24	4.01	112	.276	.345	20	.100	-1	63	3	0	0.3
	Chi A☆	10	13	.435	27	23	8-1	1	149.1	160	95	10	4	62	70	5.30	85	.274	.347	46-0-4	.174	-1	73	-12	0	-1.7
	Year	13	18	.419	35	31	12-3	1	207.2	222	125	12	6	84	94	4.94	91	.274	.347	66-0-4	.152	-3	71	-9	0	-1.4
1951	Bos A	12	9	.571	37	22	8	0	184	201	106	21	14	61	71	5.09	88	.275	.342	68-0-3	.191	-2	120	-7	0	-1.0
1952	Bos A	1	5	.167	28	8	1-1	4	76.2	79	47	8	4	35	29	4.81	82	.266	.351	18	.222	0	66	-7	0	-0.6
	†NY A	5	1	.833	9	4	1	0	34	27	11	4	1	15	13	2.91	114	.223	.314	14	.357	2	164	3	0	0.6
	Year	6	6	.500	37	12	2-1	4	110.2	106	58	12	5	50	42	4.23	89	.254	.340	32	.281	2	95	-5	0	0.0
1953	NY A	2	2	.500	25	1	0	2	54.2	52	23	4	4	26	20	3.29	112	.250	.345	12-1-1	.083	-0	144	2	0	0.2
	Det A	0	2	.000	13	0	0	2	20.2	34	24	3	3	11	12	8.27	49	.354	.436	2	.000	-0	—	-11	0	-1.2
	Year	2	4	.333	38	1	0	4	75.1	86	47	7	7	37	32	4.66	81	.283	.374	14-1-1	.071	-0	141	-10	0	-1.0
Total	10	80	85	.485	318	168	59-9	14	1428.2	1487	755	89	44	611	564	4.13	97	.267	.344	456-1-31	.186	-6	96	-19	0	-2.0
SCARCE, MAC	Guerrant McCurdy; B4.8.1949 Danville VA; BL/TL/6´3˝/(180–193); [PhiN71 8/177]; d7.10; Col Florida St.																									
1972	Phi N	1	2	.333	31	0	0	4-0	36.2	30	14	6	2	20-2	40	3.44	105	.222	.331	6	.000	-1	—	1	0	0.1
1973	Phi N	1	8	.111	52	0	0	12-2	70.2	54	23	3	1	47-14	57	2.42	157	.220	.347	5-0-1	.000	-1	—	10	0	1.4
1974	Phi N	3	8	.273	58	0	0	5-1	70.1	72	40	6	2	35-7	50	4.99	76	.275	.359	6	.000	-1	—	-7	0	-1.3
1975	NY N	0	0	ø	1	0	0	0-0	0	1	0	0	0	0-0	0	(0)	ø	1.000	1.000	0	ø	0	—	0	0	0.0
1978	Min A	1	1	.500	17	0	0	0-1	32	35	19	5	3	15-0	17	3.94	98	.292	.381	0	ø	0	—	-2	0	-0.1
Total	5	6	19	.240	159	0	0	21-4	209.2	192	96	20	8	117-23	164	3.69	102	.251	.354	17-0-1	.000	-2	—	2	0	0.1
SCHACHT, AL	Alexander; B11.11.1892 New York NY; D7.14.1984 Waterbury CT; BR/TR/5´11˝/142; d9.18; C12																									
1919	Was A	2	0	1.000	2	2	1	0	15	14	5	0	0	4	4	2.40	134	.233	.281	3-0-2	.000	0	244	1	—	0.2
1920	Was A	6	4	.600	22	11	5-1	1	99.1	130	60	2	1	30	19	4.44	84	.319	.367	26-0-1	.192	1	165	-7	—	-0.4
1921	Was A	6	6	.500	29	5	2	1	82.2	110	59	2	2	27	15	4.90	84	.332	.386	22-0-1	.227	1	138	-9	—	-1.2
Total	3	14	10	.583	53	18	8-1	2	197	254	124	4	3	61	38	4.48	86	.318	.368	51-0-4	.196	2	163	-15	—	-1.4
SCHACHT, SID	Sidney; B2.3.1918 Bogota NJ; D3.30.1991 Ft.Lauderdale FL; BR/TR/5´11˝/170; d4.23																									
1950	StL A	0	0	ø	8	1	0	0	10.2	24	22	5	0	14	7	16.03	31	.429	.543	2	.000	-0*	146	-12	0	-0.6
1951	StL A	0	0	ø	6	0	0	1	6	14	15	1	0	5	4	21.00	21	.452	.528	0	ø	0	—	-10	0	-0.5
	Bos N	0	2	.000	5	0	0	0	4.2	6	4	0	0	2	1	1.93	191	.300	.364	0	ø	0	—	0	0	-0.1
Total	2	0	2	.000	19	1	0	1	21.1	44	41	6	0	21	12	14.34	31	.411	.508	2	.000	-0	146	-22	0	-1.2
SCHACKER, HAL	Harold; B4.6.1925 Brooklyn NY; BR/TR/6´0˝/190; d5.9																									
1945	Bos N	0	1	.000	6	0	0	0	15.1	14	12	2	0	9	6	5.28	73	.241	.343	2	.000	0	—	-3	0	-0.2
SCHAEFFER, HARRY	Harry Edward "Lefty"; B6.23.1924 Reading PA; BL/TL/6´2.5˝/175; d7.28; Col East Stroudsburg																									
1952	NY A	0	1	.000	5	2	0	0	17	18	14	2	0	18	15	5.29	63	.265	.419	3	.000	-0	79	-5	0	-0.3
SCHAEFFER, MARK	Mark Philip; B6.5.1948 Santa Monica CA; BL/TL/6´5˝/215; [BosA66*2/22]; d4.18																									
1972	SD N	2	0	1.000	41	0	0	1-0	41	52	21	3	2	28-2	25	4.61	72	.319	.418	3	.000	-0	—	-5	0	-0.3
SCHAFFERNOTH, JOE	Joseph Arthur; B8.6.1937 Trenton NJ; BR/TR/6´4.5˝/195; d4.15																									
1959	Chi N	1	0	1.000	5	1	0	0	7.2	11	7	1	0	4-0	3	8.22	48	.355	.429	3	.000	-0	158	-3	55	-0.4
1960	Chi N	2	3	.400	33	0	0	3	55	46	21	2	1	17-2	33	2.78	136	.235	.295	7-0-1	.286	0	—	5	0	0.6
1961	Chi N	0	4	.000	21	0	0	0	38.1	43	29	7	1	18-2	23	6.34	66	.293	.373	5	.000	-1	—	-8	0	-0.8
	Cle A	0	1	.000	15	0	0	0	17	16	11	2	1	14-1	9	4.76	83	.242	.383	1	.000	-0	—	-2	0	-0.1
Total	3	3	8	.273	74	1	0	3	118	116	68	12	3	53-5	68	4.58	86	.264	.345	16-0-1	.125	-1	158	-8	55	-0.7
SCHALLOCK, ART	Arthur Lawrence; B4.25.1924 Mill Valley CA; BL/TL/5´9˝/(156–160); d7.16; Col Marin (CA) CC																									
1951	NY A	3	1	.750	11	6	1	0	46.1	50	20	3	1	20	19	3.88	99	.272	.346	17-0-1	.294	1	143	1	0	0.2
1952	NY A	0	0	ø	2	0	0	0	2	3	2	0	0	2	1	9.00	37	.375	.500	0	ø	0	—	-1	0	-0.1
1953	†NY A	0	0	ø	7	1	0	1	21.1	30	12	2	1	15	13	2.95	125	.345	.447	6	.333	0	144	0	0	0.0
1954	NY A	0	1	.000	6	1	1	0	17.1	20	10	3	1	11	9	4.15	83	.282	.386	3	.000	-0	26	-2	0	-0.2
1955	NY A	0	0	ø	2	0	0	0	3	4	2	1	0	1-0	2	6.00	62	.333	.385	0	ø	0	—	-1	0	0.0
	Bal A	3	5	.375	30	6	1	0	80.1	92	52	2	2	42-3	33	4.15	92	.294	.378	19-0-3	.105	-1	58	-7	0	-0.7
	Year	3	5	.375	32	6	1	0	83.1	96	54	3	2	43-3	35	4.21	90	.295	.378	19-0-3	.105	-1	58	-8	0	-0.7
Total	5	6	7	.462	58	14	3	1	170.1	199	98	11	5	91-3	77	4.02	94	.295	.381	45-0-4	.200	1	100	-10	0	-0.8

YEAR	TM LG	W	L	PCT	G	GS	CG-SHO	SV-BS	IP	H	R	HR	HB	BB-IB	SO	ERA	AERA	OAV	OOB	AB-HR-SH	AVG	PB	SUP	APR	DL	PW
Schanz, Charley	Charles Murrell; B6.8.1919 Anacortes WA; D5.28.1992 Sacramento CA; BR/TR/6´3.5˝/215; d4.20																									
1944	Phi N	13	16	.448	40	30	13-1	3	241.1	231	108	6	6	103	84	3.32	109	.254	.334	81-1-3	.148	-1	76	6	0	0.6
1945	Phi N	4	15	.211	35	21	5-1	5	144.2	165	99	5	9	87	56	4.35	88	.285	.387	39-0-5	.154	-0	66	-13	0	-1.6
1946	Phi N	6	6	.500	32	15	4	4	116.1	130	82	8	5	71	47	5.80	59	.286	.389	36-0-4	.083	-2	123	-28	0	-3.1
1947	Phi N	2	4	.333	34	6	1	2	101.2	107	59	7	3	47	42	4.16	96	.295	.380	27-0-1	.148	-1	84	-4	0	-0.3
1950	Bos A	3	2	.600	14	0	0	0	22.2	25	21	3	1	24	14	8.34	59	.281	.439	11	.091	-1	—	-7	0	-1.4
Total	5	28	43	.394	155	72	23-2	14	626.2	658	369	29	24	332	243	4.34	86	.275	.369	194-1-13	.134	-5	82	-46	0	-5.8
Schappert, John	John; B Brooklyn NY; D7.27.1917 Brooklyn NY; BR/TR/5´10˝/170; d5.3																									
1882	StL AA	8	7	.533	15	14	13	0	128	131	99	2	—	32	38	3.52	80	.248	.291	50	.180	0	135	-7	—	-0.8
Schardt, Bill	Wilburt "Big Bill"; B1.20.1886 Cleveland OH; D7.20.1964 Vermilion OH; BR/TR/6´4˝/210; d4.14																									
1911	Bro N	5	15	.250	39	22	10-1	4	195.1	190	102	4	8	91	77	3.59	93	.266	.355	59-0-3	.169	0	79	-7	—	-0.7
1912	Bro N	0	1	.000	7	0	0	1	20.2	25	13	1	2	6	7	4.35	77	.321	.384	6	.000	-1	—	-2	—	-0.1
Total	2	5	16	.238	46	22	10-1	5	216	215	115	5	10	97	84	3.67	91	.271	.358	65-0-3	.154	-1	79	-9	—	-0.8
Schattinger, Jeff	Jeffrey Charles; B10.25.1955 Fresno CA; BL/TR/6´5˝/200; [KCA79*S1/21]; d9.21; Col USC																									
1981	KC A	0	0	ø	1	0	0	0-0	3	2	0	0	2	1-0	1	0.00	ø	.182	.357	0	ø	0	—	1	0	0.1
Schatzeder, Dan	Daniel Ernest; B12.1.1954 Elmhurst IL; BL/TL/6´0˝/(185–204); [MonN76 3/57]; d9.4; Col Denver																									
1977	Mon N	2	1	.667	6	3	1-1	0-0	21.2	16	6	0	0	13-0	14	2.49	155	.203	.312	6	.333	0	77	4	0	0.5
1978	Mon N	7	7	.500	29	18	2	0-0	143.2	108	54	10	2	68-5	69	3.07	116	.213	.306	45-1-2	.222	3*	92	8	0	1.0
1979	Mon N	10	5	.667	32	21	3	1-0	162	136	57	17	1	59-2	106	2.83	131	.225	.294	51-1-1	.216	4	113	17	0	1.8
1980	Det A	11	13	.458	32	26	9-2	0-0	192.2	178	88	23	3	58-9	94	4.02	103	.246	.303	0	ø	0	91	5	21	0.5
1981	Det A	6	8	.429	17	14	1	0-0	71.1	74	49	13	2	29-1	20	6.06	63	.265	.334	0	ø	0	98	-17	0	-2.8
1982	SF N	1	4	.200	13	3	0	0-1	33.1	47	30	3	0	12-4	18	7.29	49	.333	.383	8	.125	-0	66	-13	0	-1.8
	Mon N	0	2	.000	26	1	0	0-0	36	37	16	1	2	12-5	15	3.50	106	.276	.340	5	.400	1	48	1	0	0.1
	Year	1	6	.143	39	4	0	0-1	69.1	84	46	4	2	24-9	33	5.32	68	.305	.362	13	.231	1	61	-13	0	-1.7
1983	Mon N	5	2	.714	58	2	0	2-2	87	88	34	3	5	25-6	48	3.21	113	.265	.324	10-0-1	.200	0	61	4	0	0.3
1984	Mon N	7	7	.500	36	14	1-1	1-0	136	112	44	13	2	36-1	89	2.71	128	.224	.276	35-0-5	.314	5*	78	12	0	1.7
1985	Mon N	3	5	.375	24	15	1	0-0	104.1	101	52	13	0	31-0	64	3.80	91	.259	.311	31-2-1	.194	3	96	-6	57	-0.1
1986	Mon N	3	2	.600	30	1	0	1-0	59	53	29	6	0	19-2	33	3.20	117	.240	.298	21-1-0	.429	6*	167	1	0	0.7
	Phi N	3	3	.500	25	0	0	1-0	29.1	28	14	3	0	16-7	14	3.38	116	.252	.344	5	.200	0	—	1	0	0.2
	Year	6	5	.545	55	1	0	2-0	88.1	81	43	9	0	35-9	47	3.26	117	.244	.314	26-1-0	.385	7	164	2	0	0.9
1987	Phi N	3	1	.750	26	0	0	0-0	37.2	40	21	4	0	14-7	28	4.06	106	.278	.333	12	.167	0	—	0	0	0.0
	†Min A	3	1	.750	30	1	0	0-0	43.2	64	37	8	1	18-3	30	6.39	73	.342	.399	0	ø	0	98	-10	0	-0.8
1988	Cle A	0	2	.000	15	0	0	3-1	16	26	19	6	1	2-0	10	9.56	43	.351	.377	0	ø	0	—	-9	0	-1.3
	Min A	0	1	.000	10	0	0	0-0	10.1	8	2	1	1	5-1	7	1.74	235	.216	.326	0	ø	0	—	3	0	0.2
	Year	0	3	.000	25	0	0	3-1	26.1	34	21	7	2	7-1	17	6.49	63	.306	.358	0	ø	0	—	-7	0	-1.1
1989	Hou N	4	1	.800	36	0	0	1-1	56.2	64	33	2	3	28-6	46	4.45	77	.287	.374	9	.000	-1	—	-8	49	-0.8
1990	Hou N	1	3	.250	45	2	0	0-0	64	61	23	2	0	23-4	37	2.39	156	.261	.321	4	.250	0	73	8	0	0.5
	NY N	0	0	ø	6	0	0	0-0	5.2	5	0	0	0	0-0	2	0.00	ø	.263	.263	0	ø	0	—	2	0	0.1
	Year	1	3	.250	51	2	0	0-0	69.2	66	23	2	0	23-4	39	2.20	170	.261	.317	4	.250	0	72	10	0	0.6
1991	KC A	0	0	ø	8	0	0	0-0	6.2	11	9	0	0	7-1	4	9.45	44	.367	.486	0	ø	0	—	-4	0	-0.2
Total	15	69	68	.504	504	121	18-4	10-5	1317	1257	617	128	23	475-64	748	3.74	100	.253	.319	242-5-10	.240	22	93	-1	127	-0.2
Schauer, Rube	Alexander John; B3.19.1891 Kamenka, Russia; D4.15.1957 Minneapolis MN; BR/TR/6´2˝/192; d8.27																									
1913	NY N	0	1	.000	3	1	1	0	12	14	11	0	0	9	7	7.50	42	.292	.404	3	.000	-0	24	-5	—	-0.4
1914	NY N	0	0	ø	6	0	0	0	22.1	16	10	2	0	8	6	3.22	82	.205	.279	7	.143	-0	—	-1	—	-0.1
1915	NY N	2	8	.200	32	7	4	0	105.1	101	56	4	2	35	65	3.50	73	.258	.322	26	.077	-2	58	-13	—	-1.4
1916	NY N	1	4	.200	19	3	1	0	45.2	44	22	0	2	16	24	2.96	82	.257	.328	9	.222	0	61	-4	—	-0.4
1917	Phi A	7	16	.304	33	21	10	1	215	209	116	6	3	69	62	3.14	88	.263	.324	76-0-6	.145	-2	97	-13	—	-1.6
Total	5	10	29	.256	93	32	16	1	400.1	384	215	12	7	137	164	3.35	80	.259	.324	121-0-6	.132	-4	85	-36	—	-3.9
Scheetz, Owen	Owen Franklin; B12.24.1913 New Bedford OH; D9.28.1994 Kirkersville OH; BR/TR/6´1˝/200; d4.22																									
1943	Was A	0	0	ø	6	0	0	1	9	16	7	0	0	4	5	7.00	46	.381	.435	2	.000	-0	—	-3	0	-0.2
Scheffer, Aaron	Aaron Alvin Marcus; B8.15.1975 Ypsilanti MI; BL/TR/6´2˝/165; d6.13																									
1999	Sea A	0	0	ø	4	0	0	0-0	4.2	6	5	0	1	3-0	4	1.93	248	.353	.417	0	ø	0	—	0	0	0.0
Schegg, Lefty	Gilbert Eugene (b Gilbert Eugene Price); B8.29.1889 Leesville OH; D2.27.1963 Niles OH; BL/TL/5´11˝/180; d8.20																									
1912	Was A	0	0	ø	2	1	0	0	5.1	7	5	0	0	4	3	3.38	99	.333	.440	2	.000	-0	89	-1	—	-0.1
Scheib, Carl	Carl Alvin; B1.1.1927 Gratz PA; BR/TR/6´1˝/192; d9.6; Mil 1945–46																									
1943	Phi A	0	1	.000	6	0	0	0	18.2	24	14	4	1	3	3	4.34	78	.308	.341	5	.000	-1	—	-3	0	-0.3
1944	Phi A	0	0	ø	15	0	0	0	36.1	36	18	1	4	11	13	4.21	83	.257	.329	10	.300	1	—	-2	0	0.1
1945	Phi A	0	0	ø	4	0	0	0	8.2	6	3	0	0	4	2	3.12	110	.207	.303	2	.000	-0	—	0	0	0.0
1947	Phi A	4	6	.400	21	12	6-2	0	116	121	68	11	2	55	26	5.04	76	.274	.357	45	.133	-2*	81	-13	0	-1.4
1948	Phi A	14	8	.636	32	24	15-1	0	198.2	219	90	14	1	76	44	3.94	109	.286	.351	104-2-0	.298	7*	105	10	0	2.1
1949	Phi A	9	12	.429	38	23	11-2	0	182.2	191	117	16	2	118	43	5.12	80	.275	.382	72-0-2	.236	3*	103	-21	0	-1.9
1950	Phi A	3	10	.231	43	8	1	3	106	138	96	13	0	70	37	7.22	63	.317	.411	52-1-0	.250	2*	92	-32	0	-3.3
1951	Phi A	1	12	.077	46	11	3	10	143	132	78	7	8	71	49	4.47	96	.250	.347	53-2-0	.396	8*	74	-3	0	0.8
1952	Phi A	11	7	.611	30	19	8-1	2	158	153	82	21	4	50	42	4.39	90	.253	.314	82-0-1	.220	-1*	131	-5	0	-0.6
1953	Phi A	3	7	.300	28	8	3	2	96	99	57	9	7	29	25	4.88	88	.261	.325	41	.195	-1*	80	-6	32	-0.7
1954	Phi A	0	1	.000	1	1	0	0	2	5	5	0	1	1	1	22.50	17	.500	.583	0	ø	0	68	-4	0	-0.6
	StL N	0	1	.000	3	1	0	0	4.2	6	6	3	0	5	5	11.57	36	.300	.440	2	.000	-0	87	-3	0	-0.6
Total	11	45	65	.409	267	107	47-6	17	1070.2	1130	634	99	30	493	290	4.88	85	.274	.355	468-5-3	.250	16	100	-82	32	-6.4
Scheibeck, Frank	Frank S.; B6.28.1865 Detroit MI; D10.22.1956 Detroit MI; BR/TR/5´7˝/145; d5.9; ▲																									
1887	Cle AA	0	1	.000	1	1	1	0	9	17	18	1	1	4	3	12.00	36	.362	.423	9	.222	0*	29	-7	—	-0.5
Scheible, Jack	John G.; B2.16.1866 Youngstown OH; D8.9.1897 Youngstown OH; TL; d9.8																									
1893	Cle N	1	1	.500	2	2	2-1	0	18	15	9	0	0	11	1	2.00	244	.221	.329	7	.143	-0	64	5	—	0.4
1894	Phi N	0	1	.000	1	1	0	0	0.1	6	10	0	1	2	0	189.00	3	.857	.900	0	ø	0	55	-7	—	-0.8
Total	2	1	2	.333	3	3	2-1	0	18.1	21	19	0	1	13	1	5.40	91	.280	.393	7	.143	-0	62	-2	—	-0.4
Scheid, Rich	Richard Paul; B2.3.1965 Staten Island NY; BL/TL/6´3˝/(185–200); [NYA86 2/53]; d9.11; Col Seton Hall																									
1992	Hou N	0	1	.000	7	1	0	0-0	12	14	8	2	0	6-1	8	6.00	57	.280	.357	1	.000	-0	80	-3	0	-0.3
1994	Fla N	1	3	.250	8	5	0	0-0	32.1	35	18	6	2	8-0	17	3.34	133	.269	.321	7-0-1	.000	-1	45	2	0	0.1
1995	Fla N	0	0	ø	6	0	0	0-0	10.1	14	7	1	0	7-0	10	6.10	70	.341	.429	1	.000	-0	—	-2	0	-0.1
Total	3	1	4	.200	21	6	0	0-0	54.2	63	33	9	2	21-1	35	4.45	94	.285	.351	9-0-1	.000	-1	51	-3	0	-0.3
Schelle, Jim	Gerard Anthony; B4.13.1917 Baltimore MD; D5.4.1990 Weymouth MA; BR/TR/6´3˝/204; d7.23; Col Villanova																									
1939	Phi A	0	0	ø	1	0	0	0	0	1	3	0	1	3	0	(3)	ø	1.000	1.000	0	ø	0	—	-3	0	-0.2
Schemanske, Fred	Frederick George "Buck"; B4.28.1903 Detroit MI; D2.18.1960 Detroit MI; BR/TR/6´2˝/190; d9.15																									
1923	Was A	0	0	ø	1	0	0	0	1	3	3	0	0	0	0	27.00	14	.600	.600	2	1.000	1*	—	-2	—	0.0
Schenck, Bill	William G.; B7.1854 Brooklyn NY; D1.29.1934 Brooklyn NY; 5´7˝/171; d5.29; ▲																									
1882	Lou AA	1	0	1.000	2	1	1	0	10	6	2	0	—	1	4	0.90	275	.162	.184	231	.260	0*	104	2	—	0.2
Scheneberg, John	John Bluford; B11.20.1887 Guyandotte WV; D9.26.1950 Huntington WV; BB/TR/6´1˝/180; d9.23																									
1913	Pit N	0	1	.000	1	1	0	0	6	10	5	0	0	2	1	6.00	50	.400	.444	2	.500	0	25	-2	—	-0.2
1920	StL A	0	0	ø	1	0	0	0	2	7	7	0	0	1	0	27.00	15	.583	.615	0	ø	0	—	-5	—	-0.2
Total	2	0	1	.000	2	1	0	0	8	17	12	0	0	3	1	11.25	29	.459	.500	2	.500	0	25	-7	—	-0.4

THE PITCHER REGISTER

YEAR	TM LG	W	L	PCT	G	GS	CG-SHO	SV-BS	IP	H	R	HR	HB	BB-IB	SO	ERA	AERA	OAV	OOB	AB-HR-SH	AVG	PB	SUP	APR	DL	PW
SCHERMAN, FRED	Frederick John; B7.25.1944 Dayton OH; BL/TL/6´1˝/195; d4.26; Col Ohio St.																									
1969	Det A	1	0	1.000	4	0	0	0-0	4	6	3	2	0	0-0	3	6.75	56	.333	.333	0	ø	0	—	-1	0	-0.2
1970	Det A	4	4	.500	48	0	0	1-2	69.2	61	28	5	1	28-3	58	3.23	117	.237	.314	12	.167	-0	—	4	0	0.4
1971	Det A	11	6	.647	69	1	1	20-7	113	91	38	11	5	49-7	46	2.71	134	.226	.317	24-0-2	.208	1	124	11	0	2.2
1972	†Det A	7	3	.700	57	3	0	12-6	94	91	43	5	5	53-9	53	3.64	87	.269	.371	22-0-1	.091	-1	56	-5	0	-0.8
1973	Det A	2	2	.500	34	0	0	1-1	61.2	59	30	6	3	30-4	28	4.23	97	.258	.350	0	ø	0*	—	0	0	-0.1
1974	Hou N	2	5	.286	53	0	0	4-2	61.1	67	33	5	7	26-6	35	4.11	85	.284	.370	3	.000	-0	—	-5	0	-0.7
1975	Hou N	0	1	.000	16	0	0	0-1	16.1	21	11	4	1	4-1	13	4.96	68	.318	.361	1	.000	-0	—	-4	0	-0.2
	Mon N	4	3	.571	34	7	0	0-1	76.1	84	37	3	5	41-7	43	3.54	109	.283	.374	16	.063	-1	71	1	0	0.1
	Year	4	4	.500	50	7	0	0-2	92.2	105	48	7	6	45-8	56	3.79	100	.289	.371	17	.059	-1	73	-1	0	-0.1
1976	Mon N	2	2	.500	31	0	0	1-1	40	42	25	5	3	14-3	18	4.95	76	.261	.330	4-0-1	.250	0	—	-5	0	-0.5
Total	8	33	26	.559	346	11	1	39-21	536.1	522	248	46	30	245-40	297	3.66	100	.260	.347	82-0-4	.134	-1	73	-4	0	0.2
SCHERRER, BILL	William Joseph; B1.20.1958 Tonawanda NY; BL/TL/6´4˝/(170–190); [CinN77*S1/1]; d9.7																									
1982	Cin N	0	1	.000	5	2	0	0-0	17.1	17	7	0	0	0-0	7	2.60	142	.250	.250	2-0-1	.500	1*	84	1	0	0.1
1983	Cin N	2	3	.400	73	0	0	10-6	92	73	31	6	0	33-4	57	2.74	140	.225	.291	11-0-1	.091	-0	—	11	0	0.8
1984	Cin N	1	1	.500	36	0	0	1-1	52.1	64	31	6	0	15-3	35	4.99	76	.300	.342	3-0-1	.000	-0	—	-6	15	-0.3
	†Det A	1	0	1.000	18	0	0	0-0	19	14	4	1	0	8-1	16	1.89	209	.206	.289	0	ø	0	—	5	0	0.2
1985	Det A	3	2	.600	48	0	0	0-2	66	62	35	10	1	41-13	46	4.36	94	.248	.354	0	ø	0	—	-2	0	-0.1
1986	Det A	0	1	.000	13	0	0	0-0	21	19	19	3	1	22-4	16	7.29	57	.244	.416	0	ø	0	—	-7	0	-0.4
1987	Cin N	1	1	.500	23	0	0	0-0	33	43	17	3	0	16-4	24	4.36	97	.328	.393	1	.000	-0	—	0	0	0.0
1988	Bal A	0	1	.000	4	0	0	0-0	4	8	6	2	0	3-0	3	13.50	29	.400	.478	0	ø	0	—	-4	0	-0.7
	Phi N	0	0	ø	8	0	0	0-0	6.2	7	4	0	0	2-0	3	5.40	67	.269	.321	0	ø	0	—	-1	0	-0.1
Total	7	8	10	.444	228	2	0	11-9	311.1	307	154	31	2	140-29	207	4.08	97	.260	.336	17-0-3	.118	-0	84	-3	15	-0.5
SCHESLER, DUTCH	Charles; B6.1.1900 Frankfurt, Germany; D11.19.1953 Harrisburg PA; BR/TR/6´2˝/185; d4.16																									
1931	Phi N	0	0	ø	17	0	0	0	38.1	65	39	4	4	18	14	7.28	58	.385	.455	9	.111	-0	—	-13	—	-0.6
SCHETTLER, LOU	Louis Martin; B6.12.1886 Pittsburgh PA; D5.1.1960 Youngstown OH; BR/TR/5´11˝/160; d4.25																									
1910	Phi N	2	6	.250	27	7	-3	1	107	96	53	2	2	51	62	3.20	98	.247	.337	41-0-1	.171	-1	92	-2	—	-0.3
SCHILLING, CURT	Curtis Montague; B11.14.1966 Anchorage AK; BR/TR/6´4˝/(205–235); [BosA86*2/39]; d9.7; Col Yavapai (AZ) JC																									
1988	Bal A	0	3	.000	4	4	0	0-0	14.2	22	19	3	1	10-1	4	9.82	40	.355	.434	0	ø	0	52	-10	0	-1.6
1989	Bal A	0	1	.000	5	1	0	0-0	8.2	10	6	2	0	3-0	6	6.23	61	.286	.342	0	ø	0	0	-2	0	-0.2
1990	Bal A	1	2	.333	35	0	0	3-6	46	38	13	1	0	19-0	32	2.54	150	.229	.302	0	ø	0	—	7	0	0.5
1991	Hou N	3	5	.375	56	0	0	8-3	75.2	79	35	2	0	39-7	71	3.81	93	.271	.356	3	.333	0	—	-2	0	-0.3
1992	Phi N	14	11	.560	42	26	10-4	2-1	226.1	165	67	11	1	59-4	147	2.35	150	**.201**	**.253**	64-0-8	.156	-0	89	28	0	3.0
1993	†Phi N	16	7	.696	34	34	7-2	0-0	235.1	234	114	23	4	57-6	186	4.02	99	.259	.303	75-0-13	.147	-1	109	1	0	0.0
1994	Phi N	2	8	.200	13	13	1	0-0	82.1	87	42	10	3	28-3	58	4.48	96	.270	.333	28-0-1	.107	-1	85	0	69	-0.1
1995	Phi N	7	5	.583	17	17	1	0-0	116	96	52	12	3	26-2	114	3.57	118	.220	.267	40-0-5	.175	0	91	7	75	0.6
1996	Phi N	9	10	.474	26	26	**8**-2	0-0	183.1	149	69	16	3	50-5	182	3.19	135	.223	.278	63-0-7	.175	-0*	80	24	43	2.1
1997	Phi N★	17	11	.607	35	**35**	7-2	0-0	254.1	208	96	25	5	58-3	**319**	2.97	142	.224	.271	81-0-12	.173	0	88	33	0	3.5
1998	Phi N☆	15	14	.517	35	**35**	**15**-2	0-0	**268.2**	236	101	23	6	61-3	**300**	3.25	133	.236	.282	76-0-12	.132	-1	76	33	0	3.2
1999	Phi N★	15	6	.714	24	24	8-1	0-0	180.1	159	74	25	5	44-0	152	3.54	132	.237	.287	50-0-9	.100	0	111	23	26	2.4
2000	Phi N	6	6	.500	16	16	4-1	0-0	112.2	110	49	17	1	32-4	96	3.91	117	.253	.305	30-0-2	.167	0	101	10	26	0.9
	Ari N	5	6	.455	13	13	4-1	0-0	97.2	94	41	10	0	13-0	72	3.69	130	.257	.280	31-0-7	.258	2	83	13	0	1.4
	Year	11	12	.478	29	29	**8**-2	0-0	210.1	204	90	27	1	45-4	168	3.81	123	.255	.294	61-0-9	.213	2	93	22	0	2.3
2001	†Ari N☆	**22**	6	**.786**	35	**35**	**6**-1	0-0	**256.2**	237	86	37	1	39-0	293	2.98	156	.245	**.273**	83-0-14	.133	-3	96	47	0	4.4
2002	†Ari N★	23	7	.767	36	35	5-1	0-0	259.1	218	95	29	3	33-1	316	3.23	139	.224	**.251**	86-0-8	.174	-1	112	35	0	3.6
2003	Ari N	8	9	.471	24	24	3-2	0-0	168	144	58	17	3	32-2	194	2.95	157	.230	.270	52-0-4	.058	-3	70	30	57	2.4
2004	†Bos A✳	**21**	6	**.778**	32	32	3	0-0	226.2	206	84	23	5	35-0	203	3.26	150	.239	.271	7	.143	-0	133	43	0	4.5
2005	Bos A	8	8	.500	32	11	0	9-2	93.1	121	59	12	3	22-0	87	5.69	80	.314	.352	0	ø	0	137	-10	90	-1.6
2006	Bos A	15	7	.682	31	31	0	0-0	204	220	90	28	3	28-1	183	3.97	118	.276	.303	2	.500	0	103	18	0	1.8
Total	19	207	138	.600	545	412	82-19	22-12	3110	2833	1250	326	50	688-42	3015	3.44	127	.242	.285	771-0-102	.150	-8	98	328	386	30.5
SCHILLINGS, RED	Elbert Isaiah; B3.29.1900 Deport TX; D1.7.1954 Oklahoma City OK; BR/TR/5´10˝/180; d9.11																									
1922	Phi A	0	0	ø	4	0	0	0	8	10	6	1	0	11	4	6.75	63	.313	.488	2	.000	-0	—	-2	—	-0.1
SCHIRALDI, CALVIN	Calvin Drew; B6.16.1962 Houston TX; BR/TR/6´4˝/(200–216); [NYN83 1/27]; d9.1; Col Texas																									
1984	NY N	0	2	.000	5	3	0	0-0	17.1	20	13	3	0	10-0	16	5.71	63	.286	.375	3	.000	-0	82	-4	0	-0.5
1985	NY N	2	1	.667	10	4	0	0-2	26.1	43	27	4	3	11-0	21	8.89	39	.368	.435	8	.125	-0	120	-15	15	-1.5
1986	†Bos A	4	2	.667	25	0	0	9-3	51	36	8	5	1	15-2	55	1.41	298	.201	.265	0	ø	0	—	16	0	2.3
1987	Bos A	8	5	.615	62	1	0	6-4	83.2	75	45	15	1	40-5	93	4.41	104	.240	.326	0	ø	0	20	1	0	0.2
1988	Chi N	9	13	.409	29	27	2-1	1-0	166.1	166	87	13	2	63-7	140	4.38	83	.257	.323	60-0-4	.100	-2	105	-12	30	-1.8
1989	Chi N	3	6	.333	54	0	0	4-4	78.2	60	34	7	1	50-2	54	3.78	100	.209	.326	9-0-1	.000	-1	—	1	0	0.0
	SD N	3	1	.750	5	4	0	0-0	21.1	12	6	1	0	13-0	17	2.53	139	.162	.287	7-1-1	.143	1	126	3	0	0.6
	Year	6	7	.462	59	4	0	4-4	100	72	40	8	1	63-2	71	3.51	106	.199	.319	16-1-2	.063	0	119	4	0	0.6
1990	SD N	3	8	.273	42	8	0	1-1	104	105	59	11	1	60-6	74	4.41	87	.264	.360	21-1-1	.190	2	85	-7	0	-0.6
1991	Tex A	0	1	.000	3	0	0	0-0	4.2	5	6	3	0	5-0	1	11.57	35	.263	.417	0	ø	0	—	-4	0	-0.6
Total	8	32	39	.451	235	47	2-1	21-14	553.1	522	285	62	9	267-22	471	4.28	91	.248	.334	108-2-7	.111	-1	96	-21	45	-1.9
SCHLITZER, BIFF	Victor Joseph; B12.4.1884 Rochester NY; D1.4.1948 Wellesley Hills MA; BR/TR/5´11˝/175; d4.17; Col Dayton																									
1908	Phi A	6	8	.429	24	18	11-2	0	131	110	56	1	2	45	57	3.16	81	.234	.303	46-0-1	.196	-1	80	-5	—	-0.8
1909	Phi A	0	3	.000	4	3	0	0	13.1	13	9	0	3	7	6	5.40	45	.245	.365	4	.250	0	88	-4	—	-0.7
	Bos A	4	4	.500	13	8	5	1	69.2	68	34	0	1	17	23	3.49	72	.234	.279	27-0-2	.185	0	109	-6	—	-0.7
	Year	4	7	.364	17	11	5	1	83	81	43	0	4	24	29	3.80	65	.236	.294	31-0-2	.194	1	103	-9	—	-1.4
1914	Buf F	0	0	ø	3	0	0	0	3.1	7	8	3	0	2	1	16.20	18	.438	.500	1	1.000	0	—	-5	—	-0.2
Total	3	10	15	.400	44	29	16-2	1	217.1	198	107	4	6	71	87	3.60	71	.239	.303	78-0-3	.205	0	88	-20	—	-2.4
SCHMACK, BRIAN	Brian Robert; B12.7.1973 Chicago IL; BR/TR/6´2˝/190; d8.24; Col Northern Illinois																									
2003	Det A	1	0	1.000	11	0	0	0-0	13	14	6	1	1	4-0	4	3.46	127	.292	.345	0	ø	0	—	1	0	0.1
SCHMELZ, AL	Alan George; B11.12.1943 Whittier CA; BR/TR/6´4˝/208; d9.7; Col Arizona St.																									
1967	NY N	0	0	ø	2	0	0	0	3	4	1	1	0	1-0	2	3.00	113	.364	.417	0	ø	0	—	0	0	0.0
SCHMIDT, CURT	Curtis Allen; B3.16.1970 Miles City MT; BR/TR/6´6˝/200; [MonN92 41/1135]; d4.28; Col Kansas																									
1995	Mon N	0	0	ø	11	0	0	0-0	10.1	15	8	1	2	9-0	7	6.97	62	.357	.491	0	ø	0	—	-3	0	-0.1
SCHMIDT, DAVE	David Joseph; B4.22.1957 Niles MI; BR/TR/6´1˝/(185–195); [TexA79 26/658]; d5.1; Col UCLA																									
1981	Tex A	0	1	.000	14	1	0	1-0	31.2	31	11	1	1	11-3	13	3.13	111	.258	.326	0	ø	0	52	2	0	0.1
1982	Tex A	4	6	.400	33	8	0	6-2	109.2	118	45	5	5	25-5	69	3.20	121	.279	.325	0	ø	0	79	8	0	0.7
1983	Tex A	3	3	.500	31	0	0	2-5	46.1	42	20	3	1	14-1	29	3.88	104	.241	.300	0	ø	0	—	2	27	0.2
1984	Tex A	6	6	.500	43	0	0	12-4	70.1	69	30	3	0	20-9	46	2.56	163	.262	.311	0	ø	0	—	9	0	1.8
1985	Tex A	7	6	.538	51	4	1-1	5-1	85.2	81	36	6	0	22-8	46	3.15	135	.246	.292	0	ø	0	112	9	0	1.4
1986	Chi A	3	6	.333	49	1	0	8-3	92.1	94	37	10	5	27-7	67	3.31	131	.264	.322	0	ø	0	42	10	0	1.0
1987	Bal A	10	5	.667	35	14	2-2	1-1	124	128	57	13	1	26-2	70	3.77	118	.263	.301	0	ø	0	100	9	0	0.9
1988	Bal A	8	5	.615	41	9	0	2-1	129.2	129	58	14	3	38-5	67	3.40	116	.262	.317	0	ø	0	106	6	0	0.6
1989	Bal A	10	13	.435	38	26	2	0-0	156.2	196	102	24	2	36-2	46	5.69	67	.310	.346	0	ø	0	102	-31	0	-3.9
1990	Mon N	3	3	.500	34	0	0	13-4	48	58	26	3	0	13-5	22	4.31	85	.297	.340	3	.000	-0	—	-4	93	-0.7
1991	Mon N	0	1	.000	4	0	0	0-0	4.1	9	5	2	0	2-0	3	10.38	35	.429	.478	0	ø	0	—	-3	0	-0.6
1992	Sea A	0	0	ø	3	0	0	0-0	3.1	7	7	1	0	3-0	1	18.90	21	.438	.526	0	ø	0	—	-5	0	-0.3
Total	12	54	55	.495	376	63	5-3	50-21	902	962	434	85	18	237-47	479	3.88	104	.274	.321	3	.000	-0	97	12	120	1.2

YEAR	TM LG	W	L	PCT	G	GS	CG-SHO	SV-BS	IP	H	R	HR	HB	BB-IB	SO	ERA	AERA	OAV	OOB	AB-HR-SH	AVG	PB	SUP	APR	DL	PW
SCHMIDT, FREDDY	Frederick Albert; B2.9.1916 Hartford CT; BR/TR/6´1˝/185; d4.25; Mil 1945																									
1944	†StL N	7	3	.700	37	9	3-2	5	114.1	94	48	5	1	58	58	3.15	112	.222	.317	34-0-1	.206	-0	119	4	0	0.3
1946	StL N	1	0	1.000	16	0	0	0	27.1	27	11	0	3	15	14	3.29	105	.276	.388	1	.000	-0	—	1	0	0.0
1947	StL N	0	0	ø	2	0	0	0	4	5	2	1	0	1	2	2.25	184	.333	.375	0	ø	0	—	0	0	0.0
	Phi N	5	8	.385	29	5	0	0	76.2	76	44	4	4	43	24	4.70	85	.285	.392	20	.050	-2	66	-5	0	-1.0
	Chi N	0	0	ø	1	1	0	0	3	4	3	0	0	5	0	9.00	44	.333	.529	2	.000	-0	112	-1	0	-0.1
	Year	5	8	.385	32	6	0	0	83.2	85	49	5	4	49	26	4.73	85	.289	.398	22	.045	-2	73	-6	0	-1.1
Total	3	13	11	.542	85	15	3-2	5	225.1	206	108	10	8	122	98	3.75	98	.252	.355	57-0-1	.140	-2	101	-1	0	-0.8
SCHMIDT, BILL	Frederick William; B4.1861 New Orleans LA; D5.28.1928 New Orleans LA; TR/5´8˝/152; d7.6																									
1886	Det N	5	4	.556	9	9	9	0	77	81	47	0	—	30	36	4.09	81	.259	.324	38	.184	-1*	147	-4	—	-0.5
SCHMIDT, PETE	Friedrich Christoph Herman; B7.23.1890 Lowden IA; D3.11.1973 Pembroke ON, Can.; BR/TR/5´11˝/175; d7.14																									
1913	StL A	0	0	ø	1	0	0	1	2	3	1	0	0	2	0	4.50	65	.333	.455	0	ø	0	—	0	—	0.0
SCHMIDT, HENRY	Henry Martin; B6.26.1873 Brownsville TX; D4.23.1926 Nashville TN; BR/TR/5´11˝/170; d4.17																									
1903	Bro N	22	13	.629	40	36	29-5	2	301	321	167	5	21	120	96	3.83	83	.280	.359	107-1-5	.196	3*	109	-15	—	-0.9
SCHMIDT, JASON	Jason David; B1.29.1973 Lewiston ID; BR/TR/6´5˝/(185–215); [AtlN91 8/205]; d4.28																									
1995	Atl N	2	2	.500	9	2	0	0-1	25	27	17	2	1	18-3	19	5.76	75	.287	.393	5-0-1	.200	0	52	-4	0	-0.5
1996	Atl N	3	4	.429	13	11	0	0-0	58.2	69	48	8	0	32-0	48	6.75	66	.296	.373	19-0-1	.000	-2	112	-14	46	-1.5
	Pit N	2	2	.500	6	6	1	0-0	37.2	39	19	2	2	21-0	26	4.06	108	.271	.365	12-0-1	.083	-1	130	1	0	0.0
	Year	5	6	.455	19	17	1	0-0	96.1	108	67	10	2	53-0	74	5.70	78	.286	.370	31-0-2	.032	-2	119	-13	0	-1.5
1997	Pit N	10	9	.526	32	32	2	0-0	187.2	193	106	16	9	76-2	136	4.60	93	.265	.341	56-0-9	.107	-1	94	-6	0	-0.8
1998	Pit N	11	14	.440	33	33	0	0-0	214.1	228	106	24	4	71-3	158	4.07	105	.275	.334	62-0-12	.097	-2	70	7	0	0.3
1999	Pit N	13	11	.542	33	33	2	0-0	212.2	219	110	24	3	85-4	148	4.19	110	.262	.330	60-0-12	.083	-2	88	10	0	0.6
2000	Pit N	2	5	.286	11	11	0	0-0	63.1	71	43	6	1	41-2	51	5.40	86	.284	.384	19-0-2	.000	-2	99	-6	129	-0.7
2001	Pit N	6	6	.500	14	14	1	0-0	84	81	46	11	7	28-2	77	4.61	97	.256	.328	23-1-5	.174	1	91	-1	40	-0.1
	SF N	7	1	.875	11	11	0	0-0	66.1	57	29	2	0	33-1	65	3.39	121	.230	.319	26-1-1	.154	1	158	5	0	0.5
	Year	13	7	.650	25	25	1	0-0	150.1	138	75	13	7	61-3	142	4.07	106	.244	.324	49-2-6	.163	2	119	4	0	0.4
2002	†SF N	13	8	.619	29	29	2-2	0-0	185.1	148	78	15	2	73-1	196	3.45	115	.218	.294	56-0-4	.125	-1	111	10	24	0.9
2003	†SF N★	17	5	**.773**	29	29	5-**3**	0-0	207.2	152	56	14	5	46-1	208	**2.34**	**182**	**.200**	**.250**	61-0-15	.066	-4	106	**45**	0	4.0
2004	SF N☆	18	7	.720	32	32	4-**3**	0-0	225	165	84	18	3	77-3	251	3.20	135	.202	.272	66-2-13	.136	1	98	30	12	3.1
2005	SF N	12	7	.632	29	29	0	0-0	172	160	90	16	5	85-4	165	4.40	97	.246	.334	53-1-6	.094	-2	110	-3	16	-0.6
2006	SF N☆	11	9	.550	32	32	3-1	0-0	213.1	189	94	21	6	80-6	180	3.59	124	.238	.310	66-1-6	.136	0	89	19	0	1.5
Total	12	127	90	.585	313	304	20-9	0-1	1953	1798	926	179	48	766-32	1728	3.91	110	.244	.317	584-6-88	.104	-13	98	93	267	6.7
SCHMIDT, JEFF	Jeffrey Thomas; B2.21.1971 Northfield MN; BR/TR/6´5˝/205; [CalA92 1/29]; d5.17; Col Minnesota; [DL 1997 Ana A 12, 1998 Ana A 31]																									
1996	Cal A	2	0	1.000	9	0	0	0-0	8	13	9	2	0	8-0	2	7.88	64	.394	.500	0	ø	0	—	-3	0	-0.5
SCHMIDT, WILLARD	Willard Raymond; B5.29.1928 Hays KS; BR/TR/6´1˝/(180–193); d4.19																									
1952	StL N	2	3	.400	18	3	0	1	34.2	36	20	6	2	18	30	5.19	72	.267	.361	8	.125	-0	64	-5	0	-0.6
1953	StL N	0	2	.000	6	2	0	0	17.2	21	20	1	1	13	11	9.17	46	.288	.402	4	.000	-1	52	-10	0	-0.9
1955	StL N	7	6	.538	20	15	8-1	0	129.2	89	40	7	3	57-7	86	2.78	146	.197	.289	42-0-2	.119	-3	88	20	0	1.6
1956	StL N	6	8	.429	33	21	2	1	147.2	131	69	18	1	78-7	52	3.84	99	.246	.341	43-0-3	.233	1	104	0	0	0.3
1957	StL N	10	3	.769	40	8	1	0	116.2	146	67	13	2	49-6	63	4.78	83	.312	.377	33-0-4	.212	0	158	-9	0	-0.9
1958	Cin N	3	5	.375	41	2	0	0	69.1	60	29	8	1	33-7	41	2.86	145	.235	.320	11-0-1	.091	-1	152	7	0	0.8
1959	Cin N	3	2	.600	36	4	0	0	70.2	80	36	4	1	30-4	40	3.95	103	.296	.366	12-0-1	.083	0	116	0	0	0.1
Total	7	31	29	.517	194	55	11-1	2	586.1	563	281	57	11	278-31	323	3.93	101	.258	.342	153-0-11	.163	-2	105	3	0	0.4
SCHMIT, CRAZY	Frederick M. "Germany"; B2.13.1866 Chicago IL; D10.5.1940 Chicago IL; BL/TL/5´10.5˝/165; d4.21																									
1890	Pit N	1	9	.100	11	10	9-1	0	83.1	108	98	3	8	42	35	5.83	57	.304	.390	33	.061	-3	69	-30	—	-2.7
1892	Bal N	1	4	.200	6	6	6	0	47.1	37	26	0	0	26	17	3.23	106	.207	.307	19	.105	-1*	55	2	—	0.1
1893	Bal N	3	2	.600	9	6	4	0	49	67	51	1	2	22	10	6.61	72	.316	.386	21	.238	-0	145	-10	—	-0.7
	NY N	0	2	.000	4	4	1	0	20.2	30	25	0	2	17	5	7.40	63	.330	.445	9	.444	1	146	-6	—	-0.3
	Year	3	4	.429	13	10	5	0	69.2	97	76	1	4	39	15	6.85	69	.320	.405	30	.300	1	145	-14	—	-1.0
1899	Cle N	2	17	.105	20	19	16	0	138.1	197	138	3	14	62	24	5.86	63	.334	.410	70-0-1	.157	-2*	61	-39	—	-4.1
1901	Bal A	0	2	.000	4	3	1	0	22.2	25	20	0	0	16	2	1.99	195	.278	.387	9	.222	0	116	1	—	0.1
Total	5	7	36	.163	54	48	37-1	0	361.1	464	358	7	26	185	93	5.45	69	.306	.391	161-0-1	.161	-4	87	-82	—	-7.6
SCHMITZ, JOHNNY	John Albert "Bear Tracks"; B11.27.1920 Wausau WI; BR/TL/6´0˝/(168–170); d9.6; Mil 1943–45																									
1941	Chi N	2	0	1.000	5	3	1	0	20.2	12	5	0	1	9	11	1.31	269	.182	.289	7-0-1	.571	2*	137	5	0	0.7
1942	Chi N	3	7	.300	23	10	1	2	86.2	70	41	3	3	45	51	3.43	93	.230	.335	26-0-2	.154	-1	113	-3	0	-0.2
1946	Chi N☆	11	11	.500	41	31	14-2	2	224.1	184	77	6	2	94	**135**	2.61	127	**.221**	.302	70-1-6	.129	-2*	92	17	0	1.6
1947	Chi N	13	18	.419	38	28	10-3	4	207	209	91	8	2	80	97	3.22	123	.262	.330	68-0-6	.132	-2	76	16	0	2.1
1948	Chi N★	18	13	.581	34	30	18-2	1	242	186	92	11	2	97	100	2.64	148	**.215**	.295	84-0-7	.131	-2	73	31	0	3.8
1949	Chi N	11	13	.458	36	31	9-3	3	207	227	117	11	2	92	75	4.35	93	.287	.363	70-0-3	.143	-1	85	-9	0	-0.7
1950	Chi N	10	16	.385	39	27	8-3	0	193	217	122	23	4	91	75	4.99	84	.284	.363	67-0-2	.119	-3	97	-15	0	-1.7
1951	Chi N	1	2	.333	8	3	0	0	18	22	16	1	0	15	6	8.00	51	.301	.420	6	.167	-0	43	-7	0	-0.9
	Bro N	1	4	.200	16	7	0	0	55.2	55	37	4	2	28	20	5.34	74	.259	.351	18-1-0	.222	2	125	-9	0	-0.5
	Year	2	6	.250	24	10	0	0	73.2	77	53	5	2	43	26	5.99	66	.270	.370	24-1-0	.208	1	100	-15	0	-1.4
1952	Bro N	1	1	.500	10	3	1	0	33.1	29	16	3	1	18	11	4.32	84	.238	.340	8-0-2	.125	-0	220	-2	0	-0.1
	NY A	1	1	.500	5	2	1	1	15	15	7	0	1	9	3	3.60	92	.263	.373	5	.600	2	105	-1	0	0.1
	Cin N	1	0	1.000	3	0	0	0	5	3	0	0	0	3	3	0.00	ø	.188	.316	0	ø	0	—	2	0	0.4
1953	NY A	0	0	ø	3	0	0	0	4.1	2	1	1	0	3	0	2.08	178	.143	.294	0-0-1	ø	0	—	1	0	0.1
	Was A	2	7	.222	24	13	5	4	107.2	118	52	9	4	37	39	3.68	106	.286	.351	34-0-3	.059	-4	86	1	0	-0.2
	Year	2	7	.222	27	13	5	4	112	120	53	10	4	40	39	3.62	108	.282	.349	34-0-4	.059	-4	86	2	0	-0.1
1954	Was A	11	8	.579	29	23	12-2	1	185.1	176	66	6	3	64	56	2.91	122	.255	.318	60-0-6	.117	-3	99	15	0	1.3
1955	Was A	7	10	.412	32	21	6-1	1	165	187	76	8	7	54-4	49	3.71	103	.291	.349	54-0-3	.185	0	96	3	0	0.4
1956	Bos A	0	0	ø	2	0	0	0	4.1	5	2	0	0	4-0	0	0.00	ø	.278	.409	1	.000	-0	—	1	0	0.1
	Bal A	0	3	.000	18	3	0	0	38.1	49	23	3	1	14-1	15	3.99	98	.318	.379	9-0-1	.000	-1	53	-2	0	-0.3
	Year	0	3	.000	20	3	0	0	42.2	54	25	3	1	18-1	15	3.59	111	.314	.382	10-0-1	.000	-2	52	-1	0	-0.2
Total	13	93	114	.449	366	235	86-16	19	1812.2	1766	841	97	35	757-5	746	3.55	107	.258	.335	587-2-43	.141	-14	91	44	0	6.0
SCHMOLL, STEVE	Stephen John; B2.4.1980 Silver Spring MD; BR/TR/6´2˝/200; d4.6; Col Maryland; [DL 2006 NY N 27]																									
2005	LA N	2	2	.500	48	0	0	3-1	46.2	47	29	4	3	22-2	29	5.01	83	.275	.360	1	.000	-0	—	-5	0	-0.5
SCHMUTZ, CHARLIE	Charles Otto "King"; B1.1.1891 San Diego CA; D6.27.1962 Seattle WA; BR/TR/6´1.5˝/195; d5.13																									
1914	Bro N	1	3	.250	18	5	1	0	57.1	57	29	1	1	13	21	3.30	87	.265	.310	16	.188	1	65	-2	—	-0.1
1915	Bro N	0	0	ø	1	0	0	0	4	7	5	0	0	1	1	6.75	41	.438	.471	1	.000	-0	—	-2	—	-0.1
Total	2	1	3	.250	19	5	1	0	61.1	64	34	1	1	14	22	3.52	81	.277	.321	17	.176	0	65	-4	—	-0.2
SCHNEIBERG, FRANK	Frank Fred; B3.12.1880 Milwaukee WI; D5.18.1948 Milwaukee WI; TR/6´1˝/165; d6.8																									
1910	Bro N	0	0	ø	1	0	0	0	1	5	8	0	0	4	0	63.00	5	.625	.750	0	ø	0	—	-6	—	-0.3
SCHNEIDER, DAN	Daniel Louis; B8.29.1942 Evansville IN; BL/TL/6´3˝/(170–175); d5.12; Col Arizona																									
1963	Mil N	1	0	1.000	30	3	0	0	43.2	36	20	2	0	20-5	19	3.09	104	.225	.309	7	.000	-1	116	-1	0	-0.2
1964	Mil N	1	2	.333	13	5	0	0	36.1	38	25	6	0	13-2	14	5.45	65	.270	.329	8-0-1	.000	-1*	165	-8	47	-0.6
1966	Atl N	0	0	ø	14	0	0	0	26.1	35	13	1	1	5-0	11	3.42	106	.324	.360	8	.500	1	—	0	0	0.1
1967	Hou N	0	2	.000	54	0	0	2	52.2	60	33	5	2	27-8	39	4.96	67	.296	.377	5	.200	0*	—	-10	0	-0.4
1969	Hou N	0	1	.000	6	0	0	0-0	7.1	16	12	2	0	5-2	3	13.50	26	.485	.553	1	.000	-0	—	-8	0	-0.9
Total	5	2	5	.286	117	8	0	2-0	166.1	185	103	16	3	70-17	86	4.71	72	.287	.356	29-0-1	.172	-0	148	-27	47	-2.0
SCHNEIDER, JEFF	Jeffrey Theodore; B12.6.1952 Bremerton WA; BB/TL/6´3˝/195; d8.12; Col Iowa St.																									
1981	Bal A	0	0	ø	11	0	0	1-0	24	27	15	4	1	12-1	17	4.88	75	.290	.377	0	ø	0	—	-3	0	-0.2

YEAR	TM LG	W	L	PCT	G	GS	CG-SHO	SV-BS	IP	H	R	HR	HB	BB-IB	SO	ERA	AERA	OAV	OOB	AB-HR-SH	AVG	PB	SUP	APR	DL	PW
Schneider, Pete	Peter Joseph; B8.20.1895 Los Angeles CA; D6.1.1957 Los Angeles CA; BR/TR/6´1˝/194; d6.20																									
1914	Cin N	5	13	.278	29	15	11-1	1	144.1	143	71	1	7	56	62	2.81	104	.269	.347	45-1-1	.178	1*	54	0	—	0.0
1915	Cin N	14	19	.424	48	35	16-5	2	275.2	254	110	4	7	104	108	2.48	115	.251	.325	94-2-6	.245	5	74	7	—	1.4
1916	Cin N	10	19	.345	44	31	16-2	1	274.1	259	112	4	13	82	117	2.69	96	.255	.319	89-0-4	.236	2*	88	-6	—	-0.5
1917	Cin N	20	19	.513	46	42	24	0	333.2	311	128	4	11	117	138	2.10	124	.255	.326	114-1-2	.167	0*	97	14	—	1.5
1918	Cin N	10	15	.400	33	30	17-2	0	217	213	106	2	11	117	51	3.53	76	.272	.374	83-1-3	.289	6*	115	-20	—	-1.7
1919	NY A	0	1	.000	7	4	0	0	29	19	14	1	3	22	11	3.41	94	.192	.355	9	.111	-1	92	-1	—	-0.2
Total	6	59	86	.407	207	157	84-10	4	1274	1199	541	16	52	498	487	2.66	102	.257	.336	434-5-16	.221	14	89	-6	—	0.5
Schnell, Karl	Karl Otto; B9.20.1899 Los Angeles CA; D5.31.1992 Palo Alto CA; BR/TR/6´1˝/176; d4.24; Col St. Marys (CA)																									
1922	Cin N	0	0	ø	10	0	0	0	20	21	10	0	0	18	5	2.70	148	.300	.443	4	.250	0	—	2	—	0.1
1923	Cin N	0	0	ø	1	0	0	0	1	2	4	0	0	2	0	36.00	11	.667	.800	0	ø	0	—	-3	—	-0.1
Total	2	0	0	ø	11	0	0	0	21	23	14	0	0	20	5	4.29	93	.315	.462	4	.250	0	—	-1	—	0.0
Schoen, Gerry	Gerald Thomas; B1.15.1947 New Orleans LA; BR/TR/6´3˝/215; [TexA66 25/486]; d9.14; Col Loyola–New Orleans																									
1968	Was A	0	1	.000	1	1	0	0	3.2	6	3	1	0	1-0	1	7.36	40	.400	.438	1	.000	-0	30	-2	0	-0.3
Schoeneweis, Scott	Scott David; B10.2.1973 Long Branch NJ; BL/TL/6´0˝/(185–195); [AnaA96 3/85]; d4.7; Col Duke																									
1999	Ana A	1	1	.500	31	0	0	0-0	39.1	47	27	4	0	14-1	22	5.49	89	.294	.349	0	ø	0	—	-3	0	-0.1
2000	Ana A	7	10	.412	27	27	1-1	0-0	170	183	112	21	6	67-2	78	5.45	95	.276	.346	3	.333	0	92	-6	38	-0.4
2001	Ana A	10	11	.476	32	32	1	0-0	205.1	227	122	21	14	77-2	104	5.08	92	.281	.351	0	ø	1	90	-8	0	-0.5
2002	†Ana A	9	8	.529	54	15	0	1-3	118	119	68	17	5	49-4	65	4.88	92	.264	.340	2	.000	-0	117	-5	0	-0.6
2003	Ana A	1	1	.500	39	0	0	0-1	38.2	37	19	2	3	10-3	29	3.96	111	.250	.309	0	ø	0	—	2	0	0.1
	Chi A	2	1	.667	20	0	0	0-1	26	26	16	1	1	9-2	27	4.50	102	.255	.321	0	ø	0	—	-1	0	-0.1
	Year	3	2	.600	59	0	0	0-2	64.2	63	35	3	4	19-5	56	4.18	107	.252	.314	0	ø	0	—	1	0	0.0
2004	Chi A	6	9	.400	20	19	0	0-0	112.2	129	74	17	3	49-0	69	5.59	84	.291	.364	2	.500	1	88	-11	71	-1.0
2005	Tor A	3	4	.429	80	0	0	1-3	57	54	23	2	4	25-5	43	3.32	139	.245	.333	0	ø	0	—	8	0	1.0
2006	Tor A	2	2	.500	55	0	0	1-2	37.1	39	27	3	1	16-5	18	6.51	73	.273	.350	0	ø	0	—	-6	0	-0.6
	Cin N	2	0	1.000	16	0	0	3-0	14.1	9	1	1	1	8-1	11	0.63	751	.176	.300	0	ø	0	—	6	0	1.0
Total	8	43	47	.478	374	93	2-1	6-10	818.2	870	489	89	38	324-25	466	5.01	95	.273	.345	7	.286	1	95	-24	109	-1.2
Schooler, Mike	Michael Ralph; B8.10.1962 Anaheim CA; BR/TR/6´3˝/(210–220); [SeaA85 2/35]; d6.10; Col Cal St.–Fullerton																									
1988	Sea A	5	8	.385	40	0	0	15-6	48.1	45	21	4	1	24-4	54	3.54	118	.245	.330	0	ø	0	—	3	0	0.7
1989	Sea A	1	7	.125	67	0	0	33-7	77	81	27	2	2	19-3	69	2.81	144	.266	.313	0	ø	0	—	10	0	1.8
1990	Sea A	1	4	.200	49	0	0	30-4	56	47	18	5	1	16-5	45	2.25	177	.227	.283	1	.000	-0	—	10	40	1.7
1991	Sea A	3	3	.500	34	0	0	7-3	34.1	25	14	2	0	10-0	31	3.67	113	.198	.255	0	ø	0	—	2	91	0.4
1992	Sea A	2	7	.222	53	0	0	13-5	51.2	55	29	7	1	24-6	33	4.70	85	.275	.351	0	ø	0	—	-4	37	-0.7
1993	Tex A	3	0	1.000	17	0	0	0-0	24.1	30	17	3	0	10-1	16	5.55	76	.303	.367	0	ø	0	—	-4	0	-0.4
Total	6	15	29	.341	260	0	0	98-25	291.2	283	126	23	5	103-19	248	3.49	117	.253	.316	1	.000	-0	—	17	168	3.5
Schorr, Ed	Edward Walter; B2.14.1892 Bremen OH; D9.12.1969 Atlantic City NJ; BR/TR/6´2.5˝/180; d4.26																									
1915	Chi N	0	0	ø	2	0	0	0	6	9	5	0	0	5	3	7.50	37	.409	.519	2	.500	0	—	-3	—	-0.1
Schott, Gene	Arthur Eugene; B7.14.1913 Batavia OH; D11.16.1992 Sun City Center FL; BR/TR/6´2˝/185; d4.16																									
1935	Cin N	8	11	.421	33	19	9-1	0	159	153	84	5	1	64	49	3.91	102	.253	.326	60	.200	1*	92	1	—	0.3
1936	Cin N	11	11	.500	31	22	8	1	180	184	93	7	4	73	65	3.80	101	.262	.335	60-1-1	.300	7*	90	-1	—	0.7
1937	Cin N	4	13	.235	37	16	7-2	1	154.1	150	69	2	1	48	56	2.97	125	.253	.310	49-0-2	.143	-1*	58	10	—	0.9
1938	Cin N	5	5	.500	31	4	0	2	83	89	47	8	1	32	21	4.45	82	.279	.347	24	.125	-1	116	-7	—	-0.9
1939	Phi N	0	1	.000	4	0	0	0	11	14	7	0	2	5	1	4.91	82	.326	.420	6	.333	1*	—	-1	—	0.0
Total	5	28	41	.406	136	61	24-3	4	587.1	590	300	22	9	222	192	3.72	103	.261	.329	199-1-3	.211	6	85	2	—	1.0
Schourek, Pete	Peter Alan; B5.10.1969 Austin TX; BL/TL/6´5˝/(195–220); [NYN87 2/56]; d4.9																									
1991	NY N	5	4	.556	35	8	1-1	2-1	86.1	82	49	7	2	43-4	67	4.27	86	.248	.334	22	.136	0	129	-7	0	-0.6
1992	NY N	6	8	.429	22	21	0	0-0	136	137	60	9	2	44-6	60	3.64	96	.261	.319	42-0-2	.048	-3*	82	-2	0	-0.6
1993	NY N	5	12	.294	41	18	0	0-1	128.1	168	90	13	3	45-7	72	5.96	67	.319	.370	32-0-3	.219	2	102	-25	0	-2.7
1994	Cin N	7	2	.778	22	10	0	0-0	81.1	90	39	11	3	29-4	69	4.09	102	.287	.351	23-1-1	.174	1	96	2	0	0.3
1995	†Cin N	18	7	.720	29	29	2	0-0	190.1	158	72	17	8	45-3	160	3.22	130	.228	.281	59-0-12	.220	1	110	21	0	2.7
1996	Cin N	4	5	.444	12	12	0	0-0	67.1	79	48	7	3	24-1	54	6.01	71	.293	.352	19-0-5	.263	1*	109	-12	111	-1.2
1997	Cin N	5	8	.385	18	17	0	0-0	84.2	78	59	18	4	38-0	59	5.42	79	.241	.327	24-1-6	.167	1*	87	-12	67	-1.6
1998	Hou N	7	6	.538	15	15	0	0-0	80	82	43	10	4	36-0	59	4.50	90	.269	.350	19-0-5	.211	1	107	-4	0	-0.5
	†Bos A	1	3	.250	10	8	0	0-0	44	45	21	7	1	14-1	36	4.30	110	.273	.328	0	ø	0	91	3	0	0.2
1999	Pit N	4	7	.364	30	17	0	0-0	113	128	75	20	5	49-5	94	5.34	86	.287	.358	25-0-3	.000	-2	65	-9	15	-0.9
2000	Bos A	3	10	.231	21	21	0	0-0	107.1	116	67	17	3	38-2	63	5.11	98	.278	.341	4	.500	1*	80	-1	53	0.0
2001	Bos A	1	5	.167	33	0	0	0-1	30.1	35	19	4	1	15-3	20	4.45	100	.292	.375	0	ø	0	—	-1	18	-0.2
Total	11	66	77	.462	288	176	3-1	2-3	1149	1198	642	140	39	420-36	813	4.59	91	.270	.335	269-2-37	.164	2	95	-47	264	-5.1
Schreiber, Barney	David Henry; B5.8.1882 Waverly OH; D10.6.1964 Chillicothe OH; BL/TL/6´0˝/185; d5.15																									
1911	Cin N	0	0	ø	3	0	0	1	10	19	11	2	0	2	5	5.40	61	.413	.438	3	.000	-0	—	-3	—	-0.2
Schreiber, Paul	Paul Frederick "Von"; B10.8.1902 Jacksonville FL; D1.28.1982 Sarasota FL; BR/TR/6´2˝/180; d9.2; C13																									
1922	Bro N	0	0	ø	1	0	0	0	1	2	0	0	0	0	0	0.00	ø	.500	.500	0	ø	0	—	0	—	0.0
1923	Bro N	0	0	ø	9	0	0	1	15	16	9	1	2	8	4	4.20	92	.276	.382	2	.000	-0	—	-1	—	-0.1
1945	NY A	0	0	ø	2	0	0	0	4.1	4	2	0	0	2	1	4.15	83	.267	.353	1	.000	-0	—	0	0	0.0
Total	3	0	0	ø	12	0	0	1	20.1	22	11	1	2	10	5	3.98	96	.286	.382	3	.000	-0	—	-1	0	-0.1
Schrenk, Steve	Steven Wayne; B11.20.1968 Chicago IL; BR/TR/6´3˝/(185–215); [ChiA87 4/89]; d7.3																									
1999	Phi N	1	3	.250	32	2	0	1-0	50.1	41	24	6	7	14-4	36	4.29	109	.223	.301	3-0-1	.000	-0	148	3	0	0.2
2000	Phi N	2	3	.400	20	0	0	0-0	23.1	25	20	3	1	13-0	19	7.33	63	.269	.361	0	ø	0	—	-7	0	-1.2
Total	2	3	6	.333	52	2	0	1-0	73.2	66	44	9	8	27-4	55	5.25	88	.238	.322	3-0-1	.000	-0	148	-4	0	-1.0
Schroder, Chris	Christopher Keith; B8.20.1978 Okarche OK; BR/TR/6´3˝/210; [MonN01 19/562]; d8.8; Col Oklahoma City																									
2006	Was N	0	2	.000	21	0	0	0-1	28.1	23	21	7	5	15-3	39	6.35	69	.223	.341	2	.000	-0	—	-6	0	-0.4
Schroll, Al	Albert Bringhurst "Bull"; B3.22.1932 New Orleans LA; D11.30.1999 Alexandria LA; BR/TR/6´2˝/210; d4.20; Col Tulane																									
1958	Bos A	0	0	ø	5	0	0	0	10	6	5	1	0	4-0	7	4.50	89	.176	.263	1	1.000	0	—	0	0	0.0
1959	Phi N	1	1	.500	3	0	0	0	9.1	12	9	1	0	6-0	4	8.68	47	.353	.439	4	.250	0	—	-4	0	-0.7
	Bos A	1	4	.200	14	5	1	0	46	47	29	3	1	22-1	26	4.70	86	.269	.350	9-0-2	.111	0	70	-4	0	-0.4
1960	Chi N	0	0	ø	2	0	0	0	2.2	3	3	1	0	5-0	2	10.13	37	.273	.500	1	1.000	0	—	-2	0	0.0
1961	Min A	4	4	.500	11	8	2	0	50	53	36	5	2	27-1	24	5.22	81	.266	.360	18-1-0	.278	2	104	-6	0	-0.7
Total	4	6	9	.400	35	13	3	0	118	121	82	11	3	64-2	63	5.34	77	.267	.359	33-1-2	.273	4	92	-16	0	-1.8
Schrom, Ken	Kenneth Marvin; B11.23.1954 Grangeville ID; BR/TR/6´2˝/195; [AnaA76 17/390]; d8.8; Col Idaho; [DL 1988 Cle A 81]																									
1980	Tor A	1	0	1.000	17	0	0	1-0	31	32	18	2	0	19-3	13	5.23	83	.274	.372	0	ø	0*	—	-2	0	-0.1
1982	Tor A	1	0	1.000	6	0	0	0-0	15.1	13	11	3	0	15-3	8	5.87	77	.232	.394	0	ø	0	—	-2	0	-0.1
1983	Min A	15	8	.652	33	28	6-1	0-0	196.1	196	92	14	9	80-3	80	3.71	115	.266	.341	0	ø	0*	92	11	0	1.0
1984	Min A	5	11	.313	25	21	3	0-0	137	156	75	15	1	41-2	49	4.47	95	.285	.333	0	ø	0	82	-4	50	-0.5
1985	Min A	9	12	.429	29	26	6	0-0	160.2	164	95	28	0	59-2	74	4.99	89	.272	.333	0	ø	0	82	-8	0	-0.9
1986	Cle A☆	14	7	.667	34	33	3-1	0-0	206	217	118	34	12	49-3	87	4.54	92	.271	.318	0	ø	0	113	-8	0	-0.9
1987	Cle A	6	13	.316	32	29	4-1	0-0	153.2	185	126	29	3	57-1	61	6.50	70	.298	.357	0	ø	0	91	-32	0	-3.3
Total	7	51	51	.500	176	137	22-3	1-0	900	963	535	125	25	320-17	372	4.81	90	.276	.338	0	ø	0	93	-45	131	-4.8
Schueler, Ron	Ronald Richard; B4.18.1948 Catharine KS; BR/TR/6´4˝/(185–205); [AtlN67*S3/43]; d4.16; C7																									
1972	Atl N	5	8	.385	37	18	3	2-1	144.2	122	68	16	2	60-3	96	3.67	104	.227	.304	42-0-2	.190	0	71	1	0	0.1
1973	Atl N	8	7	.533	39	20	4-2	2-2	186	179	91	24	0	66-11	124	3.87	102	.255	.317	62-0-7	.177	-1	110	1	0	0.0
1974	Phi N	11	16	.407	44	27	5	1-0	203.1	202	91	17	4	98-18	109	3.72	102	.264	.350	51-0-7	.118	-2	77	3	0	0.0
1975	Phi N	4	4	.500	46	6	1	0-0	92.2	88	55	6	1	40-4	69	5.24	72	.258	.336	13-0-1	.154	-0	117	-12	0	-1.0

YEAR	TM LG	W	L	PCT	G	GS	CG-SHO	SV-BS	IP	H	R	HR	HB	BB-IB	SO	ERA	AERA	OAV	OOB	AB-HR-SH	AVG	PB	SUP	APR	DL	PW
1976	Phi N	1	0	1.000	35	0	0	3-0	49.2	44	18	4	2	16-2	43	2.90	123	.243	.307	2-0-1	.000	-0	—	4	0	0.1
1977	Min A	8	7	.533	52	7	0	3-1	134.2	131	74	16	6	61-5	77	4.41	90	.260	.343	0	ø	0	168	-7	0	-0.7
1978	Chi A	3	5	.375	30	7	0	0-2	81.2	76	50	10	7	39-2	39	4.30	88	.251	.341	0	ø	0*	94	-8	0	-0.7
1979	Chi A	0	1	.000	8	1	0	0-0	19.2	19	16	3	2	13-1	6	7.32	58	.264	.382	0	ø	0	64	-6	83	-0.3
Total	8	40	48	.455	291	86	13-2	11-6	912.1	861	463	96	24	393-46	563	4.08	95	.253	.331	170-0-18	.159	-3	95	-24	83	-2.5
SCHULER, DAVE	David Paul; B10.4.1953 Framingham MA; BR/TL/6´4˝/(210–215); [CleA75 10/223]; d9.17; Col New Haven																									
1979	Cal A	0	0	ø	1	0	0	0-0	1.2	2	2	1	0	0-0	0	10.80	38	.333	.286	0	ø	0	—	-1	0	-0.1
1980	Cal A	0	1	.000	8	0	0	0-0	12.2	13	5	3	0	2-1	7	3.55	111	.271	.288	0	ø	0	—	1	0	0.0
1985	Atl N	0	0	ø	9	0	0	0-0	10.2	19	8	4	0	3-0	10	6.75	57	.404	.440	0	ø	0	—	-3	0	-0.2
Total	3	0	1	.000	18	0	0	0-0	25	34	15	8	0	5-1	17	5.40	73	.337	.358	0	ø	0	—	-3	0	-0.3
SCHULLSTROM, ERIK	Erik Paul; B3.25.1969 San Diego CA; BR/TR/6´5˝/(220–235); [BalA90 2/60]; d7.18; Col Cal St.–Fresno																									
1994	Min A	0	0	ø	9	0	0	1-1	13	13	7	0	1	5-0	13	2.77	178	.260	.339	0	ø	0	—	2	0	0.1
1995	Min A	0	0	ø	37	0	0	0-1	47	66	36	8	1	22-1	21	6.89	70	.332	.399	0	ø	0	—	-9	0	-0.4
Total	2	0	0	ø	46	0	0	1-2	60	79	43	8	2	27-1	34	6.00	81	.317	.387	0	ø	0	—	-7	0	-0.3
SCHULTZ, BUDDY	Charles Budd; B9.19.1950 Cleveland OH; BR/TL/6´0˝/(170–175); [ChiN72 6/135]; d9.3; Col Miami–Ohio																									
1975	Chi N	2	0	1.000	6	0	0	0-0	5.2	11	6	0	0	5-1	4	6.35	61	.367	.457	0-0-1	ø	0	—	-2	0	-0.4
1976	Chi N	1	1	.500	29	0	0	2-4	23.2	37	19	3	0	9-1	15	6.08	64	.356	.400	4	.000	-0	—	-6	0	-0.6
1977	StL N	6	1	.857	40	3	0	1-1	85.1	76	26	5	0	24-0	66	2.32	168	.245	.298	12-0-2	.167	0*	137	14	21	1.2
1978	StL N	2	4	.333	62	0	0	6-2	83	68	36	6	0	36-6	70	3.80	94	.226	.305	5-0-2	.200	1	—	0	0	0.0
1979	StL N	4	3	.571	31	0	0	3-1	42.1	40	21	7	0	14-5	38	4.46	85	.256	.312	4	.000	-0	—	-2	66	-0.4
Total	5	15	9	.625	168	3	0	12-8	240	232	108	21	0	88-13	193	3.68	103	.257	.320	25-0-5	.120	0	137	4	87	-0.2
SCHULTZ, BARNEY	George Warren; B8.15.1926 Beverly NJ; BR/TR/6´2˝/200; d4.12; C6																									
1955	StL N	1	2	.333	19	0	0	4	29.2	28	27	5	4	15-3	19	7.89	52	.259	.370	4	.000	-1	—	-12	0	-1.4
1959	Det A	1	2	.333	13	0	0	0	18.1	17	12	1	1	14-1	17	4.42	92	.254	.390	2	1.000	1	—	-1	0	-0.1
1961	Chi N	7	6	.538	41	0	0	7	66.2	57	32	6	4	25-4	59	2.70	155	.228	.307	10-0-2	.100	-1	—	7	0	1.3
1962	Chi N	5	5	.500	51	0	0	5	77.2	66	36	8	4	23-6	58	3.82	108	.231	.296	5-0-2	.000	-0	—	3	0	0.4
1963	Chi N	1	0	1.000	15	0	0	2	27.1	25	11	5	0	9-2	18	3.62	97	.263	.327	4	.000	-0	—	0	0	0.0
	StL N	2	0	1.000	24	0	0	1	35.1	36	15	5	2	8-2	26	3.57	99	.263	.311	0-0-1	ø	0	—	0	0	0.0
	Year	3	0	1.000	39	0	0	3	62.2	61	26	10	2	17-4	44	3.59	98	.263	.317	4-0-1	.000	-0	—	1	0	0.0
1964	†StL N	1	3	.250	30	0	0	14	49.1	35	14	1	0	11-3	29	1.64	232	.201	.246	6-0-1	.167	-0	—	10	0	1.4
1965	StL N	2	2	.500	34	0	0	2	42.1	39	22	8	0	11-3	38	3.83	100	.242	.289	2	.000	-0	—	-1	0	-0.1
Total	7	20	20	.500	227	0	0	35	346.2	303	169	39	15	116-24	264	3.63	109	.237	.307	33-0-6	.121	-1	—	6	0	1.5
SCHULTZ, BOB	Robert Duffy; B11.27.1923 Louisville KY; D3.31.1979 Nashville TN; BR/TL/6´3˝/200; d4.20																									
1951	Chi N	3	6	.333	17	10	2	0	77.1	75	51	9	2	51	27	5.24	78	.251	.364	29-0-1	.138	-1	101	-10	0	-1.2
1952	Chi N	6	3	.667	29	5	1	0	74	63	34	3	2	51	31	4.01	96	.232	.357	18	.222	0	51	0	0	0.0
1953	Chi N	0	2	.000	7	2	0	0	11.2	13	10	2	1	11	4	5.40	82	.289	.439	3	.000	-0	100	-2	0	-0.4
	Pit N	0	2	.000	11	2	0	0	18.2	26	19	3	2	10	5	8.20	55	.321	.409	2-0-1	.000	0	30	-7	0	-0.7
	Year	0	4	.000	18	4	0	0	30.1	39	29	5	3	21	9	7.12	63	.310	.420	5-0-1	.000	-0	65	-10	0	-1.1
1955	Det A	0	0	ø	1	0	0	0	1.1	2	3	0	0	2-0	0	20.25	19	.333	.500	0	ø	0	—	-2	0	-0.1
Total	4	9	13	.409	65	19	3	0	183	179	117	17	7	125-0	67	5.16	79	.255	.372	52-0-2	.154	-1	82	-21	0	-2.4
SCHULTZ, WEBB	Wilbert Carl; B1.31.1898 Wautoma WI; D7.26.1986 Delavan WI; BR/TR/5´11˝/172; d8.3; Col Wisconsin–La Crosse																									
1924	Chi A	0	0	ø	1	0	0	0	1	1	1	0	0	0	0	9.00	46	.250	.250	0	ø	0	—	0	—	0.0
SCHULTZ, MIKE	William Michael; B12.17.1920 Syracuse NY; D8.2.2004 East Syracuse NY; BL/TL/6´1˝/175; d4.20																									
1947	Cin N	0	0	ø	1	0	0	0	2	4	2	0	0	2	0	4.50	91	.444	.545	0	ø	0	—	0	0	0.0
SCHULTZE, JOHN	John F.; B Burlington NJ; 6´0.5˝/165; d5.6																									
1891	Phi N	0	1	.000	6	1	0	0	15	18	15	1	0	11	4	6.60	52	.286	.392	6	.167	-0	18	-5	—	-0.3
SCHULZ, AL	Albert Christopher; B5.12.1889 Toledo OH; D12.13.1931 Gallipolis OH; BR/TL/6´0˝/182; d9.25																									
1912	NY A	1	1	.500	3	1	1	0	16.1	11	8	0	0	11	8	2.20	163	.183	.310	5	.000	-0	0	2	—	0.2
1913	NY A	7	14	.333	38	22	9	0	193	197	110	4	5	69	77	3.73	80	.269	.336	63-0-2	.175	0	92	-16	—	-1.7
1914	NY A	1	3	.250	6	4	1	0	28.1	27	17	0	2	10	18	4.76	58	.237	.310	7	.000	-0	79	-6	—	-0.7
	Buf F	9	12	.429	27	23	10	2	171	160	80	3	2	77	87	3.37	88	.259	.343	56-1-2	.179	-1	92	-8	—	-1.0
1915	Buf F	21	14	.600	42	38	25-5	0	309.2	264	125	8	6	149	160	3.08	91	.238	.332	109-0-3	.165	-3	106	-7	—	-1.1
1916	Cin N	8	19	.296	44	22	10	2	215	208	100	4	5	93	95	3.14	83	.268	.350	64-0-1	.125	-3	65	-15	—	-2.3
Total	5	47	63	.427	160	110	56-5	4	933.1	867	440	19	20	409	445	3.32	85	.254	.338	304-1-8	.155	-8	91	-50	—	-6.6
SCHULZ, WALT	Walter Frederick; B4.16.1900 St.Louis MO; D2.27.1928 Prescott AZ; BR/TR/6´0˝/170; d7.8																									
1920	StL N	0	0	ø	2	0	0	0	6	10	5	0	0	2	0	6.00	50	.370	.414	2	.000	-0	—	-2	—	-0.1
SCHULZE, DON	Donald Arthur; B9.27.1962 Roselle IL; BR/TR/6´3˝/(215–230); [ChiN80 1/11]; d9.13																									
1983	Chi N	0	1	.000	4	3	0	0-0	14	19	11	1	1	7-0	8	7.07	54	.322	.403	1-0-1	.000	0	116	-4	0	-0.3
1984	Chi N	0	0	ø	1	1	0	0-0	3	8	4	0	0	1-0	2	12.00	33	.571	.563	0	ø	0	136	-2	0	-0.1
	Cle A	3	6	.333	19	14	2	0-0	85.2	105	53	9	0	27-0	39	4.83	85	.302	.349	0	ø	0	121	-8	0	-0.7
1985	Cle A	4	10	.286	19	18	1	0-0	94.1	128	75	10	4	19-2	37	6.01	69	.322	.357	0	ø	0	97	-22	0	-2.6
1986	Cle A	4	4	.500	19	13	1	0-0	84.2	88	48	9	5	34-0	33	5.00	84	.266	.342	0	ø	0	102	-5	41	-0.5
1987	NY N	1	2	.333	5	4	0	0-0	21.2	24	15	4	1	6-0	5	6.23	62	.296	.344	2-0-1	.000	0	118	-5	0	-0.5
1989	NY A	1	1	.500	2	2	0	0-0	11	12	5	1	1	5-0	5	4.09	95	.300	.375	0	ø	0	70	0	0	0.0
	SD N	2	1	.667	7	4	0	0-0	24.1	38	20	6	0	6-0	15	5.55	63	.352	.379	4-0-1	.000	-0	196	-7	0	-0.8
Total	6	15	25	.375	76	59	4	0-0	338.2	422	231	40	12	105-2	144	5.47	74	.306	.357	7-0-3	.000	0	112	-53	41	-5.5
SCHUMACHER, HAL	Harold Henry "Prince Hal"; B11.23.1910 Hinckley NY; D4.21.1993 Cooperstown NY; BR/TR/6´0˝/190; d4.15; Mil 1943–45; Col St. Lawrence																									
1931	NY N	1	1	.500	8	2	1	1	18.1	31	23	3	0	14	11	10.80	34	.387	.479	7	.143	-0	255	-14	—	-1.4
1932	NY N	5	6	.455	27	13	2-1	0	101.1	119	60	3	2	39	38	3.55	104	.288	.352	31-0-1	.226	1*	110	-3	—	-0.2
1933	†NY N☆	19	12	.613	35	33	21-7	1	258.2	199	71	9	1	84	96	2.16	149	**.214**	.280	98-0-2	.214	1*	115	33	—	4.4
1934	NY N	23	10	.697	41	36	18-2	0	297	299	131	16	2	89	112	3.18	122	.259	.313	117-6-2	.239	10*	125	22	—	3.3
1935	NY N★	19	9	.679	33	33	19-3	0	261.2	235	100	11	5	70	79	2.89	133	.238	.292	107-2-3	.196	2*	125	27	—	3.2
1936	†NY N	11	13	.458	35	30	9-2	1	215.1	234	103	15	1	69	75	3.47	112	.280	.336	74-1-0	.216	2*	102	8	—	1.1
1937	†NY N	13	12	.520	38	29	10-1	1	217.2	222	100	12	0	89	100	3.60	108	.264	.335	81-2-1	.222	3*	98	7	—	1.1
1938	NY N	13	8	.619	28	28	12-3	0	185	178	81	12	2	50	54	3.50	108	.248	.299	67-2-1	.239	4*	100	7	—	1.3
1939	NY N	13	10	.565	29	27	8	0	181.2	199	106	14	3	89	58	4.81	82	.276	.358	69-0-4	.203	1*	127	-15	—	-1.6
1940	NY N	13	13	.500	34	30	12-1	1	227	218	93	14	0	96	123	3.25	119	.251	.325	78-1-3	.192	2*	92	16	—	2.2
1941	NY N	12	10	.545	30	26	12-3	1	206	187	81	11	5	79	63	3.36	110	.243	.317	66-0-4	.152	-1*	90	11	0	1.0
1942	NY N	12	13	.480	29	29	12-3	0	216	208	81	12	3	82	49	3.04	111	.251	.321	75-1-5	.173	1*	112	10	0	1.4
1946	NY N	4	4	.500	24	13	2	1	96.2	95	50	8	0	52	48	3.91	88	.255	.347	26-0-2	.038	-2	111	-5	0	-0.6
Total	13	158	121	.566	391	329	138-26	7	2482.1	2424	1080	140	24	902	906	3.36	111	.255	.321	896-15-28	.202	24	110	104	0	15.2
SCHUMANN, HACK	Charles J.; B8.13.1884 Buffalo NY; D3.25.1946 Millgrove NY; TR/6´2˝/230; d9.19																									
1906	Phi A	0	2	.000	4	2	1	0	18	21	13	0	2	8	9	4.00	68	.296	.383	6	.000	-1	66	-3	—	-0.4
SCHUPP, FERDIE	Ferdinand Maurice; B1.16.1891 Louisville KY; D12.16.1971 Los Angeles CA; BR/TR/5´10˝/150; d8.19																									
1913	NY N	0	0	ø	5	1	0	0	12	10	3	0	0	3	2	0.75	416	.244	.295	3	.333	1	96	3	—	0.2
1914	NY N	0	0	ø	8	0	0	1	17	19	11	0	2	9	9	5.82	46	.306	.411	2	.000	-0	—	-5	—	-0.3
1915	NY N	1	0	1.000	23	1	0	0	54.2	57	37	1	3	29	28	5.10	50	.281	.379	10	.200	0	203	-15	—	-0.8
1916	NY N	9	3	.750	30	11	8-4	1	140.1	79	22	1	5	37	86	0.90	271	.167	.235	41	.098	-2	87	24	—	1.7
1917	†NY N	21	7	**.750**	36	32	25-6	0	272	202	69	7	4	70	147	1.95	131	**.209**	.265	93-0-1	.161	1	142	21	—	2.2
1918	NY N	0	1	.000	10	2	1	0	33.1	42	34	1	3	27	22	7.56	35	.328	.456	9	.111	-0	173	-19	—	-1.0
1919	NY N	1	3	.250	9	4	0	1	32	32	24	2	0	18	17	5.63	50	.269	.365	6-0-2	.333	0	113	-10	—	-1.2
	StL N	4	4	.500	10	10	6	0	69.2	55	31	2	1	30	37	3.75	75	.221	.307	20-1-1	.050	-0	88	-5	—	-0.7

YEAR	TM LG	W	L	PCT	G	GS	CG-SHO	SV-BS	IP	H	R	HR	HB	BB-IB	SO	ERA	AERA	OAV	OOB	AB-HR-SH	AVG	PB	SUP	APR	DL	PW
	Year	5	7	.417	19	14	6	1	101.2	87	55	4	1	48	54	4.34	64	.236	.326	26-1-3	.115	-0	95	-15	—	-1.9
1920	StL N	16	13	.552	38	37	17	0	250.2	246	118	5	9	127	119	3.52	85	.265	.358	86-0-4	.256	6*	139	-14	—	-1.0
1921	StL N	2	0	1.000	9	4	1	1	37.1	42	26	5	2	21	22	4.10	89	.276	.371	14-0-1	.286	0	185	-4	—	-0.2
	Bro N	3	4	.429	20	7	1	2	61	75	34	2	2	27	26	4.57	85	.310	.384	12-0-1	.083	-1	76	-3	—	-0.4
	Year	5	4	.556	29	11	2	3	98.1	117	60	7	4	48	48	4.39	87	.297	.379	26-0-2	.192	-0	114	-8	—	-0.6
1922	Chi A	4	4	.500	18	12	3-1	0	74	79	61	4	2	66	38	6.08	67	.284	.425	23	.217	1	120	-19	—	-1.7
Total	10	61	39	.610	216	121	62-11	6	1054	938	470	30	33	464	553	3.32	87	.244	.331	319-1-10	.182	5	129	-46	—	-3.2
Schurr, Wayne	Wayne Allen; B8.6.1937 Garrett IN; BR/TR/6´4˝/185; d4.15; Col Hillsdale																									
1964	Chi N	0	0	ø	26	0	0	0	48.1	57	22	3	0	11-1	29	3.72	100	.298	.333	5	.000	-0	—	0	0	0.0
Schutz, Carl	Carl James; B8.22.1971 Hammond LA; BL/TL/5´11˝/200; [AtlN93 3/96]; d9.3; Col Southeastern Louisiana																									
1996	Atl N	0	0	ø	3	0	0	0-0	3.1	3	1	0	0	2-1	5	2.70	165	.273	.385	0	ø	0	—	1	0	0.0
Schwabe, Mike	Michael Scott; B7.12.1964 Ft.Dodge IA; BR/TR/6´4˝/(200–210); [DetA87 21/547]; d5.27; Col Arizona St.																									
1989	Det A	2	4	.333	13	4	0	0-0	44.2	58	33	6	1	16-5	13	6.04	63	.307	.359	0	ø	0	71	-11	0	-1.2
1990	Det A	0	0	ø	1	0	0	0-0	3.2	5	1	0	0	0-0	1	2.45	162	.357	.357	0	ø	0	—	1	0	0.1
Total	2	2	4	.333	14	4	0	0-0	48.1	63	34	6	1	16-5	14	5.77	67	.310	.359	0	ø	0	71	-10	0	-1.1
Schwall, Don	Donald Bernard; B3.2.1936 Wilkes–Barre PA; BR/TR/6´6˝/(196–200); d5.21; Col Oklahoma																									
1961	Bos A★	15	7	.682	25	25	10-2	0	178.2	167	76	8	6	110-1	91	3.22	129	.255	.366	61-0-11	.180	-0*	121	17	0	1.9
1962	Bos A	9	15	.375	33	32	5-1	0	182.1	180	118	18	10	121-1	89	4.94	84	.260	.377	66-0-5	.136	-2*	105	-18	0	-2.3
1963	Pit N	6	12	.333	33	24	3-2	0	167.2	158	72	13	6	74-13	86	3.33	99	.255	.338	50	.160	-0	87	0	0	0.1
1964	Pit N	4	3	.571	15	9	0	0	49.2	53	28	1	0	15-1	36	4.35	81	.269	.321	19	.263	2*	136	-5	0	-0.5
1965	Pit N	9	6	.600	43	1	0	4	77	77	37	5	2	30-4	55	2.92	120	.269	.341	15	.000	-2	75	2	0	0.3
1966	Pit N	3	2	.600	11	4	0	0	41.2	31	13	3	1	21-2	24	2.16	165	.209	.312	10-0-1	.100	-0	86	6	0	0.7
	Atl N	3	3	.500	11	8	0	0	45.1	44	23	2	2	19-2	27	4.37	83	.256	.333	13	.000	-2	106	-3	0	-0.5
	Year	6	5	.545	22	12	0	0	87	75	36	5	3	40-4	51	3.31	109	.234	.323	23-0-1	.043	-2	100	2	0	0.2
1967	Atl N	0	0	ø	1	0	0	0	0.2	0	0	0	0	1-1	0	0.00	ø	.000	.500	0	ø	0	—	0	0	0.0
Total	7	49	48	.505	172	103	18-5	4	743	710	367	50	27	391-25	408	3.72	102	.257	.352	234-0-17	.145	-5	108	-1	0	-0.3
Schwamb, Blackie	Ralph Richard; B8.6.1926 Lancaster CA; D12.21.1989 Los Angeles CA; BR/TR/6´5.5˝/198; d7.25																									
1948	StL A	1	1	.500	12	5	0	0	31.2	44	34	3	0	21	7	8.53	53	.331	.422	10	.300	1	131	-13	0	-0.6
Schwarz, Jeff	Jeffrey William; B5.20.1964 Fort Pierce FL; BR/TR/6´5˝/190; [ChiN82 24/597]; d4.24																									
1993	Chi A	2	2	.500	41	0	0	0-0	51	35	21	1	3	38-2	41	3.71	114	.201	.349	0	ø	0	—	4	15	0.2
1994	Chi A	0	0	ø	9	0	0	0-0	11.1	9	10	0	0	16-0	14	6.35	74	.205	.417	0	ø	0	—	-3	0	-0.1
	Cal A	0	0	ø	4	0	0	0-0	6.2	5	3	0	0	6-0	4	4.05	121	.250	.407	0	ø	0	—	1	0	0.0
	Year	0	0	ø	13	0	0	0-0	18	14	13	0	0	22-0	18	5.50	87	.219	.414	0	ø	0	—	-2	0	-0.1
Total	2	2	2	.500	54	0	0	0-0	69	49	34	1	3	60-2	59	4.17	104	.206	.367	0	ø	0	—	2	15	0.1
Schwenck, Rudy	Rudolph Christian; B4.6.1884 Louisville KY; D11.27.1941 Anchorage KY; BL/TL/6´0˝/174; d9.23																									
1909	Chi N	1	1	.500	3	2	0	0	14	16	7	0	1	3	3	3.86	66	.308	.357	4	.250	0	83	-2	—	-0.1
Schwenk, Hal	Harold Edward; B8.23.1890 Schuylkill Haven PA; D9.3.1955 Kansas City MO; BL/TL/6´0˝/185; d9.4																									
1913	StL A	1	0	1.000	1	1	1	0	11	12	4	0	0	4	3	3.27	90	.333	.400	3	.333	1	126	0	—	0.1
Scoggins, Jim	Lynn J. "Lefty"; B7.9.1891 Killeen TX; D8.16.1923 Columbia SC; BL/TL/5´11˝/165; d8.26																									
1913	Chi A	0	1	.000	1	1	0	0	0	0	1	0	0	1	0	(0)	ø	.000	.500	0	ø	0	76	0	—	0.0
Score, Herb	Herbert Jude; B6.7.1933 Rosedale NY; BL/TL/6´2˝/(185–195); d4.15																									
1955	Cle A☆	16	10	.615	33	32	11-2	0	227.1	158	85	18	1	154-1	**245**	2.85	140	.194	.322	84-0-8	.119	-4	106	28	0	2.3
1956	Cle A★	20	9	.690	35	33	16-**5**	0	249.1	162	82	18	2	129-2	**263**	2.53	**166**	**.186**	.290	87-1-4	.184	1	98	45	0	4.9
1957	Cle A	2	1	.667	5	5	3-1	0	36	18	9	0	1	26-2	39	2.00	186	.149	.304	11	.091	-0	86	7	118	0.6
1958	Cle A	2	3	.400	12	5	2-1	3	41	29	19	1	0	34-1	48	3.95	92	.197	.346	11	.091	-0	74	-1	36	-0.2
1959	Cle A	9	11	.450	30	25	9-1	0	160.2	123	93	28	1	115-0	147	4.71	78	**.210**	.339	52	.096	-3	119	-19	0	-2.5
1960	Chi A	5	10	.333	23	22	5-1	0	113.2	91	54	10	2	87-0	78	3.72	102	.226	.363	30-0-2	.100	-0	84	0	0	-0.1
1961	Chi A	1	2	.333	8	5	1	0	24.1	22	19	3	0	24-1	14	6.66	59	.259	.411	6-0-1	.000	-1	77	-7	0	-0.8
1962	Chi A	0	0	ø	4	0	0	0	6	6	3	1	0	4-0	3	4.50	87	.261	.370	0	ø	0	—	0	0	0.0
Total	8	55	46	.545	150	127	47-11	3	858.1	609	364	79	7	573-7	837	3.36	117	.200	.326	281-1-15	.128	-8	99	53	154	4.2
Scott, Dick	Amos Richard; B2.5.1883 Bethel OH; D1.18.1911 Chicago IL; BR/TR/6´0˝/180; d6.26																									
1901	Cin N	0	2	.000	3	2	2	0	21	26	15	2	3	9	7	5.14	62	.302	.388	9	.000	-1	55	-4	—	-0.5
Scott, Darryl	Darryl Nelson; B8.6.1968 Fresno CA; BR/TR/6´1˝/185; d5.31; Col Loyola Marymount																									
1993	Cal A	1	2	.333	16	0	0	0-0	20	19	13	1	1	11-1	13	5.85	78	.250	.344	0	ø	0	—	-2	0	-0.3
Scott, George	George Wilson; B11.17.1895 Appanoose Co. IA; D12.3.1962 Philomath OR; BR/TR/6´1˝/175; d8.17																									
1920	StL N	0	0	ø	2	0	0	0	6	4	3	0	0	3	1	4.50	66	.200	.304	1	.000	-0	—	-1	—	-0.1
Scott, Jim	James "Death Valley Jim"; B4.23.1888 Deadwood SD; D4.7.1957 Jacumba CA; BR/TR/6´1˝/235; d4.25; Mil 1917–18; U2; Col Nebraska Wesleyan																									
1909	Chi A	12	12	.500	36	29	20-4	0	250.1	194	86	0	16	93	135	2.30	102	.223	.310	85-0-2	.106	-1	104	3	—	0.0
1910	Chi A	8	18	.308	41	23	14-2	1	229.2	182	99	5	4	86	135	2.43	99	.226	.303	74-0-2	.203	2	77	-3	—	0.0
1911	Chi A	14	11	.560	39	26	13-3	0	222	195	82	3	4	81	128	2.39	135	.240	.311	71-0-5	.155	-2	89	21	—	1.7
1912	Chi A	2	2	.500	6	4	2-1	0	37.2	36	16	0	1	15	23	2.15	149	.265	.342	12	.000	-2	52	3	—	0.1
1913	Chi A	20	21	.488	48	**38**	25-4	1	312.1	252	96	2	9	86	158	1.90	154	.223	.283	97-1-8	.072	-7	72	35	—	3.8
1914	Chi A	14	18	.438	43	33	12-2	1	253.1	228	109	5	5	75	138	2.84	94	.246	.306	86-0-2	.163	-0	89	-2	—	-0.2
1915	Chi A	24	11	.686	48	35	23-**7**	2	296.1	256	98	3	5	78	120	2.03	146	.238	.292	95-0-6	.126	-5	97	28	—	2.9
1916	Chi A	7	14	.333	32	21	8-1	3	165.1	155	63	3	3	53	71	2.72	101	.258	.321	52-0-4	.115	-3	85	2	—	-0.1
1917	Chi A	6	7	.462	24	17	6-2	1	125	126	37	0	6	42	37	1.87	142	.272	.341	42	.119	-2	91	10	—	0.9
Total	9	107	114	.484	317	226	123-26	9	1892	1624	686	21	53	609	945	2.30	120	.238	.305	614-1-29	.129	-21	87	97	—	9.1
Scott, Jack	John William; B4.18.1892 Ridgeway NC; D11.30.1959 Durham NC; BL/TR/6´2.5˝/199; d9.6																									
1916	Pit N	0	0	ø	1	0	0	0	5	5	6	1	0	3	4	10.80	25	.278	.381	2	.000	0*	—	-4	—	-0.2
1917	Bos N	1	2	.333	7	3	3	0	39.2	36	12	0	3	5	21	1.82	141	.255	.295	16	.125	-1	39	3	—	0.1
1919	Bos N	6	6	.500	19	12	7	1	103.2	109	47	3	1	39	44	3.13	91	.275	.341	40-0-2	.175	-1*	116	-4	—	-0.7
1920	Bos N	10	21	.323	44	33	22-3	1	291	308	148	6	13	85	94	3.53	87	.277	.336	99-0-3	.212	0	95	-19	—	-2.1
1921	Bos N	15	13	.536	**47**	28	16-2	3	233.2	258	108	9	7	57	83	3.70	99	.283	.330	88-1-1	.341	10*	121	0	—	1.0
1922	Cin N	0	0	ø	1	0	0	0	1	2	1	0	0	1	0	9.00	44	.500	.600	1	.000	-0	—	0	—	0.0
	†NY N	8	2	.800	17	10	5	2	79.2	83	42	7	2	23	37	4.41	91	.265	.320	30-0-1	.267	1	130	-1	—	-0.1
	Year	8	2	.800	18	10	5	2	80.2	85	43	7	2	24	37	4.46	90	.268	.324	31-0-1	.258	1	130	-2	—	-0.1
1923	†NY N	16	7	.696	40	25	9-3	1	220	223	104	15	4	65	79	3.89	98	.267	.323	79-1-2	.316	7	134	0	—	0.6
1925	NY N	14	15	.483	36	28	18-2	3	239.2	251	98	10	4	55	87	3.15	128	.269	.313	87-1-0	.241	6*	88	25	—	3.5
1926	NY N	13	15	.464	**50**	22	13	5	226	242	118	13	3	53	82	4.34	86	.276	.319	83-1-0	.337	9*	99	-10	—	-0.3
1927	Phi N	9	21	.300	**48**	25	17-1	1	233.1	304	154	15	4	69	69	5.09	81	.330	.379	114-1-3	.289	8*	71	-26	—	-2.1
1928	NY N	4	1	.800	16	3	3	1	50.1	59	22	3	2	11	17	3.58	109	.295	.338	15	.267	1	144	2	—	0.3
1929	NY N	7	6	.538	30	6	2	1	91.2	89	44	12	0	27	40	3.53	130	.260	.314	26	.308	3	105	10	—	1.6
Total	12	103	109	.486	356	195	115-11	19	1814.2	1969	904	94	43	493	657	3.85	96	.281	.332	680-5-12	.275	44	103	-24	—	1.6
Scott, Lefty	Marshall; B7.15.1915 Roswell NM; D3.3.1964 Houston TX; BR/TL/6´0.5˝/165; d6.15																									
1945	Phi N	0	2	.000	8	2	0	0	22.1	29	13	1	0	12	5	4.43	86	.312	.390	3-0-1	.000	-0	11	-1	0	-0.2
Scott, Mike	Michael Warren; B4.26.1955 Santa Monica CA; BR/TR/6´3˝/215; [NYN76 2/37]; d4.18; Col Pepperdine																									
1979	NY N	1	3	.250	18	9	0	0-0	52.1	59	35	4	0	20-3	21	5.33	70	.289	.351	12-0-1	.000	-1	119	-10	0	-0.8
1980	NY N	1	1	.500	6	6	1-1	0-0	29.1	40	14	1	0	8-1	13	4.30	84	.331	.369	9	.111	0	120	-1	0	-0.1
1981	NY N	5	10	.333	23	23	1	0-0	136	130	65	11	1	34-1	54	3.90	91	.261	.306	41-0-1	.073	-2	72	-4	0	-0.4
1982	NY N	7	13	.350	37	22	1	3-2	147	185	100	13	2	60-3	63	5.14	71	.321	.381	48	.146	0	97	-25	0	-2.9

YEAR	TM LG	W	L	PCT	G	GS	CG-SHO	SV-BS	IP	H	R	HR	HB	BB-IB	SO	ERA	AERA	OAV	OOB	AB-HR-SH	AVG	PB	SUP	APR	DL	PW
1983	Hou N	10	6	.625	24	24	2-2	0-0	145	143	67	8	5	46-0	73	3.72	92	.258	.318	48-0-8	.167	1	124	-4	29	-0.3
1984	Hou N	5	11	.313	31	29	0	0-0	154	179	96	7	3	43-4	83	4.68	72	.293	.337	47-0-6	.128	-0	108	-25	0	-2.4
1985	Hou N	18	8	.692	36	35	4-2	0-0	221.2	194	91	20	3	80-4	137	3.29	106	.235	.302	72-1-3	.153	2	128	6	0	0.9
1986	†Hou N★	18	10	.643	37	37	7-**5**	0-0	**275.1**	182	73	17	2	72-6	**306**	**2.22**	**162**	**.186**	**.242**	95-0-10	.126	-2*	97	**45**	0	**4.5**
1987	Hou N★	16	13	.552	36	**36**	8-3	0-0	247.2	199	94	21	4	79-6	233	3.23	122	.217	**.281**	80-0-8	.125	-1	84	22	0	2.2
1988	Hou N	14	8	.636	32	32	8-5	0-0	218.2	162	74	19	8	53-6	190	2.92	114	.204	.260	71-0-7	.085	-3	113	13	21	1.0
1989	Hou N✳	**20**	10	.667	33	32	9-2	0-0	229	180	87	23	3	62-12	172	3.10	110	.212	.267	75-1-9	.133	-1	122	8	0	0.9
1990	Hou N	9	13	.409	32	32	4-2	0-0	205.2	194	102	27	1	66-6	121	3.81	98	.246	.302	54-0-6	.130	-0	76	-4	0	-0.5
1991	Hou N	0	2	.000	2	2	0	0-0	7	11	10	2	1	4-1	3	12.86	27	.367	.457	1	.000	-0	51	-7	176	-1.1
Total	13	124	108	.534	347	319	45-22	3-2	2068.2	1858	908	173	33	627-53	1469	3.54	101	.240	.297	653-2-59	.124	-6	102	14	226	1.0
Scott, Ed	Philip Edwin; B8.12.1870 Walbridge OH; D11.1.1933 Toledo OH; BR/TR/6´3˝/?; d4.19																									
1900	Cin N	17	20	.459	42	35	31	1	315	370	192	10	14	65	87	3.86	95	.292	.334	123-1-2	.154	-5	88	-9	—	-0.9
1901	Cle A	6	6	.500	17	16	11	1	124.2	149	82	2	7	38	23	4.40	81	.293	.350	48-1-2	.208	1	96	-8	—	-0.5
Total	2	23	26	.469	59	51	42	2	439.2	519	274	12	21	103	110	4.01	91	.292	.338	171-2-4	.170	-4	90	-17	—	-1.4
Scott, Mickey	Ralph Robert; B7.25.1947 Weimar, Germany; BL/TL/6´1˝/(155–165); [NYA65 11/335]; d5.6																									
1972	Bal A	0	1	.000	15	0	0	0-1	23	23	7	2	1	5-0	11	2.74	114	.277	.319	1	.000	0	—	1	0	0.1
1973	Bal A	0	0	ø	1	0	0	0-0	1.2	2	1	1	0	2-0	2	5.40	70	.286	.444	0	ø	0	—	0	0	0.0
	Mon N	1	2	.333	22	0	0	0-1	24	27	14	3	2	9-0	11	5.25	73	.287	.362	3	.000	-0	—	-3	0	-0.3
1975	Cal A	4	2	.667	50	0	0	1-4	68.1	59	34	8	1	18-5	31	3.29	109	.233	.282	0	ø	0	—	0	0	0.0
1976	Cal A	3	0	1.000	33	0	0	3-1	39	47	17	3	0	12-4	10	3.23	104	.307	.355	0	ø	0*	—	0	27	0.0
1977	Cal A	0	2	.000	12	0	0	0-0	16	19	16	1	0	4-2	5	5.63	70	.302	.343	0	ø	0	—	-5	0	-0.5
Total	5	8	7	.533	133	0	0	4-7	172	177	89	18	4	50-11	70	3.72	95	.271	.323	4	.000	0	—	-7	27	-0.7
Scott, Dick	Richard Lewis; B3.15.1933 Portsmouth NH; BR/TL/6´2˝/(185–200); d5.8																									
1963	LA N	0	0	ø	9	0	0	2	12	17	10	6	0	3-0	6	6.75	45	.340	.370	0	ø	0	—	-5	0	-0.3
1964	Chi N	0	0	ø	3	0	0	0	4.1	10	6	2	0	1-0	1	12.46	30	.417	.440	0	ø	0	—	-4	0	-0.2
Total	2	0	0	ø	12	0	0	2	16.1	27	16	8	0	4-0	7	8.27	39	.365	.392	0	ø	0	—	-9	0	-0.5
Scott, Tim	Timothy Dale; B11.16.1966 Hanford CA; BR/TR/6´2˝/(185–205); [LAN84 2/51]; d6.25																									
1991	SD N	0	0	ø	2	0	0	0-0	1	2	2	0	0	0-0	1	9.00	42	.400	.400	0	ø	0	—	-1	0	0.0
1992	SD N	4	1	.800	34	0	0	0-1	37.2	39	24	4	1	21-6	30	5.26	68	.267	.361	0	ø	0	—	-7	0	-0.9
1993	SD N	2	0	1.000	24	0	0	0-2	37.2	38	13	1	4	15-0	30	2.39	173	.260	.341	2-0-1	.000	-0	—	6	0	0.3
	Mon N	5	2	.714	32	0	0	1-1	34	31	15	3	0	19-2	35	3.71	113	.242	.340	2	.000	-0	—	2	0	0.4
	Year	7	2	.778	56	0	0	1-3	71.2	69	28	4	4	34-2	65	3.01	138	.252	.341	4-0-1	.000	-0	—	8	0	0.7
1994	Mon N	5	2	.714	40	0	0	1-0	53.1	51	17	0	2	18-3	37	2.70	157	.251	.318	2	.000	-0	—	9	15	1.0
1995	Mon N	2	0	1.000	62	0	0	2-3	63.1	52	30	6	6	23-2	57	3.98	108	.222	.307	4	.250	0	—	2	0	0.1
1996	Mon N	3	5	.375	45	0	0	1-2	46.1	41	18	3	2	21-2	37	3.11	139	.238	.325	4	.000	-0	—	6	0	0.9
	SF N	2	2	.500	20	0	0	0-2	19.2	24	18	5	1	9-0	10	8.24	50	.316	.391	1	.000	-0	—	-8	0	-1.4
	Year	5	7	.417	65	0	0	1-4	66	65	36	8	3	30-2	47	4.64	92	.262	.345	5	.000	-1	—	-2	0	-0.5
1997	SD N	1	1	.500	14	0	0	0-1	18.1	25	17	2	3	5-0	14	7.85	50	.321	.379	0	ø	0	—	-8	0	-0.7
	Col N	0	0	ø	3	0	0	0-0	2.2	5	3	0	0	2-0	2	10.13	51	.455	.538	0	ø	0	—	-1	0	0.0
	Year	1	1	.500	17	0	0	0-1	21	30	20	2	3	7-0	16	8.14	50	.337	.400	0	ø	0	—	-9	0	-0.7
Total	7	24	13	.649	276	0	0	5-12	314	308	157	24	19	133-15	253	4.13	101	.257	.338	15-0-1	.067	-1	—	0	15	-0.3
Scudder, Scott	William Scott; B2.14.1968 Paris TX; BR/TR/6´2˝/(180–190); [CinN86 1/17]; d6.6																									
1989	Cin N	4	9	.308	23	17	0	0-0	100.1	91	54	14	1	61-11	66	4.49	80	.239	.345	24-0-4	.167	1	91	-8	0	-1.0
1990	†Cin N	5	5	.500	21	10	0	0-0	71.2	74	41	12	3	30-4	42	4.90	81	.265	.342	18-0-1	.056	-1	105	-7	0	-1.0
1991	Cin N	6	9	.400	27	14	0	1-0	101.1	91	52	6	6	56-4	51	4.35	87	.246	.352	29-1-2	.103	-0	101	-5	68	-0.7
1992	Cle A	6	10	.375	23	22	0	0-0	109	134	80	10	2	55-0	66	5.28	75	.303	.380	0	ø	0	90	-20	49	-2.6
1993	Cle A	0	1	.000	2	1	0	0-0	4	5	4	0	1	4-0	1	9.00	49	.333	.500	0	ø	0	63	-2	43	-0.3
Total	5	21	34	.382	96	64	0	1-0	386.1	395	231	42	13	206-19	226	4.80	80	.266	.358	71-1-7	.113	-0	95	-42	160	-5.6
Scurry, Rod	Rodney Grant; B3.17.1956 Sacramento CA; D11.5.1992 Reno NV; BL/TL/6´2˝/(180–195); [PitN74 1/11]; d4.17																									
1980	Pit N	0	2	.000	20	0	0	0-0	37.2	23	12	2	2	17-3	28	2.15	172	.176	.280	4	.250	0	—	5	0	0.3
1981	Pit N	4	5	.444	27	7	0	7-2	74	74	33	6	3	40-2	65	3.77	97	.261	.357	19	.158	0	45	0	0	0.0
1982	Pit N	4	5	.444	76	0	0	14-6	103.2	79	26	3	4	64-7	94	1.74	216	.212	.331	21-0-1	.238	1	—	21	0	2.4
1983	Pit N	4	9	.308	61	0	0	7-8	68	63	45	6	4	53-7	67	5.56	67	.249	.382	5	.000	-1	—	-12	0	-2.5
1984	Pit N	5	6	.455	43	0	0	4-1	46.1	28	14	1	0	22-3	48	2.53	144	.175	.275	2	.000	-0	—	6	58	1.3
1985	Pit N	0	1	.000	30	0	0	2-1	47.2	42	22	4	0	28-1	43	3.21	113	.236	.337	4	.000	-0	—	1	0	0.0
	NY A	1	0	1.000	5	0	0	1-0	12.2	5	4	2	0	10-1	17	2.84	142	.125	.300	0	ø	0	—	2	0	0.2
1986	NY A	1	2	.333	31	0	0	2-1	39.1	38	18	1	2	22-1	36	3.66	113	.252	.354	0	ø	0	—	2	73	0.2
1988	Sea A	0	2	.000	39	0	0	2-0	31.1	32	16	6	4	18-4	33	4.02	104	.258	.365	0	ø	0	—	0	0	0.0
Total	8	19	32	.373	332	7	0	39-19	460.2	384	190	31	19	274-29	431	3.24	116	.227	.339	55-0-1	.164	0	45	25	131	1.9
Seale, Johnnie	Johnny Ray "Durango Kid"; B11.14.1938 Edgewater CO; BL/TL/5´10˝/155; d9.20																									
1964	Det A	1	0	1.000	4	0	0	0	10	6	4	1	0	4-0	5	3.60	102	.171	.256	1	.000	-0	—	0	0	0.0
1965	Det A	0	0	ø	4	0	0	0	3	7	4	1	0	2-0	3	12.00	29	.500	.500	0	ø	0	—	-3	0	-0.1
Total	2	1	0	1.000	8	0	0	0	13	13	8	2	0	6-0	8	5.54	65	.265	.333	1	.000	-0	—	-3	0	-0.1
Seaman, Kim	Kim Michael; B5.6.1957 Pascagoula MS; BL/TL/6´4˝/205; [NYN76*S4/80]; d9.28; Col Mississippi Gulf Coast CC																									
1979	StL N	0	0	ø	1	0	0	0-0	2	0	0	0	0	2-0	3	0.00	ø	.000	.250	0	ø	0	—	1	0	0.0
1980	StL N	3	2	.600	26	0	0	4-1	23.2	16	9	2	0	13-1	10	3.42	110	.188	.296	1	.000	-0	—	1	0	0.3
Total	2	3	2	.600	27	0	0	4-1	25.2	16	9	2	0	15-1	13	3.16	119	.176	.292	1	.000	-0	—	2	0	0.3
Seanez, Rudy	Rudy Caballero; B10.20.1968 Brawley CA; BR/TR/5´10˝/(170–205); [CleA86 4/83]; d9.7; [DL 1992 LA N 182, 1993 Col N 102]																									
1989	Cle A	0	0	ø	5	0	0	0-0	5	1	2	0	0	4-1	7	3.60	111	.071	.250	0	ø	0	—	0	0	0.0
1990	Cle A	2	1	.667	24	0	0	0-0	27.1	22	17	2	1	25-1	24	5.60	70	.220	.378	0	ø	0	—	-4	0	-0.5
1991	Cle A	0	0	ø	5	0	0	0-1	5	10	12	2	0	7-0	7	16.20	26	.385	.515	0	ø	0	—	-7	52	-0.4
1993	SD N	0	0	ø	3	0	0	0-0	3.1	8	6	1	0	2-0	1	13.50	31	.471	.526	0	ø	0	—	-4	0	-0.2
1994	LA N	1	1	.500	17	0	0	0-1	23.2	24	7	2	1	9-1	18	2.66	150	.273	.340	1	.000	-0	—	4	0	0.3
1995	LA N	1	3	.250	37	0	0	3-1	34.2	39	27	5	1	18-3	29	6.75	57	.285	.372	1	.000	-0	—	-11	19	-1.3
1998	†Atl N	4	1	.800	34	0	0	2-2	36	25	13	2	1	16-0	50	2.75	151	.195	.286	1	.000	-0	—	5	0	0.7
1999	Atl N	6	1	.857	56	0	0	3-5	53.2	47	21	3	1	21-1	41	3.35	133	.234	.307	1	.000	0	—	7	44	0.9
2000	Atl N	2	4	.333	23	0	0	2-1	21	15	11	3	1	9-1	20	4.29	105	.192	.284	0	ø	0	—	1	132	0.1
2001	SD N	0	2	.000	26	0	0	1-2	24	15	8	3	1	15-0	24	2.63	158	.176	.304	0	ø	0	—	4	15	0.3
	†Atl N	0	0	ø	12	0	0	0-0	12	8	4	1	0	4-0	17	3.00	144	.182	.250	0	ø	0	—	2	0	0.1
	Year	0	2	.000	38	0	0	1-2	36	23	12	4	1	19-0	41	2.75	153	.178	.287	0	ø	0	—	6	0	0.4
2002	Tex A	1	3	.250	33	0	0	0-4	33	28	25	5	0	24-1	40	5.73	84	.230	.354	0	ø	0	—	-4	95	-0.4
2003	Bos A	0	1	.000	9	0	0	0-1	8.2	11	7	2	0	6-1	9	6.23	75	.297	.386	0	ø	0	—	-2	0	-0.2
2004	KC A	0	1	.000	16	0	0	0-1	23	21	10	0	0	11-2	21	3.91	119	.244	.320	0	ø	0	—	2	0	0.1
	Fla N	3	1	.750	23	0	0	0-1	23	18	7	3	0	8-1	25	2.74	150	.212	.280	0	ø	0	—	4	0	0.6
2005	†SD N	7	1	.875	57	0	0	0-2	60.1	49	19	4	2	22-4	84	2.69	146	.222	.297	0	ø	0	—	9	35	1.1
2006	Bos A	2	1	.667	41	0	0	0-1	46.2	51	28	6	1	26-1	48	4.82	97	.271	.361	0	ø	0	—	-1	0	-0.1
	†SD N	1	2	.333	8	0	0	0-1	6.1	7	4	2	0	6-3	6	5.68	73	.259	.394	0	ø	0	—	-1	0	-0.2
Total	15	30	23	.566	429	0	0	11-24	446.2	399	228	46	10	233-21	471	4.21	101	.237	.330	4	.000	-0	—	4	676	0.9
Searage, Ray	Raymond Mark; B5.1.1955 Freeport NY; BL/TL/6´1˝/(180–201); [StLN76 22/518]; d6.11; Col West Liberty St.																									
1981	NY N	1	0	1.000	26	0	0	1-0	36.2	34	16	2	0	17-3	16	3.68	96	.252	.331	1	1.000	0	—	0	0	0.0
1984	Mil A	2	1	.667	21	0	0	6-1	38.1	20	3	0	1	16-3	29	0.70	553	.155	.253	0	ø	0	—	14	0	1.5
1985	Mil A	1	4	.200	33	0	0	1-2	38	54	27	2	0	24-4	36	5.92	71	.338	.422	0	ø	0	—	-7	0	-0.8
1986	Mil A	0	1	.000	17	0	0	1-1	22	29	17	6	1	9-1	10	6.95	63	.315	.382	0	ø	0	—	-5	0	-0.2
	Chi A	1	0	1.000	29	0	0	0-0	29	15	3	1	0	19-3	26	0.62	700	.156	.291	0	ø	0	—	11	0	0.6
	Year	1	1	.500	46	0	0	1-1	51	44	20	7	1	28-4	36	3.35	130	.234	.333	0	ø	0	—	6	0	0.4
1987	Chi A	2	3	.400	58	0	0	2-3	55.2	56	28	9	1	24-3	33	4.20	110	.264	.339	0	ø	0	—	3	0	0.2

YEAR	TM LG	W	L	PCT	G	GS	CG-SHO	SV-BS	IP	H	R	HR	HB	BB-IB	SO	ERA	AERA	OAV	OOB	AB-HR-SH	AVG	PB	SUP	APR	DL	PW
1989	LA N	3	4	.429	41	0	0	0-1	35.2	29	15	1	0	18-6	24	3.53	97	.225	.313	0	ø	0	—	0	38	0.0
1990	LA N	1	0	1.000	29	0	0	0-0	32.1	30	11	1	0	10-0	19	2.78	132	.250	.299	2	.000	-0	—	4	79	0.2
Total	7	11	13	.458	254	0	0	11-8	287.2	267	120	22	3	137-23	193	3.50	115	.249	.332	3	.333	0	—	20	117	1.5
Searcy, Steve	William Steven; B6.4.1964 Knoxville TN; BL/TL/6´1˝/(185–195); [DetA85 3/80]; d8.29; Col Tennessee																									
1988	Det A	0	2	.000	2	2	0	0-0	8	8	6	3	0	4-0	5	5.63	68	.242	.324	0	ø	0	59	-2	0	-0.3
1989	Det A	1	1	.500	8	2	0	0-1	22.1	27	16	3	0	12-1	11	6.04	63	.307	.390	0	ø	0	189	-5	32	-0.4
1990	Det A	2	7	.222	16	12	1	0-0	75.1	76	44	9	0	51-3	66	4.66	85	.270	.375	0	ø	0	55	-6	0	-0.7
1991	Det A	1	2	.333	16	5	0	0-0	40.2	52	40	8	0	30-0	32	8.41	50	.313	.412	0	ø	0	101	-18	0	-1.2
	Phi N	2	1	.667	18	0	0	0-0	30.1	29	16	2	0	14-1	21	4.15	89	.252	.328	4	.000	-0	—	-2	0	-0.2
1992	Phi N	0	0	ø	10	0	0	0-0	10.1	13	9	0	0	8-0	5	6.10	58	.325	.429	0	ø	0	—	-4	0	-0.2
Total	5	6	13	.316	70	21	1	0-1	187	205	131	25	0	119-5	140	5.68	69	.283	.379	4	.000	-0	80	-37	32	-3.0
Seaton, Tom	Thomas Gordon; B8.30.1887 Blair NE; D4.10.1940 ElPaso TX; BB/TR/6´0˝/175; d4.13																									
1912	Phi N	16	12	.571	44	27	16-2	2	255	246	126	8	9	106	118	3.28	111	.261	.342	83-0-4	.217	-0	95	11	—	0.9
1913	Phi N	**27**	12	.692	52	35	21-5	1	**322.1**	262	117	6	10	136	**168**	2.60	128	.226	.313	110-1-3	.109	-5	114	25	—	2.3
1914	Bro F	25	14	.641	44	38	26-7	2	302.2	299	130	6	13	102	172	3.03	95	.259	.326	107-1-1	.206	3	100	-4	—	-0.2
1915	Bro F	11	11	.500	32	24	13	3	189.1	199	123	6	3	99	86	4.42	62	.273	.362	66-1-8	.242	4*	145	-36	—	-3.5
	New F	2	6	.250	12	10	7	1	75	61	26	1	2	21	28	2.28	112	.224	.285	26-1-0	.154	-0	98	3	—	0.3
	Year	13	17	.433	44	34	20	4	264.1	260	149	7	5	120	114	3.81	70	.260	.342	92-2-8	.217	3	132	-35	—	-3.2
1916	Chi N	6	6	.500	31	12	4	1	121	108	54	3	4	43	45	3.27	89	.246	.319	38-0-1	.184	0	122	-3	—	-0.3
1917	Chi N	5	4	.556	16	9	3-1	1	74.2	60	30	0	1	23	27	2.53	115	.227	.292	21-0-1	.238	1	92	3	—	0.5
Total	6	92	65	.586	231	155	90-15	11	1340	1235	606	30	42	530	644	3.12	99	.249	.327	451-4-18	.186	2	109	-1	—	-0.0
Seats, Tom	Thomas Edward; B9.24.1910 Farmington NC; D5.10.1992 San Ramon CA; BR/TL (BB 1940)/5´11˝/190; d5.4																									
1940	Det A	2	2	.500	26	2	0	1	55.2	67	43	4	0	21	25	4.69	101	.290	.349	12	.083	-1	129	-3	—	-0.3
1945	Bro N	10	7	.588	31	18	6-2	0	121.2	127	71	8	5	37	44	4.36	86	.261	.320	43-0-4	.209	0	135	-7	0	-0.8
Total	2	12	9	.571	57	20	6-2	1	177.1	194	114	12	5	58	69	4.47	91	.271	.329	55-0-4	.182	-1	129	-10	0	-1.1
Seaver, Tom	George Thomas "Tom Terrific"; B11.17.1944 Fresno CA; BR/TR/6´1˝/(195–210); d4.13; HF1992; Col USC																									
1967	NY N★	16	13	.552	35	34	18-2	0	251	224	85	19	5	78-6	170	2.76	123	.241	.301	77-0-6	.143	2*	94	18	0	2.4
1968	NY N★	16	12	.571	36	35	14-5	1	278	224	73	15	8	48-5	205	2.20	137	.222	.261	95-0-3	.158	0*	76	26	0	3.1
1969	†NY N☆	**25**	7	**.781**	36	35	18-5	0-0	273.1	202	75	24	7	82-9	208	2.21	166	**.207**	.272	91-0-4	.121	-0*	102	43	0	5.3
1970	NY N★	18	12	.600	37	36	19-2	0-0	290.2	230	103	21	4	83-8	**283**	**2.82**	**144**	.214	.272	95-1-7	.179	4*	87	**40**	0	4.4
1971	NY N☆	20	10	.667	36	35	21-4	0-1	286.1	210	61	18	4	61-2	**289**	**1.76**	**195**	.206	**.252**	92-1-11	.196	4*	103	**55**	0	**6.7**
1972	NY N☆	21	12	.636	35	35	13-3	0-0	262	215	92	23	5	77-2	249	2.92	116	.224	.284	89-3-6	.146	4*	80	16	0	2.5
1973	†NY N★	19	10	.655	36	36	**18**-3	0-0	290	219	74	23	4	64-5	**251**	**2.08**	**175**	**.206**	**.252**	93-1-9	.161	2*	95	**51**	0	**5.5**
1974	NY N	11	11	.500	32	32	12-5	0-0	236	199	89	19	3	75-10	201	3.20	113	.230	.293	71-0-7	.099	-2	91	14	0	1.2
1975	NY N★	**22**	9	.710	36	36	15-5	0-0	280.1	217	81	11	4	88-6	**243**	2.38	148	.214	.279	95-0-7	.179	2*	104	38	0	**4.6**
1976	NY N★	14	11	.560	35	34	13-5	0-0	271	211	83	14	4	77-9	**235**	2.59	129	.213	.272	82-0-9	.085	-2	92	**26**	0	2.3
1977	NY N	7	3	.700	13	13	5-3	0-0	96	79	33	7	0	28-3	72	3.00	127	.221	.275	31-0-2	.161	-0	96	10	0	1.0
	Cin N★	14	3	.824	20	20	14-4	0-0	165.1	120	45	12	0	38-3	124	2.34	168	.201	.248	55-3-11	.218	4	113	30	0	3.4
	Year	21	6	.778	33	33	19-**7**	0-0	261.1	199	78	19	0	66-6	196	2.58	150	**.209**	**.258**	86-3-13	.198	4	106	40	0	4.4
1978	Cin N☆	16	14	.533	36	36	8-1	0-0	259.2	218	97	26	0	89-11	226	2.88	124	.227	.289	74-0-13	.122	-0	100	18	0	1.9
1979	†Cin N	16	6	**.727**	32	32	9-**5**	0-0	215	187	85	16	0	61-6	131	3.14	118	.236	.289	76-2-4	.158	2*	116	13	0	1.4
1980	Cin N	10	8	.556	26	26	5-1	0-0	168	140	74	24	1	59-3	101	3.64	97	.225	.290	46-0-7	.130	1	113	-3	34	-0.1
1981	Cin N★	**14**	2	**.875**	23	23	6-1	0-0	166.1	120	51	10	3	66-8	87	2.54	138	.205	.285	55-1-4	.200	4	127	18	0	2.2
1982	Cin N	5	13	.278	21	21	0	0-0	111.1	136	75	14	3	44-4	62	5.50	67	.302	.367	34-0-5	.176	1*	79	-22	0	-3.1
1983	NY N	9	14	.391	34	34	5-2	0-0	231	201	104	18	4	86-5	135	3.55	104	.235	.305	64-0-6	.156	2	87	3	0	0.5
1984	Chi A	15	11	.577	34	33	10-4	0-0	236.2	216	108	27	2	61-3	131	3.95	106	.240	.288	0	ø	0	100	8	0	0.9
1985	Chi A	16	11	.593	35	33	6-1	0-0	238.2	223	103	22	8	69-6	134	3.17	137	.248	.304	0	ø	0	85	25	0	2.8
1986	Chi A	2	6	.250	12	12	1	0-0	72	66	37	9	5	27-1	31	4.38	99	.242	.319	0	ø	0	64	1	17	0.0
	Bos A	5	7	.417	16	16	1	0-0	104.1	114	46	8	2	29-1	72	3.80	111	.278	.326	0	ø	0	88	6	0	0.6
	Year	7	13	.350	28	28	2	0-0	176.1	180	83	17	7	56-2	103	4.03	106	.264	.323	0	ø	0	78	7	0	0.6
Total	20	311	205	.603	656	647	231-61	1-1	4783	3971	1674	380	76	1390-116	3640	2.86	128	.226	.283	1315-12-121	.154	27	96	434	51	49.5
Seay, Bobby	Robert Michael; B6.20.1978 Sarasota FL; BL/TL/6´2˝/(190–235); d8.14; [DL 2002 TB A 64]																									
2001	TB A	1	1	.500	12	0	0	0-0	13	13	11	3	1	5-1	12	6.23	72	.260	.339	0	ø	0	—	-3	0	-0.4
2003	TB A	0	0	ø	12	0	0	0-1	9	7	3	0	0	6-0	5	3.00	153	.226	.333	0	ø	0	—	2	40	0.1
2004	TB A	0	0	ø	21	0	0	0-0	22.2	21	6	2	2	5-1	17	2.38	196	.239	.295	0	ø	0	—	6	0	0.3
2005	Col N	0	0	ø	17	0	0	0-1	11.2	18	11	3	0	8-1	11	8.49	55	.367	.456	0	ø	0	—	-4	49	-0.2
2006	Det A	0	0	ø	14	0	0	0-0	15.1	14	11	1	3	9-1	12	6.46	69	.246	.371	0	ø	0	—	-3	0	-0.1
Total	5	1	1	.500	76	0	0	0-2	71.2	73	42	9	6	33-4	57	5.02	91	.265	.353	0	ø	0	—	-2	153	-0.3
Sebra, Bob	Robert Bush; B12.11.1961 Ridgewood NJ; BR/TR/6´2˝/(185–200); [TexA83 5/109]; d6.26; Col Nebraska																									
1985	Tex A	0	2	.000	7	4	0	0-0	20.1	26	17	4	1	14-2	13	7.52	57	.306	.402	0	ø	0	48	-6	0	-0.6
1986	Mon N	5	5	.500	17	13	3-1	0-0	91.1	82	39	9	3	25-2	66	3.55	106	.239	.294	29	.207	1*	84	3	0	-0.3
1987	Mon N	6	15	.286	36	27	4-1	0-0	177.1	184	99	15	3	67-0	156	4.42	97	.272	.337	51-0-4	.157	-0	71	-3	0	-0.3
1988	Phi N	1	2	.333	3	3	0	0-0	11.1	15	11	0	0	10-0	7	7.94	45	.333	.417	5	.000	-0	115	-5	0	-1.0
1989	Phi N	2	3	.400	6	5	0	0-0	34.1	41	20	6	4	10-2	21	4.46	81	.295	.357	10-0-1	.000	-0	79	-4	0	-0.5
	Cin N	0	0	ø	15	0	0	1-0	21	24	16	2	3	18-1	14	6.43	56	.296	.433	1	.000	-0	—	-6	0	-0.3
	Year	2	3	.400	21	5	0	1-0	55.1	65	36	8	7	28-3	35	5.20	69	.295	.388	11-0-1	.000	-1	79	-10	0	-0.8
1990	Mil A	1	2	.333	10	0	0	0-0	11	20	10	1	1	5-1	4	8.18	48	.408	.456	0	ø	0	—	-5	0	-0.9
Total	6	15	29	.341	94	52	7-2	1-0	366.2	392	212	37	15	149-8	281	4.71	85	.276	.347	96-0-5	.146	-0	76	-26	0	-3.3
Sechrist, Doc	Theodore O'Hara; B2.10.1876 Williamstown KY; D4.2.1950 Louisville KY; BR/TR/5´9˝/160; d4.28																									
1899	NY N	0	0	ø	1	0	0	0	0	0	0	0	0	2	0	(0)	ø	ø	1.000	0	ø	0	—	0	—	0.0
Secrist, Don	Donald Laverne; B2.26.1944 Seattle WA; BL/TL/6´2˝/(185–195); d4.11; Col Bradley																									
1969	Chi A	0	1	.000	19	0	0	0-0	40	35	28	7	1	14-2	23	6.07	63	.227	.296	7	.143	0	—	-9	25	-0.4
1970	Chi A	0	0	ø	9	0	0	0-0	14.2	19	9	2	0	12-0	9	5.52	70	.333	.437	0	ø	0	—	-2	0	-0.1
Total	2	0	1	.000	28	0	0	0-0	54.2	54	37	9	1	26-2	32	5.93	65	.256	.338	7	.143	0	—	-11	25	-0.5
Sedgwick, Duke	Henry Kenneth; B6.1.1898 Martins Ferry OH; D12.4.1982 Clearwater FL; BR/TR/6´0˝/175; d7.12																									
1921	Phi N	1	3	.250	16	5	1	0	71.1	81	48	3	4	32	21	4.92	86	.283	.363	24	.208	-1	82	-3	—	-0.3
1923	Was A	0	1	.000	5	2	1	0	16	27	17	1	0	6	4	7.88	48	.415	.465	5	.000	-1	99	-8	—	-0.4
Total	2	1	4	.200	21	7	2	0	87.1	108	65	4	4	38	25	5.46	76	.308	.382	29	.172	-2	85	-11	—	-0.7
Sedlacek, Shawn	Shawn Patrick; B6.29.1977 Cedar Rapids IA; BR/TR/6´4˝/200; [KCA98 14/407]; d6.18; Col Iowa St.																									
2002	KC A	3	5	.375	16	14	0	0-0	84.1	99	64	16	6	36-2	52	6.72	74	.303	.375	6	.000	-1	90	-13	0	-1.1
Seelbach, Chuck	Charles Frederick; B3.20.1948 Lakewood OH; BR/TR/6´0˝/(175–185); [DetA70 S1/12]; d6.29; Col Dartmouth																									
1971	Det A	0	0	ø	5	0	0	0-0	4	6	6	2	1	7-0	1	13.50	27	.375	.583	0	ø	0	—	-4	0	-0.2
1972	†Det A	9	8	.529	61	3	0	14-3	112	96	39	6	3	39-4	76	2.89	110	.238	.308	21-0-1	.143	1	74	4	0	0.9
1973	Det A	1	0	1.000	5	0	0	0-0	7	7	3	1	0	2-1	2	3.86	106	.250	.300	0	ø	0	—	0	53	0.1
1974	Det A	0	0	ø	4	0	0	0-0	7.2	9	4	2	1	3-0	0	4.70	82	.300	.382	0	ø	0	—	0	0	0.0
Total	4	10	8	.556	75	3	0	14-3	130.2	118	52	11	5	51-5	79	3.38	97	.247	.325	21-0-1	.143	1	74	0	53	0.8
Seelbach, Chris	Christopher Don; B12.18.1972 Lufkin TX; BR/TR/6´4˝/180; [AtlN91 4/101]; d9.9																									
2000	Atl N	0	1	.000	2	0	0	0-0	1.2	3	2	0	0	0-0	1	10.80	42	.500	.429	0	ø	0	—	-1	0	-0.2
2001	Atl N	0	0	ø	5	0	0	0-0	8	9	7	3	0	5-1	8	7.88	55	.273	.368	0	ø	0	—	-3	0	-0.1
Total	2	0	1	.000	7	0	0	0-0	9.2	12	9	3	0	5-1	9	8.38	52	.308	.378	0	ø	0	—	-4	0	-0.3
Segelke, Herman	Herman Neils; B4.24.1958 San Mateo CA; BR/TR/6´4˝/200; [ChiN76 1/7]; d4.7																									
1982	Chi N	0	0	ø	3	0	0	0-0	4.1	6	4	1	0	6-0	4	8.31	46	.316	.480	0	ø	0	—	-2	0	-0.1

YEAR	TM LG	W	L	PCT	G	GS	CG-SHO	SV-BS	IP	H	R	HR	HB	BB-IB	SO	ERA	AERA	OAV	OOB	AB-HR-SH	AVG	PB	SUP	APR	DL	PW
SEGUI, DIEGO	Diego Pablo (Gonzalez); B8.17.1937 Holguin, Cuba; BR/TR/6´0˝/(180–190); d4.12; s–David																									
1962	KC A	8	5	.615	37	13	2	6	116.2	89	53	16	1	46-2	71	3.86	109	.211	.288	34-1-1	.235	2	106	5	0	0.8
1963	KC A	9	6	.600	38	23	4-1	0	167	173	84	17	2	73-7	116	3.77	103	.267	.341	55-0-4	.218	1	95	0	0	0.1
1964	KC A	8	17	.320	40	35	5-2	0	217	219	118	30	1	94-3	155	4.56	84	.260	.333	71-1-3	.155	0	89	-16	0	-1.6
1965	KC A	5	15	.250	40	25	5-1	0	163	166	102	18	2	67-3	119	4.64	75	.261	.331	47-1-4	.191	2*	94	-24	0	-2.5
1966	Was A	3	7	.300	21	13	1-1	0	72	82	42	8	0	24-1	54	5.00	69	.291	.345	18	.111	-1	61	-11	0	-1.5
1967	KC A	3	4	.429	36	3	0	1	70	62	30	4	2	31-5	52	3.09	103	.238	.323	9	.000	-1	27	-1	0	-0.2
1968	Oak A	6	5	.545	52	0	0	6	83	51	25	7	0	32-8	72	2.39	118	.173	.254	9	.111	0	—	4	0	0.6
1969	Sea A	12	6	.667	66	8	2	12-3	142.1	127	62	14	2	61-9	113	3.35	109	.238	.317	27-0-3	.148	-0	106	4	0	0.5
1970	Oak A	10	10	.500	47	19	3-2	2-0	162	130	54	9	2	68-4	95	**2.56**	**138**	.222	.303	43-0-6	.116	-2	100	17	0	1.8
1971	†Oak A	10	8	.556	26	21	5	0-0	146.1	122	59	13	4	63-4	81	3.14	106	.229	.315	47-1-1	.085	-1	107	3	0	0.1
1972	Oak A	0	1	.000	7	3	0	0-0	22.2	25	10	2	0	7-1	11	3.57	80	.287	.340	7	.143	-0	155	-2	0	-0.2
	StL N	3	1	.750	33	0	0	9-2	55.2	47	23	2	0	32-10	54	3.07	112	.229	.332	7	.143	0	—	2	0	0.2
1973	StL N	7	6	.538	65	0	0	17-6	100.1	78	35	6	0	53-12	93	2.78	132	.211	.310	10	.000	-1	—	10	0	1.5
1974	Bos A	6	8	.429	58	0	0	10-6	108	106	54	9	1	49-10	76	4.00	96	.257	.334	0	ø	0	—	-2	0	-0.4
1975	†Bos A	2	5	.286	33	1	1	6-1	71	71	41	10	0	43-3	45	4.82	84	.270	.373	0	ø	0	0	-5	0	-0.6
1977	Sea A	0	7	.000	40	7	0	2-0	110.2	108	75	20	1	43-4	91	5.69	73	.251	.319	0	ø	0	56	-18	0	-1.1
Total	15	92	111	.453	639	171	28-7	71-18	1807.2	1656	867	185	18	786-86	1298	3.81	96	.243	.322	384-4-22	.151	-1	92	-34	0	-2.5
SEGURA, JOSE	Jose Altagracia (Mota); B1.26.1963 Fundacion, D.R.; BR/TR/5´11˝/180; d4.10																									
1988	Chi A	0	0	ø	4	0	0	0-0	8.2	19	17	1	0	8-0	2	13.50	30	.432	.519	0	ø	0	—	-10	0	-0.5
1989	Chi A	0	1	.000	7	0	0	0-1	6	13	11	2	0	3-1	4	15.00	26	.464	.500	0	ø	0	—	-7	0	-1.0
1991	SF N	0	1	.000	11	0	0	0-1	16.1	20	11	1	0	5-0	10	4.41	82	.303	.352	0	ø	0	—	-3	0	-0.2
Total	3	0	2	.000	22	0	0	0-2	31	52	39	4	0	16-1	16	9.00	42	.377	.439	0	ø	0	—	-20	0	-1.7
SEIBEL, PHIL	Philip Matthew; B1.28.1979 Louisville KY; BL/TL/6´1˝/195; [MonN00 8/225]; d4.15; Col Texas																									
2004	Bos A	0	0	ø	2	0	0	0-0	3.2	0	0	0	1	5-0	1	0.00	ø	.000	.333	0	ø	0	—	2	0	0.1
SEIBOLD, SOCKS	Harry; B5.31.1896 Philadelphia PA; D9.21.1965 Philadelphia PA; BR/TR/5´8.5˝/162; d9.18.1915; Mil 1918; ▲																									
1916	Phi A	1	1	.500	3	2	1-1	0	21.2	22	12	0	0	9	5	4.15	69	.272	.344	12	.167	-0*	106	-3	—	-0.2
1917	Phi A	4	16	.200	33	15	9-1	1	160	141	86	1	3	85	55	3.94	70	.243	.343	59-0-5	.220	2*	84	-16	—	-1.9
1919	Phi A	2	3	.400	14	4	1	0	45.2	58	34	2	4	26	19	5.32	64	.322	.419	13-0-2	.154	-1*	34	-9	—	-1.0
1929	Bos N	12	17	.414	33	27	16-1	1	205.2	228	119	17	2	80	54	4.73	99	.285	.352	70-0-2	.286	4	84	0	—	0.5
1930	Bos N	15	16	.484	36	33	20-1	2	251	288	135	16	2	85	70	4.12	120	.290	.348	90-1-1	.211	0	73	20	—	2.0
1931	Bos N	10	18	.357	33	29	10-3	0	206.1	226	122	12	3	65	50	4.67	81	.279	.335	70-0-6	.129	-4	73	-21	—	-2.8
1932	Bos N	3	10	.231	28	20	6-1	0	136.2	173	91	12	2	41	33	4.68	80	.309	.358	46-0-2	.152	-2	103	-17	—	-1.5
1933	Bos N	1	4	.200	11	5	1	1	36.2	43	18	0	0	14	10	3.68	83	.295	.356	9	.111	0	87	-3	—	-0.4
Total	8	48	85	.361	191	135	64-8	5	1063.2	1179	617	60	16	405	296	4.43	91	.284	.350	369-1-18	.198	-0	81	-49	—	-5.3
SELE, AARON	Aaron Helmer; B6.25.1970 Golden Valley MN; BR/TR/6´5˝/(215–230); [BosA91 1/23]; d6.23; Col Washington St.																									
1993	Bos A	7	2	.778	18	18	0	0-0	111.2	100	42	5	7	48-2	93	2.74	169	.237	.322	0	ø	0	94	21	0	1.4
1994	Bos A	8	7	.533	22	22	2	0-0	143.1	140	68	13	9	60-2	105	3.83	132	.261	.342	0	ø	0	94	18	0	1.6
1995	Bos A	3	1	.750	6	6	0	0-0	32.1	32	14	3	3	14-0	21	3.06	159	.252	.338	0	ø	0	102	5	131	0.6
1996	Bos A	7	11	.389	29	29	1	0-0	157.1	192	110	14	8	67-2	137	5.32	96	.303	.373	0	ø	0	100	-6	18	-0.5
1997	Bos A	13	12	.520	33	33	1	0-0	177.1	196	115	25	15	80-4	122	5.38	87	.279	.361	2	.000	-0	100	-14	0	-1.6
1998	†Tex A☆	19	11	.633	33	33	3-2	0-0	212.2	239	116	14	13	84-6	167	4.23	116	.283	.354	4	.250	0	119	12	0	1.5
1999	†Tex A	18	9	.667	33	33	2-2	0-0	205	244	115	21	12	70-3	186	4.79	108	.293	.355	4-0-1	.000	-0	112	9	0	1.0
2000	†Sea A★	17	10	.630	34	34	2-2	0-0	211.2	221	110	17	5	74-7	137	4.51	107	.271	.332	3-0-1	.000	-0	125	9	0	1.0
2001	†Sea A	15	5	.750	34	33	2-1	0-0	215	216	93	25	7	51-2	114	3.60	118	.261	.306	6-0-2	.167	0	130	17	0	1.2
2002	Ana A	8	9	.471	26	26	1-1	0-0	160	190	92	21	7	49-2	82	4.89	92	.299	.351	2	.500	0	106	-6	39	-0.7
2003	Ana A	7	11	.389	25	25	0	0-0	121.2	135	82	17	12	58-1	53	5.77	76	.284	.372	3	.333	0	99	-18	40	-2.2
2004	Ana A	9	4	.692	28	24	0	0-0	132	163	84	16	5	51-2	51	5.05	89	.310	.371	1	.000	-0	118	-11	15	-1.1
2005	Sea A	6	12	.333	21	21	1-1	0-0	116	147	76	18	5	41-2	53	5.66	74	.315	.370	3-0-1	.000	-0	84	-20	0	-2.6
2006	LA N	8	6	.571	28	15	0	0-1	103.1	120	57	11	2	30-2	57	4.53	97	.290	.340	26-0-6	.192	1	130	-2	0	-0.2
Total	14	145	110	.569	370	352	15-9	0-1	2099.1	2335	1174	220	110	777-37	1378	4.59	102	.283	.349	54-0-11	.167	1	109	14	243	-0.6
SELL, EPP	Lester Elwood; B4.26.1897 Llewellyn PA; D2.19.1961 Reading PA; BR/TR/6´0˝/175; d9.1																									
1922	StL N	4	2	.667	7	5	0	0	33	47	26	2	2	6	5	6.82	57	.338	.374	12-0-2	.333	1	139	-10	—	-1.2
1923	StL N	0	1	.000	5	1	0	0	15	16	10	1	0	8	2	6.00	65	.291	.381	7	.000	-1	189	-3	—	-0.3
Total	2	4	3	.571	12	6	0	0	48	63	36	3	2	14	7	6.56	59	.325	.376	19-0-2	.211	0	147	-13	—	-1.5
SELLERS, JEFF	Jeffrey Doyle; B5.11.1964 Compton CA; BR/TR/6´1˝/(175–195); [BosA82 8/202]; d9.15																									
1985	Bos A	2	0	1.000	4	4	1	0-0	22.1	24	10	1	0	7-1	6	3.63	119	.273	.323	0	ø	0	121	2	0	0.1
1986	Bos A	3	7	.300	14	13	1	0-0	82	90	56	13	3	40-1	51	4.94	85	.282	.365	0	ø	0	90	-9	0	-1.0
1987	Bos A	7	8	.467	25	22	4-2	0-0	139.2	161	85	10	3	61-0	99	5.28	87	.298	.368	0	ø	0	100	-9	0	-0.8
1988	Bos A	1	7	.125	18	12	1	0-0	85.2	89	49	9	3	56-3	70	4.83	85	.268	.379	0	ø	0	68	-6	63	-0.5
Total	4	13	22	.371	61	51	7-2	0-0	329.2	364	200	33	9	164-5	226	4.97	88	.285	.367	0	ø	0	92	-22	63	-2.2
SELLMAN, FRANK	Charles Francis (aka Frank C. Williams 1871-75); B1852 Baltimore MD; D5.6.1907 Baltimore MD; d5.4.1871; ▲																									
1873	Mar NA	0	1	.000	1	1	1	0	9	21	26	0	—	0	0	8.00	42	.350	.350	3	.333	0	55	-5	—	-0.3
SELLS, DAVE	David Wayne; B9.18.1946 Vacaville CA; BR/TR/5´11˝/(170–175); d8.2; Col Solano (CA) CC																									
1972	Cal A	2	0	1.000	10	0	0	0-0	16	11	6	0	0	5-1	2	2.81	104	.196	.258	0	ø	0	—	0	0	0.0
1973	Cal A	7	2	.778	51	0	0	10-3	68	72	30	2	5	35-6	25	3.71	97	.277	.368	0	ø	0	—	0	0	0.0
1974	Cal A	2	3	.400	20	0	0	2-0	39	48	19	3	3	16-0	14	3.69	94	.312	.383	0	ø	0	—	-1	0	-0.1
1975	Cal A	0	0	ø	4	0	0	0-1	8.1	9	10	3	0	8-1	7	8.64	41	.250	.386	0	ø	0	—	-5	0	-0.3
	LA N	0	2	.000	5	0	0	0-1	7	6	3	2	0	3-0	1	3.86	89	.222	.300	1	1.000	1	—	0	0	0.0
Total	4	11	7	.611	90	0	0	12-5	138.1	146	68	10	8	67-8	49	3.90	89	.274	.359	1	1.000	1	—	-6	0	-0.4
SELMA, DICK	Richard Jay; B11.4.1943 Santa Ana CA; D8.29.2001 Clovis CA; BR/TR (BB 1966p)/5´11˝/(162–185); d9.2; Col Fresno (CA) City																									
1965	NY N	2	1	.667	4	4	1-1	0	26.2	22	11	2	1	9-0	26	3.71	95	.229	.302	9	.222	0*	105	0	0	0.1
1966	NY N	4	6	.400	30	7	0	1	80.2	84	47	11	3	39-5	58	4.24	86	.274	.358	14-0-1	.071	0*	80	-7	0	-0.7
1967	NY N	2	4	.333	38	4	0	2	81.1	71	29	3	2	36-6	52	2.77	122	.241	.326	22-0-1	.091	-1*	91	5	0	0.3
1968	NY N	9	10	.474	33	23	4-3	0	170.1	148	63	11	5	54-5	117	2.75	110	.233	.297	58-0-4	.207	2*	102	3	0	0.6
1969	SD N	2	2	.500	4	3	1	0-0	22	19	10	3	0	9-0	20	4.09	87	.229	.304	7-0-1	.286	0	50	-1	0	-0.1
	Chi N	10	8	.556	36	25	4-2	1-1	168.2	137	74	13	3	72-7	161	3.63	111	.222	.305	52-0-7	.154	-0	127	8	0	0.7
	Year	12	10	.545	40	28	5-2	1-1	190.2	156	84	16	3	81-7	181	3.68	108	.223	.305	59-0-8	.169	-0	120	7	0	0.6
1970	Phi N	8	9	.471	73	0	0	22-11	134.1	108	42	8	4	59-9	153	2.75	147	.226	.315	20-0-1	.150	0	—	**20**	0	3.2
1971	Phi N	0	2	.000	17	0	0	1-0	24.2	21	9	2	2	8-0	15	3.28	108	.231	.307	1	1.000	0*	—	1	79	0.2
1972	Phi N	2	9	.182	46	10	1	3-0	98.2	91	67	13	5	73-9	58	5.56	65	.249	.375	20-0-1	.200	1*	59	-20	0	-2.2
1973	Phi N	1	1	.500	6	0	0	0-0	8	6	5	1	0	5-1	4	5.63	68	.240	.355	0	ø	0	—	-1	0	-0.2
1974	Cal A	2	2	.500	18	0	0	1-3	23	22	13	2	1	17-2	15	5.09	68	.272	.404	0	ø	0	—	-3	0	-0.5
	Mil A	0	0	ø	2	0	0	0-0	2.1	5	5	0	1	0-0	2	19.29	19	.455	.462	0	ø	0	—	-4	0	-0.2
	Year	2	2	.500	20	0	0	1-3	25.1	27	18	2	2	17-2	17	6.39	55	.293	.411	0	ø	0	—	-8	0	-0.7
Total	10	42	54	.438	307	76	11-6	31-15	840.2	734	375	69	27	381-44	681	3.62	100	.238	.325	203-0-16	.172	2	100	1	79	1.2
SEMBERA, CARROLL	Carroll William; B7.26.1941 Shiner TX; D6.15.2005 Shiner TX; BR/TR/6´0˝/155; d9.28; Col Trinity (TX)																									
1965	Hou N	0	1	.000	2	1	0	0	7.1	5	3	0	0	3-0	4	3.68	91	.185	.267	1-0-1	.000	-0	52	0	0	0.0
1966	Hou N	1	2	.333	24	0	0	1	33	36	11	3	0	16-0	21	3.00	114	.288	.366	3	.000	-0	—	2	0	0.2
1967	Hou N	2	6	.250	45	0	0	3	59.2	66	39	7	1	19-4	48	4.83	69	.269	.323	7-0-1	.143	-0	—	-11	24	-1.5
1969	Mon N	0	2	.000	23	0	0	2-1	33	28	14	1	2	24-4	15	3.55	104	.246	.383	4	.250	0	—	1	0	0.1
1970	Mon N	0	0	ø	5	0	0	0-0	6.2	14	14	2	1	11-3	6	18.90	22	.424	.578	0	ø	0	—	-10	0	-0.5
Total	5	3	11	.214	99	1	0	6-1	139.2	149	81	13	4	73-11	94	4.70	74	.274	.362	15-0-2	.133	-0	52	-18	24	-1.7

YEAR	TM LG	W	L	PCT	G	GS	CG-SHO	SV-BS	IP	H	R	HR	HB	BB-IB	SO	ERA	AERA	OAV	OOB	AB-HR-SH	AVG	PB	SUP	APR	DL	PW
Seminara, Frank	Frank Peter; B5.16.1967 Brooklyn NY; BR/TR/6´2˝/(195–205); [NYA88 12/313]; d6.2; Col Columbia																									
1992	SD N	9	4	.692	19	18	0	0-0	100.1	98	46	5	3	46-3	61	3.68	98	.257	.340	34-0-2	.118	-1	127	-1	0	-0.2
1993	SD N	3	3	.500	18	7	0	0-1	46.1	53	30	5	3	21-3	22	4.47	93	.294	.374	10-0-1	.200	0	112	-3	0	-0.4
1994	NY N	0	2	.000	10	1	0	0-0	17	20	12	2	0	8-0	7	5.82	72	.303	.373	3	.000	-0	109	-3	0	-0.4
Total	3	12	9	.571	47	26	0	0-1	163.2	171	88	12	6	75-6	90	4.12	92	.273	.353	47-0-3	.128	-1	121	-7	0	-1.0
Semproch, Ray	Roman Anthony "Baby"; B1.7.1931 Cleveland OH; BR/TR/5´11˝/(168–180); d4.15																									
1958	Phi N	13	11	.542	36	30	12-2	0	204.1	211	105	25	6	58-1	92	3.92	101	.264	.318	74-0-2	.095	-5	116	-1	0	-0.6
1959	Phi N	3	10	.231	30	18	2	3	111.2	119	76	12	3	59-1	54	5.40	76	.277	.366	34-0-2	.176	-0	79	-16	0	-1.7
1960	Det A	3	0	1.000	17	0	0	0	27	29	17	2	0	16-0	9	4.00	99	.269	.363	4-0-1	.000	-0	—	-2	0	-0.1
1961	LA A	0	0	ø	2	0	0	0	1	1	2	0	0	3-0	1	9.00	50	.333	.571	0	ø	0	—	-1	0	0.0
Total	4	19	21	.475	85	48	14-2	3	344	360	200	39	9	136-2	156	4.42	91	.269	.338	112-0-5	.116	-5	101	-20	0	-2.4
Senteney, Steve	Stephen Leonard; B8.7.1955 Indianapolis IN; D6.18.1989 Colusa CA; BR/TR/6´2˝/205; d6.6; Col St. Marys (CA)																									
1982	Tor A	0	0	ø	11	0	0	0-0	22	23	16	5	0	6-1	20	4.91	92	.247	.290	0	ø	0	—	-2	0	-0.1
Seo, Jae	Jae Weong; B5.24.1977 Kwangju, South Korea; BR/TR/6´1˝/(215–230); d7.21																									
2002	NY N	0	0	ø	1	0	0	0-0	1	0	0	0	0	0-0	1	0.00	ø	.000	.000	0	ø	0	—	0	0	0.0
2003	NY N	9	12	.429	32	31	0	0-0	188.1	193	94	18	6	46-11	110	3.82	110	.260	.307	51-0-4	.098	-1*	94	4	0	0.3
2004	NY N	5	10	.333	24	21	0	0-0	117.2	133	67	17	2	50-7	54	4.90	88	.299	.370	32-0-3	.156	1*	89	-6	0	-0.6
2005	NY N	8	2	.800	14	14	1	0-0	90.1	84	26	9	1	16-0	59	2.59	160	.251	.285	29-0-2	.103	-0	121	17	0	1.8
2006	LA N	2	4	.333	19	10	0	0-0	67	75	45	14	1	25-1	49	5.78	76	.284	.345	18-0-1	.111	-0	109	-10	0	-0.8
	TB A	1	8	.111	17	16	0	0-0	90	122	56	17	3	31-3	39	5.00	93	.331	.382	1-0-1	.000	-0	68	-4	15	-0.4
Total	5	25	36	.410	107	92	1	0-0	554.1	607	288	75	13	168-22	312	4.27	101	.281	.334	131-0-11	.115	-1	94	1	15	0.3
Seoane, Manny	Manuel Modesto; B6.26.1955 Tampa FL; BR/TR/6´3˝/(185–190); [PhiN73 6/122]; d9.18																									
1977	Phi N	0	0	ø	2	1	0	0-0	6	11	4	0	0	3-0	4	6.00	67	.407	.467	2	.500	0	110	-1	0	0.0
1978	Chi N	1	0	1.000	7	1	0	0-0	8.1	11	6	0	0	6-2	5	5.40	75	.297	.395	0	ø	0	89	-1	0	-0.2
Total	2	1	0	1.000	9	2	0	0-0	14.1	22	10	0	0	9-2	9	5.65	72	.344	.425	2	.500	0	99	-2	0	-0.2
Serad, Billy	William I.; B1863 Philadelphia PA; D11.1.1925 Chester PA; BR/TR/5´7˝/156; d5.5																									
1884	Buf N	16	20	.444	37	37	34-2	0	308	373	285	21	—	111	150	4.27	74	.281	.336	137	.175	-7	105	-38	—	-4.0
1885	Buf N	7	21	.250	30	29	27	0	241.1	299	194	5	—	80	90	4.10	73	.293	.344	104	.154	-6	72	-31	—	-3.5
1887	Cin AA	10	11	.476	22	21	20-2	1	187.1	201	139	7	8	80	34	4.08	106	.266	.343	79	.177	-4	89	4	—	-0.1
1888	Cin AA	2	3	.400	6	5	5	0	50.2	62	43	1	6	19	4	3.55	89	.291	.366	23	.130	-1	110	-5	—	-0.5
Total	4	35	55	.389	95	92	86-4	1	787.1	935	661	34	14	290	278	4.13	82	.282	.342	343	.166	-17	92	-70	—	-8.1
Serafini, Dan	Daniel Joseph; B1.25.1974 San Francisco CA; BB/TL/6´1˝/(180–195); [MinA92 1/26]; d6.25																									
1996	Min A	0	1	.000	1	1	0	0-0	4.1	7	5	1	1	2-0	1	10.38	49	.368	.435	0	ø	0	36	-2	0	-0.4
1997	Min A	2	1	.667	6	4	1	0-0	26.1	27	11	1	0	11-0	15	3.42	137	.273	.345	0	ø	0	138	3	0	0.3
1998	Min A	7	4	.636	28	9	0	0-0	75	95	58	10	1	29-1	46	6.48	74	.310	.365	1	.000	-0	103	-14	0	-1.7
1999	Chi N	3	2	.600	42	4	0	1-0	62.1	86	51	9	1	32-3	17	6.93	66	.333	.405	12-0-1	.083	0	136	-16	0	-1.1
2000	SD N	0	0	ø	3	0	0	0-0	3	9	6	2	0	2-0	3	18.00	25	.500	.550	0	ø	0	—	-4	0	-0.2
	Pit N	2	5	.286	11	11	0	0-0	62.1	70	35	9	4	26-1	32	4.91	95	.292	.368	24-0-3	.083	-2	95	-1	0	-0.2
	Year	2	5	.286	14	11	0	0-0	65.1	79	41	11	4	28-1	35	5.51	84	.306	.380	24-0-3	.083	-2	96	-6	0	-0.4
2003	Cin N	1	3	.250	10	4	0	0-0	30	41	23	5	0	14-1	13	5.40	77	.336	.399	6-0-1	.000	-1*	56	-6	0	-0.7
Total	6	15	16	.484	101	33	1	1-0	263.1	335	189	37	7	116-6	127	5.98	77	.315	.382	43-0-5	.070	-2	102	-40	0	-4.0
Serrano, Jimmy	James; B5.9.1976 Grand Junction CO; BR/TR/5´10˝/170; [MonN98 18/534]; d8.7; Col New Mexico																									
2004	KC A	1	2	.333	10	5	0	0-0	32.2	35	17	5	1	12-0	25	4.68	100	.280	.340	0	ø	0	71	1	0	0.1
Serrano, Wascar	Wascar Radames; B6.2.1978 Santo Domingo, D.R.; BR/TR/6´2˝/178; d5.12																									
2001	SD N	3	3	.500	20	5	0	0-0	46.2	60	37	7	2	21-1	39	6.56	63	.313	.382	9-0-2	.111	-0	147	-13	0	-1.4
Serum, Gary	Gary Wayne; B10.24.1956 Fargo ND; BR/TR/6´1˝/(160–175); d7.22; Col St. Cloud St.																									
1977	Min A	0	0	ø	8	0	0	0-0	22.2	22	11	4	2	10-1	14	4.37	91	.268	.362	0	ø	0	—	0	0	0.0
1978	Min A	9	9	.500	34	23	6-1	1-0	184.1	188	88	14	3	44-2	80	4.10	94	.266	.308	0	ø	0	107	-2	0	-0.2
1979	Min A	1	3	.250	20	5	0	0-0	64	93	47	10	0	20-2	31	6.61	67	.354	.398	0	ø	0	103	-13	0	-0.7
Total	3	10	12	.455	62	28	6-1	1-0	271	303	146	28	5	74-5	125	4.72	84	.288	.335	0	ø	0	105	-15	0	-0.9
Service, Scott	Scott David; B2.26.1967 Cincinnati OH; BR/TR/6´6˝/(225–250); d9.5																									
1988	Phi N	0	0	ø	5	0	0	0-0	5.1	7	1	0	1	1-0	6	1.69	214	.333	.391	0	ø	0	—	1	0	0.1
1992	Mon N	0	0	ø	5	0	0	0-0	7	15	11	1	0	5-0	11	14.14	25	.417	.488	2	.000	-0	—	-8	0	-0.4
1993	Col.N	0	0	ø	3	0	0	0-0	4.2	8	5	1	1	1-0	3	9.64	50	.400	.417	0	ø	0	—	-2	0	-0.1
	Cin N	2	2	.500	26	0	0	2-0	41.1	36	19	5	1	15-4	40	3.70	109	.235	.304	7	.143	-0*	—	1	0	0.1
	Year	2	2	.500	29	0	0	2-0	46	44	24	6	2	16-4	43	4.30	95	.254	.318	7	.143	-0	—	-1	0	0.0
1994	Cin N	1	2	.333	6	0	0	0-0	7.1	8	9	2	0	3-0	5	7.36	57	.267	.333	0	ø	0	—	-4	0	-0.7
1995	SF N	3	1	.750	28	0	0	0-0	31	18	11	4	2	20-4	30	3.19	129	.176	.317	1	.000	-0	—	4	0	0.4
1996	Cin N	1	0	1.000	34	1	0	0-0	48	51	21	7	6	18-4	46	3.94	109	.277	.359	5	.000	-1	105	3	0	0.1
1997	Cin N	0	0	ø	4	0	0	0-0	5.1	11	7	1	0	1-0	3	11.81	36	.458	.480	0	ø	0	—	-4	0	-0.2
	KC A	0	3	.000	12	0	0	0-1	17	17	9	1	0	5-0	19	4.76	100	.274	.324	0	ø	0	—	0	0	0.0
1998	KC A	6	4	.600	73	0	0	4-4	82.2	70	35	7	9	34-4	95	3.48	140	.231	.322	1	.000	-0	—	12	0	1.4
1999	KC A	5	5	.500	68	0	0	8-7	75.1	87	51	13	3	42-8	68	6.09	83	.294	.379	0	ø	0	—	-6	0	-0.8
2000	Oak A	1	2	.333	20	0	0	1-0	36.2	45	31	5	1	19-1	35	6.38	76	.302	.380	0	ø	0	—	-7	0	-0.5
2003	Ari N	0	2	.000	18	0	0	1-0	18.1	21	10	1	0	2-1	18	4.91	94	.288	.303	0	ø	0	—	0	0	0.0
	Tor A	0	0	ø	15	0	0	0-1	16	17	8	3	0	6-0	17	4.50	105	.274	.333	0	ø	0*	—	1	0	0.0
2004	Ari N	1	1	.500	21	0	0	0-2	20.1	24	17	5	2	10-2	17	7.08	64	.286	.371	1	.000	-0	—	-5	63	-0.4
Total	12	20	22	.476	338	1	0	16-15	416.1	435	245	56	26	182-28	413	4.99	92	.272	.351	17	.059	-1	105	-14	63	-1.0
Settlemire, Merle	Edgar Merle "Lefty"; B1.19.1903 Santa Fe OH; D6.12.1988 Russells Point OH; BL/TL/5´9˝/156; d4.13																									
1928	Bos A	0	6	.000	30	9	0	0	82.1	116	62	2	6	34	12	5.47	75	.345	.415	17-0-3	.176	-1*	78	-14	—	-0.8
Severinsen, Al	Albert Henry; B11.9.1944 Brooklyn NY; BR/TR/6´3˝/(205–227); d7.1; Col Wagner																									
1969	Bal A	1	1	.500	12	0	0	0-0	19.2	14	6	2	0	10-2	13	2.29	157	.206	.304	3-0-1	.333	0	—	3	0	0.3
1971	SD N	2	5	.286	59	0	0	8-6	70	77	30	4	2	30-10	31	3.47	96	.292	.365	1-0-1	.000	-0	—	0	0	0.0
1972	SD N	0	1	.000	17	0	0	1-0	21.1	13	8	1	2	7-1	9	2.53	131	.173	.259	1	.000	-0	—	1	0	0.1
Total	3	3	7	.300	88	0	0	9-6	111	104	44	7	4	47-13	53	3.08	109	.256	.335	5-0-2	.200	0	—	4	0	0.4
Seward, Ed	Edward William (b Edward William Sourhardt); B6.29.1867 Cleveland OH; D7.30.1947 Cleveland OH; TR/5´7˝/175; d9.30; U1																									
1885	Pro N	0	0	ø	1	0	0	0	6	2	0	0	—	0	1	0.00	ø	.100	.100	3	.000	-0	—	2	—	0.1
1887	Phi AA	25	25	.500	55	52	52-3	0	470.2	445	293	7	24	140	155	4.13	104	.244	.306	266-5	.188	-4*	88	16	—	0.8
1888	Phi AA	35	19	.648	57	57	57-**6**	0	518.2	388	203	4	22	127	**272**	2.01	149	.200	.258	225-2	.142	-4*	107	60	—	5.1
1889	Phi AA	21	15	.583	39	38	35-3	0	320	353	212	8	13	101	102	3.97	95	.271	.330	143-2	.217	6*	109	1	—	0.5
1890	Phi AA	6	12	.333	21	19	15-1	0	154	165	105	4	7	72	55	4.73	82	.266	.349	72	.139	-1*	101	-11	—	-1.1
1891	Cle N	2	1	.667	3	3	0	0	16.1	16	10	0	0	11	4	3.86	90	.246	.355	19	.211	0*	80	0	—	0.0
Total	6	89	72	.553	176	169	159-13	0	1485.2	1369	823	23	66	451	589	3.40	108	.237	.300	728-9	.174	-4	100	68	—	5.4
Seward, Frank	Frank Martin; B4.7.1921 Pennsauken NJ; D4.12.2004 Elmira NY; BR/TR/6´3˝/200; d9.28; Col Duke																									
1943	NY N	0	1	.000	1	1	1	0	9	12	3	0	0	5	2	3.00	115	.324	.405	4	.000	-1	49	1	0	0.0
1944	NY N	3	2	.600	25	7	2	0	78.1	98	51	8	2	32	16	5.40	68	.306	.373	24-0-1	.083	-2	128	-13	0	-1.0
Total	2	3	3	.500	26	8	3	0	87.1	110	54	8	2	37	18	5.15	71	.308	.376	28-0-1	.071	-2	118	-12	0	-1.0
Sewell, Rip	Truett Banks; B5.11.1907 Decatur AL; D9.3.1989 Plant City FL; BL/TR/6´1˝/180; d6.14; C1; Col Vanderbilt																									
1932	Det A	0	0	ø	5	0	0	0	10.2	19	15	2	0	8	2	12.66	37	.388	.474	2	.500	0	—	-8	—	-0.3
1938	Pit N	0	1	.000	17	0	0	1	38.1	41	27	3	2	21	17	4.23	90	.275	.372	12	.083	-1	—	-4	—	-0.3
1939	Pit N	10	9	.526	52	12	5-1	2	176.1	177	93	10	1	73	69	4.08	94	.265	.339	55-1-4	.200	1	110	-5	—	-0.3

THE PITCHER REGISTER

YEAR	TM LG	W	L	PCT	G	GS	CG-SHO	SV-BS	IP	H	R	HR	HB	BB-IB	SO	ERA	AERA	OAV	OOB	AB-HR-SH	AVG	PB	SUP	APR	DL	PW
1940	Pit N	16	5	.762	33	23	14-2	1	189.2	169	71	6	3	67	60	2.80	136	.238	.307	73-1-1	.192	2*	144	20	—	2.5
1941	Pit N	14	17	.452	39	32	18-2	2	249	225	126	18	3	84	76	3.72	97	.235	.299	92-1-4	.174	0*	109	-4	0	-0.3
1942	Pit N	17	15	.531	40	33	18-5	2	248	259	117	13	2	72	69	3.41	99	.265	.317	87-0-1	.149	-2*	102	-4	0	-0.6
1943	Pit N★	**21**	9	.700	35	31	**25**-2	3	265.1	267	94	6	2	75	65	2.54	137	.260	.312	105-0-1	.286	6*	121	27	0	**3.9**
1944	Pit N★	21	12	.636	38	33	24-3	2	286	263	112	15	3	99	87	3.18	117	.240	.304	112-1-2	.223	3*	109	21	0	2.6
1945	Pit N✳	11	9	.550	33	24	9-1	1	188	212	116	9	2	91	60	4.07	97	.279	.357	64-0-1	.313	6*	125	-9	0	-0.3
1946	Pit N★	8	12	.400	25	20	11-2	0	149.1	140	68	6	1	53	33	3.68	96	.245	.310	50-0-2	.180	0*	104	-1	0	-0.1
1947	Pit N	6	4	.600	24	12	4-1	0	121	121	58	11	3	36	36	3.57	118	.263	.321	40-1-0	.125	-1	94	7	0	0.5
1948	Pit N	13	3	.813	21	17	7	0	121.2	126	51	9	1	37	36	3.48	117	.262	.317	42-1-1	.143	1	105	8	0	1.1
1949	Pit N	6	1	.857	28	6	2-1	1	76	82	35	8	0	32	26	3.91	108	.280	.351	16-0-2	.063	-0	84	3	0	0.2
Total	13	143	97	.596	390	243	137-20	15	2119.1	2101	983	116	23	748	636	3.48	107	.256	.320	750-6-19	.203	16	112	51	0	8.6

SEXAUER, ELMER Elmer George; B5.21.1926 St.Louis Co. MO; BR/TR/6´4˝/220; d9.6; Col Wake Forest; [DL 1949 Phi N 77]

YEAR	TM LG	W	L	PCT	G	GS	CG-SHO	SV-BS	IP	H	R	HR	HB	BB-IB	SO	ERA	AERA	OAV	OOB	AB-HR-SH	AVG	PB	SUP	APR	DL	PW
1948	Bro N	0	0	ø	2	0	0	0	0.2	0	1	0	0	2	0	13.50	30	.000	.500	0	ø	0	—	-1	0	0.0

SEXTON, FRANK Frank Joseph; B7.8.1872 Brockton MA; D1.4.1938 Brighton MA; ?/160; d6.21; Col Michigan

YEAR	TM LG	W	L	PCT	G	GS	CG-SHO	SV-BS	IP	H	R	HR	HB	BB-IB	SO	ERA	AERA	OAV	OOB	AB-HR-SH	AVG	PB	SUP	APR	DL	PW
1895	Bos N	1	5	.167	7	5	4	0	49	59	39	2	2	22	14	5.69	89	.294	.369	26-0-1	.269	-1*	45	-1	—	-0.2

SEYFRIED, GORDON Gordon Clay; B7.4.1937 Long Beach CA; BR/TR/6´0˝/185; d9.13; Col Long Beach (CA) City

YEAR	TM LG	W	L	PCT	G	GS	CG-SHO	SV-BS	IP	H	R	HR	HB	BB-IB	SO	ERA	AERA	OAV	OOB	AB-HR-SH	AVG	PB	SUP	APR	DL	PW
1963	Cle A	0	1	.000	3	1	0	0	7.1	9	2	0	0	3-1	1	1.23	295	.300	.364	2	.000	-0	25	2	0	0.2
1964	Cle A	0	0	ø	2	0	0	0	2.1	4	0	0	0	0-0	0	0.00	ø	.444	.400	0	ø	0	—	1	0	0.0
Total	2	0	1	.000	5	1	0	0	9.2	13	2	0	0	3-1	1	0.93	388	.333	.372	2	.000	-0	25	3	0	0.2

SEYMOUR, JAKE Jacob (b Jacob Semer); B1854 Pittsburgh PA; D8.1.1897 Allegheny (now part of Pittsburgh) PA; d9.23

YEAR	TM LG	W	L	PCT	G	GS	CG-SHO	SV-BS	IP	H	R	HR	HB	BB-IB	SO	ERA	AERA	OAV	OOB	AB-HR-SH	AVG	PB	SUP	APR	DL	PW
1882	Pit AA	0	1	.000	1	1	1	0	8	16	13	0	—	2	2	7.88	33	.390	.419	4	.000	-1	59	-5	—	-0.4

SEYMOUR, CY James Bentley; B12.9.1872 Albany NY; D9.20.1919 New York NY; BL/TL/6´0˝/200; d4.22; ▲

YEAR	TM LG	W	L	PCT	G	GS	CG-SHO	SV-BS	IP	H	R	HR	HB	BB-IB	SO	ERA	AERA	OAV	OOB	AB-HR-SH	AVG	PB	SUP	APR	DL	PW
1896	NY N	2	4	.333	11	8	4	0	70.1	75	75	8	3	51	33	6.40	66	.271	.390	32	.219	-1*	135	-19	—	-1.3
1897	NY N	18	14	.563	39	34	29-2	1	286.2	257	162	4	22	168	**156**	3.27	127	**.238**	.352	141-2-1	.241	1*	101	28	—	2.9
1898	NY N	25	19	.568	45	43	39-4	0	356.2	313	199	4	32	213	**239**	3.18	109	.234	.353	297-4-2	.276	7*	113	11	—	2.1
1899	NY N	14	18	.438	32	32	31	0	268.1	247	139	5	20	170	142	3.56	106	.245	.364	159-2-5	.327	8*	100	10	—	2.0
1900	NY N	2	1	.667	13	7	2	0	53	58	54	4	10	54	19	6.96	52	.278	.447	40	.300	1*	150	-17	—	-0.6
1902	Cin N	0	0	ø	1	0	0	0	3	4	3	0	0	3	2	9.00	33	.308	.438	244-2-3	.340	0*	—	-1	—	-0.1
Total	6	61	56	.521	141	124	105-6	1	1038	954	632	25	87	659	591	3.73	102	.243	.364	913-10-11	.296	16	110	12	—	5.0

SHACKELFORD, BRIAN Brian Wesley; B8.30.1976 McAlester OK; BL/TL/6´1˝/195; [KCA98 13/377]; d6.26; Col Oklahoma

YEAR	TM LG	W	L	PCT	G	GS	CG-SHO	SV-BS	IP	H	R	HR	HB	BB-IB	SO	ERA	AERA	OAV	OOB	AB-HR-SH	AVG	PB	SUP	APR	DL	PW
2005	Cin N	1	0	1.000	37	0	0	0-0	29.2	21	9	2	6	9-1	17	2.43	176	.204	.303	1	.000	-0	—	6	0	0.3
2006	Cin N	1	0	1.000	26	0	0	0-0	16.1	18	13	4	2	10-0	15	7.16	66	.269	.380	0	ø	0	—	-4	0	-0.2
Total	2	2	0	1.000	63	0	0	0-0	46	39	22	6	8	19-1	32	4.11	108	.229	.333	1	.000	-0	—	2	0	0.1

SHAFFER, JOHN John W. "Cannon Ball"; B2.18.1864 Lock Haven PA; D11.21.1926 Endicott NY; TR/5´10˝/?; d9.13

YEAR	TM LG	W	L	PCT	G	GS	CG-SHO	SV-BS	IP	H	R	HR	HB	BB-IB	SO	ERA	AERA	OAV	OOB	AB-HR-SH	AVG	PB	SUP	APR	DL	PW
1886	NY AA	5	3	.625	8	8	8-1	0	69	40	29	0	1	29	36	1.96	167	.164	.255	25	.240	1	93	9	—	1.0
1887	NY AA	2	11	.154	13	13	13	0	112	148	119	3	11	53	22	6.19	69	.310	.391	48	.167	-3	78	-24	—	-2.0
Total	2	7	14	.333	21	21	21-1	0	181	188	148	3	12	82	58	4.57	84	.260	.346	73	.192	-2	83	-15	—	-1.0

SHALLIX, GUS August (b August Schallick); B3.29.1858 Paderborn, Prussia (now Germany); D10.28.1937 Cincinnati OH; BR/TR/5´11˝/165; d6.22

YEAR	TM LG	W	L	PCT	G	GS	CG-SHO	SV-BS	IP	H	R	HR	HB	BB-IB	SO	ERA	AERA	OAV	OOB	AB-HR-SH	AVG	PB	SUP	APR	DL	PW
1884	Cin AA	11	10	.524	23	23	23	0	199.2	163	113	6	26	53	78	3.70	90	.212	.286	84	.036	-10	110	-7	—	-1.5
1885	Cin AA	6	4	.600	13	12	7	0	91.1	95	59	1	13	33	15	3.25	100	.265	.349	39	.128	-2	113	-2	—	-0.3
Total	2	17	14	.548	36	35	30	0	291	258	172	7	39	86	93	3.56	93	.229	.306	123	.065	-12	111	-9	—	-1.8

SHANAHAN, GREG Paul Gregory; B12.11.1947 Eureka CA; BR/TR/6´2˝/190; d9.4; Col Humboldt St.

YEAR	TM LG	W	L	PCT	G	GS	CG-SHO	SV-BS	IP	H	R	HR	HB	BB-IB	SO	ERA	AERA	OAV	OOB	AB-HR-SH	AVG	PB	SUP	APR	DL	PW
1973	LA N	0	0	ø	7	0	0	1-0	15.2	14	6	2	0	4-0	11	3.45	101	.230	.277	1	.000	0	—	0	0	0.0
1974	LA N	0	0	ø	4	0	0	0-0	7	7	3	1	0	5-0	2	3.86	89	.259	.364	0	ø	0	—	0	0	0.0
Total	2	0	0	ø	11	0	0	1-0	22.2	21	9	3	0	9-0	13	3.57	97	.239	.306	1	.000	0	—	0	0	0.0

SHANK, HARVEY Harvey Tillman; B7.29.1946 Toronto ON, Can.; BR/TR/6´4˝/220; [AnaA68 10/216]; d5.16; Col Stanford

YEAR	TM LG	W	L	PCT	G	GS	CG-SHO	SV-BS	IP	H	R	HR	HB	BB-IB	SO	ERA	AERA	OAV	OOB	AB-HR-SH	AVG	PB	SUP	APR	DL	PW
1970	Cal A	0	0	ø	1	0	0	0-0	3	2	0	0	0	2-0	1	0.00	ø	.182	.308	0	ø	0	—	1	0	0.1

SHANNER, BILL Wilfred William; B11.4.1894 Oakland City IN; D12.18.1986 Evansville IN; BL/TR; d10.1

YEAR	TM LG	W	L	PCT	G	GS	CG-SHO	SV-BS	IP	H	R	HR	HB	BB-IB	SO	ERA	AERA	OAV	OOB	AB-HR-SH	AVG	PB	SUP	APR	DL	PW
1920	Phi A	0	0	ø	1	0	0	0	4	6	4	2	0	1	1	6.75	60	.353	.389	1	.000	-0	—	-1	—	-0.1

SHANTZ, BOBBY Robert Clayton; B9.26.1925 Pottstown PA; BR/TL/5´6˝/(138–154); d5.1; b–Billy

YEAR	TM LG	W	L	PCT	G	GS	CG-SHO	SV-BS	IP	H	R	HR	HB	BB-IB	SO	ERA	AERA	OAV	OOB	AB-HR-SH	AVG	PB	SUP	APR	DL	PW
1949	Phi A	6	8	.429	33	7	4-1	2	127	100	50	9	3	74	58	3.40	121	.221	.334	37-0-3	.189	1	121	12	0	1.5
1950	Phi A	8	14	.364	36	23	6-1	0	214.2	251	122	18	7	85	93	4.61	99	.294	.362	66-1-6	.167	-0*	68	-1	0	0.0
1951	Phi A☆	18	10	.643	32	25	13-3	0	205.1	213	96	15	5	70	77	3.94	108	.270	.333	72-0-8	.250	2*	107	9	0	1.5
1952	Phi A★	**24**	7	**.774**	33	33	27-5	0	279.2	230	87	21	4	63	152	2.48	160	.225	**.272**	96-0-13	.198	2*	102	**43**	0	**5.1**
1953	Phi A	5	9	.357	16	16	6	0	105.2	107	52	10	0	26	58	4.09	105	.263	.307	38-0-1	.237	1*	78	2	0	0.5
1954	Phi A	1	0	1.000	2	1	0	0	8	12	7	2	1	3	3	7.88	50	.364	.421	3	.333	0*	135	-3	95	-0.3
1955	KC A	5	10	.333	23	17	4-1	0	125	124	70	8	1	66-11	58	4.54	92	.264	.352	41-0-2	.146	-2*	86	-5	0	-0.6
1956	KC A	2	7	.222	45	2	1	9	101.1	95	51	12	3	37-4	67	4.35	99	.248	.319	22-0-2	.091	-1*	62	1	0	0.1
1957	†NY A☆	11	5	.688	30	21	9-1	5	173	157	58	15	6	40-1	72	**2.45**	**147**	.248	.296	56-0-1	.179	2*	116	21	0	2.7
1958	NY A	7	6	.538	33	13	3	0	126	127	52	8	2	35-7	80	3.36	105	.262	.312	35-0-1	.229	2	88	4	0	0.8
1959	NY A	7	3	.700	33	4	2-2	3	94.2	64	33	4	0	33-5	66	2.38	153	.189	.260	23-0-3	.217	2*	85	12	0	1.6
1960	†NY A	5	4	.556	42	0	0	11	67.2	57	24	5	2	24-4	54	2.79	128	.235	.302	10-0-2	.100	-0*	—	6	0	1.0
1961	Pit N	6	3	.667	43	6	2-1	2	89.1	91	38	5	4	26-6	61	3.32	120	.271	.328	16-0-1	.438	3*	137	6	0	1.0
1962	Hou N	1	1	.500	3	3	1	0	20.2	15	4	1	0	5-0	14	1.31	286	.208	.256	8	.000	-1*	133	6	0	0.5
	StL N	5	3	.625	28	0	0	4	57.2	45	22	7	1	20-2	47	2.18	195	.211	.282	13	.154	-0	—	10	0	1.5
	Year	6	4	.600	31	3	1	4	78.1	60	26	8	1	25-2	61	1.95	211	.211	.276	21	.095	-1	120	15	0	2.0
1963	StL N	6	4	.600	55	0	0	11	79.1	55	28	6	2	17-5	70	2.61	136	.192	.240	7-0-1	.143	0	—	7	0	1.3
1964	StL N	1	3	.250	16	0	0	0	17.1	14	6	2	0	7-3	12	3.12	122	.226	.300	0	ø	0	—	2	0	0.4
	Chi N	0	1	.000	20	0	0	1	11.1	15	7	2	0	6-2	12	5.56	67	.319	.396	0	ø	0	—	-2	0	-0.2
	Phi N	1	1	.500	14	0	0	0	32	23	10	1	0	6-3	18	2.25	154	.204	.244	5	.000	-0	—	4	0	0.3
	Year	2	5	.286	50	0	0	1	60.2	52	23	5	0	19-8	42	3.12	116	.234	.293	5	.000	0	—	4	0	0.5
Total	16	119	99	.546	537	171	78-15	48	1935.2	1795	817	151	41	643-53	1072	3.38	119	.248	.312	548-1-44	.195	11	97	134	95	18.7

SHARPLESS, JOSH Joshua David; B1.26.1981 Beaver PA; BR/TR/6´5˝/235; [PitN03 24/705]; d8.1; Col Allegheny

YEAR	TM LG	W	L	PCT	G	GS	CG-SHO	SV-BS	IP	H	R	HR	HB	BB-IB	SO	ERA	AERA	OAV	OOB	AB-HR-SH	AVG	PB	SUP	APR	DL	PW
2006	Pit N	0	0	ø	14	0	0	0-0	12	7	2	0	0	11-1	7	1.50	305	.175	.346	0	ø	0	—	4	22	0.2

SHARROTT, GEORGE George Oscar; B11.2.1869 Staten Island NY; D1.6.1932 Jamaica NY; BL/TL/5´8˝/164; d7.27

YEAR	TM LG	W	L	PCT	G	GS	CG-SHO	SV-BS	IP	H	R	HR	HB	BB-IB	SO	ERA	AERA	OAV	OOB	AB-HR-SH	AVG	PB	SUP	APR	DL	PW
1893	Bro N	4	6	.400	13	10	10	1	95	114	80	3	8	58	24	5.87	75	.289	.390	39-1	.231	0	74	-13	—	-1.0
1894	Bro N	0	1	.000	3	3	2	0	18	25	21	0	5	8	7	9.00	55	.325	.422	7	.429	1	43	-7	—	-0.2
Total	2	4	7	.364	16	13	12	1	113	139	101	3	13	66	31	6.37	71	.294	.396	46-1	.261	1	67	-20	—	-1.2

SHARROTT, JACK John Henry; B8.13.1869 Staten Island NY; D12.31.1927 Los Angeles CA; BR/TR/5´9˝/165; d4.22; ▲

YEAR	TM LG	W	L	PCT	G	GS	CG-SHO	SV-BS	IP	H	R	HR	HB	BB-IB	SO	ERA	AERA	OAV	OOB	AB-HR-SH	AVG	PB	SUP	APR	DL	PW
1890	NY N	11	10	.524	25	19	18	0	184	162	107	3	9	88	84	2.89	122	.229	.322	109	.202	-2*	96	11	—	0.9
1891	NY N	5	5	.500	10	9	6	0	69.1	47	32	2	4	35	41	2.60	123	.185	.294	30-1	.333	4	89	6	—	1.1
1892	NY N	0	0	ø	1	0	0	0	2	2	1	0	0	1	1	4.50	72	.250	.333	8	.125	-0*	—	0	—	0.0
1893	Phi N	4	2	.667	12	4	2	0	56	53	43	1	4	33	11	4.50	102	.242	.352	152-1	.250	0*	118	-1	—	-0.1
Total	4	20	17	.541	48	32	26	0	311.1	264	183	6	17	157	137	3.12	116	.222	.321	299-2	.237	2	96	16	—	1.9

SHAUTE, JOE Joseph Benjamin "Lefty"; B8.1.1899 Peckville PA; D2.21.1970 Scranton PA; BL/TL/6´0˝/190; d7.6; Col Juniata

YEAR	TM LG	W	L	PCT	G	GS	CG-SHO	SV-BS	IP	H	R	HR	HB	BB-IB	SO	ERA	AERA	OAV	OOB	AB-HR-SH	AVG	PB	SUP	APR	DL	PW
1922	Cle A	0	0	ø	2	0	0	0	3.2	7	8	2	0	3	3	19.64	20	.389	.476	5	.000	-0*	—	-6	—	-0.3
1923	Cle A	10	8	.556	33	16	7	0	172	176	93	4	1	53	61	3.51	113	.275	.332	68-0-1	.162	-4	126	5	—	0.0
1924	Cle A	20	17	.541	46	34	21-2	2	283	317	138	8	6	83	68	3.75	114	.287	.340	107-1-3	.318	9	106	19	—	3.0
1925	Cle A	4	12	.250	26	17	10-1	4	131	160	91	6	1	44	34	5.43	81	.304	.358	53	.302	3*	96	-13	—	-1.2
1926	Cle A	14	10	.583	34	25	15-1	1	206.2	215	92	9	3	65	47	3.53	115	.278	.337	73-0-7	.274	4	113	13	—	1.6
1927	Cle A	9	16	.360	45	28	14	2	230.1	255	140	9	2	75	63	4.22	100	.286	.343	83	.325	6	77	-5	—	0.0

YEAR	TM LG	W	L	PCT	G	GS	CG-SHO	SV-BS	IP	H	R	HR	HB	BB-IB	SO	ERA	AERA	OAV	OOB	AB-HR-SH	AVG	PB	SUP	APR	DL	PW
1928	Cle A	13	17	.433	36	31	21-1	2	253.2	295	145	9	6	68	81	4.04	102	.299	.348	92-0-4	.228	3	107	0	—	0.4
1929	Cle A	8	8	.500	26	24	8	0	162	211	100	6	1	52	43	4.28	104	.320	.370	58-0-5	.293	3	94	0	—	0.2
1930	Cle A	0	0	ø	4	0	0	0	4.2	8	10	0	0	4	2	15.43	31	.333	.429	0	ø	0	—	-5	—	-0.2
1931	Bro N	11	8	.579	25	19	6	0	128.2	162	87	9	1	32	50	4.83	79	.305	.346	45-0-1	.178	-0	123	-18	—	-2.3
1932	Bro N	7	7	.500	34	9	1	4	117	147	67	8	2	21	32	4.54	84	.301	.333	45-0-1	.200	1*	127	-9	—	-1.0
1933	Bro N	3	4	.429	41	4	0	2	108.1	125	63	4	1	31	26	3.49	92	.287	.336	27	.222	1	52	-9	—	-0.4
1934	Cin N	0	2	.000	8	1	0	1	17.1	19	9	1	0	3	2	4.15	98	.268	.297	4	.250	0	106	0	—	0.0
Total	13	99	109	.476	360	208	103-5	18	1818.1	2097	1043	75	24	534	512	4.15	99	.293	.345	660-1-22	.258	25	105	-28	—	-0.2
SHAVER, JEFF	Jeffrey Thomas; B7.30.1963 Beaver PA; BR/TR/6´3″/187; [OakA85 22/559]; d7.6; Col Fredonia																									
1988	Oak A	0	0	ø	1	0	0	0-0	1	0	0	0	1	0-0	0	0.00	ø	.000	.333	0	ø	0	—	0	0	0.0
SHAW, DON	Donald Wellington; B2.23.1944 Pittsburgh PA; BL/TL/6´0″/(180–191); [NYN65 21/752]; d4.11; Mil 1967; Col San Diego St.																									
1967	NY N	4	5	.444	40	0	0	3	51.1	40	19	5	0	23-5	44	2.98	114	.219	.301	3-0-1	.000	0	—	2	0	0.5
1968	NY N	0	0	ø	7	0	0	0	12	3	1	1	0	5-0	11	0.75	403	.086	.200	0	ø	0	—	3	0	0.2
1969	Mon N	2	5	.286	35	1	0	1-1	65.2	61	43	9	2	37-5	45	5.21	71	.254	.356	10	.000	-0	48	-10	0	-1.1
1971	StL N	7	2	.778	45	0	0	2-2	51	45	19	1	1	31-6	19	2.65	137	.237	.342	1-0-1	.000	-0	—	4	0	0.8
1972	StL N	0	1	.000	8	0	0	0-3	3	5	3	1	0	3-0	0	9.00	38	.417	.500	1	.000	-0	—	-2	0	-0.4
	Oak A	0	1	.000	3	0	0	0-0	5.1	12	10	2	0	2-0	4	16.88	17	.500	.500	0	ø	0	—	-8	0	-1.2
Total	5	13	14	.481	138	1	0	6-6	188.1	166	95	19	3	101-16	123	4.01	88	.243	.338	15-0-2	.000	-0	48	-11	0	-1.2
SHAW, DUPEE	Frederick Lander; B5.31.1859 Charlestown MA; D1.12.1938 Wakefield MA; BL/TL/5´8″/165; d6.18																									
1883	Det N	10	15	.400	26	25	23-1	0	227	238	135	3	—	44	73	2.50	124	.256	.290	141	.206	-3*	96	10	—	0.7
1884	Det N	9	18	.333	28	28	25	0	227.2	219	153	8	—	72	142	3.04	95	.237	.292	136-1	.191	-1*	84	-4	—	-0.4
	Bos U	21	15	.583	39	38	35-5	0	315.2	227	128	1	—	37	309	1.77	135	.188	.212	153	.242	-2*	93	20	—	1.3
1885	Pro N	23	26	.469	49	49	47-6	0	399.2	343	209	7	—	99	194	2.57	105	.209	.254	165	.133	-10	74	5	—	-0.5
1886	Was N	13	31	.295	45	44	43-1	0	385.2	384	224	12	—	91	177	3.34	97	.250	.291	148	.088	-10	75	-4	—	-1.3
1887	Was N	7	13	.350	21	20	20	0	181.1	263	177	8	3	46	47	6.45	62	.328	.366	70	.186	-2	85	-40	—	-3.3
1888	Was N	0	3	.000	3	3	3	0	25	36	24	2	0	7	8	6.48	43	.333	.374	10	.000	-1	37	-9	—	-1.0
Total	6	83	121	.407	211	207	196-13	0	1762	1710	1050	41	3	396	950	3.10	96	.239	.279	823-1	.170	-28	83	-22	—	-4.5
SHAW, JIM	James Aloysius "Grunting Jim"; B8.19.1893 Pittsburgh PA; D1.27.1962 Washington DC; BR/TR/6´0″/180; d9.15																									
1913	Was A	0	1	.000	2	1	0	0	13	8	4	0	1	7	14	2.08	142	.216	.356	2	.000	-0	0	1	—	0.1
1914	Was A	15	17	.469	48	31	15-5	**4**	257	198	99	3	8	137	164	2.70	104	.216	.324	85-1-3	.118	-3	84	3	—	0.1
1915	Was A	6	11	.353	25	18	7-1	1	133	102	50	2	2	76	78	2.50	119	.220	.333	43-0-1	.233	1	68	7	—	1.0
1916	Was A	3	8	.273	26	9	5-2	1	106.1	86	36	1	2	50	44	2.62	106	.227	.320	32-0-2	.156	-0	78	3	—	0.2
1917	Was A	15	14	.517	47	31	15-2	1	266.1	233	118	1	1	123	118	3.21	82	.242	.328	91-0-3	.154	-2	85	-15	—	-2.0
1918	Was A	16	12	.571	41	30	14-4	1	241.1	201	88	2	1	90	129	2.42	113	.228	.300	83-0-3	.133	-5	102	9	—	0.3
1919	Was A	17	17	.500	**45**	37	23-3	**5**	**306.2**	274	118	5	5	101	128	2.73	118	.244	.309	106-3-6	.160	-1	100	19	—	1.6
1920	Was A	11	18	.379	38	32	17	1	236.1	285	127	12	4	87	88	4.27	87	.314	.376	74-0-3	.189	0	83	-9	—	-1.1
1921	Was A	1	0	1.000	15	5	0	3	40.1	59	37	2	0	17	4	7.36	56	.345	.404	12-0-1	.417	2	174	-14	—	-0.5
Total	9	84	98	.462	287	194	96-17	17	1600.1	1446	677	28	24	688	767	3.07	99	.247	.329	528-4-22	.163	-8	91	4	—	-0.3
SHAW, JEFF	Jeffrey Lee; B7.7.1966 Washington Court House OH; BR/TR/6´2″/(185–200); [CleA86*1/1]; d4.30; Col Rio Grande																									
1990	Cle A	3	4	.429	12	9	0	0-0	48.2	73	38	11	0	20-0	25	6.66	59	.356	.408	0	ø	0	105	-14	0	-1.7
1991	Cle A	0	5	.000	29	1	0	1-3	72.1	72	34	6	4	27-5	31	3.36	124	.262	.332	0	ø	0	0	5	0	0.3
1992	Cle A	0	1	.000	2	1	0	0-0	7.2	7	7	2	0	4-0	3	8.22	48	.259	.355	0	ø	0	116	-3	0	-0.4
1993	Mon N	2	7	.222	55	8	0	0-1	95.2	91	47	12	7	32-2	50	4.14	101	.254	.326	15	.067	-1	54	3	0	0.1
1994	Mon N	5	2	.714	46	0	0	1-1	67.1	67	32	8	2	15-2	47	3.88	109	.254	.295	7-0-1	.286	1	—	3	0	0.4
1995	Mon N	1	6	.143	50	0	0	3-2	62.1	58	35	4	3	26-4	45	4.62	93	.250	.332	6	.000	-0	—	-2	0	-0.2
	Chi A	0	0	ø	9	0	0	0-0	9.2	12	7	2	1	1-0	6	6.52	69	.316	.350	0	ø	0	—	-2	0	-0.1
1996	Cin N	8	6	.571	78	0	0	4-7	104.2	99	34	8	2	29-11	69	2.49	172	.252	.303	5	.000	-0	—	20	0	2.5
1997	Cin N	4	2	.667	78	0	0	**42**-7	94.2	79	26	7	1	12-3	74	2.38	180	.227	.253	3-0-1	.000	-0	—	**20**	0	2.8
1998	Cin N	2	4	.333	39	0	0	23-5	49.2	40	11	2	1	12-4	29	1.81	237	.231	.282	2-0-1	.000	-0	—	13	0	2.6
	LA N★	1	4	.200	34	0	0	25-4	35.1	35	11	6	0	7-1	26	2.55	158	.252	.288	0	ø	0	—	6	0	1.3
	Year	3	8	.273	73	0	0	48-9	85	75	22	8	1	19-5	55	2.12	197	.240	.284	2-0-1	.000	-0	—	19	0	3.9
1999	LA N	2	4	.333	64	0	0	34-5	68	64	25	6	1	15-1	43	2.78	157	.242	.283	0	ø	0	—	12	0	1.9
2000	LA N	3	4	.429	60	0	0	27-7	57.1	61	29	7	1	16-3	39	4.24	105	.265	.316	0	ø	0	—	2	15	0.4
2001	LA N★	3	5	.375	77	0	0	43-9	74.2	63	32	10	2	18-8	58	3.62	114	.227	.277	0	ø	0	—	5	0	1.0
Total	12	34	54	.386	633	19	0	203-51	848	821	368	91	25	234-44	545	3.54	119	.255	.308	38-0-3	.079	-1	75	68	15	10.9
SHAW, BOB	Robert John; B6.29.1933 Bronx NY; BR/TR/6´2″/(180–195); d8.11; C1; Col St. Lawrence																									
1957	Det A	0	1	.000	7	0	0	0	9.2	11	9	2	0	7-1	4	7.45	52	.289	.400	2	.000	-0	—	-4	0	-0.4
1958	Det A	1	2	.333	11	2	0	0	26.2	32	16	2	0	13-1	17	5.06	80	.302	.375	8	.375	1*	33	-3	0	-0.1
	Chi A	4	2	.667	29	3	0	1	64	67	33	8	2	28-3	18	4.64	78	.271	.346	14	.000	-1	156	-6	0	-0.5
	Year	5	4	.556	40	5	0	1	90.2	99	49	10	2	41-4	35	4.76	79	.280	.355	22	.136	-0	105	-8	0	-0.6
1959	†Chi A	18	6	**.750**	47	26	8-3	3	230.2	217	72	15	6	54-5	89	2.69	140	.249	.295	73-0-10	.123	-2	101	31	0	2.9
1960	Chi A	13	13	.500	36	32	7-1	0	192.2	221	97	16	3	62-3	46	4.06	93	.292	.345	58-0-7	.138	-0	101	-6	0	-0.8
1961	Chi A	3	4	.429	14	10	3	0	71.1	85	40	11	1	20-5	31	3.79	103	.302	.346	18-0-2	.000	-1	97	-2	0	-0.3
	KC A	9	10	.474	26	24	6	0	150.1	165	87	14	7	58-2	60	4.31	97	.281	.348	55-0-1	.200	-1*	93	-4	0	-0.5
	Year	12	14	.462	40	34	9	0	221.2	250	127	25	8	78-7	91	4.14	99	.288	.347	73-0-3	.151	-2	95	-7	0	-0.8
1962	Mil N★	15	9	.625	38	29	12-3	2	225	223	80	20	12	44-10	124	2.80	136	.260	.303	73-0-1	.137	1	102	26	0	2.6
1963	Mil N	7	11	.389	48	16	3-3	13	159	144	51	10	4	55-12	105	2.66	121	.243	.310	41-0-7	.122	0	97	11	0	1.4
1964	SF N	7	6	.538	61	1	0	11	93.1	105	43	5	5	31-6	57	3.76	95	.286	.348	13	.000	-1	74	-2	0	-0.5
1965	SF N	16	9	.640	42	33	6-1	2	235	213	85	17	3	53-5	148	2.64	136	.236	.280	79-0-4	.101	-3	99	22	0	2.0
1966	SF N	1	4	.200	13	6	0	0	31.2	45	23	9	0	7-1	21	6.25	59	.324	.356	6-0-2	.000	-1	76	-8	0	-1.2
	NY N	11	10	.524	26	25	7-2	0	167.2	171	85	12	7	42-1	104	3.92	93	.261	.312	50-0-5	.260	3	86	-6	0	-0.3
	Year	12	14	.462	39	31	7-2	0	199.1	216	108	21	7	49-2	125	4.29	85	.272	.319	56-0-7	.232	2	84	-17	0	-1.5
1967	NY N	3	9	.250	23	13	3-1	0	98.2	105	54	9	2	28-9	49	4.29	79	.273	.325	25-0-1	.040	-2	70	-10	0	-1.4
	Chi N	0	2	.000	9	3	0	0	22.1	33	16	0	4	9-4	7	6.04	59	.351	.418	4	.250	0	99	-6	0	-0.5
	Year	3	11	.214	32	16	3-1	0	121	138	70	9	6	37-13	56	4.61	74	.289	.344	29-0-1	.069	-1	75	-15	0	-1.9
Total	11	108	98	.524	430	223	55-14	32	1778	1837	791	150	56	511-68	880	3.52	105	.267	.321	519-0-40	.133	-7	96	33	0	2.4
SHAW, SAM	Samuel E.; B5.1864 Baltimore MD; BR/TR/5´5″/140; d5.3																									
1888	Bal AA	2	4	.333	6	6	6	0	53	65	37	2	4	15	22	3.40	88	.291	.347	20	.150	-1	110	-5	—	-0.5
1893	Chi N	1	0	1.000	2	2	1	0	16	12	12	2	9	13	1	5.63	82	.203	.420	7	.286	-0	151	-1	—	-0.1
Total	2	3	4	.429	8	8	7	0	69	77	49	4	13	28	23	3.91	86	.273	.365	27	.185	-1	123	-6	—	-0.6
SHAWKEY, BOB	James Robert; B12.4.1890 Sigel PA; D12.31.1980 Syracuse NY; BR/TR/5´11″/168; d7.16; Mil 1918; M1/C1; Col Slippery Rock																									
1913	Phi A	6	5	.545	18	15	8-1	0	111.1	92	41	2	3	50	52	2.34	118	.221	.309	44-0-2	.136	-2	116	3	—	0.2
1914	†Phi A	15	8	.652	38	31	18-5	2	237	223	88	4	2	75	89	2.73	96	.262	.323	83-0-4	.205	2	122	-4	—	-0.2
1915	Phi A	6	6	.500	17	13	7-1	0	100	103	57	3	1	38	56	4.05	72	.278	.346	31-0-2	.129	-1	123	-11	—	-1.2
	NY A	4	7	.364	16	9	5-1	0	85.2	78	38	2	2	35	31	3.26	90	.265	.347	29	.241	1	61	-3	—	-0.2
	Year	10	13	.435	33	22	12-2	0	185.2	181	95	5	3	73	87	3.68	80	.272	.347	60-0-2	.183	1	97	-13	—	-1.4
1916	NY A	24	14	.632	53	27	21-4	**8**	276.2	204	78	4	6	81	122	2.21	131	.209	.273	93-0-4	.183	-1	102	24	—	3.4
1917	NY A	13	15	.464	32	26	16-2	0	236.1	207	81	2	6	72	97	2.44	110	.243	.306	84-0-4	.190	-0	99	8	—	1.2
1918	NY A	1	1	.500	3	2	1-1	0	16	7	2	0	0	10	3	1.13	251	.143	.288	4-0-1	.750	2	107	3	—	0.7
1919	NY A	20	11	.645	41	27	22-3	**5**	261.1	218	94	7	5	92	122	2.72	117	.231	.303	94-0-6	.234	-0	104	16	—	1.8
1920	NY A	20	13	.606	38	31	20-5	2	267.2	246	88	10	1	85	126	**2.45**	**156**	.248	.308	100-0-1	.230	-0	98	41	—	4.6
1921	†NY A	18	12	.600	38	31	18-3	2	245	245	131	15	7	86	126	4.08	104	.263	.329	90-1-8	.300	4	125	6	—	0.8
1922	†NY A	20	12	.625	39	34	22-3	1	299.2	286	112	16	0	98	130	2.91	138	.256	.316	115-1-7	.183	-3	103	37	—	3.3
1923	†NY A	16	11	.593	36	31	17-1	1	258.2	232	114	17	4	102	125	3.51	112	**.246**	.322	99-0-3	.202	-3	115	12	—	0.8
1924	NY A	16	11	.593	38	25	10-1	0	207.2	226	107	11	3	74	114	4.12	101	.286	.350	69-1-4	.319	8	133	2	—	0.8
1925	NY A	6	14	.300	33	19	9-1	0	186	209	101	12	5	67	81	4.11	104	.294	.359	68	.147	-4	59	2	—	-0.3
1926	†NY A	8	7	.533	29	10	3-1	3	104.1	102	49	8	2	37	63	3.62	106	.263	.330	35-0-2	.257	2	125	4	—	0.6

YEAR	TM LG	W	L	PCT	G	GS	CG-SHO	SV-BS	IP	H	R	HR	HB	BB-IB	SO	ERA	AERA	OAV	OOB	AB-HR-SH	AVG	PB	SUP	APR	DL	PW
1927	NY A	2	3	.400	19	2	0	4	43.2	44	19	1	1	16	23	2.89	134	.262	.330	11	.091	-1	130	4	—	0.4
Total	15	195	150	.565	488	333	197-33	28	2937	2722	1200	114	48	1018	1360	3.09	114	.252	.319	1049-3-48	.214	4	108	144	—	16.7
Shea, Spec	Francis Joseph "The Naugatuck Nugget" (b Francis Joseph O'Shea); B10.2.1920 Naugatuck CT; D7.19.2002 New Haven CT; BR/TR/6´0˝/195; d4.19																									
1947	†NY A★	14	5	.737	27	23	13-3	1	178.2	127	63	10	4	89	89	3.07	115	**.200**	.303	56-0-8	.196	2	128	11	0	1.2
1948	NY A	9	10	.474	28	22	8-3	1	155.2	117	66	10	2	87	71	3.41	120	**.208**	.316	47-0-5	.149	1	105	12	0	1.2
1949	NY A	1	1	.500	20	3	0	1	52.1	48	36	5	0	43	22	5.33	76	.250	.387	12	.250	1	81	-8	0	-0.3
1951	NY A	5	5	.500	25	11	2-2	0	95.2	112	59	11	4	50	38	4.33	88	.300	.389	28-1-1	.214	1	135	-9	0	-0.7
1952	Was A	11	7	.611	22	21	12-2	0	169	144	62	6	2	92	65	2.93	121	.231	.331	63-0-1	.238	2	104	12	0	1.5
1953	Was A	12	7	.632	23	23	11-1	0	164.2	151	82	11	4	75	38	3.94	99	.244	.329	62-0-4	.177	-1	120	-1	0	-0.3
1954	Was A	2	9	.182	23	11	1	0	71.1	97	54	9	2	34	22	6.18	58	.340	.412	20	.050	-2	108	-21	0	-2.9
1955	Was A	2	2	.500	27	4	1-1	2	56.1	53	31	4	1	27-0	16	3.99	96	.251	.335	10	.400	2	93	-2	0	0.0
Total	8	56	46	.549	195	118	48-12	5	943.2	849	453	66	19	497-0	361	3.80	99	.243	.339	298-1-19	.195	6	114	-6	0	-0.3
Shea, John	John Michael Joseph "Lefty"; B12.27.1904 Everett MA; D11.30.1956 Malden MA; BL/TL/5´10.5˝/171; d6.30; Col Boston College																									
1928	Bos A	0	0	ø	1	0	0	0	1	1	2	0	0	1	0	18.00	23	.250	.400	0	ø	0	—	-1	—	-0.1
Shea, Mike	Michael Joseph; B3.10.1867 New Orleans LA; D8.22.1927 New Orleans LA; TR/5´10˝/170; d4.20																									
1887	Cin AA	1	1	.500	2	2	2	0	16.2	26	25	0	0	10	0	7.02	62	.333	.409	8	.250	0	147	-6	—	-0.5
Shea, Red	Patrick Henry; B11.29.1898 Ware MA; D11.17.1981 Stafford CT; BR/TR/6´0˝/165; d5.6																									
1918	Phi A	0	0	ø	3	0	0	0	9	14	8	0	0	2	2	4.00	73	.378	.410	3	.000	-0	—	-2	—	-0.2
1921	NY N	5	2	.714	9	2	1	0	32	28	13	2	3	2	10	3.09	119	.239	.270	9	.111	-1	56	2	—	0.3
1922	NY N	0	3	.000	11	2	0	0	23	22	14	2	0	11	5	4.70	85	.256	.340	7	.000	-1	122	-2	—	-0.2
Total	3	5	5	.500	23	4	1	0	64	64	35	4	3	15	17	3.80	97	.267	.318	19	.053	-2	93	-2	—	-0.1
Shea, Steve	Steven Francis; B12.5.1942 Worcester MA; BR/TR/6´3˝/(210–215); d7.14; Col Massachusetts																									
1968	Hou N	4	4	.500	30	0	0	6	34.2	27	14	0	3	11-0	15	3.38	88	.229	.306	6	.000	-1	—	-1	0	-0.3
1969	Mon N	0	0	ø	10	0	0	0-0	15.2	18	8	2	0	8-2	11	2.87	129	.300	.371	0	ø	0	—	0	0	0.0
Total	2	4	4	.500	40	0	0	6-0	50.1	45	22	2	3	19-2	26	3.22	99	.253	.328	6	.000	-1	—	-1	0	-0.3
Shealy, Al	Albert Berley; B5.24.1900 Chapin SC; D3.7.1967 Hagerstown MD; BR/TR/5´11˝/175; d4.13; Col Newberry																									
1928	NY A	8	6	.571	23	12	3	2	96	124	64	4	1	42	39	5.06	74	.308	.375	38-1-2	.237	2	128	-15	—	-1.7
1930	Chi N	0	0	ø	24	0	0	0	27	37	24	2	0	14	14	8.00	61	.327	.402	5	.600	1	—	-8	—	-0.2
Total	2	8	6	.571	47	12	3	2	123	161	88	6	1	56	53	5.71	70	.313	.381	43-1-2	.279	4	128	-23	—	-1.9
Shearon, John	John; B1871 PA; D2.12.1932 Chicago IL; d7.28; ▲																									
1891	Cle N	1	3	.250	6	5	4	0	46	57	39	2	1	24	19	3.52	98	.292	.373	124	.242	-0*	79	-2	—	-0.1
Shears, George	George Penfield; B4.13.1890 Marshall MO; D11.12.1978 Loveland CO; BR/TL/6´3˝/180; d4.24																									
1912	NY A	0	0	ø	4	0	0	0	15	24	18	0	0	11	9	5.40	67	.364	.455	6	.167	0	—	-5	—	-0.2
Sheehan, Tom	Thomas Clancy; B3.31.1894 Grand Ridge IL; D10.29.1982 Chillicothe OH; BR/TR/6´2.5˝/190; d7.14; M1/C5																									
1915	Phi A	4	9	.308	15	13	8-1	0	102	131	73	1	1	38	22	4.15	71	.335	.395	34-0-2	.118	-3	82	-17	—	-2.2
1916	Phi A	1	16	.059	38	17	8	0	188	197	111	2	2	94	54	3.69	78	.287	.374	56-0-1	.125	-2	70	-21	—	-1.8
1921	NY A	1	0	1.000	12	1	0	1	33	43	23	1	1	19	7	5.45	78	.326	.414	8-0-2	.625	2	217	-4	—	0.0
1924	Cin N	9	11	.450	39	14	8-2	1	166.2	170	72	5	1	54	52	3.24	116	.269	.328	58	.310	4*	79	10	—	1.4
1925	Cin N	1	0	1.000	10	3	1	1	29	37	31	3	0	12	5	8.07	51	.298	.360	5-0-2	.200	1	123	-13	—	-0.5
	Pit N	1	1	.500	23	0	0	2	57.1	63	25	2	0	13	13	2.67	167	.286	.326	20	.150	-1*	—	9	—	0.3
	Year	2	1	.667	33	3	1	3	86.1	100	56	5	0	25	18	4.48	97	.291	.339	25-0-2	.160	-0	117	-2	—	-0.2
1926	Pit N	0	2	.000	9	2	1	0	31	36	24	0	2	12	16	6.68	59	.298	.370	9-0-2	.111	-1	116	-8	—	-0.5
Total	6	17	39	.304	146	50	26-3	5	607	677	359	14	7	242	169	4.00	86	.294	.362	190-0-9	.205	0	82	-44	—	-3.3
Sheets, Ben	Ben M.; B7.18.1978 Baton Rouge LA; BR/TR/6´1˝/(195–220); [MilN99 1/10]; d4.5; Col Louisiana–Monroe																									
2001	Mil N★	11	10	.524	25	25	1-1	0-0	151.1	166	89	23	5	48-6	94	4.76	90	.283	.340	42-0-2	.071	-2	105	-9	46	-1.2
2002	Mil N	11	16	.407	34	34	1	0-0	216.2	237	105	21	10	70-10	170	4.15	99	.281	.343	68-0-4	.088	-3	81	1	0	0.0
2003	Mil N	11	13	.458	34	34	1	0-0	220.2	232	122	29	6	43-2	157	4.45	97	.268	.305	66-0-5	.076	-4	103	-5	0	-1.0
2004	Mil N★	12	14	.462	34	34	5	0-0	237	201	85	25	4	32-1	264	2.70	163	.226	.255	67-0-9	.134	-1	77	41	0	4.1
2005	Mil N	10	9	.526	22	22	3	0-0	156.2	142	66	19	2	25-1	141	3.33	128	.237	.270	45-0-7	.022	-4	80	15	71	1.0
2006	Mil N	6	7	.462	17	17	0	0-0	106	105	47	9	2	11-1	116	3.82	118	.259	.278	33-0-3	.030	-2	75	9	96	0.7
Total	6	61	69	.469	166	166	11-1	0-0	1088.1	1083	514	126	29	229-21	942	3.83	112	.258	.300	321-0-30	.078	-16	87	52	213	3.6
Sheldon, Rollie	Roland Frank; B12.17.1936 Putnam CT; BR/TR/6´4˝/(190–201); d4.23; Col Connecticut																									
1961	NY A	11	5	.688	35	21	6-2	0	162.2	149	70	17	2	55-2	84	3.60	103	.246	.310	56-0-2	.125	-2*	112	3	0	0.1
1962	NY A	7	8	.467	34	16	2	1	118	136	78	12	1	28-3	54	5.49	68	.289	.324	26-0-6	.077	0	115	-23	0	-2.6
1964	†NY A	5	2	.714	19	12	3	1	102.1	92	43	18	1	18-2	57	3.61	100	.243	.276	34-0-2	.088	-2	129	1	0	-0.1
1965	NY A	0	0	ø	3	0	0	0	6.1	5	1	0	0	1-0	7	1.42	240	.238	.261	1	.000	-0	—	1	0	0.1
	KC A	10	8	.556	32	29	4-1	0	186.2	180	86	22	7	56-3	105	3.95	88	.251	.311	51-0-7	.078	-3	96	-7	0	-1.0
	Year	10	8	.556	35	29	4-1	0	193	185	87	22	7	57-3	112	3.87	90	.251	.310	52-0-7	.077	-3	96	-4	0	-0.9
1966	KC A	4	7	.364	14	13	1-1	0	69	73	31	3	1	26-3	26	3.13	109	.275	.337	23-0-2	.087	-1	82	0	0	-0.1
	Bos A	1	6	.143	23	10	1	0	79.2	106	49	15	2	23-4	38	4.97	77	.320	.367	18	.111	-1	76	-9	0	-0.8
	Year	5	13	.278	37	23	2-1	0	148.2	179	80	18	3	49-7	64	4.12	88	.300	.353	41-0-2	.098	-2	78	-8	0	-0.9
Total	5	38	36	.514	160	101	17-4	2	724.2	741	358	87	14	207-17	371	4.09	89	.266	.317	209-0-19	.096	-9	102	-34	0	-4.4
Shellenback, Frank	Frank Victor; B12.16.1898 Joplin MO; D8.17.1969 Newton MA; BR/TR/6´2˝/192; d5.8; C15; Col Santa Clara																									
1918	Chi A	9	12	.429	28	21	10-2	2	182.2	180	77	1	4	74	47	2.66	103	.262	.338	64-0-5	.130	-1*	109	-1	—	-0.5
1919	Chi A	1	3	.250	8	4	2	0	35	40	24	1	0	16	10	5.14	62	.303	.378	11	.091	-0	111	-7	—	-0.8
Total	2	10	15	.400	36	25	12-2	2	217.2	220	101	2	4	90	57	3.06	92	.269	.344	65-0-5	.123	-1	109	-8	—	-1.3
Shellenback, Jim	James Philip; B11.18.1943 Riverside CA; BL/TL/6´2˝/200; d9.15; C1																									
1966	Pit N	0	0	ø	2	0	0	0	3	3	3	2	0	3-1	0	9.00	40	.300	.462	0	ø	0	—	-2	0	-0.1
1967	Pit N	1	1	.500	6	2	1	0	23.1	23	12	1	1	12-1	11	2.70	125	.250	.343	6	.167	-0	65	0	0	0.0
1969	Pit N	0	0	ø	8	0	0	0-0	16.2	14	8	1	0	4-0	7	3.24	107	.233	.277	1	.000	-0	—	0	0	0.1
	Was A	4	7	.364	30	11	2	1-1	84.2	87	43	8	1	48-3	50	4.04	87	.268	.362	27	.185	-0	108	-5	0	-0.5
1970	Was A	6	7	.462	39	14	2-1	0-0	117.1	107	57	6	0	51-4	57	3.68	98	.246	.322	30-0-4	.067	-2*	106	-2	0	-0.4
1971	Was A	3	11	.214	40	15	3-1	0-0	120	123	56	10	3	49-5	47	3.53	96	.267	.338	30-0-1	.167	0	71	-3	0	-0.3
1972	Tex A	2	4	.333	22	6	0	1-0	57	46	24	6	2	16-0	30	3.47	88	.221	.283	10-0-1	.100	-0	58	-2	63	-0.3
1973	Tex A	0	0	ø	2	0	0	0-0	1.2	0	0	0	0	0-0	3	0.00	ø	.000	.000	0	ø	0	—	1	0	0.0
1974	Tex A	0	0	ø	11	0	0	0-0	24.2	30	18	5	1	12-0	14	5.84	61	.306	.384	0	ø	0	—	-6	26	-0.3
1977	Min A	0	0	ø	5	0	0	0-0	5.2	10	7	1	0	5-0	3	7.94	50	.385	.469	0	ø	0	—	-3	0	-0.2
Total	9	16	30	.348	165	48	8-2	2-1	454	443	228	40	8	200-14	222	3.81	91	.258	.335	104-0-6	.135	-2	88	-22	89	-2.0
Shepard, Bert	Bert Robert; B6.28.1920 Dana IN; BL/TL/5´11˝/185; d8.4; C1																									
1945	Was A	0	0	ø	1	0	0	0	5.1	3	1	0	1	1	2	1.69	184	.167	.250	3	.000	-0	—	1	0	0.0
Shepherd, Keith	Keith Wayne; B1.21.1968 Wabash IN; BR/TR/6´2˝/(197–215); [PitN86 11/264]; d9.6																									
1992	Phi N	1	1	.500	12	0	0	2-4	22	19	10	0	0	6-1	10	3.27	107	.244	.287	0	ø	0	—	0	0	0.0
1993	Col N	1	3	.250	14	1	0	1-1	19.1	26	16	4	1	4-0	7	6.98	69	.333	.369	2	.000	-0	113	-4	0	-0.7
1995	Bos A	0	0	ø	2	0	0	0-0	1	4	4	0	0	2-0	0	36.00	14	.571	.667	0	ø	0	—	-3	35	-0.1
1996	Bal A	0	1	.000	13	0	0	0-0	20.2	31	27	6	0	18-1	17	8.71	57	.341	.445	0	ø	0	—	-11	0	-0.5
Total	4	2	5	.286	41	1	0	3-5	63	80	57	10	1	30-2	34	6.71	66	.315	.383	2	.000	-0	113	-18	35	-1.3
Sherdel, Bill	William Henry "Wee Willie"; B8.15.1896 McSherrystown PA; D11.14.1968 McSherrystown PA; BL/TL/5´10˝/160; d4.22																									
1918	StL N	6	12	.333	35	16	9-1	0	182.1	174	78	3	3	49	40	2.71	100	.259	.313	62-1-2	.242	3	108	-2	—	0.2
1919	StL N	5	9	.357	36	11	7	1	137.1	137	66	3	2	42	52	3.47	80	.270	.328	48	.271	2*	101	-10	—	-0.7
1920	StL N	11	10	.524	43	7	4	**6**	170	183	72	1	11	40	74	3.28	91	.297	.350	63-1-2	.222	2*	94	-4	—	-0.2
1921	StL N	9	8	.529	38	8	5-1	1	144.1	137	62	7	3	38	57	3.18	115	.247	.299	44	.114	-2*	118	8	—	0.7

YEAR	TM LG	W	L	PCT	G	GS	CG-SHO	SV-BS	IP	H	R	HR	HB	BB-IB	SO	ERA	AERA	OAV	OOB	AB-HR-SH	AVG	PB	SUP	APR	DL	PW
1922	StL N	17	13	.567	47	31	15-3	2	242	298	132	12	5	62	79	3.87	100	.303	.348	88-1-2	.193	1*	119	-2	—	-0.4
1923	StL N	15	13	.536	39	26	14	2	225	270	127	15	6	59	78	4.32	90	.296	.343	83-1-3	.337	9*	106	-9	—	-0.3
1924	StL N	8	9	.471	35	10	6	1	168.2	188	77	9	5	38	57	3.42	111	.291	.335	75-0-1	.200	2*	99	7	—	0.8
1925	StL N	15	6	**.714**	32	21	17-2	1	200	216	77	8	3	42	53	3.11	139	.277	.316	73-1-1	.205	2*	112	29	—	2.8
1926	†StL N	16	12	.571	34	29	17-3	0	234.2	255	103	15	5	49	59	3.49	112	.278	.318	90-1-3	.244	2*	107	13	—	1.4
1927	StL N	17	12	.586	39	28	18	**6**	232.1	241	109	17	3	48	59	3.53	112	.269	.308	72-1-6	.194	1	109	12	—	1.3
1928	†StL N	21	10	.677	38	27	20	**5**	248.2	251	96	17	2	56	72	2.86	140	.261	.303	84-1-10	.226	4	112	31	—	3.9
1929	StL N	10	15	.400	33	22	11-1	0	195.2	278	144	14	2	58	69	5.93	79	.337	.382	70-1-6	.229	2	85	-26	—	-2.6
1930	StL N	3	2	.600	13	7	1	0	64	86	34	5	1	13	29	4.64	108	.325	.358	19-0-6	.105	-1	122	5	—	0.1
	Bos N	6	5	.545	21	14	7	1	119.1	131	73	10	2	30	26	4.75	104	.283	.329	42-0-2	.095	-4	105	1	—	-0.2
	Year	9	7	.563	34	21	8	1	183.1	217	107	15	3	43	55	4.71	105	.298	.340	61-0-8	.098	-5	110	6	—	-0.1
1931	Bos N	6	10	.375	27	16	8	0	137.2	163	70	13	1	35	34	4.25	89	.294	.337	46	.304	4	66	-5	—	-0.3
1932	Bos N	0	0	ø	1	0	0	0	1.2	3	3	0	0	1	0	0.00	ø	.375	.444	0	ø	0	—	-1	—	0.0
	StL N	0	0	ø	3	0	0	0	5.2	7	3	0	0	1	1	4.76	83	.304	.333	1	1.000	1	—	0	—	0.1
	Year	0	0	ø	4	0	0	0	7.1	10	6	0	0	2	1	3.68	106	.323	.364	1	1.000	1	—	-1	—	0.1
Total	15	165	146	.531	514	273	159-11	26	2709.1	3018	1326	149	54	661	839	3.72	103	.285	.330	960-9-44	.223	27	107	47	—	6.6
SHERID, ROY	Royden Richard; B1.25.1907 Norristown PA; D2.28.1982 Parker Ford PA; BR/TR/6´2˝/185; d5.11; Col Albright																									
1929	NY A	6	6	.500	33	15	9	1	154.2	165	81	6	5	55	51	3.61	107	.277	.343	50-0-3	.180	-1	120	2	—	0.0
1930	NY A	12	13	.480	37	21	8	4	184	214	122	13	5	87	59	5.23	82	.289	.368	69-0-4	.101	-6	131	-17	—	-2.5
1931	NY A	5	5	.500	17	8	3	2	74.1	94	52	4	3	24	39	5.69	70	.306	.362	30-0-5	.333	2	149	-15	—	-1.5
Total	3	23	24	.489	87	44	20	7	413	473	255	23	13	166	149	4.71	87	.288	.358	149-0-12	.174	-4	131	-30	—	-4.0
SHERMAN, JOE	Joel Powers; B11.4.1890 Yarmouth MA; D12.21.1987 Cape Coral FL; BR/TR/6´0˝/165; d9.24; Col Massachusetts																									
1915	Phi A	1	0	1.000	2	1	1	0	15	15	4	0	2	1	5	2.40	122	.259	.295	6	.333	1	100	1	—	0.1
SHERMAN, DAN	Lester Daniel "Babe"; B5.9.1890 Hubbardsville NY; D9.16.1955 Highland Park MI; BR/TR/5´6˝/145; d6.4																									
1914	Chi F	0	1	.000	1	1	0	0	0.1	0	2	0	0	2	0	0.00	ø	.000	.667	0	ø	0	103	-1	—	-0.1
SHERRILL, GEORGE	George Friederich; B4.19.1977 Memphis TN; BL/TL/6´0˝/(210–225); d7.16; Col Austin Peay																									
2004	Sea A	2	1	.667	21	0	0	0-0	23.2	24	12	3	1	9-1	16	3.80	118	.258	.327	0	ø	0	—	1	0	0.1
2005	Sea A	4	3	.571	29	0	0	0-0	19	13	12	3	1	7-2	24	5.21	80	.194	.276	0	ø	0	—	-2	0	-0.5
2006	Sea A	2	4	.333	72	0	0	1-0	40	30	19	0	0	27-4	42	4.27	103	.213	.335	0	ø	0	—	1	0	0.2
Total	3	8	8	.500	122	0	0	1-0	82.2	67	43	6	2	43-7	82	4.35	100	.223	.320	0	ø	0	—	0	0	-0.2
SHERRILL, TIM	Timothy Shawn; B9.10.1965 Harrison AR; BL/TL/5´11˝/170; [StLN87 18/462]; d8.14; Col Arkansas																									
1990	StL N	0	0	ø	8	0	0	0-0	4.1	10	5	0	0	3-0	3	6.23	62	.476	.542	0	ø	0	—	-2	0	-0.1
1991	StL N	0	0	ø	10	0	0	0-0	14.1	20	13	2	2	3-1	4	8.16	46	.339	.379	0	ø	0	—	-6	0	-0.3
Total	2	0	0	ø	18	0	0	0-0	18.2	30	18	2	2	6-1	7	7.71	49	.375	.422	0	ø	0	—	-8	0	-0.4
SHERRY, FRED	Fred Peter (b Fred Peter Schuerholz); B6.13.1889 Honesdale PA; D7.27.1975 Honesdale PA; BR/TR/6´0˝/170; d4.25; Col Villanova																									
1911	Was A	0	4	.000	10	3	2	0	52.1	63	40	1	0	19	20	4.30	76	.310	.369	19	.158	-1	66	-7	—	-0.5
SHERRY, LARRY	Lawrence; B7.25.1935 Los Angeles CA; BR/TR/6´2˝/(180–204); d4.17; C4; b–Norm																									
1958	LA N	0	0	ø	5	0	0	0	4.1	10	7	0	1	7-1	2	12.46	33	.476	.621	0	ø	0	—	-4	0	-0.2
1959	†LA N	7	2	.778	23	9	1-1	3	94.1	75	27	9	2	43-5	72	2.19	193	.218	.308	32-2-1	.219	2	101	19	0	2.1
1960	LA N	14	10	.583	57	3	1	7	142.1	125	65	14	6	82-15	114	3.79	105	.238	.346	37-1-3	.162	1	89	4	0	0.7
1961	LA N	4	4	.500	53	1	0	15	94.2	90	48	10	4	39-9	79	3.90	111	.252	.332	13	.154	-0	0	4	0	0.3
1962	LA N	7	3	.700	58	0	0	11	90	81	40	8	6	44-5	71	3.20	113	.241	.335	17-0-1	.118	-0	—	3	0	0.4
1963	LA N	2	6	.250	36	3	0	3	79.2	82	43	8	4	24-4	47	3.73	81	.265	.321	9-0-1	.111	1	67	-9	0	-0.8
1964	Det A	7	5	.583	38	0	0	11	66.1	52	29	7	3	37-2	58	3.66	100	.216	.325	14	.000	-2	—	0	59	-0.1
1965	Det A	3	6	.333	39	0	0	5	78.1	71	30	5	1	40-10	46	3.10	112	.254	.346	10-0-2	.300	2	—	3	0	0.6
1966	Det A	8	5	.615	55	0	0	20	77.2	66	38	8	3	36-2	63	3.82	91	.232	.320	10	.400	2	—	-3	0	-0.6
1967	Det A	0	1	.000	20	0	0	1	28	35	22	3	1	7-0	20	6.43	51	.289	.328	1	.000	-0	—	-10	0	-0.5
	Hou N	1	2	.333	29	0	0	6	40.2	53	26	4	1	13-2	32	4.87	68	.327	.374	5	.000	-1	—	-8	0	-0.8
1968	Cal A	0	0	ø	3	0	0	0	3	7	2	2	0	2-0	2	6.00	49	.467	.529	0	ø	0	—	-1	0	-0.1
Total	11	53	44	.546	416	16	2-1	82	799.1	747	377	78	32	374-55	606	3.67	101	.249	.336	148-3-8	.169	4	92	-2	59	1.0
SHIELDS, BEN	Benjamin Cowan "Big Ben","Lefty"; B6.17.1903 Huntersville NC; D1.24.1982 Woodruff SC; BR/TL (BB 1930–31)/6´1.5˝/195; d4.17																									
1924	NY A	0	0	ø	2	0	0	0	2	6	6	0	0	2	3	27.00	15	.545	.615	0	ø	0	—	-5	—	-0.2
1925	NY A	3	0	1.000	4	2	2	0	24	24	13	2	2	12	5	4.88	87	.267	.365	8	.125	-1	128	-1	—	-0.2
1930	Bos A	0	0	ø	3	0	0	0	10	16	11	0	0	6	1	9.00	51	.400	.478	3	.000	-1	—	-5	—	-0.2
1931	Phi N	1	0	1.000	4	0	0	0	5.1	9	9	1	0	7	0	15.19	28	.391	.533	2	.000	-0	—	-5	—	-0.8
Total	4	4	0	1.000	13	2	2	0	41.1	55	39	3	2	27	9	8.27	53	.335	.435	13	.077	-2	128	-16	—	-1.4
SHIELDS, CHARLIE	Charles Jessamine; B12.10.1879 Jackson TN; D8.27.1953 Memphis TN; BL/TL; d4.23																									
1902	Bal A	4	11	.267	23	15	10-1	1	142.1	201	102	7	2	32	28	4.24	89	.333	.368	48-0-1	.167	-1*	92	-8	—	-1.0
	StL A	3	0	1.000	4	4	3	0	30	37	16	1	0	7	6	3.30	107	.303	.341	13-0-1	.462	2	163	0	—	0.2
	Year	7	11	.389	27	19	13-1	1	172.1	238	118	8	2	39	34	4.07	92	.328	.364	61-0-2	.230	1	106	-8	—	-0.8
1907	StL N	0	2	.000	3	2	0	0	6.2	12	11	0	2	7	1	9.45	26	.444	.583	2	.000	-0	100	-5	—	-1.0
Total	2	7	13	.350	30	21	13-1	1	179	250	129	8	4	46	35	4.27	86	.332	.374	63-0-2	.222	1	103	-13	—	-1.8
SHIELDS, JAMIE	James Anthony; B12.20.1981 Newhall CA; BR/TR/6´4˝/215; [TBA00 16/466]; d5.31																									
2006	TB A	6	8	.429	21	21	1	0-0	124.2	141	69	18	5	38-5	104	4.84	96	.288	.343	8	.375	1	83	-1	0	0.1
SHIELDS, SCOT	Robert Scot; B7.22.1975 Fort Lauderdale FL; BR/TR/6´1˝/(170–175); [AnaA97 38/1137]; d5.26; Col Lincoln Memorial																									
2001	Ana A	0	0	ø	8	0	0	0-0	11	8	1	0	1	7-0	7	0.00	ø	.200	.333	0	ø	0	—	5	0	0.2
2002	†Ana A	5	3	.625	29	1	0	0-0	49	31	13	4	1	21-1	30	2.20	203	.188	.283	0	ø	0	124	12	0	1.8
2003	Ana A	5	6	.455	44	13	0	1-0	148.1	138	56	12	5	38-6	111	2.85	153	.247	.299	0	ø	0	75	24	0	1.7
2004	†Ana A	8	2	.800	60	0	0	4-3	105.1	97	42	6	3	40-5	109	3.33	134	.238	.310	1	.000	-0	—	14	0	1.2
2005	†LA A	10	11	.476	78	0	0	7-6	91.2	66	33	5	2	37-2	98	2.75	155	.201	.283	1	.000	-0	—	14	0	2.9
2006	LA A	7	7	.500	74	0	0	2-6	87.2	70	30	8	1	24-4	84	2.87	155	.217	.273	1	.000	-0	—	16	0	2.4
Total	6	35	29	.547	293	14	0	14-15	493	410	175	35	13	167-18	439	2.81	157	.225	.293	3	.000	-0	78	85	0	10.2
SHIELDS, STEVE	Stephen Mack; B11.30.1958 Gadsden AL; BR/TR/6´5˝/(220–230); [BosA77 10/247]; d6.1																									
1985	Atl N	1	2	.333	23	6	0	0-0	68	86	46	9	1	32-6	29	5.16	75	.320	.390	18	.111	-1	92	-10	0	-0.6
1986	Atl N	0	0	ø	6	0	0	0-0	12.2	13	10	4	0	7-0	6	7.11	56	.271	.364	1	.000	-0	—	-4	0	-0.2
	KC A	0	0	ø	3	0	0	0-1	8.2	3	3	1	0	4-1	2	2.08	206	.111	.212	0	ø	0	—	2	0	0.1
1987	Sea A	2	0	1.000	20	0	0	3-1	30	43	25	7	0	12-1	22	6.60	72	.333	.382	0	ø	0	—	-6	30	-0.5
1988	NY A	5	5	.500	39	0	0	0-2	82.1	96	44	8	2	30-4	55	4.37	91	.298	.360	0	ø	0	—	-4	0	-0.4
1989	Min A	0	1	.000	11	0	0	0-1	17.1	28	18	3	0	6-1	12	7.79	53	.354	.400	0	ø	0	—	-7	104	-0.4
Total	5	8	8	.500	102	6	0	3-5	219	269	146	32	3	91-13	126	5.26	77	.308	.371	19	.105	-1	92	-29	134	-2.0
SHIELDS, VINCE	Vincent William; B11.18.1900 Fredericton NB, Can.; D10.17.1952 Plaster Rock NB, Can.; BL/TR/5´11˝/185; d9.20																									
1924	StL N	1	1	.500	2	1	0	0	12	10	5	1	3	3	4	3.00	126	.227	.320	5	.400	0*	67	1	—	0.2
SHIELL, JASON	Jason Alexander; B10.19.1976 Savannah GA; BR/TR/6´0˝/180; [AtlN95 48/1328]; d9.8; [DL 2004 Bos A 183]																									
2002	SD N	0	0	ø	3	0	0	0-0	1.1	7	4	0	0	3-0	1	27.00	14	.700	.769	0	ø	0	—	-3	0	-0.2
2003	Bos A	2	0	1.000	17	0	0	1-1	23.1	23	13	4	2	17-2	23	4.63	101	.253	.382	0	ø	0	—	0	0	0.0
2006	Atl N	0	2	.000	4	3	0	0-0	15.2	23	15	5	1	9-1	14	8.62	53	.343	.423	4-0-1	.000	-0	68	-6	0	-0.6
Total	3	2	2	.500	24	3	0	1-1	40.1	53	32	9	3	29-3	38	6.92	66	.315	.423	4-0-1	.000	-0	68	-9	183	-0.8
SHIFFLETT, GARLAND	Garland Jessie "Duck"; B3.28.1935 Elkton VA; BR/TR/5´10.5˝/165; d4.22																									
1957	Was A	0	0	ø	6	1	0	0	8	6	9	0	0	10-0	2	10.13	38	.222	.421	0	ø	0	160	-5	0	-0.3
1964	Min A	0	2	.000	10	0	0	1	17.2	22	9	1	1	7-0	8	4.58	78	.297	.366	4	.000	-0	—	-1	0	-0.2
Total	2	0	2	.000	16	1	0	1	25.2	28	18	1	1	17-0	10	6.31	58	.277	.383	4	.000	-0	160	-6	0	-0.5

Shifflett, Steve Stephen Earl; B1.5.1966 Kansas City MO; BR/TR/6´1˝/205; d7.3; Col Emporia St.

YEAR	TM LG	W	L	PCT	G	GS	CG-SHO	SV-BS	IP	H	R	HR	HB	BB-IB	SO	ERA	AERA	OAV	OOB	AB-HR-SH	AVG	PB	SUP	APR	DL	PW
1992	KC A	1	4	.200	34	0	0	0-2	52	55	15	6	2	17-6	25	2.60	157	.279	.341	0	ø	0	—	9	0	0.8

Shinall, Zak Zakary Sebastien; B10.14.1968 St.Louis MO; BR/TR/6´3˝/215; [LAN87 29/742]; d5.12; Col El Camino (CA) JC

YEAR	TM LG	W	L	PCT	G	GS	CG-SHO	SV-BS	IP	H	R	HR	HB	BB-IB	SO	ERA	AERA	OAV	OOB	AB-HR-SH	AVG	PB	SUP	APR	DL	PW
1993	Sea A	0	0	ø	1	0	0	0-0	2.2	4	1	1	0	2-0	0	3.38	132	.333	.429	0	ø	0	—	0	0	0.0

Shipanoff, Dave David Noel; B11.13.1959 Edmonton AL, Can.; BR/TR/6´2˝/185; d8.10; Col Wabash Valley (IL) CC

YEAR	TM LG	W	L	PCT	G	GS	CG-SHO	SV-BS	IP	H	R	HR	HB	BB-IB	SO	ERA	AERA	OAV	OOB	AB-HR-SH	AVG	PB	SUP	APR	DL	PW
1985	Phi N	1	2	.333	26	0	0	3-0	36.1	33	15	3	1	16-3	26	3.22	115	.231	.309	3	.000	-0	—	2	0	0.1

Shipley, Joe Joseph Clark "Moses"; B5.9.1935 Morristown TN; BR/TR/6´4˝/(190–210); d7.14

YEAR	TM LG	W	L	PCT	G	GS	CG-SHO	SV-BS	IP	H	R	HR	HB	BB-IB	SO	ERA	AERA	OAV	OOB	AB-HR-SH	AVG	PB	SUP	APR	DL	PW
1958	SF N	0	0	ø	1	0	0	0	1.1	3	5	0	2	3-0	0	33.75	11	.429	.667	0	ø	0	—	-4	0	-0.2
1959	SF N	0	0	ø	10	1	0	0	18	16	11	2	1	17-0	11	4.50	85	.239	.400	3	.000	-0	70	-2	0	-0.1
1960	SF N	0	0	ø	15	0	0	0	20	20	13	2	3	9-1	9	5.40	64	.274	.372	0	ø	0	—	-4	0	-0.2
1963	Chi A	0	1	.000	3	0	0	0	4.2	9	7	0	0	6-0	3	5.79	61	.409	.536	2	.000	-0	—	-3	0	-0.6
Total	4	0	1	.000	29	1	0	0	44	48	36	4	6	35-1	23	5.93	61	.284	.422	5	.000	-1	70	-13	0	-1.1

Shirey, Duke Clair Lee; B6.20.1898 Jersey Shore PA; D9.1.1962 Hagerstown MD; BR/TR/6´1˝/175; d9.28

YEAR	TM LG	W	L	PCT	G	GS	CG-SHO	SV-BS	IP	H	R	HR	HB	BB-IB	SO	ERA	AERA	OAV	OOB	AB-HR-SH	AVG	PB	SUP	APR	DL	PW
1920	Was A	0	1	.000	2	1	0	0	4	5	4	0	1	2	0	6.75	55	.313	.421	1	.000	-0	128	-1	—	-0.3

Shirley, Tex Alvis Newman; B4.25.1918 Birthright TX; D11.7.1993 DeSoto TX; BB/TR (BR 1941–42)/6´1˝/175; d9.6

YEAR	TM LG	W	L	PCT	G	GS	CG-SHO	SV-BS	IP	H	R	HR	HB	BB-IB	SO	ERA	AERA	OAV	OOB	AB-HR-SH	AVG	PB	SUP	APR	DL	PW
1941	Phi A	0	1	.000	5	0	0	1	7.1	8	4	1	0	6	1	2.45	171	.286	.412	1	.000	-0	—	1	0	0.1
1942	Phi A	0	1	.000	15	1	0	1	35.2	37	30	0	2	22	10	5.30	71	.272	.381	9-0-1	.000	-1	136	-8	0	-0.5
1944	†StL A	5	4	.556	23	11	2-1	0	80.1	59	45	4	1	64	35	4.15	87	.203	.348	28	.143	-2*	101	-5	0	-0.8
1945	StL A	8	12	.400	32	24	10-2	0	183.2	191	79	8	1	93	77	3.63	97	.274	.360	70-0-2	.286	2*	98	0	0	0.2
1946	StL A	6	12	.333	27	18	7	0	139.2	148	89	7	1	105	45	4.96	75	.273	.391	51-0-1	.196	-0*	119	-18	0	-2.1
Total	5	19	30	.388	102	54	19-3	2	446.2	443	247	20	5	290	168	4.25	85	.261	.371	159-0-4	.214	-1	106	-30	0	-3.1

Shirley, Bob Robert Charles; B6.25.1954 Cushing OK; BR/TL/5´11˝/(180–185); [SDN76*S1/8]; d4.10; Col Oklahoma

YEAR	TM LG	W	L	PCT	G	GS	CG-SHO	SV-BS	IP	H	R	HR	HB	BB-IB	SO	ERA	AERA	OAV	OOB	AB-HR-SH	AVG	PB	SUP	APR	DL	PW
1977	SD N	12	18	.400	39	35	1	0-0	214	215	107	22	4	100-14	146	3.70	97	.259	.339	74-0-4	.122	-2	92	-6	0	-0.9
1978	SD N	8	11	.421	50	20	2	5-2	166	164	75	10	3	61-11	102	3.69	91	.262	.328	40-0-7	.125	-0	102	-5	0	-0.5
1979	SD N	8	16	.333	49	25	4-1	0-1	205	196	89	15	6	59-8	117	3.38	104	.257	.313	55-0-5	.091	-2	106	3	0	0.2
1980	SD N	11	12	.478	59	12	3	7-3	137	143	58	12	0	54-15	67	3.55	96	.276	.341	30-0-4	.033	-2	94	-1	0	-0.3
1981	StL N	6	4	.600	28	11	1	1-0	79.1	78	42	6	1	34-3	36	4.08	89	.260	.335	22-0-1	.136	-1	112	-5	0	-0.8
1982	Cin N	8	13	.381	41	20	1	0-0	152.2	138	74	17	3	73-13	89	3.60	102	.248	.335	42-0-5	.143	-1	64	-1	0	-0.2
1983	NY A	5	8	.385	25	17	1-1	0-0	108	122	71	10	0	36-3	53	5.08	78	.293	.345	0	ø	0	106	-15	0	-1.6
1984	NY A	3	3	.500	41	7	1	0-1	114.1	119	47	8	0	38-2	48	3.38	113	.274	.331	0	ø	0	77	6	0	0.3
1985	NY A	5	5	.500	48	8	2	2-2	109	103	34	5	0	26-2	55	2.64	153	.251	.293	0	ø	0	90	18	0	1.6
1986	NY A	0	4	.000	39	6	0	3-0	105.1	108	60	13	3	40-1	64	5.04	82	.271	.336	0	ø	0	48	-8	0	-0.3
1987	NY A	1	0	1.000	12	1	0	0-0	34	36	20	4	0	16-0	12	4.50	99	.277	.342	0	ø	0	82	-1	0	-0.1
	KC A	0	0	ø	3	0	0	0-0	7.1	10	12	5	0	6-0	1	14.73	31	.323	.432	0	ø	0	—	-7	0	-0.3
	Year	1	0	1.000	15	1	0	0-0	41.1	46	32	9	0	22-0	13	6.31	71	.286	.360	0	ø	0	82	-9	0	-0.4
Total	11	67	94	.416	434	162	16-2	18-9	1432	1432	689	127	20	543-72	790	3.82	97	.264	.331	263-0-26	.110	-8	91	-22	0	-2.9

Shirley, Steve Steven Brian; B10.12.1956 San Francisco CA; BL/TL/6´0˝/185; [LAN74 2/45]; d6.21

YEAR	TM LG	W	L	PCT	G	GS	CG-SHO	SV-BS	IP	H	R	HR	HB	BB-IB	SO	ERA	AERA	OAV	OOB	AB-HR-SH	AVG	PB	SUP	APR	DL	PW
1982	LA N	1	1	.500	11	0	0	0-0	12.2	15	6	0	0	7-2	8	4.26	81	.300	.386	1	1.000	0	—	-1	0	-0.1

Shocker, Urban Urban James (b Urbain Jacques Shockcor); B9.22.1890 Cleveland OH; D9.9.1928 Denver CO; BR/TR/5´10˝/170; d4.24; Mil 1918

YEAR	TM LG	W	L	PCT	G	GS	CG-SHO	SV-BS	IP	H	R	HR	HB	BB-IB	SO	ERA	AERA	OAV	OOB	AB-HR-SH	AVG	PB	SUP	APR	DL	PW
1916	NY A	4	3	.571	12	9	4-1	0	82.1	67	25	2	6	32	43	2.62	110	.230	.319	21-0-2	.190	1	102	4	—	0.5
1917	NY A	8	5	.615	26	13	7	1	145	124	59	5	0	46	68	2.61	103	.241	.303	45-0-5	.178	-1	109	0	—	0.0
1918	StL A	6	5	.545	14	9	7	2	94.2	69	26	0	1	40	33	1.81	152	.209	.296	34	.324	4	61	10	—	1.8
1919	StL A	13	11	.542	30	25	14-5	0	211	193	75	6	4	55	86	2.69	123	.244	.296	58-0-2	.138	-0	83	17	—	1.7
1920	StL A	20	10	.667	38	28	22-5	**5**	245.2	224	97	10	4	70	107	2.71	145	.248	.305	80-0-5	.225	2	98	30	—	3.7
1921	StL A	**27**	12	.692	47	38	30-4	4	326.2	345	151	21	6	86	132	3.55	126	.270	.319	104-0-7	.260	5	105	33	—	4.2
1922	StL A	24	17	.585	48	38	29-2	3	348	365	141	22	4	57	**149**	2.97	139	.272	.304	115-1-6	.191	2	97	44	—	**4.9**
1923	StL A	20	12	.625	43	35	24-3	5	277.1	292	122	12	3	49	109	3.41	122	.272	**.306**	80-0-12	.200	2	93	24	—	2.6
1924	StL A	16	13	.552	40	33	17-4	1	246.1	270	128	11	3	52	88	4.20	107	.277	.315	67-0-9	.239	5	105	11	—	1.5
1925	NY A	12	12	.500	41	30	15-2	2	244.1	278	108	17	3	58	74	3.65	117	.294	.336	64-0-10	.172	5	104	20	—	2.1
1926	†NY A	19	11	.633	41	32	18	2	258.1	272	113	13	2	71	59	3.38	114	.269	.318	76-0-20	.171	1	117	16	—	1.7
1927	NY A	18	6	.750	31	27	13-2	0	200	207	86	8	1	41	35	2.84	136	.268	.306	54-0-20	.241	3	127	20	—	2.3
1928	NY A	0	0	ø	1	0	0	0	2	3	0	0	0	0	0	0.00	ø	.429	.429	0	ø	0	—	1	—	0.0
Total	13	187	117	.615	412	317	200-28	25	2681.2	2709	1131	127	37	657	983	3.17	124	.265	.311	798-1-98	.209	28	103	230	—	27.0

Shoffner, Milt Milburn James; B11.13.1905 Sherman TX; D1.19.1978 Madison OH; BL/TL/6´1.5˝/184; d7.20

YEAR	TM LG	W	L	PCT	G	GS	CG-SHO	SV-BS	IP	H	R	HR	HB	BB-IB	SO	ERA	AERA	OAV	OOB	AB-HR-SH	AVG	PB	SUP	APR	DL	PW
1929	Cle A	2	3	.400	11	3	1	0	44.2	46	28	4	3	22	15	5.04	88	.284	.380	15	.000	-2	38	-2	—	-0.4
1930	Cle A	3	4	.429	24	10	1	0	84.2	129	86	8	1	50	17	7.97	61	.362	.442	33-1-2	.212	1	114	-26	—	-1.6
1931	Cle A	2	3	.400	12	4	1	0	41	55	34	4	2	26	12	7.24	64	.320	.415	13	.077	-1	96	-9	—	-1.0
1937	Bos N	3	1	.750	6	5	3-1	1	42.2	38	14	1	1	9	13	2.53	142	.239	.284	16-1-3	.125	1	144	5	—	0.6
1938	Bos N	8	7	.533	26	15	9-1	1	139.2	147	60	7	2	36	49	3.54	97	.270	.317	57	.211	3*	100	0	—	0.3
1939	Bos N	4	6	.400	25	11	7	1	132.1	133	56	4	1	42	51	3.13	118	.265	.324	44-0-2	.159	-0	92	8	—	0.6
	Cin N	2	2	.500	10	3	0	0	37.2	43	18	3	2	11	6	3.35	115	.289	.346	11-0-1	.091	-1	99	1	—	0.0
	Year	6	8	.429	35	14	7	1	170	176	74	7	3	53	57	3.18	117	.271	.329	55-0-3	.145	-1	94	9	—	0.6
1940	Cin N	1	0	1.000	20	0	0	0	54.1	56	35	3	0	18	17	5.63	67	.268	.326	16-0-1	.125	-1	—	-10	—	-0.6
Total	7	25	26	.490	134	51	22-2	3	577	647	331	34	12	214	180	4.59	85	.287	.352	205-2-9	.156	-0	102	-33	—	-2.1

Shore, Ernie Ernest Grady; B3.24.1891 East Bend NC; D9.24.1980 Winston–Salem NC; BR/TR/6´4˝/220; d6.20; Mil 1918; Col Guilford

YEAR	TM LG	W	L	PCT	G	GS	CG-SHO	SV-BS	IP	H	R	HR	HB	BB-IB	SO	ERA	AERA	OAV	OOB	AB-HR-SH	AVG	PB	SUP	APR	DL	PW
1912	NY N	0	0	ø	1	0	0	1	1	8	10	1	0	1	1	27.00	13	.667	.692	0	ø	0	—	-5	—	-0.6
1914	Bos A	10	5	.667	20	16	10-1	1	139.2	103	45	1	5	34	51	2.00	135	.204	.261	49-0-1	.102	-3	88	10	—	0.9
1915	†Bos A	19	8	.704	38	32	17-4	0	247	207	75	3	4	66	102	1.64	169	.228	.283	79-0-5	.101	-3	90	27	—	2.8
1916	†Bos A	16	10	.615	38	28	10-3	1	225.2	221	83	1	4	49	62	2.63	105	.259	.302	77-0-4	.091	-5	95	3	—	0.1
1917	Bos A	13	10	.565	29	27	14-1	1	226.2	201	76	1	12	55	57	2.22	116	.240	.297	78-0-4	.167	-1	94	8	—	0.8
1919	NY A	5	8	.385	20	13	3	0	95	105	50	4	1	44	24	4.17	77	.288	.366	28-0-2	.143	-2	70	-8	—	-1.2
1920	NY A	2	2	.500	14	5	2	1	44.1	61	31	1	1	21	12	4.87	78	.333	.405	11-0-2	.182	0	112	-6	—	-0.4
Total	7	65	43	.602	160	121	56-9	5	979.1	906	370	12	27	270	309	2.47	113	.247	.304	322-0-18	.121	-14	91	29	—	2.4

Shore, Ray Raymond Everett; B6.9.1921 Cincinnati OH; D8.13.1996 St.Louis MO; BR/TR/6´3˝/210; d9.21; C5

YEAR	TM LG	W	L	PCT	G	GS	CG-SHO	SV-BS	IP	H	R	HR	HB	BB-IB	SO	ERA	AERA	OAV	OOB	AB-HR-SH	AVG	PB	SUP	APR	DL	PW
1946	StL A	0	0	ø	1	0	0	0	1	3	2	0	0	1	1	18.00	21	.500	.571	0	ø	0	—	-1	0	-0.1
1948	StL A	1	2	.333	17	4	0	0	38	40	30	2	4	35	12	6.39	71	.270	.422	9	.000	-1	79	-7	0	-0.6
1949	StL A	0	1	.000	13	0	0	0	23.1	27	30	3	2	31	13	10.80	42	.297	.484	5	.000	-1	—	-14	0	-0.7
Total	3	1	3	.250	31	4	0	0	62.1	70	62	5	6	67	26	8.23	55	.286	.450	14	.000	-2	79	-22	0	-1.4

Shores, Bill William David; B5.26.1904 Abilene TX; D2.19.1984 Purcell OK; BR/TR/6´0˝/185; d4.11

YEAR	TM LG	W	L	PCT	G	GS	CG-SHO	SV-BS	IP	H	R	HR	HB	BB-IB	SO	ERA	AERA	OAV	OOB	AB-HR-SH	AVG	PB	SUP	APR	DL	PW
1928	Phi A	1	1	.500	3	2	1	0	14	13	7	0	0	7	5	3.21	125	.250	.339	5	.000	-1	53	1	—	0.0
1929	Phi A	11	6	.647	39	13	5-1	7	152.2	150	71	9	3	59	49	3.60	118	.262	.334	40-0-6	.125	-2	94	11	—	1.0
1930	†Phi A	12	4	.750	31	19	7-1	0	159	169	86	11	3	70	48	4.19	112	.276	.353	57-0-3	.193	-2	120	8	—	0.4
1931	Phi A	0	3	.000	6	2	0	0	16	26	18	3	0	10	2	5.06	89	.361	.439	3	.333	0	66	-4	—	-0.6
1933	NY N	2	1	.667	8	3	1	0	36.2	41	18	4	0	14	20	3.93	82	.291	.355	11	.273	1	121	-2	—	-0.1
1936	Chi A	0	0	ø	9	0	0	0	17	26	18	1	0	8	5	9.53	55	.356	.420	5	.200	-0	—	-7	—	-0.3
Total	6	26	15	.634	96	39	14-2	7	395.1	425	218	28	6	168	129	4.17	105	.279	.353	121-0-9	.174	-4	106	7	—	0.4

Short, Chris Christopher Joseph; B9.19.1937 Milford DE; D8.1.1991 Wilmington DE; BR/TL (BB 1970–71)/6´4˝/(195–218); d4.19; Col Bordentown Mil. Inst. (NJ) JC

YEAR	TM LG	W	L	PCT	G	GS	CG-SHO	SV-BS	IP	H	R	HR	HB	BB-IB	SO	ERA	AERA	OAV	OOB	AB-HR-SH	AVG	PB	SUP	APR	DL	PW
1959	Phi N	0	0	ø	3	2	0	0	14.1	19	13	3	1	10-0	8	8.16	50	.317	.423	6	.000	-1	141	-6	0	-0.3
1960	Phi N	6	9	.400	42	10	2	3	107.1	101	55	8	3	52-5	54	3.94	99	.249	.335	25	.000	-3	80	-2	0	-0.5
1961	Phi N	6	12	.333	39	16	1	1	127.1	157	94	12	3	71-11	80	5.94	69	.304	.390	37-0-7	.162	-1*	97	-26	0	-3.3
1962	Phi N	11	9	.550	47	12	4	3	142	149	66	13	8	56-6	91	3.42	113	.272	.347	36-0-4	.222	1*	70	5	0	0.8
1963	Phi N	9	12	.429	38	27	6-3	0	198	185	77	12	3	69-6	160	2.95	109	.248	.314	66-0-4	.106	-2	112	5	0	0.5
1964	Phi N★	17	9	.654	42	31	12-4	2	220.2	174	63	10	4	51-5	181	2.20	158	.217	.266	65-0-8	.108	-1*	96	31	0	3.6

YEAR	TM LG	W	L	PCT	G	GS	CG-SHO	SV-BS	IP	H	R	HR	HB	BB-IB	SO	ERA	AERA	OAV	OOB	AB-HR-SH	AVG	PB	SUP	APR	DL	PW
1965	Phi N	18	11	.621	47	40	15-5	2	297.1	260	102	18	5	89-8	237	2.82	123	.235	.294	99-0-8	.131	-2	92	24	0	2.0
1966	Phi N	20	10	.667	42	39	19-4	0	272	257	120	28	9	68-2	177	3.54	102	.250	.301	106-0-1	.208	1	122	1	0	0.2
1967	Phi N★	9	11	.450	29	26	8-2	1	199.1	163	55	9	4	74-7	142	2.39	142	.225	.300	66-0-4	.091	-2	90	25	34	2.4
1968	Phi N	19	13	.594	42	36	9-2	1	269.2	236	99	25	9	81-10	202	2.94	102	.236	.298	79-0-8	.152	0*	102	2	0	0.3
1969	Phi N	0	0	ø	2	2	0	0-0	10	11	8	2	1	4-0	5	7.20	50	.282	.364	3	.000	-0	112	-4	165	-0.2
1970	Phi N	9	16	.360	36	34	7-2	1-0	199	211	100	13	6	66-3	133	4.30	94	.272	.330	61-0-7	.049	-5	73	-5	0	-1.2
1971	Phi N	7	14	.333	31	26	5-2	1-0	173	182	85	22	3	63-2	95	3.85	92	.274	.339	48-0-6	.083	-1	82	-6	0	-0.9
1972	Phi N	1	1	.500	19	0	0	1-1	23	24	12	3	0	8-2	20	3.91	92	.267	.320	0	ø	0	—	-1	96	-0.1
1973	Mil A	3	5	.375	42	7	0	2-3	72	86	42	5	2	44-7	44	5.13	74	.299	.394	0	ø	0	107	-9	0	-0.9
Total	15	135	132	.506	501	308	88-24	18-4	2325	2215	991	183	61	806-74	1629	3.43	104	.252	.318	697-0-57	.126	-17	95	34	295	2.4
SHORT, BILL	William Ross; B11.27.1937 Kingston NY; BL/TL/5´9˝/(170–180); d4.23																									
1960	NY A	3	5	.375	10	10	2	0	47	49	25	5	1	30-1	14	4.79	75	.282	.390	15	.200	1	103	-5	0	-0.7
1962	Bal A	0	0	ø	5	0	0	0	4	8	7	0	1	6-0	3	15.75	23	.381	.536	1	.000	-0	—	-5	0	-0.3
1966	Bal A	2	3	.400	6	6	1-1	0	37.2	34	15	2	0	10-0	27	2.87	116	.239	.286	11	.091	-1	48	1	0	0.1
	Bos A	0	0	ø	8	0	0	0	8.1	10	6	1	0	2-0	2	4.32	88	.294	.333	1	.000	-0	—	-1	0	0.0
	Year	2	3	.400	14	6	1-1	0	46	44	21	3	0	12-0	29	3.13	109	.250	.295	12	.083	-1	47	0	0	0.1
1967	Pit N	0	0	ø	6	0	0	1	2.1	1	1	0	0	1-0	1	3.86	87	.143	.250	1	.000	-0	—	0	0	0.0
1968	NY N	0	3	.000	34	0	0	1	29.2	24	17	0	1	14-1	24	4.85	62	.220	.307	2	.000	-0	—	-6	0	-0.6
1969	Cin N	0	0	ø	4	0	0	0-0	2.1	4	4	0	0	1-0	0	15.43	24	.400	.455	1	.000	-0	—	-3	0	-0.2
Total	6	5	11	.313	73	16	3-1	2-0	131.1	130	75	8	3	64-2	71	4.73	72	.262	.346	32	.125	-1	85	-19	0	-1.7
SHOUN, CLYDE	Clyde Mitchell "Hardrock"; B3.20.1912 Mountain City TN; D3.20.1968 Mountain Home TN; BL/TL/6´1˝/188; d8.7; Mil 1945																									
1935	Chi N	1	0	1.000	5	1	0	0	12.2	14	4	2	0	5	5	2.84	138	.298	.365	3	.000	-0	43	2	—	0.1
1936	Chi N	0	0	ø	4	0	0	0	4.1	3	6	0	0	6	1	12.46	32	.200	.429	0	ø	0	—	-4	—	-0.2
1937	Chi N	7	7	.500	37	9	2	0	93	118	65	9	0	45	43	5.61	71	.309	.382	29-0-1	.138	-1	111	-17	—	-2.3
1938	StL N	6	6	.500	40	12	3	1	117.1	130	58	8	1	43	37	4.14	96	.283	.345	31-0-2	.258	0	102	1	—	0.0
1939	StL N	3	1	.750	**53**	2	0	**9**	103	98	51	4	2	42	50	3.76	109	.248	.323	26-0-2	.115	-1	117	**3**	—	0.0
1940	StL N	13	11	.542	**54**	19	13-1	5	197.1	193	96	13	2	46	82	3.92	102	.255	.299	63-0-2	.190	-1	81	3	—	0.3
1941	StL N	3	5	.375	26	6	0	0	70	98	48	9	0	20	34	5.66	67	.337	.379	22-0-3	.182	0	116	-13	0	-1.2
1942	StL N	0	0	ø	2	0	0	0	1.2	1	0	0	0	0	0	0.00	ø	.167	.167	0	ø	0	—	1	0	0.0
	Cin N	1	3	.250	34	0	0	0	72.2	55	23	2	0	24	32	2.23	147	.216	.283	13	.308	1	—	8	0	0.6
	Year	1	3	.250	36	0	0	0	74.1	56	23	2	0	24	32	2.18	151	.215	.281	13	.308	1	—	9	0	0.6
1943	Cin N	14	5	.737	45	5	2	7	147	131	52	5	0	46	61	3.06	108	.241	.300	42-0-1	.310	4	82	6	0	1.2
1944	Cin N	13	10	.565	38	21	12-1	2	202.2	193	83	10	3	42	55	3.02	116	.248	.290	67-0-5	.224	1	88	9	0	0.9
1946	Cin N	1	6	.143	27	5	0	0	79	87	42	3	1	26	20	4.10	82	.292	.351	21-0-1	.095	-1	67	-7	0	-0.8
1947	Cin N	0	0	ø	10	0	0	0	14.1	16	8	2	1	5	7	5.02	82	.320	.393	0	ø	0	—	-1	0	0.0
	Bos N	5	3	.625	26	3	1-1	1	73.2	73	41	6	0	21	23	4.40	89	.254	.305	19-0-1	.158	-1	83	-4	0	-0.5
	Year	5	3	.625	36	3	1-1	1	88	89	49	8	1	26	30	4.50	87	.264	.319	19-0-1	.158	-1	82	-5	0	-0.5
1948	Bos N	5	1	.833	36	2	1	4	74	77	37	7	0	20	25	4.01	96	.267	.315	21-0-2	.190	0	139	-2	0	-0.2
1949	Bos N	0	0	ø	1	0	0	0	1	1	0	0	0	0	0	0.00	ø	.250	.250	0	ø	0	—	0	0	0.0
	Chi A	1	1	.500	16	0	0	0	23.1	37	17	1	0	13	8	5.79	72	.370	.442	5	.200	0	—	-4	0	-0.3
Total	14	73	59	.553	454	85	34-3	29	1287	1325	631	81	10	404	483	3.91	96	.267	.324	362-0-20	.202	1	94	-19	0	-2.4
SHOUSE, BRIAN	Brian Douglas; B9.26.1968 Effingham IL; BL/TL/5´11˝/(175–190); [PitN90 13/349]; d7.31; Col Bradley; [DL 1999 Ari N 16]																									
1993	Pit N	0	0	ø	6	0	0	0-0	4	7	4	1	0	2-0	3	9.00	45	.368	.409	0	ø	0	—	-2	0	-0.1
1998	Bos A	0	1	.000	7	0	0	0-0	8	9	5	2	0	4-0	5	5.63	84	.281	.361	0	ø	0	—	-1	0	-0.1
2002	KC A	0	0	ø	23	0	0	0-0	14.2	15	10	3	2	9-1	11	6.14	81	.259	.371	0	ø	0	—	-1	15	0.0
2003	Tex A	0	1	.000	62	0	0	1-0	61	62	24	1	4	14-6	40	3.10	160	.267	.320	0	ø	0	—	11	0	0.6
2004	Tex A	2	0	1.000	53	0	0	0-0	44.1	36	12	3	1	18-3	34	2.23	221	.224	.302	0	ø	0	—	12	39	0.7
2005	Tex A	3	2	.600	64	0	0	0-2	53.1	55	37	7	3	18-4	35	5.23	87	.266	.329	0	ø	0	—	-5	0	-0.3
2006	Tex A	0	0	ø	6	0	0	0-1	4.1	6	2	1	0	1-1	3	4.15	113	.316	.350	0	ø	0	—	0	16	0.0
	Mil N	1	3	.250	59	0	0	2-2	34	34	16	3	6	17-4	20	3.97	113	.264	.373	0	ø	0	—	2	0	0.3
Total	7	6	7	.462	280	0	0	3-5	223.2	224	110	21	16	83-19	151	3.98	119	.261	.335	0	ø	0	—	16	86	1.1
SHOW, ERIC	Eric Vaughn; B5.19.1956 Riverside CA; D3.16.1994 Dulzura CA; BR/TR/6´1˝/(179–190); [SDN78 18/447]; d9.2; Col California–Riverside																									
1981	SD N	1	3	.250	15	0	0	3-3	23	17	9	2	1	9-3	22	3.13	104	.213	.300	0	ø	0	—	0	0	0.0
1982	SD N	10	6	.625	47	14	2-2	3-0	150	117	49	10	5	48-3	88	2.64	130	.217	.284	41-0-2	.146	-1	103	14	0	1.5
1983	SD N	15	12	.556	35	33	4-2	0-0	200.2	201	97	25	6	74-3	120	4.17	84	.263	.331	64-0-5	.172	1	107	-13	0	-1.6
1984	†SD N	15	9	.625	32	32	3-1	0-0	206.2	175	88	18	4	88-4	104	3.40	106	.234	.316	69-3-6	.246	6	90	4	0	1.1
1985	SD N	12	11	.522	35	35	5-2	0-0	233	212	95	27	5	87-7	141	3.09	115	.243	.314	79-1-7	.127	-1	95	10	0	0.7
1986	SD N	9	5	.643	24	22	2	0-0	136.1	109	47	11	4	69-4	94	2.97	123	.225	.326	43-0-3	.163	1	92	12	62	1.2
1987	SD N	8	16	.333	34	34	5-3	0-0	206.1	188	99	26	9	85-7	117	3.84	103	.241	.321	70-0-7	.071	-4	90	3	0	-0.2
1988	SD N	16	11	.593	32	32	13-1	0-0	234.2	201	86	22	6	53-5	144	3.26	104	.231	.279	81-0-5	.148	-0	94	7	0	0.6
1989	SD N	8	6	.571	16	16	1	0-0	106.1	113	59	9	2	39-3	66	4.23	83	.274	.336	34-0-4	.235	2*	104	-9	88	-1.0
1990	SD N	6	8	.429	39	12	0	1-0	106.1	131	74	16	4	41-9	55	5.76	67	.306	.369	25-0-1	.200	1	96	-21	0	-2.5
1991	Oak A	1	2	.333	23	5	0	0-0	51.2	62	36	5	0	17-1	20	5.92	65	.298	.345	0	ø	0	114	-13	25	-0.7
Total	11	101	89	.532	332	235	35-11	7-3	1655	1526	739	171	46	610-49	971	3.66	98	.247	.317	506-4-40	.160	3	97	-6	175	-0.9
SHREVE, LEV	Leven Lawrence; B1.14.1869 Louisville KY; D10.18.1942 Detroit MI; BR/TR/5´11˝/150; d5.2																									
1887	Bal AA	3	1	.750	5	5	4-1	0	38	33	26	0	1	19	13	3.79	108	.228	.321	24	.167	-1*	143	1	—	0.0
	Ind N	5	9	.357	14	14	14-1	0	122	141	100	5	4	65	22	4.72	88	.278	.365	49	.265	0	73	-9	—	-0.7
1888	Ind N	11	24	.314	35	35	34-1	0	297.2	352	208	23	8	93	101	4.63	64	.288	.342	115	.183	-1*	74	-49	—	-4.8
1889	Ind N	0	3	.000	3	3	1	0	15.2	25	27	3	1	12	5	13.79	30	.352	.452	7	.000	-1	145	-14	—	-1.6
Total	3	19	37	.339	57	57	53-3	0	473.1	551	361	31	14	189	141	4.89	70	.283	.351	195	.195	-3	85	-71	—	-7.1
SHRIVER, HARRY	Harry Graydon "Pop"; B9.2.1896 Wadestown WV; D1.21.1970 Morgantown WV; BR/TR/6´2˝/180; d4.14; Col West Virginia Wesleyan																									
1922	Bro N	4	6	.400	25	13	4-2	0	108.1	114	49	5	2	48	38	2.99	136	.287	.367	27-0-3	.037	-3	48	11	—	0.5
1923	Bro N	0	0	ø	1	1	0	0	4	8	3	0	0	0	1	6.75	58	.444	.444	1	.000	-0	148	-1	—	-0.1
Total	2	4	6	.400	26	14	4-2	0	112.1	122	52	5	2	48	39	3.12	130	.294	.370	28-0-3	.036	-3	54	10	—	0.4
SHUEY, PAUL	Paul Kenneth; B9.16.1970 Lima OH; BR/TR/6´3˝/215; [CleA92 1/2]; d5.8; Col North Carolina; [DL 2004 LA N 183]																									
1994	Cle A	0	1	.000	14	0	0	5-0	11.2	14	11	1	0	12-1	16	8.49	56	.280	.419	0	ø	0	—	-4	24	-0.6
1995	Cle A	0	2	.000	7	0	0	0-0	6.1	5	4	0	0	5-0	5	4.26	111	.238	.385	0	ø	0	—	0	18	0.0
1996	†Cle A	5	2	.714	42	0	0	4-3	53.2	45	19	6	0	26-3	44	2.85	171	.231	.317	0	ø	0	—	12	0	1.5
1997	Cle A	4	2	.667	40	0	0	2-1	45	52	31	5	1	28-3	46	6.20	76	.294	.389	1	.000	-0	—	-6	59	-0.7
1998	†Cle A	5	4	.556	43	0	0	2-3	51	44	19	6	3	25-5	58	3.00	159	.229	.327	1	.000	-0	—	10	66	1.5
1999	†Cle A	8	5	.615	72	0	0	6-6	81.2	68	37	8	1	40-7	103	3.53	144	.223	.314	0	ø	0	—	13	15	1.9
2000	Cle A	4	2	.667	57	0	0	0-5	63.2	51	25	4	3	30-3	69	3.39	148	.219	.312	0	ø	0	—	11	36	0.9
2001	†Cle A	5	3	.625	47	0	0	2-3	54.1	53	25	1	1	26-5	70	2.82	163	.251	.333	0	ø	0	—	8	74	1.0
2002	Cle A	3	0	1.000	39	0	0	0-2	37.1	31	11	1	0	10-1	39	2.41	184	.225	.275	0	ø	0	—	8	15	0.6
	LA N	5	2	.714	28	0	0	1-2	30.2	25	18	2	1	21-1	24	4.40	89	.217	.341	3	.333	0	—	-3	0	-0.5
2003	LA N	6	4	.600	62	0	0	0-1	69	50	24	6	4	33-3	60	3.00	137	.207	.312	2	.000	-0	—	9	22	1.3
Total	10	45	27	.625	451	0	0	22-26	504.1	438	224	40	14	256-32	534	3.57	131	.233	.327	7	.143	-0	—	58	512	6.9
SHULTZ, TOOTS	Wallace Luther; B10.10.1888 Homestead PA; D1.30.1959 McKeesport PA; BR/TR/5´10˝/175; d5.5; Col Penn																									
1911	Phi N	0	3	.000	5	3	2	0	25	30	28	5	4	15	9	9.36	37	.300	.412	8-0-1	.250	0	73	-14	—	-1.3
1912	Phi N	1	4	.200	22	4	1	1	59	75	44	2	3	35	20	4.58	79	.333	.430	21	.238	0*	157	-7	—	-0.5
Total	2	1	7	.125	27	7	3	1	84	105	72	7	7	50	29	6.00	60	.323	.424	29-0-1	.241	0	121	-21	—	-1.8
SHUMAKER, ANTHONY	Anthony Warren; B5.14.1973 Tucson AZ; BL/TL/6´5˝/222; [PhiN95 23/633]; d7.23; Col Cardinal Stritch																									
1999	Phi N	0	3	.000	8	4	0	0-0	22.2	23	17	3	1	14-0	17	5.96	78	.261	.369	5	.200	0	93	-4	0	-0.4

YEAR	TM LG	W	L	PCT	G	GS	CG-SHO	SV-BS	IP	H	R	HR	HB	BB-IB	SO	ERA	AERA	OAV	OOB	AB-HR-SH	AVG	PB	SUP	APR	DL	PW
SHUMAN, HARRY	Harry; B3.5.1915 Philadelphia PA; D10.25.1996 Philadelphia PA; BR/TR/6´2˝/195; d9.14; Col Temple																									
1942	Pit N	0	0	ø	1	0	0	0	2	0	0	0	0	1	1	0.00	ø	.000	.167	0	ø	0	—	1	0	0.0
1943	Pit N	0	0	ø	11	0	0	0	22	30	20	0	2	8	5	5.32	65	.337	.404	2	.000	-0	—	-6	0	-0.3
1944	Phi N	0	0	ø	18	0	0	0	26.2	26	15	1	0	11	4	4.05	89	.245	.316	1	.000	-0	—	-2	0	-0.1
Total	3	0	0	ø	30	0	0	0	50.2	56	35	1	2	20	10	4.44	80	.280	.351	3	.000	-0	—	-7	0	-0.4
SIEBERT, PAUL	Paul Edward; B6.5.1953 Minneapolis MN; BL/TL/6´2˝/(185–205); [HouN71 3/58]; d9.7; f–Dick																									
1974	Hou N	1	1	.500	5	5	1-1	0-0	25.1	21	12	3	0	11-0	10	3.55	98	.236	.314	6-0-2	.000	-1	110	-1	0	-0.1
1975	Hou N	0	2	.000	7	2	0	2-0	18.1	20	7	0	1	6-1	6	2.95	115	.294	.360	3	.000	-0	26	1	0	0.1
1976	Hou N	0	2	.000	19	0	0	0-0	25.2	29	10	0	1	18-7	10	3.16	102	.296	.403	2	.000	-0	—	0	0	0.0
1977	SD N	0	0	ø	4	0	0	0-0	3.2	3	4	1	0	4-1	1	2.45	146	.214	.368	0	ø	0	—	-1	0	-0.1
	NY N	2	1	.667	25	0	0	0-0	28	27	12	0	1	13-4	20	3.86	98	.257	.336	1	.000	-0	—	0	0	0.0
	Year	2	1	.667	29	0	0	0-0	31.2	30	16	1	1	17-5	21	3.69	102	.252	.340	1	.000	-0	—	-1	0	-0.1
1978	NY N	0	2	.000	27	0	0	1-1	28	30	16	2	1	21-5	12	5.14	69	.283	.406	1	.000	-0	—	-4	0	-0.3
Total	5	3	8	.273	87	7	1-1	3-1	129	130	61	6	4	73-18	59	3.77	93	.271	.366	13-0-2	.000	-2	87	-5	0	-0.4
SIEBERT, SONNY	Wilfred Charles; B1.14.1937 St.Marys MO; BR/TR/6´3˝/(190–205); d4.26; C2; Col Missouri																									
1964	Cle A	7	9	.438	41	14	3-1	3	156	142	61	15	2	57-4	144	3.23	111	.243	.310	49-2-0	.265	5*	85	7	0	1.2
1965	Cle A	16	8	.667	39	27	4-1	1	188.2	139	58	14	5	46-2	191	2.43	143	.206	**.259**	66-1-1	.106	-2*	102	22	0	2.7
1966	Cle A★	16	8	**.667**	34	32	11-1	1	241	193	89	25	6	62-3	163	2.80	123	.221	.276	85-0-5	.129	-2	111	15	0	1.3
1967	Cle A	10	12	.455	34	26	7-1	4	185.1	136	59	17	6	54-2	136	2.38	137	.202	.266	52-1-5	.135	1	80	17	0	2.2
1968	Cle A	12	10	.545	31	30	8-4	0	206	145	76	12	8	88-10	146	2.97	100	.198	.288	70-0-5	.157	1*	113	1	0	0.4
1969	Cle A	0	1	.000	2	2	0	0-0	14	10	5	1	0	8-0	6	3.21	118	.196	.305	4	.250	0	35	1	0	0.1
	Bos A	14	10	.583	43	22	2	5-3	163.1	151	93	21	4	68-1	127	3.80	101	.245	.321	53-1-4	.151	1	109	-5	0	-0.6
	Year	14	11	.560	45	24	2	5-3	177.1	161	98	22	4	76-1	133	3.76	102	.241	.320	57-1-4	.158	1	103	-4	0	-0.5
1970	Bos A	15	8	.652	33	33	7-2	0-0	222.2	207	98	29	6	60-2	142	3.44	116	.248	.302	77-0-4	.130	-2	102	13	0	1.1
1971	Bos A☆	16	10	.615	32	32	12-4	0-0	235.1	220	84	20	3	60-5	131	2.91	128	.245	.292	79-6-7	.266	9	103	19	0	3.3
1972	Bos A	12	12	.500	32	30	7-3	0-0	196.1	204	105	17	7	59-4	123	3.80	85	.264	.321	72-1-1	.236	6*	129	-16	0	-1.2
1973	Bos A	0	1	.000	2	0	0	0-1	2.1	5	2	1	0	1-0	5	7.71	52	.417	.462	0	ø	0	—	-1	0	-0.2
	Tex A	7	11	.389	25	20	1-1	2-0	119.2	120	68	11	3	37-1	76	3.99	94	.258	.314	0	ø	0	96	-6	0	-0.8
	Year	7	12	.368	27	20	1-1	2-1	122	125	70	12	3	38-1	81	4.06	93	.262	.318	0	ø	0	96	-8	0	-1.0
1974	StL N	8	8	.500	28	20	5-3	0-0	133.2	150	66	8	3	51-14	68	3.84	94	.288	.353	44-0-2	.114	-2	98	-4	23	-0.7
1975	SD N	3	2	.600	6	6	0	0-0	26.2	37	15	2	1	10-4	10	4.39	80	.330	.387	8-0-1	.375	2*	80	-2	0	-0.2
	Oak A	4	4	.500	17	13	0	0-0	61	60	28	4	0	31-3	44	3.69	99	.252	.335	1	.000	-0	97	0	40	-0.1
Total	12	140	114	.551	399	307	67-21	16-4	2152	1919	907	197	54	692-55	1512	3.21	110	.238	.301	660-12-35	.173	18	103	61	63	8.5
SIEBLER, DWIGHT	Dwight Leroy; B8.5.1937 Columbus NE; BR/TR/6´2˝/(184–195); d8.26; Col Nebraska																									
1963	Min A	2	1	.667	7	5	2	0	38.2	25	13	6	1	12-0	22	2.79	130	.182	.253	15	.133	-0	112	4	0	0.2
1964	Min A	0	0	ø	9	0	0	0	11	10	6	1	0	6-1	10	4.91	73	.256	.356	0	ø	0	—	-1	0	-0.1
1965	Min A	0	0	ø	7	1	0	0	15	11	7	2	0	11-0	15	4.20	85	.193	.324	1	.000	-0	49	-1	0	0.0
1966	Min A	2	2	.500	23	2	0	1	49.2	47	26	6	1	14-2	24	3.44	104	.253	.302	11	.000	-1	159	-1	0	-0.2
1967	Min A	0	0	ø	2	0	0	0	3	4	1	0	0	1-0	0	3.00	115	.364	.417	0	ø	0	—	0	0	0.0
Total	5	4	3	.571	48	8	2	1	117.1	97	53	15	2	44-3	71	3.45	104	.226	.298	27	.074	-1	116	1	0	-0.1
SIERRA, CANDY	Ulises (Pizarro); B3.27.1967 Rio Piedras, PR; BR/TR/6´2˝/190; d4.6																									
1988	SD N	0	1	.000	15	0	0	0-1	23.2	36	15	2	0	11-2	20	5.70	60	.379	.439	3	.000	-0	—	-5	0	-0.3
	Cin N	0	0	ø	1	0	0	0-0	4	5	2	0	0	1-0	4	4.50	79	.294	.333	1	.000	-0	—	0	0	0.0
	Year	0	1	.000	16	0	0	0-1	27.2	41	17	2	0	12-2	24	5.53	62	.366	.424	4	.000	-0	—	-6	0	-0.3
SIEVER, ED	Edward Tilden; B4.2.1875 Goddard KS; D2.4.1920 Detroit MI; BL/TL/5´11.5˝/190; d4.26																									
1901	Det A	18	14	.563	38	33	30-2	0	288.2	334	166	9	8	65	85	3.24	119	.286	.328	107-0-6	.168	-5	102	18	—	1.2
1902	Det A	8	11	.421	25	23	17-4	1	188.1	166	73	0	2	32	36	**1.91**	**191**	.237	.272	66-0-4	.152	-4	86	29	—	2.1
1903	StL A	13	14	.481	31	27	24-1	0	254	245	102	6	5	39	90	2.48	117	.253	.285	93-0-2	.140	-4	83	11	—	0.8
1904	StL A	10	15	.400	29	24	19-2	0	217	235	112	3	3	65	77	2.65	93	.277	.330	71	.155	-1*	86	-14	—	-1.7
1906	Det A	14	11	.560	30	25	20-1	0	222.2	240	95	5	10	45	71	2.71	102	.278	.321	77-0-7	.156	-3	93	-1	—	-0.6
1907	†Det A	18	11	.621	39	33	22-3	1	274.2	256	89	1	11	52	88	2.16	120	.249	.293	94-0-3	.160	-3	110	16	—	1.2
1908	Det A	2	6	.250	11	9	4-1	0	61.2	74	37	0	0	13	23	3.50	69	.302	.337	18-0-1	.167	-1	97	-8	—	-1.1
Total	7	83	82	.503	203	174	136-14	2	1507	1550	674	24	39	311	470	2.60	116	.266	.308	526-0-23	.156	-21	95	51	—	1.9
SIGNER, WALTER	Walter Donald Aloysius; B10.12.1910 New York NY; D7.23.1974 Greenwich CT; BR/TR/6´0˝/185; d9.18; Col NYU																									
1943	Chi N	2	1	.667	4	2	1	0	25	24	8	3	0	4	5	2.88	116	.245	.275	8	.250	0	38	2	0	0.3
1945	Chi N	0	0	ø	6	0	0	1	8	11	6	1	0	5	0	3.38	108	.256	.333	1	.000	-0	—	-1	0	-0.1
Total	2	2	1	.667	10	2	1	1	33	35	14	4	0	9	5	3.00	114	.248	.293	9	.222	0	38	1	0	0.2
SIGSBY, SETH	Seth De Witt (b Seth De Witt); B4.30.1874 Cobleskill NY; D9.15.1953 Schenectady NY; 6´0˝/175; d6.27																									
1893	NY N	0	0	ø	1	0	0	0	3	1	4	0	1	4	2	9.00	52	.100	.400	1	.000	-0	—	-1	—	-0.1
SIKORSKI, BRIAN	Brian Patrick; B7.27.1974 Detroit MI; BR/TR/6´1˝/190; [HouN95 4/109]; d8.16; Col Western Michigan																									
2000	Tex A	1	3	.250	10	5	0	0-0	37.2	46	31	9	1	25-1	32	5.73	89	.287	.385	0	ø	0	111	-4	0	-0.4
2006	SD N	1	1	.500	13	0	0	0-0	14.1	16	9	4	0	3-1	14	5.65	73	.281	.317	0	ø	0	—	-2	0	-0.3
	Cle A	2	1	.667	17	0	0	0-1	19.2	20	10	4	1	4-0	24	4.58	95	.267	.309	0	ø	0	—	0	0	0.0
Total	2	4	5	.444	40	5	0	0-1	71.2	82	50	17	2	32-2	70	5.40	87	.281	.354	0	ø	0	111	-6	0	-0.7
SILVA, CARLOS	Carlos; B4.23.1979 Bolivar, Venezuela; BR/TR/6´4˝/(225–250); d4.1																									
2002	Phi N	5	0	1.000	68	0	0	1-4	84	88	34	4	4	22-6	41	3.21	119	.282	.334	2	.000	0	—	5	18	0.4
2003	Phi N	3	1	.750	62	1	0	1-2	87.1	92	43	7	8	37-5	48	4.43	90	.280	.365	9-0-1	.222	1	236	-3	0	-0.1
2004	†Min A	14	8	.636	33	33	1-1	0-0	203	255	100	23	5	35-2	76	4.21	110	.310	.342	3	.000	-0	104	11	0	0.9
2005	Min A	9	8	.529	27	27	2	0-0	188.1	212	83	25	3	9-2	71	3.44	127	.290	.300	2	.000	-0	89	18	15	1.4
2006	Min A	11	15	.423	36	31	0	0-0	180.1	246	130	38	7	32-4	70	5.94	77	.324	.354	3	.333	0	112	-28	0	-3.3
Total	5	42	32	.568	226	92	3-1	2-6	743	893	390	97	27	135-19	306	4.35	101	.302	.337	19-0-1	.158	0	107	3	33	-0.7
SILVA, JOSE	Jose Leonel; B12.19.1973 Tijuana, Baja California, Mexico; BR/TR/6´5˝/(210–235); [TorA91 6/172]; d9.10																									
1996	Tor A	0	0	ø	2	0	0	0-0	2	5	3	1	0	0-0	0	13.50	37	.455	.455	0	ø	0	—	-2	0	-0.1
1997	Pit N	2	1	.667	11	4	0	0-0	36.1	52	26	4	1	16-3	30	5.94	72	.347	.406	7-0-3	.143	-0	108	-6	0	-0.5
1998	Pit N	6	7	.462	18	18	1	0-0	100.1	104	55	7	1	30-2	64	4.40	97	.271	.321	27-0-5	.037	-1	84	-1	85	-0.2
1999	Pit N	2	8	.200	34	12	0	4-1	97.1	108	70	10	3	39-0	77	5.73	80	.281	.349	20-0-2	.100	-1	122	-12	18	-1.2
2000	Pit N	11	9	.550	51	19	1	0-2	136	178	96	16	5	50-7	98	5.56	84	.317	.375	34-0-5	.176	0	97	-15	0	-1.9
2001	Pit N	3	3	.500	26	0	0	0-2	32	35	24	6	0	9-1	23	6.75	66	.271	.319	2	.000	-0	—	-7	126	-1.2
2002	Cin N	1	0	1.000	12	0	0	0-0	23.1	25	11	3	3	10-3	6	4.24	101	.294	.384	0-0-1	ø	0	—	1	133	0.1
Total	7	25	28	.472	154	53	2	4-5	427.1	507	285	47	13	154-16	298	5.41	83	.297	.357	90-0-16	.111	-3	99	-42	362	-5.0
SIMA, AL	Albert; B10.7.1921 Mahwah NJ; D8.17.1993 Suffern NY; BR/TL/6´0˝/187; d6.28																									
1950	Was A	4	5	.444	17	9	1	0	77	89	49	9	1	26	23	4.79	94	.291	.348	26-0-1	.115	-2	78	-3	0	-0.6
1951	Was A	3	7	.300	18	8	1	0	77	79	51	5	0	41	26	4.79	85	.261	.349	17-1-5	.176	1	92	-8	0	-0.8
1953	Was A	2	3	.400	31	5	1	1	68.1	63	31	7	3	31	25	3.42	114	.249	.338	17	.118	-1	82	3	0	0.1
1954	Chi A	0	1	.000	5	1	0	1	7	11	5	1	0	2	1	5.14	73	.393	.406	2	.000	-0	47	-1	0	-0.2
	Phi A	2	5	.286	29	7	1	2	79.1	101	51	9	0	32	36	5.22	75	.309	.368	20-0-2	.050	-2	58	-11	0	-1.2
	Year	2	6	.250	34	8	1	3	86.1	112	56	10	0	34	37	5.21	75	.315	.372	22-0-2	.045	-2	57	-12	0	-1.4
Total	4	11	21	.344	100	30	4	4	308.2	343	187	31	4	132	111	4.61	89	.282	.353	82-1-8	.110	-5	77	-20	0	-2.7
SIMAS, BILL	William Anthony; B11.28.1971 Hanford CA; BL/TR/6´3˝/(200–235); [CalA92 6/160]; d8.15; Col Fresno (CA) City; [DL 2001 Chi A 190]																									
1995	Chi A	1	1	.500	14	0	0	0-0	14	15	5	1	1	10-2	16	2.57	174	.273	.394	0	ø	0	—	3	0	0.3
1996	Chi A	2	8	.200	64	0	0	2-6	72.2	75	39	5	3	39-6	65	4.58	104	.265	.358	0	ø	0	—	2	0	0.2
1997	Chi A	3	1	.750	40	0	0	1-1	41.1	46	23	6	2	24-3	38	4.14	107	.279	.375	0	ø	0	—	0	61	0.0
1998	Chi A	4	3	.571	60	0	0	18-6	70.2	54	29	12	1	22-4	56	3.57	128	.206	.270	0	ø	0	—	9	0	1.1
1999	Chi A	6	3	.667	70	0	0	2-3	72	73	36	6	6	32-6	41	3.75	132	.263	.347	0	ø	0	—	8	0	0.9

YEAR	TM LG	W	L	PCT	G	GS	CG-SHO	SV-BS	IP	H	R	HR	HB	BB-IB	SO	ERA	AERA	OAV	OOB	AB-HR-SH	AVG	PB	SUP	APR	DL	PW
2000	†Chi A	2	3	.400	60	0	0	0-5	67.2	69	27	9	1	22-6	49	3.46	146	.276	.332	0	ø	0	—	13	0	0.8
Total	6	18	19	.486	308	0	0	23-21	338.1	332	159	39	14	149-27	265	3.83	124	.257	.337	0	ø	0	—	35	251	3.3
Simmons, Curt	Curtis Thomas; B5.19.1929 Egypt PA; BL/TL/6´0˝/(175–190); d9.28; Mil 1951																									
1947	Phi N	1	0	1.000	1	1	1	0	9	5	1	0	0	6	9	1.00	401	.161	.297	2-0-1	.500	0	66	3	0	0.4
1948	Phi N	7	13	.350	31	23	7	0	170	169	110	8	2	108	86	4.87	81	.266	.374	51-0-3	.137	-1	81	-18	0	-1.9
1949	Phi N	4	10	.286	38	14	2	1	131.1	133	72	7	1	55	83	4.59	86	.275	.350	41	.171	-1*	105	-9	0	-0.9
1950	Phi N	17	8	.680	31	27	11-2	1	214.2	178	93	19	2	88	146	3.40	119	.223	.302	77-0-3	.156	-1*	118	16	0	1.6
1952	Phi N★	14	8	.636	28	28	15-**6**	0	201.1	170	72	11	1	70	141	2.82	130	.227	.294	67-1-5	.164	2	100	20	0	2.2
1953	Phi N★	16	13	.552	32	30	19-4	0	238	211	102	17	3	82	138	3.21	131	.236	.302	93-0-4	.140	-3	110	25	0	2.3
1954	Phi N	14	15	.483	34	33	21-3	1	253	226	101	14	5	98	125	2.81	144	.239	.312	91-0-6	.176	-1*	95	29	0	2.9
1955	Phi N	8	8	.500	25	22	3	0	130	148	76	15	3	50-2	58	4.92	81	.290	.355	46-0-1	.174	-1*	99	-12	0	-1.4
1956	Phi N	15	10	.600	33	27	14	0	198	186	95	17	3	65-7	88	3.36	111	.248	.308	72-0-2	.236	3*	113	4	0	0.8
1957	Phi N★	12	11	.522	32	29	9-2	0	212	214	92	11	2	50-11	92	3.44	111	.264	.305	71-0-3	.239	4*	92	8	0	1.1
1958	Phi N	7	14	.333	29	27	7-1	1	168.1	196	92	11	3	40-4	78	4.38	90	.293	.332	59-0-3	.203	0*	87	-7	0	-0.9
1959	Phi N	0	0	ø	7	0	0	0	10	16	5	2	1	0-0	4	4.50	91	.400	.415	0	ø	0*	—	0	44	0.0
1960	Phi N	0	0	ø	4	2	0	0	4	13	8	3	0	6-0	4	18.00	22	.542	.633	0	ø	0	114	-6	0	-0.3
	StL N	7	4	.636	23	17	3-1	0	152	149	50	11	0	31-6	63	2.66	154	.257	.294	47-0-2	.213	1*	86	22	0	1.7
	Year	7	4	.636	27	19	3-1	0	156	162	58	14	0	37-6	67	3.06	134	.269	.309	47-0-2	.213	1	89	18	0	1.4
1961	StL N	9	10	.474	30	29	6-2	0	195.2	203	91	14	4	64-6	99	3.13	**141**	.269	.326	66-0-3	.303	5*	107	21	0	2.5
1962	StL N	10	10	.500	31	22	9-4	0	154	167	78	18	3	32-2	74	3.51	122	.280	.318	50-0-2	.160	0	112	8	0	1.0
1963	StL N	15	9	.625	32	32	11-6	0	232.2	209	82	13	6	48-3	127	2.48	143	.239	.281	81-0-3	.160	0	112	23	0	2.2
1964	†StL N	18	9	.667	34	34	12-3	0	244	233	106	24	5	49-1	104	3.43	111	.249	.288	94-0-8	.106	-3	135	11	0	0.8
1965	StL N	9	15	.375	34	32	5	0	203	229	104	19	4	54-8	96	4.08	94	.283	.330	64-0-3	.047	-5	82	-6	0	-1.2
1966	StL N	1	1	.500	10	5	1	0	33.1	35	17	3	0	14-2	14	4.59	78	.269	.338	8	.125	0	78	-3	0	-0.1
	Chi N	4	7	.364	19	10	3-1	0	77.1	79	39	7	1	21-3	24	4.07	90	.268	.317	18-0-3	.111	-0	77	-3	0	-0.4
	Year	5	8	.385	29	15	4-1	0	110.2	114	56	10	1	35-5	38	4.23	86	.268	.323	26-0-3	.115	-0	77	-7	0	-0.5
1967	Chi N	3	7	.300	17	14	3	0	82	100	54	10	2	23-4	31	4.94	72	.300	.342	28-0-1	.143	-1	112	-14	0	-1.6
	Cal A	2	1	.667	14	4	1-1	1	34.2	44	11	1	2	9-3	13	2.60	121	.321	.372	9-0-1	.222	1	118	2	0	0.3
Total	20	193	183	.513	569	462	163-36	5	3348.1	3313	1551	255	53	1063-62	1697	3.54	111	.259	.317	1135-1-57	.171	1	102	114	44	11.1
Simmons, Pat	Patrick Clement (b Patrick Clement Simoni); B11.29.1908 Watervliet NY; D7.3.1968 Albany NY; BR/TR/5´11˝/172; d4.18																									
1928	Bos A	0	2	.000	31	3	0	1	69	69	38	4	1	38	16	4.04	102	.271	.367	15	.133	-1	82	0	—	-0.1
1929	Bos A	0	0	ø	2	0	0	1	7	6	0	0	0	3	2	0.00	ø	.231	.310	1	.000	-0	—	3	—	0.1
Total	2	0	2	.000	33	3	0	2	76	75	38	4	1	41	18	3.67	112	.267	.362	16	.125	-1	82	3	—	0.0
Simons, Doug	Douglas Eugene; B9.15.1966 Bakersfield CA; BL/TL/6´0˝/(160–170); [MinA88 9/233]; d4.9; Col Pepperdine																									
1991	NY N	2	3	.400	42	1	0	1-0	60.2	55	40	5	2	19-5	38	5.19	71	.246	.305	3-0-1	.000	-0	123	-10	0	-0.8
1992	Mon N	0	0	ø	7	0	0	0-0	5.1	15	14	3	1	2-0	6	23.63	15	.500	.529	0	ø	0	—	-11	0	-0.6
Total	2	2	3	.400	49	1	0	1-0	66	70	54	8	3	21-5	44	6.68	55	.276	.332	3-0-1	.000	-0	123	-21	0	-1.4
Simontacchi, Jason	Jason William; B11.13.1973 Mountain View CA; BR/TR/6´2˝/(185–190); [KCA96 21/619]; d5.4; Col Albertson Idaho																									
2002	StL N	11	5	.688	24	24	0	0-0	143.1	134	68	18	6	54-4	72	4.02	100	.253	.327	50-0-4	.240	2*	101	1	0	0.3
2003	StL N	9	5	.643	46	16	1	1-2	126.1	153	82	21	5	41-0	74	5.56	74	.299	.355	38	.132	-1*	151	-21	0	-2.1
2004	StL N	0	0	ø	13	0	0	0-0	15.1	17	10	5	1	7-0	3	5.28	81	.304	.385	2	.500	0*	—	-2	0	0.0
Total	3	20	10	.667	83	40	1	1-2	285	304	160	44	12	102-4	149	4.77	86	.277	.343	90-0-4	.200	2	121	-22	0	-1.8
Simpson, Allan	Larry Allan; B8.26.1977 Springfield IL; BR/TR/6´4˝/(185–200); [SeaA97 8/253]; d5.17; Col Taft (CA) JC																									
2004	Col N	2	1	.667	32	0	0	0-1	39	44	26	4	4	20-0	46	5.08	94	.289	.378	1	.000	-0	—	-3	0	-0.2
2005	Cin N	0	1	.000	9	0	0	0-1	6.2	3	5	1	1	5-0	6	6.75	63	.136	.321	0	ø	0	—	-2	0	-0.2
	Col N	0	0	ø	2	0	0	0-0	0.2	3	5	0	0	3-0	0	67.50	7	.750	.750	0	ø	0	—	-4	0	-0.2
	Year	0	1	.000	11	0	0	0-1	7.1	6	10	1	1	8-0	6	12.27	35	.231	.417	0	ø	0	—	-6	0	-0.4
2006	Mil N	0	0	ø	2	0	0	0-0	2.2	1	2	0	0	4-0	5	3.38	133	.111	.357	0	ø	0	—	0	0	0.0
Total	3	2	2	.500	45	0	0	0-2	49	51	38	5	5	32-0	57	6.06	77	.273	.383	1	.000	-0	—	-9	0	-0.6
Simpson, Steve	Steven Edward; B8.30.1948 St.Joseph MO; D11.2.1989 Omaha NE; BR/TR/6´3˝/195; d9.10; Col Washburn Topeka																									
1972	SD N	0	2	.000	9	0	0	2-1	11.1	10	6	0	0	8-1	9	4.76	70	.238	.360	0	ø	0	—	-2	0	-0.3
Simpson, Duke	Thomas Leo; B9.15.1927 Columbus OH; BR/TR/6´1.5˝/190; d5.6; Col Ohio St.																									
1953	Chi N	1	2	.333	30	1	0	0	45	60	47	8	1	25	21	8.00	56	.314	.396	8	.250	0	20	-17	0	-1.0
Simpson, Wayne	Wayne Kirby; B12.2.1948 Los Angeles CA; BR/TR/6´3˝/210; [CinN67 1/8]; d4.9																									
1970	Cin N☆	14	3	.824	26	26	10-2	0-0	176	125	73	15	9	81-3	119	3.02	134	**.198**	.296	64-0-5	.094	-4*	134	18	0	1.3
1971	Cin N	4	7	.364	22	21	1	0-0	117.1	106	66	9	3	77-5	61	4.76	71	.244	.359	32-0-5	.031	-2	98	-18	0	-1.7
1972	Cin N	8	5	.615	24	22	1	0-0	130.1	124	63	17	2	49-4	70	4.14	78	.247	.316	48	.063	-3	135	-12	0	-1.6
1973	KC A	3	4	.429	16	10	1	0-0	59.2	66	39	1	1	35-0	29	5.73	72	.284	.375	0	ø	0	113	-9	0	-0.9
1975	Phi N	1	0	1.000	7	5	0	0-0	30.2	31	11	1	1	11-0	19	3.23	117	.263	.328	9	.222	0	126	2	0	0.2
1977	Cal A	6	12	.333	27	23	0	0-0	122	154	90	14	7	62-3	55	5.83	67	.308	.389	0	ø	0	94	-26	0	-3.3
Total	6	36	31	.537	122	107	13-2	0-0	636	606	342	57	23	315-15	353	4.37	85	.251	.340	153-0-10	.078	-8	116	-45	0	-6.0
Sims, Pete	Clarence; B5.24.1891 Crown City OH; D12.2.1968 Dallas TX; BR/TR/5´11.5˝/165; d9.16																									
1915	StL A	1	0	1.000	3	2	0	0	8.1	6	4	0	0	6	4	4.32	66	.214	.353	1-0-1	1.000	1	89	-1	—	0.0
Sinclair, Steve	Steven Scott; B8.2.1971 Victoria BC, Can.; BL/TL/6´2˝/190; [TorA91 28/744]; d4.25																									
1998	Tor A	0	2	.000	24	0	0	0-2	15	13	7	0	0	5-0	8	3.60	129	.232	.295	0	ø	0	—	2	0	0.2
1999	Tor A	0	0	ø	3	0	0	0-0	5.2	7	8	4	1	4-0	3	12.71	39	.304	.429	0	ø	0	—	-5	0	-0.2
	Sea A	0	1	.000	18	0	0	0-0	13.2	15	8	1	1	10-2	15	3.95	121	.268	.388	0	ø	0	—	1	0	0.0
	Year	0	1	.000	21	0	0	0-0	19.1	22	16	5	2	14-2	18	6.52	74	.278	.400	0	ø	0	—	-4	0	-0.2
Total	2	0	3	.000	45	0	0	0-2	34.1	35	23	5	2	19-2	26	5.24	91	.259	.359	0	ø	0	—	-2	0	0.0
Sincock, Bert	Herbert Sylvester; B9.8.1887 Barkerville BC, Can.; D8.1.1946 Houghton MI; BL/TL/5´10.5˝/165; d6.25; Col Michigan																									
1908	Cin N	0	0	ø	1	0	0	0	4.2	3	2	0	0	0	1	3.86	60	.176	.176	2	.000	-0	—	0	—	-0.1
Singer, Bill	William Robert "The Singer Throwing Machine"; B4.24.1944 Los Angeles CA; BR/TR/6´4˝/(190–200); d9.24; [DL 1978 Tor A 155]																									
1964	LA N	0	1	.000	2	2	0	0	14	11	5	0	0	12-1	3	3.21	101	.216	.365	6	.167	0	81	0	0	0.0
1965	LA N	0	0	ø	2	0	0	0	1	2	0	0	0	2-0	1	0.00	ø	.400	.571	0	ø	0	—	0	0	0.0
1966	LA N	0	0	ø	3	0	0	0	4	4	0	0	0	2-0	4	0.00	ø	.286	.375	0	ø	0	—	2	0	0.1
1967	LA N	12	8	.600	32	29	7-3	0	204.1	185	68	5	8	61-11	169	2.64	117	.239	.300	67-0-4	.090	-3*	92	11	0	0.8
1968	LA N	13	17	.433	37	36	12-6	0	256.1	227	97	14	5	78-10	227	2.88	96	.237	.295	81-0-3	.148	3	106	-4	0	0.0
1969	LA N★	20	12	.625	41	40	16-2	1-0	315.2	244	96	22	10	74-4	247	2.34	143	.210	.261	108-0-8	.102	-4	100	36	0	3.1
1970	LA N	8	5	.615	16	16	5-3	0-0	106.1	79	39	10	2	32-3	93	3.13	123	.203	.267	38-0-1	.132	-0	117	10	80	1.0
1971	LA N	10	17	.370	31	31	8-1	0-0	203.1	195	103	19	4	71-1	144	4.16	78	.252	.315	58-0-8	.103	-0	92	-21	0	-2.6
1972	LA N	6	16	.273	26	25	4-3	0-0	169.1	148	84	8	5	60-4	101	3.67	92	.237	.306	55-0-6	.073	-3	71	-6	21	-1.0
1973	Cal A★	20	14	.588	40	40	19-2	0-0	315.2	280	124	15	9	130-5	241	3.22	111	.235	.314	0	ø	0	102	16	0	1.5
1974	Cal A	7	4	.636	14	14	8	0-0	108.2	102	48	3	1	43-0	77	2.98	116	.250	.319	0	ø	0	127	3	116	0.3
1975	Cal A	7	15	.318	29	27	8	1-0	179	171	107	18	6	81-5	78	4.98	72	.257	.340	0	ø	0	86	-26	0	-2.9
1976	Tex A	4	1	.800	10	10	2-1	0-0	64.2	56	31	4	5	27-0	34	3.48	103	.239	.328	0	ø	0	120	0	0	0.0
	Min A	9	9	.500	26	26	5-3	0-0	172	177	88	9	6	69-4	63	3.77	95	.274	.345	0	ø	0	109	-5	0	-0.6
	Year	13	10	.565	36	36	7-4	0-0	236.2	233	119	13	11	96-4	97	3.69	97	.264	.340	0	ø	0	112	-7	0	-0.6
1977	Tor A	2	8	.200	13	12	0	0-0	59.2	71	54	5	2	39-2	33	6.79	63	.296	.392	0	ø	0	81	-17	101	-2.4
Total	14	118	127	.482	322	308	94-24	2-0	2174	1952	944	132	63	781-50	1515	3.39	100	.240	.309	413-0-30	.109	-7	99	-1	473	-2.7
Singleton, Elmer	Bert Elmer "Smoky"; B6.26.1918 Ogden UT; D1.5.1996 Ogden UT; BR/TR (BB 1957–58)/6´2˝/(174–190); d8.20																									
1945	Bos N	1	4	.200	7	5	1	0	37.1	35	22	1	1	14	14	4.82	79	.248	.321	11	.000	-1	53	-4	0	-0.6
1946	Bos N	0	1	.000	15	2	0	1	33.2	27	20	3	1	21	17	3.74	92	.221	.340	4-0-1	.000	-1*	162	-3	0	-0.2
1947	Pit N	2	2	.500	36	3	0	1	67	70	49	9	2	39	24	6.31	67	.267	.366	13-0-1	.308	1*	104	-13	0	-0.6

THE PITCHER REGISTER

YEAR	TM LG	W	L	PCT	G	GS	CG-SHO	SV-BS	IP	H	R	HR	HB	BB-IB	SO	ERA	AERA	OAV	OOB	AB-HR-SH	AVG	PB	SUP	APR	DL	PW
1948	Pit N	4	6	.400	38	5	1	2	92.1	90	52	11	1	40	53	4.97	82	.253	.330	23-0-1	.087	-2	105	-7	0	-0.8
1950	Was A	1	2	.333	21	1	0	0	36.1	39	23	4	0	17	19	5.20	86	.291	.371	7-0-1	.429	1	261	-2	0	0.0
1957	Chi N	0	1	.000	5	2	0	0	13.1	20	11	3	0	2-0	6	6.75	57	.333	.355	3-0-1	.000	-0*	91	-4	88	-0.3
1958	Chi N	1	0	1.000	2	0	0	0	4.2	1	0	0	0	1-1	2	0.00	ø	.071	.133	1	.000	-0	—	2	0	0.4
1959	Chi N	2	1	.667	21	1	0	0	43	40	15	2	0	12-2	25	2.72	145	.252	.304	6	.000	-1	23	6	0	0.3
Total	8	11	17	.393	145	19	2	4	327.2	322	192	33	5	146-3	160	4.83	83	.258	.338	68-0-5	.132	-3	99	-25	88	-1.8
SINGLETON, JOHN	John Edward "Sheriff"; B11.27.1896 Gallipolis OH; D10.23.1937 Dayton OH; BR/TR/5´11˝/171; d6.8																									
1922	Phi N	1	10	.091	22	9	3-1	0	93	127	80	6	5	38	27	5.90	79	.346	.415	36-0-1	.139	-2	97	-11	—	-1.4
SIROTKA, MIKE	Michael Robert; B5.13.1971 Houston TX; BL/TL/6´1˝/200; [ChiA93 15/425]; d7.19; Col Louisiana St.; [DL 2001 Tor A 190, 2002 Tor A 183]																									
1995	Chi A	1	2	.333	6	6	0	0-0	34.1	39	16	2	0	17-0	19	4.19	107	.298	.371	0	ø	0	83	2	0	0.1
1996	Chi A	1	2	.333	15	4	0	0-0	26.1	34	27	3	0	12-0	11	7.18	66	.315	.377	0	ø	0	117	-10	0	-0.9
1997	Chi A	3	0	1.000	7	4	0	0-0	32	36	9	4	1	5-1	24	2.25	196	.290	.323	1	.000	-0	120	8	0	0.6
1998	Chi A	14	15	.483	33	33	5	0-0	211.2	255	137	30	2	47-0	128	5.06	91	.300	.336	4	.000	-0	111	-14	0	-1.5
1999	Chi A	11	13	.458	32	32	3-1	0-0	209	236	108	24	3	57-2	125	4.00	123	.283	.327	8	.250	0	84	19	0	1.8
2000	†Chi A	15	10	.600	32	32	1	0-0	197	203	101	23	1	69-1	128	3.79	133	.269	.330	4	.000	-0	109	23	0	2.5
Total	6	45	42	.517	125	111	9-1	0-0	710.1	803	398	86	7	207-4	435	4.31	112	.286	.334	17	.118	0	102	28	373	2.6
SISCO, ANDY	Andrew Frank; B1.13.1983 Steamboat Springs CO; BL/TL/6´10˝/270; [ChiN01 2/46]; d4.4																									
2005	KC A	2	5	.286	67	0	0	0-5	75.1	68	27	6	2	42-4	76	3.11	141	.243	.343	1	.000	-0	—	11	0	0.8
2006	KC A	1	3	.250	65	0	0	1-4	58.1	66	47	8	1	40-6	52	7.10	66	.289	.391	0	ø	0	—	-14	0	-0.9
Total	2	3	8	.273	132	0	0	1-9	133.2	134	74	14	3	82-10	128	4.85	93	.264	.364	1	.000	-0	—	-3	0	-0.1
SISK, DOUG	Douglas Randall; B9.26.1957 Renton WA; BR/TR/6´2˝/210; d9.6; Col Washington St.																									
1982	NY N	0	1	.000	8	0	0	1-0	8.2	5	1	1	1	4-2	4	1.04	354	.172	.294	0	ø	0	—	3	0	0.3
1983	NY N	5	4	.556	67	0	0	11-6	104.1	88	38	1	4	59-7	33	2.24	164	.235	.342	6-0-1	.500	1	—	13	0	1.4
1984	NY N	1	3	.250	50	0	0	15-3	77.2	57	24	1	3	54-5	32	2.09	171	.215	.354	11-0-2	.091	-0	—	12	20	1.0
1985	NY N	4	5	.444	42	0	0	2-2	73	86	48	3	2	40-2	26	5.30	66	.291	.379	12	.000	-1	—	-15	0	-1.9
1986	†NY N	4	2	.667	41	0	0	1-0	70.2	77	31	0	5	31-5	31	3.06	117	.282	.366	4	.000	-0	—	3	0	0.1
1987	NY N	3	1	.750	55	0	0	3-3	78	83	38	5	3	22-4	37	3.46	111	.270	.323	5	.000	-1	—	1	0	0.1
1988	Bal A	3	3	.500	52	0	0	0-2	94.1	109	43	3	2	45-6	26	3.72	106	.306	.385	0	ø	0	—	2	25	0.1
1990	Atl N	0	0	ø	3	0	0	0-0	2.1	1	1	0	0	4-0	1	3.86	105	.143	.385	0	ø	0	—	0	31	0.0
1991	Atl N	2	1	.667	14	0	0	0-0	14.1	21	14	1	0	8-2	5	5.02	77	.333	.403	0	ø	0	—	-4	87	-0.7
Total	9	22	20	.524	332	0	0	33-16	523.1	527	238	15	20	267-33	195	3.27	113	.268	.359	38-0-3	.105	-1	—	15	163	0.4
SISK, TOMMIE	Tommie Wayne; B4.12.1942 Ardmore OK; BR/TR/6´3˝/195; d7.19																									
1962	Pit N	0	2	.000	5	3	1	0	17.2	18	9	1	1	8-1	6	4.08	97	.257	.342	5	.200	0	74	0	0	0.0
1963	Pit N	1	3	.250	57	4	1	1	108	85	42	6	1	45-10	73	2.92	113	.222	.303	16-0-1	.063	-0	78	4	0	0.2
1964	Pit N	1	4	.200	42	1	0	0	61.1	91	47	4	3	29-5	35	6.16	57	.364	.432	8	.000	-1	150	-18	0	-1.4
1965	Pit N	7	3	.700	38	12	1-1	0	111.1	103	48	6	1	50-7	66	3.40	103	.248	.328	33-0-1	.061	-2*	93	2	0	-0.1
1966	Pit N	10	5	.667	34	23	4-1	1	150	146	74	14	4	52-6	60	4.14	86	.256	.321	51-0-2	.098	-1	138	-8	0	-0.9
1967	Pit N	13	13	.500	37	31	11-2	1	207.2	196	88	6	3	78-10	85	3.34	101	.253	.321	69-0-6	.101	-2	107	1	0	-0.2
1968	Pit N	5	5	.500	33	11	0	1	96	101	40	3	3	35-8	41	3.28	89	.282	.351	24-0-2	.083	-1	116	-3	0	-0.4
1969	SD N	2	13	.133	53	13	1	6-1	143	160	81	11	1	48-8	59	4.78	75	.285	.339	25-0-4	.120	0	70	-18	0	-1.8
1970	Chi A	1	1	.500	17	1	0	0-1	33.1	37	28	6	0	13-5	16	5.40	72	.276	.338	4	.250	0	46	-8	0	-0.4
Total	9	40	49	.449	316	99	19-4	10-2	928.1	937	457	57	17	358-60	441	3.92	88	.266	.335	235-0-16	.094	-7	106	-48	0	-5.0
SISLER, DAVE	David Michael; B10.16.1931 St.Louis MO; BR/TR/6´4˝/(190–200); d4.21; b–Dick f–George; Col Princeton																									
1956	Bos A	9	8	.529	39	14	3	3	142.1	120	81	13	7	72-2	93	4.62	100	.227	.326	42-0-4	.119	-2	83	2	0	-0.1
1957	Bos A	7	8	.467	22	19	5	1	122.1	135	68	15	2	61-1	55	4.71	85	.280	.361	42-0-4	.167	-0	104	-8	0	-0.9
1958	Bos A	8	9	.471	30	25	4-1	0	149.1	157	94	22	1	79-2	71	4.94	81	.276	.361	46-0-11	.196	0	102	-14	0	-1.5
1959	Bos A	0	0	ø	3	0	0	0	6.2	9	5	3	0	1-0	3	6.75	60	.310	.333	2	.500	0	—	-2	0	-0.1
	Det A	1	3	.250	32	0	0	7	51.2	46	28	4	1	36-1	29	4.01	101	.242	.362	5-0-1	.200	-0	—	0	0	-0.1
	Year	1	3	.250	35	0	0	7	58.1	55	33	7	1	37-1	32	4.32	94	.251	.359	7-0-1	.286	0	—	-2	0	-0.2
1960	Det A	7	5	.583	41	0	0	6	80	56	23	3	2	45-1	47	2.47	160	.199	.311	16-0-1	.125	-0	—	14	0	2.2
1961	Was A	2	8	.200	45	1	0	11	60.1	55	34	6	3	48-5	30	4.18	96	.251	.390	6	.000	0	22	-2	0	-0.3
1962	Cin N	4	3	.571	35	0	0	1	43.2	44	19	4	0	26-3	27	3.92	103	.270	.370	0	ø	0	—	2	0	0.2
Total	7	38	44	.463	247	59	12-1	29	656.1	622	352	70	16	368-15	355	4.33	95	.253	.351	159-0-21	.157	-2	96	-8	0	-0.6
SISLER, GEORGE	George Harold "Georgeous George"; B3.24.1893 Manchester OH; D3.26.1973 Richmond Heights MO; BL/TL/5´11˝/170; d6.28; M3/C1; HF1939; s–Dave s–Dick; Col Michigan; ▲																									
1915	StL A	4	4	.500	15	8	6	0	70	62	26	0	4	38	41	2.83	101	.247	.355	274-3-12	.285	3*	73	2	—	0.5
1916	StL A	1	2	.333	3	3	3-1	0	27	18	4	0	1	6	12	1.00	275	.198	.255	580-4-19	.305	1*	9	5	—	0.9
1918	StL A	0	0	ø	2	1	0	1	8	10	6	0	1	4	4	4.50	61	.286	.375	452-2-9	.341	1*	165	-2	—	0.0
1920	StL A	0	0	ø	1	0	0	1	1	0	0	0	0	0	2	0.00	ø	.000	.000	631-19-13	.407	1*	—	0	—	0.1
1925	StL A	0	0	ø	1	0	0	0	2	1	0	0	0	1	1	0.00	ø	.167	.286	649-12-12	.345	0*	—	1	—	0.1
1926	StL A	0	0	ø	1	0	0	1	2	0	0	0	0	2	3	0.00	ø	.000	.286	613-7-16	.290	0*	—	1	—	0.1
1928	Bos N	0	0	ø	1	0	0	0	1	0	0	0	0	1	0	0.00	ø	.000	.333	491-4-14	.340	0*	—	0	—	0.0
Total	7	5	6	.455	24	12	9-1	3	111	91	36	0	6	52	63	2.35	123	.231	.330	3690-51-95	.335	7	64	7	—	1.7
SITTON, CARL	Charles Vetter; B9.22.1881 Pendleton SC; D9.11.1931 Valdosta GA; BR/TR/5´10.5˝/170; d4.24; Col Clemson																									
1909	Cle A	3	2	.600	14	5	3	0	50	50	22	1	2	16	16	2.88	89	.263	.327	13	.154	0	88	-1	—	-0.1
SIVESS, PETE	Peter; B9.23.1913 South River NJ; D6.1.2003 Candler NC; BR/TR/6´3.5˝/195; d6.13; Col Dickinson																									
1936	Phi N	3	4	.429	17	6	2	0	65	84	40	6	1	36	22	4.57	99	.310	.393	25	.120	-2	65	0	—	-0.3
1937	Phi N	1	1	.500	6	2	1	0	23	30	18	5	0	11	4	7.04	62	.330	.402	6	.000	-1	60	-5	—	-0.5
1938	Phi N	3	6	.333	39	8	2	3	116	143	78	12	1	69	32	5.51	71	.306	.397	32-0-1	.188	-1	76	-19	—	-1.5
Total	3	7	11	.389	62	16	5	3	204	257	136	23	2	116	58	5.38	77	.310	.396	63-0-1	.143	-4	71	-24	—	-2.3
SIWY, JIM	James Gerard; B9.20.1958 Central Falls RI; BR/TR/6´4˝/200; [ChiA80*3/59]; d8.20; Col Rhode Island																									
1982	Chi A	0	0	ø	2	1	0	0-0	7	10	8	1	0	5-0	3	10.29	40	.385	.469	0	ø	0	89	-4	0	-0.2
1984	Chi A	0	0	ø	1	0	0	0-0	4.1	3	1	0	0	2-0	1	2.08	201	.231	.313	0	ø	0	—	1	0	0.1
Total	2	0	0	ø	3	1	0	0-0	11.1	13	9	1	0	7-0	4	7.15	58	.333	.417	0	ø	0	89	-3	0	-0.1
SKALSKI, JOE	Joseph Douglas; B9.26.1964 Burnham IL; BR/TR/6´3˝/190; [CleA86 3/57]; d4.10; Col St. Xavier																									
1989	Cle A	0	2	.000	2	1	0	0-0	6.2	7	6	0	2	4-0	3	6.75	59	.259	.394	0	ø	0	46	-2	0	-0.4
SKAUGSTAD, DAVE	David Wendell; B1.10.1940 Algona IA; BL/TL/6´1˝/179; d9.25																									
1957	Cin N	0	0	ø	2	0	0	0	5.2	4	1	0	0	6-0	4	1.59	259	.190	.370	1	.000	0	—	2	0	0.1
SKEELS, DAVE	David; B12.29.1891 Addy WA; D12.2.1926 Spokane WA; BL/TR/6´1˝/187; d9.14; Col Gonzaga																									
1910	Det A	0	0	ø	1	1	0	0	6	9	8	0	1	4	2	12.00	22	.333	.438	3	.000	-0	229	-5	—	-0.3
SKOK, CRAIG	Craig Richard; B9.1.1947 Dobbs Ferry NY; BR/TL/6´0˝/(175–190); d5.4; Col Florida St.																									
1973	Bos A	0	1	.000	11	0	0	1-0	28.2	35	22	2	0	11-2	22	6.28	64	.304	.357	0	ø	0	—	-7	0	-0.4
1976	Tex A	0	1	.000	9	0	0	0-2	5	13	7	2	0	3-0	5	12.60	28	.481	.533	0	ø	0	—	-4	0	-0.8
1978	Atl N	3	2	.600	43	0	0	2-0	62	64	38	8	0	27-8	28	4.35	93	.266	.338	8	.250	0	—	-3	0	-0.2
1979	Atl N	1	3	.250	44	0	0	2-2	54.1	58	26	7	3	17-2	30	3.98	101	.282	.341	3	.000	-0	—	1	0	0.1
Total	4	4	7	.364	107	0	0	5-4	150	170	93	19	3	58-12	85	4.86	83	.289	.352	11	.182	0	—	-13	0	-1.3
SKOPEC, JOHN	John S. "Buckshot"; B5.8.1880 Chicago IL; D10.20.1912 Chicago IL; BR/TL/5´10˝/190; d4.25																									
1901	Chi A	6	3	.667	9	9	6	0	68.1	62	39	1	8	45	24	3.16	110	.239	.369	30-1-0	.333	3	136	2	—	0.6
1903	Det A	2	2	.500	6	5	3	0	39.1	46	22	0	2	13	14	3.43	85	.291	.353	13-0-2	.154	-0	79	-2	—	-0.2
Total	2	8	5	.615	15	14	9	0	107.2	108	61	1	10	58	38	3.26	101	.259	.363	43-1-2	.279	3	118	0	—	0.4

YEAR	TM LG	W	L	PCT	G	GS	CG-SHO	SV-BS	IP	H	R	HR	HB	BB-IB	SO	ERA	AERA	OAV	OOB	AB-HR-SH	AVG	PB	SUP	APR	DL	PW
Skrmetta, Matt	Matthew Leland; B11.6.1972 Biloxi MS; BB/TR/6´3˝/220; [DetA93 26/725]; d6.6; Col Jacksonville																									
2000	Mon N	0	0	ø	6	0	0	0-0	5.1	6	10	1	0	6-0	4	15.19	31	.273	.414	0	ø	0	—	-6	0	-0.3
	Pit N	2	2	.500	8	0	0	0-0	9.1	13	12	2	1	3-0	7	9.64	48	.333	.395	2	.000	-0	—	-6	0	-1.0
	Year	2	2	.500	14	0	0	0-0	14.2	19	22	3	1	9-0	11	11.66	40	.311	.403	2	.000	-0	—	-12	0	-1.3
Slagle, John	John A.; B Lawrence IN; BL/TR/?/175; d4.30																									
1891	Cin AA	0	0	ø	1	0	0	1	1.1	3	0	0	0	1	1	0.00	ø	.429	.500	1	.000	-0	—	1	—	0.1
Slagle, Roger	Roger Lee; B11.4.1953 Wichita KS; BR/TR/6´3˝/190; [NYA76 S1/19]; d9.7; Col Kansas																									
1979	NY A	0	0	ø	1	0	0	0-0	2	0	0	0	0	0-0	2	0.00	ø	.000	.000	0	ø	0	—	1	0	0.0
Slagle, Walt	Walter Jennings; B12.15.1878 Kenton OH; D6.14.1974 San Gabriel CA; BB/TR/6´0˝/165; d5.4																									
1910	Cin N	0	0	ø	1	0	0	0	1	0	1	0	1	3	0	9.00	32	.000	.571	0	ø	0	—	-1	—	0.0
Slapnicka, Cy	Cyril Charles; B3.23.1886 Cedar Rapids IA; D10.20.1979 Cedar Rapids IA; BB/TR/5´10˝/165; d9.26																									
1911	Chi N	0	2	.000	3	2	1	0	24	21	12	0	3	7	10	3.38	98	.236	.313	9	.222	-0	91	0	—	0.0
1918	Pit N	1	4	.200	7	6	4	1	49.1	50	34	2	5	22	3	4.74	61	.269	.362	14-0-2	.071	-1	101	-10	—	-1.1
Total	2	1	6	.143	10	8	5	1	73.1	71	46	2	8	29	13	4.30	70	.258	.346	23-0-2	.130	-1	97	-10	—	-1.1
Slappey, John	John Henry; B8.8.1898 Albany GA; D6.10.1957 Marietta GA; BL/TL/6´4˝/170; d8.23; Col Georgia																									
1920	Phi A	0	1	.000	3	1	0	0	6.1	15	12	0	0	4	1	7.11	57	.441	.500	2	.500	1	99	-4	—	-0.4
Slaten, Doug	Douglas; B2.4.1980 Venice CA; BL/TL/6´5˝/200; [AriN00 17/519]; d9.4; Col Los Angeles Pierce (CA) JC																									
2006	Ari N	0	0	ø	9	0	0	0-0	5.2	3	0	0	0	2-1	3	0.00	ø	.167	.250	0	ø	0	—	3	0	0.1
Slaton, Jim	James Michael; B6.19.1950 Long Beach CA; BR/TR/6´0˝/(180–192); [MilA69 15/355]; d4.14; C2; Col Antelope Valley (CA) JC																									
1971	Mil A	10	8	.556	26	23	5-4	0-0	147.2	140	67	16	1	71-9	63	3.78	92	.253	.338	46-0-4	.109	-1	98	-3	0	-0.6
1972	Mil A	1	6	.143	9	8	0	0-0	44	50	31	3	1	21-1	17	5.52	55	.287	.362	11-0-3	.091	-1	80	-12	0	-1.8
1973	Mil A	13	15	.464	38	38	13-3	0-0	276.1	266	127	30	1	99-4	134	3.71	103	.251	.314	0	ø	0	95	4	0	0.2
1974	Mil A	13	16	.448	40	35	10-3	0-0	250	255	117	22	3	102-6	126	3.92	93	.268	.339	0	ø	0	101	-7	0	-0.8
1975	Mil A	11	18	.379	37	33	10-3	0-1	217	238	129	28	2	90-6	119	4.52	85	.276	.343	0	ø	0	82	-17	0	-2.0
1976	Mil A	14	15	.483	38	38	12-2	0-0	292.2	287	126	14	6	94-12	138	3.44	102	.259	.317	0	ø	0	99	2	0	0.2
1977	Mil A☆	10	14	.417	32	31	7-1	0-0	221	223	104	25	11	77-5	104	3.58	115	.266	.333	0	ø	0	95	10	0	1.0
1978	Det A	17	11	.607	35	34	11-2	0-0	233.2	235	117	27	8	85-1	92	4.12	95	.263	.329	0	ø	0	108	-5	0	-0.7
1979	Mil A	15	9	.625	32	31	12-3	0-0	213	229	95	15	2	54-1	80	3.63	116	.278	.321	0	ø	0	112	14	0	1.4
1980	Mil A	1	1	.500	3	3	0	0-0	16.1	17	10	3	0	5-0	4	4.41	89	.270	.324	0	ø	0	168	-1	129	-0.1
1981	†Mil A	5	7	.417	24	21	0	0-0	117.1	120	60	10	2	50-2	47	4.37	79	.273	.346	0	ø	0	111	-12	0	-1.1
1982	†Mil A	10	6	.625	39	7	0	6-2	117.2	117	48	14	1	41-3	59	3.29	117	.264	.326	0	ø	0	136	7	18	1.0
1983	Mil A	14	6	.700	46	0	0	5-6	112.1	112	57	12	3	56-5	38	4.33	88	.272	.356	0	ø	0	—	-6	0	-1.1
1984	Cal A	7	10	.412	32	22	5-1	0-0	163	192	95	22	2	56-5	67	4.97	80	.295	.350	0	ø	0	101	-16	0	-1.5
1985	Cal A	6	10	.375	29	24	1	1-0	148.1	162	82	22	2	63-1	60	4.37	94	.284	.355	0	ø	0	87	-5	0	-0.5
1986	Cal A	4	6	.400	14	12	0	0-0	73.1	84	52	9	2	29-1	31	5.65	73	.295	.357	0	ø	0	102	-13	0	-1.5
	Det A	0	0	ø	22	0	0	2-1	40	46	18	5	1	11-3	12	4.05	103	.287	.333	0	ø	0	—	1	0	0.1
	Year	4	6	.400	36	12	0	2-1	113.1	130	70	14	3	40-4	43	5.08	82	.292	.349	0	ø	0	102	-11	0	-1.4
Total	16	151	158	.489	496	360	86-22	14-10	2683.2	2773	1335	277	48	1004-65	1191	4.03	95	.270	.334	57-0-7	.105	-2	100	-59	147	-7.8
Slattery, Phil	Philip Ryan; B2.25.1893 Harper IA; D3.2.1968 Long Beach CA; BR/TL/5´11˝/160; d9.16																									
1915	Pit N	0	0	ø	3	0	0	0	8	5	0	0	2	1	1	0.00	ø	.185	.267	1	.000	-0	—	2	—	0.1
Slaughter, Barney	Byron Atkins; B10.6.1884 Smyrna DE; D5.17.1961 Philadelphia PA; BR/TR/5´11.5˝/165; d8.9																									
1910	Phi N	0	1	.000	8	1	0	1	18	21	12	0	0	11	7	5.50	57	.318	.416	5	.200	0	167	-4	—	-0.2
Slaughter, Sterling	Sterling Feore; B11.18.1941 Danville IL; BR/TR/5´11˝/165; d4.19; Col Arizona St.																									
1964	Chi N	2	4	.333	20	6	1	0	51.2	64	35	8	0	32-6	32	5.75	65	.305	.393	12	.083	-0	55	-10	0	-1.2
Slayback, Bill	William Grover; B2.21.1948 Hollywood CA; BR/TR/6´4˝/185; [DetA68*7/113]; d6.26; Col Cal St.–Northridge																									
1972	Det A	5	6	.455	23	13	3-1	0-0	81.2	74	36	4	1	25-1	65	3.20	99	.239	.297	23-0-2	.174	-0	92	-2	0	-0.2
1973	Det A	0	0	ø	3	0	0	0-0	2	5	4	0	1	0-0	1	4.50	91	.417	.462	0	ø	0	—	-1	0	-0.1
1974	Det A	1	3	.250	16	4	0	0-0	54.2	57	34	1	3	26-2	23	4.77	80	.273	.351	0	ø	0	58	-6	0	-0.4
Total	3	6	9	.400	42	17	3-1	0-0	138.1	136	74	5	5	51-3	89	3.84	90	.256	.323	23-0-2	.174	-0	80	-9	0	-0.7
Slayton, Steve	Foster Herbert; B4.26.1902 Barre VT; D12.20.1984 Manchester NH; BR/TR/6´0˝/163; d7.21; Col New Hampshire																									
1928	Bos A	0	0	ø	3	0	0	0	7	6	3	0	0	3	2	3.86	107	.240	.321	2	.000	-0	—	0	—	0.0
Sleater, Lou	Louis Mortimer; B9.8.1926 St.Louis MO; BL/TL/5´10˝/185; d4.25; Col Maryland																									
1950	StL A	0	0	ø	1	0	0	0	1	0	0	0	0	0	1	0.00	ø	.000	.000	0	ø	0	—	1	0	0.0
1951	StL A	1	9	.100	20	8	4	1	81	88	53	7	5	53	33	5.11	86	.271	.381	31	.226	0*	51	-7	0	-0.8
1952	StL A	0	1	.000	4	2	0	0	8.2	9	8	1	0	5	1	7.27	54	.265	.359	2	.000	-0	111	-3	0	-0.3
	Was A	4	2	.667	14	9	3-1	0	57	56	29	4	2	30	22	3.63	98	.260	.356	20-0-1	.050	-2*	106	-2	0	-0.5
	Year	4	3	.571	18	11	3-1	0	65.2	65	37	5	2	35	23	4.11	88	.261	.357	22-0-1	.045	-2	108	-5	0	-0.8
1955	KC A	1	1	.500	16	1	0	0	25.2	33	22	3	0	21-0	11	7.71	54	.324	.429	13	.154	-1*	21	-9	0	-0.7
1956	Mil N	2	2	.500	25	1	0	2	45.2	42	22	6	0	27-9	32	3.15	110	.240	.338	10	.500	2	254	0	0	0.3
1957	Det A	3	3	.500	41	0	0	2	69.1	61	33	9	1	28-7	43	3.76	102	.237	.313	20-3-1	.250	3	—	0	0	0.3
1958	Det A	0	0	ø	4	0	0	0	5.1	3	4	2	0	6-0	4	6.75	60	.158	.360	1-1-0	1.000	1	—	-1	0	0.1
	Bal A	1	0	1.000	6	0	0	0	7	14	10	0	0	2-0	5	12.86	28	.438	.471	6	.000	-1*	—	-7	51	-0.9
	Year	1	0	1.000	10	0	0	0	12.1	17	14	2	0	8-0	9	10.22	37	.333	.424	7-1-0	.143	0	—	-8	0	-0.8
Total	7	12	18	.400	131	21	7-1	5	300.2	306	181	32	8	172-16	152	4.70	83	.263	.360	103-4-2	.204	3	86	-28	51	-2.5
Sloat, Lefty	Dwain Clifford; B12.1.1918 Nokomis IL; D4.18.2003 St.Paul MN; BR/TL/6´0˝/168; d4.24																									
1948	Bro N	0	1	.000	4	1	0	0	7.1	7	5	0	0	8	1	6.14	65	.280	.455	1-0-1	.000	-0	0	-1	0	-0.2
1949	Chi N	0	0	ø	5	1	0	0	9	14	7	0	0	3	3	7.00	58	.400	.447	0-0-1	ø	0	87	-3	0	-0.1
Total	2	0	1	.000	9	2	0	0	16.1	21	12	0	0	11	4	6.61	61	.350	.451	1-0-2	.000	-0	44	-4	0	-0.3
Slocum, Brian	Brian John; B3.27.1981 New Rochelle NY; BR/TR/6´4˝/200; [CleA02 2/63]; d4.22; Col Villanova																									
2006	Cle A	0	0	ø	8	2	0	0-0	17.2	27	11	3	1	9-0	11	5.60	77	.360	.435	0	ø	0	87	-2	0	-0.1
Slocumb, Heathcliff	Heath; B6.7.1966 Jamaica NY; BR/TR/6´3˝/(210–220); d4.11																									
1991	Chi N	2	1	.667	52	0	0	1-2	62.2	53	29	3	3	30-6	34	3.45	113	.231	.321	1	.000	-0	—	2	0	0.1
1992	Chi N	0	3	.000	30	0	0	1-0	36	52	27	3	1	21-3	27	6.50	56	.351	.430	4	.000	-0	—	-10	0	-0.9
1993	Chi N	1	0	1.000	10	0	0	0-0	10.2	7	5	0	0	4-0	4	3.38	120	.189	.262	1	.000	-0	—	1	0	0.0
	Cle A	3	1	.750	20	0	0	0-2	27.1	28	14	3	0	16-2	18	4.28	102	.272	.364	0	ø	0	—	0	0	0.0
1994	Phi N	5	1	.833	52	0	0	0-5	72.1	75	32	0	2	28-4	58	2.86	150	.262	.328	4-0-1	.250	0	—	9	0	0.7
1995	Phi N★	5	6	.455	61	0	0	32-6	65.1	64	26	2	1	35-3	63	2.89	146	.257	.351	1	.000	-0	—	8	0	1.7
1996	Bos A	5	5	.500	75	0	0	31-8	83.1	68	31	2	3	55-5	88	3.02	169	.222	.343	0	ø	0	—	19	0	3.3
1997	Bos A	0	5	.000	49	0	0	17-5	46.2	58	32	4	3	34-4	36	5.79	80	.312	.422	0	ø	0	—	-5	0	-0.8
	†Sea A	0	4	.000	27	0	0	10-1	28.1	26	13	2	1	15-1	28	4.13	110	.241	.339	0	ø	0	—	2	0	0.3
	Year	0	9	.000	76	0	0	27-6	75	84	45	6	4	49-5	64	5.16	89	.286	.393	0	ø	0	—	-4	0	-0.5
1998	Sea A	2	5	.286	57	0	0	3-1	67.2	72	40	5	1	44-1	51	5.32	88	.275	.379	0	ø	0	—	-3	0	-0.3
1999	Bal A	0	0	ø	10	0	0	0-0	8.2	15	12	2	2	9-2	12	12.46	38	.395	.531	0	ø	0	—	-7	0	-0.3
	StL N	3	2	.600	40	0	0	2-1	53.1	49	16	3	1	30-5	48	2.36	195	.243	.342	0	ø	0	—	13	23	1.1
2000	StL N	2	3	.400	43	0	0	1-0	49.2	50	32	9	1	24-1	34	5.44	85	.266	.349	1	.000	-0*	—	-4	0	-0.4
	SD N	0	1	.000	22	0	0	0-0	19	19	11	0	2	13-3	12	3.79	117	.264	.378	0	ø	0	—	0	0	0.0
	Year	2	4	.333	65	0	0	1-0	68.2	69	43	9	3	37-4	46	4.98	92	.265	.357	1	.000	-0	—	-4	0	-0.4
Total	10	28	37	.431	548	0	0	98-31	631	636	320	38	21	358-40	513	4.08	109	.263	.360	12-0-1	.083	-1	—	25	23	4.5

YEAR	TM LG	W	L	PCT	G	GS	CG-SHO	SV-BS	IP	H	R	HR	HB	BB-IB	SO	ERA	AERA	OAV	OOB	AB-HR-SH	AVG	PB	SUP	APR	DL	PW
SLUSARSKI, JOE	Joseph Andrew; B12.19.1966 Indianapolis IN; BR/TR/6'4"/195; [OakA88 2/46]; d4.11; Col New Orleans																									
1991	Oak A	5	7	.417	20	19	1	0-0	109.1	121	69	14	4	52-1	60	5.27	73	.283	.364	0	ø	0	124	-19	0	-1.8
1992	Oak A	5	5	.500	15	14	0	0-0	76	85	52	15	6	27-0	38	5.45	69	.284	.350	0	ø	0	143	-15	0	-1.7
1993	Oak A	0	0	ø	2	1	0	0-0	8.2	9	5	1	0	11-3	1	5.19	80	.300	.488	0	ø	0	67	-1	0	0.0
1995	Mil A	1	1	.500	12	0	0	0-0	15	21	11	3	2	6-1	6	5.40	93	.333	.403	0	ø	0	—	-1	0	-0.1
1999	Hou N	0	0	ø	3	0	0	0-0	3.2	1	0	0	0	3-1	3	0.00	ø	.083	.267	0	ø	0	—	2	15	0.1
2000	Hou N	2	7	.222	54	0	0	3-1	77	80	36	8	3	22-3	54	4.21	117	.268	.323	9	.111	-0	—	7	0	0.7
2001	Atl N	0	0	ø	4	0	0	0-0	6	9	6	2	0	1-0	5	9.00	48	.346	.370	0	ø	0	—	-3	28	-0.1
	Hou N	0	1	.000	8	0	0	0-0	10	16	10	2	0	3-0	6	9.00	51	.364	.396	0	ø	0	—	-4	0	-0.4
	Year	0	1	.000	12	0	0	0-0	16	25	16	4	0	4-0	11	9.00	50	.357	.387	0	ø	0	—	-7	0	-0.5
Total	7	13	21	.382	118	34	1	3-1	305.2	342	189	45	15	125-9	173	5.18	81	.285	.357	9	.111	-0	119	-34	43	-3.3
SMALL, AARON	Aaron James; B11.23.1971 Oxnard CA; BR/TR/6'5"/(200–235); [TorA89 22/575]; d6.11																									
1994	Tor A	0	0	ø	1	0	0	0-0	2	5	2	1	0	2-0	0	9.00	54	.500	.538	0	ø	0	—	-1	0	0.0
1995	Fla N	1	0	1.000	7	0	0	0-0	6.1	7	2	1	0	6-0	5	1.42	302	.269	.406	0	ø	0	—	2	0	0.2
1996	Oak A	1	3	.250	12	3	0	0-0	28.2	37	28	3	1	22-1	17	8.16	61	.308	.417	0	ø	0	87	-10	0	-1.1
1997	Oak A	9	5	.643	71	0	0	4-2	96.2	109	50	6	3	40-6	57	4.28	107	.294	.362	1	.000	-0	—	3	0	0.4
1998	Oak A	1	1	.500	24	0	0	0-0	36	51	34	3	3	14-3	19	7.25	64	.333	.398	0	ø	0	—	-11	0	-0.5
	Ari N	3	1	.750	23	0	0	0-2	31.2	32	14	5	1	8-1	14	3.69	116	.269	.320	0	ø	0	—	2	0	0.2
2002	Atl N	0	0	ø	1	0	0	0-0	0.1	2	1	0	0	2-0	1	27.00	15	.667	.800	0	ø	0	—	-1	0	0.0
2004	Fla N	0	0	ø	7	0	0	0-0	16.1	24	15	5	0	7-0	8	8.27	50	.343	.403	2	.000	-0	—	-7	0	-0.4
2005	†NY A	10	0	1.000	15	9	1-1	0-1	76	71	27	4	5	24-0	37	3.20	135	.250	.317	0	ø	0	155	11	0	1.2
2006	NY A	0	3	.000	11	3	0	0-0	27.2	42	29	9	1	12-1	12	8.46	54	.341	.401	1-0-1	.000	-0	125	-13	28	-1.1
Total	9	25	13	.658	172	15	1-1	4-5	321.2	380	202	37	14	137-12	170	5.20	86	.297	.368	4-0-1	.000	-0	133	-25	28	-1.1
SMALL, MARK	Mark Allen; B11.12.1967 Portland OR; BR/TR/6'3"/205; [HouN89 17/438]; d4.5; Col Washington St.; [DL 1997 Hou N 27]																									
1996	Hou N	0	1	.000	16	0	0	0-0	24.1	33	23	1	1	13-3	16	5.92	66	.308	.388	1	.000	-0	—	-8	0	-0.4
SMALLWOOD, WALT	Walter Clayton; B4.24.1893 Dayton MD; D4.29.1967 Baltimore MD; BR/TR/6'2"/190; d9.19; Mil 1918–19																									
1917	NY A	0	0	ø	2	0	0	0	2	1	0	0	0	1	1	0.00	ø	.167	.286	0	ø	0	—	1	—	0.0
1919	NY A	0	0	ø	6	0	0	0	21.2	20	12	1	2	9	6	4.98	64	.263	.356	5	.000	-1	—	-3	—	-0.3
Total	2	0	0	ø	8	0	0	0	23.2	21	12	1	2	10	7	4.56	69	.256	.351	5	.000	-1	—	-2	—	-0.3
SMART, J.D.	Jon David; B11.12.1973 San Saba TX; BR/TR/6'2"/(180–185); [MonN95 4/115]; d4.6; Col Texas; [DL 2000 Mon N 123]																									
1999	Mon N	0	1	.000	29	0	0	0-0	52	56	30	4	0	17-0	21	5.02	89	.276	.330	3	.000	-0	—	-2	0	-0.1
2001	Tex A	1	2	.333	15	0	0	0-2	15.1	19	11	3	0	4-0	10	6.46	74	.306	.338	0	ø	0	—	-2	99	-0.4
Total	2	1	3	.250	44	0	0	0-2	67.1	75	41	7	0	21-0	31	5.35	85	.283	.332	3	.000	-0	—	-4	222	-0.5
SMILEY, JOHN	John Patrick; B3.17.1965 Phoenixville PA; BL/TL/6'4"/(180–215); [PitN83 12/300]; d9.1; [DL 1998 Cle A 181]																									
1986	Pit N	1	0	1.000	12	0	0	0-0	11.2	4	6	2	0	4-0	9	3.86	101	.105	.190	0	ø	0	—	0	0	0.0
1987	Pit N	5	5	.500	63	0	0	4-2	75	69	49	7	0	50-8	58	5.76	72	.244	.354	7	.143	0	—	-11	0	-1.4
1988	Pit N	13	11	.542	34	32	5-1	0-0	205	185	81	15	3	46-4	129	3.25	106	.241	.284	63-0-7	.079	-2	89	5	0	0.4
1989	Pit N	12	8	.600	28	28	8-1	0-0	205.1	174	78	22	4	49-5	123	2.81	121	.226	.273	65-0-7	.138	1	100	11	0	1.1
1990	†Pit N	9	10	.474	26	25	2	0-0	149.1	161	83	15	2	36-1	86	4.64	79	.275	.317	49-0-3	.122	-0	92	-15	43	-1.7
1991	†Pit N★	**20**	8	**.714**	33	32	2-1	0-0	207.2	194	78	17	3	44-0	129	3.08	117	.251	.292	70-0-6	.100	-2	116	13	0	1.5
1992	Min A	16	9	.640	34	34	5-2	0-0	241	205	93	17	6	65-0	163	3.21	127	.231	.286	0	ø	0	91	23	0	2.3
1993	Cin N	3	9	.250	18	18	2	0-0	105.2	117	69	15	2	31-0	60	5.62	72	.286	.337	32-0-5	.250	2	101	-17	93	-1.5
1994	Cin N	11	10	.524	24	24	1-1	0-0	158.2	169	80	18	4	37-3	112	3.86	108	.275	.320	55-0-5	.200	2	122	4	0	0.7
1995	†Cin N★	12	5	.706	28	27	1	0-0	176.2	173	72	11	4	39-3	124	3.46	121	.263	.306	55-2-6	.164	2	111	15	15	1.5
1996	Cin N	13	14	.481	35	34	2-2	0-1	217.1	207	100	20	4	54-5	171	3.64	118	.256	.304	68-0-4	.191	2	90	14	0	1.7
1997	Cin N	9	10	.474	20	20	0	0-0	117	139	76	17	6	31-3	94	5.23	82	.296	.346	40-0-2	.100	-2	86	-13	15	-2.1
	Cle A	2	4	.333	6	6	0	0-0	37.1	45	23	9	1	10-0	26	5.54	85	.304	.350	0	ø	0	72	-2	8	-0.3
Total	12	126	103	.550	361	280	28-8	4-3	1907.2	1842	888	185	39	496-32	1284	3.80	103	.255	.305	504-2-45	.145	2	99	27	355	2.2
SMITH	; d6.5																									
1884	Bal U	0	0	ø	1	1	0	0	6	12	11	0	—	2	2	9.00	30	.387	.424	5	.200	-0	192	-4	—	-0.2
SMITH	; d5.31																									
1886	Cin AA	0	1	.000	1	1	1	0	9	8	8	0	0	10	1	4.00	88	.229	.400	4	.250	-0	202	-1	—	-0.1
SMITH, AL	Alfred John; B10.12.1907 Belleville IL; D4.28.1977 Brownsville TX; BL/TL/5'11"/180; d5.5; C1																									
1934	NY N	3	5	.375	30	4	0	5	66.2	70	40	2	0	21	27	4.32	90	.266	.320	14-0-1	.286	1	84	-4	—	-0.5
1935	NY N	10	8	.556	40	10	4-1	5	124	125	50	6	7	32	44	3.41	113	.263	.319	34-1-2	.118	-0	101	8	—	1.0
1936	†NY N	14	13	.519	43	30	9-**4**	2	209.1	217	116	16	4	69	89	3.78	103	.274	.335	73-0-4	.137	-1	128	-3	—	-0.5
1937	†NY N	5	4	.556	33	9	2	0	85.2	91	45	8	2	30	41	4.20	93	.275	.339	25-0-1	.120	-2	121	-2	—	-0.4
1938	Phi N	1	4	.200	37	1	0	1	86	115	70	7	0	40	46	6.28	62	.320	.388	21	.000	-2	131	-23	—	-1.4
1939	Phi N	0	0	ø	5	0	0	0	9	11	5	1	2	5	2	4.00	100	.314	.429	2	.000	-0	—	0	—	0.0
1940	Cle A	15	7	.682	31	24	11-1	2	183	187	79	12	6	55	46	3.44	122	.270	.329	62-0-1	.306	7	99	17	—	2.6
1941	Cle A	12	13	.480	29	27	13-2	0	206.2	204	95	12	1	75	76	3.83	103	.256	.321	71-1-1	.155	2*	92	4	0	0.8
1942	Cle A	10	15	.400	30	24	7-1	0	168.1	163	96	9	5	71	66	3.96	87	.251	.329	60-0-2	.250	3	94	-14	0	-1.6
1943	Cle A☆	17	7	.708	29	27	14-3	1	208.1	186	74	7	0	72	72	2.55	122	.239	.303	68-0-4	.206	3*	111	12	0	1.8
1944	Cle A	7	13	.350	28	26	7-1	0	181.2	197	83	6	3	69	44	3.42	96	.280	.347	64-0-1	.156	-1	91	-3	0	-0.4
1945	Cle A	5	12	.294	21	19	8-3	1	133.2	141	74	8	2	48	34	3.84	85	.275	.340	41-0-2	.293	4*	84	-13	0	-1.0
Total	12	99	101	.495	356	201	75-16	17	1662.1	1707	827	94	32	587	587	3.72	99	.267	.332	535-2-19	.191	14	101	-21	0	0.4
SMITH, AL	Alfred Kendricks; B12.13.1903 Norristown PA; D8.11.1995 San Diego CA; BR/TR/6'0"/170; d6.18; Col Villanova																									
1926	NY N	0	0	ø	1	0	0	0	2	4	2	0	0	2	0	9.00	42	.444	.545	0	ø	0	—	-1	—	-0.1
SMITH, ART	Arthur Laird; B6.21.1906 Boston MA; D11.22.1995 Norwalk CT; BR/TR/6'0"/175; d6.9; Col Columbia																									
1932	Chi A	0	1	.000	3	2	0	0	7	17	13	1	0	4	1	11.57	37	.500	.553	1	.000	-0	118	-7	—	-0.7
SMITH, BILLY	Billy Lavern; B9.13.1954 LaMarque TX; BR/TR/6'7"/225; [HouN77 14/352]; d6.9; Col Sam Houston St.																									
1981	†Hou N	1	1	.500	10	1	0	1-1	20.2	20	7	3	0	3-1	3	3.05	108	.263	.291	2	.000	-0	54	1	0	0.1
SMITH, BRYN	Bryn Nelson; B8.11.1955 Marietta GA; BR/TR/6'2"/(200–210); d9.8; Col Hancock (CA) JC																									
1981	Mon N	1	0	1.000	7	0	0	0-0	13	14	4	1	0	3-0	9	2.77	128	.280	.321	1-0-2	.000	-0	—	1	0	0.1
1982	Mon N	2	4	.333	47	1	0	3-0	79.1	81	43	5	0	23-5	50	4.20	88	.264	.311	8-0-1	.000	-0	0	-5	0	-0.4
1983	Mon N	6	11	.353	49	12	5-3	3-1	155.1	142	51	13	5	43-6	101	2.49	146	.248	.305	30-0-7	.167	0	83	18	0	2.0
1984	Mon N	12	13	.480	28	28	4-2	0-0	179	178	72	15	3	51-7	101	3.32	104	.259	.312	53-0-7	.132	1	93	4	0	0.7
1985	Mon N	18	5	.783	32	32	4-2	0-0	222.1	193	85	12	1	41-3	127	2.91	118	.232	.268	72-1-11	.194	3	140	11	0	1.4
1986	Mon N	10	8	.556	30	30	1	0-0	187.1	182	101	15	6	63-6	105	3.94	95	.251	.315	58-1-5	.138	1	108	-8	0	-0.5
1987	Mon N	10	9	.526	26	26	2	0-0	150.1	164	81	16	2	31-4	94	4.37	98	.274	.310	44-0-7	.136	-0	110	-1	25	-0.1
1988	Mon N	12	10	.545	32	32	1	0-0	198	179	79	15	10	32-2	122	3.00	121	.243	.282	55-0-8	.109	-1	103	12	0	1.1
1989	Mon N	10	11	.476	33	32	3-1	0-0	215.2	177	76	16	4	54-4	129	2.84	126	.223	.274	62-0-10	.065	-2	109	17	0	1.5
1990	StL N	9	8	.529	26	25	0	0-0	141.1	160	81	11	4	30-1	78	4.27	90	.286	.324	39-1-11	.256	3	97	-9	40	-0.7
1991	StL N	12	9	.571	31	31	3	0-0	198.2	188	95	16	7	45-3	94	3.85	97	.251	.297	65-0-7	.246	3	112	-3	0	0.0
1992	StL N	4	2	.667	13	1	0	0-0	21.1	20	11	3	3	5-1	9	4.64	74	.247	.315	3-0-1	.000	-0	397	-3	145	-0.6
1993	Col N	2	4	.333	11	5	0	0-1	29.2	47	29	2	3	11-1	9	8.49	56	.362	.412	6	.000	-0	79	-9	16	-1.6
Total	13	108	94	.535	365	255	23-8	6-2	1791.1	1725	808	140	48	432-43	1028	3.53	105	.253	.300	496-3-77	.153	7	108	25	226	2.9
SMITH, CHUCK	Charles Edward; B10.21.1969 Memphis TN; BR/TR/6'1"/185; d6.13; Col Indiana St.																									
2000	Fla N	6	6	.500	19	19	1	0-0	122.2	111	53	6	3	54-2	118	3.23	136	.248	.330	40-0-1	.100	-2*	95	14	0	1.0
2001	Fla N	5	5	.500	15	15	0	0-0	88	89	47	10	6	35-4	71	4.70	89	.265	.341	26-0-2	.192	1	114	-4	110	-0.4
Total	2	11	11	.500	34	34	1	0-0	210.2	200	100	16	9	89-6	189	3.84	112	.255	.335	66-0-3	.136	-2	103	10	110	0.6

YEAR	TM LG	W	L	PCT	G	GS	CG-SHO	SV-BS	IP	H	R	HR	HB	BB-IB	SO	ERA	AERA	OAV	OOB	AB-HR-SH	AVG	PB	SUP	APR	DL	PW
Smith, Charlie Charles Edwin; B4.20.1880 Cleveland OH; D1.3.1929 Wickliffe OH; BR/TR/6´1˝/185; d8.6; b–Fred																										
1902	Cle A	2	1	.667	3	3	2-1	0	20	23	9	0	0	5	5	4.05	85	.287	.329	8	.125	-0	111	0	—	0.0
1906	Was A	9	16	.360	33	22	17-2	0	235.1	250	113	2	8	75	105	2.91	91	.275	.336	87-1-1	.184	-1	86	-10	—	-1.2
1907	Was A	10	20	.333	36	31	21-3	0	258.2	254	103	0	1	51	119	2.61	93	.259	.297	84-0-5	.143	-3*	80	-3	—	-0.5
1908	Was A	9	13	.409	26	23	14-1	1	183	166	76	2	3	60	83	2.41	95	.247	.311	65-0-5	.123	-2*	92	-4	—	-0.8
1909	Was A	3	12	.200	23	15	7-1	0	145.2	140	73	4	5	37	72	3.27	74	.250	.303	45-0-1	.156	-1	60	-13	—	-1.4
	Bos A	3	0	1.000	3	3	2	0	25	23	6	2	1	2	11	2.16	116	.237	.260	10	.300	1	160	2	—	0.3
	Year	6	12	.333	26	18	9-1	0	170.2	163	79	6	6	39	83	3.11	78	.248	.297	55-0-1	.182	-0	77	-10	—	-1.1
1910	Bos A	11	6	.647	24	18	11	1	156.1	141	57	4	2	35	53	2.30	111	.248	.294	44-0-10	.114	-2	99	5	—	0.1
1911	Bos A	0	0	ø	1	1	0	0	2	2	3	1	0	1	0	9.00	36	.250	.333	0	ø	0	66	-1	—	0.0
	Chi N	3	2	.600	7	5	3-1	0	38	31	11	0	1	7	11	1.42	233	.228	.271	13-0-1	.077	-1	127	7	—	0.7
1912	Chi N	7	4	.636	20	5	1	1	94	92	56	2	3	31	47	4.21	79	.269	.335	35-0-2	.257	1*	88	-9	—	-0.8
1913	Chi N	7	9	.438	20	17	8-1	0	137.2	138	53	2	4	34	47	2.55	125	.274	.325	45-0-1	.089	-3	61	9	—	0.6
1914	Chi N	2	4	.333	16	5	1	0	53.2	49	27	3	1	15	17	3.86	72	.251	.308	11-0-1	.091	-1	57	-4	—	-0.5
Total	10	66	87	.431	212	148	87-10	3	1349.1	1309	587	22	29	353	570	2.81	94	.259	.311	447-1-27	.150	-13	84	-21	—	-3.5
Smith, Pop-Boy Clarence Ossie; B5.23.1892 Newport TN; D2.16.1924 Sweetwater TX; BR/TR/6´1˝/176; d4.19																										
1913	Chi A	0	1	.000	15	2	0	0	32	31	15	0	3	11	13	3.38	87	.263	.341	5	.000	-1	51	-1	—	-0.1
1916	Cle A	1	2	.333	5	3	0	1	25.2	25	15	1	1	11	4	3.86	78	.253	.333	7-0-1	.286	0	101	-2	—	-0.3
1917	Cle A	0	1	.000	6	0	0	0	8.2	14	11	0	1	4	3	8.31	34	.368	.442	1	.000	-0	—	-5	—	-0.5
Total	3	1	4	.200	26	5	0	1	66.1	70	41	1	5	26	20	4.21	70	.275	.353	13-0-1	.154	-1	81	-8	—	-0.9
Smith, Clay Clay Jamieson; B9.11.1914 Cambridge KS; D3.5.2002 Winfield KS; BR/TR/6´2˝/190; d9.13; Col Southwestern (KS)																										
1938	Cle A	0	0	ø	4	0	0	0	11	18	10	1	0	2	3	6.55	71	.367	.392	4	.000	-0	—	-3	—	-0.1
1940	†Det A	1	1	.500	14	1	0	0	28.1	32	18	3	1	13	14	5.08	94	.283	.362	7	.000	-1	92	-1	—	-0.1
Total	2	1	1	.500	18	1	0	0	39.1	50	28	4	1	15	17	5.49	86	.309	.371	11	.000	-1	92	-4	—	-0.2
Smith, Dan Daniel Charles; B9.15.1975 Flemington NJ; BR/TR/6´3˝/210; [TexA93 7/199]; d6.8; [DL 2004 Mon N 183]																										
1999	Mon N	4	9	.308	20	17	0	0-1	89.2	104	64	12	4	39-0	72	6.02	74	.293	.368	24-0-3	.083	-1	106	-14	0	-1.8
2000	Bos A	0	0	ø	2	0	0	0-0	3.1	2	3	0	0	3-0	1	8.10	62	.250	.357	0	ø	0	—	-1	0	-0.1
2002	Mon N	1	1	.500	33	0	0	2-0	46.2	34	18	6	1	21-0	34	3.47	126	.210	.301	3	.000	-0	—	5	0	0.2
2003	Mon N	2	2	.500	32	0	0	0-1	37.2	42	23	11	2	18-2	35	5.26	84	.280	.365	2	.000	-0	—	-3	95	-0.3
Total	4	7	12	.368	87	17	0	2-2	177.1	182	108	29	7	81-2	142	5.23	85	.270	.351	29-0-3	.069	-1	106	-13	278	-2.0
Smith, Dan Daniel Scott; B4.20.1969 St.Paul MN; BL/TL/6´5˝/(190–195); [TexA90 1/16]; d9.12; Col Creighton; [DL 1993 Tex A 33, 1995 Tex A 160]																										
1992	Tex A	0	3	.000	4	2	0	0-0	14.1	18	8	1	0	8-1	5	5.02	76	.321	.400	0	ø	0	48	-1	0	-0.3
1994	Tex A	1	2	.333	13	0	0	0-1	14.2	18	11	2	0	12-0	9	4.30	113	.281	.395	0	ø	0	—	-1	60	-0.1
Total	2	1	5	.167	17	2	0	0-1	29	36	19	3	0	20-1	14	4.66	93	.300	.397	0	ø	0	48	-2	253	-0.4
Smith, Daryl Daryl Clinton; B7.29.1960 Baltimore MD; BR/TR/6´4˝/185; [TexA80*6/141]; d9.18; Col Essex (MD) CC																										
1990	KC A	0	1	.000	2	1	0	0-0	6.2	5	3	0	0	4-0	6	4.05	95	.238	.333	0	ø	0	47	0	0	0.0
Smith, Dave David Merwin; B12.17.1914 Sellers SC; D4.1.1998 Whiteville NC; BR/TR/5´10˝/170; d6.16; Col Duke																										
1938	Phi A	2	1	.667	21	0	0	0	44.1	50	29	0	1	28	13	5.08	95	.284	.385	12	.000	-1	—	-1	—	-0.2
1939	Phi A	0	0	ø	1	0	0	0	0	1	0	0	0	2	0	(0)	ø	1.000	1.000	0	ø	0	—	0	—	0.0
Total	2	2	1	.667	22	0	0	0	44.1	51	29	0	1	30	13	5.08	95	.288	.394	12	.000	-1	—	-1	—	-0.2
Smith, Dave David Stanley; B1.21.1955 Richmond CA; BR/TR/6´1˝/195; [HouN76 8/169]; d4.11; C3; Col San Diego St.																										
1980	†Hou N	7	5	.583	57	0	0	10-5	102.2	90	24	1	4	32-7	85	1.93	170	.237	.303	12-0-2	.000	-1	—	18	0	2.1
1981	†Hou N	5	3	.625	42	0	0	8-3	75	54	26	2	2	23-4	52	2.76	119	.198	.264	8	.250	0	—	5	0	0.6
1982	Hou N	5	4	.556	49	1	0	11-3	63.1	69	30	4	0	31-4	28	3.84	87	.285	.361	2	.000	-0	186	-4	21	-0.7
1983	Hou N	3	1	.750	42	0	0	6-1	72.2	72	32	2	0	36-4	41	3.10	111	.258	.338	5-0-1	.000	-1	—	1	0	-0.1
1984	Hou N	5	4	.556	53	0	0	5-3	77.1	60	22	5	1	20-3	45	2.21	151	.214	.268	4-0-1	.000	-0	—	11	0	1.3
1985	Hou N	9	5	.643	64	0	0	27-6	79.1	69	26	3	1	17-5	40	2.27	154	.235	.279	3-0-1	.000	0	—	10	0	2.0
1986	†Hou N☆	4	7	.364	54	0	0	33-6	56	39	17	5	1	22-3	46	2.73	132	.200	.283	2	.000	-0	—	7	0	1.4
1987	Hou N	2	3	.400	50	0	0	24-5	60	39	13	0	1	21-8	73	1.65	238	.182	.257	2	.500	1	—	15	0	2.3
1988	Hou N	4	5	.444	51	0	0	27-5	57.1	60	26	1	1	19-8	38	2.67	125	.268	.327	2	.000	-0	—	1	0	0.2
1989	Hou N	3	4	.429	52	0	0	25-4	58	49	20	1	1	19-7	31	2.64	129	.233	.299	1	.000	-0	—	5	0	0.9
1990	Hou N★	6	6	.500	49	0	0	23-5	60.1	45	18	4	0	20-4	50	2.39	157	.210	.277	2	.000	0	—	9	0	1.9
1991	Chi N	0	6	.000	35	0	0	17-6	33	39	22	6	1	19-5	16	6.00	65	.302	.396	1	.000	-0	—	-6	40	-1.3
1992	Chi N	0	0	ø	11	0	0	0-0	14.1	15	4	0	0	4-2	3	2.51	145	.273	.317	0	ø	0	—	2	118	0.1
Total	13	53	53	.500	609	1	0	216-52	809.1	700	280	34	13	283-64	548	2.67	130	.234	.302	44-0-5	.068	-2	186	74	179	10.7
Smith, Dave David Wayne; B8.30.1957 Tomball TX; BR/TR/6´1˝/(190–196); [NYN79 27/668]; d9.18; Col Lamar																										
1984	Cal A	0	0	ø	1	0	0	0-0	1	4	2	1	0	0-0	0	18.00	22	.571	.571	0	ø	0	—	-1	0	-0.1
1985	Cal A	0	0	ø	4	0	0	0-0	5	5	4	1	0	1-0	3	7.20	57	.278	.300	0	ø	0	—	-2	0	-0.1
Total	2	0	0	ø	5	0	0	0-0	6	9	6	2	0	1-0	3	9.00	46	.360	.370	0	ø	0	—	-3	0	-0.2
Smith, Doug Douglass Weldon; B5.25.1892 Millers Falls MA; D9.18.1973 Greenfield MA; BL/TL/5´10˝/168; d7.10																										
1912	Bos A	0	0	ø	1	0	0	0	3	4	1	0	0	0	1	3.00	113	.364	.364	0	ø	0	—	0	—	0.0
Smith, Ed Ed; d4.18																										
1884	Bal U	3	4	.429	9	8	5	0	62	86	61	2	—	17	13	3.48	77	.308	.348	34	.147	-3	114	-8	—	-1.0
Smith, Eddie Edgar; B12.14.1913 Mansfield NJ; D1.2.1994 Willingboro NJ; BB/TL/5´10˝/174; d9.20; Mil 1944–45																										
1936	Phi A	1	1	.500	2	2	2	0	19	22	10	3	0	8	7	1.89	269	.275	.341	8	.125	-1	86	4	—	0.3
1937	Phi A	4	17	.190	38	23	14-1	5	196.2	178	100	18	4	90	79	3.94	120	.242	.327	73-0-2	.233	1*	59	17	—	1.8
1938	Phi A	3	10	.231	43	7	0	4	130.2	151	102	13	4	76	78	5.92	82	.287	.381	42-0-2	.286	3	89	-16	—	-1.1
1939	Phi A	1	0	1.000	3	0	0	0	3.2	7	4	0	0	2	3	9.82	48	.412	.474	0	ø	0	—	-2	—	-0.3
	Chi A	9	11	.450	29	22	7-1	0	176.2	161	83	11	4	90	67	3.67	129	.247	.342	52-0-5	.115	-1	72	19	—	1.7
	Year	10	11	.476	32	22	7-1	0	180.1	168	87	11	4	92	70	3.79	125	.251	.346	52-0-5	.115	-1	72	18	—	1.4
1940	Chi A	14	9	.609	32	28	12	0	207.1	179	92	16	3	95	119	3.21	138	.228	.313	69-0-8	.217	2	89	25	—	2.7
1941	Chi A★	13	17	.433	34	33	21-1	1	263.1	243	107	13	5	114	111	3.18	129	.246	.328	88-0-4	.216	4	74	28	0	3.4
1942	Chi A☆	7	20	.259	29	28	18-2	1	215	223	112	17	4	86	78	3.98	90	.269	.341	73-0-3	.123	-2	61	-10	0	-1.2
1943	Chi A	11	11	.500	25	25	14-2	0	187.2	197	85	2	5	76	66	3.69	90	.277	.351	69-1-4	.159	-1	102	-4	0	-0.6
1946	Chi A	8	11	.421	24	21	3-1	1	145.1	135	71	9	4	60	59	2.85	120	.246	.325	45	.178	0	84	4	0	0.5
1947	Chi A	1	3	.250	15	5	0	0	33.1	40	36	1	0	24	12	7.29	50	.299	.405	6	.167	-0	82	-15	0	-1.7
	Bos A	1	3	.250	8	3	0	0	17	18	14	3	0	18	15	7.41	52	.269	.424	6	.167	0	167	-6	0	-1.1
	Year	2	6	.250	23	8	0	0	50.1	58	50	4	0	42	27	7.33	51	.289	.412	12	.167	-0	116	-21	0	-2.8
Total	10	73	113	.392	282	197	91-8	12	1595.2	1554	816	106	33	739	694	3.82	108	.256	.340	531-1-28	.188	5	77	44	0	4.4
Smith, Edgar Edgar Eugene; B6.12.1862 Providence RI; D11.3.1892 Providence RI; BR/TR/5´10˝/160; d5.25; ▲																										
1883	Phi N	0	1	.000	1	1	0	0	7	18	17	0	—	3	2	15.43	20	.409	.447	4	.750	1	69	-9	—	-0.7
1884	Was AA	0	2	.000	3	2	2	0	22	27	23	0	1	5	4	4.91	62	.276	.317	57	.088	-1*	60	-5	—	-0.4
1885	Pro N	1	0	1.000	1	1	1	0	9	9	3	0	—	0	1	1.00	269	.273	.273	4	.250	0	84	1	—	0.1
1890	Cle N	1	4	.200	6	6	5	0	44	42	24	1	1	10	11	4.30	84	.243	.288	24	.292	2*	82	-1	—	0.1
Total	4	2	7	.222	11	10	8	0	82	96	67	1	2	18	18	5.05	65	.276	.315	89	.180	2	78	-14	—	-0.9
Smith, Elmer Elmer Ellsworth; B3.23.1868 Pittsburgh PA; D11.3.1945 Pittsburgh PA; BL/TL/5´11˝/178; d9.10; ▲																										
1886	Cin AA	4	4	.500	9	9	8	0	72.2	57	54	1	3	44	40	3.72	95	.211	.328	28	.286	4	125	-5	—	-0.2
1887	Cin AA	34	17	.667	52	52	49-3	0	447.1	400	224	5	9	126	176	**2.94**	**148**	**.230**	**.286**	186	.253	5	89	71	—	6.3
1888	Cin AA	22	17	.564	40	40	37-5	0	348.1	309	167	1	19	89	154	2.74	116	.229	.286	129	.225	4	93	19	—	2.0
1889	Cin AA	9	12	.429	29	22	16	0	203	253	171	11	7	101	104	4.88	80	.296	.375	83-2	.277	6	102	-21	—	-1.3
1892	Pit N	6	7	.462	17	13	12-1	0	134	140	94	2	1	58	51	3.63	91	.258	.331	511-4	.274	6*	128	-5	—	0.0
1894	Pit N	0	0	ø	1	0	0	0	4	6	2	0	1	1	0	4.50	117	.333	.400	490-6-10	.357	0*	—	1	—	0.0

YEAR	TM LG	W	L	PCT	G	GS	CG-SHO	SV-BS	IP	H	R	HR	HB	BB-IB	SO	ERA	AERA	OAV	OOB	AB-HR-SH	AVG	PB	SUP	APR	DL	PW
1898	Cin N	0	0	ø	1	0	0	0	1	2	2	0	0	3	0	18.00	21	.400	.625	486-1-6	.342	0*	—	-1	—	-0.1
Total	7	75	57	.568	149	.136	122-9	0	1210.1	1167	714	20	40	422	525	3.35	113	.244	.311	1913-13-16	.307	25	98	59	—	6.7
Smith, Frank	Frank Elmer "Nig","Piano Mover" (b Frank Elmer Schmidt); B10.28.1879 Pittsburgh PA; D11.3.1952 Pittsburgh PA; BR/TR/5´10.5˝/194; d4.22; Col Grove City																									
1904	Chi A	16	9	.640	26	23	22-4	0	202.1	157	62	0	12	58	107	2.09	117	.215	.284	72-0-3	.250	4	115	9	—	1.6
1905	Chi A	19	13	.594	39	31	27-4	0	291.2	215	97	0	8	107	171	2.13	116	.208	.287	106-1-1	.226	7*	133	12	—	2.2
1906	Chi A	5	5	.500	20	13	8-1	1	122	124	58	3	5	37	53	3.39	75	.267	.327	41-0-2	.293	5	105	-10	—	-0.2
1907	Chi A	23	10	.697	41	37	29-3	0	310	280	105	3	2	111	139	2.47	97	.243	.311	92-0-6	.196	5*	119	2	—	0.9
1908	Chi A	16	17	.485	41	35	24-3	1	297.2	213	92	2	2	73	129	2.03	114	.203	.256	106-0-6	.189	2*	106	9	—	1.5
1909	Chi A	25	17	.595	**51**	**40**	**37**-7	1	**365**	278	104	1	6	70	**177**	1.80	130	.214	.257	127-0-5	.173	6*	90	23	—	4.1
1910	Chi A	4	9	.308	19	15	9-3	0	128.2	91	43	1	2	40	50	2.03	118	.204	.272	43-0-2	.186	2*	67	6	—	1.0
	Bos A	1	2	.333	4	3	2	0	28	22	19	0	1	11	8	4.82	53	.234	.321	9-0-1	.111	-0	79	-6	—	-0.6
	Year	5	11	.313	23	18	11-3	0	156.2	113	62	1	3	51	58	2.53	96	.209	.281	52-0-3	.173	2	69	-1	—	0.4
1911	Bos A	0	0	ø	1	1	0	0	2.1	6	4	0	0	3	1	15.43	21	.500	.600	0	ø	0	308	-2	—	-0.1
	Cin N	10	14	.417	34	18	10	1	176.1	198	112	1	3	55	67	3.98	83	.289	.345	56-0-5	.214	3*	119	-16	—	-1.4
1912	Cin N	1	1	.500	7	3	1	0	22.2	34	25	1	0	15	5	6.35	53	.370	.458	6	.000	-0	167	-9	—	-0.7
1914	Bal F	10	8	.556	39	22	9-1	2	174.2	180	86	8	0	47	83	2.99	101	.259	.306	59-0-3	.203	1*	107	-3	—	-0.2
1915	Bal F	4	4	.500	17	9	2	0	88.2	108	53	5	0	31	37	4.67	61	.312	.369	29-1-1	.172	1	100	-15	—	-1.2
	Bro F	5	2	.714	15	5	4-1	0	63	69	31	2	0	18	24	3.14	87	.290	.340	20-0-1	.200	1	82	-4	—	-0.3
	Year	9	6	.600	32	14	6-1	0	151.2	177	84	7	0	49	61	4.04	70	.303	.357	49-1-2	.184	1	94	-18	—	-1.5
Total	11	139	111	.556	354	255	184-27	6	2273	1975	891	27	41	676	1051	2.59	99	.237	.297	766-2-36	.204	36	109	-4	—	6.6
Smith, Frank	Frank Thomas; B4.4.1928 Pierrepont Manor NY; D9.24.2005 Malone FL; BR/TR/6´3˝/200; d4.18																									
1950	Cin N	2	7	.222	38	4	0	3	90.2	73	43	12	8	39	55	3.87	109	.216	.312	21	.095	-2	94	4	0	0.2
1951	Cin N	5	5	.500	50	0	0	11	76	65	33	7	4	22	34	3.20	128	.230	.295	10-0-1	.000	-1	—	7	0	0.9
1952	Cin N	12	11	.522	53	2	1	7	122.1	109	56	13	7	41	77	3.75	101	.242	.315	29-0-1	.172	0	83	0	0	-0.1
1953	Cin N	8	1	.889	50	1	0	2	83.2	89	64	15	3	25	42	5.49	79	.272	.330	13-0-2	.154	-1	144	-13	0	-1.3
1954	Cin N	5	8	.385	50	0	0	20	81	60	29	15	3	29	51	2.67	157	.211	.286	10-0-2	.100	1	—	12	0	2.6
1955	StL N	3	1	.750	28	0	0	1	39	27	18	3	5	23-3	17	3.23	126	.205	.337	4-0-1	.000	-1	—	2	0	0.2
1956	Cin N	0	0	ø	2	0	0	0	3	3	4	2	0	2-0	1	12.00	33	.300	.385	0	ø	0	—	-2	0	-0.1
Total	7	35	33	.515	271	7	1	44	495.2	426	247	67	30	181-3	277	3.81	107	.234	.311	87-0-7	.115	-3	99	10	0	2.4
Smith, Fred	Frederick; B11.24.1878 New Diggings WI; D2.4.1964 Los Angeles CA; BR/TR/6´0˝/186; d6.14																									
1907	Cin N	2	7	.222	18	9	5	1	85.1	90	44	3	4	24	19	2.85	91	.274	.331	28-0-1	.107	-2	88	-4	—	-0.6
Smith, Fred	Frederick C.; B3.25.1863 Greene NY; D1.9.1941 Syracuse NY; BL/TR/5´11˝/156; d4.18																									
1890	Tol AA	19	13	.594	35	34	31-2	0	286	273	155	13	13	90	116	3.27	121	.244	.307	126	.167	-2*	88	21	—	1.8
Smith, George	George Allen "Columbia George"; B5.31.1892 Byram CT; D1.7.1965 Greenwich CT; BR/TR/6´2˝/163; d8.9; Col Columbia																									
1916	NY N	3	0	1.000	9	1	0	0	20.2	14	8	0	1	6	9	2.61	93	.197	.269	2-0-1	.000	-0	184	-1	—	-0.1
1917	NY N	0	3	.000	14	1	1	0	38	38	13	1	1	11	16	2.84	90	.270	.327	9	.000	-1	30	0	—	-0.2
1918	Cin N	2	3	.400	10	6	4-1	0	55.1	71	36	3	0	11	19	4.07	66	.329	.361	17-0-1	.000	-2	76	-10	—	-1.1
	NY N	2	3	.400	5	2	1	0	26.2	26	12	0	1	6	4	4.05	65	.255	.303	8-0-1	.250	0	58	-3	—	-0.6
	Bro N	4	1	.800	8	5	4	0	50	43	14	0	2	5	18	2.34	119	.249	.278	15-0-1	.200	0	81	4	—	0.5
	Year	8	7	.533	23	13	9-1	0	132	140	62	3	3	22	41	3.41	79	.285	.320	40-0-3	.125	-2	75	-10	—	-1.2
1919	NY N	0	2	.000	3	2	0	0	11	18	8	1	0	4	0	5.73	49	.383	.431	3	.000	-0	113	-3	—	-0.6
	Phi N	5	11	.313	31	19	11-1	0	184.2	194	94	7	3	46	42	3.22	100	.278	.326	60-0-2	.133	-3	92	-5	—	-0.8
	Year	5	13	.278	34	21	11-1	0	195.2	212	102	8	3	50	42	3.36	95	.285	.332	63-0-2	.127	-4	94	-7	—	-1.4
1920	Phi N	13	18	.419	43	28	10-1	2	250.2	265	115	10	6	51	51	3.45	99	.283	.324	72-0-8	.097	-6	77	2	—	-0.4
1921	Phi N	4	20	.167	39	28	12-1	1	221.1	303	166	12	3	52	45	4.76	89	.335	.373	71-0-1	.056	-8	69	-14	—	-2.1
1922	Phi N	5	14	.263	42	16	6-1	0	194	250	124	16	6	35	44	4.78	98	.316	.350	66	.076	-7	63	1	—	-0.7
1923	Bro N	3	6	.333	25	7	3	1	91	99	53	4	3	28	15	3.66	106	.278	.336	26-0-1	.192	-1	103	0	—	-0.2
Total	8	41	81	.336	229	115	52-5	4	1143.1	1321	643	54	26	255	263	3.89	94	.298	.340	349-0-16	.097	-29	78	-29	—	-6.3
Smith, Heinie	George Henry; B10.24.1871 Pittsburgh PA; D6.25.1939 Buffalo NY; BR/TR/5´9.5˝/160; d9.8.1897; M1; ▲																									
1901	NY N	0	1	.000	2	1	1	0	13.1	24	13	0	3	5	5	8.10	41	.387	.457	29-1-1	.207	0*	86	-6	—	-0.3
Smith, George	George Shelby; B10.27.1901 Louisville KY; D5.26.1981 Richmond VA; BR/TR/6´1˝/175; d4.21																									
1926	Det A	1	2	.333	23	1	0	0	44	55	37	3	2	33	15	6.95	58	.318	.433	5-0-1	.000	-0	41	-12	—	-0.8
1927	Det A	4	1	.800	29	0	0	0	71.1	62	38	3	2	50	32	3.91	108	.240	.368	19-2-1	.368	3	—	3	—	0.4
1928	Det A	1	1	.500	39	2	0	3	106	103	55	3	0	50	54	4.42	93	.263	.346	27-0-1	.111	-2	103	0	—	-0.3
1929	Det A	3	2	.600	14	2	1	0	35.2	42	33	1	0	36	13	5.80	74	.307	.451	12	.417	2	128	-8	—	-0.7
1930	Bos A	1	2	.333	27	2	0	0	73.2	92	62	7	1	49	21	6.60	70	.317	.418	24	.333	2*	103	-16	—	-0.6
Total	5	10	8	.556	132	7	1	3	330.2	354	225	17	5	218	135	5.28	81	.283	.392	87-2-3	.264	4	102	-33	—	-2.0
Smith, Hal	Harold Laverne; B6.30.1902 Creston IA; D9.27.1992 Ft.Lauderdale FL; BR/TR/6´3˝/195; d9.14; Col Creston (IA) JC																									
1932	Pit N	1	0	1.000	2	1	1-1	0	12	9	1	0	0	2	4	0.75	508	.209	.244	3-0-1	.000	-0	154	4	—	0.3
1933	Pit N	8	7	.533	28	19	8-2	1	145	149	66	5	5	31	40	2.86	116	.261	.305	47-0-2	.128	-2	107	4	—	0.1
1934	Pit N	3	4	.429	20	5	1	0	50	72	44	3	4	18	15	7.20	57	.343	.405	17	.059	-2	109	-16	—	-2.1
1935	Pit N	0	0	ø	1	0	0	0	3	2	1	0	0	1	0	3.00	137	.200	.273	0	ø	0	—	0	—	0.0
Total	4	12	11	.522	51	25	10-3	1	210	232	112	8	9	52	59	3.77	94	.279	.328	67-0-3	.104	-4	108	-8	—	-1.7
Smith, Harry	Harrison Morton; B8.15.1889 Union NE; D7.26.1964 Dunbar NE; BR/TR/5´9˝/160; d10.6																									
1912	Chi A	1	0	1.000	1	1	0	0	5	6	1	0	0	0	1	1.80	178	.333	.333	1-0-1	.000	-0	208	1	—	0.2
Smith, Jack	Jack Hatfield; B11.15.1935 Pikeville KY; BR/TR/6´0˝/(185–186); d9.10																									
1962	LA N	0	0	ø	8	0	0	1	10	10	6	0	0	4-1	7	4.50	81	.263	.326	1	.000	-0	—	-1	0	-0.1
1963	LA N	0	0	ø	4	0	0	0	8.1	10	7	2	2	2-0	5	7.56	40	.303	.368	2	.000	-0	—	-4	0	-0.2
1964	Mil N	2	2	.500	22	0	0	0	31	28	15	3	0	11-5	19	3.77	93	.237	.300	3	.333	0	—	-1	0	0.0
Total	3	2	2	.500	34	0	0	1	49.1	48	28	5	2	17-6	31	4.56	76	.254	.318	6	.167	-0	—	-6	0	-0.3
Smith, Jake	Jacob John (b Jacob Schmidt); B6.10.1887 Dravosburg PA; D11.7.1948 E.McKeesport PA; BB/TL/6´5˝/200; d10.3																									
1911	Phi N	0	0	ø	2	0	0	0	5	3	0	0	0	2	1	0.00	ø	.176	.263	3	.000	-0	—	2	—	0.1
Smith, Phenomenal	John Francis (b John Francis Gammon); B12.12.1864 Philadelphia PA; D4.3.1952 Manchester NH; BL/TL/5´6.5˝/161; d8.14																									
1884	Phi AA	0	1	.000	1	1	1	0	9	14	6	0	0	1	3	4.00	85	.368	.385	4	.250	-0	89	-1	—	-0.1
	Pit AA	0	1	.000	1	1	1	0	8	11	10	0	1	2	4	9.00	37	.306	.359	4	.000	-1	91	-4	—	-0.4
	Year	0	2	.000	2	2	2	0	17	25	16	0	1	3	7	6.35	53	.338	.372	8	.125	-1	90	-4	—	-0.5
1885	Bro AA	0	1	.000	1	1	1	0	8	12	18	0	1	6	2	12.38	27	.300	.404	3	.333	0	90	-8	—	-0.6
	Phi AA	0	1	.000	1	1	0	0	4	7	9	0	1	4	7	9.00	38	.368	.500	2	.000	-0	189	-3	—	-0.4
	Year	0	2	.000	2	2	1	0	12	19	27	0	2	10	9	11.25	30	.322	.437	5	.200	-0	141	-11	—	-1.0
1886	Det N	1	1	.500	3	3	3	0	25	16	9	0	—	8	15	2.16	154	.174	.240	9	.111	-1	37	3	—	0.1
1887	Bal AA	25	30	.455	58	55	54-1	0	491.1	526	369	7	14	176	206	3.79	108	.261	.325	205-1	.234	8*	95	8	—	1.3
1888	Bal AA	14	19	.424	35	32	31	0	292	249	170	5	24	137	152	3.61	83	.222	.320	109-1	.248	8	94	-18	—	-1.1
	Phi AA	2	1	.667	3	3	3	0	22	21	15	0	0	10	19	2.86	104	.241	.320	9	.333	1	123	0	—	0.1
	Year	16	20	.444	38	35	34	0	314	270	185	5	24	147	171	3.55	84	.224	.320	118-1	.254	9	97	-9	—	-1.0
1889	Phi AA	2	3	.400	5	5	5	0	43	53	31	2	3	25	12	4.40	86	.294	.389	16	.188	0	62	-2	—	-0.2
1890	Phi N	8	12	.400	24	20	19-1	0	204	209	125	5	8	89	81	4.28	86	.257	.336	86	.279	4*	93	-5	—	-0.1
	Pit N	1	3	.250	5	5	5	0	44	39	25	0	1	13	15	3.07	108	.229	.288	17	.412	2	96	1	—	0.3
	Year	9	15	.375	29	25	24-1	0	248	248	150	5	9	102	96	4.06	89	.252	.328	103	.301	6	93	-6	—	0.2
1891	Phi N	1	1	.500	3	2	0	0	19	20	15	1	0	8	3	4.26	80	.260	.329	8	.375	1	105	-2	—	-0.1
Total	8	54	74	.422	140	129	123-2	0	1169.1	1177	802	20	53	479	519	3.89	93	.251	.327	472-2	.250	23	93	-31	—	-1.2
Smith, Chick	John William (b Jan Smadt); B12.2.1892 Dayton KY; D10.11.1935 Dayton KY; BL/TL/5´8˝/165; d4.12																									
1913	Cin N	0	1	.000	5	1	0	0	17.2	15	8	1	0	11	11	3.57	91	.238	.351	4-0-1	.000	-1	23	0	—	-0.1

YEAR	TM LG	W	L	PCT	G	GS	CG-SHO	SV-BS	IP	H	R	HR	HB	BB-IB	SO	ERA	AERA	OAV	OOB	AB-HR-SH	AVG	PB	SUP	APR	DL	PW
Smith, Lee	Lee Arthur; B12.4.1957 Shreveport LA; BR/TR/6´6˝/(220–269); [ChiN75 2/28]; d9.1																									
1980	Chi N	2	0	1.000	18	0	0	0-0	21.2	21	9	0	0	14-5	17	2.91	136	.259	.365	0	ø	0	—	2	0	0.2
1981	Chi N	3	6	.333	40	1	0	1-3	66.2	57	31	2	1	31-8	50	3.51	107	.239	.327	9-0-1	.000	-1	24	1	0	0.0
1982	Chi N	2	5	.286	72	5	0	17-1	117	105	38	5	3	37-5	99	2.69	140	.245	.306	16-1-1	.063	-0	89	14	0	1.2
1983	Chi N★	4	10	.286	66	0	0	**29**-4	103.1	70	23	5	1	41-14	91	1.65	230	.194	.277	9-0-1	.111	-0	—	23	0	4.3
1984	†Chi N	9	7	.563	69	0	0	33-9	101	98	42	6	0	35-7	86	3.65	107	.255	.314	13-0-1	.077	-1	—	4	0	0.7
1985	Chi N	7	4	.636	65	0	0	33-9	97.2	87	35	9	1	32-6	112	3.04	132	.242	.305	6	.000	-0	—	10	0	1.7
1986	Chi N	9	9	.500	66	0	0	31-8	90.1	69	32	7	0	42-11	93	3.09	132	.215	.303	5	.000	-1	—	10	15	2.0
1987	Chi N★	4	10	.286	62	0	0	36-12	83.2	84	30	4	0	32-5	96	3.12	139	.259	.326	2	.000	-0*	—	11	0	2.3
1988	†Bos A	4	5	.444	64	0	0	29-8	83.2	72	34	7	1	37-6	96	2.80	148	.225	.306	0	ø	0	—	9	0	1.5
1989	Bos A	6	1	.857	64	0	0	25-5	70.2	53	30	6	0	33-6	96	3.57	115	.209	.299	0	ø	0	—	5	0	0.7
1990	Bos A	2	1	.667	11	0	0	4-1	14.1	13	4	0	0	9-2	17	1.88	218	.236	.344	0	ø	0	—	3	0	0.7
	StL N	3	4	.429	53	0	0	27-5	68.2	58	20	3	0	20-5	70	2.10	184	.227	.281	2	.000	-0	—	12	0	2.0
1991	StL N☆	6	3	.667	67	0	0	**47**-6	73	70	19	5	0	13-5	67	2.34	160	.249	.281	0	ø	0	—	12	0	2.5
1992	StL N☆	4	9	.308	70	0	0	**43**-8	75	62	28	4	0	26-4	60	3.12	110	.221	.286	0	ø	0	—	3	0	0.5
1993	StL N☆	2	4	.333	55	0	0	43-7	50	49	25	11	0	9-1	49	4.50	90	.251	.282	2	.000	-0	—	-1	0	-0.3
	NY A	0	0	ø	8	0	0	3-0	8	4	0	0	0	5-1	11	0.00	ø	.148	.273	0	ø	0	—	4	0	0.2
1994	Bal A★	1	4	.200	41	0	0	**33**-6	38.1	34	16	6	0	11-1	42	3.29	154	.239	.290	0	ø	0	—	7	0	1.2
1995	Cal A☆	0	5	.000	52	0	0	37-4	49.1	42	19	3	1	25-4	43	3.47	136	.237	.330	0	ø	0	—	8	0	1.4
1996	Cal A	0	0	ø	11	0	0	0-2	11	8	4	0	0	3-0	6	2.45	206	.205	.250	0	ø	0	—	3	20	0.1
	Cin N	3	4	.429	43	0	0	2-4	44.1	49	20	4	1	23-4	35	4.06	105	.277	.363	0	ø	0	—	2	0	0.3
1997	Mon N	0	1	.000	25	0	0	5-1	21.2	28	16	2	1	8-0	15	5.82	72	.308	.370	0	ø	0	—	-4	0	-0.3
Total	18	71	92	.436	1022	6	0	478-103	1289.1	1133	475	89	10	486-100	1251	3.03	133	.237	.306	64-1-4	.047	-4	75	138	35	22.9
Smith, Roy	Le Roy Purdy; B9.6.1961 Mt.Vernon NY; BR/TR/6´3˝/(200–217); [PhiN79 3/72]; d6.23; Col Fordham																									
1984	Cle A	5	5	.500	22	14	0	0-0	86.1	91	49	14	1	40-5	55	4.59	90	.270	.346	0	ø	0	108	-5	0	-0.5
1985	Cle A	1	4	.200	12	11	1	0-0	62.1	84	40	8	1	17-0	28	5.34	78	.321	.359	0	ø	0	123	-8	29	-0.6
1986	Min A	0	2	.000	5	0	0	0-1	10.1	13	8	1	1	5-1	8	6.97	62	.295	.380	0	ø	0	—	-3	0	-0.4
1987	Min A	1	0	1.000	7	1	0	0-1	16.1	20	10	3	2	6-0	8	4.96	94	.290	.359	0	ø	0	275	-1	0	0.0
1988	Min A	3	0	1.000	9	4	0	0-0	37	29	12	3	1	12-1	17	2.68	153	.210	.276	0	ø	0	134	6	0	0.4
1989	Min A	10	6	.625	32	26	2	1-0	172.1	180	82	22	5	51-5	92	3.92	106	.269	.324	0	ø	0	125	4	0	0.2
1990	Min A	5	10	.333	32	23	1-1	0-0	153.1	191	91	20	0	47-4	87	4.81	87	.313	.356	0	ø	0	105	-11	0	-1.1
1991	Bal A	5	4	.556	17	14	0	0-0	80.1	99	52	9	1	24-0	25	5.60	71	.311	.358	0	ø	0	110	-14	0	-1.4
Total	8	30	31	.492	136	93	4-1	1-2	618.1	707	344	80	12	202-16	320	4.60	90	.289	.343	0	ø	0	117	-32	29	-3.4
Smith, Mark	Mark Christopher; B11.23.1955 Arlington VA; BL/TR/6´2˝/215; [BalA77 9/227]; d8.12; Col American																									
1983	Oak A	1	0	1.000	8	1	0	0-0	14.2	24	11	0	1	6-1	10	6.75	58	.387	.449	0	ø	0	47	-4	0	-0.3
Smith, Matt	Matthew Joel; B6.15.1979 Las Vegas NV; BL/TL/6´5˝/225; [NYA00 4/128]; d4.14; Col Oklahoma St.																									
2006	NY A	0	0	ø	12	0	0	0-0	12	4	0	0	0	8-1	9	0.00	ø	.105	.261	0	ø	0	—	6	0	0.3
	Phi N	0	1	.000	14	0	0	0-0	8.2	3	2	0	0	4-0	12	2.08	226	.111	.226	0	ø	0	—	2	0	0.3
Total	1	0	1	.000	26	0	0	0-0	20.2	7	2	0	0	12-1	21	0.87	528	.108	.247	0	ø	0	—	8	0	0.6
Smith, Mike	Michael Anthony; B2.23.1961 Jackson MS; BR/TR/6´1˝/(170–195); d4.6; Col Hinds (MS) CC																									
1984	Cin N	1	0	1.000	8	0	0	0-0	10.1	12	6	1	0	5-0	7	5.23	73	.286	.362	0-0-1	ø	0	—	-1	0	-0.1
1985	Cin N	0	0	ø	2	0	0	0-0	3.1	2	2	2	0	1-0	2	5.40	70	.167	.231	0	ø	0	—	0	0	0.0
1986	Cin N	0	0	ø	2	1	0	0-0	3.1	7	5	0	0	1-0	1	13.50	29	.412	.444	0	ø	0	208	-3	0	-0.2
1988	Mon N	0	0	ø	5	0	0	1-0	8.2	6	3	0	0	5-0	4	3.12	117	.207	.324	2	.000	-0	—	1	0	0.0
1989	Pit N	0	1	.000	16	0	0	0-0	24	28	12	1	0	10-1	12	3.75	91	.301	.362	3	.000	-0	—	-1	0	-0.1
Total	5	1	1	.500	33	1	0	1-0	49.2	55	28	4	0	22-1	26	4.71	76	.285	.355	5-0-1	.000	-1	208	-4	0	-0.4
Smith, Mike	Michael Anthony; B10.31.1963 San Antonio TX; BR/TR/6´3˝/190; [CinN84*5/110]; d6.30; Col Ranger (TX) JC																									
1989	Bal A	2	0	1.000	13	1	0	0-0	20	25	19	3	0	14-2	12	7.65	50	.313	.411	0	ø	0	142	-9	0	-0.8
1990	Bal A	0	0	ø	2	0	0	0-0	3	4	4	2	0	1-0	2	12.00	32	.308	.357	0	ø	0	—	-3	0	-0.1
Total	2	2	0	1.000	15	1	0	0-0	23	29	23	5	0	15-2	14	8.22	46	.312	.404	0	ø	0	142	-12	0	-0.9
Smith, Mike	Michael Anthony; B9.19.1977 Norwood MA; BR/TR/5´11˝/(195–205); [TorA00 5/148]; d4.26; Col Richmond																									
2002	Tor A	0	3	.000	14	6	0	0-0	35.1	43	28	3	7	20-0	16	6.62	70	.301	.409	0	ø	0	83	-8	0	-0.5
2006	Min A	0	0	ø	1	1	0	0-0	3	5	4	1	1	3-0	1	12.00	38	.357	.500	0	ø	0	227	-2	0	-0.1
Total	2	0	3	.000	15	7	0	0-0	38.1	48	32	4	8	23-0	17	7.04	66	.306	.418	0	ø	0	103	-10	0	-0.6
Smith, Pete	Peter John; B2.27.1966 Abington MA; BR/TR/6´2˝/(183–200); [PhiN84 1/21]; d9.8																									
1987	Atl N	1	2	.333	6	6	0	0-0	31.2	39	21	3	0	14-0	11	4.83	90	.307	.371	11-0-1	.091	-1	91	-2	0	-0.3
1988	Atl N	7	15	.318	32	32	5-3	0-0	195.1	183	89	15	1	88-3	124	3.69	99	.250	.330	53-0-8	.113	-1	73	0	0	-0.3
1989	Atl N	5	14	.263	28	27	1	0-0	142	144	83	13	0	57-2	115	4.75	77	.263	.330	41-0-5	.098	-0*	74	-15	0	-2.0
1990	Atl N	5	6	.455	13	13	3	0-0	77	77	45	11	0	24-2	56	4.79	84	.260	.313	23-0-4	.087	-1	105	-6	70	-0.9
1991	Atl N	1	3	.250	14	10	0	0-0	48	48	33	5	0	22-3	29	5.06	77	.262	.335	12-0-1	.167	0	109	-7	45	-0.5
1992	†Atl N	7	0	1.000	12	11	2-1	0-0	79	63	19	3	0	28-2	43	2.05	179	.217	.285	26-0-3	.038	-1	128	14	0	1.1
1993	Atl N	4	8	.333	20	14	0	0-0	90.2	92	45	15	2	36-3	53	4.37	93	.270	.339	27-0-3	.222	1	105	-2	38	-0.1
1994	NY N	4	10	.286	21	21	1	0-0	131.1	145	83	25	2	42-4	62	5.55	75	.285	.338	37-0-6	.135	0	85	-17	19	-1.5
1995	Cin N	1	2	.333	11	2	0	0-0	24.1	30	19	8	1	7-1	14	6.66	63	.319	.362	3	.000	0	206	-7	0	-0.6
1997	SD N	7	6	.538	37	15	0	1-0	118	120	66	16	1	52-2	68	4.81	82	.267	.343	30-0-6	.167	1*	103	-10	0	-0.9
1998	SD N	3	2	.600	10	8	0	0-0	43.1	45	23	5	3	18-1	36	4.78	83	.266	.344	14-0-1	.071	-0*	153	-3	0	-0.3
	Bal A	2	3	.400	27	4	0	0-1	45	57	31	7	0	16-1	29	6.20	73	.311	.363	2	.000	-0	87	-8	0	-0.7
Total	11	47	71	.398	231	163	12-4	1-1	1025.2	1043	557	126	10	404-24	640	4.55	86	.266	.333	279-0-38	.118	-2	95	-63	172	-7.0
Smith, Pete	Peter Luke; B3.19.1940 Natick MA; BR/TR/6´2˝/190; d9.13; Mil 1963; Col Colgate; [DL 1964 Bos A 134]																									
1962	Bos A	0	1	.000	1	1	0	0	3.2	7	8	3	0	2-0	1	19.64	21	.438	.474	1	.000	-0	130	-6	0	-0.8
1963	Bos A	0	0	ø	6	1	0	0	15	11	6	2	0	6-2	6	3.60	105	.212	.293	2	.000	-0	117	1	0	0.0
Total	2	0	1	.000	7	2	0	0	18.2	18	14	5	0	8-2	7	6.75	57	.265	.338	3	.000	-0	127	-5	134	-0.8
Smith, Brian	Randall Brian; B7.19.1972 Salisbury NC; BR/TR/5´11˝/190; [TorA94 27/763]; d9.11; Col North Carolina–Wilmington																									
2000	Pit N	0	0	ø	3	0	0	0-0	4.1	6	5	1	0	2-0	3	10.38	45	.375	.421	0	ø	0	—	-3	0	-0.1
Smith, Rex	Rex (b Henry W. Schmidt); B1864 Louisville KY; D6.21.1895 Louisville KY; d7.11																									
1886	Phi AA	0	1	.000	1	1	1	0	9	15	13	0	0	5	4	7.00	50	.385	.455	4	.000	-1	68	-4	—	-0.3
Smith, Ed	Rhesa Edward; B2.21.1879 Mentone IN; D3.20.1955 Tarpon Springs FL; BR/TR/5´11˝/170; d4.27																									
1906	StL A	8	11	.421	19	18	13	0	154.2	153	90	3	8	53	45	3.72	69	.261	.331	54-0-2	.204	2	115	-19	—	-1.9
Smith, Bud	Robert Allan; B10.23.1979 Torrance CA; BL/TL/6´0˝/170; [StLN98 4/108]; d6.10; Col Los Angeles Harbor (CA) JC																									
2001	†StL N	6	3	.667	16	14	1-1	0-0	84.2	79	40	12	1	24-5	59	3.83	113	.250	.304	25-0-2	.160	-0	113	4	0	0.4
2002	StL N	1	5	.167	11	10	0	0-0	48	67	39	4	3	22-2	22	6.94	58	.338	.405	14-0-3	.214	1	92	-15	15	-1.6
Total	2	7	8	.467	27	24	1-1	0-0	132.2	146	79	16	4	46-7	81	4.95	85	.284	.344	39-0-5	.179	1	104	-11	15	-1.2
Smith, Bob	Robert Ashley (aka Robert M. Brown in 1914); B7.20.1890 Woodbury VT; D12.27.1965 West Los Angeles CA; BR/TR/5´11˝/160; d4.19; Col Tufts																									
1913	Chi A	0	0	ø	1	0	0	0	2	3	3	0	0	3	1	13.50	22	.273	.429	0	ø	0	—	-2	—	-0.1
1914	Buf F	0	0	ø	15	1	0	3	36.2	39	16	3	2	16	13	3.44	86	.281	.363	9	.222	0	70	-1	—	0.0
1915	Buf F	0	0	ø	1	0	0	0	1	1	2	0	1	2	0	18.00	16	.333	.667	0	ø	0	—	-1	—	-0.1
Total	3	0	0	ø	17	1	0	3	39.2	43	21	3	3	21	14	4.31	69	.281	.379	9	.222	0	70	-4	—	-0.2
Smith, Bob	Robert Eldridge; B4.22.1895 Rogersville TN; D7.19.1987 Waycross GA; BR/TR/5´10˝/175; d4.19.1923; ▲																									
1925	Bos N	5	3	.625	13	10	6	0	92.2	110	51	6	0	36	19	4.47	90	.304	.367	174-0-2	.282	3*	97	-3	—	0.0
1926	Bos N	10	13	.435	33	23	14-4	1	201.1	199	91	10	0	75	44	3.75	94	.269	.336	84-0-1	.298	7*	95	-1	—	0.7
1927	Bos N	10	18	.357	41	31	16-1	3	260.2	297	132	9	2	75	81	3.76	99	.301	.351	109-1-1	.248	4*	106	-3	—	0.3
1928	Bos N	13	17	.433	38	26	14	2	244.1	274	138	11	2	74	59	3.87	101	.289	.342	92-1-6	.250	3*	96	-4	—	0.0

THE PITCHER REGISTER

YEAR	TM LG	W	L	PCT	G	GS	CG-SHO	SV-BS	IP	H	R	HR	HB	BB-IB	SO	ERA	AERA	OAV	OOB	AB-HR-SH	AVG	PB	SUP	APR	DL	PW
1929	Bos N	11	17	.393	34	29	19-1	3	231	256	135	20	1	71	65	4.68	100	.285	.338	99-1-3	.172	-1*	78	1	—	0.1
1930	Bos N	10	14	.417	38	24	14-2	5	219.2	247	115	25	3	85	84	4.26	116	.290	.357	81-0-3	.235	-1*	61	17	—	1.6
1931	Chi N	15	12	.556	36	29	18-2	2	240.1	239	101	10	1	62	63	3.22	120	.256	.303	87-0-5	.218	2	105	16	—	1.9
1932	†Chi N	4	3	.571	34	11	4-1	2	119	148	64	4	3	36	35	4.61	82	.303	.355	42	.238	2*	126	-8	—	-0.2
1933	Cin N	4	4	.500	16	6	4	0	73.2	75	27	3	0	11	18	2.20	154	.260	.287	25-0-1	.200	0*	78	8	—	0.9
	Bos N	4	3	.571	14	4	3-1	1	58.2	68	24	3	0	7	16	3.22	95	.296	.316	20	.200	1	88	-1	—	0.0
	Year	8	7	.533	30	10	7-1	1	132.1	143	51	6	0	18	34	2.65	123	.276	.300	45-0-1	.200	1	82	6	—	0.9
1934	Bos N	6	9	.400	39	5	3	5	121.2	133	69	9	0	36	26	4.66	82	.277	.328	36-0-2	.250	1*	99	-10	—	-1.1
1935	Bos N	8	18	.308	46	20	8-2	5	203.1	232	105	13	3	61	58	3.94	96	.285	.337	63-0-6	.270	2*	85	-4	—	-0.3
1936	Bos N	6	7	.462	35	11	5-2	8	136	142	65	3	1	35	36	3.77	102	.264	.311	45-0-2	.222	0	80	1	—	0.2
1937	Bos N	0	1	.000	18	0	0	3	44	52	22	6	2	6	14	4.09	88	.295	.326	10	.200	0*	—	-2	—	-0.1
Total	13	106	139	.433	435	229	128-16	40	2246.1	2472	1139	132	18	670	618	3.94	100	.283	.335	967-3-32	.244	23	91	7	—	4.0

SMITH, BOB Robert Gilchrist; B2.1.1931 Woodsville NH; BR/TL/6´1.5˝/(190–195); d4.29

YEAR	TM LG	W	L	PCT	G	GS	CG-SHO	SV-BS	IP	H	R	HR	HB	BB-IB	SO	ERA	AERA	OAV	OOB	AB-HR-SH	AVG	PB	SUP	APR	DL	PW
1955	Bos A	0	0	ø	1	0	0	0	1.2	1	0	0	0	1-0	1	0.00	ø	.200	.333	0	ø	0	—	1	0	0.0
1957	StL N	0	0	ø	6	0	0	1	9.2	12	10	0	1	6-1	11	4.66	85	.267	.365	2	.000	-0	—	-3	0	-0.2
	Pit N	2	4	.333	20	4	2	0	55	48	22	3	1	25-3	35	3.11	122	.229	.314	13-0-1	.077	-1	81	4	30	0.3
	Year	2	4	.333	26	4	2	1	64.2	60	32	3	2	31-4	46	3.34	114	.235	.323	15-0-1	.067	-1	81	1	0	0.1
1958	Pit N	2	2	.500	35	4	0	1	61	61	39	6	2	31-7	24	4.43	87	.262	.352	11	.091	-1	110	-6	0	-0.4
1959	Pit N	0	0	ø	20	0	0	0	28.1	32	16	1	0	17-0	12	3.49	111	.291	.383	2	.000	-0	—	0	0	-0.1
	Det A	0	3	.000	9	0	0	0	11	20	15	5	0	3-1	10	8.18	50	.417	.451	1	.000	-0	—	-6	0	-1.2
Total	4	4	9	.308	91	8	2	2	166.2	174	102	15	4	83-12	93	4.05	95	.267	.353	29-0-1	.069	-2	95	-10	30	-1.6

SMITH, BOB Robert Walkup "Riverboat"; B5.13.1927 Clarence MO; D6.23.2003 Clarence MO; BR/TL (BB 1959)/6´0˝/180; d4.22; Col Missouri

YEAR	TM LG	W	L	PCT	G	GS	CG-SHO	SV-BS	IP	H	R	HR	HB	BB-IB	SO	ERA	AERA	OAV	OOB	AB-HR-SH	AVG	PB	SUP	APR	DL	PW
1958	Bos A	4	3	.571	17	7	1	0	66.2	61	32	4	0	45-2	43	3.78	106	.248	.362	19-0-1	.105	-1	109	2	0	0.1
1959	Chi N	0	0	ø	1	0	0	0	0.2	5	6	0	0	2-1	0	81.00	5	.833	.875	0	ø	0	—	-5	0	-0.2
	Cle A	0	1	.000	12	3	0	0	29.1	31	19	2	0	12-0	17	5.22	71	.282	.341	6	.000	-1	112	-5	0	-0.3
Total	2	4	4	.500	30	10	1	0	96.2	97	57	6	0	59-3	60	4.75	82	.268	.365	25-0-1	.080	-2	110	-8	0	-0.4

SMITH, RUFUS Rufus Frazier "Shirt"; B1.24.1905 Guilford College NC; D8.21.1984 Aiken SC; BR/TL/5´8˝/165; d10.2; Col Guilford

YEAR	TM LG	W	L	PCT	G	GS	CG-SHO	SV-BS	IP	H	R	HR	HB	BB-IB	SO	ERA	AERA	OAV	OOB	AB-HR-SH	AVG	PB	SUP	APR	DL	PW
1927	Det A	0	0	ø	1	1	0	0	8	8	4	0	1	3	2	3.38	125	.242	.324	3	.000	-1	99	1	—	0.0

SMITH, SHERRY Sherrod Malone; B2.18.1891 Monticello GA; D9.12.1949 Reidsville GA; BR/TL/6´1˝/170; d5.11; Mil 1918

YEAR	TM LG	W	L	PCT	G	GS	CG-SHO	SV-BS	IP	H	R	HR	HB	BB-IB	SO	ERA	AERA	OAV	OOB	AB-HR-SH	AVG	PB	SUP	APR	DL	PW
1911	Pit N	0	0	ø	1	0	0	0	0.2	4	5	0	0	1	0	54.00	6	.667	.714	0	ø	0	—	-4	—	-0.2
1912	Pit N	0	0	ø	3	0	0	1	4	6	3	0	0	1	3	6.75	48	.600	.636	0	ø	0	—	-1	—	-0.1
1915	Bro N	14	8	.636	29	20	11-2	2	173.2	169	71	3	5	42	52	2.59	107	.264	.315	57-0-1	.246	3	74	2	—	0.6
1916	†Bro N	14	10	.583	36	25	15-4	1	219	193	76	5	3	45	67	2.34	114	.239	.282	77-0-3	.273	5*	121	9	—	1.7
1917	Bro N	12	12	.500	38	23	15	3	211.1	210	103	5	2	51	58	3.32	84	.265	.311	77-0-1	.195	2*	95	-14	—	-1.1
1919	Bro N	7	12	.368	30	19	13-2	1	173	181	63	3	4	29	40	2.24	133	.278	.313	54-0-4	.148	-2	103	11	—	1.2
1920	†Bro N	11	9	.550	33	13	6-2	3	136.1	134	42	1	2	27	33	1.85	173	.264	.304	43	.233	2	60	18	—	3.2
1921	Bro N	7	11	.389	35	17	9	4	175.1	232	95	4	1	34	36	3.90	100	.319	.350	57-1-1	.228	1	83	-1	—	0.2
1922	Bro N	4	8	.333	28	8	3-1	2	108.2	128	71	6	7	35	15	4.56	89	.309	.373	35-1-0	.257	2	93	-8	—	-0.5
	Cle A	1	0	1.000	2	2	1	0	15.2	18	7	0	0	3	4	3.45	116	.295	.328	6	.333	1	106	1	—	0.1
1923	Cle A	9	6	.600	30	16	10-1	1	124	129	62	4	2	37	23	3.27	121	.269	.324	45-1-2	.244	1	121	7	—	1.0
1924	Cle A	12	14	.462	39	27	20-2	1	247.2	267	110	5	7	42	34	3.02	142	.277	.312	89-1-4	.202	-1*	88	31	—	2.9
1925	Cle A	11	14	.440	31	30	**22**-1	1	237	296	151	11	5	48	30	4.86	91	.306	.342	92-1-3	.304	7	120	-11	—	-0.3
1926	Cle A	11	10	.524	27	24	16-1	0	188.1	214	80	8	4	31	25	3.73	109	.292	.324	65-1-4	.215	2	85	12	—	1.5
1927	Cle A	1	4	.200	11	2	1	1	38	53	25	2	0	14	8	5.45	77	.342	.396	12	.167	-0	99	-4	—	-0.5
Total	14	114	118	.491	373	226	142-16	21	2052.2	2234	964	57	42	440	428	3.32	108	.282	.324	709-6-23	.233	22	97	48	—	9.7

SMITH, TOM Thomas Edward; B12.5.1871 Boston MA; D3.2.1929 Dorchester MA; BR/TR/5´7.5˝/165; d6.6; Col Fordham

YEAR	TM LG	W	L	PCT	G	GS	CG-SHO	SV-BS	IP	H	R	HR	HB	BB-IB	SO	ERA	AERA	OAV	OOB	AB-HR-SH	AVG	PB	SUP	APR	DL	PW
1894	Bos N	0	0	ø	2	0	0	1	6	8	14	2	4	6	2	15.00	38	.320	.514	2	.000	-0	—	-6	—	-0.2
1895	Phi N	2	3	.400	11	7	4	0	68	76	67	1	7	53	21	6.88	70	.278	.408	33	.242	-0	123	-15	—	-0.8
1896	Lou N	2	3	.400	11	5	4	0	55	73	55	2	4	25	14	5.40	80	.316	.392	39	.205	-0*	89	-8	—	-0.5
1898	StL N	0	1	.000	1	1	1	0	9	9	8	0	2	5	1	2.00	189	.257	.381	2	.500	1	94	0	—	0.1
Total	4	4	7	.364	25	13	9	1	138	166	144	5	17	89	38	6.33	72	.294	.406	76	.224	-0	107	-29	—	-1.4

SMITH, TRAVIS Travis William; B11.7.1972 Springfield OR; BR/TR/5´10˝/(165–170); [MilA95 19/516]; d6.21; Col Texas Tech

YEAR	TM LG	W	L	PCT	G	GS	CG-SHO	SV-BS	IP	H	R	HR	HB	BB-IB	SO	ERA	AERA	OAV	OOB	AB-HR-SH	AVG	PB	SUP	APR	DL	PW
1998	Mil N	0	0	ø	1	0	0	0-0	2	1	0	0	0	0-0	1	0.00	ø	.143	.143	1	.000	-0	—	1	98	0.0
2002	StL N	4	2	.667	12	10	0	0-0	54	69	44	10	3	20-0	32	7.17	56	.322	.388	18-0-2	.167	-0	119	-18	0	-1.7
2004	Atl N	2	3	.400	16	4	0	0-0	40.2	48	28	12	1	12-2	26	6.20	70	.293	.345	8	.125	-0	43	-7	0	-0.8
2005	Fla N	0	0	ø	12	0	0	0-0	10.2	17	8	1	0	5-1	9	6.75	59	.370	.423	0	ø	-0	—	-3	0	-0.2
2006	Atl N	0	1	.000	1	1	0	0-0	4.1	5	4	0	0	1-0	1	4.15	109	.313	.333	1*	.000	-0	0	-1	0	-0.1
Total	5	6	6	.500	42	15	0	0-0	111.2	140	84	23	4	38-3	69	6.53	64	.313	.371	28-0-2	.143	-1	89	-28	98	-2.8

SMITH, ROY Walter Roy; B5.18.1976 St.Petersburg FL; BR/TR/6´6˝/(210–235); [SeaA94 13/357]; d5.26

YEAR	TM LG	W	L	PCT	G	GS	CG-SHO	SV-BS	IP	H	R	HR	HB	BB-IB	SO	ERA	AERA	OAV	OOB	AB-HR-SH	AVG	PB	SUP	APR	DL	PW
2001	Cle A	0	0	ø	9	0	0	0-0	16.1	16	14	3	2	13-1	17	6.06	76	.246	.387	0	ø	0	—	-3	0	-0.2
2002	Cle A	0	0	ø	4	1	0	0-0	6	9	4	1	1	5-0	2	3.00	148	.310	.429	0	ø	0	146	0	0	0.0
Total	2	0	0	ø	13	1	0	0-0	22.1	25	18	4	3	18-1	19	5.24	87	.266	.400	0	ø	0	146	-3	0	-0.2

SMITH, BILL William Garland; B6.8.1934 Washington DC; D3.30.1997 Clinton MD; BL/TL/6´0˝/190; d9.13

YEAR	TM LG	W	L	PCT	G	GS	CG-SHO	SV-BS	IP	H	R	HR	HB	BB-IB	SO	ERA	AERA	OAV	OOB	AB-HR-SH	AVG	PB	SUP	APR	DL	PW
1958	StL N	0	1	.000	2	1	0	0	9.2	12	7	0	0	4-0	4	6.52	63	.324	.390	2	.000	-0	65	-2	0	-0.2
1959	StL N	0	0	ø	6	0	0	1	8.1	11	3	0	0	3-1	4	1.08	393	.333	.389	1	.000	-0	—	2	0	0.1
1962	Phi N	1	5	.167	24	5	0	0	50.1	59	32	8	1	10-3	26	4.29	90	.295	.329	11	.182	1	77	-5	0	-0.4
Total	3	1	6	.143	32	6	0	1	68.1	82	42	8	1	17-4	34	4.21	94	.304	.345	14	.143	0	74	-5	0	-0.5

SMITH, WILLIE Willie; B2.11.1939 Anniston AL; D1.16.2006 Anniston AL; BL/TL/6´0˝/(178–190); d6.18; ▲

YEAR	TM LG	W	L	PCT	G	GS	CG-SHO	SV-BS	IP	H	R	HR	HB	BB-IB	SO	ERA	AERA	OAV	OOB	AB-HR-SH	AVG	PB	SUP	APR	DL	PW
1963	Det A	1	0	1.000	11	2	0	2	21.2	24	13	2	0	13-2	16	4.57	82	.300	.389	8	.125	-0*	142	-2	0	-0.2
1964	LA A	1	4	.200	15	1	0	0	31.2	34	13	5	1	10-1	20	2.84	116	.293	.344	359-11-1	.301	6*	81	1	0	0.4
1968	Cle A	0	0	ø	2	0	0	0	5	2	0	0	0	1-0	1	0.00	ø	.125	.176	42	.143	0*	—	2	0	0.1
	Chi N	0	0	ø	1	0	0	0	2.2	0	0	0	0	0-0	2	0.00	ø	.000	.000	142-5-1	.275	0*	—	1	0	0.1
Total	3	2	4	.333	29	3	0	2	61	60	26	7	1	24-3	39	3.10	110	.273	.339	551-16-2	.279	6	130	2	0	0.4

SMITH, WILLIE Willie Everett; B8.27.1967 Savannah GA; BR/TR/6´6˝/250; d4.25

YEAR	TM LG	W	L	PCT	G	GS	CG-SHO	SV-BS	IP	H	R	HR	HB	BB-IB	SO	ERA	AERA	OAV	OOB	AB-HR-SH	AVG	PB	SUP	APR	DL	PW
1994	StL N	1	1	.500	8	0	0	0-1	7	9	7	4	0	3-0	7	9.00	47	.300	.364	0	ø	0	—	-3	0	-0.7

SMITH, ZANE Zane William; B12.28.1960 Madison WI; BL/TL/6´2˝/(195–207); [AtlN82 3/63]; d9.10; Col Indiana St.

YEAR	TM LG	W	L	PCT	G	GS	CG-SHO	SV-BS	IP	H	R	HR	HB	BB-IB	SO	ERA	AERA	OAV	OOB	AB-HR-SH	AVG	PB	SUP	APR	DL	PW
1984	Atl N	1	0	1.000	3	3	0	0-0	20	16	7	1	0	13-2	16	2.25	171	.219	.337	9	.556	2	76	3	0	0.4
1985	Atl N	9	10	.474	42	18	2-2	0-0	147	135	70	4	3	80-5	85	3.80	102	.254	.354	37-0-6	.162	-0*	84	1	27	0.2
1986	Atl N	8	16	.333	38	32	3-1	1-0	204.2	209	109	8	5	105-6	139	4.05	98	.275	.364	59-0-9	.085	-3*	84	-4	0	-0.5
1987	Atl N	15	10	.600	36	**36**	9-3	0-0	242	245	130	19	5	91-6	130	4.09	106	.266	.333	76-0-14	.132	-1*	109	4	0	0.4
1988	Atl N	5	10	.333	23	22	3	0-0	140.1	159	72	8	3	44-4	59	4.30	85	.292	.347	42-0-7	.167	0*	74	-8	39	-0.6
1989	Atl N	1	12	.077	17	17	0	0-0	99	102	65	5	2	33-3	58	4.45	82	.267	.325	28-0-4	.179	-0*	71	-12	0	-1.4
	Mon N	0	1	.000	31	0	0	2-1	48	39	11	2	1	19-4	35	1.50	238	.220	.299	4	.250	0*	—	10	0	0.6
	Year	1	13	.071	48	17	0	2-1	147	141	76	7	3	52-7	93	3.49	104	.252	.317	32-0-4	.188	0	72	-3	0	-0.8
1990	Mon N	6	7	.462	22	21	1	0-0	139.1	141	57	11	3	41-3	80	3.23	114	.266	.321	40-0-7	.175	1*	74	6	0	0.7
	†Pit N	6	2	.750	11	10	3-2	0-0	76	55	20	4	0	9-1	50	1.30	280	.203	.228	28-0-1	.143	0	82	17	0	1.9
	Year	12	9	.571	33	31	4-2	0-0	215.1	196	77	15	3	50-4	130	2.55	144	.245	.291	68-0-8	.162	1	76	24	0	2.6
1991	†Pit N	16	10	.615	35	35	6-3	0-0	228	234	95	15	2	29-3	120	3.20	113	.268	.292	71-0-13	.183	2*	114	9	0	1.3
1992	Pit N	8	8	.500	23	22	4-3	0-0	141	138	56	8	2	19-3	56	3.06	113	.261	.287	49-0-3	.122	-0*	100	4	62	0.5
1993	Pit N	3	7	.300	14	14	1	0-0	83	97	43	5	0	22-3	32	4.55	90	.298	.343	25-0-4	.080	-2	83	-4	96	-0.6
1994	Pit N	10	8	.556	25	24	2-1	0-0	157	162	67	18	0	34-7	57	3.27	134	.270	.307	57-0-2	.211	1*	84	17	0	2.0
1995	†Bos A	8	8	.500	24	21	0	0-0	110.2	144	78	7	1	23-1	47	5.61	87	.316	.347	0	ø	0	111	-10	38	-1.2
1996	Pit N	4	6	.400	16	16	1-1	0-0	83.1	104	53	7	4	21-4	47	5.08	86	.309	.353	26-0-2	.154	-1	105	-6	15	-0.7
Total	13	100	115	.465	360	291	35-16	3-1	1919.1	1980	933	122	31	583-55	1011	3.74	106	.271	.326	551-0-72	.158	0	94	27	277	3.0

YEAR	TM LG	W	L	PCT	G	GS	CG-SHO	SV-BS	IP	H	R	HR	HB	BB-IB	SO	ERA	AERA	OAV	OOB	AB-HR-SH	AVG	PB	SUP	APR	DL	PW
Smithberg, Roger	Roger Craig; B3.21.1966 Elgin IL; BR/TR/6´3″/210; [SDN87 2/42]; d9.1; Col Bradley																									
1993	Oak A	1	2	.333	13	0	0	3-1	19.2	13	7	2	1	7-2	4	2.75	151	.197	.284	0	ø	0	—	3	0	0.5
1994	Oak A	0	0	ø	2	0	0	0-0	2.1	6	4	1	0	1-0	3	15.43	29	.500	.538	0	ø	0	—	-3	0	-0.1
Total	2	1	2	.333	15	0	0	3-1	22	19	11	3	1	8-2	7	4.09	102	.244	.322	0	ø	0	—	0	0	0.4
Smithson, Mike	Billy Mike; B1.21.1955 Centerville TN; BL/TR/6´8″/(200–215); [BosA76 5/118]; d8.27; Col Tennessee																									
1982	Tex A	3	4	.429	8	8	3	0-0	46.2	51	26	5	3	13-2	24	5.01	78	.282	.338	0	ø	0	73	-5	0	-0.7
1983	Tex A	10	14	.417	33	33	10	0-0	223.1	233	102	14	8	71-2	135	3.91	104	.269	.327	0	ø	0	90	7	0	0.7
1984	Min A	15	13	.536	36	**36**	10-1	0-0	252	246	113	35	8	54-7	144	3.68	115	.252	.296	0	ø	0	86	15	0	1.5
1985	Min A	15	14	.517	37	**37**	8-3	0-0	257	264	134	25	15	78-1	127	4.34	102	.270	.331	0	ø	0	90	3	0	0.3
1986	Min A	13	14	.481	34	33	8-1	0-0	198	234	123	26	14	57-4	114	4.77	91	.294	.349	0	ø	0	103	-12	0	-1.4
1987	Min A	4	7	.364	21	20	0	0-0	109	126	76	17	9	38-3	53	5.94	78	.286	.351	0	ø	0	118	-14	28	-1.2
1988	†Bos A	9	6	.600	31	18	1	0-0	126.2	149	87	25	6	37-1	73	5.97	69	.292	.345	0	ø	0	125	-23	0	-2.4
1989	Bos A	7	14	.333	40	19	1-1	2-1	143.2	170	84	21	10	35-5	61	4.95	83	.297	.343	0	ø	0	108	-10	0	-1.4
Total	8	76	86	.469	240	204	41-6	2-1	1356.1	1473	745	168	73	383-25	731	4.58	93	.277	.331	0	ø	0	98	-39	28	-4.6
Smoll, Lefty	Clyde Hetrick; B4.17.1914 Quakertown PA; D8.31.1985 Quakertown PA; BB/TL/5´10″/175; d4.26																									
1940	Phi N	2	8	.200	33	9	0	0	109	145	77	6	4	36	31	5.37	73	.322	.378	31	.161	-1	59	-19	—	-1.7
Smoltz, John	John Andrew; B5.15.1967 Detroit MI; BR/TR/6´3″/(185–220); [DetA85 22/574]; d7.23; [DL 2000 Atl N 181]																									
1988	Atl N	2	7	.222	12	12	0	0-0	64	74	40	10	2	33-4	37	5.48	67	.285	.369	17-0-3	.118	-0	71	-11	0	-1.4
1989	Atl N★	12	11	.522	29	29	5	0-0	208	160	79	15	2	72-2	168	2.94	124	.212	.280	62-1-6	.113	1*	78	15	0	1.9
1990	Atl N	14	11	.560	34	34	6-2	0-0	231.1	206	109	20	1	90-3	170	3.85	105	.240	.310	74-0-7	.162	1*	102	5	0	0.7
1991	†Atl N	14	13	.519	36	36	5	0-0	229.2	206	101	16	3	77-1	148	3.80	102	.243	.305	65-0-8	.108	-1*	102	6	0	0.6
1992	†Atl N★	15	12	.556	35	**35**	9-3	0-0	246.2	206	90	17	5	80-5	**215**	2.85	129	.224	.287	75-1-10	.160	2*	99	20	0	2.4
1993	†Atl N★	15	11	.577	35	35	3-1	0-0	243.2	208	104	23	6	100-12	208	3.62	112	.230	.309	71-0-11	.183	3	110	13	0	1.6
1994	Atl N	6	10	.375	21	21	1	0-0	134.2	120	69	15	4	48-4	113	4.14	104	.239	.307	37-1-6	.162	2	83	2	0	0.4
1995	†Atl N	12	7	.632	29	29	2-1	0-0	192.2	166	76	15	4	72-8	193	3.18	136	.232	.304	56-0-6	.107	-1	93	23	0	1.9
1996	†Atl N★	**24**	8	**.750**	35	35	6-2	0-0	**253.2**	199	93	19	2	55-3	**276**	2.94	151	.216	**.260**	78-1-15	.218	3	104	40	0	5.2
1997	†Atl N	15	12	.556	35	**35**	7-2	0-0	**256**	234	97	21	1	63-9	241	3.02	139	.242	.288	79-0-6	.228	6*	98	33	0	3.9
1998	†Atl N	17	3	**.850**	26	26	2-2	0-0	167.2	145	58	10	4	44-2	173	2.90	144	.231	.285	51-0-8	.196	3	122	25	42	3.2
1999	†Atl N	11	8	.579	29	29	1-1	0-0	186.1	168	70	14	4	40-2	156	3.19	140	.245	.288	62-1-4	.274	7	104	29	34	3.4
2001	†Atl N	3	3	.500	36	5	0	10-1	59	53	24	7	2	10-2	57	3.36	128	.238	.274	7-0-2	.000	-0	120	7	88	0.8
2002	†Atl N★	3	2	.600	75	0	0	**55**-4	80.1	59	30	4	0	24-1	85	3.25	125	.206	.266	2	.000	-0	—	8	0	1.5
2003	†Atl N☆	0	2	.000	62	0	0	45-4	64.1	48	9	2	0	8-1	73	1.12	375	.204	.230	1	.000	-0	—	22	27	3.4
2004	†Atl N	0	1	.000	73	0	0	44-5	81.2	75	25	8	0	13-2	85	2.76	156	.245	.276	2	.000	-0	—	15	0	1.5
2005	†Atl N★	14	7	.667	33	33	3-1	0-0	229.2	210	83	18	1	53-7	169	3.06	138	.243	.287	68-0-12	.147	0	95	30	0	2.6
2006	Atl N	**16**	9	.640	35	**35**	3-1	0-0	232	221	93	23	9	55-4	211	3.49	130	.251	.298	64-0-18	.125	0	102	29	0	2.9
Total	18	193	137	.585	670	429	53-16	154-14	3161.1	2758	1250	257	50	937-72	2778	3.27	127	.234	.292	871-5-122	.166	26	99	311	372	36.5
Smyth, Steve	Steven Delton; B6.3.1978 Brawley CA; BL/TL/6´1″/220; [ChiN99 4/140]; d8.6; Col USC																									
2002	Chi N	1	3	.250	8	7	0	0-0	26	34	28	9	1	10-0	16	9.35	43	.321	.372	9-0-1	.222	0	140	-15	0	-1.8
Smythe, Harry	William Henry; B10.24.1904 Augusta GA; D8.28.1980 Augusta GA; BL/TL/5´10.5″/179; d7.21																									
1929	Phi N	4	6	.400	19	9	2	1	68.2	94	47	3	1	15	12	5.24	99	.330	.365	26	.192	-1*	106	-1	—	-0.1
1930	Phi N	0	3	.000	25	3	0	2	49.2	84	60	3	3	31	9	7.79	70	.368	.450	14-0-1	.286	-0	112	-15	—	-0.9
1934	NY A	0	2	.000	8	0	0	1	15	24	16	1	0	8	7	7.80	52	.381	.451	5	.200	-0	—	-7	—	-0.8
	Bro N	1	1	.500	8	0	0	0	21.1	30	19	3	1	8	5	5.91	66	.337	.398	9-0-1	.333	1*	—	-6	—	-0.3
Total	3	5	12	.294	60	12	2	4	154.2	232	142	10	5	62	33	6.40	78	.349	.408	54-0-2	.241	0	114	-29	—	-2.1
Snare, Ryan	Ryan Delbert; B2.8.1979 Clearwater FL; BL/TL/6´0″/200; [CinN00 2/63]; d8.6; Col North Carolina																									
2004	Tex A	0	0	ø	1	0	0	0-0	3.1	5	5	3	0	2-0	0	10.80	46	.333	.412	0	ø	0	—	-2	0	-0.1
Snell, Ian	Ian Dante; B10.30.1981 Dover DE; BR/TR/5´11″/(170–190); [PitN00 26/779]; d8.20																									
2004	Pit N	0	1	.000	3	1	0	0-0	12	14	10	2	0	9-0	9	7.50	58	.298	.411	2-0-1	.000	-0	86	-4	0	-0.3
2005	Pit N	1	2	.333	15	5	0	0-0	42	43	25	5	1	24-3	34	5.14	82	.267	.364	8	.000	-1	89	-4	0	-0.4
2006	Pit N	14	11	.560	32	32	0	0-0	186	198	104	29	2	74-4	169	4.74	97	.277	.344	54-0-9	.056	-3*	94	-2	0	-0.5
Total	3	15	14	.517	50	38	0	0-0	240	255	139	36	3	107-7	212	4.95	91	.276	.351	64-0-10	.047	-4	94	-10	0	-1.2
Snell, Nate	Nathaniel; B9.2.1952 Orangeburg SC; BR/TR/6´4″/(185–190); d9.20; Col Tennessee St.																									
1984	Bal A	1	1	.500	5	0	0	0-0	7.2	8	2	1	0	1-0	7	2.35	167	.258	.273	0	ø	0	—	1	0	0.3
1985	Bal A	3	2	.600	43	0	0	5-0	100.1	100	44	4	1	30-5	41	2.69	151	.260	.314	0	ø	0	—	11	30	0.6
1986	Bal A	2	1	.667	34	0	0	0-1	72.1	69	36	9	1	22-4	29	3.86	108	.257	.313	0	ø	0	—	2	0	0.1
1987	Det A	1	2	.333	22	2	0	0-0	38.2	39	20	5	0	19-3	19	3.96	108	.267	.349	0	ø	0	64	1	0	0.0
Total	4	7	6	.538	104	2	0	5-1	219	216	102	19	2	72-12	96	3.29	126	.260	.319	0	ø	0	64	15	30	1.0
Snook, Frank	Frank Walter; B3.28.1949 Somerville NJ; BR/TR/6´2″/185; [SDN71 7/148]; d7.13; Col Grand Canyon																									
1973	SD N	0	2	.000	18	0	0	1-1	27.1	19	15	4	0	18-0	13	3.62	97	.200	.319	2	.000	-0	—	-1	0	-0.1
Snover, Colonel	Colonel Lester "Bosco"; B5.16.1895 Hallstead PA; D4.30.1969 Rochester NY; BL/TL/6´0.5″/200; d9.18																									
1919	NY N	0	1	.000	2	1	0	0	9	7	5	0	1	3	4	1.00	281	.212	.297	2	.000	0	113	0	—	0.0
Snyder, Brian	Brian Robert; B2.20.1958 Flemington NJ; BL/TL/6´3″/185; [SeaA79 7/157]; d5.25; Col Clemson																									
1985	Sea A	1	2	.333	15	6	0	1-0	35.1	44	28	2	1	19-2	23	6.37	66	.306	.388	0	ø	0	97	-8	0	-0.6
1989	Oak A	0	0	ø	2	0	0	0-0	0.2	2	2	1	0	2-0	1	27.00	14	.500	.667	0	ø	0	—	-2	0	-0.1
Total	2	1	2	.333	17	6	0	1-0	36	46	30	3	1	21-2	24	6.75	62	.311	.398	0	ø	0	97	-10	0	-0.7
Snyder, Gene	Gene Walter; B3.31.1931 York PA; D6.2.1996 York PA; BR/TL/5´11″/175; d4.26																									
1959	LA N	1	1	.500	11	2	0	0-0	26.1	32	19	1	0	20-2	20	5.47	77	.299	.409	6-0-1	.000	-0	85	-4	0	-0.3
Snyder, George	George T.; B8.1848 Philadelphia PA; D8.2.1905 Philadelphia PA; d9.30																									
1882	Phi AA	1	0	1.000	1	1	1	0	9	4	3	0	—	2	0	0.00	ø	.125	.176	3	.333	0	110	2	—	0.2
Snyder, John	John Michael; B8.16.1974 Southfield MI; BR/TR/6´3″/(185–200); [CalA92 13/356]; d6.30																									
1998	Chi A	7	2	.778	15	14	1	0-0	86.1	96	49	14	2	23-1	52	4.80	96	.286	.332	0	ø	0	125	-1	0	-0.1
1999	Chi A	9	12	.429	25	25	1	0-0	129.1	167	103	27	6	49-0	67	6.68	74	.311	.371	0	ø	0	100	-23	0	-3.0
2000	Mil N	3	10	.231	23	23	0	0-0	127	147	95	8	9	77-10	69	6.17	75	.296	.395	38-0-1	.079	-1*	90	-22	46	-1.9
Total	3	19	24	.442	63	62	2	0-0	342.2	410	247	49	17	149-11	188	6.01	79	.299	.371	38-0-1	.079	-1	102	-46	46	-5.0
Snyder, Kyle	Kyle Ehren; B9.9.1977 Houston TX; BB/TR/6´8″/(215–220); [KCA99 1/7]; d5.1; Col North Carolina; [DL 2004 KC A 183]																									
2003	KC A	1	6	.143	15	15	0	0-0	85.1	94	52	11	2	21-3	39	5.17	93	.283	.321	2	.000	-0	63	-3	74	-0.2
2005	KC A	1	3	.250	13	3	0	0-0	36	55	29	3	1	10-1	19	6.75	65	.353	.391	0	ø	0	99	-9	64	-0.9
2006	KC A	0	0	ø	1	1	0	0-0	2	10	9	1	0	1-0	2	22.50	21	.556	.579	0	ø	0	321	-5	0	-0.2
	Bos A	4	5	.444	16	10	0	0-0	58.1	77	42	11	2	19-3	55	6.02	78	.314	.366	0	ø	0	73	-9	0	-1.1
	Year	4	5	.444	17	11	0	0-0	60.1	87	51	12	2	20-3	57	6.56	71	.331	.380	0	ø	0	95	-14	0	-1.3
Total	3	6	14	.300	45	29	0	0-0	181.2	236	132	26	5	51-7	115	5.94	79	.314	.356	2	.000	-0	79	-26	321	-2.4
Snyder, Bill	William Nicholas; B1.28.1898 Mansfield OH; D10.8.1934 Vicksburg MI; BR/TR; d9.4																									
1919	Was A	0	1	.000	2	1	0	0	8	6	4	0	0	3	5	1.13	285	.200	.273	2	.000	-0	73	1	—	0.1
1920	Was A	2	1	.667	16	4	1	1	54	59	33	1	6	28	17	4.17	90	.280	.380	19	.316	1	101	-3	—	-0.1
Total	2	2	2	.500	18	5	1	1	62	65	37	1	6	31	22	3.77	97	.270	.367	21	.286	1	95	-2	—	0.0
Sobkowiak, Scott	Scott; B10.26.1977 Woodstock IL; BR/TR/6´5″/230; [AtlN98 7/221]; d10.7; Col Northern Iowa																									
2001	Atl N	0	0	ø	1	0	0	0-0	1	2	1	0	0	0-0	0	9.00	48	.400	.400	0	ø	0	—	0	106	0.0
Soderstrom, Steve	Stephen Andrew; B4.3.1972 Turlock CA; BR/TR/6´3″/205; [SFN93 1/6]; d9.17; Col Cal St.–Fresno																									
1996	SF N	2	0	1.000	3	3	0	0-0	13.2	16	11	1	2	6-0	9	5.27	79	.302	.381	5	.000	-1	181	-3	0	-0.4

YEAR	TM LG	W	L	PCT	G	GS	CG-SHO	SV-BS	IP	H	R	HR	HB	BB-IB	SO	ERA	AERA	OAV	OOB	AB-HR-SH	AVG	PB	SUP	APR	DL	PW
SODOWSKY, CLINT	Clint Rea; B7.13.1972 Ponca City OK; BL/TR/6´4˝/(180–200); [DetA91 9/244]; d9.4; Col Connors St. (OK) JC																									
1995	Det A	2	2	.500	6	6	0	0-0	23.1	24	15	4	0	18-0	14	5.01	96	.258	.378	0	ø	0	68	-1	0	-0.2
1996	Det A	1	3	.250	7	7	0	0-0	24.1	40	34	5	3	20-0	9	11.84	43	.370	.481	0	ø	0	117	-18	0	-2.0
1997	Pit N	2	2	.500	45	0	0	0-2	52	49	22	6	2	34-7	51	3.63	118	.249	.362	2	.500	0	—	4	15	0.3
1998	Ari N	3	6	.333	45	6	0	0-3	77.2	86	56	5	7	39-5	42	5.68	75	.283	.375	10-0-1	.300	1*	129	-13	0	-1.2
1999	StL N	0	1	.000	3	1	0	0-0	6.1	15	11	1	0	6-0	2	15.63	29	.455	.538	1	.000	-0	140	-7	33	-0.8
Total	5	8	14	.364	106	20	0	0-5	183.2	214	138	21	12	117-12	118	6.17	72	.291	.395	13-0-1	.308	1	113	-35	48	-3.9
SOFF, RAY	Raymond John; B10.31.1958 Adrian MI; BR/TR/6´0˝/185; [ChiN79 11/272]; d7.17; Col Central Michigan																									
1986	StL N	4	2	.667	30	0	0	0-0	38.1	37	17	4	0	13-1	22	3.29	112	.255	.313	2-0-1	.000	-0	—	1	0	0.2
1987	StL N	1	0	1.000	12	0	0	0-0	15.1	18	11	3	1	5-1	9	6.46	65	.295	.353	1	.000	-0	—	-3	0	-0.2
Total	2	5	2	.714	42	0	0	0-0	53.2	55	28	7	1	18-2	31	4.19	92	.267	.325	3-0-1	.000	-0	—	-2	0	0.0
SOLANO, JULIO	Julio Cesar; B1.8.1960 Agua Blanca, D.R.; BR/TR/6´1˝/(160–170); d4.5																									
1983	Hou N	0	2	.000	4	0	0	0-0	6	5	5	1	0	4-1	3	6.00	57	.217	.333	0	ø	0	—	-2	0	-0.4
1984	Hou N	1	3	.250	31	0	0	0-2	50.2	31	13	3	0	18-1	33	1.95	171	.179	.253	3	.333	0	—	8	0	0.6
1985	Hou N	2	2	.500	20	0	0	0-0	33.2	34	13	5	0	13-2	17	3.48	100	.262	.329	2	.000	-0	—	1	0	0.0
1986	Hou N	3	1	.750	16	1	0	0-1	32	39	28	5	3	22-2	21	7.59	47	.310	.421	6-0-1	.000	-1	25	-14	0	-1.6
1987	Hou N	0	0	ø	11	0	0	0-0	20	25	17	5	0	9-0	12	7.65	51	.298	.366	2	.000	-0	—	-8	0	-0.4
1988	Sea A	0	0	ø	17	0	0	3-1	22	22	13	3	0	12-2	10	4.09	102	.268	.354	0	ø	0	—	-1	0	0.0
1989	Sea A	0	0	ø	7	0	0	0-0	9.2	6	8	1	1	4-0	6	5.59	72	.176	.282	0	ø	0	—	-2	0	-0.1
Total	7	6	8	.429	106	1	0	3-4	174	162	97	23	4	82-8	102	4.55	80	.248	.333	13-0-1	.077	-1	25	-18	0	-1.9
SOLER, ALAY	Alain; B10.9.1979 Pinar Del Rio, Cuba; BR/TR/6´1˝/240; d5.24; Col Nancy Uranga																									
2006	NY N	2	3	.400	8	8	1-1	0-0	45	50	33	7	1	21-1	23	6.00	73	.275	.350	11-0-4	.091	-1	92	-8	0	-0.8
SOLIS, MARCELINO	Marcelino; B7.19.1930 San Luis Potosi, San Luis Potosi, Mexico; D6.15.2001 Monterrey, Nuevo Leon, Mexico; BL/TL/6´1˝/185; d7.16																									
1958	Chi N	3	3	.500	15	4	0	0	52	74	41	5	4	20-1	15	6.06	65	.339	.405	20	.250	1	86	-13	0	-1.2
SOLOMON, EDDIE	Eddie "Buddy"; B2.9.1951 Perry GA; D1.12.1986 Macon GA; BR/TR/6´3˝/(185–190); d9.2																									
1973	LA N	0	0	ø	4	0	0	0-0	6.1	10	5	3	1	4-0	6	7.11	49	.357	.455	1	.000	-0	—	-2	0	-0.1
1974	†LA N	0	0	ø	4	0	0	1-0	6	5	1	1	0	2-0	2	1.50	229	.217	.280	0	ø	0	—	1	0	0.1
1975	Chi N	0	0	ø	6	0	0	0-0	6.2	7	6	1	0	6-2	3	1.35	287	.269	.406	0	ø	0	—	0	0	0.0
1976	StL N	1	1	.500	26	2	0	0-0	37	45	24	2	1	16-1	19	4.86	74	.306	.369	5	.400	1	172	-6	0	-0.1
1977	Atl N	6	6	.500	18	16	0	0-0	88.2	110	64	10	2	34-2	54	4.57	97	.305	.365	31-0-1	.129	-1	90	-6	0	-0.8
1978	Atl N	4	6	.400	37	8	0	2-2	106	98	52	12	2	50-11	64	4.08	99	.247	.334	29	.138	-1*	67	1	25	-0.1
1979	Atl N	7	14	.333	31	30	4	0-0	186	184	98	19	6	51-4	96	4.21	95	.254	.307	64-0-3	.203	1*	89	-2	0	-0.2
1980	Pit N	7	3	.700	26	12	2	0-0	100.1	96	44	8	4	37-5	35	2.69	137	.253	.322	32-0-3	.219	1*	97	6	0	0.7
1981	Pit N	8	6	.571	22	17	2	1-0	127	133	49	10	3	27-3	38	3.12	117	.278	.320	43-0-5	.163	-1*	119	8	0	0.7
1982	Pit N	2	6	.250	11	10	0	0-0	46.2	69	38	9	1	18-0	18	6.75	56	.347	.400	15-0-1	.133	-1*	111	-15	0	-2.2
	Chi A	1	0	1.000	6	0	0	0-0	7.1	7	5	1	0	2-0	2	3.68	111	.241	.290	0	ø	0	—	0	0	-0.1
Total	10	36	42	.462	191	95	8	4-2	718	764	386	76	20	247-28	337	4.00	98	.274	.335	220-0-13	.177	-1	98	-15	25	-2.1
SOMMER, JOE	Joseph John; B11.20.1858 Covington KY; D1.16.1938 Cincinnati OH; BR/TR; d7.8.1880; ▲																									
1883	Cin AA	0	0	ø	1	0	0	0	5	9	6	0	—	1	2	5.40	60	.360	.385	413-3	.278	0*	—	-1	—	-0.1
1885	Bal AA	0	0	ø	2	0	0	1	3	6	3	0	0	0	0	9.00	36	.429	.429	471-1	.251	0*	—	-1	—	-0.1
1886	Bal AA	0	0	ø	1	0	0	0	4	14	12	0	0	3	1	18.00	19	.519	.567	560-1	.209	-0*	—	-6	—	-0.2
1887	Bal AA	0	0	ø	1	0	0	0	1	2	1	0	0	1	0	9.00	46	.333	.429	463	.266	0*	—	0	—	0.0
1890	Cle N	0	0	ø	1	0	0	0	1	2	3	1	0	2	0	0.00	ø	.400	.571	35	.229	-0*	—	-1	—	0.0
Total	5	0	0	ø	6	0	0	1	14	33	25	1	0	7	3	9.64	35	.429	.476	1942-5	.248	1	—	-9	—	-0.4
SOMMERS, RUDY	Rudolph; B10.30.1886 Cincinnati OH; D3.18.1949 Louisville KY; BB/TL/5´11˝/165; d9.8																									
1912	Chi N	0	1	.000	1	0	0	0	3	4	1	0	0	2	2	3.00	111	.333	.429	1	.000	0	—	0	—	0.1
1914	Bro F	2	7	.222	23	8	2	2	82	88	54	2	3	34	40	4.06	71	.282	.358	24	.250	2	89	-13	—	-1.2
1926	Bos A	0	0	ø	2	0	0	0	2	3	3	0	0	3	0	13.50	30	.333	.500	0	ø	0	—	-2	—	-0.1
1927	Bos A	0	0	ø	7	0	0	0	14	18	15	2	0	14	2	8.36	51	.353	.492	2	.500	0	—	-6	—	-0.2
Total	4	2	8	.200	33	8	2	2	101	113	73	4	3	53	44	4.81	64	.294	.384	27	.259	2	89	-21	—	-1.4
SOMMERVILLE, ANDY	Andrew Henry (b Henry Travers Summersgill); B2.6.1876 Brooklyn NY; D6.16.1931 Richmond Hill NY; d8.8; Col Virginia																									
1894	Bro N	0	1	.000	1	1	0	0	0.1	1	6	0	0	5	0	162.00	3	.500	.857	0	ø	0	71	-5	—	-0.6
SONGER, DON	Donald C.; B1.31.1899 Walnut KS; D10.3.1962 Kansas City MO; BL/TL/6´0˝/165; d9.21																									
1924	Pit N	0	0	ø	4	1	0	1	9.1	14	7	1	0	3	3	6.75	57	.333	.378	2	.000	-0	221	-3	—	-0.1
1925	Pit N	0	1	.000	8	0	0	0	11.2	14	7	0	0	8	4	2.31	193	.298	.400	2	.000	-0	—	1	—	0.1
1926	Pit N	7	8	.467	35	15	5-1	2	126.1	118	60	4	11	52	27	3.13	126	.252	.340	38	.105	-2	96	9	—	0.7
1927	Pit N	0	0	ø	2	0	0	0	4.2	10	10	0	1	4	1	11.57	36	.526	.625	1	.000	-0	—	-5	—	-0.2
	NY N	3	5	.375	22	1	0	1	50.1	48	22	4	1	31	9	2.86	135	.261	.370	10	.300	1	44	4	—	0.8
	Year	3	5	.375	24	1	0	1	55	58	32	4	2	35	10	3.60	108	.286	.396	11	.273	1	44	-1	—	0.6
Total	4	10	14	.417	71	17	5-1	4	202.1	204	106	9	13	98	44	3.38	117	.268	.361	53	.132	-2	100	6	—	1.3
SORENSEN, LARY	Lary Alan; B10.4.1955 Detroit MI; BR/TR/6´2˝/(200–205); [MilA76 8/172]; d6.7; Col Michigan																									
1977	Mil A	7	10	.412	23	20	9	0-0	142.1	147	72	10	1	36-4	57	4.36	94	.270	.315	0	ø	0	85	-2	0	-0.2
1978	Mil A★	18	12	.600	37	36	17-3	1-0	280.2	277	111	14	5	50-4	78	3.21	118	.259	.291	0	ø	0	107	19	0	1.9
1979	Mil A	15	14	.517	34	34	16-2	0-0	235.1	250	113	30	4	42-3	63	3.98	106	.275	.309	0	ø	0	98	7	0	0.8
1980	Mil A	12	10	.545	35	29	8-2	1-0	195.2	242	91	13	2	45-6	54	3.68	106	.311	.347	0	ø	0	117	5	0	0.6
1981	StL N	7	7	.500	23	23	3-1	0-0	140.1	149	59	3	1	26-2	52	3.27	111	.271	.305	46-0-5	.065	-3	100	4	0	0.0
1982	Cle A	10	15	.400	32	30	6-1	0-0	189.1	251	130	19	3	55-6	62	5.61	74	.322	.365	0	ø	0	102	-30	0	-3.4
1983	Cle A	12	11	.522	36	34	8-1	0-0	222.2	238	112	21	2	65-9	76	4.24	101	.276	.326	0	ø	0	92	3	0	0.3
1984	Oak A	6	13	.316	46	21	2	1-1	183.1	240	117	21	6	44-4	63	4.91	77	.317	.356	0	ø	0	98	-27	0	-2.6
1985	Chi N	3	7	.300	45	3	0	0-1	82.1	86	44	8	4	24-10	34	4.26	94	.274	.331	6-0-4	.000	-0	118	-3	0	-0.4
1987	Mon N	3	4	.429	23	5	0	1-0	47.2	56	32	7	3	12-1	21	4.72	90	.286	.333	8-0-2	.000	-1	76	-4	0	-0.6
1988	SF N	0	0	ø	12	0	0	2-1	16.2	24	13	1	0	3-0	9	4.86	67	.329	.346	1-0-1	.000	-0	—	-4	0	-0.3
Total	11	93	103	.474	346	235	69-10	6-3	1736.1	1960	894	147	31	402-49	569	4.15	96	.287	.327	61-0-12	.049	-4	100	-32	0	-3.9
SORIANO, RAFAEL	Rafael; B12.19.1979 San Jose, D.R.; BR/TR/6´1˝/(175–220); d5.10																									
2002	Sea A	0	3	.000	10	8	0	1-0	47.1	45	25	8	0	16-1	32	4.56	94	.243	.303	4	.000	-0*	67	-1	30	-0.1
2003	Sea A	3	0	1.000	40	0	0	1-1	53	30	9	2	3	12-1	68	1.53	283	.162	.224	0	ø	0	—	18	0	0.9
2004	Sea A	0	3	.000	6	0	0	0-1	3.1	9	6	0	0	3-0	3	13.50	33	.450	.522	0	ø	0	—	-4	147	-0.7
2005	Sea A	0	0	ø	7	0	0	0-0	7.1	6	2	0	1	1-0	9	2.45	170	.222	.267	0	ø	0	—	2	155	0.1
2006	Sea A	1	2	.333	53	0	0	2-4	60	44	15	6	2	21-0	65	2.25	196	.204	.279	0	ø	0	—	15	15	0.7
Total	5	4	8	.333	116	8	0	4-6	171	134	57	16	6	53-2	177	2.89	150	.212	.278	4	.000	-0	67	30	347	0.9
SORRELL, VIC	Victor Garland; B4.9.1901 Morrisville NC; D5.4.1972 Raleigh NC; BR/TR/5´10˝/180; d4.22; Col Wake Forest																									
1928	Det A	8	11	.421	29	23	8	0	171	182	106	9	5	83	67	4.79	86	.277	.363	55-0-6	.109	-5	107	-11	—	-1.6
1929	Det A	14	15	.483	36	31	13-1	1	226	270	152	15	2	106	81	5.18	83	.302	.377	83-0-4	.145	-6	109	-20	—	-2.7
1930	Det A	16	11	.593	35	30	14-2	1	233.1	245	116	13	0	106	97	3.86	124	.274	.351	80-0-4	.188	-3	101	24	—	2.0
1931	Det A	13	14	.481	35	32	19-1	1	245	267	131	8	1	114	99	4.15	110	.278	.355	88-0-4	.159	-4	81	12	—	0.8
1932	Det A	14	14	.500	32	31	13-1	0	234.1	234	124	11	3	77	84	4.03	117	.259	.319	76-0-5	.118	-4*	82	18	—	1.4
1933	Det A	11	15	.423	36	28	13-1	1	232.2	233	112	18	2	78	75	3.79	114	.260	.321	74-0-4	.149	-2	83	16	—	1.3
1934	Det A	6	9	.400	28	19	6-1	2	129.2	146	76	13	3	45	46	4.79	92	.283	.345	37-0-3	.108	-1	110	-5	—	-0.5
1935	Det A	4	3	.571	12	6	4	0	51.1	65	28	2	2	25	22	4.03	103	.319	.398	18	.000	-3	167	0	—	-0.3
1936	Det A	6	7	.462	30	14	5-1	3	131.1	153	86	9	2	64	37	5.28	94	.294	.373	39-0-4	.154	1	109	-4	—	-0.1
1937	Det A	0	2	.000	7	2	0	1	17	25	18	3	0	8	11	9.00	52	.338	.402	3-0-1	.000	-0	75	-8	—	-0.8
Total	10	92	101	.477	280	216	95-8	10	1671.2	1820	949	101	20	706	619	4.43	102	.279	.351	553-0-35	.139	-27	97	22	—	-0.5

SOSA, ELIAS Elias (Martinez); B6.10.1950 LaVega, D.R.; BR/TR/6´2˝/(185–205); d9.8

YEAR	TM LG	W	L	PCT	G	GS	CG-SHO	SV-BS	IP	H	R	HR	HB	BB-IB	SO	ERA	AERA	OAV	OOB	AB-HR-SH	AVG	PB	SUP	APR	DL	PW
1972	SF N	0	1	.000	8	0	0	3-0	15.2	10	4	0	0	12-0	10	2.30	152	.189	.338	4	.000	-0	—	2	0	0.2
1973	SF N	10	4	.714	71	1	0	18-3	107	95	42	7	4	41-8	70	3.28	117	.241	.315	14-0-1	.071	-0	115	8	0	1.1
1974	SF N	9	7	.563	68	0	0	6-8	101	94	54	8	1	45-5	48	3.48	110	.252	.329	15-0-2	.067	-1	—	1	0	-0.1
1975	StL N	0	3	.000	14	1	0	0-1	27.1	22	14	3	1	14-2	15	3.95	96	.227	.319	8	.125	-0	46	0	0	-0.1
	Atl N	2	2	.500	43	0	0	2-2	62.1	70	35	3	3	29-7	31	4.48	85	.294	.376	7-0-1	.143	-0	—	-4	0	-0.3
	Year	2	5	.286	57	1	0	2-3	89.2	92	49	6	4	43-9	46	4.32	88	.275	.359	15-0-1	.133	-1	46	-4	0	-0.4
1976	Atl N	4	4	.500	21	0	0	3-4	35.1	41	26	3	1	13-2	32	5.35	71	.287	.346	7	.143	-0	—	-7	0	-1.4
	LA N	2	4	.333	24	0	0	1-0	33.2	30	16	0	0	12-4	20	3.48	98	.242	.304	0-0-1	ø	0	—	-1	0	-0.2
	Year	6	8	.429	45	0	0	4-4	69	71	42	3	1	25-6	52	4.43	81	.266	.327	7-0-1	.143	-0	—	-8	0	-1.6
1977	†LA N	2	2	.500	44	0	0	1-0	63.2	42	15	7	1	12-3	47	1.98	195	.189	.233	4-0-1	.250	0*	—	14	0	0.8
1978	Oak A	8	2	.800	68	0	0	14-4	109	106	37	5	1	44-10	61	2.64	139	.264	.337	0	ø	0	—	13	0	1.5
1979	Mon N	8	7	.533	62	0	0	18-7	96.2	77	24	2	2	37-11	59	1.96	190	.219	.297	13-0-1	.154	0	—	19	0	3.5
1980	Mon N	9	6	.600	67	0	0	9-8	93.2	104	33	5	1	19-3	58	3.07	118	.286	.320	11-0-1	.091	-1	—	7	0	1.1
1981	†Mon N	1	2	.333	32	0	0	3-2	39.1	46	16	3	1	8-0	18	3.66	97	.297	.329	2	1.000	1	—	0	0	0.1
1982	Det A	3	3	.500	38	0	0	4-3	61	64	31	11	2	18-3	24	4.43	92	.270	.327	0	ø	0	—	-1	0	-0.1
1983	SD N	1	4	.200	41	1	0	1-1	72.1	72	41	7	3	30-5	45	4.35	81	.268	.342	7	.143	-0	151	-8	0	-0.6
Total	12	59	51	.536	601	3	0	83-43	918	873	388	64	21	334-63	538	3.32	112	.255	.322	92-0-8	.130	-3	103	43	0	5.5

SOSA, JORGE Jorge Bolivar; B4.28.1977 Santo Domingo, D.R.; BR/TR/6´2˝/(175–180); d4.4

YEAR	TM LG	W	L	PCT	G	GS	CG-SHO	SV-BS	IP	H	R	HR	HB	BB-IB	SO	ERA	AERA	OAV	OOB	AB-HR-SH	AVG	PB	SUP	APR	DL	PW
2002	TB A	2	7	.222	31	14	0	0-0	99.1	88	63	16	2	54-0	48	5.53	82	.236	.332	0	ø	0	92	-10	30	-0.8
2003	TB A	5	12	.294	29	19	1-1	0-0	128.2	137	71	14	4	60-4	72	4.62	99	.278	.358	0	ø	0	80	0	0	-0.1
2004	TB A	4	7	.364	43	8	0	1-0	99.1	100	67	17	1	54-3	94	5.53	85	.259	.348	0	ø	0	84	-9	0	-0.9
2005	†Atl N	13	3	.813	44	20	0	0-0	134	122	42	12	0	64-8	85	2.55	166	.241	.325	31-0-3	.097	-1*	105	24	0	2.3
2006	Atl N	3	10	.231	26	13	0	3-3	87.1	105	61	20	1	32-5	58	5.46	83	.298	.355	20-3-6	.150	3*	85	-10	0	-1.2
	StL N	0	1	.000	19	0	0	1-0	30.2	33	18	10	0	8-1	17	5.28	82	.275	.320	4	.000	-0	—	-3	0	-0.2
	Year	3	11	.214	45	13	0	4-3	118	138	79	30	1	40-6	75	5.42	83	.292	.346	24-3-6	.125	3	86	-13	0	-1.4
Total	5	27	40	.403	192	74	1-1	5-3	579.1	585	322	89	8	272-21	374	4.61	97	.262	.342	55-3-9	.109	1	90	-8	30	-0.9

SOSA, JOSE Jose Ynocencio (b Jose Ynocencio (Sosa)); B12.28.1952 Santo Domingo, D.R.; BR/TR/5´11˝/158; d7.22

YEAR	TM LG	W	L	PCT	G	GS	CG-SHO	SV-BS	IP	H	R	HR	HB	BB-IB	SO	ERA	AERA	OAV	OOB	AB-HR-SH	AVG	PB	SUP	APR	DL	PW
1975	Hou N	1	3	.250	25	2	0	1-1	47	51	21	5	1	23-4	31	4.02	84	.291	.371	9-1-0	.333	2*	104	-3	0	-0.1
1976	Hou N	0	0	ø	9	0	0	0-0	11.2	16	9	0	3	6-2	5	6.94	46	.340	.439	0	ø	0	—	-5	0	-0.2
Total	2	1	3	.250	34	2	0	1-1	58.2	67	30	5	4	29-6	36	4.60	73	.302	.386	9-1-0	.333	2	104	-8	0	-0.3

SOTHORON, ALLEN Allen Sutton; B4.27.1893 Bradford OH; D6.17.1939 St.Louis MO; BB/TR (BR 1924–26)/5´11˝/182; d9.17; M1/C4; Col Juniata

YEAR	TM LG	W	L	PCT	G	GS	CG-SHO	SV-BS	IP	H	R	HR	HB	BB-IB	SO	ERA	AERA	OAV	OOB	AB-HR-SH	AVG	PB	SUP	APR	DL	PW
1914	StL A	0	0	ø	1	0	0	0	6	6	4	0	0	4	3	6.00	45	.261	.370	2	.000	-0	—	-2	—	-0.1
1915	StL A	0	1	.000	3	1	0	0	3.2	8	10	0	0	5	2	7.36	39	.400	.520	1	.000	-0	0	-4	—	-0.7
1917	StL A	14	19	.424	48	32	17-3	4	276.2	259	135	2	9	96	85	2.83	92	.251	.320	92-0-5	.217	3*	100	-13	—	-1.2
1918	StL A	12	12	.500	29	24	14-2	0	209	152	64	3	3	67	71	1.94	141	**.205**	.274	63-0-4	.159	-2	96	17	—	1.6
1919	StL A	20	12	.625	40	30	21-3	3	270	256	101	4	10	87	106	2.20	151	.246	.311	97-0-3	.175	-2	82	27	—	2.5
1920	StL A	8	15	.348	36	26	12-1	2	218.1	263	151	6	6	89	81	4.70	83	.307	.376	72-0-5	.222	-1	96	-22	—	-2.2
1921	StL A	1	2	.333	5	4	1	0	27.2	33	19	0	1	8	9	5.20	86	.314	.368	9-0-1	.111	-1	98	-2	—	-0.3
	Bos A	0	2	.000	2	2	0	0	6	15	10	0	0	5	2	13.50	31	.455	.526	2	.500	1	39	-6	—	-0.9
	Cle A	12	4	.750	22	16	10-2	0	144.2	146	60	0	7	58	61	3.24	132	.279	.358	58-0-3	.276	2	128	17	—	1.7
	Year	13	8	.619	29	22	11-2	0	178.1	194	89	0	8	71	72	3.89	111	.293	.368	69-0-4	.261	2	115	10	—	0.5
1922	Cle A	1	3	.250	6	4	2	0	25.1	26	22	1	2	14	8	6.39	63	.274	.378	9	.444	1	117	-7	—	-0.8
1924	StL N	10	16	.385	29	28	16-**4**	0	196.2	209	102	9	10	84	62	3.57	106	.275	.354	72-0-5	.194	-2	111	1	—	-0.3
1925	StL N	10	10	.500	28	22	8-2	0	155.2	173	86	7	6	63	67	4.05	107	.280	.353	56-0-2	.196	-1	106	3	—	0.0
1926	StL N	3	3	.500	15	4	1	0	42.2	37	22	2	0	16	19	4.22	93	.247	.319	13	.231	0	128	-1	—	-0.1
Total	11	91	99	.479	264	193	102-17	9	1582.1	1583	786	34	54	596	576	3.31	105	.264	.336	546-0-28	.207	-2	102	8	—	-0.8

SOTO, MARIO Mario Melvin; B7.12.1956 Bani, D.R.; BR/TR/6´0˝/(165–190); d7.21

YEAR	TM LG	W	L	PCT	G	GS	CG-SHO	SV-BS	IP	H	R	HR	HB	BB-IB	SO	ERA	AERA	OAV	OOB	AB-HR-SH	AVG	PB	SUP	APR	DL	PW
1977	Cin N	2	6	.250	12	10	2-1	0-0	60.2	60	38	12	3	26-4	44	5.34	74	.258	.337	13-0-1	.077	-0	90	-9	0	-1.1
1978	Cin N	1	0	1.000	5	1	0	0-0	18	13	5	1	0	13-3	13	2.50	142	.197	.329	2-0-1	.000	-0	126	2	0	0.1
1979	†Cin N	3	2	.600	25	0	0	0-0	37.1	33	25	2	1	30-2	32	5.30	70	.243	.381	7	.571	2	—	-7	0	-0.7
1980	Cin N	10	8	.556	53	12	3-1	4-1	190.1	126	72	11	2	84-10	182	3.07	115	**.187**	.276	46-0-8	.043	-4*	114	9	0	0.4
1981	Cin N	12	9	.571	25	**25**	10-3	0-0	175	142	69	13	3	61-3	151	3.29	107	.220	.289	59-0-6	.068	-4	106	5	0	0.0
1982	Cin N★	14	13	.519	35	34	13-2	0-0	257.2	202	88	19	4	71-3	274	2.79	131	.215	**.271**	84-0-11	.167	1*	92	25	0	2.7
1983	Cin N★	17	13	.567	34	34	**18**-3	0-0	273.2	207	96	28	5	95-6	242	2.70	142	.208	.278	88-0-11	.125	-2*	83	30	0	3.0
1984	Cin N★	18	7	.720	33	33	**13**	0-0	237.1	181	102	26	5	87-6	185	3.53	108	.209	.284	87-1-4	.207	3	106	7	0	0.9
1985	Cin N	12	15	.444	36	36	9-1	0-0	256.2	196	109	30	2	104-3	214	3.58	106	.211	.290	83-0-6	.133	-2*	86	8	0	0.5
1986	Cin N	5	10	.333	19	19	1-1	0-0	105	113	61	15	1	46-6	67	4.71	82	.280	.352	27-0-6	.111	-1*	84	-9	94	-1.3
1987	Cin N	3	2	.600	6	6	0	0-0	31.2	34	18	7	0	12-1	11	5.12	83	.279	.343	12	.083	-1	143	-2	150	-0.4
1988	Cin N	3	7	.300	14	14	3-1	0-0	87	88	49	8	2	28-3	34	4.66	77	.267	.326	22-0-4	.045	-1	96	-10	0	-1.2
Total	12	100	92	.521	297	224	72-13	4-1	1730.1	1395	732	172	28	657-50	1449	3.47	107	.220	.294	530-1-58	.132	-10	96	49	244	2.9

SOUZA, MARK Kenneth Mark; B2.1.1955 Redwood City CA; BL/TL/6´0˝/180; [KCA74*1/17]; d4.22; Col San Mateo (CA) [JC]

YEAR	TM LG	W	L	PCT	G	GS	CG-SHO	SV-BS	IP	H	R	HR	HB	BB-IB	SO	ERA	AERA	OAV	OOB	AB-HR-SH	AVG	PB	SUP	APR	DL	PW
1980	Oak A	0	0	ø	5	0	0	0-1	7	9	6	1	0	5-0	2	7.71	49	.310	.412	0	ø	0	—	-3	0	-0.1

SOWDERS, JOHN John; B12.10.1866 Louisville KY; D7.29.1939 Indianapolis IN; BR/TL/6´0˝/150; d6.28; b–Len b–Bill

YEAR	TM LG	W	L	PCT	G	GS	CG-SHO	SV-BS	IP	H	R	HR	HB	BB-IB	SO	ERA	AERA	OAV	OOB	AB-HR-SH	AVG	PB	SUP	APR	DL	PW
1887	Ind N	0	0	ø	1	0	0	0	3	11	13	0	0	5	0	21.00	20	.500	.593	2	.000	-0	—	-6	—	-0.3
1889	KC AA	6	16	.273	25	23	20	1	185	204	181	9	7	105	104	4.82	88	.271	.366	87	.218	-2*	78	-12	—	-1.3
1890	Bro P	19	16	.543	39	37	28-1	0	309	358	233	3	11	161	91	3.82	117	.278	.363	132-1	.189	-5*	95	19	—	1.1
Total	3	25	32	.439	65	60	48-1	1	497	573	427	12	18	271	195	4.29	102	.278	.366	221-1	.199	-7	88	1	—	-0.5

SOWDERS, BILL William Jefferson "Little Bill"; B11.29.1864 Louisville KY; D2.2.1951 Indianapolis IN; BR/TR/6´0˝/155; d4.24; b–John b–Len

YEAR	TM LG	W	L	PCT	G	GS	CG-SHO	SV-BS	IP	H	R	HR	HB	BB-IB	SO	ERA	AERA	OAV	OOB	AB-HR-SH	AVG	PB	SUP	APR	DL	PW
1888	Bos N	19	15	.559	36	35	34-2	0	317	278	155	3	9	73	132	2.07	139	.226	.275	122	.148	-4	85	19	—	1.5
1889	Bos N	1	2	.333	7	4	3	3	42	53	35	3	2	23	10	5.14	81	.299	.386	17	.235	-0	89	-5	—	-0.3
	Pit N	6	5	.545	13	11	9	0	52.2	94	55	1	4	29	33	7.35	51	.376	.449	48	.271	2*	96	-20	—	-2.7
	Year	7	7	.500	20	15	12	**3**	94.2	147	90	4	6	52	43	6.37	62	.344	.423	65	.262	2	92	-23	—	-3.0
1890	Pit N	3	8	.273	15	11	9	0	106	117	77	1	2	24	30	4.42	75	.271	.312	50	.180	-2*	71	-13	—	-1.3
Total	3	29	30	.492	71	61	55-2	3	517.2	542	322	8	17	149	205	3.34	95	.260	.314	237	.186	-4	85	-19	—	-2.8

SOWERS, JEREMY Jeremy Bryan; B5.17.1983 St.Clairsville OH; BL/TL/6´1˝/180; [CleA04 1/6]; d6.25; Col Vanderbilt

YEAR	TM LG	W	L	PCT	G	GS	CG-SHO	SV-BS	IP	H	R	HR	HB	BB-IB	SO	ERA	AERA	OAV	OOB	AB-HR-SH	AVG	PB	SUP	APR	DL	PW
2006	Cle A	7	4	.636	14	14	2-**2**	0-0	88.1	85	36	10	2	20-1	35	3.57	121	.252	.298	0	ø	0	107	9	0	1.0

SPADE, BOB Robert; B1.4.1877 Akron OH; D9.7.1924 Cincinnati OH; BR/TR/5´10˝/190; d9.22

YEAR	TM LG	W	L	PCT	G	GS	CG-SHO	SV-BS	IP	H	R	HR	HB	BB-IB	SO	ERA	AERA	OAV	OOB	AB-HR-SH	AVG	PB	SUP	APR	DL	PW
1907	Cin N	1	2	.333	3	3	3-1	0	27	21	5	0	1	9	7	1.00	260	.219	.292	7	.286	1	37	4	—	0.7
1908	Cin N	17	12	.586	35	28	22-2	1	249.1	230	111	2	5	85	74	2.74	84	.250	.317	87-0-3	.195	1	107	-12	—	-1.6
1909	Cin N	5	5	.500	14	13	8	0	98	91	38	0	4	39	31	2.85	91	.236	.313	34	.294	4	99	0	—	0.2
1910	Cin N	1	2	.333	3	3	1	0	17.1	35	19	1	1	9	1	6.75	43	.479	.542	5	.000	-1	136	-8	—	-1.1
	StL A	1	3	.250	7	5	2-1	0	34.2	34	24	1	1	17	8	4.41	56	.270	.361	11	.273	2	119	-7	—	-0.6
Total	4	25	24	.510	62	52	36-4	1	426.1	411	197	4	12	159	121	2.96	82	.257	.329	144-0-3	.222	7	104	-23	—	-2.4

SPAHN, WARREN Warren Edward; B4.23.1921 Buffalo NY; D11.24.2003 Broken Arrow OK; BL/TL/6´0˝/175; d4.19; Mil 1943–46; C3; HF1973

YEAR	TM LG	W	L	PCT	G	GS	CG-SHO	SV-BS	IP	H	R	HR	HB	BB-IB	SO	ERA	AERA	OAV	OOB	AB-HR-SH	AVG	PB	SUP	APR	DL	PW
1942	Bos N	0	0	ø	4	2	1	0	15.2	25	15	0	0	11	7	5.74	58	.368	.456	6	.167	-0	126	-6	0	-0.3
1946	Bos N	8	5	.615	24	16	8	1	125.2	107	46	6	1	36	67	2.94	117	.228	.285	43-0-2	.163	-1	105	8	0	0.6
1947	Bos N★	21	10	.677	40	35	22-**7**	3	**289.2**	245	87	15	1	84	123	**2.33**	**167**	.226	**.283**	98-0-8	.163	1*	91	**52**	0	**5.3**
1948	†Bos N	15	12	.556	36	35	16-3	1	257	237	115	19	1	77	114	3.71	103	.242	.298	90-1-7	.167	2*	113	5	0	0.7
1949	Bos N★	**21**	14	.600	38	**38**	**25**-4	0	**302.1**	283	125	27	3	86	**151**	3.07	123	.245	.299	111-2-5	.162	-0*	110	23	0	2.3
1950	Bos N☆	**21**	17	.553	41	**39**	25-1	1	293	248	123	22	1	111	**191**	3.16	122	.227	.299	106-1-5	.217	4	108	22	0	3.1
1951	Bos N☆	22	14	.611	39	36	**26-7**	0	310.2	278	111	20	1	109	**164**	2.98	123	.238	.304	116-1-4	.190	5*	124	29	0	3.6
1952	Bos N☆	14	19	.424	40	35	19-5	3	290	263	109	19	6	73	**183**	2.98	121	.240	.291	112-2-2	.161	2*	94	20	0	2.6
1953	Mil N★	**23**	7	.767	35	32	24-5	3	265.2	211	75	14	1	70	148	**2.10**	**187**	**.217**	**.270**	105-2-5	.219	5*	111	57	0	**7.0**
1954	Mil N★	21	12	.636	39	34	23-1	3	283.1	262	107	24	1	86	136	3.14	118	.245	.300	101-1-3	.208	6*	103	22	0	3.2

YEAR	TM LG	W	L	PCT	G	GS	CG-SHO	SV-BS	IP	H	R	HR	HB	BB-IB	SO	ERA	AERA	OAV	OOB	AB-HR-SH	AVG	PB	SUP	APR	DL	PW
1955	Mil N	17	14	.548	39	32	16-1	1	245.2	249	99	25	2	65-4	110	3.26	115	.265	.312	81-4-3	.210	5*	111	15	0	2.3
1956	Mil N★	20	11	.645	39	35	20-3	3	281.1	249	92	25	3	52-12	128	2.78	124	.238	.275	105-3-2	.210	6	108	**28**	0	3.7
1957	†Mil N☆	**21**	11	.656	39	35	**18**-4	3	271	241	94	23	2	78-4	111	2.69	130	.237	.291	94-2-3	.138	1	124	26	0	3.1
1958	†Mil N★	**22**	11	**.667**	38	36	**23**-2	1	**290**	257	106	29	2	76-7	150	3.07	115	.237	.287	108-2-4	.333	18*	113	18	0	**4.1**
1959	Mil N☆	**21**	15	.583	40	36	**21-4**	0	**292**	282	106	21	1	70-9	143	2.96	120	.253	.297	104-2-1	.231	7	113	23	0	3.4
1960	Mil N	**21**	10	.677	40	33	**18**-4	2	267.2	254	114	24	4	74-9	154	3.50	98	.250	.302	95-3-2	.147	3	122	0	0	0.4
1961	Mil N★	**21**	13	.618	38	34	**21-4**	0	262.2	236	96	24	4	64-1	115	**3.02**	124	.243	**.291**	94-4-2	.223	10*	100	23	0	**4.1**
1962	Mil N☆	18	14	.563	34	34	**22**	0	269.1	248	97	25	3	55-4	118	3.04	125	.246	.284	98-2-3	.184	4*	93	26	0	3.5
1963	Mil N☆	23	7	.767	33	33	**22**-7	0	259.2	241	85	23	0	49-4	102	2.60	124	.248	.282	90-2-4	.178	5	117	18	0	3.0
1964	Mil N	6	13	.316	38	25	4-1	4	173.2	204	110	23	2	52-4	78	5.29	67	.297	.345	59-1-1	.186	2*	115	-32	0	-3.2
1965	NY N	4	12	.250	20	19	5	0	126	140	70	18	2	35-1	56	4.36	81	.281	.329	35-0-2	.114	1*	76	-12	0	-1.2
	SF N	3	4	.429	16	11	3	0	71.2	70	34	8	1	21-1	34	3.39	106	.256	.308	21	.143	0	115	0	0	0.1
	Year	7	16	.304	36	30	8	0	197.2	210	104	26	3	56-2	90	4.01	89	.272	.321	56-0-2	.125	-2	90	-12	0	-1.1
Total	21	363	245	.597	750	665	382-63	29	5243.2	4830	2016	434	42	1434-60	2583	3.09	118	.244	.296	1872-35-68	.194	88	108	365	0	51.4
Spalding, Al	Albert Goodwill; B9.2.1850 Byron IL; D9.9.1915 San Diego CA; BR/TR/6´1˝/170; d5.5; M2; HF1939; ▲																									
1871	Bos NA	**19**	10	.655	31	31	22-**1**	0	257.1	333	272	2	—	38	23	3.36	124	.268	.290	144-1	.271	2	123	22	—	1.6
1872	Bos NA	**38**	8	**.826**	48	48	41-**3**	0	404.2	417	224	0	—	27	28	1.85	199	.244	.255	237	.354	18	114	**81**	—	**7.5**
1873	Bos NA	**41**	14	**.745**	**60**	**54**	46-1	3	**496.2**	643	413	5	—	36	50	2.99	116	.284	.296	323-1	.328	19	131	26	—	**3.4**
1874	Bos NA	**52**	16	**.765**	**71**	**69**	**65-4**	0	**617.1**	755	402	1	—	19	31	1.92	113	.273	.278	362	.329	21	141	17	—	**2.8**
1875	Bos NA	**54**	5	**.915**	**72**	62	52-**7**	**9**	570.2	573	241	1	—	18	75	1.59	135	.245	.251	343	.312	22*	165	33	—	**4.4**
1876	Chi N	**47**	12	**.797**	61	60	53-8	0	528.2	542	226	6	—	26	39	1.75	139	.247	.256	292	.312	9*	153	39	—	4.3
1877	Chi N	1	0	1.000	4	1	0	1	11	17	12	0	—	0	2	3.27	91	.321	.321	254	.256	0*	197	-1	—	-0.1
Total	5NA	204	53	.794	282	264	226-16	12	2346.2	2721	1552	9	—	138	207	2.21	131	.264	.274	1409-2	.323	83	135	179	—	19.7
Total	2	48	12	.800	65	61	53-8	1	539.2	559	238	6	—	26	41	1.78	138	.249	.257	546	.286	9	153	38	—	4.2
Spanswick, Bill	William Henry; B7.8.1938 Springfield MA; BL/TL/6´3˝/195; d4.18; Col Holy Cross																									
1964	Bos A	2	3	.400	29	7	0	0	65.1	75	51	9	3	44-1	55	6.89	56	.306	.412	14	.286	1	128	-19	0	-1.2
Sparks, Jeff	James Jeffrey; B4.4.1972 Houston TX; BR/TR/6´3˝/220; [CinN95 24/671]; d9.12; Col St. Marys (TX)																									
1999	TB A	0	0	ø	8	0	0	1-0	10	6	6	1	1	12-1	17	5.40	92	.171	.396	0	ø	0	—	0	0	0.0
2000	TB A	0	1	.000	15	0	0	0-0	20.1	13	8	2	2	18-1	24	3.54	138	.186	.367	0	ø	0	—	3	0	0.1
Total	2	0	1	.000	23	0	0	1-0	30.1	19	14	3	3	30-2	41	4.15	118	.181	.377	0	ø	0	—	3	0	0.1
Sparks, Steve	Stephen Lanier; B3.28.1975 Mobile AL; BR/TR/6´4˝/210; [PitN98 28/838]; d7.19; Col South Alabama																									
2000	Pit N	0	0	ø	3	0	0	0-0	4	4	3	0	0	5-0	2	6.75	69	.267	.450	0	ø	0	—	-1	0	0.0
Sparks, Steve	Steven William; B7.2.1965 Tulsa OK; BR/TR/6´0˝/(180–195); [MilA87 5/123]; d4.28; Col Sam Houston St.; [DL 1997 Mil A 181]																									
1995	Mil A	9	11	.450	33	27	3	0-0	202	210	111	17	5	86-1	96	4.63	108	.274	.346	0	ø	0	87	9	0	0.9
1996	Mil A	4	7	.364	20	13	1	0-0	88.2	103	66	19	3	52-0	21	6.60	79	.297	.392	0	ø	0	96	-11	0	-1.0
1998	Ana A	9	4	.692	22	20	0	0-0	128.2	130	66	14	5	58-0	90	4.34	109	.263	.345	1-0-1	.000	0	96	6	0	0.7
1999	Ana A	5	11	.313	28	26	0	0-0	147.2	165	101	21	9	82-0	73	5.42	90	.281	.373	3	.333	1*	87	-11	0	-0.8
2000	Det A	7	5	.583	20	15	1-1	1-0	104	108	55	7	4	29-0	53	4.07	121	.263	.317	0	ø	0	115	8	0	0.8
2001	Det A	14	9	.609	35	33	**8**-1	0-0	232	244	110	22	6	64-1	116	3.65	121	.271	.321	4	.000	-0*	98	17	0	1.6
2002	Det A	8	16	.333	32	30	3	0-0	189	238	134	23	12	67-3	98	5.52	79	.306	.366	2	.000	-0	88	-27	0	-2.7
2003	Det A	0	6	.000	42	0	0	2-2	89.2	95	57	11	3	34-4	49	4.72	93	.278	.343	0	ø	0	—	-6	0	-0.4
	†Oak A	0	0	ø	9	0	0	0-0	17.1	19	11	2	0	3-0	5	5.71	80	.271	.297	0	ø	0	—	-2	0	-0.1
	Year	0	6	.000	51	0	0	2-2	107	114	68	13	3	37-4	54	4.88	90	.277	.336	0	ø	0	—	-7	0	-0.5
2004	Ari N	3	7	.300	29	18	0	0-0	120.2	139	89	18	5	45-2	57	6.04	75	.287	.351	31-0-1	.129	-1	65	-18	0	-1.4
Total	9	59	76	.437	270	182	16-2	3-2	1319.2	1451	800	154	52	520-11	658	4.88	96	.280	.348	41-0-2	.122	-1	91	-35	181	-2.4
Sparks, Tully	Thomas Frank; B12.12.1874 Etna GA; D7.15.1937 Anniston AL; BR/TR/5´10˝/160; d9.15; Col Beloit																									
1897	Phi N	0	1	.000	1	1	1	0	8	12	9	0	0	4	0	10.13	41	.343	.410	3	.000	-1	17	-4	—	-0.4
1899	Pit N	8	6	.571	28	17	8	0	170	180	101	1	10	82	53	3.86	99	.271	.360	62	.129	-2	98	-1	—	-0.2
1901	Mil A	7	17	.292	29	26	18	0	210	228	157	5	14	93	62	3.51	102	.273	.356	71-0-3	.169	-1	82	-9	—	-1.0
1902	NY N	4	10	.286	16	14	12	1	123	142	72	2	4	41	42	4.17	67	.289	.348	40-0-2	.150	-1	78	-14	—	-1.3
	Bos A	7	9	.438	17	15	15-1	0	142.2	151	83	4	7	40	37	3.47	103	.272	.329	52-0-1	.154	-1	67	0	—	-0.1
1903	Phi N	11	15	.423	28	28	27	0	248	248	109	3	8	56	88	2.72	120	.263	.310	92-0-3	.109	-5	78	13	—	0.6
1904	Phi N	7	16	.304	26	25	19-3	0	200.2	208	109	1	5	43	67	2.65	101	.260	.302	76	.105	-5	89	-5	—	-1.3
1905	Phi N	14	11	.560	34	26	20-3	1	259.2	217	86	2	9	73	98	2.18	134	.236	.298	94-0-3	.128	-2	139	22	—	1.5
1906	Phi N	19	16	.543	42	37	29-6	3	316.2	244	99	4	10	62	114	2.16	121	.211	.257	104-0-3	.154	0	87	20	—	2.1
1907	Phi N	22	8	.733	33	31	24-3	1	265	221	78	2	7	51	90	2.00	121	.228	.271	89-0-4	.034	-8	117	13	—	0.3
1908	Phi N	16	15	.516	33	31	24-2	2	263.1	251	98	3	8	51	85	2.60	93	.257	.300	77-0-11	.052	-5	94	-3	—	-1.1
1909	Phi N	6	11	.353	24	16	6-1	0	121.2	126	54	4	3	32	40	2.96	88	.280	.332	36-0-1	.139	-1	49	-5	—	-0.8
1910	Phi N	0	2	.000	3	3	0	0	15	22	12	2	2	2	4	6.00	52	.324	.361	5	.000	-1	95	-4	—	-0.5
Total	12	121	137	.469	314	270	203-19	8	2343.2	2250	1067	33	87	630	780	2.82	104	.254	.310	801-0-31	.115	-32	90	23	—	-2.2
Sparma, Joe	Joseph Blase; B2.4.1942 Massillon OH; D5.14.1986 Columbus OH; BR/TR/6´0˝/(195–197); d5.20; Col Ohio St.																									
1964	Det A	5	6	.455	21	11	3-2	0	84	62	33	4	3	45-1	71	3.00	122	.207	.313	25	.160	1*	93	5	0	0.8
1965	Det A	13	8	.619	30	28	6	0	167	142	69	13	3	75-5	127	3.18	109	.228	.312	52-0-4	.135	-0	96	4	0	0.4
1966	Det A	2	7	.222	29	13	0	0	91.2	103	57	14	3	52-0	61	5.30	66	.288	.382	23-0-2	.217	1	109	-17	0	-1.6
1967	Det A	16	9	.640	37	37	11-5	0	217.2	186	103	20	8	85-2	153	3.76	87	.227	.305	74-0-13	.054	-5	132	-13	0	-2.1
1968	†Det A	10	10	.500	34	31	7-1	0	182.1	169	81	14	7	77-3	110	3.70	81	.246	.326	60-0-6	.133	-1	119	-13	0	-1.7
1969	Det A	6	8	.429	23	16	3-2	0-0	92.2	78	55	5	1	77-1	41	4.76	79	.231	.373	29-0-3	.138	-1	84	-10	0	-1.5
1970	Mon N	0	4	.000	9	6	1	0-0	29.1	34	25	7	2	25-3	23	7.06	59	.296	.421	6-0-1	.000	-0	47	-9	0	-1.1
Total	7	52	52	.500	183	142	31-10	0-0	864.2	774	423	77	27	436-15	586	3.94	86	.239	.332	269-0-29	.119	-6	107	-53	0	-6.8
Speck, Cliff	Robert Clifford; B8.8.1956 Portland OR; BR/TR/6´4˝/196; [NYN74 1/17]; d7.30; [DL 1985 Chi A 42]																									
1986	Atl N	2	1	.667	13	1	0	0-0	28.1	25	13	2	1	15-0	21	4.13	96	.238	.336	3-0-1	.000	-0	68	0	0	0.0
Speece, By	Byron Franklin; B1.6.1897 West Baden IN; D9.29.1974 Elgin OR; BR/TR/5´11˝/170; d4.21																									
1924	†Was A	2	1	.667	21	1	0	0	54.1	60	30	0	2	27	15	2.65	152	.303	.392	20	.150	-1	21	**4**	—	0.2
1925	Cle A	3	5	.375	28	3	3	1	90.1	106	48	0	3	28	26	4.28	103	.297	.353	31	.161	-2	51	3	—	0.1
1926	Cle A	0	0	ø	2	0	0	0	3	1	1	0	0	2	1	0.00	ø	.125	.300	0	ø	0	—	1	—	0.1
1930	Phi N	0	0	ø	11	0	0	0	19.2	41	30	1	0	4	9	13.27	41	.432	.455	3	.333	0	—	-14	—	-0.6
Total	4	5	6	.455	62	4	3	1	167.1	208	109	1	5	61	51	4.73	93	.316	.378	54	.167	-2	43	-6	—	-0.2
Speer, Floyd	Floyd Vernie; B1.27.1913 Booneville AR; D3.22.1969 Little Rock AR; BR/TR/6´0˝/180; d4.25																									
1943	Chi A	0	0	ø	1	0	0	0	1	1	1	0	0	2	1	9.00	37	.250	.500	0	ø	0	—	-1	0	0.0
1944	Chi A	0	0	ø	2	0	0	0	2	4	2	0	0	0	1	9.00	38	.500	.500	0	ø	0	—	-1	0	-0.1
Total	2	0	0	ø	3	0	0	0	3	5	3	0	0	2	2	9.00	38	.417	.500	0	ø	0	—	-2	0	-0.1
Speer, Kid	George Nathan; B6.16.1886 Corning MO; D1.13.1946 Edmonton AL, Can.; BL/TL/5´9˝/152; d4.24																									
1909	Det A	4	4	.500	12	8	4	1	76.1	88	39	2	4	13	12	2.83	89	.293	.331	25	.120	-0*	133	-5	—	-0.5
Speier, Justin	Justin James; B11.6.1973 Daly City CA; BR/TR/6´4˝/205; [ChiN95 55/1452]; d5.27; f–Chris; Col Nicholls St.																									
1998	Chi N	0	0	ø	1	0	0	0-0	1.1	2	2	0	0	1-0	2	13.50	33	.333	.429	0	ø	0	—	-1	0	-0.1
	Fla N	0	3	.000	18	0	0	0-1	19.1	25	18	7	0	12-1	15	8.38	48	.325	.411	0	ø	0	—	-9	0	-1.2
	Year	0	3	.000	19	0	0	0-1	20.2	27	20	7	0	13-1	17	8.71	47	.325	.412	0	ø	0	—	-10	0	-1.3
1999	Atl N	0	0	ø	19	0	0	0-0	28.2	28	18	8	0	13-1	22	5.65	79	.248	.323	3	.333	0	—	-3	0	-0.1
2000	Cle A	5	2	.714	47	0	0	0-1	68.1	57	27	9	4	28-3	69	3.29	152	.226	.309	2	.500	0	—	12	0	1.1
2001	Cle A	2	0	1.000	12	0	0	0-0	20.2	24	16	5	3	8-0	15	6.97	66	.293	.365	0	ø	0	—	-5	0	-0.4
	Col N	4	3	.571	42	0	0	0-1	56	47	24	8	5	12-3	47	3.70	144	.229	.283	7	.000	-1	—	9	0	0.8
2002	Col N	5	1	.833	63	0	0	1-3	62.1	51	31	9	3	19-4	47	4.33	109	.216	.282	3	.333	0	—	3	36	0.2
2003	Col N	3	1	.750	72	0	0	9-3	73.1	73	37	11	7	23-6	66	4.05	121	.257	.324	1	.000	-0	—	5	0	0.3
2004	Tor A	3	8	.273	62	0	0	7-4	69	61	32	8	5	25-6	52	3.91	125	.239	.316	1	.000	-0	—	7	28	1.0

YEAR	TM LG	W	L	PCT	G	GS	CG-SHO	SV-BS	IP	H	R	HR	HB	BB-IB	SO	ERA	AERA	OAV	OOB	AB-HR-SH	AVG	PB	SUP	APR	DL	PW
2005	Tor A	3	2	.600	65	0	0	0-4	66.2	48	20	10	3	15-2	56	2.57	179	.198	.254	0	ø	0	—	14	0	0.9
2006	Tor A	2	0	1.000	58	0	0	0-3	51.1	47	18	5	1	21-3	55	2.98	159	.235	.311	0	ø	0	—	10	32	0.5
Total	9	27	20	.574	459	0	0	17-20	517	463	243	80	31	177-29	446	4.02	120	.237	.308	17	.176	-0	—	42	96	3.0
Speier, Ryan	Ryan Andrew; B7.24.1979 Frankfort KY; BR/TR/6´7˝/200; d4.4; Col Radford																									
2005	Col N	2	1	.667	22	0	0	0-1	24.2	26	12	0	1	13-0	10	3.65	128	.277	.367	2	.000	-0	—	2	0	0.2
Spencer, Hack	Fred Calvin; B4.25.1885 St.Cloud MN; D2.5.1969 St.Anthony MN; BR/TR/5´7˝/172; d4.18																									
1912	StL A	0	0	ø	1	0	0	0	1.2	2	2	0	0	0	0	0.00	ø	.286	.286	0	ø	0	—	0	—	0.0
Spencer, George	George Elwell; B7.7.1926 Columbus OH; BR/TR/6´1˝/215; d8.17; Col Ohio St.																									
1950	NY N	1	0	1.000	10	1	1	0	25.1	12	7	3	0	7	5	2.49	165	.141	.207	4	.000	-1	108	5	0	0.2
1951	†NY N	10	4	.714	57	4	2	6	132	125	62	21	1	56	36	3.75	104	.254	.332	32-0-3	.125	-1	135	4	0	0.3
1952	NY N	3	5	.375	35	4	0	3	60	57	39	13	3	21	27	5.55	67	.251	.323	10	.200	0	138	-11	0	-1.4
1953	NY N	0	0	ø	1	0	0	0	2.1	3	2	0	0	2	1	7.71	56	.300	.417	0	ø	0	—	-1	0	0.0
1954	NY N	1	0	1.000	6	0	0	0	12.1	9	5	1	0	8	4	3.65	111	.209	.333	3	.000	-0	—	1	0	0.1
1955	NY N	0	0	ø	1	0	0	0	1.2	1	1	1	0	3-0	0	5.40	75	.167	.444	0	ø	0	—	0	0	0.0
1958	Det A	1	0	1.000	7	0	0	0	10	11	4	0	0	4-0	5	2.70	149	.289	.349	0	ø	0	—	1	0	0.1
1960	Det A	0	1	.000	5	0	0	0	7.2	10	3	1	0	5-1	4	3.52	112	.323	.417	1	.000	-0	—	1	0	0.0
Total	8	16	10	.615	122	9	3	9	251.1	228	123	40	4	106-1	82	4.05	96	.245	.324	50-0-3	.120	-2	131	0	0	-0.7
Spencer, Glenn	Glenn Edward; B9.11.1905 Corning NY; D12.30.1958 Binghamton NY; BR/TR/5´11˝/155; d4.11																									
1928	Pit N	0	0	ø	4	0	0	0	5.2	4	3	0	0	3	2	1.59	256	.200	.304	1	.000	-0	—	1	—	0.0
1930	Pit N	8	9	.471	41	11	5	4	156.2	185	110	16	2	63	60	5.40	92	.305	.372	53-0-1	.113	-4	102	-7	—	-1.1
1931	Pit N	11	12	.478	38	18	11-1	3	186.2	180	83	8	5	65	51	3.42	112	.260	.328	52-0-10	.096	-3	73	10	—	0.9
1932	Pit N	4	8	.333	39	13	5-1	1	137.2	167	104	10	3	44	35	4.97	77	.288	.341	37-0-3	.162	-1	104	-22	—	-1.8
1933	NY N	0	2	.000	17	3	1	0	47.1	52	33	3	1	26	14	5.13	63	.284	.376	12	.167	-0	95	-11	—	-0.6
Total	5	23	31	.426	139	45	22-2	8	534	588	333	37	11	201	162	4.53	91	.282	.349	155-0-14	.123	-9	90	-29	—	-2.6
Spencer, Sean	Sean James; B5.29.1975 Seattle WA; BL/TL/5´11˝/185; [SeaA96 40/1197]; d5.6; Col Washington																									
1999	Sea A	0	0	ø	2	0	0	0-0	1.2	5	4	0	0	3-0	2	21.60	22	.556	.667	0	ø	0	—	-3	0	-0.1
2000	Mon N	0	0	ø	8	0	0	0-0	6.2	7	4	2	0	3-0	6	5.40	87	.292	.357	0	ø	0	—	0	0	0.0
Total	2	0	0	ø	10	0	0	0-0	8.1	12	8	2	0	6-0	8	8.64	55	.364	.450	0	ø	0	—	-3	0	-0.1
Spencer, Stan	Stanley Roger; B8.2.1968 Vancouver WA; BR/TR/6´4˝/(205–223); [MonN90 1/35]; d8.27; Col Stanford																									
1998	SD N	1	0	1.000	6	5	0	0-0	30.2	29	16	5	1	4-0	31	4.70	85	.244	.274	9-0-3	.111	-0	148	-2	0	-0.1
1999	SD N	0	7	.000	9	8	0	0-0	38.1	56	44	11	1	11-1	36	9.16	47	.335	.380	10-0-1	.000	-1	54	-23	0	-3.0
2000	SD N	2	2	.500	8	8	0	0-0	49.2	44	22	7	2	19-1	40	3.26	137	.239	.316	12-0-2	.333	1*	80	6	103	0.6
Total	3	3	9	.250	23	21	0	0-0	118.2	129	82	23	4	34-2	107	5.54	77	.274	.328	31-0-6	.161	1	85	-19	103	-2.5
Spicer, Bob	Robert Oberton; B4.11.1925 Richmond VA; BL/TR/5´10˝/173; d4.17																									
1955	KC A	0	0	ø	2	0	0	0	2.2	9	10	2	1	4-0	2	33.75	12	.529	.636	1	.000	-0	—	-8	0	-0.4
1956	KC A	0	0	ø	2	0	0	0	2.1	6	5	1	1	1-0	0	19.29	22	.545	.615	0	ø	0	—	-3	0	-0.2
Total	2	0	0	ø	4	0	0	0	5	15	15	3	2	5-0	2	27.00	16	.536	.629	1	.000	-0	—	-11	0	-0.6
Spillner, Dan	Daniel Ray; B11.27.1951 Casper WY; BR/TR/6´1˝/(190–195); [SDN70 2/25]; d5.21																									
1974	SD N	9	11	.450	30	25	5-2	0-0	148	153	78	15	0	70-4	95	4.01	89	.267	.344	43-0-5	.023	-4	79	-9	0	-1.6
1975	SD N	5	13	.278	37	25	3	1-0	166.2	194	93	14	2	63-7	104	4.27	82	.293	.353	45-0-6	.133	1	82	-14	0	-1.3
1976	SD N	2	11	.154	32	14	0	0-1	106.2	120	70	11	0	55-8	57	5.06	65	.291	.371	25	.040	-1*	78	-23	62	-2.6
1977	SD N	7	6	.538	76	0	0	6-5	123	130	61	12	1	60-13	74	3.73	96	.280	.359	17	.118	1	—	-3	0	-0.4
1978	SD N	1	0	1.000	17	0	0	0-1	25.2	32	15	2	0	7-1	16	4.56	74	.317	.358	0-0-1	ø	0	—	-4	0	-0.2
	Cle A	3	1	.750	36	0	0	3-2	56.1	54	26	2	1	21-3	48	3.67	103	.254	.323	0	ø	0	—	1	0	0.0
1979	Cle A	9	5	.643	49	13	3	1-2	157.2	153	82	16	3	64-4	97	4.62	93	.256	.327	0	ø	0	117	-2	0	-0.2
1980	Cle A	16	11	.593	34	30	7-1	0-0	194.1	225	122	23	3	74-2	100	5.28	78	.288	.350	0	ø	0	111	-23	0	-2.9
1981	Cle A	4	4	.500	32	5	1	7-1	97.1	86	41	3	0	39-3	59	3.14	117	.240	.309	0	ø	0	97	4	0	0.4
1982	Cle A	12	10	.545	65	0	0	21-10	133.2	117	44	9	0	45-7	90	2.49	167	.235	.295	0	ø	0	—	23	0	4.2
1983	Cle A	2	9	.182	60	0	0	8-5	92.1	117	54	7	2	38-9	48	5.07	84	.315	.376	0	ø	0	—	-6	0	-0.8
1984	Cle A	0	5	.000	14	8	0	1-0	51	70	36	3	0	22-2	23	5.65	73	.332	.385	0	ø	0	74	-9	0	-0.7
	Chi A	1	0	1.000	22	0	0	1-1	48.1	51	25	7	1	14-0	26	4.10	102	.276	.328	0	ø	0*	—	0	0	0.0
	Year	1	5	.167	36	8	0	2-1	99.1	121	61	10	1	36-2	49	4.89	85	.306	.359	0	ø	0	73	-9	0	-0.7
1985	Chi A	4	3	.571	52	3	0	1-1	91.2	83	39	10	0	33-2	41	3.44	127	.245	.309	0	ø	0*	112	9	0	0.5
Total	12	75	89	.457	556	123	19-3	50-29	1492.2	1585	786	134	13	605-65	878	4.21	92	.275	.342	130-0-12	.077	-3	92	-56	62	-5.6
Spinks, Scipio	Scipio Ronald; B7.12.1947 Chicago IL; BR/TR/6´1˝/185; d9.16; Col Kennedy–King (IL) JC																									
1969	Hou N	0	0	ø	1	0	0	0-0	2	1	1	0	0	1-0	4	0.00	ø	.143	.250	0	ø	0	—	0	0	0.0
1970	Hou N	0	1	.000	5	2	0	0-0	13.2	17	15	5	0	9-0	6	9.88	39	.293	.388	3	.000	-0*	127	-9	0	-0.6
1971	Hou N	1	0	1.000	5	3	1	0-0	29.1	22	12	2	1	13-0	26	3.68	91	.210	.303	9	.222	0	132	0	0	0.0
1972	StL N	5	5	.500	16	16	6	0-0	118	96	39	5	2	59-2	93	2.67	128	.221	.317	42-0-2	.167	-1*	93	10	92	0.8
1973	StL N	1	5	.167	8	8	0	0-0	38.2	39	25	4	0	25-2	25	4.89	75	.269	.374	11-1-1	.182	1	66	-6	96	-0.6
Total	5	7	11	.389	35	29	7	0-0	201.2	175	92	16	3	107-4	154	3.70	94	.234	.331	65-1-3	.169	0	92	-5	188	-0.4
Splittorff, Paul	Paul William; B10.8.1946 Evansville IN; BL/TL/6´3˝/(195–210); [KCA68 25/575]; d9.23; Col Morningside																									
1970	KC A	0	1	.000	2	1	0	0-0	8.2	16	9	1	0	5-0	10	7.27	51	.390	.457	2	.500	0	0	-4	0	-0.3
1971	KC A	8	9	.471	22	22	6-3	0-0	144.1	129	49	4	4	35-1	80	2.68	128	.243	.292	48-0-1	.104	-1	78	12	0	1.3
1972	KC A	12	12	.500	35	33	12-2	0-1	216	189	81	11	4	67-2	140	3.13	97	.241	.301	71-0-7	.225	4	132	-1	0	0.5
1973	KC A	20	11	.645	38	38	12-3	0-0	262	279	135	19	5	78-7	110	3.98	103	.272	.325	0	ø	0	123	1	0	0.1
1974	KC A	13	19	.406	36	36	8-1	0-0	226	252	122	23	1	75-8	90	4.10	93	.285	.338	0	ø	0*	78	-8	0	-1.0
1975	KC A	9	10	.474	35	23	6-3	1-0	159	156	75	10	1	56-10	76	3.17	122	.255	.316	0	ø	0	90	7	0	1.0
1976	†KC A	11	8	.579	26	23	5-1	0-0	158.2	169	79	11	3	59-0	59	3.97	88	.277	.341	0	ø	0	106	-7	38	-0.7
1977	†KC A	16	6	**.727**	37	37	6-2	0-0	229	243	104	11	2	83-2	99	3.69	109	.278	.340	0	ø	0	122	10	0	0.9
1978	†KC A	19	13	.594	39	38	13-2	0-0	262	244	113	22	3	60-2	76	3.40	113	.247	.290	0	ø	0	112	13	0	1.5
1979	KC A	15	17	.469	36	35	11	0-0	240	248	137	25	5	77-1	77	4.24	101	.268	.324	0	ø	0	105	-3	0	-0.4
1980	†KC A	14	11	.560	34	33	4	0-0	204	236	101	17	1	43-1	53	4.15	98	.296	.329	0	ø	0	103	-1	0	0.0
1981	KC A	5	5	.500	21	15	1	0-0	99	111	48	12	1	23-4	48	4.36	83	.294	.331	0	ø	0	116	-6	0	-0.5
1982	KC A	10	10	.500	29	28	0	0-0	162	166	83	14	3	57-1	74	4.28	96	.266	.328	0	ø	0	111	-3	0	-0.3
1983	KC A	13	8	.619	27	27	4	0-0	156	159	77	9	1	52-2	61	3.63	113	.262	.319	0	ø	0	98	5	0	0.7
1984	KC A	1	3	.250	12	3	0	0-0	28	47	30	3	0	10-0	4	7.71	52	.376	.413	0	ø	0	74	-13	0	-1.5
Total	15	166	143	.537	429	392	88-17	1-1	2554.2	2644	1243	192	34	780-41	1057	3.81	101	.270	.323	121-0-8	.182	3	106	2	38	1.3
Spoljaric, Paul	Paul Nikola; B9.24.1970 Kelowna BC, Can.; BR/TL/6´3˝/(205–212); d4.6																									
1994	Tor A	0	1	.000	2	1	0	0-0	2.1	5	10	3	0	9-1	2	38.57	13	.417	.667	0	ø	0	75	-8	0	-1.1
1996	Tor A	2	2	.500	28	0	0	1-0	38	30	17	6	2	19-1	38	3.08	163	.214	.315	0	ø	0	—	7	24	0.7
1997	Tor A	0	3	.000	37	0	0	3-0	48	37	17	3	2	21-4	43	3.19	144	.215	.305	1	.000	-0	—	8	17	0.6
	†Sea A	0	0	ø	20	0	0	0-2	22.2	24	13	1	1	15-2	27	4.76	95	.276	.388	0	ø	0	—	-1	0	0.0
	Year	0	3	.000	57	0	0	3-2	70.2	61	30	4	3	36-6	70	3.69	124	.236	.333	1	.000	-0	—	7	0	0.6
1998	Sea A	4	6	.400	53	6	0	0-2	83.1	85	67	14	1	55-3	89	6.48	72	.263	.369	0	ø	0	83	-17	0	-1.7
1999	Phi N	0	3	.000	5	3	0	0-0	11.1	23	24	1	1	7-0	10	15.09	31	.426	.492	2-0-2	.000	-0	72	-14	0	-2.2
	Tor A	2	2	.500	37	2	0	0-1	62	62	41	9	2	32-2	63	4.65	106	.258	.347	0	ø	0	76	-1	0	0.0
2000	KC A	0	0	ø	13	0	0	0-0	9.2	9	7	4	0	5-0	6	6.52	80	.265	.359	0	ø	0	—	-1	23	0.0
Total	6	8	17	.320	195	12	0	4-5	277.1	275	196	41	9	163-13	278	5.52	87	.259	.359	3-0-2	.000	-0	78	-27	64	-3.7
Spongberg, Karl	Karl Gustave; B5.21.1884 Idaho Falls ID; D7.21.1938 Los Angeles CA; BR/TR/6´2˝/208; d8.1																									
1908	Chi N	0	0	ø	1	0	0	0	7	9	7	1	2	6	4	9.00	26	.321	.472	3	.667	1	—	-4	—	-0.1

YEAR	TM LG	W	L	PCT	G	GS	CG-SHO	SV-BS	IP	H	R	HR	HB	BB-IB	SO	ERA	AERA	OAV	OOB	AB-HR-SH	AVG	PB	SUP	APR	DL	PW
Spooner, Karl	Karl Benjamin; B6.23.1931 Oriskany Falls NY; D4.10.1984 Vero Beach FL; BR/TL/6´0˝/(180–185); d9.22																									
1954	Bro N	2	0	1.000	2	2	2-2	0	18	7	0	0	0	6	27	0.00	ø	.113	.191	6	.167	0	44	8	0	1.1
1955	†Bro N	8	6	.571	29	14	2-1	2	98.2	79	50	8	5	41-1	78	3.65	111	.215	.300	28-0-2	.286	3	110	3	0	0.7
Total	2	10	6	.625	31	16	4-3	2	116.2	86	50	8	5	47-1	105	3.09	132	.200	.285	34-0-2	.265	3	101	11	0	1.8
Spooneybarger, Tim	Timothy Floyd; B10.21.1979 San Diego CA; BR/TR/6´3˝/190; [AtlN98 29/881]; d9.5; Col Okaloosa–Walton (FL) CC; [DL 2004 Fla N 183, 2005 Fla N 183]																									
2001	Atl N	0	1	.000	4	0	0	0-0	4	5	1	0	0	2-1	3	2.25	192	.313	.368	0	ø	0	—	1	0	0.2
2002	Atl N	1	0	1.000	51	0	0	1-0	51.1	38	16	4	2	26-5	33	2.63	154	.207	.310	1	.000	-0	—	8	0	0.4
2003	Fla N	1	2	.333	33	0	0	0-1	42	27	21	1	1	11-0	32	4.07	101	.190	.248	3	.000	-0	—	0	0	0.0
Total	3	2	3	.400	88	0	0	1-1	97.1	70	38	5	3	39-6	68	3.24	126	.205	.288	4	.000	-0	—	9	366	0.6
Spradlin, Jerry	Jerry Carl; B6.14.1967 Fullerton CA; BB/TR/6´7˝/(230–260); [CinN88 19/488]; d7.2; Col Fullerton (CA) JC																									
1993	Cin N	2	1	.667	37	0	0	2-1	49	44	20	4	0	9-0	24	3.49	116	.249	.279	2	.000	-0	—	3	0	0.1
1994	Cin N	0	0	ø	6	0	0	0-0	8	12	11	2	0	2-0	4	10.13	41	.353	.368	0	ø	0	—	-6	0	-0.3
1996	Cin N	0	0	ø	1	0	0	0-0	0.1	0	0	0	0	0-0	0	0.00	ø	.000	.000	0	ø	0	—	0	0	0.0
1997	Phi N	4	8	.333	76	0	0	1-4	81.2	86	45	9	1	27-3	67	4.74	89	.274	.331	1	.000	-0	—	-4	0	-0.6
1998	Phi N	4	4	.500	69	0	0	1-3	81.2	63	34	9	2	20-1	76	3.53	123	.216	.270	1	1.000	1	—	7	0	0.7
1999	Cle A	0	0	ø	4	0	0	0-0	3	6	6	1	0	3-0	2	18.00	28	.400	.500	0	ø	0	—	-4	0	-0.2
	SF N	3	1	.750	59	0	0	0-1	58	59	31	4	10	29-6	52	4.19	102	.259	.367	1	.000	-0	—	0	0	-0.1
2000	KC A	4	4	.500	50	0	0	7-4	75	81	49	9	3	27-2	54	5.52	95	.283	.350	0	ø	0	—	-2	0	-0.3
	Chi N	0	1	.000	8	1	0	0-0	15	20	15	2	1	5-1	13	8.40	54	.328	.377	1	.000	-0	80	-7	0	-0.4
Total	7	17	19	.472	310	1	0	11-13	371.2	371	211	40	17	122-13	292	4.75	94	.264	.327	6	.167	0	80	-13	0	-1.1
Spragins, Homer	Homer Franklin; B11.9.1920 Grenada MS; D12.10.2002 Minter City MS; BR/TR/6´1˝/190; d9.13; Col Mississippi St.																									
1947	Phi N	0	0	ø	4	0	0	0	5.1	3	4	0	0	3	3	6.75	59	.158	.273	0	ø	0	—	-1	0	-0.1
Sprague, Charlie	Charles Wellington; B10.10.1864 Cleveland OH; D12.31.1912 Des Moines IA; BL/TL/5´11˝/150; d9.17; ▲																									
1887	Chi N	1	0	1.000	3	3	2	0	22	24	16	1	4	13	9	4.91	92	.276	.394	13	.154	-1	82	0	—	-0.1
1889	Cle N	0	2	.000	2	2	2	0	17	27	31	0	2	10	8	8.47	48	.351	.438	7	.143	-0	117	-11	—	-0.8
1890	Tol AA	9	5	.643	19	12	9	0	122.2	111	83	0	18	78	59	3.89	102	.234	.363	199-1	.236	3*	145	0	—	0.1
Total	3	10	7	.588	24	17	13	0	161.2	162	130	1	24	101	76	4.51	89	.254	.376	219-1	.228	1	130	-11	—	-0.8
Sprague, Ed	Edward Nelson Sr.; B9.16.1945 Boston MA; BR/TR/6´4˝/(190–195); d4.10; s–Ed																									
1968	Oak A	3	4	.429	47	1	0	4	68.2	51	29	5	2	34-5	34	3.28	86	.209	.309	7	.000	-1	62	-4	0	-0.5
1969	Oak A	1	1	.500	27	0	0	2-1	46.1	47	24	4	2	31-6	20	4.47	77	.267	.383	5-0-2	.200	0	—	-5	0	-0.1
1971	Cin N	1	0	1.000	7	0	0	0-1	11	8	2	0	0	1-0	7	0.00	ø	.195	.209	1	.000	-0	—	3	0	0.3
1972	Cin N	3	3	.500	33	1	0	0-0	56.2	55	33	6	3	26-3	25	4.13	79	.261	.347	7	.000	-1	82	-8	0	-0.9
1973	Cin N	1	3	.250	28	0	0	1-0	38.2	35	22	3	2	22-7	19	5.12	67	.246	.353	2-0-1	.000	-0	—	-7	0	-0.7
	StL N	0	0	ø	8	0	0	0-1	8	8	2	1	0	4-0	2	2.25	163	.276	.353	0	ø	0	—	1	0	0.1
	Year	1	3	.250	36	0	0	1-1	46.2	43	24	4	2	26-7	21	4.63	75	.251	.353	2-0-1	.000	-0	—	-5	0	-0.6
	Mil A	0	1	.000	7	0	0	1-2	9.2	13	11	0	2	14-5	3	9.31	41	.317	.492	0	ø	0	—	-6	0	-0.7
1974	Mil A	7	2	.778	20	10	3	0-0	94	94	32	3	4	31-0	57	2.39	152	.266	.327	0	ø	0	160	11	47	1.0
1975	Mil A	1	7	.125	18	11	0	1-0	67.1	81	46	5	2	40-3	21	4.68	82	.297	.389	0	ø	0	87	-9	64	-1.0
1976	Mil A	0	2	.000	3	0	0	0-0	7.2	14	7	0	0	3-1	0	7.04	50	.438	.472	0	ø	0	—	-3	41	-0.6
Total	8	17	23	.425	198	23	3	9-5	408	406	208	27	17	206-30	188	3.84	89	.263	.353	22-0-3	.045	-1	126	-27	152	-3.1
Spring, Jack	Jack Russell; B3.11.1933 Spokane WA; BR/TL/6´1˝/(167–182); d4.16; Col Washington St.																									
1955	Phi N	0	1	.000	2	0	0	0	2.2	2	2	2	0	1-0	2	6.75	59	.200	.273	1	.000	-0	—	-1	0	-0.2
1957	Bos A	0	0	ø	1	0	0	0	1	0	0	0	0	0-0	2	0.00	ø	.000	.000	0	ø	0	—	0	0	0.0
1958	Was A	0	0	ø	3	1	0	0	7	16	11	1	0	7-3	1	14.14	27	.457	.535	2	.000	-0	259	-8	0	-0.4
1961	LA A	3	0	1.000	18	4	0	0	38	35	19	4	3	15-2	27	4.26	106	.243	.323	8-0-3	.000	-1	123	2	0	0.0
1962	LA A	4	2	.667	57	0	0	6	65	66	32	7	2	30-10	31	4.02	96	.270	.353	11-0-1	.091	-1	—	0	0	-0.1
1963	LA A	3	0	1.000	45	0	0	2	38.1	40	18	3	0	9-0	13	3.05	112	.268	.310	3	.333	0	—	0	0	0.1
1964	LA A	1	0	1.000	6	0	0	0	3.1	3	1	1	0	3-1	0	2.70	122	.273	.429	0	ø	0	—	0	0	0.1
	Chi N	0	0	ø	7	0	0	0	6	4	5	0	0	2-0	1	6.00	62	.200	.261	0	ø	0	—	-2	0	-0.1
	StL N	0	0	ø	2	0	0	0	3	8	9	1	0	1-1	0	3.00	127	.471	.500	0	ø	0	—	-3	0	-0.1
	Year	0	0	ø	9	0	0	0	9	12	14	1	0	3-1	1	5.00	75	.324	.366	0	ø	0	—	-5	0	-0.2
1965	Cle A	1	2	.333	14	0	0	0	21.2	21	9	2	0	10-1	9	3.74	93	.259	.337	3-0-1	.333	0	—	0	0	0.0
Total	8	12	5	.706	155	5	0	8	186	195	106	21	5	78-18	86	4.26	90	.273	.346	28-0-5	.107	-1	167	-12	0	-0.7
Springer, Brad	Bradford Louis; B5.9.1904 Detroit MI; D1.4.1970 Birmingham MI; BL/TL/6´0˝/155; d5.1																									
1925	StL A	0	0	ø	2	0	0	0	3	1	2	0	0	7	0	3.00	156	.200	.667	0	ø	0	—	0	—	0.0
1926	Cin N	0	0	ø	1	0	0	0	1.1	2	3	0	1	2	1	6.75	55	.286	.500	1	.000	-0	—	-1	—	-0.1
Total	2	0	0	ø	3	0	0	0	4.1	3	5	0	1	9	1	4.15	105	.250	.591	1	.000	-0	—	-1	—	-0.1
Springer, Dennis	Dennis Leroy; B2.12.1965 Fresno CA; BR/TR/5´10˝/(185–190); [LAN87 21/534]; d9.13; Col Cal St.–Fresno																									
1995	Phi N	0	3	.000	4	4	0	0-0	22.1	21	15	3	1	9-1	15	4.84	87	.256	.337	8	.125	-0	75	-2	0	-0.3
1996	Cal A	5	6	.455	20	15	2-1	0-0	94.2	91	65	24	6	43-0	64	5.51	92	.251	.339	0	ø	0	104	-5	0	-0.5
1997	Ana A	9	9	.500	32	28	3-1	0-0	194.2	199	118	32	10	73-0	75	5.18	89	.267	.335	3	.000	-0	97	-10	0	-0.9
1998	TB A	3	11	.214	29	17	1	0-0	115.2	120	77	21	12	60-1	46	5.45	88	.271	.372	1	.000	-0	59	-9	0	-1.0
1999	Fla N	6	16	.273	38	29	3-2	1-0	196.1	231	121	23	7	64-4	83	4.86	90	.303	.358	50-0-3	.120	-2	83	-13	0	-1.4
2000	NY N	0	1	.000	2	2	0	0-0	11.1	20	11	2	1	5-0	5	8.74	50	.377	.441	4	.000	-0	84	-5	0	-0.4
2001	LA N	1	1	.500	4	3	0	0-0	19	19	7	3	3	2-0	7	3.32	124	.275	.324	6-0-1	.000	-1	119	2	0	0.1
2002	LA N	0	1	.000	1	0	0	0-0	1.1	1	1	0	0	2-0	1	6.75	58	.200	.429	0	ø	0	—	0	0	-0.1
Total	8	24	48	.333	130	98	9-4	1-0	655.1	702	415	108	40	258-6	296	5.18	89	.278	.351	72-0-4	.097	-4	87	-42	0	-4.5
Springer, Ed	Edward H.; B2.9.1861 CA; D4.24.1926 Los Angeles Co. CA; 6´2˝/187; d7.12																									
1889	Lou AA	0	1	.000	1	1	1	0	5	8	8	0	2	2	1	9.00	43	.348	.444	2	.000	-0	16	-3	—	-0.4
Springer, Russ	Russell Paul; B11.7.1968 Alexandria LA; BR/TR/6´4˝/(195–215); [NYA89 7/181]; d4.17; Col Louisiana St.																									
1992	NY A	0	0	ø	14	0	0	0-0	16	18	11	0	1	10-0	12	6.19	64	.281	.387	0	ø	0	—	-3	0	-0.2
1993	Cal A	1	6	.143	14	9	1	0-0	60	73	48	11	3	32-1	31	7.20	63	.303	.390	0	ø	0	90	-15	63	-1.5
1994	Cal A	2	2	.500	18	5	0	2-1	45.2	53	28	9	0	14-0	28	5.52	89	.291	.340	0	ø	0	124	-2	0	-0.2
1995	Cal A	1	2	.333	19	6	0	1-1	51.2	60	37	11	5	25-1	38	6.10	77	.290	.380	0	ø	0	115	-8	0	-0.4
	Phi N	0	0	ø	14	0	0	0-0	26.2	22	11	5	2	10-3	32	3.71	114	.227	.306	1-0-1	.000	-0	—	2	0	0.1
1996	Phi N	3	10	.231	51	7	0	0-3	96.2	106	60	12	1	38-6	94	4.66	93	.272	.336	17-0-2	.059	-1	78	-5	0	-0.8
1997	†Hou N	3	3	.500	54	0	0	3-4	55.1	48	28	4	4	27-2	74	4.23	95	.232	.329	1	.000	-0	—	-1	23	-0.1
1998	Ari N	4	3	.571	26	0	0	0-3	32.2	29	16	4	1	14-1	37	4.13	104	.232	.314	1	.000	-0	—	1	0	0.1
	Atl N	1	1	.500	22	0	0	0-1	20	22	10	0	0	16-3	19	4.05	103	.301	.422	0	ø	0	—	0	15	0.0
	Year	5	4	.556	48	0	0	0-4	52.2	51	26	4	1	30-4	56	4.10	103	.258	.357	1	.000	-0	—	1	0	0.1
1999	†Atl N	2	1	.667	49	0	0	1-0	47.1	31	20	5	2	22-2	49	3.42	131	.185	.284	0	ø	0	—	6	42	0.3
2000	Ari N	2	4	.333	52	0	0	0-2	62	63	36	11	2	34-6	59	5.08	94	.261	.354	5	.200	-0	—	-1	0	-0.1
2001	Ari N	0	0	ø	18	0	0	1-0	17.2	20	16	5	0	4-0	12	7.13	65	.274	.308	0	ø	0	—	-5	138	-0.2
2003	StL N	1	1	.500	17	0	0	0-1	17.1	19	16	8	1	6-0	11	8.31	50	.271	.338	1-0-1	.000	-0	—	-8	121	-0.8
2004	†Hou N	0	1	.000	16	0	0	0-0	13.2	15	4	1	1	6-0	9	2.63	166	.278	.355	0	ø	0	—	3	0	0.2
2005	†Hou N	4	4	.500	62	0	0	0-3	59	49	34	9	3	21-3	54	4.73	89	.222	.298	0	ø	0	—	-4	0	-0.5
2006	Hou N	1	1	.500	72	0	0	0-0	59.2	46	23	10	4	16-1	46	3.47	130	.211	.277	0	ø	0	—	8	0	0.3
Total	14	25	39	.391	518	27	1	8-19	681.1	674	398	105	30	295-29	605	4.94	90	.256	.336	26-0-4	.077	-2	103	-32	402	-3.8
Sproull, Charlie	Charles William; B1.9.1919 Taylorsville GA; D1.13.1980 Rockford IL; BR/TR/6´3˝/185; d4.19																									
1945	Phi N	4	10	.286	34	19	2	1	130.1	158	102	10	0	80	47	5.94	65	.298	.390	35-0-3	.143	-1	92	-28	0	-2.8
Sprout, Bob	Robert Samuel; B12.5.1941 Florin PA; BL/TL/6´0˝/165; d9.27																									
1961	LA A	0	0	ø	1	1	0	0	4	4	3	0	0	3-0	2	4.50	100	.267	.389	0-0-1	ø	0	157	0	0	0.0

YEAR	TM LG	W	L	PCT	G	GS	CG-SHO	SV-BS	IP	H	R	HR	HB	BB-IB	SO	ERA	AERA	OAV	OOB	AB-HR-SH	AVG	PB	SUP	APR	DL	PW
SPROWL, BOBBY	Robert John; B4.14.1956 Sandusky OH; BL/TL/6´2˝/190; [BosA77 2/39]; d9.5; Col Alabama																									
1978	Bos A	0	2	.000	3	3	0	0-0	12.2	12	10	3	0	10-0	10	6.39	64	.245	.373	0	ø	0	73	-3	0	-0.4
1979	Hou N	0	0	ø	3	0	0	0-0	4	1	0	0	0	2-0	3	0.00	ø	.083	.214	0	ø	0	—	2	0	0.1
1980	Hou N	0	0	ø	1	0	0	0-0	1	1	0	0	0	1-0	3	0.00	ø	.250	.400	0	ø	0	—	0	0	0.0
1981	Hou N	0	1	.000	15	1	0	0-0	28.2	40	20	1	0	14-1	18	5.97	55	.333	.397	6	.167	-0	162	-8	0	-0.5
Total	4	0	3	.000	22	4	0	0-0	46.1	54	30	4	0	27-1	34	5.44	65	.292	.379	6	.167	-0	101	-9	0	-0.8
SPURGEON, JAY	Jay Aaron; B7.5.1976 West Covina CA; BR/TR/6´6˝/211; [BalA97 8/255]; d8.15; Col Hawaii–Manoa																									
2000	Bal A	1	1	.500	7	4	0	0-0	24	26	16	5	2	15-0	11	6.00	78	.283	.394	0	ø	0	115	-3	0	-0.2
SPURLING, CHRIS	Christopher Michael; B6.28.1977 Dayton OH; BR/TR/6´6˝/(230–240); [NYA97 41/1246]; d4.2; Col Miami–Ohio/Sinclair (OH) CC; [DL 2004 Det A 183]																									
2003	Det A	1	3	.250	66	0	0	3-3	77	78	42	9	3	22-1	38	4.68	94	.266	.319	0	ø	0	—	-2	0	-0.2
2005	Det A	3	4	.429	56	0	0	0-1	70.2	58	30	8	2	22-6	26	3.44	124	.230	.292	0	ø	0	—	6	0	0.5
2006	Det A	0	0	ø	9	0	0	0-0	11.1	13	4	2	0	4-2	4	3.18	141	.289	.347	0	ø	0	—	2	0	0.1
	Mil N	0	0	ø	7	0	0	0-1	10	12	8	3	0	4-1	3	7.20	62	.286	.348	0	ø	0	—	-3	0	-0.1
Total	3	4	7	.364	138	0	0	3-5	169	161	84	22	5	52-10	71	4.21	103	.255	.312	0	ø	0	—	3	183	0.3
STABLEIN, GEORGE	George Charles; B10.29.1957 Inglewood CA; BR/TR/6´4˝/185; [SDN78 3/57]; d9.20; Col Cal St.–Dominguez Hills																									
1980	SD N	0	1	.000	4	2	0	0-0	11.2	16	4	0	0	3-0	4	3.09	111	.340	.380	3	.000	-0	65	1	0	0.0
STACK, EDDIE	William Edward; B10.24.1887 Chicago IL; D8.28.1958 Chicago IL; BR/TR/6´0˝/175; d6.7																									
1910	Phi N	6	7	.462	20	16	8-1	0	117	115	61	7	4	34	48	4.00	78	.266	.326	36-0-2	.083	-3	76	-8	—	-1.2
1911	Phi N	5	5	.500	13	10	5	0	77.2	67	48	3	6	41	36	3.59	96	.234	.342	24	.083	-2	85	-4	—	-0.6
1912	Bro N	7	5	.583	28	17	4	1	142	139	80	3	9	55	45	3.36	100	.264	.343	52-0-2	.135	-3	94	-3	—	-0.6
1913	Bro N	4	4	.500	23	9	4-1	0	87	79	30	0	1	32	34	2.38	138	.250	.321	25	.160	-1	97	8	—	0.5
	Chi N	4	2	.667	11	7	3-1	1	51	56	29	1	2	15	28	4.24	75	.280	.336	16-0-1	.063	-1	105	-5	—	-0.7
	Year	8	6	.571	34	16	7-2	1	138	135	59	1	3	47	62	3.07	106	.262	.327	41-0-1	.122	-2	100	5	—	-0.2
1914	Chi N	0	1	.000	7	1	0	0	16.1	13	11	0	0	11	9	4.96	56	.220	.343	4	.000	-0	0	-3	—	-0.2
Total	5	26	24	.520	102	60	24-3	2	491	469	259	14	22	188	200	3.52	93	.258	.334	157-0-5	.108	-10	88	-15	—	-2.8
STAFFORD, GENERAL	James Joseph "Jamsey"; B7.9.1868 Webster MA; D9.18.1923 Worcester MA; BR/TR/5´8˝/165; d8.27; b–John; ▲																									
1890	Buf P	3	9	.250	12	12	11	0	98	123	89	8	4	43	21	5.14	80	.294	.366	49	.143	-2*	89	-13	—	-1.2
STAFFORD, JOHN	John Henry "Doc"; B4.8.1870 Dudley MA; D7.3.1940 Worcester MA; BR/TR/5´10˝/170; d6.15; b–General; Col Holy Cross																									
1893	Cle N	0	1	.000	2	0	0	0	7	12	15	1	0	7	4	14.14	35	.364	.475	4	.000	-1	—	-6	—	-0.6
STAFFORD, BILL	William Charles; B8.13.1939 Catskill NY; D9.19.2001 Wayne MI; BR/TR/6´2˝/(185–198); d8.17																									
1960	†NY A	3	1	.750	11	8	2-1	0	60	50	17	3	1	18-0	36	2.25	159	.226	.286	22	.045	-2*	80	10	0	0.4
1961	†NY A	14	9	.609	36	25	8-3	2	195	168	65	13	5	59-4	101	2.68	139	.232	.294	67-0-3	.179	2	120	24	0	2.8
1962	†NY A	14	9	.609	35	33	7-2	0	213.1	188	95	23	4	77-6	109	3.67	102	.233	.301	78-0-4	.218	3	130	3	0	0.5
1963	NY A	4	8	.333	28	14	0	3	89.2	104	64	16	3	42-3	52	6.02	58	.287	.363	24-0-2	.292	3	117	-25	0	-2.9
1964	NY A	5	0	1.000	31	1	0	4	60.2	50	19	4	2	22-7	39	2.67	136	.231	.308	13	.077	-1	270	7	0	0.6
1965	NY A	3	8	.273	22	15	1	0	111.1	93	45	16	2	31-4	71	3.56	96	.229	.284	29-0-4	.000	-3	89	0	32	-0.3
1966	KC A	0	4	.000	9	8	0	0	39.2	42	28	2	2	12-1	31	4.99	68	.273	.327	11-0-2	.000	-1	68	-8	0	-0.9
1967	KC A	0	1	.000	14	0	0	0	16	12	4	0	0	9-2	10	1.69	189	.214	.323	1-0-1	.000	-0	—	2	0	0.1
Total	8	43	40	.518	186	104	18-6	9	785.2	707	337	77	19	270-27	449	3.52	103	.240	.306	245-0-16	.155	0	113	13	32	0.3
STALEY, GERRY	Gerald Lee; B8.21.1920 Brush Prairie WA; BR/TR/6´0˝/(185–195); d4.20																									
1947	StL N	1	0	1.000	18	1	1	0	29.1	33	11	2	1	8	14	2.76	150	.287	.339	6	.000	-1	64	4	0	0.2
1948	StL N	4	4	.500	31	3	0	0	52	61	44	5	0	21	23	6.92	59	.288	.352	9-1-1	.222	1	123	-16	0	-2.0
1949	StL N	10	10	.500	45	17	5-2	6	171.1	154	65	6	3	41	55	2.73	152	**.238**	.286	41-0-6	.122	-0	73	24	0	2.9
1950	StL N	13	13	.500	42	22	7-1	3	169.2	201	101	14	7	61	62	4.99	86	.300	.365	55-0-4	.145	-1	73	-11	0	-1.4
1951	StL N	19	13	.594	42	30	10-4	3	227	244	108	14	8	74	67	3.81	104	.275	.337	81-0-4	.160	-1	81	3	0	0.3
1952	StL N☆	17	14	.548	35	33	15	0	239.2	238	101	21	7	52	93	3.27	114	.256	.301	85-0-7	.153	-2	121	11	0	1.3
1953	StL N☆	18	9	.667	40	32	10-1	4	230	243	118	31	17	54	88	3.99	107	.269	.322	78-0-7	.103	-5	105	4	0	0.0
1954	StL N	7	13	.350	48	20	3-1	2	155.2	198	107	21	6	47	50	5.26	78	.308	.357	36-0-7	.139	-0	126	-21	0	-2.3
1955	Cin N	5	8	.385	30	18	2	0	119.2	146	72	22	3	28-3	40	4.66	91	.309	.347	36-0-4	.056	-4	97	-6	0	-0.9
	NY A	0	0	ø	2	0	0	0	2	5	5	1	0	1-0	0	13.50	28	.417	.462	0	ø	0	—	-3	0	-0.1
1956	NY A	0	0	ø	1	0	0	0	0.1	4	4	0	0	0-0	1	108.00	4	.800	.800	1	.000	-0	—	-4	0	-0.2
	Chi A	8	3	.727	26	10	5	0	101.2	98	37	11	6	20-3	25	2.92	140	.251	.297	32-0-1	.094	-2	122	13	0	1.0
	Year	8	3	.727	27	10	5	0	102	102	41	11	6	20-3	26	3.26	126	.258	.303	33-0-1	.091	-3	122	10	0	0.8
1957	Chi A	5	1	.833	47	0	0	7	105	95	27	7	0	27-9	44	2.06	182	.244	.293	22-0-4	.045	-1	—	**19**	0	1.3
1958	Chi A	4	5	.444	50	0	0	8	85.1	81	36	10	0	24-3	27	3.16	115	.259	.307	11-0-1	.000	-1	—	3	0	0.4
1959	†Chi A	8	5	.615	**67**	0	0	14	116.1	111	39	5	0	25-9	54	2.24	167	.259	.298	13-0-4	.154	0	—	**17**	0	2.3
1960	Chi A★	13	8	.619	64	0	0	10	115.1	94	40	8	3	25-7	52	2.42	156	.227	.271	17-0-1	.235	1	—	**15**	0	**3.2**
1961	Chi A	0	3	.000	16	0	0	0	18	17	10	3	0	5-1	8	5.00	78	.246	.297	0	ø	0	—	-2	0	-0.2
	KC A	1	1	.500	23	0	0	2	30	32	15	4	2	10-1	16	3.60	116	.278	.341	1	.000	0	—	1	0	0.2
	Det A	1	1	.500	13	0	0	2	13.1	15	6	1	0	6-1	8	3.38	121	.288	.356	1	.000	-0	—	1	0	0.2
	Year	2	5	.286	52	0	0	4	61.1	64	31	8	2	21-3	32	3.96	103	.271	.332	2	.000	0	—	0	0	0.2
Total	15	134	111	.547	640	186	58-9	61	1981.2	2070	946	186	63	529-37	727	3.70	108	.270	.321	525-1-51	.126	-16	101	52	0	6.2
STALEY, HARRY	Henry Eli; B11.3.1866 Jacksonville IL; D1.12.1910 Battle Creek MI; BR/TR/5´10˝/175; d6.23																									
1888	Pit N	12	12	.500	25	24	24-2	0	207.1	185	104	6	7	53	89	2.69	98	.235	.289	85	.129	-4	105	-3	—	-0.7
1889	Pit N	21	26	.447	49	47	46-1	1	420	433	254	11	8	116	159	3.51	107	.259	.310	186	.161	-7*	90	4	—	-0.1
1890	Pit P	21	25	.457	46	46	44-3	0	387.2	392	246	5	11	74	145	3.23	121	.251	**.290**	164-1	.207	1*	85	29	—	2.5
1891	Pit N	4	5	.444	9	7	6	0	71.2	77	49	4	2	11	25	2.89	114	.265	.296	31	.226	1	122	2	—	0.3
	Bos N	20	8	.714	31	30	26-1	0	252.1	236	111	12	4	69	114	2.50	146	.238	.290	102-1	.167	-2	99	32	—	2.8
	Year	24	13	.649	40	37	32-1	0	324	313	160	16	6	80	139	2.58	138	.244	**.292**	133-1	.180	-1	103	36	—	3.1
1892	†Bos N	22	10	.688	37	35	31-3	0	299.2	273	144	10	3	97	93	3.03	116	.233	.293	122-1	.131	-6*	106	18	—	1.0
1893	Bos N	18	10	.643	36	31	23	0	263	344	224	22	6	81	61	5.13	96	.307	.356	113-2	.265	3	132	-11	—	-0.7
1894	Bos N	12	10	.545	27	21	18	1	208.2	305	204	15	5	61	32	6.81	83	.337	.382	85-2-2	.235	0*	126	-18	—	-1.4
1895	StL N	6	13	.316	23	16	13	0	158.2	223	136	8	2	39	28	5.22	93	.327	.365	67-0-2	.134	-6	96	-9	—	-1.4
Total	8	136	119	.533	283	257	231-10	2	2269	2468	1472	93	48	601	746	3.80	105	.269	.317	955-7-4	.182	-19	104	44	—	2.3
STALLARD, TRACY	Evan Tracy; B8.31.1937 Coeburn VA; BR/TR/6´5˝/(204–205); d9.24																									
1960	Bos A	0	0	ø	4	0	0	0	4	0	0	0	0	2-0	6	0.00	ø	.000	.133	0	ø	0	—	2	0	0.1
1961	Bos A	2	7	.222	43	14	1	2	132.2	110	75	15	1	96-2	109	4.88	85	.229	.354	36-0-4	.083	-2	91	-7	0	-0.8
1962	Bos A	0	0	ø	1	0	0	0	1	0	0	0	0	0-0	0	0.00	ø	.000	.000	0	ø	0	—	0	0	0.0
1963	NY N	6	17	.261	39	23	5	1	154.2	156	89	23	1	77-6	110	4.71	74	.262	.344	48-0-2	.063	-3	89	-17	0	-2.8
1964	NY N	10	20	.333	36	34	11-2	0	225.2	213	111	20	6	73-3	118	3.79	94	.252	.314	79-0-1	.190	2	81	-6	0	-0.7
1965	StL N	11	8	.579	40	26	4-1	0	194.1	172	83	25	6	70-4	99	3.38	114	.235	.304	68-0-4	.088	-4	104	8	0	0.2
1966	StL N	1	5	.167	20	7	0	1	52.1	65	40	9	2	25-4	35	5.68	63	.305	.383	14	.000	-2	116	-13	0	-1.6
Total	7	30	57	.345	183	104	21-3	4	764.2	716	398	92	16	343-19	477	4.17	90	.248	.329	245-0-11	.110	-9	92	-33	0	-5.6
STANCEU, CHARLEY	Charles; B1.9.1916 Canton OH; D4.3.1969 Canton OH; BR/TR/6´2˝/190; d4.16; Mil 1942–45																									
1941	NY A	3	3	.500	22	2	0	0	48	58	41	3	1	35	21	5.63	70	.296	.405	12	.000	-2	77	-12	0	-1.5
1946	NY A	0	0	ø	3	0	0	0	4	6	4	0	0	5	3	9.00	38	.316	.458	0	ø	0	—	-2	0	-0.1
	Phi N	2	4	.333	14	11	1	0	70.1	71	35	4	0	39	23	4.22	81	.270	.364	19-0-1	.000	-2	79	-5	0	-0.6
Total	2	5	7	.417	39	13	1	0	122.1	135	80	7	1	79	47	4.93	74	.282	.385	31-0-1	.000	-4	76	-19	0	-2.2
STANDRIDGE, PETE	Alfred Peter; B4.25.1891 Black Diamond WA; D8.2.1963 San Francisco CA; BR/TR/5´10.5˝/165; d9.19																									
1911	StL N	0	0	ø	2	0	0	0	4.2	10	10	0	1	4	3	9.64	35	.435	.536	1	.000	-0	—	-5	—	-0.2
1915	Chi N	4	1	.800	29	3	2	0	112.1	120	56	2	2	36	42	3.61	77	.274	.332	40-0-1	.225	3*	268	-10	—	-0.3
Total	2	4	1	.800	31	3	2	0	117	130	66	2	3	40	45	3.85	73	.282	.343	41-0-1	.220	3	268	-15	—	-0.5

YEAR	TM LG	W	L	PCT	G	GS	CG-SHO	SV-BS	IP	H	R	HR	HB	BB-IB	SO	ERA	AERA	OAV	OOB	AB-HR-SH	AVG	PB	SUP	APR	DL	PW
STANDRIDGE, JASON	Jason Wayne; B11.9.1978 Birmingham AL; BR/TR/6´4˝/(217–230); [TBA97 1/31]; d7.29																									
2001	TB A	0	0	ø	9	1	0	0-0	19.1	19	10	5	0	14-1	9	4.66	97	.260	.379	0	ø	0	62	0	0	0.0
2002	TB A	0	0	ø	1	0	0	0-0	3	7	3	1	0	4-0	1	9.00	50	.500	.611	0	ø	0	—	-1	0	-0.1
2003	TB A	0	5	.000	8	7	1	0-0	35.1	38	25	7	1	16-0	20	6.37	72	.275	.353	0	ø	0	55	-6	0	-0.7
2004	TB A	0	0	ø	3	1	0	0-0	10	14	10	5	0	4-0	7	9.00	52	.326	.375	0	ø	0	99	-4	50	-0.2
2005	Tex A	0	0	ø	2	0	0	0-0	2.1	7	3	0	0	1-1	2	11.57	39	.467	.500	0	ø	0	—	-2	0	-0.1
	Cin N	2	2	.500	32	0	0	0-0	31	38	14	3	1	16-7	17	4.06	105	.314	.399	0	ø	0	—	1	0	0.1
2006	Cin N	1	1	.500	21	0	0	0-0	18.2	17	14	2	1	14-0	18	4.82	98	.243	.376	0	ø	0	—	-1	25	-0.1
Total	6	3	8	.273	76	9	1	0-0	119.2	140	79	23	3	69-9	74	5.64	80	.295	.387	0	ø	0	62	-13	75	-1.1
STANEK, AL	Albert Wilfred "Lefty"; B12.24.1943 Springfield MA; BL/TL/5´11.5˝/187; d4.26																									
1963	SF N	0	0	ø	11	0	0	0	13.1	10	7	1	0	12-2	5	4.73	68	.217	.379	1	.000	-0	—	-2	0	-0.1
STANFIELD, KEVIN	Kevin Bruce; B12.19.1955 Huron SD; BL/TL/6´0˝/195; [MinA76*7/126]; d9.14; Col San Bernardino Valley (CA) JC																									
1979	Min A	0	0	ø	3	0	0	0-0	3	2	2	0	0	0-0	0	6.00	73	.200	.200	0	ø	0	—	0	0	0.0
STANFORD, JASON	Jason John; B1.23.1977 Tucson AZ; BL/TL/6´2˝/200; d7.6; Col North Carolina–Charlotte; [DL 2005 Cle A 120]																									
2003	Cle A	1	3	.250	13	8	0	0-0	50	48	20	5	1	16-1	30	3.60	123	.246	.305	0	ø	0	68	6	0	0.4
2004	Cle A	0	1	.000	2	2	0	0-0	11	12	1	0	1	5-0	5	0.82	531	.279	.367	0	ø	0	11	5	171	0.4
Total	2	1	4	.200	15	10	0	0-0	61	60	21	5	2	21-1	35	3.10	143	.252	.317	0	ø	0	56	11	291	0.8
STANGE, LEE	Albert Lee; B10.27.1936 Chicago IL; BR/TR/5´10˝/(168–175); d4.15; C12; Col Drake																									
1961	Min A	1	0	1.000	7	0	0	0	12.1	15	6	1	0	10-1	10	2.92	145	.294	.410	1	.000	-0	—	1	0	0.1
1962	Min A	4	3	.571	44	6	1	3	95	98	57	14	1	39-3	70	4.45	92	.271	.342	17-0-2	.059	-1	160	-6	0	-0.5
1963	Min A	12	5	.706	32	20	7-2	0	164.2	145	53	21	0	43-1	100	2.62	139	.233	.283	52-0-3	.096	-1	130	19	0	1.8
1964	Min A	3	6	.333	14	11	2	0	79.2	78	45	13	0	19-3	54	4.74	75	.255	.297	25	.040	-1	133	-9	0	-1.0
	Cle A	4	8	.333	23	14	0	0	91.2	98	47	14	1	31-4	78	4.12	87	.270	.329	25-0-2	.080	-1*	95	-5	0	-0.8
	Year	7	14	.333	37	25	2	0	171.1	176	92	27	1	50-7	132	4.41	81	.263	.314	50-0-2	.060	-2	112	-14	0	-1.8
1965	Cle A	8	4	.667	41	12	4-2	0	132	122	50	13	1	26-6	80	3.34	104	.247	.284	28-0-4	.107	1	99	5	0	0.4
1966	Cle A	1	0	1.000	8	2	1	0	16	17	5	1	1	3-0	8	2.81	122	.279	.318	4-0-1	.250	0	64	1	0	0.1
	Bos A	7	9	.438	28	19	8-2	0	153.1	140	65	17	1	43-9	77	3.35	114	.246	.296	48-0-3	.063	-3	76	7	0	0.3
	Year	8	9	.471	36	21	9-2	0	169.1	157	70	18	2	46-9	85	3.30	114	.249	.298	52-0-4	.077	-3	75	9	0	0.4
1967	†Bos A	8	10	.444	35	24	6-2	1	181.2	171	64	14	2	32-7	101	2.77	126	.246	.281	49-0-6	.061	-3	99	13	0	0.9
1968	Bos A	5	5	.500	50	2	1	12	103	89	54	10	1	25-5	53	3.93	80	.237	.280	15-0-2	.133	0	83	-10	0	-1.3
1969	Bos A	6	9	.400	41	15	2	3-1	137	137	70	14	6	56-8	59	3.68	104	.256	.332	35-0-8	.086	-2	96	0	0	-0.3
1970	Bos A	2	2	.500	20	0	0	2-0	27.1	34	24	5	2	12-3	14	5.60	71	.301	.369	5-0-1	.000	-0	—	-6	0	-1.0
	Chi A	1	0	1.000	16	0	0	0-1	22.1	28	13	5	0	5-1	14	5.24	74	.295	.330	1	.000	-0	—	-2	0	-0.2
	Year	3	2	.600	36	0	0	2-1	49.2	62	37	10	2	17-4	28	5.44	72	.298	.352	6-0-1	.000	-0	—	-9	0	-1.2
Total	10	62	61	.504	359	125	32-8	21-2	1216	1172	553	142	16	344-51	718	3.56	102	.252	.304	305-0-32	.079	-11	105	8	0	-1.5
STANHOUSE, DON	Donald Joseph; B2.12.1951 DuQuoin IL; BR/TR/6´2˝/(185–198); [OakA69 1/9]; d4.19																									
1972	Tex A	2	9	.182	24	16	1	0-0	104.2	83	48	8	1	73-5	78	3.78	81	.223	.347	31-0-2	.129	-0*	62	-7	31	-0.7
1973	Tex A	1	7	.125	21	5	1	1-1	70	70	41	5	2	44-3	42	4.76	79	.262	.368	0	ø	0*	100	-7	0	-0.7
1974	Tex A	1	1	.500	18	0	0	0-0	31.1	38	20	4	2	17-0	26	4.88	73	.302	.390	0	ø	0	—	-5	0	-0.3
1975	Mon N	0	0	ø	4	3	0	0-0	13	19	12	1	0	11-2	5	8.31	47	.345	.448	3	.333	0	106	-5	0	-0.3
1976	Mon N	9	12	.429	34	26	8-1	1-0	184	182	84	7	4	92-10	79	3.77	100	.263	.351	52-0-4	.212	2	70	2	0	0.6
1977	Mon N	10	10	.500	47	16	1-1	10-2	158.1	147	72	12	4	84-9	89	3.41	113	.251	.346	47-1-4	.191	1	102	6	0	0.8
1978	Bal A	6	9	.400	56	0	0	24-7	74.2	60	28	0	0	52-6	42	2.89	122	.230	.348	0	ø	0	—	5	0	1.1
1979	†Bal A☆	7	3	.700	52	0	0	21-6	72.2	49	24	4	1	51-7	34	2.85	142	.202	.333	0	ø	0	—	11	0	2.1
1980	LA N	2	2	.500	21	0	0	7-5	25	30	14	4	0	16-3	5	5.04	69	.306	.400	2	.000	0	—	-4	92	-0.7
1982	Bal A	0	1	.000	17	0	0	0-0	26.2	29	16	3	2	15-1	8	5.40	75	.276	.377	0	ø	0	—	-4	45	-0.2
Total	10	38	54	.413	294	66	11-2	64-21	760.1	707	359	48	16	455-46	408	3.84	96	.252	.355	135-1-10	.185	3	80	-8	168	1.7
STANIFER, ROB	Robert Wayne; B3.10.1972 Easley SC; BR/TR/6´3˝/205; [FlaN94 12/320]; d5.3; Col Anderson																									
1997	Fla N	1	2	.333	36	0	0	1-1	45	43	23	9	3	16-0	28	4.60	88	.261	.337	3	.667	2	—	-2	0	0.0
1998	Fla N	2	4	.333	38	0	0	1-2	48	54	33	5	0	22-2	30	5.63	72	.277	.345	5	.000	-1	—	-9	0	-1.1
2000	Bos A	0	0	ø	8	0	0	0-0	13	22	19	3	0	4-1	3	7.62	66	.355	.394	0	ø	0	—	-7	0	-0.3
Total	3	3	6	.333	82	0	0	2-3	106	119	75	17	3	42-3	61	5.43	77	.282	.349	8	.250	1	—	-18	0	-1.4
STANKA, JOE	Joe Donald; B7.23.1931 Hammon OK; BR/TR/6´5˝/195; d9.2; Col Oklahoma St.																									
1959	Chi A	1	0	1.000	2	0	0	0	5.1	2	2	1	0	4-1	3	3.38	111	.111	.273	3	.333	0	—	0	0	0.1
STANLEY, BUCK	John Leonard; B11.13.1889 Washington DC; D8.13.1940 Norfolk VA; BL/TL/5´10˝/160; d9.12; b–Joe																									
1911	Phi N	0	0	ø	4	0	0	0	11.1	14	11	0	0	9	5	6.35	54	.326	.442	4	.000	-1	—	-4	—	-0.3
STANLEY, BOB	Robert William; B11.10.1954 Portland ME; BR/TR/6´4˝/(205–225); [BosA74*S1/7]; d4.16																									
1977	Bos A	8	7	.533	41	13	3-1	3-2	151	176	74	10	3	43-5	44	3.99	112	.294	.343	0	ø	0	103	7	0	0.8
1978	Bos A	15	2	.882	52	3	0	10-5	141.2	142	50	5	1	34-5	38	2.60	158	.266	.308	0	ø	0	189	20	0	2.8
1979	Bos A★	16	12	.571	40	30	9-4	1-0	216.2	250	110	14	4	44-4	56	3.99	112	.294	.330	0	ø	0	95	9	0	1.1
1980	Bos A	10	8	.556	52	17	5-1	14-3	175	186	75	11	7	52-8	71	3.39	126	.278	.335	0	ø	0	105	15	0	1.8
1981	Bos A	10	8	.556	35	1	0	0-3	98.2	110	46	3	6	38-4	28	3.83	102	.294	.365	0	ø	0	46	2	0	0.5
1982	Bos A	12	7	.632	48	0	0	14-2	168.1	161	60	11	4	50-6	83	3.10	**140**	.255	.312	0	ø	0	—	**23**	0	3.1
1983	Bos A★	8	10	.444	64	0	0	33-14	145.1	145	56	7	3	38-12	65	2.85	154	.266	.315	0	ø	0	—	21	0	3.4
1984	Bos A	9	10	.474	57	0	0	22-5	106.2	113	57	9	2	23-9	52	3.54	119	.267	.307	0	ø	0	—	4	0	0.8
1985	Bos A	6	6	.500	48	0	0	10-8	87.2	76	30	7	2	30-10	46	2.87	150	.237	.303	0	ø	0	—	14	0	2.0
1986	†Bos A	6	6	.500	66	1	0	16-5	82.1	109	48	9	0	22-8	54	4.37	96	.322	.360	0	ø	0	108	-3	0	-0.5
1987	Bos A	4	15	.211	34	20	4-1	0-2	152.2	198	96	17	1	42-7	67	5.01	91	.321	.363	0	ø	0	85	-9	18	-0.9
1988	†Bos A	6	4	.600	57	0	0	5-6	101.2	90	41	6	7	29-7	57	3.19	130	.242	.304	0	ø	0	—	10	38	0.9
1989	Bos A	5	2	.714	43	0	0	4-0	79.1	102	54	4	1	26-2	32	4.88	84	.321	.366	0	ø	0	—	-9	0	-0.7
Total	13	115	97	.542	637	85	21-7	132-55	1707	1858	797	113	41	471-87	693	3.64	118	.282	.331	0	ø	0	101	104	56	15.1
STANTON, MIKE	Michael Thomas; B9.25.1952 St.Louis MO; BB/TR/6´2˝/(200–205); [HouN73*S1/5]; d7.9; Col Miami–Dade Kendall (FL) CC																									
1975	Hou N	0	2	.000	7	2	0	1-0	17.1	20	14	1	0	20-0	16	7.27	47	.290	.449	4	.250	0	26	-7	0	-0.8
1980	Cle A	1	3	.250	51	0	0	5-1	85.2	98	58	5	3	44-1	74	5.46	76	.297	.382	0	ø	0	—	-13	0	-0.7
1981	Cle A	3	3	.500	24	0	0	2-2	43.1	43	21	4	0	18-4	34	4.36	84	.262	.333	0	ø	0	—	-2	0	-0.3
1982	Sea A	2	4	.333	56	1	0	7-3	71.1	70	37	5	0	21-3	49	4.16	103	.260	.312	0	ø	0	64	1	0	0.1
1983	Sea A	2	3	.400	50	0	0	7-2	65	65	26	3	1	28-5	47	3.32	129	.273	.349	0	ø	0	—	7	0	0.6
1984	Sea A	4	4	.500	54	0	0	8-5	61	55	28	3	2	22-4	55	3.54	113	.241	.312	0	ø	0	—	3	0	0.4
1985	Sea A	1	2	.333	24	0	0	1-1	29	32	20	4	3	21-3	17	5.28	80	.278	.403	0	ø	0	—	-4	0	-0.4
	Chi A	0	1	.000	11	0	0	0-2	11.2	15	14	2	0	8-0	12	9.26	47	.294	.383	0	ø	0	—	-6	0	-0.5
	Year	1	3	.250	35	0	0	1-3	40.2	47	34	6	3	29-3	29	6.42	66	.283	.397	0	ø	0	—	-10	0	-0.9
Total	7	13	22	.371	277	3	0	31-16	384.1	398	218	27	9	182-20	304	4.61	89	.272	.354	4	.250	0	37	-21	0	-1.6
STANTON, MIKE	William Michael; B6.2.1967 Houston TX; BL/TL/6´1˝/(190–215); [AtlN87 13/324]; d8.24; Col Southwestern (TX)																									
1989	Atl N	0	1	.000	20	0	0	7-1	24	17	4	0	0	8-1	27	1.50	244	.207	.278	0	ø	0	—	6	0	0.5
1990	Atl N	0	3	.000	7	0	0	2-1	7	16	16	1	1	4-2	7	18.00	22	.444	.512	0	ø	0	—	-10	160	-1.8
1991	†Atl N	5	5	.500	74	0	0	7-3	78	62	27	6	1	21-6	54	2.88	134	.217	.273	6	.500	2	—	9	0	1.5
1992	†Atl N	5	4	.556	65	0	0	8-3	63.2	59	32	6	2	20-2	44	4.10	89	.247	.308	2	.500	0	—	-3	0	-0.4
1993	†Atl N	4	6	.400	63	0	0	27-6	52	51	35	4	0	29-7	43	4.67	87	.255	.346	0	ø	0	—	-6	0	-1.2
1994	Atl N	3	1	.750	49	0	0	3-1	45.2	41	18	2	3	26-3	35	3.55	122	.248	.359	3-0-1	.667	1	—	5	0	0.5
1995	Atl N	1	1	.500	26	0	0	1-1	19.1	31	14	3	1	6-2	13	5.59	77	.369	.413	0	ø	0	—	-3	0	-0.3
	†Bos A	1	0	1.000	22	0	0	0-1	21	17	9	3	0	8-0	10	3.00	162	.224	.298	0	ø	0	—	4	0	0.2
1996	Bos A	4	3	.571	59	0	0	1-4	56.1	58	24	9	0	23-4	46	3.83	133	.275	.343	0	ø	0	—	9	0	1.0
	†Tex A	0	1	.000	22	0	0	0-1	22.1	20	8	2	0	4-1	14	3.22	163	.241	.276	0	ø	0	—	5	0	0.2
	Year	4	4	.500	81	0	0	1-5	78.2	78	32	11	0	27-5	60	3.66	141	.265	.325	0	ø	0	—	14	0	1.2

YEAR	TM LG	W	L	PCT	G	GS	CG-SHO	SV-BS	IP	H	R	HR	HB	BB-IB	SO	ERA	AERA	OAV	OOB	AB-HR-SH	AVG	PB	SUP	APR	DL	PW
1997	†NY A	6	1	.857	64	0	0	3-2	66.2	50	19	3	3	34-2	70	2.57	174	.205	.310	0	ø	0	—	15	0	1.5
1998	†NY A	4	1	.800	67	0	0	6-4	79	71	51	13	4	26-1	69	5.47	80	.239	.307	1	.000	-0	—	-10	0	-0.7
1999	†NY A	2	2	.500	73	1	0	0-5	62.1	71	30	5	1	18-4	59	4.33	109	.289	.337	1	.000	-0	118	4	0	0.2
2000	†NY A	2	3	.400	69	0	0	0-4	68	68	32	5	2	24-2	75	4.10	116	.263	.325	1	1.000	0	—	6	0	0.4
2001	†NY A★	9	4	.692	76	0	0	0-1	80.1	80	25	4	4	29-9	78	2.58	172	.263	.332	0	ø	0	—	17	0	2.4
2002	†NY A	7	1	.875	79	0	0	6-3	78	73	29	4	0	28-3	44	3.00	144	.256	.316	2	.000	-0	—	12	0	1.2
2003	NY N	2	7	.222	50	0	0	5-2	45.1	37	25	6	2	19-4	34	4.57	92	.219	.301	1	.000	-0	—	-2	46	-0.4
2004	NY N	2	6	.250	83	0	0	0-6	77	70	32	6	2	33-6	58	3.16	136	.237	.317	2	.500	0	—	9	0	0.9
2005	NY A	1	2	.333	28	0	0	0-0	14	17	11	1	0	6-0	12	7.07	61	.298	.359	0	ø	0	—	-4	0	-0.7
	Was N	2	1	.667	30	0	0	0-1	27.2	31	13	2	0	9-4	14	3.58	115	.292	.348	1	.000	-0	—	1	0	0.2
	Bos A	0	0	ø	1	0	0	0-0	1	1	0	0	0	0-0	1	0.00	ø	.333	.333	0	ø	0	—	0	0	0.0
2006	Was N	3	5	.375	56	0	0	0-3	44.1	47	22	1	1	21-11	30	4.47	98	.278	.356	1	.000	-0	—	0	0	0.0
	SF N	4	2	.667	26	0	0	8-3	23.1	23	8	1	1	6-0	18	3.09	144	.267	.319	1	.000	-0	—	4	0	0.7
	Year	7	7	.500	82	0	0	8-6	67.2	70	30	2	2	27-11	48	3.99	110	.275	.344	2	.000	-0	—	4	0	0.7
Total	18	67	60	.528	1109	1	0	84-56	1056.1	1011	484	87	28	402-74	855	3.81	115	.254	.324	22-0-1	.364	3	118	68	206	5.9
Stapleton, Dave	David Earl; B10.16.1961 Miami AZ; BL/TL/6´1˝/185; d9.14; Col Grand Canyon																									
1987	Mil A	2	0	1.000	4	0	0	0-0	14.2	13	3	0	0	3-0	14	1.84	251	.241	.281	0	ø	0	—	4	0	0.6
1988	Mil A	0	0	ø	6	0	0	0-0	13.2	20	9	1	1	9-1	6	5.93	68	.339	.435	0	ø	0	—	-2	141	-0.1
Total	2	2	0	1.000	10	0	0	0-0	28.1	33	12	1	1	12-1	20	3.81	113	.292	.365	0	ø	0	—	2	141	0.5
Stark, Denny	Dennis James; B10.27.1974 Hicksville OH; BR/TR/6´2˝/210; [SeaA96 4/117]; d9.15; Col Toledo; [DL 2000 Sea A 31]																									
1999	Sea A	0	0	ø	5	0	0	0-0	6.1	10	8	0	0	4-0	4	9.95	48	.370	.452	0	ø	0	—	-4	0	-0.2
2001	Sea A	1	1	.500	4	3	0	0-0	14.2	21	15	5	0	4-0	12	9.20	46	.333	.368	0	ø	0	58	-8	0	-0.8
2002	Col N	11	4	.733	32	20	0	0-1	128.1	108	69	25	5	64-4	64	4.00	118	.225	.321	41-1-3	.171	0*	122	6	0	0.7
2003	Col N	3	3	.500	17	13	0	0-0	78.2	98	57	12	3	33-2	30	5.83	84	.305	.368	22-0-1	.000	-1	125	-8	93	-0.7
2004	Col N	0	5	.000	6	6	0	0-0	26	53	43	9	0	18-3	10	11.42	42	.427	.486	8	.000	-1	111	-21	76	-2.8
Total	5	15	13	.536	64	42	0	0-1	254	290	192	51	8	123-9	120	5.78	83	.286	.363	71-1-4	.099	-2	117	-35	200	-3.8
Starkel, Con	Conrad; B11.16.1880 Red Oak IA; D1.19.1933 Tacoma WA; BR/TR/6´0˝/200; d4.19																									
1906	Was A	0	0	ø	1	0	0	0	3	7	6	1	0	2	1	18.00	15	.467	.529	0	ø	0	—	-4	—	-0.2
Starr, Ray	Raymond Francis "Iron Man"; B4.23.1906 Nowata OK; D2.9.1963 Baylis IL; BR/TR/6´1˝/178; d9.11																									
1932	StL N	1	1	.500	3	2	1-1	0	20	19	7	2	1	10	6	2.70	146	.284	.385	4-0-1	.250	0	43	3	—	0.3
1933	NY N	0	1	.000	6	2	0	0	13.1	19	11	0	1	10	2	5.40	59	.339	.448	3	.000	-0	104	-4	—	-0.3
	Bos N	0	1	.000	9	1	0	0	28	32	15	4	1	9	15	3.86	79	.296	.356	7-0-1	.143	0	81	-3	—	-0.1
	Year	0	2	.000	15	3	0	0	41.1	51	26	4	2	19	17	4.35	71	.311	.389	10-0-1	.100	-0	98	-8	—	-0.4
1941	Cin N	3	2	.600	7	4	3-2	0	34	28	10	1	1	6	11	2.65	136	.219	.259	11-0-4	.182	-0	100	4	0	0.6
1942	Cin N☆	15	13	.536	37	33	17-4	0	276.2	228	88	10	3	106	83	2.67	123	.226	.301	88-0-12	.091	-5	78	24	0	1.9
1943	Cin N	11	10	.524	36	33	9-2	1	217.1	201	93	9	5	91	42	3.64	91	.248	.328	74-0-6	.122	-4	120	-6	0	-1.0
1944	Pit N	6	5	.545	27	12	5	3	89.2	116	60	6	1	36	25	5.02	74	.314	.377	22	.136	1	135	-12	0	-1.4
1945	Pit N	0	2	.000	4	0	0	0	6.2	10	7	0	0	4	0	9.45	42	.370	.452	1	1.000	1	—	-3	0	-0.5
	Chi N	1	0	1.000	9	1	0	0	13.1	17	11	1	0	7	5	7.43	49	.298	.375	2-0-1	.500	0	255	-5	0	-0.3
	Year	1	2	.333	13	1	0	0	20	27	18	1	0	11	5	8.10	46	.321	.400	3-0-1	.667	1	248	-9	0	-0.8
Total	7	37	35	.514	138	88	35-9	4	699	670	302	33	13	279	189	3.53	96	.255	.329	212-0-25	.123	-7	105	-2	0	-0.8
Starr, Dick	Richard Eugene; B3.2.1921 Kittanning PA; BR/TR/6´3˝/190; d9.5																									
1947	NY A	1	0	1.000	4	1	1	0	12.1	12	4	1	0	8	1	1.46	242	.250	.357	3-0-1	.333	1	200	2	0	0.2
1948	NY A	0	0	ø	1	0	0	0	2	0	1	0	0	2	2	4.50	91	.000	.250	0	ø	0	—	0	0	0.0
1949	StL A	1	7	.125	30	8	1-1	0	83.1	96	46	6	1	48	44	4.32	105	.292	.384	23	.087	-1	74	2	0	0.0
1950	StL A	7	5	.583	32	16	4-1	2	123.2	140	83	11	7	74	30	5.02	99	.287	.389	36-0-4	.139	-3*	105	-2	0	-0.5
1951	StL A	2	5	.286	15	9	0	0	62	66	55	10	2	42	26	7.40	59	.273	.385	18-0-1	.222	0	92	-19	0	-1.7
	Was A	1	7	.125	11	11	1	0	61.1	76	41	12	0	24	17	5.58	73	.304	.365	17	.176	1	104	-9	0	-1.1
	Year	3	12	.200	26	20	1	0	123.1	142	96	22	2	66	43	6.49	65	.289	.375	35-0-1	.200	1	98	-28	0	-2.8
Total	5	12	24	.333	93	45	7-2	2	344.2	390	230	40	10	198	120	5.25	86	.286	.381	97-0-6	.155	-2	98	-26	0	-3.1
Starrette, Herman	Herman Paul; B11.20.1938 Statesville NC; BR/TR/6´0˝/175; d7.1; C17; Col Lenoir–Rhyne																									
1963	Bal A	0	1	.000	18	0	0	0	26	26	10	1	2	7-0	13	3.46	100	.271	.327	1-0-1	.000	0	—	1	0	0.1
1964	Bal A	1	0	1.000	5	0	0	0	11	9	3	0	0	6-0	5	1.64	218	.250	.349	3	.000	-0	—	2	0	0.1
1965	Bal A	0	0	ø	4	0	0	0	9	8	3	0	0	3-0	3	1.00	347	.258	.324	1	.000	-0	—	2	0	0.1
Total	3	1	1	.500	27	0	0	0	46	43	16	1	2	16-0	21	2.54	137	.264	.332	5-0-1	.000	-0	—	5	0	0.3
Stauffer, Ed	Charles Edward; B1.10.1898 Emsworth PA; D7.2.1979 St.Petersburg FL; BR/TR/5´11˝/185; d4.26																									
1923	Chi N	0	0	ø	1	0	0	0	2	5	3	0	0	1	0	13.50	30	.556	.600	0	ø	0	—	-2	—	-0.1
1925	StL A	0	1	.000	20	1	0	0	30.1	34	21	1	0	21	13	5.34	87	.283	.390	4	.250	-0	108	-2	—	-0.1
Total	2	0	1	.000	21	1	0	0	32.1	39	24	1	0	22	13	5.85	79	.302	.404	4	.250	-0	108	-4	—	-0.2
Stauffer, Tim	Timothy James; B6.2.1982 Portland ME; BR/TR/6´1˝/(205–215); [SDN03 1/4]; d5.11; Col Richmond																									
2005	SD N	3	6	.333	15	14	0	0-0	81	92	50	10	2	29-0	49	5.33	74	.286	.348	24-0-3	.125	-0	107	-13	0	-1.3
2006	SD N	1	0	1.000	1	1	0	0-0	6	3	2	0	0	1-0	2	1.50	277	.150	.190	2	.500	0	89	1	0	0.3
Total	2	4	6	.400	16	15	0	0-0	87	95	52	10	2	30-0	51	5.07	78	.278	.340	26-0-3	.154	-0	105	-12	0	-1.0
Stearns, Bill	William E.; B3.20.1853 Washington DC; D12.30.1898 Washington DC; TR; d6.26																									
1871	Oly NA	2	0	1.000	2	2	2	0	18	10	11	0	—	8	0	2.50	167	.149	.240	9	.000	-1	138	3	—	0.1
1872	Nat NA	0	11	.000	11	11	11	0	99	193	190	2	—	3	2	6.18	75	.339	.343	45	.244	-3	60	-13	—	-1.1
1873	Was NA	7	25	.219	32	32	32	0	283	481	395	8	—	16	5	4.61	76	.332	.340	133	.180	-6	83	-37	—	-3.0
1874	Har NA	3	14	.176	22	18	14	0	158.2	237	194	0	—	15	14	2.95	78	.297	.310	132	.159	-5*	70	-12	—	-1.3
1875	Was NA	1	14	.067	17	16	14	0	141	246	211	3	—	4	3	4.02	59	.332	.336	78	.256	-0*	52	-25	—	-2.1
Total	5NA	13	64	.169	84	79	73	0	699.2	1167	1001	13	—	46	24	4.28	74	.322	.331	397	.191	-16	73	-84	—	-7.4
Stecher, William	William Theodore; B10.20.1869 Riverside NJ; D12.26.1926 Riverside NJ; d9.6																									
1890	Phi AA	0	10	.000	10	10	9	0	68	111	110	1	14	60	18	10.32	38	.356	.479	29	.241	1	47	-48	—	-4.4
Stechschulte, Gene	Gene Urban; B8.12.1973 Lima OH; BR/TR/6´5˝/210; d4.20; Col Ashland; [DL 2003 StL N 183]																									
2000	StL N	1	0	1.000	20	0	0	0-1	25.2	24	22	6	0	17-1	12	6.31	74	.247	.353	0	ø	0	—	-6	0	-0.3
2001	†StL N	1	5	.167	67	0	0	6-2	70	71	35	10	4	30-2	51	3.86	112	.273	.354	3-1-0	.667	2*	—	3	0	0.4
2002	StL N	6	2	.750	29	0	0	0-2	32	27	19	4	1	17-1	21	4.78	84	.235	.328	2	.000	-0	—	-3	0	-0.6
Total	3	8	7	.533	116	0	0	6-5	127.2	122	76	20	5	64-4	84	4.58	94	.258	.347	5-1-0	.400	2	—	-6	183	-0.5
Steele, Elmer	Elmer Rae; B5.17.1886 Poughkeepsie NY; D3.9.1966 Rhinebeck NY; BB/TR/5´11˝/200; d9.12																									
1907	Bos A	0	1	.000	4	1	0	0	11.1	11	7	0	0	1	10	1.59	162	.256	.273	4	.000	-1	0	0	—	-0.1
1908	Bos A	5	7	.417	16	13	9-1	0	118	85	34	1	3	13	37	1.83	134	.209	.239	39-0-1	.051	-4	77	8	—	0.4
1909	Bos A	4	4	.500	16	8	2	1	75.2	75	37	1	1	15	32	2.85	88	.255	.294	22-0-1	.227	1	148	-4	—	-0.3
1910	Pit N	0	3	.000	3	3	2	0	24	19	9	0	0	3	7	2.25	138	.221	.247	7	.000	-1	32	2	—	0.2
1911	Pit N	9	9	.500	31	16	7-2	2	166	153	65	5	4	31	52	2.60	132	.256	.297	61-0-1	.180	-0	142	14	—	1.4
	Bro N	0	0	ø	5	2	0	0	23	24	10	0	0	5	9	3.13	107	.258	.296	9	.000	-1	146	1	—	0.0
	Year	9	9	.500	36	18	7-2	2	189	177	75	5	4	36	61	2.67	128	.257	.297	70-0-1	.157	-1	143	15	—	1.4
Total	5	18	24	.429	75	43	20-3	3	418	367	162	7	8	68	147	2.41	122	.241	.278	142-0-3	.127	-6	114	21	—	1.6
Steele, Bob	Robert Wesley; B3.29.1894 Cassburn ON, Can.; D1.27.1962 Ocala FL; BB/TL/5´10.5˝/175; d4.17																									
1916	StL N	5	15	.250	29	21	7-1	0	148	156	74	6	3	42	67	3.41	78	.285	.340	51	.196	-1	73	-12	—	-1.9
1917	StL N	1	3	.250	12	6	1	0	42	33	17	1	0	19	23	3.21	84	.223	.311	13	.385	2	70	-2	—	0.0
	Pit N	5	11	.313	27	19	13-1	1	179.2	158	71	0	5	53	82	2.76	103	.237	.298	76-0-1	.224	1*	73	1	—	0.0
	Year	6	14	.300	39	25	14-1	1	221.2	191	88	1	5	72	105	2.84	99	.235	.301	89-0-1	.247	2	72	-1	—	0.0
1918	Pit N	2	3	.400	10	4	2-1	1	49	44	25	2	2	17	21	3.31	87	.240	.312	16	.125	-0	79	-3	—	-0.3
	NY N	3	5	.375	12	7	5-1	1	66	56	29	1	3	11	24	2.59	101	.226	.267	21	.286	2	115	-2	—	-0.1

YEAR	TM LG	W	L	PCT	G	GS	CG-SHO	SV-BS	IP	H	R	HR	HB	BB-IB	SO	ERA	AERA	OAV	OOB	AB-HR-SH	AVG	PB	SUP	APR	DL	PW
	Year	5	8	.385	22	11	7-2	2	115	100	54	3	5	28	45	2.90	94	.232	.287	37	.216	2	101	-5	—	-0.4
1919	NY N	0	1	.000	1	0	0	0	3	3	3	0	0	2	0	6.00	47	.250	.357	1	.000	-0	—	-1	—	-0.3
Total	4	16	38	.296	91	57	28-4	3	487.2	450	219	10	13	144	217	3.05	90	.249	.310	178-0-1	.225	3	78	-19	—	-2.6
Steele, Bill	William Mitchell "Big Bill"; B10.5.1885 Milford PA; D10.19.1949 Overland MO; BR/TR/5´11"/200; d9.10																									
1910	StL N	4	4	.500	9	8	8	1	71.2	71	35	1	6	24	25	3.27	91	.264	.338	31	.258	1	119	-3	—	-0.2
1911	StL N	18	19	.486	43	34	23-1	3	287.1	287	153	8	10	113	115	3.73	91	.269	.345	101-0-3	.208	4	77	-11	—	-0.7
1912	StL N	9	13	.409	40	25	7	2	194	245	143	5	7	66	67	4.69	73	.322	.381	61-0-1	.180	1*	128	-27	—	-2.3
1913	StL N	4	4	.500	12	9	2	0	54	58	31	3	3	18	10	5.00	65	.286	.353	18-0-1	.056	-1	98	-9	—	-1.3
1914	StL N	1	2	.333	17	2	0	0	53.1	55	30	3	3	7	16	2.70	104	.274	.308	17-0-1	.294	2	90	-2	—	0.1
	Bro N	1	1	.500	8	1	0	1	16.1	17	16	1	0	7	3	5.51	52	.258	.329	3-0-1	.333	1	175	-5	—	-0.6
	Year	2	3	.400	25	3	0	1	69.2	72	46	4	3	14	19	3.36	84	.270	.313	20-0-2	.300	2	119	-6	—	-0.5
Total	5	37	43	.463	129	79	40-1	7	676.2	733	408	21	29	235	236	4.02	82	.286	.352	231-0-7	.203	8	102	-57	—	-5.0
Steen, Bill	William John; B11.11.1887 Pittsburgh PA; D3.13.1979 Signal Hill CA; BR/TR/6´0.5"/180; d4.15; Col Washington & Jefferson																									
1912	Cle A	9	8	.529	26	16	6-1	0	143.1	163	75	3	1	45	61	3.77	90	.298	.352	48-0-1	.271	2	102	-3	—	-0.2
1913	Cle A	4	5	.444	22	13	7-2	2	128.1	113	52	3	4	49	57	2.45	124	.239	.316	41-0-4	.171	-0	107	6	—	0.4
1914	Cle A	9	14	.391	30	22	13-1	0	200.2	201	74	0	4	68	97	2.60	111	.272	.337	70-0-3	.200	1	82	9	—	1.1
1915	Cle A	1	4	.200	10	7	2	0	45.1	51	30	1	2	15	22	4.96	61	.290	.352	16	.188	-0	85	-8	—	-0.7
	Det A	5	1	.833	20	7	3	4	79.1	83	35	0	1	22	28	2.72	111	.269	.319	28-0-1	.179	-1	168	1	—	0.1
	Year	6	5	.545	30	14	5	4	124.2	134	65	1	3	37	50	3.54	86	.276	.331	44-0-1	.182	-1	127	-7	—	-0.6
Total	4	28	32	.467	108	65	31-4	6	597	611	266	7	12	199	265	3.05	101	.273	.335	203-0-9	.207	1	102	5	—	0.7
Steengrafe, Milt	Milton Henry; B5.26.1898 San Francisco CA; D6.2.1977 Oklahoma City OK; BR/TR/6´0"/170; d5.5																									
1924	Chi A	0	0	ø	3	0	0	0	5.2	15	8	0	0	4	3	12.71	32	.484	.543	1	.000	-0	—	-5	—	-0.2
1926	Chi A	1	1	.500	13	1	0	0	38.1	43	22	1	2	19	10	3.99	97	.295	.383	14-0-1	.000	-2	44	-2	—	-0.3
Total	2	1	1	.500	16	1	0	0	44	58	30	1	2	23	13	5.11	76	.328	.411	15-0-1	.000	-2	44	-7	—	-0.5
Steenstra, Kennie	Kenneth Gregory; B10.13.1970 Springfield MO; BR/TR/6´5"/215; [ChiN92 12/331]; d5.21; Col Wichita St.																									
1998	Chi N	0	0	ø	4	0	0	0-0	3.1	7	4	2	0	1-0	4	10.80	41	.412	.444	0	ø	0	—	-2	0	-0.1
Steevens, Morrie	Morris Dale; B10.7.1940 Salem IL; BL/TL/6´2"/(175–180); d4.13																									
1962	Chi N	0	1	.000	12	1	0	0	15	10	4	0	1	11-0	5	2.40	173	.196	.333	1	.000	-0	63	3	0	0.2
1964	Phi N	0	0	ø	4	0	0	0	2.2	5	3	0	0	1-0	3	3.38	103	.385	.429	0	ø	0	—	-1	0	0.0
1965	Phi N	0	1	.000	6	0	0	0	2.2	5	5	1	0	4-0	3	16.88	20	.417	.563	0	ø	0	—	-4	0	-0.7
Total	3	0	2	.000	22	1	0	0	20.1	20	12	1	1	16-0	11	4.43	90	.263	.385	1	.000	-0	63	-2	0	-0.5
Stein, Ed	Edward F.; B9.5.1869 Detroit MI; D5.10.1928 Detroit MI; BR/TR/5´11"/170; d7.24																									
1890	Chi N	12	6	.667	20	18	14-1	0	160.2	147	100	9	11	83	65	3.81	96	.236	.336	59	.153	-2	99	-1	—	-0.3
1891	Chi N	7	6	.538	14	10	9-1	0	101	99	68	7	2	57	38	3.74	89	.247	.343	43	.163	-1	104	-6	—	-0.6
1892	Bro N	27	16	.628	48	42	38-6	1	377.1	310	166	6	15	150	190	2.84	111	.215	.296	144	.215	4	110	16	—	2.0
1893	Bro N	19	15	.559	37	34	28-1	0	298.1	294	190	4	8	119	81	3.77	117	.250	.323	118	.212	-3	99	20	—	1.5
1894	Bro N	26	14	.650	44	40	37-2	1	350	388	261	10	14	170	84	4.63	107	.278	.362	143-2-4	.252	4*	116	11	—	1.2
1895	Bro N	15	13	.536	32	27	24-1	1	255.1	282	163	8	6	93	55	4.72	93	.276	.340	104-0-2	.250	2	95	-5	—	-0.2
1896	Bro N	3	6	.333	17	10	6	0	90.1	130	79	6	2	51	16	4.88	84	.334	.414	39-0-1	.256	0	105	-12	—	-0.8
1898	Bro N	0	2	.000	3	2	2	0	23	39	21	0	0	9	6	5.48	65	.371	.421	10	.400	1	59	-5	—	-0.3
Total	8	109	78	.583	215	183	158-12	3	1656	1689	1048	50	58	732	535	3.97	103	.258	.338	660-2-7	.224	5	105	18	—	2.5
Stein, Irv	Irvin Michael; B5.21.1911 Madisonville LA; D1.7.1981 Covington LA; BR/TR/6´2"/170; d7.7																									
1932	Phi A	0	0	ø	1	0	0	0	3	7	4	2	0	1	0	12.00	38	.500	.533	1	.000	-0	—	-2	—	-0.1
Stein, Blake	William Blake; B8.3.1973 McComb MS; BR/TR/6´7"/(210–240); [StLN94 6/166]; d5.10; Col Spring Hill																									
1998	Oak A	5	9	.357	24	20	1-1	0-0	117.1	117	92	22	5	71-3	89	6.37	73	.255	.359	5-0-1	.000	-0	102	-22	0	-2.2
1999	Oak A	0	0	ø	1	1	0	0-0	2.2	6	5	1	0	6-0	4	16.88	28	.462	.632	0	ø	0	217	-3	0	-0.2
	KC A	1	2	.333	12	11	0	0-0	70.1	59	33	10	7	41-1	43	4.09	124	.230	.350	0	ø	0	75	8	0	0.3
	Year	1	2	.333	13	12	0	0-0	73	65	38	11	7	47-1	47	4.56	111	.241	.366	0	ø	0	86	5	0	0.1
2000	KC A	8	5	.615	17	17	1	0-0	107.2	98	57	19	3	57-1	78	4.68	112	.247	.343	2	.000	-0	108	7	92	0.7
2001	KC A	7	8	.467	36	15	0	1-1	131	112	73	20	3	79-2	113	4.74	105	.233	.342	2	.000	-0	90	4	0	0.3
2002	KC A	0	4	.000	27	2	0	1-1	46.2	59	41	6	3	27-1	42	7.91	63	.306	.394	0	ø	0	84	-12	61	-1.0
Total	5	21	28	.429	117	66	2-1	2-2	475.2	451	301	78	21	281-8	369	5.41	92	.251	.356	9-0-1	.000	-1	97	-18	153	-2.1
Stein, Randy	William Randolph; B3.7.1953 Pomona CA; BR/TR/6´4"/210; [BalA71 1/23]; d4.17																									
1978	Mil A	3	2	.600	31	1	0	1-1	72.2	78	51	5	4	39-1	42	5.33	71	.280	.371	0	ø	0	47	-14	0	-0.9
1979	Sea A	2	3	.400	23	1	0	0-3	41.1	48	29	7	1	27-4	39	5.88	74	.291	.390	0	ø	0	21	-6	0	-0.7
1981	Sea A	0	1	.000	5	0	0	0-1	9.1	18	12	1	0	8-0	6	10.61	37	.429	.510	0	ø	0	—	-6	0	-0.6
1982	Chi N	0	0	ø	6	0	0	0-0	10.1	7	4	2	0	7-2	6	3.48	109	.200	.326	0	ø	0	—	1	0	0.0
Total	4	5	6	.455	65	2	0	1-5	133.2	151	96	15	5	81-7	93	5.72	70	.290	.385	0	ø	0	34	-25	0	-2.2
Steineder, Ray	Raymond J.; B11.13.1894 Salem NJ; D8.25.1982 Vineland NJ; BR/TR/6´0.5"/160; d7.16																									
1923	Pit N	2	0	1.000	15	2	1	0	55	58	30	3	2	18	23	4.75	85	.278	.341	15-0-1	.467	3	297	-3	—	0.1
1924	Pit N	0	1	.000	5	0	0	0	2.2	6	6	0	0	5	0	13.50	28	.400	.550	0	ø	0	—	-3	—	-0.6
	Phi N	1	1	.500	9	0	0	0	28.2	31	15	1	0	16	11	4.40	101	.284	.376	10	.300	0	—	1	—	0.1
	Year	1	2	.333	14	0	0	0	31.1	37	21	1	0	21	11	5.17	85	.298	.400	10	.300	0	—	-2	—	-0.5
Total	2	3	2	.600	29	2	1	0	86.1	95	51	4	2	39	34	4.90	85	.285	.364	25-0-1	.400	3	297	-5	—	-0.4
Steirer, Rick	Ricky Francis; B8.27.1956 Baltimore MD; BR/TR/6´4"/200; [AnaA77 5/111]; d8.5																									
1982	Cal A	1	0	1.000	10	1	0	0-1	26.1	25	14	2	1	11-0	14	3.76	109	.243	.322	0	ø	0	156	0	0	0.0
1983	Cal A	3	2	.600	19	5	0	0-0	61.2	77	40	3	3	18-4	25	4.82	84	.302	.351	0	ø	0	121	-7	0	-0.5
1984	Cal A	0	1	.000	1	1	0	0-0	2.2	6	5	0	0	2-1	2	16.88	24	.500	.571	0	ø	0	90	-4	0	-0.5
Total	3	4	3	.571	30	7	0	0-1	90.2	108	59	5	4	31-5	41	4.86	83	.292	.350	0	ø	0	122	-11	0	-1.0
Stellberger, Bill	William F.; B4.22.1865 Detroit MI; D11.9.1936 Detroit MI; BL/TL/5´7"/170; d10.1																									
1885	Pro N	0	1	.000	1	1	1	0	8	14	10	0	—	4	0	7.88	34	.389	.450	4	.000	-1	126	-4	—	-0.4
Stember, Jeff	Jeffrey Alan; B3.2.1958 Elizabeth NJ; BR/TR/6´5"/210; [SFN76 26/596]; d8.5																									
1980	SF N	0	0	ø	1	1	0	0-0	3	2	3	1	0	2-0	0	3.00	117	.167	.286	1	.000	-0	229	-1	0	-0.1
Stemle, Steve	Stephen J.; B5.20.1977 Louisville KY; BR/TR/6´4"/200; [StLN98 5/138]; d5.26; Col Western Kentucky																									
2005	KC A	0	0	ø	6	0	0	0-0	10.2	10	6	0	0	4-0	9	5.06	87	.256	.326	0	ø	0*	—	-1	114	0.0
2006	KC A	0	1	.000	5	0	0	0-1	6	15	10	1	0	3-0	0	15.00	31	.455	.500	0	ø	0	—	-6	168	-0.8
Total	2	0	1	.000	11	0	0	0-1	16.2	25	16	1	0	7-0	9	8.64	52	.347	.405	0	ø	0	—	-7	282	-0.8
Stemmeyer, Bill	William "Cannon Ball"; B5.6.1865 Cleveland OH; D5.3.1945 Cleveland OH; BR/TR/6´2"/190; d10.3																									
1885	Bos N	1	1	.500	2	2	2-1	0	11	7	7	0	—	11	8	0.00	ø	.194	.383	7	.429	1	200	1	—	0.4
1886	Bos N	22	18	.550	41	41	41	0	348.2	300	218	11	—	144	239	3.02	106	.218	.292	148	.277	9	115	5	—	1.1
1887	Bos N	6	8	.429	15	14	14	1	119.1	138	107	4	2	41	41	5.20	79	.274	.331	47-1	.255	2	80	-17	—	-1.4
1888	Cle AA	0	2	.000	2	2	2	0	16	37	42	0	1	9	7	9.00	34	.435	.495	10	.400	1*	94	-14	—	-1.1
Total	4	29	29	.500	60	59	59-1	1	495	482	374	15	3	205	295	3.67	93	.241	.312	212-1	.283	14	108	-25	—	-1.0
Stenhouse, Dave	David Rotchford; B9.12.1933 Westerly RI; BR/TR/6´0"/190; d4.18; s–Mike; Col Rhode Island																									
1962	Was A★	11	12	.478	34	26	9-2	0	197	169	84	24	2	90-9	123	3.65	110	.234	.319	58-0-6	.052	-5	89	10	0	0.7
1963	Was A	3	9	.250	16	16	2-1	0	87	90	46	12	1	45-2	47	4.55	82	.260	.345	25-0-1	.080	-1	72	-6	42	-0.9
1964	Was A	2	7	.222	26	14	1	1	88	80	54	12	1	39-1	44	4.81	77	.239	.320	20-0-3	.300	2	91	-10	37	-0.8
Total	3	16	28	.364	76	56	12-3	1	372	339	184	48	4	174-12	214	4.14	94	.241	.326	103-0-10	.107	-4	84	-6	79	-1.0
Stephen, Buzz	Louis Roberts; B7.13.1944 Porterville CA; BR/TR/6´4"/197; [MinA66 S1/6]; d9.20; Col Cal St.–Fresno																									
1968	Min A	1	1	.500	2	2	0	0	11.1	11	7	0	1	7-0	4	4.76	65	.275	.388	3-0-1	.000	-0	85	-2	0	-0.4

YEAR	TM LG	W	L	PCT	G	GS	CG-SHO	SV-BS	IP	H	R	HR	HB	BB-IB	SO	ERA	AERA	OAV	OOB	AB-HR-SH	AVG	PB	SUP	APR	DL	PW
Stephens, Bryan	Bryan Maris; B7.14.1920 Fayetteville AR; D11.21.1991 Santa Ana CA; BR/TR/6´4˝/175; d5.15																									
1947	Cle A	5	10	.333	31	5	1	1	92	79	46	6	2	39	34	4.01	87	.230	.312	27-0-1	.111	-2	102	-6	0	-1.2
1948	StL A	3	6	.333	43	12	2	3	122.2	141	94	14	4	67	35	6.02	76	.289	.379	32-0-2	.125	-1	119	-20	0	-1.4
Total	2	8	16	.333	74	17	3	4	214.2	220	140	20	6	106	69	5.16	79	.264	.352	59-0-3	.119	-3	119	-26	0	-2.6
Stephens, Clarence	Clarence Wright; B8.19.1863 Cincinnati OH; D2.28.1945 Cincinnati OH; TR; d10.8																									
1886	Cin AA	1	0	1.000	1	1	1	0	8	9	8	0	1	5	6	5.63	63	.273	.385	5	.600	1	236	-2	—	-0.1
1891	Cin N	0	1	.000	1	1	1	0	8	9	9	1	0	3	3	7.88	43	.273	.333	3	.000	-0	0	-3	—	-0.3
Total	2	1	1	.500	2	2	2	0	16	18	17	1	1	8	9	6.75	51	.273	.360	8	.375	1	121	-5	—	-0.4
Stephens, Ben	George Benjamin; B9.28.1867 Romeo MI; D8.5.1896 Armada MI; TR/5´10.5˝/170; d8.5																									
1892	Bal N	1	1	.500	5	2	2	1	29	37	22	2	1	9	7	2.79	123	.298	.351	13	.000	-2	120	0	—	-0.2
	Cin N	0	1	.000	1	1	0	0	7	12	3	0	0	4	1	1.29	254	.364	.432	2	.000	-0	39	1	—	0.1
	Year	1	2	.333	6	3	2	1	36	49	25	2	1	13	8	2.50	136	.312	.368	15	.000	-2	93	1	—	-0.1
1893	Was N	0	6	.000	9	6	6	0	63.2	83	58	1	4	31	14	5.80	80	.306	.386	29	.103	-4	50	-8	—	-0.8
1894	Was N	0	0	ø	3	2	1	0	11	19	16	1	1	8	1	4.91	108	.373	.467	4	.250	-0	67	-1	—	-0.1
Total	3	1	8	.111	18	11	9	1	110.2	151	99	4	6	52	23	4.64	93	.315	.389	48	.083	-6	65	-8	—	-1.0
Stephens, John	John M.; B11.15.1979 Sydney, New South Wales, Australia; BR/TR/6´1˝/200; d7.30																									
2002	Bal A	2	5	.286	12	11	0	0-0	65	68	44	13	3	22-2	56	6.09	71	.271	.332	0	ø	0	79	-11	0	-1.0
Stephenson, Earl	Chester Earl; B7.31.1947 Benson NC; BL/TL/6´3˝/175; [ChiN67*3/39]; d4.7; Col Campbell																									
1971	Chi N	1	0	1.000	16	0	0	1-2	20.1	24	10	1	0	11-0	11	4.43	89	.316	.393	2	.000	-0	—	-1	0	0.0
1972	Mil A	3	5	.375	35	8	1	0-1	80.1	79	32	5	3	33-5	33	3.25	94	.262	.339	18	.000	-2	61	-2	0	-0.4
1977	Bal A	0	0	ø	1	0	0	0-0	3	5	3	1	0	0-0	2	9.00	43	.357	.357	0	ø	0	—	-2	0	-0.1
1978	Bal A	0	0	ø	2	0	0	0-0	9.2	10	3	0	0	5-0	4	2.79	126	.294	.375	0	ø	0	—	1	0	0.0
Total	4	4	5	.444	54	8	1	1-3	113.1	118	48	7	3	49-5	50	3.57	92	.277	.353	20	.000	-2	61	-4	0	-0.5
Stephenson, Garrett	Garrett Charles; B1.2.1972 Takoma Park MD; BR/TR/6´5˝/(185–208); [BalA92 18/492]; d7.25; Col Brigham Young–Idaho [JC]; [DL 2001 StL N 190]																									
1996	Bal A	0	1	.000	3	0	0	0-0	6.1	13	9	1	1	3-1	3	12.79	39	.433	.500	0	ø	0	—	-5	0	-0.6
1997	Phi N	8	6	.571	20	18	2	0-0	117	104	45	11	3	38-0	81	3.15	134	.244	.307	32-0-5	.094	-1	80	14	32	1.4
1998	Phi N	0	2	.000	6	6	0	0-0	23	31	24	3	0	19-0	17	9.00	48	.316	.427	6-0-1	.167	0	124	-11	0	-0.8
1999	StL N	6	3	.667	18	12	0	0-0	85.1	90	43	11	5	29-1	59	4.22	109	.275	.339	27-0-3	.074	-2	105	4	0	0.2
2000	†StL N	16	9	.640	32	31	3-2	0-0	200.1	209	105	31	7	63-0	123	4.49	103	.270	.327	59-0-13	.051	-4	115	6	0	0.2
2002	StL N	2	5	.286	12	10	0	0-0	45	48	27	4	5	25-0	34	5.40	75	.282	.388	12-0-2	.000	-1	136	-6	119	-0.9
2003	StL N	7	13	.350	32	27	1	0-0	174.1	167	94	30	13	60-3	91	4.59	90	.255	.326	44-0-7	.205	2	96	-9	0	-0.9
Total	7	39	39	.500	123	104	6-2	0-0	651.1	662	347	91	34	237-5	408	4.55	96	.267	.336	180-0-31	.100	-6	105	-7	341	-1.4
Stephenson, Jerry	Jerry Joseph; B10.6.1943 Detroit MI; BL/TR/6´2˝/(175–200); d4.14; f–Joe																									
1963	Bos A	0	0	ø	1	1	0	0	2.1	5	2	0	0	2-0	3	7.71	49	.556	.538	1	.000	-0	141	-1	0	-0.1
1965	Bos A	1	5	.167	15	8	0	0	52	62	41	7	1	33-0	49	6.23	60	.287	.382	13	.231	0	74	-13	0	-1.3
1966	Bos A	2	5	.286	15	11	1	0	66.1	68	51	6	1	44-1	50	5.83	65	.264	.370	17-0-2	.118	-1	112	-14	47	-1.5
1967	†Bos A	3	1	.750	8	6	0	1	39.2	32	18	4	1	16-2	24	3.86	90	.227	.308	16	.250	0	92	-1	0	-0.1
1968	Bos A	2	8	.200	23	7	2	0	68.2	81	51	4	2	42-3	51	5.64	56	.295	.387	17	.353	2	87	-19	0	-2.4
1969	Sea A	0	0	ø	2	0	0	0-0	2.2	6	4	0	1	3-0	1	10.13	36	.429	.556	0	ø	0	—	-2	0	-0.1
1970	LA N	0	0	ø	3	0	0	0-0	6.2	11	7	0	0	5-0	6	9.45	41	.379	.471	1	.000	-0	—	-4	0	-0.2
Total	7	8	19	.296	67	33	3	1-0	238.1	265	174	21	6	145-6	184	5.70	62	.281	.377	65-0-2	.231	2	96	-54	47	-5.7
Sterling, John	John A.; B Philadelphia PA; 6´1˝/172; d10.12																									
1890	Phi AA	0	1	.000	1	1	1	0	5	16	12	1	1	4	1	21.60	18	.516	.583	2	.000	-0	35	-8	—	-0.9
Sterling, Randy	Randall Wayne; B4.21.1951 Key West FL; BB/TR/6´2˝/195; d9.16																									
1974	NY N	1	1	.500	3	2	0	0-0	9.1	13	8	0	1	3-0	2	4.82	75	.351	.405	2	.000	0	73	-2	0	-0.4
Stevens, Dave	David James; B3.4.1970 Fullerton CA; BR/TR/6´3˝/(195–215); [ChiN89 20/512]; d5.20; Col Fullerton (CA) JC																									
1994	Min A	5	2	.714	24	0	0	0-0	45	55	35	6	1	23-2	24	6.80	73	.302	.383	0	ø	0	—	-8	0	-1.1
1995	Min A	5	4	.556	56	0	0	10-2	65.2	74	40	14	1	32-1	47	5.07	95	.285	.359	0	ø	0	—	-1	0	-0.2
1996	Min A	3	3	.500	49	0	0	11-5	58	58	31	12	0	25-2	29	4.66	110	.264	.335	0	ø	0	—	3	41	0.4
1997	Min A	1	3	.250	6	6	0	0-0	23	41	23	8	0	17-0	16	9.00	52	.383	.468	0	ø	0	121	-10	0	-1.3
	Chi N	0	2	.000	10	0	0	0-0	9.1	13	11	0	1	9-0	13	9.64	45	.333	.460	1	.000	-0	—	-5	0	-1.0
1998	Chi N	1	2	.333	31	0	0	0-0	38	42	20	6	1	17-5	31	4.74	93	.288	.364	4	.250	0	—	-1	0	-0.1
1999	Cle A	0	0	ø	5	0	0	0-0	9	10	10	1	0	8-1	6	10.00	51	.286	.409	0	ø	0	—	-4	0	-0.2
2000	Atl N	0	0	ø	2	0	0	0-0	3	5	4	2	0	1-0	4	12.00	38	.357	.400	1	.000	-0	—	-2	0	-0.1
Total	7	15	16	.484	183	6	0	21-7	251	298	174	49	4	132-11	170	6.02	80	.297	.377	6	.167	-0	121	-29	41	-3.6
Stevens, Jim	James Arthur "Steve"; B8.25.1889 Williamsburg MD; D9.25.1966 Baltimore MD; BR/TR/5´11˝/180; d8.24																									
1914	Was A	0	0	ø	2	0	0	0	3	4	3	0	1	2	0	9.00	31	.364	.500	1	.000	-0	—	-2	—	-0.1
Stewart, Dave	David Keith; B2.19.1957 Oakland CA; BR/TR/6´2˝/(200–230); [LAN75 16/384]; d9.22; C3																									
1978	LA N	0	0	ø	1	0	0	0-0	2	1	0	0	0	0-0	1	0.00	ø	.167	.167	0	ø	0	—	1	0	0.0
1981	†LA N	4	3	.571	32	0	0	6-2	43.1	40	13	3	0	14-5	29	2.49	132	.250	.305	5	.400	2	—	4	0	0.9
1982	LA N	9	8	.529	45	14	0	1-1	146.1	137	72	14	2	49-11	80	3.81	91	.249	.310	39-0-5	.179	1	98	-7	0	-0.7
1983	LA N	5	2	.714	46	1	0	8-4	76	67	28	4	2	33-7	54	2.96	122	.237	.318	7-0-1	.143	-0	171	6	0	0.6
	Tex A	5	2	.714	8	8	2	0-0	59	50	15	2	2	17-0	24	2.14	190	.233	.294	0	ø	0	62	13	0	1.5
1984	Tex A	7	14	.333	32	27	3	0-1	192.1	193	106	26	4	87-3	119	4.73	88	.258	.337	0	ø	0	75	-7	0	-0.8
1985	Tex A	0	6	.000	42	5	0	4-3	81.1	86	53	13	2	37-5	64	5.42	79	.273	.351	0	ø	0	51	-10	0	-0.7
	Phi N	0	0	ø	4	0	0	0-0	4.1	5	4	0	0	4-0	2	6.23	60	.278	.409	0	ø	0	—	-1	0	-0.1
1986	Phi N	0	0	ø	8	0	0	0-0	12.1	15	9	1	0	4-0	9	6.57	59	.306	.339	0	ø	0	—	-3	0	-0.2
	Oak A	9	5	.643	29	17	4-1	0-1	149.1	137	67	15	3	65-0	102	3.74	104	.241	.320	0	ø	0	96	4	0	0.3
1987	Oak A	**20**	13	.606	37	37	8-1	0-0	261.1	224	121	24	6	105-2	205	3.68	113	.229	.306	0	ø	0	104	14	0	1.4
1988	†Oak A	21	12	.636	37	**37**	**14**-2	0-0	**275.2**	240	111	14	3	110-5	192	3.23	118	.234	.307	0	ø	0	114	17	0	1.7
1989	†Oak A★	21	9	.700	36	**36**	8	0-0	257.2	260	105	23	6	69-0	155	3.32	112	.263	.313	0	ø	0	105	13	0	1.4
1990	†Oak A	22	11	.667	36	**36**	**11-4**	0-0	**267**	226	84	16	5	83-1	166	2.56	146	.231	.291	0	ø	0	113	37	0	4.3
1991	Oak A	11	11	.500	35	**35**	2-1	0-0	226	245	135	24	9	105-1	144	5.18	74	.278	.356	0	ø	0	134	-34	17	-3.0
1992	†Oak A	12	10	.545	31	31	2	0-0	199.1	175	96	25	8	79-1	130	3.66	103	.237	.315	0	ø	0	112	0	24	-0.1
1993	†Tor A	12	8	.600	26	26	0	0-0	162	146	86	23	4	72-0	96	4.44	99	.242	.325	0	ø	0	108	0	38	-0.1
1994	Tor A	7	8	.467	22	22	1	0-0	133.1	151	89	26	4	62-4	111	5.87	89	.285	.362	0	ø	0	99	-12	0	-1.2
1995	Oak A	3	7	.300	16	16	0	0-0	81	101	65	11	2	39-1	58	6.89	66	.305	.379	0	ø	0	102	-21	0	-2.1
Total	16	168	129	.566	523	348	55-9	19-12	2629.2	2499	1259	264	62	1034-46	1741	3.95	100	.251	.322	51-0-6	.196	2	106	14	79	3.1
Stewart, Frank	Frank "Stewy"; B9.8.1906 Minneapolis MN; D4.30.2001 Stillwater MN; BR/TR/6´1.5˝/180; d10.2																									
1927	Chi A	0	1	.000	1	1	0	0	4	5	4	0	0	4	0	9.00	45	.357	.500	1	.000	-0	62	-2	—	-0.3
Stewart, Joe	Joseph Lawrence "Ace"; B3.11.1879 Monroe NC; D2.9.1913 Youngstown OH; TR/5´11˝/175; d6.9; Col Erskine																									
1904	Bos N	0	0	ø	2	0	0	0	9.1	12	11	0	1	4	1	9.64	29	.286	.362	5	.200	-0	—	-6	—	-0.3
Stewart, Josh	Joshua Craig; B12.5.1978 Paducah KY; BL/TL/6´3˝/200; [ChiA99 5/159]; d4.6; Col Memphis																									
2003	Chi A	1	2	.333	5	5	0	0-0	25.2	28	18	4	0	16-0	13	5.96	77	.272	.367	0	ø	0	124	-4	29	-0.3
2004	Chi A	0	1	.000	3	2	0	0-0	7.2	16	13	3	0	3-0	5	15.26	31	.444	.463	0	ø	0	207	-8	0	-0.8
Total	2	1	3	.250	8	7	0	0-0	33.1	44	31	7	0	19-0	18	8.10	57	.317	.391	0	ø	0	148	-12	29	-1.1
Stewart, Sammy	Samuel Lee; B10.28.1954 Asheville NC; BR/TR/6´3˝/(207–219); d9.1; Col Montreat																									
1978	Bal A	1	1	.500	2	2	0	0-0	11.1	10	5	0	0	3-0	11	3.18	111	.238	.289	0	ø	0	140	0	0	0.0
1979	†Bal A	8	5	.615	31	3	1	1-1	117.2	96	47	11	5	71-4	71	3.52	115	.232	.349	0	ø	0	127	9	0	1.0
1980	Bal A	7	7	.500	33	3	2	3-2	118.2	103	51	9	2	60-8	78	3.56	111	.235	.328	0	ø	0	68	5	0	0.6
1981	Bal A	4	8	.333	29	3	0	4-1	112.1	89	33	8	3	57-4	57	2.32	**157**	.225	.325	0	ø	0	33	17	0	1.9

YEAR	TM LG	W	L	PCT	G	GS	CG-SHO	SV-BS	IP	H	R	HR	HB	BB-IB	SO	ERA	AERA	OAV	OOB	AB-HR-SH	AVG	PB	SUP	APR	DL	PW
1982	Bal A	10	9	.526	38	12	1-1	5-4	139	140	68	9	2	62-3	69	4.14	98	.263	.339	0	ø	0*	108	-1	23	-0.2
1983	†Bal A	9	4	.692	58	1	0	7-2	144.1	138	60	7	1	67-4	95	3.62	111	.253	.334	0	ø	0*	0	8	0	0.7
1984	Bal A	7	4	.636	60	0	0	13-3	93	81	42	7	1	47-7	56	3.29	119	.241	.332	0	ø	0	—	5	0	0.7
1985	Bal A	5	7	.417	56	1	0	9-1	129.2	117	60	15	1	66-10	77	3.61	113	.246	.336	0	ø	0	45	5	0	0.5
1986	Bos A	4	1	.800	27	0	0	0-0	63.2	64	33	7	0	48-2	47	4.38	96	.266	.381	0	ø	0	—	-1	35	-0.1
1987	Cle A	4	2	.667	25	0	0	3-4	27	25	22	4	1	21-1	25	5.67	81	.234	.362	0	ø	0	—	-4	21	-0.8
Total	10	59	48	.551	359	25	4-1	45-18	956.2	863	421	77	16	502-43	586	3.59	111	.245	.338	0	ø	0	92	43	79	4.3

STEWART, SCOTT Scott Edward; B8.14.1975 Stoughton MA; BR/TL/6´2˝/225; [TexA94 20/561]; d4.5

YEAR	TM LG	W	L	PCT	G	GS	CG-SHO	SV-BS	IP	H	R	HR	HB	BB-IB	SO	ERA	AERA	OAV	OOB	AB-HR-SH	AVG	PB	SUP	APR	DL	PW
2001	Mon N	3	1	.750	62	0	0	3-1	47.2	43	20	5	3	13-0	39	3.78	114	.243	.299	0	ø	0	—	4	22	0.4
2002	Mon N	4	2	.667	67	0	0	17-2	64	49	29	4	1	22-5	67	3.09	142	.207	.275	2	.000	-0	—	7	0	0.9
2003	Mon N	3	1	.750	51	0	0	0-1	43	52	22	5	1	13-4	29	3.98	112	.306	.357	2	.000	-0	—	2	53	0.1
2004	Cle A	0	2	.000	23	0	0	0-2	13.2	23	14	2	0	6-2	18	7.24	60	.365	.414	0	ø	0	—	-6	0	-0.7
	LA N	1	0	1.000	11	0	0	0-0	12.1	20	8	3	0	6-3	8	5.84	71	.392	.441	0	ø	0	—	-2	0	-0.2
Total	4	11	6	.647	214	0	0	20-6	180.2	187	93	19	5	60-14	161	3.99	109	.268	.326	4	.000	-0	—	5	75	0.5

STEWART, BUNKY Veston Goff; B1.7.1931 Jasper NC; BL/TL/6´0˝/155; d5.4; Col East Carolina

YEAR	TM LG	W	L	PCT	G	GS	CG-SHO	SV-BS	IP	H	R	HR	HB	BB-IB	SO	ERA	AERA	OAV	OOB	AB-HR-SH	AVG	PB	SUP	APR	DL	PW
1952	Was A	0	0	ø	1	0	0	0	1	2	2	0	0	1	1	18.00	20	.500	.600	0	ø	0	—	-2	0	-0.1
1953	Was A	0	2	.000	2	2	1	0	15.1	17	9	1	1	11	3	4.70	83	.283	.403	5	.200	-0	57	-1	0	-0.2
1954	Was A	0	2	.000	29	2	0	1	50.2	67	52	3	4	27	27	7.64	47	.324	.410	3	.000	0	99	-25	0	-1.2
1955	Was A	0	0	ø	7	1	0	0	15.1	18	7	0	0	6-1	10	4.11	93	.295	.358	2	.000	-0	93	0	0	0.0
1956	Was A	5	7	.417	33	9	1	2	105	111	77	15	5	82-4	36	5.57	78	.276	.402	28-0-4	.250	-0*	71	-15	0	-1.5
Total	5	5	11	.313	72	14	2	3	187.1	215	147	19	10	127-5	77	6.01	67	.293	.402	38-0-4	.211	-0	75	-43	0	-3.0

STEWART, LEFTY Walter Cleveland; B9.23.1900 Sparta TN; D9.26.1974 Knoxville TN; BR/TL/5´10˝/160; d4.20

YEAR	TM LG	W	L	PCT	G	GS	CG-SHO	SV-BS	IP	H	R	HR	HB	BB-IB	SO	ERA	AERA	OAV	OOB	AB-HR-SH	AVG	PB	SUP	APR	DL	PW
1921	Det A	0	0	ø	5	0	0	1	9	20	12	0	0	5	4	12.00	36	.455	.510	1	.000	-0	—	-7	—	-0.3
1927	StL A	8	11	.421	27	19	11	1	155.2	187	83	7	2	43	43	4.28	102	.310	.357	49-0-4	.306	3*	82	4	—	0.7
1928	StL A	7	9	.438	29	17	7-1	3	142.2	173	81	5	2	32	25	4.67	90	.310	.350	51	.275	3	113	-5	—	-0.2
1929	StL A	9	6	.600	23	18	8-1	0	149.2	137	67	11	4	49	47	3.25	136	.246	.312	51-0-6	.118	-4	97	17	—	1.1
1930	StL A	20	12	.625	35	33	23-1	0	271	281	119	21	1	70	79	3.45	141	.268	.315	90-0-6	.244	2	87	41	—	4.4
1931	StL A	14	17	.452	36	33	20-1	0	258	287	155	17	3	85	89	4.40	105	.277	.334	88-0-3	.250	6	93	5	—	1.2
1932	StL A	15	19	.441	41	32	18-2	1	259.2	269	148	22	3	99	86	4.61	105	.270	.338	82-0-6	.146	-2	79	10	—	0.9
1933	†Was A	15	6	.714	34	31	11-1	0	230.2	227	116	19	1	60	69	3.82	109	.256	.304	77-0-9	.143	1*	115	7	—	0.6
1934	Was A	7	11	.389	24	22	7-1	0	152	184	74	8	1	36	36	4.03	107	.303	.343	45-0-13	.156	-1*	72	6	—	0.5
1935	Was A	0	1	.000	1	1	0	0	2.2	8	9	1	0	2	1	13.50	32	.533	.588	1	.000	-0	0	-5	—	-0.7
	Cle A	6	6	.500	24	10	2	2	91	122	68	6	1	17	24	5.44	83	.312	.342	30-0-2	.200	-1	108	-11	—	-1.4
	Year	6	7	.462	25	11	2	2	93.2	130	77	7	1	19	25	5.67	79	.320	.352	31-0-2	.194	-1	98	-17	—	-2.1
Total	10	101	98	.508	279	216	107-8	8	1722	1895	932	117	18	498	503	4.19	108	.281	.332	565-0-49	.204	6	92	62	—	6.8

STEWART, MACK William Macklin; B9.23.1914 Stevenson AL; D3.21.1960 Macon GA; BR/TR/6´0˝/167; d7.7

YEAR	TM LG	W	L	PCT	G	GS	CG-SHO	SV-BS	IP	H	R	HR	HB	BB-IB	SO	ERA	AERA	OAV	OOB	AB-HR-SH	AVG	PB	SUP	APR	DL	PW
1944	Chi N	0	0	ø	8	0	0	0	12.1	11	2	1	0	4	3	1.46	242	.239	.300	1	.000	-0	—	3	0	0.1
1945	Chi N	0	1	.000	16	1	0	0	28.1	37	16	0	0	14	9	4.76	77	.322	.395	3	.333	0	70	-3	0	-0.1
Total	2	0	1	.000	24	1	0	0	40.2	48	18	1	0	18	12	3.76	96	.298	.369	4	.250	0	70	0	0	0.0

STIDHAM, PHIL Phillip Wayne; B11.18.1968 Tulsa OK; BR/TR/6´0˝/180; [DetA91 15/400]; d6.4; Col Arkansas

YEAR	TM LG	W	L	PCT	G	GS	CG-SHO	SV-BS	IP	H	R	HR	HB	BB-IB	SO	ERA	AERA	OAV	OOB	AB-HR-SH	AVG	PB	SUP	APR	DL	PW
1994	Det A	0	0	ø	5	0	0	0-0	4.1	12	12	3	0	4-1	4	24.92	20	.571	.615	0	ø	0	—	-9	0	-0.4

STIEB, DAVE David Andrew; B7.22.1957 Santa Ana CA; BR/TR/6´1˝/(185–195); [TorA78 5/106]; d6.29; Col Southern Illinois

YEAR	TM LG	W	L	PCT	G	GS	CG-SHO	SV-BS	IP	H	R	HR	HB	BB-IB	SO	ERA	AERA	OAV	OOB	AB-HR-SH	AVG	PB	SUP	APR	DL	PW
1979	Tor A	8	8	.500	18	18	7-1	0-0	129.1	139	70	11	4	48-3	52	4.31	102	.276	.342	0	ø	0*	94	1	0	0.2
1980	Tor A★	12	15	.444	34	32	14-4	0-0	242.2	232	108	12	6	83-6	108	3.71	116	.260	.324	1	.000	-0*	80	17	0	2.0
1981	Tor A★	11	10	.524	25	25	11-2	0-0	183.2	148	70	10	11	61-2	89	3.19	124	.223	.296	0	ø	0*	63	17	0	2.0
1982	Tor A	17	14	.548	38	38	**19-5**	0-0	**288.1**	271	116	27	5	75-4	141	3.25	139	.248	.298	0	ø	0	79	**36**	0	3.9
1983	Tor A★	17	12	.586	36	36	14-4	0-0	278	223	105	21	14	93-6	187	3.04	143	.219	.291	0	ø	0	94	**37**	0	3.7
1984	Tor A★	16	8	.667	35	35	11-2	0-0	**267**	215	87	19	11	88-1	198	2.83	**146**	**.221**	.292	0	ø	0	91	**40**	0	3.5
1985	†Tor A★	14	13	.519	36	36	8-2	0-0	265	206	89	22	9	96-3	167	**2.48**	**171**	**.213**	.290	0	ø	0	95	**47**	0	**4.9**
1986	Tor A	7	12	.368	37	34	1-1	1-0	205	239	128	29	15	87-1	127	4.74	90	.297	.373	0	ø	0*	101	-15	0	-1.2
1987	Tor A	13	9	.591	33	31	3-1	0-0	185	164	92	16	7	87-4	115	4.09	111	.239	.329	0	ø	0*	120	9	0	0.9
1988	Tor A★	16	8	.667	32	31	8-4	0-0	207.1	157	76	15	13	79-0	147	3.04	130	.210	.295	0	ø	0*	108	22	0	2.5
1989	†Tor A	17	8	.680	33	33	3-2	0-0	206.2	164	83	12	13	76-2	101	3.35	113	.219	.301	0	ø	0	124	12	0	1.3
1990	Tor A★	18	6	.750	33	33	2-2	0-0	208.2	179	73	11	10	64-0	125	2.93	135	.230	.296	0	ø	0	104	23	0	2.7
1991	Tor A	4	3	.571	9	9	1	0-0	59.2	52	22	4	2	23-0	29	3.17	133	.243	.321	0	ø	0	79	7	137	0.8
1992	Tor A	4	6	.400	21	14	1	0-0	96.1	98	58	9	4	43-3	45	5.04	81	.275	.355	0	ø	0	92	-9	73	-0.8
1993	Chi A	1	3	.250	4	4	0	0-0	22.1	27	17	1	0	14-0	11	6.04	70	.300	.390	0	ø	0	98	-5	23	-0.7
1998	Tor A	1	2	.333	19	3	0	2-0	50.1	58	31	6	5	17-1	27	4.83	97	.284	.351	1	.000	-0	140	-2	0	-0.1
Total	16	176	137	.562	443	412	103-30	3-0	2895.1	2572	1225	225	129	1034-36	1669	3.44	123	.239	.312	2	.000	-0	96	237	233	25.6

STIELY, FRED Fred Warren "Lefty"; B6.1.1901 Pillow PA; D1.6.1981 Valley View PA; BL/TL/5´8˝/170; d10.6

YEAR	TM LG	W	L	PCT	G	GS	CG-SHO	SV-BS	IP	H	R	HR	HB	BB-IB	SO	ERA	AERA	OAV	OOB	AB-HR-SH	AVG	PB	SUP	APR	DL	PW
1929	StL A	1	0	1.000	1	1	1	0	9	11	2	0	1	3	2	0.00	ø	.297	.366	3	.667	1	76	3	—	0.6
1930	StL A	0	1	.000	4	2	1	0	19	27	21	4	1	8	5	8.53	57	.346	.414	7	.429	1*	115	-8	—	-0.2
1931	StL A	0	0	ø	4	0	0	0	6.2	7	5	0	1	3	2	6.75	69	.269	.367	0	ø	0	—	-1	—	-0.1
Total	3	1	1	.500	9	3	2	0	34.2	45	28	4	3	14	9	5.97	79	.319	.392	10	.500	2	103	-6	—	0.3

STIGMAN, DICK Richard Lewis; B1.24.1936 Nimrod MN; BR/TL/6´3˝/200; d4.22

YEAR	TM LG	W	L	PCT	G	GS	CG-SHO	SV-BS	IP	H	R	HR	HB	BB-IB	SO	ERA	AERA	OAV	OOB	AB-HR-SH	AVG	PB	SUP	APR	DL	PW
1960	Cle A☆	5	11	.313	41	18	3	9	133.2	118	78	13	0	87-1	104	4.51	83	.238	.348	36-0-1	.222	2	79	-13	0	-1.4
1961	Cle A	2	5	.286	22	6	0	0	64.1	65	35	9	0	25-1	48	4.62	85	.264	.327	16	.125	-1	49	-4	56	-0.4
1962	Min A	12	5	.706	40	15	6	3	142.2	122	60	19	2	64-3	116	3.66	112	.233	.318	45	.044	-4	152	9	0	0.5
1963	Min A	15	15	.500	33	33	15-3	0	241	210	90	32	0	81-2	193	3.25	112	.231	.293	84-0-5	.107	-2	108	15	0	1.4
1964	Min A	6	15	.286	32	29	5-1	0	190	160	94	31	5	70-7	159	4.03	89	.225	.298	69	.101	-3	81	-8	0	-1.2
1965	Min A	4	2	.667	33	8	0	4	70	59	34	14	0	33-3	70	4.37	81	.227	.312	15-0-1	.133	-0	114	-4	0	-0.4
1966	Bos A	2	1	.667	34	10	1-1	0	81	85	51	15	1	46-5	65	5.44	70	.268	.361	17-0-2	.118	-1	79	-11	0	-0.7
Total	7	46	54	.460	235	119	30-5	16	922.2	819	442	133	8	406-22	755	4.03	93	.237	.316	282-0-9	.113	-8	97	-16	56	-2.2

STILES, ROLLIE Rolland Mays "Lena"; B11.17.1906 Ratcliff AR; BR/TR/6´1.5˝/180; d6.19; Col Southeastern Oklahoma

YEAR	TM LG	W	L	PCT	G	GS	CG-SHO	SV-BS	IP	H	R	HR	HB	BB-IB	SO	ERA	AERA	OAV	OOB	AB-HR-SH	AVG	PB	SUP	APR	DL	PW
1930	StL A	3	6	.333	20	7	3	0	102	136	77	10	1	41	25	5.91	82	.337	.399	37	.270	0	98	-11	—	-0.8
1931	StL A	3	1	.750	34	2	0	0	81	112	72	2	2	60	32	7.22	64	.352	.458	22	.045	-2	100	-19	—	-1.1
1933	StL A	3	7	.300	31	9	6-1	1	115	154	83	4	2	47	29	5.01	93	.327	.390	33-0-2	.061	-3	95	-9	—	-1.0
Total	3	9	14	.391	85	18	9-1	1	298	402	232	16	5	148	86	5.92	80	.337	.412	92-0-2	.141	-5	97	-39	—	-2.9

STIMMEL, ARCHIE Archibald May "Lumbago"; B5.30.1873 Woodsboro MD; D8.18.1958 Frederick MD; BR/TR/6´0˝/175; d7.3

YEAR	TM LG	W	L	PCT	G	GS	CG-SHO	SV-BS	IP	H	R	HR	HB	BB-IB	SO	ERA	AERA	OAV	OOB	AB-HR-SH	AVG	PB	SUP	APR	DL	PW
1900	Cin N	1	1	.500	2	1	1	0	13	18	11	1	0	4	2	6.92	53	.327	.373	5	.200	-0	0	-4	—	-0.5
1901	Cin N	4	14	.222	20	18	14-1	0	153.1	170	96	10	12	44	55	4.11	78	.279	.339	62-0-2	.081	-5*	66	-16	—	-2.1
1902	Cin N	0	4	.000	4	3	3	0	26	37	16	1	2	12	7	3.46	87	.333	.408	10	.200	-0	53	-1	—	-0.2
Total	3	5	19	.208	26	22	18-1	0	192.1	225	123	12	14	60	64	4.21	76	.290	.352	77-0-2	.104	-5	61	-21	—	-2.8

STIMSON, CARL Carl Remus; B7.18.1894 Hamburg IA; D11.9.1936 Omaha NE; BB/TR/6´5˝/190; d6.6

YEAR	TM LG	W	L	PCT	G	GS	CG-SHO	SV-BS	IP	H	R	HR	HB	BB-IB	SO	ERA	AERA	OAV	OOB	AB-HR-SH	AVG	PB	SUP	APR	DL	PW
1923	Bos A	0	0	ø	2	0	0	0	4	12	10	0	1	5	1	22.50	18	.750	.818	2	.000	-0	—	-7	—	-0.3

STINE, HARRY Harry C.; B2.20.1864 Shenandoah PA; D6.5.1924 Niagara Falls NY; TL/5´6˝/150; d7.22

YEAR	TM LG	W	L	PCT	G	GS	CG-SHO	SV-BS	IP	H	R	HR	HB	BB-IB	SO	ERA	AERA	OAV	OOB	AB-HR-SH	AVG	PB	SUP	APR	DL	PW
1890	Phi AA	0	1	.000	1	1	1	0	8	17	9	0	0	4	1	9.00	43	.415	.467	3	.000	-0	52	-4	—	-0.3

STINE, LEE Lee Elbert; B11.17.1913 Stillwater OK; D5.6.2005 Hemet CA; BR/TR/5´11˝/185; d4.17

YEAR	TM LG	W	L	PCT	G	GS	CG-SHO	SV-BS	IP	H	R	HR	HB	BB-IB	SO	ERA	AERA	OAV	OOB	AB-HR-SH	AVG	PB	SUP	APR	DL	PW
1934	Chi A	0	0	ø	4	0	0	0	11	11	10	2	1	10	8	8.18	58	.268	.423	1	.000	0	—	-3	—	-0.2
1935	Chi A	0	0	ø	2	0	0	0	2	2	2	1	0	3	1	9.00	51	.286	.500	0	ø	0	—	-1	—	0.0
1936	Cin N	3	8	.273	40	13	5-1	2	121.2	157	79	6	8	41	26	5.03	76	.318	.379	27-0-2	.296	3	107	-16	—	-1.0
1938	NY A	0	0	ø	4	0	0	0	8.2	9	1	0	0	1	4	1.04	437	.333	.357	2	.500	0	—	4	—	0.2
Total	4	3	8	.273	49	13	5-1	2	143.1	179	92	9	9	55	39	5.09	78	.315	.384	30-0-2	.300	4	107	-16	—	-1.0

YEAR	TM LG	W	L	PCT	G	GS	CG-SHO	SV-BS	IP	H	R	HR	HB	BB-IB	SO	ERA	AERA	OAV	OOB	AB-HR-SH	AVG	PB	SUP	APR	DL	PW
STIVETTS, JACK	John Elmer "Happy Jack"; B3.31.1868 Ashland PA; D4.18.1930 Ashland PA; BR/TR/6'2"/185; d6.26; ▲																									
1889	StL AA	12	7	.632	26	20	18-2	2	191.2	153	85	4	5	68	143	**2.25**	**188**	**.212**	**.285**	79	.228	-1*	72	36	—	2.8
1890	StL AA	27	21	.563	54	46	41-3	0	419.1	399	255	14	17	179	289	3.52	123	.243	.324	226-7	.288	14*	103	31	—	4.2
1891	StL AA	33	22	.600	**64**	56	40-3	1	440	357	237	15	18	232	**259**	2.86	147	.214	.317	302-7	.305	9*	95	**58**	—	**6.8**
1892	†Bos N	35	16	.686	54	48	45-3	1	415.2	346	223	12	10	171	180	3.03	116	.217	.297	240-3	.296	15*	109	18	—	3.3
1893	Bos N	20	12	.625	38	34	29-1	1	283.2	315	194	17	10	115	61	4.41	112	.273	.344	172-3	.297	7*	115	15	—	1.7
1894	Bos N	26	14	.650	45	39	30	0	338	429	278	27	13	127	76	4.90	116	.306	.369	244-8-3	.328	10*	121	22	—	2.5
1895	Bos N	17	17	.500	38	34	30	0	291	341	219	15	12	89	111	4.64	110	.288	.344	158-0-2	.190	-7*	86	15	—	0.5
1896	Bos N	22	14	.611	42	36	31-2	0	329	353	219	19	7	99	71	4.10	111	.272	.327	222-3-4	.347	12*	111	20	—	2.6
1897	†Bos N	11	4	.733	18	15	10	0	129.1	147	75	5	5	43	27	3.41	131	.284	.345	199-2-1	.367	7*	141	12	—	1.8
1898	Bos N	0	1	.000	2	1	1	0	12	17	12	2	0	7	1	8.25	45	.333	.414	111-2-4	.252	0*	58	-5	—	-0.3
1899	Cle N	0	4	.000	7	4	3	0	38	48	39	0	2	25	5	5.68	65	.308	.410	39	.205	1*	49	-11	—	-0.8
Total	11	203	132	.606	388	333	278-14	5	2887.2	2905	1836	130	99	1155	1223	3.74	121	.255	.329	1992-35-14	.298	65	104	211	—	25.1
STOBBS, CHUCK	Charles Klein; B7.2.1929 Wheeling WV; BL/TL/6'1"/(185–205); d9.15																									
1947	Bos A	0	1	.000	4	1	0	0	9	10	6	0	0	10	5	6.00	65	.294	.455	1	.000	-0	68	-2	0	-0.2
1948	Bos A	0	0	ø	6	0	0	0	7	9	5	0	0	7	4	6.43	68	.321	.457	1	.000	-0	—	-1	0	-0.1
1949	Bos A	11	6	.647	26	19	10	0	152	145	72	10	2	75	70	4.03	108	.254	.343	53-0-6	.208	0	124	7	0	0.6
1950	Bos A	12	7	.632	32	21	6	1	169.1	158	104	17	5	88	78	5.10	96	.250	.346	57-0-4	.246	3	151	-3	0	0.0
1951	Bos A	10	9	.526	34	25	6	0	170	180	100	16	5	74	75	4.76	94	.271	.349	61-0-5	.180	-2	111	-5	0	-0.7
1952	Chi A	7	12	.368	38	17	2	1	135	118	54	9	5	72	73	3.13	116	.237	.339	38-0-4	.079	-1	70	7	0	0.8
1953	Was A	11	8	.579	27	20	8	0	153	146	64	11	1	44	67	3.29	118	.246	.299	44-0-10	.227	1	128	10	0	1.3
1954	Was A	11	11	.500	31	24	10-3	0	182	189	87	6	1	67	67	4.10	87	.270	.330	51-0-9	.137	0	103	-8	0	-0.8
1955	Was A	4	14	.222	41	16	2	3	140.1	169	90	13	1	57-8	60	5.00	77	.302	.364	35-0-1	.171	2	73	-20	0	-2.0
1956	Was A	15	15	.500	37	33	15-1	1	240	264	115	29	1	54-4	97	3.60	120	.279	.316	84-0-4	.179	-2*	77	16	0	1.7
1957	Was A	8	20	.286	42	31	5-2	1	211.2	235	140	28	5	80-10	114	5.36	73	.279	.343	76-0-4	.211	1	76	-35	0	-4.1
1958	Was A	2	6	.250	19	8	0	0	56.2	87	44	7	2	16-0	23	6.04	63	.369	.405	12	.000	-2	77	-15	0	-2.0
	StL N	1	3	.250	17	0	0	0	39.2	40	16	4	0	14-1	25	3.63	114	.261	.323	4-0-1	.250	0	—	3	0	0.4
1959	Was A	1	8	.111	41	7	0	7	90.2	82	42	13	2	24-1	50	2.98	131	.238	.290	19-0-1	.105	-1	74	6	0	0.5
1960	Was A	12	7	.632	40	13	1-1	2	119.1	115	54	13	3	38-4	72	3.32	117	.252	.311	34-0-1	.088	-2	92	7	0	0.8
1961	Min A	2	3	.400	24	3	0	2	44.2	56	37	8	2	15-2	17	7.46	57	.311	.363	8	.375	1	49	-13	0	-1.3
Total	15	107	130	.451	459	238	65-7	19	1920.1	2003	1030	184	35	735-30	897	4.29	95	.269	.336	578-0-50	.176	-1	99	-46	0	-5.1
STOCK, WES	Wesley Gay; B4.10.1934 Longview WA; BR/TR/6'2"/(180–188); d4.19; C16; Col Washington St.																									
1959	Bal A	0	0	ø	7	0	0	1	12.2	16	6	1	0	2-0	8	3.55	107	.302	.327	2	.000	-0	—	0	0	0.0
1960	Bal A	2	2	.500	17	0	0	2	34.1	26	11	2	1	14-1	23	2.88	132	.218	.306	6	.000	-1	—	4	0	0.5
1961	Bal A	5	0	1.000	35	1	0	3	71.2	58	24	3	2	27-2	47	3.01	128	.225	.300	11	.000	-1	0	8	0	0.6
1962	Bal A	3	2	.600	53	0	0	3	65	50	33	7	1	36-6	34	4.43	83	.217	.326	3	.000	-0	—	-4	0	-0.2
1963	Bal A	7	0	1.000	47	0	0	1	75.1	69	41	11	0	31-7	55	3.94	88	.246	.319	10	.000	-1	—	-6	0	-0.7
1964	Bal A	2	0	1.000	14	0	0	0	20.2	17	9	5	0	8-1	14	3.92	91	.233	.305	4	.000	-0	—	0	0	-0.1
	KC A	6	3	.667	50	0	0	5	93	69	21	10	4	34-7	101	1.94	197	.213	.292	15-0-3	.200	0	—	19	0	2.0
	Year	8	3	.727	64	0	0	5	113.2	86	30	15	4	42-8	115	2.30	164	.217	.295	19-0-3	.158	-0	—	19	0	1.9
1965	KC A	0	4	.000	62	2	0	4	99.2	96	62	18	4	40-2	52	5.24	67	.251	.326	6-0-2	.000	-1	113	-18	0	-0.9
1966	KC A	2	2	.500	35	0	0	3	44	30	15	3	3	21-3	31	2.66	128	.199	.307	2	.000	-0	—	4	0	0.3
1967	KC A	0	0	ø	1	0	0	0	1	3	2	0	0	2-0	0	18.00	18	.500	.625	0	ø	0	—	-2	0	-0.1
Total	9	27	13	.675	321	3	0	22	517.1	434	224	60	15	215-29	365	3.60	101	.231	.313	59-0-5	.051	-4	73	5	0	1.4
STOCKMAN, PHIL	Phillip Matthew; B1.25.1980 Oldham, United Kingdom; BR/TR/6'8"/250; d6.15																									
2006	Atl N	0	0	ø	4	0	0	0-0	4	3	1	0	0	4-2	4	2.25	201	.231	.412	0	ø	0	—	1	100	0.1
STOCKSDALE, OTIS	Otis Hinkley "Old Gray Fox"; B8.7.1871 Arcadia MD; D3.15.1933 Pennsville NJ; BL/TR/5'10.5"/180; d7.24; Col Johns Hopkins																									
1893	Was N	2	8	.200	11	11	7	0	69	111	82	4	5	32	12	8.22	56	.352	.420	40	.300	2*	85	-24	—	-2.2
1894	Was N	5	9	.357	18	14	11	0	117.1	176	115	10	14	42	10	5.06	104	.342	.407	71-0-1	.324	1*	95	1	—	0.2
1895	Was N	6	11	.353	20	17	11	1	136	199	143	7	8	52	23	6.09	79	.336	.397	74-0-1	.311	2*	99	-18	—	-1.4
	Bos N	2	2	.500	4	4	1	0	23	31	22	2	0	8	2	5.87	87	.316	.368	15	.267	-0*	133	-2	—	-0.3
	Year	8	13	.381	24	21	12	1	159	230	165	9	8	60	25	6.06	80	.333	.393	89-0-1	.303	2	106	-25	—	-1.7
1896	Bal N	0	1	.000	1	0	0	0	1.2	4	4	0	1	2	1	16.20	26	.444	.583	3	.333	1*	—	-2	—	-0.3
Total	4	15	31	.326	54	46	30	1	347	521	366	23	28	136	48	6.20	80	.341	.405	203-0-2	.310	5	97	-45	—	-4.0
STODDARD, BOB	Robert Lyle; B3.8.1957 San Jose CA; BR/TR/6'1"/(190–200); [SeaA78 10/240]; d9.4; Col Cal St.–Fresno																									
1981	Sea A	2	1	.667	5	5	1	0-0	34.2	35	10	3	1	9-0	22	2.60	150	.269	.321	0	ø	0	97	5	0	0.4
1982	Sea A	3	3	.500	9	9	2-1	0-0	67.1	48	22	7	3	18-0	24	2.41	178	.205	.267	0	ø	0	71	13	0	1.1
1983	Sea A	9	17	.346	35	23	2-1	0-0	175.2	182	95	29	4	58-0	87	4.41	97	.274	.334	0	ø	0	60	-2	0	-0.1
1984	Sea A	2	3	.400	27	6	0	0-0	79	86	51	10	2	37-3	39	5.13	78	.278	.357	0	ø	0	86	-10	0	-0.5
1985	Det A	0	0	ø	8	0	0	1-0	13.1	15	11	3	0	5-0	11	6.75	61	.268	.328	0	ø	0	—	-4	0	-0.2
1986	SD N	1	0	1.000	18	0	0	1-1	23.1	20	7	1	1	11-1	17	2.31	158	.227	.317	1	.000	-0	—	3	0	0.2
1987	KC A	1	3	.250	17	2	0	1-0	40	51	26	3	3	22-2	23	4.27	107	.313	.402	0	ø	0	40	-1	0	0.0
Total	7	18	27	.400	119	45	5-2	3-1	433.1	437	222	56	14	160-6	223	4.03	104	.266	.334	1	.000	-0	69	4	0	0.9
STODDARD, TIM	Timothy Paul; B1.24.1953 E.Chicago IN; BR/TR/6'7"/(235–253); [ChiA75*S2/44]; d9.7; Col North Carolina St.																									
1975	Chi A	0	0	ø	1	0	0	0-0	1	2	1	1	0	0-0	0	9.00	43	.400	.400	0	ø	0	—	-1	0	0.0
1978	Bal A	0	1	.000	8	0	0	0-0	18	22	17	3	2	8-1	14	6.00	59	.301	.386	0	ø	0	—	-7	0	-0.4
1979	†Bal A	3	1	.750	29	0	0	3-3	58	44	12	3	0	19-2	47	1.71	237	.212	.278	0	ø	0	—	16	42	1.2
1980	Bal A	5	3	.625	64	0	0	26-7	86	72	27	2	1	38-1	64	2.51	158	.233	.317	0	ø	0	—	14	0	2.1
1981	Bal A	4	2	.667	31	0	0	7-4	37.1	38	16	6	2	18-0	32	3.86	95	.268	.358	0	ø	0	—	0	0	0.0
1982	Bal A	3	4	.429	50	0	0	12-3	56	53	26	4	1	29-6	42	4.02	101	.249	.337	0	ø	0	—	1	57	0.1
1983	Bal A	4	3	.571	47	0	0	9-2	57.2	65	39	10	1	29-4	50	6.09	66	.293	.371	0	ø	0	—	-12	0	-1.6
1984	†Chi N	10	6	.625	58	0	0	7-4	92	77	41	9	1	57-11	87	3.82	102	.236	.346	11-0-1	.091	-1	—	2	0	0.2
1985	SD N	1	6	.143	44	0	0	1-0	60	63	35	3	0	37-7	42	4.65	76	.269	.366	5-0-1	.000	-1	—	-7	0	-0.9
1986	SD N	1	3	.250	30	0	0	0-1	45.1	33	20	6	0	34-6	47	3.77	97	.200	.337	4-1-0	.250	1	—	0	0	0.1
	NY A	4	1	.800	24	0	0	0-1	49.1	41	23	6	0	23-3	34	3.83	108	.232	.317	0	ø	0	—	2	0	0.2
1987	NY A	4	3	.571	57	0	0	8-1	92.2	83	38	13	0	30-2	78	3.50	127	.235	.293	0	ø	0	—	10	9	0.8
1988	NY A	2	2	.500	28	0	0	3-0	55	62	41	5	2	27-1	33	6.38	62	.286	.361	0	ø	0	—	-14	21	-1.0
1989	Cle A	0	0	ø	14	0	0	0-0	21.1	25	7	1	0	7-1	12	2.95	135	.313	.356	0	ø	0	—	3	0	0.1
Total	13	41	35	.539	485	0	0	76-26	729.2	680	343	72	10	356-45	582	3.95	101	.250	.335	20-1-2	.100	-0	—	7	129	0.9
STOKES, ART	Arthur Milton; B9.13.1896 Emmitsburg MD; D6.3.1962 Titusville PA; BR/TR/5'10.5"/155; d5.5																									
1925	Phi A	1	1	.500	12	0	0	0	24.1	24	15	0	2	10	7	4.07	114	.270	.356	4	.000	-0	—	1	—	0.0
STOKES, BRIAN	Brian Alexander; B9.7.1979 Pomona CA; BR/TR/6'1"/205; d9.3; Col Riverside (CA) CC																									
2006	TB A	1	0	1.000	5	4	0	0-0	24	31	13	2	1	9-0	15	4.88	96	.320	.373	0	ø	0	111	0	0	0.0
STONE, DICK	Charles Richard; B12.5.1911 Oklahoma City OK; D2.18.1980 Oklahoma City OK; BL/TL/5'9"/153; d8.26; Col Oklahoma City																									
1945	Was A	0	0	ø	3	0	0	0	5	6	0	0	0	2	0	0.00	ø	.316	.381	0	ø	0	—	2	0	0.1
STONE, DEAN	Darrah Dean; B9.1.1930 Moline IL; BL/TL/6'4"/(195–205); d9.13																									
1953	Was A	0	1	.000	3	1	0	0	8.2	13	8	0	0	5	5	8.31	47	.361	.439	2	.000	-0	46	-4	0	-0.4
1954	Was A★	12	10	.545	31	23	10-2	0	178.2	161	76	7	1	69	87	3.22	110	.240	.310	52-1-6	.096	-0	113	6	0	0.5
1955	Was A	6	13	.316	43	24	5-1	1	180	180	98	14	3	114-5	84	4.15	92	.267	.371	46-0-10	.043	-4	80	-8	0	-1.2
1956	Was A	5	7	.417	41	21	2	3	132	148	107	10	7	93-0	86	6.27	69	.282	.395	34-0-2	.088	-1*	109	-28	0	-2.5
1957	Was A	0	0	ø	3	0	0	0	3.1	5	3	0	0	2-1	3	8.10	48	.357	.412	0	ø	0	—	-1	0	-0.1
	Bos A	1	3	.250	17	8	0	1	51.1	56	42	5	0	35-0	32	5.08	78	.284	.386	14-0-1	.000	-1	101	-10	0	-0.8
	Year	1	3	.250	20	8	0	1	54.2	61	45	5	0	37-1	35	5.27	76	.289	.387	14-0-1	.000	-1	101	-12	0	-0.9
1959	StL N	0	1	.000	18	1	0	1	30	30	15	4	0	16-4	17	4.20	101	.273	.357	4	.000	-0	0	0	0	0.0
1962	Hou N	3	2	.600	15	7	2-2	0	52.1	61	31	4	1	20-0	31	4.47	84	.295	.360	16-0-3	.250	1	107	-5	0	-0.3

YEAR	TM LG	W	L	PCT	G	GS	CG-SHO	SV-BS	IP	H	R	HR	HB	BB-IB	SO	ERA	AERA	OAV	OOB	AB-HR-SH	AVG	PB	SUP	APR	DL	PW
	Chi A	1	0	1.000	27	0	0	5	30.1	28	11	3	1	9-2	23	3.26	120	.255	.306	2	.500	1	—	3	0	0.2
1963	Bal A	1	2	.333	17	0	0	1	19.1	23	11	0	0	10-2	12	5.12	68	.307	.384	0	ø	0	—	-3	0	-0.5
Total	8	29	39	.426	215	85	19-5	12	686	705	402	47	13	373-14	380	4.47	86	.269	.360	170-1-22	.088	-6	100	-50	0	-5.1
Stone, Dwight	Dwight Ely; B8.2.1886 Holt Co. NE; D6.3.1976 Glendale CA; BR/TR/6´1.5˝/170; d4.13																									
1913	StL A	2	6	.250	18	7	4-1	0	91	94	45	0	7	46	37	3.56	82	.271	.368	33	.273	2	72	-5	—	-0.2
1914	KC F	8	14	.364	39	22	6	0	186.2	205	110	8	8	77	88	4.34	64	.281	.356	58-1-2	.121	-3	91	-30	—	-3.5
Total	2	10	20	.333	57	29	10-1	0	277.2	299	155	8	15	123	125	4.08	69	.278	.360	91-1-2	.176	-1	86	-35	—	-3.7
Stone, Arnie	Edwin Arnold; B10.9.1892 North Creek NY; D7.29.1948 Hudson Falls NY; BR/TL/6´0˝/180; d7.30																									
1923	Pit N	0	1	.000	9	0	0	0	12.1	19	12	0	0	4	2	8.03	50	.352	.397	1	.000	-0	—	-5	—	-0.4
1924	Pit N	4	2	.667	26	2	1	0	64	57	27	0	0	15	7	2.95	130	.259	.306	15	.133	-1	155	5	—	0.3
Total	2	4	3	.571	35	2	1	0	76.1	76	39	0	0	19	9	3.77	102	.277	.324	16	.125	-1	155	0	—	-0.1
Stone, George	George Heard; B7.9.1946 Ruston LA; BL/TL/6´3˝/195; [AtlN66 5/91]; d9.15; Col Louisiana Tech																									
1967	Atl N	0	0	ø	2	1	0	0	7.1	8	4	0	0	1-0	5	4.91	68	.267	.290	2	.000	-0	26	-1	0	-0.1
1968	Atl N	7	4	.636	17	10	2	0	75	63	27	9	0	19-4	52	2.76	108	.222	.271	27-0-1	.333	3	142	2	0	0.5
1969	†Atl N	13	10	.565	36	20	3	3-1	165.1	166	82	20	5	48-5	102	3.65	99	.260	.316	59-1-5	.186	1	119	-4	0	-0.4
1970	Atl N	11	11	.500	35	30	9-2	0-0	207.1	218	111	27	6	50-7	131	3.86	111	.267	.312	72-0-3	.236	4	113	4	0	1.0
1971	Atl N	6	8	.429	27	24	4-2	0-0	172.2	186	80	19	6	35-4	110	3.60	104	.274	.313	62-0-3	.177	-0*	89	2	0	0.1
1972	Atl N	6	11	.353	31	16	2-1	1-0	111	143	72	18	4	44-11	63	5.51	69	.315	.378	25-0-6	.200	1*	92	-18	0	-2.3
1973	†NY N	12	3	.800	27	20	2	1-0	148	157	53	16	0	31-3	77	2.80	130	.274	.308	48-0-3	.271	2*	111	13	0	1.6
1974	NY N	2	7	.222	15	13	1	0-0	77	103	57	10	0	21-4	29	5.03	72	.322	.362	26	.115	-1	93	-15	54	-1.7
1975	NY N	3	3	.500	13	11	1	0-0	57	75	38	3	0	21-3	21	5.05	70	.323	.378	18-0-2	.167	0	132	-11	81	-1.0
Total	9	60	57	.513	203	145	24-5	5-1	1020.2	1119	524	122	21	270-41	590	3.89	96	.278	.325	339-1-23	.212	10	108	-28	135	-2.3
Stone, Rocky	John Vernon; B8.23.1918 Redding CA; D11.12.1986 Fountain Valley CA; BR/TR/6´0˝/200; d5.2																									
1943	Cin N	0	1	.000	13	0	0	0	24.2	23	14	0	0	8	11	4.38	76	.237	.295	4	.250	0	—	-3	0	-0.2
Stone, Ricky	Ricky L.; B11.25.1975 Hamilton OH; BR/TR/6´1˝/(168–195); [LAN94 4/104]; d9.21																									
2001	Hou N	0	0	ø	6	0	0	0-0	7.2	8	3	1	0	2-1	4	2.35	196	.258	.303	0	ø	0	—	1	0	0.1
2002	Hou N	3	3	.500	78	0	0	1-1	77.1	78	36	9	1	34-3	63	3.61	120	.266	.342	4-0-1	.000	-0	—	5	0	0.3
2003	Hou N	6	4	.600	65	0	0	1-0	83	76	36	11	6	31-4	47	3.69	120	.247	.327	3	.000	-0	—	7	0	0.7
2004	Hou N	1	1	.500	16	0	0	0-0	19	26	12	5	3	7-3	16	5.68	77	.317	.391	0	ø	0	—	-2	0	-0.2
	SD N	1	1	.500	27	0	0	0-0	32.2	40	27	6	3	9-0	22	6.89	57	.301	.356	1	.000	-0	—	-12	0	-0.7
	Year	2	2	.500	43	0	0	0-0	51.2	66	39	11	6	16-3	38	6.45	64	.307	.370	1	.000	-0	—	-13	0	-0.9
2005	Cin N	0	0	ø	23	0	0	0-0	30.2	48	24	8	2	7-2	15	6.75	63	.364	.399	2	.000	-0	—	-8	0	-0.4
Total	5	11	9	.550	215	0	0	2-1	250.1	276	138	40	15	90-13	167	4.57	94	.282	.350	10-0-1	.000	-1	—	-9	0	-0.2
Stone, Steve	Steven Michael; B7.14.1947 Euclid OH; BR/TR/5´10˝/(175–178); [SFN69*S4/89]; d4.8; Col Kent St.; [DL 1982 Bal A 182]																									
1971	SF N	5	9	.357	24	19	2-2	0-0	110.2	110	56	9	3	55-4	63	4.15	82	.259	.349	34-0-3	.000	-2	89	-7	0	-1.0
1972	SF N	6	8	.429	27	16	4-1	0-1	123.2	97	48	11	2	49-2	85	2.98	117	.218	.297	34-0-6	.118	-1	95	6	0	0.6
1973	Chi A	6	11	.353	36	22	3	1-0	176.1	163	87	11	7	82-0	138	4.24	93	.245	.334	0	ø	0*	64	-2	0	-0.2
1974	Chi N	8	6	.571	38	23	1	0-0	169.2	185	92	19	4	64-4	90	4.14	93	.278	.343	58-0-5	.121	-3*	109	-5	0	-0.7
1975	Chi N	12	8	.600	33	32	6-1	0-0	214.1	198	103	24	5	80-3	139	3.95	98	.245	.314	72-0-7	.111	-2*	102	0	0	-0.2
1976	Chi N	3	6	.333	17	15	1-1	0-0	75	70	36	6	3	21-1	33	4.08	95	.250	.305	21-0-1	.143	-1	73	0	68	-0.2
1977	Chi A	15	12	.556	31	31	8	0-0	207.1	228	115	25	5	80-3	124	4.51	91	.281	.346	0	ø	0	109	-9	0	-1.0
1978	Chi A	12	12	.500	30	30	6-1	0-0	212	196	110	19	3	84-1	118	4.37	87	.247	.319	0	ø	0	98	-12	0	-1.2
1979	†Bal A	11	7	.611	32	32	3	0-0	186	173	91	31	1	73-1	96	3.77	107	.248	.320	0	ø	0	107	4	0	0.4
1980	Bal A★	**25**	7	**.781**	37	37	9-1	0-0	250.2	224	103	22	6	101-3	149	3.23	123	.240	.318	0	ø	0*	124	18	0	2.1
1981	Bal A	4	7	.364	15	12	0	0-0	62.2	63	39	7	1	27-0	30	4.60	79	.266	.342	0	ø	0	88	-8	96	-1.2
Total	11	107	93	.535	320	269	43-7	1-1	1788.1	1707	880	184	40	716-22	1065	3.97	98	.253	.326	219-0-22	.100	-9	100	-15	346	-2.6
Stoneman, Bill	William Hambly; B4.7.1944 Oak Park IL; BR/TR/5´10˝/(168–170); [ChiN66 31/595]; d7.16; Col Idaho																									
1967	Chi N	2	4	.333	28	2	0	4	63	51	24	7	0	22-4	52	3.29	108	.223	.289	13-0-3	.000	-1	99	2	0	0.1
1968	Chi N	0	1	.000	18	0	0	0	29.1	35	19	6	1	14-1	18	5.52	57	.310	.388	4	.000	-0	—	-7	0	-0.4
1969	Mon N	11	19	.367	42	36	8-5	0-0	235.2	233	133	26	12	123-4	185	4.39	84	.261	.356	73-0-8	.055	-3	93	-18	0	-2.4
1970	Mon N	7	15	.318	40	30	5-3	0-0	207.2	209	118	26	14	109-8	176	4.59	90	.263	.360	60-0-4	.100	-2*	77	-10	0	-1.2
1971	Mon N	17	16	.515	39	**39**	20-3	0-0	294.2	243	112	20	5	146-11	251	3.15	114	.225	.320	93-0-8	.129	-1*	94	15	0	1.5
1972	Mon N★	12	14	.462	36	35	13-4	0-0	250.2	213	93	15	3	102-12	171	2.98	119	.229	.305	75-0-13	.080	-4*	77	14	0	1.0
1973	Mon N	4	8	.333	29	17	0	1-0	96.2	120	77	12	6	55-6	48	6.80	56	.310	.400	20-0-2	.050	-1	110	-27	30	-3.1
1974	Cal A	1	8	.111	13	11	0	0-0	58.2	78	41	8	2	31-0	33	6.14	57	.322	.401	0	ø	0	76	-16	0	-2.1
Total	8	54	85	.388	245	170	46-15	5-0	1236.1	1182	617	120	43	602-46	934	4.08	90	.253	.342	338-0-38	.086	-13	88	-47	30	-6.6
Stoner, Lil	Ulysses Simpson Grant; B2.28.1899 Bowie TX; D6.26.1966 Enid OK; BR/TR/5´9.5˝/180; d4.15																									
1922	Det A	4	4	.500	17	7	2	0	62.2	76	53	3	3	35	18	7.04	55	.315	.409	20-0-1	.100	-1	144	-20	—	-2.2
1924	Det A	11	11	.500	36	25	10-1	0	215.2	271	130	13	5	65	66	4.72	87	.316	.367	77-2-1	.195	1*	111	-11	—	-0.9
1925	Det A	10	9	.526	34	18	8	1	152	166	79	6	9	53	51	4.26	101	.283	.352	55-0-1	.291	4	132	3	—	-0.6
1926	Det A	7	10	.412	32	22	7	0	159.2	179	115	11	3	63	57	5.47	74	.291	.359	53	.170	-2	109	-24	—	-2.3
1927	Det A	10	13	.435	38	24	13	5	215	251	118	9	3	77	63	3.98	106	.301	.362	74-0-4	.108	-6	94	6	—	-0.1
1928	Det A	5	8	.385	36	11	4	4	126.1	151	75	16	3	42	29	4.35	95	.296	.353	39-0-3	.179	-1	127	-4	—	-0.5
1929	Det A	3	3	.500	24	3	1	4	53	57	37	2	2	31	12	5.26	82	.288	.390	15	.067	-2	98	-5	—	-0.7
1930	Pit N	0	0	ø	5	0	0	0	5.2	7	3	2	0	3	1	4.76	105	.318	.400	0	ø	0	—	0	—	0.0
1931	Phi N	0	0	ø	7	1	0	0	13.2	22	13	0	0	5	2	6.59	64	.373	.422	5	.000	-1	101	-4	—	-0.3
Total	9	50	58	.463	229	111	45-1	14	1003.2	1180	623	62	28	374	299	4.76	87	.301	.366	338-2-10	.172	-7	113	-59	—	-6.4
Stoops, Jim	James Wellington; B6.30.1972 Edison NJ; BR/TR/6´2˝/180; d9.9; Col South Carolina																									
1998	Col N	1	0	1.000	3	0	0	0-0	4	5	1	1	1	3-0	0	2.25	230	.385	.529	0	ø	0	—	1	0	0.2
Stottlemyre, Mel	Melvin Leon Jr.; B12.28.1963 Prosser WA; BR/TR/6´0˝/190; [HouN85*S1/3]; d7.17; b–Todd f–Mel; Col Nevada–Las Vegas																									
1990	KC A	0	1	.000	13	2	0	0-0	31.1	35	18	3	0	12-1	14	4.88	79	.280	.343	0	ø	0	47	-3	0	-0.2
Stottlemyre, Mel	Melvin Leon Sr.; B11.13.1941 Hazleton MO; BR/TR/6´2˝/(170–192); d8.12; C22; s–Mel s–Todd; Col Yakima Valley (WA) CC																									
1964	†NY A	9	3	.750	13	12	5-2	0	96	77	26	3	2	35-3	49	2.06	176	.219	.294	37-0-1	.243	2*	113	16	0	2.3
1965	NY A☆	20	9	.690	37	37	**18**-4	0	**291**	250	99	18	7	88-3	155	2.63	129	.233	.294	99-2-9	.131	1	109	24	0	2.8
1966	NY A★	12	20	.375	37	35	9-3	1	251	239	116	18	1	82-7	146	3.80	87	.253	.311	80-1-4	.138	1	98	-12	0	-1.1
1967	NY A	15	15	.500	36	36	10-4	0	255	235	96	20	2	88-11	151	2.96	105	.248	.311	82-0-6	.098	-3	96	6	0	0.6
1968	NY A★	21	12	.636	36	36	19-6	0	278.2	243	86	21	3	65-7	140	2.45	119	.234	.280	91-0-3	.143	2	108	16	0	2.3
1969	NY A★	20	14	.588	39	39	**24**-3	0-0	303	267	105	19	6	97-11	113	2.82	125	.239	.301	101-1-4	.178	5	91	26	0	3.8
1970	NY A★	15	13	.536	37	37	14	0-0	271	262	110	23	6	84-8	126	3.09	116	.255	.313	85-2-3	.188	8*	104	14	0	2.4
1971	NY A	16	12	.571	35	35	19-7	0-0	269.2	234	100	16	4	69-6	132	2.87	115	.233	.284	94-1-3	.170	2	113	13	0	1.7
1972	NY A	14	18	.438	36	36	9-7	0-0	260	250	99	13	4	85-13	110	3.22	93	.254	.314	80-0-9	.200	3*	89	-4	0	0.0
1973	NY A	16	16	.500	38	38	19-4	0-0	273	259	112	13	5	79-3	95	3.07	121	.253	.307	0	ø	0	94	18	0	2.1
1974	NY A	6	7	.462	16	15	6	0-0	113	119	54	7	4	37-3	40	3.58	99	.272	.333	0	ø	0*	83	-1	91	-0.2
Total	11	164	139	.541	360	356	152-40	1-0	2661.1	2435	1003	171	44	809-75	1257	2.97	113	.245	.303	749-7-42	.160	20	100	116	91	16.7
Stottlemyre, Todd	Todd Vernon; B5.20.1965 Sunnyside WA; BL/TR/6´3˝/(185–215); [TorA85 S1/3]; d4.6; b–Mel f–Mel; Col Nevada–Las Vegas; [DL 2001 Ari N 190]																									
1988	Tor A	4	8	.333	28	16	0	0-1	98	109	70	15	4	46-5	67	5.69	70	.283	.363	0	ø	0	102	-19	0	-2.1
1989	†Tor A	7	7	.500	27	18	0	0-0	127.2	137	56	11	5	44-4	63	3.88	98	.282	.343	0	ø	0	80	1	0	0.0
1990	Tor A	13	17	.433	33	33	4	0-0	203	214	101	18	8	69-4	115	4.34	91	.274	.337	0	ø	0	116	-7	0	-0.9
1991	†Tor A	15	8	.652	34	34	1	0-0	219	194	97	21	12	75-3	116	3.78	112	.235	.305	0	ø	0	92	12	0	1.1
1992	†Tor A	12	11	.522	28	27	6-2	0-0	174	175	99	20	10	63-4	98	4.50	91	.262	.329	0	ø	0	118	-9	23	-1.1
1993	†Tor A	11	12	.478	30	28	1-1	0-0	176.2	204	107	11	3	69-5	98	4.84	91	.292	.353	0	ø	0	101	-10	21	-1.2
1994	Tor A	7	7	.500	26	19	3-1	1-2	140.2	149	67	19	7	48-2	105	4.22	116	.275	.339	0	ø	0	79	12	0	1.0
1995	Oak A	14	7	.667	31	31	2	0-0	209.2	228	117	26	6	80-7	205	4.55	100	.276	.343	1	.000	-0	129	-2	0	-0.2
1996	†StL N	14	11	.560	34	33	5-2	0-0	223.1	191	100	30	4	93-8	194	3.87	110	.231	.309	66-0-9	.227	3	102	12	0	1.6

YEAR	TM LG	W	L	PCT	G	GS	CG-SHO	SV-BS	IP	H	R	HR	HB	BB-IB	SO	ERA	AERA	OAV	OOB	AB-HR-SH	AVG	PB	SUP	APR	DL	PW
1997	StL N	12	9	.571	28	28	0	0-0	181	155	86	16	12	65-3	160	3.88	108	.231	.308	55-0-5	.236	6*	99	7	0	1.3
1998	StL N	9	9	.500	23	23	3	0-0	161.1	146	74	20	4	51-0	147	3.51	120	.240	.301	53-0-5	.226	2	96	11	0	1.4
	†Tex A	5	4	.556	10	10	0	0-0	60.1	68	33	5	0	30-1	57	4.33	113	.282	.358	0	ø	0	139	3	0	0.4
1999	†Ari N	6	3	.667	17	17	0	0-0	101.1	106	51	12	6	40-1	74	4.09	113	.268	.343	32-0-3	.125	0	125	6	94	0.5
2000	Ari N	9	6	.600	18	18	0	0-0	95.1	98	55	18	2	36-2	76	4.91	98	.268	.336	31-1-3	.194	2	116	-1	81	0.2
2002	Ari N	0	2	.000	5	4	0	0-0	20.1	26	17	4	0	7-0	12	7.52	60	.313	.363	4-0-1	.000	-0	62	-6	158	-0.5
Total	14	138	121	.533	372	339	25-6	1-3	2191.2	2200	1130	246	83	816-49	1587	4.28	101	.262	.330	242-1-26	.207	14	106	10	567	1.5
Stout, Allyn	Allyn McClelland "Fish Hook"; B10.31.1904 Peoria IL; D12.22.1974 Sikeston MO; BR/TR/5´10˝/167; d5.16																									
1931	StL N	6	0	1.000	30	3	1	3	72.2	87	40	2	1	34	40	4.21	93	.305	.381	19-0-2	.105	-1	189	-2	—	-0.3
1932	StL N	4	5	.444	36	3	1	1	73.2	87	40	5	4	28	32	4.40	89	.305	.375	20-0-1	.100	-1	64	-3	—	-0.4
1933	StL N	0	0	ø	1	0	0	0	2	1	0	0	0	1	1	0.00	ø	.167	.286	0	ø	0	—	1	—	0.1
	Cin N	2	3	.400	23	5	2	0	71.1	85	36	3	0	26	29	3.79	90	.295	.354	22-0-1	.182	-0	113	-2	—	-0.2
	Year	2	3	.400	24	5	2	0	73.1	86	36	3	0	27	30	3.68	92	.293	.352	22-0-1	.182	-0	113	-3	—	-0.1
1934	Cin N	6	8	.429	41	16	4	1	140.2	170	85	10	4	47	51	4.86	84	.297	.354	43-0-2	.186	0	111	-9	—	-0.8
1935	NY N	1	4	.200	40	2	0	5	88	99	58	7	4	37	29	4.91	79	.289	.365	15-1-0	.133	0	132	-12	—	-0.8
1943	Bos N	1	0	1.000	9	0	0	1	9.1	17	12	1	0	4	3	6.75	51	.378	.429	2	.000	-0	—	-5	0	-0.6
Total	6	20	20	.500	180	29	8	11	457.2	546	271	28	13	177	185	4.54	85	.299	.365	121-1-6	.149	-3	117	-32	0	-3.0
Stovall, Jesse	Jesse Cramer "Scout"; B7.24.1875 Leeds MO; D7.12.1955 San Diego CA; BL/TR/6´0˝/175; d8.31; b–George																									
1903	Cle A	5	1	.833	6	6	6-2	0	57	44	17	0	3	21	12	2.05	139	.213	.294	22	.045	-2	100	6	—	0.4
1904	Det A	2	13	.133	22	17	13-1	0	146.2	170	97	3	16	45	41	4.42	58	.291	.358	56	.196	0*	69	-29	—	-2.8
Total	2	7	14	.333	28	23	19-3	0	203.2	214	114	3	19	66	53	3.76	70	.270	.341	78	.154	-2	78	-23	—	-2.4
Stovey, Harry	Harry Duffield (b Harry Duffield Stowe); B12.20.1856 Philadelphia PA; D9.20.1937 New Bedford MA; BR/TR/5´11.5˝/175; d5.1; M2; ▲																									
1880	Wor N	0	0	ø	2	0	0	0	6	8	4	0	—	3	3	4.50	58	.308	.379	355-6	.265	0*	—	-1	—	0.0
1883	Phi AA	0	0	ø	1	0	0	0	3	5	3	0	—	0	4	9.00	39	.357	.357	421-14	.304	0*	—	-1	—	0.0
1886	Phi AA	0	0	ø	1	0	0	0	0.1	2	2	0	0	0	0	27.00	13	.667	.667	489-7	.294	0*	—	-1	—	0.0
Total	3	0	0	ø	4	0	0	0	9.1	15	9	0	0	3	7	6.75	44	.349	.391	1265-27	.289	1	—	-3	—	0.0
Stowe, Hal	Harold Rudolph; B8.29.1937 Gastonia NC; BL/TL/6´0˝/170; d9.30; Col Clemson																									
1960	NY A	0	0	ø	1	0	0	0	1	0	1	0	0	1-0	0	9.00	40	.000	.333	0	ø	0	—	-1	0	0.0
Strahler, Mike	Michael Wayne; B3.14.1947 Chicago IL; BR/TR/6´4˝/(178–180); d9.12; Col Sacramento (CA) City																									
1970	LA N	1	1	.500	6	0	0	1-0	18.2	13	6	1	0	10-0	11	1.45	266	.194	.299	8	.250	0	—	4	0	0.5
1971	LA N	0	0	ø	6	0	0	0-0	12.2	10	4	1	0	8-0	7	2.84	114	.217	.333	1	.000	-0	—	1	0	0.0
1972	LA N	1	2	.333	19	2	1	0-0	47	42	25	5	1	22-1	25	3.26	103	.237	.322	11	.182	1	105	-1	0	0.0
1973	Det A	4	5	.444	22	11	1	0-1	80.1	84	45	7	1	39-1	37	4.37	94	.273	.355	0	ø	0	95	-4	0	-0.4
Total	4	6	8	.429	53	13	2	1-1	158.2	149	80	14	2	79-2	80	3.57	106	.249	.337	20	.200	1	102	0	0	0.1
Strahs, Dick	Richard Bernard; B12.4.1923 Evanston IL; D5.26.1988 Las Vegas NV; BL/TR/6´0˝/192; d7.24																									
1954	Chi A	0	0	ø	9	0	0	1	14.1	16	10	0	0	8	8	5.65	66	.271	.358	1-0-1	.000	-0	—	-3	0	-0.2
Straker, Les	Lester Paul (Bolnalda); B10.10.1959 Ciudad Bolivar, Bolivar, Venezuela; BR/TR/6´1˝/193; d4.11																									
1987	†Min A	8	10	.444	31	26	1	0-0	154.1	150	79	24	2	59-6	76	4.37	106	.257	.325	0	ø	0	86	6	0	0.5
1988	Min A	2	5	.286	16	14	1-1	1-0	82.2	86	39	8	0	25-1	23	3.92	104	.276	.326	0	ø	0	97	1	95	0.1
Total	2	10	15	.400	47	40	2-1	1-0	237	236	118	32	2	84-7	99	4.22	106	.264	.325	0	ø	0	90	7	95	0.6
Strampe, Bob	Robert Edwin; B6.13.1950 Janesville WI; BB/TR/6´1˝/185; [DetA68 18/414]; d5.10																									
1972	Det A	0	0	ø	7	0	0	0-0	4.2	6	6	0	0	7-1	4	11.57	27	.300	.481	0	ø	0	—	-4	0	-0.2
Strand, Paul	Paul Edward; B12.19.1893 Carbonado WA; D7.2.1974 Salt Lake City UT; BL/TL/6´0.5˝/190; d5.15; ▲																									
1913	Bos N	0	0	ø	7	0	0	0	17	22	9	1	0	12	6	2.12	155	.393	.500	6	.167	-0	—	1	—	0.0
1914	Bos N	6	2	.750	16	3	1	0	55.1	47	23	1	1	23	33	2.44	113	.235	.317	24	.333	2*	164	0	—	0.3
1915	Bos N	1	1	.500	6	2	2	1	22.2	26	12	0	0	3	13	2.38	109	.295	.319	22	.091	-0*	158	-1	—	-0.2
Total	3	7	3	.700	29	5	3	1	95	95	44	2	1	38	52	2.37	119	.276	.350	52	.212	2	156	0	—	0.1
Strange, Pat	Patrick Martin; B8.23.1980 Springfield MA; BR/TR/6´5˝/243; d9.13																									
2002	NY N	0	0	ø	5	0	0	0-0	8	6	1	0	0	1-1	4	1.13	352	.207	.233	0	ø	0	—	3	0	0.1
2003	NY N	0	0	ø	6	0	0	0-0	9	13	11	4	0	11-0	5	11.00	38	.351	.500	1	.000	-0	—	-7	0	-0.3
Total	2	0	0	ø	11	0	0	0-0	17	19	12	4	0	12-1	9	6.35	64	.288	.397	1	.000	-0	—	-4	0	-0.2
Stratton, Scott	Chilton Scott; B10.2.1869 Campbellsburg KY; D3.8.1939 Louisville KY; BL/TR/6´0˝/180; d4.21; ▲																									
1888	Lou AA	10	17	.370	33	28	28-2	0	269.2	287	196	7	15	53	97	3.64	85	.263	.306	249-1	.257	5*	102	-12	—	-0.5
1889	Lou AA	3	13	.188	19	17	13	1	133.2	157	126	6	7	42	42	3.23	119	.284	.342	229-4	.288	4*	82	-5	—	0.0
1890	†Lou AA	34	14	**.708**	50	49	44-4	0	431	398	186	3	13	61	207	**2.36**	**163**	.238	**.270**	189	.323	16*	124	**74**	—	**8.9**
1891	Pit N	0	2	.000	2	2	2	0	18.1	16	9	0	0	5	5	2.45	134	.225	.276	8	.125	-1	55	2	—	0.2
	Lou AA	6	13	.316	20	20	20-1	0	172	204	112	10	7	34	52	4.08	90	.285	.324	115	.235	1*	73	-6	—	-0.3
1892	Lou N	21	19	.525	42	40	39-2	0	351.2	342	188	1	9	70	93	2.92	105	.245	.285	219	.256	10*	90	5	—	1.6
1893	Lou N	12	23	.343	37	35	34-1	0	314.2	445	253	8	8	100	43	5.43	81	.323	.373	221	.226	3*	92	-39	—	-2.6
1894	Lou N	1	5	.167	7	5	4	0	43	72	50	3	3	13	3	8.37	61	.367	.415	37	.324	2*	58	-13	—	-1.0
	Chi N	8	5	.615	16	13	12	0	128.1	205	131	5	3	42	24	5.89	96	.357	.403	99-3-0	.374	7*	123	-6	—	0.2
	Year	9	10	.474	23	18	16	0	171.1	277	181	8	6	55	27	6.51	84	.359	.406	136-3-0	.360	9	106	-19	—	-0.8
1895	Chi N	2	3	.400	5	5	3	0	30	51	42	1	4	14	4	9.60	53	.370	.442	24-0-1	.292	1*	81	-13	—	-1.3
Total	8	97	114	.460	231	214	199-10	1	1892.1	2177	1293	44	69	434	570	3.87	99	.280	.323	1390-8-1	.274	48	99	-13	—	5.2
Stratton, Monty	Monty Franklin Pierce "Gander"; B5.21.1912 Wagner TX; D9.29.1982 Greenville TX; BR/TR/6´5˝/180; d6.2; C3																									
1934	Chi A	0	0	ø	1	0	0	0	3.1	4	2	0	0	1	0	5.40	88	.333	.385	2	.000	-0	—	0	—	0.0
1935	Chi A	1	2	.333	5	5	2	0	38	40	17	0	2	9	8	4.03	115	.274	.325	14-0-1	.143	-1	75	3	—	0.2
1936	Chi A	5	7	.417	16	14	3	0	95	117	66	8	1	46	37	5.21	100	.305	.381	37-1-0	.216	1	109	-2	—	0.0
1937	Chi A*	15	5	.750	22	21	14-5	0	164.2	142	55	6	2	37	69	2.40	**191**	.234	**.280**	60-1-5	.200	-0	90	39	—	4.3
1938	Chi A	15	9	.625	26	22	17	2	186.1	186	95	18	7	56	82	4.01	122	.255	.315	79-2-2	.266	5*	133	19	—	2.7
Total	5	36	23	.610	70	62	36-5	2	487.1	489	235	32	12	149	196	3.71	130	.261	.319	192-4-8	.224	5	109	59	—	7.2
Stratton, Ed	William Edward; B Baltimore MD; d5.14																									
1873	Mar NA	0	3	.000	3	3	3	0	27	75	75	1	—	1	0	8.33	41	.412	.415	16	.125	-1*	41	-14	—	-1.0
Street, Huston	Huston Lowell; B8.2.1983 Austin TX; BR/TR/6´0˝/190; [OakA04 1/40]; d4.6; Col Texas																									
2005	Oak A	5	1	.833	67	0	0	23-4	78.1	53	17	3	2	26-4	72	1.72	254	.194	.267	0	ø	0	—	23	0	2.8
2006	†Oak A	4	4	.500	69	0	0	37-11	70.2	64	28	4	2	13-3	67	3.31	137	.238	.275	0	ø	0	—	10	20	1.8
Total	2	9	5	.643	136	0	0	60-15	149	117	45	7	4	39-7	139	2.48	180	.216	.271	0	ø	0	—	33	20	4.6
Streit, Oscar	Oscar William; B7.7.1873 Florence AL; D10.10.1935 Birmingham AL; BL/TL/6´5˝/190; d4.21																									
1899	Bos N	1	0	1.000	2	1	1	0	14.2	15	17	1	2	15	0	6.75	62	.263	.432	7	.000	-1	121	-5	—	-0.3
1902	Cle A	0	7	.000	8	7	4	0	51.2	72	54	3	3	25	10	5.23	66	.330	.407	19-0-1	.211	1	81	-14	—	-1.4
Total	2	1	7	.125	10	8	5	0	66.1	87	71	4	5	40	10	5.56	65	.316	.412	26-0-1	.154	-0	85	-19	—	-1.7
Strelecki, Ed	Edward Harold; B4.10.1905 Newark NJ; D1.9.1968 Newark NJ; BR/TR/5´11.5˝/180; d4.16																									
1928	StL A	0	2	.000	22	2	1	1	50.1	49	27	4	1	17	8	4.29	98	.269	.335	10-0-2	.200	0	71	0	—	0.0
1929	StL A	1	1	.500	7	0	0	0	11	12	8	1	1	6	2	4.91	90	.279	.380	2	.000	-0	—	-1	—	-0.2
1931	Cin N	0	0	ø	13	0	0	0	24.1	37	25	2	3	9	3	9.25	40	.394	.462	5	.200	0	—	-13	—	-0.6
Total	3	1	3	.250	42	2	1	1	85.2	98	60	7	5	32	13	5.78	71	.307	.379	17-0-2	.176	0	71	-14	—	-0.8
Stremmel, Phil	Philip; B4.16.1880 Zanesville OH; D12.26.1947 Chicago IL; BR/TR/6´0˝/175; d9.16																									
1909	StL A	0	2	.000	2	2	2	0	18	20	9	0	1	4	6	4.50	54	.308	.357	6	.000	-1	44	-3	—	-0.4
1910	StL A	0	2	.000	5	2	2	0	29	31	19	0	0	16	7	3.72	66	.287	.379	8-0-1	.125	-0	54	-4	—	-0.2
Total	2	0	4	.000	7	4	4	0	47	51	28	0	1	20	13	4.02	61	.295	.371	14-0-1	.071	-1	49	-7	—	-0.6

YEAR	TM LG	W	L	PCT	G	GS	CG-SHO	SV-BS	IP	H	R	HR	HB	BB-IB	SO	ERA	AERA	OAV	OOB	AB-HR-SH	AVG	PB	SUP	APR	DL	PW
Stricker, Cub	John A. (b John A. Streaker); B2.15.1860 Philadelphia PA; D11.19.1937 Philadelphia PA; BR/TR/5´3˝/138; d5.2; M1; ▲																									
1882	Phi AA	1	0	1.000	2	0	0	0	7	3	1	0	—	1	2	1.29	218	.120	.154	272	.217	0*	—	1	—	0.2
1884	Phi AA	0	0	ø	1	0	0	0	3	6	2	0	0	1	1	6.00	56	.333	.368	399-1	.231	0*	—	-1	—	0.0
1887	Cle AA	0	0	ø	3	0	0	1	5.2	5	5	0	0	7	2	3.18	137	.238	.429	534-2	.264	0*	—	0	—	0.0
1888	Cle AA	1	0	1.000	2	0	0	0	12	16	6	0	1	2	5	4.50	69	.308	.345	493-1	.233	0*	—	-1	—	0.0
Total	4	2	0	1.000	8	0	0	1	27.2	30	14	0	1	11	10	3.58	93	.259	.328	1698-4	.240	1	—	-1	—	0.2
Strickland, Jim	James Michael; B6.12.1946 Los Angeles CA; BL/TL/6´0˝/(175–180); d5.19																									
1971	Min A	1	0	1.000	24	0	0	1-1	31.1	20	14	2	2	18-2	21	1.44	247	.183	.303	1	.000	0	—	3	0	0.2
1972	Min A	3	1	.750	25	0	0	3-1	36	28	16	7	0	19-2	30	2.50	129	.214	.313	3	.333	1	—	1	0	0.2
1973	Min A	0	1	.000	7	0	0	0-0	5.1	11	8	0	0	5-0	6	11.81	34	.440	.516	0	ø	0	—	-4	0	-0.7
1975	Cle A	0	0	ø	4	0	0	1-0	4.2	4	1	0	1	2-0	3	1.93	198	.222	.333	0	ø	0	—	1	0	0.0
Total	4	4	2	.667	60	0	0	5-2	77.1	63	39	9	3	44-4	60	2.68	128	.223	.329	4	.250	1	—	1	0	-0.3
Strickland, Scott	Scott Michael; B4.26.1976 Houston TX; BR/TR/5´11˝/(180–195); [MonN97 10/316]; d8.14; Col New Mexico; [DL 2004 NY N 183]																									
1999	Mon N	0	1	.000	17	0	0	0-0	18	15	10	3	0	11-0	23	4.50	99	.231	.342	0	ø	0	—	0	0	0.0
2000	Mon N	4	3	.571	49	0	0	9-4	48	38	18	3	1	16-2	48	3.00	157	.215	.279	2	.000	-0	—	9	60	1.4
2001	Mon N	2	6	.250	77	0	0	9-3	81.1	67	36	9	4	41-5	85	3.21	135	.222	.322	3	.000	-0	—	8	0	0.8
2002	Mon N	0	0	ø	1	0	0	0-0	1	0	0	0	0	0-0	2	0.00	ø	.000	.000	0	ø	0	—	0	0	0.0
	NY N	6	9	.400	68	0	0	2-4	67.2	61	29	7	2	33-9	67	3.59	110	.236	.325	0	ø	0	—	3	0	0.7
	Year	6	9	.400	69	0	0	2-4	68.2	61	29	7	2	33-9	69	3.54	112	.234	.322	0	ø	0	—	3	0	0.7
2003	NY N	0	2	.000	19	0	0	0-1	20	16	6	1	1	10-1	16	2.25	186	.219	.321	1-0-1	.000	-0	—	4	141	0.4
2005	Hou N	0	0	ø	5	0	0	0-0	4	4	3	2	0	0-0	2	6.75	63	.250	.250	0	ø	0	—	-1	0	0.0
Total	6	12	21	.364	236	0	0	20-12	240	201	102	25	8	111-17	243	3.34	129	.225	.314	6-0-1	.000	-1	—	23	384	3.3
Strickland, Bill	William Goss; B3.29.1908 Ray City GA; D1.26.2000 Lakeland FL; BR/TR/6´2˝/170; d7.16; Col Georgia Tech																									
1937	StL A	0	0	ø	9	0	0	0	21.1	28	18	2	2	15	6	5.91	82	.341	.455	6	.167	-0	—	-3	—	-0.2
Stricklett, Elmer	Elmer Griffin "Spitball"; B8.29.1876 Glasco KS; D6.7.1964 Santa Cruz CA; BR/TR/5´6˝/140; d4.22; Col Santa Clara																									
1904	Chi A	0	1	.000	1	1	0	0	7	12	10	0	0	2	3	10.29	24	.375	.412	3	.000	-0	58	-6	—	-0.6
1905	Bro N	9	18	.333	33	28	25-1	1	237.1	259	143	0	14	71	77	3.34	87	.282	.343	88-0-2	.148	-1	82	-19	—	-1.6
1906	Bro N	14	18	.438	41	35	28-5	5	291.2	273	128	2	5	77	88	2.72	93	.253	.306	97-0-3	.206	5	92	-11	—	-0.1
1907	Bro N	12	14	.462	29	26	25-4	0	229.2	211	85	1	8	65	69	2.27	103	.255	.315	81-0-1	.148	1*	81	1	—	0.7
Total	4	35	51	.407	104	90	78-10	6	765.2	755	366	3	27	215	237	2.84	91	.264	.322	269-0-6	.167	4	85	-35	—	-1.6
Strike, John	John; B1865 PA; d9.24																									
1886	Phi N	1	1	.500	2	2	1	0	15	19	10	1	—	7	11	4.80	69	.311	.382	7	.000	-1	84	-1	—	-0.2
Striker, Jake	Wilbur Scott; B10.23.1933 New Washington OH; BL/TL/6´2˝/200; d9.25; Col Heidelberg																									
1959	Cle A	1	0	1.000	1	1	0	0	6.2	8	2	0	0	4-0	5	2.70	136	.296	.375	1	.000	1	192	1	0	0.2
1960	Chi A	0	0	ø	2	0	0	0	3.2	5	3	1	1	1-0	1	4.91	77	.357	.438	0	ø	0	—	-1	0	0.0
Total	2	1	0	1.000	3	1	0	0	10.1	13	5	1	1	5-0	6	3.48	107	.317	.396	1	.000	1	192	0	0	0.2
Strincevich, Nick	Nicholas "Jumbo"; B3.1.1915 Gary IN; BR/TR/6´1˝/180; d4.23																									
1940	Bos N	4	8	.333	32	14	5	1	128.2	142	89	17	8	63	54	5.53	67	.278	.367	43-0-2	.116	-2*	99	-27	—	-2.5
1941	Bos N	0	0	ø	3	0	0	0	3.1	7	5	0	1	6	1	10.80	33	.412	.583	0	ø	0	—	-3	0	-0.1
	Pit N	1	2	.333	12	3	0	0	31	35	23	4	1	13	12	5.23	69	.280	.353	7	.429	1	141	-6	0	-0.4
	Year	1	2	.333	15	3	0	0	34.1	42	28	4	2	19	13	5.77	63	.296	.387	7	.429	1	141	-9	0	-0.5
1942	Pit N	0	0	ø	7	1	0	0	22.1	19	7	2	1	9	10	2.82	120	.229	.312	4-0-1	.000	-1	50	2	0	0.0
1944	Pit N	14	7	.667	40	26	11	2	190	190	86	5	4	37	47	3.08	121	.257	.296	57-0-5	.158	-1	109	11	0	1.3
1945	Pit N	16	10	.615	36	29	18-1	2	228.1	235	94	7	3	49	74	3.31	119	.260	.301	84-0-6	.202	0	104	18	0	1.8
1946	Pit N	10	15	.400	32	22	11-3	1	176	185	77	7	4	44	49	3.58	98	.268	.316	52-0-4	.154	1	78	1	0	0.1
1947	Pit N	1	6	.143	32	7	1	0	89	111	59	9	2	37	22	5.26	80	.316	.385	21-0-1	.048	-2	84	-10	0	-0.8
1948	Pit N	0	0	ø	3	0	0	0	4.1	8	4	0	0	2	1	8.31	49	.444	.500	0	ø	0	—	-2	0	-0.1
	Phi N	0	1	.000	6	1	0	0	16.2	26	18	1	0	10	4	9.18	43	.347	.424	4	.000	-1	0	-9	0	-0.5
	Year	0	1	.000	9	1	0	0	21	34	22	1	0	12	5	9.00	44	.366	.438	4	.000	-1	0	-11	0	-0.6
Total	8	46	49	.484	203	103	46-4	6	889.2	958	462	52	24	270	274	4.05	93	.273	.329	272-0-19	.158	-4	98	-25	0	-1.2
Strohmayer, John	John Emery; B10.13.1946 Belle Fourche SD; BR/TR/6´1˝/(180–185); d4.29; Col Pacific (CA)																									
1970	Mon N	3	1	.750	42	0	0	0-2	76	85	48	7	2	39-3	74	4.86	86	.279	.364	6-0-1	.167	-0	—	-7	0	-0.4
1971	Mon N	7	5	.583	27	14	2	1-0	114	124	63	16	4	31-2	56	4.34	82	.281	.331	35-0-5	.229	0	140	-10	0	-1.0
1972	Mon N	1	2	.333	48	0	0	3-0	76.2	73	32	6	1	31-3	50	3.52	101	.256	.328	4-0-1	.000	-0	—	1	0	0.1
1973	Mon N	0	1	.000	17	3	0	0-1	34.2	34	20	4	1	22-2	15	5.19	73	.260	.370	5	.200	0	116	-4	0	-0.2
	NY N	0	0	ø	7	0	0	0-0	10	13	10	2	0	4-1	5	8.10	45	.310	.370	0	ø	0	—	-5	0	-0.2
	Year	0	1	.000	24	3	0	0-1	44.2	47	30	6	1	26-3	20	5.84	65	.272	.370	5	.200	0	117	-9	0	-0.4
1974	NY N	0	0	ø	1	0	0	0-0	1	0	0	0	0	1-0	0	0.00	ø	.000	.250	0	ø	0	—	0	0	0.0
Total	5	11	9	.550	142	17	2	4-3	312.1	329	173	35	8	128-11	200	4.47	84	.272	.344	50-0-7	.200	0	131	-25	0	-1.7
Strom, Brent	Brent Terry; B10.14.1948 San Diego CA; BR/TL/6´3˝/190; [NYN70 S1/3]; d7.31; C3; Col USC																									
1972	NY N	0	3	.000	11	5	0	0-0	30.1	34	25	7	0	15-1	20	6.82	50	.296	.374	6-0-1	.000	-1	104	-11	0	-1.1
1973	Cle A	2	10	.167	27	18	2	0-0	123	134	73	18	3	47-4	91	4.61	86	.278	.344	0	ø	0	84	-10	24	-0.8
1975	SD N	8	8	.500	18	16	6-2	0-0	120.1	103	42	6	2	33-2	56	2.54	138	.233	.287	30-0-6	.100	-1	66	13	0	1.6
1976	SD N	12	16	.429	36	33	8-1	0-0	210.2	188	100	15	2	73-8	103	3.29	100	.239	.302	63-0-10	.063	-2*	92	-6	0	-0.9
1977	SD N	0	2	.000	8	3	0	0-0	16.2	23	25	5	0	12-2	8	12.42	29	.329	.417	3-0-1	.333	0	108	-17	0	-1.7
Total	5	22	39	.361	100	75	16-3	0-0	501	482	265	51	7	180-17	278	3.95	89	.254	.318	102-0-18	.078	-3	86	-31	24	-2.9
Stromme, Floyd	Floyd Marvin "Rock"; B8.1.1916 Cooperstown ND; D2.7.1993 Wenatchee WA; BR/TR/5´11˝/170; d7.5; Col Northwestern																									
1939	Cle A	0	1	.000	5	0	0	0	13	13	8	1	0	13	4	4.85	91	.265	.419	3	.333	0	—	-1	—	0.0
Strong, Joe	Joseph Benjamin; B9.9.1962 Fairfield CA; BB/TR/6´0˝/200; [OakA84 15/376]; d5.11; Col California–Riverside																									
2000	Fla N	1	1	.500	18	0	0	1-1	19.2	26	16	3	2	12-1	18	7.32	60	.325	.426	1	.000	-0	—	-6	0	-0.6
2001	Fla N	0	0	ø	5	0	0	0-0	6.2	3	1	1	0	3-0	4	1.35	309	.136	.240	1	.000	-0	—	2	0	0.1
Total	2	1	1	.500	23	0	0	1-1	26.1	29	17	4	2	15-1	22	5.81	74	.284	.387	2	.000	-0	—	-4	0	-0.5
Stroud, Sailor	Ralph Vivian; B5.15.1885 Ironia NJ; D4.11.1970 Stockton CA; BR/TR/6´0˝/160; d4.29																									
1910	Det A	5	9	.357	28	15	7-3	1	130.1	123	54	9	7	41	63	3.25	81	.257	.325	39	.026	-4	88	-5	—	-1.2
1915	NY N	12	9	.571	32	22	8	1	184	194	76	3	6	35	62	2.79	92	.281	.321	56-0-3	.161	-1	157	-6	—	-0.7
1916	NY N	3	2	.600	10	4	0	1	46.2	47	18	1	1	9	16	2.70	90	.266	.305	14-0-1	.071	-1	131	-2	—	-0.3
Total	3	20	20	.500	70	41	15-3	3	361	364	148	13	14	85	141	2.94	88	.271	.321	109-0-4	.101	-6	128	-13	—	-2.2
Struss, Steamboat	Clarence Herbert; B2.24.1909 Riverdale IL; D9.12.1985 Grand Rapids MI; BR/TR/5´11˝/163; d9.30																									
1934	Pit N	0	1	.000	1	1	0	0	7	7	6	0	0	6	3	6.43	64	.250	.382	3	.333	0	105	-2	—	-0.2
Stryker, Dutch	Sterling Alpa; B7.29.1895 Atlantic Highlands NJ; D11.5.1964 Red Bank NJ; BR/TR/5´11.5˝/180; d4.16																									
1924	Bos N	3	8	.273	20	10	2	0	73.1	90	56	4	1	22	22	6.01	64	.314	.365	23	.217	-0	107	-18	—	-2.1
1926	Bro N	0	0	ø	2	0	0	0	2	8	8	0	0	1	0	27.00	14	.571	.600	0	ø	0	—	-5	—	-0.3
Total	2	3	8	.273	22	10	2	0	75.1	98	64	4	1	23	22	6.57	58	.326	.375	23	.217	-0	107	-23	—	-2.4
Stuart, Johnny	John Davis "Stud"; B4.27.1901 Clinton TN; D5.13.1970 Charleston WV; BR/TR/5´11˝/170; d7.27; Col Ohio St.																									
1922	StL N	0	0	ø	2	1	0	0	2	2	4	0	1	2	1	9.00	43	.222	.417	0	ø	0	148	-2	—	-0.1
1923	StL N	9	5	.643	37	10	7-1	3	149.2	139	82	11	9	70	55	4.27	91	.252	.345	57	.246	1	122	-4	—	-0.4
1924	StL N	9	11	.450	28	22	13	0	159	167	100	12	5	60	54	4.75	80	.273	.343	54-0-1	.204	-1*	127	-18	—	-2.1
1925	StL N	2	2	.500	15	1	1	0	47	52	41	6	2	24	14	6.13	71	.278	.366	16	.250	1	78	-11	—	-0.7
Total	4	20	18	.526	82	34	21-1	3	357.2	360	227	29	17	156	124	4.76	82	.265	.348	127-0-1	.228	1	122	-35	—	-3.3

YEAR	TM LG	W	L	PCT	G	GS	CG-SHO	SV-BS	IP	H	R	HR	HB	BB-IB	SO	ERA	AERA	OAV	OOB	AB-HR-SH	AVG	PB	SUP	APR	DL	PW
STUART, MARLIN	Marlin Henry; B8.8.1918 Paragould AR; D6.16.1994 Paragould AR; BL/TR/6´2˝/185; d4.26																									
1949	Det A	0	2	.000	14	2	0	0	29.2	39	33	3	0	35	14	9.10	46	.348	.503	6	.333	1*	118	-16	0	-0.9
1950	Det A	3	1	.750	19	1	0	2	43.2	59	32	6	1	22	19	5.56	84	.330	.406	12-0-1	.083	-1	96	-5	0	-0.5
1951	Det A	4	6	.400	29	15	5	1	124	119	60	9	7	71	46	3.77	111	.258	.365	43-1-1	.233	1	84	5	0	0.5
1952	Det A	3	2	.600	30	9	2	1	91.1	91	60	8	3	48	32	4.93	77	.265	.360	23-0-3	.087	-1	127	-13	0	-0.8
	StL A	1	2	.333	12	2	0	1	26	26	18	3	0	9	13	4.15	94	.260	.321	6	.000	-1	156	-2	0	-0.4
	Year	4	4	.500	42	11	2	2	117.1	117	78	11	3	57	45	4.76	81	.264	.352	29-0-3	.069	-2	132	-14	0	-1.2
1953	StL A	8	2	.800	60	2	0	7	114.1	136	62	6	1	44	46	3.94	107	.300	.363	26	.192	-1	95	1	0	0.0
1954	Bal A	1	2	.333	22	0	0	2	38.1	46	23	2	2	15	13	4.46	80	.303	.371	3	.000	-0	—	-5	0	-0.4
	NY A	3	0	1.000	10	0	0	1	18.1	28	12	0	0	12	2	5.40	64	.350	.435	6	.333	0	—	-4	0	-0.6
	Year	4	2	.667	32	0	0	3	56.2	74	35	2	2	27	15	4.76	74	.319	.393	9	.222	0	—	-9	0	-1.0
Total	6	23	17	.575	196	31	7	15	485.2	544	300	37	14	256	185	4.65	87	.289	.378	125-1-5	.176	-1	104	-39	0	-3.1
STUELAND, GEORGE	George Anton; B3.2.1899 Algona IA; D9.9.1964 Onawa IA; BB/TR/6´1.5˝/174; d9.15																									
1921	Chi N	0	1	.000	2	1	0	0	11	11	7	0	0	7	4	5.73	67	.282	.391	3	.333	0	65	-2	—	-0.1
1922	Chi N	9	4	.692	35	11	4	0	113	129	81	9	5	49	44	5.81	72	.292	.369	31-0-1	.129	-2	129	-17	—	-1.9
1923	Chi N	0	1	.000	6	0	0	0	8	11	7	0	0	5	2	5.63	71	.478	.571	0	ø	0	—	-2	—	-0.2
1925	Chi N	0	0	ø	2	0	0	0	3	2	1	0	0	3	2	3.00	144	.182	.357	1	1.000	0	—	1	—	0.1
Total	4	9	6	.600	45	12	4	0	135	153	96	9	5	64	52	5.73	73	.297	.380	35-0-1	.171	-1	124	-20	—	-2.1
STUFFEL, PAUL	Paul Harrington "Stu"; B3.22.1927 Canton OH; BR/TR/6´2˝/185; d9.16; Col Kent St.																									
1950	Phi N	0	0	ø	3	0	0	0	5	4	1	0	1	1	3	1.80	225	.211	.286	0	ø	0	—	1	0	0.1
1952	Phi N	1	0	1.000	2	1	0	0	6	5	3	0	0	7	3	3.00	122	.217	.400	2	.000	-0	171	0	0	0.0
1953	Phi N	0	0	ø	2	0	0	0	0	0	4	0	0	4	0	(4)	ø	ø	1.000	0	ø	0	—	-4	0	-0.3
Total	3	1	0	1.000	7	1	0	0	11	9	8	0	1	12	6	5.73	67	.214	.400	2	.000	-0	171	-3	0	-0.2
STULL, EVERETT	Everett James; B8.24.1971 Fort Riley KS; BR/TR/6´3˝/(195–200); [MonN92 3/71]; d4.14; Col Tennessee St.; [DL 1998 Bal A 118, 2001 Mil N 133]																									
1997	Mon N	0	1	.000	3	0	0	0-0	3.1	7	7	1	0	4-0	2	16.20	26	.438	.550	0-0-1	ø	0	—	-5	0	-0.8
1999	Atl N	0	0	ø	1	0	0	0-0	0.2	2	3	0	0	2-0	0	13.50	33	.500	.571	0	ø	0	—	-2	0	-0.1
2000	Mil N	2	3	.400	20	4	0	0-0	43.1	41	30	7	4	30-3	33	5.82	79	.256	.381	9	.000	-1	65	-5	0	-0.6
2002	Mil N	0	1	.000	2	2	0	0-0	10	15	7	0	1	9-2	7	6.30	65	.357	.481	3	.333	0	113	-2	0	-0.1
Total	4	2	5	.286	26	6	0	0-0	57.1	65	47	8	5	45-5	42	6.59	68	.293	.417	12-0-1	.083	-0	78	-14	251	-1.6
STULTS, ERIC	Eric William; B12.9.1979 Plymouth IN; BL/TL/6´0˝/215; [LAN02 15/451]; d9.5; Col Bethel (IN)																									
2006	LA N	1	0	1.000	6	2	0	0-0	17.2	17	12	4	0	7-0	5	5.60	78	.266	.338	5-0-1	.600	1	137	-2	0	-0.0
STULTZ, GEORGE	George Irvin; B6.30.1873 Louisville KY; D3.19.1955 Louisville KY; 5´10˝/150; d9.22																									
1894	Bos N	1	0	1.000	1	1	1	0	9	4	2	0	0	5	1	0.00	ø	.133	.257	3	.333	-0	37	5	—	0.5
STUMP, JIM	James Gilbert; B2.10.1932 Lansing MI; BR/TR/6´0˝/(175–188); d8.29																									
1957	Det A	1	0	1.000	6	0	0	0	13.1	11	4	0	0	8-0	2	2.03	190	.220	.328	2-0-1	.500	0	—	2	0	0.2
1959	Det A	0	0	ø	5	0	0	0	11.1	12	3	1	0	4-0	6	2.38	170	.279	.340	1	1.000	1	—	2	0	0.2
Total	2	1	0	1.000	11	0	0	0	24.2	23	7	1	0	12-0	8	2.19	180	.247	.333	3-0-1	.667	1	—	4	0	0.4
STUPER, JOHN	John Anton; B5.9.1957 Butler PA; BR/TR/6´2˝/200; [PitN78 18/460]; d6.1; Col Point Park																									
1982	†StL N	9	7	.563	23	21	2	0-0	136.2	137	55	8	0	55-5	53	3.36	110	.266	.336	42-0-4	.119	-1	83	5	0	0.3
1983	StL N	12	11	.522	40	30	6-1	1-0	198	202	95	15	2	71-3	81	3.68	99	.265	.327	59-0-7	.136	-1	109	-2	0	-0.3
1984	StL N	3	5	.375	15	12	0	0-0	61.1	73	39	4	2	20-2	19	5.28	66	.297	.351	16-0-3	.063	-1	86	-12	0	-1.5
1985	Cin N	8	5	.615	33	13	1	0-0	99	116	60	8	0	37-3	38	4.55	83	.303	.358	17-0-7	.059	-0	120	-10	0	-1.2
Total	4	32	28	.533	111	76	9-1	1-0	495	528	249	35	4	183-13	191	3.96	93	.277	.339	134-0-21	.112	-3	100	-19	0	-2.7
STURDIVANT, TOM	Thomas Virgil "Snake"; B4.28.1930 Gordon KS; BL/TR/6´1˝/(170–186); d4.14																									
1955	†NY A	1	3	.250	33	1	0	0	68.1	48	24	6	2	42-1	48	3.16	118	.203	.329	12-0-1	.083	-1	24	6	0	0.2
1956	†NY A	16	8	.667	32	17	6-2	5	158.1	134	63	15	4	52-4	110	3.30	117	.224	.291	64-0-3	.313	4	141	12	0	2.0
1957	†NY A	16	6	**.727**	28	28	7-2	0	201.2	170	65	14	4	80-2	118	2.54	141	.232	.309	71-0-4	.183	1	106	25	0	2.6
1958	NY A	3	6	.333	15	10	0	0	70.2	77	37	6	3	38-0	41	4.20	84	.274	.364	21-0-1	.190	0	99	-5	30	-0.6
1959	NY A	0	2	.000	7	3	0	0	25.1	20	16	4	0	9-0	16	4.97	73	.222	.290	6	.000	-1	48	-4	0	-0.3
	KC A	2	6	.250	36	3	0	5	71.2	70	45	9	6	34-4	57	4.65	86	.258	.347	17-0-1	.059	-2*	95	-6	0	-0.8
	Year	2	8	.200	43	6	0	5	97	90	61	13	6	43-4	73	4.73	83	.249	.333	23-0-1	.043	-3	71	-10	0	-1.1
1960	Bos A	3	3	.500	40	3	0	1	101.1	106	58	16	2	45-5	67	4.97	81	.279	.353	22-0-1	.182	-1	94	-8	0	-0.5
1961	Was A	2	6	.250	15	10	1-1	0	80	67	42	6	3	40-3	39	4.61	87	.233	.328	26-0-4	.077	-1	90	-3	0	-0.4
	Pit N	5	2	.714	13	11	6-1	1	85.2	81	29	6	1	17-3	45	2.84	141	.249	.288	32-0-1	.250	1	121	12	0	0.9
1962	Pit N	9	5	.643	49	12	2-1	2-	125.1	120	62	12	3	39-11	76	3.73	105	.260	.318	33-0-4	.182	0	87	2	0	0.2
1963	Pit N	0	0	ø	3	0	0	0	8.1	8	6	1	0	4-0	6	6.48	51	.267	.353	2	.000	-0	—	-2	0	-0.1
	Det A	1	2	.333	28	0	0	2	55	43	26	7	1	24-2	36	3.76	99	.221	.304	9	.000	-1	—	0	0	-0.1
	KC A	1	2	.333	17	3	0	0	53	47	24	3	1	17-2	26	3.74	104	.237	.300	11-0-2	.000	-1	99	1	0	-0.1
	Year	2	4	.333	45	3	0	2	108	90	50	10	2	41-4	62	3.75	102	.229	.302	20-0-2	.000	-2	101	1	0	-0.2
1964	KC A	0	0	ø	3	0	0	0	3.2	4	4	0	2	1-0	1	9.82	39	.308	.438	1	1.000	0	—	-2	0	-0.1
	NY N	0	0	ø	16	0	0	1	28.2	34	20	2	2	7-0	18	5.97	60	.306	.347	1	.000	-0	—	-7	0	-0.4
Total	10	59	51	.536	335	101	22-7	17	1137	1029	521	107	34	449-37	704	3.74	102	.244	.319	328-0-22	.183	-1	105	21	30	2.5
STURTZE, TANYON	Tanyon James; B10.12.1970 Worcester MA; BR/TR/6´5˝/(200–225); [OakA90 23/636]; d5.3; Col Quinsigamond (MA) CC																									
1995	Chi N	0	0	ø	2	0	0	0-0	2	2	2	1	0	1-0	0	9.00	46	.250	.333	0	ø	0	—	-1	0	-0.1
1996	Chi N	1	0	1.000	6	0	0	0-0	11	16	11	3	0	5-0	7	9.00	49	.348	.412	1-0-1	.000	-0	—	-5	0	-0.4
1997	Tex A	1	1	.500	9	5	0	0-0	32.2	45	30	6	0	18-0	18	8.27	59	.338	.406	0	ø	0	117	-10	0	-0.6
1999	Chi A	0	0	ø	1	1	0	0-0	6	4	0	0	0	2-0	2	0.00	ø	.200	.273	0	ø	0	19	3	0	0.2
2000	Chi A	1	2	.333	10	1	0	0-0	15.2	25	23	4	2	15-0	6	12.06	42	.379	.494	0	ø	0	37	-12	0	-1.7
	TB A	4	0	1.000	19	5	0	0-0	52.2	47	16	4	1	14-1	38	2.56	191	.236	.290	0	ø	0	126	14	35	0.9
	Year	5	2	.714	29	6	0	0-0	68.1	72	39	8	3	29-1	44	4.74	104	.272	.348	0	ø	0	111	2	0	-0.8
2001	TB A	11	12	.478	39	27	0	1-2	195.1	200	98	23	9	79-0	110	4.42	102	.271	.345	8	.125	-0	97	6	0	0.6
2002	TB A	4	18	.182	33	33	4	0-0	224	271	141	33	9	89-2	137	5.18	87	.302	.369	4-0-1	.000	-0	76	-17	0	-1.5
2003	Tor A	7	6	.538	40	8	0	0-0	89.1	107	67	14	7	43-3	54	5.94	80	.296	.380	0	ø	0	109	-12	0	-1.5
2004	†NY A	6	2	.750	28	3	0	1-0	77.1	75	49	9	6	33-2	56	5.47	84	.254	.340	3	.000	-0	154	-7	0	-0.6
2005	†NY A	5	3	.625	64	1	0	1-5	78	76	43	10	6	27-1	45	4.73	91	.257	.329	0	ø	0	280	-3	18	-0.2
2006	NY A	0	0	ø	18	0	0	0-0	10.2	17	10	3	1	6-0	6	7.59	60	.354	.429	0	ø	0	—	-4	141	-0.2
Total	11	40	44	.476	269	84	4	3-7	794.2	885	490	110	41	332-9	479	5.21	88	.285	.359	16-0-2	.063	-1	96	-48	194	-5.1
SUCH, DICK	Richard Stanley; B10.15.1944 Sanford NC; BL/TR/6´4˝/190; [TexA66*S8/101]; d4.6; C19; Col Elon																									
1970	Was A	1	5	.167	21	5	0	0-0	50	48	42	8	3	45-5	41	7.56	48	.258	.403	13	.231	1*	59	-20	0	-2.0
SUCHE, CHARLEY	Charles Morris; B8.5.1915 Cranes Mill TX; D2.11.1984 San Antonio TX; BR/TL/6´2˝/190; d9.18																									
1938	Cle A	0	0	ø	1	0	0	0	1.1	4	4	0	0	3	1	27.00	17	.571	.700	1	1.000	1	—	-3	—	-0.1
SUCHECKI, JIM	James Joseph; B8.25.1926 Chicago IL; D7.20.2000 Crofton MD; BR/TR/5´11˝/185; d5.20																									
1950	Bos A	0	0	ø	4	0	0	0	4	3	2	0	0	4	3	4.50	109	.231	.412	0	ø	0	—	0	0	0.0
1951	StL A	0	6	.000	29	6	0	0	89.2	113	64	8	1	42	47	5.42	81	.299	.371	20-0-2	.100	-2	74	-11	0	-0.8
1952	Pit N	0	0	ø	5	0	0	0	10	14	7	1	1	4	6	5.40	74	.326	.396	2	.000	0	—	-2	0	-0.1
Total	3	0	6	.000	38	6	0	0	103.2	130	73	9	2	50	56	5.38	81	.300	.374	22-0-2	.091	-2	74	-13	0	-0.9
SUDHOFF, WILLIE	John William "Wee Willie"; B9.17.1874 St.Louis MO; D5.25.1917 St.Louis MO; BR/TR/5´7˝/165; d8.20																									
1897	StL N	2	7	.222	11	9	9	0	92.2	126	72	8	4	21	19	4.47	98	.321	.362	42-0-1	.238	-1	86	-3	—	-0.3
1898	StL N	11	27	.289	41	38	35	1	315	355	205	11	27	102	65	4.34	87	.282	.349	120-0-5	.158	-6	70	-17	—	-1.9
1899	Cle N	3	8	.273	11	10	8	0	86.1	131	85	3	7	25	10	6.98	53	.347	.399	31-0-2	.065	-2	88	-30	—	-2.8
	StL N	12	10	.545	25	23	16	0	178.1	193	109	6	15	62	29	4.04	99	.276	.347	64-0-5	.203	-0	97	2	—	0.4
	Year	15	18	.455	36	33	24	0	264.2	324	194	9	22	87	39	5.00	78	.301	.365	95-0-7	.158	-2	94	-24	—	-2.4
1900	StL N	6	8	.429	16	14	13-2	0	127	128	62	3	8	37	29	2.76	132	.261	.323	106-0-1	.189	-0*	100	11	—	1.0

YEAR	TM LG	W	L	PCT	G	GS	CG-SHO	SV-BS	IP	H	R	HR	HB	BB-IB	SO	ERA	AERA	OAV	OOB	AB-HR-SH	AVG	PB	SUP	APR	DL	PW
1901	StL N	17	11	.607	38	26	25-1	2	276.1	281	142	4	18	92	78	3.52	90	.262	.331	108-1-2	.176	3	129	-10	—	-0.5
1902	StL A	12	12	.500	30	25	20	0	220	213	99	6	12	67	42	2.86	123	.254	.319	77-0-3	.169	-2*	73	14	—	1.3
1903	StL A	21	15	.583	38	35	30-5	0	293.2	262	100	4	9	56	104	2.27	128	.238	.281	110-0-3	.182	-1*	88	23	—	2.7
1904	StL A	8	15	.348	27	24	20-1	0	222.1	232	121	8	10	54	63	3.76	66	.269	.320	85-0-1	.165	0*	98	-31	—	-2.7
1905	StL A	10	20	.333	32	30	23-1	0	244	222	121	8	13	78	70	2.99	85	.244	.313	86	.186	2	77	-14	—	-1.3
1906	Was A	0	2	.000	9	5	0	0	19.2	30	25	1	2	9	7	9.15	29	.353	.427	7	.429	1	169	-14	—	-1.1
Total	10	102	135	.430	278	239	199-10	3	2075.1	2173	1141	62	125	603	516	3.60	91	.269	.329	836-1-23	.178	-7	90	-69	—	-5.2
Suggs, George	George Franklin; B7.7.1882 Kinston NC; D4.4.1949 Kinston NC; BR/TR/5´7.5˝/168; d4.21																									
1908	Det A	1	1	.500	6	1	1	1	27	32	8	0	0	2	8	1.67	145	.299	.312	10-0-1	.200	0	57	2	—	0.2
1909	Det A	1	3	.250	9	4	2	1	44.1	34	12	1	3	10	18	2.03	124	.228	.290	15-0-1	.067	-1	112	3	—	0.2
1910	Cin N	20	12	.625	35	30	23-2	3	266	248	96	6	14	48	91	2.40	121	.253	.297	85-0-2	.165	2	105	18	—	2.4
1911	Cin N	15	13	.536	36	29	17-1	0	260.2	258	110	3	10	79	91	3.00	110	.268	.330	90-0-2	.256	6	102	12	—	2.1
1912	Cin N	19	16	.543	42	36	25-5	3	303	320	132	6	11	56	104	2.94	114	.278	.318	106-1-5	.160	-1	96	16	—	1.6
1913	Cin N	8	15	.348	36	22	9-2	2	199	220	110	6	7	35	73	4.03	81	.292	.329	67-0-2	.254	2	81	-13	—	-1.1
1914	Bal F	24	14	.632	46	38	26-6	4	319.1	322	118	6	10	57	132	2.90	104	.266	.304	99-0-7	.212	3	100	10	—	1.7
1915	Bal F	11	17	.393	35	25	12	3	232.2	288	134	12	7	68	71	4.14	69	.318	.370	77-0-3	.221	1	90	-31	—	-3.3
Total	8	99	91	.521	245	185	115-16	17	1652	1722	720	40	62	355	588	3.11	100	.277	.322	549-1-23	.204	13	97	17	—	3.8
Sukla, Ed	Edward Anthony (b Edward Anthony Suckla); B3.3.1943 Long Beach CA; BR/TR/5´11˝/170; d9.17; Col Orange Coast (CA) JC																									
1964	LA A	0	1	.000	2	0	0	0	2.2	2	2	1	0	1-0	3	6.75	49	.200	.273	0	ø	0	—	-1	0	-0.2
1965	Cal A	2	3	.400	25	0	0	3	32	32	16	3	1	10-2	15	4.50	76	.264	.326	0	ø	0	—	-3	0	-0.5
1966	Cal A	1	1	.500	12	0	0	1	16.2	18	12	4	0	6-0	8	6.48	52	.281	.343	1	.000	-0	—	-5	0	-0.7
Total	3	3	5	.375	39	0	0	4	51.1	52	30	8	1	17-2	26	5.26	64	.267	.329	1	.000	-0	—	-9	0	-1.4
Sullivan, Charlie	Charles Edward; B5.23.1903 Yadkin Valley NC; D5.28.1935 Maiden NC; BL/TR/6´1˝/185; d4.21																									
1928	Det A	0	2	.000	3	2	0	0	12.1	18	12	1	0	6	2	6.57	63	.360	.429	4	.000	-1	72	-4	—	-0.5
1930	Det A	1	5	.167	40	3	2	5	93.2	112	72	9	1	53	38	6.53	73	.311	.401	24	.292	2	24	-14	—	-0.7
1931	Det A	3	2	.600	31	4	2	0	95	109	60	6	1	46	28	4.93	93	.288	.366	24	.167	-1	101	-3	—	-0.3
Total	3	4	9	.308	74	9	4	5	201	239	144	16	2	105	68	5.78	81	.303	.386	52	.212	-0	67	-21	—	-1.5
Sullivan, Jim	Daniel James; B4.25.1857 Charlestown MA; D11.29.1901 Roxbury MA; BR/TR/5´10˝/155; d4.22																									
1891	Bos N	0	0	ø	1	0	0	0	0.1	2	4	0	0	5	0	81.00	5	.667	.875	0	ø	0	—	-2	—	-0.1
	Col AA	0	1	.000	1	1	1	0	9	10	9	1	1	5	1	4.00	86	.270	.372	4	.000	-1	90	-2	—	-0.2
1895	Bos N	11	9	.550	21	19	16	0	178.1	231	133	10	16	58	45	4.74	107	.309	.371	85-0-1	.176	-6*	123	8	—	0.1
1896	Bos N	11	12	.478	31	26	21-1	1	225.1	268	148	13	6	68	33	4.03	113	.293	.346	88-1-2	.216	-2	97	15	—	0.8
1897	†Bos N	4	5	.444	13	9	8-1	2	89	91	56	1	2	26	17	3.94	113	.262	.317	33-0-1	.182	-3	80	4	—	0.1
1898	Bos N	0	1	.000	3	2	0	0	12	19	16	1	1	9	1	12.00	31	.358	.460	3	.333	0	77	-9	—	-0.6
Total	5	26	28	.481	70	57	46-2	3	514	621	366	26	26	171	97	4.50	104	.295	.356	213-1-4	.192	-11	103	14	—	0.1
Sullivan, Fleury	Florence P.; B1862 E.St.Louis IL; D2.15.1897 E.St.Louis IL; d5.3																									
1884	Pit AA	16	35	.314	51	51	51-2	0	441	496	328	15	20	96	189	4.20	79	.268	.311	189	.153	-9*	65	-44	—	-4.7
Sullivan, Frank	Franklin Leal; B1.23.1930 Hollywood CA; BR/TR/6´6.5˝/(210–215); d7.31																									
1953	Bos A	1	1	.500	14	0	0	0	25.2	24	16	3	1	11	17	5.61	75	.264	.350	4	.250	0	—	-3	0	-0.2
1954	Bos A	15	12	.556	36	26	11-3	1	206.1	185	81	19	6	66	124	3.14	131	.240	.304	68-0-3	.103	-3	106	21	0	2.5
1955	Bos A★	**18**	13	.581	35	**35**	16-3	0	**260**	235	103	23	7	100-5	129	2.91	147	.241	.313	89-0-12	.112	-4	101	34	0	3.4
1956	Bos A☆	14	7	.667	34	33	12-1	0	242	253	112	22	8	82-6	116	3.42	135	.268	.330	85-0-7	.141	-5	107	27	0	1.6
1957	Bos A	14	11	.560	31	30	14-3	0	240.2	206	76	16	7	48-4	127	2.73	146	.230	**.273**	79-0-6	.165	-2	86	**35**	0	**3.5**
1958	Bos A	13	9	.591	32	29	10-2	3	199.1	216	91	12	3	49-0	103	3.57	112	.278	.322	67-0-8	.164	-1	104	9	0	0.8
1959	Bos A	9	11	.450	30	26	5-2	1	177.2	172	86	17	7	67-2	107	3.95	103	.258	.331	60-0-7	.200	-1	94	2	0	0.1
1960	Bos A	6	16	.273	40	22	4	1	153.2	164	94	12	6	52-6	98	5.10	79	.269	.331	40-0-4	.125	-1	92	-16	0	-2.2
1961	Phi N	3	16	.158	49	18	1-1	6	159.1	161	93	19	5	55-5	114	4.29	95	.262	.326	33-0-3	.152	0	70	-7	0	-0.7
1962	Phi N	0	2	.000	19	0	0	0	23	38	21	2	2	12-2	12	6.26	62	.396	.460	0	ø	0	—	-8	0	-0.6
	Min A	4	1	.800	21	0	0	5	33.1	33	17	3	0	13-0	10	3.24	126	.258	.324	4	.000	-0	—	2	0	0.2
1963	Min A	0	1	.000	10	0	0	1	11	15	7	1	0	4-1	2	5.73	64	.349	.404	0	ø	0	—	-2	0	-0.2
Total	11	97	100	.492	351	219	73-15	18	1732	1702	797	149	52	559-31	959	3.60	116	.257	.319	529-0-50	.144	-17	97	94	0	8.2
Sullivan, Harry	Harry Andrew; B4.22.1888 Rockford IL; D9.22.1919 Rockford IL; BL/TL; d8.11; Col St. Louis																									
1909	StL N	0	0	ø	2	1	0	0	1	4	6	1	0	2	1	36.00	7	.500	.600	1	.000	-0	138	-4	—	-0.2
Sullivan, Jim	James Richard; B4.5.1894 Mine Run VA; D2.12.1972 Burtonsville MD; BR/TR/5´11˝/165; d9.27																									
1921	Phi A	0	2	.000	2	2	2	0	17	20	13	0	0	7	8	3.18	140	.294	.360	6	.000	-1	37	0	—	-0.1
1922	Phi A	0	2	.000	20	2	1	0	51.1	76	43	3	1	25	15	5.44	78	.373	.443	11-0-1	.091	-1	30	-9	—	-0.5
1923	Cle A	0	1	.000	3	0	0	0	5	10	10	0	1	5	4	14.40	28	.476	.593	1	.000	-0	—	-6	—	-0.9
Total	3	0	5	.000	25	4	3	0	73.1	106	66	3	2	37	27	5.52	78	.362	.437	18-0-1	.056	-2	35	-15	—	-1.5
Sullivan, Joe	Joe; B9.26.1910 Mason City IL; D4.8.1985 Sequim WA; BL/TL/5´11˝/175; d4.20																									
1935	Det A	6	6	.500	25	12	5	0	125.2	119	66	4	3	71	53	3.51	119	.244	.344	43-0-1	.163	-1	106	5	—	0.3
1936	Det A	2	5	.286	26	4	1	1	79.2	111	70	4	2	40	32	6.78	73	.331	.406	28-0-1	.179	-1	98	-17	—	-1.3
1939	Bos N	6	9	.400	31	11	7	2	113.2	114	57	3	2	50	46	3.64	101	.266	.346	40-0-1	.300	3*	86	-1	—	0.3
1940	Bos N	10	14	.417	36	22	7	1	177.1	157	89	9	8	89	64	3.55	105	.240	.339	71-0-3	.197	-0	110	-1	—	-0.1
1941	Bos N	2	2	.500	16	2	0	0	52.1	60	26	3	2	26	11	4.13	86	.290	.374	15	.067	-1	107	-2	0	-0.2
	Pit N	4	1	.800	16	4	0	1	39.1	40	26	2	0	22	10	2.97	121	.258	.350	11	.364	1	100	-1	0	-0.1
	Year	6	3	.667	32	6	0	1	91.2	100	52	5	2	48	21	3.63	99	.276	.364	26	.192	-0	103	-5	0	-0.3
Total	5	30	37	.448	150	55	20	5	588	601	334	25	17	298	216	4.01	99	.265	.355	208-0-6	.207	1	101	-17	0	-1.1
Sullivan, John	John Jeremiah "Lefty"; B5.31.1894 Chicago IL; D7.7.1958 Chicago IL; BL/TL/5´11˝/165; d7.18																									
1919	Chi A	0	1	.000	4	2	1	0	15	24	15	0	1	8	9	4.20	76	.364	.440	3	.000	-0	160	-4	—	-0.3
Sullivan, Mike	Michael Joseph "Big Mike"; B10.23.1866 Boston MA; D6.14.1906 Boston MA; BL/TR/6´1˝/210; d6.17; Col Boston U.																									
1889	Was N	0	3	.000	9	3	3	0	41	47	47	2	3	32	15	7.24	54	.280	.404	19	.053	-2	108	-14	—	-0.9
1890	Chi N	5	6	.455	12	12	10	0	96	108	77	3	4	58	33	4.59	80	.275	.374	40	.125	-3	82	-10	—	-1.2
1891	Phi AA	0	2	.000	2	2	2	0	18	17	13	2	3	10	7	3.50	108	.239	.357	7	.000	-1	65	0	—	-0.2
	NY N	1	2	.333	3	3	3	0	24	24	19	0	1	8	11	3.38	95	.250	.314	10	.200	-0	81	-1	—	-0.2
1892	Cin N	12	4	.750	21	16	15	0	166.1	179	90	8	9	74	56	3.08	106	.264	.344	74	.176	-2	102	2	—	-0.2
1893	Cin N	8	11	.421	27	18	14	1	183.2	200	146	5	17	103	40	5.05	95	.269	.370	79-1	.203	-3	89	-7	—	-0.8
1894	Was N	2	10	.167	20	12	11	1	117.2	166	134	10	8	74	21	6.58	80	.329	.422	57-1-1	.158	-4	100	-15	—	-1.4
	Cle N	6	5	.545	13	11	9	0	90.2	128	82	4	3	47	19	6.35	86	.329	.405	44-0-1	.295	0	105	-5	—	-0.5
	Year	8	15	.348	33	23	20	1	208.1	294	216	14	11	121	40	6.48	83	.329	.415	101-1-2	.218	-4	103	-26	—	-1.9
1895	Cle N	1	2	.333	4	3	2	0	31	42	34	1	1	16	5	8.42	59	.318	.396	15	.133	-2	119	-9	—	-0.7
1896	NY N	10	13	.435	25	22	18	0	185.1	188	131	3	13	71	42	4.66	90	.261	.338	77-0-2	.208	-3	83	-8	—	-1.0
1897	NY N	8	7	.533	23	16	11-1	2	148.2	183	113	6	14	71	35	5.09	82	.300	.386	66	.273	0	101	-11	—	-0.9
1899	Bos N	1	0	1.000	1	1	1	0	9	10	6	1	1	4	1	5.00	83	.278	.366	3	.333	0	121	-1	—	0.0
Total	10	54	65	.454	160	119	99-1	4	1111.1	1292	892	45	77	568	285	5.04	85	.284	.373	491-2-4	.196	-21	94	-79	—	-8.0
Sullivan, Lefty	Paul Thomas; B9.7.1916 Nashville TN; D11.1.1988 Scottsdale AZ; BL/TL/6´3˝/204; d5.6																									
1939	Cle A	0	1	.000	7	1	0	0	12.2	9	8	0	1	9	4	4.26	103	.214	.365	3	.000	-0	20	0	—	-0.1
Sullivan, Tom	Thomas; B3.1.1860 New York NY; D4.12.1947 Cincinnati OH; d9.27																									
1884	Col AA	2	2	.500	4	4	4	0	31	42	22	2	0	3	12	4.06	75	.318	.333	11	.091	-1	70	-4	—	-0.5
1886	Lou AA	2	7	.222	9	9	8	0	75	94	70	6	2	33	27	3.96	92	.305	.376	27	.111	-2	60	-4	—	-0.5
1888	KC AA	8	16	.333	24	24	24	0	214.2	227	146	2	24	68	84	3.40	100	.262	.332	92	.109	-6*	68	-4	—	-0.7
1889	KC AA	2	8	.200	10	10	10	0	87.1	111	88	2	7	48	24	5.67	75	.300	.391	33	.152	-1	86	-10	—	-0.9
Total	4	14	33	.298	47	47	46	0	408	474	326	12	33	152	147	4.04	89	.282	.354	163	.117	-9	71	-22	—	-2.6

YEAR	TM LG	W	L	PCT	G	GS	CG-SHO	SV-BS	IP	H	R	HR	HB	BB-IB	SO	ERA	AERA	OAV	OOB	AB-HR-SH	AVG	PB	SUP	APR	DL	PW
SULLIVAN, TOM	Thomas Augustin; B10.18.1895 Boston MA; D9.23.1962 Boston MA; BL/TL/5´11˝/178; d5.15																									
1922	Phi N	0	0	ø	3	0	0	0	8	16	11	0	1	5	2	11.25	41	.410	.489	4-1-0	.250	1	—	-4	—	-0.1
SULLIVAN, BILL	William F.; B12.1868 Providence RI; D10.8.1905 Providence RI; BR/TR; d4.19																									
1890	Syr AA	1	4	.200	6	6	4	0	42	51	50	2	6	27	13	7.93	45	.291	.404	22	.091	-2	136	-22	—	-1.9
SULLIVAN, SCOTT	William Scott; B3.13.1971 Tuscaloosa AL; BR/TR/6´3˝/210; [CinN93 2/62]; d5.6; Col Auburn; [DL 2005 KC A 183]																									
1995	Cin N	0	0	ø	3	0	0	0-0	3.2	4	2	0	0	2-0	2	4.91	85	.286	.375	1	.000	-0	—	0	0	0.0
1996	Cin N	0	0	ø	7	0	0	0-0	8	7	2	0	1	5-0	3	2.25	190	.250	.382	1	.000	-0	—	2	0	0.1
1997	Cin N	5	3	.625	59	0	0	1-1	97.1	79	36	12	7	30-8	96	3.24	132	.220	.291	7-0-2	.000	-1	—	12	0	0.8
1998	Cin N	5	5	.500	67	0	0	1-3	102	98	62	14	9	36-4	86	5.21	82	.253	.327	11-0-1	.091	-1	—	-10	0	-0.9
1999	Cin N	5	4	.556	79	0	0	3-2	113.2	88	41	10	8	47-4	78	3.01	156	.216	.307	15	.000	-2	—	21	0	1.3
2000	Cin N	3	6	.333	79	0	0	3-3	106.1	87	44	14	9	38-8	96	3.47	137	.226	.307	7	.286	0*	—	15	0	1.2
2001	Cin N	7	1	.875	79	0	0	0-3	103.1	94	44	10	8	36-8	82	3.31	139	.243	.317	3	.000	-0	—	13	0	0.8
2002	Cin N	6	5	.545	71	0	0	1-2	78.2	93	60	15	5	31-11	78	6.06	70	.294	.363	3	.333	0	—	-15	15	-2.0
2003	Cin N	6	0	1.000	50	0	0	0-1	49.2	39	22	4	5	26-4	43	3.62	115	.211	.321	0	ø	0	—	3	24	0.3
	Chi A	0	0	ø	15	0	0	0-0	14.1	9	6	2	1	6-0	13	3.77	122	.184	.281	0	ø	0	—	2	0	0.1
2004	KC A	3	4	.429	49	0	0	0-1	60.1	73	34	8	7	24-10	45	4.77	98	.308	.382	0	ø	0	—	0	39	0.0
Total	10	40	28	.588	558	0	0	9-16	737.1	671	353	89	60	281-57	622	3.98	113	.244	.324	48-0-3	.083	-3	—	43	261	1.7
SUMMERS, ED	Oron Edgar "Kickapoo Ed","Chief"; B12.5.1884 Ladoga IN; D5.12.1953 Indianapolis IN; BB/TR/6´2˝/180; d4.16; Col Wabash																									
1908	†Det A	24	12	.667	40	32	23-5	1	301	271	112	3	20	55	103	1.64	147	.242	.290	113-0-4	.124	-6	116	15	—	1.1
1909	†Det A	19	9	.679	35	32	24-3	1	281.2	243	91	4	10	52	107	2.24	113	.227	.269	94-0-3	.106	-4	109	10	—	0.6
1910	Det A	13	12	.520	30	25	18-1	0	220.1	211	83	8	5	60	82	2.53	104	.254	.308	76-2-4	.184	-0	111	2	—	0.3
1911	Det A	11	11	.500	30	20	13	1	179.1	189	108	3	11	51	65	3.66	95	.274	.334	63-0-3	.254	1	122	-7	—	-0.7
1912	Det A	1	1	.500	3	3	1	0	16.2	16	10	1	0	3	5	4.86	67	.250	.284	6	.500	1	136	-2	—	-0.1
Total	5	68	45	.602	138	112	79-9	3	999	930	404	19	46	221	362	2.42	111	.246	.296	352-2-14	.162	-9	115	18	—	1.2
SUNDIN, GORDIE	Gordon Vincent; B10.10.1937 Minneapolis MN; BR/TR/6´4˝/210; d9.19																									
1956	Bal A	0	0	ø	1	0	0	0	0	0	1	0	0	2-0	0	(1)	ø	ø	1.000	0	ø	0	—	-1	137	-0.1
SUNDRA, STEVE	Stephen Richard "Smokey"; B3.27.1910 Luxor PA; D3.23.1952 Cleveland OH; BR/TR (BB 1936–40)/6´2˝/190; d4.17; Mil 1944–45																									
1936	NY A	0	0	ø	1	0	0	0	2	2	0	0	0	2	1	0.00	ø	.286	.444	1	.000	-0	—	1	—	0.0
1938	NY A	6	4	.600	25	8	3	0	93.2	107	61	7	0	43	33	4.80	94	.291	.365	33-1-2	.182	1	141	-4	—	-0.2
1939	†NY A	11	1	.917	24	11	8-1	0	120.2	110	43	7	0	56	27	2.76	158	.240	.323	49-0-2	.265	4	162	22	—	2.3
1940	NY A	4	6	.400	27	8	2	2	99.1	121	68	11	1	42	26	5.53	73	.299	.366	29-0-1	.138	-1	101	-17	—	-1.6
1941	Was A	9	13	.409	28	23	11	0	168.1	203	108	11	1	61	50	5.29	76	.294	.352	60-0-4	.217	2	105	-20	0	-2.0
1942	Was A	1	3	.250	6	4	2	0	33.2	43	24	1	1	15	5	5.61	65	.305	.376	12	.167	-0	99	-7	0	-0.7
	StL A	8	3	.727	20	13	6	0	110.2	122	56	2	0	29	26	3.82	97	.275	.319	40-1-3	.225	3	138	-2	0	0.1
	Year	9	6	.600	26	17	8	0	144.1	165	80	3	1	44	31	4.24	87	.282	.333	52-1-3	.212	2	129	-8	0	-0.6
1943	StL A	15	11	.577	32	29	13-3	0	208	212	89	10	0	66	44	3.25	103	.266	.322	73-0-4	.219	1	104	1	0	0.2
1944	StL A	2	0	1.000	3	3	2	0	19	15	3	1	0	4	1	1.42	253	.211	.253	5	.000	-0	85	5	0	0.5
1946	StL A	0	0	ø	2	0	0	0	4	9	9	0	0	3	1	11.25	33	.409	.480	0	ø	0	—	-4	0	-0.2
Total	9	56	41	.577	168	99	47-4	2	859.1	944	461	50	3	321	214	4.17	94	.277	.340	302-2-16	.209	10	116	-25	0	-1.6
SUNKEL, TOM	Thomas Jacob "Lefty"; B8.9.1912 Paris IL; D4.6.2002 Paris IL; BL/TL/6´1˝/190; d8.26																									
1937	StL N	0	0	ø	9	1	0	1	29.1	24	11	0	0	11	9	2.76	144	.214	.285	9	.111	-1	173	4	—	0.1
1939	StL N	4	4	.500	20	11	2-1	0	85.1	79	47	4	1	56	54	4.22	98	.242	.354	28-0-1	.321	2	98	-1	—	0.0
1941	NY N	1	1	.500	2	2	1-1	0	15.1	7	5	0	1	12	14	2.93	126	.140	.317	6	.333	0	34	2	0	0.2
1942	NY N	3	6	.333	19	11	3	0	63.2	65	40	5	0	41	29	4.81	70	.269	.375	19	.105	-1	80	-10	0	-1.5
1943	NY N	0	1	.000	1	1	0	0	2.2	4	3	1	0	3	0	10.13	34	.308	.438	0	ø	0	0	-2	0	-0.3
1944	Bro N	1	3	.250	12	3	0	1	24	39	20	1	0	10	6	7.50	47	.368	.422	4-0-1	.000	-1	79	-9	0	-1.5
Total	6	9	15	.375	63	29	6-2	2	220.1	218	126	11	2	133	112	4.53	83	.256	.358	66-0-2	.212	0	84	-16	0	-3.0
SUPPAN, JEFF	Jeffrey Scot; B1.2.1975 Oklahoma City OK; BR/TR/6´2˝/(203–220); [BosA93 2/49]; d7.17																									
1995	Bos A	1	2	.333	8	3	0	0-0	22.2	29	15	4	0	5-1	19	5.96	82	.312	.343	0	ø	0	89	-2	0	-0.2
1996	Bos A	1	1	.500	8	4	0	0-0	22.2	29	19	3	1	13-0	13	7.54	68	.330	.406	0	ø	0	123	-5	36	-0.4
1997	Bos A	7	3	.700	23	22	0	0-0	112.1	140	75	12	4	36-1	67	5.69	82	.305	.358	2	.000	-0	118	-11	0	-1.0
1998	Ari N	1	7	.125	13	13	1	0-0	66	82	55	12	1	21-1	39	6.68	64	.301	.351	22-0-1	.273	1	94	-18	0	-1.6
	KC A	0	0	ø	4	1	0	0-0	12.2	9	1	1	0	1-0	12	0.71	684	.200	.217	0	ø	0	0	6	0	0.3
1999	KC A	10	12	.455	32	32	4-1	0-0	208.2	222	113	28	3	62-4	103	4.53	112	.274	.326	5	.200	0	97	13	0	1.1
2000	KC A	10	9	.526	35	33	3-1	0-0	217	240	121	36	7	84-3	128	4.94	106	.284	.351	3	.000	-0	94	9	0	0.5
2001	KC A	10	14	.417	34	34	1	0-0	218.1	227	120	26	12	74-3	120	4.37	114	.267	.333	5	.400	1	81	12	0	1.2
2002	KC A	9	16	.360	33	33	3-1	0-0	208	229	134	32	7	68-3	109	5.32	94	.279	.335	1-0-3	.000	0	83	-8	0	-0.8
2003	Pit N	10	7	.588	21	21	3-2	0-0	141	147	57	11	6	31-5	78	3.57	121	.268	.313	41-0-8	.293	4	94	13	0	1.8
	Bos A	3	4	.429	11	10	0	0-0	63	70	41	12	2	20-0	32	5.57	84	.281	.335	2-0-1	.000	-0	111	-5	0	-0.5
2004	†StL N	16	9	.640	31	31	0	0-0	188	192	98	25	8	65-1	110	4.16	102	.265	.330	57-0-7	.070	-4	118	1	0	-0.3
2005	†StL N	16	10	.615	32	32	0	0-0	194.1	206	93	24	7	63-1	114	3.57	118	.275	.335	58-1-6	.207	3	105	11	0	1.7
2006	†StL N	12	7	.632	32	32	0	0-0	190	207	100	21	8	69-6	104	4.12	106	.277	.343	55-0-9	.218	4	101	1	0	0.3
Total	12	106	101	.512	317	301	15-5	0-0	1864.2	2029	1042	247	66	612-29	1048	4.60	102	.278	.337	251-1-35	.195	8	98	17	36	2.1
SURHOFF, RICH	Richard Clifford; B10.3.1962 Bronx NY; BR/TR/6´3˝/210; [PhiN82*20/321]; d9.8; b–B.J.; Col St. Johns River (FL) CC																									
1985	Phi N	1	0	1.000	2	0	0	0-0	1	2	0	0	0	0-0	1	0.00	ø	.500	.500	0	ø	0	—	0	0	0.1
	Tex A	0	1	.000	7	0	0	2-1	8.1	12	7	2	0	3-0	8	7.56	56	.343	.395	0	ø	0	—	-3	0	-0.4
Total	1	1	1	.500	9	0	0	2-1	9.1	14	7	2	0	3-0	9	6.75	62	.359	.405	0	ø	0	—	-3	0	-0.3
SURKONT, MAX	Matthew Constantine; B6.16.1922 Central Falls RI; D10.8.1986 Largo FL; BR/TR/6´0˝/(205–215); d4.19																									
1949	Chi A	3	5	.375	44	2	0	4	96	92	61	9	3	60	38	4.78	87	.255	.366	22	.045	-1	75	-8	0	-0.8
1950	Bos N	5	2	.714	9	6	2	0	55.2	63	29	5	2	20	21	3.23	119	.285	.350	23-1-0	.435	5	142	1	0	0.7
1951	Bos N	12	16	.429	37	33	11-2	1	237	230	119	21	7	89	110	3.99	92	.252	.323	73-0-8	.151	0	98	-8	0	-1.0
1952	Bos N	12	13	.480	31	29	12-3	0	215	201	95	19	3	76	125	3.77	96	.245	.311	63-0-7	.111	-1	86	-2	0	-0.3
1953	Mil N	11	5	.688	28	24	11-2	0	170	168	82	22	0	64	83	4.18	94	.255	.321	56-0-5	.286	7	121	-1	0	0.6
1954	Pit N	9	18	.333	33	29	11	0	208.1	216	124	25	4	78	78	4.41	95	.268	.333	60-0-9	.167	0	78	-8	0	-0.8
1955	Pit N	7	14	.333	35	22	5	2	166.1	194	109	23	3	78-4	84	5.57	74	.298	.374	50-0-4	.140	-1	87	-22	0	-2.7
1956	Pit N	0	0	ø	1	0	0	0	2	2	1	0	0	3-0	1	4.50	84	.333	.500	0	ø	0	—	0	0	0.0
	StL N	0	0	ø	5	0	0	0	5.2	10	6	3	0	2-0	5	9.53	40	.417	.462	1	.000	-0	—	-3	0	-0.2
	NY N	2	2	.500	8	4	1	1	32	24	17	5	0	9-1	18	4.78	79	.202	.256	9-0-2	.111	-0	93	-3	0	-0.4
	Year	2	2	.500	14	4	1	1	39.2	36	24	8	0	14-1	24	5.45	69	.242	.303	10-0-2	.100	-0	93	-6	0	-0.6
1957	NY N	0	1	.000	5	0	0	0	6.1	9	7	2	0	2-0	8	9.95	40	.321	.367	0	ø	0	—	-4	0	-0.5
Total	9	61	76	.445	236	149	53-7	8	1194.1	1209	650	134	22	481-5	571	4.38	89	.262	.334	357-1-35	.176	8	94	-58	0	-5.4
SUSCE, GEORGE	George Daniel; B9.13.1931 Pittsburgh PA; BR/TR/6´1˝/(180–190); d4.15; f–George																									
1955	Bos A	9	7	.563	29	15	6-1	1	144.1	123	54	12	8	49-4	60	3.06	140	.232	.305	49-0-3	.143	-2	80	19	0	1.8
1956	Bos A	2	4	.333	21	6	0	0	69.2	71	54	14	4	44-1	26	6.20	74	.262	.371	18	.222	1	103	-10	0	-0.7
1957	Bos A	7	3	.700	29	5	0	1	88.1	93	45	6	3	41-5	40	4.28	93	.274	.354	25-0-1	.120	-1	85	-2	0	-0.3
1958	Bos A	0	0	ø	2	0	0	0	2	6	4	1	0	1-0	0	18.00	22	.600	.583	0	ø	0	—	-3	0	-0.1
	Det A	4	3	.571	27	10	2	1	90.2	90	45	7	3	26-1	42	3.67	110	.259	.312	24-0-2	.125	-1	89	2	0	0.0
	Year	4	3	.571	29	10	2	1	92.2	96	49	8	3	27-1	42	3.98	101	.269	.321	24-0-2	.125	-1	89	-1	0	-0.1
1959	Det A	0	0	ø	9	0	0	0	14.2	24	22	4	2	9-0	9	12.89	32	.358	.449	1	.000	-0	—	-13	0	-0.6
Total	5	22	17	.564	117	36	8-1	3	409.2	407	224	44	20	170-11	177	4.42	95	.260	.337	117-0-6	.145	-2	88	-7	0	0.1
SUTCLIFFE, RICK	Richard Lee; B6.21.1956 Independence MO; BL/TR/6´7˝/(200–240); [LAN74 1/21]; d9.29																									
1976	LA N	0	0	ø	1	1	0	0-0	5	2	0	0	0	1-0	3	0.00	ø	.125	.176	1	.000	-0	26	2	0	0.1
1978	LA N	0	0	ø	2	0	0	0-0	1.2	2	0	0	1	1-0	0	0.00	ø	.286	.444	0	ø	0	—	1	0	0.0
1979	LA N	17	10	.630	39	30	5-1	0-0	242	217	104	16	2	97-6	117	3.46	105	.243	.316	85-1-6	.247	5*	132	6	0	1.1

YEAR	TM LG	W	L	PCT	G	GS	CG-SHO	SV-BS	IP	H	R	HR	HB	BB-IB	SO	ERA	AERA	OAV	OOB	AB-HR-SH	AVG	PB	SUP	APR	DL	PW
1980	LA N	3	9	.250	42	10	1-1	5-3	110	122	73	10	1	55-2	59	5.56	62	.285	.366	27-0-3	.148	-0*	129	-25	0	-2.8
1981	LA N	2	2	.500	14	6	0	0-0	47	41	24	5	2	20-2	16	4.02	82	.238	.321	11	.182	1	72	-5	22	-0.3
1982	Cle A	14	8	.636	34	27	6-1	1-0	216	174	81	16	4	98-2	142	**2.96**	140	**.226**	.314	0	ø	0	99	27	0	2.7
1983	Cle A☆	17	11	.607	36	35	10-2	0-1	243.1	251	131	23	6	102-5	160	4.29	100	.268	.341	0	ø	0	104	-2	0	-0.1
1984	Cle A	4	5	.444	15	15	2	0-0	94.1	111	60	7	2	46-3	58	5.15	80	.298	.375	0	ø	0	115	-11	0	-0.9
	†Chi N	16	1	**.941**	20	20	7-3	0-0	150.1	123	53	9	1	39-0	155	2.69	145	.220	.271	56-0-5	.250	3	125	17	0	2.4
1985	Chi N	8	8	.500	20	20	6-3	0-0	130	119	51	12	3	44-3	102	3.18	126	.240	.304	43-1-2	.233	2	82	10	93	1.5
1986	Chi N	5	14	.263	28	27	4-1	0-0	176.2	166	92	18	1	96-8	122	4.64	88	.252	.347	53-1-4	.208	2*	71	-7	34	-0.4
1987	Chi N★	**18**	10	.643	34	34	6-1	0-0	237.1	223	106	24	4	106-14	174	3.68	118	.252	.332	81-0-11	.148	2*	113	16	0	2.3
1988	Chi N	13	14	.481	32	32	12-2	0-0	226	232	97	18	2	70-9	144	3.86	94	.269	.323	75-1-4	.160	3*	98	-1	21	0.3
1989	†Chi N★	16	11	.593	35	34	5-1	0-0	229	202	98	18	2	69-8	153	3.66	103	.240	.296	70-0-10	.143	1*	103	5	0	0.9
1990	Chi N	0	2	.000	5	5	0	0-0	21.1	25	14	2	0	12-0	7	5.91	69	.305	.385	5-0-1	.000	0	88	-3	142	-0.3
1991	Chi N	6	5	.545	19	18	0	0-0	96.2	96	52	4	0	45-2	52	4.10	95	.264	.338	32-0-5	.094	-1*	97	-3	68	-0.5
1992	Bal A	16	15	.516	36	**36**	5-2	0-0	237.1	251	123	20	7	74-4	109	4.47	91	.273	.328	0	ø	0	91	-9	0	-1.2
1993	Bal A	10	10	.500	29	28	3	0-0	166	212	112	23	6	74-5	80	5.75	79	.314	.385	0	ø	0	101	-21	19	-2.1
1994	StL N	6	4	.600	16	14	0	0-0	67.2	93	53	11	2	32-2	26	6.52	65	.331	.402	23-0-3	.130	-1	107	-17	47	-2.1
Total	18	171	139	.552	457	392	72-18	6-4	2697.2	2662	1324	236	46	1081-75	1679	4.08	98	.260	.331	562-4-54	.181	17	103	-20	446	0.6

SUTER, HARRY Harry Richard "Handsome Harry","Rube"; B9.15.1887 Independence MO; D7.24.1971 Topeka KS; BL/TL/5´10˝/190; d4.16

YEAR	TM LG	W	L	PCT	G	GS	CG-SHO	SV-BS	IP	H	R	HR	HB	BB-IB	SO	ERA	AERA	OAV	OOB	AB-HR-SH	AVG	PB	SUP	APR	DL	PW
1909	Chi A	2	3	.400	18	7	3-1	1	87.1	72	34	2	4	28	53	2.47	95	.199	.264	32-0-1	.094	-1	112	-1	—	-0.3

SUTHERLAND, DARRELL Darrell Wayne; B11.14.1941 Glendale CA; BR/TR/6´4˝/(169–175); d6.28; b–Gary; Col Stanford

YEAR	TM LG	W	L	PCT	G	GS	CG-SHO	SV-BS	IP	H	R	HR	HB	BB-IB	SO	ERA	AERA	OAV	OOB	AB-HR-SH	AVG	PB	SUP	APR	DL	PW
1964	NY N	0	3	.000	10	4	0	0	26.2	32	26	1	2	12-0	9	7.76	46	.302	.377	5	.200	0	111	-12	0	-1.2
1965	NY N	3	1	.750	18	2	0	0	48	33	16	4	4	17-2	16	2.81	125	.199	.284	13	.154	0	111	4	0	0.5
1966	NY N	2	0	1.000	31	0	0	1	44.1	60	25	6	2	25-8	23	4.87	75	.339	.422	3	.667	1	—	-5	0	-0.1
1968	Cle A	0	0	ø	3	0	0	0	3.1	6	3	0	0	4-1	2	8.10	37	.375	.500	0	ø	0	—	-2	0	-0.1
Total	4	5	4	.556	62	6	0	1	122.1	131	70	11	8	58-11	50	4.78	75	.282	.366	21	.238	1	111	-15	0	-0.9

SUTHERLAND, SUDS Harvey Scott; B2.20.1894 Eugene OR; D5.11.1972 Portland OR; BR/TR/6´0˝/180; d4.14

YEAR	TM LG	W	L	PCT	G	GS	CG-SHO	SV-BS	IP	H	R	HR	HB	BB-IB	SO	ERA	AERA	OAV	OOB	AB-HR-SH	AVG	PB	SUP	APR	DL	PW
1921	Det A	6	2	.750	13	8	3	0	58	80	43	1	0	18	18	4.97	86	.328	.374	27	.407	2*	156	-6	—	-0.3

SUTHERLAND, DIZZY Howard Alvin; B4.9.1922 Washington DC; D8.26.1979 Washington DC; BL/TL/6´0˝/200; d9.20

YEAR	TM LG	W	L	PCT	G	GS	CG-SHO	SV-BS	IP	H	R	HR	HB	BB-IB	SO	ERA	AERA	OAV	OOB	AB-HR-SH	AVG	PB	SUP	APR	DL	PW
1949	Was A	0	1	.000	1	1	0	0	1	2	5	0	0	6	0	45.00	9	.400	.727	0	ø	0	126	-4	0	-0.6

SUTTER, BRUCE Howard Bruce; B1.8.1953 Lancaster PA; BR/TR/6´2˝/(185–195); d5.9; HF2006; [DL 1987 Atl N 182, 1989 Atl N 182]

YEAR	TM LG	W	L	PCT	G	GS	CG-SHO	SV-BS	IP	H	R	HR	HB	BB-IB	SO	ERA	AERA	OAV	OOB	AB-HR-SH	AVG	PB	SUP	APR	DL	PW
1976	Chi N	6	3	.667	52	0	0	10-2	83.1	63	27	4	0	26-8	73	2.70	144	.209	.271	8	.000	-1	—	10	0	1.3
1977	Chi N✳	7	3	.700	62	0	0	31-9	107.1	69	21	5	1	23-7	129	1.34	329	.183	.231	20	.150	-0	—	31	21	4.7
1978	Chi N★	8	10	.444	64	0	0	27-14	98.2	82	44	10	1	34-7	106	3.19	127	.220	.285	13-0-4	.077	-0	—	6	0	1.3
1979	Chi N★	6	6	.500	62	0	0	**37**-10	101.1	67	29	3	0	32-5	110	2.22	187	.186	.249	12-0-2	.250	0	—	**19**	0	3.9
1980	Chi N★	5	8	.385	60	0	0	**28**-9	102.1	90	35	5	1	34-8	76	2.64	150	.242	.306	9-0-1	.111	-1	—	13	0	2.4
1981	StL N★	3	5	.375	48	0	0	**25**-7	82.1	64	24	5	1	24-8	57	2.62	138	.218	.276	9	.000	-1	—	10	0	1.4
1982	†StL N	9	8	.529	70	0	0	**36**-9	102.1	88	38	8	3	34-13	61	2.90	127	.235	.302	8-0-2	.125	-0	—	8	0	1.7
1983	StL N	9	10	.474	60	0	0	21-9	89.1	90	45	8	1	30-14	64	4.23	86	.262	.321	7-0-1	.000	-1	—	-4	0	-0.9
1984	StL N☆	5	7	.417	71	0	0	**45**-8	122.2	109	26	9	1	23-4	77	1.54	227	.245	.281	10	.000	-1	—	**26**	0	**4.4**
1985	Atl N	7	7	.500	58	0	0	23-12	88.1	91	46	13	3	29-4	52	4.48	86	.267	.328	4	.000	-0	—	-4	0	-0.9
1986	Atl N	2	0	1.000	16	0	0	3-3	18.2	17	9	3	0	9-2	16	4.34	91	.243	.329	1	.000	-0	—	0	131	0.0
1988	Atl N	1	4	.200	38	0	0	14-9	45.1	49	26	4	1	11-3	40	4.76	77	.275	.321	1	.000	0	—	-5	26	-0.8
Total	12	68	71	.489	661	0	0	300-101	1042	879	370	77	13	309-83	861	2.83	137	.230	.288	102-0-10	.088	-5	—	110	542	18.5

SUTTHOFF, JACK John Gerhard "Sunny Jack"; B6.29.1873 Cincinnati OH; D8.3.1942 Cincinnati OH; BL/TR/5´9˝/175; d9.15

YEAR	TM LG	W	L	PCT	G	GS	CG-SHO	SV-BS	IP	H	R	HR	HB	BB-IB	SO	ERA	AERA	OAV	OOB	AB-HR-SH	AVG	PB	SUP	APR	DL	PW
1898	Was N	0	0	ø	2	1	0	0	8.1	16	13	1	0	8	3	12.96	28	.400	.500	3	.333	0	194	-7	—	-0.3
1899	StL N	1	2	.333	3	3	3	0	24	29	25	0	0	15	8	4.13	97	.299	.393	10	.100	-1	121	-3	—	-0.4
1901	Cin N	1	6	.143	10	4	4	0	70.1	82	55	2	2	39	12	5.50	58	.289	.378	28-0-1	.107	-2*	78	-17	—	-1.6
1903	Cin N	16	9	.640	30	27	21-3	0	224.2	207	104	2	16	79	76	2.80	127	.246	.323	84-0-2	.143	-3	107	19	—	1.4
1904	Cin N	5	6	.455	12	10	8	0	90	83	49	1	3	43	27	2.30	127	.255	.348	33-0-1	.182	-0	120	1	—	0.0
	Phi N	6	13	.316	19	18	17	0	163.2	172	90	2	9	71	46	3.68	73	.272	.354	61-0-2	.164	-0	98	-14	—	-1.6
	Year	11	19	.367	31	28	25	0	253.2	255	139	3	12	114	73	3.19	87	.266	.352	94-0-3	.170	-1	107	-14	—	-1.6
1905	Phi N	3	4	.429	13	6	4-1	0	77.2	82	46	2	4	36	26	3.82	76	.290	.378	25-0-1	.080	-1	82	-8	—	-0.7
Total	6	32	40	.444	89	69	57-4	0	658.2	671	382	10	34	291	198	3.54	89	.268	.352	244-0-7	.143	-7	107	-29	—	-3.2

SUTTON, DON Donald Howard; B4.2.1945 Clio AL; BR/TR/6´1˝/(183–190); d4.14; HF1998; Col Gulf Coast (FL) CC

YEAR	TM LG	W	L	PCT	G	GS	CG-SHO	SV-BS	IP	H	R	HR	HB	BB-IB	SO	ERA	AERA	OAV	OOB	AB-HR-SH	AVG	PB	SUP	APR	DL	PW
1966	LA N	12	12	.500	37	35	6-2	0	225.2	192	82	19	3	52-6	209	2.99	110	.228	.274	82-0-2	.183	1*	95	10	0	1.2
1967	LA N	11	15	.423	37	34	11-3	1	232.2	223	106	18	6	57-9	169	3.95	79	.250	.299	75-0-7	.133	-0*	107	-19	0	-2.2
1968	LA N	11	15	.423	35	27	7-2	1	207.2	179	64	6	2	59-14	162	2.60	106	.232	.287	62-0-6	.177	1*	87	7	0	1.0
1969	LA N	17	18	.486	41	41	11-4	0-0	293.1	269	123	25	3	91-6	217	3.47	97	.242	.299	98-0-9	.153	-1	106	-2	0	-0.4
1970	LA N	15	13	.536	38	38	10-4	0-0	260.1	251	127	38	10	78-7	201	4.08	94	.249	.308	84-0-5	.155	3*	110	-5	0	-0.3
1971	LA N	17	12	.586	38	37	12-4	1-0	265.1	231	85	10	5	55-5	194	2.54	128	.238	.280	88-0-4	.216	3*	98	22	0	2.7
1972	LA N★	19	9	.679	33	33	18-**9**	0-0	272.2	186	78	13	4	63-1	207	2.08	161	**.189**	**.240**	91-0-11	.143	-1	105	39	0	4.0
1973	LA N★	18	10	.643	33	33	14-3	0-0	256.1	196	78	18	5	56-4	200	2.42	144	.209	.257	84-0-7	.119	-2	91	32	0	3.2
1974	†LA N	19	9	.679	40	**40**	10-5	0-0	276	241	111	23	6	80-2	179	3.23	106	.229	.287	98-0-9	.184	1	137	8	0	0.8
1975	LA N★	16	13	.552	35	35	11-4	0-0	254.1	202	87	17	3	62-5	175	2.87	119	.213	**.263**	80-0-12	.138	-1	87	18	0	1.9
1976	LA N	21	10	.677	35	34	15-4	0-0	267.2	231	98	22	3	82-6	161	3.06	111	.234	.293	84-0-9	.083	-3	100	12	0	0.8
1977	†LA N★	14	8	.636	33	33	9-3	0-0	240.1	207	93	23	3	69-2	150	3.18	121	.233	.289	73-0-10	.151	1	111	19	0	1.6
1978	†LA N	15	11	.577	34	34	12-2	0-0	238.1	228	109	29	5	54-7	154	3.55	99	.250	.294	72-0-14	.083	-3	115	-2	0	-0.7
1979	LA N	12	15	.444	33	32	6-1	1-0	226	201	109	21	1	61-6	146	3.82	95	.239	.288	77-0-8	.143	-2	106	-4	0	-0.7
1980	LA N	13	5	.722	32	31	4-2	1-0	212.1	163	56	20	2	47-5	128	**2.20**	158	.211	**.257**	64-0-8	.078	-4	87	32	0	2.2
1981	Hou N	11	9	.550	23	23	6-3	0-0	158.2	132	51	6	1	29-3	104	2.61	126	.230	**.265**	51-0-5	.137	0	105	13	0	1.7
1982	Hou N	13	8	.619	27	27	4	0-0	195	169	75	10	1	46-2	139	3.00	111	.232	.277	68-0-4	.162	-0	98	7	0	0.6
	†Mil A	4	1	.800	7	7	2-1	0-0	54.2	55	21	8	0	18-0	36	3.29	117	.263	.322	0	ø	0	200	4	0	0.4
1983	Mil A	8	13	.381	31	31	4	0-0	220.1	209	109	21	5	54-2	134	4.08	93	.246	.292	0	ø	0	101	-8	0	-0.7
1984	Mil A	14	12	.538	33	33	1	0-0	212.2	224	103	24	3	51-2	143	3.77	103	.266	.306	0	ø	0	89	2	0	0.1
1985	Oak A	13	8	.619	29	29	1-1	0-0	194.1	194	88	19	0	51-0	91	3.89	100	.256	.301	0	ø	0	111	2	0	0.2
	Cal A	2	2	.500	5	5	0	0-0	31.2	27	13	6	0	8-0	16	3.69	112	.233	.282	0	ø	0	97	2	0	0.2
	Year	15	10	.600	34	34	1-1	0-0	226	221	101	25	0	59-0	107	3.86	101	.253	.298	0	ø	0	109	5	0	0.4
1986	†Cal A	15	11	.577	34	34	3-1	0-0	207	192	93	31	3	49-2	116	3.74	111	.242	.287	0	ø	0	102	10	0	1.0
1987	Cal A	11	11	.500	35	34	1	0-0	191.2	199	101	38	7	41-0	99	4.70	92	.269	.311	0	ø	0	104	-3	0	-0.4
1988	LA N	3	6	.333	16	16	0	0-0	87.1	91	44	7	1	30-6	44	3.92	85	.270	.327	23-0-6	.087	-1	103	-6	41	-0.7
Total	23	324	256	.559	774	756	178-58	5-0	5282.1	4692	2104	472	82	1343-102	3574	3.26	108	.236	.286	1354-0-136	.144	-8	104	190	41	17.5

SUTTON, JOHN Johnny Ike; B11.13.1952 Dallas TX; BR/TR/5´11˝/185; [TexA74*3/48]; d4.7; Col Plano (TX) JC

YEAR	TM LG	W	L	PCT	G	GS	CG-SHO	SV-BS	IP	H	R	HR	HB	BB-IB	SO	ERA	AERA	OAV	OOB	AB-HR-SH	AVG	PB	SUP	APR	DL	PW
1977	StL N	2	1	.667	14	0	0	0-1	24.1	28	10	1	0	9-1	9	2.59	151	.315	.370	1	.000	-0	—	3	0	0.3
1978	Min A	0	0	ø	17	0	0	0-0	44.1	46	19	3	1	15-3	18	3.45	111	.264	.326	0	ø	0	—	2	0	0.1
Total	2	2	1	.667	31	0	0	0-1	68.2	74	29	4	1	24-4	27	3.15	123	.281	.341	1	.000	-0	—	5	0	0.4

SUZUKI, MAC Makoto; B5.31.1975 Kobe, Japan; BR/TR/6´3˝/(195–205); d7.7

YEAR	TM LG	W	L	PCT	G	GS	CG-SHO	SV-BS	IP	H	R	HR	HB	BB-IB	SO	ERA	AERA	OAV	OOB	AB-HR-SH	AVG	PB	SUP	APR	DL	PW
1996	Sea A	0	0	ø	1	0	0	0-0	1.1	2	3	0	0	2-1	1	20.25	25	.333	.500	0	ø	0	—	-2	0	-0.1
1998	Sea A	1	2	.333	6	5	0	0-0	26.1	34	23	3	0	15-0	19	7.18	65	.304	.386	0	ø	0	75	-7	0	-0.7
1999	Sea A	0	2	.000	16	4	0	0-0	42	47	47	7	4	34-2	32	9.43	51	.283	.411	0	ø	0	102	-22	0	-1.0
	KC A	2	3	.400	22	9	0	0-0	68	77	45	9	3	30-1	36	5.16	99	.287	.365	0	ø	0	79	-2	0	-0.1
	Year	2	5	.286	38	13	0	0-0	110	124	92	16	7	64-3	68	6.79	73	.286	.384	0	ø	0	87	-23	0	-1.1
2000	KC A	8	10	.444	32	29	1-1	0-0	188.2	195	100	26	3	94-6	135	4.34	120	.265	.349	5-0-1	.200	0	86	16	0	1.2
2001	KC A	2	5	.286	15	9	0	0-0	56	61	38	12	3	25-1	37	5.30	94	.277	.355	0	ø	0	91	-3	0	-0.3
	Col N	0	2	.000	3	1	0	0-0	6.1	9	12	3	1	11-0	5	15.63	34	.333	.538	1-0-1	.000	-0	52	-6	0	-1.0
	Mil N	3	5	.375	15	9	0	0-0	56	52	37	5	4	37-3	47	5.30	81	.251	.375	17-0-2	.000	-2	100	-7	0	-1.0
	Year	3	7	.300	18	10	0	0-0	62.1	61	49	8	5	48-3	52	6.35	69	.261	.397	18-0-3	.000	-2	94	-14	0	-2.0

YEAR	TM LG	W	L	PCT	G	GS	CG-SHO	SV-BS	IP	H	R	HR	HB	BB-IB	SO	ERA	AERA	OAV	OOB	AB-HR-SH	AVG	PB	SUP	APR	DL	PW
2002	KC A	0	2	.000	7	1	0	0-0	21	24	21	2	0	17-2	15	9.00	55	.296	.414	2	.500	0	56	-8	0	-0.6
Total	6	16	31	.340	117	67	1-1	0-0	465.2	501	326	67	18	265-16	327	5.72	87	.275	.370	25-0-4	.080	-1	87	-41	0	-3.6
SWAGGERTY, BILL	William David; B12.5.1956 Sanford FL; BR/TR/6´2˝/(186–200); [BalA79 26/660]; d8.13; Col Stetson																									
1983	Bal A	1	1	.500	7	2	0	0-0	21.2	23	8	1	0	6-0	7	2.91	138	.267	.315	0	ø	0	136	3	0	0.3
1984	Bal A	3	2	.600	23	6	0	0-0	57	68	41	7	0	21-3	18	5.21	75	.302	.356	0	ø	0*	104	-10	0	-0.8
1985	Bal A	0	0	ø	1	0	0	0-0	1.2	3	1	0	0	2-1	2	5.40	75	.375	.500	0	ø	0	—	0	0	0.0
1986	Bal A	0	0	ø	1	0	0	0-0	1	6	2	0	0	1-1	1	18.00	23	.750	.778	0	ø	0	—	-1	0	-0.1
Total	4	4	3	.571	32	8	0	0-0	81.1	100	52	8	0	30-5	28	4.76	83	.306	.360	0	ø	0	112	-8	0	-0.6
SWAIM, CY	John Hillary; B3.11.1874 Cadwallader (now West Chester) OH; D12.27.1945 Eustis FL; 6´6˝/180; d5.3; Col Mount Union																									
1897	Was N	9	11	.450	26	19	14	0	184	219	129	5	10	59	52	4.60	94	.293	.353	71-0-1	.225	-3	105	0	—	-0.4
1898	Was N	3	11	.214	16	13	9	1	101.1	119	77	4	4	28	30	4.26	86	.290	.342	35	.143	-3	69	-10	—	-1.4
Total	2	12	22	.353	42	32	23	1	285.1	338	206	9	14	87	82	4.48	92	.292	.349	106-0-1	.198	-6	91	-10	—	-1.8
SWAN, CRAIG	Craig Steven; B11.30.1950 Van Nuys CA; BR/TR/6´3˝/(210–225); [NYN72 3/61]; d9.3; Col Arizona St.																									
1973	NY N	0	1	.000	3	1	0	0-0	8.1	16	9	2	0	2-0	4	8.64	42	.432	.450	2	.000	-0	73	-5	0	-0.5
1974	NY N	1	3	.250	7	5	0	0-1	30.1	28	19	1	0	21-3	10	4.45	81	.255	.366	11	.364	1	116	-4	38	-0.3
1975	NY N	1	3	.250	6	6	0	0-0	31	38	22	4	1	13-2	19	6.39	55	.302	.366	7-0-2	.000	-1	71	-9	0	-1.1
1976	NY N	6	9	.400	23	22	2-1	0-0	132.1	129	64	11	5	44-3	89	3.54	95	.254	.316	39-0-6	.103	-1	100	-5	0	-0.7
1977	NY N	9	10	.474	26	24	2-1	0-0	146.2	153	76	10	1	56-3	71	4.23	90	.268	.332	48-0-6	.188	-0	99	-7	0	-1.0
1978	NY N	9	6	.600	29	28	5-1	0-0	207.1	164	62	12	2	58-8	125	**2.43**	**146**	.219	.275	65-0-8	.154	-0	96	26	0	1.8
1979	NY N	14	13	.519	35	35	10-3	0-0	251.1	241	102	20	2	57-9	145	3.29	113	.255	.296	81-0-4	.123	-1	82	12	0	1.1
1980	NY N	5	9	.357	21	21	4-1	0-0	128.1	117	59	20	0	30-3	79	3.58	101	.247	.289	32-0-7	.219	2	73	0	69	0.0
1981	NY N	0	2	.000	5	3	0	0-0	13.2	10	6	0	0	1-0	9	3.29	107	.204	.220	3	.000	-0	92	0	67	0.0
1982	NY N	11	7	.611	37	21	2	1-1	166.1	165	70	13	0	37-4	67	3.35	110	.256	.295	44-1-3	.182	3	86	7	0	1.0
1983	NY N	2	8	.200	27	18	0	1-0	96.1	112	63	14	0	42-3	43	5.51	67	.299	.366	26-0-1	.077	-2	90	-17	0	-1.9
1984	NY N	1	0	1.000	10	0	0	0-1	18.2	18	17	5	0	7-0	10	8.20	44	.247	.309	0-0-1	ø	0	—	-8	0	-0.4
	Cal A	0	1	.000	2	1	0	0-0	5	8	6	3	0	0-0	2	10.80	37	.348	.348	0	ø	0	113	-4	117	-0.5
Total	12	59	72	.450	231	185	25-7	2-3	1235.2	1199	575	115	11	368-38	673	3.74	97	.256	.309	358-1-38	.151	0	89	-14	291	-2.5
SWAN, DUCKY	Harry Gordon; B8.11.1887 Lancaster PA; D5.8.1946 Pittsburgh PA; BR/TR/5´10˝/165; d4.28																									
1914	KC F	0	0	ø	1	0	0	0	1	0	0	0	0	1	1	0.00	ø	.000	.250	0	ø	0	—	0	—	0.0
SWAN, RUSS	Russell Howard; B1.3.1964 Fremont CA; D4.26.2006 Las Vegas NV; BL/TL/6´4˝/(210–215); [SFN86 9/214]; d8.3; Col Texas A&M																									
1989	SF N	0	2	.000	2	2	0	0-0	6.2	11	10	4	0	4-0	2	10.80	31	.393	.469	2	.000	-0	92	-6	0	-1.0
1990	SF N	0	1	.000	2	1	0	0-0	2.1	6	4	0	0	4-0	1	3.86	95	.429	.556	1	.000	-0	74	-1	0	-0.3
	Sea A	2	3	.400	11	8	0	0-0	47	42	22	3	0	18-2	15	3.64	109	.244	.311	0	ø	0	89	2	55	0.2
1991	Sea A	6	2	.750	63	0	0	2-3	78.2	81	35	8	0	28-7	33	3.43	121	.269	.330	0	ø	0	—	5	15	0.5
1992	Sea A	3	10	.231	55	9	1	9-2	104.1	104	60	8	3	45-7	45	4.74	84	.262	.338	0	ø	0	61	-8	0	-1.0
1993	Sea A	3	3	.500	23	0	0	0-0	19.2	25	20	2	2	18-1	10	9.15	49	.316	.455	0	ø	0	—	-9	42	-1.7
1994	Cle A	0	1	.000	12	0	0	0-0	8	13	11	1	0	7-1	2	11.25	42	.382	.488	0	ø	0	—	-6	0	-0.6
Total	6	14	22	.389	168	20	1	11-5	266.2	282	162	26	5	124-18	108	4.83	85	.275	.353	3	.000	-0	73	-23	112	-3.9
SWANSON, RED	Arthur Leonard; B10.15.1936 Baton Rouge LA; BR/TR/6´1.5˝/175; d9.10; Col Louisiana St.																									
1955	Pit N	0	0	ø	1	0	0	0	2	2	4	1	0	3-0	0	18.00	23	.286	.500	0	ø	0	—	-3	0	-0.1
1956	Pit N	0	0	ø	9	0	0	0	11.2	21	13	1	0	8-1	5	10.03	38	.438	.492	0	ø	0*	—	-7	0	-0.3
1957	Pit N	3	3	.500	32	8	1	0	72.2	68	35	9	1	31-3	29	3.72	102	.248	.327	13	.000	-1	128	0	0	-0.1
Total	3	3	3	.500	42	8	1	0	86.1	91	52	11	1	42-4	34	4.90	77	.277	.357	13	.000	-1	128	-10	0	-0.5
SWARBACK, BILL	William (b William Schwappach); B10.1867 New York NY; D5.17.1949 Stamford CT; d7.9																									
1887	NY N	0	2	.000	2	2	2	0	16	27	23	1	1	6	6	5.06	74	.346	.400	7	.000	-1	172	-5	—	-0.5
SWARTZ, BUD	Sherwin Merle; B6.13.1929 Tulsa OK; D6.24.1991 Los Angeles CA; BL/TL/6´2.5˝/180; d7.12																									
1947	StL A	0	0	ø	5	0	0	0	5.1	9	6	1	0	7	1	6.75	57	.360	.500	1	1.000	0	—	-2	0	-0.1
SWARTZ, MONTY	Vernon Monroe "Dazzy"; B1.1.1897 Farmersville OH; D1.13.1980 Germantown OH; BR/TR/5´11˝/182; d10.3																									
1920	Cin N	0	1	.000	1	1	1	0	12	17	6	0	0	2	2	4.50	68	.333	.358	4	.500	1	78	-1	—	0.0
SWARTZBAUGH, DAVE	David Theodore; B2.11.1968 Middletown OH; BR/TR/6´2˝/(195–210); [ChiN89 9/226]; d9.3; Col Miami–Ohio																									
1995	Chi N	0	0	ø	7	0	0	0-0	7.1	5	2	0	0	3-1	5	0.00	ø	.208	.296	0	ø	0	—	3	0	0.1
1996	Chi N	0	2	.000	6	5	0	0-0	24	26	17	3	0	14-1	13	6.38	69	.277	.370	6	.000	-0	66	-4	0	-0.3
1997	Chi N	0	1	.000	2	2	0	0-0	8	12	8	1	1	7-0	4	9.00	48	.364	.476	4	.000	-0	64	-4	0	-0.4
Total	3	0	3	.000	15	7	0	0-0	39.1	43	27	4	1	24-2	22	5.72	76	.285	.384	10	.000	-1	66	-5	0	-0.6
SWARTZEL, PARK	Park B.; B11.21.1865 Knightstown IN; D1.3.1940 Los Angeles CA; BR/TR/5´10˝/?; d4.17																									
1889	KC AA	19	27	.413	48	47	45	1	410.1	481	334	21	23	117	147	4.32	98	.283	.338	174	.144	-9*	89	0	—	-0.3
SWEENEY, BRIAN	Brian Edward; B6.13.1974 Yonkers NY; BR/TR/6´2˝/(180–200); d8.16; Col Mercy (NY)																									
2003	Sea A	0	0	ø	5	0	0	0-0	9.1	7	2	0	1	1-0	7	1.93	225	.212	.257	0	ø	0	—	3	0	0.1
2004	SD N	1	0	1.000	7	2	0	0-0	14.1	20	9	1	0	2-0	10	5.65	70	.328	.349	4	.000	-0	106	-3	0	-0.2
2006	SD N	2	0	1.000	37	0	0	2-1	56.1	53	22	6	1	16-5	23	3.20	130	.249	.302	1	.000	-0	—	6	0	0.3
Total	3	3	0	1.000	49	2	0	2-1	80	80	33	7	2	19-5	40	3.49	118	.261	.306	5	.000	-1	106	6	0	0.2
SWEENEY, CHARLIE	Charles J.; B4.13.1863 San Francisco CA; D4.4.1902 San Francisco CA; BR/TR/5´10.5˝/181; d5.11.1882; ▲																									
1883	Pro N	7	7	.500	20	18	14	0	146.2	142	94	3	—	28	48	3.13	98	.237	.272	87	.218	-1*	108	0	—	0.0
1884	Pro N	17	8	.680	27	24	22-4	1	221	153	70	4	—	29	145	1.55	184	**.187**	**.215**	168-1	.298	8*	95	36	—	4.4
	StL U	24	7	.774	33	32	31-2	0	271	207	112	2	—	13	192	1.83	131	.197	.207	171-1	.316	9*	110	16	—	2.1
1885	StL N	11	21	.344	35	35	32-2	0	275	276	175	6	—	50	84	3.93	70	.250	.282	267	.206	-0*	72	-30	—	-2.8
1886	StL N	5	6	.455	11	11	11	0	93	108	73	9	—	39	28	4.16	77	.285	.352	64	.250	1*	92	-9	—	-0.6
1887	Cle AA	0	3	.000	3	3	3	0	24	42	36	0	0	13	8	8.25	53	.372	.437	133	.226	0*	59	-10	—	-0.7
Total	5	64	52	.552	129	123	113-8	1	1030.2	928	560	24	0	172	505	2.87	97	.228	.260	890-2	.252	17	93	3	—	2.4
SWEENEY, BILL	William J.; B Philadelphia PA; D8.2.1903 Philadelphia PA; TR/5´11˝/160; d6.27																									
1882	Phi AA	9	10	.474	20	20	18	0	170	178	119	4	—	42	48	2.91	96	.252	.294	88	.159	-2*	116	-8	—	-0.9
1884	Bal U	**40**	21	.656	**62**	**60**	**58**-4	0	**538**	522	294	13	—	74	374	2.59	103	.238	.263	296	.240	-10*	102	7	—	-0.6
Total	2	49	31	.613	82	80	76-4	0	708	700	413	17	—	116	422	2.67	101	.241	.270	384	.221	-12	105	-1	—	-1.5
SWEETLAND, LES	Lester Leo (Born Leo Sweetland); B8.15.1901 St.Ignace MI; D3.4.1974 Melbourne FL; BR/TL (BB 1930–31)/5´11.5˝/155; d7.4																									
1927	Phi N	2	10	.167	21	13	6	0	103.2	147	77	3	3	53	21	6.16	67	.348	.425	38-0-1	.316	3*	93	-21	—	-1.5
1928	Phi N	3	15	.167	37	18	5	2	135.1	163	111	15	15	97	23	6.58	65	.306	.426	47-0-1	.191	1*	86	-32	—	-3.4
1929	Phi N	13	11	.542	43	26	10-2	2	204.1	255	129	23	9	87	47	5.11	102	.316	.389	89-0-1	.292	3*	88	2	—	0.7
1930	Phi N	7	15	.318	34	25	8-1	0	167	271	164	24	5	60	36	7.71	71	.373	.425	57-0-4	.281	4*	100	-37	—	-3.2
1931	Chi N	8	7	.533	26	14	9	0	130.1	156	89	3	5	61	32	5.04	77	.297	.375	56-0-1	.268	5*	144	-19	—	-1.4
Total	5	33	58	.363	161	96	38-3	4	740.2	992	570	68	37	358	159	6.10	77	.329	.407	287-0-8	.272	16	100	-107	—	-8.8
SWETONIC, STEVE	Stephen Albert; B8.13.1903 Mt.Pleasant PA; D4.22.1974 Canonsburg PA; BR/TR/5´11˝/185; d4.17; Col Pittsburgh																									
1929	Pit N	8	10	.444	41	12	3	5	143.2	172	87	6	5	50	35	4.82	99	.299	.360	48-0-1	.271	3*	107	0	—	0.4
1930	Pit N	6	6	.500	23	6	3-1	5	96.2	107	53	7	0	27	35	4.47	111	.276	.323	36	.111	-3	96	7	—	0.5
1931	Pit N	0	2	.000	14	0	0	1	27.2	28	12	0	0	16	8	3.90	99	.264	.361	7	.143	-0	—	1	—	0.0
1932	Pit N	11	6	.647	24	19	11-**4**	0	162.2	134	57	11	0	55	39	2.82	135	**.221**	.286	54-0-2	.093	-4	92	21	—	1.6
1933	Pit N	12	12	.500	31	21	8-3	0	164.2	166	78	10	2	64	37	3.50	95	.260	.330	55-0-6	.200	1	100	-3	—	-0.4
Total	5	37	36	.507	133	58	25-8	11	595.1	607	287	34	7	212	154	3.81	107	.262	.326	200-0-9	.170	-3	96	26	—	2.1

Swift, Bill William Charles; B10.27.1961 Portland ME; BR/TR/6´0˝/(170–197); [SeaA84 1/2]; d6.7; Col Maine

YEAR	TM LG	W	L	PCT	G	GS	CG-SHO	SV-BS	IP	H	R	HR	HB	BB-IB	SO	ERA	AERA	OAV	OOB	AB-HR-SH	AVG	PB	SUP	APR	DL	PW
1985	Sea A	6	10	.375	23	21	0	0-0	120.2	131	71	8	5	48-5	55	4.77	89	.279	.350	0	ø	0	87	-7	0	-0.9
1986	Sea A	2	9	.182	29	17	1	0-1	115.1	148	85	5	7	55-2	55	5.46	78	.319	.397	0	ø	0	96	-18	0	-1.4
1988	Sea A	8	12	.400	38	24	6-1	0-1	174.2	199	99	10	8	65-3	47	4.59	91	.294	.362	0	ø	0	102	-7	0	-0.6
1989	Sea A	7	3	.700	37	16	0	1-0	130	140	72	7	2	38-4	45	4.43	91	.278	.329	0	ø	0	125	-5	24	-0.1
1990	Sea A	6	4	.600	55	8	0	6-1	128	135	46	4	7	21-6	42	2.39	167	.272	.309	0	ø	0	109	19	0	1.5
1991	Sea A	1	2	.333	71	0	0	17-1	90.1	74	22	3	1	26-4	48	1.99	208	.224	.283	0	ø	0	—	21	15	1.4
1992	SF N	10	4	.714	30	22	3-2	1-0	164.2	144	41	6	3	43-3	77	**2.08**	161	.239	.292	51-0-5	.157	1*	110	25	43	2.4
1993	SF N	21	8	.724	34	34	1-1	0-0	232.2	195	82	18	6	55-5	157	2.82	139	.226	.277	80-0-10	.262	6	115	28	0	4.1
1994	SF N	8	7	.533	17	17	0	0-0	109.1	109	49	10	1	31-6	62	3.38	120	.262	.313	32-0-5	.188	2*	86	7	46	1.0
1995	†Col N	9	3	.750	19	19	0	0-0	105.2	122	62	12	1	43-2	68	4.94	109	.296	.363	36-1-5	.194	0	116	5	56	0.7
1996	Col N	1	1	.500	7	3	0	2-0	18.1	23	12	1	0	5-0	5	5.40	97	.307	.346	6	.333	0	63	0	146	0.0
1997	Col N	4	6	.400	14	13	0	0-0	65.1	85	57	11	2	26-0	29	6.34	82	.317	.377	19-0-4	.211	1*	119	-10	59	-1.0
1998	Sea A	11	9	.550	29	26	0	0-0	144.2	183	103	21	10	51-2	77	5.85	80	.306	.369	5	.000	-1	131	-19	0	-2.1
Total	13	94	78	.547	403	220	11-4	27-4	1599.2	1688	801	116	53	507-42	767	3.95	106	.273	.332	229-1-29	.210	10	111	39	389	5.0

Swift, Bill William Vincent; B6.19.1908 Elmira NY; D2.23.1969 Bartow FL; BR/TR/6´1.5˝/192; d4.12

YEAR	TM LG	W	L	PCT	G	GS	CG-SHO	SV-BS	IP	H	R	HR	HB	BB-IB	SO	ERA	AERA	OAV	OOB	AB-HR-SH	AVG	PB	SUP	APR	DL	PW
1932	Pit N	14	10	.583	39	23	11	4	214.1	205	97	15	2	26	64	3.61	106	.248	.272	78-0-3	.192	-1	105	9	—	0.6
1933	Pit N	14	10	.583	37	29	13-2	0	218.1	214	96	11	4	36	64	3.13	106	.251	.285	82	.244	3	124	4	—	0.6
1934	Pit N	11	13	.458	37	25	13-1	0	212.2	244	107	15	8	46	81	3.98	103	.284	.326	84-0-1	.214	2	115	4	—	0.4
1935	Pit N	15	8	.652	39	22	11-3	1	203.2	193	76	6	1	37	74	2.70	152	.247	.282	78-0-1	.244	3	120	31	—	3.3
1936	Pit N	16	16	.500	45	31	17	2	262.1	275	132	18	5	63	92	4.01	101	.265	.310	105-2-1	.295	9	99	4	—	1.1
1937	Pit N	9	10	.474	36	17	9	3	164	160	79	14	3	34	84	3.95	98	.256	.297	54-0-2	.167	-1	79	1	—	-0.1
1938	Pit N	7	5	.583	36	9	2	4	150	155	65	9	4	40	77	3.24	117	.271	.323	50-1-2	.200	2	69	9	—	0.8
1939	Pit N	5	7	.417	36	8	2-1	4	129.2	150	60	6	3	28	56	3.89	99	.293	.333	42-0-2	.238	2	80	1	—	0.1
1940	Bos N	1	1	.500	4	0	0	1	9.1	12	7	0	0	7	7	2.89	129	.308	.413	3	.000	-0	—	-1	—	-0.2
1941	Bro N	3	0	1.000	9	0	0	1	22	26	9	4	0	7	9	3.27	112	.289	.340	5	.200	-0	—	1	0	0.1
1943	Chi A	0	2	.000	18	1	0	0	51.1	48	25	5	6	27	28	4.21	79	.246	.355	10	.100	0	25	-3	0	-0.3
Total	11	95	82	.537	336	165	78-7	20	1637.2	1682	753	103	36	351	636	3.58	108	.263	.305	591-3-12	.227	18	104	60	0	6.4

Swigart, Oad Oadis Vaughn; B2.13.1915 Archie MO; D8.8.1997 St.Joseph MO; BL/TR/6´0˝/175; d9.14; Mil 1941–45

YEAR	TM LG	W	L	PCT	G	GS	CG-SHO	SV-BS	IP	H	R	HR	HB	BB-IB	SO	ERA	AERA	OAV	OOB	AB-HR-SH	AVG	PB	SUP	APR	DL	PW
1939	Pit N	1	1	.500	3	3	1-1	0	24.1	27	14	1	0	6	8	4.44	87	.293	.337	8-0-2	.250	0	144	-2	—	-0.1
1940	Pit N	0	2	.000	7	2	0	0	22.1	27	14	1	0	10	9	4.43	86	.297	.366	5-0-1	.200	-0	57	-2	—	-0.2
Total	2	1	3	.250	10	5	1-1	0	46.2	54	28	2	0	16	17	4.44	86	.295	.352	13-0-3	.231	0	109	-4	—	-0.3

Swigler, Ad Adam William "Doc"; B9.21.1895 Philadelphia PA; D2.5.1975 Philadelphia PA; BR/TR/5´10˝/180; d9.25; Col Penn

YEAR	TM LG	W	L	PCT	G	GS	CG-SHO	SV-BS	IP	H	R	HR	HB	BB-IB	SO	ERA	AERA	OAV	OOB	AB-HR-SH	AVG	PB	SUP	APR	DL	PW
1917	NY N	0	1	.000	1	1	0	0	6	7	4	0	0	8	4	6.00	43	.333	.517	2	.000	-0	89	-2	—	-0.3

Swindell, Greg Forest Gregory; B1.2.1965 Fort Worth TX; BR/TL/6´3˝/(225–239); [CleA86 1/2]; d8.21; Col Texas

YEAR	TM LG	W	L	PCT	G	GS	CG-SHO	SV-BS	IP	H	R	HR	HB	BB-IB	SO	ERA	AERA	OAV	OOB	AB-HR-SH	AVG	PB	SUP	APR	DL	PW
1986	Cle A	5	2	.714	9	9	1	0-0	61.2	57	35	9	1	15-0	46	4.23	99	.243	.290	0	ø	0	140	-1	0	-0.1
1987	Cle A	3	8	.273	16	15	4-1	0-0	102.1	112	62	18	1	37-1	97	5.10	90	.283	.343	0	ø	0	89	-4	97	-0.4
1988	Cle A	18	14	.563	33	33	12-4	0-0	242	234	97	18	1	45-3	180	3.20	129	.252	.286	0	ø	0	89	23	0	2.9
1989	Cle A★	13	6	.684	28	28	5-2	0-0	184.1	170	71	16	0	51-1	129	3.37	118	.246	.297	0	ø	0	91	15	35	1.4
1990	Cle A	12	9	.571	34	34	3	0-0	214.2	245	110	27	1	47-2	135	4.40	90	.288	.324	0	ø	0	121	-9	0	-0.9
1991	Cle A	9	16	.360	33	33	7	0-0	238	241	112	21	3	31-1	169	3.48	120	.263	.287	0	ø	0	75	14	0	1.3
1992	Cin N	12	8	.600	31	30	5-3	0-0	213.2	210	72	14	2	41-4	138	2.70	134	.260	.295	80-0-5	.125	-2	110	20	15	1.7
1993	Hou N	12	13	.480	31	30	1-1	0-0	190.1	215	98	24	1	40-3	124	4.16	93	.283	.318	60-0-10	.183	0	98	-6	20	-0.6
1994	Hou N	8	9	.471	24	24	1	0-0	148.1	175	80	20	1	26-2	74	4.37	91	.302	.329	44-0-12	.250	3	109	-7	0	-0.5
1995	Hou N	10	9	.526	33	26	1-1	0-2	153	180	86	21	2	39-2	96	4.47	86	.297	.337	50-0-6	.240	4*	128	-11	0	-0.7
1996	Hou N	0	3	.000	8	4	0	0-2	23	35	25	5	1	11-0	15	7.83	50	.340	.405	6	.333	1	174	-12	32	-1.2
	Cle A	1	1	.500	13	2	0	0-0	28.2	31	21	8	0	8-0	21	6.59	74	.279	.325	0	ø	0	228	-5	17	-0.2
1997	Min A	7	4	.636	65	1	0	1-6	115.2	102	46	12	2	25-3	75	3.58	130	.238	.282	0	ø	0	79	15	0	1.3
1998	Min A	3	3	.500	52	0	0	2-2	66.1	67	27	10	3	18-2	45	3.66	131	.263	.317	0	ø	0	—	9	0	0.7
	†Bos A	2	3	.400	29	0	0	0-1	24	25	13	3	0	13-1	18	3.38	140	.278	.369	0	ø	0	—	2	0	0.4
	Year	5	6	.455	81	0	0	2-3	90.1	92	40	13	3	31-3	63	3.59	133	.267	.331	0	ø	0	—	11	0	1.1
1999	†Ari N	4	0	1.000	63	0	0	1-1	64.2	54	19	8	1	21-1	51	2.51	184	.230	.296	4-0-2	.000	-0	—	15	15	0.8
2000	Ari N	2	6	.250	64	0	0	1-0	76	71	29	7	1	20-5	64	3.20	150	.247	.295	1-0-1	.000	-0	—	13	0	1.2
2001	†Ari N	2	6	.250	64	0	0	2-3	53.2	51	27	12	0	8-2	42	4.53	102	.250	.277	0	ø	0	—	2	0	0.2
2002	†Ari N	0	2	.000	34	0	0	0-1	33	38	23	9	0	5-1	23	6.27	72	.279	.301	0	ø	0	—	-5	53	-0.3
Total	17	123	122	.502	664	269	40-12	7-18	2233.1	2313	1053	262	21	501-34	1542	3.86	107	.268	.308	245-0-36	.188	6	101	68	284	7.0

Swindell, Josh Joshua Ernest; B7.5.1883 Rose Hill KS; D3.19.1969 Fruita CO; BR/TR/6´0˝/180; d9.16

YEAR	TM LG	W	L	PCT	G	GS	CG-SHO	SV-BS	IP	H	R	HR	HB	BB-IB	SO	ERA	AERA	OAV	OOB	AB-HR-SH	AVG	PB	SUP	APR	DL	PW
1911	Cle A	0	1	.000	4	1	1	0	17.1	19	9	0	1	4	6	2.08	164	.257	.304	4	.250	-0	21	1	—	0.0

Swingle, Paul Paul Christopher; B12.21.1966 Inglewood CA; BR/TR/6´0˝/185; [CalA89 29/747]; d9.7; Col Grand Canyon; [DL 1994 Cal A 131]

YEAR	TM LG	W	L	PCT	G	GS	CG-SHO	SV-BS	IP	H	R	HR	HB	BB-IB	SO	ERA	AERA	OAV	OOB	AB-HR-SH	AVG	PB	SUP	APR	DL	PW
1993	Cal A	0	1	.000	9	0	0	0-0	9.2	15	9	2	0	6-0	6	8.38	54	.357	.429	0	ø	0	—	-4	0	-0.3

Switzer, Jon Jon Michael; B8.13.1979 Bowling Green KY; BL/TL/6´3˝/190; [TBA01 2/47]; d8.2; Col Arizona St.

YEAR	TM LG	W	L	PCT	G	GS	CG-SHO	SV-BS	IP	H	R	HR	HB	BB-IB	SO	ERA	AERA	OAV	OOB	AB-HR-SH	AVG	PB	SUP	APR	DL	PW
2003	TB A	0	0	ø	5	0	0	0-0	9.2	13	8	2	4	3-0	7	7.45	62	.342	.435	0	ø	0	—	-3	0	-0.1
2005	TB A	0	0	ø	2	0	0	0-0	4	5	4	0	0	7-0	5	6.75	65	.278	.480	0	ø	0	—	-1	0	-0.1
2006	TB A	2	2	.500	40	0	0	0-3	33.2	38	19	5	1	19-3	18	4.54	103	.284	.374	0	ø	0	—	0	0	0.0
Total	3	2	2	.500	47	0	0	0-3	47.1	56	31	7	5	29-3	30	5.32	87	.295	.398	0	ø	0	—	-4	0	-0.2

Swormstedt, Len Leonard Brodbeck; B10.6.1878 Cincinnati OH; D7.19.1964 Salem MA; BR/TR/5´11.5˝/165; d9.29

YEAR	TM LG	W	L	PCT	G	GS	CG-SHO	SV-BS	IP	H	R	HR	HB	BB-IB	SO	ERA	AERA	OAV	OOB	AB-HR-SH	AVG	PB	SUP	APR	DL	PW
1901	Cin N	2	1	.667	3	3	3	0	26	19	8	2	2	5	13	1.73	185	.202	.257	9	.000	-1	52	4	—	0.3
1902	Cin N	0	2	.000	2	2	2	0	18	22	11	1	0	5	3	4.00	75	.301	.346	6	.000	-1	45	-1	—	-0.2
1906	Bos A	1	1	.500	3	2	2	0	21	17	6	0	1	0	6	1.29	214	.224	.234	8	.125	-1	79	3	—	0.2
Total	3	3	4	.429	8	7	7	0	65	58	25	3	3	10	22	2.22	136	.239	.277	23	.043	-3	57	6	—	0.3

Sykes, Bob Robert Joseph; B12.11.1954 Neptune NJ; BB/TL/6´2˝/(195–200); [DetA74 19/440]; d4.9; Col Miami–Dade North (FL) CC

YEAR	TM LG	W	L	PCT	G	GS	CG-SHO	SV-BS	IP	H	R	HR	HB	BB-IB	SO	ERA	AERA	OAV	OOB	AB-HR-SH	AVG	PB	SUP	APR	DL	PW
1977	Det A	5	7	.417	32	20	3	0-1	132.2	141	74	15	2	50-0	58	4.41	98	.271	.334	0	ø	0	109	-2	0	-0.2
1978	Det A	6	6	.500	22	10	3-2	2-2	93.2	99	43	14	1	34-0	58	3.94	99	.275	.338	0	ø	0	104	1	0	0.0
1979	StL N	4	3	.571	13	11	0	0-0	67	86	49	11	1	34-2	35	6.18	62	.315	.392	21-0-2	.095	-0	137	-16	45	-1.5
1980	StL N	6	10	.375	27	19	4-3	0-1	126	134	67	12	0	54-3	50	4.64	81	.277	.348	39-0-3	.103	-2	118	-9	0	-1.4
1981	StL N	2	0	1.000	22	1	0	0-1	37.1	37	20	2	1	18-1	14	4.58	79	.266	.354	2	.000	0	172	-3	0	-0.1
Total	5	23	26	.469	116	61	10-5	2-5	456.2	497	253	54	5	190-6	215	4.65	85	.280	.349	62-0-5	.097	-2	118	-29	45	-3.2

Sylvester, Lou Louis J.; B2.14.1855 Springfield IL; D5.5.1936 Brooklyn NY; BR/TR/5´6˝/165; d4.18; ▲

YEAR	TM LG	W	L	PCT	G	GS	CG-SHO	SV-BS	IP	H	R	HR	HB	BB-IB	SO	ERA	AERA	OAV	OOB	AB-HR-SH	AVG	PB	SUP	APR	DL	PW
1884	Cin U	0	1	.000	6	1	1	1	32.2	32	27	0	—	6	7	3.58	71	.239	.271	333-2	.267	0*	100	-4	—	-0.2

Szuminski, Jason Jason Ernest; B12.11.1978 San Diego CA; BR/TR/6´4˝/220; [ChiN00 27/793]; d4.11; Col MIT

YEAR	TM LG	W	L	PCT	G	GS	CG-SHO	SV-BS	IP	H	R	HR	HB	BB-IB	SO	ERA	AERA	OAV	OOB	AB-HR-SH	AVG	PB	SUP	APR	DL	PW
2004	SD N	0	0	ø	7	0	0	0-0	10	12	9	3	2	11-2	5	7.20	55	.286	.455	1	.000	-0	—	-4	0	-0.2

Tabaka, Jeff Jeffrey Jon; B1.17.1964 Barberton OH; BR/TL/6´2˝/(195–201); [MonN86 2/43]; d4.19; Col Kent St.; [DL 1999 Pit N 182]

YEAR	TM LG	W	L	PCT	G	GS	CG-SHO	SV-BS	IP	H	R	HR	HB	BB-IB	SO	ERA	AERA	OAV	OOB	AB-HR-SH	AVG	PB	SUP	APR	DL	PW
1994	Pit N	0	0	ø	5	0	0	0-0	4	4	8	1	0	8-0	2	18.00	24	.250	.500	0	ø	0	—	-5	0	-0.3
	SD N	3	1	.750	34	0	0	1-0	37	28	21	0	0	19-3	30	3.89	106	.209	.305	1	1.000	1	—	0	0	0.1
	Year	3	1	.750	39	0	0	1-0	41	32	29	1	0	27-3	32	5.27	79	.213	.331	1	1.000	1	—	-7	0	-0.2
1995	SD N	0	0	ø	10	0	0	0-1	6.1	10	5	1	0	5-1	6	7.11	57	.370	.469	0	ø	0	—	-2	0	-0.1
	Hou N	1	0	1.000	24	0	0	0-0	24.1	17	6	1	0	12-0	19	2.22	174	.202	.302	1-0-1	.000	-0	—	5	0	0.2
	Year	1	0	1.000	34	0	0	0-1	30.2	27	11	2	0	17-1	25	3.23	121	.243	.344	1-0-1	.000	-0	—	3	0	0.1
1996	Hou N	0	2	.000	18	0	0	1-0	20.1	28	18	5	3	14-0	18	6.64	58	.322	.433	1	.000	-0	—	-7	0	-0.7
1997	Cin N	0	0	ø	3	0	0	0-0	2	1	1	1	2	1-0	1	4.50	95	.143	.400	0	ø	0	—	0	0	0.0
1998	Pit N	2	2	.500	37	0	0	0-0	50.2	37	19	6	5	22-4	40	3.02	142	.204	.305	1	.000	-0	—	7	39	0.5
2001	StL N	0	0	ø	8	0	0	0-1	3.2	6	3	1	0	1-0	3	7.36	59	.375	.412	0	ø	0	—	-1	78	0.0
Total	6	6	5	.545	139	0	0	2-2	148.1	131	81	16	10	82-8	119	4.31	95	.237	.345	4-0-1	.250	1	—	-3	299	-0.3

YEAR	TM LG	W	L	PCT	G	GS	CG-SHO	SV-BS	IP	H	R	HR	HB	BB-IB	SO	ERA	AERA	OAV	OOB	AB-HR-SH	AVG	PB	SUP	APR	DL	PW
TABER, LEFTY	Edward Timothy; B1.11.1900 Rock Island IL; D11.5.1983 Lincoln NE; BL/TL/6´0˝/180; d9.4; Col Georgetown																									
1926	Phi N	0	0	ø	6	0	0	0	8.1	8	7	0	2	5	0	7.56	55	.242	.375	1	.000	-0	—	-2	—	-0.1
1927	Phi N	0	1	.000	3	1	0	0	3.1	8	9	0	1	5	0	18.90	22	.533	.667	1	.000	-0	41	-6	—	-1.0
Total	2	0	1	.000	9	1	0	0	11.2	16	16	0	3	10	0	10.80	38	.333	.475	2	.000	-0	41	-8	—	-1.1
TABER, JOHN	John Pardon; B6.28.1868 Acushnet MA; D2.21.1940 Boston MA; BR/TR/5´8˝/?; d4.30																									
1890	Bos N	0	1	.000	2	1	1	1	13	11	8	0	0	8	3	4.15	90	.220	.328	6	.000	-1	118	0	—	-0.1
TADANO, KAZUHITO	Kazuhito; B4.25.1980 Tokyo, Japan; BR/TR/6´0˝/180; d4.27; Col Rikkyo (Japan)																									
2004	Cle A	1	1	.500	14	4	0	0-0	50.1	55	30	6	3	18-0	39	4.65	93	.272	.341	3	.333	0	160	-3	0	-0.1
2005	Cle A	0	0	ø	1	0	0	0-0	4	4	1	0	0	0-0	1	2.25	185	.250	.250	0	ø	0	—	1	0	0.0
Total	2	1	1	.500	15	4	0	0-0	54.1	59	31	6	3	18-0	40	4.47	97	.271	.335	3	.333	0	160	-2	0	-0.1
TAFF, JOHN	John Gallatin; B6.3.1890 Austin TX; D5.15.1961 Houston TX; BR/TR/6´0˝/170; d5.11																									
1913	Phi A	0	1	.000	7	1	0	1	17.2	22	13	0	0	5	9	6.62	42	.306	.351	5	.200	-0	54	-7	—	-0.4
TAKATSU, SHINGO	Shingo; B11.25.1968 Hiroshima, Japan; BR/TR/6´0˝/180; d4.9																									
2004	Chi A	6	4	.600	59	0	0	19-1	62.1	40	17	6	2	21-3	50	2.31	204	.182	.259	0	ø	0	—	16	0	3.2
2005	Chi A	1	2	.333	31	0	0	8-1	28.2	30	19	9	0	16-1	32	5.97	76	.270	.359	0	ø	0	—	-4	0	-0.5
	NY N	1	0	1.000	9	0	0	0-2	7.2	11	2	2	0	3-1	6	2.35	176	.314	.368	0	ø	0	—	2	0	0.2
Total	2	8	6	.571	99	0	0	27-4	98.2	81	38	17	2	40-5	88	3.38	136	.221	.301	0	ø	0	—	14	0	2.9
TALBOT, FRED	Frederick Lealand "Bubby"; B6.28.1941 Washington DC; BR/TR/6´2˝/(195–212); d9.28																									
1963	Chi A	0	0	ø	1	0	0	0	3	2	1	0	0	4-0	2	3.00	117	.222	.462	1	.000	-0	—	0	0	0.0
1964	Chi A	4	5	.444	17	12	3-2	0	75.1	83	31	7	4	20-0	34	3.70	93	.288	.340	19-0-2	.263	3*	99	0	0	0.2
1965	KC A	10	12	.455	39	33	2-1	0	198	188	96	25	6	86-3	117	4.14	84	.251	.330	70-0-3	.200	3*	99	-12	0	-0.9
1966	KC A	4	4	.500	11	11	0	0	67.2	65	39	6	2	28-6	37	4.79	71	.248	.324	20-0-5	.150	0	78	-10	0	-1.0
	NY A	7	7	.500	23	19	3	0	124.1	123	59	16	3	45-3	48	4.13	81	.262	.329	35-0-4	.143	1	117	-9	0	-0.8
	Year	11	11	.500	34	30	3	0	192	188	98	22	5	73-9	85	4.36	77	.257	.327	55-0-9	.145	1	103	-18	0	-1.8
1967	NY A	6	8	.429	29	22	2	0	138.2	132	78	20	6	54-5	61	4.22	74	.252	.325	38-1-2	.158	3*	111	-18	0	-1.3
1968	NY A	1	9	.100	29	11	1	0	99	89	47	6	2	42-6	67	3.36	87	.241	.319	17-1-2	.118	1	63	-7	0	-0.6
1969	NY A	0	0	ø	8	0	0	0-1	12.1	13	9	1	0	6-2	7	5.11	69	.283	.352	1-0-1	.000	-0	—	-3	0	-0.1
	Sea A	5	8	.385	25	16	1-1	0-0	114.2	125	58	12	4	41-6	67	4.16	88	.278	.342	37-2-2	.162	2*	100	-6	0	-0.4
	Oak A	1	2	.333	12	2	0	1-0	19	22	11	2	0	7-0	9	5.21	66	.297	.358	3	.333	0	141	-3	0	-0.5
	Year	6	10	.375	45	18	1-1	1-1	146	160	78	15	4	54-8	83	4.38	82	.281	.345	41-2-3	.171	2	105	-11	0	-1.0
1970	Oak A	0	1	.000	1	0	0	0-0	1.2	2	2	1	0	1-0	0	10.80	33	.286	.375	0	ø	0	—	-1	0	-0.2
Total	8	38	56	.404	195	126	12-4	1-1	853.2	844	431	96	27	334-31	449	4.12	81	.260	.331	241-4-21	.174	13	100	-69	0	-5.6
TALCOTT, ROY	Le Roy Everett; B1.16.1920 Brookline MA; D12.6.1999 Miami FL; BR/TR/6´1.5˝/180; d6.24; Col Princeton																									
1943	Bos N	0	0	ø	1	0	0	0	0.2	1	2	0	0	2	0	27.00	13	.333	.600	0	ø	0	—	-2	0	-0.1
TALLET, BRIAN	Brian Curtis; B9.21.1977 Midwest City OK; BL/TL/6´7˝/(208–220); [CleA00 2/55]; d9.16; Col Louisiana St.; [DL 2004 Cle A 113]																									
2002	Cle A	1	0	1.000	2	2	0	0-0	12	9	3	0	1	4-0	5	1.50	296	.214	.298	0	ø	0	125	4	0	0.3
2003	Cle A	0	2	.000	5	3	0	0-0	19	23	14	2	1	8-0	9	4.74	94	.303	.376	2	.000	-0	62	-2	0	-0.2
2005	Cle A	0	0	ø	2	0	0	0-0	4.2	6	4	2	1	3-0	2	7.71	54	.300	.417	0	ø	0	—	-2	0	-0.1
2006	Tor A	3	0	1.000	44	1	0	0-0	54.1	45	24	5	3	31-4	37	3.81	124	.238	.346	0	ø	0	159	6	0	0.3
Total	4	4	2	.667	53	6	0	0-0	90	83	45	9	6	46-4	53	3.90	118	.254	.352	2	.000	-0	98	6	113	0.3
TAM, JEFF	Jeffrey Eugene; B8.19.1970 Fullerton CA; BR/TR/6´1˝/(202–214); d6.30; Col Florida St.																									
1998	NY N	1	1	.500	15	0	0	0-1	14.1	13	10	2	2	4-1	8	6.28	66	.241	.317	1	.000	-0	—	-3	0	-0.4
1999	Cle A	0	0	ø	1	0	0	0-0	0.1	2	3	0	0	1-1	0	81.00	6	1.000	1.000	0	ø	0	—	-3	0	-0.1
	NY N	0	0	ø	9	0	0	0-0	11.1	6	4	3	0	3-0	8	3.18	137	.150	.209	0	ø	0	—	2	41	0.1
2000	†Oak A	3	3	.500	72	0	0	3-3	85.2	86	30	3	1	23-8	46	2.63	185	.268	.315	0	ø	0	—	21	0	1.4
2001	†Oak A	2	4	.333	70	0	0	3-3	74.2	68	27	3	3	29-9	44	3.01	151	.250	.326	0	ø	0	—	13	0	1.0
2002	Oak A	1	2	.333	40	0	0	0-4	40.1	56	26	2	2	13-5	14	5.13	87	.333	.384	0	ø	0	—	-3	0	-0.2
2003	Tor A	0	4	.000	44	0	0	1-1	44.2	58	30	5	1	25-7	26	5.64	84	.314	.396	1	1.000	1	—	-4	0	-0.2
Total	6	7	14	.333	251	0	0	7-12	271.1	289	130	18	9	98-31	146	3.91	119	.277	.342	2	.500	1	—	23	41	1.6
TAMULIS, VITO	Vitautis Casimirus; B7.11.1911 Cambridge MA; D5.5.1974 Nashville TN; BL/TL/5´9˝/170; d9.25																									
1934	NY A	1	0	1.000	1	1	1-1	0	9	7	0	0	0	1	5	0.00	ø	.219	.242	4	.250	0	107	4	—	0.6
1935	NY A	10	5	.667	30	19	9-3	1	160.2	178	80	7	2	55	57	4.09	99	.280	.339	57-1-3	.246	4	129	2	—	0.5
1938	StL A	0	3	.000	3	2	0	0	15.1	26	15	2	0	10	11	7.63	65	.366	.444	5	.400	1	80	-5	—	-0.6
	Bro N	12	6	.667	38	18	9	2	159.2	181	81	11	2	40	70	3.83	102	.288	.333	55-0-3	.127	-3*	118	1	—	-0.2
1939	Bro N	9	8	.529	39	17	8-1	4	158.2	177	81	10	8	45	83	4.37	92	.287	.343	55-0-3	.182	-1	92	-3	—	-0.4
1940	Bro N	8	5	.615	41	12	4-1	2	154.1	147	60	5	3	34	55	3.09	129	.244	.288	46-0-1	.130	-1*	96	15	—	1.0
1941	Phi N	0	1	.000	6	1	0	0	12	21	13	1	1	7	5	9.00	41	.382	.460	2	.000	-0	46	-7	0	-0.5
	Bro N	0	0	ø	12	0	0	1	22	21	10	1	0	10	8	3.68	100	.244	.323	5	.000	-1	—	0	0	-0.1
	Year	0	1	.000	18	1	0	1	34	42	23	2	1	17	13	5.56	66	.298	.377	7	.000	-1	46	-6	0	-0.6
Total	6	40	28	.588	170	70	31-6	10	691.2	758	340	37	16	202	294	3.97	101	.278	.331	229-1-10	.175	-1	109	7	0	0.3
TANANA, FRANK	Frank Daryl; B7.3.1953 Detroit MI; BL/TL/6´3˝/(185–200); [CalA71 1/13]; d9.9																									
1973	Cal A	2	2	.500	4	4	2-1	0-0	26.1	20	11	2	0	8-0	22	3.08	116	.200	.259	0	ø	0	75	1	0	0.2
1974	Cal A	14	19	.424	39	35	12-4	0-1	268.2	262	104	27	8	77-4	180	3.12	111	.255	.311	0	ø	0	83	13	0	1.6
1975	Cal A	16	9	.640	34	33	16-5	0-0	257.1	211	80	21	7	73-6	**269**	2.62	137	.226	.286	0	ø	0	117	32	0	3.2
1976	Cal A★	19	10	.655	34	34	23-2	0-0	288.1	212	88	24	9	73-5	261	2.43	138	.203	**.261**	0	ø	0*	100	31	0	3.3
1977	Cal A✳	15	9	.625	31	31	20-**7**	0-0	241.1	201	72	19	12	61-2	205	**2.54**	**155**	.227	.284	0	ø	0	110	**42**	0	4.1
1978	Cal A☆	18	12	.600	33	33	10-4	0-0	239	239	108	26	9	60-7	137	3.65	99	.258	.306	0	ø	0	117	0	0	-0.1
1979	†Cal A	7	5	.583	18	17	2-1	0-0	90.1	93	44	9	2	25-0	46	3.89	105	.264	.315	0	ø	0	108	2	57	0.2
1980	Cal A	11	12	.478	32	31	7	0-0	204	223	107	18	8	45-0	113	4.15	95	.277	.320	0	ø	0	109	-6	0	-0.6
1981	Bos A	4	10	.286	24	23	5-2	0-0	141.1	142	70	17	4	43-4	78	4.01	98	.265	.322	0	ø	0	97	0	0	0.0
1982	Tex A	7	18	.280	30	30	7	0-0	194.1	199	102	16	7	55-10	87	4.21	92	.264	.319	0	ø	0	77	-9	0	-1.0
1983	Tex A	7	9	.438	29	22	3	0-0	159.1	144	70	14	7	49-5	108	3.16	128	.240	.303	0	ø	0	79	13	0	1.4
1984	Tex A	15	15	.500	35	35	9-1	0-0	246.1	234	117	30	6	81-3	141	3.25	128	.245	.306	0	ø	0	96	18	0	2.1
1985	Tex A	2	7	.222	13	13	0	0-0	77.2	89	53	15	1	23-2	52	5.91	72	.287	.334	0	ø	0	74	-13	0	-1.2
	Det A	10	7	.588	20	20	4	0-0	137.1	131	59	13	2	34-6	107	3.34	123	.250	.296	0	ø	0	104	11	0	1.3
	Year	12	14	.462	33	33	4	0-0	215	220	112	28	3	57-8	159	4.27	97	.264	.310	0	ø	0	92	-2	0	0.1
1986	Det A	12	9	.571	32	31	3-1	0-0	188.1	196	95	23	3	65-9	119	4.16	100	.268	.328	0	ø	0	104	1	0	0.1
1987	†Det A	15	10	.600	34	34	5-3	0-0	218.2	216	106	27	5	56-5	146	3.91	109	.256	.302	0	ø	0	117	10	0	1.0
1988	Det A	14	11	.560	32	32	2	0-0	203	213	105	25	4	64-7	127	4.21	91	.267	.323	0	ø	0	98	-9	0	-0.9
1989	Det A	10	14	.417	33	33	6-1	0-0	223.2	227	105	21	8	74-8	147	3.58	107	.265	.326	0	ø	0	87	5	0	0.6
1990	Det A	9	8	.529	34	29	1	1-0	176.1	190	104	25	9	66-7	114	5.31	75	.280	.349	0	ø	0	118	-22	0	-1.8
1991	Det A	13	12	.520	33	33	3-2	0-0	217.1	217	98	26	2	78-9	107	3.77	111	.265	.327	1	.000	-0	105	10	0	1.1
1992	Det A	13	11	.542	32	31	3	0-0	186.2	188	102	22	7	90-9	91	4.39	91	.267	.351	0	ø	0	105	-10	0	-1.1
1993	NY N	7	15	.318	29	29	0	0-0	183	198	100	26	9	48-7	104	4.48	90	.278	.330	58-0-3	.155	0	93	-7	0	-0.8
	NY A	0	2	.000	3	3	0	0-0	19.2	18	10	2	0	7-1	12	3.20	131	.222	.284	0	ø	0	95	1	0	0.1
Total	21	240	236	.504	638	616	143-34	1-1	4188.1	4063	1910	448	129	1255-116	2773	3.66	106	.254	.312	59-0-3	.153	0	101	114	57	12.8
TANKERSLEY, DENNIS	Dennis Lee; B2.24.1979 Troy MO; BR/TR/6´2˝/185; [BosA98 38/1135]; d5.10; Col St. Louis–Meramec (MO) CC																									
2002	SD N	1	4	.200	17	9	0	0-0	51.1	59	46	10	6	40-3	39	8.06	48	.304	.434	13-1-0	.308	2	87	-23	0	-1.7
2003	SD N	0	1	.000	1	1	0	0-0	0	3	7	0	0	4-0	0	(7)	ø	1.000	1.000	0	ø	0	257	-7	0	-0.5
2004	SD N	0	5	.000	9	6	0	0-0	35	35	25	3	1	17-3	29	5.14	77	.254	.340	8-0-1	.250	1	55	-7	0	-0.8
Total	3	1	10	.091	27	16	0	0-0	86.1	97	78	13	7	61-6	68	7.61	51	.290	.407	21-1-1	.286	3	86	-37	0	-3.0
TANKERSLEY, TAYLOR	Taylor Mark; B3.7.1983 Missoula MT; BL/TL/6´1˝/220; [FlaN04 1/27]; d6.3; Col Alabama																									
2006	Fla N	2	1	.667	49	0	0	3-4	41	33	14	4	1	26-5	46	2.85	150	.228	.343	2	.000	-0	—	7	0	0.5

YEAR	TM LG	W	L	PCT	G	GS	CG-SHO	SV-BS	IP	H	R	HR	HB	BB-IB	SO	ERA	AERA	OAV	OOB	AB-HR-SH	AVG	PB	SUP	APR	DL	PW
TANNEHILL, JESSE	Jesse Niles "Powder"; B7.14.1874 Dayton KY; D9.22.1956 Dayton KY; BB/TL (BL 1903)/5´8˝/150; d6.17; C1; b–Lee; ▲																									
1894	Cin N	1	1	.500	5	2	1	1	29	37	30	1	1	16	7	7.14	78	.306	.391	11	.000	-2	89	-4	—	-0.4
1897	Pit N	9	9	.500	21	16	11-1	1	142	172	97	1	8	24	40	4.25	98	.297	.333	184	.266	3*	68	-3	—	0.1
1898	Pit N	25	13	.658	43	38	34-5	2	326.2	338	147	2	12	63	93	2.95	121	.265	.306	152-1-6	.289	7*	102	23	—	3.4
1899	Pit N	24	14	.632	41	36	33-3	1	322	361	139	4	14	52	65	2.82	135	.283	.318	136-0-4	.250	4*	114	36	—	4.3
1900	Pit N	20	6	.769	29	27	23-2	0	234	247	108	3	17	43	50	2.88	126	.271	.316	110-0-5	.336	8*	118	20	—	2.7
1901	Pit N	18	10	.643	32	30	25-4	1	252.1	240	94	1	10	36	118	**2.18**	150	.249	.283	135-1-3	.244	5*	106	30	—	3.3
1902	Pit N	20	6	.769	26	24	23-2	0	231	203	78	0	10	25	100	1.95	141	.236	.266	148-1-1	.291	7*	149	17	—	2.7
1903	NY A	15	15	.500	32	31	22-2	0	239.2	258	123	3	10	34	106	3.27	96	.274	.307	111-1-1	.234	5*	107	-4	—	0.2
1904	Bos A	21	11	.656	33	31	30-4	0	281.2	256	89	5	13	33	116	2.04	131	.243	.275	122-0-2	.197	3*	110	19	—	2.8
1905	Bos A	22	9	.710	37	32	27-6	0	271.2	238	91	7	13	59	113	2.48	109	.237	.288	93-1-2	.226	6	122	9	—	1.9
1906	Bos A	13	11	.542	27	26	18-2	0	196.1	207	91	9	10	39	82	3.16	87	.274	.318	79-0-1	.278	6*	113	-8	—	-0.3
1907	Bos A	6	7	.462	18	16	10-2	1	131	131	59	3	5	20	29	2.47	104	.263	.298	51-0-1	.196	1*	97	-1	—	0.1
1908	Bos A	0	0	ø	1	1	0	0	5	4	2	0	0	3	2	3.60	68	.200	.304	2	.500	0	111	0	—	0.0
	Was A	2	4	.333	10	9	5	0	71.2	77	36	0	6	23	14	3.77	61	.278	.346	43	.256	2*	116	-9	—	-0.5
	Year	2	4	.333	11	10	5	0	76.2	81	38	0	6	26	16	3.76	61	.273	.343	45	.267	2	116	-10	—	-0.5
1909	Was A	1	1	.500	3	2	2-1	0	21	19	8	1	1	5	8	3.43	71	.268	.325	36	.167	0*	73	-1	—	0.0
1911	Cin N	0	0	ø	1	0	0	0	4.1	6	7	0	0	3	1	6.23	53	.316	.409	1	.000	-0	—	-3	—	-0.1
Total	15	197	117	.627	359	321	264-34	7	2759.1	2794	1199	40	130	478	944	2.80	114	.263	.303	1414-5-26	.255	54	109	121	—	20.2
TANNER, BRUCE	Bruce Matthew; B12.9.1961 New Castle PA; BL/TR/6´3˝/220; [ChiA83 4/97]; d6.12; C5; f–Chuck; Col Florida St.																									
1985	Chi A	1	2	.333	10	4	0	0-0	27	34	17	1	2	13-3	9	5.33	82	.309	.389	0	ø	0	78	-3	0	-0.2
TAPANI, KEVIN	Kevin Ray; B2.18.1964 Des Moines IA; BR/TR/6´0˝/(180–195); [OakA86 2/40]; d7.4; Col Central Michigan																									
1989	NY N	0	0	ø	3	0	0	0-0	7.1	5	3	1	0	4-0	2	3.68	90	.192	.290	2	.000	-0	—	0	0	0.0
	Min A	2	2	.500	5	5	0	0-0	32.2	34	15	2	0	8-1	21	3.86	108	.266	.307	0	ø	0	79	1	0	0.1
1990	Min A	12	8	.600	28	28	1-1	0-0	159.1	164	75	12	2	29-2	101	4.07	102	.264	.297	0	ø	0	90	4	24	0.4
1991	†Min A	16	9	.640	34	34	4-1	0-0	244	225	84	23	2	40-0	135	2.99	143	.245	.277	0	ø	0	104	36	0	3.5
1992	Min A	16	11	.593	34	34	4-1	0-0	220	226	103	17	5	48-2	138	3.97	103	.269	.309	0	ø	0	120	4	0	0.4
1993	Min A	12	15	.444	36	35	3-1	0-0	225.2	243	123	21	6	57-1	150	4.43	100	.272	.318	0	ø	0	85	-1	0	-0.1
1994	Min A	11	7	.611	24	24	4-1	0-0	156	181	86	13	4	39-0	91	4.62	107	.291	.334	0	ø	0	94	6	0	0.6
1995	Min A	6	11	.353	20	20	3-1	0-0	133.2	155	79	21	4	34-2	88	4.92	98	.290	.335	0	ø	0	89	-1	0	-0.2
	†LA N	4	2	.667	13	11	0	0-0	57	72	37	8	1	14-2	43	5.05	77	.306	.345	17-0-3	.176	0	166	-8	0	-0.7
1996	Chi A	13	10	.565	34	34	1	0-0	225.1	236	123	34	3	76-5	150	4.59	104	.268	.326	0	ø	0	109	5	0	0.4
1997	Chi N	9	3	.750	13	13	1-1	0-0	85	77	33	7	2	23-2	55	3.39	128	.242	.296	22-0-4	.136	-0	103	9	112	1.2
1998	†Chi N	19	9	.679	35	34	2-2	0-0	219	244	120	30	5	62-4	136	4.85	91	.284	.333	75-1-5	.133	1	112	-7	0	-0.8
1999	Chi N	6	12	.333	23	23	1	0-0	136	151	81	12	4	33-2	73	4.83	95	.280	.322	39-0-5	.051	-2	85	-4	48	-0.7
2000	Chi N	8	12	.400	30	30	2	0-0	195.2	208	113	35	8	47-1	150	5.01	91	.271	.319	56-1-9	.179	2	98	-8	13	-0.6
2001	Chi N	9	14	.391	29	29	0	0-0	168.1	186	93	24	7	40-6	149	4.49	93	.279	.325	50-0-7	.240	2	91	-7	0	-0.5
Total	13	143	125	.534	361	354	26-9	0-0	2265	2407	1168	260	53	554-30	1482	4.35	102	.272	.317	261-2-33	.153	3	100	29	197	3.0
TASCHNER, JACK	Jack Gerard; B4.21.1978 Milwaukee WI; BL/TL/6´3˝/(190–205); [SFN99 2/75]; d6.11; Col Wisconsin–Oshkosh																									
2005	SF N	2	0	1.000	24	0	0	0-1	22.2	15	5	0	0	13-0	19	1.59	267	.185	.295	0	ø	0	—	6	0	0.5
2006	SF N	0	1	.000	24	0	0	0-1	19.1	31	23	4	2	7-0	15	8.38	53	.344	.396	0	ø	0	—	-10	0	-0.5
Total	2	2	1	.667	48	0	0	0-2	42	46	28	4	2	20-0	34	4.71	92	.269	.347	0	ø	0	—	-4	0	0.0
TATA, JORDAN	Jordan Arthur; B9.20.1981 Plano TX; BR/TR/6´6˝/220; [DetA03 16/460]; d4.6; Col Sam Houston St.																									
2006	Det A	0	0	ø	8	0	0	0-0	14.2	14	11	1	0	7-1	6	6.14	73	.250	.323	0	ø	0	—	-3	0	-0.1
TATE, RANDY	Randall Lee; B10.23.1952 Florence AL; BR/TR/6´3˝/190; [NYN72*5/99]; d4.14; Col Calhoun (AL) CC																									
1975	NY N	5	13	.278	26	23	2	0-0	137.2	121	73	8	5	86-3	99	4.45	79	.240	.355	41-0-5	.000	-4	84	-13	0	-2.0
TATE, STU	Stuart Douglas; B6.17.1962 Huntsville AL; BR/TR/6´3˝/205; [SFN84 8/193]; d9.20; Col Auburn																									
1989	SF N	0	0	ø	2	0	0	0-0	2.2	3	3	0	0	0-0	4	3.38	100	.250	.250	0	ø	0	—	-1	0	0.0
TATE, AL	Walter Alvin; B7.1.1918 Coleman OK; D5.8.1993 Bountiful UT; BR/TR/6´0˝/180; d9.27																									
1946	Pit N	0	1	.000	2	1	1	0	9	8	5	0	0	7	2	5.00	70	.267	.405	3	.333	0	49	-1	0	-0.1
TATIS, RAMON	Ramon Francisco (Medrano); B1.5.1973 Guayubin, D.R.; BL/TL/6´2˝/195; d4.6																									
1997	Chi N	1	1	.500	56	0	0	0-1	55.2	66	36	13	3	29-6	33	5.34	81	.308	.394	3	.000	-0	—	-6	0	-0.3
1998	TB A	0	0	ø	22	0	0	0-0	11.2	23	19	2	1	16-1	5	13.89	35	.418	.556	0	ø	0	—	-11	15	-0.5
Total	2	1	1	.500	78	0	0	0-1	67.1	89	55	15	4	45-7	38	6.82	65	.331	.430	3	.000	-0	—	-17	15	-0.8
TATUM, KEN	Kenneth Ray; B4.25.1944 Alexandria LA; BR/TR/6´2˝/(200–205); d5.28; Col Mississippi St.																									
1969	Cal A	7	2	.778	45	0	0	22-1	86.1	51	13	1	4	39-5	65	1.36	258	.172	.276	21-2-2	.286	4	—	**22**	0	4.1
1970	Cal A	7	4	.636	62	0	0	17-8	88.2	68	35	12	5	26-5	50	2.94	123	.208	.274	11-1-0	.182	1	—	6	0	1.0
1971	Bos A	2	4	.333	36	1	0	9-3	53.2	50	27	3	8	25-7	21	4.19	89	.255	.358	10-1-0	.300	2	72	-3	29	-0.1
1972	Bos A	0	2	.000	22	0	0	4-2	29.1	32	12	3	2	15-3	15	3.07	106	.283	.377	2	.000	0	—	0	40	0.0
1973	Bos A	0	0	ø	1	0	0	0-0	4	6	4	2	0	3-0	0	9.00	45	.462	.529	0	ø	0	—	-2	0	-0.1
1974	Chi A	0	0	ø	10	1	0	0-0	20.2	23	12	3	0	9-0	5	4.79	78	.274	.340	1	.000	-0	259	-2	0	-0.1
Total	6	16	12	.571	176	2	0	52-14	282.2	230	103	24	19	117-20	156	2.93	122	.224	.311	45-4-2	.244	7	174	21	69	4.8
TAUBENHEIM, TY	Ty Andrew; B11.17.1982 Bellingham WA; BR/TR/6´6˝/250; [MilN03 19/549]; d5.20; Col Edmonds (WA) CC																									
2006	Tor A	1	5	.167	12	7	0	0-0	35	40	22	5	4	18-0	26	4.89	97	.282	.373	3	.333	0	71	-1	19	-0.1
TAUSCHER, WALT	Walter Edward; B11.22.1901 LaSalle IL; D11.27.1992 Winter Park FL; BR/TR/6´1˝/186; d4.19																									
1928	Pit N	0	0	ø	17	0	0	1	29.1	28	20	0	3	12	7	4.91	83	.280	.374	6	.167	-0	—	-3	—	-0.2
1931	Was A	1	0	1.000	6	0	0	0	12	24	16	2	0	4	5	7.50	57	.429	.467	0-0-2	ø	0	—	-6	—	-0.4
Total	2	1	0	1.000	23	0	0	1	41.1	52	36	2	3	16	12	5.66	73	.333	.406	6-0-2	.167	-0	—	-9	—	-0.6
TAVAREZ, JULIAN	Julian (Carmen); B5.22.1973 Santiago, D.R.; BL/TR/6´2˝/(165–195); d8.7																									
1993	Cle A	2	2	.500	8	7	0	0-0	37	53	29	7	2	13-2	19	6.57	67	.340	.395	0	ø	0	153	-8	0	-0.8
1994	Cle A	0	1	.000	1	1	0	0-0	1.2	6	8	1	0	1-1	0	21.60	22	.500	.500	0	ø	0	97	-5	0	-0.6
1995	†Cle A	10	2	.833	57	0	0	0-4	85	76	36	7	3	21-0	68	2.44	194	.235	.286	0	ø	0	—	17	0	2.0
1996	†Cle A	4	7	.364	51	4	0	0-0	80.2	101	49	9	1	22-5	46	5.36	91	.315	.356	0	ø	0	85	-3	0	-0.3
1997	†SF N	6	4	.600	**89**	0	0	0-3	88.1	91	43	6	4	34-5	38	3.87	106	.277	.344	1	.000	-0	—	2	0	0.2
1998	SF N	5	3	.625	60	0	0	1-5	85.1	96	41	5	8	36-11	52	3.80	106	.298	.379	9-0-1	.111	-0	—	1	25	0.0
1999	SF N	2	0	1.000	47	0	0	0-2	54.2	65	38	7	8	25-3	33	5.93	72	.295	.384	5	.200	0	—	-10	31	-0.5
2000	Col N	11	5	.688	51	12	1	1-0	120	124	68	11	7	53-9	62	4.43	131	.268	.349	35-0-3	.086	-3	96	13	0	1.3
2001	Chi N	10	9	.526	34	28	0	0-0	161.1	172	98	13	11	69-4	107	4.52	93	.277	.358	41-0-11	.122	-0	112	-11	0	-1.0
2002	Fla N	10	12	.455	29	27	0	0-1	153.2	188	100	9	15	74-7	67	5.39	73	.308	.395	40-0-5	.125	-1	93	-26	24	-3.2
2003	Pit N	3	3	.500	64	0	0	11-3	83.2	75	37	1	5	27-8	39	3.66	118	.244	.314	4	.000	-0	—	6	0	0.6
2004	†StL N	7	4	.636	77	0	0	4-2	64.1	57	21	1	6	19-0	48	2.38	179	.238	.309	0	ø	0	—	12	0	2.1
2005	†StL N	2	3	.400	74	0	0	4-2	65.2	68	28	6	8	19-4	47	3.43	122	.278	.345	0-0-1	ø	0	—	6	0	0.4
2006	Bos A	5	4	.556	58	6	1	1-2	98.2	110	54	10	6	44-3	56	4.47	105	.293	.374	0	ø	0	114	1	0	0.1
Total	14	77	59	.566	700	85	2	22-24	1180	1282	650	93	84	457-62	682	4.34	102	.282	.356	135-0-21	.111	-5	106	-5	80	0.3
TAYLOR, AARON	Aaron Wade; B8.20.1977 Valdosta GA; BR/TR/6´7˝/(230–245); [AtlN96 11/332]; d9.9																									
2002	Sea A	0	0	ø	5	0	0	0-1	5	8	5	2	0	0-0	6	9.00	48	.348	.348	0	ø	0	—	-3	0	-0.1
2003	Sea A	0	0	ø	10	0	0	0-0	12.2	17	12	0	1	6-0	9	8.53	51	.315	.387	0	ø	0	—	-6	0	-0.3
2004	Sea A	0	0	ø	5	0	0	0-0	3.2	5	4	2	0	3-0	4	9.82	46	.313	.421	0	ø	0	—	-2	89	-0.1
Total	3	0	0	ø	20	0	0	0-1	21.1	30	21	4	1	9-0	19	8.86	49	.323	.385	0	ø	0	—	-11	89	-0.5
TAYLOR, ARLAS	Arlas Walter "Lefty","Foxy"; B3.16.1896 Warrick Co. IN; D9.10.1958 Dade City FL; BR/TL/5´11˝/?; d9.15																									
1921	Phi A	0	1	.000	1	1	0	0	2	7	5	1	0	2	1	22.50	20	.636	.692	0	ø	0	56	-3	—	-0.5

YEAR	TM LG	W	L	PCT	G	GS	CG-SHO	SV-BS	IP	H	R	HR	HB	BB-IB	SO	ERA	AERA	OAV	OOB	AB-HR-SH	AVG	PB	SUP	APR	DL	PW
TAYLOR, BEN	Benjamin Harrison; B4.2.1889 Paoli IN; D11.3.1946 Martin Co. IN; BR/TR/5´11˝/163; d6.28																									
1912	Cin N	0	0	ø	2	0	0	0	5.2	9	7	0	1	3	2	3.18	106	.360	.448	2	.000	0	—	-1	—	-0.1
TAYLOR, BRUCE	Bruce Bell; B4.16.1953 Holden MA; BR/TR/6´0˝/175; d8.5																									
1977	Det A	1	0	1.000	19	0	0	2-1	29.1	23	11	2	1	10-3	19	3.38	128	.219	.293	0	ø	0	—	3	0	0.2
1978	Det A	0	0	ø	1	0	0	0-0	1	0	0	0	0	0-0	0	0.00	ø	.000	.000	0	ø	0	—	0	0	0.0
1979	Det A	1	2	.333	10	0	0	0-0	18.2	16	13	1	2	7-2	8	4.82	90	.242	.325	0	ø	0	—	-2	0	-0.3
Total	3	2	2	.500	30	0	0	2-1	49	39	24	3	3	17-5	27	3.86	112	.224	.301	0	ø	0	—	1	0	-0.1
TAYLOR, CHUCK	Charles Gilbert; B4.18.1942 Murfreesboro TN; BR/TR/6´2˝/(180–195); d5.27; Col Middle Tennessee																									
1969	StL N	7	5	.583	27	13	5-1	0-0	126.2	108	39	8	3	30-5	62	2.56	140	.235	.285	39-0-2	.179	1	74	15	0	1.4
1970	StL N	6	7	.462	56	7	1-1	8-3	124.1	116	47	5	2	31-10	64	3.11	133	.256	.303	26-0-3	.115	-1	83	15	0	1.5
1971	StL N	3	1	.750	43	1	0	3-2	71.1	72	32	7	1	25-5	46	3.53	103	.267	.327	12	.167	0	146	0	0	0.0
1972	NY N	0	0	ø	20	0	0	2-0	31	44	19	2	1	9-3	9	5.52	61	.341	.386	3	.000	-0	—	-6	0	-0.3
	Mil A	0	0	ø	5	0	0	1-0	11.2	8	2	0	1	3-0	5	1.54	199	.200	.273	2	.500	0	—	2	0	0.2
1973	Mon N	2	0	1.000	8	0	0	0-1	20.1	17	4	3	0	2-1	10	1.77	216	.230	.250	4-0-2	.000	-0	—	5	0	0.4
1974	Mon N	6	2	.750	61	0	0	11-3	107.2	101	27	8	3	25-8	43	2.17	177	.256	.301	10-0-4	.300	1	—	20	0	2.0
1975	Mon N	2	2	.500	54	0	0	6-4	74	72	32	6	1	24-5	29	3.53	110	.264	.321	2	.000	-0	—	3	0	0.2
1976	Mon N	2	3	.400	31	0	0	0-0	40	38	20	4	0	13-4	14	4.50	84	.273	.333	3	.000	-0	—	-2	0	-0.3
Total	8	28	20	.583	305	21	6-2	31-13	607	576	222	43	12	162-41	282	3.07	123	.258	.309	101-0-11	.158	0	80	52	0	5.1
TAYLOR, DORN	Donald Clyde; B8.11.1958 Abington PA; BR/TR/6´2˝/180; d4.30; Col Pfeiffer																									
1987	Pit N	2	3	.400	14	8	0	0-0	53.1	48	35	10	1	28-1	37	5.74	73	.247	.342	18	.167	-0*	95	-8	27	-0.7
1989	Pit N	1	1	.500	9	0	0	0-0	10.2	14	6	0	0	5-2	3	5.06	67	.333	.404	1	.000	-0*	—	-2	0	-0.3
1990	Bal A	0	1	.000	4	0	0	0-0	3.2	4	3	0	0	2-0	4	2.45	156	.250	.333	0	ø	0	—	0	0	-0.1
Total	3	3	5	.375	27	8	0	0-0	67.2	66	44	10	1	35-3	44	5.45	74	.262	.352	19	.158	-0	95	-10	27	-1.1
TAYLOR, ED	Edgar Ruben "Rube"; B3.23.1877 Palestine TX; D1.31.1912 Dallas TX; TL; d8.8																									
1903	StL N	0	0	ø	1	0	0	0	3	0	0	0	0	0	1	0.00	ø	.000	.000	1	.000	-0	—	1	—	0.0
TAYLOR, GARY	Gary William; B10.19.1945 Detroit MI; BR/TR/6´2˝/190; [DetA65 8/163]; d9.2; Col Central Michigan																									
1969	Det A	0	1	.000	7	0	0	0-0	10.1	10	6	2	0	6-0	3	5.23	72	.244	.340	1	.000	-0	—	-1	0	-0.1
TAYLOR, HARRY	Harry Evans; B12.2.1935 San Angelo TX; BR/TR/6´0˝/185; d9.17; Col Texas																									
1957	KC A	0	0	ø	2	0	0	0	8.2	11	4	0	1	4-0	4	3.12	127	.314	.400	4	.250	0	—	0	0	0.0
TAYLOR, HARRY	James Harry; B5.20.1919 E.Glenn IN; D11.5.2000 Terre Haute IN; BR/TR/6´1˝/(175–190); d9.22																									
1946	Bro N	0	0	ø	4	0	0	1	4.2	5	2	0	0	1	6	3.86	88	.313	.353	0	ø	0	—	0	0	0.0
1947	†Bro N	10	5	.667	33	20	10-2	1	162	130	63	10	5	83	58	3.11	133	**.225**	.327	62-0-2	.129	-2	112	19	0	1.4
1948	Bro N	2	7	.222	17	13	2	0	80.2	90	55	8	3	61	32	5.36	75	.288	.408	22-0-2	.273	1	130	-12	0	-1.0
1950	Bos A	2	0	1.000	3	2	2-1	0	19	13	3	0	0	8	8	1.42	345	.197	.284	7	.286	0	92	7	0	0.7
1951	Bos A	4	9	.308	31	8	1	2	81.1	100	59	6	1	42	22	5.75	78	.307	.388	29-0-1	.103	-3	112	-11	0	-1.8
1952	Bos A	1	0	1.000	2	1	1	0	10	6	2	1	1	6	1	1.80	219	.176	.317	4	.250	0	244	2	0	0.2
Total	6	19	21	.475	90	44	16-3	4	357.2	344	184	25	10	201	127	4.10	102	.258	.359	124-0-5	.161	-3	118	5	0	-0.5
TAYLOR, JACK	John Besson "Brewery Jack"; B5.23.1873 Sandy Hill (now Stockton) MD; D2.7.1900 Staten Island NY; BR/TR/6´1˝/190; d9.16; Col Manhattan																									
1891	NY N	0	1	.000	1	1	1	0	8	4	2	1	0	3	3	1.13	285	.143	.226	2	.000	0	37	2	—	0.2
1892	Phi N	1	0	1.000	3	3	2	0	26	28	19	2	0	10	7	1.38	234	.264	.328	12	.167	-0	169	1	—	0.0
1893	Phi N	10	9	.526	25	16	14	1	170	187	113	8	10	77	41	4.24	108	.271	.353	93	.215	-2*	100	5	—	0.3
1894	Phi N	23	13	.639	41	34	31-1	1	298	347	201	13	17	96	76	4.08	126	.288	.349	145	.338	9*	105	31	—	3.5
1895	Phi N	26	14	.650	41	37	33-1	1	335	403	233	7	15	83	93	4.49	107	.293	.340	155-3-1	.290	7*	111	9	—	1.5
1896	Phi N	20	21	.488	45	41	35-1	1	359	459	282	17	20	112	97	4.79	90	.308	.365	157-0-8	.185	-7*	114	-26	—	-2.6
1897	Phi N	16	20	.444	40	37	35-2	2	317.1	376	204	5	28	76	88	4.23	99	.292	.345	139-1-2	.252	2*	96	-3	—	0.0
1898	StL N	15	29	.341	**50**	**47**	**42**	1	**397.1**	465	259	14	25	83	89	3.90	97	.290	.335	157-1-5	.242	3*	84	-12	—	-0.3
1899	Cin N	9	10	.474	25	19	16-2	2	180.1	207	110	7	11	43	35	4.09	96	.287	.337	71-0-3	.239	-1	81	-3	—	-0.4
Total	9	120	117	.506	271	235	209-7	9	2091	2476	1423	74	126	583	529	4.22	104	.291	.346	931-5-19	.252	12	100	4	—	2.2
TAYLOR, JACK	John W.; B1.14.1874 New Straitsville OH; D3.4.1938 Columbus OH; BR/TR/5´10˝/170; d9.25																									
1898	Chi N	5	0	1.000	5	5	5	0	41	32	12	0	1	10	11	2.20	163	.213	.267	15	.200	1	95	8	—	1.0
1899	Chi N	18	21	.462	41	39	39-1	0	354.2	380	223	6	22	84	67	3.76	100	.274	.325	139-0-1	.266	10*	120	1	—	1.0
1900	Chi N	10	17	.370	28	26	25-2	1	222.1	226	130	4	8	58	57	2.55	141	.263	.316	81-1-3	.235	2	63	18	—	2.0
1901	Chi N	13	19	.406	33	31	30	0	275.2	341	165	5	8	44	68	3.36	96	.302	.332	106-0-2	.217	2*	92	-7	—	-0.4
1902	Chi N	23	11	.676	37	34	34-**8**	1	333.2	273	86	2	12	45	88	**1.29**	**209**	.224	**.258**	189-0-9	.233	3*	94	**51**	—	**6.1**
1903	Chi N	21	14	.600	37	33	33-1	1	312.1	277	137	2	5	57	83	2.45	128	.235	.273	126-0-3	.222	4*	109	23	—	2.8
1904	StL N	20	19	.513	41	39	**39**-2	1	352	297	133	5	13	82	103	2.22	121	.220	.271	133-1-1	.211	4*	103	17	—	2.4
1905	StL N	15	21	.417	37	34	34-3	1	309	302	155	10	11	85	102	3.44	87	.259	.315	121-0-2	.190	4*	75	-14	—	-1.2
1906	StL N	8	9	.471	17	17	17-1	0	155	133	50	3	7	47	27	2.15	122	.227	.292	53-0-2	.208	3	86	8	—	1.3
	Chi N	12	3	.800	17	16	15-2	0	147.1	116	42	1	6	39	34	1.83	144	.223	.285	53	.208	2	121	13	—	1.6
	Year	20	12	.625	34	33	32-3	0	302.1	249	92	4	13	86	61	1.99	132	.225	.289	106-0-2	.208	5	103	20	—	2.9
1907	Chi N	7	5	.583	18	13	8	0	123	127	62	3	1	33	22	3.29	76	.268	.318	47	.191	0	101	-9	—	-0.9
Total	10	152	139	.522	311	287	279-20	5	2626	2504	1195	41	94	584	662	2.65	115	.250	.297	1063-2-23	.222	34	97	109	—	15.7
TAYLOR, KERRY	Kerry Thomas; B1.25.1971 Bemidji MN; BR/TR/6´3˝/200; d4.13; [DL 1995 SD N 31]																									
1993	SD N	0	5	.000	36	7	0	0-0	68.1	72	53	5	4	49-0	45	6.45	64	.277	.396	12-0-1	.000	-1	81	-16	0	-1.2
1994	SD N	0	0	ø	1	1	0	0-0	4.1	9	4	1	1	1-0	3	8.31	50	.409	.458	2	.000	-0	88	-2	0	-0.1
Total	2	0	5	.000	37	8	0	0-0	72.2	81	57	6	5	50-0	48	6.56	63	.287	.400	14-0-1	.000	-2	82	-18	31	-1.3
TAYLOR, DUMMY	Luther Haden; B2.21.1875 Oskaloosa KS; D8.22.1958 Jacksonville IL; BR/TR/6´1˝/160; d8.27																									
1900	NY N	4	3	.571	11	7	6	0	62.1	74	31	0	5	24	16	2.45	147	.294	.367	22-0-1	.136	-1	98	7	—	0.4
1901	NY N	18	27	.400	**45**	**43**	37-4	0	353.1	377	193	8	16	112	136	3.18	104	.271	.333	136-0-1	.132	-8	70	-1	—	-0.8
1902	Cle A	1	3	.250	4	4	4-1	0	34	37	17	0	2	8	8	1.59	217	.278	.329	10	.100	-0	52	5	—	0.5
	NY N	7	15	.318	26	25	18	0	200.2	194	98	4	15	55	87	2.29	123	.254	.317	65-0-2	.092	-5	61	5	—	-0.1
1903	NY N	13	13	.500	33	31	18-1	0	244.2	306	143	6	4	89	94	4.23	79	.314	.374	82-0-6	.146	-2	116	-19	—	-1.9
1904	NY N	21	15	.583	37	36	29-5	0	296.1	231	100	6	9	75	138	2.34	117	.214	.270	102-0-6	.157	-1*	108	15	—	1.8
1905	NY N	16	9	.640	32	28	18-4	0	213.1	200	85	5	8	51	91	2.66	110	.247	.298	69-0-10	.130	-1	125	7	—	0.7
1906	NY N	17	9	.654	31	27	13-2	0	213	186	81	3	6	57	91	2.20	119	.233	.289	76-0-2	.184	0	127	6	—	0.7
1907	NY N	11	7	.611	28	21	11-3	1	171	145	66	1	3	46	56	2.42	102	.232	.288	48-0-5	.125	-1*	94	0	—	-0.2
1908	NY N	8	5	.615	27	15	6-1	2	127.2	127	56	5	4	34	50	2.33	104	.253	.306	35-0-5	.229	2	138	-3	—	-0.2
Total	9	116	106	.523	274	237	160-21	3	1916.1	1877	870	38	72	551	767	2.75	107	.256	.314	645-0-38	.144	-17	100	22	—	0.9
TAYLOR, WILEY	Philip Wiley; B3.18.1888 Wamego KS; D7.8.1954 Westmoreland KS; BR/TR/6´1˝/175; d9.6																									
1911	Det A	0	2	.000	3	2	1	0	19	18	11	0	1	10	9	3.79	91	.247	.345	6	.000	-1	0	-1	—	-0.2
1912	Chi A	0	1	.000	3	3	0	0	20	21	12	0	0	14	4	4.95	65	.309	.427	5	.000	-1	115	-3	—	-0.2
1913	StL A	0	2	.000	5	4	1	0	31.2	33	19	0	0	16	12	4.83	61	.284	.371	10	.000	-1	120	-5	—	-0.4
1914	StL A	2	5	.286	16	8	2-1	0	50	41	24	0	2	25	20	3.42	79	.209	.305	12	.167	-0	74	-3	—	-0.5
Total	4	2	10	.167	27	17	4-1	0	120.2	113	66	0	3	65	45	4.10	72	.249	.347	33	.061	-3	81	-12	—	-1.3
TAYLOR, SCOTT	Rodney Scott; B8.2.1967 Defiance OH; BL/TL/6´1˝/(190–195); [BosA88 28/719]; d9.17; Col Bowling Green																									
1992	Bos A	1	1	.500	4	1	0	0-0	14.2	13	8	4	0	4-0	7	4.91	87	.245	.298	0	ø	0	64	-1	0	-0.1
1993	Bos A	0	1	.000	16	0	0	0-0	11	14	10	1	1	12-3	8	8.18	57	.311	.466	0	ø	0	—	-3	0	-0.3
Total	2	1	2	.333	20	1	0	0-0	25.2	27	18	5	1	16-3	15	6.31	70	.276	.383	0	ø	0	64	-4	0	-0.4
TAYLOR, RON	Ronald Wesley; B12.13.1937 Toronto ON, Can.; BR/TR/6´1˝/(180–200); d4.11																									
1962	Cle A	2	2	.500	8	4	1	0	33.1	36	23	6	1	13-4	15	5.94	65	.281	.347	11	.273	0	98	-7	0	-0.7
1963	StL N	9	7	.563	54	9	2	11	133.1	119	44	10	4	30-6	91	2.84	125	.243	.289	32-0-2	.031	-3	67	12	0	1.2
1964	†StL N	8	4	.667	63	2	0	7	101.1	109	56	15	1	33-7	69	4.62	82	.274	.329	15	.133	-0	58	-6	0	-0.8

YEAR	TM LG	W	L	PCT	G	GS	CG-SHO	SV-BS	IP	H	R	HR	HB	BB-IB	SO	ERA	AERA	OAV	OOB	AB-HR-SH	AVG	PB	SUP	APR	DL	PW
1965	StL N	2	1	.667	25	0	0	1	43.2	43	24	6	1	15-4	26	4.53	85	.261	.321	5	.400	1	—	-3	0	-0.1
	Hou N	1	5	.167	32	1	0	4	57.2	68	42	5	5	16-6	37	6.40	52	.305	.359	13	.000	-1	104	-18	0	-2.2
	Year	3	6	.333	57	1	0	5	101.1	111	66	11	6	31-10	63	5.60	64	.286	.343	18	.111	-1	98	-21	0	-2.3
1966	Hou N	2	3	.400	36	1	0	0	64.2	89	47	5	5	10-4	29	5.71	60	.333	.364	12	.167	0	77	-17	44	-1.3
1967	NY N	4	6	.400	50	0	0	8	73	60	21	1	1	23-14	46	2.34	145	.230	.290	7-0-1	.000	-1	—	9	26	1.3
1968	NY N	1	5	.167	58	0	0	13	76.2	64	24	4	1	18-9	49	2.70	112	.228	.275	9	.000	-1	—	3	0	0.4
1969	†NY N	9	4	.692	59	0	0	13-4	76	61	23	7	1	24-6	42	2.72	134	.228	.292	4	.250	0	—	9	0	1.9
1970	NY N	5	4	.556	57	0	0	13-6	66.1	65	31	5	0	16-10	28	3.93	103	.265	.305	4-0-1	.000	-0	—	2	0	0.3
1971	NY N	2	2	.500	45	0	0	2-1	69	71	28	7	1	11-6	32	3.65	94	.269	.300	4	.250	0	—	0	0	0.0
1972	SD N	0	0	ø	4	0	0	0-0	5	9	7	5	0	0-0	0	12.60	26	.375	.375	0	ø	0	—	-5	0	-0.3
Total	11	45	43	.511	491	17	3	72-11	800	794	370	76	21	209-76	464	3.93	91	.264	.312	116-0-4	.103	-5	78	-21	70	-0.3
TAYLOR, SCOTT	Scott Michael; B10.3.1966 Topeka KS; BR/TR/6´3˝/200; [SeaA88 15/383]; d7.28; Col Kansas																									
1995	Tex A	1	2	.333	3	3	0	0-0	15.1	25	16	6	0	5-0	10	9.39	52	.379	.423	0	ø	0	58	-7	0	-1.0
TAYLOR, TERRY	Terry Derrell; B7.28.1964 Crestview FL; BR/TR/6´1˝/180; [SeaA82 4/86]; d8.19; [DL 1989 Sea A 113]																									
1988	Sea A	0	1	.000	5	5	0	0-0	23	26	17	2	0	11-1	9	6.26	67	.295	.370	0	ø	0	118	-5	0	-0.3
TAYLOR, PETE	Vernon Charles; B11.26.1927 Severn MD; D11.17.2003 Annapolis MD; BR/TR/6´1˝/170; d5.2																									
1952	StL A	0	0	ø	1	0	0	0	2	4	3	0	0	3	0	13.50	29	.500	.636	0	ø	0	—	-2	0	-0.1
TAYLOR, WADE	Wade Eric; B10.19.1965 Mobile AL; BR/TR/6´1˝/185; d6.2; Col Miami																									
1991	NY A	7	12	.368	23	22	0	0-0	116.1	144	85	13	7	53-0	72	6.27	66	.314	.388	0	ø	0	91	-25	0	-3.4
TAYLOR, BILLY	William Henry "Bollicky Bill"; B1855 Washington DC; D5.14.1900 Jacksonville FL; BR/TR/5´11.5˝/204; d5.21; ▲																									
1881	Wor N	0	1	.000	1	1	1	0	8	15	13	0	—	6	0	7.88	38	.366	.447	28	.107	-0*	18	-4	—	-0.4
	Cle N	0	0	ø	1	0	0	0	3	0	0	0	—	1	2	0.00	ø	.000	.100	103	.243	-0*	—	1	—	0.0
	Year	0	1	.000	2	1	1	0	11	15	13	0	—	7	2	5.73	51	.300	.386	131	.214	-0	19	-3	—	-0.4
1882	Pit AA	0	1	.000	1	0	0	0	5	11	10	0	—	4	1	16.20	16	.407	.484	299-3	.281	0*	—	-6	—	-0.7
1883	Pit AA	4	7	.364	19	9	8	0	127	166	115	4	—	34	41	5.39	60	.296	.337	369-2	.260	3*	90	-28	—	-1.7
1884	StL U	25	4	.862	33	29	29-2	**4**	263	222	97	2	—	40	154	1.68	142	.213	.243	186-3	.366	16*	142	21	—	**2.8**
	Phi AA	18	12	.600	30	30	30-1	0	260	232	118	3	12	44	130	2.53	134	.219	.258	111	.252	3	89	21	—	2.5
1885	Phi AA	1	5	.167	6	6	6	0	52.1	68	35	0	1	9	11	3.27	105	.343	.375	21	.190	-1	63	1	—	0.0
1886	Bal AA	1	6	.143	8	8	8	0	72.1	87	63	1	2	20	37	5.72	60	.284	.332	39	.308	1*	113	-15	—	-1.0
1887	Phi AA	1	0	1.000	1	1	1	0	9	10	5	1	0	7	0	3.00	143	.286	.405	4	.250	-0	89	1	—	0.1
Total	7	50	36	.581	100	84	83-3	4	799.2	811	456	11	15	165	376	3.17	96	.248	.287	1160-8	.277	23	107	-8	—	1.6
TAYLOR, BILLY	William Howell; B10.16.1961 Monticello FL; BR/TR/6´8˝/(200–240); [TexA80*2/39]; d4.5; Col Abraham Baldwin (GA) JC; [DL 1995 Oak A 160]																									
1994	Oak A	1	3	.250	41	0	0	1-2	46.1	38	24	4	2	18-5	48	3.50	128	.220	.299	0	ø	0	—	3	16	0.2
1996	Oak A	6	3	.667	55	0	0	17-2	60.1	52	30	5	4	25-4	67	4.33	115	.231	.315	0	ø	0	—	5	28	0.9
1997	Oak A	3	4	.429	72	0	0	23-7	73	70	32	3	5	36-9	66	3.82	120	.254	.348	0	ø	0	—	7	0	1.0
1998	Oak A	4	9	.308	70	0	0	33-4	73	71	37	7	3	22-4	58	3.58	129	.255	.312	0	ø	0	—	7	0	1.3
1999	Oak A	1	5	.167	43	0	0	26-7	43	48	23	3	2	14-3	38	3.98	119	.287	.346	0	ø	0	—	3	0	0.5
	NY N	0	1	.000	18	0	0	0-1	13.1	20	12	2	0	9-5	14	8.10	54	.345	.433	0	ø	0	—	-6	0	-0.4
2000	TB A	1	3	.250	17	0	0	0-2	13.2	13	13	2	2	9-2	13	8.56	57	.255	.387	0	ø	0	—	-5	0	-0.9
2001	Pit N	0	0	ø	1	0	0	0-0	2	2	1	1	0	0-0	3	4.50	99	.250	.250	0	ø	0	—	0	0	0.0
Total	7	16	28	.364	317	0	0	100-25	324.2	314	172	27	18	133-32	307	4.21	111	.254	.332	0	ø	0	—	14	204	2.6
TEACHOUT, BUD	Arthur John; B2.27.1904 Los Angeles CA; D5.11.1985 Laguna Beach CA; BR/TL/6´2˝/183; d5.12; Col Occidental																									
1930	Chi N	11	4	.733	40	16	6	0	153	178	80	16	0	48	59	4.06	120	.296	.348	63-0-3	.270	3*	133	14	—	1.3
1931	Chi N	1	2	.333	27	3	1	0	61.1	79	40	6	1	28	14	5.72	67	.305	.375	21	.238	0*	96	-10	—	-0.5
1932	StL N	0	0	ø	1	0	0	0	1	2	1	0	0	0	0	0.00	ø	.400	.400	0	ø	0	—	0	—	0.0
Total	3	12	6	.667	68	19	7	0	215.1	259	121	22	1	76	73	4.51	102	.299	.356	84-0-3	.262	3	131	4	—	0.8
TEBEAU, GEORGE	George E. "White Wings"; B12.26.1861 St.Louis MO; D2.4.1923 Denver CO; BR/TR/5´9˝/175; d4.16; b–Patsy; ▲																									
1887	Cin AA	0	1	.000	1	1	1	0	8	21	16	0	1	3	1	13.50	32	.488	.532	318-4	.296	0*	88	-7	—	-0.5
1890	Tol AA	0	0	ø	1	0	0	0	5	9	8	0	0	5	0	9.00	44	.375	.483	381-1	.268	0*	—	-3	—	-0.1
Total	2	0	1	.000	2	1	1	0	13	30	24	0	1	8	1	11.77	36	.448	.513	699-5	.280	1	88	-10	—	-0.6
TEDROW, AL	Allen Seymour; B12.14.1891 Westerville OH; D1.23.1958 Westerville OH; BR/TL/6´0˝/180; d9.15																									
1914	Cle A	1	2	.333	4	3	1	0	22.1	19	6	0	3	14	4	1.21	239	.235	.367	6	.167	0	67	3	—	0.5
TEJEDA, ROBINSON	Robinson Garcia; B3.24.1982 Bani, D.R.; BR/TR/6´3˝/(190–230); d5.10																									
2005	Phi N	4	3	.571	26	13	0	0-0	85.2	67	36	5	8	51-4	72	3.57	122	.218	.342	20-0-5	.100	-1	109	7	0	0.4
2006	Tex A	5	5	.500	14	14	0	0-0	73.2	83	40	10	3	32-1	40	4.28	109	.288	.360	2-0-1	.000	-0	83	2	0	0.2
Total	2	9	8	.529	40	27	0	0-0	159.1	150	76	15	11	83-5	112	3.90	115	.252	.351	22-0-6	.091	-1	95	9	0	0.6
TEJERA, MICHAEL	Michael; B10.18.1976 Havana, Cuba; BL/TL/5´9˝/(175–190); [FlaN95 6/149]; d9.8; [DL 2000 Fla N 181]																									
1999	Fla N	0	0	ø	3	1	0	0-0	6.1	10	8	1	0	5-0	7	11.37	39	.385	.484	0	ø	0	105	-5	0	-0.2
2002	Fla N	8	8	.500	47	18	0	1-2	139.2	144	71	17	6	60-3	95	4.45	88	.269	.347	37-1-2	.189	2*	84	-7	0	-0.5
2003	†Fla N	3	4	.429	50	6	0	2-0	81	82	44	6	1	36-3	58	4.67	88	.267	.345	15-0-1	.067	-1	84	-5	0	-0.4
2004	Fla N	0	1	.000	2	2	0	0-0	4	6	8	0	1	6-0	3	18.00	23	.375	.565	0	ø	0	56	-6	0	-0.9
	Tex A	0	0	ø	6	0	0	0-0	5.1	9	6	1	1	3-0	7	10.13	49	.360	.448	0	ø	0	—	-3	0	-0.1
2005	Tex A	0	0	ø	3	0	0	0-0	2	5	3	1	1	1-0	2	13.50	34	.455	.538	0	ø	0	—	-2	0	-0.1
Total	5	11	13	.458	111	27	0	3-2	238.1	256	140	26	10	111-6	172	5.14	78	.278	.360	52-1-3	.154	1	82	-28	181	-2.2
TEKULVE, KENT	Kenton Charles; B3.5.1947 Cincinnati OH; BR/TR/6´4˝/(160–190); d5.20; Col Marietta																									
1974	Pit N	1	1	.500	8	0	0	0-2	9	12	6	1	1	5-2	6	6.00	58	.343	.419	0	ø	0	—	-2	0	-0.4
1975	†Pit N	1	2	.333	34	0	0	5-0	56	43	20	2	1	23-6	28	2.25	159	.215	.296	11	.091	-0	—	7	0	0.6
1976	Pit N	5	3	.625	64	0	0	9-3	102.2	91	30	3	0	25-7	68	2.45	144	.241	.287	9-0-1	.000	-1	—	13	0	1.2
1977	Pit N	10	1	.909	72	0	0	7-7	103	89	41	5	1	33-6	59	3.06	132	.236	.296	12	.250	0	—	10	0	1.3
1978	Pit N	8	7	.533	**91**	0	0	31-9	135.1	115	44	5	2	55-18	77	2.33	160	.228	.304	21	.095	-1	—	19	0	3.1
1979	†Pit N	10	8	.556	**94**	0	0	31-6	134.1	109	46	5	2	49-20	75	2.75	143	.222	.295	15-0-1	.133	-0	—	17	0	3.0
1980	Pit N☆	8	12	.400	78	0	0	21-11	93	96	39	6	1	40-16	47	3.39	109	.267	.342	9	.000	-1	—	3	0	0.6
1981	Pit N	5	5	.500	45	0	0	3-5	65	61	19	1	1	17-5	34	2.49	146	.250	.299	2	.000	-0	—	9	0	1.4
1982	Pit N	12	8	.600	**85**	0	0	20-10	128.2	113	47	7	3	46-23	66	2.87	131	.237	.305	14-0-1	.071	-1	—	12	0	2.1
1983	Pit N	7	5	.583	76	0	0	18-6	99	78	27	1	0	36-12	52	1.64	229	.223	.293	8-0-1	.000	-1	—	20	0	2.9
1984	Pit N	3	9	.250	72	0	0	13-4	88	86	30	4	1	33-12	36	2.66	137	.262	.330	7	.000	-1	—	9	0	1.5
1985	Pit N	0	0	ø	3	0	0	0-0	3.1	7	7	1	0	5-1	4	16.20	22	.467	.600	0	ø	0	—	-5	0	-0.2
	Phi N	4	10	.286	58	0	0	14-8	72.1	67	28	4	2	25-9	36	2.99	124	.246	.312	3	.000	-0	—	5	0	1.1
	Year	4	10	.286	61	0	0	14-8	75.2	74	35	5	2	30-10	40	3.57	104	.258	.330	3	.000	-0	—	1	0	0.9
1986	Phi N	11	5	.688	73	0	0	4-2	110	99	35	2	0	25-10	57	2.54	154	.240	.281	5	.000	-0	—	16	0	2.3
1987	Phi N	6	4	.600	**90**	0	0	3-3	105	96	38	8	0	29-13	60	3.09	139	.243	.293	1-0-1	.000	0	—	14	0	1.4
1988	Phi N	3	7	.300	70	0	0	4-3	80	87	34	3	2	22-11	43	3.60	100	.276	.326	2	.000	-0	—	1	19	0.1
1989	Cin N	0	3	.000	37	0	0	1-2	52	56	35	5	0	23-8	31	5.02	72	.272	.342	2	.500	0	—	-9	0	-0.5
Total	16	94	90	.511	1050	0	0	184-81	1436.2	1305	526	63	17	491-179	779	2.85	133	.244	.307	121-0-5	.083	-6	—	139	19	21.5
TELEMACO, AMAURY	Amaury (Regalado); B1.19.1974 Higuey, D.R.; BR/TR/6´3˝/(210–235); d5.16																									
1996	Chi N	5	7	.417	25	17	0	0-0	97.1	108	67	20	3	31-2	64	5.46	80	.281	.336	29-0-4	.103	-1	113	-12	15	-1.5
1997	Chi N	0	3	.000	10	5	0	0-0	38	47	26	4	0	11-0	29	6.16	70	.303	.347	9	.222	0	68	-7	0	-0.4
1998	Chi N	1	1	.500	14	0	0	0-0	27.2	23	12	5	0	13-0	18	3.90	113	.219	.305	6	.167	-0	—	2	0	0.1
	Ari N	6	9	.400	27	18	0	0-0	121	127	63	13	4	33-2	60	3.94	109	.271	.321	29-0-1	.069	-1	79	2	0	0.1
	Year	7	10	.412	41	18	0	0-0	148.2	150	75	18	4	46-2	78	3.93	109	.262	.318	35-0-1	.086	-1	78	4	0	0.2
1999	Ari N	1	0	1.000	5	0	0	0-0	6	7	5	2	0	6-1	2	7.50	62	.333	.481	0	ø	0	—	-2	33	-0.2
	Phi N	3	0	1.000	44	0	0	0-1	47	45	29	8	2	20-3	41	5.55	84	.250	.330	0	ø	0	—	-4	0	-0.2
	Year	4	0	1.000	49	0	0	0-1	53	52	34	10	2	26-4	43	5.77	81	.259	.348	0	ø	0	—	-5	0	-0.4

YEAR	TM LG	W	L	PCT	G	GS	CG-SHO	SV-BS	IP	H	R	HR	HB	BB-IB	SO	ERA	AERA	OAV	OOB	AB-HR-SH	AVG	PB	SUP	APR	DL	PW
2000	Phi N	1	3	.250	13	2	0	0-1	24.1	25	22	6	0	14-0	22	6.66	69	.275	.364	4	.000	-0	50	-7	0	-1.0
2001	Phi N	5	5	.500	24	14	1	0-0	89.1	93	59	15	9	32-3	59	5.54	74	.274	.350	21-0-2	.095	-0	119	-15	0	-1.5
2003	Phi N	1	4	.200	8	8	0	0-0	45.1	41	22	5	7	11-2	29	3.97	100	.238	.309	14-0-1	.286	2	88	0	0	0.2
2004	Phi N	0	2	.000	42	0	0	0-0	54.1	51	27	12	0	19-2	32	4.31	103	.249	.313	4	.000	-0	—	1	51	0.0
2005	Phi N	0	1	.000	7	0	0	0-0	10.2	5	5	2	0	4-0	8	4.22	103	.139	.220	0	ø	0	—	0	0	0.0
Total	9	23	35	.397	219	64	1	0-2	561	572	337	92	25	194-15	364	4.94	87	.265	.330	116-0-8	.121	-1	94	-42	99	-4.4
TELFORD, ANTHONY	Anthony Charles; B3.6.1966 San Jose CA; BR/TR/6´0˝/(175–195); [BalA87 3/65]; d8.19; Col San Jose St.																									
1990	Bal A	3	3	.500	8	8	0	0-0	36.1	43	22	4	1	19-0	20	4.95	77	.295	.375	0	ø	0	98	-5	0	-0.7
1991	Bal A	0	0	ø	9	1	0	0-0	26.2	27	12	3	0	6-1	24	4.05	98	.265	.303	0	ø	0	115	0	0	0.0
1993	Bal A	0	0	ø	3	0	0	0-0	7.1	11	8	3	1	1-0	6	9.82	46	.344	.382	0	ø	0	—	-4	0	-0.2
1997	Mon N	4	6	.400	65	0	0	1-4	89	77	34	11	5	33-4	61	3.24	129	.236	.315	15-0-1	.200	0	—	10	0	1.2
1998	Mon N	3	6	.333	77	0	0	1-4	91	85	45	9	4	36-1	59	3.86	109	.247	.322	4	.250	0	—	3	0	0.3
1999	Mon N	5	4	.556	79	0	0	2-7	96	112	52	3	3	38-3	69	3.94	113	.295	.359	2-0-2	.000	0	—	4	0	0.4
2000	Mon N	5	4	.556	64	0	0	3-2	78.1	76	38	10	5	23-1	68	3.79	124	.257	.317	2-0-1	.000	-0	—	7	14	0.7
2001	Mon N	0	1	.000	8	0	0	0-0	7	14	12	2	1	5-1	5	10.29	42	.412	.500	0	ø	0	—	-6	24	-0.7
2002	Tex A	2	1	.667	20	0	0	1-1	23.2	30	18	3	4	15-2	19	6.46	74	.316	.422	0	ø	0	—	-4	0	-0.5
Total	9	22	25	.468	333	9	0	8-18	455.1	475	241	48	24	176-13	331	4.17	104	.271	.342	23-0-4	.174	0	90	5	38	0.5
TELGHEDER, DAVE	David William; B11.11.1966 Middletown NY; BR/TR/6´3˝/(211–223); [NYN89 31/814]; d6.12; Col Massachusetts																									
1993	NY N	6	2	.750	24	7	0	0-0	75.2	82	40	10	4	21-2	35	4.76	84	.276	.331	15-0-4	.067	-0	128	-4	0	-0.4
1994	NY N	0	1	.000	6	0	0	0-0	10	11	8	2	0	8-2	4	7.20	58	.282	.404	0	ø	0	—	-3	0	-0.3
1995	NY N	1	2	.333	7	4	0	0-0	25.2	34	18	4	0	7-3	16	5.61	72	.318	.357	6-0-1	.333	1	95	-5	0	-0.4
1996	Oak A	4	7	.364	16	14	1-1	0-0	79.1	92	42	12	1	26-1	43	4.65	107	.292	.345	0	ø	0	87	4	0	0.4
1997	Oak A	4	6	.400	20	19	0	0-0	101	134	71	15	2	35-1	55	6.06	76	.324	.373	2	.000	-0	125	-15	76	-1.2
1998	Oak A	0	1	.000	8	2	0	0-0	20	19	12	4	2	6-0	5	3.60	129	.235	.303	0	ø	0	70	1	117	0.0
Total	6	15	19	.441	81	46	1-1	0-0	311.2	372	191	47	9	103-9	158	5.23	86	.297	.351	23-0-5	.130	-0	110	-22	193	-1.9
TELLMANN, TOM	Thomas John; B3.29.1954 Warren PA; BR/TR/6´3˝/(184–185); [SDN76 11/245]; d6.9; Col Grand Canyon																									
1979	SD N	0	0	ø	1	0	0	0-0	2.2	7	5	1	0	0-0	1	16.88	21	.467	.467	1	.000	-0	—	-4	0	-0.2
1980	SD N	3	0	1.000	6	2	2	1-0	22.1	23	5	0	0	8-0	9	1.61	212	.264	.326	8	.125	-0	131	4	0	0.6
1983	Mil A	9	4	.692	44	0	0	8-4	99.2	95	34	7	2	35-4	48	2.80	135	.259	.324	0	ø	0	—	12	0	1.7
1984	Mil A	6	3	.667	50	0	0	4-3	81	82	28	6	1	31-10	28	2.78	140	.272	.338	0	ø	0	—	10	21	1.2
1985	Oak A	0	0	ø	11	0	0	0-0	21.1	33	12	3	1	9-1	8	5.06	77	.347	.406	0	ø	0	—	-2	119	-0.1
Total	5	18	7	.720	112	2	2	13-7	227	240	84	17	4	83-15	94	3.05	124	.277	.341	9	.111	-0	131	20	140	3.2
TEMPLETON, CHUCK	Charles Sherman; B6.1.1932 Detroit MI; D10.9.1997 Irving TX; BR/TL/6´3˝/210; d9.9																									
1955	Bro N	0	1	.000	4	0	0	0	4.2	5	7	2	1	5-0	3	11.57	35	.294	.478	0	ø	0	—	-4	0	-0.7
1956	Bro N	0	1	.000	6	2	0	0	16.1	20	13	2	0	10-0	8	6.61	60	.294	.380	3-0-1	.000	-0	111	-4	0	-0.3
Total	2	0	2	.000	10	2	0	0	21	25	20	4	1	15-0	11	7.71	52	.294	.402	3-0-1	.000	-0	111	-8	0	-1.0
TENER, JOHN	John Kinley; B7.25.1863 Co. Tyrone, Ireland; D5.19.1946 Pittsburgh PA; BR/TR/6´4˝/180; d6.8.1885																									
1888	Chi N	7	5	.583	12	12	11-1	0	102	90	59	6	8	25	39	2.74	111	.228	.288	46	.196	-0	101	1	—	0.1
1889	Chi N	15	15	.500	35	30	28-1	0	287	302	192	16	7	105	105	3.64	114	.263	.328	150-1	.273	5*	112	14	—	1.7
1890	Pit P	3	11	.214	14	14	13	0	117	160	147	6	5	70	30	7.31	53	.312	.400	63-2	.190	2*	122	-43	—	-3.1
Total	3	25	31	.446	61	56	52-2	0	506	552	398	28	20	200	174	4.30	90	.268	.339	259-3	.239	6	112	-28	—	-1.3
TENNANT, JIM	James McDonnell; B3.3.1907 Shepherdstown WV; D4.16.1967 Trumbull CT; BR/TR/6´1˝/190; d9.28; Col George Washington																									
1929	NY N	0	0	ø	1	0	0	0	1	1	0	0	0	0	1	0.00	ø	.333	.333	0	ø	0	—	1	—	0.0
TENNEY, FRED	Fred Clay; B7.9.1859 Marlborough NH; D6.15.1919 Fall River MA; d4.28; Col Brown; ▲																									
1884	Bos U	3	1	.750	4	4	4	0	35	31	21	0	—	5	18	2.31	103	.221	.248	17	.118	-2	148	-1	—	-0.3
	Wil U	0	1	.000	1	1	1	0	8	6	5	0	—	4	10	1.13	238	.194	.286	3	.000	-1	64	1	—	0.0
	Year	3	2	.600	5	5	5	0	43	37	26	0	—	9	28	2.09	116	.216	.256	20	.100	-3	130	0	—	-0.3
TERLECKI, BOB	Robert Joseph; B2.14.1945 Trenton NJ; BR/TR/5´8˝/185; d8.16																									
1972	Phi N	0	0	ø	9	0	0	0-0	13.1	16	9	2	0	10-0	5	4.73	76	.308	.406	0	ø	0	—	-2	0	-0.1
TERLECKY, GREG	Gregory John; B3.20.1952 Culver City CA; BR/TR/6´3˝/190; [StLN70 5/109]; d6.12																									
1975	StL N	0	1	.000	20	0	0	0-0	30.1	38	16	4	0	12-5	13	4.45	85	.306	.365	3	.333	0	—	-1	0	0.0
TERPKO, JEFF	Jeffrey Michael; B10.16.1950 Sayre PA; BR/TR/6´0˝/(170–180); [TexA68 5/92]; d9.21																									
1974	Tex A	0	0	ø	3	0	0	0-0	7	6	1	0	0	4-0	3	1.29	279	.231	.333	0	ø	0	—	2	0	0.1
1976	Tex A	3	3	.500	32	0	0	0-3	52.2	42	15	3	0	29-1	24	2.39	150	.223	.321	0	ø	0	—	7	0	0.8
1977	Mon N	0	1	.000	13	0	0	0-0	20.2	28	13	2	0	15-1	14	5.66	68	.346	.448	1	.000	-0	—	-4	0	-0.2
Total	3	3	4	.429	48	0	0	0-3	80.1	76	29	5	0	48-2	41	3.14	117	.258	.357	1	.000	-0	—	5	0	0.7
TERRELL, WALT	Charles Walter; B5.11.1958 Jeffersonville IN; BL/TR/6´2˝/(205–215); [TexA80 33/764]; d9.18; Col Morehead St.																									
1982	NY N	0	3	.000	3	3	0	0-0	21	22	12	2	0	14-2	8	3.43	107	.268	.375	5-0-1	.400	1	32	-1	0	0.0
1983	NY N	8	8	.500	21	20	4-2	0-0	133.2	123	57	7	2	55-7	59	3.57	103	.251	.326	44-3-3	.182	3	77	3	0	0.7
1984	NY N	11	12	.478	33	33	3-1	0-0	215	232	99	16	4	80-1	114	3.52	102	.282	.345	75-0-1	.080	-4	106	1	0	-0.3
1985	Det A	15	10	.600	34	34	5-3	0-0	229	221	107	9	4	95-5	130	3.85	107	.255	.329	0	ø	0	102	8	0	0.9
1986	Det A	15	12	.556	34	33	9-2	0-0	217.1	199	116	30	3	98-5	93	4.56	91	.245	.328	0	ø	0	104	-7	0	-0.7
1987	†Det A	17	10	.630	35	35	10-1	0-0	244.2	254	123	30	3	94-7	143	4.05	105	.268	.333	0	ø	0	115	7	0	0.6
1988	Det A	7	16	.304	29	29	11-1	0-0	206.1	199	101	20	2	78-8	84	3.97	97	.258	.326	0	ø	0	92	-3	26	-0.3
1989	SD N	5	13	.278	19	19	4-1	0-0	123.1	134	65	14	0	26-1	63	4.01	87	.277	.313	40-0-1	.100	-0	73	-8	0	-0.9
	NY A	6	5	.545	13	13	1-1	0-0	83	102	52	9	2	24-0	30	5.20	75	.307	.356	0	ø	0	122	-12	0	-1.3
1990	Pit N	2	7	.222	16	16	0	0-0	82.2	98	59	13	4	33-1	34	5.88	62	.295	.364	28-0-1	.107	-1	118	-20	0	-2.0
	Det A	6	4	.600	13	12	0	0-0	75.1	86	39	7	8	24-3	30	4.54	88	.290	.358	0	ø	0	107	-4	0	-0.5
1991	Det A	12	14	.462	35	33	8-2	0-0	218.2	257	115	16	2	79-10	80	4.24	99	.301	.358	0	ø	0	103	-3	0	-0.3
1992	Det A	7	10	.412	36	14	1	0-1	136.2	163	86	14	3	48-10	61	5.20	77	.298	.354	0	ø	0	116	-18	0	-2.0
Total	11	111	124	.472	321	294	56-14	0-1	1986.2	2090	1031	187	37	748-60	929	4.22	94	.274	.339	192-3-7	.120	-1	102	-57	26	-6.1
TERRY, JOHN	John Burchard; B11.1.1879 Waterbury CT; D4.27.1933 Kansas City MO; d9.17																									
1902	Det A	0	1	.000	1	1	1	0	5	8	3	0	0	1	0	3.60	101	.364	.391	2	.000	-0	20	0	—	-0.1
1903	StL A	1	1	.500	3	1	1	0	17.2	21	6	0	3	4	2	2.55	114	.296	.359	9	.000	-1	245	1	—	0.0
Total	2	1	2	.333	4	2	2	0	22.2	29	9	0	3	5	2	2.78	111	.312	.366	11	.000	-2	128	1	—	-0.1
TERRY, YANK	Lancelot Yank; B2.11.1911 Bedford IN; D11.4.1979 Bloomington IN; BR/TR/6´1˝/180; d8.3																									
1940	Bos A	1	0	1.000	4	1	0	0	19.1	24	19	2	0	11	9	8.84	51	.304	.389	8	.250	0	234	-8	—	-0.4
1942	Bos A	6	5	.545	20	11	3	1	85	82	48	5	2	43	37	3.92	95	.248	.339	27-0-1	.111	-1	125	-4	0	-0.6
1943	Bos A	7	9	.438	30	22	7	1	163.2	147	70	8	1	63	63	3.52	94	.242	.314	45-0-3	.067	-3	97	-3	0	-0.6
1944	Bos A	6	10	.375	27	17	3	0	132.2	142	72	10	3	65	30	4.21	81	.276	.361	47	.234	1	114	-13	0	-1.2
1945	Bos A	0	4	.000	12	4	1	0	56.2	68	29	8	0	14	28	4.13	82	.296	.336	18	.111	-2	69	-4	0	-0.4
Total	5	20	28	.417	93	55	14	2	457.1	463	238	33	6	196	167	4.09	85	.263	.339	145-0-4	.145	-4	109	-32	0	-3.2
TERRY, RALPH	Ralph Willard; B1.9.1936 Big Cabin OK; BR/TR/6´3˝/(182–195); d8.6																									
1956	NY A	1	2	.333	3	3	0	0	13.1	17	15	2	0	11-0	8	9.45	41	.347	.459	6	.167	-0	100	-8	0	-1.3
1957	NY A	1	1	.500	7	2	1-1	0	20.2	18	7	1	0	8-1	7	3.05	118	.240	.310	4	.250	0	100	2	0	0.2
	KC A	4	11	.267	21	19	3-1	0	130.2	119	63	15	4	47-2	80	3.38	117	.239	.309	42-0-2	.143	-2*	71	4	0	0.3
	Year	5	12	.294	28	21	4-2	0	151.1	137	70	16	4	55-3	87	3.33	117	.239	.309	46-0-2	.152	-2	74	5	0	0.5
1958	KC A	11	13	.458	40	33	8-3	2	216.2	217	111	29	2	61-4	134	4.24	92	.262	.313	71-0-3	.197	-0	114	-7	0	-0.9
1959	KC A	2	4	.333	9	7	2	0	46.1	56	29	9	1	19-1	35	5.24	76	.308	.374	17-0-1	.176	-1	113	-5	0	-0.6
	NY A	3	7	.300	24	16	5-1	0	127.1	130	55	7	2	30-5	55	3.39	107	.270	.312	41-0-2	.098	-3	86	4	0	0.0
	Year	5	11	.313	33	23	7-1	0	173.2	186	84	16	3	49-6	90	3.89	96	.281	.329	58-0-3	.121	-3	95	-3	0	-0.6
1960	†NY A	10	8	.556	35	23	7-3	1	166.2	149	78	15	4	52-3	92	3.40	105	.237	.299	49-0-7	.122	-2	96	1	0	-0.1

YEAR	TM LG	W	L	PCT	G	GS	CG-SHO	SV-BS	IP	H	R	HR	HB	BB-IB	SO	ERA	AERA	OAV	OOB	AB-HR-SH	AVG	PB	SUP	APR	DL	PW
1961	†NY A	16	3	.842	31	27	9-2	0	188.1	162	74	19	1	42-0	86	3.15	118	.232	.275	66-0-5	.227	2	127	12	0	1.3
1962	†NY A☆	**23**	12	.657	43	**39**	14-3	2	**298.2**	257	123	40	3	57-1	176	3.19	117	.231	.268	106-0-11	.189	1	127	18	0	1.8
1963	†NY A	17	15	.531	40	**37**	**18**-3	1	268	246	103	29	4	39-1	114	3.22	109	.242	**.271**	87-0-9	.080	-6	103	10	0	0.5
1964	†NY A	7	11	.389	27	14	2-1	4	115	130	60	20	1	31-3	77	4.54	80	.283	.326	35-0-4	.200	1	103	-10	0	-1.4
1965	Cle A	11	6	.647	30	26	6-2	0	165.2	154	77	22	1	23-3	84	3.69	94	.242	.268	49-1-10	.143	2	116	-3	0	-0.3
1966	KC A	1	5	.167	15	10	0	0	64	65	35	7	1	15-3	33	3.80	89	.263	.305	14-0-1	.214	1	101	-5	24	-0.3
	NY N	0	1	.000	11	1	0	1	24.2	27	14	1	0	11-1	14	4.74	77	.293	.369	6	.167	-0	121	-3	0	-0.2
1967	NY N	0	0	ø	2	0	0	0	3.1	1	0	0	0	0-0	5	0.00	ø	.091	.091	0	ø	0	—	1	0	0.1
Total	12	107	99	.519	338	257	75-20	11	1849.1	1748	844	216	24	446-28	1000	3.62	102	.249	.294	593-1-55	.160	-6	108	11	24	-0.9
TERRY, SCOTT	Scott Ray; B11.21.1959 Hobbs NM; BR/TR/5´11˝/195; [CinN80 12/305]; d4.9; Col Southwestern (TX); [DL 1992 StL N 182]																									
1986	Cin N	1	2	.333	28	3	0	0-0	55.2	66	40	8	0	32-3	32	6.14	63	.300	.387	4-0-1	.250	0*	139	-13	0	-0.6
1987	StL N	0	0	ø	11	0	0	0-0	13.1	13	5	0	0	8-2	9	3.38	125	.260	.362	2	.000	-0	—	1	0	0.1
1988	StL N	9	6	.600	51	11	1	3-4	129.1	119	48	5	0	34-6	65	2.92	121	.247	.295	28-0-5	.250	2	110	8	27	1.1
1989	StL N	8	10	.444	31	24	1	2-0	148.2	142	65	14	3	43-6	69	3.57	103	.253	.308	45-2-4	.156	2*	93	2	22	0.5
1990	StL N	2	6	.250	50	2	0	2-1	72	75	45	7	4	27-5	35	4.75	81	.264	.331	11-0-1	.455	2	82	-8	0	-0.6
1991	StL N	4	4	.500	65	0	0	1-2	80.1	76	31	1	0	32-14	52	2.80	134	.249	.320	7	.143	-0	—	7	0	0.7
Total	6	24	28	.462	236	40	2	8-7	499.1	491	234	35	7	176-36	262	3.73	99	.258	.321	97-2-11	.216	5	99	-3	231	1.2
TERRY, ADONIS	William H; B8.7.1864 Westfield MA; D2.24.1915 Milwaukee WI; BR/TR/5´11.5˝/168; d5.1; U1; ▲																									
1884	Bro AA	19	35	.352	56	55	54-2	0	476	486	308	10	8	72	230	3.55	93	.247	.276	236	.233	3*	66	-14	—	-1.2
1885	Bro AA	6	17	.261	25	23	23	1	209	213	147	9	4	42	96	4.26	77	.262	.301	264-1	.170	-3*	82	-16	—	-1.6
1886	Bro AA	18	16	.529	34	34	32-5	0	288.1	263	177	1	16	115	162	3.09	113	.231	.310	299-2	.237	2*	98	12	—	1.5
1887	Bro AA	16	16	.500	40	35	35-1	**3**	318	331	230	10	9	99	138	4.02	107	.262	.320	352-3	.293	7*	100	7	—	1.2
1888	Bro AA	13	8	.619	23	23	20-2	0	195	145	79	2	9	67	138	2.03	147	**.199**	.275	115	.252	3*	100	21	—	2.2
1889	†Bro AA	22	15	.595	41	39	35-2	0	326	285	189	6	16	126	186	3.29	113	.228	.307	160-2	.300	12*	101	10	—	2.1
1890	†Bro N	26	16	.619	46	44	38-1	0	370	362	200	3	15	133	185	2.94	117	.248	.317	363-4	.278	15*	102	19	—	2.9
1891	Bro N	6	16	.273	25	22	18-1	1	194	207	139	5	7	80	65	4.22	78	.263	.336	91	.209	3*	86	-18	—	-1.3
1892	Bal N	0	1	.000	1	1	1	0	9	7	7	0	0	7	3	4.00	86	.206	.341	4	.000	-1	18	-1	—	-0.1
	Pit N	18	7	.720	30	26	24-2	1	240	185	106	3	8	106	95	2.51	131	.204	.293	100-2	.160	1*	111	23	—	2.2
	Year	18	8	.692	31	27	25-2	1	249	192	113	3	8	113	98	2.57	129	.204	.295	104-2	.154	1	107	23	—	2.1
1893	Pit N	12	8	.600	26	19	14	0	170	177	121	5	11	99	52	4.45	102	.260	.363	71	.254	2	112	2	—	0.4
1894	Pit N	0	1	.000	1	1	0	0	0.2	2	5	0	0	4	0	67.50	8	.500	.750	0	ø	0	68	-4	—	-0.5
	Chi N	5	11	.313	23	21	16	0	163.1	232	191	12	16	123	39	5.84	97	.330	.441	95	.347	4*	96	-15	—	-0.7
	Year	5	12	.294	24	22	16	0	164	234	196	12	16	127	39	6.09	93	.331	.444	95	.347	4	95	-20	—	-1.2
1895	Chi N	21	14	.600	38	34	31	0	311.1	346	228	4	17	131	88	4.80	106	.277	.354	137-1-5	.219	-6*	89	12	—	0.6
1896	Chi N	15	14	.517	30	28	25-1	0	235.2	273	166	6	10	88	75	4.43	102	.288	.354	99-0-3	.263	2	112	1	—	0.3
1897	Chi N	0	1	.000	1	1	1	0	8	11	10	0	2	6	1	10.13	44	.324	.452	3-0-1	.000	-1	64	-4	—	-0.3
Total	14	197	196	.501	440	406	367-17	6	3514.1	3525	2303	76	148	1298	1553	3.74	103	.252	.323	2389-15-9	.249	45	95	35	—	7.7
TERWILLIGER, DICK	Richard Martin; B6.27.1906 Sand Lake MI; D1.21.1969 Greenville MI; BR/TR/5´11˝/178; d8.18																									
1932	StL N	0	0	ø	1	0	0	0	3	1	0	0	1	2	2	0.00	ø	.143	.400	1	.000	-0	—	1	—	0.1
TESREAU, JEFF	Charles Monroe; B3.5.1888 Ironton MO; D9.24.1946 Hanover NH; BR/TR/6´2˝/218; d4.12; Def 1918; C1																									
1912	†NY N	17	7	.708	36	28	19-3	1	243	177	90	2	10	106	119	**1.96**	**172**	**.204**	.298	82-0-2	.146	-2	91	34	—	2.9
1913	†NY N	22	13	.629	41	**38**	17-1	0	282	222	98	7	7	119	167	2.17	144	**.220**	.306	95-0-3	.221	2	109	28	—	3.6
1914	NY N	26	10	.722	42	**41**	26-**8**	1	322.1	238	104	8	7	128	189	2.37	112	**.209**	.293	117-0-4	.239	6	144	12	—	1.9
1915	NY N	19	16	.543	43	39	24-8	3	306	235	98	4	5	75	176	2.29	112	.215	.269	103-1-2	.233	6	113	11	—	2.0
1916	NY N	14	14	.500	40	32	23-5	2	268.1	249	103	9	6	65	113	2.92	83	.250	.300	94-1-3	.191	2*	120	-13	—	-1.3
1917	†NY N	13	8	.619	33	20	11-1	2	183.2	168	71	6	3	58	85	3.09	83	.249	.312	61-0-3	.230	2	86	-8	—	-0.7
1918	NY N	4	4	.500	12	9	3-1	0	73.2	61	27	1	0	21	31	2.32	113	.227	.283	22-0-2	.318	2	106	1	—	0.4
Total	7	115	72	.615	247	207	123-27	9	1679	1350	591	37	38	572	880	2.43	114	.223	.295	574-2-19	.216	17	113	65	—	8.8
TESSMER, JAY	Jay Weldon; B12.26.1971 Meadville PA; BR/TR/6´3˝/190; [NYA95 19/534]; d8.27; Col Miami																									
1998	NY A	1	0	1.000	7	0	0	0-0	8.2	4	3	1	0	4-0	6	3.12	141	.143	.242	0	ø	0	—	1	0	0.1
1999	NY A	0	0	ø	6	0	0	0-0	6.2	16	11	1	1	4-2	3	14.85	32	.444	.512	0	ø	0	—	-7	0	-0.3
2000	NY A	0	0	ø	7	0	0	0-0	6.2	9	6	3	0	1-1	5	6.75	71	.300	.323	0	ø	0	—	-2	0	-0.1
2002	NY A	0	0	ø	2	0	0	0-0	1.1	0	1	0	0	2-0	0	6.75	64	.000	.333	0	ø	0	—	0	0	0.0
Total	4	1	0	1.000	22	0	0	0-0	23.1	29	21	5	1	11-3	14	7.71	59	.296	.369	0	ø	0	—	-8	0	-0.3
TEUT, NATE	Nathan Mark; B3.11.1976 Newton IA; BR/TL/6´7˝/220; [ChiN97 4/124]; d5.4; Col Iowa St.																									
2002	Fla N	0	1	.000	2	1	0	0-0	7.1	13	8	0	0	3-1	4	9.82	40	.394	.444	2	.000	-0	94	-5	0	-0.5
TEWKSBURY, BOB	Robert Alan; B11.30.1960 Concord NH; BR/TR/6´4˝/(180–208); [NYA81 19/493]; d4.11; Col St. Leo																									
1986	NY A	9	5	.643	23	20	2	0-0	130.1	144	58	8	5	31-0	49	3.31	125	.282	.325	0	ø	0	110	10	0	1.1
1987	NY A	1	4	.200	8	6	0	0-0	33.1	47	26	5	1	7-0	12	6.75	66	.338	.374	0	ø	0	93	-8	0	-1.0
	Chi N	0	4	.000	7	3	0	0-1	18	32	15	1	0	13-3	10	6.50	67	.421	.500	5	.000	-1	49	-4	53	-0.9
1988	Chi N	0	0	ø	1	1	0	0-0	3.1	6	5	1	0	2-0	1	8.10	45	.400	.444	2	.000	-0	268	-2	21	-0.1
1989	StL N	1	0	1.000	7	4	1-1	0-0	30	25	12	2	2	10-3	17	3.30	111	.225	.298	9	.111	-0	103	1	0	0.0
1990	StL N	10	9	.526	28	20	3-2	1-0	145.1	151	67	7	3	15-3	50	3.47	111	.267	.286	41-0-9	.171	1	83	4	0	0.6
1991	StL N	11	12	.478	30	30	3	0-0	191	206	86	13	5	38-2	75	3.25	115	.281	.317	58-0-7	.155	1	97	6	0	0.8
1992	StL N★	16	5	**.762**	33	32	5	0-0	233	217	63	15	3	20-0	91	2.16	158	.248	.265	70-0-6	.086	-2	107	32	0	2.8
1993	StL N	17	10	.630	32	32	2	0-0	213.2	258	99	15	6	20-1	97	3.83	105	.301	.318	69-0-7	.203	2*	108	6	0	1.1
1994	StL N	12	10	.545	24	24	4-1	0-0	155.2	190	97	19	3	22-1	79	5.32	80	.304	.328	54-0-4	.185	1	99	-18	0	-2.0
1995	Tex A	8	7	.533	21	21	4-1	0-0	129.2	169	75	8	3	20-4	53	4.58	106	.319	.346	1	.000	-0*	108	2	34	0.2
1996	SD N	10	10	.500	36	33	1	0-0	206.2	224	116	17	3	43-3	126	4.31	93	.275	.310	65-0-8	.031	-5	115	-10	0	-1.1
1997	Min A	8	13	.381	26	26	5-2	0-0	168.2	200	83	12	1	31-1	92	4.22	111	.297	.325	5	.200	0	73	9	50	1.2
1998	Min A	7	13	.350	26	25	1	0-0	148.1	174	82	19	6	20-1	60	4.79	100	.292	.318	1	.000	-0	69	1	53	0.2
Total	13	110	102	.519	302	277	31-7	1-1	1807	2043	884	142	41	292-22	812	3.92	105	.287	.316	380-0-41	.132	-3	98	29	211	2.9
THATCHER, GRANT	Ulysses Grant; B2.23.1877 Maytown PA; D3.17.1936 Lancaster PA; TR/5´10.5˝/180; d9.9																									
1903	Bro N	3	1	.750	4	4	4	0	28	33	12	1	0	7	9	2.89	110	.292	.333	11	.182	0	106	1	—	0.2
1904	Bro N	1	0	1.000	1	0	0	0	9	9	6	0	0	2	4	4.00	69	.281	.324	4	.250	0	—	-1	—	-0.1
Total	2	4	1	.800	5	4	4	0	37	42	18	1	0	9	13	3.16	98	.290	.331	15	.200	0	106	0	—	0.1
THAYER, GREG	Gregory Allen; B10.23.1949 Cedar Rapids IA; BR/TR/5´11˝/180; [SFN71 32/700]; d4.7; Col St. Cloud St.																									
1978	Min A	1	1	.500	20	0	0	0-2	45	40	19	5	3	30-1	30	3.80	101	.258	.380	0	ø	0	—	1	0	0.1
THEIS, JACK	John Louis; B7.23.1891 Georgetown OH; D7.6.1941 Georgetown OH; BR/TR/6´0˝/190; d7.5																									
1920	Cin N	0	0	ø	1	0	0	0	2	1	0	0	0	3	0	0.00	ø	.143	.400	0	ø	0	—	1	—	0.0
THEISS, DUANE	Duane Charles; B11.20.1953 Zanesville OH; BR/TR/6´3˝/185; [AtlN75 12/282]; d8.5; Col Marietta																									
1977	Atl N	1	1	.500	17	0	0	0-0	20.2	26	16	1	1	16-5	7	6.53	68	.338	.439	1-0-1	.000	-0	—	-4	0	-0.3
1978	Atl N	0	0	ø	3	0	0	0-0	6.1	3	1	0	1	3-0	3	1.42	284	.158	.292	1	.000	-0	—	2	0	0.1
Total	2	1	1	.500	20	0	0	0-0	27	29	17	1	2	19-5	10	5.33	82	.302	.410	2-0-1	.000	-0	—	-2	0	-0.2
THESENGA, JUG	Arnold Joseph; B4.27.1914 Jefferson SD; D12.3.2002 Wichita KS; BR/TR/6´0˝/200; d9.1																									
1944	Was A	0	0	ø	5	1	0	0	12.1	18	9	0	0	12	2	5.11	64	.340	.462	2-0-1	.000	-0	257	-3	0	-0.2
THIEL, BERT	Maynard Bert; B5.4.1926 Marion WI; BR/TR/5´10˝/185; d4.17																									
1952	Bos N	1	1	.500	4	0	0	0	7	11	7	1	2	4	6	7.71	47	.344	.447	0	ø	0	—	-3	0	-0.7
THIELMAN, HENRY	Henry Joseph; B10.3.1880 St.Cloud MN; D9.2.1942 New York NY; BR/TR/5´11˝/175; d4.17; b–Jake; Col Manhattan																									
1902	NY N	0	1	.000	2	2	0	0	6	8	10	0	0	6	5	1.50	187	.320	.452	9	.111	-0*	121	-2	—	-0.3
	Cin N	9	15	.375	25	23	22	1	211	201	111	2	19	78	49	3.24	92	.251	.332	91-0-2	.132	-4*	90	-4	—	-0.8
	Year	9	16	.360	27	25	22	1	217	209	121	2	19	84	54	3.19	94	.253	.336	100-0-2	.130	-4	92	-10	—	-1.1

YEAR	TM LG	W	L	PCT	G	GS	CG-SHO	SV-BS	IP	H	R	HR	HB	BB-IB	SO	ERA	AERA	OAV	OOB	AB-HR-SH	AVG	PB	SUP	APR	DL	PW
1903	Bro N	0	3	.000	4	3	3	0	29	31	20	3	2	14	10	4.66	69	.330	.427	23-1-0	.217	1*	35	-4	—	-0.2
Total	2	9	19	.321	31	28	25	1	246	240	141	5	21	98	64	3.37	90	.261	.346	123-1-2	.146	-3	85	-10	—	-1.3
Thielman, Jake	John Peter; B5.20.1879 St.Cloud MN; D1.28.1928 Minneapolis MN; BR/TR/5´11˝/175; d4.23; b–Henry; Col Manhattan																									
1905	StL N	15	16	.484	32	29	26	0	242	265	138	4	12	62	87	3.50	85	.281	.333	91-0-2	.231	8*	94	-18	—	-1.1
1906	StL N	0	1	.000	1	1	0	0	5	5	6	0	0	2	0	3.60	73	.263	.333	2	.500	0	139	-2	—	-0.3
1907	Cle A	11	8	.579	20	18	18-3	0	166	151	60	2	7	34	56	2.33	107	.245	.292	59-0-4	.203	1*	96	5	—	0.5
1908	Cle A	4	3	.571	11	8	5	0	61.2	59	26	2	4	9	15	3.65	65	.260	.300	23-0-3	.348	4*	125	-5	—	-0.1
	Bos A	0	0	ø	1	0	0	0	0.2	3	4	1	0	0	0	40.50	6	.600	.600	0	ø	0	—	-3	—	-0.1
	Year	4	3	.571	12	8	5	0	62.1	62	30	3	4	9	15	4.04	59	.267	.306	23-0-3	.348	4	125	-8	—	-0.2
Total	4	30	28	.517	65	56	49-3	0	475.1	483	234	9	23	107	158	3.16	86	.267	.316	175-0-9	.240	13	100	-23	—	-1.1
Thies, Dave	David Robert; B3.21.1937 Minneapolis MN; BR/TR/6´4˝/205; d4.20; Col St. Marys (MN)																									
1963	KC A	0	1	.000	9	2	0	0	25.1	26	15	2	2	12-0	9	4.62	84	.274	.364	6	.333	1	171	-2	0	0.0
Thies, Jake	Vernon Arthur; B4.1.1926 St.Louis MO; BR/TR/5´11˝/170; d4.24; Col Illinois																									
1954	Pit N	3	9	.250	33	18	3-1	0	130.1	120	70	13	3	49	57	3.87	108	.244	.312	33-0-2	.030	-2	77	2	0	0.0
1955	Pit N	0	1	.000	1	1	0	0	3.2	5	5	0	1	3-1	0	4.91	84	.357	.450	0	ø	0	65	-1	0	-0.2
Total	2	3	10	.231	34	19	3-1	0	134	125	75	13	4	52-1	57	3.90	107	.248	.317	33-0-2	.030	-2	76	1	0	-0.2
Thigpen, Bobby	Robert Thomas; B7.17.1963 Tallahassee FL; BR/TR/6´3˝/(195–222); [ChiA85 4/85]; d8.6; Col Mississippi St.																									
1986	Chi A	2	0	1.000	20	0	0	7-4	35.2	26	7	1	1	12-0	20	1.77	246	.205	.277	0	ø	0	—	10	0	0.9
1987	Chi A	7	5	.583	51	0	0	16-3	89	86	30	10	3	24-5	52	2.73	170	.256	.311	0	ø	0	—	18	0	2.8
1988	Chi A	5	8	.385	68	0	0	34-9	90	96	38	6	4	33-3	62	3.30	121	.273	.338	0	ø	0	—	7	0	1.4
1989	Chi A	2	6	.250	61	0	0	34-9	79	62	34	10	1	40-3	47	3.76	102	.218	.311	0	ø	0	—	2	0	0.3
1990	Chi A★	4	6	.400	**77**	0	0	**57**-8	88.2	60	20	5	1	32-3	70	1.83	211	.195	.271	0	ø	0	—	20	0	4.2
1991	Chi A	7	5	.583	67	0	0	30-9	69.2	63	32	10	4	38-8	47	3.49	115	.245	.348	0	ø	0	—	3	0	0.6
1992	Chi A	1	3	.250	55	0	0	22-7	55	58	29	4	3	33-5	45	4.75	82	.275	.375	0	ø	0	—	-4	0	-0.5
1993	Chi A	0	0	ø	25	0	0	1-1	34.2	51	25	5	5	12-0	19	5.71	74	.349	.410	0	ø	0	—	-6	0	-0.3
	†Phi N	3	1	.750	17	0	0	0-2	19.1	23	13	2	1	9-1	10	6.05	66	.307	.384	1	.000	-0	—	-4	0	-0.7
1994	Sea A	0	2	.000	7	0	0	0-0	7.2	12	9	3	0	5-0	4	9.39	53	.353	.436	0	ø	0	—	-4	0	-0.7
Total	9	31	36	.463	448	0	0	201-52	568.2	537	237	56	23	238-28	376	3.43	119	.252	.330	1	.000	-0	—	42	0	8.0
Thobe, J. J.	John Joseph; B11.19.1970 Covington KY; BR/TR/6´6˝/220; [CleA92 7/182]; d9.18; b–Tom; Col Santa Ana (CA) JC																									
1995	Mon N	0	0	ø	4	0	0	0-0	4	6	4	0	0	3-0	0	9.00	48	.333	.429	0	ø	-0	—	-2	0	-0.1
Thobe, Tom	Thomas Neal; B9.3.1969 Covington KY; BL/TL/6´6˝/195; [ChiN87 38/961]; d9.12; b–J.J.																									
1995	Atl N	0	0	ø	3	0	0	0-0	3.1	7	4	0	0	0-0	2	10.80	40	.412	.412	0	ø	0	—	-2	0	-0.1
1996	Atl N	0	1	.000	4	0	0	0-0	6	5	2	1	0	0-0	1	1.50	297	.217	.208	1	.000	-0	—	1	0	0.2
Total	2	0	1	.000	7	0	0	0-0	9.1	12	6	1	0	0-0	3	4.82	91	.300	.293	1	.000	-0	—	-1	0	0.1
Thoenen, Dick	Richard Crispin; B1.9.1944 Mexico MO; BR/TR/6´6˝/215; d9.16; Col Notre Dame																									
1967	Phi N	0	0	ø	1	0	0	0	1	2	1	0	0	0-0	0	9.00	38	.500	.500	0	ø	0	—	-1	0	0.0
Thomas, Tommy	Alphonse; B12.23.1899 Baltimore MD; D4.27.1988 Dallastown PA; BR/TR/5´10˝/175; d4.17; Col CC of Baltimore (MD)																									
1926	Chi A	15	12	.556	44	32	13-2	2	249	225	113	7	1	110	127	3.80	102	**.244**	.325	86-0-3	.186	-1	103	6	—	0.3
1927	Chi A	19	16	.543	40	**36**	24-3	1	**307.2**	271	110	16	1	94	107	2.98	136	.244	.303	95-1-19	.147	-3	87	**42**	—	3.8
1928	Chi A	17	16	.515	36	32	24-3	2	283	277	114	14	4	76	129	3.08	131	.259	.310	96-2-7	.219	3	93	31	—	3.5
1929	Chi A	14	18	.438	36	31	**24**-2	1	259.2	270	127	17	0	60	62	3.19	134	.269	.310	98-0-1	.255	2*	75	24	—	2.7
1930	Chi A	5	13	.278	34	27	7	0	169	229	125	13	1	44	58	5.22	89	.323	.364	56-0-4	.125	-4	91	-13	—	-1.4
1931	Chi A	10	14	.417	43	36	11-2	2	245.1	298	166	17	5	69	72	4.73	90	.292	.340	87-0-5	.241	1	108	-18	—	-1.4
1932	Chi A	3	3	.500	12	3	1	0	43.2	55	33	6	1	15	11	6.18	70	.307	.364	13-0-1	.077	-1	105	-8	—	-0.9
	Was A	8	7	.533	18	14	7-1	0	117	114	48	5	0	46	36	3.54	122	.255	.325	42-0-1	.238	1	100	12	—	1.3
	Year	11	10	.524	30	17	8-1	0	160.2	169	81	11	1	61	47	4.26	101	.270	.336	55-0-2	.200	0	101	6	—	0.4
1933	†Was A	7	7	.500	35	14	2	3	135	149	87	9	2	49	35	4.80	87	.273	.336	42-0-6	.238	1	128	-12	—	-1.1
1934	Was A	8	9	.471	33	18	7-1	1	133.1	154	87	9	3	58	42	5.47	79	.294	.368	38-0-7	.184	-0	88	-16	—	-1.8
1935	Was A	0	0	ø	1	0	0	0	0.1	3	2	0	0	0	0	54.00	8	.750	.750	0	ø	0	—	-2	—	-0.1
	Phi N	0	1	.000	4	1	0	0	12	15	9	2	0	5	3	5.25	86	.313	.377	3	.000	-0	56	-1	—	-0.1
1936	StL A	11	9	.550	36	21	8-1	0	179.2	219	132	25	4	72	40	5.26	102	.297	.362	58-0-7	.138	-3	97	-3	—	-0.6
1937	StL A	0	1	.000	17	2	0	0	30.2	46	26	2	1	10	10	7.04	69	.348	.399	4	.000	-1	117	-7	—	-0.4
	Bos A	0	2	.000	9	0	0	0	11	16	6	2	1	4	4	4.09	116	.340	.404	4	.250	-0	—	1	—	0.1
	Year	0	3	.000	26	2	0	0	41.2	62	32	4	2	14	14	6.26	77	.346	.400	8	.125	-1	118	-6	—	-0.3
Total	12	117	128	.478	398	267	128-15	12	2176.1	2341	1185	144	24	712	736	4.11	104	.275	.333	722-3-61	.195	-5	95	36	—	3.9
Thomas, Blaine	Blaine M. "Baldy"; B8.1888 Glendora CA; D8.21.1915 Payson AZ; BR/TR/5´10˝/165; d8.25																									
1911	Bos A	0	0	ø	2	2	0	0	4.2	3	2	0	1	7	0	0.00	ø	.273	.579	2	.500	0	99	1	—	0.1
Thomas, Brad	Bradley Richard; B10.22.1977 Sydney, New South Wales, Australia; BL/TL/6´4˝/(204–235); d5.26; [DL 2004 Bos A 164]																									
2001	Min A	0	2	.000	5	5	0	0-0	16.1	20	17	6	1	14-0	6	9.37	50	.303	.432	0	ø	0	79	-8	0	-0.7
2003	Min A	0	1	.000	3	0	0	0-0	4.2	6	4	1	0	3-1	2	7.71	58	.316	.409	0	ø	0	—	-2	0	-0.3
2004	Min A	0	0	ø	3	0	0	0-0	2.2	7	5	0	0	1-0	0	16.88	27	.500	.533	0	ø	0	—	-3	0	-0.2
Total	3	0	3	.000	11	5	0	0-0	23.2	33	26	7	1	18-1	8	9.89	47	.333	.441	0	ø	0	79	-13	164	-1.2
Thomas, Carl	Carl Leslie; B5.28.1932 Minneapolis MN; BR/TR/6´5˝/245; d4.19; Col Arizona																									
1960	Cle A	1	0	1.000	4	0	0	0	9.2	8	8	1	1	10-0	5	7.45	50	.229	.413	3-0-1	.333	1*	—	-4	0	-0.3
Thomas, Lefty	Clarence Fletcher; B10.4.1903 Glade Spring VA; D3.21.1952 Charlottesville VA; BL/TL/6´0˝/183; d9.26; Col Lynchburg																									
1925	Was A	0	2	.000	2	2	1	0	13	14	8	0	0	7	10	2.08	204	.264	.350	5	.000	-1	80	1	—	0.1
1926	Was A	0	0	ø	6	0	0	0	8.2	8	7	0	0	10	3	5.19	74	.267	.450	2	.000	0	—	-2	—	-0.1
Total	2	0	2	.000	8	2	1	0	21.2	22	15	0	0	17	13	3.32	123	.265	.390	7	.000	-1	80	-1	—	0.0
Thomas, Claude	Claude Alfred "Lefty"; B5.15.1890 Stanberry MO; D3.6.1946 Sulphur OK; BL/TL/6´1˝/180; d9.14																									
1916	Was A	1	2	.333	7	4	1-1	0	28.1	27	14	1	2	12	7	4.13	68	.265	.353	10	.100	-1	102	-3	—	-0.4
Thomas, Fay	Fay Wesley "Scow"; B10.10.1903 Holyrood KS; D8.12.1990 Chatsworth CA; BR/TR/6´2˝/195; d6.27; Col USC																									
1927	NY N	0	0	ø	9	0	0	0	16.1	19	10	3	1	4	11	3.31	117	.302	.353	2	.000	-0	—	0	—	-0.1
1931	Cle A	2	4	.333	16	2	1	0	48.2	63	34	2	1	32	25	5.18	89	.323	.421	13	.154	-1	64	-3	—	-0.4
1932	Bro N	0	1	.000	7	2	0	0	17	22	15	0	0	8	9	7.41	51	.306	.375	3-0-1	.000	-0	88	-6	—	-0.4
1935	StL A	7	15	.318	49	19	4	1	147	165	95	11	3	89	67	4.78	100	.289	.388	38-0-4	.105	-3	51	-2	—	-0.4
Total	4	9	20	.310	81	23	5	1	229	269	154	16	5	133	112	4.95	93	.299	.392	56-0-5	.107	-4	54	-11	—	-1.3
Thomas, Frosty	Forrest; B5.23.1881 Faucett MO; D3.18.1970 St.Joseph MO; BR/TR/6´0˝/185; d5.1																									
1905	Det A	0	1	.000	2	1	0	0	6	10	8	0	1	3	5	7.50	36	.370	.452	2	.000	0	104	-3	—	-0.5
Thomas, Larry	Larry Wayne; B10.25.1969 Miami FL; BR/TL/6´1˝/195; [ChiA91 2/69]; d8.11; Col Maine																									
1995	Chi A	0	0	ø	17	0	0	0-0	13.2	8	2	1	0	6-1	12	1.32	340	.167	.259	0	ø	0	—	5	0	0.2
1996	Chi A	2	3	.400	57	0	0	0-2	30.2	32	11	1	3	14-2	20	3.23	147	.281	.374	0	ø	0	—	6	20	0.8
1997	Chi A	0	0	ø	5	0	0	0-0	3.1	3	3	1	0	2-0	0	8.10	54	.250	.357	0	ø	0	—	-1	0	-0.1
Total	3	2	3	.400	79	0	0	0-2	47.2	43	16	3	3	22-3	32	3.02	154	.247	.342	0	ø	0	—	10	20	0.9
Thomas, Bud	Luther Baxter; B9.9.1910 Faber VA; D5.20.2001 North Garden VA; BR/TR/6´0˝/180; d9.13																									
1932	Was A	0	0	ø	2	0	0	0	3	1	0	0	0	2	1	0.00	ø	.100	.250	0	ø	0	—	1	—	0.1
1933	Was A	0	0	ø	2	0	0	0	4	11	8	1	1	2	1	15.75	27	.550	.609	1	.000	-0	—	-5	—	-0.2
1937	Phi A	8	15	.348	35	26	6-1	0	169.2	208	108	15	1	52	54	4.99	95	.295	.344	47-1-7	.128	-1	73	-4	—	-0.6
1938	Phi A	9	14	.391	42	29	7-1	0	212.1	259	138	23	2	62	48	4.92	98	.299	.347	69-0-7	.130	-3	87	-2	—	-0.5
1939	Phi A	0	1	.000	2	2	0	0	4	8	8	2	0	1	0	15.75	30	.421	.450	3	.000	-0	150	-5	—	-0.8
	Was A	0	0	ø	4	0	0	0	9	11	7	0	0	2	0	6.00	72	.306	.342	2	.000	-0	—	-2	—	-0.1

YEAR	TM LG	W	L	PCT	G	GS	CG-SHO	SV-BS	IP	H	R	HR	HB	BB-IB	SO	ERA	AERA	OAV	OOB	AB-HR-SH	AVG	PB	SUP	APR	DL	PW
	Det A	7	0	1.000	27	0	0	1	47.1	45	25	7	0	20	14	4.18	117	.254	.330	9-0-1	.111	-1	—	4	—	0.4
	Year	7	1	.875	33	2	0	1	60.1	64	40	9	0	23	14	5.22	92	.276	.341	14-0-1	.071	-2	147	-3	—	-0.5
1940	Det A	0	1	.000	3	0	0	0	4	8	5	1	0	3	0	9.00	53	.421	.500	0	ø	0	—	-2	—	-0.3
1941	Det A	1	3	.250	26	1	0	2	72.2	74	45	4	0	22	17	4.21	108	.260	.313	19-0-1	.105	-1	57	0	0	0.0
Total	7	25	34	.424	143	58	13-2	3	526	625	344	53	4	166	135	4.96	96	.292	.345	150-1-16	.120	-7	83	-15	0	-2.0
Thomas, Mike	Michael Steven; B9.2.1969 Sacramento CA; BL/TL/6´2˝/205; [NYN89 23/606]; d7.12; Col Labette (KS) CC																									
1995	Mil A	0	0	ø	1	0	0	0-0	1.1	2	0	0	0	1-0	0	0.00	ø	.333	.429	0	ø	0	—	1	17	0.0
Thomas, Myles	Myles Lewis; B10.22.1897 State College PA; D12.12.1963 Toledo OH; BR/TR/5´9.5˝/170; d4.18; Col Penn St.																									
1926	†NY A	6	6	.500	33	13	3	0	140.1	140	79	6	3	65	38	4.23	91	.271	.356	43-0-5	.116	-3	136	-6	—	-0.7
1927	NY A	7	4	.636	21	9	1	0	88.2	111	58	4	1	43	25	4.87	79	.322	.398	27-0-3	.333	2	130	-11	—	-1.0
1928	NY A	1	0	1.000	12	1	0	0	31.2	33	19	3	0	9	10	3.41	110	.277	.328	10	.400	1*	135	-1	—	0.0
1929	NY A	0	2	.000	5	1	0	0	15	27	21	1	0	9	3	10.80	36	.409	.480	7	.143	-1	87	-12	—	-1.2
	Was A	7	8	.467	22	14	7	2	125.1	139	72	3	0	48	33	3.52	121	.288	.352	48-0-1	.292	2	99	4	—	0.6
	Year	7	10	.412	27	15	7	2	140.1	166	93	4	0	57	36	4.30	98	.302	.368	55-0-1	.273	1	99	-7	—	-0.6
1930	Was A	2	2	.500	12	2	0	0	33.2	49	35	3	0	15	12	8.29	55	.358	.421	11	.182	-1*	56	-14	—	-1.4
Total	5	23	22	.511	105	40	11	2	434.2	499	284	20	4	189	121	4.64	87	.299	.372	146-0-9	.240	0	116	-40	—	-3.7
Thomas, Roy	Roy Justin; B6.22.1953 Quantico VA; BR/TR/6´6˝/(190–215); [PhiN71 1/6]; d9.21; [DL 1986 Sea A 182]																									
1977	Hou N	0	0	ø	4	0	0	0-0	6.1	5	2	0	0	3-0	4	2.84	127	.208	.296	0	ø	0	—	1	0	0.0
1978	StL N	1	1	.500	16	1	0	3-0	28.1	21	14	0	0	16-3	16	3.81	94	.216	.316	4	.250	0	76	-1	0	0.0
1979	StL N	3	4	.429	26	6	0	1-1	77	66	29	9	0	24-3	44	2.92	130	.237	.298	17-0-1	.059	-1	62	7	0	0.6
1980	StL N	2	3	.400	24	5	0	0-1	55	59	32	3	3	25-5	22	4.75	79	.274	.352	13	.154	-0	124	-6	0	-0.5
1983	Sea A	3	1	.750	43	0	0	1-3	88.2	95	44	3	2	32-3	77	3.45	124	.275	.337	0	ø	0	—	5	0	0.2
1984	Sea A	3	2	.600	21	1	0	1-0	49.2	52	33	8	4	37-1	42	5.26	76	.280	.399	0	ø	0	90	-7	22	-0.6
1985	Sea A	7	0	1.000	40	0	0	1-0	93.2	66	37	8	2	48-12	70	3.36	126	.202	.303	0	ø	0	—	9	0	0.6
1987	Sea A	1	0	1.000	8	0	0	0-0	20.2	23	12	2	1	11-0	14	5.23	91	.299	.380	0	ø	0	—	0	0	0.0
Total	8	20	11	.645	182	13	0	7-5	419.1	387	203	33	12	196-27	289	3.82	106	.250	.334	34-0-1	.118	-1	84	8	204	0.3
Thomas, Stan	Stanley Brown; B7.11.1949 Rumford ME; BR/TR/6´2˝/185; [TexA71 27/616]; d7.5; Col New Haven																									
1974	Tex A	0	0	ø	12	0	0	0-0	13.2	22	10	1	0	6-2	8	6.59	54	.379	.431	0	ø	0	—	-4	0	-0.2
1975	Tex A	4	4	.500	46	1	0	3-0	81.1	72	36	2	3	34-6	46	3.10	122	.239	.322	0	ø	0	23	5	0	0.5
1976	Cle A	4	4	.500	37	7	2	6-2	105.2	88	33	5	4	41-4	54	2.30	153	.229	.309	0	ø	0	136	13	0	1.3
1977	Sea A	2	6	.250	13	9	1	0-1	58.1	74	49	8	3	25-0	14	6.02	69	.310	.378	0	ø	0	82	-14	22	-1.7
	NY A	1	0	1.000	3	0	0	0-0	6.1	7	7	0	0	4-0	1	7.11	56	.280	.367	0	ø	0	—	-3	0	-0.4
	Year	3	6	.333	16	9	1	0-1	64.2	81	56	8	3	29-0	15	6.12	67	.307	.377	0	ø	0	82	-17	0	-2.1
Total	4	11	14	.440	111	17	3	9-3	265.1	263	135	16	10	110-12	123	3.70	101	.261	.338	0	ø	0	101	-3	22	-0.5
Thomas, Tom	Thomas Robert "Savage Tom"; B12.27.1873 Shawnee OH; D9.23.1942 Shawnee OH; BR/TR/6´4˝/195; d9.20																									
1894	Cle N	0	0	ø	1	0	0	1	0.1	0	1	0	0	2	0	27.00	20	.000	.667	0	ø	0	—	-1	—	-0.1
1899	StL N	1	1	.500	4	2	2	0	25	22	14	1	0	4	8	2.52	158	.237	.268	12	.250	0	90	3	—	0.2
1900	StL N	2	2	.500	5	1	1	0	26.1	38	22	2	1	4	7	3.76	97	.336	.364	11-0-1	.091	-1	171	-2	—	-0.4
Total	3	3	3	.500	10	3	3	1	51.2	60	37	3	1	10	15	3.31	115	.290	.326	23-0-1	.174	-1	117	0	—	-0.3
Thomason, Erskine	Melvin Erskine; B8.13.1948 Laurens SC; BR/TR/6´1˝/190; d9.18; Col Erskine																									
1974	Phi N	0	0	ø	1	0	0	0-0	1	0	0	0	0	0-0	1	0.00	ø	.000	.000	0	ø	0	—	0	0	0.0
Thompson, Art	Arthur J.; d6.17																									
1884	Was U	0	1	.000	1	1	1	0	8	10	11	0	—	3	8	6.75	36	.286	.342	3	.000	-1	18	-4	—	-0.4
Thompson, Brad	Bradley Joseph; B1.31.1982 Las Vegas NV; BR/TR/6´1˝/190; [StLN02 16/492]; d5.8; Col Dixie (UT) JC																									
2005	†StL N	4	0	1.000	40	0	0	1-0	55	46	22	5	4	15-2	29	2.95	142	.227	.293	6-0-1	.167	-0*	—	7	0	0.5
2006	†StL N	1	2	.333	43	1	0	0-0	56.2	58	23	4	5	20-3	32	3.34	130	.267	.343	2	.500	0	212	6	0	0.3
Total	2	5	2	.714	83	1	0	1-0	111.2	104	45	9	9	35-5	61	3.14	136	.248	.319	8-0-1	.250	0	212	13	0	0.8
Thompson, Forrest	David Forrest; B3.3.1918 Mooresville NC; D2.26.1979 Charlotte NC; BL/TL/5´11˝/195; d4.26																									
1948	Was A	6	10	.375	46	7	0	4	131.1	134	71	9	1	54	40	3.84	113	.262	.334	35	.286	2	74	4	0	0.7
1949	Was A	1	3	.250	9	1	1	0	16.1	22	11	1	1	9	8	4.41	97	.328	.416	5	.600	2*	21	-1	0	0.0
Total	2	7	13	.350	55	8	1	4	147.2	156	82	10	2	63	48	3.90	111	.270	.344	40	.325	4	68	3	0	0.7
Thompson, Derek	Derek Ryan; B1.8.1981 Tampa FL; BL/TL/6´2˝/180; [CleA00 1/37]; d5.28; [DL 2003 LA N 183]																									
2005	LA N	0	0	ø	4	3	0	0-0	18	16	7	0	0	10-1	13	3.50	119	.258	.356	4-0-1	.000	-0	106	2	0	0.1
Thompson, Junior	Eugene Earl; B6.7.1917 Latham IL; D8.24.2006 Scottsdale AZ; BR/TR/6´1˝/185; d4.26; Def 1943																									
1939	†Cin N	13	5	.722	42	11	5-3	2	152.1	130	51	6	3	55	87	2.54	151	.236	.309	48-0-3	.229	0	70	22	—	2.4
1940	†Cin N	16	9	.640	33	31	17-3	0	225.1	197	90	10	2	96	103	3.32	114	.233	.313	79-0-8	.228	3	107	13	—	1.6
1941	Cin N	6	6	.500	27	15	4	1	109	117	65	6	3	57	46	4.87	74	.272	.361	30-0-7	.233	1	105	-14	0	-1.2
1942	Cin N	4	7	.364	29	10	1	0	101.2	86	61	5	2	53	35	3.36	98	.226	.324	30-0-1	.267	2	107	-7	0	-0.3
1946	NY N	4	6	.400	39	1	0	4	62.2	36	18	5	0	40	31	1.29	266	.190	.332	7-0-1	.143	0	50	12	0	2.1
1947	NY N	4	2	.667	15	0	0	0	35.2	36	20	3	1	27	13	4.29	95	.279	.408	6	.000	-1	—	-1	0	-0.2
Total	6	47	35	.573	185	68	27-6	7	686.2	602	305	35	11	328	315	3.26	113	.239	.329	200-0-20	.225	6	100	25	0	4.4
Thompson, Fuller	Fuller Weidner; B5.1.1889 Los Angeles CA; D2.19.1972 Los Angeles CA; BR/TR/5´11.5˝/164; d8.19; Col Wittenberg																									
1911	Bos N	0	0	ø	3	0	0	0	4.2	5	4	0	0	2	0	3.86	99	.294	.368	0	ø	0	—	0	—	0.0
Thompson, Harry	Harold; B9.9.1889 Nanticoke PA; D2.14.1951 Reno NV; BL/TL/5´8˝/150; d4.24																									
1919	Was A	0	3	.000	12	2	0	1	43.1	48	21	0	2	8	10	3.53	91	.293	.333	32-0-2	.250	1*	37	-1	—	0.1
	Phi A	0	1	.000	3	0	0	0	12	16	9	4	0	3	1	6.75	51	.327	.365	6	.000	-1*	—	-3	—	-0.3
	Year	0	4	.000	15	2	0	1	55.1	64	30	4	2	11	11	4.23	77	.300	.341	38-0-2	.211	0	36	-5	—	-0.2
Thompson, Lee	John Dudley "Lefty"; B2.26.1898 Smithfield UT; D2.17.1963 Santa Barbara CA; BL/TL/6´1˝/185; d9.4; Col Occidental																									
1921	Chi A	0	3	.000	4	4	0	0	20.2	32	21	0	0	6	4	8.27	51	.333	.373	7-0-1	.286	0	89	-9	—	-1.0
Thompson, Gus	John Gustav; B6.22.1877 Humboldt IA; D3.28.1958 Kalispell MT; BR/TR/6´2˝/185; d8.31; Col Grinnell																									
1903	†Pit N	2	2	.500	5	4	3	0	43	52	30	1	1	16	22	3.56	91	.295	.358	16	.250	0	109	-3	—	-0.2
1906	StL N	2	11	.154	17	12	8	0	103	111	61	2	5	25	36	4.28	61	.285	.336	34	.176	-1	60	-18	—	-2.1
Total	2	4	13	.235	22	16	11	0	146	163	91	3	6	41	58	4.07	69	.288	.343	50	.200	-0	74	-21	—	-2.3
Thompson, Jocko	John Samuel; B1.17.1917 Beverly MA; D2.3.1988 Olney MD; BL/TL/6´0˝/185; d9.21; Col Northeastern																									
1948	Phi N	1	0	1.000	2	2	1	0	13	10	4	0	0	9	7	2.77	142	.233	.365	3	.000	0	135	2	0	0.2
1949	Phi N	1	3	.250	8	5	1	0	31.1	38	24	6	0	11	12	6.89	57	.314	.371	11	.182	-0*	67	-9	0	-1.0
1950	Phi N	0	0	ø	2	0	0	0	4	1	1	0	0	4	2	0.00	ø	.077	.294	0	ø	0	—	1	0	0.1
1951	Phi N	4	8	.333	29	14	3-2	1	119.1	102	55	12	2	59	60	3.85	100	.231	.325	39-0-1	.103	-1*	102	1	0	-0.1
Total	4	6	11	.353	41	21	5-2	1	167.2	151	84	18	2	83	81	4.24	91	.244	.336	53-0-1	.113	-1	96	-5	0	-0.8
Thompson, Justin	Justin Willard; B3.8.1973 San Antonio TX; BL/TL/6´4˝/(175–215); [DetA91 1/32]; d5.27; [DL 2000 Tex A 181, 2001 Tex A 190]																									
1996	Det A	1	6	.143	11	11	0	0-0	59	62	35	7	2	31-2	44	4.58	111	.267	.356	0	ø	0	58	2	75	0.3
1997	Det A★	15	11	.577	32	32	4	0-0	223.1	188	82	20	2	66-1	151	3.02	153	.233	.289	2	.000	-0	90	39	15	4.1
1998	Det A	11	15	.423	34	34	5	0-0	222	227	114	20	2	79-4	149	4.05	117	.267	.329	7	.143	-0	97	15	0	1.5
1999	Det A	9	11	.450	24	24	0	0-0	142.2	152	85	24	4	59-1	83	5.11	98	.274	.344	5	.000	-1	81	-1	49	-0.2
2005	Tex A	0	0	ø	2	0	0	0-0	1.2	4	4	2	0	0-0	1	21.60	21	.444	.444	0	ø	0	—	-3	0	-0.1
Total	5	36	43	.456	103	101	9	0-0	648.2	633	320	73	10	235-8	428	4.02	119	.258	.322	14	.071	-1	87	52	510	5.6

YEAR	TM LG	W	L	PCT	G	GS	CG-SHO	SV-BS	IP	H	R	HR	HB	BB-IB	SO	ERA	AERA	OAV	OOB	AB-HR-SH	AVG	PB	SUP	APR	DL	PW
Thompson, Mark	Mark Radford; B4.7.1971 Russellville KY; BR/TR/6´2˝/(205–213); [ColN92 2/65]; d7.26; Col Kentucky																									
1994	Col N	1	1	.500	2	2	0	0-0	9	16	9	2	1	8-0	5	9.00	55	.400	.510	4-0-1	.000	-0	91	-3	0	-0.6
1995	†Col N	2	3	.400	21	5	0	0-0	51	73	42	7	1	22-2	30	6.53	82	.349	.407	13-0-1	.385	1	94	-6	0	-0.4
1996	Col N	9	11	.450	34	28	3-1	0-1	169.2	189	109	25	13	74-1	99	5.30	98	.285	.367	58-0-5	.138	-2	99	-1	0	-0.4
1997	Col N	3	3	.500	6	6	0	0-0	29.2	40	27	8	4	13-0	9	7.89	65	.323	.399	11-1-2	.182	1	116	-7	144	-1.1
1998	Col N	1	2	.333	6	6	0	0-0	23.1	36	22	8	5	12-0	14	7.71	67	.379	.465	7	.143	-0	77	-6	144	-0.6
1999	StL N	1	3	.250	5	5	0	0-0	29.1	26	12	1	2	17-1	22	2.76	167	.241	.354	8-0-1	.000	-1	76	5	0	0.5
2000	StL N	1	1	.500	20	0	0	0-1	25	24	21	4	3	15-0	19	5.04	92	.250	.365	3	.000	-0	—	-4	66	-0.3
Total	7	18	24	.429	94	52	3-1	0-2	337	404	242	55	29	161-4	198	5.74	90	.303	.386	104-1-10	.154	-3	96	-22	354	-2.9
Thompson, Mike	Michael Paul; B11.6.1980 Walsh CO; BR/TR/6´4˝/200; [SDN99 5/172]; d5.17																									
2006	SD N	4	5	.444	19	16	0	0-0	92	103	56	13	7	30-4	35	4.99	83	.285	.350	25-0-3	.160	0	103	-10	0	-0.8
Thompson, Mike	Michael Wayne; B9.6.1949 Denver CO; BR/TR/6´3˝/(180–190); [TexA67 3/45]; d5.19																									
1971	Was A	1	6	.143	16	12	0	0-0	66.2	53	39	3	3	54-2	41	4.86	70	.222	.370	17	.118	0	84	-10	0	-1.0
1973	StL N	0	0	ø	2	2	0	0-0	4	1	0	0	0	5-0	3	0.00	ø	.077	.333	1	.000	-0	60	2	0	0.1
1974	StL N	0	3	.000	19	4	0	0-0	38.1	37	24	1	2	35-4	25	5.63	64	.274	.430	8	.000	-1	103	-7	0	-0.6
	Atl N	0	0	ø	1	1	0	0-0	4	7	2	0	0	2-0	2	4.50	84	.412	.474	1	1.000	0	115	0	0	0.0
	Year	0	3	.000	20	5	0	0-0	42.1	44	26	1	2	37-4	27	5.53	66	.289	.435	9	.111	-1	106	-7	0	-0.6
1975	Atl N	0	6	.000	16	10	0	0-0	51.2	60	32	2	0	32-0	42	4.70	80	.305	.397	14-0-2	.071	-1	81	-5	25	-0.6
Total	4	1	15	.063	54	29	0	0-0	164.2	158	97	6	5	128-6	113	4.86	74	.263	.394	41-0-2	.098	-2	85	-20	25	-2.1
Thompson, Rich	Richard Neil; B11.1.1958 New York NY; BR/TR (BB 1985)/6´3˝/(215–225); [CleA80 8/192]; d4.28; Col Amherst																									
1985	Cle A	3	8	.273	57	0	0	5-6	80	95	63	8	6	48-6	30	6.30	66	.303	.398	0	ø	0	—	-19	0	-2.6
1989	Mon N	0	2	.000	19	1	0	0-0	33	27	11	2	2	11-2	15	2.18	164	.241	.315	2	.000	0	50	4	0	0.2
1990	Mon N	0	0	ø	1	0	0	0-0	1	1	0	0	0	0-0	0	0.00	ø	.250	.250	0	ø	0	—	0	0	0.0
Total	3	3	10	.231	77	1	0	5-6	114	123	74	10	8	59-8	45	5.05	79	.286	.376	2	.000	0	50	-15	0	-2.4
Thompson, Tommy	Thomas Carl; B11.7.1889 Spring City TN; D1.16.1963 LaJolla CA; BR/TR/5´9.5˝/170; d6.5; b–Homer; Col Georgia																									
1912	NY A	0	2	.000	7	2	1	0	32.2	43	32	0	3	13	15	6.06	59	.341	.415	10-0-1	.300	1*	82	-9	—	-0.4
Thompson, Will	Will McLain; B8.30.1870 Pittsburgh PA; D6.9.1962 Pittsburgh PA; BR/TR/5´11.5˝/190; d7.9; Col Penn																									
1892	Pit N	0	1	.000	1	1	0	0	3	3	5	0	1	5	0	3.00	110	.250	.500	0	ø	0	96	-1	—	-0.1
Thomson, John	John Carl; B10.1.1973 Vicksburg MS; BR/TR/6´3˝/(175–220); [ColN93 7/212]; d5.11; Col Blinn (TX) JC; [DL 2000 Col N 181]																									
1997	Col N	7	9	.438	27	27	2-1	0-0	166.1	193	94	15	5	51-0	106	4.71	110	.296	.350	47-0-6	.213	-0	83	7	0	0.6
1998	Col N	8	11	.421	26	26	2	0-0	161	174	86	21	2	49-0	106	4.81	108	.282	.335	50-0-9	.120	-3	84	8	40	0.5
1999	Col N	1	10	.091	14	13	1	0-0	62.2	85	62	11	1	36-1	34	8.04	72	.324	.405	18	.167	-0	71	-13	0	-1.8
2001	Col N	4	5	.444	14	14	1-1	0-0	93.2	84	46	15	4	25-3	68	4.04	132	.239	.295	29-0-6	.241	1	98	11	80	1.0
2002	Col N	7	8	.467	21	21	0	0-0	127.1	136	77	21	2	27-6	76	4.88	97	.268	.304	34-0-3	.176	-0	100	-3	0	-0.2
	NY N	2	6	.250	9	9	0	0-0	54.1	65	39	7	0	17-3	31	4.31	92	.290	.336	18-0-3	.278	1	101	-7	0	-0.7
	Year	9	14	.391	30	30	0	0-0	181.2	201	116	28	2	44-9	107	4.71	96	.275	.314	52-0-6	.212	1	100	-9	0	-0.9
2003	Tex A	13	14	.481	35	35	3-1	0-0	217	234	125	27	4	49-2	136	4.85	102	.276	.316	1	.000	-0	97	3	0	0.4
2004	†Atl N	14	8	.636	33	33	0	0-0	198.1	210	93	20	6	52-5	133	3.72	116	.276	.326	66-0-10	.197	0	116	12	0	1.2
2005	†Atl N	4	6	.400	17	17	1	0-0	98.2	111	52	6	2	28-2	61	4.47	95	.284	.332	25-0-9	.200	1	95	-3	88	-0.1
2006	Atl N	2	7	.222	18	15	0	0-0	80.1	93	55	11	2	32-4	46	4.82	94	.295	.357	30-0-2	.267	2	106	-6	97	-0.3
Total	9	62	84	.425	214	210	10-3	0-0	1259.2	1385	729	154	28	366-26	797	4.69	103	.281	.332	318-0-48	.198	2	95	9	486	0.6
Thormahlen, Hank	Herbert Ehler "Lefty"; B7.5.1896 Jersey City NJ; D2.6.1955 Los Angeles CA; BL/TL/6´0˝/180; d9.29																									
1917	NY A	0	1	.000	1	1	0	0	8	9	3	0	1	4	5	2.25	119	.281	.378	2	.000	-0	27	0	—	0.0
1918	NY A	7	3	.700	16	12	5-2	0	112.2	85	39	1	6	52	22	2.48	114	.217	.318	39-0-4	.077	-3	118	4	—	0.0
1919	NY A	12	8	.600	30	25	13-2	1	188.2	155	69	10	4	61	62	2.62	122	.228	.295	59-0-3	.186	-0	103	12	—	1.1
1920	NY A	9	6	.600	29	15	6	1	143.1	178	86	5	2	43	35	4.14	92	.312	.362	45-0-5	.222	1	116	-7	—	-0.5
1921	Bos A	1	7	.125	23	9	3	0	96.1	101	56	3	6	34	17	4.48	94	.277	.349	23-0-1	.174	-1	57	-3	—	-0.3
1925	Bro N	0	3	.000	5	2	0	0	16	22	14	0	2	9	7	3.94	106	.333	.429	5	.200	0	61	-2	—	-0.2
Total	6	29	28	.509	104	64	27-4	2	565	550	267	19	21	203	148	3.33	105	.261	.332	173-0-13	.168	-3	98	4	—	0.1
Thormodsgard, Paul	Paul Gayton; B11.10.1953 San Francisco CA; BR/TR/6´2˝/(185–190); d4.10																									
1977	Min A	11	15	.423	37	37	8-1	0-0	218	236	122	25	3	65-1	94	4.62	86	.280	.331	0	ø	0	112	-15	0	-1.6
1978	Min A	1	6	.143	12	12	1	0-0	66	81	40	7	1	17-0	23	5.05	76	.308	.347	0	ø	0	72	-8	0	-0.8
1979	Min A	0	0	ø	1	0	0	0-0	1	3	1	1	0	0-0	1	9.00	49	.500	.500	0	ø	0	—	0	0	0.0
Total	3	12	21	.364	50	49	9-1	0-0	285	320	163	33	4	82-1	118	4.74	84	.288	.336	0	ø	0	102	-23	0	-2.4
Thornton, John	John; B5.22.1869 Washington DC; BL/TR/5´10.5˝/175; d8.14																									
1889	Was N	0	1	.000	1	1	1	0	9	8	11	0	0	7	3	5.00	79	.229	.357	4	.000	-1	153	-2	—	-0.2
1891	Phi N	15	16	.484	37	32	23-1	2	269	268	161	3	10	115	52	3.68	93	.250	.328	123	.138	-7*	91	-6	—	-1.2
1892	Phi N	0	2	.000	3	2	1	0	12	16	19	1	0	17	2	12.75	25	.308	.478	13	.385	1*	127	-10	—	-1.1
Total	3	15	19	.441	41	35	25-1	2	290	292	191	4	10	139	57	4.10	83	.252	.337	140	.157	-7	95	-18	—	-2.5
Thornton, Matt	Matthew J.; B9.15.1976 Three Rivers MI; BL/TL/6´6˝/(220–235); [SeaA98 1/22]; d6.27; Col Grand Valley St.; [DL 2003 Sea A 45]																									
2004	Sea A	1	2	.333	19	1	0	0-0	32.2	30	15	2	0	25-1	30	4.13	108	.250	.377	0	ø	0	41	2	0	0.1
2005	Sea A	0	4	.000	55	0	0	0-1	57	54	33	13	0	42-2	57	5.21	80	.248	.368	0	ø	0	—	-6	0	-0.4
2006	Chi A	5	3	.625	63	0	0	2-3	54	46	20	5	1	21-4	49	3.33	140	.229	.301	0	ø	0	—	8	0	1.2
Total	3	6	9	.400	137	1	0	2-4	143.2	130	68	20	1	88-7	136	4.26	104	.241	.346	0	ø	0	41	4	45	0.9
Thornton, Walter	Walter Miller; B2.18.1875 Lewiston ME; D7.14.1960 Los Angeles CA; BL/TL/6´1˝/180; d7.1; Col Cornell; ▲																									
1895	Chi N	2	0	1.000	7	2	2	1	40	58	50	3	5	31	13	6.07	84	.333	.448	22-1-0	.318	2*	196	-8	—	-0.2
1896	Chi N	2	1	.667	5	5	2	0	23.2	30	26	1	0	13	10	5.70	80	.306	.387	22	.364	2*	144	-5	—	-0.4
1897	Chi N	6	7	.462	16	16	15	0	130.1	164	91	4	6	51	55	4.70	95	.305	.371	265-0-4	.321	4*	107	0	—	0.4
1898	Chi N	13	10	.565	28	25	21-2	0	215.1	226	116	4	18	56	56	3.34	107	.268	.327	210-0-3	.295	6*	104	10	—	1.4
Total	4	23	18	.561	56	48	40-2	1	409.1	478	283	12	29	151	134	4.18	97	.289	.359	519-1-7	.312	13	114	-3	—	1.2
Thorpe, Bob	Robert Joseph; B1.12.1935 San Diego CA; D3.17.1960 San Diego CA; BR/TR/6´1˝/170; d4.17																									
1955	Chi N	0	0	ø	2	0	0	0	3	4	2	0	0	0-0	0	3.00	136	.333	.333	0	ø	0	—	0	0	0.0
Throop, George	George Lynford; B11.24.1950 Pasadena CA; BR/TR/6´7˝/(197–205); [KCA72 16/378]; d9.7; Col Cal St.–Long Beach																									
1975	KC A	0	0	ø	7	0	0	2-0	9	8	5	1	0	2-0	8	4.00	97	.250	.286	0	ø	0	—	0	0	0.0
1977	KC A	0	0	ø	4	0	0	1-0	5.1	1	2	1	0	4-0	1	3.38	120	.059	.238	0	ø	0	—	1	0	0.0
1978	KC A	1	0	1.000	1	0	0	0-0	3	2	0	0	0	3-0	2	0.00	ø	.222	.417	0	ø	0	—	1	0	0.3
1979	KC A	0	0	ø	4	0	0	0-0	2.2	7	4	0	0	5-2	1	13.50	32	.467	.600	0	ø	0	—	-2	0	-0.1
	Hou N	1	0	1.000	14	0	0	0-0	22.1	23	10	4	1	11-0	15	3.22	109	.271	.357	3	.000	-0	—	0	0	0.0
Total	4	2	0	1.000	30	0	0	3-0	42.1	41	21	6	1	25-2	27	3.83	97	.259	.360	3	.000	-0	—	0	0	0.2
Thuman, Lou	Louis Charles Frank; B12.13.1916 Baltimore MD; D12.19.2000 Baltimore MD; BR/TR/6´2˝/185; d9.8; Mil 1941–45																									
1939	Was A	0	0	ø	3	0	0	0	4	5	6	0	0	2	1	9.00	48	.278	.350	0	ø	0	—	-3	—	-0.1
1940	Was A	0	1	.000	2	0	0	0	5	10	11	0	0	7	0	14.40	29	.400	.531	2	.000	-0	—	-7	—	-0.9
Total	2	0	1	.000	5	0	0	0	9	15	17	0	0	9	1	12.00	35	.349	.462	2	.000	-0	—	-10	—	-1.0
Thurman, Corey	Corey Lamar; B11.5.1978 Augusta GA; BR/TR/6´1˝/215; [KCA96 4/109]; d4.5																									
2002	Tor A	2	3	.400	43	1	0	0-2	68	65	34	11	2	45-2	56	4.37	106	.248	.362	1-0-1	.000	-0	60	3	0	0.1
2003	Tor A	1	1	.500	6	3	0	0-0	15.1	21	11	3	0	9-1	11	6.46	74	.313	.395	0	ø	0	97	-2	0	-0.3
Total	2	3	4	.429	49	4	0	0-2	83.1	86	45	14	2	54-3	67	4.75	98	.261	.369	1-0-1	.000	-0	90	1	0	-0.2

YEAR	TM LG	W	L	PCT	G	GS	CG-SHO	SV-BS	IP	H	R	HR	HB	BB-IB	SO	ERA	AERA	OAV	OOB	AB-HR-SH	AVG	PB	SUP	APR	DL	PW
THURMAN, MIKE	Michael Richard; B7.22.1973 Corvallis OR; BR/TR/6´5˝/(210–215); [MonN94 S1/31]; d9.2; Col Oregon St.																									
1997	Mon N	1	0	1.000	5	2	0	0-0	11.2	8	9	3	1	4-0	8	5.40	77	.186	.271	2-0-1	.500	0	154	-2	0	-0.1
1998	Mon N	4	5	.444	14	13	0	0-0	67	60	38	7	3	26-2	32	4.70	89	.238	.312	23-0-2	.000	-2	119	-3	0	-0.6
1999	Mon N	7	11	.389	29	27	0	0-0	146.2	140	84	17	7	52-4	85	4.05	110	.251	.321	40-0-4	.025	-3	78	3	0	-0.1
2000	Mon N	4	9	.308	17	17	0	0-0	88.1	112	69	9	3	46-4	52	6.42	73	.315	.393	24-0-6	.042	-2	79	-16	94	-2.1
2001	Mon N	9	11	.450	28	26	0	0-0	147	172	90	21	6	50-7	96	5.33	81	.294	.351	42-0-3	.024	-3	102	-14	33	-2.0
2002	NY A	1	0	1.000	12	2	0	0-1	33	45	21	2	1	12-1	23	5.18	84	.328	.387	0	ø	0	246	-3	0	-0.2
Total	6	26	36	.419	105	87	0	0-1	493.2	537	311	59	21	190-18	296	5.05	87	.278	.346	131-0-16	.031	-10	97	-35	127	-5.1
THURMOND, MARK	Mark Anthony; B9.12.1956 Houston TX; BL/TL/6´0˝/(180–195); [SDN79 5/118]; d5.14; Col Texas A&M																									
1983	SD N	7	3	.700	21	18	2	0-0	115.1	104	40	7	2	33-2	49	2.65	132	.248	.304	37-0-6	.054	-2	113	10	0	0.7
1984	†SD N	14	8	.636	32	29	1-1	0-0	178.2	174	70	12	0	55-3	57	2.97	121	.256	.310	58-0-7	.190	1	104	11	0	1.5
1985	SD N	7	11	.389	36	23	1-1	2-1	138.1	154	70	9	3	44-5	57	3.97	90	.291	.347	34-0-9	.088	-2	89	-7	0	-1.0
1986	SD N	3	7	.300	17	15	2-1	0-0	70.2	96	58	7	0	27-5	32	6.50	56	.325	.380	24-0-2	.250	1*	93	-23	0	-2.6
	Det A	4	1	.800	25	4	0	3-1	51.2	44	13	7	0	17-2	17	1.92	217	.234	.296	0	ø	0	93	13	0	1.2
1987	†Det A	0	1	.000	48	0	0	5-2	61.2	83	32	5	0	24-4	21	4.23	101	.331	.384	0	ø	0	—	1	0	0.0
1988	Bal A	1	8	.111	43	6	0	3-0	74.2	80	43	10	2	27-3	29	4.58	86	.277	.339	0	ø	0	58	-6	0	-0.7
1989	Bal A	2	4	.333	49	2	0	4-0	90	102	43	6	1	17-2	34	3.90	98	.288	.322	0	ø	0	47	-1	0	-0.1
1990	SF N	2	3	.400	43	0	0	4-3	56.2	53	26	6	0	18-3	24	3.34	110	.257	.309	5	.000	-1	—	1	0	0.1
Total	8	40	46	.465	314	97	6-3	21-7	837.2	890	395	69	8	262-29	320	3.69	101	.277	.330	158-0-24	.139	-1	94	-1	0	-0.9
THURSTON, SLOPPY	Hollis John; B6.2.1899 Fremont NE; D9.14.1973 Los Angeles CA; BR/TR/5´11˝/165; d4.19																									
1923	StL A	0	0	ø	2	1	0	0	4	8	4	0	0	2	0	6.75	62	.421	.476	0	ø	0	139	-1	—	-0.1
	Chi A	7	8	.467	44	12	8	4	191.2	223	70	11	1	36	55	3.05	130	.308	.341	79-0-1	.316	6*	85	22	—	2.2
	Year	7	8	.467	46	13	8	4	195.2	231	74	11	1	38	55	3.13	127	.310	.345	79-0-1	.316	6	90	22	—	2.1
1924	Chi A	20	14	.588	38	36	**28**-1	1	291	330	150	17	6	60	37	3.80	108	.290	.329	122-1-5	.254	4*	117	9	—	1.5
1925	Chi A	10	14	.417	36	25	9	1	183	250	140	14	5	47	35	5.95	70	.335	.378	84-0-3	.286	7*	125	-38	—	-3.3
1926	Chi A	6	8	.429	31	13	6-1	3	134.1	164	85	10	1	36	35	5.02	77	.311	.356	61-0-1	.311	6*	99	-17	—	-1.2
1927	Was A	13	13	.500	29	28	13-2	0	205.1	254	118	16	2	60	38	4.47	91	.308	.356	92-2-4	.315	9*	98	-8	—	-0.1
1930	Bro N	6	4	.600	24	11	5-2	1	106	110	46	4	0	17	26	3.40	145	.266	.295	50-1-4	.200	-0*	74	19	—	1.6
1931	Bro N	9	9	.500	24	17	11	0	143	175	72	3	1	39	23	3.97	96	.301	.346	60-1-2	.217	2	138	-2	—	0.0
1932	Bro N	12	8	.600	28	19	10-2	0	153	174	81	14	1	38	35	4.06	94	.287	.330	56-0-2	.304	5*	134	-5	—	0.0
1933	Bro N	6	8	.429	32	15	5	3	131.1	171	70	4	6	34	22	4.52	71	.319	.366	44-0-1	.159	-1	100	-16	—	-1.6
Total	9	89	86	.509	288	177	95-8	13	1542.2	1859	836	93	23	369	306	4.24	94	.304	.346	648-5-23	.270	38	111	-37	—	-1.0
TIANT, LUIS	Luis Clemente (Vega); B11.23.1940 Marianao, Cuba; BR/TR/5´11˝/(180–205); d7.19																									
1964	Cle A	10	4	.714	19	16	9-3	1	127	94	41	13	2	47-2	105	2.83	127	.207	.283	45-1-3	.111	-1	116	13	0	1.2
1965	Cle A	11	11	.500	41	30	10-2	1	196.1	166	88	20	3	66-3	152	3.53	99	.228	.293	68-1-4	.088	-2	115	-1	0	-0.3
1966	Cle A	12	11	.522	46	16	7-**5**	8	155	121	50	16	2	50-4	145	2.79	123	.213	.279	36-0-8	.111	-1	88	13	0	1.8
1967	Cle A	12	9	.571	33	29	9-1	2	213.2	177	76	24	1	67-2	219	2.74	119	.221	.282	71-1-3	.254	5	109	12	0	1.7
1968	Cle A★	21	9	.700	34	32	19-**9**	0	258.1	152	53	16	4	73-4	264	**1.60**	**185**	**.168**	.233	87-0-11	.080	-5	96	**40**	0	**4.4**
1969	Cle A	9	20	.310	38	37	9-1	0-0	249.2	229	123	37	8	129-11	156	3.71	102	.246	.340	81-2-4	.235	5	86	0	0	0.6
1970	†Min A	7	3	.700	18	17	2-1	0-0	92.2	84	36	12	2	41-0	50	3.40	109	.246	.328	32-0-3	.406	6	132	5	63	1.2
1971	Bos A	1	7	.125	21	10	1	0-0	72.1	73	42	8	1	32-1	59	4.85	77	.259	.333	19	.158	-0	87	-8	0	-0.9
1972	Bos A	15	6	.714	43	19	12-6	3-4	179	128	45	7	0	65-5	123	**1.91**	170	.202	.275	56-0-3	.107	-2	114	25	0	2.9
1973	Bos A	20	13	.606	35	35	23	0-0	272	217	105	32	7	78-3	206	3.34	121	.219	**.278**	0	ø	0	89	23	0	2.6
1974	Bos A★	22	13	.629	38	38	25-**7**	0-0	311.1	281	106	21	4	82-3	176	2.92	132	.241	.291	0	ø	0	95	32	0	3.5
1975	†Bos A	18	14	.563	35	35	18-2	0-0	260	262	126	25	4	72-0	142	4.02	101	.264	.315	1	.000	-0	104	3	0	0.1
1976	Bos A★	21	12	.636	38	38	19-3	0-0	279	274	107	25	3	64-2	131	3.06	127	.260	.303	1	.000	-0	109	24	0	2.7
1977	Bos A	12	8	.600	32	32	3-3	0-0	188.2	210	98	26	2	51-3	124	4.53	99	.279	.325	0	ø	0	117	1	0	0.0
1978	Bos A	13	8	.619	32	31	12-5	0-0	212.1	185	80	26	5	57-4	114	3.31	125	.234	.289	0	ø	0	105	21	13	1.9
1979	NY A	13	8	.619	30	30	5-1	0-0	195.2	190	94	22	0	53-1	104	3.91	105	.251	.299	0	ø	0	117	4	0	0.4
1980	NY A	8	9	.471	25	25	3	0-0	136.1	139	79	10	1	50-3	84	4.89	81	.265	.326	0	ø	0	108	-12	22	-1.3
1981	Pit N	2	5	.286	9	9	1	0-0	57.1	54	31	3	0	19-2	32	3.92	93	.243	.303	16-0-2	.188	1	84	-3	0	-0.3
1982	Cal A	2	2	.500	6	5	0	0-0	29.2	39	20	3	0	8-0	30	5.76	71	.310	.351	0	ø	0	120	-5	0	-0.6
Total	19	229	172	.571	573	484	187-49	15-4	3486.1	3075	1400	346	49	1104-53	2416	3.30	114	.236	.297	513-5-41	.164	5	105	187	98	21.6
TIBBS, JAY	Jay Lindsey; B1.4.1962 Birmingham AL; BR/TR/6´3˝/(175–183); [NYN80 2/27]; d7.15																									
1984	Cin N	6	2	.750	14	14	3-1	0-0	100.2	87	34	4	0	33-1	40	2.86	133	.238	.302	36-0-1	.139	-1	105	10	0	0.6
1985	Cin N	10	16	.385	35	34	5-2	0-0	218	216	111	14	0	83-10	98	3.92	97	.262	.326	65-0-6	.092	-3*	96	-5	0	-0.9
1986	Mon N	7	9	.438	35	31	3-2	0-0	190.1	181	96	12	3	70-3	117	3.97	94	.256	.324	54-0-4	.130	-0*	86	-6	0	-0.5
1987	Mon N	4	5	.444	19	12	0	0-0	83	95	55	10	0	34-2	54	4.99	85	.289	.354	25	.120	0	104	-8	0	-0.7
1988	Bal A	4	15	.211	30	24	1	0-0	158.2	184	103	18	3	63-2	82	5.39	73	.293	.356	0	ø	0	82	-25	0	-2.6
1989	Bal A	5	0	1.000	10	8	1	0-0	54.1	62	17	2	0	20-0	30	2.82	136	.287	.345	0	ø	0	160	7	91	0.6
1990	Bal A	2	7	.222	10	10	0	0-0	50.2	55	34	8	0	14-1	23	5.68	67	.279	.324	0	ø	0	74	-11	0	-1.6
	Pit N	1	0	1.000	5	0	0	0-0	7	7	2	0	0	2-0	4	2.57	142	.259	.310	0	ø	0	—	1	0	0.1
Total	7	39	54	.419	158	133	13-5	0-0	862.2	887	452	68	6	319-19	448	4.20	92	.269	.333	180-0-11	.117	-4	95	-37	91	-5.0
TIDROW, DICK	Richard William; B5.14.1947 San Francisco CA; BR/TR/6´4˝/(210–215); [CleA67*S4/76]; d4.18; Col Chabot (CA) JC																									
1972	Cle A	14	15	.483	39	34	10-3	0-0	237.1	200	83	21	6	70-13	123	2.77	118	.230	.289	70-0-13	.100	-3	81	12	0	0.9
1973	Cle A	14	16	.467	42	40	13-2	0-0	274.2	289	150	31	8	95-10	138	4.42	89	.270	.332	0	ø	0	95	-14	0	-1.5
1974	Cle A	1	3	.250	4	4	0	0-0	19	21	17	4	2	13-1	8	7.11	51	.276	.387	0	ø	0	85	-7	0	-1.2
	NY A	11	9	.550	33	25	5	1-0	190.2	205	99	14	4	53-7	100	3.87	92	.279	.327	0	ø	0	117	-9	0	-0.9
	Year	12	12	.500	37	29	5	1-0	209.2	226	116	18	6	66-8	108	4.16	85	.279	.333	0	ø	0	113	-20	0	-2.1
1975	NY A	6	3	.667	37	0	0	5-4	69.1	65	27	5	3	31-6	38	3.12	119	.256	.341	0	ø	0	—	5	53	0.6
1976	†NY A	4	5	.444	47	2	0	10-3	92.1	80	29	5	1	24-1	65	2.63	130	.233	.282	0	ø	0	219	9	0	1.0
1977	†NY A	11	4	.733	49	7	0	5-2	151	143	57	20	2	41-11	83	3.16	126	.250	.300	0	ø	0	162	15	0	1.4
1978	†NY A	7	11	.389	31	25	4	0-0	185.1	191	87	13	5	53-3	73	3.84	95	.267	.320	0	ø	0	99	-3	0	-0.4
1979	NY A	2	1	.667	14	0	0	2-1	22.2	38	20	5	0	4-0	7	7.94	52	.409	.424	0	ø	0	—	-9	0	-1.1
	Chi N	11	5	.688	63	0	0	4-1	102.2	86	35	5	2	42-11	68	2.72	153	.231	.310	10-0-2	.200	0	—	15	0	2.4
1980	Chi N	6	5	.545	**84**	0	0	6-6	116	97	44	10	5	53-16	97	2.79	142	.229	.319	4	.000	-0	—	13	0	1.2
1981	Chi N	3	10	.231	51	0	0	9-4	74.2	73	45	6	1	30-15	39	5.06	74	.256	.328	5-0-1	.000	-1	—	-9	0	-1.8
1982	Chi N	8	3	.727	65	0	0	6-1	103.2	106	45	6	3	29-10	62	3.39	112	.265	.318	6	.000	-1	—	4	0	0.3
1983	†Chi A	2	4	.333	50	1	0	7-2	91.2	86	50	13	1	34-8	66	4.22	100	.242	.308	0	ø	0	108	-1	0	0.0
1984	NY N	0	0	ø	11	0	0	0-0	15.2	25	19	5	0	7-0	8	9.19	39	.357	.410	0	ø	0	—	-10	0	-0.5
Total	13	100	94	.515	620	138	32-5	55-24	1746.2	1705	807	163	43	579-112	975	3.68	102	.257	.318	95-0-16	.095	-5	99	11	53	0.4
TIEFENAUER, BOBBY	Bobby Gene; B10.10.1929 Desloge MO; D6.13.2000 Desloge MO; BR/TR/6´2˝/(185–188); d7.14; C1; [DL 1959 Cle A 172]																									
1952	StL N	0	0	ø	6	0	0	0	8	12	8	1	0	7	3	7.88	47	.343	.452	1	.000	-0	—	-4	0	-0.2
1955	StL N	1	4	.200	18	0	0	0	32.2	31	19	6	4	10-4	16	4.41	92	.261	.331	5-0-1	.000	-0	—	-2	0	-0.3
1960	Cle A	0	1	.000	6	0	0	0	9	8	2	0	0	3-0	2	2.00	187	.242	.306	1	.000	0	—	2	0	0.2
1961	StL N	0	0	ø	3	0	0	0	4.1	9	4	0	0	4-0	3	6.23	71	.450	.542	0	ø	0	—	-1	0	-0.1
1962	Hou N	2	4	.333	43	0	0	1	85	91	42	6	2	21-2	60	4.34	86	.277	.320	9	.111	0	—	-3	0	-0.3
1963	Mil N	1	1	.500	12	0	0	2	29.2	20	4	1	0	4-0	22	1.21	265	.194	.222	5-0-1	.000	-0	—	7	0	0.6
1964	Mil N	4	6	.400	46	0	0	13	73	61	33	6	3	15-2	48	3.21	110	.225	.273	14-0-1	.000	-1	—	1	0	0.0
1965	Mil N	0	1	.000	6	0	0	0	7	8	7	1	1	3-1	7	7.71	46	.286	.364	0	ø	0	—	-3	0	-0.4
	NY A	1	1	.500	10	0	0	2	20.1	19	10	3	1	5-1	15	3.54	96	.253	.301	2	.000	0	—	-1	0	-0.1
	Cle A	0	5	.000	15	0	0	4	22.1	24	17	3	1	10-3	13	4.84	72	.273	.354	1	.000	-0	—	-5	0	-1.0
	Year	1	6	.143	25	0	0	6	42.2	43	27	6	2	15-4	28	4.22	82	.264	.330	3	.000	-0	—	-5	0	-1.1
1967	Cle A	0	1	.000	5	0	0	0	11.1	9	3	0	0	3-1	6	0.79	411	.225	.279	0	ø	0	—	2	0	0.2
1968	Chi N	0	1	.000	9	0	0	1	13.1	20	12	2	0	2-1	9	6.08	52	.351	.367	1	.000	-0	—	-5	0	-0.5
Total	10	9	25	.265	179	0	0	23	316	312	161	29	12	87-15	204	3.84	94	.260	.314	39-0-3	.026	-1	—	-12	172	-1.9
TIEFENTHALER, VERLE	Verle Matthew; B7.11.1937 Breda IA; BL/TR/6´1˝/190; d8.19																									
1962	Chi A	0	0	ø	3	0	0	0	3.2	6	4	1	0	7-0	1	9.82	40	.353	.542	0	ø	0	—	-2	0	-0.1

TIERNAN, MIKE Michael Joseph "Silent Mike"; B1.21.1867 Trenton NJ; D11.7.1918 New York NY; BL/TL/5´11˝/165; d4.30; ▲

YEAR	TM LG	W	L	PCT	G	GS	CG-SHO	SV-BS	IP	H	R	HR	HB	BB-IB	SO	ERA	AERA	OAV	OOB	AB-HR-SH	AVG	PB	SUP	APR	DL	PW
1887	NY N	1	2	.333	5	0	0	**1**	19.2	33	25	2	1	7	3	8.69	43	.398	.451	407-10	.287	2*	—	-10	—	-1.1

TIETJE, LES Leslie William "Toots"; B9.11.1910 Sumner IA; D10.2.1996 Rochester MN; BR/TR/6´0.5˝/178; d9.18

YEAR	TM LG	W	L	PCT	G	GS	CG-SHO	SV-BS	IP	H	R	HR	HB	BB-IB	SO	ERA	AERA	OAV	OOB	AB-HR-SH	AVG	PB	SUP	APR	DL	PW
1933	Chi A	2	0	1.000	3	3	1	0	22.1	16	8	1	0	15	9	2.42	175	.203	.330	8-0-1	.125	0	100	4	—	0.4
1934	Chi A	5	14	.263	34	22	6-1	0	176	174	106	20	2	96	81	4.81	98	.257	.351	59-0-3	.017	-7	65	0	—	-0.6
1935	Chi A	9	15	.375	30	21	9-1	0	169.2	184	88	14	2	81	64	4.30	108	.277	.357	61-0-3	.197	-1	75	7	—	0.7
1936	Chi A	0	0	ø	2	0	0	0	2.1	6	7	0	0	5	3	27.00	19	.462	.611	0	ø	0	—	-5	—	-0.2
	StL A	3	5	.375	14	7	2	0	50.1	65	44	2	2	30	16	6.62	81	.310	.401	15-0-1	.067	-1*	87	-7	—	-1.0
	Year	3	5	.375	16	7	2	0	52.2	71	51	2	2	35	19	7.52	71	.318	.415	15-0-1	.067	-1	87	-12	—	-1.2
1937	StL A	1	2	.333	5	4	2	0	30	32	15	0	0	17	5	4.20	115	.283	.377	10-0-1	.000	-2	50	2	—	0.0
1938	StL A	2	5	.286	17	8	2-1	0	62	83	55	8	0	38	15	7.55	66	.327	.414	18-0-3	.111	-1*	95	-16	—	-1.5
Total	6	22	41	.349	105	65	22-3	0	512.2	560	323	45	6	282	193	5.11	93	.279	.369	171-0-12	.099	-12	75	-15	—	-2.2

TIFT, RAY Raymond Frank; B6.21.1884 Fitchburg MA; D3.29.1945 Verona NJ; TL/5´10.5˝/155; d8.7; Col Brown

YEAR	TM LG	W	L	PCT	G	GS	CG-SHO	SV-BS	IP	H	R	HR	HB	BB-IB	SO	ERA	AERA	OAV	OOB	AB-HR-SH	AVG	PB	SUP	APR	DL	PW
1907	NY A	0	0	ø	4	1	0	0	19	33	14	0	0	4	6	4.74	59	.384	.411	5	.000	-0	145	-3	—	-0.3

TILLMAN, JOHNNY John Lawrence "Ducky"; B10.6.1893 Bridgeport CT; D4.7.1964 Harrisburg PA; BB/TR/5´11˝/170; d9.20

YEAR	TM LG	W	L	PCT	G	GS	CG-SHO	SV-BS	IP	H	R	HR	HB	BB-IB	SO	ERA	AERA	OAV	OOB	AB-HR-SH	AVG	PB	SUP	APR	DL	PW
1915	StL A	1	0	1.000	2	1	0	0	10	6	2	0	0	4	6	0.90	318	.176	.263	3	.000	-0	76	2	—	0.2

TILLOTSON, THAD Thaddeus Asa; B12.20.1940 Merced CA; BR/TR/6´2.5˝/195; d4.14; Col Fresno (CA) City

YEAR	TM LG	W	L	PCT	G	GS	CG-SHO	SV-BS	IP	H	R	HR	HB	BB-IB	SO	ERA	AERA	OAV	OOB	AB-HR-SH	AVG	PB	SUP	APR	DL	PW
1967	NY A	3	9	.250	43	5	1	2	98.1	99	52	9	2	39-3	62	4.03	78	.261	.331	16-0-1	.063	-0	56	-10	0	-1.3
1968	NY A	1	0	1.000	7	0	0	0	10.1	11	6	0	0	7-2	1	4.35	67	.282	.383	1	.000	-0	—	-2	0	-0.2
Total	2	4	9	.308	50	5	1	2	108.2	110	58	9	2	46-5	63	4.06	77	.263	.336	17-0-1	.059	-1	56	-12	0	-1.5

TIMBERLAKE, GARY Gary Dale; B8.9.1948 Laconia IN; BR/TL/6´2˝/205; [NYA66 2/30]; d6.18; Mil 1969

YEAR	TM LG	W	L	PCT	G	GS	CG-SHO	SV-BS	IP	H	R	HR	HB	BB-IB	SO	ERA	AERA	OAV	OOB	AB-HR-SH	AVG	PB	SUP	APR	DL	PW
1969	Sea A	0	0	ø	2	2	0	0-0	6	7	6	0	0	9-0	4	7.50	49	.269	.457	1-0-1	.000	-0	121	-3	0	-0.2

TIMLIN, MIKE Michael August; B3.10.1966 Midland TX; BR/TR/6´4˝/(205–210); [TorA87 5/127]; d4.8; Col Southwestern (TX)

YEAR	TM LG	W	L	PCT	G	GS	CG-SHO	SV-BS	IP	H	R	HR	HB	BB-IB	SO	ERA	AERA	OAV	OOB	AB-HR-SH	AVG	PB	SUP	APR	DL	PW
1991	†Tor A	11	6	.647	63	3	0	3-5	108.1	94	43	6	1	50-11	85	3.16	134	.233	.317	0	ø	0	43	12	15	1.8
1992	†Tor A	0	2	.000	26	0	0	1-0	43.2	45	23	0	1	20-5	35	4.12	100	.271	.351	0	ø	0	—	-1	67	0.0
1993	†Tor A	4	2	.667	54	0	0	1-3	55.2	63	32	7	1	27-3	49	4.69	93	.284	.360	0	ø	0	—	-2	0	-0.1
1994	Tor A	0	1	.000	34	0	0	2-2	40	41	25	5	2	20-0	38	5.17	94	.261	.352	0	ø	0	—	-1	15	-0.1
1995	Tor A	4	3	.571	31	0	0	5-4	42	38	13	1	2	17-5	36	2.14	222	.242	.324	0	ø	0	—	11	57	1.9
1996	Tor A	1	6	.143	59	0	0	31-7	56.2	47	25	4	2	18-4	52	3.65	137	.229	.294	0	ø	0	—	9	0	1.6
1997	Tor A	3	2	.600	38	0	0	9-4	47	41	17	6	1	15-4	36	2.87	160	.243	.306	0	ø	0	—	9	0	1.1
	†Sea A	3	2	.600	26	0	0	1-4	25.2	28	13	2	0	5-1	9	3.86	118	.280	.314	0	ø	0	—	1	0	0.3
	Year	6	4	.600	64	0	0	10-8	72.2	69	30	8	1	20-5	45	3.22	142	.257	.309	0	ø	0	—	10	0	1.4
1998	Sea A	3	3	.500	70	0	0	19-5	79.1	78	26	5	3	16-2	60	2.95	159	.264	.306	0	ø	0	—	16	0	1.8
1999	Bal A	3	9	.250	62	0	0	27-9	63	51	30	9	5	23-3	50	3.57	132	.221	.304	0	ø	0	—	7	0	1.2
2000	Bal A	2	3	.400	37	0	0	11-4	35	37	22	6	2	15-3	26	4.89	96	.276	.355	0	ø	0	—	-2	13	-0.2
	†StL N	3	1	.750	25	0	0	1-2	29.2	30	11	2	2	20-3	26	3.34	139	.265	.382	0	ø	0	—	5	0	0.6
2001	†StL N	4	5	.444	67	0	0	3-4	72.2	78	35	6	3	19-4	47	4.09	106	.277	.327	1	.000	-0*	—	2	22	0.3
2002	StL N	1	3	.250	42	1	0	0-2	61	48	19	9	4	7-2	35	2.51	161	.215	.252	6	.000	-1	23	10	0	0.6
	Phi N	3	3	.500	30	0	0	0-2	35.2	27	16	6	1	7-0	15	3.79	101	.206	.250	0	ø	0	—	0	0	0.0
	Year	4	6	.400	72	1	0	0-4	96.2	75	35	15	5	14-2	50	2.98	133	.212	.251	6	.000	-1	23	11	0	0.6
2003	†Bos A	6	4	.600	72	0	0	2-4	83.2	77	37	11	4	9-3	65	3.55	131	.239	.268	0	ø	0	—	10	0	1.1
2004	†Bos A	5	4	.556	76	0	0	1-3	76.1	75	35	8	5	19-3	56	4.13	118	.257	.312	0	ø	0	—	8	0	0.8
2005	†Bos A	7	3	.700	**81**	0	0	13-7	80.1	86	23	2	2	20-5	59	2.24	203	.277	.319	0	ø	0	—	19	0	2.6
2006	Bos A	6	6	.500	68	0	0	9-8	64	78	33	7	2	16-4	30	4.36	107	.305	.349	0	ø	0	—	2	18	0.4
Total	16	69	68	.504	961	4	0	139-79	1099.2	1062	478	102	43	343-65	809	3.55	128	.255	.316	7	.000	-1	36	115	207	15.7

TIMMERMANN, TOM Thomas Henry; B5.12.1940 Breese IL; BR/TR/6´4˝/(210–215); d6.18; Col Southern Illinois

YEAR	TM LG	W	L	PCT	G	GS	CG-SHO	SV-BS	IP	H	R	HR	HB	BB-IB	SO	ERA	AERA	OAV	OOB	AB-HR-SH	AVG	PB	SUP	APR	DL	PW
1969	Det A	4	3	.571	31	1	1	1-1	55.2	50	22	1	2	26-4	42	2.75	137	.238	.326	9	.111	-0	94	5	0	0.5
1970	Det A	6	7	.462	61	0	0	27-5	85.1	90	44	3	2	34-11	49	4.11	92	.273	.337	16	.000	-2	—	-4	0	-0.9
1971	Det A	7	6	.538	52	2	0	4-6	84	82	36	6	3	37-3	51	3.86	94	.262	.345	19-0-2	.053	-1	136	-1	0	-0.2
1972	Det A	8	10	.444	34	25	3-2	0-0	149.2	121	57	12	5	41-1	88	2.89	110	.216	.276	44-0-2	.136	-0*	109	3	0	0.3
1973	Det A	1	1	.500	17	1	0	1-0	39	39	17	4	0	11-1	21	3.69	111	.258	.309	0	ø	0	0	2	0	0.1
	Cle A	8	7	.533	29	15	4	2-1	124.1	117	73	15	3	54-7	62	4.92	80	.251	.330	0	ø	0	110	-12	0	-1.3
	Year	9	8	.529	46	16	4	3-1	163.1	156	90	19	3	65-8	83	4.63	86	.252	.325	0	ø	0	102	-10	0	-1.2
1974	Cle A	1	1	.500	4	0	0	0-0	10	9	6	1	0	5-0	2	5.40	67	.250	.341	0	ø	0	—	-2	0	-0.3
Total	6	35	35	.500	228	44	8-2	35-13	548	508	255	42	15	208-27	315	3.78	97	.246	.317	88-0-4	.091	-4	103	-9	0	-1.8

TINCUP, BEN Austin Ben; B4.14.1893 Adair OK; D7.5.1980 Claremore OK; BL/TR/6´1˝/180; d5.22; Mil 1918; C1

YEAR	TM LG	W	L	PCT	G	GS	CG-SHO	SV-BS	IP	H	R	HR	HB	BB-IB	SO	ERA	AERA	OAV	OOB	AB-HR-SH	AVG	PB	SUP	APR	DL	PW
1914	Phi N	8	10	.444	28	17	9-3	2	155	165	71	0	4	62	108	2.61	113	.286	.359	53-0-2	.170	-1*	92	4	—	0.4
1915	Phi N	0	0	ø	10	0	0	0	31	26	8	1	0	9	10	2.03	135	.263	.324	9	.000	-1*	—	3	—	0.1
1918	Phi N	0	1	.000	8	1	0	0	16.2	24	20	0	0	6	6	7.56	40	.329	.380	8	.125	-0*	50	-9	—	-0.5
1928	Chi N	0	0	ø	2	0	0	0	9	14	7	0	0	1	3	7.00	55	.378	.395	3	.000	-0	—	-3	—	-0.2
Total	4	8	11	.421	48	18	9-3	2	211.2	229	106	1	4	78	127	3.10	95	.291	.358	73-0-2	.137	-3	90	-5	—	-0.2

TINNING, BUD Lyle Forrest; B3.12.1906 Pilger NE; D1.17.1961 Evansville IN; BB/TR (BR 1934–35)/5´11˝/198; d4.20

YEAR	TM LG	W	L	PCT	G	GS	CG-SHO	SV-BS	IP	H	R	HR	HB	BB-IB	SO	ERA	AERA	OAV	OOB	AB-HR-SH	AVG	PB	SUP	APR	DL	PW
1932	†Chi N	5	3	.625	24	7	2	0	93.1	93	34	3	2	24	30	2.80	135	.263	.313	23	.087	-1	77	10	—	0.7
1933	Chi N	13	6	.684	32	21	10-3	1	175.1	169	73	3	4	60	59	3.18	103	.255	.320	67-0-3	.209	1	135	3	—	0.2
1934	Chi N	4	6	.400	39	7	1-1	3	129.1	134	59	9	1	46	44	3.34	116	.269	.332	39-0-2	.179	-1	89	6	—	0.3
1935	StL N	0	0	ø	4	0	0	0	7.2	9	6	1	1	5	2	5.87	70	.300	.417	1	.000	-0	—	-2	—	-0.1
Total	4	22	15	.595	99	35	13-4	4	405.2	405	172	16	8	135	135	3.19	113	.262	.325	130-0-5	.177	-1	109	17	—	1.1

TIPPLE, DAN Daniel E. "Big Dan","Rusty"; B2.13.1890 Rockford IL; D3.26.1960 Omaha NE; BR/TR/6´0˝/176; d9.18

YEAR	TM LG	W	L	PCT	G	GS	CG-SHO	SV-BS	IP	H	R	HR	HB	BB-IB	SO	ERA	AERA	OAV	OOB	AB-HR-SH	AVG	PB	SUP	APR	DL	PW
1915	NY A	1	1	.500	3	2	2	0	19	14	6	1	0	11	14	0.95	310	.203	.313	6	.000	-1	99	3	—	0.1

TISING, JACK Johnnie Joseph; B10.9.1903 High Point MO; D9.5.1967 Leadville CO; BL/TR/6´2˝/180; d4.24; Col Denver

YEAR	TM LG	W	L	PCT	G	GS	CG-SHO	SV-BS	IP	H	R	HR	HB	BB-IB	SO	ERA	AERA	OAV	OOB	AB-HR-SH	AVG	PB	SUP	APR	DL	PW
1936	Pit N	1	3	.250	10	6	1	0	47	52	26	5	0	24	27	4.21	96	.272	.353	11	.273	0	77	-1	—	-0.1

TITCOMB, CANNONBALL Ledell; B8.21.1866 W.Baldwin ME; D6.8.1950 Kingston NH; BL/TL/5´6˝/157; d5.5

YEAR	TM LG	W	L	PCT	G	GS	CG-SHO	SV-BS	IP	H	R	HR	HB	BB-IB	SO	ERA	AERA	OAV	OOB	AB-HR-SH	AVG	PB	SUP	APR	DL	PW
1886	Phi N	0	5	.000	5	5	5	0	41	43	45	1	—	24	24	3.73	88	.244	.335	16	.063	-2	45	-6	—	-0.7
1887	Phi AA	1	2	.333	3	3	3	0	24	31	30	1	0	19	16	6.75	64	.298	.407	10	.000	-1	89	-8	—	-0.8
	NY N	4	3	.571	9	9	9	0	72	68	50	3	1	37	34	3.88	97	.233	.321	29	.069	-4	78	-1	—	-0.4
1888	†NY N	14	8	.636	23	23	22-4	0	197	149	91	4	5	46	129	2.24	122	.201	.253	82	.122	-4	123	10	—	0.4
1889	NY N	1	2	.333	3	3	3	0	26	27	26	1	2	16	7	6.58	60	.260	.369	12	.083	-1	74	-6	—	-0.6
1890	Roc AA	10	9	.526	20	19	19-1	0	168.2	168	123	6	14	97	73	3.74	95	.251	.358	75	.107	-5*	122	-9	—	-1.4
Total	5	30	29	.508	63	62	61-5	0	528.2	486	365	16	22	239	283	3.47	96	.233	.318	224	.098	-18	104	-20	—	-3.5

TOBIK, DAVE David Vance; B3.2.1953 Euclid OH; BR/TR/6´1˝/(190–195); [DetA75*S1/2]; d8.26; Col Ohio U.

YEAR	TM LG	W	L	PCT	G	GS	CG-SHO	SV-BS	IP	H	R	HR	HB	BB-IB	SO	ERA	AERA	OAV	OOB	AB-HR-SH	AVG	PB	SUP	APR	DL	PW
1978	Det A	0	0	ø	5	0	0	0-0	12	12	5	1	0	3-0	11	3.75	104	.261	.306	0	ø	0	—	0	0	0.0
1979	Det A	3	5	.375	37	0	0	3-5	68.2	59	34	12	0	25-5	48	4.33	101	.231	.295	0	ø	0	—	1	0	0.1
1980	Det A	1	0	1.000	17	1	0	0-0	61	61	27	7	0	21-4	34	3.98	104	.266	.325	0	ø	0	152	2	0	0.1
1981	Det A	2	2	.500	27	0	0	1-2	60.1	47	19	7	0	33-3	32	2.69	141	.215	.313	0	ø	0	—	7	0	0.4
1982	Det A	4	9	.308	51	1	0	9-3	98.2	86	45	8	1	38-8	63	3.56	115	.241	.312	0	ø	0	156	5	0	0.7
1983	Tex A	2	1	.667	27	0	0	9-0	44	36	18	2	0	13-3	30	3.68	110	.222	.278	0	ø	0	—	3	0	0.3
1984	Tex A	1	6	.143	24	0	0	5-3	42.1	44	20	5	1	17-6	30	3.61	116	.265	.337	0	ø	0	—	2	0	0.4
1985	Sea A	1	0	1.000	8	0	0	1-1	9	10	8	2	0	3-0	8	6.00	70	.286	.325	0	ø	0	—	-2	0	-0.3
Total	8	14	23	.378	196	2	0	28-14	396	355	176	44	2	153-29	256	3.70	111	.242	.310	0	ø	0	154	18	0	1.7

YEAR	TM LG	W	L	PCT	G	GS	CG-SHO	SV-BS	IP	H	R	HR	HB	BB-IB	SO	ERA	AERA	OAV	OOB	AB-HR-SH	AVG	PB	SUP	APR	DL	PW
Tobin, Jim	James Anthony "Abba Dabba"; B12.27.1912 Oakland CA; D5.19.1969 Oakland CA; BR/TR/6´0˝/185; d4.30; b–Johnny																									
1937	Pit N	6	3	.667	20	8	7	1	87	74	38	1	1	28	37	3.00	129	.226	.289	34	.441	7*	100	7	—	1.3
1938	Pit N	14	12	.538	40	33	14-2	0	241.1	254	109	17	6	66	70	3.47	109	.270	.321	103-0-1	.243	7*	99	9	—	1.5
1939	Pit N	9	9	.500	25	19	8	0	145.1	194	84	7	2	33	43	4.52	85	.319	.356	74-2-1	.243	5*	99	-11	—	-0.8
1940	Bos N	7	3	.700	15	11	9	0	96.1	102	41	8	0	24	29	3.83	97	.264	.307	43	.279	3*	132	1	—	0.4
1941	Bos N	12	12	.500	33	26	20-3	0	238	229	91	12	0	60	61	3.10	115	.253	.300	103	.184	3*	93	15	0	2.1
1942	Bos N	12	21	.364	37	33	**28**-1	0	**287.2**	283	145	20	6	96	71	3.97	84	.257	.320	114-6-0	.246	14*	86	-19	0	-0.3
1943	Bos N	14	14	.500	33	30	24-1	0	250	241	96	12	2	69	52	2.66	128	.251	.303	107-2-0	.280	6*	80	18	0	3.1
1944	Bos N★	18	19	.486	43	36	**28**-5	3	299.1	271	125	18	3	97	83	3.01	127	.240	.302	116-2-2	.190	5*	85	23	0	3.8
1945	Bos N	9	14	.391	27	25	16	0	196.2	220	101	10	5	56	38	3.84	100	.282	.334	77-3-0	.143	5*	110	-2	0	0.5
	†Det A	4	5	.444	14	6	2	1	58.1	61	31	2	4	28	14	3.55	99	.274	.365	25-2-1	.120	0*	69	-1	0	-0.2
Total	9	105	112	.484	287	227	156-12	5	1900	1929	861	107	29	557	498	3.44	106	.262	.316	796-17-5	.230	54	94	40	0	11.4
Tobin, Pat	Marion Brooks; B1.28.1916 Hermitage AR; D1.21.1975 Shreveport LA; BR/TR/6´1˝/198; d8.21																									
1941	Phi A	0	0	ø	1	0	0	0	1	4	5	0	0	2	0	36.00	12	.571	.667	0	ø	0	—	-4	0	-0.2
Todd, Frank	George Franklin; B10.18.1869 Aberdeen MD; D8.11.1919 Havre de Grace MD; TL; d7.14																									
1898	Lou N	0	2	.000	4	2	0	0	11	23	21	0	2	8	5	13.91	26	.418	.508	5	.200	0	49	-12	—	-1.5
Todd, Jackson	Jackson A; B11.20.1951 Tulsa OK; BR/TR/6´2˝/(180–190); [NYN73 2/38]; d5.5; Col Oklahoma																									
1977	NY N	3	6	.333	19	10	0	0-0	71.2	78	41	8	2	20-5	39	4.77	80	.273	.325	17	.059	-1	91	-8	0	-1.0
1979	Tor A	0	1	.000	12	1	0	0-0	32.1	40	26	7	1	7-0	14	5.85	75	.299	.333	0	ø	0	21	-6	0	-0.3
1980	Tor A	5	2	.714	12	12	4	0-0	85	90	40	14	2	30-1	44	4.02	107	.276	.340	0	ø	0	97	4	0	0.3
1981	Tor A	2	7	.222	21	13	3	0-0	97.2	94	51	10	4	31-2	41	3.96	100	.251	.313	0	ø	0	63	-1	0	0.0
Total	4	10	16	.385	64	36	7	0-0	286.2	302	158	39	9	88-8	138	4.40	93	.270	.326	17	.059	-1	81	-11	0	-1.0
Todd, Jim	James Richard; B9.21.1947 Lancaster PA; BL/TR/6´2˝/(180–195); [ChiN69 10/230]; d4.29; Col Millersville																									
1974	Chi N	4	2	.667	43	6	0	3-1	88	82	45	7	3	41-3	42	3.89	99	.252	.338	16	.063	-1	72	-1	0	-0.2
1975	†Oak A	8	3	.727	58	0	0	12-2	122	104	40	4	3	33-4	50	2.29	160	.234	.290	0	ø	0	—	17	0	2.0
1976	Oak A	7	8	.467	49	0	0	4-1	82.2	87	43	6	6	34-8	22	3.81	88	.276	.357	0	ø	0	—	-6	0	-1.0
1977	Chi N	1	1	.500	20	0	0	0-1	30.2	47	37	1	2	19-2	17	9.10	48	.336	.422	1-0-1	.000	-0	—	-15	0	-0.9
1978	Sea A	3	4	.429	49	2	0	3-2	106.2	113	52	4	0	61-4	37	3.88	99	.280	.373	0	ø	0	70	-1	0	0.0
1979	Oak A	2	5	.286	51	0	0	2-3	81	108	66	12	2	51-10	26	6.56	62	.329	.415	0	ø	0	—	-23	0	-1.8
Total	6	25	23	.521	270	8	0	24-10	511	541	283	34	16	239-31	194	4.23	90	.277	.357	17-0-1	.059	-2	73	-29	0	-1.9
Toenes, Hal	William Harrel; B10.8.1917 Mobile AL; D6.28.2004 Tampa FL; BR/TR/5´11.5˝/175; d9.17																									
1947	Was A	0	1	.000	3	1	0	0	6.2	11	5	0	0	2	5	6.75	55	.379	.419	1-0-1	.000	0	48	-2	0	-0.3
Tolar, Kevin	Kevin Anthony; B1.28.1971 Panama City FL; BR/TL/6´3˝/(225–230); [ChiA89 9/225]; d9.11																									
2000	Det A	0	0	ø	5	0	0	0-0	3	1	1	0	0	1-0	3	3.00	164	.091	.167	0	ø	0	—	1	0	0.0
2001	Det A	0	0	ø	9	0	0	0-0	10.2	7	8	0	0	13-1	11	6.75	66	.189	.400	0	ø	0	—	-2	0	-0.1
2003	Bos A	0	0	ø	6	0	0	0-0	4	5	5	1	0	2-0	3	9.00	52	.313	.389	0	ø	0	—	-2	0	-0.1
Total	3	0	0	ø	20	0	0	0-0	17.2	13	14	1	0	16-1	17	6.62	69	.203	.363	0	ø	0	—	-3	0	-0.2
Toliver, Freddie	Freddie Lee; B2.3.1961 Natchez MS; BR/TR/6´1˝/(165–170); [NYA79 3/77]; d9.15																									
1984	Cin N	0	0	ø	3	1	0	0-0	10	7	2	0	0	7-0	4	0.90	421	.206	.341	1-0-1	.000	-0	47	3	0	0.1
1985	Phi N	0	4	.000	11	3	0	1-1	25	27	15	2	0	17-1	23	4.68	79	.273	.376	4	.500	1	40	-3	0	-0.4
1986	Phi N	0	2	.000	5	5	0	0-0	25.2	28	14	0	0	11-0	20	3.51	111	.286	.358	6	.000	-0	91	0	116	0.0
1987	Phi N	1	1	.500	10	4	0	0-0	30.1	34	19	2	1	17-3	25	5.64	76	.291	.380	5-0-2	.000	-1	148	-3	0	-0.2
1988	Min A	7	6	.538	21	19	0	0-0	114.2	116	57	8	1	52-1	69	4.24	97	.270	.349	0	ø	0	101	-1	0	-0.1
1989	Min A	1	3	.250	7	5	0	0-0	29	39	26	2	1	15-0	11	7.76	53	.317	.396	0	ø	0*	52	-10	0	-1.1
	SD N	0	0	ø	9	0	0	0-0	14	17	14	5	1	9-0	14	7.07	50	.321	.422	0	ø	0	—	-6	0	-0.3
1993	Pit N	1	0	1.000	12	0	0	0-0	21.2	20	10	2	2	8-0	14	3.74	109	.267	.341	2	.000	-0	—	1	0	0.0
Total	7	10	16	.385	78	37	0	1-1	270.1	288	157	21	6	136-5	180	4.73	85	.280	.365	18-0-3	.111	-0	93	-19	116	-2.0
Tollberg, Brian	Brian Patrick; B9.16.1972 Tampa FL; BR/TR/6´3˝/195; d6.20; Col North Florida																									
2000	SD N	4	5	.444	19	19	1	0-0	118	126	58	13	5	35-4	76	3.58	124	.274	.332	32-0-6	.094	-2	81	9	0	0.4
2001	SD N	10	4	.714	19	19	0	0-0	117.1	133	58	15	2	25-3	71	4.30	97	.287	.321	40-0-5	.200	1	127	0	70	0.2
2002	SD N	1	5	.167	12	11	0	0-0	61.2	88	47	11	1	19-2	33	6.13	63	.342	.382	19-0-1	.158	1	93	-17	123	-1.3
2003	SD N	0	2	.000	3	3	0	0-0	10.1	9	11	1	0	4-0	2	6.97	58	.231	.295	2-0-1	.000	-0	86	-5	0	-0.7
Total	4	15	16	.484	53	52	1	0-0	307.1	356	174	40	8	83-9	182	4.48	94	.292	.337	93-0-13	.151	-0	100	-13	193	-1.4
Tomanek, Dick	Richard Carl "Bones"; B1.6.1931 Avon Lake OH; BL/TL/6´1˝/(165–175); d9.25																									
1953	Cle A	1	0	1.000	1	1	1	0	9	6	3	1	1	6	6	2.00	188	.176	.317	5	.000	-1	284	2	0	0.1
1954	Cle A	0	0	ø	1	0	0	0	1.2	1	1	1	0	1	0	5.40	68	.167	.286	0	ø	0	—	0	0	0.0
1957	Cle A	2	1	.667	34	2	0	0	69.2	67	51	13	1	37-3	55	5.68	65	.248	.341	13	.231	0	132	-16	0	-0.7
1958	Cle A	2	3	.400	18	6	2	0	57.2	61	37	8	2	28-2	42	5.62	65	.276	.361	17-1-1	.118	0*	111	-12	0	-0.9
	KC A	5	5	.500	36	2	1	5	72.1	69	34	5	0	28-3	50	3.61	108	.252	.321	13	.231	1	103	1	0	0.3
	Year	7	8	.467	54	8	3	5	130	130	71	13	2	56-5	92	4.50	84	.263	.339	30-1-1	.167	1	107	-10	0	-0.6
1959	KC A	1	0	1.000	16	0	0	2-3	20.2	27	15	6	2	12-1	13	6.53	61	.310	.406	2	.500	0	—	-5	71	-0.2
Total	5	10	10	.500	106	11	4	7	231	231	141	34	6	112-9	166	4.95	77	.259	.345	50-1-1	.180	1	127	-30	71	-1.4
Tomasic, Andy	Andrew John; B12.10.1919 Hokendauqua PA; BR/TR/6´0˝/175; d4.28; Col Temple																									
1949	NY N	0	1	.000	2	0	0	0	5	9	10	2	0	5	2	18.00	22	.375	.483	1	.000	-0.	—	-7	0	-1.0
Tomko, Brett	Brett Daniel; B4.7.1973 Cleveland OH; BR/TR/6´4˝/(215–225); [CinN95 2/54]; d5.27; Col Florida Southern																									
1997	Cin N	11	7	.611	22	19	0	0-0	126	106	50	14	4	47-4	95	3.43	125	.233	.305	36-0-3	.139	-0*	86	12	0	1.5
1998	Cin N	13	12	.520	34	34	1	0-0	210.2	198	111	22	7	64-3	162	4.44	97	.247	.307	65-0-9	.108	-2*	98	-3	0	-0.6
1999	Cin N	5	7	.417	33	26	1	0-0	172	175	103	31	4	60-10	132	4.92	95	.263	.325	47-0-8	.213	2	102	-4	0	-0.1
2000	†Sea A	7	5	.583	32	8	0	1-1	92.1	92	53	12	3	40-4	59	4.68	103	.264	.341	0	ø	0	90	1	16	0.0
2001	Sea A	3	1	.750	11	4	0	0-1	34.2	42	24	9	0	15-2	22	5.19	82	.288	.350	0	ø	0	169	-5	0	-0.5
2002	SD N	10	10	.500	32	32	3	0-0	204.1	212	107	31	2	60-9	126	4.49	86	.267	.317	66-0-7	.182	1	101	-12	0	-1.0
2003	StL N	13	9	.591	33	32	2	0-0	202.2	252	126	35	5	57-2	114	5.28	78	.305	.352	63-0-11	.286	6*	130	-27	0	-2.1
2004	SF N	11	7	.611	32	31	2-1	0-0	194	196	98	19	0	64-3	108	4.04	107	.260	.318	62-0-13	.113	-2*	124	5	16	0.1
2005	SF N	8	15	.348	33	30	3	1-0	190.2	205	99	20	7	57-11	114	4.48	95	.274	.329	55-0-10	.164	-0	76	-4	0	-0.5
2006	†LA N	8	7	.533	44	15	0	0-3	112.1	123	67	17	2	29-0	76	4.73	93	.276	.318	25-0-5	.120	-0*	102	-5	33	-0.7
Total	10	89	80	.527	306	231	12-1	2-5	1539.2	1601	838	210	34	493-48	1008	4.54	95	.268	.324	419-0-66	.169	4	104	-42	65	-3.9
Tomlin, Dave	David Allen; B6.22.1949 Maysville KY; BL/TL/6´3˝/(170–185); [CinN67 29/554]; d9.2																									
1972	Cin N	0	0	ø	3	0	0	0-0	4	7	4	2	0	1-0	2	9.00	36	.412	.421	0	ø	0	—	-3	0	-0.1
1973	†Cin N	1	2	.333	16	0	0	1-0	27.2	24	15	5	0	15-3	20	4.88	71	.238	.336	3	.000	-0	—	-4	0	-0.5
1974	SD N	2	0	1.000	47	0	0	2-0	58	59	29	4	2	30-10	29	4.34	83	.271	.360	4	.000	-0	—	-4	0	-0.2
1975	SD N	4	2	.667	67	0	0	1-1	83	87	38	5	2	31-9	48	3.25	108	.275	.340	5-0-2	.200	1	—	1	0	0.4
1976	SD N	0	1	.000	49	1	0	0-1	73	62	24	4	1	20-6	43	2.84	116	.235	.289	8	.000	-1	187	5	0	0.3
1977	SD N	4	4	.500	76	0	0	3-4	101.2	98	38	3	2	32-11	55	3.01	119	.259	.317	7-0-1	.286	0	—	8	0	0.7
1978	Cin N	9	1	.900	57	0	0	4-4	62.1	88	54	3	3	30-7	32	5.78	62	.326	.397	5	.200	0	—	-20	0	-3.2
1979	†Cin N	2	2	.500	53	0	0	1-1	58.1	59	29	3	1	18-5	30	2.62	141	.269	.325	2	.500	0	—	3	0	0.2
1980	Cin N	3	0	1.000	27	0	0	0-0	26	38	17	2	0	11-5	6	5.54	64	.355	.412	0	ø	0	—	-6	0	-0.6
1982	Mon N	0	0	ø	1	0	0	0-0	2	1	1	0	0	1-0	2	4.50	82	.167	.286	0	ø	0	—	0	0	0.0
1983	Pit N	0	0	ø	5	0	0	0-0	4	6	4	0	0	1-0	5	6.75	55	.316	.350	0	ø	0	—	-2	0	-0.1
1985	Pit N	0	0	ø	1	0	0	0-0	1	1	0	0	0	1-0	0	0.00	ø	.333	.500	0	ø	0	—	0	0	0.0
1986	Mon N	0	0	ø	7	0	0	0-0	10.1	13	8	1	1	7-2	6	5.23	72	.317	.420	0	ø	0	—	-2	21	-0.1
Total	13	25	12	.676	409	1	0	12-11	511.1	543	261	32	12	198-58	278	3.82	93	.277	.344	34-0-3	.147	1	187	-24	21	-3.2

YEAR	TM LG	W	L	PCT	G	GS	CG-SHO	SV-BS	IP	H	R	HR	HB	BB-IB	SO	ERA	AERA	OAV	OOB	AB-HR-SH	AVG	PB	SUP	APR	DL	PW
Tomlin, Randy	Randy Leon; B6.14.1966 Bainbridge MD; BL/TL/5´11˝/(170–182); [PitN88 18/460]; d8.6; Col Liberty																									
1990	Pit N	4	4	.500	12	12	2	0-0	77.2	62	24	5	1	12-1	42	2.55	143	.221	.254	25-0-2	.040	-1	97	10	0	1.0
1991	†Pit N	8	7	.533	31	27	4-2	0-0	175	170	75	9	6	54-4	104	2.98	121	.254	.315	52-0-13	.192	1*	129	8	0	0.9
1992	†Pit N	14	9	.609	35	33	1-1	0-0	208.2	226	85	11	5	42-4	90	3.41	102	.282	.320	65-0-7	.138	-0	111	2	0	0.3
1993	Pit N	4	8	.333	18	18	1	0-0	98.1	109	57	11	5	15-0	44	4.85	84	.291	.320	33-0-2	.182	0	84	-9	80	-0.9
1994	Pit N	0	3	.000	10	4	0	0-1	20.2	23	9	1	0	10-0	17	3.92	112	.291	.371	6	.500	1	89	1	0	0.3
Total	5	30	31	.492	106	94	8-3	0-1	580.1	590	250	37	17	133-9	297	3.43	107	.268	.312	181-0-24	.160	1	108	12	80	1.6
Tompkins, Chuck	Charles Herbert; B9.1.1889 Prescott AR; D9.20.1975 Prescott AR; BR/TR/6´0˝/185; d6.25; Col Washington and Lee																									
1912	Cin N	0	0	ø	1	0	0	0	3	5	1	0	0	0	1	0.00	ø	.357	.357	1	1.000	0	—	1	—	0.1
Tompkins, Ron	Ronald Everett "Stretch"; B11.27.1944 San Diego CA; BR/TR/6´4˝/(195–220); d9.9																									
1965	KC A	0	0	ø	5	1	0	0	10.1	9	4	0	1	3-0	4	3.48	100	.237	.310	1	.000	-0	50	0	0	0.0
1971	Chi N	0	2	.000	35	0	0	3-1	39.2	31	18	3	3	21-3	20	4.08	96	.214	.324	0-0-1	ø	0	—	0	0	0.1
Total	2	0	2	.000	40	1	0	3-1	50	40	22	3	4	24-3	24	3.96	97	.219	.321	1-0-1	.000	-0	50	0	0	0.1
Toms, Tommy	Thomas Howard; B10.15.1951 Charlottesville VA; BR/TR/6´4˝/190; [SFN73 6/126]; d5.4; Col East Carolina																									
1975	SF N	0	1	.000	7	0	0	0-0	10.1	13	8	1	0	6-5	6	6.10	63	.317	.396	0	ø	0	—	-3	0	-0.2
1976	SF N	0	1	.000	7	0	0	1-0	8.2	13	7	1	0	1-0	4	6.23	58	.351	.359	0	ø	0	—	-2	0	-0.3
1977	SF N	0	1	.000	4	0	0	0-0	4.1	7	5	0	0	2-0	2	2.08	190	.333	.391	0	ø	0	—	-1	0	-0.2
Total	3	0	3	.000	18	0	0	1-0	23.1	33	20	2	0	9-5	12	5.40	70	.333	.382	0	ø	0	—	-6	0	-0.7
Toney, Fred	Fred Alexandra; B12.11.1888 Nashville TN; D3.11.1953 Nashville TN; BR/TR/6´1˝/195; d4.15																									
1911	Chi N	1	1	.500	18	4	1	0	67	55	36	2	5	35	27	2.42	137	.229	.339	18-0-2	.111	-1	91	2	—	0.0
1912	Chi N	1	2	.333	9	2	0	0	24	21	19	0	1	11	9	5.25	63	.247	.340	4	.000	-0	33	-6	—	-0.7
1913	Chi N	2	2	.500	7	5	2	0	39	52	29	1	1	22	12	6.00	53	.327	.412	12	.250	1	95	-10	—	-0.8
1915	Cin N	17	6	.739	36	23	18-6	2	222.2	160	46	1	3	73	108	1.58	181	.207	.278	74-0-4	.095	-5	84	32	—	3.0
1916	Cin N	14	17	.452	41	38	21-3	1	300	247	98	7	8	78	146	2.28	114	.231	.288	99-0-2	.121	-4	71	10	—	0.4
1917	Cin N	24	16	.600	43	42	31-7	1	339.2	300	119	4	6	77	123	2.20	119	.238	.286	116-0-9	.112	-6	110	17	—	1.1
1918	Cin N	6	10	.375	21	19	9-1	2	136.2	148	61	2	0	31	32	2.90	92	.282	.322	42-0-3	.214	0	106	-5	—	-0.5
	NY N	6	2	.750	11	9	7-1	1	85.1	55	19	1	2	7	19	1.69	156	.192	.216	32	.188	-1	83	10	—	0.9
	Year	12	12	.500	32	28	16-2	**3**	222	203	80	3	2	38	51	2.43	109	.250	.285	74-0-3	.203	-0	99	4	—	0.4
1919	NY N	13	6	.684	24	20	14-4	1	181	157	47	6	2	35	40	1.84	152	.235	.276	66-0-5	.227	1	116	20	—	2.1
1920	NY N	21	11	.656	42	37	17-4	1	278.1	266	101	8	6	57	81	2.65	113	.259	.302	96-0-2	.240	3	111	11	—	1.5
1921	†NY N	18	11	.621	42	32	16-1	3	249.1	274	112	14	4	65	63	3.61	102	.289	.338	86-3-1	.209	2	110	4	—	0.5
1922	NY N	5	6	.455	13	12	6	0	86.1	91	44	5	2	31	10	4.17	96	.277	.343	30	.067	-3	95	0	—	-0.3
1923	StL N	11	12	.478	29	28	16-1	0	196.2	211	104	8	6	61	48	3.84	102	.282	.341	69-0-3	.116	-5	92	1	—	-0.3
Total	12	139	102	.577	336	271	158-28	12	2206	2037	835	59	46	583	718	2.69	113	.251	.305	744-3-31	.159	-18	98	86	—	6.9
Tonkin, Doc	Harry Glenville; B8.11.1881 Concord NH; D5.30.1959 Miami FL; BL/TL/5´9˝/165; d8.19; Col Maryland																									
1907	Was A	0	0	ø	1	0	0	0	2.2	6	3	0	0	5	0	6.75	36	.462	.611	2	1.000	1	—	-1	—	0.1
Toole, Steve	Stephen John; B4.9.1859 New Orleans LA; D3.28.1919 Pittsburgh PA; BR/TL/6´0˝/170; d4.20; U1																									
1886	Bro AA	6	6	.500	13	12	11	0	104	100	92	0	8	64	48	4.41	79	.246	.359	57	.351	4*	106	-11	—	-0.6
1887	Bro AA	14	10	.583	24	24	22-1	0	194	186	133	1	12	106	48	4.31	100	.254	.358	103-1	.233	-1*	104	3	—	0.2
1888	KC AA	5	6	.455	12	10	10	0	91.2	124	99	4	5	50	35	6.68	51	.312	.395	48	.208	-0*	124	-27	—	-2.4
1890	Bro AA	2	4	.333	6	6	6	0	53.1	47	32	0	4	39	10	4.05	96	.229	.363	20	.300	2	66	1	—	0.3
Total	4	27	26	.509	55	52	49-1	0	443	457	356	5	29	259	141	4.79	81	.262	.367	228-1	.263	5	104	-34	—	-2.5
Toppin, Rupe	Ruperto; B12.7.1941 Panama City, Pan; BR/TR/6´0˝/185; d7.28																									
1962	KC A	0	0	ø	2	0	0	0	2	1	3	0	0	5-0	1	13.50	31	.167	.545	1	1.000	0	—	-2	0	0.0
Torkelson, Red	Chester Leroy; B3.19.1894 Chicago IL; D9.22.1964 Chicago IL; BR/TR/6´0˝/175; d8.29; Mil 1918																									
1917	Cle A	2	1	.667	4	3	0	0	22.1	33	25	1	2	13	10	7.66	37	.333	.421	9	.222	-0	118	-11	—	-1.2
Torrealba, Pablo	Pablo Arnoldo (Torrealba); B4.28.1948 Barquisimeto, Lara, Venez.; BL/TL/5´9˝/(159–173); d4.9; s–Steve																									
1975	Atl N	0	1	.000	6	0	0	0-0	6.2	7	2	0	0	3-0	5	1.35	280	.250	.323	1	1.000	0	—	1	0	0.3
1976	Atl N	0	2	.000	36	0	0	2-1	53	67	25	0	3	22-7	33	3.57	106	.315	.387	4	.000	-0	—	1	20	0.1
1977	Oak A	4	6	.400	41	10	3	2-0	116.2	127	45	5	2	38-2	51	2.62	154	.279	.335	0	ø	0	58	16	25	1.4
1978	Chi A	2	4	.333	25	3	1-1	1-1	57.1	69	37	6	3	39-5	23	4.71	81	.301	.407	0	ø	0	87	-7	47	-0.8
1979	Chi A	0	0	ø	3	0	0	0-1	5.2	5	1	1	0	2-0	1	1.59	268	.250	.318	0	ø	0	—	2	0	0.1
Total	5	6	13	.316	111	13	4-1	5-3	239.1	275	110	12	8	104-14	113	3.27	120	.291	.364	5	.200	-0	65	13	92	1.1
Torres, Angel	Angel Rafael (Ruiz); B10.24.1952 Las Cienagas, D.R.; BL/TL/5´11˝/165; d9.12																									
1977	Cin N	0	0	ø	5	0	0	0-0	8.1	7	2	2	0	8-1	8	2.16	182	.233	.395	0	ø	0	—	2	0	0.1
Torres, Dilson	Dilson Dario; B5.31.1970 Sur Edo Aragua, Venezuela; BR/TR/6´3˝/200; d4.29																									
1995	KC A	1	2	.333	24	2	0	0-0	44.1	56	30	6	1	17-2	28	6.09	79	.311	.374	0	ø	0	107	-5	0	-0.2
Torres, Gil	Don Gilberto (Nunez); B8.23.1915 Regla, Cuba; D1.10.1983 Regla, Cuba; BR/TR/6´0˝/155; d4.25; f–Ricardo; ▲																									
1940	Was A	0	0	ø	2	0	0	0	2.2	3	1	0	0	0	1	0.00	ø	.273	.273	0	ø	0	—	1	—	0.0
1946	Was A	0	0	ø	3	0	0	1	7	9	6	0	0	3	2	7.71	43	.310	.375	185-0-4	.254	1*	—	-3	0	-0.1
Total	2	0	0	ø	5	0	0	1	9.2	12	7	0	0	3	3	5.59	64	.300	.349	185-0-4	.254	1	—	-2	0	-0.1
Torres, Salomon	Salomon (Ramirez); B3.11.1972 San Pedro de Macoris, D.R.; BR/TR/5´11˝/(150–215); d8.29																									
1993	SF N	3	5	.375	8	8	0	0-0	44.2	37	21	5	1	27-3	23	4.03	98	.231	.344	13-0-3	.231	0	63	0	0	0.0
1994	SF N	2	8	.200	16	14	1	0-0	84.1	95	55	10	7	34-2	42	5.44	75	.292	.364	26-0-3	.154	-1	74	-13	0	-1.4
1995	SF N	0	1	.000	4	1	0	0-0	8	13	8	4	0	7-0	2	9.00	46	.394	.500	1	.000	-0	66	-4	0	-0.4
	Sea A	3	8	.273	16	13	1	0-0	72	87	53	12	2	42-3	45	6.00	80	.291	.382	0	ø	0	90	-10	0	-1.2
1996	Sea A	3	3	.500	10	7	1-1	0-0	49	44	27	5	3	23-2	36	4.59	108	.242	.335	0	ø	0	120	2	0	0.2
1997	Sea A	0	0	ø	2	0	0	0-0	3.1	7	10	0	1	3-0	0	27.00	17	.412	.524	0	ø	0	—	-8	0	-0.3
	Mon N	0	0	ø	12	0	0	0-0	22.1	25	19	2	2	12-0	11	7.25	58	.284	.379	6	.000	-1	—	-7	0	-0.4
2002	Pit N	2	1	.667	5	5	0	0-0	30	28	10	2	3	13-1	12	2.70	155	.257	.352	13	.154	-0	128	5	0	0.4
2003	Pit N	7	5	.583	41	16	0	2-1	121	128	65	19	7	42-5	84	4.76	91	.276	.344	32-0-6	.063	-1*	121	-4	23	-0.4
2004	Pit N	7	7	.500	84	0	0	0-4	92	87	33	6	6	22-6	62	2.64	164	.256	.310	2	.500	1	—	16	0	2.2
2005	Pit N	5	5	.500	78	0	0	3-0	94.2	76	34	7	5	36-7	55	2.76	154	.222	.304	4	.500	1	—	14	0	1.5
2006	Pit N	3	6	.333	**94**	0	0	12-3	93.1	98	42	6	6	38-9	72	3.28	140	.274	.351	5	.200	0	—	11	0	1.2
Total	10	35	49	.417	370	64	3-1	17-8	714.2	725	377	78	43	299-38	444	4.32	101	.267	.347	102-0-12	.147	-1	97	2	23	1.4
Torrez, Mike	Michael Augustine; B8.28.1946 Topeka KS; BR/TR/6´5˝/210; d9.10																									
1967	StL N	0	1	.000	3	1	0	0	5.2	5	2	0	1	1-0	5	3.18	103	.238	.304	1	.000	-0	134	0	0	0.0
1968	StL N	2	1	.667	5	2	0	0	19	20	7	1	1	12-0	6	2.84	102	.286	.388	7	.286	0	165	0	0	0.1
1969	StL N	10	4	.714	24	15	3	0-0	107.2	96	47	7	3	62-2	61	3.59	100	.240	.345	41-0-4	.073	-2	147	1	0	-0.1
1970	StL N	8	10	.444	30	28	5-1	0-0	179.1	168	96	12	4	103-10	100	4.22	98	.248	.348	63-0-2	.270	4	90	-2	0	0.2
1971	StL N	1	2	.333	9	6	0	0-0	36	41	27	2	1	30-3	8	6.00	61	.304	.431	7-0-1	.143	1	102	-9	0	-0.6
	Mon N	0	0	ø	1	0	0	0-0	3	4	0	0	0	1-0	2	0.00	ø	.308	.357	0	ø	0	—	1	0	0.1
	Year	1	2	.333	10	6	0	0-0	39	45	27	2	1	31-3	10	5.54	66	.304	.425	7-0-1	.143	1	102	-8	0	-0.5
1972	Mon N	16	12	.571	34	33	13	0-0	243.1	215	97	15	6	103-5	112	3.33	107	.242	.323	85-0-4	.176	0	93	6	0	0.9
1973	Mon N	9	12	.429	35	34	3-1	0-0	208	207	116	17	4	115-11	90	4.46	86	.262	.357	69-0-6	.174	-1*	103	-12	0	-1.2
1974	Mon N	15	8	.652	32	30	6-1	0-0	186.1	184	90	10	3	84-3	92	3.57	108	.257	.336	64-0-3	.125	-3*	106	3	0	0.3
1975	Bal A	20	9	**.690**	36	36	16-2	0-0	270.2	238	103	15	5	133-5	119	3.06	116	.239	.331	0	ø	0	121	14	0	1.4
1976	Oak A	16	12	.571	39	39	13-4	0-0	266.1	231	93	15	6	87-2	115	2.50	135	.235	.301	0	ø	0	106	23	0	2.3
1977	Oak A	3	1	.750	4	4	2	0-0	26.1	23	14	3	1	11-0	12	4.44	91	.242	.318	0	ø	0	106	-1	0	-0.1
	†NY A	14	12	.538	31	31	15-2	0-0	217	212	99	20	6	75-1	90	3.82	104	.259	.324	0	ø	0	110	5	0	0.5
	Year	17	13	.567	35	35	17-2	0-0	243.1	235	113	23	7	86-1	102	3.88	102	.257	.323	0	ø	0	110	5	0	0.4
1978	Bos A	16	13	.552	36	36	15-2	0-0	250	272	122	19	3	99-10	120	3.96	104	.281	.347	0	ø	0	116	5	0	0.4

YEAR	TM LG	W	L	PCT	G	GS	CG-SHO	SV-BS	IP	H	R	HR	HB	BB-IB	SO	ERA	AERA	OAV	OOB	AB-HR-SH	AVG	PB	SUP	APR	DL	PW
1979	Bos A	16	13	.552	36	36	12-1	0-0	252.1	254	144	20	5	121-8	125	4.49	99	.264	.346	0	ø	0	123	-3	0	-0.3
1980	Bos A	9	16	.360	36	32	6-1	0-0	207.1	256	124	18	1	75-10	97	5.08	84	.313	.367	0	ø	0	103	-16	0	-1.6
1981	Bos A	10	3	.769	22	22	2	0-0	127.1	130	61	10	0	51-2	54	3.68	107	.267	.336	0	ø	0	121	3	0	0.2
1982	Bos A	9	9	.500	31	31	1	0-0	175.2	196	107	20	6	74-1	84	5.23	83	.282	.353	0	ø	0	120	-14	0	-1.4
1983	NY N	10	17	.370	39	34	5	0-0	222.1	227	120	16	1	113-11	94	4.37	84	.271	.356	65-0-8	.046	-5	80	-15	0	-2.2
1984	NY N	1	5	.167	9	8	0	0-0	37.2	55	25	3	2	18-0	16	5.02	71	.369	.434	10	.300	1	65	-6	0	-0.8
	Oak A	0	0	ø	2	0	0	0-0	2.1	9	7	0	0	3-0	2	27.00	14	.563	.632	0	ø	0	—	-6	0	-0.3
Total	18	185	160	.536	494	458	117-15	0-0	3043.2	3043	1501	223	59	1371-84	1404	3.96	98	.264	.343	412-0-28	.155	-4	108	-23	0	-2.2

Tost, Lou Louis Eugene; B6.1.1911 Cumberland WA; D2.21.1967 Santa Clara CA; BL/TL/6´0˝/175; d4.20; Mil 1944–45

YEAR	TM LG	W	L	PCT	G	GS	CG-SHO	SV-BS	IP	H	R	HR	HB	BB-IB	SO	ERA	AERA	OAV	OOB	AB-HR-SH	AVG	PB	SUP	APR	DL	PW
1942	Bos N	10	10	.500	35	22	5-1	0	147.2	146	66	12	4	52	43	3.53	94	.256	.322	51-0-2	.176	0	104	-3	0	-0.4
1943	Bos N	0	1	.000	3	1	0	0	6.2	10	5	2	0	4	3	5.40	63	.357	.438	1	.000	-0	25	-2	0	-0.2
1947	Pit N	0	0	ø	1	0	0	0	1	3	1	0	0	0	0	9.00	47	.600	.600	0	ø	0	—	0	0	0.0
Total	3	10	11	.476	39	23	5-1	0	155.1	159	72	14	4	56	46	3.65	92	.263	.330	52-0-2	.173	-0	100	-5	0	-0.6

Toth, Paul Paul Louis; B6.30.1935 McRoberts KY; D3.20.1999 Anaheim CA; BR/TR/6´1˝/(175–190); d4.22

YEAR	TM LG	W	L	PCT	G	GS	CG-SHO	SV-BS	IP	H	R	HR	HB	BB-IB	SO	ERA	AERA	OAV	OOB	AB-HR-SH	AVG	PB	SUP	APR	DL	PW
1962	StL N	1	0	1.000	6	1	1	0	16.2	18	10	1	0	4-0	5	5.40	79	.295	.333	5	.400	0	144	-1	0	0.0
	Chi N	3	1	.750	6	4	1	0	34	29	17	2	2	10-1	11	4.24	98	.240	.306	11-0-1	.182	0	100	0	0	0.0
	Year	4	1	.800	12	5	2	0	50.2	47	27	3	2	14-1	16	4.62	91	.258	.315	16-0-1	.250	1	109	-1	0	0.0
1963	Chi N	5	9	.357	27	14	3-2	0	130.2	115	50	9	2	35-3	66	3.10	113	.240	.291	39-0-2	.026	-3	75	6	0	0.3
1964	Chi N	0	2	.000	4	2	0	0	10.2	15	10	2	0	5-0	0	8.44	44	.341	.408	3	.333	0	59	-5	0	-0.7
Total	3	9	12	.429	43	21	5-2	0	192	177	87	14	4	54-4	82	3.80	97	.251	.305	58-0-3	.103	-2	83	0	0	-0.4

Touchstone, Clay Clayland Maffitt; B1.24.1903 Moores (now Prospect Park) PA; D4.28.1949 Beaumont TX; BR/TR/5´9˝/175; d9.4

YEAR	TM LG	W	L	PCT	G	GS	CG-SHO	SV-BS	IP	H	R	HR	HB	BB-IB	SO	ERA	AERA	OAV	OOB	AB-HR-SH	AVG	PB	SUP	APR	DL	PW
1928	Bos N	0	0	ø	5	0	0	0	8	15	8	0	1	2	1	4.50	87	.417	.462	2	.000	-0	—	-2	—	-0.1
1929	Bos N	0	0	ø	1	0	0	0	2.2	6	5	1	0	0	1	16.88	28	.429	.429	1	1.000	0	—	-3	—	-0.1
1945	Chi A	0	0	ø	6	0	0	0	10	14	10	1	1	6	4	5.40	61	.311	.404	1	.000	-0	—	-4	0	-0.2
Total	3	0	0	ø	12	0	0	0	20.2	35	23	2	2	8	6	6.53	57	.368	.429	4	.250	0	—	-9	—	-0.4

Towers, Josh Joshua Eric; B2.26.1977 Port Hueneme CA; BR/TR/6´1˝/(165–190); [BalA96 15/441]; d5.2; Col Oxnard (CA) JC

YEAR	TM LG	W	L	PCT	G	GS	CG-SHO	SV-BS	IP	H	R	HR	HB	BB-IB	SO	ERA	AERA	OAV	OOB	AB-HR-SH	AVG	PB	SUP	APR	DL	PW
2001	Bal A	8	10	.444	24	20	1-1	0-0	140.1	165	74	21	6	16-0	58	4.49	96	.296	.321	2	.000	-0	99	-1	7	-0.2
2002	Bal A	0	3	.000	5	3	0	0-0	27.1	42	24	11	0	5-0	13	7.90	55	.362	.382	0	ø	0	21	-10	0	-0.8
2003	Tor A	8	1	.889	14	8	1	1-0	64.1	67	34	15	4	7-1	42	4.48	106	.266	.294	1	.000	-0	129	2	0	0.3
2004	Tor A	9	9	.500	21	21	0	0-0	116.1	148	70	16	9	26-4	51	5.11	96	.310	.355	1-0-2	.000	-0	86	-3	0	-0.4
2005	Tor A	13	12	.520	33	33	2-1	0-0	208.2	237	101	24	6	29-2	112	3.71	124	.285	.312	6	.000	-1	99	16	0	1.8
2006	Tor A	2	10	.167	15	12	0	0-0	62	93	62	17	3	17-3	35	8.42	56	.343	.384	5	.200	0	96	-24	0	-3.5
Total	6	40	45	.471	112	97	4-2	1-0	619	752	365	104	28	100-10	311	4.89	94	.300	.332	15-0-2	.067	-1	96	-20	7	-2.8

Townsend, Ira Ira Dance "Pat"; B1.9.1894 Weimar TX; D7.21.1965 Schulenburg TX; BR/TR/6´1˝/180; d8.25

YEAR	TM LG	W	L	PCT	G	GS	CG-SHO	SV-BS	IP	H	R	HR	HB	BB-IB	SO	ERA	AERA	OAV	OOB	AB-HR-SH	AVG	PB	SUP	APR	DL	PW
1920	Bos N	0	0	ø	4	1	0	0	6.2	10	3	0	1	2	1	1.35	226	.370	.433	2	.000	-0	258	1	—	0.0
1921	Bos N	0	0	ø	4	0	0	0	7.1	11	7	1	2	4	0	6.14	59	.344	.447	2	.000	-0	—	-3	—	-0.1
Total	2	0	0	ø	8	1	0	0	14	21	10	1	3	6	1	3.86	87	.356	.441	4	.000	-1	258	-2	—	-0.1

Townsend, Happy John; B4.9.1879 Townsend DE; D12.21.1963 Wilmington DE; BR/TR/6´0˝/190; d4.19; Col Washington College

YEAR	TM LG	W	L	PCT	G	GS	CG-SHO	SV-BS	IP	H	R	HR	HB	BB-IB	SO	ERA	AERA	OAV	OOB	AB-HR-SH	AVG	PB	SUP	APR	DL	PW
1901	Phi N	9	6	.600	19	16	14-2	0	143.2	118	73	3	5	64	72	3.45	99	**.223**	.312	64	.109	-4	102	0	—	-0.5
1902	Was A	8	16	.333	27	26	22	0	220.1	233	157	12	13	89	71	4.45	83	.272	.349	87-0-3	.264	3	99	-21	—	-1.6
1903	Was A	2	11	.154	20	13	10	0	126.2	145	85	3	9	48	54	4.76	66	.287	.359	44	.045	-4	61	-20	—	-2.2
1904	Was A	5	26	.161	36	34	31-2	0	291.1	319	163	3	9	100	143	3.58	74	.279	.342	119-1-0	.168	-2*	61	-31	—	-3.4
1905	Was A	7	16	.304	34	24	22	0	263	247	117	2	15	84	102	2.63	100	.250	.318	83-0-4	.181	1	86	-2	—	-0.2
1906	Cle A	3	7	.300	17	12	8-1	0	92.2	92	45	1	6	31	31	2.91	90	.262	.332	30-0-1	.133	-1	124	-3	—	-0.5
Total	6	34	82	.293	153	125	107-5	0	1137.2	1154	640	24	57	416	473	3.59	83	.264	.336	427-1-8	.166	-8	87	-77	—	-8.4

Townsend, Leo Leo Alphonse "Lefty"; B1.15.1891 Mobile AL; D12.3.1976 Mobile AL; BL/TL/5´10˝/160; d9.8

YEAR	TM LG	W	L	PCT	G	GS	CG-SHO	SV-BS	IP	H	R	HR	HB	BB-IB	SO	ERA	AERA	OAV	OOB	AB-HR-SH	AVG	PB	SUP	APR	DL	PW
1920	Bos N	2	2	.500	7	1	1	0	24.1	18	4	1	0	2	0	1.48	206	.220	.238	6-0-1	.167	0	26	5	—	0.8
1921	Bos N	0	1	.000	1	1	0	0	1.1	2	4	0	0	3	0	27.00	14	.400	.625	0	ø	0	180	-3	—	-0.5
Total	2	2	3	.400	8	2	1	0	25.2	20	8	1	0	5	0	2.81	110	.230	.272	6-0-1	.167	0	115	2	—	0.3

Tozer, Bill William Louis; B7.3.1882 St.Louis MO; D2.23.1955 Belmont CA; BR/TR/6´0˝/200; d4.16

YEAR	TM LG	W	L	PCT	G	GS	CG-SHO	SV-BS	IP	H	R	HR	HB	BB-IB	SO	ERA	AERA	OAV	OOB	AB-HR-SH	AVG	PB	SUP	APR	DL	PW
1908	Cin N	0	0	ø	4	0	0	0	10.2	11	5	0	1	4	5	1.69	137	.268	.348	2	.000	-0	—	0	—	0.0

Traber, Billy William Henry; B9.18.1979 Torrance CA; BL/TL/6´5˝/(200–205); [NYN00 1/16]; d4.4; Col Loyola Marymount; [DL 2004 Cle A 183]

YEAR	TM LG	W	L	PCT	G	GS	CG-SHO	SV-BS	IP	H	R	HR	HB	BB-IB	SO	ERA	AERA	OAV	OOB	AB-HR-SH	AVG	PB	SUP	APR	DL	PW
2003	Cle A	6	9	.400	33	18	1-1	0-0	111.2	132	67	15	5	40-4	88	5.24	85	.293	.355	4	.000	-0	94	-7	0	-0.8
2006	Was N	4	3	.571	15	8	0	0-0	43.1	53	33	5	8	14-2	25	6.44	68	.301	.377	13-0-2	.077	-0	124	-10	0	-1.4
Total	2	10	12	.455	48	26	1-1	0-0	155	185	100	20	13	54-6	113	5.57	79	.295	.361	17-0-2	.059	-1	103	-17	183	-2.2

Tracey, Sean Sean Patrick; B11.14.1980 Upland CA; BL/TR/6´3˝/210; [ChiA02 8/240]; d6.8; Col California–Irvine

YEAR	TM LG	W	L	PCT	G	GS	CG-SHO	SV-BS	IP	H	R	HR	HB	BB-IB	SO	ERA	AERA	OAV	OOB	AB-HR-SH	AVG	PB	SUP	APR	DL	PW
2006	Chi A	0	0	ø	7	0	0	0-0	8	4	3	2	1	5-0	3	3.38	139	.143	.294	0	ø	0	—	1	0	0.1

Trachsel, Steve Stephen Christopher; B10.31.1970 Oxnard CA; BR/TR/6´4˝/(185–205); [ChiN91 8/215]; d9.19; Col Cal St.–Long Beach

YEAR	TM LG	W	L	PCT	G	GS	CG-SHO	SV-BS	IP	H	R	HR	HB	BB-IB	SO	ERA	AERA	OAV	OOB	AB-HR-SH	AVG	PB	SUP	APR	DL	PW
1993	Chi N	0	2	.000	3	3	0	0-0	19.2	16	10	4	0	3-0	14	4.58	88	.219	.247	6	.167	0	74	-1	0	0.0
1994	Chi N	9	7	.563	22	22	1	0-0	146	133	57	19	3	54-4	108	3.21	132	.242	.312	43-0-8	.186	0	94	16	15	1.8
1995	Chi N	7	13	.350	30	29	2	0-0	160.2	174	104	25	0	76-8	117	5.15	81	.277	.352	49-0-6	.265	3	102	-18	0	-1.7
1996	Chi N★	13	9	.591	31	31	3-2	0-0	205	181	82	30	8	62-3	132	3.03	144	.235	.298	66-1-6	.106	-2	90	27	0	2.4
1997	Chi N	8	12	.400	34	34	0	0-0	201.1	225	110	32	5	69-6	160	4.51	96	.287	.344	60-0-11	.117	-0	89	-5	0	-0.4
1998	Chi N	15	8	.652	33	33	1	0-0	208	204	107	27	8	84-5	149	4.46	99	.260	.334	64-1-9	.266	6	109	0	0	0.8
1999	Chi N	8	18	.308	34	34	4	0-0	205.2	226	133	32	3	64-4	149	5.56	82	.280	.330	63-0-7	.111	-3	84	-20	0	-2.3
2000	TB A	6	10	.375	23	23	3-1	0-0	137.2	160	76	16	6	49-1	78	4.58	107	.294	.356	4	.250	0	76	5	0	0.6
	Tor A	2	5	.286	11	11	0	0-0	63	72	40	10	0	25-1	32	5.29	95	.293	.357	0	ø	0	103	-1	0	-0.1
	Year	8	15	.348	34	34	3-1	0-0	200.2	232	116	26	6	74-2	110	4.80	103	.294	.356	4	.250	0	85	5	0	0.5
2001	NY N	11	13	.458	28	28	1-1	0-0	173.2	168	90	28	3	47-7	144	4.46	91	.254	.304	56-0-5	.161	-0	82	-7	0	-0.8
2002	NY N	11	11	.500	30	30	1-1	0-0	173.2	170	80	16	0	69-4	105	3.37	117	.258	.327	46-0-9	.109	-1*	97	9	21	1.0
2003	NY N	16	10	.615	33	33	2-2	0-0	204.2	204	90	26	3	65-9	111	3.78	111	.264	.320	58-0-11	.190	1*	100	10	0	1.4
2004	NY N	12	13	.480	33	33	0	0-0	202.2	203	104	25	5	83-9	117	4.00	108	.262	.334	59-0-11	.186	0*	101	5	0	0.7
2005	NY N	1	4	.200	6	6	0	0-0	37	37	20	6	1	12-0	24	4.14	100	.264	.323	15	.067	-1	76	-1	142	-0.2
2006	†NY N	15	8	.652	30	30	1	0-0	164.2	185	94	23	4	78-1	79	4.97	88	.288	.365	50-1-4	.140	2	116	-9	0	-0.9
Total	14	134	143	.484	381	380	19-7	0-0	2303.1	2358	1197	319	49	840-62	1519	4.28	101	.267	.331	639-3-87	.164	7	95	10	178	2.3

Trautman, Fred Frederick Orlando; B3.24.1892 Bucyrus OH; D2.15.1964 Bucyrus OH; BR/TR/6´1˝/175; d4.27

YEAR	TM LG	W	L	PCT	G	GS	CG-SHO	SV-BS	IP	H	R	HR	HB	BB-IB	SO	ERA	AERA	OAV	OOB	AB-HR-SH	AVG	PB	SUP	APR	DL	PW
1915	New F	0	0	ø	1	0	0	0	3	4	3	0	1	1	2	6.00	43	.364	.462	1	.000	-0	—	-1	—	-0.1

Trautwein, John John Howard; B8.7.1962 Lafayette Hill PA; BR/TR/6´3˝/195; d4.7; Col Northwestern

YEAR	TM LG	W	L	PCT	G	GS	CG-SHO	SV-BS	IP	H	R	HR	HB	BB-IB	SO	ERA	AERA	OAV	OOB	AB-HR-SH	AVG	PB	SUP	APR	DL	PW
1988	Bos A	0	1	.000	9	0	0	0-0	16	26	17	2	1	9-0	8	9.00	46	.382	.462	0	ø	0	—	-8	0	-0.5

Travers, Allan Aloysius Joseph "Joe"; B5.7.1892 Philadelphia PA; D4.19.1968 Philadelphia PA; BR/TR/6´1˝/180; d5.18

YEAR	TM LG	W	L	PCT	G	GS	CG-SHO	SV-BS	IP	H	R	HR	HB	BB-IB	SO	ERA	AERA	OAV	OOB	AB-HR-SH	AVG	PB	SUP	APR	DL	PW
1912	Det A	0	1	.000	1	1	1	0	8	26	24	0	0	7	1	15.75	21	.605	.660	3	.000	-0	45	-13	—	-0.9

Travers, Bill William Edward; B10.27.1952 Norwood MA; BL/TL/6´6˝/(185–210); [MilA70 6/127]; d5.19; [DL 1982 Cal A 182]

YEAR	TM LG	W	L	PCT	G	GS	CG-SHO	SV-BS	IP	H	R	HR	HB	BB-IB	SO	ERA	AERA	OAV	OOB	AB-HR-SH	AVG	PB	SUP	APR	DL	PW
1974	Mil A	2	3	.400	23	1	0	0-0	53	59	29	6	1	30-5	31	4.92	74	.296	.386	0	ø	0	194	-6	0	-0.6
1975	Mil A	6	11	.353	28	23	5	1-0	136.1	130	78	15	11	60-3	57	4.29	90	.251	.338	0	ø	0	78	-8	0	-0.9
1976	Mil A☆	15	16	.484	34	34	15-3	0-0	240	211	92	21	8	95-5	120	2.81	125	.237	.315	0	ø	0	76	15	0	2.0
1977	Mil A	4	12	.250	19	19	2-1	0-0	121.2	140	75	13	7	57-5	49	5.25	78	.291	.370	0	ø	0	62	-14	39	-1.5
1978	Mil A	12	11	.522	28	28	8-3	0-0	175.2	184	93	20	6	58-1	66	4.41	86	.268	.329	0	ø	0	131	-11	37	-1.2
1979	Mil A	14	8	.636	30	27	9-2	0-0	187.1	196	89	33	3	45-0	74	3.89	108	.270	.313	0-0-1	ø	0	98	7	0	0.7
1980	Mil A	12	6	.667	29	25	7-1	0-0	154.1	147	76	20	6	47-2	62	3.91	100	.249	.309	0	ø	0	127	0	0	0.0
1981	Cal A	0	1	.000	4	4	0	0-0	9.2	14	11	2	0	4-0	5	8.38	44	.333	.391	0	ø	0	104	-5	148	-0.5
1983	Cal A	0	3	.000	10	7	0	0-0	42.2	58	32	4	2	19-1	24	5.91	69	.331	.397	0	ø	0	80	-9	36	-0.6
Total	9	65	71	.478	205	168	46-10	1-0	1120.2	1139	575	134	44	415-22	488	4.10	94	.264	.333	0-0-1	ø	0	97	-31	442	-2.6

THE PITCHER REGISTER

YEAR	TM LG	W	L	PCT	G	GS	CG-SHO	SV-BS	IP	H	R	HR	HB	BB-IB	SO	ERA	AERA	OAV	OOB	AB-HR-SH	AVG	PB	SUP	APR	DL	PW
Trekell, Harry	Harry Roy; B11.18.1892 Buda IL; D11.4.1965 Spokane WA; BR/TR/6´1.5˝/170; d8.16																									
1913	StL N	0	1	.000	7	1	1	0	30	25	20	2	2	8	15	4.50	72	.221	.285	9	.111	-0	47	-5	—	-0.3
Tremel, Bill	William Leonard "Mumbles"; B7.4.1929 Lilly PA; BR/TR/5´11˝/180; d6.12																									
1954	Chi N	1	2	.333	33	0	0	4	51.1	45	27	3	0	28	21	4.21	100	.243	.338	8	.250	0	—	0	0	0.0
1955	Chi N	3	0	1.000	23	0	0	2	38.2	33	18	2	0	18-2	13	3.72	110	.239	.323	7	.286	0	—	1	0	0.1
1956	Chi N	0	0	ø	1	0	0	0	1	3	1	0	0	0-0	0	9.00	42	.600	.600	0	ø	0	—	-1	0	0.0
Total	3	4	2	.667	57	0	0	6	91	81	46	5	0	46-2	34	4.05	102	.247	.335	15	.267	1	—	0	0	0.1
Trice, Bob	Robert Lee; B8.28.1926 Newton GA; D9.16.1988 Weirton WV; BR/TR/6´3˝/190; d9.13; Negro Lg 1946–48																									
1953	Phi A	2	1	.667	3	3	1	0	23	25	14	4	0	6	4	5.48	78	.275	.320	7	.143	0	180	-2	0	-0.2
1954	Phi A	7	8	.467	19	18	8-1	0	119	146	86	14	0	48	22	5.60	70	.305	.362	42-1-0	.286	4*	103	-23	0	-2.0
1955	KC A	0	0	ø	4	0	0	0	10	14	13	4	0	6-0	2	9.00	46	.326	.400	3	.667	1	—	-6	0	-0.2
Total	3	9	9	.500	26	21	9-1	0	152	185	113	22	0	60-0	28	5.80	69	.302	.359	52-1-0	.288	5	114	-31	0	-2.4
Trimble, Joe	Joseph Gerard; B10.12.1930 Providence RI; BR/TR/6´1˝/190; d4.29																									
1955	Bos A	0	0	ø	2	0	0	0	2	0	0	0	0	3-0	1	0.00	ø	.000	.375	0	ø	0	—	1	0	0.1
1957	Pit N	0	2	.000	5	4	0	0	19.2	23	19	7	1	13-1	9	8.24	46	.291	.398	7	.143	-0	116	-9	108	-0.8
Total	2	0	2	.000	7	4	0	0	21.2	23	19	7	1	16-1	10	7.48	51	.274	.396	7	.143	-0	116	-8	108	-0.7
Trinkle, Ken	Kenneth Wayne; B12.15.1919 Paoli IN; D5.10.1976 Paoli IN; BR/TR/6´1.5˝/175; d4.25; Mil 1944–45																									
1943	NY N	1	5	.167	11	6	1	0	45.2	51	23	3	1	15	10	3.74	92	.276	.333	12	.250	1	74	-2	0	-0.1
1946	NY N	7	14	.333	**48**	13	2	2	151	146	77	8	2	74	49	3.87	89	.253	.340	38-0-2	.079	-2	124	-8	0	-1.3
1947	NY N	8	4	.667	**62**	0	0	10	93.2	100	47	3	1	48	37	3.75	109	.278	.364	16	.188	-0	—	2	0	0.4
1948	NY N	4	5	.444	53	0	0	7	70.2	66	28	6	3	41	20	3.18	124	.244	.350	8	.250	0	—	6	0	1.0
1949	Phi N	1	1	.500	42	0	0	2	74.1	79	37	3	3	30	14	4.00	99	.299	.377	6	.000	-0	—	-1	0	0.0
Total	5	21	29	.420	216	19	3	21	435.1	442	212	23	10	208	130	3.74	100	.267	.352	80-0-2	.138	-2	102	-3	0	0.0
Trlicek, Rick	Richard Alan; B4.26.1969 Houston TX; BR/TR/6´2˝/200; [PhiN87 4/104]; d4.8																									
1992	Tor A	0	0	ø	2	0	0	0-0	1.2	2	2	0	0	2-0	1	10.80	38	.286	.444	0	ø	0	—	-1	0	-0.1
1993	LA N	1	2	.333	41	0	0	1-0	64	59	32	3	2	21-4	41	4.08	95	.244	.309	4	.250	0	—	-1	0	0.0
1994	Bos A	1	1	.500	12	1	0	0-1	22.1	32	21	5	0	16-2	7	8.06	63	.330	.425	0	ø	0	36	-7	0	-0.5
1996	NY N	0	1	.000	5	0	0	0-0	5.1	3	2	0	1	3-1	3	3.38	119	.214	.389	0	ø	0	—	1	0	0.1
1997	Bos A	3	4	.429	18	0	0	0-0	23.1	26	14	2	1	18-4	10	4.63	101	.289	.409	0	ø	0	—	0	0	-0.1
	NY N	0	0	ø	9	0	0	0-1	9	10	9	2	0	5-0	4	8.00	50	.303	.395	0	ø	0	—	-4	109	-0.2
Total	5	5	8	.385	87	1	0	1-2	125.2	132	80	12	4	65-11	66	5.23	81	.273	.363	4	.250	0	36	-12	109	-0.8
Troedson, Rich	Richard La Monte; B5.1.1950 Palo Alto CA; BL/TL/6´1˝/195; d4.9; Col Santa Clara																									
1973	SD N	7	9	.438	50	18	2	1-0	152.1	167	77	12	1	59-8	81	4.25	83	.284	.347	40-0-3	.175	-0	78	-10	0	-0.9
1974	SD N	1	1	.500	15	1	0	1-0	18.2	24	18	6	1	8-1	11	8.68	41	.300	.371	1	.000	-0	24	-10	0	-1.0
Total	2	8	10	.444	65	19	2	2-0	171	191	95	18	2	67-9	92	4.74	74	.286	.350	41-0-3	.171	-0	75	-20	0	-1.9
Trombley, Mike	Michael Scott; B4.14.1967 Springfield MA; BR/TR/6´2˝/(200–210); [MinA89 14/373]; d8.19; Col Duke																									
1992	Min A	3	2	.600	10	7	0	0-0	46.1	43	20	5	1	17-0	38	3.30	124	.247	.318	0	ø	0	96	3	0	0.3
1993	Min A	6	6	.500	44	10	0	2-3	114.1	131	72	15	3	41-4	85	4.88	90	.290	.348	0	ø	0	94	-8	0	-0.7
1994	Min A	2	0	1.000	24	0	0	0-1	48.1	56	36	10	3	18-2	32	6.33	78	.287	.353	0	ø	0	—	-7	0	-0.3
1995	Min A	4	8	.333	20	18	0	0-0	97.2	107	68	18	3	42-1	68	5.62	86	.273	.346	0	ø	0	107	-9	0	-0.9
1996	Min A	5	1	.833	43	0	0	6-3	68.2	61	24	2	5	25-8	57	3.01	170	.236	.312	0	ø	0	—	16	0	1.4
1997	Min A	2	3	.400	67	0	0	1-0	82.1	77	43	7	2	31-4	74	4.37	107	.248	.317	1	.000	-0	—	3	0	0.1
1998	Min A	6	5	.545	77	1	0	1-3	96.2	90	41	16	5	41-3	89	3.63	132	.247	.331	0	ø	0	78	12	0	1.2
1999	Min A	2	8	.200	75	0	0	24-6	87.1	93	42	15	2	28-2	82	4.33	120	.272	.328	0	ø	0	—	9	0	1.3
2000	Bal A	4	5	.444	75	0	0	4-7	72	67	34	15	4	38-8	72	4.13	114	.247	.346	1	.000	-0	—	5	0	0.6
2001	Bal A	3	4	.429	50	0	0	6-3	54.2	38	23	4	2	27-2	45	3.46	125	.200	.302	0	ø	0	—	6	0	0.7
	LA N	0	4	.000	19	0	0	0-0	23.1	27	17	5	0	10-3	27	6.56	63	.290	.356	0	ø	0	—	-6	0	-0.9
2002	Min A	0	1	.000	5	0	0	0-1	4	10	7	2	0	1-0	3	15.75	28	.455	.478	0	ø	0	—	-5	0	-0.8
Total	11	37	47	.440	509	36	0	44-27	795.2	800	427	114	30	319-37	672	4.48	105	.261	.334	2	.000	-0	98	19	0	2.0
Trosky, Hal	Harold Arthur Jr. "Hoot"; B9.29.1936 Cleveland OH; BR/TR/6´3˝/205; d9.25; f–Hal																									
1958	Chi A	1	0	1.000	2	0	0	0	3	5	3	0	0	2-0	1	6.00	61	.385	.467	0	ø	0	—	-1	0	-0.2
Trotter, Bill	William Felix; B8.10.1908 Cisne IL; D8.26.1984 Arlington MA; BR/TR/6´2˝/195; d4.23																									
1937	StL A	2	9	.182	34	12	3	1	122.1	150	88	14	7	50	37	5.81	83	.304	.376	33-0-2	.030	-3	92	-12	—	-1.2
1938	StL A	0	1	.000	1	1	1	0	8	8	7	0	0	0	1	5.63	88	.242	.242	2-0-1	.000	-0	89	-1	—	-0.1
1939	StL A	6	13	.316	41	13	4	0	156.2	205	120	16	5	54	61	5.34	91	.318	.376	37-0-7	.108	-1	68	-14	—	-1.5
1940	StL A	7	6	.538	36	4	1	2	98	117	56	5	1	31	29	3.77	122	.300	.353	22-0-2	.045	-2	67	4	—	0.3
1941	StL A	4	2	.667	29	0	0	0	49.2	68	35	2	2	19	17	5.98	72	.332	.394	6-0-1	.000	-1	—	-8	0	-0.8
1942	StL A	0	1	.000	3	0	0	0	2	5	5	0	0	2	0	18.00	21	.385	.467	0	ø	0	—	-3	0	-0.6
	Was A	3	1	.750	17	0	0	0	40.2	52	29	4	0	14	13	5.75	63	.304	.357	8-0-1	.000	-0	—	-9	0	-0.8
	Year	3	2	.600	20	0	0	0	42.2	57	34	4	0	16	13	6.33	58	.310	.365	8-0-1	.000	-0	—	-12	0	-1.4
1944	StL N	0	1	.000	2	1	0	0	6	14	14	5	0	4	0	13.50	26	.467	.529	1	.000	-0	119	-8	0	-1.0
Total	7	22	34	.393	163	31	9	3	483.1	619	354	46	15	174	158	5.40	85	.313	.373	109-0-14	.055	-7	82	-51	0	-5.7
Trout, Dizzy	Paul Howard; B6.29.1915 Sandcut IN; D2.28.1972 Harvey IL; BR/TR/6´2.5˝/195; d4.25; s–Steve																									
1939	Det A	9	10	.474	33	22	6	2	162	168	82	5	4	74	72	3.61	135	.270	.351	57-0-2	.211	-0*	91	19	—	1.9
1940	†Det A	3	7	.300	33	10	1	2	100.2	125	60	4	3	54	64	4.47	106	.307	.392	31	.129	-2	100	2	—	0.1
1941	Det A	9	9	.500	37	18	6-1	2	151.2	144	76	7	2	84	88	3.74	122	.252	.350	50	.180	0*	81	11	0	1.3
1942	Det A	12	18	.400	35	29	13-1	0	223	214	98	15	4	89	91	3.43	115	.249	.322	75-1-4	.213	2*	82	14	0	2.2
1943	Det A	**20**	12	.625	44	30	18-**5**	6	246.2	204	83	6	0	101	111	2.48	142	.227	.305	91-1-4	.220	2*	98	26	0	4.1
1944	Det A☆	27	14	.659	49	**40**	**33-7**	0	**352.1**	314	104	9	4	83	144	**2.12**	**168**	.237	.284	133-5-2	.271	12*	96	**53**	0	**8.2**
1945	†Det A	18	15	.545	41	31	18-4	2	246.1	252	108	8	0	79	97	3.14	112	.267	.324	102-2-0	.245	4*	127	9	0	1.7
1946	Det A	17	13	.567	38	32	23-5	3	276.1	244	85	11	3	97	151	2.34	156	.238	.306	103-3-4	.194	3*	95	37	0	4.7
1947	Det A☆	10	11	.476	32	26	9-2	2	186.1	186	85	6	3	65	74	3.48	108	.261	.325	68-3-1	.162	3*	115	5	0	1.1
1948	Det A	10	14	.417	32	23	11-2	2	183.2	193	87	6	2	73	91	3.43	127	.269	.338	69-1-2	.217	2	94	16	0	2.1
1949	Det A	3	6	.333	33	0	0	3	59.1	68	35	2	0	21	19	4.40	95	.292	.350	14-1-0	.143	0	—	-3	0	-0.3
1950	Det A	13	5	.722	34	20	11-1	4	184.2	190	84	13	5	64	88	3.75	125	.267	.332	63-1-3	.190	1	97	19	0	1.9
1951	Det A	9	14	.391	42	22	7	5	191.2	172	98	13	1	75	89	4.04	103	.240	.312	52-1-3	.269	5	85	2	0	1.0
1952	Det A	1	5	.167	10	2	0	1	27	30	16	4	0	19	20	5.33	71	.286	.395	9-0-1	.333	1	23	-4	0	-0.6
	Bos A	9	8	.529	26	17	2	1	133.2	133	62	3	3	68	57	3.64	108	.263	.354	44-1-0	.136	-1	95	4	0	0.4
	Year	10	13	.435	36	19	2	2	160.2	163	78	7	3	87	77	3.92	100	.267	.361	53-1-1	.170	-1	88	1	0	-0.2
1957	Bal A	0	0	ø	2	0	0	0	0.1	4	3	0	0	0-0	0	81.00	4	.800	.800	0	ø	0	—	-3	0	-0.1
Total	15	170	161	.514	521	322	158-28	35	2725.2	2641	1166	112	34	1046-0	1256	3.23	124	.255	.325	961-20-26	.213	31	96	207	0	29.7
Trout, Steve	Steven Russell; B7.30.1957 Detroit MI; BL/TL/6´4˝/(189–195); [ChiA76 1/8]; d7.1; f–Dizzy																									
1978	Chi A	3	0	1.000	4	3	1	0-0	22.1	19	10	0	0	11-0	11	4.03	94	.229	.313	0	ø	0	157	0	0	0.0
1979	Chi A	11	8	.579	34	18	6-2	4-3	155	165	77	10	5	59-5	76	3.89	109	.273	.341	0	ø	0	111	7	0	0.8
1980	Chi A	9	16	.360	32	30	7-2	0-0	199.2	229	102	14	9	49-5	89	3.70	110	.290	.337	0	ø	0	85	5	0	0.7
1981	Chi A	8	7	.533	20	18	3	0-0	124.2	122	53	7	4	38-0	54	3.47	104	.261	.320	0	ø	0	106	3	0	0.4
1982	Chi A	6	9	.400	25	19	2	0-0	120.1	130	76	9	2	50-2	62	4.26	96	.273	.342	0	ø	0	94	-7	0	-0.8
1983	Chi N	10	14	.417	34	32	1	0-0	180	217	105	13	2	59-5	80	4.65	82	.305	.357	62-0-8	.194	0	97	-17	0	-1.9
1984	†Chi N	13	7	.650	32	31	6-2	0-1	190	205	80	7	2	59-7	81	3.41	115	.285	.339	61-0-5	.131	-1	116	9	0	1.0
1985	Chi N	9	7	.563	24	24	3-1	0-0	140.2	142	57	8	1	63-7	44	3.39	118	.270	.347	46-0-9	.109	-2	106	9	31	1.0
1986	Chi N	5	7	.417	37	25	0	0-0	161	184	88	6	1	78-13	69	4.75	86	.298	.375	43-0-4	.209	1	115	-9	0	-0.5
1987	Chi N	6	3	.667	11	11	3-2	0-0	75	72	27	3	1	27-0	32	3.00	144	.260	.326	26-0-3	.154	-1	105	11	43	1.2
	NY A	0	4	.000	14	9	0	0-0	46.1	51	36	4	1	37-0	27	6.60	67	.274	.397	0	ø	0	85	-11	0	-0.8
1988	Sea A	4	7	.364	15	13	0	0-0	56.1	86	53	6	5	31-2	14	7.83	53	.361	.440	0	ø	0	89	-21	65	-3.3

YEAR	TM LG	W	L	PCT	G	GS	CG-SHO	SV-BS	IP	H	R	HR	HB	BB-IB	SO	ERA	AERA	OAV	OOB	AB-HR-SH	AVG	PB	SUP	APR	DL	PW
1989	Sea A	4	3	.571	19	3	0	0-2	30	43	27	3	0	17-2	17	6.60	61	.333	.408	0	ø	0	135	-9	0	-1.7
Total	12	88	92	.489	301	236	32-9	4-6	1501.1	1665	791	90	33	578-48	656	4.18	96	.286	.351	238-0-29	.160	-2	103	-30	139	-3.9
TROWBRIDGE, BOB	Robert; B6.27.1930 Hudson NY; D4.3.1980 Hudson NY; BR/TR/6´1˝/(180–190); d4.22																									
1956	Mil N	3	2	.600	19	4	1	0	50.2	38	15	4	2	34-2	40	2.66	130	.210	.339	7-0-1	.000	-1	146	6	0	0.5
1957	†Mil N	7	5	.583	32	16	3-1	1	126	118	57	9	1	52-5	75	3.64	96	.248	.321	39-0-1	.103	-2	138	-2	0	-0.4
1958	Mil N	1	3	.250	27	4	0	1	55	53	26	4	1	26-3	31	3.93	90	.252	.332	9-0-1	.111	-1	89	-3	0	-0.3
1959	Mil N	1	0	1.000	16	0	0	1	30.1	45	25	2	0	10-2	22	5.93	60	.344	.387	4	.000	-0	—	-10	0	-0.6
1960	KC A	1	3	.250	22	1	0	2	68.1	70	41	6	1	34-3	33	4.61	86	.281	.365	18	.056	-1	111	-5	0	-0.4
Total	5	13	13	.500	116	25	4-1	5	330.1	324	164	25	5	156-15	201	3.95	91	.260	.341	77-0-3	.078	-5	128	-14	0	-1.2
TROY, BUN	Robert; B8.27.1888 Bad Wurzach, Germany; D10.7.1918 Petit Maujouym, France; BR/TR/6´4˝/195; d9.15																									
1912	Det A	0	1	.000	1	1	0	0	6.2	9	4	0	1	3	1	5.40	60	.346	.433	2	.000	-0	68	-1	—	-0.2
TRUCKS, VIRGIL	Virgil Oliver "Fire"; B4.26.1917 Birmingham AL; BR/TR/5´11˝/(190–210); d9.27; Mil 1944–45; C1																									
1941	Det A	0	0	ø	1	0	0	0	2	4	2	0	0	0	3	9.00	50	.500	.500	0	ø	0	—	-1	0	0.0
1942	Det A	14	8	.636	28	20	8-2	0	167.2	147	64	3	2	74	91	2.74	144	.231	.314	65-0-1	.123	-4	96	20	0	2.1
1943	Det A	16	10	.615	33	25	10-2	2	202.2	170	72	11	1	52	118	2.84	124	.225	.276	72	.181	-2	111	16	0	1.8
1945	†Det A	0	0	ø	1	1	0	0	5.1	3	1	0	0	2	3	1.69	208	.176	.263	2	.000	-0	145	1	0	0.1
1946	Det A	14	9	.609	32	29	15-2	0	236.2	217	94	23	3	75	161	3.23	113	.241	.302	95-0-2	.179	-1	95	12	0	0.9
1947	Det A	10	12	.455	36	26	8-2	2	180.2	186	105	14	2	79	108	4.53	83	.263	.339	70	.271	2	132	-15	0	-1.5
1948	Det A	14	13	.519	43	26	7	2	211.2	190	97	14	2	85	123	3.78	115	.240	.315	79-0-2	.165	-3	91	16	0	1.4
1949	Det A★	19	11	.633	41	32	17-**6**	4	275	209	95	16	4	124	**153**	2.81	148	.211	.301	100-0-5	.120	-6	82	42	0	3.5
1950	Det A	3	1	.750	7	7	2-1	0	48.1	45	20	6	1	21	25	3.54	133	.243	.324	20	.150	-1	113	6	0	0.4
1951	Det A	13	8	.619	37	18	6-1	1	153.2	153	81	9	5	75	89	4.33	96	.262	.350	55-0-2	.236	-0	108	-2	0	-0.2
1952	Det A	5	19	.208	35	29	8-3	1	197	190	99	12	7	82	129	3.97	96	.251	.330	64-1-2	.188	-0	62	-4	0	-0.4
1953	StL A	5	4	.556	16	12	4-2	2	88	83	37	4	4	32	47	3.07	137	.249	.322	25-0-4	.160	-1	72	9	0	0.8
	Chi A	15	6	.714	24	21	13-3	1	176.1	151	60	14	3	67	102	2.86	141	.232	.306	63-1-9	.238	2	133	24	0	3.0
	Year	20	10	.667	40	33	17-5	3	264.1	234	97	18	7	99	149	2.93	139	.238	.312	88-1-13	.216	1	110	32	0	3.8
1954	Chi A★	19	12	.613	40	33	16-**5**	3	264.2	224	87	13	1	95	152	2.79	134	.228	.296	93-0-9	.183	-1	117	30	0	3.3
1955	Chi A	13	8	.619	32	26	7-3	0	175	176	78	19	2	61-5	91	3.96	100	.260	.322	64-0-7	.125	-3	116	2	0	-0.1
1956	Det A	6	5	.545	22	16	3-1	1	120	104	56	15	6	63-5	43	3.83	108	.239	.342	45-0-2	.244	1	111	5	0	0.4
1957	KC A	9	7	.563	48	7	0	7	116	106	45	12	2	62-8	55	3.03	131	.248	.345	28-0-1	.143	-1	52	11	0	1.4
1958	KC A	0	1	.000	16	0	0	3	22	18	7	2	0	15-1	15	2.05	191	.222	.340	1	.000	-0	—	4	0	0.3
	NY A	2	1	.667	25	0	0	1	39.2	40	24	1	2	24-0	26	4.54	78	.265	.359	8	.250	0	—	-5	0	-0.4
	Year	2	2	.500	41	0	0	4	61.2	58	31	3	2	39-1	41	3.65	100	.250	.352	9	.222	0	—	-1	0	-0.1
Total	17	177	135	.567	517	328	124-33	30	2682.1	2416	1124	188	47	1088-19	1534	3.39	117	.240	.316	949-2-46	.180	-19	101	171	0	16.8
TRUJILLO, J.J.	John; B10.9.1975 Corpus Christi TX; BR/TR/6´0˝/180; d6.11; Col Dallas Baptist																									
2002	SD N	0	1	.000	4	0	0	0-0	2.2	4	3	1	1	6-0	3	10.13	38	.364	.611	0	ø	0	—	-2	0	-0.4
TRUJILLO, MIKE	Michael Andrew; B1.12.1960 Denver CO; BR/TR/6´1˝/180; [ChiA82 7/172]; d4.14; Col Northern Colorado																									
1985	Bos A	4	4	.500	27	7	1	1-0	84	112	55	7	3	23-1	19	4.82	89	.320	.365	0	ø	0	120	-7	0	-0.5
1986	Bos A	0	0	ø	3	0	0	0-0	5.2	7	6	0	0	6-2	4	9.53	44	.304	.448	0	ø	0	—	-3	0	-0.1
	Sea A	3	2	.600	11	4	1-1	1-0	41.1	32	11	5	0	15-1	19	2.40	178	.215	.285	0	ø	0	80	9	0	1.1
	Year	3	2	.600	14	4	1-1	1-0	47	39	17	5	0	21-3	23	3.26	131	.227	.309	0	ø	0	80	6	0	1.0
1987	Sea A	4	4	.500	28	7	0	1-1	65.2	70	46	12	2	26-0	36	6.17	77	.277	.346	0	ø	0	96	-8	0	-0.9
1988	Det A	0	0	ø	6	0	0	0-0	12.1	11	7	2	0	5-2	5	5.11	75	.234	.308	0	ø	0	—	-1	0	-0.1
1989	Det A	1	2	.333	8	4	1	0-0	25.2	35	17	3	0	13-0	13	5.96	64	.333	.397	0	ø	0	130	-5	0	-0.5
Total	5	12	12	.500	83	22	3-1	3-1	234.2	267	142	29	5	88-6	96	5.02	86	.288	.350	0	ø	0	107	-15	0	-1.0
TRUMBULL, ED	Edward J. (b Edward J. Trembly); B11.3.1860 Chicopee MA; D1.14.1937 Kingston PA; d5.10; ▲																									
1884	Was AA	1	9	.100	10	10	10	0	84	108	90	4	1	31	43	4.71	64	.295	.352	86	.116	-2*	88	-18	—	-1.8
TSAMIS, GEORGE	George Alex; B6.14.1967 Campbell CA; BR/TL/6´2˝/190; [MinA89 15/399]; d4.26; Col Stetson																									
1993	Min A	1	2	.333	41	0	0	1-1	68.1	86	51	9	3	27-5	30	6.19	71	.317	.378	0	ø	0	—	-13	0	-0.6
TSAO, CHIN-HUI	Chin-Hui; B6.2.1981 Hualien, Taiwan; BR/TR/6´2˝/(170–190); d7.25; [DL 2006 Col N 182]																									
2003	Col N	3	3	.500	9	8	0	0-0	43.1	48	30	11	4	20-1	29	6.02	81	.284	.373	13-0-2	.154	-0	84	-4	23	-0.5
2004	Col N	0	0	ø	10	0	0	1-1	9.1	7	4	2	0	1-0	11	3.86	123	.200	.222	0	ø	0	—	1	0	0.0
2005	Col N	1	0	1.000	10	0	0	3-1	11	16	8	3	1	5-1	4	6.55	71	.333	.400	0	ø	0	—	-2	153	-0.2
Total	3	4	3	.571	29	8	0	4-2	63.2	71	42	16	5	26-2	44	5.80	83	.282	.359	13-0-2	.154	-0	84	-5	358	-0.7
TSITOURIS, JOHN	John Philip; B5.4.1936 Monroe NC; BR/TR/6´0˝/(175–188); d6.13																									
1957	Det A	1	0	1.000	2	0	0	0	3.1	8	3	0	0	2-0	2	8.10	48	.500	.556	1	.000	-0	—	-1	0	-0.3
1958	KC A	0	0	ø	1	1	0	0	3	2	1	0	0	2-0	1	3.00	130	.182	.308	1	.000	-0	92	0	0	0.0
1959	KC A	4	3	.571	24	10	0	0	83.1	90	52	3	3	35-3	50	4.97	81	.271	.344	20-0-3	.150	-1	110	-8	0	-0.7
1960	KC A	0	2	.000	14	2	0	0	33	38	25	3	8	21-1	12	6.55	61	.297	.421	6-0-1	.000	-1	111	-8	64	-0.5
1962	Cin N	1	0	1.000	4	2	1-1	0	21.1	13	2	0	3	7-0	7	0.84	477	.181	.280	5-0-1	.000	-1	87	7	0	0.3
1963	Cin N	12	8	.600	30	21	8-3	0	191	167	73	20	11	38-1	113	3.16	106	.232	.280	62-0-3	.081	-3	83	5	0	-0.1
1964	Cin N	9	13	.409	37	24	6-1	2	175.1	178	90	20	5	75-6	146	3.80	95	.263	.338	58-0-2	.190	2	96	-6	0	-0.6
1965	Cin N	6	9	.400	31	20	3	1	131	134	87	18	9	65-1	91	4.95	76	.265	.354	43-0-3	.070	-2	120	-19	0	-2.3
1966	Cin N	0	0	ø	1	0	0	0	1	3	2	0	0	1-0	0	18.00	22	.750	.800	0	ø	0	—	-1	0	-0.1
1967	Cin N	1	0	1.000	2	1	0	0	8	4	3	1	0	6-0	4	3.38	111	.154	.313	0-0-1	ø	0	234	0	0	0.1
1968	Cin N	0	3	.000	3	3	0	0	12.2	16	10	6	1	8-0	6	7.11	44	.302	.403	2	.000	0	27	-5	0	-0.9
Total	11	34	38	.472	149	84	18-5	3	663	653	348	71	40	260-12	432	4.13	88	.257	.333	198-0-14	.111	-6	100	-36	64	-5.1
TUCKER, T.J.	Thomas John; B8.20.1978 Clearwater FL; BR/TR/6´3˝/(245–265); [MonN97 1/47]; d6.3																									
2000	Mon N	0	1	.000	2	2	0	0-0	7	11	9	5	0	3-0	2	11.57	41	.344	.400	1	1.000	0	97	-5	113	-0.5
2002	Mon N	6	3	.667	57	0	0	4-3	61.1	69	32	5	0	31-9	42	4.11	107	.290	.369	4	.750	1*	—	1	19	0.3
2003	Mon N	2	3	.400	45	7	0	0-2	80	90	49	8	4	20-1	47	4.72	94	.278	.327	19-0-1	.263	1*	106	-3	0	-0.1
2004	Mon N	4	2	.667	54	1	0	0-2	67.2	73	28	5	4	17-6	44	3.72	123	.275	.326	12	.083	-1	81	7	0	0.5
2005	Was N	1	0	1.000	13	0	0	0-0	12.2	20	9	4	0	2-0	5	6.39	64	.370	.386	0	ø	0	—	-3	143	-0.2
Total	5	13	9	.591	171	10	0	4-7	228.2	263	127	27	8	73-16	140	4.57	98	.288	.344	36-0-1	.278	2	102	-3	275	0.0
TUCKEY, TOM	Thomas Henry "Tabasco Tom"; B10.7.1884 Union City CT; D10.17.1950 New York NY; TL/5´11.5˝/190; d8.11																									
1908	Bos N	3	3	.500	8	8	3-1	0	72	60	21	2	4	20	26	2.50	96	.265	.336	20-0-1	.050	-2	80	2	—	0.0
1909	Bos N	0	9	.000	17	10	4	0	90.2	104	59	1	3	22	16	4.27	66	.295	.342	29-0-2	.138	-1	82	-13	—	-1.3
Total	2	3	12	.200	25	18	7-1	0	162.2	164	80	3	7	42	42	3.49	76	.284	.340	49-0-3	.102	-3	81	-11	—	-1.3
TUDOR, JOHN	John Thomas; B2.2.1954 Schenectady NY; BL/TL/6´0˝/185; [BosA76*S3/57]; d8.16; Col Georgia Southern																									
1979	Bos A	1	2	.333	6	6	1	0-0	28	39	23	2	0	9-1	11	6.43	69	.345	.384	0	ø	0	85	-6	0	-0.5
1980	Bos A	8	5	.615	16	13	5	0-0	92.1	81	35	4	3	31-1	45	3.02	141	.238	.304	0	ø	0	98	12	0	1.7
1981	Bos A	4	3	.571	18	11	2	1-0	78.2	74	44	11	3	28-1	44	4.58	86	.252	.319	0	ø	0	117	-5	0	-0.4
1982	Bos A	13	10	.565	32	30	6-1	0-0	195.2	215	90	20	8	59-3	146	3.63	120	.280	.336	0	ø	0	94	13	0	1.6
1983	Bos A	13	12	.520	34	34	7-2	0-0	242	236	122	32	4	81-3	136	4.09	107	.255	.316	0	ø	0	84	8	0	0.7
1984	Pit N	12	11	.522	32	32	6-1	0-0	212	200	81	19	1	56-2	117	3.27	111	.248	.295	76-0-4	.211	2*	82	11	0	1.4
1985	†StL N	21	8	.724	36	36	14-**10**	0-0	275	209	68	14	5	49-4	169	1.93	185	.209	**.249**	94-0-7	.138	1*	110	50	0	5.6
1986	StL N	13	7	.650	30	30	3	0-0	219	197	81	22	1	53-5	107	2.92	127	.244	.289	72-0-13	.153	-1	94	18	20	1.6
1987	†StL N	10	2	.833	16	16	0	0-0	96	100	43	11	1	32-1	54	3.84	109	.272	.331	35-0-3	.200	1*	107	4	101	0.6
1988	StL N	6	5	.545	21	21	4-1	0-0	145.1	131	44	5	1	31-7	55	2.29	154	.247	.287	46-0-5	.109	-1*	91	18	21	1.4
	†LA N	4	3	.571	9	9	1	0-0	52.1	58	16	5	0	10-0	32	2.41	139	.284	.318	13-0-2	.000	-1	94	6	0	0.7
	Year	10	8	.556	30	30	5-1	0-0	197.2	189	60	10	1	41-7	87	2.32	150	.257	.295	59-0-7	.085	-2	92	24	0	2.1
1989	LA N	0	0	ø	6	3	0	0-0	14.1	17	5	1	0	6-0	9	3.14	109	.309	.377	2	.000	-0	86	1	141	0.0
1990	StL N	12	4	.750	25	22	1-1	0-0	146.1	120	48	10	2	30-4	63	2.40	161	.225	.268	46-0-7	.152	0	110	21	22	2.5
Total	12	117	72	.619	281	263	50-16	1-0	1797	1677	700	156	29	475-32	988	3.12	125	.248	.299	384-0-41	.154	2	96	151	305	16.9

THE PITCHER REGISTER

YEAR	TM LG	W	L	PCT	G	GS	CG-SHO	SV-BS	IP	H	R	HR	HB	BB-IB	SO	ERA	AERA	OAV	OOB	AB-HR-SH	AVG	PB	SUP	APR	DL	PW
TUERO, OSCAR	Oscar (Monzon) (b Oscar Tuero Monzon); B12.17.1898 , Can; D10.21.1960 Houston TX; BR/TR/5´8.5˝/158; d5.30																									
1918	StL N	1	2	.333	11	3	2	0	44.1	32	12	0	3	10	13	1.02	267	.208	.269	12	.250	0*	28	7	—	0.4
1919	StL N	5	7	.417	**45**	16	4	**4**	154.2	137	71	4	10	42	45	3.20	87	.242	.306	39-0-2	.205	1	100	-8	—	-0.6
1920	StL N	0	0	ø	2	0	0	0	0.2	5	4	0	0	1	0	54.00	6	.833	.857	0	ø	0	—	-4	—	-0.2
Total	3	6	9	.400	58	19	6	4	199.2	174	87	4	13	53	58	2.88	96	.240	.303	51-0-2	.216	1	88	-5	—	-0.4
TUFTS, BOB	Robert Malcolm; B11.2.1955 Medford MA; BL/TL/6´5˝/(205–215); [SFN77 12/296]; d8.10; Col Princeton																									
1981	SF N	0	0	ø	11	0	0	0-1	15.1	20	9	1	1	6-0	12	3.52	97	.308	.370	1	.000	-0	—	-1	0	0.0
1982	KC A	2	0	1.000	10	0	0	2-1	20	24	10	3	0	3-0	13	4.50	91	.293	.314	0	ø	0	—	0	0	-0.1
1983	KC A	0	0	ø	6	0	0	0-0	6.2	16	8	1	1	5-0	3	8.10	51	.444	.524	0	ø	0	—	-3	0	-0.2
Total	3	2	0	1.000	27	0	0	2-2	42	60	27	5	2	14-0	28	4.71	81	.328	.378	1	.000	-0	—	-4	0	-0.3
TUNNELL, LEE	Byron Lee; B10.30.1960 Tyler TX; BR/TR/6´1˝/180; [PitN81 2/40]; d9.4; C1; Col Baylor; [DL 1988 StL N 8]																									
1982	Pit N	1	1	.500	5	3	0	0-0	18.1	17	8	1	2	5-0	4	3.93	95	.254	.324	4-0-1	.000	-0	126	0	0	0.0
1983	Pit N	11	6	.647	35	25	5-3	0-0	177.2	167	81	15	2	58-3	95	3.65	103	.252	.311	58-0-8	.121	-1	96	2	0	0.1
1984	Pit N	1	7	.125	26	6	0	1-4	68.1	81	44	6	0	40-6	51	5.27	69	.298	.387	12-0-3	.083	-1	93	-12	21	-1.3
1985	Pit N	4	10	.286	24	23	0	0-0	132.1	126	70	11	1	57-4	74	4.01	90	.251	.327	47	.085	-2	94	-8	0	-1.0
1987	†StL N	4	4	.500	32	9	0	0-0	74.1	90	45	5	1	34-7	49	4.84	87	.307	.377	17-0-3	.235	0*	141	-6	24	-0.5
1989	Min A	1	0	1.000	10	0	0	0-0	12	18	8	1	0	6-1	7	6.00	69	.340	.407	0	ø	0	—	-2	0	-0.2
Total	6	22	28	.440	132	66	5-3	1-4	483	499	256	39	6	200-21	280	4.23	89	.270	.341	138-0-15	.116	-4	103	-26	53	-2.9
TURBEVILLE, GEORGE	George Elkins; B8.24.1914 Turbeville SC; D10.5.1983 Salisbury NC; BR/TL/6´1˝/175; d7.20																									
1935	Phi A	0	3	.000	19	6	2	0	63.2	74	58	2	0	69	20	7.63	60	.312	.467	19-0-1	.105	-2	51	-20	—	-1.1
1936	Phi A	2	5	.286	12	6	2	0	43.2	42	36	6	6	32	10	6.39	80	.258	.398	14-0-1	.143	-1	60	-6	—	-0.9
1937	Phi A	0	4	.000	31	3	0	0	77.1	80	50	2	0	56	17	4.77	99	.266	.381	26	.231	0	117	-1	—	-0.1
Total	3	2	12	.143	62	15	4	0	184.2	196	144	10	6	157	47	6.14	77	.280	.416	59-0-2	.169	-2	69	-27	—	-2.1
TURK, LUCAS	Lucas Newton "Harlem","Chief"; B5.2.1898 Homer GA; D1.11.1994 Homer GA; BR/TR/6´0˝/165; d6.7; Col Oglethorpe																									
1922	Was A	0	0	ø	5	0	0	0	11.2	16	10	0	0	5	1	6.94	56	.340	.404	4	.250	0	—	-4	—	-0.2
TURLEY, BOB	Robert Lee "Bullet Bob"; B9.19.1930 Troy IL; BR/TR/6´2˝/(214–218); d9.29; Mil 1952–53; C1																									
1951	StL A	0	1	.000	1	1	0	0	7.1	11	6	0	0	3	5	7.36	60	.355	.412	2	.000	-0	61	-2	0	-0.2
1953	StL A	2	6	.250	10	7	3-1	0	60.1	39	24	4	2	44	61	3.28	128	.184	.329	18-1-2	.278	1	39	6	0	0.9
1954	Bal A☆	14	15	.483	35	35	14	0	247.1	178	106	7	7	181	**185**	3.46	104	**.203**	.340	81-0-6	.136	-3	82	4	0	0.2
1955	†NY A☆	17	13	.567	36	34	13-6	1	246.2	168	92	16	7	177-4	210	3.06	122	**.193**	.331	82-0-8	.134	-0	118	22	0	2.4
1956	†NY A	8	4	.667	27	21	5-1	1	132	138	76	13	4	103-0	91	5.05	77	.273	.398	46-0-3	.174	-0	152	-15	0	-1.3
1957	†NY A	13	6	.684	32	23	9-4	3	176.1	120	59	17	9	85-1	152	2.71	133	**.194**	.298	57-0-2	.088	-2	115	19	0	1.8
1958	†NY A★	**21**	7	**.750**	33	31	**19**-6	1	245.1	178	82	24	8	128-2	168	2.97	119	**.206**	.311	88-2-6	.136	-1	128	22	0	2.2
1959	NY A	8	11	.421	33	22	7-3	0	154.1	141	80	15	3	83-3	111	4.32	84	.245	.338	46-0-2	.087	-2	90	-10	0	-1.3
1960	†NY A	9	3	.750	34	24	4-1	5	173.1	138	67	14	5	87-3	87	3.27	110	.222	.319	55-0-2	.073	-4	139	9	0	0.2
1961	NY A	3	5	.375	15	12	1	0	72	74	47	11	4	51-0	48	5.75	65	.269	.390	21-0-3	.095	-1	103	-16	33	-1.6
1962	NY A	3	3	.500	24	8	0	1	69	68	45	8	4	47-2	42	4.57	82	.263	.379	12-0-3	.000	-1	110	-9	0	-0.9
1963	LA A	2	7	.222	19	12	3-2	0	87.1	71	41	5	2	51-6	70	3.30	104	.222	.331	25-1-0	.160	1	73	0	0	0.0
	Bos A	1	4	.200	11	7	0	0	41.1	42	28	6	1	28-0	35	6.10	62	.256	.366	14	.214	0	77	-9	0	-1.0
	Year	3	11	.214	30	19	3-2	0	128.2	113	69	11	3	79-6	105	4.20	84	.233	.343	39-1-0	.179	1	75	-10	0	-1.0
Total	12	101	85	.543	310	237	78-24	12	1712.2	1366	753	140	56	1068-21	1265	3.64	101	.220	.337	547-4-37	.126	-12	109	21	33	1.4
TURNBOW, DERRICK	Thomas Derrick; B1.25.1978 Union City TN; BR/TR/6´3˝/(180–210); [PhiN97 5/146]; d4.17																									
2000	Ana A	0	0	ø	24	1	0	0-0	38	36	21	7	2	36-0	25	4.74	109	.254	.409	0	ø	0	273	2	0	0.0
2003	Ana A	2	0	1.000	11	0	0	0-0	15.1	7	1	0	0	3-0	15	0.59	746	.140	.189	0	ø	0	—	7	0	0.8
2004	Ana A	0	0	ø	4	0	0	0-0	6.1	2	0	0	0	7-0	3	0.00	ø	.105	.346	1	.000	-0	—	3	0	0.2
2005	Mil N	7	1	.875	69	0	0	39-4	67.1	49	15	5	1	24-2	64	1.74	245	.199	.273	0	ø	0	—	18	0	3.8
2006	Mil N★	4	9	.308	64	0	0	24-8	56.1	56	51	8	4	39-2	69	6.87	65	.255	.375	1	.000	-0	—	-17	0	-3.2
Total	5	13	10	.565	172	1	0	63-12	183.1	150	88	20	7	109-4	176	3.78	120	.222	.335	2	.000	-0	273	13	0	1.6
TURNER, JIM	James Riley "Milkman Jim"; B8.6.1903 Antioch TN; D11.29.1998 Nashville TN; BL/TR/6´0˝/185; d4.30; C24																									
1937	Bos N	20	11	.645	33	30	**24-5**	1	256.2	228	80	13	0	52	69	**2.38**	**150**	.235	**.274**	96-0-7	.250	4*	100	**36**	—	**4.8**
1938	Bos N☆	14	18	.438	35	34	22-3	0	268	267	123	21	5	54	71	3.46	99	.259	.299	96-0-4	.229	4	87	-2	—	0.5
1939	Bos N	4	11	.267	25	22	9	0	157.2	181	83	10	4	51	50	4.28	86	.293	.351	55-1-3	.236	2	96	-9	—	-0.4
1940	†Cin N	14	7	.667	24	23	11	0	187	187	70	9	0	32	53	2.89	131	.264	.296	75-0-1	.240	3*	95	17	—	2.1
1941	Cin N	6	4	.600	23	10	3	0	113	120	49	5	1	24	34	3.11	116	.277	.317	41-0-2	.146	-1	116	5	0	0.4
1942	Cin N	0	0	ø	3	0	0	0	3.1	5	5	1	0	3	0	10.80	30	.333	.444	1	.000	-0	—	-3	0	-0.1
	†NY A	1	1	.500	5	0	0	1	7	4	1	0	0	1	2	1.29	268	.167	.200	1	.000	-0	—	2	0	0.4
1943	NY A	3	0	1.000	18	0	0	1	43.1	44	22	1	0	13	15	3.53	91	.260	.313	13	.077	-1	—	-2	0	-0.3
1944	NY A	4	4	.500	35	0	0	7	41.2	42	23	3	0	22	13	3.46	101	.264	.354	10	.200	0	—	-2	0	-0.3
1945	NY A	3	4	.429	30	0	0	**10**	54.1	45	26	4	0	31	22	3.64	95	.225	.329	11	.091	-1	—	-1	0	-0.3
Total	9	69	60	.535	231	119	69-8	20	1132	1123	482	67	10	283	329	3.22	111	.260	.307	399-1-17	.218	12	96	41	0	6.8
TURNER, KEN	Kenneth Charles; B8.17.1943 Framingham MA; BR/TL/6´2˝/190; d6.11																									
1967	Cal A	1	2	.333	13	1	0	0	17.1	16	9	4	1	4-0	6	4.15	76	.239	.292	4	.000	-0	28	-2	0	-0.3
TURNER, TED	Theodore Holhot; B5.4.1892 Lawrenceburg KY; D2.4.1958 Lexington KY; BR/TR/6´0˝/180; d4.20																									
1920	Chi N	0	0	ø	1	0	0	0	1.1	2	2	0	0	1	0	13.50	24	.400	.500	1	.000	-0	—	-1	—	-0.1
TURNER, TINK	Thomas Lovatt; B2.20.1890 Swarthmore PA; D2.25.1962 Philadelphia PA; BR/TR/6´1˝/190; d9.24; Col Penn																									
1915	Phi A	0	1	.000	1	1	0	0	2	5	6	1	0	3	0	22.50	13	.500	.615	0	ø	0	125	-4	—	-0.6
TURNER, MATT	William Matthew; B2.18.1967 Lexington KY; BR/TR/6´5˝/215; d4.23; Col Middle Georgia JC																									
1993	Fla N	4	5	.444	55	0	0	0-1	68	55	23	7	1	26-9	59	2.91	150	.227	.300	2	.000	-0	—	11	0	1.3
1994	Cle A	1	0	1.000	9	0	0	1-2	12.2	13	6	0	3	7-0	5	2.13	223	.241	.359	0	ø	0	—	3	78	0.2
Total	2	5	5	.500	64	0	0	1-3	80.2	68	29	7	4	33-9	64	2.79	159	.230	.312	2	.000	-0	—	14	78	1.5
TUTWILER, ELMER	Elmer Strange; B11.19.1905 Carbon Hill AL; D5.3.1976 Pensacola FL; BR/TR/5´11˝/158; d8.20																									
1928	Pit N	0	0	ø	2	0	0	0	3.2	4	2	0	0	0	1	4.91	83	.267	.267	1	.000	-0	—	0	—	0.0
TWINING, TWINK	Howard Earle "Doc"; B5.30.1894 Horsham PA; D6.14.1973 Lansdale PA; BR/TR/6´0˝/168; d7.9; Col Swarthmore																									
1916	Cin N	0	0	ø	1	0	0	0	2	4	3	1	1	1	0	13.50	19	.444	.545	0	ø	0	—	-2	—	-0.1
TWITCHELL, LARRY	Lawrence Grant; B2.18.1864 Cleveland OH; D8.23.1930 Cleveland OH; BR/TR/6´0˝/185; d4.30; ▲																									
1886	Det N	0	2	.000	4	4	2	0	25	35	22	1	—	12	6	6.48	51	.347	.416	16	.063	-2	101	-7	—	-0.5
1887	†Det N	11	1	.917	15	12	11	**1**	112.1	120	74	3	10	36	24	4.33	94	.268	.336	264	.333	4*	144	-2	—	0.1
1888	Det N	0	0	ø	2	0	0	1	4	6	3	1	0	0	3	6.75	41	.375	.375	524-5	.244	0*	—	-1	—	0.0
1889	Cle N	0	0	ø	1	0	0	0	1	0	0	0	0	1	0	0.00	ø	.000	.250	549-4	.275	0*	—	0	—	0.0
1890	Buf P	5	7	.417	13	12	12	0	104.1	112	77	3	15	72	29	4.57	90	.262	.387	172-2	.221	1*	77	-4	—	-0.1
1891	Col AA	1	1	.500	6	1	1	0	31	29	22	1	3	13	8	4.06	85	.240	.328	224-2	.277	2*	18	-2	—	0.0
1894	Lou N	0	0	ø	1	0	0	0	3	5	2	1	0	1	0	6.00	85	.357	.400	210-2-9	.267	0*	—	0	—	0.0
Total	7	17	11	.607	42	29	26	2	280.2	307	200	10	28	135	70	4.62	85	.272	.363	1959-15-9	.267	6	107	-16	—	-0.5
TWITCHELL, WAYNE	Wayne Lee; B3.10.1948 Portland OR; BR/TR/6´6˝/(215–225); [HouN66 1/3]; d9.7																									
1970	Mil A	0	0	ø	2	0	0	0-0	1.2	3	2	0	0	1-0	5	10.80	35	.333	.400	0	ø	0	—	-1	0	-0.1
1971	Phi N	1	0	1.000	6	1	0	0-0	16	8	4	1	1	10-0	15	0.00	ø	.145	.284	3	.000	-0	125	4	0	0.2
1972	Phi N	5	9	.357	49	15	1-1	1-1	139.2	138	72	6	2	56-6	112	4.06	89	.259	.329	28-0-1	.071	-2	54	-8	0	-1.0
1973	Phi N★	13	9	.591	34	28	10-5	0-0	223.1	172	71	16	10	99-9	169	2.50	152	.219	.312	72-0-7	.097	-4	80	31	0	2.3
1974	Phi N	6	9	.400	25	18	2	0-2	112.1	122	71	11	7	65-7	72	5.21	73	.276	.375	35-0-2	.171	-1	101	-16	49	-2.1
1975	Phi N	5	10	.333	36	20	0	0-0	134.1	132	82	10	1	78-3	101	4.42	85	.261	.358	34-0-3	.088	-2	106	-13	0	-1.6
1976	Phi N	3	1	.750	26	2	0	1-0	61.2	55	18	3	3	18-1	67	1.75	204	.241	.302	6	.167	0	62	10	0	0.7

YEAR	TM LG	W	L	PCT	G	GS	CG-SHO	SV-BS	IP	H	R	HR	HB	BB-IB	SO	ERA	AERA	OAV	OOB	AB-HR-SH	AVG	PB	SUP	APR	DL	PW
1977	Phi N	0	5	.000	12	8	0	0-0	45.2	50	27	3	0	25-1	37	4.53	89	.287	.377	11	.091	-0	72	-3	0	-0.3
	Mon N	6	5	.545	22	22	2	0-0	139	116	71	18	5	49-3	93	4.21	92	.230	.301	39-0-4	.205	2	96	-5	0	-0.1
	Year	6	10	.375	34	30	2	0-0	184.2	166	98	21	5	74-4	130	4.29	91	.244	.321	50-0-4	.180	2	90	-8	0	-0.4
1978	Mon N	4	12	.250	33	15	0	0-1	112	121	68	16	5	71-5	69	5.38	66	.286	.392	24-0-2	.083	-1	99	-20	0	-2.7
1979	NY N	5	3	.625	33	2	0	0-1	63.2	55	44	6	4	55-8	44	5.23	71	.243	.396	8-0-1	.375	1	95	-12	0	-1.3
	Sea A	0	2	.000	4	2	0	0-0	13.2	11	11	2	2	10-0	5	5.27	83	.220	.365	0	ø	0	62	-2	0	-0.3
Total	10	48	65	.425	282	133	15-6	2-5	1063	983	541	92	40	537-43	789	3.98	94	.250	.343	260-0-20	.127	-7	89	-35	49	-6.3
TWITTY, JEFF	Jeffrey Dean; B11.10.1957 Lancaster SC; BL/TL/6´2″/185; [KCA79 25/638]; d7.5; Col South Carolina																									
1980	KC A	2	1	.667	13	0	0	0-0	22.1	33	17	4	0	7-3	9	6.04	67	.351	.392	0	ø	0	—	-5	0	-0.6
TWOMBLY, CY	Edwin Parker; B6.15.1897 Groveland MA; D12.3.1974 Savannah GA; BR/TR/5´10.5″/170; d6.25; Col Springfield																									
1921	Chi A	1	2	.333	7	4	0	0	27.2	26	21	1	2	25	7	5.86	72	.283	.445	10	.000	-2	128	-5	—	-0.6
TYLER, LEFTY	George Albert; B12.14.1889 Derry NH; D9.29.1953 Lowell MA; BL/TL/6´0″/175; d9.20; b–Fred																									
1910	Bos N	0	0	ø	2	0	0	0	11.1	11	3	1	0	6	6	2.38	140	.275	.370	4	.500	1	—	1	—	0.2
1911	Bos N	7	10	.412	28	20	10-1	0	165.1	150	118	11	10	109	90	5.06	76	.243	.365	61-0-2	.164	-1	97	-19	—	-1.6
1912	Bos N	12	22	.353	42	31	15-1	0	256.1	262	150	8	10	126	144	4.18	86	.276	.366	96-0-1	.198	-1	86	-13	—	-1.4
1913	Bos N	16	17	.485	39	34	**28**-4	2	290.1	245	131	2	11	108	143	2.79	118	.235	.313	102-0-5	.206	4*	94	14	—	2.4
1914	†Bos N	16	13	.552	38	34	21-5	2	271.1	247	113	7	14	101	140	2.69	103	.249	.327	94-0-6	.202	1	93	-2	—	-0.3
1915	Bos N	10	9	.526	32	24	15-1	0	204.2	182	87	6	5	84	89	2.86	91	.243	.324	88-1-3	.261	8*	116	-6	—	0.3
1916	Bos N	17	9	.654	34	28	21-6	1	249.1	200	79	6	3	58	117	2.02	123	.226	.276	93-3-4	.204	7*	107	11	—	2.3
1917	Bos N	14	12	.538	32	28	22-4	1	239	203	81	1	6	86	98	2.52	101	.240	.314	134-0-7	.231	4*	99	2	—	1.1
1918	†Chi N	19	8	.704	33	30	22-6	1	269.1	218	72	1	5	67	102	2.00	139	.226	.279	100-0-3	.210	1*	126	27	—	3.2
1919	Chi N	2	2	.500	6	5	3	0	30	20	8	0	0	13	9	2.10	137	.196	.287	7-0-1	.143	1	94	3	—	0.6
1920	Chi N	11	12	.478	27	27	18-2	0	193	193	83	6	3	57	57	3.31	97	.268	.324	65-0-2	.262	4*	105	0	—	0.7
1921	Chi N	3	2	.600	10	6	4	0	50	59	22	2	0	14	8	3.24	118	.294	.340	26-0-1	.231	1*	115	3	—	0.3
Total	12	127	116	.523	323	267	179-30	7	2230	1990	947	51	67	829	1003	2.95	101	.245	.320	870-4-35	.217	30	102	21	—	7.8
TYNG, JIM	James Alexander; B3.27.1856 Philadelphia PA; D10.30.1931 New York NY; 5´9″/155; d9.23; Col Harvard																									
1879	Bos N	1	2	.333	3	3	3	0	27	35	25	0	—	6	7	5.00	50	.292	.325	14	.357	1	106	-7	—	-0.5
1888	Phi N	0	0	ø	1	0	0	1	4	8	4	0	1	2	2	4.50	66	.381	.458	1	.000	-0	—	-1	—	0.0
Total	2	1	2	.333	4	3	3	1	31	43	29	0	1	8	9	4.94	52	.305	.347	15	.333	1	106	-8	—	-0.5
TYRIVER, DAVE	David Burton; B10.31.1937 Oshkosh WI; D10.28.1988 Oshkosh WI; BR/TR/6´0″/175; d8.21																									
1962	Cle A	0	0	ø	4	0	0	0	10.2	10	6	2	1	7-1	7	4.22	92	.250	.375	3	.000	-0	—	-1	0	-0.1
UCHRINSCKO, JIMMY	James Emerson; B10.20.1900 W.Newton PA; D3.17.1995 Mt.Pleasant PA; BL/TR/6´0″/180; d7.20																									
1926	Was A	0	0	ø	3	0	0	0	8	13	9	0	0	8	0	10.13	38	.433	.553	2	.000	-0	—	-5	—	-0.3
UHL, BOB	Robert Ellwood "Lefty"; B9.17.1913 San Francisco CA; D8.21.1990 Santa Rosa CA; BB/TL/5´11″/175; d5.8																									
1938	Chi A	0	0	ø	1	0	0	0	2	1	0	0	0	0	0	0.00	ø	.167	.167	0	ø	0	—	1	—	0.0
1940	Det A	0	0	ø	1	0	0	0	0	4	5	0	0	2	0	(4)	ø	1.000	1.000	0	ø	0	—	-4	—	-0.3
Total	2	0	0	ø	2	0	0	0	2	5	5	0	0	2	0	18.00	27	.500	.583	0	ø	0	—	-3	—	-0.3
UHLE, GEORGE	George Ernest "The Bull"; B9.18.1898 Cleveland OH; D2.26.1985 Lakewood OH; BR/TR/6´0″/190; d4.30; C4; ▲																									
1919	Cle A	10	5	.667	26	12	7-1	0	127	129	52	1	7	43	50	2.91	115	.261	.329	43-0-1	.302	3	127	7	—	1.0
1920	†Cle A	4	5	.444	27	6	2	1	84.2	98	52	3	8	29	27	5.21	73	.296	.367	32	.344	2	94	-10	—	-0.7
1921	Cle A	16	13	.552	41	28	13-2	2	238	288	132	9	4	63	63	4.01	106	.306	.352	94-1-1	.245	3*	119	4	—	0.6
1922	Cle A	22	16	.579	50	**40**	23-**5**	3	287.1	328	147	6	13	89	82	4.07	98	.290	.348	109-0-3	.266	9*	121	-1	—	0.5
1923	Cle A	**26**	16	.619	54	**44**	**29**-1	5	**357.2**	378	167	8	12	102	109	3.77	105	.271	.326	144-0-5	.361	16*	140	16	—	**3.4**
1924	Cle A	9	15	.375	28	25	15	1	196.1	238	134	6	13	75	57	4.77	90	.306	.376	107-1-0	.308	7*	92	-13	—	-0.7
1925	Cle A	13	11	.542	29	26	17-1	0	210.2	218	118	5	8	78	68	4.10	108	.268	.339	101-0-4	.287	6*	86	6	—	1.0
1926	Cle A	**27**	11	**.711**	39	**36**	**32**-3	1	**318.1**	300	114	7	13	118	159	2.83	143	.253	.328	132-1-4	.227	4*	100	**45**	—	**5.4**
1927	Cle A	8	9	.471	25	22	10-1	1	153.1	187	88	3	9	59	69	4.34	97	.310	.379	79-0-2	.266	4*	89	-2	—	0.1
1928	Cle A	12	17	.414	31	28	18-2	1	214.1	252	121	8	8	48	74	4.07	102	.300	.344	98-1-6	.286	7*	77	0	—	0.8
1929	Det A	15	11	.577	32	30	23-1	0	249	283	141	9	2	58	100	4.08	105	.287	.328	108-0-2	.343	8*	120	4	—	1.0
1930	Det A	12	12	.500	33	29	18-1	3	239	239	110	18	5	75	117	3.65	131	.264	.323	117-2-4	.308	8*	106	31	—	3.4
1931	Det A	11	12	.478	29	18	15-2	2	193	190	88	10	4	49	63	3.50	131	.255	.304	90-2-1	.244	5*	56	23	—	2.9
1932	Det A	6	6	.500	33	15	6-1	5	146.2	152	84	15	4	42	51	4.48	105	.266	.320	55-0-2	.182	1*	103	5	—	0.4
1933	Det A	0	0	ø	1	0	0	0	0.2	2	2	1	0	0	1	27.00	16	.500	.500	0	ø	0	—	-2	—	-0.1
	NY N	1	1	.500	6	1	0	0	13.2	16	12	1	0	6	4	7.90	41	.302	.373	5	.000	-0*	26	-6	—	-0.8
	NY A	6	1	.857	12	6	4	0	61	63	42	4	3	20	26	5.16	75	.257	.321	20-0-1	.400	4	179	-10	—	-0.6
1934	NY A	2	4	.333	10	2	0	0	16.1	30	19	3	0	7	10	9.92	41	.400	.451	5	.600	2	107	-11	—	-1.7
1936	Cle A	0	1	.000	7	0	0	0	12.2	26	12	2	0	5	5	8.53	59	.419	.463	21-1-0	.381	4*	—	-4	—	0.0
Total	17	200	166	.546	513	368	232-21	25	3119.2	3417	1635	119	113	966	1135	3.99	105	.281	.340	1360-9-36	.289	92	106	82	—	15.9
UJDUR, JERRY	Gerald Raymond; B3.5.1957 Duluth MN; BR/TR/6´1″/(195–205); [DetA78 4/90]; d8.17; Col Minnesota																									
1980	Det A	1	0	1.000	9	2	0	0-0	21.1	36	20	5	1	10-2	8	7.59	54	.383	.443	0	ø	0	141	-8	0	-0.4
1981	Det A	0	0	ø	4	4	0	0-0	14	19	12	2	0	5-0	5	6.43	59	.322	.369	0	ø	0	113	-5	0	-0.2
1982	Det A	10	10	.500	25	25	7	0-0	178	150	76	29	3	69-4	86	3.69	111	.230	.304	0	ø	0	93	10	0	1.0
1983	Det A	0	4	.000	11	6	0	0-0	34	41	33	6	1	20-1	13	7.15	55	.293	.385	0	ø	0	80	-14	0	-1.4
1984	Cle A	1	2	.333	4	3	0	0-0	14.1	22	14	1	2	6-0	6	6.91	60	.355	.423	0	ø	0	110	-5	0	-0.9
Total	5	12	16	.429	53	40	7	0-0	261.2	268	155	43	7	110-7	118	4.78	85	.266	.340	0	ø	0	96	-22	0	-1.9
ULLRICH, SANDY	Carlos Santiago (Castello); B7.25.1921 Havana, Cuba; D4.21.2001 Miami FL; BR/TR/6´1″/180; d5.3																									
1944	Was A	0	0	ø	3	0	0	0	9.2	17	10	2	1	4	2	9.31	35	.386	.449	3	.333	0	—	-6	0	-0.3
1945	Was A	3	3	.500	28	6	0	1	81.1	91	45	3	0	34	26	4.54	68	.276	.343	22-0-1	.273	1	114	-12	0	-0.6
Total	2	3	3	.500	31	6	0	1	91	108	55	5	1	38	28	5.04	62	.289	.356	25-0-1	.280	1	114	-18	0	-0.9
ULRICH, DUTCH	Frank W.; B11.18.1899 Baltimore MD; D2.11.1929 Baltimore MD; BR/TR/6´2″/195; d4.18																									
1925	Phi N	3	3	.500	21	4	2-1	0	65	73	30	6	1	12	29	3.05	157	.285	.320	16	.125	-1	57	10	—	0.8
1926	Phi N	8	13	.381	45	16	8-1	1	147.2	178	85	9	1	37	52	4.08	101	.304	.347	49-0-2	.245	1	91	-1	—	0.1
1927	Phi N	8	11	.421	32	18	14-1	1	193.1	201	82	6	0	40	42	3.17	131	.271	.308	73-0-3	.123	-6	84	17	—	0.9
Total	3	19	27	.413	98	38	24-3	2	406	452	197	21	2	89	123	3.48	122	.286	.324	138-0-5	.167	-5	83	26	—	1.8
UMBACH, ARNOLD	Arnold William; B12.6.1942 Williamsburg VA; BR/TR/6´1″/180; d10.3																									
1964	Mil N	1	0	1.000	1	1	0	0	8.1	11	5	0	0	4-0	7	3.24	109	.333	.395	3	.000	0	275	0	0	-0.1
1966	Atl N	0	2	.000	22	3	0	0	40.2	40	15	1	2	18-3	23	3.10	117	.256	.339	5-0-1	.200	0	73	3	0	0.2
Total	2	1	2	.333	23	4	0	0	49	51	20	1	2	22-3	30	3.12	116	.270	.349	8-0-1	.125	0	122	3	0	0.1
UMBARGER, JIM	James Harold; B2.17.1953 Burbank CA; BL/TL/6´6″/200; [TexA74 16/362]; d4.8; Col Arizona St.																									
1975	Tex A	8	7	.533	56	12	3-2	2-0	131	134	63	11	2	59-9	50	4.12	92	.276	.353	0	ø	0	72	-2	0	-0.2
1976	Tex A	10	12	.455	30	30	10-3	0-0	197.1	208	86	12	2	54-4	105	3.15	114	.274	.321	0	ø	0	107	7	0	0.7
1977	Oak A	1	5	.167	12	8	1	0-0	44	62	40	3	4	28-2	24	6.55	62	.354	.448	0	ø	0	67	-14	0	-1.5
	Tex A	1	1	.500	3	2	0	0-0	13	14	8	2	0	4-0	5	5.54	74	.275	.321	0	ø	0	176	-2	0	-0.2
	Year	2	6	.250	15	10	1	0-0	57	76	48	5	4	32-2	29	6.32	64	.336	.421	0	ø	0	89	-16	0	-1.7
1978	Tex A	5	8	.385	32	9	1	1-2	97.2	116	58	9	2	36-4	60	4.88	77	.299	.358	0	ø	0	85	-11	0	-1.3
Total	4	25	33	.431	133	61	15-5	3-2	483	534	255	37	10	181-19	244	4.14	90	.287	.350	0	ø	0	94	-22	0	-2.5
UMBRICHT, JIM	James; B9.17.1930 Chicago IL; D4.8.1964 Houston TX; BR/TR/6´4″/(210–215); d9.26; Col Georgia																									
1959	Pit N	0	0	ø	1	1	0	0	7	7	5	3	0	4-0	3	6.43	60	.259	.355	3	.000	-0	139	-2	0	-0.1
1960	Pit N	1	2	.333	17	3	0	1	40.2	40	23	5	0	27-1	26	5.09	74	.270	.374	6	.333	0	118	-5	0	-0.4
1961	Pit N	0	0	ø	1	0	0	0	3.1	5	2	0	0	2-1	1	2.70	148	.333	.412	1	1.000	0	—	0	0	0.0
1962	Hou N	4	0	1.000	34	0	0	2	67	51	19	3	2	17-1	55	2.01	185	.213	.269	9-0-1	.111	-0	—	13	0	0.8

YEAR	TM LG	W	L	PCT	G	GS	CG-SHO	SV-BS	IP	H	R	HR	HB	BB-IB	SO	ERA	AERA	OAV	OOB	AB-HR-SH	AVG	PB	SUP	APR	DL	PW
1963	Hou N	4	3	.571	35	3	0	0	76	52	23	6	1	21-2	48	2.61	121	.195	.253	9-0-3	.111	-0	9	6	30	0.5
Total	5	9	5	.643	88	7	0	3	194	155	72	17	3	71-5	133	3.06	115	.222	.294	28-0-4	.179	-0	78	12	30	0.8
UNDERHILL, WILLIE Willie Vern; B9.6.1904 Yowell TX; D10.26.1970 Bay City TX; BR/TR/6´2˝/185; d9.8																										
1927	Cle A	0	2	.000	4	1	0	0	8.1	12	11	0	0	11	4	9.72	43	.375	.535	1-0-1	.000	-0	79	-5	—	-0.9
1928	Cle A	1	2	.333	11	3	1	0	28	33	23	0	1	20	16	4.50	92	.306	.419	11	.364	2	150	-4	—	-0.2
Total	2	1	4	.200	15	4	1	0	36.1	45	34	0	1	31	20	5.70	73	.321	.448	12-0-1	.333	1	132	-9	—	-1.1
UNDERWOOD, FRED Frederick Theodore; B10.14.1868 St.Louis Co. MO; D1.26.1906 Kansas City MO; ?/170; d7.18																										
1894	Bro N	2	4	.333	7	6	5	0	47	80	62	1	2	30	10	7.85	63	.372	.453	18	.389	2	90	-18	—	-1.3
UNDERWOOD, PAT Patrick John; B2.9.1957 Kokomo IN; BL/TL/6´0˝/(175–180); [DetA76 1/2]; d5.31; b–Tom																										
1979	Det A	6	4	.600	27	15	1	0-0	121.2	126	64	17	2	29-1	83	4.59	95	.269	.312	0	ø	0	110	-1	0	-0.1
1980	Det A	3	6	.333	49	7	0	5-0	112.2	121	51	12	2	35-7	60	3.59	115	.277	.333	0	ø	0	118	6	0	0.5
1982	Det A	4	8	.333	33	12	2	3-2	99	108	66	17	0	22-2	43	4.73	87	.269	.305	0	ø	0	97	-11	0	-1.2
1983	Det A	0	0	ø	4	0	0	0-0	10.1	11	10	1	0	6-0	2	8.71	45	.289	.386	0	ø	0	—	-5	0	-0.3
Total	4	13	18	.419	113	34	3	8-2	343.2	366	191	47	4	92-10	188	4.43	95	.272	.319	0	ø	0	107	-11	0	-1.1
UNDERWOOD, TOM Thomas Gerald; B12.22.1953 Kokomo IN; BR/TL/5´11˝/(170–185); [PhiN72 2/27]; d8.19; b–Pat																										
1974	Phi N	1	0	1.000	7	0	0	0-0	13	15	8	1	0	5-1	8	4.85	79	.313	.364	1	.000	-0	—	-2	0	-0.1
1975	Phi N	14	13	.519	35	35	7-2	0-0	219.1	221	110	12	6	84-5	123	4.14	91	.262	.331	74-0-7	.122	-2	97	-7	0	-1.2
1976	†Phi N	10	5	.667	33	25	3	2-0	155.2	154	63	9	1	63-0	94	3.53	101	.260	.331	46-0-3	.109	-1*	100	3	0	0.0
1977	Phi N	3	2	.600	14	0	0	1-0	33.1	44	21	2	0	18-2	20	5.13	79	.328	.403	3-0-1	.000	-0	—	-4	0	-0.6
	StL N	6	9	.400	19	17	1	0-0	100	104	61	7	1	57-4	66	4.95	79	.278	.372	30-0-2	.133	-0	84	-11	0	-1.5
	Year	9	11	.450	33	17	1	1-0	133.1	148	82	9	1	75-6	86	4.99	79	.291	.380	33-0-3	.121	-0	84	-16	0	-2.1
1978	Tor A	6	14	.300	31	30	7-1	0-0	197.2	201	105	23	2	87-4	139	4.10	97	.263	.339	0	ø	0	100	-7	0	-0.7
1979	Tor A	9	16	.360	33	32	12-1	0-0	227	213	113	23	9	95-3	127	3.69	119	.253	.333	0	ø	0	72	14	0	1.4
1980	†NY A	13	9	.591	38	27	2-2	2-1	187	163	85	15	4	66-4	116	3.66	108	.237	.306	0	ø	0	126	7	0	0.8
1981	NY A	1	4	.200	9	6	0	0-0	32.2	32	17	2	0	13-1	29	4.41	82	.262	.333	0	ø	0	87	-2	0	-0.4
	†Oak A	3	2	.600	16	5	1	1-1	51	37	21	4	2	25-1	46	3.18	111	.202	.305	0	ø	0	122	2	0	0.2
	Year	4	6	.400	25	11	1	1-1	83.2	69	38	6	2	38-2	75	3.66	97	.226	.316	0	ø	0	103	-1	0	-0.2
1982	Oak A	10	6	.625	56	10	2	7-6	153	136	66	11	1	68-4	79	3.29	120	.241	.321	0	ø	0	104	10	0	0.9
1983	Oak A	9	7	.563	51	15	0	4-2	144.2	156	69	13	2	50-4	62	4.04	96	.277	.332	0	ø	0	106	-1	0	-0.2
1984	Bal A	1	0	1.000	37	1	0	1-1	71.2	78	33	8	0	31-5	39	3.52	111	.282	.350	0	ø	0	46	3	0	0.2
Total	11	86	87	.497	379	203	35-6	18-11	1586	1554	772	130	28	662-38	948	3.89	101	.259	.333	154-0-13	.117	-4	97	5	0	-1.2
UPCHURCH, WOODY Jefferson Woodrow; B4.13.1911 Buies Creek NC; D10.23.1971 Buies Creek NC; BR/TL/6´0˝/180; d9.14; Col Campbell																										
1935	Phi A	0	2	.000	3	3	1	0	21.1	23	13	3	0	12	2	5.06	90	.271	.361	7	.286	0	76	-1	—	0.0
1936	Phi A	0	2	.000	7	2	1	0	22.1	36	27	7	0	14	6	9.67	53	.353	.431	7	.143	-0	86	-11	—	-0.8
Total	2	0	4	.000	10	5	2	0	43.2	59	40	10	0	26	8	7.42	65	.316	.399	14	.214	-0	80	-12	—	-0.8
UPHAM, BILL William Lawrence; B4.4.1888 Akron OH; D9.14.1959 Newark NJ; BB/TR/6´0˝/178; d4.10																										
1915	Bro F	7	8	.467	33	11	4-2	4	121	129	61	0	0	40	46	3.35	81	.274	.331	36	.111	-2	94	-9	—	-1.3
1918	Bos N	1	1	.500	3	2	2	0	20.2	28	14	2	0	1	8	5.23	51	.326	.333	9	.222	0	141	-5	—	-0.4
Total	2	8	9	.471	36	13	6-2	4	141.2	157	75	2	0	41	54	3.62	75	.282	.332	45	.133	-2	100	-14	—	-1.7
UPP, JERRY George Henry; B12.10.1883 Sandusky OH; D6.30.1937 Sandusky OH; TL; d9.2																										
1909	Cle A	2	1	.667	7	4	2	0	26.2	26	10	0	0	12	13	1.69	152	.260	.339	9	.222	0	90	2	—	0.3
UPSHAW, CECIL Cecil Lee; B10.22.1942 Spearsville LA; D2.7.1995 Lawrenceville GA; BR/TR/6´6˝/185; d10.1; Col Centenary Louisiana; [DL 1970 Atl N 165]																										
1966	Atl N	0	0	ø	1	0	0	0	3	0	0	0	0	3-0	2	0.00	ø	.000	.273	1	1.000	0	—	1	0	0.1
1967	Atl N	2	3	.400	30	0	0	8	45.1	42	14	4	4	8-4	31	2.58	129	.247	.295	6-0-2	.167	1	—	4	0	0.7
1968	Atl N	8	7	.533	52	0	0	13	116.2	98	41	6	4	24-7	74	2.47	121	.229	.275	23-0-6	.174	0	—	5	0	0.8
1969	†Atl N	6	4	.600	62	0	0	27-5	105.1	102	36	7	1	29-6	57	2.91	125	.259	.309	21-1-3	.238	2	—	9	0	1.6
1971	Atl N	11	6	.647	49	0	0	17-9	82	95	33	5	2	28-12	56	3.51	106	.292	.349	15-0-2	.000	-2	—	3	0	0.5
1972	Atl N	3	5	.375	42	0	0	13-2	53.2	50	22	5	1	19-9	23	3.69	103	.249	.315	7-0-1	.143	-0	—	2	22	0.3
1973	Atl N	0	1	.000	5	0	0	0-0	3.2	8	5	0	0	2-1	3	9.82	40	.444	.476	0	ø	0	—	-2	0	-0.5
	Hou N	2	3	.400	35	0	0	1-0	38.1	38	21	3	1	15-4	21	4.46	82	.259	.331	2	.000	-0	—	-4	0	-0.4
	Year	2	4	.333	40	0	0	1-0	42	46	26	3	1	17-5	24	4.93	75	.279	.348	2	.000	-0	—	-6	0	-0.9
1974	Cle A	0	1	.000	7	0	0	0-1	8	10	4	1	0	4-1	7	3.38	108	.345	.400	0	ø	0	—	0	0	0.0
	NY A	1	5	.167	36	0	0	6-3	59.2	53	25	1	3	24-3	27	3.02	118	.254	.339	0	ø	0	—	3	0	0.4
	Year	1	6	.143	43	0	0	6-4	67.2	63	29	2	3	28-4	34	3.06	116	.265	.347	0	ø	0	—	2	0	0.4
1975	Chi A	1	1	.500	29	0	0	1-2	47.1	49	19	5	4	21-3	22	3.23	120	.271	.359	0	ø	0	—	3	0	0.2
Total	9	34	36	.486	348	0	0	86-22	563	545	220	37	20	177-50	323	3.13	112	.258	.320	75-1-14	.160	1	—	24	187	3.7
UPTON, BILL William Ray; B6.18.1929 Esther MO; D1.2.1987 San Diego CA; BR/TR/6´0˝/167; d4.13; b–Tom																										
1954	Phi A	0	0	ø	2	0	0	1	5	6	1	1	0	1	2	1.80	217	.300	.333	0	ø	0	—	1	0	0.1
URBAN, JACK Jack Elmer; B12.5.1928 Omaha NE; D6.26.2006 Omaha NE; BR/TR/5´8˝/(155–165); d6.13																										
1957	KC A	7	4	.636	31	13	3	0	129.1	111	55	7	1	45-3	55	3.34	118	.237	.300	39-0-1	.282	2*	97	8	0	1.0
1958	KC A	8	11	.421	30	24	5-1	1	132	150	92	17	2	51-1	54	5.93	66	.286	.348	46	.152	-2*	87	-27	0	-3.6
1959	StL N	0	0	ø	8	0	0	0	10.2	18	11	1	0	7-4	4	9.28	46	.409	.490	1	.000	-0	—	-5	0	-0.3
Total	3	15	15	.500	69	37	8-1	1	272	279	158	25	3	103-8	113	4.83	82	.269	.333	86-0-1	.209	0	90	-24	0	-2.9
URBANI, TOM Thomas James; B1.21.1968 Santa Cruz CA; BL/TL/6´1˝/(190–210); [StLN90 13/357]; d4.21; Col Cal St.–Long Beach																										
1993	StL N	1	3	.250	18	9	0	0-1	62	73	44	4	0	26-2	33	4.65	87	.296	.355	16-0-2	.188	1	114	-8	0	-0.4
1994	StL N	3	7	.300	20	10	0	0-0	80.1	98	48	12	3	21-0	43	5.15	82	.302	.348	24-0-3	.250	1	84	-8	0	-0.7
1995	StL N	3	5	.375	24	13	0	0-0	82.2	99	40	11	2	21-4	52	3.70	116	.305	.351	19-1-2	.316	3	65	5	22	0.8
1996	StL N	1	0	1.000	3	2	0	0-0	11.2	15	10	3	0	4-0	1	7.71	55	.319	.365	6	.167	-0*	117	-4	0	-0.3
	Det A	2	2	.500	16	2	0	0-0	23.2	31	22	8	2	14-0	20	8.37	61	.310	.402	0	ø	0	127	-8	0	-1.0
Total	4	10	17	.370	81	36	0	0-1	260.1	316	164	38	7	86-6	149	4.98	86	.303	.357	65-1-7	.246	5	88	-23	22	-1.6
URBINA, UGUETH Ugueth Urtain (Villarreal); B2.15.1974 Caracas, Distrito Capital, Venez.; BR/TR/6´2˝/(185–205); d5.9																										
1995	Mon N	2	2	.500	7	4	0	0-0	23.1	26	17	6	0	14-1	15	6.17	70	.280	.374	6	.333	0	63	-5	0	-0.6
1996	Mon N	10	5	.667	33	17	0	0-1	114	102	54	18	1	44-4	108	3.71	117	.234	.304	29-0-3	.103	-1	80	7	0	0.6
1997	Mon N	5	8	.385	63	0	0	27-5	64.1	52	29	9	1	29-2	84	3.78	111	.214	.300	5	.000	-1	—	3	0	0.6
1998	Mon N★	6	3	.667	64	0	0	34-4	69.1	37	11	2	0	33-2	94	1.30	324	.157	.259	6	.000	-1	—	23	0	4.5
1999	Mon N	6	6	.500	71	0	0	**41**-9	75.2	59	35	6	0	36-6	100	3.69	121	.208	.295	5	.000	-1	—	7	0	1.2
2000	Mon N	0	1	.000	13	0	0	8-2	13.1	11	6	1	0	5-0	22	4.05	116	.224	.296	1	.000	-0	—	1	145	0.2
2001	Mon N	2	1	.667	45	0	0	15-3	46.2	42	24	8	0	21-1	57	4.24	102	.236	.315	1	.000	-0	—	0	0	0.0
	Bos A	0	1	.000	19	0	0	9-1	20	16	5	1	0	3-0	32	2.25	197	.219	.250	0	ø	0	—	5	0	0.6
2002	Bos A★	1	6	.143	61	0	0	40-6	60	44	21	8	0	20-5	71	3.00	149	.202	.266	0	ø	0	—	10	0	2.0
2003	Tex A	0	4	.000	39	0	0	26-4	38.2	33	19	6	0	18-2	41	4.19	119	.232	.313	0	ø	0	—	3	0	0.6
	†Fla N	3	0	1.000	33	0	0	6-2	38.1	23	6	2	0	13-0	37	1.41	291	.174	.245	0-0-1	ø	0	—	12	0	1.2
2004	Det A	4	6	.400	54	0	0	21-3	54	38	28	7	3	32-3	56	4.50	100	.194	.313	0	ø	0	—	0	0	0.0
2005	Det A	1	3	.250	25	0	0	9-2	27.1	21	9	4	1	14-2	31	2.63	162	.208	.310	0	ø	0	—	5	0	0.9
	Phi N	4	3	.571	56	0	0	1-6	52.1	35	25	8	1	25-2	66	4.13	105	.186	.280	0	ø	0	—	2	0	0.2
Total	11	44	49	.473	583	21	0	237-48	697.1	539	289	86	6	307-30	814	3.45	127	.210	.294	53-0-4	.094	-2	77	73	145	12.0
URDANETA, LINO Lino; B11.20.1979 Caracas, Distrito Capital, Venezuela; BR/TR/6´1˝/170; d9.9																										
2004	Det A	0	0	ø	1	0	0	0-0	0	5	6	0	0	1-0	0	(6)	ø	1.000	1.000	0	ø	0	—	-6	150	-0.4
URREA, JOHN John Godoy; B2.9.1955 Los Angeles CA; BR/TR/6´3˝/(195–205); [StLN74*1/14]; d4.10; Col Rio Hondo (CA) JC																										
1977	StL N	7	6	.538	41	12	2-1	4-2	139.2	126	56	13	0	35-3	81	3.16	124	.244	.291	29-0-3	.138	2	101	11	0	1.2
1978	StL N	4	9	.308	27	12	1	0-1	98.2	108	75	4	7	47-4	61	5.38	66	.284	.369	24-0-2	.125	-1	88	-23	0	-2.8
1979	StL N	0	0	ø	3	2	0	0-0	11.1	13	7	0	0	9-0	5	3.97	96	.310	.431	4	.250	0	151	-1	0	0.0

YEAR	TM LG	W	L	PCT	G	GS	CG-SHO	SV-BS	IP	H	R	HR	HB	BB-IB	SO	ERA	AERA	OAV	OOB	AB-HR-SH	AVG	PB	SUP	APR	DL	PW
1980	StL N	4	1	.800	30	1	0	3-0	64.2	57	28	2	2	41-9	36	3.48	108	.239	.352	13-0-2	.231	0	214	2	0	0.1
1981	SD N	2	2	.500	38	0	0	2-1	49	43	14	1	3	28-0	19	2.39	136	.239	.346	4	.250	0	—	5	0	0.4
Total	5	17	18	.486	139	27	3-1	9-4	363.1	347	180	20	12	160-16	202	3.74	99	.256	.337	74-0-7	.162	1	105	-6	0	-1.1
VAIL, BOB	Robert Garfield "Doc"; B9.24.1881 Linneus ME; D3.22.1942 Philadelphia PA; BR/TR/5´10˝/165; d8.27; Col Davidson																									
1908	Pit N	1	2	.333	4	1	0	0	15	15	10	0	1	7	9	6.00	38	.268	.359	3	.333	1	0	-5	—	-0.9
VALDES, MARC	Marc Christopher; B12.20.1971 Dayton OH; BR/TR/6´0˝/(170–188); [FlaN93 1/27]; d8.28; Col Florida																									
1995	Fla N	0	0	ø	3	3	0	0-0	7	17	13	1	1	9-0	2	14.14	30	.459	.563	2	.000	-0	133	-8	0	-0.4
1996	Fla N	1	3	.250	11	8	0	0-1	48.2	63	32	5	1	23-0	13	4.81	86	.315	.383	14	.000	-1	74	-5	0	-0.5
1997	Mon N	4	4	.500	48	7	0	2-0	95	84	36	2	8	39-5	54	3.13	134	.240	.326	19	.105	-1	69	12	0	0.8
1998	Mon N	1	3	.250	20	4	0	0-0	36.1	41	34	6	1	21-2	28	7.43	57	.285	.375	5	.400	1	44	-13	112	-1.1
2000	Hou N	5	5	.500	53	0	0	2-4	56.2	69	41	3	5	25-1	35	5.08	97	.301	.379	3	.000	-0	—	-4	0	-0.6
2001	Atl N	1	0	1.000	9	0	0	0-0	7	7	6	4	0	1-1	3	7.71	56	.259	.286	0	ø	0	—	-2	0	-0.3
Total	6	12	15	.444	144	22	0	4-5	250.2	281	162	21	16	118-9	135	4.95	88	.285	.366	43	.093	-1	73	-20	112	-2.1
VALDEZ, CARLOS	Carlos Luis (Lorenzo); B12.26.1971 Nizao Bani, D.R.; BR/TR/5´11˝/(175–191); d7.18																									
1995	SF N	0	1	.000	11	0	0	0-0	14.2	19	10	1	1	8-1	7	6.14	67	.322	.406	1	.000	-0	—	-3	0	-0.2
1998	Bos A	1	0	1.000	4	0	0	0-0	3.1	1	0	0	0	5-0	4	0.00	ø	.100	.375	0	ø	0	—	2	0	0.3
Total	2	1	1	.500	15	0	0	0-0	18	20	10	1	1	13-1	11	5.00	85	.290	.400	1	.000	-0	—	-1	0	0.1
VALDEZ, EFRAIN	Efrain Antonio; B7.11.1966 Nizao Bani, D.R.; BL/TL/5´11˝/170; d8.13																									
1990	Cle A	1	1	.500	13	0	0	0-0	23.2	20	10	2	0	14-3	13	3.04	130	.233	.330	0	ø	0	—	2	0	0.1
1991	Cle A	0	0	ø	7	0	0	0-0	6	5	1	0	1	3-1	1	1.50	278	.238	.346	0	ø	0	—	2	0	0.1
1998	Ari N	0	0	ø	6	0	0	0-0	4.1	7	2	2	0	1-0	2	4.15	103	.368	.400	0	ø	0	—	0	0	0.0
Total	3	1	1	.500	26	0	0	0-0	34	32	13	4	1	18-4	16	2.91	138	.254	.342	0	ø	0	—	4	0	0.2
VALDEZ, ISMAEL	Ismael (Alvarez); B8.21.1973 Ciudad Victoria, Tamaulipas, Mexico; BR/TR/6´3˝/(183–230); d6.15																									
1994	LA N	3	1	.750	21	1	0	0-0	28.1	21	10	2	0	10-2	28	3.18	125	.206	.277	2	.000	-0	160	3	0	0.4
1995	†LA N	13	11	.542	33	27	6-2	1-0	197.2	168	76	17	1	51-5	150	3.05	127	.228	.277	62-0-7	.097	-3	86	20	0	2.0
1996	†LA N	15	7	.682	33	33	0	0-0	225	219	94	20	3	54-10	173	3.32	118	.251	.294	70-0-13	.143	-1	106	17	0	1.4
1997	LA N	10	11	.476	30	30	0	0-0	196.2	171	68	16	3	47-1	140	2.65	147	.234	.282	57-0-7	.088	-2	81	27	22	2.6
1998	LA N	11	10	.524	27	27	2-2	0-0	174	171	82	17	2	66-4	122	3.98	101	.256	.323	48-0-8	.167	1	96	3	36	0.3
1999	LA N	9	14	.391	32	32	2-1	0-0	203.1	213	97	32	6	58-2	143	3.98	109	.270	.321	58-0-10	.086	-3	89	10	0	0.7
2000	Chi N	2	4	.333	12	12	0	0-0	67	71	40	17	2	27-2	45	5.37	85	.273	.344	14-0-5	.286	2*	82	-5	36	-0.2
	LA N	0	3	.000	9	8	0	0-0	40	53	29	5	1	13-0	29	6.07	73	.327	.376	11-1-2	.091	0	124	-7	0	-0.4
	Year	2	7	.222	21	20	0	0-0	107	124	69	22	3	40-2	74	5.64	80	.294	.356	25-1-7	.200	2	98	-12	0	-0.6
2001	Ana A	9	13	.409	27	27	1	0-0	163.2	177	82	20	8	50-3	100	4.45	104	.277	.338	5	.200	0	66	6	33	0.9
2002	Tex A	6	9	.400	23	23	0	0-0	146.2	135	65	19	9	36-1	75	3.93	122	.242	.297	3-0-1	.000	-0	74	15	0	1.3
	Sea A	2	3	.400	8	8	1	0-0	49.1	59	29	7	0	11-0	27	4.93	87	.299	.333	0	ø	0	140	-4	0	-0.3
	Year	8	12	.400	31	31	1	0-0	196	194	94	26	9	47-1	102	4.18	112	.257	.306	3-0-1	.000	-0	90	13	0	1.0
2003	Tex A	8	8	.500	22	22	0	0-0	115	148	83	23	5	29-0	47	6.10	81	.318	.359	4-0-2	.000	-0	90	-13	52	-1.5
2004	SD N	9	6	.600	23	20	1-1	0-0	114	141	75	21	2	31-1	37	5.53	71	.303	.347	35-0-3	.171	2	120	-21	0	-2.2
	Fla N	5	3	.625	11	11	0	0-0	56	61	30	12	0	18-2	30	4.50	91	.277	.329	17	.235	1	103	-3	0	-0.2
	Year	14	9	.609	34	31	1-1	0-0	170	202	105	33	2	49-3	67	5.19	77	.294	.341	52-0-3	.192	3	114	-21	0	-2.4
2005	Fla N	2	2	.500	14	7	0	0-0	50.2	64	32	6	5	22-6	27	5.33	75	.314	.391	13-0-3	.154	-0	91	-8	109	-0.5
Total	12	104	105	.498	325	288	13-6	1-0	1827.1	1872	892	234	47	523-39	1173	4.09	103	.265	.317	399-1-61	.130	-4	92	40	288	4.3
VALDEZ, MERKIN	Merkin R.; B11.10.1981 San Cristobal, D.R.; BR/TR/6´5˝/210; d8.1																									
2004	SF N	0	0	ø	2	0	0	0-0	1.2	4	5	1	0	3-0	2	27.00	16	.444	.583	0	ø	0	—	-4	0	-0.2
VALDEZ, RAFAEL	Rafael Emilio (Diaz); B12.17.1967 Nizao Bani, D.R.; BR/TR/5´11˝/165; d4.18																									
1990	SD N	0	1	.000	3	0	0	0-0	5.2	11	7	4	0	2-0	3	11.12	35	.393	.433	1	.000	-0	—	-4	0	-0.6
VALDEZ, RENE	Rene Gutierrez (b Rene Gutierrez (Valdez)); B6.2.1929 Guanabacoa, Cuba; BR/TR/6´3˝/175; d4.21																									
1957	Bro N	1	1	.500	5	1	0	0	13	13	8	1	0	7-1	10	5.54	75	.265	.351	3	.000	0	169	-1	0	-0.2
VALDEZ, SERGIO	Sergio Sanchez (b Sergio Sanchez (Valdez)); B9.7.1964 Elias Pina, D.R.; BR/TR/6´1˝/190; d9.10; [DL 1996 SF N 182]																									
1986	Mon N	0	4	.000	5	5	0	0-0	25	39	20	2	1	11-0	20	6.84	55	.361	.425	8	.125	-0	52	-8	0	-1.1
1989	Atl N	1	2	.333	19	1	0	0-0	32.2	31	24	5	0	17-3	26	6.06	60	.246	.336	1	1.000	0	48	-8	0	-0.7
1990	Atl N	0	0	ø	6	0	0	0-0	5.1	6	4	0	0	3-0	3	6.75	60	.273	.360	0	ø	0	—	-1	0	-0.1
	Cle A	6	6	.500	24	13	0	0-0	102.1	109	62	17	1	35-2	63	4.75	83	.276	.333	0	ø	0	123	-11	0	-1.1
1991	Cle A	1	0	1.000	6	0	0	0-0	16.1	15	11	3	0	5-1	11	5.51	76	.238	.290	0	ø	0	—	-2	0	-0.2
1992	Mon N	0	2	.000	27	0	0	0-1	37.1	25	12	2	0	12-1	32	2.41	145	.185	.252	3	.000	-0	—	4	0	0.2
1993	Mon N	0	0	ø	4	0	0	0-0	3	4	4	1	0	1-0	2	9.00	46	.308	.357	0	ø	0	—	-2	0	-0.1
1994	Bos A	0	1	.000	12	1	0	0-0	14.1	25	14	4	0	8-1	4	8.16	62	.391	.458	0	ø	0	73	-5	0	-0.2
1995	SF N	4	5	.444	13	11	1	0-0	66.1	78	43	12	3	17-3	29	4.75	87	.298	.344	21-0-3	.095	-1	92	-7	0	-0.9
Total	8	12	20	.375	116	31	1	0-1	302.2	332	194	46	5	109-11	190	5.06	78	.279	.340	33-0-3	.121	-1	98	-40	182	-4.2
VALENTINE, CORKY	Harold Lewis; B1.4.1929 Troy OH; D1.21.2005 Roswell GA; BR/TR/6´1˝/203; d4.17																									
1954	Cin N	12	11	.522	36	28	7-3	1	194.1	211	98	24	4	60	73	4.45	94	.282	.337	65-0-5	.138	-2	87	-1	0	-0.4
1955	Cin N	2	1	.667	10	5	0	0	26.2	29	23	5	1	16-2	14	7.43	57	.276	.368	7	.000	-1	118	-8	0	-0.8
Total	2	14	12	.538	46	33	7-3	1	221	240	121	29	5	76-2	87	4.81	87	.282	.341	72-0-5	.125	-3	92	-9	0	-1.2
VALENTINE, JOHN	John Gill; B11.21.1855 Brooklyn NY; D10.10.1903 Central Islip NY; d5.3																									
1883	Col AA	2	10	.167	13	12	11	0	102	130	80	0	—	17	13	3.53	87	.291	.317	60	.283	3*	70	-8	—	-0.4
VALENTINE, JOE	Joseph John; B12.24.1979 Las Vegas NV; BR/TR/6´2˝/(190–210); [ChiA99 26/789]; d8.24; Col Jefferson Davis (AL) CC																									
2003	Cin N	0	0	ø	2	0	0	0-0	2	5	4	1	0	1-0	1	18.00	23	.455	.500	0	ø	0	—	-3	0	-0.1
2004	Cin N	2	3	.400	24	1	0	4-0	29.1	23	18	4	2	25-1	29	5.22	82	.211	.368	1	.000	-0	43	-3	0	-0.5
2005	Cin N	0	1	.000	16	0	0	0-1	14.1	18	15	4	2	11-0	9	8.16	52	.295	.413	0	ø	0	—	-7	0	-0.4
Total	3	2	4	.333	42	1	0	4-1	45.2	46	37	9	4	37-1	39	6.70	64	.254	.390	1	.000	-0	43	-13	0	-1.0
VALENTINETTI, VITO	Vito John; B9.16.1928 W.New York NJ; BR/TR/6´0˝/(195–198); d6.20; Col Iona																									
1954	Chi A	0	0	ø	1	0	0	0	1	4	6	1	0	2	1	54.00	7	.571	.667	0	ø	0	—	-5	0	-0.2
1956	Chi N	6	4	.600	42	2	0	1	95.1	84	47	10	1	36-7	26	3.78	100	.243	.313	20-0-1	.100	-1	128	0	0	-0.3
1957	Chi N	0	0	ø	9	0	0	0	12	12	5	1	0	7-1	8	2.25	172	.255	.352	2	.000	0	—	1	0	0.1
	Cle A	2	2	.500	11	2	1	0	23.2	26	14	3	1	13-0	9	4.94	75	.289	.381	5	.200	-0	96	-3	0	-0.4
1958	Det A	1	0	1.000	15	0	0	2	18.2	18	7	4	1	5-0	10	3.38	120	.257	.316	0	ø	0	—	2	0	0.1
	Was A	4	6	.400	23	10	2	0	95.2	106	54	16	2	49-7	33	5.08	75	.286	.372	28-0-2	.321	2	85	-11	0	-0.8
	Year	5	6	.455	38	10	2	2	114.1	124	61	20	3	54-7	43	4.80	80	.282	.363	28-0-2	.321	2	84	-9	0	-0.7
1959	Was A	0	2	.000	7	1	0	0	10.2	16	12	0	1	10-0	7	10.13	39	.356	.482	0	ø	0	45	-6	0	-1.0
Total	5	13	14	.481	108	15	3	3	257	266	145	35	6	122-15	94	4.73	81	.273	.356	55-0-3	.218	1	89	-22	0	-2.5
VALENZUELA, FERNANDO	Fernando (Anguamea); B11.1.1960 Navojoa, Sonora, Mexico; BL/TL/5´11˝/(168–202); d9.15																									
1980	LA N	2	0	1.000	10	0	0	1-0	17.2	8	2	0	0	5-0	16	0.00	ø	.136	.200	1	.000	-0	—	6	0	0.8
1981	†LA N★	13	7	.650	25	**25**	**11-8**	0-0	**192.1**	140	55	11	1	61-4	**180**	2.48	133	.205	.270	64-0-6	.250	3	97	19	0	2.5
1982	LA N★	19	13	.594	37	37	18-4	0-0	285	247	105	13	2	83-12	199	2.87	121	.236	.292	95-1-10	.168	1*	100	19	0	2.4
1983	†LA N☆	15	10	.600	35	35	9-4	0-0	257	245	122	16	3	99-10	189	3.75	96	.255	.325	91-1-12	.187	2*	118	-1	0	0.4
1984	LA N★	12	17	.414	34	34	12-2	0-0	261	218	109	14	2	106-4	240	3.03	117	.229	.306	79-3-9	.190	4*	77	12	0	2.0
1985	†LA N★	17	10	.630	35	35	14-5	0-0	272.1	211	92	14	1	101-5	208	2.45	143	.214	.286	97-1-5	.216	4	106	31	0	3.6
1986	LA N★	**21**	11	.656	34	34	**20**-3	0-0	269.1	226	104	18	1	85-5	242	3.14	110	.226	.287	109-0-6	.220	5*	121	11	0	2.0
1987	LA N	14	14	.500	34	34	**12**-1	0-0	251	254	120	25	4	124-4	190	3.98	100	.262	.348	92-1-8	.141	-1*	92	2	0	0.3
1988	LA N	5	8	.385	23	22	3	1-0	142.1	142	71	11	0	76-4	64	4.24	79	.268	.357	44-0-7	.182	1	129	-12	57	-0.8
1989	LA N	10	13	.435	31	31	3	0-0	196.2	185	89	11	2	98-6	116	3.43	100	.251	.337	66-0-7	.182	1*	94	-2	0	-0.1
1990	LA N	13	13	.500	33	33	5-2	0-0	204	223	112	19	0	77-4	115	4.59	80	.276	.337	69-1-7	.304	8*	123	-18	0	-1.2

YEAR	TM LG	W	L	PCT	G	GS	CG-SHO	SV-BS	IP	H	R	HR	HB	BB-IB	SO	ERA	AERA	OAV	OOB	AB-HR-SH	AVG	PB	SUP	APR	DL	PW
1991	Cal A	0	2	.000	2	2	0	0-0	6.2	14	10	3	0	3-0	5	12.15	34	.452	.486	0	ø	0	0	-6	22	-0.9
1993	Bal A	8	10	.444	32	31	5-2	0-0	178.2	179	104	18	4	79-2	78	4.94	92	.266	.343	0	ø	0	95	-7	0	-0.5
1994	Phi N	1	2	.333	8	7	0	0-0	45	42	16	8	0	7-1	19	3.00	143	.247	.274	12-0-4	.250	1	67	7	0	0.5
1995	SD N	8	3	.727	29	15	0	0-0	90.1	101	53	16	0	34-2	57	4.98	82	.289	.351	32-2-3	.250	3	108	-8	0	-0.3
1996	†SD N	13	8	.619	33	31	0	0-0	171.2	177	78	17	0	67-2	95	3.62	111	.269	.334	63-0-3	.143	-1*	105	7	0	0.8
1997	SD N	2	8	.200	13	13	1	0-0	66.1	84	42	10	4	32-0	51	4.75	83	.309	.387	17-0-4	.176	0*	67	-8	0	-1.0
	StL N	0	4	.000	5	5	0	0-0	22.2	22	19	2	1	14-0	10	5.56	75	.253	.363	5-0-2	.200	0	92	-5	0	-0.7
	Year	2	12	.143	18	18	1	0-0	89	106	61	12	5	46-0	61	4.96	81	.295	.381	22-0-6	.182	0	74	-13	0	-1.7
Total	17	173	153	.531	453	424	113-31	2-0	2930	2718	1303	226	25	1151-65	2074	3.54	104	.248	.319	936-10-93	.200	32	102	47	79	9.8

Valera, Julio Julio Enrique (Torres); B10.13.1968 Aguadilla, PR; BR/TR/6´2˝/(185–215); d9.1; [DL 1994 Cal A 99]

YEAR	TM LG	W	L	PCT	G	GS	CG-SHO	SV-BS	IP	H	R	HR	HB	BB-IB	SO	ERA	AERA	OAV	OOB	AB-HR-SH	AVG	PB	SUP	APR	DL	PW
1990	NY N	1	1	.500	3	3	0	0-0	13	20	11	1	0	7-0	4	6.92	54	.351	.422	5	.200	0	136	-5	0	-0.6
1991	NY N	0	0	ø	2	0	0	0-0	2	1	0	0	0	4-1	3	0.00	ø	.143	.455	0	ø	0	—	1	0	0.0
1992	Cal A	8	11	.421	30	28	4-2	0-0	188	188	82	15	2	64-5	113	3.73	108	.262	.323	0	ø	0	84	7	0	0.5
1993	Cal A	3	6	.333	19	5	0	4-3	53	77	44	8	2	15-2	28	6.62	69	.344	.388	0	ø	0	134	-12	102	-1.9
1996	KC A	3	2	.600	31	2	0	1-0	61.1	75	44	7	2	27-3	31	6.46	78	.307	.375	0	ø	0	83	-8	0	-0.6
Total	5	15	20	.429	85	38	4-2	5-3	317.1	361	181	31	6	117-11	179	4.85	88	.289	.351	5	.200	0	91	-17	201	-2.6

Valverde, Jose Jose Rafael; B7.24.1979 San Pedro de Macoris, D.R.; BR/TR/6´4˝/(220–255); d6.1

YEAR	TM LG	W	L	PCT	G	GS	CG-SHO	SV-BS	IP	H	R	HR	HB	BB-IB	SO	ERA	AERA	OAV	OOB	AB-HR-SH	AVG	PB	SUP	APR	DL	PW
2003	Ari N	2	1	.667	54	0	0	10-1	50.1	24	16	4	2	26-2	71	2.15	215	.137	.255	1	1.000	1	—	12	0	1.1
2004	Ari N	1	2	.333	29	0	0	8-2	29.2	23	17	7	1	17-4	38	4.25	107	.213	.320	0	ø	0	—	0	112	0.1
2005	Ari N	3	4	.429	61	0	0	15-2	66.1	51	19	5	2	20-1	75	2.44	181	.211	.275	0	ø	0	—	14	29	1.9
2006	Ari N	2	3	.400	44	0	0	18-4	49.1	50	32	6	2	22-3	69	5.84	80	.256	.333	0	ø	0	—	-5	0	-0.8
Total	4	8	10	.444	188	0	0	51-9	195.2	148	84	22	7	85-10	253	3.50	130	.206	.293	1	1.000	1	—	21	141	2.3

Van Alstyne, Clay Clayton Emory "Spike"; B5.24.1900 Stuyvesant NY; D1.5.1960 Hudson NY; BR/TR/5´11˝/180; d8.20

YEAR	TM LG	W	L	PCT	G	GS	CG-SHO	SV-BS	IP	H	R	HR	HB	BB-IB	SO	ERA	AERA	OAV	OOB	AB-HR-SH	AVG	PB	SUP	APR	DL	PW
1927	Was A	0	0	ø	2	0	0	0	3	3	1	0	0	0	0	3.00	136	.250	.250	0	ø	0	—	0	—	0.0
1928	Was A	0	0	ø	4	0	0	0	21.1	26	14	0	1	13	5	5.48	73	.329	.430	8-1-0	.250	1	—	-3	—	0.0
Total	2	0	0	ø	6	0	0	0	24.1	29	15	0	1	13	5	5.18	78	.319	.410	8-1-0	.250	1	—	-3	—	0.0

Van Atta, Russ Russell "Sheriff"; B6.21.1906 Augusta NJ; D10.10.1986 Andover NJ; BL/TL/6´0˝/184; d4.25; Col Penn St.

YEAR	TM LG	W	L	PCT	G	GS	CG-SHO	SV-BS	IP	H	R	HR	HB	BB-IB	SO	ERA	AERA	OAV	OOB	AB-HR-SH	AVG	PB	SUP	APR	DL	PW
1933	NY A	12	4	.750	26	22	10-2	1	157	160	81	8	1	63	76	4.18	93	.262	.332	60-0-5	.283	4	149	-4	—	0.0
1934	NY A	3	5	.375	28	9	0	0	88	107	69	3	2	46	39	6.34	64	.307	.390	29-1-1	.207	1	100	-23	—	-1.6
1935	NY A	0	0	ø	5	0	0	0	4.2	5	5	0	0	4	3	3.86	105	.263	.391	1	.000	-0	—	-1	—	-0.1
	StL A	9	16	.360	53	17	1	3	170.1	201	116	10	3	87	87	5.34	90	.292	.374	42-0-6	.214	-1	80	-9	—	-1.3
	Year	9	16	.360	**58**	17	1	3	175	206	121	10	3	91	90	5.30	90	.291	.375	43-0-6	.209	-1	80	-11	—	-1.4
1936	StL A	4	7	.364	**52**	9	2	2	122.2	164	101	9	2	68	59	6.60	81	.320	.401	29	.172	-1*	78	-15	—	-1.1
1937	StL A	1	2	.333	16	6	1	0	58.2	74	41	2	0	32	34	5.52	87	.307	.388	13-1-0	.462	3	78	-5	—	0.1
1938	StL A	4	7	.364	25	12	3-1	0	104	118	75	7	1	61	35	6.06	82	.289	.382	30-0-3	.133	-1	61	-11	—	-1.0
1939	StL A	0	0	ø	2	1	0	0	7	9	10	0	1	7	6	11.57	42	.310	.459	2	.000	-0	127	-5	—	-0.2
Total	7	33	41	.446	207	76	17-3	6	712.1	838	498	39	10	368	339	5.60	82	.293	.376	206-2-15	.228	5	95	-73	—	-5.2

Van Benschoten, John John Wesley; B4.14.1980 San Diego CA; BR/TR/6´4˝/215; [PitN01 1/8]; d8.18; Col Kent St.; [DL 2006 Pit N 135]

YEAR	TM LG	W	L	PCT	G	GS	CG-SHO	SV-BS	IP	H	R	HR	HB	BB-IB	SO	ERA	AERA	OAV	OOB	AB-HR-SH	AVG	PB	SUP	APR	DL	PW
2004	Pit N	1	3	.250	6	5	0	0-0	28.2	33	27	3	2	19-0	18	6.91	63	.300	.406	8-1-2	.125	1	94	-10	0	-1.0

Van Brabant, Ozzie Camille Oscar; B9.28.1926 Kingsville ON, Can.; BR/TR/6´1˝/165; d4.13

YEAR	TM LG	W	L	PCT	G	GS	CG-SHO	SV-BS	IP	H	R	HR	HB	BB-IB	SO	ERA	AERA	OAV	OOB	AB-HR-SH	AVG	PB	SUP	APR	DL	PW
1954	Phi A	0	2	.000	9	2	0	0	26.2	35	23	3	1	18	10	7.09	55	.347	.446	5	.200	0	34	-9	0	-0.5
1955	KC A	0	0	ø	2	0	0	0	2	4	4	1	0	2-1	1	18.00	23	.400	.462	0	ø	0	—	-3	0	-0.1
Total	2	0	2	.000	11	2	0	0	28.2	39	27	4	1	20-1	11	7.85	50	.351	.448	5	.200	0	34	-12	0	-0.6

Van Buren, Jermaine Jermaine Russell; B7.2.1980 Laurel MS; BR/TR/6´1˝/220; [ColN98 2/60]; d8.31

YEAR	TM LG	W	L	PCT	G	GS	CG-SHO	SV-BS	IP	H	R	HR	HB	BB-IB	SO	ERA	AERA	OAV	OOB	AB-HR-SH	AVG	PB	SUP	APR	DL	PW
2005	Chi N	0	2	.000	6	0	0	0-0	6	2	2	0	0	9-2	3	3.00	146	.118	.423	0	ø	0	—	1	0	0.2
2006	Bos A	1	0	1.000	10	0	0	0-0	13	14	17	1	0	15-1	8	11.77	40	.292	.453	0	ø	0	—	-9	0	-0.6
Total	2	1	2	.333	16	0	0	0-0	19	16	19	1	0	24-3	11	9.00	51	.246	.444	0	ø	0	—	-8	0	-0.4

Vance, Dazzy Clarence Arthur; B3.4.1891 Orient IA; D2.16.1961 Homosassa Springs FL; BR/TR/6´2˝/200; d4.16; HF1955

YEAR	TM LG	W	L	PCT	G	GS	CG-SHO	SV-BS	IP	H	R	HR	HB	BB-IB	SO	ERA	AERA	OAV	OOB	AB-HR-SH	AVG	PB	SUP	APR	DL	PW
1915	Pit N	0	1	.000	1	1	0	0	2.2	3	3	0	1	5	0	10.13	27	.375	.643	1	.000	-0	54	-2	—	-0.3
	NY A	0	3	.000	8	3	1	0	28	23	14	1	2	16	18	3.54	83	.232	.350	3-0-1	.667	2	41	-2	—	0.0
1918	NY A	0	0	ø	2	0	0	0	2.1	9	5	0	0	2	0	15.43	18	.692	.733	0	ø	0	—	-3	—	-0.2
1922	Bro N	18	12	.600	36	31	16-**5**	0	245.2	259	122	9	8	94	**134**	3.70	110	.276	.347	89-0-6	.225	1	112	10	—	1.3
1923	Bro N	18	15	.545	37	35	21-3	0	280.1	263	127	10	11	100	**197**	3.50	111	.250	.322	83-1-7	.084	-3	95	17	—	1.5
1924	Bro N	**28**	6	.824	35	34	**30**-3	0	308.1	238	89	11	9	77	**262**	**2.16**	**173**	**.213**	**.269**	106-2-8	.151	-2	114	**57**	—	**5.9**
1925	Bro N	**22**	9	.710	31	31	26-**4**	0	265.1	247	115	8	10	66	**221**	3.53	118	.250	.304	98-3-2	.143	-0	115	24	—	2.5
1926	Bro N	9	10	.474	24	22	12	1	169	172	80	7	1	58	**140**	3.89	98	.271	.333	55-0-3	.182	-1	84	2	—	0.2
1927	Bro N	16	15	.516	34	32	**25**-2	1	273.1	242	98	12	6	69	**184**	2.70	147	**.239**	.291	90-0-6	.167	-2	82	38	—	3.9
1928	Bro N	22	10	.688	38	32	24-**4**	2	280.1	226	79	11	7	72	**200**	**2.09**	**191**	**.221**	**.277**	96-0-1	.177	2	85	**60**	—	**7.2**
1929	Bro N	14	13	.519	31	27	17-1	0	231.1	244	110	15	9	47	126	3.89	119	.274	.316	74-0-2	.135	-2	76	23	—	2.1
1930	Bro N	17	15	.531	35	31	20-**4**	0	258.2	241	97	15	5	55	173	**2.61**	**188**	**.246**	**.289**	89-0-3	.135	-5	83	**64**	—	**6.4**
1931	Bro N	11	13	.458	30	29	12-2	0	218.2	221	99	12	0	53	150	3.38	113	.261	.304	67-0-7	.134	-2	79	9	—	0.7
1932	Bro N	12	11	.522	27	24	9-1	1	175.2	171	90	10	1	57	103	4.20	91	.256	.315	56-0-5	.089	-4	94	-6	—	-1.1
1933	StL N	6	2	.750	28	11	2	3	99	105	42	3	1	28	67	3.55	98	.267	.318	28-0-3	.179	-1	98	1	—	0.0
1934	Cin N	0	2	.000	6	2	0	0	18	28	21	1	1	11	9	7.50	54	.350	.435	4	.250	0	63	-8	—	-0.7
	†StL N	1	1	.500	19	4	1	1	59	62	26	4	2	14	33	3.66	115	.271	.318	15-1-1	.133	-0	61	4	—	0.2
	Year	1	3	.250	25	6	1	1	77	90	47	5	3	25	42	4.56	92	.291	.350	19-1-1	.158	0	62	-3	—	-0.5
1935	Bro N	3	2	.600	20	0	0	2	51	55	29	3	3	16	28	4.41	90	.268	.330	17	.059	-2	—	-2	—	-0.4
Total	16	197	140	.585	442	349	216-29	11	2966.2	2809	1246	132	77	840	2045	3.24	125	.251	.308	971-7-55	.150	-18	92	286	—	29.2

Vance, Cory Cory Wade; B6.20.1979 Dayton OH; BL/TL/6´1˝/195; [ColN00 4/107]; d9.21; Col Georgia Tech

YEAR	TM LG	W	L	PCT	G	GS	CG-SHO	SV-BS	IP	H	R	HR	HB	BB-IB	SO	ERA	AERA	OAV	OOB	AB-HR-SH	AVG	PB	SUP	APR	DL	PW
2002	Col N	0	0	ø	2	1	0	0-0	4	4	3	2	1	4-0	1	6.75	70	.267	.450	1	.000	-0	157	-1	0	0.0
2003	Col N	1	3	.250	9	3	0	0-1	27.1	31	19	6	1	10-0	12	5.60	87	.287	.347	7-0-2	.286	0	45	-2	0	-0.2
Total	2	1	3	.250	11	4	0	0-1	31.1	35	22	8	2	14-0	13	5.74	85	.285	.362	8-0-2	.250	0	72	-3	0	-0.2

Vance, Sandy Gene Covington; B1.5.1947 Lamar CO; BR/TR/6´2˝/180; [LAN68 S2/33]; d4.26; Col Stanford

YEAR	TM LG	W	L	PCT	G	GS	CG-SHO	SV-BS	IP	H	R	HR	HB	BB-IB	SO	ERA	AERA	OAV	OOB	AB-HR-SH	AVG	PB	SUP	APR	DL	PW
1970	LA N	7	7	.500	20	18	2	0-0	115	109	47	9	1	37-2	45	3.13	123	.248	.306	37-0-4	.189	1	101	8	0	0.9
1971	LA N	2	1	.667	10	3	0	0-1	26	38	21	1	0	9-0	11	6.92	47	.355	.398	5	.000	-0	136	-11	0	-1.1
Total	2	9	8	.529	30	21	2	0-1	141	147	68	10	1	46-2	56	3.83	98	.269	.324	42-0-4	.167	0	106	-3	0	-0.2

Vance, Joe Joseph Albert "Sandy"; B9.16.1905 Devine TX; D7.4.1978 San Antonio TX; BR/TR/6´1.5˝/190; d4.18; Col Southwest Texas

YEAR	TM LG	W	L	PCT	G	GS	CG-SHO	SV-BS	IP	H	R	HR	HB	BB-IB	SO	ERA	AERA	OAV	OOB	AB-HR-SH	AVG	PB	SUP	APR	DL	PW
1935	Chi A	2	2	.500	10	0	0	0	31	36	26	1	0	21	12	6.68	69	.295	.399	11	.182	-1	—	-7	—	-0.7
1937	NY A	1	0	1.000	2	2	0	0	15	11	5	2	0	9	3	3.00	148	.204	.317	5	.000	-1	88	3	—	0.1
1938	NY A	0	0	ø	3	1	0	0	11.1	20	9	2	0	4	2	7.15	63	.408	.453	4	.750	2*	136	-3	—	0.1
Total	3	3	2	.600	15	3	0	0	57.1	67	40	5	0	34	17	5.81	79	.298	.390	20	.250	1	102	-7	—	-0.5

Van Cuyk, Chris Christian Gerald; B1.3.1927 Kimberly WI; D11.3.1992 Hudson FL; BL/TL/6´6˝/215; d7.16; b–Johnny

YEAR	TM LG	W	L	PCT	G	GS	CG-SHO	SV-BS	IP	H	R	HR	HB	BB-IB	SO	ERA	AERA	OAV	OOB	AB-HR-SH	AVG	PB	SUP	APR	DL	PW
1950	Bro N	1	3	.250	12	4	1	0	33.1	33	19	3	1	12	21	4.86	84	.266	.336	10-0-1	.100	-1	119	-3	0	-0.4
1951	Bro N	1	2	.333	9	6	0	0	29.1	33	22	4	4	11	16	5.52	71	.295	.378	8	.250	0	124	-6	0	-0.5
1952	Bro N	5	6	.455	23	16	4	1	97.2	104	58	12	5	40	66	5.16	71	.271	.347	33-0-3	.242	2	144	-15	0	-1.5
Total	3	7	11	.389	44	26	5	1	160.1	170	99	19	10	63	103	5.16	73	.274	.351	51-0-4	.216	1	134	-24	0	-2.4

Van Cuyk, Johnny John Henry; B7.7.1921 Little Chute WI; BL/TL/6´1˝/190; d9.18; b–Chris

YEAR	TM LG	W	L	PCT	G	GS	CG-SHO	SV-BS	IP	H	R	HR	HB	BB-IB	SO	ERA	AERA	OAV	OOB	AB-HR-SH	AVG	PB	SUP	APR	DL	PW
1947	Bro N	0	0	ø	2	0	0	0	3.1	5	2	0	0	1	2	5.40	77	.357	.400	0	ø	0	—	0	0	0.0
1948	Bro N	0	0	ø	3	0	0	0	5	4	3	1	0	1	1	3.60	111	.200	.238	0	ø	0	—	0	0	0.0
1949	Bro N	0	0	ø	2	0	0	0	2	3	2	0	0	1	0	9.00	46	.429	.500	0	ø	0	—	-1	0	-0.1
Total	3	0	0	ø	7	0	0	0	10.1	12	7	1	0	3	3	5.23	78	.293	.341	0	ø	0	—	-1	0	-0.1

YEAR	TM LG	W	L	PCT	G	GS	CG-SHO	SV-BS	IP	H	R	HR	HB	BB-IB	SO	ERA	AERA	OAV	OOB	AB-HR-SH	AVG	PB	SUP	APR	DL	PW
VANDE BERG, ED	Edward John; B10.26.1958 Redlands CA; BR/TL/6´2˝/(175–180); [SeaA80 13/318]; d4.7; Col Arizona St.																									
1982	Sea A	9	4	.692	**78**	0	0	5-2	76	54	21	5	2	32-7	60	2.37	181	.207	.296	0	ø	0	—	16	0	2.9
1983	Sea A	2	4	.333	68	0	0	5-4	64.1	59	32	6	1	22-6	49	3.36	128	.246	.308	0	ø	0	—	4	0	0.4
1984	Sea A	8	12	.400	50	17	2	7-5	130.1	165	76	18	0	50-4	71	4.76	84	.313	.368	0	ø	0*	78	-10	0	-1.5
1985	Sea A	2	1	.667	76	0	0	3-1	67.2	71	30	4	1	31-5	34	3.72	114	.274	.350	0	ø	0	—	4	0	0.2
1986	LA N	1	5	.167	60	0	0	0-2	71.1	83	32	8	1	33-7	42	3.41	102	.290	.364	1	.000	-0	—	0	0	0.0
1987	Cle A	1	0	1.000	55	0	0	0-1	72.1	96	42	9	0	21-2	40	5.10	90	.325	.364	0	ø	0	—	-2	0	-0.1
1988	Tex A	2	2	.500	26	0	0	2-0	37	44	19	2	0	11-4	18	4.14	99	.308	.353	0	ø	0	—	0	0	0.0
Total	7	25	28	.472	413	17	2	22-15	519	572	252	52	5	200-35	314	3.92	105	.284	.347	1	.000	-0	78	12	0	1.9
VANDENBERG, HY	Harold Harris; B3.17.1906 Abilene KS; D7.31.1994 Bloomington MN; BR/TR/6´4˝/220; d6.8																									
1935	Bos A	0	0	ø	3	0	0	0	5.1	15	12	1	0	4	2	20.25	23	.500	.559	1	1.000	0	—	-8	—	-0.3
1937	NY N	0	1	.000	1	1	1	0	8	10	7	0	0	6	2	7.88	49	.313	.421	4	.000	-1	89	-3	—	-0.3
1938	NY N	0	1	.000	6	1	0	0	18	28	16	2	0	12	7	7.50	50	.368	.455	4	.000	-1	270	-7	—	-0.3
1939	NY N	0	0	ø	2	1	0	0	6.1	10	5	0	0	6	3	5.68	69	.345	.457	2	.000	-0	134	-1	—	-0.1
1940	NY N	1	1	.500	13	3	1	1	32.1	27	15	2	1	16	17	3.90	100	.227	.324	8-0-1	.125	-0	172	0	—	0.0
1944	Chi N	7	4	.636	35	9	2	2	126.1	123	67	8	1	51	54	3.63	97	.255	.327	38-0-3	.237	1	119	-4	0	-0.3
1945	†Chi N	7	3	.700	30	7	3-1	2	95.1	91	44	4	4	33	35	3.49	105	.259	.330	32-0-1	.125	-1	99	2	0	0.1
Total	7	15	10	.600	90	22	7-1	5	291.2	304	166	17	6	128	120	4.32	85	.271	.349	89-0-5	.169	-1	126	-21	0	-1.2
VANDER MEER, JOHNNY	John Samuel "Double No-Hit","The Dutch Master"; B11.2.1914 Prospect Park NJ; D10.6.1997 Tampa FL; BB/TL/6´1˝/190; d4.22; Mil 1944–45																									
1937	Cin N	3	5	.375	19	10	4	0	84.1	63	41	0	2	69	52	3.84	97	.209	.359	23-0-1	.217	1*	92	0	—	0.2
1938	Cin N★	15	10	.600	32	29	16-3	0	225.1	177	89	12	3	103	125	3.12	117	**.213**	.302	83-0-5	.181	-2*	104	14	—	1.2
1939	Cin N☆	5	9	.357	30	21	8	0	129	128	76	7	2	95	102	4.67	82	.264	.387	36-0-7	.111	-1	110	-11	—	-1.3
1940	†Cin N	3	1	.750	10	7	2	1	48	38	24	3	1	41	41	3.75	101	.211	.360	20	.300	2*	111	-1	—	0.2
1941	Cin N	16	13	.552	33	32	18-6	0	226.1	172	83	8	1	126	**202**	2.82	127	.214	.321	76-0-9	.132	-3*	84	19	0	2.1
1942	Cin N★	18	12	.600	33	33	21-4	0	244	188	78	6	1	102	**186**	2.43	135	.208	.290	75-0-8	.147	-1*	85	25	0	3.1
1943	Cin N★	15	16	.484	36	**36**	21-3	0	289	228	102	5	3	162	**174**	2.87	116	.224	.332	95-0-8	.137	-2*	85	15	0	1.5
1946	Cin N	10	12	.455	29	25	11-4	0	204.1	175	77	11	0	78	94	3.17	105	.233	.305	73-0-1	.247	2*	73	7	0	0.9
1947	Cin N	9	14	.391	30	29	9-3	0	186	186	104	11	3	87	79	4.40	93	.261	.343	57-0-9	.088	-3*	104	-7	0	-1.0
1948	Cin N	17	14	.548	33	33	14-3	0	232	204	97	15	1	124	120	3.41	115	.239	.336	78-1-4	.141	0*	82	14	0	1.8
1949	Cin N	5	10	.333	28	24	7-3	0	159.2	172	92	12	2	85	76	4.90	85	.281	.370	52-0-8	.077	-3*	99	-9	0	-1.0
1950	Chi N	3	4	.429	32	6	0	1	73.2	60	46	10	2	59	41	3.79	111	.221	.363	16	.125	-0*	63	-1	0	-0.1
1951	Cle A	0	1	.000	1	1	0	0	3	8	6	0	0	1	2	18.00	21	.500	.529	1	.000	-0	235	-5	0	-0.7
Total	13	119	121	.496	346	286	131-29	2	2104.2	1799	915	100	21	1132	1294	3.44	107	.232	.332	685-1-60	.152	-9	92	60	0	6.9
VAN DYKE, BEN	Benjamin Harrison; B8.15.1888 Clintonville PA; D10.22.1973 Sarasota FL; BR/TL/6´1˝/150; d5.11																									
1909	Phi N	0	0	ø	2	0	0	0	7.1	7	3	0	0	4	5	3.68	71	.269	.367	3	.000	-0	—	0	—	-0.1
1912	Bos A	0	0	ø	3	1	0	0	14.1	13	10	0	1	7	8	3.14	108	.245	.344	4	.250	-0	325	-1	—	-0.1
Total	2	0	0	ø	5	1	0	0	21.2	20	13	0	1	11	13	3.32	94	.253	.352	7	.143	-0	325	-1	—	-0.2
VAN EGMOND, TIM	Timothy Layne; B5.31.1969 Shreveport LA; BR/TR/6´2˝/(180–185); [BosA91 17/460]; d6.26; Col Jacksonville St.																									
1994	Bos A	2	3	.400	7	7	1	0-0	38.1	38	27	7	0	21-3	22	6.34	80	.255	.341	0	ø	0	89	-4	0	-0.5
1995	Bos A	0	1	.000	4	1	0	0-0	6.2	9	7	2	0	6-0	5	9.45	51	.310	.429	0	ø	0	57	-3	15	-0.4
1996	Mil A	3	5	.375	12	9	0	0-0	54.2	58	35	6	1	23-2	33	5.27	99	.274	.343	0	ø	0	59	-1	0	-0.1
Total	3	5	9	.357	23	17	1	0-0	99.2	105	69	15	1	50-5	60	5.96	86	.269	.349	0	ø	0	71	-8	15	-1.0
VANGILDER, ELAM	Elam Russell; B4.23.1896 Cape Girardeau MO; D4.30.1977 Cape Girardeau MO; BR/TR/6´1˝/192; d9.18																									
1919	StL A	1	0	1.000	3	1	1	0	13	15	4	0	0	3	6	2.08	160	.306	.346	3	.667	1	71	2	—	0.2
1920	StL A	3	8	.273	24	13	4	0	104.2	131	83	7	3	40	25	5.50	71	.310	.373	30	.133	-2	94	-19	—	-1.9
1921	StL A	11	12	.478	31	21	10-1	0	180.1	196	98	10	2	67	48	3.94	114	.278	.342	65-1-2	.200	-2	82	9	—	0.7
1922	StL A	19	13	.594	43	30	19-3	4	245	248	109	13	6	48	63	3.42	121	.270	.310	93-2-9	.344	13*	141	21	—	3.8
1923	StL A	16	17	.485	41	35	20-4	1	282.1	276	129	11	6	120	74	3.06	136	.266	.345	110-1-1	.218	-0*	82	**28**	—	2.8
1924	StL A	5	10	.333	43	18	5	1	145.1	183	114	10	9	55	49	5.64	80	.317	.385	44-1-0	.295	3	114	-20	—	-1.4
1925	StL A	14	8	.636	52	16	4-1	6	193.1	225	127	11	6	92	61	4.70	99	.303	.385	71-0-3	.183	-3	102	-3	—	-0.5
1926	StL A	9	11	.450	42	19	8-1	1	181	196	121	12	2	98	40	5.17	83	.285	.376	58-0-4	.190	1	89	-16	—	-1.5
1927	StL A	10	12	.455	44	23	12-3	1	203	245	136	13	5	102	62	4.79	91	.310	.392	68-1-4	.279	2	85	-11	—	-1.0
1928	Det A	11	10	.524	38	11	7	5	156.1	163	82	4	3	68	43	3.91	105	.273	.350	58-2-1	.259	2	94	4	—	0.6
1929	Det A	0	1	.000	6	0	0	0	11.1	16	11	1	0	7	3	6.35	68	.348	.434	1	.000	-0	—	-3	—	-0.2
Total	11	99	102	.493	367	187	90-13	19	1715.2	1894	1014	92	42	700	474	4.28	100	.288	.360	601-8-24	.243	15	98	-8	—	1.6
VAN HALTREN, GEORGE	George Edward Martin "Rip"; B3.30.1866 St.Louis MO; D9.29.1945 Oakland CA; BL/TL/5´11˝/170; d6.27; M1; ▲																									
1887	Chi N	11	7	.611	20	18	18-1	**1**	161	177	113	8	16	66	76	3.86	117	.277	.359	172-3	.203	-2*	92	10	—	0.7
1888	Chi N	13	13	.500	30	24	24-4	1	245.2	263	149	15	13	60	139	3.52	86	.267	.318	318-4	.283	11*	104	-9	—	0.2
1890	Bro P	15	10	.600	28	25	23	2	223	272	190	8	21	89	48	4.28	104	.288	.362	376-5	.335	10*	109	2	—	1.0
1891	Bal AA	0	1	.000	6	1	0	0	23	38	34	1	4	10	7	5.09	73	.358	.433	566-9	.318	3*	316	-7	—	-0.2
1892	Bal N	0	0	ø	4	0	0	0	14.2	28	17	1	0	7	5	9.20	37	.389	.443	556-7	.302	2*	—	-7	—	-0.2
1895	NY N	0	0	ø	1	0	0	0	5	13	12	0	2	2	1	12.60	37	.481	.548	521-8-6	.340	0*	—	-5	—	-0.2
1896	NY N	1	0	1.000	2	0	0	0	8	5	2	1	0	1	3	2.25	187	.179	.207	562-5-4	.351	1*	—	2	—	0.3
1900	NY N	0	0	ø	1	0	0	0	3	1	0	0	0	3	0	0.00	ø	.100	.308	571-1-13	.315	0*	—	1	—	0.1
1901	NY N	0	0	ø	1	0	0	0	6	12	10	0	1	6	2	3.00	110	.414	.528	543-1-7	.335	0*	—	-2	—	-0.1
Total	9	40	31	.563	93	68	65-5	4	689.1	809	527	34	57	244	281	4.05	96	.285	.353	4185-43-30	.319	25	107	-15	—	1.6
VAN HEKKEN, ANDY	Andrew William; B7.31.1979 Holland MI; BR/TL/6´3˝/175; [SeaA98 3/95]; d9.3																									
2002	Det A	1	3	.250	5	5	1-1	0-0	30	38	13	2	0	6-0	5	3.00	146	.311	.341	0	ø	0	51	4	0	0.5
VAN LANDINGHAM, WILLIAM	William Joseph; B7.16.1970 Columbia TN; BR/TR/6´2˝/(208–210); [SFN91 5/141]; d5.21; Col Kentucky																									
1994	SF N	8	2	.800	16	14	0	0-0	84	70	37	4	2	43-4	56	3.54	115	.223	.319	31-0-4	.065	-2	120	5	0	0.2
1995	SF N	6	3	.667	18	18	1	0-0	122.2	124	58	14	2	40-2	95	3.67	112	.264	.321	46-1-1	.152	0	118	5	42	0.4
1996	SF N	9	14	.391	32	32	0	0-0	181.2	196	123	17	9	78-6	97	5.40	77	.276	.352	61-0-6	.131	-1	99	-25	0	-2.9
1997	SF N	4	7	.364	18	17	0	0-0	89	80	56	11	0	59-3	52	4.96	83	.237	.345	26-0-2	.115	-0	84	-9	0	-1.1
Total	4	27	26	.509	84	81	1	0-0	477.1	470	274	46	13	220-15	300	4.54	91	.257	.337	164-1-13	.122	-3	104	-24	42	-3.4
VAN POPPEL, TODD	Todd Matthew; B12.9.1971 Hinsdale IL; BR/TR/6´5˝/(210–235); [OakA90 1/14]; d9.11																									
1991	Oak A	0	0	ø	1	1	0	0-0	4.2	7	5	1	0	2-0	6	9.64	40	.368	.429	0	ø	0	142	-3	0	-0.1
1993	Oak A	6	6	.500	16	16	0	0-0	84	76	50	10	2	62-0	47	5.04	82	.243	.369	0	ø	0	125	-9	0	-1.1
1994	Oak A	7	10	.412	23	23	0	0-0	116.2	108	80	20	3	89-2	83	6.09	74	.250	.379	0	ø	0	110	-19	0	-2.3
1995	Oak A	4	8	.333	36	14	1	0-0	138.1	125	77	16	4	56-1	122	4.88	93	.244	.320	0	ø	0	82	-4	0	-0.3
1996	Oak A	1	5	.167	28	6	0	1-1	63	86	56	13	2	33-3	37	7.71	64	.333	.406	0	ø	0	106	-18	0	-1.5
	Det A	2	4	.333	9	9	1-1	0-0	36.1	53	51	11	1	29-0	16	11.39	45	.338	.439	0	ø	0	127	-25	0	-2.9
	Year	3	9	.250	37	15	1-1	1-1	99.1	139	107	24	3	62-3	53	9.06	55	.335	.419	0	ø	0	119	-44	0	-4.4
1998	Tex A	1	2	.333	4	4	0	0-0	19.1	26	20	5	1	10-0	10	8.84	55	.313	.389	2-0-2	.000	-0	95	-8	0	-0.9
	Pit N	1	2	.333	18	7	0	0-0	47	53	32	4	0	18-3	32	5.36	80	.286	.346	12-0-1	.250	1	111	-6	0	-0.3
2000	Chi N	4	5	.444	51	2	0	2-3	86.1	80	38	10	2	48-2	77	3.75	122	.249	.348	9-0-2	.000	-1	110	8	0	0.7
2001	Chi N	4	1	.800	59	0	0	0-0	75	63	22	9	0	38-4	90	2.52	166	.223	.316	7	.286	0	—	15	0	0.9
2002	Tex A	3	2	.600	50	0	0	1-1	72.2	80	44	14	3	29-1	85	5.45	88	.275	.346	1	.000	-0	—	-4	0	-0.3
2003	Tex A	1	0	1.000	7	1	0	0-0	12.2	20	14	1	0	9-2	9	8.53	58	.345	.433	0	ø	0	111	-5	34	-0.3
	Cin N	2	1	.667	9	4	0	0-0	35.2	31	18	7	1	6-0	25	4.54	92	.228	.266	9-0-1	.111	-0	90	-1	0	-0.1
2004	Cin N	4	6	.400	48	11	0	0-1	115.1	136	80	22	3	32-3	72	6.09	71	.298	.345	17-0-5	.176	0	108	-21	0	-1.6
Total	11	40	52	.435	359	98	2-1	4-6	907	944	587	143	22	461-21	711	5.58	81	.269	.355	57-0-11	.158	-0	109	-100	34	-10.1
VAN RYN, BEN	Benjamin Ashley; B8.9.1971 Fort Wayne IN; BL/TL/6´5˝/195; [MonN90 1/37]; d5.9																									
1996	Cal A	0	0	ø	1	0	0	0-0	1	1	0	0	0	1-0	0	0.00	ø	.250	.400	0	ø	0	—	1	0	0.0
1998	Chi N	0	0	ø	9	0	0	0-0	8	9	3	0	1	6-0	6	3.38	131	.290	.410	1	.000	-0	—	1	0	0.0
	SD N	0	1	.000	6	0	0	0-1	2.2	3	3	0	1	4-0	1	10.13	39	.273	.500	0	ø	0	—	-2	0	-0.4

YEAR	TM LG	W	L	PCT	G	GS	CG-SHO	SV-BS	IP	H	R	HR	HB	BB-IB	SO	ERA	AERA	OAV	OOB	AB-HR-SH	AVG	PB	SUP	APR	DL	PW
	Year	0	1	.000	15	0	0	0-1	10.2	12	6	0	2	10-0	7	5.06	85	.286	.436	1	.000	-0	—	-1	0	-0.4
	Tor A	0	1	.000	10	0	0	0-0	4	6	4	0	0	2-0	3	9.00	52	.400	.471	0	ø	0	—	-2	0	-0.3
Total	2	0	2	.000	26	0	0	0-1	15.2	19	10	0	2	13-0	10	5.74	77	.311	.442	1	.000	-0	—	-2	0	-0.7
VAN ZANDT, IKE	Charles Isaac; B2.1876 Brooklyn NY; D9.14.1908 Nashua NH; BL/TL; d8.5; ▲																									
1901	NY N	0	0	ø	2	0	0	0	12.2	16	15	0	1	8	2	7.11	47	.308	.410	6	.167	-0*	—	-6	—	-0.3
1905	StL A	0	0	ø	1	0	0	0	6.2	2	0	0	1	2	3	0.00	ø	.095	.208	322-1-9	.233	0*	—	2	—	0.1
Total	2	0	0	ø	3	0	0	0	19.1	18	15	0	2	10	5	4.66	65	.247	.353	328-1-9	.232	-0	—	-4	—	-0.2
VARGA, ANDY	Andrew William; B12.11.1930 Chicago IL; D11.4.1992 Orlando FL; BR/TL/6´4˝/187; d9.9; Col Bradley																									
1950	Chi N	0	0	ø	1	0	0	0	1	0	0	0	0	1	0	0.00	ø	.000	.333	0	ø	0	—	0	0	0.0
1951	Chi N	0	0	ø	2	0	0	0	3	2	1	0	0	6	1	3.00	136	.200	.500	0	ø	0	—	0	0	0.0
Total	2	0	0	ø	3	0	0	0	4	2	1	0	0	7	1	2.25	183	.167	.474	0	ø	0	—	0	0	0.0
VARGAS, CLAUDIO	Claudio (Almonte); B6.19.1978 Mao, D.R.; BR/TR/6´3˝/(210–230); d4.26																									
2003	Mon N	6	8	.429	23	20	0	0-0	114	111	59	16	7	41-5	62	4.34	102	.255	.326	30-0-4	.000	-3	77	2	40	-0.1
2004	Mon N	5	5	.500	45	14	0	0-0	118.1	120	75	26	7	64-7	89	5.25	88	.266	.363	22-0-7	.045	-2	100	-8	0	-0.8
2005	Was N	0	3	.000	4	4	0	0-0	12.2	22	15	4	0	7-2	5	9.24	44	.373	.439	2	.500	0	46	-8	38	-1.3
	Ari N	9	6	.600	21	19	0	0-0	119.2	124	66	21	7	40-3	90	4.81	92	.266	.333	34-0-7	.088	-2	117	-3	0	-0.6
	Year	9	9	.500	25	23	0	0-0	132.1	146	81	25	7	47-5	95	5.24	84	.278	.345	36-0-7	.111	-1	104	-11	0	-1.9
2006	Ari N	12	10	.545	31	30	0	0-0	167.2	185	101	27	8	52-2	123	4.83	97	.274	.332	51-0-9	.098	-2	92	-4	0	-0.7
Total	4	32	32	.500	124	87	0	0-0	532.1	562	316	94	29	204-19	369	4.92	92	.269	.341	139-0-27	.072	-8	93	-21	78	-3.5
VARGAS, JASON	Jason Matthew; B2.2.1983 Apple Valley CA; BL/TL/6´0˝/215; [FlaN04 2/68]; d7.14; Col Cal St.–Long Beach																									
2005	Fla N	5	5	.500	17	13	1	0-0	73.2	71	34	4	4	31-4	59	4.03	99	.249	.330	26	.308	3*	114	1	0	0.4
2006	Fla N	1	2	.333	12	5	0	0-0	43	50	39	9	4	30-3	25	7.33	59	.292	.402	16	.313	2	146	-15	0	-0.7
Total	2	6	7	.462	29	18	1	0-0	116.2	121	73	13	8	61-7	84	5.25	78	.265	.358	42	.310	5	123	-14	0	-0.3
VARGAS, ROBERTO	Roberto Enrique (Velez); B5.29.1929 Santurce, PR; BL/TL/5´11˝/170; d4.17; Negro Lg 1948																									
1955	Mil N	0	0	ø	25	0	0	2	24.2	39	25	4	1	14-2	13	8.76	43	.355	.432	2	.500	0	—	-14	0	-0.6
VARGUS, BILL	William Fay; B11.11.1899 N.Scituate MA; D2.12.1979 Hyannis MA; BL/TL/6´0˝/165; d6.23; Col Boston College																									
1925	Bos N	1	1	.500	11	2	1	0	36.1	45	24	1	2	13	5	3.96	101	.302	.366	12	.250	0	137	-2	—	-0.1
1926	Bos N	0	0	ø	4	0	0	0	3	4	1	0	0	1	0	3.00	118	.333	.385	0	ø	0	—	0	—	0.0
Total	2	1	1	.500	15	2	1	0	39.1	49	25	1	2	14	5	3.89	102	.304	.367	12	.250	0	137	-2	—	-0.1
VARNEY, DIKE	Lawrence Delano (b Lawrence Delano De Varney); B8.9.1880 Dover NH; D4.23.1950 Long Island City NY; BL/TL/6´0˝/165; d7.3; Col Dartmouth																									
1902	Cle A	1	1	.500	3	3	0	0	14.2	14	15	0	5	12	7	6.14	56	.250	.425	6	.167	-0	174	-4	—	-0.5
VASBINDER, CAL	Moses Calhoun; B7.19.1880 Scio OH; D12.22.1950 Cadiz OH; BR/TR/6´2˝/?; d4.27																									
1902	Cle A	0	0	ø	2	0	0	0	5	5	5	1	0	8	2	9.00	38	.263	.481	2	.500	0	—	-2	—	-0.1
VASQUEZ, JORGE	Jorge Luis; B7.16.1978 Nagua, D.R.; BR/TR/6´1˝/165; d8.13																									
2004	KC A	0	0	ø	2	0	0	0-0	3.1	4	4	1	1	1-0	4	8.10	58	.267	.353	0	ø	0	—	-2	0	-0.1
2005	Atl N	1	0	1.000	7	0	0	0-0	9	11	4	2	0	5-0	9	3.00	141	.297	.381	1	.000	-0	—	1	0	0.1
Total	2	1	0	1.000	9	0	0	0-0	12.1	15	8	3	1	6-0	13	4.38	99	.288	.373	1	.000	-0	—	-1	0	0.0
VASQUEZ, RAFAEL	Rafael; B6.28.1958 LaRomana, D.R.; BR/TR/6´0˝/162; d4.6																									
1979	Sea A	1	0	1.000	9	0	0	0-0	16	23	9	4	1	6-1	9	5.06	86	.354	.411	0	ø	0	—	-1	0	-0.1
VAUGHAN, PORTER	Cecil Porter "Lefty"; B5.11.1919 Stevensville VA; BR/TL/6´1˝/178; d6.16; Mil 1942–45; Col Richmond																									
1940	Phi A	2	9	.182	18	15	5	2	99.1	104	74	9	3	61	46	5.35	83	.264	.367	34-0-1	.235	0	95	-11	—	-1.1
1941	Phi A	0	2	.000	5	3	1	0	22.2	32	25	3	0	12	6	7.94	53	.327	.400	7	.143	-0	96	-10	0	-0.8
1946	Phi A	0	0	ø	1	0	0	0	0	1	0	0	0	1	0	(0)	ø	1.000	1.000	0	ø	0	—	0	0	0.0
Total	3	2	11	.154	24	18	6	2	122	137	99	12	3	74	52	5.83	75	.278	.375	41-0-1	.220	-0	95	-21	0	-1.9
VAUGHAN, CHARLIE	Charles Wayne; B10.6.1947 Mercedes TX; BR/TL/6´1.5˝/(170–175); [AtlN65 4/64]; d9.3																									
1966	Atl N	1	0	1.000	1	1	0	0	7	8	2	0	0	3-0	6	2.57	141	.296	.355	4	.250	0	290	1	0	0.1
1969	Atl N	0	0	ø	1	0	0	0-0	1	1	2	0	0	3-0	1	18.00	20	.250	.571	0	ø	0	—	-1	0	-0.1
Total	2	1	0	1.000	2	1	0	0-0	8	9	4	0	0	6-0	7	4.50	81	.290	.395	4	.250	0	290	0	0	0.0
VAUGHN, ROY	Clarence Leroy; B9.4.1911 Sedalia MO; D3.1.1937 Martinsville VA; BB/TR/6´0.5˝/178; d7.1																									
1934	Phi A	0	0	ø	2	0	0	0	4.1	3	2	1	0	3	1	2.08	211	.176	.300	2	.000	-0	—	1	—	0.0
VAUGHN, DE WAYNE	De Wayne Mathew; B7.22.1959 Oklahoma City OK; BR/TR/5´11˝/175; d4.17; Col Oklahoma																									
1988	Tex A	0	0	ø	8	0	0	0-0	15.1	24	15	4	0	4-0	8	7.63	54	.348	.373	0	ø	0	—	-6	0	-0.3
VAUGHN, HIPPO	James Leslie; B4.9.1888 Weatherford TX; D5.29.1966 Chicago IL; BB/TL/6´4˝/215; d6.19																									
1908	NY A	0	0	ø	2	0	0	0	2.1	1	1	0	0	4	2	3.86	64	.167	.500	1	.000	-0	—	0	—	0.0
1910	NY A	13	11	.542	30	25	18-5	1	221.2	190	76	1	10	58	107	1.83	146	.237	.297	75	.133	-2	98	14	—	1.3
1911	NY A	8	10	.444	26	19	10	0	145.2	158	92	2	7	54	74	4.39	82	.284	.354	49-0-2	.143	-1	100	-11	—	-1.2
1912	NY A	2	8	.200	15	10	5-1	0	63	66	48	1	1	37	46	5.14	70	.264	.361	21	.095	-2	109	-9	—	-1.4
	Was A	4	3	.571	12	8	4	0	81	75	33	0	4	43	49	2.89	115	.253	.356	30	.200	-1	69	5	—	0.5
	Year	6	11	.353	27	18	9-1	0	144	141	81	1	5	80	95	3.88	89	.258	.358	51	.157	-2	93	-5	—	-0.9
1913	Chi N	5	1	.833	7	6	5-2	0	56	37	13	0	2	27	36	1.45	220	.182	.284	21	.190	-1	114	10	—	1.1
1914	Chi N	21	13	.618	42	35	23-4	1	293.2	236	119	1	8	109	165	2.05	135	.222	.299	97-1-4	.144	-0	104	18	—	2.1
1915	Chi N	20	12	.625	41	34	18-4	1	269.2	240	105	4	11	77	148	2.87	97	.238	.299	86-0-2	.163	1*	110	-1	—	0.0
1916	Chi N	17	15	.531	44	35	21-4	1	294	269	94	4	7	67	144	2.20	132	.250	.298	104-0-5	.135	-4	89	20	—	1.9
1917	Chi N	23	13	.639	41	38	27-5	0	295.2	255	97	3	9	91	195	2.01	144	.235	.300	100-0-2	.160	-1	98	25	—	3.4
1918	†Chi N	**22**	10	.688	35	**33**	27-**8**	0	**290.1**	216	75	4	7	76	**148**	**1.74**	**161**	**.208**	.266	96-0-4	.240	4	95	**34**	—	**4.5**
1919	Chi N	21	14	.600	38	**37**	25-4	1	**306.2**	264	83	3	6	62	**141**	1.79	161	.234	.278	98-0-1	.173	-0	85	**36**	—	4.3
1920	Chi N	19	16	.543	40	38	24-4	0	301	301	113	8	8	81	131	2.54	126	.264	.318	102-1-2	.216	4	99	19	—	2.6
1921	Chi N	3	11	.214	17	14	7	0	109.1	153	90	8	5	31	30	6.01	64	.341	.390	41-1-1	.244	2	109	-29	—	-2.8
Total	13	178	137	.565	390	332	214-41	5	2730	2461	1039	39	85	817	1416	2.49	120	.244	.306	921-3-23	.173	-1	98	131	—	16.3
VAZQUEZ, JAVIER	Javier Carlos; B6.25.1976 Ponce, PR; BR/TR/6´2˝/(180–215); [MonN94 5/140]; d4.3																									
1998	Mon N	5	15	.250	33	32	0	0-0	172.1	196	121	31	11	68-2	139	6.06	69	.292	.364	52-0-6	.173	1	89	-31	0	-2.9
1999	Mon N	9	8	.529	26	26	3-1	0-0	154.2	154	98	20	4	52-4	113	5.00	89	.255	.316	42-0-8	.286	4	100	-10	0	-0.4
2000	Mon N	11	9	.550	33	33	2-1	0-0	217.2	247	104	24	5	61-10	196	4.05	116	.286	.335	65-0-13	.231	2	77	18	0	1.7
2001	Mon N	16	11	.593	32	32	5-**3**	0-0	223.2	197	92	24	3	44-4	208	3.42	126	.235	.274	62-0-16	.258	4	98	23	0	3.1
2002	Mon N	10	13	.435	34	34	2	0-0	230.1	243	111	28	4	49-6	179	3.91	112	.271	.310	73-0-10	.178	-0	94	12	0	1.0
2003	Mon N	13	12	.520	34	34	4-1	0-0	230.2	198	93	28	4	57-5	241	3.24	137	.229	.278	65-0-12	.154	-0	79	30	0	3.0
2004	†NY A★	14	10	.583	32	32	0	0-0	198	195	114	33	11	60-3	150	4.91	94	.255	.315	4-0-1	.250	0	91	-6	0	-0.4
2005	Ari N	11	15	.423	33	33	3-1	0-0	215.2	223	112	35	5	46-4	192	4.42	100	.266	.308	63-1-6	.238	3	79	1	0	0.5
2006	Chi A	11	12	.478	33	32	1	0-0	202.2	206	116	23	15	56-2	184	4.84	97	.259	.318	1-0-1	1.000	0	111	-3	0	-0.2
Total	9	100	105	.488	290	288	20-7	0-0	1845.2	1859	961	246	62	493-40	1602	4.34	103	.260	.312	427-1-73	.215	15	90	34	0	5.4
VEACH, AL	Alvis Lindel; B8.6.1909 Maylene AL; D9.6.1990 Charlotte NC; BR/TR/5´11˝/178; d9.22																									
1935	Phi A	0	2	.000	2	2	1	0	10	20	15	1	0	9	3	11.70	39	.417	.509	4	.000	-1	10	-8	—	-1.1
VEACH, PEEK-A-BOO	William Walter; B6.15.1862 Indianapolis IN; D11.12.1937 Indianapolis IN; 6´0˝/175; d8.24; ▲																									
1884	KC U	3	9	.250	12	12	12	0	104	95	57	1	—	10	62	2.42	92	.227	.245	82-1	.134	-2*	60	-3	—	-0.6
1887	Lou AA	0	1	.000	1	1	1	0	9	5	6	1	0	8	2	4.00	110	.172	.351	3	.000	-0	58	1	—	0.0
Total	2	3	10	.231	13	13	13	0	113	100	63	2	0	18	64	2.55	94	.223	.253	85-1	.129	-2	60	-2	—	-0.6

YEAR	TM LG	W	L	PCT	G	GS	CG-SHO	SV-BS	IP	H	R	HR	HB	BB-IB	SO	ERA	AERA	OAV	OOB	AB-HR-SH	AVG	PB	SUP	APR	DL	PW
VEALE, BOB	Robert Andrew; B10.28.1935 Birmingham AL; BB/TL/6´6˝/(210–226); d4.16; Col Benedictine																									
1962	Pit N	2	2	.500	11	6	2	1	45.2	39	25	2	0	25-1	42	3.74	105	.235	.332	16	.250	1	97	0	0	0.0
1963	Pit N	5	2	.714	34	7	3-2	3	77.2	59	15	1	1	40-2	68	1.04	316	.215	.314	23	.087	-0*	93	18	0	1.8
1964	Pit N	18	12	.600	40	38	14-1	0	279.2	222	100	8	3	124-9	**250**	2.74	128	.217	.302	96-0-6	.156	-0*	110	22	0	2.3
1965	Pit N☆	17	12	.586	39	37	14-7	0	266	221	98	5	7	119-7	276	2.84	124	.225	.312	93-0-8	.086	-4	91	20	0	1.6
1966	Pit N☆	16	12	.571	38	37	12-3	0	268.1	228	99	18	5	102-6	229	3.02	118	.232	.306	94-0-3	.138	-2	104	17	0	1.4
1967	Pit N	16	8	.667	33	31	6-1	0	203	184	90	12	5	119-10	179	3.64	93	.245	.350	69-0-3	.043	-5	121	-4	0	-1.0
1968	Pit N	13	14	.481	36	33	13-4	0	245.1	187	67	13	2	94-5	171	2.05	142	.211	.287	82-0-2	.110	-2	82	24	0	2.5
1969	Pit N	13	14	.481	34	34	9-1	0-0	225.2	232	93	8	3	91-4	213	3.23	108	.267	.336	79-0-4	.051	-5	97	6	0	0.1
1970	Pit N	10	15	.400	34	32	5-1	0-0	202	189	99	15	3	94-11	178	3.92	101	.246	.329	67-0-1	.164	1	92	0	0	0.1
1971	†Pit N	6	0	1.000	37	0	0	2-0	46.1	59	38	5	0	24-2	40	6.99	49	.314	.388	9-0-1	.333	1	—	-18	0	-2.3
1972	Pit N	0	0	ø	5	0	0	0-0	9	10	7	0	0	7-2	6	6.00	55	.313	.425	1	.000	-0	—	-3	0	-0.2
	Bos A	2	0	1.000	6	0	0	2-0	8	2	0	0	0	3-0	10	0.00	ø	.083	.185	1	.000	-0	—	3	0	0.7
1973	Bos A	2	3	.400	32	0	0	11-4	36.1	37	16	2	0	12-2	25	3.47	116	.268	.327	0	ø	0	—	2	0	0.4
1974	Bos A	0	1	.000	18	0	0	2-2	13	15	8	2	0	4-1	16	5.54	69	.283	.328	0	ø	0	—	-2	0	-0.2
Total	13	120	95	.558	397	255	78-20	21-6	1926	1684	755	91	29	858-62	1703	3.07	113	.236	.319	630-0-28	.114	-17	100	85	0	7.2
VEDDER, LOU	Louis Edward; B4.20.1897 Oakville MI; D3.9.1990 Lake Placid FL; BR/TR/5´10.5˝/175; d9.18																									
1920	Det A	0	0	ø	1	0	0	0	2	0	0	0	0	0	1	0.00	ø	.000	.000	0	ø	0	—	1	—	0.1
VEIGEL, AL	Allen Francis; B1.30.1917 Dover OH; BR/TR/6´1˝/180; d9.21																									
1939	Bos N	0	1	.000	2	2	0	0	2.2	3	6	0	0	5	1	6.75	55	.250	.471	1	.000	-0	106	-3	—	-0.5
VEIL, BUCKY	Frederick William; B8.2.1881 Tyrone PA; D4.16.1931 Altoona PA; BR/TR/5´10˝/165; d4.19; Col Bucknell																									
1903	†Pit N	5	3	.625	12	6	4	0	70.2	70	35	1	2	36	20	3.82	85	.269	.362	29	.207	-0	97	-1	—	-0.2
1904	Pit N	0	0	ø	1	1	0	0	4.2	4	3	0	1	4	1	5.79	47	.250	.429	1	1.000	0	150	-1	—	0.0
Total	2	5	3	.625	13	7	4	0	75.1	74	38	1	3	40	21	3.94	81	.268	.367	30	.233	0	102	-2	—	-0.2
VELAZQUEZ, CARLOS	Carlos (Quinones); B3.22.1948 Loiza, PR; BR/TR/5´11˝/180; d7.20																									
1973	Mil A	2	2	.500	18	0	0	2-1	38.1	46	15	5	0	10-1	12	2.58	147	.297	.337	0	ø	0	—	4	0	0.5
VENAFRO, MIKE	Michael Robert; B8.2.1973 Takoma Park MD; BL/TL/5´10˝/180; [TexA95 29/794]; d4.24; Col James Madison																									
1999	†Tex A	3	2	.600	65	0	0	0-1	68.1	63	29	4	3	22-0	37	3.29	157	.251	.317	0	ø	0	—	12	0	0.8
2000	Tex A	3	1	.750	77	0	0	1-1	56.1	64	27	2	4	21-4	32	3.83	133	.295	.362	0	ø	0	—	7	0	0.5
2001	Tex A	5	5	.500	70	0	0	4-4	60	54	35	2	7	28-4	29	4.80	100	.240	.337	0	ø	0	—	-1	0	0.0
2002	Oak A	2	2	.500	47	0	0	0-0	37	45	22	5	2	14-2	16	4.62	97	.308	.372	0	ø	0	—	-1	0	0.0
2003	TB A	1	0	1.000	24	0	0	0-0	19	24	10	1	3	3-0	9	4.74	97	.308	.353	0	ø	0	—	0	0	0.0
2004	†LA N	0	0	ø	17	0	0	0-0	9	11	5	1	2	3-1	6	4.00	104	.306	.390	0	ø	0	—	0	0	0.0
2006	Col N	1	0	1.000	7	0	0	0-0	3.2	3	1	0	0	3-0	2	2.45	196	.250	.400	0	ø	0	—	1	0	0.2
Total	7	15	10	.600	307	0	0	5-6	253.1	264	129	15	21	94-11	131	4.09	119	.274	.347	0	ø	0	—	18	0	1.5
VERAS, DARIO	Dario Antonio; B3.13.1973 Santiago, D.R.; BR/TR/6´2˝/155; d7.31																									
1996	†SD N	3	1	.750	23	0	0	0-0	29	24	10	3	1	10-4	23	2.79	144	.231	.302	0	ø	0	—	4	0	0.5
1997	SD N	2	1	.667	23	0	0	0-1	24.2	28	18	5	2	12-3	21	5.11	77	.280	.368	0	ø	0	—	-5	91	-0.5
1998	Bos A	0	1	.000	7	0	0	0-0	8	12	9	0	1	7-0	2	10.13	47	.343	.465	0	ø	0	—	-4	0	-0.5
Total	3	5	3	.625	53	0	0	0-1	61.2	64	37	8	4	29-7	46	4.67	87	.268	.355	0	ø	0	—	-5	91	-0.5
VERAS, JOSE	Jose Enger; B10.20.1980 Santo Domingo, D.R.; BR/TR/6´5˝/230; d8.5																									
2006	NY A	0	0	ø	12	0	0	1-0	11	8	5	2	0	5-0	6	4.09	111	.211	.302	0	ø	0	—	1	0	0.0
VERBANIC, JOE	Joseph Michael; B4.24.1943 Washington PA; BR/TR/6´0˝/175; d7.22; [DL 1969 NY A 124]																									
1966	Phi N	1	1	.500	17	0	0	0	14	12	9	2	0	10-3	7	5.14	70	.226	.344	0	ø	0	—	-2	0	-0.3
1967	NY A	4	3	.571	28	6	1-1	2	80.1	74	27	6	2	21-3	39	2.80	112	.249	.300	18-0-3	.111	-0	79	4	0	0.4
1968	NY A	6	7	.462	40	11	2-1	4	97	104	36	6	6	41-8	40	3.15	92	.284	.363	25-0-3	.080	-1	103	-1	0	-0.2
1970	NY A	1	0	1.000	7	0	0	0-0	15.2	20	9	1	1	12-0	8	4.60	78	.323	.440	3	.333	0	—	-2	0	0.0
Total	4	12	11	.522	92	17	3-2	6-0	207	210	81	15	9	84-14	94	3.26	95	.270	.345	46-0-6	.109	-1	91	-1	124	-0.1
VERDEL, AL	Albert Alfred "Stumpy"; B6.10.1921 Punxsutawney PA; D4.16.1991 Sarasota FL; BR/TR/5´9.5˝/186; d4.20																									
1944	Phi N	0	0	ø	1	0	0	0	1	0	0	0	0	0	0	0.00	ø	.000	.000	0	ø	0	—	0	0	0.0
VEREKER, TOMMY	John James; B12.2.1893 Baltimore MD; D4.2.1974 Baltimore MD; 5´10˝/185; d6.17																									
1915	Bal F	0	0	ø	2	0	0	0	3	3	5	1	1	2	1	15.00	19	.273	.429	0	ø	0	—	-3	—	-0.2
VERES, DAVE	David Scott; B10.19.1966 Montgomery AL; BR/TR/6´2˝/(195–220); [OakA86*4/89]; d5.10; Col Mt. Hood (OR) CC																									
1994	Hou N	3	3	.500	32	0	0	1-0	41	39	13	4	1	7-3	28	2.41	164	.247	.280	2-0-1	.500	1	—	7	0	1.0
1995	Hou N	5	1	.833	72	0	0	1-2	103.1	89	29	5	4	30-6	94	2.26	171	.241	.299	5-0-1	.000	-1	—	20	0	1.0
1996	Mon N	6	3	.667	68	0	0	4-2	77.2	85	39	10	6	32-2	81	4.17	104	.277	.353	8	.375	1	—	2	0	0.3
1997	Mon N	2	3	.400	53	0	0	1-3	62	68	28	5	2	27-3	47	3.48	120	.278	.353	1	1.000	0	—	4	30	0.3
1998	Col N	3	1	.750	63	0	0	8-5	76.1	67	26	6	2	27-2	74	2.83	183	.233	.301	3	.333	0	—	16	0	1.1
1999	Col N	4	8	.333	73	0	0	31-8	77	88	46	14	2	37-7	71	5.14	113	.290	.369	1	.000	-0	—	5	0	0.9
2000	†StL N	3	5	.375	71	0	0	29-7	75.2	65	26	6	6	25-2	67	2.85	163	.239	.315	1	.000	-0	—	15	0	2.4
2001	†StL N	3	2	.600	71	0	0	15-4	65.2	57	29	12	2	28-1	61	3.70	117	.232	.314	3-0-1	.000	-0	—	5	0	0.5
2002	†StL N	5	8	.385	71	0	0	4-4	82.2	67	34	12	2	39-4	68	3.48	116	.224	.315	3	.333	0	—	6	0	0.8
2003	†Chi N	2	1	.667	31	0	0	1-1	32.2	36	17	4	1	5-0	26	4.68	93	.290	.313	0	ø	0	—	0	95	-0.1
Total	10	36	35	.507	605	0	0	95-36	694	661	287	78	28	257-30	617	3.44	130	.253	.323	27-0-3	.259	2	—	80	125	8.2
VERES, RANDY	Randolph Ruhland; B11.25.1965 Sacramento CA; BR/TR/6´3˝/(189–210); [MilA85*S1/2]; d7.1; Col Sacramento (CA) City																									
1989	Mil A	0	1	.000	3	1	0	0-0	8.1	9	5	0	0	4-0	8	4.32	89	.290	.361	0	ø	0	23	-1	0	-0.1
1990	Mil A	0	3	.000	26	0	0	1-0	41.2	38	17	5	1	16-3	16	3.67	106	.247	.318	0	ø	0	—	2	0	0.2
1994	Chi N	1	1	.500	10	0	0	0-2	9.2	12	6	3	1	2-0	5	5.59	76	.308	.349	1	.000	-0	—	-1	0	-0.2
1995	Fla N	4	4	.500	47	0	0	1-1	48.2	46	25	6	1	22-7	31	3.88	111	.251	.329	3	.000	-0	—	1	15	0.1
1996	Det A	0	4	.000	25	0	0	0-2	30.1	38	29	6	2	23-4	28	8.31	61	.306	.414	0	ø	0	—	-10	0	-1.1
1997	KC A	4	0	1.000	24	0	0	1-2	35.1	36	17	4	3	7-1	28	3.31	143	.273	.313	0	ø	0	—	4	61	0.4
Total	6	9	13	.409	135	1	0	3-7	174	179	99	24	8	74-15	116	4.60	96	.270	.343	4	.000	-0	23	-5	76	-0.7
VERHOEVEN, JOHN	John C; B7.3.1952 Long Beach CA; BR/TR/6´5˝/(200–207); [AnaA74 12/274]; d7.6; Col La Verne																									
1976	Cal A	0	2	.000	21	0	0	4-3	37.1	35	15	2	0	14-8	23	3.38	99	.252	.320	0	ø	0	—	0	0	0.1
1977	Cal A	0	2	.000	3	0	0	0-1	4.2	4	3	0	1	4-1	3	3.86	102	.222	.391	0	ø	0	—	0	0	0.0
	Chi A	0	0	ø	6	0	0	0-0	10.1	9	3	0	0	2-0	6	2.61	156	.231	.268	0	ø	0	—	2	0	0.1
	Year	0	2	.000	9	0	0	0-1	15	13	6	0	1	6-1	9	3.00	135	.228	.313	0	ø	0	—	2	0	0.1
1980	Min A	3	4	.429	44	0	0	0-0	99.2	109	53	10	3	29-5	42	3.97	110	.289	.337	0	ø	0	—	3	0	0.2
1981	Min A	0	0	ø	25	0	0	0-1	52	57	27	4	2	14-4	16	3.98	99	.288	.335	0	ø	0	—	-1	0	0.0
Total	4	3	8	.273	99	0	0	4-5	204	214	101	16	6	63-18	90	3.79	107	.278	.332	0	ø	0	—	4	0	0.4
VERLANDER, JUSTIN	Justin B.; B2.20.1983 Manakin Sabot VA; BR/TR/6´5˝/200; [DetA04 1/2]; d7.4; Col Old Dominion																									
2005	Det A	0	2	.000	2	2	0	0-0	11.1	15	9	1	1	5-0	7	7.15	60	.313	.389	0	ø	0	22	-3	0	-0.4
2006	†Det A	17	9	.654	30	30	1-1	0-0	186	187	78	21	6	60-1	124	3.63	124	.266	.327	1-0-1	.000	-0	118	20	0	2.5
Total	2	17	11	.607	32	32	1-1	0-0	197.1	202	87	22	7	65-1	131	3.83	117	.269	.331	1-0-1	.000	-0	112	17	0	2.1
VERNON, JOE	Joseph Henry; B11.25.1889 Mansfield MA; D3.13.1955 Philadelphia PA; BR/TR/5´11˝/160; d7.20; Col Amherst																									
1912	Chi N	0	0	ø	1	0	0	0	4	4	6	0	1	6	1	11.25	30	.286	.524	2	.000	-0	—	-3	—	-0.2
1914	Bro F	0	0	ø	1	1	0	0	3.1	4	4	0	0	5	0	10.80	27	.308	.500	1	.000	-0	286	-2	—	-0.1
Total	2	0	0	ø	2	1	0	0	7.1	8	10	0	1	11	1	11.05	28	.296	.513	3	.000	-0	286	-5	—	-0.3

THE PITCHER REGISTER

YEAR	TM LG	W	L	PCT	G	GS	CG-SHO	SV-BS	IP	H	R	HR	HB	BB-IB	SO	ERA	AERA	OAV	OOB	AB-HR-SH	AVG	PB	SUP	APR	DL	PW
VESELIC, BOB	Robert Michael; B9.27.1955 Pittsburgh PA; D12.26.1995 Los Angeles CA; BR/TR/6´0˝/(175–182); [MinA76*1/9]; d9.18; Col Mt. San Antonio (CA) JC																									
1980	Min A	0	0	ø	1	0	0	0-0	4	3	2	1	0	1-0	2	4.50	97	.214	.267	0	ø	0	—	0	0	0.0
1981	Min A	1	1	.500	5	0	0	0-1	22.2	22	8	1	0	12-2	13	3.18	124	.250	.337	0	ø	0	—	2	0	0.2
Total	2	1	1	.500	6	0	0	0-1	26.2	25	10	2	0	13-2	15	3.38	119	.245	.328	0	ø	0	—	2	0	0.2
VIAU, LEE	Leon A.; B7.5.1866 Corinth VT; D12.17.1947 Hopewell NJ; BR/TR/5´4˝/160; d4.22; Col Dartmouth																									
1888	Cin AA	27	14	.659	42	42	42-1	0	387.2	331	192	7	20	110	164	2.65	120	.222	.285	149	.087	-11*	100	21	—	0.7
1889	Cin AA	22	20	.524	47	42	38-1	1	373	379	224	8	10	136	152	3.79	103	.255	.322	147	.143	-9	92	13	—	0.2
1890	Cin N	7	5	.583	13	10	7-1	0	90	97	69	8	1	39	41	4.50	79	.266	.339	36	.139	-2	87	-7	—	-0.9
	Cle N	4	9	.308	13	13	13-1	0	107	101	65	4	5	42	30	3.36	107	.241	.318	43	.163	-2	54	1	—	-0.1
	Year	11	14	.440	26	23	20-2	0	197	198	134	12	6	81	71	3.88	92	.253	.328	79	.152	-4	68	-8	—	-1.0
1891	Cle N	18	17	.514	45	38	31	0	343.2	367	239	3	15	138	130	3.01	115	.263	.336	144	.160	-3	105	9	—	0.5
1892	Cle N	0	1	.000	1	1	0	0	1	5	5	0	0	1	0	36.00	9	.625	.667	0	ø	0	56	-3	—	-0.4
	Lou N	4	11	.267	16	15	14-1	0	130.2	156	86	7	0	56	36	3.99	77	.285	.351	66	.197	1*	78	-12	—	-0.9
	Bos N	1	0	1.000	1	1	1	0	9	5	1	0	0	4	1	0.00	ø	.156	.250	3	.000	-0	144	3	—	0.3
	Year	5	12	.294	18	17	15-1	0	140.2	166	92	7	0	61	37	3.97	78	.282	.350	69	.188	1	82	-10	—	-1.0
Total	5	83	77	.519	178	162	146-5	1	1442	1441	881	37	51	526	554	3.33	105	.251	.320	588	.139	-27	93	25	—	-0.6
VICKERS, RUBE	Harry Porter; B5.17.1878 St.Marys ON, Can.; D12.9.1958 Belleville MI; BL/TR/6´2˝/225; d9.21																									
1902	Cin N	0	3	.000	3	3	3	0	21	31	20	0	1	8	6	6.00	50	.341	.400	11	.364	1*	60	-6	—	-0.7
1903	Bro N	0	1	.000	4	1	1	0	14	27	23	0	1	9	5	10.93	29	.415	.493	10	.100	-1*	63	-12	—	-0.7
1907	Phi A	2	2	.500	10	4	3-1	0	50.1	44	27	1	1	12	21	3.40	77	.238	.288	20-0-1	.150	-1	78	-4	—	-0.4
1908	Phi A	18	19	.486	53	34	21-6	1	317	264	114	0	11	71	156	2.21	116	.231	.282	106-0-4	.160	-1	88	10	—	1.0
1909	Phi A	2	2	.500	18	3	1	1	55.2	60	32	0	2	19	25	3.40	71	.274	.338	16-0-1	.063	-1	107	-7	—	-0.8
Total	5	22	27	.449	88	45	29-7	2	458	426	216	1	16	119	213	2.93	88	.250	.305	163-0-6	.160	-3	86	-19	—	-1.6
VICKERY, TOM	Thomas Gill "Vinegar Tom"; B5.5.1867 Milford NJ; D3.21.1921 Burlington NJ; TR/6´0˝/170; d4.21																									
1890	Phi N	24	22	.522	46	46	41-2	0	382	405	250	8	29	184	162	3.44	106	.263	.353	159	.208	-4	83	4	—	-0.1
1891	Chi N	6	5	.545	14	12	7	0	79.2	72	55	4	5	44	39	4.07	82	.232	.337	39	.179	-2	124	-6	—	-0.8
1892	Bal N	8	10	.444	24	21	17	0	176	189	134	3	10	87	49	3.53	97	.264	.351	74	.243	2	106	-8	—	-0.6
1893	Phi N	4	5	.444	13	11	7	0	80	100	65	1	6	37	15	5.40	85	.297	.376	35	.314	1*	90	-7	—	-0.4
Total	4	42	42	.500	97	90	72-2	0	717.2	766	504	16	50	352	265	3.75	98	.264	.353	307	.225	-3	94	-17	—	-1.9
VILLACIS, EDUARDO	Eduardo Enrique; B8.29.1979 Caracas, Distrito Capital, Venezuela; BR/TR/6´2˝/170; d5.1																									
2004	KC A	0	1	.000	1	1	0	0-0	3.1	6	5	1	0	4-0	0	13.50	35	.375	.500	0	ø	0	79	-3	0	-0.4
VILLAFUERTE, BRANDON	Brandon Paul; B12.17.1975 Hilo HI; BR/TR/5´11˝/(165–195); [NYN94 66/1587]; d5.23; Col West Valley (CA) CC																									
2000	Det A	0	0	ø	3	0	0	0-0	4.1	4	5	0	0	4-0	1	10.38	47	.250	.400	0	ø	0	—	-2	0	-0.1
2001	Tex A	0	0	ø	6	0	0	0-0	5.2	12	9	3	1	4-0	4	14.29	33	.414	.486	0	ø	0	—	-5	0	-0.3
2002	SD N	1	2	.333	31	0	0	1-0	32	29	5	2	2	12-2	25	1.41	276	.248	.326	0	ø	0	—	10	0	0.9
2003	SD N	0	2	.000	31	0	0	2-3	40.2	39	20	7	3	26-2	34	4.20	95	.252	.368	1	.000	-0	—	-1	25	0.0
2004	Ari N	0	3	.000	20	0	0	0-0	20	25	9	2	1	14-2	13	4.05	113	.313	.421	1	.000	-0	—	2	0	0.2
Total	5	1	7	.125	91	0	0	3-3	102.2	109	48	14	7	60-6	77	4.12	101	.275	.377	2	.000	-0	—	4	25	0.7
VILLANUEVA, CARLOS	Carlos Manuel (Paulino); B11.28.1983 Santiago, D.R.; BR/TR/6´2˝/190; d5.23																									
2006	Mil N	2	2	.500	10	6	0	0-0	53.2	43	22	8	4	11-1	39	3.69	122	.216	.271	15-0-2	.067	-1	69	6	0	0.3
VILLARREAL, OSCAR	Oscar Eduardo; B11.22.1981 San Nicolas de los Garza, Nuevo Leon, Mexico; BL/TR/6´0˝/(170–215); d3.31																									
2003	Ari N	10	7	.588	86	1	0	0-4	98	80	40	6	3	46-10	80	2.57	180	.222	.312	3	.000	-0	61	17	0	2.6
2004	Ari N	0	2	.000	17	0	0	0-0	18	25	14	3	1	7-1	17	7.00	65	.342	.407	0	ø	0	—	-4	147	-0.4
2005	Ari N	2	0	1.000	11	0	0	0-2	13.2	11	8	2	1	6-2	5	5.27	84	.234	.327	0	ø	0	—	-1	144	-0.1
2006	Atl N	9	1	.900	58	4	0	0-4	92.1	93	41	13	5	27-3	55	3.61	126	.261	.319	7-0-2	.000	-1	127	9	0	0.8
Total	4	21	10	.677	172	5	0	0-10	222	209	103	24	10	86-16	157	3.53	130	.250	.324	10-0-2	.000	-1	114	21	291	2.9
VILLEGAS, ISMAEL	Ismael (Diaz); B8.12.1976 Rio Piedras, PR; BR/TR/6´1˝/188; [ChiN95 5/119]; d7.3																									
2000	Atl N	0	0	ø	1	0	0	0-0	2.2	4	4	2	1	2-0	2	13.50	33	.333	.467	1	.000	-0	—	-3	0	-0.1
VILLONE, RON	Ronald Thomas; B1.16.1970 Englewood NJ; BL/TL/6´3˝/(235–245); [SeaA92 1/14]; d4.28; Col Massachusetts																									
1995	Sea A	0	2	.000	19	0	0	0-3	19.1	20	19	6	1	23-0	26	7.91	60	.270	.449	0	ø	0	—	-7	0	-0.6
	SD N	2	1	.667	19	0	0	1-1	25.2	24	12	5	0	11-0	37	4.21	97	.242	.315	1	.000	-0	—	0	0	0.0
1996	SD N	1	1	.500	21	0	0	0-1	18.1	17	6	2	1	7-0	19	2.95	137	.243	.321	0	ø	0	—	3	0	0.3
	Mil A	0	0	ø	23	0	0	2-0	24.2	14	9	4	4	18-0	19	3.28	158	.175	.346	0	ø	0	—	5	0	0.2
1997	Mil A	1	0	1.000	50	0	0	0-2	52.2	54	23	4	1	36-2	40	3.42	136	.271	.386	1	.000	-0	—	7	0	0.3
1998	Cle A	0	0	ø	25	0	0	0-0	27	30	18	3	2	22-0	15	6.00	80	.297	.425	0	ø	0	—	-3	17	-0.1
1999	Cin N	9	7	.563	29	22	0	2-0	142.2	114	70	8	5	73-2	97	4.23	111	.219	.319	43-0-5	.070	-3	90	9	0	0.6
2000	Cin N	10	10	.500	35	23	2	0-0	141	154	95	22	9	78-3	77	5.43	88	.286	.381	43-0-2	.163	-1	107	-11	0	-1.4
2001	Col N	1	3	.250	22	6	0	0-0	46.2	56	35	6	1	29-4	48	6.36	84	.295	.389	9-0-2	.000	-1	92	-4	0	-0.4
	†Hou N	5	7	.417	31	6	0	0-0	68	77	46	12	4	24-1	65	5.56	83	.282	.349	13-0-2	.077	-1	60	-7	0	-1.1
	Year	6	10	.375	53	12	0	0-0	114.2	133	81	18	5	53-5	113	5.89	83	.287	.366	22-0-4	.045	-2	79	-11	0	-1.5
2002	Pit N	4	6	.400	45	7	0	0-1	93	95	63	8	5	34-3	55	5.81	72	.270	.340	16	.250	1	60	-15	17	-1.3
2003	Hou N	6	6	.500	19	19	0	0-0	106.2	91	51	16	5	48-1	91	4.13	107	.233	.323	42-1-1	.167	1	122	4	0	0.6
2004	Sea A	8	6	.571	56	10	0	0-1	117	102	64	12	12	64-3	86	4.08	110	.232	.343	0	ø	0	116	2	0	0.2
2005	Sea A	2	3	.400	52	0	0	1-5	40.1	33	14	2	5	23-1	41	2.45	170	.226	.345	0	ø	0	—	7	0	0.8
	Fla N	3	2	.600	27	0	0	0-3	23.2	24	20	2	2	12-1	29	6.85	59	.264	.355	1	.000	-0	—	-8	0	-1.5
2006	†NY A	3	3	.500	70	0	0	0-1	80.1	75	48	9	4	51-9	72	5.04	90	.250	.362	0	ø	0	—	-4	0	-0.2
Total	12	55	57	.491	543	93	2	6-18	1027	980	593	121	61	553-30	817	4.78	96	.254	.353	169-1-12	.130	-4	101	-22	34	-3.6
VINES, BOB	Robert Earl; B2.25.1897 Waxahachie TX; D10.18.1982 Orlando FL; BR/TR/6´4˝/184; d9.3																									
1924	StL N	0	0	ø	2	0	0	0	10.2	23	13	1	0	0	0	9.28	41	.426	.426	4	.000	-1	—	-7	—	-0.4
1925	Phi N	0	0	ø	3	0	0	0	4	9	10	0	0	3	0	11.25	42	.450	.522	0	ø	0	—	-4	—	-0.2
Total	2	0	0	ø	5	0	0	0	14.2	32	23	1	0	3	0	9.82	41	.432	.455	4	.000	-1	—	-11	—	-0.6
VINEYARD, DAVE	David Kent; B2.25.1941 Clay WV; BR/TR/6´3˝/190; d7.18																									
1964	Bal A	2	5	.286	19	6	1	0	54	57	34	5	0	27-2	50	4.17	86	.274	.354	12-0-2	.167	0	71	-7	0	-0.8
VINING, KEN	Kenneth Edward; B12.5.1974 Decatur GA; BL/TL/6´0˝/180; [SFN96 4/102]; d5.23; Col Clemson																									
2001	Chi A	0	0	ø	8	0	0	0-0	6.2	15	14	3	1	7-0	3	17.55	27	.441	.548	0	ø	0	—	-9	0	-0.4
VINTON, BILL	William Miller; B4.27.1865 Winthrop MA; D9.3.1893 Pawtucket RI; BR/TR/6´1˝/160; d7.3; Col Yale																									
1884	Phi N	10	10	.500	21	21	20	0	182	166	131	6	—	35	105	2.23	134	.220	.255	78	.115	-6	110	4	—	-0.1
1885	Phi N	3	6	.333	9	9	8	0	77	90	59	0	—	23	21	3.04	92	.269	.317	30	.067	-3	113	-4	—	-0.7
	Phi AA	4	3	.571	7	7	6-2	0	55	46	41	1	4	15	34	2.45	140	.200	.261	26	.154	-0	130	3	—	0.2
Total	2	17	19	.472	37	37	34-2	0	314	302	231	7	4	73	160	2.46	122	.229	.272	134	.112	-10	115	3	—	-0.6
VIOLA, FRANK	Frank John; B4.19.1960 Hempstead NY; BL/TL/6´4˝/(195–210); [MinA81 2/37]; d6.6; Col St. Johns																									
1982	Min A	4	10	.286	22	22	3-1	0-0	126	152	77	22	0	38-2	84	5.21	82	.302	.351	0	ø	0	90	-12	0	-1.2
1983	Min A	7	15	.318	35	34	4	0-0	210	242	141	34	8	92-7	127	5.49	78	.287	.362	0	ø	0	95	-27	0	-2.5
1984	Min A	18	12	.600	35	35	10-4	0-0	257.2	225	101	28	4	73-1	149	3.21	132	.233	.289	0	ø	0	88	28	0	2.9
1985	Min A	18	14	.563	36	36	9	0-0	250.2	262	136	26	2	68-3	135	4.09	108	.268	.315	0	ø	0	84	4	0	0.4
1986	Min A	16	13	.552	37	**37**	7-1	0-0	245.2	257	136	37	3	83-0	191	4.51	96	.268	.327	0	ø	0	102	-5	0	-0.6
1987	†Min A	17	10	.630	36	36	7-1	0-0	251.2	230	91	29	6	66-1	197	2.90	160	.241	.293	0	ø	0	85	46	0	4.5
1988	Min A★	**24**	7	**.774**	35	35	7-2	0-0	255.1	236	80	20	3	54-2	193	2.64	155	.245	.286	0	ø	0	118	40	0	**4.7**
1989	Min A	8	12	.400	24	24	7-1	0-0	175.2	171	80	17	3	47-1	138	3.79	109	.256	.306	0	ø	0	86	7	0	0.7
	NY N	5	5	.500	12	12	2-1	0-0	85.1	75	35	5	1	27-3	73	3.38	98	.236	.296	23-0-5	.130	-0	110	0	0	-0.1
1990	NY N★	20	12	.625	35	**35**	7-3	0-0	**249.2**	227	83	15	2	60-2	182	2.67	141	.242	.288	85-0-7	.153	-1	103	31	0	**3.7**
1991	NY N★	13	15	.464	35	35	3	0-0	231.1	259	112	25	1	54-4	132	3.97	92	.286	.325	71-0-10	.127	-1	83	-6	0	-0.8

YEAR	TM LG	W	L	PCT	G	GS	CG-SHO	SV-BS	IP	H	R	HR	HB	BB-IB	SO	ERA	AERA	OAV	OOB	AB-HR-SH	AVG	PB	SUP	APR	DL	PW
1992	Bos A	13	12	.520	35	35	6-1	0-0	238	214	99	13	7	89-4	121	3.44	124	.242	.313	0	ø	0	75	22	0	2.4
1993	Bos A	11	8	.579	29	29	2-1	0-0	183.2	180	76	12	6	72-5	91	3.14	148	.259	.331	0	ø	0	87	27	0	2.6
1994	Bos A	1	1	.500	6	6	0	0-0	31	34	17	2	0	17-0	9	4.65	109	.296	.381	0	ø	0	94	2	100	0.1
1995	Cin N	0	1	.000	3	3	0	0-0	14.1	20	11	3	0	3-1	4	6.28	67	.333	.359	6	.167	0	87	-3	10	-0.2
1996	Tor A	1	3	.250	6	6	0	0-0	30.1	43	28	6	2	21-3	18	7.71	65	.350	.443	0	ø	0	99	-9	0	-0.9
Total	15	176	150	.540	421	420	74-16	0-0	2836.1	2827	1303	294	48	864-39	1844	3.73	113	.260	.316	185-0-22	.141	-2	92	145	110	15.7
Vitelli, Joe	Antonio Joseph; B4.12.1908 McKees Rocks PA; D2.7.1967 Pittsburgh PA; BR/TR/6´1˝/195; d5.30																									
1944	Pit N	0	0	ø	4	0	0	0	7	5	6	1	1	7	2	2.57	145	.185	.371	3	.000	-0	—	-1	0	-0.1
Vitko, Joe	Joseph John; B2.1.1970 Somerville NJ; BR/TR/6´8˝/210; [NYN89 24/632]; d9.18; Col St. Francis (PA); [DL 1993 NY N 182]																									
1992	NY N	0	1	.000	3	1	0	0-0	4.2	12	11	1	0	1-0	6	13.50	26	.444	.448	0	ø	0	155	-7	0	-1.1
Vizcaino, Luis	Luis (Arias); B8.6.1974 Bani, D.R.; BR/TR/5´11˝/(169–185); d7.23																									
1999	Oak A	0	0	ø	1	0	0	0-0	3.1	3	2	1	0	3-0	2	5.40	88	.231	.375	0	ø	0	—	0	0	0.0
2000	Oak A	0	1	.000	12	0	0	0-0	19.1	25	17	2	2	11-0	18	7.45	65	.305	.396	0	ø	0	—	-5	0	-0.2
2001	Oak A	2	1	.667	36	0	0	1-0	36.2	38	19	8	0	12-1	31	4.66	98	.266	.321	0	ø	0	—	0	0	0.0
2002	Mil N	5	3	.625	76	0	0	5-1	81.1	55	27	6	3	30-4	79	2.99	138	.192	.272	2	.000	-0	—	11	0	1.1
2003	Mil N	4	3	.571	75	0	0	0-6	62	64	45	16	1	25-3	61	6.39	68	.263	.333	0	ø	0	—	-13	0	-1.3
2004	Mil N	4	4	.500	73	0	0	1-4	72	61	35	12	1	24-3	63	3.75	117	.228	.290	0	ø	0	—	4	0	0.4
2005	Chi A	6	5	.545	65	0	0	0-3	70	74	30	8	2	29-6	43	3.73	121	.275	.349	0	ø	0	—	7	0	0.9
2006	Ari N	4	6	.400	70	0	0	0-2	65.1	51	26	8	4	29-6	72	3.58	130	.215	.311	0	ø	0	—	9	0	1.2
Total	8	25	23	.521	408	0	0	7-16	410	371	201	61	13	163-23	369	4.24	105	.241	.316	2	.000	-0	—	13	0	2.1
Vogelsong, Ryan	Ryan Andrew; B7.22.1977 Charlotte NC; BR/TR/6´3˝/(195–215); [SFN98 5/158]; d9.2; Col Kutztown; [DL 2002 Pit N 123]																									
2000	SF N	0	0	ø	4	0	0	0-0	6	4	0	0	0	2-0	6	0.00	ø	.182	.250	0	ø	0	—	3	0	0.1
2001	SF N	0	3	.000	13	0	0	0-0	28.2	29	21	5	2	14-0	17	5.65	72	.257	.346	8	.125	0	—	-6	0	-0.5
	Pit N	0	2	.000	2	2	0	0-0	6	10	10	1	0	6-1	7	12.00	37	.357	.471	2	.000	-0	103	-6	0	-0.9
	Year	0	5	.000	15	2	0	0-0	34.2	39	31	6	2	20-1	24	6.75	62	.277	.372	10	.100	-0	111	-12	0	-1.4
2003	Pit N	2	2	.500	6	5	0	0-0	22	30	19	1	2	9-3	15	6.55	66	.323	.390	6-0-2	.167	-0	113	-6	0	-0.9
2004	Pit N	6	13	.316	31	26	0	0-0	133	148	97	22	10	67-7	92	6.50	67	.285	.374	31-0-10	.226	2*	88	-28	0	-3.3
2005	Pit N	2	2	.500	44	0	0	0-1	81.1	82	43	5	8	40-1	52	4.43	96	.259	.353	9	.111	0	—	-1	0	-0.1
2006	Pit N	0	0	ø	20	0	0	0-0	38	44	27	2	7	16-2	27	6.39	72	.301	.387	3	.333	1	—	-6	0	-0.2
Total	6	10	22	.313	120	33	0	0-1	315	347	217	36	29	154-14	216	5.86	74	.281	.369	59-0-12	.186	3	93	-50	123	-5.8
Voigt, Ollie	Olen Edward "Ode"; B1.29.1899 Wheaton IL; D4.7.1970 Scottsdale AZ; BL/TR/6´1˝/170; d4.19; Col Illinois																									
1924	StL A	1	0	1.000	8	1	0	0	16.1	21	13	1	0	13	4	5.51	82	.356	.472	4	.250	1	131	-2	—	0.0
Voiselle, Bill	William Symmes "Big Bill","Ninety-Six"; B1.29.1919 Greenwood SC; D1.31.2005 Greenwood SC; BR/TR/6´4˝/200; d9.1																									
1942	NY N	0	1	.000	2	1	0	0	9	6	4	1	0	4	5	2.00	168	.176	.263	2	.000	0	50	1	0	0.1
1943	NY N	1	2	.333	4	4	3	0	31	18	10	1	0	14	19	2.03	170	.154	.244	9-0-3	.111	-1	62	4	0	0.3
1944	NY N☆	21	16	.568	43	**41**	25-1	0	**312.2**	276	138	31	4	118	**161**	3.02	121	.232	.303	105-0-9	.210	3*	103	17	0	2.0
1945	NY N	14	14	.500	41	**35**	14-4	0	232.1	249	128	15	4	97	115	4.49	87	.273	.345	79-0-7	.127	-3	105	-13	0	-1.7
1946	NY N	9	15	.375	36	25	10-2	0	178	171	88	14	0	85	89	3.74	92	.248	.330	55-0-7	.164	-1	114	-7	0	-1.0
1947	NY N	1	4	.200	11	5	1	0	42.2	44	26	4	1	22	20	4.64	88	.284	.376	15	.133	-1	100	-3	0	-0.4
	Bos N	8	7	.533	22	20	7	0	131.1	146	66	10	1	51	59	4.32	90	.280	.345	53-0-3	.170	-1	118	-4	0	-0.4
	Year	9	11	.450	33	25	8	0	174	190	92	14	2	73	79	4.40	90	.281	.352	68-0-3	.162	-1	114	-7	0	-0.8
1948	†Bos N	13	13	.500	37	30	9-2	2	215.2	226	93	18	3	90	89	3.63	106	.272	.345	72-0-7	.097	-4	89	7	0	0.3
1949	Bos N	7	8	.467	30	22	5-4	1	169.1	170	84	14	1	78	63	4.04	94	.263	.343	61	.115	-2	109	-3	0	-0.4
1950	Chi N	0	4	.000	19	7	0	0	51.1	64	39	7	1	29	25	5.79	73	.303	.390	13	.077	-1	90	-9	0	-0.7
Total	9	74	84	.468	245	190	74-13	3	1373.1	1370	676	115	15	588	645	3.83	98	.258	.334	464-0-36	.147	-10	103	-10	0	-1.9
Volquez, Edinson	Edinson; B7.3.1983 LaSegunda, D.R.; BR/TR/6´1˝/(190–200); d8.30																									
2005	Tex A	0	4	.000	6	3	0	0-0	12.2	25	22	3	2	10-0	11	14.21	32	.403	.493	0	ø	0	68	-13	0	-2.1
2006	Tex A	1	6	.143	8	8	0	0-0	33.1	52	28	7	1	17-0	15	7.29	64	.359	.427	0	ø	0	75	-9	0	-1.5
Total	2	1	10	.091	14	11	0	0-0	46	77	50	10	3	27-0	26	9.20	51	.372	.448	0	ø	0	73	-22	0	-3.6
Volz, Jake	Jacob Phillip "Silent Jake"; B4.4.1878 San Antonio TX; D8.11.1962 San Antonio TX; BR/TR/5´10˝/175; d9.28																									
1901	Bos A	1	0	1.000	1	1	1	0	7	6	9	2	0	9	5	9.00	39	.231	.429	4	.000	-1	191	-4	—	-0.4
1905	Bos N	0	2	.000	3	2	0	0	8.2	12	11	0	1	8	1	10.38	30	.364	.500	2	.000	-0	47	-6	—	-1.1
1908	Cin N	1	2	.333	7	4	1	0	22.2	16	9	1	2	12	6	3.57	65	.195	.313	4	.250	0	76	-2	—	-0.3
Total	3	2	4	.333	11	7	2	0	38.1	34	29	3	3	29	12	6.10	44	.241	.382	10	.100	-1	89	-12	—	-1.8
Von Fricken, Tony	Anthony; B5.30.1869 Brooklyn NY; D3.22.1947 Troy NY; BB/TR/5´11.5˝/160; d5.9																									
1890	Bos N	0	1	.000	1	1	1	0	8	23	16	0	0	8	2	10.13	37	.489	.564	3	.000	-1	50	-6	—	-0.5
Von Hoff, Bruce	Bruce Frederick; B11.17.1943 Oakland CA; BR/TR/6´0˝/(185–187); d9.28; Col Northern Illinois																									
1965	Hou N	0	0	ø	3	0	0	0	3	3	3	0	0	2-0	1	9.00	37	.250	.357	0	ø	0	—	-2	0	-0.1
1967	Hou N	0	3	.000	10	10	0	0	50.1	52	29	3	0	28-1	22	4.83	69	.268	.356	15-0-1	.067	-1	90	-8	0	-0.6
Total	2	0	3	.000	13	10	0	0	53.1	55	32	3	0	30-1	23	5.06	65	.267	.356	15-0-1	.067	-1	90	-10	0	-0.7
Von Ohlen, Dave	David; B10.25.1958 Flushing NY; BL/TL/6´2˝/200; [NYN76 17/397]; d5.13																									
1983	StL N	3	2	.600	46	0	0	2-2	68.1	71	27	3	3	25-8	21	3.29	111	.280	.345	7-0-1	.143	0	—	3	0	0.3
1984	StL N	1	0	1.000	27	0	0	1-1	34.2	39	13	0	0	8-3	19	3.12	112	.300	.341	1	1.000	0	—	2	0	0.2
1985	Cle A	3	2	.600	26	0	0	0-1	43.1	47	20	3	0	20-6	12	2.91	143	.288	.358	0	ø	0	—	4	18	0.4
1986	Oak A	0	3	.000	24	0	0	1-1	15.1	18	7	0	0	7-2	4	3.52	111	.300	.373	0	ø	0	—	1	0	0.1
1987	Oak A	0	0	ø	4	0	0	0-0	6	10	5	1	0	1-0	3	7.50	55	.400	.407	0	ø	0	—	-2	0	-0.1
Total	5	7	7	.500	127	0	0	4-5	167.2	185	72	7	3	61-19	59	3.33	114	.293	.353	8-0-1	.250	1	—	8	18	0.9
Vorhees, Cy	Henry Bert; B9.30.1874 Lodi OH; D2.8.1910 Perry OH; TR/6´3˝/200; d4.17; Col Syracuse																									
1902	Phi N	3	3	.500	10	5	3-1	0	53.2	63	33	1	1	20	24	3.86	73	.292	.354	20	.350	2	121	-7	—	-0.5
	Was A	0	1	.000	1	1	1	0	8	10	6	0	0	2	1	4.50	82	.303	.343	3	.667	1	39	-1	—	0.0
Total	1	3	4	.429	11	6	4-1	0	61.2	73	39	1	1	22	25	3.94	74	.293	.353	23	.391	3	103	-8	—	-0.5
Vosberg, Ed	Edward John; B9.28.1961 Tucson AZ; BL/TL/6´1˝/(190–210); [SDN83 3/64]; d9.17; Col Arizona; [DL 1998 SD N 181]																									
1986	SD N	0	1	.000	5	3	0	0-0	13.2	17	11	1	0	9-1	8	6.59	56	.304	.400	2	.000	-0	106	-4	0	-0.3
1990	SF N	1	1	.500	18	0	0	0-0	24.1	21	16	3	0	12-2	12	5.55	66	.233	.324	0	ø	0	—	-5	0	-0.4
1994	Oak A	0	2	.000	16	0	0	0-1	13.2	16	7	2	0	5-0	12	3.95	114	.320	.382	0	ø	0	—	1	0	0.1
1995	Tex A	5	5	.500	44	0	0	4-4	36	32	15	3	0	16-1	36	3.00	161	.241	.316	0	ø	0	—	6	0	1.2
1996	†Tex A	1	1	.500	52	0	0	8-1	44	51	17	4	0	21-4	32	3.27	161	.298	.373	0	ø	0	—	9	0	0.7
1997	Tex A	1	2	.333	42	0	0	0-1	41	44	23	3	2	15-6	29	4.61	105	.277	.341	0	ø	0	—	1	0	0.1
	†Fla N	1	1	.500	17	0	0	1-1	12	15	7	0	3	6-0	8	3.75	108	.313	.414	0	ø	0	—	0	0	-0.1
1999	SD N	0	0	ø	15	0	0	0-2	8.1	16	11	1	2	3-0	6	9.72	44	.421	.467	0	ø	0	—	-6	19	-0.3
	Ari N	0	1	.000	4	0	0	0-0	2.2	6	1	0	0	0-0	2	3.38	137	.462	.462	0	ø	0	—	0	0	0.1
	Year	0	1	.000	19	0	0	0-2	11	22	12	1	2	3-0	8	8.18	53	.431	.466	0	ø	0	—	-5	0	-0.2
2000	Phi N	1	1	.500	31	0	0	0-0	24	21	11	4	0	18-0	23	4.13	111	.241	.371	0	ø	0	—	2	0	0.2
2001	Phi N	0	0	ø	18	0	0	0-0	12.2	8	4	0	0	3-0	11	2.84	145	.186	.239	0	ø	0	—	2	0	0.1
2002	Mon N	0	0	ø	4	0	0	0-0	1	3	3	1	0	1-0	0	18.00	24	.429	.500	0	ø	0	—	-2	0	-0.1
Total	10	10	15	.400	266	3	0	13-10	233.1	250	126	22	7	109-14	179	4.32	106	.279	.358	2	.000	-0	106	4	200	1.3
Voss, Alex	Alexander; B5.16.1858 Roswell GA; D8.31.1906 Cincinnati OH; BR/TR/6´1˝/180; d4.17; ▲																									
1884	Was U	5	14	.263	27	20	18	0	186.1	206	136	2	—	32	112	3.57	67	.262	.291	245	.192	-6*	91	-24	—	-2.4
	KC U	0	6	.000	7	6	6	0	53	74	45	2	—	7	17	4.25	53	.310	.329	45	.089	-3*	41	-12	—	-1.3
	Year	5	20	.200	34	26	24	0	239.1	280	181	4	—	39	129	3.72	63	.273	.300	290	.176	-9	80	-36	—	-3.7
Vowinkel, Rip	John Henry; B11.18.1884 Oswego NY; D7.13.1966 Oswego NY; BR/TR/5´10˝/195; d9.5																									
1905	Cin N	3	3	.500	6	6	4	0	45.1	52	31	2	1	10	7	4.17	79	.302	.344	14-0-2	.071	-0	116	-4	—	-0.6

YEAR	TM LG	W	L	PCT	G	GS	CG-SHO	SV-BS	IP	H	R	HR	HB	BB-IB	SO	ERA	AERA	OAV	OOB	AB-HR-SH	AVG	PB	SUP	APR	DL	PW
VOYLES, BRAD	Bradley Roy; B12.30.1976 Green Bay WI; BR/TR/6´1˝/195; [AtlN98 45/1348]; d9.8; Col Lincoln Memorial; [DL 2001 Atl N 68]																									
2001	KC A	0	0	ø	7	0	0	0-0	9.1	5	4	1	1	8-0	6	3.86	129	.161	.350	0	ø	0	—	1	0	0.0
2002	KC A	0	2	.000	22	0	0	1-1	27.2	31	21	5	2	18-1	26	6.51	77	.284	.395	0	ø	0	—	-4	0	-0.3
2003	KC A	0	2	.000	11	3	0	0-0	31.1	47	29	6	1	18-1	24	7.18	67	.348	.423	1	.000	-0	96	-9	0	-0.5
Total	3	0	4	.000	40	3	0	1-1	68.1	83	54	12	4	44-2	56	6.45	76	.302	.403	1	.000	-0	96	-12	68	-0.8
VUCKOVICH, PETE	Peter Dennis; B10.27.1952 Johnstown PA; BR/TR/6´4˝/(200–225); [ChiA74 3/56]; d8.3; C4; Col Clarion; [DL 1984 Mil A 182]																									
1975	Chi A	0	1	.000	4	2	0	0-0	10.1	17	15	0	0	7-1	5	13.06	30	.386	.471	0	ø	0	193	-10	0	-0.8
1976	Chi A	7	4	.636	33	7	1	0-0	110.1	122	59	3	4	60-4	62	4.65	77	.287	.375	0	ø	0	102	-12	0	-1.1
1977	Tor A	7	7	.500	53	8	3-1	8-4	148	143	64	13	5	59-5	123	3.47	123	.257	.329	0	ø	0	87	13	0	1.2
1978	StL N	12	12	.500	45	23	6-2	1-3	198.1	187	65	9	2	59-5	149	2.54	140	.253	.308	58-0-7	.138	-1	77	22	0	2.6
1979	StL N	15	10	.600	34	32	9	0-0	233	229	108	22	3	64-4	145	3.59	106	.260	.310	79-0-8	.152	-2	115	4	0	0.1
1980	StL N	12	9	.571	32	30	7-3	1-0	222.1	203	96	18	2	68-5	132	3.40	110	.247	.304	71-0-9	.183	1	106	8	0	0.8
1981	†Mil A	**14**	4	**.778**	24	23	2-1	0-1	149.2	137	61	9	4	57-1	84	3.55	98	.249	.323	0	ø	0	129	0	0	0.0
1982	†Mil A	18	6	**.750**	30	30	9-1	0-0	223.2	234	96	14	5	102-1	105	3.34	115	.275	.354	0	ø	0	124	11	0	1.1
1983	Mil A	0	2	.000	3	3	0	0-0	14.2	15	9	0	1	10-1	10	4.91	77	.259	.377	0	ø	0	88	-2	140	-0.3
1985	Mil A	6	10	.375	22	22	1	0-0	112.2	134	74	16	7	48-2	55	5.51	76	.298	.374	0	ø	0	99	-14	24	-1.8
1986	Mil A	2	4	.333	6	6	0	0-0	32.1	33	18	3	2	11-0	12	3.06	142	.273	.336	0	ø	0	42	2	0	0.4
Total	11	93	69	.574	286	186	38-8	10-8	1455.1	1454	665	107	35	545-29	882	3.66	104	.264	.332	208-0-24	.159	-2	106	22	346	2.2
WACHTEL, PAUL	Paul Horine; B4.30.1888 Myersville MD; D12.15.1964 San Antonio TX; BR/TR/5´11˝/175; d9.18																									
1917	Bro N	0	0	ø	2	0	0	0	6	9	7	0	0	4	3	10.50	27	.375	.464	3	.333	0	—	-4	—	-0.2
WACKER, CHARLIE	Charles James; B12.8.1883 Jeffersonville IN; D8.7.1948 Evansville IN; BL/TL/5´9˝/?; d4.28																									
1909	Pit N	0	0	ø	1	0	0	0	2	2	2	0	0	1	0	0.00	ø	.400	.500	0	ø	0	—	0	—	0.0
WADDELL, RUBE	George Edward; B10.13.1876 Bradford PA; D4.1.1914 San Antonio TX; BR/TL/6´1.5˝/196; d9.8; HF1946																									
1897	Lou N	0	1	.000	2	1	1	0	14	17	6	0	1	6	5	3.21	133	.298	.375	6	.000	-1	17	2	—	0.0
1899	Lou N	7	2	.778	10	9	9-1	1	79	69	38	4	8	14	44	3.08	125	.235	.288	34	.235	-0	89	8	—	0.7
1900	†Pit N	8	13	.381	29	22	16-2	0	208.2	176	96	3	13	55	130	**2.37**	**153**	**.229**	.291	81	.173	-2*	105	24	—	1.9
1901	Pit N	0	2	.000	2	2	0	0	7.2	10	12	0	1	9	4	9.39	35	.313	.476	3	.000	-0	76	-5	—	-0.9
	Chi N	14	14	.500	29	28	26	0	243.2	239	123	5	9	66	168	2.81	115	.255	.310	98-2-0	.255	6*	102	9	—	1.8
	Year	14	16	.467	31	30	26	0	251.1	249	135	5	10	75	172	3.01	108	.257	.317	101-2-0	.248	6	101	3	—	0.9
1902	Phi A	24	7	.774	33	27	26-3	0	276.1	224	90	7	10	64	**210**	2.05	179	.222	.276	112-1-1	.286	7*	95	48	—	5.8
1903	Phi A	21	16	.568	39	38	**34**-4	0	324	274	109	3	8	85	**302**	2.44	125	.229	.284	115-0-5	.122	-6	83	23	—	1.8
1904	Phi A	25	19	.568	46	46	39-8	0	383	307	109	5	14	91	**349**	1.62	**165**	.221	.275	139-0-1	.122	-7	97	40	—	4.1
1905	Phi A	**27**	10	**.730**	**46**	34	27-7	0	328.2	231	86	5	10	90	**287**	**1.48**	**180**	**.200**	.263	116-0-6	.172	-1	106	**40**	—	**4.5**
1906	Phi A	15	17	.469	43	34	22-8	0	272.2	221	89	1	10	92	**196**	2.21	123	.225	.297	86-0-5	.163	-0	74	17	—	1.9
1907	Phi A	19	13	.594	44	33	20-7	0	284.2	234	115	2	15	73	**232**	2.15	121	.227	.287	101-0-2	.119	-5	100	8	—	0.2
1908	StL A	19	14	.576	43	36	25-5	3	285.2	223	93	0	8	90	232	1.89	127	.213	.281	91-1-3	.110	-1	101	14	—	1.5
1909	StL A	11	14	.440	31	28	16-5	0	220.1	204	78	1	7	57	141	2.37	102	.267	.323	75	.067	-5	78	1	—	-0.6
1910	StL A	3	1	.750	10	2	0	1	33	31	19	1	1	11	16	3.55	70	.242	.307	9	.111	-0	108	-4	—	-0.5
Total	13	193	143	.574	407	340	261-50	5	2961.1	2460	1063	37	115	803	2316	2.16	135	.228	.288	1066-4-23	.161	-17	93	225	—	22.2
WADDELL, TOM	Thomas David; B9.17.1958 Dundee, Scotland; BR/TR/6´1˝/190; d4.15; Col Manhattan; [DL 1986 Cle A 182]																									
1984	Cle A	7	4	.636	58	0	0	6-4	97	68	35	12	1	37-4	59	3.06	135	.202	.276	0	ø	0	—	12	0	1.3
1985	Cle A	8	6	.571	49	9	1	9-4	112.2	104	61	20	1	39-8	53	4.87	85	.246	.309	0	ø	0	133	-6	0	-0.7
1987	Cle A	0	1	.000	6	0	0	0-0	5.2	7	10	1	1	7-0	6	14.29	32	.292	.469	0	ø	0	—	-6	0	-0.8
Total	3	15	11	.577	113	9	1	15-8	215.1	179	106	33	3	83-12	118	4.30	97	.229	.300	0	ø	0	133	0	182	-0.2
WADE, BEN	Benjamin Styron; B11.25.1922 Morehead City NC; D12.2.2002 Los Angeles CA; BR/TR/6´3˝/(200–205); d4.30; b–Jake																									
1948	Chi N	0	1	.000	2	0	0	0	5	4	4	0	0	4	1	7.20	54	.211	.348	2	.000	-0	—	-2	0	-0.3
1952	Bro N	11	9	.550	37	24	5-1	3	180	166	81	19	2	94	118	3.60	101	.246	.340	60-3-2	.117	1	100	0	0	0.0
1953	†Bro N	7	5	.583	32	0	0	3	90.1	79	40	15	4	33	65	3.79	113	.232	.308	24-1-3	.167	0	—	6	0	0.6
1954	Bro N	1	1	.500	23	0	0	3	45	62	46	9	0	21	25	8.20	50	.339	.393	5-0-1	.000	-1	—	-21	0	-1.2
	StL N	0	0	ø	13	0	0	0	23	27	15	3	2	15	19	5.48	75	.303	.411	3	.000	-0	—	-3	0	-0.2
	Year	1	1	.500	36	0	0	3	68	89	61	12	2	36	44	7.28	56	.327	.399	8-0-1	.000	-1	—	-24	0	-1.4
1955	Pit N	0	1	.000	11	1	0	1	28	26	12	3	1	14-4	7	3.21	128	.252	.339	4	.000	-0	151	3	0	0.1
Total	5	19	17	.528	118	25	5-1	10	371.1	364	198	49	9	181-4	235	4.34	90	.259	.344	98-4-6	.112	-0	96	-17	0	-1.0
WADE, TERRELL	Hawatha Terrell; B1.25.1973 Rembert SC; BL/TL/6´3˝/205; d9.12																									
1995	Atl N	0	1	.000	3	0	0	0-0	4	3	2	1	0	4-0	3	4.50	96	.214	.389	0	ø	0	—	0	0	0.0
1996	†Atl N	5	0	1.000	44	8	0	1-1	69.2	57	28	9	1	47-6	79	2.97	150	.227	.350	13-0-2	.154	-0	124	10	0	0.7
1997	Atl N	2	3	.400	12	9	0	0-0	42	60	31	6	2	16-1	35	5.36	78	.349	.400	12-0-1	.250	1	112	-7	114	-0.6
1998	TB A	1	1	.500	2	2	0	0-0	10.2	14	6	3	0	2-0	8	5.06	95	.318	.348	0	ø	0	87	0	170	0.0
Total	4	8	5	.615	61	19	0	1-1	126.1	134	67	19	3	69-7	125	3.99	110	.279	.369	25-0-3	.200	1	113	3	284	0.1
WADE, JAKE	Jacob Fields "Whistling Jake"; B4.1.1912 Morehead City NC; D2.1.2006 Wildwood NC; BL/TL/6´2˝/175; d4.22; Mil 1945; b–Ben; Col North Carolina St.																									
1936	Det A	4	5	.444	13	11	4-1	0	78.1	93	60	7	1	52	30	5.29	94	.296	.398	29	.172	-0	95	-6	—	-0.6
1937	Det A	7	10	.412	33	25	7-1	0	165.1	160	106	13	3	107	69	5.39	87	.257	.368	59-0-1	.186	-1	95	-10	—	-1.0
1938	Det A	3	2	.600	27	2	0	0	70	73	56	9	0	48	23	6.56	76	.268	.378	21	.048	-2	53	-11	—	-0.9
1939	Bos A	1	4	.200	20	6	1	0	47.2	68	34	1	0	37	21	6.23	76	.358	.463	12	.000	-2	81	-6	—	-0.7
	StL A	0	2	.000	4	2	1	0	16.1	26	25	1	0	19	9	11.02	44	.356	.489	5	.000	-1	36	-12	—	-1.1
	Year	1	6	.143	24	8	2	0	64	94	59	2	0	56	30	7.45	64	.357	.470	17	.000	-3	69	-18	—	-1.8
1942	Chi A	5	5	.500	15	10	3	0	85.2	84	45	2	0	56	32	4.10	88	.255	.363	29	.241	1	93	-5	0	-0.3
1943	Chi A	3	7	.300	21	9	3-1	0	83.2	66	34	3	4	54	41	3.01	111	.222	.349	27-0-1	.148	-0	62	3	0	0.3
1944	Chi A	2	4	.333	19	5	1	2	74.2	75	46	3	0	41	35	4.82	71	.261	.354	24	.292	1	112	-11	0	-0.8
1946	NY A	2	1	.667	13	1	0	1	35.1	33	9	2	1	14	22	2.29	151	.250	.327	9	.111	-0	0	5	0	0.5
	Was A	0	0	ø	6	0	0	0	11.1	12	6	1	0	12	9	4.76	70	.279	.436	1	.000	-0	—	-1	0	-0.1
	Year	2	1	.667	19	1	0	1	46.2	45	15	3	1	26	31	2.89	118	.257	.356	10	.100	-0	0	4	0	0.4
Total	8	27	40	.403	171	71	20-3	3	668.1	690	421	42	9	440	291	5.00	84	.269	.378	216-0-2	.167	-5	89	-54	0	-4.7
WADSWORTH, JACK	John L.; B12.17.1867 Wellington OH; D7.8.1941 Elyria OH; BL/TR/?/180; d5.1																									
1890	Cle N	2	16	.111	20	19	19	0	169.2	202	139	6	6	81	26	5.20	69	.286	.364	68	.176	-3	68	-27	—	-2.4
1893	Bal N	0	3	.000	3	3	0	0	16	37	30	0	0	8	2	11.25	42	.440	.489	7	.429	1	118	-12	—	-1.3
1894	Lou N	4	18	.182	22	22	20	0	173	261	204	10	4	103	57	7.60	67	.344	.425	74-0-1	.257	0	79	-45	—	-3.6
1895	Lou N	0	1	.000	2	0	0	0	9	24	20	0	0	7	2	16.00	29	.480	.544	4-0-1	.250	-0	—	-10	—	-0.7
Total	4	6	38	.136	47	44	39	0	367.2	524	393	16	10	199	87	6.85	64	.328	.405	153-0-2	.229	-2	78	-94	—	-8.0
WAECHTER, DOUG	Douglas Michael; B1.28.1981 St.Petersburg FL; BR/TR/6´4˝/(200–210); [TBA99 3/85]; d8.27																									
2003	TB A	3	2	.600	6	5	1-1	0-0	35.1	29	13	4	1	15-0	29	3.31	138	.225	.310	0	ø	0	109	5	0	0.7
2004	TB A	5	7	.417	14	14	0	0-0	70.1	68	54	20	4	33-1	36	6.01	78	.252	.340	0	ø	0	95	-11	89	-1.6
2005	TB A	5	12	.294	29	25	0	0-0	157	191	109	29	3	38-5	87	5.62	78	.297	.337	2-0-1	.000	-0	108	-22	26	-2.1
2006	TB A	1	4	.200	11	10	0	0-0	53	67	40	6	5	19-1	25	6.62	70	.310	.370	0	ø	0	85	-10	0	-0.8
Total	4	14	25	.359	60	54	1-1	0-0	315.2	355	216	59	13	105-7	177	5.62	81	.282	.341	2-0-1	.000	-0	100	-38	115	-3.8
WAGNER, CHARLIE	Charles Thomas "Broadway"; B12.3.1912 Reading PA; D8.31.2006 Reading PA; BR/TR/5´11˝/170; d4.19; Mil 1943–45; C1																									
1938	Bos A	1	3	.250	13	6	1	0	36.2	47	36	5	1	24	14	8.35	59	.309	.407	12	.167	-1	113	-12	—	-1.1
1939	Bos A	3	1	.750	9	5	0	0	38.1	49	19	3	0	14	13	4.23	112	.320	.377	14	.071	-2*	123	3	—	0.1
1940	Bos A	1	0	1.000	12	1	0	0	29.1	45	22	5	0	8	13	5.52	81	.344	.381	5	.200	-0*	234	-4	—	-0.2
1941	Bos A	12	8	.600	29	25	12-3	0	187.1	175	76	14	1	85	51	3.07	136	.245	.326	63-0-10	.159	-1	120	22	0	2.0
1942	Bos A	14	11	.560	29	26	17-2	0	205.1	184	87	5	5	95	52	3.29	113	.247	.336	65-0-11	.077	-5	98	9	0	0.6
1946	Bos A	1	0	1.000	8	4	0	0	30.2	32	21	6	0	19	14	5.87	62	.276	.378	11-0-2	.091	-1	187	-6	0	-0.4
Total	6	32	23	.582	100	67	30-5	0	527.2	532	261	38	7	245	157	3.91	104	.264	.346	170-0-23	.118	-9	117	12	0	1.0

WAGNER, GARY Gary Edward; B6.28.1940 Bridgeport IL; BR/TR/6´4˝/(190–200); d4.18; Col Eastern Illinois

YEAR	TM LG	W	L	PCT	G	GS	CG-SHO	SV-BS	IP	H	R	HR	HB	BB-IB	SO	ERA	AERA	OAV	OOB	AB-HR-SH	AVG	PB	SUP	APR	DL	PW
1965	Phi N	7	7	.500	59	0	0	7	105	87	43	6	2	49-8	91	3.00	115	.233	.323	13-0-1	.077	-0	—	4	0	0.6
1966	Phi N	0	1	.000	5	1	0	0	6.1	8	6	1	0	5-0	2	8.53	42	.333	.433	0	ø	0	171	-3	0	-0.5
1967	Phi N	0	0	ø	1	0	0	0	2	1	0	0	0	0-0	1	0.00	ø	.167	.167	0	ø	0	—	1	0	0.0
1968	Phi N	4	4	.500	44	0	0	8	78	69	27	0	5	31-6	43	3.00	100	.243	.326	12	.083	-1	—	1	0	0.1
1969	Phi N	0	3	.000	9	2	0	0-1	19.1	31	22	3	0	7-1	8	7.91	45	.365	.404	3	.000	-0	50	-11	0	-1.5
	Bos A	1	3	.250	6	1	0	0-0	16.1	18	11	1	0	15-0	9	6.06	63	.300	.440	3-0-1	.000	-0	0	-3	0	-0.7
1970	Bos A	3	1	.750	38	0	0	7-1	40.1	36	21	3	2	19-1	20	3.35	119	.232	.320	6	.167	-0	—	1	0	0.1
Total	6	15	19	.441	162	4	0	22-2	267.1	250	130	14	9	126-16	174	3.70	93	.253	.340	37-0-2	.081	-2	70	-10	0	-1.9

WAGNER, HECTOR Hector Raul Guerrero (b Hector Raul Guerrero (Wagner)); B11.26.1968 San Juan, D.R.; BR/TR/6´3˝/(185–200); d9.10

YEAR	TM LG	W	L	PCT	G	GS	CG-SHO	SV-BS	IP	H	R	HR	HB	BB-IB	SO	ERA	AERA	OAV	OOB	AB-HR-SH	AVG	PB	SUP	APR	DL	PW
1990	KC A	0	2	.000	5	5	0	0-0	23.1	32	24	4	0	11-1	14	8.10	48	.323	.384	0	ø	0	108	-11	0	-0.8
1991	KC A	1	1	.500	2	2	0	0-0	10	16	10	2	0	3-0	5	7.20	58	.348	.388	0	ø	0	210	-4	0	-0.6
Total	2	1	3	.250	7	7	0	0-0	33.1	48	34	6	0	14-1	19	7.83	50	.331	.385	0	ø	0	139	-15	0	-1.4

WAGNER, MATT Matthew William; B4.4.1972 Cedar Falls IA; BR/TR/6´5˝/215; [SeaA94 3/77]; d6.5; Col Iowa St.; [DL 1997 Mon N 181]

YEAR	TM LG	W	L	PCT	G	GS	CG-SHO	SV-BS	IP	H	R	HR	HB	BB-IB	SO	ERA	AERA	OAV	OOB	AB-HR-SH	AVG	PB	SUP	APR	DL	PW
1996	Sea A	3	5	.375	15	14	1	0-0	80	91	62	15	3	38-2	41	6.86	72	.285	.363	0	ø	0	121	-15	0	-1.2

WAGNER, PAUL Paul Alan; B11.14.1967 Milwaukee WI; BR/TR/6´1˝/(185–211); [PitN89 12/314]; d7.26; Col Illinois St.

YEAR	TM LG	W	L	PCT	G	GS	CG-SHO	SV-BS	IP	H	R	HR	HB	BB-IB	SO	ERA	AERA	OAV	OOB	AB-HR-SH	AVG	PB	SUP	APR	DL	PW
1992	Pit N	2	0	1.000	6	1	0	0-0	13	9	1	0	0	5-0	5	0.69	501	.191	.269	3	.333	0	130	4	0	0.7
1993	Pit N	8	8	.500	44	17	1-1	2-3	141.1	143	72	15	1	42-2	114	4.27	96	.263	.314	42-0-4	.190	0	93	-3	16	-0.4
1994	Pit N	7	8	.467	29	17	1	0-0	119.2	136	69	7	8	50-4	86	4.59	95	.293	.369	37-0-2	.162	-1	76	-3	0	-0.3
1995	Pit N	5	16	.238	33	25	3-1	1-0	165	174	96	18	7	72-7	120	4.80	91	.273	.352	42-0-6	.214	2*	68	-7	18	-0.6
1996	Pit N	4	8	.333	16	15	1	0-0	81.2	86	49	10	3	39-2	81	5.40	81	.275	.360	25-0-3	.040	-2*	85	-6	97	-0.9
1997	Pit N	0	0	ø	14	0	0	0-1	16	17	7	3	0	13-3	9	3.94	109	.274	.395	1	.000	-0	—	1	108	0.0
	Mil A	1	0	1.000	2	0	0	0-0	2	3	2	1	0	0-0	0	9.00	51	.375	.375	0	ø	0	—	-1	0	-0.2
1998	Mil N	1	5	.167	13	9	0	0-0	55.2	67	49	10	1	31-1	37	7.11	61	.302	.387	19-0-1	.158	-0	66	-17	47	-1.6
1999	Cle A	1	0	1.000	3	0	0	0-0	4.1	5	4	0	2	3-0	0	4.15	122	.263	.417	0	ø	0	—	0	0	-0.1
Total	8	29	45	.392	160	84	6-2	3-4	598.2	640	349	64	22	255-19	452	4.83	89	.276	.351	169-0-16	.166	-1	78	-32	286	-3.4

WAGNER, RYAN Ryan Scott; B7.15.1982 Yoakum TX; BR/TR/6´4˝/(210–225); d7.19; Col Houston

YEAR	TM LG	W	L	PCT	G	GS	CG-SHO	SV-BS	IP	H	R	HR	HB	BB-IB	SO	ERA	AERA	OAV	OOB	AB-HR-SH	AVG	PB	SUP	APR	DL	PW
2003	Cin N	2	0	1.000	17	0	0	0-1	21.2	13	4	2	0	12-1	25	1.66	251	.173	.284	0	ø	0	—	6	0	0.5
2004	Cin N	3	2	.600	49	0	0	0-3	51.2	59	31	7	2	27-2	37	4.70	91	.284	.367	0	ø	0	—	-3	0	-0.3
2005	Cin N	3	2	.600	42	0	0	0-1	45.2	56	33	4	4	17-1	39	6.11	70	.303	.368	1-0-1	.000	-0	—	-9	87	-0.9
2006	Was N	3	3	.500	26	0	0	0-2	30.2	36	21	3	2	15-3	20	4.70	93	.293	.379	3	.333	0	—	-3	0	-0.4
Total	4	11	7	.611	134	0	0	0-7	149.2	164	89	16	8	71-7	121	4.69	91	.277	.359	4-0-1	.250	0	—	-9	87	-1.1

WAGNER, BILLY William Edward; B7.25.1971 Tannersville VA; BL/TL/5´11˝/(180–200); [HouN93 1/12]; d9.13; Col Ferrum

YEAR	TM LG	W	L	PCT	G	GS	CG-SHO	SV-BS	IP	H	R	HR	HB	BB-IB	SO	ERA	AERA	OAV	OOB	AB-HR-SH	AVG	PB	SUP	APR	DL	PW
1995	Hou N	0	0	ø	1	0	0	0-0	0.1	0	0	0	0	0-0	0	0.00	ø	.000	.000	0	ø	0	—	0	0	0.0
1996	Hou N	2	2	.500	37	0	0	9-4	51.2	28	16	6	3	30-2	67	2.44	159	.165	.298	5	.000	-1	—	9	15	0.8
1997	†Hou N	7	8	.467	62	0	0	23-6	66.1	49	23	5	3	30-1	106	2.85	141	.204	.299	1	.000	-0	—	9	0	1.8
1998	†Hou N	4	3	.571	58	0	0	30-5	60	46	19	6	0	25-1	97	2.70	150	.211	.292	3	.333	0	—	10	22	1.9
1999	†Hou N★	4	1	.800	66	0	0	39-3	74.2	35	14	5	1	23-1	124	1.57	282	.135	.208	0	ø	0	—	**25**	0	3.7
2000	Hou N	2	4	.333	28	0	0	6-9	27.2	28	19	6	1	18-0	28	6.18	79	.255	.364	2	.000	-0	—	-3	105	-0.6
2001	†Hou N★	2	5	.286	64	0	0	39-2	62.2	44	19	5	5	20-0	79	2.73	168	.198	.278	0	ø	0	—	13	15	2.6
2002	Hou N	4	2	.667	70	0	0	35-6	75	51	21	7	2	22-5	88	2.52	172	.196	.261	2	.000	-0	—	15	0	2.4
2003	Hou N★	1	4	.200	78	0	0	44-3	86	52	18	8	3	23-5	105	1.78	248	.169	.234	2	.000	0	—	25	0	3.6
2004	Phi N	4	0	1.000	45	0	0	21-4	48.1	31	16	5	2	6-1	59	2.42	183	.181	.218	2	.000	-0*	—	10	75	1.4
2005	Phi N☆	4	3	.571	75	0	0	38-3	77.2	45	17	6	3	20-2	87	1.51	288	.165	.229	3	.333	0	—	**22**	0	3.8
2006	†NY N	3	2	.600	70	0	0	40-5	72.1	59	22	7	4	21-1	94	2.24	196	.219	.285	0	ø	0	—	17	0	2.7
Total	12	37	34	.521	654	0	0	324-50	702.2	468	204	66	27	238-19	934	2.38	182	.187	.264	20	.100	-1	—	152	232	24.1

WAGNER, BULL William George; B12.25.1887 Lilley MI; D10.2.1967 Muskegon MI; BR/TR/6´0.5˝/225; d6.2

YEAR	TM LG	W	L	PCT	G	GS	CG-SHO	SV-BS	IP	H	R	HR	HB	BB-IB	SO	ERA	AERA	OAV	OOB	AB-HR-SH	AVG	PB	SUP	APR	DL	PW
1913	Bro N	4	2	.667	18	1	0	0	70.2	77	49	5	3	30	11	5.48	60	.285	.363	26	.231	0	251	-14	—	-1.1
1914	Bro N	0	1	.000	6	0	0	0	12.1	14	11	0	1	12	4	6.57	44	.311	.466	1	.000	-0	—	-4	—	-0.3
Total	2	4	3	.571	24	1	0	0	83	91	60	5	4	42	15	5.64	57	.289	.380	27	.222	0	251	-18	—	-1.4

WAINHOUSE, DAVE David Paul; B11.7.1967 Toronto ON, Can.; BL/TR/6´2˝/(185–196); [MonN88 1/19]; d8.3; Col Washington St.

YEAR	TM LG	W	L	PCT	G	GS	CG-SHO	SV-BS	IP	H	R	HR	HB	BB-IB	SO	ERA	AERA	OAV	OOB	AB-HR-SH	AVG	PB	SUP	APR	DL	PW
1991	Mon N	0	1	.000	2	0	0	0-0	2.2	2	2	0	0	4-0	1	6.75	54	.222	.429	0	ø	0	—	-1	0	-0.2
1993	Sea A	0	0	ø	3	0	0	0-0	2.1	7	7	1	1	5-0	2	27.00	17	.500	.650	0	ø	0	—	-5	0	-0.3
1996	Pit N	1	0	1.000	17	0	0	0-0	23.2	22	16	3	0	10-1	16	5.70	77	.250	.320	1	.000	-0	—	-3	0	-0.1
1997	Pit N	0	1	.000	25	0	0	0-0	28	34	28	2	3	17-0	21	8.04	53	.301	.403	2	.000	-0	—	-12	0	-0.6
1998	Col N	1	0	1.000	10	0	0	0-1	11	15	6	1	2	5-0	3	4.91	105	.341	.431	1	.000	-0	—	0	0	0.1
1999	Col N	0	0	ø	19	0	0	0-0	28.2	37	22	6	0	16-0	18	6.91	84	.330	.405	1	.000	-0	—	-2	0	-0.1
2000	StL N	0	1	.000	9	0	0	0-0	8.2	13	10	2	2	4-1	5	9.35	50	.351	.442	0	ø	0	—	-5	88	-0.4
Total	7	2	3	.400	85	0	0	0-1	105	130	91	15	8	61-2	66	7.37	65	.312	.404	5	.000	-1	—	-28	88	-1.6

WAINWRIGHT, ADAM Adam Parrish; B8.30.1981 Brunswick GA; BR/TR/6´7˝/205; [AtlN00 1/29]; d9.11

YEAR	TM LG	W	L	PCT	G	GS	CG-SHO	SV-BS	IP	H	R	HR	HB	BB-IB	SO	ERA	AERA	OAV	OOB	AB-HR-SH	AVG	PB	SUP	APR	DL	PW
2005	StL N	0	0	ø	2	0	0	0-0	2	2	3	1	0	1-0	0	13.50	31	.250	.333	0	ø	0*	—	-2	0	-0.1
2006	†StL N	2	1	.667	61	0	0	3-2	75	64	26	6	4	22-2	72	3.12	139	.230	.295	6-1-0	.500	2	—	11	0	0.8
Total	2	2	1	.667	63	0	0	3-2	77	66	29	7	4	23-2	72	3.39	128	.231	.296	6-1-0	.500	2	—	9	0	0.7

WAITS, RICK Michael Richard; B5.15.1952 Atlanta GA; BL/TL/6´3˝/(194–195); [TexA70 5/112]; d9.17; C2

YEAR	TM LG	W	L	PCT	G	GS	CG-SHO	SV-BS	IP	H	R	HR	HB	BB-IB	SO	ERA	AERA	OAV	OOB	AB-HR-SH	AVG	PB	SUP	APR	DL	PW
1973	Tex A	0	0	ø	1	0	0	1-0	1	1	1	0	0	1-0	0	9.00	42	.333	.500	0	ø	0	—	-1	0	-0.1
1975	Cle A	6	2	.750	16	7	3	1-0	70.1	57	25	3	1	25-5	34	2.94	130	.221	.292	0	ø	0	102	7	0	0.8
1976	Cle A	7	9	.438	26	22	4-2	0-0	123.2	143	60	7	0	54-1	65	4.00	88	.297	.368	0	ø	0*	83	-6	29	-0.8
1977	Cle A	9	7	.563	37	16	1	2-3	135.1	132	67	8	1	64-7	62	3.99	100	.262	.346	0	ø	0*	98	0	0	0.0
1978	Cle A	13	15	.464	34	33	15-2	0-0	230.1	206	97	16	2	86-0	97	3.20	118	.240	.309	0	ø	0*	96	12	0	1.6
1979	Cle A	16	13	.552	34	34	8-3	0-0	231	230	123	26	4	91-1	91	4.44	97	.264	.334	0	ø	0	99	-2	0	-0.2
1980	Cle A	13	14	.481	33	33	9-2	0-0	224.1	231	118	18	1	82-6	109	4.45	93	.270	.332	0	ø	0	95	-7	0	-0.7
1981	Cle A	8	10	.444	22	21	5-1	0-0	126.1	173	74	7	1	44-1	51	4.92	75	.330	.380	0	ø	0	93	-16	0	-2.0
1982	Cle A	2	13	.133	25	21	2	0-1	115	128	74	13	1	57-2	44	5.40	77	.290	.370	0	ø	0	85	-14	0	-1.6
1983	Cle A	0	1	.000	8	0	0	0-1	19.2	23	13	1	0	9-2	13	4.58	93	.307	.364	0	ø	0	—	-1	0	-0.1
	Mil A	0	2	.000	10	2	0	0-0	30	39	20	1	0	11-1	20	5.10	74	.320	.373	0	ø	0	132	-5	52	-0.3
	Year	0	3	.000	18	2	0	0-1	49.2	62	33	2	0	20-3	33	4.89	81	.315	.369	0	ø	0	125	-6	0	-0.4
1984	Mil A	2	4	.333	47	1	0	3-1	73	84	32	7	0	24-3	49	3.58	109	.297	.348	0	ø	0	70	3	18	0.3
1985	Mil A	3	2	.600	24	0	0	1-1	47	67	37	3	0	20-5	24	6.51	64	.340	.399	1	.000	-0	—	-11	0	-1.1
Total	12	79	92	.462	317	190	47-10	8-7	1427	1514	741	110	11	568-34	659	4.25	93	.277	.344	1	.000	-0	94	-41	99	-4.2

WAKEFIELD, TIM Timothy Stephen; B8.2.1966 Melbourne FL; BR/TR/6´2˝/(195–215); [PitN88 8/200]; d7.31; Col Florida Tech

YEAR	TM LG	W	L	PCT	G	GS	CG-SHO	SV-BS	IP	H	R	HR	HB	BB-IB	SO	ERA	AERA	OAV	OOB	AB-HR-SH	AVG	PB	SUP	APR	DL	PW
1992	†Pit N	8	1	.889	13	13	4-1	0-0	92	76	26	3	1	35-1	51	2.15	161	.232	.305	28-0-4	.071	-1*	106	13	0	1.2
1993	Pit N	6	11	.353	24	20	3-2	0-0	128.1	145	83	14	9	75-2	59	5.61	73	.291	.389	43-1-4	.163	1	86	-21	0	-2.3
1995	†Bos A	16	8	.667	27	27	6-1	0-0	195.1	163	76	22	9	68-0	119	2.95	165	.227	.300	0	ø	0	92	38	0	4.2
1996	Bos A	14	13	.519	32	32	6	0-0	211.2	238	151	38	12	90-0	140	5.14	99	.280	.353	0	ø	0	90	-7	0	-0.8
1997	Bos A	12	15	.444	35	29	4-2	0-0	201.1	193	109	24	16	87-5	151	4.25	110	.256	.343	1	.000	-0	96	7	21	0.7
1998	†Bos A	17	8	.680	36	33	2	0-0	216	211	123	30	14	79-1	146	4.58	103	.252	.324	2-0-2	.000	0*	129	2	0	0.1
1999	†Bos A	6	11	.353	49	17	0	15-3	140	146	93	19	5	72-2	104	5.08	98	.266	.352	3	.000	-0	88	-3	0	-0.5
2000	Bos A	6	10	.375	51	17	0	0-1	159.1	170	107	31	4	65-3	102	5.48	92	.272	.340	2-0-1	.000	-0*	118	-9	0	-0.8
2001	Bos A	9	12	.429	45	17	0	3-2	168.2	156	84	13	18	73-5	148	3.90	114	.248	.339	3-0-1	.333	0	91	9	0	1.0
2002	Bos A	11	5	.688	45	15	0	3-2	163.1	121	57	15	9	51-2	134	2.81	159	.204	.276	0	ø	0	110	30	0	2.6
2003	†Bos A	11	7	.611	35	33	0	1-0	202.1	193	106	23	12	71-0	169	4.09	114	.246	.317	0	ø	0	110	11	0	0.8
2004	†Bos A	12	10	.545	32	30	0	0-0	188.1	197	121	29	16	63-3	116	4.87	100	.264	.333	2	.000	-0	109	-2	0	-0.2
2005	†Bos A	16	12	.571	33	33	3	0-0	225.1	210	113	35	11	68-4	151	4.15	109	.245	.307	8-0-1	.250	0	98	8	0	1.0
2006	Bos A	7	11	.389	23	23	1	0-0	140	135	80	19	10	51-0	90	4.63	101	.248	.322	4	.000	-0	94	-1	57	-0.1
Total	14	151	134	.530	480	339	29-6	22-8	2432	2354	1329	315	146	948-28	1680	4.30	108	.253	.329	96-1-13	.125	-1	102	75	78	6.9

YEAR	TM LG	W	L	PCT	G	GS	CG-SHO	SV-BS	IP	H	R	HR	HB	BB-IB	SO	ERA	AERA	OAV	OOB	AB-HR-SH	AVG	PB	SUP	APR	DL	PW
WAKEFIELD, BILL	William Sumner; B5.24.1941 Kansas City MO; BR/TR/6´0˝/168; d4.18																									
1964	NY N	3	5	.375	62	4	0	2	119.2	103	57	10	9	61-6	61	3.61	99	.235	.337	24-0-3	.167	-0	98	-1	0	-0.1
WALBERG, RUBE	George Elvin; B7.27.1896 Pine City MN; D10.27.1978 Tempe AZ; BL/TL/6´1.5˝/190; d4.29																									
1923	NY N	0	0	ø	2	0	0	0	5	4	2	0	0	1	1	1.80	212	.211	.250	1	.000	-0	—	1	—	0.0
	Phi A	4	8	.333	26	10	4	0	115	122	77	10	2	60	38	5.32	77	.280	.369	41-0-3	.317	3	121	-12	—	-0.8
1924	Phi A	0	0	ø	6	2	0	0	7	10	10	0	0	10	3	12.86	33	.345	.513	2	.500	0	89	-6	—	-0.2
1925	Phi A	8	14	.364	53	20	7	7	191.2	197	99	11	2	77	82	3.99	117	.269	.340	64	.156	-4	80	14	—	1.2
1926	Phi A	12	10	.545	40	19	5-2	2	151	168	67	4	6	60	72	2.80	149	.292	.365	46-0-5	.152	-2	83	19	—	2.3
1927	Phi A	16	12	.571	46	33	14	4	249.1	257	139	18	4	91	136	3.93	108	.271	.337	87-2-2	.207	3*	120	5	—	0.8
1928	Phi A	17	12	.586	38	30	15-3	1	235.2	236	111	19	3	64	112	3.55	113	.265	.317	86-1-3	.209	1	112	12	—	1.5
1929	†Phi A	18	11	.621	40	33	20-3	4	267.2	256	115	22	0	99	94	3.60	118	.254	.320	103-1-6	.223	-0	108	24	—	2.2
1930	†Phi A	13	12	.520	38	30	12-2	1	205.1	207	121	6	2	85	100	4.69	100	.262	.335	73-0-3	.164	-3	95	1	—	-0.3
1931	†Phi A	20	12	.625	44	35	19-1	3	**291**	298	133	16	0	109	106	3.74	120	.266	.331	105-0-4	.124	-6*	92	28	—	2.0
1932	Phi A	17	10	.630	41	34	19-3	1	272	305	159	16	0	103	96	4.73	96	.282	.344	94-0-9	.170	-3	120	-7	—	-0.9
1933	Phi A	9	13	.409	40	20	10-1	4	201	224	132	12	1	95	68	4.88	88	.278	.354	68-0-7	.132	-1*	86	-14	—	-1.5
1934	Bos A	6	7	.462	30	10	2	1	104.2	118	62	5	1	41	38	4.04	119	.284	.350	32-0-1	.188	-1	98	6	—	0.6
1935	Bos A	5	9	.357	44	10	4	3	142.2	152	71	10	2	54	44	3.91	121	.273	.340	37-0-3	.162	-2	64	13	—	1.0
1936	Bos A	5	4	.556	24	9	5	0	100.1	98	53	7	1	36	49	4.40	121	.257	.323	32-0-3	.156	-1	72	11	—	0.7
1937	Bos A	5	7	.417	32	11	3	1	104.2	143	72	7	3	46	46	5.59	85	.332	.400	34-0-3	.147	-1	85	-9	—	-1.0
Total	15	155	141	.524	544	306	139-15	32	2644	2795	1423	163	27	1031	1085	4.16	107	.273	.341	905-4-52	.179	-18	99	86	—	7.6
WALDBAUER, DOC	Albert Charles; B2.22.1892 Richmond VA; D7.16.1969 Yakima WA; BR/TR/6´0˝/172; d9.24																									
1917	Was A	0	0	ø	2	0	0	1	5	10	4	0	0	2	2	7.20	36	.476	.522	1	.000	-0	—	-2	—	-0.1
WALK, BOB	Robert Vernon; B11.26.1956 Van Nuys CA; BR/TR/6´4˝/(195–217); [PhiN76 S3/52]; d5.26; Col Canyons (CA) [JC]																									
1980	†Phi N	11	7	.611	27	27	2	0-0	151.2	163	82	8	2	71-2	94	4.57	84	.276	.353	50-0-7	.140	-0	113	-10	0	-1.2
1981	Atl N	1	4	.200	12	8	0	0-0	43.1	41	25	6	0	23-0	16	4.57	77	.250	.342	7-0-3	.143	-0	120	-5	75	-0.6
1982	†Atl N	11	9	.550	32	27	3-1	0-0	164.1	179	101	19	6	59-2	84	4.87	76	.280	.344	51-0-6	.196	2	121	-21	0	-2.3
1983	Atl N	0	0	ø	1	1	0	0-0	3.2	7	3	0	0	2-0	4	7.36	53	.412	.474	1	.000	-0	137	-1	0	-0.1
1984	Pit N	1	1	.500	2	2	0	0-0	10.1	8	5	1	0	4-1	10	2.61	139	.200	.273	3	.000	-0	97	0	71	0.0
1985	Pit N	2	3	.400	9	9	1-1	0-0	58.2	60	27	3	0	18-2	40	3.68	99	.265	.318	17-0-4	.000	-2	114	-1	0	-0.3
1986	Pit N	7	8	.467	44	15	1-1	2-2	141.2	129	66	14	3	64-7	78	3.75	104	.251	.334	39-0-1	.154	0	83	2	0	0.3
1987	Pit N	8	2	.800	39	12	1-1	0-0	117	107	52	11	3	51-2	78	3.31	126	.245	.327	26-0-1	.231	1	118	9	0	0.8
1988	Pit N★	12	10	.545	32	32	1-1	0-0	212.2	183	75	6	2	65-5	81	2.71	127	.230	.288	69-0-3	.087	-2*	93	16	0	1.4
1989	Pit N	13	10	.565	33	31	2	0-1	196	208	106	15	4	65-1	83	4.41	77	.271	.330	70-0-5	.186	2	128	-22	15	-2.1
1990	†Pit N	7	5	.583	26	24	1-1	1-0	129.2	136	59	17	4	36-2	73	3.75	97	.270	.322	37-0-10	.162	1	122	0	43	0.0
1991	†Pit N	9	2	.818	25	20	0	0-1	115	104	53	10	5	35-2	67	3.60	100	.240	.302	39-1-2	.205	2	134	0	65	0.2
1992	†Pit N	10	6	.625	36	19	1	2-1	135	132	54	10	6	43-5	60	3.20	108	.258	.322	43-0-1	.093	-2	132	3	38	0.2
1993	Pit N	13	14	.481	32	32	3	0-0	187	214	121	23	5	70-5	80	5.68	72	.294	.356	58-0-7	.121	-2	103	-31	0	-4.0
Total	14	105	81	.565	350	259	16-6	5-5	1666	1671	829	143	40	606-36	848	4.03	92	.263	.329	510-1-50	.145	1	114	-61	307	-7.7
WALKER, ED	Edward Harrison; B8.11.1874 Cambois, England; D9.29.1947 Akron OH; BL/TL/6´5˝/242; d9.26																									
1902	Cle A	0	1	.000	1	1	1	0	8	11	4	0	0	3	1	3.38	102	.324	.378	3	.333	0	42	0	—	0.0
1903	Cle A	0	1	.000	3	3	0	0	12	13	12	0	0	10	4	5.25	54	.277	.404	3	.000	-0	159	-4	—	-0.3
Total	2	0	2	.000	4	4	1	0	20	24	16	0	0	13	5	4.50	69	.296	.394	6	.167	0	122	-4	—	-0.3
WALKER, DIXIE	Ewart Gladstone; B6.1.1887 Brownsville PA; D11.14.1965 Leeds AL; BL/TR/6´0˝/192; d9.17; b–Ernie s–Dixie s–Harry																									
1909	Was A	3	1	.750	4	4	4	0	36	31	12	0	0	6	25	2.50	97	.217	.248	13	.154	-0	138	0	—	0.0
1910	Was A	11	11	.500	29	26	16-3	0	199.1	177	83	2	8	68	84	3.30	76	.245	.317	69-0-1	.130	-3	80	-10	—	-1.4
1911	Was A	8	13	.381	32	24	15-2	0	185.2	205	103	2	8	50	65	3.39	97	.286	.339	66	.303	4*	102	-3	—	0.0
1912	Was A	3	6	.333	9	8	5	0	60	72	40	2	4	18	29	5.25	64	.300	.359	16	.125	1	100	-9	—	-1.1
Total	4	25	31	.446	74	62	40-5	0	481	485	238	6	20	142	203	3.52	82	.266	.326	164-0-1	.201	2	96	-22	—	-2.5
WALKER, MYSTERIOUS	Frederick Mitchell; B3.21.1884 Utica NE; D2.1.1958 Oak Park IL; BR/TR/5´10.5˝/185; d6.28; Col Chicago																									
1910	Cin N	0	0	ø	1	0	0	0	3	4	2	0	0	4	1	3.00	97	.333	.500	1	.000	-0	—	0	—	0.0
1912	Cle A	0	0	ø	1	0	0	0	1	0	0	0	0	1	0	0.00	ø	.000	.200	0	ø	0	—	0	—	0.0
1913	Bro N	1	3	.250	11	8	3	0	58.1	44	26	3	5	35	35	3.55	93	.233	.367	18-0-1	.167	-0	80	0	—	0.1
1914	Pit F	4	16	.200	35	21	12	0	169.1	197	108	3	3	74	79	4.31	67	.294	.367	53-0-2	.113	-2*	88	-29	—	-3.2
1915	Bro F	2	4	.333	13	7	2	1	65.2	61	37	3	0	22	28	3.70	73	.242	.303	27	.222	1	151	-8	—	-0.6
Total	5	7	23	.233	61	36	17	1	297.1	306	173	9	8	136	143	4.00	73	.272	.354	99-0-3	.152	-2	98	-37	—	-3.7
WALKER, GEORGE	George A.; B1863 Hamilton ON, Can.; TR/5´9˝/184; d8.1																									
1888	Bal AA	1	3	.250	4	4	4-1	0	35	36	31	2	0	14	18	5.91	50	.257	.325	13	.077	-1	68	-10	—	-1.0
WALKER, LUKE	James Luke; B9.2.1943 DeKalb TX; BL/TL/6´1.5˝/(190–195); d9.7; Col Paris (TX) JC																									
1965	Pit N	0	0	ø	2	0	0	0	5	2	0	0	0	1-0	5	0.00	ø	.118	.167	0	ø	0	—	2	0	0.1
1966	Pit N	0	1	.000	10	1	0	0	10	8	9	0	1	15-2	7	4.50	79	.205	.436	2	.000	-0	98	-3	0	-0.3
1968	Pit N	0	3	.000	39	2	0	3	62.1	42	18	1	1	39-0	66	2.02	145	.190	.314	8-0-1	.000	-1	89	6	0	0.3
1969	Pit N	4	6	.400	31	15	3-1	0-0	118.2	98	51	5	2	57-3	96	3.64	96	.226	.318	32-0-3	.000	-3	115	-1	0	-0.3
1970	†Pit N	15	6	.714	42	19	5-3	3-1	163	129	56	6	1	89-8	124	3.04	130	.219	.322	46-0-8	.130	-1	117	19	0	2.3
1971	†Pit N	10	8	.556	28	24	4-2	0-0	159.2	157	69	9	2	53-2	86	3.55	96	.262	.321	46-0-2	.022	-3	116	-2	0	-0.6
1972	†Pit N	4	6	.400	26	12	2	2-0	92.2	98	41	4	0	34-4	48	3.40	98	.278	.338	24-0-1	.083	-1	100	-1	0	-0.3
1973	Pit N	7	12	.368	37	18	2-1	1-1	122	129	75	9	1	66-8	74	4.65	76	.270	.358	30-0-3	.067	-2	99	-17	0	-2.7
1974	Det A	5	5	.500	28	9	0	0-0	92	100	56	9	2	54-1	52	4.99	77	.278	.374	0	ø	0	120	-10	24	-1.1
Total	9	45	47	.489	243	100	16-7	9-2	825.1	763	375	43	10	408-28	558	3.64	97	.247	.335	188-0-18	.059	-11	111	-7	24	-2.6
WALKER, JAMIE	James Ross; B7.1.1971 McMinnville TN; BL/TL/6´2˝/(185–195); [HouN92 10/265]; d4.2; Col Austin Peay																									
1997	KC A	3	3	.500	50	0	0	0-1	43	46	28	6	3	20-3	24	5.44	87	.271	.354	0	ø	0	—	-3	19	-0.3
1998	KC A	0	1	.000	6	2	0	0-0	17.1	30	20	5	2	3-0	15	9.87	49	.380	.412	0	ø	0	96	-9	106	-0.4
2002	Det A	1	1	.500	57	0	0	1-3	43.2	32	19	9	4	9-1	40	3.71	118	.199	.257	0	ø	0	—	4	0	0.2
2003	Det A	4	3	.571	78	0	0	3-4	65	61	30	9	2	17-1	45	3.32	132	.247	.299	0	ø	0	—	6	0	0.7
2004	Det A	3	4	.429	70	0	0	1-6	64.2	69	28	8	1	12-3	53	3.20	140	.263	.297	0	ø	0	—	8	0	0.7
2005	Det A	4	3	.571	66	0	0	0-2	48.2	49	22	5	2	13-3	30	3.70	116	.257	.309	0	ø	0	—	3	0	0.4
2006	†Det A	0	1	.000	56	0	0	0-0	48	47	15	8	0	8-3	37	2.81	159	.251	.282	0	ø	0	—	10	0	0.4
Total	7	15	16	.484	383	2	0	5-16	330.1	334	162	50	14	82-14	244	3.95	113	.258	.307	0	ø	0	96	19	125	1.7
WALKER, ROY	James Roy "Dixie"; B4.13.1893 Lawrenceburg TN; D2.10.1962 New Orleans LA; BR/TR (BB 1918, 22)/6´1.5˝/180; d9.16																									
1912	Cle A	0	0	ø	1	0	0	0	2	0	0	0	0	2	1	0.00	ø	.000	.250	0	ø	0	—	1	—	0.0
1915	Cle A	4	9	.308	25	15	4	1	131	122	73	1	7	65	57	3.98	77	.261	.360	38-0-3	.132	-2	86	-10	—	-1.4
1917	Chi N	0	1	.000	2	1	0	0	7	8	5	0	0	5	4	3.86	75	.286	.394	1	.000	-0	26	-1	—	-0.2
1918	Chi N	1	3	.250	13	7	2	1	43.1	50	27	1	1	15	20	2.70	103	.298	.359	11-0-1	.000	-1	112	-3	—	-0.4
1921	StL N	11	12	.478	38	23	11	3	170.2	194	93	10	1	53	52	4.22	87	.293	.347	54-0-4	.204	-0	100	-9	—	-1.1
1922	StL N	1	2	.333	12	2	0	0	32	34	20	1	0	15	14	4.78	81	.293	.374	7-0-1	.143	-0	84	-3	—	-0.4
Total	6	17	27	.386	91	48	17	5	386	408	218	13	9	155	148	3.99	85	.282	.355	111-0-9	.153	-4	94	-25	—	-3.5
WALKER, JERRY	Jerry Allen; B2.12.1939 Ada OK; BB/TR (BR 1963–64)/6´1˝/(185–195); d7.6; C5																									
1957	Bal A	1	0	1.000	13	3	1-1	1	27.2	24	9	1	0	14-1	13	2.93	123	.245	.336	5	.000	-1	99	3	0	0.1
1958	Bal A	0	0	ø	6	0	0	0	10.1	16	8	2	0	5-0	6	6.97	52	.340	.404	2	.000	-0	—	-4	0	-0.2
1959	Bal A★	11	10	.524	30	22	7-2	4	182	160	68	13	3	52-9	100	2.92	130	.240	.295	65-1-3	.169	-1*	92	17	0	1.9
1960	Bal A	3	4	.429	29	18	1	5	118	107	53	15	3	56-0	48	3.74	102	.247	.335	38-0-1	.368	5*	107	2	0	0.7
1961	KC A	8	14	.364	36	24	4	2	168	161	100	23	10	96-2	56	4.82	87	.253	.356	64-0-1	.250	3*	90	-10	0	-0.9
1962	KC A	8	9	.471	31	21	3-1	0	143.1	165	101	27	7	78-4	57	5.90	72	.288	.377	57-3-2	.263	5*	126	-24	0	-2.0
1963	Cle A	6	6	.500	39	2	0	1	88	92	53	15	2	36-6	41	4.91	74	.265	.334	19	.105	-0	25	-12	0	-1.6

YEAR	TM LG	W	L	PCT	G	GS	CG-SHO	SV-BS	IP	H	R	HR	HB	BB-IB	SO	ERA	AERA	OAV	OOB	AB-HR-SH	AVG	PB	SUP	APR	DL	PW
1964	Cle A	0	1	.000	6	0	0	0	9.2	9	5	1	0	4-0	5	4.66	77	.257	.333	2	.000	-0	—	-1	0	-0.1
Total	8	37	44	.457	190	90	16-4	13	747	734	397	97	25	341-22	326	4.36	90	.259	.340	252-4-7	.230	10	103	-29	0	-2.1
WALKER, KEVIN	Kevin Michael; B9.20.1976 Irving TX; BL/TL/6´4˝/(190–215); [SDN95 6/145]; d4.14																									
2000	SD N	7	1	.875	70	0	0	0-0	66.2	49	35	5	5	38-6	56	4.18	106	.206	.325	4	.250	0	—	2	0	0.2
2001	SD N	0	0	ø	16	0	0	0-1	12	5	4	0	0	8-2	17	3.00	138	.122	.265	0	ø	0	—	2	157	0.1
2002	SD N	0	1	.000	11	0	0	0-1	8	12	6	2	0	5-1	11	5.63	69	.333	.415	0	ø	0	—	-2	150	-0.2
2003	SD N	0	0	ø	11	0	0	0-0	6.2	5	4	1	0	5-0	5	5.40	74	.200	.333	0	ø	0	—	-1	71	0.0
2004	SF N	0	0	ø	5	0	0	0-0	1.2	3	3	1	1	2-0	1	16.20	27	.429	.600	0	ø	0	—	-2	0	-0.1
2005	Chi A	0	1	.000	9	0	0	0-1	7	10	7	1	0	5-1	5	9.00	50	.333	.429	0	ø	0	—	-3	0	-0.4
Total	6	7	3	.700	122	0	0	0-3	102	84	59	10	6	63-10	95	4.76	91	.223	.342	4	.250	0	—	-4	378	-0.4
WALKER, MARTY	Martin Van Buren "Buddy"; B3.27.1899 Philadelphia PA; D4.24.1978 Philadelphia PA; BL/TL/6´0˝/170; d9.30																									
1928	Phi N	0	1	.000	1	1	0	0	0	2	4	0	0	3	0	(3)	ø	1.000	1.000	0	ø	0	20	-3	—	-0.2
WALKER, MIKE	Michael Aaron; B6.23.1965 Houston TX; BR/TR/6´3˝/205; [PitN86 2/29]; d6.16; Col Houston																									
1992	Sea A	0	3	.000	5	3	0	0-0	14.2	21	14	4	0	9-3	5	7.36	54	.333	.411	0	ø	0	76	-6	0	-1.0
WALKER, MIKE	Michael Charles; B10.4.1966 Chicago IL; BR/TR/6´1˝/(175–205); [CleA86*2/27]; d9.9; Col Seminole (FL) CC																									
1988	Cle A	0	1	.000	3	1	0	0-0	8.2	8	7	0	0	10-0	7	7.27	57	.258	.439	0	ø	0	0	-3	0	-0.2
1990	Cle A	2	6	.250	18	11	0	0-0	75.2	82	49	6	6	42-4	34	4.88	81	.277	.376	0	ø	0	71	-10	0	-0.9
1991	Cle A	0	1	.000	5	0	0	0-0	4.1	6	1	0	1	2-1	2	2.08	201	.316	.409	0	ø	0	—	1	0	0.2
1995	Chi N	1	3	.250	42	0	0	1-2	44.2	45	22	2	0	24-3	20	3.22	129	.259	.342	3	.000	-0	—	3	0	0.2
1996	Det A	0	0	ø	20	0	0	1-1	27.2	40	26	10	1	17-1	13	8.46	60	.351	.433	0	ø	0	—	-9	0	-0.4
Total	5	3	11	.214	88	12	0	2-3	161	181	105	18	8	95-9	76	5.09	83	.285	.381	3	.000	-0	61	-18	0	-1.1
WALKER, PETE	Peter Brian; B4.8.1969 Beverly MA; BR/TR/6´2˝/195; [NYN90 7/199]; d6.7; Col Connecticut																									
1995	NY N	1	0	1.000	13	0	0	0-0	17.2	24	9	3	0	5-0	5	4.58	88	.329	.367	0	ø	0	—	-1	0	0.0
1996	SD N	0	0	ø	1	0	0	0-0	0.2	0	0	0	0	3-0	1	0.00	ø	.000	.600	0	ø	0	—	0	0	0.0
2000	Col N	0	0	ø	3	0	0	0-0	4.2	10	9	1	0	4-0	2	17.36	33	.435	.519	0	ø	0	—	-5	0	-0.2
2001	NY N	0	0	ø	2	0	0	0-0	6.2	6	2	0	0	0-0	4	2.70	150	.240	.240	1-0-1	.000	-0	—	1	0	0.0
2002	NY N	0	0	ø	1	0	0	0-0	1	2	1	0	0	0-0	0	9.00	44	.400	.400	0	ø	0	—	-1	0	0.0
	Tor A	10	5	.667	37	20	0	1-0	139.1	143	72	18	3	51-5	80	4.33	107	.270	.334	0	ø	0	102	5	0	0.5
2003	Tor A	2	2	.500	23	7	0	0-0	55.1	59	31	11	2	24-2	29	4.88	97	.277	.354	0	ø	0	119	0	100	0.0
2005	Tor A	6	6	.500	41	4	0	2-3	84	81	33	10	2	33-0	43	3.54	130	.254	.324	0	ø	0	65	11	0	1.4
2006	Tor A	1	1	.500	23	0	0	1-0	30	37	24	5	0	13-2	27	5.40	88	.296	.362	0	ø	0	—	-4	103	-0.2
Total	8	20	14	.588	144	31	0	4-3	339.1	362	181	48	7	133-9	191	4.48	103	.275	.342	1-0-1	.000	-0	102	6	203	1.5
WALKER, TOM	Robert Thomas; B11.7.1948 Tampa FL; BR/TR/6´1˝/(188–200); [BalA68*1/9]; d4.23; Col Brevard (FL) CC																									
1972	Mon N	2	2	.500	46	0	0	2-0	74.2	71	27	4	1	22-2	42	2.89	123	.248	.304	3	.000	-0	—	5	0	0.2
1973	Mon N	7	5	.583	54	0	0	4-2	91.2	95	52	7	3	42-12	68	3.63	105	.274	.349	7-0-1	.000	-1	—	-2	0	-0.3
1974	Mon N	4	5	.444	33	8	1	2-0	91.2	96	45	7	2	28-5	70	3.83	100	.266	.321	16-0-1	.188	0	102	0	0	0.0
1975	Det A	3	8	.273	36	9	1	0-0	115.1	116	69	16	5	40-3	60	4.45	91	.261	.325	0	ø	0	61	-6	0	-0.6
1976	StL N	1	2	.333	10	0	0	3-1	19.2	22	10	2	0	3-1	11	4.12	87	.265	.291	5	.400	1	—	-1	0	-0.2
1977	Mon N	1	1	.500	11	0	0	0-0	19	15	10	2	0	7-0	10	4.74	81	.221	.293	2-0-2	.000	-0	—	-1	0	-0.2
	Cal A	0	0	ø	1	0	0	0-0	2	3	2	2	0	0-0	1	9.00	44	.375	.375	0	ø	0	—	-1	0	-0.1
Total	6	18	23	.439	191	17	2	11-3	414	418	215	40	11	142-23	262	3.87	99	.262	.323	33-0-4	.152	-0	83	-6	0	-1.2
WALKER, TOM	Thomas William; B8.1.1881 Philadelphia PA; D7.10.1944 Woodbury Heights NJ; BR/TR/5´11˝/170; d9.27																									
1902	Phi A	0	1	.000	1	1	1	0	8	10	7	0	1	0	2	5.63	65	.303	.324	4	.250	-0	98	-2	—	-0.1
1904	Cin N	15	8	.652	24	24	22-2	0	217	196	76	2	18	53	64	2.24	131	.238	.299	77-0-2	.117	-4	85	17	—	1.2
1905	Cin N	9	7	.563	23	19	12-1	0	144.2	171	71	3	6	44	28	3.24	102	.305	.362	51-0-2	.137	-1	105	3	—	0.2
Total	3	24	16	.600	48	44	35-3	0	369.2	377	154	5	25	97	94	2.70	114	.266	.325	132-0-4	.129	-6	94	18	—	1.3
WALKER, TYLER	Tyler Lanier; B5.15.1976 San Francisco CA; BR/TR/6´3˝/(225–240); [NYN97 2/58]; d7.2; Col California																									
2002	NY N	1	0	1.000	5	1	0	0-0	10.2	11	7	3	0	5-1	7	5.91	67	.250	.327	2	.000	-0	117	-2	0	-0.2
2004	SF N	5	1	.833	52	0	0	1-0	63.2	69	31	8	1	24-1	48	4.24	102	.287	.346	7	.000	-1	—	2	0	0.0
2005	SF N	6	4	.600	67	0	0	23-5	61.2	68	31	9	3	27-6	54	4.23	100	.280	.358	1	.000	-0	—	0	18	0.0
2006	SF N	0	1	.000	6	0	0	0-2	5.1	9	9	1	0	5-0	3	15.19	29	.391	.500	0	ø	0	—	-6	0	-0.9
	TB A	1	3	.250	20	0	0	10-2	20	18	11	0	0	7-0	16	4.95	94	.240	.305	0	ø	0	—	0	111	-0.1
Total	4	13	9	.591	150	1	0	34-9	161.1	175	89	21	4	68-8	128	4.80	90	.280	.350	10	.000	-1	117	-6	129	-1.2
WALKER, BILL	William Henry; B10.7.1903 E.St.Louis IL; D6.14.1966 E.St.Louis IL; BR/TL/6´0˝/175; d9.13																									
1927	NY N	0	0	ø	3	0	0	0	4	6	6	0	0	5	4	9.00	43	.429	.579	0	ø	0	—	-3	—	-0.1
1928	NY N	3	6	.333	22	8	1	0	76.1	79	43	9	1	31	39	4.72	83	.275	.348	22-0-2	.091	-2	108	-6	—	-0.8
1929	NY N	14	7	.667	29	23	13-1	0	177.2	188	71	11	4	57	65	**3.09**	148	.274	.334	61-1-7	.115	-3	110	30	—	2.6
1930	NY N	17	15	.531	39	34	13-2	1	245.1	258	133	19	7	88	105	3.93	121	.268	.334	86-2-5	.186	-1*	96	19	—	1.9
1931	NY N	16	9	.640	37	28	19-**6**	3	239.1	212	78	6	3	64	121	**2.26**	**164**	.231	.283	77-0-3	.065	-6	102	**37**	—	2.9
1932	NY N	8	12	.400	31	22	9	2	163	177	95	23	3	55	74	4.14	90	.274	.334	52-0-1	.135	-2	111	-10	—	-1.2
1933	StL N	9	10	.474	29	20	6-2	0	158	168	71	8	1	67	41	3.42	102	.273	.346	53-1-3	.132	-2	90	1	—	-0.1
1934	†StL N	12	4	.750	24	19	10-1	0	153	160	59	11	2	66	76	3.12	136	.270	.345	54-0-3	.093	-4	90	19	—	1.3
1935	StL N★	13	8	.619	37	25	8-2	1	193.1	222	93	7	5	78	79	3.82	107	.288	.357	59-0-7	.102	-4*	95	7	—	0.2
1936	StL N	5	6	.455	21	13	4-1	1	79.2	106	62	5	2	27	22	5.87	67	.318	.373	25-0-2	.280	2*	127	-19	—	-2.0
Total	10	97	77	.557	272	192	83-15	8	1489.2	1576	711	99	28	538	626	3.59	114	.271	.335	489-4-33	.127	-23	102	75	—	4.7
WALKUP, JIM	James Elton; B12.14.1909 Havana AR; D2.7.1997 Danville AR; BR/TR/6´1˝/170; d9.22; Col Arkansas																									
1934	StL A	0	0	ø	3	0	0	0	8.1	6	4	0	0	5	6	2.16	231	.200	.314	3	.333	0	—	2	—	0.1
1935	StL A	6	9	.400	55	20	4-1	0	181.1	226	139	17	2	104	44	6.25	77	.305	.392	47-0-4	.128	-3	95	-25	—	-2.0
1936	StL A	0	3	.000	5	2	0	0	15.2	20	17	0	0	6	5	8.04	67	.308	.366	4	.000	-1	41	-5	—	-0.7
1937	StL A	9	12	.429	27	18	6	0	150.1	218	127	16	0	83	46	7.36	66	.347	.423	58-0-3	.241	-1	111	-36	—	-3.8
1938	StL A	1	12	.077	18	13	1	0	94	127	83	13	3	53	28	6.80	73	.329	.414	29-0-3	.138	-2	67	-20	—	-2.3
1939	StL A	0	1	.000	1	0	0	0	0.2	2	1	0	0	1	0	0.00	ø	.500	.600	0	ø	0	—	0	—	0.0
	Det A	0	1	.000	7	0	0	0	12	15	10	3	0	8	5	7.50	65	.319	.418	2	.500	0	—	-3	—	-0.2
	Year	0	2	.000	8	0	0	0	12.2	17	11	3	0	9	5	7.11	69	.333	.433	2	.500	0	—	-3	—	-0.2
Total	6	16	38	.296	116	53	11-1	0	462.1	614	381	49	5	260	134	6.74	72	.323	.406	143-0-10	.182	-6	91	-87	—	-8.9
WALKUP, JIM	James Huey; B11.3.1895 Havana AR; D6.12.1990 Duncan OK; BR/TL/5´8˝/150; d4.30																									
1927	Det A	0	0	ø	2	0	0	0	1.2	3	1	0	0	0	0	5.40	78	.429	.429	1	.000	-0	—	0	—	0.0
WALL, DONNE	Donnell Lee; B7.11.1967 Potosi MO; BR/TR/6´1˝/(180–205); [HouN89 18/464]; d9.2; Col Louisiana–Lafayette																									
1995	Hou N	3	1	.750	6	5	0	0-0	24.1	33	19	5	0	5-0	16	5.55	70	.320	.345	5-0-3	.000	-1	150	-6	0	-0.9
1996	Hou N	9	8	.529	26	23	2-1	0-0	150	170	84	17	6	34-3	99	4.56	85	.286	.329	44-0-8	.205	2	106	-12	0	-1.0
1997	Hou N	2	5	.286	8	8	0	0-0	41.2	53	31	8	2	16-0	25	6.26	64	.315	.382	10-0-1	.100	-0	72	-10	0	-1.4
1998	†SD N	5	4	.556	46	1	0	1-3	70.1	50	20	6	1	32-2	56	2.43	163	.202	.293	7	.286	0	69	13	0	1.6
1999	SD N	7	4	.636	55	0	0	0-6	70.1	58	31	11	0	23-3	53	3.07	139	.219	.280	1	.000	-0	—	8	0	1.1
2000	SD N	5	2	.714	44	0	0	1-4	53.2	36	20	4	0	21-1	29	3.35	133	.193	.274	1-0-1	.000	-0	—	8	29	0.9
2001	NY N	0	4	.000	32	0	0	0-0	42.2	51	24	8	1	17-6	31	4.85	83	.300	.363	0	ø	0*	—	-4	38	-0.3
2002	Ana A	0	0	ø	17	0	0	0-0	21	17	15	3	1	7-1	13	6.43	70	.221	.291	0	ø	0	—	-4	21	-0.2
Total	8	31	28	.525	234	37	2-1	2-13	474	468	244	62	11	155-16	322	4.20	97	.258	.318	68-0-13	.176	1	100	-7	88	-0.2
WALL, MURRAY	Murray Wesley; B9.19.1926 Dallas TX; D10.8.1971 Lone Oak TX; BR/TR/6´3˝/(185–205); d7.4; Col Texas																									
1950	Bos N	0	0	ø	1	0	0	0	4	6	5	0	0	2	2	9.00	43	.333	.400	1	.000	-0	—	-3	0	-0.1
1957	Bos A	3	0	1.000	11	0	0	1	24.1	21	11	3	0	2-0	13	3.33	120	.233	.247	6	.333	0	—	1	0	0.3
1958	Bos A	8	9	.471	52	1	0	10	114.1	109	51	14	5	33-4	53	3.62	111	.255	.313	28	.107	-2	67	5	0	0.8
1959	Bos A	1	4	.200	15	0	0	3	31.2	31	21	5	0	15-2	8	5.40	75	.267	.348	7	.000	-1	—	-5	0	-0.8
	Was A	0	0	ø	1	0	0	0	1.1	3	1	1	0	0-0	0	6.75	58	.600	.600	1	.000	-0	—	0	0	0.0

YEAR	TM LG	W	L	PCT	G	GS	CG-SHO	SV-BS	IP	H	R	HR	HB	BB-IB	SO	ERA	AERA	OAV	OOB	AB-HR-SH	AVG	PB	SUP	APR	DL	PW
	Bos A	1	1	.500	11	0	0	0	17.1	26	11	2	1	11-4	6	5.71	71	.371	.458	3	.000	-0	—	-3	0	-0.3
	Year	2	5	.286	27	0	0	3	50.1	60	33	8	1	26-6	14	5.54	73	.314	.395	11	.000	-1	—	-7	0	-1.1
Total	4	13	14	.481	91	1	0	14	193	196	100	25	6	63-10	82	4.20	96	.270	.330	46	.109	-3	67	-5	0	-0.1
WALL, STAN	Stanley Arthur; B6.16.1951 Butler MO; BL/TL/6´1˝/175; [LAN69 6/126]; d7.19																									
1975	LA N	0	1	.000	10	0	0	0-0	16	12	6	0	1	7-0	6	1.69	203	.222	.308	0	ø	0	—	2	0	0.1
1976	LA N	2	2	.500	31	0	0	1-1	50	50	21	5	2	15-2	27	3.60	95	.269	.325	4	.000	-0	—	-1	0	-0.1
1977	LA N	2	3	.400	25	0	0	0-0	32	36	20	3	1	13-2	22	5.34	72	.279	.350	1-0-1	.000	-0	—	-5	0	-0.7
Total	3	4	6	.400	66	0	0	1-1	98	98	47	8	4	35-4	55	3.86	92	.266	.331	5-0-1	.000	-1	—	-4	0	-0.7
WALLACE, DAVE	David William; B9.7.1947 Waterbury CT; BR/TR/5´10˝/185; d7.18; C9; Col New Haven																									
1973	Phi N	0	0	ø	4	0	0	0-0	3.2	13	9	1	0	2-0	2	22.09	17	.591	.625	0	ø	0	—	-7	0	-0.3
1974	Phi N	0	1	.000	3	0	0	0-0	3	4	4	2	0	3-1	3	9.00	42	.308	.438	0	ø	0	—	-2	0	-0.4
1978	Tor A	0	0	ø	6	0	0	0-0	14	12	6	1	0	11-0	7	3.86	103	.245	.371	0	ø	0	—	0	0	0.0
Total	3	0	1	.000	13	0	0	0-0	20.2	29	19	4	0	16-1	12	7.84	50	.345	.441	0	ø	0	—	-9	0	-0.7
WALLACE, DEREK	Derek Robert; B9.1.1971 Van Nuys CA; BR/TR/6´3˝/(185–215); [ChiN92 1/11]; d8.13; Col Pepperdine; [DL 1997 NY N 181]																									
1996	NY N	2	3	.400	19	0	0	3-0	24.2	29	12	2	0	14-2	15	4.01	100	.290	.377	0	ø	0	—	0	0	0.1
1999	KC A	0	1	.000	8	0	0	0-0	8.1	7	4	2	0	5-0	5	3.24	157	.259	.364	0	ø	0	—	1	0	0.1
Total	2	2	4	.333	27	0	0	3-0	33	36	16	4	0	19-2	20	3.82	112	.283	.374	0	ø	0	—	1	181	0.2
WALLACE, HUCK	Harry Clinton "Lefty"; B7.27.1882 Richmond IN; D7.6.1951 Cleveland OH; BL/TL/5´6˝/160; d6.5																									
1912	Phi N	0	0	ø	4	0	0	0	4.2	7	5	0	0	4	4	0.00	ø	.350	.458	0	ø	0	—	0	—	0.0
WALLACE, LEFTY	James Harold; B8.12.1921 Evansville IN; D7.28.1982 Evansville IN; BL/TL/5´11˝/160; d5.5; Mil 1943–44																									
1942	Bos N	1	3	.250	19	3	1	0	49.1	39	21	3	2	24	20	3.83	87	.217	.316	14	.143	-0	109	-1	0	-0.2
1945	Bos N	1	0	1.000	5	3	1	0	20	18	11	1	1	9	4	4.50	85	.240	.329	6-0-1	.000	-1*	96	-1	0	-0.1
1946	Bos N	3	3	.500	27	8	2	0	75.1	76	41	5	1	31	27	4.18	82	.253	.325	18	.056	-1	94	-6	0	-0.5
Total	3	5	6	.455	51	14	4	0	144.2	133	73	9	4	64	51	4.11	84	.240	.323	38-0-1	.079	-2	98	-8	0	-0.8
WALLACE, JEFF	Jeffrey Allen; B4.12.1976 Wheeling WV; BL/TL/6´2˝/(228–240); [KCA95 25/694]; d8.21; [DL 1998 Pit N 181, 2002 Bos A 114]																									
1997	Pit N	0	0	ø	11	0	0	0-1	12	8	2	0	0	8-1	14	0.75	571	.200	.327	0	ø	0	—	4	0	0.2
1999	Pit N	1	0	1.000	41	0	0	0-1	39	26	17	2	0	38-1	41	3.69	125	.195	.372	0	ø	0	—	4	47	0.2
2000	Pit N	2	0	1.000	38	0	0	0-0	35.2	42	32	5	4	34-1	27	7.07	66	.290	.432	1	.000	-0	—	-10	0	-0.5
2001	TB A	0	3	.000	29	1	0	0-0	50.1	43	26	4	1	37-0	38	3.40	133	.232	.363	0	ø	0	41	4	25	0.2
Total	4	3	3	.500	119	1	0	0-2	137	119	77	11	5	117-3	120	4.20	108	.237	.383	1	.000	0	41	2	367	0.1
WALLACE, MIKE	Michael Sherman; B2.3.1951 Gastonia NC; BL/TL/6´2˝/(185–204); [PhiN69 4/76]; d6.27																									
1973	Phi N	1	1	.500	20	3	1	1-1	33.1	38	16	1	0	15-4	20	3.78	101	.304	.373	4	.000	-0	131	0	0	0.0
1974	Phi N	1	0	1.000	8	0	0	0-0	8.1	12	6	0	0	2-0	1	5.40	70	.324	.359	0	ø	0	—	-2	0	-0.2
	NY A	6	0	1.000	23	1	0	0-0	52.1	42	18	3	0	35-3	34	2.41	147	.222	.339	0	ø	0	75	6	0	0.6
1975	NY A	0	0	ø	3	0	0	0-0	4.1	11	7	1	0	1-0	2	14.54	26	.458	.480	0	ø	0	—	-5	0	-0.2
	StL N	0	0	ø	9	0	0	0-0	8.2	9	2	0	0	5-2	6	2.08	183	.281	.378	0	ø	0	—	2	0	0.1
1976	StL N	3	2	.600	49	0	0	2-2	66.1	66	34	3	0	39-2	40	4.07	88	.264	.358	3	.333	0	—	-3	0	-0.2
1977	Tex A	0	0	ø	5	0	0	0-0	8.1	10	7	1	0	10-0	2	7.56	54	.323	.488	0	ø	0	—	-3	0	-0.1
Total	5	11	3	.786	117	4	1	3-3	181.2	188	90	9	0	107-11	105	3.91	94	.273	.367	7	.143	0	120	-5	0	0.0
WALLACE, BOBBY	Rhoderick John; B11.4.1873 Pittsburgh PA; D11.3.1960 Torrance CA; BR/TR/5´8˝/170; d9.15; M3/C1/U1; HF1953; ▲																									
1894	Cle N	2	1	.667	4	3	2	0	26	28	25	1	1	20	10	5.19	106	.272	.395	13	.154	-1	103	0	—	-0.1
1895	Cle N	12	14	.462	30	28	22-1	1	228.2	271	166	3	8	87	63	4.09	122	.290	.356	98-0-6	.214	-3	112	17	—	1.3
1896	†Cle N	10	7	.588	22	16	13-2	0	145.1	167	75	2	4	49	46	3.34	136	.286	.345	149-1-4	.235	0*	93	19	—	1.8
1902	StL A	0	0	ø	1	1	0	0	2	3	2	0	0	0	1	0.00	ø	.333	.333	494-1-6	.285	0*	82	0	—	0.0
Total	4	24	22	.522	57	48	37-3	1	402	469	268	6	13	156	120	3.87	125	.288	.355	754-2-16	.264	-3	104	36	—	3.0
WALLER, RED	John Francis; B6.16.1883 Washington DC; D2.9.1915 Secaucus NJ; BR/TR/6´0˝/175; d4.27																									
1909	NY N	0	0	ø	1	0	0	0	1	3	2	0	1	0	1	0.00	ø	.429	.500	0	ø	0	—	0	—	0.0
WALROND, LES	Leslie Dale; B11.7.1976 Muskogee OK; BL/TL/6´0˝/(190–205); [StLN98 13/378]; d6.8; Col Kansas																									
2003	KC A	0	2	.000	7	0	0	0-0	8	11	9	2	0	7-1	6	10.13	48	.324	.439	0	ø	0	—	-4	0	-0.7
2006	Chi N	0	1	.000	10	2	0	0-0	17.1	19	13	2	0	12-1	21	6.23	74	.271	.373	2-0-1	.000	-0	80	-3	0	-0.1
Total	2	0	3	.000	17	2	0	0-0	25.1	30	22	4	0	19-2	27	7.46	62	.288	.395	2-0-1	.000	-0	80	-7	0	-0.8
WALSH, AUGIE	August Sothley; B8.17.1904 Wilmington DE; D11.12.1985 San Rafael CA; BR/TR/6´0˝/175; d10.2																									
1927	Phi N	0	1	.000	1	1	1	0	10	12	5	3	0	5	0	4.50	92	.333	.415	4	.250	-0	82	0	—	0.0
1928	Phi N	4	9	.308	38	11	2	2	122.1	160	92	13	5	40	38	6.18	69	.321	.378	39-1-1	.256	2*	83	-23	—	-2.0
Total	2	4	10	.286	39	12	3	2	132.1	172	97	16	5	45	38	6.05	70	.322	.380	43-1-1	.256	2	83	-23	—	-2.0
WALSH, CONNIE	Cornelius Robert; B4.23.1882 St.Louis MO; D4.5.1953 St.Louis MO; TR; d9.16																									
1907	Pit N	0	0	ø	1	0	0	0	1	1	1	0	0	1	0	9.00	27	.250	.400	0	ø	0	—	-1	—	0.0
WALSH, DAVE	David Peter; B9.25.1960 Arlington MA; BL/TL/6´1˝/185; [TorA82 9/212]; d8.13; Col California–Santa Barbara																									
1990	LA N	1	0	1.000	20	0	0	1-1	16.1	15	12	1	0	6-1	15	3.86	96	.242	.304	0	ø	0	—	-2	0	-0.1
WALSH, ED	Edward Arthur; B2.11.1905 Meriden CT; D10.31.1937 Meriden CT; BR/TR/6´1˝/180; d7.4; f–Ed; Col Notre Dame																									
1928	Chi A	4	7	.364	14	10	3	0	78	86	45	2	5	42	32	4.96	82	.290	.387	27-0-1	.111	-2	86	-5	—	-0.8
1929	Chi A	6	11	.353	24	20	7	0	129	156	94	9	4	64	31	5.65	76	.312	.394	43-0-1	.233	2*	81	-19	—	-1.8
1930	Chi A	1	4	.200	37	4	0	0	103.2	131	67	8	4	30	37	5.38	86	.316	.367	34-0-1	.265	1*	93	-5	—	-0.1
1932	Chi A	0	2	.000	4	4	1	0	20.1	26	22	3	0	13	7	8.41	51	.299	.390	7	.286	0	98	-9	—	-0.7
Total	4	11	24	.314	79	38	11	0	331	399	228	22	13	149	107	5.57	78	.307	.384	111-0-3	.216	1	84	-38	—	-3.4
WALSH, ED	Edward Augustine "Big Ed"; B5.14.1881 Plains PA; D5.26.1959 Pompano Beach FL; BR/TR/6´1˝/193; d5.7; M1/C6/U1; HF1946; s–Ed; Col Fordham																									
1904	Chi A	6	3	.667	18	8	6-1	1	110.2	90	45	1	3	32	57	2.60	94	.223	.285	41-1-1	.220	3	120	-2	—	0.1
1905	Chi A	8	3	.727	22	13	9-1	0	136.2	121	53	0	3	29	71	2.17	113	.239	.284	58-0-1	.155	-0*	121	3	—	0.2
1906	†Chi A	17	13	.567	41	31	24-**10**	2	278.1	215	83	1	7	58	171	1.88	135	.217	.265	99-0-3	.141	-2*	90	21	—	2.6
1907	Chi A	24	18	.571	**56**	**46**	**37**-5	**4**	**422.1**	341	120	3	8	87	206	**1.60**	**150**	.223	.269	154-1-1	.162	-1*	100	**33**	—	**4.6**
1908	Chi A	**40**	15	**.727**	**66**	**49**	**42-11**	**6**	**464**	343	111	2	9	56	**269**	1.42	163	.203	.232	157-1-8	.172	2	98	**43**	—	**6.8**
1909	Chi A	15	11	.577	31	28	20-**8**	2	230.1	166	52	0	4	50	127	1.41	166	.203	**.253**	84-0-1	.214	4*	111	**25**	—	**4.1**
1910	Chi A	18	20	.474	**45**	36	33-7	**5**	369.2	242	87	5	4	61	258	**1.27**	**189**	**.187**	**.226**	138-0-5	.217	4*	71	45	—	**6.3**
1911	Chi A	27	18	.600	**56**	37	33-5	**4**	**368.2**	327	125	4	7	72	**255**	2.22	145	.239	**.280**	155-0-3	.219	-1*	117	42	—	5.5
1912	Chi A	27	17	.614	**62**	**41**	32-6	**10**	**393**	332	125	6	1	94	254	2.15	149	.231	.279	136-0-4	.243	6	94	49	—	6.5
1913	Chi A	8	3	.727	16	14	7-1	1	97.2	91	37	1	4	39	34	2.58	113	.245	.324	32-0-1	.156	-1*	96	5	—	0.5
1914	Chi A	2	3	.400	8	5	3-1	0	44.2	33	19	0	1	20	15	2.82	95	.212	.305	16-0-1	.063	-1*	60	0	—	-0.1
1915	Chi A	3	0	1.000	3	3	3-1	0	27	19	4	0	0	7	12	1.33	223	.202	.257	11-0-1	.364	1*	147	5	—	0.7
1916	Chi A	0	1	.000	2	1	0	0	3.1	4	3	0	0	3	3	2.70	102	.286	.412	0	ø	0	55	-1	—	-0.1
1917	Bos N	0	1	.000	4	3	1	0	18	22	9	0	1	9	4	3.50	73	.314	.400	4	.250	1	108	-2	—	0.0
Total	14	195	126	.607	430	315	250-57	35	2964.1	2346	873	23	52	617	1736	1.82	145	.218	.264	1085-3-30	.194	15	99	266	—	37.7
WALSH, JUNIOR	James Gerald; B3.7.1919 Newark NJ; D11.12.1990 Olyphant PA; BR/TR/5´11˝/185; d9.14																									
1946	Pit N	0	1	.000	4	2	0	0	10.1	9	6	0	1	10	2	5.23	67	.237	.408	4	.000	-1	182	-1	0	-0.2
1948	Pit N	1	0	1.000	2	0	0	0	4.1	4	5	1	0	5	0	10.38	39	.235	.409	2	.000	-0	—	-3	0	-0.5
1949	Pit N	1	4	.200	9	7	1-1	0	42.2	40	27	5	0	16	24	5.06	83	.244	.311	12	.000	-1	60	-4	0	-0.6
1950	Pit N	1	1	.500	38	2	0	2	62.1	56	36	6	1	34	33	5.05	87	.246	.346	6	.167	1	201	-3	0	0.0
1951	Pit N	1	4	.200	36	1	0	0	73.1	92	66	9	1	46	32	6.87	61	.304	.397	7	.143	0	21	-21	0	-1.2
Total	5	4	10	.286	89	12	1-1	2	193	201	140	21	3	111	91	5.88	72	.268	.365	31	.065	-1	97	-32	0	-2.5
WALSH, JIM	James Thomas; B7.10.1894 Roxbury MA; D5.13.1967 Boston MA; BL/TL/5´11˝/175; d8.25																									
1921	Det A	0	0	ø	3	0	0	0	4	2	1	0	0	1	3	2.25	190	.125	.176	0	ø	0	—	1	—	0.0

YEAR	TM LG	W	L	PCT	G	GS	CG-SHO	SV-BS	IP	H	R	HR	HB	BB-IB	SO	ERA	AERA	OAV	OOB	AB-HR-SH	AVG	PB	SUP	APR	DL	PW
WALTER, GENE	Gene Winston; B11.22.1960 Chicago IL; BL/TL/6´4˝/(200–201); [SDN82 29/720]; d8.9; Col Eastern Kentucky; [DL 1989 Sea A 182]																									
1985	SD N	0	2	.000	15	0	0	3-0	22	12	6	0	0	8-1	18	2.05	174	.158	.235	1	.000	0	—	4	0	0.4
1986	SD N	2	2	.500	57	0	0	1-1	98	89	47	7	4	49-7	84	3.86	95	.247	.341	10-0-2	.200	1	—	-2	0	0.0
1987	NY N	1	2	.333	21	0	0	0-2	19.2	18	10	1	1	13-3	11	3.20	120	.243	.360	1-0-1	.000	0	—	0	0	0.1
1988	NY N	0	1	.000	19	0	0	0-0	16.2	21	9	0	0	11-1	14	3.78	86	.309	.400	0	ø	0	—	-1	0	-0.1
	Sea A	1	0	1.000	16	0	0	0-0	26.1	21	16	0	2	15-4	13	5.13	82	.216	.330	0	ø	0	—	-2	0	-0.1
Total	4	4	7	.364	128	0	0	4-3	182.2	161	88	8	7	96-16	140	3.74	99	.238	.336	12-0-3	.167	1	—	-1	182	0.3
WALTER, BERNIE	James Bernard; B8.15.1908 Dover TN; D10.30.1988 Nashville TN; BR/TR/6´1˝/175; d8.16; Col Tennessee																									
1930	Pit N	0	0	ø	1	0	0	0	1	0	0	0	0	0	1	0.00	ø	.000	.000	0	ø	0	—	1	—	0.0
WALTERS, CHARLIE	Charles Leonard; B2.21.1947 Minneapolis MN; BR/TR/6´4˝/190; d4.11																									
1969	Min A	0	0	ø	6	0	0	0-0	6.2	6	4	1	1	3-0	2	5.40	67	.240	.345	0	ø	0	—	-1	0	-0.1
WALTERS, MIKE	Michael Charles; B10.18.1957 St.Louis MO; BR/TR/6´5˝/(195–203); [AnaA77 S1/20]; d7.8; Col Chaffey (CA) JC																									
1983	Min A	1	1	.500	23	0	0	2-0	59	52	31	4	2	20-4	21	4.12	104	.243	.311	0	ø	0	—	0	0	0.0
1984	Min A	0	3	.000	23	0	0	2-2	29	31	14	1	1	14-4	10	3.72	114	.287	.368	0	ø	0	—	1	0	0.1
Total	2	1	4	.200	46	0	0	4-2	88	83	45	5	3	34-8	31	3.99	107	.258	.331	0	ø	0	—	1	0	0.1
WALTERS, BUCKY	William Henry; B4.19.1909 Philadelphia PA; D4.20.1991 Abington PA; BR/TR/6´1˝/180; d9.18.1931; M2/C8; ▲																									
1934	Phi N	0	0	ø	2	1	0	0	7	8	3	1	1	2	7	1.29	367	.296	.367	300-4-3	.260	0*	73	2	—	0.1
1935	Phi N	9	9	.500	24	22	8-2	0	151	168	86	9	7	68	40	4.17	109	.289	.370	96-0-2	.250	1*	85	5	—	0.8
1936	Phi N	11	21	.344	40	33	15-**4**	0	258	284	146	11	5	115	66	4.26	107	.277	.353	121-1-3	.240	2*	79	9	—	1.9
1937	Phi N★	14	15	.483	37	**34**	15-3	0	246.1	292	148	14	3	86	87	4.75	91	.295	.353	137-1-2	.277	4*	101	-11	—	-0.4
1938	Phi N	4	8	.333	12	12	9-1	0	82.2	91	53	8	3	42	28	5.23	74	.276	.363	35-1-0	.286	3*	102	-11	—	-1.0
	Cin N	11	6	.647	27	22	11-2	1	168.1	168	81	5	2	66	65	3.69	99	.255	.324	64-0-2	.141	-0*	136	-1	—	0.0
	Year	15	14	.517	39	34	20-3	1	251	259	134	13	5	108	93	4.20	89	.262	.337	99-1-2	.192	3	124	-11	—	-1.0
1939	†Cin N☆	**27**	11	.711	39	**36**	**31**-2	0	**319**	250	98	15	6	109	**137**	**2.29**	**168**	**.220**	.291	120-1-5	.325	13*	110	**54**	—	**8.2**
1940	†Cin N★	**22**	10	.688	36	36	**29**-3	0	**305**	241	95	19	5	92	115	**2.48**	**153**	**.220**	.283	117-1-6	.205	2*	117	**44**	—	4.7
1941	Cin N★	19	15	.559	37	35	**27**-5	2	**302**	292	108	10	2	88	129	2.83	127	.255	.309	106-0-4	.189	2*	88	27	0	3.3
1942	Cin N★	15	14	.517	34	32	21-2	0	253.2	223	101	8	5	73	109	2.66	123	.231	.289	99-2-2	.242	6*	97	14	0	2.5
1943	Cin N	15	15	.500	34	34	21-5	0	246.1	244	105	8	1	109	80	3.54	94	.264	.342	90-1-5	.267	8*	88	-5	0	0.3
1944	Cin N★	**23**	8	.742	34	32	27-6	1	285	233	92	10	4	87	77	2.40	145	**.219**	.281	107-0-5	.280	8*	97	**34**	0	**4.7**
1945	Cin N	10	10	.500	22	22	12-3	0	168	166	62	6	2	51	45	2.68	140	.259	.316	61-3-3	.230	5*	69	18	0	2.6
1946	Cin N	10	7	.588	22	22	10-2	0	151.1	146	55	9	2	64	60	2.56	131	.258	.336	55-0-4	.127	-1*	111	12	0	1.3
1947	Cin N	8	8	.500	20	20	5-2	0	122	137	83	15	3	49	43	5.75	71	.278	.347	45-0-2	.267	3	109	-20	0	-2.0
1948	Cin N	0	3	.000	7	5	1	0	35	42	25	6	0	18	19	4.63	84	.316	.397	15	.267	0	113	-5	60	-0.3
1950	Bos N	0	0	ø	1	0	0	0	4	5	2	0	0	2	0	4.50	86	.313	.389	2	.000	-0	—	0	0	0.0
Total	16	198	160	.553	428	398	242-42	4	3104.2	2990	1343	154	51	1121	1107	3.30	115	.253	.321	1570-15-48	.246	57	99	166	60	26.7
WALTON, BRUCE	Bruce Kenneth; B12.25.1962 Bakersfield CA; BR/TR/6´2˝/195; [OakA85 16/403]; d5.11; C5; Col Hawaii–Manoa																									
1991	Oak A	1	0	1.000	12	0	0	0-1	13	11	9	3	1	6-0	10	6.23	62	.229	.321	0	ø	0	—	-3	0	-0.2
1992	Oak A	0	0	ø	7	0	0	0-0	10	17	11	1	0	3-0	7	9.90	38	.378	.408	0	ø	0	—	-6	0	-0.3
1993	Mon N	0	0	ø	4	0	0	0-0	5.2	11	6	1	0	3-0	0	9.53	44	.407	.467	1	.000	-0	—	-3	0	-0.1
1994	Col N	1	0	1.000	4	0	0	0-0	5.1	6	5	1	0	3-1	1	8.44	59	.273	.360	0	ø	0	—	-2	0	-0.3
Total	4	2	0	1.000	27	0	0	0-1	34	45	31	6	1	15-1	18	8.21	49	.317	.381	1	.000	-0	—	-14	0	-0.9
WANG, CHIEN-MING	Chien-Ming; B3.31.1980 Tainan City, Taiwan; BR/TR/6´3˝/200; d4.30; Col Taipei College of PE																									
2005	†NY A	8	5	.615	18	17	0	0-0	116.1	113	58	9	6	32-3	47	4.02	107	.256	.313	1	.000	-0	94	3	59	0.5
2006	†NY A	**19**	6	.760	34	33	2-1	1-0	218	233	92	12	2	52-4	76	3.63	125	.277	.320	4	.000	-0	116	23	0	2.5
Total	2	27	11	.711	52	50	2-1	1-0	334.1	346	150	21	8	84-7	123	3.77	118	.270	.317	5	.000	-0	108	26	59	3.0
WANTZ, DICK	Richard Carter; B4.11.1940 South Gate CA; D5.13.1965 Inglewood CA; BR/TR/6´5˝/175; d4.13; Col Cal St.–Los Angeles																									
1965	Cal A	0	0	ø	1	0	0	0	1	3	2	0	0	0-0	2	18.00	19	.500	.500	0	ø	0	—	-2	0	-0.1
WAPNICK, STEVE	Steven Lee; B9.25.1965 Los Angeles CA; BR/TR/6´2˝/200; [TorA87 30/777]; d4.14; Col Cal St.–Fresno																									
1990	Det A	0	0	ø	4	0	0	0-0	7	8	5	0	0	10-0	6	6.43	62	.296	.486	0	ø	0	—	-2	0	-0.1
1991	Chi A	0	1	.000	6	0	0	0-0	5	2	1	0	0	4-0	1	1.80	222	.111	.273	0	ø	0	—	1	0	0.2
Total	2	0	1	.000	10	0	0	0-0	12	10	6	0	0	14-0	7	4.50	89	.222	.407	0	ø	0	—	-1	0	0.1
WARD, BRYAN	Bryan Matthew; B1.28.1972 Bristol PA; BL/TL/6´2˝/(205–210); [FlaN93 20/575]; d7.3; Col South Carolina–Aiken																									
1998	Chi A	1	2	.333	28	0	0	1-3	27	30	13	4	0	7-0	17	3.33	137	.278	.319	0	ø	0	—	3	0	0.3
1999	Chi A	0	1	.000	40	0	0	0-0	39.1	63	36	10	0	11-1	35	7.55	65	.368	.404	0	ø	0	—	-11	0	-0.5
2000	Phi N	0	0	ø	20	0	0	0-0	19.1	14	5	2	0	8-0	11	2.33	197	.206	.282	0	ø	0	—	5	0	0.2
	Ana A	0	0	ø	7	0	0	0-0	8	8	6	1	0	2-0	3	5.63	92	.235	.278	0	ø	0	—	-1	0	0.0
Total	3	1	3	.250	95	0	0	1-3	93.2	115	60	17	0	28-1	66	5.09	94	.302	.346	0	ø	0	—	-4	0	0.0
WARD, COLIN	Colin Norval; B11.22.1960 Los Angeles CA; BL/TL/6´3˝/190; [DetA82 3/74]; d9.21; Col UCLA																									
1985	SF N	0	0	ø	6	2	0	0-0	12.1	10	6	0	0	7-0	8	4.38	79	.233	.333	2	.000	-0	115	-1	0	-0.1
WARD, JOHNNY	John; B East St.Louis IL; d9.19																									
1885	Pro N	0	1	.000	1	1	1	0	8	10	7	0	—	1	3	4.50	60	.286	.306	3	.000	-0	0	-2	—	-0.2
WARD, JOHN	John Montgomery; B3.3.1860 Bellefonte PA; D3.4.1925 Augusta GA; BL/TR (TL 1884p, BB 1888)/5´9˝/165; d7.15; M7; HF1964; Col Penn St.; ▲																									
1878	Pro N	22	13	.629	37	37	37-6	0	334	308	151	3	—	34	116	**1.51**	**146**	.231	.251	138-1	.196	2	95	22	—	**2.2**
1879	Pro N	**47**	19	**.712**	70	60	58-2	**1**	587	571	270	5	—	36	**239**	2.15	110	.239	.250	364-2	.286	17*	144	13	—	2.7
1880	Pro N	39	24	.619	70	67	59-**8**	1	595	501	230	5	—	45	230	1.74	127	.217	.232	356	.228	1*	108	35	—	3.5
1881	Pro N	18	18	.500	39	35	32-3	0	330	326	183	2	—	53	119	2.13	125	.242	.271	357	.244	3*	94	16	—	1.9
1882	Pro N	19	13	.594	34	33	30-4	**1**	286	268	143	6	—	36	72	2.55	111	.232	.255	355-1	.245	1*	95	11	—	1.2
1883	NY N	16	13	.552	34	25	24-1	0	277	278	165	3	—	31	121	2.70	115	.246	.267	380-7	.255	6*	97	13	—	1.7
1884	NY N	3	3	.500	9	5	5	0	60.2	72	43	2	—	18	23	3.41	87	.280	.327	482-2	.253	1*	160	-4	—	-0.2
Total	7	164	103	.614	293	262	245-24	3	2469.2	2324	1185	26	—	253	920	2.10	118	.234	.254	2432-13	.249	31	111	106	—	13.0
WARD, DICK	Richard Ole; B5.21.1909 Herrick SD; D5.30.1966 Freeland WA; BR/TR/6´1˝/198; d5.3; Col St. Martins																									
1934	Chi N	0	0	ø	3	0	0	0	6	9	6	0	0	2	1	3.00	129	.375	.423	1	.000	-0	—	-1	—	-0.1
1935	StL N	0	0	ø	1	0	0	0	0	0	1	0	0	1	0	(0)	ø	ø	1.000	0	ø	0	—	0	—	0.0
Total	2	0	0	ø	4	0	0	0	6	9	7	0	0	3	1	3.00	129	.375	.444	1	.000	-0	—	-1	—	-0.1
WARD, COLBY	Robert Colby; B1.2.1964 Lansing MI; BR/TR/6´2˝/185; [CalA86 11/285]; d7.27; Col Brigham Young																									
1990	Cle A	1	3	.250	22	0	0	1-1	36	31	17	3	1	21-4	23	4.25	93	.238	.344	0	ø	0	—	-1	0	-0.1
WARD, DUANE	Roy Duane; B5.28.1964 Park View NM; BR/TR/6´4˝/(205–225); [AtlN82 1/9]; d4.12; [DL 1994 Tor A 131]																									
1986	Atl N	0	1	.000	10	0	0	0-0	16	22	13	2	0	8-0	8	7.31	54	.349	.423	1	.000	-0	—	-5	0	-0.3
	Tor A	0	1	.000	2	1	0	0-0	2	3	4	0	1	4-0	1	13.50	31	.300	.533	0	ø	0	64	-2	0	-0.4
1987	Tor A	1	0	1.000	12	1	0	0-0	11.2	14	9	0	0	12-2	10	6.94	65	.326	.464	0	ø	0	201	-3	0	-0.2
1988	Tor A	9	3	.750	64	0	0	15-3	111.2	101	46	5	5	60-8	91	3.30	120	.245	.344	0	ø	0	—	8	0	1.0
1989	†Tor A	4	10	.286	66	0	0	15-12	114.2	94	55	4	5	58-11	122	3.77	101	.230	.326	0	ø	0	—	0	0	0.0
1990	Tor A	2	8	.200	73	0	0	11-7	127.2	101	51	9	1	42-10	112	3.45	115	.221	.287	0	ø	0	—	8	0	0.7
1991	†Tor A	7	6	.538	**81**	0	0	23-4	107.1	80	36	3	2	33-3	132	2.77	153	.207	.271	0	ø	0	—	17	0	2.5
1992	†Tor A	7	4	.636	79	0	0	12-4	101.1	76	27	5	1	39-3	103	1.95	210	.207	.282	0	ø	0	—	**22**	0	2.7
1993	†Tor A★	2	3	.400	71	0	0	**45**-6	71.2	49	17	4	1	25-2	97	2.13	205	.193	.266	0	ø	0	—	18	0	3.1
1995	Tor A	0	1	.000	4	0	0	0-0	2.2	11	10	0	1	5-0	3	27.00	18	.579	.680	0	ø	0	—	-7	122	-1.1
Total	9	32	37	.464	462	2	0	121-36	666.2	551	268	32	17	286-39	679	3.28	124	.228	.310	1	.000	-0	146	56	253	8.0
WARDEN, JON	Jonathan Edgar "Warbler"; B10.1.1946 Columbus OH; BB/TL/6´0˝/205; [DetA66*4/62]; d4.11																									
1968	Det A	4	1	.800	28	0	0	3	37.1	30	15	5	0	15-2	25	3.62	83	.217	.294	2	.000	-0	—	-2	0	-0.4

YEAR	TM LG	W	L	PCT	G	GS	CG-SHO	SV-BS	IP	H	R	HR	HB	BB-IB	SO	ERA	AERA	OAV	OOB	AB-HR-SH	AVG	PB	SUP	APR	DL	PW
WARDLE, CURT	Curtis Ray; B11.16.1960 Downey CA; BL/TL/6´5˝/220; [MinA81 3/56]; d8.30; Col California–Riverside																									
1984	Min A	0	0	ø	2	0	0	0-0	4	3	2	2	0	0-0	5	4.50	94	.200	.200	0	ø	0	—	0	0	0.0
1985	Min A	1	3	.250	35	0	0	1-4	49	49	32	9	1	28-0	47	5.51	80	.266	.364	0	ø	0	—	-5	0	-0.3
	Cle A	7	6	.538	15	12	0	0-0	66	78	51	11	1	34-0	37	6.68	62	.297	.373	0	ø	0	135	-17	0	-2.7
	Year	8	9	.471	50	12	0	1-4	115	127	83	20	2	62-0	84	6.18	69	.284	.369	0	ø	0	131	-22	0	-3.0
Total	2	8	9	.471	52	12	0	1-4	119	130	85	22	2	62-0	89	6.13	70	.281	.365	0	ø	0	131	-22	0	-3.0
WARE, JEFF	Jeffrey Allan; B11.11.1970 Norfolk VA; BR/TR/6´3˝/(190–195); [TorA91 1/35]; d9.2; Col Old Dominion																									
1995	Tor A	2	1	.667	5	5	0	0-0	26.1	28	18	2	1	21-0	18	5.47	87	.277	.407	0	ø	0	98	-2	0	-0.2
1996	Tor A	1	5	.167	13	4	0	0-0	32.2	35	34	6	2	31-1	11	9.09	55	.271	.420	0	ø	0	46	-14	0	-1.9
Total	2	3	6	.333	18	9	0	0-0	59	63	52	8	3	52-1	29	7.47	66	.274	.414	0	ø	0	74	-16	0	-2.1
WARHOP, JACK	John Milton "Chief","Crab" (b John Milton Wauhop); B7.4.1884 Hinton WV; D10.4.1960 Freeport IL; BR/TR/5´9.5˝/168; d9.19																									
1908	NY A	1	2	.333	5	4	3	0	36.1	40	19	0	4	8	11	4.46	56	.292	.349	16	.063	-1*	62	-5	—	-0.5
1909	NY A	13	15	.464	36	23	21-3	2	243.1	197	84	2	26	81	95	2.40	105	.233	.319	86-0-2	.128	-2	101	7	—	0.6
1910	NY A	14	14	.500	37	27	20	2	243	219	108	1	18	79	75	3.00	89	.246	.320	79-0-4	.177	-1	104	-8	—	-1.2
1911	NY A	12	13	.480	31	25	17-1	0	209.2	239	118	6	15	44	71	4.16	86	.286	.333	77-0-2	.156	-4*	85	-8	—	-1.3
1912	NY A	10	19	.345	39	22	16	3	258	256	121	3	16	59	110	2.86	126	.266	.319	92-0-2	.207	-1	64	17	—	1.6
1913	NY A	4	5	.444	15	7	1	0	62.1	69	42	1	12	33	11	3.75	80	.297	.412	23	.130	-0	113	-8	—	-1.1
1914	NY A	8	15	.348	37	23	15	0	216.2	182	75	8	11	44	56	2.37	117	.235	.286	71-0-2	.141	-1*	83	8	—	0.7
1915	NY A	7	9	.438	21	19	12	0	143.1	164	74	7	12	52	34	3.96	74	.309	.384	51	.137	-2	103	-14	—	-1.7
Total	8	69	92	.429	221	150	105-4	7	1412.2	1366	641	28	114	400	463	3.12	96	.262	.328	495-0-12	.156	-12	89	-11	—	-2.9
WARMOTH, CY	Wallace Walter; B2.2.1893 Bone Gap IL; D6.20.1957 Mt.Carmel IL; BL/TL/5´11˝/158; d8.31																									
1916	StL N	0	0	ø	3	0	0	0	5	12	10	0	1	4	1	14.40	18	.500	.586	2	.000	-0	—	-6	—	-0.4
1922	Was A	1	0	1.000	5	1	1	0	19	15	6	0	0	9	8	1.42	272	.205	.293	7	.143	-0	132	4	—	0.2
1923	Was A	7	5	.583	21	13	3	0	105	103	64	4	1	76	45	4.29	88	.261	.381	36-0-2	.222	2	112	-8	—	-0.5
Total	3	8	5	.615	29	14	4	0	129	130	80	4	2	89	54	4.26	88	.264	.379	45-0-2	.200	1	114	-10	—	-0.7
WARNEKE, LON	Lonnie "The Arkansas Hummingbird"; B3.28.1909 Mt.Ida AR; D6.23.1976 Hot Springs AR; BR/TR/6´2˝/185; d4,18; Mil 1944; U7																									
1930	Chi N	0	0	ø	1	0	0	0	1.1	2	5	0	0	5	0	33.75	14	.400	.700	0	ø	0	—	-4	—	-0.2
1931	Chi N	2	4	.333	20	7	3	0	64.1	67	33	1	3	37	27	3.22	120	.269	.370	19	.263	1	73	2	—	0.2
1932	†Chi N	**22**	6	**.786**	35	32	25-**4**	0	277	247	84	12	2	64	106	**2.37**	**159**	.237	.283	99-0-4	.192	-0	112	**45**	—	4.3
1933	Chi N★	18	13	.581	36	34	**26**-4	1	287.1	262	83	8	3	75	133	2.00	163	.244	.295	100-2-3	.300	10*	88	39	—	5.8
1934	Chi N★	22	10	.688	43	35	23-3	3	291.1	273	116	16	2	66	143	3.21	121	.244	.287	113-0-2	.195	-1*	115	23	—	2.2
1935	†Chi N	20	13	.606	42	30	20-1	4	261.2	257	102	19	3	50	120	3.06	128	.257	.294	91-0-7	.220	1*	111	27	—	3.3
1936	Chi N★	16	13	.552	40	29	13-**4**	1	240.1	246	108	10	4	76	113	3.45	116	.264	.322	84-1-10	.202	0	109	12	—	1.3
1937	StL N	18	11	.621	36	33	18-2	0	238.2	280	139	32	0	69	87	4.53	88	.287	.335	80-0-6	.262	4	114	-13	—	-1.0
1938	StL N	13	8	.619	31	26	12-4	0	197	199	102	14	2	64	89	3.97	100	.256	.314	71-0-3	.324	5	116	1	—	0.5
1939	StL N☆	13	7	.650	34	21	6-2	2	162	160	73	14	2	49	59	3.78	109	.259	.316	52-0-6	.192	1	126	8	—	1.0
1940	StL N	16	10	.615	33	31	17-1	0	232	235	103	17	3	47	85	3.14	127	.257	.296	86-1-7	.209	2	129	18	—	2.1
1941	StL N☆	17	9	.654	37	30	12-4	0	246	227	100	19	3	82	83	3.15	120	.249	.313	77-0-8	.117	-2	101	17	0	1.4
1942	StL N	6	4	.600	12	12	5	0	82	76	34	8	0	15	31	3.29	104	.238	.272	30-0-3	.333	3	155	2	0	0.5
	Chi N	5	7	.417	15	12	8-1	2	99	97	33	2	0	21	28	2.27	141	.259	.298	32-0-2	.188	-0	88	9	0	1.1
	Year	11	11	.500	27	24	13-1	2	181	173	67	10	0	36	59	2.73	121	.249	.286	62-0-5	.258	2	123	11	0	1.6
1943	Chi N	4	5	.444	21	10	4	0	88.1	82	40	3	0	18	30	3.16	106	.246	.285	26-0-1	.192	1	107	0	0	0.2
1945	Chi N	0	1	.000	9	1	0	0	14	16	9	0	0	1	6	3.86	95	.267	.279	2	.000	0	116	-1	0	-0.1
Total	15	192	121	.613	445	343	192-30	13	2782.1	2726	1164	175	27	739	1140	3.18	119	.255	.304	962-4-62	.223	27	112	185	0	22.6
WARNER, ED	Edward Emory; B6.20.1889 Fitchburg MA; D2.5.1954 New York NY; BR/TL/5´10.5˝/165; d7.2; Col Brown																									
1912	Pit N	1	1	.500	11	3	1-1	0	45	40	20	0	3	18	13	3.60	91	.242	.328	15	.133	-1	112	-1	—	-0.1
WARNER, JACK	Jack Dyer; B7.12.1940 Brandywine WV; BR/TR/5´11˝/195; d4.10																									
1962	Chi N	0	0	ø	7	0	0	0	7	9	7	3	0	0-0	3	7.71	54	.321	.321	0	ø	0	—	-3	0	-0.1
1963	Chi N	0	1	.000	8	0	0	0	22.2	21	7	1	0	8-2	7	2.78	126	.256	.319	4	.250	0	—	2	0	0.1
1964	Chi N	0	0	ø	7	0	0	0	9.1	12	3	0	0	4-0	6	2.89	128	.333	.390	0	ø	0	—	1	0	0.1
1965	Chi N	0	1	.000	11	0	0	0	15.2	22	16	1	0	9-1	7	8.62	43	.355	.431	1	.000	-0	—	-8	0	-0.5
Total	4	0	2	.000	33	0	0	0	54.2	64	33	5	0	21-3	23	5.10	72	.308	.366	5	.200	0	—	-8	0	-0.4
WARREN, MIKE	Michael Bruce; B3.26.1961 Inglewood CA; BR/TR/6´1˝/175; [DetA79 12/299]; d6.12																									
1983	Oak A	5	3	.625	12	9	3-1	0-0	65.2	51	33	4	1	18-1	30	4.11	95	.215	.269	0	ø	0	109	-2	0	-0.2
1984	Oak A	3	6	.333	24	12	0	0-0	90	104	52	11	3	44-1	61	4.90	77	.291	.370	0	ø	0	104	-11	0	-1.0
1985	Oak A	1	4	.200	16	6	0	0-0	49	52	42	13	4	38-0	48	6.61	59	.261	.387	0	ø	0	98	-17	0	-1.5
Total	3	9	13	.409	52	27	3-1	0-0	204.2	207	127	28	8	100-2	139	5.06	76	.261	.346	0	ø	0	104	-30	0	-2.7
WARREN, TOMMY	Thomas Gentry; B7.5.1917 Tulsa OK; D1.2.1968 Tulsa OK; BB/TL/6´1˝/190; d4.18																									
1944	Bro N	1	4	.200	22	4	2	0	68.2	74	52	4	0	40	18	4.98	71	.270	.363	43	.256	2*	100	-14	0	-0.8
WARTHEN, DAN	Daniel Dean; B12.1.1952 Omaha NE; BB/TL/6´0˝/(190–205); [MonN71 2/28]; d5.18; C8																									
1975	Mon N	8	6	.571	40	18	2	3-0	167.2	130	62	8	1	87-4	128	3.11	124	.217	.315	51-0-4	.118	-2	85	15	0	1.0
1976	Mon N	2	10	.167	23	16	2-1	0-0	90	76	59	8	2	66-2	67	5.30	71	.232	.361	27-0-1	.000	-3	82	-14	0	-2.0
1977	Mon N	2	3	.400	12	6	1	0-0	35	33	34	7	0	38-1	26	7.97	48	.262	.430	9-0-1	.111	-0	146	-16	0	-1.9
	Phi N	0	1	.000	3	0	0	0-0	3.2	4	3	0	0	5-0	1	0.00	ø	.267	.450	0	ø	0	—	0	0	0.1
	Year	2	4	.333	15	6	1	0-0	38.2	37	37	7	0	43-1	27	7.22	54	.262	.432	9-0-1	.111	-0	145	-16	0	-1.8
1978	Hou N	0	1	.000	5	1	0	0-1	10.2	10	5	3	0	2-0	2	4.22	79	.250	.279	2	.000	-0	27	-1	0	-0.1
Total	4	12	21	.364	83	41	5-1	3-1	307	253	163	26	3	198-7	224	4.31	89	.228	.344	89-0-6	.079	-6	91	-16	0	-2.9
WASDIN, JOHN	John Truman; B8.5.1972 Fort Belvoir VA; BR/TR/6´2˝/(190–196); [OakA93 1/25]; d8.24; Col Florida St.																									
1995	Oak A	1	1	.500	5	2	0	0-0	17.1	14	9	4	1	3-0	6	4.67	97	.215	.261	0	ø	0	93	0	0	0.0
1996	Oak A	8	7	.533	25	21	1	0-1	131.1	145	96	24	4	50-5	75	5.96	83	.283	.348	0	ø	0	104	-16	0	-1.5
1997	Bos A	4	6	.400	53	7	0	0-2	124.2	121	68	18	3	38-4	84	4.40	106	.251	.306	0	ø	0	82	3	0	0.1
1998	†Bos A	6	4	.600	47	8	0	0-1	96	111	57	14	2	27-8	59	5.25	90	.288	.333	0	ø	0	96	-4	0	-0.3
1999	†Bos A	8	3	.727	45	0	0	2-3	74.1	66	38	14	0	18-0	57	4.12	121	.236	.280	0	ø	0	—	7	19	0.9
2000	Bos A	1	3	.250	25	1	0	1-1	44.2	48	25	8	2	15-1	36	5.04	100	.273	.328	0	ø	0	75	1	0	0.0
	Col N	0	3	.000	14	3	1	0-0	35.2	42	23	6	3	9-2	35	5.80	100	.302	.353	8-0-1	.250	-0	37	1	0	0.0
2001	Col N	2	1	.667	18	0	0	0-3	24.1	32	19	7	1	8-2	17	7.03	76	.320	.373	3	.333	0	—	-3	0	-0.3
	Bal A	1	1	.500	26	0	0	0-2	49.2	54	25	4	5	16-4	47	4.17	103	.277	.341	0	ø	0	—	1	0	0.0
2003	Tor A	0	1	.000	3	2	0	0-0	5	16	13	2	0	4-0	5	23.40	20	.533	.571	0	ø	0	87	-9	0	-1.3
2004	Tex A	2	4	.333	15	10	0	0-0	65	83	52	18	3	23-2	36	6.78	73	.305	.363	3	.000	-0	116	-12	0	-1.0
2005	Tex A	3	2	.600	31	6	0	4-2	75.2	77	37	9	1	20-2	44	4.28	106	.261	.308	1	.000	-0	108	3	0	0.1
2006	Tex A	2	2	.500	9	5	0	0-0	30	33	19	6	4	13-0	16	5.10	92	.266	.355	0	ø	0	129	-2	19	-0.2
Total	11	38	38	.500	316	65	2	7-15	773.2	842	481	134	29	244-30	517	5.26	92	.276	.331	15-0-1	.200	0	100	-30	38	-3.5
WASHBURN, GEORGE	George Edward; B10.6.1914 Solon ME; D1.5.1979 Baton Rouge LA; BL/TR/6´1˝/175; d5.4																									
1941	NY A	0	1	.000	1	1	0	0	2	2	4	0	0	5	1	13.50	29	.286	.583	1	.000	-0	22	-2	0	-0.4
WASHBURN, GREG	Gregory James; B12.3.1946 Coal City IL; BR/TR/6´0˝/190; [CalA67 S1/19]; d6.7; Col Lewis																									
1969	Cal A	0	2	.000	8	2	0	0-0	11.1	21	11	0	1	5-0	4	7.94	44	.404	.458	0	ø	0	38	-6	0	-0.9
WASHBURN, JARROD	Jarrod Michael; B8.13.1974 LaCrosse WI; BL/TL/6´1˝/(187–200); [CalA95 2/31]; d6.2; Col Wisconsin–Oshkosh																									
1998	Ana A	6	3	.667	15	11	0	0-0	74	70	40	11	3	27-1	48	4.62	103	.248	.317	1-0-2	.000	-0	146	2	0	0.1
1999	Ana A	4	5	.444	16	10	0	0-0	61.2	61	36	6	1	26-0	39	5.25	93	.261	.335	0	ø	0	57	-1	0	-0.2
2000	Ana A	7	2	.778	14	14	0	0-0	84.1	64	38	16	1	37-0	49	3.74	138	.215	.301	3-0-2	.333	1	105	13	74	1.2
2001	Ana A	11	10	.524	30	30	1	0-0	193.1	196	89	25	7	54-4	126	3.77	123	.263	.318	5	.600	1	96	18	15	1.9
2002	†Ana A	18	6	.750	32	32	1	0-0	206	183	75	19	3	59-1	139	3.15	143	.235	.289	5	.200	0	95	32	0	3.3
2003	Ana A	10	15	.400	32	32	2	0-0	207.1	205	106	34	11	54-4	118	4.43	99	.256	.310	5	.200	0	88	1	0	0.0

YEAR	TM LG	W	L	PCT	G	GS	CG-SHO	SV-BS	IP	H	R	HR	HB	BB-IB	SO	ERA	AERA	OAV	OOB	AB-HR-SH	AVG	PB	SUP	APR	DL	PW
2004	†Ana A	11	8	.579	25	25	1-1	0-0	149.1	159	81	20	4	40-1	86	4.64	96	.269	.318	5-0-2	.400	1	134	-3	43	-0.2
2005	†LA A	8	8	.500	29	29	1-1	0-0	177.1	184	66	19	8	51-0	94	3.20	134	.274	.330	4	.000	-0	88	22	18	1.7
2006	Sea A	8	14	.364	31	31	0	0-0	187	198	103	25	7	55-2	103	4.67	94	.268	.323	2-0-1	.000	0	95	-5	0	-0.5
Total	9	83	71	.539	224	214	6-2	0-0	1340.1	1320	634	175	45	403-13	802	4.04	112	.257	.314	30-0-7	.267	3	99	79	150	7.3
Washburn, Libe	Libeus; B6.16.1874 Lyme NH; D3.22.1940 Malone NY; BB/TL/5´10˝/180; d5.30.1902; Col Brown; ▲																									
1903	Phi N	0	4	.000	4	4	4	0	35	44	23	0	0	11	9	4.37	75	.326	.377	18	.167	-0*	62	-4	—	-0.4
Washburn, Ray	Ray Clark; B5.31.1938 Pasco WA; BR/TR/6´1˝/(195–200); d9.20; Col Whitworth																									
1961	StL N	1	1	.500	3	2	1	0	20.1	10	4	1	1	7-0	12	1.77	248	.152	.243	8	.125	-1	131	6	0	0.5
1962	StL N	12	9	.571	34	25	2-1	0	175.2	187	90	25	3	58-2	109	4.10	104	.273	.331	56-0-4	.179	1	102	4	0	0.5
1963	StL N	5	3	.625	11	11	4-2	0	64.1	50	25	5	1	14-0	47	3.08	115	.212	.259	19-0-4	.053	-1	93	3	0	0.3
1964	StL N	3	4	.429	15	10	0	2	60	60	29	7	5	17-2	28	4.05	94	.264	.325	15-0-3	.133	-0	67	0	41	0.0
1965	StL N	9	11	.450	28	16	1-1	2	119.1	114	57	15	1	28-7	67	3.62	106	.254	.298	33-0-3	.152	0	77	1	0	0.1
1966	StL N	11	9	.550	27	26	4-1	0	170	183	75	15	1	44-5	98	3.76	95	.280	.324	54-1-4	.093	-1	100	-1	0	-0.2
1967	†StL N	10	7	.588	27	27	3-1	0	186.1	190	78	14	4	42-7	98	3.53	93	.265	.307	66-0-4	.091	-2	106	-3	22	-0.4
1968	†StL N	14	8	.636	31	30	8-4	0	215.1	191	67	9	1	47-7	124	2.26	128	.239	.282	60-0-11	.083	0	118	14	0	1.4
1969	StL N	3	8	.273	28	16	2	1-0	132.1	133	59	9	1	49-9	80	3.06	117	.261	.324	37-0-1	.081	-2	80	4	0	0.1
1970	†Cin N	4	4	.500	35	3	0	0-0	66.1	90	61	7	0	48-9	37	6.92	58	.324	.421	13-0-1	.000	-1	81	-22	0	-2.4
Total	10	72	64	.529	239	166	25-10	5-0	1210	1208	545	107	18	354-48	700	3.53	101	.261	.315	361-1-35	.105	-7	97	6	63	-0.1
Washer, Buck	William; B10.11.1882 Akron OH; D12.8.1955 Akron OH; BR/TR/5´10˝/175; d4.25; Col West Virginia																									
1905	Phi N	0	0	ø	1	0	0	0	3	4	2	0	0	5	0	6.00	49	.333	.529	1	.000	-0	—	-1	—	-0.1
Waslewski, Gary	Gary Lee; B7.21.1941 Meriden CT; BR/TR/6´4˝/(190–195); d6.11; Col Connecticut																									
1967	†Bos A	2	2	.500	12	8	0	0	42	34	18	3	1	20-2	20	3.21	108	.225	.314	11-0-1	.091	-1	94	1	0	0.0
1968	Bos A	4	7	.364	34	11	2	2	105.1	108	50	9	6	40-9	59	3.67	86	.269	.341	26-0-2	.038	-2*	83	-6	0	-0.8
1969	StL N	0	2	.000	12	0	0	1-0	20.2	19	9	3	1	8-4	16	3.92	91	.244	.318	1	.000	-0	—	0	0	0.0
	Mon N	3	7	.300	30	14	3-1	1-0	109.1	102	53	5	8	63-5	63	3.29	112	.252	.362	30	.033	-2	67	2	0	0.0
	Year	3	9	.250	42	14	3-1	2-0	130	121	62	8	9	71-9	79	3.39	108	.251	.355	31	.032	-2	67	1	0	0.0
1970	Mon N	0	2	.000	6	4	0	0-1	24.2	23	14	3	0	15-4	19	5.11	81	.247	.352	6-0-1	.000	-0	59	-2	0	-0.1
	NY A	2	2	.500	26	5	0	0-0	55	42	20	4	4	27-4	27	3.11	115	.219	.323	10-0-1	.100	-1	70	4	0	0.2
1971	NY A	0	1	.000	24	0	0	1-0	35.2	28	15	2	1	16-2	17	3.28	100	.214	.302	1	.000	-0	—	0	57	0.0
1972	Oak A	0	3	.000	8	0	0	0-0	17.2	12	5	3	0	8-1	8	2.04	140	.190	.282	3	.000	-0	—	1	0	0.2
Total	6	11	26	.297	152	42	5-1	5-1	410.1	368	184	32	21	197-31	229	3.44	101	.243	.336	88-0-5	.045	-6	77	0	57	-0.5
Waterbury, Steve	Steven Craig; B4.6.1952 Carbondale IL; BR/TR/6´5˝/175; d9.14																									
1976	StL N	0	0	ø	5	0	0	0-0	6	7	4	0	0	3-0	4	6.00	60	.304	.385	0	ø	0	—	-1	0	-0.1
Waters, Fred	Fred Warren; B2.2.1927 Benton MS; D8.28.1989 Pensacola FL; BL/TL/5´11˝/185; d9.20; Col Southern Mississippi																									
1955	Pit N	0	0	ø	2	0	0	0	5	7	2	1	0	2-0	0	3.60	114	.318	.375	1	.000	-0	—	0	0	0.0
1956	Pit N	2	2	.500	23	5	1	0	51	48	18	3	1	30-1	14	2.82	134	.258	.357	20	.050	-1	112	5	0	0.2
Total	2	2	2	.500	25	5	1	0	56	55	20	4	1	32-1	14	2.89	131	.264	.359	21	.048	-1	112	5	0	0.2
Watkins, Bob	Robert Cecil; B3.12.1948 San Francisco CA; BR/TR/6´1˝/170; [HouN66 22/423]; d9.6																									
1969	Hou N	0	0	ø	5	0	0	0-0	15.2	13	9	1	0	13-0	11	5.17	69	.241	.382	2	.000	-0	—	-2	0	-0.2
Watkins, Scott	Scott Allen; B5.15.1970 Tulsa OK; BL/TL/6´3˝/180; [MinA92 23/654]; d8.1; Col Oklahoma St.																									
1995	Min A	0	0	ø	27	0	0	0-2	21.2	22	14	2	0	11-1	11	5.40	89	.278	.355	0	ø	0	—	-1	0	-0.1
Watkins, Steve	Stephen Douglas; B7.19.1978 Lubbock TX; BR/TR/6´4˝/190; [SDN98 16/472]; d8.21; Col Lubbock Christian/Texas Tech																									
2004	SD N	0	0	ø	11	0	0	0-0	14.1	17	10	3	2	4-0	7	6.28	63	.293	.359	0	ø	0	—	-4	0	-0.2
Watson, Allen	Allen Kenneth; B11.18.1970 Jamaica NY; BL/TL/6´3˝/(190–212); [StLN91 1/21]; d7.8; Col New York Tech; [DL 2001 NY A 190]																									
1993	StL N	6	7	.462	16	15	0	0-1	86	90	53	11	3	28-2	49	4.60	88	.271	.330	26-0-1	.231	2	119	-7	0	-0.8
1994	StL N	6	5	.545	22	22	0	0-0	115.2	130	73	15	8	53-0	74	5.52	77	.286	.370	38-0-7	.158	1	121	-15	0	-1.2
1995	StL N	7	9	.438	21	19	0	0-0	114.1	126	68	17	5	41-0	49	4.96	86	.285	.352	36-0-3	.417	6	78	-7	31	-0.2
1996	SF N	8	12	.400	29	29	2	0-0	185.2	189	105	28	5	69-2	128	4.61	90	.273	.339	65-0-2	.231	4*	90	-8	23	-0.4
1997	Ana A	12	12	.500	35	34	0	0-0	199	220	121	37	8	73-0	141	4.93	94	.279	.344	0	ø	0	104	-8	0	-0.8
1998	Ana A	6	7	.462	28	14	1	0-0	92.1	122	67	12	3	34-0	64	6.04	79	.323	.378	0	ø	0	87	-13	50	-1.5
1999	NY N	2	2	.500	14	4	0	1-0	39.2	36	18	5	1	22-3	32	4.08	106	.252	.347	10	.300	1	85	1	0	0.2
	Sea A	0	1	.000	3	0	0	0-0	3	6	9	5	0	3-0	2	12.00	40	.400	.474	0	ø	0	—	-5	0	-0.8
	†NY A	4	0	1.000	21	0	0	0-1	34.1	30	8	3	0	10-0	30	2.10	225	.236	.292	0	ø	0	—	11	0	1.1
	Year	4	1	.800	24	0	0	0-1	37.1	36	17	8	0	13-0	32	2.89	164	.254	.314	0	ø	0	—	6	0	0.3
2000	NY A	0	0	ø	17	0	0	0-0	22	30	25	6	2	18-0	20	10.23	47	.330	.442	0	ø	0	—	-13	118	-0.6
Total	8	51	55	.481	206	137	3	1-2	892	979	547	139	35	351-7	589	5.03	87	.283	.352	175-0-13	.257	14	99	-64	412	-5.0
Watson, Doc	Charles John; B1.30.1885 Kensington OH; D12.30.1949 San Diego CA; BL/TL/6´0˝/170; d9.3																									
1913	Chi N	1	0	1.000	1	1	1	0	9	8	2	0	1	6	1	1.00	318	.242	.375	2-0-1	.000	0	166	2	—	0.2
1914	Chi F	9	8	.529	26	18	10-3	1	172	145	50	2	3	49	69	2.04	130	.236	.295	54-0-6	.093	-4	95	14	—	0.7
	StL F	3	4	.429	9	7	4-2	0	56	41	18	1	4	24	18	1.93	158	.211	.311	16-0-1	.125	-1	42	6	—	0.5
	Year	12	12	.500	35	25	14-5	1	228	186	68	3	7	73	87	2.01	137	.230	.299	70-0-7	.100	-5	79	20	—	1.2
1915	StL F	9	9	.500	33	20	6	0	135.2	132	66	1	4	58	45	3.98	72	.273	.355	40-0-2	.125	-3	77	-13	—	-2.2
Total	3	22	21	.512	69	46	21-5	1	372.2	326	136	4	12	137	133	2.70	104	.246	.322	112-0-10	.107	-8	80	9	—	-0.8
Watson, Mule	John Reaves; B10.15.1896 Arizona LA; D8.25.1949 Shreveport LA; BR/TR/6´1.5˝/185; d7.4; Col Baylor																									
1918	Phi A	7	10	.412	21	19	11-3	0	141.2	139	74	0	2	44	30	3.37	87	.288	.350	47-0-1	.128	-3	104	-8	—	-1.4
1919	Phi A	0	1	.000	4	2	0	0	14.1	17	11	2	0	7	6	6.91	50	.309	.387	6	.000	-1	103	-4	—	-0.3
1920	Bos N	0	0	ø	1	0	0	0	3	0	0	0	0	0	0	0.00	ø	.000	.000	1	.000	-0	—	1	—	0.0
	Pit N	0	0	ø	5	0	0	0	11.1	15	11	2	0	7	1	8.74	37	.326	.415	3	.000	-0	—	-6	—	-0.3
	Bos N	5	4	.556	12	10	4-2	0	71.2	79	33	0	1	17	16	3.77	81	.298	.343	23-0-1	.130	-1	67	-4	—	-0.7
	Year	5	4	.556	18	10	4-2	0	86	94	44	2	1	24	17	4.29	72	.294	.345	27-0-1	.111	-2	67	-9	—	-1.0
1921	Bos N	14	13	.519	44	31	15-1	2	259.1	269	128	11	7	57	48	3.85	95	.270	.314	87-0-6	.138	-4	105	-6	—	-1.0
1922	Bos N	8	14	.364	41	27	8-1	1	201	262	140	9	5	59	53	4.70	85	.317	.366	66-0-3	.197	-0	79	-20	—	-1.8
1923	Bos N	1	2	.333	11	4	1	1	31.1	42	26	2	0	20	10	5.17	77	.339	.431	8-0-1	.250	-0	103	-6	—	-0.5
	†NY N	8	5	.615	17	15	8	0	108.1	117	43	11	1	21	26	3.41	112	.280	.316	46-0-1	.174	-1	92	7	—	0.6
	Year	9	7	.563	28	19	9	1	139.2	159	69	13	1	41	36	3.80	101	.293	.344	54-0-2	.185	-1	94	0	—	0.1
1924	†NY N	7	4	.636	22	16	6-1	0	99.2	122	54	7	1	24	18	3.79	97	.303	.343	35-2-0	.257	4	110	-4	—	-0.1
Total	7	50	53	.485	178	124	53-8	4	941.2	1062	520	44	17	256	208	4.03	89	.293	.342	322-2-13	.165	-8	95	-50	—	-5.5
Watson, Mark	Mark Bradford; B1.23.1974 Atlanta GA; BR/TL/6´4˝/215; d5.19; Col Georgia																									
2000	Cle A	0	1	.000	6	0	0	0-0	6.1	12	7	0	1	2-0	4	8.53	59	.400	.455	0	ø	0	—	-3	0	-0.4
2002	Sea A	1	0	1.000	3	0	0	0-0	4	8	8	1	0	4-0	1	18.00	24	.421	.500	0	ø	0	—	-6	0	-1.0
2003	Cin N	0	0	ø	2	0	0	0-0	2	2	1	0	0	1-0	2	4.50	93	.250	.333	0	ø	0	—	0	38	0.0
Total	3	1	1	.500	11	0	0	0-0	12.1	22	16	1	1	7-0	7	10.95	42	.386	.455	0	ø	0	—	-9	38	-1.4
Watson, Milt	Milton Robert "Mule"; B1.10.1890 Flovilla GA; D4.10.1962 Pine Bluff AR; BR/TR/6´1˝/180; d7.26																									
1916	StL N	4	6	.400	18	13	5-2	0	103	109	51	3	4	33	27	3.06	86	.283	.346	32-0-1	.219	0	83	-6	—	-0.6
1917	StL N	10	13	.435	41	20	5-3	0	161.1	149	74	3	9	51	45	3.51	77	.252	.321	51	.098	-4	74	-14	—	-2.3
1918	Phi N	5	7	.417	23	11	6	0	112.2	126	51	1	2	36	29	3.43	87	.293	.350	40-0-1	.075	-4	99	-4	—	-0.9
1919	Phi N	2	4	.333	8	4	3	0	47	51	30	2	2	19	12	5.17	62	.282	.356	16	.063	-2	74	-8	—	-1.1
Total	4	21	30	.412	90	48	19-5	0	424	435	206	9	17	139	113	3.57	79	.274	.339	139-0-2	.115	-9	82	-32	—	-4.9
Watson, Mother	Walter L.; B1.27.1865 Middleport OH; D11.23.1898 Middleport OH; 5´9˝/145; d5.19																									
1887	Cin AA	0	1	.000	2	2	1	0	14	22	18	0	0	6	1	5.79	75	.328	.384	8	.125	-0	139	-3	—	-0.2

YEAR	TM LG	W	L	PCT	G	GS	CG-SHO	SV-BS	IP	H	R	HR	HB	BB-IB	SO	ERA	AERA	OAV	OOB	AB-HR-SH	AVG	PB	SUP	APR	DL	PW
WATT, EDDIE	Eddie Dean; B4.4.1941 Lamoni IA; BR/TR/5´10˝/(185–197); d4.12; Col Northern Iowa																									
1966	Bal A	9	7	.563	43	13	1	4	145.2	123	67	11	5	44-1	102	3.83	87	.230	.292	46-2-2	.304	6	126	-7	0	-0.3
1967	Bal A	3	5	.375	49	0	0	8	103.2	67	26	5	3	37-6	93	2.26	140	.183	.262	22-1-2	.182	2	—	12	0	1.3
1968	Bal A	5	5	.500	59	0	0	11	83.1	63	32	1	2	35-7	72	2.27	129	.209	.293	8	.000	-0	—	3	0	0.4
1969	†Bal A	5	2	.714	56	0	0	16-5	71	49	18	3	2	26-5	46	1.65	218	.194	.270	8	.000	-0	—	14	0	2.0
1970	†Bal A	7	7	.500	53	0	0	12-7	55.1	44	20	3	5	29-5	33	3.25	113	.239	.355	8	.125	-0	—	4	0	0.7
1971	†Bal A	3	1	.750	35	0	0	11-1	39.2	39	12	1	0	8-1	26	1.82	188	.260	.296	5	.000	-0	—	6	22	0.9
1972	Bal A	2	3	.400	38	0	0	7-3	45.2	30	12	2	2	20-6	23	2.17	144	.191	.286	2	.000	-0	—	5	0	0.7
1973	†Bal A	3	4	.429	30	0	0	5-2	71	62	26	8	2	21-5	38	3.30	115	.235	.296	0	ø	0	—	5	0	0.5
1974	Phi N	1	1	.500	42	0	0	6-0	38.1	39	20	3	2	26-8	23	3.99	95	.275	.385	1	.000	-0	—	-1	0	-0.1
1975	Chi N	0	1	.000	6	0	0	0-1	6	14	11	0	1	8-4	6	13.50	29	.452	.575	0	ø	0	—	-6	0	-0.9
Total	10	38	36	.514	411	13	1	80-19	659.2	530	244	37	24	254-48	462	2.91	116	.222	.301	100-3-4	.190	6	126	35	22	5.2
WATT, FRANK	Frank Marion "Kilo"; B12.15.1902 Washington DC; D8.31.1956 Washington DC; BR/TR/6´1˝/205; d4.14; b–Allie																									
1931	Phi N	5	5	.500	38	12	5	2	122.2	147	81	5	3	49	25	4.84	88	.296	.362	39	.205	0	101	-8	—	-0.7
WAUGH, JIM	James Elden; B11.25.1933 Lancaster OH; BR/TR/6´3˝/185; d4.19																									
1952	Pit N	1	6	.143	17	7	1	0	52.1	61	43	4	2	32	18	6.36	63	.285	.383	10-0-1	.100	-0	86	-13	0	-1.6
1953	Pit N	4	5	.444	29	11	1	0	90.1	108	70	21	0	56	23	6.48	69	.295	.389	22-0-1	.227	0	94	-18	0	-1.5
Total	2	5	11	.313	46	18	2	0	142.2	169	113	25	2	88	41	6.43	67	.291	.387	32-0-2	.188	0	91	-31	0	-3.1
WAYENBERG, FRANK	Frank; B8.27.1898 Franklin KS; D4.16.1975 Zanesville OH; BR/TR/6´0.5˝/172; d8.25																									
1924	Cle A	0	0	ø	2	1	0	0	6.2	7	4	0	1	5	3	5.40	79	.259	.394	2	.500	0	118	0	—	0.0
WAYNE, GARY	Gary Anthony; B11.30.1962 Dearborn MI; BL/TL/6´3˝/(185–200); [MonN84 4/93]; d4.7; Col Michigan																									
1989	Min A	3	4	.429	60	0	0	1-2	71	55	28	4	1	36-4	41	3.30	126	.212	.309	0	ø	0	—	6	0	0.6
1990	Min A	1	1	.500	38	0	0	1-1	38.2	38	19	5	1	13-0	28	4.19	99	.255	.315	0	ø	0	—	0	0	0.0
1991	Min A	1	0	1.000	8	0	0	1-0	12.1	11	7	1	1	4-0	7	5.11	84	.244	.314	0	ø	0	—	-1	0	-0.1
1992	Min A	3	3	.500	41	0	0	0-3	48	46	18	2	3	19-5	29	2.63	156	.260	.337	0	ø	0	—	6	0	0.8
1993	Col N	5	3	.625	65	0	0	1-2	62.1	68	40	8	1	26-8	49	5.05	95	.276	.339	1	1.000	0	—	-2	0	-0.2
1994	LA N	1	3	.250	19	0	0	0-2	17.1	19	13	2	3	6-2	10	4.67	85	.279	.359	1	.000	-0	—	-3	0	-0.6
Total	6	14	14	.500	231	0	0	4-10	249.2	237	125	22	10	104-19	164	3.93	109	.251	.327	2	.500	0	—	6	0	0.5
WAYNE, JUSTIN	Justin Morgan; B4.16.1979 Honolulu HI; BR/TR/6´3˝/(200–205); [MonN00 1/5]; d9.3; Col Stanford																									
2002	Fla N	2	3	.400	5	5	0	0-0	23.2	22	16	3	0	13-0	16	5.32	74	.244	.333	7-0-1	.000	-1	94	-4	0	-0.8
2003	Fla N	0	2	.000	2	2	0	0-0	5.1	9	7	1	1	5-0	1	11.81	35	.375	.484	2	.000	-0	34	-5	13	-0.7
2004	Fla N	3	3	.500	19	1	0	0-2	32.2	35	24	6	2	18-1	20	5.79	71	.282	.374	3-0-1	.000	-0	90	-7	15	-1.2
Total	3	5	8	.385	26	8	0	0-2	61.2	66	47	10	3	36-1	37	6.13	66	.277	.371	12-0-2	.000	-1	78	-16	28	-2.7
WEAFER, KEN	Kenneth Albert "Al"; B2.6.1913 Woburn MA; D6.4.2005 Guilderland NY; BR/TR/6´0.5˝/183; d5.29; Col Duke																									
1936	Bos N	0	0	ø	1	0	0	0	3	6	4	1	0	3	0	12.00	32	.375	.474	1	.000	-0	—	-3	—	-0.1
WEATHERS, DAVID	John David; B9.25.1969 Lawrenceburg TN; BR/TR/6´3˝/(205–233); [TorA88 3/82]; d8.2; Col Motlow St. (TN) CC																									
1991	Tor A	1	0	1.000	15	0	0	0-0	14.2	15	9	1	2	17-3	13	4.91	86	.263	.442	0	ø	0	—	-1	0	-0.1
1992	Tor A	0	0	ø	2	0	0	0-0	3.1	5	3	1	0	2-0	3	8.10	51	.385	.467	0	ø	0	—	-1	0	-0.1
1993	Fla N	2	3	.400	14	6	0	0-0	45.2	57	26	3	1	13-1	34	5.12	85	.306	.355	10-0-3	.100	-1	55	-3	0	-0.3
1994	Fla N	8	12	.400	24	24	0	0-0	135	166	87	13	4	59-9	72	5.27	84	.306	.376	44-0-4	.068	-2*	86	-11	0	-1.6
1995	Fla N	4	5	.444	28	15	0	0-0	90.1	104	68	8	5	52-3	60	5.98	72	.295	.391	26-0-5	.154	-1	122	-17	17	-1.6
1996	Fla N	2	2	.500	31	8	0	0-0	71.1	85	41	7	4	28-4	40	4.54	91	.302	.373	19-1-0	.158	1*	120	-4	0	-0.1
	†NY A	0	2	.000	11	4	0	0-0	17.1	23	19	1	2	14-1	13	9.35	53	.315	.433	0	ø	0	154	-9	0	-0.8
1997	NY A	0	1	.000	10	0	0	0-1	9	15	10	1	0	7-0	4	10.00	45	.375	.468	0	ø	0	—	-5	0	-0.5
	Cle A	1	2	.333	9	1	0	0-0	16.2	23	14	2	1	8-0	14	7.56	62	.343	.416	0	ø	0	39	-5	0	-0.7
	Year	1	3	.250	19	1	0	0-1	25.2	38	24	3	1	15-0	18	8.42	55	.355	.435	0	ø	0	40	-10	0	-1.2
1998	Cin N	2	4	.333	16	9	0	0-0	62.1	86	47	3	1	27-2	51	6.21	69	.330	.393	15-1-3	.067	0	117	-14	0	-1.1
	Mil N	4	1	.800	28	0	0	0-1	47.2	44	22	3	2	14-1	43	3.21	135	.246	.306	8-0-1	.125	-0	—	4	0	0.4
	Year	6	5	.545	44	9	0	0-1	110	130	69	6	3	41-3	94	4.91	88	.295	.358	23-1-4	.087	0	116	-9	0	-0.7
1999	Mil N	7	4	.636	63	0	0	2-4	93	102	49	14	2	38-3	74	4.65	99	.279	.346	7	.143	0	—	1	0	0.1
2000	Mil N	3	5	.375	69	0	0	1-6	76.1	73	29	7	2	32-8	50	3.07	151	.260	.339	1	.000	-0	—	13	19	1.1
2001	Mil N	3	4	.429	52	0	0	4-3	57.2	37	14	3	2	25-7	46	2.03	212	.188	.284	1	.000	0	—	15	0	1.8
	Chi N	1	1	.500	28	0	0	0-3	28.1	28	10	3	1	9-1	20	3.18	132	.269	.328	0	ø	0	—	4	0	0.2
	Year	4	5	.444	80	0	0	4-6	86	65	24	6	3	34-8	66	2.41	177	.216	.299	1	.000	0	—	19	0	2.0
2002	NY N	6	3	.667	71	0	0	0-5	77.1	69	30	6	3	36-7	61	2.91	136	.245	.332	1	.000	-0	—	8	0	0.9
2003	NY N	1	6	.143	77	0	0	7-2	87.2	87	33	6	6	40-6	75	3.08	136	.264	.354	3	.000	-0	—	11	0	0.9
2004	NY N	5	3	.625	32	0	0	0-1	33.2	41	19	5	2	15-0	25	4.28	100	.304	.377	0	ø	0	—	-1	0	-0.1
	Hou N	1	4	.200	26	0	0	0-3	32	31	20	5	3	13-1	26	4.78	91	.261	.348	0	ø	0	—	-2	0	-0.4
	Fla N	1	0	1.000	8	2	0	0-0	16.2	13	5	2	0	7-1	10	2.70	152	.232	.317	3	.000	-0	79	3	0	0.1
	Year	7	7	.500	66	2	0	0-4	82.1	85	44	12	5	35-2	61	4.15	103	.274	.355	3	.000	-0	76	1	0	-0.4
2005	Cin N	7	4	.636	73	0	0	15-4	77.2	71	36	7	2	29-2	61	3.94	108	.241	.312	0	ø	0	—	3	0	0.4
2006	Cin N	4	4	.500	67	0	0	12-7	73.2	61	31	12	2	34-4	50	3.54	133	.226	.314	1	.000	-0	—	10	0	1.1
Total	16	63	70	.474	754	69	0	41-40	1167.1	1236	622	113	47	519-64	845	4.37	100	.276	.355	139-2-16	.101	-3	104	-1	36	-0.4
WEAVER, FLOYD	David Floyd; B5.12.1941 Ben Franklin TX; BR/TR/6´4˝/195; d9.30; Col Paris (TX) JC																									
1962	Cle A	1	0	1.000	1	1	0	0	5	3	1	1	0	0-0	8	1.80	215	.167	.167	2	.500	0	138	1	0	0.3
1965	Cle A	2	2	.500	32	1	0	1	61.1	61	40	10	5	24-3	37	5.43	64	.265	.344	11	.091	0	277	-12	0	-0.8
1970	Chi A	1	2	.333	31	3	0	0-0	61.2	52	33	7	2	31-5	51	4.38	89	.233	.328	7-0-1	.000	-1	115	-3	0	-0.3
1971	Mil A	0	1	.000	21	0	0	0-0	27.1	33	22	3	1	18-6	12	7.24	48	.320	.416	0-0-1	ø	0	—	-10	0	-0.5
Total	4	4	5	.444	85	5	0	1-0	155.1	149	96	21	8	73-14	108	5.21	70	.260	.346	20-0-2	.100	-0	155	-24	0	-1.3
WEAVER, HARRY	Harry Abraham; B2.26.1892 Clarendon PA; D5.30.1983 Rochester NY; BR/TR/5´11˝/160; d9.18; Mil 1918																									
1915	Phi A	0	2	.000	2	2	2	0	18	18	10	1	1	10	1	3.00	98	.290	.397	6	.167	0	50	-1	—	0.0
1916	Phi A	0	0	ø	3	0	0	0	8	14	10	0	0	5	2	10.13	28	.424	.500	2	.500	0	—	-6	—	-0.3
1917	Chi N	1	1	.500	4	2	1-1	0	19.2	17	10	0	0	7	8	2.75	106	.230	.296	5	.200	-0	39	0	—	0.0
1918	Chi N	2	2	.500	8	3	1-1	1	32.2	27	13	1	0	7	9	2.20	126	.227	.270	8	.250	0	90	1	—	0.2
1919	Chi N	0	1	.000	2	1	0	0	3.1	6	7	0	1	2	1	10.80	27	.375	.474	1	.000	-0	28	-4	—	-0.7
Total	5	3	6	.333	19	8	4-2	1	81.2	82	50	2	2	31	21	3.64	79	.270	.341	22	.227	0	59	-10	—	-0.8
WEAVER, JIM	James Brian "Fluff"; B2.19.1939 Lancaster PA; BL/TL/6´0˝/(172–178); d8.13																									
1967	Cal A	3	0	1.000	13	2	0	1	30.1	26	11	2	1	9-2	20	2.67	118	.232	.293	6-0-1	.000	-1	83	1	0	0.2
1968	Cal A	0	1	.000	14	0	0	0	22.2	22	7	4	0	10-2	8	2.38	122	.259	.337	1	.000	-0	—	1	0	0.0
Total	2	3	1	.750	27	2	0	1	53	48	18	6	1	19-4	28	2.55	120	.244	.312	7-0-1	.000	-1	83	2	0	0.2
WEAVER, JIM	James Dement "Big Jim"; B11.25.1903 Obion Co. TN; D12.12.1983 Lakeland FL; BR/TR/6´6˝/230; d8.27; Col Western Kentucky																									
1928	Was A	0	0	ø	3	0	0	0	6	2	2	0	1	6	2	1.50	267	.143	.429	1	.000	-0	—	1	—	0.0
1931	NY A	2	1	.667	17	5	2	0	57.2	66	37	1	1	29	28	5.31	75	.280	.361	20-0-4	.050	-3	256	-8	—	-0.6
1934	StL A	2	0	1.000	5	5	2	0	19.2	17	14	3	0	20	11	6.41	78	.236	.402	7	.143	-0	122	-2	—	-0.1
	Chi N	11	9	.550	27	20	8-1	0	159	163	77	5	4	54	98	3.91	99	.263	.326	52-0-4	.058	-5	94	0	—	-0.6
1935	Pit N	14	8	.636	33	22	11-**4**	0	176.1	177	85	9	2	58	87	3.42	120	.254	.313	56-0-7	.071	-4	100	13	—	1.0
1936	Pit N	14	8	.636	38	31	11-1	0	225.2	239	125	12	1	74	108	4.31	94	.272	.329	79-0-6	.101	-5	111	-5	—	-1.0
1937	Pit N	8	5	.615	32	9	2-1	0	109.2	106	49	2	0	31	44	3.20	121	.255	.307	27-0-2	.148	-0	99	7	—	0.7
1938	StL A	0	1	.000	1	1	0	0	7	9	7	0	0	9	4	9.00	55	.321	.486	2	.000	-0	0	-3	—	-0.3
	Cin N	6	4	.600	30	15	2	3	129.1	109	58	6	1	54	64	3.13	117	.227	.306	44-0-4	.205	0	114	5	—	0.4
1939	Cin N	0	0	ø	3	0	0	0	3	3	1	0	0	1	3	3.00	128	.250	.308	1	.000	-0	—	0	—	0.0
Total	8	57	36	.613	189	108	38-7	3	893.1	891	455	38	10	336	449	3.88	102	.258	.326	289-0-27	.104	-17	112	8	—	-0.5

YEAR	TM LG	W	L	PCT	G	GS	CG-SHO	SV-BS	IP	H	R	HR	HB	BB-IB	SO	ERA	AERA	OAV	OOB	AB-HR-SH	AVG	PB	SUP	APR	DL	PW
Weaver, Eric	James Eric; B8.4.1973 Springfield IL; BR/TR/6´5˝/230; d5.30																									
1998	LA N	2	0	1.000	7	0	0	0-0	9.2	5	1	1	0	6-0	5	0.93	433	.179	.324	1	.000	-0	—	4	0	0.7
1999	Sea A	0	1	.000	8	0	0	0-1	9.1	14	12	2	0	8-1	14	10.61	45	.318	.423	0	ø	0	—	-6	141	-0.5
2000	Ana A	0	2	.000	17	0	0	0-1	18.1	20	16	5	0	16-1	8	6.87	75	.267	.391	0	ø	0	—	-4	0	-0.3
Total	3	2	3	.400	32	0	0	0-2	37.1	39	29	8	0	30-2	27	6.27	76	.265	.388	1	.000	-0	—	-6	141	-0.1
Weaver, Jeff	Jeffrey Charles; B8.22.1976 Northridge CA; BR/TR/6´5˝/200; [DetA98 1/14]; d4.14; b–Jered; Col Cal St.–Fresno																									
1999	Det A	9	12	.429	30	29	0	0-0	163.2	176	104	27	17	56-2	114	5.55	90	.278	.350	4-0-1	.500	1*	90	-8	0	-0.8
2000	Det A	11	15	.423	31	30	2	0-0	200	205	102	26	15	52-2	136	4.32	114	.266	.322	3	.000	-0	80	14	0	1.6
2001	Det A	13	16	.448	33	33	5	0-0	229.1	235	116	19	14	68-4	152	4.08	108	.266	.326	5-0-1	.000	-0	92	8	0	0.9
2002	Det A	6	8	.429	17	17	3-3	0-0	121.2	112	50	4	8	33-1	75	3.18	138	.243	.304	7	.286	0	65	16	0	1.8
	†NY A	5	3	.625	15	8	0	2-0	78	81	38	12	3	15-3	57	4.04	107	.260	.300	0	ø	0	134	3	0	0.3
	Year	11	11	.500	32	25	3-**3**	2-0	199.2	193	88	16	11	48-4	132	3.52	124	.250	.302	7	.286	0	87	18	0	2.1
2003	†NY A	7	9	.438	32	24	0	0-0	159.1	211	113	16	11	47-2	93	5.99	73	.320	.371	0	ø	0	104	-28	0	-2.4
2004	†LA N	13	13	.500	34	34	0	0-0	220	219	103	19	14	67-9	153	4.01	103	.260	.323	70-0-7	.214	3*	106	4	0	0.6
2005	LA N	14	11	.560	34	34	3-2	0-0	224	220	111	35	18	43-1	157	4.22	98	.256	.305	70-0-6	.229	3*	101	0	0	0.2
2006	LA A	3	10	.231	16	16	0	0-0	88.2	114	68	18	4	21-0	62	6.29	71	.309	.352	3-0-1	.333	0	79	-18	0	-2.1
	†StL N	5	4	.556	15	15	0	0-0	83.1	99	49	16	6	26-1	45	5.18	84	.297	.356	27-0-5	.111	0*	130	-7	0	-0.7
Total	8	86	101	.460	257	240	13-5	2-0	1568	1672	854	192	110	428-25	1044	4.58	97	.273	.330	189-0-21	.206	7	96	-16	0	-0.6
Weaver, Jered	Jered David; B10.4.1982 Northridge CA; BR/TR/6´7˝/205; [AnaA04 1/12]; d5.27; b–Jeff; Col Long Beach St.																									
2006	LA A	11	2	.846	19	19	0	0-0	123	94	36	15	3	33-1	105	2.56	174	.209	.266	0	ø	0	104	28	0	2.6
Weaver, Monte	Montie Morton "Prof"; B6.15.1906 Helton NC; D6.14.1994 Orlando FL; BL/TR/6´0˝/170; d9.20; Col Emory & Henry																									
1931	Was A	1	0	1.000	3	1	1	0	10	11	6	0	0	6	6	4.50	95	.268	.362	3	.000	-0	118	0	—	0.0
1932	Was A	22	10	.688	43	30	13-1	2	234	236	126	9	0	112	83	4.08	106	.261	.342	94-0-2	.287	6*	124	3	—	0.8
1933	†Was A	10	5	.667	23	21	12-1	0	152.1	147	57	3	1	53	45	3.25	129	.257	.322	56-0-1	.125	-3	107	18	—	1.2
1934	Was A	11	15	.423	31	31	11	0	204.2	255	127	16	0	63	51	4.79	90	.306	.355	80-0-4	.162	-2	103	-13	—	-1.7
1935	Was A	1	1	.500	5	2	0	0	12	16	8	1	0	6	4	5.25	82	.320	.393	3	.333	0	100	-1	—	-0.2
1936	Was A	6	4	.600	26	5	3	1	91	92	57	3	0	38	15	4.35	110	.262	.334	25	.200	1	122	2	—	0.2
1937	Was A	12	9	.571	30	26	9	0	188.2	197	102	21	0	70	44	4.20	105	.266	.330	68-0-4	.206	1	89	6	—	0.6
1938	Was A	7	6	.538	31	18	7	0	139	157	93	9	3	74	43	5.24	86	.282	.370	45-0-2	.267	4	114	-11	—	-0.5
1939	Bos A	1	0	1.000	9	1	1	1	20.1	26	15	0	1	13	6	6.64	71	.321	.421	4	.000	-1	149	-3	—	-0.3
Total	9	71	50	.587	201	135	57-2	4	1052	1137	591	62	5	435	297	4.36	101	.276	.345	378-0-13	.209	5	108	1	—	0.1
Weaver, Orlie	Orville Forest; B6.4.1886 Newport KY; D11.28.1970 New Orleans LA; BR/TR/6´0˝/180; d9.14; Col Maryville																									
1910	Chi N	1	1	.500	7	2	2	0	32	34	17	2	1	15	22	3.66	79	.270	.352	13	.154	-1	90	-3	—	-0.3
1911	Chi N	2	2	.500	6	3	1-1	0	43.2	29	12	0	4	17	20	2.06	161	.196	.296	17-0-1	.059	-1	98	7	—	0.4
	Bos N	3	12	.200	27	17	4	0	121	140	102	9	7	84	50	6.47	59	.303	.418	41-0-1	.122	-2	84	-28	—	-3.2
	Year	5	14	.263	33	20	5-1	0	164.2	169	114	9	11	101	70	5.30	70	.277	.389	58-0-2	.103	-4	88	-23	—	-2.8
Total	2	6	15	.286	40	22	7-1	0	196.2	203	131	11	12	116	92	5.03	71	.276	.383	71-0-2	.113	-4	89	-24	—	-3.1
Weaver, Roger	Roger Edward; B10.6.1954 Amsterdam NY; BR/TR/6´3˝/200; [DetA76 16/362]; d6.6; Col Oneonta																									
1980	Det A	3	4	.429	19	6	0	0-0	63.2	56	32	5	1	34-3	42	4.10	101	.247	.342	0	ø	0	87	0	21	0.0
Weaver, Sam	Samuel H.; B7.10.1855 Philadelphia PA; D2.1.1914 Philadelphia PA; BR/TR/5´10˝/175; d10.25																									
1875	Phi NA	1	0	1.000	1	1	1	0	6	6	2	0	—	2	2	1.50	152	.240	.296	4	.250	0	263	1	—	0.1
1878	Mil N	12	31	.279	45	43	39-1	0	383	371	214	2	—	21	95	1.95	135	.237	**.247**	170	.200	-3*	66	**23**	—	2.1
1882	Phi AA	26	15	.634	42	41	41-2	0	371	374	182	6	—	35	104	2.74	102	.245	.262	155	.232	2*	96	8	—	0.9
1883	Lou AA	24	22	.522	46	46	45-4	0	400.2	451	261	3	—	35	105	3.71	81	.266	.281	193	.192	0*	110	-32	—	-2.9
1884	Phi U	5	10	.333	17	17	14	0	136	206	146	3	—	11	40	5.76	40	.328	.339	84	.214	-3*	116	-52	—	-4.4
1886	Phi AA	0	2	.000	2	2	1	0	11	30	29	0	1	2	2	14.73	24	.423	.446	7	.143	-1	25	-13	—	-1.4
Total	5	67	80	.456	152	149	140-7	0	1301.2	1432	832	14	1	104	346	3.22	87	.261	.275	609	.207	-4	92	-66	—	-5.7
Webb, Brandon	Brandon Tyler; B5.9.1979 Ashland KY; BR/TR/6´3˝/(190–230); [AriN00 8/249]; d4.22; Col Kentucky																									
2003	Ari N	10	9	.526	29	28	1-1	0-0	180.2	140	65	12	13	68-4	172	2.84	163	.212	.298	50-0-7	.100	-2	93	32	15	3.0
2004	Ari N	7	16	.304	35	**35**	1	0-0	208	194	111	17	11	119-11	164	3.59	127	.248	.353	64-0-4	.094	-3	86	14	0	1.2
2005	Ari N	14	12	.538	33	33	1	0-0	229	229	98	21	2	59-4	172	3.54	125	.265	.311	62-0-13	.097	-3	82	22	0	2.1
2006	Ari N★	**16**	8	.667	33	33	5-**3**	0-0	235	216	91	15	6	50-4	178	3.10	151	.246	.289	73-0-10	.151	-0	102	38	0	3.7
Total	4	47	45	.511	130	129	8-4	0-0	852.2	779	365	65	32	296-23	686	3.28	139	.245	.313	249-0-34	.112	-9	91	106	15	10.0
Webb, Lefty	Cleon Earl; B3.1.1885 Mt.Gilead OH; D1.12.1958 Circleville OH; BB/TL/5´11˝/165; d5.23; Col Ohio Wesleyan																									
1910	Pit N	2	1	.667	7	3	2	0	27	29	17	0	2	9	6	5.67	55	.266	.333	10	.200	-0	144	-5	—	-0.6
Webb, Hank	Henry Gaylon Matthew; B5.21.1950 Copiague NY; BR/TR/6´3˝/(165–175); [NYN68 10/205]; d9.5																									
1972	NY N	0	0	ø	6	2	0	0-0	18.1	18	9	1	0	9-1	15	4.42	77	.261	.342	5	.000	-1	104	-2	0	-0.1
1973	NY N	0	0	ø	2	0	0	0-0	1.2	2	2	1	0	2-0	1	10.80	34	.286	.444	0	ø	0	—	-1	0	-0.1
1974	NY N	0	2	.000	3	2	0	0-0	10	15	9	1	1	10-0	8	7.20	50	.341	.473	3	.000	-0	85	-4	0	-0.7
1975	NY N	7	6	.538	29	15	3-1	0-0	115	102	58	12	1	62-4	38	4.07	86	.236	.331	31	.258	2*	85	-7	0	-0.6
1976	NY N	0	1	.000	8	0	0	0-1	16	17	9	2	2	7-0	7	4.50	74	.274	.366	1	.000	0	—	-2	0	-0.1
1977	LA N	0	0	ø	5	0	0	0-0	8	5	2	1	1	1-0	2	2.25	171	.192	.250	0	ø	0	—	2	0	0.1
Total	6	7	9	.438	53	19	3-1	0-1	169	159	89	18	5	91-5	71	4.31	81	.248	.345	40	.200	1	87	-14	0	-1.5
Webb, John	John Floyd; B5.23.1979 Pensacola FL; BR/TR/6´3˝/220; [ChiN99 19/590]; d8.2; Col Manatee (FL) CC																									
2004	TB A	0	0	ø	4	0	0	0-0	9	12	7	2	1	7-0	9	7.00	67	.324	.444	0	ø	0	—	-2	0	-0.1
2005	TB A	0	1	.000	1	1	0	0-0	4	6	8	1	1	4-0	2	18.00	24	.333	.478	0	ø	0	210	-6	0	-0.7
Total	2	0	1	.000	5	1	0	0-0	13	18	15	3	2	11-0	11	10.38	44	.327	.456	0	ø	0	210	-8	0	-0.8
Webb, Red	Samuel Henry; B9.25.1924 Washington DC; D2.7.1996 Hyattsville MD; BL/TR/6´0˝/175; d9.15																									
1948	NY N	2	1	.667	5	3	2	0	28	27	12	2	1	10	9	3.21	122	.248	.317	9-0-2	.222	0	120	2	0	0.2
1949	NY N	1	1	.500	20	0	0	0	44.2	41	23	3	0	21	9	4.03	99	.248	.333	10	.400	2	—	0	0	0.3
Total	2	3	2	.600	25	3	2	0	72.2	68	35	5	1	31	18	3.72	107	.248	.327	19-0-2	.316	2	120	2	0	0.5
Webb, Bill	Willie Fred; B12.12.1913 Atlanta GA; D6.1.1994 Austell GA; BR/TR/6´2˝/180; d5.15																									
1943	Phi N	0	0	ø	1	0	0	0	1	1	1	1	0	1	0	9.00	37	.333	.500	0	ø	0	—	-1	0	0.0
Webber, Les	Lester Elmer; B5.6.1915 Kelseyville CA; D11.13.1986 Santa Maria CA; BR/TR/6´0.5˝/185; d5.17																									
1942	Bro N	3	2	.600	19	3	1	1	51.2	46	17	2	0	22	23	2.96	110	.230	.306	14-0-2	.071	-1	223	3	0	0.2
1943	Bro N	2	2	.500	54	0	0	**10**	115.2	112	54	6	5	69	24	3.81	88	.264	.373	25-0-1	.120	-1	—	-5	0	-0.3
1944	Bro N	7	8	.467	48	9	1	3	140.1	157	85	9	1	64	42	4.94	72	.282	.357	39-1-2	.205	1	89	-20	0	-1.7
1945	Bro N	7	3	.700	17	7	5	0	75.1	69	37	3	1	25	30	3.58	105	.237	.300	22-0-6	.091	-1	148	2	0	0.1
1946	Bro N	3	3	.500	11	4	0	0	43	34	11	5	0	15	16	2.30	147	.225	.295	10-0-1	.100	-1	63	6	0	0.7
	Cle A	1	1	.500	4	2	0	0	5.1	13	14	0	0	5	5	23.63	14	.464	.545	1	.000	0	91	-12	0	-1.9
1948	Cle A	0	0	ø	1	0	0	0	0.2	3	3	0	0	1	1	40.50	10	.750	.800	0	ø	0	—	-3	0	-0.1
Total	6	23	19	.548	154	25	7	14	432	434	221	25	7	201	141	4.19	83	.262	.345	111-1-12	.135	-2	119	-29	0	-3.0
Weber, Ben	Benjamin Edward; B11.17.1969 Port Arthur TX; BR/TR/6´4˝/(180–210); [TorA91 20/536]; d4.3; Col Houston																									
2000	SF N	0	1	.000	9	0	0	0-2	8	16	13	0	0	4-0	6	14.63	30	.400	.455	0	ø	0	—	-9	0	-0.9
	Ana A	1	0	1.000	10	0	0	0-0	14.2	12	6	0	0	2-1	8	1.84	281	.214	.237	0	ø	0	—	4	0	0.2
2001	Ana A	6	2	.750	56	0	0	0-1	68.1	66	28	4	5	31-8	40	3.42	136	.251	.341	0	ø	0	—	9	0	1.0
2002	†Ana A	7	2	.778	63	0	0	7-4	78	70	25	4	3	22-3	43	2.54	177	.249	.308	0	ø	0	—	16	0	2.0
2003	Ana A	5	1	.833	62	0	0	0-2	80.1	84	26	7	0	22-7	46	2.69	163	.275	.323	0	ø	0	—	16	0	1.1
2004	Ana A	0	2	.000	18	0	0	0-1	22.1	37	24	4	0	15-0	11	8.06	55	.363	.444	0	ø	0	—	-11	0	-0.8
2005	Cin N	0	0	ø	10	0	0	0-0	12.1	20	11	0	1	9-1	8	8.03	53	.364	.455	0	ø	0	—	-5	96	-0.2
Total	6	19	8	.704	228	0	0	7-10	284	305	133	19	9	105-20	162	3.77	120	.277	.343	0	ø	0	—	20	96	2.4

THE PITCHER REGISTER

WEBER, CHARLIE Charles P. "Count"; B10.22.1868 Cincinnati OH; D6.13.1914 Beaumont TX; TR; d7.30

YEAR	TM LG	W	L	PCT	G	GS	CG-SHO	SV-BS	IP	H	R	HR	HB	BB-IB	SO	ERA	AERA	OAV	OOB	AB-HR-SH	AVG	PB	SUP	APR	DL	PW
1898	Was N	0	1	.000	1	1	0	0	4	9	9	0	2	1	0	15.75	23	.450	.522	2	.000	-0	58	-5	—	-0.7

WEBER, NEIL Neil Aaron; B12.6.1972 Newport Beach CA; BL/TL/6´5˝/215; [MonN93 8/230]; d9.11; Col Cuesta (CA) JC

YEAR	TM LG	W	L	PCT	G	GS	CG-SHO	SV-BS	IP	H	R	HR	HB	BB-IB	SO	ERA	AERA	OAV	OOB	AB-HR-SH	AVG	PB	SUP	APR	DL	PW
1998	Ari N	0	0	ø	4	0	0	0-0	2.1	5	3	0	0	3-0	4	11.57	37	.417	.533	0	ø	0	—	-2	0	-0.1

WEGENER, MIKE Michael Denis; B10.8.1946 Denver CO; BR/TR/6´4˝/(197–205); d4.9

YEAR	TM LG	W	L	PCT	G	GS	CG-SHO	SV-BS	IP	H	R	HR	HB	BB-IB	SO	ERA	AERA	OAV	OOB	AB-HR-SH	AVG	PB	SUP	APR	DL	PW
1969	Mon N	5	14	.263	32	26	4-1	0-1	165.2	150	92	10	4	96-6	124	4.40	84	.243	.347	54-0-3	.241	2	90	-12	0	-1.0
1970	Mon N	3	6	.333	25	16	1	0-0	104.1	100	70	16	4	56-3	35	5.26	79	.252	.349	34-0-1	.118	-2	85	-13	37	-1.2
Total	2	8	20	.286	57	42	5-1	0-1	270	250	162	26	8	152-9	159	4.73	82	.247	.347	88-0-4	.193	0	88	-25	37	-2.2

WEGMAN, BILL William Edward; B12.19.1962 Cincinnati OH; BR/TR/6´5˝/(200–238); [MilA81 5/124]; d9.14

YEAR	TM LG	W	L	PCT	G	GS	CG-SHO	SV-BS	IP	H	R	HR	HB	BB-IB	SO	ERA	AERA	OAV	OOB	AB-HR-SH	AVG	PB	SUP	APR	DL	PW
1985	Mil A	2	0	1.000	3	3	0	0-0	17.2	17	8	3	0	3-0	6	3.57	118	.246	.274	0	ø	0	166	1	0	0.1
1986	Mil A	5	12	.294	35	32	2	0-0	198.1	217	120	32	7	43-2	82	5.13	85	.279	.321	0	ø	0*	84	-12	0	-1.0
1987	Mil A	12	11	.522	34	33	7	0-1	225	229	113	31	6	53-2	102	4.24	109	.265	.310	0	ø	0	100	10	15	0.9
1988	Mil A	13	13	.500	32	31	4-1	0-0	199	207	104	24	4	50-5	84	4.12	97	.265	.309	0	ø	0*	91	-4	17	-0.5
1989	Mil A	2	6	.250	11	8	0	0-1	51	69	44	6	0	21-2	27	6.71	58	.321	.375	0	ø	0	97	-17	123	-2.1
1990	Mil A	2	2	.500	8	5	1-1	0-0	29.2	37	21	6	0	6-1	20	4.85	80	.298	.328	0	ø	0	122	-4	123	-0.5
1991	Mil A	15	7	.682	28	28	7-2	0-0	193.1	176	76	16	7	40-0	89	2.84	141	.242	.286	0	ø	0	114	21	25	2.4
1992	Mil A	13	14	.481	35	35	7	0-0	261.2	251	104	28	9	55-3	127	3.20	121	.250	.294	0	ø	0	101	19	0	2.0
1993	Mil A	4	14	.222	20	18	5	0-0	120.2	135	70	13	2	34-5	50	4.48	96	.291	.335	0	ø	0	65	-4	69	-0.4
1994	Mil A	8	4	.667	19	19	0	0-0	115.2	140	64	14	2	26-0	59	4.51	112	.303	.339	0	ø	0	114	7	26	0.7
1995	Mil A	5	7	.417	37	4	0	2-1	70.2	89	45	14	3	21-2	50	5.35	94	.312	.363	0	ø	0*	56	-2	0	-0.4
Total	11	81	90	.474	262	216	33-4	2-3	1482.2	1567	769	187	40	352-22	696	4.16	103	.271	.315	0	ø	0	97	15	398	1.2

WEHDE, BIGGS Wilbur; B11.23.1906 Holstein IA; D9.21.1970 Sioux Falls SD; BR/TR/5´10.5˝/180; d9.15

YEAR	TM LG	W	L	PCT	G	GS	CG-SHO	SV-BS	IP	H	R	HR	HB	BB-IB	SO	ERA	AERA	OAV	OOB	AB-HR-SH	AVG	PB	SUP	APR	DL	PW
1930	Chi A	0	0	ø	4	0	0	0	6.1	7	8	1	1	7	3	9.95	46	.304	.484	1	.000	-0	—	-3	—	-0.1
1931	Chi A	1	0	1.000	8	0	0	0	16	19	12	0	2	10	3	6.75	63	.333	.449	3	.000	-0	—	-4	—	-0.2
Total	2	1	0	1.000	12	0	0	0	22.1	26	20	1	3	17	6	7.66	57	.325	.460	4	.000	-1	—	-7	—	-0.3

WEHMEIER, HERM Herman Ralph; B2.18.1927 Cincinnati OH; D5.21.1973 Dallas TX; BR/TR/6´2˝/(195–204); d9.7; [DL 1959 Det A 33]

YEAR	TM LG	W	L	PCT	G	GS	CG-SHO	SV-BS	IP	H	R	HR	HB	BB-IB	SO	ERA	AERA	OAV	OOB	AB-HR-SH	AVG	PB	SUP	APR	DL	PW
1945	Cin N	0	1	.000	2	2	0	0	5	10	7	0	0	4	0	12.60	30	.435	.519	1	.000	-0*	124	-5	0	-0.7
1947	Cin N	0	0	ø	1	0	0	0	1	0	0	0	0	0	0	0.00	ø	.000	.000	0	ø	0	—	0	0	0.0
1948	Cin N	11	8	.579	33	24	6	0	147.1	179	105	21	2	75	56	5.86	67	.299	.379	55-0-3	.091	-3*	113	-31	0	-3.7
1949	Cin N	11	12	.478	33	29	11-1	0	213.1	202	119	20	7	117	80	4.68	89	.253	.353	78-0-5	.256	2*	98	-8	0	-0.7
1950	Cin N	10	18	.357	41	32	12	4	230	255	157	27	4	135	121	5.67	75	.281	.376	92-0-1	.152	-3*	97	-33	0	-3.9
1951	Cin N	7	10	.412	39	22	10-2	2	184.2	167	82	15	4	89	93	3.70	110	.241	.330	59-0-2	.288	3*	79	10	0	1.1
1952	Cin N	9	11	.450	33	26	6-1	0	190.1	197	115	23	7	103	83	5.15	73	.269	.365	64-1-2	.188	2*	99	-27	0	-2.6
1953	Cin N	1	6	.143	28	10	2	0	81.2	100	71	20	0	47	32	7.16	61	.299	.385	20	.200	-0*	82	-24	0	-1.8
1954	Cin N	0	3	.000	12	3	0	2	33.2	36	29	6	1	21	13	6.68	63	.271	.372	9-0-1	.000	-1*	57	-10	0	-0.9
	Phi N	10	8	.556	25	17	10-2	0	138	117	61	10	1	51	49	3.85	105	.231	.300	50-0-5	.120	-2	90	5	0	0.4
	Year	10	11	.476	37	20	10-2	2	171.2	153	90	16	2	72	62	4.40	92	.239	.316	59-0-6	.102	-3	84	-5	0	-0.5
1955	Phi N	10	12	.455	31	29	10-1	0	193.2	176	101	21	2	67-7	85	4.41	90	.241	.304	72-0-3	.278	4*	104	-7	0	-0.4
1956	Phi N	0	2	.000	3	3	0	0	20	18	9	2	0	11-0	8	4.05	92	.240	.333	8	.000	-1	39	0	0	-0.2
	StL N	12	9	.571	34	19	7-2	1	170.2	150	80	16	1	71-8	68	3.69	102	.240	.315	58-2-1	.224	4*	78	2	0	0.6
	Year	12	11	.522	37	22	7-2	1	190.2	168	89	18	1	82-8	76	3.73	101	.240	.317	66-2-1	.197	3	73	0	0	0.4
1957	StL N	10	7	.588	36	18	5	0	165	165	91	25	2	54-7	91	4.31	92	.253	.311	59	.203	0*	125	-7	0	-0.7
1958	StL N	0	1	.000	3	3	0	0	6	13	9	2	0	2-0	4	13.50	31	.448	.484	2	.500	1	102	-6	0	-0.7
	Det A	1	0	1.000	7	3	0	0	22.2	21	8	2	0	5-0	11	2.38	169	.241	.280	6	.000	-1	67	3	75	0.1
Total	13	92	108	.460	361	240	79-9	9	1803	1806	1044	210	31	852-22	794	4.80	84	.260	.343	633-3-23	.196	5	96	-138	108	-14.1

WEHRMEISTER, DAVE David Thomas; B11.9.1952 Berwyn IL; BR/TR/6´4˝/195; [SDN73*1/3]; d4.16; Col Truman St.

YEAR	TM LG	W	L	PCT	G	GS	CG-SHO	SV-BS	IP	H	R	HR	HB	BB-IB	SO	ERA	AERA	OAV	OOB	AB-HR-SH	AVG	PB	SUP	APR	DL	PW
1976	SD N	0	4	.000	7	4	0	0-0	19.1	27	17	0	0	11-1	10	7.45	44	.333	.409	6	.000	-1	73	-9	0	-1.6
1977	SD N	1	3	.250	30	6	0	0-0	69.2	81	53	8	3	44-4	32	6.07	59	.293	.393	12-0-2	.167	0	162	-21	0	-1.0
1978	SD N	1	0	1.000	4	0	0	0-0	7.1	8	5	1	0	5-1	2	6.14	55	.276	.382	0-0-1	ø	0	—	-2	0	-0.3
1981	NY A	0	0	ø	5	0	0	0-0	7	6	4	0	0	7-2	7	5.14	70	.240	.394	0	ø	0	—	-1	0	0.0
1984	Phi N	0	0	ø	7	0	0	0-0	15	18	12	1	1	7-2	13	7.20	51	.300	.371	2	.000	-0	—	-5	0	-0.3
1985	Chi A	2	2	.500	23	0	0	2-2	39.1	35	15	4	3	10-0	32	3.43	127	.241	.304	0	ø	0	—	4	0	0.4
Total	6	4	9	.308	76	10	0	2-2	157.2	175	106	14	7	84-10	96	5.65	66	.284	.373	20-0-3	.100	-1	120	-34	0	-2.8

WEIK, DICK Richard Henry "Legs"; B11.17.1927 Waterloo IA; D4.21.1991 Harvey IL; BR/TR/6´3.5˝/184; d9.8; Mil 1951–52; Col Illinois

YEAR	TM LG	W	L	PCT	G	GS	CG-SHO	SV-BS	IP	H	R	HR	HB	BB-IB	SO	ERA	AERA	OAV	OOB	AB-HR-SH	AVG	PB	SUP	APR	DL	PW
1948	Was A	1	2	.333	3	3	0	0	12.2	14	8	1	0	22	8	5.68	76	.311	.537	4	.750	2	69	-1	0	-0.1
1949	Was A	3	12	.200	27	14	2-2	1	95.1	78	61	5	0	103	58	5.38	79	.230	.410	28-0-2	.179	-1*	56	-10	0	-1.4
1950	Was A	1	3	.250	14	5	1	0	44	38	27	2	0	47	26	4.30	105	.236	.409	13	.154	-1	60	0	0	-0.1
	Cle A	1	3	.250	11	2	0	0	26	18	17	1	1	26	16	3.81	114	.205	.391	5	.200	0	83	0	0	0.0
	Year	2	6	.250	25	7	1	0	70	56	44	3	1	73	42	4.11	108	.225	.402	18	.167	-1	67	-1	0	-0.1
1953	Det A	0	1	.000	12	1	0	0	19.1	32	30	3	0	23	6	13.97	29	.386	.519	2-0-1	.500	1	218	-19	0	-0.9
1954	Det A	0	1	.000	9	1	0	0	16.1	23	14	3	1	16	9	7.16	52	.354	.482	1	.000	-0	382	-6	0	-0.4
Total	5	6	22	.214	76	26	3-2	1	213.2	203	157	15	2	237	123	5.90	72	.260	.433	53-0-3	.226	1	78	-36	0	-2.9

WEILAND, ED Edwin Nicholas; B11.26.1914 Evanston IL; D7.12.1971 Chicago IL; BL/TR/5´11˝/180; d5.1; Mil 1943–45; b–Bob

YEAR	TM LG	W	L	PCT	G	GS	CG-SHO	SV-BS	IP	H	R	HR	HB	BB-IB	SO	ERA	AERA	OAV	OOB	AB-HR-SH	AVG	PB	SUP	APR	DL	PW
1940	Chi A	0	0	ø	5	0	0	0	14.1	15	15	5	0	7	3	8.79	50	.263	.344	5	.200	-0	—	-6	—	-0.3
1942	Chi A	0	0	ø	5	0	0	0	9.2	18	11	0	0	3	4	7.45	48	.383	.420	2	.000	-0	—	-5	0	-0.3
Total	2	0	0	ø	10	0	0	0	24	33	26	5	0	10	7	8.25	50	.317	.377	7	.143	-0	—	-11	0	-0.6

WEILAND, BOB Robert George "Lefty"; B12.14.1905 Chicago IL; D11.9.1988 Chicago IL; BL/TL/6´4˝/215; d9.30; b–Ed

YEAR	TM LG	W	L	PCT	G	GS	CG-SHO	SV-BS	IP	H	R	HR	HB	BB-IB	SO	ERA	AERA	OAV	OOB	AB-HR-SH	AVG	PB	SUP	APR	DL	PW
1928	Chi A	1	0	1.000	1	1	1-1	0	9	7	0	0	1	5	9	0.00	ø	.212	.333	3	.333	0	21	4	—	0.5
1929	Chi A	2	4	.333	15	9	1	1	62	62	42	3	3	43	25	5.81	74	.268	.390	18-0-1	.111	-1	101	-8	—	-0.8
1930	Chi A	0	4	.000	14	3	0	0	32.2	38	31	1	2	21	15	6.61	70	.297	.404	8	.000	-1	43	-8	—	-0.9
1931	Chi A	2	7	.222	15	8	3	0	75	75	55	3	4	46	38	5.16	83	.259	.368	22	.182	1	92	-9	—	-0.7
1932	Bos A	6	16	.273	43	27	7	1	195.2	231	125	11	6	97	63	4.51	100	.295	.377	61-0-2	.148	-1	75	-3	—	-0.2
1933	Bos A	8	14	.364	39	27	12	3	216.1	197	107	19	5	100	97	3.87	113	.244	.331	65-0-6	.108	-4	65	13	—	0.7
1934	Bos A	1	5	.167	11	7	2	0	55.2	63	41	4	0	27	29	5.50	87	.293	.372	19	.105	-1	88	-4	—	-0.5
	Cle A	1	5	.167	16	7	2	0	70	71	41	5	0	30	42	4.11	111	.262	.336	24-1-1	.125	-0	57	2	—	0.1
	Year	2	10	.167	27	14	4	0	125.2	134	82	9	0	57	71	4.73	99	.276	.352	43-1-1	.116	-1	73	-4	—	-0.4
1935	StL A	0	2	.000	14	4	0	0	32	39	35	6	1	31	11	9.56	50	.298	.436	8-0-1	.000	-1	100	-14	—	-0.8
1937	StL N	15	14	.517	41	**34**	21-2	0	264.1	283	127	14	5	94	105	3.54	112	.276	.339	89-2-5	.169	0	106	11	—	1.1
1938	StL N	16	11	.593	35	29	11-1	1	228.1	248	118	14	4	67	117	3.59	110	.272	.324	80-0-10	.138	-3	112	6	—	0.3
1939	StL N	10	12	.455	32	23	6-3	1	146.1	146	69	4	6	50	63	3.57	115	.264	.331	46-0-6	.065	-4	103	7	—	0.5
1940	StL N	0	0	ø	1	0	0	0	1	3	3	1	0	0	0	27.00	15	.600	.600	0	ø	0	—	-2	—	-0.1
Total	12	62	94	.397	277	179	66-7	7	1388.1	1463	794	85	37	611	614	4.24	100	.272	.350	443-3-32	.129	-16	90	-5	—	-0.8

WEILMAN, CARL Carl Woolworth "Zeke" (b Carl Woolworth Weilenmann); B11.29.1889 Hamilton OH; D5.25.1924 Hamilton OH; BL/TL/6´5.5˝/187; d8.24

YEAR	TM LG	W	L	PCT	G	GS	CG-SHO	SV-BS	IP	H	R	HR	HB	BB-IB	SO	ERA	AERA	OAV	OOB	AB-HR-SH	AVG	PB	SUP	APR	DL	PW
1912	StL A	2	4	.333	8	6	5-2	1	48.1	42	19	0	0	3	24	2.79	119	.227	.239	17-0-1	.118	-1*	100	3	—	0.4
1913	StL A	10	19	.345	39	28	17-2	0	251.2	262	122	2	4	60	79	3.40	86	.283	.330	82-0-2	.146	-3	82	-10	—	-1.4
1914	StL A	17	12	.586	44	36	20-3	1	299	260	96	1	11	84	119	2.08	130	.237	.298	101-0-2	.149	-1	92	21	—	2.0
1915	StL A	18	19	.486	47	31	19-3	4	295.2	240	110	6	3	83	125	2.34	122	.229	.287	100-0-3	.230	2	79	17	—	2.4
1916	StL A	17	18	.486	46	31	19-1	2	276	237	90	3	8	76	91	2.15	128	.242	.301	91-0-4	.154	-1	106	17	—	2.0
1917	StL A	1	2	.333	5	3	0	0	19	19	9	1	0	6	9	1.89	137	.268	.325	4	.000	-1	74	0	—	0.0
1919	StL A	10	6	.625	20	20	12-3	0	148	133	51	3	3	45	44	2.07	160	.244	.305	47-0-4	.191	0	118	17	—	1.9
1920	StL A	9	13	.409	30	24	13-1	2	183.1	201	103	6	3	61	45	4.47	88	.291	.351	63-0-4	.175	-2	109	-7	—	-0.9
Total	8	84	93	.475	239	179	105-15	10	1521	1394	600	22	32	418	536	2.67	112	.251	.308	505-0-20	.170	-7	97	58	—	6.4

YEAR	TM LG	W	L	PCT	G	GS	CG-SHO	SV-BS	IP	H	R	HR	HB	BB-IB	SO	ERA	AERA	OAV	OOB	AB-HR-SH	AVG	PB	SUP	APR	DL	PW
WEIMER, JAKE	Jacob "Tornado Jake"; B11.29.1873 Ottumwa IA; D6.19.1928 Chicago IL; BR/TL/5´11˝/175; d4.17																									
1903	Chi N	20	8	.714	35	33	27-3	0	282	241	111	4	11	104	128	2.30	136	**.225**	.301	107-0-1	.196	2	116	28	—	2.6
1904	Chi N	20	14	.588	37	37	31-5	0	307	229	96	1	7	97	177	1.91	140	.204	.272	115-0-2	.183	-1	102	26	—	2.8
1905	Chi N	18	12	.600	33	30	26-2	1	250.1	212	84	1	12	80	107	2.26	132	.229	.299	92-0-1	.207	2	130	21	—	2.5
1906	Cin N	20	14	.588	41	39	31-6	1	304.2	263	105	0	13	99	141	2.22	124	.236	.306	108-0-2	.269	6	94	18	—	2.8
1907	Cin N	11	14	.440	29	26	19-3	0	209	165	73	6	23	63	67	2.41	108	.226	.308	72-1-4	.194	2*	88	6	—	1.1
1908	Cin N	8	7	.533	15	15	9-2	0	116.2	110	38	2	6	50	36	2.39	96	.255	.341	45-0-2	.244	2	136	1	—	0.5
1909	NY N	0	0	ø	1	0	0	0	3	7	4	0	1	0	1	9.00	28	.467	.500	1	.000	-0	—	-2	—	-0.1
Total	7	97	69	.584	191	180	143-21	2	1472.2	1227	511	14	73	493	657	2.23	125	.227	.300	540-1-12	.213	11	108	98	—	12.2
WEINERT, LEFTY	Phillip Walter; B4.21.1902 Philadelphia PA; D4.17.1973 Rockledge FL; BL/TL/6´1˝/195; d9.24																									
1919	Phi N	0	0	ø	1	0	0	0	4	11	9	0	0	2	0	18.00	18	.478	.520	2	1.000	1	—	-6	—	-0.2
1920	Phi N	1	1	.500	10	2	0	0	22	27	17	1	1	19	10	6.14	56	.333	.465	5	.000	-1	127	-5	—	-0.5
1921	Phi N	1	0	1.000	8	0	0	0	12.1	8	6	1	1	5	2	1.46	290	.216	.326	1	1.000	0	—	2	—	0.2
1922	Phi N	8	11	.421	34	22	10	1	166.2	189	103	10	5	70	58	3.40	137	.289	.362	58-0-1	.241	-0	82	13	—	1.3
1923	Phi N	4	17	.190	38	20	8	1	156	207	131	10	8	81	46	5.42	85	.327	.410	59	.322	2*	76	-18	—	-1.9
1924	Phi N	0	1	.000	8	1	0	0	14.2	10	7	0	0	11	7	2.45	182	.204	.350	4	.000	-1	38	2	—	0.1
1927	Chi N	1	1	.500	5	3	1	0	19.2	21	13	2	0	6	5	4.58	84	.259	.310	5	.200	0	118	-2	—	-0.2
1928	Chi N	1	0	1.000	10	1	0	0	17	24	10	0	1	9	8	5.29	73	.393	.479	2	.000	-0	154	-2	—	-0.2
1931	NY A	2	2	.500	17	0	0	0	24.2	31	19	2	5	19	24	6.20	64	.316	.451	6	.000	-0	—	-6	—	-0.9
Total	9	18	33	.353	131	49	19	2	437	528	315	26	21	222	160	4.59	97	.308	.393	142-0-1	.261	2	85	-22	—	-2.3
WEIR, ROY	William Franklin "Bill"; B2.25.1911 Portland ME; D9.30.1989 Anaheim CA; BL/TL/5´8.5˝/170; d6.25; Col New Hampshire																									
1936	Bos N	4	3	.571	12	7	3-2	0	57.1	53	23	0	0	24	29	2.83	136	.241	.316	18-0-1	.278	2*	63	6	—	0.9
1937	Bos N	1	1	.500	10	4	1	0	33	27	18	0	0	19	8	3.82	94	.227	.333	10	.000	-1	138	-2	—	-0.2
1938	Bos N	1	0	1.000	5	0	0	0	13.1	14	10	4	0	6	3	6.75	51	.269	.345	3	.333	0	—	-5	—	-0.3
1939	Bos N	0	0	ø	2	0	0	0	2.2	1	0	0	0	1	2	0.00	ø	.125	.222	1	.000	-0	—	1	—	0.1
Total	4	6	4	.600	29	11	4-2	0	106.1	95	51	4	0	50	42	3.55	104	.238	.323	32-0-1	.188	1	90	0	—	0.5
WELCH, TED	Floyd John; B10.17.1892 Coyville KS; D1.7.1943 Great Bend KS; BL/TR/5´9.5˝/160; d5.15																									
1914	StL F	0	0	ø	3	0	0	0	6	6	4	0	3	3	2	6.00	51	.273	.429	1	.000	-0	—	-1	—	-0.1
WELCH, JOHNNY	John Vernon; B12.2.1906 Washington DC; D9.2.1940 St.Louis MO; BL/TR/6´3˝/184; d5.22																									
1926	Chi N	0	0	ø	3	0	0	0	4.1	5	2	0	0	1	0	2.08	185	.357	.400	1	1.000	0	—	1	—	0.1
1927	Chi N	0	0	ø	1	0	0	0	1	0	1	0	0	3	1	9.00	43	.000	.500	0	ø	0	—	-1	—	0.0
1928	Chi N	0	0	ø	3	0	0	0	4	13	7	0	0	0	2	15.75	24	.591	.591	0	ø	0	—	-5	—	-0.2
1931	Chi N	2	1	.667	8	3	1	0	33.2	39	16	2	1	10	7	3.74	103	.291	.345	12	.417	2	148	1	—	0.2
1932	Bos A	4	6	.400	20	8	3-1	0	72.1	93	46	3	3	38	26	5.23	86	.312	.395	36-1-1	.250	2*	66	-4	—	-0.3
1933	Bos A	4	9	.308	47	7	1	3	129	142	81	6	2	67	68	4.60	95	.283	.370	37-0-2	.162	-1	97	-4	—	-0.5
1934	Bos A	13	15	.464	41	22	8-1	0	206.1	223	112	14	8	76	91	4.49	107	.274	.342	74-0-6	.203	-1	110	11	—	1.1
1935	Bos A	10	9	.526	31	19	10-1	2	143	155	82	4	4	53	48	4.47	106	.273	.339	50-0-2	.180	-0	96	5	—	0.6
1936	Bos A	2	1	.667	9	3	1	0	32.2	43	24	4	0	8	9	5.51	96	.305	.342	11	.273	1	127	-1	—	0.0
	Pit N	0	0	ø	9	1	0	1	22	22	12	3	0	6	5	4.50	90	.265	.315	7	.286	1	146	-1	—	0.0
Total	9	35	41	.461	172	63	24-3	6	648.1	735	383	36	18	262	257	4.66	99	.285	.355	228-1-11	.219	3	103	2	—	1.0
WELCH, MICKEY	Michael Francis "Smiling Mickey" (b Michael Francis Walsh); B7.4.1859 Brooklyn NY; D7.30.1941 Concord NH; BR/TR/5´8˝/160; d5.1; HF1973																									
1880	Tro N	34	30	.531	65	64	64-4	0	574	575	321	7	—	80	123	2.54	99	.249	.274	251	.287	10*	96	-2	—	0.5
1881	Tro N	21	18	.538	40	40	40-4	0	368	371	186	7	—	78	104	2.67	111	.255	.293	148	.203	-4	86	10	—	0.3
1882	Tro N	14	16	.467	33	33	30-5	0	281	334	221	7	—	62	53	3.46	82	.280	.315	151-1	.245	1*	96	-22	—	-1.8
1883	NY N	25	23	.521	54	52	46-4	0	426	431	271	11	—	66	144	2.73	114	.244	.272	320-2	.234	3*	97	16	—	1.4
1884	NY N	39	21	.650	65	65	62-4	0	557.1	528	275	12	—	146	345	2.50	119	.237	.284	249-3	.241	9*	106	29	—	3.2
1885	NY N	44	11	**.800**	56	55	55-7	1	492	372	170	4	—	131	258	1.66	160	.203	.256	199-2	.206	5	127	60	—	6.0
1886	NY N	33	22	.600	59	59	56-1	0	500	514	279	13	—	163	272	2.99	107	.259	.315	213	.216	1	94	10	—	0.7
1887	NY N	22	15	.595	41	40	39-2	0	346	339	191	7	5	91	115	3.36	112	.253	.303	148-2	.243	4	94	23	—	2.1
1888	†NY N	26	19	.578	47	47	47-5	0	425.1	328	156	12	14	108	167	1.93	142	.207	.263	169-2	.189	1	97	42	—	3.9
1889	†NY N	27	12	.692	45	41	39-3	2	375	340	196	14	10	149	125	3.02	130	.235	.311	156	.192	-2	120	41	—	3.1
1890	NY N	17	14	.548	37	37	33-2	0	292.1	268	145	5	12	122	97	2.99	117	.236	.317	123	.179	-3	85	24	—	1.6
1891	NY N	5	9	.357	22	15	14	1	160	177	136	7	11	97	46	4.27	75	.270	.373	71	.141	-4	92	-20	—	-1.9
1892	NY N	0	0	ø	1	1	0	0	5	11	9	0	0	4	1	14.40	22	.423	.500	3	.333	0	177	-5	—	-0.2
Total	13	307	210	.594	565	549	525-41	4	4802	4588	2556	106	52	1297	1850	2.71	113	.242	.292	2201-12	.224	21	100	206	—	18.9
WELCH, MIKE	Michael Paul; B8.25.1972 Haverhill MA; BL/TR/6´2˝/210; [NYN93 3/80]; d7.17; Col Southern Maine																									
1998	Phi N	0	2	.000	10	2	0	0-0	20.2	26	19	7	2	7-0	15	8.27	52	.310	.376	3	.000	-0	32	-8	0	-0.7
WELCH, BOB	Robert Lynn; B11.3.1956 Detroit MI; BR/TR/6´3˝/(190–198); [LAN77 1/20]; d6.20; C1; Col Eastern Michigan																									
1978	†LA N	7	4	.636	23	13	4-3	3-0	111.1	92	28	6	1	26-2	66	2.02	174	.229	.274	29-0-6	.172	0	102	19	0	1.9
1979	LA N	5	6	.455	25	12	1	5-4	81.1	82	42	7	3	32-4	64	3.98	91	.265	.339	19-0-3	.158	-0	90	-4	0	-0.5
1980	LA N★	14	9	.609	32	32	3-2	0-0	213.2	190	85	15	3	79-6	141	3.29	106	.242	.310	70-0-5	.243	3*	98	5	0	0.9
1981	†LA N	9	5	.643	23	23	2-1	0-0	141.1	141	56	11	3	41-0	88	3.44	96	.259	.313	45-0-7	.222	2	131	-1	0	0.0
1982	LA N	16	11	.593	36	36	9-3	0-0	235.2	199	94	19	5	81-5	176	3.36	103	.229	.297	85-0-7	.141	-1*	115	5	0	0.4
1983	†LA N	15	12	.556	31	31	4-3	0-0	204	164	73	13	3	72-4	156	2.65	136	.222	.291	73-1-3	.096	-2	78	22	0	2.5
1984	LA N	13	13	.500	31	29	3-1	0-1	178.2	191	86	11	2	58-7	126	3.78	94	.273	.330	51-0-8	.078	-3*	92	-4	0	-0.7
1985	†LA N	14	4	.778	23	23	8-3	0-0	167.1	141	49	16	6	35-2	96	2.31	151	.225	.272	50-0-7	.180	1*	117	24	37	2.7
1986	LA N	7	13	.350	33	33	7-3	0-0	235.2	227	95	14	7	55-6	183	3.28	106	.251	.297	76-1-5	.105	-0*	84	6	0	0.3
1987	LA N	15	9	.625	35	35	6-**4**	0-0	251.2	204	94	21	4	86-6	196	3.22	124	.221	.289	83-0-8	.157	1*	107	25	0	2.4
1988	†Oak A	17	9	.654	36	36	4-2	0-0	244.2	237	107	22	10	81-1	158	3.64	104	.257	.321	0	ø	0	111	5	0	0.5
1989	†Oak A	17	8	.680	33	33	1	0-0	209.2	191	82	13	6	78-3	137	3.00	123	.241	.312	0	ø	0	112	16	17	1.8
1990	†Oak A★	**27**	6	**.818**	35	35	2-2	0-0	238	214	90	26	5	77-4	127	2.95	127	.242	.304	0	ø	0	123	20	0	2.7
1991	Oak A	12	13	.480	35	**35**	7-1	0-0	220	220	124	25	11	91-3	101	4.58	84	.263	.341	0	ø	0*	103	-22	0	-2.2
1992	†Oak A	11	7	.611	20	20	0	0-0	123.2	114	47	13	2	43-0	47	3.27	115	.247	.312	0	ø	0	109	9	78	1.1
1993	Oak A	9	11	.450	30	28	0	0-0	166.2	208	102	25	7	56-5	63	5.29	78	.310	.368	0	ø	0	83	-21	16	-2.1
1994	Oak A	3	6	.333	25	8	0	0-1	68.2	79	56	10	1	43-2	44	7.08	63	.290	.384	1	.000	-0*	110	-20	0	-2.1
Total	17	211	146	.591	506	462	61-28	8-6	3092	2894	1310	267	79	1034-60	1969	3.47	106	.249	.312	582-2-59	.151	2	104	84	148	9.6
WELCHEL, DON	Donald Ray; B2.3.1957 Atlanta TX; BR/TR/6´4˝/205; [BalA78 7/178]; d9.15; Col Sam Houston St.																									
1982	Bal A	1	0	1.000	2	0	0	0-0	4.1	6	6	0	0	2-0	3	8.31	49	.300	.364	0	ø	0	—	-3	0	-0.5
1983	Bal A	0	2	.000	11	0	0	0-0	26.2	33	18	1	0	10-1	16	5.40	74	.297	.352	0	ø	0	—	-4	0	-0.3
Total	2	1	2	.333	13	0	0	0-0	31	39	24	1	0	12-1	19	5.81	69	.298	.354	0	ø	0	—	-7	0	-0.8
WELLEMEYER, TODD	Todd Allen; B8.30.1978 Louisville KY; BR/TR/6´3˝/(200–205); [ChiN00 4/103]; d5.15; Col Bellarmine (KY)																									
2003	Chi N	1	1	.500	15	0	0	1-0	27.2	25	22	5	0	19-1	30	6.51	67	.245	.364	1-0-1	.000	0	—	-7	0	-0.4
2004	Chi N	2	1	.667	20	0	0	0-0	24.1	27	16	1	0	20-2	30	5.92	75	.287	.405	0	ø	0	—	-3	55	-0.4
2005	Chi N	2	1	.667	22	0	0	1-0	32.1	32	23	7	0	22-1	32	6.12	71	.264	.375	4	.250	0	—	-6	0	-0.5
2006	Fla N	0	2	.000	18	0	0	0-0	21.1	20	13	1	2	13-1	17	5.48	78	.256	.365	0	ø	0	—	-2	0	-0.2
	KC A	1	2	.333	28	0	0	1-0	57	48	25	5	2	37-2	37	3.63	129	.235	.354	2	.000	-0	—	6	0	0.3
Total	4	6	7	.462	103	0	0	3-0	162.2	152	99	19	4	111-7	146	5.20	86	.254	.369	7-0-1	.143	0	—	-12	55	-1.2
WELLS, DAVID	David Lee "Boomer"; B5.20.1963 Torrance CA; BL/TL/6´4˝/(225–250); [TorA82 2/30]; d6.30																									
1987	Tor A	4	3	.571	18	2	0	1-1	29.1	37	14	0	0	12-0	32	3.99	114	.311	.374	0	ø	0	10	2	0	0.4
1988	Tor A	3	5	.375	41	0	0	4-2	64.1	65	36	12	2	31-9	56	4.62	86	.269	.354	0	ø	0	—	-4	0	-0.6
1989	†Tor A	7	4	.636	54	0	0	2-7	86.1	66	25	5	0	28-7	78	2.40	158	.207	.269	0	ø	0	—	14	0	1.8
1990	Tor A	11	6	.647	43	25	0	3-0	189	165	72	14	2	45-3	115	3.14	126	.235	.283	0	ø	0	109	16	0	1.5
1991	†Tor A	15	10	.600	40	28	2	1-1	198.1	188	88	24	2	49-1	106	3.72	114	.251	.297	0	ø	0	94	12	0	1.4
1992	†Tor A	7	9	.438	41	14	0	2-2	120	138	84	16	8	36-6	62	5.40	76	.289	.346	0	ø	0	100	-19	0	-2.3
1993	Det A	11	9	.550	32	30	0	0-0	187	183	93	26	7	42-6	139	4.19	104	.254	.300	0	ø	0	105	5	19	0.5

YEAR	TM LG	W	L	PCT	G	GS	CG-SHO	SV-BS	IP	H	R	HR	HB	BB-IB	SO	ERA	AERA	OAV	OOB	AB-HR-SH	AVG	PB	SUP	APR	DL	PW
1994	Det A	5	7	.417	16	16	5-1	0-0	111.1	113	54	13	2	24-6	71	3.96	124	.260	.302	0	ø	0	97	12	51	1.1
1995	Det A★	10	3	.769	18	18	3	0-0	130.1	120	54	17	2	37-5	83	3.04	158	.242	.297	0	ø	0	94	22	0	2.0
	†Cin N	6	5	.545	11	11	3	0-0	72.2	74	34	6	0	16-4	50	3.59	116	.265	.304	28-0-1	.143	-1	102	3	0	0.3
1996	†Bal A	11	14	.440	34	34	3	0-0	224.1	247	132	32	7	51-7	130	5.14	96	.285	.325	0	ø	0	100	-2	0	-0.1
1997	†NY A	16	10	.615	32	32	5-2	0-0	218	239	109	24	6	45-0	156	4.21	106	.278	.317	0	ø	0	95	7	0	0.8
1998	†NY A★	18	4	**.818**	30	30	8-**5**	0-0	214.1	195	86	29	1	29-0	163	3.49	126	.239	**.265**	4	.250	0	142	24	0	2.1
1999	Tor A	17	10	.630	34	34	**7**-1	0-0	**231.2**	246	132	32	6	62-2	169	4.82	102	.271	.320	6-0-1	.000	-1	112	4	0	0.4
2000	Tor A★	**20**	8	.714	35	**35**	**9**-1	0-0	229.2	266	115	23	8	31-0	166	4.11	122	.289	.316	6	.167	-0	109	23	0	2.3
2001	Chi A	5	7	.417	16	16	1	0-0	100.2	120	55	12	3	21-1	59	4.47	104	.297	.335	2	.000	-0	94	2	101	0.1
2002	†NY A	19	7	.731	31	31	2-1	0-0	206.1	210	100	21	5	45-2	137	3.75	116	.259	.300	4-0-1	.000	-0	138	12	0	1.2
2003	†NY A	15	7	.682	31	30	4-1	0-0	213	242	101	24	8	20-0	101	4.14	106	.286	.306	6	.167	0	120	9	0	0.9
2004	SD N	12	8	.600	31	31	0	0-0	195.2	203	85	23	2	20-1	101	3.73	106	.266	.285	57-0-8	.105	-1	117	7	21	0.6
2005	†Bos A	15	7	.682	30	30	2	0-0	184	220	95	21	9	21-0	107	4.45	102	.296	.321	7	.143	-0	134	3	22	0.2
2006	Bos A	2	3	.400	8	8	0	0-0	47	64	30	10	0	8-0	24	4.98	94	.327	.361	0	ø	0	113	-3	117	-0.3
	†SD N	1	2	.333	5	5	0	0-0	28.1	33	11	1	0	4-0	14	3.49	119	.292	.316	5-0-3	.200	0	53	3	0	0.2
Total	20	230	148	.608	631	460	54-12	13-13	3281.2	3434	1605	385	80	677-60	2119	4.07	110	.269	.308	125-0-14	.120	-3	111	152	331	14.5

Wells, Ed Edwin Lee "Satchelfoot"; B6.7.1900 Ashland OH; D5.1.1986 Montgomery AL; BL/TL/6´1.5˝/183; d6.16; Col Bethany

YEAR	TM LG	W	L	PCT	G	GS	CG-SHO	SV-BS	IP	H	R	HR	HB	BB-IB	SO	ERA	AERA	OAV	OOB	AB-HR-SH	AVG	PB	SUP	APR	DL	PW
1923	Det A	0	0	ø	7	0	0	0	10	11	6	0	0	6	6	5.40	72	.306	.405	1	.000	-0	—	-1	—	-0.1
1924	Det A	6	8	.429	29	15	5	4	102	117	58	2	1	42	33	4.06	101	.291	.360	33-0-2	.212	-1	79	0	—	0.0
1925	Det A	6	9	.400	35	14	5	2	134.1	190	106	8	2	62	45	6.23	69	.345	.413	43-0-1	.279	3	103	-28	—	-2.4
1926	Det A	12	10	.545	36	26	9-**4**	0	178	201	101	7	2	76	58	4.15	98	.297	.370	73	.205	0	114	-2	—	-0.4
1927	Det A	0	1	.000	8	1	0	1	20	28	16	3	0	5	5	6.75	62	.333	.371	7	.286	0	40	-4	—	-0.2
1929	NY A	13	9	.591	31	23	10-3	0	193.1	179	102	19	1	81	78	4.33	89	.248	.324	74-0-3	.230	2	156	-6	—	-0.7
1930	NY A	12	3	.800	27	21	7	0	150.2	185	101	11	4	49	46	5.20	83	.302	.358	58-0-2	.259	0*	151	-14	—	-1.2
1931	NY A	9	5	.643	27	10	6	2	116.2	130	68	7	1	37	34	4.32	92	.286	.341	45-0-2	.222	1*	194	-7	—	-0.7
1932	NY A	3	3	.500	22	0	0	2	31.2	38	19	1	0	12	13	4.26	96	.302	.362	6-0-1	.000	-1*	—	-1	—	-0.3
1933	StL A	6	14	.300	36	22	10	1	203.2	230	113	13	1	63	58	4.20	111	.278	.330	71-0-4	.197	-1*	95	7	—	0.4
1934	StL A	1	7	.125	33	8	2	1	92	108	60	7	0	35	27	4.79	104	.292	.353	22-0-1	.045	-2	89	1	—	0.0
Total	11	68	69	.496	291	140	54-7	13	1232.1	1417	750	78	12	468	403	4.65	91	.291	.355	433-0-16	.215	1	121	-55	—	-5.6

Wells, John John Frederick; B11.25.1922 Junction City KS; D10.23.1993 Olean NY; BR/TR/5´11.5˝/180; d9.14

YEAR	TM LG	W	L	PCT	G	GS	CG-SHO	SV-BS	IP	H	R	HR	HB	BB-IB	SO	ERA	AERA	OAV	OOB	AB-HR-SH	AVG	PB	SUP	APR	DL	PW
1944	Bro N	0	2	.000	4	2	0	0	15	18	9	1	0	11	7	5.40	66	.316	.426	4	.250	0	71	-2	0	-0.3

Wells, Kip Robert Kip; B4.21.1977 Houston TX; BR/TR/6´3˝/(195–205); [ChiA98 1/16]; d8.2; Col Baylor

YEAR	TM LG	W	L	PCT	G	GS	CG-SHO	SV-BS	IP	H	R	HR	HB	BB-IB	SO	ERA	AERA	OAV	OOB	AB-HR-SH	AVG	PB	SUP	APR	DL	PW
1999	Chi A	4	1	.800	7	7	0	0-0	35.2	33	17	2	3	15-0	29	4.04	122	.248	.333	0	ø	0	97	4	0	0.4
2000	Chi A	6	9	.400	20	20	0	0-0	98.2	126	76	15	2	58-4	71	6.02	84	.312	.398	2	.000	-0	107	-11	0	-1.5
2001	Chi A	10	11	.476	40	20	0	0-2	133.1	145	80	14	12	61-5	99	4.79	97	.281	.366	6	.167	-0	84	-3	0	-0.4
2002	Pit N	12	14	.462	33	33	1-1	0-0	198.1	197	92	21	7	71-11	134	3.58	117	.261	.328	63-1-13	.190	1*	88	11	0	1.4
2003	Pit N	10	9	.526	31	31	1	0-0	197.1	171	77	24	7	76-7	147	3.28	132	.233	.310	68-1-4	.191	2*	89	23	0	2.2
2004	Pit N	5	7	.417	24	24	0	0-0	138.1	145	71	14	6	66-4	116	4.55	95	.270	.352	43-0-4	.186	2*	93	-1	22	0.1
2005	Pit N	8	18	.308	33	33	1-1	0-0	182	186	116	23	12	99-8	132	5.09	83	.266	.363	57-1-3	.158	0*	75	-19	0	-2.3
2006	Pit N	1	5	.167	7	7	0	0-0	36.1	46	27	3	4	18-1	16	6.69	68	.319	.407	11-0-1	.091	-1	63	-7	76	-1.0
	Tex A	1	0	1.000	2	2	0	0-0	8	15	6	0	0	3-0	4	5.63	83	.405	.450	0	ø	0	241	-1	51	-0.1
Total	8	57	74	.435	197	177	3-2	0-2	1028	1064	562	116	53	467-40	748	4.46	99	.269	.351	250-3-25	.176	5	90	-4	149	-1.2

Wells, Bob Robert Lee; B11.1.1966 Yakima WA; BR/TR/6´0˝/(180–200); d5.16; Col Spokane Falls (WA) CC

YEAR	TM LG	W	L	PCT	G	GS	CG-SHO	SV-BS	IP	H	R	HR	HB	BB-IB	SO	ERA	AERA	OAV	OOB	AB-HR-SH	AVG	PB	SUP	APR	DL	PW
1994	Phi N	1	0	1.000	6	0	0	0-0	5	4	1	0	1	3-0	3	1.80	238	.235	.381	0	ø	0	—	1	0	0.2
	Sea A	1	0	1.000	1	0	0	0-0	4	4	1	0	0	1-0	3	2.25	219	.250	.294	0	ø	0	—	1	0	0.2
1995	†Sea A	4	3	.571	30	4	0	0-1	76.2	88	51	11	3	39-3	38	5.75	83	.284	.364	0	ø	0	68	-7	0	-0.6
1996	Sea A	12	7	.632	36	16	1-1	0-0	130.2	141	78	25	6	46-5	94	5.30	94	.274	.338	0	ø	0	121	-2	0	-0.3
1997	†Sea A	2	0	1.000	46	1	0	2-2	67.1	88	49	11	3	18-1	51	5.75	79	.314	.360	0	ø	0	203	-10	0	-0.5
1998	Sea A	2	2	.500	30	0	0	0-1	51.2	54	38	12	2	16-1	29	6.10	77	.261	.319	0	ø	0	—	-8	33	-0.5
1999	Min A	8	3	.727	**76**	0	0	1-4	87.1	79	41	8	5	28-4	44	3.81	136	.245	.312	0	ø	0	—	12	0	1.2
2000	Min A	0	7	.000	76	0	0	10-10	86.1	80	39	14	4	15-2	76	3.65	144	.247	.284	0	ø	0	—	14	0	1.2
2001	Min A	8	5	.615	65	0	0	2-2	68.2	72	39	12	10	18-2	49	5.11	91	.273	.338	0	ø	0	—	-2	0	-0.4
2002	†Min A	2	1	.667	48	0	0	0-0	58	78	41	8	1	16-1	30	5.90	76	.325	.367	0	ø	0	—	-9	41	-0.5
Total	9	40	28	.588	414	21	1-1	15-20	635.2	688	378	101	35	200-19	417	5.03	97	.276	.335	0	ø	0	116	-10	74	0.0

Wells, Terry Terry; B9.10.1963 Kankakee IL; BL/TL/6´3˝/205; [HouN85 8/196]; d7.3; Col Illinois

YEAR	TM LG	W	L	PCT	G	GS	CG-SHO	SV-BS	IP	H	R	HR	HB	BB-IB	SO	ERA	AERA	OAV	OOB	AB-HR-SH	AVG	PB	SUP	APR	DL	PW
1990	LA N	1	2	.333	5	5	0	0-0	20.2	25	23	4	0	14-0	18	7.84	47	.287	.386	7	.000	-1	123	-11	0	-1.4

Welsh, Chris Christopher Charles; B4.14.1955 Wilmington DE; BL/TL/6´2˝/185; [NYA77 21/536]; d4.12; Col South Florida

YEAR	TM LG	W	L	PCT	G	GS	CG-SHO	SV-BS	IP	H	R	HR	HB	BB-IB	SO	ERA	AERA	OAV	OOB	AB-HR-SH	AVG	PB	SUP	APR	DL	PW
1981	SD N	6	7	.462	22	19	4-2	0-0	123.2	122	55	9	1	41-4	51	3.78	86	.264	.323	41-0-3	.146	0	105	-7	0	-0.6
1982	SD N	8	8	.500	28	20	3-1	0-0	139.1	146	88	16	3	63-2	48	4.91	70	.268	.346	42-0-5	.262	4	108	-25	22	-2.1
1983	SD N	0	1	.000	7	1	0	0-0	14.1	13	5	2	0	2-0	8	2.51	140	.236	.263	4	.000	-0	25	1	0	0.0
	Mon N	0	1	.000	16	5	0	0-0	44.2	46	30	5	4	18-1	17	5.04	72	.267	.349	14	.286	1	141	-8	0	-0.2
	Year	0	2	.000	23	6	0	0-0	59	59	35	7	4	20-1	22	4.42	81	.260	.329	18	.222	1	123	-7	0	-0.2
1985	Tex A	2	5	.286	25	6	0	0-0	76.1	101	40	11	4	25-3	31	4.13	103	.316	.371	0	ø	0	71	0	0	0.0
1986	Cin N	6	9	.400	24	24	1	0-0	139.1	163	79	9	3	40-4	40	4.78	81	.301	.350	42-1-4	.119	0	112	-12	21	-1.1
Total	5	22	31	.415	122	75	8-3	0-0	537.2	591	297	52	15	189-14	192	4.45	81	.282	.344	143-1-12	.182	5	106	-51	43	-4.0

Welteroth, Dick Richard John; B8.3.1927 Williamsport PA; BR/TR/5´11˝/165; d5.16

YEAR	TM LG	W	L	PCT	G	GS	CG-SHO	SV-BS	IP	H	R	HR	HB	BB-IB	SO	ERA	AERA	OAV	OOB	AB-HR-SH	AVG	PB	SUP	APR	DL	PW
1948	Was A	2	1	.667	33	2	0	1	65.1	73	43	6	1	50	16	5.51	79	.286	.405	10	.100	-1	135	-7	0	-0.5
1949	Was A	2	5	.286	52	2	0	2	95.1	107	83	6	1	89	37	7.36	58	.296	.437	17-0-1	.059	-1	95	-30	0	-2.1
1950	Was A	0	0	ø	5	0	0	0	6	5	5	0	0	6	2	3.00	150	.217	.379	0	ø	0	—	0	0	0.0
Total	3	4	6	.400	90	4	0	3	166.2	185	131	12	2	145	55	6.48	66	.290	.422	27-0-1	.074	-2	115	-37	0	-2.6

Welzer, Tony Anton Frank; B4.5.1899 , Germany; D3.18.1971 Milwaukee WI; BR/TR/5´11˝/160; d4.13

YEAR	TM LG	W	L	PCT	G	GS	CG-SHO	SV-BS	IP	H	R	HR	HB	BB-IB	SO	ERA	AERA	OAV	OOB	AB-HR-SH	AVG	PB	SUP	APR	DL	PW
1926	Bos A	4	3	.571	39	5	1-1	0	139	167	88	5	3	53	29	4.86	84	.308	.373	38	.211	2	83	-12	—	-0.2
1927	Bos A	6	11	.353	37	19	8	1	171.2	214	109	10	4	71	56	4.72	89	.318	.386	42-0-7	.095	-2	79	-10	—	-1.0
Total	2	10	14	.417	76	24	9-1	1	310.2	381	197	15	7	124	85	4.78	87	.313	.380	80-0-7	.150	-0	81	-22	—	-1.2

Wendell, Turk Steven John; B5.19.1967 Pittsfield MA; BB/TR/6´2˝/(180–205); [AtlN88 5/112]; d6.17; Col Quinnipiac; [DL 2002 Phi N 183]

YEAR	TM LG	W	L	PCT	G	GS	CG-SHO	SV-BS	IP	H	R	HR	HB	BB-IB	SO	ERA	AERA	OAV	OOB	AB-HR-SH	AVG	PB	SUP	APR	DL	PW
1993	Chi N	1	2	.333	7	4	0	0-0	22.2	24	13	0	0	8-1	15	4.37	92	.273	.333	7	.143	-0	112	-1	0	-0.2
1994	Chi N	0	1	.000	6	2	0	0-0	14.1	22	20	3	0	10-1	9	11.93	35	.349	.432	2	.000	0	86	-12	0	-0.7
1995	Chi N	3	1	.750	43	0	0	0-0	60.1	71	35	11	2	24-4	50	4.92	85	.298	.363	7	.000	-0	—	-4	32	-0.2
1996	Chi N	4	5	.444	70	0	0	18-3	79.1	58	26	8	3	44-4	75	2.84	154	.201	.313	2-0-1	.500	1	—	14	0	2.0
1997	Chi N	3	5	.375	52	0	0	4-1	60	53	32	4	1	39-5	54	4.20	103	.238	.350	3	.000	-0	—	0	0	0.0
	NY N	0	0	ø	13	0	0	1-1	16.1	15	10	3	1	14-1	10	4.96	81	.250	.400	2	.000	-0	—	-2	0	-0.1
	Year	3	5	.375	65	0	0	5-2	76.1	68	42	7	2	53-6	64	4.36	98	.240	.361	5	.000	-0	—	-2	0	-0.1
1998	NY N	5	1	.833	66	0	0	4-4	76.2	62	25	4	2	33-9	58	2.93	140	.221	.306	4	.000	-0	—	11	0	0.8
1999	†NY N	5	4	.556	80	0	0	3-3	85.2	80	31	9	2	37-8	77	3.05	143	.245	.324	6	.000	-0	—	12	0	1.1
2000	†NY N	8	6	.571	77	0	0	1-4	82.2	60	36	9	5	41-7	73	3.59	121	.206	.312	4	.250	0	—	8	0	1.2
2001	NY N	4	3	.571	49	0	0	1-2	51.1	42	23	8	3	22-6	41	3.51	115	.223	.310	2	.000	0	—	3	0	0.3
	Phi N	0	2	.000	21	0	0	0-0	15.2	21	13	4	1	12-3	15	7.47	55	.323	.430	0	ø	0	—	-6	0	-0.6
	Year	4	5	.444	70	0	0	1-2	67	63	36	12	4	34-9	56	4.43	92	.249	.342	2	.000	-0	—	-3	0	-0.3
2003	Phi N	3	3	.500	56	0	0	1-4	64	54	24	6	6	28-5	27	3.38	118	.235	.330	2	.000	-0	—	5	15	0.4
2004	Col N	0	0	ø	12	0	0	0-1	16.2	21	13	4	2	12-1	11	7.02	68	.328	.438	2	.000	-0	—	-4	68	-0.2
Total	11	36	33	.522	552	6	0	33-23	645.2	583	301	73	28	324-55	515	3.93	108	.242	.336	43-0-1	.070	-2	101	24	298	3.8

Wengert, Don Donald Paul; B11.6.1969 Sioux City IA; BR/TR/6´2˝/(205–212); [OakA92 4/116]; d4.30; Col Iowa St.

YEAR	TM LG	W	L	PCT	G	GS	CG-SHO	SV-BS	IP	H	R	HR	HB	BB-IB	SO	ERA	AERA	OAV	OOB	AB-HR-SH	AVG	PB	SUP	APR	DL	PW
1995	Oak A	1	1	.500	19	0	0	0-0	29.2	30	14	3	1	12-2	16	3.34	136	.263	.336	0	ø	0	—	3	19	0.1
1996	Oak A	7	11	.389	36	25	1-1	0-0	161.1	200	102	29	6	60-5	75	5.58	89	.307	.368	0	ø	0	95	-9	15	-0.9
1997	Oak A	5	11	.313	49	12	1	2-1	134	177	96	21	8	41-4	68	6.04	76	.321	.372	0	ø	0	83	-21	0	-2.2
1998	SD N	0	0	ø	10	0	0	1-0	13.2	21	9	2	0	5-0	5	5.93	67	.356	.406	3	.000	-0	—	-3	0	-0.2

YEAR	TM LG	W	L	PCT	G	GS	CG-SHO	SV-BS	IP	H	R	HR	HB	BB-IB	SO	ERA	AERA	OAV	OOB	AB-HR-SH	AVG	PB	SUP	APR	DL	PW
	Chi N	1	5	.167	21	6	0	0-0	49.2	55	29	8	3	23-0	41	5.07	87	.279	.363	13-0-1	.000	-1*	104	-3	0	-0.5
	Year	1	5	.167	31	6	0	1-0	63.1	76	38	10	3	28-0	46	5.26	82	.297	.373	16-0-1	.000	-2	107	-6	0	-0.7
1999	KC A	0	1	.000	11	1	0	0-3	24.1	41	26	6	0	5-0	10	9.25	55	.376	.397	0	ø	0	92	-10	0	-0.5
2000	Atl N	0	1	.000	10	0	0	0-0	10	12	9	2	0	5-0	7	7.20	63	.286	.362	0	ø	0	—	-3	0	-0.3
2001	Pit N	0	2	.000	4	4	0	0-0	16	33	22	2	0	6-2	4	12.38	36	.429	.470	3-0-1	.000	-0	119	-13	0	-1.2
Total	7	14	32	.304	160	48	2-1	3-4	438.2	569	307	73	18	157-13	226	6.01	78	.316	.374	19-0-2	.000	-2	96	-59	34	-5.7

Wensloff, Butch Charles William; B12.3.1915 Sausalito CA; D2.18.2001 San Rafael CA; BR/TR/5´11˝/185; d5.2; Def 1944

YEAR	TM LG	W	L	PCT	G	GS	CG-SHO	SV-BS	IP	H	R	HR	HB	BB-IB	SO	ERA	AERA	OAV	OOB	AB-HR-SH	AVG	PB	SUP	APR	DL	PW
1943	NY A	13	11	.542	29	27	18-1	1	223.1	179	80	7	1	70	105	2.54	127	.219	.282	79-0-3	.177	-0	96	15	0	1.5
1947	†NY A	3	1	.750	11	5	1	0	51.2	41	17	3	0	22	18	2.61	135	.217	.299	19-0-1	.263	1	155	5	0	0.4
1948	Cle A	0	1	.000	1	0	0	0	1	2	2	1	0	3	2	10.80	38	.286	.500	0	ø	0	—	-1	0	-0.2
Total	3	16	13	.552	41	32	19-1	1	276.2	222	99	11	1	95	125	2.60	126	.219	.287	98-0-4	.194	0	105	19	0	1.7

Wenz, Fred Frederick Charles "Fireball"; B8.26.1941 Bound Brook NJ; BR/TR/6´3˝/(214–215); d6.4

YEAR	TM LG	W	L	PCT	G	GS	CG-SHO	SV-BS	IP	H	R	HR	HB	BB-IB	SO	ERA	AERA	OAV	OOB	AB-HR-SH	AVG	PB	SUP	APR	DL	PW
1968	Bos A	0	0	ø	1	0	0	0	1	0	0	0	0	2-0	3	0.00	ø	.000	.400	0	ø	0	—	0	0	0.0
1969	Bos A	1	0	1.000	8	0	0	0-0	11	9	7	7	0	10-3	11	5.73	67	.225	.380	0	ø	0	—	-2	0	-0.1
1970	Phi N	2	0	1.000	22	0	0	1-0	30.1	27	16	2	1	13-0	24	4.45	90	.237	.313	5	.000	-1	—	-1	0	-0.2
Total	3	3	0	1.000	31	0	0	1-0	42.1	36	23	9	1	25-3	38	4.68	85	.229	.333	5	.000	-0	—	-3	0	-0.3

Werden, Perry Percival Wheritt; B7.21.1865 St.Louis MO; D1.9.1934 Minneapolis MN; BR/TR/6´2˝/220; d4.24; ▲

YEAR	TM LG	W	L	PCT	G	GS	CG-SHO	SV-BS	IP	H	R	HR	HB	BB-IB	SO	ERA	AERA	OAV	OOB	AB-HR-SH	AVG	PB	SUP	APR	DL	PW
1884	StL U	12	1	.923	16	16	12-1	0	141.1	113	61	1	—	22	51	1.97	121	.204	.235	76	.237	-2*	153	7	—	0.2

Werle, Bill William George "Bugs"; B12.21.1920 Oakland CA; BL/TL/6´2.5˝/(182–192); d4.22; C1; Col California

YEAR	TM LG	W	L	PCT	G	GS	CG-SHO	SV-BS	IP	H	R	HR	HB	BB-IB	SO	ERA	AERA	OAV	OOB	AB-HR-SH	AVG	PB	SUP	APR	DL	PW
1949	Pit N	12	13	.480	35	29	10-2	0	221	243	117	23	8	51	106	4.24	99	.278	.324	77-0-2	.117	-3	93	-2	0	-0.4
1950	Pit N	8	16	.333	48	22	6	8	215.1	249	127	25	6	65	78	4.60	95	.290	.344	67-0-2	.194	1	81	-6	0	-0.3
1951	Pit N	8	6	.571	59	9	2	6	149.2	181	102	20	6	51	57	5.65	75	.304	.364	40-0-1	.300	3	116	-20	0	-1.3
1952	Pit N	0	0	ø	5	0	0	0	4	9	5	1	0	1	1	9.00	44	.429	.455	0	ø	0	—	-2	0	-0.1
	StL N	1	2	.333	19	0	0	1	39	40	23	6	1	15	23	4.85	77	.268	.339	9	.111	-0	—	-5	65	-0.3
	Year	1	2	.333	24	0	0	1	43	49	28	7	1	16	24	5.23	71	.288	.353	9	.111	-0	—	-7	0	-0.4
1953	Bos A	0	1	.000	5	0	0	0	11.2	7	3	1	0	1	4	1.54	273	.179	.200	2	.000	-0	—	3	0	0.3
1954	Bos A	0	1	.000	14	0	0	0	24.2	41	13	5	2	10	14	4.38	94	.376	.434	4	.000	-0	—	0	0	0.0
Total	6	29	39	.426	185	60	18-2	15	665.1	770	390	81	23	194	283	4.69	90	.291	.345	199-0-5	.176	1	92	-32	65	-2.1

Werley, George George William; B9.8.1938 St.Louis MO; BR/TR/6´2˝/196; d9.29

YEAR	TM LG	W	L	PCT	G	GS	CG-SHO	SV-BS	IP	H	R	HR	HB	BB-IB	SO	ERA	AERA	OAV	OOB	AB-HR-SH	AVG	PB	SUP	APR	DL	PW
1956	Bal A	0	0	ø	1	0	0	0	1	1	1	0	0	2-0	0	9.00	44	.250	.500	0	ø	0	—	-1	0	0.0

Werts, Johnny Henry Levi; B4.20.1898 Pomaria SC; D9.24.1990 Newberry SC; BR/TR/5´10˝/180; d4.14

YEAR	TM LG	W	L	PCT	G	GS	CG-SHO	SV-BS	IP	H	R	HR	HB	BB-IB	SO	ERA	AERA	OAV	OOB	AB-HR-SH	AVG	PB	SUP	APR	DL	PW
1926	Bos N	11	9	.550	32	23	7-1	0	189.1	212	85	6	10	47	65	3.28	108	.287	.338	64-1-3	.266	4	82	4	—	1.0
1927	Bos N	4	10	.286	42	15	4	1	164.1	204	95	5	4	52	39	4.55	82	.315	.369	43-0-2	.163	-0	84	-15	—	-1.2
1928	Bos N	0	2	.000	10	2	0	0	18.1	31	22	2	0	8	5	10.31	38	.369	.424	3	.333	0	87	-12	—	-1.1
1929	Bos N	0	0	ø	4	0	0	1	6	13	8	1	0	4	2	10.50	45	.433	.500	1	1.000	0	—	-4	—	-0.1
Total	4	15	21	.417	88	40	11-1	2	378	460	210	14	14	111	111	4.29	85	.307	.360	111-1-5	.234	4	82	-27	—	-1.4

Wertz, Bill William Charles; B1.15.1967 Cleveland OH; BR/TR/6´6˝/220; [CleA89 31/801]; d5.22; Col Ohio St.

YEAR	TM LG	W	L	PCT	G	GS	CG-SHO	SV-BS	IP	H	R	HR	HB	BB-IB	SO	ERA	AERA	OAV	OOB	AB-HR-SH	AVG	PB	SUP	APR	DL	PW
1993	Cle A	2	3	.400	34	0	0	0-2	59.2	54	28	5	1	32-2	53	3.62	121	.238	.333	0	ø	0	—	4	0	0.2
1994	Cle A	0	0	ø	1	0	0	0-0	4.1	9	5	0	0	1-0	1	10.38	46	.409	.435	0	ø	0	—	-2	0	-0.1
Total	2	2	3	.400	35	0	0	0-2	64	63	33	5	1	33-2	54	4.08	108	.253	.342	0	ø	0	—	2	0	0.1

West, David David Lee; B9.1.1964 Memphis TN; BL/TL/6´6˝/(207–255); [NYN83 4/84]; d9.24

YEAR	TM LG	W	L	PCT	G	GS	CG-SHO	SV-BS	IP	H	R	HR	HB	BB-IB	SO	ERA	AERA	OAV	OOB	AB-HR-SH	AVG	PB	SUP	APR	DL	PW
1988	NY N	1	0	1.000	2	1	0	0-0	6	6	2	0	0	3-0	3	3.00	109	.273	.360	2	1.000	1	381	0	0	0.2
1989	NY N	0	2	.000	11	2	0	0-0	24.1	25	20	4	1	14-2	19	7.40	45	.260	.357	5	.200	0	67	-11	0	-0.8
	Min A	3	2	.600	10	5	0	0-1	39.1	48	29	5	2	19-1	31	6.41	65	.306	.383	0	ø	0	96	-9	0	-1.0
1990	Min A	7	9	.438	29	27	2	0-0	146.1	142	88	21	4	78-1	92	5.10	82	.256	.350	0	ø	0	97	-13	27	-1.3
1991	†Min A	4	4	.500	15	12	0	0-0	71.1	66	37	13	1	28-0	52	4.54	94	.244	.314	0	ø	0	91	-1	85	-0.1
1992	Min A	1	3	.250	9	3	0	0-0	28.1	32	24	3	1	20-0	19	6.99	58	.276	.381	0	ø	0	30	-9	0	-1.1
1993	†Phi N	6	4	.600	76	0	0	3-6	86.1	60	37	6	5	51-4	87	2.92	136	.194	.316	5	.400	1	—	8	0	0.9
1994	Phi N	4	10	.286	31	14	0	0-2	99	74	44	7	1	61-2	83	3.55	121	.205	.320	28-0-1	.071	-2	73	8	0	0.7
1995	Phi N	3	2	.600	8	8	0	0-0	38	34	17	5	1	19-0	25	3.79	111	.241	.335	8-1-6	.125	1	96	2	120	0.3
1996	Phi N	2	2	.500	7	6	0	0-0	28.1	31	17	0	0	11-0	22	4.76	91	.272	.336	7-0-2	.286	1	70	-2	141	-0.1
1998	Bos A	0	0	ø	6	0	0	0-0	2	7	6	1	0	7-0	4	27.00	18	.538	.700	0	ø	0	—	-5	0	-0.2
Total	10	31	38	.449	204	78	2	3-9	569.1	525	321	65	16	311-10	437	4.66	89	.244	.341	55-1-9	.182	2	90	-32	373	-2.5

West, Hi James Hiram; B8.8.1884 Roseville IL; D5.24.1963 Los Angeles CA; BR/TR/6´0˝/185; d9.8; Col Knox

YEAR	TM LG	W	L	PCT	G	GS	CG-SHO	SV-BS	IP	H	R	HR	HB	BB-IB	SO	ERA	AERA	OAV	OOB	AB-HR-SH	AVG	PB	SUP	APR	DL	PW
1905	Cle A	2	2	.500	6	4	4-1	0	33	43	23	0	3	10	15	4.09	64	.316	.376	13	.077	-1	40	-6	—	-0.9
1911	Cle A	3	4	.429	13	8	3	1	64.2	84	35	1	3	18	17	3.76	91	.343	.395	23	.130	-2	95	-2	—	-0.4
Total	2	5	6	.455	19	12	7-1	1	97.2	127	58	1	6	28	32	3.87	81	.333	.388	36	.111	-3	80	-8	—	-1.3

West, Frank John Franklin; B1.21.1873 Johnstown PA; D9.6.1932 Wilmerding PA; TR/?/180; d7.11

YEAR	TM LG	W	L	PCT	G	GS	CG-SHO	SV-BS	IP	H	R	HR	HB	BB-IB	SO	ERA	AERA	OAV	OOB	AB-HR-SH	AVG	PB	SUP	APR	DL	PW
1894	Bos N	0	0	ø	1	0	0	0	3	5	5	0	0	2	1	9.00	63	.357	.438	1	.000	-0	—	-1	—	-0.1

West, Lefty Weldon Edison; B9.3.1915 Gibsonville NC; D7.23.1979 Hendersonville NC; BR/TL/6´0˝/165; d4.30

YEAR	TM LG	W	L	PCT	G	GS	CG-SHO	SV-BS	IP	H	R	HR	HB	BB-IB	SO	ERA	AERA	OAV	OOB	AB-HR-SH	AVG	PB	SUP	APR	DL	PW
1944	StL A	0	0	ø	11	0	0	0	24.1	34	18	1	1	19	11	6.29	57	.366	.478	7	.143	-0	—	-6	0	-0.4
1945	StL A	3	4	.429	24	8	1	0	74.1	71	37	2	0	31	38	3.63	97	.245	.318	27-0-1	.074	-3	73	-2	0	-0.6
Total	2	3	4	.429	35	8	1	0	98.2	105	55	3	1	50	49	4.29	83	.274	.359	34-0-1	.088	-3	73	-8	0	-1.0

Westbrook, Jake Jacob Cauthen; B9.29.1977 Athens GA; BR/TR/6´3˝/(185–215); [ColN96 1/21]; d6.17; [DL 2000 Cle A 30]

YEAR	TM LG	W	L	PCT	G	GS	CG-SHO	SV-BS	IP	H	R	HR	HB	BB-IB	SO	ERA	AERA	OAV	OOB	AB-HR-SH	AVG	PB	SUP	APR	DL	PW
2000	NY A	0	2	.000	3	2	0	0-0	6.2	15	10	1	0	4-1	1	13.50	35	.469	.500	0	ø	0	108	-6	0	-1.0
2001	Cle A	4	4	.500	23	6	0	0-0	64.2	79	43	6	4	22-4	48	5.85	79	.306	.363	1-0-1	.000	-0	91	-7	0	-0.7
2002	Cle A	1	3	.250	11	4	0	0-2	41.2	50	30	6	1	12-1	20	5.83	76	.296	.344	0	ø	0	63	-7	137	-0.6
2003	Cle A	7	10	.412	34	22	1	0-0	133	142	70	9	12	56-1	58	4.33	102	.281	.365	0	ø	0	95	3	0	0.4
2004	Cle A☆	14	9	.609	33	30	**5**-1	0-0	215.2	208	95	19	5	61-3	116	3.38	129	.255	.308	3-0-1	.000	-0	132	21	0	2.2
2005	Cle A	15	15	.500	34	34	2	0-0	210.2	218	121	19	7	56-3	119	4.49	93	.265	.316	2	.000	-0	103	-10	0	-1.0
2006	Cle A	15	10	.600	32	32	3-**2**	0-0	211.1	247	106	15	4	55-4	109	4.17	104	.295	.340	4-0-1	.500	1	120	5	0	0.9
Total	7	56	53	.514	170	130	11-3	0-2	883.2	959	475	75	33	266-17	471	4.35	100	.279	.334	10-0-3	.200	1	110	-1	167	0.2

Westervelt, Huyler Huyler; B10.1.1869 Tenafly NJ; D10.14.1949 Pelham Manor NY; TR/5´9˝/170; d4.21

YEAR	TM LG	W	L	PCT	G	GS	CG-SHO	SV-BS	IP	H	R	HR	HB	BB-IB	SO	ERA	AERA	OAV	OOB	AB-HR-SH	AVG	PB	SUP	APR	DL	PW
1894	NY N	7	10	.412	23	18	11-1	0	141	170	118	4	5	76	35	5.04	104	.295	.382	56-0-2	.143	-5	92	4	—	0.0

Weston, Mickey Michael Lee; B3.26.1961 Flint MI; BR/TR/6´1˝/(180–187); [NYN82 12/293]; d6.18; Col Eastern Michigan

YEAR	TM LG	W	L	PCT	G	GS	CG-SHO	SV-BS	IP	H	R	HR	HB	BB-IB	SO	ERA	AERA	OAV	OOB	AB-HR-SH	AVG	PB	SUP	APR	DL	PW
1989	Bal A	1	0	1.000	7	0	0	1-0	13	18	8	1	1	2-0	7	5.54	69	.346	.382	0	ø	0	—	-2	60	-0.2
1990	Bal A	0	1	.000	9	2	0	0-0	21	28	20	6	0	6-1	9	7.71	50	.322	.366	0	ø	0	95	-10	0	-0.5
1991	Tor A	0	0	ø	2	0	0	0-0	2	1	0	0	0	1-1	1	0.00	ø	.143	.250	0	ø	0	—	1	0	0.0
1992	Phi N	0	1	.000	1	1	0	0-0	3.2	7	5	1	0	1-0	0	12.27	29	.412	.474	2	.000	-0	26	-3	0	-0.5
1993	NY N	0	0	ø	4	0	0	0-0	5.2	11	5	0	1	1-0	2	7.94	51	.393	.433	0	ø	0	—	-2	0	-0.1
Total	5	1	2	.333	23	3	0	1-0	45.1	65	38	8	3	11-2	19	7.15	54	.340	.385	2	.000	-0	71	-16	60	-1.3

Wetteland, John John Karl; B8.21.1966 San Mateo CA; BR/TR/6´2˝/(195–215); [LAN85*S2/39]; d5.31; C1; Col San Mateo (CA) [JC]

YEAR	TM LG	W	L	PCT	G	GS	CG-SHO	SV-BS	IP	H	R	HR	HB	BB-IB	SO	ERA	AERA	OAV	OOB	AB-HR-SH	AVG	PB	SUP	APR	DL	PW
1989	LA N	5	8	.385	31	12	0	1-0	102.2	81	46	8	0	34-4	96	3.77	91	.218	.283	21-0-5	.143	-0	95	-3	0	-0.4
1990	LA N	2	4	.333	22	5	0	0-1	43	44	28	6	4	17-3	36	4.81	77	.263	.344	7-1-1	.143	1	123	-6	0	-0.8
1991	LA N	1	0	1.000	6	0	0	0-0	9	5	2	0	1	3-0	9	0.00	ø	.161	.250	0	ø	0	—	3	0	0.3
1992	Mon N	4	4	.500	67	0	0	37-9	83.1	64	27	6	4	36-3	99	2.92	120	.213	.304	5-0-1	.200	0	—	6	0	1.1
1993	Mon N	9	3	.750	70	0	0	43-6	85.1	58	17	3	2	28-3	113	1.37	305	.188	.260	4-0-1	.000	-0	—	25	18	5.1
1994	Mon N	4	6	.400	52	0	0	25-10	63.2	46	22	5	3	21-4	68	2.83	150	.202	.273	4-0-1	.250	0	—	10	16	2.0
1995	†NY A	1	5	.167	60	0	0	31-6	61.1	40	22	6	0	14-2	66	2.93	158	.185	.233	0	ø	0	—	11	0	1.9
1996	†NY A☆	2	3	.400	62	0	0	**43**-4	63.2	54	23	9	0	21-4	69	2.83	175	.224	.284	0	ø	0	—	14	24	2.6
1997	Tex A	7	2	.778	61	0	0	31-6	65	43	18	5	0	21-3	63	1.94	251	.182	.248	1	1.000	1	—	19	0	3.7
1998	†Tex A★	3	1	.750	63	0	0	42-5	62	47	17	6	0	14-1	72	2.03	241	.203	.247	0	ø	0	—	18	0	3.0

YEAR	TM LG	W	L	PCT	G	GS	CG-SHO	SV-BS	IP	H	R	HR	HB	BB-IB	SO	ERA	AERA	OAV	OOB	AB-HR-SH	AVG	PB	SUP	APR	DL	PW
1999	†Tex A★	4	4	.500	62	0	0	43-7	66	67	30	9	0	19-1	60	3.68	141	.262	.307	0	ø	0	—	10	0	1.8
2000	Tex A	6	5	.545	62	0	0	34-9	60	67	35	10	2	24-2	53	4.20	121	.285	.351	0	ø	0	—	4	0	0.7
Total	12	48	45	.516	618	17	0	330-63	765	616	287	73	16	252-30	804	2.93	148	.218	.284	42-1-9	.167	1	86	111	58	21.0
WETZEL, BUZZ	Charles Edward; B8.25.1894 Jay OK; D3.7.1941 Globe AZ; BR/TR/6´1˝/162; d7.25																									
1927	Phi A	0	0	ø	2	1	0	0	4.2	8	5	0	0	5	0	7.71	55	.400	.520	1	1.000	0	117	-2	—	0.0
WETZEL, SHORTY	George William; B1868 Philadelphia PA; D2.25.1899 Dayton OH; d8.26																									
1885	Bal AA	0	2	.000	2	2	1	0	17	27	26	0	3	9	6	8.47	38	.333	.419	7	.000	-1	45	-10	—	-0.8
WEVER, STEFAN	Stefan Matthew; B4.22.1958 Marburg, West Germany; BR/TR/6´8˝/245; [NYA79 6/155]; d9.17; Col California–Santa Barbara																									
1982	NY A	0	1	.000	1	1	0	0-0	2.2	6	9	1	0	3-0	2	27.00	15	.429	.500	0	ø	0	0	-7	0	-0.9
WEYHING, GUS	August "Cannonball"; B9.29.1866 Louisville KY; D9.4.1955 Louisville KY; BR/TR/5´10˝/145; d5.2; b–John																									
1887	Phi AA	26	28	.481	55	55	53-2	0	466.1	465	342	12	37	167	193	4.27	101	.253	.328	209	.201	-9*	94	-5	—	-1.2
1888	Phi AA	28	18	.609	47	47	45-3	0	404	314	198	4	42	111	204	2.25	133	.207	.279	184-1	.217	4*	124	30	—	3.3
1889	Phi AA	30	21	.588	54	53	50-4	0	449	382	271	15	34	212	213	2.95	128	.223	.321	191	.131	-15	98	35	—	1.6
1890	Bro P	30	16	.652	49	46	38-3	0	390	419	250	10	17	179	177	3.60	124	.263	.343	165-1	.164	-6	104	40	—	2.5
1891	Phi AA	31	20	.608	52	51	51-3	0	450	428	231	12	31	161	219	3.18	119	.242	.316	198	.111	-16*	91	29	—	1.0
1892	Phi N	32	21	.604	59	49	46-6	**3**	469.2	411	213	9	18	168	202	2.66	122	.226	.298	214	.136	-10*	104	31	—	1.6
1893	Phi N	23	16	.590	42	40	33-2	0	345.1	399	235	10	20	145	101	4.74	97	.281	.356	147	.150	-9*	117	-2	—	-1.0
1894	Phi N	16	14	.533	40	36	26-2	1	279	379	224	12	16	120	83	5.71	90	.321	.391	121-0-8	.174	-9	104	-11	—	-1.7
1895	Phi N	0	2	.000	2	2	0	0	9	23	22	0	0	13	5	20.00	24	.469	.581	4	.000	-1	104	-13	—	-1.6
	Pit N	1	0	1.000	1	1	1	0	9	10	7	0	0	5	3	1.00	451	.278	.366	4	.250	0	158	2	—	0.2
	Lou N	7	19	.269	28	25	22-1	0	213	285	205	9	8	66	53	5.41	86	.316	.368	89-1-0	.225	-0	77	-24	—	-2.1
	Year	8	21	.276	31	28	23-1	0	231	318	234	9	8	84	61	5.81	80	.322	.380	97-1-0	.216	-1	82	-38	—	-3.5
1896	Lou N	2	3	.400	5	5	4	0	42	62	46	6	2	15	9	6.64	65	.339	.395	15	.133	-1	105	-10	—	-0.9
1898	Was N	15	26	.366	45	42	39	0	361	428	232	10	16	84	92	4.51	81	.292	.338	141-0-7	.177	-5*	85	-25	—	-2.8
1899	Was N	17	21	.447	43	38	34-2	0	334.2	414	223	8	28	76	96	4.54	86	.303	.352	126-0-6	.206	-1	96	-20	—	-2.2
1900	StL N	3	2	.600	7	5	3	0	46.2	60	44	2	1	21	6	4.63	79	.311	.381	21	.095	-2	118	-8	—	-0.9
	Bro N	3	4	.429	8	8	3	0	48	66	33	1	2	20	8	4.31	89	.325	.391	18	.222	-0	146	-3	—	-0.4
	Year	6	6	.500	15	13	6	0	94.2	126	77	3	3	41	14	4.47	84	.318	.386	39	.154	-3	137	-10	—	-1.3
1901	Cle A	0	0	ø	2	1	0	0	11.1	20	11	0	4	5	0	7.94	45	.377	.468	5	.000	-1	228	-4	—	-0.3
	Cin N	0	1	.000	1	1	1	0	9	11	9	0	2	2	3	3.00	107	.297	.366	3	.000	-0	22	-2	—	-0.2
Total	14	264	232	.532	540	505	449-28	4	4337	4576	2796	120	278	1570	1667	3.88	102	.264	.335	1855-3-21	.166	-83	102	40	—	-5.1
WEYHING, JOHN	John; B6.24.1869 Louisville KY; D6.20.1890 Louisville KY; BL/TL/6´2˝/185; d7.13; b–Gus																									
1888	Cin AA	3	4	.429	8	8	7	0	65.2	52	26	0	1	17	30	1.23	257	.210	.263	23	.130	-2	66	10	—	0.8
1889	Col AA	0	0	ø	1	0	0	0	1	1	3	0	0	4	0	27.00	13	.250	.625	0	ø	0	—	-2	—	-0.1
Total	2	3	4	.429	9	8	7	0	66.2	53	29	0	1	21	30	1.62	196	.210	.274	23	.130	-2	66	8	—	0.7
WHEAT, LEE	Leroy William; B9.15.1929 Edwardsville IL; BR/TR/6´4˝/200; d4.21; Col Truman St.																									
1954	Phi A	0	2	.000	8	1	0	0	28.1	38	18	1	1	9	7	5.72	68	.304	.350	8	.125	-0	68	-5	0	-0.4
1955	KC A	0	0	ø	3	0	0	0	2	8	7	1	0	3-2	1	22.50	19	.533	.611	0	ø	0	—	-4	0	-0.2
Total	2	0	2	.000	11	1	0	0	30.1	46	25	2	1	12-2	8	6.82	57	.329	.381	8	.125	-0	68	-9	0	-0.6
WHEATLEY, CHARLIE	Charles D.; B6.27.1893 Rosedale KS; D12.10.1982 Tulsa OK; BR/TR/5´11˝/174; d9.6																									
1912	Det A	1	4	.200	5	5	2	0	35	45	27	1	2	17	14	6.17	53	.331	.413	12	.000	-2	68	-9	—	-1.2
WHEATON, WOODY	Elwood Pierce; B10.3.1914 Philadelphia PA; D12.11.1995 Lancaster PA; BL/TL/5´8.5˝/160; d9.28.1943; ▲																									
1944	Phi A	0	1	.000	11	1	1	0	38	36	17	1	1	20	15	3.55	98	.255	.352	59-0-1	.186	0*	0	0	0	0.0
WHEELER, DAN	Daniel Michael; B12.10.1977 Providence RI; BR/TR/6´3˝/(220–222); [TBA96 34/1024]; d9.1; Col Central Arizona JC																									
1999	TB A	0	4	.000	6	6	0	0-0	30.2	35	20	7	0	13-1	32	5.87	85	.287	.356	0	ø	0	78	-2	0	-0.2
2000	TB A	1	1	.500	11	2	0	0-1	23	29	14	2	2	11-2	17	5.48	89	.302	.382	0	ø	0	77	-1	0	-0.1
2001	TB A	1	0	1.000	13	0	0	0-0	17.2	30	17	3	0	5-0	12	8.66	52	.375	.402	0	ø	0	—	-7	0	-0.3
2003	NY N	1	3	.250	35	0	0	2-1	51	49	23	6	1	17-4	35	3.71	113	.253	.312	2	.000	-0	—	3	0	0.1
2004	NY N	3	1	.750	32	1	0	0-0	50.2	65	29	9	0	17-2	46	4.80	90	.307	.357	5-0-1	.200	0	173	-2	0	-0.2
	†Hou N	0	0	ø	14	0	0	0-0	14.1	11	4	1	1	3-0	9	2.51	174	.216	.273	0	ø	0	—	3	0	0.1
	Year	3	1	.750	46	1	0	0-0	65	76	33	10	1	20-2	55	4.29	101	.289	.340	5-0-1	.200	0	172	1	0	-0.1
2005	†Hou N	2	3	.400	71	0	0	3-2	73.1	53	18	7	3	19-3	69	2.21	191	.204	.265	0	ø	0	—	17	0	1.2
2006	Hou N	3	5	.375	75	0	0	9-3	71.1	58	22	5	2	24-8	68	2.52	178	.221	.288	0	ø	0	—	15	0	1.8
Total	7	11	17	.393	257	9	0	14-7	332	330	147	40	9	109-20	288	3.82	116	.258	.318	7-0-1	.143	-0	96	26	0	2.4
WHEELER, RIP	Floyd Clark; B3.2.1898 Marion KY; D9.18.1968 Marion KY; BR/TR/6´0˝/180; d9.30																									
1921	Pit N	0	0	ø	1	0	0	0	3	6	4	0	1	1	0	9.00	43	.500	.571	1	.000	-0	—	-2	—	-0.1
1922	Pit N	0	0	ø	1	0	0	0	1	1	0	0	0	2	0	0.00	ø	.333	.600	0	ø	0	—	0	—	0.0
1923	Chi N	1	2	.333	3	3	1	0	24	28	14	2	3	5	5	4.88	82	.298	.353	9	.111	-1	82	-2	—	-0.2
1924	Chi N	3	6	.333	29	4	0	0	101.1	103	53	8	0	21	16	3.91	100	.265	.303	32	.219	-1	82	0	—	-0.1
Total	4	4	8	.333	34	7	1	0	129.1	138	71	10	4	29	21	4.18	94	.278	.323	42	.190	-2	83	-4	—	-0.4
WHEELER, GEORGE	George Louis (b George Louis Heroux); B7.30.1869 Methuen MA; D3.21.1946 Santa Ana CA; BB/TR/5´9˝/180; d9.18																									
1896	Phi N	1	1	.500	3	2	2	0	16.1	18	11	0	2	5	2	3.86	112	.277	.347	9	.111	-1	124	0	—	-0.1
1897	Phi N	11	10	.524	26	19	17	0	191	229	114	3	3	62	35	3.96	106	.295	.349	79-0-1	.203	-1	91	4	—	0.4
1898	Phi N	6	8	.429	15	13	10	0	112.1	155	94	1	6	36	20	4.17	82	.325	.380	43-0-3	.186	-1	98	-16	—	-1.5
1899	Phi N	3	1	.750	6	5	3	0	39	44	30	1	3	13	3	6.00	61	.284	.351	17-1-1	.235	1	164	-8	—	-0.5
Total	4	21	20	.512	50	39	32	0	358.2	446	249	5	14	116	60	4.24	92	.303	.359	148-1-5	.196	-2	103	-20	—	-1.7
WHEELER, HARRY	Harry Eugene; B3.3.1858 Versailles IN; D10.9.1900 Cincinnati OH; BR/TR/5´11˝/165; d6.19; M1; ▲																									
1878	Pro N	6	1	.857	7	6	6	0	62	70	40	1	—	25	25	3.48	63	.275	.339	27	.148	-1	191	-6	—	-0.7
1879	Cin N	0	1	.000	1	1	0	0	1	6	10	0	—	4	0	81.00	3	.667	.769	3	.000	-0	20	-7	—	-0.8
1882	Cin AA	1	2	.333	4	1	1	0	21.2	21	17	0	—	12	10	5.40	49	.239	.330	344-1	.250	1*	156	-4	—	-0.5
1883	Col AA	0	1	.000	1	1	0	0	5	13	7	0	—	2	0	7.20	43	.448	.484	371	.226	0*	56	-2	—	-0.3
1884	KC U	0	1	.000	1	1	1	0	8	7	6	0	—	0	6	1.13	199	.219	.219	62	.258	0*	38	0	—	0.0
Total	5	7	6	.538	14	10	8	0	97.2	117	80	1	—	43	41	4.70	50	.283	.351	807-1	.235	-1	141	-19	—	-2.3
WHEELOCK, GARY	Gary Richard; B11.29.1951 Bakersfield CA; BR/TR/6´3˝/(198–200); [AnaA74 6/130]; d9.17; Col California–Irvine																									
1976	Cal A	0	0	ø	2	0	0	0-0	2	6	6	0	1	1-0	2	27.00	12	.500	.571	0	ø	0	—	-5	0	-0.3
1977	Sea A	6	9	.400	17	17	2	0-0	88.1	94	58	16	2	26-0	47	4.89	85	.268	.321	0	ø	0	85	-9	88	-1.4
1980	Sea A	0	0	ø	1	1	0	0-0	3	4	2	0	0	1-0	1	6.00	69	.333	.385	0	ø	0	64	0	0	0.0
Total	3	6	9	.400	20	18	2	0-0	93.1	104	66	16	3	28-0	50	5.40	76	.277	.332	0	ø	0	85	-14	88	-1.7
WHILLOCK, JACK	Jack Franklin; B11.4.1942 Clinton AR; BR/TR/6´3˝/194; d8.29; Col Arkansas																									
1971	Det A	0	2	.000	7	0	0	1-1	8	10	5	0	0	2-0	6	5.63	64	.323	.364	1	.000	-0	—	-2	0	-0.3
WHISENANT, MATT	Matthew Michael; B6.8.1971 Los Angeles CA; BR/TL/6´3˝/215; [PhiN89 18/456]; d7.4; Col Glendale (CA) CC																									
1997	Fla N	0	0	ø	4	0	0	0-0	2.2	4	6	0	0	6-0	4	16.88	24	.333	.556	0	ø	0*	—	-4	94	-0.2
	KC A	1	0	1.000	24	0	0	0-0	19	15	7	0	3	12-0	16	2.84	167	.211	.349	0	ø	0	—	4	0	0.2
1998	KC A	2	1	.667	70	0	0	2-3	60.2	61	37	3	3	33-2	45	4.90	99	.271	.365	0	ø	0	—	-1	0	0.0
1999	KC A	4	4	.500	48	0	0	1-3	39.2	40	28	4	7	26-1	27	6.35	80	.267	.399	0	ø	0	—	-4	0	-0.7
	SD N	0	1	.000	19	0	0	0-1	14.2	10	6	0	0	10-1	10	3.68	116	.200	.333	0	ø	0	—	1	0	0.1
2000	SD N	2	2	.500	24	0	0	0-3	21.1	16	12	1	0	17-1	12	3.80	117	.213	.351	0	ø	0	—	1	0	0.1
Total	4	9	8	.529	189	0	0	3-10	158	146	96	8	13	104-5	114	4.96	96	.250	.372	0	ø	0	—	-3	94	-0.5

YEAR	TM LG	W	L	PCT	G	GS	CG-SHO	SV-BS	IP	H	R	HR	HB	BB-IB	SO	ERA	AERA	OAV	OOB	AB-HR-SH	AVG	PB	SUP	APR	DL	PW
WHITAKER, PAT	William H.; B11.1864 St.Louis MO; D7.15.1902 St.Louis MO; TR; d10.11																									
1888	Bal AA	1	1	.500	2	2	2	0	14	13	12	0	2	6	5	5.14	58	.236	.333	6	.000	-1	68	-3	—	-0.4
1889	Bal AA	1	0	1.000	1	1	1	0	9	10	4	0	0	4	1	2.00	197	.270	.341	4	.250	-0	126	2	—	0.2
Total	2	2	1	.667	3	3	3	0	23	23	16	0	2	10	6	3.91	86	.250	.337	10	.100	-1	89	-1	—	-0.2
WHITBY, BILL	William Edward; B7.29.1943 Crewe VA; BR/TR/6´1″/180; d6.17																									
1964	Min A	0	0	ø	4	0	0	0	6.1	8	6	3	0	1-0	2	8.53	42	.308	.333	1	.000	-0	—	-3	0	-0.2
WHITCHER, BOB	Robert Arthur; B4.29.1917 Berlin NH; D5.8.1997 Akron OH; BL/TL/5´8″/165; d8.20																									
1945	Bos N	0	2	.000	6	3	0	0	15.2	12	6	1	0	12	6	2.87	133	.235	.381	3	.333	0*	37	2	0	0.2
WHITE, ABE	Adel; B5.16.1904 Winder GA; D10.1.1978 Atlanta GA; BR/TL/6´0″/185; d7.10																									
1937	StL N	0	1	.000	5	0	0	0	9.1	14	7	1	0	3	2	6.75	59	.341	.386	1	1.000	0	—	-2	—	-0.2
WHITE, ERNIE	Ernest Daniel; B9.5.1916 Pacolet Mills SC; D5.22.1974 Augusta GA; BR/TL/5´11.5″/175; d5.9; Mil 1944–45; C3																									
1940	StL N	1	1	.500	8	1	0	0	21.2	29	13	0	1	14	15	4.15	96	.315	.411	7	.429	1*	0	-1	—	0.1
1941	StL N	17	7	.708	32	25	12-3	2	210	169	72	12	6	70	117	2.40	157	.217	.287	79-0-3	.190	0*	113	28	0	3.0
1942	†StL N	7	5	.583	26	19	7-1	2	128.1	113	57	11	2	41	67	2.52	136	.232	.294	41-0-5	.195	0*	123	7	0	0.5
1943	†StL N	5	5	.500	14	10	5-1	0	78.2	78	38	4	1	33	28	3.78	89	.257	.332	28-0-2	.214	0*	124	-3	0	-0.5
1946	Bos N	0	1	.000	12	1	0	0	23.2	22	11	1	0	12	8	4.18	82	.256	.347	4	.250	0*	150	-1	0	-0.1
1947	Bos N	0	0	ø	1	1	0	0	4	1	0	0	0	1	1	0.00	ø	.083	.154	1	1.000	0	68	2	0	0.1
1948	Bos N	0	2	.000	15	0	0	2	23	13	7	0	0	17	8	1.96	196	.167	.316	3	.000	-0*	—	4	0	0.3
Total	7	30	21	.588	108	57	24-5	6	489.1	425	198	28	10	188	244	2.78	130	.231	.306	163-0-10	.209	2	115	36	0	3.4
WHITE, GABE	Gabriel Allen; B11.20.1971 Sebring FL; BL/TL/6´2″/(200–205); [MonN90 1/28]; d5.27; [DL 1996 Cin N 13]																									
1994	Mon N	1	1	.500	7	5	0	1-0	23.2	24	16	4	1	11-0	17	6.08	70	.261	.343	4-0-1	.000	-0	108	-4	0	-0.4
1995	Mon N	1	2	.333	19	1	0	0-0	25.2	26	21	7	1	9-0	25	7.01	61	.260	.319	3-0-1	.000	-0	63	-7	0	-0.8
1997	Cin N	2	2	.500	12	6	0	1-0	41	39	20	6	1	8-1	25	4.39	98	.253	.291	9-0-2	.111	-0	108	0	0	-0.1
1998	Cin N	5	5	.500	69	3	0	9-4	98.2	86	46	17	1	27-6	83	4.01	107	.231	.284	6-0-4	.167	-0	50	3	0	0.3
1999	Cin N	1	2	.333	50	0	0	0-1	61	68	31	13	2	14-1	61	4.43	106	.281	.324	0	ø	0	—	3	0	0.1
2000	Cin N	0	0	ø	1	0	0	0-0	1	2	2	1	0	1-0	2	18.00	26	.400	.500	0	ø	0	—	-1	0	-0.1
	Col N	11	2	.846	67	0	0	5-4	83	62	21	5	3	14-2	82	2.17	267	.208	.246	9-1-1	.222	1	—	27	0	4.0
	Year	11	2	.846	68	0	0	5-4	84	64	23	6	3	15-2	84	2.36	245	.211	.251	9-1-1	.222	1	—	**26**	0	3.9
2001	Col N	1	7	.125	69	0	0	0-2	67.2	70	47	18	1	26-5	47	6.25	85	.270	.337	3	.000	-0	—	-4	0	-0.5
2002	Cin N	6	1	.857	62	0	0	0-1	54.1	49	19	3	2	10-2	41	2.98	143	.238	.280	2-0-1	.000	-0	—	8	51	0.9
2003	Cin N	3	0	1.000	34	0	0	0-1	34.1	36	15	5	1	6-3	23	3.93	106	.275	.307	2	.000	-0	—	2	40	0.1
	†NY A	2	1	.667	12	0	0	0-1	12.1	8	7	2	1	2-1	6	4.38	100	.182	.229	0	ø	0	—	0	26	0.0
2004	NY A	0	1	.000	24	0	0	0-2	20.2	33	19	2	2	7-4	8	8.27	56	.355	.408	0	ø	0	—	-8	0	-0.4
	Cin N	1	2	.333	40	0	0	1-2	39	39	27	12	0	5-0	33	6.23	69	.257	.277	0	ø	0	—	-7	0	-0.6
2005	StL N	0	0	ø	6	0	0	0-0	8.1	14	2	1	0	1-1	1	2.16	194	.378	.395	0	ø	0	—	2	0	0.1
Total	11	34	26	.567	472	15	0	17-18	570.2	556	293	96	16	141-26	454	4.51	104	.254	.301	38-1-10	.105	-1	86	14	130	2.6
WHITE, DEKE	George Frederick; B9.8.1872 Albany NY; D11.5.1957 Ilion NY; BB/TL; d9.14																									
1895	Phi N	1	0	1.000	3	1	1	1	17.1	17	23	1	2	13	6	9.87	48	.254	.390	8-0-1	.125	-1	134	-9	—	-0.5
WHITE, DOC	Guy Harris; B4.9.1879 Washington DC; D2.19.1969 Silver Spring MD; BL/TL/6´1″/150; d4.22; Col Georgetown; ▲																									
1901	Phi N	14	13	.519	31	27	22	0	236.2	241	122	2	14	56	132	3.19	106	.262	.314	98-1-7	.276	5	118	3	—	0.9
1902	Phi N	16	20	.444	36	35	34-3	1	306	277	126	3	13	72	185	2.53	111	.241	.294	179-1-9	.263	4*	78	7	—	1.5
1903	Chi A	17	16	.515	37	36	29-3	0	300	258	119	4	14	69	114	2.13	132	.232	.285	99-0-2	.202	6*	95	19	—	2.8
1904	Chi A	16	12	.571	30	30	23-7	0	228	201	82	6	9	68	115	1.78	138	.238	.301	76-0-2	.158	0*	94	10	—	1.4
1905	Chi A	17	13	.567	36	33	25-4	0	260.1	204	67	2	9	58	120	1.76	140	.218	.270	90-0-4	.167	0*	86	24	—	2.9
1906	†Chi A	18	6	.750	28	24	20-7	0	219.1	160	47	2	5	38	95	**1.52**	**167**	.207	**.249**	65-0-7	.185	4*	120	28	—	**3.9**
1907	Chi A	**27**	13	.675	46	35	24-6	1	291	270	93	3	6	38	141	2.26	106	.248	.278	90-0-12	.222	4*	118	7	—	1.7
1908	Chi A	18	13	.581	41	37	24-5	0	296	262	94	3	9	69	126	2.55	91	.240	.291	109-0-9	.229	4*	104	-1	—	0.8
1909	Chi A	11	9	.550	24	21	14-3	0	177.2	149	56	1	7	31	77	1.72	136	.226	.269	192-0-13	.234	6*	80	10	—	1.9
1910	Chi A	15	13	.536	33	29	20-2	1	236.2	219	84	2	12	50	111	2.66	90	.243	.291	126-0-12	.198	2*	106	0	—	0.4
1911	Chi A	10	14	.417	34	29	16-4	2	214.1	219	91	2	9	35	72	2.98	108	.271	.309	78-0-4	.256	3*	109	8	—	1.1
1912	Chi A	8	10	.444	32	19	9-1	0	172	172	81	1	8	47	57	3.24	99	.267	.325	56-0-2	.125	-1	91	1	—	-0.2
1913	Chi A	2	4	.333	19	8	2	0	103	106	56	2	5	39	39	3.50	84	.281	.356	25-0-2	.120	-1*	73	-6	—	-0.3
Total	13	189	156	.548	427	363	262-45	5	3041	2738	1118	33	120	670	1384	2.39	112	.242	.292	1283-2-85	.217	37	100	110	—	18.8
WHITE, HAL	Harold George; B3.18.1919 Utica NY; D4.21.2001 Venice FL; BR/TR/5´10″/(165–170); d4.22; Mil 1944–45																									
1941	Det A	0	0	ø	4	0	0	0	9	11	6	0	0	6	2	6.00	76	.306	.405	2	.000	-0	—	-1	0	-0.1
1942	Det A	12	12	.500	34	25	12-4	1	216.2	212	80	6	5	82	93	2.91	136	.252	.323	77-0-3	.169	-1	109	25	0	2.5
1943	Det A	7	12	.368	32	24	7-2	2	177.2	150	84	6	1	71	58	3.39	104	.228	.304	57-0-2	.140	-1	105	1	0	0.0
1946	Det A	1	1	.500	11	1	1	0	27.1	34	20	5	0	15	12	5.60	65	.312	.395	7-0-2	.000	-1	164	-6	0	-0.5
1947	Det A	4	5	.444	35	5	0	2	84.2	91	43	5	2	47	33	3.61	104	.279	.373	18-0-1	.167	0	61	0	0	0.1
1948	Det A	2	1	.667	27	0	0	1	42.2	46	31	2	1	26	17	6.12	71	.272	.372	13	.154	0	—	-7	0	-0.5
1949	Det A	1	0	1.000	9	0	0	2	12	5	0	0	0	4	4	0.00	ø	.125	.205	3	.333	0*	—	6	0	0.7
1950	Det A	9	6	.600	42	8	3-1	1	111	96	59	7	1	65	53	4.54	103	.239	.347	33-0-2	.121	-2	103	3	0	0.2
1951	Det A	3	4	.429	38	4	0	4	76	74	45	7	2	49	23	4.74	88	.264	.378	16	.250	0	48	-5	0	-0.4
1952	Det A	1	8	.111	41	0	0	5	63.1	53	29	1	0	39	18	3.69	103	.237	.350	11	.182	-0	—	1	0	0.2
1953	StL A	0	0	ø	10	0	0	0	10.1	8	3	1	1	3	2	2.61	161	.205	.279	1	.000	0	—	2	0	0.1
	StL N	6	5	.545	49	0	0	7	84.2	84	32	5	0	39	32	2.98	143	.272	.353	16	.000	-2	—	12	0	1.4
1954	StL N	0	0	ø	4	0	0	0	5	11	11	2	1	4	2	19.80	21	.440	.533	1	.000	-0	—	-8	0	-0.4
Total	12	46	54	.460	336	67	23-7	25	920.1	875	443	47	14	450	349	3.78	106	.253	.342	255-0-10	.145	-7	99	23	0	3.3
WHITE, DEACON	James Laurie; B12.7.1847 Caton NY; D7.7.1939 Aurora IL; BL/TR/5´11″/175; d5.4.1871; M2; b–Will; ▲																									
1876	Chi N	0	0	ø	1	0	0	1	2	1	0	0	—	0	3	0.00	ø	.143	.143	303-1	.343	0*	—	1	—	0.1
1890	Buf P	0	0	ø	1	0	0	0	8	18	15	0	0	2	0	9.00	46	.429	.455	439	.260	0*	—	-5	—	-0.2
Total	2	0	0	ø	2	0	0	1	10	19	15	0	0	2	3	7.20	53	.388	.412	742-1	.294	1	—	-4	—	-0.1
WHITE, LARRY	Larry David; B9.25.1958 San Fernando CA; BR/TR/6´5″/190; [CleA79 31/756]; d9.20; Col San Francisco St.																									
1983	LA N	0	0	ø	4	0	0	0-0	7	4	1	0	0	3-0	5	1.29	281	.174	.269	0	ø	0	—	2	0	0.1
1984	LA N	0	1	.000	7	1	0	0-0	12	9	5	2	0	6-2	10	3.00	119	.209	.300	1	.000	-0	99	1	0	0.0
Total	2	0	1	.000	11	1	0	0-0	19	13	6	2	0	9-2	15	2.37	151	.197	.289	1	.000	-0	99	3	0	0.1
WHITE, MATT	Matthew Joseph; B8.19.1977 Pittsfield MA; BR/TL/6´0″/(180–205); [CleA98 15/453]; d5.27; Col Clemson																									
2003	Bos A	0	1	.000	3	0	0	0-0	3.2	10	11	1	0	3-0	0	27.00	17	.526	.565	0	ø	0	—	-8	57	-1.3
	Sea A	0	0	ø	3	0	0	0-0	2	3	3	2	0	2-0	0	13.50	32	.375	.500	0	ø	0	—	-2	0	-0.1
	Year	0	1	.000	6	0	0	0-0	5.2	13	14	3	0	5-0	0	22.24	20	.481	.545	0	ø	0	—	-10	0	-1.4
2005	Was N	0	1	.000	1	1	0	0-0	4	4	4	0	1	3-0	3	9.00	46	.267	.400	1	.000	-0	0	-2	0	-0.4
Total	2	0	2	.000	7	1	0	0-0	9.2	17	18	3	1	8-0	3	16.76	26	.405	.491	1	.000	-0	0	-12	57	-1.8
WHITE, KIRBY	Oliver Kirby "Red","Buck"; B1.3.1884 Hillsboro OH; D4.22.1943 Hillsboro OH; BL/TR/6´0″/190; d5.4																									
1909	Bos N	6	13	.316	23	19	11-1	0	148.1	134	73	5	1	80	53	3.22	88	.245	.343	50-0-3	.160	-1	69	-6	—	-0.9
1910	Bos N	1	2	.333	3	3	3	0	26	15	7	2	3	12	6	1.38	240	.188	.316	6-0-1	.333	1	45	5	—	0.7
	Pit N	10	9	.526	30	21	7-3	2	153.1	142	73	2	5	75	42	3.46	90	.258	.352	46-0-2	.261	3	106	-4	—	-0.3
	Year	11	11	.500	33	24	10-3	2	179.1	157	80	4	8	87	48	3.16	99	.249	.347	52-0-3	.269	4	98	0	—	0.4
1911	Pit N	0	1	.000	2	1	0	0	3	3	4	1	0	1	1	9.00	38	.250	.308	1	.000	-0	0	-2	—	-0.4
Total	3	17	25	.405	58	44	21-4	2	330.2	294	157	10	9	168	102	3.24	93	.247	.345	103-0-6	.214	3	83	-7	—	-0.9
WHITE, RICK	Richard Allen; B12.23.1968 Springfield OH; BR/TR/6´4″/(215–240); [PitN90 15/403]; d4.6; Col Paducah (KY) CC																									
1994	Pit N	4	5	.444	43	5	0	6-3	75.1	79	35	9	6	17-3	38	3.82	114	.280	.329	13	.077	-1	104	5	0	0.5
1995	Pit N	2	3	.400	15	9	0	0-0	55	66	33	3	2	18-0	29	4.75	92	.299	.352	15-0-2	.067	-1	104	-3	22	-0.3
1998	TB A	2	6	.250	38	3	0	0-0	68.2	66	32	8	2	23-2	39	3.80	126	.253	.315	3	.333	0	65	7	0	0.7

YEAR	TM LG	W	L	PCT	G	GS	CG-SHO	SV-BS	IP	H	R	HR	HB	BB-IB	SO	ERA	AERA	OAV	OOB	AB-HR-SH	AVG	PB	SUP	APR	DL	PW
1999	TB A	5	3	.625	63	1	0	0-2	108	132	56	8	1	38-5	81	4.08	122	.304	.358	0	ø	0	75	10	0	0.6
2000	TB A	3	6	.333	44	0	0	2-3	71.1	57	30	7	5	26-3	47	3.41	144	.220	.301	0	ø	0	—	12	0	1.3
	†NY N	2	3	.400	22	0	0	1-1	28.1	26	14	2	2	12-2	20	3.81	114	.232	.315	5	.200	0*	—	1	0	0.2
2001	NY N	4	5	.444	55	0	0	2-2	69.2	71	38	7	2	17-4	51	3.88	104	.257	.303	3	.000	-0	—	-1	36	-0.2
2002	Col N	2	6	.250	41	0	0	0-1	40.2	49	30	4	1	18-4	27	6.20	76	.310	.376	0	ø	0	—	-6	22	-1.0
	†StL N	3	1	.750	20	0	0	0-0	22	13	3	0	0	3-1	14	0.82	493	.169	.200	1	.000	-0	—	8	0	1.3
	Year	5	7	.417	61	0	0	0-1	62.2	62	33	4	1	21-5	41	4.31	104	.264	.322	1	.000	-0	—	1	0	0.3
2003	Chi A	1	2	.333	34	0	0	1-0	47.2	56	39	11	1	13-2	37	6.61	70	.295	.340	0	ø	0	—	-11	0	-0.6
	Hou N	0	0	ø	15	0	0	0-0	19.1	18	9	2	3	8-0	17	3.72	119	.243	.341	0	ø	0	—	1	0	0.0
2004	Cle A	5	5	.500	59	0	0	1-2	78.1	88	52	15	2	29-7	44	5.29	82	.293	.356	0	ø	0	—	-10	0	-1.0
2005	Pit N	4	7	.364	71	0	0	2-1	75	90	39	3	4	29-10	40	3.72	114	.308	.374	2	.000	-0	—	2	0	0.3
2006	Cin N	1	0	1.000	26	0	0	1-1	27.1	34	23	5	1	5-1	17	6.26	75	.318	.348	0	ø	0	—	-5	0	-0.2
	Phi N	3	1	.750	38	0	0	0-0	37.1	38	21	3	2	15-0	23	4.34	108	.273	.353	0	ø	0	—	1	0	0.1
	Year	4	1	.800	64	0	0	1-1	64.2	72	44	8	3	20-1	40	5.15	91	.293	.351	0	ø	0	—	-5	0	-0.1
Total	11	41	53	.436	584	18	0	16-16	824	883	454	87	34	271-44	524	4.31	105	.277	.337	42-0-2	.095	-2	95	11	80	1.7
White, Steve	Stephen Vincent; B12.21.1884 Dorchester MA; D1.29.1975 Braintree MA; BR/TR/5´10˝/160; d5.29; Col Princeton																									
1912	Was A	0	0	ø	1	0	0	0	0.2	2	2	1	0	0	1	0.00	ø	.667	.667	0	ø	0	—	0	—	0.0
	Bos N	0	0	ø	3	0	0	0	6	9	5	0	1	5	2	6.00	60	.429	.556	3	.000	-0	—	-1	—	-0.1
Total	1	0	0	ø	4	0	0	0	6.2	11	7	1	1	5	3	5.40	66	.458	.567	3	.000	-0	—	-1	—	-0.1
White, Will	William Henry "Whoop-La"; B10.11.1854 Caton NY; D8.31.1911 Port Carling ON, Can.; BB/TR/5´9.5˝/175; d7.20; M1; b–Deacon																									
1877	Bos N	2	1	.667	3	3	3-1	0	27	27	15	0	—	2	7	3.00	94	.243	.257	15	.200	-1	197	0	—	-0.1
1878	Cin N	30	21	.588	52	52	52-5	0	468	477	249	1	—	45	169	1.79	119	.252	.269	197	.142	-8	111	16	—	0.6
1879	Cin N	43	31	.581	**76**	**75**	**75**-4	0	**680**	676	404	10	—	68	232	1.99	117	.238	.256	294	.136	-17	122	22	—	0.1
1880	Cin N	18	42	.300	62	62	58-3	0	517.1	550	323	9	—	56	161	2.14	116	.255	.273	207	.169	-9	73	14	—	0.3
1881	Det N	0	2	.000	2	2	2	0	18	24	18	0	—	2	5	5.00	58	.296	.313	7	.000	-1	46	-4	—	-0.4
1882	Cin AA	**40**	12	**.769**	54	54	**52-8**	0	**480**	411	164	3	—	71	122	1.54	172	.216	.244	207	.266	6	117	**60**	—	**6.7**
1883	Cin AA	**43**	22	.662	65	64	64-**6**	0	577	473	255	16	—	104	141	**2.09**	155	.209	.244	240	.225	3	119	**75**	—	**6.9**
1884	Cin AA	34	18	.654	52	52	52-**7**	0	456	479	224	16	35	74	118	3.32	101	.255	.296	184-1	.190	-2	116	5	—	-0.1
1885	Cin AA	18	15	.545	34	34	33-2	0	293.1	295	169	9	27	64	80	3.53	92	.255	.309	118	.169	-3	97	-5	—	-0.8
1886	Cin AA	1	2	.333	3	3	3	0	26	28	23	1	6	10	6	4.15	85	.280	.379	9	.111	-1	107	-3	—	-0.4
Total	10	229	166	.580	403	401	394-36	0	3542.2	3440	1844	65	68	496	1041	2.28	120	.239	.268	1478-1	.183	-33	109	180	—	12.8
Whitehead, John	John Henderson "Silent John"; B4.27.1909 Coleman TX; D10.20.1964 Bonham TX; BR/TR/6´2˝/195; d4.19																									
1935	Chi A	13	13	.500	28	27	18-1	0	222.1	209	101	17	2	101	72	3.72	124	.250	.332	82-0-4	.146	-5	90	23	—	1.9
1936	Chi A	13	13	.500	34	32	15-1	1	230.2	254	137	9	5	98	70	4.64	112	.276	.349	87-0-7	.241	1	104	13	—	1.4
1937	Chi A	11	8	.579	26	24	8-4	0	165.2	191	84	14	5	56	45	4.07	113	.294	.354	58-0-4	.224	1	104	11	—	1.1
1938	Chi A	10	11	.476	32	24	10-2	2	183.1	218	108	12	3	80	38	4.76	103	.299	.370	60-0-5	.100	-4	71	5	—	0.1
1939	Chi A	0	3	.000	7	4	0	0	32	60	30	4	0	5	9	8.16	58	.408	.428	9	.000	-1	70	-11	—	-0.9
	StL A	1	3	.250	26	4	0	1	66	88	49	10	2	17	9	5.86	83	.321	.365	17	.059	-1	118	-7	—	-0.5
	Year	1	6	.143	33	8	0	1	98	148	79	14	2	22	18	6.61	73	.352	.387	26	.038	-3	94	-18	—	-1.4
1940	StL A	1	3	.250	15	4	1-1	0	40	46	25	3	0	14	11	5.40	85	.286	.343	12	.167	-1	72	-3	—	-0.3
1942	StL A	0	0	ø	4	0	0	0	4	8	3	0	1	1	0	6.75	55	.421	.476	0	ø	0	—	-1	0	0.0
Total	7	49	54	.476	172	119	52-9	4	944	1074	537	69	18	372	254	4.60	105	.287	.355	325-0-20	.169	-11	93	30	0	2.8
Whitehill, Earl	Earl Oliver; B2.7.1899 Cedar Rapids IA; D10.22.1954 Omaha NE; BL/TL/5´9.5˝/174; d9.15; C2																									
1923	Det A	2	0	1.000	8	3	1	0	33	22	14	2	3	15	19	2.73	142	.188	.296	11-0-1	.364	1	143	3	—	0.3
1924	Det A	17	9	.654	35	32	16-2	0	233	260	125	8	13	79	65	3.86	106	.288	.353	89-0-1	.213	1*	130	6	—	0.6
1925	Det A	11	11	.500	35	**33**	15-1	2	239.1	267	135	13	10	88	83	4.66	92	.293	.361	87-0-3	.218	0*	105	-5	—	-0.5
1926	Det A	16	13	.552	36	34	13	0	252.1	271	136	7	8	79	109	3.99	102	.277	.336	91-0-3	.253	4	98	2	—	0.5
1927	Det A	16	14	.533	41	31	17-3	3	236	238	110	4	9	105	95	3.36	125	.267	.350	78-0-6	.205	-0	93	22	—	2.4
1928	Det A	11	16	.407	31	30	12-1	0	196.1	214	131	8	1	78	93	4.31	95	.277	.344	67-0-3	.194	-1	95	-11	—	-1.4
1929	Det A	14	15	.483	38	28	18-1	1	245.1	267	147	16	3	96	103	4.62	93	.280	.348	90-3-4	.256	5	114	-7	—	-0.2
1930	Det A	17	13	.567	34	31	16	1	220.2	248	139	8	8	80	109	4.24	113	.285	.351	83-0-1	.193	-4	83	6	—	0.3
1931	Det A	13	16	.448	34	34	22	0	271.1	287	152	22	5	118	81	4.08	112	.274	.351	97-0-4	.155	-5	82	12	—	0.7
1932	Det A	16	12	.571	33	31	17-3	0	244	255	136	17	5	93	81	4.54	104	.269	.337	90-0-5	.244	1	112	9	—	1.0
1933	†Was A	22	8	.733	39	**37**	19-2	1	270	271	112	9	4	100	96	3.33	125	.262	.329	108-0-5	.222	2*	119	26	—	2.7
1934	Was A	14	11	.560	32	31	15	0	235	269	129	10	3	94	96	4.52	96	.290	.357	85-1-6	.200	4*	108	-4	—	0.0
1935	Was A	14	13	.519	34	34	19-1	0	279.1	318	149	16	7	104	102	4.29	101	.289	.354	104-0-4	.183	-1	113	1	—	0.1
1936	Was A	14	11	.560	28	28	14	0	212.1	252	124	17	2	89	63	4.87	98	.294	.362	77-0-5	.169	-0	101	2	—	0.2
1937	Cle A	8	8	.500	33	22	6-1	2	147	189	111	9	6	80	53	6.49	71	.322	.409	49-0-6	.224	1	120	-26	—	-2.2
1938	Cle A	9	8	.529	26	23	4	0	160.1	187	109	18	9	83	60	5.56	83	.289	.378	56	.125	-2	105	-15	—	-1.5
1939	Chi N	4	7	.364	24	11	2-1	1	89.1	102	59	8	5	50	42	5.14	77	.292	.389	29	.103	-2	83	-12	—	-1.5
Total	17	218	185	.541	541	473	226-16	11	3564.2	3917	2018	192	101	1431	1350	4.36	100	.282	.353	1291-4-57	.204	4	105	9	—	1.5
Whitehouse, Charlie	Charles Evis "Lefty"; B1.25.1894 Charleston IL; D7.19.1960 Indianapolis IN; BB/TL/6´0˝/152; d8.29																									
1914	Ind F	2	0	1.000	8	2	2	0	26	34	14	0	1	5	10	4.85	64	.324	.360	8	.000	-1	143	-3	—	-0.4
1915	New F	2	2	.500	11	3	1	0	39.2	46	29	0	5	17	18	4.31	59	.299	.386	10-0-1	.000	-1	127	-9	—	-1.0
1919	Was A	0	1	.000	6	1	0	0	12	13	7	1	0	6	5	4.50	71	.283	.365	1	.000	-0	98	-1	—	-0.1
Total	3	4	3	.571	25	6	3	0	77.2	93	50	1	6	28	33	4.52	63	.305	.375	19-0-1	.000	-2	129	-13	—	-1.5
Whitehouse, Len	Leonard Joseph; B9.10.1957 Burlington VT; BL/TL/5´11˝/(174–175); d9.1																									
1981	Tex A	0	1	.000	2	1	0	0-0	3.1	8	7	1	0	2-0	2	16.20	21	.500	.526	0	ø	0	52	-5	0	-0.9
1983	Min A	7	1	.875	60	0	0	2-1	73.2	70	34	6	2	44-11	44	4.15	103	.261	.365	0	ø	0	—	3	0	0.2
1984	Min A	2	2	.500	30	0	0	1-3	31.1	29	11	3	2	17-3	18	3.16	134	.254	.361	0	ø	0	—	4	0	0.5
1985	Min A	0	0	ø	5	0	0	1-0	7.1	12	9	4	0	2-0	4	11.05	40	.353	.389	0	ø	0	—	-5	0	-0.2
Total	4	9	4	.692	97	1	0	4-4	115.2	119	61	14	4	65-14	68	4.67	91	.275	.372	0	ø	0	52	-3	0	-0.4
Whitehurst, Wally	Walter Richard; B4.11.1964 Shreveport LA; BR/TR/6´3˝/(180–200); [OakA85 3/65]; d7.17; Col New Orleans																									
1989	NY N	0	1	.000	9	1	0	0-0	14	17	7	2	0	5-0	9	4.50	73	.293	.344	1-0-1	.000	0	81	-2	0	-0.1
1990	NY N	1	0	1.000	38	0	0	2-0	65.2	63	27	5	0	9-2	46	3.29	115	.251	.277	8-0-1	.250	0	—	3	0	0.2
1991	NY N	7	12	.368	36	20	0	1-0	133.1	142	67	12	4	25-3	87	4.18	88	.274	.311	33-0-5	.182	1	94	-6	15	-0.7
1992	NY N	3	9	.250	44	11	0	0-3	97	99	45	4	4	33-5	70	3.62	97	.264	.328	22-0-1	.182	1	87	-2	0	-0.2
1993	SD N	4	7	.364	21	19	0	0-0	105.2	109	47	11	3	30-5	57	3.83	108	.276	.326	24-0-10	.083	-2	79	5	88	0.4
1994	SD N	4	7	.364	13	13	0	0-0	64	84	37	8	1	26-4	43	4.92	84	.319	.383	19	.105	0	80	-5	64	-0.7
1996	NY A	1	1	.500	2	2	0	0-0	8	11	6	1	0	2-0	1	6.75	73	.324	.361	0	ø	0	75	-1	0	-0.2
Total	7	20	37	.351	163	66	0	3-3	487.2	525	236	43	12	130-19	313	4.02	95	.277	.325	107-0-18	.150	1	86	-8	167	-1.3
Whiteside, Sean	David Sean; B4.19.1971 Lakeland FL; BL/TL/6´4˝/190; [DetA92 11/308]; d4.29; Col North Carolina–Charlotte																									
1995	Det A	0	0	ø	2	0	0	0-0	3.2	7	6	1	0	4-1	2	14.73	33	.438	.500	0	ø	0	—	-4	0	-0.2
Whiteside, Matt	Matthew Christopher; B8.8.1967 Charleston MO; BR/TR/6´0˝/(185–205); [TexA90 25/678]; d8.5; Col Arkansas St.																									
1992	Tex A	1	1	.500	20	0	0	4-0	28	26	8	1	0	11-2	13	1.93	198	.245	.314	0	ø	0	—	6	0	0.5
1993	Tex A	2	1	.667	60	0	0	1-4	73	78	37	7	1	23-6	39	4.32	97	.281	.337	0	ø	0	—	0	0	0.0
1994	Tex A	2	2	.500	47	0	0	1-2	61	68	40	6	1	28-3	37	5.02	96	.286	.361	0	ø	0	—	-2	0	-0.1
1995	Tex A	5	4	.556	40	0	0	3-1	53	48	24	5	1	19-2	46	4.08	119	.242	.308	0	ø	0	—	5	16	0.8
1996	Tex A	0	1	.000	14	0	0	0-0	32.1	43	24	8	0	11-1	15	6.68	79	.321	.367	0	ø	0	—	-4	0	-0.2
1997	Tex A	4	1	.800	42	1	0	0-4	72.2	85	45	4	3	26-3	44	5.08	96	.296	.355	0	ø	0	132	-2	0	0.0
1998	Phi N	1	1	.500	10	0	0	0-0	18	27	18	6	0	5-0	14	8.50	51	.338	.376	2	.000	-0	—	-8	0	-0.8
1999	SD N	1	0	1.000	10	0	0	0-0	11	19	17	1	0	5-0	9	13.91	31	.396	.444	0	ø	0	—	-12	0	-0.9
2000	SD N	2	3	.400	28	0	0	0-0	37	32	21	6	1	17-3	27	4.14	108	.232	.318	0	ø	0	—	0	0	0.1
2001	Atl N	0	1	.000	13	0	0	0-0	16.1	23	14	5	1	7-1	10	7.16	60	.319	.383	0	ø	0	—	-5	0	-0.3
2005	Tor A	0	0	ø	2	0	0	0-0	3.2	6	8	3	1	5-0	5	19.64	23	.353	.522	0	ø	0	—	-6	0	-0.3
Total	11	18	15	.545	286	1	0	9-11	406	455	256	52	9	157-21	259	5.23	88	.285	.349	2	.000	-0	132	-28	16	-1.2

YEAR	TM LG	W	L	PCT	G	GS	CG-SHO	SV-BS	IP	H	R	HR	HB	BB-IB	SO	ERA	AERA	OAV	OOB	AB-HR-SH	AVG	PB	SUP	APR	DL	PW
Whiting, Jesse	Jesse Way; B5.30.1879 Philadelphia PA; D10.28.1937 Philadelphia PA; TR/5´10˝/154; d9.27																									
1902	Phi N	0	1	.000	1	1	1	0	9	13	8	0	0	6	0	5.00	56	.333	.422	3	.333	0	48	-3	—	-0.2
1906	Bro N	1	1	.500	3	2	2-1	0	24.2	26	10	0	1	6	7	2.92	86	.286	.337	10	.300	1	72	-1	—	0.0
1907	Bro N	0	0	ø	1	0	0	0	3	3	4	0	0	3	2	12.00	20	.273	.429	2	.000	-0*	—	-3	—	-0.2
Total	3	1	2	.333	5	3	3-1	0	36.2	42	22	0	1	15	9	4.17	62	.298	.369	15	.267	0	65	-7	—	-0.4
Whitney, Art	Arthur Wilson; B1.16.1858 Brockton MA; D8.15.1943 Lowell MA; BR/TR/5´8˝/155; d5.1.1880; b–Frank; ▲																									
1882	Det N	0	1	.000	3	2	1	0	18	31	17	1	—	8	11	6.00	49	.373	.429	115	.183	-1*	99	-5	—	-0.3
1886	Pit AA	0	0	ø	1	0	0	0	6	7	4	0	0	3	2	3.00	113	.304	.385	511	.239	0*	—	0	—	0.0
1889	†NY N	0	0	ø	1	0	0	0	4.1	1	3	0	0	4	3	2.08	190	.071	.278	473-1	.218	0*	—	0	—	0.0
Total	3	0	1	.000	5	2	1	0	28.1	39	24	1	0	15	16	4.76	67	.325	.400	1099-1	.224	-1	99	-5	—	-0.3
Whitney, Jim	James Evans "Grasshopper Jim"; B11.10.1857 Conklin NY; D5.21.1891 Binghamton NY; BL/TR/6´2˝/172; d5.2																									
1881	Bos N	**31**	33	.484	**66**	**63**	**57**-6	0	**552.1**	548	284	6	—	90	162	2.48	107	.248	.277	282	.255	11*	86	11	—	2.1
1882	Bos N	24	21	.533	49	48	46-3	0	420	404	229	3	—	41	180	2.64	109	.237	.255	251-5	.323	23*	110	7	—	2.8
1883	Bos N	37	21	.638	62	56	54-1	**2**	514	492	258	7	—	35	**345**	2.24	138	.238	.251	409-5	.281	20*	106	44	—	5.6
1884	Bos N	23	14	.622	38	37	35-6	0	336	272	140	12	—	27	270	2.09	138	.207	.223	270-3	.259	10*	100	27	—	3.6
1885	Bos N	18	32	.360	51	50	50-2	0	441.1	503	286	14	—	37	200	2.98	90	.272	.286	290	.234	7*	95	-23	—	-1.3
1886	KC N	12	32	.273	46	44	42-3	0	393	465	292	9	—	55	167	4.49	84	.284	.308	247-2	.239	5*	64	-27	—	-1.4
1887	Was N	24	21	.533	47	47	46-2	0	404.2	430	253	16	16	42	146	3.22	125	.259	.284	201-2	.264	10*	85	30	—	3.9
1888	Was N	18	21	.462	39	39	37-3	0	325	317	184	7	9	54	79	3.05	91	.245	.280	141-1	.170	-1*	92	-14	—	-1.6
1889	Ind N	2	7	.222	9	8	7	0	70	106	73	4	2	19	16	6.81	61	.339	.380	32	.375	5*	107	-19	—	-1.4
1890	Phi AA	2	2	.500	6	4	3	0	40	61	27	1	1	11	6	5.17	75	.341	.382	21	.238	-0*	108	-4	—	-0.3
Total	10	191	204	.484	413	396	377-26	2	3496.1	3598	2026	79	28	411	1571	2.97	104	.253	.275	2144-18	.261	89	93	32	—	12.0
Whitrock, Bill	William Franklin; B3.4.1870 Cincinnati OH; D7.26.1935 Derby CT; TR/5´7.5˝/170; d5.3																									
1890	StL AA	5	6	.455	16	11	10	1	105	104	62	2	7	40	39	3.51	123	.251	.327	48	.146	-3	68	8	—	0.5
1893	Lou N	2	5	.286	8	8	5	0	46.2	64	53	3	4	19	8	8.10	54	.317	.387	21	.286	1	88	-19	—	-1.8
1894	Lou N	0	1	.000	1	1	0	0	4	8	8	0	0	2	0	9.00	57	.400	.455	2	.000	-0	97	-2	—	-0.4
	Cin N	2	6	.250	11	9	9	0	79.1	121	88	7	9	46	10	6.24	89	.347	.436	65	.231	-2*	67	-9	—	-0.7
	Year	2	7	.222	12	10	9	0	83.1	129	96	7	9	48	10	6.37	87	.350	.437	67	.224	-3	69	-11	—	-1.1
1896	Phi N	0	1	.000	2	1	1	0	9	10	5	0	0	3	1	3.00	144	.278	.333	3	.000	-0	33	1	—	0.1
Total	4	9	19	.321	38	30	25	1	244	307	216	12	20	110	58	5.35	89	.300	.379	139	.201	-4	72	-21	—	-2.3
Whitson, Ed	Eddie Lee; B5.19.1955 Johnson City TN; BR/TR/6´3˝/(190–202); [PitN74 6/131]; d9.4; [DL 1992 SD N 182]																									
1977	Pit N	1	0	1.000	5	2	0	0-0	15.2	11	6	0	0	9-1	10	3.45	117	.204	.308	4	.000	-0	99	1	0	0.0
1978	Pit N	5	6	.455	43	0	0	4-3	74	66	31	5	2	37-5	64	3.28	114	.243	.333	11-0-1	.182	-0	—	4	0	0.5
1979	Pit N	2	3	.400	19	7	0	1-0	57.2	53	36	6	1	36-3	31	4.37	90	.238	.346	13-0-4	.000	-1	142	-5	0	-0.5
	SF N	5	8	.385	18	17	2	0-0	100.1	98	47	5	4	39-6	62	3.95	89	.254	.326	32-0-5	.156	-1	92	-4	0	-0.6
	Year	7	11	.389	37	24	2	1-0	158	151	83	11	5	75-9	93	4.10	89	.248	.334	45-0-9	.111	-2	107	-9	0	-1.1
1980	SF N☆	11	13	.458	34	34	6-2	0-0	211.2	222	88	7	4	56-7	90	3.10	113	.271	.318	66-0-9	.091	-4	79	8	0	0.3
1981	SF N	6	9	.400	22	22	2-1	0-0	123	130	61	10	2	47-5	65	4.02	85	.273	.339	33-0-9	.091	-1	96	-8	0	-1.1
1982	Cle A	4	2	.667	40	9	1-1	2-0	107.2	91	43	6	0	58-3	61	3.26	127	.231	.324	0	ø	0	71	11	0	0.5
1983	SD N	5	7	.417	31	21	2	1-0	144.1	143	73	23	1	50-1	81	4.30	82	.256	.316	44-0-2	.182	1	101	-12	40	-1.0
1984	†SD N	14	8	.636	31	31	1	0-0	189	181	72	16	3	42-1	103	3.24	111	.255	.296	61-0-6	.049	-5*	104	9	0	0.6
1985	NY A	10	8	.556	30	30	2-2	0-0	158.2	201	100	19	2	43-0	89	4.88	83	.309	.350	0	ø	0	133	-17	0	-1.7
1986	NY A	5	2	.714	14	4	0	0-0	37	54	37	5	0	23-1	27	7.54	55	.335	.412	0	ø	0	154	-15	21	-2.3
	SD N	1	7	.125	17	12	0	0-0	75.2	85	48	8	0	37-0	46	5.59	66	.287	.364	18-0-2	.167	-0	91	-14	0	-1.3
1987	SD N	10	13	.435	36	34	3-1	0-0	205.2	197	113	36	3	64-3	135	4.73	84	.251	.309	65-0-10	.123	-1	101	-14	0	-1.6
1988	SD N	13	11	.542	34	33	3-1	0-0	205.1	202	93	17	1	45-1	118	3.77	90	.259	.298	66-0-9	.167	1	98	-8	0	-0.8
1989	SD N	16	11	.593	33	33	5-1	0-0	227	198	77	22	5	48-6	117	2.66	132	.235	.278	72-0-7	.139	1*	99	21	0	2.5
1990	SD N	14	9	.609	32	32	6-3	0-0	228.2	215	73	13	1	47-8	127	2.60	148	.251	.289	67-1-13	.149	1*	104	**32**	0	3.3
1991	SD N	4	6	.400	13	12	2	0-0	78.2	93	47	13	0	17-3	40	5.03	76	.299	.332	24-0-2	.125	-1	87	-9	115	-1.2
Total	15	126	123	.506	452	333	35-12	8-3	2240	2240	1045	211	29	698-54	1266	3.79	97	.261	.316	576-1-79	.125	-11	101	-20	358	-4.4
Whittaker, Walt	Walter Elton "Doc"; B6.11.1894 Chelsea MA; D8.7.1965 Pembroke MA; BL/TR/5´9.5˝/165; d7.6; Col Tufts																									
1916	Phi A	0	0	ø	1	0	0	0	2	3	1	0	0	2	0	4.50	63	.375	.500	0	ø	0	—	0	—	0.0
Wickander, Kevin	Kevin Dean; B1.4.1965 Fort Dodge IA; BL/TL/6´2˝/(200–205); [CleA86 2/30]; d8.10; Col Grand Canyon																									
1989	Cle A	0	0	ø	2	0	0	0-0	2.2	6	1	0	0	2-1	0	3.38	118	.462	.533	0	ø	0	—	0	0	0.0
1990	Cle A	0	1	.000	10	0	0	0-1	12.1	14	6	0	1	4-0	10	3.65	108	.304	.358	0	ø	0	—	0	126	0.0
1992	Cle A	2	0	1.000	44	0	0	1-2	41	39	14	1	4	28-3	38	3.07	128	.258	.384	0	ø	0	—	5	0	0.2
1993	Cle A	0	0	ø	11	0	0	0-0	8.2	15	7	3	0	3-0	3	4.15	106	.366	.409	0	ø	0	—	-1	0	-0.1
	Cin N	1	0	1.000	33	0	0	0-1	25.1	32	20	5	2	19-1	20	6.75	60	.308	.424	2	.000	-0	—	-7	35	-0.4
1995	Det A	0	0	ø	21	0	0	1-2	17.1	18	6	1	1	9-4	9	2.60	185	.273	.364	0	ø	0	—	4	21	0.2
	Mil A	0	0	ø	8	0	0	0-0	6	1	0	0	0	3-1	2	0.00	ø	.059	.190	0	ø	0	—	3	0	0.1
	Year	0	0	ø	29	0	0	1-2	23.1	19	6	1	1	12-5	11	1.93	252	.229	.327	0	ø	0	—	7	0	0.3
1996	Mil A	2	0	1.000	21	0	0	0-2	25.1	26	16	2	0	17-2	19	4.97	104	.265	.368	0	ø	0	—	0	45	0.0
Total	6	5	1	.833	150	0	0	2-8	138.2	151	70	12	8	85-12	101	4.02	108	.282	.383	2	.000	-0	—	4	227	-0.0
Wicker, Kemp	Kemp Caswell (b Kemp Caswell Whicker); B8.13.1906 Kernersville NC; D6.11.1973 Kernersville NC; BR/TL/5´11˝/182; d8.14; Col North Carolina St.																									
1936	NY A	1	2	.333	7	0	0	0	20	31	18	2	0	11	5	7.65	61	.356	.429	7	.143	-0	—	-7	—	-0.8
1937	†NY A	7	3	.700	16	10	6-1	0	88	107	52	8	0	26	14	4.40	101	.296	.343	35-0-1	.114	-3	153	0	—	-0.4
1938	NY A	1	0	1.000	1	0	0	0	1	0	0	0	0	1	0	0.00	ø	.000	.250	0	ø	0	—	1	—	0.1
1941	Bro N	1	2	.333	16	2	0	1	32	30	14	3	0	14	8	3.66	100	.252	.331	4-0-3	.250	0	81	1	0	0.1
Total	4	10	7	.588	40	12	6-1	1	141	168	84	13	0	52	27	4.66	92	.294	.353	46-0-4	.130	-2	143	-5	0	-1.0
Wicker, Bob	Robert Kitridge; B5.25.1877 Bono IN; D1.22.1955 Evanston IL; BL/TR/5´11˝/210; d8.11																									
1901	StL N	0	0	ø	1	0	0	0	3	4	3	0	0	1	2	0.00	ø	.308	.357	3	.333	0*	—	0	—	0.0
1902	StL N	5	12	.294	22	16	14-1	0	152.1	159	82	1	2	45	78	3.19	86	.269	.322	77-0-2	.234	1*	67	-9	—	-0.6
1903	StL N	0	0	ø	1	0	0	0	5	4	1	0	0	3	3	0.00	ø	.174	.269	2	.000	-0	—	2	—	0.1
	Chi N	20	9	.690	32	27	24-1	1	247	236	114	3	3	74	110	3.02	104	.253	.311	98-0-1	.245	6	119	8	—	1.2
	Year	20	9	.690	33	27	24-1	1	252	240	115	3	3	77	113	2.96	106	.252	.309	100-0-1	.240	6	119	5	—	1.3
1904	Chi N	17	9	.654	30	27	23-4	0	229	201	92	6	3	58	99	2.67	100	.232	.282	155-0-3	.219	1*	112	2	—	0.0
1905	Chi N	13	6	.684	22	22	17-4	0	178	139	46	3	1	47	86	2.02	147	.221	.276	72-0-3	.139	-2*	99	22	—	1.9
1906	Chi N	3	5	.375	10	8	5	0	72.1	70	36	0	0	19	25	2.99	88	.257	.306	20	.100	-1	97	-4	—	-0.6
	Cin N	6	11	.353	20	17	14	0	150	150	69	3	1	46	69	2.70	102	.263	.319	50-0-1	.180	2	76	-1	—	-0.1
	Year	9	16	.360	30	25	19	0	222.1	220	105	3	1	65	94	2.79	97	.261	.315	70-0-1	.157	1	83	-7	—	-0.7
Total	6	64	52	.552	138	117	97-10	1	1036.2	963	443	16	10	293	472	2.73	105	.247	.301	477-0-10	.205	6	99	20	—	1.9
Wickersham, Dave	David Clifford; B9.27.1935 Erie PA; BR/TR/6´3˝/(190–195); d9.18; Col Ohio U.																									
1960	KC A	0	0	ø	5	0	0	2	8.1	4	1	0	0	1-0	3	1.08	369	.148	.179	1	.000	-0	—	3	0	0.1
1961	KC A	2	1	.667	17	0	0	2	21	25	12	0	2	5-1	10	5.14	81	.309	.360	3	.667	1	—	-1	0	-0.1
1962	KC A	11	4	.733	30	9	3	1	110	105	53	13	8	43-1	61	4.17	101	.257	.337	35-0-2	.057	-3	106	2	0	0.0
1963	KC A	12	15	.444	38	34	4-1	1	237.2	244	116	21	9	79-2	118	4.09	95	.268	.330	80-0-4	.138	-3	86	-3	0	-0.6
1964	Det A	19	12	.613	40	36	11-1	1	254	224	108	28	12	81-3	164	3.44	106	.232	.299	82-0-12	.073	-5	96	5	0	0.0
1965	Det A	9	14	.391	34	27	8-3	0	195.1	179	91	12	11	61-6	109	3.78	92	.241	.307	58-0-7	.069	-4	87	-6	0	-1.1
1966	Det A	8	3	.727	38	14	3	1	140.2	139	64	14	8	54-4	93	3.20	109	.261	.336	45-0-1	.044	-3	125	1	0	-0.2
1967	Det A	4	5	.444	36	4	0	4	85.1	72	30	6	4	33-2	44	2.74	119	.235	.315	15-0-1	.000	-2	60	4	0	0.4
1968	Pit N	1	0	1.000	11	0	0	1	20.2	21	12	0	0	13-3	9	3.48	84	.276	.362	3-0-1	.333	0	—	-2	0	-0.1
1969	KC A	2	3	.400	34	0	0	5-2	50	58	27	6	2	14-2	27	3.96	93	.294	.346	2	.000	0	—	-2	0	-0.2
Total	10	68	57	.544	283	124	29-5	18-2	1123	1071	514	100	56	384-24	638	3.66	100	.252	.320	324-0-28	.086	-18	94	1	0	-1.8

YEAR	TM LG	W	L	PCT	G	GS	CG-SHO	SV-BS	IP	H	R	HR	HB	BB-IB	SO	ERA	AERA	OAV	OOB	AB-HR-SH	AVG	PB	SUP	APR	DL	PW
WICKMAN, BOB	Robert Joe; B2.6.1969 Green Bay WI; BR/TR/6´1˝/(207–242); [ChiA90 2/44]; d8.24; Col Wisconsin–Whitewater; [DL 2003 Cle A 183]																									
1992	NY A	6	1	.857	8	8	0	0-0	50.1	51	25	2	2	20-0	21	4.11	96	.273	.344	0	ø	0	144	-1	0	-0.1
1993	NY A	14	4	.778	41	19	1-1	4-4	140	156	82	13	5	69-7	70	4.63	90	.284	.368	0	ø	0	160	-9	0	-1.0
1994	NY A	5	4	.556	**53**	0	0	6-4	70	54	26	3	1	27-3	56	3.09	149	.213	.287	0	ø	0	—	12	0	1.5
1995	†NY A	2	4	.333	63	1	0	1-9	80	77	38	6	5	33-3	51	4.05	114	.253	.335	0	ø	0	80	5	0	0.4
1996	NY A	4	1	.800	58	0	0	0-3	79	94	41	7	5	34-1	61	4.67	106	.299	.373	0	ø	0	—	4	0	0.3
	Mil A	3	0	1.000	12	0	0	0-1	16.2	12	9	3	0	10-2	14	3.24	160	.200	.314	0	ø	0	—	2	0	0.3
	Year	7	1	.875	70	0	0	0-4	95.2	106	50	10	5	44-3	75	4.42	113	.283	.363	0	ø	0	—	6	0	0.6
1997	Mil A	7	6	.538	74	0	0	1-4	95.2	89	32	8	3	41-7	78	2.73	170	.252	.333	0	ø	0	—	20	0	2.4
1998	Mil N	6	9	.400	72	0	0	25-7	82.1	79	38	5	4	39-2	71	3.72	117	.262	.352	1	.000	-0	—	5	0	1.0
1999	Mil N	3	8	.273	71	0	0	37-8	74.1	75	31	6	2	38-6	60	3.39	136	.262	.351	1	.000	-0	—	10	0	1.9
2000	Mil N★	2	2	.500	43	0	0	16-4	46	37	18	1	1	20-2	44	2.93	157	.215	.299	0	ø	0	—	8	0	1.1
	Cle A	1	3	.250	26	0	0	14-3	26.2	27	12	0	0	12-3	11	3.38	148	.270	.348	0	ø	0	—	4	0	0.8
2001	†Cle A	5	0	1.000	70	0	0	32-3	67.2	61	18	4	2	14-2	66	2.39	192	.240	.285	0	ø	0	—	17	0	2.5
2002	Cle A	1	3	.250	36	0	0	20-2	34.1	42	22	3	1	10-0	36	4.46	100	.284	.333	0	ø	0	—	-2	70	-0.4
2004	Cle A	0	2	.000	30	0	0	13-1	29.2	33	14	4	2	10-0	26	4.25	102	.282	.349	0	ø	0	—	1	93	0.1
2005	Cle A★	0	4	.000	64	0	0	**45**-5	62	57	17	9	1	21-3	41	2.47	169	.247	.310	0	ø	0	—	13	0	2.4
2006	Cle A	1	4	.200	29	0	0	15-3	28	29	15	1	1	11-0	17	4.18	104	.271	.336	0	ø	0	—	0	0	0.0
	Atl N	0	2	.000	28	0	0	18-1	26	24	7	1	0	2-0	25	1.04	436	.231	.245	0	ø	0	—	8	0	1.6
Total	14	60	57	.513	778	28	1-1	247-62	1008.2	997	445	76	35	411-41	748	3.57	126	.260	.334	2	.000	-0	141	97	346	14.8
WIDMAR, AL	Albert Joseph; B3.20.1925 Cleveland OH; D10.15.2005 Tulsa OK; BR/TR/6´3˝/185; d4.25; C17																									
1947	Bos A	0	0	ø	2	0	0	0	1.1	1	2	1	0	2	1	13.50	29	.200	.429	0	ø	0	—	-1	0	-0.1
1948	StL A	2	6	.250	49	0	0	1	82.2	88	42	4	0	48	34	4.46	102	.275	.370	10	.300	1	—	2	0	0.4
1950	StL A	7	15	.318	36	26	8-1	4	194.2	211	115	16	3	74	78	4.76	104	.271	.337	67-0-2	.149	-3	72	6	0	0.3
1951	StL A	4	9	.308	26	16	4	0	107.2	157	84	19	2	52	28	6.52	67	.344	.414	30-0-6	.167	-1	92	-22	0	-2.3
1952	Chi A	0	0	ø	1	0	0	0	2	4	1	1	0	0	2	4.50	81	.444	.444	0	ø	0	—	0	0	0.0
Total	5	13	30	.302	114	42	12-1	5	388.1	461	244	41	5	176	143	5.21	90	.294	.367	107-0-8	.168	-4	80	-15	0	-1.7
WIDNER, WILD BILL	William Waterfield; B6.3.1867 Cincinnati OH; D12.10.1908 Cincinnati OH; BR/TR/6´0˝/180; d6.8																									
1887	Cin AA	1	0	1.000	1	1	1	0	9	11	8	2	1	2	0	5.00	87	.275	.326	4	.250	-0	132	-1	—	-0.1
1888	Was N	5	7	.417	13	13	13	0	115	111	69	7	6	22	33	2.82	99	.247	.291	60	.200	-1*	89	-5	—	-0.5
1889	Col AA	12	20	.375	41	34	25-2	1	294	368	241	11	18	85	63	5.20	70	.297	.351	133-2	.211	-2	113	-46	—	-3.8
1890	Col AA	4	8	.333	13	10	8-1	0	96	103	52	3	3	24	14	3.28	109	.266	.314	41	.195	-1	86	4	—	0.4
1891	Cin AA	0	1	.000	1	1	1	0	8	13	7	0	2	4	0	7.88	52	.351	.442	4	.250	-0	61	-2	—	-0.2
Total	5	22	36	.379	69	59	48-3	1	522	606	377	23	30	137	110	4.36	79	.281	.333	242-2	.207	-3	104	-50	—	-4.2
WIEAND, TED	Franklin Delano Roosevelt; B4.4.1933 Walnutport PA; BR/TR/6´2˝/195; d9.27																									
1958	Cin N	0	0	ø	1	0	0	0	2	4	2	1	0	0-0	2	9.00	46	.400	.400	0	ø	0	—	-1	0	0.0
1960	Cin N	0	1	.000	5	0	0	0	4.1	4	5	2	0	5-1	3	10.38	37	.250	.429	0	ø	0	—	-3	0	-0.5
Total	2	0	1	.000	6	0	0	0	6.1	8	7	3	0	5-1	5	9.95	39	.308	.419	0	ø	0	—	-4	0	-0.5
WIEDEMEYER, CHARLIE	Charles John "Chick"; B1.31.1914 Chicago IL; D10.27.1979 Lake Geneva FL; BL/TL/6´3˝/180; d9.9																									
1934	Chi N	0	0	ø	4	1	0	0	8.1	16	10	0	1	4	2	9.72	40	.432	.500	1	.000	-0	156	-6	—	-0.3
WIEDMAN, STUMP	George Edward; B2.17.1861 Rochester NY; D3.2.1905 New York NY; BR/TR/5´7.5˝/165; d8.26; U1; ▲																									
1880	Buf N	0	9	.000	17	13	9	0	113.2	141	77	1	—	9	25	3.40	72	.291	.304	78	.103	-5*	57	-10	—	-1.1
1881	Det N	8	5	.615	13	13	13-1	0	115	108	48	1	—	12	26	**1.80**	**162**	.238	**.258**	47	.255	0	101	13	—	1.2
1882	Det N	25	20	.556	46	45	43-4	0	411	391	204	10	—	39	161	2.63	112	.236	.253	193	.218	-5*	86	18	—	1.2
1883	Det N	20	24	.455	52	47	41-3	**2**	402.1	435	265	8	—	72	183	3.53	88	.257	.288	313-1	.185	-8*	90	-13	—	-1.6
1884	Det N	4	21	.160	26	26	24	0	212.2	257	179	9	—	57	96	3.72	78	.273	.314	300	.163	-4*	55	-21	—	-2.2
1885	Det N	14	24	.368	38	38	37-3	0	330	343	198	7	—	63	149	3.14	91	.252	.286	153-1	.157	-4*	90	-5	—	-1.0
1886	KC N	12	36	.250	51	51	48-1	0	427.2	549	323	11	—	112	168	4.52	83	.303	.344	179	.168	-10	63	-31	—	-3.4
1887	Det N	13	7	.650	21	21	20	0	183	221	132	9	9	60	56	5.36	76	.296	.356	82-1	.207	-2	117	-18	—	-1.6
	NY AA	4	8	.333	12	12	11-1	0	97	122	84	3	1	25	37	4.64	92	.292	.333	46	.152	-2*	60	-6	—	-0.6
	NY N	0	1	.000	1	1	1	0	8	10	6	0	0	2	4	1.13	335	.286	.324	3	.333	0	52	1	—	0.1
1888	NY N	1	1	.500	2	2	2	0	18	17	20	2	2	8	5	3.50	78	.230	.321	7	.000	-0	179	-4	—	-0.4
Total	9	101	156	.393	279	269	249-13	2	2318.1	2594	1536	61	12	459	910	3.61	89	.268	.302	1401-3	.177	-41	81	-76	—	-9.4
WIENEKE, JACK	John; B3.10.1894 Saltsburg PA; D3.16.1933 Pleasant Ridge MI; BR/TL/6´0˝/182; d7.4																									
1921	Chi A	0	1	.000	10	3	0	0	25.1	39	24	4	1	17	10	8.17	52	.351	.442	9	.111	-1	66	-10	—	-0.5
WIESLER, BOB	Robert George; B8.13.1930 St.Louis MO; BB/TL/6´2˝/195; d8.3; Mil 1951–52																									
1951	NY A	0	2	.000	4	3	0	0	9.1	13	15	0	0	11	3	13.50	28	.361	.511	3	.000	-1	54	-10	0	-1.6
1954	NY A	3	2	.600	6	5	0	0	30.1	28	15	0	0	30	25	4.15	83	.259	.420	11-0-1	.273	1	97	-2	0	-0.3
1955	NY A	0	2	.000	16	7	0	0	53	39	27	1	1	49-0	22	3.91	96	.212	.380	14	.143	-1	105	-1	0	-0.1
1956	Was A	3	12	.200	37	21	3	0	123	141	98	11	3	112-1	49	6.44	67	.300	.435	33-0-4	.091	-3*	88	-27	0	-3.0
1957	Was A	1	1	.500	3	2	1	0	16.1	15	8	2	1	11-0	9	4.41	88	.250	.375	6	.167	0	126	-1	0	0.0
1958	Was A	0	0	ø	4	0	0	0	9.1	14	8	2	1	5-0	5	6.75	56	.359	.435	2	.000	-0	—	-3	0	-0.2
Total	6	7	19	.269	70	38	4	0	241.1	250	171	16	6	218-1	113	5.74	70	.279	.421	69-0-5	.130	-3	92	-44	0	-5.2
WIGGINS, SCOTT	Scott Joseph; B3.24.1976 Fort Thomas KY; BL/TL/6´3˝/205; [NYA97 7/229]; d9.11; Col Northern Kentucky																									
2002	Tor A	0	0	ø	3	0	0	0-0	2.2	5	1	1	0	1-0	3	3.38	137	.417	.462	0	ø	0	—	0	0	0.0
WIGGS, JIMMY	James Alvin "Big Jim"; B9.1.1876 Trondheim, Norway; D1.20.1963 Xenia OH; BB/TR/6´4˝/200; d4.23																									
1903	Cin N	0	1	.000	2	1	0	0	5	12	7	0	1	2	2	5.40	66	.500	.556	1	.000	-0	57	-2	—	-0.3
1905	Det A	3	3	.500	7	7	4	0	41.1	30	25	0	1	29	37	3.27	84	.205	.341	15	.133	-0	78	-4	—	-0.5
1906	Det A	0	0	ø	4	1	0	0	10.1	11	9	1	2	7	7	5.23	53	.275	.408	3	.333	0	182	-3	—	-0.1
Total	3	3	4	.429	13	9	4	0	56.2	53	41	1	4	38	46	3.81	74	.252	.377	19	.158	-0	87	-9	—	-0.9
WIGHT, BILL	William Robert "Lefty"; B4.12.1922 Rio Vista CA; BL/TL/6´1˝/(180–190); d4.17																									
1946	NY A	2	2	.500	14	4	1	0	40.1	44	22	1	1	30	11	4.46	77	.289	.410	9-0-2	.000	-1	124	-4	0	-0.5
1947	NY A	1	0	1.000	1	1	1	0	9	8	3	0	0	2	3	1.00	353	.242	.286	2-0-1	.000	0	125	2	0	0.2
1948	Chi A	9	20	.310	34	32	7-1	1	223.1	238	132	9	1	135	68	4.80	89	.278	.377	73-0-3	.082	-7	62	-13	0	-2.1
1949	Chi A	15	13	.536	35	33	14-3	1	245	254	106	9	0	96	78	3.31	126	.275	.343	85-0-9	.165	-1	96	22	0	2.2
1950	Chi A	10	16	.385	30	28	13-3	0	206	213	89	10	0	79	62	3.58	125	.270	.336	61-0-10	.000	-9	63	22	0	1.7
1951	Bos A	7	7	.500	34	17	4-2	0	118.1	128	77	5	0	63	38	5.10	88	.282	.369	41	.073	-4	95	-8	0	-1.2
1952	Bos A	2	1	.667	10	2	0	0	24.1	14	11	3	1	14	5	2.96	133	.169	.296	7	.143	-0	122	2	0	0.2
	Det A	5	9	.357	23	19	8-3	0	143.2	167	71	7	0	55	65	3.88	98	.291	.354	50-0-2	.220	1	93	-2	0	0.1
	Year	7	10	.412	33	21	8-3	0	168	181	82	10	1	69	70	3.75	102	.276	.346	57-0-2	.211	1	96	1	0	0.3
1953	Det A	0	3	.000	13	4	0	0	25.1	35	33	4	0	14	10	8.88	46	.333	.412	7	.429	1	126	-16	0	-1.5
	Cle A	2	1	.667	20	0	0	1	26.2	29	12	1	0	16	14	3.71	101	.282	.378	5	.000	-1	—	0	0	0.0
	Year	2	4	.333	33	4	0	1	52	64	45	5	0	30	24	6.23	63	.308	.395	12	.250	0	131	-16	0	-1.5
1955	Cle A	0	0	ø	17	0	0	1	24	24	8	0	0	9-1	9	2.63	152	.261	.327	0-0-1	ø	0	—	4	0	0.3
	Bal A	6	8	.429	19	14	8-2	2	117.1	111	43	6	1	39-1	54	2.45	155	.252	.311	36-0-5	.083	-2	60	16	0	1.7
	Year	6	8	.429	36	14	8-2	3	141.1	135	51	6	1	48-2	63	2.48	155	.254	.313	36-0-6	.083	-2	59	19	0	2.0
1956	Bal A	9	12	.429	35	26	7-1	0	174.2	198	92	7	6	72-3	84	4.02	98	.289	.361	60-0-2	.200	-1	92	-5	0	-0.6
1957	Bal A	6	6	.500	27	17	2	0	121	122	53	4	4	54-1	50	3.64	99	.271	.351	34-0-4	.029	-3	92	-1	0	-0.4
1958	Cin N	0	1	.000	7	0	0	0	6.2	7	4	1	0	4-0	5	4.05	102	.292	.393	0	ø	0	—	0	0	0.0
	StL N	3	0	1.000	28	1	1	2	57.1	64	35	7	0	32-1	18	5.02	82	.290	.375	10-0-1	.100	-0	109	-5	0	-0.3
	Year	3	1	.750	35	1	1	2	64	71	39	8	0	36-1	23	4.92	84	.290	.377	10-0-1	.100	-0	109	-5	0	-0.3
Total	12	77	99	.438	347	198	66-15	8	1563	1656	791	74	14	714-7	574	3.95	103	.277	.354	480-0-40	.115	-28	84	14	0	-0.2
WIGINGTON, FRED	Fred Thomas; B12.16.1897 Rogers NE; D5.8.1980 Mesa AZ; BR/TR/5´10˝/168; d4.20																									
1923	StL N	0	0	ø	4	0	0	0	8.1	11	4	0	0	5	2	3.24	121	.367	.457	1	.000	-0	—	0	—	0.0

YEAR	TM LG	W	L	PCT	G	GS	CG-SHO	SV-BS	IP	H	R	HR	HB	BB-IB	SO	ERA	AERA	OAV	OOB	AB-HR-SH	AVG	PB	SUP	APR	DL	PW
Wihtol, Sandy	Alexander Ames; B6.1.1955 Palo Alto CA; BR/TR/6´1˝/(190–195); [CleA74 S2/28]; d9.7; Col De Anza (CA) JC																									
1979	Cle A	0	0	ø	5	0	0	0-0	10.2	10	4	0	0	3-0	6	3.38	127	.238	.289	0	ø	0	—	1	0	0.1
1980	Cle A	1	0	1.000	17	0	0	1-1	35.1	35	18	2	2	14-2	20	3.57	116	.257	.333	0	ø	0	—	1	0	0.0
1982	Cle A	0	0	ø	6	0	0	0-0	11.2	9	6	1	1	7-0	8	4.63	90	.220	.340	0	ø	0	—	0	0	0.0
Total	3	1	0	1.000	28	0	0	1-1	57.2	54	28	3	3	24-2	34	3.75	111	.247	.327	0	ø	0	—	2	0	0.1
Wilcox, Milt	Milton Edward; B4.20.1950 Honolulu HI; BR/TR/6´2˝/(185–220); [CinN68 2/33]; d9.5																									
1970	†Cin N	3	1	.750	5	2	1-1	1-0	22.1	19	6	2	1	7-0	13	2.42	167	.229	.297	5-0-1	.200	0	133	4	0	0.8
1971	Cin N	2	2	.500	18	3	0	1-0	43.1	43	22	2	2	17-2	21	3.32	102	.269	.343	9	.000	-1	61	-2	0	-0.3
1972	Cle A	7	14	.333	32	27	4-2	0-0	156	145	67	18	5	72-11	90	3.40	96	.251	.336	45-0-4	.200	1	73	-3	0	-0.4
1973	Cle A	8	10	.444	26	19	4	0-0	134.1	143	90	14	8	68-9	82	5.83	68	.275	.366	0	ø	0*	105	-24	22	-2.8
1974	Cle A	2	2	.500	41	2	1	4-1	71.1	74	42	10	5	24-4	33	4.67	78	.271	.339	0	ø	0	133	-8	0	-0.5
1975	Chi N	0	1	.000	25	0	0	0-0	38.1	50	27	4	1	17-2	21	5.63	69	.323	.389	3	.333	0	—	-7	0	-0.3
1977	Det A	6	2	.750	20	13	1	0-0	106.1	96	46	13	1	37-1	82	3.64	119	.241	.305	0	ø	0	103	8	0	0.6
1978	Det A	13	12	.520	29	27	16-2	0-0	215.1	208	94	22	8	68-2	132	3.76	104	.255	.317	0	ø	0	100	5	0	0.6
1979	Det A	12	10	.545	33	29	7	0-0	196.1	201	105	18	11	73-8	109	4.35	100	.267	.338	0	ø	0	90	-1	0	0.1
1980	Det A	13	11	.542	32	31	13-1	0-1	198.2	201	112	24	6	68-5	97	4.48	92	.262	.325	0	ø	0*	130	-10	0	-1.0
1981	Det A	12	9	.571	24	24	8-1	0-0	166.1	152	61	10	6	52-3	79	3.03	125	.247	.310	0	ø	0	81	13	0	1.6
1982	Det A	12	10	.545	29	29	9-1	0-0	193.2	187	91	18	7	85-5	112	3.62	113	.257	.338	0	ø	0*	111	8	21	1.0
1983	Det A	11	10	.524	26	26	9-2	0-0	186	164	89	19	4	74-6	101	3.97	100	.237	.313	0	ø	0	110	0	31	0.1
1984	†Det A	17	8	.680	33	33	0	0-0	193.2	183	99	13	8	66-5	119	4.00	99	.252	.318	0	ø	0	137	-2	0	-0.1
1985	Det A	1	3	.250	8	8	0	0-0	39	51	24	6	0	14-2	20	4.85	85	.315	.369	0	ø	0	100	-3	116	-0.2
1986	Sea A	0	8	.000	13	10	0	0-0	55.2	74	38	11	1	28-1	26	5.50	78	.327	.399	0	ø	0	57	-7	0	-0.9
Total	16	119	113	.513	394	283	73-10	6-2	2016.2	1991	1013	204	74	770-66	1137	4.07	97	.260	.331	62-0-5	.177	0	104	-29	190	-1.7
Wiles, Randy	Randall E; B9.10.1951 Fort Belvoir VA; BL/TL/6´1˝/185; [StLN73 5/108]; d8.7; Col Louisiana St.																									
1977	Chi A	1	1	.500	5	0	0	0-0	2.2	5	3	1	0	3-1	0	10.13	40	.417	.533	0	ø	0	—	-2	0	-0.3
Wiley, Mark	Mark Eugene; B2.28.1948 National City CA; BR/TR/6´1˝/190; [MinA70 2/46]; d6.17; C15; Col Cal Poly–Pomona																									
1975	Min A	1	3	.250	15	3	1	2-1	38.2	50	30	4	1	13-1	15	6.05	63	.325	.374	0	ø	0	115	-10	0	-1.0
1978	SD N	1	0	1.000	4	1	0	0-0	7.2	11	6	1	0	1-0	1	5.87	57	.324	.343	2	.000	-0	241	-2	0	-0.3
	Tor A	0	0	ø	2	0	0	0-0	2.2	3	2	0	0	1-0	2	6.75	59	.273	.333	0	ø	0	—	-1	0	0.0
Total	2	2	3	.400	21	4	1	2-1	49	64	38	5	1	15-1	18	6.06	62	.322	.367	2	.000	-0	141	-13	0	-1.3
Wilhelm, Harry	Harry Lester; B4.7.1874 Uniontown PA; D2.20.1944 Republic PA; BR/TR/5´7˝/155; d8.12; Col Westminster (PA)																									
1899	Lou N	1	1	.500	5	3	2	0	25	36	22	1	1	3	6	6.12	63	.336	.360	12-1-0	.250	2	131	-5	—	-0.2
Wilhelm, Kaiser	Irvin Key; B1.26.1874 Wooster OH; D5.22.1936 Rochester NY; BR/TR/6´0˝/162; d4.18; M2/C1/U1																									
1903	Pit N	5	3	.625	12	9	7-1	0	86	88	51	0	3	25	20	3.24	100	.264	.321	34	.088	-2*	106	-2	—	-0.3
1904	Bos N	14	20	.412	39	36	30-3	0	288	316	150	8	7	74	73	3.69	75	.285	.333	100-0-5	.070	-8	88	-22	—	-3.2
1905	Bos N	3	23	.115	34	28	23	0	242.1	287	166	7	5	75	76	4.53	68	.295	.349	100-0-3	.160	-2*	64	-38	—	-3.7
1908	Bro N	16	22	.421	42	36	33-6	0	332	266	105	3	6	83	99	1.87	125	.217	.271	111-0-5	.108	-4	67	13	—	1.3
1909	Bro N	3	13	.188	22	17	14-1	0	163	176	92	3	2	59	45	3.26	80	.289	.353	57-0-2	.228	2	49	-18	—	-1.4
1910	Bro N	3	7	.300	15	5	0	0	68.1	88	45	3	1	18	17	4.74	64	.314	.358	19-0-2	.316	2	59	-13	—	-1.4
1914	Bal F	12	17	.414	47	27	11-1	5	243.2	263	141	10	0	81	113	4.03	75	.291	.349	84-0-4	.250	2*	82	-25	—	-2.6
1915	Bal F	0	0	ø	1	0	0	0	1	0	0	0	0	0	0	0.00	ø	.000	.000	0	ø	0	—	0	—	0.0
1921	Phi N	0	0	ø	4	0	0	0	8	11	3	0	0	3	1	3.38	125	.393	.452	2	.000	-0	—	1	—	0.0
Total	9	56	105	.348	216	158	118-12	5	1432.1	1495	753	34	24	418	444	3.44	81	.274	.328	507-0-21	.154	-11	75	-104	—	-11.3
Wilhelm, Hoyt	James Hoyt; B7.26.1922 Huntersville NC; D8.23.2002 Sarasota FL; BR/TR/6´0˝/(190–195); d4.18; HF1985																									
1952	NY N	15	3	**.833**	**71**	0	0	11	159.1	127	60	12	5	57	108	**2.43**	**152**	.220	.296	38-1-3	.158	0	—	19	0	2.3
1953	NY N☆	7	8	.467	**68**	0	0	15	145	127	61	13	4	77	71	3.04	141	.238	.339	33-0-5	.152	1	—	**18**	0	2.1
1954	†NY N	12	4	.750	57	0	0	7	111.1	77	32	5	5	52	64	2.10	192	.198	.298	21-0-1	.048	-2	—	**23**	0	3.2
1955	NY N	4	1	.800	59	0	0	0	103	104	53	10	2	40-5	71	3.93	102	.266	.333	19-0-1	.158	-1	—	1	0	0.1
1956	NY N	4	9	.308	64	0	0	8	89.1	97	45	7	2	43-10	71	3.83	99	.280	.361	9	.222	0	—	-1	0	-0.1
1957	StL N	1	4	.200	40	0	0	11	55	52	28	7	3	21-1	29	4.25	93	.254	.332	6	.000	-1	—	-1	0	-0.3
	Cle A	1	0	1.000	2	0	0	1	3.2	2	1	1	1	1-0	0	2.45	151	.154	.267	0	ø	0	—	1	0	0.1
1958	Cle A	2	7	.222	30	6	1	5	90.1	70	32	4	1	35-2	57	2.49	146	.215	.291	21-0-3	.095	-1	82	10	0	1.0
	Bal A	1	3	.250	9	4	3-1	0	40.2	25	9	2	1	10-2	35	1.99	180	.179	.238	11-0-1	.091	-1	44	8	0	0.7
	Year	3	10	.231	39	10	4-1	5	131	95	41	6	2	45-4	92	2.34	155	.204	.276	32-0-4	.094	-2	67	18	0	1.7
1959	Bal A★	15	11	.577	32	27	13-3	0	226	178	64	13	10	77-3	139	**2.19**	**173**	.224	.299	76-0-4	.053	-6	82	**40**	0	3.7
1960	Bal A	11	8	.579	41	11	3-1	7	147	125	69	13	1	39-0	107	3.31	115	.228	.279	42-0-3	.071	-3	74	5	0	0.3
1961	Bal A★	9	7	.563	51	1	0	18	109.2	89	35	5	4	41-5	87	2.30	167	.219	.296	20-0-2	.050	-1	92	18	0	3.0
1962	Bal A✳	7	10	.412	52	0	0	15	93	64	28	5	3	34-2	90	1.94	191	.197	.276	16	.125	-0	—	17	0	3.5
1963	Chi A	5	8	.385	55	3	0	21	136.1	106	47	8	4	30-1	111	2.64	133	.215	.263	29-0-3	.069	-1	68	13	0	1.5
1964	Chi A	12	9	.571	73	0	0	27	131.1	94	35	7	2	30-1	95	1.99	174	.202	.252	21-0-2	.143	-0	—	21	0	4.2
1965	Chi A	7	7	.500	66	0	0	20	144	88	34	11	2	32-7	106	1.81	176	.177	.227	22-0-4	.000	-2	—	**23**	0	2.7
1966	Chi A	5	2	.714	46	0	0	6	81.1	50	21	6	1	17-2	61	1.66	191	.178	.226	8	.125	0	—	13	48	1.3
1967	Chi A	8	3	.727	49	0	0	12	89	58	21	2	4	34-4	76	1.31	236	.183	.270	13	.077	-1	—	**16**	0	2.4
1968	Chi A	4	4	.500	72	0	0	12	93.2	69	20	4	2	24-5	72	1.73	175	.205	.261	3-0-1	.000	-0	—	14	0	1.6
1969	Cal A	5	7	.417	44	0	0	10-3	65.2	45	21	4	3	18-4	53	2.47	142	.194	.260	8	.000	-1	—	8	0	1.5
	Atl N	2	0	1.000	8	0	0	4-1	12.1	5	1	0	1	4-0	14	0.73	496	.119	.213	1	.000	-0	—	4	0	0.9
1970	Atl N☆	6	4	.600	50	0	0	13-4	78.1	69	29	7	1	39-7	67	3.10	138	.234	.323	11	.091	-0	—	10	0	1.6
	Chi N	0	1	.000	3	0	0	0-0	3.2	4	4	1	0	3-0	1	9.82	46	.286	.412	0	ø	0	—	-2	0	-0.3
	Year	6	5	.545	53	0	0	13-4	82	73	33	8	1	42-7	68	3.40	126	.236	.328	11	.091	-0	—	8	0	1.3
1971	Atl N	0	0	ø	3	0	0	0-1	2.1	6	5	2	0	1-0	1	15.43	24	.500	.538	0	ø	0	—	-3	63	-0.1
	LA N	0	1	.000	9	0	0	3-0	17.2	6	2	1	0	4-0	15	1.02	319	.111	.169	3	.000	-0	—	5	0	0.4
	Year	0	1	.000	12	0	0	3-1	20	12	7	3	0	5-0	16	2.70	123	.182	.236	3	.000	-0	—	1	0	0.3
1972	LA N	0	1	.000	16	0	0	1-0	25.1	20	16	0	0	15-0	9	4.62	73	.217	.315	1-0-1	.000	-0	—	-4	0	-0.2
Total	21	143	122	.540	1070	52	20-5	227-9	2254.1	1757	773	150	62	778-61	1610	2.52	146	.216	.288	432-1-34	.088	-21	78	276	111	37.1
Wilkie, Lefty	Aldon Jay; B10.30.1914 Zealandia SK, Can.; D8.5.1992 Tualatin OR; BL/TL/5´11.5˝/175; d4.22; Mil 1943–45																									
1941	Pit N	2	4	.333	26	6	2-1	2	79	90	42	1	1	40	16	4.56	79	.289	.372	24	.292	1	98	-6	0	-0.3
1942	Pit N	6	7	.462	35	6	3	1	107.1	112	53	4	1	37	18	4.19	81	.269	.330	38	.263	2*	99	-7	0	-0.5
1946	Pit N	0	0	ø	7	0	0	0	7.2	13	9	0	0	3	3	10.57	33	.382	.432	0	ø	0	—	-5	0	-0.3
Total	3	8	11	.421	68	12	5-1	3	194	215	104	5	2	80	37	4.59	76	.283	.352	62	.274	3	99	-18	0	-1.1
Wilkins, Dean	Dean Allan; B8.24.1966 Blue Island IL; BR/TR/6´1˝/170; [NYA86*2/51]; d8.21; Col San Diego Mesa (CA) JC																									
1989	Chi N	1	0	1.000	11	0	0	0-0	15.2	13	9	2	0	9-2	14	4.60	82	.228	.333	1-0-1	.000	-0	—	-1	0	-0.1
1990	Chi N	0	0	ø	7	0	0	1-0	7.1	11	8	1	1	7-0	3	9.82	42	.333	.463	0	ø	0	—	-4	0	-0.2
1991	Hou N	2	1	.667	7	0	0	1-1	8	16	14	0	0	10-2	4	11.25	31	.410	.531	1	.000	-0	—	-9	0	-1.6
Total	3	3	1	.750	25	0	0	2-1	31	40	31	3	1	26-4	21	7.55	50	.310	.429	2-0-1	.000	-0	—	-14	0	-1.9
Wilkins, Eric	Eric Lamoine; B12.9.1956 St.Louis MO; BR/TR/6´1˝/180; [CleA77 6/141]; d4.11; Col Washington St.																									
1979	Cle A	2	4	.333	16	14	0	0-0	69.2	77	41	4	4	38-1	52	4.39	98	.289	.384	0	ø	0	89	-2	42	-0.2
Wilkins, Marc	Marc Allen; B10.21.1970 Mansfield OH; BR/TR/5´11˝/(200–221); [PitN92 47/1323]; d5.11; Col Toledo																									
1996	Pit N	4	3	.571	47	2	0	1-4	75	75	36	6	6	36-6	62	3.84	114	.266	.357	9	.222	0	123	4	0	0.4
1997	Pit N	9	5	.643	70	0	0	2-2	75.2	65	33	7	4	33-2	47	3.69	116	.242	.333	4-0-1	.000	-0	—	6	0	0.8
1998	Pit N	0	0	ø	16	0	0	0-1	15.1	13	6	1	2	9-2	17	3.52	121	.236	.358	0	ø	0	—	2	143	0.1
1999	Pit N	2	3	.400	46	0	0	0-0	51	49	28	3	4	26-1	44	4.24	109	.257	.354	1	.000	-0	—	2	26	0.2
2000	Pit N	4	2	.667	52	0	0	0-0	60.1	54	34	4	6	43-3	37	5.07	92	.248	.376	6	.167	-0	—	-1	0	-0.1
2001	Pit N	0	1	.000	14	0	0	0-0	17.1	22	13	2	1	8-1	11	6.75	66	.319	.397	0	ø	0	—	-4	0	-0.2
Total	6	19	14	.576	245	2	0	3-7	294.2	278	150	23	23	155-15	218	4.28	104	.256	.357	20-0-1	.150	0	123	9	169	1.2

THE PITCHER REGISTER

YEAR	TM LG	W	L	PCT	G	GS	CG-SHO	SV-BS	IP	H	R	HR	HB	BB-IB	SO	ERA	AERA	OAV	OOB	AB-HR-SH	AVG	PB	SUP	APR	DL	PW
Wilkinson, Roy	Roy Hamilton; B5.8.1893 Canandaigua NY; D7.2.1956 Louisville KY; BR/TR/6´1˝/170; d4.29																									
1918	Cle A	0	0	ø	1	0	0	0	1	0	0	0	0	0	0	0.00	ø	.000	.000	0	ø	0	—	0	—	0.0
1919	†Chi A	1	1	.500	4	1	1-1	0	22	21	9	0	0	10	5	2.05	156	.266	.348	8	.375	2	172	2	—	0.4
1920	Chi A	7	9	.438	34	12	8	2	145	162	75	6	2	48	30	4.03	93	.297	.356	48-0-1	.146	-3	83	-3	—	-0.7
1921	Chi A	4	20	.167	36	23	11	3	198.1	259	135	4	4	78	50	5.13	83	.334	.397	65	.123	-4	57	-22	—	-2.4
1922	Chi A	0	1	.000	4	1	0	1	14.1	24	15	1	1	6	3	8.79	46	.393	.456	3	.000	-0	0	-7	—	-0.6
Total	5	12	31	.279	79	37	20-1	6	380.2	466	234	11	7	142	88	4.66	86	.318	.381	124-0-1	.145	-5	67	-30	—	-3.3
Wilkinson, Bill	William Carl; B8.10.1964 Greybull WY; BR/TL/5´10˝/160; [SeaA83 4/87]; d6.13; ggf–Jim Bluejacket																									
1985	Sea A	0	2	.000	2	2	0	0-0	6	8	9	2	0	6-1	5	13.50	31	.333	.467	0	ø	0	86	-6	0	-0.9
1987	Sea A	3	4	.429	56	0	0	10-2	76.1	61	33	8	0	21-1	73	3.66	130	.223	.272	0	ø	0	—	9	17	0.9
1988	Sea A	2	2	.500	30	0	0	2-1	31	28	14	3	0	15-0	25	3.48	120	.233	.316	0	ø	0	—	2	39	0.2
Total	3	5	8	.385	88	2	0	12-3	113.1	97	56	13	0	42-2	103	4.13	110	.232	.298	0	ø	0	86	5	56	0.2
Wilks, Ted	Theodore "Cork"; B11.13.1915 Fulton NY; D8.21.1989 Houston TX; BR/TR/5´9.5˝/(178–195); d4.25; C2																									
1944	†StL N	17	4	**.810**	36	21	16-4	0	207.2	173	61	12	1	49	70	2.64	133	.227	**.275**	64-0-6	.141	-1	141	25	0	2.1
1945	StL N	4	7	.364	18	16	4-1	0	98.1	103	39	9	1	29	28	2.93	128	.270	.324	30-0-1	.133	-0	76	8	0	0.7
1946	†StL N	8	0	1.000	40	4	0	1	95	88	41	13	2	38	40	3.41	101	.248	.324	24	.208	0	112	1	0	0.0
1947	StL N	4	0	1.000	37	0	0	5	50.1	57	33	10	2	11	28	5.01	83	.279	.323	6	.167	0	—	-5	0	-0.5
1948	StL N	6	6	.500	57	2	1	13	130.2	113	40	5	0	39	71	2.62	156	.235	.293	30-0-3	.167	0	163	**21**	0	2.3
1949	StL N	10	3	.769	**59**	0	0	**9**	118.1	105	52	8	0	38	71	3.73	112	.240	.301	27-0-1	.037	-3	—	7	0	0.4
1950	StL N	2	0	1.000	18	0	0	0	24.1	27	18	4	1	9	15	6.66	65	.287	.356	4	.000	-1	—	-5	42	-0.4
1951	StL N	0	0	ø	17	0	0	1	18	19	7	1	0	5	5	3.00	132	.279	.329	1	.000	-0	—	2	0	0.0
	Pit N	3	5	.375	48	1	1	12	82.2	69	31	6	2	24	43	2.83	149	.231	.292	12-0-1	.083	-1	84	12	0	1.4
	Year	3	5	.375	**65**	1	1	**13**	100.2	88	38	7	2	29	48	2.86	146	.240	.299	13-0-1	.077	-1	85	**14**	0	1.4
1952	Pit N	5	5	.500	44	0	0	4	72.1	65	32	9	2	31	24	3.61	111	.245	.329	8-0-1	.125	-0	—	3	0	0.4
	Cle A	0	0	ø	7	0	0	1	11.2	8	6	0	0	7	6	3.86	87	.186	.300	0	ø	0	—	-1	0	0.0
1953	Cle A	0	0	ø	4	0	0	0	3.2	5	4	0	0	3	2	7.36	51	.278	.381	0	ø	0	—	-2	0	-0.1
Total	10	59	30	.663	385	44	22-5	46	913	832	364	77	11	283	403	3.26	118	.244	.304	206-0-13	.131	-5	110	66	42	6.3
Willett, Ed	Robert Edgar; B3.7.1884 Norfolk VA; D5.10.1934 Wellington KS; BR/TR/6´0˝/183; d9.5																									
1906	Det A	0	3	.000	3	3	3	0	25	24	12	0	2	8	16	3.96	70	.255	.327	9	.000	-1	17	-2	—	-0.4
1907	Det A	1	5	.167	10	6	1	0	48.2	47	31	0	2	20	27	3.70	70	.255	.335	13	.077	-1	52	-6	—	-0.8
1908	Det A	15	8	.652	30	23	18-2	1	197.1	186	67	2	14	60	77	2.28	106	.261	.331	67-0-2	.164	-2	127	5	—	0.7
1909	†Det A	21	10	.677	41	34	25-3	1	292.2	239	112	5	15	76	89	2.34	108	.221	.281	112-0-3	.196	3*	134	3	—	0.6
1910	Det A	16	11	.593	37	25	18-4	0	224.1	175	85	2	17	74	65	2.37	111	.217	.296	83-0-2	.133	-2*	96	4	—	0.6
1911	Det A	13	14	.481	38	27	15-2	1	231.1	261	136	5	14	80	86	3.66	95	.295	.363	82-1-4	.268	7*	117	-8	—	-0.1
1912	Det A	17	15	.531	37	31	28-1	0	284.1	281	144	3	17	84	89	3.29	99	.262	.326	115-2-3	.165	-2	112	-2	—	-0.1
1913	Det A	13	14	.481	34	30	19	0	242	237	117	0	11	89	59	3.09	95	.263	.336	92-1-6	.283	7*	115	-5	—	0.4
1914	StL F	4	17	.190	27	22	14	0	175	208	102	5	10	56	73	4.27	71	.295	.355	64-1-2	.234	2*	73	-21	—	-1.9
1915	StL F	2	3	.400	17	2	1	2	52.2	61	36	2	3	18	19	4.61	62	.295	.360	15-0-1	.200	0	170	-11	—	-1.0
Total	10	102	100	.505	274	203	142-12	5	1773.1	1719	842	24	105	565	600	3.08	94	.259	.326	652-5-23	.199	12	109	-43	—	-2.0
Willey, Carl	Carlton Francis; B6.6.1931 Cherryfield ME; BR/TR/6´0˝/175; d4.30																									
1958	†Mil N	9	7	.563	23	19	9-**4**	0	140	110	44	14	2	53-4	74	2.70	130	.215	.289	48-0-5	.104	-2	110	15	0	1.3
1959	Mil N	5	9	.357	26	15	5-2	0	117	126	60	12	2	31-4	51	4.15	85	.273	.319	39-0-1	.103	-1	103	-8	0	-1.0
1960	Mil N	6	7	.462	28	21	2-1	0	144.2	136	78	19	7	65-5	109	4.35	79	.248	.333	48-1-5	.146	1	104	-16	0	-1.2
1961	Mil N	6	12	.333	35	22	4	0	159.2	147	71	20	2	65-9	91	3.83	98	.247	.322	54-0-3	.019	-6	85	0	0	-0.5
1962	Mil N	2	5	.286	30	6	0	1	73.1	95	49	9	1	20-3	40	5.40	70	.319	.361	11-0-1	.273	1	96	-13	0	-1.0
1963	NY N	9	14	.391	30	28	7-4	0	183	149	74	24	4	69-2	101	3.10	113	.220	.294	54-1-6	.111	-1	82	8	0	0.9
1964	NY N	0	2	.000	14	3	0	0	30	37	19	5	1	8-2	14	3.60	99	.301	.343	4-0-1	.000	-0	65	-2	51	-0.3
1965	NY N	1	2	.333	13	3	1	0	28	30	13	2	2	15-1	13	4.18	84	.270	.364	5-0-2	.000	-1	58	-1	0	-0.2
Total	8	38	58	.396	199	117	28-11	1	875.2	830	408	105	21	326-30	493	3.76	95	.250	.318	263-2-24	.099	-9	93	-17	51	-2.0
Willhite, Nick	Jon Nicholas; B1.27.1941 Tulsa OK; BL/TL/6´2˝/(175–195); d6.16																									
1963	LA N	2	3	.400	8	8	1-1	0	38	44	19	5	0	10-2	28	3.79	80	.286	.329	10-0-1	.300	1	89	-4	0	-0.4
1964	LA N	2	4	.333	10	7	2	0	43.2	43	19	4	0	13-2	24	3.71	87	.264	.315	11-0-1	.000	-0	81	-2	0	-0.2
1965	Was A	0	0	ø	5	0	0	0	6.1	10	11	2	0	4-0	3	7.11	49	.345	.424	0	ø	0	—	-5	0	-0.3
	LA N	2	2	.500	15	6	0	1	42	47	26	7	2	22-1	28	5.36	61	.288	.380	10	.400	3	103	-10	0	-0.6
1966	LA N	0	0	ø	6	0	0	0	4.1	3	1	0	0	5-0	4	2.08	159	.214	.421	0	ø	0	—	1	0	0.1
1967	Cal A	0	2	.000	10	7	0	0	39.1	39	20	8	0	16-0	22	4.35	72	.258	.329	10	.000	-1	55	-5	0	-0.4
	NY N	0	1	.000	4	1	0	0	8.1	9	8	1	0	5-0	9	8.64	39	.257	.350	2	.000	-0	259	-4	0	-0.5
Total	5	6	12	.333	58	29	3-1	1	182	195	104	27	2	75-5	118	4.55	70	.275	.345	43-0-2	.163	2	88	-29	0	-2.3
Williams, Albert	Albert Hamilton (De Souza); B5.6.1954 Laguna de Perlas, Nicaragua; BR/TR/6´4˝/(184–190); d5.7																									
1980	Min A	6	2	.750	18	9	3	1-0	77	73	33	9	0	30-1	35	3.51	125	.253	.323	0	ø	0	125	7	0	0.7
1981	Min A	6	10	.375	23	22	4	0-0	150	160	72	11	1	52-4	76	4.08	97	.276	.334	0	ø	0	97	0	0	-0.1
1982	Min A	9	7	.563	26	26	3	0-0	153.2	166	74	18	0	55-5	61	4.22	101	.276	.333	0	ø	0	98	3	0	0.2
1983	Min A	11	14	.440	36	29	4-1	1-1	193.1	196	105	21	4	68-6	68	4.14	103	.262	.325	0	ø	0	94	0	0	-0.1
1984	Min A	3	5	.375	17	11	1	0-0	68.2	75	46	9	7	22-1	22	5.77	73	.284	.351	0	ø	0	81	-10	80	-1.0
Total	5	35	38	.479	120	97	15-1	2-1	642.2	670	330	68	12	227-17	262	4.24	99	.270	.332	0	ø	0	97	0	80	-0.3
Williams, Al	Almon Edward; B5.11.1914 Valhermoso Springs AL; D7.19.1969 Groves TX; BR/TR/6´3˝/200; d4.19																									
1937	Phi A	4	1	.800	16	8	2	1	75.1	88	51	0	1	49	27	5.38	88	.300	.402	24-0-3	.083	-2	132	-4	—	-0.4
1938	Phi A	0	7	.000	30	8	1	0	93.1	128	93	6	1	54	25	6.94	70	.324	.407	25-0-1	.040	-3	71	-25	—	-1.7
Total	2	4	8	.333	46	16	3	1	168.2	216	144	6	2	103	52	6.24	77	.314	.405	49-0-4	.061	-5	101	-29	—	-2.1
Williams, Gus	Augustine H.; B1870 New York NY; D10.14.1890 New York NY; 5´11˝/170; d4.18																									
1890	Bro AA	0	1	.000	2	2	1	0	12	13	15	0	0	12	2	7.50	52	.265	.410	4	.500	1	207	-4	—	-0.3
Williams, Brian	Brian O'Neal; B2.15.1969 Lancaster SC; BR/TR/6´2˝/(195–230); [HouN90 1/31]; d9.16; Col South Carolina																									
1991	Hou N	0	1	.000	2	2	0	0-0	12	11	5	2	1	4-0	4	3.75	94	.250	.327	3-0-2	.000	-0	102	0	0	0.0
1992	Hou N	7	6	.538	16	16	0	0-0	96.1	92	44	10	0	42-1	54	3.92	87	.255	.330	30-0-5	.133	-0*	108	-5	0	-0.6
1993	Hou N	4	4	.500	42	5	0	3-3	82	76	48	7	4	38-4	56	4.83	80	.248	.335	10-0-3	.200	0	116	-8	15	-0.6
1994	Hou N	6	5	.545	20	13	0	0-0	78.1	112	64	9	4	41-4	49	5.74	69	.343	.416	23-0-5	.261	1	138	-21	11	-2.3
1995	SD N	3	10	.231	44	6	0	0-2	72	79	54	3	8	38-4	75	6.00	68	.279	.379	14	.071	-1	126	-16	0	-2.5
1996	Det A	3	10	.231	40	17	2-1	2-2	121	145	107	21	6	85-2	72	6.77	75	.304	.411	0	ø	0	88	-26	0	-2.3
1997	Bal A	0	0	ø	13	0	0	0-1	24	20	8	0	0	18-0	14	3.00	147	.220	.345	0	ø	0	—	4	0	0.2
1999	Hou N	2	1	.667	50	0	0	0-2	67.1	69	35	4	5	35-2	53	4.41	100	.272	.366	3	.333	0	—	0	0	0.1
2000	Chi N	1	1	.500	22	0	0	1-1	24.1	28	27	4	3	23-2	14	9.62	48	.304	.454	2	.500	1	—	-13	0	-1.0
	Cle A	0	0	ø	7	0	0	0-0	18	23	9	2	1	8-1	6	4.00	125	.324	.395	0	ø	0	—	2	0	0.1
Total	9	26	38	.406	256	59	2-1	6-11	595.1	655	401	62	32	332-20	397	5.37	78	.284	.378	85-0-15	.176	1	107	-83	26	-8.9
Williams, Charlie	Charles Prosek; B10.11.1947 Flushing NY; BR/TR/6´2˝/(200–210); [NYN68 7/133]; d4.23																									
1971	NY N	5	6	.455	31	9	1	0-0	90.1	92	53	7	2	41-8	53	4.78	72	.267	.343	23-0-4	.087	-1	117	-13	0	-1.7
1972	SF N	0	2	.000	3	2	0	0-0	9.1	14	10	3	0	3-0	3	8.68	40	.333	.378	2	.000	-0	38	-5	0	-0.9
1973	SF N	3	0	1.000	12	2	0	0-0	23	32	19	2	0	7-2	11	6.65	58	.330	.371	3-0-1	.333	0	229	-7	0	-0.7
1974	SF N	1	3	.250	39	7	0	0-1	100.1	93	38	6	2	31-6	48	2.78	137	.250	.308	22-0-2	.136	-1	85	11	0	0.6
1975	SF N	5	3	.625	55	2	0	3-2	98	94	41	2	4	66-14	45	3.49	109	.261	.378	16	.125	0	69	4	0	0.4
1976	SF N	2	0	1.000	48	2	0	1-1	85	80	33	4	2	39-2	34	2.96	123	.256	.340	8	.125	-0	157	6	0	0.4
1977	SF N	6	5	.545	55	8	1	0-0	119.1	116	62	9	3	60-16	41	4.00	99	.262	.352	18-0-1	.222	0	101	-1	0	-0.1
1978	SF N	1	3	.250	25	1	0	0-1	48	60	31	5	1	28-6	22	5.44	64	.314	.401	5	.000	-1	26	-10	0	-0.9
Total	8	23	22	.511	268	33	2	4-5	573.1	581	287	38	14	275-54	257	3.97	94	.269	.352	97-0-8	.134	-2	105	-15	0	-2.9

YEAR	TM LG	W	L	PCT	G	GS	CG-SHO	SV-BS	IP	H	R	HR	HB	BB-IB	SO	ERA	AERA	OAV	OOB	AB-HR-SH	AVG	PB	SUP	APR	DL	PW
Williams, Lefty	Claude Preston; B3.9.1893 Aurora MO; D11.4.1959 Laguna Beach CA; BR/TL/5´9˝/160; d9.17; Def 1918																									
1913	Det A	1	3	.250	5	4	3	1	29	34	18	0	1	4	9	4.97	59	.286	.315	10	.100	-0	82	-5	—	-0.8
1914	Det A	0	1	.000	1	1	0	0	1	3	5	0	0	2	0	0.00	ø	.429	.556	0	ø	0*	156	-1	—	-0.3
1916	Chi A	13	7	.650	43	26	10-2	1	224.1	220	99	5	8	65	138	2.89	96	.267	.327	74	.135	-0	124	-4	—	-0.7
1917	†Chi A	17	8	.680	45	29	8-1	1	230	221	94	3	9	81	85	2.97	89	.252	.321	67-0-6	.090	-3	121	-5	—	-1.1
1918	Chi A	6	4	.600	15	14	7-2	1	105.2	76	32	0	5	47	30	2.73	100	.209	.308	38-0-3	.132	-2	126	4	—	0.0
1919	†Chi A	23	11	.676	41	**40**	27-5	1	297	265	104	7	11	58	125	2.64	121	.244	.289	94-0-12	.181	1	127	20	—	2.0
1920	Chi A	22	14	.611	39	38	25	0	299	302	145	15	12	90	128	3.91	96	.271	.332	101-0-8	.218	0	95	0	—	-0.2
Total	7	82	48	.631	189	152	80-10	5	1186	1121	497	30	46	347	515	3.13	99	.255	.316	384-0-29	.159	-4	116	9	—	-1.1
Williams, Dave	David Aaron; B3.12.1979 Anchorage AK; BL/TL/6´2˝/(205–230); [PitN98 17/508]; d6.6; Col Delaware Tech (DE) CC; [DL 2003 Pit N 65]																									
2001	Pit N	3	7	.300	22	18	0	0-0	114	100	53	15	7	45-4	57	3.71	120	.244	.324	34-0-3	.118	-1	79	8	0	0.6
2002	Pit N	2	5	.286	9	9	0	0-0	43.1	38	26	9	4	24-2	33	4.98	84	.232	.342	16-1-0	.125	0*	52	-4	125	-0.4
2004	Pit N	2	3	.400	10	6	0	0-0	38.2	31	21	4	3	13-2	33	4.42	98	.215	.292	9	.111	-0	64	-1	18	-0.1
2005	Pit N	10	11	.476	25	25	1-1	0-0	138.2	137	74	20	8	58-5	88	4.41	96	.261	.342	42-0-6	.119	-1	108	-3	0	-0.4
2006	Cin N	2	3	.400	8	8	0	0-0	40	54	34	9	4	16-0	16	7.20	66	.321	.387	12	.083	-0	110	-10	0	-1.0
	NY N	3	1	.750	6	5	0	0-0	29	39	18	5	2	4-1	16	5.59	79	.333	.366	9	.222	1	139	-3	0	-0.3
	Year	5	4	.556	14	13	0	0-0	69	93	52	14	6	20-1	32	6.52	70	.326	.379	21	.143	0	121	-14	0	-1.3
Total	5	22	30	.423	80	71	1-1	0-0	403.2	399	226	62	28	160-14	243	4.64	94	.261	.339	122-1-9	.123	-2	92	-13	208	-1.6
Williams, Mutt	David Carter; B7.31.1892 Ozark AR; D3.30.1962 Fayetteville AR; BR/TR/6´3.5˝/195; d10.4																									
1913	Was A	1	0	1.000	1	1	0	0	4	4	3	1	0	2	1	4.50	66	.308	.400	2	.500	0*	251	-1	—	-0.1
1914	Was A	0	0	ø	5	0	0	1	7	5	5	0	0	4	3	5.14	55	.227	.346	0	ø	0	—	-2	—	-0.1
Total	2	1	0	1.000	6	1	0	1	11	9	8	1	0	6	4	4.91	58	.257	.366	2	.500	0	251	-3	—	-0.2
Williams, Dave	David Owen; B2.7.1881 Scranton PA; D4.25.1918 Hot Springs AR; BR/TL/5´11.5˝/167; d7.2																									
1902	Bos A	0	0	ø	3	0	0	0	18.2	22	18	0	1	11	7	5.30	67	.293	.391	9	.333	1	—	-4	—	-0.2
Williams, Don	Donald Fred; B9.14.1931 Floyd VA; BR/TR/6´2˝/180; d9.12; Col Tennessee																									
1958	Pit N	0	0	ø	2	0	0	0	4	6	3	1	0	1-0	3	6.75	57	.375	.412	0	ø	0	—	-1	0	-0.1
1959	Pit N	0	0	ø	6	0	0	0	12	17	9	1	0	3-1	3	6.75	57	.362	.377	3	.333	1	—	-3	0	-0.1
1962	KC A	0	0	ø	3	0	0	0	4	6	4	0	1	0-0	1	9.00	47	.353	.389	1	.000	-0	—	-2	0	-0.1
Total	3	0	0	ø	11	0	0	0	20	29	16	2	1	4-1	7	7.20	55	.363	.386	4	.250	1	—	-6	0	-0.3
Williams, Don	Donald Reid "Dino"; B9.2.1935 Los Angeles CA; D12.20.1991 LaJolla CA; BR/TR/6´5˝/218; d8.4																									
1963	Min A	0	0	ø	3	0	0	0	4.1	8	5	1	0	6-0	2	10.38	35	.381	.519	0	ø	0	—	-3	0	-0.1
Williams, Dale	Elisha Alphonso; B10.6.1855 Ludlow KY; D10.22.1939 Covington KY; BR/TR/5´9˝/175; d8.12																									
1876	Cin N	1	8	.111	9	9	9	0	83	123	75	1	—	4	9	4.23	52	.339	.346	35	.200	-2	43	-15	—	-1.4
Williams, Frank	Frank Lee; B2.13.1958 Seattle WA; BR/TR/6´1˝/(180–195); [SFN79 11/278]; d4.5; Col Lewis–Clark St.																									
1984	SF N	9	4	.692	61	1	1-1	3-4	106.1	88	49	2	3	51-6	91	3.55	99	.226	.319	18	.222	1	175	-1	0	0.2
1985	SF N	2	4	.333	49	0	0	0-1	73	65	39	5	6	35-7	54	4.19	83	.242	.338	3-0-1	.000	-0	—	-6	0	-0.5
1986	SF N	3	1	.750	36	0	0	1-2	52.1	35	8	0	4	21-4	33	1.20	293	.212	.314	2-0-1	.500	0	—	14	0	1.2
1987	Cin N	4	0	1.000	85	0	0	2-5	105.2	101	37	5	2	39-9	60	2.30	184	.254	.322	5-0-1	.000	-1	—	19	0	0.9
1988	Cin N	3	2	.600	60	0	0	1-1	62.2	59	24	6	2	35-4	43	2.59	138	.252	.354	1	.000	-0	—	5	0	0.4
1989	Det A	3	3	.500	42	0	0	1-1	71.2	70	37	5	3	46-10	33	3.64	105	.254	.362	0	ø	0	—	0	42	0.0
Total	6	24	14	.632	333	1	1-1	8-14	471.2	418	194	23	20	227-40	314	3.00	124	.242	.334	29-0-3	.172	1	175	31	42	2.2
Williams, Woody	Gregory Scott; B8.19.1966 Houston TX; BR/TR/6´0˝/(180–200); [TorA88 28/732]; d5.14; Col Houston																									
1993	Tor A	3	1	.750	30	0	0	0-2	37	40	18	2	1	22-3	24	4.38	100	.274	.371	0	ø	0	—	1	0	0.1
1994	Tor A	1	3	.250	38	0	0	0-0	59.1	44	24	5	2	33-1	56	3.64	134	.205	.313	0	ø	0	—	9	0	0.5
1995	Tor A	1	2	.333	23	3	0	0-1	53.2	44	23	6	2	28-1	41	3.69	129	.220	.322	0	ø	0	131	7	77	0.3
1996	Tor A	4	5	.444	12	10	1	0-0	59	64	33	8	1	21-1	43	4.73	106	.278	.340	0	ø	0	89	2	109	0.3
1997	Tor A	9	14	.391	31	31	0	0-0	194.2	201	98	31	5	66-3	124	4.35	106	.269	.329	2	.500	0	59	8	0	0.6
1998	Tor A	10	9	.526	32	32	1-1	0-0	209.2	196	112	36	2	81-3	151	4.46	104	.245	.314	6	.333	1	97	6	0	0.4
1999	SD N	12	12	.500	33	33	0	0-0	208.1	213	106	33	2	73-5	137	4.41	97	.268	.328	73-0-4	.178	2*	93	0	0	0.0
2000	SD N	10	8	.556	23	23	4	0-0	168	152	74	23	3	54-2	111	3.75	119	.239	.300	58-1-1	.259	6*	84	15	56	2.0
2001	SD N	8	8	.500	23	23	0	0-0	145	170	88	28	5	37-4	102	4.97	84	.296	.340	55-0-1	.164	2*	134	-13	0	-1.1
	†StL N	7	1	.875	11	11	3-1	0-0	75	54	22	7	3	19-1	52	2.28	190	.205	.267	27-0-1	.259	2	103	17	0	1.9
	Year	15	9	.625	34	34	3-1	0-0	220	224	110	35	8	56-5	154	4.05	104	.268	.317	82-0-2	.195	4	123	3	0	0.8
2002	†StL N	9	4	.692	17	17	1	0-0	103.1	84	30	10	4	25-2	76	2.53	160	.222	.276	29-1-5	.207	3*	93	18	92	2.6
2003	StL N★	18	9	.667	34	33	0	0-1	220.2	220	101	20	11	55-2	153	3.87	106	.256	.307	70-1-9	.243	7	141	6	0	1.4
2004	†StL N	11	8	.579	31	31	0	0-0	189.2	193	93	20	9	58-3	131	4.18	102	.262	.322	61-0-5	.180	2*	114	3	0	0.5
2005	†SD N	9	12	.429	28	28	0	0-0	159.2	174	92	24	3	51-1	106	4.85	81	.275	.330	46-0-8	.152	-1*	88	-17	34	-2.0
2006	†SD N	12	5	.706	25	24	0	0-0	145.1	152	68	21	7	35-3	72	3.65	114	.267	.314	54-0-6	.204	2*	125	6	49	0.8
Total	14	124	101	.551	391	299	10-2	0-4	2028.1	2001	982	274	60	658-35	1379	4.09	106	.257	.318	481-3-40	.206	26	101	68	417	8.3
Williams, Jeff	Jeffrey F.; B6.6.1972 Canberra, Capital Territory, Australia; BR/TL/6´0˝/185; d9.12; Col Southeastern Louisiana																									
1999	LA N	2	0	1.000	5	3	0	0-0	17.2	12	10	2	0	9-0	7	4.08	107	.190	.292	5-0-1	.200	0	197	0	0	0.0
2000	LA N	0	0	ø	7	0	0	0-1	5.2	12	11	1	0	8-0	3	15.88	28	.462	.571	0	ø	0	—	-7	67	-0.4
2001	LA N	2	1	.667	15	1	0	0-0	24.1	26	18	5	1	17-1	9	6.29	66	.295	.407	4	.000	-0	45	-6	0	-0.6
2002	LA N	0	0	ø	10	0	0	0-0	10	15	13	2	1	7-0	11	11.70	33	.333	.426	2	.500	0	—	-9	0	-0.4
Total	4	4	1	.800	37	4	0	0-1	57.2	65	52	10	2	41-1	30	7.49	56	.293	.401	11-0-1	.182	0	165	-22	67	-1.4
Williams, Jerome	Jerome Lee; B12.4.1981 Honolulu HI; BR/TR/6´3˝/(180–245); [SFN99 1/39]; d4.26																									
2003	†SF N	7	5	.583	21	21	2-1	0-0	131	116	54	10	7	49-3	88	3.30	129	.242	.319	37-0-6	.108	-1	86	13	0	0.9
2004	SF N	10	7	.588	22	22	0	0-0	129.1	123	69	14	17	44-1	80	4.24	102	.254	.332	36-0-6	.139	-1	99	0	47	-0.1
2005	SF N	0	2	.000	4	3	0	0-0	16.2	21	12	2	1	4-1	11	6.48	65	.313	.361	4	.000	-0	82	-4	0	-0.4
	Chi N	6	8	.429	18	17	0	0-0	106	98	50	12	9	45-0	59	3.91	112	.253	.339	30-0-6	.100	-1	81	5	0	0.5
	Year	6	10	.375	22	20	0	0-0	122.2	119	62	14	10	49-1	70	4.26	102	.262	.342	34-0-6	.088	-2	81	1	0	0.1
2006	Chi N	0	2	.000	5	2	0	0-0	12.1	15	12	2	1	11-1	5	7.30	63	.326	.443	2	.000	-0	40	-4	0	-0.6
Total	4	23	24	.489	70	65	2-1	0-0	395.1	373	197	40	35	153-6	243	4.03	107	.255	.335	109-0-18	.110	-4	88	10	47	0.3
Williams, Johnnie	John Brodie "Honolulu Johnnie"; B7.16.1889 Honolulu, Kingdom of Hawaii (now Hawaii); D9.8.1963 Long Beach CA; BR/TR/6´0˝/180; d4.21																									
1914	Det A	0	2	.000	4	3	1	0	11.1	17	12	0	0	5	4	6.35	44	.378	.440	3	.000	-0	95	-5	—	-0.8
Williams, Leon	Leon Theo "Lefty"; B12.2.1905 Macon GA; D11.20.1984 Atlanta GA; BL/TL/5´10.5˝/154; d6.2																									
1926	Bro N	0	0	ø	8	0	0	0	8.1	16	6	0	0	2	3	5.40	71	.421	.450	5	.200	0*	—	-1	—	0.0
Williams, Marsh	Marshall McDiarmid "Cap"; B2.21.1893 Faison NC; D2.22.1935 Tucson AZ; BR/TR/6´0˝/180; d7.7; Col North Carolina																									
1916	Phi A	0	6	.000	10	4	3	0	51.1	71	53	4	0	31	17	7.89	36	.350	.436	19	.105	-1	60	-26	—	-2.7
Williams, Matt	Matthew Evan; B7.25.1959 Houston TX; BR/TR/6´1˝/200; [TorA81 1/5]; d8.2; Col Rice																									
1983	Tor A	1	1	.500	4	3	0	0-0	8	13	13	5	1	7-0	5	14.63	30	.361	.467	0	ø	0	174	-8	0	-1.3
1985	Tex A	2	1	.667	6	3	0	0-0	26	20	7	3	0	10-0	22	2.42	176	.211	.286	0	ø	0	78	5	0	0.6
Total	2	3	2	.600	10	6	0	0-0	34	33	20	8	1	17-0	27	5.29	81	.252	.340	0	ø	0	127	-3	0	-0.7
Williams, Matt	Matthew Taylor; B4.12.1971 Virginia Beach VA; BB/TL/6´0˝/175; [CleA92 4/98]; d4.5; Col Virginia Commonwealth																									
2000	Mil N	0	0	ø	11	0	0	0-0	9	7	7	2	1	13-0	7	7.00	66	.219	.457	1	.000	-0	—	-2	0	-0.1
Williams, Mike	Michael Darren; B7.29.1968 Radford VA; BR/TR/6´2˝/(190–209); [PhiN90 14/374]; d6.30; Col VPI																									
1992	Phi N	1	1	.500	5	5	1	0-0	28.2	29	20	3	0	7-0	5	5.34	66	.259	.300	10-0-1	.400	1	155	-6	0	-0.3
1993	Phi N	1	3	.250	17	4	0	0-0	51	50	32	5	0	22-2	33	5.29	75	.253	.327	12-0-3	.083	-1	130	-7	0	-0.6
1994	Phi N	2	4	.333	12	8	0	0-0	50.1	61	31	7	0	20-3	29	5.01	86	.310	.368	12-0-5	.167	0	93	-4	0	-0.4
1995	Phi N	3	3	.500	33	8	0	0-0	87.2	78	37	10	3	29-2	57	3.29	128	.239	.304	16-0-7	.125	-0	70	8	0	0.5

YEAR	TM LG	W	L	PCT	G	GS	CG-SHO	SV-BS	IP	H	R	HR	HB	BB-IB	SO	ERA	AERA	OAV	OOB	AB-HR-SH	AVG	PB	SUP	APR	DL	PW
1996	Phi N	6	14	.300	32	29	0	0-0	167	188	107	25	6	67-6	103	5.44	79	.290	.360	51-0-6	.157	-1*	89	-18	0	-1.8
1997	KC A	0	2	.000	10	0	0	1-0	14	20	11	1	1	8-1	10	6.43	74	.333	.414	0	ø	0	—	-3	0	-0.3
1998	Pit N	4	2	.667	37	1	0	0-1	51	39	12	1	0	16-4	59	1.94	220	.211	.271	3-0-2	.000	-0	108	13	0	1.4
1999	Pit N	3	4	.429	58	0	0	23-5	58.1	63	36	9	1	37-7	76	5.09	90	.276	.378	2	.000	-0	—	-3	15	-0.4
2000	Pit N	3	4	.429	72	0	0	24-5	72	56	34	8	4	40-3	71	3.50	133	.218	.328	1	.000	-0	—	8	0	1.1
2001	Pit N	2	4	.333	40	0	0	22-2	41.2	39	18	6	0	21-2	43	3.67	122	.244	.331	0	ø	0	—	4	0	0.7
	†Hou N	4	0	1.000	25	0	0	0-1	22.1	21	10	3	0	14-1	16	4.03	114	.244	.347	0	ø	0	—	2	0	0.3
	Year	6	4	.600	65	0	0	22-3	64	60	28	9	0	35-3	59	3.80	119	.244	.337	0	ø	0	—	6	0	1.0
2002	Pit N★	2	6	.250	59	0	0	46-4	61.1	54	24	6	1	21-3	43	2.93	143	.233	.299	1	.000	0	—	7	0	1.6
2003	Pit N☆	1	3	.250	40	0	0	25-5	37.1	42	26	5	1	22-1	20	6.27	69	.282	.374	0	ø	0	—	-7	0	-1.3
	Phi N	0	4	.000	28	0	0	3-2	25.2	24	18	0	3	19-5	19	5.96	67	.247	.387	0	ø	0	—	-6	0	-0.9
	Year	1	7	.125	68	0	0	28-7	63	66	44	5	4	41-6	39	6.14	68	.268	.379	0	ø	0	—	-13	0	-2.2
Total	12	32	54	.372	468	55	1	144-25	768.1	764	416	89	20	343-40	584	4.45	97	.260	.339	108-0-24	.157	-1	94	-12	15	-0.4
Williams, Mitch	Mitchell Steven "Wild Thing"; B11.17.1964 Santa Ana CA; BL/TL/6´4˝/(200–205); [SDN82 8/187]; d4.9																									
1986	Tex A	8	6	.571	**80**	0	0	8-7	98	69	39	8	11	79-8	90	3.58	121	.202	.366	0	ø	0	—	10	0	1.4
1987	Tex A	8	6	.571	85	1	0	6-1	108.2	63	47	9	7	94-7	129	3.23	140	.175	.353	0	ø	0	121	14	0	1.8
1988	Tex A	2	7	.222	67	0	0	18-8	68	48	38	4	6	47-3	61	4.63	89	.203	.345	0	ø	0	—	-3	0	-0.5
1989	†Chi N★	4	4	.500	**76**	0	0	36-11	81.2	71	27	6	8	52-4	67	2.76	137	.238	.361	5-1-0	.200	1	—	9	0	1.7
1990	Chi N	1	8	.111	59	2	0	16-4	66.1	60	38	4	1	50-6	55	3.93	104	.239	.364	5	.000	-1	66	-1	30	-0.3
1991	Phi N	12	5	.706	69	0	0	30-9	88.1	56	24	4	8	62-5	84	2.34	158	.182	.330	1	.000	0	—	14	0	2.9
1992	Phi N	5	8	.385	66	0	0	29-7	81	69	39	4	6	64-2	74	3.78	93	.240	.386	4	.250	0	—	-3	0	-0.7
1993	†Phi N	3	7	.300	65	0	0	43-6	62	56	30	3	2	44-1	60	3.34	119	.245	.368	1	1.000	0	—	3	0	0.5
1994	Hou N	1	4	.200	25	0	0	6-2	20	21	17	4	1	24-2	21	7.65	52	.269	.442	0	ø	0	—	-8	0	-1.5
1995	Cal A	1	2	.333	20	0	0	0-1	10.2	13	10	1	2	21-0	9	6.75	70	.317	.554	0	ø	0	—	-3	0	-0.6
1997	KC A	0	1	.000	7	0	0	0-0	6.2	11	8	2	0	7-1	10	10.80	44	.367	.474	0	ø	0	—	-4	0	-0.5
Total	11	45	58	.437	619	3	0	192-56	691.1	537	317	49	52	544-39	660	3.65	111	.218	.367	16-1-0	.188	1	90	28	30	4.2
Williams, Randy	Randall Duane; B9.18.1975 Harlingen TX; BL/TL/6´3˝/195; [ChiN97 12/364]; d9.11																									
2004	Sea A	0	0	ø	6	0	0	0-0	4.2	3	3	0	0	6-0	4	5.79	77	.188	.409	0	ø	0	—	-1	0	0.0
2005	SD N	1	0	1.000	2	0	0	0-0	4.1	7	6	1	1	4-0	2	12.46	31	.350	.480	1	.000	-0	—	-4	0	-0.7
	Col N	2	1	.667	30	0	0	0-2	22	26	15	4	0	9-3	19	5.73	81	.289	.350	0	ø	0	—	-2	0	-0.3
	Year	3	1	.750	32	0	0	0-2	26.1	33	21	5	1	13-3	21	6.84	66	.300	.376	1	.000	-0	—	-6	0	-1.0
Total	2	3	1	.750	38	0	0	0-2	31	36	24	5	1	19-3	25	6.68	68	.286	.381	1	.000	-0	—	-7	0	-1.0
Williams, Steamboat	Rees Gephardt; B1.31.1892 Cascade MT; D6.29.1979 Deer River MN; BL/TR/5´11˝/170; d7.12																									
1914	StL N	0	1	.000	5	1	0	0	11	13	8	1	0	6	2	6.55	43	.295	.380	1	.000	-0	77	-3	—	-0.3
1916	StL N	6	7	.462	36	8	5	1	105	121	63	6	1	27	25	4.20	63	.291	.336	24	.208	1	92	-17	—	-2.0
Total	2	6	8	.429	41	9	5	1	116	134	71	7	1	33	27	4.42	60	.291	.340	25	.200	1	90	-20	—	-2.3
Williams, Rick	Richard Allen; B11.9.1952 Merced CA; BR/TR/6´1˝/180; d6.12; Col Merced (CA) JC																									
1978	Hou N	1	2	.333	17	1	0	0-0	34.2	43	19	2	0	10-2	17	4.67	71	.301	.342	5	.000	-1	54	-5	0	-0.5
1979	Hou N	4	7	.364	31	16	2-2	0-0	121.1	122	45	6	2	30-1	37	3.26	108	.261	.306	31-0-2	.258	3	58	6	0	0.8
Total	2	5	9	.357	48	17	2-2	0-0	156	165	64	8	2	40-3	54	3.58	97	.270	.315	36-0-2	.222	2	59	1	0	0.3
Williams, Ace	Robert Fulton; B3.18.1917 Montclair NJ; D9.16.1999 Fort Myers FL; BR/TL/6´2˝/174; d7.15; Mil 1943–45; Col Amherst																									
1940	Bos N	0	0	ø	5	0	0	0	9	21	17	0	1	12	5	16.00	23	.375	.493	2	.000	-0	—	-12	—	-0.6
1946	Bos N	0	0	ø	1	0	0	0	0	1	0	0	0	1	0	(0)	ø	1.000	1.000	0	ø	0	—	0	0	0.0
Total	2	0	0	ø	6	0	0	0	9	22	17	0	1	13	5	16.00	23	.386	.507	2	.000	-0	—	-12	0	-0.6
Williams, Shad	Shad Clayton; B3.10.1971 Fresno CA; BR/TR/6´0˝/(185–198); [CalA91 17/454]; d5.18; Col Fresno (CA) City																									
1996	Cal A	0	2	.000	13	2	0	0-0	28.1	42	34	7	2	21-4	26	8.89	57	.341	.442	0	ø	0	55	-13	0	-0.8
1997	Ana A	0	0	ø	1	0	0	0-0	1	1	0	0	0	1-0	0	0.00	ø	.250	.400	0	ø	0	—	1	0	0.0
Total	2	0	2	.000	14	2	0	0-0	29.1	43	34	7	2	22-4	26	8.59	59	.339	.441	0	ø	0	55	-12	0	-0.8
Williams, Stan	Stanley Wilson; B9.14.1936 Enfield NH; BR/TR/6´5˝/(200–230); d5.17; C14																									
1958	LA N	9	7	.563	27	21	3-2	0	119	99	58	10	7	65-1	80	4.01	102	.228	.336	40-1-3	.050	-3	92	2	0	-0.1
1959	†LA N	5	5	.500	35	15	2	0	124.2	102	64	12	9	86-7	89	3.97	106	.228	.359	36-0-1	.194	1	99	2	0	0.2
1960	LA N★	14	10	.583	38	30	9-2	1	207.1	162	84	26	5	72-1	175	3.00	133	.210	.280	64-2-7	.141	0	109	19	0	2.1
1961	LA N	15	12	.556	41	35	6-2	0	235.1	213	114	21	6	108-9	205	3.90	111	.242	.327	78-0-6	.167	-1	90	11	0	1.1
1962	LA N	14	12	.538	40	28	4-1	1	185.2	184	104	16	0	98-11	108	4.46	81	.253	.338	66-2-1	.076	-2	118	-17	0	-2.4
1963	†NY A	9	8	.529	29	21	6-1	0	146	137	59	7	6	57-1	98	3.21	110	.249	.325	49-0-1	.102	-1	126	4	0	0.4
1964	NY A	1	5	.167	21	10	1	0	82	76	39	7	0	38-2	54	3.84	94	.248	.329	21-0-1	.143	-0*	91	-2	0	-0.2
1965	Cle A	0	0	ø	3	0	0	0	4.1	6	4	1	0	3-1	1	6.23	56	.353	.450	0	ø	0	—	-2	0	-0.1
1967	Cle A	6	4	.600	16	8	2-1	1	79	64	26	6	1	24-2	75	2.62	125	.218	.277	22	.091	-1	73	6	0	0.5
1968	Cle A	13	11	.542	44	24	6-2	9	194.1	163	64	14	10	51-7	147	2.50	119	.225	.284	56-0-4	.161	1	81	10	0	1.5
1969	Cle A	6	14	.300	61	15	3	12-5	178.1	155	86	25	12	67-6	139	3.94	97	.235	.312	40-0-4	.100	-1	95	-1	0	-0.3
1970	†Min A	10	1	.909	68	0	0	15-4	113.1	85	34	8	5	32-6	76	1.99	186	.208	.272	19	.000	-2	—	20	0	2.0
1971	Min A	4	5	.444	46	1	0	4-3	78	63	44	7	8	44-7	47	4.15	85	.220	.336	10-0-1	.000	-1	127	-7	0	-1.0
	StL N	3	0	1.000	10	0	0	0-1	12.2	13	2	0	2	2-1	8	1.42	256	.265	.315	1	.000	-0	—	3	0	0.7
1972	Bos A	0	0	ø	3	0	0	0-0	4.1	5	3	0	0	1-0	3	6.23	52	.294	.333	0	ø	0	—	-1	0	-0.1
Total	14	109	94	.537	482	208	42-11	43-13	1764.1	1527	785	160	71	748-62	1305	3.48	108	.232	.315	502-5-29	.118	-10	101	47	0	4.3
Williams, Tom	Thomas C.; B8.19.1870 Minersville OH; D7.27.1940 Columbus OH; d5.1																									
1892	Cle N	1	0	1.000	2	1	1	0	9	9	4	1	0	1	3	3.00	113	.250	.270	10	.100	-1*	205	1	—	0.0
1893	Cle N	1	1	.500	5	2	2	0	24	33	18	1	1	10	6	4.88	100	.317	.383	18	.278	0*	79	1	—	0.1
Total	2	2	1	.667	7	3	3	0	33	42	22	2	1	11	9	4.36	102	.300	.355	28	.214	-0	112	2	—	0.1
Williams, Todd	Todd Michael; B2.13.1971 Syracuse NY; BR/TR/6´3˝/(185–220); [LAN90 54/1333]; d4.29; Col Onondaga (NY) CC																									
1995	LA N	2	2	.500	16	0	0	0-1	19.1	19	11	3	0	7-2	8	5.12	76	.264	.325	2	.500	0	—	-2	0	-0.3
1998	Cin N	0	1	.000	6	0	0	0-0	9.1	15	8	1	0	6-0	4	7.71	56	.341	.420	2	.000	-0	—	-3	0	-0.3
1999	Sea A	0	0	ø	13	0	0	0-0	9.2	11	5	1	1	7-0	7	4.66	103	.289	.413	0	ø	0	—	0	0	0.0
2001	NY A	1	0	1.000	15	0	0	0-0	15.1	22	9	1	2	9-2	13	4.70	95	.324	.402	0	ø	0	—	-1	61	0.0
2004	Bal A	2	0	1.000	29	0	0	0-0	31.1	26	10	2	5	9-0	13	2.87	162	.232	.317	0	ø	0	—	7	0	0.4
2005	Bal A	5	5	.500	72	0	0	1-2	76.1	72	34	5	3	26-4	38	3.30	133	.252	.317	0	ø	0	—	8	0	0.9
2006	Bal A	2	4	.333	62	0	0	1-4	57	76	36	8	2	19-3	24	4.74	95	.323	.377	0	ø	0	—	-3	26	-0.2
Total	7	12	12	.500	213	0	0	2-7	218.1	241	113	21	13	83-11	107	4.12	108	.282	.351	4	.250	0	—	6	87	0.5
Williams, Pop	Walter Merrill; B5.19.1874 Bowdoinham ME; D8.4.1959 Topsham ME; BL/TR/5´11˝/190; d9.14; Col Bowdoin																									
1898	Was N	0	2	.000	2	2	2	0	17	32	18	0	0	7	3	8.47	43	.395	.443	8	.375	1	106	-7	—	-0.5
1902	Chi N	11	16	.407	32	32	27-1	0	263.1	267	112	1	10	63	99	2.49	108	.263	.312	120-0-3	.208	3*	100	8	—	1.3
1903	Chi N	0	1	.000	1	1	1	0	5	9	3	0	0	0	2	5.40	58	.409	.409	2	.000	0*	0	-1	—	-0.1
	Phi N	1	1	.500	2	2	2	0	18	21	11	0	1	6	8	3.00	109	.304	.368	7	.286	0	103	0	—	0.0
	Bos N	4	5	.444	10	10	9-1	0	83	97	60	3	9	37	20	4.12	78	.295	.381	42-0-1	.238	-0*	97	-9	—	-0.9
	Year	5	7	.417	13	13	12-1	0	106	127	74	3	10	43	30	3.99	81	.302	.381	51-0-1	.235	0	90	-13	—	-1.0
Total	3	16	25	.390	47	47	41-2	0	386.1	426	204	4	20	113	132	3.17	91	.281	.339	179-0-4	.223	5	97	-9	—	-0.2
Williamson, Ed	Edward Nagle; B10.24.1857 Philadelphia PA; D3.3.1894 Mountain Valley Springs AR; BR/TR/5´11˝/210; d5.1.1878; ▲																									
1881	Chi N	1	1	.500	3	1	1	0	18	14	9	0	—	0	2	2.00	137	.209	.209	343-1	.268	1*	118	1	—	0.1
1882	Chi N	0	0	ø	1	0	0	0	3	9	8	1	—	1	0	6.00	48	.500	.526	348-3	.282	0*	—	-2	—	-0.1
1883	Chi N	0	0	ø	1	0	0	0	1	1	2	0	—	1	1	9.00	37	.167	.286	402-2	.276	0*	—	-1	—	0.0
1884	Chi N	0	0	ø	2	0	0	0	2	8	8	0	—	2	0	18.00	17	.500	.556	417-27	.278	1*	—	-3	—	-0.1
1885	†Chi N	0	0	ø	2	0	0	**2**	6	2	0	0	—	0	3	0.00	ø	.080	.080	407-3	.238	0*	—	2	—	0.2
1886	†Chi N	0	0	ø	2	0	0	1	3	2	2	0	—	0	1	0.00	ø	.143	.143	430-6	.216	0*	—	1	—	0.0
1887	Chi N	0	0	ø	1	0	0	0	2	2	2	0	0	1	0	9.00	50	.222	.300	439-9	.267	0*	—	-1	—	0.0
Total	7	1	1	.500	12	1	1	3	35	38	31	1	0	5	7	3.34	90	.245	.269	2786-51	.260	3	118	-3	—	0.1

YEAR	TM LG	W	L	PCT	G	GS	CG-SHO	SV-BS	IP	H	R	HR	HB	BB-IB	SO	ERA	AERA	OAV	OOB	AB-HR-SH	AVG	PB	SUP	APR	DL	PW
Williamson, Mark	Mark Alan; B7.21.1959 Corpus Christi TX; BR/TR/6´0˝/(170–198); [SDN82 4/83]; d4.8; Col San Diego St.																									
1987	Bal A	8	9	.471	61	2	0	3-7	125	122	59	12	3	41-15	73	4.03	110	.261	.322	0	ø	0	103	7	0	0.9
1988	Bal A	5	8	.385	37	10	2	2-1	117.2	125	70	14	2	40-8	69	4.90	80	.272	.332	0	ø	0	65	-12	0	-1.3
1989	Bal A	10	5	.667	65	0	0	9-6	107.1	105	35	4	2	30-9	55	2.93	130	.261	.313	0	ø	0	—	12	0	1.7
1990	Bal A	8	2	.800	49	0	0	1-4	85.1	65	25	8	0	28-2	60	2.21	172	.215	.276	0	ø	0	—	14	59	1.7
1991	Bal A	5	5	.500	65	0	0	4-3	80.1	87	42	9	0	35-7	53	4.48	89	.275	.343	0	ø	0	—	-4	18	-0.5
1992	Bal A	0	0	ø	12	0	0	1-0	18.2	16	3	1	0	10-1	14	0.96	422	.239	.338	0	ø	0	—	6	141	0.3
1993	Bal A	7	5	.583	48	1	0	0-2	88	106	54	5	0	25-8	45	4.91	92	.304	.345	0	ø	0	61	-5	0	-0.6
1994	Bal A	3	1	.750	28	2	0	1-1	67.1	75	33	9	2	17-1	28	4.01	126	.278	.323	0	ø	0	91	7	0	0.3
Total	8	46	35	.568	365	15	2	21-24	689.2	701	321	62	9	226-51	397	3.86	108	.266	.323	0	ø	0	74	25	218	2.5
Williamson, Scott	Scott Ryan; B2.17.1976 Fort Polk LA; BR/TR/6´0˝/(180–185); [CinN97 9/278]; d4.5; Col Oklahoma St.																									
1999	Cin N☆	12	7	.632	62	0	0	19-7	93.1	54	29	8	1	43-6	107	2.41	195	.171	.271	7-0-3	.000	-1	—	22	0	4.3
2000	Cin N	5	8	.385	48	10	0	6-2	112	92	45	7	3	75-7	136	3.29	145	.224	.346	16-0-4	.063	-1	77	18	13	1.9
2001	Cin N	0	0	ø	2	0	0	0-0	0.2	1	0	0	1	2-0	0	0.00	ø	.333	.667	0	ø	0	—	0	187	0.0
2002	Cin N	3	4	.429	63	0	0	8-4	74	46	27	5	2	36-5	84	2.92	146	.181	.286	0	ø	0	—	11	0	1.1
2003	Cin N	5	3	.625	42	0	0	21-5	42.1	34	15	6	1	25-4	53	3.19	131	.214	.324	0	ø	0	—	5	0	1.0
	†Bos A	0	1	.000	24	0	0	0-2	20.1	20	15	1	0	9-2	21	6.20	75	.253	.326	0	ø	0	—	-3	0	-0.1
2004	Bos A	0	1	.000	28	0	0	1-1	28.2	11	6	0	3	18-1	28	1.26	389	.115	.267	0	ø	0	—	10	93	0.5
2005	Chi N	0	0	ø	17	0	0	0-0	14.1	15	9	3	2	6-0	23	5.65	77	.273	.365	0	ø	0	—	-2	124	-0.1
2006	Chi N	2	3	.400	31	0	0	0-0	28.1	27	17	2	1	16-1	32	5.08	90	.248	.346	0	ø	0	—	-1	23	-0.2
	SD N	0	1	.000	11	0	0	0-0	11	14	9	2	0	6-0	10	7.36	56	.333	.408	0	ø	0	—	-4	27	-0.3
	Year	2	4	.333	42	0	0	0-0	39.1	41	26	4	1	22-1	42	5.72	78	.272	.364	0	ø	0	—	-5	0	-0.5
Total	8	27	28	.491	328	10	0	55-21	425	314	172	34	14	236-26	494	3.32	137	.206	.316	23-0-7	.043	-1	77	56	467	8.1
Williamson, Al	Silas Albert; B2.20.1900 Buckville AR; D11.29.1978 Hot Springs AR; BR/TR/5´11˝/160; d4.27																									
1928	Chi A	0	0	ø	1	0	0	0	2	1	0	0	0	0	0	0.00	ø	.167	.167	0	ø	0	—	1	—	0.0
Willis, Carl	Carl Blake; B12.28.1960 Danville VA; BL/TR/6´4˝/(210–213); [DetA83 23/581]; d6.9; C4; Col North Carolina–Wilmington																									
1984	Det A	0	2	.000	10	2	0	0-0	16	25	13	1	0	5-2	4	7.31	54	.362	.405	0	ø	0	103	-5	0	-0.6
	Cin N	0	1	.000	7	0	0	1-0	9.2	8	4	1	0	2-0	3	3.72	102	.222	.263	0	ø	0	—	0	0	0.0
1985	Cin N	1	0	1.000	11	0	0	1-0	13.2	21	18	3	0	5-0	6	9.22	41	.344	.382	1-0-1	.000	0	—	-9	0	-0.7
1986	Cin N	1	3	.250	29	0	0	0-1	52.1	54	29	4	1	32-9	24	4.47	86	.278	.382	3-0-1	.333	0	—	-3	0	-0.2
1988	Chi A	0	0	ø	6	0	0	0-0	12	17	12	3	0	7-1	6	8.25	49	.362	.436	0	ø	0	—	-5	0	-0.3
1991	†Min A	8	3	.727	40	0	0	2-1	89	76	31	4	1	19-1	53	2.63	163	.232	.273	0	ø	0	—	15	0	1.7
1992	Min A	7	3	.700	59	0	0	1-2	79.1	73	25	4	0	11-1	45	2.72	150	.246	.270	0	ø	0	—	12	0	1.4
1993	Min A	3	0	1.000	53	0	0	5-4	58	56	23	2	0	17-5	44	3.10	142	.259	.312	0	ø	0	—	8	39	0.4
1994	Min A	2	4	.333	49	0	0	3-4	59.1	89	48	6	0	12-5	37	5.92	83	.335	.359	0	ø	0	—	-9	0	-0.9
1995	Min A	0	0	ø	3	0	0	0-0	0.2	5	7	0	0	5-0	0	94.50	5	.833	.909	0	ø	0	—	-6	0	-0.3
Total	9	22	16	.579	267	2	0	13-12	390	424	210	28	2	115-24	222	4.25	100	.279	.327	4-0-2	.250	0	103	-2	39	0.5
Willis, Lefty	Charles William; B11.4.1905 Leetown WV; D5.10.1962 Bethesda MD; BL/TL/6´1˝/175; d10.3; Col Shepherd																									
1925	Phi A	0	0	ø	1	1	0	0	5	9	7	2	0	2	3	10.80	43	.409	.458	3	.000	-1	145	-3	—	-0.2
1926	Phi A	0	0	ø	13	1	0	1	32.1	31	9	0	1	12	13	1.39	300	.270	.344	9	.222	-0	81	9	—	0.4
1927	Phi A	3	1	.750	15	2	1	0	27	32	18	2	0	11	7	5.67	75	.308	.374	6	.000	-1	88	-3	—	-0.4
Total	3	3	1	.750	29	4	1	1	64.1	72	34	4	1	25	23	3.92	108	.299	.367	18	.111	-1	104	3	—	-0.2
Willis, Dale	Dale Jerome; B5.29.1938 Calhoun GA; BR/TR/5´11˝/165; d4.14; Col Florida																									
1963	KC A	0	2	.000	25	0	0	1	44.2	46	28	3	4	25-3	47	5.04	77	.266	.369	6	.167	-0*	—	-5	0	-0.3
Willis, Dontrelle	Dontrelle Wayne; B1.12.1982 Oakland CA; BL/TL/6´4˝/(200–240); [ChiN00 8/223]; d5.9																									
2003	†Fla N☆	14	6	.700	27	27	2-2	0-0	160.2	148	61	13	3	58-0	142	3.30	124	.245	.314	58-1-2	.241	5	104	16	0	2.2
2004	Fla N	10	11	.476	32	32	2	0-0	197	210	99	20	8	61-8	139	4.02	102	.273	.332	74-1-6	.203	4*	102	0	0	0.5
2005	Fla N★	**22**	10	.688	34	34	**7-5**	0-0	236.1	213	79	11	8	55-3	170	2.63	152	.243	.292	92-1-4	.261	8*	105	36	0	**5.8**
2006	Fla N	12	12	.500	34	34	4-1	0-0	223.1	234	106	21	19	83-6	160	3.87	111	.273	.349	64-3-6	.172	6*	82	11	0	1.8
Total	4	58	39	.598	127	127	15-8	0-0	817.1	805	345	65	38	257-17	611	3.44	120	.259	.322	288-6-18	.222	23	97	63	0	10.3
Willis, Jim	James Gladden; B3.20.1927 Doyline LA; BL/TR/6´3˝/175; d4.22; Col Northwestern Louisiana																									
1953	Chi N	2	1	.667	13	3	2	0	43.1	37	15	1	3	17	15	3.12	143	.228	.313	9-0-1	.000	-1	94	7	0	0.4
1954	Chi N	0	1	.000	14	1	0	0	23	22	10	1	3	18	5	3.91	107	.256	.402	5	.000	-1	21	1	0	0.0
Total	2	2	2	.500	27	4	2	0	66.1	59	25	2	6	35	20	3.39	129	.238	.346	14-0-1	.000	-2	77	8	0	0.4
Willis, Joe	Joseph Denk; B4.9.1890 Coal Grove OH; D12.4.1966 Ironton OH; BR/TL/6´1˝/185; d5.3																									
1911	StL A	0	1	.000	1	1	0	0	7	8	5	0	0	3	0	5.14	66	.308	.379	2	.000	0	43	-1	—	-0.1
	StL N	0	1	.000	2	2	1	0	15	13	9	0	0	4	5	4.20	80	.232	.283	5	.000	-1	56	-1	—	-0.1
1912	StL N	4	9	.308	31	17	4	2	129.2	143	83	3	5	62	55	4.44	77	.288	.372	38-0-1	.158	-2	107	-12	—	-1.2
1913	StL N	0	0	ø	7	0	0	1	9.2	9	9	0	0	11	6	7.45	43	.257	.435	3	.000	-0	—	-4	—	-0.3
Total	3	4	11	.267	41	20	5	3	161.1	173	106	3	5	80	66	4.63	74	.282	.369	48-0-1	.125	-2	99	-18	—	-1.7
Willis, Les	Lester Evans "Wimpy","Lefty"; B1.17.1908 Nacogdoches TX; D1.22.1982 Jasper TX; BL/TL/5´9.5˝/195; d4.28																									
1947	Cle A	0	2	.000	22	2	0	1	44	58	26	3	0	24	10	3.48	100	.324	.404	11-0-1	.091	-1	89	-4	0	-0.3
Willis, Mike	Michael Henry; B12.26.1950 Oklahoma City OK; BL/TL/6´2˝/(200–210); [BalA72 20/479]; d4.13; Col Vanderbilt																									
1977	Tor A	2	6	.250	43	3	0	5-4	107.1	105	48	15	0	38-6	59	3.94	108	.260	.321	0	ø	0	78	6	0	0.5
1978	Tor A	3	7	.300	44	2	1	7-2	100.2	104	55	11	0	39-2	52	4.56	87	.271	.336	0	ø	0	102	-6	0	-0.7
1979	Tor A	0	3	.000	17	1	0	0-0	26.2	35	27	1	1	16-2	8	8.44	52	.333	.419	0	ø	0	41	-11	0	-1.0
1980	Tor A	2	1	.667	20	0	0	3-1	26.1	25	6	3	1	11-4	14	1.71	253	.248	.325	0	ø	0	—	7	0	0.9
1981	Tor A	0	4	.000	20	0	0	0-1	35	43	25	6	1	20-1	16	5.91	67	.301	.386	0	ø	0	—	-6	0	-0.7
Total	5	7	21	.250	144	6	1	15-8	296	312	161	36	3	124-15	149	4.59	90	.274	.344	0	ø	0	80	-10	0	-1.0
Willis, Ron	Ronald Earl; B7.12.1943 Willisville TN; D11.21.1977 Memphis TN; BR/TR/6´2˝/(170–195); d9.20																									
1966	StL N	0	0	ø	4	0	0	1	3	1	0	0	0	1-1	2	0.00	ø	.100	.182	0	ø	0	—	1	0	0.1
1967	†StL N	6	5	.545	65	0	0	10	81	76	27	3	3	43-20	42	2.67	123	.257	.354	8	.375	1	—	6	0	1.2
1968	†StL N	2	3	.400	48	0	0	4	63.2	50	25	4	1	28-11	39	3.39	85	.213	.299	11	.000	-1	—	-2	0	-0.3
1969	StL N	1	2	.333	26	0	0	0-0	32.1	26	16	4	1	19-3	23	4.18	86	.224	.331	1	1.000	0	—	-2	0	-0.1
	Hou N	0	0	ø	3	0	0	0-0	2.1	3	0	0	0	0-0	2	0.00	ø	.300	.273	0	ø	0	—	1	0	0.0
	Year	1	2	.333	29	0	0	0-0	34.2	29	16	4	1	19-3	25	3.89	92	.230	.327	1	1.000	0	—	-1	0	-0.1
1970	SD N	2	2	.500	42	0	0	4-2	56	53	33	4	4	28-5	20	4.02	100	.247	.340	5	.000	-1	—	-2	0	-0.2
Total	5	11	12	.478	188	0	0	19-2	238.1	209	101	15	9	119-40	128	3.32	102	.237	.330	25	.160	0	—	2	0	0.7
Willis, Vic	Victor Gazaway; B4.12.1876 Cecil Co. MD; D8.3.1947 Elkton MD; BR/TR/6´2˝/185; d4.20; HF1995; Col Delaware																									
1898	Bos N	25	13	.658	41	38	29-1	0	311	264	143	5	29	148	160	2.84	130	.228	.331	117-0-2	.145	-6	100	26	—	2.2
1899	Bos N	27	8	.771	41	38	35-**5**	2	342.2	277	126	6	30	117	120	2.50	**167**	**.221**	.303	134-0-3	.216	-4	102	**58**	—	4.8
1900	Bos N	10	17	.370	32	29	22-2	0	236	258	157	11	12	106	53	4.19	98	.277	.359	88-0-3	.136	-6	94	-1	—	-0.7
1901	Bos N	20	17	.541	38	35	33-**6**	0	305.1	262	111	6	11	78	133	2.36	**153**	.230	.286	107-1-3	.187	-1	78	**39**	—	4.2
1902	Bos N	27	20	.574	**51**	**46**	**45**-4	**3**	**410**	372	142	6	14	101	**225**	2.20	129	.242	.295	150-0-1	.153	-6*	93	28	—	2.8
1903	Bos N	12	18	.400	33	32	29-2	0	278	256	121	3	10	88	125	2.98	108	.251	.317	128-0-2	.188	-1*	72	14	—	1.3
1904	Bos N	18	25	.419	43	43	**39**-2	0	350	357	174	7	14	109	196	2.85	97	.266	.327	148-0-3	.182	1*	82	-8	—	-0.4
1905	Bos N	12	29	.293	41	41	36-4	0	342	340	174	7	13	107	149	3.21	97	.265	.328	131-0-2	.153	-3*	76	-8	—	-0.8
1906	Pit N	23	13	.639	41	36	32-6	1	322	295	84	0	5	76	124	1.73	154	.250	.298	115-0-3	.174	-1	111	34	—	4.3
1907	Pit N	21	11	.656	39	37	27-6	1	292.2	234	96	4	7	69	107	2.34	104	.219	.271	103-0-5	.136	-2	137	8	—	0.7
1908	Pit N	23	11	.676	41	38	25-7	0	304.2	239	95	2	6	69	97	2.07	111	.213	.262	103-0-4	.165	-1	122	9	—	0.9
1909	†Pit N	22	11	.667	39	**35**	24-4	1	289.2	243	84	3	4	83	95	2.24	122	.231	.289	103-0-6	.136	-2	120	20	—	2.1
1910	StL N	9	12	.429	33	23	12-1	3	212	224	113	6	1	61	67	3.35	89	.275	.326	66-0-4	.167	-2	84	-14	—	-1.4
Total	13	249	205	.548	513	471	388-50	11	3996	3621	1620	66	156	1212	1651	2.63	118	.243	.307	1493-1-41	.166	-33	97	205	—	20.0

WILLOUGHBY, CLAUDE Claude William "Flunky","Weeping Willie"; B11.14.1898 Buffalo KS; D8.14.1973 McPherson KS; BR/TR/5´9.5˝/165; d9.18

YEAR	TM LG	W	L	PCT	G	GS	CG-SHO	SV-BS	IP	H	R	HR	HB	BB-IB	SO	ERA	AERA	OAV	OOB	AB-HR-SH	AVG	PB	SUP	APR	DL	PW
1925	Phi N	2	1	.667	3	3	1	0	23	26	7	0	1	11	6	1.96	244	.295	.380	8	.000	-1	71	6	—	0.6
1926	Phi N	8	12	.400	47	19	6	1	168	218	125	7	5	71	37	5.95	70	.327	.396	52-0-3	.212	-1	113	-28	—	-2.8
1927	Phi N	3	7	.300	35	6	1-1	2	97.2	126	83	7	2	53	14	6.54	63	.321	.404	26-0-1	.077	-2	106	-26	—	-2.6
1928	Phi N	6	5	.545	35	13	5-1	1	130.2	180	92	6	3	83	26	5.30	81	.340	.432	40-0-1	.150	-1	81	-16	—	-1.3
1929	Phi N	15	14	.517	49	35	14-1	4	243.1	288	156	15	5	108	50	4.99	104	.296	.370	91-0-1	.143	-5	99	3	—	0.1
1930	Phi N	4	17	.190	41	24	5-1	1	153	241	147	17	2	68	38	7.59	72	.369	.430	48	.104	-4	103	-31	—	-3.6
1931	Pit N	0	2	.000	9	2	1	0	25.2	32	21	4	0	12	4	6.31	61	.305	.376	7	.286	0	178	-7	—	-0.4
Total	7	38	58	.396	219	102	33-4	9	841.1	1111	631	56	18	406	175	5.84	81	.326	.401	272-0-6	.143	-14	104	-99	—	-10.0

WILLOUGHBY, JIM James Arthur; B1.31.1949 Salinas CA; BR/TR/6´2˝/(180–205); [SFN67 11/218]; d9.5

YEAR	TM LG	W	L	PCT	G	GS	CG-SHO	SV-BS	IP	H	R	HR	HB	BB-IB	SO	ERA	AERA	OAV	OOB	AB-HR-SH	AVG	PB	SUP	APR	DL	PW
1971	SF N	0	1	.000	2	1	0	0-0	4	8	4	0	0	1-0	3	9.00	38	.400	.429	1	.000	-0	78	-2	0	-0.4
1972	SF N	6	4	.600	11	11	7	0-0	87.2	72	25	8	2	14-4	40	2.36	148	.222	.257	27-0-5	.185	0	96	11	0	1.4
1973	SF N	4	5	.444	39	12	1-1	1-0	123	138	74	21	3	37-4	60	4.68	82	.295	.347	28-1-3	.143	1*	105	-11	0	-0.7
1974	SF N	1	4	.200	18	4	0	0-0	40.2	51	27	7	0	9-1	12	4.65	82	.304	.339	10	.100	-0*	69	-4	0	-0.5
1975	†Bos A	5	2	.714	24	0	0	8-1	48.1	46	25	6	2	16-3	29	3.54	115	.247	.311	0	ø	0	—	1	0	0.2
1976	Bos A	3	12	.200	54	0	0	10-3	99	94	38	4	8	31-12	37	2.82	138	.256	.324	1	.000	-0	—	10	0	1.7
1977	Bos A	6	2	.750	31	0	0	2-2	54.2	54	32	5	2	18-3	33	4.94	91	.258	.320	0	ø	0	—	-2	68	-0.3
1978	Chi A	1	6	.143	59	0	0	13-2	93.1	95	41	6	4	19-2	36	3.86	99	.275	.319	0	ø	0	—	1	0	0.2
Total	8	26	36	.419	238	28	8-1	34-8	550.2	558	266	57	21	145-29	250	3.79	102	.267	.319	67-1-8	.149	1	92	4	68	1.6

WILLS, FRANK Frank Lee; B10.26.1958 New Orleans LA; BR/TR/6´2˝/(200–215); [KCA80 1/16]; d7.31; Col Tulane

YEAR	TM LG	W	L	PCT	G	GS	CG-SHO	SV-BS	IP	H	R	HR	HB	BB-IB	SO	ERA	AERA	OAV	OOB	AB-HR-SH	AVG	PB	SUP	APR	DL	PW
1983	KC A	2	1	.667	6	4	0	0-0	34.2	35	17	2	0	15-0	23	4.15	99	.259	.329	0	ø	0	105	0	0	0.0
1984	KC A	2	3	.400	10	5	0	0-0	37	39	21	3	0	13-0	21	5.11	79	.271	.323	0	ø	0	89	-3	15	-0.4
1985	Sea A	5	11	.313	24	18	1	1-0	123	122	85	18	3	68-3	67	6.00	70	.266	.359	0	ø	0	93	-21	0	-2.4
1986	Cle A	4	4	.500	26	0	0	4-2	40.1	43	23	6	0	16-4	32	4.91	85	.272	.335	0	ø	0	—	-2	0	-0.5
1987	Cle A	0	1	.000	6	0	0	1-0	5.1	3	3	0	0	7-0	4	5.06	90	.176	.400	0	ø	0	—	0	0	0.0
1988	Tor A	0	0	ø	10	0	0	0-0	20.2	22	12	2	0	6-2	19	5.23	76	.272	.318	0	ø	0	—	-2	0	-0.1
1989	Tor A	3	1	.750	24	4	0	0-0	71.1	65	31	4	1	30-2	41	3.66	104	.242	.319	0	ø	0	119	2	17	0.1
1990	Tor A	6	4	.600	44	4	0	0-0	99	101	54	13	1	38-7	72	4.73	84	.266	.333	0	ø	0	98	-8	0	-0.7
1991	Tor A	0	1	.000	4	0	0	0-0	4.1	8	8	2	1	5-0	2	16.62	25	.421	.560	0	ø	0	—	-5	0	-0.9
Total	9	22	26	.458	154	35	1	6-2	435.2	438	254	50	6	198-18	281	5.06	80	.264	.341	0	ø	0	99	-39	32	-4.9

WILLS, TED Theodore Carl; B2.9.1934 Fresno CA; BL/TL/6´2˝/(190–200); d5.24; Col Cal St.–Fresno

YEAR	TM LG	W	L	PCT	G	GS	CG-SHO	SV-BS	IP	H	R	HR	HB	BB-IB	SO	ERA	AERA	OAV	OOB	AB-HR-SH	AVG	PB	SUP	APR	DL	PW
1959	Bos A	2	6	.250	9	8	2	0	56.1	68	35	9	1	24-2	24	5.27	77	.302	.369	16-0-2	.250	1	65	-7	0	-0.7
1960	Bos A	1	1	.500	15	0	0	1	30.1	38	26	4	3	16-1	28	7.42	55	.317	.404	8	.250	1*	—	-10	0	-0.6
1961	Bos A	3	2	.600	17	0	0	0	19.2	24	17	2	0	19-0	11	5.95	70	.304	.434	2	.000	-0	—	-5	0	-0.9
1962	Bos A	0	0	ø	1	0	0	0	0	2	1	0	0	1-0	0	(1)	ø	1.000	1.000	0	ø	0	—	-1	0	-0.1
	Cin N	0	2	.000	26	5	0	3	61	61	36	12	5	23-0	58	5.31	76	.266	.346	16	.313	1	148	-7	0	-0.2
1965	Chi A	2	0	1.000	15	0	0	1	19	17	8	2	1	14-2	12	2.84	112	.258	.386	2	.000	0	—	0	0	0.1
Total	5	8	11	.421	83	13	2	5	186.1	210	123	29	10	97-5	133	5.51	72	.291	.380	44-0-2	.250	3	99	-30	0	-2.4

WILMET, PAUL Paul Richard; B11.8.1958 Green Bay WI; BR/TR/5´11˝/170; d7.25; Col Des Moines Area (IA) CC

YEAR	TM LG	W	L	PCT	G	GS	CG-SHO	SV-BS	IP	H	R	HR	HB	BB-IB	SO	ERA	AERA	OAV	OOB	AB-HR-SH	AVG	PB	SUP	APR	DL	PW
1989	Tex A	0	0	ø	3	0	0	0-0	2.1	5	4	0	0	2-1	1	15.43	26	.417	.500	0	ø	0	—	-3	0	-0.1

WILSHERE, WHITEY Vernon Sprague; B8.3.1912 Poplar Ridge NY; D5.23.1985 Cooperstown NY; BL/TL/6´0˝/180; d6.24; Col Indiana

YEAR	TM LG	W	L	PCT	G	GS	CG-SHO	SV-BS	IP	H	R	HR	HB	BB-IB	SO	ERA	AERA	OAV	OOB	AB-HR-SH	AVG	PB	SUP	APR	DL	PW
1934	Phi A	0	1	.000	9	2	0	0	21.2	39	30	0	1	15	19	12.05	36	.394	.478	3	.000	-0	119	-18	—	-0.9
1935	Phi A	9	9	.500	27	18	7-3	1	142.1	136	69	8	10	78	80	4.05	112	.253	.358	43-0-5	.093	-4	90	10	—	0.7
1936	Phi A	1	2	.333	5	3	0	0	18.1	21	17	1	0	19	4	6.87	74	.288	.435	4	.000	-0	52	-4	—	-0.5
Total	3	10	12	.455	41	23	7-3	1	182.1	196	116	9	11	112	103	5.28	87	.276	.383	50-0-5	.080	-4	87	-12	—	-0.7

WILSHUSEN, TERRY Terry Wayne; B3.22.1949 Atascadero CA; D12.1.2000 Lomita CA; BR/TR/6´2˝/210; d4.7; Col Los Angeles (CA) City

YEAR	TM LG	W	L	PCT	G	GS	CG-SHO	SV-BS	IP	H	R	HR	HB	BB-IB	SO	ERA	AERA	OAV	OOB	AB-HR-SH	AVG	PB	SUP	APR	DL	PW
1973	Cal A	0	0	ø	1	0	0	0-0	0.1	0	3	0	1	2-0	0	81.00	4	.000	.750	0	ø	0	—	-3	0	-0.1

WILSON, BRIAN Brian Patrick; B3.16.1982 Londonderry NH; BR/TR/6´1˝/205; [SFN03 24/723]; d4.23; Col Louisiana St.

YEAR	TM LG	W	L	PCT	G	GS	CG-SHO	SV-BS	IP	H	R	HR	HB	BB-IB	SO	ERA	AERA	OAV	OOB	AB-HR-SH	AVG	PB	SUP	APR	DL	PW
2006	SF N	2	3	.400	31	0	0	1-1	30	32	19	1	1	21-2	23	5.40	82	.281	.386	2	.000	-0	—	-3	25	-0.5

WILSON, C.J. Christopher John; B11.18.1980 Newport Beach CA; BL/TL/6´2˝/(200–215); [TexA01 5/141]; d6.10; Col Loyola Marymount

YEAR	TM LG	W	L	PCT	G	GS	CG-SHO	SV-BS	IP	H	R	HR	HB	BB-IB	SO	ERA	AERA	OAV	OOB	AB-HR-SH	AVG	PB	SUP	APR	DL	PW
2005	Tex A	1	7	.125	24	6	0	1-0	48	63	39	5	2	18-1	30	6.94	66	.320	.379	0	ø	0	71	-12	0	-1.6
2006	Tex A	2	4	.333	44	0	0	1-1	44.1	39	23	7	5	18-1	43	4.06	115	.234	.326	0	ø	0	—	2	11	0.3
Total	2	3	11	.214	68	6	0	2-1	92.1	102	62	12	7	36-2	73	5.56	83	.280	.355	0	ø	0	71	-10	11	-1.3

WILSON, DON Donald Edward; B2.12.1945 Monroe LA; D1.5.1975 Houston TX; BR/TR/6´3˝/(202–205); d9.29; Col Compton (CA) CC

YEAR	TM LG	W	L	PCT	G	GS	CG-SHO	SV-BS	IP	H	R	HR	HB	BB-IB	SO	ERA	AERA	OAV	OOB	AB-HR-SH	AVG	PB	SUP	APR	DL	PW
1966	Hou N	1	0	1.000	1	0	0	0	6	5	2	1	0	1-0	7	3.00	114	.238	.273	2	.500	1	—	0	0	0.2
1967	Hou N	10	9	.526	31	28	7-3	0	184	141	67	10	7	69-2	159	2.79	119	.209	.288	66-0-2	.091	-2	100	10	0	0.7
1968	Hou N	13	16	.448	33	30	9-3	0	208.2	187	85	9	4	70-5	175	3.28	90	.236	.300	70-1-6	.214	4*	89	-7	0	-0.7
1969	Hou N	16	12	.571	34	34	13-1	0-0	225	210	119	16	9	97-8	235	4.00	89	.245	.326	81-0-2	.099	-1	133	-12	0	-1.6
1970	Hou N	11	6	.647	29	27	3	0-0	184.1	188	92	15	7	66-4	94	3.91	100	.259	.325	69-0-3	.116	-2*	119	-2	17	-0.5
1971	Hou N★	16	10	.615	35	34	18-3	0-0	268	195	80	15	7	79-3	180	2.45	137	**.202**	.266	91-0-6	.154	-1	92	28	0	2.5
1972	Hou N	15	10	.600	33	33	13-3	0-0	228.1	196	79	16	2	66-2	172	2.68	125	.233	.289	76-0-8	.105	-2	116	16	0	1.5
1973	Hou N	11	16	.407	37	32	10-3	2-0	239.1	187	94	21	7	92-6	149	3.20	114	.213	.291	79-0-6	.177	1	76	12	0	1.2
1974	Hou N	11	13	.458	33	27	5-4	0-1	204.2	170	80	16	4	100-2	112	3.08	113	.227	.318	63-0-9	.206	2	81	9	0	1.2
Total	9	104	92	.531	266	245	78-20	2-1	1748.1	1479	698	119	47	640-32	1283	3.15	110	.228	.299	597-1-42	.146	-1	102	54	17	4.5

WILSON, DUANE Duane Lewis; B6.29.1934 Wichita KS; BL/TL/6´1˝/185; d7.3

YEAR	TM LG	W	L	PCT	G	GS	CG-SHO	SV-BS	IP	H	R	HR	HB	BB-IB	SO	ERA	AERA	OAV	OOB	AB-HR-SH	AVG	PB	SUP	APR	DL	PW
1958	Bos A	0	0	ø	2	2	0	0	6.1	10	5	0	0	7-1	3	5.68	70	.400	.515	1-0-1	.000	-0	112	-1	0	-0.1

WILSON, FIN Finis Elbert; B12.9.1888 East Fork KY; D3.9.1959 Coral Gables FL; BL/TL/6´1˝/194; d9.26

YEAR	TM LG	W	L	PCT	G	GS	CG-SHO	SV-BS	IP	H	R	HR	HB	BB-IB	SO	ERA	AERA	OAV	OOB	AB-HR-SH	AVG	PB	SUP	APR	DL	PW
1914	Bro F	0	1	.000	2	1	1	0	7	7	7	0	0	11	4	7.71	37	.269	.486	2	.500	1	72	-3	—	-0.4
1915	Bro F	1	8	.111	18	11	5	0	102.1	85	56	2	4	53	47	3.78	72	.249	.356	35-0-1	.314	3*	87	-12	—	-0.7
Total	2	1	9	.100	20	12	6	0	109.1	92	63	2	4	64	51	4.03	68	.250	.367	37-0-1	.324	3	85	-15	—	-1.1

WILSON, ZEKE Frank Ealton; B12.24.1869 Benton AL; D4.26.1928 Montgomery AL; BR/TR/5´10˝/165; d4.23

YEAR	TM LG	W	L	PCT	G	GS	CG-SHO	SV-BS	IP	H	R	HR	HB	BB-IB	SO	ERA	AERA	OAV	OOB	AB-HR-SH	AVG	PB	SUP	APR	DL	PW
1895	Bos N	2	4	.333	6	6	4	0	45	54	48	1	0	27	5	5.20	98	.293	.384	19-1-0	.316	1	65	-4	—	-0.3
	Cle N	3	1	.750	9	8	4	0	52.2	75	38	4	4	24	20	4.27	117	.329	.402	22-0-2	.136	-3	87	3	—	0.0
	Year	5	5	.500	15	14	8	0	97.2	129	86	5	4	51	25	4.70	107	.313	.394	41-1-2	.220	-2	78	-1	—	-0.3
1896	Cle N	17	9	.654	33	29	20-1	1	240	265	150	9	8	81	56	4.01	113	.278	.339	100-0-2	.270	2	114	14	—	1.5
1897	Cle N	16	11	.593	34	30	26-1	0	263.2	323	171	9	9	83	69	4.16	108	.299	.354	116-0-3	.224	-3*	94	8	—	0.4
1898	Cle N	13	18	.419	33	31	28-1	0	254.2	307	141	4	7	51	45	3.60	100	.296	.333	118-0-7	.178	-3*	83	2	—	0.1
1899	StL N	1	1	.500	5	2	2	0	26	30	18	0	2	4	3	4.50	88	.288	.327	10	.000	-1	99	-1	—	-0.1
Total	5	52	44	.542	120	106	84-3	1	882	1054	566	27	30	270	198	4.03	106	.294	.348	385-1-14	.216	-8	95	22	—	1.6

WILSON, GARY Gary Morris; B1.1.1970 Arcata CA; BR/TR/6´3˝/190; [PitN92 18/511]; d4.28; Col Cal St.–Sacramento

YEAR	TM LG	W	L	PCT	G	GS	CG-SHO	SV-BS	IP	H	R	HR	HB	BB-IB	SO	ERA	AERA	OAV	OOB	AB-HR-SH	AVG	PB	SUP	APR	DL	PW
1995	Pit N	0	1	.000	10	0	0	0-0	14.1	13	8	2	2	5-0	8	5.02	87	.241	.328	0-0-1	ø	0	—	-1	0	0.0

WILSON, GARY Gary Steven; B11.21.1954 Camden AR; BR/TR/6´2˝/180; [HouN76*1/2]; d4.13; Col Southern Arkansas

YEAR	TM LG	W	L	PCT	G	GS	CG-SHO	SV-BS	IP	H	R	HR	HB	BB-IB	SO	ERA	AERA	OAV	OOB	AB-HR-SH	AVG	PB	SUP	APR	DL	PW
1979	Hou N	0	0	ø	6	0	0	0-0	7.1	15	11	2	0	6-0	6	12.27	29	.441	.500	0	ø	0	—	-7	0	-0.4

WILSON, TEX Gomer Russell; B7.8.1901 Trenton TX; D9.15.1946 Sulphur Springs TX; BR/TL/5´10˝/170; d9.2

YEAR	TM LG	W	L	PCT	G	GS	CG-SHO	SV-BS	IP	H	R	HR	HB	BB-IB	SO	ERA	AERA	OAV	OOB	AB-HR-SH	AVG	PB	SUP	APR	DL	PW
1924	Bro N	0	0	ø	2	0	0	0	3.2	7	6	0	0	1	1	14.73	25	.412	.444	1	.000	-0	—	-4	—	-0.2

WILSON, HIGHBALL Howard Paul; B8.9.1878 Philadelphia PA; D10.16.1934 Havre de Grace MD; TR/5´9˝/164; d9.13

YEAR	TM LG	W	L	PCT	G	GS	CG-SHO	SV-BS	IP	H	R	HR	HB	BB-IB	SO	ERA	AERA	OAV	OOB	AB-HR-SH	AVG	PB	SUP	APR	DL	PW
1899	Cle N	0	1	.000	1	1	1	0	8	12	8	0	0	5	1	9.00	41	.343	.425	3	.333	0	39	-4	—	-0.3
1902	Phi A	7	4	.636	13	10	8	0	96.1	103	44	1	9	19	18	2.43	151	.274	.324	35-0-1	.171	-1	108	11	—	0.9
1903	Was A	7	18	.280	30	28	25-1	0	242.1	269	123	7	10	43	56	3.31	95	.280	.318	85-0-2	.200	2*	70	-6	—	-0.5

YEAR	TM LG	W	L	PCT	G	GS	CG-SHO	SV-BS	IP	H	R	HR	HB	BB-IB	SO	ERA	AERA	OAV	OOB	AB-HR-SH	AVG	PB	SUP	APR	DL	PW
1904	Was A	0	3	.000	3	3	3	0	25	33	17	0	2	4	11	4.68	57	.317	.355	9-0-1	.222	1*	36	-5	—	-0.5
Total	4	14	26	.350	47	42	37-1	0	371.2	417	192	8	21	71	86	3.29	99	.283	.325	132-0-4	.197	2	77	-4	—	-0.4
WILSON, JIM	James Alger; B2.20.1922 San Diego CA; D9.2.1986 Newport Beach CA; BR/TR/6´1.5˝/(195–200); d4.18; Col San Diego St.																									
1945	Bos A	6	8	.429	23	21	8-2	0	144.1	121	61	7	1	88	50	3.30	103	.228	.339	53-0-2	.245	2*	89	2	0	0.2
1946	Bos A	0	0	ø	1	0	0	0	0.2	2	2	1	0	0	0	27.00	14	.500	.500	0	ø	0	—	-2	0	-0.1
1948	StL A	0	0	ø	4	0	0	0	2.2	5	4	0	0	5	1	13.50	34	.417	.588	0	ø	0	—	-2	0	-0.1
1949	Phi A	0	0	ø	2	0	0	0	5	7	8	2	0	5	2	14.40	29	.350	.480	3	.000	-0	—	-5	0	-0.3
1951	Bos N	7	7	.500	20	15	5	1	110	131	67	14	4	40	33	5.40	68	.294	.357	39-0-3	.179	0	152	-19	0	-2.1
1952	Bos N	12	14	.462	33	33	14	0	234	234	114	19	4	90	104	4.23	85	.262	.333	86-0-3	.163	-0	101	-13	0	-1.4
1953	Mil N	4	9	.308	20	18	5	0	114	107	59	16	3	43	71	4.34	90	.243	.315	36-1-2	.167	1	94	-4	0	-0.2
1954	Mil N☆	8	2	.800	27	19	6-4	0	127.2	129	55	12	5	36	52	3.52	106	.266	.321	44-0-2	.159	0	150	4	0	0.4
1955	Bal A☆	12	18	.400	34	31	14-4	0	235.1	200	104	17	4	87-5	96	3.44	111	.228	.297	89-0-2	.169	-2	78	10	0	1.0
1956	Bal A	4	2	.667	7	7	1	0	48.1	49	27	5	2	16-1	31	5.03	78	.268	.332	15	.267	2	91	-5	0	-0.3
	Chi A★	9	12	.429	28	21	6-3	0	159.2	149	82	15	2	70-5	82	4.06	101	.248	.328	62-1-2	.306	4	105	0	0	0.3
	Year	13	14	.481	35	28	7-3	0	208	198	109	20	4	86-6	113	4.28	95	.253	.329	77-1-2	.299	6	102	-5	0	0.0
1957	Chi A	15	8	.652	30	29	12-**5**	0	201.2	189	85	22	3	65-8	100	3.48	107	.249	.309	68-0-4	.147	-0*	115	6	0	0.5
1958	Chi A	9	9	.500	28	23	4-1	1	155.2	156	75	21	1	63-8	70	4.10	89	.268	.337	51-0-4	.078	-3	125	-7	0	-1.1
Total	12	86	89	.491	257	217	75-19	2	1539	1479	743	151	29	608-27	692	4.01	93	.254	.326	546-2-24	.181	4	108	-35	0	-3.2
WILSON, JACK	John Francis "Black Jack"; B4.12.1912 Portland OR; D4.19.1995 Edmonds WA; BR/TR/5´11˝/210; d9.9; Col Portland																									
1934	Phi A	0	1	.000	2	2	1	0	9	15	12	1	0	9	2	12.00	37	.405	.522	3-0-1	.000	-0	119	-7	—	-0.6
1935	Bos A	3	4	.429	23	6	2	1	64	72	35	0	2	36	19	4.22	112	.290	.385	16-1-1	.313	2	70	4	—	0.6
1936	Bos A	6	8	.429	43	9	2	3	136.1	152	83	4	1	86	74	4.42	120	.284	.384	50-0-1	.220	-0*	63	10	—	0.8
1937	Bos A	16	10	.615	51	21	14-1	7	221.1	209	111	13	3	119	137	3.70	128	.248	.343	85-0-2	.165	-3	118	22	—	2.1
1938	Bos A	15	15	.500	37	27	11-3	1	194.2	200	108	16	2	91	96	4.30	115	.262	.342	68-0-6	.221	0	81	13	—	1.6
1939	Bos A	11	11	.500	36	22	6	2	177.1	198	109	10	1	75	80	4.67	101	.281	.351	63-0-5	.159	-4*	103	0	—	-0.4
1940	Bos A	12	6	.667	41	16	9	5	157.2	170	104	17	3	87	102	5.08	89	.270	.362	66-2-0	.273	4	144	-13	—	-1.0
1941	Bos A	4	13	.235	27	12	4-1	1	116.1	140	82	7	5	70	55	5.03	83	.300	.397	44-0-2	.159	-1	90	-13	0	-1.7
1942	Was A	1	4	.200	12	6	1	0	42	57	34	2	1	23	18	6.64	55	.322	.403	17-0-1	.118	-1	125	-13	0	-1.4
	Det A	0	0	ø	9	0	0	0	13	20	8	3	0	5	7	4.85	81	.351	.403	1	.000	-0	—	-1	0	-0.1
	Year	1	4	.200	21	6	1	0	55	77	42	5	1	28	25	6.22	60	.329	.403	18-0-1	.111	-1	122	-14	0	-1.5
Total	9	68	72	.486	281	121	50-5	20	1131.2	1233	686	73	18	601	590	4.59	102	.276	.364	413-3-19	.199	-3	100	2	0	-0.1
WILSON, JOHN	John Nicodemus; B6.15.1890 Boonsboro MD; D9.23.1954 Annapolis MD; BR/TL/6´1˝/185; d6.11																									
1913	Was A	0	0	ø	3	0	0	0	4	4	2	0	0	3	1	4.50	66	.286	.412	0	ø	0	—	0	—	0.0
WILSON, JOHN	John Samuel; B4.25.1903 Coal City AL; D8.27.1980 Chattanooga TN; BR/TR/6´2˝/164; d5.9																									
1927	Bos A	0	2	.000	5	2	2	0	25.1	31	19	1	0	13	8	3.55	119	.326	.407	9	.111	-1	30	-1	—	-0.2
1928	Bos A	0	0	ø	2	0	0	0	5	6	5	0	0	6	1	9.00	46	.333	.500	1	.000	-0	—	-2	—	-0.1
Total	2	0	2	.000	7	2	2	0	30.1	37	24	1	0	19	9	4.45	94	.327	.424	10	.100	-1	30	-3	—	-0.3
WILSON, KRIS	Kristopher Kyle; B8.6.1976 Washington DC; BR/TR/6´4˝/(220–225); [KCA97 9/271]; d7.28; Col Georgia Tech																									
2000	KC A	0	1	.000	20	0	0	0-1	34.1	38	16	3	0	11-3	17	4.19	125	.288	.340	0	ø	0	—	4	0	0.2
2001	KC A	6	5	.545	29	15	0	1-0	109.1	132	78	26	7	32-0	67	5.19	96	.297	.352	3	.333	0	87	-6	0	-0.5
2002	KC A	2	0	1.000	12	0	0	0-2	18.2	29	18	7	2	5-0	10	8.20	61	.354	.396	0	ø	0	—	-6	56	-0.6
2003	KC A	6	3	.667	29	4	0	0-1	72.2	92	49	13	6	16-3	42	5.33	91	.305	.348	0	ø	0	81	-5	0	-0.5
2006	NY A	0	0	ø	5	1	0	0-0	8.1	14	8	4	0	4-0	6	8.64	52	.368	.429	0	ø	0	104	-4	0	-0.2
Total	5	14	9	.609	95	20	0	1-4	243.1	305	169	53	15	68-6	142	5.44	91	.306	.356	3	.333	0	86	-17	56	-1.6
WILSON, MAX	Max; B6.3.1916 Haw River NC; D1.2.1977 Greensboro NC; BL/TL/5´7˝/160; d9.10; Mil 1942–45																									
1940	Phi N	0	0	ø	3	0	0	0	7	16	13	1	0	2	3	12.86	30	.444	.474	2	.000	-0	—	-8	—	-0.4
1946	Was A	0	1	.000	9	0	0	0	12.2	16	12	1	0	9	8	7.11	47	.320	.424	2	.000	0	—	-5	0	-0.4
Total	2	0	1	.000	12	0	0	0	19.2	32	25	2	0	11	11	9.15	39	.372	.443	4	.000	-0	—	-13	0	-0.8
WILSON, PAUL	Paul Anthony; B3.28.1973 Orlando FL; BR/TR/6´5˝/(210–235); [NYN94 1/1]; d4.4; Col Florida St.; [DL 1998 NY N 181, 2006 Cin N 182]																									
1996	NY N	5	12	.294	26	26	1	0-0	149	157	102	15	10	71-11	109	5.38	75	.268	.355	50-1-4	.080	-2	99	-23	40	-2.4
2000	TB A	1	4	.200	11	7	0	0-0	51	38	20	1	4	16-2	40	3.35	146	.209	.284	0	ø	0	41	9	0	0.7
2001	TB A	8	9	.471	37	24	0	0-1	151.1	165	94	21	13	52-2	119	4.88	92	.278	.343	0	ø	0	95	-7	0	-0.7
2002	TB A	6	12	.333	30	30	1	0-0	193.2	219	113	29	13	67-2	111	4.83	94	.287	.352	5-0-1	.000	-1	89	-7	0	-0.6
2003	Cin N	8	10	.444	28	28	0	0-0	166.2	190	97	24	7	50-5	93	4.64	90	.285	.342	52-0-4	.115	-1*	101	-11	0	-1.2
2004	Cin N	11	6	.647	29	29	1	0-0	183.2	192	93	26	8	63-5	117	4.36	99	.271	.334	60-0-7	.100	-2	112	0	18	-0.2
2005	Cin N	1	5	.167	9	9	0	0-0	46.1	68	41	10	4	17-1	30	7.77	55	.343	.401	17-0-2	.176	-0	96	-17	139	-1.8
Total	7	40	58	.408	170	153	3	0-1	941.2	1029	560	126	59	336-28	619	4.86	89	.278	.345	184-1-18	.103	-5	96	-56	560	-6.2
WILSON, PETE	Peter Alex; B10.9.1885 Springfield MA; D6.5.1957 St.Petersburg FL; TL; d9.15																									
1908	NY A	3	3	.500	6	6	4-1	0	39	27	16	0	1	33	28	3.46	72	.191	.349	14-0-1	.071	-1*	55	-2	—	-0.4
1909	NY A	6	5	.545	14	13	7-1	0	93.2	82	55	2	4	43	44	3.17	80	.230	.320	34-0-1	.118	-1	114	-9	—	-1.1
Total	2	9	8	.529	20	19	11-2	0	132.2	109	71	2	5	76	72	3.26	77	.219	.329	48-0-2	.104	-2	94	-11	—	-1.5
WILSON, EARL	Robert Earl (Name Changed From Wilson, Earl Lawrence); B10.2.1934 Ponchatoula LA; D4.23.2005 Southfield MI; BR/TR/6´3˝/(214–220); d7.28																									
1959	Bos A	1	1	.500	9	4	0	0	23.2	21	17	2	0	31-0	17	6.08	67	.241	.441	8	.500	2	201	-5	0	-0.2
1960	Bos A	3	2	.600	13	9	2	0	65	61	36	4	0	48-1	40	4.71	86	.247	.367	23	.174	-0*	109	-4	0	-0.3
1962	Bos A	12	8	.600	31	28	4-1	0	191.1	163	86	21	6	111-2	137	3.90	106	.231	.338	69-3-1	.174	3*	107	8	0	1.0
1963	Bos A	11	16	.407	37	34	6-3	0	210.2	184	99	18	1	105-4	123	3.76	101	.234	.323	72-1-2	.208	5*	89	0	0	0.5
1964	Bos A	11	12	.478	33	31	5	0	202.1	213	121	37	2	73-3	166	4.49	86	.269	.328	73-5-1	.205	8*	117	-17	0	-0.9
1965	Bos A	13	14	.481	36	36	8-1	0	230.2	221	119	27	4	77-4	164	3.98	94	.250	.311	79-6-3	.177	8*	108	-6	0	0.2
1966	Bos A	5	5	.500	15	14	5-1	0	100.2	88	45	14	2	36-2	67	3.84	99	.235	.303	32-2-2	.250	3*	106	1	0	0.5
	Det A	13	6	.684	23	23	8-2	0	163.1	126	49	16	4	38-1	133	2.59	134	.213	.265	64-5-4	.234	9*	123	18	0	3.2
	Year	18	11	.621	38	37	13-3	0	264	214	94	30	6	74-3	200	3.07	117	.222	.280	96-7-6	.240	12	116	19	0	3.7
1967	Det A	**22**	11	.667	39	38	12	0	264	216	103	34	3	92-7	184	3.27	100	.224	.291	108-4-4	.185	7*	126	1	0	1.0
1968	†Det A	13	12	.520	34	33	10-3	0	224.1	192	77	20	0	65-4	168	2.85	106	.231	.287	88-7-1	.227	10*	96	4	0	1.7
1969	Det A	12	10	.545	35	35	5-1	0-0	214.2	209	93	23	4	69-4	150	3.31	114	.256	.315	76-0-2	.132	-0*	101	8	0	0.9
1970	Det A	4	6	.400	18	16	4-1	0-0	96	87	53	15	2	32-1	74	4.41	86	.238	.303	31-1-2	.194	2	93	-7	0	-0.5
	SD N	1	6	.143	15	9	0	0-0	65	82	36	5	2	19-2	29	4.85	83	.309	.356	17-1-0	.059	0	99	-5	0	-0.5
Total	11	121	109	.526	338	310	69-13	0-0	2051.2	1863	934	236	30	796-35	1452	3.69	99	.242	.313	740-35-22	.195	57	108	-4	0	6.6
WILSON, ROY	Roy Edward "Lefty"; B9.13.1896 Foster IA; D12.3.1969 Clarion IA; BL/TL/6´0˝/175; d4.18																									
1928	Chi A	0	0	ø	1	0	0	0	3.1	2	0	0	0	3	2	0.00	ø	.167	.333	1	.000	-0	—	1	—	0.1
WILSON, STEVE	Stephen Douglas; B12.13.1964 Victoria BC, Can.; BL/TL/6´4˝/(195–224); [TexA85 4/83]; d9.16; Col Portland																									
1988	Tex A	0	0	ø	3	0	0	0-0	7.2	7	5	1	0	4-1	1	5.87	70	.259	.355	0	ø	0	—	-1	0	-0.1
1989	†Chi N	6	4	.600	53	8	0	2-1	85.2	83	43	6	1	31-5	65	4.20	90	.257	.320	16-0-1	.063	-1	97	-3	0	-0.4
1990	Chi N	4	9	.308	45	15	1	1-1	139	140	77	17	2	43-6	95	4.79	85	.259	.315	37-0-5	.162	0	97	-8	0	-0.7
1991	Chi N	0	0	ø	8	0	0	0-0	12.1	13	7	1	0	5-1	9	4.38	89	.277	.340	1	.000	-0*	—	-1	0	-0.1
	LA N	0	0	ø	11	0	0	2-0	8.1	1	0	0	0	4-0	5	0.00	ø	.042	.179	1	.000	-0	—	3	0	0.2
	Year	0	0	ø	19	0	0	2-0	20.2	14	7	1	0	9-1	14	2.61	145	.197	.284	2	.000	-0	—	2	0	0.1
1992	LA N	2	5	.286	60	0	0	0-4	66.2	74	37	6	1	29-7	54	4.18	83	.282	.351	3	.333	0	—	-6	0	-0.6
1993	LA N	1	0	1.000	25	0	0	1-0	25.2	30	13	2	1	14-4	23	4.56	85	.288	.378	2	.000	-0	—	-1	0	-0.1
Total	6	13	18	.419	205	23	1	6-6	345.1	348	182	33	5	130-24	252	4.40	88	.262	.328	60-0-6	.133	-1	100	-17	0	-1.8
WILSON, TREVOR	Trevor Kirk; B6.7.1966 Torrance CA; BL/TL/6´0˝/(175–204); [SFN85 8/186]; d9.5; [DL 1994 SF N 131]																									
1988	SF N	0	2	.000	4	4	0	0-0	22	25	14	1	0	8-0	15	4.09	80	.298	.355	7-0-1	.286	1	88	-3	0	-0.3
1989	SF N	2	3	.400	14	4	0	0-0	39.1	28	20	2	4	24-0	22	4.35	78	.207	.341	8	.250	1	137	-4	0	-0.3
1990	SF N	8	7	.533	27	17	3-2	0-0	110.1	87	52	11	1	49-3	66	4.00	92	.218	.304	29-0-5	.138	0	89	-4	15	-0.4
1991	SF N	13	11	.542	44	29	2-1	0-1	202	173	87	13	5	77-4	139	3.56	101	.234	.308	51-1-8	.235	5*	97	0	0	0.7

YEAR	TM LG	W	L	PCT	G	GS	CG-SHO	SV-BS	IP	H	R	HR	HB	BB-IB	SO	ERA	AERA	OAV	OOB	AB-HR-SH	AVG	PB	SUP	APR	DL	PW
1992	SF N	8	14	.364	26	26	1-1	0-0	154	152	82	18	6	64-5	88	4.21	79	.265	.342	39-0-7	.077	-1*	84	-17	12	-2.2
1993	SF N	7	5	.583	22	18	1	0-0	110	110	45	8	6	40-3	57	3.60	109	.275	.347	29-1-8	.138	1	84	5	75	0.6
1995	SF N	3	4	.429	17	17	0	0-0	82.2	82	42	8	4	38-1	38	3.92	105	.269	.355	30-0-3	.233	1*	91	1	77	0.2
1998	Ana A	0	0	ø	15	0	0	0-2	7.2	8	4	0	1	5-2	6	3.52	135	.267	.378	0	ø	0	—	1	0	0.0
Total	8	41	46	.471	169	115	7-4	0-3	728	665	346	61	27	305-18	431	3.87	94	.249	.330	193-2-32	.176	7	91	-21	310	-1.7
WILSON, WALTER	Walter Wood; B11.24.1913 Glenn GA; D4.17.1994 Bremen GA; BL/TR/6´4˝/190; d4.17																									
1945	Det A	1	3	.250	25	4	1	0	70.1	76	40	4	3	35	28	4.61	76	.284	.373	19-0-2	.053	-2	79	-7	0	-0.5
WILSON, WILLY	William; B1.7.1884 Columbus OH; D10.28.1925 Seattle WA; BR/TR; d10.3																									
1906	Was A	0	1	.000	1	1	1	0	7	3	2	0	1	2	1	2.57	102	.130	.231	2	.000	-0	27	0	—	0.0
WILSON, MUTT	William Clarence "Lank"; B7.20.1896 Keyser (now Addor) NC; D8.31.1962 Leesburg FL; BR/TR/6´3˝/167; d9.11																									
1920	Det A	1	1	.500	3	2	1	0	13	12	10	0	0	5	4	3.46	108	.240	.309	4-0-1	.250	-0	96	-1	—	-0.2
WILSON, BILL	William Harlan; B9.21.1942 Pomeroy OH; D8.11.1993 Broken Arrow OK; BR/TR/6´2˝/(190–200); d4.8; Col Marshall																									
1969	Phi N	2	5	.286	37	0	0	6-3	62.1	53	26	6	1	36-8	48	3.32	107	.231	.336	6	.000	-0	—	2	0	0.1
1970	Phi N	1	0	1.000	37	0	0	0-1	58.1	57	35	5	0	33-0	41	4.78	84	.263	.357	4	.250	0	—	-6	0	-0.2
1971	Phi N	4	6	.400	38	0	0	7-2	58.2	39	20	4	1	22-4	40	3.07	116	.188	.266	10	.100	-1	—	4	0	0.8
1972	Phi N	1	1	.500	23	0	0	0-2	30	26	13	1	0	11-3	18	3.30	109	.234	.301	0	ø	0	—	1	103	0.1
1973	Phi N	1	3	.250	44	0	0	4-2	48.2	54	39	7	0	29-7	24	6.66	57	.293	.388	4	.000	-0	—	-14	0	-1.4
Total	5	9	15	.375	179	0	0	17-10	258	229	133	23	2	131-22	171	4.22	88	.241	.332	24	.083	-1	—	-13	103	-0.6
WILTSE, HOOKS	George Leroy; B9.7.1879 Hamilton NY; D1.21.1959 Long Beach NY; BR/TL/6´0˝/185; d4.21; C1; b–Snake																									
1904	NY N	13	3	.813	24	16	14-2	8	164.2	150	66	8	5	61	105	2.84	96	.240	.313	67-1-2	.224	3*	169	0	—	0.5
1905	NY N	15	6	.714	32	19	18-1	3	197	158	71	5	4	61	120	2.47	119	.219	.284	72-0-2	.278	7*	114	12	—	2.3
1906	NY N	16	11	.593	38	26	21-4	6	249.1	227	92	3	3	58	125	2.27	115	.241	.288	94-0-4	.191	2*	102	7	—	1.0
1907	NY N	13	12	.520	33	21	14-3	2	190.1	171	63	3	5	48	79	2.18	114	.241	.294	67-0-1	.134	0*	114	6	—	0.9
1908	NY N	23	14	.622	44	38	30-7	2	330	266	95	4	9	73	118	2.24	108	.224	.274	110-0-7	.236	6*	126	12	—	2.1
1909	NY N	20	11	.645	37	30	22-4	3	269.1	228	91	9	6	51	119	2.00	128	.233	.275	95-1-2	.200	2	133	16	—	2.0
1910	NY N	14	12	.538	36	30	18-2	2	235.1	232	96	4	2	52	88	2.72	109	.261	.303	74-0-5	.176	0	110	7	—	0.6
1911	†NY N	12	9	.571	30	24	11-4	0	187.1	177	83	7	2	39	92	3.27	103	.251	.292	69-0-2	.188	-1*	107	5	—	0.3
1912	NY N	9	6	.600	28	17	5	3	134	140	63	7	1	28	58	3.16	107	.273	.312	46-0-1	.326	4	129	5	—	0.9
1913	†NY N	0	0	ø	17	2	0	3	57.2	53	24	1	1	8	25	1.56	200	.237	.266	24	.208	0*	133	6	—	0.4
1914	NY N	1	1	.500	20	0	0	1	38	41	21	2	0	12	19	2.84	93	.289	.344	3	.667	2*	—	-3	—	0.0
1915	Bro F	3	5	.375	18	3	1	5	59.1	49	22	1	2	7	17	2.28	120	.226	.257	22	.045	-3*	26	2	—	0.0
Total	12	139	90	.607	357	226	154-27	33	2112.1	1892	787	54	40	498	965	2.47	112	.241	.290	743-2-26	.210	23	120	75	—	11.0
WILTSE, HAL	Harold James "Whitey"; B8.6.1903 Clay City IL; D11.2.1983 Bunkie LA; BL/TL/5´9˝/168; d4.13																									
1926	Bos A	8	15	.348	37	29	9-1	0	196.1	201	112	6	6	99	59	4.22	97	.273	.363	59-0-4	.085	-5	79	-5	—	-0.9
1927	Bos A	10	18	.357	36	29	13-1	1	219	276	146	5	4	76	47	5.10	83	.321	.379	77-0-2	.208	-2	72	-20	—	-2.2
1928	Bos A	0	2	.000	2	2	1	0	12	16	12	1	3	1	5	9.00	46	.314	.364	4	.000	-1	62	-6	—	-0.7
	StL A	2	5	.286	26	5	0	0	72	93	49	4	3	35	23	5.25	80	.316	.395	22-0-1	.227	0	93	-8	—	-0.6
	Year	2	7	.222	28	7	1	0	84	109	61	5	6	36	28	5.79	72	.316	.390	26-0-1	.192	-1	84	-13	—	-1.3
1931	Phi N	0	0	ø	1	0	0	0	1	3	1	0	0	0	0	9.00	47	.600	.600	0	ø	0	—	0	—	0.0
Total	4	20	40	.333	102	65	23-2	1	500.1	589	320	16	16	211	134	4.87	85	.303	.375	162-0-7	.160	-7	76	-39	—	-4.4
WILTSE, SNAKE	Lewis De Witt; B12.5.1871 Bouckville NY; D8.25.1928 Harrisburg PA; BR/TL; d5.5; b–Hooks																									
1901	Pit N	1	4	.200	7	5	3	0	44.1	57	28	2	5	13	10	4.26	77	.310	.371	19-0-1	.158	-1	82	-4	—	-0.4
	Phi A	13	5	.722	19	19	18-2	0	166	185	91	1	7	35	40	3.58	105	.279	.322	67-0-2	.373	8	122	4	—	1.2
1902	Phi A	8	8	.500	19	17	13	1	138	182	99	7	5	41	28	5.15	71	.318	.368	57	.175	-0*	113	-17	—	-1.8
	Bal A	7	11	.389	19	18	18	0	164	215	127	4	8	51	37	5.10	74	.316	.371	132-2-2	.295	6*	122	-20	—	-1.3
	Year	15	19	.441	38	35	31	1	302	397	226	11	13	92	65	5.13	73	.317	.370	189-2-2	.259	5	118	-38	—	-3.1
1903	NY A	0	3	.000	4	3	2	1	25	35	17	1	1	6	6	5.40	58	.330	.372	9	.222	0	46	-5	—	-0.5
Total	3	29	31	.483	68	62	54-2	2	537.1	674	362	15	26	146	121	4.59	80	.305	.356	284-2-5	.278	13	113	-42	—	-2.8
WINCHELL, FRED	Frederick Russell (b Frederick Cook); B1.23.1882 Arlington MA; D8.8.1958 Toronto ON, Can.; TR/5´8˝/?; d9.16; Col Princeton																									
1909	Cle A	0	3	.000	4	3	0	1	14.1	16	11	0	0	2	7	6.28	41	.296	.321	5	.200	0	74	-5	—	-0.9
WINCHESTER, SCOTT	Scott Joseph; B4.20.1973 Midland MI; BR/TR/6´2˝/210; [CleA95 14/390]; d9.8; Col Clemson; [DL 1999 Cin N 183]																									
1997	Cin N	0	0	ø	5	0	0	0-0	6	9	5	1	1	2-0	3	6.00	71	.360	.429	0	ø	0	—	-1	0	-0.1
1998	Cin N	3	6	.333	16	16	1	0-0	79	101	56	12	4	27-2	40	5.81	74	.312	.370	23-0-2	.130	-1	80	-14	0	-1.4
2000	Cin N	0	0	ø	5	0	0	0-0	7.1	10	4	1	0	2-0	3	3.68	129	.313	.343	0	ø	0	—	1	0	0.0
2001	Cin N	0	2	.000	12	1	0	0-0	24	29	19	7	3	4-3	9	4.50	102	.315	.353	3	.000	-0	81	-2	31	-0.2
Total	4	3	8	.273	38	17	1	0-0	116.1	149	84	21	8	35-5	55	5.42	81	.315	.368	26-0-2	.115	-1	79	-16	214	-1.7
WINDSOR, JASON	Jason David; B7.16.1982 San Bernardino CA; BR/TR/6´2˝/235; [OakA04 3/97]; d7.17; Col Cal St.–Fullerton																									
2006	Oak A	0	1	.000	4	3	0	0-0	13.2	21	12	2	0	5-0	6	6.59	69	.375	.413	0	ø	0	104	-4	0	-0.2
WINEAPPLE, ED	Edward "Lefty"; B8.10.1905 Boston MA; D7.23.1996 Delray Beach FL; BL/TL/6´0˝/210; d9.15; Col Providence																									
1929	Was A	0	0	ø	1	0	0	0	4	7	4	0	0	3	1	4.50	94	.467	.556	2	.000	-0	—	-1	—	-0.1
WINEGARNER, RALPH	Ralph Lee; B10.29.1909 Benton KS; D4.14.1988 Wichita KS; BR/TR/6´0˝/182; d9.20.1930; C4; Col Southwestern (KS)																									
1932	Cle A	1	0	1.000	5	1	1	0	17.1	7	4	0	0	13	5	1.04	457	.123	.286	7	.143	-0*	108	6	—	0.2
1934	Cle A	5	4	.556	22	6	4	0	78.1	91	55	1	2	39	32	5.51	82	.289	.371	51-1-0	.196	1*	108	-8	—	-0.6
1935	Cle A	2	2	.500	25	4	2	0	67.1	89	51	10	1	29	41	5.75	78	.313	.379	84-3-1	.310	4*	135	-10	—	0.0
1936	Cle A	0	0	ø	9	0	0	0	14.2	18	9	0	0	6	3	4.91	103	.295	.358	16	.125	-1*	—	0	—	-0.1
1949	StL A	0	0	ø	9	0	0	0	16.2	24	16	2	0	2	8	7.56	60	.329	.347	5-1-0	.400	2	—	-5	0	-0.1
Total	5	8	6	.571	70	11	7	0	194.1	229	135	13	3	89	89	5.33	86	.290	.364	163-5-1	.252	5	117	-17	0	-0.6
WINFORD, JIM	James Head "Cowboy"; B10.9.1909 Shelbyville TN; D12.16.1970 Miami OK; BR/TR/6´1˝/180; d9.10																									
1932	StL N	1	1	.500	4	1	0	0	8.1	9	7	0	0	5	4	6.48	61	.273	.368	3	.667	1	86	-2	—	-0.3
1934	StL N	0	2	.000	5	1	0	0	12.2	17	13	0	2	6	3	7.82	54	.327	.417	1	.000	0	41	-5	—	-0.6
1935	StL N	0	0	ø	2	1	0	0	11.1	13	5	1	0	5	7	3.97	103	.283	.353	2-0-1	.000	-0	145	0	—	0.0
1936	StL N	11	10	.524	39	23	10-1	3	192	203	90	10	5	68	72	3.80	104	.269	.333	59	.085	-4	90	4	—	-0.2
1937	StL N	2	4	.333	16	4	0	0	46.1	56	31	2	0	27	17	5.83	68	.311	.401	8	.125	-1	70	-7	—	-0.9
1938	Bro N	0	1	.000	2	1	0	0	5.2	9	10	1	0	4	4	11.12	35	.346	.433	1	.000	0	87	-5	—	-0.7
Total	6	14	18	.438	68	31	10-1	3	276.1	307	156	14	7	115	107	4.56	87	.281	.353	74-0-1	.108	-3	87	-15	—	-2.7
WINGARD, ERNIE	Ernest James "Jim"; B10.17.1900 Prattville AL; D1.17.1977 Prattville AL; BL/TL/6´2˝/176; d5.1; Col Alabama																									
1924	StL A	13	12	.520	36	26	14	1	218	215	103	6	3	85	23	3.51	129	.262	.334	77-3-4	.234	2*	76	22	—	2.2
1925	StL A	9	10	.474	32	18	8	0	145	183	111	10	3	77	20	5.52	85	.319	.403	52-1-4	.288	3*	114	-15	—	-1.1
1926	StL A	5	8	.385	39	16	7	3	169	188	86	9	5	76	30	3.57	120	.290	.369	61-0-1	.230	1*	93	10	—	1.0
1927	StL A	2	13	.133	38	17	7	0	156.1	213	132	7	2	79	28	6.56	66	.340	.415	56-3-0	.179	2*	90	-34	—	-2.5
Total	4	29	43	.403	145	77	36	4	688.1	799	432	32	13	317	101	4.64	96	.299	.377	246-7-9	.232	7	92	-17	—	-0.4
WINGFIELD, TED	Frederick Davis; B8.7.1899 Bedford VA; D7.18.1975 Johnson City TN; BR/TR/5´11˝/168; d9.23																									
1923	Was A	0	0	ø	1	0	0	0	1	0	0	0	0	0	1	0.00	ø	.000	.000	0	ø	0	—	0	—	0.0
1924	Was A	0	0	ø	4	0	0	0	7	9	2	0	0	4	2	2.57	157	.300	.382	2	.000	-0	—	1	—	0.0
	Bos A	0	2	.000	4	3	2	0	25.2	23	12	0	0	8	4	2.45	178	.240	.298	9	.333	1	64	4	—	0.3
	Year	0	2	.000	8	3	2	0	32.2	32	14	0	0	12	6	2.48	173	.254	.319	11	.273	0	65	5	—	0.3
1925	Bos A	12	19	.387	41	27	18-2	2	254.1	267	149	11	8	92	30	3.96	115	.278	.346	94-1-5	.245	1	77	13	—	1.8
1926	Bos A	11	16	.407	43	20	9-1	3	190.2	220	119	11	2	50	30	4.44	92	.298	.344	69	.217	-0	64	-12	—	-1.4
1927	Bos A	1	7	.125	20	8	2	0	74.2	105	60	2	3	27	1	5.06	83	.357	.417	18	.222	0*	57	-11	—	-0.8
Total	5	24	44	.353	113	58	31-3	5	553.1	624	342	24	13	181	68	4.18	103	.294	.353	192-1-5	.234	1	70	-5	—	-0.1

YEAR	TM LG	W	L	PCT	G	GS	CG-SHO	SV-BS	IP	H	R	HR	HB	BB-IB	SO	ERA	AERA	OAV	OOB	AB-HR-SH	AVG	PB	SUP	APR	DL	PW
WINHAM, LAVE	Lafayette Sharkey "Lefty"; B10.23.1881 Brooklyn NY; D9.12.1951 Brooklyn NY; BL/TL/5´11˝/200; d4.21																									
1902	Bro N	0	0	ø	1	0	0	0	3	4	2	0	0	2	1	0.00	ø	.308	.400	2	.000	-0	—	0	—	0.0
1903	Pit N	3	1	.750	5	4	3-1	0	36	33	20	0	0	21	22	2.25	144	.231	.329	14	.071	-1	120	2	—	0.0
Total	2	3	1	.750	6	4	3-1	0	39	37	22	0	0	23	23	2.08	154	.237	.335	16	.063	-2	120	2	—	0.0
WINKELSAS, JOE	Joseph; B9.14.1973 Buffalo NY; BR/TR/6´3˝/188; d4.10; Col Elon																									
1999	Atl N	0	0	ø	1	0	0	0-0	0.1	4	2	0	0	1-1	0	54.00	8	1.000	1.000	0	ø	0	—	-2	0	-0.1
2006	Mil N	0	1	.000	7	0	0	0-0	7	9	7	1	0	6-0	4	7.71	58	.310	.429	0	ø	0	—	-3	0	-0.3
Total	2	0	1	.000	8	0	0	0-0	7.1	13	9	1	0	7-1	4	9.82	46	.394	.500	0	ø	0	—	-5	0	-0.4
WINN, GEORGE	George Benjamin "Breezy","Lefty"; B10.26.1897 Perry GA; D11.1.1969 Roberta GA; BL/TL/5´11˝/170; d4.29; Col Mercer																									
1919	Bos A	0	0	ø	3	0	0	0	4.2	6	4	0	0	1	0	7.71	39	.353	.389	1	.000	-0	—	-2	—	-0.1
1922	Cle A	1	2	.333	8	3	1	0	33.2	44	20	2	0	5	7	4.54	88	.317	.340	9	.333	1	78	-2	—	-0.1
1923	Cle A	0	0	ø	1	0	0	0	2	0	0	0	0	1	0	0.00	ø	.000	.143	0	ø	0	—	1	—	0.0
Total	3	1	2	.333	12	3	1	0	40.1	50	24	2	0	7	7	4.69	83	.309	.337	10	.300	1	78	-3	—	-0.2
WINN, JIM	James Francis; B9.23.1959 Stockton CA; BR/TR/6´3˝/(190–219); [PitN81 1/14]; d4.10; Col John Brown																									
1983	Pit N	0	0	ø	7	0	0	0-0	11	12	9	2	0	6-0	3	7.36	51	.267	.353	0	ø	0	—	-4	0	-0.2
1984	Pit N	1	0	1.000	9	0	0	1-0	18.2	19	8	2	0	9-1	11	3.86	94	.264	.346	1	.000	-0	—	0	0	0.0
1985	Pit N	3	6	.333	30	7	0	0-1	75.2	77	45	4	2	31-2	22	5.23	69	.266	.340	18-0-2	.111	-0	66	-12	0	-1.2
1986	Pit N	3	5	.375	50	3	0	3-4	88	85	44	9	2	38-7	70	3.58	109	.258	.335	16-0-1	.063	-1	69	1	0	0.1
1987	Chi A	4	6	.400	56	0	0	6-6	94	95	54	10	6	62-5	44	4.79	97	.271	.390	0	ø	0	—	-2	0	0.0
1988	Min A	1	0	1.000	9	0	0	0-0	21	33	15	4	0	10-1	9	6.00	68	.355	.417	0	ø	0	—	-4	17	-0.2
Total	6	12	17	.414	161	10	0	10-11	308.1	321	175	31	10	156-16	159	4.67	87	.272	.361	35-0-3	.086	-1	62	-21	17	-1.5
WINSTON, DARRIN	Darrin Alexander; B7.6.1966 Passaic NJ; BR/TL/6´0˝/195; [MonN88 18/466]; d9.10; Col Rutgers																									
1997	Phi N	2	0	1.000	7	1	0	0-0	12	8	8	4	2	3-1	8	5.25	80	.178	.260	2	.500	1	44	-2	0	-0.2
1998	Phi N	2	2	.500	27	0	0	1-1	25	31	18	7	2	6-0	11	6.12	71	.298	.348	1	.000	-0	—	-5	0	-0.7
Total	2	4	2	.667	34	1	0	1-1	37	39	26	11	4	9-1	19	5.84	73	.262	.321	3	.333	1	44	-7	0	-0.9
WINSTON, HANK	Henry Rudolph; B6.15.1904 Youngsville NC; D2.4.1974 Jacksonville FL; BL/TR/6´3.5˝/226; d9.30																									
1933	Phi A	0	0	ø	1	0	0	0	6.2	7	5	0	0	6	2	6.75	63	.280	.419	3	.000	-0	—	-1	—	-0.1
1936	Bro N	1	3	.250	14	0	0	0	32.1	40	27	2	1	16	8	6.12	67	.301	.380	11	.091	-1	—	-7	—	-0.8
Total	2	1	3	.250	15	0	0	0	39	47	32	2	1	22	10	6.23	67	.297	.387	14	.071	-1	—	-8	—	-0.9
WINTER, GEORGE	George Lovington "Sassafras"; B4.27.1878 New Providence PA; D5.26.1951 Franklin Lakes NJ; BR/TR/5´8˝/155; d6.15; Col Gettysburg																									
1901	Bos A	16	12	.571	28	28	26-1	0	241	234	127	4	4	66	63	2.80	126	.252	.304	100-1-0	.190	-4	101	15	—	1.0
1902	Bos A	11	9	.550	20	20	18	0	168.1	149	77	2	7	53	51	2.99	119	.238	.305	61	.164	-2	84	12	—	1.0
1903	Bos A	9	8	.529	24	19	14	0	178.1	182	92	4	7	37	64	3.08	99	.263	.307	66-0-2	.106	-4	117	-3	—	-0.8
1904	Bos A	8	4	.667	20	16	12-1	0	135.2	126	47	4	6	27	31	2.32	115	.247	.293	43-0-4	.116	-2*	133	6	—	0.2
1905	Bos A	16	17	.485	35	27	24-2	0	264.1	249	118	5	5	54	119	2.96	91	.251	.293	92	.261	3	100	-9	—	-0.7
1906	Bos A	6	18	.250	29	22	18-1	2	207.2	215	118	8	5	38	72	4.12	67	.270	.308	69-0-2	.246	2	94	-27	—	-2.8
1907	Bos A	12	15	.444	35	27	21-4	1	256.2	198	91	2	3	61	88	2.07	124	.215	.267	94-0-1	.223	1	90	12	—	1.4
1908	Bos A	4	14	.222	22	17	8	0	147.2	150	71	3	4	34	55	3.05	81	.274	.321	49	.184	-1	72	-9	—	-1.2
	†Det A	1	5	.167	7	6	5	1	56.1	49	19	0	3	7	25	1.60	151	.240	.276	18-0-2	.111	-1	57	4	—	0.3
	Year	5	19	.208	29	23	13	1	204	199	90	3	7	41	80	2.65	93	.265	.309	67-0-2	.164	-2	68	-5	—	-0.9
Total	8	83	102	.449	220	182	146-9	4	1656	1552	760	32	44	377	568	2.87	101	.250	.297	592-1-11	.193	-8	97	1	—	-1.6
WINTERS, CLARENCE	Clarence John; B9.7.1898 Detroit MI; D6.29.1945 Detroit MI; TR; d8.28																									
1924	Bos A	0	1	.000	4	2	0	0	7	22	16	0	0	4	3	20.57	21	.512	.553	3	.333	0	145	-11	—	-1.1
WINTERS, JESSE	Jesse Franklin "Buck","T-Bone"; B12.22.1893 Stephenville TX; D6.5.1986 Abilene TX; BR/TR/6´1˝/165; d5.3; Col Hardin–Simmons																									
1919	NY N	1	2	.333	16	2	0	3	28	39	18	1	3	13	6	5.46	51	.339	.420	3	.000	-0	128	-7	—	-1.0
1920	NY N	0	0	ø	21	0	0	0	46.1	37	19	1	4	28	14	3.50	86	.233	.361	7	.000	-1	—	-1	—	-0.1
1921	Phi N	5	10	.333	18	14	10	0	114	142	73	4	4	28	22	3.63	116	.310	.355	39-0-1	.128	-3	78	3	—	0.2
1922	Phi N	6	6	.500	34	9	4	2	138.1	176	100	8	4	56	29	5.33	87	.319	.386	43-0-2	.256	0	85	-7	—	-0.5
1923	Phi N	1	6	.143	21	6	1	1	78.1	116	76	7	4	39	23	7.35	63	.348	.423	25-0-1	.160	-1	80	-20	—	-1.6
Total	5	13	24	.351	110	31	15	6	405	510	286	21	19	164	94	5.04	83	.316	.385	117-0-4	.171	-5	85	-32	—	-3.0
WIRTH, ALAN	Alan Lee; B12.8.1956 Mesa AZ; BR/TR/6´4˝/190; [SFN74 3/67]; d4.9																									
1978	Oak A	5	6	.455	16	14	2-1	0-0	81.1	72	39	6	3	34-0	31	3.43	107	.252	.333	0	ø	0	61	1	0	0.1
1979	Oak A	1	0	1.000	5	1	0	0-0	12	14	8	2	1	8-0	7	6.00	68	.298	.404	0	ø	0	112	-2	0	-0.2
1980	Oak A	0	0	ø	2	0	0	0-0	2	3	1	0	0	0-0	1	4.50	85	.333	.333	0	ø	0	—	0	0	0.0
Total	3	6	6	.500	23	15	2-1	0-0	95.1	89	48	8	4	42-0	39	3.78	98	.260	.344	0	ø	0	65	-1	0	-0.1
WISE, ARCHIE	Archibald Edwin; B7.31.1912 Waxahachie TX; D2.2.1978 Dallas TX; BR/TR/6´0˝/165; d7.24																									
1932	Chi A	0	0	ø	2	0	0	0	7.1	8	5	1	1	5	2	4.91	88	.258	.378	4	.000	-1*	—	-1	—	-0.1
WISE, MATT	Matthew John; B11.18.1975 Montclair CA; BR/TR/6´4˝/(190–200); [AnaA97 6/177]; d8.2; Col Cal St.–Fullerton; [DL 2003 Ana A 183]																									
2000	Ana A	3	3	.500	8	6	0	0-0	37.1	40	23	7	1	13-1	20	5.54	93	.272	.331	0	ø	0	79	-1	0	-0.1
2001	Ana A	1	4	.200	11	9	0	0-0	49.1	47	27	11	2	18-1	50	4.38	106	.250	.321	0	ø	0	71	1	0	0.0
2002	Ana A	0	0	ø	7	0	0	0-0	8.1	7	3	0	1	1-0	6	3.24	138	.233	.281	0	ø	0	—	1	0	0.0
2004	Mil N	1	2	.333	30	3	0	0-0	52.2	51	27	3	2	15-1	30	4.44	99	.252	.308	4-0-1	.000	-0	49	1	0	0.0
2005	Mil N	4	4	.500	49	0	0	1-2	64.1	37	25	6	3	25-5	62	3.36	127	.160	.249	1	1.000	0	—	7	23	0.8
2006	Mil N	5	6	.455	40	0	0	0-4	44.1	45	24	6	2	14-2	27	3.86	116	.268	.330	1	.000	-0	—	2	49	0.3
Total	6	14	19	.424	145	18	0	1-6	256.1	227	129	33	11	86-10	195	4.18	109	.235	.303	6-0-1	.167	-0	74	11	255	1.0
WISE, RICK	Richard Charles; B9.13.1945 Jackson MI; BR/TR/6´2˝/(195–200); d4.18																									
1964	Phi N	5	3	.625	25	8	0	0	69	78	41	7	3	25-2	39	4.04	86	.277	.341	17-0-2	.294	2	136	-7	0	-0.6
1966	Phi N	5	6	.455	22	13	3	0	99.1	100	50	5	3	24-3	58	3.71	97	.262	.308	30-0-1	.000	-4*	100	-3	0	-0.8
1967	Phi N	11	11	.500	36	25	6-3	0	181.1	177	69	8	4	45-5	111	3.28	104	.259	.307	53-0-2	.208	3	79	6	0	1.0
1968	Phi N	9	15	.375	30	30	7-1	0	182.1	210	100	12	6	37-3	97	4.54	66	.292	.330	58-2-2	.241	7	79	-29	0	-2.9
1969	Phi N	15	13	.536	33	31	14-4	0-0	220	215	100	17	2	61-3	144	3.23	110	.257	.307	74-1-6	.270	7	114	3	0	1.2
1970	Phi N	13	14	.481	35	34	5-1	0-0	220.1	253	115	15	3	65-7	113	4.17	97	.287	.337	75-2-6	.200	4*	87	-6	0	-0.1
1971	Phi N☆	17	14	.548	38	37	17-4	0-0	272.1	261	110	20	4	70-5	155	2.88	124	.254	.301	97-6-4	.237	9*	78	15	0	2.8
1972	StL N	16	16	.500	35	35	20-2	0-0	269	250	98	16	1	71-13	142	3.11	110	.251	.299	93-1-6	.172	1	96	13	0	1.7
1973	StL N★	16	12	.571	35	34	14-5	0-0	259	259	113	18	3	59-12	144	3.37	109	.257	.300	88-3-6	.193	6	99	8	0	1.4
1974	Bos A	3	4	.429	9	9	1	0-0	49	47	23	2	1	16-1	25	3.86	100	.251	.308	0	ø	0	97	0	25	0.0
1975	†Bos A	19	12	.613	35	35	17-1	0-0	255.1	262	126	34	4	72-1	141	3.95	103	.263	.313	0	ø	0	117	3	0	0.2
1976	Bos A	14	11	.560	34	34	11-4	0-0	224.1	218	100	18	2	48-1	93	3.53	110	.255	.294	0	ø	0	97	9	0	1.0
1977	Bos A	11	5	.688	26	20	4-2	0-0	128.1	151	68	19	4	28-1	85	4.77	94	.291	.332	0	ø	0	107	-1	0	-0.1
1978	Cle A	9	19	.321	33	31	9-1	0-0	211.2	226	116	22	3	59-3	106	4.34	87	.275	.322	0	ø	0	84	-14	0	-1.7
1979	Cle A	15	10	.600	34	34	9-2	0-0	231.2	229	111	24	1	68-9	108	3.73	115	.256	.307	0	ø	0	94	12	0	1.4
1980	SD N	6	8	.429	27	27	1	0-0	154.1	172	69	14	0	37-10	59	3.67	93	.285	.325	58-0-2	.138	-1*	93	-5	26	-0.5
1981	SD N	4	8	.333	18	18	0	0-0	98	116	44	10	0	19-4	27	3.77	86	.296	.327	25-0-3	.040	-2	67	-6	0	-0.8
1982	SD N	0	0	ø	1	0	0	0-0	2	3	2	0	0	0-0	0	9.00	38	.333	.333	0	ø	0	—	-1	0	-0.1
Total	18	188	181	.509	506	455	138-30	0-0	3127.1	3227	1455	261	44	804-83	1647	3.69	101	.267	.313	668-15-40	.195	34	94	-3	51	3.1
WISE, OGDEN	Roy Ogden; B11.18.1925 Springfield IL; BB/TR/6´2˝/170; d5.12; Col Illinois Wesleyan																									
1944	Pit N	0	0	ø	2	0	0	0	3	4	3	0	0	3	1	9.00	41	.333	.467	0	ø	0	—	-1	0	-0.1
WISE, BILL	William E.; B3.15.1861 Washington DC; D5.5.1940 Washington DC; d5.2																									
1882	Bal AA	1	2	.333	3	3	3	0	26	30	14	1	—	4	9	2.77	99	.270	.296	20	.100	-1*	50	0	—	-0.1
1884	Was U	23	18	.561	50	41	34-4	0	364.1	383	219	5	—	60	268	3.04	79	.252	.281	339-2	.233	-2*	94	-23	—	-2.3
1886	Was N	0	1	.000	1	1	0	0	3	6	6	0	—	2	0	9.00	36	.400	.471	3	.000	-0	19	-2	—	-0.4
Total	3	24	21	.533	54	45	37-4	0	393.1	419	239	6	—	66	277	3.07	79	.255	.284	362-2	.224	-4	90	-25	—	-2.8

YEAR	TM LG	W	L	PCT	G	GS	CG-SHO	SV-BS	IP	H	R	HR	HB	BB-IB	SO	ERA	AERA	OAV	OOB	AB-HR-SH	AVG	PB	SUP	APR	DL	PW
WISNER, JACK	John Henry; B11.5.1899 Grand Rapids MI; D12.15.1981 Jackson MI; BR/TR/6´3˝/195; d9.12; Col Eastern Michigan																									
1919	Pit N	1	0	1.000	4	1	1	0	18.2	12	3	0	1	7	4	0.96	313	.185	.274	7	.000	-1	158	4	—	0.1
1920	Pit N	1	3	.250	17	2	1	0	44.2	46	19	1	1	10	13	3.43	94	.274	.318	7	.000	-1	49	0	—	-0.1
1925	NY N	0	0	ø	25	0	0	0	40.1	33	19	4	2	14	13	3.79	106	.228	.304	7	.000	-1	—	2	—	0.0
1926	NY N	2	2	.500	5	3	2	0	28	21	12	4	0	10	5	3.54	106	.208	.279	10	.200	-0	148	1	—	0.1
Total	4	4	5	.444	51	6	4	0	131.2	112	53	9	4	41	35	3.21	111	.234	.300	31	.065	-3	114	7	—	0.1
WISTERT, WHITEY	Francis Michael; B2.20.1912 Chicago IL; D4.23.1985 Painesville OH; BR/TR/6´4˝/210; d9.11; Col Michigan																									
1934	Cin N	0	1	.000	2	1	0	0	8	5	1	1	0	5	1	1.13	363	.185	.313	3	.000	-0*	0	3	—	0.3
WITASICK, JAY	Gerald Alphonse; B8.28.1972 Baltimore MD; BR/TR/6´4˝/(205–240); [StLN93 2/58]; d7.7; Col Maryland–Baltimore Co.																									
1996	Oak A	1	1	.500	12	0	0	0-1	13	12	9	5	0	5-0	12	6.23	80	.245	.309	0	ø	0	—	-2	0	-0.2
1997	Oak A	0	0	ø	8	0	0	0-0	11	14	7	2	0	6-0	8	5.73	80	.304	.385	0	ø	0	—	-1	74	-0.1
1998	Oak A	1	3	.250	7	3	0	0-0	27	36	24	9	0	15-1	29	6.33	73	.310	.389	0	ø	0	80	-6	0	-0.8
1999	KC A	9	12	.429	32	28	1-1	0-0	158.1	191	108	23	8	83-1	102	5.57	91	.304	.387	5	.000	-1	99	-9	0	-1.1
2000	KC A	3	8	.273	22	14	2	0-0	89.1	109	65	15	4	38-0	67	5.94	88	.301	.371	4	.000	-0	118	-8	0	-0.9
	SD N	3	2	.600	11	11	0	0-0	60.2	69	42	9	3	35-5	54	5.64	79	.284	.379	22-0-2	.136	-0	99	-8	0	-0.6
2001	SD N	5	2	.714	31	0	0	1-2	38.2	31	14	3	4	15-3	53	1.86	223	.218	.311	1	.000	-0	—	8	0	1.3
	†NY A	3	0	1.000	32	0	0	0-1	40.1	47	27	5	2	18-1	53	4.69	95	.283	.356	0	ø	0	—	-3	0	-0.2
2002	†SF N	1	0	1.000	44	0	0	0-0	68.1	58	19	3	4	21-3	54	2.37	167	.234	.303	5	.000	-1	—	13	20	0.5
2003	SD N	3	7	.300	46	0	0	2-5	45.2	42	24	6	1	25-4	42	4.53	88	.244	.342	0	ø	0	—	-3	71	-0.5
2004	SD N	0	1	.000	44	0	0	1-2	61.2	57	28	8	1	26-2	57	3.21	123	.244	.319	5	.000	-1	—	4	33	0.1
2005	Col N	0	4	.000	32	0	0	0-1	35.2	27	11	2	3	12-3	40	2.52	185	.209	.292	0	ø	0	—	8	0	0.8
	Oak A	1	1	.500	28	0	0	1-2	27.2	26	15	2	3	17-2	33	3.25	135	.239	.357	0	ø	0	—	2	0	0.1
2006	Oak A	1	0	1.000	20	0	0	0-0	22.2	25	17	3	1	21-2	23	6.75	67	.281	.423	0	ø	0	—	-5	102	-0.2
Total	11	31	41	.431	369	56	3-1	5-14	700	744	410	95	34	337-27	627	4.62	99	.272	.357	42-0-2	.071	-3	112	-10	300	-1.8
WITHEM, SHANNON	Shannon Bolt; B9.21.1972 Ann Arbor MI; BR/TR/6´3˝/185; [DetA90 5/130]; d9.18																									
1998	Tor A	0	0	ø	1	0	0	0-0	3	3	1	0	0	2-0	2	3.00	155	.250	.357	0	ø	0	—	1	0	0.0
WITHEROW, CHARLES	Charles Lafayette; B4.1852 Washington DC; D7.3.1948 Washington DC; d7.1																									
1875	Was NA	0	1	.000	1	1	0	0	1	4	5	0	—	0	0	18.00	13	.444	.444	1	.000	-0	30	-1	—	-0.2
WITHERUP, ROY	Foster Leroy; B7.26.1886 N.Washington PA; D12.23.1941 New Bethlehem PA; BR/TR/6´0˝/185; d5.14																									
1906	Bos N	0	3	.000	8	3	3	0	46	59	37	2	1	19	14	6.26	43	.322	.389	15	.133	-1	63	-15	—	-1.0
1908	Was A	2	4	.333	6	6	4	0	48.1	51	21	0	1	8	31	2.98	77	.264	.297	18	.167	-1	115	-3	—	-0.4
1909	Was A	1	5	.167	12	8	5	0	68	79	41	1	0	20	26	4.24	57	.306	.356	19-0-1	.053	-2	65	-12	—	-1.3
Total	3	3	12	.200	26	17	12	0	162.1	189	99	3	2	47	71	4.44	55	.298	.348	52-0-1	.115	-3	81	-30	—	-2.7
WITT, GEORGE	George Adrian "Red"; B11.9.1933 Long Beach CA; BR/TR/6´3˝/(185–200); d9.21																									
1957	Pit N	0	1	.000	1	1	0	0	1.1	4	6	1	0	5-0	1	40.50	9	.500	.692	0	ø	0	116	-5	0	-0.7
1958	Pit N	9	2	.818	18	15	5-3	0	106	78	22	2	2	59-3	81	1.61	240	.209	.318	39-0-1	.154	-1	93	27	0	2.5
1959	Pit N	0	7	.000	15	11	0	0	50.2	58	43	7	1	32-2	30	6.93	56	.293	.394	12-0-2	.000	-1	78	-17	32	-2.1
1960	†Pit N	1	2	.333	10	6	0	0	30	33	18	3	0	12-0	15	4.20	89	.300	.363	9	.000	-1	110	-3	0	-0.4
1961	Pit N	0	1	.000	9	1	0	0	15.2	17	12	5	0	5-0	9	6.32	63	.274	.328	2-0-1	.500	1	44	-4	48	-0.2
1962	LA A	1	1	.500	5	2	0	0	10	15	12	4	0	5-0	10	8.10	48	.349	.408	3	.333	0	139	-5	0	-0.9
	Hou N	0	2	.000	8	2	0	0	15.1	20	14	2	1	9-0	10	7.04	53	.339	.423	4	.250	0	23	-6	0	-0.6
Total	6	11	16	.407	66	38	5-3	0	229	225	127	24	4	127-5	156	4.32	89	.263	.359	69-0-4	.130	-2	89	-13	80	-2.4
WITT, MIKE	Michael Atwater; B7.20.1960 Fullerton CA; BR/TR/6´7˝/(185–203); [CalA78 4/92]; d4.11; [DL 1992 NY A 182]																									
1981	Cal A	8	9	.471	22	21	7-1	0-0	129	123	60	9	11	47-4	75	3.28	112	.251	.328	0	ø	0	111	3	0	0.3
1982	†Cal A	8	6	.571	33	26	5-1	0-0	179.2	177	77	8	7	47-2	85	3.51	117	.260	.312	0	ø	0	105	11	0	0.8
1983	Cal A	7	14	.333	43	19	2	5-3	154	173	90	14	6	75-7	77	4.91	82	.293	.375	0	ø	0	102	-14	0	-1.7
1984	Cal A	15	11	.577	34	34	9-2	0-0	246.2	227	103	17	5	84-3	196	3.47	115	.244	.308	0	ø	0	93	15	0	1.4
1985	Cal A	15	9	.625	35	35	6-1	0-0	250	228	115	22	4	98-6	180	3.56	116	.243	.316	0	ø	0	91	13	0	1.2
1986	†Cal A☆	18	10	.643	34	34	14-3	0-0	269	218	95	22	3	73-2	208	2.84	145	.221	.275	0	ø	0	115	38	0	3.8
1987	Cal A☆	16	14	.533	36	36	10	0-0	247	252	128	34	4	84-4	192	4.01	108	.261	.321	0	ø	0	93	7	0	0.7
1988	Cal A	13	16	.448	34	34	12-2	0-0	249.2	263	130	14	5	87-7	133	4.15	94	.272	.332	0	ø	0	91	-9	0	-0.9
1989	Cal A	9	15	.375	33	33	5	0-0	220	252	119	26	2	48-1	123	4.54	84	.292	.326	0	ø	0	99	-17	0	-1.5
1990	Cal A	0	3	.000	10	0	0	1-2	20.1	19	9	1	1	13-2	14	1.77	217	.250	.363	0	ø	0	—	3	0	0.4
	NY A	5	6	.455	16	16	2-1	0-0	96.2	87	53	8	4	34-2	60	4.47	89	.240	.308	0	ø	0	87	-5	59	-0.5
	Year	5	9	.357	26	16	2-1	1-2	117	106	62	9	5	47-4	74	4.00	99	.241	.318	0	ø	0	87	-1	0	-0.1
1991	NY A	0	1	.000	2	2	0	0-0	5.1	8	7	1	0	1-0	0	10.13	41	.320	.346	0	ø	0	88	-4	175	-0.5
1993	NY A	3	2	.600	9	9	0	0-0	41	39	26	7	3	22-0	30	5.27	79	.248	.352	0	ø	0	122	-5	144	-0.5
Total	12	117	116	.502	341	299	72-11	6-5	2108.1	2066	1012	183	55	713-40	1373	3.83	105	.257	.320	0	ø	0	99	36	560	3.0
WITT, BOBBY	Robert Andrew; B5.11.1964 Arlington MA; BR/TR/6´2˝/(200–215); [TexA85 1/3]; d4.10; Col Oklahoma																									
1986	Tex A	11	9	.550	31	31	0	0-0	157.2	130	104	18	3	143-2	174	5.48	79	.223	.374	0	ø	0	106	-18	0	-1.9
1987	Tex A	8	10	.444	26	25	1	0-0	143	114	82	10	3	140-1	160	4.91	92	.219	.385	1	.000	-0*	89	-3	30	-0.3
1988	Tex A	8	10	.444	22	22	13-2	0-0	174.1	134	83	13	1	101-2	148	3.92	105	.216	.324	0	ø	0	83	5	0	0.4
1989	Tex A	12	13	.480	31	31	5-1	0-0	194.1	182	123	14	2	114-3	166	5.14	78	.248	.347	0	ø	0	106	-23	0	-2.6
1990	Tex A	17	10	.630	33	32	7-1	0-0	222	197	98	12	4	110-3	221	3.36	117	.238	.328	0	ø	0*	99	12	0	1.3
1991	Tex A	3	7	.300	17	16	1-1	0-0	88.2	84	66	4	1	74-1	82	6.09	67	.254	.388	0	ø	0	120	-20	66	-2.0
1992	Tex A	9	13	.409	25	25	0	0-0	161.1	152	87	14	2	95-1	100	4.46	86	.254	.354	0	ø	0	93	-10	0	-1.3
	†Oak A	1	1	.500	6	6	0	0-0	31.2	31	12	2	0	19-1	25	3.41	111	.265	.362	0	ø	0	93	2	0	0.1
	Year	10	14	.417	31	31	0	0-0	193	183	99	16	2	114-2	125	4.29	89	.256	.356	0	ø	0	93	-8	0	-1.2
1993	Oak A	14	13	.519	35	33	5-1	0-0	220	226	112	16	3	91-5	131	4.21	98	.269	.340	0	ø	0	86	-3	0	-0.2
1994	Oak A	8	10	.444	24	24	5-3	0-0	135.2	151	88	22	5	70-4	111	5.04	89	.283	.367	0	ø	0*	102	-11	0	-1.2
1995	Fla N	2	7	.222	19	19	1	0-0	110.2	104	52	8	2	47-1	95	3.90	110	.251	.328	32-0-4	.063	-2*	74	5	0	0.2
	Tex A	3	4	.429	10	10	1	0-0	61.1	81	35	4	1	21-1	46	4.55	106	.324	.376	0	ø	0	67	1	0	0.1
1996	†Tex A	16	12	.571	33	32	2	0-0	199.2	235	129	28	2	96-3	157	5.41	97	.295	.370	0	ø	0	94	-3	0	-0.4
1997	Tex A	12	12	.500	34	32	3	0-0	209	245	118	33	2	74-4	121	4.82	101	.294	.350	6-1-0	.333	2*	93	3	0	0.4
1998	Tex A	5	4	.556	14	13	0	0-0	69.1	95	62	14	0	33-1	30	7.66	64	.328	.391	1	.000	-0*	142	-19	0	-2.0
	StL N	2	5	.286	17	5	0	0-0	47.1	55	32	7	2	20-1	28	4.94	85	.289	.362	10-0-1	.200	1	61	-5	0	-0.6
1999	TB A	7	15	.318	32	32	3-2	0-0	180.1	213	130	23	3	96-1	123	5.84	85	.304	.386	2	.000	-0	80	-16	0	-1.6
2000	Cle A	0	1	.000	7	2	0	0-0	15.1	28	13	4	0	6-1	6	7.63	66	.394	.442	0	ø	0	112	-4	0	-0.2
2001	†Ari N	4	1	.800	14	7	0	0-0	43.1	36	23	6	3	25-1	31	4.78	97	.222	.333	12-0-1	.250	0	108	0	120	0.0
Total	16	142	157	.475	430	397	47-11	0-0	2465	2493	1449	252	39	1375-37	1955	4.83	91	.265	.358	64-1-6	.141	0	95	-107	216	-11.8
WITTIG, JOHNNIE	John Carl "Hans"; B6.16.1914 Baltimore MD; D2.24.1999 Nassawadox VA; BR/TR/6´0˝/180; d8.4; Def 1944–45																									
1938	NY N	2	3	.400	13	6	2	0	39.1	41	22	4	0	26	14	4.81	78	.263	.368	10-0-1	.000	-1	90	-3	—	-0.6
1939	NY N	0	2	.000	5	2	1	0	16.2	18	15	0	1	14	4	7.56	52	.281	.418	5	.000	-1	56	-6	—	-0.7
1941	NY N	3	5	.375	25	9	0	0	85.1	111	57	5	1	45	47	5.59	66	.319	.398	25-0-1	.200	-0	61	-16	0	-1.4
1943	NY N	5	15	.250	40	22	4-1	4	164	172	85	14	0	76	56	4.23	82	.273	.352	51-0-2	.098	-3	81	-13	0	-2.1
1949	Bos A	0	0	ø	1	0	0	0	2	2	2	0	0	2	0	9.00	48	.286	.444	0	ø	0	—	-1	0	0.0
Total	5	10	25	.286	84	39	7-1	4	307.1	344	181	23	2	163	121	4.89	73	.286	.372	91-0-4	.110	-6	76	-39	0	-4.8
WOHLERS, MARK	Mark Edward; B1.23.1970 Holyoke MA; BR/TR/6´4˝/207; [AtlN88 8/190]; d8.17; [DL 1999 Cin N 171, 2003 Cle A 183]																									
1991	†Atl N	3	1	.750	17	0	0	2-2	19.2	17	7	1	2	13-3	13	3.20	121	.239	.368	1	.000	-0	—	2	0	0.4
1992	†Atl N	1	2	.333	32	0	0	4-2	35.1	28	11	0	1	14-4	17	2.55	144	.235	.319	2	.000	-0	—	4	0	0.4
1993	†Atl N	6	2	.750	46	0	0	0-0	48	37	25	2	1	22-3	45	4.50	90	.218	.309	0	ø	0	—	-2	0	-0.2
1994	Atl N	7	2	.778	51	0	0	1-1	51	51	35	1	0	33-9	58	4.59	94	.264	.362	1-0-1	1.000	0	—	-4	0	-0.6
1995	†Atl N	7	3	.700	65	0	0	25-4	64.2	51	16	2	1	24-3	90	2.09	207	.211	.285	3	.000	-0	—	16	0	3.1
1996	†Atl N★	2	4	.333	77	0	0	39-5	77.1	71	30	8	2	21-3	100	3.03	147	.240	.293	3	.000	-0	—	11	0	1.7
1997	†Atl N	5	7	.417	71	0	0	33-7	69.1	57	29	4	0	38-0	92	3.50	120	.224	.321	2	.000	-0	—	6	0	1.1

YEAR	TM LG	W	L	PCT	G	GS	CG-SHO	SV-BS	IP	H	R	HR	HB	BB-IB	SO	ERA	AERA	OAV	OOB	AB-HR-SH	AVG	PB	SUP	APR	DL	PW
1998	Atl N	0	1	.000	27	0	0	8-0	20.1	18	23	2	1	33-0	22	10.18	41	.231	.464	0	ø	0	—	-13	59	-1.4
1999	Atl N	0	0	ø	2	0	0	0-0	0.2	1	2	0	0	6-0	0	27.00	17	.333	.778	0	ø	0	—	-2	0	-0.1
2000	Cin N	1	2	.333	20	0	0	0-0	28	19	14	3	0	17-0	20	4.50	106	.192	.308	0	ø	0	—	1	0	0.1
2001	Cin N	3	1	.750	30	0	0	0-1	32	36	20	5	1	7-2	21	3.94	117	.286	.326	0	ø	0	—	0	0	0.0
	†NY A	1	0	1.000	31	0	0	0-0	35.2	33	20	3	1	18-0	33	4.54	98	.241	.329	0	ø	0	—	-1	0	0.0
2002	Cle A	3	4	.429	64	0	0	7-4	71.1	71	41	6	3	26-3	46	4.79	93	.261	.330	0	ø	0	—	-3	0	-0.3
Total	12	39	29	.574	533	0	0	119-26	553.1	490	273	37	13	272-30	557	3.97	108	.238	.328	12-0-1	.083	-1	—	15	413	4.2
WOJCIECHOWSKI, STEVE	Steven Joseph; B7.29.1970 Blue Island IL; BL/TL/6´2˝/(195–202); [OakA91 4/125]; d7.18; Col St. Xavier																									
1995	Oak A	2	3	.400	14	7	0	0-0	48.2	51	28	7	1	28-1	13	5.18	87	.273	.367	0	ø	0	106	-3	0	-0.2
1996	Oak A	5	5	.500	16	15	0	0-0	79.2	97	57	10	2	28-0	30	5.65	88	.300	.358	0	ø	0*	117	-8	0	-0.8
1997	Oak A	0	2	.000	2	2	0	0-0	10.1	17	9	2	0	1-0	5	7.84	59	.386	.400	0	ø	0	50	-3	72	-0.5
Total	3	7	10	.412	32	24	0	0-0	138.2	165	94	19	3	57-1	48	5.65	85	.298	.364	0	ø	0	109	-14	72	-1.5
WOJEY, PETE	Peter Paul; B12.1.1919 Stowe PA; D4.23.1991 Mobile AL; BR/TR/5´11˝/185; d7.2																									
1954	Bro N	1	1	.500	14	1	0	1	27.2	24	13	3	2	14	21	3.25	126	.242	.348	3-0-1	.000	-0	131	2	0	0.1
1956	Det A	0	0	ø	2	0	0	0	4	2	1	0	0	1-0	1	2.25	183	.167	.231	0	ø	0	—	1	0	0.1
1957	Det A	0	0	ø	2	0	0	0	1.1	1	0	0	0	0-0	0	0.00	ø	.200	.200	0	ø	0	—	1	0	0.0
Total	3	1	1	.500	18	1	0	1	33	27	14	3	2	15-0	22	3.00	136	.233	.331	3-0-1	.000	-0	131	4	0	0.2
WOJNA, ED	Edward David; B8.20.1960 Bridgeport CT; BR/TR/6´1˝/(185–187); [PhiN80 S5/77]; d6.16; Col Indian River (FL) CC																									
1985	SD N	2	4	.333	15	7	0	0-0	42	53	35	6	3	19-0	18	5.79	61	.312	.385	12	.167	-0	110	-13	0	-1.6
1986	SD N	2	2	.500	7	7	1	0-0	39	42	19	2	1	16-3	19	3.23	113	.268	.339	14-0-2	.143	-0	118	0	0	0.0
1987	SD N	0	3	.000	5	3	0	0-0	18.1	25	12	2	1	6-0	13	5.89	67	.333	.386	5	.000	-1	23	-3	0	-0.5
1989	Cle A	0	1	.000	9	3	0	0-0	33	31	17	0	0	14-1	10	4.09	97	.254	.328	0	ø	0	99	-1	0	0.0
Total	4	4	10	.286	36	20	1	0-0	132.1	151	83	10	5	55-4	60	4.62	81	.288	.358	31-0-2	.129	-1	97	-17	0	-2.1
WOLCOTT, BOB	Robert William; B9.8.1973 Huntington Beach CA; BR/TR/6´0˝/(190–195); [SeaA92 2/52]; d8.18																									
1995	†Sea A	3	2	.600	7	6	0	0-0	36.2	43	18	6	2	14-0	19	4.42	108	.297	.360	0	ø	0	107	2	0	0.2
1996	Sea A	7	10	.412	30	28	1	0-0	149.1	179	101	26	7	54-5	78	5.73	87	.297	.360	0	ø	0	110	-12	0	-1.1
1997	Sea A	5	6	.455	19	18	0	0-0	100	129	71	22	5	29-2	58	6.03	75	.314	.365	1	.000	-0	125	-16	0	-1.5
1998	Ari N	1	3	.250	6	6	0	0-0	33	32	27	7	0	13-1	21	7.09	60	.252	.321	9	.222	0	72	-9	0	-0.9
1999	Bos A	0	0	ø	4	0	0	0-0	6.2	8	6	1	1	3-0	2	8.10	62	.333	.414	0	ø	0	—	-2	0	-0.1
Total	5	16	21	.432	66	58	1	0-0	325.2	391	223	62	15	113-8	178	5.86	81	.298	.359	10	.200	0	110	-37	0	-3.4
WOLF, ERNIE	Ernest Adolf; B2.2.1889 Newark NJ; D5.23.1964 Atlantic Highlands NJ; BR/TR/5´11˝/174; d9.10																									
1912	Cle A	0	0	ø	1	0	0	0	5.2	8	6	0	0	4	1	6.35	54	.348	.444	2	.000	-0	—	-2	—	-0.1
WOLF, RANDY	Randall Christopher; B8.22.1976 Canoga Park CA; BL/TL/6´0˝/(194–205); [PhiN97 2/54]; d6.11; Col Pepperdine																									
1999	Phi N	6	9	.400	22	21	0	0-0	121.2	126	78	20	5	67-0	116	5.55	84	.266	.362	30-0-7	.233	1	99	-10	0	-0.9
2000	Phi N	11	9	.550	32	32	1	0-0	206.1	210	107	25	8	83-2	160	4.36	105	.269	.342	57-0-10	.193	2	86	6	0	0.6
2001	Phi N	10	11	.476	28	25	4-2	0-0	163	150	74	15	10	51-4	152	3.70	111	.248	.314	45-0-5	.178	1	91	7	30	0.9
2002	Phi N	11	9	.550	31	31	3-2	0-0	210.2	172	77	23	7	63-5	172	3.20	120	.223	.285	59-1-12	.136	2*	87	18	12	1.7
2003	Phi N★	16	10	.615	33	33	2-2	0-0	200	176	101	27	6	78-4	177	4.23	94	.233	.309	70-0-6	.200	5	129	-6	0	-0.2
2004	Phi N	5	8	.385	23	23	1-1	0-0	136.2	145	73	20	5	36-4	89	4.28	104	.271	.321	45-3-8	.267	5*	112	1	59	0.5
2005	Phi N	6	4	.600	13	13	0	0-0	80	87	40	14	6	26-2	61	4.39	99	.282	.348	26-0-1	.154	0*	104	1	113	0.1
2006	Phi N	4	0	1.000	12	12	0	0-0	56.2	63	37	13	2	33-2	44	5.56	84	.285	.378	21	.190	1*	131	-5	118	-0.2
Total	8	69	60	.535	194	190	11-7	0-0	1175	1129	587	157	49	437-23	971	4.21	101	.254	.325	353-4-49	.193	18	103	12	332	2.5
WOLF, WALLY	Walter Beck; B1.5.1942 Los Angeles CA; BR/TR/6´0.5˝/(189–191); d9.27; Col USC																									
1969	Cal A	0	0	ø	2	0	0	0-0	2.1	3	3	1	0	3-0	2	11.57	30	.333	.500	0	ø	0	—	-2	0	-0.1
1970	Cal A	0	0	ø	4	0	0	0-0	5.1	3	3	1	0	4-0	5	5.06	72	.176	.333	0	ø	0	—	-1	0	0.0
Total	2	0	0	ø	6	0	0	0-0	7.2	6	6	2	0	7-0	7	7.04	51	.231	.394	0	ø	0	—	-3	0	-0.1
WOLF, LEFTY	Walter Francis; B6.10.1900 Hartford CT; D9.25.1971 New Orleans LA; BR/TL/5´10˝/163; d7.4; Col Lebanon Valley																									
1921	Phi A	0	0	ø	8	0	0	0	15	15	15	0	2	16	11	7.20	62	.273	.452	4	.250	-0	—	-4	—	-0.2
WOLF, JIMMY	William Van Winkle "Chicken"; B5.12.1862 Louisville KY; D5.16.1903 Louisville KY; BR/TR/5´9˝/190; d5.2; M1; ▲																									
1882	Lou AA	0	0	ø	1	0	0	0	6	11	11	0	—	3	1	9.00	28	.367	.424	318	.299	0*	—	-4	—	-0.2
1885	Lou AA	0	0	ø	1	0	0	0	1	1	2	0	0	0	1	9.00	36	.200	.200	483-1	.292	0*	—	-1	—	0.0
1886	Lou AA	0	0	ø	1	0	0	0	3	7	8	0	0	0	0	15.00	24	.350	.350	545-3	.272	0*	—	-3	—	-0.1
Total	3	0	0	ø	3	0	0	0	10	19	21	0	0	3	2	10.80	27	.345	.379	1346-4	.285	1	—	-8	—	-0.3
WOLFE, CHUCK	Charles Hunt; B2.15.1897 Wolfsburg PA; D11.27.1957 Schellsburg PA; BL/TR/5´7˝/175; d8.2																									
1923	Phi A	0	0	ø	3	0	0	0	9.2	6	4	1	0	8	1	3.72	110	.194	.359	3	.333	0	—	1	—	0.0
WOLFE, ED	Edward Anthony; B1.2.1928 Los Angeles CA; BR/TR/6´3˝/185; d4.19																									
1952	Pit N	0	0	ø	3	0	0	0	3.2	7	3	1	1	5	1	7.36	54	.467	.619	0	ø	0	—	-1	0	0.0
WOLFE, BARNEY	Wilbert Otto; B1.9.1876 Independence (now Allenport) PA; D2.27.1953 N.Charleroi PA; BR/TR/6´1˝/?; d4.24																									
1903	NY A	6	9	.400	20	16	12-1	0	148.1	143	66	1	6	26	48	2.97	105	.253	.293	53-0-1	.075	-4	89	3	—	-0.2
1904	NY A	0	3	.000	7	3	2	0	33.2	31	18	1	2	4	8	3.21	85	.246	.280	10-0-1	.000	-1	44	-2	—	-0.3
	Was A	6	10	.375	17	16	13-2	0	126.2	131	64	0	11	22	44	3.27	81	.268	.314	42-0-2	.119	-2	82	-9	—	-1.3
	Year	6	13	.316	24	19	15-2	0	160.1	162	82	1	13	26	52	3.26	82	.263	.307	52-0-3	.096	-3	76	-10	—	-1.6
1905	Was A	9	14	.391	28	23	17-1	1	182	162	76	1	8	37	52	2.57	103	.240	.287	63-1-0	.127	-1	66	1	—	-0.2
1906	Was A	0	3	.000	4	3	2	0	20	17	11	0	2	10	8	4.05	65	.233	.341	7	.286	0	55	-3	—	-0.3
Total	4	21	39	.350	76	61	46-4	1	510.2	484	235	3	29	99	160	2.96	94	.251	.298	175-1-4	.109	-8	75	-10	—	-2.3
WOLFE, BILL	William Franklyn; B1.14.1876 PA; d9.10																									
1902	Phi N	0	1	.000	1	1	1	0	9	11	5	0	1	4	3	4.00	70	.297	.381	3	.333	0	24	-1	—	-0.1
WOLFF, ROGER	Roger Francis; B4.10.1911 Evansville IL; D3.23.1994 Chester IL; BR/TR/6´0.5˝/208; d9.20																									
1941	Phi A	0	2	.000	2	2	2	0	17	15	6	0	0	4	2	3.18	132	.231	.275	5	.200	-0	10	2	0	0.2
1942	Phi A	12	15	.444	32	25	15-2	3	214.1	206	99	16	3	69	94	3.32	114	.249	.309	68-0-4	.088	-3	72	8	0	0.7
1943	Phi A	10	15	.400	41	26	13-2	6	221	232	97	11	4	72	91	3.54	96	.274	.334	74-0-3	.122	-4	78	-2	0	-0.8
1944	Was A	4	15	.211	33	21	5	2	155	186	107	9	6	60	73	4.99	65	.295	.362	55-0-1	.218	1	101	-32	0	-3.4
1945	Was A	20	10	.667	33	29	21-4	2	250	200	68	7	1	53	108	2.12	146	.215	**.258**	84-0-5	.107	-5	101	31	0	3.3
1946	Was A	5	8	.385	21	17	6	0	122	115	51	8	5	30	50	2.58	130	.249	.302	39-0-2	.103	-1	113	7	0	0.6
1947	Cle A	0	0	ø	7	2	0	0	16	15	7	1	2	10	5	3.94	88	.259	.386	3-0-2	.000	-0	102	-1	0	0.0
	Pit N	1	4	.200	13	6	1	0	30	49	33	4	1	18	7	8.70	49	.368	.447	9	.000	-1	129	-14	0	-2.0
Total	7	52	69	.430	182	128	63-8	13	1025.1	1018	468	56	22	316	430	3.41	100	.258	.316	337-0-17	.122	-13	92	-1	0	-1.4
WOLFGANG, MELLIE	Meldon John "Red"; B3.20.1890 Albany NY; D6.30.1947 Albany NY; BR/TR/5´9˝/160; d4.18																									
1914	Chi A	9	5	.643	24	11	9-2	0	119.1	96	42	0	0	32	50	1.89	142	.219	.272	40-0-2	.175	-0	79	9	—	1.3
1915	Chi A	2	2	.500	17	2	0	0	53.2	39	18	0	1	12	21	1.84	161	.211	.263	17-0-1	.118	-1	98	5	—	0.2
1916	Chi A	4	6	.400	27	14	6-1	0	127	103	39	2	2	42	36	1.98	139	.228	.296	40-0-2	.225	0*	90	11	—	0.9
1917	Chi A	0	0	ø	5	0	0	0	17.2	18	10	1	1	6	3	5.09	52	.305	.379	4	.000	-1	—	-3	—	-0.3
1918	Chi A	0	1	.000	4	0	0	0	8.1	12	6	0	0	3	1	5.40	51	.333	.385	2	.500	0*	—	-2	—	-0.2
Total	5	15	14	.517	77	27	15-3	0	326	268	115	3	4	95	111	2.18	127	.229	.289	103-0-5	.184	-1	85	20	—	1.9
WOLTER, HARRY	Harry Meiggs; B7.11.1884 Monterey CA; D7.6.1970 Palo Alto CA; BL/TR/5´10˝/175; d5.14; Col Santa Clara; ▲																									
1907	Pit N	0	0	ø	1	0	0	0	2	3	2	0	0	2	0	4.50	54	.333	.455	1	.000	-0	—	-1	—	-0.1
	StL N	0	2	.000	3	3	1	0	23	27	13	1	2	18	8	4.30	58	.318	.448	47	.340	1*	104	-3	—	-0.2
	Year	0	2	.000	4	3	1	0	25	30	15	1	2	20	8	4.32	58	.319	.448	48	.333	1	105	0	—	-0.3
1909	Bos A	4	4	.500	11	6	0	0	59	66	33	0	4	30	21	3.51	71	.303	.397	121-2-5	.240	2*	94	-7	—	-0.8
Total	2	4	6	.400	15	9	1	0	84	96	48	1	6	50	29	3.75	67	.308	.413	169-2-5	.266	3	97	-11	—	-1.1

YEAR	TM LG	W	L	PCT	G	GS	CG-SHO	SV-BS	IP	H	R	HR	HB	BB-IB	SO	ERA	AERA	OAV	OOB	AB-HR-SH	AVG	PB	SUP	APR	DL	PW
WOLTERS, RYNIE	Reinder Albertus; B3.17.1842 Schantz, Netherlands; D1.3.1917 Newark NJ; TR/6´0˝/165; d5.18																									
1871	Mut NA	16	16	.500	**32**	**32**	**31-1**	0	**283**	345	283	7	—	39	22	3.43	110	**.263**	.285	138	.370	20	97	12	—	2.0
1872	Cle NA	3	6	.333	12	8	5	0	75.1	115	106	3	—	7	4	6.09	59	.304	.317	69	.232	-1*	89	-23	—	-1.7
1873	Res NA	0	1	.000	1	1	1	0	9	13	23	0	—	1	1	0.00	ø	.220	.233	4	.000	-1	53	1	—	0.0
Total	3NA	19	23	.452	45	41	37-1	0	367.1	473	412	10	—	47	27	3.90	96	.271	.290	211	.318	19	94	-10	—	0.3
WOMACK, DOOLEY	Horace Guy; B8.25.1939 Columbia SC; BL/TR/6´0˝/170; d4.14																									
1966	NY A	7	3	.700	42	1	0	4	75	52	25	6	3	23-3	50	2.64	126	.198	.270	5	.200	0	53	6	0	1.0
1967	NY A	5	6	.455	65	0	0	18	97	80	33	6	3	35-14	57	2.41	130	.230	.300	14	.286	1	—	7	0	1.4
1968	NY A	3	7	.300	45	0	0	2	61.2	53	23	6	1	29-9	27	3.21	91	.244	.335	5	.200	0	—	-1	0	0.0
1969	Hou N	2	1	.667	30	0	0	0-1	51.1	49	21	1	3	20-5	32	3.51	101	.259	.338	6-0-1	.167	-0	—	1	0	0.2
	Sea A	2	1	.667	9	0	0	0-0	14.1	15	4	0	0	3-2	8	2.51	145	.273	.310	1	.000	-0	—	2	0	0.4
1970	Oak A	0	0	ø	2	0	0	0-0	3	4	5	2	0	1-0	3	15.00	24	.308	.357	0	ø	0	—	-4	0	-0.2
Total	5	19	18	.514	193	1	0	24-1	302.1	253	111	21	10	111-33	177	2.95	110	.233	.308	31-0-1	.226	1	53	11	0	2.8
WOOD, SPADES	Charles Asher; B1.13.1909 Spartanburg SC; D5.18.1986 Wichita KS; BL/TL/5´10.5˝/150; d8.16; Col Wofford																									
1930	Pit N	4	3	.571	9	7	4-2	0	58	61	34	4	0	32	23	5.12	97	.270	.360	20-0-2	.250	1	105	1	—	0.1
1931	Pit N	2	6	.250	15	10	2	0	64	69	45	2	1	46	33	6.05	64	.273	.387	22-0-1	.227	1	96	-13	—	-1.3
Total	2	6	9	.400	24	17	6-2	0	122	130	79	6	1	78	56	5.61	78	.271	.375	42-0-3	.238	1	99	-12	—	-1.2
WOOD, GEORGE	George A. "Dandy"; B11.9.1858 Boston MA; D4.4.1924 Harrisburg PA; BL/TR/5´10.5˝/175; d5.1.1880; M1/U1; ▲																									
1883	Det N	0	0	ø	1	0	0	0	5	8	9	0	—	3	0	7.20	43	.348	.423	441-5	.302	0*	—	-3	—	-0.1
1885	Det N	0	0	ø	1	0	0	0	4	5	2	0	—	1	1	0.00	ø	.333	.375	362-5	.290	0*	—	1	—	0.0
1888	Phi N	0	0	ø	2	0	0	**2**	2	3	3	0	0	1	0	4.50	66	.300	.364	433-6	.229	0*	—	-1	—	-0.1
1889	Phi N	0	0	ø	1	0	0	0	1	2	2	0	0	0	2	18.00	24	.400	.400	422-5	.251	0*	—	-1	—	0.0
Total	4	0	0	ø	5	0	0	2	12	18	16	0	0	5	3	5.25	59	.340	.397	1658-21	.267	1	—	-4	—	-0.2
WOOD, JOE	Joe "Smoky Joe" (b Howard Ellsworth Wood); B10.25.1889 Kansas City MO; D7.27.1985 West Haven CT; BR/TR/5´11˝/180; d8.24; s–Joe; ▲																									
1908	Bos A	1	1	.500	6	2	1-1	0	22.2	14	12	0	1	16	11	2.38	103	.161	.298	7	.000	-1	125	-1	—	-0.2
1909	Bos A	11	7	.611	24	19	13-4	0	160.2	121	51	1	6	43	88	2.18	114	.209	.270	55-0-1	.164	-0	93	7	—	0.5
1910	Bos A	12	13	.480	35	17	14-3	0	196.2	155	81	3	10	56	145	1.69	151	.220	.287	69-1-3	.261	5	93	9	—	1.9
1911	Bos A	23	17	.575	44	33	25-5	3	275.2	226	113	2	11	76	231	2.02	162	.223	.284	88-2-6	.261	9	105	34	—	**5.7**
1912	†Bos A	**34**	5	**.872**	43	38	**35-10**	1	344	267	104	2	12	82	258	1.91	178	.216	.272	124-1-6	.290	11	122	53	—	7.6
1913	Bos A	11	5	.688	23	18	12-1	2	145.2	120	54	0	8	61	123	2.29	129	.232	.323	56-0-1	.268	4*	148	9	—	1.8
1914	Bos A	10	3	.769	18	14	11-1	0	113.1	94	38	1	0	34	67	2.62	103	.229	.288	43-0-1	.140	-0*	110	3	—	0.4
1915	Bos A	15	5	**.750**	25	16	10-3	2	157.1	120	32	1	1	44	63	**1.49**	187	.216	.275	54-1-5	.259	4*	116	25	—	3.9
1917	Cle A	0	1	.000	5	1	0	1	15.2	17	7	0	0	7	2	3.45	82	.309	.387	6	.000	-1*	76	-1	—	-0.1
1919	Cle A	0	0	ø	1	0	0	1	0.2	0	0	0	0	0	0	0.00	ø	.000	.000	192-0-9	.255	0*	—	0	—	0.1
1920	†Cle A	0	0	ø	1	0	0	0	2	4	5	0	0	2	1	22.50	17	.444	.545	137-1-12	.270	0*	—	-4	—	-0.2
Total	11	117	57	.672	225	158	121-28	10	1434.1	1138	497	10	49	421	989	2.03	146	.220	.285	831-6-44	.249	31	114	134	—	21.4
WOOD, JOE	Joe Frank; B5.20.1916 Shohola PA; D10.10.2002 Old Saybrook CT; BR/TR/6´0˝/190; d5.1; f–Joe; Col Yale																									
1944	Bos A	0	1	.000	3	1	0	0	9.2	13	9	0	0	3	5	6.52	52	.317	.364	2	.000	-0	25	-4	0	-0.4
WOOD, JOHN	John B.; B5.1872 Harrisburg PA; D1.30.1929 Philadelphia PA; 5´7˝/142; d5.9																									
1896	StL N	0	0	ø	1	0	0	0	0	1	1	0	1	2	0	(1)	ø	1.000	1.000	0	ø	0	—	-1	—	-0.1
WOOD, KERRY	Kerry Lee; B6.16.1977 Irving TX; BR/TR/6´5˝/(220–230); [ChiN95 1/4]; d4.12; [DL 1999 Chi N 182]																									
1998	†Chi N	13	6	.684	26	26	1-1	0-0	166.2	117	69	14	11	85-1	233	3.40	129	**.196**	.306	54-2-8	.130	-0	111	17	0	1.7
2000	Chi N	8	7	.533	23	23	1	0-0	137	112	77	17	9	87-0	132	4.80	95	.226	.349	40-1-4	.250	3*	96	-3	55	0.0
2001	Chi N	12	6	.667	28	28	1-1	0-0	174.1	127	70	16	10	92-3	217	3.36	125	**.202**	.311	48-0-13	.188	1*	92	17	34	1.7
2002	Chi N	12	11	.522	33	33	4-1	0-0	213.2	169	92	22	16	97-5	217	3.66	111	.221	.320	72-1-6	.167	1	114	11	0	1.1
2003	†Chi N★	14	11	.560	32	32	4-2	0-0	211	152	77	24	21	100-2	**266**	3.20	136	.203	.312	61-2-8	.164	1	98	29	0	3.3
2004	Chi N	8	9	.471	22	22	0	0-0	140.1	127	62	16	11	51-0	144	3.72	119	.244	.321	45-1-5	.133	0	88	11	60	1.1
2005	Chi N	3	4	.429	21	10	0	0-0	66	52	32	14	2	26-0	77	4.23	103	.215	.295	18-0-2	.111	0	101	1	108	0.1
2006	Chi N	1	2	.333	4	4	0	0-0	19.2	19	13	5	1	8-0	13	4.12	111	.253	.326	6	.500	1	75	0	162	0.1
Total	8	71	56	.559	189	178	11-5	0-0	1128.2	875	492	128	81	546-11	1299	3.68	118	.215	.317	344-7-46	.172	7	100	83	601	9.1
WOOD, MIKE	Michael Burton; B4.26.1980 West Palm Beach FL; BR/TR/6´3˝/(190–220); [OakA01 10/311]; d8.21; Col North Florida																									
2003	Oak A	2	1	.667	7	1	0	0-0	13.2	24	17	1	2	7-2	15	10.54	44	.387	.465	0	ø	0	60	-9	0	-1.4
2004	KC A	3	8	.273	17	17	0	0-0	100	112	67	16	6	28-3	54	5.94	79	.286	.342	2	.000	-0	77	-11	0	-1.0
2005	KC A	5	8	.385	47	10	0	2-0	115	129	66	18	8	52-5	60	4.46	98	.287	.367	0	ø	0	97	-3	0	-0.3
2006	KC A	3	3	.500	23	7	0	0-0	64.2	86	51	10	7	23-3	29	5.71	82	.314	.379	3	.000	-0	95	-10	64	-0.8
Total	4	13	20	.394	94	35	0	2-0	293.1	351	201	45	23	110-13	158	5.52	82	.298	.367	5	.000	-1	86	-33	64	-3.5
WOOD, PETE	Peter Burke; B2.1.1857 Dundas ON, Can.; D3.15.1923 Chicago IL; TR/5´7˝/185; d7.15; b–Fred																									
1885	Buf N	8	15	.348	24	22	21	0	198.2	235	170	8	—	66	38	4.44	67	.280	.332	104	.221	-1*	102	-32	—	-3.1
1889	Phi N	1	1	.500	3	2	2	0	19	28	15	0	0	3	8	5.21	83	.333	.356	8	.000	-1	147	-1	—	-0.2
Total	2	9	16	.360	27	24	23	0	217.2	263	185	8	0	69	46	4.51	69	.285	.334	112	.205	-2	106	-33	—	-3.3
WOOD, WILBUR	Wilbur Forrester; B10.22.1941 Cambridge MA; BR/TL/6´0˝/(180–200); d6.30																									
1961	Bos A	0	0	ø	6	1	0	0	13	14	8	2	0	7-0	7	5.54	75	.269	.350	3	.000	-0	170	-1	0	-0.1
1962	Bos A	0	0	ø	1	1	0	0	7.2	6	3	0	0	3-0	3	3.52	117	.214	.290	3	.000	-0	65	1	0	0.0
1963	Bos A	0	5	.000	25	6	0	0	64.2	67	35	10	3	13-1	28	3.76	101	.270	.311	12-0-1	.000	-1	78	-2	0	-0.3
1964	Bos A	0	0	ø	4	0	0	0	5.2	13	11	1	0	3-2	5	17.47	22	.433	.485	1	.000	-0	—	-8	0	-0.4
	Pit N	0	2	.000	3	2	1	0	17.1	16	8	0	2	11-3	7	3.63	97	.246	.367	5-0-1	.000	-0	50	0	0	-0.1
1965	Pit N	1	1	.500	34	1	0	0	51.1	44	21	3	1	16-3	29	3.16	111	.237	.298	6	.000	-1	50	2	0	0.0
1967	Chi A	4	2	.667	51	8	0	4	95.1	95	34	2	1	28-4	47	2.45	126	.260	.312	16	.063	-0	91	6	0	0.4
1968	Chi A	13	12	.520	**88**	2	0	16	159	127	39	8	3	33-12	74	1.87	162	.222	.266	22-0-2	.091	-1	173	**20**	0	3.8
1969	Chi A	10	11	.476	**76**	0	0	15-7	119.2	113	48	13	3	40-15	73	3.01	128	.248	.311	15-0-2	.000	-1	—	8	0	1.5
1970	Chi A	9	13	.409	**77**	0	0	21-6	121.2	118	50	7	2	36-7	85	2.81	138	.258	.312	18-0-2	.111	-1	—	11	0	2.3
1971	Chi A☆	22	13	.629	44	42	22-7	1-0	334	272	95	21	7	62-2	210	1.91	**186**	.222	.263	96-0-17	.052	-5	92	**55**	0	**5.7**
1972	Chi A★	**24**	17	.585	49	**49**	20-8	0-0	**376.2**	325	119	28	7	74-5	193	2.51	125	.235	.276	125-0-13	.136	-2	103	25	0	2.8
1973	Chi A	**24**	20	.545	49	**48**	21-4	0-0	**359.1**	381	166	25	7	91-3	199	3.46	114	.270	.315	0	ø	0	99	15	0	1.8
1974	Chi A☆	20	19	.513	42	**42**	22-1	0-0	320.1	305	143	27	9	80-8	169	3.60	104	.254	.303	0	ø	0	105	6	0	0.8
1975	Chi A	16	20	.444	43	**43**	14-2	0-0	291.1	309	148	26	5	92-5	140	4.11	95	.272	.328	0	ø	0	98	-7	0	-0.7
1976	Chi A	4	3	.571	7	7	5-1	0-0	56.1	51	24	3	0	11-0	31	2.24	160	.242	.278	0	ø	0	91	4	145	0.6
1977	Chi A	7	8	.467	24	18	5-1	0-0	122.2	139	75	10	10	50-0	42	4.99	82	.293	.371	0	ø	0	82	-12	22	-1.1
1978	Chi A	10	10	.500	28	27	4	0-0	168	187	103	23	3	74-1	69	5.20	73	.285	.357	0	ø	0	106	-24	0	-2.4
Total	17	164	156	.512	651	297	114-24	57-13	2684	2582	1130	209	63	724-71	1411	3.24	112	.254	.306	322-0-38	.084	-13	99	99	167	14.6
WOODALL, BRAD	David Bradley; B6.25.1969 Atlanta GA; BB/TL/6´0˝/(175–181); d7.22; Col North Carolina																									
1994	Atl N	0	1	.000	1	1	0	0-0	6	5	3	2	0	2-0	2	4.50	96	.227	.292	2	.500	0	42	0	0	0.1
1995	Atl N	1	1	.500	9	0	0	0-0	10.1	13	10	1	0	8-1	5	6.10	71	.310	.412	1	1.000	0	—	-3	0	-0.5
1996	Atl N	2	2	.500	8	3	0	0-0	19.2	28	19	4	0	4-0	20	7.32	61	.333	.356	5	.200	0	128	-6	0	-1.0
1998	Mil N	7	9	.438	31	20	0	0-0	138	145	81	25	6	47-4	85	4.96	88	.273	.337	38-1-5	.237	3*	114	-8	0	-0.5
1999	Chi N	0	1	.000	6	3	0	0-0	16	17	12	5	1	6-0	7	5.63	81	.270	.338	2	.500	1	114	-2	0	0.0
Total	5	10	14	.417	55	27	0	0-0	190	208	125	37	7	67-5	119	5.31	82	.280	.343	48-1-5	.271	5	113	-19	0	-1.9
WOODARD, STEVE	Steven Larry; B5.15.1975 Hartselle AL; BL/TR/6´4˝/(217–236); [MilA94 5/123]; d7.28																									
1997	Mil A	3	3	.500	7	7	0	0-0	36.2	39	25	5	2	6-0	32	5.15	90	.269	.307	0	ø	0	60	-3	32	-0.4
1998	Mil N	10	12	.455	34	26	0	0-0	165.2	170	83	19	9	33-4	135	4.18	104	.264	.307	50-0-2	.140	-1	64	3	0	0.2
1999	Mil N	11	8	.579	31	29	2	0-0	185	219	101	23	6	36-7	119	4.52	102	.294	.330	53-0-10	.132	0	103	2	29	0.1
2000	Mil N	1	7	.125	27	11	1	0-0	93.2	125	70	16	4	33-4	65	5.96	78	.325	.381	22-0-2	.045	-1	90	-15	0	-1.2
	Cle A	3	3	.500	13	11	0	0-0	54	57	35	10	2	11-1	35	5.67	88	.269	.310	0	ø	0	126	-3	0	-0.3
2001	Cle A	3	3	.500	29	10	0	0-0	97	129	60	10	5	17-1	52	5.20	88	.325	.358	1	.000	-0	99	-6	20	-0.3

YEAR	TM LG	W	L	PCT	G	GS	CG-SHO	SV-BS	IP	H	R	HR	HB	BB-IB	SO	ERA	AERA	OAV	OOB	AB-HR-SH	AVG	PB	SUP	APR	DL	PW
2002	Tex A	0	0	ø	14	0	0	0-1	17.2	20	13	4	2	8-1	14	6.62	72	.274	.361	0	ø	0	—	-3	0	-0.1
2003	Bos A	1	0	1.000	7	0	0	0-0	17.2	23	10	3	1	5-2	12	5.09	92	.311	.358	0	ø	0	—	0	0	0.0
Total	7	32	36	.471	162	94	3	0-1	667.1	782	397	90	31	149-20	464	4.94	93	.292	.335	126-0-14	.119	-2	90	-25	81	-2.0
WOODBURN, GENE	Eugene Stewart; B8.20.1886 Bellaire OH; D1.18.1961 Sandusky OH; BR/TR/6´0˝/175; d7.27																									
1911	StL N	1	5	.167	11	6	1	0	38.1	22	32	0	6	40	23	5.40	63	.167	.382	6-0-1	.167	1	82	-10	—	-1.1
1912	StL N	1	4	.200	20	5	1	0	48.1	60	48	0	4	42	25	5.59	61	.306	.438	13	.000	-2	68	-13	—	-1.4
Total	2	2	9	.182	31	11	2	0	86.2	82	80	0	10	82	48	5.50	62	.250	.414	19-0-1	.053	-0	75	-23	—	-2.5
WOODCOCK, FRED	Fred Wayland; B5.17.1868 Winchendon MA; D8.11.1943 Ashburnham MA; BL/TL/6´2˝/190; d5.17; Col Brown																									
1892	Pit N	1	2	.333	5	4	3	0	33	42	28	1	2	17	8	3.55	93	.298	.381	15	.200	0	110	-3	—	-0.2
WOODEND, GEORGE	George Anthony; B12.9.1917 Hartford CT; D2.6.1980 Hartford CT; BR/TR/6´0˝/200; d4.22																									
1944	Bos N	0	0	ø	3	0	0	0	2	5	4	0	0	5	0	13.50	28	.556	.714	0	ø	0	—	-2	0	-0.1
WOODESHICK, HAL	Harold Joseph; B8.24.1932 Wilkes–Barre PA; BR/TL/6´3˝/200; d9.14																									
1956	Det A	0	2	.000	2	2	0	0	5.1	12	8	1	0	3-0	1	13.50	30	.444	.500	0	ø	0	130	-5	0	-0.8
1958	Cle A	6	6	.500	14	9	3	0	71.2	71	32	4	6	25-0	27	3.64	100	.265	.341	24	.167	-1	99	0	0	0.1
1959	Was A	2	4	.333	31	3	0	0	61	58	39	2	1	36-8	30	3.69	106	.253	.352	8	.000	-1*	38	-3	0	-0.3
1960	Was A	4	5	.444	41	14	1	4	115	131	67	7	3	60-3	46	4.70	83	.289	.375	29-0-6	.069	-2	126	-9	0	-0.8
1961	Was A	3	2	.600	7	6	1	0	40.1	38	19	3	3	24-0	24	4.02	100	.257	.369	16	.125	-1	99	1	0	0.1
	Det A	1	1	.500	12	2	0	0	18.1	25	17	3	0	17-1	13	7.85	52	.316	.438	4	.000	-0	65	-7	0	-0.6
	Year	4	3	.571	19	8	1	0	58.2	63	36	6	3	41-1	37	5.22	77	.278	.393	20	.100	-1	90	-7	0	-0.5
1962	Hou N	5	16	.238	31	26	2-1	0	139.1	161	84	3	3	54-1	82	4.39	85	.290	.352	37-0-3	.081	-1	72	-13	0	-1.8
1963	Hou N★	11	9	.550	55	0	0	10	114	75	29	3	6	42-6	94	1.97	160	.186	.269	23	.130	-0	—	16	0	3.2
1964	Hou N	2	9	.182	61	0	0	**23**	78.1	73	32	3	7	32-11	58	2.76	124	.249	.336	10-0-1	.000	-0	—	4	0	0.9
1965	Hou N	3	4	.429	27	0	0	3	32.1	27	13	3	0	18-5	22	3.06	110	.227	.328	6-0-1	.167	-0	—	1	0	0.2
	StL N	3	2	.600	51	0	0	15	59.2	47	14	1	2	27-11	37	1.81	212	.221	.314	8	.000	-1	—	12	0	1.8
	Year	6	6	.500	78	0	0	18	92	74	27	4	2	45-16	59	2.25	163	.223	.319	14-0-1	.071	-1	—	13	0	2.0
1966	StL N	2	1	.667	59	0	0	4	70.1	57	17	5	1	23-6	30	1.92	187	.224	.289	5	.200	0	—	13	0	0.9
1967	†StL N	2	1	.667	36	0	0	2	41.2	41	29	2	3	28-9	20	5.18	63	.252	.367	4	.000	-0	—	-10	0	-0.8
Total	11	44	62	.415	427	62	7-1	61	847.1	816	400	40	35	389-61	484	3.56	102	.254	.339	174-0-11	.092	-7	95	0	0	2.1
WOODMAN, DAN	Daniel Courtenay "Cocoa"; B7.8.1893 Danvers MA; D12.14.1962 Danvers MA; BR/TR/5´8˝/160; d7.10																									
1914	Buf F	0	0	ø	13	0	0	1	33.2	30	16	0	1	11	13	2.41	123	.246	.313	7	.143	-0	—	0	—	-0.1
1915	Buf F	0	0	ø	5	1	0	0	15.1	14	9	0	0	9	1	4.11	68	.246	.348	4	.250	-0*	125	-2	—	-0.1
Total	2	0	0	ø	18	1	0	1	49	44	25	0	1	20	14	2.94	99	.246	.325	11	.182	-0	125	-2	—	-0.2
WOODS, CLARENCE	Clarence Cofield; B6.11.1892 Woods Ridge (Ohio Co.) IN; D7.2.1969 Rising Sun IN; BR/TR/6´5˝/230; d8.8																									
1914	Ind F	0	0	ø	2	0	0	1	2	1	1	0	0	2	1	4.50	69	.167	.375	0	ø	0	—	0	—	0.0
WOODS, PINKY	George Rowland; B5.22.1915 Waterbury CT; D10.29.1982 Los Angeles CA; BR/TR/6´5˝/225; d6.20; Col Holy Cross																									
1943	Bos A	5	6	.455	23	12	2	1	100.2	109	61	6	1	55	32	4.92	67	.284	.375	36	.222	-0	102	-18	0	-1.9
1944	Bos A	4	8	.333	38	20	5-1	0	170.2	171	73	4	6	88	56	3.27	104	.266	.360	48-0-4	.146	-1	88	2	0	0.0
1945	Bos A	4	7	.364	24	12	3	2	107.1	108	56	3	1	63	36	4.19	81	.268	.368	42-0-1	.214	1	100	-9	0	-0.7
Total	3	13	21	.382	85	44	10-1	3	378.2	388	190	13	8	206	124	3.97	85	.272	.366	126-0-5	.190	-1	95	-25	0	-2.6
WOODS, JAKE	Jacob Thomas; B9.3.1981 Fresno CA; BL/TL/6´1˝/190; [AnaA01 3/89]; d4.8; Col Bakersfield (CA) JC																									
2005	LA A	1	1	.500	28	0	0	0-0	27.2	30	18	7	2	8-0	20	4.55	94	.270	.331	0	ø	0	—	-2	0	-0.2
2006	Sea A	7	4	.636	37	8	0	1-0	105	115	51	12	2	53-5	66	4.20	105	.278	.361	0	ø	0	86	3	0	0.3
Total	2	8	5	.615	65	8	0	1-0	132.2	145	69	19	4	61-5	86	4.27	102	.276	.355	0	ø	0	86	1	0	0.1
WOODS, JOHN	John Fulton "Abe"; B1.18.1898 Princeton WV; D10.4.1946 Norfolk VA; BR/TR/6´0˝/175; d9.16; Col West Virginia																									
1924	Bos A	0	0	ø	1	0	0	0	1	0	0	0	0	3	0	0.00	ø	.000	.500	0	ø	0	—	0	—	0.0
WOODS, WALT	Walter Sydney; B4.28.1875 Rye NH; D10.30.1951 Portsmouth NH; BR/TR/5´9.5˝/165; d4.20																									
1898	Chi N	9	13	.409	27	22	18-3	0	215	224	128	7	10	59	26	3.14	114	.266	.322	154-0-3	.175	-4*	98	8	—	0.3
1899	Lou N	9	13	.409	26	21	17	0	186.1	216	100	9	7	37	21	3.28	117	.290	.329	126-1-6	.151	-3*	119	12	—	1.1
1900	Pit N	0	0	ø	1	0	0	0	3	9	7	0	0	1	1	21.00	17	.500	.526	1	.000	-0	—	-5	—	-0.2
Total	3	18	26	.409	54	43	35-3	0	404.1	449	235	16	17	97	48	3.34	111	.280	.328	281-1-9	.164	-7	109	15	—	1.2
WOODSON, DICK	Richard Lee; B3.30.1945 Oelwein IA; BR/TR/6´5˝/(190–207); d4.8																									
1969	†Min A	7	5	.583	44	10	2	1-1	110.1	99	49	11	3	49-3	66	3.67	99	.237	.322	27	.074	-1	146	1	0	0.0
1970	†Min A	1	2	.333	21	0	0	1-1	30.2	29	18	2	0	19-0	22	3.82	97	.244	.345	2	.000	-0	—	-2	0	-0.2
1972	Min A	14	14	.500	36	36	9-3	0-0	251.2	193	93	19	2	101-5	150	2.72	118	.211	.290	88-0-8	.080	-5	86	13	0	0.9
1973	Min A	10	8	.556	23	23	4-2	0-0	141.1	137	68	12	2	68-0	53	3.95	101	.254	.338	0	ø	0	105	1	21	0.1
1974	Min A	1	1	.500	5	4	0	0-0	27	30	16	5	1	4-0	12	4.33	86	.273	.304	0	ø	0	88	-2	0	-0.1
	NY A	1	2	.333	8	3	0	0-0	28	34	19	6	1	12-2	12	5.79	61	.301	.370	0	ø	0	75	-6	0	-0.6
	Year	2	3	.400	13	7	0	0-0	55	64	35	11	2	16-2	24	5.07	72	.287	.339	0	ø	0	83	-9	0	-0.7
Total	5	34	32	.515	137	76	15-5	2-2	589	522	263	55	9	253-10	315	3.47	102	.236	.316	117-0-8	.077	-7	100	5	21	0.1
WOODSON, KERRY	Walter Browne; B5.18.1969 Jacksonville FL; BR/TR/6´2˝/190; [SeaA88 29/747]; d7.19; Col San Jose (CA) City; [DL 1993 Sea A 182]																									
1992	Sea A	0	1	.000	8	1	0	0-0	13.2	12	7	0	2	11-0	6	3.29	122	.245	.403	0	ø	0	68	0	44	0.0
WOODWARD, FRANK	Frank Russell; B5.17.1894 New Haven CT; D6.11.1961 New Haven CT; BR/TR/5´10˝/175; d4.17; Mil 1918																									
1918	Phi N	0	0	ø	2	0	0	0	6	6	4	0	0	4	4	6.00	50	.250	.357	3	.333	0	—	-1	—	-0.1
1919	Phi N	6	9	.400	17	12	6	0	100.2	109	63	5	5	35	27	4.74	68	.291	.359	29-0-4	.207	1	111	-15	—	-2.1
	StL N	3	5	.375	17	7	2	1	72	65	27	1	1	28	18	2.63	106	.248	.323	21-0-1	.048	-2	65	1	—	-0.1
	Year	9	14	.391	34	19	8	1	172.2	174	90	6	6	63	45	3.86	79	.273	.344	50-0-5	.140	-1	96	-14	—	-2.2
1921	Was A	0	0	ø	3	1	0	0	10.2	11	7	0	0	3	4	5.91	70	.282	.333	3	.333	0	142	-2	—	-0.1
1922	Was A	0	0	ø	1	0	0	0	2.1	3	3	0	0	3	2	11.57	33	.375	.545	1	.000	-0	—	-2	—	-0.1
1923	Chi A	0	1	.000	2	1	0	0	2	5	3	0	0	1	0	13.50	29	.500	.545	0	ø	0	63	-2	—	-0.3
Total	5	9	15	.375	42	21	8	1	193.2	199	107	6	6	74	55	4.23	74	.277	.350	57-0-5	.158	-1	97	-21	—	-2.8
WOODWARD, ROB	Robert John; B9.28.1962 Hanover NH; BR/TR/6´3˝/(185–212); [BosA81 3/70]; d9.5																									
1985	Bos A	1	0	1.000	5	2	0	0-0	26.2	17	8	0	2	9-0	16	1.69	256	.168	.250	0	ø	0	158	6	0	0.3
1986	Bos A	2	3	.400	9	6	0	0-0	35.2	46	26	4	1	11-0	14	5.30	79	.313	.360	0	ø	0	79	-5	0	-0.6
1987	Bos A	1	1	.500	9	6	0	0-0	37	53	33	6	1	15-0	15	7.05	65	.338	.394	0	ø	0	126	-11	0	-0.5
1988	Bos A	0	0	ø	1	0	0	0-0	0.2	2	1	0	0	1-0	0	13.50	31	.500	.600	0	ø	0	—	-1	0	0.0
Total	4	4	4	.500	24	14	0	0-0	100	118	68	10	4	36-0	45	5.04	87	.289	.349	0	ø	0	112	-11	0	-0.8
WOODYARD, MARK	Mark Anthony; B12.19.1978 Mobile AL; BR/TR/6´2˝/195; [DetA00 4/108]; d9.17; Col Bethune–Cookman																									
2005	Det A	0	0	ø	3	0	0	0-0	6	4	1	1	0	0-0	3	1.50	285	.182	.182	0	ø	0	—	2	0	0.1
WOOLDRIDGE, FLOYD	Floyd Lewis; B8.25.1928 Jerico Springs MO; BR/TR/6´1˝/185; d5.1																									
1955	StL N	2	4	.333	18	8	2	0	57.2	64	36	9	1	27-4	14	4.84	84	.281	.355	18-0-1	.222	0	110	-6	0	-0.6
WORDEN, FRED	Frederick Bamford; B9.4.1894 St.Louis MO; D11.9.1941 St.Louis MO; BR/TR; d9.28																									
1914	Phi A	0	0	ø	1	0	0	0	2	8	5	0	0	0	1	18.00	15	.615	.615	1	.000	-0	—	-4	—	-0.2
WORKMAN, HOGE	Harry Hallworth; B9.25.1899 Huntington WV; D5.20.1972 Ft.Myers FL; BR/TR/5´11˝/170; d6.27; Col Ohio St.																									
1924	Bos A	0	0	ø	11	0	0	0	18	25	19	2	2	11	7	8.50	51	.325	.422	2	.000	-0	—	-7	—	-0.4
WORKS, RALPH	Ralph Talmadge "Judge"; B3.16.1888 Payson IL; D8.8.1941 Pasadena CA; BL/TR/6´2.5˝/185; d5.1																									
1909	†Det A	4	1	.800	16	4	4	2	64	62	19	0	1	17	31	1.97	128	.261	.313	17	.059	-2	140	4	—	0.1
1910	Det A	3	6	.333	18	10	5	1	85.2	73	47	1	4	39	36	3.57	74	.235	.328	30-0-1	.267	1	115	-9	—	-0.9
1911	Det A	11	5	.688	30	15	9-3	0	167.1	173	93	3	6	67	68	3.87	89	.268	.342	61	.148	-3	94	-6	—	-1.0

YEAR	TM LG	W	L	PCT	G	GS	CG-SHO	SV-BS	IP	H	R	HR	HB	BB-IB	SO	ERA	AERA	OAV	OOB	AB-HR-SH	AVG	PB	SUP	APR	DL	PW
1912	Det A	5	10	.333	27	16	9-1	1	157	185	101	1	7	66	64	4.24	77	.308	.383	56-0-3	.143	-3	120	-17	—	-1.8
	Cin N	1	1	.500	3	1	1	0	9.2	4	5	0	1	5	5	2.79	120	.133	.278	5	.200	-0	262	0	—	0.0
1913	Cin N	0	1	.000	5	2	0	0	15	15	14	0	3	8	4	7.80	42	.242	.356	6	.167	-0	116	-6	—	-0.4
Total	5	24	24	.500	99	48	28-4	4	498.2	512	279	5	22	202	208	3.79	83	.271	.348	175-0-4	.160	-8	115	-34	—	-4.0
WORRELL, TIM	Timothy Howard; B7.5.1967 Pasadena CA; BR/TR/6´4˝/(215–240); [SDN89 20/520]; d6.25; b–Todd; Col Biola																									
1993	SD N	2	7	.222	21	16	0	0-0	100.2	104	63	11	0	43-5	52	4.92	84	.269	.338	31-0-2	.032	-3	109	-9	0	-1.0
1994	SD N	0	1	.000	3	3	0	0-0	14.2	9	7	0	0	5-0	14	3.68	112	.170	.237	2-0-1	.500	1	118	1	115	0.1
1995	SD N	1	0	1.000	9	0	0	0-0	13.1	16	7	2	1	6-0	13	4.73	86	.291	.371	1	.000	-0	—	-1	129	0.0
1996	†SD N	9	7	.563	50	11	0	1-1	121	109	45	9	6	39-1	99	3.05	132	.236	.304	20-0-6	.150	-0	73	14	0	1.6
1997	SD N	4	8	.333	60	10	0	3-4	106.1	116	67	14	7	50-2	81	5.16	76	.280	.363	15	.200	1	122	-15	0	-1.5
1998	Det A	2	6	.250	15	9	0	0-1	61.2	66	42	11	1	19-2	47	5.98	79	.270	.325	0	ø	0	104	-7	0	-0.8
	Cle A	0	0	ø	3	0	0	0-0	5.1	6	3	0	0	2-0	2	5.06	94	.300	.333	0	ø	0	—	0	0	0.0
	Oak A	0	1	.000	25	0	0	0-2	36	34	17	5	0	8-1	33	4.00	116	.241	.282	0	ø	0	—	3	0	0.1
	Year	2	7	.222	43	9	0	0-3	103	106	62	16	1	29-3	82	5.24	90	.262	.311	0	ø	0	105	-4	0	-0.7
1999	Oak A	2	2	.500	53	0	0	0-5	69.1	69	38	6	3	34-1	62	4.15	114	.256	.344	0	ø	0	—	3	19	0.1
2000	Bal A	2	2	.500	5	0	0	0-0	7.1	12	6	3	0	5-3	5	7.36	64	.353	.436	0	ø	0	—	-2	0	-0.4
	Chi N	3	4	.429	54	0	0	3-3	62	60	20	7	1	24-8	52	2.47	186	.252	.322	2	.000	-0	—	14	0	1.4
2001	SF N	2	5	.286	73	0	0	0-3	78.1	71	33	4	3	33-4	63	3.45	119	.240	.318	2-0-1	.000	-0	—	6	17	0.4
2002	†SF N	8	2	.800	80	0	0	0-1	72	55	21	3	0	30-2	55	2.25	176	.212	.290	3	.000	-0	—	13	0	1.7
2003	†SF N	4	4	.500	76	0	0	38-7	78.1	74	35	5	0	28-6	65	2.87	148	.246	.307	3	.000	-0	—	8	0	1.4
2004	Phi N	5	6	.455	77	0	0	19-8	78.1	75	36	10	2	21-4	64	3.68	121	.254	.303	0	ø	0	—	6	0	1.0
2005	Phi N	0	1	.000	19	0	0	1-2	17	29	17	4	1	3-0	17	7.41	59	.377	.402	0	ø	0	—	-7	59	-0.4
	Ari N	1	1	.500	32	0	0	0-1	31.2	30	13	4	1	9-2	22	2.27	195	.250	.299	1	.000	-0	—	5	0	0.3
	Year	1	2	.333	51	0	0	1-3	48.2	59	30	8	2	12-2	39	4.07	108	.299	.338	1	.000	-0	—	-1	0	-0.1
2006	SF N	3	2	.600	23	0	0	6-2	20.1	28	18	9	1	7-0	12	7.52	59	.308	.364	1	.000	-0	—	-7	113	-1.3
Total	14	48	59	.449	678	49	0	71-40	973.2	963	488	107	27	366-41	758	3.97	108	.256	.324	81-0-10	.099	-2	102	25	452	2.7
WORRELL, TODD	Todd Roland; B9.28.1959 Arcadia CA; BR/TR/6´5˝/(200–230); [StLN82 1/21]; d8.28; b–Tim; Col Biola; [DL 1991 StL N 182]																									
1985	†StL N	3	0	1.000	17	0	0	5-2	21.2	17	7	2	0	7-2	17	2.91	123	.215	.273	1	.000	-0	—	2	0	0.3
1986	StL N	9	10	.474	74	0	0	**36**-10	103.2	86	29	9	1	41-16	73	2.08	177	.229	.303	7	.143	0	—	**18**	0	3.7
1987	†StL N	8	6	.571	75	0	0	33-10	94.2	86	29	8	0	34-11	92	2.66	158	.242	.307	10-0-1	.100	-0	—	16	0	3.2
1988	StL N★	5	9	.357	68	0	0	32-9	90	69	32	7	1	34-14	78	3.00	117	.214	.287	6	.000	-0	—	6	0	1.2
1989	StL N	3	5	.375	47	0	0	20-3	51.2	42	21	4	0	26-13	41	2.96	124	.222	.315	1-0-1	.000	-0	—	3	24	0.7
1992	StL N	5	3	.625	67	0	0	3-4	64	45	15	4	1	25-5	64	2.11	162	.198	.281	0	ø	0	—	10	0	1.3
1993	LA N	1	1	.500	35	0	0	5-3	38.2	46	28	6	0	11-1	31	6.05	64	.313	.348	0	ø	0	—	-9	83	-0.6
1994	LA N	6	5	.545	38	0	0	11-8	42	37	21	4	1	12-1	44	4.29	93	.236	.291	0	ø	0	—	-1	18	-0.2
1995	LA N✳	4	1	.800	59	0	0	32-4	62.1	50	15	4	1	19-2	61	2.02	191	.221	.282	2	.000	-0	—	14	0	2.4
1996	†LA N★	4	6	.400	72	0	0	**44**-9	65.1	70	29	5	2	15-1	66	3.03	129	.265	.307	0	ø	0	—	5	0	1.0
1997	LA N	2	6	.250	65	0	0	35-9	59.2	60	38	12	0	23-1	61	5.28	74	.250	.316	0	ø	0	—	-10	0	-1.8
Total	11	50	52	.490	617	0	0	256-71	693.2	608	264	65	7	247-67	628	3.09	123	.235	.301	27-0-2	.074	-1	—	54	307	11.2
WORTHAM, RICH	Richard Cooper; B10.22.1953 Odessa TX; BR/TL/6´0˝/185; [ChiA76*S2/27]; d5.3; Col Texas																									
1978	Chi A	3	2	.600	8	8	2	0-0	59	59	24	1	0	23-0	25	3.05	125	.267	.333	0	ø	0	100	4	0	0.3
1979	Chi A	14	14	.500	34	33	5	0-0	204	195	126	21	3	100-3	119	4.90	87	.255	.339	0	ø	0	96	-13	0	-1.6
1980	Chi A	4	7	.364	41	10	0	1-2	92	102	73	4	3	58-5	45	5.97	68	.285	.383	0	ø	0	84	-21	0	-2.2
1983	Oak A	0	0	ø	1	0	0	0-0	0	3	1	0	0	1-0	0	(1)	ø	1.000	1.000	0	ø	0	—	-1	0	-0.1
Total	4	21	23	.477	84	51	7	1-2	355	359	224	26	6	182-8	189	4.89	84	.266	.352	0	ø	0	95	-31	0	-3.6
WORTHINGTON, AL	Allan Fulton "Red"; B2.5.1929 Birmingham AL; BR/TR/6´2˝/205; d7.6; C2; Col Alabama																									
1953	NY N	4	8	.333	20	17	5-2	0	102	103	55	6	2	54	52	3.44	125	.258	.349	31-0-4	.065	-2	97	5	0	0.4
1954	NY N	0	2	.000	10	1	0	0	18	21	7	0	0	15	8	3.50	115	.333	.456	4	.000	-1	155	2	0	0.1
1956	NY N	7	14	.333	28	24	4	0	165.2	158	82	20	4	74-6	95	3.97	95	.254	.335	51-1-6	.235	2	75	-3	0	-0.1
1957	NY N	8	11	.421	55	12	1-1	4	157.2	140	75	19	5	56-7	90	4.22	93	.237	.306	40-0-1	.100	-2	103	-1	0	-0.4
1958	SF N	11	7	.611	54	12	1	6	151.1	152	72	17	2	57-6	76	3.63	105	.255	.320	44-0-3	.182	0	110	2	0	0.3
1959	SF N	2	3	.400	42	3	0	2	73.1	68	34	8	5	37-4	45	3.68	103	.253	.347	13	.077	-1	133	1	0	0.0
1960	Bos A	0	1	.000	6	0	0	0	11.2	17	12	1	0	11-3	7	7.71	52	.340	.459	1	.000	-0	—	-5	0	-0.4
	Chi A	1	1	.500	4	0	0	0	5.1	3	2	0	0	4-0	1	3.38	112	.176	.318	2	1.000	1	—	0	0	0.2
	Year	1	2	.333	10	0	0	0	17	20	14	1	0	15-3	8	6.35	62	.299	.422	3	.667	1	—	-5	0	-0.2
1963	Cin N	4	4	.500	50	0	0	10	81.1	75	34	6	3	31-3	55	2.99	112	.248	.321	12-0-2	.083	-0	—	2	0	0.3
1964	Cin N	1	0	1.000	6	0	0	0	7	14	11	0	1	2-0	6	10.29	35	.400	.436	0	ø	0	—	-6	0	-0.8
	Min A	5	6	.455	41	0	0	14	72.1	47	18	4	0	28-6	59	1.37	261	.183	.262	16-0-4	.063	-1	—	16	0	2.9
1965	†Min A	10	7	.588	62	0	0	21	80.1	57	25	4	3	41-2	59	2.13	167	.207	.312	10-0-2	.100	0	—	11	0	2.6
1966	Min A	6	3	.667	65	0	0	16	91.1	66	26	6	1	27-3	93	2.46	146	.199	.260	11	.273	1	—	12	0	1.8
1967	Min A	8	9	.471	59	0	0	16	92	77	36	6	1	38-10	80	2.84	122	.229	.307	8	.000	-1	—	5	0	1.0
1968	Min A	4	5	.444	54	0	0	**18**	76.1	67	26	1	0	32-9	57	2.71	114	.238	.311	7-0-2	.000	-1	—	4	0	0.6
1969	†Min A	4	1	.800	46	0	0	3-1	61	65	31	7	0	20-2	51	4.57	80	.278	.333	5-0-1	.000	-1	—	-4	0	-0.5
Total	14	75	82	.478	602	69	11-3	110-1	1246.2	1130	546	105	27	527-61	834	3.39	110	.243	.320	255-1-25	.137	-5	100	41	0	8.0
WRIGHT, GENE	Clarence Eugene "Big Gene"; B12.11.1878 Cleveland OH; D10.29.1930 Barberton OH; BR/TR/6´2˝/185; d10.5																									
1901	Bro N	1	0	1.000	1	1	1	0	9	6	2	0	0	1	6	1.00	335	.188	.212	3	.333	0	85	2	—	0.2
1902	Cle A	7	10	.412	21	18	15-1	1	148	150	94	6	8	75	52	3.95	87	.263	.357	70-1-1	.143	-2*	132	-7	—	-1.0
1903	Cle A	3	10	.231	15	12	8	0	101.2	122	94	1	4	58	42	5.75	50	.296	.388	43-0-1	.209	2	115	-32	—	-3.1
	StL A	3	5	.375	8	8	7-1	0	61	73	29	2	4	16	37	3.69	79	.296	.348	21	.143	-1	86	-3	—	-0.4
	Year	6	15	.286	23	20	15-1	0	162.2	195	123	3	8	74	79	4.98	58	.296	.374	64-0-1	.188	2	103	-38	—	-3.5
1904	StL A	0	1	.000	1	1	0	0	4	10	6	0	0	2	3	13.50	18	.476	.522	1	.000	-0	115	-4	—	-0.6
Total	4	14	26	.350	46	40	31-2	1	323.2	361	225	9	16	152	140	4.50	70	.282	.365	138-1-2	.167	-1	117	-44	—	-4.9
WRIGHT, CLYDE	Clyde; B2.20.1941 Jefferson City TN; BR/TL/6´1˝/(185–200); [AnaA65 6/107]; d6.15; s–Jaret; Col Carson–Newman																									
1966	Cal A	4	7	.364	20	13	3-1	0	91.1	92	39	11	1	25-4	37	3.74	90	.265	.314	29-0-3	.103	-1*	93	-2	0	-0.4
1967	Cal A	5	5	.500	20	11	1	0	77.1	76	33	5	1	24-2	35	3.26	96	.260	.316	22-0-3	.273	2*	78	-1	0	0.1
1968	Cal A	10	6	.625	41	13	2-1	3	125.2	123	58	13	2	44-6	71	3.94	74	.256	.319	37-0-2	.216	2*	92	-13	0	-1.5
1969	Cal A	1	8	.111	37	5	0	0-2	63.2	66	33	4	1	30-5	31	4.10	85	.278	.361	11	.182	0*	30	-4	0	-0.5
1970	Cal A★	22	12	.647	39	39	7-2	0-0	260.2	226	97	24	7	88-4	110	2.83	128	.232	.298	105-2-4	.171	3*	122	21	0	2.9
1971	Cal A	16	17	.485	37	37	10-2	0-0	276.2	225	105	17	3	82-10	135	2.99	109	.226	.283	91-0-9	.154	2*	79	8	0	1.4
1972	Cal A	18	11	.621	35	35	15-2	0-0	251	229	101	14	4	80-6	87	2.98	99	.246	.307	83-2-6	.217	7	118	-4	0	0.5
1973	Cal A	11	19	.367	37	36	13-1	0-0	257	273	120	26	3	76-0	65	3.68	97	.273	.324	0	ø	0	96	-3	0	-0.1
1974	Mil A	9	20	.310	38	32	15	0-0	232	264	122	22	0	54-4	64	4.42	82	.284	.322	0	ø	0	88	-19	0	-2.1
1975	Tex A	4	6	.400	25	14	1	0-0	93.1	105	56	7	1	47-3	32	4.44	85	.294	.370	0	ø	0	110	-8	0	-0.7
Total	10	100	111	.474	329	235	67-9	3-2	1728.2	1679	764	143	23	550-44	667	3.50	97	.256	.314	378-4-27	.183	14	98	-25	0	-0.4
WRIGHT, DAVE	David William; B8.27.1875 Dennison OH; D1.18.1946 Dennison OH; BR/TR/6´0˝/185; d7.22																									
1895	Pit N	0	0	ø	1	0	0	0	2	6	6	0	0	1	0	27.00	17	.500	.538	1	.000	-0	—	-4	—	-0.2
1897	Chi N	1	0	1.000	1	1	1	0	7	17	14	1	2	2	4	15.43	29	.459	.512	3	.333	0	224	-7	—	-0.6
Total	2	1	0	1.000	2	1	1	0	9	23	20	1	2	3	4	18.00	25	.469	.519	4	.250	0	224	-11	—	-0.8
WRIGHT, ED	Henderson Edward; B5.15.1919 Dyersburg TN; D11.19.1995 Dyersburg TN; BR/TR/6´1˝/180; d7.29																									
1945	Bos N	8	3	.727	15	12	7-1	0	111.1	104	35	7	0	33	24	2.51	153	.254	.310	39-0-2	.128	-2	107	17	0	1.3
1946	Bos N	12	9	.571	36	21	9-2	0	176.1	164	82	8	2	71	44	3.52	97	.250	.325	59-0-4	.305	6	114	-3	0	0.3
1947	Bos N	3	3	.500	23	6	1	0	64.2	80	52	9	2	35	14	6.40	61	.305	.391	23	.130	-0	113	-19	0	-1.5
1948	Bos N	0	0	ø	3	0	0	0	4.2	9	3	0	0	2	2	1.93	199	.474	.524	0	ø	0	—	0	0	0.0
1952	Phi A	2	1	.667	24	0	0	1	41.1	55	36	6	3	20	9	6.53	61	.320	.400	7	.143	-0	—	-12	0	-0.9
Total	5	25	16	.610	101	39	17-3	1	398.1	412	208	30	7	161	93	4.00	92	.271	.344	128-0-6	.211	3	110	-17	0	-0.8

WRIGHT, JIM James "Jiggs"; B9.19.1900 Hyde, England; D4.11.1963 Oakland CA; BR/TR/6´2.5˝/195; d9.14

YEAR	TM LG	W	L	PCT	G	GS	CG-SHO	SV-BS	IP	H	R	HR	HB	BB-IB	SO	ERA	AERA	OAV	OOB	AB-HR-SH	AVG	PB	SUP	APR	DL	PW
1927	StL A	1	0	1.000	2	1	1	0	12	8	6	0	0	4	4	4.50	97	.182	.250	4	.000	-0	172	0	—	0.0
1928	StL A	0	0	ø	2	0	0	0	2	3	3	0	0	2	2	13.50	31	.375	.500	0	ø	0	—	-2	—	-0.1
Total	2	1	0	1.000	4	1	1	0	14	11	9	0	0	6	6	5.79	75	.212	.293	4	.000	-0	172	-2	—	-0.1

WRIGHT, JIM James Clifton; B12.21.1950 Reed City MI; BR/TR/6´1˝/165; [BosA69 4/83]; d4.15

YEAR	TM LG	W	L	PCT	G	GS	CG-SHO	SV-BS	IP	H	R	HR	HB	BB-IB	SO	ERA	AERA	OAV	OOB	AB-HR-SH	AVG	PB	SUP	APR	DL	PW
1978	Bos A	8	4	.667	24	16	5-3	0-0	116	122	51	8	7	24-2	56	3.57	115	.276	.321	0	ø	0	86	7	0	0.6
1979	Bos A	1	0	1.000	11	1	0	0-0	23	19	13	5	3	7-1	15	5.09	88	.226	.302	0	ø	0	81	-1	102	-0.1
Total	2	9	4	.692	35	17	5-3	0-0	139	141	64	13	10	31-3	71	3.82	109	.268	.318	0	ø	0	85	6	102	0.5

WRIGHT, JIM James Leon; B3.3.1955 St.Joseph MO; BR/TR/6´5˝/220; [PhiN73 5/98]; d4.22; C2; [DL 1979 Phi N 179]

YEAR	TM LG	W	L	PCT	G	GS	CG-SHO	SV-BS	IP	H	R	HR	HB	BB-IB	SO	ERA	AERA	OAV	OOB	AB-HR-SH	AVG	PB	SUP	APR	DL	PW
1981	KC A	2	3	.400	17	4	0	0-0	52	57	21	5	2	21-7	27	3.46	104	.277	.348	0	ø	0	75	1	0	0.1
1982	KC A	0	0	ø	7	0	0	0-0	23.2	32	18	3	0	6-0	9	5.32	77	.320	.358	0	ø	0	—	-4	0	-0.2
Total	2	2	3	.400	24	4	0	0-0	75.2	89	39	8	2	27-7	36	4.04	93	.291	.351	0	ø	0	75	-3	179	-0.1

WRIGHT, RICKY James Richard; B11.22.1958 Paris TX; BL/TL/6´3˝/175; [LAN80*S1/2]; d7.28; Col Texas

YEAR	TM LG	W	L	PCT	G	GS	CG-SHO	SV-BS	IP	H	R	HR	HB	BB-IB	SO	ERA	AERA	OAV	OOB	AB-HR-SH	AVG	PB	SUP	APR	DL	PW
1982	LA N	2	1	.667	14	5	0	0-0	32.2	28	12	1	0	20-6	24	3.03	115	.233	.340	8	.125	0	137	2	0	0.2
1983	LA N	0	0	ø	6	0	0	0-0	6.1	5	2	0	0	2-1	5	2.84	127	.227	.280	0	ø	0	—	1	0	0.0
	Tex A	0	0	ø	1	0	0	0-0	2	0	0	0	0	1-0	2	0.00	ø	.000	.167	0	ø	0	—	1	0	0.0
1984	Tex A	0	2	.000	8	1	0	0-1	14.2	20	10	3	0	11-0	6	6.14	68	.357	.463	0	ø	0	43	-2	0	-0.3
1985	Tex A	0	0	ø	5	0	0	0-0	7.2	5	4	0	0	5-1	7	4.70	91	.185	.313	0	ø	0	—	0	0	0.0
1986	Tex A	1	0	1.000	21	1	0	0-0	39.1	44	22	1	0	21-0	23	5.03	86	.284	.369	0	ø	0*	42	-2	61	-0.1
Total	5	3	3	.500	55	7	0	0-1	102.2	102	50	5	0	60-8	67	4.30	92	.265	.362	8	.125	0	100	0	61	-0.2

WRIGHT, JAMEY Jamey Alan; B12.24.1974 Oklahoma City OK; BR/TR/6´5˝/(203–236); [ColN93 1/28]; d7.3

YEAR	TM LG	W	L	PCT	G	GS	CG-SHO	SV-BS	IP	H	R	HR	HB	BB-IB	SO	ERA	AERA	OAV	OOB	AB-HR-SH	AVG	PB	SUP	APR	DL	PW
1996	Col N	4	4	.500	16	15	0	0-0	91.1	105	60	8	7	41-1	45	4.93	106	.298	.381	26-0-5	.077	-1	100	0	0	0.0
1997	Col N	8	12	.400	26	26	1	0-0	149.2	198	113	19	11	71-3	59	6.25	83	.327	.406	48-0-3	.125	-2	91	-15	24	-1.9
1998	Col N	9	14	.391	34	34	1	0-0	206.1	235	143	24	11	95-3	86	5.67	91	.294	.374	57-1-8	.175	0	91	-11	0	-0.9
1999	Col N	4	3	.571	16	16	0	0-0	94.1	110	52	10	4	54-3	49	4.87	119	.307	.400	32-0-3	.125	-2	96	9	0	0.4
2000	Mil N	7	9	.438	26	25	0	0-0	164.2	157	81	12	18	88-5	96	4.10	113	.261	.368	46-0-4	.065	-3	81	10	49	0.5
2001	Mil N	11	12	.478	33	33	1-1	0-0	194.2	201	115	26	20	98-10	129	4.90	88	.272	.370	67-0-4	.194	2*	102	-13	20	-1.1
2002	Mil N	5	13	.278	19	19	1-1	0-0	114.1	115	72	15	11	63-8	69	5.35	77	.270	.374	33-0-6	.152	0	66	-15	49	-1.9
	StL N	2	0	1.000	4	3	0	0-0	15	15	8	2	0	12-1	8	4.80	84	.259	.386	5-0-1	.000	-1	222	-1	0	-0.2
	Year	7	13	.350	23	22	1-1	0-0	129.1	130	80	17	11	75-9	77	5.29	78	.269	.375	38-0-7	.132	-0	87	-16	0	-2.1
2003	KC A	1	2	.333	4	4	2-1	0-0	25.1	23	14	1	1	11-0	19	4.26	113	.245	.330	0	ø	0	77	1	0	0.1
2004	Col N	2	3	.400	14	14	0	0-0	78.2	82	39	8	6	45-3	41	4.12	116	.266	.369	19-0-8	.053	-1	82	4	0	0.2
2005	Col N	8	16	.333	34	27	0	0-0	171.1	201	119	22	15	81-4	101	5.46	85	.296	.382	55-0-3	.145	-1*	84	-17	0	-2.3
2006	SF N	6	10	.375	34	21	0	0-0	156	167	95	16	10	64-4	79	5.19	85	.282	.359	47-0-5	.255	3*	97	-13	0	-0.8
Total	11	67	98	.406	260	237	6-3	0-0	1461.2	1609	911	163	114	723-45	781	5.14	93	.287	.377	435-1-50	.147	-6	91	-61	142	-7.9

WRIGHT, JARET Jaret Samuel; B12.29.1975 Anaheim CA; BR/TR/6´2˝/230; [CleA94 1/10]; d6.24; f–Clyde

YEAR	TM LG	W	L	PCT	G	GS	CG-SHO	SV-BS	IP	H	R	HR	HB	BB-IB	SO	ERA	AERA	OAV	OOB	AB-HR-SH	AVG	PB	SUP	APR	DL	PW
1997	†Cle A	8	3	.727	16	16	0	0-0	90.1	81	45	9	5	35-0	63	4.38	107	.238	.314	3-0-2	.000	-0	125	4	0	0.4
1998	†Cle A	12	10	.545	32	32	1-1	0-0	192.2	207	109	22	11	87-4	140	4.72	101	.277	.358	7	.429	1	108	1	0	0.2
1999	†Cle A	8	10	.444	26	26	0	0-0	133.2	144	99	18	7	77-1	91	6.06	84	.277	.376	1	.000	-0	96	-14	47	-1.6
2000	Cle A	3	4	.429	9	9	1-1	0-0	51.2	44	27	6	1	28-0	36	4.70	107	.235	.336	1-0-1	.000	-0	121	2	134	0.2
2001	Cle A	2	2	.500	7	7	0	0-0	29	36	22	2	0	22-0	18	6.52	70	.313	.420	2	.500	0	112	-6	85	-0.6
2002	Cle A	2	3	.400	8	6	0	0-0	18.1	40	34	3	2	19-0	12	15.71	28	.435	.526	0	ø	0	139	-23	111	-3.5
2003	SD N	1	5	.167	39	0	0	2-2	47.1	69	44	9	2	28-2	41	8.37	48	.348	.427	4-0-1	.250	1	—	-23	0	-2.5
	†Atl N	1	0	1.000	11	0	0	0-1	9	7	2	0	1	3-0	9	2.00	210	.226	.314	0	ø	0	—	2	0	0.2
	Year	2	5	.286	50	0	0	2-3	56.1	76	46	9	3	31-2	50	7.35	55	.332	.412	4-0-1	.250	1	—	-20	0	-2.3
2004	†Atl N	15	8	.652	32	32	0	0-0	186.1	168	79	11	3	70-5	159	3.28	131	.242	.312	57-1-6	.105	-1	115	20	0	2.1
2005	NY A	5	5	.500	13	13	0	0-0	63.2	81	51	8	6	32-1	34	6.08	71	.313	.394	0	ø	0	139	-15	113	-1.9
2006	†NY A	11	7	.611	30	27	0	0-0	140.1	157	76	10	7	57-0	84	4.49	101	.283	.355	3	.000	0*	112	1	0	0.1
Total	10	68	57	.544	223	168	2-2	2-3	962.1	1034	588	98	45	458-13	687	5.07	91	.277	.359	78-1-10	.141	0	115	-51	490	-6.9

WRIGHT, DAN Jonathan Daniel; B12.14.1977 Longview TX; BR/TR/6´5˝/(225–240); [ChiA99 2/64]; d7.27; Col Arkansas

YEAR	TM LG	W	L	PCT	G	GS	CG-SHO	SV-BS	IP	H	R	HR	HB	BB-IB	SO	ERA	AERA	OAV	OOB	AB-HR-SH	AVG	PB	SUP	APR	DL	PW
2001	Chi A	5	3	.625	13	12	0	0-0	66.1	78	45	12	2	39-1	36	5.70	82	.300	.389	0	ø	0	129	-7	0	-0.7
2002	Chi A	14	12	.538	33	33	1-1	0-0	196.1	200	124	32	6	71-1	136	5.18	87	.263	.327	4	.000	-0	110	-14	0	-1.6
2003	Chi A	1	7	.125	20	15	0	1-0	86.1	91	63	16	3	46-2	47	6.15	75	.277	.366	2	.000	-0	86	-14	36	-1.2
2004	Chi A	0	4	.000	4	4	0	0-0	17.2	24	17	5	2	11-1	6	8.15	58	.320	.420	0	ø	0	54	-7	0	-1.1
Total	4	20	26	.435	70	64	1-1	1-0	366.2	393	249	65	13	167-5	225	5.65	81	.276	.353	6	.000	-1	104	-42	36	-4.6

WRIGHT, KEN Kenneth Warren; B9.4.1946 Pensacola FL; BR/TR/6´2˝/(210–220); d4.10

YEAR	TM LG	W	L	PCT	G	GS	CG-SHO	SV-BS	IP	H	R	HR	HB	BB-IB	SO	ERA	AERA	OAV	OOB	AB-HR-SH	AVG	PB	SUP	APR	DL	PW
1970	KC A	1	2	.333	47	0	0	3-1	53.1	49	33	2	7	29-0	30	5.23	71	.261	.374	4	.000	-0	—	-8	0	-0.6
1971	KC A	3	6	.333	21	12	1-1	1-0	78	66	34	6	3	47-0	56	3.69	93	.230	.344	22-0-1	.091	-1	82	-2	21	-0.3
1972	KC A	1	2	.333	17	0	0	4-1	18.1	15	10	0	1	15-1	18	4.91	62	.231	.378	2	.000	-0	—	-3	0	-0.8
1973	KC A	6	5	.545	25	12	1	0-1	80.2	60	48	6	0	82-0	75	4.91	84	.210	.383	0	ø	0	81	-6	21	-0.8
1974	NY A	0	0	ø	3	0	0	0-0	5.2	5	2	0	0	7-0	2	3.18	112	.227	.414	0	ø	0	—	0	0	0.0
Total	5	11	15	.423	113	24	2-1	8-3	236	195	127	14	11	180-1	181	4.54	82	.230	.369	28-0-1	.071	-2	83	-19	42	-2.5

WRIGHT, MEL Melvin James; B5.11.1928 Manila AR; D5.16.1983 Houston TX; BR/TR/6´3˝/210; d4.17; C14

YEAR	TM LG	W	L	PCT	G	GS	CG-SHO	SV-BS	IP	H	R	HR	HB	BB-IB	SO	ERA	AERA	OAV	OOB	AB-HR-SH	AVG	PB	SUP	APR	DL	PW
1954	StL N	0	0	ø	9	0	0	0	10.1	16	15	2	2	11	4	10.45	39	.348	.492	1	.000	-0	—	-8	0	-0.4
1955	StL N	2	2	.500	29	0	0	1	36.1	44	26	4	1	9-2	18	6.19	66	.308	.351	6	.000	-1	—	-8	0	-0.9
1960	Chi N	0	1	.000	9	0	0	2	16.1	17	9	1	0	3-1	8	4.96	76	.279	.299	2	.000	-0	—	-2	0	-0.2
1961	Chi N	0	1	.000	11	0	0	0	21	42	26	3	0	4-0	6	10.71	39	.416	.438	2	.000	-0	—	-13	0	-0.6
Total	4	2	4	.333	58	0	0	3	84	119	76	10	3	27-3	36	7.61	53	.339	.387	11	.000	-2	—	-31	0	-2.1

WRIGHT, BOB Robert Cassius; B12.13.1891 Decatur Co. IN; D7.30.1993 Carmichael CA; BR/TR/6´1.5˝/175; d9.21

YEAR	TM LG	W	L	PCT	G	GS	CG-SHO	SV-BS	IP	H	R	HR	HB	BB-IB	SO	ERA	AERA	OAV	OOB	AB-HR-SH	AVG	PB	SUP	APR	DL	PW
1915	Chi N	0	0	ø	2	0	0	0	4	6	4	0	0	0	3	2.25	123	.353	.353	0	ø	0	—	-1	—	0.0

WRIGHT, ROY Roy Earl; B9.26.1933 Buchtel OH; BR/TR/6´2˝/170; d9.30

YEAR	TM LG	W	L	PCT	G	GS	CG-SHO	SV-BS	IP	H	R	HR	HB	BB-IB	SO	ERA	AERA	OAV	OOB	AB-HR-SH	AVG	PB	SUP	APR	DL	PW
1956	NY N	0	1	.000	1	1	0	0	2.2	8	5	1	0	2-0	0	16.88	22	.533	.588	1	.000	-0	47	-4	0	-0.6

WRIGHT, RASTY Wayne Bromley; B11.5.1895 Ceredo WV; D6.12.1948 Columbus OH; BR/TR/5´11˝/160; d6.22; Col Ohio St.

YEAR	TM LG	W	L	PCT	G	GS	CG-SHO	SV-BS	IP	H	R	HR	HB	BB-IB	SO	ERA	AERA	OAV	OOB	AB-HR-SH	AVG	PB	SUP	APR	DL	PW
1917	StL A	0	1	.000	16	1	0	0	39.2	48	31	0	1	10	5	5.45	48	.300	.345	10-0-1	.200	0	111	-12	—	-0.6
1918	StL A	8	2	.800	18	13	6-1	0	111.1	99	39	1	5	18	25	2.51	109	.244	.285	34-0-2	.294	3	106	4	—	0.6
1919	StL A	0	5	.000	24	5	2	0	63.1	79	44	1	1	20	14	5.54	60	.315	.368	12	.083	-1	66	-13	—	-1.0
1922	StL A	9	7	.563	31	16	5	5	154	148	64	7	8	50	44	2.92	142	.262	.331	50-0-4	.140	-2	113	19	—	1.8
1923	StL A	7	4	.636	20	8	4	0	82.2	107	64	6	5	34	26	6.42	65	.317	.387	27-0-3	.222	0	134	-17	—	-1.9
Total	5	24	19	.558	109	43	17-1	5	451	481	242	15	20	132	114	4.05	87	.280	.338	133-0-10	.195	1	111	-19	—	-1.1

WRIGHT, HARRY William Henry; B1.10.1835 Sheffield, England; D10.3.1895 Atlantic City NJ; BR/TR/5´9.5˝/157; d5.5; M23; HF1953; b–George b–Sam; ▲

YEAR	TM LG	W	L	PCT	G	GS	CG-SHO	SV-BS	IP	H	R	HR	HB	BB-IB	SO	ERA	AERA	OAV	OOB	AB-HR-SH	AVG	PB	SUP	APR	DL	PW
1871	Bos NA	1	0	1.000	9	0	0	**3**	18.2	34	31	0	—	4	0	6.27	66	.337	.362	147	.299	1*	—	-4	—	-0.2
1872	Bos NA	1	0	1.000	7	0	0	**4**	25.2	26	12	0	—	0	1	2.10	174	.239	.239	208	.255	0*	—	**5**	—	0.3
1873	Bos NA	2	2	.500	14	6	0	**4**	39.1	65	47	0	—	6	5	4.12	84	.328	.348	263-2	.259	2*	153	-3	—	-0.2
1874	Bos NA	0	2	.000	6	2	0	**3**	16.2	24	13	0	—	4	0	2.16	100	.324	.359	184-2	.315	2*	88	0	—	0.1
Total	4NA	4	4	.500	36	8	0	14	100.1	149	103	0	—	14	6	3.68	93	.309	.329	802-4	.278	5	132	-2	—	0.0

WRIGHT, LUCKY William Simmons "William the Red","Deacon"; B2.21.1880 Waterville OH; D7.7.1941 Tontogany OH; BR/TR/6´0˝/178; d4.18

YEAR	TM LG	W	L	PCT	G	GS	CG-SHO	SV-BS	IP	H	R	HR	HB	BB-IB	SO	ERA	AERA	OAV	OOB	AB-HR-SH	AVG	PB	SUP	APR	DL	PW
1909	Cle A	0	4	.000	5	4	3	0	28	21	16	0	0	7	5	3.21	80	.223	.277	7	.000	-1	55	-2	—	-0.4

WUERTZ, MICHAEL Michael James; B12.15.1978 Austin MN; BR/TR/6´3˝/205; [ChiN97 11/334]; d4.5

YEAR	TM LG	W	L	PCT	G	GS	CG-SHO	SV-BS	IP	H	R	HR	HB	BB-IB	SO	ERA	AERA	OAV	OOB	AB-HR-SH	AVG	PB	SUP	APR	DL	PW
2004	Chi N	1	0	1.000	31	0	0	1-0	29	22	14	4	0	17-1	30	4.34	102	.218	.325	1	.000	-0	—	1	0	0.0
2005	Chi N	6	2	.750	75	0	0	0-3	75.2	60	36	6	0	40-7	89	3.81	115	.219	.316	2	.000	-0	—	4	0	0.3
2006	Chi N	3	1	.750	41	0	0	0-1	40.2	35	14	5	1	16-2	42	2.66	173	.226	.302	0-0-1	ø	0	—	8	0	0.7
Total	3	10	3	.769	147	0	0	1-4	145.1	117	64	15	1	73-10	161	3.59	124	.221	.314	3-0-1	.000	-0	—	13	0	1.0

WUNSCH, KELLY Kelly Douglas; B7.12.1972 Houston TX; BL/TL/6´5˝/(192–225); [MilA93 1/26]; d4.3; Col Texas A&M

YEAR	TM LG	W	L	PCT	G	GS	CG-SHO	SV-BS	IP	H	R	HR	HB	BB-IB	SO	ERA	AERA	OAV	OOB	AB-HR-SH	AVG	PB	SUP	APR	DL	PW
2000	†Chi A	6	3	.667	**83**	0	0	1-4	61.1	50	22	4	2	29-1	51	2.93	172	.221	.313	0	ø	0	—	14	0	1.8
2001	Chi A	2	1	.667	33	0	0	0-2	22.1	21	19	4	6	9-1	16	7.66	61	.247	.353	0	ø	0	—	-6	112	-0.7
2002	Chi A	2	1	.667	50	0	0	0-1	31.2	26	12	3	5	19-1	22	3.41	132	.230	.365	0	ø	0	—	4	48	0.4
2003	Chi A	0	0	ø	43	0	0	0-0	36	17	13	1	7	25-4	33	2.75	167	.139	.308	0	ø	0	—	7	43	0.3
2004	Chi A	0	0	ø	3	0	0	0-0	2	2	0	0	0	1-0	1	0.00	ø	.286	.375	0	ø	0	—	1	35	0.1
2005	LA N	1	1	.500	45	0	0	0-1	23.2	20	12	2	2	14-2	22	4.56	91	.227	.346	1	.000	-0*	—	-1	87	0.0
Total	6	11	6	.647	257	0	0	1-8	177	136	78	14	22	97-9	145	3.76	125	.212	.332	1	.000	-0	—	19	325	1.9

WURM, FRANK Frank James; B4.27.1924 Cambridge NY; D9.19.1993 Glens Falls NY; BB/TL/6´1˝/175; d9.4

YEAR	TM LG	W	L	PCT	G	GS	CG-SHO	SV-BS	IP	H	R	HR	HB	BB-IB	SO	ERA	AERA	OAV	OOB	AB-HR-SH	AVG	PB	SUP	APR	DL	PW
1944	Bro N	0	0	ø	1	1	0	0	0.1	1	4	0	0	5	1	108.00	3	.500	.857	0	ø	0	142	-4	0	-0.2

WYATT, JOHN John Thomas; B4.19.1935 Chicago IL; D4.6.1998 Omaha NE; BR/TR/5´11.5˝/(195–205); d9.8

YEAR	TM LG	W	L	PCT	G	GS	CG-SHO	SV-BS	IP	H	R	HR	HB	BB-IB	SO	ERA	AERA	OAV	OOB	AB-HR-SH	AVG	PB	SUP	APR	DL	PW
1961	KC A	0	0	ø	5	0	0	1	7.1	8	3	0	1	4-0	6	2.45	170	.296	.394	0	ø	0	—	1	0	0.1
1962	KC A	10	7	.588	59	9	0	11	125	121	66	12	5	80-5	106	4.46	95	.253	.363	29	.103	-2	101	-2	0	-0.5
1963	KC A	6	4	.600	63	0	0	21	92	83	37	12	0	43-2	81	3.13	125	.239	.321	9	.000	-1	—	7	0	0.9
1964	KC A★	9	8	.529	**81**	0	0	20	128	111	53	23	1	52-5	74	3.59	106	.236	.311	14-0-4	.000	-1	—	4	0	0.5
1965	KC A	2	6	.250	65	0	0	18	88.2	78	36	8	4	53-12	70	3.25	107	.241	.350	4-0-1	.000	-0	—	2	0	0.3
1966	KC A	0	3	.000	19	0	0	2	23.2	19	14	3	2	16-4	25	5.32	64	.213	.346	0	ø	0	—	-4	0	-0.6
	Bos A	3	4	.429	42	0	0	8	71.2	59	27	3	4	27-3	63	3.14	121	.229	.308	11	.000	-1	—	5	0	0.4
	Year	3	7	.300	61	0	0	10	95.1	78	41	6	6	43-7	88	3.68	101	.225	.318	11	.000	-1	—	2	0	-0.2
1967	†Bos A	10	7	.588	60	0	0	20	93.1	71	30	6	2	39-5	68	2.60	134	.217	.303	12	.083	-0	—	9	0	1.9
1968	Bos A	1	2	.333	8	0	0	0	10.2	9	7	2	1	6-0	11	4.22	75	.231	.348	0	ø	0	—	-2	0	-0.4
	NY A	0	2	.000	7	0	0	0	8.1	7	3	1	0	9-0	6	2.16	135	.219	.381	1	.000	-0	—	0	0	0.1
	Det A	1	0	1.000	22	0	0	2	30.1	26	9	2	1	11-2	25	2.37	127	.236	.311	2	.000	-0	—	2	0	0.1
	Year	2	4	.333	37	0	0	2	49.1	42	19	5	2	26-2	42	2.74	111	.232	.333	3	.000	-0	—	1	0	-0.2
1969	Oak A	0	1	.000	4	0	0	0-0	8.1	8	5	0	2	6-1	5	5.40	64	.250	.400	1	.000	-0	—	-2	0	-0.2
Total	9	42	44	.488	435	9	0	103-0	687.1	600	290	72	23	346-39	540	3.47	108	.237	.331	83-0-5	.048	-6	101	20	0	2.6

WYATT, WHIT John Whitlow; B9.27.1907 Kensington GA; D7.16.1999 Carrollton GA; BR/TR/6´1˝/185; d9.16; Mil 1944; C13; Col Georgia Tech

YEAR	TM LG	W	L	PCT	G	GS	CG-SHO	SV-BS	IP	H	R	HR	HB	BB-IB	SO	ERA	AERA	OAV	OOB	AB-HR-SH	AVG	PB	SUP	APR	DL	PW
1929	Det A	0	1	.000	4	4	1	0	25.1	30	22	1	1	18	14	6.75	64	.309	.422	10	.100	-1	128	-6	—	-0.4
1930	Det A	4	5	.444	21	7	2	2	85.2	76	41	6	3	35	68	3.57	134	.239	.320	34-1-1	.353	3*	105	11	—	1.3
1931	Det A	0	2	.000	4	1	1	0	20.1	30	23	2	1	12	8	8.85	52	.361	.448	7	.286	0	18	-9	—	-0.7
1932	Det A	9	13	.409	43	22	10	1	205.2	228	136	12	3	102	82	5.03	93	.286	.369	78-2-1	.192	-0	100	-6	—	-0.6
1933	Det A	0	1	.000	10	0	0	0	17	20	9	1	2	9	9	4.24	102	.299	.397	2	.000	-0	—	0	—	0.0
	Chi A	3	4	.429	26	7	2	1	87.2	91	51	7	2	45	31	4.62	92	.266	.355	28-0-1	.214	0	106	-2	—	-0.1
	Year	3	5	.375	36	7	2	1	104.2	111	60	8	4	54	40	4.56	93	.271	.362	30-0-1	.200	-0	106	-2	—	-0.1
1934	Chi A	4	11	.267	23	6	2	2	67.2	83	59	10	1	37	36	7.18	66	.303	.388	26-0-1	.231	0	86	-16	—	-2.8
1935	Chi A	4	3	.571	30	1	0	5	52	65	41	6	2	25	22	6.75	68	.308	.387	13	.231	1	94	-11	—	-1.2
1936	Chi A	0	0	ø	3	0	0	1	3	3	0	0	0	0	0	0.00	ø	.273	.273	0	ø	0	—	2	—	0.1
1937	Cle A	2	3	.400	29	4	2	0	73	67	38	3	0	40	52	4.44	104	.244	.340	18-0-1	.389	3	80	3	—	0.4
1939	Bro N☆	8	3	.727	16	14	6-2	0	109	88	34	3	2	39	52	2.31	174	.224	.297	36	.167	-0	91	19	—	1.9
1940	Bro N★	15	14	.517	37	34	16-**5**	0	239.1	233	105	19	5	62	124	3.46	116	.254	.304	80-1-8	.175	-0	97	13	—	1.3
1941	†Bro N★	**22**	10	.688	38	35	23-**7**	1	288.1	223	89	10	2	82	176	2.34	157	**.212**	**.270**	109-3-8	.239	7*	114	**42**	0	**5.3**
1942	Bro N☆	19	7	.731	31	30	16	0	217.1	185	82	9	7	63	104	2.73	119	.225	.286	77-0-6	.182	1	121	11	0	1.2
1943	Bro N	14	5	.737	26	26	13-3	0	180.2	139	55	5	0	43	80	2.49	135	**.207**	**.255**	60-0-6	.283	4*	117	18	0	2.3
1944	Bro N	2	6	.250	9	9	1	0	37.2	51	37	1	2	16	4	7.17	50	.311	.379	13-0-1	.154	-0*	97	-16	0	-2.7
1945	Phi N	0	7	.000	10	10	2	0	51.1	72	38	3	0	14	10	5.26	73	.330	.371	16	.125	0	80	-8	0	-0.9
Total	16	106	95	.527	360	210	97-17	13	1761	1684	860	98	33	642	872	3.79	105	.251	.319	607-7-34	.219	18	102	45	0	4.4

WYCKOFF, WELDON John Weldon; B2.19.1892 Williamsport PA; D5.8.1961 Sheboygan Falls WI; BR/TR/6´1˝/175; d4.19; Col Bucknell

YEAR	TM LG	W	L	PCT	G	GS	CG-SHO	SV-BS	IP	H	R	HR	HB	BB-IB	SO	ERA	AERA	OAV	OOB	AB-HR-SH	AVG	PB	SUP	APR	DL	PW
1913	Phi A	2	4	.333	17	7	4	0	61.2	56	44	1	3	46	31	4.38	63	.262	.399	21	.190	-0	134	-15	—	-1.3
1914	†Phi A	11	7	.611	32	20	11	2	185	153	82	2	4	103	86	3.02	87	.228	.334	75-1-1	.147	-0*	133	-12	—	-1.4
1915	Phi A	10	22	.313	43	34	20-1	0	276	238	139	1	5	165	157	3.52	83	.246	.359	96-0-3	.125	-4*	77	-15	—	-1.9
1916	Phi A	0	1	.000	7	2	1	0	21.1	20	16	1	1	20	4	5.48	52	.247	.402	8	.375	1*	172	-6	—	-0.2
	Bos A	0	0	ø	8	0	0	1	22.2	19	13	0	0	18	18	4.76	58	.232	.370	6	.167	-0	—	-4	—	-0.3
	Year	0	1	.000	15	2	1	1	44	39	29	1	1	38	22	5.11	55	.239	.386	14	.286	1	175	-10	—	-0.5
1917	Bos A	0	0	ø	1	0	0	0	5	4	3	0	1	4	1	1.80	143	.222	.391	1	.000	-0	—	0	—	0.0
1918	Bos A	0	0	ø	1	0	0	0	2	4	1	0	0	1	2	0.00	ø	.400	.455	1	.000	-0	—	0	—	0.0
Total	6	23	34	.404	109	63	36-1	3	573.2	494	298	5	14	357	299	3.55	79	.242	.358	208-1-4	.149	-4	103	-52	—	-5.1

WYMAN, FRANK Frank H.; B5.10.1862 Haverhill MA; D2.4.1916 Everett MA; d6.10; ▲

YEAR	TM LG	W	L	PCT	G	GS	CG-SHO	SV-BS	IP	H	R	HR	HB	BB-IB	SO	ERA	AERA	OAV	OOB	AB-HR-SH	AVG	PB	SUP	APR	DL	PW
1884	KC U	0	1	.000	3	1	1	0	21	37	29	0	—	3	9	6.86	33	.363	.381	124	.218	-0*	95	-11	—	-0.5

WYNN, EARLY Early "Gus"; B1.6.1920 Hartford AL; D4.4.1999 Venice FL; BB/TR (BR 1941–44)/6´0˝/(195–220); d9.13; Mil 1944–46; C6; HF1972

YEAR	TM LG	W	L	PCT	G	GS	CG-SHO	SV-BS	IP	H	R	HR	HB	BB-IB	SO	ERA	AERA	OAV	OOB	AB-HR-SH	AVG	PB	SUP	APR	DL	PW
1939	Was A	0	2	.000	3	3	1	0	20.1	26	15	0	0	10	1	5.75	76	.313	.387	6-0-1	.167	0	108	-3	—	-0.3
1941	Was A	3	1	.750	5	5	4	0	40	35	14	1	0	10	15	1.57	257	.226	.273	15-0-1	.133	-0	111	9	0	0.8
1942	Was A	10	16	.385	30	28	10-1	0	190	246	129	6	3	73	58	5.12	71	.314	.374	69-0-2	.217	2	103	-31	0	-3.5
1943	Was A	18	12	.600	37	**33**	12-3	0	256.2	232	97	15	1	83	89	2.91	110	.240	.301	98-1-1	.296	7*	108	10	0	1.9
1944	Was A	8	17	.320	33	25	19-2	2	207.2	221	97	3	2	67	65	3.38	96	.277	.334	92-1-0	.207	2*	85	-3	0	-0.3
1946	Was A	8	5	.615	17	12	9	0	107	112	45	8	3	33	36	3.11	108	.267	.325	47-1-0	.319	7*	81	3	0	1.1
1947	Was A☆	17	15	.531	33	31	22-2	0	247	251	114	13	5	90	73	3.64	102	.262	.329	120-2-0	.275	7*	91	1	0	0.9
1948	Was A	8	19	.296	33	31	15-1	0	198	236	144	18	1	94	49	5.82	75	.295	.370	106	.217	3*	80	-31	0	-3.3
1949	Cle A	11	7	.611	26	23	6	0	164.2	186	84	8	1	57	62	4.15	96	.282	.340	70-1-2	.143	-2*	109	-3	0	-0.4
1950	Cle A	18	8	.692	32	28	14-2	0	213.2	166	88	20	4	101	143	**3.20**	135	**.212**	**.305**	77-2-4	.234	7*	118	28	0	3.7
1951	Cle A	20	13	.606	37	**34**	21-3	1	**274.1**	227	102	18	3	107	133	3.02	126	.225	.301	108-1-3	.185	2*	103	27	0	3.1
1952	Cle A	23	12	.657	42	33	19-4	3	285.2	239	103	23	1	132	153	2.90	115	.231	.318	99-0-4	.222	5*	121	18	0	2.6
1953	Cle A	17	12	.586	36	34	16-1	0	251.2	234	121	19	4	107	138	3.93	95	.245	.324	91-3-6	.275	9*	118	-4	0	0.4
1954	†Cle A	**23**	11	.676	40	**36**	20-3	2	**270.2**	225	93	21	0	83	155	2.73	135	.225	.283	93-0-5	.183	1	109	29	0	3.6
1955	Cle A★	17	11	.607	32	31	16-6	0	230	207	86	19	3	80-3	122	2.82	142	.240	.304	84-1-2	.179	1*	91	28	0	3.3
1956	Cle A★	20	9	.690	38	35	18-4	2	277.2	233	93	19	5	91-7	158	2.72	154	.228	.291	101-1-5	.228	3	105	**46**	0	**5.1**
1957	Cle A★	14	17	.452	40	**37**	13-1	1	263	270	139	32	5	104-7	**184**	4.31	86	.265	.335	86-0-3	.116	-2	107	-15	0	-1.8
1958	Chi A★	14	16	.467	40	34	11-4	2	239.2	214	115	27	6	104-3	**179**	4.13	88	.242	.323	75-0-2	.200	3	105	-11	0	-1.1
1959	†Chi A★	**22**	10	.688	37	**37**	14-5	0	**255.2**	202	106	20	9	119-5	179	3.17	119	.216	.308	90-2-2	.244	9	122	15	0	2.7
1960	Chi A★	13	12	.520	36	35	13-**4**	1	237.1	220	105	20	4	112-2	158	3.49	108	.247	.332	75-1-6	.200	7	125	7	0	1.2
1961	Chi A	8	2	.800	17	16	5	0	110.1	88	43	11	1	47-0	64	3.51	112	.220	.302	37-0-1	.162	-0	127	7	0	0.5
1962	Chi A	7	15	.318	27	26	11-3	0	167.2	171	90	15	3	56-6	91	4.46	88	.264	.325	54-0-2	.130	0	81	-10	0	-1.3
1963	Cle A	1	2	.333	20	5	1	1	55.1	50	14	2	0	15-3	29	2.28	159	.250	.300	11	.273	1	88	9	0	0.6
Total	23	300	244	.551	691	612	290-49	15	4564	4291	2037	338	64	1775-36	2334	3.54	106	.248	.320	1704-17-52	.214	72	105	126	0	19.5

WYNNE, BILLY Billy Vernon; B7.31.1943 Williamston NC; BL/TR/6´5˝/(205–206); d8.6; Col Pfeiffer

YEAR	TM LG	W	L	PCT	G	GS	CG-SHO	SV-BS	IP	H	R	HR	HB	BB-IB	SO	ERA	AERA	OAV	OOB	AB-HR-SH	AVG	PB	SUP	APR	DL	PW
1967	NY N	0	0	ø	6	1	0	0	8.2	12	4	0	0	2-0	4	3.12	109	.324	.350	1	.000	-0	130	0	0	0.0
1968	Chi A	0	0	ø	1	0	0	0	2	2	2	0	0	2-0	1	4.50	67	.250	.400	0	ø	0	—	-1	0	0.0
1969	Chi A	7	7	.500	20	20	6-1	0-0	128.2	143	63	14	3	50-8	67	4.06	95	.283	.350	41-0-7	.122	-1	80	-3	0	-0.4
1970	Chi A	1	4	.200	12	9	0	0-0	44	54	30	8	1	22-2	19	5.32	73	.298	.374	13	.077	-1	105	-7	0	-0.7
1971	Cal A	0	0	ø	3	0	0	0-0	3.2	6	2	0	0	2-0	6	4.91	66	.375	.444	0	ø	0	—	-1	0	0.0
Total	5	8	11	.421	42	30	6-1	0-0	187	217	101	22	4	78-10	97	4.33	88	.290	.359	55-0-7	.109	-2	90	-12	0	-1.1

WYNNE, BILL William Andrew; B3.27.1869 Neuse NC; D8.7.1951 Raleigh NC; BR/TR/5´11.5˝/161; d8.31; Col Wake Forest

YEAR	TM LG	W	L	PCT	G	GS	CG-SHO	SV-BS	IP	H	R	HR	HB	BB-IB	SO	ERA	AERA	OAV	OOB	AB-HR-SH	AVG	PB	SUP	APR	DL	PW
1894	Was N	0	1	.000	1	1	1	0	8	10	11	0	2	8	2	6.75	78	.303	.465	3	.000	-0	67	-2	—	-0.2

WYSE, HANK Henry Washington "Hooks"; B3.1.1918 Lunsford AR; D10.22.2000 Pryor OK; BR/TR/5´11.5˝/185; d9.7

YEAR	TM LG	W	L	PCT	G	GS	CG-SHO	SV-BS	IP	H	R	HR	HB	BB-IB	SO	ERA	AERA	OAV	OOB	AB-HR-SH	AVG	PB	SUP	APR	DL	PW
1942	Chi N	2	1	.667	4	4	1-1	0	28	33	10	1	0	6	8	1.93	166	.287	.322	8-0-2	.125	-0	171	3	0	0.3
1943	Chi N	9	7	.563	38	15	8-2	5	156	159	57	4	2	34	45	2.94	113	.264	.306	50-0-5	.080	-4*	117	8	0	0.7
1944	Chi N	16	15	.516	41	34	14-3	1	257.1	277	113	9	2	57	86	3.15	112	.278	.318	90-0-6	.178	-1	116	9	0	0.9

YEAR	TM LG	W	L	PCT	G	GS	CG-SHO	SV-BS	IP	H	R	HR	HB	BB-IB	SO	ERA	AERA	OAV	OOB	AB-HR-SH	AVG	PB	SUP	APR	DL	PW
1945	†Chi N∗	22	10	.688	38	34	23-2	0	278.1	272	95	17	5	55	77	2.68	136	.256	.296	101-0-8	.168	-2	102	32	0	3.3
1946	Chi N	14	12	.538	40	27	12-2	1	201.1	206	73	7	3	52	52	2.68	124	.265	.313	74-0-4	.243	1	107	13	0	1.9
1947	Chi N	6	9	.400	37	19	5-1	1	142	158	84	12	3	64	53	4.31	92	.286	.363	45-0-4	.111	-1	73	-8	0	-0.8
1950	Phi A	9	14	.391	41	23	4	0	170.2	192	121	16	8	87	33	5.85	78	.287	.376	59-0-3	.153	-3	97	-24	0	-2.9
1951	Phi A	1	2	.333	9	1	0	0	14.2	24	14	0	0	8	5	7.98	54	.381	.451	4	.250	-0	83	-6	0	-1.0
	Was A	0	0	ø	3	2	0	0	9.1	17	14	0	1	10	3	9.64	42	.378	.500	4	.000	-1	130	-7	0	-0.4
	Year	1	2	.333	12	3	0	0	24	41	28	0	1	18	8	8.63	49	.380	.472	8	.125	-1	113	-12	0	-1.4
Total	8	79	70	.530	251	159	67-11	8	1257.2	1338	581	66	24	373	362	3.52	105	.274	.329	435-0-32	.163	-11	104	20	0	2.0
WYSONG, BIFF	Harlan; B4.13.1905 Clarksville OH; D8.7.1951 Xenia OH; BL/TL/6´3˝/195; d8.10																									
1930	Cin N	0	1	.000	1	1	0	0	2.1	6	5	0	0	3	1	19.29	25	.545	.643	0	ø	0	0	-4	—	-0.5
1931	Cin N	0	2	.000	12	2	0	0	21.2	25	22	2	0	23	5	7.89	47	.298	.449	4	.250	0	115	-10	—	-0.8
1932	Cin N	1	0	1.000	7	0	0	0	12.1	13	7	0	0	8	5	3.65	106	.277	.382	2	.000	-0	—	0	—	0.0
Total	3	1	3	.250	20	3	0	0	36.1	44	34	2	0	34	11	7.18	54	.310	.443	6	.167	-0	74	-14	—	-1.3
YABU, KEIICHI	Keiichi; B9.28.1968 Mie, Japan; BR/TR/6´0˝/200; d4.9																									
2005	Oak A	4	0	1.000	40	0	0	1-1	58	64	34	6	8	26-3	44	4.50	97	.287	.377	1	.000	-0	—	-2	0	-0.1
YAN, ESTEBAN	Esteban Luis; B6.22.1975 Campina, D.R.; BR/TR/6´4˝/(230–255); d5.20																									
1996	Bal A	0	0	ø	4	0	0	0-0	9.1	13	7	3	0	3-1	7	5.79	86	.333	.381	0	ø	0	—	-1	0	-0.1
1997	Bal A	0	1	.000	3	2	0	0-0	9.2	20	18	3	2	7-0	4	15.83	28	.417	.500	0	ø	0	83	-13	0	-1.0
1998	TB A	5	4	.556	64	0	0	1-4	88.2	78	41	11	5	41-2	77	3.86	124	.236	.326	0	ø	0	—	9	0	0.8
1999	TB A	3	4	.429	50	1	0	0-3	61	77	41	8	9	32-4	46	5.90	84	.326	.421	0	ø	0	131	-4	28	-0.4
2000	TB A	7	8	.467	43	20	0	0-2	137.2	158	98	26	11	42-0	111	6.21	79	.285	.344	1-1-1	1.000	1	111	-18	0	-1.5
2001	TB A	4	6	.400	54	0	0	22-9	62.1	64	34	7	5	11-1	64	3.90	116	.262	.307	0	ø	0	—	3	20	0.5
2002	TB A	7	8	.467	55	0	0	19-8	69	70	35	10	3	29-1	53	4.30	105	.259	.337	0	ø	0	—	2	0	0.4
2003	Tex A	0	1	.000	15	0	0	0-0	23.1	31	19	5	2	7-1	25	6.94	72	.307	.364	0	ø	0	—	-5	0	-0.2
	StL N	2	0	1.000	39	0	0	1-0	43.1	53	29	8	5	16-4	28	6.02	68	.308	.376	1	1.000	0	—	-9	0	-0.4
2004	Det A	3	6	.333	69	0	0	7-10	87	92	43	8	4	32-5	69	3.83	117	.274	.341	0	ø	0	—	5	0	0.6
2005	†LA A	1	1	.500	49	0	0	0-0	66.2	66	36	8	0	30-4	45	4.59	93	.258	.331	0	ø	0	—	-2	0	-0.1
2006	LA A	0	0	ø	13	0	0	0-0	22.1	19	18	4	1	13-2	16	6.85	65	.232	.340	0	ø	0	—	-6	0	-0.3
	Cin N	1	0	1.000	14	0	0	1-0	15	13	7	4	0	7-2	8	3.60	131	.245	.323	0	ø	0	—	2	0	0.1
Total	11	33	39	.458	472	23	0	51-36	695.1	754	426	105	47	270-27	553	5.14	90	.277	.349	2-1-1	1.000	2	114	-37	48	-1.6
YARNALL, ED	Harvey Edward; B12.4.1975 Lima PA; BL/TL/6´3˝/234; [NYN96 3/78]; d7.15; Col Louisiana St.																									
1999	NY A	1	0	1.000	5	2	0	0-0	17	17	8	1	0	10-0	13	3.71	128	.254	.351	0	ø	0	168	2	0	0.1
2000	NY A	0	0	ø	2	1	0	0-0	3	5	5	1	1	3-0	1	15.00	32	.417	.563	0	ø	0	255	-3	0	-0.2
Total	2	1	0	1.000	7	3	0	0-0	20	22	13	2	1	13-0	14	5.40	88	.278	.387	0	ø	0	197	-1	0	-0.1
YARNALL, RUSTY	Waldo Ward; B10.22.1902 Chicago IL; D10.9.1985 Lowell MA; BR/TR/6´0˝/175; d6.30; Col Vermont																									
1926	Phi N	0	1	.000	1	0	0	0	1	3	2	0	0	1	0	18.00	23	.500	.571	1	.000	-0	—	-1	—	-0.2
YARRISON, RUBE	Byron Wardsworth; B3.9.1896 Montgomery PA; D4.22.1977 Williamsport PA; BR/TR/5´11˝/165; d4.13; Col Gettysburg																									
1922	Phi A	1	2	.333	18	1	0	0	33.2	50	32	4	2	12	10	8.29	51	.362	.421	6	.167	-0	40	-12	—	-0.9
1924	Bro N	0	2	.000	3	2	0	0	11	12	10	0	1	3	2	6.55	57	.267	.327	2	.000	-0	79	-4	—	-0.6
Total	2	1	4	.200	21	3	0	0	44.2	62	42	4	3	15	12	7.86	53	.339	.398	8	.125	-0	62	-16	—	-1.5
YATES, TYLER	Tyler Kali; B8.7.1977 Lihue HI; BR/TR/6´4˝/(220–240); [OakA98 23/675]; d4.9; Col Hawaii–Hilo; [DL 2005 NY N 183]																									
2004	NY N	2	4	.333	21	7	0	0-0	46.2	61	36	6	3	25-3	35	6.36	68	.311	.394	11-0-1	.091	-1	71	-11	0	-1.2
2006	Atl N	2	5	.286	56	0	0	1-5	50	42	23	6	0	31-8	46	3.96	114	.228	.340	0	ø	0	—	4	0	0.5
Total	2	4	9	.308	77	7	0	1-5	96.2	103	59	12	3	56-11	81	5.12	86	.271	.367	11-0-1	.091	-1	71	-7	183	-0.7
YDE, EMIL	Emil Ogden; B1.28.1900 Great Lakes IL; D12.4.1968 Leesburg FL; BB/TL (BL 1925)/5´11˝/165; d4.21																									
1924	Pit N	16	3	**.842**	33	22	14-**4**	0	194	171	70	3	6	62	53	2.83	136	.244	.311	88-1-4	.239	2*	114	22	—	2.2
1925	†Pit N	17	9	.654	33	28	13	0	207	254	125	11	2	75	41	4.13	108	.309	.369	89-0-2	.191	-2*	109	4	—	0.2
1926	Pit N	8	7	.533	37	22	12-1	0	187.1	181	97	3	2	81	34	3.65	108	.260	.339	74-0-2	.230	3*	110	4	—	0.5
1927	†Pit N	1	3	.250	9	2	0	0	29.2	45	35	1	2	15	9	9.71	42	.375	.453	18	.167	-0*	73	-17	—	-1.8
1929	Det A	7	3	.700	29	6	4-1	0	86.2	100	60	8	0	63	23	5.30	81	.296	.406	48-0-1	.333	2*	183	-9	—	-0.5
Total	5	49	25	.662	141	80	43-6	0	704.2	751	387	26	12	296	160	4.02	102	.281	.355	317-1-9	.233	5	116	4	—	0.6
YEAGER, JOE	Joseph Francis "Little Joe"; B8.28.1875 Philadelphia PA; D7.2.1937 Detroit MI; BR/TR/5´10˝/160; d4.22; ▲																									
1898	Bro N	12	22	.353	36	33	32	0	291.1	333	177	4	6	80	70	3.65	98	.285	.334	134-0-3	.172	-3*	84	-6	—	-0.7
1899	Bro N	2	2	.500	10	4	2-1	1	47.2	56	29	1	2	16	6	4.72	83	.292	.352	47-0-2	.191	1*	143	-2	—	-0.1
1900	Bro N	1	1	.500	2	2	2	0	17	21	13	1	0	5	2	6.88	56	.304	.351	9	.333	0*	90	-4	—	-0.3
1901	Det A	12	11	.522	26	25	22-2	1	199.2	209	105	4	8	46	38	2.61	147	.266	.313	125-2-2	.296	5*	85	22	—	2.9
1902	Det A	6	12	.333	19	15	14	0	140	171	90	5	5	41	28	4.82	76	.301	.353	161-1-1	.242	3*	95	-13	—	-1.0
1903	Det A	0	1	.000	1	1	1	0	9	15	7	0	0	0	1	4.00	73	.366	.366	402-0-9	.256	0*	74	-1	—	-0.1
Total	6	33	49	.402	94	80	73-3	2	704.2	805	421	15	21	188	145	3.74	99	.285	.334	878-3-17	.244	6	90	-4	—	0.7
YEARGIN, AL	James Almond; B10.16.1901 Mauldin SC; D5.8.1937 Greenville SC; BR/TR/5´11˝/170; d10.1																									
1922	Bos N	0	1	.000	1	1	1	0	7	5	3	1	0	2	1	1.29	311	.192	.250	3	.000	-0	0	1	—	0.1
1924	Bos N	1	11	.083	32	12	6	0	141.1	162	90	7	3	42	34	5.09	75	.293	.346	42-0-2	.143	-2	65	-19	—	-1.4
Total	2	1	12	.077	33	13	7	0	148.1	167	93	8	3	44	35	4.91	78	.288	.342	45-0-2	.133	-2	60	-18	—	-1.3
YELLEN, LARRY	Lawrence Alan; B1.4.1943 Brooklyn NY; BR/TR/5´11˝/190; d9.26; Col Hunter																									
1963	Hou N	0	0	ø	1	1	0	0	5	7	4	0	0	1-0	3	3.60	88	.280	.296	2	.000	-0	137	-1	0	-0.1
1964	Hou N	0	0	ø	13	1	0	0	21	27	19	4	0	10-1	9	6.86	50	.297	.363	3	.000	-0	129	-9	0	-0.5
Total	2	0	0	ø	14	2	0	0	26	34	23	4	0	11-1	12	6.23	54	.293	.349	5	.000	-0	130	-10	0	-0.6
YELLOW HORSE, CHIEF	Moses J.; B3.28.1898 Pawnee OK; D4.10.1964 Pawnee OK; BR/TR/5´10˝/180; d4.15																									
1921	Pit N	5	3	.625	10	4	1	1	48.1	45	17	1	0	13	19	2.98	129	.254	.305	17	.000	-2	75	5	—	0.5
1922	Pit N	3	1	.750	28	4	2	0	77.2	92	48	0	2	20	24	4.52	90	.305	.352	19-0-2	.316	1	120	-4	—	-0.2
Total	2	8	4	.667	38	8	3	1	126	137	65	1	2	33	43	3.93	101	.286	.335	36-0-2	.167	-2	97	1	—	0.3
YERKES, CARROLL	Charles Carroll "Lefty"; B6.13.1903 McSherrystown PA; D12.20.1950 Oakland CA; BR/TL/5´11˝/180; d5.31																									
1927	Phi A	0	0	ø	1	0	0	0	1	0	0	0	0	1	0	0.00	ø	.000	.333	0	ø	0	—	0	—	0.0
1928	Phi A	0	1	.000	2	1	1	0	8.2	7	2	0	0	2	1	2.08	193	.233	.281	3	.000	-0	0	2	—	0.2
1929	Phi A	1	0	1.000	19	2	0	1	37.1	47	20	0	1	13	11	4.58	92	.329	.389	10	.000	-2	179	0	—	-0.1
1932	Chi N	0	0	ø	2	0	0	0	9	5	3	2	0	3	4	3.00	126	.167	.242	3	.333	0	—	1	—	0.1
1933	Chi N	0	0	ø	1	0	0	0	2	2	1	0	0	1	0	4.50	73	.286	.375	0	ø	0	—	0	—	0.0
Total	5	1	1	.500	25	3	1	1	58	61	26	2	1	20	16	3.88	106	.288	.352	16	.063	-2	124	3	—	0.2
YERKES, STAN	Stanley Lewis "Yank"; B11.28.1874 Cheltenham PA; D7.28.1940 Boston MA; BR/TR/5´10˝/165; d5.3																									
1901	Bal A	0	1	.000	1	1	1	0	8	12	9	0	0	2	4	6.75	57	.343	.378	3	.333	0	70	-2	—	-0.2
	StL N	3	1	.750	4	4	4	0	34	35	14	2	1	6	15	3.18	100	.265	.302	12-0-1	.083	-1	117	1	—	0.0
1902	StL N	12	21	.364	39	37	27-1	0	272.2	341	160	1	2	79	81	3.66	75	.306	.353	91	.132	-3	93	-28	—	-3.4
1903	StL N	0	1	.000	1	1	0	0	5	8	6	0	0	0	3	1.80	181	.333	.333	2	.000	-0	124	-1	—	-0.1
Total	3	15	24	.385	45	43	32-1	0	319.2	396	189	3	3	87	103	3.66	77	.303	.348	108-0-1	.130	-4	95	-30	—	-3.7
YETT, RICH	Richard Martin; B10.6.1962 Pomona CA; BR/TR/6´2˝/(170–187); [MinA80 26/650]; d4.13																									
1985	Min A	0	0	ø	1	1	0	0-0	0.1	1	1	0	0	2-0	0	27.00	16	.333	.600	0	ø	0	144	-1	0	0.0
1986	Cle A	5	3	.625	39	3	1-1	1-3	78.2	84	48	10	1	37-4	50	5.15	81	.275	.351	0	ø	0	145	-7	0	-0.7
1987	Cle A	3	9	.250	37	11	2	1-2	97.2	96	63	21	3	49-3	59	5.25	87	.257	.346	0	ø	0	98	-6	0	-0.7
1988	Cle A	9	6	.600	23	22	0	0-0	134.1	146	72	11	1	55-1	71	4.62	90	.275	.344	0	ø	0	92	-5	34	-0.6
1989	Cle A	5	6	.455	32	12	1	0-0	99	111	56	10	2	47-1	47	5.00	80	.283	.360	0	ø	0	110	-9	0	-1.0
1990	Min A	0	0	ø	4	0	0	0-0	4.1	6	2	1	0	1-1	2	2.08	201	.353	.389	0	ø	0	—	1	0	0.0
Total	6	22	24	.478	136	49	4-1	2-5	414.1	444	242	53	7	191-10	229	4.95	85	.274	.351	0	ø	0	102	-27	34	-3.0

THE PITCHER REGISTER

YEAR	TM LG	W	L	PCT	G	GS	CG-SHO	SV-BS	IP	H	R	HR	HB	BB-IB	SO	ERA	AERA	OAV	OOB	AB-HR-SH	AVG	PB	SUP	APR	DL	PW
Yingling, Earl	Earl Hershey "Chink"; B10.29.1888 Chillicothe OH; D10.2.1962 Columbus OH; BL/TL/5´11.5˝/180; d4.12; Mil 1918																									
1911	Cle A	1	0	1.000	4	3	1	0	22.1	30	17	1	1	9	6	4.43	77	.326	.392	11	.273	0*	127	-3	—	-0.1
1912	Bro N	6	11	.353	25	16	12	0	163	186	90	10	1	56	51	3.59	93	.293	.351	64-0-1	.250	3	89	-5	—	-0.2
1913	Bro N	8	8	.500	26	13	8-2	0	146.2	158	56	2	2	10	40	2.58	128	.280	.295	60-0-2	.383	8*	97	10	—	2.0
1914	Cin N	9	13	.409	34	27	8-3	0	198	207	102	6	6	54	80	3.45	85	.274	.328	120-1-1	.192	1*	98	-9	—	-0.8
1918	Was A	1	2	.333	5	2	2	0	38	30	15	0	0	12	15	2.13	128	.238	.304	15	.467	3*	69	2	—	0.6
Total	5	25	34	.424	94	61	31-5	0	568	611	280	19	10	141	192	3.22	98	.281	.328	270-1-4	.267	16	96	-5	—	1.5
Yingling, Joe	Joseph; B2.28.1867 Baltimore MD; D10.22.1903 Baltimore MD; BR/TL/5´7.5˝/145; d5.28; b–Charlie																									
1886	Was N	0	0	ø	1	0	0	0	3	7	6	1	—	1	1	12.00	27	.412	.444	2	.000	-0	—	-3	—	-0.1
Yochim, Len	Leonard Joseph; B10.16.1928 New Orleans LA; BL/TL/6´2˝/(195–200); d9.18; b–Ray																									
1951	Pit N	1	1	.500	2	2	0	0	8.2	10	9	0	1	11	5	8.31	51	.278	.458	3-0-1	.000	-0	94	-4	0	-0.6
1954	Pit N	0	1	.000	10	1	0	0	19.2	30	17	2	0	8	7	7.32	57	.361	.409	2	.500	0	0	-6	0	-0.2
Total	2	1	2	.333	12	3	0	0	28.1	40	26	2	1	19	12	7.62	55	.336	.426	5-0-1	.200	-0	63	-10	0	-0.8
Yochim, Ray	Raymond Austin Aloysius; B7.19.1922 New Orleans LA; D1.26.2002 New Orleans LA; BR/TR/6´1˝/170; d5.2; b–Len																									
1948	StL N	0	0	ø	1	0	0	0	1	0	0	0	0	3	1	0.00	ø	.000	.500	0	ø	0	—	0	0	0.0
1949	StL N	0	0	ø	3	0	0	0	2.1	3	4	1	0	4	3	15.43	27	.273	.467	0	ø	0	—	-3	0	-0.1
Total	2	0	0	ø	4	0	0	0	3.1	3	4	1	0	7	4	10.80	38	.214	.476	0	ø	0	—	-3	0	-0.1
York, Lefty	James Edward; B11.1.1892 West Fork AR; D4.9.1961 York PA; BL/TL/5´10˝/185; d9.12																									
1919	Phi A	0	2	.000	2	2	0	0	4.1	13	13	0	0	5	2	24.92	14	.500	.581	1	.000	-0	114	-9	—	-1.3
1921	Chi N	5	9	.357	40	11	4-1	1	139	170	82	5	5	63	57	4.73	81	.308	.384	39-0-3	.128	-2	67	-13	—	-1.5
Total	2	5	11	.313	42	13	4-1	1	143.1	183	95	5	5	68	59	5.34	71	.317	.393	40-0-3	.125	-2	73	-22	—	-2.8
York, Jim	James Harlan; B8.27.1947 Maywood CA; BR/TR/6´3˝/200; [KCA69 16/381]; d9.21; Col UCLA																									
1970	KC A	1	1	.500	4	0	0	0-1	8	5	3	2	0	2-0	6	3.38	111	.179	.226	2	.000	-0	—	1	0	0.1
1971	KC A	5	5	.500	53	0	0	3-2	93.1	70	32	7	3	44-7	103	2.89	119	.203	.297	17-1-0	.118	1	—	6	0	0.8
1972	Hou N	0	1	.000	26	0	0	0-0	36	45	21	3	1	18-3	25	5.25	64	.321	.398	1	.000	-0	—	-7	0	-0.4
1973	Hou N	3	4	.429	41	0	0	6-3	53	65	26	4	1	20-5	22	4.42	83	.305	.364	5-0-1	.000	-0	—	-3	0	-0.5
1974	Hou N	2	2	.500	28	0	0	1-0	38.1	48	20	1	1	19-6	15	3.29	106	.298	.374	4	.000	-1	—	-1	0	-0.2
1975	Hou N	4	4	.500	19	4	0	0-0	46.2	43	22	1	5	25-3	17	3.86	88	.251	.358	11	.091	-0	155	-3	0	-0.5
1976	NY A	1	0	1.000	3	0	0	0-0	9.2	14	7	1	1	4-0	6	5.59	61	.333	.404	0	ø	0	—	-3	0	-0.2
Total	7	16	17	.485	174	4	0	10-6	285	290	131	19	12	132-24	194	3.79	92	.264	.346	40-1-1	.075	-1	155	-10	0	-0.9
York, Mike	Michael David; B9.6.1964 Oak Park IL; BR/TR/6´1˝/(190–192); [NYA82 40/820]; d8.17																									
1990	Pit N	1	1	.500	4	1	0	0-0	12.2	13	5	0	1	5-0	4	2.84	128	.277	.352	3	.333	0	173	1	0	0.2
1991	Cle A	1	4	.200	14	4	0	0-0	34.2	45	29	2	2	19-3	19	6.75	62	.333	.412	0	ø	0	148	-10	51	-1.2
Total	2	2	5	.286	18	5	0	0-0	47.1	58	34	2	3	24-3	23	5.70	71	.319	.397	3	.333	0	154	-9	51	-1.0
Yoshii, Masato	Masato; B4.20.1965 Osaka, Japan; BR/TR/6´2˝/(210–214); d4.5																									
1998	NY N	6	8	.429	29	29	1	0-0	171.2	166	79	22	6	53-5	117	3.93	105	.255	.315	48-0-8	.063	-2	85	4	0	0.0
1999	†NY N	12	8	.600	31	29	1	0-0	174	168	86	25	6	58-3	105	4.40	99	.260	.324	55-0-6	.164	-1	112	0	0	-0.3
2000	Col N	6	15	.286	29	29	0	0-0	167.1	201	112	32	2	53-6	88	5.86	99	.306	.357	50-1-12	.180	-1	83	1	0	0.0
2001	Mon N	4	7	.364	42	11	0	0-0	113	127	65	18	5	26-2	63	4.78	90	.279	.323	16-0-2	.125	-0	101	-6	0	-0.5
2002	Mon N	4	9	.308	31	20	1	0-0	131.1	143	66	15	4	32-2	74	4.11	107	.281	.326	35-0-5	.057	-1	100	4	0	0.2
Total	5	32	47	.405	162	118	3	0-0	757.1	805	408	112	23	222-18	447	4.62	100	.276	.329	204-1-33	.123	-5	95	3	0	-0.6
Yost, Gus	August; 6´5˝/?; d6.12																									
1893	Chi N	0	1	.000	1	1	0	0	2.2	3	4	0	0	8	1	13.50	34	.273	.579	1	.000	-0	91	-2	—	-0.3
Youman, Shane	Shane Demond; B10.11.1979 New Iberia LA; BL/TL/6´4˝/220; [PitN01 43/1280]; d9.10; Col Louisiana St.																									
2006	Pit N	0	2	.000	5	3	0	0-0	21.2	15	7	1	0	10-0	5	2.91	157	.200	.291	7	.429	1	34	4	0	0.5
Youmans, Floyd	Floyd Everett; B5.11.1964 Tampa FL; BR/TR/6´1˝/(180–200); [NYN82 2/33]; d7.1; [DL 1990 Phi N 178]																									
1985	Mon N	4	3	.571	14	12	0	0-0	77	57	27	3	1	49-1	54	2.45	140	.206	.325	19-0-3	.053	-0	96	7	0	0.5
1986	Mon N	13	12	.520	33	32	6-2	0-0	219	145	93	14	4	118-4	202	3.53	106	.188	.297	75-1-2	.160	1	96	7	0	0.7
1987	Mon N	9	8	.529	23	23	3-3	0-0	116.1	112	63	13	1	47-2	94	4.64	92	.251	.321	40-1-1	.150	1	82	-2	50	-0.3
1988	Mon N	3	6	.333	14	13	1-1	0-0	84	64	35	8	2	41-1	54	3.21	113	.213	.307	26	.154	-0	88	4	20	0.3
1989	Phi N	1	5	.167	10	10	0	0-0	42.2	50	31	7	2	25-3	20	5.70	63	.299	.391	13-0-1	.077	-1	86	-10	126	-1.3
Total	5	30	34	.469	94	90	10-6	0-0	539	428	249	45	10	280-11	424	3.74	101	.218	.316	173-2-7	.139	1	90	6	374	-0.1
Young, Anthony	Anthony Wayne; B1.19.1966 Houston TX; BR/TR/6´2˝/(200–220); [NYN87 38/978]; d8.5; Col Houston																									
1991	NY N	2	5	.286	10	8	0	0-0	49.1	48	20	4	1	12-1	20	3.10	118	.257	.303	14-0-1	.143	0	74	3	0	0.3
1992	NY N	2	14	.125	52	13	1	15-5	121	134	66	8	1	31-5	64	4.17	84	.285	.328	27-0-2	.111	-1	95	-11	0	-1.7
1993	NY N	1	16	.059	39	10	1	3-2	100.1	103	62	8	1	42-9	62	3.77	107	.265	.336	14-0-2	.143	-0	45	-3	0	-0.5
1994	Chi N	4	6	.400	20	19	0	0-0	114.2	103	57	12	0	46-2	65	3.92	108	.246	.318	34-0-5	.176	-0	103	2	32	0.2
1995	Chi N	3	4	.429	32	1	0	2-0	41.1	47	20	5	3	14-2	15	3.70	113	.288	.356	3	.667	1	108	2	77	0.3
1996	Hou N	3	3	.500	28	0	0	0-1	33.1	36	18	4	4	22-4	19	4.59	84	.279	.397	2	.000	-0	—	-2	19	-0.4
Total	6	15	48	.238	181	51	2	20-8	460	471	243	41	10	167-23	245	3.89	100	.268	.333	94-0-10	.160	-0	86	-9	128	-1.8
Young, Pete	Bryan Owen; B3.19.1968 Meadville MS; BR/TR/6´0˝/225; [MonN89 6/150]; d6.5; Col Mississippi St.																									
1992	Mon N	0	0	ø	13	0	0	0-0	20.1	18	9	0	1	9-2	11	3.98	87	.247	.329	0	ø	0	—	-1	0	-0.1
1993	Mon N	1	0	1.000	4	0	0	0-0	5.1	4	2	1	0	0-0	3	3.38	124	.211	.211	1	.000	-0	—	1	0	0.1
Total	2	1	0	1.000	17	0	0	0-0	25.2	22	11	1	1	9-2	14	3.86	94	.239	.308	1	.000	-0	—	0	0	0.0
Young, Charlie	Charles "Cy"; B1.12.1893 Philadelphia PA; D5.12.1952 Riverside NJ; BB/TR/5´10.5˝/155; d9.5																									
1915	Bal F	2	3	.400	9	5	1	0	35	39	32	0	4	21	13	5.91	49	.289	.400	9-0-1	.222	0	49	-12	—	-1.5
Young, Chris	Christopher Ryan; B5.25.1979 Dallas TX; BR/TR/6´10˝/(250–260); [PitN00 3/89]; d8.24; Col Princeton																									
2004	Tex A	3	2	.600	7	7	0	0-0	36.1	36	21	7	2	10-0	27	4.71	105	.248	.306	0	ø	0	91	1	0	0.1
2005	Tex A	12	7	.632	31	31	0	0-0	164.2	162	84	19	7	45-2	137	4.26	107	.252	.307	5	.000	-1	125	5	0	0.4
2006	†SD N	11	5	.688	31	31	0	0-0	179.1	134	72	28	6	69-4	164	3.46	120	**.206**	.287	54-0-8	.130	0	94	16	0	1.2
Total	3	26	14	.650	69	69	0	0-0	380.1	332	177	54	15	124-6	328	3.93	112	.231	.298	59-0-8	.119	-0	108	22	0	1.7
Young, Cliff	Clifford Raphael; B8.2.1964 Willis TX; D11.4.1993 Montgomery Co. TX; BL/TL/6´4˝/(200–210); [MonN83 5/120]; d7.14																									
1990	Cal A	1	1	.500	17	0	0	0-2	30.2	40	14	2	1	7-1	19	3.52	109	.325	.356	0	ø	0	—	1	0	0.1
1991	Cal A	1	0	1.000	11	0	0	0-0	12.2	12	6	3	0	3-1	6	4.26	97	.261	.306	0	ø	0	—	0	0	0.0
1993	Cle A	3	3	.500	21	7	0	1-1	60.1	74	35	9	3	18-1	31	4.62	95	.298	.352	0	ø	0	81	-2	70	-0.2
Total	3	5	4	.556	49	7	0	1-3	103.2	126	55	14	4	28-3	56	4.25	98	.302	.348	0	ø	0	81	-1	70	-0.1
Young, Curt	Curtis Allen; B4.16.1960 Saginaw MI; BR/TL/6´1˝/(175–180); [OakA81 4/92]; d6.24; C3; Col Central Michigan																									
1983	Oak A	0	1	.000	8	2	0	0-0	9	17	17	1	1	5-0	5	16.00	24	.386	.460	0	ø	0	152	-12	0	-1.1
1984	Oak A	9	4	.692	20	17	2-1	0-0	108.2	118	53	9	8	31-0	41	4.06	93	.274	.331	0	ø	0	125	-3	0	-0.3
1985	Oak A	0	4	.000	19	7	0	0-0	46	57	38	15	1	22-0	19	7.24	54	.300	.374	0	ø	0	114	-17	63	-1.3
1986	Oak A	13	9	.591	29	27	5-2	0-0	198	176	88	19	7	57-1	116	3.45	113	.236	.293	0	ø	0	98	9	0	0.9
1987	Oak A	13	7	.650	31	31	6	0-0	203	194	102	38	3	44-0	124	4.08	102	.252	.293	1	.000	-0	121	2	20	0.2
1988	†Oak A	11	8	.579	26	26	1	0-0	156.1	162	77	23	4	50-3	69	4.14	92	.275	.333	0	ø	0	103	-5	0	-0.6
1989	Oak A	5	9	.357	25	20	1	0-0	111	117	56	10	3	47-2	55	3.73	99	.264	.338	0	ø	0	88	-2	0	-0.3
1990	†Oak A	9	6	.600	26	21	0	0-0	124.1	124	70	17	2	53-1	56	4.85	77	.266	.342	0	ø	0*	120	-14	0	-1.4
1991	Oak A	4	2	.667	41	1	0	0-0	68.1	74	38	8	2	34-2	27	5.00	77	.278	.363	0	ø	0	71	-8	15	-0.6
1992	KC A	1	2	.333	10	2	0	0-1	24.1	29	14	1	0	7-1	7	5.18	79	.293	.336	0	ø	0	89	-2	0	-0.3
	NY A	3	0	1.000	13	5	0	0-1	43.1	51	21	1	2	10-1	13	3.32	119	.298	.341	0	ø	0	134	1	27	0.1
	Year	4	2	.667	23	7	0	0-2	67.2	80	35	2	2	17-2	20	3.99	100	.296	.339	0	ø	0	121	0	0	-0.2

YEAR	TM LG	W	L	PCT	G	GS	CG-SHO	SV-BS	IP	H	R	HR	HB	BB-IB	SO	ERA	AERA	OAV	OOB	AB-HR-SH	AVG	PB	SUP	APR	DL	PW
1993	Oak A	1	1	.500	3	3	0	0-0	14.2	14	7	5	0	6-0	4	4.30	96	.241	.313	0	ø	0	96	0	110	0.0
Total	11	69	53	.566	251	162	15-3	0-2	1107	1133	581	147	33	366-11	536	4.31	90	.265	.326	1	.000	-0	110	-51	235	-4.7
Young, Danny	Daniel Bracy; B11.3.1971 Smyrna TN; BR/TL/6´4˝/210; [HouN90 83/1473]; d3.30																									
2000	Chi N	0	1	.000	4	0	0	0-0	3	5	7	1	0	6-0	0	21.00	22	.357	.550	0	ø	0	—	-5	0	-0.9
Young, Cy	Denton True "Cyclone"; B3.29.1867 Gilmore OH; D11.4.1955 Newcomerstown OH; BR/TR/6´2˝/210; d8.6; M1; HF1937																									
1890	Cle N	9	7	.563	17	16	16	0	147.2	145	87	6	8	30	39	3.47	103	.249	.295	65	.123	-6	78	2	—	-0.3
1891	Cle N	27	22	.551	55	46	43	2	423.2	431	244	4	10	140	147	2.85	122	.254	.314	174-1	.167	-3	104	28	—	2.3
1892	†Cle N	**36**	12	**.750**	53	49	48-**9**	0	453	363	158	8	9	118	168	**1.93**	**176**	.211	**.266**	196-1	.158	-8	108	**74**	—	**6.4**
1893	Cle N	34	16	.680	53	46	42-1	1	422.2	442	230	10	10	103	102	3.36	145	.261	**.307**	187-1	.235	-6	102	74	—	6.5
1894	Cle N	26	21	.553	52	47	44-2	1	408.2	488	265	19	5	106	108	3.94	139	.293	.337	186-2-0	.215	-8	92	65	—	5.0
1895	†Cle N	**35**	10	.778	47	40	36-**4**	0	369.2	363	177	10	8	75	121	3.26	153	.253	**.294**	140-0-2	.214	-4	84	**73**	—	6.9
1896	†Cle N	28	15	.651	51	46	42-**5**	**3**	414.1	477	214	7	11	62	**140**	3.24	140	.286	.316	180-3-2	.289	7*	96	56	—	**5.7**
1897	Cle N	21	19	.525	46	38	35-2	0	335.2	391	189	7	9	49	88	3.78	119	.289	.318	153-0-3	.222	-4*	89	27	—	2.3
1898	Cle N	25	13	.658	46	41	40-1	0	377.2	387	167	6	9	41	101	2.53	143	.263	.287	154-2-5	.253	5*	100	40	—	4.4
1899	StL N	26	16	.619	44	42	**40**-4	1	369.1	368	173	10	6	44	111	2.58	154	.260	**.285**	148-1-6	.216	-1	101	50	—	**5.1**
1900	StL N	19	19	.500	41	35	32-**4**	0	321.1	337	144	7	3	36	115	3.00	121	.269	.291	124-1-1	.177	-2	86	28	—	2.6
1901	Bos A	**33**	10	.767	43	41	38-**5**	0	371.1	324	112	6	7	37	**158**	**1.62**	**217**	**.232**	**.256**	153-0-3	.209	0*	110	**77**	—	**7.9**
1902	Bos A	**32**	11	.744	**45**	**43**	**41**-3	0	**384.2**	350	136	6	13	53	160	2.15	166	.243	.276	148-1-1	.230	2	107	**59**	—	**6.0**
1903	†Bos A	**28**	9	**.757**	40	35	**34-7**	**2**	**341.2**	294	115	6	9	37	176	2.08	146	.232	.259	137-1-5	.321	12*	136	**34**	—	**4.8**
1904	Bos A	26	16	.619	43	41	40-**10**	1	380	327	104	6	4	29	200	1.97	136	.233	**.251**	148-1-1	.223	2	94	33	—	3.8
1905	Bos A	18	19	.486	38	33	31-4	0	320.2	248	99	3	8	30	210	1.82	148	.215	**.241**	120-2-2	.150	-2	77	25	—	2.7
1906	Bos A	13	21	.382	39	34	28	2	287.2	288	137	3	8	25	140	3.19	86	.263	.285	104-0-2	.154	-2*	74	-14	—	-1.9
1907	Bos A	21	15	.583	43	37	33-6	2	343.1	286	101	3	7	51	147	1.99	129	.229	**.263**	125-1-1	.216	0*	86	25	—	2.4
1908	Bos A	21	11	.656	36	33	30-3	2	299	230	68	1	1	37	150	1.26	195	.213	.240	115-0-2	.226	1	110	36	—	4.1
1909	Cle A	19	15	.559	35	34	30-3	0	294.1	267	110	4	8	59	109	2.26	113	.250	.294	107-0-6	.196	-0	110	9	—	0.9
1910	Cle A	7	10	.412	21	20	14-1	0	163.1	149	62	0	4	27	58	2.53	102	.252	.289	55-0-3	.145	-0	74	2	—	0.2
1911	Cle A	3	4	.429	7	7	4	0	46.1	54	28	2	1	13	20	3.88	88	.298	.349	16	.063	-2	60	-3	—	-0.5
	Bos N	4	5	.444	11	11	8-2	0	80	83	47	4	3	15	35	3.71	103	.268	.308	25-0-5	.080	-2	66	0	—	-0.3
Total	22	511	316	.618	906	815	749-76	17	7356	7092	3167	138	161	1217	2803	2.63	138	.252	.287	2960-18-50	.210	-22	97	800	—	77.0
Young, Harley	Harlan Edward "Cy the Third"; B9.28.1883 Portland IN; D3.26.1975 Jacksonville FL; BR/TR/6´2˝/?; d4.21																									
1908	Pit N	0	2	.000	8	3	0	0	48.1	40	21	0	5	10	17	2.23	103	.234	.296	12-0-1	.083	-1	61	-1	—	-0.1
	Bos N	0	1	.000	6	2	1	0	27.1	29	19	0	3	4	12	3.29	73	.269	.313	10-0-1	.200	0	117	-4	—	-0.2
	Year	0	3	.000	14	5	1	0	75.2	69	40	0	8	14	29	2.62	89	.247	.302	22-0-2	.136	-0	84	-6	—	-0.3
Young, Irv	Irving Melrose "Young Cy","Cy the Second"; B7.21.1877 Columbia Falls ME; D1.14.1935 Brewer ME; BL/TL/5´10˝/170; d4.14																									
1905	Bos N	20	21	.488	43	**42**	**41**-7	0	**378**	337	146	6	8	71	156	2.90	107	.241	.282	136-0-1	.103	-8	59	14	—	0.9
1906	Bos N	16	25	.390	43	**41**	**37**-4	0	**358.1**	349	157	7	6	83	151	2.91	92	.263	.309	125-0-2	.096	-7	72	-7	—	-1.5
1907	Bos N	10	23	.303	40	32	22-3	1	245.1	287	131	5	13	58	86	3.96	64	.306	.354	80-0-1	.162	-1	74	-33	—	-4.4
1908	Bos N	4	9	.308	16	11	7-1	0	85	94	49	2	2	19	32	2.86	84	.289	.332	32-0-1	.156	-1	101	-8	—	-1.4
	Pit N	4	3	.571	16	7	3-1	1	89.2	73	33	1	5	21	31	2.01	115	.225	.283	30	.200	1	100	1	—	0.2
	Year	8	12	.400	32	18	10-2	1	174.2	167	82	3	7	40	63	2.42	97	.257	.307	62-0-1	.177	0	101	-9	—	-1.2
1910	Chi A	4	8	.333	27	17	7-4	0	135.2	122	52	0	3	39	64	2.72	88	.247	.306	44-0-3	.114	-2	74	-2	—	-0.4
1911	Chi A	5	6	.455	24	11	3-1	2	92.2	99	61	2	0	25	40	4.37	74	.229	.271	28-0-1	.179	-0	85	-12	—	-1.3
Total	6	63	95	.399	209	161	120-21	4	1384.2	1361	629	23	37	316	560	3.11	88	.260	.307	475-0-9	.126	-18	73	-47	—	-7.9
Young, J. B.	J. B.; B Mt.Carmel PA; d6.10																									
1892	StL N	0	0	ø	1	0	0	0	2	9	13	0	2	2	1	22.50	14	.600	.647	1	.000	-0	—	-6	—	-0.3
Young, Jason	Jason Kariya; B9.28.1979 Oakland CA; BR/TR/6´5˝/(210–215); [ColN00 2/47]; d5.12; Col Stanford																									
2003	Col N	0	2	.000	8	3	0	0-0	21.1	34	22	8	1	9-0	18	8.44	58	.354	.411	7	.286	1	102	-8	0	-0.5
2004	Col N	0	1	.000	2	2	0	0-0	8.1	15	12	3	0	5-1	7	12.96	37	.385	.455	2-0-2	.000	-0	137	-7	135	-0.6
Total	2	0	3	.000	10	5	0	0-0	29.2	49	34	11	1	14-1	25	9.71	50	.363	.424	9-0-2	.222	1	115	-15	135	-1.1
Young, Kip	Kip Lane; B10.29.1954 Georgetown OH; BR/TR/5´11˝/175; [DetA76 23/529]; d7.21; Col Bowling Green																									
1978	Det A	6	7	.462	14	13	7	0-0	105.2	94	34	9	2	30-1	49	2.81	139	.246	.303	0	ø	0	92	13	0	1.5
1979	Det A	2	2	.500	13	7	0	0-0	43.2	60	32	11	1	11-0	22	6.39	68	.323	.362	0	ø	0	128	-9	0	-0.7
Total	2	8	9	.471	27	20	7	0-0	149.1	154	66	20	3	41-1	71	3.86	105	.271	.322	0	ø	0	106	4	0	0.8
Young, Matt	Matthew John; B8.9.1958 Pasadena CA; BL/TL/6´3˝/(205–210); [SeaA80 2/32]; d4.6; Col UCLA; [DL 1988 Oak A 182]																									
1983	Sea A★	11	15	.423	33	32	5-2	0-0	203.2	178	86	17	7	79-2	130	3.27	131	.236	.312	0	ø	0	67	21	0	2.6
1984	Sea A	6	8	.429	22	22	1	0-0	113.1	141	81	11	1	57-3	73	5.72	70	.307	.380	0	ø	0	125	-22	25	-2.2
1985	Sea A	12	19	.387	37	35	5-2	1-0	218.1	242	135	23	7	76-3	136	4.91	86	.282	.344	0	ø	0	95	-18	0	-2.3
1986	Sea A	8	6	.571	65	5	1	13-12	103.2	108	50	9	8	46-2	82	3.82	112	.272	.357	0	ø	0	106	5	0	0.6
1987	LA N	5	8	.385	47	0	0	11-4	54.1	62	30	3	0	17-5	42	4.47	89	.288	.339	3	.000	-0	—	-3	0	-0.7
1989	†Oak A	1	4	.200	26	4	0	0-1	37.1	42	31	2	0	31-2	27	6.75	55	.286	.408	0	ø	0	61	-13	71	-1.5
1990	Sea A	8	18	.308	34	33	7-1	0-0	225.1	198	106	15	6	107-7	176	3.51	113	.237	.325	0	ø	0	85	9	0	1.0
1991	Bos A	3	7	.300	19	16	0	0-0	88.2	92	55	4	2	53-2	69	5.18	84	.266	.365	0	ø	0	83	-7	57	-0.7
1992	Bos A	0	4	.000	28	8	1	0-0	70.2	69	42	7	3	42-2	57	4.58	93	.257	.360	0	ø	0	73	-3	16	-0.2
1993	Cle A	1	6	.143	22	8	0	0-0	74.1	75	45	8	3	57-0	65	5.21	84	.266	.394	0	ø	0	81	-6	0	-0.4
Total	10	55	95	.367	333	163	20-5	25-17	1189.2	1207	661	99	37	565-28	857	4.40	95	.265	.348	3	.000	-0	88	-37	351	-3.8
Young, Tim	Timothy R.; B10.15.1973 Gulfport MS; BL/TL/5´9˝/170; [MonN96 19/550]; d9.5; Col Alabama																									
1998	Mon N	0	0	ø	10	0	0	0-0	6	6	4	0	0	4-0	7	6.00	70	.250	.357	0	ø	0	—	-1	0	0.0
2000	Bos A	0	0	ø	8	0	0	0-0	7	7	5	3	1	2-0	6	6.43	78	.269	.345	0	ø	0	—	-1	0	0.0
Total	2	0	0	ø	18	0	0	0-0	13	13	9	3	1	6-0	13	6.23	74	.260	.351	0	ø	0	—	-2	0	0.0
Youngblood, Chief	Albert Clyde; B6.13.1900 Hillsboro TX; D7.6.1968 Amarillo TX; BL/TR/6´3˝/202; d7.16; Col Clarendon (TX) JC																									
1922	Was A	0	0	ø	2	0	0	0	4.1	9	9	0	2	7	0	14.54	27	.429	.600	2	.000	-0	—	-6	—	-0.3
Yount, Ducky	Herbert Macon "Hub"; B12.7.1885 Iredell Co. NC; D5.9.1970 Winston–Salem NC; BR/TR/6´2˝/178; d5.20																									
1914	Bal F	1	1	.500	13	1	1	0	41.1	44	28	2	2	19	19	4.14	73	.280	.365	12-0-1	.083	-1*	0	-6	—	-0.4
Yount, Larry	Lawrence King; B2.15.1950 Houston TX; BR/TR/6´2˝/185; [HouN68 5/87]; d9.15; b–Robin																									
1971	Hou N	0	0	ø	1	0	0	0-0	0	0	0	0	0	0-0	0	(0)	ø	ø	ø	0	ø	0	—	0	0	0.0
Yowell, Carl	Carl Columbus "Sundown"; B12.20.1902 Madison VA; D7.27.1985 Jacksonville TX; BL/TL/6´4˝/180; d9.5																									
1924	Cle A	1	1	.500	4	2	2	0	27	37	21	1	0	13	8	6.67	64	.343	.413	11	.182	-1	148	-6	—	-0.4
1925	Cle A	2	3	.400	12	4	1	0	36.1	40	21	1	1	17	12	4.46	99	.310	.395	8-0-1	.125	-1	57	0	—	-0.1
Total	2	3	4	.429	16	6	3	0	63.1	77	42	2	1	30	20	5.40	81	.325	.403	19-0-1	.158	-1	87	-6	—	-0.5
Yuhas, Eddie	John Edward; B8.5.1924 Youngstown OH; D7.6.1986 Winston–Salem NC; BR/TR/6´1˝/(165–180); d4.17																									
1952	StL N	12	2	.857	54	2	0	6	99.1	90	35	5	2	35	39	2.72	137	.243	.312	21-0-2	.190	1	72	11	0	1.6
1953	StL N	0	0	ø	2	0	0	0	1	3	2	0	0	0	0	18.00	24	.500	.500	0	ø	0	—	-1	140	-0.1
Total	2	12	2	.857	56	2	0	6	100.1	93	37	5	2	35	39	2.87	130	.247	.315	21-0-2	.190	1	72	10	140	1.5
Zabala, Adrian	Adrian (Rodriguez); B8.26.1916 San Antonio de los Banos, Cuba; D1.4.2002 Jacksonville FL; BL/TL/5´11˝/165; d8.11																									
1945	NY N	2	4	.333	11	5	1	0	43.1	46	25	2	0	20	14	4.78	82	.284	.363	13	.231	1	69	-4	0	-0.4
1949	NY N	2	3	.400	15	4	2-1	1	41	44	28	5	1	10	13	5.27	76	.278	.325	13	.077	-1	122	-6	0	-0.8
Total	2	4	7	.364	26	9	3-1	1	84.1	90	53	7	1	30	27	5.02	79	.281	.345	26	.154	-0	92	-10	0	-1.2

YEAR	TM LG	W	L	PCT	G	GS	CG-SHO	SV-BS	IP	H	R	HR	HB	BB-IB	SO	ERA	AERA	OAV	OOB	AB-HR-SH	AVG	PB	SUP	APR	DL	PW
ZABEL, ZIP	George Washington; B2.18.1891 Wetmore KS; D5.31.1970 Beloit WI; BR/TR/6´1.5˝/185; d10.5; Col Baker																									
1913	Chi N	1	0	1.000	1	1	0	0	5	3	0	0	0	1	0	0.00	ø	.167	.211	2	.000	0	118	2	—	0.4
1914	Chi N	4	4	.500	29	7	2	3	128	104	45	5	2	45	50	2.18	128	.235	.309	38-0-2	.184	-1	114	9	—	0.5
1915	Chi N	7	10	.412	36	17	8-3	0	163	124	80	3	4	84	60	3.20	87	.218	.323	54-0-2	.074	-4*	105	-10	—	-1.2
Total	3	12	14	.462	66	25	10-3	3	296	231	125	8	6	130	110	2.71	103	.224	.315	94-0-4	.117	-4	108	1	—	-0.3
ZACHARY, CHINK	Albert Myron (b Albert Myron Zarski); B10.19.1917 Brooklyn NY; BR/TR/5´11˝/182; d4.30																									
1944	Bro N	0	2	.000	4	2	0	0	10.1	10	11	2	1	7	3	9.58	37	.238	.360	3	.000	-0	94	-6	0	-1.0
ZACHARY, TOM	Jonathan Thompson Walton (aka Zach Walton in 1918); B5.7.1896 Graham NC; D1.24.1969 Burlington NC; BL/TL/6´1˝/187; d7.11; Mil 1918–19; Col Guilford																									
1918	Phi A	2	0	1.000	2	2	0	0	8	9	5	0	0	7	1	5.63	52	.321	.457	4	.500	1	231	-2	—	-0.3
1919	Was A	1	5	.167	17	7	0	0	61.2	68	29	0	1	20	9	2.92	110	.292	.350	15	.333	2	77	1	—	0.3
1920	Was A	15	16	.484	44	31	19-3	2	262.2	289	141	7	4	78	53	3.77	99	.285	.339	111	.261	6*	106	-2	—	0.3
1921	Was A	18	16	.529	39	30	17-2	1	250	314	130	10	6	59	53	3.96	104	.319	.361	90-0-3	.256	3	96	6	—	0.9
1922	Was A	15	10	.600	32	25	13-1	1	184.2	190	74	6	3	43	37	3.12	124	.275	.321	71-1-2	.296	5	106	18	—	2.8
1923	Was A	10	16	.385	35	29	10	0	204.1	270	117	9	4	63	40	4.49	84	.321	.372	78-0-4	.192	-0	95	-14	—	-1.6
1924	†Was A	15	9	.625	33	27	13-1	2	202.2	198	74	5	3	53	45	2.75	147	.264	.315	72-0-4	.306	4	104	30	—	3.7
1925	†Was A	12	15	.444	38	**33**	11-1	2	217.2	247	112	10	2	74	58	3.85	110	.296	.355	69-1-7	.174	-2	84	9	—	0.8
1926	StL A	14	15	.483	34	31	18-3	0	247.1	264	126	14	6	97	53	3.60	119	.288	.359	86-1-2	.267	4	81	14	—	2.1
1927	StL A	4	6	.400	13	12	6	0	78.1	110	48	4	0	27	13	4.37	100	.345	.396	28-0-2	.107	-2	94	-1	—	-0.3
	Was A	4	7	.364	15	14	5-1	0	102.2	116	54	2	2	30	13	3.94	103	.290	.343	36-0-2	.139	-2	95	1	—	-0.2
	Year	8	13	.381	28	26	11-1	0	181	226	102	6	2	57	26	4.13	102	.314	.366	64-0-4	.125	-4	95	0	—	-0.5
1928	Was A	6	9	.400	20	14	5-1	0	102.2	130	72	5	1	40	19	5.44	74	.322	.384	33-0-5	.303	1	92	-16	—	-1.8
	†NY A	3	3	.500	7	6	3	1	45.2	54	26	1	0	15	7	3.94	95	.320	.375	15-1-1	.133	-0	109	-2	—	-0.2
	Year	9	12	.429	27	20	8-1	1	148.1	184	98	6	1	55	26	4.98	79	.321	.382	48-1-6	.250	1	97	-18	—	-2.0
1929	NY A	12	0	1.000	26	11	7-2	2	119.2	131	43	5	2	30	35	2.48	155	.277	.323	42-0-5	.238	1	135	19	—	1.7
1930	NY A	1	1	.500	3	3	0	0	16.2	18	16	0	0	9	1	6.48	66	.269	.355	8	.250	1	126	-5	—	-0.4
	Bos N	11	5	.688	24	22	10-1	0	151.1	192	90	9	0	50	57	4.58	108	.317	.369	54-2-4	.241	2*	110	5	—	0.5
1931	Bos N	11	15	.423	33	28	16-3	2	229	243	87	8	1	53	64	3.10	122	.272	.314	84	.167	-1	82	19	—	2.0
1932	Bos N	12	11	.522	32	24	12-1	0	212	231	83	5	2	55	67	3.10	121	.280	.326	77	.273	5*	84	17	—	2.2
1933	Bos N	7	9	.438	26	20	6-2	2	125	134	64	1	0	35	22	3.53	87	.276	.325	42-0-3	.119	-2*	94	-11	—	-1.5
1934	Bos N	1	2	.333	5	4	2-1	0	24	27	9	1	0	8	4	3.38	113	.278	.333	8	.000	-1	34	2	—	0.1
	Bro N	5	6	.455	22	12	4	2	101.2	122	53	5	2	21	28	4.43	88	.301	.339	38	.184	1*	101	-4	—	-0.3
	Year	6	8	.429	27	16	6-1	2	125.2	149	62	6	2	29	32	4.23	92	.297	.338	46	.152	-0	85	-2	—	-0.2
1935	Bro N	7	12	.368	25	21	9-1	4	158	193	76	10	2	35	33	3.59	111	.297	.335	52-0-2	.135	-1	82	7	—	0.6
1936	Bro N	0	0	ø	1	0	0	0	0.1	2	2	0	0	1	0	54.00	8	1.000	1.000	0	ø	0	—	-2	—	-0.1
	Phi N	0	3	.000	7	2	0	1	20.1	28	20	2	0	11	8	7.97	57	.329	.406	9	.333	1*	112	-6	—	-0.7
	Year	0	3	.000	8	2	0	1	20.2	30	22	2	0	12	8	8.71	52	.345	.424	9	.333	1	112	-7	—	-0.8
Total	19	186	191	.493	533	408	186-24	22	3126.1	3580	1551	119	41	914	720	3.73	106	.294	.345	1122-6-46	.226	25	95	83	—	10.6
ZACHARY, CHRIS	William Christopher; B2.19.1944 Knoxville TN; D4.19.2003 Knoxville TN; BL/TR/6´2˝/(190–203); d4.11																									
1963	Hou N	2	2	.500	22	7	0	0	57	62	38	5	3	22-0	42	4.89	64	.272	.340	13-0-1	.000	-1	125	-12	0	-0.9
1964	Hou N	0	1	.000	1	1	0	0	4	6	5	1	0	1-0	2	9.00	38	.333	.368	1	.000	-0	77	-3	0	-0.4
1965	Hou N	0	2	.000	4	2	0	0	10.2	12	6	0	0	6-1	4	4.22	80	.273	.360	2	.000	-0	13	-1	0	-0.2
1966	Hou N	3	5	.375	10	8	0	0	55	44	22	1	1	32-2	37	3.44	100	.221	.330	18	.222	1	90	1	0	0.2
1967	Hou N	1	6	.143	9	7	0	0	36.1	42	27	5	2	12-1	18	5.70	58	.290	.352	10	.100	-0*	49	-10	0	-1.7
1969	KC A	0	1	.000	8	2	0	0-0	18.1	27	17	4	0	7-0	6	7.85	47	.346	.395	2	.500	0	60	-8	0	-0.4
1971	StL N	3	10	.231	23	12	1-1	0-1	89.2	114	58	3	4	26-7	48	5.32	68	.316	.364	33	.242	1*	116	-16	0	-2.0
1972	†Det A	1	1	.500	25	1	0	1-1	38.1	27	6	2	1	15-2	21	1.41	225	.201	.283	2	.500	1	56	8	21	0.5
1973	Pit N	0	1	.000	6	0	0	1-0	12	10	4	1	0	1-0	6	3.00	117	.222	.234	2	.000	-0	—	1	0	0.1
Total	9	10	29	.256	108	40	1-1	2-2	321.1	344	183	22	11	122-13	184	4.57	75	.275	.341	83-0-1	.181	1	91	-40	21	-4.8
ZACHRY, PAT	Patrick Paul; B4.24.1952 Richmond TX; BR/TR/6´5˝/(168–175); [CinN70 19/454]; d4.11																									
1976	†Cin N	14	7	.667	38	28	6-1	0-0	204	170	70	8	2	83-4	143	2.74	128	.228	.305	62-0-12	.113	-2	123	17	0	1.3
1977	Cin N	3	7	.300	12	12	3	0-0	75	78	45	7	1	29-1	36	5.04	78	.273	.338	22-0-4	.136	-1	87	-9	0	-1.0
	NY N	7	6	.538	19	19	2-1	0-0	119.2	129	59	14	3	48-4	63	3.76	101	.278	.347	42-0-1	.143	-2	83	-1	0	-0.4
	Year	10	13	.435	31	31	5-1	0-0	194.2	207	104	21	4	77-5	99	4.25	91	.276	.344	64-0-5	.141	-2	84	-10	0	-1.4
1978	NY N☆	10	6	.625	21	21	5-2	0-0	138	120	57	9	1	60-4	78	3.33	107	.236	.316	43-0-5	.070	-2	94	3	37	0.2
1979	NY N	5	1	.833	7	7	1	0-0	42.2	44	19	3	2	21-2	17	3.59	104	.267	.356	16	.125	-1	123	1	138	0.0
1980	NY N	6	10	.375	28	26	7-3	0-0	164.2	145	65	16	5	58-5	88	3.01	120	.240	.310	46-0-5	.043	-4	90	10	24	0.4
1981	NY N	7	14	.333	24	24	3	0-0	139	151	78	13	4	56-1	76	4.14	85	.282	.349	38-0-4	.158	0	78	-10	0	-1.4
1982	NY N	6	9	.400	36	16	2	1-2	137.2	149	69	10	0	57-5	69	4.05	91	.279	.346	38-0-2	.079	-2	98	-5	0	-0.7
1983	†LA N	6	1	.857	40	1	0	0-0	61.1	63	22	4	1	21-6	36	2.49	145	.278	.337	4	.500	1	49	7	0	0.8
1984	LA N	5	6	.455	58	0	0	2-2	82.2	84	38	3	2	51-13	55	3.81	93	.267	.367	6	.333	1	—	-1	0	-0.1
1985	Phi N	0	0	ø	10	0	0	0-0	12.2	14	7	1	0	11-1	8	4.26	87	.280	.410	1	.000	-0	—	-1	0	0.0
Total	10	69	67	.507	293	154	29-7	3-4	1177.1	1147	529	88	21	495-46	669	3.52	103	.259	.333	318-0-33	.113	-11	95	11	199	-0.9
ZACKERT, GEORGE	George Carl "Zeke"; B12.24.1884 Horton VT; D2.18.1977 Burlington IA; BL/TL/6´0˝/177; d9.22																									
1911	StL N	0	2	.000	4	1	0	0	7.1	17	13	0	0	6	6	11.05	31	.486	.561	1	.000	-0	89	-7	—	-1.2
1912	StL N	0	0	ø	1	0	0	0	1	2	2	0	1	1	0	18.00	19	.667	.800	0	ø	0*	—	-1	—	-0.1
Total	2	0	2	.000	5	1	0	0	8.1	19	15	0	1	7	6	11.88	28	.500	.587	1	.000	-0	89	-8	—	-1.3
ZAHN, GEOFF	Geoffrey Clayton; B12.19.1945 Baltimore MD; BL/TL/6´1˝/(175–185); [LAN68*S5/86]; d9.2; Col Michigan																									
1973	LA N	1	0	1.000	6	1	0	0-0	13.1	5	2	2	0	2-0	9	1.35	258	.116	.156	2	.000	-0	76	3	0	0.2
1974	LA N	3	5	.375	21	10	1	0-0	79.2	78	28	3	2	16-1	33	2.03	169	.254	.295	23-0-3	.174	-0	97	10	0	0.9
1975	LA N	0	1	.000	2	0	0	0-0	3	2	3	0	0	5-1	1	9.00	38	.222	.500	0	ø	0	—	-2	0	-0.3
	Chi N	2	7	.222	16	10	0	1-0	62.2	67	37	2	0	26-3	21	4.45	87	.282	.348	15-0-7	.133	-1	70	-5	43	-0.6
	Year	2	8	.200	18	10	0	1-0	65.2	69	40	2	0	31-4	22	4.66	83	.279	.356	15-0-7	.133	-1	71	-6	0	-0.9
1976	Chi N	0	1	.000	3	2	0	0-0	8.1	16	10	0	1	2-0	4	10.80	36	.410	.452	3	.000	-0	159	-5	0	-0.6
1977	Min A	12	14	.462	34	32	7-1	0-0	198	234	116	20	5	66-4	88	4.68	85	.299	.355	0	ø	0	109	-17	0	-1.8
1978	Min A	14	14	.500	35	35	12-1	0-0	252.1	260	101	18	4	81-2	106	3.03	127	.274	.331	0	ø	0	94	20	0	2.1
1979	Min A	13	7	.650	26	24	4	0-0	169	181	74	13	0	41-1	58	3.57	123	.279	.319	0	ø	0	100	15	31	1.7
1980	Min A	14	18	.438	38	35	13-5	0-0	232.2	273	138	17	2	66-3	96	4.41	99	.302	.347	0	ø	0	92	-4	0	-0.5
1981	Cal A	10	11	.476	25	25	9	0-0	161.1	181	93	18	0	43-2	52	4.41	83	.285	.329	0	ø	0	136	-15	0	-1.7
1982	†Cal A	18	8	.692	34	34	12-4	0-0	229.1	225	100	18	4	65-5	81	3.73	110	.259	.313	0	ø	0	124	10	0	1.0
1983	Cal A	9	11	.450	29	28	11-3	0-0	203	212	90	22	0	51-2	81	3.33	122	.269	.311	0	ø	0	96	13	31	1.1
1984	Cal A	13	10	.565	28	27	9-**5**	0-0	199.1	200	78	11	1	48-4	61	3.12	128	.263	.306	0	ø	0	103	18	31	2.0
1985	Cal A	2	2	.500	7	7	1-1	0-0	37	44	19	5	0	14-0	14	4.38	94	.299	.358	0	ø	0	110	-1	147	0.0
Total	13	111	109	.505	304	270	79-20	1-0	1849	1978	889	149	19	526-28	705	3.74	107	.278	.327	43-0-10	.140	-2	105	40	283	3.5
ZAHNISER, PAUL	Paul Vernon; B9.6.1896 Sac City IA; D9.26.1964 Klamath Falls OR; BR/TR/5´10.5˝/170; d5.18																									
1923	Was A	9	10	.474	33	21	10-1	0	177	201	103	7	3	76	52	3.86	97	.291	.364	52-0-3	.096	-1	121	-6	—	-0.8
1924	Was A	5	7	.417	24	14	5-1	0	92	98	52	2	4	49	28	4.40	92	.283	.378	31-0-1	.129	-2	90	-3	—	-0.6
1925	Bos A	5	12	.294	37	21	7-1	1	176.2	232	124	6	1	89	30	5.15	88	.327	.403	58-0-1	.138	-4	63	-10	—	-1.3
1926	Bos A	6	18	.250	30	24	7-1	0	172	213	106	5	3	69	35	4.97	82	.321	.387	49	.163	-1	59	-15	—	-1.7
1929	Cin N	0	0	ø	1	0	0	0	1	2	3	1	0	1	0	27.00	17	.400	.500	0	ø	0	—	-2	—	-0.1
Total	5	25	47	.347	125	80	29-4	1	618.2	746	388	21	11	284	145	4.66	88	.309	.384	190-0-5	.132	-8	80	-36	—	-4.5
ZAMBRANO, CARLOS	Carlos Alberto; B6.1.1981 Carabobo, Venezuela; BB/TR/6´4˝/(250–255); d8.20																									
2001	Chi N	1	2	.333	6	1	0	0-1	7.2	11	13	2	1	8-0	4	15.26	27	.355	.488	2	.000	-0	44	-9	0	-1.6
2002	Chi N	4	8	.333	32	16	0	0-0	108.1	94	53	9	4	63-2	93	3.66	111	.235	.344	30-0-2	.033	-2	80	3	28	0.2
2003	†Chi N	13	11	.542	32	32	3-1	0-0	214	188	88	9	10	94-12	168	3.11	140	.239	.326	75-2-4	.240	6	98	26	0	3.5
2004	Chi N★	16	8	.667	31	31	1-1	0-0	209.2	174	73	14	20	81-4	188	2.75	161	.225	.314	70-1-8	.229	3	120	36	0	4.3
2005	Chi N	14	6	.700	33	33	2	0-0	223.1	170	88	21	8	86-3	202	3.26	134	.212	.293	80-1-4	.300	8*	103	26	0	3.2

YEAR	TM LG	W	L	PCT	G	GS	CG-SHO	SV-BS	IP	H	R	HR	HB	BB-IB	SO	ERA	AERA	OAV	OOB	AB-HR-SH	AVG	PB	SUP	APR	DL	PW
2006	Chi N☆	**16**	7	**.696**	33	33	0	0-0	214	162	91	20	9	115-4	210	3.41	135	.208	.316	73-6-5	.151	4*	115	27	0	3.2
Total	6	64	42	.604	167	146	6-2	0-1	977	799	406	75	52	447-25	865	3.29	133	.224	.318	330-10-23	.212	19	106	109	28	12.8
Zambrano, Victor	Victor Manuel; B8.6.1975 Los Teques, Miranda, Venez.; BR/TR/6´0˝/(190–205); d6.21																									
2001	TB A	6	2	.750	36	0	0	2-4	51.1	38	21	6	3	18-0	58	3.16	143	.201	.281	0	ø	0	—	7	0	1.1
2002	TB A	8	8	.500	42	11	0	1-2	114	120	77	15	4	68-5	73	5.53	82	.278	.375	1	.000	-0	95	-13	0	-1.6
2003	TB A	12	10	.545	34	28	1	0-0	188.1	165	97	21	20	106-2	132	4.21	109	.237	.349	3-0-2	.000	-0	103	7	0	0.6
2004	TB A	9	7	.563	23	22	0	0-0	128	107	68	13	16	96-2	109	4.43	105	.230	.372	5	.200	0	105	4	0	0.5
	NY N	2	0	1.000	3	3	0	0-0	14	12	9	0	0	6-0	14	3.86	111	.218	.295	6-0-1	.167	-0	123	0	47	-0.1
2005	NY N	7	12	.368	31	27	0	0-0	166.1	170	85	12	15	77-2	112	4.17	99	.264	.353	53-0-5	.132	-1	101	-2	0	-0.3
2006	NY N	1	2	.333	5	5	0	0-0	21.1	25	16	5	0	11-0	15	6.75	65	.291	.371	5	.000	-0	109	-5	148	-0.6
Total	6	45	41	.523	174	96	1	3-6	683.1	637	373	72	58	382-11	513	4.45	100	.248	.354	73-0-8	.123	-1	103	-2	195	-0.4
Zamloch, Carl	Carl Eugene; B10.6.1889 Oakland CA; D8.19.1963 Santa Barbara CA; BR/TR/6´1˝/176; d5.7																									
1913	Det A	1	6	.143	17	5	3	1	69.2	66	31	1	3	23	28	2.45	119	.260	.329	22	.182	-1	76	2	—	0.1
Zamora, Oscar	Oscar Jose (Sosa); B9.23.1944 Camaguey, Cuba; BR/TR/5´10˝/(160–178); d6.18; Col Miami–Dade North (FL) CC																									
1974	Chi N	3	9	.250	56	0	0	10-3	83.2	82	33	6	0	19-7	38	3.12	123	.264	.301	11-0-3	.182	-0	—	7	0	1.1
1975	Chi N	5	2	.714	52	0	0	10-1	71	84	42	17	0	15-5	28	5.07	77	.298	.326	6-0-4	.167	-0	—	-7	21	-1.0
1976	Chi N	5	3	.625	40	2	0	3-2	55	70	34	8	1	17-6	27	5.24	74	.317	.365	9	.000	-1	91	-7	0	-1.1
1978	Hou N	0	0	ø	10	0	0	0-0	15	20	12	2	0	7-3	6	7.20	46	.328	.391	2	.000	-0	—	-6	0	-0.4
Total	4	13	14	.481	158	2	0	23-6	224.2	256	121	33	1	58-21	99	4.53	85	.293	.332	28-0-7	.107	-2	91	-13	21	-1.4
Zanni, Dom	Dominick Thomas; B3.1.1932 Bronx NY; BR/TR/5´11˝/(175–180); d9.28																									
1958	SF N	1	0	1.000	1	0	0	0	4	7	1	1	0	1-0	3	2.25	169	.412	.444	2	.000	-0	—	1	0	0.1
1959	SF N	0	0	ø	9	0	0	0	11	12	10	2	1	8-0	11	6.55	58	.273	.389	0	ø	0	—	-4	0	-0.1
1961	SF N	1	0	1.000	8	0	0	0	13.2	13	7	1	0	12-2	11	3.95	96	.277	.417	0	ø	0	—	0	0	0.0
1962	Chi A	6	5	.545	44	2	0	5	86.1	67	42	12	1	31-3	66	3.75	104	.214	.285	18-0-2	.278	2	57	0	0	0.3
1963	Chi A	0	0	ø	5	0	0	0	4.1	5	4	1	0	4-0	2	8.31	42	.294	.429	0	ø	0	—	-2	0	-0.1
	Cin N	1	1	.500	31	1	0	5	43	39	22	2	4	21-3	40	4.19	80	.247	.346	3	.333	0	206	-4	0	-0.2
1965	Cin N	0	0	ø	8	0	0	0	13.1	7	2	1	0	5-0	10	1.35	278	.159	.240	1	.000	-0	—	3	0	0.2
1966	Cin N	0	0	ø	5	0	0	0	7.1	5	1	0	1	3-1	5	0.00	ø	.192	.300	1	1.000	0	—	3	0	0.2
Total	7	9	6	.600	111	3	0	10	183	155	89	20	7	85-9	148	3.79	99	.233	.323	25-0-2	.280	2	102	-3	0	0.4
Zaske, Jeff	Lloyd Jeffrey; B10.6.1960 Seattle WA; BR/TR/6´5˝/180; [PitN78 27/642]; d7.21																									
1984	Pit N	0	0	ø	3	0	0	0-0	5	4	0	0	0	1-0	2	0.00	ø	.211	.250	0	ø	0	—	2	0	0.1
Zavaras, Clint	Clinton Wayne; B1.4.1967 Denver CO; BR/TR/6´1˝/175; [SeaA85 3/61]; d6.3; [DL 1990 Sea A 178]																									
1989	Sea A	1	6	.143	10	10	0	0-0	52	49	33	4	2	30-1	31	5.19	78	.253	.357	0	ø	0	70	-6	0	-0.7
Zay, William	William; d10.7																									
1886	Bal AA	0	1	.000	1	1	0	0	2	4	4	0	0	4	2	9.00	38	.333	.500	1	.000	-0	121	-1	—	-0.2
Zeiser, Matt	Mathias John; B9.25.1888 Chicago IL; D6.10.1942 Chicago IL; BR/TR/5´10˝/170; d4.27																									
1914	Bos A	0	0	ø	2	0	0	0	10	9	4	0	1	8	0	1.80	150	.281	.439	3	.000	-0	—	1	—	0.0
Zepp, Bill	William Clinton; B7.22.1946 Detroit MI; BR/TR/6´2˝/185; d8.12; Col Michigan																									
1969	Min A	0	0	ø	4	0	0	0-1	5.1	6	7	1	0	4-1	2	6.75	54	.286	.385	1	.000	-0	—	-3	0	-0.2
1970	†Min A	9	4	.692	43	20	1-1	2-2	151	154	63	9	9	51-4	64	3.22	115	.266	.334	44-0-2	.136	-1	102	8	0	0.4
1971	Det A	1	1	.500	16	4	0	2-1	31.2	41	20	2	3	17-3	15	5.12	71	.328	.412	4	.000	-0	93	-5	0	-0.4
Total	3	10	5	.667	63	24	1-1	4-4	188	201	90	12	12	72-8	81	3.64	101	.278	.350	49-0-2	.122	-2	101	0	0	-0.2
Zerbe, Chad	William Chad; B4.27.1972 Findlay OH; BL/TL/6´0˝/(190–200); [LAN91 17/455]; d9.18; Col Hillsborough (FL) CC																									
2000	SF N	0	0	ø	4	0	0	0-0	6	6	3	1	0	1-0	5	4.50	97	.273	.304	0	ø	0	—	0	0	0.0
2001	SF N	3	0	1.000	27	1	0	0-0	39	41	21	3	1	10-0	22	3.92	104	.281	.327	9-0-2	.222	0	135	0	0	0.0
2002	†SF N	2	0	1.000	50	0	0	0-1	56.1	52	22	3	4	21-2	26	3.04	130	.248	.326	6-0-1	.167	-0	—	5	0	0.2
2003	SF N	1	1	.500	33	1	0	0-1	49.2	60	26	3	1	14-2	17	4.71	90	.311	.349	5-0-1	.000	-1	66	-2	16	-0.1
Total	4	6	1	.857	114	2	0	0-2	151	159	72	10	6	46-4	70	3.87	106	.278	.333	20-0-4	.150	-0	102	3	16	0.1
Zettlein, George	George "Charmer"; B7.18.1844 Brooklyn NY; D5.23.1905 Patchogue NY; BR/TR/5´9˝/162; d5.8																									
1871	Chi NA	18	9	.667	28	28	25	0	240.2	298	233	6	—	25	22	**2.73**	**168**	.267	**.283**	128	.250	-7	93	**45**	—	**2.6**
1872	Tro NA	14	8	.636	25	22	17-2	1	187.2	207	132	2	—	8	17	2.16	169	.250	.257	114	.254	0	118	31	—	2.4
	Eck NA	1	8	.111	9	9	8	0	75.1	106	62	1	—	6	8	3.58	95	.299	.311	34	.088	-4	56	2	—	-0.1
	Year	15	16	.484	34	31	25-2	1	263	313	194	3	—	14	25	2.57	140	.265	.273	148	.216	-4	101	30	—	2.3
1873	Phi NA	36	15	.706	51	51	49	0	460	594	368	3	—	41	29	2.86	121	.284	.298	241	.207	-8	108	30	—	1.7
1874	Chi NA	27	30	.474	57	57	57-3	0	515.2	640	439	3	—	43	26	2.43	92	.273	.286	244	.193	-9	94	-13	—	-1.7
1875	Chi NA	17	14	.548	31	31	29-6	0	282	266	142	0	—	6	18	1.28	178	.230	.234	133	.218	-3*	84	31	—	2.5
	Phi NA	12	8	.600	21	21	20-1	0	181.1	209	121	0	—	10	13	2.08	109	.264	.273	83	.181	-4	113	1	—	-0.3
	Year	29	22	.569	52	52	49-**7**	0	463.1	475	263	0	—	16	31	1.59	143	.244	.250	216	.204	-7	96	24	—	2.2
1876	Phi N	4	20	.167	28	25	23-1	2	234	358	212	2	—	6	10	3.88	62	.331	.334	128	.211	-5*	73	-25	—	-2.4
Total	5NA	125	92	.576	222	219	205-12	1	1942.2	2320	1497	15	—	139	133	2.39	126	.267	.279	977	.210	-36	99	127	—	7.1
Zick, Bob	Robert George; B4.26.1927 Chicago IL; BL/TR/6´0˝/168; d5.2																									
1954	Chi N	0	0	ø	8	0	0	0	16.1	23	15	1	0	7	9	8.27	51	.343	.405	4	.250	0*	—	-6	0	-0.3
Ziegler, George	George J.; B1872 Chicago IL; D7.22.1916 Kankakee IL; 5´8˝/150; d6.19																									
1890	Pit N	0	1	.000	1	1	0	0	6	12	7	0	0	0	1	10.50	31	.400	.400	2	.000	-0	19	-4	—	-0.4
Ziem, Steve	Stephen Graeling; B10.24.1961 Milwaukee WI; BR/TR/6´2˝/210; [AtlN83 8/204]; d4.30; Col Cal Poly–Pomona																									
1987	Atl N	0	1	.000	2	0	0	0-0	2.1	4	3	0	0	1-0	0	7.71	56	.364	.417	0	ø	0	—	-1	0	-0.2
Zimmerman, Jeff	Jeffrey Ross; B8.9.1972 Kelowna BC, Can.; BR/TR/6´1˝/200; d4.13; b–Jordan; Col TCU; [DL 2002 Tex A 183, 2003 Tex A 183, 2004 Tex A 183]																									
1999	†Tex A★	9	3	.750	65	0	0	3-4	87.2	50	24	9	2	23-1	67	2.36	219	.166	.225	0	ø	0	—	26	0	3.1
2000	Tex A	4	5	.444	65	0	0	1-2	69.2	80	45	10	2	34-3	74	5.30	96	.286	.361	0	ø	0	—	-1	0	-0.2
2001	Tex A	4	4	.500	66	0	0	28-3	71.1	48	19	10	4	16-1	72	2.40	199	.192	.251	0	ø	0	—	18	0	3.0
Total	3	17	12	.586	196	0	0	32-9	228.2	178	88	29	8	73-5	213	3.27	154	.214	.280	0	ø	0	—	43	549	5.9
Zimmerman, Jordan	Jordan William; B4.28.1975 Kelowna BC, Can.; BR/TL/6´0˝/200; [SeaA94 32/889]; d5.17; b–Jeff; Col Blinn (TX) JC																									
1999	Sea A	0	0	ø	12	0	0	0-0	8	14	8	0	1	4-0	3	7.88	61	.389	.463	0	ø	0	—	-3	33	-0.1
Zink, Walter	Walter Noble; B11.21.1898 Pittsfield MA; D6.12.1964 Quincy MA; BR/TR/6´0˝/165; d7.6; Col Amherst																									
1921	NY N	0	0	ø	2	0	0	0	4	4	3	0	0	3	1	2.25	163	.235	.350	1	.000	-0	—	0	—	0.0
Zinn, Jimmy	James Edward; B1.21.1895 Benton AR; D2.26.1991 Memphis TN; BL/TR (BL 1929)/6´0.5˝/195; d9.4																									
1919	Phi A	1	3	.250	5	3	2	0	25.2	38	20	1	1	10	9	6.31	54	.365	.426	13-1-0	.308	2*	61	-7	—	-0.7
1920	Pit N	1	1	.500	6	3	2	0	31	32	14	2	1	5	18	3.48	92	.260	.295	15	.200	0*	98	-1	—	0.0
1921	Pit N	7	6	.538	32	9	5-1	4	127.1	159	63	3	2	30	49	3.68	104	.318	.359	49	.224	0*	112	2	—	0.1
1922	Pit N	0	0	ø	5	0	0	1	9.2	11	4	1	0	2	3	1.86	219	.297	.333	1	.000	-0	—	2	—	0.1
1929	Cle A	4	6	.400	18	11	6-1	2	105.1	150	75	8	3	33	29	5.04	88	.340	.390	42-1-3	.381	7*	119	-8	—	0.0
Total	5	13	16	.448	66	26	15-2	7	299	390	176	15	7	80	108	4.30	92	.324	.369	120-2-3	.283	9	109	-12	—	-0.5
Zinser, Bill	William Francis; B1.6.1918 Astoria NY; D2.16.1993 Englewood FL; BR/TR/6´1˝/185; d8.19																									
1944	Was A	0	0	ø	2	0	0	0	0.2	1	2	0	0	5	1	27.00	12	.333	.750	0	ø	0	—	-2	0	-0.1

YEAR	TM LG	W	L	PCT	G	GS	CG-SHO	SV-BS	IP	H	R	HR	HB	BB-IB	SO	ERA	AERA	OAV	OOB	AB-HR-SH	AVG	PB	SUP	APR	DL	PW
ZITO, BARRY	Barry William; B5.13.1978 Las Vegas NV; BL/TL/6´4˝/(205–215); [OakA99 1/9]; d7.22; Col USC																									
2000	†Oak A	7	4	.636	14	14	1-1	0-0	92.2	64	30	6	2	45-2	78	2.72	178	.195	.296	0	ø	0	145	23	0	2.4
2001	†Oak A	17	8	.680	35	**35**	3-2	0-0	214.1	184	92	18	13	80-0	205	3.49	131	.230	.309	5	.000	-1	117	25	0	2.6
2002	†Oak A★	**23**	5	.821	35	**35**	1	0-0	229.1	182	79	24	9	78-2	182	2.75	163	.218	.289	4-0-2	.000	-0	119	43	0	4.9
2003	†Oak A✳	14	12	.538	35	35	4-1	0-0	231.2	186	98	19	6	88-3	146	3.30	139	.219	.295	6	.000	-1	82	31	0	3.1
2004	Oak A	11	11	.500	34	34	0	0-0	213	216	116	28	9	81-2	163	4.48	103	.263	.333	4	.000	-0	88	3	0	0.3
2005	Oak A	14	13	.519	35	**35**	0	0-0	228.1	185	106	26	13	89-0	171	3.86	113	.221	.304	7	.143	-0	103	14	0	1.5
2006	†Oak A★	16	10	.615	34	**34**	0	0-0	221	211	99	27	13	99-5	151	3.83	118	.257	.344	3-0-1	.000	-0	92	18	0	1.8
Total	7	102	63	.618	222	222	9-4	0-0	1430.1	1228	620	148	65	560-14	1096	3.55	128	.232	.311	29-0-3	.034	-2	103	157	0	16.6
ZMICH, ED	Edward Albert; B10.1.1884 Cleveland OH; D8.20.1950 Cleveland OH; BL/TL/6´0˝/180; d7.23																									
1910	StL N	0	5	.000	9	6	2	0	36	38	27	0	3	29	19	6.25	48	.304	.446	13	.077	-1	67	-11	—	-1.5
1911	StL N	1	0	1.000	4	0	0	0	12.2	8	5	0	1	8	4	2.13	158	.182	.321	4	.000	-1	—	1	—	0.0
Total	2	1	5	.167	13	6	2	0	48.2	46	32	0	4	37	23	5.18	60	.272	.414	17	.059	-2	67	-10	—	-1.5
ZOLDAK, SAM	Samuel Walter "Sad Sam"; B12.8.1918 Brooklyn NY; D8.25.1966 New Hyde Park NY; BL/TL/5´11.5˝/185; d5.13; Col Fordham																									
1944	StL A	0	0	ø	18	0	0	0	38.2	49	22	1	0	19	15	3.72	97	.310	.384	6	.333	0	—	-2	0	0.0
1945	StL A	3	2	.600	26	1	1	0	69.2	74	32	3	0	18	19	3.36	105	.267	.312	20	.050	-2*	48	0	0	-0.3
1946	StL A	9	11	.450	35	21	9-2	2	170.1	166	71	11	1	57	51	3.43	109	.256	.317	52-0-3	.173	-0	72	7	0	0.8
1947	StL A	9	10	.474	35	19	6-1	1	171	162	76	7	0	76	36	3.47	112	.254	.334	58-0-1	.172	-1	90	7	0	0.8
1948	StL A	2	4	.333	11	9	0	0	54	64	30	4	1	19	13	4.67	98	.296	.356	22-0-1	.273	0	77	0	0	0.1
	Cle A	9	6	.600	23	12	4-1	0	105.2	104	37	6	0	24	17	2.81	144	.261	.303	36-0-2	.139	-2	95	16	0	1.9
	Year	11	10	.524	34	21	4-1	0	159.2	168	67	10	1	43	30	3.44	123	.274	.322	58-0-3	.190	-2	88	15	0	2.0
1949	Cle A	1	2	.333	27	0	0	0	53	60	30	4	0	18	11	4.25	94	.291	.348	8	.375	1	—	-3	0	0.1
1950	Cle A	4	2	.667	33	3	0	4	63.2	64	33	6	1	21	15	3.96	109	.259	.320	16	.188	0	97	2	0	0.2
1951	Phi A	6	10	.375	26	18	8-1	0	128	127	51	9	0	24	18	3.16	135	.257	.292	45-0-1	.156	-3	83	15	0	1.3
1952	Phi A	0	6	.000	16	10	2	1	75.1	86	41	3	0	25	12	4.06	97	.290	.345	23-0-1	.174	-1	68	-2	0	-0.1
Total	9	43	53	.448	250	93	30-5	8	929.1	956	423	54	3	301	207	3.54	112	.267	.325	286-0-9	.175	-7	82	40	0	4.8
ZUBER, BILL	William Henry "Goober"; B3.26.1913 Middle Amana IA; D11.2.1982 Cedar Rapids IA; BR/TR/6´2˝/195; d9.16																									
1936	Cle A	1	1	.500	2	2	1	0	13.2	14	11	0	0	15	5	6.59	76	.269	.433	5	.200	-0	131	-2	—	-0.2
1938	Cle A	0	3	.000	15	0	0	1	28.2	33	18	0	0	20	14	5.02	92	.295	.402	7-0-1	.000	-1	—	-1	—	-0.2
1939	Cle A	2	0	1.000	16	1	0	0	31.2	41	24	2	1	19	16	5.97	74	.323	.415	5	.200	1	160	-6	—	-0.2
1940	Cle A	1	1	.500	17	0	0	0	24	25	17	3	0	14	12	5.63	75	.260	.355	3	.333	0	—	-4	—	-0.3
1941	Was A	6	4	.600	36	7	1	2	96.1	110	63	5	2	61	51	5.42	75	.291	.392	26-0-2	.000	-3	95	-13	0	-1.5
1942	Was A	9	9	.500	37	7	3-1	1	126.2	115	66	5	0	82	64	3.84	95	.243	.355	39-0-3	.154	0	74	-3	0	-0.5
1943	NY A	8	4	.667	20	13	7	1	118	100	54	3	0	74	57	3.89	83	.234	.347	38-0-5	.184	2	167	-6	0	-0.5
1944	NY A	5	7	.417	22	13	2-1	0	107	101	54	5	1	54	59	4.21	83	.255	.346	31-0-4	.129	-2	92	-6	0	-0.9
1945	NY A	5	11	.313	21	14	7	1	127	121	50	2	0	56	50	3.19	109	.259	.338	42-0-2	.167	-1	56	5	0	0.4
1946	NY A	0	1	.000	3	0	0	0	5.2	10	9	2	0	3	3	12.71	27	.385	.448	2	.000	-0	—	-6	0	-0.9
	†Bos A	5	1	.833	15	7	2-1	0	56.2	37	20	4	0	39	29	2.54	144	.187	.321	18-0-1	.111	-1	150	6	0	0.5
	Year	5	2	.714	18	7	2-1	0	62.1	47	29	6	0	42	32	3.47	105	.210	.335	20-0-1	.100	-1	151	0	0	-0.4
1947	Bos A	1	0	1.000	20	1	0	0	50.2	60	32	4	0	31	23	5.33	73	.311	.406	13-0-2	.154	-0	114	-7	0	-0.4
Total	11	43	42	.506	224	65	23-3	6	786	767	418	35	4	468	383	4.28	87	.260	.362	229-0-20	.135	-6	103	-43	0	-4.7
ZUMAYA, JOEL	Joel Martin; B11.9.1984 Chula Vista CA; BR/TR/6´3˝/210; [DetA02 11/320]; d4.3																									
2006	†Det A	6	3	.667	62	0	0	1-5	83.1	56	20	6	2	42-2	97	1.94	231	.187	.287	0	ø	0	—	24	0	2.2
ZUVERINK, GEORGE	George; B8.20.1924 Holland MI; BR/TR/6´4˝/(195–210); d4.21																									
1951	Cle A	0	0	ø	16	0	0	0	25.1	24	17	2	1	13	14	5.33	71	.253	.349	0	ø	0	—	-5	0	-0.2
1952	Cle A	0	0	ø	1	0	0	0	1.1	1	0	0	0	0	1	0.00	ø	.200	.200	0	ø	0*	—	1	0	0.0
1954	Cin N	0	0	ø	2	0	0	0	6	10	6	1	0	1	2	9.00	47	.385	.407	2	.500	0	—	-3	0	-0.1
	Det A	9	13	.409	35	25	9-2	4	203	201	93	22	8	62	70	3.59	103	.257	.317	64-0-9	.125	-3	75	2	0	0.0
1955	Det A	0	5	.000	14	1	0	0	28.1	38	27	6	1	14-3	13	6.99	55	.309	.384	4	.000	-1	116	-11	0	-1.7
	Bal A	4	3	.571	28	5	0	4	86.1	80	28	5	4	17-1	31	2.19	174	.264	.309	23-0-1	.217	1	107	15	0	1.4
	Year	4	8	.333	42	6	0	4	114.2	118	55	11	5	31-4	44	3.38	113	.277	.331	27-0-1	.185	0	109	4	0	-0.3
1956	Bal A	7	6	.538	**62**	0	0	**16**	97.1	112	52	6	3	34-9	33	4.16	94	.294	.352	17-0-4	.118	-1	—	-4	0	-0.6
1957	Bal A	10	6	.625	**56**	0	0	9	112.2	105	37	9	4	39-13	36	2.48	145	.257	.325	23-0-2	.130	-0	—	13	0	2.0
1958	Bal A	2	2	.500	45	0	0	7	69	74	29	4	6	17-3	22	3.39	106	.286	.340	9	.222	1	—	2	0	0.3
1959	Bal A	0	1	.000	6	0	0	0	13	15	7	1	0	6-0	1	4.15	91	.306	.382	0	ø	1	—	-1	83	0.0
Total	8	32	36	.471	265	31	9-2	40	642.1	660	296	56	27	203-29	223	3.54	105	.271	.332	142-0-16	.148	-2	82	9	83	1.1

HOMETOWN HEROES: TEAM ROSTERS

Nineteenth century baseball writers often referred to their local clubs as the "hometown nine." That was both accurate and appropriate in an era when teams had very few extra players, when top pitchers started half or more of their team's games (and played in the field when they weren't pitching), and when most managers were player-managers. Moreover, baseball had little competition for the hearts of the fans from other team sports back then.

Today, with twenty-five-player active rosters, plus well-used disabled lists, plus shuttles operating almost daily between top farm teams and their parent clubs, calling a major league team the "hometown thirty-five" would be more accurate, if hardly as appealing.

Almost all players who don the uniform of a major league team, however, are truly hometown heroes—a phrase with a double meaning: Big league ballplayers are heroes where they play—their team's hometown—as well as in their individual hometowns, whether they came from large cities or from small towns.

One of the foremost goals of any encyclopedia is to present information in an accessible manner. The player registers show year-by-year information for each player's career, and the Historical Record presents detailed annual information for each league. Another important component is this Team Rosters section, which features a chronological record of all regular players and pitchers plus important reserves on each team, season-by-season, for the whole 136-year span of professional baseball history.

Roster format. In this section rosters are grouped by league for each year, with the teams in each league shown in alphabetical order. This enables quick comparisons of the various teams in a pennant race without constantly flipping from page to page. Mortal enemies like the 1951 Giants and Dodgers will be found cheek-by-jowl; and all four teams that engaged in the down-to-the-wire 1967 AL pennant race will be at most a column or two away from each other.

These team rosters provide much more complete information than typical rosters do about how each team was put together and how it utilized its players in a given season. This is especially true in the past two decades, when teams have become much more reluctant to let young pitchers learn the ropes or to let struggling players work their way out of slumps. The increasing frequency of serious injuries has also resulted in less stable lineups.

The plethora of televised games and the omnipresent and instantaneous nature of the electronic media today put tremendous pressure on major league team owners, general managers, and managers to solve problems *right now*. Of course, the enormous amount of money at stake is also a huge factor in the decreasing amount of patience exhibited by teams at every level. Big league teams, managers, and players have lived under the microscope of the media throughout baseball history, but now that media microscope broadcasts full-color video accompanied by unabashedly critical commentary, 24-7.

This intense pressure has resulted in managers using scores of different lineups and having far fewer "set" positions than in the past. This roster-coding scheme may seem complex, but it gives a much more detailed understanding of whatever team is being examined. From 1990–2005, these rosters show almost 10,000 player-seasons, with more than three-quarters of the entries using the familiar single-position codes. Because of the way these codes are defined, however, even the standard codes like SS and RF now convey more information than in other sources.

Simpler rosters that showed pitching staffs composed simply of SPs and RPs would be far less useful than rosters showing that many pitchers spent part of the season in the rotation as well as the bullpen. Rosters that showed position players only by their primary positions, or that labeled all reserves simply as utility players, would also omit much useful information. The most common combination codes are, not surprisingly, RS and SR, followed by several codes for utility players. Two-position combination codes normally show up only a few times for each team.

From top to bottom, rosters list starting pitchers first, then relief pitchers, then regular position players, then reserves. Non-playing managers are shown last. Regular players who are traded during the season will normally show up on the team where they spent the bulk of the year, though some will fail to play at least half of either team's games and, thus, not qualify for either team's roster.

Pitchers. The rosters list as many as five starting pitchers and four relief pitchers for each team. Pitcher codes are:

- *SP* – starting pitcher;
- *RP* – relief pitcher;
- *SR* – starter-reliever;
- *RS* – reliever-starter;
- *CL* – closer.

Starting pitchers qualify if they are among the top five pitchers on the team in innings pitched, provided that they have pitched at least 0.6 innings for each of their team's games played. Relief pitchers make the roster if they are among the top four pitchers on the team in innings pitched plus saves, provided that they pitched at least 0.3 innings per team game.

Pitchers are assigned codes according to the following rules:

If a starting pitcher has 0–9 games in relief, he is labeled as *SP*.

If a pitcher has 10 or more games in relief, and if at least one third of his appearances are games started, then he is labeled as *SR*.

If the pitcher has started at least 5 games and has 10 or more games in relief, he is labeled as *RS*—provided he started less than one third of the time.

If a relief pitcher has 0–4 games started, he is labeled as *RP*.

If a relief pitcher's saves total is equal to at least one third of his relief appearances, than he is labeled as *CL*.

Position Players. In order to include as clear a picture as possible of each team, every player who played in at least 50 percent of his team's games is shown, so no one who made a major impact during the regular season is missing. Position players who played in fewer than 60 percent of their team's games are marked by a dash after their position code.

Regular players are always listed in the order shown below. If a player played at least 75 percent of his team's games at one position, he is shown as the regular with the following codes:

- *C* – catcher
- *1B* – first base (1 when combined with other positions)
- *2B* – second base (2 when combined)
- *3B* – third base (3 when combined)
- *SS* – shortstop (S when combined)
- *LF*– left fielder (L when combined)
- *CF*– center fielder (M when combined)
- *RF* – right fielder (R when combined)
- *DH* – designated hitter (D when combined)

If no one played at least 75 percent of a team's games at one position, the regular shown will be the player who played the most games at that position—unless a player happened to have played the most games at two positions. If so, that player will be shown where he played the most, and the player with the second-most games at the other position will be shown as the regular. For example, for Oakland in 2001, Johnny Damon played 67 games in left and 86 in center out of a total of 154 games in the outfield. He led the team in games at both positions. Terrence Long played 62 games in left, 74 in center, and 28 in right (162 total). Damon was listed as *ML*, since he played more than 50 percent of his games in center and more than 25 percent in left. Long was listed as the regular center fielder with an *UO* code because he did not play 50 percent of his games at any one position, but he did play all three outfield spots.

In the overwhelming majority of circumstances, the regular at each position will have the standard position code or a combination code that starts with the first letter of that position (e.g., *3S* for third base/shortstop; *L1* for left field/first base). However, when a team has several players shifting among different positions during the season, the regular shown at a particular position might not have the expected code. (This usually happens on bad teams that have no set lineup.) The lineups that "fit the best" with the players who played the most are always shown.

In these rare circumstances, the "regular" third baseman might be someone who played only 40 games there, but who still played third more than anyone else on that team who wasn't a regular at another position. For example, in 1918 Fred Thomas played only 41 games at third base for the pennant-winning Red Sox, but that was still more than anyone else, so Thomas is shown as the regular.

Aside from the position codes shown above, four other codes are used for players who have played less than 75 percent of their games at one position. Details on these codes are found below:

- *OF* – outfield (*O* when used in combination);
- *IF* – infield (*I* when used in combination);
- *UT* – utility player (*U* when used in combination);
- *P* – Pitcher (when used in combination with position codes).

Combination Position Codes. If a player played between 50 percent and 75 percent of his games at one position, his primary position will be signified by the first letter of the above codes. (Exception: To avoid confusion with catcher, we have revived the old newspaper box score code *M*—for "middle outfielder"—to indicate center field).

Players with at least half their games at one position, but less than three quarters of their games at that position, are also given a secondary position code. The secondary code assigned depends on how many games they played at other positions, of course, as well as the number of other positions they played. The rules for secondary position codes are:

If a player played at least 25 percent of his other games at a position other than his primary position, the secondary position will be shown as the second letter of his position code.

If the player did not play 25 percent of his other games at any single position, but he did play at least 25 percent of his additional (i.e., non-primary position) games in the infield, the second letter of his position code will be *I*. In 2003 Desi Relaford played 141 games for Kansas City: 89 at second base, 33 at third base, 20 in the outfield, and 6 at shortstop. His 89 games at second put him in 50–75 percent range for a two-character code, with 2 as the first character. His next highest position was less than 25 percent of his total games, so his secondary code is a utility code. With 39 games at third and short combined, his second character becomes *I* and his position code becomes *2I*.

If the player did not play 25 percent of his other games at a single position, but he did play at least 25 percent of his additional games in the outfield, the second letter of his position code will be O. In 2003 Dustan Mohr of Minnesota had 30 games in left, 11 in center, and 70 in right out of a total of 121 games. Thus he qualifies for an RO code, with 50–75 percent of his games in right, less than 25 percent at any other position, but a total of 41 in left and center.

If a player's games are scattered among so many positions that none of these conditions apply, his secondary code will be *U*.

If the player's secondary position was pitcher and he pitched in at least 10 games, his second letter will be *P*. Only a few position players since 1901—the most famous being Babe Ruth, of course—have pitched in 10 games in one year while also playing in half their team's games.

If the position player has 100 innings pitched in a season and a *P* wouldn't appear as his secondary position code under the preceding rules, the *P* will take precedence. This occurs exclusively in the nineteenth century. A lowercase *p* will be used to distinguish, for example, between a right fielder who also pitched (Rp) from a relief pitcher (RP), though the location of such players on the roster will usually make this clear.

Utility Codes. No two-letter coding scheme can account for all the ways that managers can use players during a season. Therefore, a few utility codes are used to cover versatile players who didn't play 50 percent of their games at any position. (Of course, complete data on games at position for every player can be found in the player registers.) Utility codes indicating specific positions are used only for catchers and those who also pitched a substantial amount (see paragraphs immediately above). Otherwise, utility codes are assigned by the following rules:

If the player played all three outfield positions but never played the infield, he will be labeled *UO* (utility outfielder). Quinton McCracken had 115 games in 2003: 10 in left, 16 in center, and 34 in right. Since he did not have 50 percent of his games at any one position, but did play all three outfield positions, he is labeled *UO*.

If the player played two outfield positions but never played the infield, he will be labeled *OF* (outfield). In 2003 Troy O'Leary of the Chicago Cubs had 28 games in left and 24 in right out of 93 games. He is an *OF*.

If the player played three or four infield positions but never played the outfield, he will be labeled as *UI* (utility infielder). In 2003 Carlos Baerga of Arizona had 19 games at first base, 15 at second base, and 5 at third base out of 105 games total, making him a *UI*.

If the player played two infield positions but never played the outfield, he will be labeled as *IF* (infielder). In 2001 Keith Lockhart of Atlanta had 47 games at second base and 4 games at third base out of 104 total. Since he played only two infield positions with no games in the outfield and no position with at least 50 percent of his games, he qualifies as an *IF*.

If the player played two or more Outfield positions as well as at least one infield position, and he played more games in the outfield than in the Infield, he will be labeled as *OI* (outfielder-infielder). In 2003 Brian Banks had 92 games total for Florida: 23 games in left, 12 at first, and 10 in right, qualifying him as *OI*.

If the player played two or more infield positions and at least one outfield position, and he played more games in the infield than in the outfield, he will be labeled as *IO* (infielder-outfielder). In 2003 Greg Norton of Colorado had 34 games at third, 9 at first, and 3 in right field (114 games total), giving him an *IO* code.

If a player's first or second position (in terms of number of games) is catcher, but he played less than 50 percent of his games there or at any other position, he will be labeled as *IC* (infielder/catcher) or *OC* (outfielder/catcher) depending on whether he played primarily in the infield or the outfield. If he played more games at catcher than elsewhere, and he did not play another defensive position in most of his other games (i.e., he was a *DH* or a pinch hitter), he will be labeled as *UC* (utility catcher). In 2001 Shawn Wooten played 79 games for Anaheim: 27 at *DH*, 25 at catcher, 21 at first, and 1 at third. Since his second position was catcher, but he played more there than in the infield or outfield, he is listed as *UC*.

If a player doesn't fit into any of these categories, he will be labeled as *UT* (utility). Matt Franco, who was mainly a pinch hitter for Atlanta in 2003, played 112 games: 3 games at first base, 2 in right, and 1 in left. Since he played the same number of games in the infield and outfield, he gets a *UT* code.

Managers. Managers are indicated by the code *M*; see the Manager Register introduction for an explanation of who qualifies as a manager. If a team had multiple managers in a season, the order in which these managers served is shown by the number after the *M* (i.e., the first manager will be *M1*, the second *M2*, etc.). Managers' names are italicized in the rosters. Player-managers are shown with standard position code(s) and located as a player; their italicization indicates managerial status. Non-playing managers are shown at the end of the team roster.

Most of the above rules apply only to a small fraction of the players and pitchers listed in the team rosters. More than three quarters of the 40,000-plus player and pitcher seasons in this section are shown with a primary position code. Most of the remaining players are shown with two-position codes.

1871 NA

BOSTON
SP A Spalding
C C McVey
1B C Gould
2S R Barnes
SS- G Wright
3B H Schafer
LF F Cone
CF H Wright
RF D Birdsall
LU- F Barrows
2B- S Jackson

CHICAGO
SP G Zettlein
C3 C Hodes
1B B McAtee
2B J Wood
SS E Duffy
3B E Pinkham
LF F Treacey
MR T Foley
RM J Simmons
MC M King

CLEVELAND
SP A Pratt
C D White
1B J Carleton
2I G Kimball
SS J Bass
3B E Sutton
LF C Pabor
CF A Allison
RF- E White
2R- C Johnson

FT.WAYNE
SP B Mathews
C B Lennon
1B J Foran
2B T Carey
S3 W Goldsmith
3B F Sellman
LF- E Mincher
CF B Armstrong
RF B Kelly
M2 H Deane

NEW YORK
SP R Wolters
C C Mills
1B J Start
2R D Higham
SS D Pearce
32 B Ferguson
LI J Hatfield
CF D Eggler
RL D Patterson
3B- C Smith

ATHLETICS
SP D McBride
C F Malone
1B W Fisler
2B A Reach
SS J Radcliff
3B L Meyerle
LF N Cuthbert
CF C Sensenderfer
RF G Heubel
RU G Bechtel

ROCKFORD
SP C Fisher
C S Hastings
1B D Mack
2B B Addy
SS C Fulmer
3B C Anson
LF R Ham
CF G Bird
RF G Stires

TROY
SP J McMullin
C M McGeary
1R C Flynn
2U B Craver
SS D Flowers
3B S Bellan
LF S King
CF T York
R2 L Pike

OLYMPICS
SP A Brainard
C D Allison
1B E Mills
2L A Leonard
SS D Force
3B F Waterman
L2- H Berthrong
CF G Hall
RF J Glenn
M N Young

1872 NA

BALTIMORE
SP B Mathews
SP C Fisher
C B Craver
1B E Mills
2I T Carey
SS J Radcliff
3B- D Force
LF T York
CF G Hall
UT L Pike
CR D Higham

BOSTON
SP A Spalding
C C McVey
1B C Gould
2B R Barnes
SS G Wright
3B H Schafer
LF A Leonard
CF H Wright
RF F Rogers

ECKFORDS
SP P Martin
SP G Zettlein
SP J McDermott
C D Allison
1B A Allison
IO C Nelson
SS J Snyder
3B- F Fleet
LF C Gedney
CF- D Patterson
UT J Clinton
M2 J Wood

ATLANTICS
SP J Britt
C T Barlow
1B H Dehlman
2B- J Hall
SS J Burdock
3B B Ferguson
LF- A Thake
CF J Remsen
RF- J McDonald

CLEVELAND
SP A Pratt
SP R Wolters
C2 D White
1B J Simmons
2B- C Sweasy
SS J Holdsworth
3B E Sutton
LF C Pabor
CF A Allison
RF R Wolters
C2 S Hastings

MIDDLETOWN
SP C Bentley
SP F Buttery
C J Clapp
1B T Murnane
2B E Booth
SC J O'Rourke
3O G Fields
LF J Tipper
CF F McCarton
RF C Bentley
S3 H Allen

NEW YORK
SP C Cummings
C N Hicks
1B J Start
2B J Hatfield
SS D Pearce
3B B Boyd
LF J McMullin
CF D Eggler
RL G Bechtel
3S C Fulmer

ATHLETICS
SP D McBride
C1 F Malone
1S D Mack
2B W Fisler
IC M McGeary
3B C Anson
LF N Cuthbert
CF F Treacey
RF- L Meyerle
RF- A Reach

TROY
SP G Zettlein
C D Allison
1B B McAtee
2B J Wood
IO S Bellan
3S D Force
LF S King
CF- C Gedney
RF P Martin

OLYMPICS
SP A Brainard
C F Sellman
1B C Flynn
2U T Beals
S2 W Goldsmith
3B F Waterman
LF J Glenn
CF- G Heubel
RF V Robinson

NATIONALS
SP B Stearns
C B Lennon
1B P Hines
2B H Hollingshead
SS J Doyle
3B W White
LF E Mincher
CF- S Studley
RF O Bielaski
MI D Coughlin

1873 NA

MARYLANDS
SP E Stratton
SP Mc Doolan
SP F Sellman
MC B Smith
1B B Lennon
2B M Simpson
SR- L Say
3B H Kohler
LC- M Hooper
SL J Smith
IO B French

BALTIMORE
SP C Cummings
SP A Brainard
CI C McVey
1B E Mills
2B T Carey
3S J Radcliff
3S D Force
LF T York
CF G Hall
RF L Pike
CS B Craver
CM- S Hastings

BOSTON
SP A Spalding
C D White
1R J O'Rourke
2B R Barnes
SS G Wright
3B H Schafer
LF A Leonard
CF H Wright
RF- B Addy
1B- J Manning

ATLANTICS
SP J Britt
C T Barlow
1B H Dehlman
3B J Burdock
SS D Pearce
3B B Ferguson
LF C Pabor
CF J Remsen
RF B Boyd

ELIZABETH
SP H Campbell
C D Allison
1B M Campbell
2B- B Laughlin
SS- F Wordsworth
3B- A Nevin
LF E Booth
OI A Allison
MR H Austin
UI F Fleet

NEW YORK
SP B Mathews
C- N Hicks
1B J Start
2B C Nelson
SS J Holdsworth
3B J Hatfield
LF C Gedney
CF D Eggler
RF- P Martin
OI D Higham

PHILADELPHIA
SP G Zettlein
C F Malone
1B D Mack
2B J Wood
SS C Fulmer
3B L Meyerle
LF N Cuthbert
CF F Treacey
RF G Bechtel
13- J Devlin

ATHLETICS
SP D McBride
C J Clapp
1I C Anson
2B W Fisler
SS M McGeary
3B E Sutton
LF J McMullin
MI T Murnane
RF C Fisher

WASHINGTON
SP B Stearns
SP J Greason
C P Snyder
1B J Glenn
2C T Beals
SS- J Gerhardt
3B W White
LF P Hines
CF H Hollingshead
RF O Bielaski
IO J Donnelly
M N Young

1874 NA

BALTIMORE
SP A Brainard
SP J Manning
C P Snyder
1B C Gould
2B J Manning
SS- L Say
3B W White
LF J Ryan
CF H Deane
RF O Bielaski

BOSTON
SP A Spalding
C D White
1B J O'Rourke
2B R Barnes
SS G Wright
3B H Schafer
LI A Leonard
UO G Hall
RC C McVey
CF- H Wright

ATLANTICS
SP T Bond
C- J Knowdell
1B H Dehlman
C2- J Farrow
SS D Pearce
3B B Ferguson
LF E Booth
CF- B Clack
RF J Chapman

CHICAGO
SP G Zettlein
C F Malone
1R J Glenn
23 L Meyerle
S2 J Peters
3S D Force
LF N Cuthbert
CF P Hines
RM- F Treacey
1R J Devlin
M2 J Wood

HARTFORD
SP C Fisher
SP B Stearns
C S Hastings
1B E Mills
2B B Addy
SS T Barlow
3B- B Boyd
LF J Tipper
MS L Pike
CR B Barnie

NEW YORK
SP B Mathews
CR D Higham
1B J Start
2B C Nelson
SS T Carey
3B J Burdock
LF J Hatfield
CF J Remsen
RC D Allison

PHILADELPHIA
SP C Cummings
C N Hicks
1B D Mack
2B B Craver
S3 C Fulmer
3S J Holdsworth
LF T York
CF D Eggler
RF- G Bechtel

ATHLETICS
SP D McBride
CS M McGeary
1B W Fisler
2B J Battin
3S E Sutton
IO C Anson
LF C Gedney
CF J McMullin
CR J Clapp

1875 NA

BOSTON
SR A Spalding
C D White
1O C McVey
2B R Barnes
SS G Wright
3B H Schafer
LF A Leonard
M3 J O'Rourke
Rp J Manning
MO- T Beals
M H Wright

ATLANTICS
SP J Cassidy
SP J Clinton
SP J O'Neill
C J Knowdell
1B- F Crane
IC- F Fleet
SO- H Kessler
3B A Nichols
LF C Pabor
CF- B Clack
IO B Boyd

CHICAGO
SP G Zettlein
SP M Golden
CO S Hastings
1p J Devlin
2B- J Miller
SS J Peters
3B W White
L1 J Glenn
M2 P Hines
RF O Bielaski
C2 D Higham
M J Wood

HARTFORD
SP C Cummings
SP T Bond
C D Allison
1B E Mills
2B J Burdock
SS T Carey
3B B Ferguson
LF T York
CF J Remsen
RF- A Allison
CI B Harbridge

KEOKUK
SP M Golden
C P Quinn
1B J Carbine
2B J Miller
SS J Hallinan
3B W Goldsmith
LF C Jones
MU J Simmons
RF B Riley
OC B Barnie

NEW HAVEN
SP T Nichols
C T McGinley
1B- C Gould
2B E Somerville
SS S Wright
3B H Luff
LF J Ryan
CF J Tipper
RF J McKelvey
UT B Geer
M2 J Latham
M3 C Pabor

NEW YORK
SP B Mathews
C N Hicks
1B J Start
23 C Nelson
SS J Hallinan
3B J Gerhardt
LF C Gedney
MS J Holdsworth
RF E Booth

CENTENNIALS
SP G Bechtel
C T McGinley
1B J Abadie
2B E Somerville
S3 B Craver
3B G Trenwith
LF F Treacey
CF F Warner
RL C Mason

PHILADELPHIA
SP C Fisher
SP G Zettlein
SP J Borden
C P Snyder
UT T Murnane
23 L Meyerle
SS C Fulmer
UT M McGeary
LF F Treacey
ML J McMullin
RF B Addy
1B- F Malone

ATHLETICS
SP D McBride
SP L Knight
C J Clapp
1B W Fisler
2B B Craver
SS D Force
3B E Sutton
LF G Hall
CF D Eggler
RF- G Bechtel
UT C Anson
2O- J Richmond

ST. LOUIS
SP G Bradley
SP J Galvin
C T Miller
1B H Dehlman
2B J Battin
SS D Pearce
3B B Hague
LF N Cuthbert
CF J Pike
RF J Chapman
RF- C Waitt

RED STOCKINGS
SP J Blong
C S Flint
1B C Hautz
2B C Sweasy
SS B Redmon
3L T McSorley
LM A Croft
OP D Morgan
RF T Oran

WASHINGTON
SP B Stearns
C- A Thompson
1B A Allison
2S S Brady
SI J Dailey
3B H Doscher
Lp B Parks
MO H Hollingshead
R2 L Ressler

1876 NL

BOSTON
SP J Borden
SP F Bradley
C L Brown
1B T Murnane
2C J Morrill
SS G Wright
3B H Schafer
L2 A Leonard
CF J O'Rourke
Rp J Manning
LR- F Whitney
M H Wright

CHICAGO
SP A Spalding
C D White
1B C McVey
2B R Barnes
SS J Peters
3B C Anson
LF J Glenn
CF P Hines
RF- O Bielaski

CINCINNATI
SP D Dean
SP C Fisher
SP D Williams
IC A Booth
LF J Glenn
1B C Gould
2B C Sweasy
SS H Kessler
3B W Foley
LF R Snyder
CF C Jones
CR D Pierson

HARTFORD
SP T Bond
SP C Cummings
C D Allison
1B E Mills
2B J Burdock
SS T Carey
3B B Ferguson
LF T York
CF J Remsen
RF D Higham

LOUISVILLE
SP J Devlin
C P Snyder
1B J Gerhardt
2B E Somerville
SS C Fulmer
3B B Hague
LF J Ryan
CF S Hastings
R1- A Allison
M J Chapman

NEW YORK
SP B Mathews
C N Hicks
1B J Start
2B B Craver
SS J Hallinan
3B A Nichols
LF F Treacey
CF J Holdsworth
RF E Booth

PHILADELPHIA
SP L Knight
SP G Zettlein
C- F Malone
12 E Sutton
UT W Fisler
SS D Force
3B L Meyerle
LF G Hall
CF D Eggler
RC W Coon
M A Wright

ST. LOUIS
SP G Bradley
C J Clapp
1B H Dehlman
2B M McGeary
SS D Mack
3B J Battin
LF N Cuthbert
CF L Pike
RF J Blong
M1 M Graffen
M2 G McManus

1877 NL

BOSTON
SP T Bond
C L Brown
1R D White
2B G Wright
S3 E Sutton
IO J Morrill
LS A Leonard
ML J O'Rourke
R3- H Schafer
MU- T Murnane
M H Wright

CHICAGO
SP G Bradley
C3 C McVey
1B A Spalding
2B- R Barnes
SS J Peters
3C C Anson
L1 J Glenn
CF- D Eggler
OI P Hines

CINCINNATI
SP C Cummings
SP B Mathews
SP B Mitchell
C- S Hastings
1B- C Gould
2B- J Hallinan
UT J Manning
3B W Foley
1L- C Jones
M2 L Pike
RF B Addy
IC A Booth
LF C Jones

HARTFORD
SP T Larkin
C B Harbridge
1B J Start
2B J Burdock
SS T Carey
3B B Ferguson
LF T York
CF J Holdsworth
RF J Cassidy

LOUISVILLE
SP J Devlin
C P Snyder
1B J Latham
2B J Gerhardt
SS B Craver
3B B Hague
LF G Hall
CF B Crowley
RF O Shafer
M J Chapman

ST. LOUIS
SP T Nichols
C J Clapp
1B- H Dehlman
23 M McGeary
SS D Force
32 J Battin
OP J Blong
CF- J Remsen
UT M Dorgan
1L A Croft
M G McManus

1878 NL

BOSTON
SP T Bond
C P Snyder
1B J Morrill
2B J Burdock
SS G Wright
3B E Sutton
LF A Leonard
CF J O'Rourke
RF J Manning
M H Wright

CHICAGO
SP T Larkin
C B Harbridge
1B J Start
2B B McClellan
SS B Ferguson
3B F Hankinson
LF C Anson
CF J Remsen
RF J Cassidy

CINCINNATI
SP W White
SP B Mitchell
C D White
1B C Sullivan
2B J Gerhardt
SS B Geer
3B C McVey
LF C Jones
CF- L Pike
RF K Kelly

INDIANAPOLIS
SP T Nolan
SP J McCormick
SP T Healey
C S Flint
1B A Croft
2B J Quest
SS F Warner
3B E Williamson
LI J Clapp
CF R McKelvy
RF O Shafer

MILWAUKEE
SP S Weaver
CM C Bennett
1B J Goodman
2B J Peters
SS B Redmon
3B W Foley
LF A Dalrymple
Mp M Golden
RC B Holbert
2M G Creamer
M J Chapman

PROVIDENCE
SP J Ward
SP T Nichols
SP H Wheeler
C L Brown
1B T Murnane
2B C Sweasy
SS T Carey
3B B Hague
LF T York
CF P Hines
RF D Higham

1879 NL

BOSTON
SP T Bond
SP C Foley
C P Snyder
1B- E Cogswell

2B J Burdock
S3 E Sutton
31 J Morrill
LF C Jones
CF J O'Rourke
RS S Houck
M H Wright

BUFFALO
SP J Galvin
SP B McGunnigle
C J Clapp
1B O Walker
2B C Fulmer
SS D Force
3B H Richardson
LF J Hornung
CF D Eggler
RU B Crowley

CHICAGO
SP T Larkin
SP F Hankinson
C S Flint
1B C Anson
2B J Quest
SS J Peters
3B E Williamson
LF A Dalrymple
CF G Gore
RF O Shafer
M1- J Remsen

CINCINNATI
SP W White
C D White
1B C McVey
2I J Gerhardt
SS R Barnes
3R W Foley
LF B Dickerson
CF P Hotaling
UT K Kelly

CLEVELAND
SP J McCormick
SP B Mitchell
C- D Kennedy
1B B Phillips
2B J Glasscock
SS T Carey
3O F Warner
LF- B Riley
CF G Strief
RF C Eden
CL B Gilligan

PROVIDENCE
SR J Ward
SP B Mathews
C L Brown
1B J Start
2B M McGeary
SS G Wright
3B- B Hague
LF T York
CF P Hines
RI J O'Rourke

SYRACUSE
SP H McCormick
C B Holbert
13 H Carpenter
2B J Farrell
SM J Macullar
3B- R Woodhead
LF M Mansell
OI J Richmond
Rp B Purcell
IO M Dorgan

TROY
SP G Bradley
SP H Salisbury
SP F Goldsmith
C C Reilley
1B- D Brouthers
2B T Hawkes
SC E Caskin
3B H Doscher
LF- T Mansell
CF A Hall
RF J Evans
M1 H Phillips
M2 B Ferguson

1880 NL

BOSTON
SP T Bond
SP C Foley
C- P Powers
1B C Foley
2B J Burdock
S3 E Sutton
13 J Morrill
LF C Jones
CF Jo O'Rourke
UT Ji O'Rourke
M H Wright

BUFFALO
SP J Galvin
SP S Wiedman
SP T Poorman
C J Rowe
1U D Esterbrook
2S D Force
SS- M Moynahan
3B H Richardson
LF J Hornung
RC B Crowley
RC- E Stearns
M S Crane

CHICAGO
SP L Corcoran
SP F Goldsmith
C S Flint
1B C Anson
2B J Quest
SS T Burns
3B E Williamson
LF A Dalrymple
CF G Gore
RF K Kelly

CINCINNATI
SP W White
C J Clapp
1B J Reilly
2B P Smith
SS- L Say
3B H Carpenter
LF M Mansell
Mp B Purcell
RF- J Manning

CLEVELAND
SP J McCormick
SP G Gardner
C D Kennedy
1B B Phillips
2B F Dunlap
SS J Glasscock
3B F Hankinson
LF N Hanlon
CF P Hotaling
RF O Shafer

PROVIDENCE
SP J Ward
C E Gross
1B J Start
2B J Farrell
SS J Peters
3p G Bradley
LF T York
CF P Hines
RF M Dorgan
LF- S Houck
M1 M McGeary
M2 M Ward

TROY
SP M Welch
SP T Keefe
C B Holbert
1B- E Cogswell
2B B Ferguson
SS E Caskin
3B R Connor
LF P Gillespie
MR J Cassidy
RF- J Evans

WORCESTER
SP L Richmond
SP F Corey
C- C Bennett
1B- C Sullivan
2B G Creamer
SS A Irwin
3B A Whitney
LF G Wood
M1 H Stovey
RF- L Knight
M F Bancroft

1881 NL

BOSTON
SP J Whitney
SP J Fox
C P Snyder
1B J Morrill
2B J Burdock
SS R Barnes
3B E Sutton
LF J Hornung
MR B Crowley
RF- F Lewis
CU- P Deasley
M H Wright

BUFFALO
SP J Galvin
SP J Lynch
CU J Rowe
L1 D Brouthers
2S D Force
SS J Peters
3U J O'Rourke
LF- B Purcell
CF H Richardson
R1 C Foley
UT D White

CHICAGO
SP L Corcoran
SP F Goldsmith
C S Flint
1B C Anson
2B J Quest
SS T Burns
3B E Williamson
LF A Dalrymple
CF G Gore
RF K Kelly

CLEVELAND
SP J McCormick
SP T Nolan
CO J Clapp
1B B Phillips
2B F Dunlap
SS J Glasscock
3B G Bradley
LF- M Moynahan
CF- J Remsen
RF O Shafer
M1 M McGeary

DETROIT
SP G Derby
SP S Wiedman
SP F Mountain
C C Bennett
1B M Powell
2B J Gerhardt
SS S Houck
3B A Whitney
LF G Wood
CF N Hanlon
RF L Knight
M F Bancroft

PROVIDENCE
SP C Radbourn
SP B Mathews
C- E Gross
1B J Start
2B J Farrell
SO B McClellan
3B J Denny
LF T York
CF P Hines
OP J Ward
C- B Gilligan

TROY
SP T Keefe
SP M Welch
CS B Ewing
1B R Connor
2B B Ferguson
SS E Caskin
3B F Hankinson
LF P Gillespie
CF J Cassidy
RF J Evans
C- B Holbert

WORCESTER
SP L Richmond
SP H McCormick
C D Bushong
1B H Stovey
2B G Creamer
SS A Irwin
3B H Carpenter
LF B Dickerson
CF P Hotaling
Rp F Corey
1R M Dorgan

1882 AA

BALTIMORE
SP D Landis
SP T Nichols
SP E Geis
C E Whiting
1B C Householder
2B- G Pierce
SS H Myers
32 J Shetzline
LF C Waitt
CF- M Cline
RF T Brown

CINCINNATI
SP W White
SP H McCormick
C P Snyder
1U E Stearns
2B B McPhee
SS C Fulmer
3B H Carpenter
LF J Sommer
CF J Macullar
RF H Wheeler

LOUISVILLE
SP T Mullane
C D Sullivan
1p G Hecker
2S P Browning
S2 D Mack
3B B Schenck
LF L Maskrey
MU J Reccius
RF J Wolf

PHILADELPHIA
SP S Weaver
SP B Sweeney
SP F Mountain
CO J O'Brien
1B J Latham
2B C Stricker
SS L Say
3B- F Mann
LF J Birchall
CF- J Mansell
UT B Blakiston
CR- J Dorgan

PITTSBURGH
SP H Salisbury
SP D Driscoll
SP H Arundel
IC B Taylor
1B C Lane
2B G Strief
SS J Peters
3B- J Battin
LF M Mansell
RM E Swartwood
3R J Leary
M A Pratt

ST. LOUIS
SP J McGinnis
SP J Schappert
SP B Dorr
C S Sullivan
1B C Comiskey
2B B Smiley
SS B Gleason
3B J Gleason
LF N Cuthbert
CF O Walker
RU- G Seward

1882 NL

BOSTON
SP J Whitney
SP B Mathews
C P Deasley
1B J Morrill
2B J Burdock
SS S Wise
3B E Sutton
LF J Hornung
CF P Hotaling
RC E Rowen

BUFFALO
SP J Galvin
SP H Daily
CS J Rowe
1B D Brouthers
2B H Richardson
SS D Force
3B D White
LF B Purcell
CF J O'Rourke
RF C Foley

CHICAGO
SP F Goldsmith
SP L Corcoran
C S Flint
1B C Anson
2S T Burns
SR K Kelly
3B E Williamson
LF A Dalrymple
CF G Gore
RF- H Nicol
2B- J Quest

CLEVELAND
SP J McCormick
SP G Bradley
C F Briody
1B B Phillips
2B F Dunlap
SS J Glasscock
3L M Muldoon
LF- D Esterbrook
CF- J Richmond
RF O Shafer

DETROIT
SP S Wiedman
SP G Derby
C C Bennett
1B M Powell
2B- D Troy
SS- M McGeary
32 J Farrell
LF G Wood
CF N Hanlon
RF L Knight
M F Bancroft

PROVIDENCE
SP C Radbourn
C B Gilligan
1B J Start
2B J Farrell
SS- G Wright
3B J Denny
LF T York
CF P Hines
Rp J Ward
M H Wright

TROY
SP T Keefe
SP M Welch
SP J Egan
C B Holbert
1B- J Smith
2B B Ferguson
SS F Pfeffer
3C B Ewing
LF P Gillespie
1O R Connor
RF C Roseman

WORCESTER
SP L Richmond
SP F Mountain
C D Bushong
1L H Stovey
2B G Creamer
3S A Irwin
3B- F Mann
LF- J Clinton
MU J Hayes
RF J Evans
Sp F Corey
M1 F Brown
M2 T Bond
M3 J Chapman

1883 AA

BALTIMORE
SP H Henderson
SP B Emslie
SP J Fox
C- J Kelly
1B E Stearns
2B- T Manning
SS L Say
3B J McCormick
LF J Clinton
CF- D Eggler
RF D Rowe
M B Barnie

CINCINNATI
SP W White
SP R Deagle
SP H McCormick
C- P Snyder
1B J Reilly
2B B McPhee
SS C Fulmer
3B H Carpenter
LF J Sommer
CF C Jones
RF P Corkhill

COLUMBUS
SP F Mountain
SP E Dundon
SP J Valentine
C R Kemmler
1B J Field
2B P Smith
SS J Richmond
3I B Kuehne
LF H Wheeler
CF F Mann
RF T Brown
M H Phillips

LOUISVILLE
SP G Hecker
SP S Weaver
C- E Whiting
1B J Latham
2B J Gerhardt
SS- J Leary
3B J Gleason
UT P Browning
OI L Maskrey
RF J Wolf

NEW YORK
SP T Keefe
SP J Lynch
C B Holbert
1B S Brady
2B S Crane
SS C Nelson
3B D Esterbrook
LF E Kennedy
CF J O'Rourke
RF C Roseman
M J Mutrie

PHILADELPHIA
SP B Mathews
SP J Jones
SP J Bakely
CM J O'Brien
1B H Stovey
2B C Stricker
SS M Moynahan
3p G Bradley
LF J Birchall
CF- B Blakiston
RF L Knight
3p F Corey
C- E Rowen

PITTSBURGH
SP D Driscoll
SP B Barr
SP J Neagle
CU J Hayes
1M E Swartwood
2B G Creamer
S1 D Mack
3B J Battin
LF M Mansell
RM B Dickerson
Cp B Taylor
M1 A Pratt
M2 O Butler

ST. LOUIS
SP T Mullane
SP J McGinnis
C- P Deasley
1B C Comiskey
2B G Strief
SS B Gleason
3B A Latham
CO T Dolan
CF- F Lewis
RF H Nicol
M1 T Sullivan

1883 NL

BOSTON
SP J Whitney
C M Hines
1B J Morrill
2B J Burdock
SS S Wise
3B E Sutton
LF J Hornung
CF- E Smith
RM P Radford
PR C Buffinton

BUFFALO
SP J Galvin
SP G Derby
CL J Rowe
1B D Brouthers
2B H Richardson
SS D Force
3B D White
LC J O'Rourke
MO- J Lillie
RF O Shafer

CHICAGO
SP L Corcoran
SP F Goldsmith
C S Flint
1B C Anson
2B F Pfeffer
SS T Burns
3B E Williamson
LF A Dalrymple
CF G Gore
RF K Kelly

CLEVELAND
SP H Daily
SP J McCormick
SP W Sawyer
C D Bushong
1B B Phillips
2B F Dunlap
SS J Glasscock
3B M Muldoon
LF T York
CF P Hotaling
RF J Evans
M F Bancroft

DETROIT
SP S Wiedman
SP D Shaw
SP D Burns
SP J Jones
C C Bennett
1B M Powell
2C S Trott
SS S Houck
3B J Farrell
LF G Wood
CF N Hanlon
RF S Wiedman
M J Chapman

NEW YORK
SP M Welch
SP T O'Neill
CU B Ewing
1B R Connor
2B D Troy
SS E Caskin
3B F Hankinson
LF P Gillespie
Mp J Ward
RF M Dorgan
M J Clapp

PHILADELPHIA
SP J Coleman
SP A Hagan
SP J Neagle
C- E Gross
1B S Farrar
2B B Ferguson
SS B McClellan
3B- F Warner
UT B Purcell
UT B Harbridge
RF J Manning
CU F Ringo

PROVIDENCE
SP C Radbourn
SP C Sweeney
SP L Richmond
C B Gilligan
1B J Start
2B J Farrell
SS A Irwin
3B J Denny
LF- C Carroll
CF P Hines
RF J Cassidy
M H Wright

1884 AA

BALTIMORE
SP B Emslie
SP H Henderson
C S Trott
1B E Stearns
2B T Manning
SS J Macullar
3B J Sommer
LF T York
ML J Clinton
RF- G Gardner
C- B Traffley
M B Barnie

BROOKLYN
SP A Terry
SP S Kimber
SP J Conway
CU- J Corcoran
1C C Householder
2B B Greenwood
SS B Geer
3B F Warner
LF- I Benners
ML J Remsen
RF J Cassidy
OI O Walker
M G Taylor

CINCINNATI
SP W White
SP B Mountjoy
SP G Shallix
C- P Snyder
1B J Reilly
2B B McPhee
SU J Peoples
3B H Carpenter
LM- T Mansell
LM C Jones
RF P Corkhill

COLUMBUS
SP E Morris
SP F Mountain
SP E Dundon
C- R Kemmler
1B J Field
2B P Smith
SS J Richmond
3B B Kuehne
LF- J Cahill
CF F Mann
RF T Brown
C F Carroll
M G Schmelz

INDIANAPOLIS
SP L McKeon
SP B Barr
SP J Aydelott
SP A McCauley
C J Keenan
1B J Kerins
2B- E Merrill
SS M Phillips
3B- P Callaghan
LF J Peltz
CF- J Morrison
RM- P Weihe
M1 J Gifford
M2 B Watkins

LOUISVILLE
SP G Hecker
SP D Driscoll
SP R Deagle
C- D Sullivan
1B J Latham
2B J Gerhardt
SS T McLaughlin
3I P Browning
LF L Maskrey
CF M Cline
RF J Wolf
3p P Reccius
M M Walsh

NEW YORK
SP J Lynch
SP T Keefe
C- B Holbert
1B D Orr
2B D Troy
SS C Nelson
3B D Esterbrook
LF E Kennedy
CF C Roseman
RF S Brady
C- C Reipschlager
M J Mutrie

PHILADELPHIA
SP B Mathews
SP B Taylor
SP A Atkinson
C J Milligan
1B H Stovey
2B C Stricker
SS S Houck
3B F Corey
LF- J Birchall
ML H Larkin
RF L Knight

PITTSBURGH
SP F Sullivan
SP J Neagle
C- E Colgan
1B- J Knowles
2B G Creamer
SS B White
3B- J Battin
LC D Miller
CF- L Taylor
RF E Swartwood
M1 D McKnight
M2 B Ferguson
M5 H Phillips

RICHMOND
SP P Megean
SP E Dugan
C- J Hanna
1B J Powell
2B T Larkin
SS B Schenck
3B B Nash
LF E Glenn
CF D Johnston
RF M Mansell
M F Moses

ST. LOUIS
SP J McGinnis
SP D Foutz
SP D Davis
SP B Caruthers
C P Deasley
1B C Comiskey
2B J Quest
SS B Gleason
3B A Latham
Lp T O'Neill
CF F Lewis
RF H Nicol
M1 J Williams

TOLEDO
SP T Mullane
SP H O'Day
C- F Walker
1B- C Lane
2B S Barkley
SS J Miller
3B- E Brown
LF- F Olin
CF C Welch
RF T Poorman
1I- J Moffett
M C Morton

WASHINGTON
SP B Barr
SP J Hamill
CU J Humphries
1B W Prince
2B T Hawkes
SS F Fennelly
3B B Gladman
UT B Morgan
CF- H Mullin
OP- E Trumbull
M1 H Hollingshead
M2 Bickerson

1884 NL

BOSTON
SP C Buffinton
SP J Whitney
C M Hackett
1B J Morrill
2B J Burdock
SS S Wise
3B E Sutton
LF J Hornung
CF J Manning
RF B Crowley

BUFFALO
SP J Galvin
SP B Serad
CO J Rowe
1B D Brouthers
2U H Richardson
SS D Force
3B D White
LF J O'Rourke
CF- D Eggler
RF J Lillie
CO G Myers

CHICAGO
SP L Corcoran
SP F Goldsmith
SP J Clarkson
C S Flint
1B C Anson
2B F Pfeffer
SS T Burns
3B E Williamson
LF A Dalrymple
CF G Gore
RC K Kelly

CLEVELAND
SP J Harkins
SP J McCormick
SP S Moffett
C- D Bushong
1B B Phillips
2S G Smith
SS J Glasscock
3B M Muldoon
LF- W Murphy
CF P Hotaling
RL J Evans
M C Hackett

DETROIT
SP D Shaw
SP C Getzien
SP F Brill
C C Bennett
1B M Scott
2B B Geis
Sp F Meinke
3B J Farrell
LF G Wood
CF N Hanlon
Rp S Wiedman
M J Chapman

NEW YORK
SP M Welch
SP E Begley
C B Ewing
1B A McKinnon
2M R Connor
SS E Caskin
3B F Hankinson
LF P Gillespie
M2 J Ward
Rp M Dorgan
RS D Richardson
M1 J Price
M2 M Ward

PHILADELPHIA
SP C Ferguson
SP B Vinton
SP J Coleman
SP J McElroy
C- J Crowley
1B S Farrar
2B E Andrews
SS B McClellan
3B J Mulvey
LF B Purcell
MU J Fogarty
RF J Manning
M H Wright

PROVIDENCE
SP C Radbourn
SP C Sweeney
SP E Conley
C B Gilligan
1B J Start
2B J Farrell
SS A Irwin
3B J Denny
LF C Carroll
CF P Hines
RF P Radford
M F Bancroft

1884 UA

ALTOONA
SP J Murphy
SP J Leary
CR J Moore
1O F Harris
2O C Dougherty
SS G Smith
3B H Koons
LF J Murphy
OI T Shafer
PR J Brown
M E Curtis

BALTIMORE
SP B Sweeney
SP T Lee
SP A Atkinson
C E Fusselback
1B C Levis
2B D Phelan
SS L Say
3U Y Robinson
LF E Seery
CF- N Cuthbert
MR- B Graham
CO- R Sweeney
M B Henderson

BOSTON
SP J Burke
SP D Shaw
SP T Bond
C1 L Brown
1B T Murnane
2B T O'Brien
SS W Hackett
3B J Irwin
LI K Butler
CF M Slattery
OC E Crane

CHICAGO-PITT
SP H Daily
SP A Atkinson
SP J Horan
CO B Krieg
1B J Schoeneck
2B- M Hengle
SS- S Matthias
3B- W Foley
IO C Householder
CF- H Wheeler
RS J Ellick
MI- C Briggs
UT- G Gardner
CS- T Suck
M1 E Hengle
M2 J Battin

CINCINNATI
SP G Bradley
SP J McCormick
C- J Kelly
1B- M Powell
2B S Crane
S2 J Jones
3B- C Barber
LR L Sylvester
MR B Harbridge
OI B Hawes
PM D Burns
SS- J Glasscock
1B- M McQuery
M1 D O'Leary

KANSAS CITY
SP E Hickman
SP B Black
SP P Veach
SP A Voss
C K Baldwin
1B- J Sweeney
2B- C Berry
SS- C Cross
3M- P Sullivan
UT- F Wyman
UT- B McLaughlin
RF- T Shafer
M1 H Wheeler
M2 M Porter
M3 T Sullivan

MILWAUKEE
SP H Porter
SP E Cushman
CM C Broughton
1B T Griffin
2B A Myers
SS T Sexton
3B T Morrissey
LF S Behel
MP- L Baldwin
RF E Hogan
M T Loftus

PHILADELPHIA
SP J Bakely
SP S Weaver
SP Fisher
C- T Gillen
1B J McGuinness
2B E Peak
SS- H Easterday
3B J McCormick
LI B Hoover
CF B Kienzle
RF J Flynn
OC J Clements
M F Malone

ST. LOUIS
SP C Sweeney
SP B Taylor
SP P Werden
SP C Hodnett
C G Baker
1B J Quinn
2B F Dunlap
SS M Whitehead
3B J Gleason
Lp- H Boyle
CF D Rowe
RF O Shafer
CO- J Brennan
LF- B Dickerson
M1 T Sullivan

ST. PAUL
SP J Brown
SP L Galvin
C C Ganzel
1B S Dunn
2B M Hengle
SS J Werrick
3B B O'Brien
LF J Tilley
CF B Barnes
RF S Carroll
M A Thompson

WASHINGTON
SP B Wise
SP A Voss
SP C Gagus
SP A Powell
CO- C Fulmer
1B- P Joy
2B T Evers
SS- J Halpin
3B- J McCormick
LF H Moore
UT P Baker
RF B Wise
CO- J Gunson
M M Scanlon

WILMINGTON
SP J Murphy
SP T Nolan
SP D Casey
SP J Bakely
CS T Cusick
1B R Snyder
2B C Bastian
SS- H Myers
3B J Say
CL T Lynch
CF- G Fisher
RF- J Munce
M J Simmons

1885 AA

BALTIMORE
SP H Henderson
SP B Emslie
SP J Henry
C B Traffley
1B E Stearns
2B- T Manning
SS J Macullar
3B M Muldoon
LF J Sommer
CF- D Casey
Rp T Burns
MU- E Greer
M B Barnie

BROOKLYN
SP H Porter
SP J Harkins
C- J Hayes
1B B Phillips
23 G Pinkney
SS G Smith
32 B McClellan
UT E Swartwood
CF P Hotaling
RF- J Cassidy
Lp A Terry
M1 C Hackett
M2 C Byrne

CINCINNATI
SP W White
SP L McKeon
SP B Mountjoy
SP G Pechiney
SP G Shallix
C- P Snyder
1B J Reilly
2B B McPhee
SS F Fennelly
3B H Carpenter
LF C Jones
CF J Clinton
RF P Corkhill
M O Caylor

LOUISVILLE
SP G Hecker
SP N Baker
SP A Mays
SP T Ramsey
C- J Crotty
1B J Kerins
2B T McLaughlin
SS J Miller
3B P Reccius
LF L Maskrey
CF P Browning
RF J Wolf
M J Hart

NEW YORK
SP J Lynch
SP E Cushman
SP D Crothers
SP E Begley
SP B Becannon
C C Reipschlager
1B D Orr
2B- T Forster
SS C Nelson
3B F Hankinson
LF E Kennedy
CF C Roseman
RF S Brady
CU- B Holbert
M J Gifford

PHILADELPHIA
SP B Mathews
SP T Lovett
SP E Knouff
SP E Cushman
C- J Milligan
1M H Stovey
2B C Stricker
SS S Houck
3B F Corey
LF- B Purcell
ML H Larkin
RF J Coleman
CI- J O'Brien

PITTSBURGH
SP E Morris
SP P Meegan
SP H O'Day
SP J Galvin
C F Carroll
1B- J Field
2B P Smith
SS A Whitney
3B B Kuehne
LF C Eden
CF F Mann
RF T Brown
M H Phillips

ST. LOUIS
SP B Caruthers
SP D Foutz
SP J McGinnis
C D Bushong
1B C Comiskey
2B S Barkley
SS B Gleason
3B A Latham
LI Y Robinson
CF C Welch
RF H Nicol

1885 NL

BOSTON
SP J Whitney
SP C Buffinton
SP D Davis
C- T Gunning
1B J Morrill
2B- J Burdock
SU S Wise
3B E Sutton
LF- T McCarthy
CF J Manning
RF- T Poorman

BUFFALO
SP J Galvin
SP B Serad
SP P Conway
SP P Wood
C G Myers
1B D Brouthers
2S D Force
SU J Rowe
3B D White
LF B Crowley
2M H Richardson
RF J Lillie
M2 J Chapman

CHICAGO
SP J Clarkson
SP J McCormick
SP T Kennedy
C S Flint
1B C Anson
2B F Pfeffer
SS T Burns
3B E Williamson
LF A Dalrymple
CF G Gore
RC K Kelly

DETROIT
SP C Getzien
SP S Wiedman
SP L Baldwin
SP D Casey
CU C Bennett
1B M McQuery
2B S Crane
SS- M Phillips
3B- J Donnelly
LF G Wood
CF N Hanlon
RF- S Thompson
M1 C Morton
M2 B Watkins

NEW YORK
SP M Welch
SP T Keefe
SP D Richardson
C B Ewing
1B R Connor
2B J Gerhardt
SS J Ward
3B D Esterbrook
LF P Gillespie
CF J O'Rourke
RF M Dorgan
M J Mutrie

PHILADELPHIA
SP E Daily
SP C Ferguson
SP B Vinton
C- J Clements
1B S Farrar
2B A Myers
SS C Bastian
3B J Mulvey
LF E Andrews
CF J Fogarty
RF J Manning
M H Wright

PROVIDENCE
SP C Radbourn
SP D Shaw
C B Gilligan
1B J Start
2B J Farrell
SS- A Irwin
3B J Denny
LF C Carroll
CF P Hines
RF P Radford
UI C Bassett
C- C Daily
M F Bancroft

ST. LOUIS
SP H Boyle
SP J Kirby
SP H Daily
C- F Briody
1B A McKinnon
2B F Dunlap
SS J Glasscock
3B E Caskin
LF- E Seery
CF- F Lewis
RF O Shafer
OP C Sweeney
UT J Quinn
M3 F Dunlap

1886 AA

BALTIMORE
SP M Kilroy
SP J McGinnis
SP H Henderson
C- C Fulmer
1B M Scott
23 M Muldoon
SS J Macullar
3B- J Davis
LI J Sommer
CF- P O'Connell
RF J Manning
23- J Farrell
M B Barnie

BROOKLYN
SP H Porter
SP J Harkins
SP A Terry
SP H Henderson
SP S Toole
C J Peoples
1B B Phillips
2B B McClellan
SS G Smith
3B G Pinkney
LF E Burch
CF J McTamany
RF E Swartwood
CO- B Clark
M C Byrne

CINCINNATI
SP T Mullane
SP G Pechiney
SP L McKeon
C K Baldwin
1B J Reilly
2B B McPhee
SS F Fennelly
3B H Carpenter
LF C Jones
CF- F Lewis
RF P Corkhill
M O Caylor

LOUISVILLE
SP T Ramsey
SP G Hecker
C1- A Cross
C1 J Kerins
2B R Mack
SS B White
3B J Werrick
LF- J Strauss
ML P Browning
RF J Wolf
M J Hart

NEW YORK
SP J Lynch
SP A Mays
SP E Cushman
C- C Reipschlager
1B D Orr
2B- T Forster
SM C Nelson
3B F Hankinson
LM C Roseman
ML- S Behel
RF S Brady
SS- T McLaughlin
M1 J Gifford
M2 B Ferguson

PHILADELPHIA
SP A Atkinson
SP B Mathews
SP B Hart
SP T Kennedy
SP C Miller
C1 W Robinson
1M H Stovey
2B L Bierbauer
SS- C McGarr
3B- J Gleason
LF H Larkin
CF- E Greer
RF J Coleman
IC J O'Brien
C1- J Milligan
M1 L Simmons
M2 B Sharsig

PITTSBURGH
SP E Morris
SP J Galvin
SP J Handiboe
CU F Carroll
1B- O Schomberg
2B S Barkley
SS P Smith
3S A Whitney
LF- E Glenn
CF F Mann
RF T Brown
UT B Kuehne
CO- D Miller
M H Phillips

ST. LOUIS
SP D Foutz
SP B Caruthers
SP N Hudson
SP J McGinnis
C D Bushong
1B C Comiskey
2B Y Robinson
SS B Gleason
3B A Latham
LF T O'Neill
CF C Welch
RF- H Nicol

1886 NL

BOSTON
SP C Radbourn
SP B Stemmeyer
SP C Buffinton
C- C Daily
1I S Wise
2B- J Burdock
UI J Morrill
3B B Nash
LF J Hornung
CF D Johnston
RF T Poorman
UT E Sutton

CHICAGO
SP J Clarkson
SP J McCormick
SP J Flynn
C- S Flint
1B C Anson
2B F Pfeffer
SS E Williamson
3B T Burns
LF A Dalrymple
CF G Gore
OC K Kelly
UT J Ryan

DETROIT
SP L Baldwin
SP C Getzien
SP P Conway
SP B Schmidt
C- C Bennett
1B D Brouthers
2B- F Dunlap
SS J Rowe
3B D White
L2 H Richardson
CF N Hanlon
RF S Thompson
M B Watkins

KANSAS CITY
SP S Wiedman
SP J Whitney
SP P Conway
C- F Briody
1B M McQuery
2B A Myers
SS C Bassett
3B J Donnelly
LF J Lillie
CF D Rowe
RF P Radford
C- M Hackett

NEW YORK
SP T Keefe
SP M Welch
CO- B Ewing
1B R Connor
2B J Gerhardt
SS J Ward
3B D Esterbrook
LF P Gillespie
ML- D Richardson
RF M Dorgan
MC J O'Rourke
M J Mutrie

PHILADELPHIA
SP C Ferguson
SP D Casey
C- D McGuire
1B S Farrar
2B C Bastian
SS A Irwin
3B J Mulvey
LF G Wood
CF E Andrews
RF J Fogarty
Rp E Daily
M H Wright

ST. LOUIS
SP J Healy
SP J Kirby
SP H Boyle
SP C Sweeney
C G Myers
1B A McKinnon
2B- F Dunlap
SS J Glasscock
3B J Denny
LF E Seery
CF- J McGeachy
RF J Cahill
MI- J Quinn
M G Schmelz

WASHINGTON
SP D Shaw
SP B Barr
SP T Madigan
SP F Gilmore
C B Gilligan
1O P Baker
2B- J Farrell
SS- D Force
23 J Knowles
LF C Carroll
CF P Hines
RU E Crane
M1 M Scanlon
M2 J Gaffney

1887 AA

BALTIMORE
SP M Kilroy
SP P Smith
C S Trott
1B T Tucker
2B B Greenwood
S3 T Burns
3S J Davis
LF J Sommer
CF M Griffin
RF B Purcell
M B Barnie

BROOKLYN
SP H Porter
SP J Harkins
SP S Toole
SP H Henderson
C- J Peoples
1B B Phillips
2B B McClellan
SS G Smith
3B G Pinkney
LF E Greer
CF J McTamany
RF E Swartwood
OP A Terry
M C Byrne

CINCINNATI
SP E Smith
SP T Mullane
SP B Serad
C K Baldwin
1B J Reilly
2B B McPhee
SS F Fennelly
3B H Carpenter
LF G Tebeau
CF P Corkhill
RF H Nicol
M G Schmelz

CLEVELAND
SP B Crowell
SP M Morrison
SP H Daily
SP B Gilks
SP G Pechiney
C- P Snyder
1B J Toy
2B C Stricker
SS E McKean
3B- P Reccius
LR- F Mann
CF P Hotaling
LR M Allen
M J Williams

LOUISVILLE
SP T Ramsey
SP E Chamberlain
C- P Cook
1C J Kerins
2B R Mack
SS B White
3B J Werrick
LF H Collins
CF P Browning
RF J Wolf
1p G Hecker
M J Kelly

NEW YORK
SP A Mays
SP E Cushman
SP J Lynch
SP J Shaffer
SP S Wiedman
C- B Holbert
1B D Orr
2B J Gerhardt
SR P Radford

3B F Hankinson
LF D O'Brien
CF- C Jones
MO- C Roseman
M1 B Ferguson
M3 O Caylor

PHILADELPHIA
SP E Seward
SP G Weyhing
SP A Atkinson
C- W Robinson
1C J Milligan
2B L Bierbauer
SS C McGarr
3B D Lyons
LI H Larkin
OI H Stovey
RF T Poorman
M1 F Bancroft
M2 C Mason

ST. LOUIS
SP S King
C J Boyle
1B C Comiskey
2B Y Robinson
SS B Gleason
3B A Latham
LF T O'Neill
CF C Welch
Rp B Caruthers
Rp D Foutz

1887 NL

BOSTON
SP C Radbourn
SP K Madden
SP D Conway
SP B Stemmeyer
C- P Tate
1B J Morrill
2B- J Burdock
SU S Wise
3B B Nash
LF J Hornung
CF D Johnston
R2 K Kelly
UT E Sutton

CHICAGO
SP J Clarkson
SP M Baldwin
SP G Van Haltren
C- T Daly
1B C Anson
2B F Pfeffer
SS E Williamson
3B T Burns
LF M Sullivan
CF J Ryan
RM- B Sunday

DETROIT
SP C Getzien
SP L Baldwin
SP S Wiedman
SP P Conway
SP L Twitchell
C- C Ganzel
1B D Brouthers
2B- F Dunlap
SS J Rowe
3B D White
2L H Richardson
CF N Hanlon
RF S Thompson
M B Watkins

INDIANAPOLIS
SP J Healy
SP H Boyle
SP L Shreve
CU- G Myers
1B O Schomberg
2B C Bassett
SS J Glasscock
3B J Denny
LF E Seery
CF J McGeachy
RF- J Cahill
M1 W Burnham
M2 F Thomas
M3 H Fogel

NEW YORK
SP T Keefe
SP M Welch
SP B George
C- W Brown
1B R Connor
2B D Richardson
SS J Ward
3U- B Ewing
LF- P Gillespie
CF G Gore
RL M Tiernan
IC J O'Rourke
RF- M Dorgan
M J Mutrie

PHILADELPHIA
SP D Casey
SP C Buffinton
SP C Ferguson
C- J Clements
1B S Farrar
2B- B McLaughlin
SS A Irwin
3B J Mulvey
LF G Wood
CF E Andrews
RF J Fogarty
M H Wright

PITTSBURGH
SP J Galvin
SP J McCormick
SP E Morris
C D Miller
12 S Barkley
2S P Smith
SS B Kuehne
3B A Whitney
LF A Dalrymple
CF- T Brown
RF J Coleman
OC F Carroll
M H Phillips

WASHINGTON
SP J Whitney
SP H O'Day
SP F Gilmore
SP D Shaw
C C Mack
1B B O'Brien
2S A Myers
S2 J Farrell
3B J Donnelly
LF C Carroll
CF P Hines
RF E Daily
RU- G Shoch
M J Gaffney

1888 AA

BALTIMORE
SP B Cunningham
SP M Kilroy
SP P Smith
C- C Fulmer
1B T Tucker
2U B Greenwood
S2 J Farrell
3B B Shindle
LS- T Burns
CF M Griffin
RF B Purcell
UT- J Sommer
M B Barnie

BROOKLYN
SP M Hughes
SP A Terry
SP A Mays
C- D Bushong
1B D Orr
2B- J Burdock
SS G Smith
3B G Pinkney
LF D O'Brien
CF P Radford
Rp D Foutz
OP B Caruthers
2B- B McClellan
M B McGunnigle

CINCINNATI
SP L Viau
SP T Mullane
SP E Smith
C J Keenan
1B J Reilly
2B B McPhee
SS F Fennelly
3B H Carpenter
LF G Tebeau
CF P Corkhill
RF H Nicol
M G Schmelz

CLEVELAND
SP J Bakely
SP D O'Brien
SP B Crowell
C- C Zimmer
1B J Faatz
2B C Stricker
SL E McKean
S3 G Alberts
UT B Gilks
CF P Hotaling
RL- E Hogan
M1 J Williams
M2 T Loftus

KANSAS CITY
SP H Porter
SP T Sullivan
SP B Fagan
SP F Hoffman
SP S Toole
C J Donahue
1B B Phillips
2B S Barkley
SS H Easterday
3B J Davis
RL- M Cline
MR J McTamany
RF- B Hamilton
M1 D Rowe
M3 B Watkins

LOUISVILLE
SP T Ramsey
SP S Stratton
SP G Hecker
SP E Chamberlain
SP J Ewing
C- P Cook
1B- S Smith
2B R Mack
SS- B White
3B J Werrick
UT H Collins
CF P Browning
RS J Wolf
OC- J Kerins
M1 J Kelly
M2 M Davidson
M4 M Davidson

PHILADELPHIA
SP E Seward
SP G Weyhing
SP M Mattimore
C- W Robinson
1B H Larkin
2B L Bierbauer
SS B Gleason
3B D Lyons
LF H Stovey
CF C Welch
RF T Poorman
M B Sharsig

ST. LOUIS
SP S King
SP N Hudson
SP E Chamberlain
SP J Devlin
C- J Boyle
1B C Comiskey
2B Y Robinson
SS- B White
3B A Latham
LF T O'Neill
CF H Lyons
RF T McCarthy

1888 NL

BOSTON
SP J Clarkson
SP B Sowders
SP C Radbourn
SP K Madden
CR K Kelly
1B J Morrill
2B- J Quinn
SS S Wise
3B B Nash
LF J Hornung
CF D Johnston
RF T Brown

CHICAGO
SP G Krock
SP M Baldwin
SP G Van Haltren
SP J Tener
C- T Daly
1B C Anson
2B F Pfeffer
SS E Williamson
3B T Burns
LF- M Sullivan
CF J Ryan
RF- H Duffy

DETROIT
SP C Getzien
SP P Conway
SP H Gruber
SP E Beatin
C- C Bennett
1B D Brouthers
2B- H Richardson
SS J Rowe
3B D White
LF L Twitchell
CF N Hanlon
RF- C Campau
2C C Ganzel
M1 B Watkins
M2 B Leadley

INDIANAPOLIS
SP H Boyle
SP J Healy
SP L Shreve
SP B Burdick
C3- D Buckley
1B- D Esterbrook
2B C Bassett
SS J Glasscock
3B J Denny
LF E Seery
CF P Hines
RF J McGeachy
M H Spence

NEW YORK
SP T Keefe
SP M Welch
SP C Titcomb
SP E Crane
C B Ewing
1B R Connor
2B D Richardson
SS J Ward
3B A Whitney
LU J O'Rourke
CF M Slattery
RF M Tiernan
M J Mutrie

PHILADELPHIA
SP C Buffinton
SP D Casey
SP B Sanders
SP K Gleason
C J Clements
1B S Farrar
2B C Bastian
SS A Irwin
3B J Mulvey
LF G Wood
CF E Andrews
RF J Fogarty
2B- E Delahanty
M H Wright

PITTSBURGH
SP E Morris
SP J Galvin
SP H Staley
CO D Miller
1B- J Beckley
2B- F Dunlap
S2 P Smith
3S B Kuehne
LF- A Dalrymple
CF B Sunday
RF J Coleman
CL F Carroll
1R- A Maul
M H Phillips

WASHINGTON
SP H O'Day
SP J Whitney
SP W Widner
SP G Keefe
SP F Gilmore
C C Mack
1B B O'Brien
2B A Myers
SR G Shoch
3B J Donnelly
LF W Wilmot
CF D Hoy
RF E Daily
M1 W Hewett
M2 T Sullivan

1889 AA

BALTIMORE
SP M Kilroy
SP F Foreman
SP B Cunningham
C- P Tate
1B T Tucker
2B R Mack
SS- J Farrell
3B B Shindle
LF J Hornung
CF M Griffin
RF J Sommer
M B Barnie

BROOKLYN
SP B Caruthers
SP A Terry
SP T Lovett
SP M Hughes
CR- J Visner
1B D Foutz
2B H Collins
SS G Smith
3B G Pinkney
LF D O'Brien
CF P Corkhill
RF T Burns
M B McGunnigle

CINCINNATI
SP J Duryea
SP L Viau
SP T Mullane
SP E Smith
C J Keenan
1B J Reilly
2B B McPhee
SS O Beard
3B H Carpenter
LF G Tebeau
CF B Holliday
RF H Nicol
M G Schmelz

COLUMBUS
SP M Baldwin
SP W Widner
SP H Gastright
SP A Mays
C J O'Connor
1B D Orr
2B B Greenwood
SS H Easterday
UT L Marr
LF E Daily
CF J McTamany
R3 S Johnson
M A Buckenberger

KANSAS CITY
SP P Swartzel
SP J Conway
SP J Sowders
SP J McCarty
SP T Sullivan
C- C Hoover
1B E Stearns
2B- S Barkley
SS H Long
3B- J Davis
L2 J Manning
CF J Burns
RF B Hamilton
M B Watkins

LOUISVILLE
SP R Ehret
SP J Ewing
SP T Ramsey
SP S Stratton
C- P Cook
1p- G Hecker
2B D Shannon
SS P Tomney
3B H Raymond
LF- P Browning
CF F Weaver
RI J Wolf
CU F Vaughn
M1 D Esterbrook
M2 C Wolf
M4 J Chapman

PHILADELPHIA
SP G Weyhing
SP E Seward
SP S McMahon
C- W Robinson
1B H Larkin
2B L Bierbauer
SS F Fennelly
3B D Lyons
LF H Stovey
CF C Welch
RF B Purcell
M B Sharsig

ST. LOUIS
SP S King
SP E Chamberlain
SP J Stivetts
C J Boyle
1B C Comiskey
2B Y Robinson
SS S Fuller
3B A Latham
LF T O'Neill
CF C Duffee
RF T McCarthy
C- J Milligan

1889 NL

BOSTON
SP J Clarkson
SP C Radbourn
SP K Madden
C C Bennett
1B D Brouthers
2L H Richardson
S2 J Quinn
3B B Nash
LF T Brown
CF D Johnston
RF K Kelly
CR- C Ganzel
M J Hart

CHICAGO
SP B Hutchison
SP J Tener
SP F Dwyer
SP A Gumbert
C D Farrell
1B C Anson
2B F Pfeffer
SS- E Williamson
3B T Burns
LF G Van Haltren
CF J Ryan
RF H Duffy

CLEVELAND
SP D O'Brien
SP E Beatin
SP J Bakely
SP H Gruber
C C Zimmer
1B J Faatz
2B C Stricker
SS E McKean
3B P Tebeau
LF L Twitchell
CF J McAleer
RF P Radford
M T Loftus

INDIANAPOLIS
SP H Boyle
SP C Getzien
SR A Rusie
C- D Buckley
1B P Hines
2B C Bassett
SS J Glasscock
3B J Denny
LF E Seery
CF- M Sullivan
RF J McGeachy
M1 F Bancroft

NEW YORK
SP M Welch
SP T Keefe
SP E Crane
C B Ewing
1B R Connor
2B D Richardson
SS J Ward
3B A Whitney
LF J O'Rourke
CF G Gore
RF M Tiernan
M J Mutrie

PHILADELPHIA
SP C Buffinton
SP B Sanders
SP K Gleason
SP D Casey
C J Clements
1B S Farrar
2B- A Myers
SS B Hallman
3B J Mulvey
LF G Wood
CF J Fogarty
RF S Thompson
M H Wright

PITTSBURGH
SP H Staley
SP J Galvin
SP E Morris
CO D Miller
1B J Beckley
2B F Dunlap
SS- J Rowe
3B B Kuehne
LR- A Maul
CF N Hanlon
RF B Sunday
OC F Carroll
LU- J Fields
SS- P Smith
M1 H Phillips

WASHINGTON
SP A Ferson
SP G Haddock
SP G Keefe
SP H O'Day
SP J Healy
C- T Daly
1B- J Carney
2I S Wise
SS A Irwin
3B- J Irwin
LF W Wilmot
CF D Hoy
RF- E Beecher
OC C Mack
M1 J Morrill

1890 AA

BALTIMORE
SP L German
SP S McMahon
SP M O'Rourke
SP M Morrison
C- G Townsend
12 T Power
2B R Mack
SS I Ray
3B P Gilbert
LF J Sommer
CF- D Long
RF B Johnson
M B Barnie

BROOKLYN
SP C McCullough
SP M Mattimore
SP B Murphy
C- J Toy
1B B O'Brien
2B J Gerhardt
SS- C Nelson
3B- J Davis
LF H Simon
CF J Peltz
Rp E Daily
OC F Bowes
C3 H Pitz
M J Kennedy

COLUMBUS
SP H Gastright
SP F Knauss
SP J Easton
SP E Chamberlain
SP W Widner
C J O'Connor
1B M Lehane
2B J Crooks
SS- H Easterday
3B C Reilly
LR S Johnson
CF J McTamany
RF J Sneed
IC- J Doyle
M1 A Buckenberger
M2 G Schmelz
M3 J Sullivan

LOUISVILLE
SP S Stratton
SP R Ehret
SP G Meakim
SP H Goodall
SP E Daily
C J Ryan
1B H Taylor
2B T Shinnick
SS P Tomney
3B H Raymond
LF C Hamburg
CF F Weaver
RF J Wolf
M J Chapman

PHILADELPHIA
SP S McMahon
SP E Green
SP E Seward
SP D Esper
C W Robinson
1B J O'Brien
2B- T Shafer
S2 B Conroy
3B D Lyons
LF B Purcell
CF C Welch
RF O Shafer
M B Sharsig

ROCHESTER
SP B Barr
SP W Calihan
SP C Titcomb
SP B Miller
C D McGuire
1B- T O'Brien
2B B Greenwood
SS- M Phillips
3B J Knowles
LF H Lyons
CF S Griffin
RF T Scheffler
C- D McKeough
M P Powers

ST. LOUIS
SP J Stivetts
SP T Ramsey
SP B Hart
SP B Whitrock
C J Munyan
1B- E Cartwright
2B- B Higgins
SS S Fuller
M3 C Duffee
LR- C Campau
M1- C Roseman
RF T McCarthy
M2 J Kerins
M5 T McCarthy
M6 J Gerhardt

SYRACUSE
SP D Casey
SP J Keefe
SP M Morrison
SP E Mars
CM G Briggs
1B M McQuery
2B C Childs
SS B McLaughlin
C- T O'Rourke
LS B Ely
CF R Wright
RF- P Friel
3B T O'Rourke
M1 G Frazer
M2 W Fessenden
M3 G Frazer

TOLEDO
SP J Healy
SP E Cushman
SP F Smith
SP C Sprague
C H Sage
1B P Werden
2B P Nicholson
SS F Scheibeck
3B B Alvord
LF B Van Dyke
CF G Tebeau
RF E Swartwood
M C Morton

1890 NL

BOSTON
SP K Nichols
SP J Clarkson
SP C Getzien
C C Bennett
1B T Tucker
2B P Smith
SS H Long
3B C McGarr
LF M Sullivan
CF- P Hines
RF S Brodie
M F Selee

BROOKLYN
SP T Lovett
SP B Caruthers
C T Daly
1B D Foutz
2B H Collins
SS G Smith
3B G Pinkney
OP A Terry
LM D O'Brien
RF T Burns
M B McGunnigle

CHICAGO
SP B Hutchison
SP P Luby
SP E Stein
SP M Sullivan
SP R Coughlin
C M Kittridge
1B C Anson
2B- B Glenalvin
SS J Cooney
3B T Burns
LF C Carroll
CF W Wilmot
RF- J Andrews
R2 H Earl

CINCINNATI
SP B Rhines
SP J Duryea
SP T Mullane
SP F Foreman
SP L Viau
C- J Harrington
1B J Reilly
2B B McPhee
SS O Beard
IO L Marr
LF J Knight
CF B Holliday
RF- H Nicol
M T Loftus

CLEVELAND
SP E Beatin
SP J Wadsworth
SP C Young
SP E Lincoln
SP L Viau
C C Zimmer
1B- P Veach

2B J Ardner
SS E McKean
3B W Smalley
LF B Gilks
CF G Davis
RF- V Dailey
M1 G Schmelz
M2 B Leadley

NEW YORK
SP A Rusie
SP M Welch
SP J Sharrott
C- D Buckley
1B- L Whistler
2B C Bassett
SS J Glasscock
3B J Denny
L1 J Hornung
CF M Tiernan
Rp J Burkett
OC A Clarke
M J Mutrie

PHILADELPHIA
SP K Gleason
SP T Vickery
SP P Smith
C J Clements
1B A McCauley
2B A Myers
SS B Allen
3B E Mayer
LF B Hamilton
CF E Burke
RF S Thompson
M1 H Wright
M3 A Reach
M5 H Wright

PITTSBURGH
SP K Baker
SP D Anderson
SP B Sowders
SP C Schmit
C H Decker
1p G Hecker
2S S LaRoque
SS- E Sales
3U D Miller
LF- J Kelty
MR B Sunday
UT T Berger
OC B Wilson

1890 PL

BOSTON
SP C Radbourn
SP A Gumbert
SP B Daley
SP M Kilroy
C- M Murphy
1B D Brothers
2B J Quinn
SS A Irwin
3B B Nash
LF H Richardson
CF T Brown
RF H Stovey
CS K Kelly

BROOKLYN
SP G Weyhing
SP J Sowders
SP C Murphy
SP G Hemming
C- T Kinslow
1B D Orr
2B L Bierbauer
SS J Ward
3B B Joyce
LF E Seery
CF E Andrews
RM J McGeachy
Rp G Van Haltren
M M Ward

BUFFALO
SP G Haddock
SP B Cunningham
SP G Keefe
SP L Twitchell
SP G Stafford
C C Mack
31 D White
2B S Wise
SS J Rowe
3B- J Irwin
LF E Beecher
CF D Hoy
RC- J Halligan
OC- S Clark
M2 J Faatz
M3 J Rowe

CHICAGO
SP M Baldwin
SP S King
SP C Bartson
C D Farrell
1B C Comiskey
2B F Pfeffer
SS- C Bastian
3S- E Williamson
LF T O'Neill
CF J Ryan
RF H Duffy
C3 J Boyle

CLEVELAND
SP H Gruber
SP J Bakely
SP D O'Brien
SP W McGill
C S Sutcliffe
1B H Larkin
2B C Stricker
SU E Delahanty
3B P Tebeau
LF P Browning
CF J McAleer
UT P Radford
M1 T Larkin

NEW YORK
SP H O'Day
SP E Crane
SP J Ewing
SP T Keefe
C B Ewing
1B R Connor
2B D Shannon
S2 D Richardson
3S A Whitney
LM G Gore
LM M Slattery
RF J O'Rourke
3S- G Hatfield
CF- D Johnston

PHILADELPHIA
SP B Sanders
SP P Knell
SP C Buffinton
SP B Husted
SP B Cunningham
C- J Milligan
1B S Farrar
2B J Pickett
SS B Shindle
3B J Mulvey
LF G Wood
CF M Griffin
RM J Fogarty
OC B Hallman

PITTSBURGH
SP H Staley
SP A Maul
SP J Galvin
SP E Morris
SP J Tener
CL F Carroll
1B J Beckley
2B Y Robinson
SS T Corcoran
3B B Kuehne
LI J Fields
CF N Hanlon
RF J Visner

1891 AA

BALTIMORE
SP S McMahon
SP B Cunningham
SP K Madden
SP J Healy
C W Robinson
1B P Werden
2B S Wise
LS G Van Haltren
3B P Gilbert
UO B Johnson
CF C Welch
RS I Ray
M B Barnie

BOSTON
SP G Haddock
SP C Buffinton
SR D O'Brien
SP B Daley
C M Murphy
1B D Brouthers
2B C Stricker
SS P Radford
3C D Farrell
LF- H Richardson
CF T Brown
RF H Duffy
3B- B Joyce
M A Irwin

CINCINNATI
SP F Dwyer
SP E Crane
SP W Mains
SP W McGill
C K Kelly
1B J Carney
2B Y Robinson
SS J Canavan
3B A Whitney
LF E Andrews
CF D Johnston
RF E Seery

COLUMBUS
SP P Knell
SP H Gastright
SP J Dolan
SP J Easton
C- J Donahue
1B M Lehane
2B J Crooks
SS B Wheelock
3B- B Kuehne
LM C Duffee
CF- J McTamany
RF J Sneed
M G Schmelz

LOUISVILLE
SP W Fitzgerald
SP R Ehret
SP J Meekin
SP S Stratton
SP J Doran
RP E Daily
CI- J Ryan
1B H Taylor
2B T Shinnick
SS H Jennings
3B- O Beard
LF P Donovan
CF C Weaver
RF J Wolf
IC T Cahill
M J Chapman

MILWAUKEE
SP G Davies
SP F Killen
SP F Dwyer
C F Vaughn
1B J Carney
2S J Canavan
S3 G Shoch
3B- G Alberts
LF A Dalrymple
CF E Burke
RF H Earl
C3 J Grim
M C Cushman

PHILADELPHIA
SP G Weyhing
SP E Chamberlain
SP B Sanders
SP W Calihan
C1 J Milligan
1B H Larkin
2B B Hallman
SS T Corcoran
3B J Mulvey
LF G Wood
CF- P Corkhill
OC L Cross
M1 B Sharsig

ST. LOUIS
SP J Stivetts
SP W McGill
SR C Griffith
SP J Neale
SP G Rettger
C J Boyle
1B C Comiskey
2B- B Eagan
SS S Fuller
3B D Lyons
LF T O'Neill
CF D Hoy
RF T McCarthy

WASHINGTON
SP K Carsey
SP F Foreman
SP J Bakely
C D McGuire
1B- M McQuery
2B T Dowd
SS G Hatfield
3B- B Alvord
LF- E Beecher
CF- P Hines
LR L Murphy
M1 S Trott
M2 P Snyder
M3 D Shannon
M4 S Griffin

1891 NL

BOSTON
SP J Clarkson
SP K Nichols
SP H Staley
SP C Getzien
C- C Bennett
1B T Tucker
2B J Quinn
SS H Long
3B B Nash
LM B Lowe
CF S Brodie
RL H Stovey
C- C Ganzel
M F Selee

BROOKLYN
SP T Lovett
SP B Caruthers
SP G Hemming
SP A Terry
SP B Inks
C- T Kinslow
1B D Foutz
2L H Collins
SS J Ward
3B G Pinkney
LF D O'Brien
CF M Griffin
RF T Burns
M M Ward

CHICAGO
SP B Hutchison
SP A Gumbert
SP P Luby
SP E Stein
C- M Kittridge
1B C Anson
2B F Pfeffer
SS J Cooney
3O B Dahlen
LM W Wilmot
ML J Ryan
RF C Carroll

CINCINNATI
SP T Mullane
SP B Rhines
SP C Radbourn
SP E Crane
C J Harrington
1O J Reilly
2B B McPhee
SS G Smith
3B A Latham
LF- P Browning
ML B Holliday
RF- L Marr
1C- J Keenan
M T Loftus

CLEVELAND
SP C Young
SP H Gruber
SP L Viau
C C Zimmer
1B J Virtue
2B C Childs
SS E McKean
3B- P Tebeau
LF J McAleer
CF G Davis
RF- S Johnson
OC- J Doyle
M1 B Leadley

NEW YORK
SP A Rusie
SP J Ewing
SP M Welch
C- D Buckley
1B R Connor
2B D Richardson
SS J Glasscock
3B C Bassett
LF J O'Rourke
CF G Gore
RF M Tiernan
UT- L Whistler
M J Mutrie

PHILADELPHIA
SP K Gleason
SP D Esper
SP J Thornton
C J Clements
1B W Brown
2B A Myers
SS B Allen
3B B Shindle
LF B Hamilton
MU E Delahanty
RF S Thompson
M H Wright

PITTSBURGH
SP M Baldwin
SP S King
SP J Galvin
C- C Mack
1B J Beckley
2B L Bierbauer
SS- F Shugart
3B C Reilly
LF- P Browning
ML N Hanlon
RF F Carroll
IC D Miller
M2 B McGunnigle

1892 NL

BALTIMORE
SP S McMahon
SP G Cobb
SP T Vickery
SP C Buffinton
C- W Robinson
1B- S Sutcliffe
2B- C Stricker
SS- T O'Rourke
3B B Shindle
LF- H Stovey
CF- C Welch
UT G Van Haltren
C- J Gunson
UT- J McGraw
M2 J Waltz
M3 N Hanlon

BOSTON
SP K Nichols
SP J Stivetts
SP H Staley
SP J Clarkson
C- K Kelly
1B T Tucker
2B J Quinn
SS H Long
3B B Nash
LI B Lowe
CF H Duffy
RF T McCarthy
M F Selee

BROOKLYN
SP G Haddock
SP E Stein
SP D Foutz
SP B Hart
SP B Kennedy
C- C Daily
1B D Brouthers
2B J Ward
SS T Corcoran
3B B Joyce
LF D O'Brien
CF M Griffin
RF T Burns
IC T Daly
M M Ward

CHICAGO
SP B Hutchison
SP A Gumbert
SP P Luby
C P Schriver
1B C Anson
2B J Canavan
S3 B Dahlen
3B- J Parrott
LF W Wilmot
CF J Ryan
RL S Dungan
RF- G Decker

CINCINNATI
SP E Chamberlain
SP T Mullane
SP F Dwyer
SP M Sullivan
C- M Murphy
1B C Comiskey
2B B McPhee
SS G Smith
3B A Latham
LF T O'Neill
ML- P Browning
MR B Holliday
CU- F Vaughn

CLEVELAND
SP C Young
SP N Cuppy
SP J Clarkson
SP G Davies
C C Zimmer
1B J Virtue
2B C Childs
SS E McKean
3R G Davis
LF J Burkett
CF J McAleer
RU J O'Connor
3B- P Tebeau

LOUISVILLE
SP S Stratton
SP B Sanders
SP F Clausen
SP J Meekin
SP A Jones
RP L Viau
CU J Grim
1B- L Whistler
2B F Pfeffer
SS H Jennings
3B- B Kuehne
LF F Weaver
CF T Brown
UT H Taylor
3B- C Bassett
M1 J Chapman

NEW YORK
SP A Rusie
SP S King
SP E Crane
C1 J Boyle
1C B Ewing
2L- E Burke
SS S Fuller
3B D Lyons
LF J O'Rourke
CF H Lyons
RF M Tiernan
IC- J Doyle
M P Powers

PHILADELPHIA
SR G Weyhing
SP K Carsey
SP T Keefe
SP D Esper
C J Clements
1B R Connor
2B B Hallman
SS B Allen
3B- C Reilly
LF B Hamilton
CF E Delahanty
RF S Thompson
IC L Cross
M H Wright

PITTSBURGH
SP M Baldwin
SP R Ehret
SP A Terry
SP J Galvin
C C Mack
1B J Beckley
2B L Bierbauer
SS F Shugart
3B D Farrell
Lp E Smith
OC D Miller
RF- P Donovan
M1 A Buckenberger
M2 T Burns
M3 A Buckenberger

ST. LOUIS
SP K Gleason
SP T Breitenstein
SP P Hawley
SP C Getzien
SP B Hawke
C D Buckley
1B P Werden
2B J Crooks
SS J Glasscock
3B- G Pinkney
LF C Carroll
CF S Brodie
Rp B Caruthers
M2 C Stricker
M4 G Gore

WASHINGTON
SP F Killen
SP B Abbey
SP P Knell
SP J Duryea
SP J Meekin
C D McGuire
1B H Larkin
2U T Dowd
S2 D Richardson
3B- Y Robinson
LR C Duffee
CF D Hoy
UT P Radford
C1- J Milligan
M1 B Barnie
M2 A Irwin

1893 NL

BALTIMORE
SP S McMahon
SP T Mullane
SP B Hawke
SP E McNabb
SP K Baker
C W Robinson
1B H Taylor
2B H Reitz
SS J McGraw
3B B Shindle
LF- J Long
CF J Kelley
RF G Treadway
M N Hanlon

BOSTON
SP K Nichols
SP J Stivetts
SP H Staley
SP H Gastright
C- C Bennett
1B T Tucker
2B B Lowe
SS H Long
3B B Nash
LF T McCarthy
CF H Duffy
RL C Carroll
CO- C Ganzel
M F Selee

BROOKLYN
SP B Kennedy
SP E Stein
SP G Haddock
SP D Daub
SP T Lovett
RP G Sharrott
C T Kinslow
1B- D Brouthers
2B- D Richardson
SS T Corcoran
23 T Daly
L1 D Foutz
CF M Griffin
RF T Burns
UT G Shoch

CHICAGO
SP B Hutchison
SP W McGill
SP H Mauck
C- M Kittridge
1B C Anson
UT B Lange
SS B Dahlen
3B J Parrott
LF W Wilmot
CF J Ryan
RF S Dungan
UT G Decker

CINCINNATI
SP F Dwyer
SP E Chamberlain
SP M Sullivan
SP T Parrott
SP T Mullane
RP S King
CU F Vaughn
1B- C Comiskey
2B B McPhee
SS G Smith
3B A Latham
LF J Canavan
CF B Holliday
RF- J McCarthy

CLEVELAND
SP C Young
SP J Clarkson
SP N Cuppy
SP C Hastings
C- C Zimmer
1B J Virtue
2B C Childs
SS E McKean
3B- C McGarr
LF J Burkett
CF J McAleer
RF B Ewing
CM J O'Connor
UI P Tebeau

LOUISVILLE
SP G Hemming
SP S Stratton
SP B Rhodes
SP J Menefee
C J Grim
1B W Brown
2B F Pfeffer
SO T O'Rourke
3B G Pinkney
LF- P Browning
CF T Brown
RU F Weaver
M B Barnie

NEW YORK
SP A Rusie
SP M Baldwin
SP L German
CM J Doyle
1B R Connor
2B J Ward
SS S Fuller
3B G Davis
LF E Burke
CF- G Stafford
RF M Tiernan
M M Ward

PHILADELPHIA
SP G Weyhing
SP K Carsey
SP T Keefe
SP J Taylor
C J Clements
1B J Boyle
2B B Hallman
SS B Allen
3B C Reilly
LF E Delahanty
CF B Hamilton
RF S Thompson
IC L Cross
M H Wright

PITTSBURGH
SP F Killen
SP R Ehret
SP A Terry
SP A Gumbert
C- D Miller
1B J Beckley
2B L Bierbauer
SS- J Glasscock
3B D Lyons
LF E Smith
CF G Van Haltren
RF P Donovan
M A Buckenberger

ST. LOUIS
SP T Breitenstein
SP K Gleason
SP P Hawley
SP D Clarkson
C H Peitz
1B P Werden
2B J Quinn
SS- J Glasscock
3B J Crooks
LF- C Frank
CF S Brodie
OI T Dowd
M B Watkins

WASHINGTON
SP D Esper
SP A Maul
SP J Meekin
SP J Duryea
C3 D Farrell
1B H Larkin
23 S Wise
SS J Sullivan
3B- J Mulvey
L1 J O'Rourke
CF D Hoy
RF P Radford

1894 NL

BALTIMORE
SP S McMahon
SP B Hawke
SP K Gleason
SP B Inks
SP T Mullane
RP D Esper
C W Robinson
1B D Brouthers
2B H Reitz
SS H Jennings
3B J McGraw
LF J Kelley
CF S Brodie
RF W Keeler
M N Hanlon

BOSTON
SP K Nichols
SP J Stivetts
SP H Staley
SP T Lovett
C- C Ganzel
1B T Tucker
2B B Lowe
SS H Long
3B B Nash
LF T McCarthy
CF H Duffy
RF J Bannon
M F Selee

BROOKLYN
SP B Kennedy
SP E Stein
SP D Daub
SP H Gastright
C- T Kinslow
1B- D Foutz
2B T Daly
SS T Corcoran
3B B Shindle
LF G Treadway
CF M Griffin

RF T Burns
C- C Daily
1B- C LaChance

CHICAGO
SP B Hutchison
SP C Griffith
SP W McGill
SP A Terry
SP S Stratton
RP B Abbey
C P Schriver
1B C Anson
2B J Parrott
S3 B Dahlen
3S C Irwin
LF W Wilmot
CF B Lange
RF J Ryan
1O G Decker

CINCINNATI
SP F Dwyer
SP T Parrott
SP E Chamberlain
SP C Fisher
C- M Murphy
1B- C Comiskey
2B B McPhee
SS G Smith
3B A Latham
LF B Holliday
CF D Hoy
RF J Canavan
C1- F Vaughn

CLEVELAND
SP C Young
SR N Cuppy
SP J Clarkson
SP M Sullivan
C C Zimmer
1B P Tebeau
2B C Childs
SS E McKean
3B C McGarr
LF J Burkett
CF- J McAleer
RF- H Blake
CM J O'Connor

LOUISVILLE
SP G Hemming
SP P Knell
SP J Menefee
SP J Wadsworth
CI J Grim
1B- L Lutenberg
2B F Pfeffer
SS D Richardson
3B- J Denny
LF- F Clarke
CF T Brown
RF- O Smith
M B Barnie

NEW YORK
SP A Rusie
SP J Meekin
SP L German
SP H Westervelt
C D Farrell
1B J Doyle
2B J Ward
SS S Fuller
3B G Davis
LF E Burke
CF G Van Haltren
RF M Tiernan
SR- Y Murphy
M M Ward

PHILADELPHIA
SP J Taylor
SP K Carsey
SP G Weyhing
SP G Harper
CP J Clements
1B J Boyle
2B B Hallman
SS- J Sullivan
3B L Cross
LI E Delahanty
CF B Hamilton
RF S Thompson
LR T Turner
M A Irwin

PITTSBURGH
SP R Ehret
SP A Gumbert
SP F Killen
SP T Colcolough
SP J Menefee
C- C Mack
1B J Beckley
2B L Bierbauer
SS J Glasscock
3B- D Lyons
LF E Smith
CF J Stenzel
RF P Donovan
M1 A Buckenberger

ST. LOUIS
SP T Breitenstein
SR P Hawley
SP D Clarkson
IC D Miller
1B R Connor
2B J Quinn
SS B Ely
IC H Peitz
LF C Frank
CF F Shugart
RL T Dowd
M G Miller

WASHINGTON
SR W Mercer
SP A Maul
SP M Sullivan
SP O Stocksdale
SP D Esper
RP C Petty
C D McGuire
1B E Cartwright
2B P Ward
SS- F Scheibeck
3B B Joyce
OI K Selbach
ML C Abbey
R3 B Hassamaer
UT P Radford
M G Schmelz

1895 NL

BALTIMORE
SP B Hoffer
SP G Hemming
SP D Esper
SP D Clarkson
SP S McMahon
C- W Robinson
1B S Carey
2B K Gleason
SS H Jennings
3B J McGraw
LF J Kelley
CF S Brodie
RF W Keeler
C- B Clarke
23- H Reitz
M N Hanlon

BOSTON
SP K Nichols
SP J Stivetts
SP C Dolan
SP J Sullivan
C C Ganzel
1B T Tucker
2B B Lowe
SS H Long
3B B Nash
LF T McCarthy
CF H Duffy
RF J Bannon
M F Selee

BROOKLYN
SP B Kennedy
SP E Stein
SP A Gumbert
SP D Daub
SP C Lucid
C J Grim
1B C LaChance
2B T Daly
SS T Corcoran
3B B Shindle
LF J Anderson
CF M Griffin
RF G Treadway
M D Foutz

CHICAGO
SP C Griffith
SP A Terry
SP B Hutchison
C- T Donahue
1B C Anson
2B A Stewart
SS B Dahlen
3B B Everitt
LF W Wilmot
CF B Lange
RF J Ryan
UT- G Decker

CINCINNATI
SP F Dwyer
SP B Rhines
SR T Parrott
SP F Foreman
SP B Phillips
C F Vaughn
1B B Ewing
2B B McPhee
SS G Smith
3B A Latham
LM D Hoy
MO- G Hogriever
RF D Miller

CLEVELAND
SP C Young
SP N Cuppy
SP B Wallace
SP P Knell
C C Zimmer
RF- P Tebeau
2B C Childs
SS E McKean
3B C McGarr
LF J Burkett
CF J McAleer
RF H Blake
C1 J O'Connor
R1 G Tebeau

LOUISVILLE
SP B Cunningham
SP G Weyhing
SP M McDermott
SP B Inks
C- J Warner
1C- H Spies
2B J O'Brien
SS F Shugart
3B J Collins
LF F Clarke
MR- J Wright
MR- T Gettinger
M J McCloskey

NEW YORK
SP A Rusie
SP D Clarke
SP J Meekin
SP L German
C3 D Farrell
1U J Doyle
2B G Stafford
SS S Fuller
3U G Davis
LF- E Burke
CF G Van Haltren
RF M Tiernan
C- P Wilson
M3 H Watkins

PHILADELPHIA
SP K Carsey
SP J Taylor
SP W McGill
SP A Orth
C J Clements
1B J Boyle
2B B Hallman
SS J Sullivan
3B L Cross
LF E Delahanty
CF B Hamilton
RF S Thompson
M A Irwin

PITTSBURGH
SP P Hawley
SP B Hart
SP B Foreman
SP F Killen
SP J Gardner
C- B Merritt
1B J Beckley
2B L Bierbauer
SS M Cross
3B B Clingman
LF E Smith
CF J Stenzel
RF P Donovan
UT- F Genins
M C Mack

ST. LOUIS
SP T Breitenstein
SP R Ehret
SP H Staley
SR B Kissinger
SP D McDougal
C H Peitz
1B R Connor
2B J Quinn
SS B Ely
IC D Miller
LF D Cooley
CF T Brown
RM T Dowd
M1 A Buckenberger
M2 C Von Der Ahe
M4 L Phelan

WASHINGTON
SP W Mercer
SP V Anderson
SP O Stocksdale
SP A Maul
SR J Malarkey
RP J Boyd
C D McGuire
1B E Cartwright
2B J Crooks
SS- F Scheibeck
3B B Joyce
LF K Selbach
MO C Abbey
RF B Hassamaer
M G Schmelz

1896 NL

BALTIMORE
SP B Hoffer
SP A Pond
SP G Hemming
SP S McMahon
SP D Esper
C- W Robinson
1B J Doyle
2B H Reitz
SS H Jennings
3B J Donnelly
LF J Kelley
CF S Brodie
RF W Keeler
C B Clarke
M N Hanlon

BOSTON
SP K Nichols
SP J Stivetts
SP J Sullivan
SP F Klobedanz
C- M Bergen
1B T Tucker
2B- B Lowe
SS H Long
3B J Collins
LF H Duffy
CF B Hamilton
RF J Bannon
RC F Tenney
M F Selee

BROOKLYN
SP B Kennedy
SP H Payne
SP D Daub
SP B Abbey
SP E Stein
RP G Harper
C J Grim
1B C LaChance
2B- T Daly
SS T Corcoran
3B B Shindle
LF T McCarthy
CF M Griffin
RF F Jones
OI J Anderson
2B- G Shoch
M D Foutz

CHICAGO
SP C Griffith
SP D Friend
SP A Terry
SP B Briggs
C- M Kittridge
1B C Anson
2B F Pfeffer
SS B Dahlen
3O B Everitt
L1 G Decker
CF B Lange
RF J Ryan

CINCINNATI
SP F Dwyer
SP R Ehret
SP F Foreman
SR C Fisher
SP B Rhines
C- H Peitz
1B- B Ewing
2B B McPhee
SS G Smith
3B C Irwin
LF E Burke
CF D Hoy
RF D Miller
1C F Vaughn

CLEVELAND
SP C Young
SP N Cuppy
SP Z Wilson
SP B Wallace
C C Zimmer
1B P Tebeau
2B C Childs
SS E McKean
3B C McGarr
LF J Burkett
CF J McAleer
RF H Blake
C1- J O'Connor

LOUISVILLE
SP C Fraser
SP B Hill
SP B Cunningham
SP A Herman
IC D Miller
1B- J Rogers
2B- J O'Brien
SS- J Dolan
3B B Clingman
LF F Clarke
CM C Dexter
RF T McCreery
M1 J McCloskey
M2 B McGunnigle

NEW YORK
SP D Clarke
SP J Meekin
SP M Sullivan
SP E Doheny
C- P Wilson
1B- W Clark
2B K Gleason
SL F Connaughton
3S G Davis
LF- G Stafford
CF G Van Haltren
RF M Tiernan
M1 A Irwin
M2 B Joyce

PHILADELPHIA
SP J Taylor
SP A Orth
SP K Carsey
SP H Keener
SP W McGill
C- M Grady
1B- D Brouthers
2B B Hallman
SS B Hulen
3B- B Nash
LF E Delahanty
ML- D Cooley
RF S Thompson
3S L Cross

PITTSBURGH
SP F Killen
SP P Hawley
SR J Hughey
SP C Hastings
C J Sugden
1B- J Beckley
2B- D Padden
SS B Ely
3B D Lyons
LF E Smith
CF J Stenzel
RF P Donovan
C- B Merritt
M C Mack

ST. LOUIS
SP T Breitenstein
SP B Hart
SP R Donahue
SP B Kissinger
C E McFarland
1B R Connor
2M T Dowd
SS M Cross
3B B Myers
LF- J Sullivan
MO T Parrott
RL K Douglass
M1 H Diddlebock
M2 A Latham
M3 C Von Der Ahe

WASHINGTON
SP W Mercer
SP D McJames
SP L German
SP S King
C D McGuire
1B E Cartwright
2B- J O'Brien
SS De Montreville
32 B Joyce
LF K Selbach
CF T Brown
RU B Lush
RF- C Abbey
M G Schmelz

1897 NL

BALTIMORE
SP J Corbett
SP B Hoffer
SP A Pond
SP J Nops
C- B Clarke
1B J Doyle
2B H Reitz
SS H Jennings
3B J McGraw
LF J Kelley
CF J Stenzel
RF W Keeler
UT- J Quinn
M N Hanlon

BOSTON
SP K Nichols
SP F Klobedanz
SP T Lewis
SP J Stivetts
SP J Sullivan
C M Bergen
1B F Tenney
2B B Lowe
SS H Long
3B J Collins
LF H Duffy
CF B Hamilton
RF C Stahl
M F Selee

BROOKLYN
SP B Kennedy
SP H Payne
SP J Dunn
SP C Fisher
SP D Daub
C- J Grim
1B C LaChance
2B G Shoch
SS G Smith
3B B Shindle
LF J Anderson
CF M Griffin
RF F Jones
M B Barnie

CHICAGO
SP C Griffith
SP D Friend
SP B Briggs
SP W Thornton
SP R Denzer
C- M Kittridge
1B C Anson
2B- J Connor
SS- B Dahlen
3B B Everitt
L1 G Decker
CF B Lange
RF J Ryan
2p N Callahan
3S B McCormick

CINCINNATI
SP T Breitenstein
SP B Rhines
SP F Dwyer
SR R Ehret
SP B Dammann
C- H Peitz
1B J Beckley
2B B McPhee
SU C Ritchey
3B C Irwin
LF E Burke
CF D Hoy
RF D Miller
S2 T Corcoran
M B Ewing

CLEVELAND
SP C Young
SP Z Wilson
SP J Powell
SP N Cuppy
C C Zimmer
1B P Tebeau
2B C Childs
SS E McKean
3B B Wallace
LF J Burkett
OI J O'Connor
RF- C Sockalexis

LOUISVILLE
SP C Fraser
SP B Cunningham
SP B Hill
SP B Magee
C B Wilson
1B P Werden
2B- J Rogers
SS G Stafford
3B B Clingman
LF F Clarke
CF- O Pickering
RF T McCreery
OC- C Dexter

NEW YORK
SP A Rusie
SP J Meekin
SP C Seymour
SP M Sullivan
SP E Doheny
C J Warner
1B W Clark
2B K Gleason
SS G Davis
3B B Joyce
LF- D Holmes
CF G Van Haltren
RL M Tiernan

PHILADELPHIA
SP J Taylor
SP A Orth
SP J Fifield
SP G Wheeler
C1- J Boyle
1B N Lajoie
32 L Cross
SS- S Gillen
3B B Nash
LF E Delahanty
CF D Cooley
RM T Dowd
UT P Geier
M G Stallings

PITTSBURGH
SP F Killen
SP P Hawley
SP J Hughey
SP J Tannehill
SP C Hastings
RP J Gardner
C J Sugden
13 H Davis
2B D Padden
SS B Ely
3B- J Hoffmeister
LF E Smith
CF S Brodie
RF P Donovan

ST. LOUIS
SP R Donahue
SP B Hart
SP K Carsey
SP W Sudhoff
OC K Douglass
1B M Grady
2B B Hallman
SS M Cross
3B F Hartman
LF D Lally
CF D Harley
RF T Turner
2O J Houseman
M1 T Dowd
M2 H Nicol
M4 C Von Der Ahe

WASHINGTON
SP W Mercer
SP D McJames
SP C Swaim
SP S King
RS L German
C D McGuire
1B T Tucker
2B J O'Brien
SU De Montreville
3B C Reilly
LF K Selbach
CF T Brown
RF C Abbey
UT Z Wrigley
C- D Farrell
M1 G Schmelz

1898 NL

BALTIMORE
SP D McJames
SP J Hughes
SP A Maul
SP J Nops
SP F Kitson
C- W Robinson
1B D McGann
2B De Montreville
SS H Jennings
3B J McGraw
LF D Holmes
ML J Kelley
RF W Keeler
C- B Clarke
M N Hanlon

BOSTON
SP K Nichols
SP T Lewis
SP V Willis
SP F Klobedanz
C M Bergen
1B F Tenney
2B B Lowe
SS H Long
3B J Collins
LF H Duffy
CF B Hamilton
RF C Stahl
M F Selee

BROOKLYN
SP B Kennedy
SP J Dunn
SP J Yeager
SP R Miller
SP K McKenna
C- J Ryan
1S C LaChance
2B B Hallman
SS G Magoon
3B B Shindle
LF J Sheckard
CF M Griffin
RF F Jones
M1 B Barnie
M3 C Ebbets

CHICAGO
SP C Griffith
SP N Callahan
SP W Thornton
SP W Woods
SP M Kilroy
C T Donahue
1B B Everitt
2B J Connor
SS B Dahlen
3B B McCormick
LF J Ryan
CF B Lange
RU- S Mertes
M T Burns

CINCINNATI
SP P Hawley
SP T Breitenstein
SP B Hill
SP F Dwyer
SR B Dammann
C H Peitz
1B J Beckley
2B B McPhee
SS T Corcoran
3B C Irwin
LF E Smith
CF A McBride
RF D Miller
UT- H Steinfeldt
1C- F Vaughn
M B Ewing

CLEVELAND
SP C Young
SP J Powell
SP Z Wilson
SP N Cuppy
C- L Criger
12 P Tebeau
2B C Childs
SS E McKean
3B B Wallace
LF J Burkett
CF J McAleer
RF H Blake
1C J O'Connor

LOUISVILLE
SP B Cunningham
SP B Magee
SP P Dowling
SP C Fraser
C- M Kittridge
UI H Wagner
2B- H Smith
S2 C Ritchey
3S B Clingman
LF F Clarke
CF D Hoy
RF C Dexter

NEW YORK
SP C Seymour
SP J Meekin
SP A Rusie
SP E Doheny
SP C Gettig
C J Warner
1B B Joyce
2B K Gleason
SS G Davis
3B F Hartman
LF M Tiernan
CF G Van Haltren
UT- J Doyle
CO- M Grady
M2 C Anson
M3 B Joyce

PHILADELPHIA
SP W Piatt
SP R Donahue
SP A Orth
SP J Fifield
SP G Wheeler
C E McFarland
1B K Douglass
2B N Lajoie
SS M Cross
3B B Lauder

LF E Delahanty
CF D Cooley
RF E Flick
M1 G Stallings
M2 B Shettsline

PITTSBURGH
SP J Tannehill
SP B Rhines
SP J Gardner
SP F Killen
SP C Hastings
RP B Hart
C P Schriver
1B- W Clark
2B D Padden
SS B Ely
3B B Gray
LF J McCarthy
MI T O'Brien
RF P Donovan
M B Watkins

ST. LOUIS
SP J Taylor
SP W Sudhoff
SP J Hughey
SP K Carsey
C J Clements
1B- G Decker
2B- J Crooks
SS- G Smith
3B L Cross
LF D Harley
CF J Stenzel
RM T Dowd
2S J Quinn
CU- J Sugden
M T Hurst

WASHINGTON
SP G Weyhing
SP W Mercer
SP B Dinneen
SP F Killen
SP C Swaim
C1 D McGuire
1B- J Doyle
2B H Reitz
SS Z Wrigley
3I- J Smith
LF K Selbach
MU J Anderson
RF J Gettman
C1 D Farrell
M1 T Brown
M4 A Irwin

1899 NL

BALTIMORE
SP J McGinnity
SP F Kitson
SP J Nops
SP H Howell
C W Robinson
1B C LaChance
2B- De Montreville
S2 B Keister
3B J McGraw
LF D Holmes
CF S Brodie
RF J Sheckard

BOSTON
SP V Willis
SP K Nichols
SP T Lewis
SP J Meekin
SP F Killen
C- M Bergen
1B F Tenney
2B B Lowe
SS H Long
3B J Collins
LF H Duffy
CF- B Hamilton
RF C Stahl
M F Selee

BROOKLYN
SP J Dunn
SP J Hughes
SP B Kennedy
SP D McJames
C- D Farrell
1B- D McGann
2B T Daly
SS B Dahlen
3B D Casey
LF J Kelley
CF F Jones
RF W Keeler
M1 J Anderson
M N Hanlon

CHICAGO
SP J Taylor
SP C Griffith
SP N Callahan
SP N Garvin
C T Donahue
1B B Everitt
2B B McCormick
SS- De Montreville
3B H Wolverton
LF J Ryan
UT S Mertes
RF D Green
CF B Lange
M T Burns

CINCINNATI
SP N Hahn
SP P Hawley
SP B Phillips
SP T Breitenstein
SP J Taylor
C- H Peitz
1B J Beckley
2B B McPhee
SS T Corcoran
3B- C Irwin
UO- E Smith
LM K Selbach
RF- D Miller
32 H Steinfeldt
M B Ewing

CLEVELAND
SP J Hughey
SP C Knepper
SP F Bates
SP C Schmit
SP H Colliflower
C- J Sugden
1B T Tucker
2B J Quinn
SS H Lochhead
3B S Sullivan
LF D Harley
CF T Dowd
RU S McAllister
M1 L Cross

LOUISVILLE
SP B Cunningham
SP D Phillippe
SP P Dowling
SP W Woods
C- C Zimmer
1B- M Kelley
2B C Ritchey
SS B Clingman
3B T Leach
LF F Clarke
CF D Hoy
RF- C Dexter
3R H Wagner

NEW YORK
SP B Carrick
SP E Doheny
SP C Seymour
SP J Meekin
SP C Gettig
C- J Warner
1B J Doyle
2B K Gleason
SS G Davis
3B- F Hartman
LF T O'Brien
CF G Van Haltren
RF- P Foster
IC P Wilson
C3- M Grady
M1 J Day
M2 F Hoey

PHILADELPHIA
SP W Piatt
SP R Donahue
SP C Fraser
SP A Orth
SP B Bernhard
RP J Fifield
C E McFarland
1B D Cooley
2B- N Lajoie
SS M Cross
3B B Lauder
LF E Delahanty
CF R Thomas
RF E Flick
UT P Chiles
C- K Douglass
M B Shettsline

PITTSBURGH
SR S Leever
SP J Tannehill
SR T Sparks
SP B Hoffer
SP J Chesbro
C1 F Bowerman
1B- W Clark
2B- J O'Brien
SS B Ely
3B J Williams
LF J McCarthy
CF G Beaumont
RF P Donovan
UT T McCreery
C- P Schriver
M1 B Watkins

ST. LOUIS
SP J Powell
SP C Young
SP W Sudhoff
SP N Cuppy
C- L Criger
1B- P Tebeau
2B C Childs
S3 B Wallace
3B L Cross
LF J Burkett
MU H Blake
RF E Heidrick
C1- J O'Connor

WASHINGTON
SP G Weyhing
SP B Dinneen
SP D McFarlan
C- D McGuire
1B- D McGann
2B- F Bonner
S2 D Padden
3B- C Atherton
LF J O'Brien
CF J Slagle
RF B Freeman
3p W Mercer
UT- S Barry
M A Irwin

1900 NL

BOSTON
SP B Dinneen
SP V Willis
SP K Nichols
SP T Lewis
SP T Pittinger
RP N Cuppy
C- B Clarke
1B F Tenney
2B B Lowe
SS H Long
3B J Collins
RL C Stahl
CF B Hamilton
RU B Freeman
UT- S Barry
C- B Sullivan
M F Selee

BROOKLYN
SP J McGinnity
SP B Kennedy
SR F Kitson
SR H Howell
C- D Farrell
1B H Jennings
2B T Daly
SS B Dahlen
3B L Cross
LF J Sheckard
CF F Jones
RF W Keeler
L1 J Kelley
C- D McGuire
M N Hanlon

CHICAGO
SP N Callahan
SP C Griffith
SP N Garvin
SP J Taylor
SP J Menefee
C- T Donahue
1B- J Ganzel
2B C Childs
SS B McCormick
3B B Bradley
LF J McCarthy
MR D Green
RL J Ryan
M1 S Mertes
M T Loftus

CINCINNATI
SP E Scott
SP N Hahn
SP D Newton
SP B Phillips
SP T Breitenstein
C H Peitz
1B J Beckley
2B- J Quinn
SS T Corcoran
32 H Steinfeldt
LU S Crawford
CF J Barrett
RF A McBride
3U C Irwin
M B Allen

NEW YORK
SP B Carrick
SP P Hawley
SP W Mercer
SP E Doheny
C- F Bowerman
1B J Doyle
2B K Gleason
SS G Davis
3B C Hickman
LF K Selbach
CF G Van Haltren
RF E Smith
IC- M Grady
M1 B Ewing

PHILADELPHIA
SP A Orth
SP R Donahue
SP C Fraser
SP B Bernhard
SP W Piatt
C E McFarland
1B E Delahanty
2B N Lajoie
SS M Cross
3B H Wolverton
LF J Slagle
CF R Thomas
RF E Flick
UI- J Dolan
M B Shettsline

PITTSBURGH
SP D Phillippe
SP J Tannehill
SP S Leever
SP J Chesbro
SP R Waddell
C- C Zimmer
1B- D Cooley
2B C Ritchey
SS B Ely
3B J Williams
LF F Clarke
CF G Beaumont
RF H Wagner
1U T O'Brien

ST. LOUIS
SP C Young
SP C Jones
SP J Powell
SP W Sudhoff
SP J Hughey
C- L Criger
1B D McGann
2B B Keister
SS B Wallace
3B J McGraw
LF J Burkett
CF E Heidrick
RF P Donovan
OI- M Donlin
M1 P Tebeau
M2 L Heilbroner

1901 AL

BALTIMORE
SP J McGinnity
SP H Howell
SP F Foreman
SP J Nops
C R Bresnahan
1B- B Hart
2B J Williams
SS B Keister
3B- J McGraw
ML J Jackson
CF S Brodie
RF C Seymour
L1 M Donlin
3U J Dunn

BOSTON
SP C Young
SP T Lewis
SP G Winter
SP F Mitchell
SP N Cuppy
C O Schreckengost
1B B Freeman
2B H Ferris
SS F Parent
3B J Collins
LF T Dowd
CF C Stahl
RF C Hemphill
C- L Criger

CHICAGO
SP R Patterson
SP C Griffith
SP N Callahan
SP J Katoll
SP Z Harvey
C B Sullivan
1B F Isbell
2B S Mertes
SS F Shugart
3B F Hartman
LF H McFarland
CF D Hoy
RF F Jones

CLEVELAND
SP P Dowling
SP E Moore
SP B Hart
SP E Scott
SP B Hoffer
RP J Bracken
RP H McNeal
C B Wood
1B C LaChance
2B E Beck
SS F Scheibeck
3B B Bradley
LF J McCarthy
CF O Pickering
RL J O'Brien
M J McAleer

DETROIT
SP R Miller
SP E Siever
SP J Cronin
SP J Yeager
C- F Buelow
1B- P Dillon
2B K Gleason
SS K Elberfeld
3B D Casey
LF D Nance
CF J Barrett
RF D Holmes
IC S McAllister
M G Stallings

MILWAUKEE
SP B Reidy
SR N Garvin
SP B Husting
SP T Sparks
SP P Hawley
C B Maloney
1B J Anderson
2B B Gilbert
SS W Conroy
3B- J Burke
RL B Hallman
CF- H Duffy
RF- I Waldron
3O B Friel

PHILADELPHIA
SP C Fraser
SP E Plank
SP B Bernhard
SP S Wiltse
SP W Piatt
C D Powers
1B H Davis
2B N Lajoie
S3 J Dolan
3B L Cross
LF- M McIntyre
MU D Fultz
RU S Seybold
M C Mack

WASHINGTON
SP B Carrick
SP W Lee
SP C Patten
SP W Mercer
SP D Gear
C B Clarke
1C M Grady
2M J Farrell
SS B Clingman
3B B Coughlin
LF P Foster
CF- I Waldron
R1 S Dungan
M J Manning

1901 NL

BOSTON
SP K Nichols
SP B Dinneen
SP V Willis
SP T Pittinger
C M Kittridge
1B F Tenney
2B De Montreville
SS H Long
3B B Lowe
OI- D Cooley
CF B Hamilton
RF- J Slagle
M F Selee

BROOKLYN
SP B Donovan
SP F Kitson
SP J Hughes
SP D Newton
SP D McJames
RP B Kennedy
C D McGuire
1B J Kelley
2B T Daly
SS B Dahlen
3B- C Irwin
LF J Sheckard
CF T McCreery
RF W Keeler
CU- D Farrell
M N Hanlon

CHICAGO
SP T Hughes
SP J Taylor
SP R Waddell
SP M Eason
SP J Menefee
C- J Kling
1B- J Doyle
2B- C Childs
SS B McCormick
3I F Raymer
LF T Hartsel
CF D Green
RU- F Chance
UT C Dexter
M T Loftus

CINCINNATI
SP N Hahn
SP B Phillips
SP D Newton
SP A Stimmel
C B Bergen
1B J Beckley
32 H Steinfeldt
SS G Magoon
3B- C Irwin
LF D Harley
CF J Dobbs
RF S Crawford
C2- H Peitz
M B McPhee

NEW YORK
SP D Taylor
SP C Mathewson
SP B Phyle
C J Warner
1B J Ganzel
2B- R Nelson
SS G Davis
32 S Strang
LF K Selbach
CF G Van Haltren
RF- A McBride
UT C Hickman

PHILADELPHIA
SP R Donahue
SP B Duggleby
SP A Orth
SP D White
SP H Townsend
C- E McFarland
1B- H Jennings
23 B Hallman
SS M Cross
3B H Wolverton
L1 E Delahanty
CF R Thomas
RF E Flick
M B Shettsline

PITTSBURGH
SP D Phillippe
SP J Chesbro
SP J Tannehill
SP S Leever
C- C Zimmer
1B K Bransfield
2B C Ritchey
SS- B Ely
3B T Leach
LF F Clarke
CF G Beaumont
RF L Davis
UT H Wagner

ST. LOUIS
SP J Powell
SP J Harper
SR W Sudhoff
SP E Murphy
C- J Ryan
1B D McGann
2B D Padden
SS B Wallace
3B O Krueger
LF J Burkett
CF E Heidrick
RF P Donovan
CM A Nichols

1902 AL

BALTIMORE
SP J McGinnity
SP H Howell
SP S Wiltse
SP C Shields
SP J Katoll
RP I Butler
RP T Hughes
C W Robinson
1B- D McGann
2B J Williams
SS B Gilbert
IC- R Bresnahan
LF K Selbach
CF- H McFarland
RF- C Seymour
M1 J McGraw

BOSTON
SP C Young
SP B Dinneen
SP G Winter
SP T Sparks
C L Criger
1B C LaChance
2B H Ferris
SS F Parent
3B J Collins
LF P Dougherty
CF C Stahl
RF B Freeman
UT- H Gleason

CHICAGO
SP N Callahan
SP R Patterson
SP W Piatt
SP C Griffith
SP N Garvin
C- B Sullivan
1B F Isbell
2B T Daly
SS G Davis
3B S Strang
LF S Mertes
CF F Jones
RF D Green
C- E McFarland

CLEVELAND
SP E Moore
SP A Joss
SP B Bernhard
SP G Wright
C H Bemis
1B C Hickman
2B N Lajoie
SS J Gochnauer
3B B Bradley
LF J McCarthy
MO H Bay
RF E Flick
CF- O Pickering
CU- B Wood
M B Armour

DETROIT
SP W Mercer
SP G Mullin
SP E Siever
SP R Miller
SP J Yeager
C- D McGuire
1B- P Dillon
2B K Gleason
SS K Elberfeld
3B D Casey
LF D Harley
CF J Barrett
RF D Holmes
M F Dwyer

PHILADELPHIA
SP E Plank
SP R Waddell
SP B Husting
SP S Wiltse
SP F Mitchell
RP H Wilson
C- O Schreckengost
1B H Davis
2B- D Murphy
SS M Cross
3B L Cross
LF T Hartsel
CF D Fultz
RF S Seybold
C- D Powers
M C Mack

ST. LOUIS
SP J Powell
SP R Donahue
SP J Harper
SP W Sudhoff
SP B Reidy
C- J Sugden
1B J Anderson
2B D Padden
SS B Wallace
3B B McCormick
LF J Burkett
CF E Heidrick
RM C Hemphill
UT- B Friel
M J McAleer

WASHINGTON
SP A Orth
SP C Patten
SP B Carrick
SP H Townsend
C B Clarke
1B S Carey
2B- J Doyle
SS B Ely
3S B Coughlin
LF E Delahanty
CF J Ryan
UO W Lee
UT B Keister
M T Loftus

1902 NL

BOSTON
SP V Willis
SP T Pittinger
SP M Eason
SP J Malarkey
C- M Kittridge
1B F Tenney
2B De Montreville
SS H Long
3B E Gremminger
LU D Cooley
CF B Lush
RF P Carney
C- P Moran
M A Buckenberger

BROOKLYN
SP B Donovan
SP F Kitson
SP D Newton
SP J Hughes
SP R Evans
C- H Hearne
1B T McCreery
2B T Flood
SS B Dahlen
3B C Irwin
LF J Sheckard
CF C Dolan
RF W Keeler
C1- D Farrell
M N Hanlon

CHICAGO
SP J Taylor
SP P Williams
SP J Menefee
SP C Lundgren
SP B Rhoads
RP J St.Vrain
C J Kling
1C- F Chance
2B B Lowe
SS J Tinker
3B- G Schaefer
LF J Slagle
CF- J Dobbs
MR- D Jones
31- C Dexter
M F Selee

CINCINNATI
SP N Hahn
SP B Phillips
SP H Thielman
SP E Poole
SP B Ewing
C B Bergen
1B J Beckley
IC H Peitz
SS T Corcoran
3B H Steinfeldt
LF- J Dobbs
CF- D Hoy
RF S Crawford
M1 B McPhee
M2 F Bancroft
M3 J Kelley

NEW YORK
SP C Mathewson
SP D Taylor
SP R Evans
SP J McGinnity
SP T Sparks
RP J Cronin
C F Bowerman

1B- D McGann
2B H Smith
SS- J Bean
3B B Lauder
LO- J Jones
CF S Brodie
UT J Dunn
LF- G Browne
M1 H Fogel
M3 J McGraw

PHILADELPHIA
SP D White
SP B Duggleby
SP H Iburg
SP C Fraser
C R Dooin
1B- H Jennings
2B P Childs
SS R Hulswitt
3B- B Hallman
LF- G Browne
CF R Thomas
RF S Barry
1C K Douglass
M B Shettsline

PITTSBURGH
SP J Chesbro
SP D Phillippe
SP J Tannehill
SP S Leever
SP E Doheny
C- H Smith
1B K Bransfield
2B C Ritchey
SS W Conroy
3B T Leach
LF F Clarke
CF G Beaumont
UT H Wagner

ST. LOUIS
SP M O'Neill
SP S Yerkes
SP E Murphy
SP B Wicker
SP C Currie
C- J Ryan
1U R Brashear
2B J Farrell
SS O Krueger
3B F Hartman
LF G Barclay
CF H Smoot
RF P Donovan
1B- A Nichols

1903 AL

BOSTON
SP C Young
SP B Dinneen
SP T Hughes
SP N Gibson
SP G Winter
C L Criger
1B C LaChance
2B H Ferris
SS F Parent
3B J Collins
LF P Dougherty
CF- C Stahl
RF B Freeman
MU J O'Brien

CHICAGO
SP D White
SP P Flaherty
SP R Patterson
SP F Owen
C- J Slattery
1B F Isbell
2B G Magoon
SS L Tannehill
3B N Callahan
LF D Holmes
CF F Jones
RF D Green
M J Callahan

CLEVELAND
SP A Joss
SP E Moore
SP B Bernhard
SP R Donahue
SP G Wright
C H Bemis
1B C Hickman
2B N Lajoie
SS J Gochnauer
3B B Bradley
LF J McCarthy
CF H Bay
RF E Flick
C- F Abbott
M B Armour

DETROIT
SP G Mullin
SP B Donovan
SP F Kitson
SP R Kisinger
C- D McGuire
1B C Carr
2B H Smith
SU- S McAllister
3B J Yeager
LU B Lush
CF J Barrett
RL S Crawford
S2- H Long
M E Barrow

NEW YORK
SP J Chesbro
SP J Tannehill
SP C Griffith
SR H Howell
SP B Wolfe
C M Beville
1B J Ganzel
2B J Williams
SS K Elberfeld
3B W Conroy
LF L Davis
ML H McFarland
RF W Keeler
CF- D Fultz

PHILADELPHIA
SP E Plank
SP R Waddell
SP C Bender
SP W Henley
C O Schreckengost
1B H Davis
2B D Murphy
SS M Cross
3B L Cross
LF T Hartsel
CF O Pickering
RF S Seybold
LR- D Hoffman
C- D Powers
M C Mack

ST. LOUIS
SP J Powell
SP W Sudhoff
SP E Siever
SP R Donahue
C- M Kahoe
1B J Anderson
2U B Friel
SS B Wallace
3B H Hill
LF J Burkett
CF E Heidrick
RF C Hemphill
C- J Sugden
M J McAleer

WASHINGTON
SP C Patten
SP A Orth
SP H Wilson
SP H Townsend
SP D Dunkle
C- M Kittridge
1C B Clarke
2B- B McCormick
SS C Moran
3B B Coughlin
LF K Selbach
CF J Ryan
Rp- W Lee
UT R Robinson
M T Loftus

1903 NL

BOSTON
SP T Pittinger
SP V Willis
SP J Malarkey
SP W Piatt
C P Moran
1B F Tenney
2B E Abbaticchio
SS H Aubrey
3B E Gremminger
LF D Cooley
MU C Dexter
RF P Carney
OI J Stanley
M A Buckenberger

BROOKLYN
SP O Jones
SP H Schmidt
SP N Garvin
SP R Evans
SP B Reidy
C- L Ritter
1B J Doyle
2B T Flood
SS B Dahlen
3B S Strang
LF J Sheckard
CF J Dobbs
RF- W McCredie
2U- D Jordan
M N Hanlon

CHICAGO
SP J Taylor
SP J Weimer
SP B Wicker
SP C Lundgren
SP J Menefee
C J Kling
1B F Chance
2B J Evers
SS J Tinker
3B D Casey
LF J Slagle
MR D Jones
RF D Harley
M F Selee

CINCINNATI
SP N Hahn
SP B Ewing
SP J Sutthoff
SP E Poole
SP J Harper
RP B Phillips
CU H Peitz
1B J Beckley
2B- T Daly
SS T Corcoran
3B H Steinfeldt
LR M Donlin
CF C Seymour
RF C Dolan
LI J Kelley

NEW YORK
SP J McGinnity
SP C Mathewson
SP D Taylor
SP J Cronin
C J Warner
1B D McGann
2B B Gilbert
SS C Babb
3B B Lauder
LF S Mertes
MU R Bresnahan
RF G Browne
IO- J Dunn
CF- G Van Haltren
M J McGraw

PHILADELPHIA
SP B Duggleby
SP C Fraser
SP T Sparks
SP F Mitchell
SP J McFetridge
C- F Roth
1B K Douglass
2B K Gleason
SS R Hulswitt
3B H Wolverton
LF S Barry
CF R Thomas
RF B Keister
RL- J Titus
M C Zimmer

PITTSBURGH
SP D Phillippe
SP S Leever
SP E Doheny
SP B Kennedy
SP K Wilhelm
C- E Phelps
1B K Bransfield
2B C Ritchey
SS H Wagner
3B T Leach
LF F Clarke
CF G Beaumont
RF J Sebring
IO- O Krueger

ST. LOUIS
SP C McFarland
SP M Brown
SP C Currie
SP M O'Neill
SP B Rhoads
RP E Murphy
RP J Dunleavy
C- J O'Neill
1B J Hackett
2B J Farrell
S3 D Brain
3B J Burke
LF G Barclay
CF H Smoot
RF P Donovan

1904 AL

BOSTON
SP C Young
SP B Dinneen
SP J Tannehill
SP N Gibson
SP G Winter
C L Criger
1B C LaChance
2B H Ferris
SS F Parent
3B J Collins
LF K Selbach
CF C Stahl
RF B Freeman

CHICAGO
SP F Owen
SP N Altrock
SP D White
SP F Smith
SP R Patterson
RS E Walsh
C B Sullivan
1B J Donahue
2B G Dundon
SS G Davis
3B L Tannehill
LF N Callahan
CF F Jones
RF D Green
12 F Isbell
M1 J Callahan

CLEVELAND
SP B Bernhard
SP R Donahue
SP E Moore
SP A Joss
SP B Rhoads
RP O Hess
C H Bemis
21- C Hickman
2S N Lajoie
SS T Turner
3B B Bradley
LF B Lush
CF H Bay
RF E Flick
M B Armour

DETROIT
SP G Mullin
SP E Killian
SP B Donovan
SP F Kitson
SP J Stovall
C- L Drill
1B- C Carr
2B B Lowe
SS C O'Leary
3B- E Gremminger
LF M McIntyre
CF J Barrett
RF S Crawford
UT R Robinson
M1 E Barrow

NEW YORK
SP J Chesbro
SP J Powell
SP A Orth
SP T Hughes
SP C Griffith
C D McGuire
1B J Ganzel
2B J Williams
SS K Elberfeld
3B W Conroy
LF P Dougherty
OI J Anderson
RF W Keeler
CF D Fultz

PHILADELPHIA
SP R Waddell
SP E Plank
SP W Henley
SP C Bender
C O Schreckengost
1B H Davis
2B D Murphy
SS M Cross
3B L Cross
LF T Hartsel
CF O Pickering
RF S Seybold
M C Mack

ST. LOUIS
SP B Pelty
SP H Howell
SP F Glade
SP W Sudhoff
SP E Siever
C J Sugden
1B T Jones
2B D Padden
SS B Wallace
3B- C Moran
LF J Burkett
CF E Heidrick
RO C Hemphill
M J McAleer

WASHINGTON
SP C Patten
SP H Townsend
SP B Jacobson
SP B Wolfe
SP T Hughes
C- M Kittridge
1B J Stahl
2B B McCormick
SU J Cassidy
3B- H Hill
LF- F Huelsman
CF B O'Neill
RF P Donovan
C1- B Clarke

1904 NL

BOSTON
SP V Willis
SP T Pittinger
SP K Wilhelm
SR T Fisher
SP E McNichol
C- T Needham
1B F Tenney
2B F Raymer
SS E Abbaticchio
3B J Delahanty
LF D Cooley
CF P Geier
RO R Cannell
C3 P Moran
RF- P Carney
M A Buckenberger

BROOKLYN
SP O Jones
SP J Cronin
SP N Garvin
SP E Poole
SP D Scanlan
C B Bergen
1B P Dillon
2B- D Jordan
SS C Babb
3B M McCormick
LF J Sheckard
CF J Dobbs
RF H Lumley
MU D Gessler
M N Hanlon

CHICAGO
SP J Weimer
SP B Briggs
SP C Lundgren
SP B Wicker
SP M Brown
RP F Corridon
C J Kling
1B F Chance
2B J Evers
SS J Tinker
3B D Casey
LF J Slagle
CF J McCarthy
RF D Jones
M F Selee

CINCINNATI
SP N Hahn
SP J Harper
SP W Kellum
SP T Walker
SP B Ewing
C A Schlei
1B J Kelley
2B M Huggins
SS T Corcoran
3B H Steinfeldt
LF F Odwell
CF C Seymour
RU C Dolan
C- H Peitz
3I- S Woodruff

NEW YORK
SP J McGinnity
SP C Mathewson
SP D Taylor
SP H Wiltse
SP R Ames
C- J Warner
1B D McGann
2B B Gilbert
SS B Dahlen
3B A Devlin
LF S Mertes
MU R Bresnahan
RF G Browne
C- F Bowerman
M J McGraw

PHILADELPHIA
SP C Fraser
SP B Duggleby
SP T Sparks
SP J Sutthoff
SP J McPherson
RP F Mitchell
C R Dooin
1B- J Doyle
2B K Gleason
SS R Hulswitt
3B H Wolverton
LU J Titus
CF R Thomas
RF S Magee
1R J Lush
C- F Roth
M H Duffy

PITTSBURGH
SP S Leever
SP P Flaherty
SP M Lynch
SP D Phillippe
SP C Case
RP R Miller
C E Phelps
1B K Bransfield
2B C Ritchey
SS H Wagner
3B T Leach
LF- F Clarke
CF G Beaumont
RF- J Sebring
UT- O Krueger

ST. LOUIS
SP J Taylor
SP K Nichols
SP C McFarland
SP M O'Neill
SP J Corbett
C M Grady
1B J Beckley
2B J Farrell
SS D Shay
3B J Burke
LF G Barclay
CF H Smoot
RF S Shannon
UT D Brain

1905 AL

BOSTON
SP C Young
SP J Tannehill
SP G Winter
SP B Dinneen
SP N Gibson
C L Criger
1B- M Grimshaw
2B H Ferris
SS F Parent
3B J Collins
LF J Burkett
CF C Stahl
RF K Selbach
1R B Freeman

CHICAGO
SP F Owen
SP N Altrock
SP F Smith
SP D White
SP E Walsh
C B Sullivan
1B J Donahue
2B G Dundon
SS G Davis
3B L Tannehill
LU N Callahan
CF F Jones
RF D Green
LF- D Holmes
UT- F Isbell
C- E McFarland

CLEVELAND
SP A Joss
SP E Moore
SP B Rhoads
SP O Hess
SP B Bernhard
RP R Donahue
C- F Buelow
1B- C Carr
2B- N Lajoie
SS T Turner
3B B Bradley
LF J Jackson
CF H Bay
RF E Flick
12 G Stovall
M3 N Lajoie

DETROIT
SP G Mullin
SP E Killian
SP B Donovan
SP F Kitson
C- L Drill
1B- C Lindsay
2B G Schaefer
SS C O'Leary
3B B Coughlin
LF M McIntyre
CF D Cooley
R1 S Crawford
M B Armour

NEW YORK
SP A Orth
SP J Chesbro
SR B Hogg
SR J Powell
RS C Griffith
C- R Kleinow
1B H Chase
2B J Williams
SS K Elberfeld
3B J Yeager
LF P Dougherty
CF D Fultz
RF W Keeler
UT W Conroy

PHILADELPHIA
SP E Plank
SR R Waddell
SP A Coakley
SR C Bender
SP W Henley
C O Schreckengost
1B H Davis
2B D Murphy
SS- J Knight
3B L Cross
LF T Hartsel
CF D Hoffman
RF S Seybold
SS- M Cross
M C Mack

ST. LOUIS
SP H Howell
SP F Glade
SP B Pelty
SP W Sudhoff
SP J Buchanan
C- J Sugden
1B T Jones
2B I Rockenfield
SS B Wallace
3B H Gleason
LF G Stone
CF B Koehler
RF E Frisk
OI I Van Zandt
M J McAleer

WASHINGTON
SP C Patten
SP T Hughes
SR H Townsend
SP B Wolfe
SP B Jacobson
C- M Heydon
1B J Stahl
2B- C Hickman
SS J Cassidy
3B H Hill
LF F Huelsman
CF C Jones
RF J Anderson
32 R Nill
C- M Kittridge
RU- P Knoll

1905 NL

BOSTON
SP I Young
SP V Willis
SP C Fraser
SP K Wilhelm
C- P Moran
1B F Tenney
2B F Raymer
SS E Abbaticchio
3B H Wolverton
LF J Delahanty
CF R Cannell
RF C Dolan
C- T Needham

BROOKLYN
SP H McIntire
SP D Scanlan
SP E Stricklett
SP M Eason
SP O Jones
RP F Mitchell
C- L Ritter
1B D Gessler
2U C Malay
SS P Lewis
3B E Batch
LF J Sheckard
CF J Dobbs
RF H Lumley
C- B Bergen
M N Hanlon

CHICAGO
SP E Reulbach
SP J Weimer
SP M Brown
SP B Wicker
SP C Lundgren
RP B Briggs
RP B Pfeffer
C J Kling
1B F Chance
2B J Evers
SS J Tinker
3B D Casey
LF F Schulte
CF J Slagle
RF B Maloney
2U- S Hofman
M1 F Selee

CINCINNATI
SP O Overall
SP B Ewing
SR C Chech
SP J Harper
SP T Walker
C A Schlei
1B S Barry
2B M Huggins
SS T Corcoran
3B H Steinfeldt
LF- J Kelley
CF C Seymour
RL F Odwell
3U- A Bridwell

NEW YORK
SP C Mathewson
SP J McGinnity
SP R Ames
SP D Taylor
SR H Wiltse
C R Bresnahan
1B D McGann
2B B Gilbert
SS B Dahlen
3B A Devlin
LF S Mertes
CF M Donlin
RF G Browne
CU F Bowerman
UT S Strang
M J McGraw

PHILADELPHIA
SP T Pittinger
SP B Duggleby
SP T Sparks
SP F Corridon
SP K Nichols
C R Dooin
1B K Bransfield
2B K Gleason
SS M Doolan
3B E Courtney
LF S Magee
CF R Thomas
RF J Titus
M H Duffy

PITTSBURGH
SP D Phillippe
SP S Leever
SP C Case
SR M Lynch
SP P Flaherty
RP C Robitaille
C- H Peitz
1U D Howard
2B C Ritchey
SS H Wagner
3B- D Brain
LF F Clarke
CF G Beaumont
RF O Clymer
UT T Leach

ST. LOUIS
SP J Taylor
SP C McFarland
SP J Thielman
SP B Brown
SP W Egan
CU M Grady
1B J Beckley
2B H Arndt
SS- G McBride
3B J Burke
LF S Shannon
CF H Smoot

RF J Dunleavy
2S- D Shay
M1 K Nichols
M3 S Robison

1906 AL

BOSTON
SP C Young
SP J Harris
SP B Dinneen
SP G Winter
SP J Tannehill
RP R Glaze
C- C Armbruster
1B M Grimshaw
2B H Ferris
SS F Parent
3B- R Morgan
LF J Hoey
CF C Stahl
RF- J Hayden
R1 B Freeman
M1 J Collins

CHICAGO
SP F Owen
SP N Altrock
SR E Walsh
SP D White
SP R Patterson
RP F Smith
C B Sullivan
1B J Donahue
2B F Isbell
SS G Davis
3B L Tannehill
RL E Hahn
CF F Jones
RF B O'Neill
3U- G Rohe

CLEVELAND
SP O Hess
SP B Rhoads
SP A Joss
SP B Bernhard
C- H Bemis
1B C Rossman
2B N Lajoie
CF J Bates
SS T Turner
3B- B Bradley
LF J Jackson
MR E Flick
RF B Congalton
UI G Stovall

DETROIT
SP G Mullin
SP R Donahue
SP E Siever
SP B Donovan
SP E Killian
RS J Eubank
C- B Schmidt
1B C Lindsay
2B G Schaefer
SS C O'Leary
3B B Coughlin
LF M McIntyre
MO T Cobb
RF S Crawford
CF- D Jones
M B Armour

NEW YORK
SP A Orth
SP J Chesbro
SP B Hogg
SR W Clarkson
SP D Newton
C R Kleinow
1B H Chase
2B J Williams
SS K Elberfeld
3B F LaPorte
UT W Conroy
CF D Hoffman
RF W Keeler
LF- F Delahanty
M C Griffith

PHILADELPHIA
SP R Waddell
SP C Bender
SR J Dygert
SP E Plank
SP J Coombs
RP A Coakley
C O Schreckengost
1B H Davis
2B D Murphy
SS M Cross
3B- J Knight
LF T Hartsel
CF B Lord
RF S Seybold
OF H Armbruster
M C Mack

ST. LOUIS
SP H Howell
SP F Glade
SP B Pelty
SP J Powell
SP B Jacobson
RP E Smith
C- B Rickey
1B T Jones
2B P O'Brien
SS B Wallace
3B R Hartzell
LF G Stone
MR C Hemphill
RU H Niles
M J McAleer

WASHINGTON
SP C Falkenberg
SP C Patten
SR C Smith
SP T Hughes
SP F Kitson
C- H Wakefield
1B J Stahl
2B L Schlafly
SS D Altizer
3B L Cross
LF J Anderson
CF C Jones
RF C Hickman
IO- R Nill

1906 NL

BOSTON
SP I Young
SP V Lindaman
SP B Pfeffer
SP G Dorner
C- T Needham
1B F Tenney
2B A Strobel
SS A Bridwell
3B D Brain
L2 D Howard
CF J Bates
RF C Dolan

BROOKLYN
SP E Stricklett
SP D Scanlan
SP H McIntire
SP M Eason
SP J Pastorius
C B Bergen
1B T Jordan
2B W Alperman
SS P Lewis
3B D Casey
LF- J McCarthy
CF B Maloney
RF H Lumley
2U J Hummel
M P Donovan

CHICAGO
SP M Brown
SP J Pfiester
SP E Reulbach
SP C Lundgren
SP J Taylor
RP O Overall
C J Kling
1B F Chance
2B J Evers
SS J Tinker
3B H Steinfeldt
LF J Sheckard
CF J Slagle
RF F Schulte

CINCINNATI
SP J Weimer
SP B Ewing
SP C Fraser
SP B Wicker
SP C Hall
C A Schlei
1B- S Deal
2B M Huggins
SS T Corcoran
3B J Delahanty
LF J Kelley
CF- C Seymour
RF- F Jude
IO- H Lobert
M N Hanlon

NEW YORK
SP J McGinnity
SP C Mathewson
SR H Wiltse
SP D Taylor
SP R Ames
RP G Ferguson
CM R Bresnahan
1B D McGann
2B B Gilbert
SS B Dahlen
3B A Devlin
LF- S Shannon
CF- C Seymour
RF G Browne
CU F Bowerman
2O S Strang
M J McGraw

PHILADELPHIA
SP T Sparks
SR B Duggleby
SP J Lush
SR L Richie
SP T Pittinger
C R Dooin
1B K Bransfield
2B K Gleason
SS M Doolan
3B E Courtney
LF S Magee
CF R Thomas
RF J Titus
M H Duffy

PITTSBURGH
SP V Willis
SP S Leever
SP L Leifield
SP D Phillippe
SP M Lynch
C- G Gibson
1B J Nealon
2B C Ritchey
SS H Wagner
3B T Sheehan
LF F Clarke
CF- G Beaumont
RF B Ganley
UT T Leach
OI- D Meier

ST. LOUIS
SP B Brown
SP E Karger
SP F Beebe
SP J Taylor
SP C Druhot
RP G Thompson
C1 M Grady
1B- J Beckley
2B P Bennett
SS- G McBride
3B- H Arndt
LF- S Shannon
MR- H Smoot
MR- A Burch
3U A Hoelskoetter
M J McCloskey

1907 AL

BOSTON
SP C Young
SP G Winter
SR R Glaze
SR T Pruiett
SP J Tannehill
RP C Morgan
C- L Criger
1B B Unglaub
2B H Ferris
SS H Wagner
3B J Knight
LF J Barrett
CF D Sullivan
RF B Congalton
UT F Parent
M2 G Huff
M4 D McGuire

CHICAGO
SR E Walsh
SP F Smith
SR D White
SP N Altrock
SP R Patterson
C B Sullivan
1B J Donahue
2B F Isbell
SS G Davis
32 G Rohe
LF P Dougherty
CF F Jones
RF E Hahn

CLEVELAND
SP A Joss
SP G Liebhardt
SP B Rhoads
SP J Thielman
C N Clarke
1B G Stovall
2B N Lajoie
SS T Turner
3B B Bradley
LF B Hinchman
MU J Birmingham
RF E Flick

DETROIT
SP G Mullin
SP E Killian
SP E Siever
SP B Donovan
C B Schmidt
1B C Rossman
2B R Downs
SS C O'Leary
3B B Coughlin
LF D Jones
CF S Crawford
RF T Cobb
2I G Schaefer
M H Jennings

NEW YORK
SP A Orth
SP J Chesbro
SP S Doyle
SP B Hogg
SP D Newton
C- R Kleinow
1B H Chase
2B J Williams
SS K Elberfeld
3U G Moriarty
LS W Conroy
CF D Hoffman
RF W Keeler
UT F LaPorte
C- I Thomas
M C Griffith

PHILADELPHIA
SP E Plank
SR R Waddell
SR J Dygert
SP C Bender
SP J Coombs
C O Schreckengost
1B H Davis
2B D Murphy
SI S Nicholls
3B J Collins
LF T Hartsel
CF R Oldring
RF S Seybold
SS- M Cross
M C Mack

ST. LOUIS
SP H Howell
SP B Pelty
SP J Powell
SP F Glade
SP B Dinneen
C- T Spencer
1B T Jones
2B H Niles
SS B Wallace
3U J Yeager
LF G Stone
CF C Hemphill
RF O Pickering
M J McAleer

WASHINGTON
SP C Smith
SP C Patten
SP C Falkenberg
SR T Hughes
SP W Johnson
RP O Graham
C- J Warner
1L- J Anderson
23 J Delahanty
S1 D Altizer
3B- B Shipke
OI- O Clymer
MU C Jones
RL B Ganley
M J Cantillon

1907 NL

BOSTON
SP G Dorner
SP V Lindaman
SP I Young
SP P Flaherty
SP B Pfeffer
RS J Boultes
C- T Needham
1B F Tenney
2B C Ritchey
SS A Bridwell
3B D Brain
LF- N Randall
CF G Beaumont
RF J Bates

BROOKLYN
SP N Rucker
SP G Bell
SP E Stricklett
SP J Pastorius
SP H McIntire
RP D Scanlan
C L Ritter
1B T Jordan
2B W Alperman
SS P Lewis
3B D Casey
LU E Batch
CF B Maloney
RF H Lumley
UT J Hummel
M P Donovan

CHICAGO
SP O Overall
SP M Brown
SP C Lundgren
SP J Pfiester
SP E Reulbach
RP C Fraser
RP J Taylor
C J Kling
1B F Chance
2B J Evers
SS J Tinker
3B H Steinfeldt
LF J Sheckard
CF J Slagle
RF F Schulte
UT S Hofman

CINCINNATI
SP B Ewing
SP A Coakley
SP J Weimer
SP R Hitt
SP D Mason
C L McLean
1B J Ganzel
2B M Huggins
SS H Lobert
3B M Mowrey
LF F Odwell
ML A Kruger
RF M Mitchell
UT- J Kane
C- A Schlei
M N Hanlon

NEW YORK
SP C Mathewson
SR J McGinnity
SR R Ames
SR H Wiltse
SP D Taylor
C R Bresnahan
1B- D McGann
2B- L Doyle
SS B Dahlen
3B A Devlin
LF S Shannon
CF C Seymour
RF G Browne
C1 F Bowerman
UT S Strang
M J McGraw

PHILADELPHIA
SP F Corridon
SP T Sparks
SP L Moren
SP B Brown
SR L Richie
RP T Pittinger
C R Dooin
1B K Bransfield
2B O Knabe
SS M Doolan
31 E Courtney
LF S Magee
CF R Thomas
RF J Titus
M B Murray

PITTSBURGH
SP V Willis
SP L Leifield
SP S Leever
SP D Phillippe
SR H Camnitz
C G Gibson
1B J Nealon
2B E Abbaticchio
SS H Wagner
3I A Storke
LF F Clarke
MI T Leach
RU G Anderson
UO- B Hallman

ST. LOUIS
SP S McGlynn
SP E Karger
SP F Beebe
SP A Fromme
SP J Lush
C- D Marshall
1B- E Konetchy
2B- P Bennett
SS E Holly
3B B Byrne
LF R Murray
CF- J Burnett
RF- S Barry
2U A Hoelskoetter
M J McCloskey

1908 AL

BOSTON
SP C Young
SR E Cicotte
SP C Morgan
SR F Burchell
SP G Winter
RP E Steele
C- L Criger
1B- J Stahl
2B A McConnell
SS H Wagner
3B H Lord
LF J Thoney
CF D Sullivan
RF D Gessler
LU G Cravath
M1 D McGuire
M2 F Lake

CHICAGO
SR E Walsh
SP F Smith
SP D White
SR F Owen
SR N Altrock
C B Sullivan
1B- J Donahue
2U G Davis
SS F Parent
3B L Tannehill
LF P Dougherty
CF F Jones
RO E Hahn
RU J Anderson
2U- J Atz
1B- F Isbell

CLEVELAND
SP A Joss
SP B Rhoads
SR G Liebhardt
SP H Berger
SP C Chech
C N Clarke
1B G Stovall
2B N Lajoie
S3- G Perring
3B B Bradley
LF J Clarke
CF J Birmingham
UT B Hinchman
C- H Bemis

DETROIT
SP E Summers
SP G Mullin
SP B Donovan
SP E Willett
SP E Killian
C B Schmidt
1B C Rossman
2B- R Downs
UI G Schaefer
3B B Coughlin
LF M McIntyre
CF S Crawford
RF T Cobb
M H Jennings

NEW YORK
SR J Chesbro
SR J Lake
SR R Manning
SP B Hogg
SP A Orth
C R Kleinow
1B H Chase
2B H Niles
SS N Ball
3B W Conroy
LF- J Stahl
CF C Hemphill
RF- W Keeler
13 G Moriarty
M1 C Griffith
M2 K Elberfeld

PHILADELPHIA
SR R Vickers
SP E Plank
SR J Dygert
SP J Coombs
SP C Bender
RP B Schlitzer
C- O Schreckengost
1B H Davis
UT E Collins
SS S Nicholls
3B J Collins
LF T Hartsel
CF R Oldring
UT D Murphy
M C Mack

ST. LOUIS
SP H Howell
SP R Waddell
SP J Powell
SR B Dinneen
SP B Pelty
RP B Graham
RS B Bailey
C- T Spencer
1B T Jones
2B J Williams
SS B Wallace
3B H Ferris
LF G Stone
UO D Hoffman
RI R Hartzell
M J McAleer

WASHINGTON
SR T Hughes
SP W Johnson
SP C Smith
SR B Keeley
SP B Burns
RP E Cates
C G Street
1B J Freeman
2B- J Delahanty
SS G McBride
3B B Shipke
LF B Ganley
CF C Milan
RU O Pickering
RU O Clymer
M J Cantillon

1908 NL

BOSTON
SR V Lindaman
SP P Flaherty
SR G Dorner
SR G Ferguson
CU- F Bowerman
1B D McGann
2B C Ritchey
SS B Dahlen
3B B Sweeney
LF J Bates
CF G Beaumont
RF G Browne
UT- J Hannifin
M J Kelley

BROOKLYN
SP N Rucker
SP K Wilhelm
SP H McIntire
SP J Pastorius
SR G Bell
C B Bergen
1B T Jordan
2B- H Pattee
SS P Lewis
3B T Sheehan
UO A Burch
CF B Maloney
RF H Lumley
L2 J Hummel
M P Donovan

CHICAGO
SR M Brown
SR E Reulbach
SP J Pfiester
SR O Overall
SP C Fraser
RP C Lundgren
C J Kling
1B F Chance
2B J Evers
SS J Tinker
3B H Steinfeldt
LF J Sheckard
ML J Slagle
RF F Schulte
UT S Hofman
RM D Howard

CINCINNATI
SP B Ewing
SP B Spade
SP A Coakley
SR B Campbell
SP J Weimer
C- A Schlei
1B J Ganzel
2B M Huggins
SS R Hulswitt
3U H Lobert
LM D Paskert
CF J Kane
RF M Mitchell
CU L McLean

NEW YORK
SR C Mathewson
SP H Wiltse
SP D Crandall
SR J McGinnity
SP D Taylor
RP R Ames
C R Bresnahan
1B F Tenney
2B L Doyle
SS A Bridwell
3B A Devlin
LF- S Shannon
CF C Seymour
RF M Donlin
M J McGraw

PHILADELPHIA
SP G McQuillan
SP T Sparks
SP F Corridon
SR L Richie
SR L Moren
RP B Foxen
C R Dooin
1B K Bransfield
2B O Knabe
SS M Doolan
3B E Grant
LF S Magee
CF F Osborn
RF J Titus
M B Murray

PITTSBURGH
SP V Willis
SP N Maddox
SR H Camnitz
SP L Leifield
SR S Leever
C G Gibson
1B- H Swacina
2B E Abbaticchio
SS H Wagner
3B T Leach
LF F Clarke
CF R Thomas
RF C Wilson

ST. LOUIS
SR B Raymond
SP J Lush
SR F Beebe
SP E Karger
SR S Sallee
RP A Fromme
RP I Higginbotham
C- B Ludwig
1B E Konetchy
2B- B Gilbert
SS- P O'Rourke
3B B Byrne
LF J Delahanty
MU A Shaw
MR R Murray
2S C Charles
M J McCloskey

1909 AL

BOSTON
SR F Arellanes
SR E Cicotte
SP J Wood
SP C Chech
C B Carrigan
1B J Stahl
2B A McConnell
SS H Wagner
3B H Lord
LO H Niles
CF T Speaker
RF D Gessler
LF- H Hooper
M F Lake

CHICAGO
SR F Smith
SP J Scott
SP E Walsh
SP D White
SP B Burns
C B Sullivan
1B F Isbell
2B J Atz
SO F Parent
3S L Tannehill
LF P Dougherty
OI D Altizer
RF- E Hahn
32 B Purtell

CLEVELAND
SP C Young
SP H Berger
SP A Joss
SP C Falkenberg

SP B Rhoads
C T Easterly
1B G Stovall
2B N Lajoie
SS N Ball
3B B Bradley
LM B Hinchman
CF J Birmingham
RF W Good
3B- G Perring
M2 D McGuire

DETROIT
SP G Mullin
SP E Willett
SP E Summers
SP E Killian
SP B Donovan
C- B Schmidt
1B- C Rossman
2B- G Schaefer
SS D Bush
3B G Moriarty
LF M McIntyre
CF S Crawford
RF T Cobb
M H Jennings

NEW YORK
SR J Warhop
SP J Lake
SP R Manning
SP L Brockett
SP S Doyle
RP T Hughes
RS J Quinn
RP P Wilson
C- R Kleinow
1B H Chase
2B- F LaPorte
SI J Knight
3B J Austin
LF C Engle
MR R Demmitt
RF W Keeler
UT B Cree
S3 K Elberfeld
M G Stallings

PHILADELPHIA
SP E Plank
SP C Bender
SP C Morgan
SR H Krause
SP J Coombs
RS J Dygert
C- I Thomas
1B H Davis
2B E Collins
SS J Barry
3B F Baker
LF- T Hartsel
ML- R Oldring
RF D Murphy
CF- B Ganley
M C Mack

ST. LOUIS
SP J Powell
SP R Waddell
SP B Pelty
SR B Bailey
SR B Grahame
RP B Dinneen
C- L Criger
1B T Jones
2B J Williams
SS B Wallace
3B H Ferris
LF- G Stone
CF D Hoffman
RS R Hartzell
UT A Griggs
OI- J McAleese
C- J Stephens
M J McAleer

WASHINGTON
SP W Johnson
SR B Groom
SR D Gray
SP C Smith
SP T Hughes
C G Street
1B- J Donahue
2B- J Delahanty
SS G McBride
3B W Conroy
UO- J Lelivelt
MU C Milan
LR G Browne
UT B Unglaub
M J Cantillon

1909 NL

BOSTON
SR A Mattern
SP G Ferguson
SP K White
SP L Richie
SP B Brown
C- P Graham
1B- F Stem
2B- D Shean
SS- J Coffey
3B B Sweeney
LF- R Thomas
CF G Beaumont
RF B Becker
OI F Beck
M1 F Bowerman
M2 H Smith

BROOKLYN
SP N Rucker
SP G Bell
SP H McIntire
SP K Wilhelm
SP D Scanlan
RP G Hunter
C B Bergen
1B T Jordan
2B W Alperman
SS T McMillan
3B E Lennox
LF- W Clement
ML A Burch
RF- H Lumley
UT J Hummel
UT- P McElveen

CHICAGO
SR M Brown
SP O Overall
SP E Reulbach
SP J Pfiester
SP R Kroh
C- J Archer
1B F Chance
2B J Evers
SS J Tinker
3B H Steinfeldt
LF J Sheckard
CF S Hofman
RF F Schulte

CINCINNATI
SP A Fromme
SR H Gaspar
SR J Rowan
SP B Ewing
SR B Campbell
RP B Spade
C L McLean
1B D Hoblitzel
2B D Egan
SS T Downey
3B H Lobert
LF B Bescher
CF R Oakes
RF M Mitchell
OI D Paskert
M C Griffith

NEW YORK
SP C Mathewson
SP H Wiltse
SP B Raymond
SP R Ames
SP R Marquard
RS D Crandall
C- A Schlei
1B F Tenney
2B L Doyle
SS A Bridwell
3B A Devlin
LF M McCormick
CF B O'Hara
RF R Murray
1B- F Merkle
CU- C Meyers
CF- C Seymour
M J McGraw

PHILADELPHIA
SP E Moore
SP L Moren
SR G McQuillan
SP F Corridon
SP H Coveleski
RP T Sparks
C R Dooin
1B K Bransfield
2B O Knabe
SS M Doolan
3B E Grant
LF S Magee
CF- J Bates
RF J Titus
M B Murray

PITTSBURGH
SP V Willis
SR H Camnitz
SR N Maddox
SP L Leifield
SR B Adams
RP D Phillippe
C G Gibson
1B B Abstein
2B D Miller
SS H Wagner
3B- J Barbeau
LF F Clarke
CF T Leach
RF C Wilson

ST. LOUIS
SR F Beebe
SP J Lush
SP S Sallee
SP B Harmon
SP L Backman
RP S Melter
C E Phelps
1B E Konetchy
2S C Charles
SS- R Hulswitt
3B B Byrne
LF R Ellis
CF A Shaw
RF S Evans
OI J Delahanty
M R Bresnahan

1910 AL

BOSTON
SP E Cicotte
SP R Collins
SR J Wood
SR C Hall
SP E Karger
RP C Smith
RP F Arellanes
C B Carrigan
1B J Stahl
2B L Gardner
SS H Wagner
3B- H Lord
LF D Lewis
CF T Speaker
RF H Hooper
UT C Engle
M P Donovan

CHICAGO
SP E Walsh
SP D White
SR J Scott
SR F Olmstead
SR I Young
RP F Lange
RP F Smith
C- F Payne
1B- C Gandil
2S R Zeider
SS- L Blackburne
3B B Purtell
LF P Dougherty
MU- F Parent
OI S Collins
M H Duffy

CLEVELAND
SP C Falkenberg
SR W Mitchell
SP C Young
SR E Koestner
SR S Harkness
RP F Link
RP A Joss
CR T Easterly
1B G Stovall
2B N Lajoie
S3 T Turner
3B- B Bradley
UO J Graney
CF J Birmingham
RL- B Lord
M D McGuire

DETROIT
SP G Mullin
SR E Willett
SR E Summers
SP B Donovan
SR S Stroud
C- O Stanage
1B T Jones
2B J Delahanty
SS D Bush
3B G Moriarty
LF D Jones
CF T Cobb
RF S Crawford
LU- M McIntyre
M H Jennings

NEW YORK
SP R Ford
SR J Warhop
SP J Quinn
SP H Vaughn
SP T Hughes
C- E Sweeney
1B H Chase
2U F LaPorte
SI J Knight
3B J Austin
ML B Cree
MR C Hemphill
RF H Wolter
LF B Daniels
2B- E Gardner
M1 G Stallings

PHILADELPHIA
SP J Coombs
SP C Morgan
SP E Plank
SP C Bender
SP H Krause
RS J Dygert
C- J Lapp
1B H Davis
2B E Collins
SS J Barry
3B F Baker
LF- T Hartsel
CF R Oldring
RF D Murphy
M C Mack

ST. LOUIS
SP J Lake
SR B Bailey
SP B Pelty
SP F Ray
SP J Powell
C J Stephens
1B P Newnam
2B F Truesdale
S3 B Wallace
3S R Hartzell
LF G Stone
CF D Hoffman
RM A Schweitzer
UT A Griggs
M J O'Connor

WASHINGTON
SP W Johnson
SP B Groom
SP D Gray
SP D Walker
SR D Reisling
C- G Street
1B B Unglaub
2B R Killefer
SS G McBride
3B K Elberfeld
LU J Lelivelt
CF C Milan
RF D Gessler
UT W Conroy
M J McAleer

1910 NL

BOSTON
SR A Mattern
SR B Brown
SR S Frock
SR C Curtis
SP G Ferguson
C P Graham
1B B Sharpe
2B D Shean
SI B Sweeney
3B B Herzog
LF B Collins
CF F Beck
RF D Miller
M F Lake

BROOKLYN
SP N Rucker
SP G Bell
SP C Barger
SP D Scanlan
SP E Knetzer
RP R Dessau
C- B Bergen
1B J Daubert
2B J Hummel
SS T Smith
3B E Lennox
LF Z Wheat
CF B Davidson
RF- J Dalton
OI A Burch
C- T Erwin
M B Dahlen

CHICAGO
SR M Brown
SP K Cole
SP H McIntire
SP E Reulbach
SP O Overall
RS L Richie
RP J Pfiester
C- J Kling
1B- F Chance
2B J Evers
SS J Tinker
3B H Steinfeldt
LF J Sheckard
CF S Hofman
RF F Schulte
C1 J Archer
IO H Zimmerman

CINCINNATI
SR H Gaspar
SP G Suggs
SR J Rowan
SP F Beebe
SR B Burns
C L McLean
1B D Hoblitzel
2B D Egan
SS- T McMillan
3B- H Lobert
LF B Bescher
CF D Paskert
RF M Mitchell
S3 T Downey
OF- W Miller
M C Griffith

NEW YORK
SP C Mathewson
SP H Wiltse
SP L Drucke
SR D Crandall
SR R Ames
RP B Raymond
C C Meyers
1B F Merkle
2B L Doyle
SS A Bridwell
3B A Devlin
LF J Devore
ML F Snodgrass
RF R Murray
OI- B Becker
CF- C Seymour
M J McGraw

PHILADELPHIA
SR E Moore
SP B Ewing
SP L Moren
SP G McQuillan
SP E Stack
RS L Schettler
C R Dooin
1B K Bransfield
2B O Knabe
SS M Doolan
3B E Grant
LF S Magee
CF J Bates
RF J Titus
UT- J Walsh

PITTSBURGH
SP H Camnitz
SP B Adams
SR L Leifield
SP K White
RS D Phillippe
RS S Leever
C G Gibson
1B J Flynn
2B D Miller
SS H Wagner
3B B Byrne
LF F Clarke
CF T Leach
RF C Wilson
UO V Campbell

ST. LOUIS
SR B Harmon
SR J Lush
SR V Willis
SR F Corridon
SR L Backman
RP S Sallee
C E Phelps
1B E Konetchy
2B M Huggins
SS A Hauser
3B M Mowrey
LF R Ellis
CF R Oakes
RF S Evans
C- R Bresnahan

1911 AL

BOSTON
SR J Wood
SR E Cicotte
SP R Collins
SP L Pape
SP E Karger
RS C Hall
C- B Carrigan
UT C Engle
2S- H Wagner
SS S Yerkes
32 L Gardner
LF D Lewis
CF T Speaker
RF H Hooper
1C R Williams
M P Donovan

CHICAGO
SR E Walsh
SR J Scott
SP D White
SP F Lange
SR F Olmstead
RS I Young
RS J Baker
C- B Sullivan
1B S Collins
2B A McConnell
SI L Tannehill
3B H Lord
LF N Callahan
MU P Bodie
RF M McIntyre
M H Duffy

CLEVELAND
SP V Gregg
SP G Krapp
SR F Blanding
SP W Mitchell
SR G Kahler
RP C Falkenberg
C- G Fisher
1B G Stovall
2B N Ball
SS I Olson
3B T Turner
LF J Graney
CF J Birmingham
RM J Jackson
RU T Easterly
IF- N Lajoie
M1 D McGuire

DETROIT
SP G Mullin
SR E Willett
SR E Summers
SP E Lafitte
SP B Donovan
RS R Works
RP J Lively
C O Stanage
UI J Delahanty
2B- C O'Leary
SS D Bush
3B G Moriarty
LF D Jones
CF T Cobb
RF S Crawford
LF D Drake
M H Jennings

NEW YORK
SP R Ford
SR R Caldwell
SP J Warhop
SR J Quinn
SP R Fisher
RP H Vaughn
C- W Blair
1B H Chase
2B E Gardner
SI J Knight
3B R Hartzell
LF B Cree
MO B Daniels
RF H Wolter
C- E Sweeney

PHILADELPHIA
SP J Coombs
SR E Plank
SP C Morgan
SP C Bender
SP H Krause
C I Thomas
1B S McInnis
2B E Collins
SS J Barry
3B F Baker
LF B Lord
CF R Oldring
RF D Murphy
M C Mack

ST. LOUIS
SP J Lake
SP J Powell
SP B Pelty
SR E Hamilton
SR R Mitchell
RS L George
C- N Clarke
1B- J Black
2B F LaPorte
SS B Wallace
3B J Austin
LF W Hogan
CF B Shotton
RU- A Schweitzer

WASHINGTON
SP W Johnson
SP B Groom
SP T Hughes
SP D Walker
SR D Gray
C- G Street
1B G Schaefer
2B B Cunningham
SS G McBride
3B W Conroy
LF T Walker
CF C Milan
RF D Gessler
23 K Elberfeld
C1- J Henry
M J McAleer

1911 NL

BOSTON
SR B Brown
SR A Mattern
SP L Tyler
SP H Perdue
SR O Weaver
RS B Pfeffer
C- J Kling
1B F Tenney
2B B Sweeney
SS- B Herzog
UT S Ingerton
LM- A Kaiser
CF- M Donlin
RF D Miller

BROOKLYN
SR N Rucker
SP C Barger
SR E Knetzer
SR B Schardt
SP D Scanlan
RP G Bell
RS P Ragan
C- B Bergen
1B J Daubert
2B J Hummel
SS B Tooley
3B E Zimmerman
LF Z Wheat
CF- B Davidson
RF B Coulson
C- T Erwin
M B Dahlen

CHICAGO
SR M Brown
SP L Richie
SP E Reulbach
SP K Cole
SP H McIntire
RS R Richter
C J Archer
1B- V Saier
2B H Zimmerman
SS J Tinker
3B J Doyle
LF J Sheckard
M1 S Hofman
RF F Schulte
M F Chance

CINCINNATI
SP G Suggs
SR H Gaspar
SR B Keefe
SR A Fromme
SR F Smith
C L McLean
1B D Hoblitzel
2B D Egan
SS T Downey
3B E Grant
LF B Bescher
CF J Bates
RF M Mitchell
C- T Clarke
M C Griffith

NEW YORK
SP C Mathewson
SR R Marquard
SR R Ames
SR D Crandall
SP H Wiltse
C C Meyers
1B F Merkle
2B L Doyle
SS- A Bridwell
3B A Devlin
LR J Devore
CF F Snodgrass
RL R Murray
SI A Fletcher
UO- B Becker
M J McGraw

PHILADELPHIA
SR G Alexander
SP E Moore
SR G Chalmers
SP B Burns
C- R Dooin
1B F Luderus
2B O Knabe
SS M Doolan
3B H Lobert
LF S Magee
CF D Paskert
RF- F Beck
UT J Walsh

PITTSBURGH
SP L Leifield
SP B Adams
SP H Camnitz
SR E Steele
SR C Hendrix
C G Gibson
1B- N Hunter
2B D Miller
SS H Wagner
3B B Byrne
LF F Clarke
ML M Carey
RF C Wilson
CF T Leach
1I B McKechnie

ST. LOUIS
SR B Harmon
SR B Steele
SP S Sallee
SR R Geyer
SP R Golden
C J Bliss
1B E Konetchy
2B M Huggins
SS A Hauser
3B M Mowrey
LF R Ellis
CF R Oakes
RF S Evans
C- R Bresnahan
IO- W Smith

1912 AL

BOSTON
SP J Wood
SP B O'Brien
SR H Bedient
SP R Collins
SR C Hall
C- B Carrigan
1B J Stahl
2B S Yerkes
SS H Wagner
3B L Gardner
LF D Lewis
CF T Speaker
RF H Hooper

CHICAGO
SR E Walsh
SR J Benz
SR D White
SR F Lange
SP E Cicotte
RS R Peters
C- W Kuhn
13 R Zeider
2B M Rath
SS B Weaver
3O H Lord
LF N Callahan
MR P Bodie
R1 S Collins
MU- W Mattick
M J Callahan

CLEVELAND
SP V Gregg
SP F Blanding
SP G Kahler
SR W Mitchell
SR B Steen
RS J Baskette
C- S O'Neill
1B- A Griggs
2B N Lajoie
SS- R Peckinpaugh

3B T Turner
LR B Ryan
CF *J Birmingham*
RF J Jackson
IO I Olson
LF- J Graney
M1 *H Davis*

DETROIT
SP E Willett
SR J Dubuc
SP G Mullin
SR J Lake
SR R Works
C O Stanage
13 G Moriarty
2I B Louden
SS D Bush
3B- C Deal
LU D Jones
CF T Cobb
RF S Crawford
2L- J Delahanty
M *H Jennings*

NEW YORK
SP R Ford
SR J Warhop
SP R Caldwell
SP G McConnell
SP J Quinn
C E Sweeney
1B H Chase
2B H Simmons
SS- J Martin
UT R Hartzell
LR B Daniels
UT- D Sterrett
RM G Zinn
M *H Wolverton*

PHILADELPHIA
SP J Coombs
SP E Plank
SR B Brown
SR B Houck
SP C Bender
RP C Morgan
RP H Pennock
C- J Lapp
1B S McInnis
2B E Collins
SS J Barry
3B F Baker
LM A Strunk
CF R Oldring
RF B Lord
M *C Mack*

ST. LOUIS
SR E Hamilton
SP J Powell
SP G Baumgardner
SR M Allison
SR E Brown
C- J Stephens
1B G Stovall
2B D Pratt
SS B Wallace
3B J Austin
LF W Hogan
CF B Shotton
RF- G Williams
OF P Compton
UT- F LaPorte

WASHINGTON
SR W Johnson
SP B Groom
SP T Hughes
SP C Cashion
C- J Henry
1B C Gandil
2B- R Morgan
SS G McBride
3B E Foster
LF H Shanks
CF C Milan
RF D Moeller
M *C Griffith*

1912 NL

BOSTON
SR L Tyler
SP O Hess
SP H Perdue
SR W Dickson
SR E Donnelly
RS B Brown
C- J Kling
1B B Houser
2B B Sweeney
SS- F O'Rourke
3B E McDonald
LF G Jackson
CF V Campbell
RF J Titus
1I A Devlin
LU J Kirke
C- B Rariden

BROOKLYN
SR N Rucker
SR P Ragan
SP E Yingling
SR E Stack
SR E Knetzer
RP F Allen
RP C Barger
RS M Kent
C O Miller
1B J Daubert
2B G Cutshaw
SS- B Tooley
3B R Smith
LF Z Wheat
MR H Moran
UO H Northen
IO J Hummel
SS- B Fisher
M *B Dahlen*

CHICAGO
SP L Cheney
SR J Lavender
SR L Richie
SR E Reulbach
RS C Smith
C J Archer
1B V Saier
2B J Evers
SS J Tinker
3B H Zimmerman
LF J Sheckard
CF- T Leach
RF F Schulte
UO- W Miller
M *F Chance*

CINCINNATI
SP G Suggs
SR R Benton
SP A Fromme
SR B Humphries
C L McLean
1B D Hoblitzel
2B D Egan
SS- J Esmond
3B A Phelan
LF B Bescher
MU A Marsans
RF M Mitchell
SU E Grant
CF- J Bates
M *H O'Day*

NEW YORK
SP C Mathewson
SP R Marquard
SP J Tesreau
SR R Ames
SR H Wiltse
RS D Crandall
C C Meyers
1B F Merkle
2B L Doyle
SS A Fletcher
3B B Herzog
UT F Snodgrass
MU B Becker
RF R Murray
LU J Devore
UI- T Shafer
M *J McGraw*

PHILADELPHIA
SR G Alexander
SR T Seaton
SP E Moore
SP A Brennan
SP E Rixey
RP T Shultz
C- B Killefer
1B F Luderus
2B O Knabe
SS M Doolan
3B- H Lobert
LF S Magee
CF D Paskert
RO G Cravath
M *R Dooin*

PITTSBURGH
SP C Hendrix
SP H Camnitz
SP M O'Toole
SR H Robinson
SP B Adams
C G Gibson
1B D Miller
2B A McCarthy
SS H Wagner
3B B Byrne
LF M Carey
MR C Wilson
RU- M Donlin
M *F Clarke*

ST. LOUIS
SR S Sallee
SP B Harmon
SR B Steele
SR R Geyer
SR J Willis
RS G Woodburn
C I Wingo
1B E Konetchy
2B M Huggins
SS A Hauser
3B M Mowrey
LU L Magee
CF R Oakes
RF S Evans
LU R Ellis
M *R Bresnahan*

1913 AL

BOSTON
SR H Bedient
SR D Leonard
SP R Collins
SP J Wood
SR E Moseley
RP C Hall
C- B Carrigan
1B C Engle
2B S Yerkes
SS H Wagner
3B L Gardner
LF D Lewis
CF T Speaker
RF H Hooper
SI- H Janvrin
M1 *J Stahl*

CHICAGO
SR R Russell
SR J Scott
SR E Cicotte
SR J Benz
SR D White
RP E Walsh
C R Schalk
1B H Chase
2B M Rath
SS B Weaver
3B H Lord
ML P Bodie
CF- W Mattick
RF S Collins
2B- J Berger
M *J Callahan*

CLEVELAND
SR V Gregg
SP C Falkenberg
SR W Mitchell
SR F Blanding
SP B Steen
SR G Kahler
RS N Cullop
C- S O'Neill
1B D Johnston
2B N Lajoie
SS R Chapman
3U I Olson
LF J Graney
MU N Leibold
RF J Jackson
3I T Turner
C- F Carisch
M *J Birmingham*

DETROIT
SP J Dubuc
SP E Willett
SP H Dauss
SP M Hall
SR J Lake
RP F House
C- O Stanage
1B D Gainer
2B O Vitt
SS D Bush
3B G Moriarty
LF B Veach
CF T Cobb
RF S Crawford
UO- H High
M *H Jennings*

NEW YORK
SR R Fisher
SP R Ford
SR A Schulz
SR G McConnell
SR R Caldwell
RP R Keating
C E Sweeney
12- J Knight
2U R Hartzell
SS R Peckinpaugh
3B- E Midkiff
LF B Cree
CF H Wolter
RF B Daniels
M *F Chance*

PHILADELPHIA
SR C Bender
SR E Plank
SP B Brown
SR J Bush
SR B Houck
RP B Shawkey
C- J Lapp
1B S McInnis
2B E Collins
SS J Barry
3B F Baker
LF R Oldring
UO J Walsh
RF E Murphy
CF A Strunk
C- W Schang
M *C Mack*

ST. LOUIS
SP G Baumgardner
SR C Weilman
SP R Mitchell
SP E Hamilton
SP W Leverenz
C S Agnew
1B- G Stovall
2B D Pratt
SS- M Balenti
3B J Austin
LF J Johnston
CF B Shotton
RF G Williams
1U- B Brief
M3 *B Rickey*

WASHINGTON
SR W Johnson
SP B Groom
SR J Boehling
SP J Engel
RS T Hughes
RP B Gallia
C J Henry
1B C Gandil
2B R Morgan
SS G McBride
3B E Foster
LF H Shanks
CF C Milan
RF D Moeller
C- E Ainsmith
3U- F LaPorte
M *C Griffith*

1913 NL

BOSTON
SP L Tyler
SR D Rudolph
SP O Hess
SP H Perdue
SR B James
RP W Dickson
C B Rariden
1B H Myers
2B B Sweeney
SS R Maranville
3B- A Devlin
LF J Connolly
CF L Mann
RF- J Titus
3I- F Smith
C- B Whaling
M *G Stallings*

BROOKLYN
SR P Ragan
SP N Rucker
SP F Allen
SR C Curtis
SR E Yingling
RP E Reulbach
C O Miller
1B J Daubert
2B G Cutshaw
SS B Fisher
3B R Smith
LF Z Wheat
CF C Stengel
RF H Moran
M *B Dahlen*

CHICAGO
SR L Cheney
SR J Lavender
SR B Humphries
SP G Pierce
SP C Smith
C J Archer
1B V Saier
2B J Evers
SS A Bridwell
3B H Zimmerman
LF- M Mitchell
CF T Leach
RF F Schulte
LU- W Miller
23- A Phelan

CINCINNATI
SR C Johnson
SR G Suggs
SR G Packard
SP R Ames
SR M Brown
RP R Benton
RP F Harter
C T Clarke
1B D Hoblitzel
2B H Groh
SS J Tinker
3B J Dodge
LF B Bescher
UT A Marsans
RU J Bates
C- J Kling

NEW YORK
SP C Mathewson
SP R Marquard
SP J Tesreau
SP A Demaree
SR A Fromme
RP D Crandall
C C Meyers
1B F Merkle
2B L Doyle
SS A Fletcher
3B B Herzog
LF G Burns
CF F Snodgrass
RF R Murray
3I T Shafer
M *J McGraw*

PHILADELPHIA
SR T Seaton
SR G Alexander
SR A Brennan
SR E Mayer
SR E Rixey
RS G Chalmers
C B Killefer
1B F Luderus
2B O Knabe
SS M Doolan
3B H Lobert
LF S Magee
CF D Paskert
RF G Cravath
OI- B Becker
M *R Dooin*

PITTSBURGH
SP B Adams
SR C Hendrix
SR H Robinson
SR H Camnitz
SR M O'Toole
RP G McQuillan
C- M Simon
1B D Miller
2B J Viox
SS H Wagner
3B B Byrne
LF M Carey
CF- M Mitchell
RF C Wilson
IO- A Butler
M *F Clarke*

ST. LOUIS
SR S Sallee
SR B Harmon
SP D Griner
SR P Perritt
SP B Doak
RP R Geyer
C I Wingo
1B E Konetchy
2B M Huggins
SS C O'Leary
3B M Mowrey
LF L Magee
CF R Oakes
RU S Evans
UT P Whitted

1914 AL

BOSTON
SP R Collins
SR D Leonard
SP R Foster
SR H Bedient
SP E Shore
RP J Wood
RP R Johnson
C- B Carrigan
1B- D Hoblitzel
2B- S Yerkes
SS E Scott
3B L Gardner
LF D Lewis
CF T Speaker
RF H Hooper
UI H Janvrin
OF- W Rehg

CHICAGO
SR J Benz
SR E Cicotte
SR J Scott
SR R Faber
SR R Russell
RS M Wolfgang
RP B Lathrop
C R Schalk
1B J Fournier
2B L Blackburne
SS B Weaver
3B- J Breton
LF R Demmitt
CF P Bodie
RM S Collins
M *J Callahan*

CLEVELAND
SP W Mitchell
SP B Steen
SR R Hagerman
SR G Morton
SR F Blanding
RS A Collamore
RP V Gregg
C- S O'Neill
1B D Johnston
21 N Lajoie
S2 R Chapman
3B T Turner
LF J Graney
CF N Leibold
RM J Jackson
UT- I Olson
M *J Birmingham*

DETROIT
SP H Coveleski
SR H Dauss
SP J Dubuc
SR P Cavet
SR A Main
RS R Reynolds
C O Stanage
1B G Burns
2B M Kavanagh
SS D Bush
3B G Moriarty
LF B Veach
CF T Cobb
RF S Crawford
UO- H High
M *H Jennings*

NEW YORK
SR J Warhop
SP R Caldwell
SP R Fisher
SR R Keating
SP M McHale
RS K Cole
RP B Brown
C- E Sweeney
1B- C Mullen
2B L Boone
SS R Peckinpaugh
3B F Maisel
LO R Hartzell
CF- B Cree
RF D Cook
C- L Nunamaker
M1 *F Chance*

PHILADELPHIA
SP B Shawkey
SR J Bush
SR E Plank
SR W Wyckoff
SP C Bender
RS H Pennock
RS R Bressler
C W Schang
1B S McInnis
2B E Collins
SS J Barry
3B F Baker
LF R Oldring
CF A Strunk
RF E Murphy
M *C Mack*

ST. LOUIS
SP E Hamilton
SP C Weilman
SP B James
SR G Baumgardner
SR W Leverenz
RS R Mitchell
C S Agnew
1B J Leary
2B D Pratt
SS- D Lavan
3B J Austin
LF T Walker
CF B Shotton
RF G Williams
UT- I Howard
SS- B Wares
M *B Rickey*

WASHINGTON
SR W Johnson
SR D Ayers
SR J Shaw
SP J Boehling
SR J Bentley
RS J Engel
RP H Harper
C- J Henry
1B C Gandil
2B R Morgan
SS G McBride
3B E Foster
LM H Shanks
CF C Milan
RF D Moeller
CU- R Williams
M *C Griffith*

1914 FL

BALTIMORE
SP J Quinn
SP G Suggs
SR K Wilhelm
SR F Smith
SP B Bailey
RS S Conley
C F Jacklitsch
1B H Swacina
2B O Knabe
SS M Doolan
3B J Walsh
LI H Simmons
MO V Duncan
RF B Meyer
CU- H Russell

BROOKLYN
SP T Seaton
SP E Lafitte
SP H Finneran
C G Land
1B- H Myers
2U S Hofman
SS- E Gagnier
3B T Wisterzil
UO C Cooper
CF A Shaw
RO S Evans
LU G Anderson
SS- A Halt
M *B Bradley*

BUFFALO
SP F Anderson
SP R Ford
SP G Krapp
SP E Moore
SP A Schulz
RS H Moran
C W Blair
1L J Agler
2B T Downey
SS B Louden
3B F Smith
LF- F Delahanty
CF C Hanford
RF- T McDonald
UO- D Young
M *L Schlafly*

CHICAGO
SR C Hendrix
SR M Fiske
SR E Lange
SP D Watson
SR M Prendergast
RS T McGuire
RP R Johnson
C A Wilson
1B F Beck
2B J Farrell
SS J Tinker
3B R Zeider
LF M Flack
CF D Zwilling
RF A Wickland

INDIANAPOLIS
SP C Falkenberg
SP E Moseley
SP G Kaiserling
SR G Mullin
SR H Billiard
C B Rariden
1B C Carr
2B F LaPorte
SS J Esmond
3B B McKechnie
UT A Scheer
MR V Campbell
UO B Kauff
M *B Phillips*

KANSAS CITY
SP G Packard
SP N Cullop
SR D Stone
SR B Harris
SR P Henning
RS D Adams
RP C Johnson
C T Easterly
1B G Stovall
2B B Kenworthy
S3 P Goodwin
31 G Perring
LF C Chadbourne
CF A Kruger
RF G Gilmore
OI- C Coles

PITTSBURGH
SP E Knetzer
SP H Camnitz
SP W Dickson
SP C Barger
SR M Walker
RS G LeClair
C C Berry
1B H Bradley
2B J Lewis
SS E Holly
3B E Lennox
LF D Jones
CF R Oakes
RI J Savage
M1 *D Gessler*

ST. LOUIS
SP B Groom
SP D Davenport
SR H Keupper
SP M Brown
SP E Willett
RP E Herbert
C M Simon
1B H Miller
2p D Crandall
SS A Bridwell
3B A Boucher
LM W Miller
LM D Drake
RF J Tobin
2S J Misse
IC- G Hartley
M2 *F Jones*

1914 NL

BOSTON
SP D Rudolph
SP B James
SP L Tyler
SR D Crutcher
C H Gowdy
1B B Schmidt
2B J Evers
SS R Maranville
3B- C Deal
LF J Connolly
CF L Mann
RU- L Gilbert
M *G Stallings*

BROOKLYN
SP J Pfeffer
SR E Reulbach
SR P Ragan
SP R Aitchison
SR F Allen
RP N Rucker
C- L McCarty
1B J Daubert
2B G Cutshaw
SS D Egan
3B- R Smith
LF Z Wheat
CF J Dalton
RF C Stengel
M *W Robinson*

CHICAGO
SR L Cheney
SP H Vaughn
SP J Lavender
SR B Humphries
SR G Pierce
RS Z Zabel
RP C Hageman
C R Bresnahan
1B V Saier
2B B Sweeney
SS R Corriden
3B H Zimmerman
LF F Schulte

CF T Leach
RF W Good
C- J Archer
M *H O'Day*

CINCINNATI
SR R Ames
SP R Benton
SR P Douglas
SP E Yingling
SR P Schneider
C T Clarke
1B- D Hoblitzel
2B H Groh
SS *B Herzog*
3B B Niehoff
LF- G Twombly
RM- B Daniels
RF H Moran
C M Gonzalez
UO- D Miller

NEW YORK
SP J Tesreau
SP C Mathewson
SP R Marquard
SP A Demaree
RS A Fromme
C C Meyers
1B F Merkle
2B L Doyle
SS A Fletcher
3B M Stock
LR G Burns
CF B Bescher
UT F Snodgrass
3I- E Grant
C- L McLean
OF- R Murray
RU- D Robertson
M *J McGraw*

PHILADELPHIA
SP G Alexander
SR E Mayer
SR B Tincup
SR R Marshall
SR J Oeschger
RP E Rixey
C B Killefer
1B F Luderus
2B B Byrne
SS- J Martin
3B H Lobert
LO B Becker
CF D Paskert
RF G Cravath
IO S Magee
M *R Dooin*

PITTSBURGH
SP B Adams
SP W Cooper
SR G McQuillan
SP B Harmon
RS J Conzelman
C G Gibson
1B E Konetchy
2B J Viox
SS H Wagner
3B- M Mowrey
LF M Carey
OF- J Kelly
RF- M Mitchell
CF J Kelly
M *F Clarke*

ST. LOUIS
SR S Sallee
SP P Perritt
SP B Doak
SR D Griner
SP H Perdue
RS H Robinson
C F Snyder
1S D Miller
2B *M Huggins*
SS- A Butler
3B Z Beck
LU C Dolan
M1 L Magee
RF C Wilson
OF W Cruise
C- I Wingo

1915 AL

BOSTON
SP R Foster
SR E Shore
SP B Ruth
SR D Leonard
SP J Wood
RS C Mays
RS R Collins
C- P Thomas
1B D Hoblitzel
2B- H Wagner
SS E Scott
3B L Gardner
LF D Lewis
CF T Speaker
RF H Hooper
SI H Janvrin
2B- J Barry
C- H Cady
1U- D Gainer
M *B Carrigan*

CHICAGO
SR R Faber
SR J Scott
SR J Benz
SR R Russell
SR E Cicotte
C R Schalk
1L J Fournier
2B E Collins
SS B Weaver
3B L Blackburne
OI S Collins
ML H Felsch
RF- E Murphy
M *P Rowland*

CLEVELAND
SP G Morton
SP W Mitchell
SP R Hagerman
SR R Walker
SR F Coumbe
RS S Jones
RS O Harstad
C S O'Neill
1B- J Kirke
23 B Wambsganss
SS R Chapman
3B- W Barbare
LF J Graney
CF- N Leibold
RU E Smith
R1- J Jackson
M1 *J Birmingham*
M2 *L Fohl*

DETROIT
SR H Coveleski
SR H Dauss
SP J Dubuc
SR B Boland
C O Stanage
1B G Burns
2B R Young
SS D Bush
3B O Vitt
LF B Veach
CF T Cobb
RF S Crawford
IO M Kavanagh
M *H Jennings*

NEW YORK
SP R Caldwell
SP R Fisher
SP J Warhop
SP B Brown
SR C Pieh
C- L Nunamaker
1B W Pipp
2B L Boone
SS R Peckinpaugh
3B F Maisel
LF R Hartzell
ML H High
RF D Cook
M *B Donovan*

PHILADELPHIA
SP W Wyckoff
SR R Bressler
SP J Bush
SP T Sheehan
SP T Knowlson
RP B Shawkey
C J Lapp
1B S McInnis
2B N Lajoie
S3 L Kopf
IC W Schang
LF R Oldring
UT J Walsh
OI A Strunk
M *C Mack*

ST. LOUIS
SR C Weilman
SP G Lowdermilk
SP E Hamilton
SR B James
SR E Koob
RP P Perryman
C S Agnew
1U- J Leary
2B D Pratt
SS D Lavan
3B J Austin
LF B Shotton
CF T Walker
UT- D Walsh
UT I Howard
C- H Severeid
M *B Rickey*

WASHINGTON
SP W Johnson
SR B Gallia
SP J Boehling
SR D Ayers
SP J Shaw
C J Henry
1B C Gandil
2B- R Morgan
SS G McBride
32 E Foster
L3 H Shanks
CF C Milan
RF D Moeller
IC- R Williams
M *C Griffith*

1915 FL

BALTIMORE
SR J Quinn
SR G Suggs
SR B Bailey
SP C Bender
SP R Johnson
C F Owens
1B- H Swacina
2B *O Knabe*
SS M Doolan
3B J Walsh
UT V Duncan
UO J McCandless
RF- S Evans
LU G Zinn

BROOKLYN
SR H Finneran
SR D Marion
SP T Seaton
SP J Bluejacket
SP E Lafitte
RS B Upham
RP F Wilson
C G Land
1B H Myers
2B *L Magee*
SS F Smith
3S A Halt
LU C Cooper
CF B Kauff
RL G Anderson
M2 *J Ganzel*

BUFFALO
SP A Schulz
SR H Bedient
SP F Anderson
SP G Krapp
SP R Ford
RP R Marshall
RP H Ehmke
C *W Blair*
1B H Chase
2I B Louden
SS R Roach
3B *H Lord*
LF B Meyer
MI C Engle
UO J Dalton
UT S Hofman
C- N Allen
23 T Downey
RU- T McDonald
M1 *L Schlafly*

CHICAGO
SP G McConnell
SP C Hendrix
SR M Prendergast
SR M Brown
SR D Black
RP A Brennan
C A Wilson
1B F Beck
2I R Zeider
SS J Smith
3B- H Fritz
LO L Mann
CF D Zwilling
RL M Flack
C W Fischer
UO- C Hanford
M *J Tinker*

KANSAS CITY
SP N Cullop
SR G Packard
SR C Johnson
SP A Main
SR P Henning
C T Easterly
1B *G Stovall*
2B B Kenworthy
SS J Rawlings
3I G Perring
LF A Shaw
CF C Chadbourne
RF G Gilmore
C- D Brown
S2- P Goodwin
UO- A Kruger

NEWARK
SP E Reulbach
SP E Moseley
SR G Kaiserling
SR H Moran
SP C Falkenberg
C B Rariden
1B E Huhn
2B F LaPorte
SS J Esmond
3B *B McKechnie*
LF A Scheer
CF E Roush
RF V Campbell
M1 *B Phillips*

PITTSBURGH
SP F Allen
SP E Knetzer
SP C Rogge
SR B Hearn
SR C Barger
RS W Dickson
C C Berry
1B E Konetchy
2B S Yerkes
SS M Berghammer
3B M Mowrey
LF A Wickland
CF *R Oakes*
RF J Kelly
2U- J Lewis

ST. LOUIS
SP D Davenport
SP D Crandall
SR E Plank
SR B Groom
SR D Watson
C G Hartley
1B B Borton
2B B Vaughn
SS E Johnson
3B- C Deal
LF W Miller
MR D Drake
RF J Tobin
M *F Jones*

1915 NL

BOSTON
SP D Rudolph
SR T Hughes
SP P Ragan
SP L Tyler
C H Gowdy
1B B Schmidt
2B- J Evers
SS R Maranville
3B R Smith
LF J Connolly
MU S Magee
RF H Moran
2O E Fitzpatrick
UT- D Egan
M *G Stallings*

BROOKLYN
SP J Pfeffer
SR W Dell
SP J Coombs
SP S Smith
SP N Rucker
RS E Appleton
RP P Douglas
C- O Miller
1B J Daubert
2B G Cutshaw
SS O O'Mara
3B G Getz
LF Z Wheat
CF H Myers
RF C Stengel
C- L McCarty
M *W Robinson*

CHICAGO
SP H Vaughn
SR J Lavender
SR G Pierce
SP B Humphries
SR Z Zabel
RP L Cheney
RP P Standridge
RS K Adams
C J Archer
1B V Saier
23 H Zimmerman
SS B Fisher
3B A Phelan
LF F Schulte
CF C Williams
RF W Good
M *R Bresnahan*

CINCINNATI
SR G Dale
SR P Schneider
SR F Toney
SR R Benton
SR K Lear
RS L McKenry
C I Wingo
1B F Mollwitz
2B- B Rodgers
SS *B Herzog*
3B H Groh
LM R Killefer
CF T Leach
RF T Griffith
C T Clarke

NEW YORK
SP J Tesreau
SP P Perritt
SP C Mathewson
SR S Stroud
SP R Marquard
RS R Schauer
RP H Ritter
RP F Schupp
C C Meyers
1B F Merkle
2B L Doyle
SS A Fletcher
3B H Lobert
LF G Burns
CF- F Snodgrass
RF D Robertson
IO- F Brainerd
UI- E Grant
M *J McGraw*

PHILADELPHIA
SP G Alexander
SR E Mayer
SP A Demaree
SP E Rixey
SP G Chalmers
RP S Baumgartner
C B Killefer
1B F Luderus
2B B Niehoff
SS D Bancroft
3B B Byrne
LF B Becker
ML P Whitted
RF G Cravath
MU D Paskert
M *P Moran*

PITTSBURGH
SP B Harmon
SP A Mamaux
SR B Adams
SR W Cooper
SR E Kantlehner
RS G McQuillan
RP J Conzelman
C G Gibson
1B D Johnston
2B J Viox
SS H Wagner
3B D Baird
LF M Carey
CF Z Collins
RF B Hinchman
M *F Clarke*

ST. LOUIS
SR S Sallee
SP B Doak
SR L Meadows
SR D Griner
SR H Robinson
RS H Perdue
RP R Ames
C F Snyder
12 D Miller
2B *M Huggins*
SS A Butler
3B B Betzel
LF B Bescher
MR C Wilson
RM T Long
UO C Dolan
1O H Hyatt

1916 AL

BOSTON
SP B Ruth
SR D Leonard
SR C Mays
SR E Shore
SR R Foster
C P Thomas
1B D Hoblitzel
2B J Barry
SS E Scott
3B L Gardner
LF D Lewis
CF T Walker
RF H Hooper
S2 H Janvrin
C- H Cady
IO- M McNally
M *B Carrigan*

CHICAGO
SR R Russell
SR L Williams
SR R Faber
SR E Cicotte
SR J Scott
RS J Benz
RS M Wolfgang
C R Schalk
1B J Fournier
2B E Collins
SS Z Terry
3S B Weaver
LF J Jackson
CF H Felsch
RF S Collins
M *P Rowland*

CLEVELAND
SR J Bagby
SR S Coveleski
SP G Morton
SR E Klepfer
SR F Coumbe
RS A Gould
RP F Beebe
C S O'Neill
1B C Gandil
2B- I Howard
SS B Wambsganss
32 T Turner
LF J Graney
CF T Speaker
RF B Roth
UI R Chapman
RU- E Smith
M *L Fohl*

DETROIT
SP H Coveleski
SR H Dauss
SR J Dubuc
SR B James
SR G Cunningham
RS B Boland
RP W Mitchell
C O Stanage
1B G Burns
2B R Young
SS D Bush
3B O Vitt
LF B Veach
CF T Cobb
RF S Crawford
UT H Heilmann
M *H Jennings*

NEW YORK
SR B Shawkey
SP G Mogridge
SR R Fisher
SR A Russell
SP N Cullop
RP R Caldwell
RP S Love
C- L Nunamaker
1B W Pipp
2B J Gedeon
SS R Peckinpaugh
3B F Baker
LF H High
CF L Magee
RF- F Gilhooley
UT- P Baumann
M *B Donovan*

PHILADELPHIA
SP E Myers
SP J Bush
SR J Nabors
SR T Sheehan
C- B Meyer
1B S McInnis
2B N Lajoie
SS W Witt
3B C Pick
LC W Schang
CF A Strunk
RF J Walsh
M *C Mack*

ST. LOUIS
SR D Davenport
SR C Weilman
SR E Plank
SR B Groom
SR E Koob
C H Severeid
1B G Sisler
2B D Pratt
SS D Lavan
3B J Austin
LF B Shotton
CF A Marsans
RF W Miller
C- G Hartley
M *F Jones*

WASHINGTON
SR W Johnson
SR B Gallia
SP H Harper
SR D Ayers
SP J Boehling
RS J Shaw
C J Henry
1B J Judge
2B R Morgan
SS G McBride
32 E Foster
LI H Shanks
CF C Milan
RL- D Moeller
M *C Griffith*

1916 NL

BOSTON
SP D Rudolph
SP L Tyler
SP P Ragan
SR J Barnes
SP A Nehf
RS T Hughes
RP F Allen
RS E Reulbach
C H Gowdy
1B E Konetchy
2B- J Evers
SS R Maranville
3B R Smith
LF S Magee
CF F Snodgrass
RF J Wilhoit
UO- Z Collins
2U- D Egan
2R- E Fitzpatrick
M *G Stallings*

BROOKLYN
SP J Pfeffer
SP L Cheney
SR S Smith
SR R Marquard
SP J Coombs
RS W Dell
C- C Meyers
1B J Daubert
2B G Cutshaw
SS I Olson
3B M Mowrey
LF Z Wheat
CF H Myers
RF C Stengel
UO J Johnston
M *W Robinson*

CHICAGO
SP H Vaughn
SR C Hendrix
SR J Lavender
SP G McConnell
SR G Packard
RS M Prendergast
RS T Seaton
C- J Archer
1B V Saier
2B- O Knabe
SS- C Wortman
3B H Zimmerman
LO L Mann
CF C Williams
RF M Flack
32 R Zeider
M *J Tinker*

CINCINNATI
SP F Toney
SR P Schneider
SR A Schulz
SP C Mitchell
SR E Knetzer
RS E Moseley
C *I Wingo*
1U H Chase
2B B Louden
SS- *B Herzog*
3I H Groh
LM G Neale
CF- E Roush
RF T Griffith
CU- T Clarke
M3 *C Mathewson*

NEW YORK
SP J Tesreau
SR P Perritt
SP R Benton
SR F Anderson
SR F Schupp
RP S Sallee
C B Rariden
1B F Merkle
2B L Doyle
SS A Fletcher
3B- B McKechnie
LF G Burns
CF B Kauff
RF D Robertson
M *J McGraw*

PHILADELPHIA
SP G Alexander
SR E Rixey
SP A Demaree
SR E Mayer
SR C Bender
RP G McQuillan
C B Killefer
1B F Luderus
2B B Niehoff
SS D Bancroft
3B M Stock
LF P Whitted
CF D Paskert
RF G Cravath
C- E Burns
M *P Moran*

PITTSBURGH
SP A Mamaux
SR W Cooper
SR F Miller
SR B Harmon
SR E Kantlehner
RS E Jacobs
C- W Schmidt
1B D Johnston
2O- J Farmer
SU H Wagner
3U D Baird
RL- F Schulte
CF M Carey
RU B Hinchman
M *J Callahan*

ST. LOUIS
SR L Meadows
SR R Ames
SP B Doak
SP B Steele
SR H Jasper
RS S Williams
RP M Watson
C M Gonzalez
12 D Miller
2B B Betzel
SS R Corhan
3S R Hornsby
LF B Bescher
CF J Smith
RM C Wilson
RF T Long
C1 F Snyder
UT- A Butler
M *M Huggins*

1917 AL

BOSTON
SP B Ruth
SP D Leonard
SP C Mays
SP E Shore
SR R Foster
RS H Pennock
C- S Agnew
1B D Hoblitzel
2B *J Barry*
SS E Scott
3B L Gardner
LF D Lewis
CF T Walker
RF H Hooper
C- P Thomas

CHICAGO
SR E Cicotte
SR R Faber
SR L Williams
SR R Russell
SP J Scott
RS D Danforth
RP J Benz
C R Schalk
1B C Gandil
2B E Collins
SS S Risberg
3B B Weaver
LF J Jackson
CF H Felsch
RF N Leibold
RF- S Collins
M *P Rowland*

CLEVELAND
SR J Bagby
SP S Coveleski
SR E Klepfer
SR G Morton
SR O Lambeth
RS F Coumbe
C S O'Neill
1B J Harris
2B B Wambsganss
SS R Chapman
3B J Evans
LF J Graney
CF T Speaker
RF B Roth
M L Fohl

DETROIT
SP H Dauss
SR B Boland
SR H Ehmke
SR B James
SP W Mitchell
RS G Cunningham
C O Stanage
1B G Burns
2B R Young
SS D Bush
3B O Vitt
LF B Veach
CF T Cobb
RU H Heilmann
M H Jennings

NEW YORK
SP B Shawkey
SP R Caldwell
SP G Mogridge
SR N Cullop
SR U Shocker
RP R Fisher
RS S Love
RS A Russell
C L Nunamaker
1B W Pipp
2B F Maisel
SS R Peckinpaugh
3B F Baker
LF H High
UO E Miller
RU T Hendryx
M B Donovan

PHILADELPHIA
SP J Bush
SR R Schauer
SR E Myers
SR J Johnson
SP W Noyes
RS S Seibold
CU W Schang
1B S McInnis
2B R Grover
SS W Witt
3B R Bates
LF P Bodie
CF A Strunk
RF- C Jamieson
M C Mack

ST. LOUIS
SP D Davenport
SR A Sothoron
SR B Groom
SR E Koob
SP E Plank
RS T Rogers
C H Severeid
1B G Sisler
2B D Pratt
SS D Lavan
3B J Austin
LF B Shotton
RM B Jacobson
RU T Sloan
UI- E Johnson
OF- W Rumler
M F Jones

WASHINGTON
SR W Johnson
SR J Shaw
SR D Ayers
SR B Gallia
SR G Dumont
RP H Harper
C E Ainsmith
1B J Judge
2B R Morgan
SU H Shanks
32 E Foster
LF M Menosky
CF C Milan
RF S Rice
3U J Leonard
M C Griffith

1917 NL

BOSTON
SR J Barnes
SP D Rudolph
SP L Tyler
SR A Nehf
SR P Ragan
RS F Allen
C W Tragesser
1B E Konetchy
2B J Rawlings
SS R Maranville
3B R Smith
LF J Kelly
CF- R Powell
RF- W Rehg
M G Stallings

BROOKLYN
SP L Cadore
SP J Pfeffer
SP R Marquard
SR S Smith
SR L Cheney
RS J Coombs
C- O Miller
1B J Daubert
2B G Cutshaw
SS I Olson
3B- M Mowrey
LF Z Wheat
MO J Hickman
RF C Stengel
UT J Johnston
MI H Myers
M W Robinson

CHICAGO
SP H Vaughn
SR P Douglas
SR C Hendrix
SP A Demaree
SR P Carter
RS V Aldridge
RS M Prendergast
C- A Wilson
1B F Merkle
2B L Doyle
SS- C Wortman
3B C Deal
LF L Mann
CF C Williams
RL M Flack
RF H Wolter
IO R Zeider
C- R Elliott
M F Mitchell

CINCINNATI
SP F Toney
SP P Schneider
SP M Regan
SR C Mitchell
RS H Eller
C I Wingo
1B H Chase
2B D Shean
SS L Kopf
3B H Groh
LO G Neale
CF E Roush
RF T Griffith
M C Mathewson

NEW YORK
SP F Schupp
SR S Sallee
SR R Benton
SP P Perritt
SR J Tesreau
RS F Anderson
C B Rariden
1B W Holke
2B B Herzog
SS A Fletcher
3B H Zimmerman
LF G Burns
CF B Kauff
RF D Robertson
M J McGraw

PHILADELPHIA
SP G Alexander
SP E Rixey
SR J Oeschger
SR E Mayer
SR J Lavender
RS C Bender
C B Killefer
1B F Luderus
2B B Niehoff
SS D Bancroft
3B M Stock
LF P Whitted
CF D Paskert
RF G Cravath
M P Moran

PITTSBURGH
SP W Cooper
SR E Jacobs
SR F Miller
SR B Grimes
SP B Steele
RS H Carlson
CU W Fischer
1I- H Wagner
2B J Pitler
SS C Ward
3B- T Boeckel
LU C Bigbee
CF M Carey
RF L King
M1 J Callahan
M3 H Bezdek

ST. LOUIS
SP B Doak
SP L Meadows
SR R Ames
SR M Watson
RS G Packard
RS O Horstmann
C F Snyder
1B G Paulette
21 D Miller
SS R Hornsby
3B D Baird
ML W Cruise
UO J Smith
RF T Long
2U B Betzel
CU M Gonzalez
M M Huggins

1918 AL

BOSTON
SP C Mays
SP J Bush
SP S Jones
SP D Leonard
C- S Agnew
1B S McInnis
2B D Shean
SS E Scott
3B- F Thomas
LF- G Whiteman
CF A Strunk
RF H Hooper
Lp B Ruth
CU W Schang
M E Barrow

CHICAGO
SP E Cicotte
SP F Shellenback
SR J Benz
SP R Russell
SP L Williams
RS D Danforth
RP R Faber
C R Schalk
1B C Gandil
2B E Collins
SS B Weaver
3B- F McMullin
LF N Leibold
OI S Collins
RU E Murphy
IO S Risberg
M P Rowland

CLEVELAND
SP S Coveleski
SR J Bagby
SP G Morton
SP F Coumbe
SR J Enzmann
C S O'Neill
1B- D Johnston
2B B Wambsganss
SS R Chapman
3B J Evans
LU J Wood
CF T Speaker
RF B Roth
LU- J Graney
32- T Turner
M L Fohl

DETROIT
SP H Dauss
SP B Boland
SR R Kallio
SR G Cunningham
SP B James
RP E Erickson
C- A Yelle
R1 H Heilmann
2B R Young
SS D Bush
3B O Vitt
LF B Veach
CF T Cobb
RF- G Harper
3B- B Jones

CU- T Spencer
M H Jennings

NEW YORK
SR G Mogridge
SP S Love
SP R Caldwell
SP A Russell
SR H Finneran
RP H Thormahlen
C T Hannah
1B W Pipp
2B D Pratt
SS R Peckinpaugh
3B F Baker
LF P Bodie
CF- E Miller
RF F Gilhooley
C- R Walters
M M Huggins

PHILADELPHIA
SP S Perry
SP V Gregg
SR W Adams
SP M Watson
SP E Myers
RP B Geary
C W McAvoy
1B G Burns
2B- J Dykes
S2 J Dugan
3B L Gardner
LF M Kopp
CF T Walker
RF C Jamieson
C- C Perkins
S2- R Shannon
M C Mack

ST. LOUIS
SP A Sothoron
SP D Davenport
SR T Rogers
SP B Gallia
SP R Wright
RP U Shocker
RP G Lowdermilk
RP B Houck
C L Nunamaker
1B G Sisler
2B J Gedeon
S3 J Austin
3B F Maisel
LM E Smith
ML J Tobin
RF R Demmitt
UO T Hendryx
M1 F Jones
M3 J Burke

WASHINGTON
SR W Johnson
SP H Harper
SR J Shaw
SR D Ayers
C E Ainsmith
1B J Judge
2B R Morgan
SS D Lavan
3B E Foster
LR B Shotton
CF C Milan
RU F Schulte
UT H Shanks
M C Griffith

1918 NL

BOSTON
SP A Nehf
SP P Ragan
SP D Rudolph
SP B Hearn
SP D Fillingim
C A Wilson
1B E Konetchy
2B B Herzog
SU J Rawlings
3B R Smith
UT- R Massey
CF- R Powell
RF A Wickland
M G Stallings

BROOKLYN
SR B Grimes
SP R Marquard
SR L Cheney
SP J Coombs
SP D Robertson
C- O Miller
1B J Daubert
2B M Doolan
SS I Olson
3B O O'Mara
LF Z Wheat
CF H Myers

RU J Johnston
M W Robinson

CHICAGO
SP H Vaughn
SP L Tyler
SP C Hendrix
SP P Douglas
C B Killefer
1B F Merkle
2B R Zeider
SS C Hollocher
3B C Deal
LF L Mann
CF D Paskert
RF M Flack
M F Mitchell

CINCINNATI
SR H Eller
SP P Schneider
SP J Ring
SP F Toney
SP R Bressler
RP D Luque
RS M Regan
C I Wingo
1B- H Chase
2B L Magee
SS L Blackburne
3B H Groh
LU G Neale
CF E Roush
RF T Griffith
1L S Magee
M1 C Mathewson

NEW YORK
SP P Perritt
SR R Causey
SR A Demaree
SP S Sallee
SP F Toney
C L McCarty
1B W Holke
2B L Doyle
SS A Fletcher
3B H Zimmerman
LF G Burns
CF- B Kauff
RF R Youngs
C- B Rariden
MO- J Wilhoit
M J McGraw

PHILADELPHIA
SP M Prendergast
SP B Hogg
SP J Oeschger
SP E Jacobs
SR M Watson
RP E Mayer
RP D Davis
C B Adams
1B F Luderus
2B- P McGaffigan
SS D Bancroft
3B M Stock
LM I Meusel
CF C Williams
RF G Cravath
C- E Burns
LR- J Fitzgerald
M P Moran

PITTSBURGH
SP W Cooper
SP F Miller
SR R Sanders
SP E Mayer
SP B Harmon
RP R Comstock
C W Schmidt
1B F Mollwitz
2B G Cutshaw
SS H Caton
3B B McKechnie
LF C Bigbee
CF M Carey
RF- B Southworth
M H Bezdek

ST. LOUIS
SP B Doak
SP R Ames
SP G Packard
SR B Sherdel
SP L Meadows
RS J May
C M Gonzalez
1B G Paulette
2B- B Fisher
SS R Hornsby
3B D Baird
LF A McHenry
CF C Heathcote
LU- W Cruise
UT- B Betzel
M J Hendricks

1919 AL

BOSTON
SP S Jones
SP H Pennock
SP C Mays
SR A Russell
SP W Hoyt
RP R Caldwell
C W Schang
1B S McInnis
2B- R Shannon
SS E Scott
3B O Vitt
Lp B Ruth
CF- B Roth
RF H Hooper
M E Barrow

CHICAGO
SP E Cicotte
SP L Williams
SR D Kerr
SP R Faber
SP G Lowdermilk
RP D Danforth
C R Schalk
1B C Gandil
2B E Collins
SS S Risberg
3S B Weaver
LF J Jackson
CF H Felsch
RF N Leibold
M K Gleason

CLEVELAND
SP S Coveleski
SP J Bagby
SP G Morton
SP E Myers
SR G Uhle
RP T Phillips
C S O'Neill
1B D Johnston
2B B Wambsganss
SS R Chapman
3B L Gardner
LF J Graney
CF T Speaker
RF E Smith
RO- J Wood
M1 L Fohl

DETROIT
SP H Dauss
SP H Ehmke
SP B Boland
SP D Leonard
SR S Love
RS D Ayers
RP G Cunningham
C E Ainsmith
1B H Heilmann
2B R Young
SS D Bush
3B B Jones
LF B Veach
CF T Cobb
RF I Flagstead
RU C Shorten
M H Jennings

NEW YORK
SP J Quinn
SR B Shawkey
SP H Thormahlen
SR G Mogridge
SP C Mays
RP E Shore
RS A Russell
C- M Ruel
1B W Pipp
2B D Pratt
SS R Peckinpaugh
3B F Baker
LF D Lewis
CF P Bodie
RF S Vick
UT- C Fewster
C- T Hannah
M M Huggins

PHILADELPHIA
SP R Naylor
SR W Kinney
SP J Johnson
SP S Perry
SP T Rogers
C C Perkins
1R G Burns
UT W Witt
SS J Dugan
3B F Thomas
LF- M Kopp
MU T Walker
RU- A Strunk
1U- D Burrus
M C Mack

ST. LOUIS
SR A Sothoron
SP B Gallia
SP U Shocker
SP C Weilman
SP D Davenport
RS L Leifield
RP E Koob
RS R Wright
C H Severeid
1B G Sisler
2B J Gedeon
SS W Gerber
3B J Austin
LF J Tobin
MO B Jacobson
RU E Smith
RU- R Demmitt
M J Burke

WASHINGTON
SP J Shaw
SR W Johnson
SP H Harper
SP E Erickson
C- V Picinich
1B J Judge
2B- H Janvrin
S2 H Shanks
3B E Foster
LF M Menosky
CF C Milan
RF S Rice
CL P Gharrity
IO- J Leonard
MU- B Murphy
M C Griffith

1919 NL

BOSTON
SP D Rudolph
SR D Fillingim
SP A Nehf
SP R Keating
SR A Demaree
RP J Scott
C- H Gowdy
1B W Holke
2B- B Herzog
SS R Maranville
3B T Boeckel
UO- W Cruise
CF- J Riggert
RF R Powell
OI R Smith
2B- J Rawlings
C- A Wilson
M G Stallings

BROOKLYN
SP J Pfeffer
SP L Cadore
SP A Mamaux
SP B Grimes
SR S Smith
RS C Mitchell
C- E Krueger
1B E Konetchy
2U J Johnston
SS I Olson
3B- L Malone
LF Z Wheat
CF H Myers
RF T Griffith
M W Robinson

CHICAGO
SP H Vaughn
SP G Alexander
SP C Hendrix
SR S Martin
SP P Douglas
RS P Carter
C B Killefer
1B F Merkle
2B- C Pick
SS C Hollocher
3B C Deal
LF- L Mann
CF D Paskert
RF M Flack
LU- T Barber
UT- L Magee
M F Mitchell

CINCINNATI
SP H Eller
SP D Ruether
SP S Sallee
SR J Ring
SP R Fisher
RS D Luque
C- I Wingo
1B J Daubert
2B M Rath
SS L Kopf
3B H Groh
LU- R Bressler

CF E Roush
RF G Neale
C- B Rariden
M P Moran

NEW YORK
SP J Barnes
SP R Benton
SP F Toney
SP R Causey
SP A Nehf
RS J Dubuc
CU L McCarty
1B H Chase
2B L Doyle
SS A Fletcher
3B H Zimmerman
LF G Burns
CF B Kauff
RF R Youngs
M J McGraw

PHILADELPHIA
SR G Smith
SP L Meadows
SP E Rixey
SP B Hogg
SP G Packard
RP E Jacobs
RP F Woodward
C- B Adams
1B F Luderus
2B- G Paulette
SS D Bancroft
3B- L Blackburne
UO I Meusel
CF C Williams
UO- L Callahan
RU G Cravath
L2- P Whitted
M1 J Coombs

PITTSBURGH
SP W Cooper
SP B Adams
SP F Miller
SP E Hamilton
SP H Carlson
RP E Mayer
C W Schmidt
1B- F Mollwitz
2B G Cutshaw
SS Z Terry
3B W Barbare
LR B Southworth
ML C Bigbee
RF C Stengel
M H Bezdek

ST. LOUIS
SP B Doak
SR M Goodwin
SR O Tuero
SP J May
SR L Meadows
RS B Sherdel
RP E Jacobs
C V Clemons
12 D Miller
23 M Stock
SS D Lavan
3S R Hornsby
LO A McHenry
MU C Heathcote
RM J Smith
RU J Schultz
LF B Shotton
M B Rickey

1920 AL

BOSTON
SP S Jones
SP J Bush
SP H Pennock
SP H Harper
SR W Hoyt
RP A Russell
RP E Myers
C- R Walters
1B S McInnis
2B M McNally
SS E Scott
3B E Foster
LF M Menosky
CF T Hendryx
RF H Hooper
CM W Schang
3U- O Vitt
M E Barrow

CHICAGO
SP R Faber
SP E Cicotte
SP L Williams
SR D Kerr
SR R Wilkinson
C R Schalk
1B S Collins

2B E Collins
SS S Risberg
3B B Weaver
LF J Jackson
CF H Felsch
RF N Leibold
M K Gleason

CLEVELAND
SR J Bagby
SP S Coveleski
SP R Caldwell
SR G Morton
C S O'Neill
1B D Johnston
2B B Wambsganss
SS R Chapman
3B L Gardner
LF C Jamieson
CF T Speaker
RF E Smith

DETROIT
SP H Ehmke
SP H Dauss
SR R Oldham
SR D Ayers
SP D Leonard
C- O Stanage
1B H Heilmann
2B R Young
SS D Bush
3U B Pinelli
LF B Veach
CF T Cobb
RM C Shorten
RU I Flagstead
3B- B Jones
M H Jennings

NEW YORK
SP C Mays
SP B Shawkey
SP J Quinn
SR R Collins
SR H Thormahlen
RS G Mogridge
C- M Ruel
1B W Pipp
2B D Pratt
SS R Peckinpaugh
3B A Ward
LF D Lewis
CF P Bodie
RL B Ruth
UT B Meusel
C- T Hannah
M M Huggins

PHILADELPHIA
SP S Perry
SR R Naylor
SP S Harriss
SR E Rommel
SR R Moore
RS D Keefe
C C Perkins
1B I Griffin
2B J Dykes
SS C Galloway
3B- F Thomas
LF T Walker
CF F Welch
RO- A Strunk
UI J Dugan
M C Mack

ST. LOUIS
SP D Davis
SR U Shocker
SR A Sothoron
SP C Weilman
SR E Vangilder
RP B Burwell
RP B Bayne
C H Severeid
1B G Sisler
2B J Gedeon
SS W Gerber
3B- J Austin
LU K Williams
CF B Jacobson
RF J Tobin
3U E Smith
M J Burke

WASHINGTON
SR T Zachary
SR E Erickson
SP J Shaw
SR H Courtney
SP W Johnson
RS A Schacht
C P Gharrity
1B J Judge
2B B Harris
SS- J O'Neill
3U F Ellerbe
LF C Milan
CF S Rice
RF B Roth
UT H Shanks
M C Griffith

1920 NL

BOSTON
SP J Oeschger
SR J Scott
SP D Fillingim
SR H McQuillan
C M O'Neil
1B W Holke
2B C Pick
SS R Maranville
3B T Boeckel
LF L Mann
CF R Powell
RF- W Cruise
UO- E Eayrs
2I- H Ford
C- H Gowdy
RO- J Sullivan
M G Stallings

BROOKLYN
SP B Grimes
SP L Cadore
SP J Pfeffer
SR A Mamaux
SP R Marquard
RS S Smith
C- O Miller
1B E Konetchy
2B P Kilduff
SS I Olson
3B J Johnston
LF Z Wheat
CF H Myers
RF T Griffith
RU B Neis
M W Robinson

CHICAGO
SP G Alexander
SP H Vaughn
SP C Hendrix
SP L Tyler
SR S Martin
RS P Carter
C B O'Farrell
1B- F Merkle
S2 Z Terry
SS- C Hollocher
3B C Deal
LF D Robertson
CF D Paskert
RF M Flack
1U T Barber
23- B Herzog
OI- B Twombly
M F Mitchell

CINCINNATI
SP D Ruether
SP J Ring
SR H Eller
SR D Luque
SR R Fisher
RP S Sallee
C I Wingo
1B J Daubert
2B M Rath
SS L Kopf
3B H Groh
LF P Duncan
CF E Roush
RF G Neale
M P Moran

NEW YORK
SP J Barnes
SP A Nehf
SP F Toney
SR P Douglas
SP R Benton
C- F Snyder
1B G Kelly
2B L Doyle
SS D Bancroft
3B F Frisch
LF G Burns
CF L King
RF R Youngs
C- E Smith
M J McGraw

PHILADELPHIA
SP E Rixey
SR G Smith
SP L Meadows
SP R Causey
SP B Hubbell
C- M Wheat
1B G Paulette
2B J Rawlings
SS A Fletcher
3B R Miller
LR I Meusel
CF C Williams
RF C Stengel
2I D Miller
LO- B LeBourveau
M G Cravath

PITTSBURGH
SP W Cooper
SP B Adams
SP H Carlson
SR E Hamilton
SR E Ponder
C W Schmidt
1B C Grimm
2B G Cutshaw
SS H Caton
3B P Whitted
LF C Bigbee
CF M Carey
RF B Southworth
UO F Nicholson
M M Gibson

ST. LOUIS
SR J Haines
SP B Doak
SP F Schupp
SR M Goodwin
RS B Sherdel
C V Clemons
1B J Fournier
2B R Hornsby
SS D Lavan
3B M Stock
LM A McHenry
MO- J Smith
MR C Heathcote
RF J Schultz
UT- H Janvrin
M B Rickey

1921 AL

BOSTON
SP S Jones
SP J Bush
SP H Pennock
SR A Russell
SR E Myers
RS B Karr
RS H Thormahlen
C M Ruel
1B S McInnis
2B D Pratt
SS E Scott
3B E Foster
LF M Menosky
CF N Leibold
RM S Collins
3B- O Vitt
M H Duffy

CHICAGO
SP R Faber
SP D Kerr
SR R Wilkinson
RS S Hodge
RS D McWeeny
C R Schalk
1B E Sheely
2B E Collins
SS E Johnson
3B E Mulligan
LF B Falk
MR A Strunk
RF H Hooper
CF J Mostil
M K Gleason

CLEVELAND
SP S Coveleski
SR G Uhle
SR D Mails
SR J Bagby
SP A Sothoron
RS R Caldwell
RS G Morton
C S O'Neill
1B D Johnston
2B B Wambsganss
SS J Sewell
3B L Gardner
LF C Jamieson
CF T Speaker
RF E Smith
1B- G Burns

DETROIT
SP D Leonard
SP H Dauss
SR R Oldham
SP H Ehmke
SP B Cole
RS C Holling
RS J Middleton
C J Bassler
1B L Blue
2B R Young
SS D Bush
3B B Jones
LF B Veach
CF T Cobb
RF H Heilmann
SU- I Flagstead
UO- C Shorten

NEW YORK
SR C Mays
SR W Hoyt
SP B Shawkey
SR R Collins
SR J Quinn
C W Schang
1B W Pipp
2B A Ward
SR R Peckinpaugh
3B F Baker
LF B Ruth
CF- E Miller
RF B Meusel
M M Huggins

PHILADELPHIA
SR E Rommel
SR S Harriss
SP R Moore
SR B Hasty
SR R Naylor
RS D Keefe
RP H Freeman
C C Perkins
1B J Walker
2B J Dykes
SS C Galloway
3B J Dugan
LF T Walker
CF F Welch
RF W Witt
M C Mack

ST. LOUIS
SP U Shocker
SP D Davis
SR E Vangilder
SR R Kolp
RS B Bayne
RP B Burwell
C H Severeid
1B G Sisler
2B M McManus
SS W Gerber
3B F Ellerbe
LF K Williams
CF B Jacobson
RF J Tobin
M L Fohl

WASHINGTON
SP G Mogridge
SP W Johnson
SP T Zachary
SR E Erickson
SR H Courtney
RS J Acosta
RS A Schacht
C P Gharrity
1B J Judge
2B B Harris
SS F O'Rourke
3B H Shanks
LF B Miller
CF S Rice
UO C Milan
RU- F Brower
M G McBride

1921 NL

BOSTON
SR J Oeschger
SR M Watson
SR H McQuillan
SR D Fillingim
SR J Scott
C M O'Neil
1B W Holke
2B H Ford
SS W Barbare
3B T Boeckel
LF W Cruise
CF R Powell
RF B Southworth
LU- F Nicholson
M F Mitchell

BROOKLYN
SP B Grimes
SP D Ruether
SP L Cadore
SR C Mitchell
SR S Smith
RS J Miljus
C- O Miller
1B R Schmandt
2B P Kilduff
SS I Olson
3B J Johnston
LF Z Wheat
CF H Myers
RF T Griffith
OI B Neis
M W Robinson

CHICAGO
SP G Alexander
SP S Martin
SR B Freeman
SR V Cheeves
SP H Vaughn
RS L York
RP P Jones
C B O'Farrell
1B R Grimes
2B Z Terry
SS C Hollocher
3B C Deal
LO T Barber
CF G Maisel
RF M Flack
IO J Kelleher
UO- B Twombly
M1 J Evers
M2 B Killefer

CINCINNATI
SP D Luque
SP E Rixey
SP R Marquard
SR P Donohue
RS B Napier
C I Wingo
1B J Daubert
23 S Bohne
SS L Kopf
3B H Groh
LF P Duncan
CF E Roush
RU R Bressler
2U- L Fonseca
C B Hargrave
M P Moran

NEW YORK
SR J Barnes
SP A Nehf
SR F Toney
SR P Douglas
SR R Ryan
RP S Sallee
C F Snyder
1B G Kelly
2B- J Rawlings
SS D Bancroft
32 F Frisch
LF- I Meusel
LM G Burns
RF R Youngs
C- E Smith
M J McGraw

PHILADELPHIA
SP J Ring
SP B Hubbell
SR G Smith
SP L Meadows
SP J Winters
RP H Betts
C F Bruggy
1B- E Konetchy
2B- J Smith
SS F Parkinson
UT R Wrightstone
RL- I Meusel
CF C Williams
RL B LeBourveau
1R- C Lee
UI- D Miller
M1 B Donovan
M2 K Wilhelm

PITTSBURGH
SP W Cooper
SR W Glazner
SP E Hamilton
SP B Adams
SP J Morrison
RS J Zinn
RS H Carlson
C W Schmidt
1B C Grimm
2B G Cutshaw
SS R Maranville
3B C Barnhart
LF C Bigbee
CF M Carey
RF P Whitted
23 C Tierney
M M Gibson

ST. LOUIS
SP J Haines
SP B Doak
SP B Pertica
SR R Walker
SP J Pfeffer
RS B Sherdel
RP L North
C V Clemons
1B J Fournier
2B R Hornsby
SS D Lavan
3B M Stock
LF A McHenry
MU L Mann
RU J Smith
RU- J Schultz
M B Rickey

1922 AL

BOSTON
SP J Quinn
SP R Collins
SP H Pennock
SR A Ferguson
SR B Piercy
RS B Karr
RS A Russell
RP C Fullerton
C M Ruel
1B G Burns
2B D Pratt
SS- J Mitchell
3B- J Dugan
LU M Menosky
CF- N Leibold
OI S Collins
LU J Harris
M H Duffy

CHICAGO
SP R Faber
SP C Robertson
SP D Leverett
SP T Blankenship
RS S Hodge
C R Schalk
1B E Sheely
2B E Collins
SS E Johnson
3B E Mulligan
LF B Falk
CF J Mostil
RF H Hooper
3B- H McClellan
MU- A Strunk
M K Gleason

CLEVELAND
SR G Uhle
SP S Coveleski
SR G Morton
SR D Mails
SR J Bagby
RS J Lindsey
C S O'Neill
1B S McInnis
2B B Wambsganss
SS J Sewell
3B L Gardner
LF C Jamieson
CF T Speaker
RF J Wood
UT- R Stephenson

DETROIT
SR H Ehmke
SP H Pillette
SR H Dauss
SR R Oldham
SR O Olsen
RS S Johnson
C J Bassler
1B L Blue
2B G Cutshaw
SS T Rigney
3B B Jones
LF B Veach
CF T Cobb
RF H Heilmann
IO- D Clark
3U- F Haney

NEW YORK
SP B Shawkey
SR S Jones
SP W Hoyt
SP J Bush
SP C Mays
RP G Murray
C W Schang
1B W Pipp
2B A Ward
SS E Scott
3B- J Dugan
LR B Ruth
CF W Witt
RL B Meusel
M M Huggins

PHILADELPHIA
SR E Rommel
SR S Harriss
SP B Hasty
SR F Heimach
SP R Naylor
RP J Sullivan
RP C Eckert
C C Perkins
1B J Hauser
2B R Young
SS C Galloway
3B J Dykes
LF T Walker
MR B Miller
RF F Welch
MR B McGowan
M C Mack

ST. LOUIS
SR U Shocker
SR E Vangilder
SP D Davis
SR R Kolp
SR R Wright
RS H Pruett
RS B Bayne
C H Severeid
1B G Sisler
2B M McManus
SS W Gerber
3B- F Ellerbe
LF K Williams
CF B Jacobson
RF J Tobin
M L Fohl

WASHINGTON
SR W Johnson
SP G Mogridge
SR R Francis
SP T Zachary
SR E Erickson
RS J Brillheart
C P Gharrity
1B J Judge
2B B Harris
SS R Peckinpaugh
3B- B LaMotte
LF G Goslin
CF S Rice
RF F Brower
3L- H Shanks
M C Milan

1922 NL

BOSTON
SR M Watson
SP F Miller
SR R Marquard
SR J Oeschger
SR H McQuillan
RS D Fillingim
RS T McNamara
RS G Braxton
C- M O'Neil
1B W Holke
2S L Kopf
SS H Ford
3B T Boeckel
LM- A Nixon
CF R Powell
RL W Cruise
UI W Barbare
C- H Gowdy
RL- F Nicholson
M F Mitchell

BROOKLYN
SP D Ruether
SP B Grimes
SP D Vance
SP L Cadore
SR H Shriver
RS S Smith
RS A Mamaux
C- H DeBerry
1B R Schmandt
UI J Johnston
2S I Olson
3B A High
LF Z Wheat
CF H Myers
RF T Griffith
RU B Griffith
M W Robinson

CHICAGO
SP V Aldridge
SP G Alexander
SR T Osborne
SR V Cheeves
SR P Jones
RS T Kaufmann
RS G Stueland
C B O'Farrell
1B R Grimes
2B Z Terry
SS C Hollocher
3B M Krug
LF H Miller
CF J Statz
RU B Friberg
OI- T Barber
M B Killefer

CINCINNATI
SP E Rixey
SR J Couch
SP D Luque
SP P Donohue
SR C Keck
RP D Gillespie
C B Hargrave
1B J Daubert
2B S Bohne
SS I Caveney
3B B Pinelli
LF P Duncan
MR G Burns
RF G Harper
2B- L Fonseca
C- I Wingo
M P Moran

NEW YORK
SP A Nehf
SP J Barnes
SR R Ryan
SP P Douglas
RP C Jonnard
RP R Causey
RP V Barnes
C F Snyder
1B G Kelly
23 F Frisch
SS D Bancroft
3B H Groh
LF I Meusel
CF- C Stengel
RF R Youngs
CF- B Cunningham
2B- J Rawlings
C- E Smith
M J McGraw

PHILADELPHIA
SP J Ring
SP L Meadows
SR G Smith
SP B Hubbell
SR L Weinert
RS J Winters
RS J Singleton
C B Henline
1B R Leslie
2B F Parkinson
SS A Fletcher
3B G Rapp
LU C Lee
CF C Williams
RF C Walker
UI R Wrightstone
M K Wilhelm

PITTSBURGH
SP W Cooper
SR J Morrison
SP W Glazner
SP B Adams
SR E Hamilton
RS H Carlson
RP C Yellowhorse
C J Gooch
1B C Grimm
2B C Tierney
SS R Maranville
3B P Traynor
LF C Bigbee
CF M Carey
RF- R Russell
M1 M Gibson
M2 B McKechnie

ST. LOUIS
SR J Pfeffer
SR B Sherdel
SP J Haines
SP B Doak
SR B Pertica
RS L North
RP C Barfoot
C E Ainsmith
1B J Fournier
2B R Hornsby
SS S Toporcer
3B M Stock
UO J Schultz
MR J Smith
RF- M Flack
SS- D Lavan
MU- L Mann
M B Rickey

1923 AL

BOSTON
SP H Ehmke
SR J Quinn
SP A Ferguson
SP B Piercy
SR G Murray

RS C Fullerton
RP L O'Doul
C- V Picinich
1B G Burns
2S- C Fewster
SS- J Mitchell
32 H Shanks
LF J Harris
MU D Reichle
RF I Flagstead
MR S Collins
32 N McMillan
UO- M Menosky
M F Chance

CHICAGO
SP C Robertson
SP R Faber
SR M Cvengros
SR T Blankenship
SR D Leverett
RS S Thurston
C R Schalk
1B E Sheely
2B E Collins
SS H McClellan
3B W Kamm
LF- B Falk
CF J Mostil
RF H Hooper
LU- R Elsh
M K Gleason

CLEVELAND
SR G Uhle
SP S Coveleski
SR J Edwards
SR J Shaute
SR G Morton
RS S Smith
RS D Metivier
RP D Boone
C S O'Neill
1B F Brower
2B B Wambsganss
SS J Sewell
3B R Lutzke
LF C Jamieson
CF T Speaker
RF H Summa
C G Myatt
2U- R Stephenson

DETROIT
SR H Dauss
SR H Pillette
SR K Holloway
SR S Johnson
RS B Cole
RS R Francis
C J Bassler
1B L Blue
UI F Haney
SS T Rigney
3B B Jones
UO B Veach
CF T Cobb
RF H Heilmann
UO B Fothergill
LU H Manush
2I D Pratt

NEW YORK
SR J Bush
SP B Shawkey
SR S Jones
SP H Pennock
SP W Hoyt
C- W Schang
1B W Pipp
2B A Ward
SS E Scott
3B J Dugan
LR B Meusel
CF W Witt
OI B Ruth
M M Huggins

PHILADELPHIA
SR E Rommel
SP B Hasty
SR S Harriss
SR F Heimach
SP R Naylor
RS R Walberg
RP C Ogden
C C Perkins
1B J Hauser
2B J Dykes
SS C Galloway
3B S Hale
LF B Miller
CF W Matthews
RF F Welch
UO B McGowan
M C Mack

ST. LOUIS
SP E Vangilder
SP U Shocker
SP D Danforth
SR R Kolp
SP D Davis
RS H Pruett
RP C Root
C H Severeid
1B D Schliebner
2B M McManus
SS W Gerber
3B- G Robertson
LF K Williams
CF B Jacobson
RF J Tobin
CU- P Collins
3B- H Ezzell
M1 L Fohl
M2 J Austin

WASHINGTON
SP W Johnson
SP G Mogridge
SP T Zachary
SR P Zahniser
SP C Warmoth
RS A Russell
C M Ruel
1B J Judge
2B B Harris
SS R Peckinpaugh
3B O Bluege
LF G Goslin
CF N Leibold
RF S Rice
MU J Evans
IC P Gharrity
M D Bush

1923 NL

BOSTON
SP R Marquard
SR J Genewich
SP J Barnes
SR J Oeschger
SR T McNamara
RS L Benton
RS D Fillingim
RS J Cooney
C M O'Neil
1B S McInnis
2B H Ford
SS B Smith
3B T Boeckel
LF G Felix
CF R Powell
RF B Southworth
MU- A Nixon
M F Mitchell

BROOKLYN
SP B Grimes
SP D Vance
SP D Ruether
SR L Dickerman
RS A Decatur
C Z Taylor
1B J Fournier
2B- I Olson
2S J Johnston
3S A High
LF Z Wheat
MU B Neis
RF T Griffith
OI G Bailey
C- H DeBerry
LU- B Griffith
M W Robinson

CHICAGO
SP G Alexander
SP V Aldridge
SP T Kaufmann
SR T Osborne
SR V Keen
RS N Dumovich
RP F Fussell
C B O'Farrell
1B- R Grimes
2B G Grantham
SS S Adams
3B B Friberg
LF H Miller
CF J Statz
RF C Heathcote
IC- G Hartnett
M B Killefer

CINCINNATI
SP D Luque
SP E Rixey
SP P Donohue
SP R Benton
RS C Keck
C B Hargrave
1B J Daubert
23 S Bohne
SS I Caveney
3B B Pinelli
LF P Duncan
CF E Roush
RF G Burns
M P Moran

NEW YORK
SP H McQuillan
SR J Scott
SP A Nehf
SP J Bentley
SP M Watson
RS R Ryan
RP C Jonnard
RP V Barnes
C F Snyder
1B G Kelly
2B F Frisch
SS D Bancroft
3B H Groh
LF I Meusel
MU- B Cunningham
RF R Youngs
S3 T Jackson
MU- J O'Connell
M J McGraw

PHILADELPHIA
SP J Ring
SP W Glazner
SR L Weinert
SR C Mitchell
SR P Behan
RS R Head
RS B Hubbell
C B Henline
1B W Holke
2B C Tierney
SS H Sand
3I R Wrightstone
LU J Mokan
CF C Williams
RF C Walker
LR C Lee
C- J Wilson
M A Fletcher

PITTSBURGH
SP J Morrison
SP W Cooper
SP L Meadows
SP B Adams
SR E Hamilton
C W Schmidt
1B C Grimm
2B J Rawlings
SS R Maranville
3B P Traynor
LF C Bigbee
CF M Carey
RF C Barnhart
RF R Russell
M B McKechnie

ST. LOUIS
SP J Haines
SR B Sherdel
SP F Toney
SP B Doak
SP J Pfeffer
RS J Stuart
RP C Barfoot
RP L North
C- E Ainsmith
1B J Bottomley
2B R Hornsby
SS H Freigau
3B M Stock
LO J Smith
CF H Myers
RF M Flack
LF R Blades
2S S Toporcer
CF- H Mueller
M B Rickey

1924 AL

BOSTON
SP H Ehmke
SP A Ferguson
SR J Quinn
SR C Fullerton
SP B Piercy
RS G Murray
C S O'Neill
1B J Harris
2B B Wambsganss
SS- D Lee
3B D Clark
LF B Veach
CF I Flagstead
RF I Boone
OI- S Collins
3U- H Ezzell
M L Fohl

CHICAGO
SP S Thurston
SR T Lyons
SR R Faber
SR T Blankenship
SR M Cvengros
RS S Connally
RS D Leverett
RP C Robertson
C B Crouse
1B E Sheely
2B E Collins
SU B Barrett
3B W Kamm
LF B Falk
CF J Mostil
RF H Hooper
CF M Archdeacon
M1 J Evers
M2 E Walsh
M3 Collins
M4 J Evers

CLEVELAND
SR J Shaute
SR S Smith
SP S Coveleski
SP G Uhle
RS D Metivier
C G Myatt
1B G Burns
2B C Fewster
SS J Sewell
3B R Lutzke
LF C Jamieson
CF T Speaker
RF H Summa
UO P McNulty

DETROIT
SP E Whitehill
SP R Collins
SR L Stoner
SR B Cole
SR E Wells
RS K Holloway
RS H Dauss
RS S Johnson
C J Bassler
1B L Blue
21 D Pratt
SS T Rigney
3B B Jones
LF H Manush
CF T Cobb
RF H Heilmann
3U- F Haney
UO- A Wingo

NEW YORK
SP H Pennock
SP J Bush
SR W Hoyt
SR B Shawkey
SR S Jones
RP M Gaston
C W Schang
1B W Pipp
2B A Ward
SS E Scott
3B J Dugan
LR B Meusel
CF W Witt
RL B Ruth
M M Huggins

PHILADELPHIA
SP E Rommel
SR F Heimach
SR S Baumgartner
SR D Burns
SR D Gray
RS R Meeker
RS S Harriss
RP B Hasty
C C Perkins
1B J Hauser
2B- M Bishop
SS C Galloway
3B- H Riconda
LF- B Lamar
ML A Simmons
RU B Miller
2I J Dykes
RF F Welch
3U- S Hale
M C Mack

ST. LOUIS
SP U Shocker
SR D Danforth
SR E Wingard
SP D Davis
SR E Vangilder
RS R Kolp
RS G Lyons
RP H Pruett
RP B Bayne
C H Severeid
1B G Sisler
2B M McManus
SS W Gerber
3B G Robertson
LF K Williams
CF B Jacobson
RF J Tobin
UO- J Evans

WASHINGTON
SP W Johnson
SP G Mogridge
SP T Zachary
SR J Martina
SP C Ogden
RS F Marberry
RP A Russell
RP B Speece
C M Ruel
1B J Judge
2B B Harris
SS R Peckinpaugh
3B O Bluege
LF G Goslin
MU- N Leibold
RF S Rice

1924 NL

BOSTON
SP J Barnes
SP J Genewich
SR J Cooney
SR T McNamara
SR A Yeargin
RS L Benton
C M O'Neil
1B S McInnis
2B C Tierney
SS B Smith
3B E Padgett
LF B Cunningham
MU- G Felix
RF C Stengel
SS- D Bancroft
CU- F Gibson
M2 R Rudolph
M3 D Bancroft

BROOKLYN
SP B Grimes
SP D Vance
SP D Ruether
SP B Doak
SP T Osborne
RS A Decatur
C Z Taylor
1B J Fournier
2B A High
SS- J Mitchell
3B M Stock
LF Z Wheat
CF E Brown
RF T Griffith
C- H DeBerry
SU- J Johnston
UO- B Neis
M W Robinson

CHICAGO
SP V Aldridge
SR V Keen
SP T Kaufmann
SR E Jacobs
SP G Alexander
RS S Blake
RP R Wheeler
C G Hartnett
1B H Cotter
2B G Grantham
SS S Adams
3B B Friberg
LF D Grigsby
CF J Statz
RF C Heathcote
M B Killefer

CINCINNATI
SP E Rixey
SR C Mays
SP P Donohue
SP D Luque
SR T Sheehan
RS R Benton
RP J May
C B Hargrave
1B J Daubert
2B H Critz
SS I Caveney
3B B Pinelli
LF P Duncan
CF E Roush
RF C Walker
UI S Bohne
UT R Bressler
RF G Burns
M J Hendricks

NEW YORK
SP V Barnes
SP J Bentley
SP H McQuillan
SR A Nehf
SP W Dean
RS R Ryan
RP M Watson
RP C Jonnard
C F Snyder
1B G Kelly
2B F Frisch
SS T Jackson
3B H Groh
LF I Meusel
CF H Wilson
RF R Youngs
MU B Southworth
C- H Gowdy
UM- B Terry
M1 J McGraw
M2 H Jennings
M3 J McGraw

PHILADELPHIA
SP J Ring
SR H Carlson
SR B Hubbell
SP C Mitchell
SR W Glazner
RS H Betts
RS J Couch
CU B Henline
1B W Holke
2B H Ford
SS H Sand
3B R Wrightstone
LF J Mokan
CF C Williams
RF G Harper
C J Wilson
LR- J Schultz
M A Fletcher

PITTSBURGH
SP W Cooper
SR R Kremer
SR J Morrison
SP L Meadows
SR E Yde
RP A Stone
C- J Gooch
1B C Grimm
2B R Maranville
SS G Wright
3B P Traynor
LR K Cuyler
CF M Carey
RF C Barnhart
LF- C Bigbee
M B McKechnie

ST. LOUIS
SP J Haines
SP A Sothoron
SP J Stuart
SR E Dyer
SP L Dickerman
RS B Sherdel
RS H Bell
C M Gonzalez
1B J Bottomley
2B R Hornsby
SS J Cooney
3B H Freigau
RF L Blades
CF- W Holm
RO J Smith
OI- H Mueller
M B Rickey

1925 AL

BOSTON
SP H Ehmke
SR T Wingfield
SR R Ruffing
SR P Zahniser
SP J Quinn
RS B Ross
RS O Fuhr
C- V Picinich
1B P Todt
2B B Wambsganss
SS- D Lee
3B D Prothro
OF R Carlyle
CF I Flagstead
RF I Boone
OF T Vache
M L Fohl

CHICAGO
SR T Lyons
SP R Faber
SR T Blankenship
SR S Thurston
SP C Robertson
RP S Connally
RS M Cvengros
C R Schalk
1B E Sheely
2B E Collins
SS I Davis
3B W Kamm
LF B Falk
CF J Mostil
RF H Hooper
2R- B Barrett
M Collins

CLEVELAND
SP S Smith
SP G Uhle
SP B Karr
SR J Miller
SR G Buckeye
RP J Shaute
C G Myatt
1B G Burns
2B C Fewster
SS J Sewell
3B- R Lutzke
LF C Jamieson
CF T Speaker
RO P McNulty
32 F Spurgeon
RU- C Lee

DETROIT
SP E Whitehill
SP H Dauss
SR K Holloway
SR L Stoner
SP R Collins
RS E Wells
RP D Leonard
RP J Doyle
C J Bassler
1B L Blue
2B F O'Rourke
SS J Tavener
3B F Haney
LF A Wingo
CF T Cobb
RF H Heilmann
MU H Manush
2U- L Burke

NEW YORK
SR H Pennock
SR W Hoyt
SR S Jones
SR U Shocker
SR B Shawkey
RP H Johnson
RS A Ferguson
C B Bengough
1B L Gehrig
2B A Ward
SS P Wanninger
3B J Dugan
LR B Meusel
CF E Combs
RL B Ruth
UO- B Paschal
M M Huggins

PHILADELPHIA
SR E Rommel
SR S Harriss
SP D Gray
SR R Walberg
SR L Grove
RS S Baumgartner
RP J Quinn
C M Cochrane
1B J Poole
2B M Bishop
SS C Galloway
3B S Hale
LF B Lamar
CF A Simmons
RF B Miller
32 J Dykes
RU- F Welch
M C Mack

ST. LOUIS
SR M Gaston
SP J Bush
SR D Davis
SR D Danforth
SP J Giard
RS E Vangilder
RS E Wingard
C- L Dixon
1B G Sisler
2B M McManus
SS B LaMotte
3B G Robertson
LF K Williams
CF B Jacobson
RU H Rice
UO H Bennett
OI- J Tobin

WASHINGTON
SP S Coveleski
SP W Johnson
SP D Ruether
SP T Zachary
RP F Marberry
RS V Gregg
RP A Russell
C M Ruel
1B J Judge
2B B Harris
SS R Peckinpaugh
3B O Bluege
LF G Goslin
CF E McNeely
RF S Rice
1R J Harris

1925 NL

BOSTON
SP J Cooney
SP J Barnes
SR L Benton
SR J Genewich
SR S Graham
RS R Ryan
RP B Smith
RS R Marquard
RP I Kamp
C F Gibson
1B D Burrus
2B- D Gautreau
SS D Bancroft
3B W Marriott
LF D Harris
ML G Felix
RF J Welsh
MU B Neis
2I- E Padgett

BROOKLYN
SP D Vance
SP B Grimes
SR R Ehrhardt
SR T Osborne
SP J Petty
RS B Hubbell
C Z Taylor
1B J Fournier
2B M Stock
SS J Mitchell
3U J Johnston
LF Z Wheat
CF E Brown
RF D Cox
3U C Tierney
M W Robinson

CHICAGO
SP G Alexander
SP S Blake
SP W Cooper
SP T Kaufmann
SR G Bush
RS P Jones
RS V Keen
C G Hartnett
1B C Grimm
2B S Adams
SS- R Maranville
3B H Freigau
LF- A Jahn
CF- M Brooks
RF C Heathcote
M1 B Killefer
M2 W Maranville
M3 G Gibson

CINCINNATI
SP P Donohue
SP D Luque
SP E Rixey
SR R Benton
RS J May
RP H Biemiller
C- B Hargrave
1B- W Holke
2B H Critz
SS I Caveney
3B B Pinelli
LF B Zitzmann
CF E Roush
RF C Walker
1L R Bressler
LR E Smith
M J Hendricks

NEW YORK
SP J Scott
SP V Barnes
SP K Greenfield
SP J Bentley
SP A Nehf
RS W Dean
RP W Huntzinger
C F Snyder
1B B Terry
2U G Kelly

SS T Jackson
3B F Lindstrom
LF I Meusel
CF B Southworth
RF R Youngs
UI F Frisch
M1 J McGraw
M2 H Jennings
M3 J McGraw

PHILADELPHIA
SP J Ring
SP H Carlson
SP C Mitchell
SR A Decatur
RS J Knight
RS H Betts
RS J Couch
C J Wilson
1B C Hawks
2B- B Friberg
SS H Sand
3B C Huber
LF- G Burns
UO G Harper
RF C Williams
21 L Fonseca
CU B Henline
UT R Wrightstone
M A Fletcher

PITTSBURGH
SP L Meadows
SR R Kremer
SR J Morrison
SP V Aldridge
SP E Yde
RS B Adams
RP T Sheehan
C E Smith
1B G Grantham
2B E Moore
SS G Wright
3B P Traynor
LF C Barnhart
CF M Carey
RF K Cuyler
C- J Gooch
M B McKechnie

ST. LOUIS
SP J Haines
SR B Sherdel
SP F Rhem
SP A Sothoron
SP A Reinhart
RS L Dickerman
RP D Mails
C B O'Farrell
1B J Bottomley
2B R Hornsby
SS- S Toporcer
3B L Bell
LF R Blades
MU- H Mueller
RL C Hafey
RU- M Flack
UO- J Smith
M1 B Rickey

1926 AL

BOSTON
SP H Wiltse
SR T Wingfield
SP P Zahniser
SR R Ruffing
SP S Harriss
RS T Welzer
RP F Heimach
RS J Russell
RP H Ehmke
C A Gaston
1B P Todt
2B B Regan
SS T Rigney
3B F Haney
OF S Rosenthal
CF I Flagstead
MR B Jacobson
M L Fohl

CHICAGO
SP T Lyons
SR T Thomas
SP T Blankenship
SP R Faber
SR J Edwards
RS S Thurston
RS S Connally
C- R Schalk
1B E Sheely
2B E Collins
SU B Hunnefield
3B W Kamm
LF B Falk
CF J Mostil
RF B Barrett
RU- S Harris
M Collins

CLEVELAND
SP G Uhle
SP D Levsen
SP J Shaute
SP S Smith
SR G Buckeye
RS B Karr
C L Sewell
1B G Burns
2B F Spurgeon
SS J Sewell
3B R Lutzke
LF C Jamieson
CF T Speaker
RF H Summa

DETROIT
SP E Whitehill
SR S Gibson
SR E Wells
SR L Stoner
SR R Collins
RS K Holloway
RS H Dauss
RS A Johns
C- C Manion
1B L Blue
2B C Gehringer
SS J Tavener
3B J Warner
LO B Fothergill
CF H Manush
RF H Heilmann
1U J Neun
32 F O'Rourke
LU A Wingo
UO- T Cobb

NEW YORK
SP H Pennock
SP U Shocker
SR W Hoyt
SR S Jones
SR M Thomas
RS B Shawkey
RP G Braxton
C P Collins
1B L Gehrig
2B T Lazzeri
SS M Koenig
3B J Dugan
LR B Meusel
CF E Combs
LR B Ruth
UO B Paschal
M M Huggins

PHILADELPHIA
SR L Grove
SR E Rommel
SR J Quinn
SR R Walberg
SR D Gray
SP H Ehmke
RP J Pate
C M Cochrane
1B J Poole
2B M Bishop
SS C Galloway
32 J Dykes
LF B Lamar
CF A Simmons
RF W French
3U S Hale
1U J Hauser
M C Mack

ST. LOUIS
SP T Zachary
SP M Gaston
SR E Vangilder
SR E Wingard
RS W Ballou
C W Schang
1B G Sisler
2B S Melillo
SS W Gerber
32 M McManus
LF K Williams
RM H Rice
RL B Miller
UO- H Bennett
MU- C Durst
CU- P Hargrave
3U- G Robertson

WASHINGTON
SP W Johnson
SP S Coveleski
SP D Ruether
SP A Crowder
SR C Ogden
RS F Marberry
RP B Morrell
RP A Ferguson
C M Ruel
1B J Judge
2B B Harris
SS B Myer
3B O Bluege
LM E McNeely
LM G Goslin
RF S Rice
UT J Harris

1926 NL

BOSTON
SR L Benton
SR J Genewich
SR B Smith
SP J Werts
SR B Hearn
RS G Mogridge
RP H Goldsmith
C Z Taylor
1B D Burrus
2B- D Gautreau
SS D Bancroft
32 A High
ML E Brown
MO J Smith
RF J Welsh
3S E Taylor
LU- F Wilson

BROOKLYN
SP J Petty
SP B Grimes
SR D McWeeny
SR B McGraw
SP D Vance
RP J Barnes
RP R Ehrhardt
C- M O'Neil
1O B Herman
2B C Fewster
S3 J Butler
3B W Marriott
LF Z Wheat
ML G Felix
RF D Cox
UO M Jacobson
1U- J Fournier
C- C Hargreaves
SS- R Maranville
M W Robinson

CHICAGO
SR C Root
SR S Blake
SP T Kaufmann
SR P Jones
SR G Bush
RS B Osborn
C G Hartnett
1B C Grimm
2B S Adams
SS J Cooney
3B H Freigau
LF- R Stephenson
CF H Wilson
RF C Heathcote
C- M Gonzalez
OI- P Scott
M J McCarthy

CINCINNATI
SR P Donohue
SP C Mays
SP D Luque
SP E Rixey
RS J May
RS R Lucas
C B Hargrave
1B W Pipp
2B H Critz
SS- F Emmer
3B C Dressen
LU C Christensen
CF E Roush
RF C Walker
LF- R Bressler
C- V Picinich
M J Hendricks

NEW YORK
SR J Scott
SR K Greenfield
SR F Fitzsimmons
SP V Barnes
SR J Ring
RS H McQuillan
RP C Davies
C- P Florence
1B G Kelly
2B F Frisch
SS T Jackson
3B F Lindstrom
LF I Meusel
CF T Tyson
RF R Youngs
UT B Terry
UO- H Mueller
M J McGraw

PHILADELPHIA
SP H Carlson
SP W Dean
SP C Mitchell
SR C Willoughby
SR D Ulrich
RS J Knight
RS R Pierce
RP E Baecht
C- J Wilson
1U- J Bentley
2B B Friberg
SS H Sand
3B C Huber
LR J Mokan
ML F Leach
RF C Williams
C B Henline
CF A Nixon
IO R Wrightstone
M A Fletcher

PITTSBURGH
SR R Kremer
SP L Meadows
SP V Aldridge
SP E Yde
SR D Songer
RS J Morrison
RP J Bush
C E Smith
1B G Grantham
2S H Rhyne
SS G Wright
3B P Traynor
ML K Cuyler
CF- M Carey
RF P Waner
C- J Gooch
M B McKechnie

ST. LOUIS
SP F Rhem
SP B Sherdel
SR J Haines
SP V Keen
SP G Alexander
RS A Reinhart
RP B Hallahan
RS S Johnson
C B O'Farrell
1B J Bottomley
2B R Hornsby
SS T Thevenow
3B L Bell
LF R Blades
CF T Douthit
RF B Southworth
OF- C Hafey

1927 AL

BOSTON
SP H Wiltse
SP S Harriss
SR T Welzer
SR D Mac Fayden
SP R Ruffing
RS J Russell
RS D Lundgren
C G Hartley
1B P Todt
2B B Regan
SS B Myer
3U- B Rogell
LO W Shaner
CF I Flagstead
RF J Tobin
RL C Carlyle
UI J Rothrock
C- F Hofmann
3U- R Rollings
M B Carrigan

CHICAGO
SP T Lyons
SP T Thomas
SP T Blankenship
SR S Connally
SP R Faber
RS E Jacobs
RP B Cole
C- H McCurdy
1B B Clancy
2B A Ward
SU B Hunnefield
3B W Kamm
LF B Falk
CF A Metzler
RF B Barrett
C- B Crouse
M R Schalk

CLEVELAND
SR W Hudlin
SR J Shaute
SR G Buckeye
SR J Miller
SP G Uhle
RP G Grant
C L Sewell
1B G Burns
2B L Fonseca
SS J Sewell
3B R Lutzke
LF C Jamieson
CF- I Eichrodt
RF H Summa
3B- J Hodapp
M J McCallister

DETROIT
SR E Whitehill
SR L Stoner
SR K Holloway
SP S Gibson
SR R Collins
RS O Carroll
RP G Smith
C- L Woodall
1B L Blue
2B C Gehringer
SS J Tavener
3B J Warner
LF B Fothergill
CF H Manush
RF H Heilmann
UI M McManus
C- J Bassler
1U- J Neun
M G Moriarty

NEW YORK
SR W Hoyt
SP H Pennock
SP U Shocker
SP D Ruether
SP G Pipgras
RS W Moore
C- P Collins
1B L Gehrig
2I T Lazzeri
SS M Koenig
3B J Dugan
LR B Meusel
CF E Combs
RL B Ruth
M M Huggins

PHILADELPHIA
SR L Grove
SR R Walberg
SP J Quinn
SP H Ehmke
SR E Rommel
RS D Gray
RP J Pate
C M Cochrane
1I J Dykes
2B M Bishop
SS J Boley
3B S Hale
LF- B Lamar
CF A Simmons
RM T Cobb
2U E Collins
RU W French
SS- C Galloway
LU- Z Wheat
M C Mack

ST. LOUIS
SP M Gaston
SR E Vangilder
SP S Jones
SP L Stewart
SR E Wingard
RS E Nevers
C W Schang
1B G Sisler
2B S Melillo
SS W Gerber
3B F O'Rourke
LF K Williams
UO B Miller
RM H Rice
23- S Adams
UO H Bennett
M D Howley

WASHINGTON
SR H Lisenbee
SP S Thurston
SP B Hadley
SP W Johnson
SP T Zachary
RP G Braxton
RS F Marberry
RS B Burke
C M Ruel
1B J Judge
2B B Harris
SS B Reeves
3B O Bluege
LF G Goslin
CF T Speaker
RF S Rice

1927 NL

BOSTON
SR B Smith
SP K Greenfield
SR J Genewich
SR J Werts
SP C Robertson
RP G Mogridge
C- S Hogan
1B J Fournier
2U- D Gautreau
SS D Bancroft
3B A High
LF E Brown
CF J Welsh
RF L Richbourg
S2 D Farrell
UT E Moore
UO- J Smith

BROOKLYN
SP D Vance
SP J Petty
SP J Elliott
SR D McWeeny
SP B Doak
RP R Ehrhardt
RP W Clark
C- H DeBerry
1B B Herman
2B J Partridge
S3 J Butler
3B B Barrett
LF G Felix
CF J Statz
RF M Carey
R1 H Hendrick
M W Robinson

CHICAGO
SR C Root
SP S Blake
SR G Bush
SP H Carlson
SR J Brillheart
RS P Jones
RS B Osborn
C G Hartnett
1B C Grimm
2B C Beck
SS- W English
UI S Adams
LF R Stephenson
CF H Wilson
RF E Webb
RU- C Heathcote
M J McCarthy

CINCINNATI
SR R Lucas
SR J May
SP D Luque
SP E Rixey
SP P Donohue
C B Hargrave
1B W Pipp
2B H Critz
SS H Ford
3B C Dressen
LF R Bressler
MU E Allen
RF C Walker
UT- B Zitzmann
M J Hendricks

NEW YORK
SP B Grimes
SR F Fitzsimmons
SP V Barnes
SP L Benton
RS D Henry
RP D Songer
C- Z Taylor
1B B Terry
2B R Hornsby
SS T Jackson
3L F Lindstrom
LU- H Mueller
CF E Roush
RF G Harper
3U R Reese
OF- M Ott
M1 J McGraw

PHILADELPHIA
SR J Scott
SP A Ferguson
SR D Ulrich
SP H Pruett
SP L Sweetland
RS C Willoughby
RP C Mitchell
RP A Decatur
C J Wilson
1B R Wrightstone
2B F Thompson
S3 H Sand
3B B Friberg
LF D Spalding
CF F Leach
RF C Williams
M S McInnis

PITTSBURGH
SP L Meadows
SR C Hill
SP V Aldridge
SP R Kremer
RP J Morrison
RP M Cvengros
C J Gooch
1B J Harris
2B G Grantham
SS G Wright
3B P Traynor
LF C Barnhart
ML L Waner
RF P Waner
MO- K Cuyler
M D Bush

ST. LOUIS
SP J Haines
SP G Alexander
SR B Sherdel
SP F Rhem
SP B McGraw
RP H Bell
C- F Snyder
1B J Bottomley
2B F Frisch
SS- H Schuble
3B L Bell
LU C Hafey
CF T Douthit
RF B Southworth
LO W Holm
3S- S Toporcer
M B O'Farrell

1928 AL

BOSTON
SP R Ruffing
SR E Morris
SP J Russell
SP D Mac Fayden
SR S Harriss
RS M Settlemire
RP P Simmons
C- F Hofmann
1B P Todt
2B B Regan
SS W Gerber
3B B Myer
LF K Williams
CF I Flagstead
RF D Taitt
SU B Rogell
UT J Rothrock
C- C Berry
C- J Heving
M B Carrigan

CHICAGO
SP T Thomas
SR T Lyons
SP G Adkins
SP R Faber
SP T Blankenship
RS S Connally
C- B Crouse
1B B Clancy
2B B Hunnefield
SS B Cissell
3B W Kamm
LF B Falk
CF J Mostil
UO A Metzler
2S- B Redfern
RU- C Reynolds
M1 R Schalk
M2 L Blackburne

CLEVELAND
SP J Shaute
SR W Hudlin
SP G Uhle
SP J Miller
SR G Grant
RS B Bayne
RP M Harder
C L Sewell
1I- L Fonseca
2B C Lind
SS J Sewell
3B J Hodapp
LF C Jamieson
ML S Langford
RF H Summa
1U- G Burns
M R Peckinpaugh

DETROIT
SP O Carroll
SP E Whitehill
SP V Sorrell
SR K Holloway
SP S Gibson
RS E Vangilder
RS L Stoner
RP J Billings
RP G Smith
CU P Hargrave
1B- B Sweeney
2B C Gehringer
SS J Tavener
31 M McManus
LU B Fothergill
CF H Rice
RF H Heilmann
UO- A Wingo
M G Moriarty

NEW YORK
SP G Pipgras
SR W Hoyt
SP H Pennock
SP H Johnson
SR A Shealy
RP W Moore
C- J Grabowski
1B L Gehrig
2B T Lazzeri
SS M Koenig
3B J Dugan
LR B Meusel
CF E Combs
RL B Ruth
2S L Durocher
3B- G Robertson
M M Huggins

PHILADELPHIA
SP L Grove
SP R Walberg
SP J Quinn
SP G Earnshaw
SP H Ehmke
RS E Rommel
RS O Orwoll
C M Cochrane
1B J Hauser
2B M Bishop
SS J Boley
3B- S Hale
LF A Simmons
UO B Miller
RF T Cobb
31 T Foxx
IO- J Dykes
CF- M Haas
M C Mack

ST. LOUIS
SP D Gray
SR A Crowder
SP J Ogden
SR G Blaeholder
SR L Stewart
RS D Coffman
RS H Wiltse
RP E Strelecki
C- W Schang
1B L Blue
2B O Brannan
SS R Kress
3B F O'Rourke
LF H Manush
CF F Schulte
RF E McNeely
M D Howley

WASHINGTON
SP B Hadley
SP S Jones
SR G Braxton
SP M Gaston
SR L Brown
RS F Marberry
RP T Zachary
C M Ruel
1B J Judge
2B B Harris
SI B Reeves
3B O Bluege
LF G Goslin
UO S West
RF S Rice
CF R Barnes

1928 NL

BOSTON
SR B Smith
SP E Brandt
SR A Delaney
SR K Greenfield
RP F Edwards
C Z Taylor
1B G Sisler
2B R Hornsby
SS D Farrell
3B L Bell
LM E Brown
UO J Smith

RF L Richbourg
M1 J Slattery

BROOKLYN

SP D Vance
SR D McWeeny
SP J Petty
SR W Clark
SR J Elliott
RS B Doak
RS R Moss
RP R Ehrhardt
C- H DeBerry
1B D Bissonette
2B J Flowers
SS D Bancroft
3U H Hendrick
LF R Bressler
MR M Carey
RF B Herman
2I- H Riconda
MU- J Statz
M W Robinson

CHICAGO

SR P Malone
SP S Blake
SR C Root
SR G Bush
SR A Nehf
RS P Jones
RP H Carlson
C G Hartnett
1B C Grimm
2B F Maguire
SS W English
3S C Beck
LF R Stephenson
CF H Wilson
RF K Cuyler
M J McCarthy

CINCINNATI

SP E Rixey
SP D Luque
SR R Kolp
SP R Lucas
SP P Donohue
RP P Appleton
C V Picinich
1B G Kelly
2B H Critz
SS H Ford
3B C Dressen
OI B Zitzmann
CF E Allen
RF C Walker
1B W Pipp
LM- M Callaghan
M J Hendricks

NEW YORK

SP L Benton
SP F Fitzsimmons
SP J Genewich
SP C Hubbell
SP V Aldridge
RS J Faulkner
C S Hogan
1B B Terry
2B A Cohen
SS T Jackson
3B F Lindstrom
LF L O'Doul
CF J Welsh
RF M Ott
LI R Reese
RF- L Mann
M J McGraw

PHILADELPHIA

SR R Benge
SR J Ring
SR A Ferguson
SR L Sweetland
SR C Willoughby
RS A Walsh
RP B McGraw
RS R Miller
C W Lerian
1B D Hurst
2B F Thompson
SS H Sand
3B P Whitney
LU F Leach
CF D Sothern
UO C Williams
M B Shotton

PITTSBURGH

SR B Grimes
SP C Hill
SP R Kremer
SP F Fussell
SR E Brame
RS J Dawson
C- C Hargreaves
1B G Grantham
2B S Adams
SS G Wright
3B P Traynor
LU- F Brickell
CF L Waner
RF P Waner
M D Bush

ST. LOUIS

SR B Sherdel
SP G Alexander
SP J Haines
SP F Rhem
SP C Mitchell
RS S Johnson
RP H Haid
C J Wilson
1B J Bottomley
2B F Frisch
SS R Maranville
3B W Holm
LF C Hafey
CF T Douthit
RF G Harper
3U A High
M B McKechnie

1929 AL

BOSTON

SR M Gaston
SP R Ruffing
SP J Russell
SP D Mac Fayden
SP E Morris
RP E Carroll
C- C Berry
1B P Todt
2B B Regan
SS H Rhyne
3B B Reeves
LF R Scarritt
CF J Rothrock
3U- B Barrett
RU E Bigelow
S2 B Narleski
RF B Barrett
M B Carrigan

CHICAGO

SP T Thomas
SP T Lyons
SP R Faber
SR G Adkins
SP E Walsh
RS H McKain
C M Berg
1B A Shires
2B J Kerr
SS B Cissell
3B W Kamm
LF A Metzler
MU D Hoffman
RO C Reynolds
1B B Clancy
MR- J Watwood
M L Blackburne

CLEVELAND

SP W Hudlin
SR W Ferrell
SP J Miller
SP J Shaute
SR J Miljus
RS K Holloway
RP J Zinn
C L Sewell
1B L Fonseca
2B- J Hodapp
SS J Tavener
3B J Sewell
LF C Jamieson
CF E Averill
OF B Falk
RF E Morgan
SS- R Gardner
M R Peckinpaugh

DETROIT

SP G Uhle
SR E Whitehill
SP V Sorrell
SP O Carroll
RS A Prudhomme
RS E Yde
RP L Stoner
C- E Phillips
1B D Alexander
2B C Gehringer
SS- H Schuble
3B M McManus
LM R Johnson
CF H Rice
RF H Heilmann
OF B Fothergill
M B Harris

NEW YORK

SP G Pipgras
SP W Hoyt
SP E Wells
SP H Pennock
SR R Sheid
RS F Heimach
RS T Zachary
RP W Moore
C B Dickey
1B L Gehrig
2B T Lazzeri
SS L Durocher
3B- G Robertson
LR B Meusel
CF E Combs
RL B Ruth
S3 M Koenig
LO- C Durst
3U- L Lary
M1 M Huggins
M2 A Fletcher

PHILADELPHIA

SP L Grove
SP R Walberg
SR G Earnshaw
SR J Quinn
RS B Shores
RS E Rommel
C M Cochrane
1B J Foxx
2B M Bishop
SS J Boley
3B S Hale
LF A Simmons
CF M Haas
RF B Miller
S3 J Dykes
M C Mack

ST. LOUIS

SP D Gray
SP A Crowder
SP G Blaeholder
SP R Collins
SP L Stewart
RS J Ogden
RP C Kimsey
RP D Coffman
C W Schang
1B L Blue
2B S Melillo
SR R Kress
3B F O'Rourke
LF H Manush
CF F Schulte
RM B McGowan
M D Howley

WASHINGTON

SR F Marberry
SR B Hadley
SR G Braxton
SR L Brown
SR S Jones
RS B Burke
RP M Thomas
RS A Liska
C- B Tate
1B J Judge
23 B Myer
SS J Cronin
32 J Hayes
LF G Goslin
CF S West
RF S Rice
M W Johnson

1929 NL

BOSTON

SP B Smith
SP S Seibold
SR P Jones
SP E Brandt
SP B Cantwell
RS D Leverett
C A Spohrer
1B G Sisler
2B F Maguire
SS R Maranville
3B L Bell
LF G Harper
CF- E Clark
RF L Richbourg
M J Fuchs

BROOKLYN

SP W Clark
SP D Vance
SR R Moss
SR C Dudley
SR D McWeeny
RS J Morrison
RP C Moore
RP W Ballou
C V Picinich
1B D Bissonette
2S E Moore
SS D Bancroft
3B W Gilbert
LF R Bressler
CF J Frederick
RF B Herman
UT H Hendrick
M W Robinson

CHICAGO

SR G Bush
SR C Root
SR P Malone
SP S Blake
SR A Nehf
RS H Carlson
RP M Cvengros
C- Z Taylor
1B C Grimm
2B R Hornsby
SS W English
3B N McMillan
LF R Stephenson
CF H Wilson
RF K Cuyler
RU- C Heathcote
M J McCarthy

CINCINNATI

SP R Lucas
SR E Rixey
SR J May
SP P Donohue
SP D Luque
RS R Kolp
RS K Ash
RP R Ehrhardt
C- J Gooch
1B G Kelly
2B H Critz
S2 H Ford
3B C Dressen
LM E Swanson
CF E Allen
RF C Walker
SU- P Pittinger
OF- P Purdy
C- C Sukeforth
M J Hendricks

NEW YORK

SP C Hubbell
SP L Benton
SP F Fitzsimmons
SP B Walker
SR C Mays
RS D Henry
RP R Judd
C S Hogan
1B B Terry
2B A Cohen
SS T Jackson
3B F Lindstrom
LF F Leach
CF E Roush
RF M Ott
C- B O'Farrell
ML- C Fullis
M J McGraw

PHILADELPHIA

SR C Willoughby
SR L Sweetland
SR R Benge
RS P Collins
SR H Elliott
RP B McGraw
RP S Dailey
C W Lerian
1B D Hurst
2B F Thompson
SS- T Thevenow
3B P Whitney
LF L O'Doul
CF- D Sothern
RF C Klein
C S Davis
SO B Friberg
M B Shotton

PITTSBURGH

SP B Grimes
SP E Brame
SP R Kremer
SR J Petty
SR L French
RS S Swetonic
RP H Meine
RP C Hill
C C Hargreaves
1B E Sheely
2U G Grantham
S2 D Bartell
3B P Traynor
LF A Comorosky
CF L Waner
RF P Waner
C- R Hemsley
M1 D Bush
M2 J Ens

ST. LOUIS

SR B Sherdel
SR S Johnson
SP J Haines
SP C Mitchell
SR H Haid
RS F Frankhouse
RP G Alexander
RP B Hallahan
C J Wilson
1B J Bottomley
2B F Frisch
SS C Gelbert
3B A High
LF C Hafey
CF T Douthit
RU E Orsatti
RF- W Roettger
M1 B Southworth
M2 G Street
M3 B McKechnie

1930 AL

BOSTON

SP M Gaston
SP D Mac Fayden
SP H Lisenbee
SP J Russell
SR E Durham
RP G Smith
C- C Berry
1B P Todt
2B B Regan
SS H Rhyne
3U O Miller
LF R Scarritt
CF T Oliver
RF E Webb
OF C Durst
3I- B Reeves
1U- B Sweeney
M H Wagner

CHICAGO

SP T Lyons
SR P Caraway
SP R Faber
SP T Thomas
SR D Henry
RP E Walsh
RS H McKain
C- B Tate
UT J Watwood
2B B Cissell
SS- G Mulleavy
3B W Kamm
RL S Jolley
CF- R Barnes
UO C Reynolds
M D Bush

CLEVELAND

SP W Ferrell
SP W Hudlin
SP C Brown
SR M Harder
RS P Appleton
C- L Sewell
1B E Morgan
2B J Hodapp
SS J Goldman
3B J Sewell
LF C Jamieson
CF E Averill
RF D Porter
OF- B Falk
C- G Myatt
LO- B Seeds
M R Peckinpaugh

DETROIT

SP G Uhle
SP V Sorrell
SP E Whitehill
SR C Hogsett
SP W Hoyt
RP C Sullivan
C- R Hayworth
1B D Alexander
2B C Gehringer
SS- M Koenig
3B M McManus
LU J Stone
CF L Funk
RF R Johnson
S3- B Akers
M B Harris

NEW YORK

SR G Pipgras
SP R Ruffing
SR R Sherid
SR H Johnson
SP H Pennock
RP E Wells
RP L McEvoy
C B Dickey
1B L Gehrig
23 T Lazzeri
SS L Lary
32 B Chapman
UO E Combs
CF H Rice
RL B Ruth
LR- S Byrd
UO- D Cooke
2U- J Reese
M B Shawkey

PHILADELPHIA

SR L Grove
SR G Earnshaw
SP R Walberg
SR B Shores
SR R Mahaffey
RS E Rommel
RS J Quinn
C M Cochrane
1B J Foxx
2B M Bishop
SS J Boley
3B J Dykes
LF A Simmons
CF M Haas
RF B Miller
IO- E McNair
M C Mack

ST. LOUIS

SP L Stewart
SP D Coffman
SR G Blaeholder
SR R Collins
SP D Gray
RP C Kimsey
RS R Stiles
RP H Holshouser
C R Ferrell
1B L Blue
2B S Melillo
SS R Kress
3U F O'Rourke
LF G Goslin
CF F Schulte
RF- T Gullic
UO- R Badgro
M B Killefer

WASHINGTON

SP B Hadley
SP A Crowder
SR L Brown
SR F Marberry
SP S Jones
RS A Liska
C R Spencer
1B J Judge
2B B Myer
SS J Cronin
3B O Bluege
LF- H Manush
CF S West
RF S Rice
M W Johnson

1930 NL

BOSTON

SP S Seibold
SP B Smith
SR B Cantwell
SP T Zachary
SP B Sherdel
RS E Brandt
RS F Frankhouse
RS B Cunningham
C A Spohrer
1B G Sisler
2B F Maguire
SS R Maranville
3B B Chatham
LF W Berger
CF J Welsh
RF L Richbourg
UO- E Clark
OI- R Moore
1U- J Neun
M B McKechnie

BROOKLYN

SP D Vance
SR W Clark
SP D Luque
SR J Elliott
SR R Phelps
RS R Moss
RS S Thurston
C A Lopez
1B D Bissonette
2B- N Finn
SS G Wright
3B W Gilbert
LF R Bressler
CF J Frederick
RF B Herman
2U- J Flowers
M W Robinson

CHICAGO

SR P Malone
SR G Bush
SP C Root
SR S Blake
SR B Teachout
RS B Osborn
RP L Nelson
C G Hartnett
1B C Grimm
2B F Blair
3S W English
3B- L Bell
LU R Stephenson
CF H Wilson
RF K Cuyler
S2- C Beck
M1 J McCarthy
M2 R Hornsby

CINCINNATI

SR B Frey
SP R Lucas
SR L Benton
SR R Kolp
SR E Rixey
RP J May
RP S Johnson
RP A Campbell
C C Sukeforth
13 J Stripp
S2 H Ford
SS L Durocher
3B T Cuccinello
LR C Walker
LM B Meusel
RU H Heilmann
MU E Swanson
OF- M Callaghan
C- J Gooch
M D Howley

NEW YORK

SP B Walker
SP C Hubbell
SR F Fitzsimmons
SP C Mitchell
RS H Pruett
RP J Heving
C S Hogan
1B B Terry
2B H Critz
SS T Jackson
3B F Lindstrom
LF F Leach
MO W Roettger
RF M Ott
CU B O'Farrell
SI- D Marshall
M J McGraw

PHILADELPHIA

SR P Collins
SP R Benge
SP L Sweetland
SP C Willoughby
SR H Collard
RS H Elliott
RP H Smythe
C S Davis
1B D Hurst
2B F Thompson
SS T Thevenow
3B P Whitney
LF L O'Doul
CF- D Sothern
RF C Klein
UT B Friberg
CU- H McCurdy
1B- M Sherlock
M B Shotton

PITTSBURGH

SP L French
SP R Kremer
SP E Brame
SP H Meine
RS G Spencer
RS S Swetonic
C R Hemsley
1B G Suhr
2B G Grantham
SS D Bartell
3B P Traynor
LF A Comorosky
CF- L Waner
RF P Waner
C- A Bool
M J Ens

ST. LOUIS

SP B Hallahan
SP S Johnson
SP J Haines
SP B Grimes
SP F Rhem
RS H Bell
RS J Lindsey
RS A Grabowski
C J Wilson
1B J Bottomley
2B F Frisch
SS C Gelbert
3B S Adams
LF C Hafey
CF T Douthit
RU G Watkins
OF- S Fisher
M G Street

1931 AL

BOSTON

SP J Russell
SP D Mac Fayden
SR E Durham
SR H Lisenbee
SR E Morris
RS W Moore
RP M Gaston
RS B Kline
C C Berry
1B B Sweeney
2S- R Warstler
SS H Rhyne
3U O Miller
LI J Rothrock
CF T Oliver
RF E Webb
3U U Pickering
LU A Van Camp
M S Collins

CHICAGO

SR V Frasier
SP T Thomas
SR P Caraway
SR R Faber
SR T Lyons
RS H McKain
RP J Moore
RP G Braxton
C- B Tate
1B L Blue
2B J Kerr
SS B Cissell
3B- B Sullivan
LU L Fonseca
MU J Watwood
RF C Reynolds
SS L Appling
OF B Fothergill
C- F Grube
3B- I Jeffries
M D Bush

CLEVELAND

SP W Ferrell
SR W Hudlin
SP C Brown
SR M Harder
RP P Appleton
C L Sewell
1B E Morgan
2B J Hodapp
SS- E Montague
3B W Kamm
LF J Vosmik
CF E Averill
RF D Porter
S2 J Burnett
OF- B Falk
M R Peckinpaugh

DETROIT

SP E Whitehill
SP V Sorrell
SR G Uhle
SR T Bridges
SR A Herring
RS C Hogsett
RP C Sullivan
C- R Hayworth
1B D Alexander
2B C Gehringer
SS- B Rogell
3U M McManus
LF J Stone
MU- H Walker
RF R Johnson
2S M Koenig
UI M Owen
M B Harris

NEW YORK

SR L Gomez
SP R Ruffing
SR H Johnson
SP H Pennock
SR G Pipgras
RS E Wells
C B Dickey
1B L Gehrig
23 T Lazzeri

SS L Lary
3B J Sewell
LR B Chapman
CF E Combs
RL B Ruth
UO S Byrd
M J McCarthy

PHILADELPHIA
SR L Grove
SP R Walberg
SR G Earnshaw
SR R Mahaffey
SR E Rommel
RP W Hoyt
C M Cochrane
1B J Foxx
2B M Bishop
SS- D Williams
3B J Dykes
LF A Simmons
CF M Haas
RF B Miller
3I- E McNair
M C Mack

ST. LOUIS
SP D Gray
SP L Stewart
SP G Blaeholder
SR D Coffman
SP R Collins
RS W Hebert
RP C Kimsey
RP R Stiles
C R Ferrell
1B J Burns
2B S Melillo
SS J Levey
3R R Kress
LF G Goslin
CF F Schulte
RU- T Jenkins
3B- L Storti
M B Killefer

WASHINGTON
SR L Brown
SR A Crowder
SR F Marberry
SR C Fischer
SP S Jones
RS B Hadley
RS B Burke
C R Spencer
1B J Kuhel
2B B Myer
SS J Cronin
3B O Bluege
LF H Manush
CF S West
RU S Rice
RU- D Harris
M W Johnson

1931 NL

BOSTON
SP E Brandt
SP T Zachary
SP S Seibold
SR B Cantwell
SR B Sherdel
RS B Cunningham
RS F Frankhouse
RP H Haid
C A Spohrer
1B E Sheely
2B F Maguire
SS R Maranville
3B- B Urbanski
LF R Worthington
CF W Berger
RF W Schulmerich
RU L Richbourg
UT- R Moore
UL- J Neun
M B McKechnie

BROOKLYN
SP W Clark
SP D Vance
SP R Phelps
SP S Thurston
SP J Shaute
RS F Heimach
RP D Luque
CL J Quinn
RP C Moore
C A Lopez
1B D Bissonette
2B N Finn
SS- G Slade
3B W Gilbert
LF L O'Doul
CF J Frederick
RF B Herman
SS- G Wright
M W Robinson

CHICAGO
SP C Root
SP B Smith
SP P Malone
SR G Bush
SR L Sweetland
RP J May
RP B Teachout
C G Hartnett
1B C Grimm
23 R Hornsby
SS W English
3B- L Bell
UO- D Taylor
ML H Wilson
RM K Cuyler
21- F Blair
32- B Jurges
LF- R Stephenson

CINCINNATI
SP S Johnson
SP R Lucas
SR L Benton
SR B Frey
SP E Rixey
RS R Kolp
RS O Carroll
C C Sukeforth
1B H Hendrick
2B T Cuccinello
SS L Durocher
3B J Stripp
OF E Roush
CF T Douthit
RU E Crabtree
LF N Cullop
SS- H Ford
RU- C Heathcote
M D Howley

NEW YORK
SP F Fitzsimmons
SP C Hubbell
SP B Walker
SP C Mitchell
SR J Berly
C S Hogan
1B B Terry
2B- B Hunnefield
SS T Jackson
3B J Vergez
LF F Leach
UO E Allen
MR M Ott
MU- C Fullis
RF- F Lindstrom
C- B O'Farrell
M J McGraw

PHILADELPHIA
SR J Elliott
SR R Benge
SR P Collins
SP C Dudley
SR S Bolen
RS F Watt
C S Davis
1B D Hurst
2B L Mallon
SS D Bartell
3B P Whitney
LR C Klein
CF F Brickell
RF B Arlett
2I B Friberg
M B Shotton

PITTSBURGH
SP H Meine
SP L French
SP R Kremer
SR G Spencer
SP E Brame
RP B Osborn
C E Phillips
1B- G Suhr
12 G Grantham
SS T Thevenow
3B P Traynor
LF A Comorosky
CF L Waner
RF P Waner
M J Ens

ST. LOUIS
SP B Hallahan
SR P Derringer
SP B Grimes
SP F Rhem
SP S Johnson
RP J Haines
RP J Lindsey
RP A Stout
C J Wilson
1B J Bottomley
2B F Frisch
SS C Gelbert
3B S Adams
LF C Hafey
CF P Martin
RF G Watkins
1B- R Collins
M G Street

1932 AL

BOSTON
SR B Weiland
SR E Durham
SR B Kline
SP I Andrews
RP W Moore
RS J Michaels
RS L Boerner
C- B Tate
1B D Alexander
2B M Olson
SS R Warstler
3B U Pickering
LF S Jolley
CF T Oliver
RO R Johnson
OI J Watwood
23 M McManus
UO- G Stumpf
M1 S Collins

CHICAGO
SP T Lyons
SP S Jones
SP M Gaston
SP V Frasier
RS P Gregory
RS R Faber
C F Grube
1B L Blue
2B J Hayes
SI L Appling
3U C Selph
OF B Fothergill
CF L Funk
UO B Seeds
UT R Kress
1U B Sullivan
M L Fonseca

CLEVELAND
SP W Ferrell
SP C Brown
SP M Harder
SR W Hudlin
SR O Hildebrand
RS S Connally
RP J Russell
C- L Sewell
1B E Morgan
2B B Cissell
SS J Burnett
3B W Kamm
LF J Vosmik
CF E Averill
RF D Porter
C- G Myatt
M R Peckinpaugh

DETROIT
SP E Whitehill
SP V Sorrell
SR W Wyatt
SP T Bridges
SR G Uhle
RS C Hogsett
C R Hayworth
1B H Davis
2B C Gehringer
SS B Rogell
3U H Schuble
LM J Stone
ML G Walker
RF- E Webb
IO- B Rhiel
UO- J White
M B Harris

NEW YORK
SP L Gomez
SP R Ruffing
SP G Pipgras
SR J Allen
SP H Pennock
RP D Mac Fayden
RP J Brown
C B Dickey
1B L Gehrig
2B T Lazzeri
S3 F Crosetti
3B J Sewell
RL B Chapman
CF E Combs
RL B Ruth
MU S Byrd
SS- L Lary
M J McCarthy

PHILADELPHIA
SR L Grove
SP R Walberg
SP G Earnshaw
SP R Mahaffey
SP T Freitas
RP E Rommel
RP L Krausse
C M Cochrane
1B J Foxx
2B M Bishop
SS E McNair
3B J Dykes
LF A Simmons
CF M Haas
OF- D Cramer
RF B Miller
M C Mack

ST. LOUIS
SP L Stewart
SP G Blaeholder
SP B Hadley
SR D Gray
SR W Hebert
RS C Fischer
RP C Kimsey
C R Ferrell
1B J Burns
2B S Melillo
SS J Levey
3B- A Scharein
LF G Goslin
CF F Schulte
RF B Campbell
M B Killefer

WASHINGTON
SR A Crowder
SR M Weaver
SR L Brown
SP T Thomas
RS F Marberry
C R Spencer
1B J Kuhel
2B B Myer
SS J Cronin
3B O Bluege
LF H Manush
CF S West
RF C Reynolds
UO S Rice
UO- D Harris
1B- J Judge
M W Johnson

1932 NL

BOSTON
SP E Brandt
SP H Betts
SP B Brown
SP T Zachary
SP S Seibold
RS B Cantwell
RS F Frankhouse
RP B Cunningham
C A Spohrer
1B- A Shires
2B R Maranville
SS B Urbanski
3B- F Knothe
LF R Worthington
CF W Berger
RF W Schulmerich
IO R Moore
C- P Hargrave
UO- F Leach
M B McKechnie

BROOKLYN
SP W Clark
SP V Mungo
SP D Vance
SR F Heimach
SR S Thurston
RS J Shaute
RP J Quinn
RP C Moore
C A Lopez
1B- G Kelly
2B T Cuccinello
SS G Wright
31 J Stripp
LF L O'Doul
CF D Taylor
RF H Wilson
UO J Frederick
S3- G Slade
M M Carey

CHICAGO
SP L Warneke
SR G Bush
SP P Malone
SR C Root
SR B Grimes
RS B Smith
RS B Tinning
RP J May
C G Hartnett
1B C Grimm
2B B Herman
SS B Jurges
3S W English
LF R Stephenson
CF J Moore
RM K Cuyler
M1 R Hornsby

CINCINNATI
SP R Lucas
SR S Johnson
SP O Carroll
SR L Benton
SR R Kolp
RS B Frey
RS E Rixey
RP J Ogden
C E Lombardi
1B H Hendrick
2B G Grantham
SS L Durocher
3B W Gilbert
LF W Roettger
MU E Crabtree
RF B Herman
CF T Douthit
LF- C Hafey
3U- A High
S2- J Morrissey
M D Howley

NEW YORK
SP C Hubbell
SP F Fitzsimmons
SP B Walker
SR J Mooney
SR H Schumacher
RS H Bell
RS D Luque
RP W Hoyt
RS S Gibson
C S Hogan
1B B Terry
2B H Critz
SS- D Marshall
3B J Vergez
LF- J Moore
CF F Lindstrom
RF M Ott
OI C Fullis
U3- S Leslie
M1 J McGraw

PHILADELPHIA
SP E Holley
SR R Benge
SR S Hansen
SR P Collins
SP F Rhem
RS J Elliott
C S Davis
1B D Hurst
2B L Mallon
SS D Bartell
3B P Whitney
LF H Lee
CF K Davis
RF C Klein
M B Shotton

PITTSBURGH
SR L French
SR B Swift
SP H Meine
SR B Harris
SP S Swetonic
RS G Spencer
RS L Chagnon
RP E Brame
C E Grace
1B G Suhr
2B T Piet
SS A Vaughan
3B P Traynor
LU A Comorosky
CF L Waner
RF P Waner
LF D Barbee
M M Gibson

ST. LOUIS
SR D Dean
SP P Derringer
SR T Carleton
SP B Hallahan
SR S Johnson
RS J Lindsey
RP A Stout
C G Mancuso
1R R Collins
2B- J Reese
SS C Gelbert
3B- J Flowers
ML E Orsatti
CF- P Martin
UO G Watkins
23 F Frisch
RU- R Blades
1B- J Bottomley
C- J Wilson
M G Street

1933 AL

BOSTON
SP G Rhodes
SR B Weiland
SR L Brown
SP H Johnson
SR I Andrews
RS J Welch
RS B Kline
RP G Pipgras
C R Ferrell
1B D Alexander
2B J Hodapp
SS R Warstler
3I M McManus
LU S Jolley
ML D Cooke
RO R Johnson
S3 B Werber
CF T Oliver
1O- B Seeds

CHICAGO
SP T Lyons
SP S Jones
SP M Gaston
SP E Durham
SR J Miller
RS J Heving
RP P Gregory
RP C Kimsey
RP R Faber
C- F Grube
1B R Kress
2B J Hayes
SS L Appling
3B J Dykes
LF A Simmons
CF M Haas
RF E Swanson
C- C Berry
M L Fonseca

CLEVELAND
SR M Harder
SP O Hildebrand
SP W Ferrell
SR C Brown
SR W Hudlin
RP M Pearson
RP S Connally
RP B Bean
C- R Spencer
1B H Boss
2U O Hale
SS- B Knickerbocker
3B W Kamm
LF J Vosmik
CF E Averill
RF D Porter
2S B Cissell
UI- J Burnett
C- F Pytlak
M1 R Peckinpaugh
M2 B Falk
M3 W Johnson

DETROIT
SP F Marberry
SP T Bridges
SP V Sorrell
SR C Fischer
SP S Rowe
RP C Hogsett
RP V Frasier
RP A Herring
C R Hayworth
1B H Greenberg
2B C Gehringer
SS B Rogell
3B M Owen
LU G Walker
CF P Fox
RF J Stone
UO- J White
M1 B Harris
M2 D Baker

NEW YORK
SP R Ruffing
SP L Gomez
SP J Allen
SP R Van Atta
RP W Moore
RS H Pennock
C B Dickey
1B L Gehrig
2B T Lazzeri
SS F Crosetti
3B J Sewell
RL B Chapman
MU E Combs
RL B Ruth
MU D Walker
UO- S Byrd
M J McCarthy

PHILADELPHIA
SR L Grove
SP S Cain
SR R Walberg
SR R Mahaffey
SP G Earnshaw
RS J Peterson
C M Cochrane
1B J Foxx
2B M Bishop
S2 D Williams
3B P Higgins
LF B Johnson
CF D Cramer
RF E Coleman
S2- E McNair
M C Mack

ST. LOUIS
SP B Hadley
SP G Blaeholder
SP E Wells
RS D Gray
RS R Stiles
RS W Hebert
RS H McDonald
C M Shea
1B J Burns
2B S Melillo
SS J Levey
3B A Scharein
LF C Reynolds
CF S West
RF B Campbell
UT T Gullic
UO- D Garms
M1 B Killefer
M2 A Sothoron
M3 R Hornsby

WASHINGTON
SR A Crowder
SR E Whitehill
SP L Stewart
SP M Weaver
SR T Thomas
RP J Russell
RS B Burke
RP B McAfee
C L Sewell
1B J Kuhel
2B B Myer
SS J Cronin
3B O Bluege
LF H Manush
CF F Schulte
RF G Goslin
UT- D Harris

1933 NL

BOSTON
SP E Brandt
SP B Cantwell
SR F Frankhouse
SR H Betts
SP T Zachary
C S Hogan
1B B Jordan
2B R Maranville
SS B Urbanski
3B P Whitney
LF- H Lee
CF W Berger
RF R Moore
LU- J Mowry
M B McKechnie

BROOKLYN
SP B Beck
SR V Mungo
SR R Benge
SP O Carroll
SR S Thurston
RP J Shaute
RP R Ryan
C A Lopez
1B S Leslie
2B T Cuccinello
SU- G Wright
3B J Stripp
LU H Wilson
CF D Taylor
RU J Frederick
UO- B Boyle
IO- J Flowers
CU- C Outen
M M Carey

CHICAGO
SP L Warneke
SP G Bush
SP C Root
SP P Malone
SR B Tinning
C G Hartnett
1B C Grimm
2B Bi Herman
SS B Jurges
3B W English
LF R Stephenson
CF F Demaree
RF Ba Herman
UI- M Koenig

CINCINNATI
SP P Derringer
SP R Lucas
SP S Johnson
SR L Benton
SR R Kolp
RS B Frey
RP E Rixey
C E Lombardi
1B J Bottomley
2S J Morrissey
SS O Bluege
3B S Adams
LM J Moore
ML C Hafey
RF H Rice
2B- G Grantham
UO- W Roettger
M D Bush

NEW YORK
SR C Hubbell
SP H Schumacher
SP F Fitzsimmons
SP R Parmelee
RS H Bell
RP D Luque
RP G Spencer
C G Mancuso
1B B Terry
2B H Critz
SS B Ryan
3B J Vergez
LF J Moore
CF K Davis
RF M Ott
OF- L O'Doul
UO- H Peel

PHILADELPHIA
SP E Holley
SR S Hansen
SR J Elliott
SR C Moore
SP F Rhem
RS P Collins
RP A Liska
C S Davis
1B D Hurst
23 J Warner
SS D Bartell
3B- J McLeod
LF W Schulmerich
CF C Fullis
RF C Klein
M B Shotton

PITTSBURGH
SR L French
SP B Swift
SP H Meine
SR S Swetonic
SP H Smith
RS W Hoyt
RS L Chagnon
RP B Harris
C E Grace
1B G Suhr
2B T Piet
SS A Vaughan
3B P Traynor
LM L Waner
CF F Lindstrom
RF P Waner
M M Gibson

ST. LOUIS
SR D Dean
SR T Carleton
SP B Hallahan
SP B Walker
SR D Vance
RS J Haines
RP S Johnson
C J Wilson
1B R Collins
2B F Frisch
SS L Durocher
3B P Martin
LF J Medwick
CF E Orsatti
RF G Watkins
MU- E Allen
UI- P Crawford
M1 G Street

1934 AL

BOSTON

SR G Rhodes
SR J Welch
SR F Ostermueller
SP W Ferrell
SR H Johnson
RS L Grove
RS R Walberg
RP H Pennock
C R Ferrell
1B E Morgan
2B B Cissell
SS L Lary
3B B Werber
LF R Johnson
MR C Reynolds
RF- D Porter
2U M Bishop
MR M Solters
M *B Harris*

CHICAGO

SP G Earnshaw
SP T Lyons
SP M Gaston
SP S Jones
SR L Tietje
RS P Gallivan
RP J Heving
RS W Wyatt
C- E Madjeski
1B Z Bonura
2B- J Hayes
SS L Appling
3I *J Dykes*
LF A Simmons
CF M Haas
RF E Swanson
2S- B Boken
M1 *L Fonseca*

CLEVELAND

SR M Harder
SP M Pearson
SP O Hildebrand
SR W Hudlin
SR L Brown
RP B Bean
RP C Brown
C- F Pytlak
1B H Trosky
2B O Hale
SS B Knickerbocker
3B W Kamm
LF J Vosmik
CF E Averill
RU S Rice
M *W Johnson*

DETROIT

SP T Bridges
SP S Rowe
SR E Auker
SR F Marberry
SP V Sorrell
RP C Fischer
RP C Hogsett
C *M Cochrane*
1B H Greenberg
2B C Gehringer
SS B Rogell
3B M Owen
LF G Goslin
CF J White
RF P Fox
UO G Walker

NEW YORK

SP L Gomez
SP R Ruffing
SR J Murphy
SP J Broaca
SP J DeShong
RS D Mac Fayden
C B Dickey
1B L Gehrig
2U T Lazzeri
SS F Crosetti
3B J Saltzgaver
RL M Hoag
ML B Chapman
RL B Ruth
RL S Byrd
S3- R Rolfe
M *J McCarthy*

PHILADELPHIA

SP J Marcum
SP S Cain
SR B Dietrich
SR J Cascarella
SR A Benton
RS R Mahaffey
C C Berry
1B J Foxx
2B R Warstler
SS E McNair
3B P Higgins
LF B Johnson
CF D Cramer
RF E Coleman
OI L Finney
C F Hayes
RU- B Miller
M *C Mack*

ST. LOUIS

SR B Newsom
SP G Blaeholder
SP B Hadley
SR D Coffman
RS I Andrews
RS J Knott
RS E Wells
RP B McAfee
C R Hemsley
1B J Burns
2B S Melillo
SS A Strange
3B H Clift
LM R Pepper
CF S West
RF B Campbell
IO O Bejma
UO- D Garms
M *R Hornsby*

WASHINGTON

SP E Whitehill
SP M Weaver
SR B Burke
SP L Stewart
SR T Thomas
RS J Russell
RP A McColl
RS A Crowder
C- E Phillips
1B- J Kuhel
2B B Myer
SS *J Cronin*
3B C Travis
LF H Manush
CF F Schulte
RF J Stone
IO O Bluege
RU D Harris

1934 NL

BOSTON

SR E Brandt
SP F Frankhouse
SR H Betts
SP F Rhem
SP B Cantwell
RS B Smith
RP L Mangum
C A Spohrer
1B B Jordan
23 M McManus
SS B Urbanski
3B P Whitney
LF H Lee
CF W Berger
RU T Thompson
C S Hogan
OI R Moore
M *B McKechnie*

BROOKLYN

SP V Mungo
SP R Benge
SR D Leonard
SP J Babich
SR T Zachary
RS L Munns
RS O Carroll
C A Lopez
1B S Leslie
23 T Cuccinello
SS L Frey
3B J Stripp
LU D Taylor
CF L Koenecke
RO B Boyle
RU J Frederick
S2 J Jordan
M *C Stengel*

CHICAGO

SP L Warneke
SP B Lee
SR G Bush
SR P Malone
SP J Weaver
RS B Tinning
RS C Root
C G Hartnett
1B- *C Grimm*
2B Bi Herman
SS B Jurges
3B S Hack
LF C Klein
CF K Cuyler
RF Ba Herman
S3 W English
LO T Stainback

CINCINNATI

SR P Derringer
SP B Frey
SR S Johnson
SR T Freitas
SR A Stout
RS D Brennan
RP R Kolp
C E Lombardi
1B J Bottomley
IF T Piet
S2 G Slade
UI M Koenig
LF H Pool
CF C Hafey
RL A Comorosky
IF- S Adams
M1 *B O'Farrell*
M2 *B Shotton*
M3 *C Dressen*

NEW YORK

SR C Hubbell
SP H Schumacher
SP F Fitzsimmons
SP R Parmelee
RS J Bowman
RP A Smith
RP H Bell
C G Mancuso
1B *B Terry*
2B H Critz
SS T Jackson
3B J Vergez
LF J Moore
MU G Watkins
RF M Ott
3S B Ryan
OF- L O'Doul

PHILADELPHIA

SR C Davis
SP P Collins
SR C Moore
SP E Moore
RS S Hansen
RS S Johnson
RS R Grabowski
C A Todd
1B D Camilli
2U L Chiozza
SS D Bartell
3B- B Walters
LM E Allen
CF K Davis
RF J Moore
C *J Wilson*

PITTSBURGH

SR L French
SR B Swift
SR R Birkofer
SR W Hoyt
SP R Lucas
RS H Meine
RP L Chagnon
RS H Smith
C E Grace
1B G Suhr
2B- C Lavagetto
SS A Vaughan
3B *P Traynor*
LF F Lindstrom
CF L Waner
RF P Waner
23 T Thevenow
LU- W Jensen
C- T Padden
M1 *M Gibson*

ST. LOUIS

SR D Dean
SP T Carleton
SR P Dean
SP B Hallahan
SP B Walker
RS J Haines
RS J Mooney
C S Davis
1B R Collins
2B *F Frisch*
SS L Durocher
3B P Martin
LF J Medwick
CF E Orsatti
RF J Rothrock
UI B Whitehead
C B DeLancey

1935 AL

BOSTON

SP W Ferrell
SP L Grove
SR G Rhodes
SR J Welch
SP F Ostermueller
RS R Walberg
RS J Wilson
RP G Hockette
C R Ferrell
1B B Dahlgren
2B S Melillo
SS *J Cronin*
3B B Werber
LF R Johnson
CF M Almada
UO D Cooke
OF- B Miller
RF- C Reynolds

CHICAGO

SP J Whitehead
SP V Kennedy
SP T Lyons
SP L Tietje
SP S Jones
RS R Phelps
RP W Wyatt
C L Sewell
1B Z Bonura
2B- J Hayes
SS L Appling
3B *J Dykes*
LF R Radcliff
CF A Simmons
RU M Haas
RU G Washington
2B- T Piet

CLEVELAND

SP M Harder
SP W Hudlin
SR T Lee
SP M Pearson
SR O Hildebrand
RS L Brown
RP R Winegarner
RS C Brown
C- E Phillips
1B H Trosky
2B B Berger
SS B Knickerbocker
3B O Hale
LF J Vosmik
CF E Averill
RO- M Galatzer
RF- B Campbell
UI- R Hughes
M1 *W Johnson*
M2 *S O'Neill*

DETROIT

SP S Rowe
SP T Bridges
SP A Crowder
SP E Auker
SR J Sullivan
RP C Hogsett
C *M Cochrane*
1B H Greenberg
2B C Gehringer
SS B Rogell
3B M Owen
LF G Goslin
CF J White
RF P Fox
UO G Walker

NEW YORK

SP L Gomez
SP R Ruffing
SP J Broaca
SP J Allen
SR V Tamulis
RS J Murphy
RP J DeShong
RP P Malone
C B Dickey
1B L Gehrig
2B T Lazzeri
SS- F Crosetti
3B R Rolfe
LF J Hill
CF B Chapman
RF G Selkirk
LU- E Combs
M *J McCarthy*

PHILADELPHIA

SR J Marcum
SR B Dietrich
SP G Blaeholder
SP W Wilshere
SR R Mahaffey
RP G Caster
RP D Lieber
C- P Richards
1B J Foxx
2B R Warstler
SS E McNair
3B P Higgins
LF B Johnson
CF D Cramer
RF- W Moses
RU L Finney
M *C Mack*

ST. LOUIS

SR I Andrews
SR J Knott
SR J Walkup
SP S Cain
SR F Thomas
RS R Van Atta
RS D Coffman
C R Hemsley
1B J Burns
2B- T Carey
SS L Lary
3B H Clift
LF M Solters
CF S West
RF E Coleman
UT- B Bell
UO- R Pepper
M *R Hornsby*

WASHINGTON

SP E Whitehill
SP B Hadley
SP B Newsom
SR E Linke
RS J Russell
RS L Pettit
C C Bolton
1B J Kuhel
2B B Myer
S3 O Bluege
3B C Travis
LF H Manush
CF J Powell
RU J Stone
SU- R Kress
UO- F Schulte
M *B Harris*

1935 NL

BOSTON

SR F Frankhouse
SR B Cantwell
SR B Smith
SP E Brandt
SR H Betts
RP D Mac Fayden
RP L Benton
C A Spohrer
1U B Jordan
23 L Mallon
SS B Urbanski
32 P Whitney
LF H Lee
CF W Berger
RU T Thompson
RU R Moore
UI- J Coscarart
UO- J Mowry
M *B McKechnie*

BROOKLYN

SR V Mungo
SP W Clark
SP G Earnshaw
SP T Zachary
SR J Babich
RS D Leonard
RP R Benge
RS L Munns
RP D Vance
C A Lopez
1B S Leslie
23 T Cuccinello
SS L Frey
3B J Stripp
LF D Taylor
MO F Bordagaray
RF B Boyle
UT J Bucher
UI J Jordan
MU L Koenecke
M *C Stengel*

CHICAGO

SR L Warneke
SP B Lee
SR L French
SR C Root
SP T Carleton
RS R Henshaw
RP F Kowalik
C G Hartnett
1B P Cavarretta
2B B Herman
SS B Jurges
3B S Hack
LF A Galan
MR F Demaree
RF C Klein
M3- F Lindstrom
M *C Grimm*

CINCINNATI

SR P Derringer
SR A Hollingsworth
SR G Schott
SR T Freitas
SR S Johnson
RS D Brennan
RS B Frey
RS L Herrmann
CU E Lombardi
1B J Bottomley
2B A Kampouris
SS B Myers
3B L Riggs
LF- B Herman
ML S Byrd
RF I Goodman
C- G Campbell
UI- B Sullivan
M *C Dressen*

NEW YORK

SP C Hubbell
SP H Schumacher
SP R Parmelee
SP S Castleman
RS A Smith
RP A Stout
RP F Gabler
C G Mancuso
1B *B Terry*
2I M Koenig
SS D Bartell
3B T Jackson
LF J Moore
CF H Leiber
RF M Ott

PHILADELPHIA

SR C Davis
SR O Jorgens
SR S Johnson
SP B Walters
SR J Bowman
RS J Bivin
RS P Pezzullo
RS R Prim
RS H Mulcahy
C A Todd
1B D Camilli
2B L Chiozza
SS M Haslin
3B J Vergez
LF G Watkins
CF E Allen
RF J Moore
C- *J Wilson*

PITTSBURGH

SP C Blanton
SR G Bush
SR B Swift
SR J Weaver
SR R Birkofer
RS W Hoyt
RP R Lucas
C T Padden
1B G Suhr
2B P Young
SS A Vaughan
3U T Thevenow
LF W Jensen
CF L Waner
RF P Waner
C- E Grace
2U- C Lavagetto
M *P Traynor*

ST. LOUIS

SR D Dean
SR P Dean
SR B Walker
SR B Hallahan
SR J Haines
RS E Heusser
C B DeLancey
1B R Collins
2B *F Frisch*
SS L Durocher
3B P Martin
LF J Medwick
CF T Moore
RF J Rothrock
C S Davis
2U B Whitehead
UO- E Orsatti

1936 AL

BOSTON

SP W Ferrell
SP L Grove
SR F Ostermueller
SP J Marcum
SR R Walberg
RS J Wilson
C R Ferrell
1B J Foxx
2B S Melillo
S2 E McNair
3L B Werber
LF- H Manush
CF D Cramer
RU D Cooke
RU M Almada
S3- *J Cronin*
IO- J Kroner

CHICAGO

SP V Kennedy
SP J Whitehead
SP S Cain
SP T Lyons
SP M Stratton
RP C Brown
RP R Evans
C L Sewell
1B Z Bonura
2B J Hayes
SS L Appling
3B *J Dykes*
LF R Radcliff
UO M Kreevich
RF M Haas
23 T Piet
CF- L Rosenthal

CLEVELAND

SP J Allen
SP M Harder
SR O Hildebrand
SR D Galehouse
SP L Brown
RS G Blaeholder
RS T Lee
RS W Hudlin
C- B Sullivan
1B H Trosky
2B R Hughes
SS B Knickerbocker
3B O Hale
LF J Vosmik
CF E Averill
RF- R Weatherly
M *S O'Neill*

DETROIT

SP T Bridges
SP S Rowe
SP E Auker
SP V Sorrell
RS R Lawson
RP C Kimsey
C- R Hayworth
1B J Burns
2B C Gehringer
SS B Rogell
3B M Owen
LF G Goslin
CF A Simmons
RF G Walker
M1 *M Cochrane*
M2 *D Baker*
M3 *M Cochrane*

NEW YORK

SP R Ruffing
SP M Pearson
SR J Broaca
SP L Gomez
SR B Hadley
RS P Malone
C B Dickey
1B L Gehrig
2B T Lazzeri
SS F Crosetti
3B R Rolfe
UO J DiMaggio
OF- J Powell
RF G Selkirk
M *J McCarthy*

PHILADELPHIA

SP H Kelley
SP G Rhodes
SP B Ross
SR H Fink
RP R Gumpert
C F Hayes
1O L Finney
2B- R Warstler
SS S Newsome
3B P Higgins
LF B Johnson
CF W Moses
RF G Puccinelli
1U C Dean
M *C Mack*

ST. LOUIS

SR C Hogsett
SR J Knott
SR I Andrews
SR E Caldwell
SR T Thomas
RS R Van Atta
RP G Liebhardt
C R Hemsley
1B J Bottomley
2B T Carey
SS L Lary
3B H Clift
LF M Solters
CF S West
RF B Bell
U2- E Coleman
M *R Hornsby*

WASHINGTON

SP B Newsom
SP J DeShong
SP E Whitehill
SR P Appleton
SP J Cascarella
RS J Russell
C- C Bolton
1B J Kuhel
2S- O Bluege
SR C Travis
3B B Lewis
LF J Stone
CF B Chapman
RF- C Reynolds
S2 R Kress
LU- J Hill
M *B Harris*

1936 NL

BOSTON

SP D Mac Fayden
SP T Chaplin
SP J Lanning
SR B Cantwell
SP R Benge
RS B Smith
RS B Reis
C A Lopez
1B B Jordan
2B T Cuccinello
S3 B Urbanski
3B J Coscarart
LF H Lee
CF W Berger
RF G Moore
OI T Thompson
M *B McKechnie*

BROOKLYN

SP V Mungo
SP E Brandt
SR F Frankhouse
SR M Butcher
SR W Clark
RS G Jeffcoat
RS T Baker
C R Berres
1B B Hassett
2B J Jordan
SS L Frey
3B J Stripp
LU G Watkins
CF J Cooney
UT F Bordagaray
UT J Bucher
C B Phelps
M *C Stengel*

CHICAGO

SR B Lee
SR L French
SR L Warneke
SP T Carleton
SP C Davis
RS R Henshaw
RP C Root
RP C Bryant
C G Hartnett
1B P Cavarretta
2B B Herman
SS B Jurges
3B S Hack
LF- E Allen
CF A Galan
RF F Demaree
CU- K O'Dea
M *C Grimm*

CINCINNATI

SR P Derringer
SP A Hollingsworth
SP G Schott
SP B Hallahan
SR P Davis
RS B Frey
RS L Stine
RP D Brennan
C E Lombardi
1B L Scarsella
2B A Kampouris
SS B Myers
3B L Riggs
LF B Herman
MO K Cuyler
RF I Goodman
UT C Chapman

S2 T Thevenow
C- G Campbell
ML- H Walker
M C Dressen

NEW YORK
SP C Hubbell
SP H Schumacher
SR A Smith
SR F Fitzsimmons
SR H Gumbert
RS F Gabler
RS S Castleman
RP D Coffman
C G Mancuso
1B S Leslie
2B B Whitehead
SS D Bartell
3B T Jackson
LF J Moore
CF H Leiber
RF M Ott
CF J Ripple
1U- B Terry

PHILADELPHIA
SP B Walters
SR C Passeau
SR J Bowman
SR O Jorgens
RS S Johnson
RS E Moore
C- E Grace
1B D Camilli
2S C Gomez
SS L Norris
3B P Whitney
LR J Moore
ML E Sulik
CF C Klein
MI L Chiozza
CU- J Wilson

PITTSBURGH
SR B Swift
SR C Blanton
SP J Weaver
SP R Lucas
SR W Hoyt
RS M Brown
RS R Birkofer
C- T Padden
1B G Suhr
2B P Young
SS A Vaughan
3B B Brubaker
LF W Jensen
CF L Waner
RF P Waner
M P Traynor

ST. LOUIS
SR D Dean
SP R Parmelee
SR J Winford
SR J Haines
RP E Heusser
RS G Earnshaw
C S Davis
1B J Mize
2B- S Martin
SS L Durocher
3S C Gelbert
LF J Medwick
CF T Moore
RF P Martin
1U R Collins
C B Ogrodowski
2U F Frisch
UO- L King

1937 AL

BOSTON
SP L Grove
SR J Wilson
SP B Newsom
SR J Marcum
SR A McKain
RS R Walberg
C G Desautels
1B J Foxx
2B E McNair
SS J Cronin
3B P Higgins
LF B Mills
CF D Cramer
RF B Chapman

CHICAGO
SP V Kennedy
SP T Lee
SP T Lyons
SP J Whitehead
SP M Stratton
RP B Dietrich
RP C Brown
C L Sewell
1B Z Bonura
2B J Hayes
SS L Appling
3B T Piet
LF R Radcliff
CF M Kreevich
RF D Walker
M J Dykes

CLEVELAND
SP M Harder
SP D Galehouse
SR W Hudlin
SR J Allen
SP B Feller
RS E Whitehill
RP J Heving
RS L Brown
RP W Wyatt
C F Pytlak
1B H Trosky
2U- J Kroner
SS L Lary
32 O Hale
LF M Solters
CF E Averill
RF B Campbell
32 R Hughes
M S O'Neill

DETROIT
SP E Auker
SP T Bridges
SP R Lawson
SP J Wade
SR B Poffenberger
RS G Gill
RS S Coffman
C3 R York
1B H Greenberg
2B C Gehringer
SS B Rogell
3B M Owen
LR G Walker
CF J White
RO P Fox
OI- G Goslin
M1 M Cochrane
M2 D Baker
M3 M Cochrane
M4 D Baker
M5 C Perkins

NEW YORK
SP L Gomez
SP R Ruffing
SP B Hadley
SP M Pearson
RP J Murphy
RP F Makosky
C B Dickey
1B L Gehrig
2B T Lazzeri
SS F Crosetti
3B R Rolfe
LF J Powell
CF J DiMaggio
RO M Hoag
RF- G Selkirk
M J McCarthy

PHILADELPHIA
SP G Caster
SR H Kelley
SR E Smith
SP B Thomas
SP B Ross
RP L Nelson
RP H Fink
RP G Turbeville
C E Brucker
1B C Dean
23 R Peters
SS S Newsome
3B B Werber
LF B Johnson
CF- J Hill
RF W Moses
1M- L Finney
MU- J Rothrock
M1 C Mack
M2 E Mack

ST. LOUIS
SP O Hildebrand
SR J Knott
SR C Hogsett
SP J Walkup
SR J Bonetti
RS B Trotter
RS L Koupal
C R Hemsley
1B H Davis
2S T Carey
SS B Knickerbocker
3B H Clift
LF J Vosmik
CF S West
RF B Bell
MO E Allen
M1 R Hornsby
M2 J Bottomley

WASHINGTON
SP J DeShong
SP W Ferrell
SP M Weaver
SR P Appleton
RS E Linke
RP S Cohen
C- R Ferrell
1B J Kuhel
2B B Myer
SS C Travis
3B B Lewis
LF A Simmons
CF M Almada
RL J Stone
RU- F Sington
M B Harris

1937 NL

BOSTON
SP L Fette
SP J Turner
SP D Mac Fayden
SR G Bush
SR J Lanning
RS I Hutchinson
C A Lopez
1B E Fletcher
2B T Cuccinello
SS R Warstler
3B- G English
L3 D Garms
CF V DiMaggio
RF G Moore
LU- R Johnson
M B McKechnie

BROOKLYN
SR M Butcher
SR L Hamlin
SP F Frankhouse
SP W Hoyt
SP V Mungo
RS R Henshaw
RP G Jeffcoat
C B Phelps
1B B Hassett
23 C Lavagetto
SS W English
3U- J Stripp
LF T Winsett
CF J Cooney
RF H Manush
UO G Brack
UT J Bucher
M B Grimes

CHICAGO
SP B Lee
SP T Carleton
SR L French
SR C Root
RS R Parmelee
SR C Bryant
RS C Davis
RS C Shoun
C G Hartnett
1B R Collins
2B B Herman
SS B Jurges
3B S Hack
LF A Galan
CF- J Marty
RF F Demaree
OI P Cavarretta
UT- L Frey
C- K O'Dea
M C Grimm

CINCINNATI
SR L Grissom
SR P Derringer
SR P Davis
SR A Hollingsworth
SR G Schott
C E Lombardi
1B B Jordan
2B A Kampouris
SS B Myers
3B L Riggs
UO K Cuyler
OF- C Hafey
RF I Goodman
1U L Scarsella
MU- H Walker
M1 C Dressen
M2 B Wallace

NEW YORK
SP C Hubbell
SR C Melton
SP H Schumacher
SR H Gumbert
SP S Castleman
RS A Smith
RP D Coffman
C H Danning
1B J McCarthy
2B B Whitehead
SS D Bartell
3B L Chiozza
LF J Moore
OF J Ripple
R3 M Ott
C- G Mancuso
M B Terry

PHILADELPHIA
SR C Passeau
SP B Walters
SR W LaMaster
SR H Mulcahy
SR S Johnson
RS O Jorgens
RP H Kelleher
C- B Atwood
1B D Camilli
2B D Young
SS G Scharein
3B P Whitney
LF M Arnovich
CF H Martin
RL C Klein
OI E Browne
UO J Moore
2I L Norris
C- E Grace
M J Wilson

PITTSBURGH
SP C Blanton
SR R Bauers
SP E Brandt
SP B Swift
SR J Bowman
RP R Lucas
RP M Brown
RS J Weaver
C A Todd
1B G Suhr
2B L Handley
SS A Vaughan
3B B Brubaker
LM W Jensen
CF L Waner
RF P Waner
UI P Young
LU- J Dickshot
M P Traynor

ST. LOUIS
SP B Weiland
SP L Warneke
SP D Dean
SR S Johnson
SR R Harrell
RS M Ryba
C- B Ogrodowski
1B J Mize
2B J Brown
SS L Durocher
3B D Gutteridge
LF J Medwick
CF T Moore
RF D Padgett
3O F Bordagaray
OI P Martin
2U- S Martin
C- M Owen
M F Frisch

1938 AL

BOSTON
SR J Bagby
SR J Wilson
SR F Ostermueller
SP L Grove
SR E Dickman
RS A McKain
RP J Marcum
C G Desautels
1B J Foxx
2B B Doerr
SS J Cronin
3B P Higgins
LF J Vosmik
CF D Cramer
RF B Chapman
OI- R Nonnenkamp

CHICAGO
SP T Lee
SP T Lyons
SP M Stratton
SP J Whitehead
SP J Knott
RS J Rigney
C- L Sewell
1B J Kuhel
2B- J Hayes
SS- L Appling
3B M Owen
OF G Walker
CF M Kreevich
RF H Steinbacher
S2 B Berger
LF R Radcliff
M J Dykes

CLEVELAND
SP B Feller
SP M Harder
SP J Allen
SP E Whitehill
SR W Hudlin
RS D Galehouse
RS J Humphries
RS A Milnar
C F Pytlak
1B H Trosky
2B O Hale
SS L Lary
3B K Keltner
LF J Heath
CF E Averill
RF B Campbell
UO- R Weatherly
M O Vitt

DETROIT
SP V Kennedy
SP G Gill
SP E Auker
SP T Bridges
SR R Lawson
RS H Eisenstat
RS B Poffenberger
RS S Coffman
RP A Benton
C R York
1B H Greenberg
2B C Gehringer
SS B Rogell
3B- D Ross
LU D Walker
CF- C Morgan
RF P Fox
3U M Christman
UO- J White
M1 M Cochrane
M2 D Baker

NEW YORK
SP R Ruffing
SP L Gomez
SP M Pearson
SP S Chandler
SR B Hadley
CL J Murphy
RP I Andrews
C B Dickey
1B L Gehrig
2B J Gordon
SS F Crosetti
3B R Rolfe
LF G Selkirk
CF J DiMaggio
RF T Henrich
UO- M Hoag
M J McCarthy

PHILADELPHIA
SP G Caster
SR B Thomas
SP L Nelson
SP B Ross
RS E Smith
RS N Potter
RS A Williams
C F Hayes
1O L Finney
2B D Lodigiani
SS W Ambler
3B B Werber
LF S Chapman
CF B Johnson
RF W Moses
M C Mack

ST. LOUIS
SP B Newsom
SP L Mills
SP O Hildebrand
SR R Van Atta
RS E Cole
RS B Cox
C B Sullivan
1B G McQuinn
2B D Heffner
SS R Kress
3B H Clift
LF B Mills
CF M Almada
RF B Bell
UO- M Mazzera
M1 G Street
M2 S Melillo

WASHINGTON
SP D Leonard
SR K Chase
SP W Ferrell
SR H Kelley
SR M Weaver
RS P Appleton
RS J DeShong
RS J Krakauskas
RS C Hogsett
C R Ferrell
1B Z Bonura
2B B Myer
SS C Travis
3B B Lewis
LF A Simmons
CF S West
RF G Case
UO T Wright
M B Harris

1938 NL

BOSTON
SP J Turner
SP L Fette
SP D Mac Fayden
SR M Shoffner
SR J Lanning
RS I Hutchinson
RS D Errickson
C- R Mueller
1B E Fletcher
2B T Cuccinello
SS R Warstler
3B- J Stripp
LR M West
CF V DiMaggio
RO J Cooney
UT D Garms
M C Stengel

BROOKLYN
SR L Hamlin
SP F Fitzsimmons
SR T Pressnell
SR V Tamulis
SR B Posedel
RP V Mungo
RS F Frankhouse
C- B Phelps
1B D Camilli
2B J Hudson
SS L Durocher
3B C Lavagetto
LU B Hassett
OI E Koy
UO G Rosen
RO- K Cuyler
M B Grimes

CHICAGO
SP B Lee
SR C Bryant
SR L French
SP T Carleton
RS C Root
RP J Russell
C- G Hartnett
1B R Collins
2B B Herman
SS B Jurges
3B S Hack
LF A Galan
ML C Reynolds
RF F Demaree
OI- P Cavarretta
CF- J Marty
C- K O'Dea
M1 C Grimm

CINCINNATI
SP P Derringer
SP J Vander Meer
SR P Davis
SP B Walters
SR J Weaver
RP G Schott
RP J Cascarella
C E Lombardi
1B F McCormick
2B L Frey
SS B Myers
3B L Riggs
LF W Berger
CF H Craft
RF I Goodman
LU- D Cooke
M B McKechnie

NEW YORK
SP C Melton
SP H Gumbert
SP H Schumacher
SP C Hubbell
SR B Lohrman
RP D Coffman
RP J Brown
C H Danning
1B J McCarthy
2B- A Kampouris
SS D Bartell
3B M Ott
LF J Moore
CF H Leiber
RF J Ripple
U3- S Leslie
UO- B Seeds
M B Terry

PHILADELPHIA
SR H Mulcahy
SR C Passeau
SP A Hollingsworth
SP M Butcher
RS P Sivess
RP A Smith
C B Atwood
1B P Weintraub
2B H Mueller
SS D Young
3U P Whitney
LF M Arnovich
CF H Martin
RF C Klein
S2 G Scharein
3U- B Jordan
M1 J Wilson
M2 H Lobert

PITTSBURGH
SP R Bauers
SP J Tobin
SP C Blanton
SP B Klinger
SR E Brandt
RS B Swift
RP M Brown
C A Todd
1B G Suhr
2B P Young
SS A Vaughan
3B L Handley
LF J Rizzo
CF L Waner
RF P Waner
M P Traynor

ST. LOUIS
SP B Weiland
SR B McGee
SP L Warneke
SR C Davis
SR R Henshaw
RS M Macon
RS C Shoun
RP R Harrell
C M Owen
1B J Mize
2B S Martin
SS- L Myers
3S D Gutteridge
LF J Medwick
CF T Moore
RU E Slaughter
UI J Brown
RU D Padgett
OI- F Bordagaray
OI- P Martin
M1 F Frisch
M2 M Gonzalez

1939 AL

BOSTON
SP L Grove
SR J Wilson
SR F Ostermueller
SP E Auker
SR D Galehouse
RP E Dickman
RS J Heving
RS J Wade
C J Peacock
1B J Foxx
2B B Doerr
SS J Cronin
3B J Tabor
LF J Vosmik
CF D Cramer
RF T Williams
UT L Finney

CHICAGO
SP T Lee
SP J Rigney
SP E Smith
SP T Lyons
SP J Knott
RP C Brown
RP B Dietrich
C M Tresh
1B J Kuhel
2B- O Bejma
SS L Appling
3B E McNair
LF G Walker
CF M Kreevich
RU L Rosenthal
RU R Radcliff
M J Dykes

CLEVELAND
SP B Feller
SR A Milnar
SP M Harder
SP J Allen
SP W Hudlin
RS H Eisenstat
RP J Dobson
C R Hemsley
1B H Trosky
2U O Hale
SS- S Webb
3B K Keltner
LF J Heath
CF B Chapman
RF B Campbell
UI O Grimes
UO R Weatherly
M O Vitt

DETROIT
SP B Newsom
SP T Bridges
SR D Trout
SP S Rowe
SR A Benton
RS A McKain
RP B Thomas
C B Tebbetts
1B H Greenberg
2B C Gehringer
SS F Croucher
3B P Higgins
LF- E Averill
CF B McCosky
RF P Fox
CU R York
M D Baker

NEW YORK
SP R Ruffing
SP L Gomez
SP B Hadley
SP A Donald
SP M Pearson
RP O Hildebrand
RS S Sundra
RS M Russo
CL J Murphy
C B Dickey
1B B Dahlgren
2B J Gordon
SS F Crosetti
3B R Rolfe
LR G Selkirk
CF J DiMaggio
RL C Keller
RM T Henrich
M J McCarthy

PHILADELPHIA
SR L Nelson
SR N Potter
SP B Ross
SP B Beckmann
SR G Caster
RP C Dean
RP C Pippen
RS B Joyce
C F Hayes
1B D Siebert
2U J Gantenbein
SS S Newsome
3U D Lodigiani
LF B Johnson
CF S Chapman
RF W Moses
SS W Ambler
RU D Miles
23 B Nagel
M1 C Mack
M2 E Mack

ST. LOUIS
SP J Kramer
SP V Kennedy
SR R Lawson
SR L Mills
SR B Harris
RS B Trotter
RS G Gill
RP J Whitehead
C- J Glenn
1B G McQuinn
2B J Berardino
S2 D Heffner
3B H Clift
LF- J Gallagher
MU C Laabs
UO M Hoag
OI B Sullivan
SS- M Christman
M F Haney

WASHINGTON
SP D Leonard
SP K Chase
SR J Krakauskas
SP J Haynes
SR A Carrasquel
RP P Appleton
RS W Masterson
C- R Ferrell
1B- M Vernon
2B- J Bloodworth
SS C Travis
3B B Lewis
RL T Wright
OI S West
MR G Case
LF- B Estalella
2B- B Myer
M B Harris

1939 NL

BOSTON
SP B Posedel
SP D Mac Fayden
SP J Turner
SP L Fette
SR M Shoffner
RS J Lanning
RS D Errickson
RS J Sullivan
C A Lopez
1B B Hassett
2B- T Cuccinello
SS- E Miller
3B H Majeski
UO M West
CF J Cooney
R3 D Garms
LF A Simmons
UI R Warstler
M C Stengel

BROOKLYN
SP L Hamlin
SR H Casey
SR V Tamulis
SR T Pressnell
SP F Fitzsimmons
RP W Wyatt
RP I Hutchinson
RS R Evans
C B Phelps
1B D Camilli
2B P Coscarart
SS L Durocher
3B C Lavagetto
LF E Koy
CF- D Walker
RF G Moore
UI J Hudson
C- A Todd

CHICAGO
SP B Lee
SP C Passeau
SR L French
SR C Root
SR V Page
RP D Dean
RP J Russell
C G Hartnett
1B R Russell
2B B Herman
SS D Bartell
3B S Hack
LF A Galan
CF H Leiber
RU J Gleeson
C- G Mancuso
MU- C Reynolds

CINCINNATI
SP B Walters
SP P Derringer
SR W Moore
SR L Grissom
SP J Vander Meer
RS J Thompson
C E Lombardi
1B F McCormick
2B L Frey
SS B Myers
3B B Werber
LM W Berger
CF H Craft
RF I Goodman
M B McKechnie

NEW YORK
SP H Gumbert
SR C Melton
SR B Lohrman
SP H Schumacher
SR C Hubbell
RS M Salvo
RP J Brown
RP R Lynn
C H Danning
1B Z Bonura
2B B Whitehead
SS B Jurges
3B- T Hafey
LF J Moore
CF F Demaree
RF M Ott
M B Terry

PHILADELPHIA
SP H Mulcahy
SP K Higbe
SR B Beck
SR I Pearson
SP S Johnson
RP M Butcher
RS R Harrell
RP B Kerksieck
C- S Davis
1B- G Suhr
2B- R Hughes
SS G Scharein
3B P May
LF M Arnovich
MU H Martin
RU- L Scott
OI- G Brack
UT H Mueller
MO- J Marty
C- W Millies
SU- D Young
M D Prothro

PITTSBURGH
SP B Klinger
SR M Brown
SR J Bowman
SP J Tobin
RS R Sewell
RS B Swift
C- R Mueller
1B E Fletcher
2B- P Young
SS A Vaughan
3B L Handley
LF J Rizzo
CF L Waner
RF P Waner
23 B Brubaker
MO- F Bell
C- R Berres
OF- C Klein
M P Traynor

ST. LOUIS
SR C Davis
SR M Cooper
SR L Warneke
SP B McGee
SP B Weiland
RS B Bowman
RP C Shoun
C M Owen
1B J Mize
2B S Martin
S2 J Brown
3B D Gutteridge
LF J Medwick
CF T Moore
RF E Slaughter
UO- L King
OI- P Martin
CU- D Padgett
M R Blades

1940 AL

BOSTON
SR J Bagby
SR J Wilson
SP L Grove
SR F Ostermueller
SR H Hash
RS J Heving
RP D Galehouse
RS E Dickman
C- G Desautels
1C J Foxx
2B B Doerr
SS J Cronin
3B J Tabor
LF T Williams
MO D DiMaggio
MO D Cramer
R1 L Finney

CHICAGO
SP J Rigney
SP T Lee
SP E Smith
SP T Lyons
SP J Knott
RP B Dietrich
RP C Brown
RP P Appleton
C M Tresh
1B J Kuhel
2B- S Webb
SS L Appling
3B B Kennedy
LF M Solters
CF M Kreevich
RF T Wright
LU L Rosenthal
M J Dykes

CLEVELAND
SP B Feller
SP A Milnar
SP M Harder
SP A Smith
SR J Allen
RS J Dobson
RP H Eisenstat
C R Hemsley
1B H Trosky
2B R Mack
SS L Boudreau
3B K Keltner
UO B Chapman
CF R Weatherly
RF B Bell
LF J Heath
M O Vitt

DETROIT
SP B Newsom
SP T Bridges
SP S Rowe
SP J Gorsica
SP H Newhouser
RS D Trout
CL A Benton
RP T Seats
RP A McKain
C B Tebbetts
1B R York
2B C Gehringer
SS D Bartell
3B P Higgins
LF H Greenberg
CF B McCosky
RF P Fox
RU B Campbell
CU- B Sullivan
M D Baker

NEW YORK
SP R Ruffing
SP M Russo
SP S Chandler
SP M Breuer
SR A Donald
RP M Pearson
RS S Sundra
RP T Bonham
RP J Murphy
C B Dickey
1B B Dahlgren
2B J Gordon
SS F Crosetti
3B R Rolfe
LR G Selkirk
CF J DiMaggio
RL C Keller
RM- T Henrich
M J McCarthy

PHILADELPHIA
SP J Babich
SP N Potter
SR G Caster
SR C Dean
SP B Ross
RS B Beckmann
RS E Heusser
RP P Vaughan
C F Hayes
1D D Siebert
2B B McCoy
SU A Brancato
3B A Rubeling
LF B Johnson
CF S Chapman
RF W Moses
UO- D Miles
M C Mack

ST. LOUIS
SP E Auker
SP V Kennedy
SP B Harris
SP J Niggeling
SR E Bildilli
RP B Trotter
RP R Lawson
RP S Coffman
RS L Mills
C B Swift
1B G McQuinn
2B D Heffner
SS J Berardino
3B H Clift
LF R Radcliff
CF W Judnich
RU- R Cullenbine
UO C Laabs
RU- J Grace
M F Haney

WASHINGTON
SP D Leonard
SP K Chase
SP S Hudson
SR W Masterson
RS J Krakauskas
RS R Monteagudo
RS J Haynes
RP A Carrasquel
C R Ferrell
1B- Z Bonura
2B J Bloodworth
SS J Pofahl
3B C Travis
LF G Walker
CF G Case
RF B Lewis
CU- J Early
UO- J Welaj
M B Harris

1940 NL

BOSTON
SP D Errickson
SP B Posedel
SR J Sullivan
SP M Salvo
SR N Strincevich
RP J Tobin
RP A Javery
RP D Coffman
C- R Berres
1B B Hassett
2B B Rowell
SS E Miller
3B S Sisti
LF C Ross
CF J Cooney
OI M West
RF G Moore
M C Stengel

BROOKLYN
SP W Wyatt
SP L Hamlin
SR T Carleton
SP C Davis
SP F Fitzsimmons
RS V Tamulis
RS H Casey
RP T Pressnell
C B Phelps
1B D Camilli
2B P Coscarart
SS- P Reese
3B C Lavagetto
LF J Medwick
CF D Walker
UO J Vosmik
UI- J Hudson
RU- J Wasdell
M L Durocher

CHICAGO
SR C Passeau
SP L French
SP B Lee
SR V Olsen
SP J Mooty
RS K Raffensberger
SR C Root
RP V Page
C A Todd
1B- P Cavarretta
2B B Herman
SS B Mattick
3B S Hack
RL B Nicholson
MO J Gleeson
OI H Leiber
LU D Dallessandro
M G Hartnett

CINCINNATI
SP B Walters
SP P Derringer
SP J Thompson
SP J Turner
SR W Moore
RP J Beggs
RP J Hutchings
RP M Shoffner
C E Lombardi
1B F McCormick
2B L Frey
SS- B Myers
3B B Werber
UO M McCormick
CF H Craft
RF I Goodman
SS- E Joost
M B McKechnie

NEW YORK
SP H Gumbert
SP H Schumacher
SP C Hubbell
SP B Lohrman
SR C Melton
RS P Dean
RP J Brown
RP R Joiner
C H Danning
1B B Young
23- T Cuccinello
S2 M Witek
32 B Whitehead
LF J Moore
MR F Demaree
R3 M Ott
MU- J Rucker
M B Terry

PHILADELPHIA
SP K Higbe
SP H Mulcahy
SP I Pearson
SR S Johnson
SR B Beck
RS L Smoll
C B Warren
1B A Mahan
2B H Schulte
SS B Bragan
3B P May
LO J Rizzo
CF J Marty
RF C Klein
UT H Mueller
C- B Atwood
M D Prothro

PITTSBURGH
SR R Sewell
SP J Bowman
SR M Brown
SR K Heintzelman
SR B Klinger
RS M Butcher
RS J Lanning
RS D Lanahan
RS D Mac Fayden
C S Davis
1B E Fletcher
2B F Gustine
SS A Vaughan
3B L Handley
LF M Van Robays
CF V DiMaggio
RF B Elliott
3U D Garms
RU- P Waner
M F Frisch

ST. LOUIS
SP M Cooper
SP L Warneke
SP B McGee
SR C Shoun
SR B Bowman
RS M Lanier
RP J Russell
C M Owen
1B J Mize
23 J Orengo
SS M Marion
32 S Martin
LF- E Koy
CF T Moore
RF E Slaughter
UI J Brown
OI- J Hopp
OI- P Martin
C- D Padgett
M1 R Blades
M2 M Gonzalez
M3 B Southworth

1941 AL

BOSTON
SP D Newsome
SR M Harris
SP C Wagner
SP L Grove
SP J Dobson
RP M Ryba
RS J Wilson
C F Pytlak
1B J Foxx
2B B Doerr
SS J Cronin
3B J Tabor
LF T Williams
CF D DiMaggio
RU L Finney
SU S Newsome
C- J Peacock
OI- S Spence

CHICAGO
SP T Lee
SP E Smith
SP J Rigney
SP T Lyons
SP B Dietrich
RP B Ross
C M Tresh
1B J Kuhel
2B- B Knickerbocker
SS L Appling
3B- D Lodigiani
LU M Hoag
CF M Kreevich
RF T Wright
M J Dykes

CLEVELAND
SP B Feller
SP A Milnar
SP A Smith
SP J Bagby
RP C Brown
RP J Heving
C R Hemsley
1B- H Trosky
2B R Mack
SS L Boudreau
3B K Keltner
LF G Walker
CF R Weatherly
RF J Heath
MU S Campbell
M R Peckinpaugh

DETROIT
SP B Newsom
SR J Gorsica
SP H Newhouser
SR A Benton
SR D Trout
RP T Bridges
RS S Rowe
RP B Thomas
C B Tebbetts
1B R York
2B C Gehringer
SS F Croucher
3B P Higgins
LF R Radcliff
CF B McCosky
RF B Campbell
UO T Stainback
CU- B Sullivan
M D Baker

NEW YORK
SP M Russo
SP R Ruffing
SP S Chandler
SP A Donald
SP L Gomez
RP M Breuer
RP T Bonham
CL J Murphy
RP N Branch
C B Dickey
1B J Sturm
2B J Gordon
SS P Rizzuto
3B R Rolfe
LF C Keller
CF J DiMaggio
RF T Henrich
M J McCarthy

PHILADELPHIA
SP P Marchildon
SP J Knott
SP L McCrabb
SP B Beckmann
SR B Hadley
RS L Harris
RP T Ferrick
C F Hayes
1B D Siebert
2B B McCoy
SS A Brancato
3B P Suder
LF B Johnson
CF S Chapman
RF W Moses
UO- E Collins
UO- D Miles
M C Mack

ST. LOUIS
SP E Auker
SR B Muncrief
SP D Galehouse
SP B Harris
SP J Niggeling
RS G Caster
RP J Kramer
RP B Trotter
C R Ferrell
1B G McQuinn
2B D Heffner
SS J Berardino
3B H Clift
LU R Cullenbine
CF W Judnich
RO C Laabs
RF J Grace
2U J Lucadello
M1 F Haney
M2 L Sewell

WASHINGTON
SP D Leonard
SP S Hudson
SP K Chase
SP S Sundra
RS R Anderson
RS A Carrasquel
RS B Zuber
RS W Masterson
C J Early
1B M Vernon
2B J Bloodworth
SS C Travis
3U G Archie
LF G Case
CF D Cramer
R3 B Lewis
M B Harris

1941 NL

BOSTON
SP J Tobin
SP M Salvo
SR A Johnson
SR D Errickson
SR A Javery
RS T Earley
RS J Hutchings
RP F LaManna
C R Berres
1B B Hassett
2B B Rowell
SS E Miller
3B S Sisti
LF M West
CF J Cooney
RU G Moore
RU P Waner
C- P Masi
M C Stengel

BROOKLYN
SP K Higbe
SP W Wyatt
SR H Casey
SR C Davis
SR L Hamlin
C M Owen
1B D Camilli
2B B Herman
SS P Reese
3B C Lavagetto
LF J Medwick
CF P Reiser
RO D Walker
OI- J Wasdell
M L Durocher

CHICAGO
SP C Passeau
SR V Olsen
SP B Lee
SR J Mooty
SR P Erickson
RP L French
RP C Root
RP T Pressnell
RP V Page
C C McCullough
1B B Dahlgren
2B L Stringer
SS B Sturgeon
3B S Hack
OF D Dallessandro
OI P Cavarretta
RF B Nicholson
M J Wilson

CINCINNATI
SP B Walters
SP P Derringer
SP J Vander Meer
SR E Riddle
SR J Turner
RS J Thompson
RP J Beggs
RP W Moore
C E Lombardi
1B F McCormick
2B L Frey
SS E Joost
3B B Werber
LU M McCormick
CF H Craft
UO J Gleeson
M B McKechnie

NEW YORK
SP H Schumacher
SR C Melton
SP C Hubbell
SR B Lohrman
SR B Carpenter
RP B McGee
RS B Bowman
RP A Adams
RP J Brown
C H Danning
1B B Young
2B B Whitehead
SS B Jurges
3B D Bartell
LF J Moore
CF J Rucker
RF M Ott
LU- M Arnovich
M B Terry

PHILADELPHIA
SR J Podgajny
SR T Hughes
SR S Johnson
SP C Blanton
SR L Grissom
RS I Pearson
RS L Hoerst
RS B Beck
RS B Crouch
C B Warren
1B N Etten
2B- D Murtaugh
SS B Bragan
3B P May
LF D Litwhiler
CF- J Marty
RU S Benjamin
CU M Livingston
RU J Rizzo
UT H Mueller
M D Prothro

PITTSBURGH
SP R Sewell
SP M Butcher
SR K Heintzelman
SR J Lanning
RS B Klinger
RS D Dietz
C A Lopez
1B E Fletcher
2B F Gustine
SS A Vaughan
3B L Handley
LF M Van Robays
CF V DiMaggio
RF B Elliott
UT- D Garms
2U- S Martin
M F Frisch

ST. LOUIS
SP L Warneke
SP E White
SP M Cooper
SR M Lanier
SR H Gumbert
RS H Krist
RS C Shoun
RP I Hutchinson
C G Mancuso
1B J Mize
2B C Crespi
SS M Marion
3B J Brown
OI J Hopp
CF T Moore
RF E Slaughter
LU D Padgett
M B Southworth

1942 AL

BOSTON
SP T Hughson
SP C Wagner
SP J Dobson
SP D Newsome
SR O Judd
RS B Butland
RP M Brown
C- B Conroy
1B T Lupien
2B B Doerr
SS J Pesky
3B J Tabor
LF T Williams
CF D DiMaggio
RF L Finney
RF- P Fox
C- J Peacock
M J Cronin

CHICAGO
SP J Humphries
SP E Smith
SP T Lyons

SP B Dietrich
SP B Ross
RP J Haynes
C- M Tresh
1B J Kuhel
2B D Kolloway
SS L Appling
3B B Kennedy
LF- T Wright
ML M Hoag
RF W Moses
M J Dykes

CLEVELAND

SP J Bagby
SP M Harder
SP C Dean
SP A Smith
SP A Milnar
RS V Kennedy
RP T Ferrick
RP H Eisenstat
C- O Denning
1B L Fleming
2B R Mack
SS L Boudreau
3B K Keltner
LF J Heath
CF R Weatherly
RF O Hockett
UO- B Mills

DETROIT

SP A Benton
SP D Trout
SP H White
SR H Newhouser
SP T Bridges
RP V Trucks
RP R Henshaw
RP J Gorsica
C B Tebbetts
1B R York
2B J Bloodworth
SS- B Hitchcock
3B P Higgins
LF B McCosky
CF D Cramer
RF N Harris
OI- D Ross
M D Baker

NEW YORK

SP T Bonham
SP S Chandler
SP R Ruffing
SP H Borowy
SP M Breuer
RP A Donald
CL J Murphy
RP J Lindell
C- B Dickey
1B B Hassett
2B J Gordon
SS P Rizzuto
3B- F Crosetti
LF C Keller
CF J DiMaggio
RF T Henrich
M J McCarthy

PHILADELPHIA

SP P Marchildon
SP R Wolff
SP L Harris
SR R Christopher
SR D Fowler
RS H Besse
RP J Knott
C H Wagner
1B D Siebert
2B- B Knickerbocker
S3 P Suder
3B B Blair
LF B Johnson
CF M Kreevich
RF E Valo
UO D Miles
2S- C Davis
M C Mack

ST. LOUIS

SP E Auker
SP J Niggeling
SP D Galehouse
SR A Hollingsworth
SP B Muncrief
RP S Sundra
RP G Caster
C R Ferrell
1B G McQuinn
2B D Gutteridge
SS V Stephens
3B H Clift
LU G McQuillen
CF W Judnich
RL C Laabs
UO T Criscola
M L Sewell

WASHINGTON

SP S Hudson
SP B Newsom
SP E Wynn
SR A Carrasquel
SR W Masterson
RS B Zuber
C J Early
1B M Vernon
2B- E Clary
SS J Sullivan
3O B Estalella
LR G Case
CF S Spence
RU B Campbell
SI- J Pofahl
UI- B Repass
M B Harris

1942 NL

BOSTON

SP J Tobin
SP A Javery
SR L Tost
SR M Salvo
SP T Earley
RP J Sain
RS B Donovan
RP D Errickson
RP L Wallace
C E Lombardi
1L M West
2B S Sisti
SS E Miller
3L N Fernandez
LU- C Ross
CF T Holmes
RF P Waner
M C Stengel

BROOKLYN

SP K Higbe
SP W Wyatt
SP C Davis
SR L French
SR E Head
RP H Casey
RS J Allen
RP L Webber
C M Owen
1B D Camilli
2B B Herman
SS P Reese
3B A Vaughan
LF J Medwick
CF P Reiser
RF D Walker
RF- J Rizzo
M L Durocher

CHICAGO

SP C Passeau
SP B Lee
SR H Bithorn
SR V Olsen
SR B Fleming
RP L Warneke
C C McCullough
OI P Cavarretta
2B L Stringer
SS L Merullo
3B S Hack
LF L Novikoff
UO D Dallessandro
RF B Nicholson
IO R Russell
M J Wilson

CINCINNATI

SP R Starr
SP B Walters
SP J Vander Meer
SP P Derringer
SR E Riddle
RS J Thompson
RP J Beggs
RP C Shoun
C R Lamanno
1B F McCormick
2B L Frey
SS E Joost
3B B Haas
LM- E Tipton
MO G Walker
RL M Marshall
RU- I Goodman
M B McKechnie

NEW YORK

SP H Schumacher
SP B Carpenter
SP B Lohrman
SP C Hubbell
SP C Melton
RS H Feldman
RS B McGee
RP A Adams
C H Danning
1B J Mize
2B M Witek
SS B Jurges
3B B Werber
LF B Barna
LM W Marshall
RF M Ott
MU B Young
3S- D Bartell
MU- B Maynard

PHILADELPHIA

SP T Hughes
SR R Melton
SR S Johnson
SR J Podgajny
SR L Hoerst
RS I Pearson
RP S Nahem
RP E Naylor
RP B Beck
C- B Warren
1B N Etten
2B A Glossop
SU B Bragan
3B P May
LF D Litwhiler
ML E Koy
RF R Northey
UI D Murtaugh
MU L Waner
OI- S Benjamin
C- M Livingston
M H Lobert

PITTSBURGH

SP R Sewell
SR B Klinger
SP M Butcher
SP K Heintzelman
SR H Gornicki
RS D Dietz
RS J Lanning
RP L Hamlin
RS L Wilkie
C A Lopez
1B E Fletcher
2B F Gustine
SS P Coscarart
3B B Elliott
RL J Wasdell
CF V DiMaggio
RU J Barrett
C B Phelps
LF M Van Robays
UT- B Stewart
M F Frisch

ST. LOUIS

SP M Cooper
SR J Beazley
SR H Gumbert
SR M Lanier
SP E White
RS M Dickson
RS H Krist
RS H Pollet
C W Cooper
1B J Hopp
2B- C Crespi
SS M Marion
3B W Kurowski
LF S Musial
CF T Moore
RF E Slaughter
23 J Brown
1B R Sanders
M B Southworth

1943 AL

BOSTON

SP T Hughson
SP Y Terry
SP J Dobson
SP O Judd
SP D Newsome
RS M Ryba
RP M Brown
RS P Woods
C R Partee
1B T Lupien
2B B Doerr
SS S Newsome
3B J Tabor
ML- L Culberson
MR- C Metkovich
RF P Fox
LU- J Lazor
M J Cronin

CHICAGO

SP O Grove
SP J Humphries
SP E Smith
SP B Dietrich
SP B Ross
RP T Lee
RP G Maltzberger
RP J Haynes
RP B Swift
C- M Tresh
1B J Kuhel
2B- D Kolloway
SS L Appling
UT R Hodgin
LF G Curtright
CF T Tucker
RF W Moses
M J Dykes

CLEVELAND

SP J Bagby
SP A Smith
SR A Reynolds
SR V Kennedy
SP M Harder
RP J Heving
RP M Naymick
C B Rosar
1B M Rocco
2B R Mack
SS L Boudreau
3B K Keltner
LF J Heath
MO O Hockett
RF R Cullenbine
CF H Edwards
3I- R Peters

DETROIT

SR D Trout
SP V Trucks
SR H Newhouser
SP T Bridges
SP H White
RS S Overmire
RP J Gorsica
RP R Henshaw
C P Richards
1B R York
2B J Bloodworth
SS J Hoover
3B P Higgins
LF D Wakefield
CF D Cramer
RF N Harris
UT- D Ross
M S O'Neill

NEW YORK

SP S Chandler
SP T Bonham
SP B Wensloff
SP H Borowy
SP B Zuber
RP A Donald
RS M Russo
RP J Murphy
C- B Dickey
1B N Etten
2B J Gordon
SS F Crosetti
3B B Johnson
LF C Keller
RM J Lindell
RF B Metheny
SS- S Stirnweiss
CF- R Weatherly
M J McCarthy

PHILADELPHIA

SP J Flores
SR R Wolff
SP L Harris
SP D Black
SR O Arntzen
RP R Christopher
C H Wagner
1B D Siebert
2I P Suder
SS I Hall
3B E Mayo
LF B Estalella
CF J White
UO J Welaj
C- B Swift
RU- E Valo
M C Mack

ST. LOUIS

SP D Galehouse
SP S Sundra
SP B Muncrief
SR N Potter
SR A Hollingsworth
RP J Niggeling
RP G Caster
C- F Hayes
1B G McQuinn
2B D Gutteridge
SS V Stephens
3B H Clift
LF C Laabs
MO M Byrnes
RU M Chartak
UI M Christman
M L Sewell

WASHINGTON

SP E Wynn
SP D Leonard
SR M Haefner
SP M Candini
RS A Carrasquel
RS J Mertz
C J Early
1B M Vernon
2B J Priddy
SS J Sullivan
3B- E Clary
LF B Johnson
CF S Spence
RF G Case
OI G Moore
M O Bluege

1943 NL

BOSTON

SP A Javery
SP N Andrews
SP R Barrett
SP J Tobin
SP M Salvo
RP D Odom
C- P Masi
1B- J McCarthy
2B C Ryan
SS W Wietelmann
32 E Joost
LF B Nieman
CF T Holmes
RF C Workman
LF C Ross
1B- K Farrell
M1 B Coleman
M2 C Stengel

BROOKLYN

SP K Higbe
SP W Wyatt
SR E Head
SR C Davis
SR B Newsom
RP L Webber
RS R Melton
C M Owen
1B D Camilli
2B B Herman
IO- A Glossop
S3 A Vaughan
RL D Walker
MU A Galan
RU- P Waner
OI- F Bordagaray
M L Durocher

CHICAGO

SP C Passeau
SP H Bithorn
SR P Derringer
SR H Wyse
SR E Hanyzewski
RS R Prim
C- C McCullough
1B P Cavarretta
2B E Stanky
SS L Merullo
3B S Hack
LF- L Novikoff
CF P Lowrey
RF B Nicholson
OF- D Dallessandro
LU- I Goodman
M J Wilson

CINCINNATI

SP J Vander Meer
SP E Riddle
SP B Walters
SR R Starr
RS C Shoun
RP J Beggs
C R Mueller
1B F McCormick
2B L Frey
SS E Miller
3B S Mesner
LF E Tipton
MO G Walker
RF M Marshall
UO E Crabtree
IO B Haas
M B McKechnie

NEW YORK

SP C Melton
SR J Wittig
SP R Fischer
SP K Chase
RP V Mungo
RP A Adams
RS H Feldman
RP B Sayles
C G Mancuso
1B- J Orengo
2B M Witek
SU B Jurges
3S D Bartell
LF- J Medwick
CF J Rucker
RF M Ott
IO S Gordon
CU E Lombardi
OI B Maynard

PHILADELPHIA

SP A Gerheauser
SP J Kraus
SP S Rowe
SP D Barrett
SP S Johnson
RS N Kimball
C- M Livingston
1L J Wasdell
2B D Murtaugh
SU G Stewart
3B P May
LF C Triplett
CF B Adams
RF R Northey
13 B Dahlgren
M1 B Harris
M2 F Fitzsimmons

PITTSBURGH

SP R Sewell
SR M Butcher
SP B Klinger
SR W Hebert
SR H Gornicki
RS X Rescigno
RP B Brandt
C A Lopez
1B E Fletcher
2S P Coscarart
S2 F Gustine
3B B Elliott
LF J Russell
CF V DiMaggio
RU J Barrett
OI- T O'Brien
M F Frisch

ST. LOUIS

SP M Cooper
SP M Lanier
SR H Krist
SR H Brecheen
SP H Gumbert
RP H Pollet
RS M Dickson
RS R Munger
C W Cooper
1B R Sanders
2B L Klein
SS M Marion
3B W Kurowski
LF- D Litwhiler
CF H Walker
RO S Musial
UT- D Garms
OI- J Hopp
M B Southworth

1944 AL

BOSTON

SP T Hughson
SR P Woods
SP J Bowman
SP E O'Neill
SR C Hausmann
RS M Ryba
RS Y Terry
RP F Barrett
C- R Partee
1B- L Finney
2B B Doerr
SS S Newsome
3B J Tabor
LF B Johnson
M1 C Metkovich
RF P Fox
32- J Bucher
M J Cronin

CHICAGO

SP B Dietrich
SP O Grove
SP E Lopat
SR J Humphries
SR J Haynes
RP T Lee
RP G Maltzberger
C M Tresh
1B H Trosky
2B R Schalk
SS S Webb
3L R Hodgin
OI E Carnett
CF T Tucker
RF W Moses
M J Dykes

CLEVELAND

SR S Gromek
SP M Harder
SR E Klieman
SP A Smith
SP A Reynolds
RP J Heving
RS R Poat
RP P Calvert
C B Rosar
1B M Rocco
2B- R Mack
SS L Boudreau
3B K Keltner
LU P Seerey
ML O Hockett
RF R Cullenbine
2U- R Peters

DETROIT

SP D Trout
SR H Newhouser
SP R Gentry
SP S Overmire
SR J Gorsica
RP B Beck
C P Richards
1B R York
2B E Mayo
SS J Hoover
3B P Higgins
LF- D Wakefield
CF D Cramer
LR J Outlaw
RU- C Hostetler
C- B Swift
M S O'Neill

NEW YORK

SP H Borowy
SP M Dubiel
SP T Bonham
SR A Donald
SP B Zuber
RP J Page
C- M Garbark
1B N Etten
2B S Stirnweiss
SS M Milosevich
3B O Grimes
LF- H Martin
CF J Lindell
RF B Metheny
C- R Hemsley
M J McCarthy

PHILADELPHIA

SP B Newsom
SR R Christopher
SP L Hamlin
SP J Flores
SP D Black
RP L Harris
RP J Berry
C F Hayes
1B- B McGhee
2S I Hall
SS E Busch
3B G Kell
LF F Garrison
MU B Estalella
RU- J White
1L D Siebert
M C Mack

ST. LOUIS

SP J Kramer
SP N Potter
SP B Muncrief
SR S Jakucki
SP D Galehouse
RS A Hollingsworth
RP G Caster
C- F Mancuso
1B G McQuinn
2B D Gutteridge
SS V Stephens
3B M Christman
UO M Byrnes
CF M Kreevich
RF G Moore
LU A Zarilla
C- R Hayworth
M L Sewell

WASHINGTON

SP M Haefner
SP D Leonard
SP E Wynn
SP J Niggeling
SR R Wolff
RS A Carrasquel
RS M Candini
RP B Lefebvre
C R Ferrell
1B J Kuhel
2B G Myatt
SS J Sullivan
3B G Torres
LO G Case
CF S Spence
RF- R Ortiz
LR J Powell
M O Bluege

1944 NL

BOSTON

SP J Tobin
SP N Andrews
SP A Javery
SR R Barrett
RS I Hutchinson
CU- P Masi
1B B Etchison
2B- C Ryan
SS W Wietelmann
3S D Phillips
LR B Nieman
CF T Holmes
RU C Workman
1U M Macon
CU- C Kluttz
M B Coleman

BROOKLYN

SP H Gregg
SP C Davis
SR R Melton
RS L Webber
C M Owen
1B H Schultz
2S- E Stanky
SC B Bragan
3B F Bordagaray
LF A Galan
MU- G Rosen
RF D Walker
UT L Olmo
OF- P Waner
M L Durocher

CHICAGO

SP H Wyse
SP C Passeau
SR P Derringer
SR B Fleming
SP B Chipman
RS H Vandenberg
RS P Erickson
C- D Williams
1B P Cavarretta
2B D Johnson
SS- L Merullo
3B S Hack
LF D Dallessandro
CF A Pafko
RF B Nicholson
3S R Hughes
M1 J Wilson
M2 R Johnson
M3 C Grimm

CINCINNATI

SP B Walters
SR C Shoun
SP E Heusser
SR T DeLa Cruz
SP H Gumbert
RS A Carter
RP J Konstanty
C R Mueller
1B F McCormick
2B W Williams
SS E Miller
3B S Mesner
LF E Tipton
CF D Clay
RM G Walker
M B McKechnie

NEW YORK

SP B Voiselle
SR H Feldman
SR E Pyle
SR R Fischer
RP A Adams
RP A Hansen
C E Lombardi
1B P Weintraub
2B G Hausmann
SS B Kerr
32 H Luby
LF J Medwick
CF J Rucker
RF M Ott
13 N Reyes
3U- B Jurges
C- G Mancuso

PHILADELPHIA

SP K Raffensberger
SR C Schanz
SP D Barrett

SP B Lee
SP A Gerheauser
RP A Karl
C B Finley
1B T Lupien
2B M Mullen
SS- R Hamrick
3S G Stewart
LF J Wasdell
CF B Adams
RF R Northey
UI C Letchas
3U- T Cieslak
C- J Peacock
UO- C Triplett
M F Fitzsimmons

PITTSBURGH
SP R Sewell
SP F Ostermueller
SP M Butcher
SR N Strincevich
SR P Roe
RS X Rescigno
RP C Cuccurullo
C A Lopez
1B B Dahlgren
2B P Coscarart
SS F Gustine
3B B Elliott
LF J Russell
CF V DiMaggio
RM J Barrett
RU F Colman
OI- T O'Brien
UT- A Rubeling
SS- F Zak
M F Frisch

ST. LOUIS
SP M Cooper
SP M Lanier
SR T Wilks
SR H Brecheen
SR A Jurisich
RP R Munger
RS F Schmidt
RP B Donnelly
C W Cooper
1B R Sanders
2B E Verban
SS M Marion
3B W Kurowski
LF D Litwhiler
OF J Hopp
RF S Musial
OI- A Bergamo
C- K O'Dea
M B Southworth

1945 AL

BOSTON
SP D Ferriss
SP J Wilson
SR E O'Neill
SR C Hausmann
SR P Woods
RS M Ryba
RP R Heflin
RP F Barrett
C- B Garbark
1O C Metkovich
2S S Newsome
SS E Lake
3B- J Tobin
LF B Johnson
CF L Culberson
RU J Lazor
MO T McBride
2B- B Steiner
M J Cronin

CHICAGO
SP T Lee
SP O Grove
SP E Lopat
SP J Humphries
SP B Dietrich
RS E Caldwell
RP J Haynes
RP J Johnson
C M Tresh
1B K Farrell
2B R Schalk
SS C Michaels
3B T Cuccinello
LF J Dickshot
CF O Hockett
RF W Moses
UO G Curtright
3U- F Baker
M J Dykes

CLEVELAND
SP S Gromek
SR A Reynolds
SP J Bagby
SP A Smith
RS E Klieman
RS P Center
RP J Salveson
C F Hayes
1B M Rocco
2B D Meyer
SS L Boudreau
3B D Ross
LF J Heath
CF F Mackiewicz
RL P Seerey
UI A Cihocki
RU- P O'Dea

DETROIT
SP H Newhouser
SR D Trout
SP A Benton
SP S Overmire
SP L Mueller
RP W Wilson
RP G Caster
C B Swift
1B R York
2B E Mayo
SS S Webb
3B B Maier
LU J Outlaw
CF D Cramer
RF R Cullenbine
LF- H Greenberg
C- P Richards
M S O'Neill

NEW YORK
SP B Bevens
SP T Bonham
SR A Gettel
SP M Dubiel
SP H Borowy
RP B Zuber
RS J Page
RP J Turner
RP K Holcombe
C- M Garbark
1B N Etten
2B S Stirnweiss
SS F Crosetti
3B O Grimes
LF H Martin
CF T Stainback
RF B Metheny
MO- R Derry
M J McCarthy

PHILADELPHIA
SP B Newsom
SP R Christopher
SP J Flores
SR L Knerr
SP D Black
RP J Berry
RS C Gassaway
RP S Gerkin
C B Rosar
1B D Siebert
2B I Hall
SS E Busch
3B G Kell
UO- M Smith
CF B Estalella
RF H Peck
OI B McGhee
M C Mack

ST. LOUIS
SP N Potter
SP J Kramer
SP S Jakucki
SP T Shirley
SP A Hollingsworth
RS B Muncrief
RP S Zoldak
C F Mancuso
1B G McQuinn
2B D Gutteridge
SS V Stephens
3B- M Christman
OI M Byrnes
CF- M Kreevich
RF G Moore
32 L Schulte
OF- P Gray
M L Sewell

WASHINGTON
SP R Wolff
SP M Haefner
SR M Pieretti
SP D Leonard
SP J Niggeling
RS A Carrasquel
RS S Ullrich
C- R Ferrell
1B J Kuhel
2U G Myatt
SS G Torres
3B H Clift
LO G Case
MO G Binks
RF- B Lewis
2B- F Vaughn
M O Bluege

1945 NL

BOSTON
SP J Tobin
SP B Logan
SP N Andrews
SP E Wright
SP B Lee
RS J Hutchings
RP D Hendrickson
C P Masi
1B- V Shupe
2S W Wietelmann
SS D Culler
3B C Workman
OF B Nieman
LF C Gillenwater
RF T Holmes
OF- B Ramsey
M1 B Coleman
M2 D Bissonette

BROOKLYN
SP H Gregg
SR V Lombardi
SP C Davis
SP A Herring
SR T Seats
RP C King
RP R Branca
RP C Buker
CS- M Sandlock
IO A Galan
2B E Stanky
SS E Basinski
3U F Bordagaray
LU L Olmo
CF G Rosen
RF D Walker
M L Durocher

CHICAGO
SP H Wyse
SP C Passeau
SP P Derringer
SR R Prim
SP H Borowy
RS P Erickson
RS H Vandenberg
C- M Livingston
1B P Cavarretta
2B D Johnson
SS L Merullo
3B S Hack
LF P Lowrey
CF A Pafko
RF B Nicholson
M C Grimm

CINCINNATI
SP E Heusser
SP J Bowman
SP B Walters
SP V Kennedy
SP F Dasso
RS H Fox
RP H Lisenbee
C- A Lakeman
1B F McCormick
2B W Williams
SS E Miller
3B S Mesner
LF E Tipton
CF D Clay
RU A Libke
RU G Walker
OF- D Sipek
M B McKechnie

NEW YORK
SP B Voiselle
SP H Feldman
SP V Mungo
SP J Brewer
SR A Hansen
RP A Adams
RS S Emmerich
RP R Fischer
C E Lombardi
1B- P Weintraub
2B G Hausmann
SS B Kerr
3B N Reyes
LU D Gardella
CF J Rucker
RF M Ott
UO- R Treadway

PHILADELPHIA
SP D Barrett
SR C Schanz
SR C Sproull
SP D Mauney
RP A Karl
C- A Seminick
OI J Wasdell
2B- T Daniels
S2- B Mott
3B J Antonelli
LF C Triplett
CF V DiMaggio
OI V Dinges
OP R Monteagudo
UT- G Crawford
IF- J Foxx
M1 F Fitzsimmons
M2 B Chapman

PITTSBURGH
SP P Roe
SP N Strincevich
SP R Sewell
SP M Butcher
SR A Gerheauser
RS K Gables
RP X Rescigno
RP C Cuccurullo
C- A Lopez
1B B Dahlgren
2B P Coscarart
SS F Gustine
3R B Elliott
LF J Russell
MU A Gionfriddo
MR J Barrett
3B L Handley
C B Salkeld
UT- F Colman
M F Frisch

ST. LOUIS
SP R Barrett
SR K Burkhart
SP B Donnelly
SP H Brecheen
SR G Dockins
RP T Wilks
RS B Byerly
RS A Jurisich
C K O'Dea
1B R Sanders
2B E Verban
SS M Marion
3B W Kurowski
LF R Schoendienst
CF B Adams
RU J Hopp
RU A Bergamo
C- D Rice
M B Southworth

1946 AL

BOSTON
SP T Hughson
SP D Ferriss
SP M Harris
SP J Dobson
SR J Bagby
RS E Johnson
RP B Klinger
RP C Dreisewerd
C H Wagner
1B R York
2B B Doerr
SS J Pesky
3B- R Russell
LF T Williams
CF D DiMaggio
RF- C Metkovich
M J Cronin

CHICAGO
SP E Lopat
SP O Grove
SP J Haynes
SP E Smith
SR F Papish
RP E Caldwell
RS R Hamner
RP A Hollingsworth
C- M Tresh
1B- H Trosky
23 D Kolloway
SS L Appling
3B- D Lodigiani
L3 B Kennedy
CF T Tucker
RF T Wright
LU- R Hodgin
2U- C Michaels
UO- W Platt
M1 J Dykes
M2 T Lyons

CLEVELAND
SP B Feller
SP R Embree
SP A Reynolds
SP S Gromek
RS B Lemon
RS J Krakauskas
C- J Hegan
1B L Fleming
2B- D Meyer
SS L Boudreau
3B K Keltner
LF G Case
UO P Seerey
RF H Edwards
CF- F Mackiewicz

DETROIT
SP H Newhouser
SP D Trout
SP V Trucks
SP F Hutchinson
SR A Benton
RS S Overmire
C- B Tebbetts
1B H Greenberg
2B- J Bloodworth
SS E Lake
3B G Kell
LF D Wakefield
CF- H Evers
RU R Cullenbine
RF P Mullin
OI- J Outlaw
M S O'Neill

NEW YORK
SP S Chandler
SP B Bevens
SR J Page
SR R Gumpert
SP T Bonham
RS A Gettel
C A Robinson
1B N Etten
2B J Gordon
SS P Rizzuto
32 S Stirnweiss
LF C Keller
CF J DiMaggio
R1 T Henrich
OI J Lindell
3B- B Johnson
M1 J McCarthy
M2 B Dickey
M3 J Neun

PHILADELPHIA
SP P Marchildon
SP D Fowler
SR B Savage
SR J Flores
SP L Knerr
RS L Harris
RS R Christopher
C B Rosar
1B G McQuinn
2B- G Handley
S3 P Suder
3B- H Majeski
LM S Chapman
SU B Sturgeon
CF- B McCosky
RF E Valo
UO- T Stainback
M C Mack

ST. LOUIS
SP J Kramer
SP D Galehouse
SR S Zoldak
SP N Potter
SP T Shirley
RS B Muncrief
RS E Kinder
RS S Ferens
C- F Mancuso
1B C Stevens
2B J Berardino
3S V Stephens
3S M Christman
LF- J Heath
CF W Judnich
UO A Zarilla
3U- B Dillinger
RF- C Laabs
IF- J Lucadello
M1 L Sewell
M2 Z Taylor

WASHINGTON
SP M Haefner
SP B Newsom
SP D Leonard
SR R Scarborough
SR S Hudson
RP R Wolff
RP E Wynn
RP M Pieretti
C- A Evans
1B M Vernon
2B J Priddy
S3 B Hitchcock
S3 C Travis
LF- J Grace
CF S Spence
RF B Lewis
M O Bluege

1946 NL

BOSTON
SP J Sain
SP M Cooper
SR E Wright
SP B Lee
SR S Johnson
RP W Spahn
RS L Wallace
C P Masi
1B- R Sanders
2B C Ryan
SS D Culler
3U N Fernandez
LU B Rowell
MU C Gillenwater
RF T Holmes
1M J Hopp
LF- D Litwhiler
M B Southworth

BROOKLYN
SR J Hatten
SR K Higbe
SR V Lombardi
SR H Gregg
SR R Melton
RS H Behrman
RP H Casey
RP A Herring
C- B Edwards
1B E Stevens
2B E Stanky
SS P Reese
3B- C Lavagetto
LU P Reiser
CF C Furillo
RF D Walker
LI A Galan
ML D Whitman
C- F Anderson
1B- H Schultz
M L Durocher

CHICAGO
SR J Schmitz
SR H Wyse
SP H Borowy
SP P Erickson
SP C Passeau
RS E Kush
RS B Chipman
C C McCullough
1B E Waitkus
2B- D Johnson
SS- B Jurges
3B- S Hack
LO M Rickert
LM P Lowrey
R1 P Cavarretta
RF B Nicholson
SU B Sturgeon
2B- L Stringer
M C Grimm

CINCINNATI
SP J Vander Meer
SP E Blackwell
SP J Beggs
SP E Heusser
SP B Walters
RS J Hetki
RS H Gumbert
RS C Shoun
RP B Malloy
C R Mueller
1B B Haas
2B B Adams
SS- E Miller
3B G Hatton
LU E Lukon
CF D Clay
RF A Libke
2O L Frey
SS- C Corbitt
CU- R Lamanno
OI- B Usher
23- B Zientara
M1 B McKechnie
M2 H Gowdy

NEW YORK
SP D Koslo
SR M Kennedy
SR B Voiselle
SR H Schumacher
RS K Trinkle
RS M Budnick
RP J Thompson
C- W Cooper
1B J Mize
2B B Blattner
SS B Kerr
3S B Rigney
LU S Gordon
UO W Marshall
RM G Rosen
RU J Graham
MU J Rucker
UT B Young
CU- E Lombardi
23- M Witek
M M Ott

PHILADELPHIA
SR K Raffensberger
SP O Judd
SP S Rowe
SR C Schanz
SR T Hughes
RP A Karl
RS D Mulligan
C A Seminick
1B F McCormick
2B E Verban
SS S Newsome
3B J Tabor
LF D Ennis
CF J Wyrostek
RF R Northey
RO- C Gilbert
UI- R Hughes
M B Chapman

PITTSBURGH
SP F Ostermueller
SR N Strincevich
SP K Heintzelman
SP R Sewell
SR E Bahr
RS J Hallett
RS K Gables
RP A Gerheauser
C- A Lopez
1B E Fletcher
2B F Gustine
SS B Cox
3B L Handley
OI J Russell
ML R Kiner
R3 B Elliott
UI- J Brown
M1 F Frisch
M2 S Davis

ST. LOUIS
SP H Pollet
SP H Brecheen
SR M Dickson
SR A Brazle
SP J Beazley
RS K Burkhart
RP T Wilks
C- J Garagiola
1L S Musial
2B R Schoendienst
SS M Marion
3B W Kurowski
LU E Dusak
MU H Walker
RF E Slaughter
OF- B Adams
MU- T Moore
UT- D Sisler
M E Dyer

1947 AL

BOSTON
SP J Dobson
SP D Ferriss
SP T Hughson
SR E Johnson
SP D Galehouse
RS H Dorish
RP J Murphy
RP B Zuber
C- B Tebbetts
1B J Jones
2B B Doerr
SS J Pesky
3B- S Dente
LF T Williams
CF D DiMaggio
RO S Mele
RU- W Moses
M J Cronin

CHICAGO
SP E Lopat
SR F Papish
SP J Haynes
SP O Grove
SP B Gillespie
RP E Harrist
RP P Gebrian
RP G Maltzberger
RP E Caldwell
C- M Tresh
1B R York
2B D Kolloway
SS L Appling
3B F Baker
RL T Wright
ML D Philley
RF B Kennedy
23 C Michaels
C- G Dickey
MU- T Tucker
IO- J Wallaesa
M T Lyons

CLEVELAND
SP B Feller
SP D Black
SR B Lemon
SP R Embree
SR A Gettel
RP E Klieman
RS B Stephens
RS S Gromek
C J Hegan
1B E Robinson
2B J Gordon
SS L Boudreau
3B K Keltner
LM D Mitchell
CF C Metkovich
RL H Edwards
1U L Fleming
RF H Peck
LU- P Seerey

DETROIT
SP H Newhouser
SP F Hutchinson
SP D Trout
SR V Trucks
SR S Overmire
RS A Benton
RS A Houtteman
RS H White
RP J Gorsica
C B Swift
1B R Cullenbine
2B E Mayo
SS E Lake
3B G Kell
LF D Wakefield
CF H Evers
RF P Mullin
UO V Wertz
M S O'Neill

NEW YORK
SP A Reynolds
SP S Shea
SP B Bevens
SP S Chandler
SP B Newsom
RP J Page
RP V Raschi
RS R Gumpert
C- A Robinson
1B G McQuinn
2B S Stirnweiss
SS P Rizzuto
3B B Johnson
LF J Lindell
CF J DiMaggio
RF T Henrich
CO- Y Berra
M B Harris

PHILADELPHIA
SP P Marchildon
SP D Fowler
SR B McCahan
SR J Coleman
SP J Flores
RS B Savage
RP C Scheib
RP R Christopher
C B Rosar
1B F Fain
2B P Suder
SS E Joost
3B H Majeski
LF B McCosky
CF S Chapman
RF E Valo
OI G Binks
M C Mack

ST. LOUIS
SP J Kramer
SP E Kinder
SR F Sanford
SP B Muncrief
SR S Zoldak
RP C Fannin
RS N Potter
RP G Moulder
C L Moss
1B W Judnich
2B- J Berardino
SS V Stephens
3B B Dillinger
LF J Heath
CF P Lehner
RO A Zarilla
RU R Coleman
C- J Early

2I- B Hitchcock
M M Ruel

WASHINGTON
SP W Masterson
SP E Wynn
SP M Haefner
SR R Scarborough
SP S Hudson
RP M Candini
RP T Ferrick
RP S Cary
C A Evans
1B M Vernon
2B J Priddy
SS M Christman
3B E Yost
LU- J Grace
CF S Spence
RF B Lewis
LU S Robertson
M O Bluege

1947 NL

BOSTON
SP W Spahn
SP J Sain
SP R Barrett
SP B Voiselle
RS S Johnson
RP C Shoun
RP W Lanfranconi
RS E Wright
C P Masi
1B E Torgeson
2B C Ryan
SS- D Culler
3B B Elliott
LF B Rowell
CF J Hopp
RF T Holmes
SU- N Fernandez
LU- D Litwhiler
1U- F McCormick
ML- M McCormick
M B Southworth

BROOKLYN
SP R Branca
SR J Hatten
SR V Lombardi
SR H Taylor
SR H Gregg
RS H Behrman
CL H Casey
RS R Barney
C B Edwards
1B J Robinson
2B E Stanky
SS P Reese
3B S Jorgensen
ML P Reiser
CF C Furillo
RF D Walker
LF- G Hermanski
M1 C Sukeforth
M2 B Shotton

CHICAGO
SR J Schmitz
SP D Lade
SR H Borowy
SR P Erickson
SR H Wyse
RS B Chipman
RP E Kush
RP R Meers
C B Scheffing
1B E Waitkus
2B D Johnson
SS L Merullo
3B P Lowrey
LO P Cavarretta
CF A Pafko
RF B Nicholson
CU- C McCullough
S2- B Sturgeon
M C Grimm

CINCINNATI
SP E Blackwell
SP J Vander Meer
SR K Peterson
SR B Lively
SP B Walters
RS E Erautt
RP K Raffensberger
RP H Gumbert
RS J Hetki
C R Lamanno
1B B Young
2B B Zientara
SS E Miller
3B G Hatton
LF A Galan
OI B Haas
RF F Baumholtz
2B- B Adams
OF- B Lukon
MU- C Vollmer
M J Neun

NEW YORK
SR L Jansen
SP D Koslo
SR M Kennedy
SP C Hartung
RP K Trinkle
RP J Beggs
C W Cooper
1B J Mize
23 B Rigney
SS B Kerr
3B J Lohrke
LF S Gordon
CF B Thomson
RF W Marshall
M M Ott

PHILADELPHIA
SP D Leonard
SP S Rowe
SR O Judd
SP K Heintzelman
SR T Hughes
RS B Donnelly
RS A Jurisich
RS C Schanz
RS F Schmidt
C A Seminick
1B H Schultz
2B E Verban
SS S Newsome
3B L Handley
LF D Ennis
CF H Walker
RF J Wyrostek
UO- C Gilbert
M B Chapman

PITTSBURGH
SR K Higbe
SP F Ostermueller
SR T Bonham
SR P Roe
SR R Sewell
RS J Bagby
RS N Strincevich
RP E Singleton
C- D Howell
1B H Greenberg
2B- J Bloodworth
SS B Cox
3B F Gustine
LF R Kiner
CF J Russell
RF W Westlake
UO C Rikard
M1 Herman
M2 B Burwell

ST. LOUIS
SR M Dickson
SP R Munger
SP H Brecheen
SR H Pollet
SR A Brazle
RS J Hearn
RS K Burkhart
RP T Wilks
C D Rice
1B S Musial
2B R Schoendienst
SS M Marion
3B W Kurowski
LU E Slaughter
CF T Moore
RU R Northey
UO C Diering
OI E Dusak
M E Dyer

1948 AL

BOSTON
SP J Dobson
SP M Parnell
SP J Kramer
SP E Kinder
SR D Galehouse
RS D Ferriss
RP M Harris
RP E Johnson
C B Tebbetts
1B B Goodman
2B B Doerr
SS V Stephens
3B J Pesky
LF T Williams
CF D DiMaggio
RU S Spence
RU- W Moses
M J McCarthy

CHICAGO
SP B Wight
SP J Haynes
SP A Gettel
SP M Pieretti
SR F Papish
RS H Judson
RP R Gumpert
RS G Moulder
RS B Gillespie
C A Robinson
1B T Lupien
2U D Kolloway
S2 C Michaels
3S L Appling
LF P Seerey
CF D Philley
RF T Wright
3U F Baker
UO R Hodgin
M T Lyons

CLEVELAND
SP B Lemon
SP B Feller
SP G Bearden
SR S Zoldak
RS S Gromek
RP E Klieman
CL R Christopher
C J Hegan
1B E Robinson
2B J Gordon
SS L Boudreau
3B K Keltner
LF D Mitchell
CF- T Tucker
MR L Doby
RL- A Clark
OI- W Judnich

DETROIT
SP H Newhouser
SP F Hutchinson
SP V Trucks
SP D Trout
SR A Houtteman
RP S Overmire
RS B Pierce
C B Swift
1B G Vico
2B E Mayo
SS J Lipon
3B- G Kell
LR V Wertz
CF H Evers
RF P Mullin
LF D Wakefield
IF- N Berry
M S O'Neill

NEW YORK
SP A Reynolds
SP E Lopat
SP V Raschi
SP S Shea
SR T Byrne
RP J Page
RS F Hiller
C- G Niarhos
1B G McQuinn
2B S Stirnweiss
SS P Rizzuto
3B B Johnson
LF- J Lindell
CF J DiMaggio
R1 T Henrich
CR Y Berra
UT B Brown
LF- C Keller
M B Harris

PHILADELPHIA
SP P Marchildon
SP J Coleman
SP D Fowler
SP C Scheib
SR L Brissie
RP B Harris
RP B Savage
C- B Rosar
1B F Fain
2B P Suder
SS E Joost
3B H Majeski
LF B McCosky
CF S Chapman
RF E Valo
OI- D White
M C Mack

ST. LOUIS
SP F Sanford
SP C Fannin
SR N Garver
SP B Kennedy
RS B Stephens
RP F Biscan
RP A Widmar
C L Moss
1B- C Stevens
2B J Priddy
SS E Pellagrini
3B B Dillinger
LF W Platt
CF P Lehner
UO A Zarilla
SS S Dente
C- R Partee
M Z Taylor

WASHINGTON
SP E Wynn
SP W Masterson
SP R Scarborough
SR S Hudson
SP M Haefner
RS F Thompson
RP M Candini
RP T Ferrick
RP D Welteroth
C J Early
1B M Vernon
2B A Kozar
SS M Christman
3B E Yost
LF G Coan
MR- J Wooten
RM B Stewart
C A Evans
CF- C Gillenwater
OF- T McBride
SU- J Sullivan
M J Kuhel

1948 NL

BOSTON
SP J Sain
SP W Spahn
SP B Voiselle
SR V Bickford
SR R Barrett
RP B Hogue
RP C Shoun
C P Masi
1B E Torgeson
2B- E Stanky
SS A Dark
3B B Elliott
LF J Heath
CF- J Russell
RF T Holmes
UO M McCormick
ML- C Conatser
C- B Salkeld
2S- S Sisti
M B Southworth

BROOKLYN
SR R Barney
SP R Branca
SR J Hatten
SR P Roe
RS E Palica
RP H Behrman
RP P Minner
RP W Ramsdell
C- R Campanella
1C G Hodges
2B J Robinson
SS P Reese
3B- B Cox
UO- M Rackley
CF C Furillo
RF G Hermanski
CU B Edwards
23- E Miksis
M1 L Durocher
M2 R Blades
M3 B Shotton

CHICAGO
SP J Schmitz
SR R Meyer
SR D McCall
SR B Rush
SR H Borowy
RS R Hamner
RS C Chambers
RP J Dobernic
RP E Kush
C B Scheffing
1B E Waitkus
2B H Schenz
SS R Smalley
3B A Pafko
UT P Lowrey
CF H Jeffcoat
RF B Nicholson
UT P Cavarretta
LU- C Maddern
CU- R Walker
M C Grimm

CINCINNATI
SP J Vander Meer
SR K Raffensberger
SR H Fox
SP H Wehmeier
SP E Blackwell
RS K Peterson
RP H Gumbert
RP W Cress
C R Lamanno
1B T Kluszewski
2U- B Adams
SS V Stallcup
3B G Hatton
LF H Sauer
CF J Wyrostek
RO F Baumholtz
RU D Litwhiler
2I- C Corbitt
M1 J Neun
M2 B Walters

NEW YORK
SP L Jansen
SR S Jones
SR R Poat
SR C Hartung
SR D Koslo
RP M Kennedy
RS A Hansen
RP K Trinkle
C- W Cooper
1B J Mize
2B G Rigney
SS B Kerr
3B S Gordon
UO B Thomson
ML W Lockman
RF W Marshall
32 J Lohrke
M1 M Ott
M2 L Durocher

PHILADELPHIA
SP D Leonard
SP C Simmons
SR M Dubiel
SR S Rowe
SP R Roberts
RP B Donnelly
RS K Heintzelman
RP E Heusser
RP S Nahem
C A Seminick
1B D Sisler
2S G Hamner
SS E Miller
3U P Caballero
LF J Blatnik
CF R Ashburn
RF D Ennis
31 B Haas
MU H Walker
UT- B Rowell
M1 B Chapman
M2 D Cooke
M3 E Sawyer

PITTSBURGH
SP B Chesnes
SP E Riddle
SR V Lombardi
SP T Bonham
SP F Ostermueller
RS K Higbe
RP R Sewell
RS E Singleton
RS M Queen
C E Fitz Gerald
1B E Stevens
2B D Murtaugh
SS S Rojek
3B F Gustine
LF R Kiner
MR W Westlake
RF D Walker
MU J Hopp
C C Kluttz
UT- M West
M B Meyer

ST. LOUIS
SR M Dickson
SP H Brecheen
SR H Pollet
SR R Munger
SR A Brazle
RP T Wilks
RP G Staley
C D Rice
1B N Jones
2B R Schoendienst
SS M Marion
3B D Lang
LR E Slaughter
CF- T Moore
OI S Musial
UT E Dusak
RU R Northey
3B- W Kurowski
2S- R LaPointe
M E Dyer

1949 AL

BOSTON
SP M Parnell
SR E Kinder
SP J Dobson
SP C Stobbs
SP J Kramer
RP T Hughson
RP E Johnson
C B Tebbetts
1B B Goodman
2B B Doerr
SS V Stephens
3B J Pesky
LF T Williams
CF D DiMaggio
RF A Zarilla
M J McCarthy

CHICAGO
SP B Wight
SP R Gumpert
SP B Pierce
SR B Kuzava
SR H Judson
RP M Surkont
C- D Wheeler
1B C Kress
2B C Michaels
SS L Appling
3B F Baker
LU- G Zernial
CF C Metkovich
RF D Philley
UT- S Souchock
M J Onslow

CLEVELAND
SP B Lemon
SP B Feller
SR M Garcia
SP E Wynn
SR G Bearden
RS A Benton
RS S Paige
RP F Papish
RP S Zoldak
C J Hegan
1B M Vernon
2B J Gordon
S3 L Boudreau
3B- K Keltner
LF D Mitchell
CF L Doby
RF B Kennedy
SS- R Boone
OF- T Tucker

DETROIT
SP H Newhouser
SP V Trucks
SP A Houtteman
SP T Gray
SR F Hutchinson
RP D Trout
C A Robinson
1B- P Campbell
2B N Berry
SS J Lipon
3B G Kell
LM H Evers
CF J Groth
RF V Wertz
UI D Kolloway
UI E Lake
LU P Mullin
M R Rolfe

NEW YORK
SP V Raschi
SP E Lopat
SP A Reynolds
SP T Byrne
SR F Sanford
RP J Page
RP S Shea
RP C Marshall
C Y Berra
R1 T Henrich
2B J Coleman
SS P Rizzuto
3B B Brown
LU G Woodling
MR C Mapes
RO H Bauer
3U B Johnson
LF- J Lindell
M C Stengel

PHILADELPHIA
SR A Kellner
SP J Coleman
SP L Brissie
SP D Fowler
SR C Scheib
RS B Shantz
RP B Harris
C M Guerra
1B F Fain
2B P Suder
SS E Joost
3B H Majeski
LF E Valo
CF S Chapman
RF W Moses
2B- N Fox
M C Mack

ST. LOUIS
SP N Garver
SR A Papai
SP C Fannin
SP K Drews
SR R Embree
RS B Kennedy
RS J Ostrowski
RP T Ferrick
RS D Starr
C S Lollar
1B J Graham
2B J Priddy
SS- E Pellagrini
3B B Dillinger
ML R Sievers
OI S Spence
RF D Kokos
OI P Lehner
C L Moss
LU W Platt
SI J Sullivan
M Z Taylor

WASHINGTON
SR S Hudson
SP R Scarborough
SR P Calvert
SP M Harris
SR D Weik
RS L Hittle
RS J Haynes
RP D Welteroth
C A Evans
1B E Robinson
2B A Kozar
SS S Dente
3B E Yost
LO B Stewart
CF C Vollmer
RU B Lewis
LM G Coan
2U S Robertson
RM- S Mele
M J Kuhel

1949 NL

BOSTON
SP W Spahn
SP J Sain
SP V Bickford
SP B Voiselle
SR J Antonelli
RP N Potter
RP B Hogue
RS B Hall
C- B Salkeld
1B E Fletcher
2B E Stanky
SS A Dark
3B B Elliott
LR M Rickert
MU J Russell
RF T Holmes
UT S Sisti
OI- P Reiser
UI- C Ryan
UO- E Sauer
M1 B Southworth
M2 J Cooney

BROOKLYN
SP D Newcombe
SP P Roe
SP J Hatten
SP R Branca
SR R Barney
RS J Banta
RP E Palica
RP P Minner
C R Campanella
1B G Hodges
2B J Robinson
SS P Reese
3B B Cox
LU- G Hermanski
CF D Snider
RF C Furillo
M B Shotton

CHICAGO
SP J Schmitz
SP B Rush
SP D Leonard
SR M Dubiel
SR D Lade
RS W Hacker
RS B Chipman
RS D Adkins
RP B Muncrief
C- M Owen
1B H Reich
2B E Verban
SS R Smalley
3U- F Gustine
LF H Sauer
M3 A Pafko
MR H Jeffcoat
1U P Cavarretta
M1 C Grimm
M2 F Frisch

CINCINNATI
SP K Raffensberger
SP H Fox
SP H Wehmeier
SP J Vander Meer
RS E Erautt
RS B Lively
RP E Blackwell
RS K Peterson
C- W Cooper
1B T Kluszewski
2U J Bloodworth
SS V Stallcup
3B G Hatton
LF- P Lowrey
CF L Merriman
RM J Wyrostek
2U B Adams
RU D Litwhiler
OI- H Walker
M1 B Walters
M2 L Sewell

NEW YORK
SP L Jansen
SP M Kennedy
SR D Koslo
SR S Jones
SR C Hartung
RP K Higbe
RP H Behrman
RP A Hansen
C- W Westrum
1B J Mize
2B- H Thompson
SS- B Kerr
3B S Gordon
LF W Lockman
CF B Thomson
RF W Marshall
SI B Rigney
M L Durocher

PHILADELPHIA
SP K Heintzelman
SR R Roberts
SP R Meyer
SP H Borowy
SR C Simmons
RP J Konstanty
RP K Trinkle
RS S Rowe
C A Seminick
1B D Sisler
2B- E Miller
SS G Hamner
3B W Jones
LF D Ennis
CF R Ashburn
RF B Nicholson
RF- S Hollmig
CU- S Lopata
M E Sawyer

PITTSBURGH
SR M Dickson
SP B Werle
SR C Chambers
SP B Chesnes
SR V Lombardi
RS R Sewell
C- C McCullough
OI- J Hopp
2B M Basgall
SS S Rojek
3B P Castiglione
LF R Kiner
MU- D Restelli
RM W Westlake
3B- E Bockman
1B- J Hopp
UT- D Walker
M B Meyer

ST. LOUIS
SR H Pollet
SP H Brecheen
SR A Brazle
SP R Munger
SR G Staley
RP T Wilks
C- D Rice
1B N Jones
2B R Schoendienst
SS M Marion
3B- E Kazak
LF E Slaughter
CF C Diering
RM S Musial
C- J Garagiola
3B- T Glaviano
1B- R Nelson
RF- R Northey
M E Dyer

1950 AL

BOSTON
SP M Parnell
SR E Kinder
SR J Dobson
SR C Stobbs
SR M McDermott
RS W Masterson
RP W Nixon
C- B Tebbetts
1B W Dropo
2B B Doerr
SS V Stephens
3B J Pesky
LF- T Williams
CF D DiMaggio
RF A Zarilla
IO B Goodman
M1 J McCarthy
M2 S O'Neill

CHICAGO
SP B Pierce
SP B Wight
SR B Cain
SR R Gumpert
SP R Scarborough
RP H Judson
RP K Holcombe
RP L Aloma
C P Masi
1B E Robinson
2B N Fox
SS C Carrasquel
3B H Majeski
LF G Zernial
RM D Philley
RF- M Rickert
3U- F Baker
UT- G Goldsberry
M1 J Onslow
M2 R Corriden

CLEVELAND
SP B Lemon
SP B Feller
SP E Wynn
SP M Garcia
SR S Gromek
RP S Zoldak
RP A Benton
RP J Flores
RP M Pieretti
C J Hegan
1B L Easter
2B J Gordon
SS R Boone
3B A Rosen
LF D Mitchell
CF L Doby
RF B Kennedy
2B- B Avila
SS- L Boudreau

DETROIT
SP A Houtteman
SR F Hutchinson
SP H Newhouser
SR D Trout
SP T Gray
RS H White
RP P Calvert
C A Robinson
1B D Kolloway
2B J Priddy
SS J Lipon
3B G Kell
LF H Evers
CF J Groth
RF V Wertz
M R Rolfe

NEW YORK
SP V Raschi
SP A Reynolds
SP E Lopat
SP T Byrne
SP W Ford
RS F Sanford
CL J Page
RP T Ferrick
C Y Berra
1B J Collins
2B J Coleman
SS P Rizzuto
3B B Johnson
LF G Woodling
CF J DiMaggio
RL H Bauer
3B B Brown
RU C Mapes
1B- J Mize
M C Stengel

PHILADELPHIA
SR L Brissie
SP A Kellner
SR B Shantz
SR B Hooper
SR H Wyse
RS C Scheib
C- M Guerra
1B F Fain
2B B Hitchcock
SS E Joost
3B- B Dillinger
LU P Lehner
CF S Chapman
RL E Valo
RU- W Moses
3U- K Wahl
M C Mack

ST. LOUIS
SP N Garver
SR A Widmar
SR S Overmire
SR D Starr
SR H Dorish
RP C Fannin
RS D Johnson
RP C Marshall
C S Lollar
1L D Lenhardt
2B O Friend
SS T Upton
32- B Sommers
LR D Kokos
UO R Coleman
RU K Wood
1B H Arft
MU R Sievers
CU- L Moss
23 S Stirnweiss
M Z Taylor

WASHINGTON
SP S Hudson
SP B Kuzava
SP C Marrero
SP S Consuegra
SR J Haynes
RP M Harris
RP J Pearce
C- A Evans
1B- M Vernon
2B C Michaels
SS S Dente
3B E Yost
RL B Stewart
CF I Noren
RO S Mele
LF G Coan
M B Harris

1950 NL

BOSTON
SP V Bickford
SP W Spahn
SP J Sain
SR B Chipman
RP B Hogue
RS J Antonelli
RP B Hall
C W Cooper
1B E Torgeson
2B R Hartsfield
SS B Kerr
3B B Elliott
LF S Gordon
CF S Jethroe
RF T Holmes
RU W Marshall
C- D Crandall
M B Southworth

BROOKLYN
SP D Newcombe
SP P Roe
SR E Palica
SR R Branca
SP C Erskine
RS D Bankhead
C R Campanella
1B G Hodges
2B J Robinson
SS P Reese
3B B Cox
LF G Hermanski
CF D Snider
RF C Furillo
LU- J Russell
M B Shotton

CHICAGO
SP B Rush
SR P Minner
SR J Schmitz
SR F Hiller
SR D Lade
RS M Dubiel
RS J Klippstein
RP D Leonard
RS J Vander Meer
C- M Owen
1B- P Ward
2B W Terwilliger
SS R Smalley
3B B Serena
LF H Sauer
CF A Pafko
OI- B Borkowski
1B- P Cavarretta
M F Frisch

CINCINNATI
SP E Blackwell
SP K Raffensberger
SP H Wehmeier
SR H Fox
SP W Ramsdell
RP F Smith
RP E Erautt
RP J Hetki
C- D Howell
1B T Kluszewski
2B C Ryan
SS V Stallcup
3B G Hatton
LU J Adcock
CF B Usher
RF J Wyrostek
IF B Adams
CF L Merriman
LU- P Lowrey
M L Sewell

NEW YORK
SP L Jansen
SR S Maglie
SR S Jones
SR D Koslo
SP J Hearn
RS M Kennedy
RS J Kramer
RP A Hansen
C W Westrum
1B T Gilbert
2B E Stanky
SS A Dark
3B H Thompson
LF W Lockman
CF B Thomson
RF D Mueller
1R M Irvin
M L Durocher

PHILADELPHIA
SP R Roberts
SP C Simmons
SR B Miller
SP R Meyer
SR B Church
RP J Konstanty
RP K Heintzelman
C A Seminick
1B E Waitkus
2B M Goliat
SS G Hamner
3B W Jones
LF D Sisler
CF R Ashburn
RF D Ennis
M E Sawyer

PITTSBURGH
SP C Chambers
SR M Dickson
SR B Werle
SR B Macdonald
SR V Law
RS M Queen
RP V Lombardi
RP J Walsh
C C McCullough
1U J Hopp
2B D Murtaugh
SS- S Rojek
3B- N Fernandez
LF R Kiner
MU W Westlake
RF G Bell
UI P Castiglione
SS- D O'Connell
M B Meyer

ST. LOUIS
SP H Pollet
SP M Lanier
SR G Staley
SP H Brecheen
SR R Munger
RS A Brazle
RS C Boyer
RP F Martin
C D Rice
1B- R Nelson
2B R Schoendienst
SS M Marion
3B T Glaviano
OI S Musial
UO B Howerton
RF E Slaughter
CF- C Diering
3U E Kazak
M E Dyer

1951 AL

BOSTON
SP M Parnell
SR R Scarborough
SR M McDermott
SP C Stobbs
SR W Nixon
RP E Kinder
RS B Wight
RP L Kiely
RS H Taylor
C- L Moss
1B W Dropo
2B B Doerr
SS J Pesky
3B V Stephens
LF T Williams
CF D DiMaggio
RF C Vollmer
UT B Goodman
SU- L Boudreau
3U- F Hatfield
M S O'Neill

CHICAGO
SP B Pierce
SP S Rogovin
SP K Holcombe
SP J Dobson
SR R Gumpert
RP L Kretlow
RS H Judson
RP H Dorish
RP L Aloma
C- P Masi
1B E Robinson
2B N Fox
SS C Carrasquel
3B- B Dillinger
UT M Minoso
CF J Busby
RF A Zarilla
LU B Stewart
3U- F Baker
M P Richards

CLEVELAND
SP E Wynn
SP B Lemon
SR M Garcia
SP B Feller
RP L Brissie
RS S Gromek
C J Hegan
1B L Easter
2B B Avila
SS R Boone
3B A Rosen
LF D Mitchell
CF L Doby
RF B Kennedy
OI S Chapman
OI H Simpson
M A Lopez

DETROIT
SP T Gray
SR D Trout
SR F Hutchinson
SR V Trucks
SR B Cain
RS M Stuart
RP G Bearden
RP H Newhouser
RP H White
C J Ginsberg
1B D Kryhoski
2B J Priddy
SS J Lipon
3B G Kell
LM H Evers
CF J Groth
RF V Wertz
LU P Mullin
1B- D Kolloway
UT- S Souchock
M R Rolfe

NEW YORK
SP V Raschi
SP E Lopat
SR A Reynolds
SR T Morgan
SR S Shea
RP J Ostrowski
C Y Berra
1B J Collins
2B J Coleman
SS P Rizzuto
3B B Brown
LF G Woodling
CF J DiMaggio
RL H Bauer
RF M Mantle
32 G McDougald
1B J Mize
M C Stengel

PHILADELPHIA
SP A Kellner
SP B Shantz
SR B Hooper
SR M Martin
SP S Zoldak
RS C Scheib
RP D Fowler
RS J Coleman
RP J Kucab
C- J Tipton
1B F Fain
2B P Suder
SS E Joost
3B- H Majeski
LF G Zernial
CF D Philley
RF E Valo
1U L Limmer
32- B Hitchcock
M J Dykes

ST. LOUIS
SP N Garver
SR D Pillette
SP T Byrne
SR A Widmar
RP B Mahoney
RP S Paige
RS B Kennedy
C S Lollar
1B H Arft
2B B Young
SS- B Jennings
3B F Marsh
LR- R Coleman
CF J Delsing
RL K Wood
C- M Batts
M Z Taylor

WASHINGTON
SP C Marrero
SP D Johnson
SP S Hudson
SR J Moreno
SP B Porterfield
RS S Consuegra
RP M Harris
RP J Haynes
C- M Guerra
1B M Vernon
2B C Michaels
SS- P Runnels
3B E Yost
LF G Coan
CF I Noren
RU S Mele
SU- S Dente
UO- M McCormick
M B Harris

1951 NL

BOSTON
SP W Spahn
SP M Surkont
SP V Bickford
SP J Sain
SR C Nichols
RP J Wilson
RS D Cole
RP G Estock
RP B Chipman
C W Cooper
1B E Torgeson
2B R Hartsfield
SS- B Kerr
3B B Elliott
LU S Gordon
CF S Jethroe
RF W Marshall
IO S Sisti
UO- B Addis
M1 B Southworth
M2 T Holmes

BROOKLYN
SP D Newcombe
SP P Roe
SR R Branca
SR C Erskine
RP C King
RS B Podbielan
C R Campanella
1B G Hodges
2B J Robinson
SS P Reese
3B B Cox
LF- A Pafko
CF D Snider
RF C Furillo
LU- D Thompson
M C Dressen

CHICAGO
SP B Rush
SP P Minner
SR C McLish
SP F Hiller
SR T Lown
RS J Klippstein
RS B Kelly
RP D Leonard
RP M Dubiel
CU S Burgess
1B- C Connors
2B E Miksis
SS- R Smalley
3B R Jackson
LF H Sauer
UO H Jeffcoat
UO F Baumholtz
1U- P Cavarretta
M1 F Frisch

CINCINNATI
SP K Raffensberger
SP E Blackwell
SR H Fox
SP W Ramsdell
SR H Wehmeier
RS H Perkowski
RP F Smith
RP B Byerly
C- D Howell
1B T Kluszewski
2B C Ryan
SS V Stallcup
3B G Hatton
LF J Adcock
ML L Merriman
RF J Wyrostek
IO B Adams
MU B Usher
SU- R McMillan
M L Sewell

NEW YORK
SP S Maglie
SP L Jansen
SP J Hearn
SR D Koslo
RP G Spencer
RS S Jones
RS M Kennedy
RP A Gettel
C W Westrum
1B W Lockman
2B E Stanky
SS A Dark
3B- H Thompson
L1 M Irvin
CF W Mays
RF D Mueller
OI B Thomson
M L Durocher

PHILADELPHIA
SP R Roberts
SP B Church
SP R Meyer
SR J Thompson
SR K Heintzelman
RP J Konstanty
RP K Johnson
C A Seminick
1B E Waitkus
2U- P Caballero
SS G Hamner
3B W Jones
LF D Sisler
CF R Ashburn
RF D Ennis
UT- T Brown
UL- B Nicholson
2U- E Pellagrini
C- D Wilber
M E Sawyer

PITTSBURGH
SR M Dickson
SR M Queen
SR B Friend
SP H Pollet
SR V Law
RS B Werle
RP T Wilks
RP J Walsh
C- C McCullough
1B- J Phillips
2B- D Murtaugh
SS G Strickland
3B P Castiglione
L1 R Kiner
M1 C Metkovich
RF G Bell
OI- B Howerton
M B Meyer

ST. LOUIS
SR G Staley
SR T Poholsky
SP M Lanier
SP H Brecheen
SP C Chambers
RS A Brazle
RS R Munger
RP D Bokelmann
C D Rice
1B- N Jones
2B R Schoendienst
SS S Hemus
3B B Johnson
L1 S Musial
MU P Lowrey
RF E Slaughter
M M Marion

1952 AL

BOSTON
SP M Parnell
SP M McDermott
SP D Trout
SP S Hudson
SP D Brodowski
RS W Nixon
RS E Kinder
RS I Delock
RS R Scarborough
C S White
1B D Gernert
2U B Goodman
SS- J Lipon
3B- G Kell
LF H Evers
CF D DiMaggio
RU F Throneberry
23- T Lepcio
S3- V Stephens
UO- C Vollmer
M L Boudreau

CHICAGO
SP B Pierce
SP S Rogovin
SP J Dobson
SP M Grissom
SR C Stobbs
RP H Dorish
RP B Kennedy
C S Lollar
1B E Robinson
2B N Fox
SS C Carrasquel
3B H Rodriguez
UT M Minoso
UO- R Coleman
RF S Mele
LU- B Stewart
M P Richards

CLEVELAND
SP B Lemon
SR M Garcia
SP E Wynn
SP B Feller
SR S Gromek
RP L Brissie
RP M Harris
C J Hegan
1B L Easter
2B B Avila
SS R Boone
3B A Rosen
LF D Mitchell
CF L Doby
RF H Simpson
M A Lopez

DETROIT
SP T Gray
SP A Houtteman
SP V Trucks
SP H Newhouser
SP B Wight
RS B Hoeft
RP H White
RP D Littlefield
C J Ginsberg
1B W Dropo
2B- J Priddy
SS- N Berry
3B F Hatfield
LU P Mullin
CF J Groth
RF- V Wertz
RO- C Mapes
UT- S Souchock
M1 R Rolfe
M2 F Hutchinson

NEW YORK
SP A Reynolds
SP V Raschi
SR J Sain
SP E Lopat
SR B Kuzava
RP T Morgan
RS J McDonald
RP B Hogue
C Y Berra
1B J Collins
2B B Martin
SS P Rizzuto
3B G McDougald
LF G Woodling
CF M Mantle
RF H Bauer
UR- J Mize
OI I Noren
M C Stengel

PHILADELPHIA
SP B Shantz
SP A Kellner
SP H Byrd
SR C Scheib
RS B Hooper
RP J Kucab
C J Astroth
1B F Fain
2B- S Kell
SS E Joost
3B B Hitchcock
LF G Zernial
CF D Philley
RF E Valo
M J Dykes

ST. LOUIS
SP D Pillette
SP T Byrne
SP B Cain
SR G Bearden
SP N Garver
RS S Paige
RS E Harrist
RP D Madison
C C Courtney
1B D Kryhoski
2B B Young
SS- J DeMaestri
3L J Dyck
UQ J Delsing
CF J Rivera
RU B Nieman
1B- G Goldsberry
M1 R Hornsby
M2 M Marion

WASHINGTON
SP B Porterfield
SP C Marrero
SP S Shea
SP W Masterson
SP J Moreno
RP R Gumpert
RP S Consuegra
RS D Johnson
RP J Haynes
C M Grasso
1B M Vernon
2B- F Baker
SS P Runnels
3B E Yost
LF G Coan
CF J Busby
RF J Jensen
M B Harris

1952 NL

BOSTON
SP W Spahn
SP J Wilson
SP M Surkont
SP V Bickford
RS L Burdette
RP S Jones
C W Cooper
1B E Torgeson
2B J Dittmer
SS J Logan
3B E Mathews
LF S Gordon
CF S Jethroe

RU J Daniels
UT- S Sisti
RF- B Thorpe
M1 T Holmes
M2 C Grimm

BROOKLYN

SP C Erskine
SR B Loes
SR B Wade
SP P Roe
SR J Rutherford
RP J Black
RP C Van Cuyk
C R Campanella
1B G Hodges
2B J Robinson
SS P Reese
3B B Cox
LR A Pafko
CF D Snider
RF C Furillo
LU G Shuba
M C Dressen

CHICAGO

SP B Rush
SR J Klippstein
SR W Hacker
SP P Minner
SR T Lown
RS B Kelly
RP D Leonard
RS B Schultz
C T Atwell
1B D Fondy
2S E Miksis
SS- R Smalley
3B R Jackson
LF H Sauer
CF H Jeffcoat
RM F Baumholtz
RU G Hermanski
IF B Serena
UO B Addis
M P Cavarretta

CINCINNATI

SP K Raffensberger
SP H Perkowski
SP H Wehmeier
SP B Church
SR F Hiller
RP F Smith
RP E Blackwell
RS J Nuxhall
C A Seminick
1B T Kluszewski
2B G Hatton
SS R McMillan
3B B Adams
LU J Adcock
MO B Borkowski
RF W Marshall
M1 L Sewell
M2 E Brucker
M3 R Hornsby

NEW YORK

SP J Hearn
SP S Maglie
SR D Koslo
SP L Jansen
SR M Lanier
RP H Wilhelm
RS M Kennedy
RP G Spencer
C W Westrum
1B W Lockman
2B D Williams
SS A Dark
3M B Thomson
LU B Elliott
UT H Thompson
RF D Mueller
M L Durocher

PHILADELPHIA

SP R Roberts
SP R Meyer
SP K Drews
SP C Simmons
SR S Ridzik
RP J Konstanty
RP A Hansen
C S Burgess
1B E Waitkus
2B C Ryan
SS G Hamner
3B W Jones
LF D Ennis
CF R Ashburn
RF J Wyrostek
M1 E Sawyer
M2 S O'Neill

PITTSBURGH

SP M Dickson
SP H Pollet
SR B Friend
RS W Main
RP T Wilks
RP P LaPalme
C J Garagiola
1B T Bartirome
2U J Merson
SS D Groat
3B- P Castiglione
LF R Kiner
CF B Del Greco
RF G Bell
UI C Koshorek
1O C Metkovich
M B Meyer

ST. LOUIS

SP G Staley
SP V Mizell
SR J Presko
SP C Boyer
SR H Brecheen
RS A Brazle
RP E Yuhas
RS C Chambers
C D Rice
1B D Sisler
2B R Schoendienst
SS S Hemus
3B B Johnson
OI P Lowrey
MU S Musial
RF E Slaughter
LF H Rice
3U- T Glaviano
M E Stanky

1953 AL

BOSTON

SP M Parnell
SP M McDermott
SP H Brown
SR S Hudson
SP W Nixon
RP E Kinder
RS B Flowers
RP I Delock
C S White
1B D Gernert
2B B Goodman
SS M Bolling
3B G Kell
LF H Evers
CF T Umphlett
RF J Piersall
IF- F Baker
LF- G Stephens
M L Boudreau

CHICAGO

SP B Pierce
SP V Trucks
SR M Fornieles
SP S Rogovin
SR S Consuegra
RS H Dorish
RP J Dobson
RS B Keegan
RP G Bearden
C S Lollar
1B F Fain
2B N Fox
SS C Carrasquel
3B- B Elliott
LF M Minoso
CF J Rivera
RF S Mele
OF- T Wright
M P Richards

CLEVELAND

SP B Lemon
SP M Garcia
SP E Wynn
SP B Feller
SP A Houtteman
RS D Hoskins
RP B Hooper
C J Hegan
1B B Glynn
2B B Avila
SS G Strickland
3B A Rosen
LF D Mitchell
CF L Doby
RL B Kennedy
RF- H Simpson
UO- W Westlake
M A Lopez

DETROIT

SP B Hoeft
SP N Garver
SP T Gray
SP S Gromek
SP R Branca
RS D Marlowe
RP R Herbert
RP D Madison
C M Batts
1B W Dropo
2U J Pesky
SS H Kuenn
3B R Boone
LR B Nieman
CF J Delsing
RL D Lund
UI F Hatfield
OF- P Mullin
OI- S Souchock
M F Hutchinson

NEW YORK

SP W Ford
SR J Sain
SP V Raschi
SP E Lopat
SR A Reynolds
RP J McDonald
RS B Kuzava
RP T Gorman
RP R Scarborough
C Y Berra
1B J Collins
2B B Martin
SS P Rizzuto
3B G McDougald
LF G Woodling
CF M Mantle
RF H Bauer
UO I Noren
UR- J Mize
M C Stengel

PHILADELPHIA

SP H Byrd
SR M Fricano
SP A Kellner
SR C Bishop
SP B Shantz
RS M Martin
RS C Scheib
RP F Fanovich
C- J Astroth
1B E Robinson
2B C Michaels
SS J DeMaestri
3B L Babe
LF G Zernial
CF E McGhee
RF D Philley
32 P Suder
C- R Murray
M J Dykes

ST. LOUIS

SR D Larsen
SP D Pillette
SR D Littlefield
SR H Brecheen
SR B Cain
RP S Paige
RP M Stuart
RS M Blyzka
C C Courtney
1B D Kryhoski
2B B Young
SS B Hunter
OI J Dyck
LU D Kokos
CF J Groth
RF V Wertz
LU D Lenhardt
C- L Moss
1B- R Sievers
M M Marion

WASHINGTON

SP B Porterfield
SP W Masterson
SP S Shea
SP C Stobbs
SP C Marrero
RS S Dixon
RS J Schmitz
RS A Sima
RP J Lane
C- E Fitz Gerald
1B M Vernon
2B W Terwilliger
SS P Runnels
3B E Yost
LF C Vollmer
CF J Busby
RF J Jensen
M B Harris

1953 NL

BROOKLYN

SP C Erskine
SP R Meyer
SP B Loes
SP P Roe
SR J Podres
RS B Milliken
RS C Labine
RP J Hughes
RP B Wade
C R Campanella
1B G Hodges
2B J Gilliam
SS P Reese
3B B Cox
LR D Thompson
CF D Snider
RF C Furillo
L3 J Robinson
M C Dressen

CHICAGO

SP W Hacker
SP P Minner
SR J Klippstein
SP B Rush
SP H Pollet
RS T Lown
RS B Church
RP D Leonard
C- C McCullough
1B D Fondy
2S E Miksis
SS- R Smalley
3B R Jackson
LF R Kiner
MR F Baumholtz
RL H Sauer
CF H Jeffcoat
23 B Serena
M P Cavarretta

CINCINNATI

SP H Perkowski
SR B Podbielan
SP K Raffensberger
SR J Nuxhall
SP F Baczewski
RS J Collum
RP F Smith
RP C King
RS B Kelly
C A Seminick
1B T Kluszewski
2B R Bridges
SS R McMillan
3B B Adams
LF J Greengrass
CF G Bell
RF W Marshall
RU B Borkowski
UI- G Hatton
M1 R Hornsby
M2 B Mills

MILWAUKEE

SP W Spahn
SP J Antonelli
SP M Surkont
SR B Buhl
SR D Liddle
RS L Burdette
RP J Wilson
RP E Johnson
C D Crandall
1B J Adcock
2B J Dittmer
SS J Logan
3B E Mathews
LF S Gordon
CF B Bruton
RF A Pafko
LO J Pendleton
M C Grimm

NEW YORK

SP R Gomez
SP J Hearn
SR L Jansen
SP S Maglie
SP A Worthington
RP H Wilhelm
RS D Koslo
RS A Corwin
C W Westrum
1B W Lockman
2B D Williams
SU A Dark
3B H Thompson
LF M Irvin
CF B Thomson
RF D Mueller
UI D Spencer
M L Durocher

PHILADELPHIA

SP R Roberts
SP C Simmons
SR K Drews
SR J Konstanty
SR B Miller
RS S Ridzik
RP A Hansen
C S Burgess
1B E Torgeson
2S G Hamner
SS T Kazanski
3B W Jones
LF D Ennis
CF R Ashburn
RF J Wyrostek
C- S Lopata
2U- C Ryan
1U- E Waitkus
M S O'Neill

PITTSBURGH

SR M Dickson
SR P LaPalme
SP J Lindell
SP B Friend
SR B Hall
RP J Hetki
RS R Face
RP R Bowman
C- M Sandlock
1B- P Ward
2B- J O'Brien
SS- E O'Brien
32 D O'Connell
LF- H Rice
CF F Thomas
RF C Abrams
SS D Cole
1U P Smith
MO C Bernier
UI- E Pellagrini
M F Haney

ST. LOUIS

SP H Haddix
SP G Staley
SP V Mizell
SP J Presko
SR S Miller
RP A Brazle
RP H White
RS C Chambers
C D Rice
1B S Bilko
2B R Schoendienst
SS S Hemus
3B R Jablonski
LF S Musial
CF R Repulski
RF E Slaughter
UT P Lowrey
M E Stanky

1954 AL

BALTIMORE

SP B Turley
SP J Coleman
SP D Larsen
SP D Pillette
SR L Kretlow
RS B Chakales
RP M Blyzka
RP H Fox
C C Courtney
1B E Waitkus
2B B Young
SS B Hunter
3B V Stephens
LF- J Fridley
CF C Diering
RF C Abrams
OF G Coan
3U B Kennedy
1U D Kryhoski
M J Dykes

BOSTON

SR F Sullivan
SP W Nixon
SR T Brewer
SP L Kiely
SR B Henry
RP E Kinder
RS H Brown
RS S Hudson
C S White
1B H Agganis
2I T Lepcio
SS M Bolling
3B G Hatton
LF T Williams
MR J Jensen
RU J Piersall
2I B Goodman
UO K Olson
SI- B Consolo
M L Boudreau

CHICAGO

SP V Trucks
SP B Keegan
SR B Pierce
SR J Harshman
SR S Consuegra
RS D Johnson
RS H Dorish
RP M Martin
C S Lollar
1B- F Fain
2B N Fox
SS C Carrasquel
3B C Michaels
LF M Minoso
CF J Groth
RF J Rivera
M1 P Richards
M2 M Marion

CLEVELAND

SP E Wynn
SR M Garcia
SP B Lemon
SP A Houtteman
SP B Feller
RP R Narleski
RS D Mossi
RP H Newhouser
C J Hegan
1B B Glynn
2B B Avila
SS G Strickland
31 A Rosen
LU A Smith
CF L Doby
RF D Philley
1B V Wertz
LO- W Westlake
M A Lopez

DETROIT

SP S Gromek
SP N Garver
SR G Zuverink
SP B Hoeft
SR A Aber
RP D Marlowe
RP R Herbert
RP B Miller
C F House
1B W Dropo
2B F Bolling
SS H Kuenn
3B R Boone
LU J Delsing
CF B Tuttle
RF A Kaline
1B- W Belardi
2U- F Hatfield
LU- B Nieman
M F Hutchinson

NEW YORK

SP W Ford
SR B Grim
SP E Lopat
SR A Reynolds
SR T Morgan
RP H Byrd
CL J Sain
C Y Berra
1B J Collins
23 G McDougald
SS P Rizzuto
3B A Carey
OI I Noren
CF M Mantle
RF H Bauer
2S J Coleman
LF G Woodling
SS- W Miranda
UR- E Robinson
1U- B Skowron
M C Stengel

PHILADELPHIA

SP A Portocarrero
SP A Kellner
SR M Fricano
SP B Trice
SP J Gray
RS S Dixon
RP M Burtschy
RP C Bishop
RS A Sima
C- J Astroth
1U L Limmer
2B S Jacobs
SS J DeMaestri
3B J Finigan
LF G Zernial
UT V Power
RF B Renna
1U D Bollweg
OF E Valo
CF B Wilson
M E Joost

WASHINGTON

SP B Porterfield
SP M McDermott
SP J Schmitz
SP C Stobbs
SP D Stone
RP C Pascual
RP G Keriazakos
RP B Stewart
C E Fitz Gerald
1B M Vernon
2B W Terwilliger
SS P Runnels
3B E Yost
LF R Sievers
CF J Busby
RF T Umphlett
M B Harris

1954 NL

BROOKLYN

SP C Erskine
SP R Meyer
SP J Podres
SP B Loes
SP D Newcombe
RP C Labine
CL J Hughes
RP E Palica
RP B Milliken
C R Campanella
1B G Hodges
2B J Gilliam
SS P Reese
3B- D Hoak
L3 J Robinson
CF D Snider
RF C Furillo
LF- S Amoros
3B- B Cox
M W Alston

CHICAGO

SP B Rush
SP P Minner
SR W Hacker
SR J Klippstein
SP H Pollet
RS J Davis
RP H Jeffcoat
RP B Tremel
C- J Garagiola
1B D Fondy
2B G Baker
SS E Banks
3B R Jackson
LF R Kiner
CF B Talbot
RF H Sauer
MO- F Baumholtz
M S Hack

CINCINNATI

SR A Fowler
SP C Valentine
SR J Nuxhall
SP B Podbielan
SP F Baczewski
CL F Smith
RS H Judson
RS H Perkowski
RP J Collum
C- A Seminick
1B T Kluszewski
2B J Temple
SS R McMillan
3B B Adams
LF J Greengrass
CF G Bell
RF W Post
3U C Harmon
M B Tebbetts

MILWAUKEE

SP W Spahn
SP L Burdette
SP G Conley
SP J Wilson
SR C Nichols
RP D Jolly
RS B Buhl
SR E Johnson
RP R Crone
C D Crandall
1B J Adcock
2I D O'Connell
SS J Logan
3B E Mathews
LF H Aaron
CF B Bruton
RF A Pafko
M C Grimm

NEW YORK

SP J Antonelli
SP R Gomez
SP S Maglie
SR J Hearn
SP D Liddle
RP M Grissom
RP H Wilhelm
RP W McCall
C W Westrum
1B W Lockman
2B D Williams
SS A Dark
3B H Thompson
LF M Irvin
CF W Mays
RF D Mueller
C- R Katt
UO- D Rhodes
M L Durocher

PHILADELPHIA

SP R Roberts
SP C Simmons
SP M Dickson
SR B Miller
SP H Wehmeier
RS S Ridzik
RP J Konstanty
C S Burgess
1B E Torgeson
2B G Hamner
SS B Morgan
3B W Jones
LU D Schell
CF R Ashburn
OI D Ennis
RL- M Clark
C- S Lopata
RU J Wyrostek
M1 S O'Neill
M2 T Moore

PITTSBURGH

SP M Surkont
SR B Friend
SR V Law
SP D Littlefield
SR J Thies
RS B Purkey
RS P LaPalme
RP J Hetki
C T Atwell
1B B Skinner
2B C Roberts
SS G Allie
UI D Cole
UO D Hall
ML F Thomas
R3 S Gordon
UO J Lynch
IO P Ward
C- J Shepard
M F Haney

ST. LOUIS

SP H Haddix
SP V Raschi
SR B Lawrence
SR G Staley
SR T Poholsky
RP A Brazle
RP C Deal
RS J Presko
RP R Lint
C B Sarni
1B- J Cunningham
2B R Schoendienst
SS A Grammas
3B R Jablonski
LF R Repulski
CF W Moon
RF S Musial
SI S Hemus
OI- J Frazier
M E Stanky

1955 AL

BALTIMORE

SP J Wilson
SP E Palica
SP B Wight
RS R Moore
RS A Schallock
RP H Dorish
RS D Johnson
C H Smith
1C G Triandos
2B- F Marsh
SS W Miranda
3B- W Causey
RL- D Philley
CF C Diering
OI C Abrams
UO- D Pope
M P Richards

BOSTON

SP F Sullivan
SP W Nixon
SP T Brewer
SR I Delock
SR G Susce
RP L Kiely
RP T Hurd
CL E Kinder
C S White
1B N Zauchin
2B B Goodman
SS B Klaus

3B G Hatton
LF T Williams
CF J Piersall
RF J Jensen
LU G Stephens
M P Higgins

CHICAGO
SP B Pierce
SP D Donovan
SP J Harshman
SP V Trucks
SP C Johnson
RS S Consuegra
RP D Howell
RP M Martin
C S Lollar
1B W Dropo
2B N Fox
SS C Carrasquel
3B G Kell
LF M Minoso
CF J Busby
RF J Rivera
RL B Nieman
3U- B Kennedy
M M Marion

CLEVELAND
SP E Wynn
SP H Score
SP M Garcia
SP B Lemon
SR A Houtteman
RP R Narleski
RP D Mossi
C J Hegan
1B- V Wertz
2B B Avila
SS G Strickland
3B A Rosen
LF R Kiner
CF L Doby
R3 A Smith
LF- G Woodling
M A Lopez

DETROIT
SP F Lary
SP N Garver
SP B Hoeft
SP S Gromek
RP A Aber
RP B Birrer
RP P Foytack
C F House
1B- E Torgeson
2B F Hatfield
SS H Kuenn
3B R Boone
LF J Delsing
CF B Tuttle
RF A Kaline
LU B Phillips
C- R Wilson
M B Harris

KANSAS CITY
SR A Ditmar
SP A Kellner
SP B Shantz
SR A Ceccarelli
SP A Portocarrero
RP T Gorman
RP V Raschi
RS C Boyer
RP B Harrington
C J Astroth
1B V Power
23 J Finigan
SS J DeMaestri
32 H Lopez
LF G Zernial
CF H Simpson
RU E Slaughter
RU B Renna
MO B Wilson
UO E Valo
C- B Shantz
M L Boudreau

NEW YORK
SP W Ford
SP B Turley
SP T Byrne
SR J Kucks
SP D Larsen
RP J Konstanty
RP T Morgan
RP T Sturdivant
C Y Berra
1U B Skowron
2B G McDougald
SS B Hunter
3B A Carey
LF I Noren
CF M Mantle
RF H Bauer
1R J Collins
LU E Howard
SS- P Rizzuto
1U- E Robinson
M C Stengel

WASHINGTON
SR D Stone
SP B Porterfield
SR J Schmitz
SR M McDermott
SR C Stobbs
RS P Ramos
RS C Pascual
RP T Abernathy
RP S Shea
C- E Fitz Gerald
1B M Vernon
2B P Runnels
SS J Valdivielso
3B E Yost
LF R Sievers
MO T Umphlett
RU C Paula
OF E Oravetz
SS- B Kline
M C Dressen

1955 NL

BROOKLYN
SP D Newcombe
SP C Erskine
SP J Podres
SP B Loes
SR K Spooner
RS C Labine
RP E Roebuck
RP D Bessent
C R Campanella
1B G Hodges
2L J Gilliam
SS P Reese
3B J Robinson
LF S Amoros
CF D Snider
RF C Furillo
3B D Hoak
2I- D Zimmer
M W Alston

CHICAGO
SP S Jones
SP B Rush
SP W Hacker
SP P Minner
SR J Davis
RP H Jeffcoat
RS H Pollet
RP D Hillman
RP H Perkowski
C H Chiti
1B D Fondy
2B G Baker
SS E Banks
3B R Jackson
LF- H Sauer
MR E Miksis
RU J King
OF F Baumholtz
LU B Speake
M S Hack

CINCINNATI
SR J Nuxhall
SR A Fowler
SR J Klippstein
SR J Collum
SR G Staley
RS R Minarcin
RS J Black
RP H Freeman
C S Burgess
1B T Kluszewski
2B J Temple
SS R McMillan
3S R Bridges
LU- S Palys
CF G Bell
RF W Post
UT C Harmon
UL- B Thurman
M B Tebbetts

MILWAUKEE
SP W Spahn
SP L Burdette
SR B Buhl
SP G Conley
SR C Nichols
RS R Crone
RP E Johnson
RP D Jolly
C D Crandall
1B G Crowe
2B D O'Connell
SS J Logan
3B E Mathews
LF B Thomson
CF B Bruton
RU H Aaron
LU C Tanner
1B- J Adcock
RU- A Pafko
M C Grimm

NEW YORK
SP J Antonelli
SP J Hearn
SP R Gomez
SP S Maglie
SR D Liddle
RP H Wilhelm
RS W McCall
RP M Grissom
RS R Monzant
C R Katt
1B- G Harris
2B- W Terwilliger
SS A Dark
3B H Thompson
L1 W Lockman
CF W Mays
RF D Mueller
IC B Hofman
UL D Rhodes
2B- D Williams
M L Durocher

PHILADELPHIA
SP R Roberts
SP M Dickson
SP H Wehmeier
SP C Simmons
RS J Meyer
RP B Miller
C A Seminick
1U M Blaylock
2S B Morgan
SS- R Smalley
3B W Jones
LF D Ennis
CF R Ashburn
RF J Greengrass
2B G Hamner
CU S Lopata
RU- G Gorbous
M M Smith

PITTSBURGH
SR B Friend
SR V Law
SR M Surkont
SR R Kline
SR D Littlefield
RS R Face
RS L Donoso
RP D Hall
C J Shepard
1B D Long
2B- J O'Brien
SS D Groat
IF G Freese
OF- J Lynch
LM F Thomas
RF R Clemente
UI- D Cole
1U- P Ward
M F Haney

ST. LOUIS
SP H Haddix
SR L Jackson
SR L Arroyo
SP T Poholsky
SP W Schmidt
RS B Lawrence
RP P LaPalme
C B Sarni
1O S Musial
2B R Schoendienst
SS A Grammas
3B K Boyer
LU R Repulski
CF B Virdon
OI W Moon
UI S Hemus
M1 E Stanky
M2 H Walker

1956 AL

BALTIMORE
SP R Moore
SP C Johnson
SP B Wight
SR H Brown
SR E Palica
RP G Zuverink
RS M Fornieles
RS D Ferrarese
RS B Loes
C1 G Triandos
1B- B Boyd
2B B Gardner
SS W Miranda
3B G Kell
LF B Nieman
CF- D Williams
RM T Francona
1U- B Hale
CF- J Pyburn
C- H Smith
M P Richards

BOSTON
SP T Brewer
SP F Sullivan
SP W Nixon
SR D Sisler
SP M Parnell
RS I Delock
RP B Porterfield
RP T Hurd
C S White
1B M Vernon
2B B Goodman
SS D Buddin
3B B Klaus
LF T Williams
CF J Piersall
RF J Jensen
UT D Gernert
LU G Stephens
23- T Lepcio
M P Higgins

CHICAGO
SP B Pierce
SP D Donovan
SP J Harshman
SP J Wilson
SP B Keegan
RS G Staley
RP D Howell
C S Lollar
1B W Dropo
2B N Fox
SS L Aparicio
3B F Hatfield
LF M Minoso
CF L Doby
RF J Rivera
3B- S Esposito
1O- D Philley
M M Marion

CLEVELAND
SP E Wynn
SP B Lemon
SP H Score
SP M Garcia
RP D Mossi
RP R Narleski
RP C McLish
RP A Houtteman
C J Hegan
1B V Wertz
2B B Avila
SS C Carrasquel
3B A Rosen
UT A Smith
CF J Busby
RF R Colavito
LF G Woodling
UI- G Strickland
1U- P Ward
M A Lopez

DETROIT
SP F Lary
SR P Foytack
SP B Hoeft
SP V Trucks
RS S Gromek
RP A Aber
RS D Maas
RP W Masterson
C F House
1U E Torgeson
2B F Bolling
SS H Kuenn
3B R Boone
LF C Maxwell
CF B Tuttle
RF A Kaline
UT- W Belardi
C- R Wilson
M B Harris

KANSAS CITY
SR A Ditmar
SP W Burnette
SP L Kretlow
SR T Herriage
RS T Gorman
RS J Crimian
RP B Shantz
CU- T Thompson
12 V Power
23- J Finigan
SS J DeMaestri
3B H Lopez
LU- L Skizas
MO J Groth
RU H Simpson
LU G Zernial
UO- E Slaughter
M L Boudreau

NEW YORK
SP W Ford
SP J Kucks
SR D Larsen
SR T Sturdivant
SP B Turley
RS T Byrne
RP T Morgan
RS B Grim
C Y Berra
1B B Skowron
2B B Martin
SS G McDougald
3B A Carey
LC E Howard
CF M Mantle
RF H Bauer
OI J Collins
2S- J Coleman
M C Stengel

WASHINGTON
SP C Stobbs
SR C Pascual
SR P Ramos
SR D Stone
SR B Wiesler
RS B Stewart
RP B Chakales
RS H Griggs
RP C Grob
C C Courtney
12 P Runnels
2U- H Plews
SS- J Valdivielso
3B E Yost
L1 R Sievers
MU W Herzog
RF J Lemon
CU L Berberet
CF K Olson
UO- E Oravetz
M C Dressen

1956 NL

BROOKLYN
SP D Newcombe
SP R Craig
SP S Maglie
SP C Erskine
SR D Drysdale
RP C Labine
RP E Roebuck
RP D Bessent
RP K Lehman
C R Campanella
1B G Hodges
2L J Gilliam
SS P Reese
3B R Jackson
LU S Amoros
CF D Snider
RF C Furillo
3I J Robinson
M W Alston

CHICAGO
SP B Rush
SP S Jones
SR W Hacker
SP D Kaiser
RP T Lown
RS J Davis
RP V Valentinetti
RS J Brosnan
C H Landrith
1B D Fondy
2B G Baker
SS E Banks
3B D Hoak
LF M Irvin
CF P Whisenant
RF W Moryn
LU J King
UT E Miksis
M S Hack

CINCINNATI
SR B Lawrence
SP J Klippstein
SR J Nuxhall
SR A Fowler
SR H Jeffcoat
RP H Freeman
RS T Acker
RP J Black
C E Bailey
1B T Kluszewski
2B J Temple
SS R McMillan
3B R Jablonski
LF F Robinson
CF G Bell
RF W Post
CU- S Burgess
OF- B Thurman
M B Tebbetts

MILWAUKEE
SP W Spahn
SP L Burdette
SP B Buhl
SR R Crone
SR G Conley
RP E Johnson
RP B Trowbridge
C D Crandall
1B J Adcock
2B D O'Connell
SS J Logan
3B E Mathews
LF B Thomson
CF B Bruton
RF H Aaron
1B F Torre
M1 C Grimm
M2 F Haney

NEW YORK
SP J Antonelli
SP R Gomez
SP A Worthington
SR J Hearn
RS D Littlefield
RP H Wilhelm
RS S Ridzik
RP M Grissom
C- B Sarni
1B B White
2B- R Schoendienst
UI D Spencer
3B F Castleman
LF J Brandt
CF W Mays
RF D Mueller
LU D Rhodes
3U- H Thompson
M B Rigney

PHILADELPHIA
SP R Roberts
SP H Haddix
SP C Simmons
SP S Rogovin
SP S Miller
RS B Miller
RS J Meyer
RP R Negray
C1 S Lopata
1B M Blaylock
2B T Kazanski
SS G Hamner
3B W Jones
LF D Ennis
CF R Ashburn
RF E Valo
RU- J Greengrass
2U- S Hemus
M M Smith

PITTSBURGH
SP B Friend
SP R Kline
SP V Law
SR R Munger
RP R Face
RP N King
RS F Waters
C J Shepard
1B D Long
2B- B Mazeroski
SS D Groat
3L F Thomas
LR L Walls
CF B Virdon
RO R Clemente
UT B Skinner
C- H Foiles
M B Bragan

ST. LOUIS
SP V Mizell
SP T Poholsky
SP M Dickson
SR H Wehmeier
SR W Schmidt
RS L McDaniel
RP L Jackson
RP J Collum
C- H Smith
1R S Musial
2S D Blasingame
SS A Dark
3B K Boyer
LF R Repulski
CF B Del Greco
R1 W Moon
M F Hutchinson

1957 AL

BALTIMORE
SP C Johnson
SP R Moore
SR B Loes
SP H Brown
SR B O'Dell
RP G Zuverink
RS B Wight
RP K Lehman
C G Triandos
1B B Boyd
2B B Gardner
SS W Miranda
3B G Kell
LF B Nieman
CF- J Busby
RM A Pilarcik
RL T Francona
SS- J Brideweser
UO- J Durham
C- J Ginsberg
M P Richards

BOSTON
SP F Sullivan
SP T Brewer
SP W Nixon
SP M Fornieles
SP D Sisler
RP I Delock
RS B Porterfield
C S White
1U D Gernert
2B- T Lepcio
SS B Klaus
3B F Malzone
LF T Williams
CF J Piersall
RF J Jensen
LU G Stephens
1U M Vernon
C- P Daley
M P Higgins

CHICAGO
SP B Pierce
SP D Donovan
SP J Wilson
SP J Harshman
SR B Keegan
RS B Fischer
RP G Staley
RP D Howell
C S Lollar
1B- E Torgeson
2B N Fox
SS L Aparicio
3B B Phillips
LF M Minoso
CF L Doby
UO J Landis
3I S Esposito
RU J Rivera
1U W Dropo
M A Lopez

CLEVELAND
SP E Wynn
SR M Garcia
SR D Mossi
SP B Lemon
RS R Narleski
RS C McLish
RS B Daley
RP D Tomanek
C- J Hegan
1B V Wertz
2B B Avila
SS C Carrasquel
3M A Smith
LF G Woodling
CF R Maris
RF R Colavito
IO L Raines
1U- J Altobelli
2S- G Strickland
M K Farrell

DETROIT
SR J Bunning
SP F Lary
SR D Maas
SR P Foytack
SP B Hoeft
RP L Sleater
RP H Byrd
C F House
1B R Boone
2B F Bolling
SS H Kuenn
3B R Bertoia
LF C Maxwell
CF B Tuttle
RF A Kaline
M J Tighe

KANSAS CITY
SP N Garver
SP A Kellner
SP R Terry
SR J Urban
SR A Portocarrero
RS T Morgan
RS T Gorman
RS V Trucks
RS W Burnette
C H Smith
1B V Power
2S B Hunter
SS J DeMaestri
3B H Lopez
LF G Zernial
CF- W Held
R3 L Skizas
UO B Cerv
UT- I Noren
C- T Thompson
M1 L Boudreau
M2 H Craft

NEW YORK
SP T Sturdivant
SR J Kucks
SP B Turley
SP B Shantz
SP D Larsen
RS A Ditmar
RP W Ford
CL B Grim
RP T Byrne
C Y Berra
1B B Skowron
2B B Richardson
SS G McDougald
3B- A Carey
LC E Howard
CF M Mantle
RF H Bauer
UT T Kubek
LU E Slaughter
UT- J Collins
M C Stengel

WASHINGTON
SR P Ramos
SR C Stobbs
SP C Pascual
SR R Kemmerer
RS T Clevenger
RP D Hyde
RP B Byerly
C L Berberet
1I P Runnels
2B H Plews
SS R Bridges
3B E Yost
LF R Sievers
CF B Usher
RF J Lemon
U1 J Becquer
2S- M Bolling
CU- C Courtney
UT- A Schult
M1 C Dressen
M2 C Lavagetto

1957 NL

BROOKLYN
SP D Drysdale
SP D Newcombe
SP J Podres
SP D McDevitt
SR R Craig
RP C Labine
RS S Koufax
RP E Roebuck
RP S Maglie
C R Campanella
1B G Hodges
2B J Gilliam
SS C Neal
3U P Reese
LR G Cimoli
CF D Snider
RF C Furillo
LU S Amoros
OF- E Valo
UI- D Zimmer
M W Alston

CHICAGO
SP M Drabowsky
SP D Drott
SP B Rush
SR D Elston
SR D Hillman
RP T Lown
RS J Brosnan
RP D Littlefield
C C Neeman
1B D Long
2B B Morgan
SS- J Littrell

S3 E Banks
LO L Walls
OI B Speake
RF W Moryn
OI J Bolger
LM C Tanner
M *B Scheffing*

CINCINNATI

SR B Lawrence
SP H Jeffcoat
SR J Nuxhall
SR D Gross
SR J Klippstein
RS T Acker
RP H Freeman
RS A Fowler
RP R Sanchez
C E Bailey
1B G Crowe
2B J Temple
SS R McMillan
3B D Hoak
LU F Robinson
CF G Bell
RF W Post
CU- S Burgess
M *B Tebbetts*

MILWAUKEE

SP W Spahn
SP L Burdette
SP B Buhl
SR G Conley
SR B Trowbridge
RS J Pizarro
RS T Phillips
RP E Johnson
RP D McMahon
C D Crandall
1B F Torre
2B R Schoendienst
SS J Logan
3B E Mathews
LF W Covington
CF- B Bruton
RM H Aaron
UO- A Pafko
M *F Haney*

NEW YORK

SP R Gomez
SR J Antonelli
SP C Barclay
SR S Miller
SP R Crone
RS A Worthington
RP M Grissom
RP R Monzant
C- V Thomas
1B W Lockman
23 D O'Connell
SI D Spencer
3U R Jablonski
LF H Sauer
CF W Mays
RF D Mueller
3O O Virgil
1U- G Harris
OF- D Rhodes
LU- B Thomson
M *B Rigney*

PHILADELPHIA

SP R Roberts
SP J Sanford
SP C Simmons
SP H Haddix
SR D Cardwell
RP T Farrell
RP J Hearn
RP B Miller
RP S Morehead
C S Lopata
1B E Bouchee
2B G Hamner
SS C Fernandez
3B W Jones
LF H Anderson
CF R Ashburn
RL R Repulski
RF B Bowman
M *M Smith*

PITTSBURGH

SP B Friend
SP R Kline
SR B Purkey
SP V Law
RS L Arroyo
RP R Face
RS R Swanson
RP B Smith
C H Foiles
1B D Fondy
2B B Mazeroski
SS D Groat
3U G Freese
LU B Skinner
CF B Virdon
RF R Clemente
3S G Baker
UT F Thomas
OI- P Smith
M1 *B Bragan*
M2 *D Murtaugh*

ST. LOUIS

SR L Jackson
SP L McDaniel
SP S Jones
SR H Wehmeier
SR V Mizell
RS W Schmidt
RP L Merritt
RP H Wilhelm
C H Smith
1B S Musial
2B D Blasingame
SS A Dark
3B E Kasko
LR W Moon
M3 K Boyer
LR D Ennis
UT J Cunningham
MU B Smith
M *F Hutchinson*

1958 AL

BALTIMORE

SP J Harshman
SR B O'Dell
SP A Portocarrero
SR M Pappas
SP C Johnson
RS B Loes
RP H Brown
RP G Zuverink
RP K Lehman
C G Triandos
1B B Boyd
2B B Gardner
SS W Miranda
3B B Robinson
RL G Woodling
CF J Busby
RO A Pilarcik
SS F Castleman
LF B Nieman
UT D Williams
1U- J Marshall
M *P Richards*

BOSTON

SP T Brewer
SP F Sullivan
SR I Delock
SP D Sisler
RP M Wall
RS M Fornieles
RP L Kiely
C S White
1B D Gernert
21 P Runnels
SS D Buddin
3B F Malzone
LF T Williams
CF J Piersall
RF J Jensen
LU G Stephens
M *P Higgins*

CHICAGO

SP D Donovan
SP B Pierce
SP E Wynn
SP J Wilson
SR R Moore
RP G Staley
RP B Shaw
C S Lollar
1B E Torgeson
2B N Fox
SS L Aparicio
3B B Goodman
UO J Rivera
CF J Landis
LR A Smith
3U S Esposito
1B- R Boone
3O- B Phillips
M *A Lopez*

CLEVELAND

SP C McLish
SR M Grant
SR R Narleski
SR G Bell
SR D Ferrarese
RS D Mossi
RS H Wilhelm
C R Nixon
1B M Vernon
23 B Avila
SS- B Hunter
IO B Harrell
LF M Minoso
MU- L Doby
RF R Colavito
2S B Moran
OI- G Geiger
IO V Power
M1 *B Bragan*
M2 *J Gordon*

DETROIT

SP F Lary
SP P Foytack
SP J Bunning
SR B Hoeft
SR H Moford
RP H Aguirre
RP T Morgan
C R Wilson
1B G Harris
2B F Bolling
S3 B Martin
3B- R Bertoia
LF C Maxwell
CF H Kuenn
RF A Kaline
LO- J Groth
M1 *J Tighe*
M2 *B Norman*

KANSAS CITY

SP R Terry
SP N Garver
SR R Herbert
SP J Urban
SR B Grim
RS M Dickson
RP T Gorman
RP D Tomanek
RS B Daley
C H Chiti
1B- V Power
2B- M Baxes
SS J DeMaestri
23 H Lopez
LF B Cerv
MR B Tuttle
RF R Maris
UO B Martyn
IC H Smith
OI- W Herzog
1U- H Simpson
IO- P Ward
M *H Craft*

NEW YORK

SP B Turley
SP W Ford
SR A Ditmar
SR J Kucks
SR B Shantz
RP D Larsen
RP D Maas
CL R Duren
RS Z Monroe
CU Y Berra
1B B Skowron
2B G McDougald
SS T Kubek
3B A Carey
LF N Siebern
CF M Mantle
RF H Bauer
CU E Howard
3B- J Lumpe
OF- E Slaughter
M *C Stengel*

WASHINGTON

SP P Ramos
SR R Kemmerer
SP C Pascual
SR H Griggs
SR V Valentinetti
RP T Clevenger
RP D Hyde
C C Courtney
1B N Zauchin
2B- K Aspromonte
SS R Bridges
3B E Yost
LF R Sievers
CF A Pearson
RF J Lemon
OI N Chrisley
23 H Plews
SU- O Alvarez
UT- J Becquer
M *C Lavagetto*

1958 NL

CHICAGO

SR T Phillips
SP D Drott
SR D Hillman
SP M Drabowsky
SP J Briggs
RS G Hobbie
RP D Elston
RP B Henry
C S Taylor
1B D Long
2B T Taylor
SS E Banks
3B A Dark
LF W Moryn
CF B Thomson
RF L Walls
UO- J Bolger
32- J Goryl
M *B Scheffing*

CINCINNATI

SP B Purkey
SR B Lawrence
SP H Haddix
SR J Nuxhall
SP D Newcombe
RS T Acker
RP H Jeffcoat
RP W Schmidt
C E Bailey
1B G Crowe
2B J Temple
SS R McMillan
3B D Hoak
LM F Robinson
CF G Bell
RF J Lynch
CU S Burgess
S3 A Grammas
OF B Thurman
UT- D Fondy
OI- P Whisenant
M1 *B Tebbetts*
M2 *J Dykes*

LOS ANGELES

SR D Drysdale
SP J Podres
SR S Koufax
SP S Williams
RP C Labine
RS F Kipp
RP J Klippstein
RS C Erskine
C J Roseboro
1B G Hodges
2B C Neal
SS D Zimmer
3B- D Gray
UT J Gilliam
ML G Cimoli
RF C Furillo
MU D Snider
OI N Larker
M *W Alston*

MILWAUKEE

SP W Spahn
SP L Burdette
SP B Rush
SP C Willey
SP J Pizarro
RP J Jay
RS G Conley
RP D McMahon
RP B Trowbridge
C D Crandall
1B F Torre
2B R Schoendienst
SS J Logan
3B E Mathews
LF A Pafko
CF B Bruton
RF H Aaron
1U J Adcock
LF- W Covington
UT- F Mantilla
M *F Haney*

PHILADELPHIA

SP R Roberts
SP R Semproch
SR J Sanford
SP C Simmons
SP D Cardwell
RP T Farrell
RS J Meyer
RP J Hearn
C- S Lopata
1B- E Bouchee
2B S Hemus
SS C Fernandez
3B W Jones
L1 H Anderson
CF R Ashburn
RF W Post
2I T Kazanski
UO- B Bowman
UT- D Philley
OF- R Repulski
M1 *M Smith*
M2 *E Sawyer*

PITTSBURGH

SP B Friend
SP R Kline
SP V Law
SR C Raydon
SP G Witt
CL R Face
RS B Porterfield
RP D Gross
RP R Blackburn
C H Foiles
1U T Kluszewski
2B B Mazeroski
SS D Groat
3B F Thomas
LF B Skinner
CF B Virdon
RF R Clemente
M *D Murtaugh*

ST. LOUIS

SP S Jones
SR L Jackson
SP V Mizell
SR J Brosnan
SR B Mabe
RP L McDaniel
RS B Muffett
RP P Paine
RP B Wight
C- H Smith
1B S Musial
2B D Blasingame
SU E Kasko
3B K Boyer
LF D Ennis
CF C Flood
RL W Moon
1R J Cunningham
RC G Green
LU I Noren
M1 *F Hutchinson*
M2 *S Hack*

SAN FRANCISCO

SP J Antonelli
SR R Gomez
SR S Miller
SR M McCormick
SR R Monzant
RS A Worthington
RP M Grissom
C B Schmidt
1B O Cepeda
2B D O'Connell
SS D Spencer
3B J Davenport
LF- H Sauer
CF W Mays
RF W Kirkland
3U- R Jablonski
UT- W Lockman
M *B Rigney*

1959 AL

BALTIMORE

SP H Wilhelm
SP M Pappas
SR B O'Dell
SP J Walker
SR H Brown
CL B Loes
RP E Johnson
C G Triandos
1B B Boyd
2B B Gardner
SS C Carrasquel
3B- B Robinson
LR G Woodling
CF W Tasby
RF A Pilarcik
S3 B Klaus
LF B Nieman
UO- A Pearson
M *P Richards*

BOSTON

SP T Brewer
SP J Casale
SP F Sullivan
SR B Monbouquette
SR I Delock
RS F Baumann
RP M Fornieles
RP L Kiely
C S White
1U D Gernert
21 P Runnels
SS D Buddin
3B F Malzone
LO- G Stephens
ML G Geiger
RF J Jensen
MU M Keough
1U V Wertz
LU T Williams
M1 *P Higgins*
M2 *R York*
M3 *B Jurges*

CHICAGO

SP E Wynn
SR B Shaw
SP B Pierce
SP D Donovan
SR B Latman
RP G Staley
RP T Lown
C S Lollar
1B E Torgeson
2B N Fox
SS L Aparicio
3B B Phillips
LR A Smith
CF J Landis
RL- J Rivera
3U B Goodman
M *A Lopez*

CLEVELAND

SR G Bell
SP C McLish
SR M Grant
SP H Score
RS J Perry
RS M Garcia
C- R Nixon
1B V Power
2B- B Martin
S3 W Held
3S G Strickland
LF M Minoso
CF J Piersall
RF R Colavito
M1 T Francona
23- J Baxes
M *J Gordon*

DETROIT

SP J Bunning
SP P Foytack
SP D Mossi
SP F Lary
RS R Narleski
RP T Morgan
RP P Burnside
RP D Sisler
C L Berberet
1B G Harris
2B F Bolling
SS R Bridges
3B E Yost
LF C Maxwell
CF A Kaline
RF H Kuenn
1U- B Osborne
SS- C Veal
M1 *B Norman*
M2 *J Dykes*

KANSAS CITY

SR B Daley
SP N Garver
SR R Herbert
SR J Kucks
RS B Grim
RP T Sturdivant
RP M Dickson
C F House
1B K Hadley
2B- W Terwilliger
SS J DeMaestri
3I D Williams
LF B Cerv
CF B Tuttle
RF R Maris
2S J Lumpe
3U H Smith
M *H Craft*

NEW YORK

SP W Ford
SR A Ditmar
SR B Turley
SR D Maas
SP R Terry
RP D Larsen
RP J Coates
RP B Shantz
CL R Duren
C Y Berra
1B- B Skowron
2B B Richardson
SO T Kubek
3L H Lopez
LU N Siebern
CF M Mantle
RF H Bauer
IC E Howard
UI G McDougald
1U- M Throneberry
M *C Stengel*

WASHINGTON

SP C Pascual
SP P Ramos
SP R Kemmerer
SP B Fischer
RS T Clevenger
RS H Griggs
RS C Stobbs
RP H Woodeshick
C- H Naragon
1B R Sievers
2B- R Bertoia
SS- B Consolo
3B H Killebrew
LF J Lemon
CF B Allison
RU F Throneberry
U2 J Becquer
UO- L Green
S2- R Samford
M *C Lavagetto*

1959 NL

CHICAGO

SP B Anderson
SR G Hobbie
SR D Hillman
SP M Drabowsky
SP A Ceccarelli
RP B Henry
RP D Elston
RS J Buzhardt
C S Taylor
1B D Long
2B T Taylor
SS E Banks
3B A Dark
LM B Thomson
CF G Altman
RF L Walls
1U J Marshall
LF W Moryn
M *B Scheffing*

CINCINNATI

SP D Newcombe
SP B Purkey
SP J Nuxhall
SP J O'Toole
RS O Pena
RS B Lawrence
RP W Schmidt
RP T Acker
C E Bailey
1B F Robinson
2B J Temple
S3 E Kasko
3B- W Jones
LF J Lynch
CF V Pinson
RF G Bell
3L F Thomas
SS- R McMillan
M1 *M Smith*
M2 *F Hutchinson*

LOS ANGELES

SP D Drysdale
SP J Podres
SR S Koufax
SR R Craig
SR D McDevitt
RS S Williams
RP C Labine
RP A Fowler
C J Roseboro
1B G Hodges
2B C Neal
SS D Zimmer
3B J Gilliam
LF W Moon
CF D Demeter
RM D Snider
RO R Fairly
1O N Larker
SS- M Wills
M *W Alston*

MILWAUKEE

SP W Spahn
SP L Burdette
SP B Buhl
SR J Jay
SR J Pizarro
RS C Willey
RS B Rush
RP D McMahon
C D Crandall
1B J Adcock
2I F Mantilla
SS J Logan
3B E Mathews
LF W Covington
CF B Bruton
RF H Aaron
1B F Torre
M *F Haney*

PHILADELPHIA

SP R Roberts
SP J Owens
SP G Conley
SP D Cardwell
SR R Semproch
RP J Meyer
RP H Robinson
RP T Phillips
RP T Farrell
C- C Sawatski
1B E Bouchee
2B S Anderson
SS J Koppe
3B G Freese
LF H Anderson
CF R Ashburn
RF W Post
UT D Philley
M *E Sawyer*

PITTSBURGH

SP V Law
SP B Friend
SP H Haddix
SP R Kline
SR B Daniels
RP R Face
C S Burgess
1B D Stuart
2B B Mazeroski
SS D Groat
3B D Hoak
LF B Skinner
CF B Virdon
RF R Clemente
RO R Mejias
1U R Nelson
IO- D Schofield
M *D Murtaugh*

ST. LOUIS

SP L Jackson
SP V Mizell
SR E Broglio
SR G Blaylock
RS L McDaniel
RP M Bridges
C H Smith
1B S Musial
2B D Blasingame
SS A Grammas
3B K Boyer
UO G Cimoli
CF C Flood
RF J Cunningham
L1 B White
M *S Hemus*

SAN FRANCISCO

SP J Antonelli
SR S Jones
SR M McCormick
SP J Sanford
RS S Miller
RP A Worthington
C H Landrith
1B O Cepeda
2B D Spencer
SS E Bressoud
3B J Davenport
LF J Brandt
CF W Mays
RF W Kirkland
RU F Alou
UL- L Wagner
M *B Rigney*

1960 AL

BALTIMORE

SR C Estrada
SP M Pappas
SR J Fisher
SP S Barber
SR H Brown
RS H Wilhelm
RS J Walker
RP G Jones
C G Triandos
1B J Gentile
2B M Breeding
SS R Hansen
3B B Robinson
LF G Woodling
MR J Brandt
RL- G Stephens
RU A Pilarcik
CF- J Busby
CU- C Courtney
1B- W Dropo
M *P Richards*

BOSTON

SP B Monbouquette
SP T Brewer
SR F Sullivan
SP I Delock
SP B Muffett
RP M Fornieles
RP T Sturdivant
RS J Casale
RP T Borland
C- R Nixon

1B V Wertz
2B P Runnels
SS D Buddin
3B F Malzone
LF T Williams
CF W Tasby
RF L Clinton
2S P Green
RF- G Geiger
M1 B Jurges
M2 D Baker
M3 P Higgins

CHICAGO
SP E Wynn
SP B Pierce
SP B Shaw
SR F Baumann
SP H Score
RP G Staley
RS R Kemmerer
RS D Donovan
RP T Lown
C S Lollar
1B R Sievers
2B N Fox
SS L Aparicio
3B G Freese
LF M Minoso
CF J Landis
RF A Smith
U1- T Kluszewski
M A Lopez

CLEVELAND
SP J Perry
SR M Grant
SP G Bell
SR B Latman
SR D Stigman
RS B Locke
RP J Klippstein
RP D Newcombe
C J Romano
1B V Power
23 K Aspromonte
SS W Held
3B B Phillips
LF T Francona
CF J Piersall
RF H Kuenn
2B J Temple
M1 J Gordon
M2 J White
M3 J Dykes

DETROIT
SP F Lary
SP J Bunning
SP D Mossi
SR B Bruce
SR P Burnside
RS H Aguirre
RS P Foytack
RP D Sisler
RS B Fischer
C- L Berberet
1B N Cash
2B F Bolling
SS C Fernandez
3B E Yost
LF C Maxwell
CF A Kaline
RF R Colavito
OI N Chrisley
1B- S Bilko
M1 J Dykes
M2 B Hitchcock
M3 J Gordon

KANSAS CITY
SP R Herbert
SP B Daley
SP D Hall
SR N Garver
SR J Kucks
RS K Johnson
RP M Kutyna
C- P Daley
1U M Throneberry
2B J Lumpe
SS K Hamlin
3B A Carey
L1 N Siebern
CF B Tuttle
UO R Snyder
RU H Bauer
IO D Williams
RL- W Herzog
M B Elliott

NEW YORK
SP A Ditmar
SP W Ford
SR B Turley
SR R Terry
SR J Coates
RP B Shantz
RP D Maas
RP R Duren
RP J Gabler
C E Howard
1B B Skowron
2B B Richardson
SS T Kubek
3B C Boyer
LU H Lopez
CF M Mantle
RF R Maris
CO Y Berra
32 G McDougald
LU- B Cerv
M C Stengel

WASHINGTON
SP P Ramos
SR D Lee
SP C Pascual
SR J Kralick
SR H Woodeshick
RS T Clevenger
RS C Stobbs
CL R Moore
C E Battey
1U J Becquer
2B B Gardner
SS J Valdivielso
3B R Bertoia
LF J Lemon
MU L Green
RF B Allison
SS B Consolo
MO D Dobbek
13 H Killebrew
UO- F Throneberry
M C Lavagetto

1960 NL

CHICAGO
SR G Hobbie
SP B Anderson
SP D Cardwell
SP D Ellsworth
RP D Elston
RS S Morehead
RS M Freeman
RP J Schaffernoth
C- M Thacker
1B E Bouchee
2B- J Kindall
SS E Banks
3B R Santo
ML R Ashburn
OI G Altman
RF B Will
UT F Thomas
23 D Zimmer
M1 C Grimm
M2 L Boudreau

CINCINNATI
SP B Purkey
SP J Hook
SP J O'Toole
SR C McLish
RS J Nuxhall
RP J Brosnan
RP B Henry
RP C Osteen
C E Bailey
1L F Robinson
2B B Martin
SS R McMillan
32 E Kasko
LR- W Post
CF V Pinson
RL G Bell
OF J Lynch
3U- W Jones
M F Hutchinson

LOS ANGELES
SP D Drysdale
SP J Podres
SP S Williams
SR S Koufax
SP R Craig
RP L Sherry
RP E Roebuck
RS D McDevitt
C J Roseboro
1B N Larker
2B C Neal
SS M Wills
3B J Gilliam
LF W Moon
MO T Davis
RF F Howard
1B G Hodges
OF D Snider
M W Alston

MILWAUKEE
SR L Burdette
SP W Spahn
SP B Buhl
SP C Willey
SR J Jay
RP J Pizarro
RP D McMahon
RP R Piche
C D Crandall
1B J Adcock
2B C Cottier
SS J Logan
3B E Mathews
LF A Spangler
CF B Bruton
RF H Aaron
LF W Covington
M C Dressen

PHILADELPHIA
SP R Roberts
SP J Buzhardt
SP G Conley
SP J Owens
SR D Green
RP T Farrell
RS C Short
RP A Mahaffey
RP R Gomez
C- J Coker
1B P Herrera
2B T Taylor
SS- R Amaro
3B- A Dark
LU B Smith
CF B Del Greco
RF K Walters
LU T Curry
UO J Callison
CU- C Dalrymple
CF- T Gonzalez
UI- B Malkmus
M1 E Sawyer
M2 A Cohen
M3 G Mauch

PITTSBURGH
SP B Friend
SP V Law
SP H Haddix
SP V Mizell
RP R Face
RP F Green
C S Burgess
1B D Stuart
2B B Mazeroski
SS D Groat
3B D Hoak
LF B Skinner
CF B Virdon
RF R Clemente
ML G Cimoli
1B R Nelson
C- H Smith
M D Murtaugh

ST. LOUIS
SP L Jackson
SR E Broglio
RP R Sadecki
SP C Simmons
SR R Kline
RP L McDaniel
C H Smith
1B B White
2B J Javier
SS D Spencer
3B K Boyer
OI S Musial
CF C Flood
RF J Cunningham
UI A Grammas
RL- W Moryn
LU- B Nieman
C- C Sawatski
M S Hemus

SAN FRANCISCO
SP M McCormick
SP S Jones
SP J Sanford
SR B O'Dell
RS J Antonelli
RP S Miller
RP G Maranda
C B Schmidt
1U W McCovey
2B D Blasingame
SS E Bressoud
3B J Davenport
LO F Alou
CF W Mays
RF W Kirkland
32 J Amalfitano
L1 O Cepeda
S3- A Rodgers
M1 B Rigney
M2 T Sheehan

1961 AL

BALTIMORE
SP S Barber
SP C Estrada
SR J Fisher
SP M Pappas
SP H Brown
RS B Hoeft
RP H Wilhelm
RS D Hall
RP W Stock
C G Triandos
1B J Gentile
2B J Adair
SS R Hansen
3B B Robinson
LO R Snyder
CF J Brandt
RU W Herzog
LU D Williams
2B- M Breeding
OI D Philley
RF- E Robinson
M1 P Richards
M2 L Harris

BOSTON
SP B Monbouquette
SP G Conley
SP D Schwall
SP I Delock
RS T Stallard
RP M Fornieles
RS B Muffett
RP D Hillman
C J Pagliaroni
1B P Runnels
2B C Schilling
SS D Buddin
3B F Malzone
LF C Yastrzemski
CF G Geiger
RF J Jensen
SU- P Green
UO- C Hardy
C- R Nixon
1B V Wertz
M P Higgins

CHICAGO
SR J Pizarro
SR F Baumann
SR B Pierce
SP C McLish
SP R Herbert
RP T Lown
RP E Wynn
RP R Kemmerer
RP D Larsen
C S Lollar
1B R Sievers
2B N Fox
SS L Aparicio
3R A Smith
LF M Minoso
CF J Landis
RF F Robinson
13 J Martin
M A Lopez

CLEVELAND
SP M Grant
SP G Bell
SP J Perry
SR B Latman
SP W Hawkins
SP F Funk
RP B Locke
RP B Allen
RS D Stigman
C J Romano
1B V Power
2B J Temple
SS W Held
3B B Phillips
LF T Francona
CF J Piersall
RF W Kirkland
M1 J Dykes
M2 M Harder

DETROIT
SP F Lary
SP J Bunning
SP D Mossi
SR P Foytack
SR P Regan
RP T Fox
RP H Aguirre
C- D Brown
1B N Cash
2B J Wood
SS C Fernandez
3B S Boros
LF R Colavito
CF B Bruton
RF A Kaline
C- M Roarke
M B Scheffing

KANSAS CITY
SR J Archer
SR N Bass
SR J Walker
SP B Shaw
SR J Nuxhall
RS E Rakow
RP B Kunkel
RS A Ditmar
C H Sullivan
1L N Siebern
2B J Lumpe
SS D Howser
3B W Causey
LR L Posada
CF- B Del Greco
UT- D Johnson
C- J Pignatano
M1 J Gordon
M2 H Bauer

LOS ANGELES
SP K McBride
SR E Grba
SR T Bowsfield
SR R Moeller
SR R Kline
RS J Donohue
RP T Morgan
RS R Duren
RP A Fowler
C E Averill
1B S Bilko
2B- K Aspromonte
SS- J Koppe
3B- E Yost
LF L Wagner
MU K Hunt
RM A Pearson
1U T Kluszewski
R1 L Thomas
2S- R Bridges
M B Rigney

MINNESOTA
SP P Ramos
SP C Pascual
SP J Kralick
SP J Kaat
RS D Lee
RP R Moore
RP B Pleis
C E Battey
1B H Killebrew
2B B Martin
SS Z Versalles
3B B Tuttle
LF J Lemon
CF L Green
RF B Allison
M1 C Lavagetto
M2 S Mele
M3 C Lavagetto
M4 S Mele

NEW YORK
SP W Ford
SR B Stafford
SP R Terry
SR R Sheldon
SP B Daley
RP L Arroyo
RS J Coates
C E Howard
1B B Skowron
2B B Richardson
SS T Kubek
3B C Boyer
LU Y Berra
CF M Mantle
RF R Maris
CU- J Blanchard
LU- H Lopez
M R Houk

WASHINGTON
SP J McClain
SP B Daniels
SP D Donovan
SP E Hobaugh
SR P Burnside
RS M Kutyna
RP J Klippstein
RP D Sisler
CU G Green
1B D Long
2B C Cottier
SS- C Veal
32 D O'Connell
OI M Keough
CF W Tasby
RU G Woodling
RU J King
LU C Hinton
3U- B Klaus
M M Vernon

1961 NL

CHICAGO
SP D Cardwell
SP G Hobbie
SP D Ellsworth
SP J Curtis
RS B Anderson
RP D Elston
RS D Drott
RS J Brewer
C- D Bertell
1B E Bouchee
2B D Zimmer
SS E Banks
3B R Santo
LF B Williams
CF A Heist
RF G Altman
MU R Ashburn
2S J Kindall
C- S Taylor
OI- B Will
M1 V Himsl
M2 H Craft
M3 V Himsl
M4 E Tappe
M5 H Craft
M6 V Himsl
M7 E Tappe
M8 L Klein
M9 E Tappe

CINCINNATI
SP J O'Toole
SP J Jay
SP B Purkey
SP K Hunt
SR J Maloney
RP J Brosnan
CL B Henry
RS J Hook
RP S Jones
C- J Zimmerman
1B G Coleman
2B D Blasingame
SS E Kasko
3B G Freese
OF W Post
CF V Pinson
RL F Robinson
UO G Bell
OF J Lynch
M F Hutchinson

LOS ANGELES
SP S Koufax
SP D Drysdale
SP S Williams
SP J Podres
SR R Craig
RP L Sherry
RP T Farrell
RP R Perranoski
C J Roseboro
1B G Hodges
2B C Neal
SS M Wills
32 J Gilliam
LF W Moon
CF W Davis
OI T Davis
OI R Fairly
1B N Larker
RU- F Howard
RM- D Snider
M W Alston

MILWAUKEE
SP L Burdette
SP W Spahn
SP B Buhl
SR C Willey
SP B Hendley
RS D Nottebart
RP D McMahon
C J Torre
1B J Adcock
2B F Bolling
SS R McMillan
3B E Mathews
LF F Thomas
RM H Aaron
RU L Maye
M1 C Dressen
M2 B Tebbetts

PHILADELPHIA
SP A Mahaffey
SR J Buzhardt
SR F Sullivan
SR C Short
SP R Roberts
RS D Ferrarese
RS D Green
RP J Owens
RP J Baldschun
C C Dalrymple
1B P Herrera
2B T Taylor
SS R Amaro
3B C Smith
LR J Callison
MR T Gonzalez
RU- K Walters
UI B Malkmus
OI D Demeter
UO- B Smith
UT- L Walls
M G Mauch

PITTSBURGH
SP B Friend
SP J Gibbon
SP H Haddix
SP E Francis
SP V Mizell
RP R Face
RP C Labine
RS B Shantz
RP A McBean
C S Burgess
1B D Stuart
2B B Mazeroski
SS D Groat
3B D Hoak
LF B Skinner
CF B Virdon
RF R Clemente
M D Murtaugh

ST. LOUIS
SP R Sadecki
SP B Gibson
SP L Jackson
SP C Simmons
SP E Broglio
RP L McDaniel
RS B Miller
RS A Cicotte
C- J Schaffer
1B B White
2B J Javier
SU- A Grammas
3B K Boyer
LF S Musial
CF C Flood
RL C James
RF J Cunningham
UO D Taussig
S2- B Lillis
CU- C Sawatski
M1 S Hemus
M2 J Keane

SAN FRANCISCO
SP M McCormick
SP J Sanford
SP J Marichal
SR S Jones
SP B Loes
RP S Miller
RS B O'Dell
RP J Duffalo
RP B Bolin
C E Bailey
1B W McCovey
2B J Amalfitano
SS J Pagan
3B J Davenport
LI H Kuenn
CF W Mays
RL F Alou
1L O Cepeda
UO- M Alou
M A Dark

1962 AL

BALTIMORE
SP C Estrada
SP M Pappas
SP R Roberts
SP J Fisher
SP S Barber
RS D Hall
RP B Hoeft
RP H Wilhelm
RP W Stock
C- G Triandos
1B J Gentile
2B- M Breeding
SS J Adair
3B B Robinson
LF B Powell
CF J Brandt
UO R Snyder
RU W Herzog
UO- D Nicholson
CU- C Lau
UT- D Williams
M B Hitchcock

BOSTON
SP G Conley
SP B Monbouquette
SP E Wilson
SP D Schwall
RP D Radatz
RP M Fornieles
RP A Earley
RP H Kolstad
C- J Pagliaroni
1B P Runnels
2B C Schilling
SS E Bressoud
3B F Malzone
LF C Yastrzemski
CF G Geiger
RM C Hardy
RF L Clinton
C- B Tillman
M P Higgins

CHICAGO
SP R Herbert
SP J Pizarro
SP E Wynn
SP J Buzhardt
SP J Horlen
RS E Fisher
RS F Baumann
RP D Zanni
RP T Lown
C C Carreon
1B J Cunningham
2B N Fox
SS L Aparicio
3L A Smith
LR F Robinson
CF J Landis
RM M Hershberger
C- S Lollar
M A Lopez

CLEVELAND
SP D Donovan
SR P Ramos
SP J Perry
SR B Latman
SP M Grant
RS G Bell
RP F Funk
C J Romano
1B T Francona
2B J Kindall
SS W Held
3B B Phillips
LF C Essegian
CF T Cline
RF W Kirkland
LU- A Luplow
UO- D Dillard
M1 M McGaha
M2 M Harder

DETROIT
SP J Bunning
SR H Aguirre
SP D Mossi
SR P Regan
SP P Foytack
RS S Jones
RP R Kline
CL T Fox
RP R Nischwitz
C D Brown
1B N Cash
2B J Wood
SS C Fernandez
3B S Boros
LF R Colavito
CF B Bruton
RF A Kaline
23 D McAuliffe
OI- B Morton
M B Scheffing

KANSAS CITY
SP E Rakow
SR D Pfister
SR J Walker
SR B Fischer
SR D Segui
RS J Wyatt
RS D Wickersham
RP D McDevitt
C- H Sullivan
1B N Siebern
2B J Lumpe
SS- D Howser
3B E Charles
LF M Jimenez
ML B Del Greco
RF G Cimoli
UI W Causey
CF J Tartabull
OI- G Alusik
M H Bauer

LOS ANGELES
SR D Chance
SP B Belinsky
SR E Grba
SP D Lee
SP K McBride
RP T Bowsfield
RP A Fowler
RP R Duren
RP J Spring
C B Rodgers
1R L Thomas
2B B Moran
SS J Koppe
3B F Torres
LR L Wagner
CF A Pearson
RF- G Thomas
LU- E Averill
UT- T Burgess
M *B Rigney*

MINNESOTA
SP J Kaat
SP C Pascual
SP J Kralick
SR D Stigman
SR J Bonikowski
RS L Stange
RP R Moore
RP G Maranda
C E Battey
1B V Power
2B B Allen
SS Z Versalles
3B R Rollins
LF H Killebrew
CF L Green
RF B Allison
CF B Tuttle
U2- D Mincher
M *S Mele*

NEW YORK
SP R Terry
SP W Ford
SP B Stafford
SR J Bouton
SR R Sheldon
RS J Coates
RS B Daley
CL M Bridges
C E Howard
1B B Skowron
2B B Richardson
SL T Tresh
3B C Boyer
LU H Lopez
CF M Mantle
RM R Maris
OC- Y Berra
OC- J Blanchard
UO- J Reed
M *R Houk*

WASHINGTON
SP D Stenhouse
SR D Rudolph
SR T Cheney
SR B Daniels
SR P Burnside
RP C Osteen
RS S Hamilton
RP M Kutyna
RP J Hannan
C K Retzer
1B H Bright
2B C Cottier
SS K Hamlin
3S B Johnson
UT C Hinton
CF J Piersall
RU J King
UO J Hicks
IF- D O'Connell
3U- J Schaive
C- B Schmidt
M *M Vernon*

1962 NL

CHICAGO
SP B Buhl
SP D Ellsworth
SR D Cardwell
SP C Koonce
SR G Hobbie
RP B Anderson
RP B Schultz
RP D Elston
RP D Gerard
C- D Bertell
1B E Banks
2B K Hubbs
SS A Rodgers
3B R Santo
LF B Williams
CF L Brock
RF G Altman
UO- D Landrum
U1- B Will
M1 *E Tappe*
M2 *L Klein*
M3 *C Metro*

CINCINNATI
SP B Purkey
SP J Jay
SP J O'Toole
SP J Maloney
RS J Klippstein
RP J Brosnan
RS T Wills
C J Edwards
1B G Coleman
2B D Blasingame
SS L Cardenas
3B E Kasko
LF W Post
CF V Pinson
RF F Robinson
OI M Keough
LU J Lynch
M *F Hutchinson*

HOUSTON
SR T Farrell
SP K Johnson
SP B Bruce
SR J Golden
SP H Woodeshick
RP B Tiefenauer
RP D McMahon
RP R Kemmerer
RP J Umbricht
C H Smith
1B N Larker
2B J Amalfitano
SS B Lillis
3B B Aspromonte
LU A Spangler
CF C Warwick
RF R Mejias
LU J Pendleton
UI- B Goodman
M *H Craft*

LOS ANGELES
SP D Drysdale
SP J Podres
SR S Williams
SP S Koufax
RP E Roebuck
RP R Perranoski
RP L Sherry
RP P Ortega
C J Roseboro
1B R Fairly
2B L Burright
SS M Wills
23 J Gilliam
LF T Davis
CF W Davis
RF F Howard
1U- T Harkness
OI- W Moon
M *W Alston*

MILWAUKEE
SP W Spahn
SP B Shaw
SP B Hendley
SR L Burdette
SP T Cloninger
RS J Curtis
RS C Willey
RP D Nottebart
C D Crandall
1B J Adcock
2B F Bolling
SS R McMillan
3B E Mathews
ML L Maye
MR H Aaron
RF- M Jones
1B T Aaron
M *B Tebbetts*

NEW YORK
SP R Craig
SP A Jackson
SP J Hook
SR B Miller
RS C Anderson
RS B Moorhead
RP R Daviault
RP K Mac Kenzie
C- C Cannizzaro
1B M Throneberry
2S C Neal
SS E Chacon
3I F Mantilla
LF F Thomas
MO J Hickman
OI R Ashburn
UO J Christopher
UT R Kanehl
OF- G Woodling
M *C Stengel*

PHILADELPHIA
SP A Mahaffey
SR J Hamilton
SP D Bennett
SP C McLish
RS C Short
RS D Green
RP J Baldschun
RS B Smith
C C Dalrymple
1B R Sievers
2B T Taylor
SS B Wine
3M D Demeter
LU T Savage
CF T Gonzalez
RF J Callison
LF W Covington
3S B Klaus
1U F Torre
M *G Mauch*

PITTSBURGH
SP B Friend
SP A McBean
SR E Francis
SP H Haddix
SP V Law
RS T Sturdivant
CL R Face
RP D Olivo
RP J Lamabe
C S Burgess
1B D Stuart
2B B Mazeroski
SS D Groat
3B D Hoak
LF B Skinner
CF B Virdon
RF R Clemente
LO- H Goss
M *D Murtaugh*

ST. LOUIS
SP L Jackson
SP B Gibson
SP E Broglio
SP R Washburn
SP C Simmons
RP L McDaniel
RP R Sadecki
RP B Shantz
RP D Ferrarese
C G Oliver
1B B White
2B J Javier
SS J Gotay
3B K Boyer
LU S Musial
CF C Flood
RF C James
C- C Sawatski
IF R Schoendienst
LU- B Smith
M *J Keane*

SAN FRANCISCO
SP B O'Dell
SP J Sanford
SP J Marichal
SP B Pierce
RP S Miller
RS B Bolin
RP D Larsen
C- T Haller
1B O Cepeda
2B C Hiller
SS J Pagan
3B J Davenport
LF H Kuenn
CF W Mays
RF F Alou
C- E Bailey
OI- W McCovey
M *A Dark*

1963 AL

BALTIMORE
SP S Barber
SP R Roberts
SP M Pappas
SP M McCormick
SP D McNally
RP S Miller
RP D Hall
RP W Stock
C J Orsino
1B J Gentile
2B J Adair
SS L Aparicio
3B B Robinson
LF B Powell
MR J Brandt
MR R Snyder
MI B Saverine
RF A Smith
2U- B Johnson
M *B Hitchcock*

BOSTON
SP B Monbouquette
SP E Wilson
SP D Morehead
SP B Heffner
RP J Lamabe
RP D Radatz
RP A Earley
RS W Wood
C- B Tillman
1B D Stuart
2B C Schilling
SS E Bressoud
3B F Malzone
LF C Yastrzemski
MU G Geiger
RF L Clinton
MU R Mejias
C R Nixon
M *J Pesky*

CHICAGO
SR G Peters
SP R Herbert
SP J Pizarro
SP J Buzhardt
SR J Horlen
RP H Wilhelm
RS E Fisher
RP J Brosnan
RP F Baumann
C J Martin
1B T McCraw
2B N Fox
SS R Hansen
3B P Ward
LF D Nicholson
CF J Landis
RF F Robinson
C C Carreon
MR M Hershberger
UI A Weis
M *A Lopez*

CLEVELAND
SP M Grant
SP D Donovan
SP J Kralick
SR P Ramos
SR B Latman
RS G Bell
RP J Walker
RP T Abernathy
RP B Allen
C- J Azcue
1B F Whitfield
2O W Held
S2- J Kindall
3B M Alvis
LF T Francona
CF- V Davalillo
MR W Kirkland
1B- J Adcock
RU A Luplow
C- J Romano
M *B Tebbetts*

DETROIT
SP J Bunning
SP H Aguirre
SR P Regan
SR M Lolich
SP D Mossi
RP F Lary
RP T Fox
RP B Anderson
RP T Sturdivant
C G Triandos
1B N Cash
2B- J Wood
SS D McAuliffe
3B B Phillips
LF R Colavito
CF B Bruton
RF A Kaline
CU B Freehan
M1 *B Scheffing*
M2 *C Dressen*

KANSAS CITY
SP D Wickersham
SP O Pena
SP M Drabowsky
SP E Rakow
SR D Segui
RS T Bowsfield
RP J Wyatt
RP B Fischer
C- D Edwards
1B N Siebern
2B J Lumpe
SS W Causey
3B E Charles
MU B Del Greco
CF- J Tartabull
RF G Cimoli
LU C Essegian
UO- G Alusik
M *E Lopat*

LOS ANGELES
SR D Chance
SP K McBride
SR D Osinski
SR D Lee
RP J Navarro
RP A Fowler
RS P Foytack
RP M Nelson
C B Rodgers
1R L Thomas
2B B Moran
SS J Fregosi
3B F Torres
LF L Wagner
CF A Pearson
UO- B Perry
UT- B Sadowski
M *B Rigney*

MINNESOTA
SP C Pascual
SP D Stigman
SP J Kaat
SR J Perry
SR L Stange
RP B Dailey
RP B Pleis
RP G Roggenburk
C E Battey
1B V Power
2B B Allen
SS Z Versalles
3B R Rollins
LF H Killebrew
ML J Hall
RF B Allison
CF L Green
1U- D Mincher
M *S Mele*

NEW YORK
SP W Ford
SP R Terry
SR J Bouton
SP A Downing
SP S Williams
CL H Reniff
RP S Hamilton
C E Howard
1B J Pepitone
2B B Richardson
SS T Kubek
3B C Boyer
LF H Lopez
ML T Tresh
UO J Reed
RF- R Maris
M *R Houk*

WASHINGTON
SR C Osteen
SR D Rudolph
SR B Daniels
SP T Cheney
SR J Duckworth
RP R Kline
RP P Burnside
RP E Roebuck
RP J Bronstad
C- K Retzer
1U B Osborne
2B C Cottier
SS E Brinkman
3B- D Zimmer
LR C Hinton
CF D Lock
RF J King
LU M Minoso
1U D Phillips
M1 *M Vernon*
M2 *E Yost*
M3 *G Hodges*

1963 NL

CHICAGO
SP D Ellsworth
SP L Jackson
SP B Buhl
SR G Hobbie
SR P Toth
CL L McDaniel
RP D Elston
RP J Brewer
C D Bertell
1B E Banks
2B K Hubbs
SS A Rodgers
3B R Santo
LF B Williams
CF- E Burton
RF L Brock
MU- D Landrum
M *B Kennedy*

CINCINNATI
SP J Maloney
SP J O'Toole
SP J Nuxhall
SP J Tsitouris
SP J Jay
RP B Purkey
RP A Worthington
RP B Henry
C J Edwards
1B G Coleman
2B P Rose
SS L Cardenas
3B- G Freese
LF F Robinson
CF V Pinson
RU T Harper
UT- M Keough
M *F Hutchinson*

HOUSTON
SP K Johnson
SP T Farrell
SP D Nottebart
SP B Bruce
SP H Brown
RP H Woodeshick
RP D McMahon
RP J Umbricht
RS C Zachary
C J Bateman
1R R Staub
2B E Fazio
SS B Lillis
3B B Aspromonte
LM A Spangler
CF H Goss
RF C Warwick
12 P Runnels
23 J Temple
M *H Craft*

LOS ANGELES
SP D Drysdale
SP S Koufax
SP J Podres
SR B Miller
RP R Perranoski
RP L Sherry
C J Roseboro
1B R Fairly
2B J Gilliam
SS M Wills
3B- K McMullen
LF T Davis
CF W Davis
RF F Howard
UO W Moon
SS D Tracewski
1U- B Skowron
M *W Alston*

MILWAUKEE
SP W Spahn
SR D Lemaster
SR B Hendley
SR T Cloninger
SP B Sadowski
RS B Shaw
RS H Fischer
RP C Raymond
RP R Piche
C1 J Torre
1L- G Oliver
2B F Bolling
SS R McMillan
3B E Mathews
ML L Maye
MU- M Jones
RF H Aaron
S3 D Menke
C- D Crandall
M *B Bragan*

NEW YORK
SR R Craig
SP A Jackson
SP C Willey
SR T Stallard
SR J Hook
RS G Cisco
RP L Bearnarth
RP K Mac Kenzie
RP D Rowe
C C Coleman
1B T Harkness
2B R Hunt
SS A Moran
3B- C Neal
LF F Thomas
OI J Hickman
UO D Snider
UT R Kanehl
RU- E Kranepool
M *C Stengel*

PHILADELPHIA
SP C McLish
SP R Culp
SR C Short
SP A Mahaffey
SR D Green
RP J Baldschun
RP D Bennett
RP J Klippstein
RS R Duren
C C Dalrymple
1B R Sievers
2B T Taylor
SS B Wine
3B D Hoak
ML T Gonzalez
M3 D Demeter
RF J Callison
S3 R Amaro
LF W Covington
1U- F Torre
M *G Mauch*

PITTSBURGH
SP B Friend
SP D Cardwell
SP D Schwall
SR J Gibbon
RS A McBean
RP T Sisk
RP R Face
RS B Veale
C- J Pagliaroni
1B D Clendenon
2B B Mazeroski
SS D Schofield
3B B Bailey
OI W Stargell
CF B Virdon
RF R Clemente
C- S Burgess
SU- J Logan
LU- J Lynch
UO- T Savage
M *D Murtaugh*

ST. LOUIS
SP B Gibson
SP E Broglio
SP C Simmons
SP R Sadecki
RS R Taylor
RP B Shantz
RP E Bauta
C T McCarver
1B B White
2B J Javier
SS D Groat
3B K Boyer
LU C James
CF C Flood
RF G Altman
LF S Musial
M *J Keane*

SAN FRANCISCO
SP J Marichal
SP J Sanford
SP B O'Dell
SR B Pierce
RS B Bolin
RS J Fisher
RP G Perry
RS J Duffalo
C E Bailey
1B O Cepeda
2B C Hiller
SS J Pagan
3B J Davenport
LF W McCovey
CF W Mays
RF F Alou
C T Haller
OI H Kuenn
UI- E Bowman
M *A Dark*

1964 AL

BALTIMORE
SP M Pappas
SP W Bunker
SP R Roberts
SP D McNally
SR S Barber
CL S Miller
RP H Haddix
RP D Hall
RS D Vineyard
C- D Brown
1B N Siebern
2B J Adair
SS L Aparicio
3B B Robinson
LF B Powell
CF J Brandt
RF S Bowens
IO- B Johnson
C- J Orsino
M *H Bauer*

BOSTON
SP B Monbouquette
SP E Wilson
SR J Lamabe
SP D Morehead
RP D Radatz
RS B Heffner
RS P Charton
RS B Spanswick
C B Tillman
1B D Stuart
2U D Jones
SS E Bressoud
3B F Malzone
LU T Conigliaro
CF C Yastrzemski
RF L Thomas
UT F Mantilla
CU- R Nixon
M1 *J Pesky*
M2 *Herman*

CHICAGO
SP G Peters
SP J Pizarro
SP J Horlen
SP J Buzhardt
SP R Herbert
RP H Wilhelm
RP E Fisher
C J Martin
1L T McCraw
2B A Weis
SS R Hansen
3B P Ward
RF F Robinson
CF J Landis
RM M Hershberger
23 D Buford
LF- D Nicholson
UO- G Stephens
M *A Lopez*

CLEVELAND
SP J Kralick
SP S McDowell
SP D Donovan
SR S Siebert
SR P Ramos
RP L Tiant
RP D McMahon
RP G Bell
RP T Abernathy
C J Romano
1R B Chance
2B L Brown
SS D Howser
3B M Alvis
LF L Wagner
CF V Davalillo
RU T Francona
UT W Held
1B F Whitfield
C- J Azcue
R2- C Salmon
M1 *G Strickland*
M2 *B Tebbetts*

DETROIT
SP D Wickersham
SR M Lolich
SP H Aguirre
SR P Regan
SP D McLain
RS E Rakow
RP L Sherry
RP F Gladding
RP T Fox
C B Freehan
1B N Cash
2B J Lumpe
SS D McAuliffe
3B D Wert
LF G Brown
MO G Thomas
RF A Kaline
MU B Bruton
OI D Demeter
M *C Dressen*

KANSAS CITY
SP O Pena
SP D Segui
SP J O'Donoghue
SR M Drabowsky
RP J Wyatt
RS T Bowsfield
RP W Stock
RS J Santiago
C- D Edwards
1B J Gentile
2B D Green
SS W Causey
3B E Charles
UO J Tartabull

CF N Mathews
RF R Colavito
OI G Alusik
CU- B Bryan
OF- M Jimenez
M1 E Lopat
M2 M McGaha

LOS ANGELES
SR D Chance
SP F Newman
SR B Latman
SP B Belinsky
SP K McBride
RS B Lee
RP D Osinski
RS D Lee
RP B Duliba
C B Rodgers
1B J Adcock
2B B Knoop
SS J Fregosi
3U F Torres
UO W Smith
LM- J Piersall
RF- L Clinton
UO A Pearson
UI T Satriano
M B Rigney

MINNESOTA
SP C Pascual
SP J Kaat
SP D Stigman
SP M Grant
RS G Arrigo
CL A Worthington
RP J Perry
RP B Pleis
C E Battey
1O B Allison
2B- B Allen
SS Z Versalles
3B R Rollins
LF H Killebrew
CF J Hall
RF T Oliva
1U D Mincher
M S Mele

NEW YORK
SP J Bouton
SP A Downing
SP W Ford
SR R Terry
SP R Sheldon
RP P Mikkelsen
RP H Reniff
RP B Stafford
RP S Hamilton
C E Howard
1B J Pepitone
2B B Richardson
SS T Kubek
3B C Boyer
LM T Tresh
MU M Mantle
RU R Maris
UT P Linz
LO H Lopez
M Y Berra

WASHINGTON
SP C Osteen
SP B Narum
SP B Daniels
SR A Koch
RP S Ridzik
RS J Hannan
RP R Kline
RS D Rudolph
C M Brumley
1B- B Skowron
2B D Blasingame
SS E Brinkman
3S J Kennedy
LF C Hinton
CF D Lock
RF J King
1U D Phillips
UO F Valentine
3U D Zimmer
M G Hodges

1964 NL

CHICAGO
SP L Jackson
SP D Ellsworth
SP B Buhl
SR L Burdette
SP E Broglio
RP L McDaniel
RP D Elston
RS S Slaughter
C D Bertell
1B E Banks
2B J Amalfitano
SS A Rodgers
3B R Santo
LF B Williams
CF B Cowan
RU- L Gabrielson
IO J Stewart
M B Kennedy

CINCINNATI
SP J O'Toole
SP J Maloney
SP B Purkey
SR J Jay
SR J Tsitouris
RS J Nuxhall
RS S Ellis
RP B McCool
RP B Henry
C J Edwards
1B D Johnson
2B P Rose
SS L Cardenas
3B S Boros
LF T Harper
CF V Pinson
RL F Robinson
RU M Keough
1U- G Coleman
M1 F Hutchinson
M2 D Sisler
M3 F Hutchinson
M4 D Sisler

HOUSTON
SP K Johnson
SP B Bruce
SP T Farrell
SP D Nottebart
SP H Brown
RS J Owens
RS D Larsen
CL H Woodeshick
RP C Raymond
C J Grote
1R W Bond
2B N Fox
SS E Kasko
3B B Aspromonte
LF A Spangler
MU- M White
RF- J Gaines
UI B Lillis
1R- R Staub
M1 H Craft
M2 L Harris

LOS ANGELES
SP D Drysdale
SP S Koufax
SP P Ortega
SP J Moeller
RP B Miller
RP R Perranoski
RS J Brewer
C J Roseboro
1B R Fairly
2B N Oliver
SS M Wills
3U J Gilliam
LF T Davis
CF W Davis
RF F Howard
OI W Parker
23 D Tracewski
M W Alston

MILWAUKEE
SP T Cloninger
SP D Lemaster
SR W Spahn
SR B Sadowski
SP H Fischer
RS W Blasingame
RP B Tiefenauer
RP B Hoeft
RP C Olivo
C1 J Torre
1B- G Oliver
2B F Bolling
SS D Menke
3B E Mathews
LF R Carty
ML L Maye
RF H Aaron
OI F Alou
OI T Cline
C- E Bailey
M B Bragan

NEW YORK
SP J Fisher
SP T Stallard
SP A Jackson
SR G Cisco
RP B Wakefield
RP L Bearnarth
RP B Hunter
CU J Gonder
1B E Kranepool
2B R Hunt
SS R McMillan
3S C Smith
LF G Altman
ML J Hickman
RF J Christopher
UT R Kanehl
OC- H Taylor
M C Stengel

PHILADELPHIA
SP J Bunning
SR C Short
SP D Bennett
SP A Mahaffey
SR R Culp
RP J Baldschun
RP E Roebuck
RS R Wise
RP J Boozer
C C Dalrymple
1L J Herrnstein
2B T Taylor
3B B Wine
SS D Allen
LF W Covington
CF T Gonzalez
RF J Callison
S1 R Amaro
UT C Rojas
M G Mauch

PITTSBURGH
SP B Veale
SP B Friend
SP V Law
SP J Gibbon
SR S Blass
CL A McBean
RP R Face
RP R Butters
RP T Sisk
C- J Pagliaroni
1B D Clendenon
2B B Mazeroski
SS D Schofield
3O B Bailey
OI M Mota
CF B Virdon
RF R Clemente
3U G Freese
LU J Lynch
OI W Stargell
SS- G Alley
M D Murtaugh

ST. LOUIS
SP B Gibson
SP C Simmons
SP R Sadecki
SR R Craig
RP R Taylor
RS M Cuellar
CL B Schultz
C T McCarver
1B B White
2B J Javier
SS D Groat
3B K Boyer
LF L Brock
CF C Flood
RF- M Shannon
LU- C James
OF- C Warwick
M J Keane

SAN FRANCISCO
SP J Marichal
SR G Perry
SR B Bolin
SP B Hendley
SR R Herbel
RP J Sanford
RP B Shaw
RS B O'Dell
RP J Duffalo
C T Haller
1B O Cepeda
2B H Lanier
SS J Pagan
3B J Hart
LR H Kuenn
CF W Mays
RF J Alou
UO M Alou
S3 J Davenport
LU W McCovey
OF- D Snider
M A Dark

1965 AL

BALTIMORE
SP S Barber
SP M Pappas
SP D McNally
SP W Bunker
SP R Roberts
RP S Miller
RP D Hall
RP D Larsen
C- D Brown
1L B Powell
2B J Adair
SS L Aparicio
3B B Robinson
RL C Blefary
CF P Blair
UO R Snyder
1U N Siebern
RU- S Bowens
UO- J Brandt
UI- B Johnson
M H Bauer

BOSTON
SP E Wilson
SP B Monbouquette
SP D Morehead
SP J Lonborg
SR D Bennett
RP D Radatz
RP A Earley
RP J Ritchie
RP B Duliba
C B Tillman
1B L Thomas
2B F Mantilla
SS R Petrocelli
3B F Malzone
LF C Yastrzemski
MU L Green
RF T Conigliaro
SS E Bressoud
3U D Jones
CF- J Gosger
M Herman

CALIFORNIA
SP F Newman
SP D Chance
SP M Lopez
SR G Brunet
SR R May
RP B Lee
RP A Gatewood
C B Rodgers
1B V Power
2B B Knoop
SS J Fregosi
3B P Schaal
LF W Smith
CF J Cardenal
RU A Pearson
1B J Adcock
RF- L Clinton
M B Rigney

CHICAGO
SP J Horlen
SP J Buzhardt
SR T John
SP G Peters
SP B Howard
RP E Fisher
RP H Wilhelm
RP B Locker
C J Martin
1B B Skowron
2B D Buford
SS R Hansen
3B P Ward
LF D Cater
CF K Berry
RF F Robinson
1L T McCraw
C J Romano
2U A Weis
M A Lopez

CLEVELAND
SP S McDowell
SR L Tiant
SR S Siebert
SR R Terry
RS L Stange
RP G Bell
RP D McMahon
RP F Weaver
C J Azcue
1B F Whitfield
2B P Gonzalez
SS L Brown
3B M Alvis
LF L Wagner
CF V Davalillo
RF R Colavito
UT C Hinton
SU D Howser
M B Tebbetts

DETROIT
SP M Lolich
SP D McLain
SP H Aguirre
SP D Wickersham
SP J Sparma
RP T Fox
RP L Sherry
RP F Gladding
RP O Pena
C B Freehan
1B N Cash
2B J Lumpe
SS D McAuliffe
3B D Wert
LF W Horton
OI D Demeter
OI A Kaline
LU- G Brown
SU- R Oyler
M1 B Swift
M2 C Dressen

KANSAS CITY
SP F Talbot
SP R Sheldon
SP J O'Donoghue
SR D Segui
SR C Hunter
RP J Wyatt
RP W Stock
RP J Dickson
RP D Mossi
C B Bryan
1B K Harrelson
2B D Green
SS B Campaneris
3B E Charles
LF- T Reynolds
CF J Landis
RF M Hershberger
UI W Causey
C- R Lachemann
UT- S Rosario
M1 M McGaha
M2 H Sullivan

MINNESOTA
SP M Grant
SP J Kaat
SR J Perry
SP C Pascual
SR D Boswell
CL A Worthington
RP J Klippstein
RS D Stigman
RP M Nelson
C E Battey
1B D Mincher
2B J Kindall
SS Z Versalles
3B R Rollins
LF B Allison
CF J Hall
RF T Oliva
13 H Killebrew
OF S Valdespino
MU- J Nossek
C- J Zimmerman
M S Mele

NEW YORK
SP M Stottlemyre
SP W Ford
SP A Downing
SP J Bouton
SP B Stafford
RP P Ramos
RP H Reniff
RP P Mikkelsen
RP S Hamilton
C E Howard
1B J Pepitone
2B B Richardson
SS T Kubek
3B C Boyer
LF M Mantle
ML T Tresh
OI H Lopez
1U R Barker
SU P Linz
MR- R Moschitto
M J Keane

WASHINGTON
SP P Richert
SP P Ortega
SR B Narum
SR M McCormick
SR B Daniels
RP R Kline
RP S Ridzik
RS H Koplitz
RP M Bridges
C- M Brumley
1B- D Nen
2B D Blasingame
SS E Brinkman
3B K McMullen
LF F Howard
CF D Lock
UT W Held
2S K Hamlin
RU J King
RL W Kirkland
1U- J Cunningham
IC- D Zimmer
M G Hodges

1965 NL

CHICAGO
SP L Jackson
SP D Ellsworth
SP B Buhl
SR C Koonce
RP T Abernathy
RP L McDaniel
RP B Humphreys
RP B Hoeft
C- V Roznovsky
1B E Banks
2B G Beckert
SS D Kessinger
3B R Santo
UO D Clemens
CF D Landrum
RO B Williams
OI J Stewart
OI- G Altman
M1 B Kennedy
M2 L Klein

CINCINNATI
SP S Ellis
SP J Maloney
SR J Jay
SR J Nuxhall
SR J Tsitouris
RP J O'Toole
RP B McCool
RP T Davidson
RP R Craig
C J Edwards
1B T Perez
2B P Rose
SS L Cardenas
3B D Johnson
LF T Harper
CF V Pinson
RF F Robinson
1B G Coleman
M D Sisler

HOUSTON
SP B Bruce
SP T Farrell
SP D Nottebart
SP L Dierker
SP D Giusti
RS C Raymond
RP J Owens
RP R Taylor
RP M Cuellar
C R Brand
1O W Bond
2B J Morgan
SS B Lillis
3B B Aspromonte
LF L Maye
CF J Wynn
RF R Staub
OF J Gaines
1B- J Gentile
M L Harris

LOS ANGELES
SP S Koufax
SP D Drysdale
SP C Osteen
SP J Podres
RP R Perranoski
RP B Miller
RS H Reed
RP J Brewer
C J Roseboro
1B W Parker
2B J Lefebvre
SS M Wills
3B J Kennedy
LF L Johnson
CF W Davis
RF R Fairly
3U J Gilliam
M W Alston

MILWAUKEE
SP T Cloninger
SP W Blasingame
SP K Johnson
SP D Lemaster
SR B Sadowski
RP B O'Dell
RS H Fischer
RP D Osinski
RP P Niekro
C1 J Torre
UT F Alou
2B F Bolling
SS W Woodward
3B E Mathews
LF- R Carty
CF M Jones
RF H Aaron
C1 G Oliver
OI T Cline
S3- M DeLa Hoz
M B Bragan

NEW YORK
SP J Fisher
SP A Jackson
SP W Spahn
SR G Cisco
RS T McGraw
RS T Parsons
RP L Bearnarth
RS L Miller
C C Cannizzaro
1B E Kranepool
2B C Hiller
SS R McMillan
3B C Smith
LO R Swoboda
UT J Hickman
RM J Lewis
OF J Christopher
2I B Klaus
MU- B Cowan
M1 C Stengel
M2 W Westrum

PHILADELPHIA
SP C Short
SP J Bunning
SP R Culp
SP R Herbert
SR B Belinsky
RP G Wagner
RP J Baldschun
RP E Roebuck
C C Dalrymple
1B D Stuart
2B T Taylor
SS B Wine
3B D Allen
LF- A Johnson
ML T Gonzalez
RF J Callison
1S R Amaro
LU W Covington
2M C Rojas
MU- J Briggs
M G Mauch

PITTSBURGH
SP B Veale
SP D Cardwell
SP B Friend
SP V Law
SR J Gibbon
RP A McBean
RS T Sisk
RP D Schwall
RP W Wood
C J Pagliaroni
1B D Clendenon
2B B Mazeroski
S2 G Alley
3B B Bailey
LF W Stargell
CF B Virdon
RF R Clemente
UO M Mota
M H Walker

ST. LOUIS
SP B Gibson
SP C Simmons
SR T Stallard
SP R Sadecki
SR B Purkey
RS R Washburn
RP N Briles
RP H Woodeshick
RP D Dennis
C T McCarver
1B B White
2B- J Javier
SS D Groat
3B K Boyer
LF L Brock
CF C Flood
RU M Shannon
UT P Gagliano
OI- T Francona
M R Schoendienst

SAN FRANCISCO
SP J Marichal
SP B Shaw
SR G Perry
SR R Herbel
RS B Bolin
CL F Linzy
RP M Murakami
C T Haller
1B W McCovey
2B H Lanier
SS D Schofield
3B J Hart
LO M Alou
CF W Mays
RF J Alou
UI J Davenport
LF- L Gabrielson
M H Franks

1966 AL

BALTIMORE
SP D McNally
SP J Palmer
SP W Bunker
SP S Barber
SP J Miller
RS E Watt
CL S Miller
RP M Drabowsky
RP E Fisher
C A Etchebarren
1B B Powell
2B D Johnson
SS L Aparicio
3B B Robinson
LF C Blefary
CF P Blair
RF F Robinson
ML R Snyder
UO- S Bowens
M H Bauer

BOSTON
SR J Lonborg
SP J Santiago
SR B Brandon
SP L Stange
SP E Wilson
RP D McMahon
RS D Stigman
RP J Wyatt
RP D Osinski
C M Ryan
1B G Scott
2B G Smith
SS R Petrocelli
3B J Foy
LF C Yastrzemski
CF- D Demeter
RF T Conigliaro
2U D Jones
OF- L Green
M1 Herman
M2 P Runnels

CALIFORNIA
SP D Chance
SP G Brunet
SP M Lopez
SP F Newman
RP B Lee
RS J Sanford
RP M Rojas
RP L Burdette
C B Rodgers
1B N Siebern
2B B Knoop
SS J Fregosi
3B P Schaal
LF- R Reichardt
CF J Cardenal
RU E Kirkpatrick
IC T Satriano
1B- J Adcock
UR- F Malzone
OF- W Smith
M B Rigney

CHICAGO
SP T John
SP J Horlen
SP G Peters
SR J Buzhardt
SP B Howard
RS J Lamabe
RP B Locker
RP D Higgins
RS J Pizarro
C J Romano
1B T McCraw
2U A Weis
SS- L Elia
3B D Buford
LR K Berry
CF T Agee
RF F Robinson
S2 J Adair
1B B Skowron
LI- P Ward
M E Stanky

CLEVELAND
SP G Bell
SP S Siebert
SP S McDowell
SR S Hargan
SR L Tiant
RS J O'Donoghue
RP J Kralick
RP D Radatz
RP B Allen
C J Azcue

1B F Whitfield
2B P Gonzalez
SS L Brown
3B M Alvis
LF L Wagner
CF V Davalillo
RF R Colavito
UT C Hinton
UT C Salmon
UO- J Landis
M1 B Tebbetts
M2 G Strickland

DETROIT
SP D McLain
SP M Lolich
SP E Wilson
SR D Wickersham
SR J Podres
RP O Pena
RS H Aguirre
RS B Monbouquette
CL L Sherry
C B Freehan
1B N Cash
2B J Lumpe
SS D McAuliffe
3B D Wert
LF W Horton
MR A Kaline
RF J Northrup
2U J Wood
U3- G Brown
CF- M Stanley
2B- D Tracewski
M1 C Dressen
M2 B Swift
M3 F Skaff

KANSAS CITY
SR L Krausse
SP C Hunter
SP J Nash
SR P Lindblad
RP J Aker
RP K Sanders
C P Roof
1B- K Harrelson
2B D Green
SS B Campaneris
3B E Charles
LU L Stahl
MU- J Nossek
RF M Hershberger
UT D Cater
OI R Repoz
UT- O Chavarria
LM- J Gosger
M A Dark

MINNESOTA
SP J Kaat
SP M Grant
SP J Perry
SP D Boswell
SR J Merritt
RP A Worthington
RP C Pascual
RP P Cimino
RP D Siebler
C E Battey
1B D Mincher
2B B Allen
SS Z Versalles
31 H Killebrew
LO J Hall
CF T Uhlaender
RF T Oliva
2U C Tovar
3U- R Rollins
M S Mele

NEW YORK
SP M Stottlemyre
SP F Peterson
SP A Downing
SP F Talbot
SP J Bouton
RP H Reniff
RP P Ramos
RP S Hamilton
RP D Womack
C E Howard
1B J Pepitone
2B B Richardson
SU H Clarke
3S C Boyer
OI T Tresh
CF M Mantle
RF R Maris
LU R White
M1 J Keane
M2 R Houk

WASHINGTON
SP P Richert
SP M McCormick
SP P Ortega
SR J Hannan
RP C Cox
RP B Humphreys
CL R Kline
RP D Lines
C P Casanova
1B- D Nen
2I B Saverine
SS E Brinkman
3B K McMullen
LF F Howard
CF D Lock
OI F Valentine
RU J King
OF W Kirkland
M G Hodges

1966 NL

ATLANTA
SP T Cloninger
SP K Johnson
SP D Lemaster
RP C Carroll
RP C Olivo
RP T Abernathy
RP P Niekro
C J Torre
1L F Alou
2S W Woodward
SS D Menke
3B E Mathews
LF R Carty
CF M Jones
RF H Aaron
M1 B Bragan
M2 B Hitchcock

CHICAGO
SP D Ellsworth
SP K Holtzman
SR B Hands
RS F Jenkins
RS C Koonce
RS B Hendley
C R Hundley
1B E Banks
2B G Beckert
SS D Kessinger
3B R Santo
LM B Browne
CF A Phillips
RF B Williams
OI- G Altman
M L Durocher

CINCINNATI
SP J Maloney
SP S Ellis
SP M Pappas
SP J O'Toole
SR J Nuxhall
RP B McCool
RP D Nottebart
RP T Davidson
RP J Baldschun
C J Edwards
1B T Perez
2B P Rose
SS L Cardenas
3B T Helms
L1 D Johnson
CF V Pinson
RL T Harper
1U- G Coleman
CU- D Pavletich
UT- C Ruiz
OF A Shamsky
RU- D Simpson
M1 D Heffner
M2 D Bristol

HOUSTON
SR M Cuellar
SP D Giusti
SP L Dierker
SR T Farrell
SP B Bruce
RP C Raymond
RS B Latman
RP R Taylor
RP J Owens
C J Bateman
1B C Harrison
2B J Morgan
SS S Jackson
3B B Aspromonte
LF L Maye
CF J Wynn
RL R Staub
RU D Nicholson
M G Hatton

LOS ANGELES
SP S Koufax
SP D Drysdale
SP C Osteen
SP D Sutton
RP P Regan
RP B Miller
RP R Perranoski
RS J Moeller
C J Roseboro
1B W Parker
2B J Lefebvre
SS M Wills
3I J Kennedy
LR L Johnson
CF W Davis
RF R Fairly
LF T Davis
3B- J Gilliam
M W Alston

NEW YORK
SP J Fisher
SR D Ribant
SR B Shaw
SR R Gardner
RS J Hamilton
RS D Selma
RP B Hepler
RP L Bearnarth
C J Grote
1B E Kranepool
2B R Hunt
SI E Bressoud
3B K Boyer
LF R Swoboda
CF C Jones
RO A Luplow
IO C Hiller
MU- B Murphy
M W Westrum

PHILADELPHIA
SP J Bunning
SP C Short
SP L Jackson
SR B Buhl
SR R Culp
RP D Knowles
RP R Wise
RP R Herbert
C C Dalrymple
1B B White
2O C Rojas
SS D Groat
3L D Allen
LM T Gonzalez
CF- J Briggs
RF J Callison
23 T Taylor
MO- J Brandt
UT- H Kuenn
M G Mauch

PITTSBURGH
SP B Veale
SP W Fryman
SP V Law
SP S Blass
SR T Sisk
RP P Mikkelsen
RS D Cardwell
RP A McBean
RP R Face
C J Pagliaroni
1B D Clendenon
2B B Mazeroski
SS G Alley
3B B Bailey
LF W Stargell
CF M Alou
RF R Clemente
OI M Mota
3B J Pagan
M H Walker

ST. LOUIS
SP B Gibson
SP A Jackson
SP R Washburn
SR N Briles
SP L Jaster
RP J Hoerner
RP H Woodeshick
RP D Dennis
C T McCarver
1B O Cepeda
2B J Javier
SS D Maxvill
3B C Smith
LF L Brock
CF C Flood
RF M Shannon
UI J Buchek
UT- T Francona
IO- P Gagliano
M R Schoendienst

SAN FRANCISCO
SP J Marichal
SP G Perry
SP B Bolin
SR R Herbel
SP R Sadecki
RP L McDaniel
RP F Linzy
RP B Priddy
RS J Gibbon
C T Haller
1B W McCovey
2B H Lanier
S2 T Fuentes
3B J Hart
LR J Alou
CF W Mays
RF O Brown
S3 J Davenport
LU- L Gabrielson
LU- C Peterson
M H Franks

1967 AL

BALTIMORE
SP T Phoebus
SP P Richert
SR B Dillman
SP D McNally
SP J Hardin
RP E Watt
RP M Drabowsky
RP E Fisher
RP S Miller
C A Etchebarren
1B B Powell
2B D Johnson
SS L Aparicio
3B B Robinson
L1 C Blefary
CF P Blair
RU F Robinson
UO R Snyder
M H Bauer

BOSTON
SP J Lonborg
SR L Stange
SP G Bell
SR B Brandon
RS J Santiago
RP J Wyatt
RP D Osinski
C- M Ryan
1B G Scott
2B M Andrews
SS R Petrocelli
3B J Foy
LF C Yastrzemski
CF R Smith
RF- T Conigliaro
UO J Tartabull
UI- J Adair
UI- D Jones
M D Williams

CALIFORNIA
SP G Brunet
SP J McGlothlin
SP R Clark
SP J Hamilton
RP M Rojas
RP B Kelso
RP P Cimino
RP J Coates
C B Rodgers
1B D Mincher
2B B Knoop
SS J Fregosi
3B P Schaal
LF R Reichardt
ML J Cardenal
RF J Hall
IC- T Satriano
M B Rigney

CHICAGO
SP G Peters
SP J Horlen
SP T John
SR B Howard
RP B Locker
RP H Wilhelm
RS W Wood
RP D McMahon
C J Martin
1B T McCraw
2B W Causey
SS R Hansen
3B D Buford
L1 P Ward
CF T Agee
RL K Berry
LU W Williams
M E Stanky

CLEVELAND
SP S McDowell
SP S Hargan
SP L Tiant
SP S Siebert
SR J O'Donoghue
RP O Pena
RP G Culver
RP S Bailey
RP B Allen
C- J Azcue
1B T Horton
2B- P Gonzalez
SS L Brown
3B M Alvis
LF L Wagner
CF V Davalillo
RM C Hinton
OI L Maye
1U F Whitfield
UT- C Salmon
C- D Sims
M J Adcock

DETROIT
SP E Wilson
SP D McLain
SP J Sparma
SP M Lolich
RP F Gladding
RP D Wickersham
RP M Marshall
RS J Hiller
C B Freehan
1B N Cash
2B D McAuliffe
SS R Oyler
3B D Wert
ML J Northrup
CF M Stanley
RF A Kaline
LF W Horton
2U- J Lumpe
M M Smith

KANSAS CITY
SP C Hunter
SP J Nash
SP C Dobson
SR L Krausse
SR B Odom
RS P Lindblad
RS T Pierce
RP J Aker
RP D Segui
C P Roof
1U R Webster
2B J Donaldson
SS B Campaneris
UI D Green
UO J Gosger
CF R Monday
RF M Hershberger
IO D Cater
OF- J Nossek
M1 A Dark
M2 L Appling

MINNESOTA
SP D Chance
SP J Kaat
SP J Merritt
SP D Boswell
RS J Perry
RP A Worthington
RP R Kline
C J Zimmerman
1B H Killebrew
2B R Carew
SS Z Versalles
3B R Rollins
LF B Allison
CF T Uhlaender
RF T Oliva
UT C Tovar
UT- R Reese
LU S Valdespino
M1 S Mele
M2 C Ermer

NEW YORK
SP M Stottlemyre
SP A Downing
SP F Peterson
SP F Talbot
RS B Monbouquette
RP D Womack
RS T Tillotson
RS J Verbanic
C J Gibbs
1B M Mantle
2B H Clarke
SS R Amaro
3B C Smith
LF T Tresh
CF J Pepitone
RO S Whitaker
UO B Robinson
M R Houk

WASHINGTON
SP P Ortega
SP C Pascual
SP B Moore
SP J Coleman
RP D Knowles
RS B Priddy
RP B Humphreys
RP D Lines
C P Casanova
1B- M Epstein
2B- B Allen
SS E Brinkman
3B K McMullen
LF F Howard
UO F Valentine
RU C Peterson
ML H Allen
S2 T Cullen
1U D Nen
2U- B Saverine
CF- E Stroud
M G Hodges

1967 NL

ATLANTA
SR P Niekro
SP D Lemaster
SP K Johnson
SP P Jarvis
RS D Kelley
RS C Carroll
RP J Ritchie
RP R Hernandez
C J Torre
1O F Alou
2B W Woodward
SS D Menke
3B C Boyer
LU R Carty
MU M Jones
RF H Aaron
1U- T Francona
M1 B Hitchcock
M2 K Silvestri

CHICAGO
SP F Jenkins
SP R Nye
SR J Niekro
SP R Culp
RS B Hands
RP C Hartenstein
RP B Stoneman
RP C Koonce
C R Hundley
1B E Banks
2B G Beckert
SS D Kessinger
3B R Santo
LF B Williams
CF A Phillips
RU- T Savage
M L Durocher

CINCINNATI
SP G Nolan
SP M Pappas
SP J Maloney
SP M Queen
SP S Ellis
RP T Abernathy
RP D Nottebart
RS G Arrigo
RP B Lee
C- J Edwards
1L L May
2S T Helms
SS L Cardenas
3B T Perez
LF P Rose
CF V Pinson
RF T Harper
1B D Johnson
2U C Ruiz
M D Bristol

HOUSTON
SP M Cuellar
SP D Giusti
SP D Wilson
SP B Belinsky
SP L Dierker
RP B Latman
RP C Sembera
RP D Eilers
RP D Schneider
C- J Bateman
1B E Mathews
2B J Morgan
SS S Jackson
3B B Aspromonte
LU- R Davis
CF J Wynn
RF R Staub
C- R Brand
M G Hatton

LOS ANGELES
SP C Osteen
SP D Drysdale
SP D Sutton
SP B Singer
SR J Brewer
RP R Perranoski
RP P Regan
RP B Miller
C J Roseboro
1B W Parker
2B R Hunt
SS G Michael
32 J Lefebvre
LF L Johnson
CF W Davis
R1 R Fairly
3U B Bailey
RU A Ferrara
LR- L Gabrielson
SS- D Schofield
M W Alston

NEW YORK
SP T Seaver
SP J Fisher
SR D Cardwell
SR B Shaw
RP D Selma
RP R Taylor
RP D Shaw
C J Grote
1B E Kranepool
2B J Buchek
SS B Harrelson
3B E Charles
LF T Davis
MO C Jones
RF R Swoboda
OI T Reynolds
UI- B Johnson
M1 W Westrum
M2 S Parker

PHILADELPHIA
SP J Bunning
SP L Jackson
SP C Short
SR R Wise
SR D Ellsworth
RP T Farrell
RP D Hall
RP G Jackson
RS J Boozer
C C Dalrymple
1B B White
2B C Rojas
SS B Wine
3B D Allen
LO T Gonzalez
ML J Briggs
RF J Callison
CF D Lock
SU G Sutherland
UI T Taylor
C- G Oliver
M G Mauch

PITTSBURGH
SP T Sisk
SP B Veale
SR D Ribant
SR S Blass
SR W Fryman
RS A McBean
RS J Pizarro
RP R Face
RP P Mikkelsen
C J May
1B D Clendenon
2B B Mazeroski
SS G Alley
3B M Wills
L1 W Stargell
CF M Alou
RF R Clemente
OI M Mota
IO- J Pagan
M1 H Walker
M2 D Murtaugh

ST. LOUIS
SR D Hughes
SP S Carlton
SP R Washburn
SP B Gibson
SR L Jaster
RS N Briles
RS A Jackson
RP R Willis
RP J Hoerner
C T McCarver
1B O Cepeda
2B J Javier
SS D Maxvill
3B M Shannon
LF L Brock
CF C Flood
RF R Maris
OI B Tolan
RU- A Johnson
M R Schoendienst

SAN FRANCISCO
SP G Perry
SP M McCormick
SP J Marichal
SR R Sadecki
SR B Bolin
RS R Herbel
RP F Linzy
RP L McDaniel
C T Haller
1B W McCovey
2B T Fuentes
SS H Lanier
3L J Hart
LR J Alou
CF W Mays
RF O Brown
3I J Davenport
M H Franks

1968 AL

BALTIMORE
SP D McNally
SP J Hardin
SP T Phoebus
SR G Brabender
SR D Leonhard
RP E Watt
RP M Drabowsky
RP P Richert
C- A Etchebarren
1B B Powell
2B D Johnson
SS M Belanger
3B B Robinson
OI C Blefary
CF P Blair
RL F Robinson
UT D Buford
RU- D May
LU- C Motton
M1 H Bauer
M2 E Weaver

BOSTON
SP R Culp
SP G Bell
SP D Ellsworth
SP J Santiago
SP J Lonborg
RP L Stange
RP J Pizarro
RS G Waslewski
RP S Lyle
C- R Gibson
1B G Scott
2B M Andrews
SS R Petrocelli
3B J Foy
LF C Yastrzemski
CF R Smith
RF K Harrelson
1I D Jones
M D Williams

CALIFORNIA
SP G Brunet
SP J McGlothlin
SR S Ellis
SP T Murphy
RS C Wright
RP M Pattin
RS A Messersmith
RP T Burgmeier
C- B Rodgers
1B D Mincher
2B B Knoop
SS J Fregosi
3B- A Rodriguez
LF R Reichardt
CF- V Davalillo
MR R Repoz
UT C Hinton
C T Satriano
OI- E Kirkpatrick
RU- B Morton
M B Rigney

CHICAGO
SP J Horlen
SP J Fisher
SP T John
SP G Peters
SP C Carlos
RP W Wood
RS B Priddy
RP H Wilhelm
RP B Locker
C D Josephson
1B T McCraw
2I S Alomar
SS L Aparicio
3U P Ward
LF T Davis
CF K Berry
RL B Bradford
M1 E Stanky

M2 L Moss
M3 A Lopez
M4 L Moss
M5 A Lopez

CLEVELAND

SP S McDowell
SP L Tiant
SP S Siebert
SR S Williams
SP S Hargan
RP E Fisher
RS M Paul
RP V Romo
C J Azcue
1B T Horton
2B- V Fuller
SS L Brown
3B M Alvis
LU L Maye
CF J Cardenal
LR T Harper
UT C Salmon
C1 D Sims
2U- D Nelson
M A Dark

DETROIT

SP D McLain
SP E Wilson
SP M Lolich
SP J Sparma
RS P Dobson
RS J Hiller
RP D Patterson
C B Freehan
1B N Cash
2B D McAuliffe
SS R Oyler
3B D Wert
LF W Horton
CF M Stanley
RM J Northrup
RU A Kaline
SI- D Tracewski
M M Smith

MINNESOTA

SP D Chance
SP J Merritt
SP J Kaat
SP D Boswell
SR J Perry
RP A Worthington
RP R Perranoski
RP B Miller
RP J Roland
C J Roseboro
1U R Reese
2B R Carew
SS- J Hernandez
UT C Tovar
LF B Allison
CF T Uhlaender
RF T Oliva
3S R Clark
1B H Killebrew
UI- F Quilici
3U- R Rollins
M C Ermer

NEW YORK

SP M Stottlemyre
SP S Bahnsen
SP F Peterson
SP S Barber
SR F Talbot
RS J Verbanic
RP D Womack
RP S Hamilton
CL L McDaniel
C J Gibbs
1B M Mantle
2B H Clarke
SS T Tresh
3B B Cox
LU R White
UO B Robinson
RU A Kosco
CF J Pepitone
UI- D Howser
M R Houk

OAKLAND

SP C Hunter
SP B Odom
SP J Nash
SP C Dobson
SR L Krausse
RP D Segui
RP J Aker
RP E Sprague
RP P Lindblad
C- D Duncan
1B D Cater
2B J Donaldson
SS B Campaneris
3B S Bando
LR M Hershberger
CF R Monday
RF R Jackson
UO- J Gosger
M B Kennedy

WASHINGTON

SP J Coleman
SP C Pascual
SP J Hannan
SP F Bertaina
SR B Moore
RS D Bosman
RS P Ortega
RP D Higgins
RP B Humphreys
C- P Casanova
1B M Epstein
2B B Allen
SS- R Hansen
3B K McMullen
L1 F Howard
CF D Unser
RO E Stroud
OF- C Peterson
M J Lemon

1968 NL

ATLANTA

SP P Niekro
SP P Jarvis
SP R Reed
SR K Johnson
SP M Pappas
RP C Upshaw
RS J Britton
RP C Raymond
C J Torre
1B D Johnson
2B F Millan
SS S Jackson
3B- C Boyer
LU M Lum
CF F Alou
RF H Aaron
L1 T Francona
UI M Martinez
L1 T Aaron
C- B Tillman
M L Harris

CHICAGO

SP F Jenkins
SP B Hands
SP K Holtzman
SP J Niekro
SP R Nye
RP P Regan
RP J Lamabe
C R Hundley
1B E Banks
2B G Beckert
SS D Kessinger
3B R Santo
LF B Williams
CF A Phillips
RM- J Hickman
1U- D Nen
UO- A Spangler
M L Durocher

CINCINNATI

SP G Culver
SP J Maloney
SP G Arrigo
SP G Nolan
RP T Abernathy
RP C Carroll
RP B Lee
RP J Ritchie
C J Bench
1B L May
2B T Helms
SS L Cardenas
3B T Perez
LF A Johnson
CF V Pinson
RF P Rose
UO M Jones
UI- C Ruiz
US- F Whitfield
M D Bristol

HOUSTON

SP D Giusti
SP L Dierker
SP D Lemaster
SP D Wilson
SP M Cuellar
RP J Buzhardt
RP J Ray
RP T Dukes
C J Bateman
1B R Staub
2B D Menke
SS H Torres
3B D Rader
ML J Wynn
CF- R Davis
RF- N Miller
3L B Aspromonte
OI- L Thomas
M1 G Hatton
M2 H Walker

LOS ANGELES

SP B Singer
SP C Osteen
SP D Drysdale
SP D Sutton
SP M Kekich
RP M Grant
RP J Brewer
RP J Billingham
RP J Purdin
C T Haller
1B W Parker
2S P Popovich
SS Z Versalles
3B B Bailey
LR L Gabrielson
CF W Davis
R1 R Fairly
UO J Fairey
IF- K Boyer
2U- J Lefebvre
M W Alston

NEW YORK

SP T Seaver
SP J Koosman
SP D Cardwell
SR D Selma
SP N Ryan
RP C Koonce
RP R Taylor
RP D Frisella
C J Grote
1B E Kranepool
2B- P Linz
SS B Harrelson
3B E Charles
LF C Jones
CF T Agee
RF R Swoboda
LU A Shamsky
S2- A Weis
M G Hodges

PHILADELPHIA

SP C Short
SP L Jackson
SP W Fryman
SP R Wise
SR J James
RP T Farrell
RP G Wagner
RP J Boozer
RS G Jackson
C- M Ryan
1B B White
2B C Rojas
SS R Pena
3B T Taylor
LF D Allen
CF T Gonzalez
RF J Callison
OI J Briggs
UO D Lock
C- C Dalrymple
M1 G Mauch
M2 G Myatt
M3 B Skinner

PITTSBURGH

SP B Veale
SP S Blass
SP A McBean
SR B Moose
SP J Bunning
RP R Kline
RS D Ellis
RP R Face
RP L Walker
C J May
1B D Clendenon
2B B Mazeroski
SS G Alley
3B M Wills
LF W Stargell
CF M Alou
RF R Clemente
UT M Mota
M L Shepard

ST. LOUIS

SP B Gibson
SP N Briles
SP S Carlton
SP R Washburn
SR L Jaster
RS D Hughes
RP R Willis
CL J Hoerner
RP M Nelson
C T McCarver
1B O Cepeda
2B J Javier
SS D Maxvill
3B M Shannon
LF L Brock
CF C Flood
RF R Maris
CU- J Edwards
RU- B Tolan
M R Schoendienst

SAN FRANCISCO

SP J Marichal
SP G Perry
SP R Sadecki
SR M McCormick
SR B Bolin
RP F Linzy
C D Dietz
1B W McCovey
2B R Hunt
SS H Lanier
3U J Davenport
RL J Alou
CF W Mays
RF- B Bonds
OI T Cline
3L J Hart
CU- J Hiatt
M H Franks

1969 AL

BALTIMORE

SP M Cuellar
SP D McNally
SP T Phoebus
SP J Palmer
SR J Hardin
RP D Leonhard
RP E Watt
RP D Hall
RP M Lopez
C E Hendricks
1B B Powell
2B D Johnson
SS M Belanger
3B B Robinson
LF D Buford
CF P Blair
RF F Robinson
UO- M Rettenmund
M E Weaver

BOSTON

SP R Culp
SP M Nagy
SR S Siebert
SP J Lonborg
SR L Stange
RS V Romo
RP S Lyle
RS R Jarvis
RS B Landis
C- R Gibson
1U D Jones
2B M Andrews
SS R Petrocelli
31 G Scott
LF C Yastrzemski
CF R Smith
RF T Conigliaro
OI J Lahoud
3I S O'Brien
UT- D Schofield
M1 D Williams
M2 E Popowski

CALIFORNIA

SP A Messersmith
SP T Murphy
SP J McGlothlin
SR R May
SP G Brunet
CL K Tatum
RP E Fisher
RP H Wilhelm
RS C Wright
C- J Azcue
1B J Spencer
2B S Alomar
SS J Fregosi
3B A Rodriguez
LF R Reichardt
CF J Johnstone
RF B Voss
OI R Repoz
OI- B Morton
M1 B Rigney
M2 L Phillips

CHICAGO

SP J Horlen
SP T John
SP G Peters
SP B Wynne
RP W Wood
RP D Osinski
RP C Carlos
C E Herrmann
1B G Hopkins
2B B Knoop
SS L Aparicio
3B B Melton
LF C May
CF K Berry
RL W Williams
UT P Ward
RM- B Bradford
UI- R Hansen
UT- T McCraw
M1 A Lopez
M2 D Gutteridge

CLEVELAND

SP S McDowell
SP L Tiant
SP S Hargan
SR D Ellsworth
RS S Williams
RS M Paul
RP J Pizarro
RP R Law
C D Sims
1B T Horton
2B V Fuller
SS L Brown
3B- M Alvis
UO R Snyder
CF J Cardenal
RF K Harrelson
UO R Scheinblum
OI- C Hinton
3U- L Klimchock
M A Dark

DETROIT

SP D McLain
SP M Lolich
SP E Wilson
SR M Kilkenny
RS P Dobson
RS J Hiller
RP T Timmermann
C B Freehan
1B N Cash
2B- D McAuliffe
SS- T Tresh
3B D Wert
LF W Horton
MR J Northrup
RF A Kaline
MS M Stanley
23- T Matchick
M M Smith

KANSAS CITY

SP W Bunker
SR D Drago
SP B Butler
SP R Nelson
SP J Rooker
RS M Hedlund
RP M Drabowsky
RP D Wickersham
RP T Burgmeier
C- E Rodriguez
1B M Fiore
2B J Adair
SS J Hernandez
3B J Foy
LF L Piniella
UT B Oliver
RM P Kelly
UT E Kirkpatrick
2S- J Rios
M J Gordon

MINNESOTA

SR J Perry
SP D Boswell
SP J Kaat
SR T Hall
RP R Perranoski
RS B Miller
RS D Woodson
RP A Worthington
C J Roseboro
1B R Reese
2B R Carew
SS L Cardenas
31 H Killebrew
ML T Uhlaender
UT C Tovar
RF T Oliva
32 F Quilici
LU- B Allison
UO- C Manuel
LU- G Nettles
M B Martin

NEW YORK

SP M Stottlemyre
SP F Peterson
SP S Bahnsen
SP B Burbach
SR A Downing
RS M Kekich
RP L McDaniel
RP J Aker
RP S Hamilton
C- J Gibbs
1B J Pepitone
2B H Clarke
SS G Michael
3U J Kenney
LF R White
CF- R Woods
RU B Murcer
3U- B Cox
CU- F Fernandez
OI- B Robinson
M R Houk

OAKLAND

SP C Hunter
SP C Dobson
SP B Odom
SR L Krausse
SP J Nash
RS R Fingers
RP P Lindblad
RP J Roland
C P Roof
1B D Cater
2B D Green
SS B Campaneris
3B S Bando
LF T Reynolds
CF R Monday
RF R Jackson
IF- T Kubiak
M1 H Bauer
M2 J McNamara

SEATTLE

SR G Brabender
SP M Pattin
SP F Talbot
RS D Segui
RS J Gelnar
RP J Bouton
RP B Locker
C J McNertney
1B D Mincher
2B- J Donaldson
SS R Oyler
UT T Harper
LF T Davis
MR W Comer
RM- S Hovley
UI- G Gil
RU- M Hegan
M J Schultz

WASHINGTON

SP J Coleman
SP D Bosman
SP J Hannan
SP B Moore
RS C Cox
RP D Higgins
RP D Knowles
RP B Humphreys
C P Casanova
1B M Epstein
2B B Allen
SS E Brinkman
3B K McMullen
L1 F Howard
CF D Unser
UT H Allen
OI B Alyea
2B T Cullen
UO E Stroud
M T Williams

1969 NL

ATLANTA

SP P Niekro
SP R Reed
SP P Jarvis
SR G Stone
SP M Pappas
RP C Upshaw
RP G Neibauer
C B Didier
1B O Cepeda
2B F Millan
SS S Jackson
3B C Boyer
ML- T Gonzalez
CF F Alou
RF H Aaron
LF R Carty
UO M Lum
IO- B Aspromonte
SS- G Garrido
M L Harris

CHICAGO

SP F Jenkins
SP B Hands
SP K Holtzman
SR D Selma
RP P Regan
RP T Abernathy
RS R Nye
C R Hundley
1B E Banks
2B G Beckert
SS D Kessinger
3B R Santo
LF B Williams
CF D Young
RF J Hickman
OI W Smith
RU- A Spangler
M L Durocher

CINCINNATI

SP J Merritt
SP T Cloninger
SR J Maloney
SR J Fisher
SP G Nolan
RP W Granger
RP C Carroll
RS G Culver
RP P Ramos
C J Bench
1B L May
2B T Helms
SS- W Woodward
3B T Perez
LF A Johnson
MR B Tolan
RM P Rose
UT J Stewart
SS- D Chaney
IO- C Ruiz
M D Bristol

HOUSTON

SP L Dierker
SP D Lemaster
SP D Wilson
SP T Griffin
RS J Ray
CL F Gladding
RP J Billingham
RS W Blasingame
C J Edwards
1B C Blefary
2B J Morgan
SS D Menke
3B D Rader
LR J Alou
CF J Wynn
RF N Miller
LU- G Geiger
M H Walker

LOS ANGELES

SP C Osteen
SP B Singer
SP D Sutton
SP A Foster
CL J Brewer
RP P Mikkelsen
RP J Moeller
C T Haller
1B W Parker
2S T Sizemore
SS M Wills
3B B Sudakis
UO W Crawford
CF W Davis
RL A Kosco
RO B Russell
OI- L Gabrielson
UI- J Lefebvre
LF- M Mota
M W Alston

MONTREAL

SP B Stoneman
SR J Robertson
SP M Wegener
SR G Waslewski
SR H Reed
RP D McGinn
RP S Renko
RP D Shaw
RP R Face
C R Brand
1B B Bailey
2B G Sutherland
SS B Wine
3B C Laboy
LF M Jones
CF- A Phillips
RF R Staub
OI T Cline
M G Mauch

NEW YORK

SP T Seaver
SP J Koosman
SP G Gentry
SP D Cardwell
SP J McAndrew
RP T McGraw
RP C Koonce
RP R Taylor
RP J DiLauro
C J Grote
1B E Kranepool
2B K Boswell
SS B Harrelson
32 W Garrett
LF C Jones
CF T Agee
RU R Swoboda
RO R Gaspar
RU A Shamsky
S2 A Weis
M G Hodges

PHILADELPHIA

SP G Jackson
SP W Fryman
SP R Wise
SR J Johnson
SP B Champion
RP J Boozer
RP T Farrell
RP A Raffo
RP B Wilson
C M Ryan
1B D Allen
2B C Rojas
SS D Money
32 T Taylor
LM J Briggs
CF L Hisle
RF J Callison
L3 D Johnson
3U R Joseph
UO R Stone
UI- T Harmon
M1 B Skinner
M2 G Myatt

PITTSBURGH

SP B Veale
SP D Ellis
SP S Blass
SR B Moose
SP J Bunning
RS L Walker
RP C Hartenstein
RP B Dal Canton
RP J Gibbon
C M Sanguillen
1B A Oliver
2B- B Mazeroski
SS F Patek
3B R Hebner
LF W Stargell
CF M Alou
RF R Clemente
UT J Pagan
OI C Taylor
2S- G Alley
M1 L Shepard
M2 A Grammas

ST. LOUIS

SP B Gibson
SP S Carlton
SP N Briles
SR R Washburn
SR C Taylor
RP M Torrez
RS D Giusti
RP M Grant
RP J Hoerner
C T McCarver
1B J Torre
2B J Javier
SS D Maxvill
3B M Shannon
LF L Brock
CF C Flood
RF V Pinson
M R Schoendienst

SAN DIEGO

SP C Kirby
SP J Niekro
SP A Santorini
SP D Kelley
RS T Sisk
RS G Ross
RP F Reberger
RP J Baldschun
C C Cannizzaro
1B N Colbert
2S J Arcia
SS T Dean
3B E Spiezio
LU A Ferrara
CF C Gaston
RF O Brown
OI I Murrell
UI R Pena
OI- L Stahl
M P Gomez

SAN FRANCISCO

SP G Perry
SP J Marichal
SP M McCormick
SP B Bolin
SR R Sadecki

RP F Linzy
RP R Herbel
C- D Dietz
1B W McCovey
2B R Hunt
SS H Lanier
3B J Davenport
LR K Henderson
CF W Mays
RM B Bonds
UT- B Burda
LU D Marshall
UI D Mason
LU- J Hart
M *C King*

1970 AL

BALTIMORE

SP J Palmer
SP M Cuellar
SP D McNally
SR J Hardin
SP T Phoebus
RP P Richert
RP E Watt
RP D Hall
RP M Lopez
C E Hendricks
1B B Powell
2B D Johnson
SS M Belanger
3B B Robinson
LF D Buford
CF P Blair
RF F Robinson
UO M Rettenmund
OI- T Crowley
M *E Weaver*

BOSTON

SP R Culp
SP S Siebert
SP G Peters
SR K Brett
SP M Nagy
RS V Romo
RP S Lyle
C- J Moses
1L C Yastrzemski
2B M Andrews
SS R Petrocelli
31 G Scott
LO B Conigliaro
CF R Smith
RF T Conigliaro
M *E Kasko*

CALIFORNIA

SP C Wright
SP T Murphy
SP R May
SR A Messersmith
RP E Fisher
RP K Tatum
RS G Garrett
RP M Queen
C J Azcue
1B J Spencer
2B S Alomar
SS J Fregosi
3B K McMullen
LF A Johnson
MU J Johnstone
OI R Repoz
M *L Phillips*

CHICAGO

SP T John
SP J Janeski
SP J Horlen
RP W Wood
RS J Crider
RP D Murphy
RS B Moore
C- E Herrmann
1U G Hopkins
2B B Knoop
SS L Aparicio
R3 B Melton
LF C May
CF K Berry
RU W Williams
UT T McCraw
32 S O'Brien
C- D Josephson
M1 *D Gutteridge*
M2 *B Adair*
M3 *C Tanner*

CLEVELAND

SP S McDowell
SR R Hand
SR D Chance
SP S Hargan
RP D Higgins
RP P Hennigan
RS R Austin
RP F Lasher
C R Fosse
1B T Horton
2B E Leon
SS J Heidemann
3B G Nettles
LF R Foster
CF T Uhlaender
RF V Pinson
UT C Hinton
OC D Sims
M *A Dark*

DETROIT

SP M Lolich
SP J Niekro
SP L Cain
SR M Kilkenny
CL T Timmermann
RS J Hiller
RP D Patterson
RP F Scherman
C B Freehan
1B N Cash
2B D McAuliffe
SS C Gutierrez
3B D Wert
LF- W Horton
CF M Stanley
RM J Northrup
R1 A Kaline
UT E Maddox
UL- G Brown
UI- D Jones
M *M Smith*

KANSAS CITY

SP D Drago
SR B Johnson
SP J Rooker
SP B Butler
SR D Morehead
RP W Bunker
RS A Fitzmorris
RP T Burgmeier
RP T Abernathy
CU E Kirkpatrick
13 B Oliver
2B C Rojas
SS- J Hernandez
3B P Schaal
LF L Piniella
CF A Otis
RF P Kelly
M1 *C Metro*
M2 *B Lemon*

MILWAUKEE

SP M Pattin
SP L Krausse
SP S Lockwood
SR B Bolin
SP G Brabender
RP K Sanders
RP J Gelnar
C P Roof
1B M Hegan
2S T Kubiak
SS R Pena
3B T Harper
LF D Walton
CF D May
UO R Snyder
C J McNertney
OI T Savage
M *D Bristol*

MINNESOTA

SP J Perry
SR J Kaat
SP B Blyleven
SR B Zepp
RS T Hall
RP R Perranoski
RP S Williams
C G Mitterwald
1B R Reese
2B- D Thompson
SS L Cardenas
3B H Killebrew
LM J Holt
CF C Tovar
RF T Oliva
2I F Quilici
LF- B Alyea
UT- R Renick
M *B Rigney*

NEW YORK

SP M Stottlemyre
SP F Peterson
SP S Bahnsen
SP S Kline
SR M Kekich
RP L McDaniel
RP R Klimkowski
CL J Aker
RS G Waslewski
C T Munson
1B D Cater
2B H Clarke
SS G Michael
3B J Kenney
LF R White
CF B Murcer
RF C Blefary
RU- J Lyttle
RU- R Woods
M *R Houk*

OAKLAND

SP C Dobson
SP C Hunter
SR D Segui
SP B Odom
SR R Fingers
RP M Grant
RP P Lindblad
RP M Lachemann
RP B Locker
C- F Fernandez
1B D Mincher
2B D Green
SS B Campaneris
3B S Bando
LR F Alou
CF R Monday
RF R Jackson
L1 J Rudi
C- D Duncan
M *J McNamara*

WASHINGTON

SP D Bosman
SR J Coleman
SP C Cox
SR J Hannan
SP G Brunet
RP D Knowles
RS J Shellenback
RP J Grzenda
RP H Pina
C P Casanova
1B M Epstein
2B T Cullen
SS E Brinkman
3B A Rodriguez
L1 F Howard
CF E Stroud
UO D Unser
2B B Allen
OI R Reichardt
RU- L Maye
M *T Williams*

1970 NL

ATLANTA

SP P Jarvis
SP P Niekro
SP J Nash
SP G Stone
SP R Reed
RP H Wilhelm
RP B Priddy
C- B Tillman
1B O Cepeda
2B F Millan
SS S Jackson
3B C Boyer
LF R Carty
CF T Gonzalez
RF H Aaron
SS G Garrido
UO M Lum
CU- H King
M *L Harris*

CHICAGO

SP F Jenkins
SP K Holtzman
SP B Hands
SP M Pappas
SP J Decker
RP P Regan
RS J Colborn
C- R Hundley
1B- E Banks
2B G Beckert
SS D Kessinger
3B R Santo
LF B Williams
OI J Hickman
RF J Callison
CF C James
UT- W Smith
M *L Durocher*

CINCINNATI

SP G Nolan
SP J Merritt
SP J McGlothlin
SP W Simpson
SR T Cloninger
RP C Carroll
CL W Granger
RP D Gullett
RP R Washburn
C J Bench
1B L May
2B T Helms
SS D Concepcion
3B T Perez
LF B Carbo
CF B Tolan
RF P Rose
UT J Stewart
SS W Woodward
M *S Anderson*

HOUSTON

SP L Dierker
SR J Billingham
SP D Wilson
SR D Lemaster
SP T Griffin
RP J Ray
RP F Gladding
RS R Cook
RS J Bouton
C J Edwards
1B- B Watson
2B J Morgan
SS D Menke
3B D Rader
ML J Wynn
CF- C Cedeno
RF J Alou
RF- N Miller
M *H Walker*

LOS ANGELES

SP D Sutton
SP C Osteen
SP A Foster
SR J Moeller
SP S Vance
CL J Brewer
RP B Singer
RP P Mikkelsen
RP F Norman
C T Haller
1B W Parker
2B- T Sizemore
SS M Wills
3S B Grabarkewitz
LF M Mota
CF W Davis
RL W Crawford
2U J Lefebvre
RM- B Russell
1C- B Sudakis
M *W Alston*

MONTREAL

SP C Morton
SP S Renko
SR B Stoneman
SR D McGinn
SP M Wegener
CL C Raymond
RP H Reed
RP J Strohmayer
RS M Marshall
C J Bateman
1B R Fairly
2B G Sutherland
SS B Wine
3B C Laboy
LF M Jones
CF- A Phillips
RF R Staub
IO B Bailey
2B M Staehle
UO- J Fairey
MO- J Gosger
LO- D Hahn
M *G Mauch*

NEW YORK

SP T Seaver
SP J Koosman
SP G Gentry
SP J McAndrew
SP R Sadecki
RP N Ryan
RP T McGraw
RP R Taylor
RP D Frisella
C J Grote
1B D Clendenon
2B K Boswell
SS B Harrelson
3B J Foy
LF C Jones
CF T Agee
RF R Swoboda
32 W Garrett
OI A Shamsky
OF- D Marshall
M *G Hodges*

PHILADELPHIA

SP R Wise
SP J Bunning
SP C Short
SP G Jackson
SP W Fryman
RP D Selma
RS B Lersch
RS L Palmer
RP J Hoerner
C- M Ryan
1B D Johnson
2B D Doyle
SS L Bowa
3B D Money
LU J Briggs
MR L Hisle
OI R Stone
RO B Browne
IO T Taylor
MR- O Gamble
M *F Lucchesi*

PITTSBURGH

SP D Ellis
SP B Veale
SP S Blass
SP B Moose
SR L Walker
RP D Giusti
RS B Dal Canton
C M Sanguillen
1B B Robertson
2B B Mazeroski
SS G Alley
3B R Hebner
LF W Stargell
CF M Alou
RF R Clemente
1R A Oliver
UO- J Jeter
3U- J Pagan
SS- F Patek
M *D Murtaugh*

ST. LOUIS

SP B Gibson
SP S Carlton
SP M Torrez
SP J Reuss
SR N Briles
RS Ch Taylor
RP F Linzy
RP S Campisi
C- T Simmons
1R J Hague
2B J Javier
SS D Maxvill
C3 J Torre
LF L Brock
CF J Cardenal
RU L Lee
13 D Allen
UO V Davalillo
UT Ca Taylor
M *R Schoendienst*

SAN DIEGO

SP P Dobson
SP C Kirby
SP D Coombs
SR D Roberts
SP M Corkins
RP R Herbel
RP T Dukes
RP G Ross
RP R Willis
C C Cannizzaro
1B N Colbert
2B D Campbell
SI J Arcia
3B E Spiezio
LU A Ferrara
CF C Gaston
RF O Brown
OI I Murrell
S3 S Huntz
UT- R Webster
M *P Gomez*

SAN FRANCISCO

SP G Perry
SP J Marichal
SR R Robertson
SR F Reberger
RP D McMahon
RS R Bryant
RP J Johnson
C D Dietz
1B W McCovey
2U R Hunt
SS H Lanier
3B A Gallagher
LF K Henderson
CF W Mays
RF B Bonds
2S T Fuentes
M1 *C King*
M2 *C Fox*

1971 AL

BALTIMORE

SP M Cuellar
SP P Dobson
SP J Palmer
SP D McNally
RS G Jackson
C E Hendricks
1B B Powell
2B D Johnson
SS M Belanger
3B B Robinson
LF D Buford
CF P Blair
RL M Rettenmund
R1 F Robinson
M *E Weaver*

BOSTON

SP R Culp
SP S Siebert
SP G Peters
SP J Lonborg
RP B Lee
RP B Bolin
RP S Lyle
RP K Tatum
C- D Josephson
1B G Scott
2B D Griffin
SS L Aparicio
3B R Petrocelli
LF C Yastrzemski
CF B Conigliaro
MR R Smith
RU J Lahoud
M *E Kasko*

CALIFORNIA

SP A Messersmith
SP C Wright
SP T Murphy
SP R May
RP E Fisher
RP L Allen
RP D LaRoche
RP M Queen
C J Stephenson
1B J Spencer
2B S Alomar
SU J Fregosi
3B K McMullen
LU T Gonzalez
CF K Berry
RO R Repoz
SU- S O'Brien
M *L Phillips*

CHICAGO

SP W Wood
SP T Bradley
SP T John
SR J Horlen
RS B Johnson
RP S Kealey
RP V Romo
RP T Forster
C E Herrmann
1B C May
2U M Andrews
SU L Alvarado
3B B Melton
LF R Reichardt
MO J Johnstone
RL W Williams
2U R McKinney
C- T Egan
SI- R Morales
SS- L Richard
M *C Tanner*

CLEVELAND

SP S McDowell
SP S Dunning
SR A Foster
SR R Lamb
SR S Hargan
RS V Colbert
RP P Hennigan
RP E Farmer
RP S Mingori
C R Fosse
1B C Chambliss
2B E Leon
SS- J Heidemann
3B G Nettles
LO T Uhlaender
MR V Pinson
RL R Foster
UT- C Hinton
M1 *A Dark*
M2 *J Lipon*

DETROIT

SP M Lolich
SP J Coleman
SP L Cain
SR J Niekro
RP F Scherman
RP T Timmermann
RP B Denehy
C B Freehan
1B N Cash
2B D McAuliffe
SS E Brinkman
3B A Rodriguez
LF W Horton
CF M Stanley
RF A Kaline
ML J Northrup
LU- G Brown
UT- D Jones
M *B Martin*

KANSAS CITY

SP D Drago
SP M Hedlund
SP P Splittorff
SP B Dal Canton
SR A Fitzmorris
RP T Burgmeier
CL T Abernathy
RP J York
C- J May
1B G Hopkins
2B C Rojas
SS F Patek
3B P Schaal
LF L Piniella
CF A Otis
RF J Keough
OC E Kirkpatrick
1R B Oliver
M *B Lemon*

MILWAUKEE

SP M Pattin
SP B Parsons
SP S Lockwood
SR L Krausse
SP J Slaton
SR K Sanders
RP J Morris
C E Rodriguez
OI J Briggs
2B R Theobald
SS- R Auerbach
3B- T Matchick
L3 T Harper
MR D May
RU B Voss
UT A Kosco
UI R Pena
2S- T Kubiak
M *D Bristol*

MINNESOTA

SP B Blyleven
SP J Perry
SP J Kaat
RS R Corbin
RS T Hall
RP S Williams
C G Mitterwald
1B R Reese
2B R Carew
SS L Cardenas
3I S Braun
LR C Tovar
MU J Holt
RF T Oliva
13 H Killebrew
M *B Rigney*

NEW YORK

SP F Peterson
SP M Stottlemyre
SP S Bahnsen
SP S Kline
SR M Kekich
RP L McDaniel
RP J Aker
C T Munson
13 D Cater
2B H Clarke
SS G Michael
3B J Kenney
LF R White
CF B Murcer
OI F Alou
1B- J Ellis
M *R Houk*

OAKLAND

SP V Blue
SP C Hunter
SP C Dobson
SP D Segui
SP B Odom
RS R Fingers
RP B Locker
RP D Knowles
C D Duncan
1B M Epstein,
2B D Green
SS B Campaneris
3B S Bando
LF J Rudi
CF R Monday
RF R Jackson
MO- A Mangual
M *D Williams*

WASHINGTON

SP D Bosman
SP D McLain
SP P Broberg
SR B Gogolewski
SR J Shellenback
RS C Cox
RP P Lindblad
RP J Grzenda
RP D Riddleberger
C- P Casanova
1B D Mincher
2S T Cullen
SS T Harrah
3B- D Nelson
L1 F Howard
MU E Maddox
MR D Unser
IF B Allen
CO D Billings
OI T McCraw
M *T Williams*

1971 NL

ATLANTA

SP P Niekro
SP R Reed
SP G Stone
SR P Jarvis
SP T Kelley
RS J Nash
CL C Upshaw
RP S Barber
RP B Priddy
IC E Williams
1R H Aaron
2B F Millan
SS M Perez
3B- D Evans
LF R Garr
CF S Jackson
RU M Lum
CU- H King
M *L Harris*

CHICAGO

SP F Jenkins
SP M Pappas
SP B Hands
SP K Holtzman
SP J Pizarro
RP P Regan
RP B Bonham
C- C Cannizzaro
1B J Pepitone
2B G Beckert
SS D Kessinger
3B R Santo
LF B Williams
CF B Davis
RF J Callison
R1 J Hickman
UI- P Popovich
M *L Durocher*

CINCINNATI

SP G Nolan
SP D Gullett
SP J McGlothlin
SP R Grimsley
SP W Simpson
RP W Granger
RP C Carroll
RS J Merritt
RP J Gibbon
C J Bench
1B L May
2B T Helms
SS D Concepcion
3B T Perez
LM H McRae
CF G Foster
RF P Rose
LF B Carbo
S3 W Woodward
M *S Anderson*

HOUSTON

SP D Wilson
SP J Billingham
SR K Forsch
SP L Dierker
SP W Blasingame
RP G Culver
RP J Ray
RP F Gladding
RP D Lemaster
C J Edwards
1I D Menke
2B J Morgan
SS R Metzger
3B D Rader

RL J Alou
CF C Cedeno
RM J Wynn
L1 B Watson
LU- C Geronimo
M H Walker

LOS ANGELES
SP D Sutton
SP A Downing
SP C Osteen
SP B Singer
CL J Brewer
RP P Mikkelsen
RP J Moeller
C- D Sims
1B W Parker
2B J Lefebvre
SS M Wills
3B- S Garvey
IO D Allen
CF W Davis
RF B Buckner
LF W Crawford
UT B Valentine
C- T Haller
LR- M Mota
UT- B Russell
M W Alston

MONTREAL
SP B Stoneman
SP S Renko
SP C Morton
SP E McAnally
SR J Strohmayer
RP M Marshall
RS D McGinn
RP H Reed
RP C Raymond
C J Bateman
1B R Fairly
2B R Hunt
SS B Wine
3B B Bailey
LU- J Fairey
CF B Day
RF R Staub
2S G Sutherland
M G Mauch

NEW YORK
SP T Seaver
SP G Gentry
SP J Koosman
SR R Sadecki
SP N Ryan
RP T McGraw
RP D Frisella
RS C Williams
RP R Taylor
C J Grote
1B E Kranepool
2B K Boswell
SS B Harrelson
3B B Aspromonte
LF C Jones
CF T Agee
RU K Singleton
23- T Foli
CF D Hahn
OF D Marshall
1B- D Clendenon
M G Hodges

PHILADELPHIA
SP R Wise
SP B Lersch
SP C Short
SR K Reynolds
SR W Fryman
RS J Bunning
RS B Champion
RP B Brandon
RP J Hoerner
C T McCarver
1B D Johnson
2B- D Doyle
SS L Bowa
3B- J Vukovich
LR- O Gamble
CF W Montanez
RF R Freed
3L D Money
OI- R Stone
M F Lucchesi

PITTSBURGH
SP S Blass
SP D Ellis
SP B Johnson
SP L Walker
SR B Moose
RS N Briles
CL D Giusti
RP M Grant
C M Sanguillen
1B B Robertson
2B D Cash
SS G Alley
3B R Hebner
LF W Stargell
CF A Oliver
RF R Clemente
UO- G Clines
OI V Davalillo
SS- J Hernandez
M D Murtaugh

ST. LOUIS
SP S Carlton
SP B Gibson
SP R Cleveland
SP J Reuss
RP C Taylor
RP M Drabowsky
RP F Linzy
RP D Shaw
C T Simmons
1R J Hague
2S T Sizemore
SS D Maxvill
3B J Torre
LF L Brock
OI M Alou
RF- J Cardenal
CF- J Cruz
2B- J Javier
RO- L Melendez
M R Schoendienst

SAN DIEGO
SP D Roberts
SP C Kirby
SP S Arlin
SP T Phoebus
SP F Norman
RP A Severinsen
RP B Miller
RP D Kelley
C B Barton
1B N Colbert
2B D Mason
SS E Hernandez
3B E Spiezio
OI L Stahl
CF C Gaston
RF O Brown
23 D Campbell
LU I Murrell
M P Gomez

SAN FRANCISCO
SP G Perry
SP J Marichal
SR J Cumberland
SP R Bryant
SP S Stone
RP J Johnson
RP D McMahon
RS R Robertson
C D Dietz
1B W McCovey
2B T Fuentes
SS C Speier
3B A Gallagher
LF K Henderson
M1 W Mays
RF B Bonds
3B H Lanier
MU- J Rosario
M C Fox

1972 AL

BALTIMORE
SP J Palmer
SP P Dobson
SP M Cuellar
SP D McNally
RS D Alexander
RP R Harrison
C- J Oates
1B B Powell
2B D Johnson
SS M Belanger
3B B Robinson
LF D Buford
CF P Blair
RF M Rettenmund
OI D Baylor
RU T Crowley
S2 B Grich
M E Weaver

BOSTON
SP M Pattin
SP S Siebert
SR L Tiant
SP J Curtis
SP L McGlothen
RP R Culp
RP B Lee
RP G Peters
RS L Krausse
C C Fisk
1B- D Cater
2B D Griffin
SS L Aparicio
3B R Petrocelli
L1 C Yastrzemski
CF T Harper
RF R Smith
OF B Oglivie
ML- R Miller
M E Kasko

CALIFORNIA
SP N Ryan
SP C Wright
SP R May
SP A Messersmith
SR R Clark
RS L Allen
RP E Fisher
RP S Barber
C- A Kusnyer
1B B Oliver
2B S Alomar
SS L Cardenas
3B K McMullen
LF V Pinson
CF K Berry
RF L Stanton
UT- J Spencer
M D Rice

CHICAGO
SP W Wood
SP T Bradley
SP S Bahnsen
SR D Lemonds
RP T Forster
RP R Gossage
RP S Kealey
RP V Romo
C E Herrmann
1B D Allen
2B M Andrews
SS R Morales
3B- E Spiezio
LF C May
CF J Johnstone
RF P Kelly
SS L Alvarado
CF R Reichardt
RU- W Williams
M C Tanner

CLEVELAND
SP G Perry
SP D Tidrow
SP M Wilcox
SP S Dunning
RS R Lamb
RP P Hennigan
RP E Farmer
RP S Mingori
C R Fosse
1B C Chambliss
2B J Brohamer
SS F Duffy
3B G Nettles
LF A Johnson
MO D Unser
OI B Bell
OI T McCraw
IF- E Leon
M K Aspromonte

DETROIT
SP M Lolich
SP J Coleman
SP T Timmermann
SP W Fryman
RP C Seelbach
RP F Scherman
C B Freehan
1B N Cash
2B D McAuliffe
SS E Brinkman
3B A Rodriguez
LF W Horton
CF M Stanley
RL J Northrup
LU G Brown
RF A Kaline
2B- T Taylor
M B Martin

KANSAS CITY
SP D Drago
SP P Splittorff
SR R Nelson
SR B Dal Canton
SR M Hedlund
RP A Fitzmorris
RP T Burgmeier
RP T Abernathy
C E Kirkpatrick
1B J Mayberry
2B C Rojas
SS F Patek
3B P Schaal
LF L Piniella
CF A Otis
RF R Scheinblum
UO S Hovley
M B Lemon

MILWAUKEE
SP J Lonborg
SP B Parsons
SP S Lockwood
SP K Brett
SP G Ryerson
RS J Colborn
RP K Sanders
RP F Linzy
RS E Stephenson
C E Rodriguez
1B G Scott
2B R Theobald
SS R Auerbach
3B M Ferraro
LU J Briggs
CF D May
RL J Lahoud
23 B Heise
UO- B Davis
M1 D Bristol
M2 R McMillan
M3 D Crandall

MINNESOTA
SP B Blyleven
SP D Woodson
SP J Perry
SR R Corbin
SP J Kaat
RP W Granger
RP D LaRoche
C- P Roof
1B H Killebrew
2B R Carew
SS D Thompson
3B E Soderholm
LU S Brye
MR B Darwin
RL C Tovar
3I S Braun
MU J Nettles
1U R Reese
M1 B Rigney
M2 F Quilici

NEW YORK
SP M Stottlemyre
SP F Peterson
SP S Kline
SP M Kekich
SP R Gardner
RP S Lyle
RP L McDaniel
RP F Beene
C T Munson
1B R Blomberg
2B H Clarke
SS G Michael
3B- C Sanchez
LF R White
CF B Murcer
RF- J Callison
1B F Alou
3U- B Allen
RF- R Torres
M R Houk

OAKLAND
SP C Hunter
SP K Holtzman
SP B Odom
SP V Blue
SR D Hamilton
RP R Fingers
RP B Locker
RS J Horlen
RP D Knowles
C D Duncan
1B M Epstein
2B- T Cullen
SS B Campaneris
3B S Bando
LF J Rudi
MR R Jackson
RO- A Mangual
1U M Hegan
CU- G Tenace
M D Williams

TEXAS
SR P Broberg
SP D Bosman
SP R Hand
SR M Paul
SR B Gogolewski
RP P Lindblad
RP D Stanhouse
RP J Panther
RP H Pina
CL D Billings
1U F Howard
2B- L Randle
SS T Harrah
3B D Nelson
OI L Biittner
MO J Lovitto
RF T Ford
MO E Maddox
M T Williams

1972 NL

ATLANTA
SP P Niekro
SP R Reed
SR R Schueler
SR T Kelley
SR G Stone
RS P Jarvis
RP C Upshaw
C E Williams
1B H Aaron
2B F Millan
SS M Perez
3B D Evans
LF- R Carty
CF D Baker
LR R Garr
RO M Lum
M1 L Harris
M2 E Mathews

CHICAGO
SP F Jenkins
SP B Hooton
SP M Pappas
SP B Hands
SR R Reuschel
RP T Phoebus
CL J Aker
RP D McGinn
C R Hundley
1U J Hickman
2B G Beckert
SS D Kessinger
3B R Santo
LF B Williams
CF R Monday
RF J Cardenal
IO- C Fanzone
M1 L Durocher
M2 W Lockman

CINCINNATI
SP J Billingham
SP R Grimsley
SP G Nolan
SR J McGlothlin
SR D Gullett
RP P Borbon
RP C Carroll
RS T Hall
RP W Simpson
C J Bench
1B T Perez
2B J Morgan
SS D Concepcion
3B D Menke
LF P Rose
CF B Tolan
RF C Geronimo
SS- D Chaney
M S Anderson

HOUSTON
SP D Wilson
SP L Dierker
SP D Roberts
SP J Reuss
SP K Forsch
RP G Culver
RP J Ray
RS T Griffin
RP F Gladding
C J Edwards
1B L May
2B T Helms
SS R Metzger
3B D Rader
LF B Watson
CF C Cedeno
RF J Wynn
M1 H Walker
M2 S Parker
M3 L Durocher

LOS ANGELES
SP D Sutton
SP C Osteen
SP A Downing
SP T John
SP B Singer
RP J Brewer
RP P Mikkelsen
RP P Richert
RP M Strahler
C- C Cannizzaro
1B W Parker
2B- L Lacy
SS B Russell
3B S Garvey
LF M Mota
CF W Davis
RF F Robinson
OI B Buckner
LR W Crawford
UT B Valentine
M W Alston

MONTREAL
SP B Stoneman
SP M Torrez
SP C Morton
SP E McAnally
SP B Moore
RP M Marshall
RS S Renko
RP J Strohmayer
RP T Walker
C- J Boccabella
1U M Jorgensen
2B R Hunt
SS T Foli
3B B Bailey
LF K Singleton
CF B Day
UO- C Mashore
R1 R Fairly
MU R Woods
UO- J Fairey
2U- H Torres
M G Mauch

NEW YORK
SP T Seaver
SP J Matlack
SP G Gentry
SR J Koosman
SP J McAndrew
RP T McGraw
RP D Frisella
RP R Sadecki
C D Dyer
1B E Kranepool
2B K Boswell
SS B Harrelson
3B J Fregosi
LF J Milner
CF T Agee
RF- R Staub
3U W Garrett
UT T Martinez
LU C Jones
M Y Berra

PHILADELPHIA
SP S Carlton
SR K Reynolds
SP B Champion
SP W Fryman
RS W Twitchell
RS B Brandon
RS D Selma
RS B Lersch
C- J Bateman
1R T Hutton
2B D Doyle
SS L Bowa
3B D Money
LF G Luzinski
CF W Montanez
UO- B Robinson
1U D Johnson
M1 F Lucchesi
M2 P Owens

PITTSBURGH
SP S Blass
SP B Moose
SP N Briles
SP D Ellis
SR B Kison
RS B Johnson
CL D Giusti
RP R Hernandez
RP B Miller
C M Sanguillen
1U W Stargell
2B D Cash
SS G Alley
3B R Hebner
LO V Davalillo
CF A Oliver
RF R Clemente
UO G Clines
1B R Robertson
UT R Stennett
M B Virdon

ST. LOUIS
SP B Gibson
SP R Wise
SP R Cleveland
SR A Santorini
SP S Spinks
RP D Segui
C T Simmons
1R M Alou
2B T Sizemore
SS D Maxvill
3B J Torre
LF L Brock
MU J Cruz
MR L Melendez
RF B Carbo
UI E Crosby
M R Schoendienst

SAN DIEGO
SP S Arlin
SP C Kirby
SR F Norman
SR M Caldwell
SR B Greif
RS M Corkins
RP G Ross
RP E Acosta
C- F Kendall
1B N Colbert
2S D Thomas
SS E Hernandez
3B D Roberts
LF L Lee
CF J Jeter
RU C Gaston
OI J Morales
OI L Stahl
23 G Jestadt
M1 P Gomez
M2 D Zimmer

SAN FRANCISCO
SP R Bryant
SR J Barr
SP J Marichal
SP S McDowell
SR S Stone
RP F Reberger
RP J Johnson
RP R Moffitt
RP D McMahon
C D Rader
1B- W McCovey
2B T Fuentes
SS C Speier
3B- A Gallagher
LU K Henderson
CF G Maddox
RF B Bonds
IO D Kingman
M C Fox

1973 AL

BALTIMORE
SP J Palmer
SP M Cuellar
SP D McNally
SP D Alexander
SP J Jefferson
RP B Reynolds
RP G Jackson
RP E Watt
C1 E Williams
1B B Powell
2B B Grich
SS M Belanger
3B B Robinson
LF D Baylor
CF P Blair
RM R Coggins
DH T Davis
LR A Bumbry
RF- M Rettenmund
M E Weaver

BOSTON
SP B Lee
SP L Tiant
SP J Curtis
SP M Pattin
SR R Moret
CL B Bolin
C C Fisk
1U C Yastrzemski
2B D Griffin
SS L Aparicio
3B R Petrocelli
LF T Harper
UO R Miller
RF D Evans
DH O Cepeda
CF R Smith
M1 E Kasko
M2 E Popowski

CALIFORNIA
SP N Ryan
SP B Singer
SP C Wright
SP R May
RP S Barber
RP D Sells
C J Torborg
1B- M Epstein
2B S Alomar
SS R Meoli
3B A Gallagher
LM V Pinson
CF K Berry
RL L Stanton
DH F Robinson
OI T McCraw
IO B Oliver
M B Winkles

CHICAGO
SP W Wood
SP S Bahnsen
SR S Stone
SR E Fisher
RS T Forster
CL C Acosta
RP R Gossage
C E Herrmann
1B T Muser
2B J Orta
SS E Leon
3B B Melton
DL C May
UO- J Jeter
RF P Kelly
OF- K Henderson
M C Tanner

CLEVELAND
SP G Perry
SP D Tidrow
SP M Wilcox
SR T Timmermann
SP B Strom
RP T Hilgendorf
RP R Lamb
RP J Johnson
C- D Duncan
1B C Chambliss
2B J Brohamer
SS F Duffy
3B B Bell
LU C Spikes
CF G Hendrick
RM R Torres
DR O Gamble
CD J Ellis
UT J Lowenstein
LD W Williams
M K Aspromonte

DETROIT
SP M Lolich
SP J Coleman
SP J Perry
SP W Fryman
RP J Hiller
RP F Scherman
RP L LaGrow
C B Freehan
1B N Cash
2B D McAuliffe
SS E Brinkman
3B A Rodriguez
LF W Horton
CF M Stanley
RL J Northrup
DH G Brown
DH- F Howard
R1- A Kaline
RF- D Sharon
2B- T Taylor
M1 B Martin
M2 J Schultz

KANSAS CITY
SP P Splittorff
SP S Busby
SP D Drago
RS G Garber
RP D Bird
RP S Mingori
C- F Healy
1B J Mayberry
2B C Rojas
SS F Patek
3B P Schaal
LF L Piniella
CF A Otis
RO E Kirkpatrick
RD H McRae
UT K Bevacqua
RO S Hovley
M J McKeon

MILWAUKEE
SP J Colborn
SP J Slaton
SP J Bell
SR S Lockwood
RS B Champion
RS E Rodriguez
RP F Linzy
RS C Short
C D Porter
1B G Scott
2B P Garcia
SS T Johnson
3B D Money
LF J Briggs
CF D May
RO B Coluccio
DH- O Brown
OF- J Lahoud

C- E Rodriguez
M D Crandall

MINNESOTA
SP B Blyleven
SP J Kaat
SP J Decker
SR B Hands
SP D Woodson
RS R Corbin
RS D Goltz
RS E Bane
RP B Campbell
C G Mitterwald
1B J Lis
2B R Carew
SS D Thompson
3B S Braun
L1 J Holt
ML L Hisle
RF B Darwin
DH T Oliva
SI J Terrell
CF- S Brye
M F Quilici

NEW YORK
SP M Stottlemyre
SP D Medich
SP F Peterson
SP P Dobson
RP L McDaniel
CL S Lyle
C T Munson
1U- F Alou
2B H Clarke
SS G Michael
3B G Nettles
LF R White
CF B Murcer
R1 M Alou
DH J Hart
D1 R Blomberg
M R Houk

OAKLAND
SP K Holtzman
SP V Blue
SP C Hunter
SP B Odom
RP R Fingers
RS D Knowles
RP H Pina
RP P Lindblad
C R Fosse
1B G Tenace
2B D Green
SS B Campaneris
3B S Bando
LF J Rudi
CF B North
RF R Jackson
DH D Johnson
2B T Kubiak
M D Williams

TEXAS
SP J Bibby
SR J Merritt
SP S Siebert
SP P Broberg
RP B Gogolewski
RS M Paul
RP J Brown
RP S Foucault
C- K Suarez
1B J Spencer
2B D Nelson
SS- J Mason
S3 T Harrah
LD- R Carty
MI V Harris
RL J Burroughs
DL A Johnson
MO E Maddox
OI- L Biittner
C- D Billings
IO- B Sudakis
M1 W Herzog
M2 D Wilber
M3 B Martin

1973 NL

ATLANTA
SP C Morton
SR P Niekro
SR R Schueler
SR R Harrison
SP R Reed
RP T House
C- J Oates
1L M Lum
2B D Johnson
SS M Perez
3B D Evans
LU H Aaron
CF D Baker
RF R Garr
OI S Jackson
C- P Casanova
IC- D Dietz
M E Mathews

CHICAGO
SP F Jenkins
SP B Hooton
SP R Reuschel
SP M Pappas
SR B Bonham
RP B Locker
RP J Aker
RP R Burris
RP D LaRoche
C R Hundley
1U- J Hickman
2B G Beckert
SS D Kessinger
3B R Santo
LF B Williams
CF R Monday
RF J Cardenal
UO G Hiser
2B P Popovich
M W Lockman

CINCINNATI
SP J Billingham
SP R Grimsley
SR D Gullett
SP F Norman
RP P Borbon
RS T Hall
RS C Carroll
C J Bench
1B T Perez
2B J Morgan
SS- D Concepcion
3B D Menke
LF P Rose
MU C Geronimo
MR B Tolan
SU D Chaney
3B D Driessen
M S Anderson

HOUSTON
SP J Reuss
SP D Roberts
SP D Wilson
SR K Forsch
SR T Griffin
RP J Crawford
RP J Ray
RP J York
C- S Jutze
1B L May
2B T Helms
SS R Metzger
3B D Rader
LF B Watson
CF C Cedeno
RF J Wynn
UO- T Agee
M L Durocher

LOS ANGELES
SP D Sutton
SP A Messersmith
SP C Osteen
SP T John
SP A Downing
CL J Brewer
RP C Hough
RP D Rau
RP P Richert
C J Ferguson
1L B Buckner
2B D Lopes
SS B Russell
3B R Cey
LF- M Mota
CF W Davis
RF W Crawford
1U S Garvey
OI- T Paciorek
M W Alston

MONTREAL
SP S Renko
SP M Torrez
SP B Moore
SP E McAnally
SP S Rogers
RP M Marshall
RP T Walker
C J Boccabella
1B M Jorgensen
2B R Hunt
SS T Foli
3B B Bailey
LF R Fairly
MU R Woods
RF K Singleton
1U H Breeden
UO B Day
IO P Frias
M G Mauch

NEW YORK
SP T Seaver
SP J Koosman
SP J Matlack
SP G Stone
SR R Sadecki
RP T McGraw
RS H Parker
C- J Grote
1U J Milner
2B F Millan
SS B Harrelson
3B W Garrett
LF- C Jones
CF- D Hahn
RF R Staub
1L E Kranepool
UT- T Martinez
M Y Berra

PHILADELPHIA
SP S Carlton
SP W Twitchell
SP K Brett
SP J Lonborg
SP D Ruthven
RP B Lersch
RP M Scarce
RP B Brandon
RP B Wilson
C B Boone
1R W Montanez
2B D Doyle
SS L Bowa
3B M Schmidt
LF G Luzinski
CF D Unser
RM B Robinson
1U T Hutton
UT- C Tovar
RU- M Anderson
M D Ozark

PITTSBURGH
SP N Briles
SP B Moose
SP D Ellis
SR J Rooker
SR L Walker
RP D Giusti
RP R Hernandez
RP B Johnson
CR M Sanguillen
1B B Robertson
2B D Cash
SS- D Maxvill
3B R Hebner
LF W Stargell
M1 A Oliver
RU R Zisk
UO G Clines
C M May
2S R Stennett
M1 B Virdon
M2 D Murtaugh

ST. LOUIS
SP R Wise
SP R Cleveland
SP A Foster
SP B Gibson
RP D Segui
RS R Folkers
RP O Pena
RP A Hrabosky
C T Simmons
1B J Torre
2B T Sizemore
SS M Tyson
3B K Reitz
LF L Brock
MO L Melendez
MR J Cruz
RF B Carbo
1U T McCarver
M R Schoendienst

SAN DIEGO
SP B Greif
SP C Kirby
SP S Arlin
SR R Troedson
SP R Jones
RS M Caldwell
RS M Corkins
RP V Romo
RP G Ross
C F Kendall
1B N Colbert
2B- R Morales
S2 D Thomas
3B D Roberts
LU L Lee
CF J Grubb
RF C Gaston
UO J Morales
OI- I Murrell
M D Zimmer

SAN FRANCISCO
SP R Bryant
SP J Barr
SP T Bradley
SP J Marichal
RP E Sosa
RS J Willoughby
RP R Moffitt
RP D Carrithers
C D Rader
1B W McCovey
2B T Fuentes
SS C Speier
3B E Goodson
LF G Matthews
CF G Maddox
RF B Bonds
31 D Kingman
UT G Thomasson
M C Fox

1974 AL

BALTIMORE
SP R Grimsley
SP M Cuellar
SP D McNally
SP J Palmer
SR D Alexander
RP G Jackson
RP B Reynolds
RP D Hood
RP J Jefferson
C1 E Williams
1B B Powell
2B B Grich
SS M Belanger
3B B Robinson
LF D Baylor
CF P Blair
RF R Coggins
DH T Davis
LU- A Bumbry
M E Weaver

BOSTON
SP L Tiant
SP B Lee
SR R Cleveland
SR D Drago
SR R Moret
RP D Segui
C- B Montgomery
1L C Yastrzemski
2B- D Griffin
SS- M Guerrero
3B R Petrocelli
OF B Carbo
CF J Beniquez
RF D Evans
LD T Harper
SS R Burleson
MU R Miller
1D C Cooper
23 D McAuliffe
M D Johnson

CALIFORNIA
SP N Ryan
SP F Tanana
SP A Hassler
SP D Lange
SP B Singer
RS E Figueroa
RP S Lockwood
C E Rodriguez
1B- J Doherty
2B D Doyle
S3 D Chalk
3B- P Schaal
LR J Lahoud
CF M Rivers
RF L Stanton
DH F Robinson
13 B Oliver
LS B Valentine
M1 B Winkles
M2 W Herzog
M3 D Williams

CHICAGO
SP W Wood
SP J Kaat
SP S Bahnsen
SP B Johnson
RP T Forster
RS S Pitlock
RP R Gossage
C E Herrmann
1B D Allen
2B J Orta
SS B Dent
3B B Melton
LF C May
CF K Henderson
RF B Sharp
DR P Kelly
CR B Downing
1B T Muser
UI R Santo
M C Tanner

CLEVELAND
SP G Perry
SP J Perry
SP F Peterson
SP D Bosman
RP T Buskey
RP F Beene
RP M Wilcox
C D Duncan
1C J Ellis
2B J Brohamer
SS F Duffy
3B B Bell
LI J Lowenstein
CF G Hendrick
RF C Spikes
DH O Gamble
UO R Torres
M K Aspromonte

DETROIT
SP M Lolich
SP J Coleman
SP L LaGrow
SP W Fryman
RP J Hiller
RP J Ray
C- J Moses
1C B Freehan
2B G Sutherland
SS E Brinkman
3B A Rodriguez
LF- W Horton
CF M Stanley
RF- J Northrup
DH A Kaline
LU- B Oglivie
M R Houk

KANSAS CITY
SP S Busby
SP P Splittorff
SP A Fitzmorris
SP B Dal Canton
SR M Pattin
RS L McDaniel
RP N Briles
RP D Bird
RP S Mingori
C F Healy
1B J Mayberry
2B C Rojas
SS F Patek
3B G Brett
LF J Wohlford
CF A Otis
RF V Pinson
DL H McRae
RO A Cowens
2S F White
1U- T Solaita
M J McKeon

MILWAUKEE
SP J Slaton
SP C Wright
SP J Colborn
SR K Kobel
SP B Champion
RP T Murphy
RS E Rodriguez
RP B Travers
C D Porter
1B G Scott
2B P Garcia
SS R Yount
3B D Money
LF J Briggs
MO B Coluccio
RF D May
DO- B Mitchell
CF K Berry
UT- M Hegan
S2- T Johnson
M D Crandall

MINNESOTA
SP B Blyleven
SP J Decker
SP D Goltz
SR V Albury
SR R Corbin
RP B Campbell
RS B Hands
RS B Butler
RP T Burgmeier
C G Borgmann
1B- C Kusick
2B R Carew
SS- D Thompson
3B E Soderholm
LM L Hisle
CF S Brye
RF B Darwin
DH T Oliva
LF S Braun
UT H Killebrew
IO J Terrell
SS- L Gomez
M F Quilici

NEW YORK
SP P Dobson
SP D Medich
SP D Tidrow
SP R May
SP M Stottlemyre
RP S Lyle
RP C Upshaw
RP M Wallace
C T Munson
1B C Chambliss
2B- S Alomar
SS J Mason
3B G Nettles
LU L Piniella
CF E Maddox
RM B Murcer
DU- R Blomberg
UT R White
2S- G Michael
IF- B Sudakis
M B Virdon

OAKLAND
SP C Hunter
SP V Blue
SP K Holtzman
SR D Hamilton
RP R Fingers
RP P Lindblad
RS B Odom
RP D Knowles
C- L Haney
1C G Tenace
2B D Green
SS B Campaneris
3B S Bando
LF J Rudi
CF B North
RF R Jackson
OF- J Alou
2I T Kubiak
OI A Mangual
LS- H Washington
M A Dark

TEXAS
SP F Jenkins
SP J Bibby
SP J Brown
SR S Hargan
SP D Clyde
RP S Foucault
C J Sundberg
1U M Hargrove
2B D Nelson
SS T Harrah
32 L Randle
ML C Tovar
CF J Lovitto
RF J Burroughs
1D J Spencer
LD A Johnson
OI- T Grieve
M B Martin

1974 NL

ATLANTA
SP P Niekro
SP C Morton
SR B Capra
SP R Reed
SP R Harrison
RP T House
RP M Leon
RP L Krausse
C J Oates
12 D Johnson
2B M Perez
SS C Robinson
3B D Evans
LF H Aaron
RF D Baker
LR R Garr
CF R Office
1O M Lum
M1 E Mathews
M2 C King

CHICAGO
SP B Bonham
SP R Reuschel
SR B Hooton
SR S Stone
RS K Frailing
RP D LaRoche
RP O Zamora
RS J Todd
C- S Swisher
1B A Thornton
2B- V Harris
SS D Kessinger
3B B Madlock
LR J Morales
CF R Monday
RF J Cardenal
1L B Williams
OI- C Ward
M1 W Lockman
M2 J Marshall

CINCINNATI
SP D Gullett
SP C Kirby
SP J Billingham
SP F Norman
RP P Borbon
RP C Carroll
RP T Hall
C J Bench
1B T Perez
2B J Morgan
SS D Concepcion
3B D Driessen
LF P Rose
CF C Geronimo
RM G Foster
32 D Chaney
OI- T Crowley
RF- K Griffey
M S Anderson

HOUSTON
SP L Dierker
SP T Griffin
SP D Roberts
SP D Wilson
SP C Osteen
RP K Forsch
RP M Cosgrove
RP F Scherman
C M May
1B L May
2B T Helms
SS R Metzger
3B D Rader
LF B Watson
CF C Cedeno
RF G Gross
RU B Gallagher
2B L Milbourne
IC- C Johnson
M P Gomez

LOS ANGELES
SP A Messersmith
SP D Sutton
SP D Rau
SP T John
RP M Marshall
RP C Hough
C- S Yeager
1B S Garvey
2B D Lopes
SS B Russell
3B R Cey
LF B Buckner
CF J Wynn
RF W Crawford
CR J Ferguson
UO- V Joshua
LM- T Paciorek
M W Alston

MONTREAL
SP S Rogers
SP S Renko
SP M Torrez
SP D Blair
SP E McAnally
RP C Taylor
RS T Walker
RP J Montague
RP D Murray
C B Foote
1U M Jorgensen
2B- J Cox
SS T Foli
32 R Hunt
L3 B Bailey
CF W Davis
RF K Singleton
1U R Fairly
2S L Lintz
UO- R Woods
M G Mauch

NEW YORK
SP J Koosman
SP J Matlack
SP T Seaver
SR H Parker
RS B Apodaca
RS R Sadecki
RP T McGraw
RP B Miller
C- J Grote
1B J Milner
2B F Millan
SS B Harrelson
3B W Garrett
LF C Jones
CF D Hahn
RF R Staub
SU T Martinez
UT- K Boswell
OI- E Kranepool
MO- D Schneck
M Y Berra

PHILADELPHIA
SP S Carlton
SP J Lonborg
SP D Ruthven
SR R Schueler
SP W Twitchell
RP M Scarce
C B Boone
1B W Montanez
2B D Cash
SS L Bowa
3B M Schmidt
LF- G Luzinski
CF D Unser
RF M Anderson
UO B Robinson
UT- T Hutton
M D Ozark

PITTSBURGH
SP J Rooker
SP J Reuss
SP K Brett
SP D Ellis
SR B Kison
RP D Giusti
RP R Hernandez
RP J Morlan
C M Sanguillen
1U- B Robertson
2B R Stennett
SS F Taveras
3B R Hebner
LF W Stargell
M1 A Oliver
RF R Zisk
UO G Clines
1U E Kirkpatrick
SS- M Mendoza
M D Murtaugh

ST. LOUIS
SP B Gibson
SP L McGlothen
SP J Curtis
SP A Foster
SP S Siebert
RP B Forsch
RP A Hrabosky
RP R Folkers
RP M Garman
C T Simmons
1B J Torre
2B T Sizemore
SS M Tyson
3B K Reitz
LF L Brock
CF B McBride
RF R Smith
OI J Cruz
OI- L Melendez
M R Schoendienst

SAN DIEGO
SP B Greif
SP D Freisleben
SP R Jones
SP D Spillner
RP L Hardy
RP V Romo
RP D Tomlin
RP M Corkins
C F Kendall
1B W McCovey
2U D Thomas
SS E Hernandez
3B D Roberts
LO D Winfield
CF J Grubb
RF- B Tolan
1L N Colbert
OF C Gaston
M J McNamara

SAN FRANCISCO
SR J Barr
SP J D'Acquisto
SP M Caldwell
SP T Bradley
SR R Bryant
RP R Moffitt
RP E Sosa
RS C Williams
C D Rader
1B D Kingman
2B T Fuentes
SS C Speier
3U S Ontiveros
LF G Matthews
CF G Maddox

RF B Bonds
1U E Goodson
UI M Phillips
OI G Thomasson
M1 C Fox
M2 W Westrum

1975 AL

BALTIMORE

SP J Palmer
SP M Torrez
SP M Cuellar
SP R Grimsley
SR D Alexander
RP W Garland
RP G Jackson
C D Duncan
1B L May
2B B Grich
SS M Belanger
3B B Robinson
LF D Baylor
CF P Blair
RF K Singleton
DH T Davis
OI A Bumbry
C- E Hendricks
1B- T Muser
MU- J Northrup
M E Weaver

BOSTON

SP B Lee
SP L Tiant
SP R Wise
SR R Cleveland
SR R Moret
CL D Drago
RP D Segui
RP J Willoughby
RP J Burton
C- C Fisk
1B C Yastrzemski
2B D Griffin
SS R Burleson
3B R Petrocelli
OF B Carbo
CF F Lynn
RF D Evans
LD J Rice
D1 C Cooper
2B- D Doyle
M D Johnson

CALIFORNIA

SP F Tanana
SP E Figueroa
SP N Ryan
SP B Singer
SR A Hassler
RS D Lange
RP D Kirkwood
RP M Scott
C- E Rodriguez
1B B Bochte
2B J Remy
SS- M Miley
3B D Chalk
UO M Nettles
CF M Rivers
RF L Stanton
DU- T Harper
LF- D Collins
M D Williams

CHICAGO

SP J Kaat
SP W Wood
SP C Osteen
SP J Jefferson
SR R Gossage
RP D Hamilton
RP O Osborn
RP B Gogolewski
C B Downing
UT C May
2B J Orta
SS B Dent
3B B Melton
LO N Nyman
CF K Henderson
RF P Kelly
D1 D Johnson
M C Tanner

CLEVELAND

SR D Eckersley
SP F Peterson
SR D Hood
SP R Harrison
SP G Perry
RS J Bibby
RP D LaRoche
RP T Buskey
RP J Brown
C- A Ashby
1B B Powell
2B- D Kuiper
SS F Duffy
3B B Bell
LU O Gamble
MR R Manning
MR G Hendrick
DU R Carty
RL C Spikes
C- J Ellis
UT- J Lowenstein
M F Robinson

DETROIT

SP M Lolich
SP J Coleman
SP V Ruhle
SP L LaGrow
SP R Bare
RS T Walker
RS D Lemanczyk
CL J Hiller
C B Freehan
1B- J Pierce
2B G Sutherland
SS T Veryzer
3B A Rodriguez
LF B Oglivie
CF R LeFlore
RF L Roberts
DH W Horton
L1 D Meyer
M R Houk

KANSAS CITY

SP S Busby
SP A Fitzmorris
SP D Leonard
SR M Pattin
SR P Splittorff
RP D Bird
RP N Briles
RP L McDaniel
RP S Mingori
C- B Martinez
1B J Mayberry
2B C Rojas
SS F Patek
3B G Brett
LF H McRae
CF A Otis
RM A Cowens
DH H Killebrew
RU V Pinson
2S F White
RL J Wohlford
UT- T Solaita
M1 J McKeon
M2 W Herzog

MILWAUKEE

SP P Broberg
SP J Slaton
SP J Colborn
SP B Travers
SR B Champion
RS T Hausman
RP E Rodriguez
CL T Murphy
C D Porter
1B G Scott
2B P Garcia
SS R Yount
3B D Money
ML B Sharp
CF G Thomas
RF S Lezcano
DH H Aaron
32 K Bevacqua
OI- M Hegan
LF- B Mitchell
M1 D Crandall
M2 H Kuenn

MINNESOTA

SP B Blyleven
SP J Hughes
SP D Goltz
SR V Albury
RS B Campbell
RP T Burgmeier
C G Borgmann
1B- C Kusick
2B R Carew
SS D Thompson
3B E Soderholm
LF S Braun
CF D Ford
RM L Bostock
DH T Oliva
IO J Terrell
1O- J Briggs
RO- S Brye
SS- L Gomez
UO- L Hisle
M F Quilici

NEW YORK

SP C Hunter
SP D Medich
SP R May
SP P Dobson
SP L Gura
RP S Lyle
RP D Tidrow
C T Munson
1B C Chambliss
2B S Alomar
SS- J Mason
3B G Nettles
LF R White
CF- E Maddox
RM B Bonds
UC- E Herrmann
S2 F Stanley
OI- W Williams
M1 B Virdon
M2 B Martin

OAKLAND

SP V Blue
SP K Holtzman
SP D Bosman
SR G Abbott
SP S Bahnsen
RP R Fingers
RP J Todd
RP P Lindblad
C G Tenace
1L J Rudi
2B P Garner
SS B Campaneris
3B S Bando
LF C Washington
CF B North
RF R Jackson
DH B Williams
1U J Holt
C- R Fosse
UO- D Hopkins
S2- T Martinez
M A Dark

TEXAS

SP F Jenkins
SP S Hargan
SP G Perry
SP B Hands
RS J Umbarger
RP S Foucault
RP S Thomas
C J Sundberg
1B J Spencer
2M L Randle
SS T Harrah
3B R Howell
L1 M Hargrove
CF- D Moates
RF J Burroughs
DO C Tovar
UO T Grieve
M1 B Martin
M2 F Lucchesi

1975 NL

ATLANTA

SP C Morton
SP P Niekro
RP M Leon
RP T House
RP M Beard
RS R Sadecki
C V Correll
1B E Williams
2B M Perez
SS L Blanks
3B D Evans
LF R Garr
CF R Office
RF D Baker
UT M Lum
2U- R Gilbreath
UO- D May
M1 C King
M2 C Ryan

CHICAGO

SP R Burris
SP R Reuschel
SP B Bonham
SP S Stone
RP D Knowles
RS T Dettore
RP O Zamora
RP K Frailing
C- S Swisher
1B A Thornton
2B M Trillo
SS D Kessinger
3B B Madlock
LF J Cardenal
CF R Monday
RF J Morales
1U P LaCock
CU- G Mitterwald
M J Marshall

CINCINNATI

SP G Nolan
SP J Billingham
SP F Norman
SP D Gullett
SP P Darcy
RP P Borbon
CL R Eastwick
RP C Kirby
RP W McEnaney
C J Bench
1B T Perez
2B J Morgan
SS D Concepcion
3B P Rose
LO G Foster
CF C Geronimo
RF K Griffey
UT- D Driessen
UI- D Flynn
OI- M Rettenmund
M S Anderson

HOUSTON

SP L Dierker
SP J Richard
SP D Roberts
SP D Konieczny
RS K Forsch
SP J Niekro
RP J Crawford
RP W Granger
C M May
1B B Watson
2B R Andrews
SS R Metzger
3B D Rader
UO W Howard
CF C Cedeno
OF G Gross
UT E Cabell
RU J Cruz
IC C Johnson
IF- K Boswell
M1 P Gomez
M2 B Virdon

LOS ANGELES

SP A Messersmith
SP D Rau
SP D Sutton
SP B Hooton
SR R Rhoden
RP M Marshall
RP C Hough
C S Yeager
1B S Garvey
2B D Lopes
SS- B Russell
3B R Cey
LF- B Buckner
CF J Wynn
RF W Crawford
UT L Lacy
SS- R Auerbach
M W Alston

MONTREAL

SP S Rogers
SP S Renko
SR D Warthen
SP D Blair
SR W Fryman
RP D Murray
RP D Carrithers
RP D DeMola
RP C Taylor
C B Foote
1B M Jorgensen
2B P Mackanin
SS T Foli
3B L Parrish
UO L Biittner
CF P Mangual
RC G Carter
LU B Bailey
UT- J Morales
UO- T Scott
M G Mauch

NEW YORK

SP T Seaver
SP J Koosman
SP J Matlack
SP R Tate
SR H Webb
RP R Baldwin
RP B Apodaca
RP T Hall
C J Grote
1B E Kranepool
2B F Millan
SS M Phillips
3B W Garrett
L1 D Kingman
CF D Unser
RF R Staub
3U J Torre
UO- G Clines
OI- J Milner
M1 Y Berra
M2 R McMillan

PHILADELPHIA

SP S Carlton
SP T Underwood
SP L Christenson
SP J Lonborg
SR W Twitchell
RP G Garber
RP T McGraw
RP T Hilgendorf
RS R Schueler
C- B Boone
1B D Allen
2B D Cash
SS L Bowa
3B M Schmidt
LF G Luzinski
CF G Maddox
RF M Anderson
1U T Hutton
RF J Johnstone
RL- O Brown
C- J Oates
M D Ozark

PITTSBURGH

SP J Reuss
SP J Rooker
SP B Kison
SP D Ellis
SP J Candelaria
RS L Demery
RP K Brett
RP D Giusti
RP R Hernandez
C M Sanguillen
1B W Stargell
2B R Stennett
SS F Taveras
3B R Hebner
LF R Zisk
CF A Oliver
RF D Parker
UT- E Kirkpatrick
UO- B Robinson
M D Murtaugh

ST. LOUIS

SP L McGlothen
SP B Forsch
SP R Reed
SR J Curtis
SP J Denny
CL A Hrabosky
RP B Gibson
RP M Garman
C T Simmons
R1 R Smith
2B T Sizemore
SS M Tyson
3B K Reitz
LF L Brock
CF B McBride
RU W Davis
1U R Fairly
UO L Melendez
M R Schoendienst

SAN DIEGO

SP R Jones
SP J McIntosh
SP D Freisleben
SR D Spillner
SP B Strom
RS R Folkers
RP D Frisella
RP D Tomlin
RP B Greif
C F Kendall
1B W McCovey
2B T Fuentes
SS E Hernandez
3U- T Kubiak
LU B Tolan
CF J Grubb
RF D Winfield
13 M Ivie
LU G Locklear
S3 H Torres
UO- D Sharon
M J McNamara

SAN FRANCISCO

SP J Barr
SP J Montefusco
SP P Falcone
SR M Caldwell
SP E Halicki
RP C Williams
RP G Lavelle
RP R Moffitt
RP D Heaverlo
C D Rader
1B W Montanez
2B D Thomas
SS C Speier
3B S Ontiveros
LF G Matthews
CF V Joshua
RF B Murcer
3I B Miller
OI G Thomasson
M W Westrum

1976 AL

BALTIMORE

SP J Palmer
SR W Garland
SP R May
SP R Grimsley
SP M Cuellar
RP D Miller
C- D Duncan
1B T Muser
2B B Grich
SS M Belanger
3B D DeCinces
LR K Singleton
CF P Blair
RF R Jackson
1D L May
LM A Bumbry
M E Weaver

BOSTON

SP L Tiant
SP R Wise
SP F Jenkins
SR R Cleveland
SR D Pole
RP J Willoughby
RS R Jones
RP T Murphy
C C Fisk
1L C Yastrzemski
2B D Doyle
SS R Burleson
3B- B Hobson
LD J Rice
CF F Lynn
RF D Evans
1D C Cooper
UO R Miller
3B- R Petrocelli
M1 D Johnson
M2 D Zimmer

CALIFORNIA

SP F Tanana
SP N Ryan
SP G Ross
SR P Hartzell
SP D Kirkwood
RS S Monge
RP D Drago
C A Etchebarren
OI B Bochte
2B J Remy
S3 D Chalk
3B R Jackson
UO- L Stanton
CF R Torres
RF B Bonds
DH- T Davis
LU D Collins
IF B Melton
IF- M Guerrero
M1 D Williams
M2 N Sherry

CHICAGO

SP R Gossage
SP B Johnson
SP K Brett
SR F Barrios
SR T Forster
RS P Vuckovich
RP D Hamilton
RP C Carroll
C B Downing
1B J Spencer
3B J Brohamer
SS B Dent
3B- K Bell
OI J Orta
CF C Lemon
UO R Garr
DU P Kelly
IO B Stein
UT- L Johnson
M P Richards

CLEVELAND

SP P Dobson
SP D Eckersley
SP J Brown
SR J Bibby
SP R Waits
RP J Kern
RP D LaRoche
RS S Thomas
RP T Buskey
C- A Ashby
1B- B Powell
2B D Kuiper
SS F Duffy
3B B Bell
LF G Hendrick
CF R Manning
RF C Spikes
DH R Carty
S2 L Blanks
C- R Fosse
OI- J Lowenstein
M F Robinson

DETROIT

SP D Roberts
SP M Fidrych
SP V Ruhle
SP R Bare
RP J Hiller
RS J Crawford
RP S Grilli
C- B Kimm
1B J Thompson
2B- P Garcia
SS T Veryzer
3B A Rodriguez
LU A Johnson
CF R LeFlore
RF R Staub
DH W Horton
UT D Meyer
OI B Oglivie
UT- M Stanley
M R Houk

KANSAS CITY

SP D Leonard
SP A Fitzmorris
SR D Bird
SP P Splittorff
SR M Pattin
RP M Littell
RP A Hassler
RP S Mingori
C- B Martinez
1B J Mayberry
2B F White
SS F Patek
3B G Brett
LF T Poquette
CF A Otis
RF A Cowens
DH H McRae
LF J Wohlford
M W Herzog

MILWAUKEE

SP J Slaton
SP B Travers
SP J Colborn
SR J Augustine
RS E Rodriguez
RP B Castro
RP D Frisella
C D Porter
1B G Scott
2B T Johnson
SS R Yount
3B D Money
UO S Lezcano
CF V Joshua
MR G Thomas
DH- H Aaron
CL- C Moore
M A Grammas

MINNESOTA

SP D Goltz
SR J Hughes
SP B Singer
SP P Redfern
RP B Campbell
RS S Luebber
RP T Burgmeier
RP V Albury
C B Wynegar
1B R Carew
2B B Randall
SS R Smalley
3B M Cubbage
LF L Hisle
CF L Bostock
RF D Ford
DU C Kusick
DO S Braun
MO- S Brye
UT- J Terrell
M G Mauch

NEW YORK

SP C Hunter
SP E Figueroa
SP D Ellis
SP K Holtzman
SP D Alexander
RP S Lyle
RP D Tidrow
RP G Jackson
C T Munson
1B C Chambliss
2B W Randolph
SS F Stanley
3B G Nettles
LF R White
CF M Rivers
RF O Gamble
DH- C May
OF L Piniella
SS- J Mason
M B Martin

OAKLAND

SP V Blue
SP M Torrez
SR S Bahnsen
SP P Mitchell
SR D Bosman
RP R Fingers
RP P Lindblad
RP J Todd
C- L Haney
1C G Tenace
2B P Garner
SS B Campaneris
3B S Bando
LF J Rudi
CF B North
RF C Washington
DH B Williams
OI D Baylor
IO K McMullen
M C Tanner

TEXAS

SP G Perry
SP N Briles
SP B Blyleven
SP J Umbarger
RS S Hargan
RP S Foucault
RP M Bacsik
RP J Terpko
C J Sundberg
1B M Hargrove
2B L Randle
SS T Harrah
3B R Howell
LF G Clines
CF J Beniquez
RF J Burroughs
DL T Grieve
UO- D Moates
M F Lucchesi

1976 NL

ATLANTA

SP P Niekro
SP D Ruthven
SP A Messersmith
SP C Morton
SP F LaCorte
RP A Devine
RP B Dal Canton
RP P Torrealba
C- V Correll
1B W Montanez
2B R Gilbreath
SS D Chaney
3B J Royster
LM J Wynn
CF R Office
RF K Henderson
OF D May
UT T Paciorek
M D Bristol

CHICAGO

SP R Reuschel
SP R Burris
SP B Bonham
SP S Renko
RP B Sutter
RP P Reuschel
RP J Coleman
RP D Knowles
C S Swisher
1U P LaCock
2B M Trillo
SS M Kelleher
3B B Madlock
LF J Cardenal
MU R Monday
RF J Morales
CU G Mitterwald
MU J Wallis
SS- D Rosello
OI- C Summers
M J Marshall

CINCINNATI

SP G Nolan
SR P Zachry
SP F Norman
SP J Billingham
SP S Alcala
RP R Eastwick
RP P Borbon

RP D Gullett
RP W McEnaney
C J Bench
1B T Perez
2B J Morgan
SS D Concepcion
3B P Rose
LF G Foster
CF C Geronimo
RF K Griffey
UT D Driessen
2I- D Flynn
UO- M Lum
M S Anderson

HOUSTON
SP J Richard
SP L Dierker
SP J Andujar
SR J Niekro
CL K Forsch
RP G Pentz
RP J Sambito
C- E Herrmann
1B B Watson
2B R Andrews
SS R Metzger
3B E Cabell
LO J Cruz
CF C Cedeno
RF G Gross
CU C Johnson
IO- K Boswell
OI- W Howard
LU- L Roberts
M B Virdon

LOS ANGELES
SP D Sutton
SP D Rau
SP B Hooton
SP T John
SP R Rhoden
RP C Hough
RP M Marshall
RP S Wall
C S Yeager
1B S Garvey
2B D Lopes
SS B Russell
3B R Cey
LF B Buckner
MU D Baker
RF- R Smith
IO- E Goodson
2B- T Sizemore
M1 W Alston
M2 T Lasorda

MONTREAL
SP S Rogers
SP W Fryman
SP D Stanhouse
SR D Carrithers
RP D Murray
RS S Dunning
RP C Lang
RP J Kerrigan
C B Foote
1O M Jorgensen
2B P Mackanin
SS T Foli
3B L Parrish
UO- D Unser
MU J White
MR- E Valentine
IC J Morales
CR- G Carter
M1 K Kuehl
M2 C Fox

NEW YORK
SP T Seaver
SP J Matlack
SP J Koosman
SP M Lolich
SP C Swan
CL S Lockwood
RP B Apodaca
C J Grote
1O E Kranepool
2B F Millan
SS B Harrelson
3B- R Staiger
LF J Milner
CF- D Unser
RF D Kingman
1U J Torre
UO B Boisclair
SI- M Phillips
M J Frazier

PHILADELPHIA
SP S Carlton
SP J Kaat
SP J Lonborg
SP L Christenson
SP T Underwood
RP R Reed
RP T McGraw
RP G Garber
RP W Twitchell
C B Boone
1B- D Allen
2B D Cash
SS L Bowa
3B M Schmidt
LF G Luzinski
CF G Maddox
RF J Johnstone
LO J Martin
UT B Tolan
RF- O Brown
1B- T Hutton
IC- T McCarver
M D Ozark

PITTSBURGH
SP J Candelaria
SP J Reuss
SP J Rooker
SP B Kison
SP D Medich
RS L Demery
RP K Tekulve
RP B Moose
RP D Giusti
C M Sanguillen
1B W Stargell
2B R Stennett
SS F Taveras
3B R Hebner
LF R Zisk
CF A Oliver
RF D Parker
UT B Robinson
UT- E Kirkpatrick
M D Murtaugh

ST. LOUIS
SP P Falcone
SP J Denny
SP L McGlothen
SP B Forsch
SR E Rasmussen
RS J Curtis
RP A Hrabosky
RP M Wallace
RP B Greif
C T Simmons
1B K Hernandez
2B- M Tyson
SS D Kessinger
3B H Cruz
LF L Brock
MU J Mumphrey
RF W Crawford
UT- V Harris
OI- M Anderson
M R Schoendienst

SAN DIEGO
SP R Jones
SP B Strom
SR D Freisleben
SR D Spillner
RP B Metzger
RP D Tomlin
RP R Folkers
C F Kendall
1B M Ivie
2B T Fuentes
SS E Hernandez
3B D Rader
LR J Grubb
CF W Davis
RF D Winfield
LU J Turner
UI- T Kubiak
UO- M Rettenmund
M J McNamara

SAN FRANCISCO
SP J Montefusco
SP J Barr
SP E Halicki
SP R Dressler
SP J D'Acquisto
RP G Lavelle
RP R Moffitt
RS M Caldwell
RP C Williams
C- D Rader
1B- D Evans
2B- M Perez
SS C Speier
3B K Reitz
LF G Matthews
CF L Herndon
RF B Murcer
OI G Thomasson
2B- D Thomas
M B Rigney

1977 AL

BALTIMORE
SP J Palmer
SP R May
SP M Flanagan
SP R Grimsley
RS D Martinez
RS S McGregor
RP T Martinez
C- R Dempsey
1D L May
2B B Smith
SS M Belanger
3B D DeCinces
LF P Kelly
CF A Bumbry
RF K Singleton
D1 E Murray
1U T Muser
2B- R Dauer
M E Weaver

BOSTON
SP F Jenkins
SP R Cleveland
SP L Tiant
SR B Lee
SP R Wise
RP B Campbell
RS B Stanley
RS M Paxton
RP J Willoughby
C C Fisk
1B G Scott
2B D Doyle
SS R Burleson
3B B Hobson
LF C Yastrzemski
CF F Lynn
RM- R Miller
DO J Rice
RU- B Carbo
M D Zimmer

CALIFORNIA
SP N Ryan
SP F Tanana
SR P Hartzell
SP K Brett
SP W Simpson
RP D Miller
RP D LaRoche
RP M Barlow
C T Humphrey
1B T Solaita
2B J Remy
SS- R Mulliniks
3B D Chalk
LF- J Rudi
UO G Flores
RF B Bonds
OI D Baylor
IO R Jackson
IF- M Guerrero
M1 N Sherry
M2 D Garcia

CHICAGO
SP F Barrios
SP S Stone
SP K Kravec
SP C Knapp
SP W Wood
RP L LaGrow
RP D Hamilton
C J Essian
1B J Spencer
2B J Orta
SS A Bannister
3B E Soderholm
LF R Garr
CF C Lemon
RU R Zisk
DR O Gamble
D1 L Johnson
M B Lemon

CLEVELAND
SP W Garland
SP D Eckersley
SP J Bibby
SR R Waits
SR P Dobson
RP A Fitzmorris
RP J Kern
RS D Hood
C F Kendall
1B A Thornton
2B D Kuiper
SS F Duffy
3B B Bell
L1 B Bochte
MR J Norris
UT P Dade
DH R Carty
SI L Blanks
OI- J Lowenstein
M1 F Robinson
M2 J Torborg

DETROIT
SP D Rozema
SR F Arroyo
SR B Sykes
SP D Roberts
SP M Wilcox
RS J Hiller
RS J Crawford
RP S Foucault
RP S Grilli
C M May
1B J Thompson
2B T Fuentes
SS T Veryzer
3B- A Rodriguez
LF S Kemp
CF R LeFlore
RF B Oglivie
DH R Staub
3B- P Mankowski
M R Houk

KANSAS CITY
SP D Leonard
SP J Colborn
SP P Splittorff
SP A Hassler
RS D Bird
RS M Pattin
RS M Littell
RS L Gura
C D Porter
1B J Mayberry
2B F White
SS F Patek
3B G Brett
LR T Poquette
CF A Otis
RF A Cowens
DL H McRae
LF J Zdeb
UT- P LaCock
M W Herzog

MILWAUKEE
SP J Slaton
SP J Augustine
SP M Haas
SP L Sorensen
SP B Travers
RS E Rodriguez
RP B Castro
RP B McClure
SP S Hinds
C C Moore
1B C Cooper
2B D Money
SS R Yount
3B S Bando
LF J Wohlford
CF V Joshua
RF S Lezcano
DU- J Quirk
UO- S Brye
M A Grammas

MINNESOTA
SP D Goltz
SP P Thormodsgard
SP G Zahn
SP P Redfern
RP T Johnson
RS R Schueler
RP T Burgmeier
RS D Johnson
C B Wynegar
1B R Carew
2B R Randall
SS R Smalley
3B M Cubbage
UO L Hisle
ML L Bostock
RF D Ford
DU C Kusick
DU R Chiles
OF- G Adams
3U- J Terrell
M G Mauch

NEW YORK
SP E Figueroa
SP M Torrez
SP R Guidry
SP D Gullett
SP C Hunter
RP S Lyle
RS D Tidrow
RP K Clay
C T Munson
1B C Chambliss
2B W Randolph
SS B Dent
3B G Nettles
LF R White
CF M Rivers
RF R Jackson
DH- C May
OI L Piniella
MR- P Blair
M B Martin

OAKLAND
SP V Blue
SP R Langford
SP D Medich
RS J Coleman
RP B Lacey
RS P Torrealba
RP D Bair
C- J Newman
1B- D Allen
2B M Perez
SS R Picciolo
3B W Gross
LF M Page
MR T Armas
RU- J Tyrone
CD M Sanguillen
2S R Scott
UC E Williams
UT- M Alexander
UT- R McKinney
OI- L Murray
M1 J McKeon
M2 B Winkles

SEATTLE
SP G Abbott
SP D Pole
RS J Montague
RP E Romo
RS D Segui
RP M Kekich
C B Stinson
1B D Meyer
2B- J Baez
SS C Reynolds
3B B Stein
LU S Braun
CF R Jones
RU L Stanton
DI- J Bernhardt
LD D Collins
RF C Lopez
UI- L Milbourne
M D Johnson

TEXAS
SP G Perry
SP D Alexander
SP B Blyleven
SP D Ellis
SR N Briles
RP A Devine
RP P Lindblad
RP D Knowles
C J Sundberg
1B M Hargrove
2B B Wills
SS B Campaneris
3B T Harrah
LM C Washington
CF J Beniquez
RF D May
DH W Horton
M1 F Lucchesi
M2 E Stanky
M3 C Ryan
M4 B Hunter

TORONTO
SP D Lemanczyk
SP J Garvin
SP J Jefferson
RS P Vuckovich
RP M Willis
RP J Johnson
RP T Murphy
C A Ashby
1B D Ault
2B- S Staggs
S2- H Torres
3B- R Howell
LF A Woods
OI B Bailor
RU O Velez
UT R Fairly
OI S Ewing
RM- S Bowling
UI- D McKay
IO- D Rader
M R Hartsfield

1977 NL

ATLANTA
SP P Niekro
SP D Ruthven
SR B Capra
SP A Messersmith
RP D Campbell
RP R Camp
RS M Leon
RS D Collins
C B Pocoroba
1B W Montanez
2B R Gilbreath
SS- P Rockett
3B J Moore
LF G Matthews
CF R Office
RF J Burroughs
M3 B Bonnell
IO J Royster
UO- B Asselstine
M1 D Bristol
M2 T Turner
M3 V Benson
M4 D Bristol

CHICAGO
SP R Reuschel
SP R Burris
SP B Bonham
SP M Krukow
RP B Sutter
RP W Hernandez
RP P Reuschel
RP D Moore
C G Mitterwald
1B B Buckner
2B M Trillo
SS I DeJesus
3B S Ontiveros
LU J Cardenal
CF J Morales
RF B Murcer
1L L Biittner
UO G Gross
UO G Clines
M H Franks

CINCINNATI
SP F Norman
SP T Seaver
SR J Billingham
SP P Moskau
SP D Capilla
RP P Borbon
RP D Murray
C J Bench
1B D Driessen
2B J Morgan
SS D Concepcion
3B P Rose
LF G Foster
CF C Geronimo
RF K Griffey
OI- M Lum
M S Anderson

HOUSTON
SP J Richard
SP M Lemongello
SP J Andujar
SP F Bannister
RS J Niekro
RP J Sambito
RS K Forsch
RS B McLaughlin
C J Ferguson
1B B Watson
2B A Howe
SS- R Metzger
3B E Cabell
LF- T Puhl
CF C Cedeno
RF J Cruz
S2 J Gonzalez
LU- W Howard
M B Virdon

LOS ANGELES
SP D Sutton
SP B Hooton
SP T John
SP R Rhoden
SP D Rau
RP C Hough
RP M Garman
RP E Sosa
C S Yeager
1B S Garvey
2B D Lopes
SS B Russell
3B R Cey
LF D Baker
CF R Monday
RF R Smith
CF- G Burke
M T Lasorda

MONTREAL
SP S Rogers
SR J Brown
SR D Stanhouse
SP W Twitchell
SP S Bahnsen
RS S Alcala
RP J Kerrigan
RP B Atkinson
RP W McEnaney
C G Carter
1B T Perez
2B D Cash
SS C Speier
3B L Parrish
LF W Cromartie
CF A Dawson
RF E Valentine
OI D Unser
M D Williams

NEW YORK
SP J Koosman
SP N Espinosa
SP J Matlack
SP C Swan
SP P Zachry
RP S Lockwood
RP B Apodaca
RP B Myrick
RP R Baldwin
C J Stearns
1U J Milner
2B- F Millan
SS B Harrelson
3B L Randle
LF S Henderson
CF L Mazzilli
RF M Vail
OI E Kranepool
OI B Boisclair
S2- D Flynn
M1 J Frazier
M2 J Torre

PHILADELPHIA
SP S Carlton
SP L Christenson
SP R Lerch
SP J Kaat
SP J Lonborg
RP R Reed
RP G Garber
RP T McGraw
RP W Brusstar
C B Boone
1B R Hebner
2B T Sizemore
SS L Bowa
3B M Schmidt
LF G Luzinski
CF G Maddox
RF J Johnstone
1U T Hutton
OI J Martin
RU- B McBride
IC- T McCarver
M D Ozark

PITTSBURGH
SP J Candelaria
SP J Reuss
SP J Rooker
SP B Kison
SR O Jones
RP R Gossage
RP K Tekulve
RP G Jackson
RS L Demery
C- D Dyer
1L B Robinson
2B R Stennett
SS F Taveras
32 P Garner
LF A Oliver
CF O Moreno
RF D Parker
C E Ott
M C Tanner

ST. LOUIS
SP E Rasmussen
SP B Forsch
SP J Denny
SP P Falcone
SP T Underwood
RS J Urrea
RP B Metzger
RP A Hrabosky
RP C Carroll
C T Simmons
1B K Hernandez
2B M Tyson
SS G Templeton
3B K Reitz
LF L Brock
UO J Mumphrey
RU H Cruz
RF- M Anderson
CF- T Scott
M V Rapp

SAN DIEGO
SP B Shirley
SP B Owchinko
SR T Griffin
SP R Jones
SR D Freisleben
RP R Fingers
RP D Spillner
RS R Sawyer
RP D Tomlin
CI G Tenace
1B M Ivie
2B M Champion
SS B Almon
3B- T Ashford
OI G Richards
CF G Hendrick
RF D Winfield
OI M Rettenmund
LU J Turner
C- D Roberts
M1 J McNamara
M2 B Skinner
M3 A Dark

SAN FRANCISCO
SP E Halicki
SP J Barr
SP B Knepper
SP J Montefusco
RP G Lavelle
RS C Williams
RP D Heaverlo
RP R Moffitt
C M Hill
1B W McCovey
2B R Andrews
SS T Foli
3B B Madlock
OI G Thomasson
MI D Thomas
RF J Clark
L1 D Evans
UO T Whitfield
M J Altobelli

1978 AL

BALTIMORE
SP J Palmer
SP M Flanagan
SP D Martinez
SP S McGregor
CL D Stanhouse
RP J Kerrigan
RP T Martinez
C R Dempsey
1B E Murray
23 R Dauer
SS M Belanger
3B D DeCinces
LU P Kelly
CF L Harlow
RF K Singleton
DH L May
RM C Lopez
2B- B Smith
M E Weaver

BOSTON
SP D Eckersley
SP M Torrez
SP L Tiant
SP B Lee
SP J Wright
RP B Stanley
RP D Drago
RP T Burgmeier
RP B Campbell
C C Fisk
1B G Scott
2B J Remy
SS R Burleson
3B B Hobson
OI C Yastrzemski
CF F Lynn
RF D Evans
LD J Rice
IF- J Brohamer
M D Zimmer

CALIFORNIA
SP F Tanana
SP N Ryan
SP C Knapp
SP D Aase
RS P Hartzell
CL D LaRoche
RS K Brett
RP D Miller
C B Downing
1B- R Fairly
2B B Grich
SI D Chalk
3B C Lansford
LF J Rudi
MR R Miller
RM L Bostock
DU D Baylor
13 R Jackson
UO- K Landreaux
M1 D Garcia
M2 J Fregosi

CHICAGO
SP S Stone
SP K Kravec
SP F Barrios
SP W Wood
RP J Willoughby
RP L LaGrow
RP R Hinton
RS R Schueler
C B Nahorodny
1B- M Squires
2B J Orta
SS D Kessinger
3B E Soderholm
LF R Garr
CF C Lemon
RO- C Washington
1U L Johnson
UO B Molinaro
UI- G Pryor
M1 B Lemon
M2 L Doby

CLEVELAND
SP R Waits
SP R Wise
SP M Paxton
SR D Hood
SP D Clyde
RP J Kern
RP S Monge
RP D Spillner
CD- G Alexander
1B A Thornton
2B D Kuiper
SS T Veryzer
3B B Bell
LF J Grubb
CF R Manning
RF- P Dade
DH- B Carbo
OI J Norris
UT- T Cox
M J Torborg

DETROIT
SP J Slaton
SP M Wilcox
SP D Rozema
SP J Billingham
SP K Young
RP J Hiller
RS J Morris
C M May
1B J Thompson
2B L Whitaker
SS A Trammell
3B A Rodriguez
LF S Kemp
CF R LeFlore
RF T Corcoran
DH R Staub
3B- P Mankowski
C- L Parrish
M R Houk

KANSAS CITY
SP D Leonard
SP P Splittorff
SP L Gura
SP R Gale
RS D Bird
CL A Hrabosky
RS M Pattin
RP S Mingori
C D Porter
1B P LaCock
2B F White
SS F Patek
3B G Brett
LM W Wilson
CF A Otis
RF A Cowens
DH H McRae
UT C Hurdle
M W Herzog

MILWAUKEE
SP M Caldwell
SP L Sorensen
SP J Augustine
SP B Travers
SR A Replogle
RS E Rodriguez
RP B McClure
RP R Stein
RP B Castro
C- C Moore
1B C Cooper
2I P Molitor
SS R Yount
3B S Bando
LU B Oglivie
CF G Thomas
RF S Lezcano
UO L Hisle
UI D Money
C- B Martinez
M G Bamberger

MINNESOTA
SP R Erickson
SP G Zahn
SP D Goltz
SR G Serum
RP M Marshall
C B Wynegar
1B R Carew
2B R Randall
SS R Smalley
3B M Cubbage
LF W Norwood
CF D Ford
RF H Powell
DH G Adams
DH J Morales
RL B Rivera
LU- R Chiles
2B- R Wilfong
3B- L Wolfe
M G Mauch

NEW YORK
SP R Guidry
SP E Figueroa
SP D Tidrow
SP J Beattie
SP C Hunter
RP R Gossage
RP S Lyle
RS K Clay
C T Munson
1B C Chambliss
2B W Randolph
SS B Dent
3B G Nettles
LU L Piniella
CF M Rivers
RD R Jackson
DC- C Johnson
LU R White
SS- F Stanley
M1 B Martin
M2 D Howser
M3 B Lemon

OAKLAND
SP M Keough
SP J Johnson
SR R Langford
SP P Broberg
SP S Renko
RP D Heaverlo
RP B Lacey
RP E Sosa
C J Essian
1B D Revering
2B M Edwards
SS M Guerrero
3B W Gross
LF M Page
OI M Dilone
RM- T Armas
DH- G Alexander
3B T Duncan
C1 J Newman
MR- J Wallis
M1 B Winkles
M2 J McKeon

SEATTLE
SP P Mitchell
SP G Abbott
SP R Honeycutt
SP J Colborn
SP B McLaughlin
RP E Romo
RS T House
RP S Rawley
RP J Todd
C B Stinson
1B D Meyer
2B J Cruz
SS C Reynolds
3B B Stein
LD B Bochte
CF R Jones
RF L Roberts
UO J Hale
UI- L Milbourne
DL- L Stanton
M D Johnson

TEXAS
SP J Matlack
SP F Jenkins
SP D Alexander
SP D Medich
SP D Ellis
RS S Comer
RP R Cleveland
RP L Barker
C J Sundberg
1B M Hargrove
2B B Wills
SS B Campaneris
3S T Harrah
LF A Oliver
CF J Beniquez
RF B Bonds
OF R Zisk
3U- K Bevacqua
1B- M Jorgensen
M1 B Hunter
M2 P Corrales

TORONTO
SP J Jefferson
SP T Underwood
SP J Clancy
SP J Garvin
SR B Moore
RP D Lemanczyk
RP M Willis
RP T Murphy
RP J Coleman
C- R Cerone
1B J Mayberry
2B D McKay
SS L Gomez
3B R Howell
OI- O Velez
CF R Bosetti
RU B Bailor
DH R Carty
C- A Ashby
OI- W Upshaw
M R Hartsfield

1978 NL

ATLANTA
SP P Niekro
SP P Hanna
SR M Mahler
SP L McWilliams
RS E Solomon
CL G Garber
RS J Easterly
RP R Camp
C- B Pocoroba
1B D Murphy
2S J Royster
SS- D Chaney
3B- B Horner
LF J Burroughs
CF R Office
RF G Matthews
UT B Beall
OI B Bonnell
32 R Gilbreath
CU- J Nolan
M B Cox

CHICAGO
SP R Reuschel
SP D Lamp
SP R Burris
SR D Roberts
SP M Krukow
RP B Sutter
RP D Moore
RP L McGlothen
RP W Hernandez
C D Rader
1B B Buckner
2B M Trillo
SS I DeJesus
3B- S Ontiveros
LF D Kingman
ML G Gross
RF B Murcer
1U L Biittner
UO G Clines
M H Franks

CINCINNATI
SP T Seaver
SP F Norman
SR T Hume
SP P Moskau
SP B Bonham
RP M Sarmiento
RP D Bair
RP P Borbon
RP D Tomlin
C J Bench
1B D Driessen
2B J Morgan
SS D Concepcion
3B P Rose
LF G Foster
CF C Geronimo
RF K Griffey
UO D Collins
2B- J Kennedy
3U- R Knight
OI- M Lum
M S Anderson

HOUSTON
SP J Richard
SP M Lemongello
SP J Niekro
SR T Dixon
SR J Andujar
RS K Forsch
RS F Bannister
RP J Sambito
C- L Pujols
1B B Watson
2B A Howe
SU- J Sexton
3B E Cabell
LU D Walling
ML T Puhl
RF J Cruz
1L D Bergman
OI- W Howard
M B Virdon

LOS ANGELES
SP D Sutton
SP B Hooton
SP T John
SP D Rau
SP R Rhoden
RS B Welch
RP C Hough
CL T Forster
RP L Rautzhan
C- S Yeager
1B S Garvey
2B D Lopes
SS B Russell
3B R Cey
LF D Baker
CF B North
RF R Smith
UT L Lacy
MR R Monday
M T Lasorda

MONTREAL
SP R Grimsley
SP S Rogers
SP R May
SR D Schatzeder
SR W Twitchell
RS H Dues
RP S Bahnsen
RP D Knowles
RP M Garman
C G Carter
1B T Perez
2B D Cash
SS C Speier
3B L Parrish
LF W Cromartie
CF A Dawson
RF E Valentine
UT D Unser
M D Williams

NEW YORK
SP J Koosman
SP C Swan
SP N Espinosa
SP P Zachry
SP M Bruhert
RS K Kobel
RP S Lockwood
RP D Murray
C J Stearns
1B W Montanez
2B D Flynn
SS T Foli
3B L Randle
LF S Henderson
CF L Mazzilli
R3 E Maddox
RU B Boisclair
UT J Youngblood
M J Torre

PHILADELPHIA
SP S Carlton
SP L Christenson
SP R Lerch
SP D Ruthven
SP J Kaat
RP R Reed
RP J Lonborg
RP T McGraw
RP W Brusstar
C B Boone
1B R Hebner
2B T Sizemore
SS L Bowa
3B M Schmidt
LF G Luzinski
CF G Maddox
RF B McBride
UO J Martin
1U- J Cardenal
IC- T McCarver
M D Ozark

PITTSBURGH
SP B Blyleven
SP D Robinson
SP J Candelaria
SP J Rooker
SR J Bibby
RP K Tekulve
RP G Jackson
RP E Whitson
C E Ott
1B W Stargell
2B R Stennett
SS F Taveras
23 P Garner
LF B Robinson
CF O Moreno
RF D Parker
L1 J Milner
IC- M Sanguillen
M C Tanner

ST. LOUIS
SP J Denny
SP B Forsch
SR P Vuckovich
SP S Martinez
SR J Urrea
RP M Littell
RP B Schultz
RP A Lopez
RP T Bruno
C T Simmons
1B K Hernandez
2B M Tyson
SS G Templeton
3B K Reitz
LF- L Brock
CF G Hendrick
RM J Morales
UO J Mumphrey
UO- T Scott
M1 V Rapp
M2 J Krol
M3 K Boyer

SAN DIEGO
SP G Perry
SP R Jones
SP B Owchinko
SR B Shirley
SP E Rasmussen
RP R Fingers
RP J D'Acquisto
RP M Lee
C- R Sweet
1C G Tenace
2B F Gonzalez
SS O Smith
3B B Almon
LU G Richards
RM D Winfield
RL O Gamble
M2 D Thomas
UO J Turner
M R Craig

SAN FRANCISCO
SP B Knepper
SP V Blue
SP J Montefusco
SP E Halicki
SP J Barr
RP G Lavelle
RP R Moffitt
RP J Curtis
C M Hill
1B W McCovey
2B B Madlock
SS J LeMaster
3B D Evans
LF T Whitfield
CF L Herndon
RF J Clark
1U M Ivie
M J Altobelli

1979 AL

BALTIMORE
SP D Martinez
SP M Flanagan
SP S Stone
SP S McGregor
SP J Palmer
RP S Stewart
CL D Stanhouse
RP T Martinez
RP T Stoddard
C R Dempsey
1B E Murray
23 R Dauer
SS K Garcia
3B D DeCinces
LF G Roenicke
CF A Bumbry
RF K Singleton
DH L May
SS M Belanger
UT J Lowenstein
M E Weaver

BOSTON
SP M Torrez
SP D Eckersley
SR B Stanley
SP S Renko
SP C Rainey
RP D Drago
RP T Burgmeier
RP B Campbell
C G Allenson
1D- B Watson
2B- J Remy
SS R Burleson
3B B Hobson
LF J Rice
CF F Lynn
RF D Evans
UT C Yastrzemski
UC- C Fisk
M D Zimmer

CALIFORNIA
SP D Frost
SP N Ryan
SR J Barr
SP D Aase
RP M Clear
RP D LaRoche
RP M Barlow
C B Downing
1B R Carew
2B B Grich
SS- B Campaneris
3B C Lansford
LF- J Rudi
CF R Miller
RF D Ford
OI D Baylor
UT W Aikens
SS- J Anderson
M J Fregosi

CHICAGO
SP K Kravec
SP R Wortham
SP R Baumgarten
SR S Trout
RS R Scarbery
RS M Proly
CL E Farmer
RS F Howard
C- M May
1B M Squires
UT A Bannister
SS G Pryor
3B- K Bell
UO- R Torres
CF C Lemon
RF C Washington
D2 J Orta
LU R Garr
1D L Johnson
LU- J Moore
M1 D Kessinger
M2 T LaRussa

CLEVELAND
SP R Wise
SP R Waits
SP M Paxton
SR L Barker
RS D Spillner
RP S Monge
RP V Cruz
C G Alexander
1B A Thornton
2B D Kuiper
SS T Veryzer
3B T Harrah
UO J Norris
CF R Manning
RF B Bonds
DH- C Johnson
L1 M Hargrove
M1 J Torborg
M2 D Garcia

DETROIT
SP J Morris
SP M Wilcox
SR J Billingham
SR P Underwood
SP D Petry
RP A Lopez
RP D Rozema
RP J Hiller
RP D Tobik
C L Parrish
1B J Thompson
2B L Whitaker
SS A Trammell
3B A Rodriguez
LF S Kemp
CF R LeFlore
RO J Morales
DH- R Staub
UO- L Jones
RU- C Summers
IC- J Wockenfuss
M1 L Moss
M2 D Tracewski
M3 S Anderson

KANSAS CITY
SP P Splittorff
SP D Leonard
SP L Gura
SP R Gale
RP A Hrabosky
RP E Rodriguez
C D Porter
1B P LaCock
2B F White
SS F Patek
3B G Brett
LF W Wilson
CF A Otis
RF A Cowens
DH H McRae
UI U Washington
1C- J Wathan
M W Herzog

MILWAUKEE
SP M Caldwell
SP L Sorensen
SP J Slaton
SP B Travers
SP M Haas
RP J Augustine
RP R Cleveland
RP B McClure
RP B Galasso
C C Moore
1B C Cooper
2B P Molitor
SS R Yount
3B S Bando
LU B Oglivie
CF G Thomas
RF S Lezcano
DL- D Davis
UI- D Money
M G Bamberger

MINNESOTA
SP J Koosman
SP D Goltz
SP G Zahn
SP P Hartzell
SP R Erickson
RP M Marshall
RS P Redfern
RP M Bacsik
C B Wynegar
1B R Jackson
2B R Wilfong
SS R Smalley
3B J Castino
LR B Rivera
ML K Landreaux
RF H Powell
DH- J Morales
OF G Adams
3U- M Cubbage
UO- D Edwards
OF- W Norwood
M G Mauch

NEW YORK
SP T John
SP R Guidry
SP L Tiant
SP E Figueroa
SP C Hunter
RP R Davis
RS K Clay
CL R Gossage
RS D Hood
C T Munson
1B C Chambliss
2B W Randolph
SS B Dent
3B G Nettles
LU L Piniella
CF- B Murcer
RF R Jackson
DU J Spencer
UT- R White
M1 B Lemon
M2 B Martin

OAKLAND
SP R Langford
SP S McCatty
SP M Keough
SR M Norris
SR C Minetto
RP B Kingman
RP D Heaverlo
RS D Hamilton
RP J Todd
C1 J Newman
1B D Revering
2B M Edwards
SS R Picciolo
3B W Gross
LM- R Henderson
CF D Murphy
RO L Murray
DH M Page
CU J Essian
M J Marshall

SEATTLE
SP M Parrott
SP R Honeycutt
SP F Bannister
SP O Jones
SP G Abbott
RS B McLaughlin
RP J Montague
RS R Dressler
RP S Rawley
C L Cox
1B B Bochte
2B J Cruz
SS M Mendoza
3U D Meyer
OF L Roberts
CF R Jones
RO J Simpson
DH W Horton
S2 L Milbourne
OI T Paciorek
3B- B Stein
C- B Stinson
M D Johnson

TEXAS
SP F Jenkins
SP S Comer
SR D Medich
SP D Alexander
RP J Kern
RP S Lyle
RP D Rajsich
C J Sundberg
1U P Putnam
2B B Wills
SS N Norman
3B B Bell
LU B Sample
ML A Oliver
RF R Zisk
D1 J Ellis
UO J Grubb
1U- M Jorgensen
M P Corrales

TORONTO
SP T Underwood
SP P Huffman
SP D Lemanczyk
SR B Moore
SP D Stieb
RS J Jefferson
RP D Freisleben
RP T Buskey
C R Cerone
1B J Mayberry
2B- D Ainge
SS A Griffin
3B R Howell
LF A Woods
CF R Bosetti
RF B Bailor
DH R Carty
OI O Velez
M R Hartsfield

1979 NL

ATLANTA
SP P Niekro
SP E Solomon
SP R Matula
SP T Brizzolara
SP M Mahler
RP G Garber
RP J McLaughlin
RP A Devine
RP C Skok
C- B Benedict
1C D Murphy
2B G Hubbard
SS P Frias
31 B Horner
LF J Burroughs
CF R Office
RF G Matthews
UT M Lum
LM B Bonnell
32 J Royster
C- J Nolan
M B Cox

CHICAGO
SP R Reuschel
SR L McGlothen
SP D Lamp
SP M Krukow
SP K Holtzman
RP B Sutter
RP D Tidrow
RP W Hernandez
RP D Moore
C B Foote
1B B Buckner
2B T Sizemore

SS I DeJesus
3B S Ontiveros
LF D Kingman
CF J Martin
RO S Thompson
OI L Biittner
2U- S Dillard
OI- M Vail
M1 H Franks
M2 J Amalfitano

CINCINNATI

SP T Seaver
SP M LaCoss
SP F Norman
SP B Bonham
SP P Moskau
RS T Hume
RP D Bair
RP D Tomlin
C J Bench
1B D Driessen
2B J Morgan
SS D Concepcion
3B R Knight
LF G Foster
CF C Geronimo
RF- K Griffey
OI D Collins
2U- J Kennedy
M J McNamara

HOUSTON

SP J Richard
SP J Niekro
SR J Andujar
SP K Forsch
SR R Williams
CL J Sambito
RS R Niemann
C A Ashby
1M C Cedeno
2B R Landestoy
SS C Reynolds
3B E Cabell
LF J Cruz
MR T Puhl
RU J Leonard
23 A Howe
OF- D Walling
M B Virdon

LOS ANGELES

SP R Sutcliffe
SP D Sutton
SP B Hooton
SR J Reuss
RS C Hough
RP D Patterson
C S Yeager
1B S Garvey
2B D Lopes
SS B Russell
3B R Cey
LF D Baker
CF D Thomas
MR G Thomasson
CR J Ferguson
UO- V Joshua
UI- T Martinez
M T Lasorda

MONTREAL

SP S Rogers
SP B Lee
SR S Sanderson
SR D Schatzeder
SP R Grimsley
RS D Palmer
RP E Sosa
RP S Bahnsen
RS R May
C G Carter
1B T Perez
2S R Scott
SS C Speier
3B L Parrish
LF W Cromartie
CF A Dawson
RF E Valentine
UT- T Hutton
UO- J White
M D Williams

NEW YORK

SP C Swan
SP P Falcone
SP K Kobel
RS N Allen
RP D Murray
RS A Hassler
RP E Glynn
C J Stearns
1B W Montanez
2B D Flynn
SS F Taveras
3B R Hebner
LF S Henderson
CF L Mazzilli
RL J Youngblood
UT- E Kranepool
OI- E Maddox
M J Torre

PHILADELPHIA

SP S Carlton
SP R Lerch
SP N Espinosa
SP D Ruthven
SP L Christenson
RP R Reed
RP T McGraw
RP R Eastwick
RP K Saucier
C B Boone
1B P Rose
2B M Trillo
SS L Bowa
3B M Schmidt
LF G Luzinski
CF G Maddox
RF B McBride
UO G Gross
OI- D Unser
M1 D Ozark
M2 D Green

PITTSBURGH

SP B Blyleven
SP J Candelaria
SP B Kison
SP D Robinson
SR J Bibby
RP K Tekulve
RP E Romo
RP J Rooker
RP G Jackson
C E Ott
1B W Stargell
2B R Stennett
SS T Foli
3B- B Madlock
LF B Robinson
CF O Moreno
RF D Parker
23 P Garner
L1 J Milner
UT- L Lacy
M C Tanner

ST. LOUIS

SP P Vuckovich
SP B Forsch
SP S Martinez
SP J Denny
SP J Fulgham
RP M Littell
RS R Thomas
RR W McEnaney
RP D Knowles
C T Simmons
1B K Hernandez
2B K Oberkfell
SS G Templeton
3B K Reitz
LF L Brock
CF T Scott
RF G Hendrick
LO J Mumphrey
M K Boyer

SAN DIEGO

SP R Jones
SP G Perry
SR B Shirley
SR E Rasmussen
SR B Owchinko
RS J D'Acquisto
RP R Fingers
RS S Mura
RP M Lee
C- B Fahey
C1 G Tenace
2B F Gonzalez
SS O Smith
3B- P Dade
LF J Turner
MU G Richards
RF D Winfield
2S B Almon
3U K Bevacqua
UT D Briggs
M R Craig

SAN FRANCISCO

SP V Blue
SP B Knepper
SP J Montefusco
SR E Halicki
SP J Curtis
RP G Lavelle
RS P Nastu
RP E Whitson
RP T Griffin
C- D Littlejohn
1U M Ivie
2B- J Strain
SS J LeMaster
3B D Evans
ML L Herndon
CF B North
RF J Clark
1B W McCovey
LF T Whitfield
SS- R Metzger
M1 J Altobelli
M2 D Bristol

1980 AL

BALTIMORE

SP S McGregor
SP M Flanagan
SP S Stone
SP J Palmer
SR D Martinez
RP S Stewart
CL T Stoddard
RP T Martinez
RP D Ford
C R Dempsey
1B E Murray
2B R Dauer
SS M Belanger
3B D DeCinces
LR G Roenicke
CF A Bumbry
RF K Singleton
DU- T Crowley
SS K Garcia
LF J Lowenstein
C- D Graham
OF- P Kelly
M E Weaver

BOSTON

SP M Torrez
SP D Eckersley
SP S Renko
RS B Stanley
RS D Drago
RP T Burgmeier
C C Fisk
1B T Perez
2B D Stapleton
SS R Burleson
3B G Hoffman
LF J Rice
CF F Lynn
RF D Evans
OI C Yastrzemski
OI- J Dwyer
3D- B Hobson
M1 D Zimmer
M2 J Pesky

CALIFORNIA

SP F Tanana
SR D Aase
SP A Martinez
SR C Knapp
RS D LaRoche
RP M Clear
RP A Hassler
RP J Montague
C- T Donohue
1U R Carew
2B B Grich
SS- F Patek
3B C Lansford
LF J Rudi
CF R Miller
RM L Harlow
UT J Thompson
OF- D Baylor
M J Fregosi

CHICAGO

SP B Burns
SP S Trout
SP R Dotson
SP R Baumgarten
SR L Hoyt
RP M Proly
RP E Farmer
RS R Wortham
C B Kimm
1B M Squires
2B J Morrison
SS- T Cruz
3B- K Bell
OF W Nordhagen
CF C Lemon
RF H Baines
1D L Johnson
UT B Molinaro
S3 G Pryor
M T LaRussa

CLEVELAND

SP L Barker
SP R Waits
SP D Spillner
SP W Garland
SR B Owchinko
RP J Denny
RP S Monge
RP V Cruz
RP M Stanton
C R Hassey
1B M Hargrove
2B- J Brohamer
SS T Veryzer
3B T Harrah
LO M Dilone
CF R Manning
RF J Orta
LD J Charboneau
S2 J Dybzinski
2R- A Bannister
M D Garcia

DETROIT

SP J Morris
SP M Wilcox
SP D Schatzeder
SP D Petry
RS D Rozema
RP A Lopez
RS P Underwood
C L Parrish
13 R Hebner
2B L Whitaker
SS A Trammell
3B T Brookens
LD S Kemp
MU R Peters
RF A Cowens
DO C Summers
UT J Wockenfuss
1U- T Corcoran
M S Anderson

KANSAS CITY

SP L Gura
SP D Leonard
SP P Splittorff
SP R Gale
SR R Martin
RP D Quisenberry
RP M Pattin
CD D Porter
1B W Aikens
2B F White
SS U Washington
3B G Brett
LM W Wilson
CF A Otis
RF C Hurdle
DH H McRae
1B P LaCock
CO J Wathan
M J Frey

MILWAUKEE

SP M Haas
SP M Caldwell
SP L Sorensen
SP B Travers
RS R Cleveland
RS B McClure
RP B Castro
RP J Augustine
C C Moore
1B C Cooper
2B P Molitor
SS R Yount
32 J Gantner
LF B Oglivie
CF G Thomas
RF S Lezcano
DR D Davis
3U- D Money
M1 B Rodgers
M2 G Bamberger
M3 B Rodgers

MINNESOTA

SP J Koosman
SP G Zahn
SP R Erickson
SP D Jackson
SP P Redfern
RP D Corbett
RP J Verhoeven
C B Wynegar
1B R Jackson
2B R Wilfong
SS R Smalley
3B J Castino
LM R Sofield
ML K Landreaux
RF H Powell
DH J Morales
DH G Adams
13 M Cubbage
2S P Mackanin
ML- D Edwards
M1 G Mauch
M2 J Goryl

NEW YORK

SP T John
SP R Guidry
SR T Underwood
SR R May
SP L Tiant
RP R Davis
RP R Gossage
RP D Bird
C R Cerone
1B B Watson
2B W Randolph
SS B Dent
3B- G Nettles
LF L Piniella
MO B Brown
RD R Jackson
D3- E Soderholm
OF B Murcer
1B- J Spencer
CF- R Jones
M D Howser

OAKLAND

SP R Langford
SP M Norris
SP M Keough
SP S McCatty
SP B Kingman
RP B Lacey
C- J Essian
1B D Revering
23 D McKay
SS M Guerrero
3B W Gross
LF R Henderson
CF D Murphy
RF T Armas
DH M Page
IC J Newman
CD- M Heath
S2- R Picciolo
M B Martin

SEATTLE

SP F Bannister
SP G Abbott
SP R Honeycutt
SP J Beattie
SR R Dressler
RP S Rawley
RP B McLaughlin
RP D Heaverlo
RP D Roberts
C L Cox
1B B Bochte
2B J Cruz
SS M Mendoza
3B- T Cox
LF D Meyer
OI J Simpson
RO L Roberts
DH- W Horton
S3 J Anderson
UI L Milbourne
OI T Paciorek
M1 D Johnson
M2 M Wills

TEXAS

SP J Matlack
SP D Medich
SP F Jenkins
SP G Perry
RP D Darwin
RP S Lyle
RP J Kern
C J Sundberg
1B P Putnam
2B B Wills
SS P Frias
3B B Bell
LF A Oliver
CF M Rivers
OI J Norris
DR R Zisk
RU J Grubb
IO D Roberts
D1 R Staub
SS- B Harrelson
UO B Sample
M P Corrales

TORONTO

SP J Clancy
SP D Stieb
SR P Mirabella
SR J Jefferson
RS J McLaughlin
RP J Garvin
RP T Buskey
RP B Moore
C E Whitt
1B J Mayberry
2B D Garcia
SS A Griffin
3B R Howell
UT B Bailor
UO B Bonnell
RF L Moseby
DH O Velez
LF A Woods
C- B Davis
M B Mattick

1980 NL

ATLANTA

SP P Niekro
SP D Alexander
SP T Boggs
SP R Matula
SP L McWilliams
RP R Camp
RP G Garber
RP P Hanna
RP A Hrabosky
C B Benedict
1B C Chambliss
2B G Hubbard
SS L Gomez
3B B Horner
LU J Burroughs
CF D Murphy
RF G Matthews
IO J Royster
UO- B Asselstine
S3- L Blanks
UT- M Lum
M B Cox

CHICAGO

SP R Reuschel
SP M Krukow
SP D Lamp
SR L McGlothen
RP B Sutter
RP B Caudill
RP D Tidrow
RS W Hernandez
C T Blackwell
1L B Buckner
2B M Tyson
SS I DeJesus
3B L Randle
LF- D Kingman
MR J Martin
RU M Vail
UT L Biittner
32 S Dillard
UO J Figueroa
23 M Kelleher
RU S Thompson
M1 P Gomez
M2 J Amalfitano

CINCINNATI

SP F Pastore
SP C Leibrandt
SP M LaCoss
SP T Seaver
SR P Moskau
RS M Soto
RP T Hume
RS J Price
RP D Bair
C J Bench
1B D Driessen
2B J Kennedy
SS D Concepcion
3B R Knight
LF G Foster
CF D Collins
RF K Griffey
CF C Geronimo
2B R Oester
M J McNamara

HOUSTON

SP J Niekro
SP N Ryan
SP K Forsch
SP V Ruhle
SR J Andujar
RP J Richard
RP D Smith
RP J Sambito
RP F LaCorte
C A Ashby
1I A Howe
2B J Morgan
SS C Reynolds
3B E Cabell
LF J Cruz
CF C Cedeno
RF T Puhl
2S R Landestoy
1U D Walling
1U- D Bergman
RU- J Leonard
M B Virdon

LOS ANGELES

SP J Reuss
SP B Welch
SP D Sutton
SP B Hooton
SP D Goltz
RS R Sutcliffe
RP B Castillo
RP S Howe
RP J Beckwith
C- S Yeager
1B S Garvey
2B D Lopes
SS B Russell
3B R Cey
LF D Baker
CF R Law
RF- R Smith
RU J Johnstone
UT D Thomas
UO- R Monday
M T Lasorda

MONTREAL

SP S Rogers
SP S Sanderson
SP B Gullickson
SP D Palmer
SP B Lee
RP C Lea
RP E Sosa
RS F Norman
RP W Fryman
C G Carter
1B W Cromartie
2B R Scott
SS C Speier
3B L Parrish
LF R LeFlore
CF A Dawson
RO R Office
LU J White
IF- T Bernazard
RF- E Valentine
M D Williams

NEW YORK

SP R Burris
SP P Zachry
SR M Bomback
SR P Falcone
SP C Swan
RP T Hausman
CL N Allen
RP J Reardon
RP E Glynn
C A Trevino
1M L Mazzilli
2B D Flynn
SS F Taveras
3B E Maddox
LF S Henderson
RM J Youngblood
RL- C Washington
1O M Jorgensen
MU- J Morales
C- J Stearns
M J Torre

PHILADELPHIA

SP S Carlton
SP D Ruthven
SP B Walk
SP R Lerch
CL T McGraw
RP R Reed
RP D Noles
RP K Saucier
C B Boone
1B P Rose
2B M Trillo
SS L Bowa
3B M Schmidt
LF G Luzinski
CF G Maddox
RF B McBride
OI G Gross
LO L Smith
UT- D Unser
M D Green

PITTSBURGH

SP J Bibby
SP J Candelaria
SP B Blyleven
SP D Robinson
SP R Rhoden
RP E Romo
RP K Tekulve
RS E Solomon
RP G Jackson
C E Ott
1U J Milner
2B P Garner
SS T Foli
3B B Madlock
LR M Easler
CF O Moreno
RF D Parker
LF L Lacy
UT B Robinson
3S- D Berra
M C Tanner

ST. LOUIS

SP P Vuckovich
SP B Forsch
SP B Sykes
SP S Martinez
RS J Kaat
RS D Hood
RP J Littlefield
RP J Urrea
C T Simmons
1B K Hernandez
2B K Oberkfell
SS G Templeton
3B K Reitz
LU- B Bonds
CF T Scott
RF G Hendrick
UT D Iorg
OI- L Durham
OC- T Kennedy
M1 K Boyer
M2 J Krol
M3 W Herzog
M4 R Schoendienst

SAN DIEGO

SP J Curtis
SS S Mura
SP R Jones
SP R Wise
SR G Lucas
RS B Shirley
RP R Fingers
RS E Rasmussen
RP D Kinney
C G Tenace
1B W Montanez
2B D Cash
SS O Smith
3B- A Rodriguez
LF G Richards
CF J Mumphrey
RF D Winfield
C- B Fahey
23- T Flannery
OF- J Turner
M J Coleman

SAN FRANCISCO

SP V Blue
SP B Knepper
SP E Whitson
SP J Montefusco
SP A Ripley
RP G Minton
RP G Lavelle
RP T Griffin
RP A Holland
C M May
1B- M Ivie
2B R Stennett
SS J LeMaster
3B D Evans
UO L Herndon
CF B North
RF J Clark
LF T Whitfield
OI- J Wohlford
M D Bristol

1981 AL

BALTIMORE

SP D Martinez
SP S McGregor
SP J Palmer
SP M Flanagan
RP S Stewart
RP T Martinez
RP T Stoddard
RP D Ford
C R Dempsey
1B E Murray
2B R Dauer
SS M Belanger
3B D DeCinces
LF J Lowenstein
CF A Bumbry
RL G Roenicke
DU T Crowley
LR J Dwyer
RD K Singleton
CU- D Graham
S2- L Sakata
M E Weaver

BOSTON

SP D Eckersley
SP F Tanana
SP M Torrez
SP J Tudor
SP B Ojeda
RP B Stanley
RP M Clear
RP T Burgmeier
RP B Campbell
C- R Gedman
1D T Perez
2B J Remy
SS G Hoffman
3B C Lansford
LF J Rice

CF R Miller
RF D Evans
D1 C Yastrzemski
UI D Stapleton
M *R Houk*

CALIFORNIA
SP G Zahn
SP K Forsch
SP M Witt
SP S Renko
RP A Hassler
RS J Jefferson
RP D Aase
RP L Sanchez
C E Ott
1B R Carew
2B B Grich
SS R Burleson
3B B Hobson
LC B Downing
CF F Lynn
RF D Ford
DH D Baylor
ML- J Beniquez
3B- B Campaneris
M1 *J Fregosi*
M2 *G Mauch*

CHICAGO
SP B Burns
SP R Dotson
SR D Lamp
SP S Trout
SP R Baumgarten
RP L Hoyt
RP E Farmer
RP K Hickey
C C Fisk
1B M Squires
2B T Bernazard
SS B Almon
3B J Morrison
LF R LeFlore
CF C Lemon
RF H Baines
DH G Luzinski
UO R Kuntz
RL W Nordhagen
M *T LaRussa*

CLEVELAND
SP B Blyleven
SP L Barker
SP J Denny
SP R Waits
RS D Spillner
RP S Monge
RP M Stanton
C- R Hassey
1B M Hargrove
2B D Kuiper
SS T Veryzer
3B T Harrah
LF M Dilone
CF R Manning
RF J Orta
DH A Thornton
UT A Bannister
C B Diaz
M *D Garcia*

DETROIT
SP J Morris
SP M Wilcox
SP D Petry
SP D Schatzeder
RS D Rozema
RP A Lopez
CL K Saucier
RP D Tobik
C L Parrish
1B R Hebner
2B L Whitaker
SS A Trammell
3B T Brookens
LF S Kemp
CF A Cowens
UO K Gibson
D1 J Wockenfuss
RU L Jones
3I- M Kelleher
1R- R Leach
MD- R Peters
DR- C Summers
M *S Anderson*

KANSAS CITY
SP D Leonard
SP L Gura
SP R Gale
SP P Splittorff
SP M Jones
RP D Quisenberry
RP R Martin
RP K Brett
C J Wathan
1B W Aikens
2B F White
SS U Washington
3B G Brett
LF W Wilson
CF A Otis
RF- C Geronimo
DH H McRae
M1 *J Frey*
M2 *D Howser*

MILWAUKEE
SP P Vuckovich
SP M Caldwell
SP M Haas
SP J Slaton
SP R Lerch
RP R Fingers
RP R Cleveland
RP J Easterly
RP J Augustine
C T Simmons
1B C Cooper
2B J Gantner
SS R Yount
3B- D Money
LF B Oglivie
OF G Thomas
RF- M Brouhard
DH- L Hisle
3U R Howell
MD- P Molitor
M *B Rodgers*

MINNESOTA
SP A Williams
SP P Redfern
SP F Arroyo
SP J Koosman
SP R Erickson
RP D Corbett
RP B Havens
RP D Cooper
RP J Verhoeven
C- S Butera
1U- D Goodwin
2B R Wilfong
SD- R Smalley
3B J Castino
LU G Ward
CF M Hatcher
RF D Engle
DH G Adams
UI P Mackanin
RU H Powell
1U- R Jackson
M1 *J Goryl*
M2 *B Gardner*

NEW YORK
SP R May
SP T John
SP R Guidry
SP D Righetti
SP R Reuschel
RP R Davis
CL R Gossage
RP D LaRoche
C R Cerone
1B- B Watson
2B W Randolph
SS B Dent
3B G Nettles
LF D Winfield
CF J Mumphrey
RD R Jackson
DU- B Murcer
OF O Gamble
SI- L Milbourne
OF- L Piniella
M1 *G Michael*
M2 *B Lemon*

OAKLAND
SP R Langford
SP S McCatty
SP M Norris
SP M Keough
SP B Kingman
RP J Jones
RP B Owchinko
C M Heath
1B- J Spencer
2B- S Babitt
SS R Picciolo
3B W Gross
LF R Henderson
CF D Murphy
RF T Armas
DH C Johnson
32 D McKay
C1 J Newman
SS F Stanley
M *B Martin*

SEATTLE
SP G Abbott
SP F Bannister
SP K Clay
SR M Parrott
SP J Gleaton
RS B Clark
RP G Rawley
RP L Andersen
RP J Beattie
C J Narron
1B B Bochte
2B J Cruz
SS J Anderson
32 L Randle
LF T Paciorek
CF J Simpson
RF J Burroughs
DH R Zisk
UT G Gray
3U D Meyer
C- B Bulling
MR- D Henderson
M1 *M Wills*
M2 *R Lachemann*

TEXAS
SP D Darwin
SP D Medich
SP R Honeycutt
SP F Jenkins
SP J Matlack
RP S Comer
RS C Hough
RP D Schmidt
C J Sundberg
1B P Putnam
2B B Wills
SS M Mendoza
3B B Bell
LF B Sample
CF M Rivers
RL L Roberts
DH A Oliver
RF J Grubb
M *D Zimmer*

TORONTO
SP D Stieb
SR L Leal
SP J Clancy
SP J Todd
SP M Bomback
RP J Berenguer
RP J McLaughlin
RP R Jackson
RP J Garvin
C E Whitt
1B J Mayberry
2B D Garcia
SS A Griffin
3B D Ainge
LF A Woods
CF L Moseby
RM B Bonnell
DH O Velez
2I G Iorg
OF- G Bell
UT- W Upshaw
M *B Mattick*

1981 NL

ATLANTA
SP G Perry
SP T Boggs
SP P Niekro
SR R Mahler
SR J Montefusco
RP R Camp
RP G Garber
RP P Hanna
RP A Hrabosky
C B Benedict
1B C Chambliss
2B G Hubbard
SS R Ramirez
3B B Horner
LF R Linares
CF D Murphy
RF C Washington
IF- J Royster
OF- B Asselstine
IC- B Pocoroba
M *B Cox*

CHICAGO
SP M Krukow
SR R Martz
SP R Reuschel
SR K Kravec
SP D Bird
RP D Tidrow
RS B Caudill
RP L Smith
RS L McGlothen
C- J Davis
1B B Buckner
2U- M Tyson
SS I DeJesus
3B K Reitz
LF S Henderson
MO J Morales
RF L Durham
C- T Blackwell
OI- S Thompson
M *J Amalfitano*

CINCINNATI
SP M Soto
SP T Seaver
SP F Pastore
SP B Berenyi
SP M LaCoss
RP T Hume
RP J Price
RP P Moskau
RP D Bair
C J Nolan
1B D Driessen
2B R Oester
SS D Concepcion
3B R Knight
LF G Foster
CF K Griffey
RF D Collins
RU S Mejias
C- M O'Berry
M *J McNamara*

HOUSTON
SP J Niekro
SP D Sutton
SP B Knepper
SP N Ryan
SP V Ruhle
RP D Smith
RP J Sambito
RP F LaCorte
C A Ashby
1M C Cedeno
2U- J Pittman
SS C Reynolds
3B A Howe
LF J Cruz
CF- T Scott
RU T Puhl
UT- D Walling
RU- G Woods
M *B Virdon*

LOS ANGELES
SP F Valenzuela
SP J Reuss
SP B Hooton
SP B Welch
RS D Goltz
RP S Howe
RP B Castillo
RP D Stewart
C M Scioscia
1B S Garvey
2B- D Lopes
SS B Russell
3B R Cey
LF D Baker
CF K Landreaux
RU P Guerrero
UT D Thomas
OI- J Johnstone
RU R Monday
M *T Lasorda*

MONTREAL
SP S Rogers
SP B Gullickson
SP S Sanderson
SP R Burris
RS B Lee
RP S Bahnsen
RP W Fryman
RP J Reardon
C G Carter
1R W Cromartie
2B R Scott
SS C Speier
3B L Parrish
LF T Raines
CF A Dawson
UO- J White
UT T Wallach
M1 *D Williams*
M2 *J Fanning*

NEW YORK
SP P Zachry
SP M Scott
SP E Lynch
SP G Harris
RS P Falcone
RP N Allen
RP D Miller
RP R Searage
C J Stearns
1L D Kingman
2B D Flynn
SS F Taveras
3B H Brooks
LM L Mazzilli
MU M Wilson
RF- E Valentine
U1 M Cubbage
UT M Jorgensen
1U R Staub
C- A Trevino
M *J Torre*

PHILADELPHIA
SP S Carlton
SP D Ruthven
SP L Christenson
SP N Espinosa
RP S Lyle
RP R Reed
RP M Proly
RP T McGraw
C B Boone
1B P Rose
2B M Trillo
SS L Bowa
3B M Schmidt
LF G Matthews
CF G Maddox
RF- B McBride
UO G Gross
C- K Moreland
UO- L Smith
UT- D Unser
M *D Green*

PITTSBURGH
SP R Rhoden
SP E Solomon
SP J Bibby
SP P Perez
RS R Scurry
RP K Tekulve
RP E Romo
RP D Robinson
C T Pena
1B J Thompson
2B- P Garner
SS T Foli
3B B Madlock
LF M Easler
CF O Moreno
RF D Parker
3S D Berra
OI L Lacy
C- S Nicosia
M *C Tanner*

ST. LOUIS
SP L Sorensen
SP B Forsch
SP J Martin
SP S Martinez
SR B Shirley
RP B Sutter
RP J Kaat
RP M Littell
RP B Sykes
C- D Porter
1B K Hernandez
2B T Herr
SS G Templeton
3B K Oberkfell
LU D Iorg
RM G Hendrick
OF S Lezcano
LR T Landrum
CU- G Tenace
M *W Herzog*

SAN DIEGO
SP J Eichelberger
SP S Mura
SP C Welsh
SP R Wise
SR T Lollar
RP G Lucas
RS J Curtis
RP J Littlefield
RP D Boone
C T Kennedy
1B B Perkins
2B J Bonilla
SS O Smith
3B L Salazar
LF G Richards
CF R Jones
RF J Lefebvre
1U R Bass
RU- D Edwards
UI- B Evans
M *F Howard*

SAN FRANCISCO
SP D Alexander
SP T Griffin
SP V Blue
SP E Whitson
SP A Ripley
RP A Holland
RP G Minton
RP F Breining
RP G Lavelle
C M May
1U E Cabell
2B J Morgan
SS J LeMaster
3B D Evans
LF L Herndon
CF J Martin
RF J Clark
1U- D Bergman
M *F Robinson*

1982 AL

BALTIMORE
SP D Martinez
SP M Flanagan
SP J Palmer
SP S McGregor
RS S Stewart
RP T Martinez
RS S Davis
RP T Stoddard
C R Dempsey
1B E Murray
2B R Dauer
2S L Sakata
S3 C Ripken
LR G Roenicke
CF A Bumbry
RF D Ford
DH K Singleton
LF J Lowenstein
M *E Weaver*

BOSTON
SP D Eckersley
SP J Tudor
SP M Torrez
SP C Rainey
SP B Hurst
RP B Stanley
RP M Clear
RP T Burgmeier
RP L Aponte
C- G Allenson
1I D Stapleton
2B J Remy
SS G Hoffman
3B C Lansford
LF J Rice
CF R Miller
RF D Evans
DH C Yastrzemski
IO W Boggs
C- R Gedman
ML- R Nichols
M *R Houk*

CALIFORNIA
SP G Zahn
SP K Forsch
SP M Witt
SP S Renko
SR B Kison
RP L Sanchez
RP A Hassler
RP D Corbett
RP D Aase
C B Boone
1B R Carew
2B B Grich
SS T Foli
3B D DeCinces
LF B Downing
CF F Lynn
RF R Jackson
DH D Baylor
UO J Beniquez
RO B Clark
M *G Mauch*

CHICAGO
SP L Hoyt
SP R Dotson
SR D Lamp
SR J Koosman
SP B Burns
RP S Barojas
RP S Trout
RP K Hickey
RP C Escarrega
C C Fisk
1B M Squires
2B T Bernazard
SS B Almon
3B A Rodriguez
LF S Kemp
MU R Law
RF H Baines
DH G Luzinski
S3 V Law
1B T Paciorek
UO- J Hairston
CF- R LeFlore
M *T LaRussa*

CLEVELAND
SP L Barker
SP R Sutcliffe
SP L Sorensen
SP J Denny
SP R Waits
RP D Spillner
RS E Whitson
RP E Glynn
C R Hassey
1B M Hargrove
2B- J Perconte
SS M Fischlin
3B T Harrah
LF M Dilone
CF R Manning
RF V Hayes
DH A Thornton
UT A Bannister
2B- L Milbourne
M *D Garcia*

DETROIT
SP J Morris
SP D Petry
SP M Wilcox
SP J Ujdur
SR P Underwood
RP D Tobik
RP E Sosa
RP D Rucker
C L Parrish
13 E Cabell
2B L Whitaker
SS A Trammell
3B T Brookens
LF L Herndon
CF- G Wilson
RU C Lemon
DH- M Ivie
1U- R Leach
DU- J Turner
M *S Anderson*

KANSAS CITY
SP L Gura
SP V Blue
SP P Splittorff
SP D Leonard
RP D Quisenberry
RP M Armstrong
RP D Hood
C J Wathan
1B W Aikens
2B F White
SS U Washington
3B G Brett
LF W Wilson
CF A Otis
RF J Martin
DH H McRae
M *D Howser*

MILWAUKEE
SP M Caldwell
SP P Vuckovich
SP M Haas
SP B McClure
SP R Lerch
RS J Slaton
CL R Fingers
RP D Bernard
C T Simmons
1B C Cooper
2B J Gantner
SS R Yount
3B P Molitor
LF B Oglivie
CF G Thomas
RF C Moore
DH R Howell
DI- D Money
M1 *B Rodgers*
M2 *H Kuenn*

MINNESOTA
SR B Castillo
SP B Havens
SP A Williams
SP J O'Connor
SP F Viola
RP R Davis
RS T Felton
RP J Pacella
RP P Boris
C- T Laudner
1B K Hrbek
2B J Castino
SS R Washington
3B G Gaetti
LF G Ward
CF B Mitchell
RF T Brunansky
DH- R Johnson
SS- L Faedo
OI- M Hatcher
M *B Gardner*

NEW YORK
SP R Guidry
SP T John
SP D Righetti
SR S Rawley
SP M Morgan
CL R Gossage
RP G Frazier
RS R May
RP D LaRoche
C- R Cerone
1B- J Mayberry
2B W Randolph
S3 R Smalley
3B G Nettles
LF D Winfield
CF J Mumphrey
RF K Griffey
DR O Gamble
OI D Collins
DR L Piniella
M1 *B Lemon*
M2 *G Michael*
M3 *C King*

OAKLAND
SP R Langford
SP M Keough
SP M Norris
SP S McCatty
SP B Kingman
RS T Underwood
RP B Owchinko
RP D Beard
C M Heath
UT D Meyer
2B D Lopes
SS F Stanley
3B W Gross
LF R Henderson
CF D Murphy
RF T Armas
DU- C Johnson
OF J Burroughs
M *B Martin*

SEATTLE
SP F Bannister
SP G Perry
SP J Beattie
SP M Moore
SP G Nelson
CL B Caudill
RS B Clark
RP L Andersen
RP E Vande Berg
C- R Sweet
1B- G Gray
2B J Cruz
SS T Cruz
3B M Castillo
LU B Bochte
CF D Henderson
RF A Cowens
DH R Zisk
ML J Simpson
M *R Lachemann*

TEXAS
SP C Hough
SP F Tanana
SP R Honeycutt
SR J Matlack
SP D Medich
RS D Schmidt
RP S Comer
RP D Darwin
RP P Mirabella
C J Sundberg
1B D Hostetler
2B M Richardt
SS- M Wagner
3B B Bell
LF- B Sample
CF G Wright
RF L Parrish
DU L Johnson
OF J Grubb
2S- D Flynn
IO- B Stein
M1 *D Zimmer*
M2 *D Johnson*

TORONTO
SP D Stieb
SP J Clancy
SP L Leal
SP J Gott
RP D Murray
RP R Jackson
RP J McLaughlin
RP J Garvin
C E Whitt
1B W Upshaw
2B D Garcia
SS A Griffin
3B R Mulliniks
LM B Bonnell
CF L Moseby
RF J Barfield
DH- D Revering
3B G Iorg
RU H Powell
C- B Martinez
LF- A Woods
M *B Cox*

1982 NL

ATLANTA

SP P Niekro
SP R Mahler
SR R Camp
SP B Walk
RP S Bedrosian
RP G Garber
C B Benedict
1B C Chambliss
2B G Hubbard
SS R Ramirez
3B B Horner
LU- R Linares
ML D Murphy
RF C Washington
3U J Royster
CF- B Butler
OF- L Whisenton
M *J Torre*

CHICAGO

SP F Jenkins
SP D Bird
SP D Noles
SP R Martz
SP A Ripley
RS L Smith
RP D Tidrow
RP B Campbell
RP W Hernandez
C J Davis
1B B Buckner
2B B Wills
SS L Bowa
3B R Sandberg
OC K Moreland
ML G Woods
RM L Durham
RL J Johnstone
2S J Kennedy
LF- S Henderson
M *L Elia*

CINCINNATI

SP M Soto
SP B Berenyi
SP F Pastore
SR B Shirley
SP T Seaver
RS C Leibrandt
RS G Harris
CL T Hume
RP J Kern
C A Trevino
1B D Driessen
2B R Oester
SS D Concepcion
3B J Bench
LR E Milner
CF C Cedeno
RF P Householder
OI- L Biittner
3U- W Krenchicki
UO- D Walker
M1 *J McNamara*
M2 *R Nixon*

HOUSTON

SP J Niekro
SP N Ryan
SP D Sutton
SP B Knepper
SR V Ruhle
RS M LaCoss
RP F LaCorte
RP D Smith
C A Ashby
13 R Knight
2B P Garner
SS D Thon
31 A Howe
LF J Cruz
CF T Scott
RF T Puhl
OI- D Heep
OI- D Walling
M1 *B Virdon*
M2 *B Lillis*

LOS ANGELES

SP F Valenzuela
SP J Reuss
SP B Welch
SP B Hooton
RS D Stewart
RP S Howe
RP T Forster
RP T Niedenfuer
C M Scioscia
1B S Garvey
2B S Sax
SS B Russell
3B R Cey
LF D Baker
CF K Landreaux
RM P Guerrero
OI R Monday
UO R Roenicke
OF- J Orta
C- S Yeager
M *T Lasorda*

MONTREAL

SP S Rogers
SP B Gullickson
SP S Sanderson
SP C Lea
SR R Burris
RP J Reardon
RP W Fryman
RP B Smith
C G Carter
1B A Oliver
2B- D Flynn
SS C Speier
3B T Wallach
LF T Raines
CF A Dawson
RF W Cromartie
M *J Fanning*

NEW YORK

SR P Falcone
SR C Puleo
SR C Swan
SR M Scott
SR P Zachry
RS E Lynch
RP J Orosco
RP R Jones
CL N Allen
C J Stearns
1B D Kingman
2B- W Backman
SS R Gardenhire
3B H Brooks
LF G Foster
CF M Wilson
RU E Valentine
S2 B Bailor
UT M Jorgensen
OI R Staub
M *G Bamberger*

PHILADELPHIA

SP S Carlton
SP L Christenson
SP M Krukow
SP D Ruthven
RP R Reed
RP E Farmer
RP S Monge
C B Diaz
1B P Rose
2B M Trillo
SS I DeJesus
3B M Schmidt
LF G Matthews
CF G Maddox
RF G Vukovich
UO G Gross
MR B Dernier
M *P Corrales*

PITTSBURGH

SP R Rhoden
SP D Robinson
SP J Candelaria
SR M Sarmiento
SP L McWilliams
RP K Tekulve
RP R Scurry
RP E Romo
C T Pena
1B J Thompson
2B J Ray
SS D Berra
3B B Madlock
LF M Easler
CF O Moreno
RL L Lacy
M *C Tanner*

ST. LOUIS

SP J Andujar
SP B Forsch
SP S Mura
SR D LaPoint
SP J Stuper
RP B Sutter
RP D Bair
RP J Kaat
RS J Martin
C D Porter
1B K Hernandez
2B T Herr
SS O Smith
3B K Oberkfell
LF L Smith
CF W McGee
RF G Hendrick
UT D Iorg
IO M Ramsey
M *W Herzog*

SAN DIEGO

SP T Lollar
SP J Montefusco
SP J Eichelberger
SP C Welsh
SP J Curtis
RS E Show
RP L DeLeon
RP G Lucas
RS D Dravecky
C T Kennedy
1B B Perkins
2B T Flannery
SS G Templeton
3B L Salazar
LF G Richards
CF R Jones
RF S Lezcano
UT J Lefebvre
M *D Williams*

SAN FRANCISCO

SP B Laskey
SP A Hammaker
SP R Gale
SP R Martin
RP G Minton
RS F Breining
RS A Holland
RS J Barr
C M May
1B R Smith
2B J Morgan
SS J LeMaster
31 D Evans
LU- J Leonard
CF C Davis
RF J Clark
1U D Bergman
U3 D Kuiper
LU- J Wohlford
3B- T O'Malley
M *F Robinson*

1983 AL

BALTIMORE

SP S McGregor
SP S Davis
SP M Boddicker
SP D Martinez
SP M Flanagan
RP S Stewart
RP T Martinez
RP T Stoddard
C R Dempsey
1B E Murray
2B R Dauer
SS C Ripken
3B- T Cruz
LF J Lowenstein
CF J Shelby
RF D Ford
OI J Dwyer
CF A Bumbry
LO G Roenicke
DH K Singleton
M *J Altobelli*

BOSTON

SP J Tudor
SP B Hurst
SP D Eckersley
SP B Ojeda
SP M Brown
RP B Stanley
RP M Clear
RP O Boyd
RP L Aponte
C- G Allenson
1B D Stapleton
2B J Remy
SS G Hoffman
3B W Boggs
LF J Rice
CF T Armas
RF D Evans
DH C Yastrzemski
OI R Miller
OI R Nichols
C- R Gedman
M *R Houk*

CALIFORNIA

SP T John
SP K Forsch
SP G Zahn
SR M Witt
SP B Kison
RP L Sanchez
RP J Curtis
C B Boone
1U R Carew
2B B Grich
SS- T Foli
3B- D DeCinces
LU B Downing
CF F Lynn
RF- E Valentine
DR Re Jackson
UT Ro Jackson
1D D Sconiers
UO- J Beniquez
M *J McNamara*

CHICAGO

SP L Hoyt
SP R Dotson
SP F Bannister
SP B Burns
SR J Koosman
RS D Lamp
RP S Barojas
RP D Tidrow
C C Fisk
1B M Squires
2B J Cruz
SS J Dybzinski
3B V Law
LF R Kittle
CF R Law
RF H Baines
DH G Luzinski
SS S Fletcher
UO J Hairston
1L T Paciorek
1U G Walker
M *T LaRussa*

CLEVELAND

SP R Sutcliffe
SP L Sorensen
SP B Blyleven
SR N Heaton
SP L Barker
RS J Eichelberger
RP D Spillner
RP B Anderson
RP J Easterly
C R Hassey
1B M Hargrove
2B- M Trillo
SS J Franco
3B T Harrah
UT A Bannister
CF G Thomas
RF G Vukovich
DH A Thornton
LU P Tabler
2U- M Fischlin
M1 *M Ferraro*
M2 *P Corrales*

DETROIT

SP J Morris
SP D Petry
SP M Wilcox
SR J Berenguer
SR D Rozema
RP A Lopez
RP H Bailey
RP D Bair
C L Parrish
1B E Cabell
2B L Whitaker
SS A Trammell
3I T Brookens
LF L Herndon
CF C Lemon
RF G Wilson
DO K Gibson
1U R Leach
UC- J Wockenfuss
M *S Anderson*

KANSAS CITY

SP L Gura
SP B Black
SP P Splittorff
SP S Renko
RP D Quisenberry
RP M Armstrong
C1 J Wathan
1B W Aikens
2B F White
SS U Washington
3B G Brett
ML W Wilson
MR A Otis
UO P Sheridan
DH H McRae
UO- L Roberts
1O- J Simpson
C- D Slaught
M *D Howser*

MILWAUKEE

SP M Caldwell
SP D Sutton
SP M Haas
SP B McClure
SP C Porter
RP J Slaton
RP T Tellmann
RS B Gibson
CL P Ladd
C- N Yost
1B C Cooper
2B J Gantner
SS R Yount
3B P Molitor
LF B Oglivie
CF R Manning
RF C Moore
CD T Simmons
M *H Kuenn*

MINNESOTA

SP F Viola
SP K Schrom
SP A Williams
SP B Castillo
RP R Lysander
CL R Davis
RP L Whitehouse
RP M Walters
CU D Engle
1B K Hrbek
2B J Castino
SS R Washington
3B G Gaetti
LF G Ward
CF- D Brown
RF T Brunansky
DH R Bush
UT M Hatcher
M *B Gardner*

NEW YORK

SP R Guidry
SP S Rawley
SP D Righetti
SP B Shirley
RP G Frazier
CL R Gossage
RP D Murray
C- B Wynegar
1B K Griffey
2B W Randolph
SI R Smalley
3B G Nettles
LF D Winfield
CF- J Mumphrey
RF S Kemp
DH D Baylor
SS A Robertson
UT- D Mattingly
M *B Martin*

OAKLAND

SP C Codiroli
SR S McCatty
SR T Conroy
SP B Krueger
RS T Underwood
RP T Burgmeier
RP K Atherton
RP D Beard
C B Kearney
13 W Gross
2B D Lopes
S2 T Phillips
3B- C Lansford
LF R Henderson
CF D Murphy
RF M Davis
DH J Burroughs
UT B Almon
OI G Hancock
C- M Heath
M *S Boros*

SEATTLE

SP M Young
SP J Beattie
SR B Stoddard
SR B Clark
SP M Moore
RP G Perry
CL B Caudill
RP R Thomas
RP M Stanton
C- R Sweet
1B P Putnam
2B- T Bernazard
SS- S Owen
3B- J Allen
LF S Henderson
MR D Henderson
RD A Cowens
DH- R Zisk
3U- M Castillo
UO- J Moses
RL R Nelson
M1 *R Lachemann*
M2 *D Crandall*

TEXAS

SP C Hough
SP M Smithson
SP D Darwin
SP R Honeycutt
SP F Tanana
RS J Butcher
RP O Jones
C J Sundberg
1B P O'Brien
2B W Tolleson
SS B Dent
3B B Bell
LF B Sample
CF G Wright
RF L Parrish
DH- D Hostetler
DU- M Rivers
M *D Rader*

TORONTO

SP D Stieb
SP J Clancy
SP L Leal
SP J Gott
SP D Alexander
RS J Acker
RP R Jackson
RP J McLaughlin
RP R Moffitt
C E Whitt
1B W Upshaw
2B D Garcia
SS A Griffin
3B R Mulliniks
LR B Bonnell
CF L Moseby
RF J Barfield
DH C Johnson
LF D Collins
32 G Iorg
DU J Orta
C- B Martinez
M *B Cox*

1983 NL

ATLANTA

SP C McMurtry
SP P Perez
SP P Niekro
SR R Camp
SR P Roenicke
RP S Bedrosian
RP K Dayley
RP T Forster
RP D Moore
C B Benedict
1B C Chambliss
2B G Hubbard
SS R Ramirez
3B B Horner
LM B Butler
CF D Murphy
RF C Washington
3U- R Johnson
32- J Royster
M *J Torre*

CHICAGO

SP C Rainey
SP S Trout
SP F Jenkins
SP D Ruthven
SP D Noles
RP L Smith
RP B Campbell
RS C Lefferts
RP M Proly
C J Davis
1B B Buckner
2B R Sandberg
SS L Bowa
3B R Cey
LM L Durham
CF M Hall
RF K Moreland
OF- J Johnstone
OI- G Woods
M1 *L Elia*
M2 *C Fox*

CINCINNATI

SP M Soto
SP B Berenyi
SP F Pastore
SP J Price
SP C Puleo
RS T Power
RP B Scherrer
RS R Gale
RP B Hayes
C D Bilardello
1B D Driessen
2B R Oester
SS D Concepcion
3B- N Esasky
LF G Redus
CF E Milner
RM P Householder
IO J Bench
RU C Cedeno
OF D Walker
M *R Nixon*

HOUSTON

SP J Niekro
SP B Knepper
SP N Ryan
SP M Scott
SR M LaCoss
RS V Ruhle
RP B Dawley
CL F DiPino
RP D Smith
C- A Ashby
1B R Knight
2B B Doran
SS D Thon
3B P Garner
LF J Cruz
CF- O Moreno
RF T Puhl
UT D Walling
RU- K Bass
M *B Lillis*

LOS ANGELES

SP F Valenzuela
SP J Reuss
SP B Welch
SP A Pena
SP B Hooton
RP T Niedenfuer
CL S Howe
RP D Stewart
RP J Beckwith
C S Yeager
1B G Brock
2B S Sax
SS B Russell
3B P Guerrero
LF D Baker
CF K Landreaux
RF M Marshall
UT D Thomas
OI R Monday
RO- R Roenicke
M *T Lasorda*

MONTREAL

SP S Rogers
SP B Gullickson
SP C Lea
SR R Burris
RS B Smith
RP J Reardon
RP D Schatzeder
RP B James
C G Carter
1B A Oliver
2S D Flynn
SS- C Speier
3B T Wallach
LF T Raines
CF A Dawson
RF W Cromartie
OI T Francona
S2 B Little
RU- J Wohlford
M *B Virdon*

NEW YORK

SP T Seaver
SP M Torrez
SP E Lynch
SP W Terrell
RP J Orosco
RP D Sisk
RS S Holman
RP C Diaz
C R Hodges
1B- K Hernandez
2B B Giles
SS J Oquendo
3B H Brooks
LF G Foster
CF M Wilson
RF D Strawberry
S2 B Bailor
OI D Heep
1U D Kingman
UT R Staub
M1 *G Bamberger*
M2 *F Howard*

PHILADELPHIA

SP S Carlton
SP J Denny
SP C Hudson
SP M Bystrom
CL A Holland
RP R Reed
RP W Hernandez
RP T McGraw
C B Diaz
1U P Rose
2B J Morgan
SS I DeJesus
3B M Schmidt
LF G Matthews
CF- G Maddox
RM V Hayes
LO G Gross
RU J Lefebvre
MR B Dernier
2S- K Garcia
1B- T Perez
M1 *P Corrales*
M2 *P Owens*

PITTSBURGH

SP R Rhoden
SP L McWilliams
SP J Candelaria
SR L Tunnell
SP J DeLeon
RP K Tekulve
RP C Guante
RP M Sarmiento
RP R Scurry
C T Pena
1B J Thompson
2B J Ray
SS D Berra
3B B Madlock
LF M Easler
CF M Wynne
RF D Parker
LR L Lacy
OI L Mazzilli
M *C Tanner*

ST. LOUIS

SP J Andujar
SR J Stuper
SP D LaPoint
SP B Forsch
SP N Allen
CL B Sutter
RP J Lahti
RP D Von Ohlen
RS J Martin
C D Porter
1R G Hendrick
2B- T Herr
SS O Smith
3B K Oberkfell
LF L Smith
CF W McGee
RO D Green
2I- M Ramsey
UT A Van Slyke
M *W Herzog*

SAN DIEGO

SP E Show
SP D Dravecky
SP T Lollar
SR E Whitson
SP A Hawkins
RP L DeLeon
RP M Thurmond
RP G Lucas
RP S Monge
C T Kennedy
1B S Garvey
2B J Bonilla
SS G Templeton
3B L Salazar
OI A Wiggins
CF R Jones
RF- S Lezcano
3I- T Flannery
RL- T Gwynn
LU- G Richards
M *D Williams*

SAN FRANCISCO

SP F Breining
SP M Krukow
SP A Hammaker
SP B Laskey
SR A McGaffigan
RP G Minton
RP M Davis
CL G Lavelle
RP J Barr
C B Brenly
1B D Evans
2B- B Wellman
SS J LeMaster
3B T O'Malley
LF J Leonard
CF C Davis
RF J Clark
2U J Youngblood
1U- D Bergman
UO- M Venable
M *F Robinson*

1984 AL

BALTIMORE

SP M Boddicker
SP M Flanagan
SP S Davis
SP S McGregor
SR D Martinez
RP T Martinez
RP S Stewart
RP T Underwood

RS B Swaggerty
C R Dempsey
1B E Murray
2B R Dauer
SS C Ripken
3B W Gross
LR G Roenicke
CF J Shelby
RL M Young
DH K Singleton
MU A Bumbry
LU J Lowenstein
3B- T Cruz
C- F Rayford
2B- L Sakata
M J Altobelli

BOSTON
SP B Hurst
SP B Ojeda
SP O Boyd
SP A Nipper
SP R Clemens
RP B Stanley
RP M Clear
RP J Johnson
RP S Crawford
C R Gedman
1B B Buckner
2B M Barrett
SS J Gutierrez
3B W Boggs
LF J Rice
CF T Armas
RF D Evans
DH M Easler
OI- R Miller
M R Houk

CALIFORNIA
SP M Witt
SP R Romanick
SP G Zahn
SP T John
SR J Slaton
RP L Sanchez
RP D Corbett
RP C Kaufman
C B Boone
1B- R Carew
2B R Wilfong
SS D Schofield
3B D DeCinces
LF B Downing
CF G Pettis
RF F Lynn
DH R Jackson
LR J Beniquez
2B B Grich
SS- R Picciolo
M J McNamara

CHICAGO
SP R Dotson
SP T Seaver
SP L Hoyt
SP F Bannister
SR B Burns
RP R Reed
RP J Agosto
C C Fisk
1U G Walker
2B J Cruz
SS S Fletcher
3B V Law
LF R Kittle
CF R Law
RF H Baines
DH G Luzinski
UO J Hairston
1O T Paciorek
1U M Squires
SS- J Dybzinski
M T LaRussa

CLEVELAND
SP B Blyleven
SP N Heaton
SP S Comer
SR S Farr
RP E Camacho
RP T Waddell
RP M Jeffcoat
RP J Easterly
C- J Willard
1B M Hargrove
2B T Bernazard
SS J Franco
3B B Jacoby
LF- M Hall
CF B Butler
RF G Vukovich
DH A Thornton
IO P Tabler
RF- C Castillo
2I- M Fischlin
M P Corrales

DETROIT
SP J Morris
SP D Petry
SP M Wilcox
SP J Berenguer
SR D Rozema
RP W Hernandez
RP A Lopez
RP D Bair
C L Parrish
1B D Bergman
2B L Whitaker
SS A Trammell
3B H Johnson
LF L Herndon
CF C Lemon
RF K Gibson
IF D Evans
3I T Brookens
1U B Garbey
OF- J Grubb
UO- R Kuntz
M S Anderson

KANSAS CITY
SP B Black
SP M Gubicza
SP L Gura
SR B Saberhagen
SP C Leibrandt
RP D Quisenberry
RP J Beckwith
RP M Huismann
C D Slaught
1B S Balboni
2B F White
SS- O Concepcion
3B G Pryor
LR D Motley
CF W Wilson
RM P Sheridan
DH H McRae
3B G Brett
DU J Orta
C1- J Wathan
M D Howser

MILWAUKEE
SP D Sutton
SP M Haas
SP J Cocanower
SP B McClure
SR M Caldwell
RP P Ladd
RP T Tellmann
RP R Waits
C J Sundberg
1B C Cooper
2B J Gantner
SS R Yount
3S E Romero
LF B Oglivie
CF R Manning
RO D James
D1 T Simmons
M R Lachemann

MINNESOTA
SP F Viola
SP M Smithson
SP J Butcher
SP K Schrom
SR E Hodge
RS P Filson
CL R Davis
RP R Lysander
C D Engle
1B K Hrbek
2B T Teufel
SS H Jimenez
3B G Gaetti
LU M Hatcher
CF K Puckett
RF T Brunansky
DH R Bush
OF- D Brown
C- T Laudner
SS- R Washington
M B Gardner

NEW YORK
SP P Niekro
SP R Guidry
SR R Fontenot
SP D Rasmussen
CL D Righetti
RS B Shirley
RP J Howell
RS J Rijo
C B Wynegar
1B D Mattingly
2B W Randolph
SS B Meacham
3B- T Harrah
OI K Griffey
CF O Moreno
RF D Winfield
DH D Baylor
LF- S Kemp
M Y Berra

OAKLAND
SP R Burris
SR L Sorensen
SP S McCatty
SP B Krueger
SP C Young
CL B Caudill
RP K Atherton
C M Heath
1B B Bochte
2B J Morgan
S2 T Phillips
3B C Lansford
LF R Henderson
CF D Murphy
RF M Davis
DH D Kingman
UT B Almon
SI- M Wagner
M1 S Boros
M2 J Moore

SEATTLE
SP M Langston
SP M Moore
SP J Beattie
SR E Vande Berg
SP M Young
RP D Beard
RS B Stoddard
RP E Nunez
RP P Mirabella
C B Kearney
1B A Davis
2B J Perconte
SS S Owen
3B- J Presley
ML P Bradley
CF D Henderson
RF A Cowens
DH K Phelps
LO B Bonnell
UT S Henderson
M1 D Crandall
M2 C Cottier

TEXAS
SP C Hough
SP F Tanana
SP D Darwin
SP D Stewart
SR M Mason
RP D Schmidt
RP O Jones
C- D Scott
1B P O'Brien
2B W Tolleson
SS C Wilkerson
3B B Bell
LM B Sample
MR G Wright
UO G Ward
RD L Parrish
UO M Rivers
M D Rader

TORONTO
SP D Stieb
SP D Alexander
SP L Leal
SP J Clancy
SR J Gott
RP R Jackson
RP D Lamp
RP J Acker
RP J Key
C E Whitt
1B W Upshaw
2B D Garcia
SS A Griffin
3B R Mulliniks
LF D Collins
CF L Moseby
RL G Bell
DH C Johnson
RU J Barfield
3B G Iorg
C B Martinez
DH- W Aikens
SS- T Fernandez
M B Cox

1984 NL

ATLANTA
SP R Mahler
SP P Perez
SP C McMurtry
SR R Camp
SP L Barker
RS P Falcone
RP G Garber
RP S Bedrosian
RP J Dedmon
C- B Benedict
1B C Chambliss
2B G Hubbard
SS R Ramirez
3B- R Johnson
RL- B Komminsk
CF D Murphy
RF C Washington
1L G Perry
LU- A Hall
IO- J Royster
M J Torre

CHICAGO
SP S Trout
SP D Eckersley
SP R Sutcliffe
SP S Sanderson
SP D Ruthven
RP L Smith
RP T Stoddard
RS R Bordi
RP W Brusstar
C J Davis
1B L Durham
2B R Sandberg
SS L Bowa
3B R Cey
LF G Matthews
CF B Dernier
RI K Moreland
UO H Cotto
OI- G Woods
M J Frey

CINCINNATI
SP M Soto
SP J Russell
SP J Price
SP J Tibbs
RP T Power
RS T Hume
RP B Owchinko
RP J Franco
C B Gulden
1B- D Driessen
2B R Oester
S3 D Concepcion
3U N Esasky
LF G Redus
CF E Milner
RF D Parker
OI C Cedeño
SS T Foley
3U- W Krenchicki
LO- D Walker
M1 V Rapp
M2 P Rose

HOUSTON
SP J Niekro
SP B Knepper
SP N Ryan
SP M Scott
SR M LaCoss
RP B Dawley
RS V Ruhle
RP F DiPino
RP D Smith
C M Bailey
1B E Cabell
2B B Doran
SS C Reynolds
32 P Garner
LF J Cruz
CF J Mumphrey
RF T Puhl
OF K Bass
31- R Knight
3U- D Walling
M B Lillis

LOS ANGELES
SP F Valenzuela
SP A Pena
SR O Hershiser
SP R Honeycutt
SP B Welch
RS B Hooton
RS J Reuss
RP P Zachry
RP K Howell
C M Scioscia
1B- G Brock
2B S Sax
SS D Anderson
3B- G Rivera
LF M Marshall
CF K Landreaux
RM C Maldonado
3R P Guerrero
SU- B Russell
1O- F Stubbs
UO- T Whitfield
M T Lasorda

MONTREAL
SP B Gullickson
SP C Lea
SP B Smith
SP S Rogers
SR D Schatzeder
CL J Reardon
RP B James
RP D Palmer
RP G Lucas
C G Carter
1B- T Francona
2S D Flynn
SS- A Salazar
3B T Wallach
OI- J Wohlford
CF T Raines
RF A Dawson
SL D Thomas
U1- M Dilone
2B- B Little
UT- P Rose
M1 B Virdon
M2 J Fanning

NEW YORK
SP D Gooden
SP W Terrell
SP R Darling
SP B Berenyi
RS E Lynch
CL J Orosco
RP D Sisk
RP B Gaff
C M Fitzgerald
1B K Hernandez
2B W Backman
SS- J Oquendo
3B H Brooks
LF G Foster
CF M Wilson
RF D Strawberry
OI D Heep
M D Johnson

PHILADELPHIA
SP S Carlton
SP J Koosman
SP C Hudson
SP J Denny
SP S Rawley
RS K Gross
RP A Holland
RP L Andersen
RP B Campbell
C O Virgil
1B L Matuszek
2B J Samuel
SS I DeJesus
3B M Schmidt
LU G Wilson
CF V Hayes
RF S Lezcano
1U T Corcoran
OI G Gross
IC- J Wockenfuss
M P Owens

PITTSBURGH
SP R Rhoden
SP L McWilliams
SP J Tudor
SP J DeLeon
SP J Candelaria
RP D Robinson
RP K Tekulve
RS L Tunnell
C T Pena
1B J Thompson
2B J Ray
SS D Berra
3B B Madlock
RL L Lacy
CF M Wynne
RF D Frobel
LU L Mazzilli
32 J Morrison
M C Tanner

ST. LOUIS
SP J Andujar
SP D LaPoint
SP D Cox
SR R Horton
SP K Kepshire
RP B Sutter
RP N Allen
RP J Lahti
RP D Rucker
C D Porter
1B D Green
2B T Herr
SS O Smith
3B- T Pendleton
LF L Smith
CF W McGee
RF G Hendrick
LO T Landrum
UT A Van Slyke
OI- S Braun
3I- A Howe
M W Herzog

SAN DIEGO
SP E Show
SP T Lollar
SP E Whitson
SP M Thurmond
SR A Hawkins
RS D Dravecky
RP R Gossage
RP C Lefferts
RP G Booker
C T Kennedy
1B S Garvey
2B A Wiggins
SS G Templeton
3B G Nettles
LF C Martinez
CF K McReynolds
RF T Gwynn
UO- B Brown
UI- T Flannery
3O- L Salazar
M D Williams

SAN FRANCISCO
SP B Laskey
SP M Krukow
SR M Davis
SP J Robinson
RP G Minton
RP G Lavelle
RP F Williams
RP R Lerch
C B Brenly
1U S Thompson
2B M Trillo
SS J LeMaster
3B J Youngblood
LF J Leonard
CF- D Gladden
UO C Davis
OF D Baker
IF- D Kuiper
1B- A Oliver
UO- G Richards
2S- B Wellman
M1 F Robinson
M2 D Ozark

1985 AL

BALTIMORE
SP S McGregor
SP M Boddicker
SP D Martinez
SP S Davis
SR K Dixon
RP S Stewart
RP N Snell
RP D Aase
RP T Martinez
C R Dempsey
1B E Murray
2B- A Wiggins
SS C Ripken Jr
3C F Rayford
LD M Young
CF F Lynn
RF L Lacy
DH L Sheets
OF J Dwyer
3U W Gross
LU G Roenicke
2B- R Dauer
M1 J Altobelli
M2 C Ripken Sr
M3 E Weaver

BOSTON
SP O Boyd
SP B Hurst
SP A Nipper
SR B Ojeda
RP S Crawford
RP B Stanley
RP M Clear
C R Gedman
1B B Buckner
2B M Barrett
SS J Gutierrez
3B W Boggs
LF J Rice
CF S Lyons
RF D Evans
DH M Easler
MU T Armas
SS- G Hoffman
M J McNamara

CALIFORNIA
SP M Witt
SP R Romanick
SP K McCaskill
SP J Slaton
RP D Moore
RP S Cliburn
RP P Clements
RP L Sanchez
C B Boone
1B R Carew
2B B Grich
SS D Schofield
3B D DeCinces
LF B Downing
CF G Pettis
UO R Jones
RD R Jackson
UT J Beniquez
2B- R Wilfong
M G Mauch

CHICAGO
SP T Seaver
SP B Burns
SP F Bannister
SR G Nelson
RP B James
RP D Spillner
RP J Agosto
C C Fisk
1B G Walker
2B- J Cruz
SS O Guillen
3B T Hulett
LF R Law
CF- D Boston
RF H Baines
UT R Kittle
UI S Fletcher
M3 L Salazar
UT- J Hairston
M T LaRussa

CLEVELAND
SP N Heaton
SP B Blyleven
SR V Ruhle
RS T Waddell
RS J Easterly
RP R Thompson
RS J Reed
C J Willard
1B P Tabler
2B T Bernazard
SS J Franco
3B B Jacoby
LF J Carter
CF B Butler
RF G Vukovich
DH A Thornton
1B M Hargrove
LM O Nixon
M P Corrales

DETROIT
SP J Morris
SP D Petry
SP W Terrell
SP F Tanana
RP W Hernandez
RP A Lopez
RP B Scherrer
RP D Bair
C L Parrish
1U D Evans
2B L Whitaker
SS A Trammell
3B T Brookens
LF L Herndon
CF C Lemon
RF K Gibson
OF- J Grubb
UT- B Garbey
M S Anderson

KANSAS CITY
SP C Leibrandt
SP B Saberhagen
SP D Jackson
SP B Black
SP M Gubicza
RP D Quisenberry
RP J Beckwith
RP M Jones
C J Sundberg
1B S Balboni
2B F White
SS O Concepcion
3B G Brett
LF L Smith
CF W Wilson
RL D Motley
DH H McRae
LR L Jones
DH J Orta
SS- B Biancalana
M D Howser

MILWAUKEE
SR D Darwin
SP T Higuera
SP R Burris
SP M Haas
SP J Cocanower
RP P Vuckovich
RP B Gibson
RP B McClure
CL R Fingers
C C Moore
1B C Cooper
2B J Gantner
SS E Riles
3B P Molitor
RL B Oglivie
LM R Yount
RM- P Householder
DU T Simmons
UT- E Romero
M G Bamberger

MINNESOTA
SP M Smithson
SP F Viola
SP J Butcher
SP K Schrom
SP B Blyleven
RS P Filson
CL R Davis
RP F Eufemia
RP R Lysander
C M Salas
1B K Hrbek
2B T Teufel
SS G Gagne
3B G Gaetti
LF M Hatcher
CF K Puckett
RF T Brunansky
UI R Smalley
OI- R Bush
OI- M Stenhouse
M1 B Gardner
M2 R Miller

NEW YORK
SP R Guidry
SP P Niekro
SP J Cowley
SP E Whitson
SP D Rasmussen
RP D Righetti
RP B Fisher
RS B Shirley
RP R Bordi
C B Wynegar
1B D Mattingly
2B W Randolph
SS B Meacham
3B M Pagliarulo
LF K Griffey
CF R Henderson
RF D Winfield
DH D Baylor
C- R Hassey
M1 Y Berra
M2 B Martin

OAKLAND
SP C Codiroli
SP D Sutton
SP B Krueger
SP T Birtsas
RP J Howell
RP K Atherton
RS S McCatty
RP S Ontiveros
C M Heath
1B B Bochte
2B D Hill
SS A Griffin
3B C Lansford
LF D Collins
CF D Murphy
RF M Davis
DH D Kingman
1L D Baker
LU- S Henderson
M J Moore

SEATTLE
SP M Moore
SP M Young
SP M Langston
SP F Wills
SP B Swift
RP E Nunez
RP R Thomas
RP E Vande Berg
C B Kearney
1B A Davis
2B J Perconte
SS S Owen
3B J Presley
LF P Bradley
CF D Henderson
RF A Cowens
DH G Thomas
M C Cottier

TEXAS
SP C Hough
SP M Mason
SP B Hooton
SR D Noles
RP G Harris
RP D Rozema
RP D Schmidt

RS D Stewart
C D Slaught
1B P O'Brien
2B T Harrah
SS C Wilkerson
3B- B Bell
LF G Ward
CF O McDowell
RM G Wright
DH- C Johnson
SI W Tolleson
OI- B Jones
RU- L Parrish
M1 D Rader
M2 B Valentine

TORONTO
SP D Stieb
SP D Alexander
SP J Key
SP J Clancy
RP D Lamp
RP J Acker
RP B Caudill
RP G Lavelle
C E Whitt
1B W Upshaw
2B D Garcia
SS T Fernandez
3B R Mulliniks
LF G Bell
CF L Moseby
RF J Barfield
DH- J Burroughs
3B G Iorg
M B Cox

1985 NL

ATLANTA
SP R Mahler
SP S Bedrosian
SR Z Smith
RP R Camp
CL B Sutter
RP G Garber
RP J Dedmon
C- R Cerone
13 B Horner
2B G Hubbard
SS R Ramirez
3B K Oberkfell
LF T Harper
CF D Murphy
RF C Washington
UL C Chambliss
RL B Komminsk
1U G Perry
2S- P Zuvella
M1 E Haas
M2 B Wine

CHICAGO
SP D Eckersley
SR R Fontenot
SP S Trout
SP R Sutcliffe
SP S Sanderson
RP L Smith
RP L Sorensen
RP W Brusstar
RP G Frazier
C J Davis
1B L Durham
2B R Sandberg
SS- S Dunston
3B R Cey
LF- G Matthews
CF B Dernier
RF K Moreland
UO T Bosley
UT D Lopes
S3 C Speier
IO- R Hebner
LU- G Woods
M J Frey

CINCINNATI
SP T Browning
SP M Soto
SP J Tibbs
SR R Robinson
SR J Stuper
RP J Franco
CL T Power
RP T Hume
RS J Price
C- D Van Gorder
1B P Rose
2B R Oester
SS D Concepcion
3B- B Bell
LM G Redus
CF E Milner
RF D Parker
IO N Esasky
L1- C Cedeno
3U- W Krenchicki

HOUSTON
SP B Knepper
SP N Ryan
SP M Scott
SP J Niekro
CL D Smith
RP B Dawley
RP F DiPino
RP J Calhoun
C M Bailey
1B G Davis
2B B Doran
SS C Reynolds
3B P Garner
LF J Cruz
MR K Bass
RM J Mumphrey
UT D Walling
SS- D Thon
M B Lillis

LOS ANGELES
SP F Valenzuela
SP O Hershiser
SP J Reuss
SP B Welch
SP R Honeycutt
RP T Niedenfuer
RP K Howell
RP C Diaz
RS B Castillo
C M Scioscia
1B G Brock
2B S Sax
SS M Duncan
3S- D Anderson
UO C Maldonado
CF K Landreaux
RF M Marshall
L3 P Guerrero
M T Lasorda

MONTREAL
SP B Smith
SP B Gullickson
SP J Hesketh
SP D Palmer
SP D Schatzeder
CL J Reardon
RP T Burke
RP B Roberge
RP G Lucas
C M Fitzgerald
1B- D Driessen
2B V Law
SS H Brooks
3B T Wallach
LF T Raines
CF H Winningham
RF A Dawson
1O T Francona
M B Rodgers

NEW YORK
SP D Gooden
SP R Darling
SP E Lynch
SP S Fernandez
SP R Aguilera
RP R McDowell
RP J Orosco
RP D Sisk
RP T Leach
C G Carter
1B K Hernandez
2B W Backman
SS R Santana
3B H Johnson
LF G Foster
CF- M Wilson
RF D Strawberry
CF- L Dykstra
OI- D Heep
3B- R Knight
M D Johnson

PHILADELPHIA
SP J Denny
SP K Gross
SP S Rawley
SR C Hudson
SP J Koosman
RP D Carman
RP K Tekulve
RP D Rucker
RP L Andersen
C O Virgil
13 M Schmidt
2B J Samuel
SS- S Jeltz
3B R Schu
CF V Hayes
CF G Maddox
RF G Wilson
1U T Corcoran
SI- L Aguayo
OI- G Gross
LU- J Russell
LF- J Stone
M J Felske

PITTSBURGH
SP R Rhoden
SP R Reuschel
SP J DeLeon
SP L Tunnell
SR L McWilliams
RP C Guante
RS D Robinson
RS J Winn
RP J Candelaria
C T Pena
1B J Thompson
2B J Ray
SS- S Khalifa
3B B Madlock
ML J Orsulak
CF M Wynne
RF- G Hendrick
UT- B Almon
LU- S Kemp
UT- L Mazzilli
3U- J Morrison
M C Tanner

ST. LOUIS
SP J Tudor
SP J Andujar
SP D Cox
SP K Kepshire
SR B Forsch
RP R Horton
CL J Lahti
RP K Dayley
RP B Campbell
C- T Nieto
1B J Clark
2B T Herr
SS O Smith
3B T Pendleton
LF V Coleman
CF W McGee
RF A Van Slyke
RF- T Landrum
C- D Porter
M W Herzog

SAN DIEGO
SP E Show
SP A Hawkins
SP D Dravecky
SP L Hoyt
SR M Thurmond
CL R Gossage
RP C Lefferts
RP T Stoddard
C T Kennedy
1B S Garvey
2B T Flannery
SS G Templeton
3B G Nettles
LF C Martinez
CF K McReynolds
RF T Gwynn
23- J Royster
M D Williams

SAN FRANCISCO
SP D LaPoint
SP M Krukow
SP A Hammaker
SP J Gott
SR V Blue
RP M Davis
RP S Garrelts
RP B Laskey
RP G Minton
C B Brenly
1U D Green
2B M Trillo
SS J Uribe
3B C Brown
LF J Leonard
CF D Gladden
RM C Davis
OI- J Youngblood
M1 J Davenport
M2 R Craig

1986 AL

BALTIMORE
SP M Boddicker
SP S McGregor
SP K Dixon
SP M Flanagan
SP S Davis
CL D Aase
RP R Bordi
RP B Havens
RP N Snell
C R Dempsey
1B E Murray
23 J Bonilla
SS C Ripken
3B- F Rayford
UO J Shelby
CF F Lynn
RF L Lacy
DO L Sheets
UT J Beniquez
LD M Young
OI- J Dwyer
M E Weaver

BOSTON
SP R Clemens
SP O Boyd
SP B Hurst
SP A Nipper
SP T Seaver
RP B Stanley
RP S Stewart
RP S Crawford
CL C Schiraldi
C R Gedman
1B B Buckner
2B M Barrett
SS E Romero
3B W Boggs
LF J Rice
CF T Armas
RF D Evans
DH D Baylor
M J McNamara

CALIFORNIA
SP M Witt
SP K McCaskill
SP D Sutton
SP R Romanick
CL D Moore
RP D Corbett
C B Boone
1B W Joyner
2B- R Wilfong
SS D Schofield
3B D DeCinces
LF B Downing
CF G Pettis
RF R Jones
DH R Jackson
2B B Grich
RF G Hendrick
UI- R Burleson
M G Mauch

CHICAGO
SP R Dotson
SP F Bannister
SP J Cowley
SP N Allen
SP J Davis
SP G Nelson
RP B Dawley
RP D Schmidt
RP B James
CU C Fisk
1B- G Walker
2B- J Cruz
SS O Guillen
32 T Hulett
OI- R Nichols
MU J Cangelosi
RF H Baines
DU- R Kittle
UT J Hairston
3B- W Tolleson
M1 T LaRussa
M2 D Rader
M3 J Fregosi

CLEVELAND
SP T Candiotti
SP P Niekro
SP K Schrom
RS S Bailes
RP R Yett
CL E Camacho
RP B Oelkers
C A Allanson
1B P Tabler
2B T Bernazard
SS J Franco
3B B Jacoby
LF M Hall
CF B Butler
OI J Carter
DH A Thornton
LF O Nixon
RS C Snyder
C- C Bando
UT- C Castillo
M P Corrales

DETROIT
SP J Morris
SP W Terrell
SP F Tanana
SR E King
SP D Petry
RS R O'Neal
CL W Hernandez
RP B Campbell
RP M Thurmond
C- L Parrish
1D D Evans
2B L Whitaker
SS A Trammell
3B D Coles
LU D Collins
CF C Lemon
RF K Gibson
DU- J Grubb
UT T Brookens
LF L Herndon
MR P Sheridan
M S Anderson

KANSAS CITY
SP C Leibrandt
SP D Leonard
SP D Jackson
SR M Gubicza
SP B Saberhagen
RP B Black
RP S Bankhead
RP S Farr
RP D Quisenberry
C J Sundberg
1B S Balboni
2B F White
SS A Salazar
3B G Brett
LF L Smith
CF W Wilson
LR- R Law
DH J Orta
SS B Biancalana
DU H McRae
M1 D Howser
M2 M Ferraro

MILWAUKEE
SP T Higuera
SP B Wegman
SP T Leary
SP J Nieves
SR D Darwin
RP D Plesac
RP M Clear
RP B Clutterbuck
C- C Moore
1B- B Robidoux
2B J Gantner
SS E Riles
3B P Molitor
UO- R Manning
CF R Yount
RF R Deer
1D C Cooper
OF B Oglivie
3I- D Sveum
M1 G Bamberger
M2 T Trebelhorn

MINNESOTA
SP B Blyleven
SP F Viola
SP M Smithson
SP N Heaton
SR M Portugal
RP K Atherton
RP R Jackson
RP F Pastore
C- M Salas
1B K Hrbek
2B S Lombardozzi
SS G Gagne
3B G Gaetti
LU R Bush
CF K Puckett
RF T Brunansky
DH R Smalley
UT M Hatcher
M1 R Miller
M2 T Kelly

NEW YORK
SP D Rasmussen
SP R Guidry
SP D Drabek
SP B Tewksbury
SP J Niekro
RP D Righetti
RS B Shirley
RP B Fisher
RP T Stoddard
C- B Wynegar
1B D Mattingly
2B W Randolph
SS- W Tolleson
3B M Pagliarulo
LU D Pasqua
CF R Henderson
RF D Winfield
DH M Easler
M L Piniella

OAKLAND
SP C Young
SR J Rijo
SP J Andujar
SR D Stewart
SR E Plunk
RS B Mooneyham
RP S Ontiveros
CL J Howell
C- M Tettleton
1B B Bochte
23 T Phillips
SS A Griffin
31 C Lansford
LF J Canseco
CF D Murphy
RF M Davis
DH D Kingman
23 D Hill
OI- D Baker
M1 J Moore
M2 J Newman
M3 T LaRussa

SEATTLE
SP M Moore
SP M Langston
SP M Morgan
SR B Swift
RS M Young
RP M Huismann
RP P Ladd
RP L Guetterman
C- B Kearney
1U A Davis
2B H Reynolds
SS S Owen
3B J Presley
LF P Bradley
CF J Moses
RU D Tartabull
DH- G Thomas
OF D Henderson
UT K Phelps
M1 C Cottier
M2 M Martinez
M3 D Williams

TEXAS
SP C Hough
SP E Correa
SP J Guzman
SP B Witt
SP M Mason
RP G Harris
RP M Williams
RP D Mohorcic
RP J Russell
C- D Slaught
1B P O'Brien
2B- T Harrah
SS S Fletcher
3B S Buechele
RL R Sierra
CF O McDowell
RU P Incaviglia
DH L Parrish
LF G Ward
2S C Wilkerson
UT- T Paciorek
M B Valentine

TORONTO
SP J Key
SP J Clancy
SP D Stieb
SR J Cerutti
SP D Alexander
RP M Eichhorn
CL T Henke
RP D Lamp
RS J Acker
C E Whitt
1B W Upshaw
2B D Garcia
SS T Fernandez
3B R Mulliniks
LF G Bell
CF L Moseby
RF J Barfield
DH C Johnson
32 G Iorg
OI R Leach
UT- K Gruber
C- B Martinez
M J Williams

1986 NL

ATLANTA
SP R Mahler
SP D Palmer
SP Z Smith
SP D Alexander
RP J Dedmon
CL G Garber
RS C McMurtry
RP P Assenmacher
C O Virgil
1B B Horner
2B G Hubbard
SS A Thomas
3B K Oberkfell
LU T Harper
CF D Murphy
RO O Moreno
U1 C Chambliss
S3 R Ramirez
RU- B Sample
M C Tanner

CHICAGO
SP D Eckersley
SP R Sutcliffe
SP S Sanderson
SR S Trout
SR E Lynch
CL L Smith
RS G Hoffman
RP D Gumpert
RP J Baller
C J Davis
1B L Durham
2B R Sandberg
SS S Dunston
3B R Cey
LF G Matthews
CF B Dernier
RF K Moreland
ML J Mumphrey
UO- T Bosley
OI- T Francona
3I- C Speier
3U- M Trillo
M1 J Frey
M2 J Vukovich
M3 G Michael

CINCINNATI
SP B Gullickson
SP T Browning
SP J Denny
SP C Welsh
SP M Soto
RP R Robinson
RP J Franco
RS T Power
RP S Terry
C B Diaz
1L N Esasky
2B R Oester
SS K Stillwell
3B B Bell
LM E Davis
CF E Milner
RF D Parker
UO M Venable
SI- D Concepcion
M P Rose

HOUSTON
SP M Scott
SP B Knepper
SP N Ryan
SP J Deshaies
RP C Kerfeld
CL D Smith
RP A Lopez
RP L Andersen
C A Ashby
1B G Davis
2B B Doran
SS D Thon
3B D Walling
LF J Cruz
ML B Hatcher
RF K Bass
3B P Garner
SS C Reynolds
RU- T Puhl
CF- T Walker
M H Lanier

LOS ANGELES
SP F Valenzuela
SP B Welch
SP O Hershiser
SP R Honeycutt
RP K Howell
RP T Niedenfuer
RP E Vande Berg
RS D Powell
C M Scioscia
1B G Brock
2B S Sax
SS M Duncan
3B B Madlock
LF F Stubbs
MR R Williams
RF M Marshall
1U E Cabell
MU K Landreaux
UT B Russell
3S- D Anderson
OI- L Matuszek
CU- A Trevino
M T Lasorda

MONTREAL
SP F Youmans
SP J Tibbs
SP B Smith
SP D Martinez
RS A McGaffigan
CL J Reardon
RP T Burke
RP B McClure
C- D Bilardello
1B A Galarraga
2B V Law
SS- H Brooks
3B T Wallach
LF T Raines
CF M Webster
RF A Dawson
IO W Krenchicki
2U- A Newman
MU- H Winningham
M B Rodgers

NEW YORK
SP D Gooden
SP R Darling
SP B Ojeda
SP S Fernandez
SP R Aguilera
RP R McDowell
CL J Orosco
RP D Sisk
C G Carter
1B K Hernandez
2B W Backman
SS R Santana
3B R Knight
LM M Wilson
CF L Dykstra
RF D Strawberry
UT K Mitchell
LU- D Heep
3S- H Johnson
2B- T Teufel
M D Johnson

PHILADELPHIA
SP K Gross
SP S Rawley
SP B Ruffin
SR C Hudson
RS D Carman
CL S Bedrosian
RP K Tekulve
RP T Hume
C- J Russell
1B V Hayes
2B J Samuel
SS S Jeltz
3B M Schmidt
LF- G Redus
CF- M Thompson
RF G Wilson
MO R Roenicke
OI- G Gross
3U- R Schu
OF- J Stone
M J Felske

PITTSBURGH
SP R Rhoden
SP R Reuschel
SP M Bielecki
SR B Walk
SP B Kipper
RS L McWilliams
RP J Winn
RP D Robinson
RP C Guante
C T Pena
1B S Bream
2B J Ray
SS R Belliard
3B J Morrison
LR R Reynolds
CF B Bonds
RM J Orsulak
L3 B Almon
UT- M Diaz
RF- M Brown
M J Leyland

ST. LOUIS
SP B Forsch
SP D Cox
SP J Tudor
SP G Mathews
SP T Conroy
RP T Worrell
RS R Horton
RP P Perry
C M LaValliere
1B- J Clark
2B T Herr
SS O Smith
3B T Pendleton
LF V Coleman
CF W McGee
R1 A Van Slyke
OF- C Ford
RU- T Landrum
M W Herzog

SAN DIEGO
SP A Hawkins
SP D Dravecky
SR L Hoyt
SP E Show
RS L McCullers
RP C Lefferts
RP G Walter
CL R Gossage
C T Kennedy
1B S Garvey
2B T Flannery
SS G Templeton
3B G Nettles
ML K McReynolds
CF M Wynne
RF T Gwynn
LU J Kruk
LU C Martinez
2B B Roberts
3B J Royster
IO- D Iorg
M S Boros

SAN FRANCISCO
SP M Krukow
SP M LaCoss
SR S Garrelts
SP V Blue
RP J Robinson
RP M Davis
RP J Berenguer
RP G Minton
C3 B Brenly
1B W Clark
2B R Thompson
SS J Uribe
3B C Brown
OI C Maldonado
CF D Gladden
RF C Davis
UT- J Youngblood
UT- M Aldrete
LF- J Leonard
C- B Melvin
M R Craig

1987 AL

BALTIMORE
SP M Boddicker
SP E Bell
SR D Schmidt
SR J Habyan
SR K Dixon
RP M Williamson
RP T Niedenfuer
RP T Arnold
C T Kennedy
1B E Murray
2B- B Ripken
SS C Ripken Jr
3B R Knight
LM- K Gerhart
CF F Lynn
LR L Sheets
OF M Young
OF- J Dwyer
RF- L Lacy
D2- A Wiggins
M C Ripken Sr

BOSTON
SP R Clemens
SP B Hurst
SP A Nipper
SR B Stanley
SP J Sellers
RP W Gardner
RP C Schiraldi
RP S Crawford
RP T Bolton
C- M Sullivan
1R D Evans
2B M Barrett
SS S Owen
3B W Boggs
LF J Rice
CF E Burks
LU M Greenwell
DH D Baylor
UI- E Romero
M J McNamara

CALIFORNIA
SP M Witt
SP D Sutton
SR W Fraser
SR J Lazorko
SP J Candelaria
RP D Buice
RP C Finley
RP G Minton
RP G Lucas
C B Boone
1B W Joyner
2B M McLemore
SS D Schofield
3B D DeCinces
L3 J Howell
CF G Pettis
RF D White
DH B Downing
LO- R Jones
M G Mauch

CHICAGO
SP F Bannister
SP R Dotson
SP J DeLeon
SP B Long
RP B Thigpen
RP J Winn
RP B James
RP R Searage
C C Fisk
1B G Walker
2B F Manrique
SS O Guillen
3B- T Hulett
LO G Redus
CF K Williams
RF I Calderon
DH H Baines
OF D Boston
2B D Hill
M J Fregosi

CLEVELAND
SP T Candiotti
SP K Schrom
SR S Bailes
SP P Niekro
SP S Carlton
RP G Swindell
RP D Jones
RS R Yett
RP R Vande Berg
C- C Bando
1L J Carter
2B- T Bernazard
SS J Franco
3B B Jacoby
LF M Hall
CF B Butler
RF C Snyder
1D P Tabler
OF- C Castillo
M1 P Corrales
M2 D Edwards

DETROIT
SP J Morris
SP W Terrell
SP F Tanana
SP D Petry
SP J Robinson
RP E King
RP M Henneman
RP M Thurmond
RP W Hernandez
C M Nokes
1D D Evans
2B L Whitaker
SS A Trammell
3B T Brookens
LF K Gibson
CF C Lemon
RF P Sheridan
D1- B Madlock
1U- D Bergman
CO- M Heath
OF- L Herndon
M S Anderson

KANSAS CITY
SP B Saberhagen
SP M Gubicza
SP C Leibrandt
SP D Jackson
SR B Black
RP S Farr
RP D Quisenberry
RP J Gleaton
C J Quirk
1U G Brett
2B F White
SS A Salazar
3B K Seitzer
LF B Jackson
CF W Wilson
RF D Tartabull
UT S Balboni
M1 B Gardner
M2 J Wathan

MILWAUKEE
SP T Higuera
SP B Wegman
SP J Nieves
SR C Bosio
RS C Crim
CL D Plesac
RP M Clear
RP J Aldrich
C B Surhoff
1B G Brock
2B J Castillo
SS D Sveum
3B- E Riles
LU R Deer
CF R Yount
RF G Braggs
DH- C Cooper
LU M Felder
RO- R Manning
IF P Molitor
23- J Gantner
M T Trebelhorn

MINNESOTA
SP B Blyleven
SP F Viola
SP L Straker
SP M Smithson
RS J Berenguer
CL J Reardon
RP G Frazier
RP K Atherton
C T Laudner
1B K Hrbek
2B S Lombardozzi
SS G Gagne
3B G Gaetti
LF D Gladden
CF K Puckett
RL T Brunansky
DU R Smalley
RU R Bush
UO M Davidson
S2 A Newman
UT- G Larkin
M T Kelly

NEW YORK
SP T John
SP R Rhoden
SR C Hudson
SP D Rasmussen
SP R Guidry
CL D Righetti
RP T Stoddard
RP P Clements
C R Cerone
1B D Mattingly
2B W Randolph
SS W Tolleson
3B M Pagliarulo
OI G Ward
MU C Washington
RF D Winfield
LU D Pasqua
OF- R Henderson
M L Piniella

OAKLAND
SP D Stewart
SP C Young
SR S Ontiveros
RP D Eckersley
RS G Nelson
RS D Lamp
RP D Leiper
C T Steinbach
1B M McGwire
2B T Phillips
SS A Griffin
3B C Lansford
LF J Canseco
ML L Polonia
RF M Davis
DU R Jackson
MO- S Javier
CF- D Murphy
C- M Tettleton
M T LaRussa

SEATTLE
SP M Langston
SP M Moore
SP M Morgan
SP S Bankhead
SP L Guetterman
RP J Reed
RP B Wilkinson
RS M Trujillo
C S Bradley
1B A Davis
2B H Reynolds
SS R Quinones
3B J Presley
LF P Bradley
CF J Moses
RF M Kingery
DH K Phelps
MR- M Brantley
C- D Valle
M D Williams

TEXAS
SP C Hough
SP J Guzman
SP B Witt
SR C Harris
RP D Mohorcic
RP M Williams
RP J Russell
RS M Loynd
C- D Slaught
1B P O'Brien
2B J Browne
SS S Fletcher
3B S Buechele
LF P Incaviglia
CF O McDowell
RF R Sierra
DH L Parrish
ML B Brower
CI G Petralli
UC- D Porter
UI- C Wilkerson
M B Valentine

TORONTO
SP J Key
SP J Clancy
SP D Stieb
SR J Cerutti
RP M Eichhorn
CL T Henke
RS J Nunez
RP J Musselman
C E Whitt
1B W Upshaw
2U G Iorg
SS T Fernandez
3B K Gruber
LF G Bell
CF L Moseby
RF J Barfield
DH F McGriff
OI R Leach
3B R Mulliniks
DU- C Fielder
M J Williams

1987 NL

ATLANTA
SP Z Smith
SR R Mahler
SP D Palmer
SR C Puleo
SP D Alexander
RP J Acker
RP J Dedmon
RP G Garber
RP P Assenmacher
C O Virgil
1B G Perry
2B G Hubbard
SS- A Thomas
3B K Oberkfell
LF K Griffey
MU D James
RF D Murphy
IF G Nettles
MU- A Hall
M C Tanner

CHICAGO
SP R Sutcliffe
SP J Moyer
SP G Maddux
SR S Sanderson
SP L Lancaster
CL L Smith
RS E Lynch
RP F DiPino
RP D Noles
C J Davis
1B L Durham
2B R Sandberg
SS- S Dunston
3B K Moreland
LU J Mumphrey
CF D Martinez
RF A Dawson
LU B Dayett
UI M Trillo
CF- B Dernier
LU- R Palmeiro
M1 G Michael
M2 F Lucchesi

CINCINNATI
SP T Power
SP T Browning
SP B Gullickson
SR G Hoffman
SR R Robinson
CL J Franco
RP F Williams
RP R Murphy
RP B Landrum
C B Diaz
1B N Esasky
2B- R Oester
SS B Larkin
3B B Bell
UO T Jones
CF E Davis
RF D Parker
21 D Concepcion
LF K Daniels
1U T Francona
UI K Stillwell
OI- P O'Neill
M P Rose

HOUSTON
SP M Scott
SP N Ryan
SP D Darwin
SP B Knepper
SP J Deshaies
RP L Andersen
CL D Smith
RP D Meads
C A Ashby
1B G Davis
2B B Doran
SS C Reynolds
3U D Walling
LF J Cruz
ML B Hatcher
RF K Bass
UO- T Puhl
M H Lanier

LOS ANGELES
SP O Hershiser
SP B Welch
SP F Valenzuela
SP R Honeycutt
RS T Leary
CL A Pena
RP B Holton
RP M Young
C M Scioscia
1B F Stubbs
2B S Sax
SS- M Duncan
UT M Hatcher
L1 P Guerrero
CF J Shelby
RF M Marshall
S3 D Anderson
UO K Landreaux
M T Lasorda

MONTREAL
SP N Heaton
SP B Sebra
SP B Smith
SP D Martinez
SP F Youmans
RP A McGaffigan
RP T Burke
RP R St.Claire
RP J Parrett
C M Fitzgerald
1B A Galarraga
2B V Law
SS H Brooks
3B T Wallach
LF T Raines
CF H Winningham
RF M Webster
UT C Candaele
UI T Foley
M B Rodgers

NEW YORK
SP R Darling
SP D Gooden
SP S Fernandez
SP R Aguilera
SP J Mitchell
RS T Leach
CL R McDowell
RP D Cone
RP J Orosco
C G Carter
1B K Hernandez
2B- T Teufel
SS R Santana
3B H Johnson
LF K McReynolds
CF L Dykstra
RF D Strawberry
MO M Wilson
2B- W Backman
3U- D Magadan
OI- L Mazzilli
M D Johnson

PHILADELPHIA
SP S Rawley
SP D Carman
SP B Ruffin
SP K Gross
CL S Bedrosian
RS M Jackson
RP K Tekulve
RS T Hume
C L Parrish
1B V Hayes
2B J Samuel
SS S Jeltz
3B M Schmidt
LF C James
CF M Thompson
RF G Wilson
OI G Gross
SS- L Aguayo
IF- R Schu
M1 J Felske
M2 L Elia

PITTSBURGH
SR B Fisher
SP R Reuschel
SP D Drabek
SP M Dunne
SP B Kipper
RS B Walk
RP J Smiley
RP D Robinson
C M LaValliere
1B S Bream
2B J Ray
SS- A Pedrique
3O B Bonilla
LM B Bonds
MU A Van Slyke
RU R Reynolds
UO J Cangelosi
OI M Diaz
SS- R Belliard
3B- J Morrison
M J Leyland

ST. LOUIS
SP D Cox
SP G Mathews
SP B Forsch
SP J Magrane
RS R Horton
CL T Worrell
RP B Dawley
RS L Tunnell
C T Pena
1B J Clark
2B T Herr
SS O Smith
3B T Pendleton
LF V Coleman
CF W McGee
RU- C Ford
RU J Morris
UT J Oquendo
M W Herzog

SAN DIEGO
SP E Show
SP E Whitson
SP J Jones
SP A Hawkins
SP M Grant
RP L McCullers
RP G Booker
RP M Davis
RP R Gossage
C B Santiago
1U J Kruk
2B T Flannery
SS G Templeton
IO R Ready
ML S Jefferson
CF S Mack
RF T Gwynn
L1 C Martinez
UO M Wynne
UT- L Salazar
M L Bowa

SAN FRANCISCO
SR K Downs
SR M LaCoss
SP A Hammaker
SP M Krukow
SP D Dravecky
RP S Garrelts
RP J Robinson
RP J Gott
C B Brenly
1B W Clark
2B R Thompson
SS- J Uribe
3B- K Mitchell
LF J Leonard
CF C Davis
RF C Maldonado
OI M Aldrete
CF E Milner
UI C Speier
C- B Melvin
IF- H Spilman
SS- M Williams
M R Craig

1988 AL

BALTIMORE
SP J Bautista
SP J Tibbs
SP J Ballard
SP M Boddicker
RS D Schmidt
RS M Williamson
RP D Sisk
RS M Thurmond
C- M Tettleton
1D J Traber
2B B Ripken
SS C Ripken Jr
3B- R Gonzales
LF- P Stanicek
MU- F Lynn
RL J Orsulak
1D E Murray
OI L Sheets
ML K Gerhart
C- T Kennedy
3B- R Schu
M1 C Ripken Sr
M2 F Robinson

BOSTON
SP R Clemens
SP B Hurst
SR W Gardner
SP O Boyd
SR M Smithson
CL L Smith
RP B Stanley
RP D Lamp
C- R Gedman
1R T Benzinger
2B M Barrett
SS J Reed
3B W Boggs
LF M Greenwell
CF E Burks
R1 D Evans
DH J Rice
C- R Cerone
SS- S Owen
M1 J McNamara
M2 J Morgan

CALIFORNIA
SP M Witt
SP W Fraser
SP C Finley
SP K McCaskill
SP D Petry
CL B Harvey
RP G Minton
RP S Cliburn
C B Boone
1B W Joyner
2L J Ray
SS D Schofield
3B J Howell
LM T Armas
CF D White
RF C Davis
DH B Downing
M1 C Rojas
M2 M Stubing

CHICAGO
SP M Perez
SP J Reuss
SR B Long
SP D LaPoint
SP J McDowell
CL B Thigpen
RS R Horton
RP J Davis
RS J Bittiger
C- C Fisk
1B G Walker
2B F Manrique
SS O Guillen
3B S Lyons
UO D Boston
CF D Gallagher
LR D Pasqua
DH H Baines
2U- D Hill
M J Fregosi

CLEVELAND
SP G Swindell
SP T Candiotti
SP J Farrell
SR S Bailes
SP R Yett
CL D Jones
RP D Gordon
RP B Havens
C A Allanson
1B W Upshaw
2B J Franco
SS- J Bell
3B B Jacoby
LF M Hall
CF J Carter
RF C Snyder
DH- R Kittle
M D Edwards

DETROIT
SP J Morris
SP D Alexander
SP W Terrell
SP F Tanana
SP J Robinson
CL M Henneman
RP P Gibson
RP W Hernandez
RS E King
C M Nokes
1U R Knight
2B L Whitaker
SS A Trammell
3B T Brookens
LU P Sheridan
CF G Pettis
RF C Lemon
D1 D Evans
1D D Bergman
UT L Salazar
C- M Heath
2U- J Walewander
M S Anderson

KANSAS CITY
SP M Gubicza
SP B Saberhagen
SP C Leibrandt
SP F Bannister
RP S Farr
RP J Montgomery
C- J Quirk
1B G Brett
2B F White
SS K Stillwell
3B K Seitzer
LF B Jackson
CF W Wilson
RF D Tartabull
UT- B Buckner
UO- J Eisenreich
UT- B Pecota
UT- P Tabler
M J Wathan

MILWAUKEE
SP T Higuera
SP B Wegman
SR C Bosio
SP D August
SP M Birkbeck
RP C Crim
RS J Nieves
RP T Filer
RP O Jones
C B Surhoff
1B G Brock
2B J Gantner
SS D Sveum
3D P Molitor
LF- J Leonard
CF R Yount
RL R Deer
D1 J Meyer
M T Trebelhorn

MINNESOTA
SP F Viola
SP B Blyleven
SP A Anderson
SP C Lea
SP F Toliver
CL J Reardon
RP J Berenguer
RP K Atherton
RP M Portugal
C T Laudner
1D K Hrbek
2B S Lombardozzi
SS G Gagne
3B G Gaetti
LF D Gladden
CF K Puckett
RF R Bush
D1 G Larkin
RF M Davidson
UO J Moses
3S A Newman
2B- T Herr
M T Kelly

NEW YORK
SP R Rhoden
SP T John
SP R Dotson
SP J Candelaria
SR C Hudson
RP N Allen
CL D Righetti
RP C Guante
RP S Shields
C D Slaught
1B D Mattingly
2B W Randolph
SS R Santana
3B M Pagliarulo
LF R Henderson
CF C Washington
RF D Winfield
DU J Clark
C- J Skinner
UT- G Ward

M1 B Martin
M2 L Piniella

OAKLAND
SP D Stewart
SP B Welch
SP S Davis
SP C Young
SP T Burns
CL D Eckersley
RP G Nelson
RP R Honeycutt
RP E Plunk
C R Hassey
1B M McGwire
2B G Hubbard
SS W Weiss
3B C Lansford
LM S Javier
CF D Henderson
RF J Canseco
DH- D Baylor
2S M Gallego
DL D Parker
C T Steinbach
LF- L Polonia
M T LaRussa

SEATTLE
SP M Langston
SP M Moore
SR B Swift
SP S Bankhead
SP M Campbell
RP M Jackson
RP J Reed
CL M Schooler
C S Bradley
1B A Davis
2B H Reynolds
SS R Quinones
3B J Presley
LF M Brantley
CF H Cotto
RF- G Wilson
DH- K Phelps
D1 S Balboni
C- D Valle
M1 D Williams
M2 J Snyder

TEXAS
SP C Hough
SP J Guzman
SP P Kilgus
SR J Russell
SP B Witt
RP M Williams
RP C McMurtry
RP D Mohorcic
CU G Petralli
1B P O'Brien
2I C Wilkerson
SS S Fletcher
3B S Buechele
UT C Espy
CF O McDowell
RF R Sierra
DH- L Parrish
LF P Incaviglia
UO- B Brower
CU- M Stanley
M B Valentine

TORONTO
SP M Flanagan
SP D Stieb
SP J Clancy
SP J Key
RP D Ward
RS J Cerutti
CL T Henke
RP M Eichhorn
C E Whitt
1B F McGriff
2B M Lee
SS T Fernandez
3B K Gruber
LF G Bell
CF L Moseby
RF J Barfield
DH R Mulliniks
2B N Liriano
OI- R Leach
M J Williams

1988 NL

ATLANTA
SP R Mahler
SP T Glavine
SP P Smith
SP Z Smith
RP C Puleo
RP J Alvarez
RP P Assenmacher
C O Virgil
1B G Perry
2B R Gant
SS A Thomas
3B K Oberkfell
LM D James
MU- A Hall
RF D Murphy
C- B Benedict
M1 C Tanner
M2 R Nixon

CHICAGO
SP G Maddux
SP R Sutcliffe
SP J Moyer
SP C Schiraldi
SR J Pico
RP F DiPino
RP L Lancaster
C- D Berryhill
1B M Grace
2B R Sandberg
SS S Dunston
3B V Law
LF R Palmeiro
UO D Jackson
RF A Dawson
C- J Davis
M D Zimmer

CINCINNATI
SP D Jackson
SP T Browning
SR J Rijo
CL J Franco
RP R Murphy
RP T Birtsas
RP F Williams
C- B Diaz
1B N Esasky
2B J Treadway
SS B Larkin
3B C Sabo
LF K Daniels
CF E Davis
RF P O'Neill
OI D Collins
2I- D Concepcion
M1 P Rose
M2 T Helms
M3 P Rose

HOUSTON
SP N Ryan
SP M Scott
SP J Deshaies
SR D Darwin
SP B Knepper
RP J Agosto
RP L Andersen
CL D Smith
C- A Trevino
1B G Davis
2B B Doran
SS R Ramirez
3B- B Bell
LF B Hatcher
CF G Young
RF K Bass
UO T Puhl
M H Lanier

LOS ANGELES
SP O Hershiser
SP T Leary
SP T Belcher
SP F Valenzuela
RP A Pena
RP B Holton
CL J Howell
RP T Crews
C M Scioscia
1U F Stubbs
2B S Sax
SS- A Griffin
3B J Hamilton
LF K Gibson
CF J Shelby
R1 M Marshall
SU D Anderson
RU M Davis
UT- M Hatcher
OI- D Heep
M T Lasorda

MONTREAL
SP D Martinez
SP B Smith
SP P Perez
SP J Dopson
SP B Holman
RP T Burke
RP J Parrett
RP A McGaffigan
RP J Hesketh
C- N Santovenia
1B A Galarraga
2S T Foley
SS L Rivera
3B T Wallach
LF T Raines
ML- O Nixon
RF H Brooks
IF- W Johnson
MO- M Webster
M B Rodgers

NEW YORK
SP D Gooden
SP R Darling
SP D Cone
SP B Ojeda
SP S Fernandez
RP R McDowell
RP T Leach
CL R Myers
C G Carter
1B- K Hernandez
2B W Backman
SS K Elster
3B H Johnson
LF K McReynolds
CF L Dykstra
RF D Strawberry
13 D Magadan
MO M Wilson
2B- T Teufel
M D Johnson

PHILADELPHIA
SP K Gross
SP D Carman
SP S Rawley
SP D Palmer
RS B Ruffin
RP G Harris
CL S Bedrosian
RP K Tekulve
C L Parrish
1B V Hayes
2B J Samuel
SS S Jeltz
3B M Schmidt
LF P Bradley
CF M Thompson
RU C James
OI G Gross
M1 L Elia
M2 J Vukovich

PITTSBURGH
SP D Drabek
SP B Walk
SP J Smiley
SP M Dunne
SR B Fisher
RP J Robinson
CL J Gott
RP B Kipper
RP B Jones
C M LaValliere
1B S Bream
2B J Lind
SS R Belliard
3B B Bonilla
LF B Bonds
CF A Van Slyke
RU R Reynolds
M J Leyland

ST. LOUIS
SP J DeLeon
SP J Magrane
SP J Tudor
SR L McWilliams
SR B Forsch
RS S Terry
CL T Worrell
RP K Dayley
RP J Costello
C T Pena
1B- B Horner
2B- L Alicea
SS O Smith
3B T Pendleton
LF V Coleman
CF W McGee
RF T Brunansky
UT J Oquendo
OI- C Ford
IC- T Pagnozzi
M W Herzog

SAN DIEGO
SP E Show
SP A Hawkins
SP E Whitson
SP J Jones
SP D Rasmussen
RP M Davis
RP L McCullers
RS M Grant
RP G Booker
C B Santiago
1L K Moreland
2B R Alomar
SS G Templeton
3B- C Brown
OI C Martinez
ML M Wynne
RF T Gwynn
1O J Kruk
3U R Ready
SU- D Thon
M1 L Bowa
M2 J McKeon

SAN FRANCISCO
SP R Reuschel
SR D Robinson
SP K Downs
SR A Hammaker
SP M Krukow
RP M LaCoss
RP S Garrelts
RP C Lefferts
RP J Price
C- B Melvin
1B W Clark
2B R Thompson
SS J Uribe
3L K Mitchell
LR M Aldrete
CF B Butler
RF C Maldonado
23- C Speier
UO- J Youngblood
M R Craig

1989 AL

BALTIMORE
SP B Milacki
SP J Ballard
SR D Schmidt
SP P Harnisch
RS B Holton
RP M Williamson
CL G Olson
RP M Thurmond
CD M Tettleton
1B R Milligan
2B B Ripken
SS C Ripken
3B C Worthington
LF P Bradley
MR M Devereaux
RU J Orsulak
DH L Sheets
CF- B Anderson
RM- S Finley
C- B Melvin
1B- J Traber
M F Robinson

BOSTON
SP R Clemens
SP M Boddicker
SP J Dopson
SR M Smithson
RP D Lamp
RP R Murphy
CL L Smith
RP B Stanley
C R Cerone
1B N Esasky
2B- M Barrett
SS- L Rivera
3B W Boggs
LF M Greenwell
CF- E Burks
MR- K Romine
RD D Evans
RU D Heep
S2 J Reed
C- R Gedman
M J Morgan

CALIFORNIA
SP B Blyleven
SP M Witt
SP K McCaskill
SP C Finley
SP J Abbott
RP G Minton
RP W Fraser
CL B Harvey
RP B McClure
C L Parrish
1B W Joyner
2B J Ray
SS- D Schofield
3B J Howell
LF C Davis
CF D White
RF C Washington
DH B Downing
SS- K Anderson
M D Rader

CHICAGO
SP M Perez
SP E King
SR S Rosenberg
SP G Hibbard
SP J Reuss
RS S Hillegas
CL B Thigpen
RS B Long
RP R Dotson
C C Fisk
1D- G Walker
21 S Lyons
SS O Guillen
31 C Martinez
LU D Boston
CF D Gallagher
RU I Calderon
DR- H Baines
M J Torborg

CLEVELAND
SP B Black
SP J Farrell
SP T Candiotti
SP G Swindell
SR R Yett
RS S Bailes
CL D Jones
RP J Orosco
C A Allanson
1B P O'Brien
2B J Browne
SS F Fermin
3B B Jacoby
ML J Carter
CF- B Komminsk
RF C Snyder
DU D Clark
M1 D Edwards
M2 J Hart

DETROIT
SP F Tanana
SP D Alexander
SP J Morris
RS P Gibson
RP M Henneman
RP F Williams
RP E Nunez
C M Heath
1B D Bergman
2B L Whitaker
SS A Trammell
3B R Schu
LD F Lynn
CF G Pettis
RF C Lemon
D1- K Moreland
OI G Ward
UT- M Brumley
CD- M Nokes
OI- K Williams
M S Anderson

KANSAS CITY
SP B Saberhagen
SP M Gubicza
SP C Leibrandt
SR L Aquino
RS T Gordon
RP J Montgomery
CL S Farr
RP T Leach
C B Boone
1B G Brett
2B F White
SS K Stillwell
3B K Seitzer
LF B Jackson
CF W Wilson
MR J Eisenreich
RD D Tartabull
UT P Tabler
2S B Wellman
M J Wathan

MILWAUKEE
SP C Bosio
SP D August
SP T Higuera
SP J Navarro
RP C Crim
RS M Knudson
RS B Krueger
CL D Plesac
C B Surhoff
1B G Brock
2B J Gantner
SS B Spiers
3U P Molitor
LF G Braggs
CF R Yount
RF R Deer
D1- J Meyer
OI M Felder
1D- T Francona
SU- G Sheffield
M T Trebelhorn

MINNESOTA
SP A Anderson
SP F Viola
SP R Smith
SP S Rawley
RP J Berenguer
CL J Reardon
RP G Wayne
C B Harper
1B K Hrbek
23 A Newman
SS G Gagne
3B G Gaetti
LF D Gladden
CF K Puckett
RU R Bush
DH- J Dwyer
UT G Larkin
CU T Laudner
OI J Moses
2B- W Backman
RU- C Castillo
M T Kelly

NEW YORK
SP A Hawkins
SP C Parker
SP D LaPoint
SR C Cary
RP L Guetterman
CL D Righetti
RP L McCullers
RS E Plunk
C D Slaught
1B D Mattingly
2B S Sax
SS A Espinoza
3B- M Pagliarulo
OF M Hall
CF R Kelly
RF J Barfield
DU S Balboni
DU- K Phelps
M1 D Green
M2 B Dent

OAKLAND
SP D Stewart
SP M Moore
SP B Welch
SP S Davis
SP C Young
RP T Burns
CL D Eckersley
RP R Honeycutt
RP G Nelson
C T Steinbach
1B M McGwire
23 T Phillips
S2 M Gallego
3B C Lansford
LF- R Henderson
CF D Henderson
RM S Javier
DH D Parker
C- R Hassey
SS- W Weiss
M T LaRussa

SEATTLE
SP S Bankhead
SP B Holman
SP R Johnson
SR B Swift
SP E Hanson
CL M Schooler
RP M Jackson
RP J Reed
C- D Valle
1B A Davis
2B H Reynolds
SS O Vizquel
3B J Presley
LF G Briley
CF K Griffey
RI D Coles
CU S Bradley
LM H Cotto
DH J Leonard
M J Lefebvre

TEXAS
SP N Ryan
SP B Witt
SP K Brown
SP C Hough
SP M Jeffcoat
CL J Russell
RP K Rogers
RP C Guante
RP D Hall
C- C Kreuter
1B R Palmeiro
2B J Franco
SS- S Fletcher
3B S Buechele
LF P Incaviglia
CF C Espy
RF R Sierra
DH- H Baines
3D J Kunkel
OI R Leach
M B Valentine

TORONTO
SP J Key
SP D Stieb
SP J Cerutti
SP M Flanagan
SP T Stottlemyre
RP D Ward
RP T Henke
RP D Wells
RP F Wills
C E Whitt
1B F McGriff
2B N Liriano
SS T Fernandez
3B K Gruber
LF G Bell
CF L Moseby
RF J Felix
D3 R Mulliniks
IO M Lee
CU- P Borders
M1 J Williams
M2 C Gaston

1989 NL

ATLANTA
SP J Smoltz
SP T Glavine
SP D Lilliquist
SP P Smith
SP M Clary
RP J Boever
RP J Acker
RP Z Smith
RP M Eichhorn
C- J Davis
1B- G Perry
2B J Treadway
SS A Thomas
32 J Blauser
LF L Smith
CF- O McDowell
MR D Murphy
IF D Evans
OI T Gregg
OF- G Berroa
M R Nixon

CHICAGO
SP G Maddux
SP R Sutcliffe
SP M Bielecki
SR P Kilgus
SR S Sanderson
CL M Williams
RS J Pico
RS S Wilson
RP C Schiraldi
C- D Berryhill
1B M Grace
2B R Sandberg
SS S Dunston
3B V Law
LR D Smith
CF J Walton
RF A Dawson
LO M Webster
UT- L McClendon
IF- D Ramos
M D Zimmer

CINCINNATI
SP T Browning
SP R Mahler
SP D Jackson
SP J Rijo
SP S Scudder
CL J Franco
RP R Dibble
RP N Charlton
RP T Birtsas
C J Reed
1B T Benzinger
2B R Oester
SS- B Larkin
3B- C Sabo
UO R Roomes
CF E Davis
RF P O'Neill
LU K Griffey
23- L Quinones
UO H Winningham
M1 P Rose
M2 T Helms

HOUSTON
SP M Scott
SP J Deshaies
SP J Clancy
SP B Knepper
SR B Forsch
RP D Darwin
RP M Portugal
RP L Andersen
RP J Agosto
C C Biggio
1B G Davis
2B B Doran
SS R Ramirez
3B K Caminiti
LF B Hatcher
CF G Young
RL T Puhl
IO C Reynolds
RL- K Bass
M A Howe

LOS ANGELES
SP O Hershiser
SP T Belcher
SP F Valenzuela
SR M Morgan
SP T Leary
CL J Howell
RS J Wetteland
RP R Martinez
RP A Pena
C M Scioscia
1B E Murray
2B W Randolph
SS A Griffin
3B J Hamilton
LF- K Gibson
CF J Shelby
RF M Marshall
UI- D Anderson
MR- J Gonzalez
UT- M Hatcher
M T Lasorda

MONTREAL
SP De Martinez
SP B Smith
SP K Gross
SP P Perez
SP M Langston
CL T Burke
RP A McGaffigan
C- N Santovenia
1B A Galarraga
2B T Foley
SS S Owen
3B T Wallach
LF T Raines
CF Da Martinez
RF H Brooks
C M Fitzgerald
MU O Nixon
UT- R Hudler
US- W Johnson
M B Rodgers

NEW YORK
SP D Cone
SP S Fernandez
SP R Darling
SP B Ojeda
SP D Gooden
CL R Myers
RP R Aguilera
RP D Aase
C- B Lyons
1U D Magadan
2B G Jefferies
SS K Elster
3B H Johnson
LF K McReynolds
CF- J Samuel
RF D Strawberry
IF- T Teufel
M D Johnson

PHILADELPHIA
SP K Howell
SR D Carman
SP B Ruffin
SR L McWilliams
SP D Cook
RP J Parrett
RP T Mulholland
RP G Harris
CL R McDowell
C D Daulton
1B R Jordan
2B T Herr
SS D Thon
3B- C Hayes
LF- J Kruk
CF- L Dykstra
RF V Hayes
UT C Ford
S3 S Jeltz
UO B Dernier
UO D Murphy
M N Leyva

PITTSBURGH
SP D Drabek
SP J Smiley
SP B Walk
SR N Heaton
SR J Robinson
RS R Kramer
CL B Landrum
RP B Kipper
RP D Bair

C- J Ortiz
1U- G Redus
2B J Lind
SS- J Bell
3B B Bonilla
LF B Bonds
CF A Van Slyke
RO R Reynolds
UO J Cangelosi
RF G Wilson
1U- B Distefano
M J Leyland

ST. LOUIS
SP J DeLeon
SP J Magrane
SP K Hill
SP S Terry
RP F DiPino
RP K Dayley
RP D Quisenberry
CL T Worrell
C T Pena
1B P Guerrero
2B J Oquendo
SS O Smith
3B T Pendleton
LF V Coleman
CF M Thompson
RF T Brunansky
UO- J Morris
M W Herzog

SAN DIEGO
SP B Hurst
SP E Whitson
SP D Rasmussen
SP W Terrell
SP E Show
RS G Harris
CL M Davis
RP M Grant
C B Santiago
1B J Clark
2B R Alomar
SS G Templeton
3B- L Salazar
LR- C James
UO M Wynne
MR T Gwynn
L1 C Martinez
UT B Roberts
M J McKeon

SAN FRANCISCO
SP R Reuschel
SP D Robinson
SP S Garrelts
SR M LaCoss
RP C Lefferts
RP J Brantley
RS A Hammaker
CL S Bedrosian
C T Kennedy
1B W Clark
2B R Thompson
SS J Uribe
3U E Riles
LF K Mitchell
CF B Butler
RF C Maldonado
C- K Manwaring
UO- D Nixon
UI- K Oberkfell
3B- M Williams
M R Craig

1990 AL

BALTIMORE
SP P Harnisch
SP D Johnson
SP B Milacki
SR J Ballard
SP B McDonald
RP J Mitchell
CL G Olson
RP M Williamson
RP J Price
CD M Tettleton
1B R Milligan
2B B Ripken
SS C Ripken
3B C Worthington
LF- P Bradley
CF M Devereaux
RM S Finley
DH- S Horn
RU J Orsulak
UO- B Anderson
C- B Melvin
M F Robinson

BOSTON
SP M Boddicker
SP R Clemens
SP G Harris
SP D Kiecker
SP T Bolton
RP D Lamp
RS W Gardner
CL J Reardon
RP R Murphy
C T Pena
1B C Quintana
2B J Reed
SS L Rivera
3B W Boggs
LF M Greenwell
CF E Burks
RF T Brunansky
DH D Evans
M J Morgan

CALIFORNIA
SP C Finley
SP M Langston
SP J Abbott
SP K McCaskill
SP B Blyleven
RP M Eichhorn
CL B Harvey
RP W Fraser
RP M Fetters
C L Parrish
1B- W Joyner
2B J Ray
SS D Schofield
3B J Howell
UO D Bichette
CF D White
RF D Winfield
DH- B Downing
DL C Davis
2I D Hill
LU L Polonia
UO- M Venable
M D Rader

CHICAGO
SP G Hibbard
SP J McDowell
SP M Perez
SP E King
CL B Thigpen
RS W Edwards
RP D Pall
RP B Jones
C C Fisk
1B- C Martinez
2B S Fletcher
SS O Guillen
3B R Ventura
LF I Calderon
CF L Johnson
RF S Sosa
DO D Pasqua
D1- R Kittle
1U- S Lyons
M J Torborg

CLEVELAND
SP G Swindell
SP T Candiotti
SP B Black
SR S Valdez
CL D Jones
RP S Olin
RP J Orosco
C S Alomar
31 B Jacoby
2B J Browne
SS F Fermin
UI C Baerga
LR C Maldonado
MU M Webster
RF C Snyder
DH C James
UT- D James
M J McNamara

DETROIT
SP J Morris
SP F Tanana
SP D Petry
SP J Robinson
RP M Henneman
RP P Gibson
RP J Gleaton
RP E Nunez
C M Heath
1B C Fielder
2B L Whitaker
SS A Trammell
32 T Phillips
LU G Ward
CF L Moseby
RF C Lemon
D1 D Bergman
OF L Sheets
M S Anderson

KANSAS CITY
SP T Gordon
SP K Appier
SP B Saberhagen
SP S Davis
RS S Farr
RP J Montgomery
RP S Crawford
RP M Davis
C M Macfarlane
1U G Brett
2B- F White
SS K Stillwell
3B K Seitzer
UO W Wilson
ML B Jackson
RL J Eisenreich
D1 G Perry
2I- B Pecota
RD- D Tartabull
M J Wathan

MILWAUKEE
SP T Higuera
SP M Knudson
SR J Navarro
SP R Robinson
SP C Bosio
SP B Krueger
RP C Crim
CL D Plesac
RS T Edens
C B Surhoff
1B G Brock
2B- J Gantner
SS B Spiers
3B G Sheffield
LR M Felder
CF R Yount
RF R Deer
DH D Parker
21 P Molitor
LF G Vaughn
SS- E Diaz
UO- D Hamilton
M T Trebelhorn

MINNESOTA
SP A Anderson
SP K Tapani
SP R Smith
SP D West
SP M Guthrie
RP S Erickson
RP J Berenguer
CL R Aguilera
RP T Drummond
C B Harper
1B K Hrbek
2S A Newman
SS G Gagne
3B G Gaetti
LF D Gladden
CF K Puckett
UO S Mack
UT G Larkin
OI J Moses
M T Kelly

NEW YORK
SP T Leary
SP A Hawkins
SP D LaPoint
SP C Cary
RS G Cadaret
RP L Guetterman
CL D Righetti
RP J Robinson
C B Geren
1B D Mattingly
2B S Sax
SS A Espinoza
3B- R Velarde
LU- O Azocar
CF R Kelly
RF J Barfield
DU S Balboni
OF M Hall
3B- J Leyritz
CD- M Nokes
M1 B Dent
M2 S Merrill

OAKLAND
SP D Stewart
SP B Welch
SP S Sanderson
SP M Moore
SP C Young
CL D Eckersley
RP T Burns
RP G Nelson
RP R Honeycutt
CU T Steinbach
1B M McGwire
2B- W Randolph
SS W Weiss
3B C Lansford
LF R Henderson
CF D Henderson
RL F Jose
RD J Canseco
2S M Gallego
UT- L Blankenship
CU- R Hassey
M T LaRussa

SEATTLE
SP E Hanson
SP M Young
SP R Johnson
SP B Holman
RS B Swift
CL M Schooler
RP M Jackson
RP K Comstock
C D Valle
1B P O'Brien
2B H Reynolds
SS- O Vizquel
3B E Martinez
RL G Briley
CF K Griffey
RL H Cotto
D1 A Davis
CU S Bradley
LD J Leonard
M J Lefebvre

TEXAS
SP B Witt
SP C Hough
SP N Ryan
SP K Brown
RS M Jeffcoat
RP K Rogers
RS J Moyer
RP B Arnsberg
C G Petralli
1B R Palmeiro
2B J Franco
SS J Huson
3B- S Buechele
LF P Incaviglia
CF G Pettis
RF R Sierra
DH H Baines
OI J Daugherty
SI J Kunkel
CU M Stanley
M B Valentine

TORONTO
SP D Stieb
SP T Stottlemyre
SR D Wells
SP J Key
SP J Cerutti
RP D Ward
CL T Henke
RP F Wills
RP J Acker
C P Borders
1B F McGriff
2B M Lee
SS T Fernandez
3B K Gruber
LD G Bell
CF M Wilson
RF J Felix
DH J Olerud
UO- G Hill
C- G Myers
M C Gaston

1990 NL

ATLANTA
SP J Smoltz
SP T Glavine
SP C Leibrandt
SR M Clary
SP S Avery
RP T Castillo
RP M Grant
RP R Luecken
C G Olson
1R D Justice
2B J Treadway
SS J Blauser
3B J Presley
LF L Smith
ML R Gant
RF- D Murphy
UT T Gregg
UI M Lemke
MU O McDowell
SS- A Thomas
M1 R Nixon
M2 B Cox

CHICAGO
SP G Maddux
SP M Harkey
SP M Bielecki
RS S Wilson
RS L Lancaster
RP P Assenmacher
RS J Pico
C J Girardi
1B M Grace
2B R Sandberg
SS S Dunston
3B L Salazar
LM D Dascenzo
CF J Walton
RF A Dawson
3U D Ramos
LU D Smith
UM- D Clark
MU- M Wynne
M D Zimmer

CINCINNATI
SP T Browning
SP J Rijo
SP J Armstrong
SR R Mahler
SP D Jackson
RS N Charlton
CL R Myers
RP R Dibble
RP T Layana
C J Oliver
1B T Benzinger
2B M Duncan
SS B Larkin
3B C Sabo
LM B Hatcher
ML E Davis
RF P O'Neill
1U H Morris
UI- L Quinones
MU- H Winningham
M L Piniella

HOUSTON
SP J Deshaies
SP M Scott
SP M Portugal
SP B Gullickson
SR D Darwin
RP J Agosto
CL D Smith
RP L Andersen
RS J Clancy
C C Biggio
1B- G Davis
2B B Doran
SS R Ramirez
3B K Caminiti
UT F Stubbs
MS E Yelding
RF G Wilson
UT C Candaele
RU- E Anthony
M A Howe

LOS ANGELES
SP R Martinez
SP M Morgan
SP F Valenzuela
SP T Belcher
RP T Crews
CL J Howell
RS M Hartley
RP J Gott
C M Scioscia
1B E Murray
2B J Samuel
SS A Griffin
3B M Sharperson
LF K Daniels
MU S Javier
RF H Brooks
UO J Gonzalez
UO C Gwynn
32 L Harris
CF- K Gibson
IO- M Hatcher
M T Lasorda

MONTREAL
SP De Martinez
SP O Boyd
SP K Gross
SP M Gardner
SP Z Smith
CL T Burke
RP B Sampen
RP S Frey
RP D Hall
C M Fitzgerald
1B A Galarraga
2B D DeShields
SS S Owen
3B T Wallach
LF T Raines
CF Da Martinez
RF L Walker
UO M Grissom
MU O Nixon
OI- M Aldrete
UT- J Noboa
M B Rodgers

NEW YORK
SP F Viola
SP D Gooden
SP D Cone
SP S Fernandez
SR R Darling
RS B Ojeda
CL J Franco
RP A Pena
RP W Whitehurst
C M Sasser
1B D Magadan
2B G Jefferies
SS- K Elster
3S H Johnson
LF K McReynolds
CF D Boston
RF D Strawberry
UO- M Carreon
MU- K Miller
IF- T O'Malley
M1 D Johnson
M2 B Harrelson

PHILADELPHIA
SP P Combs
SP T Mulholland
SP B Ruffin
SP J DeJesus
SP K Howell
RS D Cook
RP R McDowell
RP D Akerfelds
RP D Carman
C D Daulton
1B- R Jordan
2B T Herr
SS D Thon
3B C Hayes
OI J Kruk
CF L Dykstra
RL V Hayes
UT R Ready
M N Leyva

PITTSBURGH
SP D Drabek
SP J Smiley
SP N Heaton
SP B Walk
RS B Patterson
RP B Landrum
RP S Belinda
RP B Kipper
C- M LaValliere
1B S Bream
2B J Lind
SS J Bell
3B J King
LF B Bonds
CF A Van Slyke
RF B Bonilla
3U W Backman
1B- G Redus
UO- R Reynolds
C- D Slaught
M J Leyland

ST. LOUIS
SP J Magrane
SP J DeLeon
SP B Tewksbury
SP J Tudor
SP B Smith
CL L Smith
RP F DiPino
RP K Dayley
RP S Terry
CU T Zeile
1B P Guerrero
2B J Oquendo
SS O Smith
3B T Pendleton
LF V Coleman
CF W McGee
RU M Thompson
UT D Collins
UT- R Hudler
M1 W Herzog
M2 R Schoendienst
M3 J Torre

SAN DIEGO
SP E Whitson
SP B Hurst
SP A Benes
SP D Rasmussen
SP G Harris
RS E Show
RS C Schiraldi
CL C Lefferts
C B Santiago
1B J Clark
2B R Alomar
SS G Templeton
3B M Pagliarulo
L3 B Roberts
ML J Carter
RF T Gwynn
1U P Stephenson
UO- S Abner
UO- F Lynn
M1 J McKeon
M2 G Riddoch

SAN FRANCISCO
SP J Burkett
SP S Garrelts
SP D Robinson
SR T Wilson
CL J Brantley
RP S Bedrosian
RS A Hammaker
RP M Thurmond
C T Kennedy
1B W Clark
2B R Thompson
SS J Uribe
3B M Williams
LF K Mitchell
CF B Butler
RU M Kingery
C- G Carter
UT- G Litton
UI- E Riles
M R Craig

1991 AL

BALTIMORE
SP B Milacki
SP B McDonald
SP J Ballard
SP J Mesa
SP J Robinson
CL G Olson
RP M Flanagan
RP T Frohwirth
RP M Williamson
C C Hoiles
1B R Milligan
2B B Ripken
SS C Ripken
3B L Gomez
LO B Anderson
CF M Devereaux
LR J Orsulak
DH S Horn
2B J Bell
RU D Evans
UT- D Segui
M1 F Robinson
M2 J Oates

BOSTON
SP R Clemens
SP G Harris
SR J Hesketh
SP M Gardiner
SP T Bolton
CL J Reardon
RP D Lamp
RP J Gray
RP T Fossas
C T Pena
1B C Quintana
2B J Reed
SS L Rivera
3B W Boggs
LF M Greenwell
CF E Burks
RF T Brunansky
DH J Clark
UT- S Lyons
M J Morgan

CALIFORNIA
SP M Langston
SP J Abbott
SP C Finley
SP K McCaskill
CL B Harvey
RP M Eichhorn
RP J Robinson
RP S Bailes
C L Parrish
1B W Joyner
2B L Sojo
SS D Schofield
3B G Gaetti
LF L Polonia
MR- D Gallagher
RF D Winfield
DH D Parker
UO- M Venable
M1 D Rader
M2 B Rodgers

CHICAGO
SP J McDowell
SP C Hough
SP G Hibbard
SP A Fernandez
RS M Perez
CL B Thigpen
RP S Radinsky
RP D Pall
C C Fisk
1R D Pasqua
2B- S Fletcher
SS O Guillen
3B R Ventura
LF T Raines
CF L Johnson
RF S Sosa
D1 F Thomas
2B J Cora
UI C Grebeck
M J Torborg

CLEVELAND
SP G Swindell
SP C Nagy
SP E King
SR R Nichols
SP T Candiotti
RP D Otto
RP S Hillegas
CL S Olin
RP J Shaw
C J Skinner
1B- B Jacoby
2S- M Lewis
SS F Fermin
32 C Baerga
LD A Belle
CF A Cole
RF- M Whiten
DO C James
IO J Browne
1U- M Aldrete
M1 J McNamara
M2 M Hargrove

DETROIT
SP B Gullickson
SP W Terrell
SP F Tanana
SR M Leiter
CL M Henneman
RP P Gibson
RS J Cerutti
RP J Gleaton
C M Tettleton
1U- D Bergman
2B L Whitaker
SS A Trammell
3S T Fryman
LF- L Moseby
CF M Cuyler
RF R Deer
1B C Fielder
LD- P Incaviglia
UT T Phillips
M S Anderson

KANSAS CITY
SP K Appier
SP B Saberhagen
SP M Boddicker
SR L Aquino
SP M Gubicza
RS T Gordon
CL J Montgomery
RS S Davis
RS M Davis
C- B Mayne
1B- T Benzinger
2B T Shumpert
SS K Stillwell
3B B Pecota
OI J Eisenreich
CF B McRae
RF D Tartabull
DH G Brett
LU K Gibson
S2- D Howard
C- M Macfarlane
3B- K Seitzer
M1 J Wathan
M2 B Schaefer
M3 H McRae

MILWAUKEE
SP J Navarro
SP C Bosio
SP B Wegman
SP D August
RS D Plesac
RP C Crim
RP J Machado
RP D Holmes
C B Surhoff
1B F Stubbs
2B W Randolph
SS B Spiers
32 J Gantner
LF G Vaughn
CF R Yount
RF D Bichette
D1 P Molitor
UO D Hamilton
S3- D Sveum
M T Trebelhorn

MINNESOTA
SP J Morris
SP K Tapani
SP S Erickson
SP A Anderson
CL R Aguilera
RS M Guthrie

RP C Willis
RP S Bedrosian
C B Harper
1B K Hrbek
2B C Knoblauch
SS G Gagne
3B M Pagliarulo
LF D Gladden
CF K Puckett
RL S Mack
DH C Davis
UT G Larkin
3U S Leius
IO A Newman
OI- R Bush
M T Kelly

NEW YORK
SP S Sanderson
SP J Johnson
SR T Leary
SP W Taylor
RS G Cadaret
RS E Plunk
RP L Guetterman
CL S Farr
C M Nokes
1B D Mattingly
2B S Sax
SS A Espinoza
3B- P Kelly
ML R Kelly
CF- B Williams
UO M Hall
DU K Maas
RF- J Barfield
LU- H Meulens
M S Merrill

OAKLAND
SP D Stewart
SP B Welch
SP M Moore
SP J Slusarski
CL D Eckersley
RP C Young
RP S Chitren
RP J Klink
C T Steinbach
1B M McGwire
2B M Gallego
SS- M Bordick
3I E Riles
LF R Henderson
CF D Henderson
RF J Canseco
DH H Baines
UO W Wilson
2O- L Blankenship
M T LaRussa

SEATTLE
SP R Johnson
SP B Holman
SP R DeLucia
SP E Hanson
SR B Krueger
RP B Swift
RP M Jackson
RP R Swan
C D Valle
1B P O'Brien
2B H Reynolds
SS O Vizquel
3B E Martinez
LR G Briley
CF K Griffey
RF J Buhner
DH A Davis
C- S Bradley
S3- J Schaefer
M J Lefebvre

TEXAS
SP K Brown
SP N Ryan
SP J Guzman
RS K Rogers
CL J Russell
RS G Alexander
RS J Barfield
C- I Rodriguez
1B R Palmeiro
2B J Franco
SS J Huson
3B S Buechele
ML J Gonzalez
CF G Pettis
RF R Sierra
DH B Downing
OF K Reimer
SI- M Diaz
3L- D Palmer
C- G Petralli
CU- M Stanley
M B Valentine

TORONTO
SP T Stottlemyre
SP J Key
SR D Wells
SP J Guzman
SP T Candiotti
RP D Ward
RP M Timlin
RP J Acker
CL T Henke
C G Myers
1B J Olerud
2B R Alomar
SS M Lee
3B K Gruber
LF- C Maldonado
CF D White
RL J Carter
DH- R Mulliniks
C P Borders
DU- P Tabler
OF- M Wilson
M1 C Gaston
M2 G Tenace
M3 C Gaston

1991 NL

ATLANTA
SP T Glavine
SP C Leibrandt
SP J Smoltz
SP S Avery
RP M Stanton
CL J Berenguer
RP K Mercker
C G Olson
1B- B Hunter
2B M Lemke
SS R Belliard
3B T Pendleton
UO O Nixon
CF R Gant
RF D Justice
SI J Blauser
LF L Smith
2B J Treadway
1B- S Bream
M B Cox

CHICAGO
SP G Maddux
SP M Bielecki
SP S Boskie
SP F Castillo
SP R Sutcliffe
RS L Lancaster
RP P Assenmacher
RS B Scanlan
RP C McElroy
C- R Wilkins
1B M Grace
2B R Sandberg
SS S Dunston
3B L Salazar
LF G Bell
CF J Walton
RF A Dawson
ML D Dascenzo
UT C Walker
UO- D Smith
3S- J Vizcaino
M1 D Zimmer
M2 J Altobelli
M3 J Essian

CINCINNATI
SP T Browning
SP J Rijo
SP J Armstrong
SR S Scudder
SP C Hammond
RS R Myers
CL R Dibble
RS N Charlton
RP T Power
C- J Oliver
1B H Morris
2B B Doran
SS B Larkin
3B C Sabo
LM B Hatcher
CF- E Davis
RF P O'Neill
2S M Duncan
UI- L Quinones
MU H Winningham
LR- G Braggs
C- J Reed
M L Piniella

HOUSTON
SP P Harnisch
SP M Portugal
SP J Deshaies
SR D Kile
SP J Jones
RP A Osuna
RP C Schilling
RP J Corsi
RP D Henry
C C Biggio
1B J Bagwell
2U C Candaele
SS- E Yelding
3B K Caminiti
LF L Gonzalez
MU G Young
CF S Finley
UI R Ramirez
UO- M Davidson
M A Howe

LOS ANGELES
SP M Morgan
SP R Martinez
SP T Belcher
SP B Ojeda
SP O Hershiser
RS K Gross
RP T Crews
RP J Gott
CL J Howell
C M Scioscia
1B E Murray
2B J Samuel
SS A Griffin
3B L Harris
LF K Daniels
CF B Butler
RF D Strawberry
CU G Carter
OI S Javier
3I M Sharperson
UO- C Gwynn
M T Lasorda

MONTREAL
SP De Martinez
SP M Gardner
SP B Barnes
SP C Nabholz
SP O Boyd
RP B Jones
RS B Sampen
RP S Ruskin
RP J Fassero
C- G Reyes
1B A Galarraga
2B D DeShields
SS S Owen
3B T Wallach
LF I Calderon
CF M Grissom
UO Da Martinez
R1 L Walker
S1- T Foley
M1 B Rodgers
M2 T Runnells

NEW YORK
SP D Cone
SP F Viola
SP D Gooden
SR W Whitehurst
SP R Darling
RS P Schourek
CL J Franco
RP J Innis
RP A Pena
C- R Cerone
1B D Magadan
23 G Jefferies
SS K Elster
3U H Johnson
LF K McReynolds
MR D Boston
RF H Brooks
UO M Carreon
2O K Miller
OC- M Sasser
M1 B Harrelson
M2 M Cubbage

PHILADELPHIA
SP T Mulholland
SP T Greene
SP J DeJesus
SR B Ruffin
SP D Cox
CL M Williams
RP J Boever
RP R McDowell
RP D Akerfelds
C- D Daulton
1O J Kruk
2B M Morandini
SS D Thon
3B C Hayes
LF W Chamberlain
ML- V Hayes
RF D Murphy
1U R Jordan
IF- W Backman
UO- J Morris
M1 N Leyva
M2 J Fregosi

PITTSBURGH
SP D Drabek
SP Z Smith
SP J Smiley
SP R Tomlin
SP B Walk
RP S Belinda
RP B Landrum
RS V Palacios
RP N Heaton
C M LaValliere
1B O Merced
2B J Lind
SS J Bell
R3 B Bonilla
LF B Bonds
CF A Van Slyke
OI G Varsho
UT G Redus
OI- L McClendon
UI- C Wilkerson
M J Leyland

ST. LOUIS
SP B Smith
SP B Tewksbury
SP K Hill
SP O Olivares
SP J DeLeon
CL L Smith
RP J Agosto
RP S Terry
RP C Carpenter
C T Pagnozzi
1B P Guerrero
2B J Oquendo
SS O Smith
3B T Zeile
LU M Thompson
CF R Lankford
RF F Jose
UT R Hudler
2B G Pena
1U G Perry
LF- B Gilkey
M J Torre

SAN DIEGO
SP A Benes
SP B Hurst
SP D Rasmussen
SP G Harris
RP M Maddux
CL C Lefferts
RP R Rodriguez
C B Santiago
1B F McGriff
2O B Roberts
SS T Fernandez
3B- J Howell
LU J Clark
MU D Jackson
RF T Gwynn
UO T Howard
23- T Teufel
M G Riddoch

SAN FRANCISCO
SP B Black
SP J Burkett
SR T Wilson
SR D Robinson
RS K Downs
RP J Brantley
CL D Righetti
RP F Oliveras
C- S Decker
1B W Clark
2B R Thompson
SS- J Uribe
3B M Williams
UT M Felder
MR W McGee
RU K Bass
SI D Anderson
LF K Mitchell
OI- M Kingery
M R Craig

1992 AL

BALTIMORE
SP M Mussina
SP R Sutcliffe
SP B McDonald
SP B Milacki
RP T Frohwirth
RP A Mills
CL G Olson
RP S Davis
C- C Hoiles
1B R Milligan
2B B Ripken
SS C Ripken
3B L Gomez
LF B Anderson
CF M Devereaux
RF J Orsulak
DH G Davis
2U M McLemore
1B D Segui
RU- C Martinez
M J Oates

BOSTON
SP R Clemens
SP F Viola
SP J Hesketh
SP J Dopson
SR M Gardiner
RS D Darwin
RP G Harris
RS M Young
RP P Quantrill
C T Pena
1B M Vaughn
2B J Reed
SS L Rivera
3B W Boggs
LF- B Hatcher
ML B Zupcic
RU T Brunansky
DH- J Clark
13 S Cooper
OF H Winningham
RU P Plantier
M B Hobson

CALIFORNIA
SP M Langston
SP J Abbott
SP C Finley
SP J Valera
SP B Blyleven
CL J Grahe
RP C Crim
RP M Eichhorn
C- M Fitzgerald
1B L Stevens
2B L Sojo
SS G DiSarcina
31 G Gaetti
LD L Polonia
CF J Felix
UO C Curtis
DH- H Brooks
32 R Gonzales
RF- V Hayes
M1 B Rodgers
M2 J Wathan
M3 B Rodgers

CHICAGO
SP J McDowell
SP K McCaskill
SP A Fernandez
SP G Hibbard
SP C Hough
RS W Alvarez
RP R Hernandez
CL B Thigpen
RP T Leach
C R Karkovice
1B F Thomas
2B S Sax
SS- C Grebeck
3B R Ventura
LF T Raines
CF L Johnson
RF- S Abner
DH G Bell
RF- D Pasqua
M G Lamont

CLEVELAND
SP C Nagy
SR J Armstrong
SP D Cook
SP S Scudder
CL S Olin
RS R Nichols
RP T Power
RP E Plunk
C- S Alomar
1B P Sorrento
2B C Baerga
SS M Lewis
3B B Jacoby
LO T Howard
CF K Lofton
RF M Whiten
DL A Belle
UO G Hill
C- J Ortiz
M M Hargrove

DETROIT
SP B Gullickson
SP F Tanana
SR W Terrell
SR M Leiter
RS J Doherty
CL M Henneman
RP L Lancaster
RP K Knudsen
CD M Tettleton
1U- D Bergman
2B L Whitaker
SS T Fryman
3B S Livingstone
LF D Gladden
CF- M Cuyler
RF R Deer
1D C Fielder
LU M Carreon
UT T Phillips
UT- S Barnes
M S Anderson

KANSAS CITY
SP K Appier
SP H Pichardo
SP M Gubicza
SP R Reed
CL J Montgomery
RS T Gordon
RP R Meacham
RS M Boddicker
C M Macfarlane
1B W Joyner
2B K Miller
SS- D Howard
3B G Jefferies
LF K McReynolds
CF B McRae
RU J Eisenreich
DH G Brett
S2 C Wilkerson
C- B Mayne
RU- G Thurman
M H McRae

MILWAUKEE
SP B Wegman
SP J Navarro
SP C Bosio
SP R Bones
SP C Eldred
CL D Henry
RP D Plesac
RP M Fetters
RP J Austin
C B Surhoff
1U- F Stubbs
2B S Fletcher
SS P Listach
3B K Seitzer
LF G Vaughn
CF R Yount
RM D Hamilton
D1 P Molitor
RF D Bichette
23 J Gantner
M P Garner

MINNESOTA
SP J Smiley
SP K Tapani
SP S Erickson
SP B Krueger
CL R Aguilera
RP M Guthrie
RP C Willis
RP T Edens
C B Harper
1B K Hrbek
2B C Knoblauch
SS G Gagne
3B S Leius
LF S Mack
CF K Puckett
RF P Munoz
DH C Davis
OI R Bush
UT G Larkin
M T Kelly

NEW YORK
SP M Perez
SP S Sanderson
SP S Kamieniecki
RS G Cadaret
RP R Monteleone
CL S Farr
RP J Habyan
C M Nokes
1B D Mattingly
2B P Kelly
S2 A Stankiewicz
3B C Hayes
LU M Hall
ML R Kelly
RD D Tartabull
DU K Maas
SU R Velarde
M B Showalter

OAKLAND
SP M Moore
SP R Darling
SP D Stewart
SP B Welch
CL D Eckersley
RP J Parrett
RS K Campbell
RP G Nelson
C T Steinbach
1B M McGwire
2S M Bordick
SS W Weiss
3B C Lansford
LF R Henderson
CF W Wilson
RF- J Canseco
DH H Baines
2O L Blankenship
3O J Browne
M T LaRussa

SEATTLE
SP D Fleming
SP R Johnson
SP E Hanson
RS R Swan
RP J Nelson
RP M Schooler
RP C Jones
C D Valle
1D P O'Brien
2B H Reynolds
SS O Vizquel
3B E Martinez
LM H Cotto
CF K Griffey
RF J Buhner
1D T Martinez
LD K Mitchell
UT- G Briley
M B Plummer

TEXAS
SP K Brown
SP J Guzman
SP B Witt
SP N Ryan
RS T Burns
RP K Rogers
CL J Russell
C I Rodriguez
1B R Palmeiro
2I A Newman
SS- D Thon
3B D Palmer
LU K Reimer
CF J Gonzalez
RF R Sierra
DH B Downing
S2 J Huson
CU- G Petralli
M1 B Valentine
M2 T Harrah

TORONTO
SP J Morris
SP J Key
SP J Guzman
SP T Stottlemyre
SR D Wells
RP D Ward
CL T Henke
RP P Hentgen
C P Borders
1B J Olerud
2B R Alomar
SS M Lee
3B K Gruber
LF C Maldonado
CF D White
RF J Carter
DH D Winfield
M C Gaston

1992 NL

ATLANTA
SP J Smoltz
SP S Avery
SP T Glavine
SP C Leibrandt
RP K Mercker
RP M Stanton
RP M Freeman
C- G Olson
1B S Bream
2B M Lemke
SS R Belliard
3B T Pendleton
LF R Gant
CF O Nixon
RF D Justice
C D Berryhill
SS J Blauser
1B B Hunter
MU- D Sanders
UM- L Smith
M B Cox

CHICAGO
SP G Maddux
SP M Morgan
SP F Castillo
SP D Jackson
RP B Scanlan
RS J Bullinger
RP C McElroy
RS J Robinson
C- J Girardi
1B M Grace
2B R Sandberg
SS- R Sanchez
3B- S Buechele
LF D May
MO D Dascenzo
RF A Dawson
UT L Salazar
UO D Smith
S3- J Vizcaino
C- R Wilkins
M J Lefebvre

CINCINNATI
SP T Belcher
SP G Swindell
SP J Rijo
SP C Hammond
CL N Charlton
CL R Dibble
RP D Henry
RP S Bankhead
C J Oliver
1B H Morris
2B B Doran
SS B Larkin
3B- C Sabo
ML R Sanders
CF D Martinez
RF P O'Neill
UT B Roberts
LR- G Braggs
M L Piniella

HOUSTON
SP P Harnisch
SP B Henry
SP J Jones
SP D Kile
SP M Portugal
RP D Jones
RP X Hernandez
RP J Boever
RS W Blair
C E Taubensee
1B J Bagwell
2B C Biggio
SS- A Cedeno
3B K Caminiti
LF L Gonzalez
CF S Finley
RF E Anthony
UT C Candaele
LR P Incaviglia
M A Howe

LOS ANGELES
SP O Hershiser
SP K Gross
SP T Candiotti
SP B Ojeda
SP R Martinez
RP R McDowell
RP J Gott
RP T Crews
RP S Wilson
C M Scioscia
1B E Karros
2I L Harris
SS J Offerman
3B D Hansen
LF- E Davis
CF B Butler
UO M Webster
OI T Benzinger
UI M Sharperson
M T Lasorda

MONTREAL
SP D Martinez
SP K Hill
SP C Nabholz
SP M Gardner
SP B Barnes
CL J Wetteland
RP M Rojas
RP J Fassero
RP B Sampen
C- G Carter
31 T Wallach
2B D DeShields
SS S Owen
3U B Barberie
LU M Alou
CF M Grissom
RF L Walker
LU J Vander Wal
1U- A Cianfrocco
C- D Fletcher
M1 T Runnells
M2 F Alou

NEW YORK
SP S Fernandez
SP D Gooden
SP D Cone
SP P Schourek
RS A Young
RS W Whitehurst
RP J Innis
RP P Gibson
C T Hundley
1B E Murray
2B- W Randolph
SS D Schofield
3B D Magadan
LU D Boston
CF H Johnson
RF B Bonilla
UO D Gallagher
UI B Pecota
UT C Walker
IC- M Sasser
M *J Torborg*

PHILADELPHIA
SP T Mulholland
SR C Schilling
SR K Abbott
SP B Rivera
CL M Williams
RS C Brantley
RP M Hartley
RP B Jones
C D Daulton
1B J Kruk
2B M Morandini
SS- J Bell
3B D Hollins
IO M Duncan
CF- L Dykstra
RO R Amaro
ML- S Javier
1U- R Jordan
M *J Fregosi*

PITTSBURGH
SP D Drabek
SP R Tomlin
SP Z Smith
SR B Walk
RP R Mason
RP S Belinda
RS D Neagle
RP B Patterson
C- M LaValliere
1B O Merced
2B J Lind
SS J Bell
3B- S Buechele
LF B Bonds
CF A Van Slyke
RO C Espy
3I J King
UO G Varsho
RU- L McClendon
C- D Slaught
M *J Leyland*

ST. LOUIS
SP B Tewksbury
SP O Olivares
SP R Cormier
SP D Osborne
SP M Clark
CL L Smith
RS J DeLeon
RP M Perez
RP C Carpenter
C T Pagnozzi
1B- A Galarraga
2B- L Alicea
SS O Smith
3B T Zeile
LF B Gilkey
CF R Lankford
RF F Jose
UO M Thompson
UR- G Perry
M *J Torre*

SAN DIEGO
SP A Benes
SP B Hurst
SP C Lefferts
SP G Harris
SP F Seminara
CL R Myers
RP R Rodriguez
RP J Melendez
RP M Maddux
C B Santiago
1B F McGriff
2B K Stillwell
SS T Fernandez
3B G Sheffield
LF J Clark
CF D Jackson
RF T Gwynn
OF O Azocar
23 T Teufel
UO- K Ward
M1 *G Riddoch*
M2 *J Riggleman*

SAN FRANCISCO
SP J Burkett
SP B Black
SP B Swift
SP T Wilson
RP R Beck
RP J Brantley
RP B Hickerson
RP M Jackson
C K Manwaring
1B W Clark
2B R Thompson
SS R Clayton
3B M Williams
OI M Felder
CF D Lewis
RU W McGee
LU C James
UT C Snyder
LU- K Bass
M *R Craig*

1993 AL

BALTIMORE
SP B McDonald
SP F Valenzuela
SP M Mussina
SP R Sutcliffe
SP J Moyer
RP A Mills
RP T Frohwirth
RP M Williamson
RP J Poole
C C Hoiles
1B D Segui
2B H Reynolds
SS C Ripken
3B- T Hulett
LF B Anderson
CF M Devereaux
RF M McLemore
DH H Baines
M *J Oates*

BOSTON
SP D Darwin
SP R Clemens
SP F Viola
SP J Dopson
SP A Sele
RS P Quantrill
RP G Harris
RP S Bankhead
RS J Hesketh
C T Pena
1B M Vaughn
2B S Fletcher
SS J Valentin
3B S Cooper
LF M Greenwell
CF B Hatcher
UO B Zupcic
DH A Dawson
1R C Quintana
UI- E Riles
M *B Hobson*

CALIFORNIA
SP M Langston
SP C Finley
SP S Sanderson
RP J Grahe
RP K Patterson
RS J Valera
RP G Nelson
C G Myers
1B J Snow
2B T Lovullo
SS G DiSarcina
31 R Gonzales
LF L Polonia
CF C Curtis
RF T Salmon
DH C Davis
UT- S Javier
M *B Rodgers*

CHICAGO
SP J McDowell
SP A Fernandez
SP W Alvarez
SP J Bere
SR K McCaskill
CL R Hernandez
RP D Pall
RP S Radinsky
RP J Schwarz
C R Karkovice
1B F Thomas
2B J Cora
SS O Guillen
3B R Ventura
LF T Raines
CF L Johnson
RF E Burks
DH G Bell
OF- B Jackson
M *G Lamont*

CLEVELAND
SP J Mesa
SP T Kramer
SR M Clark
RP E Plunk
RP J Hernandez
RP D Lilliquist
RP J Dipoto
C- J Ortiz
1B P Sorrento
2B C Baerga
SS F Fermin
3B A Espinoza
LF A Belle
CF K Lofton
RF W Kirby
DH R Jefferson
IF- J Treadway
M *M Hargrove*

DETROIT
SP M Moore
SP D Wells
SP J Doherty
SP B Gullickson
SR M Leiter
RS T Bolton
CL M Henneman
RS B Krueger
RP R Mac Donald
C C Kreuter
1B C Fielder
2B L Whitaker
S3 A Trammell
S3 T Fryman
UT T Phillips
CF- M Cuyler
RF- R Deer
DM K Gibson
3D S Livingstone
IC M Tettleton
UT- S Barnes
LF- D Gladden
M *S Anderson*

KANSAS CITY
SP D Cone
SP K Appier
SP H Pichardo
SP C Haney
RS T Gordon
CL J Montgomery
RS M Gubicza
C M Macfarlane
1B W Joyner
2B J Lind
SS G Gagne
3B- G Gaetti
LF K McReynolds
CF B McRae
RF F Jose
DH G Brett
LU C Gwynn
3B- P Hiatt
M *H McRae*

MILWAUKEE
SP C Eldred
SP J Navarro
SP R Bones
SP B Wegman
SP A Miranda
RP D Henry
RP J Orosco
RP G Lloyd
RP M Fetters
C D Nilsson
1B J Jaha
2B B Spiers
SS P Listach
3B B Surhoff
LD G Vaughn
CF R Yount
RM D Hamilton
DO K Reimer
2S- J Bell
UI- D Thon
M *P Garner*

MINNESOTA
SP K Tapani
SP S Erickson
SP W Banks
SP J Deshaies
RS M Trombley
CL R Aguilera
RP M Hartley
RP G Tsamis
C B Harper
1B K Hrbek
2B C Knoblauch
SP P Meares
3B- M Pagliarulo
LR P Munoz
ML S Mack
MR K Puckett
DU D Winfield
OI D McCarty
S3 J Reboulet
M *T Kelly*

NEW YORK
SP J Key
SP J Abbott
SP M Perez
SR S Kamieniecki
SR B Wickman
RR R Monteleone
RP S Howe
C M Stanley
1B D Mattingly
2B P Kelly
SS S Owen
3B W Boggs
LF D James
CF B Williams
RL P O'Neill
DR D Tartabull
UI M Gallego
UT- J Leyritz
LS- R Velarde
M *B Showalter*

OAKLAND
SP B Witt
SP R Darling
SP B Welch
RS K Downs
CL D Eckersley
RP J Boever
RP E Nunez
C T Steinbach
1U- M Aldrete
2B B Gates
SS M Bordick
3B C Paquette
LF- R Henderson
MD D Henderson
RF R Sierra
D1 T Neel
MI- L Blankenship
C- S Hemond
M *T LaRussa*

SEATTLE
SP R Johnson
SP E Hanson
SP T Leary
SP D Fleming
SP C Bosio
RP J Nelson
RP D Henry
C D Valle
1B T Martinez
2I R Amaral
SS O Vizquel
3B M Blowers
LF M Felder
CF K Griffey
RF J Buhner
DU- P O'Brien
OI- M Sasser
M *L Piniella*

TEXAS
SP K Brown
SP K Rogers
SP R Pavlik
SP C Leibrandt
CL T Henke
RS B Bohanon
RS C Lefferts
RP M Whiteside
C I Rodriguez
1B R Palmeiro
2B D Strange
SS- M Lee
3B D Palmer
LF J Gonzalez
CF D Hulse
RF- J Canseco
DH J Franco
M *K Kennedy*

TORONTO
SP J Guzman
SP P Hentgen
SP T Stottlemyre
SP D Stewart
SP J Morris
CL D Ward
RS A Leiter
RP D Cox
RP M Eichhorn
C P Borders
1B J Olerud
2B R Alomar
SS- T Fernandez
3B E Sprague
OI- T Ward
CF D White
RL J Carter
DH P Molitor
M *C Gaston*

1993 NL

ATLANTA
SP G Maddux
SP J Smoltz
SP T Glavine
SP S Avery
RP G McMichael
CL M Stanton
RS K Mercker
RP J Howell
C D Berryhill
1B S Bream
2B M Lemke
SS J Blauser
3B T Pendleton
LF R Gant
CF O Nixon
RF D Justice
S2- R Belliard
C- G Olson
MU- D Sanders
M *B Cox*

CHICAGO
SP M Morgan
SP J Guzman
SP G Hibbard
SP M Harkey
SP F Castillo
CL R Myers
RS J Bautista
RP B Scanlan
RP S Boskie
C R Wilkins
1B M Grace
2B R Sandberg
SS R Sanchez
3B S Buechele
LF D May
UO D Smith
RM S Sosa
S3 J Vizcaino
CF W Wilson
M *J Lefebvre*

CINCINNATI
SP J Rijo
SP T Pugh
SP T Belcher
SP T Browning
SP J Smiley
RS B Ayala
RP J Reardon
RP J Spradlin
C J Oliver
1B H Morris
2U J Samuel
SS B Larkin
3B C Sabo
LF- K Mitchell
MO J Brumfield
RF R Sanders
UI J Branson
1U- R Milligan
2B- B Roberts
M1 *T Perez*
M2 *D Johnson*

COLORADO
SP A Reynoso
SR W Blair
RS B Ruffin
CL D Holmes
RP S Reed
RS J Parrett
C- J Girardi
1B A Galarraga
2L E Young
SS V Castilla
3B C Hayes
L1 J Clark
MU A Cole
RF D Bichette
UO D Boston
MU- C Jones
C- D Sheaffer
UT- J Tatum
M *D Baylor*

FLORIDA
SP C Hough
SP J Armstrong
SP C Hammond
SP R Bowen
SR L Aquino
CL B Harvey
RP R Lewis
RP M Turner
C B Santiago
1B O Destrade
2B B Barberie
SS W Weiss
3B- G Sheffield
LF J Conine
CF C Carr
RF- D Whitmore
UO G Briley
IO R Renteria
UI- A Arias
M *R Lachemann*

HOUSTON
SP D Drabek
SP P Harnisch
SP M Portugal
SP G Swindell
SP D Kile
CL D Jones
RP X Hernandez
RS B Williams
RP T Edens
C- E Taubensee
1B J Bagwell
2B C Biggio
SS A Cedeno
3B K Caminiti
LF L Gonzalez
CF S Finley
RF E Anthony
UO K Bass
UI- C Donnels
C- S Servais
M *A Howe*

LOS ANGELES
SP O Hershiser
SP T Candiotti
SP R Martinez
SP K Gross
SP P Astacio
RP P Martinez
CL J Gott
RP R McDowell
RP R Trlicek
C M Piazza
1B E Karros
2B J Reed
SS J Offerman
3B T Wallach
LF E Davis
CF B Butler
RF C Snyder
IO L Harris
U2- D Hansen
UO- M Webster
M *T Lasorda*

MONTREAL
SP D Martinez
SP K Hill
SP C Nabholz
RS J Fassero
CL J Wetteland
RS B Barnes
RP M Rojas
C D Fletcher
1B- G Colbrunn
2B D DeShields
SS W Cordero
3B S Berry
LF M Alou
CF M Grissom
RF L Walker
UT L Frazier
3S M Lansing
UT J Vander Wal
13- F Bolick
M *F Alou*

NEW YORK
SP D Gooden
SP F Tanana
SP E Hillman
SP B Saberhagen
SR P Schourek
RP S Fernandez
RS A Young
RP J Innis
RP M Maddux
C T Hundley
1B E Murray
2B J Kent
SS- T Bogar
3B- H Johnson
LF- V Coleman
OI J Orsulak
R3 B Bonilla
OI D Gallagher
UI J McKnight
UT C Walker
RU- J Burnitz
M1 *J Torborg*
M2 *D Green*

PHILADELPHIA
SP C Schilling
SP D Jackson
SP T Greene
SP T Mulholland
SP B Rivera
CL M Williams
RP D West
RP L Andersen
RP M Williams
C D Daulton
1B J Kruk
2B M Morandini
SS- K Stocker
3B D Hollins
LF M Thompson
CF L Dykstra
RF J Eisenreich
2S M Duncan
LF P Incaviglia
RF- W Chamberlain
UM- R Jordan
M *J Fregosi*

PITTSBURGH
SP S Cooke
SP B Walk
SR P Wagner
SP T Wakefield
RP B Minor
RS D Neagle
RS D Otto
RP J Johnston
C D Slaught
1B K Young
2B C Garcia
SS J Bell
3B J King
LM A Martin
CF- A Van Slyke
RF O Merced
OF D Clark
UI- T Foley
RU- L McClendon
LU- L Smith
M *J Leyland*

ST. LOUIS
SP B Tewksbury
SP R Arocha
SP D Osborne
SR R Cormier
SP J Magrane
RS O Olivares
CL L Smith
RP M Perez
RP R Murphy
C- T Pagnozzi
1B G Jefferies
2B L Alicea
SS O Smith
3B T Zeile
LF B Gilkey
CF R Lankford
RF M Whiten
OI R Brewer
C- E Pappas
UT- G Perry
M *J Torre*

SAN DIEGO
SP A Benes
SP Gr Harris
SP D Brocail
SP W Whitehurst
SP T Worrell
CL Ge Harris
RS K Taylor
RP T Hoffman
RP R Mason
C- K Higgins
1B- F McGriff
2B J Gardner
SS R Gutierrez
3B- G Sheffield
LF P Plantier
CF D Bell
RF T Gwynn
UT P Clark
UT C Shipley
OI- B Bean
3B- A Cianfrocco
2U- T Teufel
M *J Riggleman*

SAN FRANCISCO
SP B Swift
SP J Burkett
SP T Wilson
CL R Beck
RS B Hickerson
RS J Brantley
RS D Burba
C K Manwaring
1B W Clark
2B R Thompson
SS R Clayton
3B M Williams
LF B Bonds
CF D Lewis
RF W McGee
IO- T Benzinger
UO- D Martinez
M *D Baker*

1994 AL

BALTIMORE
SP M Mussina
SP B McDonald
SP J Moyer
SP S Fernandez
RP M Eichhorn
CL L Smith
RP M Williamson
RP A Mills
C C Hoiles
1B R Palmeiro
2B M McLemore
SS C Ripken
3B L Gomez
LM B Anderson
CF M Devereaux
RF J Hammonds
DH H Baines
3O C Sabo
RL- J Voigt
M *J Oates*

BOSTON
SP R Clemens
SP A Sele
SP J Hesketh
SP D Darwin
RP K Ryan
RP G Harris
RP C Howard
RP S Bankhead
C D Berryhill
1B M Vaughn
2B- S Fletcher
SS J Valentin
3B S Cooper
LF M Greenwell
CF O Nixon
RL- T Brunansky
DH A Dawson
2I T Naehring
S2- C Rodriguez
UO L Tinsley
M *B Hobson*

CALIFORNIA
SP C Finley
SP M Langston
SP P Leftwich
SP B Anderson
SP J Magrane
RS M Leiter
RS J Dopson
RP J Grahe
RS R Springer
C- C Turner
1B- J Snow
2B H Reynolds
SS G DiSarcina
3B S Owen
LO J Edmonds
CF C Curtis
RF T Salmon
DH C Davis
32 D Easley
LU B Jackson
M1 *B Rodgers*
M2 *B Knoop*
M3 *M Lachemann*

CHICAGO
SP J McDowell
SP A Fernandez
SP W Alvarez
SP J Bere
SP S Sanderson
RP J DeLeon
RP R Hernandez
RP K McCaskill
C R Karkovice
1B F Thomas
2B J Cora
SS O Guillen
3B R Ventura
LF T Raines
CF L Johnson
RF D Jackson
DH J Franco
C- M LaValliere
OF- W Newson
M *G Lamont*

CLEVELAND
SP D Martinez
SP C Nagy
SP J Morris
SP M Clark
SP J Grimsley
RP J Mesa
RP E Plunk
C S Alomar
1B P Sorrento
2B C Baerga
SS O Vizquel
3B J Thome
LF A Belle

CF K Lofton
RF M Ramirez
DH E Murray
UI A Espinoza
RU W Kirby
M *M Hargrove*

DETROIT
SP T Belcher
SP M Moore
SP B Gullickson
SP D Wells
SP J Doherty
RP J Boever
RP M Gardiner
RP S Davis
RP M Henneman
C- C Kreuter
1B C Fielder
2B L Whitaker
SS A Trammell
3B T Fryman
LF T Phillips
ML- M Cuyler
RF J Felix
DO K Gibson
S2 C Gomez
IC M Tettleton
UT- J Samuel
M *S Anderson*

KANSAS CITY
SP D Cone
SP K Appier
SP T Gordon
SP M Gubicza
CL J Montgomery
RP H Pichardo
RP R Meacham
RP S Belinda
C M Macfarlane
1B W Joyner
2B J Lind
SS G Gagne
3B G Gaetti
LF V Coleman
CF B McRae
RF F Jose
DU B Hamelin
23- T Shumpert
M *H McRae*

MILWAUKEE
SP C Eldred
SP R Bones
SP B Wegman
SR B Scanlan
SR J Navarro
CL M Fetters
RP G Lloyd
RS M Ignasiak
RP J Orosco
CD D Nilsson
1B J Jaha
2B J Reed
SS J Valentin
31 K Seitzer
LF G Vaughn
ML T Ward
RF M Mieske
DC- B Harper
MR A Diaz
IO B Spiers
M *P Garner*

MINNESOTA
SP K Tapani
SP S Erickson
SP J Deshaies
SP P Mahomes
SP C Pulido
CL R Aguilera
RP C Willis
RP M Guthrie
RP M Trombley
C M Walbeck
1B K Hrbek
2B C Knoblauch
SS P Meares
3B S Leius
LF S Mack
CF A Cole
RF K Puckett
DH D Winfield
LR P Munoz
SI J Reboulet
IO- C Hale
M *T Kelly*

NEW YORK
SP J Key
SP J Abbott
SP M Perez
SP T Mulholland
SP S Kamieniecki
RP B Wickman
CL S Howe
RS S Hitchcock
RP X Hernandez
C M Stanley
1B D Mattingly
2B P Kelly
SS M Gallego
3B W Boggs
LF L Polonia
CF B Williams
RF P O'Neill
DH D Tartabull
IC J Leyritz
S3 R Velarde
UO- G Williams
M *B Showalter*

OAKLAND
SP R Darling
SP B Witt
SP T Van Poppel
SR S Ontiveros
RS C Reyes
RS B Welch
CL D Eckersley
RP J Briscoe
C T Steinbach
1D T Neel
2B- B Gates
SS M Bordick
3B S Brosius
LF R Henderson
CF S Javier
RF R Sierra
OI G Berroa
OI M Aldrete
IC S Hemond
M *T LaRussa*

SEATTLE
SP R Johnson
SP C Bosio
SP D Fleming
SP G Hibbard
CL B Ayala
RP B Risley
RP T Davis
RP R Gossage
C D Wilson
1B T Martinez
2U R Amaral
SS F Fermin
3D E Martinez
LF E Anthony
CF K Griffey
RF J Buhner
DU- R Jefferson
3U M Blowers
2S- L Sojo
M *L Piniella*

TEXAS
SP K Brown
SP K Rogers
SP H Fajardo
RP C Carpenter
RP M Whiteside
CL T Henke
RP D Oliver
C I Rodriguez
1B W Clark
2B- J Frye
SS M Lee
3B D Palmer
LF J Gonzalez
CF D Hulse
RM R Greer
DH J Canseco
2U D Strange
MR- O McDowell
M *K Kennedy*

TORONTO
SP P Hentgen
SP J Guzman
SP T Stottlemyre
SP D Stewart
SP A Leiter
RP T Castillo
RP W Williams
RP M Timlin
C P Borders
1B J Olerud
2B R Alomar
SS D Schofield
3B E Sprague
LO M Huff
CF D White
RF J Carter
DH P Molitor
M *C Gaston*

1994 NL

ATLANTA
SP G Maddux
SP T Glavine
SP S Avery
SP J Smoltz
SP K Mercker
CL G McMichael
RP M Wohlers
RP M Stanton
RP S Bedrosian
C J Lopez
1B F McGriff
2B M Lemke
SS J Blauser
3B T Pendleton
LF R Klesko
CF- R Kelly
RF D Justice
OF T Tarasco
LF D Gallagher
IO- B Pecota
M *B Cox*

CHICAGO
SP S Trachsel
SP W Banks
SP A Young
SP K Foster
SP M Morgan
RS J Bullinger
RP J Bautista
RP C Crim
CL R Myers
C R Wilkins
1B M Grace
2B- R Sandberg
SS S Dunston
3B S Buechele
LF D May
UO G Hill
RF S Sosa
MU K Rhodes
2S R Sanchez
UT- E Zambrano
M *T Trebelhorn*

CINCINNATI
SP J Rijo
SP J Smiley
SP E Hanson
SP J Roper
SR P Schourek
RP J Brantley
RP J Ruffin
RP C McElroy
RP H Carrasco
C B Dorsett
1B H Morris
2B B Boone
SS B Larkin
3B T Fernandez
LF K Mitchell
CF- D Sanders
RF R Sanders
UI- J Branson
UO- J Brumfield
IO- L Harris
UO T Howard
C- E Taubensee
M *D Johnson*

COLORADO
SR G Harris
SP D Nied
SP M Freeman
SR M Harkey
SP L Painter
RP W Blair
RP K Ritz
RP B Ruffin
RP S Reed
C J Girardi
1B A Galarraga
2B N Liriano
SS W Weiss
3B C Hayes
LU H Johnson
MU M Kingery
RF D Bichette
UO- J Cangelosi
UT J Vander Wal
LU E Young
M *D Baylor*

FLORIDA
SP D Weathers
SP P Rapp
SP C Hough
SP M Gardner
SP C Hammond
CL R Nen
RP R Lewis
RP L Aquino
RP T Mathews
C B Santiago
1B- G Colbrunn
2B B Barberie
SS K Abbott
3B- D Hollins
3O J Browne
LF J Conine
CF C Carr
RF G Sheffield
UO M Carrillo
3U D Magadan
IF- A Arias
M *R Lachemann*

HOUSTON
SP D Drabek
SP D Kile
SP G Swindell
SR S Reynolds
SP P Harnisch
RP T Jones
RP B Williams
CL J Hudek
RP T Edens
C S Servais
1B J Bagwell
2B C Biggio
SS A Cedeno
3B K Caminiti
LF L Gonzalez
CF S Finley
RF J Mouton
RU K Bass
UO- M Felder
M *T Collins*

LOS ANGELES
SP R Martinez
SP K Gross
SP T Candiotti
SP P Astacio
SP O Hershiser
RP T Worrell
RP R McDowell
RP J Gott
C M Piazza
1B E Karros
2B D DeShields
SS J Offerman
3B T Wallach
LF H Rodriguez
CF B Butler
RF R Mondesi
LI C Snyder
LU M Webster
OF- C Gwynn
M *T Lasorda*

MONTREAL
SP K Hill
SP P Martinez
SP J Fassero
SP B Henry
SP K Rueter
RP M Rojas
CL J Wetteland
RP G Heredia
RP J Shaw
C D Fletcher
1B C Floyd
2B M Lansing
SS W Cordero
3B S Berry
LR M Alou
CF M Grissom
R1 L Walker
UT L Frazier
C- L Webster
M *F Alou*

NEW YORK
SP B Saberhagen
SP B Jones
SP P Smith
SR M Gozzo
CL J Franco
RP R Mason
RP D Linton
RP J Manzanillo
C T Hundley
1B D Segui
2B J Kent
SS J Vizcaino
3B B Bonilla
UO- J Cangelosi
CF R Thompson
RO J Orsulak
IO F Vina
M *D Green*

PHILADELPHIA
SP D Jackson
SP B Munoz
SR D West
SP S Boskie
SP C Schilling
CL D Jones
RP H Slocumb
C D Daulton
1B J Kruk
2B M Morandini
SS K Stocker
3B- D Hollins
LF M Thompson
CL J Dykstra
RF J Eisenreich
UI M Duncan
LF P Incaviglia
1U R Jordan
3S- K Batiste
OF T Longmire
M *J Fregosi*

PITTSBURGH
SP Z Smith
SP D Neagle
SP S Cooke
SR P Wagner
SP J Lieber
RS R White
RP M Dewey
RP R Manzanillo
C D Slaught
1B B Hunter
2B C Garcia
SS J Bell
3B J King
LF A Martin
CF A Van Slyke
R1 O Merced
RU D Clark
UI- T Foley
OI- G Varsho
13- K Young
M *J Leyland*

ST. LOUIS
SP B Tewksbury
SR V Palacios
SP A Watson
SR T Urbani
SP O Olivares
RS R Arocha
RP B Eversgerd
RP R Rodriguez
RP J Habyan
C T Pagnozzi
1B G Jefferies
2U G Pena
SS O Smith
3B T Zeile
LF B Gilkey
CF R Lankford
RF M Whiten
2U L Alicea
U2- G Perry
M *J Torre*

SAN DIEGO
SP A Benes
SP A Ashby
SP S Sanders
SP J Hamilton
CL T Hoffman
RP P Martinez
RP T Mauser
RP A Sager
C B Ausmus
1B- E Williams
2B B Roberts
SS R Gutierrez
3I C Shipley
LF P Plantier
CF D Bell
RF T Gwynn
OI B Bean
S2 L Lopez
31- A Cianfrocco
UT- P Clark
3B- S Livingstone
M *J Riggleman*

SAN FRANCISCO
SP J Burkett
SP M Portugal
SP B Swift
SR B Hickerson
SP S Torres
RP Van
Landingham
CL R Beck
RP D Burba
RP M Jackson
C K Manwaring
1B T Benzinger
2U J Patterson
SS R Clayton
3B M Williams
LF B Bonds
CF D Lewis
R1 D Martinez
M *D Baker*

1995 AL

BALTIMORE
SP M Mussina
SP K Brown
SP J Moyer
SP S Erickson
CL D Jones
RP M Oquist
RP J Orosco
RP A Benitez
C C Hoiles
1B R Palmeiro
2B M Alexander
SS C Ripken
3B J Manto
LF B Anderson
CF C Goodwin
OF K Bass
DH H Baines
2B B Barberie
M *P Regan*

BOSTON
SP T Wakefield
SP E Hanson
SP R Clemens
SP Z Smith
RS R Cormier
RP M Maddux
RP S Belinda
RP J Hudson
C M Macfarlane
1B M Vaughn
2B L Alicea
SS J Valentin
3B T Naehring
LF M Greenwell
CF L Tinsley
RF T O'Leary
DH J Canseco
M *K Kennedy*

CALIFORNIA
SP C Finley
SP M Langston
SP S Boskie
SP B Anderson
CL L Smith
RP T Percival
RP M James
RP B Patterson
C- J Fabregas
1B J Snow
2B D Easley
SS G DiSarcina
3L T Phillips
LF G Anderson
CF J Edmonds
RF T Salmon
DH C Davis
2O- R Hudler
CU- G Myers
UI- S Owen
M *M Lachemann*

CHICAGO
SP A Fernandez
SP W Alvarez
SP J Bere
SP J Abbott
SR B Keyser
CL R Hernandez
RP K McCaskill
RP J DeLeon
C R Karkovice
OI D Martinez
2B R Durham
SS O Guillen
3B R Ventura
LF T Raines
CF L Johnson
RF M Devereaux
1D F Thomas
UT- N Martin
M1 *G Lamont*
M2 *T Bevington*

CLEVELAND
SP D Martinez
SP C Nagy
SP O Hershiser
SP M Clark
SP C Ogea
CL J Mesa
RP J Tavarez
RP E Plunk
RP J Poole
C T Pena
1B P Sorrento
2B C Baerga
SS O Vizquel
3B J Thome
LF A Belle
CF K Lofton
RF M Ramirez
DH E Murray
UO W Kirby
M *M Hargrove*

DETROIT
SR F Lira
SP S Bergman
SP M Moore
SP D Wells
RP J Doherty
RS B Bohanon
RP J Boever
RP M Christopher
C J Flaherty
1D C Fielder
2B- L Whitaker
SS C Gomez
3B T Fryman
RL B Higginson
CF C Curtis
RF D Bautista
DH- K Gibson
IO- J Samuel
SS- A Trammell
M *S Anderson*

KANSAS CITY
SP M Gubicza
SP K Appier
SP T Gordon
CL J Montgomery
RP H Pichardo
RP R Meacham
RP B Brewer
C B Mayne
1B W Joyner
2U K Lockhart
SS G Gagne
3B G Gaetti
LF- V Coleman
ML T Goodwin
RF J Nunnally
DH- B Hamelin
UT D Howard
M *B Boone*

MILWAUKEE
SP S Sparks
SP R Bones
SP S Karl
SP B Givens
RP B Wegman
RP M Kiefer
C J Oliver
1B J Jaha
2B F Vina
SS J Valentin
3B J Cirillo
LM D Hulse
CF D Hamilton
RF M Mieske
DH G Vaughn
2S P Listach
31 K Seitzer
OI B Surhoff
C- M Matheny
RU- D Nilsson
M *P Garner*

MINNESOTA
SP B Radke
SP K Tapani
SP M Trombley
SP F Rodriguez
SP S Erickson
RS P Mahomes
RS E Guardado
RP D Stevens
RP R Robertson
C M Walbeck
1U S Stahoviak
2B C Knoblauch
SS P Meares
3B S Leius
LF M Cordova
CF R Becker
RF K Puckett
DU P Munoz
CU- M Merullo
UI J Reboulet
M *T Kelly*

NEW YORK
SP J McDowell
SP A Pettitte
SP S Hitchcock
SP D Cone
SP S Kamieniecki
CL J Wetteland
RP B Wickman
RP S Howe
RP R Mac Donald
C M Stanley
1B D Mattingly
2B P Kelly
SS T Fernandez
3B W Boggs
LR G Williams
CF B Williams
RF P O'Neill
DH- R Sierra
2S R Velarde
OI- D James
CU- J Leyritz
M *B Showalter*

OAKLAND
SP T Stottlemyre
SR T Van Poppel
SP S Ontiveros
SP R Darling
CL D Eckersley
RP C Reyes
RP M Acre
RP J Corsi
C T Steinbach
1B M McGwire
2B B Gates
SS M Bordick
3U C Paquette
LF R Henderson
CF S Javier
RF- R Sierra
DR G Berroa
UT S Brosius
M *T LaRussa*

SEATTLE
SP R Johnson
SP T Belcher
SP C Bosio
RP B Ayala
RP J Nelson
RP B Wells
CL N Charlton
C D Wilson
1B T Martinez
2B J Cora
SS L Sojo
3B M Blowers
LM R Amaral
MU A Diaz
RF J Buhner
DH E Martinez
S2- F Fermin
CF- K Griffey
3U- D Strange
M *L Piniella*

TEXAS
SP K Rogers
SP R Pavlik
SP K Gross
SP B Tewksbury
RP R McDowell
RP M Whiteside
RP D Cook
RP T Burrows
C I Rodriguez
1B W Clark
2B J Frye
SS B Gil
3B- M Pagliarulo
L2 M McLemore
CF O Nixon
RF R Greer
DH J Gonzalez
OI M Tettleton
M *J Oates*

TORONTO
SP P Hentgen
SP A Leiter
SP J Guzman
SP D Cone
RP T Castillo
RP W Williams
RP D Cox
C- L Parrish
1B J Olerud
2B R Alomar
SS A Gonzalez
3B E Sprague
LF J Carter
CF D White
RF S Green
DH P Molitor
M *C Gaston*

1995 NL

ATLANTA
SP G Maddux
SP T Glavine
SP J Smoltz
SP S Avery
SP K Mercker
CL M Wohlers
RP G McMichael
RP B Clontz
C J Lopez
1B F McGriff
2B M Lemke
SS J Blauser
3B C Jones
LF R Klesko
CF M Grissom
RF D Justice
LO M Kelly
OF D Smith
S2- R Belliard
M *B Cox*

CHICAGO
SP J Navarro
SP F Castillo
SP K Foster
SP S Trachsel
SP J Bullinger
CL R Myers
RP M Perez
RP T Wendell
RP M Walker
C- S Servais
1B M Grace
2B R Sanchez
SS S Dunston
3B- T Zeile
LF- L Gonzalez

CF B McRae
RF S Sosa
LU S Bullett
UI J Hernandez
IO H Johnson
LU- O Timmons
M J Riggleman

CINCINNATI

SP P Schourek
SP J Smiley
SR T Pugh
CL J Brantley
RP X Hernandez
RP H Carrasco
RP M Jackson
C- B Santiago
1B H Morris
2B B Boone
SS B Larkin
3B J Branson
LF R Gant
OI J Walton
RF R Sanders
UT L Harris
UO T Howard
3B- M Lewis
C- E Taubensee
M D Johnson

COLORADO

SP K Ritz
SP B Swift
SP M Freeman
SP A Reynoso
RP C Leskanic
RP S Reed
RS R Bailey
RP D Holmes
C J Girardi
1B A Galarraga
2I J Bates
SS W Weiss
3B V Castilla
LF D Bichette
CF M Kingery
RF L Walker
MU E Burks
UT J Vander Wal
2U E Young
M D Baylor

FLORIDA

SP J Burkett
SP P Rapp
SP C Hammond
SP B Witt
SR D Weathers
RS M Gardner
CL R Nen
RP T Mathews
RP R Veres
C C Johnson
1B G Colbrunn
2B Q Veras
SS K Abbott
3B T Pendleton
LF J Conine
CF C Carr
RF- G Sheffield
UI A Arias
UT- J Browne
RU- A Dawson
OI- T Gregg
M R Lachemann

HOUSTON

SP S Reynolds
SP D Drabek
SP G Swindell
SP M Hampton
SP D Kile
RP T Jones
RP D Veres
RS D Brocail
RP J Dougherty
C T Eusebio
1B J Bagwell
2B C Biggio
SS O Miller
3B D Magadan
UO J Mouton
CF- B Hunter
RM D Bell
UO J Cangelosi
3U C Shipley
UO M Thompson
LU- D May
M T Collins

LOS ANGELES

SP R Martinez
SP I Valdes
SP H Nomo
SP T Candiotti
RS P Astacio
CL T Worrell
RP A Osuna
C M Piazza
1B E Karros
2B D DeShields
SS J Offerman
3B T Wallach
LF- B Ashley
LM R Kelly
RF R Mondesi
UT C Fonville
3U D Hansen
M T Lasorda

MONTREAL

SP P Martinez
SP J Fassero
SP C Perez
SP B Henry
SR G Heredia
CL M Rojas
RP T Scott
RP J Shaw
RP G Harris
C D Fletcher
1B D Segui
2B M Lansing
SS W Cordero
3B S Berry
LR M Alou
CF R White
RF T Tarasco
31- S Andrews
UI- M Grudzielanek
M F Alou

NEW YORK

SP B Jones
SP D Mlicki
SP B Pulsipher
SP P Harnisch
SP B Saberhagen
RP J Isringhausen
RP J Dipoto
CL J Franco
RP D Henry
C T Hundley
1B R Brogna
2B J Kent
SS J Vizcaino
32 E Alfonzo
LR J Orsulak
CF B Butler
RF- C Everett
IO- T Bogar
3L- B Bonilla
OI- C Jones
C- K Stinnett
MR- R Thompson
M D Green

PHILADELPHIA

SP P Quantrill
SP T Green
SR M Mimbs
SP C Schilling
CL H Slocumb
RP R Bottalico
RS M Williams
RP T Borland
C D Daulton
1B- D Hollins
2B M Morandini
SS K Stocker
3B C Hayes
CF- A Van Slyke
CF- L Dykstra
RL J Eisenreich
1L G Jefferies
OF- G Varsho
M J Fregosi

PITTSBURGH

SP D Neagle
SP E Loaiza
SP P Wagner
SP J Ericks
CL D Miceli
RP M Dyer
RP D Plesac
RP J McCurry
C- M Parent
1B- M Johnson
2B C Garcia
SS J Bell
31 J King
LF A Martin
CF J Brumfield
RF O Merced
2U N Liriano
OF- D Clark
UO- S Pegues
M J Leyland

ST. LOUIS

SP M Petkovsek
SP A Watson
SP D Osborne
SP K Hill
SP M Morgan
RP D Jackson
CL T Henke
RP R DeLucia
RP J Parrett
C- D Sheaffer
1O J Mabry
2S J Oquendo
SS T Cromer
3B S Cooper
LF B Gilkey
CF R Lankford
RF B Jordan
M1 J Torre
M2 M Jorgensen

SAN DIEGO

SP J Hamilton
SP A Ashby
SP A Benes
SP G Dishman
SP S Sanders
RS W Blair
RS F Valenzuela
CL T Hoffman
RP B Williams
C B Ausmus
1B E Williams
3B J Reed
SS A Cedeno
3B K Caminiti
LU M Nieves
CF S Finley
RF T Gwynn
UI S Livingstone
1U R Petagine
OI- P Clark
L2- B Roberts
M B Bochy

SAN FRANCISCO

SP M Leiter
SP T Mulholland
SP Van
Landingham
SP M Portugal
RS J Bautista
CL R Beck
RP C Hook
RP S Barton
C K Manwaring
1U M Carreon
2B R Thompson
SS R Clayton
3B- M Williams
LF B Bonds
CF- D Lewis
RF G Hill
2U J Patterson
1B J Phillips
3I- S Scarsone
M D Baker

1996 AL

BALTIMORE

SP M Mussina
SP D Wells
SP S Erickson
SP R Coppinger
CL R Myers
RP R McDowell
RP A Mills
RP J Orosco
C C Hoiles
1B R Palmeiro
2B R Alomar
SS C Ripken
3U B Surhoff
UO M Devereaux
CF B Anderson
RD B Bonilla
DH- E Murray
M D Johnson

BOSTON

SP R Clemens
SP T Gordon
SP T Wakefield
SP A Sele
CL H Slocumb
RS V Eshelman
RS M Maddux
RP M Stanton
C M Stanley
1B M Vaughn
2B J Frye
SS J Valentin
3B T Naehring
LF- M Greenwell
CF- L Tinsley
RL T O'Leary
DH- J Canseco
UT R Jefferson
M K Kennedy

CALIFORNIA

SP C Finley
SP S Boskie
SP J Abbott
SR J Grimsley
SP M Langston
CL T Percival
RP M James
C- J Fabregas
1B J Snow
2B R Velarde
SS G DiSarcina
3B- G Arias
LF G Anderson
CF J Edmonds
RF T Salmon
DH C Davis
2U- R Hudler
M1 M Lachemann
M2 J McNamara

CHICAGO

SP A Fernandez
SP K Tapani
SP W Alvarez
SP J Baldwin
CL R Hernandez
RP B Simas
RP B Keyser
RP M Karchner
C R Karkovice
1B F Thomas
2B R Durham
SS O Guillen
3B R Ventura
LF T Phillips
CF D Lewis
RF D Tartabull
DH H Baines
MR D Martinez
OF- L Mouton
M T Bevington

CLEVELAND

SP C Nagy
SP O Hershiser
SP J McDowell
SP C Ogea
SP D Martinez
CL J Mesa
RP J Tavarez
RP E Plunk
RP P Shuey
C S Alomar
1B J Franco
2B C Baerga
SS O Vizquel
3B J Thome
LF A Belle
CF K Lofton
RF M Ramirez
DH- E Murray
M M Hargrove

DETROIT

SP F Lira
SP O Olivares
SR B Williams
RP R Lewis
RP J Lima
RP M Myers
C- B Ausmus
1B T Clark
2B M Lewis
SS- A Cedeno
3B T Fryman
UO B Higginson
CF C Curtis
RU M Nieves
DU- E Williams
CF K Bartee
1D C Fielder
OF- C Pride
M B Bell

KANSAS CITY

SP T Belcher
SP C Haney
SP K Appier
SP M Gubicza
SP J Rosado
RP D Linton
CL J Montgomery
RP H Pichardo
RP J Valera
C M Macfarlane
12 J Offerman
23 K Lockhart
SS D Howard
3B J Randa
ML T Goodwin
MR J Damon
RL M Tucker
DH- J Vitiello
IO C Paquette
D1- B Hamelin
2U- B Roberts
M B Boone

MILWAUKEE

SP B McDonald
SP S Karl
SP R Bones
RS A Miranda
CL M Fetters
RP R Garcia
RP G Lloyd
C M Matheny
IF K Seitzer
2B F Vina
SS J Valentin
3B J Cirillo
LF G Vaughn
CF- P Listach
RF M Mieske
1D J Jaha
C J Levis
OI D Nilsson
UO- D Hulse
M P Garner

MINNESOTA

SP B Radke
SP F Rodriguez
SP R Robertson
SP S Aldred
SP R Aguilera
RP E Guardado
RP G Hansell
RP M Trombley
RS J Parra
C- G Myers
1B S Stahoviak
2B C Knoblauch
SS P Meares
3B D Hollins
LF M Cordova
CF R Becker
RM R Kelly
DH P Molitor
UT J Reboulet
1U- R Coomer
IO- C Hale
M T Kelly

NEW YORK

SP A Pettitte
SP K Rogers
SP D Gooden
SP J Key
RP M Rivera
CL J Wetteland
RP B Wickman
RP J Nelson
C J Girardi
1B T Martinez
2B M Duncan
SS D Jeter
3B W Boggs
LU G Williams
CF B Williams
RF P O'Neill
DL- R Sierra
23 A Fox
CU- J Leyritz
M J Torre

OAKLAND

SR D Wengert
SR D Johns
SP J Wasdin
SP A Prieto
RS C Reyes
RP M Mohler
RP B Groom
RP J Corsi
C T Steinbach
1B M McGwire
2S- R Bournigal
SS M Bordick
3B S Brosius
LF- P Plantier
CF E Young
RF J Herrera
DR G Berroa
UT J Giambi
M A Howe

SEATTLE

SP S Hitchcock
SP B Wolcott
SR B Wells
RP N Charlton
RP R Carmona
RP M Jackson
RP B Ayala
C D Wilson
1B P Sorrento
2B J Cora
SS A Rodriguez
3B- R Davis
LO R Amaral
CF K Griffey
RF J Buhner
DH E Martinez
UT- D Strange
M L Piniella

TEXAS

SP K Hill
SP R Pavlik
SP B Witt
SP D Oliver
SP K Gross
RP G Heredia
RP D Cook
RP J Russell
C I Rodriguez
1B W Clark
2B M McLemore
SS K Elster
3B D Palmer
LF R Greer
CF D Hamilton
RF J Gonzalez
DH M Tettleton
UO- D Buford
RU- W Newson
M J Oates

TORONTO

SP P Hentgen
SP E Hanson
SP J Guzman
SR P Quantrill
CL M Timlin
RP T Castillo
RP T Crabtree
RP C O'Brien
1B J Olerud
2B- T Perez
SS A Gonzalez
3B E Sprague
L1 J Carter
CF O Nixon
RF S Green
DH C Delgado
UO- J Brumfield
LR- R Perez
M C Gaston

1996 NL

ATLANTA

SP J Smoltz
SP G Maddux
SP T Glavine
SP S Avery
CL M Wohlers
RP G McMichael
RP B Clontz
RS M Bielecki
C J Lopez
1B F McGriff
2B M Lemke
SS- J Blauser
3B C Jones
LF R Klesko
CF M Grissom
RL J Dye
OF D Smith
SU- R Belliard
M B Cox

CHICAGO

SP J Navarro
SP S Trachsel
SP F Castillo
SR J Bullinger
RP T Adams
RP T Wendell
RP R Myers
RP K Bottenfield
C S Servais
1B M Grace
2B R Sandberg
SS- R Sanchez
3B L Gomez
LF L Gonzalez
CF B McRae
RF S Sosa
UO S Bullett
S3 J Hernandez
M J Riggleman

CINCINNATI

SP J Smiley
SP D Burba
SP M Portugal
SP K Jarvis
SR R Salkeld
CL J Brantley
RP J Shaw
RP H Carrasco
RP J Ruffin
C J Oliver
1B H Morris
2B B Boone
SS B Larkin
3U W Greene
UO T Howard
CF E Davis
RF- R Sanders
UI J Branson
UT L Harris
C E Taubensee
LU- E Owens
M R Knight

COLORADO

SP K Ritz
SP M Thompson
SP A Reynoso
SP M Freeman
CL B Ruffin
RP C Leskanic
RP D Holmes
RP S Reed
C J Reed
1B A Galarraga
2B E Young
SS W Weiss
3B V Castilla
LF E Burks
MU Q McCracken
RF D Bichette
OI J Vander Wal
UI- J Bates
MR- L Walker
M D Baylor

FLORIDA

SP K Brown
SP A Leiter
SP P Rapp
SP J Burkett
CL R Nen
RS C Hammond
RP J Powell
RS D Weathers
C C Johnson
1B G Colbrunn
2B- Q Veras
SS E Renteria
3B T Pendleton
LF J Conine
CF D White
RF G Sheffield
UI K Abbott
3U A Arias
OI J Orsulak
UO J Tavarez
M1 R Lachemann
M2 C Rojas
M3 J Boles

HOUSTON

SP S Reynolds
SP D Kile
SP D Drabek
SP M Hampton
SP D Wall
RP X Hernandez
RP T Jones
RP B Wagner
RP D Brocail
C- R Wilkins
1B J Bagwell
2B C Biggio
SS O Miller
3B S Berry
LO J Mouton
CF B Hunter
RF D Bell
OF J Cangelosi
LU D May
3U B Spiers
SS- R Gutierrez
M T Collins

LOS ANGELES

SP H Nomo
SP I Valdes
SP P Astacio
SP R Martinez
SP T Candiotti
RS C Park
CL T Worrell
RP A Osuna
RP M Guthrie
C M Piazza
1B E Karros
2B D DeShields
SS G Gagne
3B- M Blowers
LF T
Hollandsworth
MO- R Cedeno
RF R Mondesi
UT C Fonville
M1 T Lasorda
M2 B Russell

MONTREAL

SP J Fassero
SP P Martinez
SP R Cormier
SR U Urbina
CL M Rojas
RS O Daal
RP B Manuel
RP D Veres
C D Fletcher
1B D Segui
2B M Lansing
SS M Grudzielanek
3B S Andrews
L1 H Rodriguez
MO F Santangelo
RF M Alou
LU C Floyd
RU- S Obando
3U- D Silvestri
CF- R White
M F Alou

NEW YORK

SP M Clark
SP B Jones
SP P Harnisch
SP J Isringhausen
SP P Wilson
RP D Mlicki
RP D Henry
CL J Franco
RP J Dipoto
C T Hundley
1R B Huskey
2B- J Vizcaino
SS R Ordonez
3B- J Kent
LF B Gilkey
CF L Johnson
RF- A Ochoa
23 E Alfonzo
UO C Everett
UI- T Bogar
OI- C Jones
M1 D Green
M2 B Valentine

PHILADELPHIA

SP C Schilling
SP M Williams
SP T Mulholland
SP M Mimbs
CL R Bottalico
RP K Ryan
RS R Springer
RP T Borland
C B Santiago
1L G Jefferies
2B M Morandini
SS K Stocker
3B T Zeile
LU P Incaviglia
CF R Otero
UO J Eisenreich
M J Fregosi

PITTSBURGH

SP D Neagle
SP D Darwin
RS J Lieber
RS F Cordova
RS D Miceli
RP D Plesac
C J Kendall
1B M Johnson
2B C Garcia
SS J Bell
3B C Hayes
LF A Martin
MU M Kingery
RF O Merced
12 J King
UI N Liriano
OF- D Clark
UT- J Wehner
M J Leyland

ST. LOUIS

SP An Benes
SP T Stottlemyre
SP D Osborne
SP Al Benes
SP M Morgan
CL D Eckersley
RP T Mathews
RS M Petkovsek
RP C Bailey
C T Pagnozzi
1B J Mabry
2B L Alicea
SS R Clayton
3B G Gaetti
LF R Gant
CF R Lankford
RF B Jordan
OI W McGee
OI M Sweeney
SU- O Smith
M T LaRussa

SAN DIEGO

SP J Hamilton
SP B Tewksbury
SP F Valenzuela
SP A Ashby
SR S Sanders
CL T Hoffman
RS T Worrell
RS S Bergman
RP W Blair
C- J Flaherty
1B W Joyner
2B J Reed
SS- C Gomez
3B K Caminiti
LF R Henderson

CF S Finley
RF T Gwynn
IF S Livingstone
OI- C Gwynn
C- B Johnson
OI- M Newfield
M B Bochy

SAN FRANCISCO
SP A Watson
SP Van Landingham
SP M Gardner
SP O Fernandez
SP M Leiter
CL R Beck
RP M Dewey
RP J Bautista
RP R DeLucia
C- T Lampkin
1B- M Carreon
2U S Scarsone
SS R Aurilia
3B M Williams
LF B Bonds
CF M Benard
RF G Hill
SS- S Dunston
1U- D McCarty
M D Baker

1997 AL

ANAHEIM
SP J Dickson
SP A Watson
SP D Springer
SP C Finley
RS S Hasegawa
RP P Harris
CL T Percival
RP M James
C- C Kreuter
1B D Erstad
2B L Alicea
SS G DiSarcina
3B D Hollins
LF G Anderson
CF J Edmonds
RF T Salmon
DH- E Murray
UT T Phillips
CU- J Leyritz
M T Collins

BALTIMORE
SP M Mussina
SP S Erickson
SP J Key
SP S Kamieniecki
CL R Myers
RP A Rhodes
RP A Benitez
RS S Boskie
C L Webster
1B R Palmeiro
2B R Alomar
SS M Bordick
3B C Ripken
LF B Surhoff
CF B Anderson
UO J Hammonds
DR- G Berroa
C C Hoiles
2I J Reboulet
RU T Tarasco
M D Johnson

BOSTON
SP T Wakefield
SR T Gordon
SP A Sele
SP J Suppan
RS J Wasdin
RS B Henry
RS C Hammond
RP J Corsi
C S Hatteberg
1B M Vaughn
2U J Frye
SS N Garciaparra
3B- T Naehring
LF W Cordero
CF D Bragg
RF T O'Leary
DH R Jefferson
D1- M Stanley
23 J Valentin
M J Williams

CHICAGO
SP J Navarro
SP J Baldwin
SP D Drabek
SP W Alvarez
SP D Darwin
RP M Karchner
RP C Castillo
RP T Castillo
RP C McElroy
C J Fabregas
1D F Thomas
2B R Durham
SS O Guillen
3B- C Snopek
LF A Belle
CF M Cameron
R1 D Martinez
DH- H Baines
CF- D Lewis
RU- L Mouton
M T Bevington

CLEVELAND
SP C Nagy
SP O Hershiser
SP C Ogea
RP J Mesa
RP M Jackson
RS A Lopez
RP E Plunk
C S Alomar
1B J Thome
2B T Fernandez
SS O Vizquel
3B M Williams
LO B Giles
CF M Grissom
RF M Ramirez
LD D Justice
M M Hargrove

DETROIT
SP J Thompson
SP W Blair
SP B Moehler
SP O Olivares
CL T Jones
RP A Sager
RP D Miceli
RP D Brocail
C R Casanova
1B T Clark
2B D Easley
SS D Cruz
3B T Fryman
LR B Higginson
CF B Hunter
RF M Nieves
DH B Hamelin
UT- P Nevin
M B Bell

KANSAS CITY
SP K Appier
SP T Belcher
SP J Rosado
SP G Rusch
SP J Pittsley
RP J Montgomery
RP H Pichardo
C- M Macfarlane
1B J King
2B J Offerman
SS J Bell
3B- C Paquette
LF B Roberts
CF T Goodwin
UO J Damon
DH C Davis
C- M Sweeney
M1 B Boone
M2 T Muser

MILWAUKEE
SP C Eldred
SP S Karl
SP J Mercedes
SP J D'Amico
SP B McDonald
CL D Jones
RP B Wickman
RS J Adamson
RP M Fetters
C M Matheny
UT D Nilsson
2B- F Vina
SS J Valentin
3B J Cirillo
RL- M Mieske
CF G Williams
RF J Burnitz
D1- J Franco
C J Levis
UI M Loretta
UT- J Huson
M P Garner

MINNESOTA
SP B Radke
SP B Tewksbury
SP R Robertson
SR F Rodriguez
SP L Hawkins
RP G Swindell
CL R Aguilera
RP M Trombley
RP T Ritchie
C T Steinbach
1B- S Stahoviak
2B C Knoblauch
SS P Meares
3B R Coomer
LF M Cordova
CF R Becker
UO M Lawton
DH P Molitor
UT D Hocking
M T Kelly

NEW YORK
SP A Pettitte
SP D Wells
SP D Cone
SP K Rogers
SR R Mendoza
CL M Rivera
RP D Gooden
RP J Nelson
RP M Stanton
C J Girardi
1B T Martinez
2B- L Sojo
SS D Jeter
3B C Hayes
LM- C Curtis
CF B Williams
RF P O'Neill
DH C Fielder
3U W Boggs
M J Torre

OAKLAND
SP S Karsay
SP A Prieto
SP M Oquist
SP D Telgheder
RS D Wengert
RS M Mohler
RP A Small
RP B Taylor
C- B Mayne
1B M McGwire
2B S Spiezio
SS- R Bournigal
3B S Brosius
UT J Giambi
CF- D Mashore
OI M Stairs
CF- J McDonald
IF D Magadan
DR J Canseco
M A Howe

SEATTLE
SP J Fassero
SP R Johnson
SP J Moyer
SP B Wolcott
RP B Ayala
RP N Charlton
RP B Wells
RS S Sanders
C D Wilson
1B P Sorrento
2B J Cora
SS A Rodriguez
3B R Davis
LR- R Ducey
CF K Griffey
RF J Buhner
DH E Martinez
UT- R Amaral
M L Piniella

TEXAS
SP B Witt
SP D Oliver
SP J Burkett
SP K Hill
SR J Santana
CL J Wetteland
RP M Whiteside
RP D Patterson
RP E Gunderson
C I Rodriguez
1B W Clark
2B- M McLemore
SS B Gil
3B- D Palmer
LF R Greer
CF D Buford
RU- W Newson
DR J Gonzalez
2S D Cedeno
UT L Stevens
M J Oates

TORONTO
SP R Clemens
SP P Hentgen
SP W Williams
SP R Person
RP P Quantrill
RP D Plesac
C- B Santiago
1B C Delgado
2B C Garcia
SS A Gonzalez
3B E Sprague
OF S Green
CF O Nixon
RF O Merced
OI J Carter
M1 C Gaston
M2 M Queen

1997 NL

ATLANTA
SP J Smoltz
SP T Glavine
SP G Maddux
SP D Neagle
CL M Wohlers
RP M Bielecki
RP P Byrd
C J Lopez
1B F McGriff
2B M Lemke
SS J Blauser
3B C Jones
LF R Klesko
RM A Jones
RL M Tucker
2U T Graffanino
CF K Lofton
IF- K Lockhart
M B Cox

CHICAGO
SP S Trachsel
SP T Mulholland
SP K Foster
SP J Gonzalez
RP T Adams
RP K Bottenfield
RP M Rojas
RP T Wendell
C S Servais
1B M Grace
2B R Sandberg
SS S Dunston
3B K Orie
LF D Glanville
CF B McRae
RF S Sosa
OF D Clark
IO J Hernandez
S2- R Sanchez
3U- D Hansen
M J Riggleman

CINCINNATI
SP M Morgan
SP D Burba
SP K Mercker
SP B Tomko
SP J Smiley
CL J Shaw
RS M Remlinger
RP S Belinda
RP S Sullivan
C J Oliver
1B- H Morris
2B B Boone
SS P Reese
3O W Greene
UO- C Goodwin
ML D Sanders
RF- R Sanders
UT L Harris
1U E Perez
CU E Taubensee
M1 R Knight
M2 J McKeon

COLORADO
SP R Bailey
SP J Thomson
SP J Wright
SP K Ritz
RP J Dipoto
RS D Holmes
RP M DeJean
RP S Reed
C K Manwaring
1B A Galarraga
2B E Young
SS W Weiss
3B V Castilla
LF D Bichette
CF Q McCracken
RF L Walker
ML E Burks
S2- N Perez
C- J Reed
M D Baylor

FLORIDA
SP K Brown
SP A Fernandez
SP A Leiter
SP T Saunders
SP P Rapp
CL R Nen
RP J Powell
RS R Helling
RP D Cook
C C Johnson
1B J Conine
2B- L Castillo
SS E Renteria
3B B Bonilla
LM M Alou
CF- D White
RF G Sheffield
UO J Cangelosi
OI J Eisenreich
2U- K Abbott
M J Leyland

HOUSTON
SP D Kile
SP M Hampton
SP C Holt
SP S Reynolds
SR R Garcia
CL B Wagner
RP J Lima
RP T Martin
RP R Springer
C B Ausmus
1B J Bagwell
2B C Biggio
SS- T Bogar
3B- S Berry
LF L Gonzalez
UO T Howard
RM D Bell
SI R Gutierrez
3I B Spiers
UO- J Mouton
M L Dierker

LOS ANGELES
SP H Nomo
SP I Valdes
SP C Park
SP P Astacio
SR T Candiotti
RP R Martinez
CL T Worrell
RP M Guthrie
RP D Dreifort
C M Piazza
1B E Karros
2B W Guerrero
SS G Gagne
3B T Zeile
LF T Hollandsworth
OF B Butler
RF R Mondesi
M B Russell

MONTREAL
SP P Martinez
SP C Perez
SP D Hermanson
SR J Bullinger
SP J Juden
RS M Valdes
CL U Urbina
RP A Telford
RP D Veres
C- C Widger
1B D Segui
2B M Lansing
SS M Grudzielanek
3B D Strange
LF H Rodriguez
CF R White
UT F Santangelo
OI J Orsulak
C- D Fletcher
RF- V Guerrero
OI- R McGuire
M F Alou

NEW YORK
SP R Reed
SP D Mlicki
SP B Jones
SP M Clark
CL J Franco
RP G McMichael
RP C Lidle
C T Hundley
1B J Olerud
2B C Baerga
SS R Ordonez
3B E Alfonzo
LF B Gilkey
MR C Everett
RI B Huskey
IO M Franco
RU A Ochoa
M B Valentine

PHILADELPHIA
SP C Schilling
SP M Leiter
SP M Beech
SP G Stephenson
CL R Bottalico
RP J Spradlin
RP R Blazier
RP R Harris
C M Lieberthal
1B R Brogna
2B M Morandini
SS K Stocker
3B S Rolen
LF G Jefferies
OI R Amaro
RF- D Daulton
UI- K Jordan
RU- D May
M T Francona

PITTSBURGH
SP E Loaiza
SP J Lieber
SP J Schmidt
SP F Cordova
SP S Cooke
CL R Loiselle
RP M Wilkins
RP R Rincon
RP M Ruebel
C J Kendall
1B- K Young
2B T Womack
SS- K Polcovich
3B J Randa
LF A Martin
CF J Allensworth
RF J Guillen
UI D Sveum
M G Lamont

ST. LOUIS
SP M Morris
SP T Stottlemyre
SP An Benes
SP Al Benes
RP M Petkovsek
CL D Eckersley
RP J Frascatore
RP R Beltran
C- M Difelice
1U D Young
2B D DeShields
SS R Clayton
3B G Gaetti
LF R Gant
CF R Lankford
UO W McGee
C T Lampkin
R1 J Mabry
M T LaRussa

SAN DIEGO
SP A Ashby
SP J Hamilton
SP S Hitchcock
SR P Smith
CL T Hoffman
RS T Worrell
RS S Bergman
RS W Cunnane
C J Flaherty
1B W Joyner
2B Q Veras
SS C Gomez
3B K Caminiti
LF G Vaughn
CF S Finley
RF T Gwynn
IO- A Cianfrocco
LO- R Henderson
UO- C Jones
M B Bochy

SAN FRANCISCO
SP S Estes
SP K Rueter
SP M Gardner
CL R Beck
RP J Tavarez
RP D Henry
RP J Roa
C- R Wilkins
1B J Snow
2B J Kent
SS J Vizcaino
3B B Mueller
LF B Bonds
CF D Hamilton
RM S Javier
RF G Hill
3U M Lewis
UO- M Benard
M D Baker

1998 AL

ANAHEIM
SP C Finley
SR O Olivares
SP S Sparks
SP J Dickson
SP K Hill
CL T Percival
RP S Hasegawa
RP R DeLucia
RP P Harris
C M Walbeck
1D C Fielder
2B- J Baughman
SS G DiSarcina
3B D Hollins
1L D Erstad
CF J Edmonds
RF G Anderson
DH T Salmon
M T Collins

BALTIMORE
SP S Erickson
SP M Mussina
SR S Ponson
SP D Drabek
RP A Benitez
RS D Johns
RP A Rhodes
RP A Mills
C L Webster
1B R Palmeiro
2B R Alomar
SS M Bordick
3B C Ripken
LF B Surhoff
CF B Anderson
OF E Davis
DH H Baines
C- C Hoiles
RD- J Carter
M R Miller

BOSTON
SP P Martinez
SP T Wakefield
SP B Saberhagen
SR S Avery
RS D Lowe
CL T Gordon
RS J Wasdin
RP J Corsi
C S Hatteberg
1B M Vaughn
2I M Benjamin
SS N Garciaparra
3B J Valentin
LF T O'Leary
MR D Lewis
RF D Bragg
DH- R Jefferson
CF- D Buford
C- J Varitek
M J Williams

CHICAGO
SP M Sirotka
SR J Navarro
SR J Baldwin
SP J Parque
SR S Eyre
RP C Castillo
RP B Simas
RP K Foulke
RP B Howry
C- C Kreuter
1B- W Cordero
2B R Durham
SS M Caruso
3B R Ventura
LF A Belle
CF M Cameron
RF M Ordonez
DH F Thomas
1B G Norton
UO- J Abbott
M J Manuel

CLEVELAND
SP C Nagy
SP D Burba
SP B Colon
SP J Wright
SP D Gooden
CL M Jackson
RP J Mesa
RP P Shuey
C S Alomar
1B J Thome
2B D Bell
SS O Vizquel
3B T Fryman
LF B Giles
CF K Lofton
RF M Ramirez
DH D Justice
UO- M Whiten
M M Hargrove

DETROIT
SP J Thompson
SP B Moehler
SR B Florie
SP S Greisinger
SP F Castillo
CL T Jones
RP D Bochtler
RP D Brocail
RP A Sager
C- P Bako
1B T Clark
2B D Easley
SS D Cruz
3B J Randa
LF L Gonzalez
CF B Hunter
RF B Higginson
DU- G Berroa
UI- F Catalanotto
M1 B Bell
M2 L Parrish

KANSAS CITY
SP T Belcher
SP P Rapp
SR J Rosado
SP G Rusch
SP H Pichardo
RS C Haney
CL J Montgomery
RP S Service
RP J Pittsley
C- M Sweeney
1B J King
2B J Offerman
SS- M Lopez
3B D Palmer
LR- J Conine
CF J Damon
OI L Sutton
D3- T Pendleton
UT H Morris
SS- S Halter
M T Muser

MINNESOTA
SP B Radke
SP L Hawkins
SP E Milton
SP B Tewksbury
CL R Aguilera
RP M Trombley
RS D Serafini
RP G Swindell
C T Steinbach
1B- D Ortiz
2B T Walker
SS P Meares
3U B Gates
LF M Cordova
CF O Nixon
RM M Lawton
DH P Molitor
31 R Coomer
UT D Hocking
RO- A Ochoa
M T Kelly

NEW YORK
SP A Pettitte
SP D Wells
SP D Cone
SP H Irabu
SP O Hernandez
RS R Mendoza
CL M Rivera
RP M Stanton
RP D Holmes
C J Posada
1B T Martinez
2B C Knoblauch
SS D Jeter
3B S Brosius
LM C Curtis
CF B Williams
RF P O'Neill
DH D Strawberry
DL T Raines
M J Torre

OAKLAND
SP K Rogers
SP T Candiotti
SP J Haynes
SP M Oquist
SP B Stein
CL B Taylor
RP T Mathews
RP M Mohler
RP B Groom
C A Hinch
1B J Giambi
2B S Spiezio
SS M Tejada
3B M Blowers
LF R Henderson
CF R Christenson
RF B Grieve
DH M Stairs
2S- R Bournigal
M A Howe

SEATTLE
SP J Moyer
SP J Fassero
SP R Johnson
SP K Cloude
SP B Swift
RP M Timlin
RP B Ayala
RS P Spoljaric
RP H Slocumb
C- D Wilson
1B D Segui
2B J Cora
SS A Rodriguez
3B R Davis
LF- G Hill
CF K Griffey
RO R Ducey
DH E Martinez
M *L Piniella*

TAMPA BAY
SP R Arrojo
SP T Saunders
SP W Alvarez
SR J Santana
SR D Springer
CL R Hernandez
RP E Yan
RP J Mecir
RP A Lopez
C- J Flaherty
1B F McGriff
2B M Cairo
SS K Stocker
3B B Smith
ML Q McCracken
MO R Winn
OF M Kelly
DU P Sorrento
3D W Boggs
C- M Difelice
SI- A Ledesma
RF- D Martinez
M *L Rothschild*

TEXAS
SP R Helling
SP A Sele
SP J Burkett
SP D Oliver
CL J Wetteland
RP T Crabtree
RP E Gunderson
RP D Patterson
C I Rodriguez
1B W Clark
2B M McLemore
SS- K Elster
3B- F Tatis
LF R Greer
CF T Goodwin
RF J Gonzalez
D1 L Stevens
IO L Alicea
OI- M Simms
M *J Oates*

TORONTO
SP R Clemens
SP W Williams
SP P Hentgen
SP C Carpenter
SP J Guzman
RP P Quantrill
RP B Risley
RP D Plesac
RP D Stieb
C D Fletcher
1B C Delgado
2B C Grebeck
SS A Gonzalez
3B E Sprague
LF S Stewart
CF J Cruz
RF S Green
DL J Canseco
23 T Fernandez
DU M Stanley
M *T Johnson*

1998 NL

ARIZONA
SP A Benes
SP B Anderson
SR O Daal
SP W Blair
SP A Telemaco
CL G Olson
RS C Sodowsky
C- K Stinnett
1B T Lee
2B- A Stankiewicz
SS J Bell
3B M Williams
LF D Dellucci
CF D White
RF K Garcia
UI T Batista
OI B Brede
UT A Fox
LU- Y Benitez
M *B Showalter*

ATLANTA
SP G Maddux
SP T Glavine
SP D Neagle
SP K Millwood
SP J Smoltz
CL K Ligtenberg
RS D Martinez
C J Lopez
1B A Galarraga
2B K Lockhart
SS- W Weiss
3B C Jones
LF R Klesko
CF A Jones
UO G Williams
2B T Graffanino
RF M Tucker
LU- D Bautista
SS- O Guillen
M *B Cox*

CHICAGO
SP K Tapani
SP M Clark
SP S Trachsel
SP K Wood
SP J Gonzalez
CL R Beck
RS T Mulholland
RP T Adams
RS D Wengert
C S Servais
1B M Grace
2B M Morandini
SS J Blauser
UT J Hernandez
LF H Rodriguez
ML B Brown
RF S Sosa
IO M Alexander
CU- T Houston
CF- L Johnson
M *J Riggleman*

CINCINNATI
SP B Tomko
SP P Harnisch
SP M Remlinger
SP S Parris
RP G White
RP S Sullivan
RP D Graves
CL J Shaw
C E Taubensee
1B- S Casey
2B B Boone
SS B Larkin
3O W Greene
L1 D Young
MR R Sanders
RM- J Nunnally
LI C Stynes
OF- M Nieves
1U- E Perez
UO- P Watkins
M *J McKeon*

COLORADO
SP D Kile
SP P Astacio
SP J Wright
SP J Thomson
SR B Jones
RP J Dipoto
RP D Veres
RP C Leskanic
RP M DeJean
C K Manwaring
1B T Helton
2B M Lansing
SS N Perez
3B V Castilla
LF D Bichette
CF E Burks
RF L Walker
MU C Goodwin
C J Reed
OI- J Vander Wal
M *D Baylor*

FLORIDA
SP L Hernandez
SP B Meadows
SP J Sanchez
RS K Ojala
RP A Alfonseca
RP V Darensbourg
RP M Mantei
C G Zaun
1B D Lee
2B C Counsell
SS E Renteria
3B- T Zeile
LF C Floyd
CF T Dunwoody
RM M Kotsay
UO J Cangelosi
UT R Jackson
UI- D Berg
M *J Leyland*

HOUSTON
SP J Lima
SP S Reynolds
SP M Hampton
SP S Bergman
CL B Wagner
RP D Henry
RP C Nitkowski
RP S Elarton
C B Ausmus
1B J Bagwell
2B C Biggio
SS R Gutierrez
3B B Spiers
LF M Alou
CF C Everett
RF D Bell
3B S Berry
OF- D Clark
M *L Dierker*

LOS ANGELES
SP C Park
SP D Dreifort
SP I Valdes
SP D Mlicki
SP R Martinez
RP S Radinsky
RP A Osuna
RP M Guthrie
C C Johnson
1B E Karros
2B E Young
SS- J Vizcaino
3B- A Beltre
OI- T Hubbard
MR R Mondesi
RF- G Sheffield
UO R Cedeno
S2- J Castro
M1 *B Russell*
M2 *G Hoffman*

MILWAUKEE
SP S Karl
SP S Woodard
SP J Juden
SR B Woodall
SP C Eldred
CL B Wickman
RP B Patrick
RP D Jones
RP C Fox
C M Matheny
1S M Loretta
2B F Vina
SS J Valentin
3B J Cirillo
UO D Jackson
CF M Grissom
RF J Burnitz
UT B Hamelin
UT D Nilsson
C- B Hughes
LF- G Jenkins
LU- M Newfield
M *P Garner*

MONTREAL
SP D Hermanson
SP J Vazquez
SP C Perez
SP C Pavano
RS M Batista
CL U Urbina
RP S Bennett
RP A Telford
C C Widger
1B B Fullmer
2U- J Vidro
SS M Grudzielanek
3B S Andrews
L2 F Santangelo
CF- R White
RF V Guerrero
1L R McGuire
LU- D May
M *F Alou*

NEW YORK
SP R Reed
SP B Jones
SP A Leiter
SP M Yoshii
CL J Franco
RP T Wendell
RP D Cook
RP M Rojas
C M Piazza
1B J Olerud
2B C Baerga
SS R Ordonez
3B E Alfonzo
LF- B Gilkey
CF B McRae
RF B Huskey
UT M Franco
UT L Lopez
M *B Valentine*

PHILADELPHIA
SP C Schilling
SP M Portugal
SP T Green
SP C Loewer
SP M Beech
RP M Leiter
RP W Gomes
RP J Spradlin
RP Y Perez
C- M Lieberthal
1B R Brogna
2B M Lewis
SS D Relaford
3B S Rolen
LF G Jefferies
CF D Glanville
RF B Abreu
UI K Jordan
UT K Sefcik
UO- R Amaro
M *T Francona*

PITTSBURGH
SP F Cordova
SP J Schmidt
SP J Lieber
SR C Peters
SP J Silva
RP R Rincon
RS E Dessens
CL R Loiselle
RP J Christiansen
C J Kendall
1B K Young
2B T Womack
SS L Collier
3B- A Ramirez
LF A Martin
UO T Ward
RF J Guillen
SI- K Polcovich
UI- D Strange
M *G Lamont*

ST. LOUIS
SP K Mercker
SP T Stottlemyre
SR K Bottenfield
SP M Morris
RS J Acevedo
RS M Petkovsek
RP J Frascatore
RP J Brantley
C- E Marrero
1B M McGwire
2B D DeShields
SS- R Clayton
3B- G Gaetti
LF R Gant
CF R Lankford
RF B Jordan
UT J Mabry
OI W McGee
CU- T Lampkin
M *T LaRussa*

SAN DIEGO
SP K Brown
SP A Ashby
SP J Hamilton
SR S Hitchcock
CL T Hoffman
RP B Boehringer
RP D Miceli
RP D Wall
C C Hernandez
1B W Joyner
2B Q Veras
SS C Gomez
3B K Caminiti
LF G Vaughn
CF S Finley
RF T Gwynn
OI M Sweeney
UI- E Giovanola
RF- R Rivera
UI- A Sheets
M *B Bochy*

SAN FRANCISCO
SP M Gardner
SP O Hershiser
SP K Rueter
SP D Darwin
SP S Estes
CL R Nen
RP J Johnstone
RP J Tavarez
RP R Rodriguez
C B Johnson
1B J Snow
2B J Kent
SS R Aurilia
3B B Mueller
LF B Bonds
CF- D Hamilton
RO S Javier
RU M Benard
IF C Hayes
S2 R Sanchez
C- B Mayne
M *D Baker*

1999 AL

ANAHEIM
SP C Finley
SP S Sparks
SP T Belcher
SP O Olivares
SP K Hill
CL T Percival
RP A Levine
RP M Petkovsek
RP S Hasegawa
C M Walbeck
1L D Erstad
2B- R Velarde
SS- G DiSarcina
3B T Glaus
LR O Palmeiro
MU G Anderson
RF T Salmon
1D M Vaughn
OF- T Greene
IO- J Huson
SS- A Sheets
M1 *T Collins*
M2 *J Maddon*

BALTIMORE
SP S Erickson
SP S Ponson
SP M Mussina
SP J Guzman
SP J Johnson
CL M Timlin
RS D Johns
RP S Kamieniecki
RP A Rhodes
C C Johnson
1U J Conine
2B- D DeShields
SS M Bordick
3B- C Ripken
LF B Surhoff
CF B Anderson
RF A Belle
DH H Baines
32 J Reboulet
UT- R Amaral
M *R Miller*

BOSTON
SP P Martinez
SR T Wakefield
SP M Portugal
SR P Rapp
SP B Saberhagen
RP D Lowe
RP J Wasdin
RP R Cormier
C J Varitek
1B M Stanley
2B J Offerman
SS N Garciaparra
3B J Valentin
LF T O'Leary
MR D Lewis
RF T Nixon
DU- R Jefferson
1D B Daubach
CF- D Buford
M *J Williams*

CHICAGO
SP M Sirotka
SP J Baldwin
SP J Parque
SP J Navarro
SP J Snyder
RP K Foulke
CL B Howry
RP S Lowe
RP B Simas
RP B Fordyce
1D P Konerko
2B R Durham
SS M Caruso
3B G Norton
LF C Lee
CF C Singleton
RF M Ordonez
D1 F Thomas
3I C Wilson
M *J Manuel*

CLEVELAND
SP D Burba
SP B Colon
SP C Nagy
SP J Wright
SP D Gooden
CL M Jackson
RP P Shuey
RP S Karsay
RS M Langston
C E Diaz
UT R Sexson
2B R Alomar
SS O Vizquel
3B- T Fryman
LD D Justice
CF K Lofton
RF M Ramirez
1B J Thome
3S E Wilson
M *M Hargrove*

DETROIT
SP B Moehler
SP D Mlicki
SP J Weaver
SP J Thompson
SR W Blair
CL T Jones
RP D Brocail
RS C Nitkowski
RS N Cruz
C B Ausmus
1B T Clark
2B D Easley
SS D Cruz
3B D Palmer
LF J Encarnacion
CF G Kapler
RF B Higginson
OF- L Polonia
UI F Catalanotto
RL- K Garcia
M *L Parrish*

KANSAS CITY
SP J Suppan
SP J Rosado
SP J Witasick
SP K Appier
RP S Service
RP J Montgomery
RP A Morman
C C Kreuter
UT M Sweeney
2B C Febles
SS R Sanchez
3B J Randa
LF J Damon
CF C Beltran
RF J Dye
D1- J Giambi
UO- S Pose
M *T Muser*

MINNESOTA
SP B Radke
SP E Milton
SP L Hawkins
SR J Mays
RP M Trombley
RP B Wells
RP B Sampson
RP H Carrasco
C T Steinbach
1B D Mientkiewicz
2U T Walker
SS C Guzman
3U C Koskie
LF C Allen
CF T Hunter
RF M Lawton
DO M Cordova
13 R Coomer
32 B Gates
UT D Hocking
CF- J Jones
M *T Kelly*

NEW YORK
SP O Hernandez
SP D Cone
SP A Pettitte
SP R Clemens
SP H Irabu
RS R Mendoza
CL M Rivera
RP J Grimsley
RP M Stanton
C J Posada
1B T Martinez
2B C Knoblauch
SS D Jeter
3B S Brosius
LF- C Curtis
CF B Williams
RF P O'Neill
DH C Davis
LF- R Ledee
M1 *D Zimmer*
M2 *J Torre*

OAKLAND
SP G Heredia
SP J Haynes
SP M Oquist
SP T Hudson
SP K Rogers
RP D Jones
RP T Worrell
RP T Mathews
RP B Rigby
C- M Macfarlane
1B J Giambi
2M T Phillips
SS M Tejada
3B E Chavez
LF B Grieve
CF R Christenson
RF M Stairs
DH J Jaha
ML J McDonald
31- O Saenz
UI- S Spiezio
M *A Howe*

SEATTLE
SP J Moyer
SP F Garcia
SR J Halama
SP J Fassero
CL J Mesa
RP J Paniagua
RS F Rodriguez
RS P Abbott
C D Wilson
1B- D Segui
2B D Bell
SS A Rodriguez
3B R Davis
LF B Hunter
CF K Griffey
RF- J Buhner
DH E Martinez
OI- R Ibanez
UT- J Mabry
M *L Piniella*

TAMPA BAY
SP B Witt
SP W Alvarez
SP R Rupe
SP R Arrojo
CL R Hernandez
RP R White
RP A Lopez
RP E Yan
C J Flaherty
1B F McGriff
2B M Cairo
SS- K Stocker
3B- W Boggs
LU- B Trammell
CF- R Winn
RM D Martinez
DH J Canseco
L1 P Sorrento
S3- A Ledesma
M *L Rothschild*

TEXAS
SP R Helling
SP A Sele
SP J Burkett
SP M Morgan
SR E Loaiza
CL J Wetteland
RP J Zimmerman
RP M Venafro
RP T Crabtree
C I Rodriguez
1B L Stevens
2B M McLemore
SS R Clayton
3B T Zeile
LF R Greer
CF T Goodwin
RF J Gonzalez
DH R Palmeiro
UO- R Kelly
M *J Oates*

TORONTO
SP D Wells
SP P Hentgen
SP K Escobar
SP C Carpenter
SR R Halladay
CL B Koch
RP G Lloyd
RP P Spoljaric
RP P Munro
C D Fletcher
1B C Delgado
2B H Bush
SS T Batista
3B T Fernandez
LF S Stewart
CF J Cruz
RF S Green
DU- W Greene
M *J Fregosi*

1999 NL

ARIZONA
SP R Johnson
SP O Daal
SP A Benes
SP A Reynoso
SR B Anderson
RP T Stottlemyre
RP G Olson
RP G Swindell
RP D Holmes
C- K Stinnett
1B T Lee
2B J Bell
SS A Fox
3B M Williams
LF L Gonzalez
CF S Finley
RF T Womack
OF- B Gilkey
C- D Miller
M *B Showalter*

ATLANTA
SP T Glavine
SP K Millwood
SP G Maddux
SP J Smoltz
CL J Rocker
RP M Remlinger
RP K McGlinchy
RP R Seanez
C E Perez
1B B Hunter
2B B Boone
SS W Weiss
3B C Jones
LF G Williams
CF A Jones
RF B Jordan
1L R Klesko
IF K Lockhart
SU- O Guillen
LU- O Nixon
1B- R Simon
M *B Cox*

CHICAGO
SP S Trachsel
SP J Lieber
SP K Tapani
SP K Farnsworth
SR T Mulholland
RS S Sanders
RP T Adams
RP R Myers
RP D Serafini
C B Santiago
1B M Grace
2B M Morandini
SS J Hernandez
3U G Gaetti
LF H Rodriguez
CF- L Johnson
RF S Sosa
IO J Blauser
OF G Hill
3U T Houston
IO- M Alexander
OF- C Goodwin
M *J Riggleman*

CINCINNATI
SP P Harnisch
SP B Tomko
SP R Villone
SP S Parris
SP D Neagle
RP D Graves
RP S Sullivan
RP S Williamson
RP D Reyes
C E Taubensee
1B S Casey
2B P Reese
SS B Larkin
3B A Boone
LF G Vaughn
CF M Cameron
RF M Tucker
UO J Hammonds
RU D Young
3U- M Lewis
M *J McKeon*

COLORADO
SP P Astacio
SP B Bohanon
SP D Kile
SR B Jones

CL D Veres
RP J Dipoto
RP C Leskanic
RP M DeJean
C- H Blanco
1B T Helton
2U- K Abbott
SS N Perez
3B V Castilla
LF D Bichette
CF- D Hamilton
RF L Walker
OI A Echevarria
UT- L Harris
2U- T Shumpert
M J Leyland

FLORIDA

SP D Springer
SP B Meadows
SP R Dempster
SP A Fernandez
SP L Hernandez
RP A Alfonseca
RP B Edmondson
RP B Looper
RS J Sanchez
C- M Redmond
1B K Millar
2B L Castillo
SS A Gonzalez
3B- M Lowell
LU B Aven
MO P Wilson
RF M Kotsay
IO D Berg
C- J Fabregas
M J Boles

HOUSTON

SP J Lima
SP M Hampton
SP S Reynolds
SP C Holt
SR S Elarton
CL B Wagner
RP S Bergman
RP J Powell
RP B Williams
C T Eusebio
1B J Bagwell
2B C Biggio
SS T Bogar
3B- K Caminiti
LF R Hidalgo
CF C Everett
RF D Bell
3O B Spiers
MU- G Barker
SS- R Gutierrez
UI- R Johnson
M1 L Dierker
M2 M Galante
M3 L Dierker

LOS ANGELES

SP K Brown
SP I Valdes
SP C Park
SP D Dreifort
CL J Shaw
RP A Mills
RP J Arnold
RP O Masaoka
C T Hundley
1B E Karros
2B E Young
SS M Grudzielanek
3B A Beltre
LF G Sheffield
CF D White
RF R Mondesi
IO D Hansen
OI- T Hollandsworth
OI- T Hubbard
IO- J Vizcaino
M D Johnson

MILWAUKEE

SP S Karl
SP S Woodard
SP H Nomo
CL B Wickman
RP D Weathers
RS R Roque
RP E Plunk
C D Nilsson
UI M Loretta
2B R Belliard
SS- J Valentin
3B J Cirillo
LF G Jenkins
CF M Grissom
RF J Burnitz
IC B Banks
1U S Berry
UO A Ochoa
UO- R Becker
M1 P Garner
M2 J Lefebvre

MONTREAL

SP D Hermanson
SP J Vazquez
SP M Thurman
SR M Batista
SP C Pavano
CL U Urbina
RP A Telford
RP S Kline
RP B Ayala
C C Widger
1B B Fullmer
2B J Vidro
SS O Cabrera
3B S Andrews
LM R White
CF M Martinez
RF V Guerrero
3C M Barrett
UT W Guerrero
UI M Mordecai
1O- R McGuire
UT- O Merced
UO- J Mouton
M F Alou

NEW YORK

SP A Leiter
SP O Hershiser
SP M Yoshii
SP R Reed
RP A Benitez
RP T Wendell
RP D Cook
RP P Mahomes
C M Piazza
1B J Olerud
2B E Alfonzo
SS R Ordonez
3B R Ventura
LF R Henderson
CF- B McRae
RF R Cedeno
UO B Agbayani
UT M Franco
M B Valentine

PHILADELPHIA

SP P Byrd
SP C Schilling
SP C Ogea
SP R Person
SP R Wolf
RP W Gomes
RP S Montgomery
RS M Grace
RP S Schrenk
C M Lieberthal
1B R Brogna
2B M Anderson
SS A Arias
3B S Rolen
LF R Gant
CF D Glanville
RF B Abreu
2B D Doster
UO R Ducey
32 K Jordan
OI K Sefcik
M T Francona

PITTSBURGH

SP J Schmidt
SP K Benson
SP T Ritchie
SP F Cordova
SR P Schourek
RS J Silva
CL M Williams
RP S Sauerbeck
RP B Clontz
C- J Kendall
1B K Young
2B W Morris
SS M Benjamin
3B E Sprague
LF A Martin
CF B Giles
RM A Brown
OI B Brown
SU- A Nunez
M G Lamont

ST. LOUIS

SP D Oliver
SP K Bottenfield
SP J Jimenez
SP K Mercker
RS J Acevedo
RP M Aybar
RP R Bottalico
RP R Croushore
C E Marrero
1B M McGwire
2O J McEwing
SS E Renteria
3B F Tatis
LF R Lankford
CF J Drew
OI W McGee
OF T Howard
UO- D Bragg
C- A Castillo
2B- P Polanco
M T LaRussa

SAN DIEGO

SP W Williams
SP A Ashby
SP S Hitchcock
SP M Clement
CL T Hoffman
RP C Reyes
RP D Miceli
RP D Wall
C- B Davis
1B W Joyner
2B Q Veras
SS D Jackson
3U P Nevin
UT E Owens
CF R Rivera
LR R Sanders
RF T Gwynn
IF D Magadan
OI J Vander Wal
M B Bochy

SAN FRANCISCO

SP R Ortiz
SP S Estes
SP K Rueter
SP M Gardner
SP C Brock
CL R Nen
RP J Johnstone
RP F Rodriguez
RP A Embree
C B Mayne
1B J Snow
2B J Kent
SS R Aurilia
3B B Mueller
LF B Bonds
CF M Benard
RF E Burks
UO S Javier
UT F Santangelo
3U- C Hayes
M D Baker

2000 AL

ANAHEIM

SP S Schoeneweis
SP K Bottenfield
SP R Ortiz
RP S Hasegawa
RS A Levine
RP M Petkovsek
CL T Percival
C B Molina
1B M Vaughn
2B A Kennedy
SS B Gil
3B T Glaus
LU D Erstad
CF G Anderson
RF T Salmon
UT S Spiezio
UO O Palmeiro
M M Scioscia

BALTIMORE

SP M Mussina
SP S Ponson
SP P Rapp
SR J Mercedes
SR J Johnson
RP M Trombley
RP B Groom
RP C McElroy
C- C Johnson
1B- W Clark
2L D DeShields
SS M Bordick
3B- C Ripken
LF B Surhoff
MO B Anderson
RF A Belle
DH- H Baines
UT J Conine
M M Hargrove

BOSTON

SP P Martinez
SR J Fassero
SP R Martinez
SP P Schourek
RS T Wakefield
CL D Lowe
RP R Garces
RP R Cormier
C J Varitek
1D- M Stanley
21 J Offerman
SS N Garciaparra
3I M Alexander
LF T O'Leary
CF C Everett
RF T Nixon
1D B Daubach
UO- D Lewis
CU- S Hatteberg
M J Williams

CHICAGO

SP M Sirotka
SP J Parque
SP J Baldwin
SP C Eldred
SP K Wells
CL K Foulke
RP B Howry
RS S Lowe
RP B Simas
C- M Johnson
1B P Konerko
2B R Durham
3U J Valentin
3B H Perry
LF C Lee
CF C Singleton
RF M Ordonez
DH F Thomas
M J Manuel

CLEVELAND

SP C Finley
SP D Burba
SP B Colon
RP S Karsay
RP J Speier
RP P Shuey
RP S Reed
C- S Alomar
1D- D Segui
2B R Alomar
SS O Vizquel
3B T Fryman
L1- R Sexson
CF K Lofton
RF M Ramirez
1D J Thome
UT J Cabrera
M C Manuel

DETROIT

SP J Weaver
SP H Nomo
SP B Moehler
SR W Blair
SP D Mlicki
RS C Nitkowski
CL T Jones
RP S Sparks
RP M Anderson
C B Ausmus
1B- T Clark
2B D Easley
SS D Cruz
3B D Palmer
LF B Higginson
CF J Encarnacion
RM- R Becker
RD J Gonzalez
31 S Halter
RO- W Magee
M P Garner

KANSAS CITY

SP J Suppan
SP M Suzuki
SR D Reichert
SP B Stein
RP R Bottalico
RP J Spradlin
RP J Santiago
C- G Zaun
1D M Sweeney
2B C Febles
SS R Sanchez
3B J Randa
OF J Damon
CF C Beltran
RF J Dye
LD M Quinn
1U D McCarty
M T Muser

MINNESOTA

SP B Radke
SP E Milton
SP J Mays
SP M Redman
RP L Hawkins
RP B Wells
RS J Santana
RP H Carrasco
C- M LeCroy
1B R Coomer
2B J Canizaro
SS C Guzman
3B C Koskie
LM J Jones
CF T Hunter
RL M Lawton
DU D Ortiz
UT D Hocking
M T Kelly

NEW YORK

SP A Pettitte
SP R Clemens
SP O Hernandez
SP D Cone
CL M Rivera
RP J Grimsley
RP J Nelson
RP M Stanton
C J Posada
1B T Martinez
2B C Knoblauch
SS D Jeter
3B S Brosius
LR- D Justice
CF B Williams
RF P O'Neill
OF- S Spencer
UT C Bellinger
M J Torre

OAKLAND

SP T Hudson
SP G Heredia
SP K Appier
SP M Mulder
SP O Olivares
CL J Isringhausen
RP J Tam
RP D Jones
RP T Mathews
C R Hernandez
1B Ja Giambi
2B R Velarde
SS M Tejada
3B E Chavez
LF B Grieve
CF T Long
RD M Stairs
OI Je Giambi
LO R Christenson
M A Howe

SEATTLE

SP A Sele
SP P Abbott
SP J Halama
SP J Moyer
SP F Garcia
CL K Sasaki
RS B Tomko
RP J Paniagua
RP J Mesa
C- D Wilson
1B J Olerud
2B M McLemore
SS A Rodriguez
32 D Bell
OI S Javier
CF M Cameron
RF J Buhner
DH E Martinez
3B- C Guillen
LF- R Henderson
OI- R Ibanez
M L Piniella

TAMPA BAY

SR A Lopez
SP B Rekar
SR E Yan
SP S Trachsel
SR C Lidle
CL R Hernandez
RP R White
RP D Creek
RS T Sturtze
C J Flaherty
1B F McGriff
2B M Cairo
SS F Martinez
3B- V Castilla
LD G Vaughn
CF G Williams
RF J Guillen
DH- J Canseco
OI S Cox
M L Rothschild

TEXAS

SP K Rogers
SP R Helling
SP D Oliver
SP E Loaiza
SR M Perisho
RS D Davis
CL J Wetteland
RP T Crabtree
RP F Cordero
C- I Rodriguez
1D R Palmeiro
2B L Alicea
SS R Clayton
3B M Lamb
LF R Greer
MR G Kapler
OF C Curtis
D1- D Segui
IO F Catalanotto
M J Oates

TORONTO

SP D Wells
SR K Escobar
SP C Carpenter
SP F Castillo
CL B Koch
RP P Quantrill
RP J Frascatore
RP L Painter
C D Fletcher
1B C Delgado
2B- H Bush
SS A Gonzalez
3B T Batista
LF S Stewart
CF J Cruz
RF- R Mondesi
DH B Fullmer
M J Fregosi

2000 NL

ARIZONA

SP R Johnson
SP B Anderson
SP A Reynoso
RP M Morgan
RP B Kim
RP G Swindell
RP R Springer
C D Miller
1B G Colbrunn
2B J Bell
SS T Womack
3B- M Williams
LF L Gonzalez
CF S Finley
RF- D Bautista
M B Showalter

ATLANTA

SP G Maddux
SP T Glavine
SP K Millwood
SR T Mulholland
SP J Burkett
RP M Remlinger
CL J Rocker
RP K Ligtenberg
C J Lopez
1B A Galarraga
2B- Q Veras
SS R Furcal
3B C Jones
LR R Sanders
CF A Jones
RF B Jordan
LU B Bonilla
UT W Joyner
2U K Lockhart
M B Cox

CHICAGO

SP J Lieber
SP K Tapani
SP K Wood
RP T Van Poppel
RS K Farnsworth
RP D Garibay
RP T Worrell
C J Girardi
1B M Grace
2B E Young
SS R Gutierrez
3B W Greene
LF- H Rodriguez
CF D Buford
RF S Sosa
UI- J Nieves
C- J Reed
M D Baylor

CINCINNATI

SP S Parris
SR E Dessens
SR R Villone
SP R Bell
SP P Harnisch
CL D Graves
RP D Neagle
RS S Williamson
RP S Sullivan
C- B Santiago
1B S Casey
2B P Reese
SS B Larkin
3B- A Boone
OI M Tucker
CF K Griffey
RF D Bichette
LR A Ochoa
3U C Stynes
LU D Young
S2- J Castro
C- E Taubensee
M J McKeon

COLORADO

SP P Astacio
SP B Bohanon
SP M Yoshii
SP K Jarvis
SP R Arrojo
RS J Tavarez
RP J Jimenez
RP G White
RP M DeJean
C B Mayne
1B T Helton
2B- M Lansing
SS N Perez
3B J Cirillo
RL- L Walker
CF- T Goodwin
RL J Hammonds
IO T Shumpert
M B Bell

FLORIDA

SP R Dempster
SP J Sanchez
SP R Cornelius
SP C Smith
SP B Penny
CL A Alfonseca
RP R Bones
RP B Looper
RP V Darensbourg
C- M Redmond
1B D Lee
2B L Castillo
SS A Gonzalez
3B M Lowell
LF C Floyd
CF P Wilson
RF M Kotsay
UT K Millar
OF M Smith
SI- D Berg
M J Boles

HOUSTON

SP C Holt
SP J Lima
SP S Elarton
SP S Reynolds
SP W Miller
RS O Dotel
RP J Slusarski
RP J Cabrera
RP M Valdes
C M Meluskey
1B J Bagwell
2B C Biggio
SS T Bogar
3B- C Truby
RL M Alou
CF R Hidalgo
RL L Berkman
S2 J Lugo
UT B Spiers
OI D Ward
CF- G Barker
M L Dierker

LOS ANGELES

SP K Brown
SP C Park
SP D Dreifort
SP C Perez
SP E Gagne
RP M Herges
RP T Adams
CL J Shaw
RP A Osuna
C- T Hundley
1B E Karros
2B M Grudzielanek
SS A Cora
3B A Beltre
LF G Sheffield
CF- T Hollandsworth
RF S Green
IO D Hansen
OI- F Santangelo
M D Johnson

MILWAUKEE

SP J Haynes
SP J Wright
SP J D'Amico
SP J Snyder
SP J Bere
RP C Leskanic
RP J Acevedo
RP D Weathers
RP V DeLos Santos
C- H Blanco
1B- R Sexson
2B R Belliard
SS- M Loretta
3B J Hernandez
LF G Jenkins
CF M Grissom
RF J Burnitz
IF C Hayes
IF T Houston
C- R Casanova
UO- J Mouton
M D Lopes

MONTREAL

SP J Vazquez
SP D Hermanson
RS F Lira
RS M Johnson
RP S Kline
RP A Telford
C- C Widger
1B L Stevens
2B J Vidro
SS O Cabrera
3I- M Mordecai
LO T Jones
CF P Bergeron
RF V Guerrero
UI G Blum
OI W Guerrero
3C- M Barrett
IF- A Tracy
M F Alou

NEW YORK

SP M Hampton
SP A Leiter
SP G Rusch
SP R Reed
SP B Jones
CL A Benitez
RS P Mahomes
RP T Wendell
RP D Cook
C M Piazza
1B T Zeile
2B E Alfonzo
SS- M Bordick
3B R Ventura
LF B Agbayani
CF J Payton
RF D Bell
IO M Franco
UT- J McEwing
M B Valentine

PHILADELPHIA

SP R Wolf
SP R Person
SP C Schilling
SP A Ashby
RS C Brock
RP W Gomes
CL J Brantley
C M Lieberthal
1L P Burrell
2B- M Morandini
SS- D Relaford
3B S Rolen
LF- R Gant
CF D Glanville
RF B Abreu
UI K Jordan
UO K Sefcik
UT- B Hunter
M T Francona

PITTSBURGH

SP K Benson
SP T Ritchie
SP J Anderson
SR J Silva
RP M Williams
RP S Sauerbeck
RP M Wilkins
RP J Manzanillo
C J Kendall
1B K Young
2B W Morris
SS P Meares
RU- A Ramirez
LF- W Cordero
MU A Brown
UO B Giles
OI J Vander Wal
UI- M Benjamin
M G Lamont

ST. LOUIS

SP D Kile
SP G Stephenson
SP P Hentgen
SP R Ankiel
SP A Benes
CL D Veres
RP M Morris
RP M James

RP H Slocumb
C M Matheny
1B- M McGwire
2B F Vina
SS E Renteria
3B- F Tatis
LF R Lankford
CF J Edmonds
RO J Drew
UT S Dunston
3I C Paquette
UI P Polanco
RF- E Davis
OI- T Howard
M *T LaRussa*

SAN DIEGO
SP M Clement
SP W Williams
SP A Eaton
SP B Meadows
SP B Tollberg
CL T Hoffman
RP C Almanzar
RP K Walker
RP D Wall
C- W Gonzalez
1B R Klesko
2B B Boone
S2 D Jackson
3B P Nevin
LF- A Martin
CF R Rivera
OI E Owens
RU- K DeHaan
UI- D Magadan
M *B Bochy*

SAN FRANCISCO
SP L Hernandez
SP R Ortiz
SP S Estes
SP K Rueter
SR M Gardner
CL R Nen
RP F Rodriguez
RP A Fultz
RP A Embree
C B Estalella
1B J Snow
2B J Kent
SS R Aurilia
3B B Mueller
LF B Bonds
CF M Benard
RF E Burks
CF C Murray
RU A Rios
UT- F Crespo
S2- R Martinez
C- D Mirabelli
M *D Baker*

2001 AL

ANAHEIM
SP R Ortiz
SP S Schoeneweis
SP J Washburn
SP P Rapp
SP I Valdes
CL T Percival
RP L Pote
RP A Levine
RP B Weber
C- B Molina
1B S Spiezio
2B A Kennedy
SS D Eckstein
3B T Glaus
LF G Anderson
CF D Erstad
RF T Salmon
UC- S Wooten
IO B Gil
UO O Palmeiro
M *M Scioscia*

BALTIMORE
SP J Johnson
SP J Mercedes
SP J Towers
SP S Ponson
SR W Roberts
RP B Groom
RP M Trombley
RP B Ryan
RP J Wasdin
C- B Fordyce
1O J Conine
2B J Hairston
SS- M Bordick
3B C Ripken
RL B Anderson
MS M Mora
RM C Richard
IF- T Batista
1B- D Segui
M *M Hargrove*

BOSTON
SP H Nomo
SR T Wakefield
SP F Castillo
SP D Cone
SP P Martinez
CL D Lowe
RS R Arrojo
RP R Beck
RP R Garces
C- S Hatteberg
1B B Daubach
21 J Offerman
S2 M Lansing
3B S Hillenbrand
LR T O'Leary
CF C Everett
RM T Nixon
DL M Ramirez
OF D Bichette
UO- D Lewis
IO- C Stynes
M1 *J Williams*
M2 *J Kerrigan*

CHICAGO
SP M Buehrle
SR K Wells
SP R Biddle
SR J Garland
SP D Wells
RS S Lowe
CL K Foulke
RS G Glover
RP B Howry
C- S Alomar
1B P Konerko
2B R Durham
SS R Clayton
3U- H Perry
LF C Lee
CF C Singleton
RF M Ordonez
DH- J Canseco
3S J Valentin
UT- J Liefer
M *J Manuel*

CLEVELAND
SP B Colon
SP C Sabathia
SP D Burba
SP C Finley
CL B Wickman
RS J Westbrook
RP R Rincon
RP P Shuey
C E Diaz
1B J Thome
2B R Alomar
SS O Vizquel
3B T Fryman
LO M Cordova
CF K Lofton
RF J Gonzalez
DH E Burks
3L R Branyan
UT J Cabrera
LU- W Cordero
M *C Manuel*

DETROIT
SP S Sparks
SP J Weaver
SP C Holt
SP J Lima
CL M Anderson
RS V Santos
RP D Patterson
RP H Murray
C- B Inge
1D T Clark
2B D Easley
SS D Cruz
3U J Macias
LF B Higginson
MR R Cedeno
RM J Encarnacion
DH- D Palmer
CU R Fick
3S S Halter
UO- W Magee
1D- R Simon
M *P Garner*

KANSAS CITY
SP J Suppan
SP C Durbin
SR B Stein
SP D Reichert
SR K Wilson
CL R Hernandez
RP J Grimsley
RP D Henry
RP C Bailey
C- H Ortiz
1U D McCarty
2B- C Febles
SS R Sanchez
3B J Randa
OF M Quinn
CF C Beltran
RF- J Dye
1D M Sweeney
OF B Grieve
DL G Vaughn
2U L Alicea
LU D Brown
UT R Ibanez
M *T Muser*

MINNESOTA
SP J Mays
SP B Radke
SP E Milton
RP E Guardado
CL L Hawkins
RP H Carrasco
RP B Wells
C A Pierzynski
1B D Mientkiewicz
2B L Rivas
SS C Guzman
3B C Koskie
LF J Jones
CF T Hunter
RF M Lawton
DH- D Ortiz
UT D Hocking
M *T Kelly*

NEW YORK
SP M Mussina
SP R Clemens
SP A Pettitte
SP T Lilly
CL M Rivera
RP R Mendoza
RP M Stanton
C J Posada
1B T Martinez
2B A Soriano
SS D Jeter
3B S Brosius
LF C Knoblauch
CF B Williams
RF P O'Neill
DH D Justice
M *J Torre*

OAKLAND
SP T Hudson
SP M Mulder
SP B Zito
SP C Lidle
SP G Heredia
CL J Isringhausen
RP J Tam
RP J Mecir
RP M Magnante
C R Hernandez
1B J Giambi
2B F Menechino
SS M Tejada
3B E Chavez
ML J Damon
UO T Long
RF- J Dye
1B J Giambi
D1 O Saenz
OI J Giambi
M *A Howe*

SEATTLE
SP F Garcia
SP A Sele
SP J Moyer
SP P Abbott
SR J Halama
CL K Sasaki
RP R Franklin
RP A Rhodes
RP J Nelson
C D Wilson
1B J Olerud
2B B Boone
SS C Guillen
3B D Bell
LO- S Javier
CF M Cameron
RF I Suzuki
DH E Martinez
LU A Martin
L3 M McLemore
UT- C Gipson
M *L Piniella*

TAMPA BAY
SR T Sturtze
SR P Wilson
SP R Rupe
SP B Rekar
SP A Lopez
RP J Kennedy
CL E Yan
RP T Phelps
RP D Creek
C- J Flaherty
1U S Cox
2B- B Abernathy
SS- F Martinez
3U A Huff
LM J Tyner
UO R Winn
OF B Grieve
DL G Vaughn
1B- F McGriff
UI- R Johnson
2O- D Rolls
M1 *L Rothschild*
M2 *H McRae*

TEXAS
SP R Helling
SP D Davis
SP D Oliver
SP K Rogers
SP R Bell
RP P Mahomes
CL J Zimmerman
RP M Petkovsek
RP M Venafro
C I Rodriguez
1D R Palmeiro
2B M Young
SS A Rodriguez
3B- M Lamb
LU F Catalanotto
CF G Kapler
RF- R Ledee
DR- R Sierra
M1 *J Oates*
M2 *J Narron*

TORONTO
SP C Carpenter
SP E Loaiza
SP J Hamilton
SP C Michalak
SP S Parris
RS K Escobar
RP R Halladay
CL B Koch
RP P Quantrill
C D Fletcher
1B C Delgado
2B- H Bush
SS A Gonzalez
3B- T Batista
LF S Stewart
CF J Cruz
RF R Mondesi
DH B Fullmer
M *B Martinez*

2001 NL

ARIZONA
SP C Schilling
SP R Johnson
SR M Batista
SP B Anderson
RP B Kim
RP G Swindell
RP E Sabel
RP T Brohawn
C D Miller
1B M Grace
23 J Bell
SS T Womack
3B M Williams
LF L Gonzalez
CF S Finley
RF R Sanders
UO D Bautista
UI C Counsell
UO D Dellucci
UT- E Durazo
M *B Brenly*

ATLANTA
SP G Maddux
SP J Burkett
SP T Glavine
SR J Marquis
SP K Millwood
RP M Remlinger
RS J Smoltz
RP J Cabrera
RP K Ligtenberg
C J Lopez
1B W Helms
2B- Q Veras
SS- R Furcal
3B C Jones
LF B Surhoff
CF A Jones
RF B Jordan
IF K Lockhart
OI D Martinez
M *B Cox*

CHICAGO
SP J Lieber
SP J Bere
SP K Wood
SP K Tapani
SP J Tavarez
RP J Fassero
RP K Farnsworth
RP T Van Poppel
C- J Girardi
1U M Stairs
2B E Young
SS R Gutierrez
31 R Coomer
LF- R White
CF G Matthews
RF S Sosa
M *D Baylor*

CINCINNATI
SP E Dessens
SP C Reitsma
SP L Davis
RS J Brower
CL D Graves
RP S Sullivan
RP H Mercado
C J LaRue
1B S Casey
2B- T Walker
S2 P Reese
3B A Boone
L1 D Young
CF K Griffey
RF- A Ochoa
MO R Rivera
UI- J Castro
UO- B Clark
UO- M Tucker
M *B Boone*

COLORADO
SP M Hampton
SP D Neagle
SP S Chacon
SP P Astacio
RP J Jimenez
RP K Davis
RP G White
RP J Speier
C- B Petrick
1B T Helton
2B- T Walker
SS- N Perez
3B J Cirillo
LR- A Ochoa
CF J Pierre
RF L Walker
UT G Norton
IO T Shumpert
M *B Bell*

FLORIDA
SP R Dempster
SP B Penny
SP A Burnett
SP M Clement
RP V Nunez
CL A Alfonseca
RP B Looper
RP R Bones
C C Johnson
1B D Lee
2B L Castillo
SS A Gonzalez
3B M Lowell
LF C Floyd
CF P Wilson
RM E Owens
UT K Millar
UI- D Berg
OI- J Mabry
M1 *J Boles*
M2 *T Perez*

HOUSTON
SP W Miller
SP S Reynolds
SP R Oswalt
SP S Elarton
RP O Dotel
CL B Wagner
RP N Cruz
RP M Jackson
C B Ausmus
1B J Bagwell
2B C Biggio
SS J Lugo
3B V Castilla
LF L Berkman
CF R Hidalgo
RF M Alou
UI J Vizcaino
UT- O Merced
OI- D Ward
M *L Dierker*

LOS ANGELES
SP C Park
SR T Adams
SP E Gagne
SP L Prokopec
SP K Brown
CL J Shaw
RP M Herges
RP G Carrara
C P LoDuca
1B E Karros
2B M Grudzielanek
SS A Cora
3B A Beltre
LF G Sheffield
MU M Grissom
RF S Green
MU T Goodwin
IF- D Hansen
SI- J Reboulet
M *J Tracy*

MILWAUKEE
SP J Wright
SP J Haynes
SP B Sheets
SR A Levrault
RP M DeJean
RP C Leskanic
RP C Fox
RP D Weathers
C H Blanco
1B R Sexson
2B R Belliard
SS J Hernandez
3B- T Houston
LF G Jenkins
MU D White
RF J Burnitz
23 M Loretta
3I- L Lopez
M *D Lopes*

MONTREAL
SP J Vazquez
SP T Armas
SP M Thurman
RS M Yoshii
RS B Reames
RP S Strickland
RP G Lloyd
C M Barrett
1B L Stevens
2B J Vidro
SS O Cabrera
IO G Blum
LU- M Smith
CF P Bergeron
RF V Guerrero
IO- M Mordecai
M1 *F Alou*
M2 *J Torborg*

NEW YORK
SP K Appier
SP A Leiter
SP G Rusch
SP S Trachsel
SP R Reed
CL A Benitez
RP R White
RP J Franco
RP T Wendell
C M Piazza
1B T Zeile
2B E Alfonzo
SS R Ordonez
3B R Ventura
LF- B Agbayani
CF J Payton
UO T Shinjo
UT L Harris
UT J McEwing
UI D Relaford
RU- T Perez
M *B Valentine*

PHILADELPHIA
SP R Person
SP O Daal
SP R Wolf
CL J Mesa
RP R Bottalico
RP J Santiago
RP R Cormier
C- J Estrada
1B T Lee
2B M Anderson
SS J Rollins
3B S Rolen
LF P Burrell
CF D Glanville
RF B Abreu
UO- B Hunter
M *L Bowa*

PITTSBURGH
SP T Ritchie
SP J Anderson
SR J Beimel
SP D Williams
RS O Olivares
RP J Manzanillo
RP S Sauerbeck
C J Kendall
1B K Young
2B- P Meares
SS J Wilson
3B A Ramirez
LF B Giles
OF- E Brown
RU- J Vander Wal
IO A Nunez
UT- R Mackowiak
UT- C Wilson
M *L McClendon*

ST. LOUIS
SP D Kile
SP M Morris
SP D Hermanson
SP A Benes
RS M Matthews
RP S Kline
RP D Veres
RP G Stechschulte
C M Matheny
1B- M McGwire
2B F Vina
SS E Renteria
3S P Polanco
LF- R Lankford
CF J Edmonds
RF J Drew
UT C Paquette
UT A Pujols
UO K Robinson
UT- B Bonilla
C- E Marrero
M *T LaRussa*

SAN DIEGO
SP B Jones
SP K Jarvis
SP W Williams
SP A Eaton
SP B Tollberg
RS B Lawrence
CL T Hoffman
RP J Nunez
RP D Lee
C B Davis
1B R Klesko
2B D Jackson
SS- D Jimenez
3B P Nevin
LF R Henderson
CF M Kotsay
RU B Trammell
RM M Darr
UI- D Magadan
M *B Bochy*

SAN FRANCISCO
SP L Hernandez
SP R Ortiz
SP K Rueter
SP S Estes
CL R Nen
RP F Rodriguez
RP T Worrell
RP A Fultz
C B Santiago
1B J Snow
2B J Kent
SS R Aurilia
3B- P Feliz
LF B Bonds
CF C Murray
MR M Benard
32 R Martinez
OI- S Dunston
RF- A Rios
M *D Baker*

2002 AL

ANAHEIM
SP R Ortiz
SP J Washburn
SP K Appier
SP A Sele
SP J Lackey
RS S Schoeneweis
CL T Percival
RP B Weber
RP A Levine
C B Molina
1B S Spiezio
2B A Kennedy
SS D Eckstein
3B T Glaus
LF G Anderson
CF D Erstad
RF T Salmon
DU B Fullmer
UO O Palmeiro
M *M Scioscia*

BALTIMORE
SP R Lopez
SP S Ponson
SP S Erickson
SR T Driskill
SP J Johnson
CL J Julio
RP R Bauer
RP W Roberts
RP B Groom
C G Gil
1B J Conine
2B J Hairston
SS M Bordick
3B T Batista
UT M Mora
CF C Singleton
RO G Matthews
LD M Cordova
RU J Gibbons
M *M Hargrove*

BOSTON
SP D Lowe
SP P Martinez
SP J Burkett
SR F Castillo
RS T Wakefield
RS C Fossum
CL U Urbina
RS R Arrojo
C J Varitek
1B- T Clark
2B R Sanchez
SS N Garciaparra
3B S Hillenbrand
LU- R Henderson
CF J Damon
RF T Nixon
LD M Ramirez
UT B Daubach
2B- L Merloni
M *G Little*

CHICAGO
SP M Buehrle
SP D Wright
SP J Garland
SR G Glover
SP T Ritchie
RP K Foulke
RS R Biddle
RP A Osuna
RP D Marte
C- M Johnson
1B P Konerko
2B- R Durham
SS R Clayton
3S J Valentin
LF C Lee
ML A Rowand
RF M Ordonez
DH F Thomas
CF- K Lofton
M *J Manuel*

CLEVELAND
SP C Sabathia
SR D Baez
SP R Drese
SP B Colon
SP C Finley
RP M Wohlers
RP D Riske
C E Diaz
1B J Thome
2B- R Gutierrez
SS O Vizquel
3B T Fryman
LR- C Magruder
CF M Bradley
RU M Lawton
DH E Burks
2I- J McDonald
M1 *C Manuel*
M2 *J Skinner*

DETROIT
SP M Redman
SP S Sparks
SP M Maroth
SP J Weaver
SR A Bernero
CL J Acevedo
RP J Farnsworth
RP J Santana
C- B Inge
1B- C Pena
2B- D Easley
SI S Halter
3B- C Truby
LF B Higginson
CF W Magee
RF R Fick
D1 R Simon
2U- D Jackson
M1 *P Garner*
M2 *L Pujols*

KANSAS CITY
SP P Byrd
SP J Suppan
SP D May
SR M Asencio

RS J Affeldt
CL R Hernandez
RP J Grimsley
RS D Reichert
C B Mayne
1B M Sweeney
2B C Febles
SS N Perez
3B J Randa
LF- C Knoblauch
CF C Beltran
UT M Tucker
OI R Ibanez
IO- L Alicea
M1 T Muser
M2 J Mizerock
M3 A Pena

MINNESOTA
SP R Reed
SP K Lohse
SP E Milton
SP B Radke
SR J Santana
CL E Guardado
RP T Fiore
RP J Romero
RP L Hawkins
C A Pierzynski
1B D Mientkiewicz
2B- L Rivas
SS C Guzman
3B C Koskie
LF J Jones
CF T Hunter
RF D Mohr
DH D Ortiz
2I D Hocking
OI B Kielty
M R Gardenhire

NEW YORK
SP M Mussina
SP D Wells
SP R Clemens
SP O Hernandez
SP A Pettitte
RP S Karsay
RP R Mendoza
RP M Stanton
C J Posada
1D N Johnson
2B A Soriano
SS D Jeter
3B R Ventura
LF R White
CF B Williams
RL- S Spencer
1D J Giambi
RU- J Vander Wal
M J Torre

OAKLAND
SP T Hudson
SP B Zito
SP M Mulder
SP C Lidle
CL B Koch
RP C Bradford
RP J Mecir
C R Hernandez
1D S Hatteberg
2B M Ellis
SS M Tejada
3B E Chavez
LO- E Byrnes
CF T Long
RF J Dye
DH- R Durham
OF D Justice
1L- J Mabry
M A Howe

SEATTLE
SP J Moyer
SP F Garcia
SP J Pineiro
SP J Baldwin
RS R Franklin
RS J Halama
CL K Sasaki
RP A Rhodes
C D Wilson
1B J Olerud
2B B Boone
SS C Guillen
3B J Cirillo
LF M McLemore
CF M Cameron
RF I Suzuki
DH- E Martinez
UT D Relaford
OF R Sierra
M L Piniella

TAMPA BAY
SP T Sturtze
SP J Kennedy
SP P Wilson
SR J Sosa
RS V Zambrano
CL E Yan
RS T Harper
RP S Kent
C- T Hall
1U S Cox
2B B Abernathy
SS C Gomez
3B J Sandberg
LF- C Crawford
CF R Winn
RF B Grieve
IF A Huff
M H McRae

TEXAS
SP K Rogers
SP I Valdes
SP C Park
SP D Burba
RP T Van Poppel
RP J Powell
C I Rodriguez
UT M Lamb
2B M Young
SS A Rodriguez
3B H Perry
RL K Mench
CF- R Rivera
UO C Everett
1D R Palmeiro
M J Narron

TORONTO
SP R Halladay
SP E Loaiza
SR P Walker
SP J Miller
CL K Escobar
RP C Thurman
RP S Cassidy
RP S Eyre
C- K Huckaby
1B C Delgado
2B- O Hudson
SS- C Woodward
3B E Hinske
LD S Stewart
CF V Wells
UO J Cruz
DH- J Phelps
UT D Berg
SS- F Lopez
CU- T Wilson
M1 B Martinez
M2 C Tosca

2002 NL

ARIZONA
SP R Johnson
SP C Schilling
SP M Batista
SP R Helling
SR B Anderson
CL B Kim
RP M Koplove
C D Miller
1B M Grace
2B J Spivey
SS T Womack
3B C Counsell
LF L Gonzalez
CF S Finley
RM Q McCracken
UO- D Dellucci
M B Brenly

ATLANTA
SP T Glavine
SP K Millwood
SP G Maddux
SP D Moss
SP J Marquis
CL J Smoltz
RP C Hammond
RP M Remlinger
RP K Ligtenberg
C J Lopez
1B J Franco
2U K Lockhart
SS R Furcal
3B V Castilla
LF C Jones
CF A Jones
RF G Sheffield
UO D Bragg
C- H Blanco
1U- M Franco
13- W Helms
M B Cox

CHICAGO
SP K Wood
SP M Clement
SP J Lieber
SP M Prior
SR C Zambrano
RP J Borowski
RS J Cruz
RP A Alfonseca
RP J Fassero
C- J Girardi
1B F McGriff
2I M Bellhorn
SS A Gonzalez
3B B Mueller
LF M Alou
CF C Patterson
RF S Sosa
UO R Brown
IF C Stynes
C- T Hundley
M1 D Baylor
M2 B Kimm

CINCINNATI
SP J Haynes
SP E Dessens
SR C Reitsma
SR J Hamilton
RP D Graves
RP S Williamson
RP S Sullivan
RS J Rijo
C J LaRue
1B S Casey
2B T Walker
SS B Larkin
3B A Boone
L1 A Dunn
ML R Taylor
RF A Kearns
IO- R Branyan
MR- J Encarnacion
M B Boone

COLORADO
SP J Jennings
SP M Hampton
SP D Neagle
SR D Stark
SR J Thomson
RP S Chacon
CL J Jimenez
RP T Jones
RP J Speier
C- G Bennett
1B T Helton
23 B Butler
SS J Uribe
3B T Zeile
LF- T Hollandsworth
CF J Pierre
RF L Walker
IO G Norton
2U T Shumpert
M1 B Bell
M2 C Hurdle

FLORIDA
SP A Burnett
SP J Tavarez
SR M Tejera
SP B Penny
SP R Dempster
RP V Nunez
RP J Beckett
RP B Looper
C- C Johnson
1B D Lee
2B L Castillo
SS A Fox
3B M Lowell
LU K Millar
CF P Wilson
LR E Owens
UT T Raines
RU- C Floyd
C- M Redmond
M J Torborg

HOUSTON
SP R Oswalt
SP W Miller
SP C Hernandez
CL B Wagner
RP O Dotel
RS N Cruz
RP R Stone
C B Ausmus
1B J Bagwell
2B C Biggio
SS- J Lugo
3B G Blum
LF D Ward
CF L Berkman
RF R Hidalgo
CF B Hunter
UT O Merced
UI J Vizcaino
M J Williams

LOS ANGELES
SP O Perez
SP H Nomo
SP A Ashby
SR O Daal
SP K Ishii
CL E Gagne
RP G Carrara
RP P Quantrill
RP G Mota
C P LoDuca
1B E Karros
2B M Grudzielanek
SS C Izturis
3B A Beltre
LF B Jordan
CF D Roberts
RF S Green
S2 A Cora
ML M Grissom
IF- D Hansen
M J Tracy

MILWAUKEE
SP B Sheets
SP G Rusch
SP R Quevedo
SP J Wright
RS J Cabrera
CL M DeJean
RP L Vizcaino
RP R King
C- P Bako
1B R Sexson
2B E Young
SS J Hernandez
3B- T Houston
LF- G Jenkins
CF A Sanchez
MR J Hammonds
IF R Belliard
IO L Harris
OF M Stairs
3U- M Loretta
RU- A Ochoa
M1 D Lopes
M2 J Royster

MONTREAL
SP J Vazquez
SP T Ohka
SP T Armas
SR M Yoshii
SP B Colon
RP S Stewart
RP M Herges
RS B Reames
RP T Tucker
C M Barrett
1B A Galarraga
2B J Vidro
SS O Cabrera
3B F Tatis
LU- T O'Leary
OI B Wilkerson
RF V Guerrero
MI- J Macias
M F Robinson

NEW YORK
SP A Leiter
SP P Astacio
SP S Trachsel
SP J D'Amico
SP S Estes
CL A Benitez
RP D Weathers
RP S Strickland
C M Piazza
1B M Vaughn
2B R Alomar
SS R Ordonez
3B E Alfonzo
LF R Cedeno
MO T Perez
RF J Burnitz
UT J McEwing
UI J Valentin
CF- J Payton
M B Valentine

PHILADELPHIA
SP R Wolf
SP V Padilla
SP B Duckworth
SR T Adams
CL J Mesa
RP C Silva
RS D Coggin
RP R Cormier
C M Lieberthal
1B T Lee
2B M Anderson
SS J Rollins
3B S Rolen
LF P Burrell
CF D Glanville
RF B Abreu
UT- J Giambi
UO- R Ledee
OI- J Michaels
2I- T Perez
M L Bowa

PITTSBURGH
SP K Wells
SP J Fogg
SP J Anderson
SP K Benson
CL M Williams
RS R Villone
RS J Beimel
RP B Boehringer
C J Kendall
1B K Young
2B P Reese
SS J Wilson
3B A Ramirez
LF B Giles
RM R Mackowiak
R1 C Wilson
3I M Benjamin
IF A Nunez
MU- A Brown
M L McClendon

ST. LOUIS
SP M Morris
SP J Simontacchi
SP W Williams
CL J Isringhausen
RP D Veres
RS L Hackman
RP S Kline
C M Matheny
1B T Martinez
2B F Vina
SS E Renteria
3B- P Polanco
L3 A Pujols
CF J Edmonds
RF J Drew
UT M Cairo
OC E Marrero
UO K Robinson
UT- E Perez
M T LaRussa

SAN DIEGO
SP B Lawrence
SP B Tomko
SP B Jones
CL T Hoffman
RP J Fikac
C T Lampkin
1B R Klesko
2S R Vazquez
SS D Cruz
31 P Nevin
LF R Gant
CF M Kotsay
RF B Trammell
LF R Gant
UT- T Hubbard
23- D Jimenez
RL- E Kingsale
LU- R Lankford
M B Bochy

SAN FRANCISCO
SP L Hernandez
SP R Ortiz
SP K Rueter
SP J Schmidt
SP R Jensen
CL R Nen
RP T Worrell
RP F Rodriguez
RP J Witasick
C B Santiago
1B J Snow
2B J Kent
SS R Aurilia
3B D Bell
LF B Bonds
CF T Shinjo
RF R Sanders
1U- D Minor
M D Baker

2003 AL

ANAHEIM
SP J Washburn
SP J Lackey
SP R Ortiz
SP A Sele
RS S Shields
RP F Rodriguez
CL T Percival
RP B Weber
C B Molina
13 S Spiezio
2B A Kennedy
SS D Eckstein
3B- T Glaus
LF G Anderson
UO E Owens
RM J DaVanon
RD T Salmon
IF S Wooten
M M Scioscia

BALTIMORE
SP J Johnson
SP P Hentgen
SP S Ponson
SP R Lopez
SP R Helling
CL J Julio
RP R Bauer
RP K Ligtenberg
RP B Ryan
C B Fordyce
1B J Conine
2B B Roberts
SS D Cruz
3B T Batista
LF- L Bigbie
CF L Matos
RF J Gibbons
DH- D Segui
LO- M Mora
OI- B Surhoff
M M Hargrove

BOSTON
SP D Lowe
SP T Wakefield
SP P Martinez
SP J Burkett
CL B Kim
RP M Timlin
RP B Lyon
RS R Mendoza
C J Varitek
1U K Millar
2B T Walker
SS N Garciaparra
3B B Mueller
LF M Ramirez
CF J Damon
RF T Nixon
D1 D Ortiz
UT D Jackson
M G Little

CHICAGO
SP B Colon
SP M Buehrle
SP E Loaiza
SP J Garland
RP D Marte
RP T Gordon
RP B Koch
C M Olivo
1B P Konerko
2B- D Jimenez
SS J Valentin
3B J Crede
LF C Lee
ML- A Rowand
RF M Ordonez
DH F Thomas
UT- B Daubach
UI- T Graffanino
M J Manuel

CLEVELAND
SP C Sabathia
SP J Davis
SP B Anderson
SR J Westbrook
SR B Traber
CL D Baez
RP T Mulholland
RP D Riske
RP J Boyd
C- J Bard
1B B Broussard
2B B Phillips
SS- J Peralta
3B C Blake
ML C Crisp
CF M Bradley
UO J Gerut
DH- E Burks
LU M Lawton
UT- T Hafner
UI- J McDonald
M E Wedge

DETROIT
SP N Cornejo
SP M Maroth
SP J Bonderman
SP A Bernero
RS M Roney
RP S Sparks
RS W Ledezma
RP C Spurling
C B Inge
1B C Pena
2B- W Morris
S2 R Santiago
3B E Munson
LR C Monroe
CF A Sanchez
RF B Higginson
UT D Young
IO S Halter
IO- K Witt
M A Trammell

KANSAS CITY
SP D May
SR J Affeldt
CL M Mac Dougal
RP D Carrasco
RP J Grimsley
RP K Wilson
C B Mayne
1U K Harvey
2I D Relaford
SS A Berroa
3B J Randa
LF R Ibanez
CF C Beltran
RF A Guiel
D1 M Sweeney
UO M Tucker
M A Pena

MINNESOTA
SP B Radke
SP K Lohse
SP K Rogers
SR J Santana
SP R Reed
RS J Mays
CL E Guardado
RP J Rincon
RP L Hawkins
C A Pierzynski
1B D Mientkiewicz
2B L Rivas
SS C Guzman
3B C Koskie
LU J Jones
CF T Hunter
RO D Mohr
DU M LeCroy
UT- D Hocking
M R Gardenhire

NEW YORK
SP M Mussina
SP D Wells
SP R Clemens
SP A Pettitte
SP J Weaver
CL M Rivera
RP C Hammond
RP A Osuna
RP S Hitchcock
C J Posada
1D- N Johnson
2B A Soriano
SS D Jeter
3B- R Ventura
LM H Matsui
CF B Williams
RF R Mondesi
1D J Giambi
M J Torre

OAKLAND
SP T Hudson
SP B Zito
SP M Mulder
SP T Lilly
SR J Halama
CL K Foulke
RP C Bradford
RP R Rincon
C R Hernandez
1B S Hatteberg
2B M Ellis
SS M Tejada
3B E Chavez
ML E Byrnes
CF C Singleton
LR T Long
DH E Durazo
M K Macha

SEATTLE
SP J Moyer
SP R Franklin
SP J Pineiro
SP F Garcia
SP G Meche
RP S Hasegawa
RP J Mateo
RP A Rhodes
RP R Soriano
C- D Wilson
1B J Olerud
2B B Boone
S3 C Guillen
3B- J Cirillo
LF R Winn
CF M Cameron
RF I Suzuki
DH E Martinez
IO M McLemore
UT- W Bloomquist
M B Melvin

TAMPA BAY
SP V Zambrano
SP J Gonzalez
SR J Kennedy
SR J Sosa
SP R Bell
CL L Carter
RP T Harper
RP J Colome
RP A Levine
C T Hall
1B T Lee
2B M Anderson
SS J Lugo
3R D Rolls
LF C Crawford
CF R Baldelli
RU A Huff
DU A Martin
M L Piniella

TEXAS
SP J Thomson
SP C Lewis
SR R Dickey
SP I Valdes
SP J Benoit
RP F Cordero
RP A Fultz
RP B Shouse
RP J Powell
C E Diaz
1B M Teixeira
2B M Young
SS A Rodriguez
3B H Blalock
LR- C Everett
CF- R Christenson
RD- J Gonzalez
D1 R Palmeiro
M B Showalter

TORONTO
SP R Halladay
SP C Lidle
SR K Escobar
SP M Hendrickson
RS T Sturtze
RP A Lopez
RP C Politte
RP T Miller
CU G Myers
1B C Delgado
2B O Hudson
SS C Woodward
3B E Hinske
OI F Catalanotto
CF V Wells
RL R Johnson
DH J Phelps
SI M Bordick
C- T Wilson
M C Tosca

2003 NL

ARIZONA
SP M Batista
SP B Webb
SP E Dessens
SP C Schilling
SP R Johnson
RP O Villarreal
CL M Mantei
RP S Randolph
RP J Valverde
C- R Barajas
1B- L Overbay
2B J Spivey
SS A Cintron
3S- C Counsell
LF L Gonzalez
CF S Finley
RU- D Bautista
UI C Baerga
UO Q McCracken
13- S Hillenbrand
M B Brenly

ATLANTA
SP G Maddux
SP R Ortiz
SP M Hampton
SP H Ramirez
SP S Reynolds
CL J Smoltz
RP T Hodges
RP R Hernandez
RP R King
C J Lopez
1B R Fick
2B M Giles
SS R Furcal
3B V Castilla
LF C Jones

- CF A Jones
- RF G Sheffield
- UO D Bragg
- IO M DeRosa
- 1U J Franco
- UT M Franco
- *M B Cox*

CHICAGO

- SP C Zambrano
- SP M Prior
- SP K Wood
- SP M Clement
- SP S Estes
- CL J Borowski
- RP K Farnsworth
- RP M Remlinger
- RP A Alfonseca
- C D Miller
- 1B E Karros
- 2B M Grudzielanek
- SS A Gonzalez
- 3B- A Ramirez
- LF M Alou
- CF- C Patterson
- RF S Sosa
- UI R Martinez
- UO- T Goodwin
- OF- T O'Leary
- *M D Baker*

CINCINNATI

- SP D Graves
- SP P Wilson
- SP R Dempster
- RS J Riedling
- RP C Reitsma
- RP F Heredia
- RP B Reith
- C J LaRue
- 1B S Casey
- 2B- D Jimenez
- SS- B Larkin
- 3B A Boone
- LF A Dunn
- RM- A Kearns
- RO- J Guillen
- UI J Castro
- UO R Taylor
- *M1 B Boone*
- *M2 R Knight*
- *M3 D Miley*

COLORADO

- SP J Jennings
- SP D Oliver
- SP S Chacon
- SR A Cook
- RS J Jimenez
- RP J Speier
- RP B Fuentes
- RP S Reed
- C C Johnson
- 1B T Helton
- 2B R Belliard
- SS- J Uribe
- 3B C Stynes
- LF J Payton
- CF P Wilson
- RF L Walker
- IO G Norton
- *M C Hurdle*

FLORIDA

- SP C Pavano
- SP B Penny
- SP M Redman
- SP D Willis
- SP J Beckett
- CL B Looper
- RS M Tejera
- RS T Phelps
- RP A Almanza
- C I Rodriguez
- 1B D Lee
- 2B L Castillo
- SS A Gonzalez
- 3B M Lowell
- LU- T Hollandsworth
- CF J Pierre
- RF J Encarnacion
- OI- B Banks
- L3- M Cabrera
- *M1 J Torborg*
- *M2 J McKeon*

HOUSTON

- SP W Miller
- SP T Redding
- SP J Robertson
- SP R Oswalt
- SP R Villone
- CL B Wagner
- RP O Dotel
- RP B Lidge
- RP R Stone
- C B Ausmus
- 1B J Bagwell
- 2B J Kent
- SS A Everett
- 3B M Ensberg
- LF L Berkman
- CF C Biggio
- RF R Hidalgo
- 3I G Blum
- UT O Merced
- UI- J Vizcaino
- *M J Williams*

LOS ANGELES

- SP H Nomo
- SP K Brown
- SP O Perez
- SP K Ishii
- CL E Gagne
- RP G Mota
- RP P Quantrill
- RP P Shuey
- C P LoDuca
- 1B- F McGriff
- 2B A Cora
- SS C Izturis
- 3B A Beltre
- LF- B Jordan
- CF D Roberts
- RF S Green
- UT J Cabrera
- UT- M Kinkade
- *M J Tracy*

MILWAUKEE

- SP B Sheets
- SP W Franklin
- SP M Kinney
- SR G Rusch
- RP M DeJean
- RP L Estrella
- RP L Vizcaino
- RP B Kieschnick
- C E Perez
- 1B R Sexson
- 2B E Young
- SS R Clayton
- 3B W Helms
- LF G Jenkins
- CF S Podsednik
- RU B Clark
- IO K Ginter
- RU J Vander Wal
- *M N Yost*

MONTREAL

- SP L Hernandez
- SP J Vazquez
- SP T Ohka
- SP Z Day
- SP C Vargas
- CL R Biddle
- RS T Tucker
- RP L Ayala
- RP J Eischen
- C B Schneider
- 1B W Cordero
- 2B J Vidro
- SS O Cabrera
- 3U J Carroll
- LM B Wilkerson
- CF E Chavez
- RF V Guerrero
- UO R Calloway
- UT J Macias
- UT H Mateo
- *M F Robinson*

NEW YORK

- SP S Trachsel
- SP J Seo
- SP T Glavine
- SP A Leiter
- RP D Weathers
- CL A Benitez
- RP D Wheeler
- C- V Wilson
- 1U J Phillips
- 2B- R Alomar
- SS- J Reyes
- 3B T Wigginton
- LF C Floyd
- UO T Perez
- RF R Cedeno
- 1U T Clark
- UO R Gonzalez
- UT J McEwing
- *M A Howe*

PHILADELPHIA

- SP K Millwood
- SP V Padilla
- SP R Wolf
- SP B Myers
- RP C Silva
- RP R Cormier
- CL J Mesa
- RP T Adams
- C M Lieberthal
- 1B J Thome
- 2B P Polanco
- SS J Rollins
- 3B- D Bell
- LF P Burrell
- CF M Byrd
- RF B Abreu
- UO R Ledee
- UI T Perez
- *M L Bowa*

PITTSBURGH

- SP K Wells
- SP J D'Amico
- SP J Fogg
- SP J Suppan
- SR S Torres
- RP K Benson
- RP J Tavarez
- RS B Meadows
- RP J Beimel
- C J Kendall
- 1B- R Simon
- 2B- J Reboulet
- SS J Wilson
- 3B- A Ramirez
- LF B Giles
- CF- K Lofton
- RL R Sanders
- 2U A Nunez
- OI M Stairs
- OI C Wilson
- *M L McClendon*

ST. LOUIS

- SP W Williams
- SP B Tomko
- SP G Stephenson
- SP M Morris
- SR J Simontacchi
- RS J Fassero
- RP C Eldred
- RP S Kline
- C M Matheny
- 1B T Martinez
- 2B- B Hart
- SS E Renteria
- 3B S Rolen
- L1 A Pujols
- CF J Edmonds
- UO O Palmeiro
- RM J Drew
- RU E Perez
- UO K Robinson
- UT- M Cairo
- *M T LaRussa*

SAN DIEGO

- SP B Lawrence
- SP J Peavy
- SP A Eaton
- SP O Perez
- RP L Hackman
- RP M Matthews
- RP S Linebrink
- C- G Bennett
- 1B R Klesko
- 2B M Loretta
- SS R Vazquez
- 3B S Burroughs
- LF R White
- CF M Kotsay
- RF X Nady
- OI B Buchanan
- UI D Hansen
- UO G Matthews
- *M B Bochy*

SAN FRANCISCO

- SP J Schmidt
- SP K Rueter
- SP J Williams
- SP D Moss
- SP J Foppert
- CL T Worrell
- RS J Brower
- RP J Nathan
- RP F Rodriguez
- C B Santiago
- 1B J Snow
- 2B R Durham
- SS R Aurilia
- 3B E Alfonzo
- LF B Bonds
- CF M Grissom
- RF J Cruz
- 1U A Galarraga
- UI N Perez
- 3U- P Feliz
- *M F Alou*

2004 AL

ANAHEIM

- SP B Colon
- SP K Escobar
- SP J Lackey
- SP J Washburn
- SP A Sele
- RS R Ortiz
- RP S Shields
- RP F Rodriguez
- RP K Gregg
- C- B Molina
- 1B D Erstad
- 2B A Kennedy
- SS D Eckstein
- 3M C Figgins
- LF J Guillen
- CF G Anderson
- RF V Guerrero
- DU- T Salmon
- UO J DaVanon
- *M M Scioscia*

BALTIMORE

- SP S Ponson
- SR R Lopez
- SP D Cabrera
- SP E Bedard
- CL J Julio
- RP B Ryan
- RP J Parrish
- RP R Bauer
- C J Lopez
- 1B R Palmeiro
- 2B B Roberts
- SS M Tejada
- 3B M Mora
- LF L Bigbie
- CF- L Matos
- OI B Surhoff
- UT- D Newhan
- RU- J Gibbons
- UT- J Hairston
- *M L Mazzilli*

BOSTON

- SP C Schilling
- SP P Martinez
- SP T Wakefield
- SP D Lowe
- SP B Arroyo
- CL K Foulke
- RP M Timlin
- RP A Embree
- C J Varitek
- OI K Millar
- 2B M Bellhorn
- S2- P Reese
- 3B B Mueller
- LF M Ramirez
- CF J Damon
- RO G Kapler
- DH D Ortiz
- 1U- D McCarty
- *M T Francona*

CHICAGO

- SP M Buehrle
- SP J Garland
- SP E Loaiza
- SP S Schoeneweis
- SP F Garcia
- RP S Takatsu
- RP D Marte
- RP N Cotts
- RP J Adkins
- C- B Davis
- 1B P Konerko
- 2U W Harris
- SS J Valentin
- 3B J Crede
- LF C Lee
- CF A Rowand
- UO T Perez
- DH- F Thomas
- UT R Gload
- 2S J Uribe
- *M O Guillen*

CLEVELAND

- SP J Westbrook
- SP C Sabathia
- SP C Lee
- SP S Elarton
- SP J Davis
- RP D Riske
- RP R White
- RP R Betancourt
- RP M Miller
- C V Martinez
- 1B B Broussard
- 2B R Belliard
- SS O Vizquel
- 3B C Blake
- LF M Lawton
- ML C Crisp
- RF J Gerut
- DH T Hafner
- *M E Wedge*

DETROIT

- SP M Maroth
- SP N Robertson
- SP J Johnson
- SP J Bonderman
- SR G Knotts
- RP E Yan
- CL U Urbina
- RP A Levine
- RP J Walker
- C I Rodriguez
- 1B C Pena
- 2U O Infante
- SS C Guillen
- 3B E Munson
- LR C Monroe
- CF- A Sanchez
- RF B Higginson
- DI D Young
- 3C B Inge
- LD R White
- *M A Trammell*

KANSAS CITY

- SP D May
- SP B Anderson
- SP J Gobble
- SP Z Greinke
- SP M Wood
- RS D Reyes
- CL J Affeldt
- RP S Camp
- RP S Sullivan
- C- J Buck
- 1D K Harvey
- 2B- T Graffanino
- SS A Berroa
- 3B J Randa
- CF- D DeJesus
- CF- C Beltran
- OI M Stairs
- 1D M Sweeney
- UT D Relaford
- *M T Pena*

MINNESOTA

- SP J Santana
- SP B Radke
- SP C Silva
- SP K Lohse
- SR T Mulholland
- CL J Nathan
- RP J Rincon
- RP J Romero
- RP J Roa
- C H Blanco
- 1B- D Mientkiewicz
- 2B L Rivas
- SS C Guzman
- 3B C Koskie
- LM L Ford
- CF T Hunter
- RF J Jones
- DU- J Offerman
- UT M Cuddyer
- UC- M LeCroy
- LF- S Stewart
- *M R Gardenhire*

NEW YORK

- SP J Vazquez
- SP J Lieber
- SP M Mussina
- SP K Brown
- CL M Rivera
- RP P Quantrill
- RP T Gordon
- RP T Sturtze
- C J Posada
- 1B T Clark
- 2B M Cairo
- SS D Jeter
- 3B A Rodriguez
- LF H Matsui
- MD B Williams
- RF G Sheffield
- DO R Sierra
- CF- K Lofton
- 2B- E Wilson
- *M J Torre*

OAKLAND

- SP M Mulder
- SP B Zito
- SP M Redman
- SP R Harden
- SP T Hudson
- RP J Duchscherer
- CL O Dotel
- RP C Bradford
- RP C Hammond
- C D Miller
- 1B S Hatteberg
- 2B M Scutaro
- SS B Crosby
- 3B E Chavez
- LF E Byrnes
- CF M Kotsay
- RF J Dye
- DH E Durazo
- LR- B Kielty
- *M K Macha*

SEATTLE

- SP J Moyer
- SP R Franklin
- SP J Pineiro
- SP G Meche
- SP F Garcia
- RS R Villone
- RP J Putz
- RP S Hasegawa
- RP J Mateo
- C D Wilson
- 1B- J Olerud
- 2B B Boone
- SS- R Aurilia
- 31 S Spiezio
- LF R Ibanez
- CF R Winn
- RF I Suzuki
- DH E Martinez
- UT J Cabrera
- UT- W Bloomquist
- *M B Melvin*

TAMPA BAY

- SP M Hendrickson
- SP V Zambrano
- SP R Bell
- SP D Brazelton
- SR J Halama
- RS J Sosa
- CL D Baez
- RP L Carter
- RP T Harper
- C T Hall
- 1B T Martinez
- 2B- R Sanchez
- SS J Lugo
- 32 G Blum
- LF C Crawford
- CF R Baldelli
- RF J Cruz
- 3U A Huff
- *M L Piniella*

TEXAS

- SP K Rogers
- SP R Drese
- SR R Dickey
- SR J Benoit
- CL F Cordero
- RP C Almanzar
- RP R Mahay
- RP D Brocail
- C R Barajas
- 1B M Teixeira
- 2B A Soriano
- SS M Young
- 3B H Blalock
- LF D Dellucci
- CF L Nix
- UO K Mench
- DH- B Fullmer
- UT E Young
- RF- G Matthews
- *M B Showalter*

TORONTO

- SP M Batista
- SP T Lilly
- SP R Halladay
- SP J Towers
- SP D Bush
- RP J Frasor
- RP J Speier
- RP V Chulk
- RP K Ligtenberg
- C G Zaun
- 1B C Delgado
- 2B O Hudson
- SU C Gomez
- 3B E Hinske
- UO R Johnson
- CF V Wells
- RF A Rios
- DH- J Phelps
- *M1 C Tosca*
- *M2 J Gibbons*

2004 NL

ARIZONA

- SP R Johnson
- SP B Webb
- SP C Fossum
- SR S Sparks
- RP M Koplove
- RS E Dessens
- RS S Randolph
- RP R Choate
- C- J Brito
- 1B S Hillenbrand
- 2B S Hairston
- SS A Cintron
- 3B C Tracy
- LF L Gonzalez
- CF S Finley
- RF D Bautista
- *M1 B Brenly*
- *M2 A Pedrique*

ATLANTA

- SP R Ortiz
- SP J Thomson
- SP J Wright
- SP M Hampton
- SP P Byrd
- CL J Smoltz
- RP C Reitsma
- RP A Alfonseca
- RP J Cruz
- C J Estrada
- 1B A LaRoche
- 2B M Giles
- SS R Furcal
- 3U C Jones
- LR- E Marrero
- CF A Jones
- RF J Drew
- 3U M DeRosa
- 1U J Franco
- 2B- N Green
- LF- C Thomas
- *M B Cox*

CHICAGO

- SP G Maddux
- SP C Zambrano
- SP M Clement
- SP K Wood
- SR G Rusch
- RP M Prior
- RP L Hawkins
- RP K Farnsworth
- RP K Mercker
- C M Barrett
- 1B D Lee
- 2U T Walker
- SI R Martinez
- 3B A Ramirez
- LF M Alou
- CF C Patterson
- RF S Sosa
- UT J Macias
- 2B- M Grudzielanek
- *M D Baker*

CINCINNATI

- SP P Wilson
- SP A Harang
- SR J Acevedo
- SP C Lidle
- RS T Van Poppel
- CL D Graves
- RP J Riedling
- RP P Norton
- C J LaRue
- 1B S Casey
- 2B D Jimenez
- SS B Larkin
- 3S J Castro
- LF A Dunn
- UO W Pena
- UT R Freel
- OI- J Cruz
- CF- K Griffey
- CU- J Valentin
- *M D Miley*

COLORADO

- SP S Estes
- SP J Jennings
- SP J Kennedy
- RS J Fassero
- CL S Chacon
- RP S Reed
- RP T Harikkala
- C C Johnson
- 1B T Helton
- 2B A Miles
- SS R Clayton
- 3B V Castilla
- LF M Holliday
- CF- P Wilson
- RM J Burnitz
- UT L Gonzalez
- OI M Sweeney
- *M C Hurdle*

FLORIDA

- SP C Pavano
- SP D Willis
- SP J Beckett
- SP B Penny
- SP A Burnett
- CL A Benitez
- RP N Bump
- C- M Redmond
- 1B- H Choi
- 2B L Castillo
- SS A Gonzalez
- 3B M Lowell
- L1 J Conine
- CF J Pierre
- RL M Cabrera
- IO D Easley
- *M J McKeon*

HOUSTON

- SP R Oswalt
- SP R Clemens
- SR T Redding
- SP P Munro
- CL B Lidge
- RP D Miceli
- RS B Backe
- RP C Harville
- C B Ausmus
- 1B J Bagwell
- 2B J Kent
- SS A Everett
- 3B M Ensberg
- LM C Biggio
- CF- C Beltran
- RL L Berkman
- 3U M Lamb
- OI J Lane
- UO O Palmeiro
- UI J Vizcaino
- *M1 J Williams*
- *M2 P Garner*

LOS ANGELES

- SP J Weaver
- SP O Perez
- SP K Ishii
- SR J Lima
- SR W Alvarez
- CL E Gagne
- RP D Sanchez
- RP G Mota
- RP G Carrara
- C- P LoDuca
- 1R S Green
- 2B A Cora
- SS C Izturis
- 3B A Beltre
- LU- J Werth
- MO M Bradley
- RF- J Encarnacion
- OI J Grabowski
- IF R Ventura
- 2I- J Hernandez
- *M J Tracy*

MILWAUKEE

- SP B Sheets
- SP D Davis
- SP V Santos
- SP W Obermueller
- CL D Kolb
- RP L Vizcaino
- RP D Burba
- RP J Bennett
- C C Moeller
- 1B L Overbay
- 2B- J Spivey
- SS C Counsell
- 3U- W Helms
- LF G Jenkins
- CF S Podsednik
- RF B Clark
- IO K Ginter
- RU B Grieve
- UI B Hall
- *M N Yost*

MONTREAL

- SP L Hernandez
- SR S Kim
- SP Z Day
- RS C Vargas
- RP C Cordero
- RP L Ayala
- RS R Biddle
- C B Schneider
- 1L B Wilkerson
- 2B J Vidro
- SS O Cabrera
- 3B T Batista
- LR T Sledge
- CF E Chavez
- RF J Rivera
- 2U J Carroll
- *M F Robinson*

NEW YORK

- SP T Glavine
- SP S Trachsel
- SP A Leiter
- SP J Seo
- CL B Looper
- RP M Stanton
- RP R Bottalico
- RP D Wheeler
- C1 J Phillips
- 1C M Piazza
- 2B- D Garcia
- SS K Matsui
- 3B- D Wright
- LF C Floyd
- CF M Cameron
- RF- R Hidalgo
- OI E Valent
- IF T Zeile

3B- T Wigginton
M A Howe

PHILADELPHIA
SP E Milton
SP B Myers
SP K Millwood
SP R Wolf
SP V Padilla
RP T Worrell
RP R Cormier
RP R Madson
RP R Hernandez
C M Lieberthal
1B J Thome
2B P Polanco
SS J Rollins
3B D Bell
LF P Burrell
CF M Byrd
RF B Abreu
UO J Michaels
MU- D Glanville
UI- T Perez
2U- C Utley
M L Bowa

PITTSBURGH
SP O Perez
SP J Fogg
SP K Wells
SP R Vogelsong
SP K Benson
CL J Mesa
RP S Torres
RP B Meadows
RP J Grabow
C J Kendall
1B- D Ward
2B J Castillo
SS J Wilson
3B- C Stynes
LF J Bay
CF T Redman
R3 R Mackowiak
IF B Hill
UI A Nunez
R1 C Wilson
M L McClendon

ST. LOUIS
SP M Morris
SP J Marquis
SP W Williams
SP J Suppan
SP C Carpenter
CL J Isringhausen
RP C Eldred
RP J Tavarez
RP R King
C M Matheny
1B A Pujols
2B T Womack
SS E Renteria
3B S Rolen
UO S Taguchi
CF J Edmonds
RL R Sanders
UT M Anderson
OF- R Cedeno
LU- R Lankford
UT- H Luna
UT- J Mabry
M T LaRussa

SAN DIEGO
SP B Lawrence
SP A Eaton
SP D Wells
SP J Peavy
SP I Valdez
CL T Hoffman
RP S Linebrink
RP A Otsuka
RP J Witasick
C R Hernandez
1B P Nevin
2B M Loretta
SS K Greene
3B S Burroughs
LF R Klesko
CF J Payton
RF B Giles
UO T Long
M B Bochy

SAN FRANCISCO
SP J Schmidt
SP B Tomko
SP K Rueter
SR D Hermanson
SP J Williams
RP J Brower
RP M Herges
RP T Walker
RP S Eyre
C A Pierzynski
1B J Snow
2B R Durham
SS D Cruz
3B E Alfonzo
LF B Bonds
CF M Grissom
RF M Tucker
UT P Feliz
UO D Mohr
S2 N Perez
M F Alou

2005 AL

BALTIMORE
SP R Lopez
SP B Chen
SP D Cabrera
SP E Bedard
SP S Ponson
CL B Ryan
RP T Williams
RP J Julio
RP S Kline
CD J Lopez
1B R Palmeiro
2B B Roberts
SS M Tejada
3B M Mora
OI- D Newhan
CF L Matos
RD S Sosa
RD J Gibbons
UI- C Gomez
LU- B Surhoff
M1 L Mazzilli
M2 S Perlozzo

BOSTON
SP T Wakefield
SP B Arroyo
SP M Clement
SP D Wells
CL C Schilling
RP M Timlin
RP J Gonzalez
C J Varitek
1B K Millar
2B- M Bellhorn
SS E Renteria
3B B Mueller
LF M Ramirez
CF J Damon
RF T Nixon
DH D Ortiz
1B- J Olerud
M T Francona

CHICAGO
SP M Buehrle
SP F Garcia
SP J Garland
SP J Contreras
SP O Hernandez
CL D Hermanson
RP L Vizcaino
RP C Politte
RP N Cotts
C A Pierzynski
1B P Konerko
2B T Iguchi
SS J Uribe
3B J Crede
LF S Podsednik
CF A Rowand
RF J Dye
DH C Everett
M O Guillen

CLEVELAND
SP J Westbrook
SP C Lee
SP C Sabathia
SP K Millwood
SP S Elarton
CL B Wickman
RP B Howry
RP D Riske
RP R Betancourt
C V Martinez
1B B Broussard
2B R Belliard
SS J Peralta
3B A Boone
LF C Crisp
CF G Sizemore
RF C Blake
DH T Hafner
13- J Hernandez
M E Wedge

DETROIT
SP J Johnson
SP M Maroth
SP N Robertson
SP J Bonderman
RP C Spurling
RP F German
RP J Walker
C I Rodriguez
1B C Shelton
2B- P Polanco
SS- C Guillen
3B B Inge
RL C Monroe
CF N Logan
RF- M Ordonez
DU D Young
2S O Infante
LD- R White
M A Trammell

KANSAS CITY
SP Z Greinke
SP J Lima
SP R Hernandez
SP D Carrasco
RS M Wood
RP M Mac Dougal
RP A Sisco
RP A Burgos
C J Buck
1D M Stairs
2B- R Gotay
SS A Berroa
3B M Teahen
LF T Long
CF D DeJesus
RF E Brown
D1 M Sweeney
UT- J McEwing
M1 T Pena
M2 B Schaefer
M3 B Bell

LOS ANGELES
SP B Colon
SP J Lackey
SP P Byrd
SP J Washburn
SP E Santana
CL F Rodriguez
RP S Shields
RP E Yan
RP B Donnelly
C B Molina
1B D Erstad
2B A Kennedy
SS O Cabrera
3B- D McPherson
UO J Rivera
CF S Finley
RF V Guerrero
LD G Anderson
UO J DaVanon
UT C Figgins
M M Scioscia

MINNESOTA
SP J Santana
SP B Radke
SP C Silva
SP K Lohse
SP J Mays
CL J Nathan
RP J Crain
RP J Rincon
RP M Guerrier
C J Mauer
1B J Morneau
2S N Punto
SS- J Castro
3B M Cuddyer
LF S Stewart
UO L Ford
RF J Jones
DU M LeCroy
CF T Hunter
M R Gardenhire

NEW YORK
SP R Johnson
SP M Mussina
SP C Wang
SP C Pavano
CL M Rivera
RP T Gordon
RP T Sturtze
C J Posada
1B T Martinez
2B R Cano
SS D Jeter
3B A Rodriguez
LU H Matsui
CF B Williams
RF G Sheffield
1D J Giambi
OI T Womack
M J Torre

OAKLAND
SP B Zito
SP D Haren
SP J Blanton
SP K Saarloos
SP R Harden
CL H Street
RP J Duchscherer
RP K Yabu
RP K Calero
C J Kendall
1B D Johnson
2B M Ellis
SS- B Crosby
3B E Chavez
LR B Kielty
CF M Kotsay
RF N Swisher
D1 S Hatteberg
S2 M Scutaro
M K Macha

SEATTLE
SP J Moyer
SP R Franklin
SP J Pineiro
SP G Meche
SP A Sele
CL E Guardado
RP J Mateo
RP S Hasegawa
RP J Putz
C- M Olivo
1B R Sexson
2B- B Boone
SS- M Morse
3B A Beltre
LF R Winn
CF J Reed
RF I Suzuki
DL R Ibanez
UT- W Bloomquist
M M Hargrove

TAMPA BAY
SP S Kazmir
SP M Hendrickson
SR C Fossum
SP D Waechter
SR S McClung
CL D Baez
RP H Nomo
RP T Harper
RP L Carter
C T Hall
1B T Lee
2B N Green
SS J Lugo
3B A Gonzalez
LF C Crawford
MR D Hollins
RU A Huff
OF J Gomes
23 J Cantu
M L Piniella

TEXAS
SP K Rogers
SP C Young
SP C Park
CL F Cordero
RS K Loe
RS J Benoit
RS J Wasdin
C R Barajas
1B M Teixeira
2B A Soriano
SS M Young
3B H Blalock
LF K Mench
MU G Matthews
RF- R Hidalgo
DL D Dellucci
M B Showalter

TORONTO
SP J Towers
SP G Chacin
SP R Halladay
SP D Bush
SP T Lilly
CL M Batista
RP P Walker
RP J Frasor
RP V Chulk
C G Zaun
IF S Hillenbrand
2B O Hudson
SS R Adams
3B- C Koskie
LF R Johnson
CF V Wells
RF A Rios
1D E Hinske
LF F Catalanotto
UI A Hill
M J Gibbons

2005 NL

ARIZONA
SP B Webb
SP J Vazquez
SP B Halsey
SP S Estes
SP C Vargas
RP R Ortiz
RP J Valverde
RP L Cormier
RP M Koplove
C C Snyder
1U T Clark
2B C Counsell
SS R Clayton
3B T Glaus
LF L Gonzalez
CF- L Terrero
RF S Green
UI A Cintron
UO Q McCracken
1R C Tracy
M B Melvin

ATLANTA
SP J Smoltz
SP H Ramirez
SP T Hudson
SR J Sosa
SP J Thomson
RP C Reitsma
RP D Kolb
C J Estrada
1B A LaRoche
2B M Giles
SS R Furcal
3B C Jones
LF- K Johnson
CF A Jones
UO R Langerhans
3U W Betemit
1U J Franco
IO P Orr
M B Cox

CHICAGO
SP G Maddux
SP C Zambrano
SP M Prior
SR G Rusch
SP J Williams
CL R Dempster
RP M Wuertz
C M Barrett
1B D Lee
2B T Walker
SS N Perez
3B A Ramirez
LF T
Hollandsworth
CF C Patterson
RF J Burnitz
UT J Hairston
UT J Macias
M D Baker

CINCINNATI
SP A Harang
SP E Milton
SP R Ortiz
SP B Claussen
RP D Weathers
RS M Belisle
RP K Mercker
RP T Coffey
C J LaRue
1B S Casey
2S R Aurilia
SS F Lopez
3B- J Randa
LF A Dunn
CF K Griffey
RF A Kearns
OI J Cruz
UT R Freel
RM W Pena
M1 D Miley
M2 J Narron

COLORADO
SP J Francis
SP J Wright
SR B Kim
SP J Jennings
CL B Fuentes
RS J Acevedo
RP D Cortes
RP M Carvajal
C- J Closser
1B T Helton
2I L Gonzalez
SS- C Barmes
3B G Atkins
LF M Holliday
MU C Sullivan
RF B Hawpe
2B A Miles
RO D Mohr
M C Hurdle

FLORIDA
SP D Willis
SP A Burnett
SP J Beckett
SR B Moehler
CL T Jones
RP G Mota
C P LoDuca
1B C Delgado
2B L Castillo
SS A Gonzalez
3B M Lowell
LF M Cabrera
CF J Pierre
RF J Encarnacion
OI J Conine
UI D Easley
UT- L Harris
M J McKeon

HOUSTON
SP R Oswalt
SP A Pettitte
SP R Clemens
SP B Backe
SP W Rodriguez
CL B Lidge
RP C Qualls
RP D Wheeler
RP R Springer
C B Ausmus
1L L Berkman
2B C Biggio
SS A Everett
3B M Ensberg
LF C Burke
CF W Taveras
RF J Lane
1U M Lamb
UO O Palmeiro
UI J Vizcaino
UT- E Bruntlett
M P Garner

LOS ANGELES
SP J Weaver
SP D Lowe
SP B Penny
SR D Houlton
SP O Perez
RP Y Brazoban
RP D Sanchez
RP G Carrara
RS E Dessens
C J Phillips
1U H Choi
2B J Kent
SS C Izturis
UI O Robles
LR J Werth
UO J Repko
RM- J Drew
LU R Ledee
IO A Perez
1U O Saenz
UT- M Edwards
M J Tracy

MILWAUKEE
SP D Davis
SP C Capuano
SP B Sheets
SP V Santos
SP T Ohka
CL D Turnbow
RP M Wise
C D Miller
1B L Overbay
2B- R Weeks
SS J Hardy
UI B Hall
LF C Lee
CF B Clark
RF G Jenkins
UO C Magruder
3U- R Branyan
IF- W Helms
M N Yost

NEW YORK
SP P Martinez
SP T Glavine
SP K Benson
SP V Zambrano
RS A Heilman
CL B Looper
RP R Hernandez
C M Piazza
1B- D Mientkiewicz
2B M Cairo
SS J Reyes
3B D Wright
LF C Floyd
CF C Beltran
RF- V Diaz
UT M Anderson
C R Castro
2B- K Matsui
UT- C Woodward
M W Randolph

PHILADELPHIA
SP J Lieber
SP B Myers
SP C Lidle
SP V Padilla
CL B Wagner
RP R Madson
RP A Fultz
RP G Geary
C M Lieberthal
1B- R Howard
2B C Utley
SS J Rollins
3B D Bell
LF P Burrell
CF K Lofton
RF B Abreu
MO J Michaels
UO- E Chavez
UI- T Perez
M C Manuel

PITTSBURGH
SP K Wells
SP M Redman
SP J Fogg
SP D Williams
SP O Perez
RP S Torres
CL J Mesa
RP R Vogelsong
RP R White
C- H Cota
1B D Ward
2B J Castillo
SS J Wilson
UI F Sanchez
LF J Bay
MU T Redman
RF M Lawton
UT R Mackowiak
M1 L McClendon
M2 P Mackanin

ST. LOUIS
SP C Carpenter
SP J Marquis
SP M Mulder
SP J Suppan
SP M Morris
CL J Isringhausen
RP J Tavarez
RP A Reyes
RP B Thompson
C Y Molina
1B A Pujols
2B M Grudzielanek
SS D Eckstein
3I A Nunez
UO S Taguchi
CF J Edmonds
RF L Walker
UT J Mabry
LF- R Sanders
M T LaRussa

SAN DIEGO
SP J Peavy
SP B Lawrence
SP W Williams
SP A Eaton
CL T Hoffman
RP S Linebrink
RP A Otsuka
RP R Seanez
C R Hernandez
1B- P Nevin
2B M Loretta
SS K Greene
3B- S Burroughs
LF R Klesko
CF D Roberts
RF B Giles
UT D Jackson
UT X Nady
UT M Sweeney
IC- R Fick
M B Bochy

SAN FRANCISCO
SP N Lowry
SP B Tomko
SP J Schmidt
SP B Hennessey
SP K Rueter
RS J Fassero
CL T Walker
RP S Eyre
C M Matheny
1B J Snow
2B R Durham
SS O Vizquel
3B E Alfonzo
3L P Feliz
MO J Ellison
LR M Alou
1U L Niekro
RU M Tucker
UI- D Cruz
M F Alou

WASHINGTON
SP L Hernandez
SP E Loaiza
SP J Patterson
SP T Armas
CL C Cordero
RS H Carrasco
RP G Majewski
RP L Ayala
C B Schneider
1B N Johnson
2B- J Vidro
SS C Guzman
3B V Castilla
LO R Church
ML B Wilkerson
RF J Guillen
2S J Carroll
UI- C Baerga
M F Robinson

2006 AL

BALTIMORE
SP E Bedard
SP R Lopez
SP K Benson
SP D Cabrera
SP A Loewen
RS B Chen
CL C Ray
RP L Hawkins
RP T Williams
C R Hernandez
1U K Millar
2B B Roberts
SS M Tejada
3B M Mora
1L J Conine
CF C Patterson
RF N Markakis
DC- J Lopez
LI- B Fahey
DR- J Gibbons
M S Perlozzo

BOSTON
SP J Beckett
SP C Schilling
SP T Wakefield
CL J Papelbon
RS J Tavarez
RP M Timlin
RP M Delcarmen
C J Varitek
1B K Youkilis
2B M Loretta
SS A Gonzalez
3B M Lowell
LF M Ramirez
CF C Crisp
RF T Nixon
DH D Ortiz
SI- A Cora
UO- W Pena
M T Francona

CHICAGO
SP F Garcia
SP J Garland
SP M Buehrle
SP J Vazquez
SP J Contreras
CL B Jenks
RP B McCarthy
RP M Thornton
RP N Cotts
C A Pierzynski
1B P Konerko
2B T Iguchi
SS J Uribe
3B J Crede
LF S Podsednik
CF B Anderson
RF J Dye
DH J Thome
ML R Mackowiak
UI- A Cintron
M O Guillen

CLEVELAND
SP J Westbrook
SP C Lee
SP C Sabathia
SP P Byrd
RS F Carmona
RP F Cabrera
RP R Betancourt
RP J Davis
C V Martinez
1B- B Broussard
2B- R Belliard
SS J Peralta
3B A Boone
LF J Michaels
CF G Sizemore
RF C Blake
DH T Hafner
M E Wedge

DETROIT
SP J Bonderman
SP N Robertson
SP K Rogers

SP J Verlander
CL T Jones
RP J Zumaya
RP F Rodney
RP J Grilli
C I Rodriguez
1B C Shelton
2B P Polanco
SS C Guillen
3B B Inge
LF C Monroe
CF C Granderson
RF M Ordonez
OF M Thames
M J Leyland

KANSAS CITY

SP M Redman
SP S Elarton
SP R Hernandez
SR L Hudson
RP A Burgos
RS J Gobble
RP J Peralta
RS M Wood
C J Buck
1B- D Mientkiewicz
2B M Grudzielanek
SS A Berroa
3B M Teahen
LR E Brown
CF- J Gathright
LM D DeJesus
DH- M Sweeney
UT E German
RF- R Sanders
M B Bell

LOS ANGELES

SP J Lackey
SP E Santana
SP K Escobar
SP J Weaver
CL F Rodriguez
RP H Carrasco
RP S Shields
RP K Gregg
C M Napoli
1B- K Morales
2B A Kennedy
SS O Cabrera
3B M Izturis
UO J Rivera
MI C Figgins
RF V Guerrero
DU- T Salmon
LD G Anderson
1U- R Quinlan
M M Scioscia

MINNESOTA

SP J Santana
SP C Silva
SP B Radke
SR F Liriano
SP B Bonser
CL J Nathan
RP J Crain
RP J Rincon
RP M Guerrier
C J Mauer
1B J Morneau
2B L Castillo
SS J Bartlett
3I N Punto
LO L Ford
CF T Hunter
RF M Cuddyer
DL R White
M R Gardenhire

NEW YORK

SP C Wang
SP R Johnson
SP M Mussina
SP J Wright
CL M Rivera
RP S Proctor
RP R Villone
RP K Farnsworth
C J Posada
1B A Phillips
2B R Cano
SS D Jeter
3B A Rodriguez
LF M Cabrera
CF J Damon
UO B Williams
D1 J Giambi
2I- M Cairo
M J Torre

OAKLAND

SP D Haren
SP B Zito
SP J Blanton
SP E Loaiza
SR K Saarloos
CL H Street
RS B Halsey
RP C Gaudin
RP J Duchscherer
C J Kendall
1L N Swisher
2B M Ellis
SS- B Crosby
3B E Chavez
UO J Payton
CF M Kotsay
RF- M Bradley
DH F Thomas
S2 M Scutaro
1B- D Johnson
LR- B Kielty
M K Macha

SEATTLE

SP F Hernandez
SP G Meche
SP J Washburn
SR J Pineiro
SP J Moyer
CL J Putz
RS J Woods
RP R Soriano
RP J Mateo
C K Johjima
1B R Sexson
2B J Lopez
SS Y Betancourt
3B A Beltre
LF R Ibanez
CF- J Reed
RF I Suzuki
DH- C Everett
UT W Bloomquist
M M Hargrove

TAMPA BAY

SP S Kazmir
SP C Fossum
SP J Shields
SR S McClung
RP R Lugo
RP S Camp
RP B Meadows
C- T Hall
1B T Lee
2B J Cantu
SS- J Lugo
3B- A Huff
LF C Crawford
CF- R Baldelli
RM D Hollins
DH J Gomes
OI G Norton
UT T Perez
UT T Wigginton
M J Maddon

TEXAS

SP K Millwood
SP V Padilla
SP J Koronka
CL A Otsuka
RP J Benoit
RP R Bauer
RP R Mahay
C- R Barajas
1B M Teixeira
2B I Kinsler
SS M Young
3B H Blalock
LF- B Wilkerson
CF G Matthews
RU- K Mench
DH- P Nevin
UT M DeRosa
M B Showalter

TORONTO

SP R Halladay
SP T Lilly
SP A Burnett
CL B Ryan
RS S Downs
RP B Tallet
RP J Speier
C B Molina
1B L Overbay
2S A Hill
SS J McDonald
3B T Glaus
LO R Johnson
CF V Wells
RF A Rios
DI- S Hillenbrand
LF F Catalanotto
CU G Zaun
2S- R Adams
M J Gibbons

2006 NL

ARIZONA

SP B Webb
SP M Batista
SP C Vargas
SP E Gonzalez
RP B Medders
RP B Lyon
CL J Valverde
RP L Vizcaino
C J Estrada
1B C Jackson
2B O Hudson
SS C Counsell
3B C Tracy
LF L Gonzalez
CF E Byrnes
RF S Green
UO- J DaVanon
IO- D Easley
M B Melvin

ATLANTA

SP J Smoltz
SP T Hudson
SP C James
RP O Villarreal
RS L Cormier
RP K Ray
RP M McBride
C B McCann
1B A LaRoche
2B M Giles
SS E Renteria
3B C Jones
LF R Langerhans
CF A Jones
RF J Francoeur
LF M Diaz
IF P Orr
UI- W Betemit
M B Cox

CHICAGO

SP C Zambrano
SP G Maddux
SP S Marshall
SP R Hill
RP R Dempster
RP B Howry
RP R Novoa
RP W Ohman
C M Barrett
UT J Mabry
2I- N Perez
SS R Cedeno
3B A Ramirez
LF M Murton
CF J Pierre
RF J Jones
IF- T Walker
M D Baker

CINCINNATI

SP B Arroyo
SP A Harang
SP E Milton
SP E Ramirez
RP T Coffey
RP D Weathers
C- D Ross
1B S Hatteberg
2B B Phillips
SS- F Lopez
3B E Encarnacion
LF A Dunn
CF K Griffey
UT R Freel
UI R Aurilia
RF- A Kearns
CU- J Valentin
M J Narron

COLORADO

SP A Cook
SP J Jennings
SP J Francis
SP J Fogg
SP B Kim
CL B Fuentes
RP J Mesa
RP R Ramirez
RP T Martin
C- Y Torrealba
1B T Helton
2B J Carroll
SS C Barmes
3B G Atkins
LF M Holliday
CF C Sullivan
RF B Hawpe
MU- C Freeman
M C Hurdle

FLORIDA

SP D Willis
SP S Olsen
SP J Johnson
SR R Nolasco
SP B Moehler
RP A Sanchez
CL J Borowski
RP M Herges
RP R Messenger
C M Olivo
1B M Jacobs
2B D Uggla
SS H Ramirez
3B M Cabrera
LF J Willingham
CF R Abercrombie
RF J Hermida
MI A Amezaga
RU J Borchard
1U W Helms
UO- C Ross
M J Girardi

HOUSTON

SP R Oswalt
SP A Pettitte
SP W Rodriguez
SP T Buchholz
SP R Clemens
CL B Lidge
RS F Nieve
RP C Qualls
RP D Wheeler
C B Ausmus
1R L Berkman
2B C Biggio
SS A Everett
3B M Ensberg
LF P Wilson
CF W Taveras
RF J Lane
2M C Burke
13 M Lamb
OF O Palmeiro
M P Garner

LOS ANGELES

SP D Lowe
SP B Penny
SR B Tomko
SR A Sele
RP T Saito
RP J Broxton
RP J Beimel
RS H Kuo
C R Martin
1B N Garciaparra
2B J Kent
SS R Furcal
3B- W Betemit
LF A Ethier
CF K Lofton
RF J Drew
IF O Saenz
UO- J Cruz
IO- R Martinez
M G Little

MILWAUKEE

SP C Capuano
SP D Bush
SP D Davis
SP B Sheets
CL D Turnbow
RP J Capellan
C D Miller
1B P Fielder
2B- R Weeks
SS B Hall
3B- C Koskie
LF C Lee
CF B Clark
RF G Jenkins
UI J Cirillo
UO G Gross
OI- C Hart
M N Yost

NEW YORK

SP T Glavine
SP S Trachsel
SP P Martinez
SP O Hernandez
CL B Wagner
RP A Heilman
RP D Oliver
RP C Bradford
C P LoDuca
1B C Delgado
2U J Valentin
SS J Reyes
3B D Wright
LF- C Floyd
CF C Beltran
UO E Chavez
IF- J Franco
UT- C Woodward
M W Randolph

PHILADELPHIA

SP B Myers
SP J Lieber
SR R Madson
SP C Hamels
SP C Lidle
CL T Gordon
RP G Geary
RP A Fultz
RP R Franklin
C- M Lieberthal
1B R Howard
2B C Utley
SS J Rollins
3B- D Bell
LF P Burrell
UO S Victorino
CF A Rowand
RF B Abreu
OF D Dellucci
3U A Nunez
M C Manuel

PITTSBURGH

SP Z Duke
SP I Snell
SP P Maholm
SP V Santos
RP S Torres
RP M Capps
CL M Gonzalez
RP J Grabow
C R Paulino
1B- S Casey
2B J Castillo
SS J Wilson
3I F Sanchez
LF J Bay
UT J Bautista
RF J Burnitz
UO N McLouth
CF- C Duffy
IF- J Randa
1R- C Wilson
M J Tracy

ST. LOUIS

SP C Carpenter
SP J Marquis
SP J Suppan
CL J Isringhausen
RP J Hancock
RP A Wainwright
RP B Looper
C Y Molina
1B A Pujols
2S A Miles
SS D Eckstein
3B S Rolen
LM S Taguchi
CF J Edmonds
RF J Encarnacion
OF J Rodriguez
IO S Spiezio
LR- C Duncan
M T LaRussa

SAN DIEGO

SP J Peavy
SP C Hensley
SP C Young
SP W Williams
SP C Park
CL T Hoffman
RP S Linebrink
RP B Sweeney
RP J Adkins
C M Piazza
1B A Gonzalez
2B J Barfield
SS K Greene
3B- V Castilla
LF D Roberts
CF M Cameron
RF B Giles
IO M Bellhorn
IO G Blum
C- J Bard
CU- R Bowen
M B Bochy

SAN FRANCISCO

SP J Schmidt
SP M Morris
SP M Cain
SP N Lowry
SR J Wright
RS B Hennessey
RP K Correia
RP S Kline
C- E Alfonzo
1B- L Niekro
2B R Durham
SS O Vizquel
3B P Feliz
LF B Bonds
CF S Finley
RM R Winn
RF M Alou
UT M Sweeney
LO- J Ellison
M F Alou

WASHINGTON

SP R Ortiz
SP T Armas
SP L Hernandez
SP M O'Connor
CL C Cordero
RP J Rauch
RS J Bergmann
RP S Rivera
C B Schneider
1B N Johnson
2B J Vidro
SS- R Clayton
3B R Zimmerman
LF A Soriano
MO- M Byrd
RF- J Guillen
UT M Anderson
M F Robinson

THE MEN IN THE DUGOUT: THE MANAGERS

Vin Scully, on the flap of the dust jacket for Leonard Koppett's 1993 book *The Man in the Dugout*, praised the author by saying, "If there would be a degree in baseball, Leonard Koppett would be a professor."

True enough. The late, great Koppett was certainly a professor of the National Pastime, and he was writing about men who had hard-earned Ph.D.'s in the game. The men in the dugout are perhaps the least understood of the important "players" in the game today. Manager's roles have changed greatly in recent decades; partly because of the prominence of millionaire superstars, but mostly due to the increasingly visible intrusion of the business of baseball into the game on the field.

In the early days, baseball was not nearly as studied a tactical game as it would later become and, when players did get "scientific," it was usually in the heat of battle rather than in any planned fashion. At this time, a manager's job involved mostly keeping his players under contract, on-time, on the train, and out of the bars. Players generally knew their roles, particularly in the days where regulars, including pitchers, played nearly every game.

Many of the great early managers—such as Cap Anson, Harry Wright, John Ward, and Charlie Comiskey—were thought of not only as leaders of men but also as particularly brainy players and sharp businessmen.

As baseball became more specialized in the 1890s, different managerial skills came into vogue. Managers began to make more of the decisions to bunt, steal, and the like, instead of letting the players play as they thought best. Furthermore, while teams always had a need to find and evaluate talent, the reserve clause now forced clubs to look into the "minor" leagues for new players. Well-traveled players and former players, who knew many different leagues, became especially valuable. Many of them—such as Hughie Jennings, John McGraw, and Wilbert Robinson—ended up as longtime managers.

In the 1890s, approximately half of managers were playing managers. Their experience on the field also helped these men manage ballplayers. Even at this time, rarely could a skipper become "one of the boys." Managers have long been expected to keep a fair distance from their players, because—as Sparky Anderson would comment many years later—"You take a guy out for a pinch hitter, he ain't gonna be your friend."

Most of the best managers—Joe McCarthy, Casey Stengel, Ned Hanlon, Frank Selee, Connie Mack, John McGraw, Earl Weaver, Walter Alston, Bill McKechnie, and others—respected their players and tried to treat them fairly, even if they weren't necessarily nice people to be around. Many of the greatest managers, especially in the early days, were also great teachers who showed younger men how to play the game as well as how to conduct their lives.

True renegades (e.g., Leo Durocher, Billy Martin, and Paul Richards) were impetuous, conniving, and often devious or deceitful. While many of their players didn't like them, the results were often positive—at least in the short term.

By the 1910s, managers were required to be better tacticians, not just shepherds of hard-bitten players. Relief pitchers, pinch hitters, and even platooning had come into use. As managing became more involved, fewer players were thought to be able to simultaneously handle the increased responsibility.

When the power era began in the 1920s, many a manager found himself less able to influence the game through tactical decisions and instead had to configure his lineup and rotation to provide the best offense and the most reliable pitching. Moreover, most managers were no longer the locus of player procurement. Clubs were now using general managers and, as a result, much of the personnel decisions were now out of the field manager's hands. The field manager also didn't necessarily control the salaries or the contracts of his players, taking away much of his power.

Managers ever since have had to deal with open revolt, dissension, and disobedience while maintaining order amidst changing social mores. Player salaries began to rise in the 1930s, and star players soon made as much as or more money than the manager. How, then, to keep the respect of the players? The more successful and famous managers of the 1940s—Lou Boudreau, Leo Durocher, and Billy Southworth, for example—would have expressed very different opinions.

Increasing expectations of success during the postwar boom also meant that managers were being fired more often. Some of the most successful managers of the 1950s—Casey Stengel, Chuck Dressen, Charlie Grimm, and Fred Haney—lost their jobs when things got rocky.

Stengel, Al Lopez, and Walter Alston were tremendous managers, and all had different ways of winning. Lopez was largely focused on power and starting pitching, while Stengel kept the entire roster involved and always had strong defensive teams. The unflappable Alston used one-run offensive strategies and depended heavily on pitching, defense and, later, Dodger Stadium to keep opponents from scoring.

The success of the quiet, dignified Lopez and Alston was not lost among managers of the 1960s, who generally became less confrontational (with exceptions like Durocher and Alvin Dark). Most of the top managers of that time—Alston, Red Schoendienst, Ralph Houk, Gil Hodges—met this standard. However, highly qualified "Nervous Nellies"—tough, involved guys like Gene Mauch, Harry Walker, Dick Williams, and Dave Bristol—also enjoyed success, usually when brought in to turn around underachieving teams with fire and brimstone.

Free agency in the late 1970s meant even more challenges for managers trying to keep their highly paid and mobile stars in line. The kindly old man in the dugout was largely a character of the past. Instead, tough little guys—firebrands like Williams, Sparky Anderson, Earl Weaver, Billy Martin, and Whitey Herzog—became the game's top skippers in the 1970s and early 1980s. Much of their success came from a lack of fear of using untested players. The successful skippers of the era were never big stars; some had never even reached the majors. Therefore, they knew—as did Joe McCarthy, John McGraw, and Connie Mack before them—that plenty of talent was trapped in the minor leagues, just waiting to be given a chance.

By the 1980s and 1990s, the best managers had learned that lesson as a new type of manager evolved. True; there were some tough guys, like in the 1970s, but they were also more "nice guys." The *personalities* of winners like Tony La Russa, Tommy Lasorda, Bobby Cox, Jim Leyland, and Davey Johnson were very different. What they had in common, though, was an ability to keep a lid on the clubhouse full of millionaire players and million-dollar egos.

Keeping clubhouse dissension and other 'private matters' out of the public eye became an important mark of most successful teams. Baseball people now saw the media as even more of an enemy, largely because the rise in salaries had caused a rift between the press and the players, and because the media was working harder to break juicy stories rather than just report the games. Modern managers were able to get their players to buy into the team concept. Different managers did this in various ways, either through enthusiastic positive reinforcement, a caring demeanor, or simply excellent personnel management. Many teams continued to hire the older "pepperpot" type of manager, though few of them were now successful.

Today's managers must balance the skills and egos of their players, the omnipresence of the media, and their relationship with the front office to succeed on the field—but they have to do it with a decreasing amount of perceived authority. The contemporary game's ever-changing finances mean that few managers can count on a consistently high payroll. It's a tough job to do, and the most successful managers of today—such as Cox, La Russa, Dusty Baker, Lou Piniella, and Joe Torre—do it through by earning respect and building consensus.

This Manager Register includes everyone who has ever managed a major league baseball team, from 1871 to the present, from the National Association to the Federal League to the American League, from Bill Adair to Ted Turner to Don Zimmer. Identifying managers, however, has not always been so obvious as it would seem, so there are some important things to note about this section.

First, a quick tongue-twister: A manager has to have managed to be listed as a manager, but he doesn't have to have been called a manager to have managed. In the early days of baseball history, the term "team manager" did not mean what it does now. Then, the person called the manager was what would now be called a general manager or a vice president. If those official team manager's duties did not include traveling with the club, making out the lineups, deciding when to change pitchers, arguing with the umpires, and the like, then this register does not include him. The "real" field manager of the team back then may have been the team captain; if so, this register will show him as the manager regardless of his title. This is a record of those who did the job of a baseball manager, not those who had the title of manager.

Sometimes baseball managers have been referred to as coaches, as they are in other sports. The most famous recent example comes from P.K. Wrigley's rotating "College of Coaches" that ran the Cubs for five seasons during the 1960s. In that case, the coach referred to as head coach by the team is listed herein as the Cubs' manager for the period he was head coach.

Managers do not necessarily manage every single game in a season, of course. Managers are human beings, and they do occasionally miss a few games when they fall ill, get suspended, or attend to their families. In those cases, the coach left in charge does not become the manager in any real sense. Though the coach may make the moves, he is in most cases simply carrying out the manager's wishes.

When a long absence occurs, however, the situation gets muddier. This section uses a reasonable, though admittedly arbitrary, requirement of 30 consecutive days of managing the team in these cases for a substitute to qualify as the *de facto* manager.

When a manager is fired, however, the situation requires a different standard. When the manager's position is left vacant for any reason, the interim manager *is* definitely in charge. Thus, even if his managerial career lasts but one day, he is considered to have been a manager.

This register shows the date of birth for all managers, plus full biographical information for managers who were not major leaguer players (and are, therefore, not listed in the batter or pitcher registers). Managers who never played professional baseball are shown with a "DNP" code (Did Not Play). If a manager played in the minors but not in the majors, his primary position is showed in parentheses.

For each manager, the register shows the team(s) he managed in each season, along with that team's won-lost record and winning percentage during when he was manager. A lowercase e, w, or c after the league code indicates the team's division (East, West, or Central, respectively) from 1969–present. Player-managers are indicated by boldface years in the first column. Further information is available under the following headings:

The **Mgr/Yr** column gives results for clubs with multiple managers in a single season. If the team had more than one manager in the season listed, two numbers are shown, separated by a slash. In these cases, the second number indicates how many managers the team employed that season, and the first number indicating which of these the listed manager was. For example, Jack McKeon is listed in 2003 as 2/2, because he was the second of two managers for the Florida Marlins.

The **Finish** column indicates how the team did under that manager. For managers who guided the team all season, the number gives the team's standing at year's end. If manager B took over from manager A *during* the season, the first number indicates the team's standing when manager B took over, and the second number the team's standing at the end of the season. Three or more managers in one season for a team would produce a three-number entry for the manager(s) in the middle: the team's standing before, during, and after said manager was running the club.

Symbols after the finish show if the team that finished first won any postseason series. A solid star (★) indicates the team won the World Series (including the NL-AA World Series in the nineteenth century). A solid diamond (u) indicates the team won their LCS but lost the World Series (1969–present). A (●) solid bullet indicates a team won the NL championship in the 1890s (i.e., the 1892 series between the first- and second-place teams, the 1894–97 Temple Cup, or the 1900 *Chronicle-Telegraph* Cup). A hollow star (☆) indicates the team won a Division Series but lost in their LCS (1995–present). A cross (✚) indicates a Wild Card team. A solid triangle (▲) indicates the team was tied at the end of the regular season for first place or the Wild Card and played a one-game or three-game playoff. A t after the finish indicates a tie in the standings below first place (e.g., 4t means the team tied for fourth place that year).

The plus/minus column (**+/-**) indicates how many games the team won compared to how many the team was projected to win based on its run production. In other words, a 6.5 rating for a manager for a season indicates that his team won $6^1/_2$ games more than could have been expected. A rating below zero indicates a disappointing performance, worse than expected given the team's runs scored and allowed.

On the career line, the manager's lifetime won-lost record and winning percentage are shown along with the number of seasons he managed and how many games his teams won compared to their projections.

ADAIR, BILL Marion Danne; B2.10.1913 Mobile, AL; D6.17.2002 Bay Minette, AL BR/TR/5´8˝/190(2B)

YEAR TM LG	W	L	PCT	FINISH	MGR/YR	+/-
1970 Chi A w	4	6	.400	6-6-6	2/3	0.2

ADCOCK, JOE B10.30.1927

YEAR TM LG	W	L	PCT	FINISH	MGR/YR	+/-
1967 Cle A	75	87	.463	8	—	0.0

ADDY, BOB B2.1845

YEAR TM LG	W	L	PCT	FINISH	MGR/YR	+/-
1875 Phi NA	3	4	.429	4-5	2/2	-1.3
1877 Cin N	5	19	.208	6-6-6	2/3	-0.3
Total 2	8	23	.258	—	—	-1.6

ALLEN, BOB B7.10.1867

YEAR TM LG	W	L	PCT	FINISH	MGR/YR	+/-
1890 Phi N	25	10	.714	3-2-3	4/5	4.8
1900 Cin N	62	77	.446	7	—	-3.5
Total 2	87	87	.500	—	—	1.3

ALLISON, ANDY B1848

YEAR TM LG	W	L	PCT	FINISH	MGR/YR	+/-
1872 Eck NA	0	11	.000	10-9	1/3	1.2

ALLISON, DOUG B7.12.1846

YEAR TM LG	W	L	PCT	FINISH	MGR/YR	+/-
1873 Res NA	2	21	.087	8	—	5.0

ALOU, FELIPE B5.12.1935

YEAR TM LG	W	L	PCT	FINISH	MGR/YR	+/-
1992 Mon N e	70	55	.560	4-2	2/2	1.9
1993 Mon N e	94	68	.580	2	—	7.9
1994 Mon N e	74	40	.649	1	—	4.0
1995 Mon N e	66	78	.458	5	—	-4.3
1996 Mon N e	88	74	.543	2	—	-0.4
1997 Mon N e	78	84	.481	4	—	1.9
1998 Mon N e	65	97	.401	4	—	-1.9
1999 Mon N e	68	94	.420	4	—	0.0
2000 Mon N e	67	95	.414	4	—	1.5
2001 Mon N e	21	33	.389	5-5	1/2	-1.3
2003 SF N w	100	61	.621	1	—	7.6
2004 SF N w	91	71	.562	2	—	2.4
2005 SF N w	75	87	.463	3	—	3.8
2006 SF N w	76	85	.472	3	—	-0.2
Total 14	1033	1022	.503	—	—	22.8

ALSTON, WALTER B12.1.1911

YEAR TM LG	W	L	PCT	FINISH	MGR/YR	+/-
1954 Bro N	92	62	.597	2	—	11.4
1955 Bro N	98	55	.641	1★	—	1.6
1956 Bro N	93	61	.604	1	—	3.8
1957 Bro N	84	70	.545	3	—	-3.3
1958 LA N	71	83	.461	7	—	3.2
1959 LA N	88	68	.564	1▲★	—	6.5
1960 LA N	82	72	.532	4	—	-2.3
1961 LA N	89	65	.578	2	—	8.3
1962 LA N	102	63	.618	2▲	—	5.3
1963 LA N	99	63	.611	1★	—	8.0
1964 LA N	80	82	.494	6t	—	-5.7
1965 LA N	97	65	.599	1★	—	6.1
1966 LA N	95	67	.586	1	—	0.6
1967 LA N	73	89	.451	8	—	0.7
1968 LA N	76	86	.469	7t	—	-0.2
1969 LA N w	85	77	.525	4	—	-5.2
1970 LA N w	87	74	.540	2	—	-0.0
1971 LA N w	89	73	.549	2	—	-0.2
1972 LA N w	85	70	.548	3	—	1.1
1973 LA N w	95	66	.590	2	—	2.6
1974 LA N w	102	60	.630	1◆	—	-3.6
1975 LA N w	88	74	.543	2	—	-5.7
1976 LA N w	90	68	.570	2-2	1/2	3.9
Total 23	2040	1613	.558	—	—	36.8

ALTOBELLI, JOE B5.26.1932

YEAR TM LG	W	L	PCT	FINISH	MGR/YR	+/-
1977 SF N w	75	87	.463	4	—	-2.1
1978 SF N w	89	73	.549	3	—	5.9
1979 SF N w	61	79	.436	4-4	1/2	-2.1
1983 Bal A e	98	64	.605	1★	—	2.3
1984 Bal A e	85	77	.525	5	—	2.5
1985 Bal A e	29	26	.527	4-4	1/3	-0.3
1991 Chi N e	0	1	.000	4-5-4	2/3	-0.5
Total 7	437	407	.518	—	—	5.8

AMALFITANO, JOEY B1.23.1934

YEAR TM LG	W	L	PCT	FINISH	MGR/YR	+/-
1979 Chi N e	2	5	.286	5-5	2/2	-1.5
1980 Chi N e	26	46	.361	6-6	2/2	-4.7
1981-1 Chi N e	15	37	.288	6	—	-1.5
1981-2 Chi N e	23	28	.451	5	—	-1.5
Total 3	66	116	.363	—	—	-9.3

ANDERSON, SPARKY B2.22.1934

YEAR TM LG	W	L	PCT	FINISH	MGR/YR	+/-
1970 Cin N w	102	60	.630	1◆	—	11.6
1971 Cin N w	79	83	.488	4t	—	-2.6
1972 Cin N w	95	59	.617	1◆	—	2.3
1973 Cin N w	99	63	.611	1	—	5.6
1974 Cin N w	98	64	.605	2	—	2.2
1975 Cin N w	108	54	.667	1★	—	1.3
1976 Cin N w	102	60	.630	1★	—	-1.2
1977 Cin N w	88	74	.543	2	—	-0.5
1978 Cin N w	92	69	.571	2	—	9.3
1979 Det A e	56	50	.528	5-5	3/3	0.9
1980 Det A e	84	78	.519	5	—	-4.0
1981-1 Det A e	31	26	.544	4	—	3.0
1981-2 Det A e	29	23	.558	2t	—	3.0
1982 Det A e	83	79	.512	4	—	-2.5
1983 Det A e	92	70	.568	2	—	0.0
1984 Det A e	104	58	.642	1★	—	4.5
1985 Det A e	84	77	.522	3	—	-0.6
1986 Det A e	87	75	.537	3	—	-2.2
1987 Det A e	98	64	.605	1	—	1.8
1988 Det A e	88	74	.543	2	—	2.3
1989 Det A e	59	103	.364	7	—	-1.9
1990 Det A e	79	83	.488	3	—	-1.6
1991 Det A e	84	78	.519	2t	—	0.8
1992 Det A e	75	87	.463	6	—	-5.7
1993 Det A e	85	77	.525	3t	—	-1.7
1994 Det A e	53	62	.461	5	—	-2.8
1995 Det A e	60	84	.417	4	—	5.7
Total 26	2194	1834	.545	—	—	26.9

ANSON, CAP B4.17.1852

YEAR TM LG	W	L	PCT	FINISH	MGR/YR	+/-
1875 Ath NA	4	2	.667	2-2	2/2	-0.9
1879 Chi N	41	21	.661	2-4	1/2	8.1
1880 Chi N	67	17	.798	1	—	4.0
1881 Chi N	56	28	.667	1	—	-1.3
1882 Chi N	55	29	.655	1	—	-9.3
1883 Chi N	59	39	.602	2	—	-1.8
1884 Chi N	62	50	.554	4t	—	-9.5
1885 Chi N	87	25	.777	1★	—	-1.1
1886 Chi N	90	34	.726	1	—	-2.5
1887 Chi N	71	50	.587	3	—	2.1
1888 Chi N	77	58	.570	2	—	2.5
1889 Chi N	67	65	.508	3	—	-3.5
1890 Chi N	84	53	.613	2	—	1.5
1891 Chi N	82	53	.607	2	—	5.4
1892-1 Chi N	31	39	.443	8	—	6.8
1892-2 Chi N	39	37	.513	7	—	6.8
1893 Chi N	56	71	.441	9	—	-3.8
1894 Chi N	57	75	.432	8	—	-7.2
1895 Chi N	72	58	.554	4	—	6.0
1896 Chi N	71	57	.555	5	—	6.1
1897 Chi N	59	73	.447	9	—	-1.7
1898 NY N	9	13	.409	6-7-7	2/3	-2.5
Total 21	1296	947	.578	—	—	4.1

APPLING, LUKE B4.2.1907

YEAR TM LG	W	L	PCT	FINISH	MGR/YR	+/-
1967 KC A	10	30	.250	10-10	2/2	-6.5

ARMOUR, BILL William Reginald; B9.3.1869 Homestead, PA; D12.2.1922 Minneapolis, MN (DNP)

YEAR TM LG	W	L	PCT	FINISH	MGR/YR	+/-
1902 Cle A	69	67	.507	5	—	-0.8
1903 Cle A	77	63	.550	3	—	0.9
1904 Cle A	86	65	.570	4	—	-7.8
1905 Det A	79	74	.516	3	—	12.8
1906 Det A	71	78	.477	6	—	5.3
Total 5	382	347	.524	—	—	10.4

ASPROMONTE, KEN B9.22.1931

YEAR TM LG	W	L	PCT	FINISH	MGR/YR	+/-
1972 Cle A e	72	84	.462	5	—	-0.4
1973 Cle A e	71	91	.438	6	—	4.4
1974 Cle A e	77	85	.475	4	—	-0.7
Total 3	220	260	.458	—	—	3.3

AUSTIN, JIMMY B12.8.1879

YEAR TM LG	W	L	PCT	FINISH	MGR/YR	+/-
1913 StL A	2	6	.250	7-7-8	2/3	-1.3
1918 StL A	7	9	.438	6-6-5	2/3	-0.7
1923 StL A	22	29	.431	3-5	2/2	-2.4
Total 3	31	44	.413	—	—	-4.5

BAKER, DEL B5.3.1892

YEAR TM LG	W	L	PCT	FINISH	MGR/YR	+/-
1933 Det A	2	0	1.000	5-5	2/2	1.0
1936 Det A	18	16	.529	3-4-2	2/3	0.0
1937 Det A	34	20	.630	3-3-2	2/5	4.1
1937 Det A	7	3	.700	2-2-2	4/5	1.5
1938 Det A	37	19	.661	5-4	2/2	6.8
1939 Det A	81	73	.526	5	—	-4.1
1940 Det A	90	64	.584	1	—	-2.9
1941 Det A	75	79	.487	4t	—	3.6
1942 Det A	73	81	.474	5	—	-4.2
1960 Bos A	2	5	.286	8-8-7	2/3	-1.0
Total 9	419	360	.538	—	—	4.7

BAKER, DUSTY B6.15.1949

YEAR TM LG	W	L	PCT	FINISH	MGR/YR	+/-
1993 SF N w	103	59	.636	2	—	4.7
1994 SF N w	55	60	.478	2	—	-2.9
1995 SF N w	67	77	.465	4	—	6.8
1996 SF N w	68	94	.420	4	—	-2.5
1997 SF N w	90	72	.556	1	—	9.9
1998 SF N w	89	74	.546	2▲	—	-2.7
1999 SF N w	86	76	.531	2	—	1.2
2000 SF N w	97	65	.599	1	—	-0.6
2001 SF N w	90	72	.556	2	—	4.0
2002 SF N w	95	66	.590	2◆✜	—	-2.6
2003 Chi N c	88	74	.543	1☆	—	2.8
2004 Chi N c	89	73	.549	3	—	-4.4
2005 Chi N c	79	83	.488	4	—	-0.9
2006 Chi N c	66	96	.407	6	—	-3.6
Total 14	1162	1041	.527	—	—	9.3

BAMBERGER, GEORGE B8.1.1923

YEAR TM LG	W	L	PCT	FINISH	MGR/YR	+/-
1978 Mil A e	93	69	.574	3	—	-3.4
1979 Mil A e	95	66	.590	2	—	6.2
1980 Mil A e	47	45	.511	2-4-3	2/3	-6.2
1982 NY N e	65	97	.401	6	—	-4.1
1983 NY N e	16	30	.348	6-6	1/2	-3.8
1985 Mil A e	71	90	.441	6	—	1.5
1986 Mil A e	71	81	.467	6-6	1/2	1.4
Total 7	458	478	.489	—	—	-8.3

BANCROFT, DAVE B4.20.1891

YEAR TM LG	W	L	PCT	FINISH	MGR/YR	+/-
1924 Bos N	27	38	.415	6-8	1/3	6.6
1924 Bos N	15	35	.300	8-8	3/3	-0.7
1925 Bos N	70	83	.458	5	—	2.5
1926 Bos N	66	86	.434	7	—	-0.4
1927 Bos N	60	94	.390	7	—	-5.1
Total 4	238	336	.415	—	—	2.9

BANCROFT, FRANK Frank Carter; B5.9.1846 Lancaster, MA; D3.30.1921 Cincinnati, OH (DNP)

YEAR TM LG	W	L	PCT	FINISH	MGR/YR	+/-
1880 Wor N	40	43	.482	5	—	-5.7
1881 Det N	41	43	.488	4	—	-2.0
1882 Det N	42	41	.506	6	—	8.0
1883 Cle N	55	42	.567	4	—	3.2
1884 Pro N	84	28	.750	1★	—	0.7
1885 Pro N	53	57	.482	4	—	7.0
1887 Phi AA	26	29	.473	6-5	1/2	-1.6
1889 Ind N	25	43	.368	7-7	1/2	-5.8
1902 Cin N	9	7	.563	6-6-4	2/3	0.2
Total 9	375	333	.530	—	—	4.0

BARKLEY, SAM B5.24.1858

YEAR TM LG	W	L	PCT	FINISH	MGR/YR	+/-
1888 KC AA	21	36	.368	8-8-8	2/3	4.8

BARNIE, BILLY B1.26.1853

YEAR TM LG	W	L	PCT	FINISH	MGR/YR	+/-
1883 Bal AA	28	68	.292	8	—	2.9
1884 Bal AA	63	43	.594	6	—	-1.1
1885 Bal AA	41	68	.376	8	—	-0.7
1886 Bal AA	48	83	.366	8	—	5.6
1887 Bal AA	77	58	.570	3	—	0.0
1888 Bal AA	57	80	.416	5	—	0.2
1889 Bal AA	70	65	.519	5	—	2.9
1890 Bal AA	15	19	.441	8	—	-1.0
1891 Bal AA	71	64	.526	3	—	-1.0
1892-1 Was N	0	2	.000	11t-7	1/2	-0.8
1893 Lou N	50	75	.400	11	—	2.4
1894 Lou N	36	94	.277	12	—	-2.4
1897 Bro N	61	71	.462	6t	—	-1.3
1898 Bro N	15	20	.429	9-10	1/3	1.5
Total 14	632	810	.438	—	—	7.0

BARROW, ED Edward Grant "Cousin Ed"; B5.10.1868 Springfield, IL; D12.15.1953 Port Chester, NY (DNP)

YEAR TM LG	W	L	PCT	FINISH	MGR/YR	+/-
1903 Det A	65	71	.478	5	—	-6.0
1904 Det A	32	46	.410	7-7	1/2	0.1
1918 Bos A	75	51	.595	1★	—	1.2
1919 Bos A	66	71	.482	6	—	-3.8
1920 Bos A	72	81	.471	5	—	0.4
Total 5	310	320	.492	—	—	-8.1

BARRY, JACK B4.26.1887

YEAR TM LG	W	L	PCT	FINISH	MGR/YR	+/-
1917 Bos A	90	62	.592	2	—	2.2

BATTIN, JOE B11.11.1851

YEAR TM LG	W	L	PCT	FINISH	MGR/YR	+/-
1883 Pit AA	2	11	.154	7-7	3/3	-2.2
1884 Pit AA	6	7	.462	11-10-10	3/5	3.1
1884 CP U	1	5	.167	5-5	2/3	-1.7
Total 2	9	23	.281	—	—	-0.9

BAUER, HANK B7.31.1922

YEAR TM LG	W	L	PCT	FINISH	MGR/YR	+/-
1961 KC A	35	67	.343	8-9t	2/2	-4.9
1962 KC A	72	90	.444	9	—	-0.2
1964 Bal A	97	65	.599	3	—	3.8
1965 Bal A	94	68	.580	3	—	6.1
1966 Bal A	97	63	.606	1★	—	1.1
1967 Bal A	76	85	.472	6t	—	-11.2
1968 Bal A	43	37	.538	3-2	1/2	-1.7
1969 Oak A w	80	69	.537	2-2	1/2	-0.3
Total 8	594	544	.522	—	—	-7.2

BAYLOR, DON B6.28.1949

YEAR TM LG	W	L	PCT	FINISH	MGR/YR	+/-
1993 Col N w	67	95	.414	6	—	5.2
1994 Col N w	53	64	.453	3	—	0.6
1995 Col N w	77	67	.535	2✜	—	4.8
1996 Col N w	82	79	.509	3	—	2.3
1997 Col N w	83	79	.512	3	—	0.7
1998 Col N w	77	85	.475	4	—	-1.3
2000 Chi N c	65	97	.401	6	—	-2.9
2001 Chi N c	88	74	.543	3	—	-0.5
2002 Chi N c	39	49	.443	5-4	1/2	-2.1
Total 9	631	689	.478	—	—	6.6

BELL, BUDDY B8.27.1951

YEAR TM LG	W	L	PCT	FINISH	MGR/YR	+/-
1996 Det A e	53	109	.327	5	—	0.1
1997 Det A e	79	83	.488	3	—	-1.4
1998 Det A c	52	85	.380	5-5	1/2	-5.1
2000 Col N w	82	80	.506	4	—	-5.3
2001 Col N w	73	89	.451	5	—	-9.5
2002 Col N w	6	16	.273	5-4	1/2	-3.5
2005 KC A c	43	69	.384	5-5	3/3	2.3
2006 KC A c	62	100	.383	5	—	0.7
Total 8	450	631	.416	—	—	-21.7

BENSON, VERN B9.19.1924

YEAR TM LG	W	L	PCT	FINISH	MGR/YR	+/-
1977 Atl N w	1	0	1.000	6-6-6	3/4	0.6

BERRA, YOGI B5.12.1925

YEAR TM LG	W	L	PCT	FINISH	MGR/YR	+/-
1964 NY A	99	63	.611	1	—	1.7
1972 NY N e	83	73	.532	3	—	10.6
1973 NY N e	82	79	.509	1◆	—	-0.7
1974 NY N e	71	91	.438	5	—	-1.9
1975 NY N e	56	53	.514	3-3t	1/2	-0.0
1984 NY A e	87	75	.537	3	—	-2.0
1985 NY A e	6	10	.375	7-2	1/2	-3.7
Total 7	484	444	.522	—	—	4.0

BEVINGTON, TERRY Terry Paul; B7.7.1956 Akron, OH; BR/TR/6´2˝/190(C)

YEAR TM LG	W	L	PCT	FINISH	MGR/YR	+/-
1995 Chi A c	57	56	.504	4-3	2/2	0.7
1996 Chi A c	85	77	.525	2	—	-5.7
1997 Chi A c	80	81	.497	2	—	4.6
Total 3	222	214	.509	—	—	-0.3

YEAR TM LG	W	L	PCT	FINISH	MGR/YR	+/-
Bezdek, Hugo Hugo Frank; B4.1.1884 Prague, Czechoslovakia; D9.19.1952 Atlantic City, NJ (DNP)						
1917 Pit N	30	59	.337	8-8	3/3	-5.8
1918 Pit N	65	60	.520	4	—	-3.6
1919 Pit N	71	68	.511	4	—	0.8
Total 3	166	187	.470	—	—	-8.6
Bickerson (DNP)						
1884 Was AA	0	1	.000	12-12	2/2	-0.2
Birmingham, Joe B8.6.1884						
1912 Cle A	21	7	.750	6-5	2/2	7.1
1913 Cle A	86	66	.566	3	—	-0.6
1914 Cle A	51	102	.333	8	—	-7.3
1915 Cle A	12	16	.429	6-7	1/2	0.6
Total 4	170	191	.471	—	—	-0.2
Bissonette, Del B9.6.1899						
1945 Bos N	25	34	.424	7-6	2/2	-4.2
Blackburne, Lena B10.23.1886						
1928 Chi A	40	40	.500	6-5	2/2	3.6
1929 Chi A	59	93	.388	7	—	-0.8
Total 2	99	133	.427	—	—	2.8
Blades, Ray B8.6.1896						
1939 StL N	92	61	.601	2	—	1.0
1940 StL N	14	24	.368	6-3	1/3	-6.2
1948 Bro N	1	0	1.000	5-5-3	2/3	0.5
Total 3	107	85	.557	—	—	-4.7
Blair, Walter B10.13.1883						
1915 Buf F	1	1	.500	8-8-6	2/3	0.1
Bluege, Ossie B10.24.1900						
1943 Was A	84	69	.549	2	—	0.1
1944 Was A	64	90	.416	8	—	-5.4
1945 Was A	87	67	.565	2	—	3.5
1946 Was A	76	78	.494	4	—	9.1
1947 Was A	64	90	.416	7	—	6.5
Total 5	375	394	.488	—	—	13.7
Bochy, Bruce B4.16.1955						
1995 SD N w	70	74	.486	3	—	-1.6
1996 SD N w	91	71	.562	1	—	1.1
1997 SD N w	76	86	.469	4	—	3.9
1998 SD N w	98	64	.605	1◆	—	5.3
1999 SD N w	74	88	.457	4	—	0.0
2000 SD N w	76	86	.469	5	—	-1.1
2001 SD N w	79	83	.488	4	—	0.2
2002 SD N w	66	96	.407	5	—	0.2
2003 SD N w	64	98	.395	5	—	-2.0
2004 SD N w	87	75	.537	3	—	-0.3
2005 SD N w	82	80	.506	1	—	5.3
2006 SD N w	88	74	.543	2✤	—	1.7
Total 12	951	975	.494	—	—	15.0
Boles, John John; B8.19.1948 Chicago, IL; BL/TR/5´10˝/165(OF)						
1996 Fla N e	40	35	.533	4-3	3/3	3.2
1999 Fla N e	64	98	.395	5	—	-1.3
2000 Fla N e	79	82	.491	3	—	4.9
2001 Fla N e	22	26	.458	3-4	1/2	-1.9
Total 4	205	241	.460	—	—	4.8
Bond, Tommy B4.2.1856						
1882 Wor N	2	4	.333	8-8-8	2/3	0.7
Boone, Bob B11.19.1947						
1995 KC A c	70	74	.486	2	—	4.1
1996 KC A c	75	86	.466	5	—	-1.6
1997 KC A c	36	46	.439	4-5	1/2	-1.4
2001 Cin N c	66	96	.407	5	—	-4.0
2002 Cin N c	78	84	.481	3	—	3.4
2003 Cin N c	46	58	.442	5-5	1/3	5.8
Total 6	371	444	.455	—	—	6.4
Boros, Steve B9.3.1936						
1983 Oak A w	74	88	.457	4	—	0.3
1984 Oak A w	20	24	.455	5-4	1/2	-0.5
1986 SD N w	74	88	.457	4	—	-0.1
Total 3	168	200	.457	—	—	-0.3
Bottomley, Jim B4.23.1900						
1937 StL A	21	56	.273	7-8	2/2	-3.7
Boudreau, Lou B7.17.1917						
1942 Cle A	75	79	.487	4	—	5.3
1943 Cle A	82	71	.536	3	—	3.0
1944 Cle A	72	82	.468	5t	—	-1.5
1945 Cle A	73	72	.503	5	—	-0.5
1946 Cle A	68	86	.442	6	—	2.0
1947 Cle A	80	74	.519	4	—	-7.4
1948 Cle A	97	58	.626	1▲★	—	-7.7
1949 Cle A	89	65	.578	3	—	1.4
1950 Cle A	92	62	.597	4	—	0.1
1952 Bos A	76	78	.494	6	—	-2.0
1953 Bos A	84	69	.549	4	—	5.0
1954 Bos A	69	85	.448	4	—	-5.2
1955 KC A	63	91	.409	6	—	11.9
1956 KC A	52	102	.338	8	—	-4.3
1957 KC A	36	67	.350	8-7	1/2	-5.2
1960 Chi N	54	83	.394	7-7	2/2	-1.9
Total 16	1162	1224	.487	—	—	-6.9

YEAR TM LG	W	L	PCT	FINISH	MGR/YR	+/-
Bowa, Larry B12.6.1945						
1987 SD N w	65	97	.401	6	—	-6.4
1988 SD N w	16	30	.348	5-3	1/2	-7.3
2001 Phi N e	86	76	.531	2	—	2.3
2002 Phi N e	80	81	.497	3	—	0.9
2003 Phi N e	86	76	.531	3	—	-4.3
2004 Phi N e	86	76	.531	2	—	-0.6
Total 6	419	436	.490	—	—	-15.4
Bowerman, Frank B12.5.1868						
1909 Bos N	22	54	.289	8-8	1/2	-2.2
Boyd, Bill B12.22.1852						
1875 Atl NA	0	2	.000	12-12	2/2	0.2
Boyer, Ken B5.20.1931						
1978 StL N e	62	81	.434	6-5	3/3	-4.1
1979 StL N e	86	76	.531	3	—	1.1
1980 StL N e	18	33	.353	6-4	1/4	-8.4
Total 3	166	190	.466	—	—	-11.3
Bradley, Bill B2.13.1878						
1905 Cle A	20	21	.488	1t-2-5	2/3	0.2
1914 Bro F	77	77	.500	5	—	1.5
Total 2	97	98	.497	—	—	1.7
Bragan, Bobby B10.30.1917						
1956 Pit N	66	88	.429	7	—	-4.1
1957 Pit N	36	67	.350	7-7t	1/2	-7.8
1958 Cle A	31	36	.463	6-4	1/2	-5.1
1963 Mil N	84	78	.519	6	—	-4.9
1964 Mil N	88	74	.543	5	—	1.3
1965 Mil N	86	76	.531	5	—	-2.8
1966 Atl N	52	59	.468	7-5	1/2	-10.3
Total 7	443	478	.481	—	—	-33.8
Brenly, Bob B2.25.1954						
2001 Ari N w	92	70	.568	1★	—	-2.9
2002 Ari N w	98	64	.605	1	—	2.7
2003 Ari N w	84	78	.519	3	—	-0.3
2004 Ari N w	29	50	.367	5-5	1/2	3.1
Total 4	303	262	.536	—	—	2.6
Bresnahan, Roger B6.11.1879						
1909 StL N	54	98	.355	7	—	-6.8
1910 StL N	63	90	.412	7	—	-5.5
1911 StL N	75	74	.503	5	—	7.9
1912 StL N	63	90	.412	6	—	2.9
1915 Chi N	73	80	.477	4	—	1.9
Total 5	328	432	.432	—	—	0.5
Bristol, Dave James David; B6.23.1933 Macon, GA; BR/TR/5´11˝/175(2B)						
1966 Cin N	39	38	.506	8-7	2/2	1.0
1967 Cin N	87	75	.537	4	—	1.4
1968 Cin N	83	79	.512	4	—	0.2
1969 Cin N w	89	73	.549	3	—	5.1
1970 Mil A w	65	97	.401	4t	—	-1.7
1971 Mil A w	69	92	.429	6	—	-3.1
1972 Mil A e	10	20	.333	6-6	1/3	-2.8
1976 Atl N w	70	92	.432	6	—	-2.6
1977 Atl N w	8	21	.276	6-6	1/4	-2.8
1977 Atl N w	52	79	.397	6-6	4/4	3.4
1979 SF N w	10	12	.455	4-4	2/2	0.1
1980 SF N w	75	86	.466	5	—	1.2
Total 11	657	764	.462	—	—	-0.5
Brown, Freeman Freeman; B1.31.1845 Hubbardston, MA; D12.27.1916 Worcester, MA (DNP)						
1882 Wor N	9	32	.220	8-8	1/3	-0.1
Brown, Mordecai B10.19.1876						
1914 StL F	50	63	.442	7-8	1/2	3.9
Brown, Tom B9.21.1860						
1897 Was N	52	46	.531	11-6t	2/2	3.8
1898 Was N	12	26	.316	11-11	1/4	-1.6
Total 2	64	72	.471	—	—	2.2
Brucker, Earle B5.6.1901						
1952 Cin N	3	2	.600	7-7-6	2/3	0.6
Buckenberger, Al Albert C.; B1.31.1861 Detroit, MI; D7.1.1917 Syracuse, NY (DNP)						
1889 Col AA	60	78	.435	6	—	3.5
1890 Col AA	39	41	.488	5-2	1/3	-12.9
1892-1 Pit N	15	14	.517	7-6	1/2	0.4
1892-2 Pit N	38	27	.585	10-4	2/2	5.3
1893 Pit N	81	48	.628	2	—	-0.3
1894 Pit N	53	55	.491	7-7	1/2	0.0
1895 StL N	16	34	.320	11-11	1/4	-0.0
1902 Bos N	73	64	.533	3	—	-1.6
1903 Bos N	58	80	.420	6	—	1.0
1904 Bos N	55	98	.359	7	—	5.9
Total 9	488	539	.475	—	—	1.2
Buffinton, Charlie B6.14.1861						
1890 Phi P	61	54	.530	5-5	2/2	-2.6
Burdock, Jack B4.1852						
1883 Bos N	30	24	.556	4-1	1/2	-7.4

YEAR TM LG	W	L	PCT	FINISH	MGR/YR	+/-
Burke, Jimmy B10.12.1874						
1905 StL N	34	56	.378	7-6-6	2/3	1.2
1918 StL A	29	31	.483	6-5	3/3	0.2
1919 StL A	67	72	.482	5	—	1.1
1920 StL A	76	77	.497	4	—	-3.4
Total 4	206	236	.466	—	—	-0.9
Burnham, George George Walter "Watch"; B5.20.1860 Albion, MI; D11.18.1902 Detroit, MI (DNP)						
1887 Ind N	6	22	.214	8-8	1/3	-1.7
Burns, Tom B3.30.1857						
1892-1 Pit N	22	25	.468	7-6	2/2	-1.7
1892-2 Pit N	5	7	.417	10-4	1/2	-1.0
1898 Chi N	85	65	.567	4	—	-4.2
1899 Chi N	75	73	.507	8	—	-3.6
Total 3	187	170	.524	—	—	-10.5
Burwell, Bill B3.27.1895						
1947 Pit N	1	0	1.000	8-7t	2/2	0.5
Bush, Donie B10.8.1887						
1923 Was A	75	78	.490	4	—	1.1
1927 Pit N	94	60	.610	1	—	1.6
1928 Pit N	85	67	.559	4	—	-3.5
1929 Pit N	67	51	.568	2-2	1/2	-0.7
1930 Chi A	62	92	.403	7	—	-0.6
1931 Chi A	56	97	.366	8	—	1.2
1933 Cin N	58	94	.382	8	—	-1.8
Total 7	497	539	.480	—	—	-2.7
Butler, Ormond Ormond Hook; B11.1854 WV; D9.12.1915 Mt.Hope, MD (DNP)						
1883 Pit AA	17	36	.321	6-6-7	2/3	-0.3
Byrne, Charlie Charles H.; B9.1843 New York, NY; D1.4.1898 New York, NY (DNP)						
1885 Bro AA	38	37	.507	7-5t	2/2	2.0
1886 Bro AA	76	61	.555	3	—	7.5
1887 Bro AA	60	74	.448	6	—	-5.8
Total 3	174	172	.503	—	—	3.7
Callahan, Nixey B3.18.1874						
1903 Chi A	60	77	.438	7	—	1.7
1904 Chi A	23	18	.561	4-3	1/2	-1.1
1912 Chi A	78	76	.506	4	—	1.9
1913 Chi A	78	74	.513	5	—	3.2
1914 Chi A	70	84	.455	6t	—	1.5
1916 Pit N	65	89	.422	6	—	-0.3
1917 Pit N	20	40	.333	8-8	1/3	-4.1
Total 7	394	458	.462	—	—	2.8
Campau, Count B10.17.1863						
1890 StL AA	27	14	.659	5-2-3	4/6	2.9
Cantillon, Joe Joseph D. "Pongo Joe"; B8.19.1861 Janesville, WI; D1.31.1930 Hickman, KY (DNP)						
1907 Was A	49	102	.325	8	—	-6.4
1908 Was A	67	85	.441	7	—	-2.0
1909 Was A	42	110	.276	8	—	-1.9
Total 3	158	297	.347	—	—	-10.2
Carey, Max B1.11.1890						
1932 Bro N	81	73	.526	3	—	3.5
1933 Bro N	65	88	.425	6	—	-3.4
Total 2	146	161	.476	—	—	0.1
Carey, Tom B3.1846						
1873 Bal NA	14	9	.609	3-3	2/2	-2.9
1874 Mut NA	13	12	.520	3-2	1/2	-3.4
Total 2	27	21	.563	—	—	-6.3
Carrigan, Bill B10.22.1883						
1913 Bos A	40	30	.571	5-4	2/2	4.0
1914 Bos A	91	62	.595	2	—	5.5
1915 Bos A	101	50	.669	1★	—	6.9
1916 Bos A	91	63	.591	1★	—	5.8
1927 Bos A	51	103	.331	8	—	-0.7
1928 Bos A	57	96	.373	8	—	-1.2
1929 Bos A	58	96	.377	8	—	0.7
Total 7	489	500	.494	—	—	21.0
Caruthers, Bob B1.5.1864						
1892-2 StL N	16	32	.333	12-11	3/3	-1.5
Cavarretta, Phil B7.19.1916						
1951 Chi N	27	47	.365	7-8	2/2	-3.4
1952 Chi N	77	77	.500	5	—	0.3
1953 Chi N	65	89	.422	7	—	7.7
Total 3	169	213	.442	—	—	4.6
Caylor, O.P. Oliver Perry; B12.17.1849 Near Dayton, OH; D10.19.1897 Winona, MN (DNP)						
1885 Cin AA	63	49	.563	2	—	0.9
1886 Cin AA	65	73	.471	5	—	-5.5
1887 NY AA	35	60	.368	7-7	3/3	7.4
Total 3	163	182	.472	—	—	2.7
Chance, Frank B9.9.1876						
1905 Chi N	55	33	.625	4-3	2/2	-3.5
1906 Chi N	116	36	.763	1	—	3.4
1907 Chi N	107	45	.704	1★	—	8.9
1908 Chi N	99	55	.643	1★	—	3.3
1909 Chi N	104	49	.680	2	—	-1.1

YEAR	TM LG	W	L	PCT	FINISH	MGR/YR	+/-
1910	Chi N	104	50	.675	1	—	4.2
1911	Chi N	92	62	.597	2	—	-0.3
1912	Chi N	91	59	.607	3	—	7.4
1913	NY A	57	94	.377	7	—	-3.6
1914	NY A	60	74	.448	7-6t	1/2	-5.7
1923	Bos A	61	91	.401	8	—	7.4
Total	11	946	648	.593	—	—	20.4

Chapman, Jack B5.8.1843

YEAR	TM LG	W	L	PCT	FINISH	MGR/YR	+/-
1876	Lou N	30	36	.455	5	—	3.4
1877	Lou N	35	25	.583	2	—	0.2
1878	Mil N	15	45	.250	6	—	-3.0
1882	Wor N	7	30	.189	8-8	3/3	-1.2
1883	Det N	40	58	.408	7	—	2.1
1884	Det N	28	84	.250	8	—	-0.9
1885	Buf N	31	57	.352	7-7	2/2	5.7
1889	Lou AA	1	6	.143	8-8	4/4	-0.5
1890	Lou AA	88	44	.667	1	—	0.5
1891	Lou AA	54	83	.394	7	—	1.1
1892-1	Lou N	21	33	.389	10-11	1/2	-0.6
Total	11	350	501	.411	—	—	6.8

Chapman, Ben B12.25.1908

YEAR	TM LG	W	L	PCT	FINISH	MGR/YR	+/-
1945	Phi N	28	57	.329	8-8	2/2	2.8
1946	Phi N	69	85	.448	5	—	7.2
1947	Phi N	62	92	.403	7t	—	-4.8
1948	Phi N	37	42	.468	7-6	1/3	4.7
Total	4	196	276	.415	—	—	10.0

Chase, Hal B2.13.1883

YEAR	TM LG	W	L	PCT	FINISH	MGR/YR	+/-
1910	NY A	10	4	.714	3-2	2/2	2.3
1911	NY A	76	76	.500	6	—	3.9
Total	2	86	80	.518	—	—	6.2

Clapp, John B7.17.1851

YEAR	TM LG	W	L	PCT	FINISH	MGR/YR	+/-
1872	Man NA	5	19	.208	8	—	0.9
1878	Ind N	24	36	.400	5	—	-2.7
1879	Buf N	46	32	.590	3	—	4.2
1880	Cin N	21	59	.262	8	—	-1.6
1881	Cle N	32	41	.438	6-7	2/2	-2.6
1883	NY N	46	50	.479	6	—	2.2
Total	6	174	237	.423	—	—	0.3

Clarke, Fred B10.3.1872

YEAR	TM LG	W	L	PCT	FINISH	MGR/YR	+/-
1897	Lou N	35	54	.393	9-11	2/2	2.3
1898	Lou N	70	81	.464	9	—	4.4
1899	Lou N	75	76	.497	9	—	-5.8
1900	Pit N	79	60	.568	2	—	-2.2
1901	Pit N	90	49	.647	1	—	-3.2
1902	Pit N	103	36	.741	1	—	-0.9
1903	Pit N	91	49	.650	1	—	3.9
1904	Pit N	87	66	.569	4	—	1.8
1905	Pit N	96	57	.627	2	—	6.7
1906	Pit N	93	60	.608	3	—	-0.7
1907	Pit N	91	63	.591	2	—	0.2
1908	Pit N	98	56	.636	2t	—	7.5
1909	Pit N	110	42	.724	1★	—	6.3
1910	Pit N	86	67	.562	3	—	1.1
1911	Pit N	85	69	.552	3	—	-11.4
1912	Pit N	93	58	.616	2	—	-1.5
1913	Pit N	78	71	.523	4	—	-5.8
1914	Pit N	69	85	.448	7	—	-3.7
1915	Pit N	73	81	.474	5	—	-8.2
Total	19	1602	1180	.576	—	—	-9.1

Clements, Jack B7.24.1864

YEAR	TM LG	W	L	PCT	FINISH	MGR/YR	+/-
1890	Phi N	13	6	.684	1-2-3	2/5	2.0

Cobb, Ty B12.18.1886

YEAR	TM LG	W	L	PCT	FINISH	MGR/YR	+/-
1921	Det A	71	82	.464	6	—	-8.3
1922	Det A	79	75	.513	3	—	-1.4
1923	Det A	83	71	.539	2	—	-2.5
1924	Det A	86	68	.558	3	—	4.1
1925	Det A	81	73	.526	4	—	-2.7
1926	Det A	79	75	.513	6	—	5.5
Total	6	479	444	.519	—	—	-5.3

Cochrane, Mickey B4.6.1903

YEAR	TM LG	W	L	PCT	FINISH	MGR/YR	+/-
1934	Det A	101	53	.656	1	—	1.2
1935	Det A	93	58	.616	1★	—	-6.1
1936	Det A	29	24	.547	3-2	1/3	1.0
1936	Det A	36	31	.537	4-2	3/3	0.6
1937	Det A	16	13	.552	3-2	1/5	-0.1
1937	Det A	26	20	.565	3-2-2	3/5	0.5
1938	Det A	47	51	.480	5-4	1/2	-5.9
Total	5	348	250	.582	—	—	-8.8

Cohen, Andy B10.25.1904

YEAR	TM LG	W	L	PCT	FINISH	MGR/YR	+/-
1960	Phi N	1	0	1.000	6t-4t-8	2/3	0.6

Coleman, Jerry B9.14.1924

YEAR	TM LG	W	L	PCT	FINISH	MGR/YR	+/-
1980	SD N w	73	89	.451	6	—	-1.2

Coleman, Bob B9.26.1890

YEAR	TM LG	W	L	PCT	FINISH	MGR/YR	+/-
1943	Bos N	21	25	.457	6-6	1/2	3.0
1944	Bos N	65	89	.422	6	—	-3.5
1945	Bos N	42	51	.452	7-6	1/2	-4.1
Total	3	128	165	.437	—	—	-4.6

Collins, Eddie B5.2.1887

YEAR	TM LG	W	L	PCT	FINISH	MGR/YR	+/-
1924	Chi A	14	13	.519	6	3/4	1.6
1925	Chi A	79	75	.513	5	—	-1.8
1926	Chi A	81	72	.529	5	—	-2.0
Total	3	174	160	.521	—	—	-2.3

Collins, Jimmy B1.16.1870

YEAR	TM LG	W	L	PCT	FINISH	MGR/YR	+/-
1901	Bos A	79	57	.581	2	—	-3.4
1902	Bos A	77	60	.562	3	—	2.2
1903	Bos A	91	47	.659	1★	—	1.1
1904	Bos A	95	59	.617	1	—	1.7
1905	Bos A	78	74	.513	4	—	0.5
1906	Bos A	35	79	.307	8-8	1/2	-2.3
Total	6	455	376	.548	—	—	-0.3

Collins, Shano B12.4.1885

YEAR	TM LG	W	L	PCT	FINISH	MGR/YR	+/-
1931	Bos A	62	90	.408	6	—	3.2
1932	Bos A	11	44	.200	8-8	1/2	-4.4
Total	2	73	134	.353	—	—	-1.2

Collins, Terry Terry Lee; B5.27.1949 Midland, MI; BL/TR/5´8˝/160(2B)

YEAR	TM LG	W	L	PCT	FINISH	MGR/YR	+/-
1994	Hou N c	66	49	.574	2	—	-1.1
1995	Hou N c	76	68	.528	2	—	-3.0
1996	Hou N c	82	80	.506	2	—	4.8
1997	Ana A w	84	78	.519	2	—	-0.3
1998	Ana A w	85	77	.525	2	—	3.6
1999	Ana A w	51	82	.383	4-4	1/2	-6.3
Total	6	444	434	.506	—	—	-2.3

Comiskey, Charlie B8.15.1859

YEAR	TM LG	W	L	PCT	FINISH	MGR/YR	+/-
1883	StL AA	12	7	.632	2-2	2/2	-0.1
1884	StL AA	16	7	.696	5-4	2/2	2.2
1885	StL AA	79	33	.705	1	—	2.7
1886	StL AA	93	46	.669	1★	—	-8.3
1887	StL AA	95	40	.704	1	—	-2.5
1888	StL AA	92	43	.681	1	—	-3.7
1889	StL AA	89	46	.659	2	—	-1.9
1890	Chi P	75	62	.547	4	—	-3.5
1891	StL AA	85	51	.625	2	—	-2.0
1892-1	Cin N	44	31	.587	4	—	3.6
1892-2	Cin N	38	37	.507	8	—	3.6
1893	Cin N	65	63	.508	6t	—	5.8
1894	Cin N	55	75	.423	10	—	3.2
Total	12	838	541	.608	—	—	-0.9

Connor, Roger B7.1.1857

YEAR	TM LG	W	L	PCT	FINISH	MGR/YR	+/-
1896	StL N	8	37	.178	11-11-11	4/5	-4.3

Cooke, Dusty B6.23.1907

YEAR	TM LG	W	L	PCT	FINISH	MGR/YR	+/-
1948	Phi N	6	6	.500	7-6-6	2/3	1.1

Coombs, Jack B11.18.1882

YEAR	TM LG	W	L	PCT	FINISH	MGR/YR	+/-
1919	Phi N	18	44	.290	8-8	1/2	-4.3

Cooney, Johnny B3.18.1901

YEAR	TM LG	W	L	PCT	FINISH	MGR/YR	+/-
1949	Bos N	20	25	.444	4-4	2/2	-2.1

Corrales, Pat B3.20.1941

YEAR	TM LG	W	L	PCT	FINISH	MGR/YR	+/-
1978	Tex A w	1	0	1.000	2t-2t	2/2	0.5
1979	Tex A w	83	79	.512	3	—	-3.2
1980	Tex A w	76	85	.472	4	—	-4.9
1982	Phi N e	89	73	.549	2	—	6.9
1983	Phi N e	43	42	.506	1-1◆	1/2	-2.9
1983	Cle A e	30	32	.484	7-7	2/2	2.1
1984	Cle A e	75	87	.463	6	—	-5.5
1985	Cle A e	60	102	.370	7	—	-8.4
1986	Cle A e	84	78	.519	5	—	3.9
1987	Cle A e	31	56	.356	7-7	1/2	-1.8
Total	9	572	634	.474	—	—	-13.2

Corriden, Red B9.4.1887

YEAR	TM LG	W	L	PCT	FINISH	MGR/YR	+/-
1950	Chi A	52	72	.419	8-6	2/2	0.1

Cottier, Chuck B1.8.1936

YEAR	TM LG	W	L	PCT	FINISH	MGR/YR	+/-
1984	Sea A w	15	12	.556	7-5t	2/2	3.0
1985	Sea A w	74	88	.457	6	—	2.6
1986	Sea A w	9	19	.321	6-7	1/3	-3.0
Total	3	98	119	.452	—	—	2.6

Cox, Bobby B5.21.1941

YEAR	TM LG	W	L	PCT	FINISH	MGR/YR	+/-
1978	Atl N w	69	93	.426	6	—	3.6
1979	Atl N w	66	94	.412	6	—	-4.6
1980	Atl N w	81	80	.503	4	—	3.7
1981-1	Atl N w	25	29	.463	4	—	-0.7
1981-2	Atl N w	25	27	.481	5	—	-0.7
1982	Tor A e	78	84	.481	6t	—	2.2
1983	Tor A e	89	73	.549	4	—	1.2
1984	Tor A e	89	73	.549	2	—	2.6
1985	Tor A e	99	62	.615	1	—	0.8
1990	Atl N w	40	57	.412	6-6	2/2	-0.3
1991	Atl N w	94	68	.580	1◆	—	2.3
1992	Atl N w	98	64	.605	1◆	—	4.8
1993	Atl N w	104	58	.642	1	—	1.2
1994	Atl N e	68	46	.596	2	—	1.4
1995	Atl N e	90	54	.625	1★	—	7.0
1996	Atl N e	96	66	.593	1◆	—	2.3
1997	Atl N e	101	61	.623	1☆	—	-1.7
1998	Atl N e	106	56	.654	1☆	—	0.1
1999	Atl N e	103	59	.636	1◆	—	4.4
2000	Atl N e	95	67	.586	1	—	4.6
2001	Atl N e	88	74	.543	1☆	—	-1.9
2002	Atl N e	101	59	.631	1	—	5.7
2003	Atl N e	101	61	.623	1	—	4.3
2004	Atl N e	96	66	.593	1	—	1.6
2005	Atl N e	90	72	.556	1	—	-0.6
2006	Atl N e	79	83	.488	3	—	-6.1
Total	25	2171	1686	.563	—	—	37.2

Craft, Harry B4.19.1915

YEAR	TM LG	W	L	PCT	FINISH	MGR/YR	+/-
1957	KC A	23	27	.460	8-7	2/2	3.0
1958	KC A	73	81	.474	7	—	3.2
1959	KC A	66	88	.429	7	—	-3.3
1961	Chi N	4	8	.333	6t-7-7	2/9	-1.2
1961	Chi N	3	1	.750	7-7-7	5/9	1.3
1962	Hou N	64	96	.400	8	—	-2.8
1963	Hou N	66	96	.407	9	—	5.2
1964	Hou N	61	88	.409	9-9	1/2	0.4
Total	7	360	485	.426	—	—	6.0

Craig, Roger B2.17.1930

YEAR	TM LG	W	L	PCT	FINISH	MGR/YR	+/-
1978	SD N w	84	78	.519	4	—	3.8
1979	SD N w	68	93	.422	5	—	-4.2
1985	SF N w	6	12	.333	6-6	2/2	-1.6
1986	SF N w	83	79	.512	3	—	-6.4
1987	SF N w	90	72	.556	1	—	-2.4
1988	SF N w	83	79	.512	4	—	-2.7
1989	SF N w	92	70	.568	1◆	—	0.5
1990	SF N w	85	77	.525	3	—	3.1
1991	SF N w	75	87	.463	4	—	-1.0
1992	SF N w	72	90	.444	5	—	-1.0
Total	10	738	737	.500	—	—	-11.9

Crandall, Del B3.5.1930

YEAR	TM LG	W	L	PCT	FINISH	MGR/YR	+/-
1972	Mil A e	54	70	.435	6-6	3/3	1.2
1973	Mil A e	74	88	.457	5	—	-4.7
1974	Mil A e	76	86	.469	5	—	-3.6
1975	Mil A e	67	94	.416	5-5	1/2	-1.9
1983	Sea A w	34	55	.382	7-7	2/2	0.1
1984	Sea A w	59	76	.437	7-5t	1/2	-0.8
Total	6	364	469	.437	—	—	-9.7

Crane, Sam B1.2.1854

YEAR	TM LG	W	L	PCT	FINISH	MGR/YR	+/-
1880	Buf N	24	58	.293	7	—	-0.6
1884	Cin U	49	21	.700	5-3	2/2	-0.2
Total	2	73	79	.480	—	—	-0.8

Cravath, Gavy B3.23.1881

YEAR	TM LG	W	L	PCT	FINISH	MGR/YR	+/-
1919	Phi N	29	46	.387	8-8	2/2	2.0
1920	Phi N	62	91	.405	8	—	1.0
Total	2	91	137	.399	—	—	2.9

Craver, Bill B6.1844

YEAR	TM LG	W	L	PCT	FINISH	MGR/YR	+/-
1871	Tro NA	12	12	.500	7-6	2/2	0.6
1872	Bal NA	27	13	.675	2-2	1/2	-2.6
1875	Cen NA	2	12	.143	11	—	0.3
1876	NY N	21	35	.375	6	—	6.3
Total	4	62	72	.463	—	—	4.6

Creamer, George B1855

YEAR	TM LG	W	L	PCT	FINISH	MGR/YR	+/-
1884	Pit AA	0	8	.000	10-10-10	4/5	-1.8

Cronin, Joe B10.12.1906

YEAR	TM LG	W	L	PCT	FINISH	MGR/YR	+/-
1933	Was A	99	53	.651	1	—	5.4
1934	Was A	66	86	.434	7	—	-2.7
1935	Bos A	78	75	.510	4	—	2.9
1936	Bos A	74	80	.481	6	—	-4.0
1937	Bos A	80	72	.526	5	—	-0.3
1938	Bos A	88	61	.591	2	—	-0.1
1939	Bos A	89	62	.589	2	—	4.9
1940	Bos A	82	72	.532	4t	—	0.8
1941	Bos A	84	70	.545	2	—	-3.7
1942	Bos A	93	59	.612	2	—	0.2
1943	Bos A	68	84	.447	7	—	-3.2
1944	Bos A	77	77	.500	4	—	-6.3
1945	Bos A	71	83	.461	7	—	1.9
1946	Bos A	104	50	.675	1	—	7.1
1947	Bos A	83	71	.539	3	—	0.9
Total	15	1236	1055	.540	—	—	3.7

Crooks, Jack B11.9.1865

YEAR	TM LG	W	L	PCT	FINISH	MGR/YR	+/-
1892-1	StL N	24	22	.522	11-9	3/3	7.2
1892-2	StL N	3	11	.214	12-11	1/3	-2.1

Cross, Lave B5.12.1866

YEAR	TM LG	W	L	PCT	FINISH	MGR/YR	+/-
1899	Cle N	8	30	.211	12-12	1/2	4.7

Cubbage, Mike B7.21.1950

YEAR	TM LG	W	L	PCT	FINISH	MGR/YR	+/-
1991	NY N e	3	4	.429	3-5	2/2	-0.5

Curtis, Ed Edwin Russell; B8.29.1843 Hartford, CT; D8.6.1914 Bath, NY (DNP)

YEAR	TM LG	W	L	PCT	FINISH	MGR/YR	+/-
1884	Alt U	6	19	.240	6	—	4.3

Cushman, Charlie Charles H.; B5.25.1850 New York, NY; D6.29.1909 Milwaukee, WI (DNP)

YEAR	TM LG	W	L	PCT	FINISH	MGR/YR	+/-
1891	Mil AA	21	15	.583	5	—	-3.5

Cuthbert, Ned B6.20.1845

YEAR	TM LG	W	L	PCT	FINISH	MGR/YR	+/-
1882	StL AA	37	43	.463	5	—	5.7

Dahlen, Bill B1.5.1870

YEAR	TM LG	W	L	PCT	FINISH	MGR/YR	+/-
1910	Bro N	64	90	.416	6	—	1.1
1911	Bro N	64	86	.427	7	—	1.9
1912	Bro N	58	95	.379	7	—	-9.3
1913	Bro N	65	84	.436	6	—	-7.6
Total	4	251	355	.414	—	—	-13.8

Dark, Alvin B1.7.1922

YEAR	TM LG	W	L	PCT	FINISH	MGR/YR	+/-
1961	SF N	85	69	.552	3	—	-3.7
1962	SF N	103	62	.624	1▲	—	2.2
1963	SF N	88	74	.543	3	—	-1.7
1964	SF N	90	72	.556	4	—	1.5
1966	KC A	74	86	.463	7	—	3.2

YEAR TM LG	W	L	PCT	FINISH	MGR/YR	+/-
1967 KC A	52	69	.430	10-10	1/2	2.0
1968 Cle A	86	75	.534	3	—	4.1
1969 Cle A e	62	99	.385	6	—	-3.2
1970 Cle A e	76	86	.469	5	—	-2.3
1971 Cle A e	42	61	.408	6-6	1/2	4.3
1974 Oak A w	90	72	.556	1★	—	-6.0
1975 Oak A w	98	64	.605	1	—	1.3
1977 SD N w	48	65	.425	4-5	3/3	1.2
Total 13	994	954	.510	—	—	2.9

Davenport, Jim B8.17.1933

YEAR TM LG	W	L	PCT	FINISH	MGR/YR	+/-
1985 SF N w	56	88	.389	6-6	1/2	-4.6

Davidson, Mordecai Mordecai H.; B11.30.1846 Port Washington, OH; D9.6.1940 Louisville, KY (DNP)

YEAR TM LG	W	L	PCT	FINISH	MGR/YR	+/-
1888 Lou AA	1	2	.333	8-8-7	2/4	-0.1
1888 Lou AA	34	52	.395	8-7	4/4	1.3

Davis, George B8.23.1870

YEAR TM LG	W	L	PCT	FINISH	MGR/YR	+/-
1895 NY N	16	17	.485	8-9	1/3	-0.9
1900 NY N	39	37	.513	8-8	2/2	6.5
1901 NY N	52	85	.380	7	—	4.4
Total 3	107	139	.435	—	—	10.0

Davis, Harry B7.19.1873

YEAR TM LG	W	L	PCT	FINISH	MGR/YR	+/-
1912 Cle A	54	71	.432	6-5	1/2	-8.2

Davis, Spud B12.20.1904

YEAR TM LG	W	L	PCT	FINISH	MGR/YR	+/-
1946 Pit N	1	2	.333	7-7	2/2	-0.3

Day, John John B.; B9.23.1847 Colchester, CT; D1.25.1925 Cliffside, NJ (DNP)

YEAR TM LG	W	L	PCT	FINISH	MGR/YR	+/-
1899 NY N	29	35	.453	9-10	1/2	2.0

Deane, Harry B5.6.1846

YEAR TM LG	W	L	PCT	FINISH	MGR/YR	+/-
1871 Kek NA	2	3	.400	7-8	2/2	1.4

Dent, Bucky B11.25.1951

YEAR TM LG	W	L	PCT	FINISH	MGR/YR	+/-
1989 NY A e	18	22	.450	6-5	2/2	0.3
1990 NY A e	18	31	.367	7-7	1/2	-1.9
Total 2	36	53	.404	—	—	-1.6

Dickey, Bill B6.6.1907

YEAR TM LG	W	L	PCT	FINISH	MGR/YR	+/-
1946 NY A	57	48	.543	2-3-3	2/3	-5.4

Diddlebock, Harry Henry H.; B6.27.1854 Philadelphia, PA; D2.5.1900 Philadelphia, PA (DNP)

YEAR TM LG	W	L	PCT	FINISH	MGR/YR	+/-
1896 StL N	7	10	.412	10-11	1/5	2.4

Dierker, Larry B9.22.1946

YEAR TM LG	W	L	PCT	FINISH	MGR/YR	+/-
1997 Hou N c	84	78	.519	1	—	-8.8
1998 Hou N c	102	60	.630	1	—	-4.1
1999 Hou N c	37	23	.617	1-1	1/3	1.6
1999 Hou N c	47	28	.627	1t-1	3/3	2.7
2000 Hou N c	72	90	.444	4	—	-8.5
2001 Hou N c	93	69	.574	1	—	4.6
Total 5	435	348	.556	—	—	-12.4

Doby, Larry B12.13.1923

YEAR TM LG	W	L	PCT	FINISH	MGR/YR	+/-
1978 Chi A w	37	50	.425	5-5	2/2	-1.1

Donovan, Patsy B3.16.1865

YEAR TM LG	W	L	PCT	FINISH	MGR/YR	+/-
1897 Pit N	60	71	.458	8	—	8.8
1899 Pit N	69	58	.543	10-7	2/2	-0.1
1901 StL N	76	64	.543	4	—	-3.6
1902 StL N	56	78	.418	6	—	7.2
1903 StL N	43	94	.314	8	—	3.0
1904 Was A	37	97	.276	8-8	2/2	-0.3
1906 Bro N	66	86	.434	5	—	4.3
1907 Bro N	65	83	.439	5	—	0.1
1908 Bro N	53	101	.344	7	—	-6.4
1910 Bos A	81	72	.529	4	—	-3.9
1911 Bos A	78	75	.510	5	—	-2.3
Total 11	684	879	.438	—	—	6.8

Donovan, Bill B10.13.1876

YEAR TM LG	W	L	PCT	FINISH	MGR/YR	+/-
1915 NY A	69	83	.454	5	—	-6.6
1916 NY A	80	74	.519	4	—	1.2
1917 NY A	71	82	.464	6	—	-1.6
1921 Phi N	25	62	.287	8-8	1/2	-2.3
Total 4	245	301	.449	—	—	-9.3

Dooin, Red B6.12.1879

YEAR TM LG	W	L	PCT	FINISH	MGR/YR	+/-
1910 Phi N	78	75	.510	4	—	-2.1
1911 Phi N	79	73	.520	4	—	4.1
1912 Phi N	73	79	.480	5	—	-1.2
1913 Phi N	88	63	.583	2	—	6.6
1914 Phi N	74	80	.481	6	—	0.7
Total 5	392	370	.514	—	—	8.0

Dorgan, Mike B10.2.1853

YEAR TM LG	W	L	PCT	FINISH	MGR/YR	+/-
1879 Syr N	17	26	.395	6-7	1/3	6.1
1880 Pro N	26	12	.684	3-2	3/3	1.3
1881 Wor N	24	32	.429	7-8	1/2	1.1
Total 3	67	70	.489	—	—	8.6

Dowd, Tommy B4.20.1869

YEAR TM LG	W	L	PCT	FINISH	MGR/YR	+/-
1896 StL N	25	38	.397	11-11	5/5	7.8
1897 StL N	6	22	.214	12-12	1/4	0.9
Total 2	31	60	.341	—	—	8.8

Doyle, Jack B10.25.1869

YEAR TM LG	W	L	PCT	FINISH	MGR/YR	+/-
1895 NY N	32	31	.508	8-9-9	2/3	-0.2
1898 Was N	8	9	.471	11-10-11	2/4	1.9
Total 2	40	40	.500	—	—	1.7

Dressen, Chuck B9.20.1898

YEAR TM LG	W	L	PCT	FINISH	MGR/YR	+/-
1934 Cin N	21	39	.350	8-8	3/3	-0.7
1935 Cin N	68	85	.444	6	—	4.0
1936 Cin N	74	80	.481	5	—	0.7
1937 Cin N	51	78	.395	8-8	1/2	-5.4
1951 Bro N	97	60	.618	2▲	—	0.8
1952 Bro N	96	57	.627	1	—	2.2
1953 Bro N	105	49	.682	1	—	3.5
1955 Was A	53	101	.344	8	—	-4.9
1956 Was A	59	95	.383	7	—	7.6
1957 Was A	4	16	.200	8-8	1/2	-3.4
1960 Mil N	88	66	.571	2	—	4.4
1961 Mil N	71	58	.550	3-4	1/2	1.8
1963 Det A	55	47	.539	9-5t	2/2	4.2
1964 Det A	85	77	.525	4	—	1.8
1965 Det A	65	55	.542	3-4	2/2	-1.2
1966 Det A	16	10	.615	3-3	1/3	2.7
Total 16	1008	973	.509	—	—	18.1

Duffy, Hugh B11.26.1866

YEAR TM LG	W	L	PCT	FINISH	MGR/YR	+/-
1901 Mil A	48	89	.350	8	—	-3.2
1904 Phi N	52	100	.342	8	—	-2.4
1905 Phi N	83	69	.546	4	—	-3.8
1906 Phi N	71	82	.464	4	—	-1.4
1910 Chi A	68	85	.444	6	—	-5.8
1911 Chi A	77	74	.510	4	—	-8.1
1921 Bos A	75	79	.487	5	—	0.8
1922 Bos A	61	93	.396	8	—	1.2
Total 8	535	671	.444	—	—	-22.7

Dunlap, Fred B5.21.1859

YEAR TM LG	W	L	PCT	FINISH	MGR/YR	+/-
1882 Cle N	42	36	.538	8-5	2/2	3.8
1884 StL U	66	16	.805	1-1	2/2	-4.3
1885 StL N	21	29	.420	5-8	1/3	5.5
1885 StL N	9	11	.450	8-8	3/3	2.8
1889 Pit N	7	10	.412	6-7-5	2/3	-0.6
Total 4	145	102	.587	—	—	7.1

Durocher, Leo B7.27.1905

YEAR TM LG	W	L	PCT	FINISH	MGR/YR	+/-
1939 Bro N	84	69	.549	3	—	1.1
1940 Bro N	88	65	.575	2	—	3.7
1941 Bro N	100	54	.649	1	—	0.8
1942 Bro N	104	50	.675	2	—	2.7
1943 Bro N	81	72	.529	3	—	0.4
1944 Bro N	63	91	.409	7	—	-0.4
1945 Bro N	87	67	.565	3	—	3.2
1946 Bro N	96	60	.615	2▲	—	4.2
1948 Bro N	35	37	.486	5-3	1/3	-4.5
1948 NY N	41	38	.519	4-5	2/2	-2.3
1949 NY N	73	81	.474	5	—	-8.3
1950 NY N	86	68	.558	3	—	-0.2
1951 NY N	98	59	.624	1▲	—	5.5
1952 NY N	92	62	.597	2	—	6.6
1953 NY N	70	84	.455	5	—	-9.0
1954 NY N	97	57	.630	1★	—	1.1
1955 NY N	80	74	.519	3	—	0.1
1966 Chi N	59	103	.364	10	—	-5.5
1967 Chi N	87	74	.540	3	—	-1.7
1968 Chi N	84	78	.519	3	—	2.9
1969 Chi N e	92	70	.568	2	—	-0.4
1970 Chi N e	84	78	.519	2	—	-9.6
1971 Chi N e	83	79	.512	3t	—	3.2
1972 Chi N e	46	44	.511	4-2	1/2	-6.3
1972 Hou N w	16	15	.516	2-2	3/3	-1.0
1973 Hou N w	82	80	.506	4	—	0.1
Total 24	2008	1709	.540	—	—	-13.6

Dwyer, Frank B3.25.1868

YEAR TM LG	W	L	PCT	FINISH	MGR/YR	+/-
1902 Det A	52	83	.385	7	—	-6.4

Dyer, Eddie B10.11.1899

YEAR TM LG	W	L	PCT	FINISH	MGR/YR	+/-
1946 StL N	98	58	.628	1▲★	—	2.3
1947 StL N	89	65	.578	2	—	-2.5
1948 StL N	85	69	.552	2	—	-1.6
1949 StL N	96	58	.623	2	—	3.8
1950 StL N	78	75	.510	5	—	-0.8
Total 5	446	325	.578	—	—	1.2

Dykes, Jimmy B11.10.1896

YEAR TM LG	W	L	PCT	FINISH	MGR/YR	+/-
1934 Chi A	49	88	.358	8-8	2/2	0.4
1935 Chi A	74	78	.487	5	—	-0.8
1936 Chi A	81	70	.536	3	—	1.4
1937 Chi A	86	68	.558	3	—	4.2
1938 Chi A	65	83	.439	6	—	-4.9
1939 Chi A	85	69	.552	4	—	6.3
1940 Chi A	82	72	.532	4t	—	-1.3
1941 Chi A	77	77	.500	3	—	1.1
1942 Chi A	66	82	.446	6	—	-0.3
1943 Chi A	82	72	.532	4	—	7.3
1944 Chi A	71	83	.461	7	—	6.8
1945 Chi A	71	78	.477	6	—	0.4
1946 Chi A	10	20	.333	7-5	1/2	-4.3
1951 Phi A	70	84	.455	6	—	-6.1
1952 Phi A	79	75	.513	4	—	7.9
1953 Phi A	59	95	.383	7	—	-1.4
1954 Bal A	54	100	.351	7	—	-2.7
1958 Cin N	24	17	.585	8-4	2/2	1.5
1959 Det A	74	63	.540	8-4	2/2	7.2
1960 Det A	44	52	.458	6-6	1/3	-3.3
1960 Cle A	26	32	.448	4-4	3/3	-2.0
1961 Cle A	77	83	.481	5-5	1/2	-1.5
Total 21	1406	1541	.477	—	—	15.7

Ebbets, Charlie Charles Hercules; B10.29.1859 New York, NY; D4.18.1925 New York, NY (DNP)

YEAR TM LG	W	L	PCT	FINISH	MGR/YR	+/-
1898 Bro N	38	68	.358	9-10	3/3	-2.8

Edwards, Doc B12.10.1936

YEAR TM LG	W	L	PCT	FINISH	MGR/YR	+/-
1987 Cle A e	30	45	.400	7-7	2/2	1.7
1988 Cle A e	78	84	.481	6	—	3.6
1989 Cle A e	65	78	.455	6-6	1/2	-1.7
Total 3	173	207	.455	—	—	3.6

Elberfeld, Kid B4.13.1875

YEAR TM LG	W	L	PCT	FINISH	MGR/YR	+/-
1908 NY A	27	71	.276	6-8	2/2	-4.4

Elia, Lee B7.16.1937

YEAR TM LG	W	L	PCT	FINISH	MGR/YR	+/-
1982 Chi N e	73	89	.451	5	—	-4.6
1983 Chi N e	54	69	.439	5-5	1/2	-6.1
1987 Phi N e	51	50	.505	5-4t	2/2	3.4
1988 Phi N e	60	92	.395	6-6	1/2	-2.5
Total 4	238	300	.442	—	—	-9.8

Ellick, Joe B4.3.1854

YEAR TM LG	W	L	PCT	FINISH	MGR/YR	+/-
1884 CP U	6	6	.500	5-5	3/3	0.6

Elliott, Bob B11.26.1916

YEAR TM LG	W	L	PCT	FINISH	MGR/YR	+/-
1960 KC A	58	96	.377	8	—	-4.8

Ens, Jewel B8.24.1889

YEAR TM LG	W	L	PCT	FINISH	MGR/YR	+/-
1929 Pit N	21	14	.600	2-2	2/2	0.9
1930 Pit N	80	74	.519	5	—	6.2
1931 Pit N	75	79	.487	5	—	3.6
Total 3	176	167	.513	—	—	10.8

Ermer, Cal B11.10.1923

YEAR TM LG	W	L	PCT	FINISH	MGR/YR	+/-
1967 Min A	66	46	.589	6-2t	2/2	3.9
1968 Min A	79	83	.488	7	—	-3.8
Total 2	145	129	.529	—	—	0.1

Essian, Jim B1.2.1951

YEAR TM LG	W	L	PCT	FINISH	MGR/YR	+/-
1991 Chi N e	59	63	.484	5-4	3/3	1.0

Esterbrook, Dude B6.20.1857

YEAR TM LG	W	L	PCT	FINISH	MGR/YR	+/-
1889 Lou AA	2	8	.200	7-8	1/4	-0.2

Evers, Johnny B7.21.1881

YEAR TM LG	W	L	PCT	FINISH	MGR/YR	+/-
1913 Chi N	88	65	.575	3	—	2.4
1921 Chi N	41	55	.427	6-7	1/2	-0.6
1924 Chi A	10	11	.476	6	1/4	0.3
1924 Chi A	41	61	.402	8	4/4	-6.0
Total 3	180	192	.484	—	—	-3.9

Ewing, Buck B10.17.1859

YEAR TM LG	W	L	PCT	FINISH	MGR/YR	+/-
1890 NY P	74	57	.565	3	—	-2.8
1895 Cin N	66	64	.508	8	—	-3.0
1896 Cin N	77	50	.606	3	—	-1.3
1897 Cin N	76	56	.576	4	—	4.7
1898 Cin N	92	60	.605	3	—	7.4
1899 Cin N	83	67	.553	6	—	0.2
1900 NY N	21	41	.339	8-8	1/2	-5.5
Total 7	489	395	.553	—	—	-0.3

Faatz, Jay B10.24.1860

YEAR TM LG	W	L	PCT	FINISH	MGR/YR	+/-
1890 Buf P	9	24	.273	8-8-8	2/3	0.4

Falk, Bibb B1.27.1899

YEAR TM LG	W	L	PCT	FINISH	MGR/YR	+/-
1933 Cle A	1	0	1.000	5-5-4	2/3	0.5

Fanning, Jim B9.14.1927

YEAR TM LG	W	L	PCT	FINISH	MGR/YR	+/-
1981-2 Mon N e	16	11	.593	2-1☆	2/2	1.2
1982 Mon N e	86	76	.531	3	—	-3.5
1984 Mon N e	14	16	.467	5-5	2/2	-1.2
Total 3	116	103	.530	—	—	-3.5

Farrell, Jack B7.5.1857

YEAR TM LG	W	L	PCT	FINISH	MGR/YR	+/-
1881 Pro N	24	27	.471	4-2	1/2	-2.7

Farrell, Kerby B9.3.1913

YEAR TM LG	W	L	PCT	FINISH	MGR/YR	+/-
1957 Cle A	76	77	.497	6	—	3.5

Felske, John B5.30.1942

YEAR TM LG	W	L	PCT	FINISH	MGR/YR	+/-
1985 Phi N e	75	87	.463	5	—	-5.4
1986 Phi N e	86	75	.534	2	—	2.9
1987 Phi N e	29	32	.475	5-4t	1/2	0.3
Total 3	190	194	.495	—	—	-2.2

Ferguson, Bob B1.31.1845

YEAR TM LG	W	L	PCT	FINISH	MGR/YR	+/-
1871 Mut NA	16	17	.485	4	—	0.3
1872 Atl NA	9	28	.243	6	—	6.7
1873 Atl NA	17	37	.315	6	—	3.5
1874 Atl NA	22	33	.400	6	—	6.7
1875 Har NA	54	28	.659	3	—	-6.8
1876 Har N	47	21	.691	3	—	-2.9
1877 Har N	31	27	.534	3	—	-0.7
1878 Chi N	30	30	.500	4	—	-3.5
1879 Tro N	7	22	.241	8-8	2/2	0.2
1880 Tro N	41	42	.494	4	—	3.9
1881 Tro N	39	45	.464	5	—	-0.3
1882 Tro N	35	48	.422	7	—	1.7
1883 Phi N	4	13	.235	8-8	1/2	1.9
1884 Pit AA	11	31	.262	9-11-10	2/5	1.6
1886 NY AA	48	70	.407	8-7	2/2	0.3
1887 NY AA	6	24	.200	8-7	1/3	-2.7
Total 16	417	516	.447	—	—	9.7

Ferraro, Mike B8.18.1944

YEAR TM LG	W	L	PCT	FINISH	MGR/YR	+/-
1983 Cle A e	40	60	.400	7-7	1/2	-5.1
1986 KC A w	36	38	.486	4-3t	2/2	-0.1
Total 2	76	98	.437	—	—	-5.1

Fessenden, Wallace Wallace Clifton; B10.5.1860 Windham, NH; D5.16.1935 Brooklyn, NY (DNP)

YEAR TM LG	W	L	PCT	FINISH	MGR/YR	+/-
1890 Syr AA	4	7	.364	7-7-6	2/3	-0.5

Fitzsimmons, Freddie B7.28.1901

YEAR TM LG	W	L	PCT	FINISH	MGR/YR	+/-
1943 Phi N	26	38	.406	7-7	2/2	-1.4
1944 Phi N	61	92	.399	8	—	-2.7
1945 Phi N	18	51	.261	8-8	1/2	-2.4
Total 3	105	181	.367	—	—	-6.5

Fletcher, Art B1.5.1885

YEAR TM LG	W	L	PCT	FINISH	MGR/YR	+/-
1923 Phi N	50	104	.325	8	—	-3.8
1924 Phi N	55	96	.364	7	—	-4.1
1925 Phi N	68	85	.444	6t	—	2.0
1926 Phi N	58	93	.384	8	—	2.3
1929 NY A	6	5	.545	2-2	2/2	-0.3
Total 5	237	383	.382	—	—	-4.0

Flint, Silver B8.3.1855

YEAR TM LG	W	L	PCT	FINISH	MGR/YR	+/-
1879 Chi N	5	12	.294	2-4	2/2	-4.0

Fogarty, Jim B2.12.1864

YEAR TM LG	W	L	PCT	FINISH	MGR/YR	+/-
1890 Phi P	7	9	.438	5-5	1/2	-1.9

Fogel, Horace Horace S.; B3.2.1861 Macungie, PA; D11.15.1928 Philadelphia, PA (DNP)

YEAR TM LG	W	L	PCT	FINISH	MGR/YR	+/-
1887 Ind N	20	49	.290	8-8	3/3	1.1
1902 NY N	18	23	.439	4-8	1/3	4.2
Total 2	38	72	.345	—	—	5.4

Fohl, Lee B11.28.1876

YEAR TM LG	W	L	PCT	FINISH	MGR/YR	+/-
1915 Cle A	45	79	.363	6-7	2/2	-5.6
1916 Cle A	77	77	.500	6	—	-3.0
1917 Cle A	88	66	.571	3	—	6.4
1918 Cle A	73	54	.575	2	—	3.2
1919 Cle A	44	34	.564	3-2	1/2	-0.7
1921 StL A	81	73	.526	3	—	4.9
1922 StL A	93	61	.604	2	—	-5.5
1923 StL A	52	49	.515	3-5	1/2	3.6
1924 Bos A	67	87	.435	7	—	-3.2
1925 Bos A	47	105	.309	8	—	-2.5
1926 Bos A	46	107	.301	8	—	-3.3
Total 11	713	792	.474	—	—	-5.6

Fonseca, Lew B1.21.1899

YEAR TM LG	W	L	PCT	FINISH	MGR/YR	+/-
1932 Chi A	49	102	.325	7	—	-5.0
1933 Chi A	67	83	.447	6	—	4.5
1934 Chi A	4	11	.267	8-8	1/2	-1.3
Total 3	120	196	.380	—	—	-1.8

Foutz, Dave B9.7.1856

YEAR TM LG	W	L	PCT	FINISH	MGR/YR	+/-
1893 Bro N	65	63	.508	6t	—	6.9
1894 Bro N	70	61	.534	5	—	4.2
1895 Bro N	71	60	.542	5t	—	2.1
1896 Bro N	58	73	.443	9t	—	-1.0
Total 4	264	257	.507	—	—	12.2

Fox, Charlie B10.7.1921

YEAR TM LG	W	L	PCT	FINISH	MGR/YR	+/-
1970 SF N w	67	53	.558	4-3	2/2	6.7
1971 SF N w	90	72	.556	1	—	2.6
1972 SF N w	69	86	.445	5	—	-9.8
1973 SF N w	88	74	.543	3	—	3.3
1974 SF N w	34	42	.447	5-5	1/2	0.3
1976 Mon N e	12	22	.353	6-6	2/2	-0.4
1983 Chi N e	17	22	.436	5-5	2/2	-2.1
Total 7	377	371	.504	—	—	0.5

Francona, Terry B4.22.1959

YEAR TM LG	W	L	PCT	FINISH	MGR/YR	+/-
1997 Phi N e	68	94	.420	5	—	3.9
1998 Phi N e	75	87	.463	3	—	3.3
1999 Phi N e	77	85	.475	3	—	-3.5
2000 Phi N e	65	97	.401	5	—	-4.1
2004 Bos A e	98	64	.605	2★✜	—	0.3
2005 Bos A e	95	67	.586	2✜	—	4.3
2006 Bos A e	86	76	.531	3	—	5.5
Total 7	564	570	.497	—	—	9.7

Franks, Herman B1.4.1914

YEAR TM LG	W	L	PCT	FINISH	MGR/YR	+/-
1965 SF N	95	67	.586	2	—	4.5
1966 SF N	93	68	.578	2	—	7.3
1967 SF N	91	71	.562	2	—	-1.1
1968 SF N	88	74	.543	2	—	-1.0
1977 Chi N e	81	81	.500	4	—	4.7
1978 Chi N e	79	83	.488	3	—	4.2
1979 Chi N e	78	77	.503	5-5	1/2	0.6
Total 7	605	521	.537	—	—	19.2

Frazer, George George Kasson; B1.7.1861 Syracuse, NY; D2.5.1913 New York, NY (DNP)

YEAR TM LG	W	L	PCT	FINISH	MGR/YR	+/-
1890 Syr AA	31	40	.437	7-6	1/3	2.0
1890 Syr AA	20	25	.444	7-6	3/3	1.6

Frazier, Joe B10.6.1922

YEAR TM LG	W	L	PCT	FINISH	MGR/YR	+/-
1976 NY N e	86	76	.531	3	—	-3.7
1977 NY N e	15	30	.333	6-6	1/2	-5.2
Total 2	101	106	.488	—	—	-8.9

Fregosi, Jim B4.4.1942

YEAR TM LG	W	L	PCT	FINISH	MGR/YR	+/-
1978 Cal A w	62	54	.534	3-2t	2/2	2.1
1979 Cal A w	88	74	.543	1	—	-2.3
1980 Cal A w	65	95	.406	6	—	-5.3
1981-1 Cal A w	22	25	.468	4-4	1/2	-2.5
1986 Chi A w	45	51	.469	5-5	3/3	0.4
1987 Chi A w	77	85	.475	5	—	-4.2
1988 Chi A w	71	90	.441	5	—	3.4
1991 Phi N e	74	75	.497	6-3	2/2	4.5
1992 Phi N e	70	92	.432	6	—	-7.8
1993 Phi N e	97	65	.599	1◆	—	3.0
1994 Phi N e	54	61	.470	4	—	-5.9
1995 Phi N e	69	75	.479	2t	—	1.3
1996 Phi N e	67	95	.414	5	—	0.1
1999 Tor A e	84	78	.519	3	—	1.1
2000 Tor A e	83	79	.512	3	—	6.3
Total 15	1028	1094	.484	—	—	-5.9

Frey, Jim James Gottfried; B5.26.1931 Cleveland, OH; BL/TL/5´9˝/170(OF)

YEAR TM LG	W	L	PCT	FINISH	MGR/YR	+/-
1980 KC A w	97	65	.599	1◆	—	4.7
1981-1 KC A w	20	30	.400	5	—	-0.6
1981-2 KC A w	10	10	.500	2t-1	1/2	0.2
1984 Chi N e	96	65	.596	1	—	5.0
1985 Chi N e	77	84	.478	4	—	0.9
1986 Chi N e	23	33	.411	5-5	1/3	-1.5
Total 5	323	287	.530	—	—	8.6

Frisch, Frankie B9.9.1898

YEAR TM LG	W	L	PCT	FINISH	MGR/YR	+/-
1933 StL N	36	26	.581	5-5	2/2	1.7
1934 StL N	95	58	.621	1★	—	4.5
1935 StL N	96	58	.623	2	—	-0.9
1936 StL N	87	67	.565	2t	—	9.9
1937 StL N	81	73	.526	4	—	-1.4
1938 StL N	63	72	.467	6-6	1/2	-4.8
1940 Pit N	78	76	.506	4	—	-1.4
1941 Pit N	81	73	.526	4	—	-0.8
1942 Pit N	66	81	.449	5	—	-2.6
1943 Pit N	80	74	.519	4	—	-3.7
1944 Pit N	90	63	.588	2	—	5.3
1945 Pit N	82	72	.532	4	—	-1.6
1946 Pit N	62	89	.411	7-7	1/2	-1.3
1949 Chi N	42	62	.404	7-8	2/2	2.2
1950 Chi N	64	89	.418	7	—	0.3
1951 Chi N	35	45	.438	7-8	1/2	2.1
Total 16	1138	1078	.514	—	—	7.4

Fuchs, Judge Emil Edwin; B4.17.1878 Hamburg, Germany; D12.5.1961 Boston, MA (DNP)

YEAR TM LG	W	L	PCT	FINISH	MGR/YR	+/-
1929 Bos N	56	98	.364	8	—	-0.2

Gaffney, John John H.; B6.29.1855 Roxbury, MA; D8.8.1913 New York, NY (DNP)

YEAR TM LG	W	L	PCT	FINISH	MGR/YR	+/-
1886 Was N	15	25	.375	8	2/2	6.0
1887 Was N	46	76	.377	7	—	5.0
Total 2	61	101	.377	—	—	11.0

Galante, Matt Matthew Joseph; B3.22.1944 Brooklyn, NY; BR/TR/5´6˝/175(2B)

YEAR TM LG	W	L	PCT	FINISH	MGR/YR	+/-
1999 Hou N c	13	14	.481	1t-1	2/3	-2.9

Galvin, Jim B12.25.1856

YEAR TM LG	W	L	PCT	FINISH	MGR/YR	+/-
1885 Buf N	7	17	.292	7-7	1/2	0.1

Ganzel, John B4.7.1874

YEAR TM LG	W	L	PCT	FINISH	MGR/YR	+/-
1908 Cin N	73	81	.474	5	—	2.4
1915 Bro F	17	18	.486	7-7	2/2	0.1
Total 2	90	99	.476	—	—	2.5

Garcia, Dave David; B9.15.1920 E.St.Louis, IL; BR/TR/6´0˝/180(2B)

YEAR TM LG	W	L	PCT	FINISH	MGR/YR	+/-
1977 Cal A w	35	46	.432	5-5	2/2	-4.5
1978 Cal A w	25	21	.543	3-2t	1/2	1.3
1979 Cle A e	38	28	.576	6-6	2/2	6.8
1980 Cle A e	79	81	.494	6	—	5.7
1981-1 Cle A e	26	24	.520	6	—	1.6
1981-2 Cle A e	26	27	.491	5	—	1.6
1982 Cle A e	78	84	.481	6t	—	3.6
Total 6	307	311	.497	—	—	16.1

Gardenhire, Ron B10.24.1957

YEAR TM LG	W	L	PCT	FINISH	MGR/YR	+/-
2002 Min A c	94	67	.584	1☆	—	8.0
2003 Min A c	90	72	.556	1	—	4.8
2004 Min A c	92	70	.568	1	—	4.6
2005 Min A c	83	79	.512	3	—	-0.7
2006 Min A c	96	66	.593	1	—	3.3
Total 5	455	354	.562	—	—	20.0

Gardner, Billy B7.19.1927

YEAR TM LG	W	L	PCT	FINISH	MGR/YR	+/-
1981-1 Min A w	6	14	.300	6-7	2/2	-1.9
1981-2 Min A w	24	29	.453	4	—	-1.9
1982 Min A w	60	102	.370	7	—	-4.9
1983 Min A w	70	92	.432	5	—	0.0
1984 Min A w	81	81	.500	2	—	0.2
1985 Min A w	27	35	.435	6-4	1/2	-1.1
1987 KC A w	62	64	.492	4-2	1/2	-2.9
Total 6	330	417	.442	—	—	-12.5

Garner, Phil B4.30.1949

YEAR TM LG	W	L	PCT	FINISH	MGR/YR	+/-
1992 Mil A e	92	70	.568	2	—	-3.2
1993 Mil A e	69	93	.426	7	—	-6.2
1994 Mil A c	53	62	.461	5	—	-0.8
1995 Mil A c	65	79	.451	4	—	-6.3
1996 Mil A c	80	82	.494	3	—	-0.5
1997 Mil A c	78	83	.484	3	—	3.7
1998 Mil N c	74	88	.457	5	—	3.3
1999 Mil N c	52	60	.464	5-5	1/2	0.6
2000 Det A c	79	83	.488	3	—	-1.6
2001 Det A c	66	96	.407	4	—	-0.5
2002 Det A c	0	6	.000	5-5	1/2	-1.9
2004 Hou N c	48	26	.649	5-2☆✜	2/2	6.3
2005 Hou N c	89	73	.549	2◆✜	—	-0.9
2006 Hou N c	82	90	.477	2	—	-0.6
Total 14	927	991	.483	—	—	-8.8

Gaston, Cito B3.17.1944

YEAR TM LG	W	L	PCT	FINISH	MGR/YR	+/-
1989 Tor A e	77	49	.611	6-1	2/2	7.6
1990 Tor A e	86	76	.531	2	—	-5.7
1991 Tor A e	66	54	.550	1-1	1/3	1.1
1991 Tor A e	6	3	.667	1-1	3/3	1.1
1992 Tor A e	96	66	.593	1★	—	5.2
1993 Tor A e	95	67	.586	1★	—	3.9
1994 Tor A e	55	60	.478	3	—	-1.3
1995 Tor A e	56	88	.389	5	—	-3.1
1996 Tor A e	74	88	.457	4	—	-2.9
1997 Tor A e	72	85	.459	5-5	1/2	-2.5
Total 9	683	636	.518	—	—	3.6

Gerhardt, Joe B2.14.1855

YEAR TM LG	W	L	PCT	FINISH	MGR/YR	+/-
1883 Lou AA	52	45	.536	5	—	3.3
1890 StL AA	20	16	.556	2-3	6/6	-1.2
Total 2	72	61	.541	—	—	2.2

Gessler, Doc B12.23.1880

YEAR TM LG	W	L	PCT	FINISH	MGR/YR	+/-
1914 Pit F	3	8	.273	8-7	1/2	-1.8

Gibbons, John B6.8.1962

YEAR TM LG	W	L	PCT	FINISH	MGR/YR	+/-
2004 Tor A e	20	20	.500	5-5	2/2	2.5
2005 Tor A e	80	82	.494	3	—	-7.9
2006 Tor A e	87	75	.537	2	—	0.7
Total 3	187	177	.514	—	—	-4.8

Gibson, George B7.22.1880

YEAR TM LG	W	L	PCT	FINISH	MGR/YR	+/-
1920 Pit N	79	75	.513	4	—	4.5
1921 Pit N	90	63	.588	2	—	3.4
1922 Pit N	32	33	.492	5-3t	1/2	-5.6
1925 Chi N	12	14	.462	7-8	3/3	-0.2
1932 Pit N	86	68	.558	2	—	10.0
1933 Pit N	87	67	.565	2	—	5.0
1934 Pit N	27	24	.529	4-5	1/2	0.8
Total 7	413	344	.546	—	—	17.9

Gifford, Jim James H.; B10.18.1845 Warren, NY; D12.19.1901 Columbus, OH (DNP)

YEAR TM LG	W	L	PCT	FINISH	MGR/YR	+/-
1884 Ind AA	25	60	.294	10-11	1/2	3.5
1885 NY AA	44	64	.407	7	—	4.5
1886 NY AA	5	12	.294	8-7	1/2	-1.9
Total 3	74	136	.352	—	—	6.1

Girardi, Joe B10.14.1964

YEAR TM LG	W	L	PCT	FINISH	MGR/YR	+/-
2006 Fla N e	78	84	.481	4	—	-1.6

Glasscock, Jack B7.22.1857

YEAR TM LG	W	L	PCT	FINISH	MGR/YR	+/-
1889 Ind N	34	32	.515	7-7	2/2	4.1
1892-1 StL N	1	3	.250	10-9	1/3	-0.5
Total 2	35	35	.500	—	—	3.7

Gleason, Kid B10.26.1866

YEAR TM LG	W	L	PCT	FINISH	MGR/YR	+/-
1919 Chi A	88	52	.629	1	—	4.4
1920 Chi A	96	58	.623	2	—	6.4
1921 Chi A	62	92	.403	7	—	1.6
1922 Chi A	77	77	.500	5	—	0.0
1923 Chi A	69	85	.448	7	—	-3.1
Total 5	392	364	.519	—	—	9.3

Gomez, Preston B4.20.1923

YEAR TM LG	W	L	PCT	FINISH	MGR/YR	+/-
1969 SD N w	52	110	.321	6	—	1.5
1970 SD N w	63	99	.389	6	—	-7.3
1971 SD N w	61	100	.379	6	—	-5.2
1972 SD N w	4	7	.364	4-6	1/2	-0.1
1974 Hou N w	81	81	.500	4	—	-2.2
1975 Hou N w	47	80	.370	6-6	1/2	-12.7
1980 Chi N e	38	52	.422	6-6	1/2	-0.4
Total 7	346	529	.395	—	—	-26.5

Gonzalez, Mike B9.24.1890

YEAR TM LG	W	L	PCT	FINISH	MGR/YR	+/-
1938 StL N	8	8	.500	6-6	2/2	-0.0
1940 StL N	1	5	.167	6-7-3	2/3	-2.2
Total 2	9	13	.409	—	—	-2.2

Gordon, Joe B2.18.1915

YEAR TM LG	W	L	PCT	FINISH	MGR/YR	+/-
1958 Cle A	46	40	.535	6-4	2/2	-0.4
1959 Cle A	89	65	.578	2	—	2.1
1960 Cle A	49	46	.516	4-4	1/3	3.1
1960 Det A	26	31	.456	6-6	3/3	-2.1
1961 KC A	26	33	.441	8-9t	1/2	2.9
1969 KC A w	69	93	.426	4	—	-1.1
Total 5	305	308	.498	—	—	4.6

Gore, George B5.3.1857

YEAR TM LG	W	L	PCT	FINISH	MGR/YR	+/-
1892-2 StL N	6	9	.400	12-12-11	2/3	0.5

Goryl, Johnny B10.21.1933

YEAR TM LG	W	L	PCT	FINISH	MGR/YR	+/-
1980 Min A w	23	13	.639	4-3	2/2	6.2
1981-1 Min A w	11	25	.306	6-7	1/2	-3.2
Total 2	34	38	.472	—	—	3.0

THE MANAGER REGISTER

YEAR TM LG	W	L	PCT	FINISH	MGR/YR	+/-
GOULD, CHARLIE B8.21.1847						
1875 NH NA	2	21	.087	11-8	1/3	0.1
1876 Cin N	9	56	.138	8	—	5.4
Total 2	11	77	.125	—	—	5.5
GOWDY, HANK B8.24.1889						
1946 Cin N	3	1	.750	6-6	2/2	1.1
GRAFFEN, MASE Samuel Mason; B1845 Philadelphia, PA; D11.18.1883 Silver City, NM (DNP)						
1876 StL N	39	17	.696	2-2	1/2	-2.3
GRAMMAS, ALEX B4.3.1926						
1969 Pit N e	4	1	.800	3-3	2/2	1.3
1976 Mil A e	66	95	.410	6	—	-5.3
1977 Mil A e	67	95	.414	6	—	-1.2
Total 3	137	191	.418	—	—	-5.1
GREEN, DALLAS B8.4.1934						
1979 Phi N e	19	11	.633	5-4	2/2	4.7
1980 Phi N e	91	71	.562	1★	—	0.8
1981-1 Phi N e	34	21	.618	1	—	3.6
1981-2 Phi N e	25	27	.481	3	—	3.6
1989 NY A e	56	65	.463	6-5	1/2	2.5
1993 NY N e	46	78	.371	7-7	2/2	-10.4
1994 NY N e	55	58	.487	3	—	0.5
1995 NY N e	69	75	.479	2t	—	-6.9
1996 NY N e	59	72	.450	4-4	1/2	-3.9
Total 8	454	478	.487	—	—	-5.6
GRIFFIN, MIKE B3.20.1865						
1898 Bro N	1	3	.250	9-9-10	2/3	-0.5
GRIFFIN, SANDY B10.24.1858						
1891 Was AA	2	4	.333	8-8	4/4	0.4
GRIFFITH, CLARK B11.20.1869						
1901 Chi A	83	53	.610	1	—	-2.3
1902 Chi A	74	60	.552	4	—	-0.2
1903 NY A	72	62	.537	4	—	4.4
1904 NY A	92	59	.609	2	—	8.5
1905 NY A	71	78	.477	6	—	0.2
1906 NY A	90	61	.596	2	—	4.0
1907 NY A	70	78	.473	5	—	2.4
1908 NY A	24	32	.429	6-8	1/2	6.0
1909 Cin N	77	76	.503	4	—	-0.3
1910 Cin N	75	79	.487	5	—	4.6
1911 Cin N	70	83	.458	6	—	-4.1
1912 Was A	91	61	.599	2	—	2.7
1913 Was A	90	64	.584	2	—	9.3
1914 Was A	81	73	.526	3	—	-2.1
1915 Was A	85	68	.556	4	—	-0.4
1916 Was A	76	77	.497	7	—	0.3
1917 Was A	74	79	.484	5	—	-0.0
1918 Was A	72	56	.563	3	—	2.3
1919 Was A	56	84	.400	7	—	-10.0
1920 Was A	68	84	.447	6	—	-0.5
Total 20	1491	1367	.522	—	—	24.9
GRIMES, BURLEIGH B8.18.1893						
1937 Bro N	62	91	.405	6	—	1.1
1938 Bro N	69	80	.463	7	—	-4.9
Total 2	131	171	.434	—	—	-3.8
GRIMM, CHARLIE B8.28.1898						
1932 Chi N	37	18	.673	2-1	2/2	6.4
1933 Chi N	86	68	.558	3	—	-2.9
1934 Chi N	86	65	.570	3	—	3.8
1935 Chi N	100	54	.649	1	—	-1.5
1936 Chi N	87	67	.565	2t	—	-5.4
1937 Chi N	93	61	.604	2	—	3.6
1938 Chi N	45	36	.556	3-1	1/2	-1.9
1944 Chi N	74	69	.517	8-4	3/3	-0.6
1945 Chi N	98	56	.636	1	—	-0.3
1946 Chi N	82	71	.536	3	—	0.7
1947 Chi N	69	85	.448	6	—	7.9
1948 Chi N	64	90	.416	8	—	-1.8
1949 Chi N	19	31	.380	7-8	1/2	-0.1
1952 Bos N	51	67	.432	7-7	2/2	-1.2
1953 Mil N	92	62	.597	2	—	-0.4
1954 Mil N	89	65	.578	3	—	-0.1
1955 Mil N	85	69	.552	2	—	0.6
1956 Mil N	24	22	.522	5-2	1/2	-3.4
1960 Chi N	6	11	.353	7-7	1/2	-0.9
Total 19	1287	1067	.547	—	—	2.4
GROH, HEINIE B9.18.1889						
1918 Cin N	7	3	.700	4-3	2/2	1.7
GUILLEN, OZZIE B1.20.1964						
2004 Chi A c	83	79	.512	2	—	-1.2
2005 Chi A c	99	63	.611	1★	—	8.2
2006 Chi A c	90	72	.556	3	—	2.1
Total 3	272	214	.560	—	—	9.1
GUTTERIDGE, DON B6.19.1912						
1969 Chi A w	60	85	.414	4-5	2/2	-3.4
1970 Chi A w	49	87	.360	6-6	1/3	-3.1
Total 2	109	172	.388	—	—	-6.5
HAAS, EDDIE B5.26.1935						
1985 Atl N w	50	71	.413	5-5	1/2	0.8
HACK, STAN B12.6.1909						
1954 Chi N	64	90	.416	7	—	-6.6
1955 Chi N	72	81	.471	6	—	4.4
1956 Chi N	60	94	.390	8	—	-5.4
1958 StL N	3	7	.300	5-5t	2/2	-1.4
Total 4	199	272	.423	—	—	-9.1
HACKETT, CHARLIE Charles Michael; B1855 Lee, MA; D8.1.1898 Holyoke, MA (DNP)						
1884 Cle N	35	77	.313	7	—	3.0
1885 Bro AA	15	22	.405	7-5t	1/2	-2.7
Total 2	50	99	.336	—	—	0.3
HALLMAN, BILL B3.31.1867						
1897 StL N	13	36	.265	12-12-12	3/4	4.2
HANEY, FRED B4.25.1898						
1939 StL A	43	111	.279	8	—	-7.1
1940 StL A	67	87	.435	6	—	1.6
1941 StL A	15	29	.341	7-6t	1/2	-5.4
1953 Pit N	50	104	.325	8	—	-1.6
1954 Pit N	53	101	.344	8	—	4.6
1955 Pit N	60	94	.390	8	—	4.2
1956 Mil N	68	40	.630	5-2	2/2	3.7
1957 Mil N	95	59	.617	1★	—	2.0
1958 Mil N	92	62	.597	1	—	0.7
1959 Mil N	86	70	.551	2▲	—	-2.3
Total 10	629	757	.454	—	—	0.4
HANLON, NED B8.22.1857						
1889 Pit N	26	18	.591	7-5	3/3	6.2
1890 Pit P	60	68	.469	6	—	0.7
1891 Pit N	31	47	.397	8-8	1/2	-4.5
1892-1 Bal N	17	39	.304	12-12	3/3	-3.0
1892-2 Bal N	26	46	.361	10	—	-6.5
1893 Bal N	60	70	.462	8	—	1.0
1894 Bal N	89	39	.695	1	—	-1.9
1895 Bal N	87	43	.669	1	—	-8.8
1896 Bal N	90	39	.698	1●	—	-2.7
1897 Bal N	90	40	.692	2●	—	-0.1
1898 Bal N	96	53	.644	2	—	-7.8
1899 Bro N	100	47	.680	1	—	5.2
1900 Bro N	82	54	.603	1●	—	5.4
1901 Bro N	79	57	.581	3	—	-2.8
1902 Bro N	75	63	.543	2	—	1.1
1903 Bro N	70	66	.515	5	—	3.4
1904 Bro N	56	97	.366	6	—	-7.4
1905 Bro N	48	104	.316	8	—	3.0
1906 Cin N	64	87	.424	6	—	-6.0
1907 Cin N	66	87	.431	6	—	-11.3
Total 19	1312	1164	.530	—	—	-36.6
HARDER, MEL B10.15.1909						
1961 Cle A	1	0	1.000	5-5	2/2	0.5
1962 Cle A	2	0	1.000	6-6	2/2	1.1
Total 2	3	0	1.000	—	—	1.6
HARGROVE, MIKE B10.26.1949						
1991 Cle A e	32	53	.376	7-7	2/2	-0.5
1992 Cle A e	76	86	.469	4t	—	2.3
1993 Cle A e	76	86	.469	6	—	-2.8
1994 Cle A c	66	47	.584	2	—	-1.1
1995 Cle A c	100	44	.694	1◆	—	5.9
1996 Cle A c	99	62	.615	1	—	1.7
1997 Cle A c	86	75	.534	1◆	—	0.6
1998 Cle A c	89	73	.549	1☆	—	1.3
1999 Cle A c	97	65	.599	1	—	2.8
2000 Bal A e	74	88	.457	4	—	4.0
2001 Bal A e	63	98	.391	4	—	-3.6
2002 Bal A e	67	95	.414	4	—	-3.3
2003 Bal A e	71	91	.438	4	—	-2.5
2005 Sea A w	69	93	.426	4	—	-6.8
2006 Sea A w	78	84	.481	4	—	0.5
Total 15	1143	1140	.501	—	—	-1.4
HARRAH, TOBY B10.26.1948						
1992 Tex A w	32	44	.421	3-4	2/2	-2.6
HARRELSON, BUD B6.6.1944						
1990 NY N e	71	49	.592	4-2	2/2	-1.3
1991 NY N e	74	80	.481	3-5	1/2	-2.4
Total 2	145	129	.529	—	—	-3.7
HARRIS, LUM B1.17.1915						
1961 Bal A	17	10	.630	3-3	2/2	1.7
1964 Hou N	5	8	.385	9-9	2/2	-0.3
1965 Hou N	65	97	.401	9	—	-0.8
1968 Atl N	81	81	.500	5	—	4.1
1969 Atl N w	93	69	.574	1	—	5.7
1970 Atl N w	76	86	.469	5	—	-1.5
1971 Atl N w	82	80	.506	3	—	6.8
1972 Atl N w	47	57	.452	4-4	1/2	2.0
Total 8	466	488	.488	—	—	17.7
HARRIS, BUCKY B11.8.1896						
1924 Was A	92	62	.597	1★	—	0.6
1925 Was A	96	55	.636	1	—	5.3
1926 Was A	81	69	.540	4	—	2.2
1927 Was A	85	69	.552	3	—	3.0
1928 Was A	75	79	.487	4	—	-3.3
1929 Det A	70	84	.455	6	—	-6.8
1930 Det A	75	79	.487	5	—	2.6
1931 Det A	61	93	.396	7	—	1.9
1932 Det A	76	75	.503	5	—	-0.6
1933 Det A	73	79	.480	5-5	1/2	-1.9
1934 Bos A	76	76	.500	4	—	-4.2
1935 Was A	67	86	.438	6	—	-2.3
1936 Was A	82	71	.536	4	—	-2.6
1937 Was A	73	80	.477	6	—	4.4
1938 Was A	75	76	.497	5	—	4.8
1939 Was A	65	87	.428	6	—	-1.9
1940 Was A	64	90	.416	7	—	1.1
1941 Was A	70	84	.455	6t	—	-0.3
1942 Was A	62	89	.411	7	—	2.3
1943 Phi N	38	52	.422	7-7	1/2	-0.5
1947 NY A	97	57	.630	1★	—	-2.9
1948 NY A	94	60	.610	3	—	-4.6
1950 Was A	67	87	.435	5	—	1.9
1951 Was A	62	92	.403	7	—	-6.0
1952 Was A	78	76	.506	5	—	2.1
1953 Was A	76	76	.500	5	—	-7.5
1954 Was A	66	88	.429	6	—	-6.1
1955 Det A	79	75	.513	5	—	-9.5
1956 Det A	82	72	.532	5	—	-3.7
Total 29	2157	2218	.493	—	—	-32.5
HART, JIM James Aristotle; B7.10.1855 Fairview, PA; D7.18.1919 Chicago, IL (DNP)						
1885 Lou AA	53	59	.473	5t	—	0.2
1886 Lou AA	66	70	.485	4	—	-4.4
1889 Bos N	83	45	.648	2	—	0.8
Total 3	202	174	.537	—	—	-3.4
HART, JOHN John Henry (b John Henry Reen); B7.21.1948 Tampa, FL; BR/TR/6´1˝/180(C)						
1989 Cle A e	8	11	.421	6-6	2/2	-0.9
HARTNETT, GABBY B12.20.1900						
1938 Chi N	44	27	.620	3-1	2/2	2.9
1939 Chi N	84	70	.545	4	—	2.4
1940 Chi N	75	79	.487	5	—	-6.6
Total 3	203	176	.536	—	—	-1.3
HARTSFIELD, ROY B10.25.1925						
1977 Tor A e	54	107	.335	7	—	-4.6
1978 Tor A e	59	102	.366	7	—	-2.4
1979 Tor A e	53	109	.327	7	—	-3.2
Total 3	166	318	.343	—	—	-10.3
HASTINGS, SCOTT B8.10.1847						
1871 Rok NA	4	21	.160	9	—	-4.8
1872 Cle NA	6	14	.300	6-7	1/2	0.9
Total 2	10	35	.222	—	—	-3.9
HATFIELD, JOHN B7.20.1847						
1872 Mut NA	24	14	.632	4-3	2/2	-3.6
1873 Mut NA	11	17	.393	5-4	1/2	-4.6
Total 2	35	31	.530	—	—	-8.1
HATTON, GRADY B10.7.1922						
1966 Hou N	72	90	.444	8	—	-0.2
1967 Hou N	69	93	.426	9	—	-0.0
1968 Hou N	23	38	.377	10-10	1/2	-4.1
Total 3	164	221	.426	—	—	-4.3
HECKER, GUY B4.3.1856						
1890 Pit N	23	113	.169	8	—	7.5
HEFFNER, DON B2.8.1911						
1966 Cin N	37	46	.446	8-7	1/2	-4.0
HEILBRONER, LOUIE Louis Wilbur; B7.4.1861 Ft.Wayne, IN; D12.21.1933 Ft.Wayne, IN (DNP)						
1900 StL N	23	25	.479	7-5t	2/2	-0.9
HELMS, TOMMY B5.5.1941						
1988 Cin N w	12	15	.444	4-4-2	2/3	-2.3
1989 Cin N w	16	21	.432	4t-5	2/2	-1.1
Total 2	28	36	.438	—	—	-3.4
HEMUS, SOLLY B4.17.1923						
1959 StL N	71	83	.461	7	—	2.5
1960 StL N	86	68	.558	3	—	6.6
1961 StL N	33	41	.446	6-5	1/2	-5.7
Total 3	190	192	.497	—	—	3.3
HENDERSON, BILL William C.; (DNP)						
1884 Bal U	58	47	.552	4	—	2.5
HENDRICKS, JACK B4.9.1875						
1918 StL N	51	78	.395	8	—	-5.5
1924 Cin N	83	70	.542	4	—	-0.9
1925 Cin N	80	73	.523	3	—	-1.3
1926 Cin N	87	67	.565	2	—	0.3
1927 Cin N	75	78	.490	5	—	-0.5
1928 Cin N	78	74	.513	5	—	5.9
1929 Cin N	66	88	.429	7	—	-3.7
Total 7	520	528	.496	—	—	-5.7
HENGLE, ED Edward Siegfried; B Chicago, IL; D11.4.1927 Norwich, England (DNP)						
1884 CP U	34	39	.466	5	1/3	0.9
HERMAN, BILLY B7.7.1909						
1947 Pit N	61	92	.399	8-7t	1/2	-8.7
1964 Bos A	2	0	1.000	8-8	2/2	1.1
1965 Bos A	62	100	.383	9	—	-6.8
1966 Bos A	64	82	.438	9-9	1/2	-2.0
Total 4	189	274	.408	—	—	-16.4

Herzog, Buck B7.9.1885

YEAR	TM LG	W	L	PCT	FINISH	MGR/YR	+/-
1914	Cin N	60	94	.390	8	—	-3.8
1915	Cin N	71	83	.461	7	—	1.9
1916	Cin N	34	49	.410	8-7t	1/3	-0.7
Total	3	165	226	.422	—	—	-2.6

Herzog, Whitey B11.9.1931

YEAR	TM LG	W	L	PCT	FINISH	MGR/YR	+/-
1973	Tex A w	47	91	.341	6-6	1/3	-2.9
1974	Cal A w	2	2	.500	6-6-6	2/3	0.1
1975	KC A w	41	25	.621	2-2	2/2	5.4
1976	KC A w	90	72	.556	1	—	-1.7
1977	KC A w	102	60	.630	1	—	4.0
1978	KC A w	92	70	.568	1	—	-0.2
1979	KC A w	85	77	.525	2	—	0.7
1980	StL N e	38	35	.521	6-5-4	3/4	0.2
1981-1	StL N e	30	20	.600	2	—	3.2
1981-2	StL N e	29	23	.558	2	—	3.2
1982	StL N e	92	70	.568	1★	—	2.9
1983	StL N e	79	83	.488	4	—	1.2
1984	StL N e	84	78	.519	3	—	2.3
1985	StL N e	101	61	.623	1◆	—	1.6
1986	StL N e	79	82	.491	3	—	-0.4
1987	StL N e	95	67	.586	1◆	—	3.6
1988	StL N e	76	86	.469	5	—	1.0
1989	StL N e	86	76	.531	3	—	2.4
1990	StL N e	33	47	.412	6-6	1/3	-1.8
Total	18	1281	1125	.532	—	—	24.8

Hewett, Walter Walter F.; B1861 Washington, DC; D10.7.1944 Washington, DC (DNP)

YEAR	TM LG	W	L	PCT	FINISH	MGR/YR	+/-
1888	Was N	10	29	.256	8-8	1/2	-2.2

Hicks, Nat B4.19.1845

YEAR	TM LG	W	L	PCT	FINISH	MGR/YR	+/-
1874	Phi NA	29	29	.500	4	—	-3.6
1875	Mut NA	30	38	.441	7	—	4.9
Total	2	59	67	.468	—	—	1.3

Higgins, Pinky B5.27.1909

YEAR	TM LG	W	L	PCT	FINISH	MGR/YR	+/-
1955	Bos A	84	70	.545	4	—	-3.2
1956	Bos A	84	70	.545	4	—	4.2
1957	Bos A	82	72	.532	3	—	-0.3
1958	Bos A	79	75	.513	3	—	1.4
1959	Bos A	31	42	.425	8-8	1/3	-6.9
1960	Bos A	48	57	.457	8-7	3/3	3.3
1961	Bos A	76	86	.469	6	—	1.2
1962	Bos A	76	84	.475	8	—	0.9
Total	8	560	556	.502	—	—	0.6

Higham, Dick B7.24.1851

YEAR	TM LG	W	L	PCT	FINISH	MGR/YR	+/-
1874	Mut NA	29	11	.725	3-2	2/2	2.8

Himsl, Vedie Avitus Bernard; B4.2.1917 Plevna, MT; D3.1.2004 Chicago, IL BR/TR/6´1˝/200(P)

YEAR	TM LG	W	L	PCT	FINISH	MGR/YR	+/-
1961	Chi N	5	6	.455	6-6t	1/9	0.3
1961	Chi N	5	12	.294	7-7-7	3/9	-2.3
1961	Chi N	0	3	.000	7-7-7	6/9	-1.3

Hitchcock, Billy B7.31.1916

YEAR	TM LG	W	L	PCT	FINISH	MGR/YR	+/-
1960	Det A	1	0	1.000	6-6-6	2/3	0.5
1962	Bal A	77	85	.475	7	—	-1.1
1963	Bal A	86	76	.531	4	—	2.5
1966	Atl N	33	18	.647	7-5	2/2	4.4
1967	Atl N	77	82	.484	7-7	1/2	-1.6
Total	5	274	261	.512	—	—	4.8

Hobson, Butch B8.17.1951

YEAR	TM LG	W	L	PCT	FINISH	MGR/YR	+/-
1992	Bos A e	73	89	.451	7	—	-0.5
1993	Bos A e	80	82	.494	5	—	0.2
1994	Bos A e	54	61	.470	4	—	3.0
Total	3	207	232	.472	—	—	2.7

Hodges, Gil B4.4.1924

YEAR	TM LG	W	L	PCT	FINISH	MGR/YR	+/-
1963	Was A	42	79	.347	10-10	3/3	-0.6
1964	Was A	62	100	.383	9	—	-2.7
1965	Was A	70	92	.432	8	—	2.7
1966	Was A	71	88	.447	8	—	2.6
1967	Was A	76	85	.472	6t	—	5.1
1968	NY N	73	89	.451	9	—	-4.8
1969	NY N e	100	62	.617	1★	—	8.9
1970	NY N e	83	79	.512	3	—	-4.8
1971	NY N e	83	79	.512	3t	—	-2.3
Total	9	660	753	.467	—	—	4.1

Hoey, Fred Frederick Chamberlain; B1866 New York, NY; D12.7.1933 Paris, France (DNP)

YEAR	TM LG	W	L	PCT	FINISH	MGR/YR	+/-
1899	NY N	31	55	.360	9-10	2/2	-5.3

Hoffman, Glenn B7.7.1958

YEAR	TM LG	W	L	PCT	FINISH	MGR/YR	+/-
1998	LA N w	47	41	.534	3-3	2/2	3.5

Holbert, Bill B3.14.1855

YEAR	TM LG	W	L	PCT	FINISH	MGR/YR	+/-
1879	Syr N	0	1	.000	6-6-7	2/3	-0.3

Hollingshead, Holly B1.17.1853

YEAR	TM LG	W	L	PCT	FINISH	MGR/YR	+/-
1875	Was NA	4	16	.200	8-10	1/2	6.4
1884	Was AA	12	50	.194	12-12	1/2	1.2
Total	2	16	66	.195	—	—	7.6

Holmes, Tommy B3.29.1917

YEAR	TM LG	W	L	PCT	FINISH	MGR/YR	+/-
1951	Bos N	48	47	.505	5-4	2/2	-3.3
1952	Bos N	13	22	.371	7-7	1/2	-2.5
Total	2	61	69	.469	—	—	-5.8

Hornsby, Rogers B4.27.1896

YEAR	TM LG	W	L	PCT	FINISH	MGR/YR	+/-
1925	StL N	64	51	.557	8-4	2/2	2.0
1926	StL N	89	65	.578	1★	—	-1.5
1927	NY N	22	10	.688	4-3	2/2	4.1
1928	Bos N	39	83	.320	7-7	2/2	-3.2
1930	Chi N	4	0	1.000	2-2	2/2	1.7
1931	Chi N	84	70	.545	3	—	-4.3
1932	Chi N	53	46	.535	2-1	1/2	-2.2
1933	StL A	19	33	.365	8-8	3/3	-2.0
1934	StL A	67	85	.441	6	—	3.2
1935	StL A	65	87	.428	7	—	8.5
1936	StL A	57	95	.375	7	—	3.5
1937	StL A	25	52	.325	7-8	1/2	0.3
1952	StL A	22	29	.431	8-7	1/2	0.9
1952	Cin N	27	24	.529	7-6	3/3	3.0
1953	Cin N	64	82	.438	6-6	1/2	-2.2
Total	14	701	812	.463	—	—	11.9

Houk, Ralph B8.9.1919

YEAR	TM LG	W	L	PCT	FINISH	MGR/YR	+/-
1961	NY A	109	53	.673	1★	—	6.3
1962	NY A	96	66	.593	1★	—	1.5
1963	NY A	104	57	.646	1	—	5.6
1966	NY A	66	73	.475	10-10	2/2	-3.4
1967	NY A	72	90	.444	9	—	2.2
1968	NY A	83	79	.512	5	—	1.4
1969	NY A e	80	81	.497	5	—	2.3
1970	NY A e	93	69	.574	2	—	4.8
1971	NY A e	82	80	.506	4	—	0.3
1972	NY A e	79	76	.510	4	—	-1.9
1973	NY A e	80	82	.494	4	—	-4.3
1974	Det A e	72	90	.444	6	—	6.2
1975	Det A e	57	102	.358	6	—	-0.3
1976	Det A e	74	87	.460	5	—	4.0
1977	Det A e	74	88	.457	4	—	-3.3
1978	Det A e	86	76	.531	5	—	-1.3
1981-1	Bos A e	30	26	.536	5	—	1.3
1981-2	Bos A e	29	23	.558	2t	—	1.3
1982	Bos A e	89	73	.549	3	—	4.0
1983	Bos A e	78	84	.481	6	—	2.0
1984	Bos A e	86	76	.531	4	—	0.6
Total	20	1619	1531	.514	—	—	29.0

Howard, Frank B8.8.1936

YEAR	TM LG	W	L	PCT	FINISH	MGR/YR	+/-
1981-1	SD N w	23	33	.411	6	—	-6.1
1981-2	SD N w	18	36	.333	6	—	-6.1
1983	NY N e	52	64	.448	6-6	2/2	2.1
Total	2	93	133	.412	—	—	-10.0

Howe, Art B12.15.1946

YEAR	TM LG	W	L	PCT	FINISH	MGR/YR	+/-
1989	Hou N w	86	76	.531	3	—	7.3
1990	Hou N w	75	87	.463	4t	—	3.0
1991	Hou N w	65	97	.401	6	—	-4.2
1992	Hou N w	81	81	.500	4	—	6.4
1993	Hou N w	85	77	.525	3	—	-5.0
1996	Oak A w	78	84	.481	3	—	0.5
1997	Oak A w	65	97	.401	4	—	0.8
1998	Oak A w	74	88	.457	4	—	-1.2
1999	Oak A w	87	75	.537	2	—	1.7
2000	Oak A w	91	70	.565	1	—	-1.7
2001	Oak A w	102	60	.630	2✤	—	-2.3
2002	Oak A w	103	59	.636	1	—	7.4
2003	NY N e	66	95	.410	5	—	-3.1
2004	NY N e	71	91	.438	4	—	-5.2
Total	14	1129	1137	.498	—	—	4.5

Howley, Dan B10.16.1885

YEAR	TM LG	W	L	PCT	FINISH	MGR/YR	+/-
1927	StL A	59	94	.386	7	—	-0.8
1928	StL A	82	72	.532	3	—	2.1
1929	StL A	79	73	.520	4	—	1.0
1930	Cin N	59	95	.383	7	—	0.3
1931	Cin N	58	96	.377	8	—	-3.7
1932	Cin N	60	94	.390	8	—	-2.4
Total	6	397	524	.431	—	—	-3.5

Howser, Dick B5.14.1936

YEAR	TM LG	W	L	PCT	FINISH	MGR/YR	+/-
1978	NY A e	0	1	.000	3-4-1★▲	2/3	-0.6
1980	NY A e	103	59	.636	1	—	6.3
1981-2	KC A w	20	13	.606	2t-1	2/2	3.8
1982	KC A w	90	72	.556	2	—	2.4
1983	KC A w	79	83	.488	2	—	5.1
1984	KC A w	84	78	.519	1	—	4.3
1985	KC A w	91	71	.562	1★	—	5.0
1986	KC A w	40	48	.455	4-3t	1/2	-2.9
Total	8	507	425	.544	—	—	23.4

Huff, George George A. "Gee"; B6.11.1872 Champaign, IL; D10.1.1936 Champaign, IL (DNP)

YEAR	TM LG	W	L	PCT	FINISH	MGR/YR	+/-
1907	Bos A	2	6	.250	4t-6-7	2/4	-1.4

Huggins, Miller B3.27.1878

YEAR	TM LG	W	L	PCT	FINISH	MGR/YR	+/-
1913	StL N	51	99	.340	8	—	-0.5
1914	StL N	81	72	.529	3	—	2.5
1915	StL N	72	81	.471	6	—	-3.3
1916	StL N	60	93	.392	7t	—	0.6
1917	StL N	82	70	.539	3	—	10.0
1918	NY A	60	63	.488	4	—	-3.4
1919	NY A	80	59	.576	3	—	2.7
1920	NY A	95	59	.617	3	—	-2.3
1921	NY A	98	55	.641	1	—	-0.4
1922	NY A	94	60	.610	1	—	2.9
1923	NY A	98	54	.645	1★	—	2.4
1924	NY A	89	63	.586	2	—	0.3
1925	NY A	69	85	.448	7	—	-1.4
1926	NY A	91	63	.591	1	—	1.3
1927	NY A	110	44	.714	1★	—	-2.4
1928	NY A	101	53	.656	1★	—	4.4
1929	NY A	82	61	.573	2-2	1/2	0.0
Total	17	1413	1134	.555	—	—	13.5

Hunter, Billy B6.4.1928

YEAR	TM LG	W	L	PCT	FINISH	MGR/YR	+/-
1977	Tex A w	60	33	.645	5-2	4/4	7.1
1978	Tex A w	86	75	.534	2t-2t	1/2	-0.8
Total	2	146	108	.575	—	—	6.4

Hurdle, Clint B7.30.1957

YEAR	TM LG	W	L	PCT	FINISH	MGR/YR	+/-
2002	Col N w	67	73	.479	5-4	2/2	6.7
2003	Col N w	74	88	.457	4	—	-3.4
2004	Col N w	68	94	.420	4	—	-4.8
2005	Col N w	67	95	.414	5	—	-2.4
2006	Col N w	76	86	.469	5	—	-5.1
Total	5	352	436	.447	—	—	-9.0

Hurst, Tim Timothy Carroll; B6.30.1865 Ashland, PA; D6.4.1915 Pottsville, PA 5-5/(DNP)

YEAR	TM LG	W	L	PCT	FINISH	MGR/YR	+/-
1898	StL N	39	111	.260	12	—	-1.6

Hutchinson, Fred B8.12.1919

YEAR	TM LG	W	L	PCT	FINISH	MGR/YR	+/-
1952	Det A	27	55	.329	8-8	2/2	-4.0
1953	Det A	60	94	.390	6	—	4.4
1954	Det A	68	86	.442	5	—	-0.5
1956	StL N	76	78	.494	4	—	1.0
1957	StL N	87	67	.565	2	—	2.9
1958	StL N	69	75	.479	5-5t	1/2	5.1
1959	Cin N	39	35	.527	7-5t	2/2	0.8
1960	Cin N	67	87	.435	6	—	-4.7
1961	Cin N	93	61	.604	1	—	10.3
1962	Cin N	98	64	.605	3	—	5.4
1963	Cin N	86	76	.531	5	—	-0.9
1964	Cin N	54	45	.545	3-2t	1/4	-1.8
1964	Cin N	6	4	.600	4-3-2t	3/4	0.4
Total	12	830	827	.501	—	—	18.5

Irwin, Arthur B2.14.1858

YEAR	TM LG	W	L	PCT	FINISH	MGR/YR	+/-
1889	Was N	28	45	.384	8-8	2/2	4.8
1891	Bos AA	93	42	.689	1	—	-4.8
1892-1	Was N	35	39	.473	11t-7	2/2	4.3
1892-2	Was N	11	21	.344	11-12	1/2	-2.3
1894	Phi N	71	57	.555	4	—	-6.6
1895	Phi N	78	53	.595	3	—	4.0
1896	NY N	36	53	.404	10-7	1/2	-9.0
1898	Was N	10	19	.345	11-11	4/4	-0.4
1899	Was N	54	98	.355	11	—	-0.4
Total	8	416	427	.493	—	—	-10.4

Jennings, Hughie B4.2.1869

YEAR	TM LG	W	L	PCT	FINISH	MGR/YR	+/-
1907	Det A	92	58	.613	1	—	-0.2
1908	Det A	90	63	.588	1	—	2.7
1909	Det A	98	54	.645	1	—	2.8
1910	Det A	86	68	.558	3	—	-1.0
1911	Det A	89	65	.578	2	—	7.0
1912	Det A	69	84	.451	6	—	-2.0
1913	Det A	66	87	.431	6	—	-1.3
1914	Det A	80	73	.523	4	—	3.8
1915	Det A	100	54	.649	2	—	4.7
1916	Det A	87	67	.565	3	—	2.1
1917	Det A	78	75	.510	4	—	-5.1
1918	Det A	55	71	.437	7	—	0.6
1919	Det A	80	60	.571	4	—	5.9
1920	Det A	61	93	.396	7	—	1.5
1924	NY N	32	12	.727	3-1-1	2/3	4.0
1925	NY N	21	11	.656	1-1-2	2/3	4.3
Total	16	1184	995	.543	—	—	29.9

Johnson, Darrell B8.25.1928

YEAR	TM LG	W	L	PCT	FINISH	MGR/YR	+/-
1974	Bos A e	84	78	.519	3	—	-0.6
1975	Bos A e	95	65	.594	1◆	—	6.5
1976	Bos A e	41	45	.477	5-3	1/2	-5.1
1977	Sea A w	64	98	.395	6	—	5.9
1978	Sea A w	56	104	.350	7	—	-2.1
1979	Sea A w	67	95	.414	6	—	-3.4
1980	Sea A w	39	65	.375	6-7	1/2	-1.0
1982	Tex A w	26	40	.394	6-6	2/2	-0.2
Total	8	472	590	.444	—	—	0.1

Johnson, Davey B1.30.1943

YEAR	TM LG	W	L	PCT	FINISH	MGR/YR	+/-
1984	NY N e	90	72	.556	2	—	11.5
1985	NY N e	98	64	.605	2	—	3.4
1986	NY N e	108	54	.667	1★	—	5.8
1987	NY N e	92	70	.568	2	—	-1.2
1988	NY N e	100	60	.625	1	—	1.5
1989	NY N e	87	75	.537	2	—	-3.4
1990	NY N e	20	22	.476	4-2	1/2	-5.3
1993	Cin N w	53	65	.449	5-5	2/2	-1.5
1994	Cin N c	66	48	.579	1	—	-2.5
1995	Cin N c	85	59	.590	1☆	—	0.9
1996	Bal A e	88	74	.543	2☆✤	—	2.9
1997	Bal A e	98	64	.605	1☆	—	4.1
1999	LA N w	77	85	.475	3	—	-4.6
2000	LA N w	86	76	.531	2	—	-1.7
Total	14	1148	888	.564	—	—	9.8

Johnson, Roy B10.1.1895

YEAR	TM LG	W	L	PCT	FINISH	MGR/YR	+/-
1944	Chi N	0	1	.000	8-8-4	2/3	-0.5

Johnson, Tim B7.22.1949

YEAR	TM LG	W	L	PCT	FINISH	MGR/YR	+/-
1998	Tor A e	88	74	.543	3	—	2.4

YEAR	TM LG	W	L	PCT	FINISH	MGR/YR	+/-
JOHNSON, WALTER B11.6.1887							
1929	Was A	71	81	.467	5	—	-0.6
1930	Was A	94	60	.610	2	—	-2.0
1931	Was A	92	62	.597	3	—	0.4
1932	Was A	93	61	.604	3	—	4.3
1933	Cle A	48	51	.485	5-4	3/3	-0.5
1934	Cle A	85	69	.552	3	—	3.2
1935	Cle A	46	48	.489	5-3	1/2	-3.2
Total 7		529	432	.550	—	—	1.6
JONES, FIELDER B8.13.1871							
1904	Chi A	66	47	.584	4-3	2/2	-0.4
1905	Chi A	92	60	.605	2	—	-2.6
1906	Chi A	93	58	.616	1★	—	4.7
1907	Chi A	87	64	.576	3	—	-1.7
1908	Chi A	88	64	.579	3	—	4.1
1914	StL F	12	26	.316	7-8	2/2	-3.5
1915	StL F	87	67	.565	2	—	-1.9
1916	StL A	79	75	.513	5	—	-2.8
1917	StL A	57	97	.370	7	—	-0.9
1918	StL A	22	24	.478	6-5	1/3	-0.1
Total 10		683	582	.540	—	—	-5.0
JOOST, EDDIE B6.5.1916							
1954	Phi A	51	103	.331	8	—	7.2
JORGENSEN, MIKE B8.16.1948							
1995	StL N c	42	54	.438	4-4	2/2	0.5
JOYCE, BILL B9.21.1865							
1896	NY N	28	14	.667	10-7	2/2	6.8
1897	NY N	83	48	.634	3	—	-0.6
1898	NY N	22	21	.512	6-7	1/3	-0.5
1898	NY N	46	39	.541	7-7	3/3	1.6
Total 3		179	122	.595	—	—	7.3
JURGES, BILLY B5.9.1908							
1959	Bos A	44	36	.550	8-5	3/3	2.5
1960	Bos A	15	27	.357	8-7	1/3	-2.9
Total 2		59	63	.484	—	—	-0.4
KASKO, EDDIE B6.27.1932							
1970	Bos A e	87	75	.537	3	—	-0.3
1971	Bos A e	85	77	.525	3	—	1.5
1972	Bos A e	85	70	.548	2	—	5.4
1973	Bos A e	88	73	.547	2-2	1/2	-1.8
Total 4		345	295	.539	—	—	4.8
KEANE, JOHNNY John Joseph; B11.3.1911 St.Louis, MO; D1.6.1967 Houston, TX BR/TR/5´10˝/165(SS)							
1961	StL N	47	33	.587	6-5	2/2	5.2
1962	StL N	84	78	.519	6	—	-8.1
1963	StL N	93	69	.574	2	—	-0.3
1964	StL N	93	69	.574	1★	—	5.5
1965	NY A	77	85	.475	6	—	-4.8
1966	NY A	4	16	.200	10-10	1/2	-6.0
Total 6		398	350	.532	—	—	-8.5
KELLEY, JOE B12.9.1871							
1902	Cin N	34	26	.567	6-4	3/3	1.0
1903	Cin N	74	65	.532	4	—	-5.8
1904	Cin N	88	65	.575	3	—	-4.3
1905	Cin N	79	74	.516	5	—	-1.2
1908	Bos N	63	91	.409	6	—	-4.6
Total 5		338	321	.513	—	—	-14.9
KELLY, TOM B8.15.1950							
1986	Min A w	12	11	.522	7-6	2/2	1.8
1987	Min A w	85	77	.525	1★	—	5.9
1988	Min A w	91	71	.562	2	—	1.2
1989	Min A w	80	82	.494	5	—	-1.2
1990	Min A w	74	88	.457	7	—	-0.6
1991	Min A w	95	67	.586	1★	—	1.5
1992	Min A w	90	72	.556	2	—	-0.6
1993	Min A w	71	91	.438	5t	—	3.4
1994	Min A c	53	60	.469	4	—	4.9
1995	Min A c	56	88	.389	5	—	0.8
1996	Min A c	78	84	.481	4	—	-0.9
1997	Min A c	68	94	.420	4	—	-4.6
1998	Min A c	70	92	.432	4	—	-2.9
1999	Min A c	63	97	.394	5	—	-1.5
2000	Min A c	69	93	.426	5	—	0.5
2001	Min A c	85	77	.525	2	—	3.5
Total 16		1140	1244	.478	—	—	11.3
KELLY, KICK B10.31.1856							
1887	Lou AA	76	60	.559	4	—	-0.5
1888	Lou AA	10	29	.256	8-7	1/4	-4.8
Total 2		86	89	.491	—	—	-5.3
KELLY, KING B12.31.1857							
1887	Bos N	49	43	.533	5-5	1/2	0.3
1890	Bos P	81	48	.628	1	—	-1.9
1891	Cin AA	43	57	.430	6	—	1.3
Total 3		173	148	.539	—	—	-0.3
KENNEDY, JIM James C.; B1867 New York, NY; D4.20.1904 Brighton Beach, NY (DNP)							
1890	Bro AA	26	73	.263	8	—	-2.3
KENNEDY, KEVIN Kevin Curtis; B9.26.1954 Los Angeles, CA; BR/TR/6´3˝/220(C)							
1993	Tex A w	86	76	.531	2	—	-3.1
1994	Tex A w	52	62	.456	1	—	2.4
1995	Bos A e	86	58	.597	1	—	5.3

YEAR	TM LG	W	L	PCT	FINISH	MGR/YR	+/-
1996	Bos A e	85	77	.525	3	—	3.4
Total 4		309	273	.531	—	—	8.1
KENNEDY, BOB B8.18.1920							
1963	Chi N	82	80	.506	7	—	1.9
1964	Chi N	76	86	.469	8	—	2.7
1965	Chi N	24	32	.429	9-8	1/2	-0.8
1968	Oak A	82	80	.506	6	—	-1.9
Total 4		264	278	.487	—	—	1.9
KERINS, JOHN B7.15.1858							
1888	Lou AA	3	4	.429	8-8-7	3/4	0.3
1890	StL AA	9	8	.529	4-4-3	2/6	-1.0
Total 2		12	12	.500	—	—	-0.6
KERRIGAN, JOE B1.30.1954							
2001	Bos A e	17	26	.395	2-2	2/2	-5.2
KESSINGER, DON B7.17.1942							
1979	Chi A	46	60	.434	5-5	1/2	-5.8
KILLEFER, BILL B10.10.1887							
1921	Chi N	23	34	.404	6-7	2/2	-1.7
1922	Chi N	80	74	.519	5	—	6.5
1923	Chi N	83	71	.539	4	—	0.9
1924	Chi N	81	72	.529	5	—	4.6
1925	Chi N	33	42	.440	7-8	1/3	-2.2
1930	StL A	64	90	.416	6	—	-0.6
1931	StL A	63	91	.409	5	—	-0.1
1932	StL A	63	91	.409	6	—	0.9
1933	StL A	34	57	.374	8-8	1/3	-2.7
Total 9		524	622	.457	—	—	5.7
KIMM, BRUCE B6.29.1951							
2002	Chi N c	28	46	.378	3-4	2/2	-6.6
KING, CLYDE B5.23.1924							
1969	SF N w	90	72	.556	2	—	1.0
1970	SF N w	19	23	.452	4-3	1/2	-2.1
1974	Atl N w	38	25	.603	4-3	2/2	2.3
1975	Atl N w	58	76	.433	5-5	1/2	4.6
1982	NY A e	29	33	.468	5t-5	3/3	-1.7
Total 5		234	229	.505	—	—	4.1
KITTRIDGE, MALACHI B10.12.1869							
1904	Was A	1	16	.059	8-8	1/2	-3.7
KLEIN, LOU B10.22.1918							
1961	Chi N	5	6	.455	7-7-7	8/9	0.3
1962	Chi N	12	18	.400	9-9-9	2/3	0.6
1965	Chi N	48	58	.453	9-8	2/2	1.0
Total 3		65	82	.442	—	—	1.9
KLING, JOHNNY B11.13.1875							
1912	Bos N	52	101	.340	8	—	-7.7
KNABE, OTTO B6.12.1884							
1914	Bal F	84	70	.545	3	—	5.2
1915	Bal F	47	107	.305	8	—	-8.4
Total 2		131	177	.425	—	—	-3.2
KNIGHT, LON B6.16.1853							
1883	Phi AA	66	32	.673	1	—	2.6
1884	Phi AA	61	46	.570	7	—	-6.1
Total 2		127	78	.620	—	—	-3.5
KNIGHT, RAY B12.28.1952							
1996	Cin N c	81	81	.500	3	—	-0.5
1997	Cin N c	43	56	.434	4-3	1/2	0.5
2003	Cin N c	1	0	1.000	5-5-5	2/3	0.6
Total 3		125	137	.477	—	—	0.6
KNOOP, BOBBY B10.18.1938							
1994	Cal A w	1	1	.500	3-2-4	2/3	0.2
KROL, JACK John Thomas; B7.5.1936 Chicago, IL; D5.30.1994 Winston-Salem, NC BR/TR/5´11˝/175(2B)							
1978	StL N e	1	1	.500	6-6-5	2/3	0.1
1980	StL N e	0	1	.000	6-6-4	2/4	-0.5
Total 2		1	2	.333	—	—	-0.4
KUEHL, KARL Karl Otto; B9.5.1937 Monterey Park, CA; BL/TL/5´11˝/175(1B)							
1976	Mon N e	43	85	.336	6-6	1/2	-3.8
KUENN, HARVEY B12.4.1930							
1975	Mil A e	1	0	1.000	5-5	2/2	0.6
1982	Mil A e	72	43	.626	5-1◆	2/2	2.7
1983	Mil A e	87	75	.537	5	—	0.4
Total 3		160	118	.576	—	—	3.7
KUHEL, JOE B6.25.1906							
1948	Was A	56	97	.366	7	—	1.4
1949	Was A	50	104	.325	8	—	0.7
Total 2		106	201	.345	—	—	2.1
LACHEMANN, MARCEL B6.13.1941							
1994	Cal A w	30	44	.405	2-4	3/3	-0.0
1995	Cal A w	78	67	.538	2▲	—	-4.2
1996	Cal A w	52	59	.468	4	1/2	8.0
Total 3		160	170	.485	—	—	3.8
LACHEMANN, RENE B5.4.1945							
1981-1	Sea A w	15	18	.455	7-6	2/2	1.4
1981-2	Sea A w	23	29	.442	5	—	-0.8
1982	Sea A w	76	86	.469	4	—	1.3
1983	Sea A w	26	47	.356	7-7	1/2	-1.8

YEAR	TM LG	W	L	PCT	FINISH	MGR/YR	+/-
1984	Mil A e	67	94	.416	7	—	-4.0
1993	Fla N e	64	98	.395	6	—	-1.9
1994	Fla N e	51	54	.486	5	—	4.3
1995	Fla N e	67	76	.469	4	—	-4.5
1996	Fla N e	39	47	.453	4-3	1/3	-3.2
Total 8		428	549	.438	—	—	-9.1
LAJOIE, NAP B9.5.1874							
1905	Cle A	37	21	.638	1t-5	1/3	9.0
1905	Cle A	19	36	.345	2-5	3/3	-7.6
1906	Cle A	89	64	.582	3	—	-7.7
1907	Cle A	85	67	.559	4	—	8.3
1908	Cle A	90	64	.584	2	—	0.1
1909	Cle A	57	57	.500	4-6	1/2	3.4
Total 5		377	309	.550	—	—	5.4
LAKE, FRED B10.16.1866							
1908	Bos A	22	17	.564	6-5	2/2	1.0
1909	Bos A	88	63	.583	3	—	6.8
1910	Bos N	53	100	.346	8	—	-1.1
Total 3		163	180	.475	—	—	6.8
LAMONT, GENE B12.25.1946							
1992	Chi A w	86	76	.531	3	—	0.1
1993	Chi A w	94	68	.580	1	—	1.7
1994	Chi A c	67	46	.593	1	—	-2.3
1995	Chi A c	11	20	.355	4-3	1/2	-4.4
1997	Pit N c	79	83	.488	2	—	1.5
1998	Pit N c	69	93	.426	6	—	-5.0
1999	Pit N c	78	83	.484	3	—	-1.8
2000	Pit N c	69	93	.426	5	—	-3.2
Total 8		553	562	.496	—	—	-13.3
LANIER, HAL B7.4.1942							
1986	Hou N w	96	66	.593	1	—	5.7
1987	Hou N w	76	86	.469	3	—	-1.9
1988	Hou N w	82	80	.506	5	—	2.5
Total 3		254	232	.523	—	—	6.4
LARKIN, HENRY B1.12.1860							
1890	Cle P	34	45	.430	7-7	1/2	3.1
LARUSSA, TONY B10.4.1944							
1979	Chi A w	27	27	.500	5-5	2/2	0.6
1980	Chi A w	70	90	.438	5	—	4.2
1981-1	Chi A w	31	22	.585	3	—	-4.5
1981-2	Chi A w	23	30	.434	6	—	-4.5
1982	Chi A w	87	75	.537	3	—	-1.5
1983	Chi A w	99	63	.611	1	—	3.0
1984	Chi A w	74	88	.457	5t	—	-1.2
1985	Chi A w	85	77	.525	3	—	2.4
1986	Chi A w	26	38	.406	6-5	1/3	-3.7
1986	Oak A w	45	34	.570	7-3t	3/3	6.9
1987	Oak A w	81	81	.500	3	—	-1.6
1988	Oak A w	104	58	.642	1◆	—	4.8
1989	Oak A w	99	63	.611	1★	—	3.5
1990	Oak A w	103	59	.636	1◆	—	4.8
1991	Oak A w	84	78	.519	4	—	4.6
1992	Oak A w	96	66	.593	1	—	7.6
1993	Oak A w	68	94	.420	7	—	-0.3
1994	Oak A w	51	63	.447	2	—	-2.2
1995	Oak A w	67	77	.465	4	—	-2.1
1996	StL N c	88	74	.543	1☆	—	1.7
1997	StL N c	73	89	.451	4	—	-6.1
1998	StL N c	83	79	.512	3	—	-0.7
1999	StL N c	75	86	.466	4	—	-2.8
2000	StL N c	95	67	.586	1☆	—	3.1
2001	StL N c	93	69	.574	2✤	—	-0.8
2002	StL N c	97	65	.599	1☆	—	2.0
2003	StL N c	85	77	.525	3	—	-3.5
2004	StL N c	105	57	.648	1◆	—	4.8
2005	StL N c	100	62	.617	1☆	—	1.8
2006	StL N c	83	78	.516	1★	—	0.7
Total 28		2297	1986	.536	—	—	20.9
LASORDA, TOM B9.22.1927							
1976	LA N w	2	2	.500	2-2	2/2	-0.2
1977	LA N w	98	64	.605	1◆	—	-2.4
1978	LA N w	95	67	.586	1◆	—	-2.3
1979	LA N w	79	83	.488	3	—	-4.2
1980	LA N w	92	71	.564	2▲	—	2.7
1981-1	LA N w	36	21	.632	1★	—	-2.4
1981-2	LA N w	27	26	.509	4	—	-2.4
1982	LA N w	88	74	.543	2	—	-1.4
1983	LA N w	91	71	.562	1	—	5.1
1984	LA N w	79	83	.488	4	—	0.2
1985	LA N w	95	67	.586	1	—	2.9
1986	LA N w	73	89	.451	5	—	-3.7
1987	LA N w	73	89	.451	4	—	-3.8
1988	LA N w	94	67	.584	1★	—	4.1
1989	LA N w	77	83	.481	4	—	-5.1
1990	LA N w	86	76	.531	2	—	0.6
1991	LA N w	93	69	.574	2	—	1.1
1992	LA N w	63	99	.389	6	—	-8.2
1993	LA N w	81	81	.500	4	—	-1.4
1994	LA N w	58	56	.509	1	—	-1.3
1995	LA N w	78	66	.542	1	—	3.4
1996	LA N w	41	35	.539	1-2	1/2	0.5
Total 21		1599	1439	.526	—	—	-17.9
LATHAM, JUICE B9.6.1852							
1875	NH NA	4	14	.222	11-8-8	2/3	2.5
1882	Phi AA	41	34	.547	2	—	1.9
Total 2		45	48	.484	—	—	4.4

LATHAM, ARLIE B3.15.1860

YEAR	TM LG	W	L	PCT	FINISH	MGR/YR	+/-
1896	StL N	0	3	.000	10-10-11	2/5	-0.8

LAVAGETTO, COOKIE B12.1.1912

YEAR	TM LG	W	L	PCT	FINISH	MGR/YR	+/-
1957	Was A	51	83	.381	8-8	2/2	1.7
1958	Was A	61	93	.396	8	—	4.2
1959	Was A	63	91	.409	8	—	-5.6
1960	Was A	73	81	.474	5	—	-1.6
1961	Min A	19	30	.388	8-7	1/4	-3.4
1961	Min A	4	6	.400	9-9-7	3/4	-0.6
Total 5		271	384	.414	—	—	-5.3

LEADLEY, BOB Robert H.; B11.11.1858 Brooklyn, NY; D5.19.1936 Los Angeles, CA (DNP)

YEAR	TM LG	W	L	PCT	FINISH	MGR/YR	+/-
1888	Det N	19	19	.500	3-5	2/2	-2.5
1890	Cle N	23	33	.411	7-7	2/2	2.8
1891	Cle N	34	34	.500	4-5	1/2	2.2
Total 3		76	86	.469	—	—	2.5

LEFEBVRE, JIM B1.7.1942

YEAR	TM LG	W	L	PCT	FINISH	MGR/YR	+/-
1989	Sea A w	73	89	.451	6	—	-4.6
1990	Sea A w	77	85	.475	5	—	0.2
1991	Sea A w	83	79	.512	5	—	-0.9
1992	Chi N e	78	84	.481	4	—	0.4
1993	Chi N e	84	78	.519	4	—	3.1
1999	Mil N c	22	27	.449	5-5	2/2	-0.5
Total 6		417	442	.485	—	—	-2.2

LEMON, JIM B3.23.1928

YEAR	TM LG	W	L	PCT	FINISH	MGR/YR	+/-
1968	Was A	65	96	.404	10	—	0.1

LEMON, BOB B9.22.1920

YEAR	TM LG	W	L	PCT	FINISH	MGR/YR	+/-
1970	KC A w	46	64	.418	5-4t	2/2	-2.3
1971	KC A w	85	76	.528	2	—	0.4
1972	KC A w	76	78	.494	4	—	-4.9
1977	Chi A w	90	72	.556	3	—	2.1
1978	Chi A w	34	40	.459	5-5	1/2	1.6
1978	NY A e	48	20	.706	4-1★▲	3/3	7.3
1979	NY A e	34	31	.523	4-4	1/2	-1.0
1981-2	NY A e	11	14	.440	4-6	2/2	-3.5
1982	NY A e	6	8	.429	4t-5	1/3	-0.9
Total 8		430	403	.516	—	—	-1.4

LENNON, BILL B1848

YEAR	TM LG	W	L	PCT	FINISH	MGR/YR	+/-
1871	Kek NA	5	9	.357	7-8	1/2	3.2

LEYLAND, JIM James Richard; B12.15.1944 Toledo, OH; BR/TR/5´11˝/170(C)

YEAR	TM LG	W	L	PCT	FINISH	MGR/YR	+/-
1986	Pit N e	64	98	.395	6	—	-13.2
1987	Pit N e	80	82	.494	4t	—	1.1
1988	Pit N e	85	75	.531	2	—	1.3
1989	Pit N e	74	88	.457	5	—	-2.4
1990	Pit N e	95	67	.586	1	—	2.2
1991	Pit N e	98	64	.605	1	—	3.1
1992	Pit N e	96	66	.593	1	—	4.6
1993	Pit N e	75	87	.463	5	—	3.7
1994	Pit N c	53	61	.465	3t	—	7.3
1995	Pit N c	58	86	.403	5	—	-3.6
1996	Pit N c	73	89	.451	5	—	-2.6
1997	Fla N e	92	70	.568	2★✣	—	3.8
1998	Fla N e	54	108	.333	5	—	-2.5
1999	Col N w	72	90	.444	5	—	1.6
2006	Det A c	95	67	.586	2✣◆	—	-0.5
Total 15		1164	1198	.493	—	—	3.8

LEYVA, NICK Nicholas Tomas; B8.16.1953 Ontario, CA; BR/TR/5´11˝/165(3B)

YEAR	TM LG	W	L	PCT	FINISH	MGR/YR	+/-
1989	Phi N e	67	95	.414	6	—	-3.0
1990	Phi N e	77	85	.475	4t	—	4.5
1991	Phi N e	4	9	.308	6-3	1/2	-2.1
Total 3		148	189	.439	—	—	-0.5

LILLIS, BOB B6.2.1930

YEAR	TM LG	W	L	PCT	FINISH	MGR/YR	+/-
1982	Hou N w	28	23	.549	5-5	2/2	4.3
1983	Hou N w	85	77	.525	3	—	4.3
1984	Hou N w	80	82	.494	2t	—	-7.6
1985	Hou N w	83	79	.512	3t	—	0.5
Total 4		276	261	.514	—	—	1.5

LIPON, JOHNNY B11.10.1922

YEAR	TM LG	W	L	PCT	FINISH	MGR/YR	+/-
1971	Cle A e	18	41	.305	6-6	2/2	-3.6

LITTLE, GRADY William Grady; B3.3.1950 Abilene, TX; BR/TR/5´11˝/190(C)

YEAR	TM LG	W	L	PCT	FINISH	MGR/YR	+/-
2002	Bos A e	93	69	.574	2	—	-7.0
2003	Bos A e	95	67	.586	2☆✣	—	0.2
2006	LA N w	88	74	.543	1	—	0.4
Total 3		276	210	.568	—	—	-6.4

LOBERT, HANS B10.18.1881

YEAR	TM LG	W	L	PCT	FINISH	MGR/YR	+/-
1938	Phi N	0	2	.000	8-8	2/2	-0.6
1942	Phi N	42	109	.278	8	—	1.2
Total 2		42	111	.275	—	—	0.6

LOCKMAN, WHITEY B7.25.1926

YEAR	TM LG	W	L	PCT	FINISH	MGR/YR	+/-
1972	Chi N e	39	26	.600	4-2	2/2	1.3
1973	Chi N e	77	84	.478	5	—	0.9
1974	Chi N e	41	52	.441	5-6	1/2	3.4
Total 3		157	162	.492	—	—	5.5

LOFTUS, TOM B11.15.1856

YEAR	TM LG	W	L	PCT	FINISH	MGR/YR	+/-
1884	Mil U	8	4	.667	2	—	-0.1
1888	Cle AA	30	38	.441	8-6	2/2	4.7
1889	Cle N	61	72	.459	6	—	0.5
1890	Cin N	77	55	.583	4	—	-0.2
1891	Cin N	56	81	.409	7	—	0.9
1900	Chi N	65	75	.464	5t	—	6.3
1901	Chi N	53	86	.381	6	—	-4.5
1902	Was A	61	75	.449	6	—	0.6
1903	Was A	43	94	.314	8	—	1.3
Total 9		454	580	.439	—	—	9.6

LOPAT, ED B6.21.1918

YEAR	TM LG	W	L	PCT	FINISH	MGR/YR	+/-
1963	KC A	73	89	.451	8	—	1.4
1964	KC A	17	35	.327	10-10	1/2	-2.1
Total 2		90	124	.421	—	—	-0.7

LOPES, DAVEY B5.3.1945

YEAR	TM LG	W	L	PCT	FINISH	MGR/YR	+/-
2000	Mil N c	73	89	.451	3	—	0.3
2001	Mil N c	68	94	.420	4	—	-6.6
2002	Mil N c	3	12	.200	6-6	1/2	-2.7
Total 3		144	195	.425	—	—	-9.0

LOPEZ, AL B8.20.1908

YEAR	TM LG	W	L	PCT	FINISH	MGR/YR	+/-
1951	Cle A	93	61	.604	2	—	5.4
1952	Cle A	93	61	.604	2	—	0.2
1953	Cle A	92	62	.597	2	—	0.7
1954	Cle A	111	43	.721	1	—	8.3
1955	Cle A	93	61	.604	2	—	6.0
1956	Cle A	88	66	.571	2	—	-2.6
1957	Chi A	90	64	.584	2	—	-1.8
1958	Chi A	82	72	.532	2	—	3.0
1959	Chi A	94	60	.610	1	—	8.4
1960	Chi A	87	67	.565	3	—	-2.5
1961	Chi A	86	76	.531	4	—	1.1
1962	Chi A	85	77	.525	5	—	-1.1
1963	Chi A	94	68	.580	2	—	-2.2
1964	Chi A	98	64	.605	2	—	1.1
1965	Chi A	95	67	.586	2	—	3.9
1968	Chi A	6	5	.545	9-9-8t	3/5	1.0
1968	Chi A	15	21	.417	9-8t	5/5	-1.3
1969	Chi A w	8	9	.471	4-5	1/2	0.6
Total 17		1410	1004	.584	—	—	28.3

LORD, HARRY B3.8.1882

YEAR	TM LG	W	L	PCT	FINISH	MGR/YR	+/-
1915	Buf F	60	49	.550	8-6	3/3	10.1

LOWE, BOBBY B7.10.1865

YEAR	TM LG	W	L	PCT	FINISH	MGR/YR	+/-
1904	Det A	30	44	.405	7-7	2/2	-0.3

LUCCHESI, FRANK Frank Joseph; B4.24.1927 San Francisco, CA; BR/TR/5´8˝/175(OF)

YEAR	TM LG	W	L	PCT	FINISH	MGR/YR	+/-
1970	Phi N e	73	88	.453	5	—	6.7
1971	Phi N e	67	95	.414	6	—	0.1
1972	Phi N e	26	50	.342	6-6	1/2	-4.9
1975	Tex A w	35	32	.522	4-3	2/2	2.3
1976	Tex A w	76	86	.469	4t	—	-1.1
1977	Tex A w	31	31	.500	3t-2	1/4	-4.3
1987	Chi N e	8	17	.320	5-6	2/2	-3.3
Total 7		316	399	.442	—	—	-4.4

LUMLEY, HARRY B9.29.1880

YEAR	TM LG	W	L	PCT	FINISH	MGR/YR	+/-
1909	Bro N	55	98	.359	6	—	-0.6

LYONS, TED B12.28.1900

YEAR	TM LG	W	L	PCT	FINISH	MGR/YR	+/-
1946	Chi A	64	60	.516	7-5	2/2	4.9
1947	Chi A	70	84	.455	6	—	4.6
1948	Chi A	51	101	.336	8	—	0.6
Total 3		185	245	.430	—	—	10.1

MACHA, KEN B9.29.1950

YEAR	TM LG	W	L	PCT	FINISH	MGR/YR	+/-
2003	Oak A w	96	66	.593	1	—	2.3
2004	Oak A w	91	71	.562	2	—	5.0
2005	Oak A w	88	74	.543	2	—	-4.5
2006	Oak A w	93	69	.574	1☆	—	7.7
Total 4		368	280	.568	—	—	10.5

MACK, CONNIE B12.22.1862

YEAR	TM LG	W	L	PCT	FINISH	MGR/YR	+/-
1894	Pit N	12	10	.545	7-7	2/2	1.2
1895	Pit N	71	61	.538	7	—	3.6
1896	Pit N	66	63	.512	6	—	-2.5
1901	Phi A	74	62	.544	4	—	2.0
1902	Phi A	83	53	.610	1	—	2.0
1903	Phi A	75	60	.556	2	—	-0.7
1904	Phi A	81	70	.536	5	—	-0.7
1905	Phi A	92	56	.622	1	—	3.0
1906	Phi A	78	67	.538	4	—	3.1
1907	Phi A	88	57	.607	2	—	7.4
1908	Phi A	68	85	.444	6	—	0.3
1909	Phi A	95	58	.621	2	—	4.1
1910	Phi A	102	48	.680	1★	—	1.1
1911	Phi A	101	50	.669	1★	—	0.5
1912	Phi A	90	62	.592	3	—	2.2
1913	Phi A	96	57	.627	1★	—	-0.6
1914	Phi A	99	53	.651	1	—	-0.2
1915	Phi A	43	109	.283	8	—	0.8
1916	Phi A	36	117	.235	8	—	-5.5
1917	Phi A	55	98	.359	8	—	-4.2
1918	Phi A	52	76	.406	8	—	2.0
1919	Phi A	36	104	.257	8	—	-4.8
1920	Phi A	48	106	.312	8	—	-1.3
1921	Phi A	53	100	.346	8	—	-1.0
1922	Phi A	65	89	.422	7	—	-0.1
1923	Phi A	69	83	.454	6	—	2.8
1924	Phi A	71	81	.467	5	—	4.0
1925	Phi A	88	64	.579	2	—	0.9
1926	Phi A	83	67	.553	3	—	-3.1
1927	Phi A	91	63	.591	2	—	3.1
1928	Phi A	98	55	.641	2	—	0.6
1929	Phi A	104	46	.693	1★	—	1.9
1930	Phi A	102	52	.662	1★	—	7.0
1931	Phi A	107	45	.704	1	—	8.6
1932	Phi A	94	60	.610	2	—	-3.5
1933	Phi A	79	72	.523	3	—	1.5
1934	Phi A	68	82	.453	5	—	-0.1
1935	Phi A	58	91	.389	8	—	-1.8
1936	Phi A	53	100	.346	8	—	5.9
1937	Phi A	39	80	.328	7-7	1/2	-9.0
1938	Phi A	53	99	.349	8	—	-2.1
1939	Phi A	25	37	.403	6-7	1/2	5.3
1940	Phi A	54	100	.351	8	—	-1.9
1941	Phi A	64	90	.416	8	—	-1.0
1942	Phi A	55	99	.357	8	—	3.5
1943	Phi A	49	105	.318	8	—	-4.4
1944	Phi A	72	82	.468	5t	—	2.7
1945	Phi A	52	98	.347	8	—	-7.1
1946	Phi A	49	105	.318	8	—	-11.8
1947	Phi A	78	76	.506	5	—	-1.0
1948	Phi A	84	70	.545	4	—	7.6
1949	Phi A	81	73	.526	5	—	3.9
1950	Phi A	52	102	.338	8	—	-2.3
Total 53		3731	3948	.486	—	—	13.6

MACK, DENNY B1851

YEAR	TM LG	W	L	PCT	FINISH	MGR/YR	+/-
1882	Lou AA	42	38	.525	3	—	-6.7

MACK, EARLE B2.1.1890

YEAR	TM LG	W	L	PCT	FINISH	MGR/YR	+/-
1937	Phi A	15	17	.469	7-7	2/2	2.1
1939	Phi A	30	60	.333	6-7	2/2	1.4
Total 2		45	77	.369	—	—	3.5

MACKANIN, PETE B8.1.1951

YEAR	TM LG	W	L	PCT	FINISH	MGR/YR	+/-
2005	Pit N c	12	14	.462	6-6	2/2	0.4

MACULLAR, JIMMY B1.16.1855

YEAR	TM LG	W	L	PCT	FINISH	MGR/YR	+/-
1879	Syr N	5	21	.192	6-7	3/3	-1.6

MADDON, JOE Joseph John; B2.8.1954 Hazleton, PA; BR/TR/5´11˝/190(C)

YEAR	TM LG	W	L	PCT	FINISH	MGR/YR	+/-
1999	Ana A w	19	10	.655	4-4	2/2	6.5
2006	TB A e	61	101	.377	5	—	-3.8
Total 2		80	111	.419	—	—	2.7

MAGEE, LEE B6.4.1889

YEAR	TM LG	W	L	PCT	FINISH	MGR/YR	+/-
1915	Bro F	53	64	.453	7-7	1/2	-3.5

MALONE, FERGY B1842

YEAR	TM LG	W	L	PCT	FINISH	MGR/YR	+/-
1873	Phi NA	36	27	.571	2	—	0.1
1874	Chi NA	18	18	.500	4-5	1/2	2.9
1884	Phi U	21	46	.313	7	—	-2.1
Total 3		75	91	.452	—	—	0.9

MANNING, JIMMY B1.31.1862

YEAR	TM LG	W	L	PCT	FINISH	MGR/YR	+/-
1901	Was A	61	72	.459	6	—	2.7

MANNING, JACK B12.20.1853

YEAR	TM LG	W	L	PCT	FINISH	MGR/YR	+/-
1877	Cin N	7	12	.368	6-6	3/3	2.8

MANUEL, CHARLIE B1.4.1944

YEAR	TM LG	W	L	PCT	FINISH	MGR/YR	+/-
2000	Cle A c	90	72	.556	2	—	-3.2
2001	Cle A c	91	71	.562	1	—	3.0
2002	Cle A c	39	48	.448	3-3	1/2	0.6
2005	Phi N e	88	74	.543	2	—	-0.9
2006	Phi N e	85	77	.525	2	—	-0.9
Total 5		393	342	.535	—	—	-1.5

MANUEL, JERRY B12.23.1953

YEAR	TM LG	W	L	PCT	FINISH	MGR/YR	+/-
1998	Chi A c	80	82	.494	2	—	5.3
1999	Chi A c	75	86	.466	2	—	3.3
2000	Chi A c	95	67	.586	1	—	1.5
2001	Chi A c	83	79	.512	3	—	1.7
2002	Chi A c	81	81	.500	2	—	-5.4
2003	Chi A c	86	76	.531	2	—	-2.5
Total 6		500	471	.515	—	—	3.9

MARANVILLE, RABBIT B11.11.1891

YEAR	TM LG	W	L	PCT	FINISH	MGR/YR	+/-
1925	Chi N	23	30	.434	7-7-8	2/3	-1.8

MARION, MARTY B12.1.1917

YEAR	TM LG	W	L	PCT	FINISH	MGR/YR	+/-
1951	StL N	81	73	.526	3	—	2.8
1952	StL A	42	61	.408	8-7	2/2	-0.7
1953	StL A	54	100	.351	8	—	-0.3
1954	Chi A	3	6	.333	3-3	2/2	-2.7
1955	Chi A	91	63	.591	3	—	-3.5
1956	Chi A	85	69	.552	3	—	-6.1
Total 6		356	372	.489	—	—	-10.5

MARSHALL, JIM B5.25.1931

YEAR	TM LG	W	L	PCT	FINISH	MGR/YR	+/-
1974	Chi N e	25	44	.362	5-6	2/2	-2.9
1975	Chi N e	75	87	.463	5t	—	5.2
1976	Chi N e	75	87	.463	4	—	6.2
1979	Oak A w	54	108	.333	7	—	2.0
Total 4		229	326	.413	—	—	10.5

MARTIN, BILLY B5.16.1928

YEAR	TM LG	W	L	PCT	FINISH	MGR/YR	+/-
1969	Min A w	97	65	.599	1	—	-1.5
1971	Det A e	91	71	.562	2	—	4.2
1972	Det A e	86	70	.551	1	—	3.0
1973	Det A e	71	63	.530	3-3	1/2	6.8
1973	Tex A w	9	14	.391	6-6	3/3	0.7
1974	Tex A w	84	76	.525	2	—	4.8
1975	Tex A w	44	51	.463	4-3	1/2	-2.4
1975	NY A e	30	26	.536	3-3	2/2	-1.5
1976	NY A e	97	62	.610	1◆	—	1.3
1977	NY A e	100	62	.617	1★	—	1.1

YEAR TM LG	W	L	PCT	FINISH	MGR/YR	+/-
1978 NY A e	52	42	.553	3-1★▲	1/3	-4.3
1979 NY A e	55	40	.579	4-4	2/2	3.8
1980 Oak A w	83	79	.512	2	—	-2.6
1981-1 Oak A w	37	23	.617	1☆	—	3.6
1981-2 Oak A w	27	22	.551	2	—	3.6
1982 Oak A w	68	94	.420	5	—	-0.4
1983 NY A e	91	71	.562	3	—	3.3
1985 NY A e	91	54	.628	7-2	2/2	2.6
1988 NY A e	40	28	.588	2-5	1/2	5.0
Total 16	1253	1013	.553	—	—	31.2

Martin, Phonney B8.4.1845

YEAR TM LG	W	L	PCT	FINISH	MGR/YR	+/-
1872 Eck NA	1	8	.111	10-9	3/3	2.0

Martinez, Buck B11.7.1948

YEAR TM LG	W	L	PCT	FINISH	MGR/YR	+/-
2001 Tor A e	80	82	.494	3	—	-2.4
2002 Tor A e	20	33	.377	4-3	1/2	-6.0
Total 2	100	115	.465	—	—	-8.4

Martinez, Marty B8.23.1941

YEAR TM LG	W	L	PCT	FINISH	MGR/YR	+/-
1986 Sea A w	0	1	.000	6-6-7	2/3	-0.4

Mason, Charlie B6.25.1853

YEAR TM LG	W	L	PCT	FINISH	MGR/YR	+/-
1887 Phi AA	38	40	.487	6-5	2/2	-1.1

Mathews, Eddie B10.13.1931

YEAR TM LG	W	L	PCT	FINISH	MGR/YR	+/-
1972 Atl N w	23	27	.460	4-4	2/2	1.4
1973 Atl N w	76	85	.472	5	—	-6.9
1974 Atl N w	50	49	.505	4-3	1/2	-6.1
Total 3	149	161	.481	—	—	-11.6

Mathewson, Christy B8.12.1880

YEAR TM LG	W	L	PCT	FINISH	MGR/YR	+/-
1916 Cin N	25	43	.368	8-7t	3/3	-3.4
1917 Cin N	78	76	.506	4	—	2.1
1918 Cin N	61	57	.517	4-3	1/2	-1.3
Total 3	164	176	.482	—	—	-2.7

Mattick, Bobby B12.5.1915

YEAR TM LG	W	L	PCT	FINISH	MGR/YR	+/-
1980 Tor A e	67	95	.414	7	—	0.2
1981-1 Tor A e	16	42	.276	7	—	-1.0
1981-2 Tor A e	21	27	.438	7	—	-1.0
Total 2	104	164	.388	—	—	-1.8

Mauch, Gene B11.18.1925

YEAR TM LG	W	L	PCT	FINISH	MGR/YR	+/-
1960 Phi N	58	94	.382	4t-8	3/3	-2.8
1961 Phi N	47	107	.305	8	—	-8.7
1962 Phi N	81	80	.503	7	—	5.9
1963 Phi N	87	75	.537	4	—	-1.0
1964 Phi N	92	70	.568	2t	—	4.6
1965 Phi N	85	76	.528	6	—	5.9
1966 Phi N	87	75	.537	4	—	0.1
1967 Phi N	82	80	.506	5	—	-2.4
1968 Phi N	27	27	.500	6t-7t	1/3	2.7
1969 Mon N e	52	110	.321	6	—	-7.5
1970 Mon N e	73	89	.451	6	—	3.9
1971 Mon N e	71	90	.441	5	—	1.6
1972 Mon N e	70	86	.449	5	—	2.7
1973 Mon N e	79	83	.488	4	—	1.5
1974 Mon N e	79	82	.491	4	—	-2.0
1975 Mon N e	75	87	.463	5t	—	3.5
1976 Min A w	85	77	.525	3	—	0.1
1977 Min A w	84	77	.522	4	—	-5.0
1978 Min A w	73	89	.451	4	—	-6.8
1979 Min A w	82	80	.506	4	—	-2.9
1980 Min A w	54	71	.432	4-3	1/2	-4.2
1981-1 Cal A w	9	4	.692	4-4	2/2	2.2
1981-2 Cal A w	20	30	.400	7	—	-6.4
1982 Cal A w	93	69	.574	1	—	-2.3
1985 Cal A w	90	72	.556	2	—	6.1
1986 Cal A w	92	70	.568	1	—	0.8
1987 Cal A w	75	87	.463	6t	—	-2.8
Total 26	1902	2037	.483	—	—	-13.2

Mazzilli, Lee B3.25.1955

YEAR TM LG	W	L	PCT	FINISH	MGR/YR	+/-
2004 Bal A e	78	84	.481	3	—	-4.1
2005 Bal A e	51	56	.477	4-4	1/2	2.1
Total 2	129	140	.480	—	—	-2.0

McAleer, Jimmy B7.10.1864

YEAR TM LG	W	L	PCT	FINISH	MGR/YR	+/-
1901 Cle A	54	82	.397	7	—	1.0
1902 StL A	78	58	.574	2	—	8.8
1903 StL A	65	74	.468	6	—	-1.7
1904 StL A	65	87	.428	6	—	3.0
1905 StL A	54	99	.353	8	—	-11.8
1906 StL A	76	73	.510	5	—	-5.5
1907 StL A	69	83	.454	6	—	-5.4
1908 StL A	83	69	.546	4	—	-0.1
1909 StL A	61	89	.407	7	—	1.7
1910 Was A	66	85	.437	7	—	-3.7
1911 Was A	64	90	.416	7	—	1.1
Total 11	735	889	.453	—	—	-12.7

McBride, George B11.20.1880

YEAR TM LG	W	L	PCT	FINISH	MGR/YR	+/-
1921 Was A	80	73	.523	4	—	6.8

McBride, Dick B1845

YEAR TM LG	W	L	PCT	FINISH	MGR/YR	+/-
1871 Ath NA	21	7	.750	1	—	0.1
1872 Ath NA	30	14	.682	4	—	-5.1
1873 Ath NA	28	23	.549	5	—	-2.7
1874 Ath NA	33	23	.589	3	—	-2.2
1875 Ath NA	49	18	.731	2-2	1/2	-6.1
Total 5	161	85	.654	—	—	-16.0

McCallister, Jack John; B1.19.1879 Marietta, OH; D10.18.1946 Columbus, OH (DNP)

YEAR TM LG	W	L	PCT	FINISH	MGR/YR	+/-
1927 Cle A	66	87	.431	6	—	-0.9

McCarthy, Joe Joseph Vincent "Marse Joe"; B4.21.1887 Philadelphia, PA; D1.13.1978 Buffalo, NY BR/TR/5´8.5˝/190(2B)

YEAR TM LG	W	L	PCT	FINISH	MGR/YR	+/-
1926 Chi N	82	72	.532	4	—	-3.3
1927 Chi N	85	68	.556	4	—	-0.3
1928 Chi N	91	63	.591	3	—	3.9
1929 Chi N	98	54	.645	1	—	1.9
1930 Chi N	86	64	.573	2-2	1/2	0.2
1931 NY A	94	59	.614	2	—	-9.3
1932 NY A	107	47	.695	1★	—	4.9
1933 NY A	91	59	.607	2	—	1.7
1934 NY A	94	60	.610	2	—	0.4
1935 NY A	89	60	.597	2	—	-3.4
1936 NY A	102	51	.667	1★	—	-3.9
1937 NY A	102	52	.662	1★	—	-3.5
1938 NY A	99	53	.651	1★	—	-0.5
1939 NY A	106	45	.702	1★	—	-8.5
1940 NY A	88	66	.571	3	—	-3.1
1941 NY A	101	53	.656	1★	—	4.5
1942 NY A	103	51	.669	1	—	-4.3
1943 NY A	98	56	.636	1★	—	7.4
1944 NY A	83	71	.539	3	—	0.1
1945 NY A	81	71	.533	4	—	-2.2
1946 NY A	22	13	.629	2-3	1/3	1.2
1948 Bos A	96	59	.619	2▲	—	1.2
1949 Bos A	96	58	.623	2	—	-2.6
1950 Bos A	31	28	.525	4-3	1/2	-5.9
Total 24	2125	1333	.615	—	—	-23.6

McCarthy, Tommy B7.24.1863

YEAR TM LG	W	L	PCT	FINISH	MGR/YR	+/-
1890 StL AA	11	11	.500	4-3	1/6	-1.9
1890 StL AA	4	1	.800	2-2-3	5/6	1.1

McClendon, Lloyd B1.11.1959

YEAR TM LG	W	L	PCT	FINISH	MGR/YR	+/-
2001 Pit N c	62	100	.383	6	—	0.7
2002 Pit N c	72	89	.447	4	—	0.7
2003 Pit N c	75	87	.463	4	—	-1.4
2004 Pit N c	72	89	.447	5	—	-2.0
2005 Pit N c	55	81	.404	6-6	1/2	-5.5
Total 5	336	446	.430	—	—	-7.5

McCloskey, John John Joseph "Honest John"; B4.4.1862 Louisville, KY; D11.17.1940 Louisville, KY (DNP)

YEAR TM LG	W	L	PCT	FINISH	MGR/YR	+/-
1895 Lou N	35	96	.267	12	—	1.6
1896 Lou N	2	17	.105	12-12	1/2	-3.2
1906 StL N	52	98	.347	7	—	-7.5
1907 StL N	52	101	.340	8	—	-2.3
1908 StL N	49	105	.318	8	—	1.9
Total 5	190	417	.313	—	—	-9.4

McCormick, Jim B11.3.1856

YEAR TM LG	W	L	PCT	FINISH	MGR/YR	+/-
1879 Cle N	27	55	.329	6	—	-0.5
1880 Cle N	47	37	.560	3	—	-0.1
1882 Cle N	0	4	.000	8-5	1/2	-2.0
Total 3	74	96	.435	—	—	-2.6

McGaha, Mel Fred Melvin; B9.26.1926 Bastrop, LA; D2.3.2002 Tulsa, OK BR/TR/6´2˝/210(OF)

YEAR TM LG	W	L	PCT	FINISH	MGR/YR	+/-
1962 Cle A	78	82	.488	6-6	1/2	4.3
1964 KC A	40	70	.364	10-10	2/2	-0.3
1965 KC A	5	21	.192	10-10	1/2	-5.2
Total 3	123	173	.416	—	—	-1.2

McGeary, Mike B1851

YEAR TM LG	W	L	PCT	FINISH	MGR/YR	+/-
1875 Phi NA	34	27	.557	4-5	1/2	-3.8
1880 Pro N	8	7	.533	4-2	1/3	-1.7
1881 Cle N	4	7	.364	6-7	1/2	-1.2
Total 3	46	41	.529	—	—	-6.7

McGraw, John B4.7.1873

YEAR TM LG	W	L	PCT	FINISH	MGR/YR	+/-
1899 Bal N	86	62	.581	4	—	-0.9
1901 Bal A	68	65	.511	5	—	0.6
1902 Bal A	26	31	.456	7-8	1/2	2.5
1902 NY N	25	38	.397	8-8	3/3	3.8
1903 NY N	84	55	.604	2	—	-1.6
1904 NY N	106	47	.693	1	—	0.3
1905 NY N	105	48	.686	1★	—	-0.2
1906 NY N	96	56	.632	2	—	7.2
1907 NY N	82	71	.536	4	—	-1.8
1908 NY N	98	56	.636	2t	—	-1.2
1909 NY N	92	61	.601	3	—	7.0
1910 NY N	91	63	.591	2	—	-1.4
1911 NY N	99	54	.647	1	—	0.4
1912 NY N	103	48	.682	1	—	2.4
1913 NY N	101	51	.664	1	—	6.7
1914 NY N	84	70	.545	2	—	-3.2
1915 NY N	69	83	.454	8	—	-2.1
1916 NY N	86	66	.566	4	—	-0.5
1917 NY N	98	56	.636	1	—	0.7
1918 NY N	71	53	.573	2	—	1.7
1919 NY N	87	53	.621	2	—	2.4
1920 NY N	86	68	.558	2	—	-5.8
1921 NY N	94	59	.614	1★	—	-2.1
1922 NY N	93	61	.604	1★	—	-2.7
1923 NY N	95	58	.621	1	—	1.9
1924 NY N	16	13	.552	3-1	1/3	-2.4
1924 NY N	45	35	.563	1-1	3/3	-5.9
1925 NY N	10	4	.714	1-2	1/3	2.7
1925 NY N	55	51	.519	1-2	3/3	-0.3
1926 NY N	74	77	.490	5	—	-1.0
1927 NY N	70	52	.574	4-3	1/2	1.7
1928 NY N	93	61	.604	2	—	0.9
1929 NY N	84	67	.556	3	—	-8.9
1930 NY N	87	67	.565	3	—	-2.8
1931 NY N	87	65	.572	2	—	-6.0
1932 NY N	17	23	.425	8-6t	1/2	-4.2
Total 33	2763	1948	.586	—	—	-11.9

McGuire, Deacon B11.18.1863

YEAR TM LG	W	L	PCT	FINISH	MGR/YR	+/-
1898 Was N	21	47	.309	10-11-11	3/4	-3.3
1907 Bos A	45	61	.425	8-7	4/4	-0.4
1908 Bos A	53	62	.461	6-5	1/2	-8.8
1909 Cle A	14	25	.359	4-6	2/2	-4.3
1910 Cle A	71	81	.467	5	—	7.0
1911 Cle A	6	11	.353	7-3	1/2	-2.3
Total 6	210	287	.423	—	—	-12.2

McGunnigle, Bill B1.1.1855

YEAR TM LG	W	L	PCT	FINISH	MGR/YR	+/-
1888 Bro AA	88	52	.629	2	—	1.0
1889 Bro AA	93	44	.679	1	—	-0.4
1890 Bro N	86	43	.667	1★	—	-1.7
1891 Pit N	24	33	.421	8-8	2/2	-1.9
1896 Lou N	36	76	.321	12-12	2/2	5.1
Total 5	327	248	.569	—	—	2.1

McInnis, Stuffy B9.19.1890

YEAR TM LG	W	L	PCT	FINISH	MGR/YR	+/-
1927 Phi N	51	103	.331	8	—	-4.9

McKechnie, Bill B8.7.1886

YEAR TM LG	W	L	PCT	FINISH	MGR/YR	+/-
1915 New F	54	45	.545	6-5	2/2	2.8
1922 Pit N	53	36	.596	5-3t	2/2	1.5
1923 Pit N	87	67	.565	3	—	1.3
1924 Pit N	90	63	.588	3	—	-0.6
1925 Pit N	95	58	.621	1★	—	0.4
1926 Pit N	84	69	.549	3	—	-0.4
1928 StL N	95	59	.617	1	—	1.2
1929 StL N	34	29	.540	4-4	3/3	1.5
1930 Bos N	70	84	.455	6	—	6.5
1931 Bos N	64	90	.416	7	—	2.8
1932 Bos N	77	77	.500	5	—	0.6
1933 Bos N	83	71	.539	4	—	3.6
1934 Bos N	78	73	.517	4	—	5.6
1935 Bos N	38	115	.248	8	—	-11.3
1936 Bos N	71	83	.461	6	—	2.6
1937 Bos N	79	73	.520	5	—	0.5
1938 Cin N	82	68	.547	4	—	-1.9
1939 Cin N	97	57	.630	1	—	2.5
1940 Cin N	100	53	.654	1★	—	4.5
1941 Cin N	88	66	.571	3	—	5.4
1942 Cin N	76	76	.500	4	—	2.0
1943 Cin N	87	67	.565	2	—	2.8
1944 Cin N	89	65	.578	3	—	8.0
1945 Cin N	61	93	.396	7	—	0.8
1946 Cin N	64	86	.427	6-6	1/2	-5.8
Total 25	1896	1723	.524	—	—	37.0

McKeon, Jack John Aloysius; B11.23.1930 South Amboy, NJ; BR/TR/5´8˝/205(C)

YEAR TM LG	W	L	PCT	FINISH	MGR/YR	+/-
1973 KC A w	88	74	.543	2	—	6.7
1974 KC A w	77	85	.475	5	—	-4.5
1975 KC A w	50	46	.521	2-2	1/2	-1.7
1977 Oak A w	26	27	.491	5t-7	1/2	4.4
1978 Oak A w	45	78	.366	1-6	2/2	-3.4
1988 SD N w	67	48	.583	5-3	2/2	8.6
1989 SD N w	89	73	.549	2	—	6.3
1990 SD N w	37	43	.463	4-5	1/2	-3.0
1997 Cin N c	33	30	.524	4-3	2/2	6.0
1998 Cin N c	77	85	.475	4	—	-3.0
1999 Cin N c	96	67	.589	2▲	—	-0.4
2000 Cin N c	85	77	.525	2	—	-1.8
2003 Fla N e	74	49	.602	4-2✤★	2/2	8.0
2004 Fla N e	83	79	.512	3	—	0.2
2005 Fla N e	83	79	.512	3t	—	3.5
Total 15	1010	940	.518	—	—	25.9

McKinnon, Alex B8.14.1856

YEAR TM LG	W	L	PCT	FINISH	MGR/YR	+/-
1885 StL N	6	32	.158	5-8-8	2/3	-5.8

McKnight, Denny Harmar Denny; B4.29.1848 Pittsburgh, PA; D5.5.1900 Pittsburgh, PA (DNP)

YEAR TM LG	W	L	PCT	FINISH	MGR/YR	+/-
1884 Pit AA	4	8	.333	9-10	1/5	1.3

McManus, George George; B6.28.1846 Ireland; D10.2.1918 New York, NY (DNP)

YEAR TM LG	W	L	PCT	FINISH	MGR/YR	+/-
1876 StL N	6	2	.750	2-2	2/2	0.1
1877 StL N	28	32	.467	4	—	1.2
Total 2	34	34	.500	—	—	1.3

McManus, Marty B3.14.1900

YEAR TM LG	W	L	PCT	FINISH	MGR/YR	+/-
1932 Bos A	32	67	.323	8-8	2/2	4.2
1933 Bos A	63	86	.423	7	—	-5.9
Total 2	95	153	.383	—	—	-1.7

McMillan, Roy B7.17.1929

YEAR TM LG	W	L	PCT	FINISH	MGR/YR	+/-
1972 Mil A e	1	1	.500	6-6-6	2/3	0.1
1975 NY N e	26	27	.491	3-3t	2/2	-1.2
Total 2	27	28	.491	—	—	-1.1

McNamara, John John Francis; B6.4.1932 Sacramento, CA; BR/TR/5´10˝/175(C)

YEAR TM LG	W	L	PCT	FINISH	MGR/YR	+/-
1969 Oak A w	8	5	.615	2-2	2/2	1.0
1970 Oak A w	89	73	.549	2	—	-1.1
1974 SD N w	60	102	.370	6	—	8.8
1975 SD N w	71	91	.438	4	—	4.2
1976 SD N w	73	89	.451	5	—	2.0
1977 SD N w	20	28	.417	4-5	1/3	0.1

YEAR TM LG	W	L	PCT	FINISH	MGR/YR	+/-
1979 Cin N w	90	71	.559	1	—	0.6
1980 Cin N w	89	73	.549	3	—	4.2
1981-1 Cin N w	35	21	.625	2	—	9.5
1981-2 Cin N w	31	21	.596	2	—	9.5
1982 Cin N w	34	58	.370	6-6	1/2	-4.8
1983 Cal A w	70	92	.432	5t	—	-5.4
1984 Cal A w	81	81	.500	2t	—	0.1
1985 Bos A e	81	81	.500	5	—	-7.9
1986 Bos A e	95	66	.590	1◆	—	4.8
1987 Bos A e	78	84	.481	5	—	-4.6
1988 Bos A e	43	42	.506	4-1	1/2	-5.9
1990 Cle A e	77	85	.475	4	—	-3.5
1991 Cle A e	25	52	.325	7-7	1/2	-4.4
1996 Cal A w	18	32	.360	4	2/2	-1.8
Total 19	1168	1247	.484	—	—	5.5

McPhee, Bid B11.1.1859

YEAR TM LG	W	L	PCT	FINISH	MGR/YR	+/-
1901 Cin N	52	87	.374	8	—	7.2
1902 Cin N	27	37	.422	6-4	1/3	-8.2
Total 2	79	124	.389	—	—	-0.9

McRae, Hal B7.10.1945

YEAR TM LG	W	L	PCT	FINISH	MGR/YR	+/-
1991 KC A w	66	58	.532	7-6	3/3	3.6
1992 KC A w	72	90	.444	5t	—	-2.9
1993 KC A w	84	78	.519	3	—	5.0
1994 KC A c	64	51	.557	3	—	2.4
2001 TB A e	58	90	.392	5-5	2/2	3.0
2002 TB A e	55	106	.342	5	—	-2.1
Total 6	399	473	.458	—	—	9.0

McVey, Cal B8.30.1849

YEAR TM LG	W	L	PCT	FINISH	MGR/YR	+/-
1873 Bal NA	20	13	.606	3-3	1/2	-4.3
1878 Cin N	37	23	.617	2	—	2.1
1879 Cin N	34	28	.548	4-5	2/2	1.6
Total 3	91	64	.587	—	—	-0.6

Mele, Sam B1.21.1922

YEAR TM LG	W	L	PCT	FINISH	MGR/YR	+/-
1961 Min A	2	5	.286	8-9-7	2/4	-1.2
1961 Min A	45	49	.479	9-7	4/4	2.1
1962 Min A	91	71	.562	2	—	1.6
1963 Min A	91	70	.565	3	—	-6.5
1964 Min A	79	83	.488	6t	—	-8.0
1965 Min A	102	60	.630	1	—	3.1
1966 Min A	89	73	.549	2	—	-0.9
1967 Min A	25	25	.500	6-2t	1/2	-2.7
Total 7	524	436	.546	—	—	-12.4

Melillo, Ski B8.4.1899

YEAR TM LG	W	L	PCT	FINISH	MGR/YR	+/-
1938 StL A	2	7	.222	7-7	2/2	-1.4

Melvin, Bob B10.28.1961

YEAR TM LG	W	L	PCT	FINISH	MGR/YR	+/-
2003 Sea A w	93	69	.574	2	—	-3.9
2004 Sea A w	63	99	.389	4	—	-5.8
2005 Ari N w	77	85	.475	2	—	11.5
2006 Ari N w	76	86	.469	4	—	-3.6
Total 4	309	339	.477	—	—	-1.7

Merrill, Stump Carl Harrison; B2.25.1944 Brunswick, ME; BL/TR/5´8˝/190(C)

YEAR TM LG	W	L	PCT	FINISH	MGR/YR	+/-
1990 NY A e	49	64	.434	7-7	2/2	3.1
1991 NY A e	71	91	.438	5	—	0.3
Total 2	120	155	.436	—	—	3.4

Metro, Charlie B4.28.1919

YEAR TM LG	W	L	PCT	FINISH	MGR/YR	+/-
1962 Chi N	43	69	.384	9-9	3/3	0.5
1970 KC A w	19	33	.365	5-4t	1/2	-3.8
Total 2	62	102	.378	—	—	-3.3

Meyer, Billy B1.14.1893

YEAR TM LG	W	L	PCT	FINISH	MGR/YR	+/-
1948 Pit N	83	71	.539	4	—	5.5
1949 Pit N	71	83	.461	6	—	1.7
1950 Pit N	57	96	.373	8	—	-2.8
1951 Pit N	64	90	.416	7	—	1.9
1952 Pit N	42	112	.273	8	—	-6.3
Total 5	317	452	.412	—	—	0.0

Michael, Gene B6.2.1938

YEAR TM LG	W	L	PCT	FINISH	MGR/YR	+/-
1981-1 NY A e	34	22	.607	1◆	—	-3.3
1981-2 NY A e	14	12	.538	4-6	1/2	-1.1
1982 NY A e	44	42	.512	4t-5t-5	2/3	1.4
1986 Chi N e	46	56	.451	5-5	3/3	1.4
1987 Chi N e	68	68	.500	5-6	1/2	6.7
Total 4	206	200	.507	—	—	5.1

Milan, Clyde B3.25.1887

YEAR TM LG	W	L	PCT	FINISH	MGR/YR	+/-
1922 Was A	69	85	.448	6	—	-2.3

Miley, Dave David Allen; B4.3.1962 Tampa, FL; BL/TR/6´3˝/220(C)

YEAR TM LG	W	L	PCT	FINISH	MGR/YR	+/-
2003 Cin N c	22	35	.386	5-5	3/3	-0.0
2004 Cin N c	76	86	.469	4	—	9.7
2005 Cin N c	27	43	.386	6	1/2	-5.2
Total 3	125	164	.433	—	—	4.5

Miller, Doggie B8.15.1864

YEAR TM LG	W	L	PCT	FINISH	MGR/YR	+/-
1894 StL N	56	76	.424	9	—	5.2

Miller, Ray Raymond Roger; B4.30.1945 Takoma Park, MD; BR/TR/6´3˝/215(P)

YEAR TM LG	W	L	PCT	FINISH	MGR/YR	+/-
1985 Min A w	50	50	.500	6-4	2/2	4.7
1986 Min A w	59	80	.424	7-6	1/2	-2.4
1998 Bal A e	79	83	.488	4	—	-5.1
1999 Bal A e	78	84	.481	4	—	-6.4
Total 4	266	297	.472	—	—	-9.1

Mills, Buster B9.16.1908

YEAR TM LG	W	L	PCT	FINISH	MGR/YR	+/-
1953 Cin N	4	4	.500	6-6	2/2	0.4

Mills, Everett B1.20.1845

YEAR TM LG	W	L	PCT	FINISH	MGR/YR	+/-
1872 Bal NA	8	6	.571	2-2	2/2	-2.3

Mitchell, Fred B6.5.1878

YEAR TM LG	W	L	PCT	FINISH	MGR/YR	+/-
1917 Chi N	74	80	.481	5	—	-1.3
1918 Chi N	84	45	.651	1	—	3.2
1919 Chi N	75	65	.536	3	—	-0.7
1920 Chi N	75	79	.487	5t	—	-0.3
1921 Bos N	79	74	.516	4	—	0.1
1922 Bos N	53	100	.346	8	—	-1.2
1923 Bos N	54	100	.351	7	—	-7.0
Total 7	494	543	.476	—	—	-7.2

Mizerock, John B12.8.1960

YEAR TM LG	W	L	PCT	FINISH	MGR/YR	+/-
2002 KC A c	5	8	.385	4-4-4	2/3	-0.3

Moore, Jackie B2.19.1939

YEAR TM LG	W	L	PCT	FINISH	MGR/YR	+/-
1984 Oak A w	57	61	.483	5-4	2/2	2.1
1985 Oak A w	77	85	.475	4t	—	-1.1
1986 Oak A w	29	44	.397	6t-3t	1/3	-6.2
Total 3	163	190	.462	—	—	-5.2

Moore, Terry B5.27.1912

YEAR TM LG	W	L	PCT	FINISH	MGR/YR	+/-
1954 Phi N	35	42	.455	3-4	2/2	-5.8

Moran, Pat B2.7.1876

YEAR TM LG	W	L	PCT	FINISH	MGR/YR	+/-
1915 Phi N	90	62	.592	1	—	-0.4
1916 Phi N	91	62	.595	2	—	4.0
1917 Phi N	87	65	.572	2	—	2.2
1918 Phi N	55	68	.447	6	—	1.9
1919 Cin N	96	44	.686	1★	—	6.0
1920 Cin N	82	71	.536	3	—	-2.0
1921 Cin N	70	83	.458	6	—	-3.3
1922 Cin N	86	68	.558	2	—	0.2
1923 Cin N	91	63	.591	2	—	6.0
Total 9	748	586	.561	—	—	14.6

Morgan, Joe B11.19.1930

YEAR TM LG	W	L	PCT	FINISH	MGR/YR	+/-
1988 Bos A e	46	31	.597	4-1	2/2	1.7
1989 Bos A e	83	79	.512	3	—	-1.8
1990 Bos A e	88	74	.543	1	—	3.4
1991 Bos A e	84	78	.519	2t	—	1.1
Total 4	301	262	.535	—	—	4.3

Moriarty, George B7.7.1885

YEAR TM LG	W	L	PCT	FINISH	MGR/YR	+/-
1927 Det A	82	71	.536	4	—	1.8
1928 Det A	68	86	.442	6	—	-3.3
Total 2	150	157	.489	—	—	-1.5

Morrill, John B2.19.1855

YEAR TM LG	W	L	PCT	FINISH	MGR/YR	+/-
1882 Bos N	45	39	.536	3t	—	-2.4
1883 Bos N	33	11	.750	4-1	2/2	2.5
1884 Bos N	73	38	.658	2	—	-3.1
1885 Bos N	46	66	.411	5	—	-4.2
1886 Bos N	56	61	.479	5	—	-2.1
1887 Bos N	12	17	.414	5-5	2/2	-3.3
1888 Bos N	70	64	.522	4	—	-1.9
1889 Was N	13	38	.255	8-8	1/2	-3.2
Total 8	348	334	.510	—	—	-17.7

Morton, Charlie B10.12.1854

YEAR TM LG	W	L	PCT	FINISH	MGR/YR	+/-
1884 Tol AA	46	58	.442	8	—	4.6
1885 Det N	7	31	.184	8-6	1/2	-9.7
1890 Tol AA	68	64	.515	4	—	-2.6
Total 3	121	153	.442	—	—	-7.8

Moses, Felix Felix Inglesby; B5.13.1853 Charleston, SC; D5.5.1888 Sheffield, AL (DNP)

YEAR TM LG	W	L	PCT	FINISH	MGR/YR	+/-
1884 Ric AA	12	30	.286	12	—	0.2

Moss, Les B5.14.1925

YEAR TM LG	W	L	PCT	FINISH	MGR/YR	+/-
1968 Chi A	0	2	.000	9-9-8t	2/5	-0.9
1968 Chi A	12	22	.353	9-9-8t	4/5	-3.4
1979 Det A e	27	26	.509	5-5	1/3	-0.5
Total 2	39	50	.438	—	—	-4.8

Murnane, Tim B6.4.1852

YEAR TM LG	W	L	PCT	FINISH	MGR/YR	+/-
1884 Bos U	58	51	.532	5	—	-3.6

Murray, Billy William Jeremiah; B4.13.1864 Peabody, MA; D3.25.1937 Youngstown, OH (DNP)

YEAR TM LG	W	L	PCT	FINISH	MGR/YR	+/-
1907 Phi N	83	64	.565	3	—	5.1
1908 Phi N	83	71	.539	4	—	-1.2
1909 Phi N	74	79	.484	5	—	-2.3
Total 3	240	214	.529	—	—	1.7

Murtaugh, Danny B10.8.1917

YEAR TM LG	W	L	PCT	FINISH	MGR/YR	+/-
1957 Pit N	26	25	.510	7-7t	2/2	4.3
1958 Pit N	84	70	.545	2	—	1.3
1959 Pit N	78	76	.506	4	—	4.0
1960 Pit N	95	59	.617	1★	—	3.5
1961 Pit N	75	79	.487	6	—	-3.9
1962 Pit N	93	68	.578	4	—	4.2
1963 Pit N	74	88	.457	8	—	-3.9
1964 Pit N	80	82	.494	6t	—	-3.9
1967 Pit N	39	39	.500	6-6	2/2	0.7
1970 Pit N e	89	73	.549	1	—	1.3
1971 Pit N e	97	65	.599	1★	—	-3.4
1973 Pit N e	13	13	.500	2-3	2/2	-0.2
1974 Pit N e	88	74	.543	1	—	-2.6
1975 Pit N e	92	69	.571	1	—	-4.2
1976 Pit N e	92	70	.568	2	—	2.9
Total 15	1115	950	.540	—	—	0.2

Muser, Tony B8.1.1947

YEAR TM LG	W	L	PCT	FINISH	MGR/YR	+/-
1997 KC A c	31	48	.392	4-5	2/2	-5.1
1998 KC A c	72	89	.447	3	—	9.0
1999 KC A c	64	97	.398	4	—	-10.6
2000 KC A c	77	85	.475	4	—	0.6
2001 KC A c	65	97	.401	5	—	-3.6
2002 KC A c	8	15	.348	4-4	1/3	-1.4
Total 6	317	431	.424	—	—	-11.1

Mutrie, Jim James J. "Truthful Jim"; B6.13.1851 Chelsea, MA; D1.24.1938 New York, NY (DNP)

YEAR TM LG	W	L	PCT	FINISH	MGR/YR	+/-
1883 NY AA	54	42	.563	4	—	-3.1
1884 NY AA	75	32	.701	1	—	-7.5
1885 NY N	85	27	.759	2	—	-2.3
1886 NY N	75	44	.630	3	—	2.8
1887 NY N	68	55	.553	4	—	-1.6
1888 NY N	84	47	.641	1★	—	-0.3
1889 NY N	83	43	.659	1★	—	0.8
1890 NY N	63	68	.481	6	—	-3.9
1891 NY N	71	61	.538	3	—	1.1
Total 9	658	419	.611	—	—	-14.1

Myatt, George B6.14.1914

YEAR TM LG	W	L	PCT	FINISH	MGR/YR	+/-
1968 Phi N	1	0	1.000	6t-5-7t	2/3	0.5
1969 Phi N e	19	35	.352	5-5	2/2	-4.6
Total 2	20	35	.364	—	—	-4.0

Myers, Henry B5.1858

YEAR TM LG	W	L	PCT	FINISH	MGR/YR	+/-
1882 Bal AA	19	54	.260	6	—	4.8

Narron, Jerry B1.15.1956

YEAR TM LG	W	L	PCT	FINISH	MGR/YR	+/-
2001 Tex A w	62	72	.463	4-4	2/2	0.7
2002 Tex A w	72	90	.444	4-4	—	-5.4
2005 Cin N c	46	46	.500	5	2/2	3.6
2006 Cin N c	80	82	.494	3	—	4.0
Total 4	260	290	.473	—	—	3.0

Nash, Billy B6.24.1865

YEAR TM LG	W	L	PCT	FINISH	MGR/YR	+/-
1896 Phi N	62	68	.477	8	—	-2.9

Neun, Johnny B10.28.1900

YEAR TM LG	W	L	PCT	FINISH	MGR/YR	+/-
1946 NY A	8	6	.571	3-3	3/3	-0.3
1947 Cin N	73	81	.474	5	—	3.3
1948 Cin N	44	56	.440	7-7	1/2	4.8
Total 3	125	143	.466	—	—	7.8

Newman, Jeff B9.11.1948

YEAR TM LG	W	L	PCT	FINISH	MGR/YR	+/-
1986 Oak A w	2	8	.200	6t-7-3t	2/3	-2.8

Nichols, Kid B9.14.1869

YEAR TM LG	W	L	PCT	FINISH	MGR/YR	+/-
1904 StL N	75	79	.487	5	—	-2.8
1905 StL N	5	9	.357	7-6	1/3	-0.1
Total 2	80	88	.476	—	—	-2.9

Nicol, Hugh B1.1.1858

YEAR TM LG	W	L	PCT	FINISH	MGR/YR	+/-
1897 StL N	8	32	.200	12-12-12	2/4	0.8

Nixon, Russ B2.19.1935

YEAR TM LG	W	L	PCT	FINISH	MGR/YR	+/-
1982 Cin N w	27	43	.386	6-6	2/2	-2.5
1983 Cin N w	74	88	.457	6	—	2.1
1988 Atl N w	42	79	.347	6-6	2/2	-3.7
1989 Atl N w	63	97	.394	6	—	-6.7
1990 Atl N w	25	40	.385	6-6	1/2	-2.0
Total 5	231	347	.400	—	—	-12.8

Norman, Bill B7.16.1910

YEAR TM LG	W	L	PCT	FINISH	MGR/YR	+/-
1958 Det A	56	49	.533	8-5	2/2	-0.3
1959 Det A	2	15	.118	8-4	1/2	-6.3
Total 2	58	64	.475	—	—	-6.6

Oakes, Rebel B12.17.1883

YEAR TM LG	W	L	PCT	FINISH	MGR/YR	+/-
1914 Pit F	61	78	.439	8-7	2/2	0.4
1915 Pit F	86	67	.562	3	—	1.9
Total 2	147	145	.503	—	—	2.3

Oates, Johnny B1.21.1946

YEAR TM LG	W	L	PCT	FINISH	MGR/YR	+/-
1991 Bal A e	54	71	.432	7-6	2/2	-0.1
1992 Bal A e	89	73	.549	3	—	2.9
1993 Bal A e	85	77	.525	3t	—	-0.0
1994 Bal A e	63	49	.563	2	—	-1.9
1995 Tex A w	74	70	.514	3	—	4.8
1996 Tex A w	90	72	.556	1	—	-2.9
1997 Tex A w	77	85	.475	3	—	-2.5
1998 Tex A w	88	74	.543	1	—	0.8
1999 Tex A w	95	67	.586	1	—	6.3
2000 Tex A w	71	91	.438	4	—	1.3
2001 Tex A w	11	17	.393	4	1/2	-1.8
Total 11	797	746	.517	—	—	6.9

O'Connor, Jack B6.2.1869

YEAR TM LG	W	L	PCT	FINISH	MGR/YR	+/-
1910 StL A	47	107	.305	8	—	1.9

O'Day, Hank B7.8.1862

YEAR TM LG	W	L	PCT	FINISH	MGR/YR	+/-
1912 Cin N	75	78	.490	4	—	5.1
1914 Chi N	78	76	.506	4	—	4.5
Total 2	153	154	.498	—	—	9.6

O'Farrell, Bob B10.19.1896

YEAR TM LG	W	L	PCT	FINISH	MGR/YR	+/-
1927 StL N	92	61	.601	2	—	6.7
1934 Cin N	30	60	.333	8-8	1/3	-2.5
Total 2	122	121	.502	—	—	4.2

O'Leary, Dan B10.22.1856

YEAR TM LG	W	L	PCT	FINISH	MGR/YR	+/-
1884 Cin U	20	15	.571	5-3	1/2	-4.6

YEAR	TM LG	W	L	PCT	FINISH	MGR/YR	+/-
O'Neill, Steve B7.6.1891							
1935	Cle A	36	23	.610	5-3	2/2	5.1
1936	Cle A	80	74	.519	5	—	-2.3
1937	Cle A	83	71	.539	4	—	1.4
1943	Det A	78	76	.506	5	—	-6.8
1944	Det A	88	66	.571	2	—	2.8
1945	Det A	88	65	.575	1★	—	4.2
1946	Det A	92	62	.597	2	—	0.6
1947	Det A	85	69	.552	2	—	0.6
1948	Det A	78	76	.506	5	—	3.6
1950	Bos A	63	32	.663	4-3	2/2	3.5
1951	Bos A	87	67	.565	3	—	2.5
1952	Phi N	59	32	.648	6-4	2/2	6.9
1953	Phi N	83	71	.539	3t	—	1.0
1954	Phi N	40	37	.519	3-4	1/2	-0.8
Total 14		1040	821	.559	—	—	22.2
Onslow, Jack B10.13.1888							
1949	Chi A	63	91	.409	6	—	-5.1
1950	Chi A	8	22	.267	8-6	1/2	-4.6
Total 2		71	113	.386	—	—	-9.7
O'Rourke, Jim B9.1.1850							
1881	Buf N	45	38	.542	3	—	4.1
1882	Buf N	45	39	.536	3t	—	-0.5
1883	Buf N	52	45	.536	5	—	0.2
1884	Buf N	64	47	.577	3	—	2.0
1893	Was N	40	89	.310	12	—	0.8
Total 5		246	258	.488	—	—	6.7
Orr, Dave B9.29.1859							
1887	NY AA	3	5	.375	8-7-7	2/3	0.7
Ott, Mel B3.2.1909							
1942	NY N	85	67	.559	3	—	1.2
1943	NY N	55	98	.359	8	—	-5.2
1944	NY N	67	87	.435	5	—	-1.1
1945	NY N	78	74	.513	5	—	5.3
1946	NY N	61	93	.396	8	—	-8.5
1947	NY N	81	73	.526	4	—	-2.5
1948	NY N	37	38	.493	4-5	1/2	-4.1
Total 7		464	530	.467	—	—	-14.8
Owens, Paul Paul Francis; B2.7.1924 Salamanca, NY; D12.26.2003 Woodbury, NJ BR/TR/6´3˝/185(1B)							
1972	Phi N e	33	47	.412	6-6	2/2	0.5
1983	Phi N e	47	30	.610	1-1◆	2/2	5.5
1984	Phi N e	81	81	.500	4	—	-3.1
Total 3		161	158	.505	—	—	2.9
Ozark, Danny Daniel Leonard (b Daniel Leonard Orzechowski); B11.26.1923 Buffalo, NY; BR/TR/6´3˝/210(1B)							
1973	Phi N e	71	91	.438	6	—	-2.2
1974	Phi N e	80	82	.494	3	—	1.6
1975	Phi N e	86	76	.531	2	—	0.9
1976	Phi N e	101	61	.623	1	—	-2.3
1977	Phi N e	101	61	.623	1	—	2.4
1978	Phi N e	90	72	.556	1	—	-4.0
1979	Phi N e	65	67	.492	5-4	1/2	1.9
1984	SF N w	24	32	.429	6-6	2/2	0.3
Total 8		618	542	.533	—	—	-1.4
Pabor, Charlie B9.24.1846							
1871	Cle NA	10	19	.345	7	—	1.6
1875	Atl NA	2	40	.048	12-12	1/2	5.3
1875	NH NA	1	5	.167	8-8	3/3	0.5
Total 2		13	64	.169	—	—	7.5
Parker, Salty B7.8.1912							
1967	NY N	4	7	.364	10-10	2/2	-0.2
1972	Hou N w	1	0	1.000	2-2	2/3	0.5
Total 2		5	7	.417	—	—	0.3
Parks, Bill B6.4.1849							
1875	Was NA	1	7	.125	8-10	2/2	2.0
Parrish, Larry B11.10.1953							
1998	Det A c	13	12	.520	5-5	2/2	2.6
1999	Det A c	69	92	.429	3	—	1.2
Total 2		82	104	.441	—	—	3.8
Pearce, Dickey B2.29.1836							
1872	Mut NA	10	6	.625	4-3	1/2	-1.6
1875	StL NA	39	29	.574	4	—	3.4
Total 2		49	35	.583	—	—	1.8
Peckinpaugh, Roger B2.5.1891							
1914	NY A	10	10	.500	7-6t	2/2	0.2
1928	Cle A	62	92	.403	7	—	0.0
1929	Cle A	81	71	.533	3	—	6.8
1930	Cle A	81	73	.526	4	—	6.2
1931	Cle A	78	76	.506	4	—	-3.7
1932	Cle A	87	65	.572	4	—	1.9
1933	Cle A	26	25	.510	5-4	1/3	1.0
1941	Cle A	75	79	.487	4t	—	-2.9
Total 8		500	491	.505	—	—	9.5
Pedrique, Al B8.11.1960							
2004	Ari N w	22	61	.265	5-5	2/2	-5.2
Pena, Tony B6.4.1957							
2002	KC A c	49	77	.389	4-4	3/3	-2.7
2003	KC A c	83	79	.512	3	—	4.9
2004	KC A c	58	104	.358	5	—	-5.5

YEAR	TM LG	W	L	PCT	FINISH	MGR/YR	+/-
2005	KC A c	8	25	.242	5-5	1/3	-4.0
Total 4		198	285	.410	—	—	-7.3
Perez, Tony B5.14.1942							
1993	Cin N w	20	24	.455	5-5	1/2	-0.3
2001	Fla N e	54	60	.474	3-4	2/2	-2.9
Total 2		74	84	.468	—	—	-3.2
Perkins, Cy B2.27.1896							
1937	Det A	6	9	.400	2-2	5/5	-2.3
Perlozzo, Sam B3.4.1951							
2005	Bal A e	23	32	.418	4-4	2/2	-2.1
2006	Bal A e	70	92	.432	4	—	1.3
Total 2		93	124	.429	—	—	-0.9
Pesky, Johnny B9.27.1919							
1963	Bos A	76	85	.472	7	—	-0.6
1964	Bos A	70	90	.438	8-8	1/2	0.3
1980	Bos A e	1	4	.200	3-4	2/2	-1.5
Total 3		147	179	.451	—	—	-1.8
Pfeffer, Fred B3.17.1860							
1892-1	Lou N	9	14	.391	10-11	2/2	-0.2
1892-2	Lou N	33	42	.440	9	—	2.1
Phelan, Lou Louis A.; B3.1864 St.Louis, MO; D11.2.1933 Los Angeles, CA (DNP)							
1895	StL N	11	30	.268	11-11	4/4	-2.1
Phillips, Lefty Harold Ross; B6.16.1919 Los Angeles, CA; D6.12.1972 Fullerton, CA BL/TL/5´11˝/192(P)							
1969	Cal A w	60	63	.488	6-3	2/2	9.0
1970	Cal A w	86	76	.531	3	—	4.9
1971	Cal A w	76	86	.469	4	—	2.5
Total 3		222	225	.497	—	—	16.4
Phillips, Horace Horace B.; B5.14.1853 Salem, OH; (DNP)							
1879	Tro N	12	34	.261	8-8	1/2	1.2
1883	Col AA	32	65	.330	6	—	-0.4
1884	Pit AA	9	24	.273	10-10	5/5	1.6
1885	Pit AA	56	55	.505	3	—	-0.3
1886	Pit AA	80	57	.584	2	—	-3.7
1887	Pit N	55	69	.444	6	—	4.7
1888	Pit N	66	68	.493	6	—	3.9
1889	Pit N	28	43	.394	6-5	1/3	-3.9
Total 8		338	415	.449	—	—	3.1
Phillips, Bill B11.9.1868							
1914	Ind F	88	65	.575	1	—	-2.6
1915	New F	26	27	.491	6-5	1/2	-1.4
Total 2		114	92	.553	—	—	-4.0
Pike, Lip B5.25.1845							
1871	Tro NA	1	3	.250	7-6	1/2	-0.9
1874	Har NA	16	37	.302	7	—	-3.0
1877	Cin N	3	11	.214	6-6	1/3	-0.1
Total 3		20	51	.282	—	—	-4.0
Piniella, Lou B8.28.1943							
1986	NY A e	90	72	.556	2	—	3.2
1987	NY A e	89	73	.549	4	—	5.1
1988	NY A e	45	48	.484	2-5	2/2	-2.9
1990	Cin N w	91	71	.562	1★	—	-0.2
1991	Cin N w	74	88	.457	5	—	-6.8
1992	Cin N w	90	72	.556	2	—	3.5
1993	Sea A w	82	80	.506	4	—	0.7
1994	Sea A w	49	63	.438	3	—	-2.7
1995	Sea A w	79	66	.545	1☆▲	—	-1.7
1996	Sea A w	85	76	.528	2	—	-4.1
1997	Sea A w	90	72	.556	1	—	0.6
1998	Sea A w	76	85	.472	3	—	-4.9
1999	Sea A w	79	83	.488	3	—	2.2
2000	Sea A w	91	71	.562	2☆✤	—	-1.8
2001	Sea A w	116	46	.716	1☆	—	5.9
2002	Sea A w	93	69	.574	3	—	0.7
2003	TB A e	63	99	.389	5	—	-4.8
2004	TB A e	70	91	.435	4	—	1.9
2005	TB A e	67	95	.414	5	—	3.3
Total 19		1519	1420	.517	—	—	-2.6
Plummer, Bill B3.21.1947							
1992	Sea A w	64	98	.395	7	—	-5.1
Popowski, Eddie Edward Joseph; B8.20.1913 Sayreville, NJ; D12.4.2001 Sayreville, NJ BR/TR/5´4.5˝/145(2B)							
1969	Bos A e	5	4	.556	3-3	2/2	0.5
1973	Bos A e	1	0	1.000	2-2	2/2	0.4
Total 2		6	4	.600	—	—	0.9
Porter, Matthew B							
1884	KC U	3	13	.188	8-8-8	2/3	0.5
Powers, Pat Patrick Thomas; B6.27.1860 Trenton, NJ; D8.29.1925 Belmar, NJ (DNP)							
1890	Roc AA	63	63	.500	5	—	0.2
1892-1	NY N	31	43	.419	10	—	-3.1
1892-2	NY N	40	37	.519	6	—	-3.1
Total 2		134	143	.484	—	—	-6.1

YEAR	TM LG	W	L	PCT	FINISH	MGR/YR	+/-
Pratt, Al B11.19.1848							
1882	Pit AA	39	39	.500	4	—	-0.9
1883	Pit AA	12	20	.375	6-7	1/3	1.6
Total 2		51	59	.464	—	—	0.6
Price, Jim James Lyman; B9.20.1847 New York, NY; D10.24.1925 Oak Park, IL (DNP)							
1884	NY N	56	42	.571	4-4t	1/2	1.5
Prothro, Doc B7.16.1893							
1939	Phi N	45	106	.298	8	—	-0.6
1940	Phi N	50	103	.327	8	—	0.4
1941	Phi N	43	111	.279	8	—	-3.7
Total 3		138	320	.301	—	—	-3.9
Pujols, Luis B11.18.1955							
2002	Det A c	55	100	.355	5-5	2/2	5.4
Purcell, Blondie B							
1883	Phi N	13	68	.160	8-8	2/2	3.0
Queen, Mel B3.26.1942							
1997	Tor A e	4	1	.800	5-5	2/2	1.6
Quilici, Frank B5.11.1939							
1972	Min A w	41	43	.488	3-3	2/2	-1.1
1973	Min A w	81	81	.500	3	—	-4.6
1974	Min A w	82	80	.506	3	—	0.6
1975	Min A w	76	83	.478	4	—	-2.3
Total 4		280	287	.494	—	—	-7.5
Quinn, Joe B12.25.1864							
1895	StL N	11	28	.282	11-11-11	3/4	-1.5
1899	Cle N	12	104	.103	12-12	2/2	2.0
Total 2		23	132	.148	—	—	0.5
Rader, Doug B7.30.1944							
1983	Tex A w	77	85	.475	3	—	-7.3
1984	Tex A w	69	92	.429	7	—	-5.5
1985	Tex A w	9	23	.281	7-7	1/2	-3.6
1986	Chi A w	1	1	.500	6-5-5	2/3	0.1
1989	Cal A w	91	71	.562	3	—	0.2
1990	Cal A w	80	82	.494	4	—	0.6
1991	Cal A w	61	63	.492	7-7	1/2	-1.3
Total 7		388	417	.482	—	—	-16.9
Randolph, Willie B7.6.1954							
2005	NY N e	83	79	.512	3t	—	-5.6
2006	NY N e	97	65	.599	1☆	—	6.1
Total 2		180	144	.556	—	—	0.4
Rapp, Vern Vernon Fred; B5.11.1928 St.Louis, MO; BR/TR/6´0˝/195(C)							
1977	StL N e	83	79	.512	3	—	-3.0
1978	StL N e	6	11	.353	6-5	1/3	-1.9
1984	Cin N w	51	70	.421	5-5	1/2	-0.3
Total 3		140	160	.467	—	—	-5.1
Reach, Al B5.25.1840							
1890	Phi N	4	7	.364	2-3-3	3/5	-2.4
Regan, Phil B4.6.1937							
1995	Bal A e	71	73	.493	3	—	-7.3
Rice, Del B10.27.1922							
1972	Cal A w	75	80	.484	5	—	6.9
Richards, Paul B11.21.1908							
1951	Chi A	81	73	.526	4	—	-3.1
1952	Chi A	81	73	.526	3	—	-0.6
1953	Chi A	89	65	.578	3	—	-0.8
1954	Chi A	91	54	.628	3-3	1/2	-0.5
1955	Bal A	57	97	.370	7	—	2.3
1956	Bal A	69	85	.448	6	—	6.0
1957	Bal A	76	76	.500	5	—	-1.0
1958	Bal A	74	79	.484	6	—	3.6
1959	Bal A	74	80	.481	6	—	4.6
1960	Bal A	89	65	.578	2	—	4.1
1961	Bal A	78	57	.578	3-3	1/2	1.3
1976	Chi A w	64	97	.398	6	—	0.1
Total 12		923	901	.506	—	—	15.9
Richardson, Danny B1.25.1863							
1892-2	Was N	12	31	.279	11-12	2/2	-5.9
Rickey, Branch B12.20.1881							
1913	StL A	5	6	.455	7-8	3/3	0.4
1914	StL A	71	82	.464	5	—	4.8
1915	StL A	63	91	.409	6	—	3.2
1919	StL N	54	83	.394	7	—	-4.7
1920	StL N	75	79	.487	5t	—	-1.3
1921	StL N	87	66	.569	3	—	-1.8
1922	StL N	85	69	.552	3t	—	4.0
1923	StL N	79	74	.516	5	—	1.1
1924	StL N	65	89	.422	6	—	-11.0
1925	StL N	13	25	.342	8-4	1/2	-7.5
Total 10		597	664	.473	—	—	-12.7
Riddoch, Greg Gregory Lee; B7.17.1945 Greeley, CO; BR/TR/5´11˝/175(SS)							
1990	SD N w	38	44	.463	4-5	2/2	-3.0
1991	SD N w	84	78	.519	3	—	4.1
1992	SD N w	78	72	.520	3-3	1/2	4.9
Total 3		200	194	.508	—	—	6.0

RIGGLEMAN, JIM James David; B11.9.1952 Fort Dix, NJ; BR/TR/5´11˝/175(3B)

YEAR	TM LG	W	L	PCT	FINISH	MGR/YR	+/-
1992	SD N w	4	8	.333	3-3	2/2	-1.8
1993	SD N w	61	101	.377	7	—	-10.7
1994	SD N w	47	70	.402	4	—	-6.2
1995	Chi N c	73	71	.507	3	—	-1.1
1996	Chi N c	76	86	.469	4	—	-5.1
1997	Chi N c	68	94	.420	5	—	-5.8
1998	Chi N c	90	73	.552	2✤▲	—	4.8
1999	Chi N c	67	95	.414	6	—	2.2
Total	8	486	598	.448	—	—	-23.8

RIGNEY, BILL B1.29.1918

YEAR	TM LG	W	L	PCT	FINISH	MGR/YR	+/-
1956	NY N	67	87	.435	6	—	1.9
1957	NY N	69	85	.448	6	—	-2.1
1958	SF N	80	74	.519	3	—	0.1
1959	SF N	83	71	.539	3	—	-3.4
1960	SF N	33	25	.569	2-5	1/2	2.4
1961	LA A	70	91	.435	8	—	-6.6
1962	LA A	86	76	.531	3	—	3.8
1963	LA A	70	91	.435	9	—	-3.7
1964	LA A	82	80	.506	5	—	1.8
1965	Cal A	75	87	.463	7	—	-1.2
1966	Cal A	80	82	.494	6	—	3.2
1967	Cal A	84	77	.522	5	—	5.7
1968	Cal A	67	95	.414	8	—	-0.6
1969	Cal A w	11	28	.282	6-3	1/2	-5.2
1970	Min A w	98	64	.605	1	—	2.5
1971	Min A w	74	86	.463	5	—	-4.3
1972	Min A w	36	34	.514	3-3	1/2	0.9
1976	SF N w	74	88	.457	4	—	2.7
Total	18	1239	1321	.484	—	—	-2.0

RIPKEN, CAL Calvin Edwin Sr.; B12.17.1935 Aberdeen, MD; D3.25.1999 Baltimore, MD BR/TR/6´0˝/175(C)

YEAR	TM LG	W	L	PCT	FINISH	MGR/YR	+/-
1985	Bal A e	1	0	1.000	4-4-4	2/3	0.5
1987	Bal A e	67	95	.414	6	—	0.4
1988	Bal A e	0	6	.000	7-7	1/2	-2.1
Total	3	68	101	.402	—	—	-1.2

ROBINSON, FRANK B8.31.1935

YEAR	TM LG	W	L	PCT	FINISH	MGR/YR	+/-
1975	Cle A	79	80	.497	4	—	1.0
1976	Cle A	81	78	.509	4	—	1.5
1977	Cle A e	26	31	.456	5-5	1/2	-0.2
1981-1	SF N w	27	32	.458	5	—	-0.9
1981-2	SF N w	29	23	.558	3	—	-0.9
1982	SF N w	87	75	.537	3	—	7.4
1983	SF N w	79	83	.488	5	—	-1.0
1984	SF N w	42	64	.396	6-6	1/2	-2.9
1988	Bal A e	54	101	.348	7-7	2/2	0.4
1989	Bal A e	87	75	.537	2	—	3.7
1990	Bal A e	76	85	.472	5	—	-1.5
1991	Bal A e	13	24	.351	7-6	1/2	-3.0
2002	Mon N e	83	79	.512	2	—	0.3
2003	Mon N e	83	79	.512	4	—	2.5
2004	Mon N e	67	95	.414	5	—	-0.3
2005	Was N e	81	81	.500	5	—	3.6
2006	Was N e	71	91	.438	5	—	2.0
Total	16	1065	1176	.475	—	—	11.7

ROBINSON, WILBERT B6.29.1863

YEAR	TM LG	W	L	PCT	FINISH	MGR/YR	+/-
1902	Bal A	24	57	.296	7-8	2/2	-9.5
1914	Bro N	75	79	.487	5	—	-2.4
1915	Bro N	80	72	.526	3	—	6.7
1916	Bro N	94	60	.610	1	—	3.9
1917	Bro N	70	81	.464	7	—	-0.0
1918	Bro N	57	69	.452	5	—	6.1
1919	Bro N	69	71	.493	5	—	-2.3
1920	Bro N	93	61	.604	1	—	1.7
1921	Bro N	77	75	.507	5	—	2.4
1922	Bro N	76	78	.494	6	—	0.1
1923	Bro N	76	78	.494	6	—	-2.2
1924	Bro N	92	62	.597	2	—	11.2
1925	Bro N	68	85	.444	6*t*	—	-1.2
1926	Bro N	71	82	.464	6	—	2.9
1927	Bro N	65	88	.425	6	—	-3.0
1928	Bro N	77	76	.503	6	—	-2.1
1929	Bro N	70	83	.458	6	—	5.7
1930	Bro N	86	68	.558	4	—	-3.3
1931	Bro N	79	73	.520	4	—	2.2
Total	19	1399	1398	.500	—	—	16.8

ROBISON, STAN Matthew Stanley; B3.30.1859 Pittsburgh, PA; D3.24.1911 Cleveland, OH (DNP)

YEAR	TM LG	W	L	PCT	FINISH	MGR/YR	+/-
1905	StL N	19	31	.380	6-6	3/3	0.8

RODGERS, BUCK B8.16.1938

YEAR	TM LG	W	L	PCT	FINISH	MGR/YR	+/-
1980	Mil A e	26	21	.553	2-3	1/3	-1.2
1980	Mil A e	13	10	.565	4-3	3/3	-0.3
1981-1	Mil A e	31	25	.554	3	—	4.0
1981-2	Mil A e	31	22	.585	1	—	4.0
1982	Mil A e	23	24	.489	5-1◆	1/2	-5.3
1985	Mon N e	84	77	.522	3	—	3.8
1986	Mon N e	78	83	.484	4	—	2.8
1987	Mon N e	91	71	.562	3	—	7.9
1988	Mon N e	81	81	.500	3	—	-3.9
1989	Mon N e	81	81	.500	4	—	-0.2
1990	Mon N e	85	77	.525	3	—	-2.9
1991	Mon N e	20	29	.408	6-6	1/2	-2.0
1991	Cal A w	20	18	.526	7-7	2/2	0.9
1992	Cal A w	19	20	.487	5-5*t*	1/3	1.9
1992	Cal A w	14	20	.412	5-5*t*	3/3	-0.9
1993	Cal A w	71	91	.438	5*t*	—	-1.4
1994	Cal A w	16	23	.410	3-4	1/3	0.2
Total	13	784	773	.504	—	—	7.5

ROGERS, JIM B4.9.1872

YEAR	TM LG	W	L	PCT	FINISH	MGR/YR	+/-
1897	Lou N	17	24	.415	9-11	1/2	1.9

ROJAS, COOKIE B3.6.1939

YEAR	TM LG	W	L	PCT	FINISH	MGR/YR	+/-
1988	Cal A w	75	79	.487	4-4	1/2	3.4
1996	Fla N e	1	0	1.000	4-4-3	2/3	0.5
Total	2	76	79	.490	—	—	3.9

ROLFE, RED B10.17.1908

YEAR	TM LG	W	L	PCT	FINISH	MGR/YR	+/-
1949	Det A	87	67	.565	4	—	0.4
1950	Det A	95	59	.617	2	—	6.2
1951	Det A	73	81	.474	5	—	1.5
1952	Det A	23	49	.319	8-8	1/2	-4.2
Total	4	278	256	.521	—	—	3.9

ROSE, PETE B4.14.1941

YEAR	TM LG	W	L	PCT	FINISH	MGR/YR	+/-
1984	Cin N	19	22	.463	5-5	2/2	1.6
1985	Cin N	89	72	.553	2	—	7.4
1986	Cin N	86	76	.531	2	—	3.5
1987	Cin N w	84	78	.519	2	—	-0.0
1988	Cin N w	11	12	.478	4-2	1/3	-1.2
1988	Cin N w	64	47	.577	4-2	3/3	5.1
1989	Cin N w	59	66	.472	4*t*-5	1/2	1.3
Total	6	412	373	.525	—	—	17.7

ROSEMAN, CHIEF B1856

YEAR	TM LG	W	L	PCT	FINISH	MGR/YR	+/-
1890	StL AA	7	8	.467	4-5-3	3/6	-1.8

ROTHSCHILD, LARRY B3.12.1954

YEAR	TM LG	W	L	PCT	FINISH	MGR/YR	+/-
1998	TB A e	63	99	.389	5	—	-4.5
1999	TB A e	69	93	.426	5	—	1.1
2000	TB A e	69	92	.429	5	—	-1.0
2001	TB A e	4	10	.286	5-5	1/2	-1.2
Total	4	205	294	.411	—	—	-5.6

ROWE, DAVE B10.9.1854

YEAR	TM LG	W	L	PCT	FINISH	MGR/YR	+/-
1886	KC N	30	91	.248	7	—	3.9
1888	KC AA	14	36	.280	8-8	1/3	-0.2
Total	2	44	127	.257	—	—	3.7

ROWE, JACK B12.8.1856

YEAR	TM LG	W	L	PCT	FINISH	MGR/YR	+/-
1890	Buf P	22	58	.275	8-8	1/3	1.1
1890	Buf P	5	14	.263	8-8	3/3	0.0

ROWLAND, PANTS Clarence Henry; B2.12.1879 Platteville, WI; D5.17.1969 Chicago, IL BR/TR/5´9˝/168(C)

YEAR	TM LG	W	L	PCT	FINISH	MGR/YR	+/-
1915	Chi A	93	61	.604	3	—	-6.2
1916	Chi A	89	65	.578	2	—	0.3
1917	Chi A	100	54	.649	1★	—	1.5
1918	Chi A	57	67	.460	6	—	-6.2
Total	4	339	247	.578	—	—	-10.7

ROYSTER, JERRY B10.18.1952

YEAR	TM LG	W	L	PCT	FINISH	MGR/YR	+/-
2002	Mil N c	53	94	.361	6-6	2/2	-2.8

RUDOLPH, DICK B8.25.1887

YEAR	TM LG	W	L	PCT	FINISH	MGR/YR	+/-
1924	Bos N	11	27	.289	6-8-8	2/3	-0.9

RUEL, MUDDY B2.20.1896

YEAR	TM LG	W	L	PCT	FINISH	MGR/YR	+/-
1947	StL A	59	95	.383	8	—	0.5

RUNNELLS, TOM B4.17.1955

YEAR	TM LG	W	L	PCT	FINISH	MGR/YR	+/-
1991	Mon N e	51	61	.455	6-6	2/2	0.7
1992	Mon N e	17	20	.459	4-2	1/2	-3.2
Total	2	68	81	.456	—	—	-2.4

RUNNELS, PETE B1.28.1928

YEAR	TM LG	W	L	PCT	FINISH	MGR/YR	+/-
1966	Bos A	8	8	.500	9-9	2/2	0.8

RUSSELL, BILL B10.21.1948

YEAR	TM LG	W	L	PCT	FINISH	MGR/YR	+/-
1996	LA N w	49	37	.570	1-2✤	2/2	3.2
1997	LA N w	88	74	.543	2	—	-2.9
1998	LA N w	36	38	.486	3-3	1/2	-0.6
Total	3	173	149	.537	—	—	-0.3

RYAN, CONNIE B2.27.1920

YEAR	TM LG	W	L	PCT	FINISH	MGR/YR	+/-
1975	Atl N w	9	18	.333	5-5	2/2	-1.8
1977	Tex A w	2	4	.333	3-5-2	3/4	-1.4
Total	2	11	22	.333	—	—	-3.2

SAWYER, EDDIE Edwin Milby; B9.10.1910 Westerly, RI; D9.22.1997 Phoenixville, PA BR/TR/6´0˝/210(OF)

YEAR	TM LG	W	L	PCT	FINISH	MGR/YR	+/-
1948	Phi N	23	40	.365	6-6	3/3	-2.7
1949	Phi N	81	73	.526	3	—	4.6
1950	Phi N	91	63	.591	1	—	4.0
1951	Phi N	73	81	.474	5	—	-4.4
1952	Phi N	28	35	.444	6-4	1/2	-8.1
1958	Phi N	30	40	.429	8-8	2/2	-0.6
1959	Phi N	64	90	.416	8	—	-0.1
1960	Phi N	0	1	.000	6*t*-8	1/3	-0.4
Total	8	390	423	.480	—	—	-7.8

SCANLON, MIKE Michael B.; B11.1843 Cork, Ireland; D1.18.1929 Washington, DC (DNP)

YEAR	TM LG	W	L	PCT	FINISH	MGR/YR	+/-
1884	Was U	47	65	.420	6	—	0.7
1886	Was N	13	67	.162	8-8	1/2	-5.0
Total	2	60	132	.313	—	—	-4.3

SCHAEFER, BOB Robert Walden; B5.22.1944 Putnam, CT; BL/TR/5´11˝/180(SS)

YEAR	TM LG	W	L	PCT	FINISH	MGR/YR	+/-
1991	KC A w	1	0	1.000	7-7-6	2/3	0.5
2005	KC A c	5	12	.294	5-5-5	2/3	-1.2
Total	2	6	12	.333	—	—	-0.7

SCHALK, RAY B8.12.1892

YEAR	TM LG	W	L	PCT	FINISH	MGR/YR	+/-
1927	Chi A	70	83	.458	5	—	-1.9
1928	Chi A	32	42	.432	6-5	1/2	-1.7
Total	2	102	125	.449	—	—	-3.6

SCHEFFING, BOB B8.11.1913

YEAR	TM LG	W	L	PCT	FINISH	MGR/YR	+/-
1957	Chi N	62	92	.403	7*t*	—	-5.4
1958	Chi N	72	82	.468	5*t*	—	-3.4
1959	Chi N	74	80	.481	5*t*	—	-1.5
1961	Det A	101	61	.623	2	—	3.3
1962	Det A	85	76	.528	4	—	-2.1
1963	Det A	24	36	.400	9-5t	1/2	-5.9
Total	6	418	427	.495	—	—	-15.1

SCHLAFLY, LARRY B9.19.1878

YEAR	TM LG	W	L	PCT	FINISH	MGR/YR	+/-
1914	Buf F	80	71	.530	4	—	2.6
1915	Buf F	13	28	.317	8-6	1/3	-5.8
Total	2	93	99	.484	—	—	-3.2

SCHMELZ, GUS Gustavius Heinrich; B9.26.1850 Columbus, OH; D10.13.1925 Columbus, OH (DNP)

YEAR	TM LG	W	L	PCT	FINISH	MGR/YR	+/-
1884	Col AA	69	39	.639	2	—	2.7
1886	StL N	43	79	.352	6	—	-2.3
1887	Cin AA	81	54	.600	2	—	0.8
1888	Cin AA	80	54	.597	4	—	1.9
1889	Cin AA	76	63	.547	4	—	-4.7
1890	Cle N	21	55	.276	7-7	1/2	-6.4
1890	Col AA	38	13	.745	5-2	2/3	4.9
1891	Col AA	61	76	.445	6	—	-0.6
1894	Was N	45	87	.341	11	—	-2.5
1895	Was N	43	85	.336	10	—	-4.1
1896	Was N	58	73	.443	9*t*	—	1.0
1897	Was N	9	25	.265	11-6*t*	1/2	-7.7
Total	11	624	703	.470	—	—	-17.1

SCHOENDIENST, RED B2.2.1923

YEAR	TM LG	W	L	PCT	FINISH	MGR/YR	+/-
1965	StL N	80	81	.497	7	—	-3.9
1966	StL N	83	79	.512	6	—	2.7
1967	StL N	101	60	.627	1★	—	5.7
1968	StL N	97	65	.599	1	—	2.9
1969	StL N e	87	75	.537	4	—	-0.2
1970	StL N e	76	86	.469	4	—	-4.7
1971	StL N e	90	72	.556	2	—	5.0
1972	StL N e	75	81	.481	4	—	0.5
1973	StL N e	81	81	.500	2	—	-4.3
1974	StL N e	86	75	.534	2	—	1.9
1975	StL N e	82	80	.506	3t	—	3.8
1976	StL N e	72	90	.444	5	—	-4.6
1980	StL N e	18	19	.486	5-4	4/4	-1.1
1990	StL N e	13	11	.542	6-6-6	2/3	2.6
Total	14	1041	955	.522	—	—	6.2

SCHULTZ, JOE B8.29.1918

YEAR	TM LG	W	L	PCT	FINISH	MGR/YR	+/-
1969	Sea A w	64	98	.395	6	—	-0.8
1973	Det A e	14	14	.500	3-3	2/2	0.6
Total	2	78	112	.411	—	—	-0.3

SCIOSCIA, MIKE B11.27.1958

YEAR	TM LG	W	L	PCT	FINISH	MGR/YR	+/-
2000	Ana A w	82	80	.506	3	—	1.5
2001	Ana A w	75	87	.463	3	—	-2.0
2002	Ana A w	99	63	.611	2★✤	—	-2.4
2003	Ana A w	77	85	.475	3	—	-3.3
2004	Ana A w	92	70	.568	1	—	1.2
2005	LA A w	95	67	.586	1☆	—	2.0
2006	LA A w	89	73	.549	2	—	4.6
Total	7	609	525	.537	—	—	1.4

SELEE, FRANK Frank Gibson; B10.26.1859 Amherst, NY; D7.5.1909 Denver, CO (DNP)

YEAR	TM LG	W	L	PCT	FINISH	MGR/YR	+/-
1890	Bos N	76	57	.571	5	—	-6.5
1891	Bos N	87	51	.630	1	—	0.7
1892-1	Bos N	52	22	.703	1	—	6.7
1892-2	Bos N	50	26	.658	2●	—	6.7
1893	Bos N	86	43	.667	1	—	4.3
1894	Bos N	83	49	.629	3	—	1.0
1895	Bos N	71	60	.542	5*t*	—	-1.3
1896	Bos N	74	57	.565	4	—	-0.4
1897	Bos N	93	39	.705	1	—	-3.5
1898	Bos N	102	47	.685	1	—	2.7
1899	Bos N	95	57	.625	2	—	-1.4
1900	Bos N	66	72	.478	4	—	-6.6
1901	Bos N	69	69	.500	5	—	2.7
1902	Chi N	68	69	.496	5	—	-4.8
1903	Chi N	82	56	.594	3	—	3.6
1904	Chi N	93	60	.608	2	—	7.5
1905	Chi N	37	28	.569	4-3	1/2	-6.2
Total	16	1284	862	.598	—	—	5.2

SEWELL, LUKE B1.5.1901

YEAR	TM LG	W	L	PCT	FINISH	MGR/YR	+/-
1941	StL A	55	55	.500	7-6t	2/2	3.9
1942	StL A	82	69	.543	3	—	-2.8
1943	StL A	72	80	.474	6	—	-3.1
1944	StL A	89	65	.578	1	—	1.9
1945	StL A	81	70	.536	3	—	0.1
1946	StL A	53	71	.427	7-7	1/2	-1.6
1949	Cin N	1	2	.333	7-7	2/2	-0.2
1950	Cin N	66	87	.431	6	—	-2.5
1951	Cin N	68	86	.442	6	—	2.5
1952	Cin N	39	59	.398	7-6	1/3	-7.1
Total	10	606	644	.485	—	—	-9.0

YEAR TM LG	W	L	PCT	FINISH	MGR/YR	+/-
SHANNON, DAN B3.23.1865						
1889 Lou AA	10	46	.179	8-8-8	3/4	-2.1
1891 Was AA	15	34	.306	7-8-8	3/4	2.0
Total 2	25	80	.238	—	—	-0.1
SHARSIG, BILL William A.; B1855 Philadelphia, PA; D2.1.1902 Philadelphia, PA (DNP)						
1886 Phi AA	22	17	.564	6-6	2/2	6.7
1888 Phi AA	81	52	.609	3	—	-7.1
1889 Phi AA	75	58	.564	3	—	0.5
1890 Phi AA	54	78	.409	7	—	8.6
1891 Phi AA	6	11	.353	7-4	1/2	-2.8
Total 5	238	216	.524	—	—	5.9
SHAWKEY, BOB B12.4.1890						
1930 NY A	86	68	.558	3	—	-4.8
SHEEHAN, TOM B3.31.1894						
1960 SF N	46	50	.479	2-5	2/2	-4.6
SHEPARD, LARRY Lawrence William; B4.3.1919 Lakewood, OH; BR/TR/5´11˝/180(P)						
1968 Pit N	80	82	.494	6	—	-6.9
1969 Pit N e	84	73	.535	3-3	1/2	-1.8
Total 2	164	155	.514	—	—	-8.6
SHERRY, NORM B7.16.1931						
1976 Cal A w	37	29	.561	6-4*t*	2/2	7.7
1977 Cal A w	39	42	.481	5-5	1/2	-0.5
Total 2	76	71	.517	—	—	7.2
SHETTSLINE, BILL William Joseph; B10.25.1863 Philadelphia, PA; D2.22.1933 Philadelphia, PA (DNP)						
1898 Phi N	59	44	.573	8*t*-6	2/2	5.0
1899 Phi N	94	58	.618	3	—	2.2
1900 Phi N	75	63	.543	3	—	4.4
1901 Phi N	83	57	.593	2	—	0.2
1902 Phi N	56	81	.409	7	—	4.8
Total 5	367	303	.548	—	—	16.6
SHOTTON, BURT B10.18.1884						
1928 Phi N	43	109	.283	8	—	-5.7
1929 Phi N	71	82	.464	5	—	5.9
1930 Phi N	52	102	.338	8	—	-4.4
1931 Phi N	66	88	.429	6	—	2.8
1932 Phi N	78	76	.506	4	—	-3.4
1933 Phi N	60	92	.395	7	—	-0.7
1934 Cin N	1	0	1.000	8-8-8	2/3	0.6
1947 Bro N	92	60	.605	1*t*-1	2/2	5.6
1948 Bro N	48	33	.593	5-3	3/3	3.6
1949 Bro N	97	57	.630	1	—	-1.8
1950 Bro N	89	65	.578	2	—	0.4
Total 11	697	764	.477	—	—	3.0
SHOWALTER, BUCK William Nathaniel; B5.23.1956 DeFuniak Springs, FL; BL/TL/5´9˝/195(1B)						
1992 NY A e	76	86	.469	4*t*	—	-3.7
1993 NY A e	88	74	.543	2	—	1.2
1994 NY A e	70	43	.619	1	—	1.0
1995 NY A e	79	65	.549	2✤	—	1.2
1998 Ari N w	65	97	.401	5	—	-1.4
1999 Ari N w	100	62	.617	1	—	-3.3
2000 Ari N w	85	77	.525	3	—	0.3
2003 Tex A w	71	91	.438	4	—	2.9
2004 Tex A w	89	73	.549	3	—	1.8
2005 Tex A w	79	83	.488	3	—	-2.6
2006 Tex A w	80	82	.494	3	—	-5.8
Total 11	882	833	.514	—	—	-8.4
SILVESTRI, KEN B5.3.1916						
1967 Atl N	0	3	.000	7-7	2/2	-1.5
SIMMONS, JOE B6.13.1845						
1875 Wes NA	1	12	.077	13	—	-1.5
1884 Wil U	2	16	.111	8	—	1.2
Total 2	3	28	.097	—	—	-0.2
SIMMONS, LEW Lewis; B8.27.1838 New Castle, PA; D9.2.1911 Jamestown, PA (DNP)						
1886 Phi AA	41	55	.427	6-6	1/2	3.3
SISLER, GEORGE B3.24.1893						
1924 StL A	74	78	.487	4	—	1.6
1925 StL A	82	71	.536	3	—	6.0
1926 StL A	62	92	.403	7	—	0.6
Total 3	218	241	.475	—	—	8.2
SISLER, DICK B11.2.1920						
1964 Cin N	3	3	.500	3-4-2*t*	2/4	-0.4
1964 Cin N	29	18	.617	3-2*t*	4/4	2.5
1965 Cin N	89	73	.549	4	—	-3.8
Total 2	121	94	.563	—	—	-1.7
SKAFF, FRANK B9.30.1910						
1966 Det A	40	39	.506	2-3	3/3	-0.5
SKINNER, JOEL B2.21.1961						
2002 Cle A c	35	40	.467	3-3	2/2	1.9
SKINNER, BOB B10.3.1931						
1968 Phi N	48	59	.449	5-7*t*	3/3	-0.2
1969 Phi N e	44	64	.407	5-5	1/2	-3.2
1977 SD N w	1	0	1.000	4-4-5	2/3	0.6
Total 3	93	123	.431	—	—	-2.7
SLATTERY, JACK B1.6.1878						
1928 Bos N	11	20	.355	7-7	1/2	0.3
SMITH, MAYO B1.17.1915						
1955 Phi N	77	77	.500	4	—	-0.9
1956 Phi N	71	83	.461	5	—	1.0
1957 Phi N	77	77	.500	5	—	3.5
1958 Phi N	39	45	.464	8-8	1/2	2.3
1959 Cin N	35	45	.438	7-5*t*	1/2	-6.3
1967 Det A	91	71	.562	2*t*	—	-0.3
1968 Det A	103	59	.636	1★	—	1.8
1969 Det A e	90	72	.556	2	—	-1.6
1970 Det A e	79	83	.488	4	—	4.6
Total 9	662	612	.520	—	—	4.0
SMITH, HEINIE B10.24.1871						
1902 NY N	5	27	.156	4-8-8	2/3	-5.7
SMITH, HARRY B10.31.1874						
1909 Bos N	23	54	.299	8-8	2/2	-1.6
SMITH, BILL B						
1873 Mar NA	0	6	.000	9	—	3.9
SNYDER, POP B10.6.1854						
1882 Cin AA	55	25	.688	1	—	-6.6
1883 Cin AA	61	37	.622	3	—	-10.6
1884 Cin AA	24	14	.632	5-5	2/2	-2.5
1891 Was AA	23	46	.333	6-7-8	2/4	4.7
Total 4	163	122	.572	—	—	-14.9
SNYDER, JIM B8.15.1932						
1988 Sea A w	45	60	.429	6-7	2/2	-2.2
SOTHORON, ALLEN B4.27.1893						
1933 StL A	2	6	.250	8-8-8	2/3	-1.2
SOUTHWORTH, BILLY B3.9.1893						
1929 StL N	43	45	.489	4-4	1/3	-2.3
1940 StL N	69	40	.633	7-3	3/3	11.1
1941 StL N	97	56	.634	2	—	5.6
1942 StL N	106	48	.688	1★	—	-0.3
1943 StL N	105	49	.682	1	—	5.4
1944 StL N	105	49	.682	1★	—	-1.8
1945 StL N	95	59	.617	2	—	0.2
1946 Bos N	81	72	.529	4	—	0.5
1947 Bos N	86	68	.558	3	—	1.3
1948 Bos N	91	62	.595	1	—	-1.4
1949 Bos N	55	54	.505	4-4	1/2	1.4
1950 Bos N	83	71	.539	4	—	1.3
1951 Bos N	28	31	.475	5-4	1/2	-3.8
Total 13	1044	704	.597	—	—	17.2
SPALDING, AL B9.2.1850						
1876 Chi N	52	14	.788	1	—	-11.1
1877 Chi N	26	33	.441	5	—	-2.7
Total 2	78	47	.624	—	—	-13.9
SPEAKER, TRIS B4.4.1888						
1919 Cle A	40	21	.656	3-2	2/2	5.0
1920 Cle A	98	56	.636	1★	—	0.3
1921 Cle A	94	60	.610	2	—	-2.6
1922 Cle A	78	76	.506	4	—	5.6
1923 Cle A	82	71	.536	3	—	-7.5
1924 Cle A	67	86	.438	6	—	-4.0
1925 Cle A	70	84	.455	6	—	-3.7
1926 Cle A	88	66	.571	2	—	-1.8
Total 8	617	520	.543	—	—	-8.7
SPENCE, HARRY Harrison L.; B2.2.1856 New York, NY; D5.17.1908 Chicago, IL (DNP)						
1888 Ind N	50	85	.370	7	—	-5.2
STAHL, CHICK B1.10.1873						
1906 Bos A	14	26	.350	8-8	2/2	0.9
STAHL, JAKE B4.13.1879						
1905 Was A	64	87	.424	7	—	-4.6
1906 Was A	55	95	.367	7	—	-4.4
1912 Bos A	105	47	.691	1★	—	3.1
1913 Bos A	39	41	.488	5-4	1/2	-2.2
Total 4	263	270	.493	—	—	-8.0
STALLINGS, GEORGE B11.17.1867						
1897 Phi N	55	77	.417	10	—	-7.5
1898 Phi N	19	27	.413	8*t*-6	1/2	-5.1
1901 Det A	74	61	.548	3	—	2.2
1909 NY A	74	77	.490	5	—	-1.7
1910 NY A	78	59	.569	3-2	1/2	2.7
1913 Bos N	69	82	.457	5	—	-1.5
1914 Bos N	94	59	.614	1★	—	5.7
1915 Bos N	83	69	.546	2	—	2.9
1916 Bos N	89	63	.586	3	—	2.4
1917 Bos N	72	81	.471	6	—	-2.7
1918 Bos N	53	71	.427	7	—	-4.0
1919 Bos N	57	82	.410	6	—	-1.6
1920 Bos N	62	90	.408	7	—	1.8
Total 13	879	898	.495	—	—	-6.6
STANKY, EDDIE B9.3.1916						
1952 StL N	88	66	.571	3	—	6.2
1953 StL N	83	71	.539	3*t*	—	0.6
1954 StL N	72	82	.468	6	—	-5.8
1955 StL N	17	19	.472	5-7	1/2	1.4
1966 Chi A	83	79	.512	4	—	-4.6
1967 Chi A	89	73	.549	4	—	3.2
1968 Chi A	34	45	.430	9-8	1/5	-1.7
1977 Tex A w	1	0	1.000	3*t*-3-2	2/4	0.4
Total 8	467	435	.518	—	—	-0.3
START, JOE B10.14.1842						
1873 Mut NA	18	7	.720	5-4	2/2	4.1
STENGEL, CASEY B7.30.1890						
1934 Bro N	71	81	.467	6	—	-0.6
1935 Bro N	70	83	.458	5	—	-1.1
1936 Bro N	67	87	.435	7	—	-1.0
1938 Bos N	77	75	.507	5	—	7.2
1939 Bos N	63	88	.417	7	—	-3.3
1940 Bos N	65	87	.428	7	—	1.2
1941 Bos N	62	92	.403	7	—	-1.8
1942 Bos N	59	89	.399	7	—	-1.0
1943 Bos N	47	60	.439	6-6	2/2	5.1
1949 NY A	97	57	.630	1★	—	1.3
1950 NY A	98	56	.636	1★	—	0.2
1951 NY A	98	56	.636	1★	—	3.5
1952 NY A	95	59	.617	1★	—	0.3
1953 NY A	99	52	.656	1★	—	-2.0
1954 NY A	103	51	.669	2	—	1.6
1955 NY A	96	58	.623	1	—	-0.7
1956 NY A	97	57	.630	1★	—	-1.8
1957 NY A	98	56	.636	1	—	1.2
1958 NY A	92	62	.597	1★	—	-3.6
1959 NY A	79	75	.513	3	—	-2.1
1960 NY A	97	57	.630	1	—	8.0
1962 NY N	40	120	.250	10	—	-8.1
1963 NY N	51	111	.315	10	—	-0.8
1964 NY N	53	109	.327	10	—	-6.4
1965 NY N	31	64	.326	10-10	1/2	-0.1
Total 25	1905	1842	.508	—	—	-4.8
STOVALL, GEORGE B11.23.1877						
1911 Cle A	74	62	.544	7-3	2/2	7.7
1912 StL A	41	74	.357	8-7	2/2	-0.1
1913 StL A	50	84	.373	7-8	1/3	-6.1
1914 KC F	67	84	.444	6	—	-4.5
1915 KC F	81	72	.529	4	—	4.9
Total 5	313	376	.454	—	—	1.9
STOVEY, HARRY B12.20.1856						
1881 Wor N	8	18	.308	7-8	2/2	-2.6
1885 Phi AA	55	57	.491	4	—	-7.1
Total 2	63	75	.457	—	—	-9.7
STREET, GABBY B9.30.1882						
1929 StL N	1	0	1.000	4-4-4	2/3	0.5
1930 StL N	92	62	.597	1	—	-4.4
1931 StL N	101	53	.656	1★	—	4.2
1932 StL N	72	82	.468	6*t*	—	-1.7
1933 StL N	46	45	.505	5-5	1/2	-4.3
1938 StL A	53	90	.371	7-7	1/2	-0.9
Total 6	365	332	.524	—	—	-6.6
STRICKER, CUB B2.15.1860						
1892-1 StL N	6	17	.261	10-11-9	2/3	-2.4
STRICKLAND, GEORGE B1.10.1926						
1964 Cle A	33	39	.458	8-6*t*	1/2	-2.8
1966 Cle A	15	24	.385	3-5	2/2	-4.2
Total 2	48	63	.432	—	—	-7.0
STUBING, MOOSE B3.31.1938						
1988 Cal A w	0	8	.000	4-4	2/2	-3.7
SUKEFORTH, CLYDE B11.30.1901						
1947 Bro N	2	0	1.000	1*t*-1	1/2	0.9
SULLIVAN, HAYWOOD B12.15.1930						
1965 KC A	54	82	.397	10-10	2/2	0.9
SULLIVAN, PAT Patrick Joseph; B3.24.1854 Lewisburg, VA; D2.26.1896 Columbus, OH (DNP)						
1890 Col AA	2	1	.667	5-5-2	3/3	0.1
SULLIVAN, TED B1851						
1883 StL AA	53	26	.671	2-2	1/2	2.7
1884 StL U	28	3	.903	1-1	1/2	1.4
1884 KC U	13	46	.220	8-8	3/3	3.9
1888 Was N	38	57	.400	8-8	2/2	8.2
Total 3	132	132	.500	—	—	16.2
SULLIVAN, BILLY B2.1.1875						
1909 Chi A	78	74	.513	4	—	-1.4
SWEASY, CHARLIE B11.2.1847						
1875 RS NA	4	15	.211	9	—	3.4
SWIFT, BOB B3.6.1915						
1965 Det A	24	18	.571	3-4	1/2	0.8
1966 Det A	32	25	.561	3-2-3	2/3	2.8
Total 2	56	43	.566	—	—	3.6
TANNER, CHUCK B7.4.1929						
1970 Chi A w	3	13	.188	6-6	3/3	-3.1
1971 Chi A w	79	83	.488	3	—	-4.2
1972 Chi A w	87	67	.565	2	—	6.9
1973 Chi A w	77	85	.475	5	—	1.5
1974 Chi A w	80	80	.500	4	—	3.8
1975 Chi A w	75	86	.466	5	—	-0.5
1976 Oak A w	87	74	.540	2	—	-2.8
1977 Pit N e	96	66	.593	2	—	8.0
1978 Pit N e	88	73	.547	2	—	2.6

YEAR	TM LG	W	L	PCT	FINISH	MGR/YR	+/-
1979	Pit N e	98	64	.605	1★	—	3.6
1980	Pit N e	83	79	.512	3	—	-0.1
1981-1	Pit N e	25	23	.521	4	—	-3.1
1981-2	Pit N e	21	33	.389	6	—	-3.1
1982	Pit N e	84	78	.519	4	—	0.2
1983	Pit N e	84	78	.519	2	—	1.8
1984	Pit N e	75	87	.463	6	—	-11.3
1985	Pit N e	57	104	.354	6	—	-8.6
1986	Atl N w	72	89	.447	6	—	2.3
1987	Atl N w	69	92	.429	5	—	-3.6
1988	Atl N w	12	27	.308	6-6	1/2	-2.7
Total	19	1352	1381	.495	—	—	-12.7

TAPPE, EL B5.21.1927

YEAR	TM LG	W	L	PCT	FINISH	MGR/YR	+/-
1961	Chi N	2	0	1.000	7-7-7	4/9	1.1
1961	Chi N	35	43	.449	7-7-7	7/9	1.5
1961	Chi N	5	11	.313	7-7	9/9	-1.9
1962	Chi N	4	16	.200	9-9	1/3	-3.6
Total	2	46	70	.397	—	—	-2.9

TAYLOR, GEORGE George J.; B11.22.1852 NY; D10.28.1911 New York, NY (DNP)

YEAR	TM LG	W	L	PCT	FINISH	MGR/YR	+/-
1884	Bro AA	40	64	.385	9	—	3.7

TAYLOR, ZACK B7.27.1898

YEAR	TM LG	W	L	PCT	FINISH	MGR/YR	+/-
1946	StL A	13	17	.433	7-7	2/2	-0.2
1948	StL A	59	94	.386	6	—	-0.4
1949	StL A	53	101	.344	7	—	-0.9
1950	StL A	58	96	.377	7	—	2.6
1951	StL A	52	102	.338	8	—	1.1
Total	5	235	410	.364	—	—	2.2

TEBBETTS, BIRDIE B11.10.1912

YEAR	TM LG	W	L	PCT	FINISH	MGR/YR	+/-
1954	Cin N	74	80	.481	5	—	0.3
1955	Cin N	75	79	.487	5	—	-9.5
1956	Cin N	91	63	.591	3	—	2.5
1957	Cin N	80	74	.519	4	—	6.2
1958	Cin N	52	61	.460	8-4	1/2	-10.1
1961	Mil N	12	13	.480	3-4	2/2	-1.4
1962	Mil N	86	76	.531	5	—	-1.6
1963	Cle A	79	83	.488	5t	—	5.0
1964	Cle A	46	44	.511	8-6t	2/2	1.2
1965	Cle A	87	75	.537	5	—	0.7
1966	Cle A	66	57	.537	3-5	1/2	5.5
Total	11	748	705	.515	—	—	-1.3

TEBEAU, PATSY B12.5.1864

YEAR	TM LG	W	L	PCT	FINISH	MGR/YR	+/-
1890	Cle P	21	30	.412	7-7	2/2	1.0
1891	Cle N	31	40	.437	4-5	2/2	-2.2
1892-1	Cle N	40	33	.548	5	—	-4.9
1892-2	Cle N	53	23	.697	1	—	-4.9
1893	Cle N	73	55	.570	3	—	-2.0
1894	Cle N	68	61	.527	6	—	0.6
1895	Cle N	84	46	.646	2●	—	2.3
1896	Cle N	80	48	.625	2	—	-1.2
1897	Cle N	69	62	.527	5	—	-4.9
1898	Cle N	81	68	.544	5	—	1.8
1899	StL N	84	67	.556	5	—	0.9
1900	StL N	42	50	.457	7-5t	1/2	-3.8
Total	11	726	583	.555	—	—	-17.1

TENACE, GENE B10.10.1946

YEAR	TM LG	W	L	PCT	FINISH	MGR/YR	+/-
1991	Tor A e	19	14	.576	1-1-1	2/3	1.2

TENNEY, FRED B11.26.1871

YEAR	TM LG	W	L	PCT	FINISH	MGR/YR	+/-
1905	Bos N	51	103	.331	7	—	2.7
1906	Bos N	49	102	.325	8	—	0.9
1907	Bos N	58	90	.392	7	—	0.3
1911	Bos N	44	107	.291	8	—	-2.4
Total	4	202	402	.334	—	—	1.5

TERRY, BILL B10.30.1898

YEAR	TM LG	W	L	PCT	FINISH	MGR/YR	+/-
1932	NY N	55	59	.482	8-6t	2/2	-5.5
1933	NY N	91	61	.599	1★	—	1.6
1934	NY N	93	60	.608	2	—	-1.4
1935	NY N	91	62	.595	3	—	5.1
1936	NY N	92	62	.597	1	—	2.8
1937	NY N	95	57	.625	1	—	5.8
1938	NY N	83	67	.553	3	—	1.1
1939	NY N	77	74	.510	5	—	-0.3
1940	NY N	72	80	.474	6	—	-4.4
1941	NY N	74	79	.484	5	—	1.4
Total	10	823	661	.555	—	—	6.3

THOMAS, FRED Frederick L.; B IN; (DNP)

YEAR	TM LG	W	L	PCT	FINISH	MGR/YR	+/-
1887	Ind N	11	18	.379	8-8-8	2/3	3.1

THOMPSON, ANDREW Andrew M.; B11.9.1845 Seward, IL; D2.17.1895 Pecatonica, IL (DNP)

YEAR	TM LG	W	L	PCT	FINISH	MGR/YR	+/-
1884	Stp U	2	6	.250	7	—	1.3

TIGHE, JACK John Thomas; B8.9.1913 Kearny, NJ; D8.1.2002 Pompano Beach, FL BR/TR/5´8˝/170(C)

YEAR	TM LG	W	L	PCT	FINISH	MGR/YR	+/-
1957	Det A	78	76	.506	4	—	1.0
1958	Det A	21	28	.429	8-5	1/2	-5.3
Total	2	99	104	.488	—	—	-4.3

TINKER, JOE B7.27.1880

YEAR	TM LG	W	L	PCT	FINISH	MGR/YR	+/-
1913	Cin N	64	89	.418	7	—	-1.2
1914	Chi F	87	67	.565	2	—	-1.6
1915	Chi F	86	66	.566	1	—	-1.1
1916	Chi N	67	86	.438	5	—	-7.1
Total	4	304	308	.497	—	—	-10.9

TORBORG, JEFF B11.26.1941

YEAR	TM LG	W	L	PCT	FINISH	MGR/YR	+/-
1977	Cle A e	45	59	.433	5-5	2/2	-2.9
1978	Cle A e	69	90	.434	6	—	-4.8
1979	Cle A e	43	52	.453	6-6	1/2	-1.9
1989	Chi A w	69	92	.429	7	—	-5.8
1990	Chi A w	94	68	.580	2	—	7.8
1991	Chi A w	87	75	.537	2	—	-1.8
1992	NY N e	72	90	.444	5	—	-3.2
1993	NY N e	13	25	.342	7-7	1/2	-4.3
2001	Mon N e	47	61	.435	5-5	2/2	2.4
2002	Fla N e	79	83	.488	4	—	4.4
2003	Fla N e	17	22	.436	4-2✤★	1/2	-3.9
Total	11	635	717	.470	—	—	-13.9

TORRE, JOE B7.18.1940

YEAR	TM LG	W	L	PCT	FINISH	MGR/YR	+/-
1977	NY N	49	68	.419	6-6	2/2	-3.6
1978	NY N e	66	96	.407	6	—	-6.2
1979	NY N e	63	99	.389	6	—	-6.0
1980	NY N e	67	95	.414	5	—	-4.4
1981-1	NY N e	17	34	.333	5	—	-1.3
1981-2	NY N e	24	28	.462	4	—	-1.3
1982	Atl N w	89	73	.549	1	—	4.3
1983	Atl N w	88	74	.543	2	—	-3.9
1984	Atl N w	80	82	.494	2t	—	1.4
1990	StL N e	24	34	.414	6-6	3/3	-1.2
1991	StL N e	84	78	.519	2	—	2.7
1992	StL N e	83	79	.512	3	—	-0.9
1993	StL N e	87	75	.537	3	—	4.6
1994	StL N c	53	61	.465	3t	—	4.1
1995	StL N c	20	27	.426	4-4	1/2	-0.3
1996	NY A e	92	70	.568	1★	—	3.1
1997	NY A e	96	66	.593	2✤	—	-4.5
1998	NY A e	114	48	.704	1★	—	3.7
1999	NY A e	77	49	.611	1-1★	2/2	1.6
2000	NY A e	87	74	.540	1★	—	1.2
2001	NY A e	95	65	.594	1◆	—	6.1
2002	NY A e	103	58	.640	1	—	3.4
2003	NY A e	101	61	.623	1◆	—	4.5
2004	NY A e	101	61	.623	1☆	—	11.8
2005	NY A e	95	67	.586	1	—	4.9
2006	NY A e	97	65	.599	1	—	0.9
Total	25	1952	1687	.536	—	—	24.9

TOSCA, CARLOS Carlos; B9.29.1953 Pinar Del Rio, Cuba; 5-7/158(DNP)

YEAR	TM LG	W	L	PCT	FINISH	MGR/YR	+/-
2002	Tor A e	58	51	.532	4-3	2/2	4.5
2003	Tor A e	86	76	.531	3	—	-1.3
2004	Tor A e	47	74	.388	5-5	1/2	-5.9
Total	3	191	201	.487	—	—	-2.7

TRACEWSKI, DICK B2.3.1935

YEAR	TM LG	W	L	PCT	FINISH	MGR/YR	+/-
1979	Det A e	2	0	1.000	5-5-5	2/3	1.0

TRACY, JIM B12.31.1955

YEAR	TM LG	W	L	PCT	FINISH	MGR/YR	+/-
2001	LA N w	86	76	.531	3	—	3.6
2002	LA N w	92	70	.568	3	—	3.7
2003	LA N w	85	77	.525	2	—	2.0
2004	LA N w	93	69	.574	1	—	4.3
2005	LA N w	71	91	.438	4	—	-3.0
2006	Pit N c	67	95	.414	5	—	-3.5
Total	6	494	478	.508	—	—	7.1

TRAMMELL, ALAN B2.21.1958

YEAR	TM LG	W	L	PCT	FINISH	MGR/YR	+/-
2003	Det A c	43	119	.265	5	—	-5.0
2004	Det A c	72	90	.444	4	—	-7.4
2005	Det A c	71	91	.438	4	—	-3.7
Total	3	186	300	.383	—	—	-16.1

TRAYNOR, PIE B11.11.1898

YEAR	TM LG	W	L	PCT	FINISH	MGR/YR	+/-
1934	Pit N	47	52	.475	4-5	2/2	-3.9
1935	Pit N	86	67	.562	4	—	-0.1
1936	Pit N	84	70	.545	4	—	-1.3
1937	Pit N	86	68	.558	3	—	3.2
1938	Pit N	86	64	.573	2	—	3.2
1939	Pit N	68	85	.444	6	—	-3.0
Total	6	457	406	.530	—	—	-1.8

TREBELHORN, TOM Thomas Lynn; B1.27.1948 Portland, OR; BL/TR/5´11˝/178(C)

YEAR	TM LG	W	L	PCT	FINISH	MGR/YR	+/-
1986	Mil A e	6	3	.667	6-6	2/2	1.9
1987	Mil A e	91	71	.562	3	—	5.8
1988	Mil A e	87	75	.537	3t	—	-1.0
1989	Mil A e	81	81	.500	4	—	-2.9
1990	Mil A e	74	88	.457	6	—	-4.2
1991	Mil A e	83	79	.512	3	—	-3.3
1994	Chi N c	49	64	.434	5	—	-2.7
Total	7	471	461	.505	—	—	-6.4

TROTT, SAM B3.1859

YEAR	TM LG	W	L	PCT	FINISH	MGR/YR	+/-
1891	Was AA	4	7	.364	6-9	1/4	1.1

TURNER, TED Robert Edward; B11.19.1938 Cincinnati, OH; (DNP)

YEAR	TM LG	W	L	PCT	FINISH	MGR/YR	+/-
1977	Atl N w	0	1	.000	6-6-6	2/4	-0.4

UNGLAUB, BOB B7.31.1881

YEAR	TM LG	W	L	PCT	FINISH	MGR/YR	+/-
1907	Bos A	9	20	.310	6-8-7	3/4	-3.4

VALENTINE, BOBBY B5.13.1950

YEAR	TM LG	W	L	PCT	FINISH	MGR/YR	+/-
1985	Tex A w	53	76	.411	7-7	2/2	2.2
1986	Tex A w	87	75	.537	2	—	3.3
1987	Tex A w	75	87	.463	6t	—	-3.6
1988	Tex A w	70	91	.435	6	—	-0.4
1989	Tex A w	83	79	.512	4	—	3.9
1990	Tex A w	83	79	.512	3	—	4.1
1991	Tex A w	85	77	.525	3	—	2.6
1992	Tex A w	45	41	.523	3-4	1/2	5.8
1996	NY N e	12	19	.387	4-4	2/2	-2.9
1997	NY N e	88	74	.543	3	—	0.3
1998	NY N e	88	74	.543	2	—	0.7
1999	NY N e	97	66	.595	2☆▲✤	—	1.7
2000	NY N e	94	68	.580	2◆✤	—	6.3
2001	NY N e	82	80	.506	3	—	8.4
2002	NY N e	75	86	.466	5	—	-4.2
Total	15	1117	1072	.510	—	—	28.1

VANHALTREN, GEORGE B3.30.1866

YEAR	TM LG	W	L	PCT	FINISH	MGR/YR	+/-
1892-1	Bal N	1	10	.091	12-12	1/3	-2.9

VERNON, MICKEY B4.22.1918

YEAR	TM LG	W	L	PCT	FINISH	MGR/YR	+/-
1961	Was A	61	100	.379	9t	—	-3.4
1962	Was A	60	101	.373	10	—	-8.2
1963	Was A	14	26	.350	10-10	1/3	-0.1
Total	3	135	227	.373	—	—	-11.7

VIRDON, BILL B6.9.1931

YEAR	TM LG	W	L	PCT	FINISH	MGR/YR	+/-
1972	Pit N e	96	59	.619	1	—	-0.8
1973	Pit N e	67	69	.493	2-3	1/2	-1.9
1974	NY A e	89	73	.549	2	—	2.9
1975	NY A e	53	51	.510	3-3	1/2	-5.4
1975	Hou N w	17	17	.500	6-6	2/2	1.0
1976	Hou N w	80	82	.494	3	—	2.4
1977	Hou N w	81	81	.500	3	—	-3.1
1978	Hou N w	74	88	.457	5	—	-3.9
1979	Hou N w	89	73	.549	2	—	7.9
1980	Hou N w	93	70	.571	1▲	—	6.2
1981-1	Hou N w	28	29	.491	3	—	-1.4
1981-2	Hou N w	33	20	.623	1	—	-1.4
1982	Hou N w	49	62	.441	5-5	1/2	-2.6
1983	Mon N e	82	80	.506	3	—	-2.3
1984	Mon N e	64	67	.489	5-5	1/2	-2.2
Total	13	995	921	.519	—	—	-4.5

VITT, OSSIE B1.4.1890

YEAR	TM LG	W	L	PCT	FINISH	MGR/YR	+/-
1938	Cle A	86	66	.566	3	—	4.0
1939	Cle A	87	67	.565	3	—	0.7
1940	Cle A	89	65	.578	2	—	4.6
Total	3	262	198	.570	—	—	9.3

VONDER AHE, CHRIS Christian Frederick Wilhelm; B10.7.1851 Hille, Prussia; D6.5.1913 St.Louis, MO (DNP)

YEAR	TM LG	W	L	PCT	FINISH	MGR/YR	+/-
1895	StL N	1	0	1.000	11-11-11	2/4	0.7
1896	StL N	0	2	.000	10-11-11	3/5	-0.5
1897	StL N	2	12	.143	12-12	4/4	-0.5
Total	3	3	14	.176	—	—	-0.4

VUKOVICH, JOHN B7.31.1947

YEAR	TM LG	W	L	PCT	FINISH	MGR/YR	+/-
1986	Chi N e	1	1	.500	5-5-5	2/3	0.1
1988	Phi N e	5	4	.556	6-6	2/2	1.3
Total	2	6	5	.545	—	—	1.4

WAGNER, HEINIE B9.23.1880

YEAR	TM LG	W	L	PCT	FINISH	MGR/YR	+/-
1930	Bos A	52	102	.338	8	—	-5.1

WAGNER, HONUS B2.24.1874

YEAR	TM LG	W	L	PCT	FINISH	MGR/YR	+/-
1917	Pit N	1	4	.200	8-8-8	2/3	-1.0

WALKER, HARRY B10.22.1916

YEAR	TM LG	W	L	PCT	FINISH	MGR/YR	+/-
1955	StL N	51	67	.432	5-7	2/2	-0.2
1965	Pit N	90	72	.556	3	—	-1.3
1966	Pit N	92	70	.568	3	—	-1.0
1967	Pit N	42	42	.500	6-6	1/2	0.8
1968	Hou N	49	52	.485	10-10	2/2	4.1
1969	Hou N w	81	81	.500	5	—	-0.8
1970	Hou N w	79	83	.488	4	—	-0.1
1971	Hou N w	79	83	.488	4t	—	-4.0
1972	Hou N w	67	54	.554	2-2	1/3	0.7
Total	9	630	604	.511	—	—	-1.9

WALLACE, BOBBY B11.4.1873

YEAR	TM LG	W	L	PCT	FINISH	MGR/YR	+/-
1911	StL A	45	107	.296	8	—	-6.6
1912	StL A	12	27	.308	8-7	1/2	-1.9
1937	Cin N	5	20	.200	8-8	2/2	-5.9
Total	3	62	154	.287	—	—	-14.5

WALSH, ED B5.14.1881

YEAR	TM LG	W	L	PCT	FINISH	MGR/YR	+/-
1924	Chi A	1	2	.333	6	2/4	-0.4

WALSH, MIKE Michael John; B4.29.1850 Ireland; D2.2.1929 Louisville, KY (DNP)

YEAR	TM LG	W	L	PCT	FINISH	MGR/YR	+/-
1884	Lou AA	68	40	.630	3	—	-0.7

WALTERS, BUCKY B4.19.1909

YEAR	TM LG	W	L	PCT	FINISH	MGR/YR	+/-
1948	Cin N	20	33	.377	7-7	2/2	-0.8
1949	Cin N	61	90	.404	7-7	1/2	-0.4
Total	2	81	123	.397	—	—	-1.2

WALTZ, JOHN John William; B1.12.1860 MD; D4.27.1931 Baltimore, MD (DNP)

YEAR	TM LG	W	L	PCT	FINISH	MGR/YR	+/-
1892-1	Bal N	2	6	.250	12-12-12	2/3	-0.9

WARD, JOHN B3.3.1860

YEAR	TM LG	W	L	PCT	FINISH	MGR/YR	+/-
1880	Pro N	18	13	.581	4-3-2	2/3	-2.1
1884	NY N	6	8	.429	4-4t	2/2	-1.8
1890	Bro P	76	56	.576	2	—	4.3
1891	Bro N	61	76	.445	6	—	-2.6
1892-1	Bro N	51	26	.662	2	—	-0.7
1892-2	Bro N	44	33	.571	3	—	-0.7
1893	NY N	68	64	.515	5	—	-5.9

YEAR TM LG	W	L	PCT	FINISH	MGR/YR	+/-
1894 NY N	88	44	.667	2●	—	8.4
Total 7	412	320	.563	—	—	-1.1
WATERMAN, FRED B12.1845						
1872 Oly NA	2	7	.222	10	—	3.1
WATHAN, JOHN B10.4.1949						
1987 KC A w	21	15	.583	4-2	2/2	2.5
1988 KC A w	84	77	.522	3	—	-2.3
1989 KC A w	92	70	.568	2	—	5.2
1990 KC A w	75	86	.466	6	—	-5.3
1991 KC A w	15	22	.405	7-6	1/3	-3.6
1992 Cal A w	39	50	.438	5-5-5t	2/3	-0.0
Total 6	326	320	.505	—	—	-3.6
WATKINS, HARVEY Harvey L.; (DNP)						
1895 NY N	18	17	.514	9-9	3/3	0.1
WATKINS, BILL B5.5.1858						
1884 Ind AA	4	18	.182	10-11	2/2	-1.6
1885 Det N	34	36	.486	8-6	2/2	3.2
1886 Det N	87	36	.707	2	—	-1.0
1887 Det N	79	45	.637	1★	—	-4.4
1888 Det N	49	44	.527	3-5	1/2	-3.7
1888 KC AA	8	17	.320	8-8	3/3	0.9
1889 KC AA	55	82	.401	7	—	1.1
1893 StL N	57	75	.432	10	—	-1.6
1898 Pit N	72	76	.486	8	—	4.1
1899 Pit N	7	15	.318	10-7	1/2	-5.0
Total 9	452	444	.504	—	—	-8.0
WEAVER, EARL Earl Sidney; B8.14.1930 St.Louis, MO; BR/TR/5´7˝/180(2B)						
1968 Bal A	48	34	.585	3-2	2/2	2.2
1969 Bal A e	109	53	.673	1◆	—	0.2
1970 Bal A e	108	54	.667	1★	—	4.5
1971 Bal A e	101	57	.639	1◆	—	-0.4
1972 Bal A e	80	74	.519	3	—	-7.8
1973 Bal A e	97	65	.599	1	—	-4.3
1974 Bal A e	91	71	.562	1	—	5.0
1975 Bal A e	90	69	.566	2	—	-3.4
1976 Bal A e	88	74	.543	2	—	4.7
1977 Bal A e	97	64	.602	2t	—	9.7
1978 Bal A e	90	71	.559	4	—	6.7
1979 Bal A e	102	57	.642	1◆	—	4.4
1980 Bal A e	100	62	.617	2	—	2.4
1981-1 Bal A e	31	23	.574	2	—	7.3
1981-2 Bal A e	28	23	.549	4	—	7.3
1982 Bal A e	94	68	.580	2	—	4.3
1985 Bal A e	53	52	.505	4-4	3/3	-2.9
1986 Bal A e	73	89	.451	7	—	-2.8
Total 17	1480	1060	.583	—	—	37.2
WEDGE, ERIC B1.27.1968						
2003 Cle A c	68	94	.420	4	—	-5.2
2004 Cle A c	80	82	.494	3	—	-1.1
2005 Cle A c	93	69	.574	2	—	-2.9
2006 Cle A c	78	84	.481	4	—	-11.3
Total 4	319	329	.492	—	—	-20.4
WESTRUM, WES B11.28.1922						
1965 NY N	19	48	.284	10-10	2/2	-2.9
1966 NY N	66	95	.410	9	—	3.5
1967 NY N	57	94	.377	10-10	1/2	-0.4
1974 SF N w	38	48	.442	5-5	2/2	-0.1
1975 SF N w	80	81	.497	3	—	0.8
Total 5	260	366	.415	—	—	0.9
WHEELER, HARRY B3.3.1858						
1884 KC U	0	4	.000	8-8	1/3	-0.6
WHITE, DEACON B12.7.1847						
1872 Cle NA	0	2	.000	6-7	2/2	-0.5
1879 Cin N	9	9	.500	4-5	1/2	-0.4
Total 2	9	11	.450	—	—	-0.9
WHITE, JO-JO B6.1.1909						
1960 Cle A	1	0	1.000	4-4-4	2/3	0.5
WHITE, WILL B10.11.1854						
1884 Cin AA	44	27	.620	5	1/2	-5.6
WHITE, WARREN B1844						
1872 Nat NA	0	11	.000	11	—	1.2
1874 Bal NA	9	38	.191	8	—	6.6
Total 2	9	49	.155	—	—	7.8
WILBER, DEL B2.24.1919						
1973 Tex A w	1	0	1.000	6-6-6	2/3	0.6
WILHELM, KAISER B1.26.1874						
1921 Phi N	26	41	.388	8-8	2/2	5.0
1922 Phi N	57	96	.373	7	—	-2.9
Total 2	83	137	.377	—	—	2.1

YEAR TM LG	W	L	PCT	FINISH	MGR/YR	+/-
WILLIAMS, JIMMY James Andrew; B1.4.1847 Catawba, OH; D10.23.1918 Westbury, NY (DNP)						
1884 StL AA	51	33	.607	5-4	1/2	0.5
1887 Cle AA	39	92	.298	8	—	4.4
1888 Cle AA	20	44	.313	8-6	1/2	-3.8
Total 3	110	169	.394	—	—	1.1
WILLIAMS, JIMY B10.4.1943						
1986 Tor A e	86	76	.531	4	—	-2.4
1987 Tor A e	96	66	.593	2	—	-3.7
1988 Tor A e	87	75	.537	3t	—	-2.3
1989 Tor A e	12	24	.333	6-1	1/2	-7.8
1997 Bos A e	78	84	.481	4	—	-2.4
1998 Bos A e	92	70	.568	2✤	—	-3.0
1999 Bos A e	94	68	.580	2☆✤	—	1.6
2000 Bos A e	85	77	.525	2	—	-0.6
2001 Bos A e	65	53	.551	2-2	1/2	4.1
2002 Hou N c	84	78	.519	2	—	-2.4
2003 Hou N c	87	75	.537	2	—	-6.7
2004 Hou N c	44	44	.500	5-2☆✤	1/2	-5.6
Total 12	910	790	.535	—	—	-31.5
WILLIAMS, DICK B5.7.1929						
1967 Bos A	92	70	.568	1	—	-0.3
1968 Bos A	86	76	.531	4	—	4.7
1969 Bos A e	82	71	.536	3-3	1/2	4.8
1971 Oak A w	101	60	.627	1	—	6.9
1972 Oak A w	93	62	.600	1★	—	-1.4
1973 Oak A w	94	68	.580	1★	—	-1.7
1974 Cal A w	36	48	.429	6-6	3/3	-3.8
1975 Cal A w	72	89	.447	6	—	1.3
1976 Cal A w	39	57	.406	6-4t	1/2	-3.7
1977 Mon N e	75	87	.463	5	—	1.2
1978 Mon N e	76	86	.469	4	—	-7.4
1979 Mon N e	95	65	.594	2	—	2.3
1980 Mon N e	90	72	.556	2	—	2.2
1981-1 Mon N e	30	25	.545	3	—	0.7
1981-2 Mon N e	14	12	.538	2-1☆	1/2	-0.3
1982 SD N w	81	81	.500	4	—	-1.8
1983 SD N w	81	81	.500	4	—	0.0
1984 SD N w	92	70	.568	1◆	—	5.5
1985 SD N w	83	79	.512	3t	—	-1.0
1986 Sea A w	58	75	.436	6-7	3/3	0.8
1987 Sea A w	78	84	.481	4	—	1.0
1988 Sea A w	23	33	.411	6-7	1/2	-2.2
Total 21	1571	1451	.520	—	—	8.0
WILLIAMS, TED B8.30.1918						
1969 Was A e	86	76	.531	4	—	-0.2
1970 Was A e	70	92	.432	6	—	-4.4
1971 Was A e	63	96	.396	5	—	-3.1
1972 Tex A w	54	100	.351	6	—	-4.2
Total 4	273	364	.429	—	—	-11.8
WILLS, MAURY B10.2.1932						
1980 Sea A w	20	38	.345	6-7	2/2	-2.3
1981-1 Sea A w	6	18	.250	7-6	1/2	-3.9
Total 2	26	56	.317	—	—	-6.2
WILSON, JIMMIE B7.23.1900						
1934 Phi N	56	93	.376	7	—	-7.1
1935 Phi N	64	89	.418	7	—	5.2
1936 Phi N	54	100	.351	8	—	-9.2
1937 Phi N	61	92	.399	7	—	-1.9
1938 Phi N	45	103	.304	8-8	1/2	-0.7
1941 Chi N	70	84	.455	6	—	-6.6
1942 Chi N	68	86	.442	6	—	-1.2
1943 Chi N	74	79	.484	5	—	-6.0
1944 Chi N	1	9	.100	8-4	1/3	-4.2
Total 9	493	735	.401	—	—	-31.8
WINE, BOBBY B9.17.1938						
1985 Atl N w	16	25	.390	5-5	2/2	-0.7
WINGO, IVEY B7.8.1890						
1916 Cin N	1	1	.500	8-8-7t	2/3	0.2
WINKLES, BOBBY Bobby Brooks; B3.11.1930 Tuckerman, AR; BR/TR/5´9˝/170(SS)						
1973 Cal A w	79	83	.488	4	—	1.0
1974 Cal A w	30	44	.405	6-6	1/3	-5.1
1977 Oak A w	37	71	.343	5t-7	2/2	-7.0
1978 Oak A w	24	15	.615	1-6	1/2	8.7
Total 4	170	213	.444	—	—	-2.5
WOLF, JIMMY B5.12.1862						
1889 Lou AA	14	51	.215	8-8-8	2/4	-0.0
WOLVERTON, HARRY B12.6.1873						
1912 NY A	50	102	.329	8	—	-5.5
WOOD, GEORGE B11.9.1858						
1891 Phi AA	67	55	.549	7-4	2/2	4.2

YEAR TM LG	W	L	PCT	FINISH	MGR/YR	+/-
WOOD, JIMMY B12.1.1842						
1871 Chi NA	19	9	.679	2	—	0.8
1872 Tro NA	15	10	.600	5	—	-3.2
1872 Eck NA	2	7	.222	10-10-9	2/3	3.0
1874 Chi NA	10	13	.435	4-5	2/2	0.4
1875 Chi NA	30	37	.448	6	—	-0.2
Total 4	76	76	.500	—	—	0.8
WRIGHT, AL Alfred Hector; B3.30.1842 Cedar Grove, NJ; D4.20.1905 New York, NY (DNP)						
1876 Phi N	14	45	.237	7	—	-3.5
WRIGHT, GEORGE B1.28.1847						
1879 Pro N	59	25	.702	1	—	-5.9
WRIGHT, HARRY B1.10.1835						
1871 Bos NA	20	10	.667	3	—	-1.2
1872 Bos NA	39	8	.830	1	—	-6.0
1873 Bos NA	43	16	.729	1	—	-5.2
1874 Bos NA	52	18	.743	1	—	-6.9
1875 Bos NA	71	8	.899	1	—	-7.2
1876 Bos N	39	31	.557	4	—	2.3
1877 Bos N	42	18	.700	1	—	-2.0
1878 Bos N	41	19	.683	1	—	5.3
1879 Bos N	54	30	.643	2	—	-7.5
1880 Bos N	40	44	.476	6	—	1.8
1881 Bos N	38	45	.458	6	—	2.8
1882 Pro N	52	32	.619	2	—	-0.3
1883 Pro N	58	40	.592	3	—	-9.1
1884 Phi N	39	73	.348	6	—	6.7
1885 Phi N	56	54	.509	3	—	0.8
1886 Phi N	71	43	.623	4	—	2.0
1887 Phi N	75	48	.610	2	—	-3.4
1888 Phi N	69	61	.531	3	—	1.2
1889 Phi N	63	64	.496	3	—	0.0
1890 Phi N	14	8	.636	1-3	1/5	1.3
1890 Phi N	22	23	.489	2-3	5/5	-4.0
1891 Phi N	68	69	.496	4	—	1.0
1892-1 Phi N	46	30	.605	3	—	-5.6
1892-2 Phi N	41	36	.532	5	—	-5.6
1893 Phi N	72	57	.558	4	—	-6.2
Total 23	1225	885	.581	—	—	-45.1
YORK, RUDY B8.17.1913						
1959 Bos A	0	1	.000	8-8-5	2/3	-0.5
YORK, TOM B7.13.1850						
1878 Pro N	33	27	.550	3	—	1.6
1881 Pro N	23	10	.697	4-2	2/2	5.7
Total 2	56	37	.602	—	—	7.3
YOST, NED B8.19.1954						
2003 Mil N c	68	94	.420	6	—	2.2
2004 Mil N c	67	94	.416	6	—	-0.9
2005 Mil N c	81	81	.500	3	—	-2.9
2006 Mil N c	75	87	.463	4	—	3.9
Total 4	291	356	.450	—	—	2.3
YOST, EDDIE B10.13.1926						
1963 Was A	0	1	.000	10-10-10	2/3	-0.4
YOUNG, CY B3.29.1867						
1907 Bos A	3	3	.500	4t-7	1/4	0.4
YOUNG, NICK Nicholas Ephraim; B9.12.1840 Fort Johnson, NY; D10.31.1916 Washington, DC (OF)						
1871 Oly NA	15	15	.500	5	—	-0.5
1873 Was NA	8	31	.205	7	—	2.2
Total 2	23	46	.333	—	—	1.7
ZIMMER, CHIEF B11.23.1860						
1903 Phi N	49	86	.363	7	—	-6.9
ZIMMER, DON B1.17.1931						
1972 SD N w	54	88	.380	4-6	2/2	1.0
1973 SD N w	60	102	.370	6	—	2.4
1976 Bos A e	42	34	.553	5-3	2/2	1.3
1977 Bos A e	97	64	.602	2t	—	2.4
1978 Bos A e	99	64	.607	2▲	—	3.5
1979 Bos A e	91	69	.569	3	—	-1.5
1980 Bos A e	82	73	.529	3-4	1/2	5.4
1981-1 Tex A w	33	22	.600	2	—	-2.2
1981-2 Tex A w	24	26	.480	3	—	-2.2
1982 Tex A w	38	58	.396	6-6	1/2	-0.2
1988 Chi N e	77	85	.475	4	—	-0.5
1989 Chi N e	93	69	.574	1	—	3.7
1990 Chi N e	77	85	.475	4t	—	4.4
1991 Chi N e	18	19	.486	4-4	1/3	0.4
1999 NY A e	21	15	.583	1-1	1/2	-0.6
Total 14	906	873	.509	—	—	17.4

UNSUNG MAJOR LEAGUE MENTORS: THE COACHES

The first person specifically hired to be a coach was Arlie Latham in 1900. However, it wasn't until the 1910s before a majority of teams employed a fulltime coach. Originally, coaches had no special assignments. The first level of specialization was, naturally, the hiring of dedicated batting and pitching coaches. As more coaches were employed, some were formally designated as first base and third base coaches—though these coaches always had other assigned responsibilities (like outfield or infield instruction, coaching the catchers, or teaching baserunning and basestealing). In the last two decades, big-league teams have added bench coaches and bullpen coaches to the traditional ranks of hitting, pitching, first base, and third base coaches.

Key. The large majority of major league coaches (86.5 percent) were former big-league players or managers. Coaches who played in the majors are indicated by a solid star (★) for position players or hollow star (☆) for pitchers. Their bio info can be found in the player registers. A triangle (▲) indicates the coach was also a manager; their bio info can be found in the Manager Register. Coaches marked with a bullet (●) never played or managed in the majors; their biographical info is at the end of the Coach Register.

Aaron, Tommie★ Atl N 1979-84
Abbott, Spencer● Was A 1935
Acosta, Oscar● Chi N 2000-01, Tex A 2002
Acta, Manny● Mon N 2002-04, NY N 2005-06
Adair, Jimmy★ Chi A 1951-52, Bal A 1957-61, Hou N 1962-65
Adair, Jerry★ Oak A 1972-74, Cal A 1975
Adair, Bill▲ Mil N 1962, Atl N 1967, Chi A 1970, Mon N 1976
Adair, Rick● Cle A 1992-93, Det A 1996-99
Adams, Red☆ LA N 1969-80
Adams, Bobby★ Chi N 1961-65, 1973
Aguirre, Hank☆ Chi N 1972-74
Aker, Jack☆ Cle A 1985-87
Akerfelds, Darrel☆ SD N 2001-06
Aldrete, Mike★ Sea A 2004, Ari N 2005-06
Alejo, Bob● Oak A 1997
Alfonso, Carlos● SF N 1992, 1997-99
Allenson, Gary★ Bos A 1992-94, Mil N 2000-02
Alomar, Sandy★ SD N 1986-90, Chi N 2000-02, Col N 2003-04, NY N 2005-06
Alou, Felipe★ Mon N 1979-80, 1984, 1992, Det A 2002
Alou, Jesus★ Hou N 1979
Altobelli, Joe★ NY A 1981-82, 1986, Chi N 1988-91
Altrock, Nick☆ Was A 1912-53
Amalfitano, Joey★ Chi N 1967-71, SF N 1972-75, SD N 1976-77, Chi N 1978-80, Cin N 1982, LA N 1983-98
Amaro, Ruben★ Phi N 1980-81, Chi N 1983-86
Anderson, Sparky★ SD N 1969
Anderson, Rick☆ Min A 2002-06
Apodaca, Bob☆ NY N 1996-99, Mil N 2000-01, Col N 2003-06
Appling, Luke★ Det A 1960, Cle A 1960-61, Bal A 1963, KC A 1964-67, Chi A 1970-71
Arnsberg, Brad☆ Mon N 2000-01, Fla N 2002-03, Tor A 2005-06
Arsenault, Pierre● Mon N 1992-2001
Ashby, Alan★ Hou N 1997
Auferio, Tony● StL N 1973
Austin, Jimmy★ StL A 1923-32, Chi A 1933-40
Babe, Loren★ NY A 1967, Chi A 1980-81, 1983
Bader, Lore☆ Bos N 1926
Bailey, Mark★ Hou N 2002-06
Bailey, Buddy● Bos A 2000
Bailor, Bob★ Tor A 1992-95
Baines, Harold★ Chi A 2004-06
Baker, Del★ Det A 1933-38, Cle A 1943-44, Bos A 1945-48, 1953-60
Baker, Gene★ Pit N 1963
Baker, Floyd★ Min A 1961-64
Baker, Dusty★ SF N 1988-92
Baker, Bill★ Chi N 1950
Balsley, Darren● SD N 2003-06
Bamberger, George☆ Bal A 1968-77
Bancroft, Dave★ NY N 1930-32
Bando, Chris★ Mil A 1996-97, Mil N 1998
Bando, Sal★ Mil A 1980-81
Banks, Ernie★ Chi N 1967-73
Barfield, Jesse★ Hou N 1995, Sea A 1998-99
Barnett, Mike● Tor A 2002-05, KC A 2006
Bartell, Dick★ NY N 1946, Det A 1949-52, Cin N 1954-55
Bartirome, Tony★ Atl N 1986-88
Basgall, Monty★ LA N 1973-86
Bassler, Johnny★ Cle A 1938-40, StL A 1941
Bauer, Hank★ Bal A 1963
Baylor, Don★ Mil A 1990-91, StL N 1992, Atl N 1999, NY N 2003-04, Sea A 2005
Bearnarth, Larry☆ Mon N 1976, 1985-91, Col N 1993-95
Beasley, Tony● Was N 2006
Beauchamp, Jim★ Atl N 1991-98
Beck, Boom-Boom☆ Was A 1957-59
Becker, Joe★ Bro N 1955-57, LA N 1958-64, StL N 1965-66, Chi N 1967-70
Bedell, Howie★ KC A 1984, Sea A 1988
Bell, Buddy★ Cle A 1994-95, 2003-05
Bell, Jay★ Ari N 2005-06
Belliard, Rafael★ Det A 2006
Benavides, Freddie★ Cin N 2003
Bender, Chief☆ Chi A 1925-26, NY N 1931, Phi A 1951-53
Benedict, Bruce★ NY N 1997-99
Bengough, Benny★ Was A 1940-43, Bos N 1944-45, Phi N 1946-58
Benson, Vern★ StL N 1961-64, NY A 1965-66, Cin N 1966-69, StL N 1970-75, Atl N 1976-77, SF N 1980
Berardino, Johnny★ StL A 1951
Berardino, Dick● Bos A 1989-91
Berg, Moe★ Bos A 1940-41
Beringer, C. B.● LA N 1967-72, Phi N 1973-78
Bernhardt, Carlos● Bal A 1998
Berra, Yogi★ NY A 1963, NY N 1965-71, NY A 1976-83, Hou N 1986-89
Berres, Ray★ Chi A 1949-66, 1968-69
Berry, Charlie★ Phi A 1936-40
Berry, Sean★ Hou N 2006
Berry, Mark● Cin N 2003-06
Bevington, Terry▲ Chi A 1989-95, Tor A 1999-2001
Biagini, Greg● Bal A 1992-94
Bialas, Dave● SD N 1993-94, Chi N 1995-99, 2002
Bissonette, Del★ Bos N 1945, Pit N 1946
Black, Bud☆ Ana A 2000-04, LA A 2005-06
Blackburn, Wayne● Det A 1963-64
Blackburne, Lena★ Chi A 1927-28, StL A 1930, Phi A 1933-40, 1942-43
Blades, Ray★ StL N 1930-32, Cin N 1942, Bro N 1947-48, StL N 1951, Chi N 1953-56
Blaylock, Gary☆ KC A 1984-87
Bloomfield, Jack● SD N 1974, Chi N 1975-76, 1977-78
Bluege, Ossie★ Was A 1940-42
Bochy, Bruce★ SD N 1993-94
Boggs, Wade★ TB A 2001
Bombard, Marc● Cin N 1996, Phi N 2005-06
Bonds, Bobby★ Cle A 1984-87, SF N 1993-96
Booker, Greg☆ SD N 1997-2003
Boone, Bob★ Cin N 1994
Boros, Steve★ KC A 1975-79, Mon N 1981-82, KC A 1993-94, Bal A 1995
Bosio, Chris☆ TB A 2003
Bosley, Thad★ Oak A 1999-2003
Bosman, Dick☆ Chi A 1986-87, Bal A 1992-94, Tex A 1995-2000
Bottomley, Jim★ StL A 1937
Bowa, Larry★ Phi N 1988-96, Ana A 1997-99, Sea A 2000, NY A 2006
Boyer, Clete★ Oak A 1980-85, NY A 1988, 1992-94
Boyer, Cloyd☆ NY A 1975, 1977, Atl N 1978-81, KC A 1982-83
Boyer, Ken★ StL N 1971-72
Bragan, Jimmy● Cin N 1967-69, Mon N 1970-72, Mil A 1976-77
Bragan, Bobby★ LA N 1960, Hou N 1962
Brantley, Mickey★ NY N 1999, Tor A 2005-06
Braun, Steve★ StL N 1990
Brecheen, Harry☆ Bal A 1954-67
Breeden, Scott● Cin N 1986-89
Breeden, Joe● Fla N 1995-96, 1999-2001, Tor A 2004
Brenly, Bob★ SF N 1992-95
Bresnahan, Roger★ NY N 1925-28, Det A 1930-31
Brewer, Jim☆ Mon N 1977-79
Bridges, Rocky★ LA A 1962-63, Cal A 1968-71, SF N 1985
Bridges, Tommy☆ Det A 1946, Cin N 1951
Brinkman, Ed★ Det A 1979, SD N 1981, Chi A 1983-88
Bristol, Dave▲ Cin N 1966, Mon N 1973-75, SF N 1978-79, Phi N 1982-85, 1988, Cin N 1989, 1993
Brown, Hal☆ Bal A 1964
Brown, Jackie☆ Tex A 1979-82, Chi A 1992-95, TB A 2002
Brown, Jimmy★ Bos N 1949-51
Brown, Mace☆ Bos A 1965
Brown, Mike☆ Cle A 2002
Brown, Gates★ Det A 1978-84
Brucker, Earle★ Phi A 1941-49, StL A 1950, Cin N 1952
Bryant, Clay☆ LA N 1961, Cle A 1967, 1974
Bryant, Don★ Bos A 1974-76, Sea A 1977-80
Buckner, Bill★ Chi A 1996-97
Buford, Don★ SF N 1981-84, Bal A 1994, Was N 2005
Bumbry, Al★ Bos A 1988-93, Bal A 1995, Cle A 1998, 2002
Bundy, Lorenzo● Fla N 1998, Col N 1999, Ari N 2004
Burdette, Lew☆ Atl N 1972-73
Burgess, Tom★ NY N 1977, Atl N 1978
Burgmeier, Tom☆ KC A 1991, 1998-2000
Burke, Jimmy★ Det A 1914-17, Bos A 1921-23, Chi N 1926-30, NY A 1931-33
Burkett, Jesse★ NY N 1921
Burleson, Rick★ Oak A 1991, Bos A 1992-93, Cal A 1995-96
Burns, George★ NY N 1931
Burns, Jack★ Bos A 1955-59
Burris, Ray☆ Mil A 1990-91, Tex A 1992
Burwell, Bill☆ Bos A 1944, Pit N 1947-48, 1958-62
Busby, Jim★ Bal A 1961, Hou N 1962, 1963-67, Atl N 1968-75, Chi A 1976, Sea A 1977-78
Butcher, Mike☆ TB A 2006
Butera, Sal★ Tor A 1998-99
Butler, Brett★ Ari N 2005
Butler, Johnny★ Chi A 1932
Butterfield, Brian● NY A 1994-95, Ari N 1998-2000, Tor A 2002-06
Camacho, Joe● Was A 1969-71, Tex A 1972
Camilli, Doug★ Was A 1968-69, Bos A 1970-73
Campbell, Bill☆ Mil N 1999
Cannizzaro, Chris★ Atl N 1976-78
Cardenal, Jose★ Cin N 1993, StL N 1994-95, NY A 1996-99, TB A 2000-01, Cin N 2002-03
Carew, Rod★ Cal A 1992-96, Ana A 1997-99, Mil N 2000-01
Carey, Max★ Pit N 1930
Carey, P. J.● Col N 1997
Carey, Tom★ Bos A 1946-47
Carisch, Fred★ Det A 1923-24
Carlucci, Dave● Bos A 1996
Carnevale, Danny● KC A 1970
Carter, Dick● Phi N 1959-60
Case, George★ Was A 1961-63, Min A 1968
Cash, Dave★ Phi N 1996, Bal A 2005-06
Castro, Bill☆ Mil A 1992-95, NY A 1996, Mil A 1997, Mil N 1998-2006
Cavarretta, Phil★ Det A 1961-63, NY N 1978

Cepeda, Orlando★ Chi A 1980
Chambliss, Chris★ NY A 1988, StL N 1993-95, NY A 1997-2000, NY N 2002, Cin N 2004-06
Chandler, Spud☆ KC A 1957-58
Chapman, Ben★ Cin N 1952
Chaves, Rafael● Sea A 2006
Chesbro, Jack☆ Was A 1924
Chiti, Dom● Cle A 1991-93, Tex A 2006
Cisco, Galen☆ KC A 1971-79, Mon N 1980-84, SD N 1985-87, Tor A 1988, 1990-95, Phi N 1997-2000
Clark, Dave★ Pit N 2001-02
Clark, Jack★ LA N 2001-03
Clark, Ron★ Chi A 1988-90, Sea A 1991, Cle A 1992-93
Clarke, Fred★ Pit N 1925
Clarke, Tommy★ NY N 1932-35, 1938
Clary, Ellis★ Was A 1955-60, Tor A 1989
Clear, Bob● Cal A 1976-87
Clines, Gene★ Chi N 1979-81, Hou N 1988, Sea A 1989-92, Mil A 1993-94, SF N 1997-2002, Chi N 2003-06
Cloninger, Tony☆ NY A 1992-2001, Bos A 2002-03
Cluck, Bob● Hou N 1979, 1990-93, Oak A 1996-97, Det A 2003-05
Clymer, Bill★ Cin N 1925
Cochrane, Mickey★ Phi A 1950
Cockrell, Alan★ Col N 2002
Cohen, Andy★ Phi N 1960
Colavito, Rocky★ Cle A 1973, 1976-78, KC A 1982-83
Colborn, Jim☆ LA N 2001-05, Pit N 2006
Cole, Dick★ Chi N 1961
Coleman, Joe☆ Cal A 1988-90, StL N 1991-94, Cal A 1996, Ana A 1997-99
Coleman, Bob★ Bos A 1926, Det A 1932, Bos N 1943
Collins, Dave★ StL N 1991-92, Cin N 1999-2000, Mil N 2002, Col N 2003-06
Collins, Eddie★ Phi A 1931-32
Collins, Ripper★ Chi N 1961-63
Collins, Terry▲ Pit N 1992-93, TB A 2001
Combs, Earle★ NY A 1936-44, StL A 1947, Bos A 1948-52, Phi N 1954
Combs, Merl★ Tex A 1974-75
Comer, Steve☆ Cle A 1987
Connor, Mark● NY A 1984-85, 1986-87, 1990-93, Ari N 1998-2000, Tor A 2001-02, Tex A 2003-06
Connors, Billy☆ KC A 1980-81, Chi N 1982-86, Sea A 1987-88, NY A 1989-90, Chi N 1991-93, NY A 1994-95, 2000
Conroy, Wid★ Phi N 1922
Consolo, Billy★ Det A 1979-92, 1995
Conti, Guy● NY N 2005-06
Contreras, Nardi☆ NY A 1995, Sea A 1997-98, Chi A 1998-2002
Cooke, Dusty★ Phi N 1948-52
Coombs, Jack☆ Det A 1920
Cooney, Johnny★ Bos N 1940-42, 1946-49, 1950-52, Mil N 1953-55, Chi A 1957-64
Cooper, Cecil★ Mil N 2002, Hou N 2005-06
Cooper, Don☆ Chi A 1995, 2003-06
Cooper, Walker★ StL N 1957, KC A 1960
Cora, Joey★ Chi A 2004-06
Corrales, Pat★ Tex A 1975-78, NY A 1989, Atl N 1990-2006
Corriden, Red★ Chi N 1932-40, Bro N 1941-46, NY A 1947-48, Chi A 1950
Cottier, Chuck★ NY N 1979-81, Sea A 1982-84, Chi N 1988-94, Bal A 1995, Phi N 1997-2000
Couchee, Mike☆ Cal A 1996
Courtney, Clint★ Hou N 1965
Cox, Jeff★ KC A 1995, Mon N 2000-01, Fla N 2002-05, Pit N 2006
Cox, Larry★ Chi N 1988-89
Cox, Bobby★ NY A 1977
Crabtree, Estel★ Cin N 1943-44
Craft, Harry★ KC A 1955-57, Chi N 1960-61
Craig, Roger☆ SD N 1969-72, Hou N 1974-75, SD N 1976-77, Det A 1980-84
Cramer, Doc★ Det A 1948, Chi A 1951-53
Crandall, Del★ Cal A 1977
Crandall, Doc☆ Pit N 1931-34
Crandall, Jimmie● StL A 1953
Cravath, Gavvy★ Phi N 1923
Cresse, Mark● LA N 1977-98
Crosetti, Frankie★ NY A 1947-68, Sea A 1969, Min A 1970-71
Crowley, Terry★ Bal A 1985-88, Min A 1991-98, Bal A 1999-2006
Cruz, Jose★ Hou N 1997-2006
Cubbage, Mike★ NY N 1990-91, 1992-96, Hou N 1997-2001, Bos A 2002-03
Cuccinello, Tony★ Cin N 1949-51, Cle A 1952-56, Chi A 1957-66, Det A 1967-68, Chi A 1969
Cuellar, Bobby☆ Sea A 1995-96, Mon N 1997-2000, Tex A 2001, Pit N 2006
Culp, Benny★ Phi N 1946-47
Cumberland, John☆ Bos A 1995, 1999-2001, KC A 2002-04
Cunningham, Joe★ StL N 1982
Cunningham, Bill★ Chi A 1932
Cuyler, Kiki★ Chi N 1941-43, Bos A 1949
Dahlgren, Babe★ KC A 1964
Dal Canton, Bruce☆ Chi A 1978, Atl N 1987-90
Daly, Tom★ Bos A 1933-46
Daly, Tom★ NY A 1914
Dancy, Bill● Phi N 2005-06,
Dark, Alvin★ Chi N 1965, 1977
Datz, Jeff★ Cle A 2002-06
Dauer, Rich★ Cle A 1990-91, KC A 1997-2002, Mil N 2003-05
Daulton, Darren★ TB A 2001
Davenport, Jim★ SF N 1970, SD N 1974-75, SF N 1976-82, 1984, Phi N 1986-87, Cle A 1989, SF N 1996
David, Andre★ KC A 2005-06
Davis, Doug★ Fla N 2003-04
Davis, Harry★ Phi A 1913-17, 1919
Davis, Tommy★ Sea A 1981
Davis, Mark☆ Ari N 2003-05
Davis, Brandy★ Phi N 1972
Davis, Spud★ Pit N 1942-46, Chi N 1950-53
Deal, Cot☆ Cin N 1959-60, Hou N 1962-64, NY A 1965, KC A 1966-67, Cle A 1970-71, Det A 1973-74, Hou N 1983-85
Dean, Dizzy☆ Chi N 1941
DeArmas, Roly● Chi A 1995-96, Tor A 2000
Debus, Jon● LA N 2005
DeJohn, Mark★ StL N 1996-2001
DeMars, Billy★ Phi N 1969-81, Mon N 1982-84, Cin N 1985-87
DeMerritt, Marty● SF N 1989, Chi N 1999
Demeter, Steve★ Pit N 1985
Dempsey, Rick★ LA N 1999-2000, Bal A 2002-06
Denbo, Gary● NY A 2001
Dent, Bucky★ StL N 1991-94, Tex A 1995-2001, Cin N 2006
DeTore, George★ Pit N 1959
Devlin, Art★ Bos N 1926, 1928
Dews, Bobby● Atl N 1979-81, 1985, 1997-2006
Dickey, Bill★ NY A 1949-57, 1960
Didier, Bob★ Oak A 1984-86, Sea A 1989-90
DiMaggio, Joe★ Oak A 1968-69
Dixon, Walt● Chi N 1964-65
Dobson, Pat☆ Mil A 1982-84, SD N 1988-90, KC A 1991, Bal A 1996
Doby, Larry★ Mon N 1971-73, Cle A 1974, Mon N 1976, Chi A 1977-78
Doerr, Bobby★ Bos A 1967-69, Tor A 1977-81
Dolan, Cozy★ NY N 1922-24
Donnelly, Rich● Tex A 1980, 1983-85, Pit N 1986-95, Fla N 1997-98, Col N 1999-2002, Mil N 2003-05, LA N 2006
Donovan, Bill☆ Det A 1918
Doolan, Mickey★ Chi N 1926-29, Cin N 1930-32
Doran, Bill★ Cin N 2001, KC A 2005-06
Dorante, Luis● Fla N 2005
Dorish, Fritz☆ Bos A 1963, Atl N 1968-71
Douglas, Otis● Cin N 1961-62
Down, Rick● Cal A 1987-88, NY A 1993-95, Bal A 1996-98, LA N 1999-2000, Bos A 2001, NY A 2002-03, NY N 2005-06
Drabowsky, Moe☆ Chi A 1986, Chi N 1994
Dressen, Chuck★ Bro N 1939-42, 1943-46, NY A 1947-48, LA N 1958-59
Dubee, Rich● Fla N 1998-2001, Phi N 2005-06
Dubuc, Jean☆ Det A 1930-31
Duffy, Hugh★ Bos A 1932
Dugey, Oscar★ Bos N 1920, Chi N 1921-24
Duncan, Dave★ Cle A 1978-81, Sea A 1982, Chi A 1983-86, Oak A 1986-95, StL N 1996-2006
Duncan, Mariano★ LA N 2006
Dunlop, Harry● KC A 1969-75, Chi N 1976, Cin N 1979-82, SD N 1983-87, Cin N 1998, Fla N 2005
Durocher, Leo★ LA N 1961-64
Dusan, Gene● NY N 1983
Dyer, Duffy★ Chi N 1983, Mil A 1989-95, Oak A 1996-98
Dykes, Jimmy★ Phi A 1949-50, Cin N 1955-58, Pit N 1959, Mil N 1962, KC A 1963-64
Earnshaw, George☆ Phi N 1949-50
Easler, Mike★ Mil A 1992, Bos A 1993-94, StL N 1999-2001
Easter, Luke★ Cle A 1969
Ebel, Dino● LA A 2006
Edwards, Doc★ Phi N 1970-72, Cle A 1985-87, NY N 1990-91
Egan, Ben★ Bro N 1925, Chi A 1926
Egan, Dick☆ Tex A 1988-89
Elia, Lee★ Phi N 1980-81, 1985-87, NY A 1989, Sea A 1993-97, Tor A 2000, TB A 2003-05, Bal A 2006
Elliott, Bob★ LA A 1961
Ellis, Sammy☆ NY A 1982, 1983-84, 1986, Chi A 1989-91, Chi N 1992, Sea A 1993-94, Bos A 1996, Bal A 2000
Emery, Cal★ Chi A 1988
Engle, Dave★ Hou N 1998, NY N 2001-02
Ens, Jewel★ Pit N 1926-29, Det A 1932, Cin N 1933, Bos N 1934, Pit N 1935-39, Cin N 1941
Ermer, Cal★ Bal A 1962, Mil A 1970-71, Oak A 1977
Espy, Duane● SD N 2000-02, Col N 2003-06
Estrada, Chuck☆ Tex A 1973, SD N 1978-81, Cle A 1983
Etchebarren, Andy★ Cal A 1977, Mil A 1985-91, Bal A 1996-97
Evans, Darrell★ NY A 1990
Evans, Dwight★ Col N 1994, Bos A 2002
Evers, Johnny★ NY N 1920, Chi A 1922-23, Bos N 1929-32
Evers, Hoot★ Cle A 1970
Evers, Bill● TB A 2006
Ezell, Glenn● Tex A 1983-85, KC A 1989-94, Det A 1996, TB A 2001-02
Faber, Red☆ Chi A 1946-48
Fahey, Bill★ SF N 1986-91
Falk, Bibb★ Cle A 1933, Bos A 1934
Fanning, Jim★ Atl N 1967
Farrell, Duke★ NY A 1909, 1911, 1915-17
Farrell, Kerby★ Chi A 1966-69, Cle A 1970-71
Felske, John★ Tor A 1980-81, Phi N 1984
Ferguson, Joe★ Tex A 1986-87, LA N 1988-89, 1992-93
Ferraro, Mike★ NY A 1979-82, KC A 1984-86, NY A 1987-88, 1989-91, Bal A 1993
Ferrell, Rick★ Was A 1946-49, Det A 1950-53
Ferrick, Tom☆ Cin N 1954-58, Phi N 1959, Det A 1960-63, KC A 1964-65
Ferriss, Dave☆ Bos A 1955-59
Fields, Bruce★ Det A 2003-05
Fischer, Brad● Oak A 1996-2006
Fischer, Bill☆ Cin N 1979-83, Bos A 1985-91, TB A 2000-01
Fitz Gerald, Ed★ Cle A 1960, KC A 1961, Min A 1962-64
Fitzgerald, Joe● Was A 1947-56
Fitzpatrick, John● Pit N 1953-56, Mil N 1958-59
Fitzsimmons, Freddie☆ Bro N 1942, Bos N 1948, NY N 1949-53, 1954-55, Chi N 1957-59, KC A 1960, Chi N 1966
Flanagan, Mike☆ Bal A 1995, 1998
Flannery, Tim★ SD N 1996-2002
Fletcher, Art★ NY A 1927-45
Flowers, Jake★ Pit N 1940-45, Bos N 1946, Cle A 1951-52

Floyd, Bobby★ NY N 2001, 2004
Fohl, Lee★ StL A 1920
Foley, Marv★ Chi N 1994, Bal A 1999
Foley, Tom★ TB A 2002-06
Foli, Tim★ Tex A 1986-87, Mil A 1992-95, KC A 1996, Cin N 2001-03
Foote, Barry★ Chi A 1991, NY N 1992-93
Ford, Whitey☆ NY A 1964, 1968, 1974-75
Fowler, Art☆ LA A 1964, Min A 1969, Det A 1971-73, Tex A 1973-75, NY A 1977-79, Oak A 1980-82, NY A 1983, 1988
Fox, Charlie★ SF N 1965-68, NY A 1989
Fox, Nellie★ Hou N 1965, 1966-67, Was A 1968-71, Tex A 1972
Foxx, Jimmie★ Chi N 1944
Francona, Terry★ Det A 1996, Tex A 2002, Oak A 2003
Franks, Herman★ NY N 1949-55, SF N 1958, 1964, Chi N 1970
Fraser, Chick☆ Pit N 1923
Freese, George★ Chi N 1964-65
Frey, Jim▲ Bal A 1970-79, NY N 1982-83
Friel, Bill★ StL A 1920
Friend, Owen★ KC A 1969
Frisch, Frankie★ NY N 1949
Funk, Frank☆ SF N 1976, Sea A 1980-81, 1983-84, KC A 1988-90, Col N 1996-98
Gaetti, Gary★ Hou N 2004-06
Galan, Augie★ Phi A 1954
Galante, Matt★ Hou N 1985-96, 1998-2001, NY N 2002-04
Gale, Rich☆ Bos A 1992-93
Gallego, Mike★ Col N 2002, 2005-06
Gamboa, Tom● Chi N 1998-99, KC A 2001-03
Gantner, Jim★ Mil A 1996-97
Garcia, Carlos★ Sea A 2005-06
Garcia, Dave▲ SD N 1970-73, Cle A 1975-76, Cal A 1977, Cle A 1979, Mil A 1983-84
Gardenhire, Ron★ Min A 1991-2001
Gardner, Mark☆ SF N 2003-06
Gardner, Billy★ Bos A 1965-66, Mon N 1977-78, Min A 1981
Garner, Phil★ Hou N 1989-91
Garrett, Adrian★ KC A 1988-92
Garrison, Ford★ Cin N 1953
Gaston, Cito★ Tor A 1982-89, 2000-01
Gebhard, Bob☆ Mon N 1982
Gehringer, Charlie★ Det A 1942
Geren, Bob★ Oak A 2003-06
Gernert, Dick★ Tex A 1975-76
Gharrity, Patsy★ Was A 1929-32, Cle A 1933-35
Gibbons, John★ Tor A 2002-04
Gibson, George★ Was A 1923, Chi N 1925, 1926
Gibson, Kirk★ Det A 2003-05
Gibson, Bob☆ NY N 1981, Atl N 1982-84, StL N 1995
Gilbert, Andy★ SF N 1972-75
Gilliam, Jim★ LA N 1965-78
Girardi, Joe★ NY A 2005
Gladding, Fred☆ Det A 1976-78
Gleason, Kid★ Phi N 1908-11, Chi A 1912-14, 1916-17, Phi A 1926-32
Gleeson, Jim★ KC A 1957, NY A 1964
Glynn, Gene● Col N 1994, 1995-98, Mon N 1999, Chi N 2000-02, SF N 2003-06
Goff, Mike● Sea A 2005-06
Gomez, Orlando● Tex A 1991-92, TB A 1998-2000, Sea A 2003-04
Gomez, Preston★ LA N 1965-68, Hou N 1973, StL N 1976, LA N 1977-79, Cal A 1981-84
Gonzalez, Fredi● Fla N 1999-2001, Atl N 2003-06
Gonzalez, Mike★ StL N 1934-46
Gooch, Johnny★ Pit N 1937-39
Goodman, Billy★ Atl N 1968-70
Gordon, Joe★ Det A 1956
Goryl, Johnny★ Min A 1968-69, 1979-80, Cle A 1982-88, 1997-98
Gowdy, Hank★ Bos N 1929-37, Cin N 1938-42, 1945-46, NY N 1947-48
Graff, Milt★ Pit N 1985
Graham, Brian● Cle A 1999, Bal A 2000
Grammas, Alex★ Chi N 1964, Pit N 1965-69, Cin N 1970-75, 1978, Atl N 1979, Det A 1980-91
Greenwell, Mike★ Cin N 2001
Gregson, Glenn● LA N 1998, Bos A 2003
Griffey, Ken★ Sea A 1993, Col N 1996, Cin N 1997-2001, 2001
Griffin, Alfredo★ Tor A 1996-97, Ana A 2000-04, LA A 2005-06
Grimes, Burleigh★ KC A 1955
Grimm, Charlie★ Chi N 1941, 1961-63
Grissom, Marv☆ LA A 1961-65, Cal A 1966, Chi A 1967-68, Cal A 1969, Min A 1970-71, Chi N 1975-76, Cal A 1977-78
Grodzicki, Johnny☆ Det A 1979
Gross, Greg★ Phi N 2001-04
Guerrero, Epy● Tor A 1981
Guidry, Ron☆ NY A 2006
Guillen, Ozzie★ Mon N 2001, Fla N 2002-03
Gullett, Don☆ Cin N 1993-2005
Gumpert, Randy☆ NY A 1957
Gustine, Frankie★ Pit N 1950
Gutteridge, Don★ Chi A 1955-66, 1968-69
Haas, Eddie★ Atl N 1974-77, 1984
Haas, Mule★ Chi A 1940-46
Hack, Stan★ StL N 1957-58, Chi N 1965
Hacker, Rich★ StL N 1986-90, Tor A 1991-94
Haddix, Harvey☆ NY N 1966-67, Cin N 1969, Bos A 1971, Cle A 1975-78, Pit N 1979-84
Haines, Jesse☆ Bro N 1938
Hairston, Sammy★ Chi A 1978
Hale, DeMarlo● Tex A 2002-05, Bos A 2006
Haller, Tom★ SF N 1977-79
Hamilton, Steve☆ Det A 1975
Hancken, Buddy★ Hou N 1968-72
Haney, Fred★ Mil N 1956
Haney, Larry★ Mil A 1978-91
Hansen, Guy● KC A 1991-93, 1996-97, 2005
Hansen, Roger● Sea A 1992
Hansen, Ron★ Mil A 1980-83, Mon N 1985-89
Harder, Mel☆ Cle A 1947, 1948-63, NY N 1964, Chi N 1965, Cin N 1966-68, KC A 1969
Hardy, Larry☆ Tex A 1995-2001
Hargrove, Mike★ Cle A 1990-91
Harkey, Mike☆ Fla N 2006
Harmon, Tom● Chi N 1982
Harper, Tommy★ Bos A 1980-84, Mon N 1990-99, Bos A 2000-02
Harrah, Toby★ Tex A 1989-92, Cle A 1996, Col N 2000-02
Harrelson, Bud★ NY N 1982, 1985-90
Harris, Lum☆ Chi A 1951-54, Bal A 1955-61, Hou N 1962-64
Hart, John▲ Bal A 1988
Hartenstein, Chuck☆ Cle A 1979, Mil A 1987-89
Hartley, Grover★ Cle A 1928-30, Pit N 1931-33, StL A 1934-36, NY N 1946
Hartnett, Gabby★ Chi N 1938, NY N 1941, KC A 1965
Hartsfield, Roy★ LA N 1969-72, Atl N 1973
Haselman, Bill★ Bos A 2005-06
Hassey, Ron★ Col N 1993-95, StL N 1996, Sea A 2005-06
Hatcher, Mickey★ Tex A 1993-94, LA N 1998, Ana A 2000-04, LA A 2005-06
Hatcher, Billy★ TB A 1998-2005
Hatfield, Fred★ Det A 1977-78
Hatton, Grady★ Chi N 1960, Hou N 1973-74
Hayes, Bill★ Col N 1998
Haynes, Joe☆ Was A 1953-55
Hayworth, Ray★ Bro N 1945, Chi N 1955
Hebner, Richie★ Bos A 1989-91, Phi N 2001
Heffner, Don★ KC A 1958-60, Det A 1961, NY N 1964-65, Cal A 1967-68
Hegan, Jim★ NY A 1960-73, Det A 1974-78, NY A 1979-80
Heilmann, Harry★ Cin N 1932
Heist, Al★ Hou N 1966-67, SD N 1980
Helms, Tommy★ Tex A 1981-82, Cin N 1983-89
Hemsley, Rollie★ Phi A 1954, Was A 1961-62
Hemus, Solly★ NY N 1962-63, Cle A 1964-65
Henderson, Ramon● Phi N 1998-2006
Henderson, Steve★ Hou N 1994-96, TB A 1998, 2006
Hendrick, George★ StL N 1996-97, Ana A 1998-99, LA N 2003, TB A 2006
Hendricks, Elrod★ Bal A 1978-2005
Henrich, Tommy★ NY A 1951, NY N 1957, Det A 1958-59
Herman, Babe★ Pit N 1951
Herman, Billy★ Bro N 1952-57, Mil N 1958-59, Bos A 1960-64, Cal A 1967, SD N 1978-79
Hernandez, Chuck● Cal A 1992-96, TB A 2004-05, Det A 2006
Herndon, Larry★ Det A 1992-98
Hershiser, Orel☆ Tex A 2002-05
Herzog, Whitey★ KC A 1965, NY N 1966, Cal A 1974-75
Hiatt, Jack★ Chi N 1981
Hickey, Jim● Hou N 2004-06
High, Andy★ Bro N 1937-38
Hill, Marc★ Hou N 1988, NY A 1991
Hill, Perry● Tex A 1992-94, 1995, Det A 1997-99, Mon N 2000-01, Fla N 2002-06
Hiller, Chuck★ Tex A 1973, KC A 1976-79, StL N 1981-83, SF N 1985, NY N 1990
Hilton, Dave★ Mil A 1987-88
Himsl, Vedie▲ Chi N 1960-64
Hinchman, Bill★ Pit N 1923
Hines, Ben● Sea A 1984, LA N 1986, 1988-93, Hou N 1994
Hines, Bruce● Cal A 1991
Hisle, Larry★ Tor A 1992-95
Hitchcock, Billy★ Det A 1955-60, Atl N 1966
Hoak, Don★ Phi N 1967
Hoffman, Glenn★ LA N 1999-2005, SD N 2006
Hofman, Bobby★ KC A 1966-67, Was A 1968, Oak A 1969-70, Cle A 1971-72, Oak A 1974-75, 1978
Hofmann, Fred★ StL A 1938-49, 1951
Holke, Walter★ StL A 1940
Hollingsworth, Al☆ StL N 1957-58
Holmberg, Dennis● Tor A 1994-95
Holmquist, Doug● NY A 1984, 1985
Holt, Goldie● Pit N 1948-50, Chi N 1961-65
Honeycutt, Rick☆ LA N 2006
Hooton, Burt☆ Hou N 2000-04
Hopp, Johnny★ Det A 1954, StL N 1956
Hornsby, Rogers★ Chi N 1958-59, NY N 1962
Horton, Willie★ NY A 1985, Chi A 1986
Hoscheit, Vern● Bal A 1968, Oak A 1969-74, Cal A 1976, NY N 1984-87
Hough, Charlie☆ LA N 1998-99, NY N 2001-02
Houk, Ralph★ NY A 1954, 1958-60
House, Tom☆ Tex A 1985-92
Howard, Elston★ NY A 1969-79
Howard, Frank★ Mil A 1977-80, NY N 1982-83, 1984, Mil A 1985-86, Sea A 1987-88, NY A 1989, 1991-93, NY N 1994-96, TB A 1998-99
Howe, Art★ Tex A 1985-88, Col N 1995
Howley, Dan★ Det A 1919, 1921-22
Howser, Dick★ NY A 1969-78
Hriniak, Walt★ Mon N 1974-75, Bos A 1977-88, Chi A 1989-95
Hubbard, Glenn★ Atl N 1999-2006
Hubbard, Jack● StL N 1993, Tor A 1998
Hudgens, Dave★ Oak A 1999, 2003-05
Hudlin, Willis☆ Det A 1957-59
Hudson, Sid☆ Was A 1961-65, 1968-71, Tex A 1972, 1975-78
Hulswitt, Rudy★ Bos A 1931-33
Hume, Tom☆ Cin N 1996-2006
Hundley, Randy★ Chi N 1977
Hunter, Newt★ Phi N 1928-31, 1933
Hunter, Billy★ Bal A 1964-77
Huppert, Dave★ Was N 2005
Hurdle, Clint★ Col N 1997-2002
Iorg, Garth★ Tor A 2001-02
Isaac, Luis● Cle A 1987-91, 1994-2006
Jackson, Al☆ Bos A 1977-79, Bal A 1989-91, NY N 1999-2000
Jackson, Grant☆ Pit N 1984-85, Cin N 1994-95

Jackson, Sonny★ Atl N 1982-83, SF N 1997-2002
Jackson, Ron★ Chi A 1995-98, Mil N 1999, Bos A 2003-06
Jackson, Travis★ NY N 1939-40, 1947-48
Jacoby, Brook★ Tex A 2006
Jansen, Larry☆ NY N 1954, SF N 1961-71, Chi N 1972-73
Jaramillo, Rudy● Hou N 1990-93, Tex A 1995-2005, 2006
Jauss, Dave● Bos A 1997-99, LA N 2006
Jenkins, Fergie☆ Chi N 1995-96
Jennings, Hughie★ NY N 1921-25
Jewett, Trent● Pit N 2000-02
Johnson, Darrell★ StL N 1960-61, Bal A 1962, Bos A 1968-69, Tex A 1981-82, NY N 1993
Johnson, Deron★ Cal A 1979-80, NY N 1981, Phi N 1982-84, Sea A 1985-86, Chi A 1987, Cal A 1989-92
Johnson, Lamar★ Mil A 1995-97, Mil N 1998, KC A 1999-2002, Sea A 2003
Johnson, Roy☆ Chi N 1935-39, 1944-53
Johnson, Syl☆ Phi N 1937-40
Johnson, Tim★ Mon N 1993-94, Bos A 1995-96
Johnson, Wallace★ Chi A 1998-2002
Johnston, Jimmy★ Bro N 1931
Jones, Clarence★ Atl N 1985, 1988-98, Cle A 1999-2001
Jones, Gary● Oak A 1998
Jones, Gordon☆ Hou N 1966-67
Jones, Deacon★ Hou N 1976-82, SD N 1984-87
Jones, Jeff☆ Det A 1995, 1998-99, 2000, 2002
Jones, Joe● KC A 1987, 1992, Pit N 1997-2000, KC A 2005
Jones, Lynn★ KC A 1991-92, Fla N 2001, Bos A 2004-05
Jones, Bobby★ Tex A 2000-01, 2006
Jones, Tommy● Ari N 2004
Jonnard, Bubber★ Phi N 1935, NY N 1942-46
Joshua, Von★ Chi A 1998-2001
Judge, Joe★ Was A 1945-46
Jurges, Billy★ Chi N 1947-48, Was A 1956-59
Kaat, Jim☆ Cin N 1984-85
Kahn, Lou● StL N 1955
Katt, Ray★ StL N 1959-60, Cle A 1962
Kaufmann, Tony☆ StL N 1947-50
Keane, Johnny▲ StL N 1959-61
Keefe, Dave☆ Phi A 1940-49
Keely, Bob★ Bos N 1946-52, Mil N 1953-57
Kelleher, Mick★ Pit N 1986, Det A 2003-05
Keller, Charlie★ NY A 1957, 1959
Kelley, Joe★ Bro N 1926
Kelly, Mike● Chi A 1930-31, Chi N 1934, Bos N 1937-39, Pit N 1940-41
Kelly, George★ Cin N 1935-37, Bos N 1938-43, Cin N 1947-48
Kelly, Tom★ Min A 1983-86
Kendall, Fred★ Det A 1996-98, Col N 2000-02, KC A 2006
Kennedy, Kevin▲ Mon N 1992
Kennedy, Bob★ Chi N 1962-65, Atl N 1967
Kerr, John★ Was A 1935
Kerrigan, Joe☆ Mon N 1983-86, 1992-96, Bos A 1997-2001, Phi N 2003-04, NY A 2006
Killefer, Bill★ StL N 1926, StL A 1927-29, Bro N 1939, Phi N 1942
Kim, Wendell● SF N 1989-96, Bos A 1997-2000, Mon N 2002, Chi N 2003-04
Kimm, Bruce★ Cin N 1984-88, Pit N 1989, SD N 1991-92, Fla N 1997-98, Col N 1999, Chi A 2003
King, Clyde☆ Cin N 1959, Pit N 1965-67, NY A 1978, 1981, 1982, 1988
Kipper, Bob☆ Bos A 2002
Kison, Bruce☆ KC A 1992-98, Bal A 1999
Kissell, George● StL N 1969-75
Kittle, Hub● Hou N 1971-75, StL N 1981-83
Klein, Chuck★ Phi N 1942-45
Klein, Lou★ Chi N 1960-65
Kluszewski, Ted★ Cin N 1970-78
Kniffin, Chuck● Ari N 2002-04
Knight, Ray★ Cin N 1993-95, 2002-03
Knoop, Bobby★ Chi A 1977-78, Cal A 1979-96, Tor A 2000
Knorr, Randy★ Was N 2006
Knowles, Darold☆ StL N 1983, Phi N 1989-90
Koenig, Fred● Cal A 1970-71, StL N 1976, Tex A 1977-82, Chi N 1983, Cle A 1985-86
Kranitz, Rick● Chi N 2002, Fla N 2006
Kress, Red★ Det A 1940, NY N 1946-49, Cle A 1953-60, LA A 1961, NY N 1962
Krol, Jack▲ StL N 1977-80, SD N 1981-86
Krug, Chris★ SD N 1969
Kuehl, Karl▲ Min A 1977-82
Kuenn, Harvey★ Mil A 1971-82
Kuntz, Rusty★ Sea A 1989-92, Fla N 1995-96, 1999-2000, Pit N 2003-05
Kusnyer, Art★ Chi A 1980-87, Oak A 1989-95, Chi A 1997-2006
Lachemann, Marcel☆ Cal A 1984-92, Fla N 1993-94, Ana A 1997-98, Col N 2000-01
Lachemann, Rene★ Bos A 1985-86, Oak A 1987-92, StL N 1997-99, Chi N 2000-02, Sea A 2003-04, Oak A 2005-06
Lachemann, Bill● Cal A 1995-96
Lakeman, Al★ Bos A 1963-64, 1967-69
Lamont, Gene★ Pit N 1986-91, 1996, Bos A 2001, Hou N 2002-04, Det A 2006
Land, Grover★ Pit N 1914, Cin N 1925-28, Chi N 1929-30
Landestoy, Rafael★ Mon N 1989, NY N 1996, Det A 2002
Landrith, Hobie★ Was A 1964
Langford, Rick☆ Tor A 2000
Lanier, Hal★ StL N 1981-85, Phi N 1990-91
Lansford, Carney★ Oak A 1994-95, StL N 1997
LaRoche, Dave☆ Chi A 1989-91, NY N 1992-93
LaRussa, Tony★ Chi A 1978
Lasorda, Tommy☆ LA N 1973-76
Latham, Arlie★ Cin N 1900, NY N 1909
Lau, Charley★ Bal A 1969, Oak A 1970, KC A 1971-74, 1975-78, NY A 1979-81, Chi A 1982-83
Lauder, Billy★ Chi A 1925
Lavagetto, Cookie★ Bro N 1951-53, Was A 1955-57, NY N 1962-63, SF N 1964-67
Law, Vern☆ Pit N 1968-69
Lazzeri, Tony★ Chi N 1938
Lefebvre, Jim★ LA N 1978-79, SF N 1980-82, Oak A 1987-88, 1994-95, Mil N 1999, Cin N 2002
Lefebvre, Joe★ SF N 2002-06
Leifield, Lefty☆ StL A 1920-23, Bos A 1924-26, Det A 1927-28
Lemon, Jim★ Min A 1965-67, 1981-84
Lemon, Bob☆ Cle A 1960, Phi N 1961, Cal A 1967-68, KC A 1970, NY A 1976
Lenhardt, Don★ Bos A 1970-73
Leonard, Dutch☆ Chi N 1954-56
Leppert, Don★ Pit N 1968-76, Tor A 1977-79, Hou N 1980-85
Lett, Jim● Cin N 1988-89, 1996, Tor A 1997-99, LA N 2001-05, Pit N 2006
Levy, Lenny● Pit N 1957-63
Lewallyn, Dennis☆ Ari N 2004
Lewis, Duffy★ Bos N 1931-35
Lewis, Johnny★ StL N 1973-76, 1985-89
Leyland, Jim▲ Chi A 1982-85
Leyva, Nick★ Ln@ 1 84-8, RaJ 1 93-9
Liddle, Steve● Min A 2002-06
Lillis, Bob★ Hou N 1967, 1973-82, SF N 1986-96
Linares, Julio● Hou N 1994-96
Lind, Jack★ Pit N 1997-2000
Lipon, Johnny★ Cle A 1968-71
Little, Bryan★ Chi A 1998-2000
Little, Grady▲ SD N 1996, Bos A 1997-99, Cle A 2000-01
Litwhiler, Danny★ Cin N 1951
Livingston, Paddy★ Phi A 1919
Llenas, Winston★ Tor A 1988
Lobe, Bill● Cle A 1951-56
Lobert, Hans★ NY N 1928, Phi N 1934-41, Cin N 1943-44
Lockman, Whitey★ Cin N 1960, SF N 1961-64, Chi N 1965-66
Lodigiani, Dario★ KC A 1961-62
Lollar, Sherm★ Bal A 1964-67, Oak A 1968
Long, Dale★ NY A 1963
Lonnett, Joe★ Chi A 1971-75, Oak A 1976, Pit N 1977-84
Lopat, Ed☆ NY A 1960, Min A 1961, KC A 1962
Lopes, Davey★ Tex A 1988-91, Bal A 1992-94, SD N 1995-99, 2003-05, Was N 2006
Lopez, Juan● SF N 1999-2002, Chi N 2003-06
Lowe, Q. V.● Chi N 1972
Lowrey, Peanuts★ Phi N 1960-66, SF N 1967-68, Mon N 1969, Chi N 1970-71, Cal A 1972, Chi N 1977-79, 1981
Lucchesi, Frank▲ Tex A 1974-75, 1979-80
Lum, Mike★ Chi A 1985, KC A 1988-89
Lumpe, Jerry★ Oak A 1971
Lund, Don★ Det A 1957-58
Luque, Dolf☆ NY N 1935-38, 1941-45
Lutz, Joe★ Cle A 1971-73
Luzinski, Greg★ Oak A 1993, KC A 1995-97
Lyons, Eddie★ Min A 1976
Lyons, Ted☆ Det A 1949-53, Bro N 1954
Macha, Ken★ Mon N 1987-91, Cal A 1992-94, Oak A 1999-2002
Mack, Earle★ Phi A 1924-50
Mackanin, Peter★ Mon N 1997-2000, Pit N 2003-05
MacKenzie, Gordy★ KC A 1980-81, Chi N 1982, SF N 1986-88, Cle A 1991
Macko, Joe● Chi N 1964
Maddon, Joe▲ Cal A 1994-96, Ana A 1997-2004, LA A 2005
Maddux, Mike☆ Mil N 2003, 2005-06
Madlock, Bill★ Det A 2000-01
Magadan, Dave★ SD N 2003-06
Maglie, Sal☆ Bos A 1960-62, 1966-67, Sea A 1969
Mahoney, Jim★ Chi A 1972-76, Sea A 1985-86
Majtyka, Roy● Atl N 1988-90
Malmberg, Harry★ Bos A 1963-64
Maloof, Jack● SD N 1990, Fla N 1999-2001
Maltzberger, Gordon☆ Min A 1962-64
Mancuso, Gus★ Cin N 1950
Mansolino, Doug● Chi A 1992-96, Mil N 1998-99, Det A 2000-02, Hou N 2005-06
Mantle, Mickey★ NY A 1970
Manto, Jeff★ Pit N 2006
Manuel, Charlie★ Cle A 1988-89, 1994-99
Manuel, Jerry★ Mon N 1991-96, Fla N 1997, NY N 2005-06
Manush, Heinie★ Was A 1953-54
Marion, Marty★ StL A 1952, Chi A 1954
Marshall, Jim★ Chi N 1974
Martin, Billy★ Min A 1965-68
Martin, Fred☆ Chi N 1961-65, Chi A 1979
Martin, Pepper★ Chi N 1956
Martin, J. C.★ Chi N 1974
Martinez, Jose★ KC A 1980-87, Chi N 1988-94
Martinez, Marty★ Sea A 1984-86, 1992
Mason, Marty● StL N 2000-06
Mason, Mike☆ KC A 2004
Mathews, Eddie★ Atl N 1971-72
Mathews, Harry● Cle A 1926-27, NY A 1929
Mathews, Rick● Col N 1993, 1995, 2003-06
Mathewson, Christy☆ NY N 1919-20
Matlack, Jon☆ Det A 1996
Matthews, Gary★ Tor A 1998-99, Mil N 2002, Chi N 2003-06
Mattingly, Don★ NY A 2004-06
Mauch, Gene★ KC A 1995
Maxvill, Dal★ Oak A 1975, NY N 1978, StL N 1979-80, Atl N 1982-84
May, Lee★ KC A 1984-86, Cin N 1988-89, KC A 1992-93, Bal A 1995, TB A 2001-02
May, Milt★ Pit N 1987-96, Fla N 1997-98, Col N 1999, TB A 2002
Mayberry, John★ KC A 1989-90
Mayo, Eddie★ Bos A 1951, Phi N 1952-54
Mays, Willie★ NY N 1974-79
Mazeroski, Bill★ Pit N 1973, Sea A 1979-80
Mazzilli, Lee★ NY A 2000-03, 2006
Mazzone, Leo● Atl N 1985, 1990-2005, Bal A 2006
McBride, George★ Det A 1925-26, 1929
McBride, Ken☆ Mil A 1975
McCall, Larry☆ Bal A 2006

McCallister, Jack▲ Cle A 1920-26, Bos A 1930
McCatty, Steve☆ Det A 2002
McClendon, Lloyd★ Pit N 1997-2000, Det A 2006
McClure, Bob☆ Fla N 1994, KC A 2006
McCormick, Frank★ Cin N 1956-57
McCrabb, Les☆ Phi A 1950-54
McCraw, Tom★ Cle A 1975, 1979-82, SF N 1983-85, Bal A 1989-91, NY N 1992-96, Hou N 1997-99, 1999-2000, Mon N 2002-04, Was N 2005
McCullough, Clyde★ Was A 1960, Min A 1961, NY N 1963, SD N 1982
McDermott, Mickey☆ Cal A 1968
McDonnell, Maje● Phi N 1951-57
McDowell, Roger☆ Atl N 2006
McGaha, Mel▲ Cle A 1961, KC A 1963-64, Hou N 1968-70
McGinnity, Joe☆ Bro N 1926
McGuire, Deacon★ Det A 1911-16
McKay, Dave★ Oak A 1984-95, StL N 1996-2006
McKechnie, Bill★ Pit N 1922, StL N 1927, Cle A 1947-49, Bos A 1952-53
McKee, J. R.● Pit N 1947
McKeon, Jack▲ Oak A 1978
McLaren, John● Tor A 1986-90, Bos A 1991, Cin N 1992, Sea A 1993-2002, TB A 2003-05
McLish, Cal☆ Phi N 1965-66, Mon N 1969-75, Mil A 1976-82
McMahon, Don☆ SF N 1973-75, Min A 1976-77, SF N 1980-82, Cle A 1983-85
McMillan, Roy★ Mil A 1970-72, NY N 1973-76
McNamara, John▲ Oak A 1968-69, SF N 1971-73, Cal A 1978
McNeely, Earl★ StL A 1931, Was A 1936-37
McNertney, Jerry★ NY A 1984, Bos A 1988
McRae, Hal★ KC A 1987, Mon N 1990-91, Cin N 1995-96, Phi N 1997-2000, TB A 2001, StL N 2005-06
Meacham, Bobby★ Fla N 2006
Mejias, Sammy★ Sea A 1993-99
Mele, Sam★ Was A 1959-60, Min A 1961
Melillo, Ski★ StL A 1938, Cle A 1939-40, 1942, 1945-48, 1950, Bos A 1952-53, KC A 1955-56
Melvin, Bob★ Mil N 1999, Det A 2000, Ari N 2001-02
Mendoza, Minnie★ Bal A 1988
Menke, Denis★ Tor A 1980-81, Hou N 1983-88, Phi N 1989-96, Cin N 1997-2000
Mercado, Orlando★ Ana A 2003-04, LA A 2005-06
Merkle, Fred★ NY A 1925-26
Merrill, Stump▲ NY A 1985, 1986-87
Metro, Charlie★ Chi N 1962, Chi A 1965, Oak A 1982
Meusel, Irish★ NY N 1930
Meyer, Benny★ Phi N 1924-26, Det A 1928-30
Meyer, Russ★ NY A 1992
Michael, Gene★ NY A 1976-77, 1978, 1984-86, 1988, 1989
Milan, Clyde★ Was A 1928-29, 1938-52
Miley, Dave▲ Cin N 1993
Miller, Dyar☆ Chi A 1987-88
Miller, Bing★ Bos A 1937, Det A 1938-41, Chi A 1942-49, Phi A 1950-53
Miller, Otto★ Bro N 1926-36
Miller, Ray▲ Bal A 1978-85, Pit N 1987-96, Bal A 1997, 2004-05
Miller, Bob☆ Tor A 1977-79, SF N 1985
Milliken, Bob☆ StL N 1965-70, 1976
Mills, Art☆ Det A 1944-48
Mills, Buster★ Cle A 1946, Chi A 1947-50, Cin N 1953, Bos A 1954
Mills, Brad★ Phi N 1997-2000, Mon N 2003, Bos A 2004-06
Minoso, Minnie★ Chi A 1976-78, 1980
Mitchell, Clarence★ NY N 1932-33
Mitchell, Fred★ Bos N 1914-16
Mitterwald, George★ Oak A 1979-82, NY A 1988
Mize, Johnny★ KC A 1961
Mizerock, John★ KC A 2002-04
Molitor, Paul★ Min A 2000-01, 2003, Sea A 2004
Monbouquette, Bill☆ NY N 1982-83, NY A 1985
Monchak, Al★ Chi A 1971-75, Oak A 1976, Pit N 1977-84, Atl N 1986-88
Monteleone, Rich☆ NY A 2002-05
Moon, Wally★ SD N 1969
Moore, Jackie★ Mil A 1970-72, Tex A 1973-74, 1975-76, Tor A 1977-79, Tex A 1980, Oak A 1981-84, Mon N 1987-89, Cin N 1990-92, Tex A 1993-94, Col N 1996-98
Moore, Terry★ StL N 1949-52, 1956-58
Morales, Jose★ SF N 1986-88, Cle A 1990-93, Fla N 1995-96
Morales, Jerry★ Mon N 2002-04
Morales, Rich★ Atl N 1986-87
Morgan, Joe★ Pit N 1972, Bos A 1985-88
Morgan, Tom☆ Cal A 1972-74, SD N 1975, NY A 1979, Cal A 1981-83
Morgan, Vern★ Min A 1969-75
Moseby, Lloyd★ Tor A 1999
Moses, John★ Sea A 2000-03, Cin N 2005-06
Moses, Wally★ Phi A 1952-54, Phi N 1955-58, Cin N 1959-60, NY A 1961-62, 1966, Det A 1967-70
Moss, Les★ Chi A 1967-68, 1969-70, Chi N 1981, Hou N 1982-84, 1985-89
Mota, Manny★ LA N 1980-89, 2004, 2006
Motton, Curt★ Bal A 1991
Mozzali, Mo● StL N 1977-78
Mueller, Ray★ NY N 1956, Chi N 1957
Muffett, Billy☆ StL N 1967-70, Cal A 1974-77, Det A 1985-94
Mulcahy, Hugh☆ Chi A 1970
Mull, Jack● SF N 1985
Mulleavy, Greg★ Bro N 1957, LA N 1958-60, 1962-64
Mullin, Pat★ Det A 1963-66, Cle A 1967, Mon N 1979-81
Mungo, Van☆ Bro N 1940
Murphy, Danny★ Phi A 1920-24, Phi N 1927
Murphy, Dwayne★ Ari N 1998-2003
Murray, Eddie★ Bal A 1998-2001, Cle A 2002-05, LA N 2006
Murtaugh, Danny★ Pit N 1956-57
Muser, Tony★ Mil A 1985-89, Chi N 1993-97, SD N 2003-06
Myatt, George★ Was A 1950-54, Chi A 1955-56, Chi N 1957-59, Mil N 1960-61, Det A 1962-63, Phi N 1964-72
Myers, Dave● Sea A 2001-04
Napoleon, Ed● Cle A 1983-85, KC A 1987-88, Hou N 1989, NY A 1992-93, Tex A 1995-2000
Naragon, Hal★ Min A 1963-66, Det A 1967-69
Narron, Jerry★ Bal A 1993-94, Tex A 1995-2001, Bos A 2003, Cin N 2004-05
Narron, Sam★ Pit N 1952-64
Natal, Bob★ Mon N 2002-04, Was N 2005
Neale, Greasy★ StL N 1929
Nelson, Dave★ Chi A 1981-84, Cle A 1992-97, Mil N 2003-06
Nettles, Graig★ NY A 1991, SD N 1995
Neun, Johnny★ NY A 1944-46
Newman, Al★ Min A 2002-03, 2004-05
Newman, Jeff★ Oak A 1986, Cle A 1992-99, Bal A 2000, Sea A 2005
Niarhos, Gus★ KC A 1962-64
Nichols, Reid★ Tex A 2001
Niehoff, Bert★ NY N 1929
Niemann, Randy☆ NY N 1997-99, 2001-02
Nipper, Al☆ Bos A 1995-96, KC A 2001-02, Bos A 2006
Nixon, Russ★ Cin N 1976-82, Mon N 1984-85, Atl N 1986-87, Sea A 1992
Noren, Irv★ Oak A 1971-74, Chi N 1975
Norman, Bill★ StL A 1952-53
Norman, Nelson★ Bos A 2001
Northey, Ron★ Pit N 1961-63
Nossek, Joe★ Mil A 1973-75, Min A 1976, Cle A 1977-81, KC A 1982-83, Chi A 1984-85, 1986, 1991-2003
Nottle, Ed● Oak A 1983
Oates, Johnny★ Chi N 1984-87, Bal A 1989-91
O'Brien, Eddie★ Sea A 1969
Oceak, Frank● Pit N 1958-64, Cin N 1965, Pit N 1970-72
O'Connell, Danny★ Was A 1963-64
O'Connor, Paddy★ NY A 1918-21
Oester, Ron★ Cin N 1993, Det A 1996, Cin N 1997-2001
Oglivie, Ben★ SD N 2000
Okrie, Len★ Bos A 1961-62, 1965-66, Det A 1970
Oldis, Bob★ Phi N 1964-66, Min A 1968, Mon N 1969
O'Leary, Charley★ StL N 1913, NY A 1920-30, Chi N 1931-33, StL A 1934-37
Oliva, Tony★ Min A 1976-78, 1985-91
Oliveras, Mako● Cal A 1994, Chi N 1995-97
Oliver, Dave★ Tex A 1987-94, Bos A 1995-96
Oliver, Tom★ Phi A 1951-53, Bal A 1954
Olson, Ivy★ Bro N 1924, 1930-31, NY N 1932
O'Neil, Mickey★ Cle A 1930
O'Neil, Buck● Chi N 1962-65
O'Neill, Steve★ Cle A 1935, Det A 1941, Cle A 1949, Bos A 1950
Onslow, Jack★ Pit N 1925-26, Was A 1927, StL N 1928, Phi N 1931-32, Bos A 1934
Oquendo, Jose★ StL N 1999-2006
Osborn, Don● Pit N 1963-64, 1970-72, 1974-76
Osteen, Claude☆ StL N 1977-80, Phi N 1982-88, Tex A 1993-94, LA N 1999-2000
Otero, Regie★ Cin N 1959-65, Cle A 1966
Otis, Amos★ SD N 1988-90, Col N 1993
Ott, Ed★ Hou N 1989-93, Det A 2001-02
Overmire, Stubby☆ Det A 1963-66
Owen, Mickey★ Bos A 1955-56
Owens, Jim☆ Hou N 1967-72
Ozark, Danny▲ LA N 1965-72, 1980-82, SF N 1983-84
Pacheco, Tony● Cle A 1974, Hou N 1976-79, 1982
Paepke, Jack● LA A 1961-64, Cal A 1965-66
Pafko, Andy★ Mil N 1960-62
Pagan, Jose★ Pit N 1974-78
Page, Mitchell★ KC A 1995-97, StL N 2001-04, Was N 2006
Page, Phil☆ Cin N 1947-52
Paige, Satchell☆ Atl N 1968-69
Parker, Dave★ Ana A 1997, StL N 1998
Parker, Salty★ SF N 1958-61, Cle A 1962, LA A 1964, Cal A 1965-66, NY N 1967, Hou N 1968-72, Cal A 1973-74
Parrish, Lance★ Det A 1999-2001, 2003-05
Parrish, Larry★ Det A 1997-98
Pascual, Camilo☆ Min A 1978-80
Patkin, Max● Cle A 1946-47, StL A 1951, Chi A 1976, 1978
Patterson, Gil☆ Tor A 2001-04
Patterson, Hank★ Bos A 1932
Pattin, Marty☆ Tor A 1989
Paul, Mike☆ Oak A 1987-88, Sea A 1989-91, Oak A 1993
Pavlick, Greg● NY N 1985-86, 1988-91, 1994-96
Pazik, Mike☆ Chi A 1995-98
Peden, Les★ Chi N 1965
Pedrique, Al★ Ari N 2004
Peitz, Heinie★ Cin N 1912, StL N 1913, Cin N 1916
Pena, Tony★ Hou N 2002, NY A 2006
Pendleton, Terry★ Atl N 2002-06
Pennock, Herb☆ Bos A 1936-39
Pentland, Jeff● Fla N 1996, Chi N 1997-2002, KC A 2003-05, Sea A 2006
Pepitone, Joe★ NY A 1982
Perez, Tony★ Cin N 1987-92
Perkins, Cy★ NY A 1932-33, Det A 1934-39, Phi N 1946-54
Perlozzo, Sam★ NY N 1987-89, Cin N 1990-92, Sea A 1993-95, Bal A 1996-2005
Perranoski, Ron☆ LA N 1981-94, SF N 1997-99
Perry, Gerald★ Sea A 2000-02, Pit N 2003-05, Oak A 2006
Pesky, Johnny★ Pit N 1965-67, Bos A 1975-84
Peterson, Rick● Pit N 1984-85, Chi A 1994-95, Oak A 1998-2003, NY N 2004-06
Pettini, Joe★ StL N 2002-06
Pettis, Gary★ Chi A 2001-02, NY N 2003-04
Pevey, Marty★ Tor A 1999, 2005-06
Pfister, George★ Bro N 1952
Phillips, Lefty▲ LA N 1965-68
Phillips, Dick★ SD N 1980
Picciolo, Rob★ SD N 1990-2005
Piche, Ron☆ Mon N 1976
Picinich, Val★ Cin N 1934
Piersall, Jimmy★ Tex A 1975
Pignatano, Joe★ Was A 1965-67, NY N 1968-81, Atl N 1982-84

THE COACH REGISTER

Piniella, Lou★ NY A 1984-85
Pinson, Vada★ Sea A 1977-80, Chi A 1981, Sea A 1982-83, Det A 1985-91, Fla N 1993-94
Pitler, Jake★ Bro N 1947-57
Pitts, Gaylen★ StL N 1991-95
Plaza, Ron● Sea A 1969, Cin N 1978-83, Oak A 1986
Plummer, Bill★ Sea A 1982-83, 1988-91, Col N 1993
Podres, Johnny☆ SD N 1973, Bos A 1980, Min A 1981-85, Phi N 1991-96
Poldberg, Brian● KC A 2002, 2004-06
Pole, Dick☆ Chi N 1988-91, SF N 1993-97, Bos A 1998, Ana A 1999, Cle A 2000-01, Mon N 2002, Chi N 2003-06
Pollet, Howie☆ StL N 1959-64, Hou N 1965
Popowski, Eddie▲ Bos A 1967-76
Poquette, Tom★ KC A 1997-98
Posedel, Bill☆ Pit N 1949-53, StL N 1954-57, Phi N 1958, SF N 1959-60, Oak A 1968-72, SD N 1974
Presley, Jim★ Ari N 1998-2000, Fla N 2006
Price, Bryan● Sea A 2000-05, Ari N 2006
Pujols, Luis★ Mon N 1993-2000, Det A 2002, SF N 2003-06
Quade, Mike● Oak A 2000-02, Chi N 2006
Queen, Mel☆ Cle A 1982, Tor A 1996-99
Quilici, Frank★ Min A 1971-72
Quirk, Jamie★ StL N 1984, KC A 1994-2001, Tex A 2002, Col N 2003-06
Rader, Doug★ SD N 1978-79, Chi A 1986-87, Oak A 1992, Fla N 1993-94, Chi A 1997
Radison, Dan● SD N 1993-94, Chi N 1995-99
Ragan, Pat☆ Phi N 1924
Raines, Tim★ Mon N 2003, Chi A 2005-06
Ramos, Bobby★ Ana A 2000-02, TB A 2006
Randall, Bobby★ Min A 1980
Randolph, Willie★ NY A 1994-2004
Rapp, Vern▲ Mon N 1979-83
Reberger, Frank☆ Cal A 1991, Fla N 1993-94
Redys, Ed● StL A 1950-51
Reese, Pee Wee★ LA N 1959
Reese, Jimmie★ Cal A 1973-94
Regan, Phil☆ Sea A 1984-86, Cle A 1994, Chi N 1997-98, Cle A 1999
Reiser, Pete★ LA N 1960-64, Chi N 1966-69, Cal A 1970-71, Chi N 1972-74
Renick, Rick★ KC A 1981, Mon N 1985-86, Min A 1987-90, Pit N 1997-2000, Mon N 2001, Fla N 2002
Resinger, Grover● Atl N 1966, Chi A 1967-68, Det A 1969-70, Cal A 1975-76
Rettenmund, Merv★ Cal A 1980-82, Tex A 1983-85, Oak A 1989-90, SD N 1991-99, Atl N 2000-01, Det A 2002, SD N 2006
Reyes, Cananea● Sea A 1981
Reynolds, Tommie★ Oak A 1989-95, StL N 1996
Rice, Del★ StL N 1959, LA A 1962-64, Cal A 1965-66, Cle A 1967
Rice, Jim★ Bos A 1994-2000
Ricketts, Dave★ Pit N 1971-73, StL N 1974-75, 1978-91
Riddle, Johnny★ Pit N 1948-50, StL N 1952-55, Mil N 1956-57, Cin N 1958, Phi N 1959
Riddoch, Greg▲ SD N 1987-90, TB A 1998-99
Riggins, Mark● StL N 1995
Riggleman, Jim▲ StL N 1989-90, Cle A 2000, LA N 2001-04
Righetti, Dave☆ SF N 2000-06
Rigney, Bill★ SD N 1975
Rigoli, Joe● Phi N 1996-97
Ripken, Cal▲ Bal A 1976-86, 1989-92
Rippelmeyer, Ray☆ Phi N 1970-78
Rivera, Luis☆ Cle A 2006
Roarke, Mike★ Det A 1965-66, Cal A 1967-69, Det A 1970, Chi N 1978-80, StL N 1984-90, SD N 1991-93, Bos A 1994
Roberts, Dave☆ Cle A 1987
Roberts, Leon★ TB A 1999-2000
Roberts, Mel● Phi N 1992-95
Robertson, Sherry★ Min A 1970
Robinson, Brooks★ Bal A 1977
Robinson, Dewey☆ Chi A 1993-94
Robinson, Frank★ Cal A 1977, Bal A 1978-80, 1985-87
Robinson, Sheriff● NY N 1964, 1965-67, 1972
Robinson, Wilbert★ NY N 1911-13
Robinson, Eddie★ Bal A 1957-59
Robinson, Bill★ NY N 1984-89, Fla N 2002-05
Robson, Tom★ Tex A 1986-92, NY N 1997-99, 2000, 2002, Cin N 2003
Rodgers, Bob★ Min A 1970-74, SF N 1976, Mil A 1978-80
Rodriguez, Eddie● Cal A 1996, Tor A 1998, Ari N 2001-03, Mon N 2004, Was N 2005-06
Roenicke, Ron★ Ana A 2000-04, LA A 2005-06
Roessler, Pat● Mon N 2000-01
Rojas, Euclides● Bos A 2003-04
Rojas, Cookie★ Chi N 1978-81, Fla N 1993-96, NY N 1997-2000, Tor A 2001-02
Rolfe, Red★ NY A 1946
Rommel, Eddie☆ Phi A 1933-34
Roof, Gene★ Det A 1992-95
Roof, Phil★ SD N 1978, Sea A 1983-88, Chi N 1990-91
Root, Charlie☆ Chi N 1951-53, Mil N 1956-57, Chi N 1960
Roseboro, John★ Was A 1970-71, Cal A 1972-74
Rosenbaum, Glen● Chi A 1973-75, 1986-88
Rosenthal, Wayne☆ Fla N 2003-04
Roth, Frank★ Pit N 1917, NY A 1921-22, Cle A 1923-25, Chi A 1927
Rothschild, Larry☆ Cin N 1990-93, Fla N 1995-97, Chi N 2002-06
Roush, Edd★ Cin N 1938
Rowe, Don☆ Chi A 1988, Mil A 1992-97, Mil N 1998
Rowe, Ken☆ Bal A 1985-86
Rowe, Schoolboy☆ Det A 1954-55
Rowe, Ralph● Min A 1972-75, Bal A 1981-84
Royster, Jerry★ Col N 1993, Mil N 2000-02
Ruberto, Sonny★ StL N 1977-78
Rudi, Joe★ Oak A 1986-87
Rudolph, Dick☆ Bos N 1921-27
Ruel, Muddy★ Chi A 1935-45, Cle A 1948-50
Ruffing, Red☆ NY N 1962
Ruhle, Vern☆ Hou N 1997-2000, Phi N 2001-02, NY N 2003, Cin N 2004
Runnells, Tom★ Mon N 1990-91
Runnels, Pete★ Bos A 1965-66
Russell, John★ Pit N 2003-05
Russell, Bill★ LA N 1987-91, 1994-96, TB A 2000
Ruth, Babe★ Bro N 1938
Ryan, Connie★ Mil N 1957, Atl N 1971, 1973-75, Tex A 1977-79
Ryan, Jack★ Was A 1912-13, Bos A 1923-27
Ryan, Mike★ Phi N 1980-95
Ryba, Mike☆ StL N 1951-54
Sain, Johnny☆ KC A 1959, NY A 1961-63, Min A 1965-66, Det A 1967-69, Chi A 1971-75, Atl N 1977, 1985-86
St.Claire, Randy☆ Mon N 2003-04, Was N 2005-06
Salazar, Luis★ Mil N 2001
Samuel, Juan★ Det A 1999-2005
Sandt, Tommy★ Pit N 1987-96, Fla N 1997-98, Col N 1999, Pit N 2000-02
Sanford, Jack☆ Cle A 1968-69
Santana, Rafael★ Chi A 2003-04
Sarni, Bill★ NY N 1957
Sauer, Hank★ SF N 1959
Saul, Jim● Chi N 1975-76, Oak A 1979
Scarborough, Ray☆ Bal A 1968
Schacht, Al☆ Was A 1925-34, Bos A 1935-36
Schaefer, Bob▲ KC A 1988-91, 2002-05
Schaefer, Germany★ NY A 1916
Schaffer, Jim★ Tex A 1978, KC A 1980-88
Schalk, Ray★ Chi N 1930-31
Schang, Wally★ Cle A 1936-38
Scheffing, Bob★ StL A 1952-53, Chi N 1954-55, Mil N 1960
Scherger, George● Cin N 1970-78, 1982-86
Schoendienst, Red★ StL N 1961-64, Oak A 1977-78, StL N 1979-89
Schreiber, Paul☆ NY A 1942, Bos A 1947-58
Schu, Rick★ Ari N 2004
Schueler, Ron☆ Chi A 1979-82, Oak A 1983-84, Pit N 1986
Schulte, Johnny★ Chi N 1933, NY A 1934-48, Bos A 1949-50
Schultz, Barney☆ StL N 1971-75, Chi N 1977
Schultz, Joe★ StL A 1949, StL N 1963-68, KC A 1970, Det A 1971-76
Scioscia, Mike★ LA N 1997-98
Scott, Tony★ Phi N 2001-03
Seminick, Andy★ Phi N 1957-58, 1967-69
Sewell, Luke★ Cle A 1939-41, Cin N 1949
Sewell, Joe★ NY A 1934-35
Sewell, Rip☆ Pit N 1948
Shanks, Howie★ Cle A 1928-32
Shaughnessy, Shag★ Det A 1928
Shaw, Bob☆ Mil A 1973
Shawkey, Bob☆ NY A 1929
Shea, Merv★ Det A 1939-42, Phi N 1944-45, Chi N 1948-49
Sheehan, Tom☆ Cin N 1935-37, Bro N 1938, Bos N 1944
Shelby, John★ LA N 1998-2005, Pit N 2006
Shellenback, Frank☆ StL A 1939, Bos A 1940-44, Det A 1946-47, NY N 1949-55
Shellenback, Jim☆ Min A 1983
Shelton, Derek● Cle A 2005-06
Shepard, Bert☆ Was A 1946
Shepard, Larry▲ Phi N 1967, Cin N 1970-78, SF N 1979
Sherlock, Glenn● Ari N 1998-2006
Sherry, Larry☆ Pit N 1977-78, Cal A 1979-80
Sherry, Norm★ Cal A 1970-71, 1976, Mon N 1978-81, SD N 1982-84, SF N 1986-91
Shore, Ray☆ Cin N 1963-67
Shotton, Burt★ StL N 1923-25, Cin N 1934, Cle A 1942-45
Showalter, Buck▲ NY A 1990-91
Siebert, Sonny☆ SD N 1994-95
Sievers, Roy★ Cin N 1966
Silvera, Charlie★ Min A 1969, Det A 1971-73, Tex A 1973-75
Silverio, Luis★ KC A 2003-06
Silvestri, Ken★ Phi N 1959-60, Mil N 1963-65, Atl N 1966-75, Chi A 1976, 1982
Simmons, Al★ Phi A 1940-42, 1944-49, Cle A 1950-51
Sinatro, Matt★ Sea A 1995-2002, TB A 2003-05
Sisler, George★ Bos N 1930
Sisler, Dick★ Cin N 1961-64, StL N 1966-70, SD N 1975-76, NY N 1979-80
Sisti, Sibby★ Mil N 1954, Sea A 1969
Skaff, Frank★ Bal A 1954, Det A 1965-66, 1971
Skinner, Joel★ Cle A 2001-02, 2003-06
Skinner, Bob★ SD N 1970-73, Pit N 1974-76, SD N 1977, Cal A 1978, Pit N 1979-85, Atl N 1986-88
Slaton, Jim☆ Sea A 2005-06
Slattery, Jack★ Bos N 1918-19
Slaught, Don★ Det A 2006
Slider, Rac● Bos A 1987-90
Smith, Al☆ NY N 1933
Smith, Billy● Tor A 1984-88
Smith, Reggie★ LA N 1994-98
Smith, Dave☆ SD N 1999-2001
Smith, Hal★ StL N 1962, Pit N 1965-67, Cin N 1968-69, Mil A 1976-77
Smith, Red★ Chi N 1945-48
Smith, Steve● Sea A 1996-99, Tex A 2002-06
Snider, Duke★ Mon N 1974-75
Snitker, Brian● Atl N 1985, 1988-90
Snyder, Frank★ NY N 1933-41
Snyder, Jim★ Chi N 1987, Sea A 1988, SD N 1991-92
Sojo, Luis★ NY A 2004-05
Sommers, Denny● NY N 1977-78, Cle A 1980-85, SD N 1988-90
Sothoron, Allen☆ StL N 1927-28, StL A 1932-33
Southworth, Billy★ NY N 1933
Spahn, Warren☆ NY N 1965, Cle A 1972-73
Spalding, Dick★ Phi N 1934-36, Chi N 1941-43
Spangler, Al★ Chi N 1970-71, 1974
Sparks, Joe● Chi A 1979, Cin N 1984, Mon N 1989, NY A 1990
Speier, Chris★ Mil N 2000, Ari N 2001, Oak A 2004, Chi N 2005-06
Spencer, Tom★ Cle A 1988-89, NY N 1991, Hou N 1992-93

Spilman, Harry★ Hou N 1999, 2000-04
Squires, Mike★ Tor A 1989-91, Chi A 1992
Staller, George★ Bal A 1962, 1968-75
Stanage, Oscar★ Pit N 1927-31
Stange, Lee☆ Bos A 1969, 1972-74, Min A 1975, Oak A 1977-79, Bos A 1981-84
Stanky, Eddie★ Cle A 1957-58
Stanley, Fred★ Mil A 1991
Stanley, Mike★ Bos A 2002
Stargell, Willie★ Pit N 1985, Atl N 1986-88
Starrette, Herm☆ Atl N 1974-76, SF N 1977-78, Phi N 1979-81, SF N 1983-84, Mil A 1985-86, Chi N 1987, Bal A 1988, Bos A 1995, 1996-97
Staub, Rusty★ NY N 1982
Stearns, John★ NY A 1989, Bal A 1996-97, NY N 2000-01
Stelmaszek, Rick★ Min A 1981-2006
Stengel, Casey★ Bro N 1932-33
Stevens, Ed★ SD N 1981
Stewart, Dave☆ SD N 1998, Tor A 2000, Mil N 2002
Stock, Milt★ Chi N 1944-48, Bro N 1949-50, Pit N 1951-52
Stock, Wes☆ KC A 1967, Mil A 1970-72, Oak A 1972-76, Sea A 1977-81, Oak A 1984-86
Stottlemyre, Mel☆ NY N 1984-93, Hou N 1994-95, NY A 1996-2000, 2001-05
Stratton, Monty☆ Chi A 1939-41
Street, Gabby★ StL N 1929, StL A 1937
Strickland, George★ Min A 1962, Cle A 1963-69, KC A 1970-72
Strom, Brent☆ Hou N 1996, KC A 2000-01
Stubing, Moose★ Cal A 1985-88, 1989-90
Such, Dick☆ Tex A 1983-85, Min A 1985-2001
Sugden, Joe★ StL N 1921-25, Phi N 1926-27
Sukeforth, Clyde★ Bro N 1943-51, Pit N 1952-57
Sullivan, John★ KC A 1979, Atl N 1980-81, Tor A 1982-93
Summers, Champ★ NY A 1989-90
Susce, George★ Cle A 1941-47, 1948-49, Bos A 1950-54, KC A 1955-56, Mil N 1958-59, Was A 1961-67, 1969-71, Tex A 1972
Sveum, Dale★ Bos A 2004-05, Mil N 2006
Sweeney, Bill★ Det A 1947-48
Sweet, Rick★ Sea A 1984, Hou N 1996
Swift, Bob★ Det A 1953-54, KC A 1957-59, Was A 1960, Det A 1963-66
Swisher, Steve★ NY N 1993-96
Tamargo, John★ Hou N 1999-2004
Tannehill, Jesse☆ Phi N 1920
Tanner, Bruce☆ Pit N 2001-05
Tappe, El★ Chi N 1958-65
Taylor, Tony★ Phi N 1977-79, 1988-89, Fla N 1999-2001, 2004
Taylor, Zack★ Bro N 1936, StL A 1941-46, Pit N 1947
Temple, Johnny★ Cin N 1964
Tenace, Gene★ Hou N 1986-87, Tor A 1990-97
Terwilliger, Wayne★ Was A 1969-71, Tex A 1972, 1981-85, Min A 1986-94
Tesreau, Jeff☆ Chi A 1928
Testa, Nick★ SF N 1958
Thomas, George★ Bos A 1970
Thomas, Ira★ Phi A 1914-17, 1925-26
Thomas, Lee★ StL N 1972, 1983
Thomas, Roy★ StL N 1922
Thompson, Tim★ StL N 1981
Thompson, Milt★ Phi N 2004-06
Thompson, Robby★ SF N 2000-01, Cle A 2002, 2005
Tiefenauer, Bobby☆ Phi N 1979
Tighe, Jack▲ Det A 1942, 1955-56
Tincup, Ben☆ Bro N 1940
Tinsley, Lee★ Ari N 2006
Tobin, Jack★ StL A 1949-51
Tolan, Bobby★ SD N 1980-83, Sea A 1987
Torborg, Jeff★ Cle A 1975-77, NY A 1979-88
Torchia, Tony● Bos A 1985
Torgeson, Earl★ NY A 1961
Torres, Hector★ Tor A 1990-91
Tosca, Carlos▲ Ari N 1998-2000, Tor A 2002, Ari N 2005-06
Tracewski, Dick★ Det A 1972-95
Tracy, Jim★ Mon N 1995-98, LA N 1999-2000
Trammell, Alan★ Det A 1999, SD N 2000-02
Trebelhorn, Tom▲ Mil A 1984, 1986, Chi N 1992-93, Bal A 2001-06
Treuel, Ralph● Det A 1995, Bos A 2001
Trucks, Virgil☆ Pit N 1963
Tuck, Gary● Fla N 2006
Tunnell, Lee☆ Cin N 2006
Turley, Bob☆ Bos A 1964
Turner, Jim☆ NY A 1949-59, Cin N 1961-65, NY A 1966-73
Turner, Terry★ StL N 1924
Uhlaender, Ted★ Cle A 2000-01
Uhle, George☆ Cle A 1936-37, Chi N 1940, Was A 1944
Ullger, Scott★ Min A 1995-2006
Unser, Del★ Phi N 1985-88
Upshaw, Willie★ Tex A 1993-94, Tor A 1996-97
Valentine, Bobby★ NY N 1983-85, Cin N 1993
Valo, Elmer★ Cle A 1963-64
Van Ornum, John● SF N 1980-84
Van Slyke, Andy★ Det A 2006
Varsho, Gary★ Phi N 2002-06
Vavra, Joe● Min A 2006
Vernon, Mickey★ Pit N 1960, 1964, StL N 1965, Mon N 1977-78, NY A 1982
Vincent, Al● Det A 1943-44, Bal A 1955-59, Phi N 1961-63, KC A 1966-67
Virdon, Bill★ Pit N 1968-71, 1986, Hou N 1997, Pit N 2001-02
Virgil, Ozzie★ SF N 1969-72, 1974-75, Mon N 1976-81, SD N 1982-85, Sea A 1986-88
Vuckovich, Pete☆ Pit N 1997-2000
Vukovich, John★ Chi N 1982-87, Phi N 1988, 1989-2004
Wagner, Heinie★ Bos A 1916-19, 1927-29
Wagner, Charley☆ Bos A 1970
Wagner, Honus★ Pit N 1933-51
Waits, Rick☆ NY N 2003, 2004
Wakamatsu, Don★ Tex A 2003-06
Walker, Rube★ LA N 1958, Was A 1965-67, NY N 1968-81, Atl N 1982-84
Walker, Dixie★ StL N 1953, 1955, Mil N 1963-65
Walker, Gee★ Cin N 1946
Walker, Greg★ Chi A 2003-06
Walker, Harry★ StL N 1959-62
Walker, Jerry☆ NY A 1981-82, Hou N 1983-85
Walker, Verlon● Chi N 1961-70
Wallace, Dave☆ LA N 1995-97, NY N 1999-2000, Bos A 2003-06
Wallace, Bobby★ Cin N 1926
Wallach, Tim★ LA N 2004-05
Waller, Ty★ SD N 1995, 2006
Walling, Denny★ Oak A 1996-98, NY N 2003-04
Walls, Lee★ Oak A 1979-82, NY A 1983
Walsh, Ed☆ Chi A 1923-25, 1928-30
Walters, Bucky☆ Bos N 1950-52, Mil N 1953-55, NY N 1956-57
Walton, Jim● Mil A 1973-75
Walton, Bruce☆ Tor A 2002-06
Waner, Paul★ Phi N 1965
Ward, Gary★ Chi A 2001-03
Ward, Jay★ NY A 1987, Mon N 1991-92
Ward, Pete★ Atl N 1978
Wares, Buzzy★ StL N 1930-35, 1937-52
Warner, Harry● Tor A 1977-79, 1980, Mil A 1981-82
Warthen, Dan☆ Sea A 1991-92, SD N 1996-97, Det A 1999-2002
Washington, Ron★ Oak A 1996-2006
Wathan, John★ KC A 1986, Cal A 1992-93, Bos A 1994
Watson, Bob★ Oak A 1986-88
Weaver, Earl▲ Bal A 1968
Webb, Billy★ Chi A 1935-39
Welch, Bob☆ Ari N 2001
Werle, Bill☆ SF N 1966
West, Sam★ Was A 1947-49
Westrum, Wes★ SF N 1958-63, NY N 1964-65, SF N 1968-71
Wetteland, John☆ Was N 2006
Whisenant, Pete★ Cin N 1961-62
Whisler, Randy● Cin N 2004-05
White, Ernie☆ Bos N 1947-48, NY N 1963
White, Frank★ Bos A 1994-96, KC A 1997-2001
White, Jerry★ Min A 1995, Det A 1997-98, Min A 1999-2006
White, Jo-Jo★ Cle A 1958-60, Det A 1960, KC A 1961-62, Mil N 1963-65, Atl N 1966, KC A 1969
White, Roy★ NY A 1983-84, 1986, 2004-05
Whitehill, Earl☆ Cle A 1941, Phi N 1943
Whitmer, Dan★ Det A 1992-94
Whitt, Ernie★ Tor A 2005-06
Widmar, Al☆ Phi N 1962-64, 1968-69, Mil A 1973-74, Tor A 1980-88, 1989
Wietelmann, Whitey★ Cin N 1966-67, SD N 1969-79
Wilber, Del★ Chi A 1955-56, Was A 1970, Tex A 1973
Wiley, Mark☆ Bal A 1987, Cle A 1988-91, 1995-98, KC A 1999, Bal A 2001-04, Fla N 2005
Wilhelm, Kaiser☆ Phi N 1921
Wilks, Ted☆ Cle A 1960, KC A 1961
Williams, Billy★ Chi N 1980-82, Oak A 1983-85, Chi N 1986-87, 1992-2001
Williams, Dallas★ Col N 2000-02, Bos A 2003
Williams, Dan● Cle A 1993, 1995-2002
Williams, Davey★ NY N 1956-57
Williams, Don● SD N 1977-80
Williams, Spin● Pit N 1994-2005
Williams, Jimmy● Hou N 1975, Bal A 1981-87
Williams, Jimy★ Tor A 1980-85, Atl N 1990-96
Williams, Otto★ Det A 1925, StL N 1926, StL A 1927, Cin N 1930
Williams, Rick● Fla N 1995-96, TB A 1998-2000
Williams, Dick★ Mon N 1970
Williams, Stan☆ Bos A 1975-76, Chi A 1977-78, NY A 1980-81, 1982, Cin N 1984, NY A 1987, 1988, Cin N 1990-91, Sea A 1998-99
Williams, Walt★ Chi A 1988
Willis, Carl☆ Cle A 2003-06
Wilson, Jimmy★ Cin N 1939-40, 1944-46
Wilson, Mookie★ NY N 1997-2002
Wiltse, Hooks☆ NY A 1925
Wine, Bobby★ Phi N 1972-83, Atl N 1985, 1988-90, NY N 1993-96
Winegarner, Ralph☆ StL A 1948-51
Wingo, Ivey★ Cin N 1928-29, 1936
Winkles, Bobby▲ Cal A 1972, Oak A 1974-75, SF N 1976-77, Chi A 1979-81, Mon N 1986-88
Wolgamot, Earl● Cle A 1931-33
Woodall, Larry★ Bos A 1942-48
Woodling, Gene★ Bal A 1964-67
Worthington, Al☆ Min A 1972-73
Wotus, Ron★ SF N 1998-2006
Wright, Jim☆ Phi N 1996, Col N 2002
Wright, Mel☆ Chi N 1963-64, 1971, Pit N 1973, NY A 1974-75, Hou N 1976-82, Mon N 1983
Wyatt, Whit☆ Phi N 1955-57, Mil N 1958-65, Atl N 1966-67
Wynegar, Butch★ Mil N 2003-06
Wynn, Early☆ Cle A 1964-66, Min A 1967-69
York, Rudy★ Bos A 1959-62
Yost, Ned★ Atl N 1991-2002
Yost, Eddie★ LA A 1962, Was A 1963-67, NY N 1968-76, Bos A 1977-84
Young, Curt☆ Oak A 2004-06
Youngblood, Joel★ Cin N 1994-97, Mil N 1998
Yount, Robin★ Ari N 2002-04, Mil N 2006
Zarilla, Al★ Was A 1971
Zeller, Bart★ StL N 1970
Zimmer, Don★ Mon N 1971, SD N 1972, Bos A 1974-76, NY A 1983, Chi N 1984-86, NY A 1986, SF N 1987, Bos A 1992, Col N 1993-95, NY A 1996-2003
Zimmer, Tom● StL N 1976
Zimmerman, Gerry★ Min A 1967, Mon N 1969-75, Min A 1976-80
Zuvella, Paul★ Col N 1996
Zwilling, Dutch★ Cle A 1941

Biographical Information for Other Coaches *(i.e., those who do not appear in the batter, pitcher, or manager registers.)*

Abbott, Spencer; Spencer Arthur; B8.27.1877 Chicago IL; D12.18.1951 Washington DC; BL/TL/1B
Acosta, Oscar; Oscar Carlos; B3.21.1957 Portales NM; D4.19.2006 Santo Domingo, D.R.; BR/TR/6'1"/175; P
Acta, Manny; Manuel Elias (Pena); B1.11.1969 San Pedro de Macoris, D.R.; BR/TR/6'2"/205; 2B
Adair, Rick; Michael Richard; B1.19.1958 Spartanburg SC; BL/TL/6'0"/185; P
Alejo, Bob; Robert Kevin; B11.19.1957 Sacramento CA; BR/TR/5'10"/185; DNP
Alfonso, Carlos; Carlos; B12.18.1950 Havana, Cuba; BR/TR/6'2"/205; P
Arsenault, Pierre; Pierre Jean; B10.12.1963 Roberval QC, Can.; BR/TR/5'11"/180; C
Auferio, Tony; Anthony Patrick; B6.13.1947 Orange NJ; BR/TR/5'10"/185; 3B
Bailey, Buddy; Welby Sheldon; B3.28.1957 Norristown PA; BR/TR/6'0"/193; C
Balsley, Darren; Darren Wayne; B10.27.1964 Newport Beach CA; BR/TR/6'3"/205; P
Barnett, Mike; Michael Lee; B2.1.1959 Columbus OH; BR/TR/5'11"/175; DNP
Beasley, Tony; Anthony Wayne; B12.5.1966 Fredericksburg VA; BR/TR/5'8"/165; 2B
Berardino, Dick; Richard J.; B7.2.1937 Cambridge MA; BR/TR/6'1"/190; OF
Beringer, C. B.; Carroll James; B8.14.1928 Bellwood NE; BR/TR/6'0"/195; P
Bernhardt, Carlos; Carlos; B9.9.1950 San Pedro de Macoris, D.R.; BR/TR/5'11"/195; P
Berry, Mark; Mark William; B9.22.1962 Oxnard CA; BR/TR/6'0"/190; C
Biagini, Greg; Gregory Peter; B5.12.1952 Chicago IL; BB/TR/6'2"/205; 1B-OF
Bialas, Dave; David Bruce; B3.6.1954 Houston TX; BR/TR/6'1"/210; OF
Blackburn, Wayne; Wayne Clark; B7.10.1916 Mount Joy OH; D2.16.2000 Portsmouth OH; BL/TR/5'10"/165; OF-3B-2B
Bloomfield, Jack; Gordon Leigh; B8.7.1932 Monte Alto TX; BL/TR/6'2"/185; 2B
Bombard, Marc; Marc; B11.15.1949 Tampa FL; BR/TL/5'8"/180; P
Bragan, Jimmy; James Alton; B3.12.1929 Birmingham AL; D6.2.2001 Sterrett AL; BR/TR/6'0"/198; 2B; b-Bobby Bragan
Breeden, Scott; Harold Scott; B9.17.1937 Charlottesville VA; BR/TR/6'2"/210; P
Breeden, Joe; Joseph Thomas; B10.11.1956 Newport News VA; BR/TR/5'11"/195; C
Bundy, Lorenzo; Charles Lorenzo; B11.6.1959 Philadelphia PA; BL/TR/6'2"/205; 1B
Butterfield, Brian; Brian James; B3.9.1958 Bangor ME; BB/TR/6'0"/200; 2B
Camacho, Joe; Joseph Gomes; B5.29.1928 New Bedford MA; BR/TR/6'0"/185; SS-2B
Carey, P. J.; Paul Jerome; B11.4.1953 Scranton PA; BR/TR/6'1"/190; C
Carlucci, Dave; David Mario; B5.1.1963 Milford MA; BR/TR/6'1"/195; C
Carnevale, Danny; Daniel Joseph; B2.8.1918 Buffalo NY; D12.29.2005 Buffalo NY; BR/TR/6'0"/195; SS
Carter, Dick; Richard Joseph; B8.31.1916 Philadelphia PA; D9.11.1969 Philadelphia PA; BR/TR/5'10"/190; P-OF
Chaves, Rafael; Rafael; B11.1.1968 Isabela PR; BR/TR/6'0"/195; P
Chiti, Dom; Harry Dominic; B12.10.1958 Independence MO; BL/TL/6'2"/200; P
Clear, Bob; Elwood Robert; B12.14.1927 Denver CO; BR/TR/5'10"/170; P
Cluck, Bob; Robert Alton; B1.10.1946 San Diego CA; BL/TL/6'2"/195; P
Connor, Mark; Mark Peter; B5.27.1949 Brooklyn NY; BR/TR/6'3"/195; P
Conti, Guy; Guy Clyle; B3.9.1942 Vero Beach FL; BR/TR/5'11"/195; C
Crandall, Jimmie; James Mark; B12.7.1912 Wadena IN; D2.1.1983 Bullhead City AZ; BB/TR/5'11"/190; P-C; f-Doc Crandall
Cresse, Mark; Mark Emery; B9.21.1951 St.Albans NY; BR/TR/6'3"/220; C
Dancy, Bill; William Woodruff; B11.10.1951 St.Augustine FL; BB/TR/6'0"/215; SS
DeArmas, Roly; Rolando Jesus; B12.29.1951 New York NY; BR/TR/6'1"/190; C
Debus, Jon; Jon Eric; B8.31.1958 Chicago Heights IL; BR/TR/6'3"/215; C
DeMerritt, Marty; Martin Gordon; B3.4.1953 San Francisco CA; BR/TR/6'2.5"/205; P
Denbo, Gary; Gary Brian; B12.9.1960 Princeton IN; BR/TR; 2B
Dews, Bobby; Robert Walter; B3.23.1938 Clinton IA; BR/TR/6'1"/175; SS
Dixon, Walt; Walter Edward; B11.25.1920 Mount Vernon Springs NC; D9.25.2003 Florence SC; BR/TR/6'2"/220; P
Donnelly, Rich; Richard Francis; B8.3.1946 Steubenville OH; BL/TR/6'0"/185; C
Dorante, Luis; Luis Alberto; B10.25.1968 Estado Falcon, Venez.; BR/TR/6'0"/180; C
Douglas, Otis; Otis Whitfield; B7.25.1911 Reedville VA; D3.21.1989 Kilmarnock VA; BR/TR/6'1"/230; DNP
Down, Rick; Richard John; B12.14.1950 Wyandotte MI; BR/TR/5'11"/220; OF
Dubee, Rich; Richard Peter; B10.19.1957 Brockton MA; BB/TR/6'2"/200; P
Dunlop, Harry; Harry Alexander; B9.6.1933 Sacramento CA; BL/TR/6'3"/200; C
Dusan, Gene; Eugene Paul; B11.9.1949 Los Angeles CA; BB/TR/6'0"/200; C
Ebel, Dino; Dino Alex; B3.20.1966 Barstow CA; BR/TR/5'9"/170; SS
Espy, Duane; Duane; B6.23.1952 Aberdeen WA; BR/TR/6'0"/210; 2B
Evers, Bill; William; B1.29.1954 New York NY; BR/TR/5'10"/210; C
Ezell, Glenn; Glenn Wayne; B10.29.1944 Kentwood LA; BR/TR/6'0"/190; C
Fischer, Brad; Bradley James; B6.28.1956 Toledo OH; BR/TR/6'3"/198; C
Fitzgerald, Joe; Joseph Patrick; B3.17.1897 Washington DC; D8.29.1967 Orlando FL; BR/TR/5'11"/200; C
Fitzpatrick, John; John Arthur; B3.19.1904 LaSalle IL; D11.19.1990 San Diego CA; BR/TR/6'1.5"/185; C
Gamboa, Tom; Thomas Harold; B2.28.1948 Los Angeles CA; BL/TL/5'10"/175; OF
Glynn, Gene; Eugene Patrick; B9.22.1956 Waseca MN; BR/TR/5'9"/165; SS
Goff, Mike; Michael Roger; B9.30.1962 Mobile AL; BR/TR/6'0"/175; 2B
Gomez, Orlando; Juan Alejandro; B6.24.1946 Juana Diaz PR; BR/TR/6'0"/190; C
Gonzalez, Fredi; Fredi Jesus; B1.28.1964 Havana, Cuba; BR/TR/5'11"/200; C
Graham, Brian; John Brian; B4.9.1960 San Diego CA; BR/TR/6'1"/195; 2B
Gregson, Glenn; Glenn; B2.10.1950 Hamlet NC; BB/TR/6'3"/185; P
Guerrero, Epy; Epifanio Obdulio (Abud); B1.3.1942 Santo Domingo, D.R.; BR/TR/5'11"/168; OF; b-Mario Guerrero
Hale, De; De Marlo; B7.16.1961 Chicago IL; BR/TR/6'2"/185; 1B
Hansen, Guy; Guy Christopher; B11.12.1947 Los Angeles CA; BR/TR/6'0"/170; P
Hansen, Roger; Roger Christian; B8.28.1961 Johnstown PA; BR/TR/6'0"/200; C
Harmon, Tom; Thomas Harold; B12.16.1948 Lubbock TX; BL/TR/5'11"/185; C
Henderson, Ramon; Ramon Gaspar; B8.18.1963 Moncion, D.R.; BR/TR/5'11"/175; 3B
Hernandez, Chuck; Carlo Amado; B11.11.1960 Tampa FL; BL/TL/6'3"/200; P
Hickey, Jim; James Joseph; B10.12.1961 Chicago IL; BR/TR/6'2"/215; P
Hill, Perry; Perry Wendell; B3.19.1952 Salina KS; BR/TR/5'10"/170; 2B
Hines, Ben; Benjamin Thortan; B11.7.1935 Yeager OK; BR/TR/5'11"/205; 3B-C; s-Bruce Hines
Hines, Bruce; Bruce Edwin; B11.7.1957 Pomona CA; BB/TR/5'10"/180; 2B; f-Ben Hines
Holmberg, Dennis; Dennis Nels; B8.2.1951 Fremont NE; BL/TR/6'0"/190; 3B
Holmquist, Doug; Douglas Leonard; B10.4.1941 Bridgeport CT; D2.27.1988 Altamonte Springs FL; BR/TR/6'2"/195; C
Holt, Goldie; Golden Desmond; B3.22.1902 Enloe TX; D6.11.1991 Sherman Oaks CA; BR/TR/5'7.5"/165; 3B-OF-2B
Hoscheit, Vern; Vernard Arthur; B4.1.1922 Brunswick NE; BR/TR/5'9"/185; C
Hubbard, Jack; John H.; B10.4.1950 Rock Hall MD; BR/TR/5'11"/175; DNP
Isaac, Luis; Luis (Aponte); B6.19.1946 Rio Piedras PR; BR/TR/5'11.5"/195; C
Jaramillo, Rudy; Rudolph; B9.20.1950 Beeville TX; BL/TR/5'11"/180; OF
Jauss, Dave; David Patrick; B1.16.1957 Chicago IL; BR/TR/5'11"/170; DNP
Jewett, Trent; Philip Trent; B3.3.1964 Dallas TX; BR/TR/6'0"/240; C
Jones, Gary; Gary Wayne; B11.11.1960 Henderson TX; BL/TR/5'9"/163; 2B
Jones, Joe; Joseph Carmack; B12.13.1941 Lebanon TN; BR/TR/5'9"/155; 2B
Jones, Tommy; Thomas M.; B10.13.1964 Stockton CA; BR/TR/6'1"/180; OF
Kahn, Lou; Louis; B12.4.1916 St.Louis MO; D3.13.2002 Albany GA; BR/TR/5'11"/195; C
Kelly, Mike; Bernard Francis; B5.1.1896 Indianapolis IN; D10.23.1968 Indianapolis IN; BR/TR/6'0"/198; 1B
Kim, Wendell; Wendell Kealohapauloe; B3.9.1951 Honolulu HI; BR/TR/5'5"/160; 2B
Kissell, George; George Marshall; B9.9.1921 Watertown NY; BR/TR/5'8"/175; 3B
Kittle, Hub; Hubert Milton; B2.19.1917 Los Angeles CA; D2.10.2004 Yakima WA; BR/TR/6'1"/195; P
Kniffin, Chuck; Charles; B10.28.1950 Rockville Centre NY; BR/TL/5'11"/200; P
Koenig, Fred; Fred Carl; B4.27.1931 St.Louis MO; D1.12.1993 Wagoner OK; BR/TR/6'3"/200; 1B-3B
Kranitz, Rick; Richard Alan; B9.15.1958 San Rafael CA; BR/TR/5'11"/170; P
Lachemann, Bill; William Charles; B4.5.1934 Los Angeles CA; BL/TR/5'9"/195; C
Lett, Jim; James Curtis; B1.3.1951 Charleston WV; BR/TR/6'2"/185; 3B
Levy, Lenny; Leonard Howard; B6.11.1913 Pittsburgh PA; D2.2.1993 Palm Desert CA; BR/TR/5'10.5"/190; C
Liddle, Steve; Steven Michael; B3.4.1959 Nashville TN; BR/TR/6'4"/220; C
Linares, Julio; Julio Mairenu (Rijo); B12.26.1940 San Pedro de Macoris, D.R.; BR/TR/5'9"/165; 3B
Lobe, Bill; William Charles; B3.24.1912 Cleveland OH; D1.7.1969 Cleveland OH; BR/TR/5'9.5"/178; C
Lopez, Juan; Juan Enrique; B5.16.1962 Bayamon PR; BR/TR/5'10"/187; C
Lowe, Q. V.; Q. V.; B1.15.1945 Red Level AL; BR/TR/6'1"/185; P
Macko, Joe; Joseph John; B2.19.1928 Port Clinton OH; BR/TR/6'2"/195; 1B; s-Steve Macko
Majtyka, Roy; Le Roy Walter; B6.1.1939 Buffalo NY; BR/TR/5'10"/170; 2B
Maloof, Jack; Jack Garth; B10.12.1949 Redlands CA; BL/TL/6'0"/175; 1B-OF
Mansolino, Doug; Douglas; B9.20.1956 Plainfield NJ; BR/TR/5'7"/155; IF
Mason, Marty; Martin Lee; B4.4.1958 Central City KY; BR/TR/6'1"/175; P
Mathews, Harry; Henry; B7.23.1876 Newport KY; BR/TR; C
Mathews, Rick; Rick Ray; B10.9.1947 Centerville IA; BR/TR/5'11"/180; P
Mazzone, Leo; Leo David; B10.16.1948 Keyser WV; BL/TL/5'10"/185; P
McDonnell, Maje; Robert A.; B7.20.1920 Philadelphia PA; BR/TR/5'6"/135; P
McKee, J. R.; John R.;
McLaren, John; John Lowell; B9.29.1951 Galveston TX; BR/TR/6'0"/200; C
Mozzali, Mo; Maurice Joseph; B12.12.1922 Louisville KY; D3.2.1987 Lakeland FL; BL/TL/5'10"/160; 1B
Mull, Jack; Jack Leroy; B9.29.1943 Chambersburg PA; BR/TR/5'10"/188; C
Myers, Dave; David; B8.8.1959 York PA; BR/TR/6'4"/190; 3B
Napoleon, Ed; Edward George; B9.17.1937 Baltimore MD; BR/TR/5'8"/165; OF-3B-1B
Nottle, Ed; Edward William; B10.22.1939 Philadelphia PA; BR/TR/5'10"/180; P
Oceak, Frank; Frank John "Fez"; B9.8.1912 Pocahontas VA; D3.19.1983 Johnstown PA; BR/TR/5'9"/172; 2B
Oliveras, Mako; Max; B9.10.1946 Santurce PR; BR/TR/6'0"/195; 2B
O'Neil, Buck; John Jordan; B11.13.1911 Carrabelle FL; D 10.06.2006 Kansas City MO; BR/TR/6'2"/190; 1B
Osborn, Don; Donald Edwin; B6.3.1908 Sandpoint ID; D3.23.1979 Torrance CA; BR/TR/6'0"/185; P
Pacheco, Tony; Antonio Aristides; B8.9.1927 Havana, Cuba; D3.23.1987 Miami Beach FL; BR/TR/6'0"/190; 2B
Paepke, Jack; Jack; B8.28.1922 Provo UT; BR/TR/6'2.5"/220; C-P; s-Dennis Paepke
Patkin, Max; Max O.; B1.10.1920 Philadelphia PA; D10.30.1999 Paoli PA; BR/TR/6'2"/170; P
Pavlick, Greg; Gregory Michael; B3.10.1950 Washington DC; BR/TR/6'3"/205; P
Pentland, Jeff; Jeffrey William; B9.18.1946 Hollywood CA; BL/TL/5'10"/185; 1B
Peterson, Rick; Eric Harding; B10.30.1954 New Brunswick NJ; BL/TL/6'0"/175; P; f-Harding Peterson
Plaza, Ron; Ronald Charles; B8.24.1934 Passaic NJ; BL/TR/6'0"/180; 3B
Poldberg, Brian; Brian John; B5.16.1957 Omaha NE; BR/TR/6'4 1"/90; C
Price, Bryan; Bryan Roberts; B6.22.1962 San Francisco CA; BL/TL/6'2"/200; P
Quade, Mike; Gregory Mike; B3.12.1957 Evanston IL; BR/TR/6'0"/182; OF
Radison, Dan; Daniel John; B8.24.1950 St.Louis MO; BR/TR/6'2"/190; C
Redys, Ed; Edward; B6.23.1921 Detroit MI; BR/TR/6'0"/185; P
Resinger, Grover; Grover S; B10.20.1915 St.Louis MO; D1.11.1986 St.Louis MO; BR/TR/5'9"/180; 3B
Reyes, Cananea; Benjamin (Chavez); B2.18.1937 Nacozari, Mex.; D11.11.1991 Hermosillo, Mex.; BR/TR/OF
Riggins, Mark; Mark Alan; B1.3.1957 Jasper IN; BR/TL/5'10"/180; P
Rigoli, Joe; Joseph M.; B12.14.1956 New York NY; BR/TR/6'2"/190; C
Roberts, Mel; Melvin Henry; B1.18.1943 Abington PA; BR/TR/6'0"/180; OF
Robinson, Sheriff; Warren Grant; B9.8.1921 Cambridge MD; D4.5.2002 Cambridge MD; BR/TR/6'1"/195; C
Rodriguez, Eddie; Eduardo; B3.11.1959 Havana, Cuba; BR/TR/5'8"/165; SS
Roessler, Pat; Patrick Alan; B12.27.1959 Phoenix AZ; BR/TR/6'0"/200; IF
Rojas, Euclides; Euclides; B8.25.1967 Havana, Cuba; BL/TR/6'0"/210; P
Rosenbaum, Glen; Glen Otis; B6.14.1936 Union Mills IN; BR/TR/5'11"/180; P
Rowe, Ralph; Ralph Emanuel; B7.14.1924 Newberry SC; D2.29.1996 Newberry SC; BL/TR/5'6"/160; OF
Saul, Jim; James Allen; B11.24.1939 Bristol VA; BL/TR/6'3"/210; C
Scherger, George; George Richard; B11.20.1920 Dickinson ND; BR/TR/5'8"/170; 2B
Shelton, Derek; Derek Lee; B7.30.1970 Carbondale IL; BR/TR/6'0"/190; C
Sherlock, Glenn; Glenn Patrick; B9.26.1960 Nahant MA; BL/TR/6'1"/200; C
Slider, Rac; Rachel W.; B12.23.1933 Simms TX; BL/TR/5'8"/160; SS
Smith, Billy; Billy Franklin; B1.14.1930 High Point NC; BL/TL/5'9"/160; 1B-OF
Smith, Steve; Steven J.; B7.21.1953 Canton OH; BR/TR/5'11"/180; 2B-SS
Snitker, Brian; Brian Gerald; B10.17.1955 Decatur IL; BR/TR/6'1"/192; C
Sommers, Denny; Dennis James; B7.12.1940 New London WI; BL/TR/6'2"/205; C
Sparks, Joe; Joseph Everett; B3.15.1938 McComas WV; BR/TR/6'0"/195; 3B-2B
Torchia, Tony; Anthony Lewis; B12.13.1943 Chicago IL; BR/TL/5'10"/180; 1B-OF
Treuel, Ralph; Ralph Martin; B6.7.1955 Elyria OH; BR/TR/6'4"/220; P
Tuck, Gary; Gary Robert; B9.6.1954 Amsterdam NY; BR/TR/6'1"/215; C
VanOrnum, John; John Clayton; B10.20.1939 Pasadena CA; BR/TR/5'11"/175; C
Vavra, Joe; Joseph Alan; B11.16.1959 Chippewa Falls WI; BL/TR/5'11"/190; 3B
Vincent, Al; Albert Linder; B12.23.1906 Birmingham AL; D12.14.2000 Beaumont TX; BR/TR/5'9.5"/170; 2B
Walker, Verlon; Verlon Lee "Rube"; B3.7.1929 Lenoir NC; D3.24.1971 Chicago IL; BL/TR/6'0"/210; C; b-Rube Walker
Walton, Jim; James Robert; B9.5.1935 Shattuck OK; BR/TR/6'2"/190; P
Warner, Harry; Harry Clinton; B12.11.1928 Reeders PA; BL/TR/6'2"/215; 1B
Whisler, Randy; Randy Keith; B6.16.1962 Harbor City CA; BB/TR/5'9"/185; 3B
Williams, Dan; Daniel Lawrence; B9.3.1966 San Gabriel CA; BR/TR/6'3"/245; C
Williams, Don; Donald Ellis; B12.24.1937 Paragould AR; BR/TR/5'10"/185; SS
Williams, Spin; Donald Ray; B1.5.1956 Davenport IA; BL/TL/6'3"/230; P
Williams, Jimmy; James Bernard; B5.15.1926 Toronto ON, Can.; BR/TR/5'10"/180; OF
Williams, Rick; Richard Anthony; B11.21.1956 Ft.Worth TX; BL/TL/6'1"/205; P; f-Dick Williams
Wolgamot, Earl; Clinton Earl; B12.21.1895 Fairbank IA; D4.25.1970 Independence IA; BR/TR/5'8"/155; C
Zimmer, Tom; Thomas Jeffrey; B6.30.1952 Mobile AL; BR/TR/5'8"/165; C; f-Don Zimmer

BLACK BASEBALL AND THE NEGRO LEAGUES

As it flowed from its origin, part of the river of baseball history diverged at one point and formed a separate branch that paralleled the main stream for a half-century. Finally the waters were rejoined, making the river whole again.

During this separation, baseball was not complete. The majority of Americans went with the flow of the main stream, following its course intently, with only an occasional excursion to see the parallel branch.

Thus for a half-century, white Americans sat watching Major League Baseball, only vaguely aware of the shadowy world of black baseball that existed beyond the scope of their vision. To most white baseball observers, black ballplayers were as unreal as the shadows on Plato's wall. In this world of reflected images, there existed exceptionally talented players whose ability was unsurpassed anywhere.

Best known among these great black ballplayers in today's baseball world are Hall of Famers Satchel Paige and Josh Gibson. But as Satchel himself said, "There were many Satchels, many Joshs." And indeed there were. There, in the shadows of black baseball, were players who were yesteryear's equivalent of Hank Aaron, Willie Mays, Barry Bonds, Lou Brock, Bob Gibson, Reggie Jackson, Lee Smith, David Justice, Gary Sheffield, Cecil Fielder, Tony Gwynn, Ken Griffey Jr., Frank Thomas, Barry Larkin, Fred McGriff, Albert Belle, Ricky Henderson, Mo Vaughn, Derek Jeter, Andruw Jones, C.C. Sabathia, and so many others. The list is almost endless.

Try to imagine post-World War II baseball without its black stars. Visualize baseball today without black stars complementing the white stars. Obviously, all great black ballplayers were not born after 1947 when Jackie Robinson re-integrated Major League Baseball. They were always there, required by custom and circumstance to play in their separate leagues.

This period of separation is remote from the memory of the majority of the current populace. Today's younger generation, as well as most of the older generation now, do not fully understand the sociological factors which prohibited black and white baseball players from engaging in competition together. Consequently, they know and understand even less about the men who were destined to demonstrate their abilities to a comparatively small segment of American society. Just who were these men who displayed their talent in virtual obscurity?

During the half-century of dual baseball development, more than 4,000 men plied their trade in the arenas of black baseball, many of whom were of major league caliber. Many of these possessed sufficient skills to have been first-line players in the major leagues, and the best of this group would have achieved stardom. Approximately two dozen of these stars shone with such magnificence as to have merited selection to the National Baseball Hall of Fame.

Extrapolating the past from the present, if the black leagues and the white leagues had been merged into a 30-team configuration, an average black team during this period of separation would have had 14 players on their roster who possessed major league talent. Seven of the first nine could have won starting positions in the major leagues, with the top three players being "stars." For any given year, two out of every three teams would have a player in their line-up with Hall of Fame qualifications. The better teams would have exceeded these parameters, while lesser teams would have failed to meet them.

Still, the greats, the near-greats, and the not-so-greats were there, unnoticed by the vast majority of America, until Jackie Robinson broke the color barrier in 1947 and finally opened the National Pastime to all men, regardless of the color of their skin.

What little exposure most white fans in larger cities got to the Negro Leagues came in the form of exhibition games against white major leaguers during barnstorming tours held during the off-season.

White major leaguers, looking to augment their baseball salaries, played exhibitions against black teams made up of the best Negro League players. That the black players not only held their own, but often beat the white teams, would hardly have been a surprise in a perfect world. Since that perfect world didn't exist, there was a lot on the line for the Negro Leaguers in those games. Buck O'Neil, black baseball's most famous spokesman, described the dynamics of these games in an interview with MLB.com:

"What a lot of people don't know is that we won a majority of those ballgames," O'Neil recalled. "Now that didn't mean we were better players than the Major Leaguers. We won the majority of the ballgames because the Major Leaguers were just making a payday. We wanted to prove to the world that they weren't superior because they were Major Leaguers and we weren't inferior because we played in the Negro Leagues. We stretched that single into a double, that double into a triple. We stole home. The Major Leaguers couldn't afford to twist an ankle or break a finger in an exhibition ballgame, but, honey, we went all out."

In smaller cities and towns, black teams would often play against factory-league teams or local semi-pro teams—many of which were good enough to be considered of minor league quality. These exhibitions would take place both during and after the regular season.

Baseball was originally a gentleman's game played by members of rival athletic clubs for recreation. In the aftermath of the Civil War, baseball enjoyed a great surge in interest, activity, and growth. Americans of all classes, creeds, and races joined in the game that quickly grew to become our National Pastime. Baseball was then an amateur sport: some black Americans played on all-black clubs, while others played on integrated teams.

However, black ballplayers were excluded from participation by the National Association of Base Ball Players on December 11, 1868 when the governing body voted unanimously to bar "any club which may be composed of one or more colored persons." This was the first appearance of an official color line in baseball.

When baseball openly admitted the professional status of top clubs in subsequent seasons, pro teams were not bound by the amateur association's ruling. Thus, during the nineteenth century, black ballplayers appeared on integrated teams and some black teams played in integrated leagues. Two brothers—Moses Fleetwood Walker and Welday Walker—even played in the major leagues in 1884 for Toledo of the American Association. Gradually, however, black players began to be excluded from the white leagues and, by the beginning of the new century, there were no black players in what was grandiloquently called Organized Baseball.

Nevertheless, black Americans continued to play baseball. By necessity they played on all-black teams and, eventually, formed all-black leagues. The first black professional team was the Cuban Giants in 1885, but black teams played as independent clubs until the first black league was organized in 1920. In the decade prior to the founding of the first black major league, many independent black clubs had developed impressive enough rosters to be considered of big-league quality. The critical change was the first great migration of African-Americans from the rural South to the industrial cities of the Northeast and Midwest during and after World War I. That massive social change ensured that there were large enough concentrations of black Americans to support organized leagues.

That year Rube Foster, considered the father of black baseball, founded the Negro National League. Three years later, in 1923, Ed Bolden formed the Eastern Colored League. These two leagues operated successfully for several years before they fell victim to financial difficulties. Three other black major leagues—the American Negro League (1929), the Negro Southern League (1932) and the East-West League (1932) operated for a single season but were not able to continue on a sound fiscal basis.

Many of the best players in the original Negro National League migrated to the Negro Southern League after the NNL's break-up; the NSL operated before and after 1932 as a minor league. And most of those players left the NSL after only one year to return to a newly reformed Negro National League, which began play in 1933. The Chicago American Giants played in both incarnations of the Negro National League, as well as the NSL in 1932. The Indianapolis ABCs also played in the first NNL and the NSL

The new NNL and the Negro American League (chartered in 1937) both thrived until the color line was broken. During their existence, the Negro Leagues played eleven World Series (1924–27 and 1942–48) and created their own All-Star Game in 1933. The East-West Game became the biggest black sports attraction in the country.

The most famous of the Negro League clubs were the Homestead Grays and the Kansas City Monarchs, the latter ironically owned by a white businessman. Homestead, which featured such great players as Josh Gibson, Buck Leonard and Cool Papa Bell, won three Negro League World Series (1943, 1944, and 1948), and nine straight NNL pennants from 1937–45. That unparalleled streak included five years in which the Grays won both halves of a split season schedule. In three other years (1939, 1940, and 1942), the NNL did not play a split season, leaving 1941 as the only year in which Homestead failed to dominate the entire season—and in that year the Grays easily bested the New York Cubans in four games in the league's Championship Series.

Kansas City won the first Negro League World Series in 1924 over the Hilldale Daisies, and had many star players in its history, including Buck O'Neil. O'Neil, who would later go on to become the first black coach in the big leagues, signed future Hall of Famers Lou Brock and Ernie Banks while working for the Cubs as a scout. The Monarchs sent a host of players on to the big leagues, including Banks, Satchel Paige, and Elston Howard, the first black to play for the legendary New York Yankees.

During most of the Negro Leagues existence, two leagues, one based in the east and one in the west, were dominant. The original Negro National League was comprised of teams from Pittsburgh west, while the Eastern Colored League, the NNL's main competition, featured teams based in eastern Pennsylvania, Baltimore, New York City, and New Jersey. From 1933 on, the new Negro National League became the predominant circuit in the eastern part of the country, while the Negro American League ruled the west.

That clear geographical division was one of the reasons why the East-West All-Star Game was so hotly contested by the players and so highly anticipated by the fans of black baseball. The game was held yearly in Chicago's Comiskey Park from 1933 to 1953, with additional East-West games played in the east in six years. Competition in these games was intense, and fan interest was always high, as the contests in the Windy City drew 30,000 or more people 11 times, including six crowds of more than 45,000. The paying customers got their money's worth as 19 of the 28 games were decided by four runs or less.

The Negro National League folded following the 1948 season and, although the Negro American League survived more than another decade and other black touring teams continued to play until the early 1960s, they were of greatly diminished quality after 1950 and certainly not of major league caliber after 1954. The demise of the Negro Leagues was inevitable as the best young black players were signed by Organized Baseball clubs.

The Negro Leagues would not have been able to survive even that long had racial prejudices not prevailed long after Jackie Robinson's big-league debut. Even after Robinson's immensely successful rookie season in 1947, many AL and NL clubs were hesitant to sign black players, having incorrectly assumed that Robinson's success with the Dodgers in 1947 was a fluke. It wasn't until after Robinson, and Larry Doby, the first black to play in the American League, equaled or bettered Robinson's rookie year in 1948 that other big-league clubs began to actively seek out black players.

Even so, many of the best Negro League players never got a shot in the big leagues, since most clubs wouldn't sign black players who were older than 28. There were some exceptions, Satchel Paige being the most famous; however, many other truly great ballplayers were denied entry into the majors, having been born a couple of years too early.

Josh Gibson, the greatest slugger in black baseball history, might have had a chance, like Paige, to play in the big leagues near the end of his career. Gibson led the NNL in home runs in 1945, hit .361 and slugged .958 in 1946, and had at least one meeting with Washington Senators owner Clark Griffith about joining the perennial AL basement dwellers. However, the powerful home run hitter suffered a massive stroke and died in January 1947 when he was but thirty-five years old.

Despite the immediate success of black players in the majors, baseball wasn't fully integrated until well into the 1960s. In 1953, six years after Robinson debuted with Brooklyn, and the year he, Roy Campanella, and Jim Gilliam helped the Dodgers win their second straight pennant, only seven big-league clubs featured black players—not even half of the teams had the wisdom and the integrity to see what the future held.

For a half-century the best black players were not allowed to play on the same field with the best white players, and it was during this era of separation that two parallel baseball universes co-existed. The history of the white major leagues has been well chronicled, but only in recent years has the history of the black major leagues started to get the recognition that it deserves. The Negro Leagues showcased some of the greatest baseball talent of all-time, with a special essence that was all its own.

This section is designed to help preserve the fragmentary record of this segment of baseball history. It is respectfully dedicated to the men who played during this segregated era, so that they will be remembered as more than just a name in an obscure box score or as bits of dust caught in the cobwebs of the receding memory of old men.

Key to Negro Leagues Section. James A. Riley, renowned black baseball historian and consultant to the Negro Leagues Baseball Museum, has selected the greatest black baseball and Negro League players of all-time. Players are grouped into five categories—The Titans, The Elites, All-Time Greats, Long and Distinguished Careers, and Short but Brilliant Careers. An alphabetical index is included before the biographies to make it easier to find individual players.

In all five groups, players are shown in order of merit. Most of the early selections for the Hall of Fame, titans like Josh Gibson and Buck Leonard, are in the top group. Other elite Hall of Famers fall into the second group, including most of those inducted in 2006. Two all-time greats who made it to Cooperstown in 2006—ahead of others we judge as better—can be found in the third grouping. Biographical information for the five Negro Leagues executives and pioneers inducted in 2006 can be found at the end of the Hall of Fame section, along with Frank Grant. While Grant was elected as a player, he played long before the Negro Leagues era and was really more of a pioneer.

The teams that players are most commonly associated with are indicated by bold type.

Also included are synopses of top-level independent black baseball and Negro League seasons from 1910–1950, year-by-year standings, and results of any postseason intraleague championship series or interleague World Series. In the many years where some or all of the standings are unknown, the team that was declared the champion is listed first with other teams listed in alphabetical order. Ex Post Facto Most Valuable Player, Pitcher of the Year, and Rookie of the Year awards have been selected for the Negro major leagues from 1920–50, for the 1910–1919 period when there were four or more teams of big-league caliber, and during selected seasons when clubs that were major league caliber played independently in the east. During the non-league seasons the top performer is referred to as Player of the Year.

The All-Star Game list shows the results of every East-West All-Star Game played, including two games in 1938 that have rarely been mentioned. Most accounts of East-West games leave out several of the "second" games played; this is the first time a complete list has been published. There was only one year when an official MVP was selected for the East-West Game (1945). Therefore, we have chosen Ex Post Facto MVPs for all other East-West Games.

Finally, at the end of this section is a list of Negro League home ballparks, organized by the metropolitan area the ballparks were located in. Negro League teams played thousands of games at neutral sites, in between official league games during the season, as well as on off-season barnstorming tours. In fact, teams frequently played doubleheaders where the first game was an official league contest but the nightcap was just an exhibition—a distinction that was often conveniently ignored when promoting the games to draw a bigger crowd for the second game.

Negro Major Leagues

NNL	Negro National League 1920–31
ECL	Eastern Colored League 1923–28
NSL	Negro Southern League 1932
ANL	American Negro League 1929
EWL	East-West League 1932
NNL	Negro National League 1933–48
NAL	Negro American League 1937–54

Negro Major League Teams and Big-League Caliber Independent Teams

AC	All Cubans (Touring) 1921 Ind.
Atl	Atlanta Black Crackers 1938 NAL
Bac	Bacharach Giants (Atlantic City NJ) 1923–28 ECL; 1929 ANL
Bal BS	Baltimore Black Sox 1922 Ind.; 1923–28 ECL; 1929 ANL; 1930–31 Ind.; 1932 EWL; 1933–34 NNL
Bal EG	Baltimore Elite Giants 1938–48 NNL; 1949–51 NAL
Bir	Birmingham Black Barons 1924–25 NNL; 1927–30 NNL; 1932 NSL; 1937–38, 1940–54 NAL
Bow	Bowser's ABCs (Indianapolis) 1916 Ind.
Bro E	Brooklyn Eagles 1935 NNL
Bro RG	Brooklyn Royal Giants 1905–14, 1916–22 Ind.; 1923–27 ECL; 1928–32 Ind.; 1933 NNL
Chi AG[1]	Chicago American Giants 1920–31 NNL; 1932 NSL; 1933–35 NNL; 1936 Ind.; 1937–52 NAL
Chi CG	Chicago Columbia Giants 1899–1900 Ind.
Chi G	Chicago Giants 1920–21 NNL
Chi LG	Chicago Leland Giants 1905–10 Ind.
Chi UG	Chicago Union Giants 1901–04 Ind.
Chi U	Chicago Unions 1888–1900 Ind.
Cin Bu	Cincinnati Buckeyes 1942 NAL
Cin	Cincinnati Tigers 1937 NAL
Cle Be	Cleveland Bears 1939–40 NAL
Cle Br	Cleveland Browns 1924 NNL
Cle Bu	Cleveland Buckeyes 1943–48, 1950 NAL
Cle C	Cleveland Cubs 1931 NNL
Cle E	Cleveland Elites 1926 NNL
Cle G	Cleveland Giants 1933 NNL
Cle H	Cleveland Hornets 1927 NNL
Cle RS	Cleveland Red Sox 1934 NNL
Cle S	Cleveland Stars 1932 EWL
Cle TS	Cleveland Tate Stars 1922 NNL
Cle T	Cleveland Tigers 1928 NNL
Col BB	Columbus Blue Birds 1933 NNL
Col B	Columbus Buckeyes 1921 NNL
Col EG	Columbus Elite Giants 1935 NNL
Cub HD[2]	Cuban House of David (Touring) 1931–32 Ind.; 1932 EWL
Cub SE	Cuban Stars [East] (Touring/New York) 1923–28 ECL; 1929 ANL
Cub SW[3]	Cuban Stars [West] (Touring) 1920–30 NNL
Cub XG	Cuban X-Giants (Touring/Philadelphia) 1897–1908 Ind.
Day	Dayton Marcos [I] 1920 NNL; [II] 1926 NNL
Det S	Detroit Stars [I] 1920–31 NNL; [II] 1933 NNL; [III] 1937 NAL
Det W	Detroit Wolves 1932 EWL
Eth	Ethiopian Clowns (Miami/Touring) 1940–42 Ind.
GCT	GCT (Grand Central Terminal) Red Caps (New York City) 1918–19 Ind.
Har G	Harrisburg Giants 1924–27 ECL
Har S	Harlem Stars (New York City) 1931 Ind.
Hil	Hilldale Daisies 1923–28 ECL; 1929 ANL; 1930–31 Ind.; 1932 EWL
Hom[4]	Homestead Grays (Pittsburgh) 1929 ANL; 1930–31 Ind.; 1932 EWL; 1933–34 Ind.; 1935–48 NNL
Hou	Houston Eagles 1949–50 NAL
Ind ABC	Indianapolis ABCs [I] 1920–26 NNL; [II] 1931 NNL; 1932 NSL; [III] 1933 NNL; [IV] 1938–39 NAL
Ind A	Indianapolis Athletics 1937 NAL
Ind Cl[5]	Indianapolis Clowns 1943–54 NAL
Ind Cr	Indianapolis Crawfords 1940 NAL
Jac	Jacksonville Red Caps 1938, 1941–42 NAL
Jew	Jewell's ABCs (Indianapolis) 1917 Ind.
KC	Kansas City Monarchs 1920–31 NNL; 1932–36 Ind.; 1937–54 NAL
Lin	Lincoln Giants (New York City) 1923–26 ECL; 1927 Ind.; 1928 ECL; 1929 ANL
Lou BCa	Louisville Black Caps 1932 NSL
Lou BCo	Louisville Black Colonels 1954 NAL
Lou Bu	Louisville Buckeyes 1949 NAL
Lou WS	Louisville White Sox 1931 NNL
Mem	Memphis Red Sox 1924–25, 1927, 1929–30 NNL; 1932 NSL; 1937–54 NAL
Mil	Milwaukee Bears 1923 NNL
Moh	Mohawk Giants (Schenectady NY) 1913–15 Ind.
Mon M	Monroe Monarchs 1932 NSL
Mon GS	Montgomery Grey Sox 1932 NSL
Nas	Nashville Elite Giants 1930 NNL; 1932 NSL; 1933–34 NNL
NO	New Orleans Eagles 1951 NAL
NY BY[6]	New York Black Yankees 1936–48 NNL
NY C	New York Cubans 1935–36, 1939–48 NNL; 1949–50 NAL
NY LS	New York Lincoln Stars 1914–16 Ind.
New B	Newark Browns 1932 EWL
New D	Newark Dodgers 1934–35 NNL
New E	Newark Eagles 1936–48 NNL
New S	Newark Stars 1926 ECL
Pen	Penn (Pennsylvania) Red Caps of New York 1917–19 Ind.
PF	Page Fence Giants (Adrian MI) 1894–98 Ind.
Phi BG	Philadelphia Bacharach Giants 1934 NNL
Phi G	Philadelphia Giants 1902–16 Ind.
Phi S	Philadelphia Stars 1934–48 NNL; 1949–52 NAL
Phi T	Philadelphia Tigers 1928 ECL
Pit C	Pittsburgh Crawfords 1933–38 NNL
Pit K	Pittsburgh Keystones 1922 NNL
Qua	Quaker Giants (Philadelphia) 1909 Ind.
StL G	St. Louis Giants 1920–21 NNL
StL S[7]	St. Louis Stars [I] 1922–31 NNL; [II] 1937 NAL; [III] 1939 NAL; 1940 Ind.; 1941 NAL; 1943 NNL
Tol C	Toledo Crawfords 1939 NAL
Tol T	Toledo Tigers 1923 NNL
Was BS	Washington Black Senators 1938 NNL
Was EG	Washington Elite Giants 1936–37 NNL
Was Pi	Washington Pilots 1932 EWL
Was Po	Washington Potomacs 1924 ECL
Wil	Wilmington Potomacs 1925 Ind.
Zul	Zulu Cannibal Giants (Touring) 1934–37 Ind.

Notes

[1] played as Cole's American Giants, 1932–35
[2] also known as Cuban Stars when playing in 1932 EWL
[3] based in Cincinnati as Cincinnati Cuban Stars, 1921
[4] played home games in both Pittsburgh PA and Washington DC, 1937–48
[5] played selected home games in Cincinnati OH, 1943–45
[6] played home games in Rochester NY in 1948
[7] played selected home games in New Orleans LA in 1941 and Harrisburg PA in 1943
Ind. Independent Team of Major League Caliber

THE NEGRO LEAGUES

Top 100 Black baseball/Negro League Players

Alpha List

Allen, Newt	Elite-18	Charleston, Oscar	Titan-3	Grant, Leroy	LDC-1	Mendez, Jose	ATG-5	Smith, Hilton	Elite-13
Bankhead, Sam	ATG-12	Cooper, Andy	ATG-14	Harris, Vic	ATG-8	Monroe, Bill	ATG-10	Stearnes, Turkey	Elite-7
Barnhill, Dave	ATG-33	Crutchfield, Jimmie	ATG-27	Hill, Pete	Elite-4	Moore, Dobie	SBC-4	Strong, Ted	ATG-40
Beckwith, John	Elite-19	Dandridge, Ray	Elite-3	Holland, Bill	LDC-8	Oms, Alejandro	ATG-22	Suttles, Mule	Elite-12
Bell, Cool Papa	Titan-9	Davis, Piper	ATG-2	Hughes, Sammy T.	Elite-23	O'Neil, Buck	ATG-11	Taylor, Ben	Elite-17
Bell, William Sr.	LDC-5	Davis, Steel Arm	LDC-7	Irvin, Monte	Elite-2	Paige, Satchel	Titan-2	Thomas, Clint	ATG-7
Benjamin, Jerry	LDC-12	Day, Leon	Elite-10	Jenkins, Fats	ATG-15	Parnell, Roy	ATG-38	Tiant, Luis	ATG-36
Benson, Gene	ATG-25	DeMoss, Bingo	Elite-21	Johnson, Heavy	ATG-44	Petway, Bruce	ATG-16	Torriente, Cristobal	Elite-6
Brewer, Chet	ATG-34	Dihigo, Martin	Titan-12	Johnson, Home Run	Elite-26	Poles, Spot	Elite-16	Trent, Ted	ATG-30
Brooks, Chester	ATG-21	Dismukes, Dizzy	ATG-29	Johnson, Judy	Elite-11	Radcliffe, Alex	ATG-3	Warfield, Frank	ATG-19
Brown, Barney	ATG-37	Dixon, Rap	ATG-13	Jones, Slim	SBC-5	Radcliffe, Double Duty	ATG-1	Wells, Willie	Titan-7
Brown, Dave	SBC-2	Donaldson, John	ATG-4	Kimbro, Henry	ATG-24	Redding, Dick	Elite-15	White, Chaney	ATG-26
Brown, Larry	ATG-18	Duncan, Frank	ATG-17	Leonard, Buck	Titan-5	Robinson, Neil	ATG-23	Wickware, Frank	ATG-35
Brown, Ray	Elite-20	Duncan, Frank	LDC-11	Lloyd, John Henry	Titan-4	Rogan, Bullet	Titan-8	Williams, Smokey Joe	Titan-6
Brown, Willard	Elite-14	Earle, Frank	ATG-43	Lundy, Dick	Elite-5	Rogers, Nat	LDC-9	Wilson, Artie	SBC-6
Byrd, Bill	Elite-25	Easterling, Howard	ATG-42	Lyons, Jimmie	ATG-20	Sampson, Tommy	ATG-41	Wilson, Jud	Elite-8
Campanella, Roy	SBC-1	Foster, Rube	Elite-1	Mackey, Biz	Titan-11	Santop, Louis	Elite-9	Winters, Nip	ATG-6
Cannady, Rev	LDC-2	Foster, Willie	Titan-10	Malarcher, Dave	ATG-47	Scales, George	ATG-9	Wright, Bill	Elite-22
Carr, George	ATG-39	Francis, Bill	LDC-10	Marcelle, Oliver H.	Elite-24	Seay, Dick	LDC-3		
		Gardner, Jelly	ATG-28	Mathis, Verdell	ATG-32	Shively, George	ATG-31		
		Gibson, Josh	Titan-1	McNair, Hurley	LDC-6	Smith, Chino	SBC-3		

Titan Greatest of the Great Elite Hall of Fame-Caliber Career ATG All-Time Great LDC Long and Distinguished Career SBC Short but Brilliant Career

The Titans

GIBSON, JOSH Joshua; B12.21.1911 Buena Vista GA; D1.20.1947 Pittsburgh PA; BR/TR/6-4/210; d1929; HF 1972; b-Jerry; s-Josh Jr; C, OF, 3b, 1b

Hom 1929–31; Pit C 1932–36; [Dom 1937]; **Hom** 1937–40; [Mexico 1940–41]; **Hom** 1942–46

Legendary hitting feats and fine all-around defensive skills lend weight to the argument that Gibson was the greatest catcher ever, black or white. Gibson, anchor of the great Homestead Grays and Pittsburgh Crawfords clubs, stroked out at 36, still a remarkable hitter but no longer in shape to catch.

PAIGE, SATCHEL Robert LeRoy; B7.7.1906 Mobile AL; D6.8.1982 Kansas City MO; BR/TR/6´4˝/180; d1927; HF 1971; ML 1948–49; 1951–53;1965; P

Bir 1927–30; Bal BS 1930; Cle C 1931; **Pit C** 1931–37; KC 1935–36; [Dom 1937] Santo Domingo All-Stars 1937; New E 1938; [Mexico 1938]; [Satchel Paige's All-Stars 1939]; **KC** 1939–48; NY BY 1943; Mem 1943; PhiS 1946; KC 1950; Phi S 1950; Chi AG 1951; KC 1955; [OB minors 1956–58 1961 1965–66]

The most famous and probably greatest Negro Leagues moundsman, the seemingly ageless Paige toiled for 25 years in baseball's Jim Crow era. Paige, a right-hander with great control of a humming fastball, curve, and change-up, was the model of a pitcher for many years—and not just for black fans.

CHARLESTON, OSCAR Oscar McKinley "Charlie"; B10.14.1896 Indianapolis IN D10.5.1954 Philadelphia PA; BL/TL/6-0/190; d1915 HF 1976; CF, 1B, M

Ind ABC 1915–18; Lin S 1915–16; Bow ABC 1916; Chi AG 1919; **Ind ABC** 1920; StL G 1921; **Ind ABC** 1922–23; **Har** 1924–27; Hil 1928–29; Hom 1930–31; **Pit C** 1932–38; Tol C 1939; Ind C 1940; Phi S 1941 1942–44 1946–50

Was Charleston the greatest center fielder in baseball history? He could do it all in every facet of the game, and gained well-deserved comparisons to Ruth, Cobb, and Speaker. Winning titles in several different leagues, he played 27 years and was as famous in Latin America as in the U.S.

LLOYD, JOHN HENRY "Pop","El Cuchara"; B4.25.1884 Palatka FL; D3.19.1964 Atlantic City NJ; BL/TR/5-11/180; d1906; HF 1977; SS, 2b, 1b, C, M

Cub X 1906; Phi G 1907–09; Chi LG 1910; **Lin** 1911–15; Chi AG 1914–17; Lin S 1915 Bro RG 1918–20; Bac 1919; Col B 1921; Bac 1922; Hil 1923; Bac 1924–25; **Lin** 1926–30; Har S 1931; Bac 1931–32

A great shortstop comparable to Honus Wagner, Lloyd was the Dead Ball Era's top Negro Leaguer. He combined smarts and skills in every area of the game into a dominating; package, slashing hits all over the field and fielding flawlessly. Babe Ruth once called Lloyd the greatest baseball player ever.

LEONARD, BUCK Walter Fenner; B9.8.1907 Rocky Mount NC; D11.27.1997 Rocky Mount NC; BL/TL/5-10/185; d1933; HF 1972; 1b, OF

Bro RG 1933; **Hom** 1934–50; [Mexico 1951 1955]; [OB minors 1953]

A popular left-handed-batting first baseman who played 17 years for the Homestead Grays, Leonard hit for average and power, took walks, fielded his position as well as anyone in any league, and possessed smarts and character. He was a star south of the border as well as in the U.S.

WILLIAMS, SMOKEY JOE Joseph "Joe", "Cyclone", "Yank"; B4.6.1886; Seguin TX; D2.25.1951; New York; NY; BR/TR/6-4/190; d1911; HF 1999; P, M Chi G 1910–11

Lin 1912–23; Moh 1913; Chi AG 1914; Bac 1916; Hil 1917; Bro RG 1924; **Hom** 1925–32; Det W 1932

The right-handed Williams was early black baseball's best pitcher, as famous in his time as Satchel Paige became. In early years, with the Lincoln Giants, "Cyclone" threw harder than anyone, and years later, with Homestead, won with smarts and command. Williams was especially good in competition against white major leaguers.

WELLS, WILLIE James "The Devil","El Diablo"; B8.10.1905; Austin TX; D1.22.1989; Austin TX; BR/TR/5-8/160; d1924; HF 1997; s-Willie Jr; SS, 3b, 2b

StL S 1924–31; Det W 1932; Hom 1932; KC 1932; Chi AG 1933–34; KC 1934; Chi AG 1935; **New E** 1936–39; [Mex 1940–41]; **New E** 1942; [Mex 1943–44]; Chi AG 1944; Mem 1944; NY BY 1945–46; Bal EG 1946; Ind/Cin 1947; Mem 1948; [Can 1949–51]; Bir 1954

Wells succeeded "Pop" Lloyd as the Negro Leagues' greatest shortstop. He won three titles with the St. Louis Stars, then contributed to other great teams (Homestead, Kansas City, Chicago, and Newark). While not blessed with a great throwing arm, Wells played excellent defense, hit the ball, worked hard, and knew the game.

ROGAN, BULLET Wilbur; B7.28.1889; Oklahoma City OK; D3.4.1967; Kansas City MO; BR/TR/5-7/180; d1920; HF 1998; P, OF, 1b, 2b, SS, M, U

KC 1920–38

Some feel that Rogan was the hardest thrower in black baseball. A star for nearly 20 years with the Kansas City Monarchs, the durable righty threw several pitches with great efficiency and also hit well enough to play the outfield. In addition, he served as player-manager for several years.

BELL, COOL PAPA James Thomas; B5.17.1903; Starkville MS; D3.7.1991; St. Louis MO; BB/TL/5-11/150 d1922; HF 1974; b-Fred; CF, LF, 1b, P

StL S 1922–31; Det W 1932; KC 1932; **Hom** 1932; **Pit C** 1933–38; KC 1934; [Dom 1937]; [Mexico 1938–41]; Chi AG 1942; Mem 1942; **Hom** 1943–46

Speed was Bell's key marker, and he used it on the basepaths and in center field. Arguably the fastest player ever, the well-liked Bell didn't hit with power, but drove opponents to; distraction anyway. He played for champions in St. Louis and Pittsburgh and also starred during his four years in Mexico.

FOSTER, WILLIE William Hendrick "Bill"; B6.12.1904; Calvert TX; D9.16.1978; Lorman MS; BB/TL/6.1/195; d1923; HF 1996; b-Rube; Col Alcorn; P, M

Mem 1923–24; Bir 1925; **Chi AG** 1923–30; Hom 1931; KC 1931; **Chi AG** 1932–35; Pit C 1936; **Chi AG** 1937; Mem 1938

This tall lefty pitched for the Chicago American Giants (for a time under his half-brother, Rube Foster) for more than a decade. An early proponent of the slider, he was fast with good control. Foster was also a member of the 1931 Homestead Grays, considered by many to be black baseball's greatest team.

MACKEY, BIZ Raleigh; B7.27.1897; Eagle Pass TX; D9.22.1965; Los Angeles CA; BB/TR/6-0/200; d1920; HF 2006; C, SS, 3b, M

Ind ABC 1920; Lin 1920; **Hil** 1923–31; Phi S 1933–35; New D 1935; Was EG 1936–37; Bal EG 1938–39; New E 1939–41 1945–47 1950

No one played better defense behind the plate than Mackey, who was blessed with a great arm, agility, and strong baseball smarts (he later managed). In addition, he was a fearsome switch-hitter with some power. Mackey played organized black baseball from age 21 until he was past 50.

DIHIGO, MARTIN B5.25.1905; Matanzas, Cuba; D5.22.1971; Cienfuegos, Cuba; BR/TR/6-3/190; d1923; HF 1977; 2b, OF, P, 1b, 3b, SS, C, M

Cub SE 1923–27; Hom 1928; Hil 1929–30; Cub SE 1930; Hil 1931; Bal BS 1931; [Venezuela 1933]; NY C 1935–36; [Dom 1937]; [Mexico 1940–44]; NY C 1945 Dihigo could—and did—play every position on the diamond in his 22-year career, much of it spent in Mexico and his native Cuba. An all-around hitter with power and speed who also won over 200 games as a pitcher, Dihigo later served as minister of sports for Fidel Castro.

The Elites

FOSTER, RUBE Andrew "Jock"; B9.17.1879; Calvert TX; D12.9.1930; Kankakee IL; BR/TR/6-2/200; d1902; HF 1981; b-Willie; P, 1b, OF, M

Chi UG 1902; Cub XG 1903; Phi G 1904–06; Chi LG 1907–10; **Chi AG** 1911–26

He was a great pitcher, but Foster is most lauded for his managing skill and founding of the Negro National League. Finished on the mound by the early 1910s, Foster excelled as; manager of the Chicago American Giants. He later organized the NNL and ran the league until stepping down in 1926.

IRVIN, MONTE Monford Merrill; B2.25.1919 Halesburg AL; BR/TR/6-1/190 d1937 HF1973 Col Lincoln Mil 1943–45 ML 1949–56; CF, SS, 3b

New E 1937–42; [Mexico 1942]; **New E** 1945–48; [OB minors 1949–50, 1957]

A star with the Newark Eagles by age 21, Irvin had the speed and defensive ability to play center field and shortstop, and hit for power as well as average. Irvin played in several Negro All-Star games, won championships in Latin America, and had an excellent career in the majors.

DANDRIDGE, RAY Raymond Emmitt "Dannie","Hooks","Squatty","Talua","Mamerto"; B8.31.1913; Richmond VA; D2.12.1994; Palm Bay FL; d1933; HF 1987; BR/TR/5-7/170; 3b,2b,SS
Det S 1933; Nas 1933; New D 1933–35; **New E** 1936–39; [Ven 1939]; [Mex 1940–41]; **New E** 1942; [Mex 1942–43]; **New E** 1944; [Mex 1945–48]; NY C 1949; [OB minors 1949–53]
Dandridge was really a shortstop playing third, as Willie Wells had short covered for Newark in the 1930s. In addition to being the greatest defensive player at the hot corner in Negro Leagues history, Dandridge was a fine spray hitter who made contact. He played several full seasons in Latin America.

HILL, PETE Joseph Preston; B10.12.1880; Pittsburgh PA; D11.26.1951; Buffalo NY; BL/TR/6-1/215; d1899; HF 2006; CF, LF, RF, 1b, 2b, M
Pit K 1899–1900; Cub XG 1901–02; **Phi G** 1903–07; Chi LG 1907–10; **Chi AG** 1911–18; Det S 1919–21; Mil 1923; Bal BS 1924–25
Black baseball's first great outfielder, and a great comparison for Ty Cobb, Hill starred for two decades after the turn of the century. Blessed with speed, the range to play center field, and a strong arm, Hill also drove pitchers crazy on the bases and hit for a high average.

LUNDY, DICK Richard "King Richard"; B7.10.1898; Jacksonville FL; D1.5.1965; Jacksonville; FL; BB/TR/5-11/180; d1916; SS, 3b, 2b, C, M
Bac 1916–18; Hil 1917–19; **Bac** 1920–28; Bal BS 1929–32; Phil S 1933; New D 1934–35; NY C 1935; New E 1936–37; Atl 1938; New E1938–39
A decade-long star for the Bacharach Giants, Lundy was the Negro Leagues' top shortstop of the 1920s, during which he played on three pennant winners. A switch-hitter with pop who played gracefully and athletically in the field, "King Richard" was a natural leader and a successful playing manager.

TORRIENTE, CRISTOBAL B11.16.1893; Cienfuegas, Cuba; D4.15.1938; New York NY; BL/TL/5-9/190; d1913; HF 2006; CF, LF, RF, P
Cub SW 1913–18; **Chi AG** 1918–25; KC 1926; Det S 1927–28
A Cuban-born center fielder with a power bat and excellent defensive skills, Torriente excelled for nearly a decade with Rube Foster's American Giants. He wasn't easy to manage—he loved the nightlife, had anger issues, and swung at bad balls—but Torriente was a "franchise player" for many great teams.

STEARNES, TURKEY Norman Thomas; B5.8.1901; Nashville TN; D9.4.1979; Detroit MI; BL/TL/6.0/175; d1923; HF 2000; CF, LF, 1b
Det S 1923–30; Lin 1930; **Det S** 1931; KC 1931; Chi AG 1932–35; Det S 1933; KC 1934; Phi S 1936; Det S 1937; Chi AG 1938; KC 1938–41
Stearnes had the speed to lead off as well as the power to hit cleanup, and he did both during a 20-year career. The hard-nosed Stearnes, a lefty batter, was a fine center fielder; most of his fame came in Detroit, but he also starred for Chicago and Kansas City.

WILSON, JUD Ernest Judson "Boojum"; B2.28.1899; Remington VA; D6.26.1963; Washington DC; BL/TR/5-8/185; d1922; HF 2006; Mil 1918; 3b, 1b, 2b, SS, OF, M
Bal BS 1922–30; **Hom** 1931–32; Pit C 1932; **Phi S** 1933–39; **Hom** 1940–45
"Boojum" was one of the game's top batters in the 1930s, rapping out hit after hit for several great teams. Tough, pugnacious, and ill-tempered, Wilson argued constantly and was not strong defensively at any position (he played mostly at third) but was a truly fearsome hitter.

SANTOP, LOUIS Louis Santop Loftin "Top","Big Bertha"; B1.17.1890; Tyler TX; D1.6.1942; Philadelphia PA; BL/TR/6-4/240; d1909; HF 2006; Mil 1918–19; C, LF, RF, 1b, 3b, M
Phi G 1909–10; **Lin** 1911–14; **Bro RG** 1914; Chi AG 1915; NY LS 1915–16; **Bro RG** 1916–19; **Hil** 1917–26
The strong-armed, lefty-swinging catcher starred mostly for East Coast teams. Popular, well-paid, and genial, Santop showed an excellent power bat and was celebrated for his glove work. A key error in the 1924 Negro World Series, however, ushered in the decline phase of his great career.

DAY, LEON B10.30.1916; Alexandria VA; D3.13.1995; Baltimore MD; BR/TR/5-9/170; d1934; HF 1995; Mil 1944–45; P, 2b, OF
Bal BS 1934; Bro E 1935; **New E** 1936–39; [Ven 1940]; [Mex 1940]; **New E** 1941–43 1946; [Mex 1947–48]; Bal EG 1949–50; [OB minors 1950–54]
With the Newark Eagles in the late 1930s and 1940s, Day was black baseball's best pitcher. He threw hard but also deceived hitters with movement and by changing speeds. He could hit, too, and was fast and agile enough to play other positions (center field and second base) when needed.

JOHNSON, JUDY William Julius; B10.26.1899; Snow Hill MD; D6.15.1989; Wilmington DE; BR/TR/5-11/150; d1918; HF 1974; 3b, SS, M
Bac 1918; **Hil** 1921–29; Hom 1930; Hil 1931–32; **Pit C** 1932–36; Hom 1937
William Julius Johnson played a great third base, hit for high averages, and served as playing manager for the Homestead Grays and Hilldale Daisies. His career started during World War I and lasted through 1937, and Johnson would live another 50 years, some of which he spent as a big-league scout.

SUTTLES, MULE George; B3.31.1900; Brockton LA; D7.9.1966; Newark NJ; BR/TR/6-3/215; d1918; ; HF 2006; 1b, LF, RF, M, U
Bir 1923–25; **StL S** 1926–1930; Bal BS 1930; **StL S** 1931; Det W 1932; Was Pi 1932; Chi AG 1933–35; **New E** 1936–39; Ind ABC 1939; **New E** 1940; NY BY 1941–42; **New E** 1942–44
While Suttles wasn't much in the field (first base and left field were his positions), he showed prodigious home run power and was particularly dangerous in All-Star competition. He may have struck out a little too often, but when he made contact, Suttles was unstoppable.

SMITH, HILTON Lee; B2.27.1912; Giddings TX; D11.18.1983; Kansas City MO; BR/TR/6-2/180; d1932; HF 2001; Col Prairie View A&M; P, OF, 1b
Mon M 1932–35; **KC** 1936–48
Smith threw several pitches, the best a curve that nobody in black baseball (and maybe all baseball) could match. A 13-year star for Kansas City, he had as much talent as teammate Satchel Paige but never the acclaim. While not strong afield, Smith hit enough to play the outfield when needed.

BROWN, WILLARD Jesse "Home Run","Esse Hombre","Willie","Sonny"; B6.26.1911; Shreveport; LA; D8.8.1996; Houston TX; BR/TR/6-0/195; d1935; HF 2006; CF, LF, SS KC 1935–40; [Mex 1940]
KC 1941–43 1946–51; Military 1944–45; ML 1947; [OB minors 1950 1953–56]
The top black power hitter of the 1940s, "Home Run" Brown had a huge strike zone but hit enough to play into his forties. Signed by the St. Louis Browns in 1947 at age 36, he hit the first home run ever by an AL black player, but questions lingered about his desire.

REDDING, DICK Richard "Cannonball"; B1891; Atlanta; D1948; Islip NY; BR/TR/6-4/210; d1911; Mil 1918–19; P, OF, 1b, M
Phi G 1911; **Lin** 1911–14; Lin S 1915; Ind ABC 1915; **Lin** 1915–16; **Bro RG** 1916; Chi AG 1917–18; **Bro RG** 1918; Bac 1919–22; **Bro RG** 1923–32,1938
"Cannonball Dick" pitched with blazing speed but also had a crazy-making "hesitation pitch" that froze batters who were waiting for yet another high, hard one. Durable, hard-working, and very successful, Redding was sought by many owners and changed teams often. In his latter years, he was a playing manager.

POLES, SPOT Spottswood; B11.7.1889; Winchester VA; D9.12.1962; Harrisburg PA; BB/TR/5-7/165; d1909; Mil 1918; CF
Phi G 1909–10; **Lin** 1911–12; Bro RG 1912; **Lin** 1913–14; Lin S 1914–16; **Lin** 1917; Hil 1917; Bac 1919; **Lin** 1919; Hil 1920; **Lin** 1920–23
The early-century center fielder drove pitchers crazy with his speed, bunting ability, and confidence on the bases. A high-average leadoff hitter, Poles, one of black baseball's earliest stars, spent his entire career on the east coast. He was celebrated as one of the greatest athletes of his day.

TAYLOR, BEN Benjamin; B7.1.1888; Anderson SC; D1.24.1953; Baltimore MD; BL/TL/6-1/190; d1910; b-C.I. b-Jim b-Johnny; 1b, P, M, U
StL G 1911–12; Lin 1912; Chi AG 1913–14; **Ind ABC** 1914–18; Hil 1919; Bac 1919; **Ind ABC** 1920–22; Was Po 1923–24; Har 1925; Bal BS 1916–28; Bac 1929; Was Pi 1932; Bro E 1935; Was BS 1938; NY C 1940
Hitting for average and making good contact, fielding flawlessly at first base, and excelling at "inside baseball," Taylor did all the things a good Dead Ball Era player was asked to do. When the lively ball came around, Taylor's batting numbers improved. He also was a longtime manager and umpire.

ALLEN, NEWT Newton Henry "Colt"; B5.19.1901; Austin TX; D6.11.1988; Cincinnati OH; BR/TR/5-8/160; d1922; HF 2006; 2b, 3b, SS, OF, 1b, M
KC 1922–1931; StL S 1931; Det W 1932; Hom 1932; **KC** 1932–44; Ind C 1947
"Colt" ranks as one of the greatest second basemen in black baseball history. Fast, aggressive, and nimble in the field, Allen was also the prototypical #2 hole batter due to his bunting, slashing, and bat control skills. His smarts and all-around ability made Allen perhaps the ultimate Kansas City Monarchs player.

BECKWITH, JOHN B6.20.1902; Louisville KY; D1.4.1956; New York NY; BR/TR/6-3/220; d1916; SS, 3b, C, OF, 1b, M
Chi UG 1916; Chi G 1916–23; Chi AG 1922–23; Hom 1924; Bal BS 1924–26; Har 1926–27; Hom 1928–29; Lin 29–30; Bal BS 1930–31; New B 1931–32; NY BY 1933–34; New D 1934; Hom 1935; Bro RG 1938
Despite a huge frame, Beckwith was agile enough to play any position, and in fact was a fine defensive shortstop. But defense was just a bonus—he had fantastic power, even though he was a rank pull hitter. Unfortunately, Beckwith also had a temper and didn't play "inside baseball."

BROWN, RAY Raymond; B2.23.1908; Ashland Grove OH; D1965; Canada; BB/TR/6-1/195; d1930; HF 2006; P, OF, M
Day 1930; Ind ABC 1931; Det W 1932; **Hom** 1932–39; [Mex 1939]; **Hom** 1940–45; [Mex 1946–47]; **Hom** 1947–48; [Mex 1948–49]; [Can 1950–53]
A master of deception and movement, Brown had a full arsenal of pitches headed by a devastating curve. Brown, a star in Latin America and even Canada, sometimes played the outfield when he wasn't pitching. Many in the African-American press felt he would have been an ideal major-league pitcher.

DEMOSS, BINGO Elwood; B9.5.1889; Topeka; KS; D1.26.1965; Chicago IL; BR/TR/6-2/175 d1910; 2b, SS, OF, M
Chi G 1913; **Chi AG** 1913; Ind ABC 1915–16; Bow ABC 1916; **Chi AG** 1917–25; Ind ABC 1926; Det S 1927–30; Cle 1933
DeMoss could do it all—run the bases, play sterling second base, hit for average and bunt, and outwit opponents. A perfect Dead Ball-Era player, he was highly celebrated and may be the greatest second sacker in the history of black baseball. DeMoss also spent nearly a decade as a manager.

WRIGHT, BILL Burnis "Wild Bill"; B6.6.1914; Milan TN; D8.3.1996; Aquascalientes, Mexico; BB/TR/6-4/220; d1932; CF, RF, LF
Nas 1932–1934; Col EG 1935; Was EG 1936–37; **Bal EG** 1938–39; [Mex 1940–41]; **Bal EG** 1942; [Mex 1943–44]; **Bal EG** 1945; [Mex 1946–56]
A seven-time All-Star who could play both center field (excellent range) and right field (a strong arm), Wright was a capable #3 or #4 hitter with power and speed who rarely struck out. Wright started his career as a pitcher, but soon switched to the outfield. He won the 1943 Triple Crown in Mexico.

HUGHES, SAMMY T. Samuel Thomas; B10.20.1910; Louisville TX; D8.9.1981; Los Angeles CA; BR/TR/6-3/190; d1931; Mil 1943–46; 2b, SS
Lou WS 1929–31; Was Pi 1932; Nas 1933–34; Col EG 1935; Was EG 1936–37; **Bal EG** 1938–40; [Mex 1941]; **Bal EG** 1942, 1946
An excellent second baseman who saw his action before the Second World War, Hughes did everything well both offensively and defensively and had good speed, though he was not a home-run hitter. In 1946, his final season, he tutored Jim Gilliam to take over his position in Baltimore.

MARCELLE, OLIVER H. [Marcell] [Marcel] "Ghost"; B6.24.1897; Thibedeaux; LA; D6.12.1949; Denver CO; BR/TR/5-9/160; d1918; s-Everett; 3b, SS
Bro RG 1918–19; Det S 1919; **Bac** 1920–22; Lin 1923–25; **Bac** 1925–28; Bal BS 1929; Bro RG 1930
Considered the best third baseman of the 1920s, Marcelle was a spectacular defender and a good enough hitter to bat second or third for many quality teams. "Ghost" had a temper and was easily riled, and lost part of his nose in a fight over a dice game.

BYRD, BILL William "Daddy"; B7.15.1907; Canton GA; D1.4.1991; Philadelphia; PA; BB/TR/6-1/210; d1932; P, 1b, OF
Col T 1932; Col BB 1933; Nas 1933; Cle RS 1934; Col EG 1935; Was EG 1936–37; **Bal EG** 1938–39; [Ven 1940]; **Bal EG** 1941–50
"Daddy" Byrd was a beneficiary of the "grandfather" clause that allowed veteran pitchers to throw spitballs. He also used the knuckleball to great effect, and in his later years became a mentor to younger teammates. Byrd was slow afoot, but could hit and sometimes played first base and the outfield.

JOHNSON, HOME RUN Grant; B1874; Findlay OH; D1964; Buffalo NY; BR/TR/5-10/170; d1895; SS, 2b, M
[OB minors 1894]; PF 1895–98; Chi CG 1899; Chi U 1900 Cub XG 1903–04; Phi G 1905–06; Bro RG 1906–09; Chi L 1910; Chi G 1911; Lin 1911; Bro RG 1912; Lin 1912–13; Moh 1913; Lin S 1916
Black baseball's first great shortstop played with the best teams of his era, earning his nickname with power blasts as well as high averages. While not as slick defensively as others, he was solid with the glove. A stickler for conditioning, Johnson played until he was fifty-eight.

All-Time Greats

RADCLIFFE, DOUBLE DUTY Theodore Roosevelt "Ted"; B7.7.1902; Mobile AL; BR/TR/5-10/190; d1928; b-Alex; C, P, M
Det S 1928–29; StL S 1930; Det S 1931; Hom 1931; Pit C 1932; Col BB 1933; Cle G 1933; NY BY 1933; Hom 1933; Chi AG 1934; [Bismarck 1934–35]; Bro E 1935; Hom 1936; Cin T 1936–37; Mem 1938–39; [Mex 1940]; Chi AG 1941–43; Bir 1942–45; KC 1945; Bir 1946; Hom 1946; Lou B 1949; Chi AG 1949–50
As both a pitcher and catcher, "Duty" was a valuable member of the 1931 Homestead Grays, perhaps black baseball's greatest club. He had strong receiving skills and hit for power, and on the hill he mastered various quasi-legal deliveries. Radcliffe's colorful nature makes him a witty raconteur to this day.

DAVIS, PIPER Lorenzo; B7.3.1917; Piper AL; D5.21.1997; Birmingham AL; BR/TR/6-3/186; d1942; 2b, 1b, SS, M
Bir 1942–50; [OB minors 1950–58]
For nearly a decade, Davis was one of the game's top second basemen. Steady and dependable in the field, he turned the double play well and made solid contact at bat with some power. The Boston Red Sox made him their first black player, but Davis never made the majors.

RADCLIFFE, ALEX Alexander "Alec"; B7.26.1905; Mobile AL; D7.18.1983; Chicago IL; BR/TR/6.0/205; d1932; b-"Double Duty"; 3b, SS, OF
Chi AG 1932–35; NY C 1936; **Chi AG** 1936–39, 1941–42; Bir 1942; **Chi AG** 1943–44; Ind/Cin 1944–45; Mem 1946; **Chi AG** 1949
"Double Duty's" younger brother, a fearsome clutch hitter, might be the Negro Leagues' greatest All-Star performer, starring in 11 midsummer classics. Perhaps the NAL's best-ever third baseman, he was considered lazy by some observers but had a penchant to play his hardest for the biggest crowds.

DONALDSON, JOHN Wesley; B2.20.1892; Glasgow MO; D4.14.1970; Chicago IL; BL/TL/6-0/185; d1913; Mil 1917; P, OF
[**All Nations** 1913–1917]; Ind ABC 1918; Bro RG 1918; Lin 1918; Det S 1919; **KC** 1920–24 1931 1934
The best black left-handed pitcher of the 1910s, Donaldson threw a baffling curve; when his arm went bad, he relied on control and smarts to star for the Kansas City Monarchs. When not pitching, Donaldson filled in capably in the lineup, and transferred full-time to the outfield when his arm finally died.

MENDEZ, JOSE (Baez) "Joe","The Black Diamond"; B3.19.1887; Cardenas, Mantanzas, Cuba; BR/TR/5-8/160; d1908; HF 2006; P, SS, 3b, 2b, OF, M
Bro RG 1908; Cub SW 1909–12; [All Nations 1912–17]; Chi AG 1918; Det S 1919; KC 1920–26
"The Black Diamond" made his name both in Cuba and later in Kansas City for a blazing fastball, a good curve, an unmatched ability to change speeds, and a smooth, rapid delivery now called "quick-pitching." Mendez' fastball was so powerful that he once accidentally killed a teammate in practice.

WINTERS, NIP James H. Jr. "Jessee","Nipper","Jim"; B4.29.1899; Washington DC; D12.12.1971; Hockessin DE; BL/TL/6-5/225; d1920; P, 1b, OF
Bal BS 1920; Bac 1921–22; **Hil** 1922–28; Hom 1928; Lin 1928–29; Bal BS 1929; New B 1931; Hil 1931; Bac 1931; Was Pi 1932; Bac 1932–33; Phi S 1933
Spending his entire career in the East, southpaw Winters threw a curveball that broke sharply (sometimes well out of the strike zone). A mighty carouser, Winters was devastating when on his game, and also hit well enough to occasionally play first base. He was very successful against major leaguers in exhibitions.

THOMAS, CLINT Clinton Cyrus "Hawk","Buckeye"; B11.25.1896; Greenup KY; D12.2.1990; Charleston WV; BR/TR/5-8/180; d1920; Mil 1918–19; CF, RF, 2b
Bro RG 1920; Col B 1921; Det S 1922; **Hil** 1923–28; Bac 1928–29; Lin 1930; Har S 1931; Ind ABC 1932; **NY BY** 1932–35; New E 1936; **NY BY** 1937–38
Regarded as a complete player, "Hawk" flagged down everything hit to him in the outfield and hit for average and power. Popular with fans and teammates, Thomas was nicknamed "The Black DiMaggio" for his balance of skills. He once homered off Fidel Castro in an exhibition game in Cuba.

HARRIS, VIC Elander Victor; B6.10.1905; Pensacola FL; D2.23.1978; San Fernando CA; BL/TR/5-10/168; d1923; Def 1943; LF, RF, CF, 1b
Cle TS 1923; Tol T 1923; Cle B 1924; Chi AG 1924–25; **Hom** 1925–31; Det W 1932; **Hom** 1932–33; Pit C 1934; **Hom** 1935–48; Bal EG 1949; Bir 1950
A lefty swinger who made solid contact and hit the ball all over the field, Harris played all three outfield positions with skill. Speedy and pugnacious, "Vicious Vic" ran the bases with abandon and never shied from a fight, but also was a steady and patient player-manager in his later years.

SCALES, GEORGE Walter "Tubby"; B8.16.1900; Talladega AL; D4.1976 Los Angeles CA; BR/TR/5-11/195; 2b, 3b, 1b, SS, OF, M
Pit K 1921; StL G 1921; StL S 1922; Lin 1923–25; Hom 1925–26; New S 1926; Lin 1926–29; Hom 1929–31; NY BY 1932–34; Hom 1935; NY BY 1936; Bal EG 1938; NY BY 1939–40; Phi S 1940; Bal EG 1940–44; NY BY 1945; Bal EG 1946–48
"Tubby" lacked range at second base, but knew the hitters and used a very strong arm to turn the double play. He hit fifth for the 1931 Homestead Grays, supplying power and average, and continued to hit well into his forties. A real character, Scales was pugnacious and a tough manager.

MONROE, BILL William; B1876; D3.16.1915; Chicago IL; BR/TR; d1896; 2b, 3b, SS, 1b
Chi U 1896–1900; Cub XG 1900; Phi G 1903–06; Bro RG 1907; [Qua G 1908]; Bro RG 1908–10; Chi AG 1911–13; Chi G 1913; Chi AG 1914
John McGraw said Monroe, whose career was only halted by death, was the greatest player ever. He could play any infield position with grace and style and had the skills to bat both leadoff and fourth. A handsome man, Monroe was the toast of black baseball audiences in Chicago and New York.

O'NEIL, BUCK John Jordan; "Nancy"; B11.13.1911; Carabelle FL; D10.6.2006 Kansas City MO; BR/TR/6-2/190; d1937; Mil 1943–45; 1b, M
Mem 1937; **KC** 1938–43 1946–55
Famous for longevity, humor, and grace, O'Neil was also a fine player, especially in Kansas City. A slick-fielding first baseman who hit for high averages, O'Neil punched the ball the opposite way, making him a natural hit-and-run man. O'Neil later became the first black major league scout and signed Ernie Banks and Lou Brock to contracts for the Chicago Cubs.

BANKHEAD, SAM Samuel Howard; B9.18.1905; Empire AL; D7.24.1976; Pittsburgh PA; BR/TR/5-8/175; d1830; b-Dan; b-Fred; b-Joe; b-Garnett; SS, CF, 2b, LF, RF, 3b
Bir 1929; Nas 1930; Bir 1931–32; Lou BC 1932; Nas 1932–34; KC 1934; Pit C 1935–36; [Dom 1937]; Bir 1938; Pit C 1938; Tol C 1939; **Hom** 1939; [Mex 1940–41]; **Hom** 1942–50; [Can 1951]
He had the range and arm to play both shortstop and center field, and would fill in wherever needed. The speedy Bankhead had some power but was more of a high-average hitter. While he starred in Cuba and against major-league players, Bankhead enjoyed his greatest fame in Pittsburgh.

DIXON, RAP Herbert Albert; B9.2.1902; Kingston GA; D7.20.1944; Detroit MI; BR/TR/6-2/185; d1922; RF, CF, LF, M
Har 1922–23; Was Po 1924; Har 1924–27; Bal BS 1928–30; Chi AG 1930–31; Bal BS 1931; Hil 1931; Pit C 1932; Was Pi 1932; Phi S 1933; Bal BS 1934; Pit C 1934; Bro E 1935; NY C 1935; Hom 1936; Pit C 1937
Famous for his disciplined batting approach, Dixon put the ball in play and racked up high averages and good power totals.; He had the arm to play right field and the range to excel in center, and did both. Injuries and illness curtailed his career, and Dixon died young.

COOPER, ANDY Andrew L. "Lefty"; B.4.4.1896; Waco TX; D6.3.1841; Waco TX; BR/TL/6-2/220; d1920; HF 2006; P, M
Det S 1920–27; **KC** 1928–30; **Det S** 1930; **KC** 1931–41
Using a solid repertoire, command, and smarts, Cooper remained an effective pitcher into his forties. He did all the things that make lefty pitchers helpful—he had a great pickoff move, changed speeds, and had a great screwball. Just prior to his premature death, Cooper was a successful manger for Kansas City.

JENKINS, FATS Clarence; B1.19.1898; New York NY; D12.6.1968; Philadelphia PA; BL/TL/5-7/180; d1920; OF, M
Lin 1920; Bac 1922; Har G 1923–27; Lin 1928; Hil 1928; Bac 1928–29; Bal BS 1930; Lin 1930; Har S 1931; Pit C 1932; NY BY 1932–34; Bro E 1935; NY BY 1936–38; Pit C 1938; Tol C 1939; Bro RG 1939–40; NY BY 1940; Phi S 1940
A solid corner outfielder and leadoff man with speed, bat control, and smarts at bat and on the bases, Jenkins was also a superb basketball player as well as a famed musician who sang and played piano. A hustling player, Jenkins spent most of his career in New York.

PETWAY, BRUCE "Buddy"; B1883; Nashville TN; D7.4.1941; Chicago IL; BB/TR/5-11/170; d1906; b-Howard; C, 1b, OF, M
Cub XG 1906; Phi G 1907–09; Chi L 1910; **Chi AG** 1911–18; Det S 1919–25
The best defensive catcher in the game during black baseball's early years, the surprisingly lean and athletic Petway kept opposing runners close to the base but was an excellent basestealer himself. His bat skills and speed made him that unusual specimen—a catcher who sometimes batted leadoff.

DUNCAN, FRANK B2.14.1901; Kansas City MO; D12.4.1973; Kansas City MO; BR/TR/6-0/175; d1920; s-Frank III; C, 1b, M
Chi G 1920–21; **KC** 1921–31; NY BY 1931; Pit C 1932; Hom 1932; **KC** 1932–34; NY C 1935–37; **KC** 1937; Chi AG 1938 1940; **KC** 1941–47
A superb handler of pitchers who caught Paige, Rogan, Donaldson, and others for Kansas City, Duncan also had a strong arm and agility behind the plate. He was slow and only a mediocre hitter, but the very tough—almost mean—Duncan later served as a patient and effective manager.

BROWN, LARRY "Iron Man"; B9.5.1905; Pratt City; AL; D4.7.1972; Memphis TN; BB/TR/5-8/180; d1919; C, M

Bir 1919; Ind ABC 1921–23; Pit K 1922; **Mem** 1923–25; Det S 1926; Chi AG 1927; **Mem** 1927–29; Chi AG 1929; Lin 1930; **Mem** 1931; Har S 1931; NY BY 1932; Chi AG 1932–35; Phi S 1936–38; **Mem** 1938–40; Chi AG 1940; **Mem** 1941–48

Good enough to play on several championship clubs despite only an average bat, Brown was a fine defensive catcher. Although Brown was a heavy drinker, he gained the nickname "Iron Man" and played into his forties. He was tough on umpires but played the game hard.

WARFIELD, FRANK Francis Xavier "The Weasel"; B1895; Indianapolis IN D7.24.1932; Pittsburgh PA; BR/TR/5-7/160; d1915; 2b, SS, 3b, OF, M

StL G 1914–15; Ind ABC 1915; StL G 1915–16; Bow ABC 1916; Ind ABC 1917–18; Day 1919; Det S 1919–21; KC 1921; Det S 1922; **Hil** 1923–28; **Bal BS** 1929–31; Was Pi 1932

A hustling middle infielder with fine leadoff skills and all the defensive tools (arm, range, hands, and an underhand "snap" throw), Warfield was a pariah with fellow players due to a; violent nature that led to arguments. He carried a knife and bit off part of Oliver Marcelle's nose in a fight.

LYONS, JIMMIE B11.6.1892; Chicago IL; D10.1963; Chicago IL; BL/TR/5-8/175; d1910; Mil 1918–19 LF, CF, RF, M

StL G 1910–11; Lin 1911; StL G 1912; Bro RG 1914; StL G 1915–16; Bow ABC 1916; Ind ABC 1916–17; StL G 1917; Chi G 1917; StL G 1919; Det S 1920; Bac 1920; **Chi AG** 1921–23; Was Po 1924; Cle B 1924; **Chi AG** 1924–25; Lou BC 1932

Lyons' skill set was much valued in the early 20th century—he was one of the fastest players in baseball history and could bunt his way on base almost at will. Lyons was a star at times, but lacked power and was not exceptional defensively, and suffered from injuries.

BROOKS, CHESTER "Irving","Beattie"; B Nassau, Bahamas; BR/TR; d1918; CF, RF

Bro RG 1918–33

Rube Foster discovered him pitching in the late teens, but Brooks spent most of his career as a center fielder. He had the arm to play right field and enough power to hit fourth, but played his entire career with Brooklyn, who rarely contended for a championship.

OMS, ALEJANDRO "El Caballero","Walla Walla","Papa"; B3.13.1895; Santa Clara, Cuba; D11.9.1946; BL/TL/5-9/190; d1917; CF, LF, RF

Cub SE 1917–1922–33; AC 1935

A showy player with a terrific power stroke, Oms was a key member of the Cuban Stars of the 1920s. He played a solid center field and could steal bases when needed. "El Caballero," who played for several championship clubs, was elected to the Cuban HOF.

ROBINSON, NEIL Cornelius Randall "Shadow"; B7.7.1908; Grand Rapids MI; D7.23.1983; Cincinnati OH; BR/TR/5–11/182; d1934; CF, LF, RF, SS, 3b

Hom 1934; Cin T 1936–37; **Mem** 1938–52

A perennial All-Star, the popular Robinson (nicknamed "Shadow") was one of the game's top outfielders due to his fearsome power. While he was only average defensively, struck out too often, and struggled with the bottle, Robinson made undeniable offensive contributions in the NAL.

KIMBRO, HENRY Allen "Kimmie","Jimbo"; B2.19.1912; Nashville TN; D1.31.2001; Philadelphia PA; BL/TR/5-8/175; d1937; CF, LF, M

Was EG 1937; **Bal EG** 1938–1940; NYBY 1941; **Bal EG** 1942–51

On the field, Kimbro was nearly flawless, playing a solid center field with good range and doing it all at bat. The offensive leader boards perennially boasted his name in several; categories. Perhaps he was not more celebrated due to an aloof and brooding nature that invited little intimacy.

BENSON, GENE Eugene "Spider"; B10.2.1913 Pittsburgh PA; D.4.6.1999; Philadelphia PA BL/TL/5-8/180; d1933; CF, LF

Was EG 1936; **Phi S** 1937; Pit C 1938; Hom 1938; **Phi S** 1938–41; New E 1942; **Phi S** 1942–48

An unusual player, Benson was a left-handed batter who hit lefties better than righties.; He used a slap approach but still generated good power. The Philly Star also was a fine; outfielder with excellent range who made "circus" catches. Later he was a winter-ball roommate and counselor to Jackie Robinson.

WHITE, CHANEY S "Reindeer","Liz"; B4.15.1894; Dallas TX; D2.1.1967; Philadelphia PA; BR/TL/5-10/195; d1919; OF

Hil 1919; Chi AG 1920; Hil 20–22; **Bac** 1923–24; Was Po 1924; Wil 1925; **Bac** 1925–28; Hil 1928; **Bac** 1929; Hom 1930; Hil 1930–32; Bal BS 1932; Phi S 1933–35; NY C 1936

White hit for high averages with moderate power. Fast and strong, he ran the bases with reckless abandon, which gave him the label of a "dirty" player. Off the field, he was well liked. Despite his speed and good hands, White was best in left field because of a weak arm.

CRUTCHFIELD, JIMMIE John William; B3.15.1910; Ardmore MO; D3.31.1993; Chicago IL; BL/TR/5-7/150; d1930; Mil 1943–44 CF, RF, LF

Bir 1930; Ind ABC 1931; **Pit C** 1931–33; Phi S 1933; **Pit C** 1934–36; New E 1937–38; Tol C 1939; Ind C 1940; Chi AG 1941–42; Cle Bu 1944; Chi AG 1944–45

Small in size but big in heart, Crutchfield was a team man all the way who played excellent "little ball." A superb outfielder, he was popular both for his defensive ability and entertaining stunts. While not exactly a batting threat, he did hit for average and made other contributions.

GARDNER, JELLY Floyd; B9.27.1895; Russellville AK; D3.1.1977; Chicago IL; BL/TR/5-7/160; d1919; RF, CF, LF, 1b

Det S 1919; **Chi AG** 1920–1930; Lin G 1927; Hom 1928; Det S 1931; Hom 1932; **Chi AG** 1933

An excellent outfielder blessed with speed, bunting skills, and a line-drive bat, Gardner also worked pitchers for walks, which made him a better leadoff man than some of his; contemporaries. Gardner did have trouble with breaking pitches, and was a carouser with a combative nature.

DISMUKES, DIZZY William; B3.15.1890; Birmingham AL; D6.30.1961; Campbell OH; BR/TR/6-0/180; d1910 Mil 1917–18; P, M

StL G 1912; Phi G 1913; Bro RG 1913–14; Lin S 1914; Ind ABC 1915–16; Chi AG 1916; Ind ABC 1917–18; Day 1918–19; Ind ABC 1920–21; Pit K 1921–23; Ind ABC 1923–24; Bir 1924; Mem 1925; StL S 1926–29; Chi AG 1930; Det W 1932; Col BB 1933–34; Chi AG 1935; StL S 1936–37; Bir 1938; Atl 1939; Hom 1940; KC 1941–42; Mem 1942; KC 1943–51

This college-educated, submarining hurler, who pitched with smarts and breaking stuff, is said to have tutored Carl Mays. He pitched for more than two decades and later served as a manager, Negro League club and league executive, and even as a major league scout.

TRENT, TED Theodore "Highpockets","Stringbean","Big Florida"; B12.17.1903; Jacksonville FL; D1.10.1944; Chicago IL; BR/TR/6-3/185; d1927; P

StL S 1927–31; Was Pi 1932; Det W 1932 H om 1932; Bal BS 1932; KC 1932; NY BY 1933–34; Chi AG 1934–35; **Chi AG** 1936–39

The tall righty had his share of nicknames as well as strikeout stuff—a fastball, a variety of baffling curves, and a sharp slider. A great big-game pitcher, Trent was one of the best; pitchers in black baseball, but his career and life were shortened by a weak immune system brought about by the bottle.

SHIVELY, GEORGE Anner "Rabbit" B1893; Lebanon KY; D6.7.1962; Bloomington; IN; BL/TR; d1910; OF

Ind ABC 1914–15; Bow ABC 1916; **Ind ABC** 1916–18; Bac 1919–20; **Ind ABC** 1920–21; Bac 1921–22; **Ind ABC** 1923; Bro RG 1924; Was Po 1924; Bac 1924–25

"The Rabbit" ran the bases at will and with great success. While Shively could run down fly balls, bunt for hits, and even show power on occasion, he was never one of the game's biggest stars in a time where these skills were almost a requirement to play.

MATHIS, VERDELL "Lefty"; B11.18.1914; Crawfordsville AK; D10.30.1998; Memphis TN; BL/TL/5-11/150; d1940 P, OF, 1b

Mem 1940–50; Phi S 1943

The NAL's best lefty during the 1940s, Mathis' signature pitch was his curve, but he also threw hard and boasted a screwball and an excellent pickoff move. A big workload took its toll, however—after World War II he underwent elbow surgery to remove bone chips and never again excelled.

BARNHILL, DAVE David "Impo","Skinny"; B10.30.1914; Greenville NC; D1.8.1983; Miami FL; BB/TR/5-7/145; d1937; P

Zul 1937; Eth 1937–40; **NY C** 1941–49; [OB minors 1949–53]

He played four years with the Ethiopian Clowns, who were as much a comedy club as a competitive team, but Barnhill had a serious fastball. When he went to New York in 1941, "Skinny" immediately became a dominating strikeout pitcher. Barnhill also could help at bat and on the bases.

BREWER, CHET Chester Arthur; B1.14.1907; Leavenworth KS; D3.26.1990; Whittier CA; BB/TR/6-4/187; d1925; P

KC 1925–31; Was Pi 1932; **KC** 1932–35; [Bismarck 1935–36]; NY C 1936; **KC** 1937; [Dom 1937]; [Mex 1938–39]; **KC** 1940–41; Phi S 1941; Cle Bu 1942–43; [Mex 1944]; Chi AG 1946; Cle Bu 1946–48; [OB minors 1952]

While Brewer was a finesse pitcher, using a screwball, slider, curve, or emery ball to get hitters out, he also would throw fastballs inside. He played all around the world, including in Asia, and was the first black American to play in Mexico. Brewer lived a full and fascinating life.

WICKWARE, FRANK "Smokey","Rawhide","The Red Ant","Smiley"; B3.8.1888; Coffeeville KS; D11.2.1967; Schenectady NY; BR/TR; d1910; Mil 1918–19; P

Chi L 1909–10; Chi AG 1911–12; Bro RG 1912–13; Moh 1913–14; Lou WS 1914; Bro RG 1914; Chi AG 1914–16; Ind ABC 1916; Jew ABC 1917; Chi AG 1917–18; Det S 1919; Lin 1920; Chi AG 1920–21; [Can 1921]; Lin 1925

A fastballer with excellent mechanics and command, Wickware was, as one of the top pitchers of the teens, a tremendous gate attraction who—as was the practice—often jumped; contracts to get more money. Unfortunately, he was also a drinker, and his habits shortened his brilliant career.

TIANT, LUIS Eleuterio Sr. "Lefty","Sir","Skinny"; B8.27.1906; Havana, Cuba; D12.10.1976; Milton MA; BL/TL/5-11/175; d1930; s-Luis; P

Cub SW 1930–32; Cub HD 1934; NY C 1935–36 1939–40 1943 1945–47

Using a herky-jerky motion, as his son would decades later, the elder Tiant had control of three power pitches (fastball, curve, slider) but his best pitch was a screwball.; He worked with a junkballer's attitude and his mix of skills and approach served him well, especially in big games.

BROWN, BARNEY [Brownez] "Brinquitos"; B10.23.1908; Hartsville SC; D10.1.1985; Philadelphia PA; BL/TL/5-9/165; d1931; Mil 1943; P, OF

Cub HD 1931–32; NY BY 1936–37; **Phi S** 1937; NY BY 1937–39; [Mex 1939–41]; **Phi S** 1942–44; [Mex 1945]; **Phi S** 1945–49; [Mex 1950–52]; [OB minors 1952–53]

With good command and a screwball, Brown starred on the East Coast in the 30s and 40s, appearing in several All-Star contests. He also was a big winner in Puerto Rican winter ball. Brown was nearly as good at the plate as on the mound despite a small frame.

PARNELL, ROY "Red"; B9.17.1905; Austin TX; D6.1.1969; Terrell TX; BR/TR/5-10/180; d1926; LF, RF, CF, 1b, P, M

Bir 1926–28; Mon M 1932; Nas 1934; Col EG 1935; **Phi S** 1936–43; [Dom 1937]; NY BY 1937; Pit C 1946; Hou 1950

Unlike many Negro League stars, Parnell did not run particularly well or have a strong throwing arm. What he did was hit, both for average and power, and catch everything he reached in the outfield. Another drinking man, he batted #2 in the lineup for most of his long career.

CARR, GEORGE Henry "Tank" B1895; California; D1.14.1948; Los Angeles CA; BB/TR/6-2/230; d1917; 1b, 3b, OF, 2b, C
KC 1920–22; **Hil** 1923–28; Lin 1928; **Bac** 1928–29 1933; Phi S 1933–34
A very productive hitter for power and high average in the 20s, Carr had some speed but was used almost exclusively at first base. He had a high arc, but Carr's career declined quickly because of a serious drinking problem and some resulting disciplinary issues.

STRONG, TED T.R.; B1.2.1914; South Bend IL; D3.1.1978; Chicago IL; BB/TR/6-6/210; d1937; Mil 1943–45; RF, 1b, LF, SS, CF, 3b
Ind A 1937; Ind ABC 1938; **KC** 1937–39; [Mex 1940]; KC 1941–42 1946–47; Ind C 1948; [OB minors 1950]; Chi AG 1951
As his name suggests, Strong was a power hitter who disdained "little ball." A good right fielder with defensive tools, he won homer and RBI crowns, and hit for average, despite a; free-swinging approach. Strong also played for the original Globetrotters basketball team. Drinking and womanizing shortened his career.

SAMPSON, TOMMY Thomas "Toots"; B8.31.1912; Calhoun AL; BR/TR/6-1/180; d1940; 2b, 1b, OF, M
Bir 1940–47; Chi AG 1948; NY C 1949
"Toots" made four consecutive All-Star appearances at second base. Despite losing his right index finger in a coal mining accident, Sampson played strong defense and had fine bat control. He hit for average and stole bases, but a broken leg suffered in a 1944 car crash shortened his career.

EASTERLING, HOWARD B11.26.1911; Mount Olive MS; D9.6.1993; Collins MS; BB/TR/5-10,175; d1936; Mil 1944–45; 3b, 2b, SS, OF
Cin T 1936–37; Chi AG 1938; Hom 1940–43 1946–47; NY C 1949; [Mex 1951–1952 1954]
Voted an All-Star both as a third baseman and shortstop, Easterling was a five-tool player who batted from both sides. Since he only started his organized black baseball career at 25, and he missed two years due to World War II, Easterling's star does not shine as bright as it might have.

EARLE, FRANK Charles [Frank] [Earl] [Charles Babcock] [Frank Peles]; BR/TR; d1906; LF, RF, CF, P, M
Bro RG 1909–14; StL G 1915; Lin 1915; Bro RG 1916–17; GCT 1918–19; Bac 1919; Pen 1919
The respected outfielder could run and hit, and was also the best pitcher on the 1909 championship Royal Giants club. An excellent table-setter, he spent most of his career in the East. Like many stars of his era, he is plagued by a lack of documentation of his greatness.

JOHNSON, HEAVY Oscar; B11.2.1896; Atchison KS; D1.1964; Cleveland OH; BR/TR/6-0/250; d1922; OF, C, 2b
KC 1922–24; Bal BS 1925–26; Har 1927; Cle T 1928; Mem 1928–33
One of the heaviest players of his time, Johnson was a premier power producer who nonetheless played the outfield (though with little speed or grace) for quality teams. The oft-told stories of just-awoken Negro League players homering with fungo bats seems somehow more believable in Johnson's case.

Long and Distinguished Careers

GRANT, LEROY BR/TR/6-4/215; d1911; Mil1918–19; 1b
Chi AG 1911; Lin 1912–15; Moh 1913; **Chi AG** 1916–25; Ind ABC 1923; Cle B 1924
The burly, plodding first sacker was slow and hit low in the order, but connected for big power, ran the bases intelligently, and usually played excellent defense. A key part of Rube Foster's American Giants dynasty, Grant also played with the New York Lincoln Giants early in his career.

CANNADY, REV Walter; B3.6.1904; Lake City FL; D12.3.1981; Ft. Myers FL; BR/TR/6-0/180; d1921; 2b, 3b, SS, OF, 1b, P, M
Col B 1921; Cle TS 1922; Hom 1923–24; Har 1925–27; Lin 1926–28; Hil 1928; Hom 1929; Lin 1930; Hil 1931; Pit C 1932; NYBY 1933–35; Pit C 1936; NYBY 1936–39; Bro RG 1940; Chi AG 1942; Ind/Cin 1943–44; Hom 1944; NY C 1945
A good hitter who excelled at pounding curve balls, Cannady had the defensive skills to man any infield spot, but played mostly at second base. He was mean, angry, and moody, not a favorite of other players, and never stayed in one place for very long.

SEAY, DICK Richard William; B11.30.1904; West New York NY; D4.6.1981; Jersey City NJ; BR/TR/5-8/156; d1925; Mil 1943–45; 2b, SS, 3b
Bro RG 1925; New S 1926; Bal BS 1926; Bro RG 1927–31; New B 1931; Bal BS 1932–33; Phi S 1933–36; Pit C 1935–36; NYBY 1936; New E 1937–40; NY BY 1941–42 1946–47
The slightly-built Seay, one of black baseball's all-time best defensive second basemen, played a key role for several championship teams. While a relatively weak hitter, Seay had the ability to bunt and hit-and-run, and his glove work was good enough to make up for his bat.

MALARCHER, DAVE David Julius "Gentleman Dave","Cap","Preacher"; B10.18.1894; Whitehall LA; D5.11.1982; Chicago IL; BB/TR/5-7/148; d1916; Mil 1918–19; 3b,2b,SS,RF,C,P,M
Ind ABC 1916–18; Det S 1919; **Chi AG** 1920–28; Chi AG 1931–35
Malarcher, an outstanding defensive third baseman, did everything well enough to help teams win but was not a world-class hitter. Most of his offensive value came from bunting, place-hitting, and speed. A clean-living man, Malarcher was an intelligent player who later managed.

BELL, WILLIAM Sr.; B8.31.1897; Lavaca County TX; D3.16.1969; El Campo TX; BR/TR/5-11/185; d1923; s-William Jr.; P, OF, M
KC 1923–30; Har S 1931; Det W 1932; Hom 1932; Pit C 1932–35; New D 1935; New E 1936–37 1948
A winning pitcher with good command of a fastball, curve, and change, Bell made a positive impact on several pennant races, especially in Kansas City. Bell hit well enough to play the outfield, taught younger pitchers, and always took the ball.; After his playing career, he was a coach and manager.

MCNAIR, HURLEY Alen "Mac","Bugger"; B10.28.1888; Marshall TX; D12.2.1948; Kansas City MO; BB/TR/5-6/150; d1911; RF, LF, CF, P, U
Chi G 1911–12; Chi UG 1914; Chi AG 1915–16; Chi UG 1916; [All Nations 1917]; Det S 1919; **KC** 1920–27; Det S 1928; KC 1934; Cin T 1937
A star outfielder for Kansas City, McNair was a patient hitter with power who could run and field. While he was haunted by a reputation for self-centeredness, McNair taught young players, including Willie Wells, then later umpired in the NAL—carrying a knife to emphasize his point.

HOLLAND, BILL Elvis William; B2.2.1901; Indianapolis IN; D New York NY; BB/TR/5-9/180; d1920; P, M
Det S 1920–22; Chi AG 1921; Lin 1923–24; Bro RG 1925–27; Hil 1927; Lin 1927–30; Har S 1931; **NY BY** 1932–41; Phi S 1941
After an impressive first three years with Detroit, power pitcher Holland's career nosedived until his 1929 comeback. In 1930, he went 29-2 with the Lincoln Giants in their last season, becoming the first black player to pitch in Yankee Stadium and then the ace of Black Yankees staff in the 1930s.

ROGERS, NAT [Rodgers] William Nathaniel; B6.7.1893; Spartanburg SC; D12.1981 Memphis TN; BL/TR/5-11/160; d1923; RF, LF, 1b
Bro RG 1923; Phi G 1924; Har 1924–25; **Mem** 1924–30; Chi AG 1927–28; Bir 1930; KC 1931; Chi AG 1931–34; Bro E 1935; Chi AG 1944
Hard-nosed and slightly built, Rogers was a powerful line-drive hitter as well as a good baserunner and bunter. His 31-game hitting streak propelled Chicago to a 1927 World Series victory; he also hit cleanup in 1932–33 for the pennant-winning American Giants. Defensively, Rogers was adequate with a plus arm.

DAVIS, STEEL ARM Walter C.; B1902.Madison WI; D1935; Chicago IL; BL/TL/6-1/175; d1923; OF, 1b
Det S 1923; **Chi AG** 1924–30; Chi AG 1931–35; Nas 1934; Bro E 1935
A hot-tempered, hard-playing, high-average hitter with power, Davis' nickname derived from his career start as a pitcher. Because of his ability at the plate, however, he ended up as an All-Star outfielder and a middle-of-the-order hitter for the powerful American Giants. Davis was shot to death in a barroom brawl.

FRANCIS, BILL William "Billy","Brodie","Ducky"; BR/TR/5-5/140; d1904; 3b, SS, M
Phi G 1904–1910; Lin 1911–13; Moh 1913; Chi AG 1914–1919; Hil 1920–22; Bac 1923; Cle B 1924; Wil 1925; Chi AG 1925; Chi G 1925
Called one of the best black ballplayers of his era by legendary umpire Jocko Conlan, the stocky but speedy third sacker played on many great early teams. Soft hands and quick reflexes enabled him to play shallow at third; offensively he drew plenty of walks, and hit .396 in 1914.

DUNCAN, FRANK "Pete","Dunk"; BL/TR; d1909; LF, RF, CF, M
Phi G 1909; Chi L 1910; **Chi** AG 1911–18; Det S 1919; Chi G 1920; Tol T 1923; Mil 1923; Cle E 1926; Cle H 1927; Cle T 1928
Not to be confused with the catcher with the same name, he was an exceptional outfielder with Rube Foster's American Giants and a prototypical leadoff hitter, who dazzled opponents with his bunting, speed and basestealing ability. He hit a career-best .389 in 1910, and managed after his playing days finished.

BENJAMIN, JERRY Charles [Christopher]; B11.9.1909; Montgomery AL; D11.23.1974; Detroit MI; BB/TR/5-9/165; d1932; CF
Mem 1932; Det S 1933; Bir 1934; Hom 1935–48; New E 1939; Tol C 1939; NY C 1948
An integral part of the Homestead Grays dynasty, Benjamin and Cool Papa Bell formed a fearsome pair of basestealers. A three-time East-West All-Star, he wowed home crowds with a .485 average (.392 overall) in 1943. Benjamin played for Toledo in 1939 using an alias in protest after being dealt to Newark.

Short but Brilliant Careers

CAMPANELLA, ROY "Campy"; B11.19.1921; Philadelphia PA; D6.26.1921; Woodland Hills CA; BR/TR/5-9.5/195; d1937; HF1969; ML 1948–1957; C, 3b, OF
Bal EG 1937–42; [Mex 1943]; **Bal EG** 1944–45; [OB minors 1946–48]; [ML 1948–57]
A baseball prodigy who began his pro career at 15, playing only on the weekends, Campanella had a tryout with the Phillies scheduled as a teenager, until the club discovered his race. A career .353 hitter, most observers thought he should have jumped straight from black ball to the big leagues.

BROWN, DAVE David "Dave","Lefty"; B1896; San Marcos TX; D. Denver CO; BL/TL/5-10/170; d1918; P
Chi AG 1918–22; Lin 1923–25
A dazzling pitcher in his prime, Brown used outstanding control of his fastball, curve and drop to go 29-6 combined in 1920–22. His career ended abruptly when he killed a man and fled New York to avoid arrest. Rumors had him playing as "Lefty Wilson" in the 1930s for Midwestern semipro teams.

SMITH, CHINO Charles "Charlie"; B.1903; Greenwood SC; D.1.16.1932; BL/TR/5-6/168; d1925; OF, 2b
Bro RG 1925–28; Lin 1929–30; Bro RG 1931
A line-drive power hitter, Smith was one of the best sluggers during his time. A lifetime .423 batter, Smith's top mark was .468 in 1931; he also led the ANL in batting and home runs in that league's only season. He died suddenly at age 29 after contracting yellow fever

MOORE, DOBIE Walter "Freckles","Scoops"; B.2.27.1890; Rome GA; D.4.1.1963; Detroit MI; BR/TR/5-11/230; d1920; SS, OF
KC 1920–26
Recommended to Kansas City by Casey Stengel, Moore was outstanding at the plate and in the field. Offensively, he hit well over .300 after his first two seasons. As a shortstop, he displayed outstanding range and a powerful, accurate arm. A bullet wound broke two leg bones, ending his career.

JONES, SLIM Stuart; B.5.6.1913; Baltimore MD; D.12.1938; Baltimore MD; BL/TL/6-6/185; d1932; P
Bal BS 1932–33; Phi S 1934–38
A towering presence on the mound, the fireballing Jones was an electrifying hurler. He was said to throw as hard as Lefty Grove, and dueled often with Satchel Paige, including a 10-inning dogfight in 1934, often considered the best Negro League game ever, stopped by darkness in a 1-1 tie.

WILSON, ARTIE Arthur Lee "Snoop"; B10.28.1916; Springville AL; BL/TR/5-10/160; d1944 ML 1951; SS
Bir 1944–48; [OB minors 1949–57 1962]
One of his league's top stolen base threats, Wilson used his opposite field approach at the plate to capture two NAL batting titles and two other second place finishes. He received but 22 at-bats in the major leagues, despite hitting.312 during the nine years he played in the Pacific Coast League.

Black Baseball/Negro League Season Synopses, 1910–1950

1910 Rube Foster's Chicago Leland Giants, featuring John Henry Lloyd, Pete Hill, Grant "Home Run" Johnson, and Bruce Petway, were black baseball's first "super team." Following their regular season, they traveled to Cuba where they played the best Cuban teams. When the touring Detroit Tigers (with Ty Cobb and Sam Crawford) and Philadelphia Athletics (with Eddie Plank and Chief Bender) arrived, the Cuban teams added Lloyd, Hill, Johnson, and Petway to their rosters to play against the white major leaguers.

1911 Rube Foster changed his team's name to the Chicago American Giants and continued their dominance in the West for the remainder of the decade. Jess McMahon, a white entrepreneur, formed the New York Lincoln Giants, and after enticing John Henry Lloyd to join his team, the Lincolns became the top club in the East.

1912 With John Henry Lloyd at the helm and joined in the lineup by slugger Louis Santop, speedster Spot Poles, and pitching greats Cyclone Joe Williams and Cannonball Dick Redding, the Lincoln Giants were again the top team in the East. Foster's American Giants continued as the top team in the West.

1913 The Chicago American Giants and the New York Lincoln Giants, who enjoyed their best season ever, remained the best teams in their regions. Cyclone Joe Williams defeated Grover Cleveland Alexander and the Philadelphia Phillies in a postseason exhibition game.

1914 Rube Foster lured John Henry Lloyd back to Chicago, and the American Giants fielded one of their strongest teams. In Lloyd's absence, the Brooklyn Royal Giants wrested the Eastern title from the Lincoln Giants.

1915 Parity was beginning to manifest itself in both the East and West. C. I. Taylor's Indianapolis ABCs waged a heated battle against Foster's American Giants for the Western title, while Jess McMahon left the Lincoln Giants to form a new franchise, the New York Lincoln Stars, and challenged his old team.

1916 Taylor's Indianapolis ABCs succeeded in their battle against Foster's American Giants to take the Western title, while the New York Lincoln Stars took the Eastern title.

1917 John Henry Lloyd returned to the Chicago American Giants and the Western championship returned with him. In the East the Lincoln Giants and Brooklyn Royal Giants were the top teams.

1918 John Henry Lloyd jumped back east again, this time to Nat Strong's Brooklyn Royal Giants. This gave the East three competitive teams, along with the Lincoln Giants and Hilldale, a new entry into the Eastern scene. The Chicago American Giants remained the top club in the West.

1919 Rube Foster's Chicago American Giants were challenged by the Detroit Stars under Foster's former star Pete Hill, who took the Stars helm as a player-manager. There was no dominant team in the East, with the Lincoln Giants, Bacharach Giants, and Hilldale all contending on relatively even terms.

1920 Rube Foster founded the first black league, the Negro National League, comprised of eight Midwestern teams. He also served as league president and, recognizing the need for a measure of parity, oversaw the transfer of players from stronger teams to weaker franchises. Despite losing players from his own team in this action, Foster's Chicago American Giants won the NNL's inaugural pennant to continue their dominance from the previous decade of independent blackball. The Detroit Stars and Kansas City Monarchs proved to be the other strong franchises.

1921 The NNL began the season with seven of the original teams and one replacement franchise. Rube Foster's Chicago American Giants, with what was called a "race horse" style of play, nosed out the Kansas City Monarchs to repeat as champions. Key players were ace left-hander Dave Brown and Cristobal Torriente, who provided the power. Envisioning future eastward expansion, Foster played postseason series against two top eastern teams, Hilldale and the Bacharach Giants.

1922 Following the death of Indianapolis ABCs owner-manager C. I. Taylor, his brother Ben Taylor assumed the role of player-manager. Behind the hitting of Oscar Charleston, the team challenged the Chicago American Giants, who captured their third straight NNL title. Chicago played a September series against the Bacharach Giants, a top eastern team, with the final game going 20 innings before Chicago eked out a 1-0 victory. Harold Treadwell went the entire distance in taking the loss, while Dave Brown pitched the last 14 innings to get the win.

1923 The big story of the year was the formation of the Eastern Colored League by Hilldale owner Ed Bolden, whose team won the inaugural pennant. Many NNL players jumped to eastern teams, including American Giants ace Dave Brown. His defection contributed to the Kansas City Monarchs' ending Chicago's skein of NNL titles. The nucleus of the NNL remained solid, though the raids on its teams created a war between the leagues that precluded a true Negro World Series being played.

1924 The ECL and NNL pennant races produced the same two winners as the previous season, but this year Hilldale and the Kansas City Monarchs faced each other in the first Negro World Series. The best five-of-nine series included a tie to make a total of ten games played in four different cities before the Monarchs emerged victorious. In the final game, Monarchs manager Jose Mendez, long past his prime as a player, fashioned a masterful three-hit shutout to seal the historic victory. His gem nullified the efforts of Nip Winters, who had posted three wins to get Hilldale to the final game.

1925 Hilldale won the ECL pennant, finishing ahead of a strong Harrisburg team. For the first time, the NNL featured a split-season format, with the winners of each half meeting in a playoff for the pennant. The Kansas City Monarchs defeated the St. Louis Stars in the first NNL League Championship Series. For both champions, it was their third consecutive pennant and it set up a repeat of the inaugural Negro World Series. Rogan, who had won three games in the LCS, injured his knee and missed the Series, enabling Hilldale to win the rematch.

1926 Rube Foster became mentally incapacitated, so his protege Dave Malarcher took the helm to direct the Chicago American Giants to victory over the Kansas City Monarchs in the NNL's LCS. In a dramatic finish, needing wins in both ends of a doubleheader, Willie Foster pitched dual shutouts to beat Bullet Rogan twice and take the pennant. Meanwhile, player-manager Dick Lundy guided the Bacharach Giants to the ECL pennant, and the ensuing Negro World Series produced a historic event when the Bacharachs' Red Grier hurled the first Series no-hitter. Still, eleven games were required before a winner was determined. Foster again rose to the occasion with two wins, including a 1-0 victory in the final game.

1927 The Chicago American Giants swept the Birmingham Black Barons in four straight games to win the NNL's championship series. Birmingham rookie Satchel Paige pitched in two games without a decision. For the first time, the ECL also played a split-season schedule, but the Bacharachs won both halves to avoid a playoff. Chicago prevailed again in the Negro World Series rematch, as Willie Foster won twice, including in the final game. His one loss was also notable, as it came in a second World Series no-hitter. Luther Farrell's historic no-hit performance was less than masterful, as he was clinging to a 3-2 lead when darkness ended the game in the 7th inning.

1928 The St. Louis Stars battled the Chicago American Giants in the NNL's championship series, as Willie Wells' pair of homers in the final game of the best-of-nine series gave the Stars a hard-fought victory. There was no Negro World Series due to the demise of the ECL, whose decline had accelerated after Ed Bolden's nervous breakdown. After starting with a shaky five-team alignment, the ECL disbanded early in the season, although some teams continued to play as independent clubs.

1929 Owner Cum Posey's Homestead Grays, long an outstanding independent team that had eschewed league play, joined five teams from the nucleus of the ECL to form the American Negro League. However, the replacement eastern league would last only one season. The ANL and the established NNL both employed a split-season format; in each loop, strong teams won both halves. The Kansas City Monarchs were NNL champions, while the Baltimore Black Sox were ANL champions. No interleague postseason series was played, and there would be no more Negro World Series until 1942.

1930 The St. Louis Stars edged the Detroit Stars in seven games to win the NNL's LCS. With no league in the east, the Homestead Grays beat the New York Lincoln Giants in a ten-game challenge series for the Eastern Championship. In one of these games, Grays rookie Josh Gibson smashed a homer that almost went out of Yankee Stadium. The Grays played a night game under the portable lighting system of pioneering Kansas City Monarchs owner J. L. Wilkinson. The game featured a 12-inning, 1-0, duel between the Monarchs' Chet Brewer and the Grays' Smokey Joe Williams. Brewer allowed four hits and fanned 19, while Williams yielded only one hit and struck out 25 in taking the win. In December, legendary owner, promoter, and future Hall of Famer Rube Foster died in an asylum.

1931 The St. Louis Stars repeated as champions in the NNL's final season by taking both halves of the split season, as the NNL fell victim to the Great Depression after struggling for years. The Homestead Grays and Hilldale were the top eastern teams. The powerful 1931 Grays—featuring Hall of Fame sluggers Josh Gibson and Oscar Charleston, Hall of Fame pitchers Willie Foster and Smokey Joe Williams, as well as other greats like Jud "Boojum" Wilson and "Double Duty" Radcliffe—are considered to be one of black baseball's all-time greatest teams. With Foster winning three games, the Grays defeated

THE NEGRO LEAGUES

the Kansas City Monarchs in what was falsely hyped as a championship series. Slugging outfielder Chino Smith's brief but brilliant career ended in the spring when he died of yellow fever at age 31.

1932 The 1932 season was one of depression-era chaos. Cum Posey's newly formed East-West League dissolved in midseason, with the Baltimore Black Sox in first place. Only the Negro Southern League, which had strengthened its rosters by adding players from the defunct NNL as well as assimilated select surviving franchises, completed the season. A longtime Negro minor league circuit, the NSL is considered to have been of big-league caliber for that one season. Willie Foster won the final two games as the Chicago American Giants edged the Nashville Elite Giants to win the NSL's seven-game League Championship Series.

1933 Pittsburgh Crawfords owner Gus Greenlee took two actions that gave impetus to black baseball's revival. First, he organized a new Negro National League and, although the first season was surrounded by controversy, he managed to salvage a viable league. The Chicago American Giants won the first half title. However, the second half schedule was not completed and discord intensified when Greenlee, who also served as league president, awarded his own team the championship. By contrast, Greenlee's promotion of the first East-West All-Star game proved an instant success, as Willie Foster pitched a complete game to give the West a victory in the inaugural contest. The annual Classic quickly became the most popular and prosperous black sporting event in the country.

1934 There were three strong teams in the NNL and, although the Pittsburgh Crawfords may have been the best, they were the team left out of the playoffs. The Philadelphia Stars edged the Chicago American Giants, four games to three, in the LCS, with ace left-hander Slim Jones pitching a 2-0 shutout in the final game. Jones and Satchel Paige were the two best pitchers in the league, and a highly publicized showdown between the pair at Yankee Stadium was ended by darkness after ten innings in a 1-1 deadlock—a game considered to be the greatest game ever played in Negro League history. At the prestigious annual semi-pro tournament sponsored by the *Denver Post*, an integrated House of David team led by Satchel Paige took the championship, besting the Kansas City Monarchs—the first all-black team to ever be allowed to compete in the tourney.

1935 The 1935 Pittsburgh Crawfords roster included no less than five future Hall of Famers (Satchel Paige, Josh Gibson, Oscar Charleston, Cool Papa Bell, and Judy Johnson) and are generally regarded as the greatest black team of all-time. Paige jumped the team to play with a semi-pro team in Bismarck, North Dakota, but Leroy Matlock filled the departed superstar pitcher's role and finished with a 17-0 mark. The Crawfords defeated the New York Cubans in a seven-game LCS by winning each of the last three games by one run. The 1935 East-West Classic produced the most exciting All-Star game ever, as the winner was not decided until the bottom of the 12th inning, when Mule Suttles smashed a three-run homer off Martin Dihigo to give the West an 11-8 victory.

1936 When the Chicago American Giants dropped out of the league and Tom Wilson moved his Elite Giants to Washington, the NNL became an entirely eastern league. The move must have agreed with the Elites, as they won the first half title, while the Pittsburgh Crawfords won the second half. The pennant race was interrupted when the NNL took an all-star team to the *Denver Post* Tournament, where their domination of the white opposition generated much greater awareness and recognition for the skill levels of black ballplayers. Hall of Famer Buck Leonard later said it was the best team he ever played on.

1937 The Negro American League was founded with teams from the Midwest and South. The Kansas City Monarchs defeated the Chicago American Giants in a championship series to win the first NAL pennant. In the east, Satchel Paige led a defection from the Crawfords to the Dominican Republic, which decimated Greenlee's team. NNL officials responded by banning the jumpers, except for Josh Gibson, who had received owner Cum Posey's permission. When he returned, Gibson teamed with Buck Leonard to power the Homestead Grays to their first of nine consecutive NNL pennants. Paige also returned after pitching Ciudad Trujillo to the championship, thumbing his nose at the Negro Leagues establishment and leading a barnstorming All-Star team of top black talent to the 1937 *Denver Post* tournament championship.

1938 The *New York Daily News* and the *Pittsburgh Courier*, a black newspaper, boldly published articles saying that the Giants and Pirates, respectively, would be guaranteed to win the NL pennant if they would sign selected star black players. Three Homestead Grays (Josh Gibson, Buck Leonard, and ace right-handed pitcher Ray Brown, who helped the Grays win another NNL pennant) were included on both lists. Southern teams prevailed in the NAL, as the Memphis Red Sox and the Atlanta Black Crackers won the two halves of the split season. They were recognized as co-champions when the LCS was cancelled after two games because of friction between the rival team officials.

1939 The Homestead Grays finished first in the NNL pennant race and, since there was no playoff, a postseason elimination tournament was held with the top four teams. The Grays beat the Philadelphia Stars and the Baltimore Elite Giants beat the Newark Eagles to advance to the final round, where the Elites upset the Grays to win the tournament trophy. In the NAL, the Kansas City Monarchs edged the St. Louis Stars in the LCS to begin a streak of four straight pennants.

1940 Mexican League officials lured many Negro League stars south of the border. Among the defectors were Josh Gibson, Ray Dandridge, Willie Wells, Leon Day, Cool Papa Bell, and Bill Wright. The loss of this top talent weakened the leagues considerably. In the absence of Gibson, Buck Leonard's bat and Ray Brown's pitching carried the Homestead Grays to a first place finish in the NNL pennant race. In the NAL, the Kansas City Monarchs edged the St. Louis Stars in the LCS to repeat as champions.

1941 Both Negro leagues were still suffering from talent depletion from the loss of so many players to Mexico. Monte Irvin had an outstanding year and was being touted by NNL owners as the player to break the color barrier in what was then arrogantly called "Organized Baseball." The Homestead Grays and the Kansas City Monarchs repeated as champions in their respective leagues. The Grays defeated the New York Cuban Stars in the split-season NNL's LCS, while the superlative pitching combination of Satchel Paige and Hilton Smith pitched the Monarchs to the NAL championship without a playoff.

1942 The onset of World War II and local draft boards contributed to a return of many players from Mexico. Josh Gibson's return reunited the "Thunder Twins," as he and Leonard were dubbed by the press. The Grays and Monarchs again won their league championships to establish themselves as the two dominant dynasties in the Negro Leagues. Finally, after a 15-year hiatus, there would be another Negro World Series. In the classic match-up of pitching versus power, the Monarchs swept the Series with Satchel Paige getting three wins and Hilton Smith one. Leon Day, the star of the East-West game, beat Satchel as a "ringer" in the Series, but the win was not allowed.

1943 World War II sent many African-American players into military service and the quality of the leagues suffered accordingly. The Kansas City Monarchs suffered more adversely than some teams, as their streak of four straight pennants was broken essentially by the draft. The Birmingham Black Barons defeated the Chicago American Giants in the LCS to win the NAL pennant. The Homestead Grays were less affected by the draft and fared better, winning the NNL's pennant and besting Birmingham in a hard-fought seven-game Negro World Series. Ray Brown and Johnny Wright won two games apiece, with Brown taking the final-game victory.

1944 Another war year saw a reprise for both the league champions and the Negro World Series. The Homestead Grays and Birmingham Black Barons each won both halves of their respective split schedules to create a rematch in the World Series. The outcome was the same, but this time around the Grays required only five games to defeat the Black Barons and win their second consecutive World Championship of black baseball.

1945 In the final year of World War II, the Homestead Grays won both halves of the NNL season to win their ninth straight pennant, while the Cleveland Buckeyes won both halves of the NAL split-season to win their first pennant. The veteran Grays were favored, but Manager Quincy Trouppe's upstart Cleveland club swept the Negro World Series in four games.

1946 With the end of World War II, soldiers traded their military uniforms for baseball uniforms, and the leagues returned to their pre-war strength. Leon Day wasted no time and pitched an opening day no-hitter for the Newark Eagles. Monte Irvin and Larry Doby returned from the Army and Navy, respectively, and provided the firepower that elevated the Eagles to the top of the league, ending the long line of Grays NNL pennants. The Kansas City Monarchs returning servicemen included Willard Brown, Buck O'Neil, and Joe Greene, and their presence in the lineup brought KC another NAL pennant. The Negro World Series was a closely contested seven-game series, with Newark winning. No one foresaw it, but this was Josh Gibson's last season.

1947 The death knell for the Negro Leagues was sounded when Jackie Robinson put on a Brooklyn Dodgers uniform, but it took a couple of years before the full impact was felt. In the NNL Newark started where it had left off, winning the first-half title before their momentum was stalled with the loss of Larry Doby to the major leagues. The New York Cubans captured the second-half title and were awarded the league pennant based on the total record for the season. The Cleveland Buckeyes won the NAL pennant but lost to the Cubans in the Negro World Series. The immortal Josh Gibson died tragically in January, going out as Jackie Robinson was finally smashing the racist barrier that had for so long excluded Gibson and other great black Americans from the white-owned National Pastime.

1948 After Jackie Robinson's successful rookie season, the press and fans virtually deserted the Negro Leagues. The handwriting was on the wall; only the foolish couldn't read it—integration had killed the Negro Leagues. Fittingly, the Homestead Grays were the last team to win a Negro World Series, defeating the Birmingham Black Barons. In symbolic contrast, future Hall of Famer Buck Leonard was the star for the Grays during the season, while a teenaged Willie Mays made his debut with Birmingham to serve as a catalyst for their pennant race. The NNL folded after the season.

1949 The mounting financial losses that forced the collapse of the NNL were still a pressing reality, but the NAL absorbed four of the surviving franchises from their late "sister" league and began the season with two five-team divisions in anticipation of continuing the same general geographic structure that had existed since 1937. The Baltimore Elite Giants won both halves of the Eastern Division season and swept the Western Division second-half champion Chicago American Giants in four straight games to win the NAL pennant. However, the nails were being driven into the Negro Leagues' coffin. Reflecting the continuing decline of the talent on Negro League team rosters was the Kansas City Monarchs refusal to play Chicago for the Western Division title due to the loss of many of their best players to OB.

1950 After the success that Jackie Robinson and other pioneering black players had generated both on the field and at the box office, major league owners were inspired to accelerate their search for "another Robinson." Consequently, doors in Organized Baseball were now opening wide for young black players, and a mass exodus of African-American talent flowed into the major leagues in the 1950s—most into the National League. In 1950, the Indianapolis Clowns and Kansas City Monarchs won their divisional titles, but no League Championship Series was played.

1951-54 The NAL soldiered on into the 1950s despite a depleted talent pool, with the Monarchs and the Clowns clearly the class of the league. By 1953, the struggling loop could field only four teams, as every good black player who wasn't too old was now playing in "Organized Baseball." Historians disagree about where to divide the post-integration Negro Leagues into "major" and "minor"; we have chosen to do so after 1954 when only Kansas City and Indianapolis remained as links to the glory days of the 1940s. Though few now remember it, the Negro American League staggered on for another seven years before it finally collapsed after 1961.

Independent Award Winners (Pre-League Era)

1910

Player: Pete Hill
Pitcher: Frank Wickware
Rookie: Frank Wickware

1911

Player: John Henry Lloyd
Pitcher: Dick Redding
Rookie: Dick Redding

1912

Player: Louis Santop
Pitcher: Dick Redding
Rookie: Johnny Pugh

1913

Player: Joe Williams
Pitcher: Joe Williams
Rookie: Cristobal Torriente

1914

Player: John Henry Lloyd
Pitcher: Joe Williams
Rookie: George Shively

1915

Player: John Henry Lloyd
Pitcher: Dizzy Dismukes
Rookie: Oscar Charleston

1916

Player: John Henry Lloyd
Pitcher: John Donaldson
Rookie: Dick Lundy

1917

Player: Louis Santop
Pitcher: Tom Johnson
Rookie: Alejandro Oms

1918

Player: Oscar Charleston
Pitcher: Richard Whitworth
Rookie: Oliver Marcelle

1919

Player: Oscar Charleston
Pitcher: Joe Williams
Rookie: Dave Brown

1920

NNL

TEAM	W	L	PCT
Chi AG	32	13	.711
Det S	35	23	.603
KC	41	29	.586
Ind ABC	39	35	.527
StL G	25	32	.439
Cub SW	21	24	.467
Day	8	18	.308
Chi G	4	24	.143

MVP: Cristobal Torriente
Pitcher: Dave Brown
Rookie: Bullet Rogan

EASTERN INDEPENDENT TEAMS

Player: Chester Brooks
Pitcher: Dick Redding
Rookie: Fats Jenkins

1921

NNL

TEAM	W	L	PCT
Chi AG	41	21	.661
KC	50	31	.617
StL G	33	23	.589
Det S	30	27	.526
Ind ABC	30	29	.508
Col B	24	38	.387
Cub SW	23	39	.371
Chi G	10	32	.329

MVP: Oscar Charleston
Pitcher: Dave Brown
Rookie: Crush Holloway

EASTERN INDEPENDENT TEAMS

Player: Louis Santop
Pitcher: Joe Williams
Rookie: Nip Winters

1922

NNL

TEAM	W	L	PCT
Chi AG	36	23	.610
Ind ABC	46	33	.582
Det S	43	32	.573
KC	44	33	.571
StL S	23	23	.500
Pit K	16	21	.432
Cub SW	19	30	.388
Cle TS	17	29	.370

MVP: Cristobal Torriente
Pitcher: Dave Brown
Rookie: Heavy Johnson

EASTERN INDEPENDENT TEAMS

Player: John Henry Lloyd
Pitcher: Phil Cockrell
Rookie: Jud Wilson

1923

NNL

TEAM	W	L	PCT
KC	57	33	.633
Det S	40	27	.597
Chi AG	41	29	.586
Ind ABC	45	34	.570
Cub SW	27	31	.466
StL S	23	31	.426
Tol T†	11	15	.423
Mil‡	14	32	.304

†Folded July 15
‡Folded late in season
MVP: Bullet Rogan
Pitcher: Tom Williams
Rookie: Turkey Stearnes

ECL

TEAM	W	L	PCT
Hil	32	17	.673
Cub SE	23	17	.575
Bro RG	18	28	.500
Bac	19	23	.452
Lin	16	22	.421
Bal BS	19	30	.388

MVP: Biz Mackey
Pitcher: Nip Winters
Rookie: Rats Henderson

1924

NNL

TEAM	W	L	PCT
KC	55	22	.714
Chi AG	49	24	.671
Det S	37	27	.578
StL S	40	36	.526
Bir	32	37	.464
Mem†	29	37	.439
Cub SW	16	33	.327
Cle Br	15	34	.306

†started season as Indianapolis ABCs
MVP: Bullet Rogan
Pitcher: Bullet Rogan
Rookie: Willie Bobo

ECL

TEAM	W	L	PCT
Hil	47	22	.681
Bal BS	30	19	.612
Lin	31	25	.554
Bac	30	29	.508
Har	26	28	.481
Bro RG	16	25	.390
Was Po	21	37	.362
Cub SE	15	31	.326

MVP: Biz Mackey
Pitcher: Nip Winters
Rookie: Joe Strong

1925

NNL

First half

TEAM	W	L	PCT
KC	31	9	.775
StL S	31	14	.689
Det S	26	20	.565
Chi AG	26	22	.542
Cub SW	12	13	.480
Mem	18	24	.429
Ind ABC	13	24	.351
Bir	14	33	.298

Second half

TEAM	W	L	PCT
StL S	38	12	.760
KC	31	11	.738
Chi AG	28	18	.609
Det S	27	20	.574
Cub SW	10	12	.454
Bir	10	16	.384
Mem	12	24	.333
Ind ABC	4	33	.108

MVP: Bullet Rogan
Pitcher: Bullet Rogan
Rookie: Nelson Dean

ECL

TEAM	W	L	PCT
Hil	45	13	.775
Har	37	18	.673
Bal BS	31	19	.620
Bac	26	26	.500
Bro RG	13	20	.394
Cub SE	15	26	.366
Lin	7	39	.152

MVP: Oscar Charleston
Pitcher: Nip Winters
Rookie: Chino Smith

1926

NNL

First half

TEAM	W	L	PCT
KC	35	12	.745
Det S	33	17	.660
Chi AG	28	16	.636
StL S	29	18	.617
Ind ABC	28	18	.609
Cub SW	6	27	.182
Day	7	32	.179
Cle E	5	32	.135

Second Half

TEAM	W	L	PCT
Chi AG	29	7	.806
KC	21	7	.750
StL S	20	11	.645
Ind ABC	15	25	.375
Det S	13	23	.361
Cub SW	10	20	.333

MVP: Willie Foster
Pitcher: Willie Foster
Rookie: Hallie Harding

ECL

TEAM	W	L	PCT
Bac	34	20	.629
Har	25	17	.595
Hil	34	24	.586
Cub SE	28	21	.572
Lin	19	22	.463
Bal BS	18	29	.383
Bro RG	7	20	.260
New S†	1	10	.091

†Folded in mid-season
MVP: Dick Lundy
Pitcher: Rats Henderson
Rookie: Romando Garcia

1927

NNL

First half

TEAM	W	L	PCT
Chi AG	32	14	.696
KC	36	18	.667
StL S	32	19	.627
Det S	28	18	.609
Bir	23	29	.442
Mem	19	25	.432
Cub SW	15	23	.395
Cle H	10	37	.213

Second half

Bir†
Chi AG
Cle H
Cub SW
Det S
KC
Mem
StL S

†Pennant winner; standings not published
MVP: Willie Wells
Pitcher: Willie Foster
Rookie: Red Parnell

ECL

First half

TEAM	W	L	PCT
Bac	29	17	.630
Bal BS	23	17	.575
Cub SE	24	19	.558
Har	25	20	.556
Hil	17	28	.378
Bro RG	10	21	.323

Second half

TEAM	W	L	PCT
Bac	25	18	.581
Har	16	12	.572
Hil	19	17	.528
Cub SE	9	13	.409
Bal BS	12	18	.400
Bro RG	5	10	.333

MVP: Jud Wilson
Pitcher: Rats Henderson
Rookie: Tetelo Vargas

1928

NNL

First half	***Second half***
StL S†	Chi AG†
Bir	Bir
Chi AG	Cub SW
Cub SW	Det S
Det S	StL S

†Pennant winners; standings not published
MVP: Mule Suttles
Pitcher: Ted Trent
Rookie: Double Duty Radcliffe

ECL†

TEAM	W	L	PCT
Bal BS	5	2	.714
Lin	3	2	.600
Cub SE	2	2	.500
Phi T	2	3	.400
Bac	2	5	.286

†League disbanded early in the season

EASTERN INDEPENDENT TEAMS

Player: Oscar Charleston
Pitcher: Laymon Yokely
Rookie: Ramon Bragana

1929

NNL

First half

TEAM	W	L	PCT
KC	28	11	.718
StL S	28	14	.667
Det S	24	16	.600
Bir	20	24	.454
Chi AG	22	29	.431
Mem	14	22	.389
Cub SW	6	14	.300

Second half

TEAM	W	L	PCT
KC	34	6	850
Chi AG	26	9	743
StL S	28	16	.636
Cub SW	12	12	.500
Det S	10	23	.303
Bir	9	27	.250
Mem	5	22	.185

MVP: Willie Wells
Pitcher: Chet Brewer
Rookie: Leroy Matlock

ANL

First half

TEAM	W	L	PCT
Bal BS	24	11	.686
Lin	22	11	.667
Hom	15	13	.536
Hil	15	20	.429
Bac	11	20	.355
Cub SE	6	16	.273

Second half

TEAM	W	L	PCT
Bal BS	25	10	.714
Hil	24	15	.615
Lin	18	15	.545
Hom	19	16	.543
Cub SE	9	23	.281
Bac	8	25	.242

MVP: Chino Smith
Pitcher: Connie Rector
Rookie: Buddy Burbage

1930

NNL

First half

TEAM	W	L	PCT
StL S	41	15	.732
KC	31	14	.689
Mem	20	17	.541
Bir	30	27	.526
Det S	26	26	.500
Cub SW	17	23	.425
Chi AG	24	39	.381
Nas	13	35	.271

Second half

TEAM	W	L	PCT
Det S	24	7	.774
StL S	22	7	.759
Chi AG	19	12	.613
KC	8	12	.400
Nas	7	12	.368
Cub SW	6	12	.333
Mem	7	14	.333
Bir	10	20	.333

MVP: Willie Wells
Pitcher: Eggie Hensley
Rookie: Jimmie Crutchfield

EASTERN INDEPENDENT TEAMS

Player: Chino Smith
Pitcher: Bill Holland
Rookie: Josh Gibson

1931

NNL

StL S†
Chi AG
Cle C
Det S
Ind ABC
Lou WS
KC‡

†Won both halves; standings not published
‡KC re-joined league in 2nd half
MVP: Cool Papa Bell
Pitcher: Ted Trent
Rookie: Ray Brown

EASTERN INDEPENDENT TEAMS

Player: Josh Gibson
Pitcher: Willie Foster
Rookie: Chester Williams

1932

NSL

First half

TEAM	W	L	PCT
Chi AG	34	7	.829
Mon M	33	7	.825
Nas	24	13	.649
Mon GS	22	17	.564
Mem	22	22	.500
Lou BCa	13	17	.433
Ind ABC	14	19	.424

Second half

TEAM	W	L	PCT
Nas†	12	0	1.000
Chi AG			
Col T			
Ind ABC			
Mem			
Mon GS			
Mon M			

†leading the league when it folded in June
MVP: Turkey Stearnes
Pitcher: Willie Foster
Rookie: Alec Radcliffe

EWL

TEAM	W	L	PCT
Bal BS	20	9	.690
Det W†	20	6	.769
Hom	16	8	.667
Cub HD	12	15	.444
Was Pi	13	18	.419
Hil	10	17	.370
Cle S	8	16	.333
New B	3	14	.176

†Left league to merge with Homestead
MVP: Cool Papa Bell
Pitcher: Bert Hunter
Rookie: Cliff Allen
@StandYearFirst:1933

NNL

First half

TEAM	W	L	PCT
Chi AG	21	7	.750
Pit C	20	8	.714
Bal BS	10	9	.526
Nas	12	13	.480
Det S	13	20	.394
Col BB	11	18	.379

Second half†

†schedule not completed
MVP: Josh Gibson
Pitcher: Willie Foster
Rookie: Ray Dandridge

1934

NNL

First half

TEAM	W	L	PCT
Chi AG	17	6	.739
Pit C	14	8	.636
Phi S	12	9	.571
New D	6	5	.545
Nas	9	11	.450
Cle RS	2	22	.083

Second half

Phi S	11	4	.733
Nas	6	3	.667
Pit C	15	9	.625
Chi AG	11	9	.550
Cle RS	2	3	.400
New D	5	9	.357
Phi BG†	3	12	.200
Bal BS†	1	6	.143

†joined league in second half

MVP: Jud Wilson

Pitcher: Slim Jones

Rookie: Buck Leonard

1935

NNL

First half

Pit C	26	6	.785
Col EG	17	11	.607
Hom	14	13	.519
Bro E	15	15	.500
Chi AG	14	16	.467
Phi S	14	17	.452
NY C	10	16	.385
New D	8	20	.286

Second half

NY C	20	7	.741
Pit C	13	9	.591
Phi S	14	10	.583
Col EG	10	10	.500
Hom	9	10	.474
Bro E	13	16	.448
Chi AG	7	13	.350
New D	9	21	.300

MVP: Josh Gibson

Pitcher: Leroy Matlock

Rookie: Johnny Taylor

1936

NNL

First half

Was EG	14	10	.583
Phi S	15	12	.556
Pit C	16	15	.516
New E	15	18	.455
NY C	9	11	.450
Hom	10	13	.435

Second half

Pit C	20	9	.690
New E	15	11	.577
NY BY	8	7	.533
NY C	13	12	.520
Hom	12	14	.462
Phi S	10	18	.357
Was EG	7	14	.333

MVP: Josh Gibson

Pitcher: Satchel Paige

Rookie: Henry Spearman

1937

NNL

First half

Hom	21	9	.700
New E	19	14	.576
Phi S	12	11	.522
Was EG	11	15	.423
Pit C	11	16	.407
NY BY	11	17	.393

Second half

Hom†
New E
NY BY
Phi S
Pit C
Was EG

†overall winner; second half standings not published

MVP: Buck Leonard

Pitcher: Leon Day

Rookie: Henry Kimbro

NAL

First half

KC	19	8	.704
Chi AG	18	8	.692
Cin	15	11	.577
Mem	13	13	.500
Det S	12	15	.444
Bir	10	17	.370
Ind A	9	18	.333
StL S	5	22	.185

Second half

Chi AG†
Bir
Cin
Det S
Ind A
KC
Mem
StL S

†No standings published; played Kansas City in playoff

MVP: Newt Allen

Pitcher: Ted Trent

Rookie: Ted Strong

1938

NNL

First half

Hom	26	6	.813
Phi S	20	11	.645
New E	11	11	.500
Pit C	14	14	.500
Bal EG	12	14	.462
NY BY	4	17	.190
Was BS	1	20	.048

Second half

Hom†
Phi S
Pit C
Bal EG
New E
NY BY
Was BS‡

†Records not available; teams listed in order of finish

‡Folded in second half

MVP: Josh Gibson

Pitcher: Ray Brown

Rookie: Jimmy Hill

NAL

First half

Mem	21	4	.840
KC	19	5	.792
Ind ABC†	6	6	.500
Atl†	9	10	.474
Jac†	3	4	.429
Chi AG†	8	13	.381
Bir†	3	11	.214

@StandNote2:†Last reported records; final results not available

Second half

Atl	12	4	.750
Chi AG	17	7	.708
KC	13	10	.565
Ind ABC	8	13	.381
Mem	8	15	.348
Bir	5	12	.294

MVP: Neil Robinson

Pitcher: Hilton Smith

Rookie: Joe Greene

1939

NNL

Hom	33	14	.702
New E	29	20	.592
Bal EG	25	21	.543
Phi S	31	32	.492
NY BY	15	21	.417
NY C	5	22	.185

MVP: Bill Wright

Pitcher: Bill Byrd

Rookie: Pedro Pages

NAL

First half

KC	17	7	.708
Chi AG	17	11	.607
Mem	11	11	.500
Cle Be	9	9	.500
StL S	10	12	.455
Ind ABC†			

†left league shortly after start of season

Second half

StL S†
Chi AG
Cle Be
KC
Mem
Tol C

†final standings not published; St. Louis played Kansas City in LCS

MVP: Turkey Stearnes

Pitcher: Hilton Smith

Rookie: Chin Green

1940

NNL

Hom	28	13	.683
Bal EG	25	14	.641
New E	25	17	.595
NY C	12	19	.387
Phi S	16	31	.340
NY BY	10	22	.313

MVP: Buck Leonard

Pitcher: Ray Brown

Rookie: Frank Coimbre

NAL

First half

KC	12	7	.632
Cle Be	10	10	.500
Mem	12	12	.500
Bir	9	9	.500
Chi AG	9	15	.429
Ind Cr	3	5	.375

Second half

Bir†
Chi AG
Cle Be
Ind Cr
Mem
KC

†final standings not published; KC declared league champion

MVP: Buck O'Neil

Pitcher: Jack Matchett

Rookie: Tommy Sampson

1941

NNL

First half

Hom	17	9	.654
New E	11	6	.647
Bal EG	13	10	.565
NY C	7	10	.412
Phi S	10	18	.357
NY BY	7	13	.350

Second half

NY C	4	2	.667
New E	8	5	.615
Bal EG	8	5	.615
Hom	8	8	.500
NY BY	5	5	.500
Phi S	2	8	.200

MVP: Monte Irvin

Pitcher: Dave Barnhill

Rookie: Dave Barnhill

NAL

Bir†
Chi AG
Jac
KC
Mem
StL S

†final standings not published

MVP: Ted Strong

Pitcher: Hilton Smith

Rookie: Gready McKinnis

1942

NNL

Hom	21	11	.656
Bal EG	21	12	.636
New E	18	16	.529
Phi S	16	18	.471
NY C	8	14	.364
NY BY	7	20	.259

MVP: Josh Gibson

Pitcher: Leon Day

Rookie: Louis Louden

NAL

KC†
Bir
Chi AG
Cin Bu
Jac

†final standings not published

MVP: Willard Brown

Pitcher: Satchel Paige

Rookie: Bonnie Serrell

1943

NNL

First half

Hom	17	4	.810
NY C	13	6	.684
StL S	5	4	.556
New E	9	10	.474
Phi S	11	16	.407
Bal EG	9	15	.375
NY BY	2	11	.154

Second half

Hom	9	3	.750
New E	9	4	.692
NY C	4	3	.571
Bal EG	5	6	.455
Phi S	7	9	.438
NY BY	0	10	.000
StL S†			

†Suspended for second half by league

MVP: Josh Gibson

Pitcher: Johnny Wright

Rookie: Bill Cash

NAL

First half

Bir†
Chi AG
Ind Cl
Cle Bu
KC
Mem

†first half winner; final standings not published

Second half

Chi AG	13	5	.722
Bir	5	3	.625
Cle Bu	8	5	.615
KC	6	7	.462
Ind Cl	3	7	.300
Mem	4	11	.267

MVP: Piper Davis

Pitcher: John Markham

Rookie: Hank Thompson

1944

NNL

First half

Hom	15	8	.652
New E	13	9	.591
NY C	12	10	.545
Bal EG	12	11	.522
Phi S	7	11	.389
NY BY	2	13	.133

Second half

Hom	12	4	.750
Phi S	12	7	.632
Bal EG	12	9	.571
NY C	4	4	.500
New E	6	13	.316
NY BY	2	11	.154

MVP: Ray Dandridge

Pitcher: Ray Brown

Rookie: Frank Austin

NAL

First half

Bir	24	9	.727
Ind Cl	18	13	.581
Cle Bu	20	20	.500
Mem	20	23	.465
KC	12	19	.387
Chi AG	10	20	.333

Second half

Bir	24	13	.649
Ind Cl	22	18	.550
Chi AG	22	19	.537
Cle Bu	20	21	.488
Mem	24	28	.462
KC	11	23	.324

MVP: Artie Wilson

Pitcher: Gentry Jessup

Rookie: Artie Wilson

1945

NNL

First half

Hom	18	7	.720
Phi S	14	9	.609
Bal EG	13	9	.591
New E	11	9	.550
NY C	3	11	.214
NY BY	2	16	.111

Second half

Hom	14	6	.700
Bal EG	12	8	.600
New E	10	8	.556
Phi S	7	10	.412
NY BY	5	10	.333
NY C	3	9	.250

MVP: Josh Gibson

Pitcher: Roy Welmaker

Rookie: Garnet Blair

NAL

First half

Cle Bu	31	9	.775
Bir	26	11	.703
KC	17	18	.486
Chi AG	17	24	.415
Ind Cl	15	26	.366
Mem	13	31	.295

Second half

Cle Bu	22	7	.759
Chi AG	22	11	.667
KC	15	12	.556
Ind Cl	15	13	.536
Bir	13	19	.406
Mem	4	30	.118

MVP: Sam Jethroe

Pitcher: Willie Jefferson

Rookie: Jackie Robinson

1946

NNL

First half

New E	25	9	.735
Phi S	17	12	.586
Hom	18	15	.545
NY C	13	13	.500
Bal EG	14	17	.451
NY BY	3	24	.111

Second half

New E	22	7	.759
NY C	15	8	.652
Bal EG	14	14	.500
Hom	9	13	.409
Phi S	10	17	.370
NY BY	5	16	.238

MVP: Monte Irvin

Pitcher: Leon Day

Rookie: Junior Gilliam

NAL

First half

KC	27	8	.771
Bir	22	15	.595
Cle Bu	14	17	.452
Ind Cl	15	19	.441
Mem	16	21	.432
Chi AG	14	28	.333

Second half

KC†
Bir
Chi AG
Cle Bu
Ind Cl
Mem

†second half winner; final standings not published

MVP: Willard Brown

Pitcher: Dan Bankhead

Rookie: Leon Kellman

1947

NNL

First half

New E	27	15	.643
NY C	20	12	.625
Bal EG	23	20	.535
Hom	19	20	.487
Phi S	13	16	.448
NY BY	6	25	.193

Second half

NY C	22	6	.786
Bal EG	17	16	.526
Hom	13	14	.481
Phi S	13	15	.464
New E	19	22	.463
NY BY	4	15	.267

MVP: Luis Marquez

Pitcher: Luis Tiant

Rookie: Luke Easter

NAL

Cle Bu	54	23	.701
KC	38	22	.633
Bir	35	27	.565
Mem	35	43	.449
Chi AG	27	51	.346
Ind Cl	22	45	.328

MVP: Sam Jethroe

Pitcher: Vibert Clarke

Rookie: John Ritchey

1948

NNL

Hom†	38	20	.655
Bal EG‡	45	26	.634
New E	29	28	.509
Phi S	24	28	.462
NY C	16	26	.381
NY BY	8	32	.200

†First half winner

‡Second half winner

MVP: Buck Leonard

Pitcher: Max Manning

Rookie: Charles Gary

NAL

First half

Bir	38	14	.731
Cle Bu	31	21	.596
KC	24	18	.571
Chi AG	20	31	.392
Ind Cl	20	33	.377
Mem	13	29	.310

Second half

KC	19	7	.731
Bir	17	7	.708
Mem	20	15	.571
Ind Cl	7	13	.350
Cle Bu	10	21	.323
Chi AG	7	17	.292

MVP: Willard Brown

Pitcher: Lefty LaMarque

Rookie: Gene Baker

1949

NAL EASTERN DIVISION

First Half

Bal EG	33	16	.673
NY C	17	15	.531
Ind Cl	22	30	.423
Phi S	17	24	.415
Lou Bu	12	39	.235

Second Half

Bal EG	30	16	.652
NY C	9	5	.643
Phi S	11	11	.500
Ind Cl	22	22	.476
Lou Bu	7	26	.212

NAL WESTERN DIVISION

First Half

KC	31	20	.608
Chi AG	32	23	.582
Bir	29	21	.580
Hou	19	21	.475
Mem	13	29	.310

Second Half

Chi AG	19	12	.613
KC	23	17	.575
Hou	16	14	.533
Bir	18	21	.462
Mem	19	28	.404

MVP: Piper Davis

Pitcher: Bill Byrd

1950

NAL EASTERN DIVISION

First Half

Ind Cl	29	17	.630
Bal EG	10	9	.526
NY C	12	13	.480
Phi S	10	21	.323
Cle Bu	3	37	.075

Second Half

NY C	6	3	.667
Bal EG	14	11	.560
Ind Cl†	18	21	.462
Phi S	5	7	.417
Cle Bu‡	0	2	.000

†Awarded second-half title; league required champion to play 30 games per half

‡Dropped out after July 6

NAL WESTERN DIVISION

First Half

KC	30	11	.732
Bir	38	14	.731
Hou	18	21	.462
Mem	19	23	.452
Chi AG	13	16	.448

Second Half

Mem	23	9	.719
KC	22	10	.688
Bir	14	11	.560
Hou	5	20	.200
Chi AG	2	15	.118

MVP: Sam Hairston

Pitcher: Bill Powell

1951

NAL EASTERN DIVISION

First Half

Ind Cl	29	12	.707
Bir	15	21	.417
Phi S	12	17	.414
Bal EG	13	24	.351

Second Half

Ind Cl	24	14	.632
Bal EG	15	12	.556
Phi S	6	11	.353
Bir	9	19	.321

NAL WESTERN DIVISION

First Half

KC	28	15	.651
Chi AG	21	16	.568
Mem	13	17	.433
NO	17	26	.395

Second Half

Chi AG	13	8	.619
NO	22	18	.550
KC	14	13	.519
Mem	9	17	.346

1952

NAL

First Half

Ind Cl	26	14	.650
Bir	28	21	.571
Chi AG	16	16	.500
KC	12	12	.500
Mem	15	22	.405
Phi S	11	23	.324

Second Half

Bir	21	15	.583
Ind Cl	18	16	.529
Chi AG	16	15	.516
KC	11	14	.440
Mem	14	18	.438
Phi S	11	15	.423

1953

NAL

KC	56	21	.727
Bir	28	34	.452
Ind Cl	31	43	.419
Mem	20	37	.351

1954

NAL

Ind Cl	43	22	.662
Mem	49	34	.590
Bir	41	38	.519
Det S	23	31	.426
Lou BCo	19	30	.388
KC	23	43	.348

All Star Games

YEAR/NO.	SITE	PLAYERS	SCORE (INNINGS)	ATTENDANCE	E-W RECORD	MVP (TEAM) [EPF]
1933	Comiskey Park	23	W 11, E 7	19,568	0-1	[Willie Foster (Chi AG)]
1934	Comiskey Park	26	E 1, W 0	30,000	1-1	[Satchel Paige (Pit C)]
1935	Comiskey Park	32	W 11, E 8 (11)	25,000	1-2	[Mule Suttles (Chi AG)]
1936	Comiskey Park	34	E 10, W 2	26,400	2-2	[Cool Papa Bell (Pit C)]
1937	Comiskey Park	28	E 7, W 2	25,000	3-2	[Bill Wright (Was EG); Buck Leonard (Hom)]
1938 G1	Comiskey Park	25	W 5, E 4	30,000	3-3	[Neil Robinson (Mem)]
1938 G2	Penmar Park†	22	E 14, W 3	12,000	4-3	[Bill Wright (Bal EG)]
1938 G3	Polo Grounds**	23	E 5, W 4 (10)	15,000	5-3	[Bill Wright (Bal EG)]
1939 G1	Comiskey Park	27	W 4, E 2	40,000	5-4	[Dan Wilson (StL S); Hilton Smith (KC)]
1939 G2	Yankee Stadium**	27	E 10, W 2	20,000	6-4	[Josh Gibson (Hom)]
1940	Comiskey Park	31	E 11, W 0	25,000	7-4	[Buck Leonard (Hom)]
1941	Comiskey Park	37	E 8, W 3	50,256	8-4	[Buck Leonard (Hom)]
1942 G1	Comiskey Park	32	E 5, W 2	45,179	9-4	[Leon Day (New E)]
1942 G2	Municipal Stadium‡	29	E 9, W 2	10,791	10-4	[Willie Wells (New E)]
1943	Comiskey Park	31	W 2, E 1	51,723	10-5	[Satchel Paige (KC)]
1944	Comiskey Park	28	W 7, E 4	46,247	10-6	[Ted Radcliffe (Bir)]
1945	Comiskey Park	30	W 9, E 6	33,088	10-7	Roy Campanella (Bal EG)***
1946 G1	Griffith Stadium*	37	E 6, W 3	16,268	11-7	[Howard Easterling (Hom); Bill Byrd (Bal EG)]
1946 G2	Comiskey Park	26	W 4, E 1	45,474	11-8	[Felix Evans (Mem)]
1947 G1	Comiskey Park	29	W 5, E 2	48,112	11-9	[Gentry Jessup (Chi AG)]
1947 G2	Polo GroundsH	32	W 8, E 2	38,402	11-10	[Artie Wilson (Bir)]
1948 G1	Comiskey Park	26	W 3, E 0	42,099	11-11	[Gentry Jessup (Chi AG); Bob Boyd (Mem)]
1948 G2	Yankee Stadium**	31	E 6, W 1	17,928	12-11	[Luis Marquez (Hom); Minnie Minoso (NY C)]
1949	Comiskey Park	30	E 4, W 0	31,097	13-11	[Bob Griffith (Phi S)]
1950	Comiskey Park	29	W 5, E 3	24,614	13-12	[Jesse Douglas (Chi AG)]
1951	Comiskey Park	27	E 3, W 1	21,312	14-12	[Norman Robinson (Bir)]
1952	Comiskey Park	25	W 7, E 3	18,279	14-13	[Hank Baylis (KC)]
1953	Comiskey Park	31	W 5, E 1	10,000	14-14	[John Jackson (KC)]

*† Philadelphia ‡ Cleveland * Washington, DC ** New York City *** Only year when ASG MVP was chosen*

NNL LCS

YEAR	TEAM GAMES WON	GAME SCORES
1925	Kansas City 4, St. Louis 3	8-6, 3-6, 2-3, 5-4, 1-2, 9-3, 4-0
1926	Chicago 5, Kansas City 4	3-4, 5-6, 0-5, 4-3, 5-11, 2-0, 4-3, 1-0, 5-0
1927	Chicago 4, Birmingham 1	5-0, 10-5, 5-6, 6-4, 6-2
1928	St. Louis 5, Chicago 4	3-7, 0-3, 6-4, 5-4, 3-5, 12-7, 7-9, 19-4, 9-2
1930	St. Louis 4, Detroit 3	5-4, 7-11, 7-2, 4-5, 5-7, 4-3, 13-7
1934	Philadelphia 4, Chicago 3	3-4, 0-3, 5-3, 1-2, 1-0, 4-1, 4-4, 2-0
1935	Pittsburgh 4, New York Cubans 3	2-6, 0-4, 3-0, 1-6, 3-2, 7-6, 8-7
1941	Homestead 4, New York Cubans 1	5-4, 6-0, 4-5, 20-0, 5-0
1948	Homestead 3, Baltimore 1	6-0, 5-3, 3-11, 9-0 (forfeit)

NAL LCS

YEAR	TEAM GAMES WON	GAME SCORES
1937	Kansas City 4, Chicago 1	4-5, 8-7, 6-5, 2-2, 6-4, 2-1
1938	Memphis 2, Atlanta 0	6-1, 11-6*
1939	Kansas City 3, St. Louis 1	4-1, 6-5, 1-5, 7-0
1943	Birmingham 3, Chicago 2	2-3, 16-5, 4-5, 4-1, 1-0
1948	Birmingham 4, Kansas City 3	5-4, 6-5, 4-3, 1-3, 3-3 (5 inn.; rain), 5-1, 3-5
1949	Baltimore 4, Chicago 0	

** Series not completed; teams declared co-champions by NAL*

NNL Postseason Tournament 1939

ROUND	TEAM GAMES WON	GAME SCORES
1st	Homestead 3, Philadelphia 2	9-12, 15-9, 6-4, 3-5, 3-0
1st	Baltimore 3, Newark 1	6-8, 11-3, 7-3, 5-2
2nd	Baltimore 3, Homestead 1 (one tie)	1-2, 7-5, 1-1, 10-5, 2-0

NSL LCS

YEAR	TEAM GAMES WON	GAME SCORES
1932	Chicago 4, Nashville 3	5-6, 3-4, 5-3, [W], [L], 10-5, 9-2

World Series

NNL-ECL Negro World Series

YEAR	TEAM (LEAGUE) GAMES WON	GAME SCORES
1924	Kansas City (NNL) 5, Hilldale (ECL) 4	6-2, 0-11, 6-6, 3-4, 3-5, 6-5, 4-3, 3-2, 3-5, 5-0
1925	Hilldale (ECL) 5, Kansas City (NNL) 1	5-2, 3-5, 3-1, 7-3, 2-1, 5-2
1926	Chicago (NNL) 5, Bacharach (ECL) 3	3-3, 7-6, 0-10, 4-4, 5-7, 5-4, 0-3, 6-3, 13-0, 1-0
1927	Chicago (NNL) 5, Bacharach (ECL) 3	6-2, 11-1, 7-0, 9-1, 2-3, 1-1, 1-8, 5-6, 11-4

NNL-NAL Negro World Series

YEAR	TEAM (LEAGUE) GAMES WON	GAME SCORES
1942	Kansas City (NAL) 4, Homestead (NNL) 0	8-0, 8-4, 9-3, 9-5
1943	Homestead (NNL) 4, Birmingham (NAL) 3	2-4, 4-3, 9-0, 10-11, 8-0, 0-1, 8-4
1944	Homestead (NNL) 4, Birmingham (NAL) 1	8-5, 6-1, 9-0, 0-6, 4-2
1945	Cleveland (NAL) 4, Homestead (NNL) 0	2-1, 4-2, 4-0, 5-0
1946	Newark (NNL) 4, Kansas City (NAL) 3	1-2, 7-4, 5-15, 8-1, 1-5, 9-7, 3-2
1947	NY Cubans (NNL) 4, Cleveland (NAL) 1	7-10, 6-0, 9-4, 9-2, 6-5
1948	Homestead (NNL) 4, Birmingham (NAL) 1	3-2, 5-3, 3-4, 14-1, 10-6

Fields of Segregated Dreams

The tremendous amount of research done on the Negro Leagues in recent decades has dramatically increased knowledge of black and Latino ballplayers. Using Philip Lowry's *Green Cathedrals*, Michael Benson's *Ballparks of North America*, and other sources, we have collected information on the home parks for all big league-caliber Negro League teams from 1920–54.

Listed for each city are park names, years used by Negro League tenants, and any other available information such as capacity or outfield dimensions. Miscellaneous notes of interest are included for some parks. A dagger (†) indicates that the venue was the home park for a major league team; an asterisk (*) indicates that the park is still standing today. (See the Ballparks section of the encyclopedia for full explanation of capacity and dimensions data.)

Not included here are home parks for independent black baseball clubs of big-league caliber, parks used by touring teams, neutral fields where teams played when barnstorming, or parks that hosted All-Star contests or exhibitions with major leaguers. A list of such venues might well include almost every ballpark in the lower 48 states, Mexico, South America, and Canada.

During the peak years of the great Negro Leagues, only 11 U.S. cities had major-league teams (counting Brooklyn). Of those cities, all but one—Boston—also boasted at least one big league-caliber Negro League club. Way back in 1887, the National Colored Base Ball League, the first Negro League, did include a Boston club—the Resolutes—but the loop quickly crumbled. Aside from a couple of black semi-pro teams in the 1940s, Beantown was bereft of the glories of black baseball in the first half of the twentieth century.

While black ballplayers were prohibited by the game's racist white power structure from playing in "Organized Baseball," many major league teams had no compunctions about taking in the green dollars of black baseball fans. The White Sox, Indians, Yankees, Senators, Giants, Pirates, Reds, and Dodgers rented out their home parks to Negro League clubs at some point from 1920–50; the Cubs, Athletics, Browns, Tigers, and Phillies (before they moved to Connie Mack Stadium) did not. (The Cardinals were the tenants of the Browns; the Phillies were tenants of the A's from mid-1938 onward.) Because NL and AL clubs shared one field in St. Louis and Philadelphia, there were few open dates. In lily-white Boston, the last major league city to integrate, neither the Braves or Red Sox had to make such a choice.

Between the years of 1925 and 1945, only one new major league park opened: Municipal Stadium in Cleveland. Afterward, the Indians' old stomping grounds in League Park were given over to weekday AL games and Negro League contests. Even as a second-fiddle facility, that was a relatively good place to play. In many cities, black players had to play on badly maintained fields, many of them not even real ballparks.

Many Negro League games and exhibitions—featuring some of the greatest athletes ever to don a uniform—were held on fields laid out over horse-racing tracks, polo grounds, football fields, track-and-field layouts, or worse—in the case of New York City's 59th Street Stadium, a pitch of dirt under a bridge. Not that this took the zing out of black baseball. The modernist credo of "Clean living in difficult circumstances" could well have been applied to most of the hardy and oft-times heroic souls who played and watched Negro League baseball.

Negro League Home Ballparks by City

PARK	YEARS	TENANTS	NOTES
ATLANTIC CITY, NJ			
Bacharach Park	1923–28	ECL Bacharach Giants	*aka Bacharachs Athletic Park*
	1929	ANL Bacharach Giants	ø
ATLANTA			
Ponce de Leon Park	1938	NAL Black Crackers	Cap 15,000; Dim 365–525/448/?–324
BALTIMORE			
Maryland Baseball Park	1923–28	ECL Black Sox	ø
	1929	ANL Black Sox	ø
Druid Hill	1925	ECL Black Sox	ø
Bugle Field	1932	EWL Black Sox	*aka Moore's Field*
	1933	NNL Black Sox	ø
Oriole Park V	1938–44	NNL Elite Giants	Cap 14,000; Dim 305–?/412/?–310
Venable Stadium	1944–48	NNL Elite Giants	Cap 58,917; Dim 291–?/?/?–291; Football stadium
	1949–50	NAL Elite Giants	ø
Westport Park	1950–51	NAL Elite Giants	ø
BIRMINGHAM, AL			
Rickwood Field	1924–25, 1927–30	NNL Black Barons	Cap 9,312; Dim 405–?/470/?–334
	1932	NSL Black Barons	ø
	1937–38, 1940–54	NAL Black Barons	ø
BROOKLYN			
Dexter Park	1923–27	ECL Royal Giants	ø
Ebbets Field†	1935	NNL Eagles	Cap 28,000; Dim 356–365/399/352–318
CHICAGO			
South Side Park (III)	1920–21	NNL Giants	Cap 15,000
	1920–31	NNL American Giants	Cap 15,000
	1932	NSL American Giants	Cap 15,000
	1933–35	NNL American Giants	Cap 15,000
	1937–40	NAL American Giants	Cap 15,000
Leland Giants Field	1920s	NNL American Giants	ø
Asbury Ball Park	1920s	NNL American Giants	ø
67th and Langley Sts. Park	1920s	NNL American Giants	ø
37th and Butler Sts. Park	1920s	NNL American Giants	ø
Pyott's Park	1920s	NNL American Giants	Short LF porch
Normal Field	1920s	NNL American Giants	Football stadium
Soldier Field*	1920s	NNL American Giants	Football stadium
Comiskey Park (I)†	1941–52	NAL American Giants	Cap 47,400; Dim 352–375/415/382–352; Lights 1939
CINCINNATI			
Redland Field/Crosley Field†	1920–21	NNL Cuban Stars West	Cap 25,000; Dim 320–380/420/?–384
	1937	NAL Tigers	Cap 33,000; Dim 339–380/407/?–377
	1942	NAL Buckeyes	Cap 33,000; Dim 328–380/387/?–342
	1943–45	NAL Clowns	Cap 33,000; Dim 328–380/390/?–342
Northside Park	1921	NNL Cuban Stars West	ø
CLEVELAND			
Tate Park	1922	NNL Tate Stars	ø
	1924	NNL Browns	ø
	1926	NNL Elites	ø
Hooper Field	1927	NNL Hornets	ø
Cubs Stadium	1931	NNL Cubs	ø
	1932	EWL Stars	ø
Hardware Field	1931	NNL Cubs	ø
Luna Bowl	1928	NNL Tigers	Football stadium
	1933	NNL Giants	ø
	1934	NNL Red Sox	ø
League Park (II)†	1939–40	NAL Bears	Cap 22,500; Dim 347–?/420/400–290
	1943–48, 1950	NAL Buckeyes	Cap 22,500; Dim 349–?/420/400–290
COLUMBUS, OH			
Neil Park (II)	1921	NNL Buckeyes	
	1932	NSL Turfs	
Red Bird Stadium	1933	NNL Blue Birds	Dim 415–?/450/337–315
	1935	NNL Elite Giants	Dim 415–?/450/337–315
DAYTON, OH			
Ducks Park	1920, 1926	NNL Marcos	Cap 5,000; Dim 360–360/360/360–360
DETROIT			
Mack Park	1920–29	NNL Stars	
Hamtramck Stadium	1930–31, 1933	NNL Stars	[Hamtramck] Dim 315–?/?/?–407; Lights 1930
	1932	EWL Wolves	
Dequindre Park	1937	NAL Stars	
Briggs Stadium†*	1954	NAL Stars	Cap 54,000; Dim 340–365/440/370–325
HARRISBURG, PA			
West End Grounds	1924–27	ECL Giants	
Island Stadium	1943	NNL Stars	Cap 3,700
HOUSTON			
Buff Stadium	1949–50	NAL Eagles	Cap 14,000; Dim 345–?/440/?–325
INDIANAPOLIS			
ABCs Field	1920–26	NNL ABCs [I]	*aka Washington Park and Greenlawn Park*
	1931	NNL ABCs [II]	
	1937	NAL Athletics	
	1939	NAL ABCs [IV]	
	1943–54	NAL Clowns	
Perry Stadium/Victory Field	1932	NSL ABCs [II]	Cap 13,000;
	1938	NAL ABCs [III]	Dim 350–?/497/?–350
	1944	NAL Clowns	Cap 13,254;
	1940	NAL Crawfords	Dim 335–?/500/?–335
JACKSONVILLE, FL			
Red Cap Stadium	1938, 1941–42	NAL Red Caps	Cap 4,564; Dim 350–?/400/?–309

PARK	YEARS	TENANTS	NOTES
Kansas City			
Association Park (II)	1920–22	NNL Monarchs	
Paradeway Park	1920s	NNL Monarchs	
Muehlebach Field	1923–27, 1929–30	NNL Monarchs	Cap 17,476; Dim 350–408/450/?–350; Lights 1929
	1937–54	NAL Monarchs	Dim 350–408/432/?–350; *Ruppert Stadium 1938–42; Blues Stadium 1943–54*
Louisville			
Parkway Field	1931	NNL White Sox	Dim 329–512/467/?–345
	1932	NSL Black Caps	Dim 329–512/467/?–345
	1949	NAL Buckeyes	Dim 329–512/467/?–345
	1954	NAL Black Colonels	Cap 13,496
Memphis			
Martin Park	1924–25, 1927, 1929–30	NNL Red Sox	
	1932	NSL Red Sox	
	1937–54	NAL Red Sox	
Milwaukee			
Borchert Field	1923	NNL Bears	Cap 10,000; Dim 266–?/395/?–266
Monroe, LA			
Casino Park	1932	NSL Monarchs	Dim 360–?/450/?–330
Montgomery, AL			
Cramton Bowl	1932	NSL Grey Sox	Cap 10,000; Dim 420–?/600/?–600; Football stadium
College Hill Park	1932	NSL Grey Sox	
Nashville			
Wilson Park	1930	NNL Elite Giants	
	1932	NSL Elite Giants	
Sulphur Dell	1933–34	NNL Elite Giants	Cap 7,000; Dim 334–?/421/?–262; Field full of inclines
Newark			
Newark Schools Stadium	1926	ECL Stars	Football stadium
Sprague Field	1932	EWL Browns	[Bloomfield NJ] *aka General Electric Field*
Meadowbrook Oval	1934–35	NNL Dodgers	Dim 300–?/380/?–300
Ruppert Stadium	1936–48	NNL Eagles	Cap 19,000; Dim 305–?/410/?–305
New Orleans			
Pelican Stadium	1941	NAL Stars	Dim 427–?/405/?–418 (New Orleans/St. Louis)
	1951	NAL Eagles	
New York City			
Dyckman Oval	1923–28	ECL Cuban Stars East	Lights 1930
	1923	ECL Bacharach Giants	
	1929	ANL Cuban Stars East	
	1932	EWL Cuban Stars East	
Catholic Protectory Oval	1923–26, 1928	ECL Lincoln Giants	
	1935–36	NNL Cubans	
Capital Texture	1929	ANL Lincoln Giants	*aka Olympic Park*
Hinchliffe Stadium	1936–37, 1939–1945	NNL Black Yankees	Football stadium [Patterson, NJ]
Triborough Stadium	1938	NNL Black Yankees	Cap 21,141; Football stadium
59th Street Stadium	1939	NNL Cubans	Underneath Queensboro Bridge

PARK	YEARS	TENANTS	NOTES
Polo Grounds†	1940s	NNL Cubans	Cap 47,000; Dim 280–455/484/449–258; Lights 1940
Grove Street Oval	1940–48	NNL Cubans	Dim 240–/360/–280
	1949–50	NAL Cubans	
Yankee Stadium†'	1946–47	NNL Black Yankees	Cap 70,000; Dim 301–457/461/407–296; Lights 1946
Philadelphia			
Hilldale Park	1923–27	ECL Hilldale	Dim 315–?/400/?–370 [Yeadon PA]
	1929	ANL Hilldale	Dim 315–?/400/?–370 [Yeadon PA]
	1932	EWL Hilldale	Dim 315–?/400/?–370 [Yeadon PA]
Passon Field	1934–35	NNL Stars	
	1934	NNL Bacharach Giants	
Penncoyd Field	1928	ECL Tigers	
Penmar Park	1936–48	NNL Stars	330–?/410/?–310
	Lights 1933		
	1949–1952		NAL Stars
330–?/410/?–310			
Pittsburgh			
Ammon Field	1922	NNL Keystones	
Grays Field	1929	ANL Homestead Grays	
Gus Greenlee Field	1932	EWL Homestead Grays	
	1933–38	NNL Crawfords	Lights 1933
	1935–38	NNL Homestead Grays	
Point Stadium	1930s	NNL Homestead Grays	Dim 270–?/475/?–250 [Johnstown PA]
Cycler Park	1930s	NNL Homestead Grays	Dim 393–?/440/?–325 [McKeesport PA]
Page Park	1930s	NNL Homestead Grays	[Monessen PA]
Forbes Field†	1939–48	NNL Homestead Grays	Cap 33,730; Dim 335–355/435/408–300; Lights 1940
Rochester			
Red Wing Stadium	1948	NNL Black Yankees	
St. Louis			
Giants Field	1920–21	NNL Giants	
	1922	NNL Stars	
Stars Park	1922–31	NNL Stars	Cap 10,000; Dim 250–?/422/?–?
Metropolitan Park	1937	NAL Stars	
South End Park	1939	NAL Stars	
Mounds Ballfield	1941	NAL Stars	[Mounds IL] (New Orleans/St. Louis)
Toledo, OH			
Swayne Field	1923	NNL Tigers	Cap 10,000; Dim 472–?/448/?–347
	1939	NAL Crawfords	Cap 12,500; Dim 472–?/448/?–347
Washington, DC			
Griffith Stadium†	1924	ECL Potomacs	Cap 32,000; Dim 424–391/421/378/326
	1932	EWL Pilots	Cap 32,000 Dim 407–391/421/378–320
	1936–37	NNL Elite Giants	Cap 30,171; Dim 402–391/421/378/320
	1937–48	NNL Homestead Grays	Cap 25,048; Dim 402–391/421/378–320
	1938	NNL Black Senators	Cap 30,171; Dim 402–391/421/378–320

MIDSUMMER CLASSICS: THE ALL-STAR GAMES

The All-Star Game was born in 1933, initially conceived as a one-time event to bring sports fans to Chicago's Century of Progress Exposition. Arch Ward, the sports editor of the Chicago Tribune, thought up the idea of "the game of the century." After experiencing opposition from Commissioner Landis as well as the two leagues, Ward ultimately convinced baseball's hierarchy, as well as sportswriters across the country, to make it happen.

The very first All-Star game was played at Comiskey Park—a coin-flip winner over Wrigley Field—on July 6, 1933 before 49,200 fans. The game featured a fairy-tale AL victory, sparked by a Babe Ruth home run that sent straw boaters flying in the grandstands. As remains the case today, each manager (John McGraw and Connie Mack in the first game) was the defending league champion's skipper.

The unexpected success of this special event persuaded everyone to make the game an annual affair, and only in 1945 has the summer not featured an All-Star Game; the game was cancelled due to wartime travel restrictions after attendance had dipped dramatically in previous two years. Baseball held two games each season from 1959–62, largely because players wanted the extra gate and television proceeds for their pension fund. The two-game format was never popular, and it was abolished when the owners agreed to a new formula for contributions to the players' pension fund.

The debate over who should elect or select the All-Star teams, over how to vote, and over whom to vote for has become an annual tradition. Over the years, the All-Star franchise has switched back and forth between fans, managers, and players. Initially, the manager of each team chose the entire squad, but fans were finally enfranchised in 1947.

The oft-told scandal surrounding the 1957 NL All-Star voting, in which Cincinnati fans stuffed ballot boxes with pre-printed votes for Reds players and elected their hometown heroes to seven of the eight starting spots, resulted in the fans being denied the vote from 1958 through 1969. During those seasons, players, managers, and coaches selected the All-Stars. Unfortunately, the lack of fan input at this critical time, when football, basketball, and hockey were making inroads into baseball's fan base, helped turn some interest away from baseball.

In 1968, MLB moved the All-Star Game to the evening to increase TV viewership. Prior to then, all All-Star Games had been daytime contests (except for 1943). For the 1970 game, fans were again granted the privilege of picking the starting lineup. That same season, Pete Rose steamrolled over AL catcher Ray Fosse at home plate in the game's deciding play, providing a classic and enduring All-Star image.

Fans and pundits, meanwhile, have constantly debated about whether the most popular players—as opposed to simply the best players—should be voted onto the teams, as well as whether voting should be based on a player's current season performance or on his entire career. The fairly recent practice appointing of aging or recently retired stars as honorary captains for each team has somewhat addressed this issue.

Wall-to-wall national and regional television coverage of regular-season baseball in recent decades has made the All-Star Game less of a special event, as dramatically declining Nielsen ratings have shown. The advent of interleague play in 1997 has also clearly diminished interest in what was once "must-see" TV.

Nevertheless, Major League Baseball's annual Midsummer Classic is still by far the most popular all-star contest in American sports. Football's Pro Bowl is a thoroughly irrelevant post-Super-Bowl Hawaiian vacation; the NBA's All-Star game is little more than a shooting exhibition where style counts as much as the result; and the NHL's midseason game features almost no defensive play, leading to ridiculously high scores. While some purists decry the 2003 change that gave World Series home-field advantage to the All-Star Game-winning league, this decision at least puts something at stake besides league pride. In an era where interleague trades are commonplace through the end of July, where even the best players frequently change teams in the prime of their careers, and where distinctions between the so-called Senior Circuit and the Junior League have been substantially eroded, the All-Star Game is not nearly so special.

As the luster of the game itself has dulled, MLB has effectively increased interest in the event by turning it into a weeklong fan festival that includes a very popular home run-hitting contest (started in 1985) and a "Futures Game" showcase of top minor league talent (first held in 1999). For a brief period in the 1980s, an old-timers' game was also part of the National Pastime's annual midsummer break.

The embarrassing 2002 incident in which both leagues ran out of pitchers at Miller Park, forcing Commissioner Selig to declare a tie game after 11 innings on his home turf, was another black eye for baseball. Media critics also have focused in recent years on the "must carry" rule mandating that at least one player from each big-league team be picked for the All-Star squad while more deserving candidates on other clubs are left home. Conversely, it is always an issue whenever an All-Star manager brings along six or seven of his own pitchers or reserve players at the expense of other players having better seasons.

It is a healthy indicator that MLB's All-Star Game continues to inspire spirited debate among baseball fans while no one cares much about such games in other major sports. It is also healthy that the patterns of success in the All-Star Game reflect the way that the game is played in general. The AL won 12 of the first 16 classics before the NL—bolstered by its far larger talent base of African-American players—reeled off a dominating 30-6-1 string starting in 1950.

In 1983, however, the AL clobbered the NL 13-3 at Comiskey Park in the 50th anniversary game as Fred Lynn slugged the first-ever All-Star Game grand slam. Since then, the Junior League has dominated the Midsummer Classic, party due to an edge in international scouting and partly due to the return to the traditionally AL power-based style of play in both leagues. The Americans have now won 9 of the last 10 games while losing only 3 of the last 19.

In recent years, the National Pastime has enjoyed some excellent Midsummer Classics, notably those in 1994, 1995, 1997, and 2003. Despite constant interest from baseball fans, and the advent of Internet voting on MLB.com to determine the final roster slot on each team, the era of the All-Star Game as a major event in the country's cultural framework may be over. Several ideas have been proposed in recent years to reinvigorate the game, the most popular being a "U.S. versus the World" format where major league stars from Latin America and Asia would square off against American players, as in the Futures Game.

The 2006 and 2007 games will mark the first time since 1952-53 that the ASG host has not alternated between the leagues. In 1951, the game was moved from Philadelphia to Detroit to help the Motor City celebrate its 250th anniversary. So the AL hosted the 1950 and 1951 games, with the NL hosting the 1952 and 1953 classics. Afterward, the alternating host pattern continued unbroken until this year.

The All-Star Game table below shows the results of all 76 Midsummer Classics. The **Site** column shows the ballpark names as of the date of each game, so the first two games played at Tiger Stadium are properly shown as being played at Briggs Stadium. The **Rosters** column shows the size of each league's All-Star squad, not including players replaced due to injury. **Innings** are shown in the **Score** column only if the game went into extra innings or was shortened by rain. The **AL-NL Record** column shows the cumulative balance of power between the leagues (including ties starting with 1961's second game). **Ex Post Facto MVP** choices are shown in brackets prior to the inception of the official award in 1962; **MVPs** are italicized if they played for the losing league.

Most All-Star Selections

Hitters				Pitchers			
Hank Aaron	25	Pete Rose	17	Warren Spahn	17	Rich Gossage	9
Willie Mays	24	Warren Spahn	17	Tom Seaver	12	Carl Hubbell	9
Stan Musial	24	Tony Gwynn	16	Roger Clemens	11	Early Wynn	9
Mickey Mantle	20	Roberto Clemente	15	Steve Carlton	10	Bob Feller	8
Cal Ripken	19	Nellie Fox	15	Don Drysdale	10	Catfish Hunter	8
Ted Williams	19	Ozzie Smith	15	Whitey Ford	10	Sandy Koufax	8
Yogi Berra	18	Ernie Banks	14	Tom Glavine	10	Greg Maddux	8
Rod Carew	18	Johnny Bench	14	Randy Johnson	10	Pedro Martinez	8
Al Kaline	18	Reggie Jackson	14	Juan Marichal	10	Mariano Rivera	8
Brooks Robinson	18	Frank Robinson	14	Jim Bunning	9	Nolan Ryan	8
Carl Yastrzemski	18			Bob Gibson	9	Hoyt Wilhelm	8

MIDSUMMER CLASSICS: THE ALL-STAR GAMES

YEAR NO.	HOST	SITE	ROSTERS	SCORE (INNINGS)	ATTENDANCE	AL-NL RECORD	MVP/TEAM [EX POST FACTO]
1933	Chicago AL	Comiskey Park	18	AL 4, NL 2	49,200	1-0	[Lefty Gomez NY]
1934	New York NL	Polo Grounds	20	AL 9, NL 7	48,363	2-0	[Carl Hubbell NY]
1935	Cleveland AL	Lakefront Stadium	20	AL 4, NL 1	69,812	3-0	[Jimmie Foxx Phi]
1936	Boston NL	Braves Field	21	NL 4, AL 3	25,534	3-1	[Dizzy Dean StL]
1937	Washington AL	Griffith Stadium	23	AL 8, NL 3	31,391	4-1	[Lou Gehrig NY]
1938	Cincinnati NL	Crosley Field	23	NL 4, AL 1	27,607	4-2	[Johnny Vander Meer Cin]
1939	New York AL	Yankee Stadium	25	AL 3, NL 1	62,892	5-2	[Bob Feller Cle]
1940	St.Louis NL	Sportsman's Park	25	NL 4, AL 0	32,373	5-3	[Billy Herman Chi]
1941	Detroit AL	Briggs Stadium	25	AL 7, NL 5	54,674	6-3	[Ted Williams Bos]
1942	New York NL	Polo Grounds	25	AL 3, NL 1	33,694	7-3	[Spud Chandler NY]
1943	Philadelphia AL	Shibe Park	25	AL 5, NL 3	31,938	8-3	[Bobby Doerr Bos]
1944	Pittsburgh NL	Forbes Field	25	NL 7, AL 1	29,589	8-4	[Rip Sewell Pit]
1946	Boston AL	Fenway Park	25	AL 12, NL 0	34,906	9-4	[Ted Williams Bos]
1947	Chicago NL	Wrigley Field	25	AL 2, NL 1	41,123	10-4	[Hal Newhouser Det]
1948	St.Louis AL	Sportsman's Park	25	AL 5, NL 2	34,009	11-4	[Vic Raschi NY]
1949	Brooklyn NL	Ebbets Field	25	AL 11, NL 7	32,577	12-4	[Joe DiMaggio NY]
1950	Chicago AL	Comiskey Park	25	NL 4, AL 3 (14)	46,127	12-5	[Red Schoendienst StL]
1951	Detroit AL	Briggs Stadium	25	NL 8, AL 3	52,075	12-6	[Richie Ashburn Phi]
1952	Philadelphia NL	Shibe Park	25	NL 3, AL 2 (5)	32,785	12-7	[Hank Sauer Chi]
1953	Cincinnati NL	Crosley Field	25	NL 5, AL 1	30,846	12-8	[Enos Slaughter StL]
1954	Cleveland AL	Municipal Stadium	25	AL 11, NL 9	68,751	13-8	[Al Rosen Cle]
1955	Milwaukee NL	County Stadium	25	NL 6, AL 5 (12)	45,314	13-9	[Stan Musial StL]
1956	Washington AL	Griffith Stadium	25	NL 7, AL 3	28,843	13-10	[Willie Mays NY]
1957	St.Louis NL	Busch Stadium	25	AL 6, NL 5	30,693	14-10	[Jim Bunning Det]
1958	Baltimore AL	Memorial Stadium	25	AL 4, NL 3	48,829	15-10	[Billy O'Dell Bal]
1959 G1	Pittsburgh NL	Forbes Field	25	NL 5, AL 4	35,277	15-11	[Hank Aaron Mil]
1959 G2	Los Angeles NL	Memorial Coliseum	25	AL 5, NL 3	55,105	16-11	[Yogi Berra NY]
1960 G1	Kansas City AL	Municipal Stadium	25	NL 5, AL 3	30,619	16-12	[Ernie Banks Chi]
1960 G2	New York AL	Yankee Stadium	25	NL 6, AL 0	38,362	16-13	[Willie Mays SF]
1961 G1	San Francisco NL	Candlestick Park	25	NL 5, AL 4 (10)	44,115	16-14	[Roberto Clemente Pit]
1961 G2	Boston AL	Fenway Park	25	AL 1, NL 1	31,851	16-14-1	[No Selection]
1962 G1	Washington AL	District of Columbia Stadium	25	NL 3, AL 1	45,480	16-15-1	Maury Wills LA
1962 G2	Chicago NL	Wrigley Field	25	AL 9, NL 4	38,359	17-15-1	Leon Wagner LA
1963	Cleveland AL	Municipal Stadium	25	NL 5, AL 3	44,160	17-16-1	Willie Mays SF
1964	New York NL	Shea Stadium	25	NL 7, AL 4	50,850	17-17-1	Johnny Callison Phi
1965	Minnesota AL	Metropolitan Stadium	25	NL 6, AL 5	46,706	17-18-1	Juan Marichal SF
1966	St.Louis NL	Busch Memorial Stadium	25	NL 2, AL 1 (10)	49,936	17-19-1	Brooks Robinson Bal
1967	California AL	Anaheim Stadium	25	NL 2, AL 1 (15)	46,309	17-20-1	Tony Perez Cin
1968	Houston NL	Astrodome	25	NL 1, AL 0	48,321	17-21-1	Willie Mays SF
1969	Washington AL	Robert F. Kennedy Memorial Stadium	28	NL 9, AL 3	45,259	17-22-1	Willie McCovey SF
1970	Cincinnati NL	Riverfront Stadium	28	NL 5, AL 4 (12)	51,838	17-23-1	Carl Yastrzemski Bos
1971	Detroit AL	Tiger Stadium	28	AL 6, NL 4	53,559	18-23-1	Frank Robinson Bal
1972	Atlanta NL	Atlanta-Fulton County Stadium	28	NL 4, AL 3 (10)	53,107	18-24-1	Joe Morgan Cin
1973	Kansas City AL	Royals Stadium	28	NL 7, AL 1	40,849	18-25-1	Bobby Bonds SF
1974	Pittsburgh NL	Three Rivers Stadium	28	NL 7, AL 2	50,706	18-26-1	Steve Garvey LA
1975	Milwaukee AL	County Stadium	28	NL 6, AL 3	51,480	18-27-1	Bill Madlock Chi; Jon Matlack NY
1976	Philadelphia NL	Veterans Stadium	28	NL 7, AL 1	63,974	18-28-1	George Foster Cin
1977	New York AL	Yankee Stadium	28	NL 7, AL 5	56,683	18-29-1	Don Sutton LA
1978	San Diego NL	San Diego Stadium	28	NL 7, AL 3	51,549	18-30-1	Steve Garvey LA
1979	Seattle AL	Kingdome	28	NL 7, AL 6	58,905	18-31-1	Dave Parker Pit
1980	Los Angeles NL	Dodger Stadium	28	NL 4, AL 2	56,088	18-32-1	Ken Griffey Cin
1981	Cleveland AL	Cleveland Stadium	28	NL 5, AL 4	72,086	18-33-1	Gary Carter Mon
1982	Montreal NL	Olympic Stadium	28	NL 4, AL 1	59,057	18-34-1	Dave Concepcion Cin
1983	Chicago AL	Comiskey Park	28	AL 13, NL 3	43,801	19-34-1	Fred Lynn Cal
1984	San Francisco NL	Candlestick Park	28	NL 3, AL 1	57,756	19-35-1	Gary Carter Mon
1985	Minnesota AL	Metrodome	28	NL 6, AL 1	54,960	19-36-1	La Marr Hoyt SD
1986	Houston NL	Astrodome	28	AL 3, NL 2	45,774	20-36-1	Roger Clemens Bos
1987	Oakland AL	Oakland Coliseum	28	NL 2, AL 0 (12)	49,671	20-37-1	Tim Raines Mon
1988	Cincinnati NL	Riverfront Stadium	28	AL 2, NL 1	55,837	21-37-1	Terry Steinbach Oak
1989	California AL	Anaheim Stadium	28	AL 5, NL 3	64,036	22-37-1	Bo Jackson KC
1990	Chicago NL	Wrigley Field	28	AL 2, NL 0	39,071	23-37-1	Julio Franco Tex
1991	Toronto AL	SkyDome	28	AL 4, NL 2	52,383	24-37-1	Cal Ripken Bal
1992	San Diego NL	Jack Murphy Stadium	28	AL 13, NL 6	59,372	25-37-1	Ken Griffey Jr. Sea
1993	Baltimore AL	Oriole Park at Camden Yards	28	AL 9, NL 3	48,147	26-37-1	Kirby Puckett Min
1994	Pittsburgh NL	Three Rivers Stadium	28	NL 8, AL 7 (10)	59,568	26-38-1	Fred McGriff Atl
1995	Texas AL	The Ballpark in Arlington	28	NL 3, AL 2	50,920	26-39-1	Jeff Conine Fla
1996	Philadelphia NL	Veterans Stadium	28	NL 6, AL 0	62,670	26-40-1	Mike Piazza LA
1997	Cleveland AL	Jacobs Field	28	AL 3, NL 1	44,916	27-40-1	Sandy Alomar Jr. Cle
1998	Colorado NL	Coors Field	30	AL 13, NL 8	51,267	28-40-1	Roberto Alomar Bal
1999	Boston AL	Fenway Park	30	AL 4, NL 1	34,187	29-40-1	Pedro Martinez Bos
2000	Atlanta NL	Turner Field	30	AL 6, NL 3	51,323	30-40-1	Derek Jeter NY
2001	Seattle AL	SAFECO Field	30	AL 4, NL 1	47,364	31-40-1	Cal Ripken Bal
2002	Milwaukee NL	Miller Park	30	AL 7, NL 7 (11)	41,871	31-40-2	(No Selection)
2003	Chicago AL	U.S. Cellular Field	32	AL 7, NL 6	47,609	32-40-2	Garret Anderson Ana
2004	Houston NL	Minute Maid Park	32	AL 9, NL 4	41,886	33-40-2	Alfonso Soriano Tex
2005	Detroit AL	Comerica Park	32	AL 7, NL 5	41,617	34-40-2	Miguel Tejada Bal
2006	Pittsburgh NL	PNC Park	32	AL 3, NL 2	38,904	35-40-2	Michael Young Tex

OCTOBER CLASSICS: POSTSEASON SERIES AND PLAYOFFS

The 2004 postseason showed that, on its 101st anniversary, the World Series had come full circle since the Boston Americans (as the 2004 champion Red Sox were then called) had defeated the Pittsburgh Pirates in the 1903 Fall Classic. While the 1903 affair was certainly the first series of its kind, it was definitely not the first World Series.

Postseason play is almost as old as Organized Baseball itself. In the 1870s, National Association teams would play exhibition games against local teams after the regular season was over. The first series between two league champions occurred in 1882, when National League champion Chicago faced American Association champion St. Louis in two exhibition games. Starting in 1884, the regular-season winners of these two competing leagues officially met to determine the championship of professional baseball in the United States—and, thus, the world.

These nineteenth century championship series, often referred to today as "World Series" since they pitted two league winners against each other, were played in a variety of formats. The 1884 Series was a simple best-of-five arrangement; the 1885 and 1886 Series changed to a best out of seven games. The 1887 Series was stretched to an epic best-of-15 affair, with the NL Detroit Wolverines and the AA St. Louis Browns playing in ten different cities! Even *after* the Wolverines clinched the Series with their eighth win in the 11th game, the two teams still played out the final four games, largely to bring in gate receipts. The 1888 battle between the NL Giants and the AA Browns was downsized to a 10-game series played in four cities. The last year for this nineteenth century World Series was 1890, as the collapse of the American Association in 1891 left the National League as the only major league standing.

Without another league, the NL—conscious of the lucrative purses that could be generated by an end-of-year tournament—tried several different formats for postseason play. In 1892 the season was deliberately divided into two halves for the only time in big-league history, with the winner of the first half facing the second-half winner in an NL championship series. From 1894–97, the first place team in the NL faced the second place team in a postseason trophy series sponsored by wealthy sportsman William Temple. While the "Temple Cup" format did attract paying fans to the ballpark, it never generated that much excitement. (Not too surprising, as the first-place team had already shown itself superior during the regular season. Nevertheless, the second-place team did win three of the four Temple Cups.) After the demise of the Temple Cup, Pittsburgh's *Chronicle-Telegraph* newspaper sponsored a five-game match-up in 1900 between the second-place Pirates and the first-place Brooklyn Superbas.

In 1901 the American League emerged as an alternative major league. By outbidding the senior National League for most of the game's best players, ending the scourge of syndicate ownership, and putting a more refined game on the field, the AL quickly surpassed the NL in popularity. By 1903 the established league agreed to a ceasefire with its upstart rival. This agreement allowed the NL champion Pittsburgh Pirates to challenge AL champion Boston.

This first modern World Series was an enormous success in virtually every way, with Boston winning the series, five games to three. Baseball fans fully expected—but did not get—another World Series the next year. The 1903 arrangement was the result of a bilateral agreement between the two clubs involved, and was not officially sanctioned by either league. New York was the runaway NL winner in 1904, but Giants manager John McGraw—who disliked the AL and despised its president, Ban Johnson—had no intention of playing an AL team in the postseason.

Giants owner John Brush, who had problems of his own with the AL and with Ban Johnson, backed McGraw's stand in 1904. Then—perhaps bowing to public sentiment and perhaps lured by the financial possibilities—Brush changed his mind in the off-season and proposed an annual, officially sanctioned World Series, starting in 1905. The National Commission, which had been formed to oversee the two leagues as a result of the 1903 ceasefire agreement, adopted most of Brush's suggestions. So the World Series became a permanent fixture of the National Pastime.

While the early World Series were marked with roughhouse play from even the game's biggest stars—the leagues truly didn't like each other back then—both sides on the field (and in the front offices) recognized the financial and public-relations value of the enterprise.

To be sure, the Fall Classic has provided more than its share of great moments. From Christy Mathewson's three shutouts to Willie Mays' amazing catch, from series-ending homers by Bill Mazeroski and Joe Carter to the memorable long balls of Carlton Fisk, Casey Stengel, and Reggie Jackson, individual efforts have brightened the Series stage. Classic World Series battles like 2002 have enthralled the American public as well as fans worldwide.

The World Series has run relatively smoothly since 1905, with few major crises affecting the Fall Classic. In 1918 the two leagues chose to shut down the season early during World War I, and the resulting Cubs-Red Sox World Series had only one travel day. Players nearly went on strike before Game Five to protect their already-meager postseason shares.

The next year, however, featured a far more serious scandal. The 1919 World Series, featuring the heavily favored Chicago White Sox and the Cincinnati Reds, ended in an upset as the Reds won the best-of-nine in eight contests. After a year full of rumors about game-fixing, late in the 1920 pennant race, the very core of the White Sox club was implicated in a plot to throw the previous year's series. The 1919 series had been expanded to a best-of-nine to bring in more profits for the owners, as the greed of the era manifested itself on all sides. Following the 1921 series, the Fall Classic was shrunk back to its current seven-game schedule.

The public shock and outcry over the White Sox' actions severely damaged the credibility of the World Series and of professional baseball itself. Only the harsh actions of new commissioner Judge Landis (who banned eight Chicago players from the game for life) and Babe Ruth's emergence as an international superstar kept the major leagues from falling from grace.

Even World War II couldn't cancel the World Series, though the level of play in 1944 and 1945 was predictably poor with most big-leaguers off at war. Labor problems, though, knocked out the games in 1994, as the titanic dispute between owners and players resulted in a strike—the most disastrous in major league history. In September acting Commissioner Bud Selig did the unthinkable: he canceled the 1994 World Series, marking the first time in eighty-nine years that the Series had not been played. Baseball fans were more than angry—they were appalled and incredulous that the *World Series* wouldn't be played—a sad commentary on the times. Nevertheless, the Grand Old Game came back again in the late 1990s, revived by the great home run chase of 1998 and by some excellent postseason and World Series tussles.

Old-time fans remember the days when the World Series was the only time, besides the All-Star game, that the two leagues would meet. For more than sixty years after the modern World Series was founded, baseball's postseason stayed the course with little significant change. In the 1960s, however, baseball faced increasing competition from other sports, its own declining popularity, and the demands of expansion. The AL and NL separately expanded to ten teams in the early 1960s without changing the postseason.

As both leagues planned to go to 12 teams in 1969, MLB felt that the leagues could no longer maintain their traditional structures and keep most of the fans interested in the pennant races ("You can't sell a twelfth-place team," it was said, ignoring the fact that it wasn't possible to sell an eighth-place team before expansion, either.) Therefore, each league was split into East and West Divisions (though geography didn't always determine which division teams were placed in), and new League Championship Series were created to determine the pennant winners.

Initially, the LCS match-ups were best-of-five affairs; in 1985, MLB expanded the postseason to a best-of-seven format. The previous season, 1984, saw the Chicago Cubs attempting to reach the World Series for the first time in nearly forty years. The Cubbies fell short, however, losing the final three games on the road in San Diego. In 1985, the Kansas City Royals, down 3-1 to the Toronto Blue Jays, took advantage of the new format, storming back to win the final three ALCS contests on the way to their only World Championship.

The other anomalous postseason in the twentieth century resulted from the 1981 strike and its ad hoc split season. First-half winners in each division faced second-half winners in best-of-five series in order to qualify for the LCS. The expanded format not only rewarded teams who played well before the work stoppage, but also created some extra revenue after the lost summer of the strike. And generated a lot of anguish in St. Louis and Cincinnati as the team with the best overall record in each NL division were shut out of postseason play.

The 1993 NL expansion gave each league 14 teams, with further expansion expected soon. A year later, therefore, baseball owners decided to add another postseason round, ushering in the era of Division Series. In 1994 MLB adopted a three-division structure out of which the division winners and one "Wild Card" team from each league would reach the postseason. This meant that a World Series champion would now have to win three short series: a best-of-five Division series, a best-of-seven League Championship Series, and the best-of-seven World Series. Since a wild card team has won the World Series in three out of the first nine years this system has been in place, it is clear that winning a regular-season title is no longer necessary.

While many traditionalists have been disappointed by the way the expanded postseason has reduced the importance of the regular season, MLB, the punditocracy, and most fans feel that the Wild Card has boosted interest in many cities late in the season. The remarkably tight 2003 NL Wild Card race—in which seven teams were competing well into the final month of the reason—added fuel to the discussion about expanding the postseason even further by adding more Wild Card berths.

While there is little question that a Wild Card race fueled interest in places like South Florida during 2003, the long-term damage to the pennant races and to the postseason is substantial, even though less clear. Division Series attendance has been mediocre at best in many places as fans wait to see if their team will survive the lightning round and play for the pennant. Even worse, the magnitude of baseball's showcase event, the World Series, has dimmed dramatically since the 1980s.

One thing that has not changed that much over the last 100 years of postseason history is the home-field advantage. The winning percentage for home teams has always hovered around 55 percent in the World Series, and even in the "old days" home games were not a walk in the park. In four of the first five Fall Classics, in fact, the visiting team won a majority of contests. The advantage hovers at 53–54 percent for the Division Series and LCS.

Among the Division Series, only one has featured a home-team sweep (1995 AL); in the LCS, every game has been won by the home team only three times (1982 AL, 1984 NL, and 2004 NL). Three World Series have been swept by the home teams: 1987, 1991, and 2001. Never in *any* postseason series—even a best-of-three—has the visiting team won every contest.

In 1998, the Division Series format was overhauled after complaints because the home-field advantage was being determined on a rotating basis rather than on the basis of the best record. After almost 30 years of LCS play, home-field advantage in the championship series was also now given to the team with the better record.

Furthermore, the format of the Division Series was changed from "2-3" format to "2-2-1" so that the team with the home-field advantage didn't have to play the first two games on the road.

Key to Postseason and Playoff Tables. The first World Series Most Valuable Player Award was created in 1949 by the New York chapter of the Baseball Writers Association of America in honor of Babe Ruth, who had died the previous year. In 1955 the editors of SPORT Magazine started choosing their own World Series MVP. That MVP Award often came with a Corvette, courtesy of General Motors' Chevrolet division.

Eventually, the winners of the *SPORT* award came to be determined by baseball writers and executives present at the World Series. Now MLB's official World Series MVP Award greatly overshadows the Babe Ruth Award, whose winner is generally not selected until several weeks after the Series ends. *SPORT*'s involvement with the World Series MVP Award ended with the magazine's demise in 2000. We have selected Ex Post Facto MVPs for all World Series prior to 1955 to honor the players who we think would have won the World Series MVP Award, had it existed. Selections in italics designate MVPs from losing teams. A single entry in the MVP column for the World Series means that the same player won both the SPORT/MLB award and the Babe Ruth Award.

MVPs for the League Championship Series have been awarded by the NL since 1977 and the AL since 1980. No MVP Award has been established for the more recent Division Series. We have made Ex Post Facto MVP picks for all Division Series and for the ALCS and NLCS played prior to the league awards.

The following tables show the results of all postseason series in baseball history, as well as; the four NL playoff series and the six-single game playoffs. Prior to the advent of divisional play in 1969, NL first-place ties were broken by playing a three-game series, while the AL used a single-game playoff format. Since 1969 all ties for postseason qualification have been broken by one-game playoffs. MLB considers any playoff game or series that determines which club advances to the postseason to be part of the regular season.

Also note that game scores for each contest in every postseason series since 1884 are included. These scores appear in chronological order, with the scores given in reference to which team won the series. Therefore, "5-0"-indicates that the team that won the series won that game, while an "0-5" score means that the team that *lost* the series won that game.

National League Playoff Series

YEAR	TEAM GAMES WON (SCORES)
1946	St. Louis 2, Brooklyn 0 (4-2, 8-4)
1951	New York 2, Brooklyn 1 (3-1, 0-10, 5-4)
1959	Los Angeles 2, Milwaukee 0 (3-2, 6-5)
1962	San Francisco 2, Los Angeles 1 (8-0, 7-8, 6-4)

Single-Game Playoffs

YEAR	TITLE	TEAM (DIVISION) SCORE
1948	AL Pennant	Cleveland 8, Boston 3
1978	AL East Title	New York 5, Boston 4
1980	NL West Title	Houston 7, Los Angeles 1
1995	AL West Title	Seattle 9, California 1
1998	NL Wild Card	Chicago (C) 5, San Francisco (W) 3
1999	NL Wild Card	New York (E) 5, Cincinnati (C) 0

American League Division Series

YEAR	TEAM (DIVISION WC) GAMES WON	GAME SCORES	[EX POST FACTO MVP]
1981	New York (E/1H) 3, Milwaukee (E/2H) 2	5-3,3-0,3-5,1-2,7-3	[Goose Gossage]
1981	Oakland (W/1H) 3, Kansas City (W/2H) 0	4-0,2-1,4-1	[Dwayne Murphy]
1995	Cleveland (C) 3, Boston (E) 0	5-4,4-0,8-2	[Eddie Murray]
1995	Seattle (W) 3, New York (E†) 2	6-9,5-7,7-4,11-8,6-5	[Edgar Martinez]
1996	Baltimore (E†) 3, Cleveland (C) 1	10-4,7-4,4-9,4-3	[Brady Anderson]
1996	New York (E) 3, Texas (W) 1	2-6,5-4,3-2,6-4	[Juan Gonzalez]
1997	Cleveland (C) 3, New York (E†) 2	6-8,7-5,1-6,3-2,4-3	[Mike Mussina]
1997	Baltimore (E) 3, Seattle (W) 1	9-3,9-3,2-4,3-1	[Omar Vizquel]
1998	New York (E) 3, Texas (W) 0	2-0,3-1,4-0	[Scott Brosius]
1998	Cleveland (C) 3, Boston (E†) 1	3-11,9-5,4-3,2-1	[Manny Ramirez]
1999	New York (E) 3, Texas (W) 0	8-0,3-1,3-0	[Bernie Williams]
1999	Boston (E†) 3, Cleveland (C) 2	2-3,1-11,9-3,23-7,12-8	[Pedro Martinez]
2000	New York (E) 3, Oakland (W) 2	3-5,4-0,4-2,1-11,7-5	[Mariano Rivera]
2000	Seattle (W†) 3, Chicago (C) 0	7-4,5-2,2-1	[Edgar Martinez]
2001	Seattle (W) 3, Cleveland (C) 2	7-4,1-0,6-2	[Edgar Martinez]
2001	New York (E) 3, Oakland (W†) 2	1-0,1-4,5-3,1-4,2-1	[Derek Jeter]
2002	Minnesota (C) 3, Oakland (W) 2	7-5,1-9,3-6,11-2,5-4	[A.J. Pierzynski]
2002	Anaheim (W†) 3, New York (E) 1	5-8,8-6,9-6,9-5	[Scott Spiezio]
2003	Boston (E†) 3, Oakland (W) 2	4-5,1-5,3-1,5-4,4-3	[Todd Walker]
2003	New York (E) 3, Minnesota (C) 1	1-3,4-1,3-1,8-1	[Derek Jeter]
2004	New York (E) 3, Minnesota (C) 1	0-2,7-6,8-4,6-5	[Alex Rodriguez]
2004	Boston (E†) 3, Anaheim (W) 0	9-3,8-3,8-6	[David Ortiz]
2005	Los Angeles (W) 3, New York (E) 2	2-4,5-3,11-7,2-3,5-3	[Bengie Molina]
2005	Chicago (C) 3, Boston (E†) 0	14-2,5-4,5-3	[A.J. Pierzynski]
2006	Detroit (C†) 3, New York (E) 1	4-8,4-3,6-0,8-3	[Carlos Guillen]
2006	Oakland (W) 3, Minnesota (C) 0	3-2,5-2,8-3	[Frank Thomas]

National League Division Series

YEAR	TEAM (DIVISION/WC) GAMES WON	GAME SCORES	[EX POST FACTO MVP]
1981	Montreal (E/2H) 3, Philadelphia (E/1H) 2	3-1,3-1,2-6,5-6,3-0	[Steve Rogers]
1981	Los Angeles (W/1H) 3, Houston (W/2H) 2	1-3,0-1,6-1,2-1,4-0	[Jerry Reuss]
1995	Atlanta (E) 3, Colorado (W†) 1	5-4,7-4,5-7,10-4	[Marquis Grissom]
1995	Cincinnati (C) 3, Los Angeles (W) 0	7-2,5-4,10-1	[Hal Morris]
1996	Atlanta (E) 3, Los Angeles (W†) 0	2-1,3-2,5-2	[Mark Wohlers]
1996	St. Louis (C) 3, San Diego (W) 0	3-1,5-4,7-5	[Brian Jordan]
1997	Florida (E†) 3, San Francisco (W) 0	2-1,7-6,6-2	[Gary Sheffield]
1997	Atlanta (E) 3, Houston (C) 0	2-1,13-3,4-1	[Chipper Jones]
1998	Atlanta (E) 3, Chicago (C†) 0	7-1,2-1,6-2	[Javy Lopez]
1998	San Diego (W) 3, Houston (C) 1	2-1,4-5,2-1,6-1	[Kevin Brown]
1999	New York (E†) 3, Arizona (W) 1	8-4,1-7,9-2,4-3	[Edgardo Alfonzo]
1999	Atlanta (W) 3, Houston (C) 1	1-6,5-1,5-3,7-5	[Brian Jordan]
2000	St. Louis (C) 3, Atlanta (E) 0	7-5,10-4,7-1	[Jim Edmonds]
2000	New York (E†) 3, San Francisco (W) 1	1-5,5-4,3-2,4-0	[Bobby Jones]
2001	Atlanta (E) 3, Houston (C) 0	0-5,5-1,2-17,6-2,3-1	[Chipper Jones]
2001	Arizona (W) 3, St. Louis (C†) 2	3-5,0-2,1-0,9-2,5-3	[Curt Schilling]
2002	St. Louis (C) 3, Arizona (W) 0	12-2,2-1,6-3	[Fernando Vina]
2002	San Francisco (W†) 3, Atlanta (E) 2	8-5,3-7,2-10,8-3,3-1	[Barry Bonds]
2003	Florida (E) 3, San Francisco (W†) 1	0-2,9-5,4-3,7-6	[Ivan Rodriguez]
2003	Chicago (C) 3, Atlanta (E) 2	4-2,3-5,3-1,4-6,5-1	[Kerry Wood]
2004	St. Louis (C) 3, Los Angeles (W) 1	8-3,8-3,0-4,6-2	[Edgar Renteria]
2004	Houston (C†) 3, Atlanta (E) 2	9-3,2-4,8-5,5-6,12-3	[Carlos Beltran]
2005	St. Louis (C) 3, San Diego (W) 0	8-5,6-2,7-4	[Reggie Sanders]
2005	Houston (C†) 3, Atlanta (E) 1	16-5,1-7,7-3,7-6	[Lance Berkman]
2006	New York (E) 3, Los Angeles (W†) 0	6-5,4-1,9-5	[Paul Lo Duca]
2006	St. Louis (C) 3, San Diego (W) 1	5-1,2-0,1-3,6-2	[Chris Carpenter]

E East Division C Central Division W West Division † Wild Card 1H First-half winner 2H Second-half winner

Nineteenth Century National League Championship Series

YEAR	TEAM GAMES WON	GAME SCORES	[EX POST FACTO MVP]	
1892	Boston (1H) 5, Cleveland (2H) 0, 1 tie	0-0,4-3,3-2,4-0,12-7,8-3	[Hugh Duffy]	
1894	New York (2) 4, Baltimore (1) 0	4-1,9-6,4-1,16-3	[Amos Rusie]	Temple Cup
1895	Cleveland (2) 4, Baltimore (1) 1	5-4,7-2,7-1,0-5,5-2	[Cy Young]	Temple Cup
1896	Baltimore (1) 4, Cleveland (2) 0	7-1,7-2,6-2,5-0	[Willie Keeler]	Temple Cup
1897	Baltimore (2) 4, Boston (1) 1	12-13,13-11,8-3,12-11,9-3	[Jack Doyle]	Temple Cup
1900	Brooklyn (1) 3, Pittsburgh (2) 1	5-2,4-2,0-10,6-1	[Joe McGinnity]	Chronicle-Telegraph Cup

1 Finished first in regular season 2 Finished second in regular season 1H First-half winner 2H Second-half winner

American League Championship Series

YEAR	TEAM (DIVISION/WC) GAMES WON	GAME SCORES	MVP [EX POST FACTO]
1969	Baltimore (E) 3, Minnesota (W) 0	4-3,1-0,11-2	[Dave McNally]
1970	Baltimore (E) 3, Minnesota (W) 0	10-6,11-3,6-1	[Boog Powell]
1971	Baltimore (E) 3, Oakland (W) 0	5-3,5-1,5-3	[Boog Powell]
1972	Oakland (W) 3, Detroit (E) 2	3-2,5-0,0-3,3-4,2-1	[Blue Moon Odom]
1973	Oakland (W) 3, Baltimore (E) 2	0-6,6-3,2-1,4-5,3-0	[Catfish Hunter]
1974	Oakland (W) 3, Baltimore (E) 1	3-6,5-0,1-0,2-1	[Sal Bando]
1975	Boston (E) 3, Oakland (W) 0	7-1,6-3,5-3	[Carl Yastrzemski]
1976	New York (E) 3, Kansas City (W) 2	4-1,3-7,5-3,4-7,7-6	[Chris Chambliss]
1977	New York (E) 3, Kansas City (W) 2	2-7,6-2,2-6,4-5,3	[Sparky Lyle]
1978	New York (E) 3, Kansas City (W) 1	7-1,4-10,6-5,2-1	[Reggie Jackson]
1979	Baltimore (E) 3, California (W) 1	6-3,9-8,3-4,8-0	[Eddie Murray]
1980	Kansas City (W) 3, New York (E) 0	7-2,3-2,4-2	Frank White
1981	New York (E) 3, Oakland (W) 0	3-1,13-3,4-0	Graig Nettles
1982	Milwaukee (E) 3, California (W) 2	3-8,2-4,5-3,9-5,4-3	Fred Lynn
1983	Baltimore (E) 3, Chicago (W) 1	1-2,4-0,11-1,3-0	Mike Boddicker
1984	Detroit (E) 3, Kansas City (W) 0	8-1,5-3,1-0	Kirk Gibson
1985	Kansas City (W) 4, Toronto (E) 3	1-6,5-6,6-5,1-3,2-0,5-3,6-2	George Brett
1986	Boston (E) 4, California (W) 3	1-8,9-2,3-5,3-4,7-6,10-4,8-1	Marty Barrett
1987	Minnesota (W) 4, Detroit (E) 1	8-5,6-3,6-7,5-3,9-5	Gary Gaetti
1988	Oakland (W) 4, Boston (E) 0	2-1,4-3,10-6,4-1	Dennis Eckersley
1989	Oakland (W) 4, Toronto (E) 1	7-3,6-3,3-7,6-5,4-3	Rickey Henderson
1990	Oakland (W) 4, Boston (E) 0	9-1,4-1,4-1,3-1	Dave Stewart
1991	Minnesota (W) 4, Toronto (E) 1	5-4,2-5,3-2,9-3,8-5	Kirby Puckett
1992	Toronto (E) 4, Oakland (W) 2	3-4,3-1,7-5,7-6,2-6,9-2	Roberto Alomar
1993	Toronto (E) 4, Chicago (W) 2	7-3,3-1,1-6,4-7,5-3,6-3	Dave Stewart
1995	Cleveland (C) 4, Seattle (W) 2	2-3,5-2,2-5,7-0,3-2,4-0	Orel Hershiser
1996	New York (E) 4, Baltimore (E†) 1	5-4,3-5,5-2,8-4,6-4	Bernie Williams
1997	Cleveland (C) 4, Baltimore (E) 2	0-3,5-4,2-1,8-7,2-4,1-0	Marquis Grissom
1998	New York (E) 4, Cleveland (C) 2	7-2,1-4,1-6,4-0,5-3,9-5	David Wells
1999	New York (E) 4, Boston (E†) 1	4-3,3-2,1-13,9-2,6-1	Orlando Hernandez
2000	New York (E) 4, Seattle (W) 2	6-2,6-5,2-8,10-6,7-0	David Justice
2001	New York (E) 4, Seattle (W) 1	2-0,1-8,5-1,11-4,3-2	Alfonso Soriano
2002	Anaheim (W†) 4, Minnesota (C) 1	1-2,6-3,2-1,7-1,13-5	Adam Kennedy
2003	New York (E) 4, Boston (E†) 3	2-5,6-2,4-3,2-3,4-2,6-9,6-5	Mariano Rivera
2004	Boston (E†) 4, New York (E) 3	7-10,1-3,8-19,6-4,5-4,4-2,10-3	David Ortiz
2005	Chicago (C) 4, Los Angeles (W) 1	2-3,2-1,5-2,8-2,6-3	Paul Konerko
2006	Detroit (C†) 4, Oakland (W) 0	5-1,8-5,3-0,6-3	Placido Polanco

National League Championship Series

YEAR	TEAM (DIVISION/WC) GAMES WON	GAME SCORES	MVP [EX POST FACTO]
1969	New York (E) 3, Atlanta (W) 0	9-5,11-6,7-4	[Ken Boswell]
1970	Cincinnati (W) 3, Pittsburgh (E) 0	3-0,3-1,3-2	[Bobby Tolan]
1971	Pittsburgh (E) 3, San Francisco (W) 1	4-5,9-4,2-1,9-5	[Bob Robertson]
1972	Cincinnati (W) 3, Pittsburgh (E) 2	1-5,5-3,2-3,7-1,4-3	[Johnny Bench]
1973	New York (E) 3, Cincinnati (W) 2	1-2,5-0,9-2,1-2,7-2	[Rusty Staub]
1974	Los Angeles (W) 3, Pittsburgh (E) 1	3-0,5-2,0-7,12-1	[Don Sutton]
1975	Cincinnati (W) 3, Pittsburgh (E) 0	8-3,6-1,5-3	[Tony Perez]
1976	Cincinnati (W) 3, Philadelphia (E) 0	6-3,6-2,7-6	[Pete Rose]
1977	Los Angeles (W) 3, Philadelphia (E) 1	5-7,7-1,6-5,4-1	Dusty Baker
1978	Los Angeles (W) 3, Philadelphia (E) 1	9-5,4-0,4-9,4-3	Steve Garvey
1979	Pittsburgh (E) 3, Cincinnati (W) 0	5-2,3-2,7-1	Willie Stargell
1980	Philadelphia (E) 3, Houston (W) 2	3-1,4-7,0-1,5-3,8-7	Manny Trillo
1981	Los Angeles (W) 3, Montreal (E) 2	5-1,0-3,1-4,7-1,2-1	Burt Hooton
1982	St. Louis (E) 3, Atlanta (W) 0	7-0,4-3,6-2	Darrell Porter
1983	Philadelphia (E) 3, Los Angeles (W) 1	1-0,1-4,7-2,7-2	Gary Matthews
1984	San Diego (W) 3, Chicago (E) 2	0-13,2-4,7-1,7-5,6-3	Steve Garvey
1985	St. Louis (E) 4, Los Angeles (W) 2	1-4,2-8,4-2,12-2,3-2,7-5	Ozzie Smith
1986	New York (E) 4, Houston (W) 2	0-1,5-1,6-5,1-3,2-1,7-6	Mike Scott
1987	St. Louis (E) 4, San Francisco (W) 3	5-3,0-5,6-5,2-4,3-6,1-0,6-0	Jeffrey Leonard
1988	Los Angeles (W) 4, New York (E) 3	2-3,6-3,4-8,5-4,7-4,1-5,6-0	Orel Hershiser
1989	San Francisco (W) 4, Chicago (E) 1	11-3,5-9,5-4,6-4,3-2	Will Clark
1990	Cincinnati (W) 4, Pittsburgh (E) 2	3-4,2-1,6-3,5-3,2-3,2-1	Rob Dibble; Randy Myers
1991	Atlanta (W) 4, Pittsburgh (E) 3	1-5,1-0,10-3,2-3,0-1,1-0,4-0	Steve Avery
1992	Atlanta (W) 4, Pittsburgh (E) 3	5-1,13-5,2-3,6-4,1-7,4-13,3-2	John Smoltz
1993	Philadelphia (E) 4, Atlanta (W) 2	4-3,3-14,4-9,2-1,4-3,6-3	Curt Schilling
1995	Atlanta (E) 4, Cincinnati (C) 0	2-1,6-2,5-2,6-0	Mike Devereaux
1996	Atlanta (E) 4, St. Louis (C) 3	4-2,3-8,2-3,3-4,14-0,3-1,15-0	Javier Lopez
1997	Florida (E†) 4, Atlanta (E) 2	5-3,1-7,5-2,0-4,2-1,7-4	Livan Hernandez
1998	San Diego (W) 4, Atlanta (E) 2	3-2,3-0,4-1,3-8,6-7,5-0	Sterling Hitchcock
1999	Atlanta (E) 4, New York (E†) 2	4-2,4-3,1-0,2-3,3-4,10-9	Eddie Perez
2000	New York (E†) 4, St. Louis (C) 1	0-2,7-1,8-2,5-0,2-6,9-7	Mike Hampton
2001	Arizona (W) 4, Atlanta (E) 1	4-2,3-2,3-14,3-1,12-3	Craig Counsell
2002	San Francisco (W†) 4, St. Louis (C) 1	9-6,4-1,4-5,4-3,2-1	Benito Santiago
2003	Florida (E†) 4, Chicago (C) 3	9-8,3-12,4-5,3-8,4-0,8-3,9-6	Ivan Rodriguez
2004	St. Louis (C) 4, Houston (C†) 3	10-7,6-4,2-5,5-6,0-3,6-4,5-2	Albert Pujols
2005	Houston (C†) 4, St. Louis (C) 2	3-5,4-1, 4-3,2-1,4-5,5-1	Roy Oswalt
2006	St. Louis (C) 4, New York (E) 3	0-2,9-6,5-0,5-12,4-2,2-4,3-1	Jeff Suppan

E East Division C Central Division W West Division † Wild Card

Nineteenth Century World Series (American Association vs. National League)

YEAR	TEAM (LEAGUE) GAMES WON	GAME SCORES	MVP [EX POST FACTO]
1884	Providence (N) 3, New York (AA) 0	6-0,3-1,12-2	[Charles Radbourn]
1885	St. Louis (AA) 3, Chicago (N) 3, 1 tie	5-5,5-4,4-7,2-39-2,9-2,4-13	[Cap Anson]
1886	St. Louis (AA) 4, Chicago (N) 2	0-6,12-0,4-11,8-5,10-3,4-3	[Bob Caruthers]
1887	Detroit (N) 10, St. Louis (AA) 5	1-6,5-3,2-1,8-0,2-5,9-0,3-1,9-2,4-2,4-11,13-3,1-5,6-3,4-3,2-9	[Lady Baldwin]
1888	New York (N) 6, St. Louis (AA) 4	2-1,0-3,4-2,6-3,6-4,12-5,5-7,11-3,11-14,7-18	[Tim Keefe]
1889	New York (N) 6, Brooklyn (AA) 3	10-12,6-2,7-8,7-10,11-3,2-1,11-7,16-7,3-2	[John Ward]
1890	Brooklyn (N) 3, Louisville (AA) 3, 1 tie	9-0,5-3,7-7,4-5,7-2,8-9,2-6	[Red Ehret]

World Series

YEAR	TEAM (LEAGUE) GAMES WON	GAME SCORES	MVP [EX POST FACTO] BABE RUTH AWARD*
1903	Boston (A) 5, Pittsburgh (N) 3	3-7,3-0,2-4,4-5,11-2, 6-3, 7-3,3-0	[Bill Dineen]
1904	[No World Series held]		
1905	New York (N) 4, Philadelphia (A) 1	3-0,0-3,9-0,1-0,2-0	[Christy Mathewson]
1906	Chicago (A) 4, Chicago (N) 2	2-1,1-7,3-0,0-1,8-6,8-3	[George Davis]
1907	Chicago (N) 4, Detroit (A) 0, 1 tie	3-3,3-1,5-1,6-1,2-0	[Harry Steinfeldt]
1908	Chicago (N) 4, Detroit (A) 1	10-6,6-1,3-8,3-0,2-0	[Orval Overall]
1909	Pittsburgh (N) 4, Detroit (A) 3	4-1,2-7,8-6,0-5,8-4, 4-5,8-0	[Babe Adams]
1910	Philadelphia (A) 4, Chicago (N) 1	4-1,9-3,12-5,3-4,7-2	[Jack Coombs]
1911	Philadelphia (A) 4, New York (N) 2	1-2,3-1,3-2,4-2,3-4,13-2	[Frank Baker]
1912	Boston (A) 4, New York (N) 3, 1 tie	4-3,6-6,1-2,3-1,2-1,2-5, 4-11,3-2	[Joe Wood]
1913	Philadelphia (A) 4, New York (N) 1	6-4,0-3,8-2,6-5,3-1	[Frank Baker]
1914	Boston (N) 4, Philadelphia (A) 0	7-1,1-0,5-4,3-1	[Hank Gowdy]
1915	Boston (A) 4, Philadelphia (N) 1	1-3,2-1,2-1,2-1,5-4	[Harry Hooper]
1916	Boston (A) 4, Brooklyn (N) 1	6-5,2-1,3-4,6-2,4-1	[Ernie Shore]
1917	Chicago (A) 4, New York (N) 2	2-1,7-2,0-2,0-5,8-5,4-2	[Red Faber]
1918	Boston (A) 4, Chicago (N) 2	1-0,1-3,2-1,3-2,0-3,2-1	[Carl Mays]
1919	Cincinnati (N) 5, Chicago (A) 3	9-1,4-2,0-3,2-0,5-0,4-5, 1-4,10-5	[Hod Eller]
1920	Cleveland (A) 5, Brooklyn (N) 2	3-1,0-3,1-2,5-1,8-1,1-0, 3-0	[Stan Coveleski]
1921	New York (N) 5, New York (A) 3	0-3,0-3,13-5,4-2,1-3,8-5, 2-1,1-0	[Waite Hoyt]
1922	New York (N) 4, New York (A) 0, 1 tie	3-2,3-3,3-0,4-3,5-3	[Irish Meusel]
1923	New York (A) 4, New York (N) 2	4-5,4-2,0-1,8-4,8-1,6-4	[Babe Ruth]
1924	Washington (A) 4, New York (N) 3	3-4,4-3,4-6,7-4,2-6,2-1,4-3	[Goose Goslin]
1925	Pittsburgh (N) 4, Washington (A) 3	1-4,3-2,3-4,0-4,6-3,3-2,9-7	[Max Carey]
1926	St.Louis (N) 4, New York (A) 3	1-2,6-2,4-0,5-10,2-3,10-2,3-2	[Grover Alexander]
1927	New York (A) 4, Pittsburgh (N) 0	5-4,6-2,8-1,4-3	[Babe Ruth]
1928	New York (A) 4, St.Louis (N) 0	4-1,9-3,7-3,7-3	[Lou Gehrig]
1929	Philadelphia (A) 4, Chicago (N) 1	3-1,9-3,1-3,10-8,3-2	[Jimmie Foxx]
1930	Philadelphia (A) 4, St.Louis (N) 2	5-2,6-1,0-5,1-3,2-0,7-1	[George Earnshaw]
1931	St.Louis (N) 4, Philadelphia (A) 3	2-6,2-0,5-2,0-3,5-1,1-8,4-2	[Pepper Martin]
1932	New York (A) 4, Chicago (N) 0	12-6,5-2,7-5,13-6	[Lou Gehrig]
1933	New York (N) 4, Washington (A) 1	4-2,6-1,0-4,2-1,4-3	[Carl Hubbell]
1934	St.Louis (N) 4, Detroit (A) 3	8-3,2-3,4-1,4-10,1-3,4-3,11-0	[Dizzy Dean]
1935	Detroit (A) 4, Chicago (N) 2	0-3,8-3,6-5,2-1,1-3,4-3	[Tommy Bridges]
1936	New York (A) 4, New York (N) 2	1-6,18-4,2-1,5-2,4-5,13-5	[Jake Powell]
1937	New York (A) 4, New York (N) 1	8-1,8-1,5-1,3-7,4-2	[Lefty Grove]
1938	New York (A) 4, Chicago (N) 0	3-1,6-3,5-2,8-3	[Joe Gordon]
1939	New York (A) 4, Cincinnati (N) 0	2-1,4-0,7-3,7-4	[Charlie Keller]
1940	Cincinnati (N) 4, Detroit (A) 3	2-7,5-3,4-7,5-2,0-8,4-0,2-1	[Jimmy Ripple]
1941	New York (A) 4, Brooklyn (N) 1	3-2,2-3,2-1,7-4,3-1	[Charlie Keller]
1942	St. Louis (N) 4, New York (A) 1	4-7,4-3,2-0,9-6,4-2	[Johnny Beazley]
1943	New York (A) 4, St .Louis (N) 1	4-2,3-4,6-2,2-1,2-0	[Spud Chandler]
1944	St .Louis (N) 4, St. Louis (A) 2	1-2,3-2,2-6,5-1,2-0,3-1	[Mort Cooper]
1945	Detroit (A) 4, Chicago (N) 3	0-9,4-1,0-3,4-1,8-4,7-8,9-3	[Hank Greenberg]
1946	St. Louis (N) 4, Boston (A) 3	2-3,3-0,0-4,12-3,3-6,4-1,4-3	[Harry Brecheen]
1947	New York (A) 4, Brooklyn (N) 3	5-3,10-3,8-9,2-3,2-1,6-8,5-2	[Johnny Lindell]
1948	Cleveland (A) 4, Boston (N) 2	0-1,4-1,2-0,2-1,5-11,4-3	[Bob Lemon]
1949	New York (A) 4, Brooklyn (N) 1	1-0,0-1,4-3,6-4,10-6	[Allie Reynolds] Joe Page*
1950	New York (A) 4, Philadelphia (N) 0	1-0,2-1,3-2,5-2	[Jerry Coleman]
1951	New York (A) 4, New York (N) 2	1-5,3-1,2-6,6-2,13-1,4-3	[Ed Lopat] Phil Rizzuto*
1952	New York (A) 4, Brooklyn (N) 3	2-4,7-1,3-5,2-0,5-6,3-2,4-2	[Mickey Mantle] Johnny Mize
1953	New York (A) 4, Brooklyn (N) 2	9-5,4-2,2-3,3-7,11-7,4-3	[Billy Martin]
1954	New York (N) 4, Cleveland (A) 0	5-2,3-1,6-2,7-4	[Dusty Rhodes]
1955	Brooklyn (N) 4, New York (A) 3	5-6,2-4,8-3,8-5,5-3,1-5,2-0	Johnny Podres
1956	New York (A) 4, Brooklyn (N) 3	3-6,8-13,5-3,6-2,2-0,0-1,9-0	Don Larsen
1957	Milwaukee (N) 4, New York (A) 3	1-3,4-2,3-12,7-5,1-0,2-3,5-0	Lew Burdette
1958	New York (A) 4, Milwaukee (N) 3	3-4,5-13,4-0,0-3,7-0,4-3,6-2	Bob Turley Elston Howard*
1959	Los Angeles (N) 4, Chicago (A) 2	0-11,4-3,3-1,5-4,0-1,9-3	Larry Sherry
1960	Pittsburgh (N) 4, New York (A) 3	6-4,3-16,0-10,3-2,5-2, 0-12,10-9	*Bobby Richardson* Bill Mazeroski
1961	New York (A) 4, Cincinnati (N) 1	2-0,2-6,3-2,7-0,13-5	Whitey Ford
1962	New York (A) 4, San Francisco (N) 3	6-2,0-2,3-2,3-7,5-3,2-5,1-0	Ralph Terry
1963	Los Angeles (N) 4, New York (A) 0	5-2,4-1,1-0,2-1	Sandy Koufax
1964	St.Louis (N) 4, New York (A) 3	9-5,3-8,1-2,4-3,5-2,3-8,7-5	Bob Gibson
1965	Los Angeles (N) 4, Minnesota (A) 3	2-8,1-5,4-0,7-2,7-0,1-5,2-0	Sandy Koufax
1966	Baltimore (A) 4, Los Angeles (N) 0	5-2,6-0,1-0,1-0	Frank Robinson
1967	St. Louis (N) 4, Boston (A) 3	2-1,0-5,5-2,6-0,1-3,4-8,7-2	Bob Gibson Lou Brock*
1968	Detroit (A) 4, St.Louis (N) 3	0-4,8-1,3-7,1-10,5-3,13-1,4-1	Mickey Lolich
1969	New York (N) 4, Baltimore (A) 1	1-4,2-1,5-0,2-1,5-3	Donn Clendenon Al Weis*
1970	Baltimore (A) 4, Cincinnati (N) 1	4-3,6-5,9-3,5-6,9-3	Brooks Robinson
1971	Pittsburgh (N) 4, Baltimore (A) 3	3-5,3-11,5-1,4-3,4-0,2-3,2-1	Roberto Clemente
1972	Oakland (A) 4, Cincinnati (N)3	3-2,2-1,0-1,3-2,4-5,1-8,3-2	Gene Tenace
1973	Oakland (A) 4, New York (N) 3	2-1,7-10,3-2,1-6,0-2,3-1,5-2	Reggie Jackson Bert Campaneris*
1974	Oakland (A) 4, Los Angeles (N) 1	3-2,2-3,3-2,5-2,3-2	Rollie Fingers Dick Green*
1975	Cincinnati (N) 4, Boston (A) 3	0-6,3-2,6-5,4-5,6-2,6-7,4-3	Pete Rose *Luis Tiant**
1976	Cincinnati (N) 4, New York (A) 0	5-1,4-3,6-2,7-2	Johnny Bench
1977	New York (A) 4, Los Angeles (N) 2	4-3,1-6,5-3,4-2,4-10,8-4	Reggie Jackson
1978	New York (A) 4, Los Angeles (N) 2	5-11,3-4,5-1,4-3,12-2,7-2	Bucky Dent
1979	Pittsburgh (N) 4, Baltimore (A) 3	4-5,3-2,4-8,6-9,7-1,4-0,4-1	Willie Stargell
1980	Philadelphia (N) 4, Kansas City (A) 2	7-6,6-4,3-4,3-5,4-3,4-1	Mike Schmidt Tug McGraw*
1981	Los Angeles (N) 4, New York (A) 2	3-5,0-3,5-4,8-7,2-1,9-2	Ron Cey Pedro Guerrero Steve Yeager Ron Cey*
1982	St. Louis (N) 4, Milwaukee (A) 3	0-10,5-4,6-2,5-7,4-6,13-1,6-3	Darrell Porter Bruce Sutter*
1983	Baltimore (A) 4, Philadelphia (N) 1	1-2,4-1,3-2,5-4,5-0	Rick Dempsey
1984	Detroit (A) 4, San Diego (N) 1	3-2,3-5,5-2,4-2,8-4	Alan Trammell Jack Morris*
1985	Kansas City (A) 4, St. Louis (N) 3	1-3,2-4,6-1,0-3,6-1,2-1,11-0	Bret Saberhagen
1986	New York (N) 4, Boston (A) 3	0-1,3-9,7-1,6-2,2-4,6-5,8-5	Ray Knight
1987	Minnesota (A) 4, St. Louis (N) 3	10-1,8-4,1-3,2-7,2-4,11-5,4-2	Frank Viola
1988	Los Angeles (N) 4, Oakland (A) 1	5-4,6-0,1-2,4-3,5-2	Orel Hershiser
1989	Oakland (A) 4, San Francisco (N) 0	5-0,5-1,13-7,9-6	Dave Stewart
1990	Cincinnati (N) 4, Oakland (A) 0	7-0,5-4,8-3,2-1	Jose Rijo Billy Hatcher*
1991	Minnesota (A) 4, Atlanta (N) 3	5-2,3-2,4-5,2-3,5-14,4-3,1-0	Jack Morris
1992	Toronto (A) 4, Atlanta (N) 2	1-3,5-4,3-2,2-1,2-7,4-3	Pat Borders Dave Winfield*
1993	Toronto (A) 4, Philadelphia (N) 2	8-5,4-6,10-3,15-14,0-2,8-6	Paul Molitor
1994	[World Series canceled]		
1995	Atlanta (N) 4, Cleveland (A) 2	3-2,4-3,6-7,5-2,4-5,1-0	Tom Glavine
1996	New York (A) 4, Atlanta (N) 2	1-12,0-4,5-2,8-6,1-0,3-2	John Wetteland Cecil Fielder*
1997	Florida (N) 4, Cleveland (A) 3	7-4,1-6,14-11,3-10,8-7, 1-4,3-2	Livan Hernandez Moises Alou*
1998	New York (A) 4, San Diego (N) 0	9-6,9-3,5-4,3-0	Scott Brosius
1999	New York (A) 4, Atlanta (N) 0	4-1,7-2,6-5,4-1	Mariano Rivera
2000	New York (A) 4, New York (N) 1	4-3,6-5,2-4,3-2,4-2	Derek Jeter
2001	Arizona (N) 4, New York (A) 3	9-1,4-0,1-2,3-4,2-3,15-2,3-2	Randy Johnson Curt Schilling
2002	Anaheim (A) 4, San Francisco (N) 3	3-4,11-10,10-4,3-4,4-16, 6-5,4-1	Troy Glaus
2003	Florida (N) 4, New York (A) 2	3-2,1-6,1-6,4-3,6-4,2-0	Josh Beckett
2004	Boston (A) 4, St. Louis (N) 0	11-9,6-2,4-1,3-0	Manny Ramirez Keith Foulke*
2005	Chicago (A) 4, Houston (N) 0	1-0,7-5,7-6,5-3	Jermaine Dye
2006	St. Louis (N) 4, Detroit (A) 1	7-2,1-3,5-0,5-4,4-2	David Eckstein

All-Time World Series Leaders

GAMES

1	Yogi Berra	75
2	Mickey Mantle	65
3	Elston Howard	54
4	Hank Bauer	53
	Gil McDougald	53
6	Phil Rizzuto	52
7	Joe DiMaggio	51
8	Frankie Frisch	50
9	Pee Wee Reese	44
10	Roger Maris	41
	Babe Ruth	41
12	Carl Furillo	40
13	Jim Gilliam	39
	Gil Hodges	39
	Bill Skowron	39
16	Bill Dickey	38
	Jackie Robinson	38
18	Tony Kubek	37
19	Joe Collins	36
	David Justice	36
	Bobby Richardson	36
	Duke Snider	36

AT-BATS

1	Yogi Berra	259
2	Mickey Mantle	230
3	Joe DiMaggio	199
4	Frankie Frisch	197
5	Gil McDougald	190
6	Hank Bauer	188
7	Phil Rizzuto	183
8	Elston Howard	171
9	Pee Wee Reese	169
10	Roger Maris	152
11	Jim Gilliam	147
12	Tony Kubek	146
13	Bill Dickey	145
14	Jackie Robinson	137
15	Bill Skowron	133
	Duke Snider	133
17	Gil Hodges	131
	Bobby Richardson	131
19	Pete Rose	130
20	Goose Goslin	129
	Derek Jeter	129
	Bob Meusel	129
	Babe Ruth	129

RUNS

1	Mickey Mantle	42
2	Yogi Berra	41
3	Babe Ruth	37
4	Lou Gehrig	30
5	Joe DiMaggio	27
	Derek Jeter	27
7	Roger Maris	26
8	Elston Howard	25
9	Gil McDougald	23
10	Jackie Robinson	22
11	Hank Bauer	21
	Reggie Jackson	21
	Phil Rizzuto	21
	Duke Snider	21
	Gene Woodling	21
16	Eddie Collins	20
	Pee Wee Reese	20
18	Bill Dickey	19
	Frank Robinson	19
	Bill Skowron	19

HITS

1	Yogi Berra	71
2	Mickey Mantle	59
3	Frankie Frisch	58
4	Joe DiMaggio	54
5	Hank Bauer	46
	Pee Wee Reese	46
7	Gil McDougald	45
	Phil Rizzuto	45
9	Lou Gehrig	43
10	Eddie Collins	42
	Elston Howard	42
	Babe Ruth	42
13	Bobby Richardson	40
14	Derek Jeter	39
	Bill Skowron	39
16	Duke Snider	38
17	Bill Dickey	37
	Goose Goslin	37
19	Steve Garvey	36
20	Gil Hodges	35
	Reggie Jackson	35
	Tony Kubek	35
	Pete Rose	35

DOUBLES

1	Yogi Berra	10
	Frankie Frisch	10
3	Jack Barry	9
	Pete Fox	9
	Carl Furillo	9
6	Lou Gehrig	8
	Lonnie Smith	8
	Duke Snider	8
9	Frank Baker	7
	Lou Brock	7
	Eddie Collins	7
	Rick Dempsey	7
	Hank Greenberg	7
	Chick Hafey	7
	Elston Howard	7
	Reggie Jackson	7
	Marty Marion	7
	Pepper Martin	7
	Danny Murphy	7
	Stan Musial	7
	Terry Pendleton	7
	Jackie Robinson	7
	Devon White	7

TRIPLES

1	Billy Johnson	4
	Tommy Leach	4
	Tris Speaker	4
4	Hank Bauer	3
	Bobby Brown	3
	Dave Concepcion	3
	Buck Freeman	3
	Frankie Frisch	3
	Lou Gehrig	3
	Dan Gladden	3
	Mark Lemke	3
	Billy Martin	3
	Tim McCarver	3
	Bob Meusel	3
	Freddy Parent	3
	Chick Stahl	3
	Devon White	3
18	Kitty Bransfield	2
	Lou Brock	2
	Eddie Collins	2
	Jimmy Collins	2
	Jake Daubert	2
	Tommy Davis	2
	Patsy Dougherty	2
	Larry Gardner	2
	Hank Greenberg	2
	Heinie Groh	2
	Rickey Henderson	2
	Gene Hermanski	2
	Buck Herzog	2

HOME RUNS

1	Mickey Mantle	18
2	Babe Ruth	15
3	Yogi Berra	12
4	Duke Snider	11
5	Lou Gehrig	10
	Reggie Jackson	10
7	Joe DiMaggio	8
	Frank Robinson	8
	Bill Skowron	8
10	Hank Bauer	7
	Goose Goslin	7
	Gil McDougald	7
13	Lenny Dykstra	6
	Roger Maris	6
	Al Simmons	6
	Reggie Smith	6
17	Johnny Bench	5
	Bill Dickey	5
	Hank Greenberg	5
	Gil Hodges	5
	Elston Howard	5
	Charlie Keller	5
	Billy Martin	5
	Bernie Williams	5

RBIS

1	Mickey Mantle	40
2	Yogi Berra	39
3	Lou Gehrig	35
4	Babe Ruth	33
5	Joe DiMaggio	30
6	Bill Skowron	29
7	Duke Snider	26
8	Hank Bauer	24
	Bill Dickey	24
	Reggie Jackson	24
	Gil McDougald	24
12	Hank Greenberg	22
13	Gil Hodges	21
	David Justice	21
15	Goose Goslin	19
	Elston Howard	19
	Tony Lazzeri	19
	Billy Martin	19
19	Frank Baker	18
	Charlie Keller	18
	Roger Maris	18

WALKS

1	Mickey Mantle	43
2	Babe Ruth	33
3	Yogi Berra	32
4	Phil Rizzuto	30
5	Lou Gehrig	26
	David Justice	26
7	Mickey Cochrane	25
8	Jim Gilliam	23
9	Jackie Robinson	21
10	Gil McDougald	20
	Bernie Williams	20
12	Joe DiMaggio	19
	Gene Woodling	19
14	Roger Maris	18
	Pee Wee Reese	18
16	Gil Hodges	17
	Gene Tenace	17
	Ross Youngs	17
19	Paul O'Neill	16
	Pete Rose	16

STRIKEOUTS

1	Mickey Mantle	54
2	Elston Howard	37
3	Derek Jeter	33
	Duke Snider	33
5	David Justice	30
	Babe Ruth	30
7	Gil McDougald	29
8	Bill Skowron	26
	Bernie Williams	26
10	Hank Bauer	25
11	Reggie Jackson	24
	Bob Meusel	24
	Jorge Posada	24
14	Joe DiMaggio	23
	George Kelly	23
	Tony Kubek	23
	Frank Robinson	23
	Devon White	23
19	Jim Bottomley	22
	Joe Collins	22
	Gil Hodges	22
	Lonnie Smith	22

STOLEN BASES

1	Lou Brock	14
	Eddie Collins	14
3	Frank Chance	10
	Davey Lopes	10
	Phil Rizzuto	10
6	Frankie Frisch	9
	Kenny Lofton	9
	Honus Wagner	9
9	Johnny Evers	8
10	Roberto Alomar	7
	Rickey Henderson	7
	Pepper Martin	7
	Joe Morgan	7
	Joe Tinker	7
15	Vince Coleman	6
	Chuck Knoblauch	6
	Jackie Robinson	6
	Jimmy Slagle	6
	Bobby Tolan	6
	Omar Vizquel	6
	Maury Wills	6

AVERAGE

(50 AT-BATS MINIMUM)

1	Pepper Martin	.418
	Paul Molitor	.418
3	Lou Brock	.391
4	Marquis Grissom	.390
5	Thurman Munson	.373
6	George Brett	.373
7	Hank Aaron	.364
8	Frank Baker	.363
9	Roberto Clemente	.362
10	Lou Gehrig	.361
11	Reggie Jackson	.357
12	Carl Yastrzemski	.352
13	Earle Combs	.350
14	Stan Hack	.348
15	Joe Jackson	.345
16	Jimmie Foxx	.344
17	Rickey Henderson	.339
18	Billy Martin	.333
	Julian Javier	.333
	David Eckstein	.333

SLUGGING AVERAGE

(50 AT-BATS MINIMUM)

1	Reggie Jackson	.755
2	Babe Ruth	.744
3	Lou Gehrig	.731
4	Lenny Dykstra	.700
5	Al Simmons	.658
6	Lou Brock	.655
7	Pepper Martin	.636
	Paul Molitor	.636
9	Hank Greenberg	.623
10	Charlie Keller	.611
11	Jimmie Foxx	.609
12	Rickey Henderson	.607
13	Dave Henderson	.606
14	Hank Aaron	.600
15	Duke Snider	.594
16	Dwight Evans	.580
17	Steve Yeager	.579
18	Willie Stargell	.574
19	Billy Martin	.566
20	Carl Yastrzemski	.556

ON-BASE PERCENTAGE

(50 AT-BATS MINIMUM)

1	Lou Gehrig	.477
2	Paul Molitor	.475
3	Pepper Martin	.467
	Babe Ruth	.467
5	Reggie Jackson	.457
6	Rickey Henderson	.448
7	Earle Combs	.444
8	Gene Woodling	.442
9	Marquis Grissom	.440
10	George Brett	.439
11	Carl Yastrzemski	.438
12	Jimmy Ripple	.433
13	Jimmie Foxx	.425
14	Lou Brock	.424
15	Lenny Dykstra	.424
16	Hank Greenberg	.420
17	Hank Aaron	.417
	Thurman Munson	.417
19	Dave Henderson	.410
20	Stan Hack	.408

OPS

(50 AT-BATS MINIMUM)

1	Reggie Jackson	1.212
2	Babe Ruth	1.211
3	Lou Gehrig	1.208
4	Lenny Dykstra	1.124
5	Paul Molitor	1.112
6	Pepper Martin	1.103
7	Lou Brock	1.079
8	Rickey Henderson	1.055
9	Hank Greenberg	1.043
10	Jimmie Foxx	1.034
11	Al Simmons	1.033
12	Hank Aaron	1.017
13	Dave Henderson	1.015
14	Carl Yastrzemski	.993
15	Charlie Keller	.978
16	Dwight Evans	.977
17	Gene Woodling	.972
18	George Brett	.968
19	Willie Stargell	.955
20	Duke Snider	.945

WINS

1	Whitey Ford	10
2	Bob Gibson	7
	Allie Reynolds	7
	Red Ruffing	7
5	Chief Bender	6
	Lefty Gomez	6
	Waite Hoyt	6
8	Mordecai Brown	5
	Jack Coombs	5
	Catfish Hunter	5
	Christy Mathewson	5
	Herb Pennock	5
	Vic Raschi	5
14	Harry Brecheen	4
	Tommy Bridges	4
	Lew Burdette	4
	George Earnshaw	4
	Tom Glavine	4
	Lefty Grove	4
	Ken Holtzman	4
	Carl Hubbell	4
	Sandy Koufax	4
	Don Larsen	4
	Ed Lopat	4
	Dave McNally	4
	Jack Morris	4
	Art Nehf	4
	Jim Palmer	4
	Monte Pearson	4
	Johnny Podres	4
	Warren Spahn	4
	Bob Turley	4

SAVES

1	Mariano Rivera	9
2	Rollie Fingers	6
3	Johnny Murphy	4
	Robb Nen	4
	Allie Reynolds	4
	John Wetteland	4
7	Roy Face	3
	Firpo Marberry	3
	Will McEnaney	3
	Tug McGraw	3
	Herb Pennock	3
	Troy Percival	3
	Kent Tekulve	3
	Todd Worrell	3
15	Rick Aguilera	2
	Rich Gossage	2
	Lefty Grove	2
	Dick Hall	2
	Tom Henke	2
	Willie Hernandez	2
	Bobby Jenks	2
	Darold Knowles	2
	Bob Kuzava	2
	Clem Labine	2
	Tippy Martinez	2
	Bob McClure	2
	Jose Mesa	2
	Jesse Orosco	2
	Joe Page	2
	Larry Sherry	2
	Bruce Sutter	2
	Ron Taylor	2
	Ugueth Urbina	2
	Duane Ward	2
	Mark Wohlers	2

INNINGS

1	Whitey Ford	146.0
2	Christy Mathewson	101.2
3	Red Ruffing	85.2
4	Chief Bender	85.0
5	Waite Hoyt	83.2
6	Bob Gibson	81.0
7	Art Nehf	79.0
8	Allie Reynolds	77.1
9	Andy Pettitte	66.0
10	Jim Palmer	64.2
11	Catfish Hunter	63.0
12	George Earnshaw	62.2
13	Joe Bush	60.2
14	Vic Raschi	60.1
15	Rube Marquard	58.2
16	Tom Glavine	58.1
17	George Mullin	58.0
18	Mordecai Brown	57.2
19	Carl Mays	57.1
20	Sandy Koufax	57.0
	Dave Stewart	57.0

STRIKEOUTS

1	Whitey Ford	94
2	Bob Gibson	92
3	Allie Reynolds	62
4	Sandy Koufax	61
	Red Ruffing	61
6	Chief Bender	59
7	George Earnshaw	56
8	John Smoltz	52
9	Roger Clemens	49
	Waite Hoyt	49
11	Christy Mathewson	48
12	Andy Pettitte	46
	Bob Turley	46
14	Jim Palmer	44
15	Vic Raschi	43
16	Jack Morris	40
17	Curt Schilling	39
18	Tom Glavine	38
19	Don Gullett	37
20	Don Drysdale	36
	Lefty Grove	36
	Orlando Hernandez	36
	George Mullin	36

ERA

(30 INNINGS MINIMUM)

1	Harry Brecheen	0.83
2	Babe Ruth	0.87
3	Sherry Smith	0.89
4	Sandy Koufax	0.95
5	Monte Pearson	1.01
6	Christy Mathewson	1.06
7	Mariano Rivera	1.16
8	Eddie Plank	1.32
9	Rollie Fingers	1.35
10	Bill Hallahan	1.36
11	George Earnshaw	1.58
12	Spud Chandler	1.62
13	Jesse Haines	1.67
14	Ron Guidry	1.69
15	Max Lanier	1.71
16	Stan Coveleski	1.74
17	Lefty Grove	1.75
	Orval Overall	1.75
19	Carl Hubbell	1.79
20	Ernie Shore	1.82

All-Time Postseason Leaders

GAMES

1	Bernie Williams	121
2	Derek Jeter	119
3	David Justice	112
4	Tino Martinez	99
5	Chipper Jones	92
	Jorge Posada	92
7	Paul O'Neill	85
8	Kenny Lofton	84
9	Manny Ramirez	81
10	Reggie Jackson	77
11	Yogi Berra	75
	Andruw Jones	75
13	Pete Rose	67
14	Chuck Knoblauch	66
	John Olerud	66
	Terry Pendleton	66
17	Mickey Mantle	65
18	Reggie Sanders	64
19	Lonnie Smith	63
20	Ryan Klesko	62
	Mark Lemke	62

AT-BATS

1	Derek Jeter	478
2	Bernie Williams	465
3	David Justice	398
4	Tino Martinez	356
5	Kenny Lofton	349
6	Chipper Jones	333
7	Jorge Posada	307
	Manny Ramirez	307
9	Paul O'Neill	299
10	Reggie Jackson	281
11	Pete Rose	268
12	Yogi Berra	259
13	Chuck Knoblauch	244
14	Andruw Jones	238
15	John Olerud	237
16	Mark Lemke	232
17	Roberto Alomar	230
	Mickey Mantle	230
	Terry Pendleton	230
20	Omar Vizquel	228

RUNS

1	Derek Jeter	85
2	Bernie Williams	83
3	Kenny Lofton	61
4	Chipper Jones	58
5	David Justice	55
6	Rickey Henderson	47
7	Tino Martinez	44
	Manny Ramirez	44
9	Andruw Jones	43
10	Mickey Mantle	42
11	Yogi Berra	41
	Reggie Jackson	41
13	Jorge Posada	40
14	Paul O'Neill	39
	Albert Pujols	39
16	Babe Ruth	37
17	Fred McGriff	36
18	Marquis Grissom	34
	John Olerud	34
20	Barry Bonds	33

HITS

1	Derek Jeter	150
2	Bernie Williams	128
3	Chipper Jones	96
4	David Justice	89
5	Pete Rose	86
6	Kenny Lofton	85
	Paul O'Neill	85
8	Tino Martinez	83
9	Manny Ramirez	79
10	Reggie Jackson	78
11	Steve Garvey	75
12	Jorge Posada	74
13	Roberto Alomar	72
14	Yogi Berra	71
15	Marquis Grissom	69
16	John Olerud	66
17	Andruw Jones	65
18	Rickey Henderson	63
	Chuck Knoblauch	63
	Mark Lemke	63

DOUBLES

1	Bernie Williams	29
2	Derek Jeter	22
3	Chipper Jones	18
	Jorge Posada	18
5	David Justice	17
	Paul O'Neill	17
7	Roberto Alomar	16
8	Jim Edmonds	15
	Tino Martinez	15
10	Reggie Jackson	14
	Javy Lopez	14
	Hal McRae	14
	Lonnie Smith	14
14	Hideki Matsui	13
	Pete Rose	13
16	Edgardo Alfonzo	12
	Rickey Henderson	12
	Terry Pendleton	12
	Manny Ramirez	12
	Edgar Renteria	12
	Devon White	12

TRIPLES

1	George Brett	5
2	Mariano Duncan	4
	Rickey Henderson	4
	Billy Johnson	4
	Tommy Leach	4
	Kenny Lofton	4
	Tris Speaker	4
	Omar Vizquel	4
	Devon White	4
10	Hank Bauer	3
	Johnny Bench	3
	Bobby Brown	3
	Dave Concepcion	3
	Buck Freeman	3
	Frankie Frisch	3
	Steve Garvey	3
	Lou Gehrig	3
	Dan Gladden	3
	Marquis Grissom	3
	Derek Jeter	3
	Mark Lemke	3
	Keith Lockhart	3
	Davey Lopes	3
	Billy Martin	3
	Tim McCarver	3
	Willie McGee	3
	Bob Meusel	3
	Paul Molitor	3
	Joe Morgan	3
	Freddy Parent	3

HOME RUNS

1	Bernie Williams	22
2	Manny Ramirez	20
3	Reggie Jackson	18
	Mickey Mantle	18
5	Derek Jeter	17
	Jim Thome	17
7	Babe Ruth	15
8	David Justice	14
9	Jim Edmonds	13
	Chipper Jones	13
	Albert Pujols	13
12	Yogi Berra	12
13	Carlos Beltran	11
	Steve Garvey	11
	Paul O'Neill	11
	Duke Snider	11
17	Johnny Bench	10
	George Brett	10
	Lenny Dykstra	10
	Lou Gehrig	10
	Andruw Jones	10
	Ryan Klesko	10
	Javy Lopez	10
	Fred McGriff	10
	Frank Robinson	10

RBIS

1	Bernie Williams	80
2	David Justice	63
3	Reggie Jackson	48
	Derek Jeter	48
	Manny Ramirez	48
6	Chipper Jones	47
7	Jim Edmonds	41
8	Mickey Mantle	40
9	Yogi Berra	39
	Paul O'Neill	39
11	Tino Martinez	38
12	Fred McGriff	37
13	Jim Thome	36
14	Lou Gehrig	35
	Albert Pujols	35
16	John Olerud	34
17	Roberto Alomar	33
	Andruw Jones	33
	Babe Ruth	33
20	David Ortiz	32

WALKS

1	Chipper Jones	72
2	Bernie Williams	71
3	David Justice	64
4	Jorge Posada	55
5	Barry Bonds	52
6	Derek Jeter	51
7	Mickey Mantle	43
	Manny Ramirez	43
9	Tino Martinez	41
10	Gary Sheffield	39
11	Joe Morgan	38
	Paul O'Neill	38
13	Rickey Henderson	37
14	Kenny Lofton	35
15	Andruw Jones	34
16	Reggie Jackson	33
	Albert Pujols	33
	Babe Ruth	33
19	Yogi Berra	32
20	John Olerud	31

STRIKEOUTS

1	Derek Jeter	92
2	Bernie Williams	85
3	David Justice	79
	Reggie Sanders	79
5	Jorge Posada	74
6	Tino Martinez	72
	Manny Ramirez	72
8	Jim Edmonds	70
	Reggie Jackson	70
10	Kenny Lofton	64
11	Jim Thome	61
12	Chipper Jones	60
13	Mickey Mantle	54
14	Andruw Jones	50
15	Devon White	48
16	Jeff Blauser	46
	Scott Brosius	46
	Ryan Klesko	46
19	Alfonso Soriano	45
20	Willie McGee	43

STOLEN BASES

1	Rickey Henderson	33
2	Kenny Lofton	32
3	Omar Vizquel	23
4	Roberto Alomar	20
	Davey Lopes	20
6	Derek Jeter	16
7	Joe Morgan	15
8	Lou Brock	14
	Eddie Collins	14
10	Vince Coleman	13
	Ron Gant	13
	Willie Wilson	13
13	Marquis Grissom	12
14	Rafael Furcal	11
	Chuck Knoblauch	11
	Otis Nixon	11
17	Bert Campaneris	10
	Frank Chance	10
	Johnny Damon	10
	Phil Rizzuto	10
	Alfonso Soriano	10

AVERAGE

(50 AT-BATS MINIMUM)

1	Pepper Martin	.418
2	Fred Lynn	.407
3	Billy Hatcher	.404
4	Lou Brock	.391
5	Bob Watson	.371
6	Carl Yastrzemski	.369
7	Paul Molitor	.368
8	Carlos Beltran	.366
9	Frank Baker	.363
10	Hank Aaron	.362
11	Lou Gehrig	.361
12	Thurman Munson	.357
13	Mike Stanley	.356
14	Earle Combs	.350
	Vinny Castilla	.350
16	Stan Hack	.348
17	John Valentin	.347
	Troy Glaus	.347
19	Joe Jackson	.345
20	Carlos Guillen	.344

SLUGGING AVERAGE

(50 AT-BATS MINIMUM)

1	Troy Glaus	.819
2	Carlos Beltran	.817
3	Babe Ruth	.744
4	Juan Gonzalez	.742
5	Lou Gehrig	.731
6	Hank Aaron	.710
7	Gary Matthews	.677
8	Lenny Dykstra	.661
9	Bob Robertson	.660
10	Al Simmons	.658
11	Lou Brock	.655
12	Billy Hatcher	.654
13	Ken Griffey	.644
14	John Valentin	.639
15	Pepper Martin	.636
16	Todd Walker	.635
17	George Brett	.627
18	Hank Greenberg	.623
	Jay Buhner	.623
20	Craig Monroe	.620

ON-BASE PERCENTAGE

(50 AT-BATS MINIMUM)

1	Carlos Beltran	.485
2	Lou Gehrig	.477
3	Pepper Martin	.467
	Babe Ruth	.467
5	Billy Hatcher	.466
6	Fred Lynn	.450
7	Carl Yastrzemski	.447
8	Earle Combs	.444
9	Gene Woodling	.442
10	Paul Molitor	.435
11	Mike Stanley	.434
12	Jimmy Ripple	.433
13	Lenny Dykstra	.433
14	Barry Bonds	.433
15	Jason Giambi	.431
16	Albert Pujols	.429
17	Troy Glaus	.427
18	Lance Berkman	.426
19	Jimmie Foxx	.425
	Robin Yount	.425

OPS

(50 AT-BATS MINIMUM)

1	Carlos Beltran	1.302
2	Troy Glaus	1.246
3	Babe Ruth	1.211
4	Lou Gehrig	1.208
5	Billy Hatcher	1.119
6	Hank Aaron	1.116
7	Pepper Martin	1.103
8	Lenny Dykstra	1.094
9	Gary Matthews	1.090
10	Lou Brock	1.079
11	Juan Gonzalez	1.075
12	Paul Molitor	1.051
13	Carl Yastrzemski	1.047
14	John Valentin	1.046
15	Hank Greenberg	1.043
16	Fred Lynn	1.043
17	Jimmie Foxx	1.034
18	Al Simmons	1.033
19	Ken Griffey	1.026
20	Vinny Castilla	1.026

WINS

1	John Smoltz	15
2	Tom Glavine	14
	Andy Pettitte	14
4	Roger Clemens	12
5	Greg Maddux	11
6	Whitey Ford	10
	Dave Stewart	10
	David Wells	10
9	Orlando Hernandez	9
	Catfish Hunter	9
11	David Cone	8
	Orel Hershiser	8
	Jim Palmer	8
	Mariano Rivera	8
	Curt Schilling	8
16	Bob Gibson	7
	Randy Johnson	7
	Dave McNally	7
	Jack Morris	7
	Mike Mussina	7
	Allie Reynolds	7
	Red Ruffing	7

SAVES

1	Mariano Rivera	34
2	Dennis Eckersley	15
3	Jason Isringhausen	11
	Robb Nen	11
5	Rollie Fingers	9
	Mark Wohlers	9
7	Rich Gossage	8
	Tug McGraw	8
	Randy Myers	8
10	Troy Percival	7
	John Wetteland	7
12	Brad Lidge	6
	Jose Mesa	6
	Jeff Reardon	6
15	Rick Aguilera	5
	Ken Dayley	5
	Dave Giusti	5
	Tom Henke	5
	Duane Ward	5
20	Armando Benitez	4
	Trevor Hoffman	4
	Mike Jackson	4
	Bobby Jenks	4
	Todd Jones	4
	Johnny Murphy	4
	Alejandro Pena	4
	Allie Reynolds	4
	John Smoltz	4
	Ugueth Urbina	4
	Adam Wainwright	4
	Todd Worrell	4
	Kazuhiro Sasaki	4

INNINGS

1	Tom Glavine	218.1
2	Andy Pettitte	212.0
3	John Smoltz	207.0
4	Roger Clemens	196.2
5	Greg Maddux	194.0
6	Whitey Ford	146.0
7	Mike Mussina	135.0
8	Dave Stewart	133.0
9	Catfish Hunter	132.1
10	Orel Hershiser	132.0
11	David Wells	125.0
12	Jim Palmer	124.1
13	Randy Johnson	121.0
14	Mariano Rivera	112.2
15	David Cone	111.1
16	Curt Schilling	109.1
17	Orlando Hernandez	106.0
18	Christy Mathewson	101.2
19	Don Sutton	100.1
20	Steve Carlton	99.1

STRIKEOUTS

1	John Smoltz	194
2	Roger Clemens	172
3	Tom Glavine	143
4	Mike Mussina	142
5	Andy Pettitte	134
6	Randy Johnson	132
7	Greg Maddux	122
8	Orlando Hernandez	107
9	Curt Schilling	104
10	Orel Hershiser	97
11	David Cone	94
	Whitey Ford	94
13	Bob Gibson	92
14	Jim Palmer	90
15	Mariano Rivera	87
16	Steve Carlton	84
17	David Wells	83
18	Pedro Martinez	80
19	Dave Stewart	73
20	Kevin Brown	71

ERA

(30 INNINGS MINIMUM)

1	Mariano Rivera	0.80
2	Harry Brecheen	0.83
3	Babe Ruth	0.87
4	Sherry Smith	0.89
5	Sandy Koufax	0.95
6	Monte Pearson	1.01
7	Christy Mathewson	1.06
8	Blue Moon Odom	1.13
9	Eddie Plank	1.32
10	Bill Hallahan	1.36
11	Clay Carroll	1.39
12	Mickey Lolich	1.57
13	George Earnshaw	1.58
14	Spud Chandler	1.62
15	Scott McGregor	1.63
16	Jesse Haines	1.67
17	Max Lanier	1.71
18	Stan Coveleski	1.74
19	Lefty Grove	1.75
	Orval Overall	1.75

THE GLORY OF THEIR TIMES: THE LIFETIME LEADERS

The history of baseball is so appealing partly because it is possible to compare achievements from eras that are many years apart. While baseball has certainly evolved over time, it has not undergone radical changes that would make the sport unrecognizable. A fan from 1903 magically transported to a big-league game of today would not have a problem understanding what was happening on the field (though he might not be carrying a week's wages to pay for a hot dog).

The unchanging nature of the game is why the leaders section is often the first place a reader turns upon opening a book such as this. Most baseball statistics have maintained enough of their meaning over time so as to make comparisons between players of different eras possible, either directly or indirectly (by comparing to the league average). Only a few statistical categories have changed continually in one direction over baseball history. Those few include innings pitched, which has generally declined on a seasonal basis along with parallel statistics such as complete games; fielding average, which has risen due to improvements in gloves, better groundskeeping, and more lenient official scoring; and strikeouts, which have risen due to changes in the style of play. Most other statistics rise and fall with variances in the balance between offense and defense but haven't fundamentally changed over the years.

Some of the lists in this section are divided by time period in order to more clearly highlight the standout performers of each era. Eight significant eras in baseball history have been defined for this purpose—each is distinguished by major rules changes, by large changes in the number of leagues or teams, or by other important factors.

- The first era covers 1876–91, a period that started with the formation of the National League and ended with the collapse of the American Association;
- The next period, 1892–1900, marks the short period during which the National League stood unchallenged by any rival major league;
- The third era, 1901–20, covers the Dead Ball Era, World War I, the banning of the spitball, and the Black Sox scandal. It concludes as offensive levels start to jump (which came later in the NL than in the AL);
- The next period, 1921–42, takes the major leagues through the period in which offense dominated until World War II started to seriously deplete the majors;
- The fifth era, 1943–60, starts with the peak war years and continues through baseball's integration and the migration of the major leagues to the West Coast;
- The next period, 1961–72, is highlighted by the expansion of both leagues as well the change to division play, the expansion of the strike zone (and its subsequent reversion), and the resulting collapse of offense;
- The seventh era, 1973–1987, starts with the implementation of the designated hitter rule and includes the heyday of the multipurpose stadiums. This era is highlighted by the return of offense—as well as significantly higher attendance—to the game;
- The current era, which covers 1988 to the present, is marked by the explosion of home runs, the wave of retro ballparks, and a new period of expansion.

Players are only eligible to be listed in only one era each, even if their careers spanned several eras. They are placed in the era during which they played the most games or pitched the most innings. *However, their lifetime totals or averages are used to rank them in the era they played the most.*

A quick perusal of these leader lists will reveal the names of all of the National Pastime's immortals along with the all-time greats and numerous perennial all-stars. They recount the exploits of more than a few lucky players who happened to catch lightning in a bottle once or twice. The greatest players live on in the memories of most baseball fans; the lucky ones sometimes live on only in the pages of the record books. Regardless of the type of player, the vast majority of ballplayers who show up on these lists were truly the glory of their times.

The Glory of Their Times is one of the greatest baseball books ever published. In its pages, Lawrence Ritter captured the sweet essence of men in the twilight of their lives—men whose glory may have faded but whose memories have not. By recording the names of these all-time leaders, we hope to honor them as well as the game they played so well.

A few notes about some of the leader lists:

On-Base Percentage is calculated by the current official definition for every season since 1954. However, since a distinct sacrifice fly category was not kept before 1954, they are not included in the calculations for seasons before 1954, except for the years during which sacrifice flies were not counted as sacrifice hits. (1908–30 and 1939 were the other years when sac flies were awarded; in other years pre–1954, a sacrifice fly was counted as an at bat.)

Plate Appearances count every time a batter completes an at bat, including hits, outs, walks, sacrifices, hit-by-pitches, etc.

Strikeout Percentage divides strikeouts by at bats to indicate what percentage of the time a batter strikes out.

At Bats per Strikeout indicates how infrequently a batter strikes out.

Relative Batting Average is a player's batting average compared to the league's batting average (where the latter is 1.0).

Home Run Percentage divides home runs by at bats to show the percentage of times a batter hits a home run.

Runs/150 Games and **RBI/150 Games** show a player's typical production in a full season. While today the regular season lasts 162 games, for most of baseball history the regular season was 154 games or less.

Total Chances consist of assists plus putouts plus errors.

Relief Wins and **Relief Losses** include only decisions for pitchers who did not start the game.

Blown Saves and **Save Percentage** are available for 1969 to the present only.

The minimums for Single-Season leaders include:

- Starting Pitchers (for rate statistics): 1 inning pitched per scheduled game;
- Relief Pitchers (for rate statistics): 0.5 inning pitched per scheduled game;
- Pitcher Winning Percentage: 15 wins;
- Save Percentage: 20 saves;
- Batters (for rate statistics): 3.1 plate appearances per scheduled game;
- Pinch-Hit Batting Average: 30 at bats;
- Pitcher Batting Average: 20 hits;
- Stolen Base Percentage: 20 stolen bases;
- Fielding Statistics: 0.66 games played per scheduled game (exception: for outfielders with a 1.000 Fielding Average, a minimum of 250 total chances, and for pitchers with a 1.000 Fielding Average, a minimum of 50 total chances);
- Catcher Fielding Statistics: 0.5 games played per scheduled game.

The minimums for Career leaders include:

- Starting Pitchers (for rate statistics): 1,500 innings pitched;
- Relief Pitchers (for rate statistics): 750 innings pitched;
- Save Percentage: 50 Saves;
- Batters (for rate statistics): 1,000 games;
- Pinch-Hit Batting Average: 150 at bats;
- Pitcher Batting Average: 80 hits;
- Stolen Base Percentage: 100 stolen bases.

GAMES

1	Pete Rose	3562
2	Carl Yastrzemski	3308
3	Hank Aaron	3298
4	Rickey Henderson	3081
5	Ty Cobb	3034
6	Eddie Murray	3026
	Stan Musial	3026
8	Cal Ripken	3001
9	Willie Mays	2992
10	Dave Winfield	2973
11	Rusty Staub	2951
12	Brooks Robinson	2896
13	**Barry Bonds**	**2860**
14	Robin Yount	2856
15	Al Kaline	2834
16	Rafael Palmeiro	2831
17	Harold Baines	2830
18	Eddie Collins	2826
19	Reggie Jackson	2820
20	Frank Robinson	2808
21	Honus Wagner	2794
22	Tris Speaker	2789
23	Tony Perez	2777
24	Mel Ott	2730
25	**Craig Biggio**	**2709**
26	George Brett	2707
27	Graig Nettles	2700
28	Darrell Evans	2687
29	Paul Molitor	2683
30	Rabbit Maranville	2670
31	Joe Morgan	2649
32	Andre Dawson	2627
33	Lou Brock	2616
34	Dwight Evans	2606
35	Luis Aparicio	2599
36	Willie McCovey	2588
37	Ozzie Smith	2573
38	Paul Waner	2549
39	**Steve Finley**	**2540**
40	Ernie Banks	2528
41	Bill Buckner	2517
	Sam Crawford	2517
43	Gary Gaetti	2507
44	Babe Ruth	2503
45	Tim Raines	2502
46	Carlton Fisk	2499
47	Dave Concepcion	2488
	Billy Williams	2488
49	Nap Lajoie	2480
50	Max Carey	2476
51	**Julio Franco**	**2472**
52	Rod Carew	2469
	Vada Pinson	2469
54	Dave Parker	2466
55	Fred McGriff	2460
56	Ted Simmons	2456
57	Bill Dahlen	2444
58	**Omar Vizquel**	**2443**
59	Ron Fairly	2442
60	Wade Boggs	2440
	Tony Gwynn	2440
62	Chili Davis	2436
63	Harmon Killebrew	2435
64	Roberto Clemente	2433
65	Willie Davis	2429
66	Luke Appling	2422
67	Zack Wheat	2410
68	Mickey Vernon	2409
69	Buddy Bell	2405
70	Sam Rice	2404
	Mike Schmidt	2404
72	Mickey Mantle	2401
73	Eddie Mathews	2391
74	Lou Whitaker	2390
75	Jake Beckley	2389
76	Bobby Wallace	2383
77	Enos Slaughter	2380
78	Roberto Alomar	2379
79	George Davis	2372
80	Al Oliver	2368
81	Nellie Fox	2367
82	Willie Stargell	2360
83	Jose Cruz	2353
84	Brian Downing	2344
85	Steve Garvey	2332
86	Bert Campaneris	2328
87	Frank White	2324
88	Charlie Gehringer	2323
89	Jimmie Foxx	2317
90	**Luis Gonzalez**	**2316**
91	B.J. Surhoff	2313
92	Frankie Frisch	2311
93	Harry Hooper	2309
94	Gary Carter	2296
95	Alan Trammell	2293
96	Don Baylor	2292
	Ted Williams	2292
98	Goose Goslin	2287
99	Jimmy Dykes	2282
100	Lave Cross	2278

PLATE APPEARANCES

1	Pete Rose	15861
2	Carl Yastrzemski	13991
3	Hank Aaron	13940
4	Rickey Henderson	13346
5	Ty Cobb	13068
6	Cal Ripken	12883
7	Eddie Murray	12817
8	Stan Musial	12712
9	Willie Mays	12493
10	Dave Winfield	12358
11	Robin Yount	12249
12	Paul Molitor	12160
13	**Barry Bonds**	**12129**
14	Rafael Palmeiro	12046
15	Eddie Collins	12037
16	Tris Speaker	11988
17	**Craig Biggio**	**11948**
18	Brooks Robinson	11782
19	Honus Wagner	11748
20	Frank Robinson	11743
21	George Brett	11624
22	Al Kaline	11597
23	Reggie Jackson	11416
24	Mel Ott	11337
25	Joe Morgan	11329
26	Rabbit Maranville	11256
27	Lou Brock	11235
28	Luis Aparicio	11230
29	Rusty Staub	11229
30	Harold Baines	11092
31	Tony Perez	10861
32	Ozzie Smith	10778
33	Max Carey	10770
34	Andre Dawson	10769
35	Paul Waner	10762
36	Wade Boggs	10740
37	Darrell Evans	10737
38	Babe Ruth	10617
39	Sam Crawford	10594
40	Dwight Evans	10569
41	Rod Carew	10550
42	Billy Williams	10519
43	Jake Beckley	10504
44	Nap Lajoie	10460
45	Bill Dahlen	10405
46	Vada Pinson	10403
47	Roberto Alomar	10400
48	Ernie Banks	10395
49	Tim Raines	10359
50	**Steve Finley**	**10358**
51	Nellie Fox	10349
52	Sam Rice	10246
53	Harry Hooper	10244
54	Luke Appling	10243
55	Charlie Gehringer	10237
56	Tony Gwynn	10232
57	Graig Nettles	10226
58	Roberto Clemente	10212
59	**Omar Vizquel**	**10207**
60	Dave Parker	10184
61	George Davis	10178
62	Fred McGriff	10174
63	Cap Anson	10123
64	Eddie Mathews	10101
65	Frankie Frisch	10100
66	Mike Schmidt	10062
67	Bill Buckner	10033
68	Buddy Bell	10009
69	Chili Davis	9996
	Zack Wheat	9996
71	Lou Whitaker	9967
72	Doc Cramer	9933
73	Mickey Mantle	9909
74	Carlton Fisk	9853
75	Fred Clarke	9838
76	Mickey Vernon	9834
77	Harmon Killebrew	9831
78	Willie Davis	9822
	Goose Goslin	9822
80	Gary Gaetti	9817
81	Ted Williams	9791
82	Al Oliver	9778
83	Lave Cross	9742
84	Richie Ashburn	9736
85	Willie McCovey	9686
86	Ted Simmons	9685
87	Jimmie Foxx	9670
88	Lou Gehrig	9660
89	Dave Concepcion	9640
90	Bert Campaneris	9625
	Julio Franco	**9625**
92	Jesse Burkett	9620
93	**Luis Gonzalez**	**9618**
94	Bobby Wallace	9612
95	Willie Keeler	9610
96	**Gary Sheffield**	**9560**
97	Brett Butler	9545
98	**Ken Griffey Jr.**	**9544**
99	Al Simmons	9515
100	Rogers Hornsby	9475

AT BATS

1	Pete Rose	14053
2	Hank Aaron	12364
3	Carl Yastrzemski	11988
4	Cal Ripken	11551
5	Ty Cobb	11434
6	Eddie Murray	11336
7	Robin Yount	11008
8	Dave Winfield	11003
9	Stan Musial	10972
10	Rickey Henderson	10961
11	Willie Mays	10881
12	Paul Molitor	10835
13	Brooks Robinson	10654
14	Rafael Palmeiro	10472
15	Honus Wagner	10439
16	**Craig Biggio**	**10359**
17	George Brett	10349
18	Lou Brock	10332
19	Luis Aparicio	10230
20	Tris Speaker	10195
21	Al Kaline	10116
22	Rabbit Maranville	10078
23	Frank Robinson	10006
24	Eddie Collins	9949
25	Andre Dawson	9927
26	Harold Baines	9908
27	Reggie Jackson	9864
28	Tony Perez	9778
29	Rusty Staub	9720
30	Vada Pinson	9645
31	Nap Lajoie	9589
32	Sam Crawford	9570
33	Jake Beckley	9538
34	**Barry Bonds**	**9507**
35	Paul Waner	9459
36	Mel Ott	9456
37	Roberto Clemente	9454
38	Ernie Banks	9421
39	Bill Buckner	9397
40	Ozzie Smith	9396
41	Max Carey	9363
42	Dave Parker	9358
43	Billy Williams	9350
44	Rod Carew	9315
45	**Steve Finley**	**9303**
46	Tony Gwynn	9288
47	Joe Morgan	9277
48	Sam Rice	9269
49	Nellie Fox	9232
50	Wade Boggs	9180
51	Willie Davis	9174
52	Doc Cramer	9140
53	Frankie Frisch	9112
54	Zack Wheat	9106
55	Cap Anson	9104
56	Lave Cross	9085
57	Roberto Alomar	9073
58	Al Oliver	9049
59	George Davis	9045
60	Bill Dahlen	9036
61	Dwight Evans	8996
62	Buddy Bell	8995
63	Graig Nettles	8986
64	Darrell Evans	8973
65	**Omar Vizquel**	**8966**
66	Gary Gaetti	8951
67	Tim Raines	8872
68	Charlie Gehringer	8860
69	Luke Appling	8856
70	Steve Garvey	8835
71	Tommy Corcoran	8812
72	Harry Hooper	8785
73	Al Simmons	8759
74	Fred McGriff	8757
75	Carlton Fisk	8756
76	Mickey Vernon	8731
77	Dave Concepcion	8723
78	Bert Campaneris	8684
79	Ted Simmons	8680
80	Chili Davis	8673
81	Goose Goslin	8656
82	Bobby Wallace	8618
83	Willie Keeler	8591
84	**Julio Franco**	**8587**
85	Fred Clarke	8584
86	Lou Whitaker	8570
87	Eddie Mathews	8537
88	Red Schoendienst	8479
89	Jesse Burkett	8426
90	Joe Carter	8422
91	Larry Bowa	8418
92	Sammy Sosa	8401
93	Babe Ruth	8399
94	Ryne Sandberg	8385
95	Richie Ashburn	8365
96	**Luis Gonzalez**	**8352**
	Mike Schmidt	8352
98	Bid McPhee	8304
99	**Ken Griffey Jr.**	**8298**
100	Alan Trammell	8288

RUNS

1	Rickey Henderson	2295
2	Ty Cobb	2246
3	Hank Aaron	2174
	Babe Ruth	2174
5	Pete Rose	2165
6	**Barry Bonds**	**2152**
7	Willie Mays	2062
8	Stan Musial	1949
9	Lou Gehrig	1888
10	Tris Speaker	1882
11	Mel Ott	1859
12	Frank Robinson	1829
13	Eddie Collins	1821
14	Carl Yastrzemski	1816
15	Ted Williams	1798
16	Paul Molitor	1782
17	**Craig Biggio**	**1776**
18	Charlie Gehringer	1774
19	Jimmie Foxx	1751
20	Honus Wagner	1739
21	Cap Anson	1722
22	Jesse Burkett	1720
23	Willie Keeler	1719
24	Billy Hamilton	1697
25	Bid McPhee	1684
26	Mickey Mantle	1677
27	Dave Winfield	1669
28	Rafael Palmeiro	1663
29	Joe Morgan	1650
30	Cal Ripken	1647
31	Jimmy Ryan	1643
32	George Van Haltren	1642
33	Robin Yount	1632
34	Eddie Murray	1627
	Paul Waner	1627
36	Fred Clarke	1622
	Al Kaline	1622
38	Roger Connor	1620
39	Lou Brock	1610
40	Jake Beckley	1602
41	Ed Delahanty	1600
42	Bill Dahlen	1590
43	George Brett	1583
44	Rogers Hornsby	1579
45	Tim Raines	1571
46	Hugh Duffy	1554
47	Reggie Jackson	1551
48	Max Carey	1545
	George Davis	1545
50	Frankie Frisch	1532
51	Dan Brouthers	1523
	Tom Brown	1523
53	Jeff Bagwell	1517
54	Sam Rice	1514
55	Wade Boggs	1513
56	Eddie Mathews	1509
57	Roberto Alomar	1508
58	Al Simmons	1507
59	Mike Schmidt	1506
60	Nap Lajoie	1504
61	Harry Stovey	1492
62	Goose Goslin	1483
63	Arlie Latham	1481
64	Dwight Evans	1470
65	**Ken Griffey Jr.**	**1467**
66	Herman Long	1456
67	Jim O'Rourke	1446
68	**Kenny Lofton**	**1442**
69	**Steve Finley**	**1434**
70	**Gary Sheffield**	**1433**
71	Harry Hooper	1429
	Dummy Hoy	1429
73	Rod Carew	1424
74	Sammy Sosa	1422
75	Joe Kelley	1421
76	Roberto Clemente	1416
77	John Ward	1410
	Billy Williams	1410
79	Mike Griffin	1406
80	**Frank Thomas**	**1404**
81	Sam Crawford	1391
82	Joe DiMaggio	1390
83	Lou Whitaker	1386
84	Tony Gwynn	1383
85	Andre Dawson	1373
86	Vada Pinson	1366
	Bernie Williams	**1366**
88	Brett Butler	1359
89	**Alex Rodriguez**	**1358**
90	Doc Cramer	1357
	King Kelly	1357
92	Tommy Leach	1355
	Larry Walker	1355
94	Fred McGriff	1349
95	Darrell Evans	1344
96	Lave Cross	1338
	Pee Wee Reese	1338
98	Luis Aparicio	1335
99	Barry Larkin	1329
100	George Gore	1327

RUNS BY ERA

1988–2006

1	Rickey Henderson	2295
2	**Barry Bonds**	**2152**
3	Paul Molitor	1782
4	**Craig Biggio**	**1776**
5	Rafael Palmeiro	1663
6	Cal Ripken	1647
7	Tim Raines	1571
8	Jeff Bagwell	1517
9	Wade Boggs	1513
10	Roberto Alomar	1508

1973–87

1	Pete Rose	2165
2	Dave Winfield	1669
3	Joe Morgan	1650
4	Robin Yount	1632
5	Eddie Murray	1627
6	George Brett	1583
7	Reggie Jackson	1551
8	Mike Schmidt	1506
9	Dwight Evans	1470
10	Rod Carew	1424

1961–72

1	Hank Aaron	2174
2	Willie Mays	2062
3	Frank Robinson	1829
4	Carl Yastrzemski	1816
5	Al Kaline	1622
6	Lou Brock	1610
7	Roberto Clemente	1416
8	Billy Williams	1410
9	Vada Pinson	1366
10	Luis Aparicio	1335

1943–60

1	Stan Musial	1949
2	Ted Williams	1798
3	Mickey Mantle	1677
4	Eddie Mathews	1509
5	Pee Wee Reese	1338
6	Richie Ashburn	1322
7	Nellie Fox	1279
8	Duke Snider	1259
9	Enos Slaughter	1247
10	Red Schoendienst	1223

1921–42

1	Babe Ruth	2174
2	Lou Gehrig	1888
3	Mel Ott	1859
4	Charlie Gehringer	1774
5	Jimmie Foxx	1751
6	Paul Waner	1627
7	Rogers Hornsby	1579
8	Frankie Frisch	1532
9	Sam Rice	1514
10	Al Simmons	1507

1901–20

1	Ty Cobb	2246
2	Tris Speaker	1882
3	Eddie Collins	1821
4	Honus Wagner	1739
5	Willie Keeler	1719
6	Fred Clarke	1622
7	Bill Dahlen	1590
8	Max Carey	1545
9	Nap Lajoie	1504
10	Harry Hooper	1429

1893–1900

1	Jesse Burkett	1720
2	Billy Hamilton	1697
3	Jimmy Ryan	1643
4	George Van Haltren	1642
5	Jake Beckley	1602
6	Ed Delahanty	1600
7	Hugh Duffy	1554
8	George Davis	1545
9	Herman Long	1456
10	Dummy Hoy	1429

1876–92

1	Cap Anson	1722
2	Bid McPhee	1684
3	Roger Connor	1620
4	Dan Brouthers	1523
	Tom Brown	1523
6	Harry Stovey	1492
7	Arlie Latham	1481
8	Jim O'Rourke	1446
9	John Ward	1410
10	King Kelly	1357

RUNS/150 GAMES BY ERA

1988–2006

1	**Alex Rodriguez**	**116.7**
2	**Derek Jeter**	**114.1**
3	**Barry Bonds**	**112.9**
4	Rickey Henderson	111.7
5	**Kenny Lofton**	**110.0**
6	**Todd Helton**	**107.2**
7	**Nomar Garciaparra**	**106.5**
8	Jeff Bagwell	105.8
9	**Carlos Beltran**	**105.4**
10	**Johnny Damon**	**104.6**

1973–87

1	Bobby Bonds	102.1
2	Ron LeFlore	99.8
3	Mike Schmidt	94.0
4	Joe Morgan	93.4
5	Pete Rose	91.2
6	Kirk Gibson	90.4
7	Jim Rice	89.7
8	George Brett	87.7
9	Lou Whitaker	87.0
10	Rod Carew	86.5

1961–72

1	Willie Mays	103.4
2	Hank Aaron	98.9
3	Frank Robinson	97.7
4	Dick Allen	94.3
5	Lou Brock	92.3
6	Roberto Clemente	87.3
7	Jimmy Wynn	86.3
8	Al Kaline	85.9
9	Billy Williams	85.0
10	Roger Maris	84.7

1943–60

1	Ted Williams	117.7
2	Dom DiMaggio	112.2
3	Mickey Mantle	104.8
4	Jackie Robinson	102.8
5	Johnny Pesky	102.4
6	Ralph Kiner	98.9
7	Eddie Stanky	96.6
8	Stan Musial	96.6
9	Eddie Mathews	94.7
10	Larry Doby	93.9

1921–42

1	Lou Gehrig	130.9
2	Babe Ruth	130.3
3	Earle Combs	122.3
4	Red Rolfe	120.3
5	Joe DiMaggio	120.1
6	Charlie Gehringer	114.6
7	Jimmie Foxx	113.4
8	Hank Greenberg	113.1
9	Earl Averill	110.0
10	Max Bishop	108.3

1901–20

1	Willie Keeler	121.5
2	Ty Cobb	111.0
3	Fred Clarke	108.3
4	Roy Thomas	103.2
5	Tris Speaker	101.2
6	Fielder Jones	99.0
7	Donie Bush	98.7
8	Chick Stahl	98.7
9	Joe Jackson	98.3
10	Ginger Beaumont	97.9

1893–1900

1	Billy Hamilton	159.7
2	John McGraw	139.8
3	Mike Griffin	139.4
4	Hugh Duffy	134.1
5	Mike Tiernan	133.6
6	Ed Delahanty	130.6
7	Cupid Childs	125.0
8	Jesse Burkett	124.8
9	George Van Haltren	123.8
10	Jimmy Ryan	122.4

1876–92

1	George Gore	151.9
2	Harry Stovey	150.6
3	King Kelly	139.9
4	Dan Brouthers	136.6
5	Arlie Latham	136.4
6	Sam Thompson	134.3
7	Buck Ewing	128.8
8	Tom Brown	127.8
9	Hardy Richardson	126.2
10	Tommy McCarthy	125.6

HITS

1	Pete Rose	4256
2	Ty Cobb	4189
3	Hank Aaron	3771
4	Stan Musial	3630
5	Tris Speaker	3514
6	Honus Wagner	3420
7	Carl Yastrzemski	3419
8	Paul Molitor	3319
9	Eddie Collins	3315
10	Willie Mays	3283
11	Eddie Murray	3255
12	Nap Lajoie	3242
13	Cal Ripken	3184
14	George Brett	3154
15	Paul Waner	3152
16	Robin Yount	3142
17	Tony Gwynn	3141
18	Dave Winfield	3110
19	Rickey Henderson	3055
20	Rod Carew	3053
21	Lou Brock	3023
22	Rafael Palmeiro	3020
23	Cap Anson	3012
24	Wade Boggs	3010
25	Al Kaline	3007
26	Roberto Clemente	3000
27	Sam Rice	2987
28	Sam Crawford	2961
29	Frank Robinson	2943
30	Jake Beckley	2934
31	Willie Keeler	2932
32	**Craig Biggio**	**2930**
	Rogers Hornsby	2930
34	Al Simmons	2927
35	Zack Wheat	2884
36	Frankie Frisch	2880
37	Mel Ott	2876
38	Babe Ruth	2873
39	Harold Baines	2866
40	Jesse Burkett	2850
41	Brooks Robinson	2848
42	**Barry Bonds**	**2841**
43	Charlie Gehringer	2839
44	George Sisler	2812
45	Andre Dawson	2774
46	Vada Pinson	2757
47	Luke Appling	2749
48	Al Oliver	2743
49	Goose Goslin	2735
50	Tony Perez	2732
51	Roberto Alomar	2724
52	Lou Gehrig	2721
53	Rusty Staub	2716
54	Bill Buckner	2715
55	Dave Parker	2712
56	Billy Williams	2711
57	Doc Cramer	2705
58	Fred Clarke	2678
59	Luis Aparicio	2677
60	Max Carey	2665
	George Davis	2665
62	Nellie Fox	2663
63	Harry Heilmann	2660
64	Ted Williams	2654
65	Lave Cross	2651
66	Jimmie Foxx	2646
67	Rabbit Maranville	2605
	Tim Raines	2605
69	Steve Garvey	2599
70	Ed Delahanty	2597
71	Reggie Jackson	2584
72	Ernie Banks	2583
73	Richie Ashburn	2574
74	**Julio Franco**	**2566**
75	Willie Davis	2561
76	George Van Haltren	2544
77	**Steve Finley**	**2531**
78	Heinie Manush	2524
79	Joe Morgan	2517
80	Buddy Bell	2514
81	Jimmy Ryan	2513
82	Mickey Vernon	2495
83	Fred McGriff	2490
84	Ted Simmons	2472
	Omar Vizquel	**2472**
86	Joe Medwick	2471
87	Roger Connor	2467
88	Harry Hooper	2466
89	Bill Dahlen	2461
90	Ozzie Smith	2460
91	Lloyd Waner	2459
92	Jim Rice	2452
93	Red Schoendienst	2449
94	Dwight Evans	2446
95	Mark Grace	2445
96	Pie Traynor	2416
97	Mickey Mantle	2415
98	**Ken Griffey Jr.**	**2412**
99	Stuffy McInnis	2405
100	**Gary Sheffield**	**2390**

DOUBLES

1	Tris Speaker	792
2	Pete Rose	746
3	Stan Musial	725
4	Ty Cobb	724
5	George Brett	665
6	Nap Lajoie	657
7	Carl Yastrzemski	646
8	Honus Wagner	643
9	**Craig Biggio**	**637**
10	Hank Aaron	624
11	Paul Molitor	605
	Paul Waner	605
13	Cal Ripken	603
14	**Barry Bonds**	**587**
15	Rafael Palmeiro	585
16	Robin Yount	583
17	Wade Boggs	578
18	Charlie Gehringer	574
19	Eddie Murray	560
20	**Luis Gonzalez**	**547**
21	Tony Gwynn	543
22	Harry Heilmann	542
23	Rogers Hornsby	541
24	Joe Medwick	540
	Dave Winfield	540
26	Al Simmons	539
27	Lou Gehrig	534
28	Cap Anson	529
	Al Oliver	529
30	Frank Robinson	528
31	Dave Parker	526
32	Ted Williams	525
33	Willie Mays	523
34	Ed Delahanty	522
35	Joe Cronin	515
36	Edgar Martinez	514
37	Mark Grace	511
38	Rickey Henderson	510
39	Babe Ruth	506
40	Tony Perez	505
41	Roberto Alomar	504
42	Andre Dawson	503
43	**Jeff Kent**	**501**
44	Goose Goslin	500
	John Olerud	500
46	Rusty Staub	499
47	Bill Buckner	498
	Al Kaline	498
	Sam Rice	498
50	Heinie Manush	491
51	Mickey Vernon	490
52	Jeff Bagwell	488
	Harold Baines	488
	Mel Ott	488
55	Lou Brock	486
	Billy Herman	486
57	Vada Pinson	485
58	Hal McRae	484
59	Dwight Evans	483
	Ted Simmons	483
61	Brooks Robinson	482
62	Zack Wheat	476
63	Jake Beckley	473
	Ivan Rodriguez	**473**
65	Larry Walker	471
66	Frankie Frisch	466
67	Jim Bottomley	465
68	Reggie Jackson	463
69	Dan Brouthers	460
70	Sam Crawford	458
	Jimmie Foxx	458
	Frank Thomas	**458**
73	George Davis	453
	Jimmy Dykes	453
75	Paul O'Neill	451
	Jimmy Ryan	451
77	**Ken Griffey Jr.**	**449**
	Joe Morgan	449
	Bernie Williams	**449**
80	**Steve Finley**	**446**
81	Rod Carew	445
82	George Burns	444
	Andres Galarraga	444
84	Gary Gaetti	443
85	Dick Bartell	442
	Don Mattingly	442
87	Roger Connor	441
	Barry Larkin	441
	Fred McGriff	441
90	Luke Appling	440
	Will Clark	440
	Roberto Clemente	440
	Steve Garvey	440
	B.J. Surhoff	440
95	Eddie Collins	438
	Manny Ramirez	**438**
97	Cesar Cedeno	436
	Joe Sewell	436
99	Wally Moses	435
100	Billy Williams	434

DOUBLES BY ERA

1988–2006

1	**Craig Biggio**	**637**
2	Paul Molitor	605
3	Cal Ripken	603
4	**Barry Bonds**	**587**
5	Rafael Palmeiro	585
6	Wade Boggs	578
7	**Luis Gonzalez**	**547**
8	Tony Gwynn	543
9	Edgar Martinez	514
10	Mark Grace	511

1973–87

1	Pete Rose	746
2	George Brett	665
3	Robin Yount	583
4	Eddie Murray	560
5	Dave Winfield	540
6	Al Oliver	529
7	Dave Parker	526
8	Tony Perez	505
9	Andre Dawson	503
10	Rusty Staub	499

1961–72

1	Carl Yastrzemski	646
2	Hank Aaron	624
3	Frank Robinson	528
4	Willie Mays	523
5	Al Kaline	498
6	Lou Brock	486
7	Vada Pinson	485
8	Brooks Robinson	482
9	Roberto Clemente	440
10	Billy Williams	434

1943–60

1	Stan Musial	725
2	Ted Williams	525
3	Mickey Vernon	490
4	Red Schoendienst	427
5	Enos Slaughter	413
6	Lou Boudreau	385
	George Kell	385
8	Bob Elliott	382
9	Bobby Doerr	381
10	Dixie Walker	376

1921–42

1	Paul Waner	605
2	Charlie Gehringer	574
3	Harry Heilmann	542
4	Rogers Hornsby	541
5	Joe Medwick	540
6	Al Simmons	539
7	Lou Gehrig	534
8	Joe Cronin	515
9	Babe Ruth	506
10	Goose Goslin	500

1901–20

1	Tris Speaker	792
2	Ty Cobb	724
3	Nap Lajoie	657
4	Honus Wagner	643
5	Zack Wheat	476
6	Sam Crawford	458
7	Eddie Collins	438
8	Sherry Magee	425
9	Max Carey	419
10	Bill Dahlen	413

1893–1900

1	Ed Delahanty	522
2	Jake Beckley	473
3	George Davis	453
4	Jimmy Ryan	451
5	Lave Cross	412
6	Joe Kelley	358
7	Herman Long	342
8	Hugh Duffy	325
9	Jesse Burkett	320
10	Jack Doyle	316

1876–92

1	Cap Anson	529
2	Dan Brouthers	460
3	Roger Connor	441
4	Jim O'Rourke	414
5	Paul Hines	368
6	King Kelly	359
7	Harry Stovey	347
8	Sam Thompson	343
9	Jack Glasscock	313
10	Bid McPhee	303
	Hardy Richardson	303

TRIPLES

1	Sam Crawford	309
2	Ty Cobb	295
3	Honus Wagner	252
4	Jake Beckley	244
5	Roger Connor	233
6	Tris Speaker	222
7	Fred Clarke	220
8	Dan Brouthers	205
9	Joe Kelley	194
10	Paul Waner	191
11	Bid McPhee	189
12	Eddie Collins	187
13	Ed Delahanty	186
14	Sam Rice	184
15	Jesse Burkett	182
	Ed Konetchy	182
	Edd Roush	182
18	Buck Ewing	178
19	Rabbit Maranville	177
	Stan Musial	177
21	Harry Stovey	174
22	Goose Goslin	173
23	Tommy Leach	172
	Zack Wheat	172
25	Rogers Hornsby	169
26	Joe Jackson	168
27	Roberto Clemente	166
	Sherry Magee	166
29	Jake Daubert	165
30	Elmer Flick	164
	George Sisler	164
	Pie Traynor	164
33	Bill Dahlen	163
	George Davis	163
	Lou Gehrig	163
	Nap Lajoie	163
37	Mike Tiernan	162
38	Sam Thompson	161
	George Van Haltren	161
40	Harry Hooper	160
	Heinie Manush	160
42	Max Carey	159
	Joe Judge	159
44	Ed McKean	158
45	Kiki Cuyler	157
	Jimmy Ryan	157
47	Tommy Corcoran	155
48	Earle Combs	154
49	Jim Bottomley	151
	Harry Heilmann	151
51	Kip Selbach	149
	Al Simmons	149
53	Wally Pipp	148
	Enos Slaughter	148
55	Bobby Veach	147
	Willie Wilson	147
57	Charlie Gehringer	146
58	Harry Davis	145
	Willie Keeler	145
60	Bobby Wallace	143
61	Lou Brock	141
62	Willie Mays	140
63	John Reilly	139
64	Tom Brown	138
	Willie Davis	138
	Frankie Frisch	138
	Jimmy Williams	138
68	George Brett	137
69	Lave Cross	136
	Babe Ruth	136
	Jimmy Sheckard	136
	Elmer Smith	136
73	Pete Rose	135
74	Shano Collins	133
75	Jim O'Rourke	132
	George Wood	132
77	Brett Butler	131
	Joe DiMaggio	131
	Buck Freeman	131
80	Buddy Myer	130
81	Tommy Burns	129
	Larry Gardner	129
83	Earl Averill	128
	Arky Vaughan	128
85	Vada Pinson	127
86	Hardy Richardson	126
	Robin Yount	126
88	Jimmie Foxx	125
89	John Anderson	124
	Cap Anson	124
	Hal Chase	124
	Steve Finley	**124**
	Frank Schulte	124
94	Larry Doyle	123
	Duke Farrell	123
96	Dummy Hoy	121
97	Fred Pfeffer	120
	Mickey Vernon	120
99	Hugh Duffy	119
100	Joe Cronin	118
	Chick Stahl	118
	Lloyd Waner	118

TRIPLES BY ERA

1988–2006

1	Brett Butler	131
2	**Steve Finley**	**124**
3	Lance Johnson	117
4	Paul Molitor	114
5	Tim Raines	113
6	**Kenny Lofton**	**110**
7	Juan Samuel	102
8	Willie McGee	94
9	Tony Fernandez	92
10	Andy Van Slyke	91

1973–87

1	Willie Wilson	147
2	George Brett	137
3	Pete Rose	135
4	Robin Yount	126
5	Rod Carew	112
6	Garry Templeton	106
7	Larry Bowa	99
8	Andre Dawson	98
9	Joe Morgan	96
10	Jose Cruz	94

1961–72

1	Roberto Clemente	166
2	Lou Brock	141
3	Willie Mays	140
4	Willie Davis	138
5	Vada Pinson	127
6	Hank Aaron	98
7	Luis Aparicio	92
8	Ernie Banks	90
9	Johnny Callison	89
10	Billy Williams	88

1943–60

1	Stan Musial	177
2	Enos Slaughter	148
3	Mickey Vernon	120
4	Nellie Fox	112
5	Richie Ashburn	109
6	Bill Bruton	102
	Jeff Heath	102
8	Phil Cavarretta	99
9	Dixie Walker	96
10	Bob Elliott	94

1921–42

1	Paul Waner	191
2	Sam Rice	184
3	Edd Roush	182
4	Rabbit Maranville	177
5	Goose Goslin	173
6	Rogers Hornsby	169
7	George Sisler	164
	Pie Traynor	164
9	Lou Gehrig	163
10	Heinie Manush	160

1901–20

1	Sam Crawford	309
2	Ty Cobb	295
3	Honus Wagner	252
4	Tris Speaker	222
5	Fred Clarke	220
6	Eddie Collins	187
7	Ed Konetchy	182
8	Tommy Leach	172
	Zack Wheat	172
10	Joe Jackson	168

1893–1900

1	Jake Beckley	244
2	Joe Kelley	194
3	Ed Delahanty	186
4	Jesse Burkett	182
5	George Davis	163
6	Mike Tiernan	162
7	George Van Haltren	161
8	Ed McKean	158
9	Jimmy Ryan	157
10	Tommy Corcoran	155

1876–92

1	Roger Connor	233
2	Dan Brouthers	205
3	Bid McPhee	189
4	Buck Ewing	178
5	Harry Stovey	174
6	Sam Thompson	161
7	John Reilly	139
8	Tom Brown	138
9	Jim O'Rourke	132
	George Wood	132

HOME RUNS

1	Hank Aaron	755
2	**Barry Bonds**	**734**
3	Babe Ruth	714
4	Willie Mays	660
5	Sammy Sosa	588
6	Frank Robinson	586
7	Mark McGwire	583
8	Harmon Killebrew	573
9	Rafael Palmeiro	569
10	**Ken Griffey Jr.**	**563**
	Reggie Jackson	563
12	Mike Schmidt	548
13	Mickey Mantle	536
14	Jimmie Foxx	534
15	Willie McCovey	521
	Ted Williams	521
17	Ernie Banks	512
	Eddie Mathews	512
19	Mel Ott	511
20	Eddie Murray	504
21	Lou Gehrig	493
	Fred McGriff	493
23	**Frank Thomas**	**487**
24	Stan Musial	475
	Willie Stargell	475
26	**Jim Thome**	**472**
27	**Manny Ramirez**	**470**
28	Dave Winfield	465
29	**Alex Rodriguez**	**464**
30	Jose Canseco	462
31	**Gary Sheffield**	**455**
32	Carl Yastrzemski	452
33	Jeff Bagwell	449
34	Dave Kingman	442
35	Andre Dawson	438
36	Juan Gonzalez	434
37	Cal Ripken	431
38	Billy Williams	426
39	**Mike Piazza**	**419**
40	Darrell Evans	414
41	**Carlos Delgado**	**407**
	Duke Snider	407
43	Andres Galarraga	399
	Al Kaline	399
45	Dale Murphy	398
46	Joe Carter	396
47	Graig Nettles	390
48	Johnny Bench	389
49	Dwight Evans	385
50	Harold Baines	384
51	Larry Walker	383
52	Frank Howard	382
	Jim Rice	382
54	Albert Belle	381
55	Orlando Cepeda	379
	Tony Perez	379
57	Matt Williams	378
58	Norm Cash	377
59	Carlton Fisk	376
60	Rocky Colavito	374
61	Gil Hodges	370
62	Ralph Kiner	369
63	Joe DiMaggio	361
64	Gary Gaetti	360
65	Johnny Mize	359
66	Yogi Berra	358
67	**Chipper Jones**	**357**
68	Greg Vaughn	355
69	Lee May	354
70	Ellis Burks	352
71	Dick Allen	351
72	Chili Davis	350
	Jim Edmonds	**350**
	Jason Giambi	**350**
75	George Foster	348
76	**Jeff Kent**	**345**
77	**Andruw Jones**	**342**
	Ron Santo	342
79	Jack Clark	340
80	Tino Martinez	339
	Dave Parker	339
	Boog Powell	339
83	Don Baylor	338
	Vladimir Guerrero	**338**
85	Joe Adcock	336
86	Darryl Strawberry	335
87	Bobby Bonds	332
88	**Luis Gonzalez**	**331**
	Hank Greenberg	331
90	Mo Vaughn	328
91	Willie Horton	325
92	Gary Carter	324
	Lance Parrish	324
94	Ron Gant	321
95	**Vinny Castilla**	**320**
96	**Moises Alou**	**319**
	Cecil Fielder	319
98	**Shawn Green**	**318**
	Roy Sievers	318
100	George Brett	317

HOME RUNS BY ERA

1988–2006

1	**Barry Bonds**	**734**
2	Sammy Sosa	588
3	Mark McGwire	583
4	Rafael Palmeiro	569
5	**Ken Griffey Jr.**	**563**
6	Fred McGriff	493
7	**Frank Thomas**	**487**
8	**Jim Thome**	**472**
9	**Manny Ramirez**	**470**
10	**Alex Rodriguez**	**464**

1973–87

1	Reggie Jackson	563
2	Mike Schmidt	548
3	Eddie Murray	504
4	Dave Winfield	465
5	Dave Kingman	442
6	Andre Dawson	438
7	Darrell Evans	414
8	Dale Murphy	398
9	Graig Nettles	390
10	Johnny Bench	389

1961–72

1	Hank Aaron	755
2	Willie Mays	660
3	Frank Robinson	586
4	Harmon Killebrew	573
5	Willie McCovey	521
6	Ernie Banks	512
7	Willie Stargell	475
8	Carl Yastrzemski	452
9	Billy Williams	426
10	Al Kaline	399

1943–60

1	Mickey Mantle	536
2	Ted Williams	521
3	Eddie Mathews	512
4	Stan Musial	475
5	Duke Snider	407
6	Gil Hodges	370
7	Ralph Kiner	369
8	Yogi Berra	358
9	Joe Adcock	336
10	Roy Sievers	318

1921–42

1	Babe Ruth	714
2	Jimmie Foxx	534
3	Mel Ott	511
4	Lou Gehrig	493
5	Joe DiMaggio	361
6	Johnny Mize	359
7	Hank Greenberg	331
8	Al Simmons	307
9	Rogers Hornsby	301
10	Chuck Klein	300

1901–20

1	Zack Wheat	132
2	Gavy Cravath	119
3	Tilly Walker	118
4	Ty Cobb	117
	Tris Speaker	117
6	Honus Wagner	101
7	Sam Crawford	97
8	Frank Baker	96
9	Frank Schulte	92
10	Bill Dahlen	84
	Fred Luderus	84

1893–1900

1	Jimmy Ryan	118
2	Hugh Duffy	106
	Mike Tiernan	106
4	Ed Delahanty	101
5	Herman Long	91
6	Jake Beckley	87
7	Jesse Burkett	75
8	George Davis	73
9	Bobby Lowe	71
10	Bill Joyce	70

1876–92

1	Roger Connor	138
2	Sam Thompson	126
3	Harry Stovey	122
4	Dan Brouthers	106
5	Cap Anson	97
6	Fred Pfeffer	94
7	Jack Clements	77
8	Jerry Denny	74
9	Buck Ewing	71
10	Hardy Richardson	70

HOME RUN PCT.

1	Mark McGwire	9.42
2	Babe Ruth	8.50
3	**Barry Bonds**	**7.72**
4	**Jim Thome**	**7.36**
5	**Manny Ramirez**	**7.15**
6	Ralph Kiner	7.09
7	Harmon Killebrew	7.03
8	Sammy Sosa	7.00
9	**Alex Rodriguez**	**6.86**
10	**Ken Griffey Jr.**	**6.78**
11	Ted Williams	6.76
12	**Carlos Delgado**	**6.72**
13	Juan Gonzalez	6.62
14	Dave Kingman	6.62
15	Mickey Mantle	6.62
16	Jimmie Foxx	6.57
17	**Frank Thomas**	**6.56**
18	Mike Schmidt	6.56
19	Jose Canseco	6.55
20	Albert Belle	6.51
21	**Richie Sexson**	**6.48**
22	Hank Greenberg	6.37
23	**Troy Glaus**	**6.36**
24	Willie McCovey	6.36
25	**Mike Piazza**	**6.35**
26	**David Ortiz**	**6.30**
27	**Jason Giambi**	**6.23**
28	Cecil Fielder	6.19
29	Jay Buhner	6.18
30	Darryl Strawberry	6.18
31	Lou Gehrig	6.16
32	**Vladimir Guerrero**	**6.14**
33	Hank Aaron	6.11
34	**Lance Berkman**	**6.10**
35	Willie Mays	6.07
36	Hank Sauer	6.01
37	Eddie Mathews	6.00
38	Willie Stargell	5.99
39	Mo Vaughn	5.93
40	Rob Deer	5.93
41	**Jim Edmonds**	**5.93**
42	Frank Howard	5.89
43	**Andruw Jones**	**5.86**
44	Frank Robinson	5.86
45	Greg Vaughn	5.82
46	Bob Horner	5.77
47	Jeff Bagwell	5.76
48	Roy Campanella	5.76
49	Rocky Colavito	5.75
50	Gus Zernial	5.74
51	Gorman Thomas	5.73
52	Reggie Jackson	5.71
53	Dick Stuart	5.70
54	Duke Snider	5.68
55	**Gary Sheffield**	**5.66**
56	Kevin Mitchell	5.66
57	Fred McGriff	5.63
58	Norm Cash	5.62
59	Dean Palmer	5.61
60	**Todd Helton**	**5.60**
61	**Chipper Jones**	**5.59**
62	Johnny Mize	5.57
63	Larry Walker	5.55
64	**Tony Clark**	**5.54**
65	Dick Allen	5.54
66	**Jeromy Burnitz**	**5.52**
67	Ernie Banks	5.43
68	Rafael Palmeiro	5.43
69	David Justice	5.42
70	Mel Ott	5.40
71	Matt Williams	5.40
72	Roger Maris	5.39
73	**Paul Konerko**	**5.37**
74	Todd Hundley	5.36
75	Eric Davis	5.30
76	Joe DiMaggio	5.29
77	Gil Hodges	5.26
78	Wally Post	5.24
79	Danny Tartabull	5.23
80	Mickey Tettleton	5.21
81	**Matt Stairs**	**5.19**
82	**Ryan Klesko**	**5.18**
83	Al Rosen	5.15
84	Hack Wilson	5.13
85	Glenn Davis	5.11
86	Bob Allison	5.09
87	Joe Adcock	5.09
88	Johnny Bench	5.08
89	Boog Powell	5.07
90	**Derrek Lee**	**5.07**
91	Jesse Barfield	5.06
92	Nate Colbert	5.06
93	**Tim Salmon**	**5.04**
94	**Eric Chavez**	**5.03**
95	**Aramis Ramirez**	**5.03**
96	Glenallen Hill	5.01
97	Dale Murphy	5.00
98	Charlie Keller	4.99
99	Roy Sievers	4.98
100	Ron Gant	4.98

HOME RUN PCT. BY ERA

1988–2006

1	Mark McGwire	9.42
2	**Barry Bonds**	**7.72**
3	**Jim Thome**	**7.36**
4	**Manny Ramirez**	**7.15**
5	Sammy Sosa	7.00
6	**Alex Rodriguez**	**6.86**
7	**Ken Griffey Jr.**	**6.78**
8	**Carlos Delgado**	**6.72**
9	Juan Gonzalez	6.62
10	**Frank Thomas**	**6.56**

1973–87

1	Dave Kingman	6.62
2	Mike Schmidt	6.56
3	Bob Horner	5.77
4	Gorman Thomas	5.73
5	Reggie Jackson	5.71
6	Johnny Bench	5.08
7	Jesse Barfield	5.06
8	Dale Murphy	5.00
9	Cliff Johnson	4.97
10	Jack Clark	4.97

1961–72

1	Harmon Killebrew	7.03
2	Willie McCovey	6.36
3	Hank Aaron	6.11
4	Willie Mays	6.07
5	Willie Stargell	5.99
6	Frank Howard	5.89
7	Frank Robinson	5.86
8	Rocky Colavito	5.75
9	Dick Stuart	5.70
10	Norm Cash	5.62

1943–60

1	Ralph Kiner	7.09
2	Ted Williams	6.76
3	Mickey Mantle	6.62
4	Hank Sauer	6.01
5	Eddie Mathews	6.00
6	Roy Campanella	5.76
7	Gus Zernial	5.74
8	Duke Snider	5.68
9	Gil Hodges	5.26
10	Wally Post	5.24

1921–42

1	Babe Ruth	8.50
2	Jimmie Foxx	6.57
3	Hank Greenberg	6.37
4	Lou Gehrig	6.16
5	Johnny Mize	5.57
6	Mel Ott	5.40
7	Joe DiMaggio	5.29
8	Hack Wilson	5.13
9	Rudy York	4.70
10	Wally Berger	4.69

1901–20

1	Gavy Cravath	3.01
2	Tilly Walker	2.33
3	Elmer Smith	2.19
4	Buck Freeman	1.95
5	Fred Luderus	1.73
6	Frank Baker	1.60
7	Charlie Hickman	1.48
8	Zack Wheat	1.45
9	Frank Schulte	1.41
10	Casey Stengel	1.40

1893–1900

1	Mike Tiernan	1.79
2	Hugh Duffy	1.50
3	Jimmy Ryan	1.44
4	Ed Delahanty	1.34
5	Herman Long	1.19
6	Bobby Lowe	1.00
7	Ed McKean	0.97
8	Joe Kelley	0.93
9	Duke Farrell	0.92
10	Jake Beckley	0.91

1876–92

1	Sam Thompson	2.10
2	Harry Stovey	1.99
3	Jack Clements	1.79
4	Roger Connor	1.77
5	Dan Brouthers	1.58
6	Jerry Denny	1.50
7	John Reilly	1.47
8	Denny Lyons	1.44
9	Charlie Bennett	1.44
10	Fred Pfeffer	1.43

EXTRA BASE HITS

1	Hank Aaron	1477
2	**Barry Bonds**	**1398**
3	Stan Musial	1377
4	Babe Ruth	1356
5	Willie Mays	1323
6	Rafael Palmeiro	1192
7	Lou Gehrig	1190
8	Frank Robinson	1186
9	Carl Yastrzemski	1157
10	Ty Cobb	1136
11	Tris Speaker	1131
12	George Brett	1119
13	Jimmie Foxx	1117
	Ted Williams	1117
15	Eddie Murray	1099
16	Dave Winfield	1093
17	Cal Ripken	1078
18	Reggie Jackson	1075
19	Mel Ott	1071
20	**Ken Griffey Jr.**	**1048**
21	Pete Rose	1041
22	Andre Dawson	1039
23	Mike Schmidt	1015
24	Rogers Hornsby	1011
25	Ernie Banks	1009
26	Honus Wagner	996
27	Al Simmons	995
28	Sammy Sosa	987
29	Al Kaline	972
30	**Craig Biggio**	**970**
31	Jeff Bagwell	969
32	Tony Perez	963
33	Robin Yount	960
34	Fred McGriff	958
35	**Frank Thomas**	**956**
36	Paul Molitor	953
	Willie Stargell	953
38	Mickey Mantle	952
39	Billy Williams	948
40	**Luis Gonzalez**	**943**
41	Dwight Evans	941
42	Dave Parker	940
43	Eddie Mathews	938
44	**Manny Ramirez**	**924**
45	Harold Baines	921
	Goose Goslin	921
47	Willie McCovey	920
48	Larry Walker	916
49	Paul Waner	909
50	Charlie Gehringer	904
51	Nap Lajoie	902
52	**Gary Sheffield**	**897**
53	**Jeff Kent**	**891**
54	Harmon Killebrew	887
55	Joe Carter	881
	Joe DiMaggio	881
57	Harry Heilmann	876
58	Andres Galarraga	875
59	**Steve Finley**	**873**
	Rickey Henderson	873
61	Vada Pinson	868
62	Sam Crawford	864
63	Joe Medwick	858
64	**Alex Rodriguez**	**854**
65	Duke Snider	850
66	Juan Gonzalez	847
67	Roberto Clemente	846
	Jim Thome	**846**
69	Carlton Fisk	844
70	Gary Gaetti	842
71	Mark McGwire	841
72	Edgar Martinez	838
	Rusty Staub	838
74	**Carlos Delgado**	**837**
75	Jim Bottomley	835
76	Jim Rice	834
77	Al Oliver	825
78	Orlando Cepeda	823
79	Brooks Robinson	818
80	Ellis Burks	817
81	Jose Canseco	816
82	Joe Morgan	813
83	Roger Connor	812
84	Ed Delahanty	809
	Johnny Mize	809
86	Jake Beckley	804
	Chili Davis	804
88	Joe Cronin	803
89	Roberto Alomar	794
	Johnny Bench	794
91	**Ruben Sierra**	**793**
92	**Ivan Rodriguez**	**792**
93	Albert Belle	791
	Bernie Williams	**791**
95	Dale Murphy	787
96	Mickey Vernon	782
97	Hank Greenberg	781
98	Zack Wheat	780
99	Darrell Evans	779
	Bob Johnson	779

TOTAL BASES

1	Hank Aaron	6856
2	Stan Musial	6134
3	Willie Mays	6066
4	Ty Cobb	5854
5	Babe Ruth	5793
6	**Barry Bonds**	**5784**
7	Pete Rose	5752
8	Carl Yastrzemski	5539
9	Eddie Murray	5397
10	Rafael Palmeiro	5388
11	Frank Robinson	5373
12	Dave Winfield	5221
13	Cal Ripken	5168
14	Tris Speaker	5101
15	Lou Gehrig	5060
16	George Brett	5044
17	Mel Ott	5041
18	Jimmie Foxx	4956
19	Ted Williams	4884
20	Honus Wagner	4870
21	Paul Molitor	4854
22	Al Kaline	4852
23	Reggie Jackson	4834
24	Andre Dawson	4787
25	Robin Yount	4730
26	Rogers Hornsby	4712
27	Ernie Banks	4706
28	Al Simmons	4685
29	**Ken Griffey Jr.**	**4622**
30	Harold Baines	4604
31	Billy Williams	4599
32	Rickey Henderson	4588
33	Tony Perez	4532
34	**Craig Biggio**	**4514**
35	Mickey Mantle	4511
	Sammy Sosa	4511
37	Roberto Clemente	4492
38	Paul Waner	4478
39	Nap Lajoie	4471
40	Fred McGriff	4458
41	Dave Parker	4405
42	Mike Schmidt	4404
43	Eddie Mathews	4349
44	Sam Crawford	4328
45	Goose Goslin	4325
46	Brooks Robinson	4270
47	Eddie Collins	4268
48	Vada Pinson	4264
49	Tony Gwynn	4259
50	Charlie Gehringer	4257
51	Lou Brock	4238
52	Dwight Evans	4230
53	**Gary Sheffield**	**4221**
54	Willie McCovey	4219
55	Jeff Bagwell	4213
56	**Frank Thomas**	**4203**
57	Willie Stargell	4190
58	Rusty Staub	4185
59	Jake Beckley	4156
60	Harmon Killebrew	4143
61	**Steve Finley**	**4134**
62	Jim Rice	4129
63	Zack Wheat	4100
64	Al Oliver	4083
65	Cap Anson	4080
66	Wade Boggs	4064
67	Harry Heilmann	4053
68	**Luis Gonzalez**	**4043**
69	Andres Galarraga	4038
70	Roberto Alomar	4018
71	Carlton Fisk	3999
72	Rod Carew	3998
73	Joe Morgan	3962
74	Orlando Cepeda	3959
75	Sam Rice	3955
76	Joe DiMaggio	3948
77	**Manny Ramirez**	**3946**
78	Steve Garvey	3941
79	Frankie Frisch	3937
80	Chili Davis	3914
81	Joe Carter	3910
82	Larry Walker	3904
83	Gary Gaetti	3881
84	**Alex Rodriguez**	**3875**
85	George Sisler	3871
86	Darrell Evans	3866
87	Duke Snider	3865
88	Joe Medwick	3852
89	Bill Buckner	3833
90	**Jeff Kent**	**3815**
91	Ed Delahanty	3794
92	Ted Simmons	3793
93	Roger Connor	3788
94	Ryne Sandberg	3787
95	Graig Nettles	3779
	Ron Santo	3779
97	Willie Davis	3778
98	Tim Raines	3771
99	Jesse Burkett	3759
100	**Bernie Williams**	**3756**

RUNS BATTED IN

1	Hank Aaron	2297
2	Babe Ruth	2213
3	Lou Gehrig	1995
4	Stan Musial	1951
5	Ty Cobb	1938
6	**Barry Bonds**	**1930**
7	Jimmie Foxx	1922
8	Eddie Murray	1917
9	Willie Mays	1903
10	Cap Anson	1880
11	Mel Ott	1860
12	Carl Yastrzemski	1844
13	Ted Williams	1839
14	Rafael Palmeiro	1835
15	Dave Winfield	1833
16	Al Simmons	1827
17	Frank Robinson	1812
18	Honus Wagner	1733
19	Reggie Jackson	1702
20	Cal Ripken	1695
21	Tony Perez	1652
22	Ernie Banks	1636
23	Harold Baines	1628
24	Goose Goslin	1609
25	**Ken Griffey Jr.**	**1608**
26	Nap Lajoie	1599
27	George Brett	1595
	Mike Schmidt	1595
29	Andre Dawson	1591
30	Rogers Hornsby	1584
	Harmon Killebrew	1584
32	Al Kaline	1583
33	**Frank Thomas**	**1579**
34	Jake Beckley	1578
35	Sammy Sosa	1575
36	Willie McCovey	1555
37	Fred McGriff	1550
38	Willie Stargell	1540
39	Harry Heilmann	1539
40	Joe DiMaggio	1537
41	Jeff Bagwell	1529
	Tris Speaker	1529
43	Sam Crawford	1525
44	**Manny Ramirez**	**1516**
45	Mickey Mantle	1509
46	**Gary Sheffield**	**1501**
47	Dave Parker	1493
48	Billy Williams	1475
49	Ed Delahanty	1466
	Rusty Staub	1466
51	Eddie Mathews	1453
52	Jim Rice	1451
53	Joe Carter	1445
54	George Davis	1440
55	Yogi Berra	1430
56	Charlie Gehringer	1427
57	Andres Galarraga	1425
58	Joe Cronin	1424
59	Jim Bottomley	1422
60	Mark McGwire	1414
61	Jose Canseco	1407
62	Robin Yount	1406
63	Juan Gonzalez	1404
64	Ted Simmons	1389
65	Dwight Evans	1384
66	Joe Medwick	1383
67	**Jeff Kent**	**1380**
68	Lave Cross	1378
69	Johnny Bench	1376
70	Chili Davis	1372
71	Orlando Cepeda	1365
72	Brooks Robinson	1357
73	Darrell Evans	1354
74	**Alex Rodriguez**	**1347**
75	Gary Gaetti	1341
76	Johnny Mize	1337
77	Duke Snider	1333
78	Ron Santo	1331
79	Carlton Fisk	1330
80	Al Oliver	1326
81	**Luis Gonzalez**	**1324**
82	Roger Connor	1323
83	**Ruben Sierra**	**1322**
84	Graig Nettles	1314
	Pete Rose	1314
86	Mickey Vernon	1311
	Larry Walker	1311
88	Paul Waner	1309
89	Steve Garvey	1308
90	Paul Molitor	1307
91	Roberto Clemente	1305
	Sam Thompson	1305
93	Enos Slaughter	1304
94	Hugh Duffy	1302
	Jim Thome	**1302**
96	Eddie Collins	1300
97	Dan Brouthers	1296
98	**Mike Piazza**	**1291**
99	**Carlos Delgado**	**1287**
100	Del Ennis	1284

RUNS BATTED IN BY ERA

1988–2006

1	**Barry Bonds**	**1930**
2	Rafael Palmeiro	1835
3	Cal Ripken	1695
4	Harold Baines	1628
5	**Ken Griffey Jr.**	**1608**
6	**Frank Thomas**	**1579**
7	Sammy Sosa	1575
8	Fred McGriff	1550
9	Jeff Bagwell	1529
10	**Manny Ramirez**	**1516**

1973–87

1	Eddie Murray	1917
2	Dave Winfield	1833
3	Reggie Jackson	1702
4	Tony Perez	1652
5	George Brett	1595
	Mike Schmidt	1595
7	Andre Dawson	1591
8	Dave Parker	1493
9	Rusty Staub	1466
10	Jim Rice	1451

1961–72

1	Hank Aaron	2297
2	Willie Mays	1903
3	Carl Yastrzemski	1844
4	Frank Robinson	1812
5	Ernie Banks	1636
6	Harmon Killebrew	1584
7	Al Kaline	1583
8	Willie McCovey	1555
9	Willie Stargell	1540
10	Billy Williams	1475

1943–60

1	Stan Musial	1951
2	Ted Williams	1839
3	Mickey Mantle	1509
4	Eddie Mathews	1453
5	Yogi Berra	1430
6	Duke Snider	1333
7	Mickey Vernon	1311
8	Enos Slaughter	1304
9	Del Ennis	1284
10	Gil Hodges	1274

1921–42

1	Babe Ruth	2213
2	Lou Gehrig	1995
3	Jimmie Foxx	1922
4	Mel Ott	1860
5	Al Simmons	1827
6	Goose Goslin	1609
7	Rogers Hornsby	1584
8	Harry Heilmann	1539
9	Joe DiMaggio	1537
10	Charlie Gehringer	1427

1901–20

1	Ty Cobb	1938
2	Honus Wagner	1733
3	Nap Lajoie	1599
4	Tris Speaker	1529
5	Sam Crawford	1525
6	Eddie Collins	1300
7	Zack Wheat	1248
8	Bill Dahlen	1234
9	Sherry Magee	1176
10	Bobby Veach	1166

1893–1900

1	Jake Beckley	1578
2	Ed Delahanty	1466
3	George Davis	1440
4	Lave Cross	1378
5	Hugh Duffy	1302
6	Joe Kelley	1194
7	Tommy Corcoran	1135
8	Ed McKean	1124
9	Jimmy Ryan	1093
10	Herman Long	1055

1876–92

1	Cap Anson	1880
2	Roger Connor	1323
3	Sam Thompson	1305
4	Dan Brouthers	1296
5	Bid McPhee	1072
6	Fred Pfeffer	1021
7	Jim O'Rourke	1010
8	Billy Nash	979
9	King Kelly	950
10	Harry Stovey	908

RBI/150 GAMES BY ERA

1988–2006

1	**Manny Ramirez**	**125.2**
2	Juan Gonzalez	124.7
3	Albert Belle	120.8
4	**Alex Rodriguez**	**115.7**
5	Mark McGwire	113.2
6	**Frank Thomas**	**113.0**
7	**Carlos Delgado**	**112.8**
8	Jose Canseco	111.8
9	**Richie Sexson**	**110.1**
10	**David Ortiz**	**109.7**

1973–87

1	Jim Rice	104.2
2	Bob Horner	100.7
3	Mike Schmidt	99.5
4	Johnny Bench	95.6
5	Eddie Murray	95.0
6	George Foster	94.0
7	Dave Kingman	93.5
8	Kent Hrbek	93.2
9	Greg Luzinski	92.9
10	Dave Winfield	92.5

1961–72

1	Hank Aaron	104.5
2	Dick Stuart	100.2
3	Willie Stargell	97.9
4	Harmon Killebrew	97.6
5	Ernie Banks	97.1
6	Frank Robinson	96.8
7	Orlando Cepeda	96.4
8	Dick Allen	96.0
9	Willie Mays	95.4
10	Rocky Colavito	94.4

1943–60

1	Ted Williams	120.4
2	Roy Campanella	105.7
3	Ralph Kiner	103.4
4	Al Rosen	103.0
5	Vern Stephens	102.4
6	Del Ennis	101.2
7	Yogi Berra	101.2
8	Bobby Doerr	100.3
9	Charlie Keller	97.4
10	Jackie Jensen	96.9

1921–42

1	Lou Gehrig	138.3
2	Hank Greenberg	137.3
3	Joe DiMaggio	132.8
4	Babe Ruth	132.6
5	Jimmie Foxx	124.4
6	Al Simmons	123.7
7	Hack Wilson	118.3
8	Bob Meusel	113.8
9	Hal Trosky	112.7
10	Rudy York	107.8

1901–20

1	Nap Lajoie	96.7
2	Bobby Veach	96.0
3	Ty Cobb	95.8
4	Buck Freeman	95.0
5	Frank Baker	94.0
6	Honus Wagner	93.0
7	Sam Mertes	90.9
8	Sam Crawford	90.9
9	John Anderson	89.7
10	Gavy Cravath	88.4

1893–1900

1	Ed Delahanty	119.7
2	Hugh Duffy	112.4
3	Ed McKean	101.9
4	Jake Beckley	99.1
5	Hughie Jennings	98.1
6	Joe Kelley	96.7
7	Patsy Tebeau	94.5
8	Steve Brodie	93.9
9	Jack Doyle	92.8
10	George Davis	91.1

1876–92

1	Sam Thompson	138.8
2	Cap Anson	123.8
3	Dan Brouthers	116.2
4	Tip O'Neill	107.9
5	Henry Larkin	105.9
6	Tommy Burns	105.3
7	Denny Lyons	101.0
8	Buck Ewing	100.7
9	Roger Connor	99.3
10	Dave Foutz	99.0

WALKS

1	**Barry Bonds**	**2426**
2	Rickey Henderson	2190
3	Babe Ruth	2062
4	Ted Williams	2021
5	Joe Morgan	1865
6	Carl Yastrzemski	1845
7	Mickey Mantle	1733
8	Mel Ott	1708
9	Eddie Yost	1614
10	Darrell Evans	1605
11	Stan Musial	1599
12	Pete Rose	1566
13	Harmon Killebrew	1559
14	**Frank Thomas**	**1547**
15	Lou Gehrig	1508
16	Mike Schmidt	1507
17	Eddie Collins	1499
18	Willie Mays	1464
19	Jimmie Foxx	1452
20	Eddie Mathews	1444
21	Frank Robinson	1420
22	Wade Boggs	1412
23	Hank Aaron	1402
24	Jeff Bagwell	1401
25	Dwight Evans	1391
26	Tris Speaker	1381
27	Reggie Jackson	1375
28	**Jim Thome**	**1364**
29	Rafael Palmeiro	1353
30	Willie McCovey	1345
31	Eddie Murray	1333
32	Tim Raines	1330
33	Tony Phillips	1319
34	Mark McGwire	1317
35	Fred McGriff	1305
36	Luke Appling	1302
37	**Gary Sheffield**	**1293**
38	Edgar Martinez	1283
39	Al Kaline	1277
40	John Olerud	1275
41	Ken Singleton	1263
42	Jack Clark	1262
43	Rusty Staub	1255
44	Ty Cobb	1249
45	Willie Randolph	1243
46	Jimmy Wynn	1224
47	Dave Winfield	1216
48	Pee Wee Reese	1210
49	Richie Ashburn	1198
50	Brian Downing	1197
	Lou Whitaker	1197
52	Chili Davis	1194
53	Billy Hamilton	1189
54	Charlie Gehringer	1186
55	Donie Bush	1158
56	Max Bishop	1156
57	Toby Harrah	1153
58	**Craig Biggio**	**1137**
59	Harry Hooper	1136
60	Jimmy Sheckard	1135
61	Brett Butler	1129
	Cal Ripken	1129
63	Ron Santo	1108
64	George Brett	1096
65	Paul Molitor	1094
66	Lu Blue	1092
	Stan Hack	1092
68	Paul Waner	1091
69	**Jason Giambi**	**1089**
70	Graig Nettles	1088
71	Bobby Grich	1087
72	**Ken Griffey Jr.**	**1077**
73	Mark Grace	1075
	Bob Johnson	1075
	Robin Ventura	1075
76	Ozzie Smith	1072
77	Harlond Clift	1070
	Keith Hernandez	1070
	Chipper Jones	**1070**
80	**Bernie Williams**	**1069**
81	Bill Dahlen	1064
82	Harold Baines	1062
83	Joe Cronin	1059
84	**Luis Gonzalez**	**1058**
85	**Manny Ramirez**	**1054**
86	Ron Fairly	1052
87	Billy Williams	1045
88	Norm Cash	1043
	Eddie Joost	1043
90	Roy Thomas	1042
91	Max Carey	1040
92	Rogers Hornsby	1038
93	Jim Gilliam	1036
94	Roberto Alomar	1032
95	Sal Bando	1031
96	Jesse Burkett	1029
97	Rod Carew	1018
	Enos Slaughter	1018
99	Ron Cey	1012
100	Ralph Kiner	1011

WALK PERCENTAGE (BB/PA)

1	Ted Williams	20.64
2	Max Bishop	20.00
3	**Barry Bonds**	**20.00**
4	Babe Ruth	19.42
5	Ferris Fain	18.43
6	Eddie Stanky	18.33
7	Roy Cullenbine	17.82
8	Gene Tenace	17.81
9	Eddie Yost	17.59
10	Mickey Mantle	17.49
11	**Jim Thome**	**17.29**
12	Mark McGwire	17.19
13	Charlie Keller	17.03
14	John McGraw	16.92
15	**Frank Thomas**	**16.89**
16	Mickey Tettleton	16.52
17	Joe Morgan	16.46
18	Rickey Henderson	16.41
19	Earl Torgeson	16.23
20	Bernie Carbo	16.20
21	Ralph Kiner	16.16
22	Harmon Killebrew	15.86
23	Roy Thomas	15.85
24	**Brian Giles**	**15.78**
25	**Jason Giambi**	**15.76**
26	**Bobby Abreu**	**15.75**
27	Billy Hamilton	15.63
28	Lou Gehrig	15.61
29	Harlond Clift	15.52
30	Joe Ferguson	15.51
31	**Lance Berkman**	**15.47**
32	Elmer Valo	15.47
33	Eddie Joost	15.38
34	Jack Clark	15.34
35	Jimmy Wynn	15.28
36	Lu Blue	15.15
37	Mel Ott	15.07
38	Jimmie Foxx	15.02
39	Mike Schmidt	14.98
40	Darrell Evans	14.95
41	Dolph Camilli	14.91
42	Jeff Bagwell	14.86
43	Edgar Martinez	14.79
44	Ken Singleton	14.76
45	Joe Cunningham	14.75
46	Miller Huggins	14.75
47	John Cangelosi	14.72
48	Cupid Childs	14.65
49	Elbie Fletcher	14.61
50	Darren Daulton	14.51
51	Tony Phillips	14.48
52	Merv Rettenmund	14.48
53	Dave Magadan	14.47
54	Topsy Hartsel	14.45
55	Mike Hargrove	14.42
56	Jason Thompson	14.35
57	Wayne Garrett	14.34
58	Eddie Mathews	14.30
59	Dwayne Murphy	14.25
60	**Todd Helton**	**14.23**
61	**Chipper Jones**	**14.19**
62	John Kruk	14.10
63	John Olerud	14.07
64	Augie Galan	13.98
65	Hank Greenberg	13.98
66	Gene Woodling	13.93
67	Andy Thornton	13.92
68	Willie McCovey	13.89
69	Larry Doby	13.82
70	Mickey Cochrane	13.81
71	**Tim Salmon**	**13.78**
72	Darrell Porter	13.77
73	Johnny Briggs	13.71
74	David Justice	13.68
75	Alvin Davis	13.67
76	John Mayberry	13.67
77	**Jorge Posada**	**13.60**
78	Paul Radford	13.57
79	Billy North	13.57
80	**Manny Ramirez**	**13.54**
81	**Gary Sheffield**	**13.53**
82	**Troy Glaus**	**13.48**
83	Steve Braun	13.48
84	Dave Hansen	13.48
85	Norm Siebern	13.44
86	Bob Allison	13.43
87	Al Rosen	13.42
88	**Carlos Delgado**	**13.42**
89	Jay Buhner	13.36
90	Bob Johnson	13.36
91	Lee Mazzilli	13.29
92	Roger Bresnahan	13.29
93	Donie Bush	13.26
94	Bobby Grich	13.22
95	Wally Schang	13.22
96	Mike Jorgensen	13.19
97	Carl Yastrzemski	13.19
98	Norm Cash	13.19
99	Rick Ferrell	13.16
100	Tommy Henrich	13.16

STRIKEOUTS

1	Reggie Jackson	2597
2	Sammy Sosa	2194
3	Andres Galarraga	2003
4	Jose Canseco	1942
5	Willie Stargell	1936
6	**Jim Thome**	**1909**
7	Mike Schmidt	1883
8	Fred McGriff	1882
9	Tony Perez	1867
10	Dave Kingman	1816
11	Bobby Bonds	1757
12	Dale Murphy	1748
13	Lou Brock	1730
14	Mickey Mantle	1710
15	Harmon Killebrew	1699
16	Chili Davis	1698
17	Dwight Evans	1697
18	Rickey Henderson	1694
19	Dave Winfield	1686
20	**Craig Biggio**	**1641**
21	Gary Gaetti	1602
22	**Reggie Sanders**	**1599**
23	Mark McGwire	1596
24	Lee May	1570
25	Jeff Bagwell	1558
26	Dick Allen	1556
27	Ray Lankford	1550
	Willie McCovey	1550
29	Dave Parker	1537
30	Frank Robinson	1532
31	Lance Parrish	1527
32	Willie Mays	1526
	Devon White	1526
34	Eddie Murray	1516
35	Rick Monday	1513
	Greg Vaughn	1513
37	**Jim Edmonds**	**1512**
38	Andre Dawson	1509
39	Tony Phillips	1499
40	Greg Luzinski	1495
41	**Ken Griffey Jr.**	**1494**
42	Eddie Mathews	1487
43	**Barry Bonds**	**1485**
44	**Carlos Delgado**	**1483**
45	Frank Howard	1460
46	**Manny Ramirez**	**1451**
47	Jay Bell	1443
48	Juan Samuel	1442
49	Harold Baines	1441
	Jack Clark	1441
51	Mo Vaughn	1429
52	Jimmy Wynn	1427
53	Jim Rice	1423
54	George Foster	1419
55	George Scott	1418
56	Ron Gant	1411
57	Darrell Evans	1410
58	Rob Deer	1409
	Jeff Kent	**1409**
60	Jay Buhner	1406
61	**Alex Rodriguez**	**1404**
62	Eric Davis	1398
63	Carl Yastrzemski	1393
64	**Jose Hernandez**	**1391**
65	Joe Carter	1387
66	Carlton Fisk	1386
67	Hank Aaron	1383
68	**Jeromy Burnitz**	**1376**
69	Travis Fryman	1369
70	Matt Williams	1363
71	**Royce Clayton**	**1362**
	Danny Tartabull	1362
73	**Tim Salmon**	**1360**
74	Larry Parrish	1359
75	Darryl Strawberry	1352
76	Robin Yount	1350
77	Rafael Palmeiro	1348
78	Ron Santo	1343
79	Ellis Burks	1340
	Mike Cameron	**1340**
81	Gorman Thomas	1339
82	Dean Palmer	1332
83	Babe Ruth	1330
84	**Julio Franco**	**1318**
	Deron Johnson	1318
86	Cecil Fielder	1316
87	Willie Horton	1313
88	Jimmie Foxx	1311
89	Mickey Tettleton	1307
	Tim Wallach	1307
91	Cal Ripken	1305
92	Bret Boone	1295
	Steve Finley	**1295**
94	Kirk Gibson	1285
95	Todd Zeile	1279
96	Johnny Bench	1278
	Bobby Grich	1278
98	Pete Incaviglia	1277
99	Juan Gonzalez	1273
100	Benito Santiago	1270

AT BATS PER STRIKEOUT

1	Joe Sewell	62.6
2	Lloyd Waner	44.9
3	Nellie Fox	42.7
4	Tommy Holmes	40.9
5	Andy High	33.8
6	Sam Rice	33.7
7	Frankie Frisch	33.5
8	Dale Mitchell	33.5
9	Johnny Cooney	31.5
10	Frank McCormick	30.3
11	Don Mueller	29.9
12	Billy Southworth	29.5
13	Rip Radcliff	28.9
14	Edd Roush	28.3
15	Pie Traynor	27.2
16	Doc Cramer	26.5
17	Carson Bigbee	26.0
18	Hank Severeid	25.5
19	George Sisler	25.3
20	Paul Waner	25.2
21	Sparky Adams	24.9
22	Lou Finney	24.9
23	Deacon White	24.8
24	Jack Rowe	24.8
25	Irish Meusel	24.6
26	Ezra Sutton	24.6
27	Red Schoendienst	24.5
28	Vic Power	24.5
29	Arky Vaughan	24.0
30	Felix Millan	23.9
31	Mickey Cochrane	23.8
32	Charlie Gehringer	23.8
33	John Ward	23.5
34	George Kell	23.4
35	George Cutshaw	23.2
36	Jack Tobin	23.1
37	Taffy Wright	23.1
38	Hughie Critz	23.1
39	Mark Koenig	22.5
40	Ernie Lombardi	22.3
41	Heinie Manush	22.2
42	Bobby Richardson	22.2
43	Jo-Jo Moore	22.0
44	Earl Sheely	21.8
45	Bill Dickey	21.8
46	Johnny Pesky	21.8
47	Rick Ferrell	21.8
48	Glenn Beckert	21.4
49	Tony Gwynn	21.4
50	Dick Siebert	21.2

STRIKEOUT PERCENTAGE

1	Rob Deer	36.31
2	Pete Incaviglia	30.17
3	**Jose Hernandez**	**30.12**
4	**Jim Thome**	**29.79**
5	Gorman Thomas	28.63
6	Jay Buhner	28.05
7	Mickey Tettleton	27.82
8	Jose Canseco	27.52
9	**Mike Cameron**	**27.45**
10	Dave Kingman	27.20
11	Danny Tartabull	27.18
12	Dean Palmer	27.17
13	Cory Snyder	27.13
14	**Preston Wilson**	**27.11**
15	Ray Lankford	26.97
16	**Richie Sexson**	**26.74**
17	Gary Pettis	26.40
18	Nate Colbert	26.36
19	Reggie Jackson	26.33
20	**Troy Glaus**	**26.31**
21	Eric Davis	26.27
22	Todd Hundley	26.21
23	**Tony Clark**	**26.16**
24	Sammy Sosa	26.12
25	Charles Johnson	25.99
26	Jesse Barfield	25.93
27	**Reggie Sanders**	**25.92**
28	Mo Vaughn	25.83
29	Mark McGwire	25.80
30	**Jim Edmonds**	**25.60**
31	Cecil Fielder	25.52
32	John Vander Wal	25.37
33	**Geoff Jenkins**	**25.13**
34	Lee Stevens	24.97
35	Darryl Strawberry	24.95
36	Bobby Bonds	24.95
37	Greg Vaughn	24.79
38	Andres Galarraga	24.74
39	Paul Sorrento	24.74
40	Rick Monday	24.66
41	Dick Allen	24.57
42	Donn Clendenon	24.53
43	**Carlos Delgado**	**24.50**
44	Mack Jones	24.46
45	Willie Stargell	24.42
46	**Phil Nevin**	**24.33**
47	**Derrek Lee**	**24.33**
48	**Jose Cruz**	**24.28**
49	**Jorge Posada**	**24.16**
50	**Jeromy Burnitz**	**24.10**

BATTING AVERAGE

1	Ty Cobb	.366
2	Rogers Hornsby	.358
3	Joe Jackson	.356
4	Ed Delahanty	.346
5	Tris Speaker	.345
6	Billy Hamilton	.344
7	Ted Williams	.344
8	Dan Brouthers	.342
9	Babe Ruth	.342
10	Harry Heilmann	.342
11	Pete Browning	.341
12	Willie Keeler	.341
13	Bill Terry	.341
14	George Sisler	.340
15	Lou Gehrig	.340
16	Jesse Burkett	.338
17	Tony Gwynn	.338
18	Nap Lajoie	.338
19	Riggs Stephenson	.336
20	Al Simmons	.334
21	John McGraw	.334
22	Paul Waner	.333
23	Eddie Collins	.333
24	**Todd Helton**	**.333**
25	Mike Donlin	.333
26	Sam Thompson	.331
27	Cap Anson	.331
28	Stan Musial	.331
29	Heinie Manush	.330
30	Wade Boggs	.328
31	Rod Carew	.328
32	Honus Wagner	.328
33	Tip O'Neill	.326
34	Hugh Duffy	.326
35	Bob Fothergill	.325
36	Jimmie Foxx	.325
37	Earle Combs	.325
38	**Vladimir Guerrero**	**.325**
39	Joe DiMaggio	.325
40	Babe Herman	.324
41	Joe Medwick	.324
42	Edd Roush	.323
43	Sam Rice	.322
44	Ross Youngs	.322
45	Kiki Cuyler	.321
46	Charlie Gehringer	.320
47	Chuck Klein	.320
48	Pie Traynor	.320
49	Mickey Cochrane	.320
50	Ken Williams	.319
51	**Nomar Garciaparra**	**.318**
52	Kirby Puckett	.318
53	Earl Averill	.318
54	Arky Vaughan	.318
55	Roberto Clemente	.317
56	Chick Hafey	.317
57	Joe Kelley	.317
58	Zack Wheat	.317
59	**Derek Jeter**	**.317**
60	Roger Connor	.316
61	Lloyd Waner	.316
62	George Van Haltren	.316
63	Frankie Frisch	.316
64	Goose Goslin	.316
65	Bibb Falk	.314
66	**Manny Ramirez**	**.314**
67	Cecil Travis	.314
68	Hank Greenberg	.313
69	Jack Fournier	.313
70	Elmer Flick	.313
71	Larry Walker	.313
72	Bill Dickey	.313
73	Dale Mitchell	.312
74	Johnny Mize	.312
75	Joe Sewell	.312
76	Fred Clarke	.312
77	Barney McCosky	.312
78	Hughie Jennings	.312
79	Edgar Martinez	.312
80	Freddie Lindstrom	.311
81	Bing Miller	.311
82	Jackie Robinson	.311
83	Baby Doll Jacobson	.311
84	Taffy Wright	.311
85	Rip Radcliff	.311
86	Ginger Beaumont	.311
87	Mike Tiernan	.311
88	Luke Appling	.310
89	Irish Meusel	.310
90	Elmer Smith	.310
91	Denny Lyons	.310
92	Bobby Veach	.310
93	Jim O'Rourke	.310
94	Jim Bottomley	.310
95	John Stone	.310
96	Sam Crawford	.309
97	**Mike Piazza**	**.309**
98	Bob Meusel	.309
99	Jack Tobin	.309
100	Spud Davis	.308

BATTING AVERAGE BY ERA

1988–2006

1	Tony Gwynn	.338
2	**Todd Helton**	**.333**
3	Wade Boggs	.328
4	**Vladimir Guerrero**	**.325**
5	**Nomar Garciaparra**	**.318**
6	Kirby Puckett	.318
7	**Derek Jeter**	**.317**
8	**Manny Ramirez**	**.314**
9	Larry Walker	.313
10	Edgar Martinez	.312

1973–87

1	Rod Carew	.328
2	Ralph Garr	.306
3	George Brett	.305
4	Bill Madlock	.305
5	Al Oliver	.303
6	Pete Rose	.303
7	Pedro Guerrero	.300
8	Bake McBride	.299
9	Cecil Cooper	.298
10	Jim Rice	.298

1961–72

1	Roberto Clemente	.317
2	Matty Alou	.307
3	Hank Aaron	.305
4	Tony Oliva	.304
5	Manny Mota	.304
6	Willie Mays	.302
7	Rico Carty	.299
8	Joe Torre	.297
9	Al Kaline	.297
10	Orlando Cepeda	.297

1943–60

1	Ted Williams	.344
2	Stan Musial	.331
3	Dale Mitchell	.312
4	Barney McCosky	.312
5	Jackie Robinson	.311
6	Richie Ashburn	.308
7	Johnny Pesky	.307
8	George Kell	.306
9	Dixie Walker	.306
10	Harvey Kuenn	.303

1921–42

1	Rogers Hornsby	.358
2	Babe Ruth	.342
3	Harry Heilmann	.342
4	Bill Terry	.341
5	George Sisler	.340
6	Lou Gehrig	.340
7	Riggs Stephenson	.336
8	Al Simmons	.334
9	Paul Waner	.333
10	Heinie Manush	.330

1901–20

1	Ty Cobb	.366
2	Joe Jackson	.356
3	Tris Speaker	.345
4	Willie Keeler	.341
5	Nap Lajoie	.338
6	Eddie Collins	.333
7	Mike Donlin	.333
8	Honus Wagner	.328
9	Zack Wheat	.317
10	Elmer Flick	.313

1893–1900

1	Ed Delahanty	.346
2	Billy Hamilton	.344
3	Jesse Burkett	.338
4	John McGraw	.334
5	Hugh Duffy	.326
6	Joe Kelley	.317
7	George Van Haltren	.316
8	Hughie Jennings	.312
9	Mike Tiernan	.311
10	Elmer Smith	.310

1876–92

1	Dan Brouthers	.342
2	Pete Browning	.341
3	Sam Thompson	.331
4	Cap Anson	.331
5	Tip O'Neill	.326
6	Roger Connor	.316
7	Denny Lyons	.310
8	Jim O'Rourke	.310
9	King Kelly	.308
10	Deacon White	.303

ON-BASE PERCENTAGE

1	Ted Williams	.482
2	Babe Ruth	.474
3	John McGraw	.466
4	Billy Hamilton	.455
5	Lou Gehrig	.447
6	**Barry Bonds**	**.443**
7	Rogers Hornsby	.434
8	Ty Cobb	.433
9	**Todd Helton**	**.430**
10	Jimmie Foxx	.428
	Tris Speaker	.428
12	Eddie Collins	.424
	Ferris Fain	.424
	Frank Thomas	**.424**
15	Max Bishop	.423
	Dan Brouthers	.423
	Joe Jackson	.423
18	Mickey Mantle	.421
19	Mickey Cochrane	.419
20	Edgar Martinez	.418
21	Stan Musial	.417
22	**Lance Berkman**	**.416**
	Cupid Childs	.416
24	Wade Boggs	.415
	Jesse Burkett	.415
26	Mel Ott	.414
27	**Jason Giambi**	**.413**
	Roy Thomas	.413
29	**Bobby Abreu**	**.412**
	Hank Greenberg	.412
31	Ed Delahanty	.411
	Manny Ramirez	**.411**
33	Harry Heilmann	.410
	Charlie Keller	.410
	Eddie Stanky	.410
36	Jackie Robinson	.409
	Jim Thome	**.409**
38	Jeff Bagwell	.408
	Roy Cullenbine	.408
	Brian Giles	**.408**
41	Denny Lyons	.407
	Riggs Stephenson	.407
43	Arky Vaughan	.406
44	Charlie Gehringer	.404
	Paul Waner	.404
46	Pete Browning	.403
	Joe Cunningham	.403
48	Lu Blue	.402
	Chipper Jones	**.402**
	Joe Kelley	.402
51	Rickey Henderson	.401
52	Larry Walker	.400
53	Luke Appling	.399
	Ross Youngs	.399
55	Joe DiMaggio	.398
	Ralph Kiner	.398
	John Olerud	.398
	Gary Sheffield	**.398**
	Elmer Smith	.398
	Elmer Valo	.398
61	Earle Combs	.397
	Roger Connor	.397
	John Kruk	.397
	Johnny Mize	.397
65	Cap Anson	.396
	Richie Ashburn	.396
	Mike Hargrove	.396
68	Earl Averill	.395
	Hack Wilson	.395
70	Frank Chance	.394
	Stan Hack	.394
	Mark McGwire	.394
	Johnny Pesky	.394
	Eddie Yost	.394
75	Rod Carew	.393
	Bob Johnson	.393
	Wally Schang	.393
	Bill Terry	.393
	Ken Williams	.393
80	Jack Fournier	.392
	George Grantham	.392
	Joe Morgan	.392
	Tip O'Neill	.392
	Mike Tiernan	.392
85	Hughie Jennings	.391
	Joe Sewell	.391
	Honus Wagner	.391
88	Harlond Clift	.390
	Joe Cronin	.390
	Carlos Delgado	**.390**
	Augie Galan	.390
	Vladimir Guerrero	**.390**
	Dave Magadan	.390
94	Elmer Flick	.389
	Minnie Minoso	.389
	Buddy Myer	.389
	Frank Robinson	.389
98	Dolph Camilli	.388
	Mike Griffin	.388
	Tony Gwynn	.388
	Derek Jeter	**.388**
	Willie Keeler	.388
	Ken Singleton	.388
	Gene Tenace	.388

SLUGGING AVERAGE

1	Babe Ruth	.690
2	Ted Williams	.634
3	Lou Gehrig	.632
4	Jimmie Foxx	.609
5	**Barry Bonds**	**.608**
6	Hank Greenberg	.605
7	**Manny Ramirez**	**.600**
8	**Todd Helton**	**.593**
9	Mark McGwire	.588
10	**Vladimir Guerrero**	**.583**
11	Joe DiMaggio	.579
12	Rogers Hornsby	.577
13	**Alex Rodriguez**	**.573**
14	**Lance Berkman**	**.567**
15	**Frank Thomas**	**.566**
16	Larry Walker	.565
17	**Jim Thome**	**.565**
18	Albert Belle	.564
19	Johnny Mize	.562
20	Juan Gonzalez	.561
21	Stan Musial	.559
22	**Carlos Delgado**	**.558**
23	Willie Mays	.557
24	**Ken Griffey Jr.**	**.557**
25	Mickey Mantle	.557
26	Hank Aaron	.555
27	**Mike Piazza**	**.551**
28	**David Ortiz**	**.550**
29	Ralph Kiner	.548
30	Hack Wilson	.545
31	Chuck Klein	.543
32	**Chipper Jones**	**.542**
33	**Jason Giambi**	**.541**
34	Jeff Bagwell	.540
35	**Nomar Garciaparra**	**.540**
36	Duke Snider	.540
37	**Jim Edmonds**	**.539**
38	Frank Robinson	.537
39	Sammy Sosa	.537
40	Al Simmons	.535
41	Dick Allen	.534
42	Earl Averill	.534
43	Mel Ott	.533
44	Babe Herman	.532
45	Ken Williams	.530
46	Willie Stargell	.529
47	Mike Schmidt	.527
48	**Richie Sexson**	**.526**
49	Chick Hafey	.526
50	**Gary Sheffield**	**.525**
51	**Brian Giles**	**.525**
52	Mo Vaughn	.523
53	Hal Trosky	.522
54	Wally Berger	.522
55	Harry Heilmann	.520
56	Kevin Mitchell	.520
57	Dan Brouthers	.519
58	Charlie Keller	.518
59	Joe Jackson	.517
60	**Moises Alou**	**.516**
61	Edgar Martinez	.515
62	**Scott Rolen**	**.515**
63	Willie McCovey	.515
64	Jose Canseco	.515
65	Rafael Palmeiro	.515
66	**Magglio Ordonez**	**.513**
67	Ty Cobb	.512
68	Ellis Burks	.510
69	Eddie Mathews	.509
70	Fred McGriff	.509
71	Jeff Heath	.509
72	Harmon Killebrew	.509
73	**Ryan Klesko**	**.507**
74	**Bobby Abreu**	**.507**
75	Bob Johnson	.506
76	Bill Terry	.506
77	Darryl Strawberry	.505
78	Sam Thompson	.505
79	**Andruw Jones**	**.505**
80	Ed Delahanty	.505
81	Joe Medwick	.505
82	**Jeff Kent**	**.504**
83	**Troy Glaus**	**.503**
84	Jim Rice	.502
85	Tris Speaker	.500
86	David Justice	.500
87	Jim Bottomley	.500
88	**Derrek Lee**	**.500**
89	Goose Goslin	.500
90	Roy Campanella	.500
91	Ernie Banks	.500
92	Orlando Cepeda	.499
93	Bob Horner	.499
94	**Geoff Jenkins**	**.499**
95	Dante Bichette	.499
96	**Shawn Green**	**.499**
97	Andres Galarraga	.499
98	Frank Howard	.499
99	**Tim Salmon**	**.498**
100	Ted Kluszewski	.498

ON-BASE PLUS SLUGGING

1	Babe Ruth	1164
2	Ted Williams	1116
3	Lou Gehrig	1079
4	**Barry Bonds**	**1051**
5	Jimmie Foxx	1037
6	**Todd Helton**	**1023**
7	Hank Greenberg	1017
8	Rogers Hornsby	1011
	Manny Ramirez	**1011**
10	**Frank Thomas**	**990**
11	**Lance Berkman**	**983**
12	Mark McGwire	982
13	Mickey Mantle	978
14	Joe DiMaggio	977
15	Stan Musial	976
16	**Jim Thome**	**974**
17	**Vladimir Guerrero**	**973**
18	Larry Walker	965
19	Johnny Mize	959
	Alex Rodriguez	**959**
21	**Jason Giambi**	**954**
22	Jeff Bagwell	948
	Carlos Delgado	**948**
24	Mel Ott	947
25	Ralph Kiner	946
26	Ty Cobb	945
27	**Chipper Jones**	**944**
28	Dan Brouthers	942
29	Willie Mays	941
30	Joe Jackson	940
	Hack Wilson	940
32	Albert Belle	933
	Brian Giles	**933**
	Edgar Martinez	933
35	**Ken Griffey Jr.**	**931**
36	**Mike Piazza**	**930**
37	Harry Heilmann	930
38	Hank Aaron	929
	Earl Averill	929
40	Charlie Keller	928
	Tris Speaker	928
42	Frank Robinson	926
43	**David Ortiz**	**924**
44	**Gary Sheffield**	**923**
	Ken Williams	923
46	Chuck Klein	922
47	**Jim Edmonds**	**921**
48	Duke Snider	920
49	**Bobby Abreu**	**919**
50	Ed Delahanty	916
51	Al Simmons	915
52	Babe Herman	915
53	Dick Allen	912
54	**Nomar Garciaparra**	**907**
55	Mike Schmidt	907
56	Mo Vaughn	906
57	Juan Gonzalez	904
58	Bob Johnson	899
	Bill Terry	899
60	Chick Hafey	898
61	Mickey Cochrane	897
62	Hal Trosky	893
63	**Scott Rolen**	**890**
64	Willie McCovey	889
	Willie Stargell	889
	Sam Thompson	889
67	Billy Hamilton	887
68	Goose Goslin	887
69	Fred McGriff	886
70	Rafael Palmeiro	886
71	Harmon Killebrew	885
	Eddie Mathews	885
73	Charlie Gehringer	884
74	**Moises Alou**	**884**
75	Roger Connor	883
	Jackie Robinson	883
	Tim Salmon	**883**
78	Sammy Sosa	882
79	Wally Berger	881
	Will Clark	881
81	Dolph Camilli	880
	Kevin Mitchell	880
	Riggs Stephenson	880
84	**Ryan Klesko**	**879**
85	Jeff Heath	879
	Al Rosen	879
87	David Justice	878
88	Paul Waner	877
89	Larry Doby	876
	Richie Sexson	**876**
91	John McGraw	876
92	Jack Fournier	875
	Magglio Ordonez	**875**
94	Ellis Burks	873
	Tommy Henrich	873
96	Pete Browning	870
	Mike Sweeney	**870**
98	Jim Bottomley	869
99	Jose Canseco	868
	Bill Dickey	868

ADJUSTED OPS

1	Babe Ruth	209
2	Ted Williams	186
3	**Barry Bonds**	**182**
	Lou Gehrig	182
5	Rogers Hornsby	176
6	Mickey Mantle	173
7	Dan Brouthers	169
	Joe Jackson	169
9	Ty Cobb	167
10	Pete Browning	164
11	Mark McGwire	163
12	Jimmie Foxx	161
13	**Frank Thomas**	**160**
14	Hank Greenberg	157
	Johnny Mize	157
	Stan Musial	157
17	Hank Aaron	156
	Dick Allen	156
	Joe DiMaggio	156
	Willie Mays	156
	Tris Speaker	156
22	Mel Ott	155
	Manny Ramirez	**155**
24	Roger Connor	154
25	Frank Robinson	153
26	Ed Delahanty	152
	Charlie Keller	152
28	**Vladimir Guerrero**	**150**
	Nap Lajoie	150
	Honus Wagner	150
31	Jeff Bagwell	149
	Gavy Cravath	149
	Elmer Flick	149
34	**Jason Giambi**	**148**
	Harry Heilmann	148
	Ralph Kiner	148
	Willie McCovey	148
	Jim Thome	**148**
39	Edgar Martinez	147
	Mike Piazza	**147**
	Willie Stargell	147
42	Mike Schmidt	146
	Sam Thompson	146
44	**Lance Berkman**	**145**
	Eddie Mathews	145
	Gary Sheffield	**145**
	Hack Wilson	145
48	Albert Belle	144
	Alex Rodriguez	**144**
50	Sam Crawford	143
	Jack Fournier	143
	Frank Howard	143
53	Eddie Collins	142
	Mike Donlin	142
	Chipper Jones	**142**
	Harmon Killebrew	142
	Henry Larkin	142
	Kevin Mitchell	142
59	**Carlos Delgado**	**141**
	Brian Giles	**141**
	Ken Griffey Jr.	**141**
	Babe Herman	141
	Harry Stovey	141
64	Wally Berger	140
	Jesse Burkett	140
	Jeff Heath	140
	Tip O'Neill	140
68	**Bobby Abreu**	**139**
	Cap Anson	139
	Billy Hamilton	139
	Todd Helton	**139**
	Reggie Jackson	139
	Bob Johnson	139
74	Norm Cash	138
	Pedro Guerrero	138
	Denny Lyons	138
	Al Rosen	138
	Duke Snider	138
	Darryl Strawberry	138
	Mike Tiernan	138
81	Jack Clark	137
	Will Clark	137
	Larry Doby	137
	Sherry Magee	137
	Gene Tenace	137
	Bill Terry	137
87	Frank Baker	136
	King Kelly	136
	Reggie Smith	136
	Arky Vaughan	136
	Larry Walker	136
	Ken Williams	136
93	Tommy Burns	135
	Frank Chance	135
	Chuck Klein	135
	John McGraw	135
97	George Brett	134
	Dolph Camilli	134
	Jim Edmonds	**134**
	George Gore	134
	Al Kaline	134
	John Kruk	134
	Boog Powell	134

ADJUSTED BATTING WINS

1	Babe Ruth	135.3
2	**Barry Bonds**	**124.1**
3	Ty Cobb	103.4
4	Ted Williams	103.0
5	Hank Aaron	95.1
6	Lou Gehrig	93.7
7	Stan Musial	92.5
8	Mickey Mantle	89.4
9	Rogers Hornsby	87.6
10	Willie Mays	86.9
11	Tris Speaker	82.9
12	Frank Robinson	78.4
13	Mel Ott	78.2
14	Jimmie Foxx	70.0
15	**Frank Thomas**	**68.6**
16	Honus Wagner	66.0
17	Eddie Collins	64.4
18	Jeff Bagwell	60.3
19	Eddie Mathews	58.3
20	Nap Lajoie	57.9
21	Willie McCovey	57.3
22	Mark McGwire	56.8
23	Mike Schmidt	56.5
24	**Gary Sheffield**	**56.0**
25	Dan Brouthers	53.4
26	Reggie Jackson	53.3
27	Edgar Martinez	53.3
28	Rickey Henderson	52.8
29	**Manny Ramirez**	**52.7**
30	Harry Heilmann	52.7
31	Carl Yastrzemski	52.3
32	Joe Morgan	51.7
33	Harmon Killebrew	51.3
34	Willie Stargell	51.2
35	Joe DiMaggio	50.2
36	Dick Allen	49.7
37	Johnny Mize	49.5
38	Al Kaline	49.5
39	George Brett	49.0
40	Sam Crawford	48.7
41	Ed Delahanty	48.5
42	Roger Connor	48.3
43	Rafael Palmeiro	47.3
44	**Jim Thome**	**47.1**
45	**Ken Griffey Jr.**	**46.8**
46	Paul Waner	46.6
47	Eddie Murray	46.3
48	Joe Jackson	45.0
49	Tony Gwynn	44.7
50	Dave Winfield	44.4
51	Wade Boggs	44.2
52	**Mike Piazza**	**43.2**
53	Jesse Burkett	43.1
54	**Jason Giambi**	**42.3**
55	Fred McGriff	42.1
56	Rod Carew	42.0
57	**Alex Rodriguez**	**41.9**
58	**Chipper Jones**	**41.4**
59	Hank Greenberg	40.8
60	Jack Clark	39.9
61	Will Clark	39.7
62	Duke Snider	39.6
63	Cap Anson	39.6
64	Billy Williams	39.4
65	Pete Rose	39.2
66	**Vladimir Guerrero**	**38.8**
67	Norm Cash	37.9
68	Frank Howard	37.9
69	Bob Johnson	37.7
70	Ken Singleton	37.7
71	**Carlos Delgado**	**37.6**
72	John Olerud	37.5
73	Larry Walker	37.0
74	Billy Hamilton	36.9
75	Reggie Smith	36.8
76	Roberto Clemente	36.7
77	Ralph Kiner	36.5
78	Rusty Staub	36.1
79	Elmer Flick	35.9
80	Arky Vaughan	35.8
81	Orlando Cepeda	35.7
82	Sherry Magee	35.7
83	Fred Clarke	35.6
84	Zack Wheat	34.8
85	Dwight Evans	34.8
86	Albert Belle	34.7
87	**Albert Pujols**	**34.6**
88	**Brian Giles**	**34.3**
89	**Bobby Abreu**	**34.2**
90	Pete Browning	34.0
91	Al Simmons	33.6
92	Keith Hernandez	33.4
93	Boog Powell	33.3
94	Paul Molitor	33.1
95	Tim Raines	33.1
96	Bill Terry	32.6
97	Goose Goslin	32.4
98	**Todd Helton**	**32.1**
99	Charlie Gehringer	32.0
100	Joe Medwick	32.0

ADJUSTED BATTING WINS

101	Babe Herman	31.7
102	Jimmy Wynn	31.6
103	Jack Fournier	31.2
104	Sammy Sosa	31.2
105	Joe Torre	31.0
106	Minnie Minoso	30.7
107	Rocky Colavito	30.6
108	Hack Wilson	30.4
109	Joe Kelley	30.3
110	**Jim Edmonds**	**30.2**
111	Jose Canseco	30.1
112	Sam Thompson	29.9
113	Chuck Klein	29.9
114	**Bernie Williams**	**29.6**
115	Charlie Keller	29.3
116	Darryl Strawberry	29.3
117	Pedro Guerrero	29.1
118	Ron Santo	28.9
119	Larry Doby	28.7
120	Bobby Bonds	28.5
121	Brian Downing	28.3
122	Gene Tenace	28.2
123	Tony Perez	28.1
124	Darrell Evans	28.1
125	Johnny Bench	28.1
126	Jim Rice	27.8
127	Earl Averill	27.7
128	Jake Beckley	27.6
129	Greg Luzinski	27.6
130	Fred Lynn	27.5
131	Harold Baines	27.4
132	Mike Tiernan	27.2
133	Bobby Grich	27.1
134	Willie Keeler	27.1
135	**Jeff Kent**	**27.1**
136	Dolph Camilli	26.9
137	Ernie Banks	26.9
138	Gavy Cravath	26.8
139	Wally Berger	26.6
140	**Lance Berkman**	**26.6**
141	Harry Stovey	26.5
142	Enos Slaughter	26.5
143	Frank Baker	26.4
144	Jim O'Rourke	26.3
145	Bob Elliott	26.2
146	**Moises Alou**	**26.1**
147	Don Mattingly	26.1
148	Bob Watson	26.0
149	Jeff Heath	25.9
150	**Tim Salmon**	**25.8**
151	Chili Davis	25.7
152	Roy Thomas	25.4
153	Tony Oliva	25.3
154	Jimmy Sheckard	25.2
155	Bill Nicholson	25.1
156	Rico Carty	25.1
157	Stan Hack	25.1
158	Bobby Bonilla	25.1
159	Kiki Cuyler	25.1
160	Juan Gonzalez	25.1
161	Jackie Robinson	24.9
162	**Luis Gonzalez**	**24.8**
163	Mark Grace	24.7
164	George Davis	24.6
165	Mo Vaughn	24.6
166	Jose Cruz	24.4
167	George Sisler	24.3
168	Yogi Berra	24.3
169	Jim Bottomley	24.2
170	George Foster	24.2
171	Cesar Cedeno	24.2
172	Bill Dickey	24.0
173	**Ryan Klesko**	**23.9**
174	Al Oliver	23.9
175	**Craig Biggio**	**23.8**
176	Edd Roush	23.8
177	Kevin Mitchell	23.7
178	Ken Williams	23.6
179	Dave Parker	23.5
180	Gabby Hartnett	23.5
181	Ron Cey	23.4
182	Kent Hrbek	23.4
183	Bobby Veach	23.4
184	Ellis Burks	23.4
185	Paul O'Neill	23.3
186	Danny Tartabull	23.2
187	Mickey Cochrane	23.2
188	John McGraw	23.1
189	Bobby Murcer	23.1
190	Dale Murphy	23.1
191	**Scott Rolen**	**23.0**
192	David Justice	23.0
193	**Derek Jeter**	**22.6**
194	King Kelly	22.5
195	Lou Whitaker	22.5
196	Sid Gordon	22.4
197	Paul Hines	22.4
198	Roy White	22.4
199	Augie Galan	22.4
200	Earle Combs	22.4

PINCH HITS

1	Lenny Harris	212
2	Manny Mota	150
3	Smoky Burgess	145
4	Greg Gross	143
5	Dave Hansen	139
6	**Mark Sweeney**	**139**
7	John Vander Wal	126
8	Jose Morales	123
9	Jerry Lynch	116
10	Red Lucas	114
11	Steve Braun	113
12	Terry Crowley	108
	Denny Walling	108
14	Gates Brown	107
15	**Orlando Palmeiro**	**105**
16	Mike Lum	103
17	Jim Dwyer	102
18	Rusty Staub	100
19	Dave Clark	96
20	Larry Biittner	95
	Vic Davalillo	95
	Gerald Perry	95
23	Jerry Hairston	94
24	Dave Philley	93
	Joel Youngblood	93

PINCH HIT AVERAGE

(150 AT-BATS MINIMUM)

1	Alex Arias	.320
2	Tommy Davis	.320
3	Frenchy Bordagaray	.312
4	Harold Baines	.311
5	Greg Colbrunn	.310
6	Frankie Baumholtz	.307
7	Sid Bream	.306
8	Mark Carreon	.306
9	Red Schoendienst	.303
10	Bob Fothergill	.300
11	Dave Philley	.299
12	Manny Mota	.297
13	Ted Easterly	.296
14	Harvey Hendrick	.295
15	Larry Herndon	.294
16	Rance Mulliniks	.292
17	**Marlon Anderson**	**.291**
18	Terry Puhl	.289
19	Chip Hale	.289
20	Manny Sanguillen	.288
21	Midre Cummings	.287
	Glenallen Hill	.287
23	Carlos Baerga	.286
24	Smoky Burgess	.286
25	Rick Miller	.286

PINCH HIT HOME RUNS

1	Cliff Johnson	20
2	Jerry Lynch	18
	John Vander Wal	17
4	Gates Brown	16
	Smoky Burgess	16
	Willie McCovey	16
7	Dave Hansen	15
8	George Crowe	14
9	Glenallen Hill	13
	Mark Sweeney	**13**
11	Joe Adcock	12
	Bob Cerv	12
	Jose Morales	12
	Graig Nettles	12
	Craig Wilson	**12**
16	Jeff Burroughs	11
	Jay Johnstone	11
	Candy Maldonado	11
	Orlando Merced	11
	Fred Whitfield	11
	Cy Williams	11
23	Mark Carreon	10
	Dave Clark	10
	Jim Dwyer	10
	Ricky Ledee	**10**
	Mike Lum	10
	Ken McMullen	10
	Don Mincher	10
	Greg Norton	**10**
	Wally Post	10
	Olmedo Saenz	**10**
	Matt Stairs	**10**
	Champ Summers	10
	Jerry Turner	10
	Gus Zernial	10

STOLEN BASES

1	Rickey Henderson	1406
2	Lou Brock	938
3	Billy Hamilton	914
4	Ty Cobb	897
5	Tim Raines	808
6	Vince Coleman	752
7	Arlie Latham	742
8	Eddie Collins	741
9	Max Carey	738
10	Honus Wagner	723
11	Joe Morgan	689
12	Willie Wilson	668
13	Tom Brown	657
14	Bert Campaneris	649
15	Otis Nixon	620
16	George Davis	619
17	**Kenny Lofton**	**599**
18	Dummy Hoy	596
19	Maury Wills	586
20	George Van Haltren	583
21	Ozzie Smith	580
22	Hugh Duffy	574
23	Bid McPhee	568
24	Brett Butler	558
25	Davey Lopes	557
26	Cesar Cedeno	550
27	Bill Dahlen	548
28	John Ward	540
29	Herman Long	537
30	Patsy Donovan	518
	Jack Doyle	518
32	**Barry Bonds**	**509**
	Fred Clarke	509
	Harry Stovey	509
35	Luis Aparicio	506
36	Paul Molitor	504
37	Willie Keeler	495
	Clyde Milan	495
39	Omar Moreno	487
40	Roberto Alomar	474
41	Mike Griffin	473
42	Tommy McCarthy	468
43	Jimmy Sheckard	465
	Eric Young	**465**
45	Delino DeShields	463
46	Bobby Bonds	461
47	Ed Delahanty	455
	Ron LeFlore	455
49	Curt Welch	453
50	Steve Sax	444
51	Joe Kelley	443
52	Sherry Magee	441
53	John McGraw	436
	Tris Speaker	436
55	Marquis Grissom	429
56	Bob Bescher	428
	Mike Tiernan	428
58	Frankie Frisch	419
	Jimmy Ryan	419
60	Charlie Comiskey	416
61	**Craig Biggio**	**410**
62	Tommy Harper	408
63	Chuck Knoblauch	407
64	Donie Bush	406
65	Frank Chance	403
66	Bill Lange	400
67	Willie Davis	398
68	Sam Mertes	396
	Juan Samuel	396
70	Dave Collins	395
	Billy North	395
72	Jesse Burkett	389
73	Tommy Corcoran	387
74	Tom Daly	385
	Freddie Patek	385
76	George Burns	383
	Hugh Nicol	383
	Fred Pfeffer	383
	Walt Wilmot	383
80	Nap Lajoie	380
81	Barry Larkin	379
82	Harry Hooper	375
	George Sisler	375
84	Jack Glasscock	372
85	Lonnie Smith	370
86	Tom Goodwin	369
87	Tommy Dowd	368
	King Kelly	368
89	Sam Crawford	367
90	**Omar Vizquel**	**366**
91	Hal Chase	363
	Tony Womack	**363**
93	Tommy Leach	361
94	Hughie Jennings	359
	Fielder Jones	359
96	Buck Ewing	354
	Gary Pettis	354
98	Rod Carew	353
99	Willie McGee	352
	Tommy Tucker	352

STOLEN BASE AVERAGE

1	**Carlos Beltran**	**87.6**
2	Pokey Reese	84.7
3	Tim Raines	84.7
4	Eric Davis	84.1
5	Henry Cotto	83.3
6	Willie Wilson	83.3
7	Barry Larkin	83.1
8	**Tony Womack**	**83.1**
9	Davey Lopes	83.0
10	**Carl Crawford**	**82.8**
11	Stan Javier	82.8
12	Doug Glanville	82.4
13	Julio Cruz	81.5
14	Brian Hunter	81.0
15	Joe Morgan	81.0
16	Vince Coleman	80.9
17	Rickey Henderson	80.8
18	Roberto Alomar	80.6
19	Andy Van Slyke	80.6
20	**Orlando Cabrera**	**80.6**
21	**Dave Roberts**	**80.5**
22	**Corey Patterson**	**80.4**
23	**Ichiro Suzuki**	**80.2**
24	Mickey Mantle	80.1
25	**Alex Rodriguez**	**80.1**
26	**Derek Jeter**	**80.1**
27	**Jimmy Rollins**	**79.9**
28	Lenny Dykstra	79.8
29	Ozzie Smith	79.7
30	**Kenny Lofton**	**79.7**
31	Enzo Hernandez	79.6
32	Gary Redus	79.5
33	Paul Molitor	79.4
34	R. J. Reynolds	79.0
35	Luis Aparicio	78.8
36	Marquis Grissom	78.7
37	**Mike Cameron**	**78.6**
38	Amos Otis	78.6
39	Kirk Gibson	78.5
40	**Aaron Boone**	**78.4**
41	**Barry Bonds**	**78.3**
42	**Johnny Damon**	**78.3**
43	Alan Wiggins	78.1
44	**Miguel Cairo**	**77.9**
45	Devon White	77.9
46	Tommy Harper	77.9
47	Rudy Law	77.8
48	Joe Carter	77.8
	Mike Felder	77.8
	Alfonso Soriano	**77.8**

BASE STEALING WINS

1	Rickey Henderson	18.7
2	Tim Raines	12.7
3	Vince Coleman	10.6
4	Lou Brock	10.4
5	Willie Wilson	10.0
6	Joe Morgan	9.8
7	Davey Lopes	8.5
8	Ozzie Smith	7.9
9	Bert Campaneris	7.7
10	**Kenny Lofton**	**7.5**
11	Otis Nixon	7.1
12	Luis Aparicio	6.7
13	Paul Molitor	6.3
14	Roberto Alomar	6.2
15	**Barry Bonds**	**6.1**
16	Cesar Cedeno	6.1
17	Maury Wills	5.9
18	Barry Larkin	5.6
19	Eric Davis	5.4
20	Marquis Grissom	5.3
21	**Tony Womack**	**5.3**
22	Tommy Harper	5.2
23	Ron LeFlore	5.1
24	Delino DeShields	5.0
25	Julio Cruz	4.9
26	**Craig Biggio**	**4.7**
27	Chuck Knoblauch	4.6
28	Omar Moreno	4.5
29	Willie Davis	4.4
30	Amos Otis	4.4
31	Bobby Bonds	4.3
32	Gary Redus	4.3
33	**Eric Young**	**4.3**
34	Gary Pettis	4.2
35	Devon White	4.1
36	Freddie Patek	4.1
37	Ryne Sandberg	3.9
38	Dave Collins	3.9
39	Mookie Wilson	3.9
40	Willie Mays	3.9
41	George Case	3.9
42	Lenny Dykstra	3.8
43	Tom Goodwin	3.8
44	Juan Samuel	3.8
45	**Carlos Beltran**	**3.7**
46	Steve Sax	3.7
47	Willie McGee	3.6
48	Stan Javier	3.6
49	**Johnny Damon**	**3.5**
50	Larry Bowa	3.5

PITCHER BATTING AVERAGE BY ERA

1988–2006

1	Mike Hampton	.242
2	**Livan Hernandez**	**.234**
3	**Javier Vazquez**	**.215**
4	**Russ Ortiz**	**.208**
5	**Woody Williams**	**.206**
6	Orel Hershiser	.201
7	Mark Portugal	.198
8	Doc Gooden	.196
9	Jose Rijo	.191
10	**Tom Glavine**	**.186**

1973–87

1	Ken Brett	.262
2	Rick Rhoden	.238
3	Don Robinson	.231
4	Steve Renko	.215
5	Bob Forsch	.213
6	Jim Rooker	.201
7	Steve Carlton	.201
8	Fernando Valenzuela	.200
9	Dave Roberts	.194
10	Mike Krukow	.193

1961–72

1	Catfish Hunter	.226
2	Gary Peters	.222
3	Bob Gibson	.206
4	Camilo Pascual	.205
5	Juan Pizarro	.202
6	Jim Maloney	.201
7	Jim Perry	.199
8	Rick Wise	.195
9	Earl Wilson	.195
10	Tony Cloninger	.192

1943–60

1	Fred Hutchinson	.276
2	Don Newcombe	.266
3	Mickey McDermott	.250
	Carl Scheib	.250
5	Tommy Byrne	.246
6	Johnny Sain	.245
7	Willard Nixon	.242
8	Don Larsen	.240
9	Bob Lemon	.233
10	Murry Dickson	.231

1921–42

1	George Uhle	.286
2	Wes Ferrell	.284
3	Jack Scott	.276
4	Sloppy Thurston	.270
5	Red Ruffing	.269
6	Carl Mays	.268
7	Johnny Marcum	.265
8	Dutch Ruether	.264
9	Joe Shaute	.260
10	Schoolboy Rowe	.257

1901–20

1	Babe Ruth	.299
2	Doc Crandall	.279
3	Al Orth	.277
4	George Mullin	.262
5	Jesse Tannehill	.256
6	Joe Wood	.241
7	Claude Hendrix	.241
8	Ray Caldwell	.241
9	Frank Kitson	.240
10	Wilbur Cooper	.239

1893–1900

1	Cy Seymour	.280
2	Win Mercer	.261
3	Brickyard Kennedy	.261
4	Nixey Callahan	.260
5	Jack Taylor	.252
6	Al Maul	.246
7	Jack Dunn	.244
8	Jouett Meekin	.243
9	Frank Killen	.241
10	Pink Hawley	.241

1876–92

1	Guy Hecker	.297
2	Jack Stivetts	.295
3	Jim Devlin	.293
4	Charlie Ferguson	.288
5	Charlie Sweeney	.284
6	Bob Caruthers	.276
7	Ben Sanders	.275
8	Scott Stratton	.275
9	Ad Gumbert	.274
10	Dave Foutz	.262

PITCHER BATTING RUNS

1	Red Ruffing	143
2	Bob Caruthers	111
3	Wes Ferrell	100
4	Walter Johnson	99
5	Red Lucas	98
6	George Uhle	92
7	Guy Hecker	90
	Bob Lemon	90
9	Jim Whitney	89
10	Warren Spahn	88
11	George Mullin	87
12	Don Newcombe	79
13	Babe Ruth	78
14	Schoolboy Rowe	76
15	Early Wynn	72
16	Bob Gibson	65
	Jack Stivetts	65
18	Carl Mays	64
19	Al Orth	63
20	Don Drysdale	60
21	Christy Mathewson	59
22	Gary Peters	57
	Bucky Walters	57
	Earl Wilson	57
25	Doc Crandall	54
	Mike Hampton	54
	Jesse Tannehill	54
	Jim Tobin	54
29	Ad Gumbert	53
30	Burleigh Grimes	52
31	Claude Hendrix	50
	Tony Mullane	50
33	Joe Bush	49
	Charlie Ferguson	49
35	Steve Carlton	48
	Scott Stratton	48
37	Bob Forsch	47
38	Don Larsen	46
39	Dave Foutz	45
	Vern Law	45
	Dutch Ruether	45
	Adonis Terry	45
43	Frank Killen	44
	Rick Rhoden	44
	Jack Scott	44
46	**Livan Hernandez**	**43**
47	Tommy Byrne	41
	Jim Kaat	41
49	Don Robinson	40
	Johnny Sain	40
51	Wilbur Cooper	39
	Fred Hutchinson	39
53	Claude Osteen	38
	Charley Radbourn	38
	Sloppy Thurston	38
56	Dolf Luque	37
	Doc White	37
58	Jack Coombs	36
	Mickey McDermott	36
60	Clark Griffith	35
	Harvey Haddix	35
	Win Mercer	35
	Frank Smith	35
64	**Tom Glavine**	**34**
	Art Nehf	34
	Robin Roberts	34
	Jack Taylor	34
	Rick Wise	34
69	Chief Bender	33
	Erv Brame	33
	Catfish Hunter	33
	Ben Sanders	33
73	Ken Brett	32
	Hooks Dauss	32
	Orel Hershiser	32
	Ted Lyons	32
	Al Maul	32
	Fernando Valenzuela	32
79	Ray Caldwell	31
	Russ Ortiz	**31**
	Dizzy Trout	31
	John Ward	31
	Joe Wood	31
84	Ed Brandt	30
	Lew Burdette	30
	Lefty Tyler	30
87	Doc Gooden	29
	Jack Harshman	29
	Ed Lopat	29
	Jouett Meekin	29
	Camilo Pascual	29
	Juan Pizarro	29
93	Jack Bentley	28
	Joe Nuxhall	28
	Urban Shocker	28
96	Charlie Buffinton	27
	Whitey Ford	27
	Brickyard Kennedy	27
	Frank Kitson	27
	Tom Seaver	27
	Bill Sherdel	27
	Lon Warneke	27

GAMES

FIRST BASE

1	Eddie Murray	2413
2	Jake Beckley	2380
3	Fred McGriff	2239
4	Mickey Vernon	2237
5	Mark Grace	2162
6	Rafael Palmeiro	2139
7	Lou Gehrig	2137
8	Charlie Grimm	2131
9	Jeff Bagwell	2111
10	Andres Galarraga	2106

SECOND BASE

1	Eddie Collins	2650
2	Joe Morgan	2527
3	Roberto Alomar	2320
4	Lou Whitaker	2308
5	Nellie Fox	2295
6	Charlie Gehringer	2206
7	Willie Randolph	2152
8	Frank White	2151
9	Bid McPhee	2129
10	Bill Mazeroski	2094

SHORTSTOP

1	Luis Aparicio	2581
2	Ozzie Smith	2511
3	**Omar Vizquel**	**2427**
4	Cal Ripken	2302
5	Larry Bowa	2222
6	Luke Appling	2218
7	Dave Concepcion	2178
8	Rabbit Maranville	2153
9	Alan Trammell	2139
10	Bill Dahlen	2133

THIRD BASE

1	Brooks Robinson	2870
2	Graig Nettles	2412
3	Gary Gaetti	2282
4	Wade Boggs	2215
5	Mike Schmidt	2212
6	Buddy Bell	2183
7	Eddie Mathews	2181
8	Ron Santo	2130
9	Tim Wallach	2054
10	Eddie Yost	2008

OUTFIELD

1	Ty Cobb	2934
2	Willie Mays	2842
3	Rickey Henderson	2826
4	**Barry Bonds**	**2764**
5	Hank Aaron	2760
6	Tris Speaker	2698
7	Lou Brock	2507
8	Al Kaline	2488
9	Dave Winfield	2469
10	**Steve Finley**	**2459**
11	Max Carey	2421
12	Vada Pinson	2403
13	Roberto Clemente	2370
14	Zack Wheat	2337
15	Tony Gwynn	2326
16	Willie Davis	2323
	Andre Dawson	2323
18	Mel Ott	2313
19	Sam Crawford	2299
20	Paul Waner	2288

CATCHER

1	Carlton Fisk	2226
2	Bob Boone	2225
3	Gary Carter	2056
4	Tony Pena	1950
5	**Ivan Rodriguez**	**1934**
6	Jim Sundberg	1927
7	Al Lopez	1918
8	Benito Santiago	1917
9	Lance Parrish	1818
10	Rick Ferrell	1806

PITCHER

1	Jesse Orosco	1252
2	John Franco	1119
3	**Mike Stanton**	**1109**
4	Dennis Eckersley	1071
5	Hoyt Wilhelm	1070
6	Dan Plesac	1064
7	Kent Tekulve	1050
8	Lee Smith	1022
9	Mike Jackson	1005
10	Rich Gossage	1002

FIELDING AVERAGE

FIRST BASE

1	**Travis Lee**	**.997**
2	Steve Garvey	.996
3	Don Mattingly	.996
4	**Todd Helton**	**.996**
5	Wes Parker	.996
6	**J.T. Snow**	**.996**
7	David Segui	.995
8	John Olerud	.995
9	**Sean Casey**	**.995**
10	Tino Martinez	.995

SECOND BASE

1	Ryne Sandberg	.989
2	Tom Herr	.989
3	Mickey Morandini	.989
4	Jose Lind	.988
5	Jody Reed	.988
6	Bret Boone	.986
7	Jim Gantner	.985
8	**Jose Vidro**	**.985**
9	**Craig Biggio**	**.984**
10	Bobby Grich	.984

SHORTSTOP

1	**Omar Vizquel**	**.984**
2	Mike Bordick	.982
3	Larry Bowa	.980
4	Tony Fernandez	.980
5	Cal Ripken	.979
6	Ozzie Smith	.978
7	Deivi Cruz	.978
8	**Orlando Cabrera**	**.978**
9	**Neifi Perez**	**.978**
10	Alex Rodriguez	.977

THIRD BASE

1	**Mike Lowell**	**.977**
2	Brooks Robinson	.971
3	Ken Reitz	.970
4	George Kell	.969
5	Steve Buechele	.968
6	Don Money	.968
7	**Eric Chavez**	**.968**
8	Don Wert	.968
9	Willie Kamm	.967
10	Heinie Groh	.967

OUTFIELD

1	Darryl Hamilton	.995
2	Darren Lewis	.994
3	Terry Puhl	.993
4	Brett Butler	.993
5	Pete Rose	.991
6	Tom Goodwin	.991
7	Amos Otis	.991
8	**Randy Winn**	**.991**
9	Doug Glanville	.991
10	Joe Rudi	.991
11	Mickey Stanley	.991
12	**Torii Hunter**	**.991**
13	Robin Yount	.990
14	Jim Piersall	.990
15	**Andruw Jones**	**.990**
16	**Bernie Williams**	**.990**
17	Brian McRae	.990
18	Jim Landis	.989
19	Ken Berry	.989
20	Otis Nixon	.989

CATCHER

1	Dan Wilson	.995
2	**Mike Matheny**	**.994**
3	**Brad Ausmus**	**.994**
4	Charles Johnson	.993
5	Darrin Fletcher	.993
6	Bill Freehan	.993
7	Brent Mayne	.993
8	**Jason Varitek**	**.993**
9	Elston Howard	.993
10	Jim Sundberg	.993

PITCHER

1	Don Mossi	.990
2	Gary Nolan	.990
3	Rick Rhoden	.989
4	**Russ Ortiz**	**.988**
5	Lon Warneke	.988
6	Jim Wilson	.988
7	Kirk Rueter	.988
8	Woodie Fryman	.988
9	**Brad Radke**	**.987**
10	Larry Gura	.986

DOUBLE PLAYS

FIRST BASE

1	Mickey Vernon	2044
2	Eddie Murray	2033
3	Rafael Palmeiro	1782
4	Fred McGriff	1775
5	Joe Kuhel	1769
6	Charlie Grimm	1733
7	Chris Chambliss	1687
8	Keith Hernandez	1654
9	Andres Galarraga	1648
10	Jeff Bagwell	1618

SECOND BASE

1	Bill Mazeroski	1706
2	Nellie Fox	1619
3	Willie Randolph	1547
4	Lou Whitaker	1527
5	Bobby Doerr	1507
6	Joe Morgan	1505
7	Charlie Gehringer	1444
8	Roberto Alomar	1407
9	Frank White	1382
10	Red Schoendienst	1368

SHORTSTOP

1	Ozzie Smith	1590
2	**Omar Vizquel**	**1567**
3	Cal Ripken	1565
4	Luis Aparicio	1553
5	Luke Appling	1424
6	Alan Trammell	1307
7	Roy McMillan	1304
8	Dave Concepcion	1290
9	Larry Bowa	1265
10	Pee Wee Reese	1246

THIRD BASE

1	Brooks Robinson	618
2	Graig Nettles	470
3	Gary Gaetti	460
4	Mike Schmidt	450
5	Buddy Bell	430
6	Wade Boggs	423
7	Aurelio Rodriguez	408
8	Ron Santo	395
9	Eddie Mathews	369
10	Robin Ventura	359

OUTFIELD

1	Tris Speaker	139
2	Ty Cobb	107
3	Max Carey	86
4	Tom Brown	85
5	Harry Hooper	81
6	Jimmy Sheckard	80
7	Mike Griffin	75
8	Dummy Hoy	72
9	Jimmy Ryan	71
10	Fielder Jones	70
11	Patsy Donovan	69
12	Sam Rice	67
13	George Van Haltren	64
14	Jesse Burkett	62
15	Sam Thompson	61
16	Willie Keeler	60
	Willie Mays	60
	Tommy McCarthy	60
	Mel Ott	60
20	Sam Crawford	59

CATCHER

1	Ray Schalk	226
2	Steve O'Neill	193
3	Yogi Berra	175
4	Gabby Hartnett	163
5	Tony Pena	156
6	Bob Boone	154
7	Jimmie Wilson	153
8	Gary Carter	149
	Wally Schang	149
10	Carlton Fisk	147

PITCHER

1	**Greg Maddux**	**89**
2	Phil Niekro	83
3	Warren Spahn	82
4	Freddie Fitzsimmons	79
5	Bob Lemon	78
6	Bucky Walters	76
7	Burleigh Grimes	74
8	Walter Johnson	72
9	Tommy John	69
10	Jim Kaat	65

ASSISTS (INFIELD)

FIRST BASE

1	Eddie Murray	1865
2	Jeff Bagwell	1704
3	Keith Hernandez	1682
4	Mark Grace	1665
5	Rafael Palmeiro	1587
6	George Sisler	1529
7	Wally Joyner	1470
8	Mickey Vernon	1448
9	Fred McGriff	1447
10	John Olerud	1418
11	Andres Galarraga	1376
12	Fred Tenney	1363
13	Eric Karros	1359
14	Bill Buckner	1351
	Chris Chambliss	1351
16	Norm Cash	1317
17	Jake Beckley	1316
18	Joe Judge	1301
19	Will Clark	1294
20	Ed Konetchy	1292
21	Gil Hodges	1281
22	Stuffy McInnis	1238
23	Jimmie Foxx	1222
	Willie McCovey	1222
25	Charlie Grimm	1214

SECOND BASE

1	Eddie Collins	7630
2	Charlie Gehringer	7068
3	Joe Morgan	6967
4	Bid McPhee	6919
5	Bill Mazeroski	6685
6	Lou Whitaker	6653
7	Roberto Alomar	6524
8	Nellie Fox	6373
9	Ryne Sandberg	6363
10	Willie Randolph	6336
11	Nap Lajoie	6267
12	Frank White	6253
13	Frankie Frisch	6026
14	Bobby Doerr	5710
15	Billy Herman	5681
16	Bobby Grich	5381
17	Red Schoendienst	5243
18	**Craig Biggio**	**5181**
19	Rogers Hornsby	5166
20	Hughie Critz	5138
21	Johnny Evers	5124
22	Fred Pfeffer	5108
23	Del Pratt	5075
24	**Jeff Kent**	**4968**
25	Steve Sax	4805

SHORTSTOP

1	Ozzie Smith	8375
2	Luis Aparicio	8016
3	Bill Dahlen	7505
4	Rabbit Maranville	7354
5	Luke Appling	7218
6	Tommy Corcoran	7110
7	Cal Ripken	6977
8	**Omar Vizquel**	**6924**
9	Larry Bowa	6857
10	Dave Concepcion	6594
11	Dave Bancroft	6561
12	Roger Peckinpaugh	6337
13	Bobby Wallace	6303
14	Don Kessinger	6212
15	Roy McMillan	6191
16	Alan Trammell	6172
17	Germany Smith	6166
18	Bert Campaneris	6160
19	Herman Long	6137
20	Donie Bush	6119
21	Garry Templeton	6041
	Honus Wagner	6041
23	Pee Wee Reese	5891
24	Barry Larkin	5858
25	Joe Tinker	5856

THIRD BASE

1	Brooks Robinson	6205
2	Graig Nettles	5279
3	Mike Schmidt	5045
4	Buddy Bell	4925
5	Ron Santo	4581
6	Gary Gaetti	4531
7	Eddie Mathews	4322
8	Wade Boggs	4246
9	Aurelio Rodriguez	4150
10	Ron Cey	4018
11	Tim Wallach	3992
12	Terry Pendleton	3891
13	Sal Bando	3720
14	Lave Cross	3715
15	Jimmy Collins	3702
16	George Brett	3674
17	Eddie Yost	3659
18	Ken Boyer	3652
19	Robin Ventura	3552
20	Arlie Latham	3546
21	Pie Traynor	3521
22	Stan Hack	3494
23	Larry Gardner	3408
24	Matt Williams	3376
25	Willie Kamm	3345

ASSISTS/GAME (INFIELD)

FIRST BASE

1	Bill Buckner	0.87
2	Ferris Fain	0.84
3	Keith Hernandez	0.84
4	**Todd Helton**	**0.83**
5	Vic Power	0.83
6	Jeff Bagwell	0.81
7	Eric Karros	0.81
8	Mark Grace	0.78
9	Eddie Murray	0.78
10	Pete O'Brien	0.78
11	George Sisler	0.78
12	Wally Joyner	0.77
13	Rudy York	0.77
14	Fred Tenney	0.76
15	Mike Hargrove	0.75
16	Rafael Palmeiro	0.75
17	Dick Stuart	0.75
18	**Derrek Lee**	**0.74**
19	Willie Upshaw	0.74
20	Elbie Fletcher	0.71
21	George McQuinn	0.71
22	Bill Terry	0.71
23	Frank McCormick	0.70
24	John Olerud	0.70
25	George Stovall	0.70

SECOND BASE

1	Hughie Critz	3.54
2	Frankie Frisch	3.42
3	Ski Melillo	3.38
4	Lou Bierbauer	3.35
5	Glenn Hubbard	3.34
6	Fred Pfeffer	3.33
7	Rogers Hornsby	3.31
8	Bid McPhee	3.25
9	Tony Cuccinello	3.23
10	Cupid Childs	3.22
11	Charlie Gehringer	3.21
12	Bill Mazeroski	3.20
13	Ryne Sandberg	3.19
14	Bobby Lowe	3.17
15	Max Bishop	3.14
16	Billy Herman	3.14
17	Hobe Ferris	3.10
18	Joe Gordon	3.10
19	Manny Trillo	3.10
20	Bobby Doerr	3.09
21	Nap Lajoie	3.08
22	Bucky Harris	3.07
23	Miller Huggins	3.07
24	Julio Cruz	3.06
25	Tony Lazzeri	3.06

SHORTSTOP

1	Germany Smith	3.70
2	Art Fletcher	3.55
3	Bill Dahlen	3.52
4	Dave Bancroft	3.51
5	Bones Ely	3.50
6	Travis Jackson	3.50
7	George Davis	3.49
8	Jack Glasscock	3.46
9	Bobby Wallace	3.46
10	Tommy Corcoran	3.43
11	Herman Long	3.42
12	Rabbit Maranville	3.42
13	Freddy Parent	3.36
14	Joe Tinker	3.36
15	Ozzie Smith	3.34
16	Dick Bartell	3.33
17	Glenn Wright	3.31
18	Donie Bush	3.28
19	Luke Appling	3.26
20	Mickey Doolan	3.26
21	Rick Burleson	3.25
22	George McBride	3.25
23	Robin Yount	3.25
24	Joe Sewell	3.24
25	3 players tied	3.23

THIRD BASE

1	Mike Schmidt	2.29
2	Billy Shindle	2.27
3	Buddy Bell	2.26
4	Arlie Latham	2.26
5	Clete Boyer	2.24
6	Jimmy Collins	2.20
7	Graig Nettles	2.19
8	George Brett	2.18
9	Terry Pendleton	2.18
10	Darrell Evans	2.17
11	Brooks Robinson	2.17
12	Lave Cross	2.16
13	Ron Santo	2.16
14	Doug Rader	2.15
15	Billy Nash	2.14
16	Bill Bradley	2.12
17	Billy Werber	2.12
18	Harlond Clift	2.11
19	Jerry Denny	2.11
20	Frank Malzone	2.11
21	Aurelio Rodriguez	2.10
22	Doug DeCinces	2.09
23	Art Devlin	2.09
24	Ken McMullen	2.08
25	**Scott Rolen**	**2.08**

TOTAL CHANCES/GAME (INF)

FIRST BASE

1	Tom Jones	11.38
2	George Stovall	11.30
3	George Kelly	11.09
4	Wally Pipp	11.05
5	Ed Konetchy	11.04
6	Candy LaChance	11.04
7	George Burns	10.92
8	Bill Terry	10.91
9	Cap Anson	10.85
10	Walter Holke	10.83
11	Bill Phillips	10.83
12	Fred Tenney	10.83
13	Hal Chase	10.82
14	Charlie Comiskey	10.82
15	Dan Brouthers	10.74
16	Roger Connor	10.74
17	Jake Beckley	10.73
18	Lu Blue	10.73
19	Stuffy McInnis	10.71
20	Fred Luderus	10.69
21	Fred Merkle	10.68
22	John Reilly	10.68
23	Kitty Bransfield	10.67
24	Dan McGann	10.65
25	Jack Doyle	10.63

SECOND BASE

1	Fred Pfeffer	6.95
2	Bid McPhee	6.70
3	Cub Stricker	6.59
4	Lou Bierbauer	6.49
5	Cupid Childs	6.32
6	Ski Melillo	6.16
7	Hughie Critz	6.07
8	Frankie Frisch	6.05
9	Nap Lajoie	6.01
10	Bobby Lowe	6.01
11	Bucky Harris	6.00
12	Billy Herman	5.97
13	Jerry Priddy	5.93
14	Bobby Doerr	5.86
15	Kid Gleason	5.83
16	Hobe Ferris	5.82
17	Buddy Myer	5.79
18	Tony Cuccinello	5.78
19	Charlie Gehringer	5.78
20	Joe Quinn	5.78
21	Tom Daly	5.77
22	Bill Wambsganss	5.77
23	George Cutshaw	5.75
24	Bill Hallman	5.70
25	Bill Mazeroski	5.67

SHORTSTOP

1	Herman Long	6.38
2	Dave Bancroft	6.33
3	Bill Dahlen	6.26
4	George Davis	6.22
5	Rabbit Maranville	6.10
6	Bobby Wallace	6.10
7	Tommy Corcoran	6.09
8	Monte Cross	6.06
9	Bones Ely	6.06
10	Honus Wagner	5.99
11	Germany Smith	5.98
12	Travis Jackson	5.96
13	Dick Bartell	5.92
14	Joe Tinker	5.88
15	Art Fletcher	5.87
16	Donie Bush	5.82
17	Mickey Doolan	5.81
18	Doc Lavan	5.81
19	Ivy Olson	5.81
20	Freddy Parent	5.77
21	George McBride	5.75
22	Jack Glasscock	5.71
23	Glenn Wright	5.69
24	Joe Sewell	5.64
25	Luke Appling	5.53

THIRD BASE

1	Jerry Denny	4.21
2	Billy Shindle	4.15
3	Billy Nash	4.07
4	Arlie Latham	4.04
5	Denny Lyons	3.98
6	Jimmy Collins	3.89
7	Hick Carpenter	3.81
8	Jimmy Austin	3.74
9	Lave Cross	3.73
10	Frank Baker	3.64
11	Bill Bradley	3.63
12	Harry Steinfeldt	3.57
13	George Pinkney	3.56
14	Doc Casey	3.48
15	Art Devlin	3.48
16	Bobby Byrne	3.44
17	Harlond Clift	3.44
18	Red Smith	3.42
19	Billy Werber	3.42
20	Eddie Foster	3.41
21	Willie Kamm	3.40
22	Clete Boyer	3.38
23	Larry Gardner	3.32
24	Mike Mowrey	3.31
25	Pie Traynor	3.30

PUTOUTS (OUTFIELD)

OUTFIELD

1	Willie Mays	7095
2	Tris Speaker	6788
3	Rickey Henderson	6468
4	Max Carey	6363
5	Ty Cobb	6361
6	Richie Ashburn	6089
7	**Steve Finley**	**5618**
8	Hank Aaron	5539
9	**Barry Bonds**	**5475**
10	Willie Davis	5449
11	Doc Cramer	5412
12	Brett Butler	5296
13	Andre Dawson	5158
14	Vada Pinson	5097
15	**Ken Griffey Jr.**	**5083**
16	Willie Wilson	5060
17	Al Kaline	5035
18	Zack Wheat	4996
19	Chet Lemon	4993
20	Al Simmons	4988
21	Dave Winfield	4975
22	Amos Otis	4936
23	Marquis Grissom	4880
24	Paul Waner	4872
25	Lloyd Waner	4860
26	Fred Clarke	4795
27	Goose Goslin	4792
28	Sam Rice	4774
29	Devon White	4739
30	**Bernie Williams**	**4710**
31	Roberto Clemente	4696
32	**Kenny Lofton**	**4586**
33	Fred Lynn	4556
34	Edd Roush	4537
35	Joe DiMaggio	4516
36	Tony Gwynn	4512
37	Mel Ott	4511
38	Sammy Sosa	4490
39	Garry Maddox	4449
40	Babe Ruth	4444
41	Mickey Mantle	4438
42	Lou Brock	4394
43	Kirby Puckett	4392
44	Jose Cruz	4391
45	Dwight Evans	4371
46	Paul Blair	4343
47	Sam West	4300
48	Willie McGee	4260
49	Jimmy Sheckard	4203
50	Tim Raines	4201
51	Cy Williams	4180
52	Ted Williams	4158
53	**Luis Gonzalez**	**4155**
54	Cesar Cedeno	4131
55	Duke Snider	4099
56	Clyde Milan	4095
57	**Andruw Jones**	**4090**
58	Reggie Jackson	4062
59	Dale Murphy	4053
60	Kiki Cuyler	4034
61	Curt Flood	4021
62	Bob Johnson	4003
63	Wally Moses	4000
64	Joe Medwick	3994
65	Harry Hooper	3981
66	Frank Robinson	3978
67	Earl Averill	3968
68	Dummy Hoy	3964
69	Jesse Burkett	3961
70	Carl Yastrzemski	3941
71	Enos Slaughter	3925
72	George Burns	3918
73	Jimmy Wynn	3912
74	Bill Bruton	3905
75	**Johnny Damon**	**3897**
76	**Jim Edmonds**	**3896**
77	Dom DiMaggio	3859
78	Jim Piersall	3851
79	Heinie Manush	3841
80	Rick Manning	3831
81	George Foster	3809
82	Sherry Magee	3800
83	Dave Parker	3791
84	Bill Virdon	3777
85	Lloyd Moseby	3765
86	Bobby Veach	3754
87	George Hendrick	3751
88	Dode Paskert	3734
89	Stan Musial	3730
90	Paul O'Neill	3724
91	Brady Anderson	3713
92	Jimmy Ryan	3701
93	Reggie Smith	3676
94	Joe Carter	3669
95	Dusty Baker	3663
96	Gee Walker	3661
97	Bobby Bonds	3659
98	**Mike Cameron**	**3640**
99	Tom Brown	3629
100	Sam Crawford	3626

PUTOUTS/GAME (OUTFIELD)

OUTFIELD

1	Taylor Douthit	3.01
2	Richie Ashburn	2.90
3	Dom DiMaggio	2.82
4	Dwayne Murphy	2.82
5	Mike Kreevich	2.81
6	Sam Chapman	2.74
7	Sam West	2.74
8	Fred Schulte	2.70
9	Lloyd Waner	2.68
10	Billy North	2.65
11	**Carlos Beltran**	**2.64**
12	Garry Maddox	2.64
13	Max Carey	2.63
14	Joe DiMaggio	2.63
15	Vince DiMaggio	2.63
16	Terry Moore	2.63
17	Robin Yount	2.63
18	**Mike Cameron**	**2.62**
19	Gary Pettis	2.62
20	Chet Lemon	2.60
21	Kirby Puckett	2.59
22	**Torii Hunter**	**2.58**
23	Omar Moreno	2.58
24	Wally Berger	2.57
25	Jim Busby	2.57
26	**Andruw Jones**	**2.57**
27	Amos Otis	2.57
28	Lenny Dykstra	2.55
29	Rick Manning	2.55
30	Ruppert Jones	2.54
31	Devon White	2.54
32	Doc Cramer	2.53
33	Baby Doll Jacobson	2.53
34	Lance Johnson	2.53
35	Larry Doby	2.52
36	Mickey Rivers	2.52
37	Tris Speaker	2.52
38	Bill Bruton	2.51
39	Gorman Thomas	2.51
40	Earl Averill	2.50
41	Fred Lynn	2.50
42	Willie Mays	2.50
43	Willie Wilson	2.50
44	Earle Combs	2.49
45	Lloyd Moseby	2.47
46	Brett Butler	2.46
47	Hy Myers	2.46
48	Edd Roush	2.46
49	Ethan Allen	2.45
50	Bill Virdon	2.45
51	**Bernie Williams**	**2.45**
52	**Jim Edmonds**	**2.44**
53	Mule Haas	2.44
54	**Randy Winn**	**2.44**
55	Ron LeFlore	2.43
56	Jimmy McAleer	2.43
57	Mookie Wilson	2.43
58	Cesar Cedeno	2.41
59	**Ken Griffey Jr.**	**2.41**
60	Dave Henderson	2.41
61	**Kenny Lofton**	**2.41**
62	Barney McCosky	2.41
63	Al Bumbry	2.40
64	Ira Flagstead	2.40
65	Mike Griffin	2.40
66	**Johnny Damon**	**2.39**
67	Jim Piersall	2.39
68	Tony Armas	2.37
69	George Case	2.37
70	Curt Flood	2.37
71	Tommy Leach	2.37
72	Bobby Thomson	2.37
73	Brian McRae	2.36
74	Willie Davis	2.35
75	Marquis Grissom	2.34
76	Ben Chapman	2.33
77	Hoot Evers	2.33
78	Al Simmons	2.33
79	Paul Blair	2.32
80	Mike Devereaux	2.32
81	Jim Landis	2.32
82	Tommy Holmes	2.30
83	Roy Thomas	2.30
84	Cy Williams	2.30
85	**Steve Finley**	**2.29**
86	Rickey Henderson	2.29
87	Dode Paskert	2.29
88	Carl Reynolds	2.29
89	**Mark Kotsay**	**2.28**
90	Al Oliver	2.28
91	Ken Williams	2.28
92	Cliff Heathcote	2.27
93	Bob Johnson	2.27
94	Bill Tuttle	2.27
95	Gee Walker	2.27
96	Roberto Kelly	2.26
97	Carson Bigbee	2.24
98	Kiki Cuyler	2.24
99	Rick Miller	2.24
100	Wally Moses	2.24
101	Hack Wilson	2.24

FIELDING RUNS (BY POSITION)

FIRST BASE

1	Keith Hernandez	133
2	Fred Tenney	130
3	Vic Power	123
4	Bill Buckner	114
5	**Todd Helton**	**113**
6	Jeff Bagwell	95
7	George Sisler	93
8	Rafael Palmeiro	81
9	Darrell Evans	75
	Richie Sexson	**75**

SECOND BASE

1	Bill Mazeroski	364
2	Nap Lajoie	343
3	Bid McPhee	283
4	Fred Pfeffer	240
5	Glenn Hubbard	213
6	Bobby Doerr	175
7	Manny Trillo	170
8	Bobby Knoop	169
9	Ski Melillo	149
10	Bobby Grich	139

SHORTSTOP

1	Ozzie Smith	279
2	Bill Dahlen	273
3	Jack Glasscock	256
4	George Davis	182
5	Joe Tinker	181
6	Dave Bancroft	177
7	**Neifi Perez**	**175**
8	George McBride	171
9	Art Fletcher	170
10	Tim Foli	159

THIRD BASE

1	Mike Schmidt	236
2	Buddy Bell	227
3	Clete Boyer	184
4	Ron Santo	162
5	Terry Pendleton	160
6	Lave Cross	136
7	Tim Wallach	134
8	**Scott Rolen**	**133**
9	Darrell Evans	132
10	Aurelio Rodriguez	129

OUTFIELD

1	Tris Speaker	160
2	Max Carey	127
3	Richie Ashburn	121
4	Roberto Clemente	116
5	Jesse Barfield	101
6	Jimmy Sheckard	100
7	Jim Fogarty	97
8	Johnny Callison	91
9	Ed Delahanty	84
	Rickey Henderson	84
11	Bob Johnson	83
12	Sam West	80
13	**Andruw Jones**	**76**
	Curt Welch	76
15	Al Kaline	75
16	Kip Selbach	71
	Carl Yastrzemski	71
18	Orator Shafer	70
19	Harry Hooper	69
20	Fred Clarke	66

CATCHER

1	**Ivan Rodriguez**	**203**
2	Tony Pena	184
3	Chief Zimmer	164
4	Gary Carter	156
5	Pop Snyder	144
6	Lou Criger	137
7	Johnny Bench	127
8	Lance Parrish	124
9	Ray Schalk	122
10	Jim Sundberg	119

PITCHER

1	**Greg Maddux**	**108**
2	Ed Walsh	80
3	Carl Mays	72
4	**Kenny Rogers**	**66**
5	Christy Mathewson	65
6	Tommy John	62
7	Freddie Fitzsimmons	60
8	Bob Lemon	58
9	Burleigh Grimes	57
10	**Tom Glavine**	**52**

FIELDING WINS

1	Bill Mazeroski	37.8
2	Nap Lajoie	34.4
3	Bill Dahlen	29.2
4	Ozzie Smith	29.1
5	Bid McPhee	24.5
6	Mike Schmidt	24.4
7	Buddy Bell	23.4
8	Glenn Hubbard	22.1
9	George Davis	21.9
10	Jack Glasscock	21.8
11	Fred Pfeffer	21.4
12	Darrell Evans	21.2
13	Clete Boyer	21.0
14	**Neifi Perez**	**20.4**
15	Bobby Wallace	20.2
16	**Ivan Rodriguez**	**19.3**
17	Joe Tinker	19.0
18	Tony Pena	18.8
19	George McBride	18.2
20	Bobby Knoop	18.1
21	Dave Bancroft	18.1
22	Art Fletcher	18.0
23	Rey Sanchez	17.9
24	Manny Trillo	17.5
25	Bobby Doerr	17.4
26	Tim Foli	17.4
27	Mickey Doolan	17.2
28	Ron Santo	17.2
29	Dick Bartell	16.8
30	Terry Pendleton	16.3
31	Tris Speaker	16.1
32	Lee Tannehill	16.1
33	Gary Carter	15.4
34	Gene Alley	15.4
35	Frank White	15.1
36	Lave Cross	14.6
37	Red Schoendienst	14.4
38	Ski Melillo	14.2
39	Chief Zimmer	14.2
40	Aurelio Rodriguez	14.1
41	Vic Power	13.8
42	Keith Hernandez	13.8
43	Tim Wallach	13.7
44	Lou Criger	13.5
45	Lou Boudreau	13.4
46	**Orlando Hudson**	**13.3**
47	Willie Randolph	13.3
48	Fred Tenney	13.3
49	Frankie Frisch	13.1
50	Joe Gerhardt	13.0
51	**Scott Rolen**	**13.0**
52	Max Carey	12.9
53	Pop Snyder	12.9
54	Billy Jurges	12.8
55	Rabbit Maranville	12.8
56	Graig Nettles	12.8
57	Rick Burleson	12.8
58	Bobby Grich	12.8
59	Hughie Jennings	12.8
60	Danny Richardson	12.4
61	Lance Parrish	12.3
62	Ray Schalk	12.3
63	Fred Dunlap	12.3
64	Jim Sundberg	12.3
65	Harold Reynolds	12.1
66	Hughie Critz	12.1
67	Richie Ashburn	12.1
68	Mark Belanger	12.0
69	Roberto Clemente	12.0
70	Phil Rizzuto	11.7
71	Jimmy Collins	11.7
72	Germany Smith	11.7
73	Bill Holbert	11.6
74	Bill Buckner	11.5
75	**Brad Ausmus**	**11.3**
76	Gary Gaetti	11.2
77	Everett Scott	11.1
78	Lou Bierbauer	11.0
79	Luis Aparicio	10.9
80	John Ward	10.8
81	**Jack Wilson**	**10.8**
82	Brooks Robinson	10.8
83	Jim Hegan	10.8
84	Gil McDougald	10.7
85	**Todd Helton**	**10.6**
86	Mike Scioscia	10.6
87	**Craig Counsell**	**10.4**
88	Bobby Wine	10.4
89	Julio Cruz	10.4
90	Gabby Hartnett	10.4
91	**Placido Polanco**	**10.2**
92	Hobe Ferris	10.2
93	Ryne Sandberg	10.2
94	Johnny Edwards	10.1
95	**Jose Valentin**	**10.1**
96	Mike Benjamin	10.0
97	Jesse Barfield	10.0
98	Ron Hansen	10.0
99	Jody Reed	9.9
100	Carlton Fisk	9.9

FIELDING WINS

101	Roger Peckinpaugh	9.8
102	Don Kessinger	9.7
103	Del Pratt	9.6
104	Rennie Stennett	9.6
105	Roy McMillan	9.5
106	Burgess Whitehead	9.4
107	Jerry Denny	9.4
108	Johnny Callison	9.4
109	Johnny Logan	9.4
110	Jeff Bagwell	9.4
111	Yogi Berra	9.1
112	George Sisler	9.1
113	Buddy Kerr	9.0
114	**Rafael Furcal**	**9.0**
115	Hardy Richardson	9.0
116	Buck Ewing	9.0
117	Charlie Bennett	9.0
118	**Omar Vizquel**	**9.0**
119	Miller Huggins	8.9
120	Joe Sewell	8.9
121	Rocky Bridges	8.8
122	Jimmy Sheckard	8.8
123	Eddie Miller	8.7
124	Thurman Munson	8.7
125	Travis Jackson	8.7
126	Dick Groat	8.7
127	Bill Killefer	8.6
128	Art Devlin	8.6
129	Buck Herzog	8.6
130	Pokey Reese	8.6
131	Matt Williams	8.6
132	Johnny Bench	8.6
133	Robin Ventura	8.5
134	Honus Wagner	8.5
135	Dave Cash	8.5
136	Ted Sizemore	8.5
137	Davy Force	8.4
138	Steve Yeager	8.4
139	Frank Malzone	8.2
140	Carl Yastrzemski	8.2
141	Rick Dempsey	8.2
142	Billy Shindle	8.2
143	Rickey Henderson	8.2
144	Jerry Grote	8.2
145	Wade Boggs	8.1
146	Cupid Childs	8.1
147	Charlie O'Brien	8.0
148	Pinky May	8.0
149	Tony Kubek	8.0
150	Bill Bergen	7.9
151	Hal Lanier	7.9
152	Rollie Hemsley	7.8
153	Scott Fletcher	7.8
154	John Valentin	7.8
155	Tommy Corcoran	7.7
156	Rafael Palmeiro	7.7
157	Doug Rader	7.6
158	**Miguel Tejada**	**7.6**
159	Al Kaline	7.6
160	John Farrell	7.6
161	Bob Johnson	7.5
162	**Damian Miller**	**7.5**
163	Babe Pinelli	7.5
164	Billy Rogell	7.4
165	Sid Bream	7.4
166	Ernie Whitt	7.4
167	**Juan Uribe**	**7.4**
168	Sam West	7.3
169	**Andruw Jones**	**7.3**
170	Willie Kamm	7.3
171	Billy Clingman	7.2
172	Nellie Fox	7.2
173	Jim Fogarty	7.2
174	Bob Boone	7.2
175	Wid Conroy	7.2
176	Harlond Clift	7.1
177	Ken Boyer	7.1
178	Tommy Leach	7.1
179	Al Lopez	7.0
180	Jerry Priddy	7.0
181	Bill Sweeney	7.0
182	Harry Hooper	6.9
183	Bill Terry	6.9
184	Muddy Ruel	6.9
185	Earl Battey	6.8
186	Mike Bordick	6.8
187	Freddie Maguire	6.7
188	**Henry Blanco**	**6.7**
189	Alvaro Espinoza	6.7
190	Eric Karros	6.7
191	Marty Marion	6.7
192	Kip Selbach	6.6
193	Danny O'Connell	6.6
194	Jerry Royster	6.6
195	Eddie Murray	6.5
196	Pinky Whitney	6.5
197	Luke Appling	6.5
198	**Richie Sexson**	**6.5**
199	Johnny Roseboro	6.5
200	Curt Welch	6.5

BFW BY ERA

1988–2006

1	**Barry Bonds**	**124.7**
2	Rickey Henderson	70.2
3	Jeff Bagwell	52.9
4	**Alex Rodriguez**	**52.5**
5	Wade Boggs	50.5
6	**Frank Thomas**	**49.5**
7	**Ken Griffey Jr.**	**46.8**
8	Edgar Martinez	44.6
9	Cal Ripken	43.3
10	**Mike Piazza**	**42.6**
	Gary Sheffield	**42.6**
12	**Ivan Rodriguez**	**42.1**
13	Barry Larkin	41.9
14	**Manny Ramirez**	**39.5**
15	Tony Gwynn	38.5
16	Tim Raines	38.1
17	**Scott Rolen**	**37.4**
18	Ryne Sandberg	36.8
19	**Jeff Kent**	**36.7**
20	Paul Molitor	36.6
21	Roberto Alomar	36.1
22	**Jim Thome**	**35.9**
23	Rafael Palmeiro	35.8
24	**Jim Edmonds**	**35.6**
25	**Vladimir Guerrero**	**35.2**

1973–87

1	Mike Schmidt	77.3
2	Joe Morgan	68.5
3	Bobby Grich	50.6
4	Ozzie Smith	44.9
5	George Brett	42.8
6	Johnny Bench	42.4
7	Darrell Evans	41.4
8	Robin Yount	40.0
9	Rod Carew	39.5
10	Gary Carter	38.8
	Carlton Fisk	38.8
12	Reggie Jackson	38.7
13	Willie Randolph	36.0
14	Lou Whitaker	35.2
15	Eddie Murray	35.1
16	Keith Hernandez	33.5
17	Reggie Smith	31.5
18	Alan Trammell	31.1
19	Dave Winfield	30.1
20	Jack Clark	29.6
21	Buddy Bell	28.0
22	Bobby Bonds	27.2
23	Gene Tenace	26.1
24	Thurman Munson	25.0
25	Dwight Evans	24.7

1961–72

1	Willie Mays	84.4
2	Hank Aaron	83.0
3	Frank Robinson	65.0
4	Ron Santo	44.7
5	Al Kaline	43.8
6	Carl Yastrzemski	42.7
7	Willie McCovey	39.3
8	Dick Allen	39.0
9	Roberto Clemente	35.4
10	Bill Mazeroski	35.2
11	Harmon Killebrew	32.0
12	Norm Cash	30.4
13	Jimmy Wynn	29.6
14	Willie Stargell	29.5
15	Ernie Banks	27.8
16	Jim Fregosi	25.5
17	Billy Williams	24.6
18	Joe Torre	22.8
19	Rocky Colavito	22.3
20	Frank Howard	21.9
21	Tony Oliva	20.5
22	Ken Boyer	20.4
23	Gene Alley	19.1
24	Bill Freehan	18.8
25	Orlando Cepeda	18.4

1943–60

1	Ted Williams	86.5
2	Stan Musial	76.0
3	Mickey Mantle	71.8
4	Eddie Mathews	53.0
5	Lou Boudreau	43.6
6	Bobby Doerr	40.3
7	Yogi Berra	40.2
8	Jackie Robinson	34.3
9	Joe Gordon	28.8
10	Roy Campanella	24.6
11	Ralph Kiner	24.2
	Gil McDougald	24.2
13	Richie Ashburn	22.8
14	Charlie Keller	22.3
15	Duke Snider	22.2
16	Bob Elliott	21.4
17	Minnie Minoso	21.3
18	Vern Stephens	20.7
19	Eddie Stanky	20.1
20	Roy Cullenbine	18.8
	Ferris Fain	18.8
22	Phil Rizzuto	18.7
23	Larry Doby	17.8
24	Jeff Heath	17.2
	Bill Nicholson	17.2

BFW BY ERA

1921–42

1	Babe Ruth	112.0
2	Rogers Hornsby	86.0
3	Lou Gehrig	70.9
4	Mel Ott	60.7
5	Jimmie Foxx	58.3
6	Joe DiMaggio	45.8
7	Charlie Gehringer	45.1
8	Gabby Hartnett	44.4
9	Arky Vaughan	43.3
10	Luke Appling	42.4
11	Joe Cronin	39.6
12	Bill Dickey	38.5
13	Johnny Mize	37.7
14	Frankie Frisch	37.3
15	Dave Bancroft	36.2
16	Bob Johnson	35.7
17	Joe Sewell	35.2
18	Mickey Cochrane	34.7
19	Paul Waner	33.8
20	Harry Heilmann	33.2
21	Hank Greenberg	32.6
22	Billy Herman	31.6
23	Stan Hack	29.4
24	Dick Bartell	28.2
25	Bill Terry	26.7

1901–20

1	Nap Lajoie	95.2
2	Ty Cobb	85.7
3	Tris Speaker	82.7
4	Honus Wagner	82.2
5	Eddie Collins	72.5
6	Bill Dahlen	48.5
7	Joe Jackson	38.3
8	Bobby Wallace	35.4
9	Frank Baker	33.7
10	Heinie Groh	30.4
11	Elmer Flick	29.7
12	Sam Crawford	29.3
13	Fred Clarke	27.9
14	Art Fletcher	27.2
15	Sherry Magee	26.2
16	Zack Wheat	24.1
17	Jimmy Collins	23.0
	Fred Tenney	23.0
19	Roy Thomas	22.7
20	Frank Chance	22.6
21	Roger Bresnahan	22.5
	Del Pratt	22.5
23	Miller Huggins	22.4
24	Ed Konetchy	21.2
25	Jimmy Sheckard	20.7

1893–1900

1	George Davis	50.7
2	Ed Delahanty	42.8
3	Cupid Childs	30.4
4	Jesse Burkett	27.9
5	Billy Hamilton	27.2
6	Hughie Jennings	26.8
7	Jake Beckley	23.0
8	Joe Kelley	20.7
	Chief Zimmer	20.7
10	John McGraw	19.5
11	Bill Joyce	19.3
12	Mike Griffin	18.3
13	Lave Cross	16.4
14	Mike Tiernan	14.4
15	Kip Selbach	13.9
16	Jimmy Ryan	12.8
17	Ed McFarland	10.3
18	George Van Haltren	10.2
19	Heinie Peitz	10.1
20	Jack Crooks	9.9
21	Duke Farrell	9.8
22	Bill Lange	7.8
	Elmer Smith	7.8
24	Mike Grady	7.6
25	Perry Werden	7.0

1876–92

1	Roger Connor	43.4
2	Dan Brouthers	43.2
3	Bid McPhee	38.3
4	Jack Glasscock	36.6
5	Cap Anson	35.4
6	Sam Thompson	29.5
7	Buck Ewing	29.1
8	King Kelly	28.9
9	Fred Dunlap	28.1
10	Pete Browning	28.0
11	Hardy Richardson	26.7
12	Charlie Bennett	23.9
13	Harry Stovey	21.5
14	Fred Pfeffer	20.6
15	Denny Lyons	19.6
16	Charley Jones	19.4
17	Jim O'Rourke	16.0
18	Henry Larkin	15.2
19	Paul Hines	14.4
20	Dave Orr	13.8
21	Jocko Milligan	13.6
22	George Gore	13.5
23	Jack Clements	12.9
24	Fred Carroll	12.6
25	Orator Shafer	12.0

BATTER-FIELDER WINS

1	**Barry Bonds**	**124.7**
2	Babe Ruth	112.0
3	Nap Lajoie	95.2
4	Ted Williams	86.5
5	Rogers Hornsby	86.0
6	Ty Cobb	85.7
7	Willie Mays	84.4
8	Hank Aaron	83.0
9	Tris Speaker	82.7
10	Honus Wagner	82.2
11	Mike Schmidt	77.3
12	Stan Musial	76.0
13	Eddie Collins	72.5
14	Mickey Mantle	71.8
15	Lou Gehrig	70.9
16	Rickey Henderson	70.2
17	Joe Morgan	68.5
18	Frank Robinson	65.0
19	Mel Ott	60.7
20	Jimmie Foxx	58.3
21	Eddie Mathews	53.0
22	Jeff Bagwell	52.9
23	**Alex Rodriguez**	**52.5**
24	George Davis	50.7
25	Bobby Grich	50.6
26	Wade Boggs	50.5
27	**Frank Thomas**	**49.5**
28	Bill Dahlen	48.5
29	**Ken Griffey Jr.**	**46.8**
30	Joe DiMaggio	45.8
31	Charlie Gehringer	45.1
32	Ozzie Smith	44.9
33	Ron Santo	44.7
34	Edgar Martinez	44.6
35	Gabby Hartnett	44.4
36	Al Kaline	43.8
37	Lou Boudreau	43.6
38	Roger Connor	43.4
39	Cal Ripken	43.3
	Arky Vaughan	43.3
41	Dan Brouthers	43.2
42	George Brett	42.8
	Ed Delahanty	42.8
44	Carl Yastrzemski	42.7
45	**Mike Piazza**	**42.6**
	Gary Sheffield	**42.6**
47	Luke Appling	42.4
	Johnny Bench	42.4
49	**Ivan Rodriguez**	**42.1**
50	Barry Larkin	41.9
51	Darrell Evans	41.4
52	Bobby Doerr	40.3
53	Yogi Berra	40.2
54	Robin Yount	40.0
55	Joe Cronin	39.6
56	Rod Carew	39.5
	Manny Ramirez	**39.5**
58	Willie McCovey	39.3
59	Dick Allen	39.0
60	Gary Carter	38.8
	Carlton Fisk	38.8
62	Reggie Jackson	38.7
63	Bill Dickey	38.5
	Tony Gwynn	38.5
65	Joe Jackson	38.3
	Bid McPhee	38.3
67	Tim Raines	38.1
68	Johnny Mize	37.7
69	**Scott Rolen**	**37.4**
70	Frankie Frisch	37.3
71	Ryne Sandberg	36.8
72	**Jeff Kent**	**36.7**
73	Jack Glasscock	36.6
	Paul Molitor	36.6
75	Dave Bancroft	36.2
76	Roberto Alomar	36.1
77	Willie Randolph	36.0
78	**Jim Thome**	**35.9**
79	Rafael Palmeiro	35.8
80	Bob Johnson	35.7
81	**Jim Edmonds**	**35.6**
82	Cap Anson	35.4
	Roberto Clemente	35.4
	Bobby Wallace	35.4
85	**Vladimir Guerrero**	**35.2**
	Bill Mazeroski	35.2
	Joe Sewell	35.2
	Lou Whitaker	35.2
89	Eddie Murray	35.1
90	Mark McGwire	35.0
91	Mickey Cochrane	34.7
92	Jackie Robinson	34.3
93	Paul Waner	33.8
94	Frank Baker	33.7
95	Keith Hernandez	33.5
96	Harry Heilmann	33.2
97	**Craig Biggio**	**32.9**
98	Larry Walker	32.7
99	Hank Greenberg	32.6
100	Harmon Killebrew	32.0
101	Billy Herman	31.6
102	Reggie Smith	31.5
103	**Todd Helton**	**31.3**
104	Alan Trammell	31.1
105	Norm Cash	30.4
	Cupid Childs	30.4
	Heinie Groh	30.4
	Albert Pujols	**30.4**
109	Dave Winfield	30.1
110	**Brian Giles**	**29.9**
111	Elmer Flick	29.7
112	Jack Clark	29.6
	Jimmy Wynn	29.6
114	Willie Stargell	29.5
	Sam Thompson	29.5
116	**Bobby Abreu**	**29.4**
	Albert Belle	29.4
	Stan Hack	29.4
119	Sam Crawford	29.3
120	Buck Ewing	29.1
121	King Kelly	28.9
122	Joe Gordon	28.8
123	Dick Bartell	28.2
124	Fred Dunlap	28.1
125	Buddy Bell	28.0
	Pete Browning	28.0
127	Jesse Burkett	27.9
	Fred Clarke	27.9
129	Ernie Banks	27.8
130	**Miguel Tejada**	**27.5**
131	Bobby Bonds	27.2
	Art Fletcher	27.2
	Billy Hamilton	27.2
134	**Chipper Jones**	**27.1**
135	Hughie Jennings	26.8
136	Hardy Richardson	26.7
	Bill Terry	26.7
138	Harlond Clift	26.3
139	Sherry Magee	26.2
140	Gene Tenace	26.1
141	Joe Medwick	25.6
142	Jim Fregosi	25.5
143	Sammy Sosa	25.3
144	Thurman Munson	25.0
145	**Nomar Garciaparra**	**24.8**
	George Sisler	24.8
147	Dwight Evans	24.7
	Robin Ventura	24.7
	Bernie Williams	**24.7**
150	Roy Campanella	24.6
	Billy Williams	24.6
152	Jack Fournier	24.4
	John Olerud	24.4
	Pete Rose	24.4
155	Will Clark	24.2
	Ralph Kiner	24.2
	Gil McDougald	24.2
158	**Jason Giambi**	**24.1**
	Zack Wheat	24.1
160	Charlie Bennett	23.9
161	Kirby Puckett	23.4
162	Jose Canseco	23.3
	Goose Goslin	23.3
164	Lenny Dykstra	23.1
	Rusty Staub	23.1
166	Jake Beckley	23.0
	Jimmy Collins	23.0
	Jorge Posada	**23.0**
	Al Simmons	23.0
	Fred Tenney	23.0
171	Richie Ashburn	22.8
	Joe Torre	22.8
173	Roy Thomas	22.7
174	Frank Chance	22.6
	Andruw Jones	**22.6**
176	Roger Bresnahan	22.5
	Del Pratt	22.5
	Darryl Strawberry	22.5
179	Miller Huggins	22.4
180	Cesar Cedeno	22.3
	Rocky Colavito	22.3
	Charlie Keller	22.3
	Lance Parrish	22.3
184	Fred McGriff	22.2
	Duke Snider	22.2
186	Travis Jackson	22.0
187	Frank Howard	21.9
188	**Tim Salmon**	**21.8**
189	Ted Simmons	21.7
190	Harry Stovey	21.5
191	Bob Elliott	21.4
192	**Carlos Delgado**	**21.3**
	Minnie Minoso	21.3
194	Ron Cey	21.2
	Ed Konetchy	21.2
	Graig Nettles	21.2
197	Chuck Klein	21.1
	Javy Lopez	**21.1**
199	Wally Berger	21.0
200	Tony Fernandez	20.9
201	Joe Kelley	20.7
	Ernie Lombardi	20.7
	Jimmy Sheckard	20.7
	Vern Stephens	20.7
	Chief Zimmer	20.7
206	Fred Pfeffer	20.6
207	Jose Cruz	20.5
	Eric Davis	20.5
	Glenn Hubbard	20.5
	Tony Oliva	20.5
	Darrell Porter	20.5
212	**Lance Berkman**	**20.4**
	Ken Boyer	20.4
	Wally Schang	20.4
215	Ken Caminiti	20.3
	Kevin Mitchell	20.3
217	Eddie Stanky	20.1
218	Art Devlin	20.0
	Brian Downing	20.0
220	Ken Singleton	19.8
221	Denny Lyons	19.6
222	John McGraw	19.5
	Joe Tinker	19.5
224	Charley Jones	19.4
225	Bill Joyce	19.3
226	Toby Harrah	19.2
	Fred Lynn	19.2
228	Gene Alley	19.1
229	Roy Cullenbine	18.8
	Ferris Fain	18.8
	Bill Freehan	18.8
	Luis Gonzalez	**18.8**
233	Tony Phillips	18.7
	Phil Rizzuto	18.7
	Matt Williams	18.7
236	George Foster	18.6
237	**Jason Kendall**	**18.5**
	Chet Lemon	18.5
239	Orlando Cepeda	18.4
	Gavy Cravath	18.4
	Jim Rice	18.4
	Pie Traynor	18.4
243	Mike Griffin	18.3
244	Mike Scioscia	18.2
	Hack Wilson	18.2
246	Rico Carty	18.1
	Juan Gonzalez	18.1
248	Max Carey	18.0
	Dave Concepcion	18.0
250	Bobby Veach	17.9
251	Larry Doby	17.8
	Tony Lazzeri	17.8
253	**Eric Chavez**	**17.6**
254	Babe Herman	17.5
	Derek Jeter	**17.5**
	Ken Williams	17.5
257	Pedro Guerrero	17.4
	Ray Lankford	17.4
259	Earl Averill	17.3
	Rafael Furcal	**17.3**
	Bobby Knoop	17.3
	Boog Powell	17.3
263	Andre Dawson	17.2
	Jeff Heath	17.2
	Chief Meyers	17.2
	Bill Nicholson	17.2
	John Valentin	17.2
268	**Kenny Lofton**	**16.9**
	Roy Smalley	16.9
270	Rick Burleson	16.8
	Pee Wee Reese	16.8
	Andy Van Slyke	16.8
273	Ellis Burks	16.6
	Ray Chapman	16.6
275	Paul O'Neill	16.5
	Red Schoendienst	16.5
277	Lave Cross	16.4
278	Bobby Bonilla	16.3
279	Johnny Logan	16.2
	Al Rosen	16.2
281	**Carlos Beltran**	**16.1**
	Ray Schalk	16.1
283	Jim O'Rourke	16.0
284	Johnny Evers	15.9
285	**Moises Alou**	**15.8**
	Mike Hargrove	15.8
	David Justice	15.8
288	Brett Butler	15.7
	Willie Kamm	15.7
290	Luis Aparicio	15.6
	Earl Battey	15.6
	Rico Petrocelli	15.6
293	Ron Hansen	15.5
	Johnny Pesky	15.5
295	Jay Bell	15.4
	Don Mattingly	15.4
	Jimmy Williams	15.4
298	Chili Davis	15.3
	Augie Galan	15.3
300	Henry Larkin	15.2
301	Dwayne Murphy	15.1
	Enos Slaughter	15.1
303	Tommy Henrich	15.0
	Willie Keeler	15.0
305	Don Buford	14.9
306	Sid Gordon	14.8
	Roy White	14.8
308	Nellie Fox	14.6
	Jose Valentin	**14.6**
310	Ben Chapman	14.5
	Julio Franco	**14.5**
	Brooks Robinson	14.5
	Ichiro Suzuki	**14.5**
314	Paul Hines	14.4
	Johnny Kling	14.4
	Mike Tiernan	14.4
317	Buddy Myer	14.3
	Roger Peckinpaugh	14.3
319	Doug DeCinces	14.2
	J.D. Drew	**14.2**
321	Kid Elberfeld	14.0
	Orlando Hudson	**14.0**
	Dave Parker	14.0
324	Kip Selbach	13.9
325	Jesse Barfield	13.8
	Hal McRae	13.8
	Dave Orr	13.8
328	Bob Allison	13.7
	Tom Haller	13.7
	Gil Hodges	13.7
	Davey Johnson	13.7
	John Titus	13.7
333	Lonny Frey	13.6
	Jocko Milligan	13.6
335	Kiki Cuyler	13.5
	George Gore	13.5
	Chick Hafey	13.5
	Red Smith	13.5
339	Dolph Camilli	13.4
	Bert Campaneris	13.4
341	Harold Baines	13.3
	Rudy York	13.3
343	Hank Gowdy	13.2
	Roy Sievers	13.2
345	**Travis Hafner**	**13.1**
	Tony Pena	13.1
	Riggs Stephenson	13.1
	Danny Tartabull	13.1
349	Sherm Lollar	13.0
350	Jack Clements	12.9
	Stan Spence	12.9
	Robby Thompson	12.9
353	Jimmy Ryan	12.8
354	Mark Grace	12.7
	Ken Keltner	12.7
356	Fred Carroll	12.6
	Lefty O'Doul	12.6
	Maury Wills	12.6
359	**Richie Sexson**	**12.5**
360	Dick McAuliffe	12.4
	Dan McGann	12.4
	George Stone	12.4
363	**Mike Cameron**	**12.3**
	Ron Hunt	12.3
365	Smoky Burgess	12.2
	Dick Groat	12.2
	Joe Harris	12.2
	Tommy Holmes	12.2
	John Kruk	12.2
370	Davey Lopes	12.1
	Greg Luzinski	12.1
	David Ortiz	**12.1**
	Lonnie Smith	12.1
374	Earle Combs	12.0
	Darren Daulton	12.0
	Harry Hooper	12.0
	Tommy Leach	12.0
	Orator Shafer	12.0
	Andy Thornton	12.0
380	Lou Criger	11.9
	Cliff Floyd	**11.9**
	Jim Gentile	11.9
	Kirk Gibson	11.9
	Bob Watson	11.9
385	Johnny Romano	11.8
	Gene Woodling	11.8
387	Tony Cuccinello	11.7
	Joe Ferguson	11.7
	Jerry Priddy	11.7
	Dixie Walker	11.7
391	Walker Cooper	11.6
	Kal Daniels	11.6
	Kent Hrbek	11.6
	Heinie Zimmerman	11.6
395	Rick Ferrell	11.5
	Ryan Klesko	**11.5**
	Amos Otis	11.5
	Jim Sundberg	11.5
399	Oscar Gamble	11.4
	Chris Hoiles	11.4
	Dale Murphy	11.4
	Tim Wallach	11.4
403	Billy Nash	11.3
	Deacon White	11.3
	Ernie Whitt	11.3
406	**Alfonso Soriano**	**11.2**
	Vic Wertz	11.2
	Ross Youngs	11.2
409	Elston Howard	11.1
	Placido Polanco	**11.1**
411	Tommy Burns	11.0
	Mike Donlin	11.0
	Ed Swartwood	11.0
414	Max Bishop	10.9
	Bill Bradley	10.9
	Jake Daubert	10.9
	Harry Davis	10.9
	Troy Glaus	**10.9**
	Benny Kauff	10.9
	Derrek Lee	**10.9**
421	Solly Hemus	10.8
422	Dave Cash	10.7
	Charlie Hickman	10.7
	Tip O'Neill	10.7
425	Larry Doyle	10.6
	Buck Herzog	10.6
	Sixto Lezcano	10.6
	Reggie Sanders	**10.6**
	Ed Williamson	10.6
430	Johnny Callison	10.5
	Snuffy Stirnweiss	10.5
432	**Jason Varitek**	**10.4**
	Richie Zisk	10.4
434	**Marcus Giles**	**10.3**
	Wally Joyner	10.3
	Rabbit Maranville	10.3
	Roger Maris	10.3
	Ed McFarland	10.3
	Melvin Mora	**10.3**
	Andy Seminick	10.3
	Bump Wills	10.3
442	Don Baylor	10.2
	Pinky May	10.2
	Tim McCarver	10.2
	Kevin McReynolds	10.2
	Bob O'Farrell	10.2
	Cecil Travis	10.2
	George Van Haltren	10.2
	Jimmy Wolf	10.2
450	Dom DiMaggio	10.1
	Heinie Peitz	10.1
	Johnny Ray	10.1
453	Tony Perez	10.0
	Jody Reed	10.0
	Johnny Roseboro	10.0
456	Jack Crooks	9.9
	Ken Griffey Sr.	9.9
	Freddie Lindstrom	9.9
	Bob Nieman	9.9
	Doug Rader	9.9
	Cy Seymour	9.9
462	**Miguel Cabrera**	**9.8**
	Duke Farrell	9.8
464	Clete Boyer	9.7
	Shawn Green	**9.7**
	Larry Hisle	9.7
	Marty McManus	9.7
	Danny Murphy	9.7
	Edd Roush	9.7
	Mike Sweeney	**9.7**
	Quilvio Veras	9.7
	Omar Vizquel	**9.7**
	Billy Werber	9.7
474	Jackie Jensen	9.6
	Chris Speier	9.6
	Mickey Tettleton	9.6
477	Topsy Hartsel	9.5
	Bill Sweeney	9.5
	Cy Williams	9.5
480	Donie Bush	9.4
	Bernie Carbo	9.4
	Charlie Hollocher	9.4
483	**Geoff Jenkins**	**9.3**
	Billy Jurges	9.3
	Socks Seybold	9.3
	Frank White	9.3
487	Sal Bando	9.2
	Don Money	9.2
	Maggio Ordonez	**9.2**
490	**Adam Dunn**	**9.1**
	Von Hayes	9.1
	Kevin Seitzer	9.1
493	Jerry Denny	9.0
	Art Wilson	9.0
495	Alvin Davis	8.9
	Larry Gardner	8.9
	Freddie Patek	8.9
	Garry Templeton	8.9
499	4 players tied	8.8

WINS

1	Cy Young	511
2	Walter Johnson	417
3	Grover Alexander	373
	Christy Mathewson	373
5	Warren Spahn	363
6	Jim Galvin	361
	Kid Nichols	361
8	**Roger Clemens**	**348**
9	Tim Keefe	342
10	**Greg Maddux**	**333**
11	Steve Carlton	329
12	John Clarkson	328
13	Eddie Plank	326
14	Nolan Ryan	324
	Don Sutton	324
16	Phil Niekro	318
17	Gaylord Perry	314
18	Tom Seaver	311
19	Charley Radbourn	309
20	Mickey Welch	307
21	Lefty Grove	300
	Early Wynn	300
23	**Tom Glavine**	**290**
24	Tommy John	288
25	Bert Blyleven	287
26	Robin Roberts	286
27	Fergie Jenkins	284
	Tony Mullane	284
29	Jim Kaat	283
30	**Randy Johnson**	**280**
31	Red Ruffing	273
32	Burleigh Grimes	270
33	Jim Palmer	268
34	Bob Feller	266
	Eppa Rixey	266
36	Jim McCormick	265
37	Gus Weyhing	264
38	Ted Lyons	260
39	Red Faber	254
	Jack Morris	254
41	Carl Hubbell	253
42	Bob Gibson	251
43	Vic Willis	249
44	Jack Quinn	247
45	Joe McGinnity	246
	Amos Rusie	246
47	Dennis Martinez	245
	Jack Powell	245
49	Juan Marichal	243
50	Herb Pennock	241
51	Frank Tanana	240
52	Mordecai Brown	239
	Mike Mussina	**239**
54	Clark Griffith	237
	Waite Hoyt	237
56	Whitey Ford	236
57	Charlie Buffinton	233
58	**David Wells**	**230**
59	Sam Jones	229
	Luis Tiant	229
	Will White	229
62	George Mullin	228
63	Jim Bunning	224
	Catfish Hunter	224
65	Hooks Dauss	223
	Paul Derringer	223
	Mel Harder	223
68	Jerry Koosman	222
69	Joe Niekro	221
70	Jerry Reuss	220
71	Bob Caruthers	218
	Earl Whitehill	218
73	Freddie Fitzsimmons	217
	Mickey Lolich	217
75	Wilbur Cooper	216
	Charlie Hough	216
	Jamie Moyer	**216**
78	Stan Coveleski	215
	Jim Perry	215
80	Rick Reuschel	214
81	Chief Bender	212
82	Kevin Brown	211
	Bobo Newsom	211
	Billy Pierce	211
	Bob Welch	211
86	Jesse Haines	210
87	Vida Blue	209
	Eddie Cicotte	209
	Don Drysdale	209
	Milt Pappas	209
91	Carl Mays	208
92	Bob Lemon	207
	Hal Newhouser	207
	Kenny Rogers	**207**
	Curt Schilling	**207**
96	**Pedro Martinez**	**206**
97	Orel Hershiser	204
	Al Orth	204
99	Lew Burdette	203
	Silver King	203
	Jack Stivetts	203

LOSSES

1	Cy Young	316
2	Jim Galvin	308
3	Nolan Ryan	292
4	Walter Johnson	279
5	Phil Niekro	274
6	Gaylord Perry	265
7	Don Sutton	256
8	Jack Powell	254
9	Eppa Rixey	251
10	Bert Blyleven	250
11	Robin Roberts	245
	Warren Spahn	245
13	Steve Carlton	244
	Early Wynn	244
15	Jim Kaat	237
16	Frank Tanana	236
17	Gus Weyhing	232
18	Tommy John	231
19	Bob Friend	230
	Ted Lyons	230
21	Fergie Jenkins	226
22	Tim Keefe	225
	Red Ruffing	225
24	Bobo Newsom	222
25	Tony Mullane	220
26	Jack Quinn	218
27	Sam Jones	217
28	Charlie Hough	216
29	Jim McCormick	214
30	Red Faber	213
31	Paul Derringer	212
	Chick Fraser	212
	Burleigh Grimes	212
34	Mickey Welch	210
35	Jerry Koosman	209
36	Grover Alexander	208
	Kid Nichols	208
38	Tom Seaver	205
	Vic Willis	205
40	Joe Niekro	204
	Jim Whitney	204
42	**Greg Maddux**	**203**
43	George Mullin	196
	Adonis Terry	196
45	Claude Osteen	195
46	Eddie Plank	194
	Charley Radbourn	194
48	Dennis Martinez	193
49	**Tom Glavine**	**191**
	Mickey Lolich	191
	Rick Reuschel	191
	Jerry Reuss	191
	Tom Zachary	191
54	Al Orth	189
55	Christy Mathewson	188
56	Mel Harder	186
	Mike Morgan	186
	Jack Morris	186
59	Earl Whitehill	185
60	Jim Bunning	184
	Joe Bush	184
62	Larry Jackson	183
	Curt Simmons	183
64	Danny Darwin	182
	Hooks Dauss	182
	Waite Hoyt	182
67	Murry Dickson	181
	Dutch Leonard	181
	Rick Wise	181
70	Lee Meadows	180
71	Pink Hawley	179
	Dolf Luque	179
73	John Clarkson	178
	Roger Clemens	**178**
	Wilbur Cooper	178
76	Bill Dinneen	177
	Rube Marquard	177
78	Mike Moore	176
79	Red Donahue	175
80	Doyle Alexander	174
	Bob Gibson	174
	Tom Hughes	174
	Jim Perry	174
	Amos Rusie	174
85	Chuck Finley	173
86	Luis Tiant	172
87	Dennis Eckersley	171
	Larry French	171
89	Ted Breitenstein	170
	Camilo Pascual	170
91	Billy Pierce	169
92	Red Ames	167
	Jim Clancy	167
	Bert Cunningham	167
	Red Ehret	167
96	Don Drysdale	166
	Howard Ehmke	166
	Catfish Hunter	166
	Jamie Moyer	**166**
	George Uhle	166
	Will White	166

WINNING PERCENTAGE

1	**Pedro Martinez**	**.691**
2	Dave Foutz	.690
3	Whitey Ford	.690
4	Bob Caruthers	.688
5	Lefty Grove	.680
6	Vic Raschi	.667
7	Larry Corcoran	.665
8	Christy Mathewson	.665
9	**Tim Hudson**	**.665**
10	**Roger Clemens**	**.662**
11	Sam Leever	.660
12	Sal Maglie	.657
13	**Randy Johnson**	**.656**
14	Sandy Koufax	.655
15	Johnny Allen	.654
16	Ron Guidry	.651
17	Lefty Gomez	.649
18	John Clarkson	.648
19	Mordecai Brown	.648
20	Dizzy Dean	.644
21	Grover Alexander	.642
22	**Andy Pettitte**	**.641**
23	**Mike Mussina**	**.641**
24	Jim Palmer	.638
25	Kid Nichols	.634
26	Deacon Phillippe	.634
27	Joe McGinnity	.634
28	Doc Gooden	.634
29	Ed Reulbach	.632
30	Juan Marichal	.631
31	Mort Cooper	.631
32	Allie Reynolds	.630
33	Jesse Tannehill	.627
34	Ray Kremer	.627
35	Firpo Marberry	.627
36	Eddie Plank	.627
37	Tommy Bond	.627
38	Chief Bender	.625
39	Don Newcombe	.623
40	Nig Cuppy	.623
41	Carl Mays	.623
42	Addie Joss	.623
43	Fred Goldsmith	.622
44	Doc Crandall	.622
45	Carl Hubbell	.622
46	Bob Feller	.621
47	**Greg Maddux**	**.621**
48	Mel Parnell	.621
49	**Freddy Garcia**	**.620**
50	John Tudor	.619
51	Clark Griffith	.619
52	Bob Lemon	.618
53	Cy Young	.618
54	**Bartolo Colon**	**.617**
55	Urban Shocker	.615
56	Jeff Tesreau	.615
57	Jim Maloney	.615
58	Charley Radbourn	.614
59	John Ward	.614
60	Jimmy Key	.614
61	Lon Warneke	.613
62	Gary Nolan	.611
63	Schoolboy Rowe	.610
64	Carl Erskine	.610
65	**David Wells**	**.608**
66	Ed Walsh	.607
67	Charlie Ferguson	.607
68	Dave McNally	.607
69	Hooks Wiltse	.607
70	David Cone	.606
71	Jack Stivetts	.606
72	Ramon Martinez	.605
73	Art Nehf	.605
74	Charlie Buffinton	.605
75	Orval Overall	.603
76	Tim Keefe	.603
77	**Tom Glavine**	**.603**
78	Tom Seaver	.603
79	Stan Coveleski	.602
80	Preacher Roe	.602
81	Wes Ferrell	.601
82	J.R. Richard	.601
83	Jack Chesbro	.600
	Curt Schilling	**.600**
85	Walter Johnson	.599
86	**Kenny Rogers**	**.598**
87	Herb Pennock	.598
88	Freddie Fitzsimmons	.598
89	Ed Lopat	.597
90	Warren Spahn	.597
91	Rip Sewell	.596
92	**Chris Carpenter**	**.595**
93	Kevin Brown	.594
94	Mike Garcia	.594
95	Mickey Welch	.594
96	Jack McDowell	.593
97	Pat Malone	.593
98	Alvin Crowder	.592
99	John Candelaria	.592
100	Harry Brecheen	.591

GAMES

1	Jesse Orosco	1252
2	John Franco	1119
3	**Mike Stanton**	**1109**
4	Dennis Eckersley	1071
5	Hoyt Wilhelm	1070
6	Dan Plesac	1064
7	Kent Tekulve	1050
8	Lee Smith	1022
9	Mike Jackson	1005
10	Rich Gossage	1002
11	Lindy McDaniel	987
12	**Jose Mesa**	**966**
13	**Mike Timlin**	**961**
14	**Roberto Hernandez**	**960**
15	Rollie Fingers	944
16	Gene Garber	931
17	Cy Young	906
18	Sparky Lyle	899
19	Jim Kaat	898
20	Paul Assenmacher	884
21	Jeff Reardon	880
22	**Todd Jones**	**874**
	Don McMahon	874
24	Phil Niekro	864
25	Charlie Hough	858
26	Roy Face	848
27	Doug Jones	846
28	Paul Quantrill	841
29	Steve Reed	833
30	Tug McGraw	824
31	**Trevor Hoffman**	**821**
32	**Mike Myers**	**811**
33	**Tom Gordon**	**809**
34	Nolan Ryan	807
35	Walter Johnson	802
36	**Jeff Nelson**	**798**
37	Rick Honeycutt	797
38	Buddy Groom	786
39	**Eddie Guardado**	**781**
40	**Bob Wickman**	**778**
41	Gaylord Perry	777
42	Don Sutton	774
43	Mark Guthrie	765
	Darold Knowles	765
45	Tommy John	760
46	Jack Quinn	756
47	**David Weathers**	**754**
48	Ron Reed	751
49	Warren Spahn	750
50	Tom Burgmeier	745
	Gary Lavelle	745
52	Willie Hernandez	744
53	Steve Carlton	741
54	Ron Perranoski	737
55	Ron Kline	736
56	Rick Aguilera	732
	Steve Bedrosian	732
58	Clay Carroll	731
59	**Steve Kline**	**728**
	Randy Myers	728
61	Mike Marshall	723
	Roger McDowell	723
63	**Kenny Rogers**	**721**
64	**Jeff Fassero**	**720**
	Mariano Rivera	**720**
66	Dave Righetti	718
67	Danny Darwin	716
68	Eric Plunk	714
69	Johnny Klippstein	711
70	Greg Minton	710
71	**Alan Embree**	**708**
72	Rod Beck	704
	Stu Miller	704
74	Greg Harris	703
75	Joe Niekro	702
76	Bill Campbell	700
	Jeff Montgomery	700
	Julian Tavarez	**700**
79	Larry Andersen	699
	Armando Benitez	**699**
81	Bob McClure	698
82	Jim Galvin	697
83	Grover Alexander	696
	Craig Lefferts	696
85	Bob Miller	694
86	Bert Blyleven	692
	Grant Jackson	692
	Dennis Martinez	692
	Eppa Rixey	692
90	**Roger Clemens**	**691**
	Early Wynn	691
92	Eddie Fisher	690
93	**Terry Mulholland**	**685**
94	Ted Abernathy	681
95	**Tim Worrell**	**678**
96	**Rheal Cormier**	**677**
	Greg Maddux	**677**
	Kent Mercker	**677**
99	Robin Roberts	676
100	Waite Hoyt	674
	Dan Quisenberry	674

GAMES STARTED

1	Cy Young	815
2	Nolan Ryan	773
3	Don Sutton	756
4	Phil Niekro	716
5	Steve Carlton	709
6	Tommy John	700
7	**Roger Clemens**	**690**
	Gaylord Perry	690
9	Bert Blyleven	685
10	Jim Galvin	681
11	**Greg Maddux**	**673**
12	Walter Johnson	666
13	Warren Spahn	665
14	Tom Seaver	647
15	**Tom Glavine**	**635**
16	Jim Kaat	625
17	Frank Tanana	616
18	Early Wynn	612
19	Robin Roberts	609
20	Grover Alexander	600
21	Fergie Jenkins	594
	Tim Keefe	594
23	Dennis Martinez	562
	Kid Nichols	562
25	Eppa Rixey	554
26	Christy Mathewson	552
27	Mickey Welch	549
28	Jerry Reuss	547
29	**Randy Johnson**	**546**
30	Red Ruffing	538
31	Eddie Plank	529
	Rick Reuschel	529
33	Jerry Koosman	527
	Jack Morris	527
35	Jim Palmer	521
36	Jim Bunning	519
37	John Clarkson	518
	Jamie Moyer	**518**
39	Jack Powell	516
40	Gus Weyhing	505
41	Tony Mullane	504
42	Charley Radbourn	502
43	Joe Niekro	500
44	Bob Friend	497
	Burleigh Grimes	497
46	Mickey Lolich	496
47	Claude Osteen	488
48	Sam Jones	487
49	Jim McCormick	485
50	Bob Feller	484
	Ted Lyons	484
	Luis Tiant	484
53	Red Faber	483
	Bobo Newsom	483
55	Bob Gibson	482
56	Kevin Brown	476
	Catfish Hunter	476
58	**Mike Mussina**	**475**
59	Vida Blue	473
	Earl Whitehill	473
61	Vic Willis	471
62	Chuck Finley	467
63	Orel Hershiser	466
64	Don Drysdale	465
	Milt Pappas	465
66	Doyle Alexander	464
67	Curt Simmons	462
	Bob Welch	462
69	**David Wells**	**460**
70	Mike Torrez	458
71	Lefty Grove	457
	Juan Marichal	457
73	Rick Wise	455
74	Jim Perry	447
75	Paul Derringer	445
76	Jack Quinn	443
77	Charlie Hough	440
	Mike Moore	440
79	Whitey Ford	438
80	Mel Harder	433
	Carl Hubbell	433
	Kenny Rogers	**433**
83	Billy Pierce	432
84	Larry Jackson	429
	John Smoltz	**429**
86	Mark Langston	428
	George Mullin	428
88	Amos Rusie	427
89	Freddie Fitzsimmons	425
	Waite Hoyt	425
91	Fernando Valenzuela	424
92	John Burkett	423
93	Bob Forsch	422
94	Frank Viola	420
95	David Cone	419
	Herb Pennock	419
97	Bob Knepper	413
98	**Curt Schilling**	**412**
	Dave Stieb	412
100	Mike Morgan	411

GAMES STARTED BY ERA

1988–2006

1 Roger Clemens ... 690
2 Greg Maddux ... 673
3 Tom Glavine ... 635
4 Randy Johnson ... 546
5 Jamie Moyer ... 518
6 Kevin Brown ... 476
7 Mike Mussina ... 475
8 Chuck Finley ... 467
9 Orel Hershiser ... 466
10 David Wells ... 460

1973–87

1 Nolan Ryan ... 773
2 Don Sutton ... 756
3 Phil Niekro ... 716
4 Steve Carlton ... 709
5 Tommy John ... 700
6 Gaylord Perry ... 690
7 Bert Blyleven ... 685
8 Tom Seaver ... 647
9 Frank Tanana ... 616
10 Fergie Jenkins ... 594

1961–72

1 Jim Kaat ... 625
2 Jim Bunning ... 519
3 Mickey Lolich ... 496
4 Claude Osteen ... 488
5 Bob Gibson ... 482
6 Catfish Hunter ... 476
7 Don Drysdale ... 465
Milt Pappas ... 465
9 Juan Marichal ... 457
10 Jim Perry ... 447

1943–60

1 Warren Spahn ... 665
2 Early Wynn ... 612
3 Robin Roberts ... 609
4 Bob Friend ... 497
5 Bob Feller ... 484
6 Curt Simmons ... 462
7 Whitey Ford ... 438
8 Billy Pierce ... 432
9 Dutch Leonard ... 375
10 Hal Newhouser ... 374

1921–42

1 Eppa Rixey ... 554
2 Red Ruffing ... 538
3 Burleigh Grimes ... 497
4 Sam Jones ... 487
5 Ted Lyons ... 484
6 Red Faber ... 483
Bobo Newsom ... 483
8 Earl Whitehill ... 473
9 Lefty Grove ... 457
10 Paul Derringer ... 445

1901–20

1 Cy Young ... 815
2 Walter Johnson ... 666
3 Grover Alexander ... 600
4 Christy Mathewson ... 552
5 Eddie Plank ... 529
6 Jack Powell ... 516
7 Vic Willis ... 471
8 George Mullin ... 428
9 Rube Marquard ... 407
10 Wilbur Cooper ... 406

1893–1900

1 Kid Nichols ... 562
2 Amos Rusie ... 427
3 Clark Griffith ... 372
4 Brickyard Kennedy ... 354
5 Pink Hawley ... 344
6 Ted Breitenstein ... 342
7 Frank Dwyer ... 318
8 Bert Cunningham ... 311
9 Red Ehret ... 309
10 Jouett Meekin ... 308

1876–92

1 Jim Galvin ... 681
2 Tim Keefe ... 594
3 Mickey Welch ... 549
4 John Clarkson ... 518
5 Gus Weyhing ... 505
6 Tony Mullane ... 504
7 Charley Radbourn ... 502
8 Jim McCormick ... 485
9 Adonis Terry ... 406
10 Will White ... 401

COMPLETE GAMES

1 Cy Young ... 749
2 Jim Galvin ... 639
3 Tim Keefe ... 554
4 Kid Nichols ... 532
5 Walter Johnson ... 531
6 Mickey Welch ... 525
7 Charley Radbourn ... 488
8 John Clarkson ... 485
9 Tony Mullane ... 468
10 Jim McCormick ... 466
11 Gus Weyhing ... 449
12 Grover Alexander ... 437
13 Christy Mathewson ... 435
14 Jack Powell ... 422
15 Eddie Plank ... 410
16 Will White ... 394
17 Amos Rusie ... 393
18 Vic Willis ... 388
19 Warren Spahn ... 382
20 Jim Whitney ... 377
21 Adonis Terry ... 367
22 Ted Lyons ... 356
23 George Mullin ... 353
24 Charlie Buffinton ... 351
25 Chick Fraser ... 342
26 Clark Griffith ... 337
27 Red Ruffing ... 335
28 Silver King ... 328
29 Al Orth ... 324
30 Bill Hutchison ... 321
31 Burleigh Grimes ... 314
Joe McGinnity ... 314
33 Red Donahue ... 312
Guy Hecker ... 312
35 Bill Dinneen ... 306
36 Robin Roberts ... 305
37 Gaylord Perry ... 303
38 Ted Breitenstein ... 301
39 Bob Caruthers ... 298
Lefty Grove ... 298
41 Pink Hawley ... 297
Ed Morris ... 297
43 Mark Baldwin ... 295
44 Tommy Bond ... 294
Brickyard Kennedy ... 294
46 Eppa Rixey ... 290
Early Wynn ... 290
48 Bill Donovan ... 289
Bobby Mathews ... 289
50 Bert Cunningham ... 287
51 Wilbur Cooper ... 279
Bob Feller ... 279
Sadie McMahon ... 279
Jack Taylor ... 279
55 Jack Stivetts ... 278
56 Charlie Getzien ... 277
57 Red Faber ... 273
58 Mordecai Brown ... 271
Frank Dwyer ... 271
60 Jouett Meekin ... 270
61 Fergie Jenkins ... 267
62 Elton Chamberlain ... 264
Matt Kilroy ... 264
Jesse Tannehill ... 264
65 Doc White ... 262
66 Rube Waddell ... 261
67 Jack Chesbro ... 260
Red Ehret ... 260
Carl Hubbell ... 260
70 Larry Corcoran ... 256
71 Chief Bender ... 255
Bob Gibson ... 255
73 Steve Carlton ... 254
74 Frank Killen ... 253
Win Mercer ... 253
76 Paul Derringer ... 251
77 Sam Jones ... 250
Ed Walsh ... 250
79 Eddie Cicotte ... 249
Stump Wiedman ... 249
81 Herb Pennock ... 247
82 Bobo Newsom ... 246
83 George Bradley ... 245
Hooks Dauss ... 245
Phil Niekro ... 245
John Ward ... 245
87 Harry Howell ... 244
Juan Marichal ... 244
89 Jack Quinn ... 243
90 Bert Blyleven ... 242
Deacon Phillippe ... 242
Bucky Walters ... 242
93 Sam Leever ... 241
94 Kid Gleason ... 240
95 Addie Joss ... 234
96 George Uhle ... 232
97 Carl Mays ... 231
Tom Seaver ... 231
Harry Staley ... 231
100 Earl Moore ... 230

COMPLETE GAMES BY ERA

1988–2006

1 Roger Clemens ... 118
2 Greg Maddux ... 108
3 Randy Johnson ... 98
4 Curt Schilling ... 82
5 Mark Langston ... 81
6 Mike Moore ... 79
7 Bret Saberhagen ... 76
8 Frank Viola ... 74
9 Kevin Brown ... 72
10 Tom Candiotti ... 68
Doc Gooden ... 68
Orel Hershiser ... 68

1973–87

1 Gaylord Perry ... 303
2 Fergie Jenkins ... 267
3 Steve Carlton ... 254
4 Phil Niekro ... 245
5 Bert Blyleven ... 242
6 Tom Seaver ... 231
7 Nolan Ryan ... 222
8 Jim Palmer ... 211
9 Luis Tiant ... 187
10 Don Sutton ... 178

1961–72

1 Bob Gibson ... 255
2 Juan Marichal ... 244
3 Mickey Lolich ... 195
4 Catfish Hunter ... 181
5 Jim Kaat ... 180
6 Mike Cuellar ... 172
7 Don Drysdale ... 167
8 Mel Stottlemyre ... 152
9 Jim Bunning ... 151
10 Larry Jackson ... 149

1943–60

1 Warren Spahn ... 382
2 Robin Roberts ... 305
3 Early Wynn ... 290
4 Bob Feller ... 279
5 Hal Newhouser ... 212
6 Billy Pierce ... 193
7 Dutch Leonard ... 192
8 Bob Lemon ... 188
9 Ed Lopat ... 164
10 Bob Friend ... 163
Curt Simmons ... 163

1921–42

1 Ted Lyons ... 356
2 Red Ruffing ... 335
3 Burleigh Grimes ... 314
4 Lefty Grove ... 298
5 Eppa Rixey ... 290
6 Red Faber ... 273
7 Carl Hubbell ... 260
8 Paul Derringer ... 251
9 Sam Jones ... 250
10 Herb Pennock ... 247

1901–20

1 Cy Young ... 749
2 Walter Johnson ... 531
3 Grover Alexander ... 437
4 Christy Mathewson ... 435
5 Jack Powell ... 422
6 Eddie Plank ... 410
7 Vic Willis ... 388
8 George Mullin ... 353
9 Chick Fraser ... 342
10 Al Orth ... 324

1893–1900

1 Kid Nichols ... 532
2 Amos Rusie ... 393
3 Clark Griffith ... 337
4 Ted Breitenstein ... 301
5 Pink Hawley ... 297
6 Brickyard Kennedy ... 294
7 Bert Cunningham ... 287
8 Frank Dwyer ... 271
9 Jouett Meekin ... 270
10 Red Ehret ... 260

1876–92

1 Jim Galvin ... 639
2 Tim Keefe ... 554
3 Mickey Welch ... 525
4 Charley Radbourn ... 488
5 John Clarkson ... 485
6 Tony Mullane ... 468
7 Jim McCormick ... 466
8 Gus Weyhing ... 449
9 Will White ... 394
10 Jim Whitney ... 377

SHUTOUTS

1 Walter Johnson ... 110
2 Grover Alexander ... 90
3 Christy Mathewson ... 79
4 Cy Young ... 76
5 Eddie Plank ... 69
6 Warren Spahn ... 63
7 Nolan Ryan ... 61
Tom Seaver ... 61
9 Bert Blyleven ... 60
10 Don Sutton ... 58
11 Jim Galvin ... 57
Ed Walsh ... 57
13 Bob Gibson ... 56
14 Mordecai Brown ... 55
Steve Carlton ... 55
16 Jim Palmer ... 53
Gaylord Perry ... 53
18 Juan Marichal ... 52
19 Rube Waddell ... 50
Vic Willis ... 50
21 Don Drysdale ... 49
Fergie Jenkins ... 49
Luis Tiant ... 49
Early Wynn ... 49
25 Kid Nichols ... 48
26 Roger Clemens ... 46
Tommy John ... 46
Jack Powell ... 46
29 Whitey Ford ... 45
Addie Joss ... 45
Phil Niekro ... 45
Robin Roberts ... 45
Red Ruffing ... 45
Doc White ... 45
35 Babe Adams ... 44
Bob Feller ... 44
37 Milt Pappas ... 43
38 Catfish Hunter ... 42
Bucky Walters ... 42
40 Mickey Lolich ... 41
Hippo Vaughn ... 41
Mickey Welch ... 41
43 Chief Bender ... 40
Jim Bunning ... 40
Larry French ... 40
Sandy Koufax ... 40
Claude Osteen ... 40
Ed Reulbach ... 40
Mel Stottlemyre ... 40
50 Tim Keefe ... 39
Sam Leever ... 39
Jerry Reuss ... 39
53 Stan Coveleski ... 38
Billy Pierce ... 38
Nap Rucker ... 38
56 Vida Blue ... 37
John Clarkson ... 37
Larry Jackson ... 37
Randy Johnson ... 37
Eppa Rixey ... 37
Steve Rogers ... 37
62 Mike Cuellar ... 36
Bob Friend ... 36
Carl Hubbell ... 36
Sam Jones ... 36
Camilo Pascual ... 36
Allie Reynolds ... 36
Curt Simmons ... 36
Will White ... 36
70 Tommy Bond ... 35
Joe Bush ... 35
Jack Chesbro ... 35
Eddie Cicotte ... 35
Jack Coombs ... 35
Wilbur Cooper ... 35
Bill Donovan ... 35
Burleigh Grimes ... 35
Lefty Grove ... 35
Greg Maddux ... 35
George Mullin ... 35
Herb Pennock ... 35
Charley Radbourn ... 35
83 Bill Doak ... 34
Earl Moore ... 34
Frank Tanana ... 34
Jesse Tannehill ... 34
87 Tommy Bridges ... 33
Lew Burdette ... 33
Dean Chance ... 33
Mort Cooper ... 33
Jerry Koosman ... 33
Dutch Leonard ... 33
Jim McCormick ... 33
Dave McNally ... 33
Hal Newhouser ... 33
Bob Shawkey ... 33
Virgil Trucks ... 33
98 Paul Derringer ... 32
Lefty Leifield ... 32
Joe McGinnity ... 32
Jim Perry ... 32

SAVES

1 Trevor Hoffman ... 482
2 Lee Smith ... 478
3 John Franco ... 424
4 Mariano Rivera ... 413
5 Dennis Eckersley ... 390
6 Jeff Reardon ... 367
7 Randy Myers ... 347
8 Rollie Fingers ... 341
9 John Wetteland ... 330
10 Roberto Hernandez ... 326
11 Troy Percival ... 324
Billy Wagner ... 324
13 Jose Mesa ... 320
14 Rick Aguilera ... 318
15 Robb Nen ... 314
16 Tom Henke ... 311
17 Rich Gossage ... 310
18 Jeff Montgomery ... 304
19 Doug Jones ... 303
20 Bruce Sutter ... 300
21 Rod Beck ... 286
22 Armando Benitez ... 280
23 Todd Jones ... 263
24 Todd Worrell ... 256
25 Dave Righetti ... 252
26 Jason Isringhausen ... 249
27 Bob Wickman ... 247
28 Dan Quisenberry ... 244
29 Sparky Lyle ... 238
30 Ugueth Urbina ... 237
31 Hoyt Wilhelm ... 227
32 Gene Garber ... 218
33 Gregg Olson ... 217
34 Dave Smith ... 216
35 Jeff Shaw ... 203
36 Bobby Thigpen ... 201
37 Roy Face ... 193
Mike Henneman ... 193
39 Mitch Williams ... 192
40 Keith Foulke ... 190
41 Mike Marshall ... 188
42 Jeff Russell ... 186
43 Steve Bedrosian ... 184
Kent Tekulve ... 184
45 Eddie Guardado ... 183
46 Danny Graves ... 182
47 Tug McGraw ... 180
48 Ron Perranoski ... 179
49 Bryan Harvey ... 177
50 Jeff Brantley ... 172
Lindy McDaniel ... 172
52 Billy Koch ... 163
53 Eric Gagne ... 161
54 Roger McDowell ... 159
55 Dan Plesac ... 158
56 Jay Howell ... 155
57 Stu Miller ... 154
John Smoltz ... 154
59 Don McMahon ... 153
60 Tom Gordon ... 150
Greg Minton ... 150
62 Ted Abernathy ... 148
63 Willie Hernandez ... 147
64 Dave Giusti ... 145
65 Jesse Orosco ... 144
Mike Williams ... 144
67 Clay Carroll ... 143
Darold Knowles ... 143
69 Mike Jackson ... 142
70 Mike Timlin ... 139
71 Gary Lavelle ... 136
72 Francisco Cordero ... 133
73 Jim Brewer ... 132
Steve Farr ... 132
Bob Stanley ... 132
76 Ron Davis ... 130
77 Kazuhiro Sasaki ... 129
78 Terry Forster ... 127
79 Bill Campbell ... 126
Dave LaRoche ... 126
Mel Rojas ... 126
82 John Hiller ... 125
83 Joe Nathan ... 124
84 Jack Aker ... 123
85 Dick Radatz ... 122
86 Antonio Alfonseca ... 121
Duane Ward ... 121
88 Mark Wohlers ... 119
89 Ricky Bottalico ... 116
90 Tippy Martinez ... 115
91 Danys Baez ... 111
Frank Linzy ... 111
93 Jose Jimenez ... 110
Al Worthington ... 110
95 Fred Gladding ... 109
96 Wayne Granger ... 108
Ron Kline ... 108
98 Johnny Murphy ... 107
99 Bill Caudill ... 106
Francisco Rodriguez ... 106

SAVES BY ERA

1988–2006

1	**Trevor Hoffman**	**482**
2	John Franco	424
3	**Mariano Rivera**	**413**
4	Randy Myers	347
5	John Wetteland	330
6	**Roberto Hernandez**	**326**
7	Troy Percival	324
	Billy Wagner	**324**
9	**Jose Mesa**	**320**
10	Rick Aguilera	318

1973–87

1	Lee Smith	478
2	Dennis Eckersley	390
3	Jeff Reardon	367
4	Rollie Fingers	341
5	Rich Gossage	310
6	Bruce Sutter	300
7	Dave Righetti	252
8	Dan Quisenberry	244
9	Sparky Lyle	238
10	Gene Garber	218

1961–72

1	Ron Perranoski	179
2	Lindy McDaniel	172
3	Don McMahon	153
4	Ted Abernathy	148
5	Dave Giusti	145
6	Clay Carroll	143
	Darold Knowles	143
8	Jim Brewer	132
9	Jack Aker	123
10	Dick Radatz	122

1943–60

1	Hoyt Wilhelm	227
2	Roy Face	193
3	Stu Miller	154
4	Al Worthington	110
5	Ron Kline	108
6	Ellis Kinder	102
7	Clem Labine	96
8	Bill Henry	90
9	Joe Page	76
10	Jim Konstanty	74

1921–42

1	Johnny Murphy	107
2	Firpo Marberry	101
3	Al Benton	66
4	Clint Brown	64
5	Joe Heving	63
6	Jack Quinn	57
7	Hugh Casey	55
	Lefty Grove	55
9	Waite Hoyt	52
10	Wilcy Moore	49

1901–20

1	Mordecai Brown	49
2	Allan Russell	42
3	Hooks Dauss	39
4	Red Ames	36
	Slim Sallee	36
6	Ed Walsh	35
7	Chief Bender	34
	Walter Johnson	34
9	Hooks Wiltse	33
10	Grover Alexander	32

1893–1900

1	Kid Nichols	17
2	Win Mercer	10
3	Brickyard Kennedy	9
	Jack Taylor	9
5	Clark Griffith	8
6	Frank Dwyer	6
	George Hemming	6
8	Nig Cuppy	5
	Duke Esper	5
	Amos Rusie	5

1876–92

1	Tony Mullane	15
2	Kid Gleason	6
	Silver King	6
	Adonis Terry	6
	Jack Manning	6
6	Mark Baldwin	5
	John Clarkson	5
	Jack Stivetts	5
9	Charlie Ferguson	4
	Frank Foreman	4
	Dave Foutz	4
	Bill Hutchison	4
	Sadie McMahon	4
	Hank O'Day	4
	Billy Taylor	4
	Mickey Welch	4
	Gus Weyhing	4
	Bill Daley	4
	Herb Goodall	4
	Cal McVey	4

SAVE PERCENTAGE

1	**Eric Gagne**	**96.41**
2	**John Smoltz**	**91.67**
3	**Joe Nathan**	**89.86**
4	**Trevor Hoffman**	**89.59**
5	**Mariano Rivera**	**88.25**
6	**Billy Wagner**	**86.63**
7	Troy Percival	85.94
8	**Chad Cordero**	**85.85**
9	Kazuhiro Sasaki	85.43
10	Robb Nen	85.33
11	Randy Myers	85.26
12	Mike Williams	85.21
13	Tom Henke	84.97
14	**Jason Isringhausen**	**84.69**
15	Bryan Harvey	84.62
16	Dennis Eckersley	84.60
17	**Armando Benitez**	**84.59**
18	**Brad Lidge**	**84.55**
19	Billy Koch	84.46
20	**Keith Foulke**	**84.44**
21	**Francisco Rodriguez**	**84.13**
22	**Derrick Turnbow**	**84.00**
23	John Wetteland	83.97
24	Rod Beck	83.87
25	**Jose Mesa**	**83.77**
26	**Brian Fuentes**	**83.33**
27	Ugueth Urbina	83.16
28	**Ryan Dempster**	**83.10**
29	Matt Mantei	83.04
30	Lee Smith	82.27
31	Jose Jimenez	82.09
32	Mark Wohlers	82.07
33	**Danny Graves**	**81.61**
34	**Eddie Guardado**	**80.97**
35	**Kelvim Escobar**	**80.82**
36	John Franco	80.76
37	Dave Smith	80.60
38	Jeff Russell	80.52
39	Rick Aguilera	80.51
40	Jeff Montgomery	80.42
41	Mike Henneman	80.42
42	Dan Quisenberry	80.26
43	John Rocker	80.00
	Billy Taylor	80.00
45	**Todd Jones**	**79.94**
46	**Bob Wickman**	**79.94**
47	Jeff Shaw	79.92
48	**Jorge Julio**	**79.84**
49	Doug Jones	79.74
50	Mike Schooler	79.67

BLOWN SAVES

1	Rich Gossage	112
2	Rollie Fingers	109
3	Jeff Reardon	106
4	Lee Smith	103
5	John Franco	101
	Bruce Sutter	101
7	**Roberto Hernandez**	**93**
8	Sparky Lyle	86
9	Gene Garber	82
10	Kent Tekulve	81
11	Gary Lavelle	80
12	**Mike Timlin**	**79**
13	Rick Aguilera	77
	Doug Jones	77
15	Jesse Orosco	76
16	Mike Marshall	74
	Jeff Montgomery	74
	Dan Plesac	74
	Dave Righetti	74
20	Bill Campbell	72
21	Dennis Eckersley	71
	Todd Worrell	71
23	**Todd Jones**	**66**
24	John Wetteland	63
25	Darold Knowles	62
	Jose Mesa	**62**
	Bob Wickman	**62**
28	John Hiller	60
	Randy Myers	60
	Dan Quisenberry	60
31	Paul Assenmacher	59
	Mike Jackson	59
33	Steve Bedrosian	57
34	**Trevor Hoffman**	**56**
	Gregg Olson	56
	Mike Stanton	**56**
	Mitch Williams	56
38	Rod Beck	55
	Tom Henke	55
	Roger McDowell	55
	Mariano Rivera	**55**
	Bob Stanley	55
43	Greg Minton	54
	Robb Nen	54
45	Troy Percival	53
46	Dave Smith	52
	Bobby Thigpen	52
48	**Armando Benitez**	**51**
	Jeff Shaw	51
50	2 players tied	50

INNINGS PITCHED

1	Cy Young	7356.0
2	Jim Galvin	5941.1
3	Walter Johnson	5914.1
4	Phil Niekro	5404.0
5	Nolan Ryan	5386.0
6	Gaylord Perry	5350.0
7	Don Sutton	5282.1
8	Warren Spahn	5243.2
9	Steve Carlton	5217.2
10	Grover Alexander	5190.0
11	Kid Nichols	5067.1
12	Tim Keefe	5049.2
13	Bert Blyleven	4970.0
14	**Roger Clemens**	**4817.2**
15	Mickey Welch	4802.0
16	Christy Mathewson	4788.2
17	Tom Seaver	4783.0
18	Tommy John	4710.1
19	Robin Roberts	4688.2
20	**Greg Maddux**	**4616.1**
21	Early Wynn	4564.0
22	John Clarkson	4536.1
23	Tony Mullane	4531.1
24	Jim Kaat	4530.1
25	Charley Radbourn	4527.1
26	Fergie Jenkins	4500.2
27	Eddie Plank	4495.2
28	Eppa Rixey	4494.2
29	Jack Powell	4389.0
30	Red Ruffing	4344.0
31	Gus Weyhing	4337.0
32	Jim McCormick	4275.2
33	Frank Tanana	4188.1
34	Burleigh Grimes	4180.0
35	Ted Lyons	4161.0
36	**Tom Glavine**	**4149.2**
37	Red Faber	4086.2
38	Dennis Martinez	3999.2
39	Vic Willis	3996.0
40	Jim Palmer	3948.0
41	Lefty Grove	3940.2
42	Jack Quinn	3920.1
43	Bob Gibson	3884.1
44	Sam Jones	3883.0
45	Jerry Koosman	3839.1
46	Bob Feller	3827.0
47	Jack Morris	3824.0
48	Charlie Hough	3801.1
49	**Randy Johnson**	**3798.2**
50	Amos Rusie	3778.2
51	Waite Hoyt	3762.1
52	Jim Bunning	3760.1
53	Bobo Newsom	3759.1
54	George Mullin	3686.2
55	Jerry Reuss	3669.2
56	Paul Derringer	3645.0
57	Mickey Lolich	3638.1
58	Bob Friend	3611.0
59	Carl Hubbell	3590.1
60	Joe Niekro	3584.1
61	Herb Pennock	3571.2
62	Earl Whitehill	3564.2
63	Rick Reuschel	3548.1
64	Will White	3542.2
65	Adonis Terry	3514.1
66	Juan Marichal	3507.0
67	Jim Whitney	3496.1
68	Luis Tiant	3486.1
69	Wilbur Cooper	3480.0
70	Claude Osteen	3460.2
71	Catfish Hunter	3449.1
72	Joe McGinnity	3441.1
73	Don Drysdale	3432.0
74	Mel Harder	3426.1
75	Charlie Buffinton	3404.0
76	Hooks Dauss	3390.2
77	Clark Griffith	3385.2
78	Doyle Alexander	3367.2
79	Chick Fraser	3364.0
80	Al Orth	3354.2
81	**Jamie Moyer**	**3351.0**
82	Curt Simmons	3348.1
83	Vida Blue	3343.1
84	Rube Marquard	3306.2
	Billy Pierce	3306.2
86	Dennis Eckersley	3285.2
	Jim Perry	3285.2
88	**David Wells**	**3281.2**
89	Larry Jackson	3262.2
90	Kevin Brown	3256.1
91	Eddie Cicotte	3226.0
92	Freddie Fitzsimmons	3223.2
93	Dolf Luque	3220.1
94	Dutch Leonard	3218.1
95	**Mike Mussina**	**3210.1**
96	Jesse Haines	3208.2
97	Red Ames	3198.0
98	Chuck Finley	3197.1
	Charlie Root	3197.1
100	Milt Pappas	3186.0

INNINGS PITCHED BY ERA

1988–2006

1	**Roger Clemens**	**4817.2**
2	**Greg Maddux**	**4616.1**
3	**Tom Glavine**	**4149.2**
4	**Randy Johnson**	**3798.2**
5	**Jamie Moyer**	**3351.0**
6	**David Wells**	**3281.2**
7	Kevin Brown	3256.1
8	**Mike Mussina**	**3210.1**
9	Chuck Finley	3197.1
10	**John Smoltz**	**3161.1**

1973–87

1	Phil Niekro	5404.0
2	Nolan Ryan	5386.0
3	Gaylord Perry	5350.0
4	Don Sutton	5282.1
5	Steve Carlton	5217.2
6	Bert Blyleven	4970.0
7	Tom Seaver	4783.0
8	Tommy John	4710.1
9	Fergie Jenkins	4500.2
10	Frank Tanana	4188.1

1961–72

1	Jim Kaat	4530.1
2	Bob Gibson	3884.1
3	Jim Bunning	3760.1
4	Mickey Lolich	3638.1
5	Juan Marichal	3507.0
6	Claude Osteen	3460.2
7	Catfish Hunter	3449.1
8	Don Drysdale	3432.0
9	Jim Perry	3285.2
10	Larry Jackson	3262.2

1943–60

1	Warren Spahn	5243.2
2	Robin Roberts	4688.2
3	Early Wynn	4564.0
4	Bob Feller	3827.0
5	Bob Friend	3611.0
6	Curt Simmons	3348.1
7	Billy Pierce	3306.2
8	Dutch Leonard	3218.1
9	Whitey Ford	3170.1
10	Lew Burdette	3067.1

1921–42

1	Eppa Rixey	4494.2
2	Red Ruffing	4344.0
3	Burleigh Grimes	4180.0
4	Ted Lyons	4161.0
5	Red Faber	4086.2
6	Lefty Grove	3940.2
7	Jack Quinn	3920.1
8	Sam Jones	3883.0
9	Waite Hoyt	3762.1
10	Bobo Newsom	3759.1

1901–20

1	Cy Young	7356.0
2	Walter Johnson	5914.1
3	Grover Alexander	5190.0
4	Christy Mathewson	4788.2
5	Eddie Plank	4495.2
6	Jack Powell	4389.0
7	Vic Willis	3996.0
8	George Mullin	3686.2
9	Wilbur Cooper	3480.0
10	Joe McGinnity	3441.1

1893–1900

1	Kid Nichols	5067.1
2	Amos Rusie	3778.2
3	Clark Griffith	3385.2
4	Brickyard Kennedy	3030.0
5	Pink Hawley	3012.2
6	Ted Breitenstein	2973.1
7	Frank Dwyer	2819.0
8	Red Ehret	2754.1
9	Bert Cunningham	2734.2
10	Jouett Meekin	2605.1

1876–92

1	Jim Galvin	5941.1
2	Tim Keefe	5049.2
3	Mickey Welch	4802.0
4	John Clarkson	4536.1
5	Tony Mullane	4531.1
6	Charley Radbourn	4527.1
7	Gus Weyhing	4337.0
8	Jim McCormick	4275.2
9	Will White	3542.2
10	Adonis Terry	3514.1

FEWEST HITS/GAME

1	Nolan Ryan	6.56
2	Sandy Koufax	6.79
3	**Pedro Martinez**	**6.85**
4	Sid Fernandez	6.85
5	J.R. Richard	6.88
6	Andy Messersmith	6.94
7	Hoyt Wilhelm	7.01
8	Sam McDowell	7.03
9	Ed Walsh	7.12
10	**Randy Johnson**	**7.14**
11	Bob Turley	7.18
12	Orval Overall	7.22
13	Jeff Tesreau	7.24
14	Ed Reulbach	7.24
15	Mario Soto	7.26
16	Addie Joss	7.30
17	Jose DeLeon	7.38
18	Jim Maloney	7.39
19	Rich Gossage	7.45
20	Tom Seaver	7.47
21	Walter Johnson	7.48
22	Rube Waddell	7.48
23	Bob Gibson	7.60
24	Don Wilson	7.61
25	**Roger Clemens**	**7.63**
26	Jim Palmer	7.63
27	Larry Cheney	7.68
28	Mordecai Brown	7.68
29	Sam Jones	7.68
30	Bob Feller	7.69
31	Johnny Vander Meer	7.69
32	Catfish Hunter	7.72
33	Al Downing	7.72
34	Jim Scott	7.73
35	Charlie Hough	7.77
36	David Cone	7.77
37	Bobby Bolin	7.79
38	Stan Williams	7.79
39	Rollie Fingers	7.80
40	Dean Chance	7.81
41	Frank Smith	7.82
42	Tug McGraw	7.83
43	Barney Pelty	7.84
44	**John Smoltz**	**7.85**
45	Whitey Ford	7.85
46	Denny McLain	7.85
47	Bob Veale	7.87
48	Chief Bender	7.89
49	George McQuillan	7.89
50	Jack Coombs	7.89
51	Moe Drabowsky	7.90
52	Tim Keefe	7.91
53	Vida Blue	7.91
54	Nap Rucker	7.92
55	Allie Reynolds	7.92
56	Eddie Plank	7.92
57	Christy Mathewson	7.93
58	Luis Tiant	7.94
59	Rudy May	7.94
60	Ray Culp	7.95
61	Bill Donovan	7.99
62	Howie Camnitz	7.99
63	Don Sutton	7.99
64	Juan Pizarro	7.99
65	Dave Stieb	7.99
66	Gary Bell	8.01
67	**Tom Gordon**	**8.02**
68	Earl Moore	8.02
69	Hideo Nomo	8.02
70	Sonny Siebert	8.03
71	Ramon Martinez	8.03
72	Lefty Tyler	8.03
73	Hal Newhouser	8.04
74	Claude Hendrix	8.06
75	Steve Carlton	8.06
76	Hooks Wiltse	8.06
77	Amos Rusie	8.07
78	Willie Mitchell	8.07
79	Larry Corcoran	8.08
80	Bill Singer	8.08
81	Bob Lemon	8.08
82	Eddie Cicotte	8.08
83	Mike Scott	8.08
84	Don Drysdale	8.09
85	Gary Nolan	8.09
86	Stu Miller	8.09
87	Juan Marichal	8.09
88	Al Leiter	8.10
89	Doc White	8.10
90	Virgil Trucks	8.11
91	Hippo Vaughn	8.11
92	Blue Moon Odom	8.12
93	Kirby Higbe	8.13
94	Jim Shaw	8.13
95	Mike Cuellar	8.13
96	Billy Pierce	8.14
97	Mort Cooper	8.15
98	Red Ames	8.15
99	Vic Willis	8.16
100	Harry Brecheen	8.17

FEWEST HITS/GAME BY ERA

1988–2006

1	**Pedro Martinez**	**6.85**
2	Sid Fernandez	6.85
3	**Randy Johnson**	**7.14**
4	Jose DeLeon	7.38
5	**Roger Clemens**	**7.63**
6	David Cone	7.77
7	**John Smoltz**	**7.85**
8	**Tom Gordon**	**8.02**
9	Hideo Nomo	8.02
10	Ramon Martinez	8.03

1973–87

1	Nolan Ryan	6.56
2	J.R. Richard	6.88
3	Andy Messersmith	6.94
4	Mario Soto	7.26
5	Rich Gossage	7.45
6	Tom Seaver	7.47
7	Jim Palmer	7.63
8	Charlie Hough	7.77
9	Rollie Fingers	7.80
10	Tug McGraw	7.83

1961–72

1	Sandy Koufax	6.79
2	Sam McDowell	7.03
3	Jim Maloney	7.39
4	Bob Gibson	7.60
5	Don Wilson	7.61
6	Catfish Hunter	7.72
7	Al Downing	7.72
8	Bobby Bolin	7.79
9	Stan Williams	7.79
10	Dean Chance	7.81

1943–60

1	Hoyt Wilhelm	7.01
2	Bob Turley	7.18
3	Sam Jones	7.68
4	Bob Feller	7.69
5	Johnny Vander Meer	7.69
6	Whitey Ford	7.85
7	Allie Reynolds	7.92
8	Hal Newhouser	8.04
9	Bob Lemon	8.08
10	Stu Miller	8.09

1921–42

1	Kirby Higbe	8.13
2	Mort Cooper	8.15
3	Lefty Gomez	8.23
4	Van Mungo	8.34
5	Tommy Bridges	8.52
6	Dazzy Vance	8.52
7	Johnny Allen	8.53
8	Whit Wyatt	8.61
9	Bucky Walters	8.67
10	Carl Hubbell	8.68

1901–20

1	Ed Walsh	7.12
2	Orval Overall	7.22
3	Jeff Tesreau	7.24
4	Ed Reulbach	7.24
5	Addie Joss	7.30
6	Walter Johnson	7.48
7	Rube Waddell	7.48
8	Larry Cheney	7.68
9	Mordecai Brown	7.68
10	Jim Scott	7.73

1893–1900

1	Amos Rusie	8.07
2	Kid Nichols	8.75
3	Ed Stein	9.18
4	Billy Rhines	9.33
5	Ted Breitenstein	9.39
6	Brickyard Kennedy	9.75
7	Clark Griffith	9.76
8	Frank Killen	9.78
9	Jouett Meekin	9.80
10	Nixey Callahan	9.81

1876–92

1	Tim Keefe	7.91
2	Larry Corcoran	8.08
3	Ed Morris	8.29
4	Dave Foutz	8.30
5	Toad Ramsey	8.32
6	Charlie Ferguson	8.33
7	Tony Mullane	8.33
8	John Ward	8.47
9	Bob Caruthers	8.52
10	John Clarkson	8.52

FEWEST HR ALL./GAME BY ERA

1988–2006

1	Zane Smith	0.57
2	Kevin Brown	0.57
3	Danny Jackson	0.58
4	**Greg Maddux**	**0.62**
5	Mark Gubicza	0.63
6	Bill Swift	0.65
7	**Roger Clemens**	**0.66**
8	Doc Gooden	0.67
9	Orel Hershiser	0.68
10	**Tom Glavine**	**0.70**

1973–87

1	J.R. Richard	0.41
2	Steve Rogers	0.48
3	Mike LaCoss	0.51
4	Nolan Ryan	0.54
5	Steve Trout	0.54
6	Rick Reuschel	0.56
7	John Denny	0.57
8	Tommy John	0.58
9	Rich Gossage	0.59
10	Dock Ellis	0.59

1961–72

1	Bob Veale	0.43
2	Dean Chance	0.51
3	Bill Singer	0.55
4	Steve Barber	0.56
5	Mel Stottlemyre	0.58
6	Bob Miller	0.59
7	Sam McDowell	0.59
8	Bob Gibson	0.60
9	Don Wilson	0.61
10	Blue Moon Odom	0.61

1943–60

1	Max Lanier	0.36
2	Dizzy Trout	0.37
3	Hal Newhouser	0.41
4	Bill Wight	0.43
5	Johnny Vander Meer	0.43
6	Dutch Leonard	0.44
7	Allie Reynolds	0.48
8	Johnny Schmitz	0.48
9	Rip Sewell	0.49
10	Mike Garcia	0.50

1921–42

1	Eppa Rixey	0.18
2	Stan Coveleski	0.19
3	Jakie May	0.20
4	Dutch Ruether	0.23
5	Jack Quinn	0.23
6	Lee Meadows	0.24
7	Red Faber	0.24
8	Sherry Smith	0.25
9	Al Hollingsworth	0.28
10	Pete Donohue	0.29

1901–20

1	Ed Killian	0.05
2	Ed Walsh	0.07
3	Addie Joss	0.07
4	Willie Mitchell	0.08
5	Eddie Plank	0.08
6	Eddie Cicotte	0.09
7	Cy Falkenberg	0.09
8	Bill Donovan	0.09
9	Orval Overall	0.09
10	Harry Howell	0.09

1893–1900

1	Billy Rhines	0.12
2	Amos Rusie	0.18
3	Pink Hawley	0.18
4	Nixey Callahan	0.19
5	Frank Killen	0.20
6	Clark Griffith	0.20
7	Bert Cunningham	0.20
8	Red Ehret	0.21
9	Jouett Meekin	0.23
10	Win Mercer	0.23

1876–92

1	Terry Larkin	0.07
2	John Ward	0.09
3	Tommy Bond	0.10
4	Jumbo McGinnis	0.12
5	Hardie Henderson	0.13
6	Tim Keefe	0.13
7	Ed Morris	0.14
8	Lee Richmond	0.15
9	Guy Hecker	0.15
10	George Bradley	0.16

WALKS

1	Nolan Ryan	2795
2	Steve Carlton	1833
3	Phil Niekro	1809
4	Early Wynn	1775
5	Bob Feller	1764
6	Bobo Newsom	1732
7	Amos Rusie	1707
8	Charlie Hough	1665
9	Gus Weyhing	1570
10	**Roger Clemens**	**1549**
11	Red Ruffing	1541
12	Bump Hadley	1442
13	Warren Spahn	1434
14	Earl Whitehill	1431
15	**Randy Johnson**	**1409**
16	Tony Mullane	1408
17	**Tom Glavine**	**1399**
18	Sam Jones	1396
19	Jack Morris	1390
	Tom Seaver	1390
21	Gaylord Perry	1379
22	Bobby Witt	1375
23	Mike Torrez	1371
24	Walter Johnson	1363
25	Don Sutton	1343
26	Chick Fraser	1338
27	Bob Gibson	1336
28	Chuck Finley	1332
29	Bert Blyleven	1322
30	Sam McDowell	1312
31	Jim Palmer	1311
32	Mark Baldwin	1307
33	Adonis Terry	1298
34	Mickey Welch	1297
35	Burleigh Grimes	1295
36	Mark Langston	1289
37	Kid Nichols	1272
38	Joe Bush	1263
39	Joe Niekro	1262
40	Allie Reynolds	1261
41	Tommy John	1259
42	Frank Tanana	1255
43	Bob Lemon	1251
44	Hal Newhouser	1249
45	George Mullin	1238
46	Tim Keefe	1233
47	Cy Young	1217
48	Red Faber	1213
49	Vic Willis	1212
50	Ted Breitenstein	1207
51	Brickyard Kennedy	1203
52	Jerry Koosman	1198
53	Tommy Bridges	1192
54	John Clarkson	1191
55	Lefty Grove	1187
56	Vida Blue	1185
57	Billy Pierce	1178
58	Dennis Martinez	1165
59	Al Leiter	1163
60	Mike Moore	1156
61	Jack Stivetts	1155
62	Fernando Valenzuela	1151
63	David Cone	1137
64	Bill Hutchison	1132
	Johnny Vander Meer	1132
66	Jerry Reuss	1127
67	Ted Lyons	1121
	Bucky Walters	1121
69	Mel Harder	1118
70	Earl Moore	1108
71	Bob Buhl	1105
72	Luis Tiant	1104
73	Mickey Lolich	1099
74	Lefty Gomez	1095
75	Virgil Trucks	1088
76	Whitey Ford	1086
77	Jim Kaat	1083
78	Eppa Rixey	1082
79	Rick Sutcliffe	1081
80	**Kenny Rogers**	**1079**
81	Eddie Plank	1072
82	Camilo Pascual	1069
83	Bob Turley	1068
84	Hooks Dauss	1067
85	Elton Chamberlain	1065
86	Bert Cunningham	1064
87	Curt Simmons	1063
88	Bill Donovan	1059
89	Murry Dickson	1058
90	Jouett Meekin	1056
91	Vern Kennedy	1049
92	Dizzy Trout	1046
93	Howard Ehmke	1042
94	Wes Ferrell	1040
95	Tommy Byrne	1037
96	Red Ames	1034
	Dave Stewart	1034
	Dave Stieb	1034
	Bob Welch	1034
100	Rube Walberg	1031

STRIKEOUTS

1	Nolan Ryan	5714
2	**Roger Clemens**	**4604**
3	**Randy Johnson**	**4544**
4	Steve Carlton	4136
5	Bert Blyleven	3701
6	Tom Seaver	3640
7	Don Sutton	3574
8	Gaylord Perry	3534
9	Walter Johnson	3509
10	Phil Niekro	3342
11	Fergie Jenkins	3192
12	**Greg Maddux**	**3169**
13	Bob Gibson	3117
14	**Curt Schilling**	**3015**
15	**Pedro Martinez**	**2998**
16	Jim Bunning	2855
17	Mickey Lolich	2832
18	Cy Young	2803
19	**John Smoltz**	**2778**
20	Frank Tanana	2773
21	David Cone	2668
22	Chuck Finley	2610
23	Warren Spahn	2583
24	Bob Feller	2581
25	**Mike Mussina**	**2572**
26	Tim Keefe	2564
27	Jerry Koosman	2556
28	Christy Mathewson	2507
29	Don Drysdale	2486
30	**Tom Glavine**	**2481**
31	Jack Morris	2478
32	Mark Langston	2464
33	Jim Kaat	2461
34	Sam McDowell	2453
35	Luis Tiant	2416
36	Dennis Eckersley	2401
37	Kevin Brown	2397
38	Sandy Koufax	2396
39	Charlie Hough	2362
40	Robin Roberts	2357
41	Early Wynn	2334
42	Rube Waddell	2316
43	Juan Marichal	2303
44	Doc Gooden	2293
45	Lefty Grove	2266
46	Eddie Plank	2246
47	Tommy John	2245
48	Jim Palmer	2212
49	Grover Alexander	2198
50	Vida Blue	2175
51	Camilo Pascual	2167
52	Dennis Martinez	2149
53	**David Wells**	**2119**
54	Bobo Newsom	2082
55	Fernando Valenzuela	2074
56	Dazzy Vance	2045
57	Rick Reuschel	2015
58	Orel Hershiser	2014
59	Catfish Hunter	2012
60	Andy Benes	2000
61	Billy Pierce	1999
62	Kevin Appier	1994
63	**Jamie Moyer**	**1992**
64	Red Ruffing	1987
65	John Clarkson	1978
66	Al Leiter	1974
67	Bob Welch	1969
68	Whitey Ford	1956
69	Bobby Witt	1955
70	Amos Rusie	1950
71	Danny Darwin	1942
72	Hideo Nomo	1915
73	Jerry Reuss	1907
74	Kid Nichols	1881
75	**Tom Gordon**	**1870**
76	**Kenny Rogers**	**1850**
	Mickey Welch	1850
78	Frank Viola	1844
79	Charley Radbourn	1830
80	Tony Mullane	1803
81	Jim Galvin	1799
82	Hal Newhouser	1796
83	Ron Guidry	1778
84	John Burkett	1766
85	Rudy May	1760
86	Joe Niekro	1747
87	Sid Fernandez	1743
88	Dave Stewart	1741
89	Ed Walsh	1736
90	Tom Candiotti	1735
91	Bob Friend	1734
92	Joe Coleman	1728
	Milt Pappas	1728
	Jason Schmidt	**1728**
95	Kevin Gross	1727
96	Floyd Bannister	1723
97	Bret Saberhagen	1715
98	Chief Bender	1711
99	Larry Jackson	1709
100	Jim McCormick	1704

STRIKEOUTS/GAME

1	**Randy Johnson**	**10.77**
2	**Pedro Martinez**	**10.20**
3	Nolan Ryan	9.55
4	Sandy Koufax	9.28
5	Sam McDowell	8.86
6	Hideo Nomo	8.74
7	**Curt Schilling**	**8.73**
8	**Roger Clemens**	**8.60**
9	Sid Fernandez	8.40
10	J.R. Richard	8.37
11	David Cone	8.28
12	**Tom Gordon**	**8.26**
13	**Jason Schmidt**	**7.96**
14	Bob Veale	7.96
15	**John Smoltz**	**7.91**
16	Jim Maloney	7.81
17	**Javier Vazquez**	**7.81**
18	**Chan Ho Park**	**7.77**
19	Jose Rijo	7.69
20	Jose DeLeon	7.56
21	Mario Soto	7.54
22	Sam Jones	7.54
23	Mark Langston	7.49
24	Rich Gossage	7.47
25	Al Leiter	7.43
26	Doc Gooden	7.37
27	Chuck Finley	7.35
28	**Kevin Millwood**	**7.29**
29	**Jeff Fassero**	**7.27**
30	Bob Gibson	7.22
31	**Mike Mussina**	**7.21**
32	Andy Benes	7.18
33	Bobby Witt	7.14
34	Steve Carlton	7.13
35	Dave Burba	7.08
36	Shane Reynolds	7.05
37	Rube Waddell	7.04
38	**Bartolo Colon**	**7.03**
39	Mickey Lolich	7.01
40	Darryl Kile	6.93
41	Kevin Appier	6.91
42	**Chris Carpenter**	**6.89**
43	Rollie Fingers	6.87
44	Tom Seaver	6.85
45	Wilson Alvarez	6.85
46	Jim Bunning	6.83
47	**Pedro Astacio**	**6.82**
48	Erik Hanson	6.80
49	Ramon Martinez	6.77
50	Denny Neagle	6.74
51	Juan Pizarro	6.73
52	Bobby Bolin	6.71
53	Bert Blyleven	6.70
54	Ron Guidry	6.69
55	Ray Culp	6.69
56	Stan Williams	6.66
57	Camilo Pascual	6.65
58	Bob Turley	6.65
59	**Andy Pettitte**	**6.63**
60	Kevin Brown	6.62
61	Don Wilson	6.60
62	Tug McGraw	6.59
63	**Freddy Garcia**	**6.58**
64	Dennis Eckersley	6.58
65	Denny Lemaster	6.57
66	Andy Messersmith	6.56
67	**Shawn Estes**	**6.56**
68	Don Drysdale	6.52
69	Todd Stottlemyre	6.52
70	Al Downing	6.50
71	Floyd Bannister	6.49
72	Toad Ramsey	6.49
73	**Russ Ortiz**	**6.48**
74	Diego Segui	6.46
75	Dean Chance	6.43
76	Hoyt Wilhelm	6.43
77	**Eric Milton**	**6.42**
78	Mark Gardner	6.41
79	Alex Fernandez	6.40
80	Mike Scott	6.39
81	**Jon Lieber**	**6.39**
82	Fergie Jenkins	6.38
83	Moe Drabowsky	6.37
84	Fernando Valenzuela	6.37
85	Earl Wilson	6.37
86	Harvey Haddix	6.34
87	Sonny Siebert	6.32
88	Chris Short	6.31
89	**Tim Hudson**	**6.30**
90	Bruce Hurst	6.29
91	Pete Harnisch	6.28
92	Bill Singer	6.27
93	**Matt Morris**	**6.26**
94	Kevin Gross	6.25
95	Jack McDowell	6.25
96	**Rick Helling**	**6.24**
97	Luis Tiant	6.24
98	**Tim Wakefield**	**6.22**
99	Turk Farrell	6.21
100	Greg Swindell	6.21

EARNED RUN AVERAGE

1	Ed Walsh	1.82
2	Addie Joss	1.89
3	Mordecai Brown	2.06
4	John Ward	2.10
5	Christy Mathewson	2.13
6	Rube Waddell	2.16
7	Walter Johnson	2.17
8	Orval Overall	2.23
9	Tommy Bond	2.25
10	Ed Reulbach	2.28
	Will White	2.28
12	Jim Scott	2.30
13	Eddie Plank	2.35
14	Larry Corcoran	2.36
15	Eddie Cicotte	2.38
	Ed Killian	2.38
	George McQuillan	2.38
18	Doc White	2.39
19	Nap Rucker	2.42
20	Terry Larkin	2.43
	Jim McCormick	2.43
	Jeff Tesreau	2.43
23	Chief Bender	2.46
24	Sam Leever	2.47
	Lefty Leifield	2.47
	Hooks Wiltse	2.47
27	Bob Ewing	2.49
	Hippo Vaughn	2.49
29	George Bradley	2.50
30	Hoyt Wilhelm	2.52
31	Noodles Hahn	2.55
32	Grover Alexander	2.56
	Slim Sallee	2.56
34	Deacon Phillippe	2.59
	Frank Smith	2.59
36	Ed Siever	2.60
37	Bob Rhoads	2.61
38	Red Ames	2.63
	Tim Keefe	2.63
	Barney Pelty	2.63
	Vic Willis	2.63
	Cy Young	2.63
43	Claude Hendrix	2.65
	Jack Taylor	2.65
45	Joe McGinnity	2.66
	Dick Rudolph	2.66
47	Nick Altrock	2.67
	Charlie Ferguson	2.67
	Carl Weilman	2.67
50	Jack Chesbro	2.68
	Cy Falkenberg	2.68
	Charley Radbourn	2.68
53	Bill Donovan	2.69
	Fred Toney	2.69
55	Larry Cheney	2.70
56	Mickey Welch	2.71
57	Fred Goldsmith	2.73
58	Harry Howell	2.74
59	Howie Camnitz	2.75
	Whitey Ford	2.75
	Dummy Taylor	2.75
62	Babe Adams	2.76
	Sandy Koufax	2.76
	Dutch Leonard	2.76
65	Jeff Pfeffer	2.77
66	Jack Coombs	2.78
	Earl Moore	2.78
68	Phil Douglas	2.80
	Jesse Tannehill	2.80
70	John Clarkson	2.81
	Pedro Martinez	**2.81**
72	Ray Fisher	2.82
	Ed Morris	2.82
	George Mullin	2.82
	Tully Sparks	2.82
76	Bob Caruthers	2.83
77	Dave Foutz	2.84
78	Andy Messersmith	2.86
	Jim Palmer	2.86
	Tom Seaver	2.86
81	Jim Galvin	2.87
	George Winter	2.87
83	Willie Mitchell	2.88
84	Wilbur Cooper	2.89
	Stan Coveleski	2.89
	Juan Marichal	2.89
87	Rollie Fingers	2.90
88	Bob Gibson	2.91
89	Harry Brecheen	2.92
	Dean Chance	2.92
	Doc Crandall	2.92
	Carl Mays	2.92
93	Dave Davenport	2.93
	Guy Hecker	2.93
95	Don Drysdale	2.95
	Jumbo McGinnis	2.95
	Lefty Tyler	2.95
98	Charlie Buffinton	2.96
	Kid Nichols	2.96
100	Mort Cooper	2.97
	Jack Powell	2.97
	Mel Stottlemyre	2.97
	Jim Whitney	2.97

ADJUSTED EARNED RUN AVG.

1	**Pedro Martinez**	**160**
2	Lefty Grove	148
3	Walter Johnson	147
4	Hoyt Wilhelm	146
5	Ed Walsh	145
6	**Roger Clemens**	**144**
7	Addie Joss	142
8	**Randy Johnson**	**139**
	Kid Nichols	139
10	Cy Young	138
11	Mordecai Brown	137
12	**Greg Maddux**	**136**
	Christy Mathewson	136
14	Grover Alexander	135
	Rube Waddell	135
16	John Clarkson	134
17	Harry Brecheen	133
	Whitey Ford	133
	Noodles Hahn	133
20	Sandy Koufax	131
21	Dizzy Dean	130
	Carl Hubbell	130
	Hal Newhouser	130
	Amos Rusie	130
25	**Tim Hudson**	**129**
26	Kevin Brown	128
	Stan Coveleski	128
	Tom Seaver	128
29	Nig Cuppy	127
	Bob Gibson	127
	Sal Maglie	127
	Curt Schilling	**127**
	John Smoltz	**127**
34	Tommy Bridges	126
	Rich Gossage	126
	Jim Palmer	126
	Bret Saberhagen	126
38	Lefty Gomez	125
	Tim Keefe	125
	Max Lanier	125
	Mike Mussina	**125**
	Mel Parnell	125
	John Tudor	125
	Dazzy Vance	125
45	Dave Foutz	124
	Urban Shocker	124
	Dizzy Trout	124
48	Bob Caruthers	123
	Eddie Cicotte	123
	Mort Cooper	123
	Larry Corcoran	123
	Sam Leever	123
	Orval Overall	123
	Dave Stieb	123
55	Kevin Appier	122
	Bob Feller	122
	Charlie Ferguson	122
	Jimmy Key	122
	Silver King	122
	Juan Marichal	122
	Eddie Plank	122
	Ed Reulbach	122
	Eddie Rommel	122
64	Don Drysdale	121
	Clark Griffith	121
	Andy Messersmith	121
	Jose Rijo	121
	Jack Stivetts	121
69	Tiny Bonham	120
	David Cone	120
	Rollie Fingers	120
	Tom Glavine	**120**
	Ron Guidry	120
	Derek Lowe	**120**
	Joe McGinnity	120
	Deacon Phillippe	120
	Charley Radbourn	120
	Jim Scott	120
	Hippo Vaughn	120
	Will White	120
81	Dean Chance	119
	Red Faber	119
	Thornton Lee	119
	Bob Lemon	119
	Dutch Leonard	119
	Carl Mays	119
	Andy Pettitte	**119**
	Billy Pierce	119
	Nap Rucker	119
	Bobby Shantz	119
	Lon Warneke	119
92	Babe Adams	118
	Bert Blyleven	118
	Ted Lyons	118
	Sadie McMahon	118
	Tony Mullane	118
	Warren Spahn	118
	Bob Stanley	118
	John Ward	118
	Vic Willis	118

ADJUSTED ERA BY ERA

1988–2006

1	**Pedro Martinez**	**160**
2	**Roger Clemens**	**144**
3	**Randy Johnson**	**139**
4	**Greg Maddux**	**136**
5	**Tim Hudson**	**129**
6	Kevin Brown	128
7	**Curt Schilling**	**127**
	John Smoltz	**127**
9	Bret Saberhagen	126
10	**Mike Mussina**	**125**

1973–87

1	Tom Seaver	128
2	Rich Gossage	126
	Jim Palmer	126
4	John Tudor	125
5	Dave Stieb	123
6	Andy Messersmith	121
7	Rollie Fingers	120
	Ron Guidry	120
9	Bert Blyleven	118
	Bob Stanley	118

1961–72

1	Sandy Koufax	131
2	Bob Gibson	127
3	Juan Marichal	122
4	Don Drysdale	121
5	Dean Chance	119
6	Gary Nolan	116
7	Jim Maloney	115
8	Jim Bunning	114
	Bill Hands	114
10	Larry Jackson	113
	Sam McDowell	113
	Mel Stottlemyre	113
	Bob Veale	113

1943–60

1	Hoyt Wilhelm	146
2	Harry Brecheen	133
	Whitey Ford	133
4	Hal Newhouser	130
5	Sal Maglie	127
6	Max Lanier	125
	Mel Parnell	125
8	Dizzy Trout	124
9	Bob Feller	122
10	Tiny Bonham	120

1921–42

1	Lefty Grove	148
2	Dizzy Dean	130
	Carl Hubbell	130
4	Stan Coveleski	128
5	Tommy Bridges	126
6	Lefty Gomez	125
	Dazzy Vance	125
8	Urban Shocker	124
9	Mort Cooper	123
10	Eddie Rommel	122

1901–20

1	Walter Johnson	147
2	Ed Walsh	145
3	Addie Joss	142
4	Cy Young	138
5	Mordecai Brown	137
6	Christy Mathewson	136
7	Grover Alexander	135
	Rube Waddell	135
9	Noodles Hahn	133
10	Eddie Cicotte	123
	Sam Leever	123
	Orval Overall	123

1893–1900

1	Kid Nichols	139
2	Amos Rusie	130
3	Nig Cuppy	127
4	Clark Griffith	121
5	Frank Dwyer	115
6	Billy Rhines	114
7	Ted Breitenstein	109
	Nixey Callahan	109
	Frank Killen	109
10	Pink Hawley	107
	Win Mercer	107

1876–92

1	John Clarkson	134
2	Tim Keefe	125
3	Dave Foutz	124
4	Bob Caruthers	123
	Larry Corcoran	123
6	Charlie Ferguson	122
	Silver King	122
8	Jack Stivetts	121
9	Charley Radbourn	120
	Will White	120

OPPONENT BATTING AVG.

1	Nolan Ryan	.204
2	Sandy Koufax	.205
3	Sid Fernandez	.209
	Pedro Martinez	**.209**
5	Andy Messersmith	.212
	J.R. Richard	.212
7	Sam McDowell	.215
8	Hoyt Wilhelm	.216
9	**Randy Johnson**	**.217**
10	Ed Walsh	.218
11	Mario Soto	.220
	Bob Turley	.220
13	Addie Joss	.223
	Orval Overall	.223
	Jeff Tesreau	.223
16	Jose DeLeon	.224
	Jim Maloney	.224
	Ed Reulbach	.224
19	Larry Corcoran	.226
	Tim Keefe	.226
	Tom Seaver	.226
22	Walter Johnson	.227
23	**Roger Clemens**	**.228**
	Bob Gibson	.228
	Rich Gossage	.228
	Rube Waddell	.228
	Don Wilson	.228
28	Sam Jones	.230
	Jim Palmer	.230
30	Bobby Bolin	.231
	Bob Feller	.231
	Catfish Hunter	.231
33	David Cone	.232
	Al Downing	.232
	Johnny Vander Meer	.232
	Stan Williams	.232
37	Mordecai Brown	.233
	Charlie Ferguson	.233
	Charlie Hough	.233
40	Dean Chance	.234
	Larry Cheney	.234
	Denny McLain	.234
	Toad Ramsey	.234
	Amos Rusie	.234
	John Smoltz	**.234**
	John Ward	.234
47	Ray Culp	.235
	Rollie Fingers	.235
	Whitey Ford	.235
	Dave Foutz	.235
	Ed Morris	.235
	Tony Mullane	.235
53	Moe Drabowsky	.236
	Christy Mathewson	.236
	Don Sutton	.236
	Luis Tiant	.236
	Bob Veale	.236
58	Vida Blue	.237
	Juan Marichal	.237
	Tug McGraw	.237
	Juan Pizarro	.237
	Frank Smith	.237
63	**Tom Gordon**	**.238**
	Rudy May	.238
	Allie Reynolds	.238
	Jim Scott	.238
	Sonny Siebert	.238
68	Gary Bell	.239
	Chief Bender	.239
	Bill Donovan	.239
	Don Drysdale	.239
	Ramon Martinez	.239
	Hal Newhouser	.239
	Gary Nolan	.239
	Hideo Nomo	.239
	Barney Pelty	.239
	Eddie Plank	.239
	Dupee Shaw	.239
	Dave Stieb	.239
	Will White	.239
81	Steve Carlton	.240
	Bob Caruthers	.240
	John Clarkson	.240
	Mort Cooper	.240
	Billy Pierce	.240
	Mike Scott	.240
	Bill Singer	.240
	Virgil Trucks	.240
89	Jack Coombs	.241
	Kirby Higbe	.241
	Bob Lemon	.241
	George McQuillan	.241
	Earl Moore	.241
	Charley Radbourn	.241
	Hooks Wiltse	.241
96	11 players tied	.242

OPPONENT ON-BASE PCT.

1	John Ward	.254
2	Addie Joss	.260
3	George Bradley	.262
4	Terry Larkin	.263
5	Larry Corcoran	.264
	Ed Walsh	.264
7	Tommy Bond	.267
8	Will White	.268
9	Charlie Ferguson	.270
	Pedro Martinez	**.270**
11	Christy Mathewson	.273
	Ed Morris	.273
13	Jim McCormick	.274
14	Fred Goldsmith	.275
	Tim Keefe	.275
	Sandy Koufax	.275
	Jim Whitney	.275
18	Juan Marichal	.277
19	Mordecai Brown	.278
	Charley Radbourn	.278
21	Walter Johnson	.279
	Dupee Shaw	.279
23	Guy Hecker	.281
	Jumbo McGinnis	.281
25	Deacon Phillippe	.283
	Tom Seaver	.283
27	Babe Adams	.284
	Jim Galvin	.284
29	Bob Caruthers	.285
	Catfish Hunter	.285
	Bobby Mathews	.285
	Gary Nolan	.285
	Curt Schilling	**.285**
34	Sid Fernandez	.286
	Dave Foutz	.286
	Don Sutton	.286
37	Fergie Jenkins	.287
	Andy Messersmith	.287
	Cy Young	.287
40	Grover Alexander	.288
	Rube Waddell	.288
	Hoyt Wilhelm	.288
43	Tiny Bonham	.289
	Henry Boyle	.289
	Noodles Hahn	.289
	Jack Lynch	.289
	Bret Saberhagen	.289
48	Dennis Eckersley	.290
	Greg Maddux	**.290**
	Denny McLain	.290
	Hooks Wiltse	.290
52	Nick Altrock	.291
	John Clarkson	.291
	Carl Hubbell	.291
55	Chief Bender	.292
	Charlie Buffinton	.292
	Rollie Fingers	.292
	Ron Guidry	.292
	Robin Roberts	.292
	John Smoltz	**.292**
	Mickey Welch	.292
	Doc White	.292
63	Don Drysdale	.293
	Sam Leever	.293
	Mike Mussina	**.293**
	Eddie Plank	.293
67	**Roger Clemens**	**.294**
	George McQuillan	.294
	Jim Palmer	.294
	Mario Soto	.294
	Ralph Terry	.294
72	John Candelaria	.295
	Toad Ramsey	.295
	Jeff Tesreau	.295
75	**Randy Johnson**	**.296**
	Gaylord Perry	.296
	Warren Spahn	.296
78	Jim Bunning	.297
	Jack Chesbro	.297
	Eddie Cicotte	.297
	Mike Cuellar	.297
	Eddie Fisher	.297
	Bob Gibson	.297
	Don Mossi	.297
	Mike Scott	.297
	Frank Smith	.297
	Jack Taylor	.297
	Luis Tiant	.297
	George Winter	.297
90	Harry Brecheen	.298
	Dizzy Dean	.298
	Tony Mullane	.298
	Don Newcombe	.298
	Orval Overall	.298
	Fritz Peterson	.298
	Lee Richmond	.298
	Dick Rudolph	.298
98	Joe Horlen	.299
	Ed Reulbach	.299
	Slim Sallee	.299
	John Tudor	.299
	Don Wilson	.299

ADJUSTED PITCHING WINS

1	Cy Young	77.8
2	**Roger Clemens**	**73.1**
3	Walter Johnson	70.8
4	Lefty Grove	60.8
5	**Greg Maddux**	**56.2**
6	Kid Nichols	55.1
7	Grover Alexander	55.0
8	**Pedro Martinez**	**50.5**
9	**Randy Johnson**	**50.3**
10	Tom Seaver	47.3
11	Christy Mathewson	41.3
12	John Clarkson	39.6
13	Warren Spahn	38.2
14	Carl Hubbell	38.2
15	Bob Gibson	37.0
16	Jim Palmer	36.2
17	Bert Blyleven	34.8
18	Whitey Ford	34.6
19	Amos Rusie	33.9
20	**Curt Schilling**	**33.2**
21	Tim Keefe	33.1
22	**Tom Glavine**	**33.0**
23	Gaylord Perry	32.7
24	Kevin Brown	32.6
25	**Mike Mussina**	**32.4**
26	Bob Feller	32.3
27	**John Smoltz**	**32.0**
28	Ed Walsh	30.0
29	Hal Newhouser	29.7
30	Eddie Plank	29.1
31	Hoyt Wilhelm	28.8
32	Steve Carlton	28.7
33	Dazzy Vance	28.5
34	Charley Radbourn	27.8
35	Mordecai Brown	27.7
36	Ted Lyons	27.3
37	Phil Niekro	27.2
38	Robin Roberts	27.2
39	Stan Coveleski	27.0
40	Tommy Bridges	26.8
41	Bret Saberhagen	26.6
42	Fergie Jenkins	26.4
43	Sandy Koufax	25.9
44	Juan Marichal	25.7
45	Don Drysdale	25.2
46	Nolan Ryan	25.1
47	Billy Pierce	24.6
48	Red Faber	24.6
49	Rube Waddell	24.4
50	Dave Stieb	24.3
51	Eppa Rixey	23.7
52	Tony Mullane	23.5
53	Lefty Gomez	23.4
54	Clark Griffith	23.3
55	Urban Shocker	23.1
56	David Cone	23.0
57	Addie Joss	22.9
58	Dennis Eckersley	22.9
59	Kevin Appier	22.7
60	Silver King	22.3
61	Jimmy Key	22.1
62	**Mariano Rivera**	**21.8**
63	Harry Brecheen	21.5
64	Eddie Cicotte	21.5
65	Vic Willis	21.4
66	Dizzy Trout	21.3
67	Jim Bunning	21.1
68	Dolf Luque	20.8
69	Joe McGinnity	20.7
70	Dutch Leonard	20.6
71	Eddie Rommel	20.5
72	Chuck Finley	20.2
73	Don Sutton	20.2
74	Luis Tiant	19.9
75	Dizzy Dean	19.9
76	Ron Guidry	19.8
77	Bob Lemon	19.7
78	Carl Mays	19.6
79	Rick Reuschel	19.5
80	Bob Caruthers	19.4
81	Jim McCormick	19.4
82	Red Ruffing	19.2
83	Mickey Welch	19.1
84	Nig Cuppy	19.1
85	Lon Warneke	19.0
86	**Tim Hudson**	**18.5**
87	Noodles Hahn	18.1
88	Jack Stivetts	18.1
89	Tommy John	18.0
90	**Roy Oswalt**	**18.0**
91	Babe Adams	17.9
92	Steve Rogers	17.9
93	Sam Leever	17.7
94	Virgil Trucks	17.6
95	Wes Ferrell	17.5
96	Waite Hoyt	17.5
97	Bucky Walters	17.2
98	Ed Reulbach	17.0
99	Will White	16.9
100	Sal Maglie	16.9

RELIEF WINS

1	Hoyt Wilhelm	124
2	Lindy McDaniel	119
3	Rich Gossage	115
4	Rollie Fingers	107
5	Sparky Lyle	99
6	Roy Face	96
7	Gene Garber	94
	Kent Tekulve	94
9	Mike Marshall	92
10	John Franco	90
	Don McMahon	90
12	Tug McGraw	89
13	Clay Carroll	88
14	Jesse Orosco	87
15	Bob Stanley	85
16	Bill Campbell	80
	Gary Lavelle	80
18	Tom Burgmeier	79
	Stu Miller	79
	Ron Perranoski	79
21	Johnny Murphy	73
	Jeff Reardon	73
23	John Hiller	72
24	Mark Clear	71
	Dick Hall	71
	Lee Smith	71
27	Willie Hernandez	70
	Roger McDowell	70
29	Pedro Borbon	69
30	Bruce Sutter	68
	Mike Timlin	**68**
32	**Mike Stanton**	**67**
33	Doug Jones	66
34	Steve Bedrosian	65
35	Al Hrabosky	64
36	**Roberto Hernandez**	**63**
	Darold Knowles	63
	Clem Labine	63
	Dave LaRoche	63
	Eric Plunk	63
41	Jim Brewer	62
	Turk Farrell	62
	Eddie Fisher	62
	Grant Jackson	62
	Paul Lindblad	62
	Frank Linzy	62
	Dan Plesac	62
48	Paul Assenmacher	61
	Mike Jackson	61
50	Joe Heving	60

RELIEF LOSSES

1	Gene Garber	108
2	Hoyt Wilhelm	103
3	Rollie Fingers	101
4	Mike Marshall	98
5	Kent Tekulve	90
6	Lindy McDaniel	88
7	John Franco	87
	Lee Smith	87
9	Rich Gossage	85
10	Roy Face	82
11	Doug Jones	78
	Jesse Orosco	78
13	Jeff Reardon	77
14	Sparky Lyle	76
15	Gary Lavelle	75
16	Ron Perranoski	74
17	Darold Knowles	71
	Bruce Sutter	71
19	Roger McDowell	69
	Tug McGraw	69
21	**Roberto Hernandez**	**68**
22	Stu Miller	67
	Dan Plesac	67
24	Clay Carroll	66
	Jose Mesa	**66**
	Don McMahon	66
	Mike Timlin	**66**
28	Bill Campbell	65
29	Mike Jackson	63
30	Greg Minton	62
31	Steve Bedrosian	61
	Bob Stanley	61
33	**Mike Stanton**	**60**
34	John Hiller	58
35	**Todd Jones**	**57**
	Frank Linzy	57
	Randy Myers	57
38	Mitch Williams	56
39	Willie Hernandez	55
	Trevor Hoffman	**55**
41	Craig Lefferts	54
42	Tom Burgmeier	53
	Ron Davis	53
	Greg Harris	53
	Dave Smith	53
46	Rick Aguilera	52
	Jim Kern	52
	Randy Moffitt	52
	Dave Righetti	52
	Todd Worrell	52

RELIEF GAMES

1	Jesse Orosco	1248
2	John Franco	1119
3	**Mike Stanton**	**1108**
4	Dan Plesac	1050
	Kent Tekulve	1050
6	Hoyt Wilhelm	1018
7	Lee Smith	1016
8	Mike Jackson	998
9	Rich Gossage	965
10	**Roberto Hernandez**	**957**
	Mike Timlin	**957**
12	Gene Garber	922
13	Lindy McDaniel	913
14	Rollie Fingers	907
15	Sparky Lyle	899
16	Paul Assenmacher	883
17	Jeff Reardon	880
18	**Todd Jones**	**873**
19	Don McMahon	872
20	**Jose Mesa**	**871**
21	Doug Jones	842
22	Steve Reed	833
23	Roy Face	821
	Trevor Hoffman	**821**
25	**Mike Myers**	**811**
26	**Jeff Nelson**	**798**
27	Tug McGraw	785
28	Paul Quantrill	777
29	Buddy Groom	771
30	Darold Knowles	757
31	**Eddie Guardado**	**756**
32	**Bob Wickman**	**750**
33	Tom Burgmeier	742
	Gary Lavelle	742
35	Ron Perranoski	736
36	Willie Hernandez	733
37	**Steve Kline**	**727**
38	Mark Guthrie	722
39	Roger McDowell	721
40	Randy Myers	716
41	Dennis Eckersley	710
	Mariano Rivera	**710**
43	Rod Beck	704
	Alan Embree	**704**
45	Clay Carroll	703
	Greg Minton	703
47	**Armando Benitez**	**699**
	Mike Marshall	699
	Jeff Montgomery	699
50	Larry Andersen	698

RELIEF INNINGS PITCHED

1	Hoyt Wilhelm	1871.0
2	Lindy McDaniel	1694.0
3	Rich Gossage	1556.2
4	Rollie Fingers	1500.1
5	Gene Garber	1452.2
6	Kent Tekulve	1436.2
7	Sparky Lyle	1390.1
8	Tug McGraw	1301.1
9	Don McMahon	1297.0
10	Jesse Orosco	1277.0
11	Mike Marshall	1259.1
12	Lee Smith	1252.1
13	Tom Burgmeier	1248.2
14	John Franco	1245.2
15	Roy Face	1212.1
16	Clay Carroll	1204.2
17	Eddie Fisher	1186.0
18	Bill Campbell	1177.1
19	Ron Perranoski	1170.2
20	Bob Stanley	1159.0
21	Mike Jackson	1154.2
22	Jeff Reardon	1132.1
23	Doug Jones	1097.1
24	Stu Miller	1094.2
25	Greg Minton	1087.1
26	**Mike Timlin**	**1080.2**
27	Gary Lavelle	1077.2
28	Darold Knowles	1052.1
	Mike Stanton	**1052.1**
30	Paul Lindblad	1043.1
	Dan Quisenberry	1043.1
32	Bruce Sutter	1042.0
33	Johnny Klippstein	1040.2
34	Roger McDowell	1039.2
35	Pedro Borbon	1016.1
36	**Roberto Hernandez**	**1013.2**
37	Dan Plesac	1003.0
38	Willie Hernandez	994.1
39	Bob Miller	992.2
40	Larry Andersen	990.2
41	Dave LaRoche	976.0
42	Ted Abernathy	970.0
43	**Todd Jones**	**964.2**
44	John Hiller	962.2
45	**Jose Mesa**	**933.1**
46	Steve Bedrosian	931.0
47	Greg Harris	922.1
48	Eric Plunk	920.0
49	Elias Sosa	905.0
50	Dale Murray	901.1

ADJUSTED RELIEVER RUNS

1	Hoyt Wilhelm	252
2	**Mariano Rivera**	**235**
3	Rich Gossage	185
4	**Billy Wagner**	**151**
5	Dan Quisenberry	148
6	John Franco	145
7	**Roberto Hernandez**	**143**
	Trevor Hoffman	**143**
	Kent Tekulve	143
10	Lee Smith	138
11	John Wetteland	135
12	Tom Henke	132
13	Rollie Fingers	131
14	Mark Eichhorn	127
15	**Keith Foulke**	**126**
16	Mike Jackson	124
	Jesse Orosco	124
18	Sparky Lyle	123
19	Doug Jones	121
20	Bob Stanley	117
	Mike Timlin	**117**
22	Tug McGraw	116
	Paul Quantrill	116
24	**Armando Benitez**	**115**
25	**Bob Wickman**	**114**
26	Dennis Eckersley	112
	Bruce Sutter	112
28	**Tom Gordon**	**111**
	John Hiller	111
	Jeff Montgomery	111
31	Troy Percival	108
32	Lindy McDaniel	107
33	Mike Marshall	105
34	Robb Nen	100
35	Clay Carroll	99
	Steve Reed	99
37	**Jeff Nelson**	**98**
38	Gary Lavelle	97
39	Rick Aguilera	94
40	Ellis Kinder	93
41	Greg Harris	92
42	Gene Garber	88
	Ron Perranoski	88
44	Jeff Reardon	87
45	Tom Burgmeier	86
	Willie Hernandez	86
	Don McMahon	86
48	Stu Miller	85
49	Shigetoshi Hasegawa	84
	Eric Plunk	84

RELIEF RANKING

1	**Mariano Rivera**	**425**
2	Hoyt Wilhelm	366
3	Rich Gossage	318
4	**Trevor Hoffman**	**269**
5	John Franco	263
6	**Roberto Hernandez**	**256**
7	John Wetteland	251
8	**Billy Wagner**	**241**
9	Lee Smith	223
10	Dan Quisenberry	219
11	Rollie Fingers	218
12	Tom Henke	214
13	Robb Nen	205
	Kent Tekulve	205
15	Doug Jones	194
16	Sparky Lyle	190
17	Dennis Eckersley	189
18	Mike Marshall	187
19	Jesse Orosco	183
20	John Hiller	181
21	Rick Aguilera	178
22	Jeff Montgomery	175
	Bruce Sutter	175
24	**Bob Wickman**	**174**
25	**Armando Benitez**	**172**
26	Troy Percival	168
27	**Tom Gordon**	**167**
	Tug McGraw	167
29	**Keith Foulke**	**165**
30	**Mike Timlin**	**159**
31	Bob Stanley	158
32	Ellis Kinder	154
	Ron Perranoski	154
34	Mike Jackson	148
35	Gary Lavelle	147
36	Lindy McDaniel	145
37	Stu Miller	141
38	Mark Eichhorn	138
39	Roy Face	137
40	Gregg Olson	135
	Dan Plesac	135
	Jeff Reardon	135
43	Randy Myers	134
	Paul Quantrill	134
45	Mike Henneman	133
46	Gene Garber	129
	Jason Isringhausen	**129**
	Dave Righetti	129
49	Clay Carroll	128
50	Ugueth Urbina	127

PITCHER WINS BY ERA

1988–2006

1	**Roger Clemens**	**73.2**
2	**Greg Maddux**	**64.7**
3	**Pedro Martinez**	**49.9**
4	**Randy Johnson**	**48.5**
5	**Tom Glavine**	**41.3**
6	**Mariano Rivera**	**41.2**
7	**John Smoltz**	**36.5**
8	**Mike Mussina**	**34.2**
9	Kevin Brown	33.7
10	**Curt Schilling**	**30.5**

1973–87

1	Tom Seaver	49.5
2	Jim Palmer	35.0
3	Steve Carlton	34.0
4	Gaylord Perry	32.9
5	Bert Blyleven	31.8
6	Dennis Eckersley	30.5
7	Fergie Jenkins	30.4
8	Rich Gossage	29.7
9	Phil Niekro	29.1
10	Dave Stieb	25.6

1961–72

1	Bob Gibson	45.0
2	Don Drysdale	32.4
3	Juan Marichal	27.7
4	Sandy Koufax	22.3
5	Mel Stottlemyre	16.7
6	Jim Bunning	16.4
	Jim Kaat	16.4
8	Larry Jackson	16.0
9	Ron Perranoski	14.7
10	Wilbur Wood	14.6

1943–60

1	Warren Spahn	51.4
2	Whitey Ford	37.2
	Hal Newhouser	37.2
4	Hoyt Wilhelm	37.1
5	Bob Lemon	34.2
6	Bob Feller	31.6
7	Robin Roberts	30.3
8	Dizzy Trout	29.7
9	Billy Pierce	25.6
10	Harry Brecheen	24.9

1921–42

1	Lefty Grove	59.1
2	Carl Hubbell	40.2
3	Ted Lyons	33.5
4	Red Ruffing	31.4
5	Wes Ferrell	31.1
6	Dazzy Vance	29.2
7	Tommy Bridges	27.3
8	Urban Shocker	27.0
9	Bucky Walters	26.7
10	Dolf Luque	26.2

1901–20

1	Walter Johnson	89.9
2	Cy Young	77.0
3	Grover Alexander	62.9
4	Christy Mathewson	56.3
5	Ed Walsh	37.7
6	Mordecai Brown	32.7
7	Carl Mays	31.7
8	Eddie Plank	30.3
9	Eddie Cicotte	24.3
10	Addie Joss	23.0

1893–1900

1	Kid Nichols	56.2
2	Amos Rusie	36.7
3	Clark Griffith	28.3
4	Nig Cuppy	20.4
5	Frank Dwyer	13.6
6	Ted Breitenstein	10.9
	Frank Killen	10.9
8	Nixey Callahan	9.3
9	Pink Hawley	8.3
10	Win Mercer	8.0

1876–92

1	John Clarkson	42.5
2	Tim Keefe	35.6
3	Charley Radbourn	31.5
4	Tony Mullane	30.2
5	Bob Caruthers	30.0
6	Jack Stivetts	25.1
7	Silver King	23.0
8	Guy Hecker	22.5
9	Jim McCormick	21.1
10	Charlie Buffinton	19.6

PITCHER WINS

1 Walter Johnson 89.9
2 Cy Young 77.0
3 Roger Clemens 73.2
4 Greg Maddux 64.7
5 Grover Alexander 62.9
6 Lefty Grove 59.1
7 Christy Mathewson 56.3
8 Kid Nichols 56.2
9 Warren Spahn 51.4
10 Pedro Martinez 49.9
11 Tom Seaver 49.5
12 Randy Johnson 48.5
13 Bob Gibson 45.0
14 John Clarkson 42.5
15 Tom Glavine 41.3
16 Mariano Rivera 41.2
17 Carl Hubbell 40.2
18 Ed Walsh 37.7
19 Whitey Ford 37.2
Hal Newhouser 37.2
21 Hoyt Wilhelm 37.1
22 Amos Rusie 36.7
23 John Smoltz 36.5
24 Tim Keefe 35.6
25 Jim Palmer 35.0
26 Bob Lemon 34.2
Mike Mussina 34.2
28 Steve Carlton 34.0
29 Kevin Brown 33.7
30 Ted Lyons 33.5
31 Gaylord Perry 32.9
32 Mordecai Brown 32.7
33 Don Drysdale 32.4
34 Bert Blyleven 31.8
35 Carl Mays 31.7
36 Bob Feller 31.6
37 Charley Radbourn 31.5
38 Red Ruffing 31.4
39 Wes Ferrell 31.1
40 Dennis Eckersley 30.5
Curt Schilling 30.5
42 Fergie Jenkins 30.4
43 Eddie Plank 30.3
Robin Roberts 30.3
45 Tony Mullane 30.2
46 Bob Caruthers 30.0
47 Rich Gossage 29.7
Dizzy Trout 29.7
49 Dazzy Vance 29.2
50 Phil Niekro 29.1
51 Clark Griffith 28.3
52 Bret Saberhagen 27.9
53 Juan Marichal 27.7
54 Tommy Bridges 27.3
55 Urban Shocker 27.0
56 Bucky Walters 26.7
57 Trevor Hoffman 26.6
58 John Franco 26.2
Dolf Luque 26.2
60 Stan Coveleski 26.0
61 Billy Pierce 25.6
Dave Stieb 25.6
63 Jack Stivetts 25.1
64 Harry Brecheen 24.9
65 Eddie Cicotte 24.3
66 Eppa Rixey 24.2
67 Billy Wagner 24.1
68 Dan Quisenberry 23.6
69 Roberto Hernandez 23.4
70 Red Faber 23.3
Jimmy Key 23.3
72 David Cone 23.2
Rick Reuschel 23.2
74 Addie Joss 23.0
Silver King 23.0
Eddie Rommel 23.0
77 Lee Smith 22.9
78 Rollie Fingers 22.7
79 Lon Warneke 22.6
80 Guy Hecker 22.5
81 Dizzy Dean 22.3
Sandy Koufax 22.3
83 Dutch Leonard 22.2
Nolan Ryan 22.2
Rube Waddell 22.2
86 Tom Henke 21.7
87 Luis Tiant 21.6
88 Red Lucas 21.5
Kent Tekulve 21.5
90 Joe Wood 21.4
91 Jim McCormick 21.1
92 John Hiller 21.0
John Wetteland 21.0
94 Ron Guidry 20.5
95 Nig Cuppy 20.4
Tommy John 20.4
97 Kevin Appier 20.3
98 Chuck Finley 20.2
Jesse Tannehill 20.2
100 Lefty Gomez 20.1

PITCHER WINS

101 Vic Willis 20.0
102 Wilbur Cooper 19.7
103 Charlie Buffinton 19.6
Doug Jones 19.6
105 Robb Nen 19.5
Early Wynn 19.5
107 Orel Hershiser 19.4
Sparky Lyle 19.4
Mike Marshall 19.4
Roy Oswalt 19.4
Andy Pettitte 19.4
Jack Quinn 19.4
113 Spud Chandler 19.1
114 Freddie Fitzsimmons 19.0
115 Joe McGinnity 18.9
Jesse Orosco 18.9
Mickey Welch 18.9
118 Schoolboy Rowe 18.8
Doc White 18.8
120 Bobby Shantz 18.7
121 Tom Gordon 18.6
Ed Lopat 18.6
Don Newcombe 18.6
124 Bruce Sutter 18.5
125 Doc Gooden 18.4
126 Burleigh Grimes 18.3
127 Curt Davis 18.2
128 Tim Hudson 18.1
129 Babe Adams 17.7
130 Andy Messersmith 17.6
Johan Santana 17.6
132 Don Sutton 17.5
133 Jeff Montgomery 17.4
134 Rick Aguilera 17.3
Ed Reulbach 17.3
136 Dave Foutz 17.2
137 John Candelaria 17.0
Noodles Hahn 17.0
Mel Harder 17.0
Babe Ruth 17.0
141 John Tudor 16.9
142 Larry French 16.8
Virgil Trucks 16.8
144 Bob Shawkey 16.7
Mel Stottlemyre 16.7
146 Barry Zito 16.6
147 Armando Benitez 16.4
Jim Bunning 16.4
Jim Kaat 16.4
150 Hippo Vaughn 16.3
151 Murry Dickson 16.2
152 Sam Leever 16.1
153 Larry Jackson 16.0
Derek Lowe 16.0
155 Keith Foulke 15.9
George Uhle 15.9
157 Thornton Lee 15.8
158 Mike Garcia 15.7
Waite Hoyt 15.7
Max Lanier 15.7
Jack Taylor 15.7
Mike Timlin 15.7
Frank Viola 15.7
164 Jerry Koosman 15.6
Troy Percival 15.6
Deacon Phillippe 15.6
167 Mel Parnell 15.5
Kenny Rogers 15.5
Steve Rogers 15.5
Nap Rucker 15.5
171 Johnny Antonelli 15.4
172 Stu Miller 15.3
173 Ned Garver 15.2
Hal Schumacher 15.2
175 Bob Stanley 15.1
176 Randy Myers 15.0
177 Chief Bender 14.9
Ellis Kinder 14.9
Claude Passeau 14.9
180 Bob Wickman 14.8
181 Ron Perranoski 14.7
182 Tug McGraw 14.6
Wilbur Wood 14.6
184 Dave Righetti 14.5
David Wells 14.5
186 Mort Cooper 14.3
Charlie Ferguson 14.3
Claude Hendrix 14.3
Brad Radke 14.3
190 Mark Eichhorn 14.2
Gregg Olson 14.2
192 Mike Jackson 14.1
193 Bartolo Colon 14.0
Roy Halladay 14.0
195 Jeff Reardon 13.9
Jose Rijo 13.9
197 Sal Maglie 13.8
198 Fred Hutchinson 13.7
Firpo Marberry 13.7
Claude Osteen 13.7

PITCHER WINS

201 Frank Dwyer 13.6
Jim Maloney 13.6
203 Gary Lavelle 13.5
Charlie Root 13.5
205 Mike Hampton 13.4
206 Vida Blue 13.2
Roy Face 13.2
Gene Garber 13.2
209 Lindy McDaniel 13.0
Sadie McMahon 13.0
John Ward 13.0
212 Willie Hernandez 12.9
Milt Pappas 12.9
214 Frank Tanana 12.8
Will White 12.8
Carlos Zambrano 12.8
217 Gary Peters 12.7
218 Orval Overall 12.6
219 Larry Corcoran 12.5
Harry Howell 12.5
Dan Plesac 12.5
222 Steve Farr 12.4
Mike Henneman 12.4
Charlie Hough 12.4
Frank Lary 12.4
Joe Nathan 12.4
227 Alex Fernandez 12.3
Howie Pollet 12.3
229 Clay Carroll 12.2
Jeff Pfeffer 12.2
Jake Weimer 12.2
232 Van Mungo 12.1
233 Jon Matlack 12.0
Ugueth Urbina 12.0
Jim Whitney 12.0
236 Mark Buehrle 11.9
Mark Langston 11.9
Frank Linzy 11.9
George Mullin 11.9
240 Dennis Martinez 11.8
241 Bryan Harvey 11.6
242 Tom Burgmeier 11.5
243 Harvey Haddix 11.4
Dick Radatz 11.4
Jim Tobin 11.4
246 Bill Hutchison 11.3
247 Francisco Cordero 11.2
Jim Devlin 11.2
Jason Isringhausen 11.2
Al Leiter 11.2
Johnny Sain 11.2
Todd Worrell 11.2
253 Jamie Moyer 11.1
Jim Perry 11.1
Curt Simmons 11.1
256 Jack Chesbro 11.0
Hooks Wiltse 11.0
258 Ted Breitenstein 10.9
Eric Gagne 10.9
Frank Killen 10.9
Don McMahon 10.9
Jeff Nelson 10.9
Jeff Shaw 10.9
264 Tiny Bonham 10.8
Teddy Higuera 10.8
266 Jim Brewer 10.7
Ray Kremer 10.7
Dave Smith 10.7
269 Tom Zachary 10.6
270 Jay Howell 10.5
Johnny Murphy 10.5
272 Rod Beck 10.4
Tex Hughson 10.4
Greg Minton 10.4
275 Al Brazle 10.3
Dontrelle Willis 10.3
277 Ewell Blackwell 10.2
Jack McDowell 10.2
Dutch Ruether 10.2
Slim Sallee 10.2
Scot Shields 10.2
282 Jim Kern 10.1
Lefty Leifield 10.1
284 Bob Ewing 10.0
Francisco Rodriguez 10.0
Brandon Webb 10.0
287 Mike Boddicker 9.9
Mark Gubicza 9.9
Sam McDowell 9.9
Camilo Pascual 9.9
Monte Pearson 9.9
292 Sid Fernandez 9.8
Jim Galvin 9.8
Catfish Hunter 9.8
Ed Morris 9.8
Fernando Valenzuela 9.8
297 5 players tied 9.7

PLAYER OVERALL WINS BY ERA

1988–2006

1 Barry Bonds 124.7
2 Roger Clemens 73.2
3 Rickey Henderson 70.2
4 Greg Maddux 64.7
5 Jeff Bagwell 52.9
6 Alex Rodriguez 52.5
7 Wade Boggs 50.5
8 Pedro Martinez 49.9
9 Frank Thomas 49.5
10 Randy Johnson 48.5
11 Ken Griffey Jr. 46.8
12 Edgar Martinez 44.6
13 Cal Ripken 43.3
14 Mike Piazza 42.6
Gary Sheffield 42.6
16 Ivan Rodriguez 42.1
17 Barry Larkin 41.9
18 Tom Glavine 41.3
19 Mariano Rivera 41.2
20 Manny Ramirez 39.5
21 Tony Gwynn 38.5
22 Tim Raines 38.1
23 Scott Rolen 37.4
24 Ryne Sandberg 36.8
25 Jeff Kent 36.7

1973–87

1 Mike Schmidt 77.3
2 Joe Morgan 68.5
3 Bobby Grich 50.6
4 Tom Seaver 49.5
5 Ozzie Smith 44.9
6 George Brett 42.8
7 Johnny Bench 42.4
8 Darrell Evans 41.4
9 Robin Yount 40.0
10 Rod Carew 39.5
11 Gary Carter 38.8
Carlton Fisk 38.8
13 Reggie Jackson 38.7
14 Willie Randolph 36.0
15 Lou Whitaker 35.2
16 Eddie Murray 35.1
17 Jim Palmer 35.0
18 Steve Carlton 34.0
19 Keith Hernandez 33.5
20 Gaylord Perry 32.9
21 Bert Blyleven 31.8
22 Reggie Smith 31.5
23 Alan Trammell 31.1
24 Dennis Eckersley 30.5
25 Fergie Jenkins 30.4

1961–72

1 Willie Mays 84.4
2 Hank Aaron 83.0
3 Frank Robinson 65.0
4 Bob Gibson 45.0
5 Ron Santo 44.7
6 Al Kaline 43.8
7 Carl Yastrzemski 42.7
8 Willie McCovey 39.3
9 Dick Allen 39.0
10 Roberto Clemente 35.4
11 Bill Mazeroski 35.2
12 Don Drysdale 32.4
13 Harmon Killebrew 32.0
14 Norm Cash 30.4
15 Jimmy Wynn 29.6
16 Willie Stargell 29.5
17 Ernie Banks 27.8
18 Juan Marichal 27.7
19 Jim Fregosi 25.5
20 Billy Williams 24.6
21 Joe Torre 22.8
22 Rocky Colavito 22.7
23 Sandy Koufax 22.3
24 Frank Howard 21.9
25 Tony Oliva 20.5

1943–60

1 Ted Williams 86.5
2 Stan Musial 76.0
3 Mickey Mantle 71.8
4 Eddie Mathews 53.0
5 Warren Spahn 51.4
6 Lou Boudreau 43.6
7 Bobby Doerr 40.3
8 Yogi Berra 40.2
9 Whitey Ford 37.2
Hal Newhouser 37.2
11 Hoyt Wilhelm 37.1
12 Jackie Robinson 34.3
13 Bob Lemon 34.0
14 Bob Feller 31.6
15 Robin Roberts 30.3
16 Dizzy Trout 29.7
17 Joe Gordon 28.8
18 Billy Pierce 25.6
19 Harry Brecheen 24.9
20 Roy Campanella 24.6
21 Ralph Kiner 24.2
Gil McDougald 24.2
23 Richie Ashburn 22.8
24 Charlie Keller 22.3
25 Dutch Leonard 22.2
Duke Snider 22.2

PLAYER OVERALL WINS BY ERA

1921–42

1 Babe Ruth 129.0
2 Rogers Hornsby 86.0
3 Lou Gehrig 70.9
4 Mel Ott 60.7
5 Lefty Grove 59.1
6 Jimmie Foxx 58.7
7 Joe DiMaggio 45.8
8 Charlie Gehringer 45.1
9 Gabby Hartnett 44.4
10 Arky Vaughan 43.3
11 Luke Appling 42.4
12 Carl Hubbell 40.2
13 Joe Cronin 39.6
14 Bill Dickey 38.5
15 Johnny Mize 37.7
16 Frankie Frisch 37.3
17 Dave Bancroft 36.2
18 Bob Johnson 35.7
19 Joe Sewell 35.2
20 Mickey Cochrane 34.7
21 Paul Waner 33.8
22 Ted Lyons 33.5
23 Harry Heilmann 33.2
24 Hank Greenberg 32.6
25 Billy Herman 31.6

1901–20

1 Nap Lajoie 95.2
2 Walter Johnson 89.9
3 Ty Cobb 85.8
4 Tris Speaker 82.7
5 Honus Wagner 82.3
6 Cy Young 77.0
7 Eddie Collins 72.5
8 Grover Alexander 62.9
9 Christy Mathewson 56.3
10 Bill Dahlen 48.5
11 Bobby Wallace 38.4
12 Joe Jackson 38.3
13 Ed Walsh 37.7
14 Frank Baker 33.7
15 Mordecai Brown 32.7
16 Carl Mays 31.7
17 Heinie Groh 30.4
18 Eddie Plank 30.3
19 Elmer Flick 29.7
20 Sam Crawford 29.3
21 Fred Clarke 27.9
22 Art Fletcher 27.2
23 Sherry Magee 26.2
24 Eddie Cicotte 24.3
25 Zack Wheat 24.1

1893–1900

1 Kid Nichols 56.2
2 George Davis 50.1
3 Ed Delahanty 42.8
4 Amos Rusie 36.7
5 Cupid Childs 30.4
6 Clark Griffith 28.3
7 Billy Hamilton 27.2
8 Hughie Jennings 26.8
9 Jesse Burkett 25.9
10 Jake Beckley 22.6
11 Joe Kelley 20.7
Chief Zimmer 20.7
13 Nig Cuppy 20.4
14 John McGraw 19.5
15 Bill Joyce 19.3
16 Mike Griffin 18.3
17 Lave Cross 16.4
18 Elmer Smith 14.5
19 Kip Selbach 13.9
20 Frank Dwyer 13.6
21 Mike Tiernan 13.3
22 Jimmy Ryan 13.2
23 George Van Haltren 11.8
24 Ted Breitenstein 10.9
Frank Killen 10.9

1876–92

1 Roger Connor 43.4
2 John Clarkson 42.5
Dan Brouthers 42.5
4 Bid McPhee 38.3
5 Jack Glasscock 36.5
6 Tim Keefe 35.6
7 Cap Anson 35.3
8 Bob Caruthers 33.6
Bob Caruthers 33.6
10 Charley Radbourn 31.5
11 Tony Mullane 30.0
12 Sam Thompson 29.5
13 Buck Ewing 29.3
14 King Kelly 28.4
15 Fred Dunlap 28.0
16 Pete Browning 27.7
17 Hardy Richardson 26.6
18 Charlie Bennett 23.9
19 Jack Stivetts 23.7
20 Silver King 23.0
21 Guy Hecker 21.9
22 Harry Stovey 21.5
23 Jim McCormick 21.1
24 Fred Pfeffer 20.8
25 John Ward 20.7

PLAYER OVERALL WINS ALPHA

Hank Aaron	83.0
Bobby Abreu	**29.4**
Babe Adams	17.7
Rick Aguilera	17.3
Grover Alexander	62.9
Dick Allen	39.0
Gene Alley	19.1
Roberto Alomar	36.1
Moises Alou	**15.8**
Cap Anson	35.3
Johnny Antonelli	15.4
Luis Aparicio	15.6
Kevin Appier	20.3
Luke Appling	42.4
Richie Ashburn	22.8
Earl Averill	17.3
Jeff Bagwell	52.9
Frank Baker	33.7
Dave Bancroft	36.2
Ernie Banks	27.8
Dick Bartell	28.2
Earl Battey	15.6
Jake Beckley	22.6
Buddy Bell	28.0
Jay Bell	15.4
Albert Belle	29.4
Carlos Beltran	**16.1**
Johnny Bench	42.4
Chief Bender	14.9
Armando Benitez	**16.4**
Charlie Bennett	23.9
Wally Berger	21.0
Lance Berkman	**20.4**
Yogi Berra	40.2
Craig Biggio	**32.9**
Bert Blyleven	31.8
Wade Boggs	50.5
Barry Bonds	**124.7**
Bobby Bonds	27.2
Bobby Bonilla	16.3
Lou Boudreau	43.6
Ken Boyer	20.4
Harry Brecheen	24.9
Roger Bresnahan	22.8
George Brett	42.8
Tommy Bridges	27.3
Dan Brouthers	42.5
Kevin Brown	33.7
Mordecai Brown	32.7
Pete Browning	27.7
Charlie Buffinton	16.2
Don Buford	14.9
Jim Bunning	16.4
Jesse Burkett	25.9
Ellis Burks	16.6
Rick Burleson	16.8
Brett Butler	15.7
Ken Caminiti	20.3
Roy Campanella	24.6
John Candelaria	17.0
Jose Canseco	23.2
Rod Carew	39.5
Max Carey	18.0
Steve Carlton	34.0
Gary Carter	38.8
Rico Carty	18.1
Bob Caruthers	33.6
Norm Cash	30.4
Cesar Cedeno	22.3
Orlando Cepeda	18.4
Ron Cey	21.2
Frank Chance	22.6
Spud Chandler	19.1
Ray Chapman	16.6
Ben Chapman	14.4
Eric Chavez	**17.6**
Cupid Childs	30.4
Eddie Cicotte	24.3
Jack Clark	29.6
Will Clark	24.2
Fred Clarke	27.9
John Clarkson	42.5
Roger Clemens	**73.2**
Roberto Clemente	35.4
Harlond Clift	26.3
Ty Cobb	85.8
Mickey Cochrane	34.7
Rocky Colavito	22.7
Eddie Collins	72.5
Jimmy Collins	23.0
Dave Concepcion	18.0
David Cone	23.2
Roger Connor	43.4
Wilbur Cooper	19.7
Stan Coveleski	26.0
Gavy Cravath	18.4
Sam Crawford	29.3
Joe Cronin	39.6
Lave Cross	16.4
Jose Cruz	20.5

PLAYER OVERALL WINS ALPHA

Roy Cullenbine	18.8
Nig Cuppy	20.4
Bill Dahlen	48.5
Curt Davis	18.2
Chili Davis	15.4
Eric Davis	20.5
George Davis	50.1
Andre Dawson	17.2
Dizzy Dean	22.3
Ed Delahanty	42.8
Carlos Delgado	**21.3**
Art Devlin	20.0
Bill Dickey	38.5
Murry Dickson	16.2
Joe DiMaggio	45.8
Larry Doby	17.8
Bobby Doerr	40.3
Brian Downing	20.0
Don Drysdale	32.4
Fred Dunlap	28.0
Lenny Dykstra	23.1
Dennis Eckersley	30.5
Jim Edmonds	**35.6**
Bob Elliott	21.4
Darrell Evans	41.4
Dwight Evans	24.7
Johnny Evers	15.9
Buck Ewing	29.3
Red Faber	23.3
Ferris Fain	18.8
Bob Feller	31.6
Tony Fernandez	20.9
Wes Ferrell	31.2
Rollie Fingers	22.7
Chuck Finley	20.2
Carlton Fisk	38.8
Freddie Fitzsimmons	19.0
Art Fletcher	27.2
Elmer Flick	29.7
Whitey Ford	37.2
George Foster	18.6
Keith Foulke	**15.9**
Jack Fournier	24.4
Nellie Fox	14.6
Jimmie Foxx	58.7
John Franco	26.2
Julio Franco	**14.5**
Bill Freehan	18.8
Jim Fregosi	25.5
Larry French	16.8
Frankie Frisch	37.3
Rafael Furcal	**17.3**
Augie Galan	15.3
Mike Garcia	15.7
Nomar Garciaparra	**24.8**
Ned Garver	15.2
Lou Gehrig	70.9
Charlie Gehringer	45.1
Jason Giambi	**24.1**
Bob Gibson	45.0
Brian Giles	**29.9**
Jack Glasscock	36.5
Tom Glavine	**41.3**
Lefty Gomez	20.1
Juan Gonzalez	18.1
Luis Gonzalez	**18.8**
Doc Gooden	18.4
Tom Gordon	**18.6**
Joe Gordon	28.8
Sid Gordon	14.8
Goose Goslin	23.3
Rich Gossage	29.7
Hank Greenberg	32.6
Bobby Grich	50.6
Ken Griffey Jr.	**46.8**
Mike Griffin	18.3
Clark Griffith	28.3
Burleigh Grimes	18.3
Heinie Groh	30.4
Lefty Grove	59.1
Pedro Guerrero	17.4
Vladimir Guerrero	**35.2**
Ron Guidry	20.5
Tony Gwynn	38.5
Stan Hack	29.4
Noodles Hahn	17.0
Billy Hamilton	27.2
Ron Hansen	15.5
Mel Harder	17.0
Mike Hargrove	15.8
Toby Harrah	19.2
Gabby Hartnett	44.4
Jeff Heath	17.2
Guy Hecker	21.9
Harry Heilmann	33.2
Todd Helton	**31.3**
Rickey Henderson	70.2
Tom Henke	21.7
Tommy Henrich	15.0
Babe Herman	17.5

PLAYER OVERALL WINS ALPHA

Billy Herman	31.6
Roberto Hernandez	**23.4**
Keith Hernandez	33.5
Orel Hershiser	19.4
John Hiller	21.0
Paul Hines	14.4
Trevor Hoffman	**26.6**
Rogers Hornsby	86.0
Frank Howard	21.9
Waite Hoyt	15.7
Glenn Hubbard	20.5
Carl Hubbell	40.2
Tim Hudson	**18.1**
Miller Huggins	22.4
Larry Jackson	16.0
Joe Jackson	38.3
Reggie Jackson	38.7
Travis Jackson	22.0
Fergie Jenkins	30.4
Hughie Jennings	26.8
Derek Jeter	**17.5**
Tommy John	20.4
Randy Johnson	**48.5**
Walter Johnson	89.9
Bob Johnson	35.7
Doug Jones	19.6
Andruw Jones	**22.6**
Charley Jones	19.4
Chipper Jones	**27.1**
Addie Joss	23.0
Bill Joyce	19.3
David Justice	15.8
Jim Kaat	16.4
Al Kaline	43.8
Willie Kamm	15.7
Tim Keefe	35.6
Willie Keeler	15.0
Charlie Keller	22.3
Joe Kelley	20.7
King Kelly	28.4
Jason Kendall	**18.5**
Jeff Kent	**36.7**
Jimmy Key	23.3
Harmon Killebrew	32.0
Ellis Kinder	14.9
Ralph Kiner	24.2
Silver King	23.0
Chuck Klein	21.1
Johnny Kling	14.4
Bobby Knoop	17.3
Ed Konetchy	21.2
Jerry Koosman	15.6
Sandy Koufax	22.3
Nap Lajoie	95.2
Max Lanier	15.7
Ray Lankford	17.4
Barry Larkin	41.9
Henry Larkin	15.2
Tony Lazzeri	17.8
Thornton Lee	15.8
Sam Leever	16.1
Bob Lemon	34.0
Chet Lemon	18.5
Dutch Leonard	22.2
Kenny Lofton	**16.9**
Johnny Logan	16.2
Ernie Lombardi	20.7
Ed Lopat	18.6
Javy Lopez	**21.1**
Derek Lowe	**16.0**
Red Lucas	20.8
Dolf Luque	26.2
Sparky Lyle	19.4
Fred Lynn	19.2
Ted Lyons	33.5
Denny Lyons	19.6
Greg Maddux	**64.7**
Sherry Magee	26.2
Mickey Mantle	71.8
Juan Marichal	27.7
Mike Marshall	19.4
Pedro Martinez	**49.9**
Edgar Martinez	44.6
Eddie Mathews	53.0
Christy Mathewson	56.3
Don Mattingly	15.4
Carl Mays	31.7
Willie Mays	84.4
Bill Mazeroski	35.2
Jim McCormick	21.1
Willie McCovey	39.3
Gil McDougald	24.2
Joe McGinnity	18.9
Tug McGraw	14.6
John McGraw	19.5
Fred McGriff	22.2
Mark McGwire	35.0
Bid McPhee	38.3
Joe Medwick	25.6
Andy Messersmith	17.6

PLAYER OVERALL WINS ALPHA

Chief Meyers	17.2
Stu Miller	15.3
Minnie Minoso	21.3
Kevin Mitchell	20.3
Johnny Mize	37.7
Paul Molitor	36.6
Jeff Montgomery	17.4
Joe Morgan	68.5
Tony Mullane	30.0
Thurman Munson	25.0
Dwayne Murphy	15.1
Eddie Murray	35.1
Stan Musial	76.0
Mike Mussina	**34.2**
Randy Myers	15.0
Robb Nen	19.5
Graig Nettles	21.2
Don Newcombe	18.6
Hal Newhouser	37.2
Kid Nichols	56.2
Bill Nicholson	17.2
Phil Niekro	29.1
John Olerud	24.4
Tony Oliva	20.5
Paul O'Neill	16.4
Jesse Orosco	18.9
Jim O'Rourke	16.0
Roy Oswalt	**19.4**
Mel Ott	60.7
Rafael Palmeiro	35.8
Jim Palmer	35.0
Mel Parnell	15.5
Lance Parrish	22.3
Claude Passeau	14.9
Troy Percival	15.6
Ron Perranoski	14.7
Gaylord Perry	32.9
Johnny Pesky	15.5
Rico Petrocelli	15.6
Andy Pettitte	**19.4**
Fred Pfeffer	20.8
Deacon Phillippe	15.6
Tony Phillips	18.7
Mike Piazza	**42.6**
Billy Pierce	25.6
Eddie Plank	30.3
Darrell Porter	20.5
Jorge Posada	**23.0**
Boog Powell	17.3
Del Pratt	22.5
Kirby Puckett	23.4
Albert Pujols	**30.4**
Jack Quinn	19.4
Dan Quisenberry	23.6
Charley Radbourn	31.5
Tim Raines	38.1
Manny Ramirez	**39.5**
Willie Randolph	36.0
Pee Wee Reese	16.8
Ed Reulbach	17.3
Rick Reuschel	23.2
Jim Rice	18.4
Hardy Richardson	26.6
Dave Righetti	14.5
Cal Ripken	43.3
Mariano Rivera	**41.2**
Eppa Rixey	24.2
Phil Rizzuto	18.7
Robin Roberts	30.3
Brooks Robinson	14.5
Frank Robinson	65.0
Jackie Robinson	34.3
Alex Rodriguez	**52.5**
Ivan Rodriguez	**42.1**
Kenny Rogers	**15.5**
Steve Rogers	15.5
Scott Rolen	**37.4**
Eddie Rommel	23.0
Pete Rose	24.4
Al Rosen	16.2
Schoolboy Rowe	18.8
Nap Rucker	15.5
Red Ruffing	31.2
Amos Rusie	36.7
Babe Ruth	129.0
Nolan Ryan	22.2
Bret Saberhagen	27.9
Tim Salmon	**21.8**
Ryne Sandberg	36.8
Johan Santana	**17.6**
Ron Santo	44.7
Ray Schalk	16.1
Wally Schang	20.4
Curt Schilling	**30.5**
Mike Schmidt	77.3
Red Schoendienst	16.5
Hal Schumacher	15.2
Mike Scioscia	18.2
Tom Seaver	49.5
Joe Sewell	35.2

PLAYER OVERALL WINS ALPHA

Cy Seymour	14.9
Bobby Shantz	18.7
Bob Shawkey	16.7
Jimmy Sheckard	20.7
Gary Sheffield	**42.6**
Urban Shocker	27.0
Al Simmons	23.0
Ted Simmons	21.7
Ken Singleton	19.8
George Sisler	26.5
Enos Slaughter	15.1
Roy Smalley	16.9
Lee Smith	22.9
Reggie Smith	31.5
Ozzie Smith	44.9
John Smoltz	**36.5**
Duke Snider	22.2
Sammy Sosa	25.3
Warren Spahn	51.4
Tris Speaker	82.7
Eddie Stanky	20.1
Bob Stanley	15.1
Willie Stargell	29.5
Rusty Staub	23.1
Vern Stephens	20.7
Dave Stieb	25.6
Jack Stivetts	23.7
Mel Stottlemyre	16.7
Harry Stovey	21.5
Darryl Strawberry	22.5
Bruce Sutter	18.5
Don Sutton	17.5
Ichiro Suzuki	**14.5**
Jesse Tannehill	20.0
Jack Taylor	15.7
Miguel Tejada	**27.5**
Kent Tekulve	21.5
Gene Tenace	26.1
Fred Tenney	22.9
Bill Terry	26.7
Frank Thomas	**49.5**
Roy Thomas	22.7
Jim Thome	**35.9**
Sam Thompson	29.5
Luis Tiant	21.6
Mike Timlin	**15.7**
Joe Tinker	19.5
Joe Torre	22.8
Alan Trammell	31.1
Pie Traynor	18.4
Dizzy Trout	29.7
Virgil Trucks	16.8
John Tudor	16.9
George Uhle	15.9
John Valentin	17.2
Jose Valentin	**14.6**
Dazzy Vance	29.2
Andy Van Slyke	16.8
Arky Vaughan	43.3
Hippo Vaughn	16.3
Bobby Veach	17.9
Robin Ventura	24.7
Frank Viola	15.7
Rube Waddell	22.2
Billy Wagner	**24.1**
Honus Wagner	82.3
Larry Walker	32.7
Bobby Wallace	38.4
Ed Walsh	37.7
Bucky Walters	24.8
Paul Waner	33.8
John Ward	20.7
Lon Warneke	22.6
Mickey Welch	18.9
David Wells	**14.5**
John Wetteland	21.0
Zack Wheat	24.1
Lou Whitaker	35.2
Doc White	19.3
Roy White	14.8
Bob Wickman	**14.8**
Hoyt Wilhelm	37.1
Bernie Williams	**24.7**
Billy Williams	24.6
Jimmy Williams	15.4
Ken Williams	17.5
Matt Williams	18.7
Ted Williams	86.5
Vic Willis	20.0
Hack Wilson	18.2
Dave Winfield	30.1
Joe Wood	22.1
Wilbur Wood	14.6
Early Wynn	19.5
Jimmy Wynn	29.6
Carl Yastrzemski	42.7
Cy Young	77.0
Robin Yount	40.0
Chief Zimmer	20.7
Barry Zito	**16.6**

PLAYER OVERALL WINS

1	Babe Ruth	129.0
2	**Barry Bonds**	**124.7**
3	Nap Lajoie	95.2
4	Walter Johnson	89.9
5	Ted Williams	86.5
6	Rogers Hornsby	86.0
7	Ty Cobb	85.8
8	Willie Mays	84.4
9	Hank Aaron	83.0
10	Tris Speaker	82.7
11	Honus Wagner	82.3
12	Mike Schmidt	77.3
13	Cy Young	77.0
14	Stan Musial	76.0
15	**Roger Clemens**	**73.2**
16	Eddie Collins	72.5
17	Mickey Mantle	71.8
18	Lou Gehrig	70.9
19	Rickey Henderson	70.2
20	Joe Morgan	68.5
21	Frank Robinson	65.0
22	**Greg Maddux**	**64.7**
23	Grover Alexander	62.9
24	Mel Ott	60.7
25	Lefty Grove	59.1
26	Jimmie Foxx	58.7
27	Christy Mathewson	56.3
28	Kid Nichols	56.2
29	Eddie Mathews	53.0
30	Jeff Bagwell	52.9
31	**Alex Rodriguez**	**52.5**
32	Warren Spahn	51.4
33	Bobby Grich	50.6
34	Wade Boggs	50.5
35	George Davis	50.1
36	**Pedro Martinez**	**49.9**
37	Tom Seaver	49.5
	Frank Thomas	**49.5**
39	**Randy Johnson**	**48.5**
	Bill Dahlen	48.5
41	**Ken Griffey Jr.**	**46.8**
42	Joe DiMaggio	45.8
43	Charlie Gehringer	45.1
44	Bob Gibson	45.0
45	Ozzie Smith	44.9
46	Ron Santo	44.7
47	Edgar Martinez	44.6
48	Gabby Hartnett	44.4
49	Al Kaline	43.8
50	Lou Boudreau	43.6
51	Roger Connor	43.4
52	Cal Ripken	43.3
	Arky Vaughan	43.3
54	George Brett	42.8
	Ed Delahanty	42.8
56	Carl Yastrzemski	42.7
57	**Mike Piazza**	**42.6**
	Gary Sheffield	**42.6**
59	John Clarkson	42.5
	Dan Brouthers	42.5
61	Luke Appling	42.4
	Johnny Bench	42.4
63	**Ivan Rodriguez**	**42.1**
64	Barry Larkin	41.9
65	Darrell Evans	41.4
66	**Tom Glavine**	**41.3**
67	**Mariano Rivera**	**41.2**
68	Bobby Doerr	40.3
69	Carl Hubbell	40.2
	Yogi Berra	40.2
71	Robin Yount	40.0
72	Joe Cronin	39.6
73	Rod Carew	39.5
	Manny Ramirez	**39.5**
75	Willie McCovey	39.3
76	Dick Allen	39.0
77	Gary Carter	38.8
	Carlton Fisk	38.8
79	Reggie Jackson	38.7
80	Bill Dickey	38.5
	Tony Gwynn	38.5
82	Bobby Wallace	38.4
83	Joe Jackson	38.3
	Bid McPhee	38.3
85	Tim Raines	38.1
86	Ed Walsh	37.7
	Johnny Mize	37.7
88	**Scott Rolen**	**37.4**
89	Frankie Frisch	37.3
90	Whitey Ford	37.2
	Hal Newhouser	37.2
92	Hoyt Wilhelm	37.1
93	Ryne Sandberg	36.8
94	Amos Rusie	36.7
	Jeff Kent	**36.7**
96	Paul Molitor	36.6
97	**John Smoltz**	**36.5**
	Jack Glasscock	36.5
99	Dave Bancroft	36.2
100	Roberto Alomar	36.1

PLAYER OVERALL WINS

101	Willie Randolph	36.0
102	**Jim Thome**	**35.9**
103	Rafael Palmeiro	35.8
104	Bob Johnson	35.7
105	Tim Keefe	35.6
	Jim Edmonds	**35.6**
107	Roberto Clemente	35.4
108	Cap Anson	35.3
109	**Vladimir Guerrero**	**35.2**
	Bill Mazeroski	35.2
	Joe Sewell	35.2
	Lou Whitaker	35.2
113	Eddie Murray	35.1
114	Jim Palmer	35.0
	Mark McGwire	35.0
116	Mickey Cochrane	34.7
117	Jackie Robinson	34.3
118	**Mike Mussina**	**34.2**
119	Steve Carlton	34.0
	Bob Lemon	34.0
121	Paul Waner	33.8
122	Kevin Brown	33.7
	Frank Baker	33.7
124	Bob Caruthers	33.6
125	Ted Lyons	33.5
	Keith Hernandez	33.5
127	Harry Heilmann	33.2
128	Gaylord Perry	32.9
	Craig Biggio	**32.9**
130	Mordecai Brown	32.7
	Larry Walker	32.7
132	Hank Greenberg	32.6
133	Don Drysdale	32.4
134	Harmon Killebrew	32.0
135	Bert Blyleven	31.8
136	Carl Mays	31.7
137	Bob Feller	31.6
	Billy Herman	31.6
139	Charley Radbourn	31.5
	Reggie Smith	31.5
141	**Todd Helton**	**31.3**
142	Wes Ferrell	31.2
	Red Ruffing	31.2
144	Alan Trammell	31.1
145	Dennis Eckersley	30.5
	Curt Schilling	**30.5**
147	Fergie Jenkins	30.4
	Norm Cash	30.4
	Cupid Childs	30.4
	Heinie Groh	30.4
	Albert Pujols	**30.4**
152	Eddie Plank	30.3
	Robin Roberts	30.3
154	Dave Winfield	30.1
155	Tony Mullane	30.0
156	**Brian Giles**	**29.9**
157	Rich Gossage	29.7
	Dizzy Trout	29.7
	Elmer Flick	29.7
160	Jack Clark	29.6
	Jimmy Wynn	29.6
162	Willie Stargell	29.5
	Sam Thompson	29.5
164	**Bobby Abreu**	**29.4**
	Albert Belle	29.4
	Stan Hack	29.4
167	Sam Crawford	29.3
	Buck Ewing	29.3
169	Dazzy Vance	29.2
170	Phil Niekro	29.1
171	Joe Gordon	28.8
172	King Kelly	28.4
173	Clark Griffith	28.3
174	Dick Bartell	28.2
175	Buddy Bell	28.0
	Fred Dunlap	28.0
177	Bret Saberhagen	27.9
	Fred Clarke	27.9
179	Ernie Banks	27.8
180	Juan Marichal	27.7
	Pete Browning	27.7
182	**Miguel Tejada**	**27.5**
183	Tommy Bridges	27.3
184	Bobby Bonds	27.2
	Art Fletcher	27.2
	Billy Hamilton	27.2
187	**Chipper Jones**	**27.1**
188	Urban Shocker	27.0
189	Hughie Jennings	26.8
190	Bill Terry	26.7
191	**Trevor Hoffman**	**26.6**
	Hardy Richardson	26.6
193	George Sisler	26.5
194	Harlond Clift	26.3
195	John Franco	26.2
	Dolf Luque	26.2
	Sherry Magee	26.2
198	Gene Tenace	26.1
199	Stan Coveleski	26.0
200	Jesse Burkett	25.9

PLAYER OVERALL WINS

201	Billy Pierce	25.6
	Dave Stieb	25.6
	Joe Medwick	25.6
204	Jim Fregosi	25.5
205	Sammy Sosa	25.3
206	Thurman Munson	25.0
207	Harry Brecheen	24.9
208	Bucky Walters	24.8
	Nomar Garciaparra	**24.8**
210	Dwight Evans	24.7
	Robin Ventura	24.7
	Bernie Williams	**24.7**
213	Roy Campanella	24.6
	Billy Williams	24.6
215	Jack Fournier	24.4
	John Olerud	24.4
	Pete Rose	24.4
218	Eddie Cicotte	24.3
219	Eppa Rixey	24.2
	Will Clark	24.2
	Ralph Kiner	24.2
	Gil McDougald	24.2
223	**Billy Wagner**	**24.1**
	Jason Giambi	**24.1**
	Zack Wheat	24.1
226	Charlie Bennett	23.9
227	Jack Stivetts	23.7
228	Dan Quisenberry	23.6
229	**Roberto Hernandez**	**23.4**
	Kirby Puckett	23.4
231	Red Faber	23.3
	Jimmy Key	23.3
	Goose Goslin	23.3
234	David Cone	23.2
	Rick Reuschel	23.2
	Jose Canseco	23.2
237	Lenny Dykstra	23.1
	Rusty Staub	23.1
239	Addie Joss	23.0
	Silver King	23.0
	Eddie Rommel	23.0
	Jimmy Collins	23.0
	Jorge Posada	**23.0**
	Al Simmons	23.0
245	Lee Smith	22.9
	Fred Tenney	22.9
247	Richie Ashburn	22.8
	Roger Bresnahan	22.8
	Joe Torre	22.8
250	Rollie Fingers	22.7
	Rocky Colavito	22.7
	Roy Thomas	22.7
253	Lon Warneke	22.6
	Jake Beckley	22.6
	Frank Chance	22.6
	Andruw Jones	**22.6**
257	Del Pratt	22.5
	Darryl Strawberry	22.5
259	Miller Huggins	22.4
260	Dizzy Dean	22.3
	Sandy Koufax	22.3
	Cesar Cedeno	22.3
	Charlie Keller	22.3
	Lance Parrish	22.3
265	Dutch Leonard	22.2
	Nolan Ryan	22.2
	Rube Waddell	22.2
	Fred McGriff	22.2
	Duke Snider	22.2
270	Joe Wood	22.1
271	Travis Jackson	22.0
272	Guy Hecker	21.9
	Frank Howard	21.9
274	**Tim Salmon**	**21.8**
275	Tom Henke	21.7
	Ted Simmons	21.7
277	Luis Tiant	21.6
278	Kent Tekulve	21.5
	Harry Stovey	21.5
280	Bob Elliott	21.4
281	**Carlos Delgado**	**21.3**
	Minnie Minoso	21.3
283	Ron Cey	21.2
	Ed Konetchy	21.2
	Graig Nettles	21.2
286	Jim McCormick	21.1
	Chuck Klein	21.1
	Javy Lopez	**21.1**
289	John Hiller	21.0
	John Wetteland	21.0
	Wally Berger	21.0
292	Tony Fernandez	20.9
293	Red Lucas	20.8
	Fred Pfeffer	20.8
295	John Ward	20.7
	Joe Kelley	20.7
	Ernie Lombardi	20.7
	Jimmy Sheckard	20.7
	Vern Stephens	20.7
	Chief Zimmer	20.7

PLAYER OVERALL WINS

301	Ron Guidry	20.5
	Jose Cruz	20.5
	Eric Davis	20.5
	Glenn Hubbard	20.5
	Tony Oliva	20.5
	Darrell Porter	20.5
307	Nig Cuppy	20.4
	Tommy John	20.4
	Lance Berkman	**20.4**
	Ken Boyer	20.4
	Wally Schang	20.4
312	Kevin Appier	20.3
	Ken Caminiti	20.3
	Kevin Mitchell	20.3
315	Chuck Finley	20.2
316	Lefty Gomez	20.1
	Eddie Stanky	20.1
318	Jesse Tannehill	20.0
	Vic Willis	20.0
	Art Devlin	20.0
	Brian Downing	20.0
322	Ken Singleton	19.8
323	Wilbur Cooper	19.7
324	Doug Jones	19.6
	Denny Lyons	19.6
326	Robb Nen	19.5
	Early Wynn	19.5
	John McGraw	19.5
	Joe Tinker	19.5
330	Orel Hershiser	19.4
	Sparky Lyle	19.4
	Mike Marshall	19.4
	Roy Oswalt	**19.4**
	Andy Pettitte	**19.4**
	Jack Quinn	19.4
	Charley Jones	19.4
337	Doc White	19.3
	Bill Joyce	19.3
339	Toby Harrah	19.2
	Fred Lynn	19.2
341	Spud Chandler	19.1
	Gene Alley	19.1
343	Freddie Fitzsimmons	19.0
344	Joe McGinnity	18.9
	Jesse Orosco	18.9
	Mickey Welch	18.9
347	Schoolboy Rowe	18.8
	Roy Cullenbine	18.8
	Ferris Fain	18.8
	Bill Freehan	18.8
	Luis Gonzalez	**18.8**
352	Bobby Shantz	18.7
	Tony Phillips	18.7
	Phil Rizzuto	18.7
	Matt Williams	18.7
356	**Tom Gordon**	**18.6**
	Ed Lopat	18.6
	Don Newcombe	18.6
	George Foster	18.6
360	Bruce Sutter	18.5
	Jason Kendall	**18.5**
	Chet Lemon	18.5
363	Doc Gooden	18.4
	Orlando Cepeda	18.4
	Gavy Cravath	18.4
	Jim Rice	18.4
	Pie Traynor	18.4
368	Burleigh Grimes	18.3
	Mike Griffin	18.3
370	Curt Davis	18.2
	Mike Scioscia	18.2
	Hack Wilson	18.2
373	**Tim Hudson**	**18.1**
	Rico Carty	18.1
	Juan Gonzalez	18.1
376	Max Carey	18.0
	Dave Concepcion	18.0
378	Bobby Veach	17.9
379	Larry Doby	17.8
	Tony Lazzeri	17.8
381	Babe Adams	17.7
382	Andy Messersmith	17.6
	Johan Santana	**17.6**
	Eric Chavez	**17.6**
385	Don Sutton	17.5
	Babe Herman	17.5
	Derek Jeter	**17.5**
	Ken Williams	17.5
389	Jeff Montgomery	17.4
	Pedro Guerrero	17.4
	Ray Lankford	17.4
392	Rick Aguilera	17.3
	Ed Reulbach	17.3
	Earl Averill	17.3
	Rafael Furcal	**17.3**
	Bobby Knoop	17.3
	Boog Powell	17.3
398	Andre Dawson	17.2
	Jeff Heath	17.2
	Chief Meyers	17.2

PLAYER OVERALL WINS

	Bill Nicholson	17.2
	John Valentin	17.2
403	John Candelaria	17.0
	Noodles Hahn	17.0
	Mel Harder	17.0
406	John Tudor	16.9
	Kenny Lofton	**16.9**
	Roy Smalley	16.9
409	Larry French	16.8
	Virgil Trucks	16.8
	Rick Burleson	16.8
	Pee Wee Reese	16.8
	Andy Van Slyke	16.8
414	Bob Shawkey	16.7
	Mel Stottlemyre	16.7
416	**Barry Zito**	**16.6**
	Ellis Burks	16.6
	Ray Chapman	16.6
419	Red Schoendienst	16.5
420	**Armando Benitez**	**16.4**
	Jim Bunning	16.4
	Jim Kaat	16.4
	Lave Cross	16.4
	Paul O'Neill	16.4
425	Hippo Vaughn	16.3
	Bobby Bonilla	16.3
427	Charlie Buffinton	16.2
	Murry Dickson	16.2
	Johnny Logan	16.2
	Al Rosen	16.2
431	Sam Leever	16.1
	Carlos Beltran	**16.1**
	Ray Schalk	16.1
434	Larry Jackson	16.0
	Derek Lowe	**16.0**
	Jim O'Rourke	16.0
437	**Keith Foulke**	**15.9**
	George Uhle	15.9
	Johnny Evers	15.9
440	Thornton Lee	15.8
	Moises Alou	**15.8**
	Mike Hargrove	15.8
	David Justice	15.8
444	Mike Garcia	15.7
	Waite Hoyt	15.7
	Max Lanier	15.7
	Jack Taylor	15.7
	Mike Timlin	**15.7**
	Frank Viola	15.7
	Brett Butler	15.7
	Willie Kamm	15.7
452	Jerry Koosman	15.6
	Troy Percival	15.6
	Deacon Phillippe	15.6
	Luis Aparicio	15.6
	Earl Battey	15.6
	Rico Petrocelli	15.6
458	Mel Parnell	15.5
	Kenny Rogers	**15.5**
	Steve Rogers	15.5
	Nap Rucker	15.5
	Ron Hansen	15.5
	Johnny Pesky	15.5
464	Johnny Antonelli	15.4
	Jay Bell	15.4
	Chili Davis	15.4
	Don Mattingly	15.4
	Jimmy Williams	15.4
469	Stu Miller	15.3
	Augie Galan	15.3
471	Ned Garver	15.2
	Hal Schumacher	15.2
	Henry Larkin	15.2
474	Bob Stanley	15.1
	Dwayne Murphy	15.1
	Enos Slaughter	15.1
477	Randy Myers	15.0
	Tommy Henrich	15.0
	Willie Keeler	15.0
480	Chief Bender	14.9
	Ellis Kinder	14.9
	Claude Passeau	14.9
	Don Buford	14.9
	Cy Seymour	14.9
485	**Bob Wickman**	**14.8**
	Sid Gordon	14.8
	Roy White	14.8
488	Ron Perranoski	14.7
489	Tug McGraw	14.6
	Wilbur Wood	14.6
	Nellie Fox	14.6
	Jose Valentin	**14.6**
493	Dave Righetti	14.5
	David Wells	**14.5**
	Julio Franco	**14.5**
	Brooks Robinson	14.5
	Ichiro Suzuki	**14.5**
498	Ben Chapman	14.4
	Paul Hines	14.4
	Johnny Kling	14.4

PLATE APPEARANCES

1 Lenny Dykstra, 1993 773
2 Pete Rose, 1974 770
3 Dave Cash, 1975 766
4 Pete Rose, 1975 764
5 Ichiro Suzuki, 2004.... 762
6 Maury Wills, 1962 759
Pete Rose, 1976 759
8 Wade Boggs, 1985 758
Jimmy Rollins, 2006 .. 758
10 Frankie Crosetti, 1938 757
Pete Rose, 1965 757
Omar Moreno, 1979 757
13 Dom DiMaggio, 1948 756
14 Woody English, 1930 755
15 Bobby Richardson, 1962 754
16 Taylor Douthit, 1928 752
Pete Rose, 1973 752
Mo Vaughn, 1996 752
Derek Jeter, 2005...... 752
Ichiro Suzuki, 2006.... 752
21 Paul Molitor, 1982 751
Grady Sizemore, 2006 751
23 Juan Pierre, 2006 750
24 Paul Molitor, 1991 749
Brady Anderson, 1992 749
Craig Biggio, 1999 749
27 Taylor Douthit, 1930 748
Augie Galan, 1935 748
Derek Jeter, 1997 748
Alex Rodriguez, 1998 748
Juan Pierre, 2004 748
Michael Young, 2006 . 748
33 Rabbit Maranville, 1922 747
Darin Erstad, 2000..... 747
35 Matty Alou, 1969 746
Jim Rice, 1978 746
Juan Pierre, 2003 746
38 Dave Bancroft, 1922 745
Lyn Lary, 1936 745
Tommy Harper, 1965 745
Bobby Bonds, 1970 745
Dave Cash, 1974 745
Omar Moreno, 1980 745
Willie Wilson, 1980 745
45 Jo-Jo Moore, 1935 744
Dwight Evans, 1985 744
Kirby Puckett, 1985 744
Craig Biggio, 1997 744
49 Frankie Crosetti, 1939 743
Pee Wee Reese, 1949 743
Felix Millan, 1975 743
52 Charlie Jamieson, 1923 .. 742
Don Mattingly, 1986 742
Wade Boggs, 1989 742
55 Kiki Cuyler, 1930 741
Lyn Lary, 1937 741
Ron LeFlore, 1978 741
Johnny Damon, 2000 741
Alfonso Soriano, 2002 741
60 Frankie Crosetti, 1936 740
Red Rolfe, 1937 740
62 Curt Flood, 1964 739
Sandy Alomar, 1971 739
Derek Jeter, 1999 739
Michael Young, 2004 . 739
Ichiro Suzuki, 2005.... 739
Chase Utley, 2006...... 739
68 Lou Gehrig, 1931 738
Chuck Schilling, 1961 738
Bobby Bonds, 1973 738
Al Bumbry, 1980 738
Dwight Evans, 1984 738
Brian Hunter, 1997 738
Craig Biggio, 1998 738
Ichiro Suzuki, 2001.... 738
76 Don Kessinger, 1969 737
Juan Samuel, 1984 737
Harold Reynolds, 1990 ... 737
79 Brooks Robinson, 1961 .. 736
Kenny Lofton, 1996 736
Rafael Furcal, 2006 ... 736
82 Billy Herman, 1935 735
Phil Rizzuto, 1950 735
Dick Howser, 1964 735
Sandy Alomar, 1970 735
Pete Rose, 1980 735
Doug Glanville, 1998 735
Vernon Wells, 2003.... 735
89 Eddie Yost, 1952 734
Sal Bando, 1969 734
Rusty Staub, 1978 734
Nomar Garciaparra, 1997 .. 734
Rafael Furcal, 2003 ... 734
Alfonso Soriano, 2003 734
Brian Roberts, 2004 .. 734
96 Buddy Lewis, 1937 733
Darrell Evans, 1973 733
Tony Phillips, 1992 733
Jose Reyes, 2005...... 733
100 9 players tied 732

AT BATS

1 Willie Wilson, 1980 705
2 Ichiro Suzuki, 2004.... 704
3 Juan Samuel, 1984 701
4 Dave Cash, 1975 699
Juan Pierre, 2006 699
6 Matty Alou, 1969 698
7 Woody Jensen, 1936 696
Alfonso Soriano, 2002 696
Jose Reyes, 2005...... 696
10 Maury Wills, 1962 695
Omar Moreno, 1979 695
Ichiro Suzuki, 2006.... 695
13 Bobby Richardson, 1962 692
Ichiro Suzuki, 2001.... 692
15 Kirby Puckett, 1985 691
Michael Young, 2006 . 691
17 Neifi Perez, 1999 690
Michael Young, 2004 . 690
19 Lou Brock, 1967 689
Sandy Alomar, 1971 689
Jimmy Rollins, 2006 .. 689
22 Dave Cash, 1974 687
Tony Fernandez, 1986 687
24 Horace Clarke, 1970 686
Alex Rodriguez, 1998 686
26 Nomar Garciaparra, 1997 .. 684
27 Lance Johnson, 1996 682
Alfonso Soriano, 2003 682
29 Lloyd Waner, 1931 681
Jo-Jo Moore, 1935 681
31 Pete Rose, 1973 680
Frank Taveras, 1979 680
Kirby Puckett, 1986 680
34 Harvey Kuenn, 1953 679
Curt Flood, 1964 679
Bobby Richardson, 1964 679
Ichiro Suzuki, 2003.... 679
Ichiro Suzuki, 2005.... 679
39 Dick Groat, 1962 678
Doug Glanville, 1998 678
Vernon Wells, 2003.... 678
Juan Pierre, 2004 678
43 Matty Alou, 1970 677
Jim Rice, 1978 677
Don Mattingly, 1986 677
Jimmy Rollins, 2005 .. 677
47 Felix Millan, 1975 676
Omar Moreno, 1980 676
Darin Erstad, 2000..... 676
50 Rennie Stennett, 1974 673
Bill Buckner, 1985 673
B.J. Surhoff, 1999 673
53 Rabbit Maranville, 1922 672
Tony Oliva, 1964 672
Sandy Alomar, 1970 672
Garry Templeton, 1979 ... 672
Garret Anderson, 2001 672
58 Jack Tobin, 1921 671
Marquis Grissom, 1996 .. 671
60 Al Simmons, 1932 670
Pete Rose, 1965 670
Buddy Bell, 1979 670
Cesar Izturis, 2004 670
64 Vada Pinson, 1965 669
Larry Bowa, 1974 669
66 Buddy Lewis, 1937 668
Brooks Robinson, 1961 .. 668
Ralph Garr, 1973 668
Juan Pierre, 2003 668
Michael Young, 2005 . 668
71 Carl Furillo, 1951 667
72 Billy Herman, 1935 666
Zoilo Versalles, 1965 666
Felipe Alou, 1966 666
Dave Cash, 1976 666
Ron LeFlore, 1978 666
Paul Molitor, 1982 666
Michael Young, 2003 . 666
79 Tommy Davis, 1962 665
Pete Rose, 1976 665
Paul Molitor, 1991 665
82 Taylor Douthit, 1930 664
Bobby Richardson, 1965 664
Don Kessinger, 1969 664
Lou Brock, 1970 664
Rafael Furcal, 2003 ... 664
87 Jake Wood, 1961 663
Bill Virdon, 1962 663
Bobby Bonds, 1970 663
Rick Burleson, 1977 663
Cal Ripken, 1983 663
Juan Samuel, 1985 663
Joe Carter, 1986 663
Carlos Beltran, 1999 . 663
95 11 players tied 662

RUNS

1 Billy Hamilton, 1894 198
2 Tom Brown, 1891 177
Babe Ruth, 1921 177
4 Tip O'Neill, 1887 167
Lou Gehrig, 1936 167
6 Billy Hamilton, 1895 166
7 Willie Keeler, 1894 165
Joe Kelley, 1894 165
9 Arlie Latham, 1887 163
Babe Ruth, 1928 163
Lou Gehrig, 1931 163
12 Willie Keeler, 1895 162
13 Hugh Duffy, 1890 161
14 Fred Dunlap, 1884 160
Hugh Duffy, 1894 160
Jesse Burkett, 1896 160
17 Hughie Jennings, 1895 ... 159
18 Bobby Lowe, 1894 158
Babe Ruth, 1920 158
Babe Ruth, 1927 158
Chuck Klein, 1930 158
22 John McGraw, 1894 156
Rogers Hornsby, 1929 156
24 King Kelly, 1886 155
Kiki Cuyler, 1930 155
26 Dan Brouthers, 1887 153
Jesse Burkett, 1895 153
Billy Hamilton, 1896 153
Willie Keeler, 1896 153
30 Arlie Latham, 1886 152
Mike Griffin, 1889 152
Harry Stovey, 1889 152
Billy Hamilton, 1897 152
Lefty O'Doul, 1929 152
Woody English, 1930 152
Al Simmons, 1930 152
Chuck Klein, 1932 152
Jeff Bagwell, 2000 152
39 Babe Ruth, 1923 151
Jimmie Foxx, 1932 151
Joe DiMaggio, 1937 151
42 George Gore, 1886 150
Bill Dahlen, 1894 150
Jake Stenzel, 1894 150
Babe Ruth, 1930 150
Ted Williams, 1949 150
47 Herman Long, 1893 149
Ed Delahanty, 1895 149
Lou Gehrig, 1927 149
Babe Ruth, 1931 149
51 Hub Collins, 1890 148
Ed Delahanty, 1894 148
Joe Kelley, 1895 148
Joe Kelley, 1896 148
55 Mike Tiernan, 1889 147
Hugh Duffy, 1893 147
Patsy Donovan, 1894 147
Ty Cobb, 1911 147
59 Darby O'Brien, 1889 146
Tom Brown, 1890 146
Hack Wilson, 1930 146
Rickey Henderson, 1985 146
Craig Biggio, 1997 146
Sammy Sosa, 2001 146
65 Jesse Burkett, 1893 145
Cupid Childs, 1893 145
Ed Delahanty, 1893 145
Willie Keeler, 1897 145
Nap Lajoie, 1901 145
Harlond Clift, 1936 145
71 Hugh Duffy, 1889 144
Billy Hamilton, 1889 144
Ty Cobb, 1915 144
Kiki Cuyler, 1925 144
Charlie Gehringer, 1930 144
Al Simmons, 1932 144
Charlie Gehringer, 1936 144
Hank Greenberg, 1938 ... 144
79 Cupid Childs, 1894 143
John McGraw, 1898 143
Babe Ruth, 1924 143
Babe Herman, 1930 143
Lou Gehrig, 1930 143
Earle Combs, 1932 143
Red Rolfe, 1937 143
Lenny Dykstra, 1993 143
Larry Walker, 1997 143
Jeff Bagwell, 1999 143
89 Mike Griffin, 1887 142
Harry Stovey, 1890 142
Jesse Burkett, 1901 142
Paul Waner, 1928 142
Ted Williams, 1946 142
Ellis Burks, 1996 142
95 Billy Hamilton, 1891 141
Rogers Hornsby, 1922 141
Ted Williams, 1942 141
Alex Rodriguez, 1996 141
99 9 players tied 140

RUNS BY ERA

1988–2006

1 Jeff Bagwell, 2000 152
2 Craig Biggio, 1997 146
Sammy Sosa, 2001 146
4 Lenny Dykstra, 1993 143
Larry Walker, 1997 143
Jeff Bagwell, 1999 143
7 Ellis Burks, 1996 142
8 Alex Rodriguez, 1996 141
9 Chuck Knoblauch, 1996 . 140
10 Roberto Alomar, 1999 138
Todd Helton, 2000 138

1973–87

1 Rickey Henderson, 1985 146
2 Paul Molitor, 1982 136
3 Willie Wilson, 1980 133
Tim Raines, 1983 133
5 Bobby Bonds, 1973 131
Dale Murphy, 1983 131
7 Pete Rose, 1976 130
Rickey Henderson, 1986 130
9 Robin Yount, 1982 129
10 Rod Carew, 1977 128

1961–72

1 Billy Williams, 1970 137
2 Frank Robinson, 1962 134
Bobby Bonds, 1970 134
4 Mickey Mantle, 1961 132
Roger Maris, 1961 132
6 Willie Mays, 1962 130
Maury Wills, 1962 130
8 Willie Mays, 1961 129
Rocky Colavito, 1961 129
10 Hank Aaron, 1962 127

1943–60

1 Ted Williams, 1949 150
2 Ted Williams, 1946 142
3 Tommy Henrich, 1948 138
4 Johnny Mize, 1947 137
5 Stan Musial, 1948 135
6 Pee Wee Reese, 1949 132
Duke Snider, 1953 132
Mickey Mantle, 1956 132
9 Dom DiMaggio, 1950 131
Vada Pinson, 1959 131

1921–42

1 Babe Ruth, 1921 177
2 Lou Gehrig, 1936 167
3 Babe Ruth, 1928 163
Lou Gehrig, 1931 163
5 Babe Ruth, 1927 158
Chuck Klein, 1930 158
7 Rogers Hornsby, 1929 156
8 Kiki Cuyler, 1930 155
9 Lefty O'Doul, 1929 152
Woody English, 1930 152
Al Simmons, 1930 152
Chuck Klein, 1932 152

1901–20

1 Babe Ruth, 1920 158
2 Ty Cobb, 1911 147
3 Nap Lajoie, 1901 145
4 Ty Cobb, 1915 144
5 Jesse Burkett, 1901 142
6 Ginger Beaumont, 1903 . 137
Eddie Collins, 1912 137
Tris Speaker, 1920 137
George Sisler, 1920 137
10 Tris Speaker, 1912 136

1893–1900

1 Billy Hamilton, 1894 198
2 Billy Hamilton, 1895 166
3 Willie Keeler, 1894 165
Joe Kelley, 1894 165
5 Willie Keeler, 1895 162
6 Hugh Duffy, 1894 160
Jesse Burkett, 1896 160
8 Hughie Jennings, 1895 ... 159
9 Bobby Lowe, 1894 158
10 John McGraw, 1894 156

1876–92

1 Tom Brown, 1891 177
2 Tip O'Neill, 1887 167
3 Arlie Latham, 1887 163
4 Hugh Duffy, 1890 161
5 Fred Dunlap, 1884 160
6 King Kelly, 1886 155
7 Dan Brouthers, 1887 153
8 Arlie Latham, 1886 152
Mike Griffin, 1889 152
Harry Stovey, 1889 152

HITS

1 Ichiro Suzuki, 2004.... 262
2 George Sisler, 1920 257
3 Lefty O'Doul, 1929 254
Bill Terry, 1930 254
5 Al Simmons, 1925 253
6 Rogers Hornsby, 1922 250
Chuck Klein, 1930 250
8 Ty Cobb, 1911 248
9 George Sisler, 1922 246
10 Ichiro Suzuki, 2001.... 242
11 Heinie Manush, 1928 241
Babe Herman, 1930 241
13 Jesse Burkett, 1896 240
Wade Boggs, 1985 240
Darin Erstad, 2000..... 240
16 Willie Keeler, 1897 239
Rod Carew, 1977 239
18 Ed Delahanty, 1899 238
Don Mattingly, 1986 238
20 Hugh Duffy, 1894 237
Harry Heilmann, 1921 237
Paul Waner, 1927 237
Joe Medwick, 1937 237
24 Jack Tobin, 1921 236
25 Rogers Hornsby, 1921 235
26 Lloyd Waner, 1929 234
Kirby Puckett, 1988 234
28 Joe Jackson, 1911 233
29 Nap Lajoie, 1901 232
Earl Averill, 1936 232
31 Earle Combs, 1927 231
Freddie Lindstrom, 1928 231
Freddie Lindstrom, 1930 231
Matty Alou, 1969 231
35 Stan Musial, 1948 230
Tommy Davis, 1962 230
Joe Torre, 1971 230
Pete Rose, 1973 230
Willie Wilson, 1980 230
40 Rogers Hornsby, 1929 229
41 Kiki Cuyler, 1930 228
Stan Musial, 1946 228
43 Nap Lajoie, 1910 227
Rogers Hornsby, 1924 227
Jim Bottomley, 1925 227
Sam Rice, 1925 227
Billy Herman, 1935 227
Charlie Gehringer, 1936 227
Lance Johnson, 1996 227
50 Jesse Burkett, 1901 226
Joe Jackson, 1912 226
Ty Cobb, 1912 226
Bill Terry, 1929 226
Chuck Klein, 1932 226
55 Tip O'Neill, 1887 225
Billy Hamilton, 1894 225
Jesse Burkett, 1895 225
Ty Cobb, 1917 225
Harry Heilmann, 1925 225
Johnny Hodapp, 1930 225
Bill Terry, 1932 225
Paul Molitor, 1996 225
63 Eddie Collins, 1920 224
George Sisler, 1925 224
Joe Medwick, 1935 224
Tommy Holmes, 1945 224
Ichiro Suzuki, 2006.... 224
68 Frankie Frisch, 1923 223
Lloyd Waner, 1927 223
Paul Waner, 1928 223
Chuck Klein, 1933 223
Joe Medwick, 1936 223
Hank Aaron, 1959 223
Kirby Puckett, 1986 223
75 Sam Thompson, 1893 222
Tris Speaker, 1912 222
Charlie Jamieson, 1923 .. 222
78 Jesse Burkett, 1899 221
Zack Wheat, 1925 221
Lloyd Waner, 1928 221
Heinie Manush, 1933 221
Richie Ashburn, 1951 221
Juan Pierre, 2004 221
Michael Young, 2005 . 221
85 Pete Browning, 1887 220
Jimmy Williams, 1899 220
Kiki Cuyler, 1925 220
Lou Gehrig, 1930 220
Stan Musial, 1943 220
Tony Gwynn, 1997 220
91 Ed Delahanty, 1893 219
Willie Keeler, 1894 219
Cy Seymour, 1905 219
Chuck Klein, 1929 219
Lefty O'Doul, 1932 219
Paul Waner, 1937 219
Ralph Garr, 1971 219
Cecil Cooper, 1980 219
Dante Bichette, 1998 219
Derek Jeter, 1999 219

DOUBLES

1	Earl Webb, 1931	67
2	George Burns, 1926	64
	Joe Medwick, 1936	64
4	Hank Greenberg, 1934	63
5	Paul Waner, 1932	62
6	Charlie Gehringer, 1936	60
7	Tris Speaker, 1923	59
	Chuck Klein, 1930	59
	Todd Helton, 2000	**59**
10	Billy Herman, 1935	57
	Billy Herman, 1936	57
	Carlos Delgado, 2000	**57**
13	Joe Medwick, 1937	56
	George Kell, 1950	56
	Craig Biggio, 1999	**56**
	Garret Anderson, 2002	**56**
	Nomar Garciaparra, 2002	**56**
18	Ed Delahanty, 1899	55
	Gee Walker, 1936	55
	Lance Berkman, 2001	**55**
21	Hal McRae, 1977	54
	John Olerud, 1993	54
	Alex Rodriguez, 1996	**54**
	Mark Grudzielanek, 1997	**54**
	Todd Helton, 2001	**54**
26	Tris Speaker, 1912	53
	Al Simmons, 1926	53
	Paul Waner, 1936	53
	Stan Musial, 1953	53
	Don Mattingly, 1986	53
	Jeff Cirillo, 2000	**53**
	Lyle Overbay, 2004	**53**
	Freddy Sanchez, 2006	**53**
	Grady Sizemore, 2006	**53**
35	Tip O'Neill, 1887	52
	Tris Speaker, 1921	52
	Tris Speaker, 1926	52
	Lou Gehrig, 1927	52
	Johnny Frederick, 1929	52
	Enos Slaughter, 1939	52
	Albert Belle, 1995	52
	Edgar Martinez, 1995	52
	Edgar Martinez, 1996	52
	Luis Gonzalez, 2006	**52**
	Michael Young, 2006	**52**
46	Hugh Duffy, 1894	51
	Nap Lajoie, 1910	51
	Baby Doll Jacobson, 1926	51
	George Burns, 1927	51
	Johnny Hodapp, 1930	51
	Beau Bell, 1937	51
	Joe Cronin, 1938	51
	Stan Musial, 1944	51
	Mickey Vernon, 1946	51
	Frank Robinson, 1962	51
	Pete Rose, 1978	51
	Wade Boggs, 1989	51
	Mark Grace, 1995	51
	Craig Biggio, 1998	**51**
	Jose Vidro, 2000	**51**
	Nomar Garciaparra, 2000	**51**
	Alfonso Soriano, 2002	**51**
	Albert Pujols, 2003	**51**
	Albert Pujols, 2004	**51**
65	Tris Speaker, 1920	50
	Harry Heilmann, 1927	50
	Paul Waner, 1928	50
	Kiki Cuyler, 1930	50
	Chuck Klein, 1932	50
	Charlie Gehringer, 1934	50
	Odell Hale, 1936	50
	Ben Chapman, 1936	50
	Hank Greenberg, 1940	50
	Stan Musial, 1946	50
	Stan Spence, 1946	50
	Juan Gonzalez, 1998	50
	Bobby Abreu, 2002	**50**
	Brian Roberts, 2004	**50**
	Derrek Lee, 2005	**50**
	Miguel Tejada, 2005	**50**
	Miguel Cabrera, 2006	**50**
82	Ed Williamson, 1883	49
	Ed Delahanty, 1895	49
	Nap Lajoie, 1904	49
	George Sisler, 1920	49
	Heinie Manush, 1930	49
	Riggs Stephenson, 1932	49
	Hank Greenberg, 1937	49
	Robin Yount, 1980	49
	Rafael Palmeiro, 1991	49
	Tony Gwynn, 1997	**49**
	Jeff Kent, 2001	**49**
	Marcus Giles, 2003	**49**
	Shawn Green, 2003	**49**
	Todd Helton, 2003	**49**
	Scott Rolen, 2003	**49**
	Garret Anderson, 2003	**49**
	Vernon Wells, 2003	**49**
	Todd Helton, 2004	**49**
100	21 players tied	48

DOUBLES BY ERA

1988–2006

1	**Todd Helton, 2000**	**59**
2	**Carlos Delgado, 2000**	**57**
3	**Craig Biggio, 1999**	**56**
	Garret Anderson, 2002	**56**
	Nomar Garciaparra, 2002	**56**
6	**Lance Berkman, 2001**	**55**
7	John Olerud, 1993	54
	Alex Rodriguez, 1996	**54**
	Mark Grudzielanek, 1997	**54**
	Todd Helton, 2001	**54**

1973–87

1	Hal McRae, 1977	54
2	Don Mattingly, 1986	53
3	Pete Rose, 1978	51
4	Robin Yount, 1980	49
5	Keith Hernandez, 1979	48
	Don Mattingly, 1985	48
7	Pete Rose, 1975	47
	Fred Lynn, 1975	47
	Cal Ripken, 1983	47
	Wade Boggs, 1986	47

1961–72

1	Frank Robinson, 1962	51
2	Wes Parker, 1970	47
3	Lou Brock, 1968	46
4	Floyd Robinson, 1962	45
	Zoilo Versalles, 1965	45
	Carl Yastrzemski, 1965	45
7	Lee Maye, 1964	44
	Rusty Staub, 1967	44
9	Carl Yastrzemski, 1962	43
	Dick Groat, 1963	43
	Tony Oliva, 1964	43

1943–60

1	George Kell, 1950	56
2	Stan Musial, 1953	53
3	Stan Musial, 1944	51
	Mickey Vernon, 1946	51
5	Stan Musial, 1946	50
	Stan Spence, 1946	50
7	Stan Musial, 1943	48
8	Tommy Holmes, 1945	47
	Vada Pinson, 1959	47
10	Stan Musial, 1948	46
	Hank Aaron, 1959	46

1921–42

1	Earl Webb, 1931	67
2	George Burns, 1926	64
	Joe Medwick, 1936	64
4	Hank Greenberg, 1934	63
5	Paul Waner, 1932	62
6	Charlie Gehringer, 1936	60
7	Tris Speaker, 1923	59
	Chuck Klein, 1930	59
9	Billy Herman, 1935	57
	Billy Herman, 1936	57

1901–20

1	Tris Speaker, 1912	53
2	Nap Lajoie, 1910	51
3	Tris Speaker, 1920	50
4	Nap Lajoie, 1904	49
	George Sisler, 1920	49
6	Nap Lajoie, 1901	48
	Nap Lajoie, 1906	48
8	Harry Davis, 1905	47
	Ty Cobb, 1911	47
10	John Anderson, 1901	46
	Tris Speaker, 1914	46

1893–1900

1	Ed Delahanty, 1899	55
2	Hugh Duffy, 1894	51
3	Ed Delahanty, 1895	49
4	Joe Kelley, 1894	48
5	Walt Wilmot, 1894	45
	Sam Thompson, 1895	45
	Honus Wagner, 1899	45
	Honus Wagner, 1900	45
9	Ed Delahanty, 1896	44
10	Jake Stenzel, 1897	43
	Nap Lajoie, 1898	43

1876–92

1	Tip O'Neill, 1887	52
2	Ed Williamson, 1883	49
3	Denny Lyons, 1887	43
4	Dan Brouthers, 1883	41
	King Kelly, 1889	41
	Sam Thompson, 1890	41
7	Orator Shafer, 1884	40
	Dan Brouthers, 1886	40
	Jack Glasscock, 1889	40
	Pete Browning, 1890	40

TRIPLES

1	Chief Wilson, 1912	36
2	Dave Orr, 1886	31
	Heinie Reitz, 1894	31
4	Perry Werden, 1893	29
5	Sam Thompson, 1894	28
	Harry Davis, 1897	28
7	George Davis, 1893	27
	Jimmy Williams, 1899	27
9	John Reilly, 1890	26
	George Treadway, 1894	26
	Joe Jackson, 1912	26
	Sam Crawford, 1914	26
	Kiki Cuyler, 1925	26
14	Roger Connor, 1894	25
	Buck Freeman, 1899	25
	Sam Crawford, 1903	25
	Larry Doyle, 1911	25
	Tom Long, 1915	25
19	Ed McKean, 1893	24
	Ty Cobb, 1911	24
	Ty Cobb, 1917	24
22	Harry Stovey, 1884	23
	Sam Thompson, 1887	23
	Elmer Smith, 1893	23
	Dan Brouthers, 1894	23
	Nap Lajoie, 1897	23
	Ty Cobb, 1912	23
	Sam Crawford, 1913	23
	Earle Combs, 1927	23
	Adam Comorosky, 1930	23
	Dale Mitchell, 1949	23
32	Roger Connor, 1887	22
	Bid McPhee, 1890	22
	Jake Beckley, 1890	22
	Joe Visner, 1890	22
	Willie Keeler, 1894	22
	Kip Selbach, 1895	22
	John Anderson, 1898	22
	Honus Wagner, 1900	22
	Tommy Leach, 1902	22
	Sam Crawford, 1902	22
	Bill Bradley, 1903	22
	Elmer Flick, 1906	22
	Mike Mitchell, 1911	22
	Birdie Cree, 1911	22
	Tris Speaker, 1913	22
	Hy Myers, 1920	22
	Jake Daubert, 1922	22
	Paul Waner, 1926	22
	Earle Combs, 1930	22
	Snuffy Stirnweiss, 1945	22
52	Dave Orr, 1885	21
	Mike Tiernan, 1890	21
	Billy Shindle, 1890	21
	Tom Brown, 1891	21
	Ed Delahanty, 1892	21
	Sam Thompson, 1895	21
	Mike Tiernan, 1895	21
	Tom McCreery, 1896	21
	George Van Haltren, 1896	21
	Bobby Wallace, 1897	21
	Jimmy Williams, 1901	21
	Bill Keister, 1901	21
	Jimmy Williams, 1902	21
	Cy Seymour, 1905	21
	Frank Schulte, 1911	21
	Frank Baker, 1912	21
	Sam Crawford, 1912	21
	Vic Saier, 1913	21
	Joe Jackson, 1916	21
	Edd Roush, 1924	21
	Earle Combs, 1928	21
	Willie Wilson, 1985	21
	Lance Johnson, 1996	21
75	37 players tied	20

TRIPLES BY ERA

1988–2006

1	Lance Johnson, 1996	21
2	Cristian Guzman, 2000	20
3	**Carl Crawford, 2004**	**19**
4	Tony Fernandez, 1990	17
	Chone Figgins, 2004	**17**
	Jose Reyes, 2005	**17**
	Jose Reyes, 2006	**17**
8	**Carl Crawford, 2006**	**16**
9	Andy Van Slyke, 1988	15
	Ray Lankford, 1991	15
	Carl Crawford, 2005	**15**

1973–87

1	Willie Wilson, 1985	21
2	George Brett, 1979	20
3	Garry Templeton, 1979	19
	Juan Samuel, 1984	19
	Ryne Sandberg, 1984	19
6	Garry Templeton, 1977	18
	Willie McGee, 1985	18
8	Ralph Garr, 1974	17
9	Rod Carew, 1977	16
	Paul Molitor, 1979	16

1961–72

1	Johnny Callison, 1965	16
	Willie Davis, 1970	16
3	Gino Cimoli, 1962	15
4	Jake Wood, 1961	14
	Vada Pinson, 1963	14
	Dick Allen, 1965	14
	Roberto Clemente, 1965	14
	Donn Clendenon, 1965	14
	Lou Brock, 1968	14
	Don Kessinger, 1970	14

1943–60

1	Dale Mitchell, 1949	23
2	Snuffy Stirnweiss, 1945	22
3	Stan Musial, 1943	20
	Stan Musial, 1946	20
	Willie Mays, 1957	20
6	Johnny Barrett, 1944	19
7	Stan Musial, 1948	18
	Minnie Minoso, 1954	18
9	Jim Gilliam, 1953	17
10	Bob Elliott, 1944	16
	Snuffy Stirnweiss, 1944	16
	Johnny Lindell, 1944	16
	Hank Edwards, 1946	16
	Harry Walker, 1947	16
	Jim Rivera, 1953	16

1921–42

1	Kiki Cuyler, 1925	26
2	Earle Combs, 1927	23
	Adam Comorosky, 1930	23
4	Jake Daubert, 1922	22
	Paul Waner, 1926	22
	Earle Combs, 1930	22
7	Edd Roush, 1924	21
	Earle Combs, 1928	21
9	Rabbit Maranville, 1924	20
	Goose Goslin, 1925	20
	Curt Walker, 1926	20
	Lou Gehrig, 1926	20
	Jim Bottomley, 1928	20
	Heinie Manush, 1928	20
	Lloyd Waner, 1929	20
	Bill Terry, 1931	20
	Joe Vosmik, 1935	20
	Jeff Heath, 1941	20

1901–20

1	Chief Wilson, 1912	36
2	Joe Jackson, 1912	26
	Sam Crawford, 1914	26
4	Sam Crawford, 1903	25
	Larry Doyle, 1911	25
	Tom Long, 1915	25
7	Ty Cobb, 1911	24
	Ty Cobb, 1917	24
9	Ty Cobb, 1912	23
	Sam Crawford, 1913	23

1893–1900

1	Heinie Reitz, 1894	31
2	Perry Werden, 1893	29
3	Sam Thompson, 1894	28
	Harry Davis, 1897	28
5	George Davis, 1893	27
	Jimmy Williams, 1899	27
7	George Treadway, 1894	26
8	Roger Connor, 1894	25
	Buck Freeman, 1899	25
10	Ed McKean, 1893	24

1876–92

1	Dave Orr, 1886	31
2	John Reilly, 1890	26
3	Harry Stovey, 1884	23
	Sam Thompson, 1887	23
5	Roger Connor, 1887	22
	Bid McPhee, 1890	22
	Jake Beckley, 1890	22
	Joe Visner, 1890	22
9	Dave Orr, 1885	21
	Mike Tiernan, 1890	21
	Billy Shindle, 1890	21
	Tom Brown, 1891	21
	Ed Delahanty, 1892	21

HOME RUNS

1	**Barry Bonds, 2001**	**73**
2	Mark McGwire, 1998	70
3	Sammy Sosa, 1998	66
4	Mark McGwire, 1999	65
5	Sammy Sosa, 2001	64
6	Sammy Sosa, 1999	63
7	Roger Maris, 1961	61
8	Babe Ruth, 1927	60
9	Babe Ruth, 1921	59
10	Mark McGwire, 1997	58
	Jimmie Foxx, 1932	58
	Hank Greenberg, 1938	58
	Ryan Howard, 2006	**58**
14	**Luis Gonzalez, 2001**	**57**
	Alex Rodriguez, 2002	**57**
16	Hack Wilson, 1930	56
	Ken Griffey Jr., 1997	**56**
	Ken Griffey Jr., 1998	**56**
19	Babe Ruth, 1920	54
	Babe Ruth, 1928	54
	Ralph Kiner, 1949	54
	Mickey Mantle, 1961	54
	David Ortiz, 2006	**54**
24	Mickey Mantle, 1956	52
	Willie Mays, 1965	52
	George Foster, 1977	52
	Mark McGwire, 1996	52
	Alex Rodriguez, 2001	**52**
	Jim Thome, 2002	**52**
30	Ralph Kiner, 1947	51
	Johnny Mize, 1947	51
	Willie Mays, 1955	51
	Cecil Fielder, 1990	51
	Andruw Jones, 2005	**51**
35	Jimmie Foxx, 1938	50
	Albert Belle, 1995	50
	Brady Anderson, 1996	50
	Greg Vaughn, 1998	50
	Sammy Sosa, 2000	50
40	Babe Ruth, 1930	49
	Lou Gehrig, 1934	49
	Lou Gehrig, 1936	49
	Ted Kluszewski, 1954	49
	Willie Mays, 1962	49
	Harmon Killebrew, 1964	49
	Frank Robinson, 1966	49
	Harmon Killebrew, 1969	49
	Andre Dawson, 1987	49
	Mark McGwire, 1987	49
	Ken Griffey Jr., 1996	**49**
	Larry Walker, 1997	49
	Albert Belle, 1998	49
	Barry Bonds, 2000	**49**
	Shawn Green, 2001	**49**
	Todd Helton, 2001	**49**
	Jim Thome, 2001	**49**
	Sammy Sosa, 2002	49
	Albert Pujols, 2006	**49**
59	Jimmie Foxx, 1933	48
	Harmon Killebrew, 1962	48
	Frank Howard, 1969	48
	Willie Stargell, 1971	48
	Dave Kingman, 1979	48
	Mike Schmidt, 1980	48
	Albert Belle, 1996	48
	Ken Griffey Jr., 1999	**48**
	Adrian Beltre, 2004	**48**
	Alex Rodriguez, 2005	**48**
69	Babe Ruth, 1926	47
	Lou Gehrig, 1927	47
	Ralph Kiner, 1950	47
	Eddie Mathews, 1953	47
	Ted Kluszewski, 1955	47
	Ernie Banks, 1958	47
	Willie Mays, 1964	47
	Reggie Jackson, 1969	47
	Hank Aaron, 1971	47
	George Bell, 1987	47
	Kevin Mitchell, 1989	47
	Andres Galarraga, 1996	47
	Juan Gonzalez, 1996	47
	Rafael Palmeiro, 1999	47
	Jeff Bagwell, 2000	47
	Troy Glaus, 2000	**47**
	Rafael Palmeiro, 2001	47
	Jim Thome, 2003	**47**
	Alex Rodriguez, 2003	**47**
	David Ortiz, 2005	**47**
89	19 players tied	46

HOME RUNS BY ERA

1988–2006

1 Barry Bonds, 2001 73
2 Mark McGwire, 1998 70
3 Sammy Sosa, 1998 66
4 Mark McGwire, 1999 65
5 Sammy Sosa, 2001 64
6 Sammy Sosa, 1999 63
7 Mark McGwire, 1997 58
Ryan Howard, 2006 58
9 Luis Gonzalez, 2001 57
Alex Rodriguez, 2002 57

1973–87

1 George Foster, 1977 52
2 Andre Dawson, 1987 49
Mark McGwire, 1987 49
4 Dave Kingman, 1979 48
Mike Schmidt, 1980 48
6 George Bell, 1987 47
7 Jim Rice, 1978 46
8 Mike Schmidt, 1979 45
Gorman Thomas, 1979 45
10 Willie Stargell, 1973 44
Dale Murphy, 1987 44

1961–72

1 Roger Maris, 1961 61
2 Mickey Mantle, 1961 54
3 Willie Mays, 1965 52
4 Willie Mays, 1962 49
Harmon Killebrew, 1964 49
Frank Robinson, 1966 49
Harmon Killebrew, 1969 49
8 Harmon Killebrew, 1962 48
Frank Howard, 1969 48
Willie Stargell, 1971 48

1943–60

1 Ralph Kiner, 1949 54
2 Mickey Mantle, 1956 52
3 Ralph Kiner, 1947 51
Johnny Mize, 1947 51
Willie Mays, 1955 51
6 Ted Kluszewski, 1954 49
7 Ralph Kiner, 1950 47
Eddie Mathews, 1953 47
Ted Kluszewski, 1955 47
Ernie Banks, 1958 47

1921–42

1 Babe Ruth, 1927 60
2 Babe Ruth, 1921 59
3 Jimmie Foxx, 1932 58
Hank Greenberg, 1938 58
5 Hack Wilson, 1930 56
6 Babe Ruth, 1928 54
7 Jimmie Foxx, 1938 50
8 Babe Ruth, 1930 49
Lou Gehrig, 1934 49
Lou Gehrig, 1936 49

1901–20

1 Babe Ruth, 1920 54
2 Babe Ruth, 1919 29
3 Gavy Cravath, 1915 24
4 Frank Schulte, 1911 21
5 Gavy Cravath, 1913 19
Gavy Cravath, 1914 19
George Sisler, 1920 19
8 Fred Luderus, 1913 18
Vic Saier, 1914 18
10 Hal Chase, 1915 17
Tilly Walker, 1920 17

1893–1900

1 Buck Freeman, 1899 25
2 Ed Delahanty, 1893 19
3 Hugh Duffy, 1894 18
Sam Thompson, 1895 18
5 Jack Clements, 1893 17
Bill Joyce, 1894 17
Bobby Lowe, 1894 17
Bill Joyce, 1895 17
9 Bill Dahlen, 1894 15
Jimmy Collins, 1898 15

1876–92

1 Ed Williamson, 1884 27
2 Fred Pfeffer, 1884 25
3 Abner Dalrymple, 1884 22
4 Cap Anson, 1884 21
5 Sam Thompson, 1889 20
6 Billy O'Brien, 1887 19
Bug Holliday, 1889 19
Harry Stovey, 1889 19
9 Jerry Denny, 1889 18
10 Roger Connor, 1887 17
Jimmy Ryan, 1889 17

HOME RUN PCT.

1 Barry Bonds, 2001 15.34
2 Mark McGwire, 1998 13.75
3 Mark McGwire, 1999 12.48
4 Mark McGwire, 1996 12.29
5 Barry Bonds, 2004 12.06
6 Babe Ruth, 1920 11.79
7 Barry Bonds, 2003 11.54
8 Barry Bonds, 2002 11.41
9 Babe Ruth, 1927 11.11
10 Sammy Sosa, 2001 11.09
11 Babe Ruth, 1921 10.93
12 Jim Thome, 2002 10.83
13 Mark McGwire, 1997 10.74
14 Mickey Mantle, 1961 10.51
15 Hank Greenberg, 1938 10.43
16 Roger Maris, 1961 10.34
17 Sammy Sosa, 1998 10.26
18 Barry Bonds, 2000 10.21
19 Sammy Sosa, 1999 10.08
20 Babe Ruth, 1928 10.07
21 Ryan Howard, 2006 9.98
22 Jimmie Foxx, 1932 9.91
23 Ralph Kiner, 1949 9.84
24 Mickey Mantle, 1956 9.76
25 Jeff Bagwell, 1994 9.75
26 Kevin Mitchell, 1994 9.68
David Ortiz, 2006 9.68
28 Matt Williams, 1994 9.66
29 Hack Wilson, 1930 9.57
30 Frank Thomas, 1994 9.52
31 Babe Ruth, 1926 9.49
Hank Aaron, 1971 9.49
33 Jim Gentile, 1961 9.47
34 Barry Bonds, 1994 9.46
35 Babe Ruth, 1930 9.46
36 Willie Stargell, 1971 9.39
37 Luis Gonzalez, 2001 9.36
38 Willie Mays, 1965 9.32
39 Jim Thome, 2001 9.32
40 Travis Hafner, 2006 9.25
41 Ken Griffey Jr., 1994 9.24
42 Babe Ruth, 1929 9.22
43 Ken Griffey Jr., 1997 9.21
44 Boog Powell, 1964 9.20
45 Willie McCovey, 1969 9.16
46 Albert Pujols, 2006 9.16
47 Albert Belle, 1995 9.16
48 Alex Rodriguez, 2002 9.13
49 Ted Williams, 1957 9.05
50 Ralph Kiner, 1947 9.03
51 Dave Kingman, 1979 9.02
52 Mark McGwire, 1992 8.99
53 Ken Griffey Jr., 1996 8.99
54 Babe Ruth, 1932 8.97
55 Cecil Fielder, 1990 8.90
56 Jimmie Foxx, 1938 8.85
57 Ken Griffey Jr., 1998 8.85
58 Harmon Killebrew, 1969 8.83
59 Sammy Sosa, 2002 8.81
60 Mark McGwire, 1987 8.80
61 Willie Mays, 1955 8.79
62 Mike Schmidt, 1980 8.76
63 Mike Schmidt, 1981 8.76
64 Harmon Killebrew, 1963 8.74
Albert Belle, 1994 8.74
66 Greg Vaughn, 1998 8.73
67 Jim Edmonds, 2003 8.72
68 Johnny Mize, 1947 8.70
Andruw Jones, 2005 8.70
70 Babe Ruth, 1924 8.70
Harmon Killebrew, 1962 8.70
72 Juan Gonzalez, 1996 8.69
73 Manny Ramirez, 2000 8.66
74 Kevin Mitchell, 1989 8.66
75 Brady Anderson, 1996 8.64
76 Larry Walker, 1997 8.63
77 Babe Ruth, 1922 8.62
78 Babe Ruth, 1931 8.61
79 Ralph Kiner, 1950 8.59
80 Gary Sheffield, 2000 8.58
81 Juan Gonzalez, 1993 8.58
82 Jim Thome, 2006 8.57
83 Reggie Jackson, 1969 8.56
84 Ted Kluszewski, 1954 8.55
85 Barry Bonds, 1993 8.53
86 Jay Buhner, 1995 8.51
87 Frank Robinson, 1966 8.51
88 Harmon Killebrew, 1961 8.50
89 Harmon Killebrew, 1964 8.49
90 Lou Gehrig, 1934 8.46
Lou Gehrig, 1936 8.46
92 George Foster, 1977 8.46
93 Larry Walker, 1999 8.45
94 Jim Edmonds, 2004 8.43
95 Jason Giambi, 2000 8.43
96 Willie Stargell, 1973 8.43
Manny Ramirez, 1999 8.43
98 Hank Greenberg, 1946 8.41
99 Eddie Mathews, 1954 8.40
100 Lance Berkman, 2006 8.40

HOME RUN PCT. BY ERA

1988–2006

1 Barry Bonds, 2001 15.34
2 Mark McGwire, 1998 13.75
3 Mark McGwire, 1999 12.48
4 Mark McGwire, 1996 12.29
5 Barry Bonds, 2004 12.06
6 Barry Bonds, 2003 11.54
7 Barry Bonds, 2002 11.41
8 Sammy Sosa, 2001 11.09
9 Jim Thome, 2002 10.83
10 Mark McGwire, 1997 10.74

1973–87

1 Dave Kingman, 1979 9.02
2 Mark McGwire, 1987 8.80
3 Mike Schmidt, 1980 8.76
4 Mike Schmidt, 1981 8.76
5 George Foster, 1977 8.46
6 Willie Stargell, 1973 8.43
7 Jack Clark, 1987 8.35
8 Mike Schmidt, 1979 8.32
9 Gorman Thomas, 1979 8.08
10 Reggie Jackson, 1980 7.98

1961–72

1 Mickey Mantle, 1961 10.51
2 Roger Maris, 1961 10.34
3 Hank Aaron, 1971 9.49
4 Jim Gentile, 1961 9.47
5 Willie Stargell, 1971 9.39
6 Willie Mays, 1965 9.32
7 Boog Powell, 1964 9.20
8 Willie McCovey, 1969 9.16
9 Harmon Killebrew, 1969 8.83
10 Harmon Killebrew, 1963 8.74

1943–60

1 Ralph Kiner, 1949 9.84
2 Mickey Mantle, 1956 9.76
3 Ted Williams, 1957 9.05
4 Ralph Kiner, 1947 9.03
5 Willie Mays, 1955 8.79
6 Johnny Mize, 1947 8.70
7 Ralph Kiner, 1950 8.59
8 Ted Kluszewski, 1954 8.55
9 Hank Greenberg, 1946 8.41
10 Eddie Mathews, 1954 8.40

1921–42

1 Babe Ruth, 1927 11.11
2 Babe Ruth, 1921 10.93
3 Hank Greenberg, 1938 10.43
4 Babe Ruth, 1928 10.07
5 Jimmie Foxx, 1932 9.91
6 Hack Wilson, 1930 9.57
7 Babe Ruth, 1926 9.49
8 Babe Ruth, 1930 9.46
9 Babe Ruth, 1929 9.22
10 Babe Ruth, 1932 8.97

1901–20

1 Babe Ruth, 1920 11.79
2 Babe Ruth, 1919 6.71
3 Gavy Cravath, 1915 4.60
4 Gavy Cravath, 1914 3.81
5 Frank Schulte, 1911 3.64
6 Gavy Cravath, 1913 3.62
7 Sherry Magee, 1911 3.37
8 Vic Saier, 1914 3.35
9 Sam Crawford, 1901 3.11
10 Socks Seybold, 1902 3.07

1893–1900

1 Bill Joyce, 1894 4.79
2 Jack Clements, 1893 4.52
3 Buck Freeman, 1899 4.25
4 Jim Canavan, 1894 3.57
5 Bill Joyce, 1895 3.55
6 Sam Thompson, 1895 3.35
7 Hugh Duffy, 1894 3.34
8 Ed Delahanty, 1893 3.19
9 Bill Dahlen, 1894 2.96
10 Sam Thompson, 1894 2.88

1876–92

1 Ed Williamson, 1884 6.47
2 Fred Pfeffer, 1884 5.35
3 Cap Anson, 1884 4.42
4 Abner Dalrymple, 1884 4.22
5 Billy O'Brien, 1887 4.19
6 Sam Thompson, 1889 3.75
7 Roger Connor, 1887 3.61
8 Dan Brouthers, 1884 3.52
9 Harry Stovey, 1889 3.42
10 Bug Holliday, 1889 3.37

EXTRA BASE HITS

1 Babe Ruth, 1921 119
2 Lou Gehrig, 1927 117
3 Chuck Klein, 1930 107
Barry Bonds, 2001 107
5 Todd Helton, 2001 105
6 Chuck Klein, 1932 103
Hank Greenberg, 1937 103
Stan Musial, 1948 103
Albert Belle, 1995 103
Todd Helton, 2000 103
Sammy Sosa, 2001 103
12 Rogers Hornsby, 1922 102
13 Lou Gehrig, 1930 100
Jimmie Foxx, 1932 100
Luis Gonzalez, 2001 100
16 Babe Ruth, 1920 99
Babe Ruth, 1923 99
Hank Greenberg, 1940 99
Larry Walker, 1997 99
Albert Belle, 1998 99
Carlos Delgado, 2000 99
Albert Pujols, 2004 99
Derrek Lee, 2005 99
24 Hank Greenberg, 1935 98
25 Babe Ruth, 1927 97
Hack Wilson, 1930 97
Joe Medwick, 1937 97
Juan Gonzalez, 1998 97
29 Hank Greenberg, 1934 96
Hal Trosky, 1936 96
Joe DiMaggio, 1937 96
32 Lou Gehrig, 1934 95
Joe Medwick, 1936 95
Albert Pujols, 2003 95
35 Rogers Hornsby, 1929 94
Chuck Klein, 1929 94
Babe Herman, 1930 94
Jimmie Foxx, 1933 94
Lance Berkman, 2001 94
40 Jim Bottomley, 1928 93
Al Simmons, 1930 93
Lou Gehrig, 1936 93
Ellis Burks, 1996 93
Ken Griffey Jr., 1997 93
45 Babe Ruth, 1924 92
Lou Gehrig, 1931 92
Jimmie Foxx, 1938 92
Stan Musial, 1953 92
Hank Aaron, 1959 92
Frank Robinson, 1962 92
Brady Anderson, 1996 92
Ken Griffey Jr., 1998 92
Alfonso Soriano, 2002 92
Grady Sizemore, 2006 92
55 Babe Ruth, 1928 91
Alex Rodriguez, 1996 91
Mark McGwire, 1998 91
David Ortiz, 2004 91
59 Rogers Hornsby, 1925 90
Stan Musial, 1949 90
Willie Mays, 1962 90
Willie Stargell, 1973 90
63 Hal Trosky, 1934 89
Duke Snider, 1954 89
Andres Galarraga, 1996 89
Albert Belle, 1996 89
Sammy Sosa, 1999 89
Richard Hidalgo, 2000 89
Sammy Sosa, 2000 89
Alfonso Soriano, 2006 89
71 Joe DiMaggio, 1936 88
Barry Bonds, 1993 88
Barry Bonds, 1998 88
Albert Pujols, 2001 88
Garret Anderson, 2002 88
David Ortiz, 2005 88
77 Tris Speaker, 1923 87
Kiki Cuyler, 1925 87
Lou Gehrig, 1928 87
Ripper Collins, 1934 87
Charlie Gehringer, 1936 87
Johnny Mize, 1940 87
Willie Mays, 1954 87
Robin Yount, 1982 87
Kevin Mitchell, 1989 87
Chipper Jones, 1999 87
Mark McGwire, 1999 87
Shawn Green, 1999 87
Frank Thomas, 2000 87
Jason Giambi, 2001 87
Alex Rodriguez, 2001 87
Todd Helton, 2003 87
Vernon Wells, 2003 87
Manny Ramirez, 2004 87
Mark Teixeira, 2005 87
96 17 players tied 86

TOTAL BASES

1 Babe Ruth, 1921 457
2 Rogers Hornsby, 1922 450
3 Lou Gehrig, 1927 447
4 Chuck Klein, 1930 445
5 Jimmie Foxx, 1932 438
6 Stan Musial, 1948 429
7 Sammy Sosa, 2001 425
8 Hack Wilson, 1930 423
9 Chuck Klein, 1932 420
10 Lou Gehrig, 1930 419
Luis Gonzalez, 2001 419
12 Joe DiMaggio, 1937 418
13 Babe Ruth, 1927 417
14 Babe Herman, 1930 416
Sammy Sosa, 1998 416
16 Barry Bonds, 2001 411
17 Lou Gehrig, 1931 410
18 Rogers Hornsby, 1929 409
Lou Gehrig, 1934 409
Larry Walker, 1997 409
21 Joe Medwick, 1937 406
Jim Rice, 1978 406
23 Chuck Klein, 1929 405
Hal Trosky, 1936 405
Todd Helton, 2000 405
26 Jimmie Foxx, 1933 403
Lou Gehrig, 1936 403
28 Todd Helton, 2001 402
29 Hank Aaron, 1959 400
30 George Sisler, 1920 399
Babe Ruth, 1923 399
Albert Belle, 1998 399
33 Jimmie Foxx, 1938 398
34 Lefty O'Doul, 1929 397
Hank Greenberg, 1937 397
Sammy Sosa, 1999 397
37 Albert Pujols, 2003 394
38 Ken Griffey Jr., 1997 393
Alex Rodriguez, 2001 393
Derrek Lee, 2005 393
41 Al Simmons, 1925 392
Bill Terry, 1930 392
Al Simmons, 1930 392
Ellis Burks, 1996 392
45 Babe Ruth, 1924 391
46 Hank Greenberg, 1935 389
Alex Rodriguez, 2002 389
Albert Pujols, 2004 389
49 Babe Ruth, 1920 388
George Foster, 1977 388
Don Mattingly, 1986 388
52 Ken Griffey Jr., 1998 387
53 Earl Averill, 1936 385
54 Hank Greenberg, 1940 384
Alex Rodriguez, 1998 384
56 Mark McGwire, 1998 383
Sammy Sosa, 2000 383
Ryan Howard, 2006 383
59 Stan Musial, 1949 382
Willie Mays, 1955 382
Willie Mays, 1962 382
Jim Rice, 1977 382
Juan Gonzalez, 1998 382
64 Rogers Hornsby, 1925 381
Alfonso Soriano, 2002 381
66 Babe Ruth, 1928 380
Hank Greenberg, 1938 380
Frank Robinson, 1962 380
Vinny Castilla, 1998 380
70 Babe Ruth, 1930 379
Ernie Banks, 1958 379
Alex Rodriguez, 1996 379
Vladimir Guerrero, 2000 379
74 Rogers Hornsby, 1921 378
Duke Snider, 1954 378
Carlos Delgado, 2000 378
77 Willie Mays, 1954 377
Albert Belle, 1995 377
79 Mickey Mantle, 1956 376
Andres Galarraga, 1996 376
Adrian Beltre, 2004 376
82 Albert Belle, 1996 375
83 Hugh Duffy, 1894 374
Babe Ruth, 1931 374
Hal Trosky, 1934 374
Tony Oliva, 1964 374
87 Rogers Hornsby, 1924 373
Al Simmons, 1929 373
Bill Terry, 1932 373
Billy Williams, 1970 373
Vernon Wells, 2003 373
92 Lou Gehrig, 1932 370
Duke Snider, 1953 370
Hank Aaron, 1963 370
Don Mattingly, 1985 370
Mo Vaughn, 1996 370
Shawn Green, 2001 370
Mark Teixeira, 2005 370
99 8 players tied 369

RUNS BATTED IN

1	Hack Wilson, 1930	191
2	Lou Gehrig, 1931	184
3	Hank Greenberg, 1937	183
4	Lou Gehrig, 1927	175
	Jimmie Foxx, 1938	175
6	Lou Gehrig, 1930	174
7	Babe Ruth, 1921	171
8	Chuck Klein, 1930	170
	Hank Greenberg, 1935	170
10	Jimmie Foxx, 1932	169
11	Joe DiMaggio, 1937	167
12	Sam Thompson, 1887	166
13	Sam Thompson, 1895	165
	Al Simmons, 1930	165
	Lou Gehrig, 1934	165
	Manny Ramirez, 1999	**165**
17	Babe Ruth, 1927	164
18	Babe Ruth, 1931	163
	Jimmie Foxx, 1933	163
20	Hal Trosky, 1936	162
21	Sammy Sosa, 2001	160
22	Hack Wilson, 1929	159
	Lou Gehrig, 1937	159
	Ted Williams, 1949	159
	Vern Stephens, 1949	159
26	Sammy Sosa, 1998	158
27	Al Simmons, 1929	157
	Juan Gonzalez, 1998	157
29	Jimmie Foxx, 1930	156
30	Ken Williams, 1922	155
	Joe DiMaggio, 1948	155
32	Babe Ruth, 1929	154
	Joe Medwick, 1937	154
34	Babe Ruth, 1930	153
	Tommy Davis, 1962	153
36	Rogers Hornsby, 1922	152
	Lou Gehrig, 1936	152
	Albert Belle, 1998	152
39	Mel Ott, 1929	151
	Lou Gehrig, 1932	151
	Al Simmons, 1932	151
42	Hank Greenberg, 1940	150
	Andres Galarraga, 1996	150
	Miguel Tejada, 2004	**150**
45	Rogers Hornsby, 1929	149
	George Foster, 1977	149
	Ryan Howard, 2006	**149**
48	Johnny Bench, 1970	148
	Albert Belle, 1996	148
	Rafael Palmeiro, 1999	148
	David Ortiz, 2005	**148**
52	Cap Anson, 1886	147
	Sam Thompson, 1894	147
	Ken Griffey Jr., 1997	**147**
	Mark McGwire, 1998	147
	Mark McGwire, 1999	147
	Todd Helton, 2000	**147**
58	Hardy Richardson, 1890	146
	Ed Delahanty, 1893	146
	Babe Ruth, 1926	146
	Hank Greenberg, 1938	146
	Ken Griffey Jr., 1998	**146**
	Todd Helton, 2001	**146**
64	Hugh Duffy, 1894	145
	Chuck Klein, 1929	145
	Ted Williams, 1939	145
	Al Rosen, 1953	145
	Don Mattingly, 1985	145
	Manny Ramirez, 1998	**145**
	Edgar Martinez, 2000	145
	Carlos Delgado, 2003	**145**
72	Walt Dropo, 1950	144
	Vern Stephens, 1950	144
	Juan Gonzalez, 1996	144
	Vinny Castilla, 1998	**144**
	Mike Sweeney, 2000	**144**
	Manny Ramirez, 2005	**144**
	Mark Teixeira, 2005	**144**
79	Rogers Hornsby, 1925	143
	Earl Averill, 1931	143
	Don Hurst, 1932	143
	Jimmie Foxx, 1936	143
	Ernie Banks, 1959	143
	Mo Vaughn, 1996	143
	Frank Thomas, 2000	**143**
86	Lou Gehrig, 1928	142
	Babe Ruth, 1928	142
	Hal Trosky, 1934	142
	Roy Campanella, 1953	142
	Orlando Cepeda, 1961	142
	Roger Maris, 1961	142
	Rafael Palmeiro, 1996	142
	Matt Williams, 1999	142
	Luis Gonzalez, 2001	**142**
	Alex Rodriguez, 2002	**142**
96	Ted Kluszewski, 1954	141
	Jim Gentile, 1961	141
	Willie Mays, 1962	141
	Dante Bichette, 1996	141
	Tino Martinez, 1997	141
	Sammy Sosa, 1999	141
	Bret Boone, 2001	141
	Preston Wilson, 2003	**141**

RUNS BATTED IN BY ERA

1988–2006

1	**Manny Ramirez, 1999**	**165**
2	Sammy Sosa, 2001	160
3	Sammy Sosa, 1998	158
4	Juan Gonzalez, 1998	157
5	Albert Belle, 1998	152
6	Andres Galarraga, 1996	150
	Miguel Tejada, 2004	**150**
8	**Ryan Howard, 2006**	**149**
9	Albert Belle, 1996	148
	Rafael Palmeiro, 1999	148
	David Ortiz, 2005	**148**

1973–87

1	George Foster, 1977	149
2	Don Mattingly, 1985	145
3	Jim Rice, 1978	139
	Don Baylor, 1979	139
5	Andre Dawson, 1987	137
6	George Bell, 1987	134
7	Hal McRae, 1982	133
8	Greg Luzinski, 1977	130
	Jim Rice, 1979	130
10	Johnny Bench, 1974	129

1961–72

1	Tommy Davis, 1962	153
2	Johnny Bench, 1970	148
3	Orlando Cepeda, 1961	142
	Roger Maris, 1961	142
5	Jim Gentile, 1961	141
	Willie Mays, 1962	141
7	Rocky Colavito, 1961	140
	Harmon Killebrew, 1969	140
9	Joe Torre, 1971	137
10	Frank Robinson, 1962	136

1943–60

1	Ted Williams, 1949	159
	Vern Stephens, 1949	159
3	Joe DiMaggio, 1948	155
4	Al Rosen, 1953	145
5	Walt Dropo, 1950	144
	Vern Stephens, 1950	144
7	Ernie Banks, 1959	143
8	Roy Campanella, 1953	142
9	Ted Kluszewski, 1954	141
10	Johnny Mize, 1947	138

1921–42

1	Hack Wilson, 1930	191
2	Lou Gehrig, 1931	184
3	Hank Greenberg, 1937	183
4	Lou Gehrig, 1927	175
	Jimmie Foxx, 1938	175
6	Lou Gehrig, 1930	174
7	Babe Ruth, 1921	171
8	Chuck Klein, 1930	170
	Hank Greenberg, 1935	170
10	Jimmie Foxx, 1932	169

1901–20

1	Babe Ruth, 1920	137
2	Frank Baker, 1912	130
3	Gavy Cravath, 1913	128
4	Ty Cobb, 1911	127
5	Honus Wagner, 1901	126
6	Nap Lajoie, 1901	125
7	Sherry Magee, 1910	123
8	George Sisler, 1920	122
	Baby Doll Jacobson, 1920	122
10	Buck Freeman, 1902	121
	Cy Seymour, 1905	121
	Joe Jackson, 1920	121

1893–1900

1	Sam Thompson, 1895	165
2	Sam Thompson, 1894	147
3	Ed Delahanty, 1893	146
4	Hugh Duffy, 1894	145
5	Ed Delahanty, 1899	137
6	George Davis, 1897	135
7	Steve Brodie, 1895	134
	Joe Kelley, 1895	134
9	Ed McKean, 1893	133
	Ed Delahanty, 1894	133

1876–92

1	Sam Thompson, 1887	166
2	Cap Anson, 1886	147
3	Hardy Richardson, 1890	146
4	Roger Connor, 1889	130
5	Tommy Burns, 1890	128
6	Dave Orr, 1890	124
	Dan Brouthers, 1892	124
8	Tip O'Neill, 1887	123
9	Jake Beckley, 1890	120
	Cap Anson, 1891	120

WALKS

1	**Barry Bonds, 2004**	**232**
2	**Barry Bonds, 2002**	**198**
3	**Barry Bonds, 2001**	**177**
4	Babe Ruth, 1923	170
5	Ted Williams, 1947	162
	Ted Williams, 1949	162
	Mark McGwire, 1998	162
8	Ted Williams, 1946	156
9	Eddie Yost, 1956	151
	Barry Bonds, 1996	**151**
11	Babe Ruth, 1920	150
12	Eddie Joost, 1949	149
	Jeff Bagwell, 1999	149
14	Eddie Stanky, 1945	148
	Jimmy Wynn, 1969	148
	Barry Bonds, 2003	**148**
17	Jimmy Sheckard, 1911	147
	Ted Williams, 1941	147
19	Mickey Mantle, 1957	146
20	Babe Ruth, 1921	145
	Ted Williams, 1942	145
	Harmon Killebrew, 1969	145
	Barry Bonds, 1997	**145**
24	Babe Ruth, 1926	144
	Eddie Stanky, 1950	144
	Ted Williams, 1951	144
27	Babe Ruth, 1924	142
	Gary Sheffield, 1996	**142**
29	Eddie Yost, 1950	141
30	**Frank Thomas, 1991**	**138**
31	Babe Ruth, 1927	137
	Babe Ruth, 1928	137
	Eddie Stanky, 1946	137
	Roy Cullenbine, 1947	137
	Ralph Kiner, 1951	137
	Willie McCovey, 1970	137
	Jason Giambi, 2000	**137**
38	Jack Crooks, 1892	136
	Babe Ruth, 1930	136
	Ferris Fain, 1949	136
	Ted Williams, 1954	136
	Jack Clark, 1987	136
	Frank Thomas, 1995	**136**
44	Eddie Yost, 1959	135
	Jeff Bagwell, 1996	135
	Brian Giles, 2002	**135**
47	Ferris Fain, 1950	133
	Mark McGwire, 1999	133
49	Lou Gehrig, 1935	132
	Frank Howard, 1970	132
	Joe Morgan, 1975	132
	Jack Clark, 1989	132
	Tony Phillips, 1993	132
54	Bob Elliott, 1948	131
	Eddie Yost, 1954	131
	Harmon Killebrew, 1967	131
57	Babe Ruth, 1932	130
	Lou Gehrig, 1936	130
	Barry Bonds, 1998	**130**
60	Eddie Yost, 1952	129
	Mickey Mantle, 1958	129
	Lenny Dykstra, 1993	129
	Jason Giambi, 2001	**129**
	Jason Giambi, 2003	**129**
65	Billy Hamilton, 1894	128
	Max Bishop, 1929	128
	Max Bishop, 1930	128
	Babe Ruth, 1931	128
	Harmon Killebrew, 1970	128
	Carl Yastrzemski, 1970	128
	Mike Schmidt, 1983	128
	Adam Dunn, 2002	**128**
73	Lu Blue, 1931	127
	Lou Gehrig, 1937	127
	Eddie Stanky, 1951	127
	Jimmy Wynn, 1976	127
	Barry Bonds, 1992	**127**
	Jeff Bagwell, 1997	127
	Jim Thome, 1999	**127**
	Bobby Abreu, 2004	**127**
	Lance Berkman, 2004	**127**
	Todd Helton, 2004	**127**
83	Lu Blue, 1929	126
	Ted Williams, 1948	126
	Eddie Yost, 1951	126
	Mickey Mantle, 1961	126
	Darrell Evans, 1974	126
	Rickey Henderson, 1989	126
	Barry Bonds, 1993	**126**
	Chipper Jones, 1999	**126**
91	Richie Ashburn, 1954	125
	Eddie Yost, 1960	125
	Gene Tenace, 1977	125
	Wade Boggs, 1988	125
	Rickey Henderson, 1996	125
	Tony Phillips, 1996	125
	John Olerud, 1999	125
98	**Bobby Abreu, 2006**	**124**
	John McGraw, 1899	124
	Norm Cash, 1961	124
	Eddie Mathews, 1963	124
	Darrell Evans, 1973	124

WALK PERCENTAGE (BB/PA)

1	**Barry Bonds, 2004**	**37.60**
2	**Barry Bonds, 2002**	**32.35**
3	**Barry Bonds, 2003**	**26.91**
4	**Barry Bonds, 2001**	**26.66**
5	Ted Williams, 1954	25.86
6	Jack Clark, 1987	24.37
7	Babe Ruth, 1920	24.35
8	Babe Ruth, 1923	24.32
9	Mickey Mantle, 1962	24.30
10	Ted Williams, 1941	24.26
11	Mark McGwire, 1998	23.79
12	Mickey Mantle, 1957	23.43
13	Ted Williams, 1947	23.38
14	Jack Crooks, 1892	23.33
15	Ted Williams, 1946	23.21
16	John McGraw, 1899	23.01
17	Jimmy Wynn, 1969	22.66
18	Roy Cullenbine, 1947	22.57
19	**Barry Bonds, 1996**	**22.37**
20	Jack Clark, 1989	22.26
21	Ted Williams, 1949	22.19
22	Babe Ruth, 1926	22.09
23	Eddie Yost, 1956	22.08
24	Babe Ruth, 1932	22.07
25	Max Bishop, 1926	21.93
26	Eddie Joost, 1949	21.85
27	Mickey Tettleton, 1994	21.85
28	Ted Williams, 1957	21.79
29	Max Bishop, 1930	21.77
30	Jimmy Wynn, 1976	21.75
31	Toby Harrah, 1985	21.69
32	Ted Williams, 1942	21.61
33	Gene Tenace, 1977	21.51
34	Willie McCovey, 1970	21.47
35	Max Bishop, 1927	21.47
36	Eddie Stanky, 1946	21.34
37	Ted Williams, 1951	21.33
38	Mark McGwire, 1996	21.17
39	**Frank Thomas, 1994**	**21.08**
40	Max Bishop, 1932	21.07
41	**Frank Thomas, 1995**	**21.02**
42	**Barry Bonds, 1997**	**21.01**
43	Max Bishop, 1933	20.99
44	**Gary Sheffield, 1996**	**20.97**
45	**Brian Giles, 2002**	**20.96**
46	Jack Crooks, 1893	20.93
47	Babe Ruth, 1921	20.92
48	Jimmy Sheckard, 1911	20.88
49	Willie Mays, 1971	20.86
50	Babe Ruth, 1924	20.85
51	Eddie Stanky, 1950	20.84
52	Jimmy Wynn, 1975	20.79
53	**Gary Sheffield, 1997**	**20.79**
54	Max Bishop, 1929	20.78
55	Rickey Henderson, 1996	20.76
56	**Barry Bonds, 1992**	**20.75**
57	Joe Morgan, 1975	20.66
58	**Jason Giambi, 2000**	**20.63**
59	Yank Robinson, 1889	20.49
60	Harmon Killebrew, 1969	20.45
61	Ralph Kiner, 1951	20.45
62	Jeff Bagwell, 1999	20.44
63	Elmer Valo, 1952	20.40
64	Hank Greenberg, 1947	20.39
65	Eddie Stanky, 1945	20.39
66	Ted Williams, 1956	20.28
67	Ferris Fain, 1949	20.24
68	Ferris Fain, 1950	20.21
69	**Jim Thome, 1999**	**20.19**
70	Mark McGwire, 1999	20.12
71	Babe Ruth, 1930	20.12
72	Babe Ruth, 1928	20.03
73	Eddie Yost, 1959	20.00
74	**Jim Thome, 2002**	**19.90**
75	Yank Robinson, 1888	19.90
76	Babe Ruth, 1927	19.83
77	Babe Ruth, 1933	19.83
78	**Jason Giambi, 2005**	**19.82**
79	Ted Williams, 1948	19.75
80	Mickey Mantle, 1958	19.72
81	**Frank Thomas, 1991**	**19.71**
82	Bill Joyce, 1890	19.71
83	Mel Ott, 1943	19.71
84	Cupid Childs, 1893	19.70
85	Mel Ott, 1939	19.69
86	Rickey Henderson, 1993	19.67
87	Eddie Yost, 1960	19.65
88	Lou Gehrig, 1935	19.64
89	Gene Tenace, 1978	19.61
90	Danny Tartabull, 1992	19.58
91	Mickey Tettleton, 1995	19.56
92	Mickey Cochrane, 1933	19.56
93	Luke Appling, 1949	19.55
94	John McGraw, 1897	19.53
95	Mickey Mantle, 1961	19.50
96	Eddie Stanky, 1951	19.45
97	Johnny Evers, 1910	19.42
98	Willie McCovey, 1969	19.42
99	Bob Elliott, 1948	19.41
100	Edgar Martinez, 1996	19.40

STRIKEOUTS

1	**Adam Dunn, 2004**	**195**
2	**Adam Dunn, 2006**	**194**
3	Bobby Bonds, 1970	189
4	**Jose Hernandez, 2002**	**188**
5	Bobby Bonds, 1969	187
	Preston Wilson, 2000	**187**
7	Rob Deer, 1987	186
8	Pete Incaviglia, 1986	185
	Jose Hernandez, 2001	**185**
	Jim Thome, 2001	**185**
11	Cecil Fielder, 1990	182
	Jim Thome, 2003	**182**
13	Mo Vaughn, 2000	181
	Ryan Howard, 2006	**181**
15	Mike Schmidt, 1975	180
16	Rob Deer, 1986	179
17	**Richie Sexson, 2001**	**178**
18	**Jose Hernandez, 2003**	**177**
	Mark Bellhorn, 2004	**177**
20	**Mike Cameron, 2002**	**176**
21	Dave Nicholson, 1963	175
	Gorman Thomas, 1979	175
	Jose Canseco, 1986	175
	Rob Deer, 1991	175
	Jay Buhner, 1997	175
26	Sammy Sosa, 1997	174
	Curtis Granderson, 2006	**174**
28	Jim Presley, 1986	172
	Bo Jackson, 1989	172
30	Reggie Jackson, 1968	171
	Sammy Sosa, 1998	171
	Sammy Sosa, 1999	171
	Jim Thome, 1999	**171**
	Jim Thome, 2000	**171**
35	Gorman Thomas, 1980	170
	Adam Dunn, 2002	**170**
37	Andres Galarraga, 1990	169
	Rob Deer, 1993	169
	Craig Wilson, 2004	**169**
40	Juan Samuel, 1984	168
	Pete Incaviglia, 1987	168
	Sammy Sosa, 2000	168
	Corey Patterson, 2004	**168**
	Adam Dunn, 2005	**168**
45	**Jim Edmonds, 2000**	**167**
	Richie Sexson, 2005	**167**
47	Gary Alexander, 1978	166
	Steve Balboni, 1985	166
	Cory Snyder, 1987	166
50	**Derrek Lee, 2002**	**164**
51	Donn Clendenon, 1968	163
	Troy Glaus, 2000	**163**
53	Butch Hobson, 1977	162
	Juan Samuel, 1987	162
	Ron Gant, 1997	162
	Pat Burrell, 2001	**162**
	Bill Hall, 2006	**162**
58	Dick Allen, 1968	161
	Reggie Jackson, 1971	161
	Brad Wilkerson, 2002	**161**
61	Mickey Tettleton, 1990	160
	Henry Rodriguez, 1996	160
	Pat Burrell, 2005	**160**
	Alfonso Soriano, 2006	**160**
65	Mark McGwire, 1997	159
	Richie Sexson, 2000	**159**
	Jay Buhner, 1996	159
	Jose Canseco, 1998	159
	Ben Grieve, 2001	159
70	Bo Jackson, 1987	158
	Andres Galarraga, 1989	158
	Rob Deer, 1989	158
	Jose Canseco, 1990	158
	Melvin Nieves, 1996	158
	Jeromy Burnitz, 1998	**158**
	Troy Glaus, 2001	**158**
77	Danny Tartabull, 1986	157
	Jose Canseco, 1987	157
	Jim Presley, 1987	157
	Andres Galarraga, 1996	157
	Melvin Nieves, 1997	157
	Lee Stevens, 2001	157
	Alfonso Soriano, 2002	**157**
84	Tommie Agee, 1970	156
	Dave Kingman, 1982	156
	Reggie Jackson, 1982	156
	Tony Armas, 1984	156
	Danny Tartabull, 1993	156
	Preston Wilson, 1999	**156**
	Jason Bay, 2006	**156**
91	Frank Howard, 1967	155
	Jeff Burroughs, 1975	155
	Mark McGwire, 1998	155
	Mike Cameron, 2001	**155**
	Brad Wilkerson, 2003	**155**
96	Willie Stargell, 1971	154
	Larry Parrish, 1987	154
	Dean Palmer, 1992	154
	Dean Palmer, 1993	154
	Mo Vaughn, 1996	154
	Mo Vaughn, 1997	154
	Richie Sexson, 2006	**154**

STRIKEOUT PERCENTAGE

1988–2006

1 Rob Deer, 1991 .... 39.06
2 Rob Deer, 1993 .... 36.27
3 Mickey Tettleton, 1990. 36.04
4 Jose Hernandez, 2002 .. 35.81
5 Benji Gil, 1995 .... 35.42
6 Jim Thome, 2001 .... 35.17
7 Jim Thome, 1999 .... 34.62
8 Adam Dunn, 2006 ... 34.58
9 Adam Dunn, 2004 ... 34.33
10 Jose Hernandez, 2001 .. 34.13

1973–87

1 Rob Deer, 1987 .... 39.24
2 Rob Deer, 1986 .... 38.41
3 Pete Incaviglia, 1986 ... 34.26
4 Gary Alexander, 1978.. 33.33
5 Jack Clark, 1987 .... 33.17
6 Pete Incaviglia, 1987 ... 33.01
7 Mike Schmidt, 1975 ...... 32.03
8 Gorman Thomas, 1979 31.42
9 Danny Tartabull, 1986.. 30.72
10 Dave Kingman, 1975 ... 30.48

1961–72

1 Dave Nicholson, 1963 . 38.98
2 Dick Allen, 1969 .... 32.88
3 Reggie Jackson, 1970 . 31.69
4 Larry Hisle, 1969 .... 31.54
5 Reggie Jackson, 1968 . 30.92
6 Dick Allen, 1968 .... 30.90
7 Willie Stargell, 1971 ...... 30.14
8 Bobby Bonds, 1969 ...... 30.06
9 Frank Howard, 1967 .... 29.87
10 Rick Monday, 1968 ...... 29.67

1943–60

1 Pancho Herrera, 1960 . 26.56
2 Jim Lemon, 1956 .... 25.65
3 Dick Stuart, 1960 .... 24.43
4 Frank Howard, 1960 .... 24.11
5 Harmon Killebrew, 1960 ... 23.98
6 Jim Lemon, 1958 .... 23.95
7 Mickey Mantle, 1960 .... 23.72
8 Larry Doby, 1953 .... 23.59
9 Pat Seerey, 1945 .... 23.43
10 Mickey Mantle, 1959 .... 23.29

1921–42

1 Vince DiMaggio, 1938 . 24.81
2 Vince DiMaggio, 1937 . 22.52
3 Chet Ross, 1940 .... 22.32
4 Dolph Camilli, 1941 ...... 21.74
5 Joe Orengo, 1940 .... 21.69
6 Jimmie Foxx, 1941 ...... 21.15
7 Boze Berger, 1935 ...... 21.04
8 Jimmie Foxx, 1936 ...... 20.34
9 Dolph Camilli, 1938 ...... 19.84
10 Babe Ruth, 1922 .... 19.70

1901–20

1 Gus Williams, 1914 ...... 24.05
2 Grover Gilmore, 1914 .. 20.38
3 Gavy Cravath, 1916 ...... 19.87
4 Ed McDonald, 1912 ...... 19.83
5 Art Wilson, 1914 .... 18.18
6 Gavy Cravath, 1912 ...... 17.66
7 Cozy Dolan, 1914 .... 17.58
8 Max Carey, 1911 .... 17.56
9 Danny Moeller, 1913 .... 17.49
10 Babe Ruth, 1920 .... 17.47

1893–1900

1 Billy Lush, 1896 .... 13.92
2 Tom Daly, 1893 .... 13.83
3 Tom Brown, 1894 .... 13.68
4 Tom McCreery, 1896 ... 13.15
5 Tom Brown, 1895 .... 12.27
6 Billy Clingman, 1896 .... 12.06
7 Tom Brown, 1893 .... 11.91
8 Bill Joyce, 1895 .... 11.69
9 Tom Daly, 1895 .... 11.30
10 Tom Brown, 1896 .... 11.26

1876–92

1 Frank Meinke, 1884 ..... 26.10
2 Jim Galvin, 1883 .... 24.53
3 Sam Wise, 1884 .... 24.41
4 Jim Galvin, 1879 .... 21.13
5 Charlie Bastian, 1885 .. 21.08
6 Will White, 1878 .... 20.81
7 Silver Flint, 1883 .... 20.78
8 John Morrill, 1884 .... 19.86
9 John Morrill, 1885 .... 19.80
10 Charlie Bastian, 1886 .. 19.57

BATTING AVERAGE

1 Hugh Duffy, 1894 .... .440
2 Tip O'Neill, 1887 .... .435
3 Ross Barnes, 1876 .... .429
4 Nap Lajoie, 1901 .... .426
5 Willie Keeler, 1897 .... .424
6 Rogers Hornsby, 1924 .... .424
7 George Sisler, 1922 .... .420
8 Ty Cobb, 1911 .... .420
9 Sam Thompson, 1894 .... .415
10 Fred Dunlap, 1884 .... .412
11 Ed Delahanty, 1899 .... .410
12 Jesse Burkett, 1896 .... .410
13 Ty Cobb, 1912 .... .409
14 Joe Jackson, 1911 .... .408
15 George Sisler, 1920 .... .407
16 Ted Williams, 1941 .... .406
17 Jesse Burkett, 1895 .... .405
18 Ed Delahanty, 1895 .... .404
19 Ed Delahanty, 1894 .... .404
20 Billy Hamilton, 1894 .... .403
21 Rogers Hornsby, 1925 .... .403
22 Harry Heilmann, 1923 .... .403
23 Pete Browning, 1887 .... .402
24 Rogers Hornsby, 1922 .... .401
25 Bill Terry, 1930 .... .401
26 Hughie Jennings, 1896 ... .401
27 Ty Cobb, 1922 .... .401
28 Cap Anson, 1881 .... .399
29 Lefty O'Doul, 1929 .... .398
30 Harry Heilmann, 1927 .... .398
31 Rogers Hornsby, 1921 .... .397
32 Ed Delahanty, 1896 .... .397
33 Jesse Burkett, 1899 .... .396
34 Joe Jackson, 1912 .... .395
35 Tony Gwynn, 1994 ..... .394
36 Harry Heilmann, 1921 .... .394
37 Babe Ruth, 1923 .... .393
38 Harry Heilmann, 1925 .... .393
39 Babe Herman, 1930 .... .393
40 Joe Kelley, 1894 .... .393
41 Sam Thompson, 1895 .... .392
42 John McGraw, 1899 .... .391
43 Ty Cobb, 1913 .... .390
44 Al Simmons, 1931 .... .390
45 George Brett, 1980 .... .390
46 Fred Clarke, 1897 .... .390
47 Tris Speaker, 1925 .... .389
48 Bill Lange, 1895 .... .389
49 Billy Hamilton, 1895 .... .389
50 Ty Cobb, 1921 .... .389
51 Ted Williams, 1957 .... .388
52 King Kelly, 1886 .... .388
53 Rod Carew, 1977 .... .388
54 Luke Appling, 1936 .... .388
55 Tris Speaker, 1920 .... .388
56 Lave Cross, 1894 .... .387
57 Deacon White, 1877 .... .387
58 Al Simmons, 1925 .... .387
59 Rogers Hornsby, 1928 .... .387
60 Tris Speaker, 1916 .... .386
61 Willie Keeler, 1896 .... .386
62 Chuck Klein, 1930 .... .386
63 Hughie Jennings, 1895 .... .386
64 Willie Keeler, 1898 .... .385
65 Arky Vaughan, 1935 .... .385
66 Rogers Hornsby, 1923 .... .384
67 Ty Cobb, 1919 .... .384
68 Nap Lajoie, 1910 .... .384
69 Ty Cobb, 1910 .... .383
70 Jesse Burkett, 1897 .... .383
71 Tris Speaker, 1912 .... .383
72 Ty Cobb, 1917 .... .383
73 Lefty O'Doul, 1930 .... .383
74 Joe Jackson, 1920 .... .382
75 Ty Cobb, 1918 .... .382
76 Honus Wagner, 1900 .... .381
77 Babe Herman, 1929 .... .381
78 Joe DiMaggio, 1939 .... .381
79 Al Simmons, 1930 .... .381
80 Paul Waner, 1927 .... .380
81 Rogers Hornsby, 1929 .... .380
82 Billy Hamilton, 1893 .... .380
83 Tris Speaker, 1923 .... .380
84 Goose Goslin, 1928 .... .379
85 Freddie Lindstrom, 1930 ...... .379
86 Larry Walker, 1999 .... .379
87 Willie Keeler, 1899 .... .379
88 Lou Gehrig, 1930 .... .379
89 John Cassidy, 1877 .... .378
90 Pete Browning, 1882 .... .378
91 Ty Cobb, 1925 .... .378
92 Babe Ruth, 1924 .... .378
93 Sam Crawford, 1911 .... .378
94 Tris Speaker, 1922 .... .378
95 Earl Averill, 1936 .... .378
96 Babe Ruth, 1921 .... .378
97 Heinie Manush, 1928 .... .378
98 Heinie Manush, 1926 .... .378
99 Ed Delahanty, 1897 .... .377
100 Willie Keeler, 1895 .... .377

BATTING AVERAGE BY ERA

1988–2006

1 Tony Gwynn, 1994 ..... .394
2 Larry Walker, 1999 .... .379
3 Todd Helton, 2000 ...... .372
4 Nomar Garciaparra, 2000 .. .372
5 Ichiro Suzuki, 2004 .... .372
6 Tony Gwynn, 1997 ..... .372
7 Andres Galarraga, 1993 .370
8 Barry Bonds, 2002 ..... .370
9 Tony Gwynn, 1995 ..... .368
10 Jeff Bagwell, 1994 .... .368

1973–87

1 George Brett, 1980 .... .390
2 Rod Carew, 1977 .... .388
3 Tony Gwynn, 1987 ..... .370
4 Wade Boggs, 1985 .... .368
5 Rod Carew, 1974 .... .364
6 Wade Boggs, 1987 .... .363
7 Wade Boggs, 1983 .... .361
8 Rod Carew, 1975 .... .359
9 Wade Boggs, 1986 .... .357
10 Bill Madlock, 1975 .... .354

1961–72

1 Rico Carty, 1970 .... .366
2 Joe Torre, 1971 .... .363
3 Norm Cash, 1961 .... .361
4 Roberto Clemente, 1967 .357
5 Roberto Clemente, 1961 .351
6 Pete Rose, 1969 .... .348
7 Tommy Davis, 1962 .... .346
8 Roberto Clemente, 1969 .345
9 Ralph Garr, 1971 .... .343
10 Vada Pinson, 1961 .... .343

1943–60

1 Ted Williams, 1957 .... .388
2 Stan Musial, 1948 .... .376
3 Ted Williams, 1948 .... .369
4 Stan Musial, 1946 .... .365
5 Mickey Mantle, 1957 .... .365
6 Harry Walker, 1947 .... .363
7 Dixie Walker, 1944 .... .357
8 Stan Musial, 1943 .... .357
9 Phil Cavarretta, 1945 .... .355
10 Lou Boudreau, 1948 .... .355

1921–42

1 Rogers Hornsby, 1924 .... .424
2 George Sisler, 1922 .... .420
3 Ted Williams, 1941 .... .406
4 Rogers Hornsby, 1925 .... .403
5 Harry Heilmann, 1923 .... .403
6 Rogers Hornsby, 1922 .... .401
7 Bill Terry, 1930 .... .401
8 Ty Cobb, 1922 .... .401
9 Lefty O'Doul, 1929 .... .398
10 Harry Heilmann, 1927 .... .398

1901–20

1 Nap Lajoie, 1901 .... .426
2 Ty Cobb, 1911 .... .420
3 Ty Cobb, 1912 .... .409
4 Joe Jackson, 1911 .... .408
5 George Sisler, 1920 .... .407
6 Joe Jackson, 1912 .... .395
7 Ty Cobb, 1913 .... .390
8 Tris Speaker, 1920 .... .388
9 Tris Speaker, 1916 .... .386
10 Ty Cobb, 1919 .... .384

1893–1900

1 Hugh Duffy, 1894 .... .440
2 Willie Keeler, 1897 .... .424
3 Sam Thompson, 1894 .... .415
4 Ed Delahanty, 1899 .... .410
5 Jesse Burkett, 1896 .... .410
6 Jesse Burkett, 1895 .... .405
7 Ed Delahanty, 1895 .... .404
8 Ed Delahanty, 1894 .... .404
9 Billy Hamilton, 1894 .... .403
10 Hughie Jennings, 1896 .. .401

1876–92

1 Tip O'Neill, 1887 .... .435
2 Ross Barnes, 1876 .... .429
3 Fred Dunlap, 1884 .... .412
4 Pete Browning, 1887 .... .402
5 Cap Anson, 1881 .... .399
6 King Kelly, 1886 .... .388
7 Deacon White, 1877 .... .387
8 John Cassidy, 1877 .... .378
9 Pete Browning, 1882 .... .378
10 Dan Brouthers, 1883 .... .374

RELATIVE BATTING AVG.

1 Ross Barnes, 1876 ...... 1.608
2 Tip O'Neill, 1887 .... 1.564
3 Nap Lajoie, 1910 .... 1.537
4 Ty Cobb, 1910 .... 1.534
5 Pete Browning, 1882 ... 1.526
6 Cap Anson, 1881 .... 1.512
7 King Kelly, 1886 .... 1.508
8 Roger Connor, 1885 .... 1.506
9 Tris Speaker, 1916 .... 1.506
10 Ty Cobb, 1917 .... 1.501
11 Ty Cobb, 1912 .... 1.501
12 Nap Lajoie, 1901 .... 1.501
13 Nap Lajoie, 1904 .... 1.499
14 Ty Cobb, 1911 .... 1.493
15 Ty Cobb, 1909 .... 1.492
16 Ted Williams, 1957 .... 1.476
17 Ty Cobb, 1913 .... 1.475
18 Ted Williams, 1941 .... 1.472
19 Ty Cobb, 1918 .... 1.469
20 George Gore, 1880 .... 1.462
21 Rogers Hornsby, 1924. 1.461
22 Rod Carew, 1977 .... 1.458
23 Dan Brouthers, 1885 ... 1.455
24 Joe Jackson, 1911 .... 1.452
25 Joe Jackson, 1912 .... 1.451
26 Dan Brouthers, 1882 ... 1.449
27 Dave Orr, 1884 .... 1.448
28 George Brett, 1980 .... 1.448
29 Ty Cobb, 1915 .... 1.448
30 Pete Browning, 1887 ... 1.446
31 Ty Cobb, 1916 .... 1.445
32 Cap Anson, 1886 .... 1.442
33 Pete Browning, 1885 ... 1.439
34 Dan Brouthers, 1886 ... 1.439
35 Tony Gwynn, 1994 .. 1.436
36 Honus Wagner, 1908 .. 1.434
37 George Sisler, 1922 .... 1.433
38 Cap Anson, 1882 .... 1.428
39 Cy Seymour, 1905 .... 1.425
40 Willie Keeler, 1897 .... 1.423
41 Ed Delahanty, 1899 .... 1.414
42 Wade Boggs, 1988 .... 1.413
43 King Kelly, 1884 .... 1.411
44 Joe Jackson, 1913 .... 1.411
45 Rod Carew, 1974 .... 1.408
46 Wade Boggs, 1985 .... 1.407
47 Tris Speaker, 1912 .... 1.406
48 Deacon White, 1877 .... 1.405
49 Dan Brouthers, 1883 ... 1.401
50 Jimmy Wolf, 1890 .... 1.401
51 George Stone, 1906 .... 1.400
52 Stan Musial, 1948 .... 1.400
53 Cap Anson, 1888 .... 1.399
54 George Sisler, 1920 .... 1.398
55 Joe Torre, 1971 .... 1.397
56 Hugh Duffy, 1894 .... 1.393
57 Stan Musial, 1946 .... 1.393
58 Ed Swartwood, 1883 ... 1.392
59 Ty Cobb, 1919 .... 1.392
60 Rod Carew, 1975 .... 1.391
61 Barry Bonds, 2002 .. 1.391
62 Tommy Tucker, 1889 .... 1.391
63 Nap Lajoie, 1906 .... 1.390
64 John Reilly, 1884 .... 1.389
65 Harry Heilmann, 1923 .. 1.389
66 Mickey Mantle, 1957 .... 1.388
67 Willie Keeler, 1898 .... 1.387
68 Honus Wagner, 1907 ... 1.387
69 Roberto Clemente, 1967 .. 1.385
70 George Sisler, 1917 .... 1.383
71 Jim O'Rourke, 1884 .... 1.383
72 Pete Browning, 1886 ... 1.382
73 Tris Speaker, 1917 .... 1.380
74 Ezra Sutton, 1884 .... 1.380
75 Ty Cobb, 1907 .... 1.379
76 Hick Carpenter, 1882 ... 1.379
77 Roger Connor, 1886 .... 1.378
78 Jesse Burkett, 1896 .... 1.378
79 Paul Hines, 1879 .... 1.377
80 Tony Gwynn, 1987 .. 1.375
81 Ichiro Suzuki, 2004 . 1.375
82 Larry Walker, 1999 .... 1.375
83 Pete Browning, 1884 ... 1.374
84 Tris Speaker, 1913 .... 1.374
85 Tony Gwynn, 1997 .. 1.374
86 Kirby Puckett, 1988 .... 1.374
87 John Cassidy, 1877 .... 1.373
88 Eddie Collins, 1909 .... 1.373
89 Honus Wagner, 1905 ... 1.372
90 Dave Orr, 1886 .... 1.372
91 Rico Carty, 1970 .... 1.372
92 George Hall, 1876 .... 1.372
93 Tip O'Neill, 1888 .... 1.370
94 Wade Boggs, 1987 .... 1.370
95 Ty Cobb, 1922 .... 1.370
96 Cap Anson, 1880 .... 1.368
97 Norm Cash, 1961 .... 1.368
98 Jesse Burkett, 1899 .... 1.367
99 Andres Galarraga, 1993 ... 1.366
100 Jesse Burkett, 1901 .... 1.365

ON-BASE PERCENTAGE

1 Barry Bonds, 2004 ..... .609
2 Barry Bonds, 2002 ..... .582
3 Ted Williams, 1941 .... .553
4 John McGraw, 1899 .... .547
5 Babe Ruth, 1923 .... .545
6 Babe Ruth, 1920 .... .532
7 Barry Bonds, 2003 ..... .529
8 Ted Williams, 1957 .... .526
9 Billy Hamilton, 1894 .... .522
10 Babe Ruth, 1926 .... .516
11 Barry Bonds, 2001 ..... .515
12 Ted Williams, 1954 .... .513
13 Babe Ruth, 1924 .... .513
14 Babe Ruth, 1921 .... .512
15 Mickey Mantle, 1957 .... .512
16 Rogers Hornsby, 1924 .... .507
17 John McGraw, 1900 .... .505
18 Joe Kelley, 1894 .... .502
19 Hugh Duffy, 1894 .... .502
20 Ed Delahanty, 1895 .... .500
21 Ted Williams, 1942 .... .499
22 Ted Williams, 1947 .... .499
23 Rogers Hornsby, 1928 .... .498
24 Ted Williams, 1946 .... .497
25 Ted Williams, 1948 .... .497
26 Bill Joyce, 1894 .... .496
27 Babe Ruth, 1931 .... .495
28 Babe Ruth, 1930 .... .493
29 Arky Vaughan, 1935 .... .491
30 Ted Williams, 1949 .... .490
31 Billy Hamilton, 1895 .... .490
32 Billy Hamilton, 1893 .... .490
33 Tip O'Neill, 1887 .... .490
34 Rogers Hornsby, 1925 .... .489
Babe Ruth, 1932 .... .489
36 Frank Thomas, 1994 .. .487
37 Norm Cash, 1961 .... .487
38 Ty Cobb, 1915 .... .486
39 Mickey Mantle, 1962 .... .486
40 Babe Ruth, 1927 .... .486
41 Tris Speaker, 1920 .... .483
42 King Kelly, 1886 .... .483
43 Jesse Burkett, 1895 .... .482
44 Harry Heilmann, 1923 .... .481
45 Billy Hamilton, 1898 .... .480
46 Tris Speaker, 1925 .... .479
Ted Williams, 1956 .... .479
48 Edgar Martinez, 1995 .... .479
49 Billy Hamilton, 1896 .... .478
50 Lou Gehrig, 1936 .... .478
51 Jason Giambi, 2001 ... .477
52 Jason Giambi, 2000 ... .476
53 Wade Boggs, 1988 .... .476
54 Cupid Childs, 1894 .... .475
55 John McGraw, 1898 .... .475
56 Ed Delahanty, 1894 .... .475
57 Harry Heilmann, 1927 .... .475
58 Tris Speaker, 1922 .... .474
59 Lou Gehrig, 1927 .... .474
60 Luke Appling, 1936 .... .474
61 Lou Gehrig, 1930 .... .473
62 Lou Gehrig, 1937 .... .473
63 John Olerud, 1993 .... .473
64 Hughie Jennings, 1896 .... .472
65 Ed Delahanty, 1896 .... .472
66 John McGraw, 1897 .... .471
67 Dan Brouthers, 1891 .... .471
68 Tris Speaker, 1916 .... .470
69 Bill Joyce, 1896 .... .470
70 Mark McGwire, 1998 .... .470
71 Carlos Delgado, 2000 ...... .470
72 Joe Kelley, 1896 .... .469
73 Tris Speaker, 1923 .... .469
74 Jimmie Foxx, 1932 .... .469
75 Todd Helton, 2004 ..... .469
76 Jesse Burkett, 1897 .... .468
77 Ty Cobb, 1925 .... .468
78 Joe Jackson, 1911 .... .468
79 Lou Gehrig, 1928 .... .467
80 Ty Cobb, 1913 .... .467
81 Mark McGwire, 1996 .... .467
82 George Sisler, 1922 .... .467
83 Cupid Childs, 1896 .... .467
84 Ty Cobb, 1911 .... .467
85 Joe Morgan, 1975 .... .466
86 Dan Brouthers, 1890 .... .466
87 Lou Gehrig, 1935 .... .466
88 Gary Sheffield, 1996 .465
89 Lou Gehrig, 1934 .... .465
90 Lefty O'Doul, 1929 .... .465
91 Mike Griffin, 1894 .... .465
92 Sam Thompson, 1894 .... .465
93 Jimmie Foxx, 1939 .... .464
94 Tris Speaker, 1912 .... .464
95 Ed Delahanty, 1899 .... .464
96 Pete Browning, 1887 .... .464
97 Mickey Mantle, 1956 .... .464
98 Edgar Martinez, 1996 .... .464
99 Ted Williams, 1951 .... .464
100 Willie Keeler, 1897 .... .464

SLUGGING AVERAGE

1	**Barry Bonds, 2001**	**.863**
2	Babe Ruth, 1920	.847
3	Babe Ruth, 1921	.846
4	**Barry Bonds, 2004**	**.812**
5	**Barry Bonds, 2002**	**.799**
6	Babe Ruth, 1927	.772
7	Lou Gehrig, 1927	.765
8	Babe Ruth, 1923	.764
9	Rogers Hornsby, 1925	.756
10	Mark McGwire, 1998	.752
11	Jeff Bagwell, 1994	.750
12	Jimmie Foxx, 1932	.749
	Barry Bonds, 2003	**.749**
14	Babe Ruth, 1924	.739
15	Babe Ruth, 1926	.737
16	Sammy Sosa, 2001	.737
17	Ted Williams, 1941	.735
18	Babe Ruth, 1930	.732
19	Ted Williams, 1957	.731
20	Mark McGwire, 1996	.730
21	**Frank Thomas, 1994**	**.729**
22	Hack Wilson, 1930	.723
23	Rogers Hornsby, 1922	.722
24	Lou Gehrig, 1930	.721
25	Larry Walker, 1997	.720
26	Albert Belle, 1994	.714
27	Larry Walker, 1999	.710
28	Babe Ruth, 1928	.709
29	Al Simmons, 1930	.708
30	Lou Gehrig, 1934	.706
31	Mickey Mantle, 1956	.705
32	Jimmie Foxx, 1938	.704
33	Jimmie Foxx, 1933	.703
34	Stan Musial, 1948	.702
35	Babe Ruth, 1931	.700
36	**Todd Helton, 2000**	**.698**
37	Babe Ruth, 1929	.697
38	**Manny Ramirez, 2000**	**.697**
39	Mark McGwire, 1999	.697
40	Sam Thompson, 1894	.696
41	Lou Gehrig, 1936	.696
42	Rogers Hornsby, 1924	.696
43	Hugh Duffy, 1894	.694
44	Jimmie Foxx, 1939	.694
45	Tip O'Neill, 1887	.691
46	Albert Belle, 1995	.690
47	**Luis Gonzalez, 2001**	**.688**
48	**Barry Bonds, 2000**	**.688**
49	Mickey Mantle, 1961	.687
50	Chuck Klein, 1930	.687
51	**Todd Helton, 2001**	**.685**
52	Hank Greenberg, 1938	.683
53	Kevin Mitchell, 1994	.681
54	Rogers Hornsby, 1929	.679
55	Babe Herman, 1930	.678
56	**Barry Bonds, 1993**	**.677**
57	**Jim Thome, 2002**	**.677**
58	**Ken Griffey Jr., 1994**	**.674**
59	Joe DiMaggio, 1937	.673
60	Babe Ruth, 1922	.672
61	**Albert Pujols, 2006**	**.671**
62	Joe DiMaggio, 1939	.671
63	Hank Greenberg, 1940	.670
64	Hank Aaron, 1971	.669
65	Hank Greenberg, 1937	.668
66	Ted Williams, 1946	.667
67	Willie Mays, 1954	.667
68	**Albert Pujols, 2003**	**.667**
69	Mickey Mantle, 1957	.665
70	**Carlos Delgado, 2000**	**.664**
71	**Vladimir Guerrero, 2000**	**.664**
72	George Brett, 1980	.664
73	**Manny Ramirez, 1999**	**.663**
74	Lou Gehrig, 1931	.662
75	Larry Walker, 2001	.662
76	Norm Cash, 1961	.662
77	**Derrek Lee, 2005**	**.662**
78	Babe Ruth, 1932	.661
79	**Jason Giambi, 2001**	**.660**
80	**Ryan Howard, 2006**	**.659**
81	Willie Mays, 1955	.659
82	**Travis Hafner, 2006**	**.659**
83	Ralph Kiner, 1949	.658
84	Chuck Klein, 1929	.657
85	Babe Ruth, 1919	.657
86	**Albert Pujols, 2004**	**.657**
87	Willie McCovey, 1969	.656
88	Albert Belle, 1998	.655
89	Sam Thompson, 1895	.654
90	Jimmie Foxx, 1934	.653
91	Chick Hafey, 1930	.652
92	Ted Williams, 1949	.650
93	Bill Joyce, 1894	.648
94	Lou Gehrig, 1928	.648
95	Ted Williams, 1942	.648
96	Duke Snider, 1954	.647
97	**Barry Bonds, 1994**	**.647**
	Jason Giambi, 2000	**.647**
99	Sammy Sosa, 1998	.647
100	**Manny Ramirez, 2002**	**.647**

ON-BASE PLUS SLUGGING

1	**Barry Bonds, 2004**	**1422**
2	**Barry Bonds, 2002**	**1381**
3	Babe Ruth, 1920	1379
4	**Barry Bonds, 2001**	**1379**
5	Babe Ruth, 1921	1359
6	Babe Ruth, 1923	1309
7	Ted Williams, 1941	1287
8	**Barry Bonds, 2003**	**1278**
9	Babe Ruth, 1927	1258
10	Ted Williams, 1957	1257
11	Babe Ruth, 1926	1253
12	Babe Ruth, 1924	1252
13	Rogers Hornsby, 1925	1245
14	Lou Gehrig, 1927	1240
15	Babe Ruth, 1930	1225
16	Mark McGwire, 1998	1222
17	Jimmie Foxx, 1932	1218
18	**Frank Thomas, 1994**	**1217**
19	Rogers Hornsby, 1924	1203
20	Jeff Bagwell, 1994	1201
21	Mark McGwire, 1996	1198
22	Hugh Duffy, 1894	1196
23	Babe Ruth, 1931	1195
24	Lou Gehrig, 1930	1194
25	Rogers Hornsby, 1922	1181
26	Tip O'Neill, 1887	1180
27	Hack Wilson, 1930	1177
28	Mickey Mantle, 1957	1177
29	Sammy Sosa, 2001	1174
30	Lou Gehrig, 1936	1174
31	Babe Ruth, 1928	1172
32	Larry Walker, 1997	1172
33	Lou Gehrig, 1934	1172
34	Mickey Mantle, 1956	1169
35	Larry Walker, 1999	1168
36	Jimmie Foxx, 1938	1166
37	Ted Williams, 1946	1164
38	**Todd Helton, 2000**	**1162**
39	Sam Thompson, 1894	1161
40	Jimmie Foxx, 1939	1158
41	**Manny Ramirez, 2000**	**1154**
42	Jimmie Foxx, 1933	1153
43	Stan Musial, 1948	1152
44	Albert Belle, 1994	1152
45	Babe Ruth, 1932	1150
46	Norm Cash, 1961	1148
47	Ted Williams, 1954	1148
48	Ted Williams, 1942	1147
49	Bill Joyce, 1894	1143
50	Ted Williams, 1949	1141
51	Rogers Hornsby, 1929	1139
52	**Jason Giambi, 2001**	**1137**
53	**Barry Bonds, 1993**	**1136**
54	Mickey Mantle, 1961	1135
55	**Carlos Delgado, 2000**	**1134**
56	Ted Williams, 1947	1133
57	Babe Herman, 1930	1132
58	Al Simmons, 1930	1130
59	Rogers Hornsby, 1928	1130
60	Babe Ruth, 1929	1128
61	**Barry Bonds, 2000**	**1127**
62	Chuck Klein, 1930	1123
63	**Jason Giambi, 2000**	**1123**
64	**Jim Thome, 2002**	**1122**
65	Hank Greenberg, 1938	1122
66	Mark McGwire, 1999	1120
67	Joe DiMaggio, 1939	1119
68	George Brett, 1980	1118
69	Ed Delahanty, 1895	1117
70	**Luis Gonzalez, 2001**	**1117**
71	**Todd Helton, 2001**	**1116**
72	Lou Gehrig, 1937	1116
73	Lou Gehrig, 1928	1115
74	Babe Ruth, 1919	1114
75	Harry Heilmann, 1923	1113
76	Ted Williams, 1948	1112
77	Larry Walker, 2001	1111
78	Kevin Mitchell, 1994	1110
79	Willie McCovey, 1969	1108
80	Lou Gehrig, 1931	1108
81	Edgar Martinez, 1995	1107
82	Nap Lajoie, 1901	1106
83	Babe Ruth, 1922	1106
84	**Albert Pujols, 2003**	**1106**
85	**Manny Ramirez, 1999**	**1105**
86	Hank Greenberg, 1937	1105
87	Joe Kelley, 1894	1104
88	Hank Greenberg, 1940	1103
89	Ed Delahanty, 1896	1103
90	**Albert Pujols, 2006**	**1102**
91	Jimmie Foxx, 1934	1102
92	Arky Vaughan, 1935	1098
93	**Travis Hafner, 2006**	**1097**
94	Rogers Hornsby, 1921	1097
95	**Manny Ramirez, 2002**	**1097**
96	Jimmie Foxx, 1935	1096
97	Albert Belle, 1995	1091
98	Mickey Mantle, 1962	1091
99	Harry Heilmann, 1927	1091
100	**Gary Sheffield, 1996**	**1090**

ADJUSTED OPS

1	**Barry Bonds, 2002**	**269**
2	**Barry Bonds, 2001**	**263**
3	**Barry Bonds, 2004**	**255**
4	Babe Ruth, 1920	252
5	Babe Ruth, 1923	238
6	Babe Ruth, 1921	236
7	Ted Williams, 1941	232
8	Babe Ruth, 1927	229
9	Pete Browning, 1882	229
10	Babe Ruth, 1926	228
11	Ted Williams, 1957	227
12	**Barry Bonds, 2003**	**226**
13	Lou Gehrig, 1927	224
14	Babe Ruth, 1919	224
15	Babe Ruth, 1931	223
16	Mickey Mantle, 1957	223
17	Rogers Hornsby, 1924	223
18	Ross Barnes, 1876	222
19	Babe Ruth, 1924	221
20	Jeff Bagwell, 1994	219
21	Mark McGwire, 1998	217
22	Babe Ruth, 1930	216
23	Ted Williams, 1942	214
24	Lou Gehrig, 1934	213
25	Mickey Mantle, 1956	213
26	**Frank Thomas, 1994**	**212**
27	Willie McCovey, 1969	211
28	Ted Williams, 1946	211
29	Babe Ruth, 1928	211
30	Mickey Mantle, 1961	210
31	Rogers Hornsby, 1922	210
32	Ty Cobb, 1917	210
33	George Hall, 1876	208
34	Rogers Hornsby, 1925	208
35	**Barry Bonds, 1993**	**207**
36	Lou Gehrig, 1930	207
37	Babe Ruth, 1932	206
38	Tip O'Neill, 1887	205
39	**Barry Bonds, 1992**	**205**
40	Honus Wagner, 1908	205
41	Rogers Hornsby, 1928	204
42	Sammy Sosa, 2001	204
43	Nap Lajoie, 1904	204
44	Ty Cobb, 1912	203
45	Jimmie Foxx, 1932	203
46	Roger Connor, 1885	203
47	Dan Brouthers, 1886	203
48	Ty Cobb, 1910	202
49	George Brett, 1980	201
50	Frank Robinson, 1966	200
51	Jimmie Foxx, 1933	199
52	Mark McGwire, 1996	199
53	Ted Williams, 1947	199
54	Lou Gehrig, 1931	199
55	Dan Brouthers, 1885	199
56	Babe Ruth, 1929	199
57	Norm Cash, 1961	198
58	Mickey Mantle, 1962	198
59	Dick Allen, 1972	198
60	Dan Brouthers, 1882	198
61	Nap Lajoie, 1910	198
62	Ed Swartwood, 1882	197
63	Lou Gehrig, 1928	197
64	Stan Musial, 1948	196
65	**Jason Giambi, 2001**	**196**
66	Ty Cobb, 1918	196
67	Ty Cobb, 1913	196
68	Nap Lajoie, 1901	196
69	Orator Shafer, 1878	196
70	George Stone, 1906	195
71	Harry Heilmann, 1923	195
72	Dave Orr, 1884	195
73	Kevin Mitchell, 1989	194
74	Dave Orr, 1886	193
75	Mike Schmidt, 1981	193
76	Lou Gehrig, 1936	193
77	**Barry Bonds, 2000**	**193**
78	Ed Delahanty, 1899	193
79	Ty Cobb, 1911	193
80	Ted Williams, 1954	193
81	Joe Jackson, 1911	192
82	Ed Delahanty, 1896	192
83	Rogers Hornsby, 1921	191
84	Ty Cobb, 1909	190
85	**Gary Sheffield, 1996**	**190**
86	**Jim Thome, 2002**	**190**
87	Joe Jackson, 1913	190
88	Pete Browning, 1885	190
89	Deacon White, 1877	190
90	Joe Jackson, 1912	190
91	Rogers Hornsby, 1920	190
92	Hank Aaron, 1971	190
93	Albert Belle, 1994	190
94	Dave Orr, 1885	189
95	Jim Gentile, 1961	189
96	Cupid Childs, 1890	189
97	Carl Yastrzemski, 1967	189
98	Mickey Mantle, 1958	189
99	Frank Robinson, 1967	189
100	Cap Anson, 1881	189

ADJUSTED BATTING WINS

1	**Barry Bonds, 2001**	**12.4**
2	**Barry Bonds, 2002**	**12.0**
3	**Barry Bonds, 2004**	**11.2**
4	Babe Ruth, 1923	11.1
5	Babe Ruth, 1921	10.6
6	Babe Ruth, 1920	10.2
7	Lou Gehrig, 1927	10.0
8	Babe Ruth, 1927	9.9
9	Babe Ruth, 1926	9.6
10	Ted Williams, 1941	9.5
11	Babe Ruth, 1924	9.5
12	Rogers Hornsby, 1924	9.5
13	Babe Ruth, 1931	9.4
14	Mickey Mantle, 1957	9.4
15	Mark McGwire, 1998	9.2
16	Rogers Hornsby, 1922	9.1
17	Lou Gehrig, 1934	9.0
18	Ted Williams, 1942	8.9
19	Ted Williams, 1946	8.9
20	Sammy Sosa, 2001	8.9
21	Babe Ruth, 1930	8.8
22	**Barry Bonds, 1993**	**8.7**
23	Lou Gehrig, 1930	8.7
24	Babe Ruth, 1928	8.6
25	Mickey Mantle, 1956	8.5
26	Ted Williams, 1957	8.4
27	Ted Williams, 1947	8.3
28	Mickey Mantle, 1961	8.3
29	**Barry Bonds, 2003**	**8.3**
30	Lou Gehrig, 1931	8.2
31	Jimmie Foxx, 1932	8.2
32	Ty Cobb, 1917	8.2
33	Willie McCovey, 1969	8.1
34	Frank Robinson, 1966	8.1
35	Norm Cash, 1961	8.0
36	Stan Musial, 1948	8.0
37	Rogers Hornsby, 1928	7.9
38	Lou Gehrig, 1936	7.8
39	**Jason Giambi, 2001**	**7.8**
40	**Barry Bonds, 1992**	**7.8**
41	Lou Gehrig, 1928	7.8
42	Rogers Hornsby, 1925	7.7
43	Babe Ruth, 1919	7.7
44	Rogers Hornsby, 1921	7.6
45	Ted Williams, 1949	7.6
46	Jimmie Foxx, 1933	7.6
47	Hank Aaron, 1959	7.5
48	Jeff Bagwell, 1996	7.5
49	**Gary Sheffield, 1996**	**7.5**
50	**Albert Pujols, 2003**	**7.5**
51	Nap Lajoie, 1910	7.4
52	Honus Wagner, 1908	7.4
53	Babe Ruth, 1932	7.3
54	Carl Yastrzemski, 1967	7.2
55	Rogers Hornsby, 1920	7.2
56	Dick Allen, 1972	7.2
57	Harry Heilmann, 1923	7.2
58	**Barry Bonds, 1996**	**7.2**
59	Mickey Mantle, 1958	7.1
60	Reggie Jackson, 1969	7.1
61	Lou Gehrig, 1932	7.1
62	John Olerud, 1993	7.1
63	**Barry Bonds, 1998**	**7.1**
64	**Mike Piazza, 1997**	**7.0**
65	Ty Cobb, 1912	7.0
66	Hank Aaron, 1963	7.0
67	Tris Speaker, 1923	7.0
68	Kevin Mitchell, 1989	7.0
69	Nap Lajoie, 1904	6.9
70	Jeff Bagwell, 1994	6.9
71	**Frank Thomas, 1991**	**6.9**
72	Ty Cobb, 1915	6.9
73	**Carlos Delgado, 2000**	**6.9**
74	**Jason Giambi, 2000**	**6.9**
75	Ty Cobb, 1911	6.9
76	Stan Musial, 1951	6.8
77	Stan Musial, 1946	6.8
78	Joe Jackson, 1911	6.8
79	Rogers Hornsby, 1929	6.8
80	Ralph Kiner, 1951	6.7
81	George Stone, 1906	6.7
82	Ed Delahanty, 1899	6.7
83	**Frank Thomas, 1994**	**6.7**
84	**Barry Bonds, 2000**	**6.7**
85	Ted Williams, 1948	6.7
86	Rod Carew, 1977	6.7
87	**Frank Thomas, 1997**	**6.7**
88	Edgar Martinez, 1995	6.7
89	Frank Howard, 1969	6.7
90	Al Rosen, 1953	6.6
91	Lou Gehrig, 1937	6.6
92	Tris Speaker, 1912	6.6
93	Jimmie Foxx, 1934	6.6
94	Babe Ruth, 1929	6.6
95	Lou Gehrig, 1935	6.6
96	Joe Medwick, 1937	6.6
97	Carl Yastrzemski, 1970	6.6
98	Ty Cobb, 1910	6.6
99	Hack Wilson, 1930	6.6
100	**Frank Thomas, 1992**	**6.6**

PINCH HITS

1	John Vander Wal, 1995	28
2	Lenny Harris, 1999	26
3	Jose Morales, 1976	25
4	Dave Philley, 1961	24
	Vic Davalillo, 1970	24
	Rusty Staub, 1983	24
	Gerald Perry, 1993	24
8	**Greg Norton, 2003**	**23**
9	Sam Leslie, 1932	22
	Peanuts Lowrey, 1953	22
	Red Schoendienst, 1962	22
	Wallace Johnson, 1988	22
	Mark Sweeney, 1997	**22**
	Lenny Harris, 2002	22
	Daryle Ward, 2006	**22**
16	Doc Miller, 1913	21
	Smoky Burgess, 1966	21
	Merv Rettenmund, 1977	21
Len	y Harris, 2001	21
20	Ed Coleman, 1936	20
	Frenchy Bordagaray, 1938	20
	Joe Frazier, 1954	20
	Smoky Burgess, 1965	20
	Ken Boswell, 1976	20
	Jerry Turner, 1978	20
	Thad Bosley, 1985	20
	Chris Chambliss, 1986	20
	Dave Clark, 1997	20
	Jacob Cruz, 2005	20
	Orlando Palmeiro, 2006	**20**

PINCH HIT AVERAGE

(30 AT-BATS MINIMUM)

1	Ed Kranepool, 1974	.486
2	Smead Jolley, 1931	.467
3	Frenchy Bordagaray, 1938	.465
4	Rick Miller, 1983	.457
5	Bill Spiers, 1997	.455
	Jorge Piedra, 2005	**.455**
7	Jose Pagan, 1969	.452
8	Elmer Valo, 1955	.452
	Mark Johnson, 1996	.452
10	Gates Brown, 1968	.450
11	Ted Easterly, 1912	.433
	Milt Thompson, 1985	.433
	Randy Bush, 1986	.433
14	Joe Cronin, 1943	.429
	Don Dillard, 1961	.429
16	Candy Maldonado, 1986	.425
17	Richie Ashburn, 1962	.419
	Dick Williams, 1962	.419
19	Merritt Ranew, 1963	.415
	Carl Taylor, 1969	.415
21	Kurt Bevacqua, 1983	.412
22	Jerry Turner, 1978	.408
23	Bob Bowman, 1958	.406
	Chico Walker, 1991	.406
	Sid Bream, 1994	.406

PINCH HIT HOME RUNS

1	Dave Hansen, 2000	7
	Craig Wilson, 2001	**7**
3	Johnny Frederick, 1932	6
4	Joe Cronin, 1943	5
	Butch Nieman, 1945	5
	Gene Freese, 1959	5
	Jerry Lynch, 1961	5
	Cliff Johnson, 1974	5
	Lee Lacy, 1978	5
	Jerry Turner, 1978	5
	Billy Ashley, 1996	5
	David Dellucci, 2001	**5**
	Erubiel Durazo, 2001	5
	Mark Sweeney, 2004	**5**
15	Ernie Lombardi, 1946	4
	Del Wilber, 1953	4
	Bill Taylor, 1955	4
	Bob Thurman, 1957	4
	Rip Repulski, 1958	4
	George Crowe, 1959	4
	George Crowe, 1960	4
	Johnny Blanchard, 1961	4
	Carl Sawatski, 1961	4
	Jerry Lynch, 1963	4
	Don Mincher, 1964	4
	Hal Breeden, 1973	4
	Mike Ivie, 1978	4
	Del Unser, 1979	4
	Jeff Burroughs, 1982	4
	Danny Heep, 1983	4
	Candy Maldonado, 1986	4
	Mark Carreon, 1989	4
	Tommy Gregg, 1990	4
	Ernest Riles, 1990	4
	Howard Johnson, 1994	4
	John Vander Wal, 1995	4
	Jack Howell, 1996	4
	Mark Johnson, 1996	4
	Bob Hamelin, 1998	4
	Angelo Echevarria, 1999	4
Gle	allen Hill, 1999	4
	Bubba Trammell, 2000	4
	Orlando Merced, 2001	4
	Greg Norton, 2003	**4**
	Matthew LeCroy, 2004	**4**
	Javier Valentin, 2006	**4**
	Daryle Ward, 2006	**4**

STOLEN BASES

1	Hugh Nicol, 1887	138
2	Rickey Henderson, 1982	130
3	Arlie Latham, 1887	129
4	Lou Brock, 1974	118
5	Charlie Comiskey, 1887	117
6	John Ward, 1887	111
	Billy Hamilton, 1889	111
	Billy Hamilton, 1891	111
9	Vince Coleman, 1985	110
10	Arlie Latham, 1888	109
	Vince Coleman, 1987	109
12	Rickey Henderson, 1983	108
13	Vince Coleman, 1986	107
14	Tom Brown, 1891	106
15	Maury Wills, 1962	104
16	Pete Browning, 1887	103
	Hugh Nicol, 1888	103
18	Jim Fogarty, 1887	102
	Billy Hamilton, 1890	102
20	Billy Hamilton, 1894	100
	Rickey Henderson, 1980	100
22	Jim Fogarty, 1889	99
23	Harry Stovey, 1890	97
	Billy Hamilton, 1895	97
	Ron LeFlore, 1980	97
26	Ty Cobb, 1915	96
	Omar Moreno, 1980	96
28	Bid McPhee, 1887	95
	Curt Welch, 1888	95
30	Mike Griffin, 1887	94
	Maury Wills, 1965	94
32	Tommy McCarthy, 1888	93
	Rickey Henderson, 1988	93
34	Darby O'Brien, 1889	91
35	Tim Raines, 1983	90
36	Curt Welch, 1887	89
	Herman Long, 1889	89
38	Tom Poorman, 1887	88
	Blondie Purcell, 1887	88
	John Ward, 1892	88
	Clyde Milan, 1912	88
42	Harry Stovey, 1888	87
	Arlie Latham, 1891	87
	Joe Kelley, 1896	87
	Rickey Henderson, 1986	87
46	Cub Stricker, 1887	86
47	Tommy Tucker, 1887	85
	Hub Collins, 1890	85
	Hugh Duffy, 1891	85
50	King Kelly, 1887	84
	Chippy McGarr, 1887	84
	Billy Sunday, 1890	84
	Bill Lange, 1896	84
54	Tommy McCarthy, 1890	83
	Billy Hamilton, 1896	83
	Ty Cobb, 1911	83
	Willie Wilson, 1979	83
58	Dummy Hoy, 1888	82
	John Reilly, 1888	82
60	Eddie Collins, 1910	81
	Bob Bescher, 1911	81
	Vince Coleman, 1988	81
63	Emmett Seery, 1888	80
	Hugh Nicol, 1889	80
	Rickey Henderson, 1985	80
	Eric Davis, 1986	80
67	Tom Brown, 1890	79
	Dave Collins, 1980	79
	Willie Wilson, 1980	79
70	Hugh Duffy, 1890	78
	Tom Brown, 1892	78
	John McGraw, 1894	78
	Ron LeFlore, 1979	78
	Tim Raines, 1982	78
	Marquis Grissom, 1992	78
76	Ted Scheffler, 1890	77
	Jimmy Sheckard, 1899	77
	Davey Lopes, 1975	77
	Omar Moreno, 1979	77
	Rudy Law, 1983	77
	Rickey Henderson, 1989	77
	Vince Coleman, 1990	77
83	Ed McKean, 1887	76
	Walt Wilmot, 1890	76
	Walt Wilmot, 1894	76
	Dusty Miller, 1896	76
	Ty Cobb, 1909	76
	Marquis Grissom, 1991	76
89	Yank Robinson, 1887	75
	George Van Haltren, 1891	75
	Clyde Milan, 1913	75
	Benny Kauff, 1914	75
	Billy North, 1976	75
	Tim Raines, 1984	75
	Kenny Lofton, 1996	**75**
96	Frank Fennelly, 1887	74
	Harry Stovey, 1887	74
	Fritz Maisel, 1914	74
	Lou Brock, 1966	74
	Brian Hunter, 1997	74

STOLEN BASE AVERAGE

1	Kevin McReynolds, 1988	100.0
	Paul Molitor, 1994	100.0
3	Brady Anderson, 1994	96.9
	Carlos Beltran, 2001	**96.9**
5	**Chris Duffy, 2006**	**96.3**
6	Max Carey, 1922	96.2
7	Ken Griffey Sr., 1980	95.8
8	**Ichiro Suzuki, 2006**	**95.7**
9	**Jason Bay, 2005**	**95.5**
10	Stan Javier, 1988	95.2
11	Doug Glanville, 1999	94.4
12	Amos Otis, 1970	94.3
13	Jack Perconte, 1985	93.9
14	**Alfonso Soriano, 2005**	**93.8**
15	**Carlos Beltran, 2004**	**93.3**
16	Miguel Dilone, 1984	93.1
	Bob Dernier, 1986	93.1
18	Kirk Gibson, 1990	92.9
	Barry Larkin, 1994	92.9
20	**Dave Roberts, 2004**	**92.7**
21	**Rafael Furcal, 2003**	**92.6**
	Brandon Phillips, 2006	**92.6**
23	Don Baylor, 1972	92.3
	Oddibe McDowell, 1987	92.3
	Orlando Cabrera, 2003	**92.3**
26	Davey Lopes, 1985	92.2
27	Eric Davis, 1988	92.1
28	Cesar Cedeno, 1978	92.0
	Delino DeShields, 2001	92.0
	Henry Cotto, 1992	92.0
	Mike Cameron, 1997	**92.0**
32	Bobby Bonds, 1969	91.8
	Davey Lopes, 1978	91.8
34	Davey Lopes, 1979	91.7
	Marquis Grissom, 1990	91.7
36	Jimmy Wynn, 1965	91.5
37	Larry Bowa, 1977	91.4
	Derek Jeter, 2002	**91.4**
39	Ryne Sandberg, 1987	91.3
	Alan Trammell, 1987	91.3
	Rich Amaral, 1995	91.3
	Orlando Cabrera, 2005	**91.3**
43	Jerry Mumphrey, 1980	91.2
44	Tom Herr, 1985	91.2
45	**Carlos Beltran, 2003**	**91.1**
46	Barry Larkin, 1995	91.1
47	7 players tied	90.9

BASE STEALING WINS

1	Vince Coleman, 1986	2.0
2	Maury Wills, 1962	1.8
3	Rickey Henderson, 1983	1.7
4	Vince Coleman, 1985	1.6
5	Vince Coleman, 1987	1.6
6	Rickey Henderson, 1988	1.6
7	Ron LeFlore, 1980	1.6
8	Tim Raines, 1983	1.5
9	Lou Brock, 1974	1.5
10	Eric Davis, 1986	1.4
11	Willie Wilson, 1980	1.4
12	Rickey Henderson, 1982	1.4
13	Willie Wilson, 1979	1.4
14	Rickey Henderson, 1985	1.4
15	Marquis Grissom, 1992	1.4
16	Tim Raines, 1984	1.3
17	Davey Lopes, 1975	1.3
18	Rudy Law, 1983	1.3
19	Rickey Henderson, 1980	1.3
20	Tim Raines, 1985	1.3
21	Tim Raines, 1986	1.3
22	Rickey Henderson, 1986	1.3
23	Tim Raines, 1981	1.3
24	Tim Raines, 1982	1.2
25	Rickey Henderson, 1989	1.2
26	Ron LeFlore, 1979	1.2
27	Vince Coleman, 1989	1.2
28	Bert Campaneris, 1969	1.1
29	Joe Morgan, 1975	1.1
30	Fritz Maisel, 1914	1.1
31	Vince Coleman, 1990	1.1
32	Marquis Grissom, 1991	1.1
33	Juan Samuel, 1984	1.1
34	Davey Lopes, 1976	1.1
35	**Scott Podsednik, 2004**	**1.1**
36	**Tony Womack, 1999**	**1.1**
37	Lou Brock, 1968	1.1
38	Mickey Rivers, 1975	1.1
39	Rickey Henderson, 1990	1.1
40	**Tony Womack, 1997**	**1.1**
41	Dave Collins, 1980	1.1
42	**Kenny Lofton, 1992**	**1.0**
43	Lou Brock, 1966	1.0
44	Alan Wiggins, 1983	1.0
45	Maury Wills, 1965	1.0
46	Joe Morgan, 1976	1.0
47	Tommy Harper, 1969	1.0
48	Willie Wilson, 1983	1.0
49	Jerry Mumphrey, 1980	1.0
50	Omar Moreno, 1980	1.0

PITCHER BATTING AVERAGE BY ERA

1988–2006

1	Orel Hershiser, 1993	.356
2	**Mike Hampton, 2002**	**.344**
3	**Mike Hampton, 1999**	**.311**
4	**Jason Marquis, 2005**	**.310**
5	Fernando Valenzuela, 1990	.304
6	**Carlos Zambrano, 2005**	**.300**
7	**Livan Hernandez, 2001**	**.296**
8	**Jason Marquis, 2004**	**.292**
9	**Mike Hampton, 2001**	**.291**
10	**Tom Glavine, 1996**	**.289**

1973–87

1	Rick Rhoden, 1984	.333
2	Ken Brett, 1974	.310
3	Bob Forsch, 1975	.308
	Rick Rhoden, 1976	.308
5	Jim Rooker, 1974	.305
6	Rick Mahler, 1984	.296
7	Bob Forsch, 1980	.295
8	Tom Griffin, 1974	.294
9	Steve Carlton, 1978	.291
10	Don Robinson, 1982	.282

1961–72

1	Catfish Hunter, 1971	.350
2	Curt Simmons, 1961	.303
3	Bob Gibson, 1970	.303
4	Don Drysdale, 1965	.300
5	Claude Osteen, 1972	.273
6	Gary Peters, 1971	.271
7	Rick Wise, 1969	.270
8	Camilo Pascual, 1962	.268
9	Blue Moon Odom, 1969	.266
	Sonny Siebert, 1971	.266

1943–60

1	Don Newcombe, 1955	.359
2	Gene Bearden, 1952	.354
3	Johnny Sain, 1947	.346
4	Warren Spahn, 1958	.333
5	Fritz Ostermueller, 1946	.328
6	Fred Hutchinson, 1950	.326
7	Oscar Judd, 1946	.316
8	Fred Hutchinson, 1946	.315
9	Rip Sewell, 1945	.313
	Tom Sturdivant, 1956	.313

1921–42

1	Walter Johnson, 1925	.433
2	Jack Bentley, 1923	.427
3	Curt Davis, 1939	.381
4	Red Ruffing, 1930	.374
5	George Uhle, 1923	.361
6	Erv Brame, 1930	.353
7	Dutch Ruether, 1921	.351
8	Wes Ferrell, 1935	.347
9	Wilbur Cooper, 1924	.346
	Dolf Luque, 1926	.346

1901–20

1	Snake Wiltse, 1901	.373
2	Doc Crandall, 1910	.342
3	Bill Phillips, 1902	.342
4	Nixey Callahan, 1901	.331
5	Babe Ruth, 1917	.325
6	Frank Foreman, 1901	.325
	George Mullin, 1902	.325
8	Al Orth, 1907	.324
9	Claude Hendrix, 1912	.322
10	Cy Young, 1903	.321

1893–1900

1	Ad Gumbert, 1895	.361
2	Ted Breitenstein, 1899	.352
3	Kid Gleason, 1894	.349
4	Adonis Terry, 1894	.347
5	Jack Stivetts, 1896	.347
6	Tom Parrott, 1895	.343
7	Jack Taylor, 1894	.338
8	Jesse Tannehill, 1900	.336
9	Al Orth, 1897	.329
10	Jack Stivetts, 1894	.328

1876–92

1	Billy Taylor, 1884	.366
2	Guy Hecker, 1886	.341
3	Charlie Ferguson, 1887	.337
4	Bob Caruthers, 1886	.334
5	Scott Stratton, 1890	.323
6	Jim Whitney, 1882	.323
7	Charlie Sweeney, 1884	.316
8	Jim Devlin, 1876	.315
9	Ed Crane, 1890	.315
	Curry Foley, 1879	.315

PITCHER BATTING RUNS

1	Guy Hecker, 1884	27.5
2	Bob Caruthers, 1886	23.4
3	Jim Whitney, 1882	22.2
4	Don Drysdale, 1965	21.6
5	Wes Ferrell, 1935	20.2
6	Don Newcombe, 1955	19.6
7	Guy Hecker, 1886	18.4
8	Jim Whitney, 1883	17.7
9	Schoolboy Rowe, 1943	17.4
10	Warren Spahn, 1958	17.4
11	Charlie Ferguson, 1885	17.1
12	Wes Ferrell, 1931	16.9
13	Babe Ruth, 1917	16.5
14	Scott Stratton, 1890	16.4
15	George Uhle, 1923	16.4
16	Red Ruffing, 1930	16.4
17	Walter Johnson, 1925	16.2
18	Tony Mullane, 1884	16.2
19	Bob Lemon, 1950	16.1
20	Bob Caruthers, 1889	15.7
21	Bob Caruthers, 1887	15.7
22	Red Lucas, 1930	15.4
23	Bob Lemon, 1949	15.0
24	Jack Bentley, 1923	15.0
25	Babe Ruth, 1915	15.0
26	John Ward, 1879	15.0
27	Claude Hendrix, 1912	14.8
28	Don Newcombe, 1959	14.7
29	Red Ruffing, 1936	14.3
30	Jim Tobin, 1942	14.3
31	Red Lucas, 1932	14.2
32	Frank Killen, 1893	14.2
33	Robin Roberts, 1955	13.9
34	Jack Stivetts, 1892	13.8
35	Pink Hawley, 1895	13.7
36	Scott Stratton, 1888	13.4
37	Pete Conway, 1888	13.4
38	Charlie Ferguson, 1887	13.3
39	Red Ruffing, 1932	13.2
40	Jack Coombs, 1911	13.1
41	Clark Griffith, 1901	13.1
42	Jack Stivetts, 1890	13.1
43	Joe Bush, 1924	13.1
44	Babe Ruth, 1916	13.0
45	Adonis Terry, 1890	13.0
46	Schoolboy Rowe, 1935	12.9
47	Bob Lemon, 1948	12.9
48	Red Ruffing, 1935	12.9
49	Elam Vangilder, 1922	12.9
50	Dave Foutz, 1887	12.9
51	Terry Larkin, 1878	12.8
52	Red Lucas, 1933	12.7
53	Bucky Walters, 1939	12.7
54	Red Ruffing, 1928	12.4
55	Catfish Hunter, 1971	12.3
56	Ad Gumbert, 1891	12.2
57	Johnny Sain, 1947	12.0
58	Joe Bowman, 1939	12.0
59	Jouett Meekin, 1896	11.8
60	Doc Crandall, 1915	11.8
61	Babe Ruth, 1918	11.8
62	Jim Whitney, 1887	11.7
63	Bob Gibson, 1970	11.7
64	Cy Young, 1903	11.7
65	George Mullin, 1904	11.7
66	Curt Davis, 1939	11.6
67	Red Lucas, 1931	11.6
68	Charley Radbourn, 1883	11.5
69	Jim Whitney, 1881	11.5
70	Tim Keefe, 1884	11.4
71	Wes Ferrell, 1936	11.3
72	Red Lucas, 1929	11.3
73	Erv Brame, 1929	11.3
74	Billy Taylor, 1884	11.3
75	Dizzy Trout, 1944	11.3
76	Adonis Terry, 1889	11.2
77	Schoolboy Rowe, 1934	11.2
78	Frank Foreman, 1891	11.2
79	Dutch Ruether, 1921	11.2
80	Jack Stivetts, 1896	11.1
81	Charlie Ferguson, 1886	11.1
82	Ad Gumbert, 1895	11.1
83	Guy Hecker, 1883	11.0
84	Red Ruffing, 1941	10.9
85	Bob Caruthers, 1891	10.9
86	Jack Scott, 1921	10.9
87	Charlie Buffinton, 1884	10.8
88	Ben Sanders, 1892	10.8
89	Blue Moon Odom, 1969	10.8
90	Guy Hecker, 1887	10.8
91	Scott Stratton, 1892	10.8
92	Carl Mays, 1921	10.7
93	Erv Brame, 1930	10.7
94	Dave Ferriss, 1945	10.6
95	Tony Mullane, 1882	10.5
96	**Mike Hampton, 1999**	**10.5**
97	Ken Brett, 1974	10.5
98	Claude Hendrix, 1915	10.5
99	Al Maul, 1893	10.5
100	George Van Haltren, 1888	10.4

FIELDING AVERAGE

FIRST BASE

1	Steve Garvey, 1984	1.000
2	Stuffy McInnis, 1921	.999
3	Frank McCormick, 1946	.999
4	David Segui, 1998	.999
5	**J.T. Snow, 1998**	**.999**
6	Steve Garvey, 1981	.999
7	Jim Spencer, 1973	.999
8	Wes Parker, 1968	.999

SECOND BASE

1	**Mark Ellis, 2006**	**.997**
2	Bret Boone, 1997	.997
3	Bobby Grich, 1985	.997
4	Jose Oquendo, 1990	.996
5	Ryne Sandberg, 1991	.995
6	Jody Reed, 1994	.995
7	**Jamey Carroll, 2006**	**.995**
8	Rob Wilfong, 1980	.995
9	**Placido Polanco, 2004**	**.995**
10	Bobby Grich, 1973	.995

SHORTSTOP

1	Mike Bordick, 2002	.998
2	Cal Ripken, 1990	.996
3	**Omar Vizquel, 2000**	**.995**
4	Rey Sanchez, 2000	.994
5	Rey Ordonez, 1999	.994
6	**Omar Vizquel, 2006**	**.993**
7	**Omar Vizquel, 1998**	**.993**
8	Tony Fernandez, 1989	.992
9	Rey Sanchez, 2001	.991
10	Larry Bowa, 1979	.991

THIRD BASE

1	Tony Fernandez, 1994	.991
2	Don Money, 1974	.989
3	Hank Majeski, 1947	.988
4	**Eric Chavez, 2006**	**.987**
5	Aurelio Rodriguez, 1978	.987
6	**Mike Lowell, 2006**	**.987**
7	**Vinny Castilla, 2004**	**.987**
8	Willie Kamm, 1933	.984
9	Steve Buechele, 1991	.983
10	Gary Gaetti, 1998	.983

OUTFIELD (250 CHANCES ACCEPTED)

1	Danny Litwhiler, 1942	1.000
	Tony Gonzalez, 1962	1.000
	Rocky Colavito, 1965	1.000
	Curt Flood, 1966	1.000
	Mickey Stanley, 1968	1.000
	Mickey Stanley, 1970	1.000
	Roy White, 1971	1.000
	Ken Berry, 1972	1.000
	Carl Yastrzemski, 1977	1.000
	Terry Puhl, 1979	1.000
	Brian Downing, 1982	1.000
	Brian Downing, 1984	1.000
	Brett Butler, 1991	1.000
	Darryl Hamilton, 1992	1.000
	Brett Butler, 1993	1.000
	Darren Lewis, 1993	1.000
	Lance Johnson, 1994	1.000
	Stan Javier, 1995	1.000
	Darryl Hamilton, 1996	1.000
	Paul O'Neill, 1996	1.000
	Darryl Hamilton, 1999	1.000
	B.J. Surhoff, 1999	1.000
	Eric Owens, 2000	1.000
	Bernie Williams, 2000	**1.000**
	Luis Gonzalez, 2001	**1.000**
	Dave Roberts, 2002	**1.000**
	Juan Encarnacion, 2003	**1.000**
	Carlos Lee, 2004	**1.000**
	Shawn Green, 2005	**1.000**
	Vernon Wells, 2005	**1.000**

CATCHER

1	Spud Davis, 1939	1.000
	Buddy Rosar, 1946	1.000
	Lou Berberet, 1957	1.000
	Pete Daley, 1957	1.000
	Yogi Berra, 1958	1.000
	Rick Cerone, 1988	1.000
	Charles Johnson, 1997	1.000
	Chris Hoiles, 1997	1.000
	Mike Matheny, 2003	**1.000**

PITCHER (90 CHANCES ACCEPTED)

1	Kid Nichols, 1896	1.000
	Frank Owen, 1904	1.000
	Mordecai Brown, 1908	1.000
	Grover Alexander, 1913	1.000
	Walter Johnson, 1913	1.000
	Eppa Rixey, 1917	1.000
	Walter Johnson, 1917	1.000
	Grover Alexander, 1919	1.000
	Jesse Barnes, 1921	1.000
	Hal Schumacher, 1935	1.000
	Larry Jackson, 1964	1.000
	Randy Jones, 1976	1.000
	Greg Maddux, 1990	**1.000**

TOTAL CHANCES/GAME (INF)

FIRST BASE
1 Joe Gerhardt, 1876 ..... 13.28
2 Jiggs Donahue, 1907 .. 12.73
3 Oscar Walker, 1879 ..... 12.60
4 Joe Start, 1878 .... 12.54
5 Tim Murnane, 1878 ..... 12.52
6 Joe Start, 1879 .... 12.49
7 Jake Goodman, 1878 .. 12.45
8 Herman Dehlman, 1876 ... 12.36
9 Phil Todt, 1926 .... 12.36
10 Joe Start, 1877 .... 12.35
11 George Burns, 1914 .... 12.32
12 George Stovall, 1908 ... 12.20
13 Stuffy McInnis, 1918 ... 12.19
14 Juice Latham, 1877 ..... 12.19
15 Bill Phillips, 1888 .... 12.12
16 Joe Start, 1880 .... 12.11
17 Tom Jones, 1905 .... 12.09
18 George Kelly, 1920 ...... 12.08
19 Gene Paulette, 1918 .... 12.08
20 George Stovall, 1907 ... 12.08
21 Hal Chase, 1919 .... 12.07
22 Cap Anson, 1885 .... 12.04
23 Bill Everitt, 1899 .... 12.01
24 Charlie Comiskey, 1883 .... 11.96
25 Jiggs Donahue, 1905 .. 11.95

SECOND BASE
1 Thorny Hawkes, 1879 .... 8.44
2 Chick Fulmer, 1879 .... 8.34
3 Jack Burdock, 1878 .... 8.30
4 Ed Somerville, 1876 ...... 8.28
5 Joe Gerhardt, 1877 .... 8.12
6 Fred Pfeffer, 1884 .... 8.08
7 Jack Burdock, 1879 .... 7.88
8 Joe Quest, 1878 .... 7.81
9 Pop Smith, 1885 .... 7.74
10 Joe Quest, 1879 .... 7.73
11 Jack Farrell, 1879 .... 7.67
12 Pop Smith, 1883 .... 7.66
13 Joe Gerhardt, 1883 .... 7.65
14 Hardy Richardson, 1883 7.62
15 Jack Burdock, 1880 .... 7.59
16 Bid McPhee, 1886 .... 7.56
17 Bid McPhee, 1884 .... 7.54
18 Fred Pfeffer, 1883 .... 7.53
19 Cub Stricker, 1882 .... 7.53
20 Jack Burdock, 1877 .... 7.53
21 Joe Gerhardt, 1884 .... 7.51
22 Fred Dunlap, 1882 .... 7.48
23 George Wright, 1877 ..... 7.47
24 Hardy Richardson, 1882 7.45
25 Bob Ferguson, 1880 ...... 7.40

SHORTSTOP
1 Herman Long, 1889 ...... 7.27
2 Hughie Jennings, 1895 .. 7.16
3 Dave Bancroft, 1918 ...... 7.14
4 Phil Tomney, 1889 .... 7.12
5 George Davis, 1899 .... 7.10
6 Hughie Jennings, 1896 .. 7.07
7 Hughie Jennings, 1897 .. 7.03
8 Bobby Wallace, 1901 ..... 6.97
9 Monte Cross, 1897 .... 6.97
10 Bill Dahlen, 1895 .... 6.93
11 Gene DeMontreville, 1897 ... 6.91
12 Rabbit Maranville, 1919 .... 6.89
13 Bill Dahlen, 1893 .... 6.82
George Davis, 1898 .... 6.82
15 Herman Long, 1893 .... 6.81
16 Bob Allen, 1890 .... 6.81
17 Hughie Jennings, 1894 .. 6.79
18 George Davis, 1900 .... 6.77
19 Kid Elberfeld, 1901 .... 6.77
20 Honus Wagner, 1903 ...... 6.76
21 Herman Long, 1896 .... 6.74
22 Bill Dahlen, 1898 .... 6.73
23 Monte Cross, 1898 .... 6.73
24 Bill Dahlen, 1900 .... 6.71
25 Rabbit Maranville, 1914 .... 6.71
Dave Bancroft, 1922 ...... 6.71

THIRD BASE
1 Al Nichols, 1876 .... 5.81
2 Bob Ferguson, 1877 .... 5.61
3 Jumbo Davis, 1888 .... 5.13
4 Billy Alvord, 1891 .... 5.03
5 Cap Anson, 1876 .... 5.03
6 George Bradley, 1880 .... 4.93
7 Billy Shindle, 1892 .... 4.93
8 Jack Gleason, 1882 .... 4.90
9 Bill Bradley, 1900 .... 4.87
10 Will Foley, 1877 .... 4.79
11 Levi Meyerle, 1876 .... 4.78
12 Joe Battin, 1876 .... 4.76
13 Harry Schafer, 1876 .... 4.73
14 Jerry Denny, 1882 .... 4.73
15 Patsy Tebeau, 1890 .... 4.69
16 Joe Battin, 1883 .... 4.68
17 Arlie Latham, 1884 .... 4.67
18 Frank Hankinson, 1878 . 4.65
19 Ed Williamson, 1883 .... 4.64
20 Billy Shindle, 1889 .... 4.61
21 Arlie Latham, 1891 .... 4.61
22 Billy Shindle, 1891 .... 4.59
23 Hick Carpenter, 1880 ..... 4.58
24 Charlie Reilly, 1890 .... 4.58
25 Jerry Denny, 1881 .... 4.55

ASSISTS (INFIELD)

FIRST BASE
1 Bill Buckner, 1985 184
2 Mark Grace, 1990 180
3 Mark Grace, 1991 167
4 Sid Bream, 1986 166
5 Bill Buckner, 1983 161
6 Bill Buckner, 1982 159
7 Bill Buckner, 1986 157
8 Todd Helton, 2003 156
9 Mickey Vernon, 1949 155
10 Fred Tenney, 1905 152
Eddie Murray, 1985 152
12 Ferris Fain, 1952 150
13 Rudy York, 1943 149
Keith Hernandez, 1986 ... 149
Keith Hernandez, 1987 ... 149
Todd Helton, 2000 149
17 Keith Hernandez, 1983 ... 147
Eric Karros, 1993 147
Rafael Palmeiro, 1993 147
Jeff King, 1997 147
21 Rudy York, 1942 146
Keith Hernandez, 1979 ... 146
Pete O'Brien, 1987 146
Todd Helton, 1998 146

SECOND BASE
1 Frankie Frisch, 1927 641
2 Hughie Critz, 1926 588
3 Rogers Hornsby, 1927 582
4 Ski Melillo, 1930 572
5 Ryne Sandberg, 1983 571
6 Rabbit Maranville, 1924 568
7 Frank Parkinson, 1922 ... 562
8 Tony Cuccinello, 1936 559
9 Johnny Hodapp, 1930 557
10 Lou Bierbauer, 1892 555
11 Pep Young, 1938 554
12 Burgess Whitehead, 1936 552
13 Sparky Adams, 1925 551
14 Ryne Sandberg, 1984 550
15 Rogers Hornsby, 1929 547
16 Hod Ford, 1924 543
Ski Melillo, 1931 543
Bill Mazeroski, 1964 543
19 Hughie Critz, 1925 542
Charlie Gehringer, 1933 542
Woody Williams, 1944 542
Jerry Priddy, 1950 542
23 Hughie Critz, 1933 541
24 Glenn Hubbard, 1985 539
Ryne Sandberg, 1992 539

SHORTSTOP
1 Ozzie Smith, 1980 621
2 Glenn Wright, 1924 601
3 Dave Bancroft, 1920 598
4 Tommy Thevenow, 1926 . 597
5 Ivan DeJesus, 1977 595
6 Cal Ripken, 1984 583
7 Whitey Wietelmann, 1943 581
8 Dave Bancroft, 1922 579
9 Rabbit Maranville, 1914 574
10 Don Kessinger, 1968 573
11 Roy Smalley, 1979 572
12 Terry Turner, 1906 570
Joe Tinker, 1908 570
Leo Cardenas, 1969 570
Ozzie Guillen, 1988 570
16 Heinie Wagner, 1908 569
Ed Brinkman, 1970 569
18 George McBride, 1908 568
19 Donie Bush, 1909 567
20 Art Fletcher, 1917 565
21 Luis Aparicio, 1969 563
22 Germany Smith, 1892 561
Tommy Corcoran, 1898 .. 561
24 Larry Bowa, 1971 560
Bill Russell, 1973 560

THIRD BASE
1 Graig Nettles, 1971 412
2 Graig Nettles, 1973 410
Brooks Robinson, 1974 .. 410
4 Harlond Clift, 1937 405
Brooks Robinson, 1967 .. 405
6 Mike Schmidt, 1974 404
7 Doug DeCinces, 1982 399
8 Brandon Inge, 2006 ... 398
9 Clete Boyer, 1962 396
Mike Schmidt, 1977 396
Buddy Bell, 1982 396
12 Ron Santo, 1967 393
13 Terry Pendleton, 1989 392
14 Ron Santo, 1966 391
15 Aurelio Rodriguez, 1974 389
Vinny Castilla, 1996 .. 389
17 Ossie Vitt, 1916 385
18 Graig Nettles, 1976 383
Buddy Bell, 1983 383
Tim Wallach, 1985 383
21 Billy Shindle, 1892 382
22 Darrell Evans, 1975 381
23 Graig Nettles, 1975 379
24 Frank Malzone, 1958 378
Ron Santo, 1968 378
Brandon Inge, 2005 ... 378

ASSISTS/GAME (INFIELD)

FIRST BASE
1 Mark Grace, 1990 .... 1.18
2 Bill Buckner, 1986 .... 1.14
3 Bill Buckner, 1985 .... 1.14
4 Jeff Bagwell, 1995 .... 1.13
5 Bill Buckner, 1983 .... 1.12
6 Jeff Bagwell, 1994 .... 1.10
7 Sid Bream, 1986 .... 1.08
8 Eric Karros, 1994 .... 1.08
9 Cecil Fielder, 1994 .... 1.06
10 Ferris Fain, 1951 .... 1.05
11 Mark Grace, 1991 .... 1.04
12 Ferris Fain, 1952 .... 1.04
13 Wally Joyner, 1993 .... 1.04
14 Fred Tenney, 1905 .... 1.03
15 Keith Hernandez, 1983 .. 1.02
16 Bob Robertson, 1971 ...... 1.02
17 Sid Bream, 1988 .... 1.01
18 Mickey Vernon, 1949 ...... 1.01
19 Darrell Evans, 1985 .... 1.01
20 Roy Cullenbine, 1947 ..... 1.01
21 Vic Power, 1961 .... 1.01
22 Keith Hernandez, 1986 .. 1.00
Todd Helton, 1998 .... 1.00
24 Bill Buckner, 1982 .... 0.99
25 Eddie Murray, 1985 .... 0.99

SECOND BASE
1 Joe Gerhardt, 1877 .... 4.28
2 Frankie Frisch, 1927 ...... 4.19
3 Thorny Hawkes, 1879 .... 4.13
4 Hughie Critz, 1933 .... 4.07
5 Frank Parkinson, 1922 .. 4.04
6 Joe Quest, 1879 .... 3.99
7 Chick Fulmer, 1879 .... 3.96
8 Ed Somerville, 1876 .... 3.92
9 Ski Melillo, 1930 .... 3.86
10 Glenn Hubbard, 1985 ..... 3.85
11 Frankie Frisch, 1930 ...... 3.85
12 Jack Farrell, 1883 .... 3.84
13 Sparky Adams, 1925 ...... 3.83
14 Freddie Maguire, 1928 .. 3.80
15 Hughie Critz, 1926 .... 3.79
16 Fred Pfeffer, 1884 .... 3.77
17 Hughie Critz, 1925 .... 3.76
18 Danny Richardson, 1891 ..... 3.76
19 John Kerr, 1929 .... 3.76
20 Frankie Frisch, 1924 ...... 3.76
21 Rogers Hornsby, 1927 ... 3.75
22 Hod Ford, 1924 .... 3.74
23 Hardy Richardson, 1883 3.74
24 Rabbit Maranville, 1924 .... 3.74
25 Charley Bassett, 1887 ... 3.73

SHORTSTOP
1 Germany Smith, 1885 ... 4.21
2 Arthur Irwin, 1880 .... 4.13
3 Art Fletcher, 1919 .... 4.10
4 Bill Dahlen, 1895 .... 4.09
5 Phil Tomney, 1889 .... 4.05
6 Bobby Wallace, 1901 ...... 4.04
7 Jack Glasscock, 1887 .... 4.04
8 Germany Smith, 1892 ... 4.04
9 Henry Easterday, 1888 .. 3.99
10 Dave Bancroft, 1920 .... 3.99
11 Rogers Hornsby, 1918 ... 3.98
12 Robin Yount, 1981 .... 3.98
13 Germany Smith, 1894 ... 3.98
14 Bob Ferguson, 1878 .... 3.96
15 Shorty Fuller, 1895 .... 3.96
16 George Davis, 1900 .... 3.95
17 Ozzie Smith, 1980 .... 3.93
18 Glenn Wright, 1924 .... 3.93
19 Garry Templeton, 1980 .. 3.92
20 Monte Cross, 1897 .... 3.91
21 Art Fletcher, 1918 .... 3.90
22 Hughie Jennings, 1894 .. 3.90
23 Sadie Houck, 1885 .... 3.89
24 Bill Dahlen, 1900 .... 3.89
25 Davy Force, 1876 .... 3.89

THIRD BASE
1 Jumbo Davis, 1888 .... 2.96
2 Buddy Bell, 1981 .... 2.93
3 George Bradley, 1880 .... 2.89
4 Bill Hague, 1878 .... 2.85
5 Billy Shindle, 1892 .... 2.85
6 Bob Ferguson, 1877 .... 2.77
7 Ed Williamson, 1879 .... 2.76
8 Arlie Latham, 1884 .... 2.75
9 Bill Bradley, 1900 .... 2.75
10 Arlie Latham, 1891 .... 2.74
11 Buddy Bell, 1982 .... 2.73
12 Brooks Robinson, 1974 . 2.68
13 Aaron Ward, 1920 .... 2.66
14 Mike Schmidt, 1977 .... 2.66
15 Joe Battin, 1883 .... 2.63
16 Harlond Clift, 1937 .... 2.61
17 Arlie Latham, 1883 .... 2.61
18 Graig Nettles, 1973 .... 2.61
19 Doug DeCinces, 1982 .... 2.61
20 Graig Nettles, 1971 .... 2.61
21 Billy Nash, 1892 .... 2.60
22 Ed Williamson, 1883 .... 2.60
23 Charlie Reilly, 1890 .... 2.58
24 Ron Santo, 1966 .... 2.57
25 Brooks Robinson, 1967 . 2.56

DOUBLE PLAYS

FIRST BASE
1 Ferris Fain, 1949 194
2 Ferris Fain, 1950 192
3 Donn Clendenon, 1966 .. 182
4 Andres Galarraga, 1997 . 176
5 Ron Jackson, 1979 175
Albert Pujols, 2005 175
7 Gil Hodges, 1951 171
8 Mickey Vernon, 1949 168
9 Ted Kluszewski, 1954 166
Carlos Delgado, 2001 166

SECOND BASE
1 Bill Mazeroski, 1966 161
2 Jerry Priddy, 1950 150
3 Bill Mazeroski, 1961 144
4 Nellie Fox, 1957 141
Dave Cash, 1974 141
6 Buddy Myer, 1935 138
Bill Mazeroski, 1962 138
Carlos Baerga, 1992 138
9 Jerry Coleman, 1950 137
Jackie Robinson, 1951 137
Red Schoendienst, 1954 137

SHORTSTOP
1 Rick Burleson, 1980 147
2 Roy Smalley, 1979 144
3 Bobby Wine, 1970 137
4 Lou Boudreau, 1944 134
5 Spike Owen, 1986 133
6 Mike Bordick, 1999 132
7 Rafael Ramirez, 1982 130
8 Roy McMillan, 1954 129
Jack Wilson, 2004 129
10 Hod Ford, 1928 128
Vern Stephens, 1949 128
Gene Alley, 1966 128

THIRD BASE
1 Graig Nettles, 1971 54
2 Harlond Clift, 1937 50
3 Johnny Pesky, 1949 48
Paul Molitor, 1982 48
5 Sammy Hale, 1927 46
Clete Boyer, 1965 46
Gary Gaetti, 1983 46
8 Eddie Yost, 1950 45
Frank Malzone, 1961 45
Darrell Evans, 1974 45
Jeff Cirillo, 1998 45

OUTFIELD
1 Happy Felsch, 1919 15
2 Jimmy Sheckard, 1899 14
3 Tom Brown, 1893 13
4 Tom Brown, 1886 12
Tommy McCarthy, 1888 12
Jimmy Bannon, 1894 12
Mike Griffin, 1895 12
Danny Green, 1899 12
Cy Seymour, 1905 12
Ginger Beaumont, 1907 ... 12
Ty Cobb, 1907 12
Tris Speaker, 1909 12
Jimmy Sheckard, 1911 12
Tris Speaker, 1914 12
Mel Ott, 1929 12
16 Sam Thompson, 1886 11
Tommy McCarthy, 1889 11
Billy Sunday, 1890 11
Sam Thompson, 1896 11
Bill Lange, 1899 11
Fielder Jones, 1902 11
Jimmy Sebring, 1903 11
Phil Geier, 1904 11
Ben Koehler, 1905 11
Burt Shotton, 1913 11
Chief Wilson, 1914 11

CATCHER
1 Steve O'Neill, 1916 36
2 Frankie Hayes, 1945 29
3 Ray Schalk, 1916 25
Yogi Berra, 1951 25
5 Jack Lapp, 1915 23
Muddy Ruel, 1924 23
Tom Haller, 1968 23
8 Steve O'Neill, 1914 22
Bob O'Farrell, 1922 22
10 Gabby Hartnett, 1927 21
Wes Westrum, 1950 21

PITCHER
1 Bob Lemon, 1953 15
2 Eddie Rommel, 1924 12
Curt Davis, 1934 12
Randy Jones, 1976 12
5 Scott Perry, 1919 11
Tom Rogers, 1919 11
Art Nehf, 1920 11
Burleigh Grimes, 1925 11
Gene Bearden, 1948 11
Kirk Rueter, 2001 11

PUTOUTS (OUTFIELD)

OUTFIELD
1 Taylor Douthit, 1928 547
2 Richie Ashburn, 1951 538
3 Richie Ashburn, 1949 514
4 Chet Lemon, 1977 512
5 Dwayne Murphy, 1980 507
6 Dom DiMaggio, 1948 503
Richie Ashburn, 1956 503
8 Richie Ashburn, 1957 502
9 Richie Ashburn, 1953 496
10 Richie Ashburn, 1958 495
11 Andruw Jones, 1999 .. 492
12 Jim Busby, 1954 491
13 Omar Moreno, 1979 490
14 Baby Doll Jacobson, 1924 488
Bobby Thomson, 1949 ... 488
Al Bumbry, 1980 488
17 Mike Cameron, 2003 . 485
18 Lloyd Waner, 1931 484
19 Richie Ashburn, 1954 483
20 Jim Busby, 1953 482
Willie Wilson, 1980 482
22 Omar Moreno, 1980 479
23 Tom Oliver, 1930 477
24 Dwayne Murphy, 1984 474
25 Lloyd Moseby, 1984 473
26 Jim Busby, 1952 472
27 Rick Manning, 1983 471
28 Lenny Dykstra, 1993 469
29 Johnny Lindell, 1944 468
30 Rick Bosetti, 1979 466
31 Ruppert Jones, 1977 465
Kirby Puckett, 1985 465
33 Ken Henderson, 1974 462
Gary Pettis, 1986 462
35 Andruw Jones, 2001 .. 461
36 George Wright, 1983 460
Torii Hunter, 2001 460
38 Wally Berger, 1935 458
39 Wally Berger, 1931 457
Vince DiMaggio, 1943 457
41 Jim Piersall, 1956 455
Gorman Thomas, 1980 ... 455
43 Sam Rice, 1920 454
44 Ruppert Jones, 1979 453
45 Dwayne Murphy, 1982 452
Darin Erstad, 2002 452
47 Carden Gillenwater, 1945 451
48 Max Carey, 1923 450
Lloyd Waner, 1929 450
Sam West, 1932 450
Sam Chapman, 1949 450
Kirby Puckett, 1988 450
53 Max Carey, 1922 449
Eddie Brown, 1925 449
Sam West, 1935 449
Buster Adams, 1944 449
57 Willie Mays, 1954 448
Brett Butler, 1984 448
59 Al Simmons, 1925 447
Gus Bell, 1953 447
Paul Blair, 1974 447
62 Johnny Mostil, 1925 446
Dain Clay, 1945 446
Cesar Cedeno, 1974 446
65 Garry Maddox, 1978 444
Joe Carter, 1988 444
Robin Yount, 1988 444
68 Doc Cramer, 1936 443
Devon White, 1992 443
70 Taylor Douthit, 1929 442
Sam West, 1936 442
Dave Philley, 1952 442
Bill Tuttle, 1955 442
74 Joe DiMaggio, 1948 441
Garry Maddox, 1976 441
76 Max Carey, 1917 440
Happy Felsch, 1917 440
Taylor Douthit, 1926 440
Johnny Mostil, 1926 440
Ron LeFlore, 1978 440
81 Dom DiMaggio, 1942 439
Gorman Thomas, 1983 ... 439
Rickey Henderson, 1985 439
Lenny Dykstra, 1990 439
Devon White, 1991 439
86 Jigger Statz, 1923 438
Kirby Puckett, 1984 438
Kirby Puckett, 1989 438
Ray Lankford, 1992 438
Andruw Jones, 2000 .. 438
91 Billy North, 1974 437
Brett Butler, 1985 437
Rocco Baldelli, 2003 . 437
94 Harry Craft, 1938 436
Darrin Jackson, 1992 436
96 Gorman Thomas, 1979 ... 435
Andre Dawson, 1983 435
98 Stan Spence, 1944 434
Brett Butler, 1986 434
100 Tom Oliver, 1931 433
Fred Schulte, 1933 433
Garry Maddox, 1979 433
Lance Johnson, 1992 433

PUTOUTS/GAME (OUTFIELD)

OUTFIELD

1	Taylor Douthit, 1928	3.55
2	Fred Treacey, 1876	3.54
3	Richie Ashburn, 1951	3.49
4	Thurman Tucker, 1944	3.45
5	Chet Lemon, 1977	3.44
6	Kirby Puckett, 1984	3.42
7	Richie Ashburn, 1949	3.34
8	Irv Noren, 1951	3.33
9	Sam West, 1935	3.33
10	**Mike Cameron, 2003**	**3.30**
11	Jim Busby, 1952	3.28
12	Richie Ashburn, 1956	3.27
13	Richie Ashburn, 1958	3.26
14	Lloyd Waner, 1932	3.25
15	Dom DiMaggio, 1948	3.25
16	Carden Gillenwater, 1945	3.22
17	Richie Ashburn, 1957	3.22
18	Jim Busby, 1953	3.21
19	Baby Doll Jacobson, 1924	3.21
20	Dwayne Murphy, 1980	3.21
21	Taylor Douthit, 1926	3.19
22	Richie Ashburn, 1953	3.18
23	Andre Dawson, 1981	3.17
24	Taylor Douthit, 1927	3.17
25	Jim Busby, 1954	3.17
26	Billy North, 1974	3.17
27	Sam West, 1931	3.17
28	Lloyd Waner, 1931	3.16
29	**Darin Erstad, 2002**	**3.16**
30	Richie Ashburn, 1954	3.16
31	Sam West, 1932	3.15
32	Terry Moore, 1936	3.14
33	Johnny Lindell, 1944	3.14
34	Devon White, 1988	3.14
35	**Torii Hunter, 2001**	**3.13**
36	Bobby Thomson, 1949	3.13
37	Sam Chapman, 1948	3.12
38	Rickey Henderson, 1985	3.11
39	Fred Schulte, 1929	3.11
40	Billy North, 1973	3.11
41	Max Carey, 1921	3.10
42	Dwayne Murphy, 1984	3.10
43	Tom Oliver, 1930	3.10
44	Garry Maddox, 1979	3.09
45	Kiddo Davis, 1932	3.09
46	Rick Bosetti, 1978	3.09
47	Dom DiMaggio, 1947	3.08
48	Lance Johnson, 1994	3.08
49	Dwayne Murphy, 1981	3.08
50	Dwayne Murphy, 1982	3.07
51	Wally Berger, 1935	3.07
52	Ruppert Jones, 1978	3.07
53	Garry Maddox, 1976	3.06
54	Sam Chapman, 1950	3.06
55	Rickey Henderson, 1981	3.06
56	Redleg Snyder, 1876	3.05
57	Al Bumbry, 1980	3.05
	Chet Lemon, 1984	3.05
59	Jim Rivera, 1952	3.05
60	Fred Schulte, 1933	3.05
61	Mike Mansell, 1879	3.04
62	Billy North, 1975	3.04
63	Jigger Statz, 1927	3.04
64	**Andruw Jones, 1999**	**3.04**
65	Lloyd Moseby, 1984	3.03
66	Willie Wilson, 1980	3.03
67	Amos Otis, 1981	3.03
68	Terry Moore, 1935	3.03
69	Omar Moreno, 1979	3.02
70	Thurman Tucker, 1943	3.02
71	Gary Pettis, 1986	3.02
72	Gary Pettis, 1985	3.02
73	Mike Kreevich, 1939	3.01
74	Johnny Groth, 1953	3.01
75	Johnny Mostil, 1928	3.01
76	Kiddo Davis, 1934	3.00
	Ruppert Jones, 1977	3.00
	Otis Nixon, 1992	3.00
	Bernie Williams, 1995	**3.00**
80	Johnny Mostil, 1926	2.99
81	Mickey Rivers, 1976	2.99
82	Willie Wilson, 1984	2.99
83	Sam Chapman, 1939	2.99
84	Jimmy Welsh, 1930	2.99
85	Sam West, 1936	2.99
86	Wally Judnich, 1946	2.99
87	Taylor Douthit, 1931	2.98
88	Freddie Lindstrom, 1933	2.98
89	Mike Kreevich, 1938	2.98
90	Rick Miller, 1979	2.98
91	**Mike Cameron, 1997**	**2.98**
92	Rick Manning, 1983	2.98
93	Lloyd Waner, 1929	2.98
94	Ira Flagstead, 1925	2.98
95	Dave Philley, 1948	2.98
96	Buster Adams, 1944	2.97
97	Mike Kreevich, 1940	2.97
98	Amos Otis, 1974	2.97
99	Eric Davis, 1987	2.97
100	Sam Rice, 1920	2.97

FIELDING RUNS

FIRST BASE

1	Bill Buckner, 1985	25
2	Mark Grace, 1990	25
3	Chick Gandil, 1914	23
4	Fred Tenney, 1905	22
5	Bill Buckner, 1983	22
6	Sid Bream, 1986	21
7	Jeff King, 1997	21
8	Jiggs Donahue, 1907	20
9	Jake Beckley, 1892	20
10	Vic Power, 1960	20

SECOND BASE

1	Glenn Hubbard, 1985	60
2	Bill Mazeroski, 1963	55
3	Frankie Frisch, 1927	49
4	Freddie Maguire, 1928	49
5	Nap Lajoie, 1908	45
6	Hughie Critz, 1933	45
7	**Orlando Hudson, 2003**	**45**
8	Ryne Sandberg, 1983	44
9	Danny Richardson, 1891	43
10	Fred Pfeffer, 1884	43

SHORTSTOP

1	Rabbit Maranville, 1914	50
2	George Davis, 1899	46
3	Ivan DeJesus, 1977	45
4	Dick Bartell, 1936	43
5	Everett Scott, 1921	41
6	Ozzie Guillen, 1988	41
7	Germany Smith, 1885	40
8	Freddie Patek, 1973	40
9	Cal Ripken, 1984	39
10	Jack Glasscock, 1887	39

THIRD BASE

1	Graig Nettles, 1971	46
2	Harlond Clift, 1937	41
3	Billy Shindle, 1892	40
4	Buddy Bell, 1982	38
5	Billy Shindle, 1888	38
6	Arlie Latham, 1884	37
7	Tommy Leach, 1904	36
8	Tim Wallach, 1985	36
9	Lave Cross, 1899	36
10	Terry Pendleton, 1989	35

OUTFIELD

1	Jim Fogarty, 1887	30
2	Tom Brown, 1893	26
3	Tommy McCarthy, 1888	26
4	Jimmy Sheckard, 1903	25
5	Mike Mitchell, 1907	25
6	Richie Ashburn, 1957	24
7	Ed Delahanty, 1893	24
8	Dave Parker, 1977	23
9	Chet Lemon, 1977	23
10	Tris Speaker, 1914	23
11	Dick Johnston, 1887	23
12	Hardy Richardson, 1881	22
13	Johnny Callison, 1962	22
14	Max Carey, 1916	22
15	Richie Ashburn, 1951	21
16	Roberto Clemente, 1958	21
17	Max Carey, 1917	21
18	Chuck Klein, 1930	21
19	Al Kaline, 1958	20
20	**Andruw Jones, 1998**	**20**

CATCHER

1	Bill Holbert, 1883	34
2	**Paul LoDuca, 2003**	**33**
3	Jim Sundberg, 1977	32
4	John Warner, 1897	32
5	**Damian Miller, 2001**	**30**
6	Tom Daly, 1887	28
7	Duke Farrell, 1894	27
8	John Kerins, 1886	27
9	Rick Dempsey, 1979	27
10	Morgan Murphy, 1891	27

PITCHER

1	Ed Walsh, 1907	21
2	Harry Howell, 1905	17
3	Ed Walsh, 1911	14
4	Ed Walsh, 1908	13
5	Will White, 1882	12
6	John Clarkson, 1889	11
7	Tony Mullane, 1882	10
8	Sadie McMahon, 1890	10
9	Carl Mays, 1926	10
10	Ed Walsh, 1910	10

FIELDING WINS

1	Glenn Hubbard, 1985	6.3
2	Bill Mazeroski, 1963	6.1
3	Rabbit Maranville, 1914	5.4
4	Nap Lajoie, 1908	5.3
5	Graig Nettles, 1971	4.9
6	Nap Lajoie, 1907	4.9
7	Freddie Maguire, 1928	4.8
8	Frankie Frisch, 1927	4.8
9	Hughie Critz, 1933	4.8
10	Ryne Sandberg, 1983	4.7
11	Ivan DeJesus, 1977	4.6
12	Dave Shean, 1910	4.6
13	Bill Dahlen, 1908	4.3
14	Bill Mazeroski, 1966	4.3
15	Freddie Patek, 1972	4.3
16	**Orlando Hudson, 2003**	**4.3**
17	Danny Richardson, 1892	4.2
18	Ozzie Guillen, 1988	4.2
19	George Davis, 1899	4.2
20	Dick Bartell, 1936	4.1
21	Glenn Hubbard, 1986	4.1
22	Bill Mazeroski, 1962	4.1
23	Ozzie Smith, 1980	4.1
24	Freddie Patek, 1973	4.1
25	Bobby Knoop, 1964	4.0
26	Danny Richardson, 1891	4.0
27	Nap Lajoie, 1903	4.0
28	**Jamey Carroll, 2006**	**3.9**
29	Dave Bancroft, 1920	3.9
30	Cal Ripken, 1984	3.9
31	Everett Scott, 1921	3.9
32	Art Fletcher, 1915	3.9
33	Joe Cassidy, 1905	3.9
34	Fred Pfeffer, 1884	3.8
35	Miller Huggins, 1905	3.8
36	Rey Sanchez, 2001	3.8
37	Buck Weaver, 1913	3.8
38	Tommy Leach, 1904	3.8
39	Tim Wallach, 1985	3.8
40	Harlond Clift, 1937	3.8
41	Garry Templeton, 1980	3.7
42	Ozzie Smith, 1982	3.7
43	Buddy Bell, 1982	3.7
44	Terry Pendleton, 1989	3.7
45	George McBride, 1908	3.7
46	Bill Mazeroski, 1961	3.7
47	Heinie Wagner, 1908	3.7
48	Fred Pfeffer, 1888	3.7
49	Bill Mazeroski, 1964	3.7
50	Red Schoendienst, 1952	3.7
51	Tim Foli, 1974	3.7
52	George McBride, 1910	3.6
53	Germany Smith, 1885	3.6
54	Lee Tannehill, 1906	3.6
55	Buck Herzog, 1914	3.6
56	Lee Tannehill, 1911	3.6
57	Mickey Doolan, 1914	3.6
58	Buddy Bell, 1981	3.6
59	Spike Owen, 1986	3.6
60	Eddie Mayo, 1944	3.5
61	Billy Shindle, 1888	3.5
62	Zoilo Versalles, 1962	3.5
63	Brooks Robinson, 1967	3.5
64	Donie Bush, 1914	3.5
65	Dick Bartell, 1937	3.5
66	**Neifi Perez, 2000**	**3.5**
67	Garry Templeton, 1978	3.5
68	Clete Boyer, 1962	3.4
69	Bobby Knoop, 1969	3.4
70	Luis Aparicio, 1969	3.4
71	Luis Aparicio, 1960	3.4
72	Mickey Doolan, 1915	3.4
73	Billy Shindle, 1892	3.4
74	Joe Gerhardt, 1890	3.4
75	Horace Clarke, 1968	3.4
76	Buck Herzog, 1915	3.4
77	John Farrell, 1902	3.4
78	Bruno Betzel, 1916	3.4
79	Ron Santo, 1967	3.3
80	Graig Nettles, 1973	3.3
81	Arlie Latham, 1884	3.3
82	Mike Benjamin, 1999	3.3
83	Ozzie Smith, 1984	3.3
84	**Paul LoDuca, 2003**	**3.3**
85	**David Eckstein, 2005**	**3.3**
86	**Vinny Castilla, 1996**	**3.3**
87	Ski Melillo, 1931	3.3
88	Ed Brinkman, 1970	3.3
89	Jack Glasscock, 1889	3.3
90	Cupid Childs, 1896	3.3
91	Jack Glasscock, 1887	3.3
92	Eddie Collins, 1910	3.3
93	Mike Bordick, 1999	3.3
94	Darrell Evans, 1975	3.3
95	Lave Cross, 1899	3.2
96	**Alex Gonzalez, 2001**	**3.2**
97	Dave Cash, 1974	3.2
98	Jim Sundberg, 1977	3.2
99	Roy Smalley, 1979	3.2
100	Ozzie Smith, 1978	3.2

BATTER-FIELDER WINS

1	**Barry Bonds, 2001**	**11.7**
2	**Barry Bonds, 2002**	**11.5**
3	**Barry Bonds, 2004**	**10.7**
4	Babe Ruth, 1923	10.1
5	Babe Ruth, 1921	9.4
	Cal Ripken, 1984	9.4
7	Babe Ruth, 1920	9.3
	Rogers Hornsby, 1924	9.3
9	Nap Lajoie, 1910	8.9
	Rogers Hornsby, 1922	8.9
11	Babe Ruth, 1927	8.8
12	Sammy Sosa, 2001	8.6
13	Babe Ruth, 1926	8.5
	Ted Williams, 1941	8.5
	Ted Williams, 1942	8.5
	Cal Ripken, 1991	8.5
17	Babe Ruth, 1924	8.4
	Lou Gehrig, 1927	8.4
19	**Craig Biggio, 1997**	**8.2**
	Barry Bonds, 2003	**8.2**
21	Nap Lajoie, 1901	8.1
	Nap Lajoie, 1903	8.1
	Babe Ruth, 1931	8.1
	Ted Williams, 1946	8.1
	Mickey Mantle, 1956	8.1
	Joe Morgan, 1975	8.1
27	Nap Lajoie, 1908	8.0
	Mickey Mantle, 1957	8.0
	Barry Bonds, 1993	**8.0**
30	Rogers Hornsby, 1920	7.9
	George Sisler, 1920	7.9
	Lou Gehrig, 1934	7.9
	Barry Bonds, 1992	**7.9**
34	Rogers Hornsby, 1917	7.8
35	Rogers Hornsby, 1921	7.7
	Lou Gehrig, 1930	7.7
	Ron Santo, 1967	7.7
	Rickey Henderson, 1990	7.7
	Jeff Bagwell, 1994	7.7
	Mike Piazza, 1997	**7.7**
41	Nap Lajoie, 1906	7.6
	Babe Ruth, 1930	7.6
	Norm Cash, 1961	7.6
	Ron Santo, 1966	7.6
	Rico Petrocelli, 1969	7.6
	Barry Bonds, 1996	**7.6**
47	Honus Wagner, 1905	7.5
	Lou Boudreau, 1944	7.5
	Mickey Mantle, 1961	7.5
50	Nap Lajoie, 1904	7.4
	Ty Cobb, 1917	7.4
	Harlond Clift, 1937	7.4
	Al Rosen, 1953	7.4
	Joe Morgan, 1973	7.4
	Ken Caminiti, 1996	7.4
	Alex Rodriguez, 2002	**7.4**
57	Tris Speaker, 1914	7.3
	Babe Ruth, 1919	7.3
	Jackie Robinson, 1951	7.3
	Ted Williams, 1957	7.3
	Mike Schmidt, 1974	7.3
62	Honus Wagner, 1906	7.2
	Tris Speaker, 1912	7.2
	Frankie Frisch, 1927	7.2
	Snuffy Stirnweiss, 1945	7.2
	Ted Williams, 1947	7.2
	Stan Musial, 1948	7.2
68	Fred Dunlap, 1884	7.1
	Joe Jackson, 1912	7.1
	Babe Ruth, 1928	7.1
	Lou Boudreau, 1948	7.1
	Ron Santo, 1964	7.1
	Mike Schmidt, 1981	7.1
	Robin Yount, 1982	7.1
	Jeff Bagwell, 1996	7.1
	Mark McGwire, 1998	7.1
	Albert Pujols, 2003	**7.1**
78	Nap Lajoie, 1907	7.0
	Eddie Collins, 1910	7.0
	Eddie Collins, 1913	7.0
	Joe Morgan, 1974	7.0
	Cal Ripken, 1983	7.0
83	Honus Wagner, 1908	6.9
	Eddie Collins, 1914	6.9
	Joe Cronin, 1930	6.9
	Jimmie Foxx, 1933	6.9
	Willie Mays, 1965	6.9
	Carl Yastrzemski, 1967	6.9
	Rod Carew, 1974	6.9
	Toby Harrah, 1975	6.9
	Rickey Henderson, 1985	6.9
	Alex Rodriguez, 2001	**6.9**
93	Cupid Childs, 1890	6.8
	Dan Brouthers, 1892	6.8
	Rogers Hornsby, 1925	6.8
	Rogers Hornsby, 1927	6.8
	Rogers Hornsby, 1929	6.8
	Lou Boudreau, 1943	6.8
	Snuffy Stirnweiss, 1944	6.8
	Willie Mays, 1955	6.8

BATTER-FIELDER WINS

	Mike Schmidt, 1980	6.8
	Gary Carter, 1982	6.8
	Barry Bonds, 2000	**6.8**
104	Hughie Jennings, 1896	6.7
	Honus Wagner, 1907	6.7
	Jimmie Foxx, 1932	6.7
	Rod Carew, 1975	6.7
	Joe Morgan, 1976	6.7
	Barry Bonds, 1998	**6.7**
	Alex Rodriguez, 2003	**6.7**
111	Art Devlin, 1906	6.6
	Ty Cobb, 1911	6.6
	Frank Baker, 1913	6.6
	Eddie Collins, 1915	6.6
	Arky Vaughan, 1935	6.6
	Lou Gehrig, 1936	6.6
	Joe DiMaggio, 1941	6.6
	Hank Aaron, 1959	6.6
	Ryne Sandberg, 1984	6.6
	George Brett, 1985	6.6
	Alex Rodriguez, 2000	**6.6**
	Miguel Tejada, 2004	**6.6**
123	Joe Jackson, 1911	6.5
	Frank Baker, 1912	6.5
	Tris Speaker, 1913	6.5
	Tris Speaker, 1923	6.5
	Babe Ruth, 1932	6.5
	Eddie Lake, 1945	6.5
	Red Schoendienst, 1953	6.5
	Willie McCovey, 1969	6.5
	Willie McCovey, 1970	6.5
	Johnny Bench, 1972	6.5
	Rod Carew, 1977	6.5
	George Brett, 1980	6.5
	Wade Boggs, 1987	6.5
136	Eddie Collins, 1912	6.4
	Mel Ott, 1938	6.4
	Arky Vaughan, 1938	6.4
	Ted Williams, 1949	6.4
	Ernie Banks, 1959	6.4
	Bobby Grich, 1975	6.4
	Mike Schmidt, 1977	6.4
	Mike Schmidt, 1983	6.4
	Wade Boggs, 1988	6.4
	Barry Bonds, 1990	**6.4**
	Jeff Kent, 2000	**6.4**
	Scott Rolen, 2004	**6.4**
148	Hughie Jennings, 1895	6.3
	Cupid Childs, 1896	6.3
	Ty Cobb, 1910	6.3
	George Sisler, 1922	6.3
	Luke Appling, 1943	6.3
	Frank Robinson, 1966	6.3
	Carl Yastrzemski, 1968	6.3
	Reggie Jackson, 1969	6.3
	Darrell Evans, 1973	6.3
	Mike Schmidt, 1982	6.3
	Jason Giambi, 2001	**6.3**
	Derrek Lee, 2005	**6.3**
160	Joe Sewell, 1923	6.2
	Willie Mays, 1954	6.2
	Willie Mays, 1958	6.2
	Ron Santo, 1965	6.2
	Dickie Thon, 1983	6.2
	Kevin Mitchell, 1989	6.2
	Barry Larkin, 1991	6.2
	Barry Bonds, 1997	**6.2**
	Todd Helton, 2004	**6.2**
169	George Davis, 1899	6.1
	Rogers Hornsby, 1928	6.1
	Jimmie Foxx, 1934	6.1
	Charlie Gehringer, 1936	6.1
	Dick Bartell, 1937	6.1
	Stan Musial, 1951	6.1
	Eddie Mathews, 1953	6.1
	Willie Mays, 1962	6.1
	Alan Trammell, 1987	6.1
	Roberto Alomar, 1996	6.1
179	Fred Pfeffer, 1884	6.0
	Ed Delahanty, 1896	6.0
	Ty Cobb, 1909	6.0
	Harry Heilmann, 1923	6.0
	Frankie Frisch, 1924	6.0
	Lou Gehrig, 1931	6.0
	Charlie Gehringer, 1934	6.0
	Joe Medwick, 1937	6.0
	Nellie Fox, 1957	6.0
	Eddie Mathews, 1959	6.0
	Ernie Banks, 1960	6.0
	Willie Mays, 1963	6.0
	Bobby Grich, 1974	6.0
	Gary Sheffield, 1992	**6.0**
	Barry Larkin, 1996	6.0
	Jeff Bagwell, 1997	6.0
	Ken Griffey Jr., 1997	**6.0**
	Mike Piazza, 1998	**6.0**
	Alex Rodriguez, 2005	**6.0**
198	17 players tied	5.9

THE SEASON LEADERS

WINS

1	Charley Radbourn, 1884	59
2	John Clarkson, 1885	53
3	Guy Hecker, 1884	52
4	John Clarkson, 1889	49
5	Charley Radbourn, 1883	48
	Charlie Buffinton, 1884	48
7	Al Spalding, 1876	47
	John Ward, 1879	47
9	Jim Galvin, 1883	46
	Jim Galvin, 1884	46
	Matt Kilroy, 1887	46
12	George Bradley, 1876	45
	Jim McCormick, 1880	45
	Silver King, 1888	45
15	Mickey Welch, 1885	44
	Bill Hutchison, 1891	44
17	Billy Taylor, 1884	43
	Tommy Bond, 1879	43
	Will White, 1879	43
	Larry Corcoran, 1880	43
	Will White, 1883	43
22	Lady Baldwin, 1886	42
	Tim Keefe, 1886	42
	Bill Hutchison, 1890	42
25	Charlie Sweeney, 1884	41
	Tim Keefe, 1883	41
	Dave Foutz, 1886	41
	Ed Morris, 1886	41
	Jack Chesbro, 1904	41
30	Jim McCormick, 1884	40
	Tommy Bond, 1877	40
	Tommy Bond, 1878	40
	Will White, 1882	40
	Bill Sweeney, 1884	40
	Bob Caruthers, 1885	40
	Bob Caruthers, 1889	40
	Ed Walsh, 1908	40
38	John Ward, 1880	39
	Mickey Welch, 1884	39
	Ed Morris, 1885	39
41	Toad Ramsey, 1886	38
	John Clarkson, 1887	38
	Kid Gleason, 1890	38
44	Jim Galvin, 1879	37
	Jim Whitney, 1883	37
	Tim Keefe, 1884	37
	Jack Lynch, 1884	37
	Toad Ramsey, 1887	37
	Christy Mathewson, 1908	37
50	Jim McCormick, 1882	36
	Tony Mullane, 1884	36
	John Clarkson, 1886	36
	Sadie McMahon, 1890	36
	Bill Hutchison, 1892	36
	Cy Young, 1892	36
	Frank Killen, 1893	36
	Amos Rusie, 1894	36
	Walter Johnson, 1913	36
59	Jim Devlin, 1877	35
	Tony Mullane, 1883	35
	Larry Corcoran, 1884	35
	Tim Keefe, 1887	35
	Tim Keefe, 1888	35
	Ed Seward, 1888	35
	Silver King, 1889	35
	Sadie McMahon, 1891	35
	Kid Nichols, 1892	35
	Jack Stivetts, 1892	35
	Cy Young, 1895	35
	Joe McGinnity, 1904	35
71	Mickey Welch, 1880	34
	Larry Corcoran, 1883	34
	Ed Morris, 1884	34
	Will White, 1884	34
	Elmer Smith, 1887	34
	Scott Stratton, 1890	34
	George Haddock, 1891	34
	Kid Nichols, 1893	34
	Cy Young, 1893	34
	Joe Wood, 1912	34
81	Charley Radbourn, 1882	33
	Dave Foutz, 1885	33
	Henry Porter, 1885	33
	Mickey Welch, 1886	33
	Tony Mullane, 1886	33
	John Clarkson, 1888	33
	Mark Baldwin, 1890	33
	John Clarkson, 1891	33
	Amos Rusie, 1891	33
	Jack Stivetts, 1891	33
	Amos Rusie, 1893	33
	Jouett Meekin, 1894	33
	Cy Young, 1901	33
	Christy Mathewson, 1904	33
	Walter Johnson, 1912	33
	Grover Alexander, 1916	33
97	10 players tied	32

WINS BY ERA

1988–2006

1	Bob Welch, 1990	27
2	Frank Viola, 1988	24
	John Smoltz, 1996	**24**
	Randy Johnson, 2002	**24**
5	Orel Hershiser, 1988	23
	Danny Jackson, 1988	23
	Bret Saberhagen, 1989	23
	Pedro Martinez, 1999	**23**
	Curt Schilling, 2002	**23**
	Barry Zito, 2002	**23**

1973–87

1	Catfish Hunter, 1974	25
	Fergie Jenkins, 1974	25
	Ron Guidry, 1978	25
	Steve Stone, 1980	25
5	Ron Bryant, 1973	24
	Wilbur Wood, 1973	24
	Steve Carlton, 1980	24
	La Marr Hoyt, 1983	24
	Doc Gooden, 1985	24
	Roger Clemens, 1986	**24**

1961–72

1	Denny McLain, 1968	31
2	Sandy Koufax, 1966	27
	Steve Carlton, 1972	27
4	Sandy Koufax, 1965	26
	Juan Marichal, 1968	26
6	Whitey Ford, 1961	25
	Don Drysdale, 1962	25
	Sandy Koufax, 1963	25
	Juan Marichal, 1963	25
	Juan Marichal, 1966	25
	Jim Kaat, 1966	25
	Tom Seaver, 1969	25
	Mickey Lolich, 1971	25

1943–60

1	Hal Newhouser, 1944	29
2	Robin Roberts, 1952	28
3	Dizzy Trout, 1944	27
	Don Newcombe, 1956	27
5	Hal Newhouser, 1946	26
	Bob Feller, 1946	26
7	Hal Newhouser, 1945	25
	Dave Ferriss, 1946	25
	Mel Parnell, 1949	25
10	Johnny Sain, 1948	24
	Bobby Shantz, 1952	24

1921–42

1	Lefty Grove, 1931	31
2	Dizzy Dean, 1934	30
3	Dazzy Vance, 1924	28
	Lefty Grove, 1930	28
	Dizzy Dean, 1935	28
6	Carl Mays, 1921	27
	Urban Shocker, 1921	27
	Eddie Rommel, 1922	27
	Dolf Luque, 1923	27
	George Uhle, 1926	27
	Bucky Walters, 1939	27
	Bob Feller, 1940	27

1901–20

1	Jack Chesbro, 1904	41
2	Ed Walsh, 1908	40
3	Christy Mathewson, 1908	37
4	Walter Johnson, 1913	36
5	Joe McGinnity, 1904	35
6	Joe Wood, 1912	34
7	Cy Young, 1901	33
	Christy Mathewson, 1904	33
	Walter Johnson, 1912	33
	Grover Alexander, 1916	33

1893–1900

1	Frank Killen, 1893	36
	Amos Rusie, 1894	36
3	Cy Young, 1895	35
4	Kid Nichols, 1893	34
	Cy Young, 1893	34
6	Amos Rusie, 1893	33
	Jouett Meekin, 1894	33
8	Kid Nichols, 1894	32
9	Pink Hawley, 1895	31
	Bill Hoffer, 1895	31
	Kid Nichols, 1897	31
	Kid Nichols, 1898	31

1876–92

1	Charley Radbourn, 1884	59
2	John Clarkson, 1885	53
3	Guy Hecker, 1884	52
4	John Clarkson, 1889	49
5	Charley Radbourn, 1883	48
	Charlie Buffinton, 1884	48
7	Al Spalding, 1876	47
	John Ward, 1879	47
9	Jim Galvin, 1883	46
	Jim Galvin, 1884	46
	Matt Kilroy, 1887	46

LOSSES

1	John Coleman, 1883	48
2	Will White, 1880	42
3	Larry McKeon, 1884	41
4	George Bradley, 1879	40
	Jim McCormick, 1879	40
6	Henry Porter, 1888	37
	Kid Carsey, 1891	37
	George Cobb, 1892	37
9	Stump Wiedman, 1886	36
	Bill Hutchison, 1892	36
11	Jim Devlin, 1876	35
	Jim Galvin, 1880	35
	Fleury Sullivan, 1884	35
	Adonis Terry, 1884	35
	Hardie Henderson, 1885	35
	Red Donahue, 1897	35
17	Bobby Mathews, 1876	34
	Bob Barr, 1884	34
	Matt Kilroy, 1886	34
	Al Mays, 1887	34
	Mark Baldwin, 1889	34
	Amos Rusie, 1890	34
23	Hardie Henderson, 1883	33
	Dupee Shaw, 1884	33
	Harry McCormick, 1879	33
	Jim Whitney, 1881	33
	Lee Richmond, 1882	33
	Frank Mountain, 1883	33
	Jersey Bakely, 1888	33
30	Lee Richmond, 1880	32
	John Harkins, 1884	32
	Jim Whitney, 1885	32
	Jim Whitney, 1886	32
34	Sam Weaver, 1878	31
	Will White, 1879	31
	Charley Radbourn, 1886	31
	Dupee Shaw, 1886	31
	Billy Crowell, 1887	31
	Amos Rusie, 1892	31
40	Mickey Welch, 1880	30
	Jim McCormick, 1881	30
	Jim McCormick, 1882	30
	Jersey Bakely, 1884	30
	Jack Lynch, 1886	30
	Phenomenal Smith, 1887	30
	Toad Ramsey, 1888	30
	John Ewing, 1889	30
	Ed Beatin, 1890	30
	Ted Breitenstein, 1895	30
	Jim Hughey, 1899	30
51	Tommy Bond, 1880	29
	Doc Landis, 1882	29
	Jim Galvin, 1883	29
	John Healy, 1887	29
	Hank O'Day, 1888	29
	Bert Cunningham, 1888	29
	Red Ehret, 1889	29
	Silver King, 1891	29
	Bill Hart, 1896	29
	Jack Taylor, 1898	29
	Vic Willis, 1905	29
62	Jim McCormick, 1880	28
	Hank O'Day, 1884	28
	Hugh Daily, 1884	28
	Gus Weyhing, 1887	28
	Mark Baldwin, 1891	28
	Duke Esper, 1893	28
	Bill Hill, 1896	28
69	Jim Galvin, 1879	27
	Tim Keefe, 1881	27
	Tim Keefe, 1883	27
	Charlie Buffinton, 1885	27
	Al Mays, 1886	27
	Tony Mullane, 1886	27
	Toad Ramsey, 1886	27
	Toad Ramsey, 1887	27
	Park Swartzel, 1889	27
	Phil Knell, 1891	27
	Mark Baldwin, 1892	27
	Pink Hawley, 1894	27
	Chick Fraser, 1896	27
	Bill Hart, 1897	27
	Willie Sudhoff, 1898	27
	Bill Carrick, 1899	27
	Dummy Taylor, 1901	27
	George Bell, 1910	27
	Paul Derringer, 1933	27
88	20 players tied	26

WINNING PERCENTAGE

1	Roy Face, 1959	.947
2	Johnny Allen, 1937	.938
3	**Greg Maddux, 1995**	**.905**
4	**Randy Johnson, 1995**	**.900**
5	Ron Guidry, 1978	.893
6	Freddie Fitzsimmons, 1940	.889
7	Lefty Grove, 1931	.886
8	Bob Stanley, 1978	.882
9	Preacher Roe, 1951	.880
10	Fred Goldsmith, 1880	.875
11	Joe Wood, 1912	.872
12	David Cone, 1988	.870
	Roger Clemens, 2001	**.870**
14	Orel Hershiser, 1985	.864
15	Bill Donovan, 1907	.862
	Whitey Ford, 1961	.862
17	Doc Gooden, 1985	.857
	Roger Clemens, 1986	**.857**
19	**Pedro Martinez, 1999**	**.852**
20	Chief Bender, 1914	.850
	John Smoltz, 1998	**.850**
22	Lefty Grove, 1930	.848
23	**Mike Hampton, 1999**	**.846**
24	Tom Hughes, 1916	.842
	Emil Yde, 1924	.842
	Schoolboy Rowe, 1940	.842
	Sandy Consuegra, 1954	.842
	Ralph Terry, 1961	.842
	Ron Perranoski, 1963	.842
30	Lefty Gomez, 1934	.839
31	Bill Hoffer, 1895	.838
	Denny McLain, 1968	.838
33	Walter Johnson, 1913	.837
34	Henry Boyle, 1884	.833
	King Cole, 1910	.833
	Spud Chandler, 1943	.833
	Hoyt Wilhelm, 1952	.833
	Sandy Koufax, 1963	.833
	Randy Johnson, 1997	**.833**
	Pedro Martinez, 2002	**.833**
41	Charley Radbourn, 1884	.831
42	**Randy Johnson, 2002**	**.828**
43	Ed Reulbach, 1906	.826
	Elmer Riddle, 1941	.826
	Greg Maddux, 1997	**.826**
46	Jay Hughes, 1899	.824
	Jack Chesbro, 1902	.824
	Dazzy Vance, 1924	.824
49	Chief Bender, 1910	.821
	Bob Purkey, 1962	.821
	Barry Zito, 2002	**.821**
52	Sal Maglie, 1950	.818
	Bob Welch, 1990	.818
	Mark Portugal, 1993	.818
	David Wells, 1998	**.818**
	Roger Clemens, 2004	**.818**
57	Joe McGinnity, 1904	.814
58	Mordecai Brown, 1906	.813
	Russ Ford, 1910	.813
	Eddie Plank, 1912	.813
	Carl Hubbell, 1936	.813
62	Dizzy Dean, 1934	.811
63	Ed Reulbach, 1907	.810
	Doc Crandall, 1910	.810
	Johnny Allen, 1932	.810
	Ted Wilks, 1944	.810
	Phil Niekro, 1982	.810
	Jimmy Key, 1994	.810
	Paul Abbott, 2001	.810
70	Alvin Crowder, 1928	.808
	Bobo Newsom, 1940	.808
	Tiny Bonham, 1942	.808
	Larry Jansen, 1947	.808
	Dave McNally, 1971	.808
	Catfish Hunter, 1973	.808
	Chris Carpenter, 2005	**.808**
77	Christy Mathewson, 1909	.806
	Howie Camnitz, 1909	.806
	Dave Ferriss, 1946	.806
	Juan Marichal, 1966	.806
81	Eddie Cicotte, 1919	.806
82	Mickey Welch, 1885	.800
	Ed Doheny, 1902	.800
	Sam Leever, 1905	.800
	Bert Humphries, 1913	.800
	Stan Coveleski, 1925	.800
	Firpo Marberry, 1931	.800
	Robin Roberts, 1952	.800
	Ed Lopat, 1953	.800
	Don Newcombe, 1955	.800
	Jim Palmer, 1969	.800
	John Candelaria, 1977	.800
	Larry Gura, 1978	.800
	Tommy Greene, 1993	.800
	Denny Neagle, 1997	.800
96	Al Spalding, 1876	.797
97	Don Newcombe, 1956	.794
98	Jocko Flynn, 1886	.793
	Ellis Kinder, 1949	.793
	Sal Maglie, 1951	.793
	Bret Saberhagen, 1989	.793

GAMES

1	Mike Marshall, 1974	106
2	Kent Tekulve, 1979	94
	Salomon Torres, 2006	**94**
4	Mike Marshall, 1973	92
5	Kent Tekulve, 1978	91
6	Wayne Granger, 1969	90
	Mike Marshall, 1979	90
	Kent Tekulve, 1987	90
9	Mark Eichhorn, 1987	89
	Julian Tavarez, 1997	**89**
	Steve Kline, 2001	**89**
	Paul Quantrill, 2003	89
	Jim Brower, 2004	**89**
14	Wilbur Wood, 1968	88
	Mike Myers, 1997	**88**
	Sean Runyan, 1998	88
17	Rob Murphy, 1987	87
18	Paul Quantrill, 2002	86
	Oscar Villarreal, 2003	**86**
	Ray King, 2004	**86**
	Paul Quantrill, 2004	86
	Scott Eyre, 2005	**86**
23	Kent Tekulve, 1982	85
	Frank Williams, 1987	85
	Mitch Williams, 1987	85
	Matt Capps, 2006	**85**
	Jon Rauch, 2006	**85**
28	Ted Abernathy, 1965	84
	Enrique Romo, 1979	84
	Dick Tidrow, 1980	84
	Dan Quisenberry, 1985	84
	Stan Belinda, 1997	84
	Graeme Lloyd, 2001	84
	Billy Koch, 2002	84
	Rheal Cormier, 2004	**84**
	Chris Reitsma, 2004	**84**
	Salomon Torres, 2004	**84**
	Bob Howry, 2006	**84**
39	Ken Sanders, 1971	83
	Craig Lefferts, 1986	83
	Eddie Guardado, 1996	**83**
	Mike Myers, 1996	**83**
	Steve Kline, 2000	**83**
	Kelly Wunsch, 2000	83
	Octavio Dotel, 2002	**83**
	Scott Eyre, 2004	**83**
	Mike Stanton, 2004	**83**
	Scott Proctor, 2006	**83**
49	Eddie Fisher, 1965	82
	Bill Campbell, 1983	82
	Juan Agosto, 1990	82
	Paul Quantrill, 1998	82
	Steve Kline, 1999	**82**
	Jeff Fassero, 2001	**82**
	Ray King, 2001	**82**
	Mike Stanton, 2006	**82**
57	Ugueth Urbina, 2005	81
	John Wyatt, 1964	81
	Dale Murray, 1976	81
	Jeff Robinson, 1987	81
	Duane Ward, 1991	81
	Joe Boever, 1992	81
	Kenny Rogers, 1992	**81**
	Mike Jackson, 1993	81
	Brad Clontz, 1996	81
	Mike Stanton, 1996	**81**
	Rod Beck, 1998	81
	Greg Swindell, 1998	81
	J.C. Romero, 2002	**81**
	Luis Ayala, 2004	81
	Mike Timlin, 2005	**81**
	Todd Coffey, 2006	**81**
	Geoff Geary, 2006	**81**
	Chad Qualls, 2006	**81**
75	Mudcat Grant, 1970	80
	Pedro Borbon, 1973	80
	Willie Hernandez, 1984	80
	Mitch Williams, 1986	80
	Doug Jones, 1992	80
	Greg Harris, 1993	80
	Turk Wendell, 1999	80
	Felix Rodriguez, 2001	**80**
	David Weathers, 2001	**80**
	Paul Quantrill, 2001	80
	Tim Worrell, 2002	**80**
	Ray King, 2003	**80**
	Tom Martin, 2003	**80**
	Brad Lidge, 2004	**80**
	Tom Gordon, 2004	**80**
	Scott Schoeneweis, 2005	**80**
91	20 players tied	79

GAMES BY ERA

1988–2006

1	**Salomon Torres, 2006**	**94**
2	**Julian Tavarez, 1997**	**89**
	Steve Kline, 2001	**89**
	Paul Quantrill, 2003	89
	Jim Brower, 2004	**89**
6	**Mike Myers, 1997**	**88**
	Sean Runyan, 1998	88
8	Paul Quantrill, 2002	86
	Oscar Villarreal, 2003	**86**
	Ray King, 2004	**86**
	Paul Quantrill, 2004	86
	Scott Eyre, 2005	**86**

1973–87

1	Mike Marshall, 1974	106
2	Kent Tekulve, 1979	94
3	Mike Marshall, 1973	92
4	Kent Tekulve, 1978	91
5	Mike Marshall, 1979	90
	Kent Tekulve, 1987	90
7	Mark Eichhorn, 1987	89
8	Rob Murphy, 1987	87
9	Kent Tekulve, 1982	85
	Frank Williams, 1987	85
	Mitch Williams, 1987	85

1961–72

1	Wayne Granger, 1969	90
2	Wilbur Wood, 1968	88
3	Ted Abernathy, 1965	84
4	Ken Sanders, 1971	83
5	Eddie Fisher, 1965	82
6	John Wyatt, 1964	81
7	Mudcat Grant, 1970	80
8	Dick Radatz, 1964	79
9	Hal Woodeshick, 1965	78
	Ted Abernathy, 1968	78

1943–60

1	Jim Konstanty, 1950	74
2	Hoyt Wilhelm, 1952	71
3	Ace Adams, 1943	70
	Mike Fornieles, 1960	70
5	Ellis Kinder, 1953	69
	Don Elston, 1958	69
7	Hoyt Wilhelm, 1953	68
	Roy Face, 1956	68
	Roy Face, 1960	68
10	Andy Karl, 1945	67
	Turk Lown, 1957	67
	Gerry Staley, 1959	67

1921–42

1	Firpo Marberry, 1926	64
2	Clint Brown, 1939	61
	Ace Adams, 1942	61
4	Garland Braxton, 1927	58
	Russ Van Atta, 1935	58
6	Eddie Rommel, 1923	56
	Firpo Marberry, 1927	56
	Hugh Mulcahy, 1937	56
9	Firpo Marberry, 1925	55
	Bump Hadley, 1931	55
	Jim Walkup, 1935	55

1901–20

1	Ed Walsh, 1908	66
2	Ed Walsh, 1912	62
3	Dave Davenport, 1916	59
4	Ed Walsh, 1907	56
	Christy Mathewson, 1908	56
	Ed Walsh, 1911	56
	Reb Russell, 1916	56
8	Joe McGinnity, 1903	55
	Jack Chesbro, 1904	55
	Dave Davenport, 1915	55

1893–1900

1	Amos Rusie, 1893	56
	Ted Breitenstein, 1894	56
	Pink Hawley, 1895	56
4	Frank Killen, 1893	55
	Ted Breitenstein, 1895	55
6	Amos Rusie, 1894	54
7	Cy Young, 1893	53
	Pink Hawley, 1894	53
	Jouett Meekin, 1894	53
10	Kid Nichols, 1893	52
	Cy Young, 1894	52
	Frank Killen, 1896	52

1876–92

1	Will White, 1879	76
	Jim Galvin, 1883	76
	Charley Radbourn, 1883	76
4	Charley Radbourn, 1884	75
	Guy Hecker, 1884	75
	Bill Hutchison, 1892	75
7	Jim McCormick, 1880	74
	Lee Richmond, 1880	74
9	John Clarkson, 1889	73
10	Jim Galvin, 1884	72

GAMES STARTED BY ERA

1988–2006

1	Dave Stewart, 1988	37
	Tom Browning, 1989	37
	Greg Maddux, 1991	**37**
4	Frank Viola, 1989	36
	Tom Browning, 1988	36
	Rick Reuschel, 1988	36
	Bob Welch, 1988	36
	Jose DeLeon, 1989	36
	Mark Gubicza, 1989	36
	Bob Milacki, 1989	36
	Dave Stewart, 1989	36
	Jack Morris, 1990	36
	Dave Stewart, 1990	36
	Tom Browning, 1991	36
	Charlie Leibrandt, 1991	36
	John Smoltz, 1991	**36**
	Mike Moore, 1992	36
	Rick Sutcliffe, 1992	36
	Tom Glavine, 1993	**36**
	Greg Maddux, 1993	**36**
	Jose Rijo, 1993	36
	Cal Eldred, 1993	36
	Mike Moore, 1993	36
	Tom Glavine, 1996	**36**
	Mike Mussina, 1996	**36**
	Scott Erickson, 1998	**36**
	Tom Glavine, 2002	**36**
	Greg Maddux, 2003	**36**
	Roy Halladay, 2003	**36**

1973–87

1	Wilbur Wood, 1973	48
2	Phil Niekro, 1979	44
3	Wilbur Wood, 1975	43
	Phil Niekro, 1977	43
5	Stan Bahnsen, 1973	42
	Mickey Lolich, 1973	42
	Wilbur Wood, 1974	42
	Phil Niekro, 1978	42
9	8 players tied	41

1961–72

1	Wilbur Wood, 1972	49
2	Mickey Lolich, 1971	45
3	Don Drysdale, 1963	42
	Jack Sanford, 1963	42
	Don Drysdale, 1965	42
	Jim Kaat, 1965	42
	Fergie Jenkins, 1969	42
	Wilbur Wood, 1971	42
9	14 players tied	41

1943–60

1	Bob Feller, 1946	42
	Bob Friend, 1956	42
3	Bill Voiselle, 1944	41
	Robin Roberts, 1953	41
5	Dizzy Trout, 1944	40
6	Johnny Sain, 1948	39
	Robin Roberts, 1950	39
	Warren Spahn, 1950	39
	Vern Bickford, 1950	39
	Robin Roberts, 1951	39
	Ron Kline, 1956	39
	Lew Burdette, 1959	39

1921–42

1	George Uhle, 1923	44
2	Stan Coveleski, 1921	40
	George Uhle, 1922	40
	George Caster, 1938	40
	Bobo Newsom, 1938	40
	Bob Feller, 1941	40
7	7 players tied	39

1901–20

1	Jack Chesbro, 1904	51
2	Ed Walsh, 1908	49
3	Joe McGinnity, 1903	48
4	Vic Willis, 1902	46
	Christy Mathewson, 1904	46
	Rube Waddell, 1904	46
	Ed Walsh, 1907	46
	Dave Davenport, 1915	46
9	2 players tied	45

1893–1900

1	Amos Rusie, 1893	52
2	Ted Breitenstein, 1895	51
3	Ted Breitenstein, 1894	50
	Amos Rusie, 1894	50
	Pink Hawley, 1895	50
	Frank Killen, 1896	50
7	Jouett Meekin, 1894	49
8	Frank Killen, 1893	48
9	3 players tied	47

1876–92

1	Will White, 1879	75
	Jim Galvin, 1883	75
3	Jim McCormick, 1880	74
4	Charley Radbourn, 1884	73
	Guy Hecker, 1884	73
6	Jim Galvin, 1884	72
	John Clarkson, 1889	72
8	John Clarkson, 1885	70
	Bill Hutchison, 1892	70
10	Matt Kilroy, 1887	69

COMPLETE GAMES

1	Will White, 1879	75
2	Charley Radbourn, 1884	73
3	Jim McCormick, 1880	72
	Jim Galvin, 1883	72
	Guy Hecker, 1884	72
6	Jim Galvin, 1884	71
7	Tim Keefe, 1883	68
	John Clarkson, 1885	68
	John Clarkson, 1889	68
10	Bill Hutchison, 1892	67
11	Jim Devlin, 1876	66
	Charley Radbourn, 1883	66
	Matt Kilroy, 1886	66
	Toad Ramsey, 1886	66
	Matt Kilroy, 1887	66
16	Jim Galvin, 1879	65
	Jim McCormick, 1882	65
	Bill Hutchison, 1890	65
19	Mickey Welch, 1880	64
	Will White, 1883	64
	Tony Mullane, 1884	64
	Silver King, 1888	64
23	Jim McCormick, 1884	63
	George Bradley, 1876	63
	Charlie Buffinton, 1884	63
	Ed Morris, 1885	63
	Ed Morris, 1886	63
28	Mickey Welch, 1884	62
	Tim Keefe, 1886	62
30	Jim Devlin, 1877	61
	Toad Ramsey, 1887	61
32	Dupee Shaw, 1884	60
	Jersey Bakely, 1888	60
34	Billy Taylor, 1884	59
	Tommy Bond, 1879	59
	Jim McCormick, 1879	59
	John Ward, 1880	59
	John Coleman, 1883	59
	Larry McKeon, 1884	59
	Hardie Henderson, 1885	59
	Amos Rusie, 1892	59
42	Tommy Bond, 1877	58
	John Ward, 1879	58
	Will White, 1880	58
	Bill Sweeney, 1884	58
46	Tommy Bond, 1878	57
	Terry Larkin, 1879	57
	Larry Corcoran, 1880	57
	Lee Richmond, 1880	57
	Jim McCormick, 1881	57
	Jim Whitney, 1881	57
	Frank Mountain, 1883	57
	Larry Corcoran, 1884	57
	Charley Radbourn, 1886	57
	Ed Seward, 1888	57
56	Terry Larkin, 1878	56
	Tim Keefe, 1884	56
	Hugh Daily, 1884	56
	Mickey Welch, 1886	56
	John Clarkson, 1887	56
	Amos Rusie, 1890	56
	Bill Hutchison, 1891	56
63	Bobby Mathews, 1876	55
	Terry Larkin, 1877	55
	George Derby, 1881	55
	Mickey Welch, 1885	55
	Lady Baldwin, 1886	55
	Dave Foutz, 1886	55
	Tony Mullane, 1886	55
	Matt Kilroy, 1889	55
	Sadie McMahon, 1890	55
72	Jim Whitney, 1883	54
	Adonis Terry, 1884	54
	Tim Keefe, 1887	54
	Phenomenal Smith, 1887	54
	Ed Morris, 1888	54
	Mark Baldwin, 1889	54
	Kid Gleason, 1890	54
79	Charlie Sweeney, 1884	53
	Al Spalding, 1876	53
	George Bradley, 1879	53
	Jack Lynch, 1884	53
	Bob Caruthers, 1885	53
	Henry Porter, 1885	53
	Gus Weyhing, 1887	53
	John Clarkson, 1888	53
	Henry Porter, 1888	53
	Ed Beatin, 1890	53
	Mark Baldwin, 1890	53
	Sadie McMahon, 1891	53
91	Will White, 1878	52
	Will White, 1882	52
	Will White, 1884	52
	Ed Seward, 1887	52
	Bob Barr, 1890	52
	Amos Rusie, 1891	52
97	Tony Mullane, 1882	51
	Larry Corcoran, 1883	51
	Guy Hecker, 1883	51
	Fleury Sullivan, 1884	51
	Guy Hecker, 1885	51
	Gus Weyhing, 1891	51

COMPLETE GAMES BY ERA

1988–2006

1	Orel Hershiser, 1988	15
	Danny Jackson, 1988	15
	Jack McDowell, 1991	15
	Curt Schilling, 1998	**15**
5	**Roger Clemens, 1988**	**14**
	Dave Stewart, 1988	14
7	Eric Show, 1988	13
	Bobby Witt, 1988	13
	Roger Clemens, 1991	**13**
	Jack McDowell, 1992	13
	Chuck Finley, 1993	13
	Pedro Martinez, 1997	**13**

1973–87

1	Catfish Hunter, 1975	30
2	Gaylord Perry, 1973	29
	Fergie Jenkins, 1974	29
4	Gaylord Perry, 1974	28
	Rick Langford, 1980	28
6	Mickey Lolich, 1974	27
7	Nolan Ryan, 1973	26
	Nolan Ryan, 1974	26
9	Bert Blyleven, 1973	25
	Luis Tiant, 1974	25
	Jim Palmer, 1975	25
	Gaylord Perry, 1975	25
	Randy Jones, 1976	25

1961–72

1	Juan Marichal, 1968	30
	Fergie Jenkins, 1971	30
	Steve Carlton, 1972	30
4	Mickey Lolich, 1971	29
	Gaylord Perry, 1972	29
6	Bob Gibson, 1968	28
	Denny McLain, 1968	28
	Bob Gibson, 1969	28
9	Sandy Koufax, 1965	27
	Sandy Koufax, 1966	27
	Juan Marichal, 1969	27

1943–60

1	Bob Feller, 1946	36
2	Dizzy Trout, 1944	33
	Robin Roberts, 1953	33
4	Robin Roberts, 1952	30
5	Hal Newhouser, 1945	29
	Hal Newhouser, 1946	29
	Robin Roberts, 1954	29
8	Jim Tobin, 1944	28
	Johnny Sain, 1948	28
	Bob Lemon, 1952	28

1921–42

1	Burleigh Grimes, 1923	33
2	Red Faber, 1921	32
	George Uhle, 1926	32
4	Red Faber, 1922	31
	Wes Ferrell, 1935	31
	Bobo Newsom, 1938	31
	Bucky Walters, 1939	31
	Bob Feller, 1940	31
9	Burleigh Grimes, 1921	30
	Carl Mays, 1921	30
	Urban Shocker, 1921	30
	Dazzy Vance, 1924	30
	Burleigh Grimes, 1924	30
	Ted Lyons, 1927	30
	Thornton Lee, 1941	30

1901–20

1	Jack Chesbro, 1904	48
2	Vic Willis, 1902	45
3	Joe McGinnity, 1903	44
4	George Mullin, 1904	42
	Ed Walsh, 1908	42
6	Noodles Hahn, 1901	41
	Cy Young, 1902	41
	Irv Young, 1905	41
9	Cy Young, 1904	40
10	Joe McGinnity, 1901	39
	Bill Dinneen, 1902	39
	Vic Willis, 1904	39
	Jack Taylor, 1904	39
	Rube Waddell, 1904	39

1893–1900

1	Amos Rusie, 1893	50
2	Ted Breitenstein, 1895	47
3	Ted Breitenstein, 1894	46
4	Amos Rusie, 1894	45
5	Cy Young, 1894	44
	Pink Hawley, 1895	44
	Frank Killen, 1896	44
8	Kid Nichols, 1893	43
	Kid Nichols, 1895	43
10	4 players tied	42

1876–92

1	Will White, 1879	75
2	Charley Radbourn, 1884	73
3	Jim McCormick, 1880	72
	Jim Galvin, 1883	72
	Guy Hecker, 1884	72
6	Jim Galvin, 1884	71
7	Tim Keefe, 1883	68
	John Clarkson, 1885	68
	John Clarkson, 1889	68
10	Bill Hutchison, 1892	67

SHUTOUTS

1	George Bradley, 1876	16
	Grover Alexander, 1916	16
3	Jack Coombs, 1910	13
	Bob Gibson, 1968	13
5	Jim Galvin, 1884	12
	Ed Morris, 1886	12
	Grover Alexander, 1915	12
8	Tommy Bond, 1879	11
	Charley Radbourn, 1884	11
	Dave Foutz, 1886	11
	Christy Mathewson, 1908	11
	Ed Walsh, 1908	11
	Walter Johnson, 1913	11
	Sandy Koufax, 1963	11
	Dean Chance, 1964	11
16	Jim McCormick, 1884	10
	John Clarkson, 1885	10
	Cy Young, 1904	10
	Ed Walsh, 1906	10
	Joe Wood, 1912	10
	Dave Davenport, 1915	10
	Carl Hubbell, 1933	10
	Mort Cooper, 1942	10
	Bob Feller, 1946	10
	Bob Lemon, 1948	10
	Juan Marichal, 1965	10
	Jim Palmer, 1975	10
	John Tudor, 1985	10
29	Tommy Bond, 1878	9
	George Derby, 1881	9
	Cy Young, 1892	9
	Joe McGinnity, 1904	9
	Mordecai Brown, 1906	9
	Addie Joss, 1906	9
	Mordecai Brown, 1908	9
	Addie Joss, 1908	9
	Orval Overall, 1909	9
	Grover Alexander, 1913	9
	Walter Johnson, 1914	9
	Cy Falkenberg, 1914	9
	Babe Ruth, 1916	9
	Stan Coveleski, 1917	9
	Grover Alexander, 1919	9
	Bill Lee, 1938	9
	Bob Porterfield, 1953	9
	Luis Tiant, 1968	9
	Denny McLain, 1969	9
	Don Sutton, 1972	9
	Nolan Ryan, 1972	9
	Bert Blyleven, 1973	9
	Ron Guidry, 1978	9
52	Al Spalding, 1876	8
	John Ward, 1880	8
	Will White, 1882	8
	Charlie Buffinton, 1884	8
	Tim Keefe, 1888	8
	Ben Sanders, 1888	8
	John Clarkson, 1889	8
	Jack Taylor, 1902	8
	Christy Mathewson, 1902	8
	Jack Chesbro, 1902	8
	Rube Waddell, 1904	8
	Christy Mathewson, 1905	8
	Ed Killian, 1905	8
	Lefty Leifield, 1906	8
	Rube Waddell, 1906	8
	Orval Overall, 1907	8
	Christy Mathewson, 1907	8
	Eddie Plank, 1907	8
	Mordecai Brown, 1909	8
	Christy Mathewson, 1909	8
	Ed Walsh, 1909	8
	Russ Ford, 1910	8
	Walter Johnson, 1910	8
	Reb Russell, 1913	8
	Jeff Tesreau, 1914	8
	Al Mamaux, 1915	8
	Jeff Tesreau, 1915	8
	Joe Bush, 1916	8
	Grover Alexander, 1917	8
	Jim Bagby, 1917	8
	Walter Johnson, 1917	8
	Hippo Vaughn, 1918	8
	Walter Johnson, 1918	8
	Carl Mays, 1918	8
	Babe Adams, 1920	8
	Hal Newhouser, 1945	8
	Steve Barber, 1961	8
	Camilo Pascual, 1961	8
	Whitey Ford, 1964	8
	Sandy Koufax, 1965	8
	Don Drysdale, 1968	8
	Juan Marichal, 1969	8
	Vida Blue, 1971	8
	Steve Carlton, 1972	8
	Wilbur Wood, 1972	8
	Fernando Valenzuela, 1981	8
	Doc Gooden, 1985	8
	Orel Hershiser, 1988	8
	Roger Clemens, 1988	**8**
	Tim Belcher, 1989	8

SAVES

1 Bobby Thigpen, 1990 57
2 John Smoltz, 2002........55
Eric Gagne, 2003........55
4 Randy Myers, 1993 53
Trevor Hoffman, 1998 .53
Mariano Rivera, 2004..53
7 Eric Gagne, 2002........52
8 Dennis Eckersley, 1992..... 51
Rod Beck, 1998................ 51
10 Mariano Rivera, 2001..50
11 Francisco Cordero, 2004.... 49
12 Dennis Eckersley, 1990.... 48
Rod Beck, 1993................ 48
Jeff Shaw, 1998................ 48
15 Lee Smith, 1991 47
Armando Benitez, 2004...... 47
Jason Isringhausen, 2004 .. 47
Chad Cordero, 2005 47
Francisco Rodriguez, 2006 . 47
20 Lee Smith, 1993 46
Dave Righetti, 1986........... 46
Bryan Harvey, 1991 46
Jose Mesa, 1995.........46
Tom Gordon, 1998........46
Mike Williams, 2002.......... 46
Trevor Hoffman, 2006 .46
27 Dan Quisenberry, 1983 45
Bruce Sutter, 1984 45
Dennis Eckersley, 1988 45
Bryan Harvey, 1993........... 45
Jeff Montgomery, 1993..... 45
Duane Ward, 1993 45
Randy Myers, 1997 45
Mariano Rivera, 1999..45
Antonio Alfonseca, 2000.... 45
Robb Nen, 2001 45
Kazuhiro Sasaki, 2001 45
Jose Mesa, 2002.........45
Eddie Guardado, 2002.45
John Smoltz, 2003........45
Eric Gagne, 2004........45
Francisco Rodriguez, 2005 . 45
Bob Wickman, 2005.......45
44 Dan Quisenberry, 1984 44
Mark Davis, 1989 44
Jeff Brantley, 1996............ 44
Todd Worrell, 1996 44
Billy Koch, 2002................ 44
Billy Wagner, 2003.......44
John Smoltz, 2004.......44
Joe Nathan, 2004 44
52 Doug Jones, 1990............. 43
Dennis Eckersley, 1991 43
Lee Smith, 1992 43
John Wetteland, 1993....... 43
Mitch Williams, 1993......... 43
John Wetteland, 1996....... 43
Mariano Rivera, 1997..43
Roberto Hernandez, 1999... 43
John Wetteland, 1999....... 43
Trevor Hoffman, 2000 .43
Armando Benitez, 2001...... 43
Trevor Hoffman, 2001 .43
Jeff Shaw, 2001................. 43
Robb Nen, 2002 43
Keith Foulke, 2003.......43
Jose Mesa, 2004..........43
Trevor Hoffman, 2005 .43
Joe Nathan, 2005 43
Mariano Rivera, 2005..43
71 Jeff Reardon, 1988........... 42
Rick Aguilera, 1991 42
Trevor Hoffman, 1996 .42
Jeff Shaw, 1997................. 42
Troy Percival, 1998 42
John Wetteland, 1998....... 42
Todd Jones, 2000 42
Derek Lowe, 2000.........42
Jose Mesa, 2001..........42
Keith Foulke, 2001.......42
Brad Lidge, 2005 42
82 Jeff Reardon, 1985........... 41
Rick Aguilera, 1992 41
Ugueth Urbina, 1999 41
Armando Benitez, 2000...... 41
Robb Nen, 2000 41
Jose Jimenez, 2002 41
Eddie Guardado, 2003.41
Danny Graves, 2004....41
Trevor Hoffman, 2004 .41
Danys Baez, 2005........41
Bobby Jenks, 2006.......41
93 Steve Bedrosian, 1987..... 40
Jeff Reardon, 1991 40
Tom Henke, 1993 40
Robb Nen, 1998................. 40
Mike Jackson, 1998........... 40
Trevor Hoffman, 1999 .40
Troy Percival, 2002 40
Ugueth Urbina, 2002 40
Mariano Rivera, 2003..40
Todd Jones, 2005 40
Billy Wagner, 2006.......40

SAVES BY ERA

1988–2006

1 Bobby Thigpen, 1990 57
2 John Smoltz, 2002........55
Eric Gagne, 2003........55
4 Randy Myers, 1993 53
Trevor Hoffman, 1998 .53
Mariano Rivera, 2004..53
7 Eric Gagne, 2002........52
8 Dennis Eckersley, 1992..... 51
Rod Beck, 1998................ 51
10 Mariano Rivera, 2001..50

1973–87

1 Dave Righetti, 1986.......... 46
2 Dan Quisenberry, 1983 45
Bruce Sutter, 1984 45
4 Dan Quisenberry, 1984 44
5 Jeff Reardon, 1985........... 41
6 Steve Bedrosian, 1987...... 40
7 John Hiller, 1973.............. 38
8 Rollie Fingers, 1978 37
Bruce Sutter, 1979 37
Dan Quisenberry, 1985 37

1961–72

1 Clay Carroll, 1972............. 37
2 Wayne Granger, 1970 35
Sparky Lyle, 1972............. 35
4 Ron Perranoski, 1970....... 34
5 Jack Aker, 1966................ 32
6 Ted Abernathy, 1965......... 31
Ron Perranoski, 1969....... 31
Ken Sanders, 1971........... 31
9 Dave Giusti, 1971 30
10 Luis Arroyo, 1961 29
Dick Radatz, 1964............ 29
Ron Kline, 1965................ 29
Fred Gladding, 1969......... 29
Lindy McDaniel, 1970........ 29
Terry Forster, 1972 29

1943–60

1 Joe Page, 1949 27
Ellis Kinder, 1953............... 27
3 Lindy McDaniel, 1960....... 26
4 Jim Hughes, 1954 24
Roy Face, 1960 24
6 Jim Konstanty, 1950 22
Johnny Sain, 1954............ 22
8 Frank Smith, 1954 20
Roy Face, 1958 20
Ryne Duren, 1958 20

1921–42

1 Firpo Marberry, 1926........ 22
2 Johnny Murphy, 1939 19
3 Clint Brown, 1937 18
Clint Brown, 1939 18
5 Al Benton, 1940................ 17
6 Firpo Marberry, 1924........ 15
Firpo Marberry, 1925........ 15
Jack Quinn, 1931.............. 15
Johnny Murphy, 1941 15
10 Wilcy Moore, 1927............ 13
Garland Braxton, 1927 13
Firpo Marberry, 1932........ 13
Jack Russell, 1933 13
Hugh Casey, 1942............ 13

1901–20

1 Mordecai Brown, 1911 13
Chief Bender, 1913........... 13
3 Larry Cheney, 1913.......... 11
4 Ed Walsh, 1912 10
Hugh Bedient, 1915.......... 10
6 Tom Hughes, 1915 9
Dave Danforth, 1917 9
8 Frank Arellanes, 1909 8
Red Ames, 1916.................. 8
Bob Shawkey, 1916............ 8

1893–1900

1 Tony Mullane, 1894 4
Kid Nichols, 1898 4
Frank Kitson, 1900 4
4 Bill Hawke, 1894................. 3
Win Mercer, 1894 3
Kid Nichols, 1895 3
Tom Parrott, 1895............... 3
Cy Young, 1896 3
Win Mercer, 1897 3
Kid Nichols, 1897 3
Sam Leever, 1899 3

1876–92

1 Jack Manning, 1876 5
Tony Mullane, 1889 5
3 Billy Taylor, 1884................ 4
Herb Goodall, 1890 4
5 Lee Richmond, 1880 3
Tommy Burns, 1885 3
Adonis Terry, 1887 3
Bill Sowders, 1889.............. 3
Hank O'Day, 1890 3
George Hemming, 1890...... 3
John Clarkson, 1891 3
Kid Nichols, 1891 3
Joe Neale, 1891 3
Gus Weyhing, 1892 3

SAVE PERCENTAGE

1 Rod Beck, 1994........... 100.0
Eric Gagne, 2003....100.0
Mike Gonzalez, 2006 .... 100.0
4 Trevor Hoffman, 1998..... 98.1
5 Tom Gordon, 1998.......97.9
6 Randy Myers, 1997 .... 97.8
7 Willie Hernandez, 1984 . 97.0
8 Dennis Eckersley, 1990 . 96.0
9 Jose Mesa, 1995.......95.8
10 Eric Gagne, 2004......95.7
11 Ken Tatum, 1969............ 95.7
12 Billy Wagner, 2001.....95.1
13 Tom Henke, 1995 .... 94.7
Doug Jones, 1997 .... 94.7
Joe Nathan, 2006 .....94.7
16 Dennis Eckersley, 1992 . 94.4
17 Ryan Dempster, 2005 ...... 94.3
18 Billy Wagner, 2003....93.6
Joe Nathan, 2004 .....93.6
20 Armando Benitez, 2001.....93.5
Trevor Hoffman, 2001 ..... 93.5
Trevor Hoffman, 2005 ..... 93.5
23 Keith Foulke, 2001.....93.3
24 John Smoltz, 2002.....93.2
25 Doug Jones, 1994 .... 93.1
26 Trevor Hoffman, 1999 ..... 93.0
27 Mariano Rivera, 2004 ...... 93.0
28 John Franco, 1988 .... 92.9
Billy Wagner, 1999.....92.9
Troy Percival, 2001 .... 92.9
Eric Gagne, 2002......92.9
32 Trevor Hoffman, 2002 ...... 92.7
Billy Wagner, 2005....92.7
34 Clay Carroll, 1972.......... 92.5
Kazuhiro Sasaki, 2000 .. 92.5
36 Mudcat Grant, 1970........ 92.3
Tom Burgmeier, 1980 ..... 92.3
Dave Righetti, 1990 .... 92.3
Rod Beck, 1993............... 92.3
Troy Percival, 1996 .... 92.3
Takashi Saito, 2006..92.3
42 Armando Benitez, 2004.... 92.2
Francisco Rodriguez, 2006 92.2
44 Mike Williams, 2002....... 92.0
45 Tom Henke, 1992 .... 91.9
Mariano Rivera, 2006 ..... 91.9
47 Bryan Harvey, 1993........ 91.8
Mariano Rivera, 1999 ..... 91.8
Antonio Alfonseca, 2000..91.8
John Smoltz, 2003....91.8

BLOWN SAVES

1 Rollie Fingers, 1976 14
Bruce Sutter, 1978 14
Bob Stanley, 1983 14
Ron Davis, 1984............... 14
5 John Hiller, 1976............... 13
Rich Gossage, 1983.......... 13
Jeff Reardon, 1986........... 13
Dan Plesac, 1987 13
Dave Righetti, 1987 13
10 Mike Marshall, 1973 12
Mike Marshall, 1974 12
Enrique Romo, 1978 12
Bruce Sutter, 1985 12
Dan Quisenberry, 1985 12
Matt Young, 1986.............. 12
Lee Smith, 1987 12
Duane Ward, 1989 12
Mark Leiter, 1998.............. 12
Ambiorix Burgos, 2006 12
20 Francisco Cordero, 2006.... 11
Ron Perranoski, 1969 11
Dick Selma, 1970 11
Darold Knowles, 1970 11
Ron Perranoski, 1970....... 11
Rollie Fingers, 1977 11
Bill Campbell, 1977 11
Bill Campbell, 1978 11
Kent Tekulve, 1980 11
Ed Farmer, 1980............... 11
Joey McLaughlin, 1983 11
Rich Gossage, 1984.......... 11
Rich Gossage, 1986.......... 11
Greg Harris, 1986.............. 11
Lance McCullers, 1987..... 11
Tim Burke, 1989 11
Mitch Williams, 1989......... 11
Jeff Reardon, 1989 11
Greg McMichael, 1997 11
Norm Charlton, 1997 11
Scott Radinsky, 1998......... 11
Rick Aguilera, 1998 11
Huston Street, 2006....11
43 52 players tied 10

INNINGS PITCHED

1 Will White, 1879........... 680.0
2 Charley Radbourn, 1884 .. 678.2
3 Guy Hecker, 1884......... 670.2
4 Jim McCormick, 1880.. 657.2
5 Jim Galvin, 1883........... 656.1
6 Jim Galvin, 1884........... 636.1
7 Charley Radbourn, 1883 .. 632.1
8 John Clarkson, 1885 .... 623.0
9 Jim Devlin, 1876........... 622.0
Bill Hutchison, 1892...... 622.0
11 John Clarkson, 1889 .... 620.0
12 Tim Keefe, 1883 .... 619.0
13 Bill Hutchison, 1890...... 603.0
14 Jim McCormick, 1882.. 595.2
15 John Ward, 1880 .... 595.0
16 Jim Galvin, 1879........... 593.0
17 Lee Richmond, 1880 ... 590.2
18 Matt Kilroy, 1887........... 589.1
19 Toad Ramsey, 1886...... 588.2
20 John Ward, 1879 .... 587.0
Charlie Buffinton, 1884 ..... 587.0
22 Silver King, 1888 .... 584.2
23 Matt Kilroy, 1886........... 583.0
24 Ed Morris, 1885............ 581.0
25 Will White, 1883............ 577.0
26 Mickey Welch, 1880...... 574.0
27 George Bradley, 1876.. 573.0
28 Jim McCormick, 1884.. 569.0
29 Tony Mullane, 1884...... 567.0
30 Toad Ramsey, 1887...... 561.0
Bill Hutchison, 1891...... 561.0
32 Jim Devlin, 1877........... 559.0
33 Mickey Welch, 1884...... 557.1
34 Tommy Bond, 1879 ...... 555.1
Ed Morris, 1886............ 555.1
36 Jim Whitney, 1881 .... 552.1
37 Amos Rusie, 1890........ 548.2
38 Jim McCormick, 1879.. 546.1
39 Dupee Shaw, 1884 ...... 543.1
40 Amos Rusie, 1892........ 541.0
41 Hardie Henderson, 1885 .. 539.1
42 John Coleman, 1883 .... 538.1
43 Bill Sweeney, 1884 ...... 538.0
44 Larry Corcoran, 1880 .. 536.1
45 Tim Keefe, 1886 .... 535.0
46 Tommy Bond, 1878 ...... 532.2
Jersey Bakely, 1888 .... 532.2
48 Tony Mullane, 1886...... 529.2
49 Al Spalding, 1876 .... 528.2
50 Jim McCormick, 1881.. 526.0
51 Billy Taylor, 1884.......... 523.0
John Clarkson, 1887 ... 523.0
53 Tommy Bond, 1877 ...... 521.0
54 Ed Seward, 1888.......... 518.2
55 Will White, 1880........... 517.1
56 Larry Corcoran, 1884 .. 516.2
57 Bobby Mathews, 1876. 516.0
58 Jim Whitney, 1883 .... 514.0
59 Mark Baldwin, 1889...... 513.2
60 Terry Larkin, 1879 .... 513.1
61 Larry McKeon, 1884..... 512.0
62 Charley Radbourn, 1886 .. 509.1
63 Sadie McMahon, 1890 509.0
64 Terry Larkin, 1878 .... 506.0
Kid Gleason, 1890........ 506.0
66 Dave Foutz, 1886 .... 504.0
67 Frank Mountain, 1883.. 503.0
Sadie McMahon, 1891 503.0
69 Terry Larkin, 1877 .... 501.0
70 Hugh Daily, 1884 .... 500.2
71 Amos Rusie, 1891........ 500.1
72 Mickey Welch, 1886...... 500.0
73 Jack Lynch, 1884.......... 496.0
74 George Derby, 1881 .... 494.2
75 Bob Barr, 1890 .... 493.1
76 Tommy Bond, 1880 ...... 493.0
77 Charlie Sweeney, 1884 492.0
Mickey Welch, 1885...... 492.0
Mark Baldwin, 1890...... 492.0
80 Phenomenal Smith, 1887 . 491.1
81 George Bradley, 1879.. 487.0
Lady Baldwin, 1886...... 487.0
83 John Clarkson, 1888 ... 483.1
84 Tim Keefe, 1884 .... 483.0
85 Bob Caruthers, 1885 ... 482.1
86 Amos Rusie, 1893........ 482.0
87 Henry Porter, 1885 ...... 481.2
88 Matt Kilroy, 1889.......... 480.2
89 Will White, 1882........... 480.0
Guy Hecker, 1885......... 480.0
Ed Morris, 1888............ 480.0
92 Tim Keefe, 1887 .... 476.2
93 Adonis Terry, 1884 .... 476.0
94 Ed Beatin, 1890............ 474.1
95 Jim Galvin, 1881........... 474.0
Henry Porter, 1888 ...... 474.0
97 Larry Corcoran, 1883 .. 473.2
98 Ed Seward, 1887 .... 470.2
99 Gus Weyhing, 1892...... 469.2
100 Guy Hecker, 1883........ 469.0

INNINGS PITCHED BY ERA

1988–2006

1 Dave Stewart, 1988..... 275.2
2 Randy Johnson, 1999 ... 271.2
3 Roger Clemens, 1991 ... 271.1
4 Mark Gubicza, 1988..... 269.2
5 Curt Schilling, 1998 268.2
6 Greg Maddux, 1992 268.0
7 Orel Hershiser, 1988 ... 267.0
Dave Stewart, 1990..... 267.0
Greg Maddux, 1993 267.0
10 Roy Halladay, 2003.266.0

1973–87

1 Wilbur Wood, 1973...... 359.1
2 Gaylord Perry, 1973..... 344.0
3 Phil Niekro, 1979 .... 342.0
4 Phil Niekro, 1978 .... 334.1
5 Nolan Ryan, 1974........ 332.2
6 Phil Niekro, 1977 .... 330.1
7 Fergie Jenkins, 1974 ... 328.1
8 Catfish Hunter, 1975.... 328.0
9 Nolan Ryan, 1973........ 326.0
10 Bert Blyleven, 1973 ..... 325.0

1961–72

1 Wilbur Wood, 1972...... 376.2
2 Mickey Lolich, 1971 ..... 376.0
3 Steve Carlton, 1972..... 346.1
4 Gaylord Perry, 1972..... 342.2
5 Denny McLain, 1968 .... 336.0
6 Sandy Koufax, 1965 .... 335.2
7 Wilbur Wood, 1971 ...... 334.0
8 Gaylord Perry, 1970..... 328.2
9 Mickey Lolich, 1972 ..... 327.1
10 Juan Marichal, 1968 .... 325.2

1943–60

1 Bob Feller, 1946 .... 371.1
2 Dizzy Trout, 1944......... 352.1
3 Robin Roberts, 1953.... 346.2
4 Robin Roberts, 1954.... 336.2
5 Robin Roberts, 1952.... 330.0
6 Robin Roberts, 1951.... 315.0
7 Johnny Sain, 1948....... 314.2
8 Bob Friend, 1956......... 314.1
9 Hal Newhouser, 1945.. 313.1
10 Bill Voiselle, 1944 .... 312.2

1921–42

1 George Uhle, 1923....... 357.2
2 Red Faber, 1922.......... 352.0
3 Urban Shocker, 1922... 348.0
4 Bob Feller, 1941 .... 343.0
5 Carl Mays, 1921 .... 336.2
6 Red Faber, 1921.......... 330.2
Burleigh Grimes, 1928 330.2
8 Bobo Newsom, 1938... 329.2
9 Wilbur Cooper, 1921.... 327.0
Burleigh Grimes, 1923 327.0
Alvin Crowder, 1932 .... 327.0

1901–20

1 Ed Walsh, 1908 .... 464.0
2 Jack Chesbro, 1904..... 454.2
3 Joe McGinnity, 1903.... 434.0
4 Ed Walsh, 1907 .... 422.1
5 Vic Willis, 1902 .... 410.0
6 Joe McGinnity, 1904.... 408.0
7 Ed Walsh, 1912 .... 393.0
8 Dave Davenport, 1915 392.2
9 Christy Mathewson, 1908 . 390.2
10 Jack Powell, 1904 .... 390.1

1893–1900

1 Amos Rusie, 1893....... 482.0
2 Ted Breitenstein, 1894. 447.1
3 Pink Hawley, 1895....... 444.1
4 Amos Rusie, 1894....... 444.0
5 Ted Breitenstein, 1895. 438.2
6 Frank Killen, 1896....... 432.1
7 Kid Nichols, 1893 .... 425.0
8 Cy Young, 1893 .... 422.2
9 Jouett Meekin, 1894..... 418.0
10 Frank Killen, 1893....... 415.0

1876–92

1 Will White, 1879.......... 680.0
2 Charley Radbourn, 1884 .. 678.2
3 Guy Hecker, 1884......... 670.2
4 Jim McCormick, 1880.. 657.2
5 Jim Galvin, 1883.......... 656.1
6 Jim Galvin, 1884.......... 636.1
7 Charley Radbourn, 1883 .. 632.1
8 John Clarkson, 1885 ... 623.0
9 Jim Devlin, 1876.......... 622.0
Bill Hutchison, 1892..... 622.0

FEWEST HITS/GAME

1	Nolan Ryan, 1972	5.26
2	Luis Tiant, 1968	5.30
3	Nolan Ryan, 1991	5.31
4	**Pedro Martinez, 2000**	**5.31**
5	Ed Reulbach, 1906	5.33
6	Dutch Leonard, 1914	5.57
7	Carl Lundgren, 1907	5.65
8	Sid Fernandez, 1985	5.71
9	Tommy Byrne, 1949	5.74
10	Dave McNally, 1968	5.77
11	Sandy Koufax, 1965	5.79
12	Russ Ford, 1910	5.83
13	Tim Keefe, 1880	5.83
14	Hideo Nomo, 1995	5.83
15	Al Downing, 1963	5.84
16	Herb Score, 1956	5.85
17	Bob Gibson, 1968	5.85
18	Sam McDowell, 1965	5.87
19	Ed Walsh, 1910	5.89
20	**Pedro Martinez, 1997**	**5.89**
21	Mike Scott, 1986	5.95
22	Mario Soto, 1980	5.96
23	Floyd Youmans, 1986	5.96
24	Nolan Ryan, 1977	5.96
25	Nolan Ryan, 1974	5.98
26	Nolan Ryan, 1981	5.98
27	Nolan Ryan, 1986	6.02
28	Sam McDowell, 1966	6.02
29	Vida Blue, 1971	6.03
30	Walter Johnson, 1913	6.03
31	Nolan Ryan, 1990	6.04
32	Grover Alexander, 1915	6.05
33	Sam McDowell, 1968	6.06
34	Joe Horlen, 1964	6.07
35	Andy Messersmith, 1969	6.08
36	Nolan Ryan, 1989	6.09
37	Stan Coveleski, 1917	6.09
38	Catfish Hunter, 1972	6.09
39	Nolan Ryan, 1976	6.11
40	Sid Fernandez, 1988	6.11
41	Bob Turley, 1957	6.12
42	Bob Turley, 1955	6.13
43	Don Sutton, 1972	6.14
44	Nolan Ryan, 1983	6.14
45	Ron Guidry, 1978	6.15
46	**Johan Santana, 2004**	**6.16**
47	Mordecai Brown, 1908	6.17
48	Sandy Koufax, 1963	6.19
49	**Randy Johnson, 1997**	**6.21**
50	Jack Pfiester, 1906	6.21
51	Sandy Koufax, 1964	6.22
52	Roger Nelson, 1972	6.23
53	Herb Score, 1955	6.26
54	Cy Morgan, 1909	6.26
55	Dean Chance, 1964	6.27
56	Christy Mathewson, 1909	6.28
	J.R. Richard, 1978	6.28
58	Art Fromme, 1909	6.28
59	**Greg Maddux, 1995**	**6.31**
60	Walter Johnson, 1912	6.32
61	**Kerry Wood, 1998**	**6.32**
62	Jack Coombs, 1910	6.32
63	Rube Waddell, 1905	6.33
64	Vean Gregg, 1911	6.33
65	Jeff Robinson, 1988	6.33
66	Larry Cheney, 1916	6.33
67	Sonny Siebert, 1968	6.33
68	Allie Reynolds, 1943	6.34
69	**Roger Clemens, 1986**	**6.34**
70	Willie Mitchell, 1913	6.35
71	Jose DeLeon, 1989	6.36
72	Pascual Perez, 1988	6.37
73	Walter Johnson, 1910	6.37
74	Dave Boswell, 1966	6.38
75	Harry Krause, 1909	6.38
76	Dutch Leonard, 1915	6.38
77	Eddie Cicotte, 1917	6.39
78	Wayne Simpson, 1970	6.39
79	Al Leiter, 1996	6.39
80	Babe Ruth, 1916	6.40
81	Spec Shea, 1947	6.40
82	Jim Bibby, 1973	6.42
83	Ed Reulbach, 1905	6.42
84	Gaylord Perry, 1974	6.42
85	Eddie Fisher, 1965	6.42
86	Addie Joss, 1908	6.42
87	Mordecai Brown, 1906	6.43
88	**Roger Clemens, 2005**	**6.43**
89	Luis Tiant, 1972	6.44
90	Frank Smith, 1908	6.44
91	Doc Gooden, 1985	6.44
92	Orval Overall, 1909	6.44
93	Sid Fernandez, 1989	6.44
94	Denny McLain, 1968	6.46
95	Mordecai Brown, 1909	6.46
96	Ray Caldwell, 1914	6.46
97	Fred Toney, 1915	6.47
98	Gary Peters, 1967	6.47
99	Christy Mathewson, 1908	6.47
100	Bob Turley, 1954	6.48

FEWEST HITS/GAME BY ERA

1988–2006

1	Nolan Ryan, 1991	5.31
2	**Pedro Martinez, 2000**	**5.31**
3	Hideo Nomo, 1995	5.83
4	**Pedro Martinez, 1997**	**5.89**
5	Nolan Ryan, 1990	6.04
6	Nolan Ryan, 1989	6.09
7	Sid Fernandez, 1988	6.11
8	**Johan Santana, 2004**	**6.16**
9	**Randy Johnson, 1997**	**6.21**
10	**Greg Maddux, 1995**	**6.31**

1973–87

1	Sid Fernandez, 1985	5.71
2	Mike Scott, 1986	5.95
3	Mario Soto, 1980	5.96
4	Floyd Youmans, 1986	5.96
5	Nolan Ryan, 1977	5.96
6	Nolan Ryan, 1974	5.98
7	Nolan Ryan, 1981	5.98
8	Nolan Ryan, 1986	6.02
9	Nolan Ryan, 1976	6.11
10	Nolan Ryan, 1983	6.14

1961–72

1	Nolan Ryan, 1972	5.26
2	Luis Tiant, 1968	5.30
3	Dave McNally, 1968	5.77
4	Sandy Koufax, 1965	5.79
5	Al Downing, 1963	5.84
6	Bob Gibson, 1968	5.85
7	Sam McDowell, 1965	5.87
8	Sam McDowell, 1966	6.02
9	Vida Blue, 1971	6.03
10	Sam McDowell, 1968	6.06

1943–60

1	Tommy Byrne, 1949	5.74
2	Herb Score, 1956	5.85
3	Bob Turley, 1957	6.12
4	Bob Turley, 1955	6.13
5	Herb Score, 1955	6.26
6	Allie Reynolds, 1943	6.34
7	Spec Shea, 1947	6.40
8	Bob Turley, 1954	6.48
9	Sam Jones, 1955	6.52
10	Bob Turley, 1958	6.53

1921–42

1	Mort Cooper, 1942	6.69
2	Hal Newhouser, 1942	6.71
3	Johnny Vander Meer, 1941	6.84
4	Bob Feller, 1940	6.88
5	Bob Feller, 1939	6.89
6	Hal Schumacher, 1933	6.92
7	Johnny Vander Meer, 1942	6.93
8	Dazzy Vance, 1924	6.95
9	Whit Wyatt, 1941	6.96
10	Bucky Walters, 1939	7.05

1901–20

1	Ed Reulbach, 1906	5.33
2	Dutch Leonard, 1914	5.57
3	Carl Lundgren, 1907	5.65
4	Russ Ford, 1910	5.83
5	Ed Walsh, 1910	5.89
6	Walter Johnson, 1913	6.03
7	Grover Alexander, 1915	6.05
8	Stan Coveleski, 1917	6.09
9	Mordecai Brown, 1908	6.17
10	Jack Pfiester, 1906	6.21

1893–1900

1	Vic Willis, 1899	7.28
2	Kid Nichols, 1898	7.33
3	Rube Waddell, 1900	7.59
4	Vic Willis, 1898	7.64
5	Ted Lewis, 1898	7.67
6	Jay Hughes, 1899	7.71
7	Al Maul, 1898	7.77
8	Doc McJames, 1898	7.87
9	Cy Seymour, 1898	7.90
10	Jay Hughes, 1898	8.02

1876–92

1	Tim Keefe, 1880	5.83
2	Guy Hecker, 1882	6.49
3	Tim Keefe, 1888	6.57
4	Charlie Sweeney, 1884	6.59
5	Adonis Terry, 1888	6.69
6	Silver King, 1888	6.70
7	Frank Knauss, 1890	6.73
8	Ed Seward, 1888	6.73
9	Tim Keefe, 1885	6.75
10	Tony Mullane, 1892	6.77

FEWEST HR ALLOWED/GAME BY ERA

1988–2006

1	**Greg Maddux, 1994**	**0.18**
2	Joe Magrane, 1989	0.19
3	**Greg Maddux, 1992**	**0.24**
4	**Tom Glavine, 1992**	**0.24**
5	Bob Walk, 1988	0.25
6	**Andy Pettitte, 1997**	**0.26**
7	Danny Jackson, 1992	0.27
8	**Roger Clemens, 1990**	**0.28**
9	Kevin Brown, 1998	0.28
10	Bob Ojeda, 1988	0.28

1973–87

1	Nolan Ryan, 1981	0.12
2	Reggie Cleveland, 1976	0.16
3	Bill Gullickson, 1981	0.17
4	Ron Reed, 1975	0.18
5	Burt Hooton, 1981	0.19
6	Lary Sorensen, 1981	0.19
7	Randy Jones, 1978	0.21
8	Bruce Berenyi, 1981	0.21
9	Ken Brett, 1976	0.22
10	Al Fitzmorris, 1976	0.25

1961–72

1	Bob Veale, 1965	0.17
2	Bill Singer, 1967	0.22
3	Claude Osteen, 1966	0.22
4	Dean Chance, 1964	0.23
5	Bob Veale, 1964	0.26
6	Tommie Sisk, 1967	0.26
	Don Sutton, 1968	0.26
8	Bob Moose, 1968	0.26
9	Andy Messersmith, 1972	0.27
10	Sam McDowell, 1965	0.30

1943–60

1	Ewell Blackwell, 1946	0.05
2	Rube Melton, 1944	0.05
3	Stubby Overmire, 1944	0.09
4	Eddie Smith, 1943	0.10
5	Jack Kramer, 1944	0.11
6	Allie Reynolds, 1944	0.11
7	Marino Pieretti, 1945	0.12
8	Oscar Judd, 1943	0.12
9	Max Lanier, 1943	0.13
10	Early Wynn, 1944	0.13

1921–42

1	Allen Sothoron, 1921	0.00
2	Slim Harriss, 1926	0.00
3	Eppa Rixey, 1921	0.03
4	Sam Jones, 1921	0.03
5	Stan Coveleski, 1926	0.04
6	Babe Adams, 1922	0.05
7	Dolf Luque, 1923	0.06
8	George Mogridge, 1924	0.08
9	Herb Pennock, 1928	0.09
10	Eppa Rixey, 1923	0.09

1901–20

1	Walter Johnson, 1916	0.00
2	Jack Coombs, 1910	0.00
3	Ed Killian, 1904	0.00
4	Babe Ruth, 1916	0.00
5	Vic Willis, 1906	0.00
6	Rube Vickers, 1908	0.00
7	Ed Killian, 1905	0.00
8	Jake Weimer, 1906	0.00
9	Frank Smith, 1905	0.00
10	Cy Morgan, 1910	0.00

1893–1900

1	Billy Rhines, 1898	0.00
2	Brownie Foreman, 1895	0.00
3	Clark Griffith, 1898	0.03
4	Bill Hoffer, 1896	0.03
5	Chick Fraser, 1899	0.03
6	Jerry Nops, 1899	0.03
7	Ed Doheny, 1898	0.04
8	Harry Howell, 1899	0.04
9	Ned Garvin, 1899	0.05
10	Pink Hawley, 1896	0.05

1876–92

1	Jersey Bakely, 1884	0.00
2	Lon Knight, 1876	0.00
3	Frank Hankinson, 1879	0.00
4	Candy Cummings, 1876	0.00
5	Denny Driscoll, 1882	0.00
6	Joe Blong, 1877	0.00
7	Ren Deagle, 1883	0.00
8	Bobby Mathews, 1877	0.00
	John Kirby, 1885	0.00
10	John Fox, 1881	0.00

WALKS

1	Amos Rusie, 1890	289
2	Mark Baldwin, 1889	274
3	Amos Rusie, 1892	270
4	Amos Rusie, 1891	262
5	Mark Baldwin, 1890	249
6	Jack Stivetts, 1891	232
7	Mark Baldwin, 1891	227
8	Phil Knell, 1891	226
9	Bob Barr, 1890	219
10	Amos Rusie, 1893	218
11	Cy Seymour, 1898	213
12	Gus Weyhing, 1889	212
13	Ed Crane, 1890	208
	Bob Feller, 1938	208
15	Toad Ramsey, 1886	207
16	Elton Chamberlain, 1891	206
17	Mike Morrison, 1887	205
18	Henry Gruber, 1890	204
	Nolan Ryan, 1977	204
20	Ed Crane, 1891	203
	John Clarkson, 1889	203
22	Nolan Ryan, 1974	202
23	Bert Cunningham, 1890	201
24	Amos Rusie, 1894	200
25	Bill Hutchison, 1890	199
26	Mark Baldwin, 1892	194
	Bob Feller, 1941	194
28	Bobo Newsom, 1938	192
29	Ted Breitenstein, 1894	191
30	Bill Hutchison, 1892	190
31	Ed Crane, 1892	189
	Tony Mullane, 1893	189
33	Tony Mullane, 1891	187
	Kid Gleason, 1893	187
35	Ed Beatin, 1890	186
36	Sam Jones, 1955	185
37	Tom Vickery, 1890	184
38	Nolan Ryan, 1976	183
39	Matt Kilroy, 1886	182
	Frank Killen, 1892	182
	Ted Breitenstein, 1895	182
42	Willie McGill, 1893	181
	Bob Harmon, 1911	181
	Bob Turley, 1954	181
45	Jack Stivetts, 1890	179
	Gus Weyhing, 1890	179
	Tommy Byrne, 1949	179
48	Bill Hutchison, 1891	178
49	Bob Turley, 1955	177
50	Phenomenal Smith, 1887	176
	Jouett Meekin, 1894	176
52	George Hemming, 1893	175
53	Silver King, 1892	171
	Jack Stivetts, 1892	171
	Bump Hadley, 1932	171
56	Elton Chamberlain, 1892	170
	Ed Stein, 1894	170
	Cy Seymour, 1899	170
59	Gus Weyhing, 1892	168
	Brickyard Kennedy, 1893	168
	Cy Seymour, 1897	168
	Elmer Myers, 1916	168
63	Toad Ramsey, 1887	167
	Gus Weyhing, 1887	167
	Darby O'Brien, 1889	167
	Kid Gleason, 1890	167
	Bill Daley, 1890	167
	Bobo Newsom, 1937	167
69	Tony Mullane, 1886	166
	Sadie McMahon, 1890	166
	Phil Knell, 1890	166
	Chick Fraser, 1896	166
73	Elton Chamberlain, 1889	165
	Dan Casey, 1890	165
	Kid Gleason, 1891	165
	Weldon Wyckoff, 1915	165
77	Earl Moore, 1911	164
	Phil Niekro, 1977	164
79	Mickey Welch, 1886	163
	Silver King, 1890	163
	Willie McGill, 1891	163
	George Haddock, 1892	163
83	Johnny Vander Meer, 1943	162
	Nolan Ryan, 1973	162
85	Hank O'Day, 1890	161
	John Sowders, 1890	161
	Kid Carsey, 1891	161
	Gus Weyhing, 1891	161
89	Tommy Byrne, 1950	160
90	George Hemming, 1894	159
	Amos Rusie, 1895	159
	Marty O'Toole, 1912	159
93	Ed Doheny, 1899	158
	Joe Coleman, 1974	158
95	Matt Kilroy, 1887	157
	Bert Cunningham, 1888	157
	Pink Hawley, 1896	157
	Grover Lowdermilk, 1915	157
	Nolan Ryan, 1972	157
100	Ted Breitenstein, 1893	156
	Duke Esper, 1893	156
	Bill Hutchison, 1893	156
	Sadie McMahon, 1893	156

STRIKEOUTS

1	Matt Kilroy, 1886	513
2	Toad Ramsey, 1886	499
3	Hugh Daily, 1884	483
4	Dupee Shaw, 1884	451
5	Charley Radbourn, 1884	441
6	Charlie Buffinton, 1884	417
7	Guy Hecker, 1884	385
8	Nolan Ryan, 1973	383
9	Sandy Koufax, 1965	382
10	Bill Sweeney, 1884	374
11	**Randy Johnson, 2001**	**372**
12	Jim Galvin, 1884	369
13	Mark Baldwin, 1889	368
14	Nolan Ryan, 1974	367
15	**Randy Johnson, 1999**	**364**
16	Tim Keefe, 1883	359
17	Toad Ramsey, 1887	355
18	Rube Waddell, 1904	349
19	Bob Feller, 1946	348
20	**Randy Johnson, 2000**	**347**
21	Hardie Henderson, 1884	346
22	Jim Whitney, 1883	345
	Mickey Welch, 1884	345
24	Jim McCormick, 1884	343
25	Amos Rusie, 1890	341
	Nolan Ryan, 1977	341
27	Charlie Sweeney, 1884	337
	Amos Rusie, 1891	337
29	Tim Keefe, 1888	335
30	Tim Keefe, 1884	334
	Randy Johnson, 2002	**334**
32	**Randy Johnson, 1998**	**329**
	Nolan Ryan, 1972	329
34	Nolan Ryan, 1976	327
35	Ed Morris, 1886	326
36	Tony Mullane, 1884	325
	Sam McDowell, 1965	325
38	Lady Baldwin, 1886	323
39	**Curt Schilling, 1997**	**319**
40	Sandy Koufax, 1966	317
41	**Curt Schilling, 2002**	**316**
42	Charley Radbourn, 1883	315
43	Bill Hutchison, 1892	314
44	John Clarkson, 1886	313
	Walter Johnson, 1910	313
	J.R. Richard, 1979	313
	Pedro Martinez, 1999	**313**
48	Steve Carlton, 1972	310
49	Larry McKeon, 1884	308
	John Clarkson, 1885	308
	Mickey Lolich, 1971	308
	Randy Johnson, 1993	**308**
53	Sandy Koufax, 1963	306
	Mike Scott, 1986	306
55	**Pedro Martinez, 1997**	**305**
56	Amos Rusie, 1892	304
	Sam McDowell, 1970	304
58	Walter Johnson, 1912	303
	J.R. Richard, 1978	303
60	Ed Morris, 1884	302
	Rube Waddell, 1903	302
62	Vida Blue, 1971	301
	Nolan Ryan, 1989	301
64	**Curt Schilling, 1998**	**300**
65	Ed Morris, 1885	298
66	Tim Keefe, 1886	297
67	**Randy Johnson, 1995**	**294**
68	**Curt Schilling, 2001**	**293**
69	Jack Lynch, 1884	292
	Roger Clemens, 1997	**292**
71	Sadie McMahon, 1890	291
	Roger Clemens, 1988	**291**
	Randy Johnson, 1997	**291**
74	**Randy Johnson, 2004**	**290**
75	Bill Hutchison, 1890	289
	Jack Stivetts, 1890	289
	Tom Seaver, 1971	289
78	Rube Waddell, 1905	287
79	Bobby Mathews, 1884	286
	Bobby Mathews, 1885	286
	Steve Carlton, 1980	286
	Steve Carlton, 1982	286
83	Billy Taylor, 1884	284
	John Clarkson, 1889	284
	Pedro Martinez, 2000	**284**
86	Dave Foutz, 1886	283
	Sam McDowell, 1968	283
	Tom Seaver, 1970	283
89	Denny McLain, 1968	280
90	Jim Galvin, 1883	279
	Sam McDowell, 1969	279
92	Bob Veale, 1965	276
	Doc Gooden, 1984	276
	John Smoltz, 1996	**276**
95	Hal Newhouser, 1946	275
	Steve Carlton, 1983	275
97	Bob Gibson, 1970	274
	Fergie Jenkins, 1970	274
	Mario Soto, 1982	274
100	Fergie Jenkins, 1969	273

STRIKEOUTS/GAME

1 Randy Johnson, 2001 ... 13.41
2 Pedro Martinez, 1999 ... 13.20
3 Kerry Wood, 1998 ... 12.58
4 Randy Johnson, 2000 ... 12.56
5 Randy Johnson, 1995 ... 12.35
6 Randy Johnson, 1997 ... 12.30
7 Randy Johnson, 1998 ... 12.12
8 Randy Johnson, 1999 ... 12.06
9 Pedro Martinez, 2000 ... 11.78
10 Randy Johnson, 2002 ... 11.56
11 Nolan Ryan, 1987 ... 11.48
12 Doc Gooden, 1984 ... 11.39
13 Pedro Martinez, 1997 ... 11.37
14 Kerry Wood, 2003 ... 11.35
15 Nolan Ryan, 1989 ... 11.32
16 Curt Schilling, 1997 11.29
17 Kerry Wood, 2001 ... 11.20
18 Hideo Nomo, 1995 ... 11.10
19 Oliver Perez, 2004 .. 10.97
20 Curt Schilling, 2002 10.97
21 Randy Johnson, 1993 ... 10.86
22 Pedro Martinez, 2002 ... 10.79
23 Sam McDowell, 1965 ... 10.71
24 Randy Johnson, 1994 ... 10.67
25 Randy Johnson, 2004 ... 10.62
26 Nolan Ryan, 1973 ... 10.57
27 Nolan Ryan, 1991 ... 10.56
28 Sandy Koufax, 1962 ... 10.55
29 Johan Santana, 2004 ... 10.46
30 Mark Prior, 2003 ... 10.43
31 Nolan Ryan, 1972 ... 10.43
32 Sam McDowell, 1966 .. 10.42
33 Roger Clemens, 1998 ... 10.39
34 Curt Schilling, 2003 10.39
35 Nolan Ryan, 1976 ... 10.35
36 Randy Johnson, 1992 ... 10.31
37 Curt Schilling, 2001 10.27
38 Nolan Ryan, 1977 ... 10.26
39 David Cone, 1997 ... 10.25
40 Sandy Koufax, 1965 ... 10.24
41 Nolan Ryan, 1990 ... 10.24
42 Randy Johnson, 1991 ... 10.19
43 Mark Prior, 2005 ... 10.15
44 Bartolo Colon, 2000 ... 10.15
45 Sandy Koufax, 1960 ... 10.13
46 Hideo Nomo, 1997 ... 10.11
47 Curt Schilling, 1998 10.05
48 Jason Schmidt, 2004 ... 10.04
49 Ben Sheets, 2004 ... 10.03
50 Mike Scott, 1986 ... 10.00
51 Hideo Nomo, 2001 ... 10.00
52 Rick Ankiel, 2000 ... 9.98
53 Nolan Ryan, 1978 ... 9.97
54 Roger Clemens, 1997 ... 9.95
55 Pedro Martinez, 2003 ... 9.93
56 Nolan Ryan, 1974 ... 9.93
57 Roger Clemens, 1988 ... 9.92
58 David Cone, 1990 ... 9.91
59 J.R. Richard, 1978 ... 9.90
60 Andy Benes, 1994 ... 9.87
61 Nolan Ryan, 1986 ... 9.81
62 John Smoltz, 1996 ... 9.79
63 Herb Score, 1955 ... 9.70
64 Pedro Martinez, 1998 ... 9.67
65 Nolan Ryan, 1984 ... 9.65
66 J.R. Richard, 1979 ... 9.64
67 Roger Clemens, 2002 ... 9.60
68 Jake Peavy, 2005 ... 9.58
69 Mario Soto, 1982 ... 9.57
70 Jake Peavy, 2006 ... 9.56
71 Tom Griffin, 1969 ... 9.56
72 Roger Clemens, 1996 ... 9.53
73 Jim Maloney, 1963 ... 9.53
74 Jason Schmidt, 2002 9.52
75 Sid Fernandez, 1985 ... 9.51
76 Herb Score, 1956 ... 9.49
77 Sandy Koufax, 1961 ... 9.47
78 Sam McDowell, 1968 ... 9.47
79 Matt Clement, 2004 .. 9.45
80 Matt Clement, 2002 .. 9.44
81 Johan Santana, 2006 9.44
82 Pedro Martinez, 2004 ... 9.41
83 David Cone, 1992 ... 9.41
84 Frank Tanana, 1975 ... 9.41
85 Javier Vazquez, 2003 ... 9.40
86 Don Wilson, 1969 ... 9.40
87 Jake Peavy, 2004 ... 9.36
88 Bob Veale, 1965 ... 9.34
89 Nolan Ryan, 1988 ... 9.33
90 David Cone, 1991 ... 9.32
91 John Smoltz, 1998 ... 9.29
92 Johan Santana, 2005 9.25
93 Luis Tiant, 1967 ... 9.22
94 Hideo Nomo, 1996 ... 9.22
95 Pedro Martinez, 1996 ... 9.22
96 Brandon Duckworth, 2002 9.22
97 Mark Langston, 1986 ... 9.21
98 Luis Tiant, 1968 ... 9.20
99 Dave Boswell, 1966 ... 9.19
100 Sam McDowell, 1964 ... 9.19

EARNED RUN AVERAGE

1 Tim Keefe, 1880 ... 0.86
2 Dutch Leonard, 1914 ... 0.96
3 Mordecai Brown, 1906 .. 1.04
4 Bob Gibson, 1968 ... 1.12
5 Christy Mathewson, 1909 ... 1.14
6 Walter Johnson, 1913 ... 1.14
7 Jack Pfiester, 1907 ... 1.15
8 Addie Joss, 1908 ... 1.16
9 Carl Lundgren, 1907 ... 1.17
10 Denny Driscoll, 1882 ... 1.21
11 Grover Alexander, 1915. 1.22
12 George Bradley, 1876 ... 1.23
13 Cy Young, 1908 ... 1.26
14 Ed Walsh, 1910 ... 1.27
15 Walter Johnson, 1918 ... 1.27
16 Christy Mathewson, 1905 ... 1.28
17 Jack Taylor, 1902 ... 1.29
18 Guy Hecker, 1882 ... 1.30
19 Jack Coombs, 1910 ... 1.30
20 Mordecai Brown, 1909 .. 1.31
21 Walter Johnson, 1910 ... 1.36
22 George Bradley, 1880 ... 1.38
23 Charley Radbourn, 1884 1.38
24 Walter Johnson, 1912 ... 1.39
25 Mordecai Brown, 1907 .. 1.39
26 Harry Krause, 1909 ... 1.39
27 Ed Walsh, 1909 ... 1.41
28 Ed Walsh, 1908 ... 1.42
29 Ed Reulbach, 1905 ... 1.42
30 Orval Overall, 1909 ... 1.42
31 Christy Mathewson, 1908 ... 1.43
32 Fred Anderson, 1917 ... 1.44
33 Mordecai Brown, 1908 .. 1.47
34 Rube Waddell, 1905 ... 1.48
35 Joe Wood, 1915 ... 1.49
36 Walter Johnson, 1919 ... 1.49
37 Jack Pfiester, 1906 ... 1.51
38 John Ward, 1878 ... 1.51
39 Harry McCormick, 1882 1.52
40 Doc White, 1906 ... 1.52
41 George McQuillan, 1908 1.53
42 Doc Gooden, 1985 ... 1.53
43 Eddie Cicotte, 1917 ... 1.53
44 Will White, 1882 ... 1.54
45 Cy Morgan, 1910 ... 1.55
46 Grover Alexander, 1916. 1.55
47 Walter Johnson, 1915 ... 1.55
48 Howie Camnitz, 1908 ... 1.56
49 Greg Maddux, 1994 .. 1.56
50 Jim Devlin, 1876 ... 1.56
51 Tim Keefe, 1885 ... 1.58
52 Fred Toney, 1915 ... 1.58
53 Eddie Cicotte, 1913 ... 1.58
54 Rube Marquard, 1916 ... 1.58
55 Chief Bender, 1910 ... 1.58
56 Barney Pelty, 1906 ... 1.59
57 Addie Joss, 1904 ... 1.59
58 Ed Walsh, 1907 ... 1.60
59 Luis Tiant, 1968 ... 1.60
60 Joe McGinnity, 1904 ... 1.61
61 Ray Collins, 1910 ... 1.62
62 Rube Waddell, 1904 ... 1.62
63 Howie Camnitz, 1909 ... 1.62
64 Cy Young, 1901 ... 1.62
65 Greg Maddux, 1995 .. 1.63
66 Silver King, 1888 ... 1.63
67 Spud Chandler, 1943 ... 1.64
68 Ernie Shore, 1915 ... 1.64
69 Ed Summers, 1908 ... 1.64
70 Dean Chance, 1964 ... 1.65
71 Walter Johnson, 1908 ... 1.65
72 Ed Reulbach, 1906 ... 1.65
73 Russ Ford, 1910 ... 1.65
74 Chief Bender, 1909 ... 1.66
75 Sam Leever, 1907 ... 1.66
76 Carl Hubbell, 1933 ... 1.66
77 Mickey Welch, 1885 ... 1.66
78 Candy Cummings, 1876 1.67
79 Tommy Bond, 1876 ... 1.68
80 Orval Overall, 1907 ... 1.68
81 Ed Reulbach, 1907 ... 1.69
82 Claude Hendrix, 1914 ... 1.69
83 Nolan Ryan, 1981 ... 1.69
84 Jim McCormick, 1878 ... 1.69
85 Joe Wood, 1910 ... 1.69
86 Rube Foster, 1914 ... 1.70
87 Charlie Sweeney, 1884 .. 1.70
Bill Burns, 1908 ... 1.70
89 Addie Joss, 1909 ... 1.71
90 Ed Killian, 1909 ... 1.71
91 Walter Johnson, 1914 ... 1.72
92 Ned Garvin, 1904 ... 1.72
93 Doc White, 1909 ... 1.72
94 Bill Doak, 1914 ... 1.72
95 Addie Joss, 1906 ... 1.72
Grover Alexander, 1919. 1.72
97 Sandy Koufax, 1966 ... 1.73
98 Bob Ewing, 1907 ... 1.73
99 Vic Willis, 1906 ... 1.73
100 Sandy Koufax, 1964 ... 1.74

EARNED RUN AVG. BY ERA

1988–2006

1 Greg Maddux, 1994 .. 1.56
2 Greg Maddux, 1995 .. 1.63
3 Pedro Martinez, 2000 ... 1.74
4 Roger Clemens, 2005 ... 1.87
5 Kevin Brown, 1996 ... 1.89
6 Pedro Martinez, 1997 ... 1.90
7 Roger Clemens, 1990 ... 1.93
8 Roger Clemens, 1997 ... 2.05
9 Pedro Martinez, 1999 ... 2.07
10 Bill Swift, 1992 ... 2.08

1973–87

1 Doc Gooden, 1985 ... 1.53
2 Nolan Ryan, 1981 ... 1.69
3 Ron Guidry, 1978 ... 1.74
4 John Tudor, 1985 ... 1.93
5 Orel Hershiser, 1985 ... 2.03
6 Tom Seaver, 1973 ... 2.08
7 Jim Palmer, 1975 ... 2.09
8 Bob Knepper, 1981 ... 2.18
9 Don Sutton, 1980 ... 2.20
10 Mike Scott, 1986 ... 2.22

1961–72

1 Bob Gibson, 1968 ... 1.12
2 Luis Tiant, 1968 ... 1.60
3 Dean Chance, 1964 ... 1.65
4 Sandy Koufax, 1966 ... 1.73
5 Sandy Koufax, 1964 ... 1.74
6 Tom Seaver, 1971 ... 1.76
7 Sam McDowell, 1968 ... 1.81
8 Vida Blue, 1971 ... 1.82
9 Phil Niekro, 1967 ... 1.87
10 Joe Horlen, 1964 ... 1.88

1943–60

1 Spud Chandler, 1943 ... 1.64
2 Hal Newhouser, 1945 ... 1.81
3 Max Lanier, 1943 ... 1.90
4 Hal Newhouser, 1946 ... 1.94
5 Billy Pierce, 1955 ... 1.97
6 Whitey Ford, 1958 ... 2.01
7 Al Benton, 1945 ... 2.02
8 Allie Reynolds, 1952 ... 2.06
9 Howie Pollet, 1946 ... 2.10
10 Spud Chandler, 1946 ... 2.10

1921–42

1 Carl Hubbell, 1933 ... 1.66
2 Mort Cooper, 1942 ... 1.78
3 Dolf Luque, 1923 ... 1.93
4 Lon Warneke, 1933 ... 2.00
5 Lefty Grove, 1931 ... 2.06
6 Dazzy Vance, 1928 ... 2.09
7 Ted Lyons, 1942 ... 2.10
8 Johnny Beazley, 1942 ... 2.13
9 Hal Schumacher, 1933 .. 2.16
10 Dazzy Vance, 1924 ... 2.16

1901–20

1 Dutch Leonard, 1914 ... 0.96
2 Mordecai Brown, 1906 .. 1.04
3 Christy Mathewson, 1909 ... 1.14
4 Walter Johnson, 1913 ... 1.14
5 Jack Pfiester, 1907 ... 1.15
6 Addie Joss, 1908 ... 1.16
7 Carl Lundgren, 1907 ... 1.17
8 Grover Alexander, 1915. 1.22
9 Cy Young, 1908 ... 1.26
10 Ed Walsh, 1910 ... 1.27

1893–1900

1 Clark Griffith, 1898 ... 1.88
2 Al Maul, 1898 ... 2.10
3 Kid Nichols, 1898 ... 2.13
4 Doc McJames, 1898 ... 2.36
5 Rube Waddell, 1900 ... 2.37
6 Ned Garvin, 1900 ... 2.41
7 Al Maul, 1895 ... 2.45
Billy Rhines, 1896 ... 2.45
9 Nixey Callahan, 1898 ... 2.46
10 Vic Willis, 1899 ... 2.50

1876–92

1 Tim Keefe, 1880 ... 0.86
2 Denny Driscoll, 1882 ... 1.21
3 George Bradley, 1876 ... 1.23
4 Guy Hecker, 1882 ... 1.30
5 George Bradley, 1880 ... 1.38
6 Charley Radbourn, 1884 1.38
7 John Ward, 1878 ... 1.51
8 Harry McCormick, 1882 1.52
9 Will White, 1882 ... 1.54
10 Jim Devlin, 1876 ... 1.56

ADJ. EARNED RUN AVG.

1 Tim Keefe, 1880 ... 294
2 Pedro Martinez, 2000 288
3 Dutch Leonard, 1914 ... 280
4 Greg Maddux, 1994 ... 277
5 Greg Maddux, 1995 ... 265
6 Walter Johnson, 1913 ... 258
7 Bob Gibson, 1968 ... 258
8 Mordecai Brown, 1906 ... 254
9 Pedro Martinez, 1999 241
10 Walter Johnson, 1912 ... 240
11 Christy Mathewson, 1905 ... 230
12 Doc Gooden, 1985 ... 229
13 Roger Clemens, 2005 225
14 Grover Alexander, 1915 .. 225
15 Roger Clemens, 1997 224
16 Christy Mathewson, 1909 ... 223
17 Pedro Martinez, 1997 220
18 Lefty Grove, 1931 ... 218
19 Kevin Brown, 1996 ... 218
20 Cy Young, 1901 ... 217
21 Jack Pfiester, 1907 ... 216
22 Denny Driscoll, 1882 ... 216
23 Walter Johnson, 1919 ... 216
24 Walter Johnson, 1918 ... 215
25 Carl Lundgren, 1907 ... 213
26 Roger Clemens, 1990 212
27 Pedro Martinez, 2003 210
28 Ed Reulbach, 1905 ... 210
29 Ron Guidry, 1978 ... 210
30 Jack Taylor, 1902 ... 209
31 Charley Radbourn, 1884 206
32 Addie Joss, 1908 ... 206
33 Billy Pierce, 1955 ... 201
34 Dolf Luque, 1923 ... 200
35 Silver King, 1888 ... 200
36 Dean Chance, 1964 ... 199
37 Randy Johnson, 1997 199
38 Pedro Martinez, 2002 198
39 Spud Chandler, 1943 ... 197
40 Al Maul, 1895 ... 196
41 Tom Seaver, 1971 ... 195
42 Cy Young, 1908 ... 195
43 Hal Newhouser, 1945 ... 194
44 Nolan Ryan, 1981 ... 194
45 Mordecai Brown, 1909 ... 193
46 Randy Johnson, 2002 193
47 Carl Hubbell, 1933 ... 193
48 Mort Cooper, 1942 ... 193
49 Randy Johnson, 1995 193
50 Walter Johnson, 1915 ... 191
51 Monty Stratton, 1937 ... 191
52 Guy Hecker, 1882 ... 191
53 Lefty Gomez, 1937 ... 191
54 Sandy Koufax, 1966 ... 191
55 Ed Siever, 1902 ... 191
56 Clark Griffith, 1898 ... 191
57 Dazzy Vance, 1928 ... 191
58 Greg Maddux, 1997 ... 191
59 Amos Rusie, 1894 ... 189
60 Lefty Grove, 1936 ... 189
61 Vean Gregg, 1911 ... 189
62 Ed Walsh, 1910 ... 189
63 Hal Newhouser, 1946 ... 189
64 Dazzy Vance, 1930 ... 188
65 Billy Rhines, 1896 ... 188
66 Jack Stivetts, 1889 ... 188
67 Greg Maddux, 1998 ... 187
68 Joe Wood, 1915 ... 187
69 Warren Spahn, 1953 ... 187
70 Sandy Koufax, 1964 ... 187
71 Randy Johnson, 2001 186
72 Wilbur Wood, 1971 ... 186
73 Randy Johnson, 1999 186
74 Lefty Grove, 1939 ... 186
75 Eddie Cicotte, 1913 ... 185
76 Luis Tiant, 1968 ... 185
77 John Tudor, 1985 ... 185
78 Lefty Grove, 1930 ... 184
79 Hank Aguirre, 1962 ... 184
80 Joe Horlen, 1964 ... 184
81 Vida Blue, 1971 ... 183
82 Walter Johnson, 1910 ... 183
83 Harry Brecheen, 1948 ... 183
84 Henry Boyle, 1886 ... 183
85 Steve Carlton, 1972 ... 183
86 Billy Rhines, 1890 ... 183
87 Jack Coombs, 1910 ... 182
88 Jason Schmidt, 2003 . 182
89 Fred Toney, 1915 ... 182
90 Randy Johnson, 2000 181
91 Johnny Allen, 1937 ... 181
92 Kevin Appier, 1993 ... 180
93 Rube Waddell, 1905 ... 180
94 Mordecai Brown, 1907 ... 179
95 Bret Saberhagen, 1989 .. 179
96 Mark Prior, 2003 ... 179
97 Orval Overall, 1909 ... 179
98 Rube Waddell, 1902 ... 179
99 Joe Wood, 1912 ... 178
100 Phil Niekro, 1967 ... 178

ADJ. EARNED RUN AVG.

101 Johan Santana, 2004 178
102 Max Lanier, 1943 ... 177
103 Roger Clemens, 1994 177
104 Andy Pettitte, 2005 ... 177
105 Roger Clemens, 1992 177
106 Fred Anderson, 1917 ... 177
107 Roger Clemens, 1998 176
108 Cy Young, 1892 ... 176
109 Johnny Antonelli, 1954 ... 176
110 Whitey Ford, 1958 ... 176
111 Lefty Grove, 1935 ... 176
112 Tom Seaver, 1973 ... 175
113 Randy Johnson, 2004 175
114 Jack Pfiester, 1906 ... 175
115 Eddie Cicotte, 1919 ... 175
116 Mel Harder, 1934 ... 174
117 Lefty Gomez, 1934 ... 174
118 Harry McCormick, 1882 . 174
119 Al Benton, 1945 ... 174
120 George Bradley, 1876 ... 174
121 Jim Devlin, 1876 ... 174
122 Eddie Cicotte, 1917 ... 174
123 Jeff D'Amico, 2000 ... 174
124 Jake Peavy, 2004 ... 174
125 Dazzy Vance, 1924 ... 173
126 Derek Lowe, 2002 ... 173
127 Kid Nichols, 1898 ... 173
128 Thornton Lee, 1941 ... 173
129 Walter Johnson, 1911 ... 173
130 Hoyt Wilhelm, 1959 ... 173
131 Orel Hershiser, 1985 ... 173
132 Kevin Brown, 2003 ... 173
133 Harry Krause, 1909 ... 172
134 Jeff Tesreau, 1912 ... 172
135 Kevin Brown, 2000 ... 172
136 John Candelaria, 1977 ... 172
137 Will White, 1882 ... 172
138 Ted Lyons, 1942 ... 172
139 Greg Maddux, 1993 ... 172
140 Guy Hecker, 1884 ... 172
141 Juan Guzman, 1996 ... 171
142 Ted Lyons, 1939 ... 171
143 Grover Alexander, 1916 .. 171
144 David Cone, 1994 ... 171
145 Dave Stieb, 1985 ... 171
146 Red Faber, 1921 ... 171
147 Jim McCormick, 1883 ... 171
148 Gaylord Perry, 1972 ... 170
149 Al Maul, 1898 ... 170
150 Tim Hudson, 2003 ... 170
151 Rube Marquard, 1916 ... 170
152 Whitey Ford, 1964 ... 170
153 Jim Palmer, 1975 ... 170
154 Noodles Hahn, 1902 ... 170
155 Luis Tiant, 1972 ... 170
156 Tim Keefe, 1885 ... 169
157 Roger Clemens, 1986 169
158 Mike Garcia, 1949 ... 169
159 Ernie Shore, 1915 ... 169
160 Joe McGinnity, 1904 ... 169
161 Steve Ontiveros, 1994 ... 169
162 Christy Mathewson, 1908 ... 169
163 Kid Nichols, 1897 ... 169
164 Wilcy Moore, 1927 ... 169
165 Christy Mathewson, 1911 ... 169
166 Danny Darwin, 1990 ... 169
167 Juan Marichal, 1965 ... 169
168 Carl Hubbell, 1936 ... 169
169 Kid Nichols, 1890 ... 169
170 Tom Glavine, 1998 ... 168
171 Dizzy Trout, 1944 ... 168
172 Carl Hubbell, 1934 ... 168
173 Grover Alexander, 1920 .. 168
174 Bobo Newsom, 1940 ... 168
175 Howie Camnitz, 1909 ... 168
176 Bucky Walters, 1939 ... 168
177 Doc White, 1906 ... 167
178 Rick Honeycutt, 1983 ... 167
179 Grover Alexander, 1919 .. 167
180 Dick Donovan, 1961 ... 167
181 Juan Marichal, 1969 ... 167
182 Allan Anderson, 1988 ... 167
183 Ed Crane, 1891 ... 167
184 Warren Spahn, 1947 ... 167
185 Gene Bearden, 1948 ... 167
186 Al Leiter, 1998 ... 167
187 Kevin Brown, 1998 ... 167
188 Vic Willis, 1899 ... 167
189 Dick Ellsworth, 1963 ... 167
190 Kevin Millwood, 1999 167
191 Buzz Capra, 1974 ... 166
192 Ray Kremer, 1927 ... 166
193 Herb Score, 1956 ... 166
194 Ed Walsh, 1909 ... 166
195 Bill Bernhard, 1902 ... 166
196 Greg Maddux, 1992 ... 166
197 Charlie Ferguson, 1886 .. 166
198 Cy Young, 1902 ... 166
199 Tom Seaver, 1969 ... 166
200 Lefty Grove, 1926 ... 166

OPPONENT BATTING AVG.

1 Pedro Martinez, 2000 .167
2 Luis Tiant, 1968 .168
3 Nolan Ryan, 1972 .171
4 Nolan Ryan, 1991 .172
5 Ed Reulbach, 1906 .175
6 Tim Keefe, 1880 .178
7 Sandy Koufax, 1965 .179
8 Dutch Leonard, 1914 .180
9 Sid Fernandez, 1985 .181
10 Hideo Nomo, 1995 .182
11 Dave McNally, 1968 .182
12 Tommy Byrne, 1949 .183
13 Pedro Martinez, 1997 .184
14 Al Downing, 1963 .184
15 Bob Gibson, 1968 .184
16 Sam McDowell, 1965 .185
17 Carl Lundgren, 1907 .185
18 Herb Score, 1956 .186
19 Mike Scott, 1986 .186
20 Nolan Ryan, 1989 .187
21 Ed Walsh, 1910 .187
22 Mario Soto, 1980 .187
23 Nolan Ryan, 1981 .188
24 Russ Ford, 1910 .188
25 Nolan Ryan, 1986 .188
26 Nolan Ryan, 1990 .188
27 Floyd Youmans, 1986 .188
28 Sam McDowell, 1966 .188
29 Guy Hecker, 1882 .188
30 Sandy Koufax, 1963 .189
31 Sam McDowell, 1968 .189
32 Don Sutton, 1972 .189
33 Catfish Hunter, 1972 .189
34 Vida Blue, 1971 .189
35 Walter Johnson, 1913 .190
36 Nolan Ryan, 1974 .190
37 Andy Messersmith, 1969 .190
38 Joe Horlen, 1964 .190
39 Sid Fernandez, 1988 .191
40 Grover Alexander, 1915 .191
41 Sandy Koufax, 1964 .191
42 Johan Santana, 2004 .192
43 Bob Turley, 1955 .193
44 Nolan Ryan, 1977 .193
45 Fred Beebe, 1908 .193
46 Charlie Sweeney, 1884 .193
47 Ron Guidry, 1978 .193
48 Stan Coveleski, 1917 .194
49 Bob Turley, 1957 .194
50 Randy Johnson, 1997 .194
51 Herb Score, 1955 .194
52 Jack Pfiester, 1906 .194
53 Mordecai Brown, 1908 .195
54 Nolan Ryan, 1976 .195
55 Nolan Ryan, 1983 .195
56 Dean Chance, 1964 .195
57 Roger Clemens, 1986 .195
58 Tim Keefe, 1888 .196
59 Kerry Wood, 1998 .196
60 Walter Johnson, 1912 .196
61 Roger Nelson, 1972 .196
62 J.R. Richard, 1978 .196
63 Pascual Perez, 1988 .196
64 Greg Maddux, 1995 .197
65 Jeff Robinson, 1988 .197
66 Lady Baldwin, 1885 .197
67 Jose DeLeon, 1989 .197
68 Dave Boswell, 1966 .197
69 Sandy Koufax, 1962 .197
70 Randy Johnson, 2004 .197
71 Addie Joss, 1908 .197
72 Christy Mathewson, 1908 .197
73 Roger Clemens, 1998 .197
74 Sonny Siebert, 1968 .198
75 Sid Fernandez, 1989 .198
76 Toad Ramsey, 1886 .198
77 Larry Cheney, 1916 .198
78 Wayne Simpson, 1970 .198
79 Pedro Martinez, 2002 .198
80 Roger Clemens, 2005 .198
81 Orval Overall, 1909 .198
82 Gary Peters, 1967 .199
83 Larry Corcoran, 1880 .199
84 Adonis Terry, 1888 .199
85 Nolan Ryan, 1987 .199
86 Mordecai Brown, 1904 .199
87 Silver King, 1888 .200
88 Christy Mathewson, 1909 .200
89 Rube Waddell, 1905 .200
90 Denny McLain, 1968 .200
91 Larry Corcoran, 1882 .200
92 Bobby Bolin, 1968 .200
Jim Palmer, 1969 .200
Sid Fernandez, 1990 .200
95 Jason Schmidt, 2003 .200
96 Spec Shea, 1947 .200
97 Ed Seward, 1888 .200
98 Tony Mullane, 1892 .201
99 Art Fromme, 1909 .201
100 Babe Ruth, 1916 .201

OPPONENT ON-BASE PCT.

1 Guy Hecker, 1882 .199
2 Charlie Sweeney, 1884 .211
3 Tim Keefe, 1880 .212
4 Pedro Martinez, 2000 .214
5 Henry Boyle, 1884 .215
6 George Bradley, 1880 .217
7 Denny Driscoll, 1882 .218
8 Addie Joss, 1908 .218
9 Walter Johnson, 1913 .220
10 Christy Mathewson, 1908 .222
11 Jim Whitney, 1884 .223
12 George Bradley, 1876 .224
13 Greg Maddux, 1995 .225
14 Guy Hecker, 1884 .226
15 Ed Walsh, 1910 .226
16 Tommy Bond, 1876 .227
17 Lady Baldwin, 1885 .228
18 Sandy Koufax, 1965 .228
19 Christy Mathewson, 1909 .228
20 Sandy Koufax, 1963 .230
21 Juan Marichal, 1966 .230
22 John Ward, 1880 .232
23 Mordecai Brown, 1908 .232
24 Ed Walsh, 1908 .232
25 Luis Tiant, 1968 .233
26 Bob Gibson, 1968 .233
27 Grover Alexander, 1915 .234
28 Dave McNally, 1968 .234
29 Larry Corcoran, 1882 .234
30 Charley Radbourn, 1884 .234
31 Ed Morris, 1884 .234
32 Perry Werden, 1884 .235
33 Jim Devlin, 1876 .235
34 Jack Lynch, 1884 .236
35 Larry Corcoran, 1880 .236
36 Roger Nelson, 1972 .236
37 Silver King, 1888 .237
38 Charlie Getzien, 1884 .237
39 Tim Keefe, 1883 .237
40 Tony Mullane, 1883 .238
41 John Clarkson, 1885 .239
42 Tim Keefe, 1884 .239
43 Mordecai Brown, 1909 .239
44 Fred Corey, 1880 .239
45 Juan Marichal, 1965 .240
46 Cy Young, 1908 .240
47 Don Sutton, 1972 .240
48 Cy Young, 1905 .241
49 Babe Adams, 1919 .241
50 Sandy Koufax, 1964 .241
51 Catfish Hunter, 1972 .242
52 Randy Johnson, 2004 .243
53 Pete Conway, 1888 .243
54 Harry McCormick, 1882 .243
55 Denny McLain, 1968 .243
56 Tim Keefe, 1888 .243
57 Lady Baldwin, 1886 .243
58 Mike Scott, 1986 .244
59 Charley Radbourn, 1883 .244
60 Will White, 1883 .244
61 Charlie Ferguson, 1886 .244
62 Charlie Buffinton, 1888 .244
63 Will White, 1882 .244
64 Charlie Buffinton, 1884 .244
65 Russ Ford, 1910 .245
66 Grover Alexander, 1919 .245
67 Christy Mathewson, 1905 .245
68 Greg Maddux, 1994 .245
69 Dutch Leonard, 1914 .246
70 Bobby Mathews, 1882 .246
71 Jim Galvin, 1884 .246
72 Sam Weaver, 1878 .247
73 Charley Radbourn, 1882 .247
74 Charlie Gagus, 1884 .247
75 Christy Mathewson, 1907 .247
76 Warren Hacker, 1952 .247
77 Jim McCormick, 1880 .247
78 Ed Morris, 1885 .247
79 Fred Goldsmith, 1880 .247
80 Dupee Shaw, 1884 .247
81 Eddie Cicotte, 1917 .248
82 Walter Johnson, 1912 .248
83 Doc White, 1906 .249
84 John Clarkson, 1884 .249
85 Jumbo McGinnis, 1883 .249
86 John Tudor, 1985 .249
87 Pedro Martinez, 1999 .249
88 Henry Gruber, 1888 .249
89 Hugh Daily, 1884 .250
90 Ron Guidry, 1978 .250
91 Joe Horlen, 1964 .250
92 Pedro Martinez, 1997 .250
93 Terry Larkin, 1879 .250
94 Johan Santana, 2004 .250
95 John Ward, 1879 .250
96 John Ward, 1878 .251
97 Johan Santana, 2005 .251
98 Billy Taylor, 1884 .251
99 Jason Schmidt, 2003 .251
100 Candy Cummings, 1876 .251

RELIEF WINS

1 Roy Face, 1959 18
2 John Hiller, 1974 17
Bill Campbell, 1976 17
4 Jim Konstanty, 1950 16
Ron Perranoski, 1963 16
Dick Radatz, 1964 16
Tom Johnson, 1977 16
8 Mace Brown, 1938 15
Hoyt Wilhelm, 1952 15
Luis Arroyo, 1961 15
Dick Radatz, 1963 15
Eddie Fisher, 1965 15
Mike Marshall, 1974 15
Dale Murray, 1975 15
15 Joe Page, 1947 14
Joe Black, 1952 14
Hersh Freeman, 1956 14
Stu Miller, 1961 14
Stu Miller, 1965 14
Phil Regan, 1966 14
Frank Linzy, 1969 14
Mike Marshall, 1972 14
Mike Marshall, 1973 14
Ron Davis, 1979 14
Mark Clear, 1982 14
Jim Slaton, 1983 14
Roger McDowell, 1986 14
Mark Eichhorn, 1986 14
29 Dick Tidrow, 1979 13
Wilcy Moore, 1927 13
Earl Caldwell, 1946 13
Clyde Shoun, 1943 13
Joe Page, 1949 13
Clyde King, 1951 13
Lindy McDaniel, 1959 13
Larry Sherry, 1960 13
Gerry Staley, 1960 13
Lindy McDaniel, 1963 13
Ak Hrabosky, 1975 13
Rollie Fingers, 1976 13
Bill Campbell, 1977 13
Sparky Lyle, 1977 13
Gary Lavelle, 1978 13
Bob Stanley, 1978 13
Ron Reed, 1979 13
Jim Kern, 1979 13
Aurelio Lopez, 1980 13
Jesse Orosco, 1983 13
Rich Gossage, 1983 13
50 34 players tied 12

RELIEF LOSSES

1 Gene Garber, 1979 16
2 Darold Knowles, 1970 14
John Hiller, 1974 14
Mike Marshall, 1975 14
Mike Marshall, 1979 14
6 Wilbur Wood, 1970 13
Rollie Fingers, 1978 13
Skip Lockwood, 1978 13
9 Roy Face, 1956 12
Roy Face, 1961 12
Ken Sanders, 1971 12
Mike Marshall, 1974 12
Gene Garber, 1975 12
Jim Willoughby, 1976 12
Charlie Hough, 1977 12
Mike Marshall, 1978 12
Kent Tekulve, 1980 12
Ken Howell, 1986 12
Roger Mason, 1993 12
Luis Ayala, 2004 12
21 Nels Potter, 1949 11
Frank Funk, 1961 11
Dick Radatz, 1965 11
Frank Linzy, 1966 11
Wilbur Wood, 1968 11
Wilbur Wood, 1969 11
Mike Marshall, 1973 11
Rollie Fingers, 1976 11
Rich Gossage, 1978 11
Dave Heaverlo, 1979 11
Mark Clear, 1980 11
Greg Minton, 1983 11
Ron Davis, 1984 11
Mark Davis, 1985 11
Joe Boever, 1989 11
Jose Paniagua, 1999 11
Scot Shields, 2005 11
38 49 players tied 10

RELIEF GAMES

1 Mike Marshall, 1974 106
2 Kent Tekulve, 1979 94
Salomon Torres, 2006 94
4 Mike Marshall, 1973 92
5 Kent Tekulve, 1978 91
6 Wayne Granger, 1969 90
Kent Tekulve, 1987 90
8 Mike Marshall, 1979 89
Mark Eichhorn, 1987 89
Julian Tavarez, 1997 89
Steve Kline, 2001 89
Paul Quantrill, 2003 89
Jim Brower, 2004 89
14 Mike Myers, 1997 88
Sean Runyan, 1998 88
16 Rob Murphy, 1987 87
17 Wilbur Wood, 1968 86
Paul Quantrill, 2002 86
Ray King, 2004 86
Paul Quantrill, 2004 86
Scott Eyre, 2005 86
22 Kent Tekulve, 1982 85
Frank Williams, 1987 85
Oscar Villarreal, 2003 85
Matt Capps, 2006 85
Jon Rauch, 2006 85
27 Ted Abernathy, 1965 84
Enrique Romo, 1979 84
Dick Tidrow, 1980 84
Dan Quisenberry, 1985 84
Mitch Williams, 1987 84
Stan Belinda, 1997 84
Graeme Lloyd, 2001 84
Billy Koch, 2002 84
Rheal Cormier, 2004 84
Chris Reitsma, 2004 84
Salomon Torres, 2004 84
Bob Howry, 2006 84
39 Ken Sanders, 1971 83
Craig Lefferts, 1986 83
Eddie Guardado, 1996 83
Mike Myers, 1996 83
Steve Kline, 2000 83
Kelly Wunsch, 2000 83
Octavio Dotel, 2002 83
Scott Eyre, 2004 83
Mike Stanton, 2004 83
Scott Proctor, 2006 83
49 8 players tied 82

RELIEF INNINGS PITCHED

1 Mike Marshall, 1974 208.1
2 Mike Marshall, 1973 179.0
3 Bob Stanley, 1982 168.1
4 Bill Campbell, 1976 167.2
5 Andy Karl, 1945 166.2
6 Eddie Fisher, 1965 165.1
7 Hoyt Wilhelm, 1952 159.1
8 Dick Radatz, 1964 157.0
Mark Eichhorn, 1986 157.0
10 Jim Konstanty, 1950 152.0
11 John Hiller, 1974 150.0
12 Tom Johnson, 1977 146.2
13 Garland Braxton, 1927 146.0
14 Bob Stanley, 1983 145.1
15 Hoyt Wilhelm, 1953 145.0
Wilbur Wood, 1968 145.0
17 Allan Russell, 1923 144.2
Wayne Granger, 1969 144.2
19 Steve Foucault, 1974 144.1
20 Hoyt Wilhelm, 1965 144.0
21 Jim Kern, 1979 143.0
22 Charlie Hough, 1976 142.2
23 Rich Gossage, 1975 141.2
24 Mike Marshall, 1979 140.2
25 Sammy Stewart, 1983 140.1
Willie Hernandez, 1984 140.1
27 Bill Campbell, 1977 140.0
28 Jack Lamabe, 1963 139.2
29 Pedro Borbon, 1974 139.0
Dan Quisenberry, 1983 139.0
31 Lindy McDaniel, 1973 138.1
32 Aurelio Lopez, 1984 137.2
33 Clay Carroll, 1966 137.1
34 Sparky Lyle, 1977 137.0
Tom Hume, 1980 137.0
36 Dan Quisenberry, 1982 136.2
37 Ted Abernathy, 1965 136.1
Ken Sanders, 1971 136.1
Doug Corbett, 1980 136.1
40 Mudcat Grant, 1970 135.1
Joe Page, 1949 135.1
Ted Abernathy, 1968 135.1
Kent Tekulve, 1978 135.1
44 Clay Carroll, 1968 135.0
45 Phil Regan, 1968 134.2
Rollie Fingers, 1976 134.2
47 Bill Henry, 1959 134.1
Dick Selma, 1970 134.1
Rich Gossage, 1978 134.1
Kent Tekulve, 1979 134.1

ADJUSTED RELIEVER RUNS

1 Mark Eichhorn, 1986 44.0
2 Jim Kern, 1979 39.0
3 John Hiller, 1973 35.0
Doug Corbett, 1980 35.0
Mariano Rivera, 1996 35.0
6 Rich Gossage, 1977 34.0
Willie Hernandez, 1984 34.0
8 Dan Quisenberry, 1983 33.0
9 Keith Foulke, 1999 32.0
10 Rich Gossage, 1975 31.0
Bruce Sutter, 1977 31.0
12 Lindy McDaniel, 1960 29.8
13 Mudcat Grant, 1970 28.0
Sid Monge, 1979 28.0
Tim Burke, 1987 28.0
Derek Lowe, 1999 28.0
Eric Gagne, 2003 28.0
Jonathan Papelbon, 2006 28.0
19 Wilcy Moore, 1927 27.3
20 Ellis Kinder, 1951 27.1
21 Aurelio Lopez, 1979 27.0
Roberto Hernandez, 1996 27.0
Guillermo Mota, 2003 27.0
24 Bob Lee, 1964 26.8
25 Mike Marshall, 1979 26.7
26 Dick Radatz, 1962 26.0
Dick Radatz, 1963 26.0
Dick Radatz, 1964 26.0
Ted Abernathy, 1967 26.0
Sparky Lyle, 1977 26.0
Bruce Sutter, 1984 26.0
Jeff Montgomery, 1989 26.0
Jeff Zimmerman, 1999 26.0
Gabe White, 2000 26.0
Octavio Dotel, 2002 26.0
Damaso Marte, 2003 26.0
Brad Lidge, 2004 26.0
B.J. Ryan, 2006 26.0
39 Ellis Kinder, 1953 25.0
Bob James, 1985 25.0
Dan Quisenberry, 1985 25.0
Dennis Eckersley, 1990 25.0
John Wetteland, 1993 25.0
Jose Mesa, 1995 25.0
Billy Wagner, 1999 25.0
Derek Lowe, 2000 25.0
Billy Wagner, 2003 25.0
Shigetoshi Hasegawa, 2003 25.0
49 20 players tied 24.0

RELIEF RANKING

1 Jim Kern, 1979 62.0
2 John Hiller, 1973 61.5
3 Rich Gossage, 1977 59.6
4 Mark Eichhorn, 1986 55.9
5 Roberto Hernandez, 1996 54.0
6 Mike Marshall, 1979 53.3
7 Lindy McDaniel, 1960 52.8
8 Sid Monge, 1979 51.5
9 John Wetteland, 1993 50.0
10 Eric Gagne, 2003 48.6
11 Dick Radatz, 1963 48.2
12 Robb Nen, 1998 48.0
Mariano Rivera, 2005 48.0
14 Jonathan Papelbon, 2006 47.9
15 Ellis Kinder, 1953 47.8
16 Donnie Moore, 1985 47.6
17 Mariano Rivera, 2004 47.4
18 Keith Foulke, 2003 47.3
19 Dick Radatz, 1964 46.9
20 Rich Gossage, 1975 46.3
21 Jesse Orosco, 1983 46.1
22 Doug Jones, 1997 46.0
Ugueth Urbina, 1998 46.0
Mariano Rivera, 1999 46.0
Mariano Rivera, 2006 46.0
26 Doug Corbett, 1980 45.5
27 Bob James, 1985 44.9
28 Dennis Eckersley, 1990 44.6
29 Bruce Sutter, 1977 44.2
30 Mike Marshall, 1972 44.0
Jeff Montgomery, 1993 44.0
Scott Williamson, 1999 44.0
33 Tom Murphy, 1974 43.9
34 Trevor Hoffman, 1998 43.9
35 Jose Mesa, 1995 43.6
36 Dan Quisenberry, 1985 43.6
37 Stu Miller, 1965 43.5
38 Mariano Rivera, 2003 43.0
39 Joe Nathan, 2006 42.9
40 Joe Page, 1949 42.4
41 Rollie Fingers, 1981 42.2
42 Bill Campbell, 1977 42.1
43 Dan Spillner, 1982 42.0
44 8 players tied 42.0

ADJUSTED PITCHING WINS

1	Charley Radbourn, 1884	10.5
2	Amos Rusie, 1894	9.7
3	Guy Hecker, 1884	9.7
4	Silver King, 1888	9.4
5	Walter Johnson, 1912	9.4
6	Walter Johnson, 1913	9.3
7	Lefty Grove, 1931	8.6
8	John Clarkson, 1889	8.5
9	**Pedro Martinez, 2000**	**8.2**
10	**Pedro Martinez, 1999**	**7.9**
11	Cy Young, 1901	7.9
12	**Roger Clemens, 1997**	**7.7**
13	Dolf Luque, 1923	7.3
14	Jim Galvin, 1884	7.3
15	Bob Gibson, 1968	7.3
16	Red Faber, 1921	7.1
17	Toad Ramsey, 1886	7.1
18	Will White, 1883	7.0
19	Lefty Gomez, 1937	7.0
20	Charley Radbourn, 1883	7.0
21	Grover Alexander, 1915	7.0
22	Cy Young, 1892	7.0
23	John Clarkson, 1885	7.0
24	Silver King, 1890	7.0
25	Christy Mathewson, 1905	7.0
26	Scott Stratton, 1890	7.0
27	Sandy Koufax, 1966	7.0
28	Lefty Grove, 1930	6.9
29	Steve Carlton, 1972	6.9
30	Cy Young, 1895	6.9
31	John Clarkson, 1887	6.9
32	Dazzy Vance, 1930	6.9
33	Cy Young, 1893	6.9
34	Doc Gooden, 1985	6.8
35	Hal Newhouser, 1945	6.8
36	Bob Feller, 1940	6.8
37	Lefty Grove, 1936	6.8
38	Dave Foutz, 1886	6.7
39	Dazzy Vance, 1928	6.7
40	Kid Nichols, 1897	6.7
41	Kevin Brown, 1996	6.7
42	Carl Hubbell, 1933	6.7
43	Billy Rhines, 1890	6.5
44	Gaylord Perry, 1972	6.5
45	Amos Rusie, 1893	6.5
46	**Greg Maddux, 1994**	**6.5**
47	Dean Chance, 1964	6.4
48	Walter Johnson, 1915	6.4
49	Walter Johnson, 1918	6.4
50	Ron Guidry, 1978	6.4
51	Walter Johnson, 1919	6.4
52	Hal Newhouser, 1946	6.4
53	Kid Nichols, 1898	6.3
54	**Greg Maddux, 1995**	**6.3**
55	Grover Alexander, 1920	6.3
56	Bucky Walters, 1939	6.3
57	Robin Roberts, 1953	6.3
58	Warren Spahn, 1953	6.3
59	Dizzy Trout, 1944	6.3
60	Elmer Smith, 1887	6.2
61	Tom Seaver, 1971	6.2
62	Dazzy Vance, 1924	6.2
63	Carl Hubbell, 1936	6.2
64	Wilbur Wood, 1971	6.1
65	**Roger Clemens, 1990**	**6.1**
66	Grover Alexander, 1916	6.1
67	**Randy Johnson, 2002**	**6.1**
68	Cy Young, 1902	6.0
69	Clark Griffith, 1898	6.0
70	Pink Hawley, 1895	6.0
71	Mickey Welch, 1885	6.0
72	Lefty Grove, 1932	6.0
73	Matt Kilroy, 1887	6.0
74	Ted Breitenstein, 1893	6.0
75	**Derek Lowe, 2002**	**6.0**
76	Jouett Meekin, 1894	6.0
77	**Pedro Martinez, 1997**	**6.0**
78	Lefty Grove, 1935	6.0
79	Lefty Gomez, 1934	5.9
80	Walter Johnson, 1914	5.9
81	Thornton Lee, 1941	5.9
82	Juan Marichal, 1965	5.9
83	Vida Blue, 1971	5.9
84	Dizzy Dean, 1934	5.9
85	Jack Stivetts, 1891	5.9
86	Joe Wood, 1912	5.9
87	Mordecai Brown, 1906	5.8
88	George Bradley, 1876	5.8
89	**Randy Johnson, 2001**	**5.8**
90	Kid Nichols, 1893	5.8
91	Kid Nichols, 1890	5.8
92	Jim Devlin, 1876	5.8
93	Jack Coombs, 1910	5.8
94	Carl Hubbell, 1934	5.7
95	Mel Harder, 1934	5.7
96	Bob Caruthers, 1885	5.7
97	Bob Feller, 1946	5.7
98	Christy Mathewson, 1908	5.7
99	Eddie Cicotte, 1917	5.7
100	Will White, 1882	5.7

PITCHER WINS

1	Guy Hecker, 1884	12.9
2	Walter Johnson, 1913	10.9
3	Charley Radbourn, 1884	10.7
4	Walter Johnson, 1912	10.6
5	Silver King, 1888	10.2
	Amos Rusie, 1894	10.2
7	John Clarkson, 1889	8.9
	Scott Stratton, 1890	8.9
9	Christy Mathewson, 1905	8.5
10	**Pedro Martinez, 2000**	**8.4**
11	Charley Radbourn, 1883	8.3
12	Lefty Grove, 1931	8.2
	Bucky Walters, 1939	8.2
	Dizzy Trout, 1944	8.2
15	**Pedro Martinez, 1999**	**8.1**
16	Cy Young, 1901	7.9
	Roger Clemens, 1997	**7.9**
18	Dave Foutz, 1886	7.6
	Joe Wood, 1912	7.6
	Walter Johnson, 1918	7.6
	Dolf Luque, 1923	7.6
	Hal Newhouser, 1945	7.6
	Bob Gibson, 1968	7.6
	Doc Gooden, 1985	7.6
25	John Clarkson, 1887	7.5
	Grover Alexander, 1915	7.5
27	Pink Hawley, 1895	7.4
	Walter Johnson, 1915	7.4
	Steve Carlton, 1972	7.4
30	John Clarkson, 1885	7.3
	Carl Hubbell, 1933	7.3
32	Bob Caruthers, 1886	7.2
	Matt Kilroy, 1887	7.2
	Walter Johnson, 1914	7.2
	Grover Alexander, 1916	7.2
	Dazzy Vance, 1928	7.2
37	Tony Mullane, 1884	7.1
38	Warren Spahn, 1953	7.0
39	Will White, 1883	6.9
	Cy Young, 1895	6.9
	Kid Nichols, 1897	6.9
	Grover Alexander, 1920	6.9
	Lefty Grove, 1930	6.9
	Kevin Brown, 1996	6.9
45	Jack Stivetts, 1891	6.8
	Amos Rusie, 1893	6.8
	Ed Walsh, 1908	6.8
	Red Faber, 1921	6.8
	Wes Ferrell, 1935	6.8
	Lefty Gomez, 1937	6.8
	Bob Feller, 1940	6.8
	Gaylord Perry, 1972	6.8
	Greg Maddux, 1994	**6.8**
54	Will White, 1882	6.7
	Toad Ramsey, 1886	6.7
	Walter Johnson, 1919	6.7
	Tom Seaver, 1971	6.7
	John Hiller, 1973	6.7
59	Silver King, 1890	6.6
	Christy Mathewson, 1909	6.6
	Lefty Grove, 1936	6.6
	Bob Lemon, 1948	6.6
63	Charlie Sweeney, 1884	6.5
	Charlie Ferguson, 1886	6.5
	Cy Young, 1893	6.5
	Christy Mathewson, 1908	6.5
	Ed Walsh, 1912	6.5
	Thornton Lee, 1941	6.5
	Greg Maddux, 1995	**6.5**
70	Cy Young, 1892	6.4
	Kid Nichols, 1898	6.4
	Dazzy Vance, 1930	6.4
	Hal Newhouser, 1946	6.4
	Robin Roberts, 1953	6.4
	Rich Gossage, 1977	6.4
	Ron Guidry, 1978	6.4
	Greg Maddux, 1998	**6.4**
78	Jim Galvin, 1884	6.3
	Bob Caruthers, 1885	6.3
	Elmer Smith, 1887	6.3
	Ed Walsh, 1910	6.3
	Bob Gibson, 1969	6.3
	Jim Kern, 1979	6.3
84	George Bradley, 1876	6.2
	Jim Devlin, 1876	6.2
	Jouett Meekin, 1894	6.2
	Carl Hubbell, 1936	6.2
	Roger Clemens, 1990	**6.2**
	Derek Lowe, 2002	**6.2**
90	Jack Taylor, 1902	6.1
	Jack Chesbro, 1904	6.1
	Mordecai Brown, 1906	6.1
	Dizzy Dean, 1934	6.1
	Hal Newhouser, 1944	6.1
	Sandy Koufax, 1966	6.1
96	Tim Keefe, 1883	6.0
	Mickey Welch, 1885	6.0
	Guy Hecker, 1885	6.0
	Billy Rhines, 1890	6.0
	Cy Young, 1902	6.0

PITCHER WINS

	Bob Feller, 1939	6.0
	Juan Marichal, 1965	6.0
	Greg Maddux, 1992	**6.0**
104	Bob Caruthers, 1887	5.9
	Kid Nichols, 1890	5.9
	Amos Rusie, 1890	5.9
	Amos Rusie, 1897	5.9
	Clark Griffith, 1898	5.9
	Dazzy Vance, 1924	5.9
	Dolf Luque, 1925	5.9
	Wes Ferrell, 1930	5.9
	Lefty Grove, 1932	5.9
	Carl Hubbell, 1934	5.9
114	Charlie Buffinton, 1884	5.8
	Rube Waddell, 1902	5.8
	Jack Coombs, 1910	5.8
	Lon Warneke, 1933	5.8
	Juan Marichal, 1966	5.8
	Mark Eichhorn, 1986	5.8
	Pedro Martinez, 1997	**5.8**
	Dontrelle Willis, 2005	**5.8**
122	Lady Baldwin, 1886	5.7
	Jesse Duryea, 1889	5.7
	Matt Kilroy, 1889	5.7
	Cy Young, 1896	5.7
	Christy Mathewson, 1911	5.7
	Joe Wood, 1911	5.7
	Babe Ruth, 1916	5.7
	Eddie Cicotte, 1917	5.7
	Curt Davis, 1934	5.7
	Mel Harder, 1934	5.7
	Wilbur Wood, 1971	5.7
	Jim Palmer, 1975	5.7
	Randy Johnson, 2002	**5.7**
	Roger Clemens, 2005	**5.7**
136	Jim Whitney, 1883	5.6
	Ted Breitenstein, 1893	5.6
	Bob Lemon, 1949	5.6
	Dean Chance, 1964	5.6
	Fergie Jenkins, 1971	5.6
	John Tudor, 1985	5.6
	Randy Johnson, 1997	**5.6**
	Tom Glavine, 1998	**5.6**
	Johan Santana, 2004	**5.6**
145	Tony Mullane, 1883	5.5
	Tim Keefe, 1884	5.5
	Frank Killen, 1893	5.5
	Kid Nichols, 1893	5.5
	Nig Cuppy, 1896	5.5
	Walter Johnson, 1910	5.5
	Ed Walsh, 1911	5.5
	Eddie Cicotte, 1919	5.5
	Stan Coveleski, 1920	5.5
	Lefty Gomez, 1934	5.5
	Lefty Grove, 1935	5.5
	Gene Bearden, 1948	5.5
	Sandy Koufax, 1965	5.5
	Tom Seaver, 1973	5.5
	Steve Carlton, 1977	5.5
	Esteban Loaiza, 2003	**5.5**
161	Kid Nichols, 1896	5.4
	Joe McGinnity, 1904	5.4
	Walter Johnson, 1911	5.4
	Claude Hendrix, 1914	5.4
	Grover Alexander, 1917	5.4
	Carl Mays, 1921	5.4
	George Uhle, 1926	5.4
	Johnny Sain, 1946	5.4
	Bob Feller, 1946	5.4
	Mike Marshall, 1979	5.4
	Randy Johnson, 2001	**5.4**
172	Billy Taylor, 1884	5.3
	George Haddock, 1891	5.3
	Mordecai Brown, 1909	5.3
	Christy Mathewson, 1910	5.3
	Christy Mathewson, 1912	5.3
	Whit Wyatt, 1941	5.3
	Spud Chandler, 1943	5.3
	Warren Spahn, 1947	5.3
	Harry Brecheen, 1948	5.3
	Johnny Sain, 1948	5.3
	Johnny Antonelli, 1954	5.3
	Billy Pierce, 1955	5.3
	Tom Seaver, 1969	5.3
	Vida Blue, 1971	5.3
	Bert Blyleven, 1973	5.3
	Rick Reuschel, 1977	5.3
	Bret Saberhagen, 1989	5.3
	Roger Clemens, 1992	**5.3**
	Greg Maddux, 1993	**5.3**
	Greg Maddux, 1997	**5.3**
	Mike Hampton, 1999	**5.3**
	Randy Johnson, 2004	**5.3**
194	13 players tied	5.2

PITCHER WINS BY ERA

1988–2006

1	**Pedro Martinez, 2000**	**8.4**
2	**Pedro Martinez, 1999**	**8.1**
3	**Roger Clemens, 1997**	**7.9**
4	Kevin Brown, 1996	6.9
5	**Greg Maddux, 1994**	**6.8**
6	**Greg Maddux, 1995**	**6.5**
7	**Greg Maddux, 1998**	**6.4**
8	**Roger Clemens, 1990**	**6.2**
	Derek Lowe, 2002	**6.2**
10	**Greg Maddux, 1992**	**6.0**

1973–87

1	Doc Gooden, 1985	7.6
2	John Hiller, 1973	6.7
3	Rich Gossage, 1977	6.4
	Ron Guidry, 1978	6.4
5	Jim Kern, 1979	6.3
6	Mark Eichhorn, 1986	5.8
7	Jim Palmer, 1975	5.7
8	John Tudor, 1985	5.6
9	Tom Seaver, 1973	5.5
	Steve Carlton, 1977	5.5

1961–72

1	Bob Gibson, 1968	7.6
2	Steve Carlton, 1972	7.4
3	Gaylord Perry, 1972	6.8
4	Tom Seaver, 1971	6.7
5	Bob Gibson, 1969	6.3
6	Sandy Koufax, 1966	6.1
7	Juan Marichal, 1965	6.0
8	Juan Marichal, 1966	5.8
9	Wilbur Wood, 1971	5.7
10	Dean Chance, 1964	5.6
	Fergie Jenkins, 1971	5.6

1943–60

1	Dizzy Trout, 1944	8.2
2	Hal Newhouser, 1945	7.6
3	Warren Spahn, 1953	7.0
4	Bob Lemon, 1948	6.6
5	Hal Newhouser, 1946	6.4
	Robin Roberts, 1953	6.4
7	Hal Newhouser, 1944	6.1
8	Bob Lemon, 1949	5.6
9	Gene Bearden, 1948	5.5
10	Johnny Sain, 1946	5.4
	Bob Feller, 1946	5.4

1921–42

1	Lefty Grove, 1931	8.2
	Bucky Walters, 1939	8.2
3	Dolf Luque, 1923	7.6
4	Carl Hubbell, 1933	7.3
5	Dazzy Vance, 1928	7.2
6	Lefty Grove, 1930	6.9
7	Red Faber, 1921	6.8
	Wes Ferrell, 1935	6.8
	Lefty Gomez, 1937	6.8
	Bob Feller, 1940	6.8

1901–20

1	Walter Johnson, 1913	10.9
2	Walter Johnson, 1912	10.6
3	Christy Mathewson, 1905	8.5
4	Cy Young, 1901	7.9
5	Joe Wood, 1912	7.6
	Walter Johnson, 1918	7.6
7	Grover Alexander, 1915	7.5
8	Walter Johnson, 1915	7.4
9	Walter Johnson, 1914	7.2
	Grover Alexander, 1916	7.2

1893–1900

1	Amos Rusie, 1894	10.2
2	Pink Hawley, 1895	7.4
3	Cy Young, 1895	6.9
	Kid Nichols, 1897	6.9
5	Amos Rusie, 1893	6.8
6	Cy Young, 1893	6.5
7	Kid Nichols, 1898	6.4
8	Jouett Meekin, 1894	6.2
9	Amos Rusie, 1897	5.9
	Clark Griffith, 1898	5.9

1876–92

1	Guy Hecker, 1884	12.9
2	Charley Radbourn, 1884	10.7
3	Silver King, 1888	10.2
4	John Clarkson, 1889	8.9
	Scott Stratton, 1890	8.9
6	Charley Radbourn, 1883	8.3
7	Dave Foutz, 1886	7.6
8	John Clarkson, 1887	7.5
9	John Clarkson, 1885	7.3
10	Bob Caruthers, 1886	7.2
	Matt Kilroy, 1887	7.2

PLAYER OVERALL WINS ALPHA

Hank Aaron, 1959	6.6
Grover Alexander, 1915	7.5
Grover Alexander, 1916	7.2
Grover Alexander, 1920	6.9
Roberto Alomar, 1996	6.1
Luke Appling, 1943	6.3
Jeff Bagwell, 1994	7.7
Jeff Bagwell, 1996	7.1
Jeff Bagwell, 1997	6.0
Frank Baker, 1912	6.5
Frank Baker, 1913	6.6
Ernie Banks, 1959	6.4
Ernie Banks, 1960	6.0
Dick Bartell, 1937	6.1
Johnny Bench, 1972	6.5
Craig Biggio, 1997	**8.2**
Wade Boggs, 1987	6.5
Wade Boggs, 1988	6.4
Barry Bonds, 1990	**6.4**
Barry Bonds, 1992	**7.9**
Barry Bonds, 1993	**8.0**
Barry Bonds, 1996	**7.6**
Barry Bonds, 1997	**6.2**
Barry Bonds, 1998	**6.7**
Barry Bonds, 2000	**6.8**
Barry Bonds, 2001	**11.7**
Barry Bonds, 2002	**11.5**
Barry Bonds, 2003	**8.2**
Barry Bonds, 2004	**10.7**
Lou Boudreau, 1943	6.8
Lou Boudreau, 1944	7.5
Lou Boudreau, 1948	7.1
George Bradley, 1876	6.2
George Brett, 1980	6.5
George Brett, 1985	6.6
Dan Brouthers, 1892	6.8
Mordecai Brown, 1906	6.1
Kevin Brown, 1996	6.9
Ken Caminiti, 1996	7.4
Rod Carew, 1974	6.9
Rod Carew, 1975	6.7
Rod Carew, 1977	6.5
Steve Carlton, 1972	7.4
Gary Carter, 1982	6.8
Bob Caruthers, 1885	6.3
Bob Caruthers, 1886	7.2
Norm Cash, 1961	7.6
Jack Chesbro, 1904	6.1
Cupid Childs, 1890	6.8
Cupid Childs, 1896	6.3
John Clarkson, 1885	7.3
John Clarkson, 1887	7.5
John Clarkson, 1889	8.9
Roger Clemens, 1990	**6.2**
Roger Clemens, 1997	**7.9**
Harlond Clift, 1937	7.4
Ty Cobb, 1909	6.0
Ty Cobb, 1910	6.3
Ty Cobb, 1911	6.6
Ty Cobb, 1917	7.4
Eddie Collins, 1910	7.0
Eddie Collins, 1912	6.4
Eddie Collins, 1913	7.0
Eddie Collins, 1914	6.9
Eddie Collins, 1915	6.6
Joe Cronin, 1930	6.9
George Davis, 1899	6.1
Dizzy Dean, 1934	6.1
Ed Delahanty, 1896	6.0
Jim Devlin, 1876	6.2
Art Devlin, 1906	6.6
Joe DiMaggio, 1941	6.6
Fred Dunlap, 1884	7.1
Darrell Evans, 1973	6.3
Red Faber, 1921	6.8
Bob Feller, 1939	6.0
Bob Feller, 1940	6.8
Charlie Ferguson, 1886	6.5
Wes Ferrell, 1935	6.8
Dave Foutz, 1886	7.6
Nellie Fox, 1957	6.0
Jimmie Foxx, 1932	6.7
Jimmie Foxx, 1933	6.9
Jimmie Foxx, 1934	6.1
Frankie Frisch, 1924	6.0
Frankie Frisch, 1927	7.2
Jim Galvin, 1884	6.3
Lou Gehrig, 1927	8.4
Lou Gehrig, 1930	7.7
Lou Gehrig, 1931	6.0
Lou Gehrig, 1934	7.9
Lou Gehrig, 1936	6.6
Charlie Gehringer, 1934	6.0
Charlie Gehringer, 1936	6.1
Jason Giambi, 2001	**6.3**
Bob Gibson, 1968	7.6
Bob Gibson, 1969	6.3
Lefty Gomez, 1937	6.8
Doc Gooden, 1985	7.6
Rich Gossage, 1977	6.4

PLAYER OVERALL WINS ALPHA (CONT.)

Bobby Grich, 1974	6.0
Bobby Grich, 1975	6.4
Ken Griffey Jr., 1997	**6.0**
Lefty Grove, 1930	6.9
Lefty Grove, 1931	8.2
Lefty Grove, 1936	6.6
Ron Guidry, 1978	6.4
Toby Harrah, 1975	6.9
Pink Hawley, 1895	7.4
Guy Hecker, 1884	12.9
Guy Hecker, 1885	6.0
Harry Heilmann, 1923	6.0
Todd Helton, 2004	**6.2**
Rickey Henderson, 1985	6.9
Rickey Henderson, 1990	7.7
John Hiller, 1973	6.7
Rogers Hornsby, 1917	7.8
Rogers Hornsby, 1920	7.9
Rogers Hornsby, 1921	7.7
Rogers Hornsby, 1922	8.9
Rogers Hornsby, 1924	9.3
Rogers Hornsby, 1925	6.8
Rogers Hornsby, 1927	6.8
Rogers Hornsby, 1928	6.1
Rogers Hornsby, 1929	6.8
Carl Hubbell, 1933	7.3
Carl Hubbell, 1936	6.2
Joe Jackson, 1911	6.5
Joe Jackson, 1912	7.1
Reggie Jackson, 1969	6.3
Hughie Jennings, 1895	6.3
Hughie Jennings, 1896	6.7
Walter Johnson, 1912	10.6
Walter Johnson, 1913	10.9
Walter Johnson, 1914	7.2
Walter Johnson, 1915	7.4
Walter Johnson, 1918	7.6
Walter Johnson, 1919	6.7
Tim Keefe, 1883	6.0
Jeff Kent, 2000	**6.4**
Jim Kern, 1979	6.3
Matt Kilroy, 1887	7.2
Silver King, 1888	10.2
Silver King, 1890	6.6
Sandy Koufax, 1966	6.1
Nap Lajoie, 1901	8.1
Nap Lajoie, 1903	8.1
Nap Lajoie, 1904	7.4
Nap Lajoie, 1906	7.6
Nap Lajoie, 1907	7.0
Nap Lajoie, 1908	8.0
Nap Lajoie, 1910	8.9
Eddie Lake, 1945	6.5
Barry Larkin, 1991	6.2
Barry Larkin, 1996	6.0
Thornton Lee, 1941	6.5
Derrek Lee, 2005	**6.3**
Bob Lemon, 1948	6.6
Derek Lowe, 2002	**6.2**
Dolf Luque, 1923	7.6
Greg Maddux, 1992	**6.0**
Greg Maddux, 1994	**6.8**
Greg Maddux, 1995	**6.5**
Greg Maddux, 1998	**6.4**
Mickey Mantle, 1956	8.1
Mickey Mantle, 1957	8.0
Mickey Mantle, 1961	7.5
Juan Marichal, 1965	6.0
Pedro Martinez, 1999	**8.1**
Pedro Martinez, 2000	**8.4**
Eddie Mathews, 1953	6.1
Eddie Mathews, 1959	6.0
Christy Mathewson, 1905	8.5
Christy Mathewson, 1908	6.5
Christy Mathewson, 1909	6.6
Willie Mays, 1954	6.2
Willie Mays, 1955	6.8
Willie Mays, 1958	6.2
Willie Mays, 1962	6.1
Willie Mays, 1963	6.0
Willie Mays, 1965	6.9
Willie McCovey, 1969	6.5
Willie McCovey, 1970	6.5
Mark McGwire, 1998	7.1
Joe Medwick, 1937	6.0
Jouett Meekin, 1894	6.2
Kevin Mitchell, 1989	6.2
Joe Morgan, 1973	7.4
Joe Morgan, 1974	7.0
Joe Morgan, 1975	8.1
Joe Morgan, 1976	6.7
Tony Mullane, 1884	7.1
Stan Musial, 1948	7.2
Stan Musial, 1951	6.1
Hal Newhouser, 1944	6.1
Hal Newhouser, 1945	7.6
Hal Newhouser, 1946	6.4
Kid Nichols, 1897	6.9
Kid Nichols, 1898	6.4
Mel Ott, 1938	6.4

PLAYER OVERALL WINS ALPHA (CONT.)

Gaylord Perry, 1972	6.8
Rico Petrocelli, 1969	7.6
Fred Pfeffer, 1884	6.0
Mike Piazza, 1997	**7.7**
Mike Piazza, 1998	**6.0**
Albert Pujols, 2003	**7.1**
Charley Radbourn, 1883	8.3
Charley Radbourn, 1884	10.7
Toad Ramsey, 1886	6.7
Billy Rhines, 1890	6.0
Cal Ripken, 1983	7.0
Cal Ripken, 1984	9.4
Cal Ripken, 1991	8.5
Robin Roberts, 1953	6.4
Jackie Robinson, 1951	7.3
Frank Robinson, 1966	6.3
Alex Rodriguez, 2000	**6.6**
Alex Rodriguez, 2001	**6.9**
Alex Rodriguez, 2002	**7.4**
Alex Rodriguez, 2003	**6.7**
Alex Rodriguez, 2005	**6.0**
Scott Rolen, 2004	**6.4**
Al Rosen, 1953	7.4
Amos Rusie, 1893	6.8
Amos Rusie, 1894	10.2
Babe Ruth, 1919	8.7
Babe Ruth, 1920	9.3
Babe Ruth, 1921	9.4
Babe Ruth, 1923	10.1
Babe Ruth, 1924	8.4
Babe Ruth, 1926	8.5
Babe Ruth, 1927	8.8
Babe Ruth, 1928	7.1
Babe Ruth, 1930	7.6
Babe Ruth, 1931	8.1
Babe Ruth, 1932	6.5
Ryne Sandberg, 1984	6.6
Ron Santo, 1964	7.1
Ron Santo, 1965	6.2
Ron Santo, 1966	7.6
Ron Santo, 1967	7.7
Mike Schmidt, 1974	7.3
Mike Schmidt, 1977	6.4
Mike Schmidt, 1980	6.8
Mike Schmidt, 1981	7.1
Mike Schmidt, 1982	6.3
Mike Schmidt, 1983	6.4
Red Schoendienst, 1953	6.5
Tom Seaver, 1971	6.7
Joe Sewell, 1923	6.2
Gary Sheffield, 1992	**6.0**
George Sisler, 1920	7.9
George Sisler, 1922	6.3
Elmer Smith, 1887	6.3
Sammy Sosa, 2001	8.6
Warren Spahn, 1953	7.0
Tris Speaker, 1912	7.2
Tris Speaker, 1913	6.5
Tris Speaker, 1914	7.3
Tris Speaker, 1923	6.5
Snuffy Stirnweiss, 1944	6.8
Snuffy Stirnweiss, 1945	7.2
Jack Stivetts, 1891	6.8
Scott Stratton, 1890	8.9
Charlie Sweeney, 1884	6.5
Jack Taylor, 1902	6.1
Miguel Tejada, 2004	**6.6**
Dickie Thon, 1983	6.2
Alan Trammell, 1987	6.1
Dizzy Trout, 1944	8.2
Dazzy Vance, 1928	7.2
Dazzy Vance, 1930	6.4
Arky Vaughan, 1935	6.6
Arky Vaughan, 1938	6.4
Honus Wagner, 1905	7.5
Honus Wagner, 1906	7.2
Honus Wagner, 1907	6.7
Honus Wagner, 1908	6.9
Ed Walsh, 1908	6.8
Ed Walsh, 1910	6.3
Ed Walsh, 1912	6.5
Bucky Walters, 1939	8.2
Mickey Welch, 1885	6.0
Will White, 1882	6.7
Will White, 1883	6.9
Ted Williams, 1941	8.5
Ted Williams, 1942	8.5
Ted Williams, 1946	8.1
Ted Williams, 1947	7.2
Ted Williams, 1949	6.4
Ted Williams, 1957	7.3
Joe Wood, 1912	7.6
Carl Yastrzemski, 1967	6.9
Carl Yastrzemski, 1968	6.3
Cy Young, 1892	6.4
Cy Young, 1893	6.5
Cy Young, 1895	6.9
Cy Young, 1901	7.9
Cy Young, 1902	6.0
Robin Yount, 1982	7.1

PLAYER OVERALL WINS

1	Guy Hecker, 1884	12.9
2	**Barry Bonds, 2001**	**11.7**
3	**Barry Bonds, 2002**	**11.5**
4	Walter Johnson, 1913	10.9
5	Charley Radbourn, 1884	10.7
	Barry Bonds, 2004	**10.7**
7	Walter Johnson, 1912	10.6
8	Silver King, 1888	10.2
	Amos Rusie, 1894	10.2
10	Babe Ruth, 1923	10.1
11	Babe Ruth, 1921	9.4
	Cal Ripken, 1984	9.4
13	Babe Ruth, 1920	9.3
	Rogers Hornsby, 1924	9.3
15	John Clarkson, 1889	8.9
	Scott Stratton, 1890	8.9
	Nap Lajoie, 1910	8.9
	Rogers Hornsby, 1922	8.9
19	Babe Ruth, 1927	8.8
20	Babe Ruth, 1919	8.7
21	Sammy Sosa, 2001	8.6
22	Christy Mathewson, 1905	8.5
	Babe Ruth, 1926	8.5
	Ted Williams, 1941	8.5
	Ted Williams, 1942	8.5
	Cal Ripken, 1991	8.5
27	**Pedro Martinez, 2000**	**8.4**
	Babe Ruth, 1924	8.4
	Lou Gehrig, 1927	8.4
30	Charley Radbourn, 1883	8.3
31	Lefty Grove, 1931	8.2
	Bucky Walters, 1939	8.2
	Dizzy Trout, 1944	8.2
	Craig Biggio, 1997	**8.2**
	Barry Bonds, 2003	**8.2**
36	**Pedro Martinez, 1999**	**8.1**
	Nap Lajoie, 1901	8.1
	Nap Lajoie, 1903	8.1
	Babe Ruth, 1931	8.1
	Ted Williams, 1946	8.1
	Mickey Mantle, 1956	8.1
	Joe Morgan, 1975	8.1
43	Nap Lajoie, 1908	8.0
	Mickey Mantle, 1957	8.0
	Barry Bonds, 1993	**8.0**
46	Cy Young, 1901	7.9
	Roger Clemens, 1997	**7.9**
	Rogers Hornsby, 1920	7.9
	George Sisler, 1920	7.9
	Lou Gehrig, 1934	7.9
	Barry Bonds, 1992	**7.9**
52	Rogers Hornsby, 1917	7.8
53	Rogers Hornsby, 1921	7.7
	Lou Gehrig, 1930	7.7
	Ron Santo, 1967	7.7
	Rickey Henderson, 1990	7.7
	Jeff Bagwell, 1994	7.7
	Mike Piazza, 1997	**7.7**
59	Dave Foutz, 1886	7.6
	Joe Wood, 1912	7.6
	Walter Johnson, 1918	7.6
	Dolf Luque, 1923	7.6
	Hal Newhouser, 1945	7.6
	Bob Gibson, 1968	7.6
	Doc Gooden, 1985	7.6
	Nap Lajoie, 1906	7.6
	Babe Ruth, 1930	7.6
	Norm Cash, 1961	7.6
	Ron Santo, 1966	7.6
	Rico Petrocelli, 1969	7.6
	Barry Bonds, 1996	**7.6**
72	John Clarkson, 1887	7.5
	Grover Alexander, 1915	7.5
	Honus Wagner, 1905	7.5
	Lou Boudreau, 1944	7.5
	Mickey Mantle, 1961	7.5
77	Pink Hawley, 1895	7.4
	Walter Johnson, 1915	7.4
	Steve Carlton, 1972	7.4
	Nap Lajoie, 1904	7.4
	Ty Cobb, 1917	7.4
	Harlond Clift, 1937	7.4
	Al Rosen, 1953	7.4
	Joe Morgan, 1973	7.4
	Ken Caminiti, 1996	7.4
	Alex Rodriguez, 2002	**7.4**
87	John Clarkson, 1885	7.3
	Carl Hubbell, 1933	7.3
	Tris Speaker, 1914	7.3
	Jackie Robinson, 1951	7.3
	Ted Williams, 1957	7.3
	Mike Schmidt, 1974	7.3
93	Bob Caruthers, 1886	7.2
	Matt Kilroy, 1887	7.2
	Walter Johnson, 1914	7.2
	Grover Alexander, 1916	7.2
	Dazzy Vance, 1928	7.2
	Honus Wagner, 1906	7.2
	Tris Speaker, 1912	7.2
	Frankie Frisch, 1927	7.2

PLAYER OVERALL WINS

	Snuffy Stirnweiss, 1945	7.2
	Ted Williams, 1947	7.2
	Stan Musial, 1948	7.2
104	Tony Mullane, 1884	7.1
	Fred Dunlap, 1884	7.1
	Joe Jackson, 1912	7.1
	Babe Ruth, 1928	7.1
	Lou Boudreau, 1948	7.1
	Ron Santo, 1964	7.1
	Mike Schmidt, 1981	7.1
	Robin Yount, 1982	7.1
	Jeff Bagwell, 1996	7.1
	Mark McGwire, 1998	7.1
	Albert Pujols, 2003	**7.1**
115	Warren Spahn, 1953	7.0
	Nap Lajoie, 1907	7.0
	Eddie Collins, 1910	7.0
	Eddie Collins, 1913	7.0
	Joe Morgan, 1974	7.0
	Cal Ripken, 1983	7.0
121	Will White, 1883	6.9
	Cy Young, 1895	6.9
	Kid Nichols, 1897	6.9
	Grover Alexander, 1920	6.9
	Lefty Grove, 1930	6.9
	Kevin Brown, 1996	6.9
	Honus Wagner, 1908	6.9
	Eddie Collins, 1914	6.9
	Joe Cronin, 1930	6.9
	Jimmie Foxx, 1933	6.9
	Willie Mays, 1965	6.9
	Carl Yastrzemski, 1967	6.9
	Rod Carew, 1974	6.9
	Toby Harrah, 1975	6.9
	Rickey Henderson, 1985	6.9
	Alex Rodriguez, 2001	**6.9**
137	Jack Stivetts, 1891	6.8
	Amos Rusie, 1893	6.8
	Ed Walsh, 1908	6.8
	Red Faber, 1921	6.8
	Wes Ferrell, 1935	6.8
	Lefty Gomez, 1937	6.8
	Bob Feller, 1940	6.8
	Gaylord Perry, 1972	6.8
	Greg Maddux, 1994	**6.8**
	Cupid Childs, 1890	6.8
	Dan Brouthers, 1892	6.8
	Rogers Hornsby, 1925	6.8
	Rogers Hornsby, 1927	6.8
	Rogers Hornsby, 1929	6.8
	Lou Boudreau, 1943	6.8
	Snuffy Stirnweiss, 1944	6.8
	Willie Mays, 1955	6.8
	Mike Schmidt, 1980	6.8
	Gary Carter, 1982	6.8
	Barry Bonds, 2000	**6.8**
157	Will White, 1882	6.7
	Toad Ramsey, 1886	6.7
	Walter Johnson, 1919	6.7
	Tom Seaver, 1971	6.7
	John Hiller, 1973	6.7
	Hughie Jennings, 1896	6.7
	Honus Wagner, 1907	6.7
	Jimmie Foxx, 1932	6.7
	Rod Carew, 1975	6.7
	Joe Morgan, 1976	6.7
	Barry Bonds, 1998	**6.7**
	Alex Rodriguez, 2003	**6.7**
169	Silver King, 1890	6.6
	Christy Mathewson, 1909	6.6
	Lefty Grove, 1936	6.6
	Bob Lemon, 1948	6.6
	Art Devlin, 1906	6.6
	Ty Cobb, 1911	6.6
	Frank Baker, 1913	6.6
	Eddie Collins, 1915	6.6
	Arky Vaughan, 1935	6.6
	Lou Gehrig, 1936	6.6
	Joe DiMaggio, 1941	6.6
	Hank Aaron, 1959	6.6
	Ryne Sandberg, 1984	6.6
	George Brett, 1985	6.6
	Alex Rodriguez, 2000	**6.6**
	Miguel Tejada, 2004	**6.6**
185	Charlie Sweeney, 1884	6.5
	Charlie Ferguson, 1886	6.5
	Cy Young, 1893	6.5
	Christy Mathewson, 1908	6.5
	Ed Walsh, 1912	6.5
	Thornton Lee, 1941	6.5
	Greg Maddux, 1995	**6.5**
	Joe Jackson, 1911	6.5
	Frank Baker, 1912	6.5
	Tris Speaker, 1913	6.5
	Tris Speaker, 1923	6.5
	Babe Ruth, 1932	6.5
	Eddie Lake, 1945	6.5
	Red Schoendienst, 1953	6.5
	Willie McCovey, 1969	6.5
	Willie McCovey, 1970	6.5

PLAYER OVERALL WINS

	Johnny Bench, 1972	6.5
	Rod Carew, 1977	6.5
	George Brett, 1980	6.5
	Wade Boggs, 1987	6.5
205	Cy Young, 1892	6.4
	Kid Nichols, 1898	6.4
	Dazzy Vance, 1930	6.4
	Hal Newhouser, 1946	6.4
	Robin Roberts, 1953	6.4
	Rich Gossage, 1977	6.4
	Ron Guidry, 1978	6.4
	Greg Maddux, 1998	**6.4**
	Eddie Collins, 1912	6.4
	Mel Ott, 1938	6.4
	Arky Vaughan, 1938	6.4
	Ted Williams, 1949	6.4
	Ernie Banks, 1959	6.4
	Bobby Grich, 1975	6.4
	Mike Schmidt, 1977	6.4
	Mike Schmidt, 1983	6.4
	Wade Boggs, 1988	6.4
	Barry Bonds, 1990	**6.4**
	Jeff Kent, 2000	**6.4**
	Scott Rolen, 2004	**6.4**
225	Jim Galvin, 1884	6.3
	Bob Caruthers, 1885	6.3
	Elmer Smith, 1887	6.3
	Ed Walsh, 1910	6.3
	Bob Gibson, 1969	6.3
	Jim Kern, 1979	6.3
	Hughie Jennings, 1895	6.3
	Cupid Childs, 1896	6.3
	Ty Cobb, 1910	6.3
	George Sisler, 1922	6.3
	Luke Appling, 1943	6.3
	Frank Robinson, 1966	6.3
	Carl Yastrzemski, 1968	6.3
	Reggie Jackson, 1969	6.3
	Darrell Evans, 1973	6.3
	Mike Schmidt, 1982	6.3
	Jason Giambi, 2001	**6.3**
	Derrek Lee, 2005	**6.3**
243	George Bradley, 1876	6.2
	Jim Devlin, 1876	6.2
	Jouett Meekin, 1894	6.2
	Carl Hubbell, 1936	6.2
	Roger Clemens, 1990	**6.2**
	Derek Lowe, 2002	**6.2**
	Joe Sewell, 1923	6.2
	Willie Mays, 1954	6.2
	Willie Mays, 1958	6.2
	Ron Santo, 1965	6.2
	Dickie Thon, 1983	6.2
	Kevin Mitchell, 1989	6.2
	Barry Larkin, 1991	6.2
	Barry Bonds, 1997	**6.2**
	Todd Helton, 2004	**6.2**
258	Jack Taylor, 1902	6.1
	Jack Chesbro, 1904	6.1
	Mordecai Brown, 1906	6.1
	Dizzy Dean, 1934	6.1
	Hal Newhouser, 1944	6.1
	Sandy Koufax, 1966	6.1
	George Davis, 1899	6.1
	Rogers Hornsby, 1928	6.1
	Jimmie Foxx, 1934	6.1
	Charlie Gehringer, 1936	6.1
	Dick Bartell, 1937	6.1
	Stan Musial, 1951	6.1
	Eddie Mathews, 1953	6.1
	Willie Mays, 1962	6.1
	Alan Trammell, 1987	6.1
	Roberto Alomar, 1996	6.1
274	Tim Keefe, 1883	6.0
	Mickey Welch, 1885	6.0
	Guy Hecker, 1885	6.0
	Billy Rhines, 1890	6.0
	Cy Young, 1902	6.0
	Bob Feller, 1939	6.0
	Juan Marichal, 1965	6.0
	Greg Maddux, 1992	**6.0**
	Fred Pfeffer, 1884	6.0
	Ed Delahanty, 1896	6.0
	Ty Cobb, 1909	6.0
	Harry Heilmann, 1923	6.0
	Frankie Frisch, 1924	6.0
	Lou Gehrig, 1931	6.0
	Charlie Gehringer, 1934	6.0
	Joe Medwick, 1937	6.0
	Nellie Fox, 1957	6.0
	Eddie Mathews, 1959	6.0
	Ernie Banks, 1960	6.0
	Willie Mays, 1963	6.0
	Bobby Grich, 1974	6.0
	Gary Sheffield, 1992	**6.0**
	Barry Larkin, 1996	6.0
	Jeff Bagwell, 1997	6.0
	Ken Griffey Jr., 1997	**6.0**
	Mike Piazza, 1998	**6.0**
	Alex Rodriguez, 2005	**6.0**

THE NATURALS: THE HALL OF FAME

While lesser sports have copied the National Baseball Hall of Fame and Museum, no other athletic Hall of Fame commands nearly so much respect, interest, or passion. In a cynical modern era when very few athletic heroes are idolized, those fortunate few inducted into Cooperstown have achieved a kind of immortality. Many of these bronze demigods were *naturals* in the true sense of the word, whether they triumphed over their demons like Robert Redford in Barry Levinson's 1984 film *The Natural*—or whether they succumbed like Roy Hobbs in Bernard Malamud's classic novella on which the movie was based.

In 1934 in the middle of the Great Depression, Alexander Cleland, a civic leader in Cooperstown, New York, came up with an idea to boost tourism in his small city: He decided that Cooperstown could benefit from building a baseball museum. Cooperstown was (and still is) an out-of-the-way place. However, the town was home to a rich foundation—Cleland's employer, the Clark Foundation—that would support these types of projects, and it was also the supposed birthplace of baseball. Even then, many people realized that Abner Doubleday most certainly did *not* invent baseball in Cooperstown, and that neither the famous general nor the picturesque town had even played a role in the development of baseball. Nonetheless, creation myths are very powerful, and Cooperstown has been able to take great advantage of its part in this fictional tale.

Once Cooperstown officials were convinced of the wisdom of building a baseball museum, they contacted Major League Baseball. Coincidentally, NL President Ford Frick had come up with an idea of his own that would enhance any baseball museum: a Hall of Fame. Frick had recently visited the Hall of Fame for Great Americans at New York University and been inspired to do something similar for baseball's legendary stars.

While the phrase "Hall of Fame" was well known at the time, it was almost always used as a metaphor. Today there are more Halls of Fame in the United States than anyone has the patience to count—there's even a Shuffleboard Hall of Fame in Texas—but the Hall for Great Americans was the first of its kind when it opened in 1900. The Baseball Hall of Fame would be the first such institution devoted to a sport. So Cooperstown leaders and baseball officials reached an agreement to build the National Baseball Hall of Fame and Museum in upstate New York.

Though the museum would not be ready to open until 1939, the process of electing players to the Hall began in 1936. Two groups were formed to elect players—a large group of more than 200 writers from the Baseball Writers Association of America and a 78-member Old-Timers Committee. While the Old-Timers Committee was formed specifically to evaluate long-retired players, the two sets of voters were given almost no further guidance on whom to elect. Several active players received significant support from the BBWAA, while other players received votes from both the writers and the Old Timers. A 75-percent vote of either group was needed to earn induction in the Hall. In the end, the writers selected five of the all-time greats: Ty Cobb, Babe Ruth, Honus Wagner Christy Mathewson, and Walter Johnson. A divided and confused Old-Timers Committee elected no one.

The BBWAA would hold three more elections before the official opening of the Hall of Fame, electing Nap Lajoie, Tris Speaker, and Cy Young in 1937, Grover Cleveland Alexander in 1938, and George Sisler, Eddie Collins, and Willie Keeler in 1939. Afterward, the BBWAA held a vote only once every three years. The organization went back to having an annual election in 1946, then reduced the frequency of their balloting to every two years after 1956. Finally, the BBWAA permanently returned to an annual election in 1966. In 1954, it was decided that all future candidates would not appear on the BBWAA ballot until five years after retirement. After Roberto Clemente's death in 1972, the rules were modified so that any player who died before eligibility could be considered by the writers only six months later.

After the failure of the Old-Timers Committee to elect anyone in 1936, a smaller Centennial Commission was formed to elect executives, managers, and other pioneers. This commission elected Morgan B. Bulkeley, Ban Johnson, Connie Mack, John McGraw, and George Wright in 1937, and added Alexander Cartwright (though not Abner Doubleday) and Henry Chadwick in 1938. The idea of an Old-Timers Committee was revived in 1939, electing various players and officials in 1939, 1944, 1945, 1946, and 1949. The committee's election of 21 players and executives in 1945 and 1946 started a long tradition of questionable choices, which didn't stop the formation of a permanent Veterans Committee in 1953. The Veterans Committee continued to elect managers and executives—as well as players that the writers had passed over—until it was disbanded after 2001.

While the Veterans Committee certainly made some worthy selections, its voting process was politicized from the start: The number of friends or teammates a player under consideration had on the committee was often the best indicator of whether he would be elected. Separate committees for the Negro Leagues and for the nineteenth century did a much better job dealing with leagues and eras of which previous voters showed little knowledge. However, even the Negro Leagues Committee was criticized for relying too much on the opinion of one man, Buck O'Neil.

A new Veterans Committee (which includes all living Hall of Famers and all living recipients of either the Frick or the Spink awards) has now been assembled to consider players every two years; the group also votes on umpires, managers, and executives every four years. No one came remotely close to winning induction into the Hall in the new committee's voting in 2003 and 2005. Unless the rules or composition of the committee is changed, it seems unlikely that it will elect many candidates since Hall of Famers usually want the Hall to be more exclusive after they've been elected. In a group far too big for the kind of personal politicking that was so effective on the old Veterans Committee, it will probably be very hard to reach consensus. In 2005, a new 12-member committee of Negro League historians was appointed to vote in February 2006 on a pre-selected group of 30 Negro League players and 9 pre-Negro League pioneers. Candidates receiving 75 percent of that vote will be inducted into the Hall in summer 2006 along with Bruce Sutter.

What follows is a listing of every member of the Hall of Fame. Also listed are those not in the Hall of Fame who have ever received a vote (not including 2006), plus the leading vote-getters each year. The first and last years of everyone's **Career** is shown, regardless of whether their seasons were consecutive. Voting totals include the candidate's first-year percentage of votes **(1st Yr/Pct)** and the final year totals **(Last Yr/Pct)** through 2005, as well as the year the player received his highest vote total and the percentage of that vote he received (**Max Yr/Pct**). (Hall of Fame election results for 2006 were announced as this edition went to press; therefore, only the voting for new HOF member Bruce Sutter is reflected in this section.) For Hall of Fame members, their actual **Votes** received are also shown alongside the number of votes **Needed** to be elected. The Year-by-Year section includes the totals of all candidates who received at least 25 percent of the BBWAA votes in a given year; also provided are the number of votes (which fluctuate each year) required to gain induction.

Hall of Famers and other candidates are listed by their primary position (**Pos**); non-players are listed as executives (*Exe*), managers (*Mgr*), pioneers (*Pio*), or umpires (*Ump*). Special elections and abbreviations include *1936V* (for Veteran's Election) and *1946N* (for Nominating Ballot, where no one was to be elected). The Negro Leagues Committee is represented by an *N*, while *C* stands for Centennial, *V* for Veterans, and *S* for Special. An *R* after a year indicates a run-off election, held after no one was elected on the regular ballot. A maximum of one player could be elected in the three run-off elections, even if more than one received 75 percent of the run-off vote.

MEMBER	CAREER	POS	ELECTED	MAX YR	PCT	VOTES	NEEDED	1ST YR	PCT	VOTES	NEEDED	LAST YR	PCT	VOTES	NEEDED
MEMBERS OF THE HALL OF FAME															
Hank Aaron	1954–76	RF	1982	1982	97.8	406	312								
Grover Alexander	1911–30	P	1938	1938	80.9	212	197	1936	24.3	55	170	1938	80.9	212	197
Walter Alston	1954–76	Mgr	1983V												
Sparky Anderson	1970–95	Mgr	2000V												
Cap Anson	1871–97	1B	1939O	1936V	51.3	40	59								
Luis Aparicio	1956–73	SS	1984	1984	84.6	341	303	1979	27.8	120	324	1984	84.6	341	303
Luke Appling	1930–50	SS	1964	1964R	83.6	189	170	1953	0.8	2	198	1964R	83.6	189	170
Richie Ashburn	1948–62	CF	1995V	1978	41.7	158	285	1968	2.1	6	213	1982	30.4	126	312
Earl Averill	1929–41	CF	1975V	1958	5.3	14	200	1949	0.7	1	115	1962	1.9	3	120
Frank Baker	1908–22	3B	1955V	1947	30.4	49	121	1936	0.4	1	170	1951	3.5	8	170
Dave Bancroft	1915–30	SS	1971V	1958	16.2	43	200	1937	1.5	3	151	1960	11.2	30	202
Ernie Banks	1953–71	1B	1977	1977	83.8	321	288								
Al Barlick	1940–71	Ump	1989V												
Ed Barrow	1903–47	Exe	1953V												
Jake Beckley	1888–1907	1B	1971V	1936V	1.3	1	59	1936V	1.3	1	59	1942	0.4	1	175
Cool Papa Bell	1922–46	CF	1974N												
Johnny Bench	1967–83	C	1989	1989	96.4	431	336								
Chief Bender	1903–17	P	1953V	1947	44.7	72	121	1936	0.9	2	170	1953	39.4	104	198
Yogi Berra	1946–65	C	1972	1972	85.6	339	297	1971	67.2	242	270	1972	85.6	339	297
Wade Boggs	1982–99	3B	2005	2005	91.9	474	387								
Jim Bottomley	1922–37	1B	1974V	1960	33.1	89	202	1948	3.3	4	91	1962	12.5	20	120
Lou Boudreau	1938–52	SS	1970	1970	77.3	232	225	1956	1.0	2	145	1970	77.3	232	225
Roger Bresnahan	1897–1915	C	1945O	1945	53.8	133	186	1936	20.8	47	170	1945	53.8	133	186
George Brett	1973–93	3B	1999	1999	98.2	488	373								
Lou Brock	1961–79	LF	1985	1985	79.7	315	297								
Dan Brouthers	1879–96	1B	1945O	1936V	2.6	2	59								
Mordecai Brown	1903–16	P	1949O	1946N	27.7	56	152	1936	2.7	6	170	1946	18.3	48	198
Ray Brown	1930–53	P	2006N												
Willard Brown	1935–56	CF	2006N												
Morgan Bulkeley	1876–76	Exe	1937C												
Jim Bunning	1955–71	P	1996V	1988	74.2	317	321	1977	38.1	146	288	1991	63.7	282	333
Jesse Burkett	1890–1905	LF	1946O	1942	1.7	4	175	1936V	1.3	1	59	1946N	1.0	2	152
Roy Campanella	1948–57	C	1969	1969	79.4	270	255	1964	57.2	115	151	1969	79.4	270	255
Rod Carew	1967–85	1B	1991	1991	90.5	401	333								
Max Carey	1910–29	CF	1961V	1958	51.1	136	200	1937	3.0	6	151	1958	51.1	136	200
Steve Carlton	1965–88	P	1994	1994	95.8	436	342								
Gary Carter	1974–92	C	2003	2003	78.0	387	372	1998	42.3	200	355	2003	78.0	387	372
Alexander Cartwright	1845–48	Pio	1938C												
Orlando Cepeda	1958–74	1B	1999V	1994	73.6	335	342	1980	12.5	48	289	1994	73.6	335	342
Henry Chadwick	1858–1908	Pio	1938C												
Frank Chance	1898–1914	1B	1946O	1945	72.5	179	186	1936	2.2	5	170	1946	57.0	150	198
Happy Chandler	1945–51	Exe	1982V												
Oscar Charleston	1915–40	CF	1976N												
Jack Chesbro	1899–1909	P	1946O	1939	2.2	6	206	1937	0.5	1	151	1946N	0.5	1	152
Nestor Chylak	1954–78	Ump	1999V												
Fred Clarke	1894–1915	LF	1945O	1942	24.9	58	175	1936V	11.5	9	59	1945	21.5	53	186
John Clarkson	1882–94	P	1963V	1936V	6.4	5	59	1936V	6.4	5	59	1946N	0.5	1	152
Roberto Clemente	1955–72	RF	1973S												
Ty Cobb	1905–28	CF	1936	1936	98.2	222	170								
Mickey Cochrane	1925–37	C	1947	1947	79.5	128	121	1936	35.4	80	170	1947	79.5	128	121
Eddie Collins	1906–30	2B	1939	1939	77.7	213	206	1936	26.5	60	170	1939	77.7	213	206
Jimmy Collins	1895–1908	3B	1945O	1945	49.0	121	186	1936V	10.3	8	59	1945	49.0	121	186
Earle Combs	1924–35	CF	1970V	1960	16.0	43	202	1937	2.0	4	151	1962	3.8	6	120
Charlie Comiskey	1882–94	Exe	1939O	1936V	7.7	6	59								
Jocko Conlan	1941–64	Ump	1974V												
Tommy Connolly	1898–1931	Ump	1953V												
Roger Connor	1880–97	1B	1976V												
Andy Cooper	1920–41	P	2006N												
Stan Coveleski	1912–28	P	1969V	1958	12.8	34	200	1938	0.4	1	197	1958	12.8	34	200
Sam Crawford	1899–1917	RF	1957V	1946N	4.5	9	152	1936	0.4	1	170	1946N	4.5	9	152
Joe Cronin	1926–45	SS	1956	1956	78.8	152	145	1947	3.7	6	121	1956	78.8	152	145
Candy Cummings	1872–77	Pio	1939O												
Kiki Cuyler	1921–38	RF	1968V	1958	33.8	90	200	1948	2.5	3	91	1962	19.4	31	120
Ray Dandridge	1933–49	3B	1987V												
George Davis	1890–1909	SS	1998V												
Leon Day	1934–50	P	1995V												
Dizzy Dean	1930–40	P	1953	1953	79.2	209	198	1936	0.4	1	170	1953	79.2	209	198
Ed Delahanty	1888–1903	LF	1945O	1939	52.9	145	206	1936V	28.2	22	59	1945	44.9	111	186
Bill Dickey	1928–46	C	1954	1954	80.2	202	189	1945	6.9	17	186	1954	80.2	202	189
Martin Dihigo	1923–45	2B	1977N												
Joe DiMaggio	1936–51	CF	1955	1955	88.8	223	189	1945	0.4	1	186	1955	88.8	223	189
Larry Doby	1947–59	CF	1998V	1967	3.4	10	219	1966	2.3	7	227	1967R	0.3	1	230
Bobby Doerr	1937–51	2B	1986V	1970	25.0	75	225	1953	0.8	2	198	1971	21.7	78	270
Don Drysdale	1956–69	P	1984	1984	78.4	316	303	1975	21.0	76	272	1984	78.4	316	303
Hugh Duffy	1888–1906	CF	1945O	1942	33.0	77	175	1936V	5.1	4	59	1945	25.9	64	186
Leo Durocher	1939–73	Mgr	1994V	1958	10.5	28	200	1948	0.8	1	91	1964R	0.9	2	170
Dennis Eckersley	1975–98	P	2004	2004	83.2	421	380								
Billy Evans	1906–27	Ump	1973V												
Johnny Evers	1902–29	2B	1946O	1946N	64.4	130	152	1936	2.7	6	170	1946	41.8	110	198
Buck Ewing	1880–97	C	1939O	1936V	51.3	40	59	1936V	51.3	40	59	1939	0.7	2	206
Red Faber	1914–33	P	1964V	1960	30.9	83	202	1937	1,5	3	151	1962	18.8	30	120
Bob Feller	1936–56	P	1962	1962	93.8	150	120								
Rick Ferrell	1929–47	C	1984V	1956	0.5	1	145	1956	0.5	1	145	1960	0.4	1	202
Rollie Fingers	1968–85	P	1992	1992	81.2	349	323	1991	65.7	291	333	1992	81.2	349	323
Carlton Fisk	1969–93	C	2000	2000	79.6	397	375	1999	66.4	330	373	2000	79.6	397	375
Elmer Flick	1898–1910	RF	1963V	1938	0.4	1	197								
Whitey Ford	1950–67	P	1974	1974	77.8	284	274	1973	67.1	255	285	1974	77.8	284	274
Bill Foster	1923–37	P	1996V												
Rube Foster	1902–26	Mgr	1981V												
Nellie Fox	1947–65	2B	1997V	1985	74.7	295	297	1971	10.8	39	270	1985	74.7	295	297
Jimmie Foxx	1925–45	1B	1951	1951	79.2	179	170	1936	9.3	21	170	1951	79.2	179	170
Ford Frick	1934–65	Exe	1970V												
Frankie Frisch	1919–37	2B	1947	1947	84.5	136	121	1936	6.2	14	170	1947	84.5	136	121
Jim Galvin	1875–92	P	1965V												
Lou Gehrig	1923–39	1B	1939S	1936	22.6	51	170								
Charlie Gehringer	1924–42	2B	1949	1949R	85.0	159	141	1936	0.4	1	170	1949R	85.0	159	141
Josh Gibson	1930–46	C	1972N												
Bob Gibson	1959–75	P	1981	1981	84.0	337	301								
Warren Giles	1946–69	Exe	1979V												
Lefty Gomez	1930–43	P	1972V	1956	46.1	89	145	1945	2.8	7	186	1962	12.5	20	120
Goose Goslin	1921–38	LF	1968V	1956	13.5	26	145	1948	0.8	1	91	1962	8.8	14	120
Frank Grant	1886–1903	2B	2006N												

MEMBER	CAREER	POS	ELECTED	MAX YR	PCT	VOTES	NEEDED	1ST YR	PCT	VOTES	NEEDED	LAST YR	PCT	VOTES	NEEDED
Hank Greenberg	1930–47	1B	1956	1956	85.0	164	145	1945	1.2	3	186	1956	85.0	164	145
Clark Griffith	1891–1907	Exe	1946O	1945	43.7	108	186	1937	2.0	4	151	1946	31.2	82	198
Burleigh Grimes	1916–34	P	1964V	1960	34.2	92	202	1937	0.5	1	151	1962	26.9	43	120
Lefty Grove	1925–41	P	1947	1947	76.4	123	121	1936	5.3	12	170	1947	76.4	123	121
Tony Gwynn	1982–2001	RF	2007	2007	97.6	532	409								
Chick Hafey	1924–37	LF	1971V	1960	10.8	29	202	1948	0.8	1	91	1962	4.4	7	120
Jesse Haines	1918–37	P	1970V	1958	8.3	22	200	1939	0.4	1	206	1962	1.9	3	120
Billy Hamilton	1888–1901	CF	1961V	1936V	2.6	2	59	1936V	2.6	2	59	1942	0.4	1	175
Ned Hanlon	1889–1907	Mgr	1996V												
Will Harridge	1931–59	Exe	1972V												
Bucky Harris	1924–56	Mgr	1975V	1958	16.9	45	200	1938	0.4	1	197	1960	11.5	31	202
Gabby Hartnett	1922–41	C	1955	1955	77.7	195	189	1936	0.4	1	170	1955	77.7	195	189
Harry Heilmann	1914–32	RF	1952	1952	86.8	203	176	1937	5.0	10	151	1952	86.8	203	176
Billy Herman	1931–47	2B	1975V	1967	20.2	59	219	1948	0.8	1	91	1967R	4.6	14	230
Pete Hill	1899–1925	CF	2006N												
Harry Hooper	1909–25	RF	1971V	1937	3.0	6	151	1937	3.0	6	151	1951	1.3	3	170
Rogers Hornsby	1915–37	2B	1942	1942	78.1	182	175	1936	46.5	105	170	1942	78.1	182	175
Waite Hoyt	1918–38	P	1969V	1956	19.2	37	145	1939	0.4	1	206	1962	11.3	18	120
Cal Hubbard	1936–51	Ump	1976V												
Carl Hubbell	1928–43	P	1947	1947	87.0	140	121	1945	9.7	24	186	1947	87.0	140	121
Miller Huggins	1913–29	Mgr	1964V	1946N	63.9	129	152	1937	2.5	5	151	1950	1.2	2	126
William Hulbert	1877–82	Exe	1995V												
Catfish Hunter	1965–79	P	1987	1987	76.3	315	310	1985	53.7	212	297	1987	76.3	315	310
Monte Irvin	1939–56	LF	1973N												
Reggie Jackson	1967–87	LF	1993	1993	93.6	396	318								
Travis Jackson	1922–36	SS	1982V	1956	7.3	14	145	1948	4.1	5	91	1962	0.6	1	120
Fergie Jenkins	1965–83	P	1991	1991	75.4	334	333	1989	52.3	234	336	1991	75.4	334	333
Hughie Jennings	1891–1903	SS	1945O	1945	37.2	92	186	1936V	14.1	11	59	1945	37.2	92	186
Ban Johnson	1901–27	Exe	1937C												
Judy Johnson	1921–38	3B	1975N												
Walter Johnson	1907–27	P	1936	1936	83.6	189	170								
Addie Joss	1902–10	P	1978V	1942	14.2	33	175	1937	5.5	11	151	1960	0.4	1	202
Al Kaline	1953–74	RF	1980	1980	88.3	340	289								
Tim Keefe	1880–93	P	1964V	1936V	1.3	1	59								
Willie Keeler	1892–1910	RF	1939	1939	75.5	207	206	1936V	42.3	33	59	1939	75.5	207	206
George Kell	1943–57	3B	1983V	1977	36.8	141	288	1964	16.4	33	151	1977	36.8	141	288
Joe Kelley	1891–1908	LF	1971V	1942	0.4	1	175	1939	0.4	1	206	1942	0.4	1	175
George Kelly	1915–32	1B	1973V	1960	1.9	5	202	1947	0.6	1	121	1962	0.6	1	120
King Kelly	1878–93	C	1945O	1936V	19.2	15	59								
Harmon Killebrew	1954–75	1B	1984	1984	83.1	335	303	1981	59.6	239	301	1984	83.1	335	303
Ralph Kiner	1946–55	LF	1975	1975	75.4	273	272	1962	3.1	5	120	1975	75.4	273	272
Chuck Klein	1928–44	RF	1980V	1964	27.9	56	151	1948	2.5	3	91	1964R	8.0	18	170
Bill Klem	1905–41	Ump	1953V												
Sandy Koufax	1955–66	P	1972	1972	86.9	344	297								
Nap Lajoie	1896–1916	2B	1937	1937	83.6	168	151	1936V	2.6	2	59	1937	83.6	168	151
Judge Landis	1920–44	Exe	1944O												
Tom Lasorda	1976–96	Mgr	1997V												
Tony Lazzeri	1926–39	2B	1991V	1956	33.2	64	145	1945	0.4	1	186	1962	5.0	8	120
Bob Lemon	1941–58	P	1976	1976	78.6	305	291	1964	11.9	24	151	1976	78.6	305	291
Buck Leonard	1933–50	1B	1972N												
Freddie Lindstrom	1924–36	3B	1976V	1962	4.4	7	120	1949	0.7	1	115	1962	4.4	7	120
John Henry Lloyd	1905–31	SS	1977N												
Ernie Lombardi	1931–47	C	1986V	1964	16.4	33	151	1950	1.8	3	126	1967R	8.2	25	230
Al Lopez	1928–47	Mgr	1977V	1967	39.0	114	219	1949	0.7	1	115	1967R	16.3	50	230
Ted Lyons	1923–46	P	1955	1955	86.5	217	189	1945	1.6	4	186	1955	86.5	217	189
Connie Mack	1894–1950	Mgr	1937C	1936	0.4	1	170								
Biz Mackey	1920–50	C	2006N												
Larry MacPhail	1934–47	Exe	1978V												
Lee MacPhail	1941–85	Exe	1998V												
Effa Manley	1935–48	Exe	2006N												
Mickey Mantle	1951–68	CF	1974	1974	88.2	322	274								
Heinie Manush	1923–39	LF	1964V	1962	9.4	15	120	1948	0.8	1	91	1962	9.4	15	120
Rabbit Maranville	1912–35	SS	1954	1954	82.9	209	189	1937	12.4	25	151	1954	82.9	209	189
Juan Marichal	1960–75	P	1983	1983	83.7	313	281	1981	58.1	233	301	1983	83.7	313	281
Rube Marquard	1908–25	P	1971V	1955	13.9	35	189	1936	0.4	1	170	1955	13.9	35	189
Eddie Mathews	1952–68	3B	1978	1978	79.4	301	285	1974	32.3	118	274	1978	79.4	301	285
Christy Mathewson	1900–16	P	1936	1936	90.7	205	170								
Willie Mays	1951–73	CF	1979	1979	94.7	409	324								
Bill Mazeroski	1956–72	2B	2001V	1992	42.3	182	323	1978	6.1	23	285	1992	42.3	182	323
Joe McCarthy	1926–50	Mgr	1957V	1947	1.2	2	121	1939	1.1	3	206	1958	0.8	2	200
Tommy McCarthy	1884–96	RF	1946O	1936V	1.3	1	59								
Willie McCovey	1959–80	1B	1986	1986	81.4	346	319								
Joe McGinnity	1899–1908	P	1946O	1946N	26.2	53	152	1937	6.0	12	151	1946	17.9	47	198
Bill McGowan	1925–54	Ump	1992V												
John McGraw	1891–1906	Mgr	1937C	1936V	21.8	17	59	1936V	21.8	17	59	1937	17.4	35	151
Bill McKechnie	1922–46	Mgr	1962V	1951	3.5	8	170	1945	0.8	2	186	1951	3.5	8	170
Bid McPhee	1882–99	2B	2000V												
Joe Medwick	1932–48	LF	1968	1968	84.8	240	213	1948	0.8	1	91	1968	84.8	240	213
Jose Mendez	1908–26	P	2006N												
Johnny Mize	1936–53	1B	1981V	1971	43.6	157	270	1960	16.7	45	202	1973	41.3	157	285
Paul Molitor	1978–98	DH	2004	2004	85.2	431	380								
Joe Morgan	1963–84	2B	1990	1990	81.8	363	333								
Eddie Murray	1977–97	1B	2003	2003	85.3	423	372								
Stan Musial	1941–63	LF	1969	1969	93.2	317	255								
Hal Newhouser	1939–55	P	1992V	1975	42.8	155	272	1962	2.5	4	120	1975	42.8	155	272
Kid Nichols	1890–1906	P	1949O	1936V	3.8	3	59	1936V	3.8	3	59	1946N	0.5	1	152
Phil Niekro	1964–87	P	1997	1997	80.3	380	355	1993	65.7	278	318	1997	80.3	380	355
Jim O'Rourke	1872–93	LF	1945O												
Mel Ott	1926–47	RF	1951	1951	87.2	197	170	1949	61.4	94	115	1951	87.2	197	170
Satchel Paige	1927–53	P	1971N	1951	0.4	1	170								
Jim Palmer	1965–84	P	1990	1990	92.6	411	333								
Herb Pennock	1912–34	P	1948	1948	77.7	94	91	1937	7.5	15	151	1948	77.7	94	91
Tony Perez	1964–86	1B	2000	2000	77.2	385	375	1992	50.0	215	323	2000	77.2	385	375
Gaylord Perry	1962–83	P	1991	1991	77.2	342	333	1989	68.0	304	336	1991	77.2	342	333
Eddie Plank	1901–17	P	1946O	1942	27.0	63	175	1937	11.4	23	151	1946N	16.8	34	152
Alex Pompez	1916–50	Exe	2006N												
Cum Posey	1911–46	Exe	2006N												
Kirby Puckett	1984–95	CF	2001	2001	82.1	423	387								
Charley Radbourn	1880–91	P	1939O	1936V	20.5	16	59								
Pee Wee Reese	1940–58	SS	1984V	1976	47.9	186	291	1964	36.3	73	151	1978	44.6	169	285
Sam Rice	1915–34	RF	1963V	1960	53.2	143	202	1938	0.4	1	197	1962	50.6	81	120
Branch Rickey	1913–65	Exe	1967V	1942	1.3	3	175	1942	1.3	3	175	1945	0.8	2	186
Cal Ripken	1981–2001	SS	2007	2007	98.5	537	409								

THE HALL OF FAME

MEMBER	CAREER	POS	ELECTED	MAX YR	PCT	VOTES	NEEDED	1ST YR	PCT	VOTES	NEEDED	LAST YR	PCT	VOTES	NEEDED
Eppa Rixey	1912–33	P	1963V	1960	52.8	142	202	1937	0.5	1	151	1962	30.6	49	120
Phil Rizzuto	1941–56	SS	1994V	1976	38.4	149	291	1956	0.5	1	145	1976	38.4	149	291
Robin Roberts	1948–66	P	1976	1976	86.9	337	291	1973	56.1	213	285	1976	86.9	337	291
Brooks Robinson	1955–77	3B	1983	1983	92.0	344	281								
Frank Robinson	1956–76	RF	1982	1982	89.2	370	312								
Jackie Robinson	1947–56	2B	1962	1962	77.5	124	120								
Wilbert Robinson	1886–1902	Mgr	1945O	1942	38.2	89	175	1936V	7.7	6	59	1945	32.8	81	186
Bullet Joe Rogan	1920–38	P	1998V												
Edd Roush	1913–31	CF	1962V	1960	54.3	146	202	1936	0.9	2	170	1960	54.3	146	202
Red Ruffing	1924–47	P	1967	1967R	86.9	266	230	1948	3.3	4	91	1967R	86.9	266	230
Amos Rusie	1889–1901	P	1977V	1936V	15.4	12	59	1936V	15.4	12	59	1945	0.4	1	186
Babe Ruth	1914–35	RF	1936	1936	95.1	215	170								
Nolan Ryan	1966–93	P	1999	1999	98.8	491	373								
Ryne Sandberg	1981–97	2B	2005	2005	76.2	393	387	2003	49.2	244	372	2005	76.2	393	387
Louis Santop	1909–26	C	2006N												
Ray Schalk	1912–29	C	1955V	1955	45.0	113	189	1936	1.8	4	170	1955	45.0	113	189
Mike Schmidt	1972–89	3B	1995	1995	96.5	444	345								
Red Schoendienst	1945–63	2B	1989V	1980	42.6	164	289	1969	19.1	65	255	1983	39.0	146	281
Tom Seaver	1967–86	P	1992	1992	98.8	425	323								
Frank Selee	1890–1905	Mgr	1999V												
Joe Sewell	1920–33	SS	1977V	1960	8.6	23	202	1937	0.5	1	151	1960	8.6	23	202
Al Simmons	1924–44	LF	1953	1953	75.4	199	198	1936	1.8	4	170	1953	75.4	199	198
George Sisler	1915–30	1B	1939	1939	85.8	235	206	1936	34.1	77	170	1939	85.8	235	206
Enos Slaughter	1938–59	RF	1985V	1978	68.9	261	285	1966	33.1	100	227	1979	68.8	297	324
Hilton Smith	1933–48	P	2001V												
Ozzie Smith	1978–96	SS	2002	2002	91.7	433	354								
Duke Snider	1947–64	CF	1980	1980	86.5	333	289	1970	17.0	51	225	1980	86.5	333	289
Warren Spahn	1942–65	P	1973	1973	83.2	316	285								
Al Spalding	1871–78	Pio	1939O	1936V	5.1	4	59								
Tris Speaker	1907–28	CF	1937	1937	82.1	165	151	1936	58.8	133	170	1937	82.1	165	151
Willie Stargell	1962–82	LF	1988	1988	82.4	352	321								
Turkey Stearnes	1923–40	CF	2000V												
Casey Stengel	1934–65	Mgr	1966V	1953	23.1	61	198	1938	0.8	2	197	1953	23.1	61	198
Bruce Sutter	1976–88	P	2006	2006	76.9	400	390	1994	24.0	109	342	2006	76.9	400	390
Mule Suttles	1918–44	1B	2006N												
Don Sutton	1966–88	P	1998	1998	81.6	386	355	1994	56.9	259	342	1998	81.6	386	355
Ben Taylor	1910–29	1B	2006N												
Bill Terry	1923–36	1B	1954	1954	77.4	195	189	1936	4.0	9	170	1954	77.4	195	189
Sam Thompson	1885–98	RF	1974V												
Joe Tinker	1902–16	SS	1946O	1946N	27.2	55	152	1937	7.5	15	151	1946	17.1	45	198
Cristobal Torriente	1913–28	RF	2006N												
Pie Traynor	1920–37	3B	1948	1948	76.9	93	91	1936	7.1	16	170	1948	76.9	93	91
Dazzy Vance	1915–35	P	1955	1955	81.7	205	189	1936	0.4	1	170	1955	81.7	205	189
Arky Vaughan	1932–48	SS	1985V	1968	29.0	82	213	1953	0.4	1	198	1968	29.0	82	213
Bill Veeck	1933–80	Exe	1991V												
Rube Waddell	1897–1910	P	1946O	1939	65.3	179	206	1936	14.6	33	170	1946	33.1	87	198
Honus Wagner	1897–1917	SS	1936	1936	95.1	215	170	1936V	6.4	5	59	1936	95.1	215	170
Bobby Wallace	1894–1918	SS	1953V	1938	2.7	7	197	1936V	1.3	1	59	1945	1.2	3	186
Ed Walsh	1904–17	P	1946O	1946N	56.9	115	152	1936	8.8	20	170	1946	40.3	106	198
Lloyd Waner	1927–45	CF	1967V	1964	23.4	47	151	1949	2.0	3	115	1964R	5.3	12	170
Paul Waner	1926–45	RF	1952	1952	83.3	195	176	1946N	2.0	4	152	1952	83.3	195	176
John Ward	1878–94	SS	1964V	1936V	3.8	3	59								
Earl Weaver	1968–86	Mgr	1996V												
George Weiss	1932–71	Exe	1971V												
Mickey Welch	1880–92	P	1973V												
Willie Wells	1924–48	SS	1997V												
Zack Wheat	1909–27	LF	1959V	1947	23.0	37	121	1937	2.5	5	151	1956	13.5	26	145
Sol White	1887–1926	Pio	2006N												
Hoyt Wilhelm	1952–72	P	1985	1985	83.8	331	297	1978	41.7	158	285	1985	83.8	331	297
J.L. Wilkinson	1920–48	Exe	2006N												
Billy Williams	1959–76	LF	1987	1987	85.7	354	310	1982	23.4	97	312	1987	85.7	354	310
Joe Williams	1910–32	P	1999V												
Ted Williams	1939–60	LF	1966	1966	93.4	282	227								
Vic Willis	1898–1910	P	1995V												
Jud Wilson	1922–45	3B	2006N												
Hack Wilson	1923–34	CF	1979V	1956	38.3	74	145	1937	0.5	1	151	1962	24.4	39	120
Dave Winfield	1973–95	RF	2001	2001	84.5	435	387								
George Wright	1871–82	Pio	1937C	1936V	7.7	6	59								
Harry Wright	1871–93	Pio	1953V												
Early Wynn	1939–63	P	1972	1972	76.0	301	297	1969	27.9	95	255	1972	76.0	301	297
Tom Yawkey	1933–76	Exe	1980V												
Carl Yastrzemski	1961–83	LF	1989	1989	94.6	423	336								
Cy Young	1890–1911	P	1937	1937	76.1	153	151	1936V	41.0	32	59	1937	76.1	153	151
Ross Youngs	1917–26	RF	1972V	1947	22.4	36	121	1936	4.4	10	170	1956	9.8	19	145
Robin Yount	1974–93	SS	1999	1999	77.5	385	373								

Non–Hall of Famers Who Have Received Votes

CANDIDATE	CAREER	POS	MAX YR (PCT)	1ST YEAR (PCT)	LAST YR (PCT)
Jim Abbott	1989–99	P	2005 (2.5)		
Babe Adams	1906–26	P	1947 (13.7)	1937 (4.0)	1955 (9.6)
Sparky Adams	1922–34	2B	1958 (0.4)	1958 (0.4)	1960 (0.4)
Bobby Adams	1946–59	2B	1966 (0.3)		
Rick Aguilera	1985–2000	P	2006 (0.6)		
Dick Allen	1963–77	1B	1996 (18.9)	1983 (3.7)	1997 (16.7)
Johnny Allen	1932–44	P	1955 (0.4)		
Doug Allison	1871–83	C	1936V (1.3)		
Felipe Alou	1958–74	RF	1980 (0.8)		
Jesus Alou	1963–79	LF	1985 (0.3)		
Matty Alou	1960–74	CF	1980 (1.3)		
Nick Altrock	1898–1909	P	1958 (7.5)	1937 (1.5)	1960 (6.7)
Jimmy Archer	1904–18	C	1937 (3.0)	1937 (3.0)	1939 (1.1)
Jimmy Austin	1909–22	3B	1958 (0.4)		
Bob Bailey	1962–78	3B	1984 (0.2)		
Harold Baines	1980–2001	DH	2007 (5.3)		
Dusty Baker	1968–86	LF	1992 (0.9)		
Sal Bando	1966–81	3B	1987 (0.7)		
Ross Barnes	1871–81	2B	1936V (3.8)		
Jack Barry	1908–19	SS	1938 (1.1)	1938 (1.1)	1939 (0.4)
Dick Bartell	1927–46	SS	1948 (0.8)	1948 (0.8)	1960 (0.4)
Joe Battin	1871–90	3B	1936V (1.3)		
Don Baylor	1970–88	DH	1994 (2.6)	1994 (2.6)	1995 (2.6)
Hank Bauer	1948–61	RF	1967 (7.9)	1967 (7.9)	1967R (2.9)
Ginger Beaumont	1899–1910	CF	1946N (0.5)	1938 (0.4)	1946N (0.5)
Glenn Beckert	1965–75	2B	1981 (0.2)		
Steve Bedrosian	1981–95	P	2001 (0.2)		
Mark Belanger	1965–82	SS	1988 (3.7)		
Buddy Bell	1972–89	3B	1995 (1.7)		
George Bell	1981–93	LF	1999 (1.2)		
Albert Belle	1989–2000	LF	2006 (7.7)	2006 (7.7)	2007 (3.5)
Charlie Bennett	1878–93	C	1936V (3.8)		
Larry Benton	1923–35	P	1958 (0.4)		
Moe Berg	1923–39	C	1960 (1.9)	1958 (1.1)	1960 (1.9)
Marty Bergen	1896–99	C	1937 (1.0)	1937 (1.0)	1939 (0.4)
Wally Berger	1930–40	CF	1958 (0.8)	1956 (0.5)	1958 (0.8)
Charlie Berry	1925–38	C	1958 (1.1)	1955 (0.4)	1958 (1.1)
Jim Bibby	1972–84	P	1990 (0.2)		
Dante Bichette	1988–2001	RF	2007 (0.6)		
Carson Bigbee	1916–26	LF	1948 (0.8)		
Jack Billingham	1968–80	P	1986 (0.2)		
Max Bishop	1924–35	2B	1960 (1.9)	1955 (0.4)	1960 (1.9)
Ewell Blackwell	1942–55	P	1970 (4.7)	1968 (1.8)	1970 (4.7)
Ray Blades	1922–32	LF	1958 (0.4)	1958 (0.4)	1960 (0.4)
Paul Blair	1964–80	CF	1986 (1.9)		
Steve Blass	1964–74	P	1980 (0.5)		
Lu Blue	1921–33	1B	1954 (0.4)		
Vida Blue	1969–86	P	1993 (8.7)	1992 (5.3)	1995 (5.7)
Ossie Bluege	1922–39	3B	1948 (1.7)	1948 (1.7)	1960 (1.1)
Bert Blyleven	1970–92	P	2006 (53.3)	1998 (17.5)	2007 (47.7)
Ping Bodie	1911–21	CF	1937 (1.0)	1937 (1.0)	1949 (0.7)
Joe Boley	1927–32	SS	1942 (0.4)		
Tommy Bond	1874–84	P	1936V (1.3)		
Bobby Bonds	1968–81	RF	1993 (10.6)	1987 (5.8)	1997 (4.2)
Bobby Bonilla	1986–2001	RF	2007 (0.4)		
Bob Boone	1972–90	C	1996 (7.7)	1996 (7.7)	2000 (4.2)
Jim Bouton	1962–70	P	1984 (0.7)		
Larry Bowa	1970–85	SS	1991 (2.5)		
Clete Boyer	1955–71	3B	1979 (0.7)	1978 (0.3)	1979 (0.7)
Ken Boyer	1955–69	3B	1988 (25.5)	1975 (2.5)	1994 (11.9)
Bill Bradley	1899–1915	3B	1937 (2.5)	1936 (0.4)	1946N (0.5)
Harry Brecheen	1940–53	P	1960 (2.6)	1960 (2.6)	1973 (0.8)
Ted Breitenstein	1891–1901	P	1937 (0.5)		
Jim Brewer	1960–76	P	1982 (0.5)		
Tommy Bridges	1930–46	P	1964 (7.5)	1956 (1.6)	1966 (5.3)
Gates Brown	1963–75	LF	1981 (0.2)		
Tom Browning	1984–95	P	2001 (0.2)		
Bill Bruton	1953–64	CF	1971 (0.3)		
Bill Buckner	1969–90	1B	1996 (2.1)		
Jay Buhner	1987–2001	LF	2007 (0.2)		
Lew Burdette	1950–67	P	1984 (24.1)	1973 (3.2)	1987 (23.2)
Smoky Burgess	1949–67	C	1974 (0.5)	1973 (0.3)	1974 (0.5)
George J. Burns	1911–25	LF	1937 (1.5)	1937 (1.5)	1950 (1.2)
Jeff Burroughs	1970–85	RF	1991 (0.2)		
Guy Bush	1923–45	P	1956 (1.0)		
Joe Bush	1912–28	P	1958 (1.9)		
Donie Bush	1908–23	SS	1946N (1.0)	1937 (0.5)	1953 (0.4)
Brett Butler	1981–97	CF	2003 (0.4)		
Leon Cadore	1915–24	P	1948 (0.8)		
Johnny Callison	1958–73	RF	1979 (0.2)		
Dolf Camilli	1933–45	1B	1958 (1.5)	1948 (0.8)	1960 (1.1)
Ken Caminiti	1987–2001	3B	2007 (0.4)		
Howie Camnitz	1904–15	P	1945 (0.4)		
Bert Campaneris	1964–83	SS	1989 (3.1)		
Bill Campbell	1973–87	P	1993 (0.2)		
John Candelaria	1975–93	P	1999 (0.2)		
Tom Candiotti	1983–99	P	2005 (0.4)		
Jose Canseco	1985–2001	RF	2007 (1.1)		
Jose Cardenal	1963–80	CF	1986 (0.2)		
Leo Cardenas	1960–75	SS	1981 (0.2)	1981 (0.2)	1982 (0.2)
Chico Carrasquel	1950–59	SS	1966 (0.3)		
Bill Carrigan	1913–29	Mgr	1937 (2.5)	1937 (2.5)	1945 (1.2)
Clay Carroll	1964–78	P	1984 (0.2)		
Joe Carter	1983–98	LF	2004 (3.8)		
Rico Carty	1963–79	LF	1985 (0.3)		
George Case	1937–47	LF	1964 (1.0)	1958 (0.4)	1964 (1.0)
Dave Cash	1969–80	2B	1986 (0.5)		
Norm Cash	1958–74	1B	1980 (1.6)		
Phil Cavaretta	1934–55	1B	1975 (35.6)	1962 (1.3)	1975 (35.6)
Cesar Cedeno	1970–86	CF	1992 (0.5)		
Ron Cey	1971–87	3B	1993 (1.9)		
Spud Chandler	1937–47	P	1964 (3.0)	1950 (1.2)	1964 (3.0)
Ben Chapman	1930–46	CF	1949 (0.7)	1949 (0.7)	1952 (0.4)
Ray Chapman	1912–20	SS	1938 (0.4)		
Sam Chapman	1938–51	CF	1958 (0.4)		
Hal Chase	1905–19	1B	1937 (9.0)	1936 (4.9)	1937 (9.0)
Bill Cissell	1938–38	2B	1937 (0.5)		
Jack Clark	1975–92	RF	1998 (1.5)		
Watty Clark	1924–37	P	1958 (0.4)		
Will Clark	1986–2000	1B	2006 (4.4)		
Andy Coakley	1902–11	P	1938 (0.4)		
Rocky Colavito	1955–68	RF	1974 (0.5)	1974 (0.5)	1975 (0.3)
Vince Coleman	1985–97	LF	2003 (0.6)		
Shano Collins	1910–25	RF	1937 (0.5)		
Dave Concepcion	1970–88	SS	1998 (16.9)	1994 (6.8)	2007 (13.6)
Wid Conroy	1901–11	3B	1945 (0.4)		
Jack Coombs	1906–20	P	1948 (1.7)	1937 (1.0)	1951 (0.4)
Mort Cooper	1938–49	P	1958 (1.1)	1956 (1.0)	1969 (0.9)
Walker Cooper	1940–57	C	1976 (14.4)	1968 (2.8)	1977 (11.7)
Wilbur Cooper	1912–26	P	1955 (4.4)	1938 (0.4)	1955 (4.4)
Clint Courtney	1951–61	C	1967 (0.3)		
Billy Cox	1941–55	3B	1962 (0.6)		
Doc Cramer	1929–48	CF	1964 (6.0)	1956 (2.1)	1964 (6.0)
Del Crandall	1949–66	C	1976 (3.9)	1976 (3.9)	1979 (2.1)
Doc Crandall	1908–18	P	1938 (0.4)		
Gavy Cravath	1908–20	Exe	1947 (1.2)	1937 (1.0)	1947 (1.2)
Lou Criger	1896–1912	C	1937 (8.0)	1936V (1.3)	1946N (3.0)
Hughie Critz	1924–35	2B	1956 (1.0)		
Frank Crosetti	1932–48	SS	1968 (5.3)	1950 (0.6)	1968 (5.3)
Lave Cross	1887–1907	3B	1942 (0.4)	1939 (0.4)	1942 (0.4)
Al Crowder	1926–36	P	1958 (0.4)	1958 (0.4)	1960 (0.4)
Walt Cruise	1914–24	LF	1938 (0.4)		
Jose Cruz	1970–88	LF	1994 (0.4)		
Tony Cuccinello	1930–45	2B	1958 (1.1)	1956 (0.5)	1958 (1.1)
Bill Dahlen	1891–1911	SS	1936V (1.3)	1936V (1.3)	1938 (0.4)
Harry Danning	1933–42	C	1958 (0.4)	1958 (0.4)	1960 (0.4)
Alvin Dark	1946–60	SS	1979 (18.5)	1966 (5.6)	1980 (11.2)
Ron Darling	1983–95	P	2001 (0.2)		
Jake Daubert	1910–24	1B	1937 (1.0)	1936 (0.4)	1955 (0.4)
Darren Daulton	1983–97	C	2003 (0.2)		
Chili Davis	1981–99	CF	2005 (0.6)		
Curt Davis	1934–46	P	1958 (0.4)		
Eric Davis	1984–2001	CF	2007 (0.6)		
Harry Davis	1895–1911	1B	1946N (1.0)	1945 (0.4)	1946N (1.0)
Mark Davis	1980–97	P	2003 (0.2)		
Tommy Davis	1959–76	LF	1982 (1.2)		
Spud Davis	1928–45	C	1948 (0.8)	1948 (0.8)	1949 (0.7)
Andre Dawson	1976–96	RF	2006 (61.0)	2002 (45.3)	2007 (56.7)
Doug DeCinces	1973–87	3B	1993 (0.5)		
Rick Dempsey	1969–92	C	1998 (0.2)		
Jerry Denny	1881–94	3B	1936V (7.7)		
Bucky Dent	1973–84	SS	1990 (0.7)		
Paul Derringer	1931–45	P	1956 (6.2)	1948 (0.8)	1960 (3.0)
Jim Deshaies	1984–95	P	2001 (0.2)		
Dom DiMaggio	1940–53	CF	1973 (11.3)	1960 (1.5)	1973 (11.3)
Bill Dinneen	1898–1909	P	1939 (2.6)	1938 (1.5)	1946N (0.5)
Bill Doak	1912–29	P	1958 (1.1)		
Mike Donlin	1899–1914	RF	1937 (3.0)	1937 (3.0)	1945 (0.4)
Bill Donovan	1898–1918	P	1946N (2.0)	1937 (1.5)	1946N (2.0)
Red Dooin	1902–16	C	1937 (0.5)	1937 (0.5)	1938 (0.4)
Brian Downing	1973–92	LF	1998 (0.4)		
Jack Doyle	1889–1905	1B	1936V (1.3)		
Larry Doyle	1907–20	2B	1938 (1.5)	1937 (1.0)	1939 (0.4)
Doug Drabek	1986–98	P	2004 (0.4)		
Walt Dropo	1949–61	1B	1967 (0.3)		
Joe Dugan	1917–31	3B	1960 (3.0)	1937 (0.5)	1960 (3.0)
Fred Dunlap	1880–91	2B	1936V (2.6)		
Jack Dunn	1907–28	Exe	1946N (0.5)	1942 (0.4)	1946N (0.5)
Eddie Dyer	1946–50	Mgr	1947 (0.6)		
Jimmy Dykes	1918–39	3B	1960 (10.0)	1948 (4.1)	1962 (3.8)
Lenny Dykstra	1985–96	CF	2002 (0.2)		
George Earnshaw	1928–36	P	1948 (2.5)	1948 (2.5)	1956 (1.6)
Hank Edwards	1941–53	RF	1960 (0.7)		
Howard Ehmke	1915–30	P	1960 (4.5)	1938 (0.4)	1960 (4.5)
Jim Eisenreich	1982–98	RF	2004 (0.6)		
Kid Elberfeld	1898–1914	SS	1945 (0.8)	1936 (0.4)	1945 (0.8)
Jumbo Elliott	1923–34	P	1958 (0.4)		
Bob Elliott	1939–53	3B	1964 (2.0)	1960 (0.7)	1964 (2.0)
Dock Ellis	1968–79	P	1985 (0.3)		
Del Ennis	1946–59	RF	1966 (1.0)	1966 (1.0)	1967 (0.7)
Jewel Ens	1929–31	Mgr	1950 (0.6)		
Carl Erskine	1948–59	P	1968 (3.2)	1966 (2.0)	1974 (3.0)
Darrell Evans	1969–89	3B	1995 (1.7)		
Dwight Evans	1972–91	RF	1998 (10.4)	1997 (5.9)	1999 (3.6)
Elroy Face	1953–69	P	1987 (18.9)	1976 (5.9)	1990 (11.3)
Ron Fairly	1959–78	1B	1985 (0.8)		
Cy Falkenberg	1903–17	P	1937 (0.5)		
Sid Fernandez	1983–97	P	2003 (0.4)		
Tony Fernandez	1983–2001	SS	2007 (0.7)		
Wes Ferrell	1927–41	P	1956 (3.6)	1948 (0.8)	1962 (0.6)
Cecil Fielder	1985–98	1B	2004 (0.2)		
Fred Fitzsimmons	1925–43	P	1958 (6.0)	1948 (1.7)	1962 (0.6)
Mike Flanagan	1975–92	P	1998 (0.4)		
Art Fletcher	1909–22	SS	1948 (2.5)	1937 (1.0)	1951 (1.8)
Curt Flood	1956–71	CF	1996 (15.1)	1977 (4.2)	1996 (15.1)
Lew Fonseca	1921–33	1B	1950 (1.2)	1948 (0.8)	1960 (1.1)
Bob Forsch	1974–89	P	1995 (0.4)		
Eddie Foster	1910–23	2B	1938 (0.8)		
George Foster	1969–86	LF	1993 (6.9)	1992 (5.6)	1995 (4.1)
Chick Fraser	1896–1909	P	1939 (0.4)		
Bill Freehan	1961–76	C	1982 (0.5)		
Jim Fregosi	1961–78	SS	1984 (1.0)		
Carl Furillo	1946–60	RF	1971 (1.4)	1966 (0.7)	1972 (0.5)
Gary Gaetti	1981–2000	3B	2006 (0.8)		
Augie Galan	1934–49	LF	1970 (1.0)	1968 (0.7)	1970 (1.0)
Phil Garner	1973–88	2B	1994 (0.4)		
Ned Garver	1948–61	P	1967 (0.3)		

CANDIDATE	CAREER	POS	MAX YR (PCT)	1ST YEAR (PCT)	LAST YR (PCT)
Steve Garvey	1969–87	1B	1995 (42.6)	1993 (41.6)	2007 (21.1)
Charlie Gelbert	1929–40	SS	1949 (1.3)	1947 (0.6)	1951 (0.4)
Kirk Gibson	1979–95	LF	2001 (2.5)		
Dave Giusti	1962–77	P	1983 (0.3)		
Jack Glasscock	1879–95	SS	1936V (2.6)		
Kid Gleason	1888–1912	2B	1937 (0.5)	1937 (0.5)	1945 (0.4)
Mike Gonzales	1912–32	C	1958 (1.1)	1950 (0.6)	1960 (0.7)
Dwight Gooden	1984–2000	P	2006 (3.3)		
Joe Gordon	1938–50	2B	1969 (28.5)	1945 (0.4)	1970 (26.3)
Rich Gossage	1972–94	P	2007 (71.2)	2000 (33.3)	2007 (71.2)
Hank Gowdy	1910–30	C	1955 (35.9)	1937 (1.0)	1960 (14.1)
Eddie Grant	1905–15	2B	1942 (1.3)	1938 (0.4)	1946N (0.5)
George Grantham	1922–34	2B	1958 (0.4)		
Mike Greenwell	1985–96	LF	2002 (0.4)		
Bobby Grich	1970–86	2B	1992 (2.6)		
Ken Griffey Sr.	1973–91	RF	1997 (4.7)		
Charlie Grimm	1916–36	1B	1958 (9.8)	1939 (0.4)	1962 (1.3)
Marv Grissom	1946–59	P	1966 (0.7)		
Dick Groat	1952–67	SS	1973 (1.8)	1973 (1.8)	1978 (0.8)
Heinie Groh	1912–27	3B	1955 (2.0)	1937 (0.5)	1960 (0.4)
Steve Gromek	1941–57	P	1964 (0.5)		
Orval Grove	1940–49	P	1960 (2.6)	1958 (1.9)	1960 (2.6)
Pedro Guerrero	1978–92	1B	1998 (1.3)		
Ron Guidry	1975–88	P	2000 (8.8)	1994 (5.3)	2002 (4.9)
Ozzie Guillen	1985–2000	SS	2006 (1.0)		
Bill Gullickson	1979–94	P	2000 (0.2)		
Frank Gustine	1939–50	3B	1958 (1.1)		
Mule Haas	1925–38	CF	1956 (0.5)	1955 (0.4)	1960 (0.4)
Stan Hack	1932–47	3B	1950 (4.8)	1948 (1.7)	1960 (2.2)
Harvey Haddix	1952–65	P	1985 (3.8)	1971 (2.8)	1985 (3.8)
Noodles Hahn	1899–1906	P	1939 (0.4)		
Bill Hallahan	1925–38	P	1948 (0.8)	1948 (0.8)	1960 (0.7)
Mel Harder	1928–47	P	1964 (25.4)	1949 (2.6)	1967R (4.6)
Bubbles Hargrave	1913–30	C	1947 (0.6)	1947 (0.6)	1960 (0.4)
Mike Hargrove	1974–85	1B	1991 (0.2)		
Toby Harrah	1969–86	3B	1992 (0.2)		
Bud Harrelson	1965–80	SS	1986 (0.2)		
Grady Hatton	1946–60	3B	1966 (1.3)	1966 (1.3)	1967 (0.3)
Jim Hearn	1947–59	P	1967 (0.3)	1966 (0.3)	1967 (0.3)
Richie Hebner	1968–85	3B	1991 (0.2)		
Jim Hegan	1941–60	C	1966 (1.7)	1966 (1.7)	1967 (0.7)
Tommy Helms	1964–77	2B	1983 (0.3)		
Solly Hemus	1949–59	SS	1966 (0.3)		
Dave Henderson	1981–94	CF	2000 (0.4)		
Tom Henke	1982–95	P	2001 (1.2)		
Tommy Henrich	1937–50	RF	1970 (20.7)	1952 (1.7)	1970 (20.7)
Babe Herman	1926–37	RF	1956 (5.7)	1942 (0.4)	1960 (2.6)
Keith Hernandez	1974–90	1B	1998 (10.8)	1996 (5.1)	2004 (4.3)
Willie Hernandez	1977–89	P	1995 (0.4)		
Orel Hershiser	1983–2000	P	2006 (11.2)	2006 (11.2)	2007 (4.4)
Buck Herzog	1908–20	2B	1938 (0.4)		
Jim Hickman	1962–74	CF	1980 (0.3)		
Pinky Higgins	1930–46	3B	1958 (2.3)	1950 (1.2)	1960 (1.1)
John Hiller	1965–80	P	1986 (2.6)		
Bill Hinchman	1905–20	RF	1937 (0.5)		
Gil Hodges	1943–63	1B	1983 (63.4)	1969 (24.1)	1983 (63.4)
Tommy Holmes	1942–52	RF	1958 (0.8)	1958 (0.8)	1960 (0.7)
Ken Holtzman	1965–79	P	1986 (1.2)	1985 (1.0)	1986 (1.2)
Rick Honeycutt	1977–97	P	2003 (0.4)		
Burt Hooton	1971–85	P	1991 (0.2)		
Willie Horton	1963–80	LF	1986 (0.9)		
Charlie Hough	1970–94	P	2000 (0.8)		
Art Houtteman	1945–57	P	1964 (1.0)		
Elston Howard	1955–68	C	1981 (20.7)	1974 (5.2)	1988 (12.4)
Frank Howard	1958–73	LF	1979 (1.4)		
Al Hrabosky	1970–82	P	1988 (0.2)		
Kent Hrbek	1981–94	1B	2000 (1.0)		
Bruce Hurst	1980–94	P	2000 (0.2)		
Fred Hutchinson	1939–53	P	1964 (5.0)	1962 (0.6)	1964 (5.0)
Charlie Irwin	1893–1902	3B	1938 (0.4)	1938 (0.4)	1939 (0.4)
Joe Jackson	1908–20	LF	1946N (1.0)	1936 (0.9)	1946N (1.0)
Sonny Jackson	1963–74	SS	1980 (0.3)		
Greg Jefferies	1987–2000	1B	2006 (0.4)		
Jackie Jensen	1950–61	RF	1968 (1.1)	1967 (1.0)	1972 (0.3)
Tommy John	1963–89	P	2006 (29.6)	1995 (21.3)	2007 (22.9)
Bob Johnson	1933–45	LF	1948 (0.8)	1948 (0.8)	1956 (0.5)
Dave Johnson	1965–78	2B	1984 (0.7)		
Doug Jones	1982–2000	P	2006 (0.4)		
Fielder Jones	1896–1908	CF	1946N (0.5)		
Sam Jones	1914–35	P	1956 (0.5)	1939 (0.4)	1956 (0.5)
Tim Jordan	1901–10	1B	1951 (0.4)		
Mike Jorgensen	1968–85	1B	1991 (0.2)		
Joe Judge	1915–34	1B	1960 (5.6)	1937 (0.5)	1960 (5.6)
Billy Jurges	1931–47	SS	1949 (1.3)	1949 (1.3)	1958 (0.4)
Jim Kaat	1959–83	P	1993 (29.6)	1989 (19.5)	2003 (26.2)
Willie Kamm	1923–35	3B	1958 (1.1)	1958 (1.1)	1960 (0.4)
Charlie Keller	1939–52	LF	1972 (6.1)	1953 (0.4)	1972 (6.1)
Ken Keltner	1937–55	3B	1958 (0.4)	1958 (0.4)	1960 (0.4)
Terry Kennedy	1978–91	C	1997 (0.2)		
Dickie Kerr	1919–25	P	1955 (10.0)	1937 (0.5)	1955 (10.0)
Don Kessinger	1964–79	SS	1985 (0.5)		
Jimmy Key	1984–98	P	2004 (0.6)		
Daryl Kile	1991–2002	P	2003 (1.4)		
Bill Killefer	1909–21	C	1946N (0.5)		
Matt Kilroy	1886–98	P	1936V (1.3)		
Ellis Kinder	1946–57	P	1964 (1.5)		
Dave Kingman	1971–86	LF	1992 (0.7)		
Johnny Kling	1900–13	C	1937 (10.0)	1936 (3.5)	1953 (0.4)
Ted Kluszewski	1947–61	1B	1977 (14.4)	1967 (3.1)	1981 (14.0)
Otto Knabe	1905–16	2B	1946N (0.5)	1939 (0.4)	1946N (0.5)
Ray Knight	1974–88	3B	1994 (0.2)		
Jerry Koosman	1967–85	P	1991 (0.9)		
Ray Kremer	1924–33	P	1948 (0.8)	1948 (0.8)	1958 (0.8)
Red Kress	1927–40	SS	1960 (1.1)	1958 (0.4)	1960 (1.1)
John Kruk	1986–95	1B	2001 (0.2)		
Mike Krukow	1976–89	P	1995 (0.2)		
Harvey Kuenn	1952–66	SS	1988 (39.3)	1977 (14.9)	1991 (22.6)
Joe Kuhel	1930–47	1B	1956 (0.5)		
Bob Kuzava	1946–57	P	1964 (0.5)		
Bill Lange	1893–99	CF	1936V (7.7)	1936V (7.7)	1953 (0.4)
Hal Lanier	1964–73	SS	1979 (0.2)		
Carney Lansford	1978–92	3B	1998 (0.6)		
Don Larsen	1953–67	P	1979 (12.3)	1974 (7.9)	1988 (7.3)
Arlie Latham	1880–99	3B	1936V (1.3)	1936V (1.3)	1942 (0.4)
Cookie Lavagetto	1934–47	3B	1958 (1.5)	1958 (1.5)	1960 (0.7)
Vern Law	1950–67	P	1973 (2.4)	1973 (2.4)	1979 (2.1)
Fred Leach	1923–32	LF	1958 (0.8)	1958 (0.8)	1960 (0.4)
Tommy Leach	1898–1918	CF	1937 (0.5)	1937 (0.5)	1939 (0.4)
Bill Lee	1969–82	P	1988 (0.7)		
Sam Leever	1898–1910	P	1937 (0.5)		
Chet Lemon	1975–90	CF	1996 (0.2)		
Dennis Leonard	1974–86	P	1992 (0.2)		
Emil Leonard	1933–53	P	1968 (1.8)	1960 (0.7)	1973 (1.6)
Duffy Lewis	1910–21	LF	1955 (13.5)	1937 (1.5)	1955 (13.5)
Hans Lobert	1903–17	3B	1937 (1.0)	1937 (1.0)	1960 (0.4)
Whitey Lockman	1945–60	1B	1966 (1.3)		
Mickey Lolich	1963–79	P	1988 (25.5)	1985 (19.7)	1999 (5.2)
Jim Lonborg	1965–79	P	1985 (0.8)	1985 (0.8)	1986 (0.7)
Herman Long	1889–1904	SS	1936V(20.5)	1936V(20.5)	1946N (0.5)
Ed Lopat	1944–55	P	1971 (1.1)	1968 (0.7)	1972 (0.5)
Davey Lopes	1972–87	2B	1993 (0.5)		
Bobby Lowe	1890–1907	2B	1936V (2.6)	1936V (2.6)	1945 (0.8)
John Lowenstein	1970–85	LF	1991 (0.2)		
Red Lucas	1923–38	P	1949 (1.3)	1949 (1.3)	1958 (0.4)
Dolph Luque	1919–35	P	1958 (5.6)	1937 (0.5)	1960 (1.5)
Greg Luzinski	1970–84	LF	1990 (0.2)		
Sparky Lyle	1967–82	P	1988 (13.1)	1988 (13.1)	1991 (3.4)
Fred Lynn	1974–90	CF	1996 (5.5)	1996 (5.5)	1997 (4.7)
Bill Madlock	1973–87	3B	1993 (4.5)		
Sherry Magee	1904–19	LF	1937 (1.0)	1937 (1.0)	1951 (0.9)
Sal Maglie	1945–58	P	1964 (6.5)	1964 (6.5)	1968 (3.9)
Jim Maloney	1960–71	P	1978 (0.5)	1978 (0.5)	1979 (0.5)
Gus Mancuso	1928–45	C	1958 (0.4)		
Firpo Marberry	1923–36	P	1958 (1.9)	1938 (0.4)	1962 (1.3)
Marty Marion	1940–53	SS	1970 (40.0)	1956 (0.5)	1973 (33.4)
Roger Maris	1957–68	RF	1988 (43.1)	1974 (21.4)	1988 (43.1)
Mike Marshall	1967–81	P	1987 (1.5)		
Billy Martin	1950–61	2B	1967 (0.3)		
Pepper Martin	1928–44	CF	1958 (17.3)	1942 (0.9)	1964R (2.2)
Morrie Martin	1949–59	P	1966 (0.7)		
Dennis Martinez	1976–98	P	2004 (3.2)		
Don Mattingly	1982–95	1B	2001 (28.2)	2001 (28.2)	2007 (9.9)
Lee May	1965–82	1B	1988 (0.5)		
Carl Mays	1915–29	P	1958 (2.3)		
Jim McAleer	1889–1902	CF	1936V (1.3)		
Tim McCarver	1959–80	C	1986 (3.8)		
Frank McCormick	1934–48	1B	1964 (3.0)	1956 (1.6)	1968 (1.1)
Lindy McDaniel	1955–75	P	1982 (0.7)	1981 (0.2)	1982 (0.7)
Gil McDougald	1951–60	2B	1966 (1.7)	1966 (1.7)	1974 (0.8)
Jack McDowell	1987–99	P	2005 (0.8)		
Willie McGee	1982–99	CF	2005 (5.0)	2005 (5.0)	2006 (2.3)
Tug McGraw	1965–84	P	1990 (1.4)		
Mark McGwire	1986–2001	1B	2007 (23.5)		
Stuffy McInnis	1909–27	1B	1949 (5.2)	1937 (0.5)	1951 (1.3)
Denny McLain	1963–72	P	1979 (0.7)	1978 (0.3)	1985 (0.5)
Larry McLean	1901–15	C	1937 (0.5)		
Don McMahon	1957–74	P	1980 (0.3)		
Marty McManus	1920–34	2B	1958 (0.8)	1958 (0.8)	1960 (0.7)
Roy McMillan	1951–66	SS	1972 (2.3)	1972 (2.3)	1974 (1.1)
Dave McNally	1962–75	P	1986 (2.8)	1981 (1.2)	1986 (2.8)
Cal McVey	1871–79	1B	1936V (1.3)		
Lee Meadows	1915–29	P	1958 (0.8)		
Andy Messersmith	1968–79	P	1985 (0.8)	1985 (0.8)	1986 (0.7)
Bob Meusel	1920–30	LF	1948 (5.0)	1937 (0.5)	1960 (3.7)
Eddie Miksis	1944–58	2B	1964 (0.5)		
Clyde Milan	1907–22	CF	1955 (2.4)	1938 (0.4)	1955 (2.4)
Felix Millan	1966–77	2B	1983 (0.3)		
Bing Miller	1921–36	RF	1960 (2.2)	1958 (0.4)	1960 (2.2)
Dots Miller	1909–21	1B	1948 (0.8)		
Hack Miller	1916–25	LF	1937 (0.5)		
Minnie Minoso	1949–64	LF	1988 (21.1)	1969 (1.8)	1999 (14.7)
Kevin Mitchell	1984–98	LF	2004 (0.4)		
Rick Monday	1966–84	CF	1990 (0.5)		
Don Money	1968–83	3B	1989 (0.2)		
Jeff Montgomery	1987–99	P	2005 (0.4)		
Wally Moon	1954–65	LF	1971 (0.6)		
Jo–Jo Moore	1930–41	LF	1950 (0.6)		
Terry Moore	1935–48	CF	1968 (11.7)	1950 (0.6)	1968 (11.7)
Pat Moran	1901–14	C	1937 (0.5)	1937 (0.5)	1945 (0.4)
Hal Morris	1988–2000	1B	2006 (1.0)		
Jack Morris	1977–94	P	2006 (41.2)	2000 (22.2)	2007 (37.1)
Wally Moses	1935–51	RF	1971 (1.9)	1958 (0.4)	1971 (1.9)
Johnny Mostil	1918–29	CF	1956 (0.5)	1956 (0.5)	1958 (0.4)
Manny Mota	1962–82	LF	1988 (4.2)	1988 (4.2)	1989 (2.0)
Hugh Mulcahy	1935–47	P	1948 (0.8)		
Van Mungo	1931–45	P	1948 (0.8)	1945 (0.4)	1960 (0.7)
Thurman Munson	1969–79	C	1981 (15.5)	1981 (15.5)	1995 (6.5)
Bobby Murcer	1965–83	RF	1989 (0.7)		
Dale Murphy	1976–93	CF	2000 (23.2)	1999 (19.3)	2007 (9.2)
Danny Murphy	1900–15	2B	1937 (0.5)	1937 (0.5)	1945 (0.4)
Red Murray	1906–17	RF	1937 (0.5)	1937 (0.5)	1938 (0.4)
Buddy Myer	1925–41	2B	1949 (0.7)		
Randy Myers	1985–98	P	2004 (0.2)		
Art Nehf	1915–29	P	1958 (4.9)	1937 (1.5)	1958 (4.9)
Graig Nettles	1967–88	3B	1994 (8.4)	1994 (8.4)	1997 (4.7)
Don Newcombe	1949–60	P	1980 (15.3)	1966 (2.3)	1980 (15.3)
Bobo Newsom	1929–53	P	1969 (9.4)	1960 (2.2)	1973 (8.7)
Bill Nicholson	1936–53	RF	1960 (0.4)		

CANDIDATE	CAREER	POS	MAX YR (PCT)	1ST YEAR (PCT)	LAST YR (PCT)
Joe Niekro	1967–88	P	1994 (1.3)		
Ron Northey	1942–57	RF	1964 (0.5)		
Jim Northrup	1964–75	RF	1981 (0.2)		
Lefty O'Doul	1919–34	LF	1960 (16.7)	1948 (3.3)	1962 (8.1)
Joe Oeschger	1914–25	P	1948 (0.8)		
Bob O'Farrell	1915–35	C	1950 (2.4)	1950 (2.4)	1960 (1.1)
Charlie O'Leary	1904–13	SS	1953 (0.4)	1953 (0.4)	1960 (0.4)
Tony Oliva	1962–76	RF	1988 (47.3)	1982 (15.2)	1996 (36.2)
Al Oliver	1968–85	CF	1991 (4.3)		
Paul O'Neill	1985–2001	RF	2007 (2.2)		
Steve O'Neill	1911–28	C	1953 (4.9)	1948 (1.7)	1958 (3.8)
Claude Osteen	1957–75	P	1981 (0.5)		
Charlie Pabor	1871–75	LF	1936V (1.3)		
Andy Pafko	1943–59	CF	1966 (0.7)	1966 (0.7)	1967 (0.3)
Milt Pappas	1957–73	P	1979 (1.2)		
Dave Parker	1973–91	RF	1998 (24.5)	1997 (17.5)	2007 (11.4)
Lance Parrish	1977–95	C	2001 (1.7)		
Larry Parrish	1974–88	3B	1994 (0.4)		
Camilo Pascual	1954–71	P	1977 (0.8)	1977 (0.8)	1978 (0.3)
Dode Paskert	1907–21	CF	1937 (0.5)		
Monte Pearson	1932–41	P	1958 (0.4)		
Roger Peckinpaugh	1910–27	SS	1937 (1.5)	1937 (1.5)	1955 (0.4)
Heinie Peitz	1893–1906	C	1939 (0.4)		
Tony Pena	1980–97	C	2003 (0.4)		
Terry Pendleton	1984–98	3B	2004 (0.2)		
Hub Perdue	1911–15	P	1938 (0.4)	1938 (0.4)	1939 (0.4)
Cy Perkins	1915–31	C	1958 (0.8)		
Ron Perranoski	1961–73	P	1979 (1.4)		
Jim Perry	1959–75	P	1983 (1.9)	1981 (1.5)	1983 (1.9)
Johnny Pesky	1942–54	SS	1960 (0.4)		
Rico Petrocelli	1963–76	SS	1982 (0.7)		
Deacon Phillippe	1899–1911	P	1945 (0.8)	1939 (0.4)	1946N (0.5)
Tony Phillips	1982–99	LF	2005 (0.2)		
Billy Pierce	1945–64	P	1971 (1.9)	1970 (1.7)	1974 (1.1)
Lip Pike	1871–81	CF	1936V (1.3)		
Lou Piniella	1964–84	LF	1990 (0.5)		
Vada Pinson	1958–75	CF	1988 (15.7)	1981 (4.5)	1996 (10.9)
Wally Pipp	1913–28	1B	1958 (0.4)		
Johnny Podres	1953–69	P	1975 (0.8)	1975 (0.8)	1977 (0.8)
Bob Porterfield	1948–59	P	1966 (0.3)		
Boog Powell	1961–77	1B	1983 (1.3)		
Vic Power	1954–65	1B	1972 (0.8)	1971 (0.6)	1972 (0.8)
Herb Pruett	1922–32	P	1949 (0.7)	1949 (0.7)	1953 (0.4)
Terry Puhl	1977–91	RF	1997 (0.2)		
Jack Quinn	1909–33	P	1958 (3.4)	1948 (1.7)	1960 (0.7)
Dan Quisenberry	1979–90	P	1996 (3.8)		
Willie Randolph	1975–92	2B	1998 (1.1)		
Vic Raschi	1946–55	P	1975 (10.2)	1962 (0.6)	1975 (10.2)
Bugs Raymond	1904–11	P	1937 (0.5)		
Jeff Reardon	1979–94	P	2000 (4.8)		
Pete Reiser	1940–52	CF	1960 (3.0)	1958 (2.3)	1960 (3.0)
Jack Remsen	1872–84	CF	1936V (1.3)		
Jerry Remy	1975–84	2B	1990 (0.2)		
Rick Reuschel	1972–91	P	1997 (0.4)		
Jerry Reuss	1969–90	P	1996 (0.4)		
Allie Reynolds	1942–54	P	1968 (33.6)	1956 (0.5)	1974 (27.7)
Del Rice	1945–61	C	1966 (0.7)		
Jim Rice	1974–89	LF	2006 (64.8)	1995 (29.8)	2007 (63.5)
J. R. Richard	1971–80	P	1986 (1.6)		
Hardy Richardson	1879–92	2B	1936V (1.3)		
Bobby Richardson	1955–66	2B	1972 (2.0)	1972 (2.0)	1974 (1.4)
Dave Righetti	1979–95	P	2001 (0.4)		
Jose Rijo	1984–95	P	2001 (0.2)		
Jimmy Ring	1917–28	P	1949 (0.7)		
Claude Ritchey	1897–1909	2B	1945 (0.4)		
Mickey Rivers	1970–84	CF	1990 (0.5)		
Dave Robertson	1912–22	RF	1953 (0.4)		
Preacher Roe	1938–54	P	1971 (0.8)	1960 (0.4)	1972 (0.5)
Red Rolfe	1931–42	3B	1958 (4.9)	1950 (4.2)	1962 (0.6)
Eddie Rommel	1920–32	P	1960 (4.5)	1948 (2.5)	1960 (4.5)
Charlie Root	1923–41	P	1948 (2.5)	1945 (0.4)	1960 (0.7)
Pete Rose	1963–86	RF	1992 (9.5)	1992 (9.5)	2000 (3.4)
Schoolboy Rowe	1933–49	P	1969 (5.0)	1958 (4.5)	1969 (5.0)
Nap Rucker	1907–16	P	1942 (6.4)	1936 (0.4)	1946N (6.4)
Dick Rudolph	1910–23	P	1937 (0.5)	1937 (0.5)	1951 (0.4)
Muddy Ruel	1915–34	C	1956 (8.3)	1946N (0.5)	1960 (3.3)
Bill Russell	1969–86	SS	1992 (0.7)		
Bret Saberhagen	1984–2001	P	2007 (1.3)		
Ray Sadecki	1960–77	P	1983 (0.5)		
Johnny Sain	1942–55	P	1975 (34.0)	1962 (0.6)	1975 (34.0)
Juan Samuel	1983–98	2B	2004 (0.4)		
Manny Sanguillen	1967–80	C	1986 (0.5)		
Ron Santo	1960–74	3B	1998 (43.1)	1980 (3.9)	1998 (43.1)
Hank Sauer	1941–59	LF	1966 (1.3)		
Steve Sax	1981–94	2B	2000 (0.4)		
Al Schacht	1919–21	P	1951 (1.8)	1939 (0.4)	1956 (0.5)
Germany Schaefer	1901–18	2B	1942 (0.4)	1942 (0.4)	1953 (0.4)
Wally Schang	1913–31	C	1960 (4.1)	1948 (0.8)	1960 (4.1)
Ossie Schreck	1897–1908	C	1937 (1.0)	1937 (1.0)	1939 (0.7)
Frank Schulte	1904–18	RF	1937 (0.5)		
Hal Schumacher	1931–46	P	1964 (5.0)	1948 (0.8)	1964 (5.0)
Everett Scott	1914–26	SS	1955 (3.2)	1937 (1.0)	1956 (0.5)
George Scott	1969–79	1B	1986 (0.2)		
Jack Scott	1916–29	P	1958 (0.4)		
Mike Scott	1979–91	P	1997 (0.4)		
George Selkirk	1934–42	LF	1951 (0.9)	1948 (0.8)	1953 (0.4)
Hank Severeid	1911–26	C	1948 (0.8)		
Luke Sewell	1921–42	C	1958 (1.1)	1948 (0.8)	1962 (0.6)
Rip Sewell	1932–49	P	1962 (0.6)	1958 (0.4)	1964 (0.5)
Cy Seymour	1896–1913	CF	1945 (0.4)		
Bobby Shantz	1949–64	P	1970 (2.3)	1970 (2.3)	1974 (0.8)
Jim Sheckard	1897–1913	LF	1946N (0.5)	1938 (0.4)	1946N (0.5)
Bill Sherdel	1918–32	P	1948 (0.8)	1948 (0.8)	1960 (0.7)
Urban Shocker	1916–28	P	1958 (1.5)	1938 (0.4)	1958 (1.5)
Chris Short	1959–73	P	1979 (0.2)		
Sonny Siebert	1964–75	P	1981 (0.2)		
Roy Sievers	1949–65	1B	1971 (1.1)	1971 (1.1)	1972 (0.8)
Curt Simmons	1947–67	P	1973 (1.3)	1973 (1.3)	1974 (0.8)
Ted Simmons	1968–88	C	1994 (3.7)		
Sibby Sisti	1939–54	2B	1960 (0.4)		
Roy Smalley	1948–58	SS	1964 (0.5)		
Earl Smith	1919–30	C	1948 (0.8)	1948 (0.8)	1956 (0.5)
Lee Smith	1980–97	P	2006 (45.0)	2003 (42.3)	2007 (39.8)
Lonnie Smith	1978–94	LF	2000 (0.2)		
Reggie Smith	1966–82	RF	1988 (0.7)		
Sherry Smith	1911–27	P	1948 (0.8)		
Billy Southworth	1940–51	Mgr	1958 (6.8)	1945 (0.4)	1958 (6.8)
Tully Sparks	1897–1910	P	1946N (0.5)		
Chris Speier	1971–89	SS	1995 (0.2)		
Jake Stahl	1903–13	1B	1938 (0.4)	1938 (0.4)	1939 (0.4)
Eddie Stanky	1943–53	2B	1960 (1.1)		
Mickey Stanley	1964–78	CF	1984 (0.5)		
Rusty Staub	1963–85	RF	1994 (7.9)	1991 (6.3)	1997 (3.8)
Terry Steinbach	1986–99	C	2005 (0.2)		
Harry Steinfeldt	1898–1911	3B	1937 (0.5)	1937 (0.5)	1942 (0.4)
Riggs Stephenson	1921–34	LF	1960 (1.5)	1956 (1.0)	1962 (0.6)
Dave Stewart	1978–95	P	2001 (7.4)	2001 (7.4)	2002 (4.9)
Dave Stieb	1979–98	P	2004 (1.4)		
Mel Stottlemyre	1964–74	P	1980 (0.8)		
Harry Stovey	1880–93	1B	1936V (7.7)		
Darryl Strawberry	1983–99	RF	2005 (1.2)		
Gabby Street	1904–12	C	1937 (0.5)	1937 (0.5)	1953 (0.4)
Gus Suhr	1930–40	1B	1956 (0.5)	1956 (0.5)	1960 (0.4)
Clyde Sukeforth	1926–34	C	1958 (0.4)		
Billy Sullivan	1899–1916	C	1937 (0.5)	1937 (0.5)	1946N (0.5)
Jim Sundberg	1974–89	C	1995 (0.2)		
Rick Sutcliffe	1976–94	P	2000 (1.8)		
Bill Sweeney	1907–14	2B	1945 (0.4)		
Jess Tannehill	1894–1911	P	1946N (0.5)		
Danny Tartabull	1984–97	RF	2003 (0.2)		
Birdie Tebbetts	1936–52	C	1958 (3.0)	1958 (3.0)	1960 (0.4)
Kent Tekulve	1974–89	P	1995 (1.3)		
Gary Templeton	1976–91	SS	1997 (0.4)		
Gene Tenace	1969–83	C	1989 (0.2)		
Fred Tenney	1894–1911	1B	1938 (3.1)	1936V (1.3)	1946N (0.5)
Tommy Thevenow	1924–38	SS	1950 (1.2)		
Ira Thomas	1906–15	C	1938 (0.4)		
Bobby Thomson	1946–60	CF	1968 (4.6)	1966 (4.0)	1979 (2.5)
Andre Thornton	1973–87	DH	1993 (0.5)		
Luis Tiant	1964–82	P	1988 (30.9)	1988 (30.9)	2002 (18.0)
Jim Tobin	1914–27	RF	1956 (1.0)		
Fred Toney	1911–23	P	1949 (0.7)		
Earl Torgeson	1947–61	1B	1967 (0.7)		
Joe Torre	1960–77	C	1997 (22.2)	1983 (5.3)	1997 (22.2)
Mike Torrez	1967–84	P	1990 (0.2)		
Alan Trammell	1977–96	SS	2006 (17.7)	2002 (15.7)	2007 (13.4)
Dizzy Trout	1939–52	P	1964 (0.5)		
Virgil Trucks	1941–58	P	1964 (2.0)		
John Tudor	1979–90	P	1996 (0.4)		
Jim Turner	1937–45	P	1956 (0.5)		
Terry Turner	1901–19	SS	1947 (1.2)		
George Uhle	1919–36	P	1958 (1.5)	1956 (0.5)	1960 (1.5)
Ellis Valentine	1975–85	RF	1991 (0.2)		
Fernando Valenzuela	1980–97	P	2003 (6.3)	2003 (6.3)	2004 (3.8)
Elmer Valo	1940–61	RF	1967 (0.7)		
Johnny Vander Meer	1937–51	P	1967 (29.8)	1945 (0.4)	1971 (27.2)
George Van Haltren	1887–1903	CF	1936V (1.3)		
Bobby Veach	1912–25	LF	1937 (0.5)		
Mickey Vernon	1939–60	1B	1980 (24.9)	1966 (6.6)	1980 (24.9)
Frank Viola	1982–96	P	2002 (0.4)		
Bill Virdon	1955–68	CF	1974 (0.8)	1974 (0.8)	1975 (0.3)
Rube Walberg	1923–37	P	1958 (0.4)	1958 (0.4)	1960 (0.4)
Dixie Walker	1931–49	RF	1964 (3.0)	1962 (0.6)	1969 (2.6)
Harry Walker	1940–51	CF	1958 (0.4)		
Tim Wallach	1980–96	3B	2002 (0.2)		
Bucky Walters	1931–50	P	1968 (23.7)	1950 (2.4)	1970 (9.7)
Bill Wambsganss	1914–26	2B	1955 (2.0)	1942 (0.4)	1956 (0.5)
Lon Warneke	1930–45	P	1964 (6.5)	1949 (1.3)	1964 (6.5)
Bob Watson	1966–84	1B	1990 (0.7)		
Walt Weiss	1987–2000	SS	2006 (0.2)		
Bob Welch	1978–94	P	2000 (0.2)		
Billy Werber	1930–42	3B	1958 (1.1)	1949 (0.7)	1958 (1.1)
Vic Wertz	1947–63	RF	1975 (1.4)	1970 (0.7)	1978 (1.1)
Sam West	1927–42	CF	1948 (0.8)		
Wes Westrum	1947–57	C	1964 (1.0)		
John Wetteland	1989–2000	P	2006 (0.8)		
Lou Whitaker	1977–95	2B	2001 (2.9)		
Deacon White	1871–90	3B	1936V (1.3)		
Frank White	1973–90	2B	1996 (3.8)		
Will White	1877–86	P	1975 (1.9)	1975 (1.9)	1977 (1.0)
Burgess Whitehead	1933–46	2B	1956 (0.5)		
Earl Whitehill	1923–39	P	1960 (1.1)	1956 (0.5)	1960 (1.1)
Fred Williams	1912–30	CF	1956 (5.7)	1938 (0.4)	1960 (4.1)
Ken Williams	1915–29	LF	1956 (0.5)	1956 (0.5)	1958 (0.4)
Ned Williamson	1878–90	3B	1936V (2.6)		
Maury Wills	1959–72	SS	1981 (40.6)	1978 (30.3)	1992 (25.6)
Jimmie Wilson	1923–40	C	1956 (8.8)	1948 (6.6)	1962 (2.5)
Jim Wilson	1945–58	P	1964 (1.0)		
Willie Wilson	1976–94	CF	2000 (2.0)		
Whitey Witt	1916–26	CF	1949 (0.7)		
Joe Wood	1908–22	P	1947 (18.0)	1937 (6.5)	1951 (2.2)
Wilbur Wood	1961–78	P	1988 (7.0)	1984 (3.5)	1989 (3.1)
Glenn Wright	1924–35	SS	1960 (6.7)	1948 (1.7)	1962 (0.6)
Whit Wyatt	1929–45	P	1958 (0.4)		
Steve Yeager	1972–86	C	1992 (0.5)		
Steve Yerkes	1909–16	2B	1945 (0.4)		
Rudy York	1934–48	1B	1964 (5.0)	1962 (0.6)	1964 (5.0)
Pep Young	1933–45	2B	1958 (0.4)		
Tom Zachary	1918–36	P	1958 (0.4)	1958 (0.4)	1960 (0.4)
Chief Zimmer	1884–1903	C	1938 (0.4)		

Top Vote-Getters by Year

1936 VETERANS
NEEDED TO ELECT: 59

Cap Anson ... 40
Buck Ewing ... 40
Willie Keeler ... 33
Cy Young ... 32
Ed Delahanty ... 22

1936
NEEDED TO ELECT: 170

Ty Cobb ... 222
Babe Ruth ... 215
Honus Wagner ... 215
Christy Mathewson 205
Walter Johnson ... 189
Nap Lajoie ... 146
Tris Speaker ... 133
Cy Young ... 111
Rogers Hornsby ... 105
Mickey Cochrane ... 80
George Sisler ... 77
Eddie Collins ... 60
Jimmy Collins ... 58

1937
NEEDED TO ELECT: 151

Nap Lajoie ... 168
Tris Speaker ... 165
Cy Young ... 153
Grover Alexander ... 125
Eddie Collins ... 115
Willie Keeler ... 115
George Sisler ... 106
Ed Delahanty ... 70
Rube Waddell ... 67
Jimmy Collins ... 66
Ed Walsh ... 56
Rogers Hornsby ... 53

1938
NEEDED TO ELECT: 197

Grover Alexander ... 212
George Sisler ... 179
Willie Keeler ... 177
Eddie Collins ... 175
Rube Waddell ... 148
Frank Chance ... 133
Ed Delahanty ... 132
Ed Walsh ... 110
Johnny Evers ... 91
Jimmy Collins ... 79
Rabbit Maranville ... 73
Roger Bresnahan ... 67

1939
NEEDED TO ELECT: 206

George Sisler ... 235
Eddie Collins ... 213
Willie Keeler ... 207
Rube Waddell ... 179
Rogers Hornsby ... 176
Frank Chance ... 158
Ed Delahanty ... 145
Ed Walsh ... 132
Johnny Evers ... 107
Miller Huggins ... 97
Rabbit Maranville ... 82
Jimmy Collins ... 72

1942
NEEDED TO ELECT: 175

Rogers Hornsby ... 182
Frank Chance ... 136
Rube Waddell ... 126
Ed Walsh ... 113
Miller Huggins ... 111
Ed Delahanty ... 104
Johnny Evers ... 91
Wilbert Robinson ... 89
Mickey Cochrane ... 88
Frankie Frisch ... 84
Hugh Duffy ... 77
Herb Pennock ... 72
Clark Griffith ... 71
Jimmy Collins ... 68
Rabbit Maranville ... 66
Hughie Jennings ... 64
Mordecai Brown ... 63
Eddie Plank ... 63
Joe McGinnity ... 59

1945
NEEDED TO ELECT: 186

Frank Chance ... 179
Rube Waddell ... 154
Ed Walsh ... 137
Johnny Evers ... 134
Roger Bresnahan ... 133
Miller Huggins ... 133
Mickey Cochrane ... 125
Jimmy Collins ... 121
Ed Delahanty ... 111
Clark Griffith ... 108
Frankie Frisch ... 101
Hughie Jennings ... 92
Wilbert Robinson ... 81
Pie Traynor ... 81
Hugh Duffy ... 64

1946 NOMINATING
TOTAL VOTING 202

Frank Chance ... 144
Johnny Evers ... 130
Miller Huggins ... 129
Rube Waddell ... 122
Ed Walsh ... 115
Frankie Frisch ... 104
Carl Hubbell ... 101
Mickey Cochrane ... 80
Clark Griffith ... 73
Lefty Grove ... 71
Pie Traynor ... 65
Mordecai Brown ... 56
Joe Tinker ... 55
Joe McGinnity ... 53

1946
NEEDED TO ELECT: 198

Frank Chance ... 150
Johnny Evers ... 110
Miller Huggins ... 106
Ed Walsh ... 106
Rube Waddell ... 87
Clark Griffith ... 82
Carl Hubbell ... 75
Frankie Frisch ... 67

1947
NEEDED TO ELECT: 121

Carl Hubbell ... 140
Frankie Frisch ... 136
Mickey Cochrane ... 128
Lefty Grove ... 123
Pie Traynor ... 119
Charlie Gehringer ... 105
Rabbit Maranville ... 91
Dizzy Dean ... 88
Herb Pennock ... 86
Chief Bender ... 72
Harry Heilmann ... 65
Ray Schalk ... 50
Dazzy Vance ... 50
Frank Baker ... 49
Bill Terry ... 46

1948
NEEDED TO ELECT: 91

Herb Pennock ... 94
Pie Traynor ... 93
Al Simmons ... 60
Charlie Gehringer ... 52
Bill Terry ... 52
Paul Waner ... 51
Jimmie Foxx ... 50
Dizzy Dean ... 40
Harry Heilmann ... 40
Bill Dickey ... 39
Rabbit Maranville ... 38
Gabby Hartnett ... 33

1949
NEEDED TO ELECT: 115

Charlie Gehringer ... 102
Mel Ott ... 94
Al Simmons ... 89
Dizzy Dean ... 88
Jimmie Foxx ... 85
Bill Terry ... 81
Paul Waner ... 73
Hank Greenberg ... 67
Bill Dickey ... 65
Harry Heilmann ... 59
Rabbit Maranville ... 58

1949 RUN OFF
NEEDED TO ELECT: 141
ONE PLAYER MAXIMUM

Charlie Gehringer ... 159
Mel Ott ... 128
Jimmie Foxx ... 89
Dizzy Dean ... 81
Al Simmons ... 76
Paul Waner ... 63
Harry Heilmann ... 52
Bill Terry ... 48

1950
NEEDED TO ELECT: 126

Mel Ott ... 115
Bill Terry ... 105
Jimmie Foxx ... 103
Paul Waner ... 95
Al Simmons ... 90
Harry Heilmann ... 87
Dizzy Dean ... 85
Bill Dickey ... 78
Rabbit Maranville ... 66
Hank Greenberg ... 64
Gabby Hartnett ... 54
Dazzy Vance ... 52
Ted Lyons ... 42

1951
NEEDED TO ELECT: 170

Mel Ott ... 197
Jimmie Foxx ... 179
Paul Waner ... 162
Harry Heilmann ... 153
Bill Terry ... 148
Dizzy Dean ... 145
Bill Dickey ... 118
Al Simmons ... 116
Rabbit Maranville ... 110
Ted Lyons ... 71
Dazzy Vance ... 70
Hank Greenberg ... 67
Gabby Hartnett ... 57

1952
NEEDED TO ELECT: 176

Harry Heilmann ... 203
Paul Waner ... 195
Bill Terry ... 155
Dizzy Dean ... 152
Al Simmons ... 141
Bill Dickey ... 139
Rabbit Maranville ... 133
Dazzy Vance ... 105
Ted Lyons ... 101
Gabby Hartnett ... 77
Hank Greenberg ... 75
Chief Bender ... 70

1953
NEEDED TO ELECT: 198

Dizzy Dean ... 209
Al Simmons ... 199
Bill Terry ... 191
Bill Dickey ... 179
Rabbit Maranville ... 164
Dazzy Vance ... 150
Ted Lyons ... 139
Joe DiMaggio ... 117
Chief Bender ... 104
Gabby Hartnett ... 104
Hank Greenberg ... 80
Joe Cronin ... 69

1954
NEEDED TO ELECT: 189

Rabbit Maranville ... 209
Bill Dickey ... 202
Bill Terry ... 195
Joe DiMaggio ... 175
Ted Lyons ... 170
Dazzy Vance ... 158
Gabby Hartnett ... 151
Hank Greenberg ... 97
Joe Cronin ... 85

1955
NEEDED TO ELECT: 189

Joe DiMaggio ... 223
Ted Lyons ... 217
Dazzy Vance ... 205
Gabby Hartnett ... 195
Hank Greenberg ... 157
Joe Cronin ... 135
Max Carey ... 119
Ray Schalk ... 113
Edd Roush ... 97
Hank Gowdy ... 90
Hack Wilson ... 81
Lefty Gomez ... 71
Tony Lazzeri ... 66

1956
NEEDED TO ELECT: 145

Hank Greenberg ... 164
Joe Cronin ... 152
Red Ruffing ... 97
Edd Roush ... 91
Lefty Gomez ... 89
Hack Wilson ... 74
Max Carey ... 65
Tony Lazzeri ... 64
Kiki Cuyler ... 55
Hank Gowdy ... 49

1958
NEEDED TO ELECT: 200

Max Carey ... 136
Edd Roush ... 112
Red Ruffing ... 99
Hack Wilson ... 94
Kiki Cuyler ... 90
Sam Rice ... 90
Tony Lazzeri ... 80
Luke Appling ... 77
Lefty Gomez ... 76
Burleigh Grimes ... 71
Red Faber ... 68

1960
NEEDED TO ELECT: 202

Edd Roush ... 146
Sam Rice ... 143
Eppa Rixey ... 142
Burleigh Grimes ... 92
Jim Bottomley ... 89
Red Ruffing ... 86
Red Faber ... 83
Luke Appling ... 72
Kiki Cuyler ... 72
Hack Wilson ... 72

1962
NEEDED TO ELECT: 120

Bob Feller ... 150
Jackie Robinson ... 124
Sam Rice ... 81
Red Ruffing ... 72
Eppa Rixey ... 49
Luke Appling ... 48
Phil Rizzuto ... 44
Burleigh Grimes ... 43

1964
NEEDED TO ELECT: 151

Luke Appling ... 142
Red Ruffing ... 141
Roy Campanella ... 115
Joe Medwick ... 108
Pee Wee Reese ... 73
Lou Boudreau ... 68
Al Lopez ... 57
Chuck Klein ... 56
Johnny Mize ... 54
Mel Harder ... 51
Johnny Vander Meer ... 51

1964 RUN OFF
NEEDED TO ELECT: 170
ONE PLAYER MAXIMUM

Luke Appling ... 189
Red Ruffing ... 184
Roy Campanella ... 138
Joe Medwick ... 130

1966
NEEDED TO ELECT: 227

Ted Williams ... 282
Red Ruffing ... 208
Roy Campanella ... 197
Joe Medwick ... 187
Lou Boudreau ... 115
Al Lopez ... 109
Enos Slaughter ... 100
Pee Wee Reese ... 95
Marty Marion ... 86
Johnny Mize ... 81

1967
NEEDED TO ELECT: 219

Joe Medwick ... 212
Red Ruffing ... 212
Roy Campanella ... 204
Lou Boudreau ... 143
Ralph Kiner ... 124
Enos Slaughter ... 123
Al Lopez ... 114
Marty Marion ... 90
Johnny Mize ... 89
Pee Wee Reese ... 89
Johnny Vander Meer ... 87
Allie Reynolds ... 77

1967 RUN OFF
NEEDED TO ELECT: 230
ONE PLAYER MAXIMUM

Red Ruffing ... 266
Joe Medwick ... 248
Roy Campanella ... 170

1968
NEEDED TO ELECT: 213

Joe Medwick ... 240
Roy Campanella ... 205
Lou Boudreau ... 146
Enos Slaughter ... 129
Ralph Kiner ... 118
Johnny Mize ... 103
Allie Reynolds ... 95
Marty Marion ... 89
Arky Vaughan ... 82
Pee Wee Reese ... 81
Johnny Vander Meer ... 79
Joe Gordon ... 77
Phil Rizzuto ... 74

1969
NEEDED TO ELECT: 255

Stan Musial ... 317
Roy Campanella ... 270
Lou Boudreau ... 218
Ralph Kiner ... 137
Enos Slaughter ... 128
Johnny Mize ... 116
Marty Marion ... 112
Allie Reynolds ... 98
Joe Gordon ... 97
Johnny Vander Meer ... 95
Early Wynn ... 95
Pee Wee Reese ... 89

1970
NEEDED TO ELECT: 225

Lou Boudreau ... 232
Ralph Kiner ... 167
Gil Hodges ... 145
Early Wynn ... 140
Enos Slaughter ... 133
Johnny Mize ... 126
Marty Marion ... 120
Pee Wee Reese ... 97
Red Schoendienst ... 97
George Kell ... 90
Allie Reynolds ... 89
Johnny Vander Meer ... 88
Hal Newhouser ... 80
Joe Gordon ... 79
Phil Rizzuto ... 79
Bobby Doerr ... 75

1971
NEEDED TO ELECT: 270

Yogi Berra ... 242
Early Wynn ... 240
Ralph Kiner ... 212
Gil Hodges ... 180
Enos Slaughter ... 165
Johnny Mize ... 157
Pee Wee Reese ... 127
Marty Marion ... 123
Red Schoendienst ... 123
Allie Reynolds ... 110
George Kell ... 105
Johnny Vander Meer ... 98
Hal Newhouser ... 94
Phil Rizzuto ... 92
Bob Lemon ... 90

1972
NEEDED TO ELECT: 297

Sandy Koufax ... 344
Yogi Berra ... 339
Early Wynn ... 301
Ralph Kiner ... 235
Gil Hodges ... 161
Johnny Mize ... 157
Enos Slaughter ... 149
Pee Wee Reese ... 129
Marty Marion ... 120
Bob Lemon ... 117
George Kell ... 115
Allie Reynolds ... 105
Red Schoendienst ... 104
Phil Rizzuto ... 103

1973
NEEDED TO ELECT: 285

Warren Spahn ... 316
Whitey Ford ... 255
Ralph Kiner ... 235
Gil Hodges ... 218
Robin Roberts ... 213
Bob Lemon ... 177
Johnny Mize ... 157
Enos Slaughter ... 145
Marty Marion ... 127
Pee Wee Reese ... 126
George Kell ... 114
Phil Rizzuto ... 111
Duke Snider ... 101
Red Schoendienst ... 96

1974
NEEDED TO ELECT: 274

Mickey Mantle ... 322
Whitey Ford ... 284
Robin Roberts ... 224
Ralph Kiner ... 215
Gil Hodges ... 198
Bob Lemon ... 190
Enos Slaughter ... 145
Pee Wee Reese ... 141
Eddie Mathews ... 118
Phil Rizzuto ... 111
Duke Snider ... 111
Red Schoendienst ... 110
Allie Reynolds ... 101
George Kell ... 94

1975
NEEDED TO ELECT: 272

Ralph Kiner ... 273
Robin Roberts ... 263
Bob Lemon ... 233
Gil Hodges ... 188
Enos Slaughter ... 177
Hal Newhouser ... 155
Pee Wee Reese ... 154
Eddie Mathews ... 148
Phil Cavaretta ... 129
Duke Snider ... 129
Johnny Sain ... 123
Phil Rizzuto ... 117
George Kell ... 114
Red Schoendienst ... 94

1976
NEEDED TO ELECT: 291

Robin Roberts ... 337
Bob Lemon ... 305
Gil Hodges ... 233
Enos Slaughter ... 197
Eddie Mathews ... 189
Pee Wee Reese ... 186
Nellie Fox ... 174
Duke Snider ... 159
Phil Rizzuto ... 149
George Kell ... 129
Red Schoendienst ... 129
Don Drysdale ... 114

1977
NEEDED TO ELECT: 288

Ernie Banks ... 321
Eddie Mathews ... 239
Gil Hodges ... 224
Enos Slaughter ... 222
Duke Snider ... 212
Don Drysdale ... 197
Pee Wee Reese ... 163
Nellie Fox ... 152
Jim Bunning ... 146
George Kell ... 141
Richie Ashburn ... 139
Red Schoendienst ... 105

1978
NEEDED TO ELECT: 285

Eddie Mathews ... 301
Enos Slaughter ... 261
Duke Snider ... 254
Gil Hodges ... 226
Don Drysdale ... 219
Jim Bunning ... 181
Pee Wee Reese ... 169
Richie Ashburn ... 158
Hoyt Wilhelm ... 158
Nellie Fox ... 149
Red Schoendienst ... 130
Maury Wills ... 115

1979
NEEDED TO ELECT: 324

Willie Mays ... 409
Duke Snider ... 308
Enos Slaughter ... 297
Gil Hodges ... 242
Don Drysdale ... 233
Nellie Fox ... 174
Hoyt Wilhelm ... 168
Maury Wills ... 166
Red Schoendienst ... 159
Jim Bunning ... 147
Richie Ashburn ... 130
Roger Maris ... 127
Luis Aparicio ... 120

1980
NEEDED TO ELECT: 289

Al Kaline 340
Duke Snider........... 333
Don Drysdale.............238
Gil Hodges..................230
Hoyt Wilhelm...............209
Jim Bunning................177
Red Schoendienst.......164
Nellie Fox....................161
Maury Wills..................146
Richie Ashburn............134
Luis Aparicio...............124
Roger Maris.................111

1981
NEEDED TO ELECT: 301

Bob Gibson............ 337
Don Drysdale..............243
Gil Hodges..................241
Harmon Killebrew........239
Hoyt Wilhelm...............238
Juan Marichal..............233
Nellie Fox....................168
Red Schoendienst.......166
Jim Bunning................164
Maury Wills..................163
Richie Ashburn............142

1982
NEEDED TO ELECT: 312

Hank Aaron............ 406
Frank Robinson...... 370
Juan Marichal..............305
Harmon Killebrew........246
Hoyt Wilhelm...............236
Don Drysdale..............233
Gil Hodges..................205
Luis Aparicio...............174
Jim Bunning................138
Red Schoendienst.......135
Nellie Fox....................127
Richie Ashburn............126

1983
NEEDED TO ELECT: 281

Brooks Robinson.... 344
Juan Marichal......... 313
Harmon Killebrew........269
Luis Aparicio...............252
Hoyt Wilhelm...............243
Don Drysdale..............242
Gil Hodges..................237
Nellie Fox....................173
Billy Williams...............153
Red Schoendienst.......146
Jim Bunning................138

1984
NEEDED TO ELECT: 303

Luis Aparicio......... 341
Harmon Killebrew.. 335
Don Drysdale......... 316
Hoyt Wilhelm...............290
Nellie Fox....................246
Billy Williams...............202
Jim Bunning................201
Orlando Cepeda...........124
Tony Oliva...................124
Roger Maris.................107
Harvey Kuenn..............106
Maury Wills..................104

1985
NEEDED TO ELECT: 297

Hoyt Wilhelm......... 331
Lou Brock............. 315
Nellie Fox....................295
Billy Williams...............252
Jim Bunning................214
Catfish Hunter.............212
Roger Maris.................128
Harvey Kuenn..............125
Orlando Cepeda...........114
Tony Oliva...................114

1986
NEEDED TO ELECT: 319

Willie McCovey....... 346
Billy Williams...............315
Catfish Hunter.............289
Jim Bunning................279
Roger Maris.................177
Tony Oliva...................154
Orlando Cepeda...........152
Harvey Kuenn..............144
Maury Wills..................124

1987
NEEDED TO ELECT: 310

Billy Williams......... 354
Catfish Hunter........ 315
Jim Bunning................289
Orlando Cepeda...........179
Roger Maris.................176
Tony Oliva...................160
Harvey Kuenn..............144
Bill Mazeroski..............125
Maury Wills..................113

1988
NEEDED TO ELECT: 321

Willie Stargell........ 352
Jim Bunning................317
Tony Oliva...................202
Orlando Cepeda...........199
Roger Maris.................184
Harvey Kuenn..............168
Bill Mazeroski..............143
Luis Tiant....................132
Maury Wills..................127
Ken Boyer....................109
Mickey Lolich...............109
Ron Santo....................108

1989
NEEDED TO ELECT: 336

Johnny Bench........ 431
Carl Yastrzemski.... 423
Gaylord Perry..............304
Jim Bunning................283
Fergie Jenkins.............234
Orlando Cepeda...........176
Tony Oliva...................135
Bill Mazeroski..............134
Harvey Kuenn..............115

1990
NEEDED TO ELECT: 333

Jim Palmer............ 411
Joe Morgan............ 363
Gaylord Perry..............320
Fergie Jenkins.............296
Jim Bunning................257
Orlando Cepeda...........211
Tony Oliva...................142
Bill Mazeroski..............131

1991
NEEDED TO ELECT: 333

Rod Carew............. 401
Gaylord Perry......... 342
Fergie Jenkins........ 334
Rollie Fingers..............291
Jim Bunning................282
Orlando Cepeda...........192
Tony Oliva...................160
Bill Mazeroski..............142
Ron Santo....................116

1992
NEEDED TO ELECT: 323

Tom Seaver............ 425
Rollie Fingers......... 349
Orlando Cepeda...........246
Tony Perez...................215
Bill Mazeroski..............182
Tony Oliva...................175
Ron Santo....................136
Jim Kaat......................114
Maury Wills..................110

1993
NEEDED TO ELECT: 318

Reggie Jackson...... 396
Phil Niekro..................278
Orlando Cepeda...........252
Tony Perez...................233
Steve Garvey...............176
Tony Oliva...................157
Ron Santo....................155
Jim Kaat......................125

1994
NEEDED TO ELECT: 342

Steve Carlton......... 436
Orlando Cepeda...........335
Phil Niekro..................273
Tony Perez...................263
Don Sutton...................259
Steve Garvey...............166
Tony Oliva...................158
Ron Santo....................150

1995
NEEDED TO ELECT: 345

Mike Schmidt......... 444
Phil Niekro..................286
Don Sutton...................264
Tony Perez...................259
Steve Garvey...............196
Tony Oliva...................149
Ron Santo....................139
Jim Rice.......................137
Bruce Sutter.................137

1996
NEEDED TO ELECT: 353

Phil Niekro..................321
Tony Perez...................309
Don Sutton...................300
Steve Garvey...............175
Ron Santo....................174
Tony Oliva...................170
Jim Rice.......................166
Bruce Sutter.................137

1997
NEEDED TO ELECT: 355

Phil Niekro............. 380
Don Sutton...................346
Tony Perez...................312
Ron Santo....................186
Jim Rice.......................178
Steve Garvey...............167
Bruce Sutter.................130

1998
NEEDED TO ELECT: 355

Don Sutton............. 386
Tony Perez...................321
Ron Santo....................204
Jim Rice.......................203
Gary Carter..................200
Steve Garvey...............195
Bruce Sutter.................147
Tommy John................129
Jim Kaat......................129

1999
NEEDED TO ELECT: 373

Nolan Ryan............ 491
George Brett.......... 488
Robin Yount........... 385
Carlton Fisk.................330
Tony Perez...................302
Gary Carter..................168
Steve Garvey...............150
Jim Rice.......................146

2000
NEEDED TO ELECT: 375

Carlton Fisk........... 397
Tony Perez............. 385
Jim Rice.......................257
Gary Carter..................248
Bruce Sutter.................192
Rich Gossage..............166
Steve Garvey...............160
Tommy John................135
Jim Kaat......................125

2001
NEEDED TO ELECT: 387

Dave Winfield.......... 435
Kirby Puckett......... 423
Gary Carter..................334
Jim Rice.......................298
Bruce Sutter.................245
Rich Gossage..............228
Steve Garvey...............176
Tommy John................146
Don Mattingly...............145
Jim Kaat......................139

2002
NEEDED TO ELECT: 354

Ozzie Smith........... 433
Gary Carter..................343
Jim Rice.......................260
Bruce Sutter.................238
Andre Dawson..............214
Rich Gossage..............203
Steve Garvey...............134
Tommy John................127
Bert Blyleven...............124

2003
NEEDED TO ELECT: 372

Eddie Murray......... 423
Gary Carter............ 387
Bruce Sutter.................266
Jim Rice.......................259
Andre Dawson..............248
Ryne Sandberg............244
Lee Smith....................210
Rich Gossage..............209
Bert Blyleven...............145
Steve Garvey...............138
Jim Kaat......................130

2004
NEEDED TO ELECT: 380

Paul Molitor........... 431
Dennis Eckersley... 421
Ryne Sandberg............309
Bruce Sutter.................301
Jim Rice.......................276
Andre Dawson..............253
Rich Gossage..............206
Lee Smith....................185
Bert Blyleven...............179
Jack Morris..................133

2005
NEEDED TO ELECT: 387

Wade Boggs........... 474
Ryne Sandberg....... 393
Bruce Sutter.................344
Jim Rice.......................307
Rich Gossage..............285
Andre Dawson..............270
Bert Blyleven...............211
Lee Smith....................200
Jack Morris..................172

2006
NEEDED TO ELECT: 390

Bruce Sutter.......... 400
Jim Rice.......................337
Rich Gossage..............336
Andre Dawson..............317
Bert Blyleven...............277
Lee Smith....................234
Jack Morris..................214
Tommy John................154
Steve Garvey...............135

2007
NEEDED TO ELECT: 409

Cal Ripken............. 537
Tony Gwynn........... 532
Rich Gossage..............388
Jim Rice.......................346
Andre Dawson..............309
Bert Blyleven...............260
Lee Smith....................217
Jack Morris..................202

Biographical Information for Other Hall of Famers

Biographical and career information is shown on this page for all Hall of Famers who were neither major-league players nor managers nor great Negro League players. This includes all those elected to the Hall of Fame as Pioneers, Executives, or Umpires.

Note that Frank Grant and Sol White—both inducted in 2006 after the special election on the Negro Leagues and pre-Negro Leagues—are also included here. White, although he was both a notable player and manager, was elected as a Pioneer/Executive. Both Grant and White played all of their careers in the pre-Negro Leagues era (mostly in the nineteenth century) when statistics and information about black ballplayers was even more sketchy than during the Negro Leagues era from the 1920s to the 1950s. And neither Grant nor White was one of the Top 100 players of all-time as picked in our Black Baseball and the Negro Leagues section.

Al Barlick Albert Joseph; B4.2.1915 Springfield IL; D12.27.1995 Springfield IL; 5-6/195; HF 1989
Umpire, National League, 1940–71

Morgan Bulkeley Morgan; B12.26.1837 East Haddam CT; D11.6.1922 Hartford CT; HF 1937; Col Yale; Trinity College
Organizer and President, National League, 1876

Alexander Cartwright Alexander Joy Jr.; B4.17.1820 New York NY; D7.12.1892 Honolulu HI; HF 1939
One of the Fathers of Baseball; Organizer, Secretary, and Vice President of Knickerbocker Base Ball Club, 1845

Henry Chadwick Henry; B10.5.1824 Exeter, England; D4.29.1908 Brooklyn NY; HF 1938
One of the Fathers of Baseball; Sportswriter for *New York Clipper*, *New York Herald*, and *Brooklyn Daily Eagle*, 1858–1908; Chairman of Rules Committee, National Association of Base Ball Players; Editor, The Spalding Guide, 1881–1908

Albert "Happy" Chandler Albert B.; B7.14.1898 Corydon KY; D6.15.1991 Versailles KY; HF 1982
Commissioner of Baseball, 1945–51

Nestor Chylak Nestor; B5.11.1922 Oliphant PA; D2.17.1982 Dunmore PA; 6-0/200; HF 1999
Umpire, American League, 1954–78; Asst. Supervisor of Umpires, American League, 1978–84

Tommy Connolly Thomas Francis; B12.31.1870 Manchester, England; D4.28.1961 Natick MA; 5-7/170; HF 1953
Umpire, National League, 1898–1900; Umpire; American League, 1901–31; Umpire-in-Chief, American League, 1931–54

Billy Evans William G.; B2.10.1884 Chicago IL; D1.23.1956 Miami FL 5-11.5/225; HF 1973
Umpire, American League, 1906–27; GM, Cle A, 1928–35; Farm Director, Bos A, 1936–40; GM, Det A, 1947–51

Ford Frick Ford; B12.19.1894 Wawaka IN; D4.8.1978 Bronxville NY; HF 1970
PR Director, National League, 1934; President, National League, 1934–51; Proposed founding of National Baseball Hall of Fame and Museum, 1939; Commissioner of Baseball, 1951–65

Warren Giles Warren; B5.28.1896 Tiskilwa IL; D2.7.1979 Cincinnati OH; HF 1979
GM, Cin N, 1936–51; President, National League, 1951–69

Frank Grant Ulysses F.; B8.1.1865 Pittsfield MA; D5.27.1937 New York NY; BR/TR/5'7.5"/155; d1889; HF 2006; 2b, SS, P, OF, 3b, C.
Player [OB minors 1886-88, 1890]; Cub G 1889, 1891-97, 1899; PF 1891; Cub X 1899; Phi G 1902-03
One of the premier black ballplayers of the nineteenth century, Grant played against white players in the minors for several seasons before segregation was complete. A superb second baseman with a strong arm as well as a swift baserunner, Grant could hit for both average and power plus steal bases.

Will Harridge William; B10.16.1883 Chicago IL; D4.9.1971 Evanston IL; HF 1972
President, American League, 1931–58; Chairman, American League, 1958–71

Cal Hubbard Robert Calvin; B10.31.1900 Keytesville MO; D10.17.1977 St. Petersburg FL; 6-2.5/265; HF 1976; Col Centenary; Geneva
Umpire, American League, 1936–51; Asst. Supervisor of Umpires, American League, 1952–54; Supervisor of Umpires, American League, 1954–70

William Hulbert William A.; B10.23.1832 Burlington Flats NY; D4.10.1882 Chicago IL; HF 1995; Col Beloit
Owner, Chi NA, 1875; Owner, Chi N, 1876–82; Founder, National League, 1876; President, National League, 1877–82

Ban Johnson Byron Bancroft; B1.5.1864 Norwalk OH; D3.28.1931 St. Louis MO; HF 1937; Col Marietta; Cincinnati Law School
President, Western League, 1894–99; President, (minor league) American League, 1900; Founder/Organizer, American League 1901; President, American League, 1901–27; Member, National Commission, 1903–20

Bill Klem William J.; B2.22.1874 Rochester NY; D9.1.1951 Miami FL; 5-7.5/157; HF 1953
Umpire, National League, 1905–40; Chief of Umpires, National League, 1941–51

Kenesaw Mountain Landis Kenesaw Mountain; B11.20.1866 Millville OH; D11.25.1944 Chicago IL; 5-6/135; HF 1945; Col YMCA Law School of Cincinnati; Union Law School
Commissioner of Baseball, 1920–44

Larry MacPhail Leland Stanford; B2.3.1890 Cass City MI; D10.1.1975 Miami FL; HF 1978; s-Lee; Col Beloit; Michigan; George Washington
GM, Cin N, 1935; GM, Bro N, 1938–45; GM, NY A, 1946–47

Lee MacPhail Leland Stanford Jr.; B10.25.1917 Nashville TN; HF 1998; f-Larry
GM, Bal A, 1958–66; GM, NY A, 1966–73; President, American League, 1974–84

Effa Manley B3.27.1897 Philadelphia PA; D4.16.1981 Los Angeles CA; HF 2006
Co-owner/executive, Bro E 1935; New E 1936-48

Bill McGowan William A.; B1.18.1896 Wilmington DE; D12.9.1954 Silver Spring MD; 5-9/178; HF 1992
Umpire, American League, 1925–54

Alex Pompez Alejandro; B5.14.1890 Key West FL; D3.14.1974 New York NY; HF 2006
Owner/Executive, Cub SE 1920-33; NY C 1935-36, 1938-50; Vice President, NNL 1946-48

Cum Posey Cumberland Willis Jr.; B6.20.1890 Homestead PA; D3.28.1946 Pittsburgh PA; HF 2006
Manager/Executive/Owner Hom 1912-46; Secretary, NNL

Bill Veeck William Louis Jr.; B2.9.1914 Chicago IL; D1.2.1986 Chicago IL; HF 1991; Col Kenyon
Owner, Cle A, 1946–49; Owner, Stl A, 1951–53; Owner, Chi A, 1959–61, 1975–80

George Weiss George; B6.23.1895 New Haven CT; D8.13.1972 Greenwich CT; HF 1971
Owner, New Haven EL, 1920–29; Owner, Bal IL, 1929–32; Farm Director, NY A, 1932–47; GM, NY A, 1948–60; President and GM, NY N, 1961–66; Director, NY N, 1966–71

Sol White King Solomon; B6.12.1868 Bellaire OH; D8.26.1955 Central Islip NY; HF 2006
Player/Manager/Pioneer/Executive [OB minors 1887, 1892, 1895] Cub G 1889-91. 1893-94; PF 1895; Cub XG 1896-99, 1901; Phi G 1902-09; Bro RG 1910; Col B 1920; Cle B 1924; New S 1926

J.L. Wilkinson James Leslie; B5.14.1878 Algona IA; D8.21.1964 Kansas City MO; HF 2006
Owner, KC 1920-47; Secretary, NNL; Treasurer NAL

Tom Yawkey Thomas Austin; B2.21.1903 Detroit MI; D7.9.1976 Boston MA; HF 1980
Owner, Bos A, 1933–76; Vice President, American League, 1956–73

THE BOYS OF SUMMER: AWARDS AND OTHER HONORS

Roger Kahn's 1971 masterwork about baseball and life struck a deep chord with Americans. As a result, the term *Boys of Summer* established itself forever in the popular lexicon. Merely playing in the big leagues, even for a moment, is certainly a tremendous accomplishment. However, the boys of our fondest summer memories are typically the stars whose ability, skill, and determination make them rise above the ordinary and place them ahead of their peers. Recognition by others in their field usually follows.

Most of this encyclopedia—indeed, most of any baseball encyclopedia—is filled with statistics. This section, however, is different: It records what the people who have watched baseball for a living thought about the players who produced the statistics. Who was the most valuable player? The *best* player? The best pitcher? The most impressive rookie? Which managers did the best job? Who were the best minor league prospects? Which players were leaders in their communities?

If you look carefully at the players who won the major awards, you'll also see signs of how the game has evolved. Different eras have brought different skills to the forefront, and the weight that the voters have given the various aspects of baseball has changed significantly over time. The major awards shown in this section represent the collective opinions of writers, editors, managers, coaches, and ballplayers over the past century, from the Chalmers Award in 1911 to last year's Rookie of the Year Award. Unanimous selections for all awards are indicated by asterisks.

Lists of "Ex Post Facto" awards for Most Valuable Player, Cy Young, and Rookie of the Year are also presented. Going back in time, we have chosen the players that we think would have won the major awards if they had been given out then (or if the awards had been given out in both leagues). Note that these Ex Post Facto awards do not necessarily represent who we think *should* have won. Instead, we have tried to apply the standards of times past and, based on what the writers historically valued, we have chosen who we think *would have won* had the writers of the time been given the opportunity to vote.

Most Valuable Player Award

The most important award in baseball is undoubtedly the Most Valuable Player Award. No other annual sports award generates as much debate as much as the AL and NL MVPs. Furthermore, no other award in American sports has as long and controversial a history.

The first incarnation of the MVP award was the Chalmers Award, named after Hugh Chalmers, an automobile manufacturer who decided in 1910 that it would be great publicity to give one of his company's automobiles to the player with the highest batting average in each league at the season's end. Unfortunately for the sponsor, the AL batting race that year ended in a white-hot controversy as the St. Louis Browns allowed Nap Lajoie to lay down 7 bunt hits on the last day of the season to give him an edge over the widely disliked Ty Cobb. AL President Ban Johnson ruled that a recalculation showed that Cobb had won the race anyway, and Chalmers ended up awarding cars to both Lajoie and Cobb.

To avoid this type of embarrassment, Chalmers decided in 1911 to change the rules of the contest, constituting a committee of baseball writers to determine—following the season—the "most important and useful player to his club and to the league." This was clearly the first Most Valuable Player Award. However, the Chalmers Award did not prove to be the hoped-for marketing bonanza, and the award was discontinued after 1914.

In 1922 the American League created a new award to honor "the baseball player who is of greatest all-around service to his club." Regrettably, the league saddled the new award with several rules that led to widespread dissatisfaction. Voters were required to select one (and only one) player from each team and were not allowed to vote for player-managers. Moreover, previous award winners were disqualified from consideration. Flawed from its inception, the award was dropped in 1929. The National League, which had in 1924 instituted its own contest (without the controversial restrictions), again followed the AL's lead and eliminated its award in 1930.

After a brief interregnum the Baseball Writers Association of America created the modern MVP award in 1931, adopting the same system that the NL had used for its abandoned MVP award. One writer in each league city was asked to fill out a ten-place ballot; ten points was awarded to the recipient of a first-place vote, nine points for a second-place vote, and so on, with one point awarded for a tenth place vote. In 1938 the BBWAA began polling three writers in each league city and raised the number of points for first-place votes to fourteen. The only significant change in the MVP balloting since then has been the reduction of writers polled to two per league city in 1961.

Despite continuing debate, the BBWAA has never spelled out the definition of the Most Valuable Player. Is the MVP simply the *best* player? Should candidates on pennant winners get special consideration? Must the MVP play on a contending team? Should starting pitchers qualify for the honor despite not participating in the great majority of their team's games? What about relief pitchers? Can any player be "most valuable" if his team finishes last?

While there have never been official answers to these questions, it is clear that the voting patterns of the BBWAA have changed over time. In the 1950s, for example, MVP voting favored "up the middle" players: center fielders, middle infielders, and catchers. Players like Nellie Fox (who won the 1959 AL MVP) and Dick Groat (1960 NL MVP) would not be serious candidates for the award today; in the last twenty-five years, writers have valued sluggers with high RBI totals (e.g., Juan Gonzalez and Jeff Kent) more highly than any other type of player. It is difficult to tell whether these voting patterns will persist; the argument over whether Alex Rodriguez of the last-place Rangers deserved the 2003 AL MVP is a perfect example of the utter lack of definition for the award.

Award voting, especially MVP balloting, frequently seems to stir up more controversy than it used to. Voters in the last twenty years have made some very debatable selections, including some outright mistakes, but it's wise to recall that their counterparts in earlier times were perfectly capable of picking less-than-qualified winners. Glamour statistics, mostly RBIs, have always tended to help players that are having otherwise modest seasons win prestigious trophies. Jackie Jensen, Hank Sauer, Frank McCormick, and Jeff Burroughs—MVP winners all—are good examples. Furthermore, decent but otherwise unspectacular players having that one "career year" (e.g., Zoilo Versalles, Bobby Shantz, and Bob Elliott) have copped awards despite clearly superior competition. Compared to some of the stranger BBWAA decisions of earlier times, the record-setting seventh MVP and Cy Young Awards given to Barry Bonds and Roger Clemens in 2004 seem like no-brainers.

Chalmers Award

AMERICAN LEAGUE		NATIONAL LEAGUE	
1911	Ty Cobb*, Det	1911	Frank Schulte, Chi
1912	Tris Speaker, Bos	1912	Larry Doyle, NY
1913	Walter Johnson, Was	1913	Jake Daubert, Bro
1914	Eddie Collins, Phi	1914	Johnny Evers, Bos

League Award

AMERICAN LEAGUE		NATIONAL LEAGUE	
1922	George Sisler, StL		
1923	Babe Ruth*, NY		
1924	Walter Johnson, Was	1924	Dazzy Vance, Bro
1925	Roger Peckinpaugh, Was	1925	Rogers Hornsby, StL
1926	George Burns, Cle	1926	Bob O'Farrell, StL
1927	Lou Gehrig, NY	1927	Paul Waner, Pit
1928	Mickey Cochrane, Phi	1928	Jim Bottomley, StL
		1929	Rogers Hornsby, Chi

BBWAA AL & NL MVP Awards

AMERICAN LEAGUE		NATIONAL LEAGUE	
1931	Lefty Grove, Phi	1931	Frankie Frisch, StL
1932	Jimmie Foxx, Phi	1932	Chuck Klein, Phi
1933	Jimmie Foxx, Phi	1933	Carl Hubbell, NY
1934	Mickey Cochrane, Det	1934	Dizzy Dean, StL
1935	Hank Greenberg*, Det	1935	Gabby Hartnett, Chi
1936	Lou Gehrig, NY	1936	Carl Hubbell*, NY
1937	Charlie Gehringer, Det	1937	Joe Medwick, StL
1938	Jimmie Foxx, Bos	1938	Ernie Lombardi, Cin
1939	Joe DiMaggio, NY	1939	Bucky Walters, Cin
1940	Hank Greenberg, Det	1940	Frank McCormick, Cin
1941	Joe DiMaggio, NY	1941	Dolph Camilli, Bro
1942	Joe Gordon, NY	1942	Mort Cooper, StL
1943	Spud Chandler, NY	1943	Stan Musial, StL
1944	Hal Newhouser, Det	1944	Marty Marion, StL
1945	Hal Newhouser, Det	1945	Phil Cavarretta, Chi
1946	Ted Williams, Bos	1946	Stan Musial, StL
1947	Joe DiMaggio, NY	1947	Bob Elliott, Bos
1948	Lou Boudreau, Cle	1948	Stan Musial, StL
1949	Ted Williams, Bos	1949	Jackie Robinson, Bro
1950	Phil Rizzuto, NY	1950	Jim Konstanty, Phi
1951	Yogi Berra, NY	1951	Roy Campanella, Bro
1952	Bobby Shantz, Phi	1952	Hank Sauer, Chi
1953	Al Rosen*, Cle	1953	Roy Campanella, Bro
1954	Yogi Berra, NY	1954	Willie Mays, NY

1955	Yogi Berra, NY	1955	Roy Campanella, Bro
1956	Mickey Mantle*, NY	1956	Don Newcombe, Bro
1957	Mickey Mantle, NY	1957	Hank Aaron, Mil
1958	Jackie Jensen, Bos	1958	Ernie Banks, Chi
1959	Nellie Fox, Chi	1959	Ernie Banks, Chi
1960	Roger Maris, NY	1960	Dick Groat, Pit
1961	Roger Maris, NY	1961	Frank Robinson*, Cin
1962	Mickey Mantle, NY	1962	Maury Wills, LA
1963	Elston Howard, NY	1963	Sandy Koufax, LA
1964	Brooks Robinson, Bal	1964	Ken Boyer, StL
1965	Zoilo Versalles, Min	1965	Willie Mays, SF
1966	Frank Robinson*, Bal	1966	Roberto Clemente, Pit
1967	Carl Yastrzemski, Bos	1967	Orlando Cepeda*, StL
1968	Denny McLain*, Det	1968	Bob Gibson, StL
1969	Harmon Killebrew, Min	1969	Willie McCovey, SF
1970	Boog Powell, Bal	1970	Johnny Bench, Cin
1971	Vida Blue, Oak	1971	Joe Torre, StL
1972	Dick Allen, Chi	1972	Johnny Bench, Cin
1973	Reggie Jackson*, Oak	1973	Pete Rose, Cin
1974	Jeff Burroughs, Tex	1974	Steve Garvey, LA
1975	Fred Lynn, Bos	1975	Joe Morgan, Cin
1976	Thurman Munson, NY	1976	Joe Morgan, Cin
1977	Rod Carew, Min	1977	George Foster, Cin
1978	Jim Rice, Bos	1978	Dave Parker, Pit
1979	Don Baylor, Cal	1979	Keith Hernandez, StL
		(tie)	Willie Stargell, Pit
1980	George Brett, KC	1980	Mike Schmidt*, Phi
1981	Rollie Fingers, Mil	1981	Mike Schmidt, Phi
1982	Robin Yount, Mil	1982	Dale Murphy, Atl
1983	Cal Ripken, Bal	1983	Dale Murphy, Atl
1984	Willie Hernandez, Det	1984	Ryne Sandberg, Chi
1985	Don Mattingly, NY	1985	Willie McGee, StL
1986	Roger Clemens, Bos	1986	Mike Schmidt, Phi
1987	George Bell, Tor	1987	Andre Dawson, Chi
1988	Jose Canseco*, Oak	1988	Kirk Gibson, LA
1989	Robin Yount, Mil	1989	Kevin Mitchell, SF
1990	Rickey Henderson, Oak	1990	Barry Bonds, Pit
1991	Cal Ripken, Bal	1991	Terry Pendleton, Atl
1992	Dennis Eckersley, Oak	1992	Barry Bonds, Pit
1993	Frank Thomas*, Chi	1993	Barry Bonds, SF
1994	Frank Thomas, Chi	1994	Jeff Bagwell*, Hou
1995	Mo Vaughn, Bos	1995	Barry Larkin, Cin
1996	Juan Gonzalez, Tex	1996	Ken Caminiti*, SD
1997	Ken Griffey Jr.*, Sea	1997	Larry Walker, Col
1998	Juan Gonzalez, Tex	1998	Sammy Sosa, Chi
1999	Ivan Rodriguez, Tex	1999	Chipper Jones, Atl
2000	Jason Giambi, Oak	2000	Jeff Kent, SF
2001	Ichiro Suzuki, Sea	2001	Barry Bonds, SF
2002	Miguel Tejada, Oak	2002	Barry Bonds, SF
2003	Alex Rodriguez, Tex	2003	Barry Bonds, SF
2004	Vladimir Guerrero, Ana	2004	Barry Bonds, SF
2005	Alex Rodriguez, NY	2005	Albert Pujols, StL
2006	Ryan Howard, Phi	2006	Justin Morneau, Min

Ex Post Facto MVP Award

NATIONAL ASSOCIATION	
1871	Levi Meyerle, Ath
1872	Ross Barnes, Bos
1873	Ross Barnes, Bos
1874	Cal McVey, Bos
1875	Cal McVey, Bos

AMERICAN ASSOCIATION	
1882	Hick Carpenter, Cin
1883	Harry Stovey, Phi
1884	Guy Hecker, Lou
1885	Bob Caruthers, StL
1886	Bob Caruthers, StL
1887	Tip O'Neill, StL
1888	Silver King, StL
1889	Harry Stovey, Phi
1890	Jimmy Wolf, Lou
1891	Dan Brouthers, Bos

UNION ASSOCIATION	
1884	Fred Dunlap, StL

PLAYERS LEAGUE	
1890	Hardy Richardson, Bos

FEDERAL LEAGUE	
1914	Benny Kauff, Ind
1915	Ed Konetchy, Pit

NATIONAL LEAGUE	
1876	Ross Barnes, Chi
1877	Deacon White, Bos
1878	Paul Hines, Pro
1879	Paul Hines, Pro
1880	George Gore, Chi
1881	Cap Anson, Chi
1882	Cap Anson, Chi
1883	Jim Whitney, Bos
1884	Charley Radbourn, Pro
1885	John Clarkson, Chi
1886	King Kelly, Chi
1887	Sam Thompson, Det
1888	Buck Ewing, NY
1889	John Clarkson, Bos
1890	Jack Glasscock, NY
1891	Billy Hamilton, Phi
1892	Dan Brouthers, Bro
1893	Ed Delahanty, Phi
1894	Hugh Duffy, Bos
1895	Hughie Jennings, Bal
1896	Hughie Jennings, Bal
1897	Willie Keeler, Bal
1898	Jimmy Collins, Bos
1899	Ed Delahanty, Phi
1900	Honus Wagner, Pit
1901	Honus Wagner, Pit
1902	Honus Wagner, Pit
1903	Honus Wagner, Pit
1904	Joe McGinnity, NY
1905	Christy Mathewson, NY
1906	Frank Chance, Chi
1907	Honus Wagner, Pit
1908	Christy Mathewson, NY
1909	Honus Wagner, Pit
1910	Sherry Magee, Phi
[1911–14	See Chalmers Awards]
1915	Grover Alexander, Phi
1916	Grover Alexander, Phi
1917	Grover Alexander, Phi
1918	Hippo Vaughn, Chi
1919	Edd Roush, Cin
1920	Rogers Hornsby, StL
1921	Rogers Hornsby, StL
1922	Rogers Hornsby, StL
1923	Dolf Luque, Cin
[1924–29	See NL Awards]
1930	Hack Wilson, Chi

AMERICAN LEAGUE	
1901	Nap Lajoie, Phi
1902	Cy Young, Bos
1903	Nap Lajoie, Cle
1904	Jack Chesbro, NY
1905	Rube Waddell, Phi
1906	Nap Lajoie, Cle
1907	Ty Cobb, Det
1908	Ed Walsh, Chi
1909	Ty Cobb, Det
1910	Jack Coombs, Phi
[1911–14	See Chalmers Awards]
1915	Ty Cobb, Det
1916	Ty Cobb, Det
1917	Eddie Cicotte, Chi
1918	Babe Ruth, Bos
1919	Eddie Cicotte, Chi
1920	Babe Ruth, NY
1921	Babe Ruth, NY
[1922–28	See AL Awards]
1929	Lew Fonseca, Cle
1930	Joe Cronin, Was

BBWAA Cy Young Award

In 1956 the BBWAA, prodded by Commissioner Ford Frick, created the Cy Young Award in order to annually honor the best pitcher in the major leagues. The award was named after Cy Young, the all-time leader in pitching wins (and losses), who had died in 1955. The impetus for the award's creation was the lack of support pitchers had been receiving in MVP balloting. Ironically, the creation of the Cy Young would further reduce that support. In 1967 voters began selecting one Cy Young winner in each league. In 1970 a three-place ballot replaced the original one-place ballot.

There's no debating the goal of the Cy Young Award; voters do not give extra credit to pitchers on contenders, and you'll rarely hear talk about a pitcher's leadership skills from the electorate. However, there has been one major change over the last forty years in the voting pattern—the rise in the status of relief pitchers. No relief pitcher had ever appeared in the Cy Young results until Lindy McDaniel in 1960. It would not be until 1974 that a relief pitcher, in this case Mike Marshall, would capture a Cy Young Award. No reliever has yet won one unanimously, though Eric Gagne came within two first-place votes of doing so in 2003. Some baseball writers have argued that it would be more appropriate for relievers to compete against everyday players in the MVP race rather than against starting pitchers for the Cy Young.

Cy Young Award

1956	Don Newcombe, Bro NL
1957	Warren Spahn, Mil NL
1958	Bob Turley, NY AL
1959	Early Wynn, Chi AL
1960	Vern Law, Pit NL
1961	Whitey Ford, NY AL
1962	Don Drysdale, LA NL
1963	Sandy Koufax*, LA NL
1964	Dean Chance, LA AL
1965	Sandy Koufax*, LA NL
1966	Sandy Koufax*, LA NL

AL & NL Cy Young Awards

	AL	NL
1967	Jim Lonborg, Bos	Mike McCormick, SF
1968	Denny McLain*, Det	Bob Gibson*, StL
1969	Mike Cuellar, Bal	Tom Seaver, NY
(tie)	Denny McLain, Det	
1970	Jim Perry, Min	Bob Gibson, StL
1971	Vida Blue, Oak	Fergie Jenkins, Chi
1972	Gaylord Perry, Cle	Steve Carlton*, Phi
1973	Jim Palmer, Bal	Tom Seaver, NY
1974	Catfish Hunter, Oak	Mike Marshall, LA
1975	Jim Palmer, Bal	Tom Seaver, NY
1976	Jim Palmer, Bal	Randy Jones, SD
1977	Sparky Lyle, NY	Steve Carlton, Phi
1978	Ron Guidry*, NY	Gaylord Perry, SD
1979	Mike Flanagan, Bal	Bruce Sutter, Chi
1980	Steve Stone, Bal	Steve Carlton, Phi
1981	Rollie Fingers, Mil	Fernando Valenzuela, LA
1982	Pete Vuckovich, Mil	Steve Carlton, Phi
1983	La Marr Hoyt, Chi	John Denny, Phi
1984	Willie Hernandez, Det	Rick Sutcliffe*, Chi
1985	Bret Saberhagen, KC	Dwight Gooden*, NY
1986	Roger Clemens*, Bos	Mike Scott, Hou
1987	Roger Clemens, Bos	Steve Bedrosian, Phi
1988	Frank Viola, Min	Orel Hershiser*, LA
1989	Bret Saberhagen, KC	Mark Davis, SD
1990	Bob Welch, Oak	Doug Drabek, Pit
1991	Roger Clemens, Bos	Tom Glavine, Atl
1992	Dennis Eckersley, Oak	Greg Maddux, Chi
1993	Jack McDowell, Chi	Greg Maddux, Atl
1994	David Cone, KC	Greg Maddux*, Atl
1995	Randy Johnson, Sea	Greg Maddux*, Atl
1996	Pat Hentgen, Tor	John Smoltz, Atl
1997	Roger Clemens, Tor	Pedro Martinez*, Mon
1998	Roger Clemens*, Tor	Tom Glavine, Atl
1999	Pedro Martinez*, Bos	Randy Johnson, Ari
2000	Pedro Martinez*, Bos	Randy Johnson, Ari
2001	Roger Clemens, NY	Randy Johnson, Ari
2002	Barry Zito, Oak	Randy Johnson*, Ari
2003	Roy Halladay, Tor	Eric Gagne, LA
2004	Johan Santana*, Min	Roger Clemens, Hou
2005	Bartolo Colon, LA	Chris Carpenter, StL
2006	Johan Santana*, Min	Brandon Webb, Ari

Ex Post Facto Cy Young Awards

NATIONAL ASSOCIATION	
1871	George Zettlein, Chi
1872	Al Spalding, Bos
1873	Al Spalding, Bos
1874	Al Spalding, Bos
1875	Al Spalding, Bos

AMERICAN ASSOCIATION	
1882	Will White, Cin
1883	Will White, Cin
1884	Guy Hecker, Lou
1885	Bob Caruthers, StL
1886	Dave Foutz, StL
1887	Matt Kilroy, Bal
1888	Silver King, StL
1889	Bob Caruthers, Bro
1890	Scott Stratton, Lou
1891	George Haddock, Bos

UNION ASSOCIATION	
1884	Bill Sweeney, Bal

PLAYERS LEAGUE	
1890	Silver King, Chi

FEDERAL LEAGUE	
1914	Claude Hendrix, Chi
1915	George McConnell, Chi

UE	
	George Bradley, StL
	Tommy Bond, Bos
	Tommy Bond, Bos
	Tommy Bond, Bos
80	Larry Corcoran, Chi
1881	Larry Corcoran, Chi
1882	Charley Radbourn, Pro
1883	Charley Radbourn, Pro
1884	Charley Radbourn, Pro
1885	John Clarkson, Chi
1886	Lady Baldwin, Det
1887	John Clarkson, Chi
1888	Tim Keefe, NY
1889	John Clarkson, Bos
1890	Bill Hutchison, Chi
1891	Bill Hutchison, Chi
1892	Cy Young, Cle
1893	Amos Rusie, NY
1894	Amos Rusie, NY
1895	Cy Young, Cle
1896	Kid Nichols, Bos
1897	Kid Nichols, Bos
1898	Kid Nichols, Bos
1899	Vic Willis, Bos
1900	Joe McGinnity, Bro
1901	Deacon Phillippe, Pit
1902	Jack Chesbro, Pit
1903	Christy Mathewson, NY
1904	Joe McGinnity, NY
1905	Christy Mathewson, NY
1906	Mordecai Brown, Chi
1907	Orval Overall, Chi
1908	Christy Mathewson, NY
1909	Mordecai Brown, Chi
1910	Christy Mathewson, NY
1911	Christy Mathewson, NY
1912	Rube Marquard, NY
1913	Christy Mathewson, NY
1914	Bill James, Bos
1915	Grover Alexander, Phi
1916	Grover Alexander, Phi
1917	Grover Alexander, Phi
1918	Hippo Vaughn, Chi
1919	Hippo Vaughn, Chi
1920	Pete Alexander, Chi
1921	Burleigh Grimes, Bro
1922	Wilbur Cooper, Pit
1923	Dolf Luque, Cin
1924	Dazzy Vance, Bro
1925	Dazzy Vance, Bro
1926	Ray Kremer, Pit
1927	Charles Root, Chi
1928	Burleigh Grimes, Pit
1929	Burleigh Grimes, Pit
1930	Pat Malone, Chi
1931	Ed Brandt, Bos
1932	Lou Warneke, Chi
1933	Carl Hubbell, NY
1934	Dizzy Dean, StL
1935	Dizzy Dean, StL
1936	Carl Hubbell, NY
1937	Carl Hubbell, NY
1938	Bill Lee, Chi
1939	Bucky Walters, Cin
1940	Bucky Walters, Cin
1941	Whit Wyatt, Bro
1942	Mort Cooper, StL
1943	Mort Cooper, StL
1944	Bucky Walters, Cin
1945	Red Barrett, Bos-StL
1946	Howie Pollet, StL
1947	Ewell Blackwell, Cin
1948	Johnny Sain, Bos
1949	Warren Spahn, Bos
1950	Jim Konstanty, Phi
1951	Sal Maglie, NY
1952	Robin Roberts, Phi
1953	Warren Spahn, Mil
1954	Johnny Antonelli, NY
1955	Robin Roberts, Phi
1958	Warren Spahn, Mil
1959	Sam Jones, SF
1961	Warren Spahn, Mil
1964	Sandy Koufax, LA

AMERICAN LEAGUE	
1901	Cy Young, Bos
1902	Cy Young, Bos
1903	Cy Young, Bos
1904	Jack Chesbro, NY
1905	Rube Waddell, Phi
1906	Al Orth, NY
1907	Bill Donovan, Det
1908	Ed Walsh, Chi
1909	George Mullin, Det
1910	Jack Coombs, Phi
1911	Walter Johnson, Was
1912	Walter Johnson, Was
1913	Walter Johnson, Was
1914	Walter Johnson, Was
1915	Walter Johnson, Was
1916	Babe Ruth, Bos
1917	Eddie Cicotte, Chi
1918	Walter Johnson, Was
1919	Eddie Cicotte, Chi
1920	Jim Bagby, Cle
1921	Red Faber, Chi
1922	Eddie Rommel, Phi
1923	George Uhle, Cle
1924	Walter Johnson, Was
1925	Stan Coveleski, Was
1926	George Uhle, Cle
1927	Waite Hoyt, NY
1928	Lefty Grove, Phi
1929	Lefty Grove, Phi
1930	Lefty Grove, Phi
1931	Lefty Grove, Phi
1932	Lefty Grove, Phi
1933	Lefty Grove, Phi
1934	Lefty Gomez, NY
1935	Wes Ferrell, Bos
1936	Tommy Bridges, Det
1937	Lefty Gomez, NY
1938	Red Ruffing, NY
1939	Bob Feller, Cle
1940	Bob Feller, Cle
1941	Bob Feller, Cle
1942	Tex Hughson, Bos
1943	Spud Chandler, NY
1944	Hal Newhouser, Det
1945	Hal Newhouser, Det
1946	Hal Newhouser, Det
1947	Bob Feller, Cle
1948	Bob Lemon, Cle
1949	Mel Parnell, Bos
1950	Bob Lemon, Cle
1951	Ed Lopat, NY
1952	Bobby Shantz, Phi
1953	Billy Pierce, Chi
1954	Bob Lemon, Cle
1955	Whitey Ford, NY
1956	Billy Pierce, Chi
1957	Jim Bunning, Det
1960	Chuck Estrada, Bal
1962	Dick Donovan, Cle
1963	Whitey Ford, NY
1965	Mudcat Grant, Min
1966	Jim Kaat, Min

BBWAA Rookie of the Year Award

Inspired by its Chicago branch, which had been honoring top rookies since 1940, the Baseball Writers Association of America took the Rookie of the Year awards national starting in 1947. After honoring only one rookie in 1947 and 1948, the BBWAA started giving the award to a rookie in each league in 1949. In the early days of the award, there was significant confusion over which players qualified as rookies. The first set of standards dealing with this was established in 1957. The current standards, which say that any player who has accumulated more than 130 at bats, 50 innings, or a certain amount of time on the major league roster is no longer a rookie, took effect in 1971. Writers used a one-place ballot for most the award's history until 1980, when voters shifted over to a three-place ballot.

Though there's no longer any debate over which players are technically rookies, there is discussion as to whether certain players should be *considered* rookies. Hideki Matsui lost the 2003 AL Rookie of the Year Award because two voters purposely left him off their ballots as a result of his Japanese pro experience. Ironically, the first BBWAA Rookie of the Year Award winner, Jackie Robinson, and many of the other players who won the award in its first decade of existence, came from the high-level Negro Leagues and thus had a similar baseball background to the Japanese players of today who are competing for MLB's rookie awards.

A more general issue is whether voters should favor younger rookies who show greater potential over older rookies who perform better in their first years but have much lower ceilings. With more Japanese players entering the majors, this issue will remain a hot topic, but it appears unlikely that the rules will be altered anytime soon.

ROOKIE OF THE YEAR AWARD	
1947	Jackie Robinson, Bro NL
1948	Alvin Dark, Bos NL

AL ROOKIE OF THE YEAR AWARD		NL ROOKIE OF THE YEAR AWARD	
1949	Roy Sievers, StL	1949	Don Newcombe, Bro
1950	Walt Dropo, Bos	1950	Sam Jethroe, Bos
1951	Gil McDougald, NY	1951	Willie Mays, NY
1952	Harry Byrd, Phi	1952	Joe Black, Bro
1953	Harvey Kuenn, Det	1953	Jim Gilliam, Bro
1954	Bob Grim, NY	1954	Wally Moon, StL
1955	Herb Score, Cle	1955	Bill Virdon, StL
1956	Luis Aparicio, Chi	1956	Frank Robinson*, Cin
1957	Tony Kubek*, NY	1957	Jack Sanford, Phi
1958	Albie Pearson, Was	1958	Orlando Cepeda*, SF
1959	Bob Allison, Was	1959	Willie McCovey*, SF
1960	Ron Hansen, Bal	1960	Frank Howard, LA
1961	Don Schwall, Bos	1961	Billy Williams, Chi
1962	Tom Tresh, NY	1962	Ken Hubbs, Chi
1963	Gary Peters, Chi	1963	Pete Rose, Cin
1964	Tony Oliva, Min	1964	Richie Allen, Phi
1965	Curt Blefary, Bal	1965	Jim Lefebvre, LA
1966	Tommie Agee, Chi	1966	Tommy Helms, Cin
1967	Rod Carew, Min	1967	Tom Seaver, NY
1968	Stan Bahnsen, NY	1968	Johnny Bench, Cin
1969	Lou Piniella, KC	1969	Ted Sizemore, LA
1970	Thurman Munson, NY	1970	Carl Morton, Mon
1971	Chris Chambliss, Cle	1971	Earl Williams, Atl
1972	Carlton Fisk, Bos	1972	Jon Matlack, NY
1973	Al Bumbry, Bal	1973	Gary Matthews, SF
1974	Mike Hargrove, Tex	1974	Bake McBride, StL
1975	Fred Lynn*, Bos	1975	John Montefusco, SF
1976	Mark Fidrych, Det	1976	Pat Zachary, Cin
		(tie)	Butch Metzger, SD
1977	Eddie Murray, Bal	1977	Andre Dawson, Mon
1978	Lou Whitaker, Det	1978	Bob Horner, Atl
1979	Alfredo Griffin, Tor	1979	Rick Sutcliffe, LA
(tie)	John Castino, Min		
1980	Joe Charboneau, Cle	1980	Steve Howe, LA
1981	Dave Righetti, NY	1981	Fernando Valenzuela, LA
1982	Cal Ripken, Bal	1982	Steve Sax, LA
1983	Ron Kittle, Chi	1983	Darryl Strawberry, NY
1984	Alvin Davis, Sea	1984	Dwight Gooden, NY
1985	Ozzie Guillen, Chi	1985	Vince Coleman*, StL
1986	Jose Canseco, Oak	1986	Todd Worrell, StL
1987	Mark McGwire*, Oak	1987	Benito Santiago*, SD
1988	Walt Weiss, Oak	1988	Chris Sabo, Cin
1989	Gregg Olson, Bal	1989	Jerome Walton, Chi
1990	Sandy Alomar Jr.*, Cle	1990	David Justice, Atl
1991	Chuck Knoblauch, Min	1991	Jeff Bagwell, Hou
1992	Pat Listach, Mil	1992	Eric Karros, LA
1993	Tim Salmon*, Cal	1993	Mike Piazza*, LA
1994	Bob Hamelin, KC	1994	Raul Mondesi*, LA
1995	Marty Cordova, Min	1995	Hideo Nomo, LA
1996	Derek Jeter*, NY	1996	Todd Hollandsworth, LA
1997	Nomar Garciaparra, Bos	1997	Scott Rolen*, Phi
1998	Ben Grieve, Oak	1998	Kerry Wood, Chi
1999	Carlos Beltran, KC	1999	Scott Williamson, Cin
2000	Kazuhiro Sasaki, Sea	2000	Rafael Furcal, Atl
2001	Ichiro Suzuki, Sea	2001	Albert Pujols*, StL
2002	Eric Hinske, Tor	2002	Jason Jennings, Col
2003	Angel Berroa, KC	2003	Dontrelle Willis, Fla
2004	Bobby Crosby, Oak	2004	Jason Bay, Pit
2005	Huston Street, Oak	2005	Ryan Howard, Phi
2006	Justin Verlander, Det	2006	Hanley Ramirez , Fla

Ex Post Facto Rookie of the Year Award

NATIONAL ASSOCIATION	
1872	Candy Cummings, Mut
1873	Paul Hines, Was
1874	Tommy Bond, Atl
1875	George Bradley, StL

AMERICAN ASSOCIATION	
1882	Pete Browning, Lou
1883	Arlie Latham, StL
1884	Dave Orr, NY
1885	Norm Baker, Lou
1886	Matt Kilroy, Bal
1887	Mike Griffin, Bal
1888	Mickey Hughes, Bro
1889	Jesse Duryea, Cin
1890	Cupid Childs, Syr
1891	Willard Mains, Cin

UNION ASSOCIATION	
1884	Harry Moore, Was

PLAYERS LEAGUE	
1890	Phil Knell, Phi

FEDERAL LEAGUE	
1914	Benny Kauff, Ind
1915	Jim Kelly, Pit

NATIONAL LEAGUE	
1876	Charley Jones, Cin
1877	Terry Larkin, Har
1878	Abner Dalrymple, Mil
1879	John O'Rourke, Bos
1880	Roger Connor, Tro
1881	Jim Whitney, Bos
1882	Mike Muldoon, Cle
1883	Charlie Buffinton, Bos
1884	John Clarkson, Chi
1885	Ed Daily, Phi
1886	Jocko Flynn, Chi
1887	Mark Baldwin, Chi
1888	Ben Sanders, Phi
1889	Patsy Tebeau, Cle
1890	Billy Rhines, Cin
1891	Bill Dahlen, Chi
1892	Nig Cuppy, Cle
1893	Heinie Reitz, Bal
1894	Win Mercer, Was
1895	Bill Hoffer, Bal

1896	Gene DeMontreville, Was
1897	Chick Stahl, Bos
1898	Elmer Flick, Phi
1899	Jimmy Williams, Pit
1900	Jimmy Barrett, Cin
1901	Christy Mathewson, NY
1902	Homer Smoot, StL
1903	Jake Weimer, Chi
1904	Harry Lumley, Bro
1905	George Stone, StL
1906	Jack Pfiester, Chi
1907	Nap Rucker, Bro
1908	George McQuillan, Phi
1909	Harry Gaspar, Cin
1910	King Cole, Chi
1911	Grover Alexander, Phi
1912	Larry Cheney, Chi
1913	Jim Vlox, Pit
1914	Jeff Pfeffer, Bro
1915	Tom Long, StL
1916	Rogers Hornsby, StL
1917	Leon Cadore, Bro
1918	Charlie Hollocher, Chi
1919	Oscar Tuero, StL
1920	Pat Duncan, Cin
1921	Ray Grimes, Chi
1922	Hack Miller, Chi
1923	George Grantham, Chi
1924	Kiki Cuyler, Pit
1925	Jimmy Welsh, Bos
1926	Paul Waner, Pit
1927	Lloyd Waner, Pit
1928	Del Bissonette, Bro
1929	Johnny Frederick, Bro
1930	Wally Berger, Bos
1931	Paul Derringer, StL
1932	Dizzy Dean, StL
1933	Frank Demaree, Chi
1934	Curt Davis, Phi
1935	Cy Blanton, Pit
1936	Johnny Mize, StL
1937	Cliff Melton, NY
1938	Johnny Rizzo, Pit
1939	Bob Bowman, StL
1940	Babe Young, NY
1941	Elmer Riddle, Cin
1942	Johnny Beazley, StL
1943	Lou Klein, StL
1944	Bill Voiselle, NY
1945	Ken Burkhart, StL
1946	Del Ennis, Phi

AMERICAN LEAGUE

1901	Socks Seybold, Phi
1902	Addie Joss, Cle
1903	Chief Bender, Phi
1904	Fred Glade, StL
1905	George Stone, StL
1906	Claude Rossman, Cle
1907	Glenn Liebhardt, Cle
1908	Ed Summers, Det
1909	Frank Baker, Phi
1910	Russ Ford, NY
1911	Vean Gregg, Cle
1912	Del Pratt, StL
1913	Reb Russell, Chi
1914	George Burns, Det
1915	Babe Ruth, Bos
1916	Jim Bagby, Cle
1917	Joe Harris, Cle
1918	Scott Perry, Phi
1919	Dickie Kerr, Chi
1920	Bob Meusel, NY
1921	Joe Sewell, Cle
1922	Herman Pillette, Det
1923	Homer Summa, Cle
1924	Ike Boone, Bos
1925	Earle Combs, NY
1926	Tony Lazzeri, NY
1927	Wilcy Moore, NY
1928	Ed Morris, Bos
1929	Dale Alexander, Det
1930	Smead Jolley, Chi
1931	Joe Vosmik, Cle
1932	Johnny Allen, NY
1933	Bob Johnson, Phi
1934	Hal Trosky, Cle
1935	Jake Powell, Was
1936	Joe DiMaggio, NY
1937	Rudy York, Det
1938	Ken Keltner, Cle
1939	Ted Williams, Bos
1940	Walt Judnich, StL
1941	Phil Rizzuto, NY
1942	Johnny Pesky, Bos
1943	Billy Johnson, NY
1944	Joe Berry, Phi
1945	Dave Ferriss, Bos
1946	Hoot Evers, Det
1947	Spec Shea, NY
1948	Gene Bearden, Cle

BBWAA Manager of the Year Award

The Baseball Writers Association of America was a latecomer to honoring the major leagues' best managers, but today the trophy given to the BBWAA's Manager of the Year is the most prestigious of its kind. Voting is done with the same three-place ballot that the BBWAA uses for the Cy Young and Rookie of the Year.

	AL	NL
1983	Tony La Russa, Chi	Tommy Lasorda, LA
1984	Sparky Anderson, Det	Jim Frey, Chi
1985	Bobby Cox, Tor	Whitey Herzog, StL
1986	John McNamara, Bos	Hal Lanier, Hou
1987	Sparky Anderson, Det	Buck Rodgers, Mon
1988	Tony La Russa, Oak	Tommy Lasorda, La
1989	Frank Robinson, Bal	Don Zimmer, Chi
1990	Jeff Torborg, Chi	Jim Leyland, Pit
1991	Tom Kelly, Min	Bobby Cox, Atl
1992	Tony La Russa, Oak	Jim Leyland, Pit
1993	Gene Lamont, Chi	Dusty Baker, SF
1994	Buck Showalter, NY	Felipe Alou, Mon
1995	Lou Piniella, Sea	Don Baylor, Col
1996	Johnny Oates, Tex	Bruce Bochy, SD
(tie)	Joe Torre, NY	
	AL	**NL**
1997	Davey Johnson, Bal	Dusty Baker, SF
1998	Joe Torre, NY	Larry Dierker, Hou
1999	Jimy Williams, Bos	Jack McKeon, Cin
2000	Jerry Manuel, Chi	Dusty Baker, SF
2001	Lou Piniella, Sea	Larry Bowa, Phi
2002	Mike Scioscia, Ana	Tony La Russa, StL
2003	Tony Pena, KC	Jack McKeon, Fla
2004	Buck Showalter, Tex	Bobby Cox, Atl
2005	Ozzie Guillen, Chi	Bobby Cox, Atl
2006	Jim Leyland, Det	Joe Girardi, Fla

The Sporting News Player and Pitcher of the Year Awards

The Sporting News was once known as "Baseball's Bible." (Some especially avid baseball fans referred to the Bible as "*The Sporting News* of religion.") That reputation endowed *The Sporting News*' awards with a great deal of prestige. Many fans held the newspaper's selections in equal or even higher regard than the choices made by the BBWAA. That time is long gone, but *The Sporting News* still gives out more baseball awards than any other organization, and the long tradition of these awards gives them unmatched historical value.

The Sporting News started its tradition of awards in 1929 after the American League abandoned choosing a Most Valuable Player. Over the following twenty years, *The Sporting News* alternated between competing with the BBWAA's MVP awards and endorsing them. In 1948, *The Sporting News* started annually selecting Players and Pitchers of the Year in each league as well as continuing their Major League Player of the Year, which had been selected annually since 1935. In 1992, *The Sporting News* decided to drop its AL and NL Player of the Year Awards in order to focus exclusively on its Major League Player of the Year Award, which would heretofore be selected by big league players. The remaining *Sporting News* awards are still selected by the magazine's editors.

	AL PLAYER	AL PITCHER	NL PLAYER	NL PITCHER	ML PLAYER
1929	Al Simmons, Phi				
1930	Joe Cronin, Was		Bill Terry, NY		
1931	Lou Gehrig, NY		Chuck Klein, Phi		
1932	Jimmie Foxx, Phi		Chuck Klein, Phi		
1933	Jimmie Foxx, Phi			Carl Hubbell, NY	
1934	Lou Gehrig, NY			Dizzy Dean, StL	
1935	Hank Greenberg, Det		Arky Vaughan, Pit		
1936	Lou Gehrig, NY			Carl Hubbell, NY	Carl Hubbell, NY
1937	Charlie Gehringer, Det	Johnny Allen, Cle	Joe Medwick, StL		Johnny Allen, Cle
1938	Jimmie Foxx, Bos		Ernie Lombardi, Cin	Johnny Vander Meer, Cin	Johnny Vander Meer, Cin
1939	Joe DiMaggio, NY			Bucky Walters, Cin	Joe DiMaggio, NY
1940	Hank Greenberg, Det	Bob Feller, Cle	Frank McCormick, Cin		Bob Feller, Cle
1941	Joe DiMaggio, NY		Dolf Camilli, Bro		Ted Williams, Bos
1942	Joe Gordon, NY			Mort Cooper, StL	Ted Williams, Bos
1943		Spud Chandler, NY	Stan Musial, StL		Spud Chandler, NY
1944	Bobby Doerr, Bos	Hal Newhouser, Det	Marty Marion, StL	Bill Voiselle, NY	Marty Marion, StL
1945	Eddie Mayo, Det	Hal Newhouser, Det	Tommy Holmes, Bos	Hank Borowy, Chi	Hal Newhouser, Det
1946			Stan Musial, StL		Stan Musial, StL
1947	Ted Williams, Bos				Ted Williams, Bos
1948	Lou Boudreau, Cle	Bob Lemon, Cle	Stan Musial, StL	Johnny Sain, Bos	Lou Boudreau, Cle
1949	Ted Williams, Bos	Ellis Kinder, Bos	Enos Slaughter, StL	Howie Pollet, StL	Ted Williams, Bos
1950	Phil Rizzuto, NY	Bob Lemon, Cle	Ralph Kiner, Pit	Jim Konstanty, Phi	Phil Rizzuto, NY
1951	Ferris Fain, Phi	Bob Feller, Cle	Stan Musial, StL	Preacher Roe, Bro	Stan Musial, StL
1952	Luke Easter, Cle	Bobby Shantz, Phi	Hank Sauer, Chi	Robin Roberts, Phi	Robin Roberts, Phi
1953	Al Rosen, Cle	Bob Porterfield, Was	Roy Campanella, Bro	Warren Spahn, Mil	Al Rosen, Cle
1954	Bobby Avila, Cle	Bob Lemon, Cle	Willie Mays, NY	John Antonelli, NY	Willie Mays, NY
1955	Al Kaline, Det	Whitey Ford, NY	Duke Snider, Bro	Robin Roberts, Phi	Duke Snider, Bro
1956	Mickey Mantle, NY	Billy Pierce, Chi	Hank Aaron, Mil	Don Newcombe, Bro	Mickey Mantle, NY
1957	Ted Williams, Bos	Billy Pierce, Chi	Stan Musial, StL	Warren Spahn, Mil	Ted Williams, Bos
1958	Jackie Jensen, Bos	Bob Turley, NY	Ernie Banks, Chi	Warren Spahn, Mil	Bob Turley, NY
1959	Nellie Fox, Chi	Early Wynn, Chi	Ernie Banks, Chi	Sam Jones, SF	Early Wynn, Chi
1960	Roger Maris, NY	Chuck Estrada, Bal	Dick Groat, Pit	Vern Law, Pit	Bill Mazeroski, Pit
1961	Roger Maris, NY	Whitey Ford, NY	Frank Robinson, Cin	Warren Spahn, Mil	Roger Maris, NY
1962	Mickey Mantle, NY	Dick Donovan, Cle	Maury Wills, LA	Don Drysdale, LA	Don Drysdale, LA
1963	Al Kaline, Det	Whitey Ford, NY	Hank Aaron, Mil	Sandy Koufax, LA	Sandy Koufax, LA
1964	Brooks Robinson, Bal	Dean Chance, LA	Ken Boyer, StL	Sandy Koufax, LA	Ken Boyer, StL
1965	Tony Oliva, Min	Mudcat Grant, Min	Willie Mays, SF	Sandy Koufax, LA	Sandy Koufax, LA
1966	Frank Robinson, Bal	Jim Kaat, Min	Roberto Clemente, Pit	Sandy Koufax, LA	Frank Robinson, Bal
1967	Carl Yastrzemski, Bos	Jim Lonborg, Bos	Orlando Cepeda, StL	Mike McCormick, SF	Carl Yastrzemski, Bos

AWARDS

1968	Ken Harrelson, Bos	Denny McLain, Det	Pete Rose, Cin	Bob Gibson, StL	Denny McLain, Det
1969	Harmon Killebrew, Min	Denny McLain, Det	Willie McCovey, SF	Tom Seaver, NY	Willie McCovey, SF
1970	Harmon Killebrew, Min	Sam McDowell, Cle	Johnny Bench, Cin	Bob Gibson, StL	Johnny Bench, Cin
1971	Tony Oliva, Min	Vida Blue, Oak	Joe Torre, StL	Fergie Jenkins, Chi	Joe Torre, StL
1972	Dick Allen, Chi	Wilbur Wood, Chi	Billy Williams, Chi	Steve Carlton, Phi	Billy Williams, Chi
1973	Reggie Jackson, Oak	Jim Palmer, Bal	Bobby Bonds, SF	Ron Bryant, SF	Reggie Jackson, Oak
1974	Jeff Burroughs, Tex	Catfish Hunter, Oak	Lou Brock, StL	Mike Marshall, LA	Lou Brock, StL
1975	Fred Lynn, Bos	Jim Palmer, Bal	Joe Morgan, Cin	Tom Seaver, NY	Joe Morgan, Cin
1976	Thurman Munson, NY	Jim Palmer, Bal	George Foster, Cin	Randy Jones, SD	Joe Morgan, Cin
1977	Rod Carew, Min	Nolan Ryan, Cal	George Foster, Cin	Steve Carlton, Phi	Rod Carew, Min
1978	Jim Rice, Bos	Ron Guidry, NY	Dave Parker, Pit	Vida Blue, SF	Ron Guidry, NY
1979	Don Baylor, Cal	Mike Flanagan, Bal	Keith Hernandez, StL	Joe Niekro, Hou	Willie Stargell, Pit
1980	George Brett, KC	Steve Stone, Bal	Mike Schmidt, Phi	Steve Carlton, Phi	George Brett, KC
1981	Tony Armas, Oak	Jack Morris, Det	Andre Dawson, Mon	Fernando Valenzuela, LA	Fernando Valenzuela, LA
1982	Robin Yount, Mil	Dave Stieb, Tor	Dale Murphy, Atl	Steve Carlton, Phi	Robin Yount, Mil
1983	Cal Ripken, Bal	La Marr Hoyt, Chi	Dale Murphy, Atl	John Denny, Phi	Cal Ripken, Bal
1984	Don Mattingly, NY	Willie Hernandez, Det	Ryne Sandberg, Chi	Rick Sutcliffe, Chi	Ryne Sandberg, Chi
1985	Don Mattingly, NY	Bret Saberhagen, KC	Willie McGee, StL	Dwight Gooden, NY	Don Mattingly, NY
1986	Don Mattingly, NY	Roger Clemens, Bos	Mike Schmidt, Phi	Mike Scott, Hou	Roger Clemens, Bos
1987	George Bell, Tor	Jimmy Key, Tor	Andre Dawson, Chi	Rick Sutcliffe, Chi	George Bell, Tor
1988	Jose Canseco, Oak	Frank Viola, Min	Andy Van Slyke, Pit	Orel Hershiser, LA	Orel Hershiser, LA
1989	Ruben Sierra, Tex	Bret Saberhagen, KC	Kevin Mitchell, SF	Mark Davis, SD	Kevin Mitchell, SF
1990	Cecil Fielder, Det	Bob Welch, Oak	Barry Bonds, Pit	Doug Drabek, Pit	Barry Bonds, Pit
1991	Cal Ripken, Bal	Roger Clemens, Bos	Barry Bonds, Pit	Tom Glavine, Atl	Cal Ripken, Bal
1992		Dennis Eckersley, Oak		Greg Maddux, Chi	Gary Sheffield, SD
1993		Jack McDowell, Chi		Greg Maddux, Atl	Frank Thomas, Chi
1994		Jimmy Key, NY		Greg Maddux, Atl	Jeff Bagwell, Hou
1995		Randy Johnson, Sea		Greg Maddux, Atl	Albert Belle, Cle
1996		Pat Hentgen, Tor		John Smoltz, Atl	Alex Rodriguez, Sea
1997		Roger Clemens, Tor		Pedro Martinez, Mon	Ken Griffey Jr., Sea
1998		Roger Clemens, Tor		Kevin Brown, SD	Sammy Sosa, Chi
1999		Pedro Martinez, Bos		Mike Hampton, Hou	Rafael Palmeiro, Tex
2000		Pedro Martinez, Bos		Tom Glavine, Atl	Carlos Delgado, Tor
2001		Roger Clemens, NY		Curt Schilling, Ari	Barry Bonds, SF
2002		Barry Zito, Oak		Curt Schilling, Ari	Alex Rodriguez, Tex
2003		Roy Halladay, Oak		Eric Gagne, LA	Albert Pujols, StL
2004		Johan Santana, Min		Jason Schmidt, SF	Barry Bonds, SF
2005		Bartolo Colon, Cle		Chris Carpenter, StL	Andruw Jones, Atl
2006		Johan Santana, Min		Chris Carpenter, StL	Ryan Howard, Phi

The Sporting News Rookie Player and Pitcher of the Year Awards

The Sporting News started selecting a Rookie of the Year in 1946, and moved tentatively to selecting one player from each league in 1949. It selected a separate Rookie Pitcher of the Year in 1957, one in each league in 1958 and 1961, and no pitchers at all in 1959, 1960, and 1962, Finally, in 1963, *The Sporting News* settled on annually picking both a Rookie Player of the Year and a Rookie Pitcher of the Year from each league. In 2004, however, *The Sporting News* eliminated its Rookie Pitcher of the Year awards. (The top rookie—if a pitcher—is listed under the pitcher heading before 1957 and after 2003 but, in those cases, the pitcher is simply *The Sporting News* Rookie of the Year for his league.)

	AL PLAYER	AL PITCHER	NL PLAYER	NL PITCHER
1946			Del Ennis, Phi	
1947			Jackie Robinson, Bro	
1948			Richie Ashburn, Phi	
1949	Roy Sievers, StL			Don Newcombe, Bro
1950		Whitey Ford, NY		
1951	Minnie Minoso, Chi		Willie Mays, NY	
1952	Clint Courtney, StL			Joe Black, Bro
1953	Harvey Kuenn, Det		Junior Gilliam, Bro	
1954		Bob Grim, NY	Wally Moon, StL	
1955		Herb Score, Cle	Bill Virdon, StL	
1956	Luis Aparicio, Chi		Frank Robinson, Cin	
1957	Tony Kubek, NY		Ed Bouchee, Phi	Jack Sanford, Phi
1958	Albie Pearson, Was	Ryne Duren, NY	Orlando Cepeda, SF	Carlton Willey, Mil
1959	Bob Allison, Was		Willie McCovey, SF	
1960	Ron Hansen, Bal		Frank Howard, LA	
1961	Dick Howser, KC	Don Schwall, Bos	Billy Williams, Chi	Ken Hunt, Cin
1962	Tom Tresh, NY		Ken Hubbs, Chi	
1963	Pete Ward, Chi	Gary Peters, Chi	Pete Rose, Cin	Ray Culp, Phi
1964	Tony Oliva, Min	Wally Bunker, Bal	Richie Allen, Phi	Billy McCool, Cin
1965	Curt Blefary, Bal	Marcelino Lopez, Cal	Joe Morgan, Hou	Frank Linzy, SF
1966	Tommie Agee, Chi	Jim Nash, KC	Tommy Helms, Cin	Don Sutton, La
1967	Rod Carew, Min	Tom Phoebus, Bal	Lee May, Cin	Dick Hughes, StL
1968	Del Unser, Was	Stan Bahnsen, NY	Johnny Bench, Cin	Jerry Koosman, NY
1969	Carlos May, Chi	Mike Nagy, Bos	Coco Laboy, Mon	Tom Griffin, Hou
1970	Roy Foster, Cle	Bert Blyleven, Min	Bernie Carbo, Cin	Carl Morton, Mon
1971	Chris Chambliss, Cle	Bill Parsons, Mil	Earl Williams, Atl	Reggie Cleveland, StL
1972	Carlton Fisk, Bos	Dick Tidrow, Cle	Dave Rader, SF	Jon Matlack, NY
1973	Al Bumbry, Bal	Steve Busby, KC	Gary Matthews, SF	Steve Rogers, Mon
1974	Mike Hargrove, Tex	Frank Tanana, Cal	Greg Gross, Hou	John D'Acquisto, SF
1975	Fred Lynn, Bos	Dennis Eckersley, Cle	Gary Carter, Mon	John Montefusco, SF
1976	Butch Wynegar, Min	Mark Fidrych, Det	Larry Herndon, SF	Butch Metzger, SD
1977	Mitchell Page, Oak	Dave Rozema, Det	Andre Dawson, Mon	Bob Owchinko, SD
1978	Paul Molitor, Mil	Rich Gale, KC	Bob Horner, Atl	Don Robinson, Pit
1979	Pat Putnam, Tex	Mark Clear, Cal	Jeff Leonard, Hou	Rick Sutcliffe, LA
1980	Joe Charboneau, Cle	Britt Burns, Chi	Lonnie Smith, Phi	Bill Gullickson, Mon
1981	Rich Gedman, Bos	Dave Righetti, NY	Tim Raines, Mon	Fernando Valenzuela, LA
1982	Cal Ripken, Bal	Ed Vande Berg, Sea	Johnny Ray, Pit	Steve Bedrosian, Atl
1983	Ron Kittle, Chi	Mike Boddicker, Bal	Darryl Strawberry, NY	Craig McMurtry, Atl
1984	Alvin Davis, Sea	Mark Langston, Sea	Juan Samuel, Phi	Dwight Gooden, NY
1985	Ozzie Guillen, Chi	Ted Higuera, Mil	Vince Coleman, StL	Tom Browning, Cin
1986	Jose Canseco, Oak	Mark Eichhorn, Tor	Robby Thompson, SF	Todd Worrell, StL
1987	Mark McGwire, Oak	Mike Henneman, Det	Benito Santiago, SD	Mike Dunne, Pit
1988	Walt Weiss, Oak	Bryan Harvey, Cal	Mark Grace, Chi	Tim Belcher, LA
1989	Craig Worthington, Bal	Tom Gordon, KC	Jerome Walton, Chi	Andy Benes, SD
1990	Sandy Alomar Jr., Cle	Kevin Appier, KC	Dave Justice, Atl	Mike Harkey, Chi
1991	Chuck Knoblauch, Min	Juan Guzman, Tor	Jeff Bagwell, Hou	Al Osuna, Hou
1992	Pat Listach, Mil	Cal Eldred, Mil	Eric Karros, LA	Tim Wakefield, Pit
1993	Tim Salmon, Cal	Aaron Sele, Bos	Mike Piazza, LA	Kirk Rueter, Mon
1994	Bob Hamelin, KC	Brian Anderson, Cal	Raul Mondesi, LA	Steve Trachsel, Chi
1995	Garret Anderson, Cal	Julian Tavarez, Cle	Chipper Jones, Atl	Hideo Nomo, LA
1996	Derek Jeter, NY	James Baldwin, Chi	Jason Kendall, Pit	Alan Benes, StL

1997	Nomar Garciaparra, Bos	Jason Dickson, Ana	Scott Rolen, Phi	Matt Morris, StL
1998	Ben Grieve, Oak	Rolando Arrojo, TB	Todd Helton, Col	Kerry Wood, Chi
1999	Carlos Beltran, KC	Tim Hudson, Oak	Preston Wilson, Fla	Scott Williamson, Cin
2000	Mark Quinn, KC	Kazuhiro Sasaki, Sea	Rafael Furcal, Atl	Rick Ankiel, StL
2001	Ichiro Suzuki, Sea	C.C. Sabathia, Cle	Albert Pujols, StL	Roy Oswalt, Hou
2002	Eric Hinske, Tor	Rodrigo Lopez, Bal	Brad Wilkerson, Mon	Jason Jennings, Col
2003	Jody Gerut, Cle	Rafael Soriano, Sea	Scott Podsednik, Mil	Dontrelle Willis, Fla
2004	Bobby Crosby, Oak		Jason Bay, Pit	
2005		Huston Street, Oak	Willy Tavares, Hou	
2006		Justin Verlander, Det	Dan Uggla, Flo	

The Sporting News Manager of the Year Award

The Sporting News has honored a Manager of the Year since 1936, forty-six years before the BBWAA first gave a comparable award. In response to the BBWAA's selection of a Manager of the Year for each major league, *The Sporting News* started doing the same in 1986.

1936	Joe McCarthy, NY AL	1961	Ralph Houk, NY AL
1937	Bill McKechnie, Bos NL	1962	Bill Rigney, LA AL
1938	Joe McCarthy, NY AL	1963	Walt Alston, LA NL
1939	Leo Durocher, Bro NL	1964	Johnny Keane, StL NL
1940	Bill McKechnie, Cin NL	1965	Sam Mele, Min AL
1941	Billy Southworth, StL NL	1966	Hank Bauer, Bal AL
1942	Billy Southworth, StL NL	1967	Dick Williams, Bos AL
1943	Joe McCarthy, NY AL	1968	Mayo Smith, Det AL
1944	Luke Sewell, StL AL	1969	Gil Hodges, NY NL
1945	Ossie Bluege, Was AL	1970	Danny Murtaugh, Pit NL
1946	Eddie Dyer, StL NL	1971	Charlie Fox, SF NL
1947	Bucky Harris, NY AL	1972	Chuck Tanner, Chi AL
1948	Billy Meyer, Pit NL	1973	Gene Mauch, Mon NL
1949	Casey Stengel, NY AL	1974	Bill Virdon, NY AL
1950	Red Rolfe, Det AL	1975	Darrell Johnson, Bos AL
1951	Leo Durocher, NY NL	1976	Danny Ozark, Phi NL
1952	Eddie Stanky, StL NL	1977	Earl Weaver, Bal AL
1953	Casey Stengel, NY AL	1978	George Bamberger, Mil AL
1954	Leo Durocher, NY NL	1979	Earl Weaver, Bal AL
1955	Walt Alston, Bro NL	1980	Bill Virdon, Hou NL
1956	Birdie Tebbetts, Cin NL	1981	Billy Martin, Oak AL
1957	Fred Hutchinson, StL NL	1982	Whitey Herzog, StL NL
1958	Casey Stengel, NY AL	1983	Tony La Russa, Chi AL
1959	Walt Alston, LA NL	1984	Jim Frey, Chi NL
1960	Danny Murtaugh, Pit NL	1985	Bobby Cox, Tor AL

	AL	NL
1986	John McNamara, Bos	Hal Lanier, Hou
1987	Sparky Anderson, Det	Buck Rodgers, Mon
1988	Tony La Russa, Oak	Jim Leyland, Pit
1989	Frank Robinson, Bal	Don Zimmer, Chi
1990	Jeff Torborg, Chi	Jim Leyland, Pit
1991	Tom Kelly, Min	Bobby Cox, Atl
1992	Tony La Russa, Oak	Jim Leyland, Pit
1993	Johnny Oates, Bal	Bobby Cox, Atl
1994	Buck Showalter, NY	Felipe Alou, Mon
1995	Mike Hargrove, Cle	Don Baylor, Col
1996	Johnny Oates, Tex	Bruce Bochy, SD
1997	Davey Johnson, Bal	Dusty Baker, SF
1998	Joe Torre, NY	Bruce Bochy, SD
1999	Jimy Williams, Bos	Bobby Cox, Atl
2000	Jerry Manuel, Chi	Dusty Baker, SF
2001	Lou Piniella, Sea	Larry Bowa, Phi
2002	Mike Scioscia, Ana	Bobby Cox, Atl
2003	Tony Peña, KC	Bobby Cox, Atl
2004	Ron Gardenhire, Min	Bobby Cox, Atl
(tie)	Buck Showalter, Tex	
2005	Ozzie Guillen, Chi	Bobby Cox, Atl
2006	Jim Leyland, Det	Joe Girardi, Fla

The Sporting News Comeback Player of the Year Award

Other organizations have selected Comeback Player of the Year awards, but only *The Sporting News* version has stood the test of time. No one has ever really defined a "comeback" for the purposes of this award, but it's safe to say that no other award for on-field achievement in baseball honors players with a higher average age.

	AL	NL
1965	Norm Cash, Det	Vern Law, Pit
1966	Boog Powell, Bal	Phil Regan, LA
1967	Dean Chance, Min	Mike McCormick, SF
1968	Ken Harrelson, Bos	Alex Johnson, Cin
1969	Tony Conigliaro, Bos	Tommie Agee, NY
1970	Clyde Wright, Cal	Jim Hickman, Chi
1971	Norm Cash, Det	Al Downing, LA
1972	Luis Tiant, Bos	Bobby Tolan, Cin
1973	John Hiller, Det	Davey Johnson, Atl
1974	Ferguson Jenkins, Tex	Jimmy Wynn, LA
1975	Boog Powell, Cle	Randy Jones, SD
1976	Dock Ellis, NY	Tommy John, LA
1977	Eric Soderholm, Chi	Willie McCovey, SF
1978	Mike Caldwell, Mil	Willie Stargell, Pit
1979	Willie Horton, Sea	Lou Brock, StL
1980	Matt Keough, Oak	Jerry Reuss, LA
1981	Richie Zisk, Sea	Bob Knepper, Hou
1982	Andre Thornton, Cle	Joe Morgan, SF
1983	Alan Trammell, Det	John Denny, Phi
1984	Dave Kingman, Oak	Joaquin Andujar, StL
1985	Gorman Thomas, Sea	Rick Reuschel, Pit
1986	John Candelaria, Cal	Ray Knight, NY
1987	Bret Saberhagen, KC	Rick Sutcliffe, Chi
1988	Storm Davis, Oak	Tim Leary, LA
1989	Bert Blyleven, Cal	Lonnie Smith, Atl
1990	Dave Winfield, Cal	John Tudor, StL
1991	Jose Guzman, Tex	Terry Pendleton, Atl
1992	Rick Sutcliffe, Bal	Gary Sheffield, SD
1993	Bo Jackson, Chi	Andres Galarraga, Col
1994	Jose Canseco, Tex	Tim Wallach, LA
1995	Tim Wakefield, Bos	Ron Gant, Cin
1996	Kevin Elster, Tex	Eric Davis, Cin
1997	David Justice, Cle	Darren Daulton, Phi-Fla
1998	Bret Saberhagen, Bos	Greg Vaughn, SD
1999	John Jaha, Oak	Rickey Henderson, NY
2000	Frank Thomas, Chi	Andres Galarraga, Atl
2001	Ruben Sierra, Tex	Matt Morris, StL
2002	Tim Salmon, Phi	Mike Lieberthal, Phi
2003	Gil Meche, Sea	Javy Lopez, Atl
2004	Paul Konerko, Chi	Chris Carpenter, SL
2005	Jason Giambi, NY	Ken Griffey Jr., Cin
2006	Jim Thome, Chi	Nomar Garciaparra LA

The Sporting News Fireman/Reliever of the Year Award

No comparison of baseball teams these days is complete without a discussion about relief pitchers, especially closers. Many baseball fans today view closers as one of their team's most valuable commodities, and blown leads by relievers earn the ire of baseball fans unlike any other failure in the game. Contrast that to the first half of the twentieth century, when relief pitchers were an anonymous and unappreciated lot. When *The Sporting News* created their Fireman of the Year award in 1960, no reliever had ever received a Cy Young vote, and only one, Hoyt Wilhelm in 1952, had ever finished in the top ten in MVP voting. The Fireman award winner was originally selected based on a strict statistical formula, devised by Jerome Holtzman, which added relief wins and saves. Today, the award winner (called Reliever of the Year as of 2001) is chosen by the magazine's editors.

	AL	NL
1960	Mike Fornieles, Bos	Lindy McDaniel, StL
1961	Luis Arroyo, NY	Stu Miller, SF
1962	Dick Radatz, Bos	Roy Face, Pit
1963	Stu Miller, Bal	Lindy McDaniel, Chi
1964	Dick Radatz, Bos	Al McBean, Pit
1965	Eddie Fisher, Chi	Ted Abernathy, Chi
1966	Jack Aker, KC	Phil Regan, LA
1967	Minnie Rojas, Cal	Ted Abernathy, Cin
1968	Wilbur Wood, Chi	Phil Regan, Chi
1969	Ron Perranoski, Min	Wayne Granger, Cin
1970	Ron Perranoski, Min	Wayne Granger, Cin
1971	Ken Sanders, Mil	Dave Giusti, Pit
1972	Sparky Lyle, NY	Clay Carroll, Cin
1973	John Hiller, Det	Mike Marshall, Mon
1974	Terry Forster, Chi	Mike Marshall, LA
1975	Rich Gossage, Chi	Al Hrabosky, StL
1976	Bill Campbell, Min	Rawly Eastwick, Cin
1977	Bill Campbell, Bos	Rollie Fingers, SD
1978	Rich Gossage, NY	Rollie Fingers, SD
1979	Jim Kern, Tex	Bruce Sutter, Chi
(tie)	Mike Marshall, Min	
1980	Dan Quisenberry, KC	Rollie Fingers, SD
(tie)		Tom Hume, Cin
1981	Rollie Fingers, Mil	Bruce Sutter, StL
1982	Dan Quisenberry, KC	Bruce Sutter, StL
1983	Dan Quisenberry, KC	Al Holland, Phi
(tie)		Lee Smith, Chi
1984	Dan Quisenberry, KC	Bruce Sutter, StL
1985	Dan Quisenberry, KC	Jeff Reardon, Mon
1986	Dave Righetti, NY	Todd Worrell, StL
1987	Jeff Reardon, Min	Steve Bedrosian, Phi
(tie)	Dave Righetti, NY	
1988	Dennis Eckersley, Oak	John Franco, Cin
1989	Jeff Russell, Tex	Mark Davis, SD
1990	Bobby Thigpen, Chi	John Franco, NY
1991	Dennis Eckersley, Oak	Lee Smith, StL
(tie)	Bryan Harvey, Cal	
1992	Dennis Eckersley, Oak	Doug Jones, Hou
(tie)		Lee Smith, StL
1993	Jeff Montgomery, KC	Randy Myers, Chi
1994	Lee Smith, Bal	John Franco, NY
1995	Jose Mesa, Cle	Randy Myers, Chi
1996	John Wetteland, NY	Trevor Hoffman, SD
1997	Mariano Rivera, NY	Jeff Shaw, Cin
1998	Tom Gordon, Bos	Trevor Hoffman, SD
1999	Mariano Rivera, NY	Ugueth Urbina, Mon
2000	Todd Jones, Det	Antonio Alfonseca, Fla

	AL	NL
2001 (tie)	Mariano Rivera, NY	Armando Benitez, NY Robb Nen, SF
2002	Billy Koch, Oak	John Smoltz, Atl
2003	Keith Foulke, Oak	Eric Gagne, LA
2004	Mariano Rivera, NY	Eric Gagne, LA
2005 (tie)	Mariano Rivera, NY Joe Nathan, Min	Chad Cordero, Was
2006	Francisco Rodriguez, LA	Trevor Hoffman, SD

The Sporting News Major League Executive of the Year Award

Nearly all baseball awards honor on-field performance, but there may be no one more responsible for a team's on-field performance than its top executive. This *Sporting News* award has long honored the men behind the scenes who build baseball teams. While many of today's fans are familiar with their team's top front office personnel, this was not the case when the award was created. The most frequent recipient of this award was George Weiss, who was selected four times while running the Yankees during their most successful dynasty from the late 1940s to the early 1960s.

1936	Branch Rickey, StL NL	1972	Roland Hemond, Chi AL
1937	Ed Barrow, NY AL	1973	Bob Howsam, Cin NL
1938	Warren Giles, Cin NL	1974	Gabe Paul, NY AL
1939	Larry MacPhail, Bro NL	1975	Dick O'Connell, Bos AL
1940	Walter Briggs Sr., Det AL	1976	Joe Burke, KC AL
1941	Ed Barrow, NY AL	1977	Bill Veeck, Chi AL
1942	Branch Rickey, StL NL	1978	Spec Richardson, SF NL
1943	Calvin Griffith, Was AL	1979	Hank Peters, Bal AL
1944	William DeWitt, StL AL	1980	Tal Smith, Hou NL
1945	Phil Wrigley, Chi NL	1981	John McHale, Mon NL
1946	Tom Yawkey, Bos AL	1982	Harry Dalton, Mil AL
1947	Branch Rickey, Bro NL	1983	Hank Peters, Bal AL
1948	Bill Veeck, Cle AL	1984	Dallas Green, Chi NL
1949	Bob Carpenter, Phi NL	1985	John Schuerholz, KC AL
1950	George Weiss, NY AL	1986	Frank Cashen, NY NL
1951	George Weiss, NY AL	1987	Al Rosen, SF NL
1952	George Weiss, NY AL	1988	Fred Claire, LA NL
1953	Lou Perini, Mil NL	1989	Roland Hemond, Bal AL
1954	Horace Stoneham, NY NL	1990	Bob Quinn, Cin NL
1955	Walter O'Malley, Bro NL	1991	Andy MacPhail, Min AL
1956	Gabe Paul, Cin NL	1992	Dan Duquette, Mon NL
1957	Frank Lane, StL NL	1993	Lee Thomas, Phi NL
1958	Joe Brown, Pit NL	1994	John Hart, Cle AL
1959	Buzzie Bavasi, LA NL	1995	John Hart, Cle AL
1960	George Weiss, NY AL	1996	Doug Melvin, Tex AL
1961	Dan Topping, NY AL	1997	Cam Bonifay, Pit NL
1962	Fred Haney, LA AL	1998	Gerry Hunsicker, Hou NL
1963	Bing Devine, StL NL	1999	Billy Beane, Oak AL
1964	Bing Devine, StL NL	2000	Walt Jocketty, StL NL
1965	Calvin Griffith, Min AL	2001	Pat Gillick, Sea AL
1966	Lee MacPhail, MLB	2002	Terry Ryan, Min AL
1967	Dick O'Connell, Bos AL	2003	Brian Sabean, SF NL
1968	Jim Campbell, Det AL	2004	Walt Jocketty, StL NL
1969	Johnny Murphy, NY NL	2005	Mark Shapiro, Cle AL
1970	Harry Dalton, Bal AL	2006	Terry Ryan, Min AL
1971	Cedric Tallis, KC AL		

Rolaids Relief Man of the Year Award

The owners of Rolaids® antacids created this award for relief pitchers in order to impress upon potential customers that Rolaids® did indeed "spell relief" for heartburn and indigestion. This marketing effort proved enormously successful, raising the profile of both the antacid and the pitchers. The winners of the award have always been determined by a statistical formula, which originally took into account saves, wins, and losses, and later included blown saves as well as tough saves. Rolaids® has expanded this promotional award throughout the minor leagues.

	AL	NL
1976	Bill Campbell, Min	Rawly Eastwick, Cin
1977	Bill Campbell, Bos	Rollie Fingers, SD
1978	Rich Gossage, NY	Rollie Fingers, SD
1979	Jim Kern, Tex	Bruce Sutter, Chi
1980	Dan Quisenberry, KC	Rollie Fingers, SD
1981	Rollie Fingers, Mil	Bruce Sutter, StL
1982	Dan Quisenberry, KC	Bruce Sutter, StL
1983	Dan Quisenberry, KC	Al Holland, Phi
1984	Dan Quisenberry, KC	Bruce Sutter, StL
1985	Dan Quisenberry, KC	Jeff Reardon, Mon
1986	Dave Righetti, NY	Todd Worrell, StL
1987	Dave Righetti, NY	Steve Bedrosian, Phi
1988	Dennis Eckersley, Oak	John Franco, Cin
1989	Jeff Russell, Tex	Mark Davis, SD
1990	Bobby Thigpen, Chi	John Franco, NY
1991	Bryan Harvey, Cal	Lee Smith, StL
1992	Dennis Eckersley, Oak	Lee Smith, StL
1993	Jeff Montgomery, KC	Randy Myers, Chi
1994	Lee Smith, Bal	Rod Beck, SF
1995	Jose Mesa, Cle	Tom Henke, StL
1996	John Wetteland, NY	Jeff Brantley, Cin
1997	Randy Myers, Bal	Jeff Shaw, Cin
1998	Tom Gordon, Bos	Trevor Hoffman, SD

	AL	NL
1999	Mariano Rivera, NY	Billy Wagner, Hou
2000	Todd Jones, Det	Antonio Alfonseca, Fla
2001	Mariano Rivera, NY	Armando Benitez, NY
2002	Billy Koch, Oak	John Smoltz, Atl
2003	Keith Foulke, Oak	Eric Gagne, LA
2004	Mariano Rivera, NY	Eric Gagne, LA
2005	Mariano Rivera, NY	Chad Cordero, Was
2006	Francisco Rodriguez, LA	Trevor Hoffman, SD

GOLD GLOVE AWARDS

MLB Gold Gloves

Defense is the most difficult skill in baseball to judge by sight alone. The way a player looks when he makes plays is often misleading, because positioning is very important and poor defenders can make easy plays look hard. Defense is also the hardest act in baseball to statistically measure. The Gold Glove Awards were created to systematically use subjective analysis to bring recognition to the best fielders at each position.

Rawlings, the manufacturer of the great majority of big-leaguers' gloves at the time, teamed up in 1957 to present the Gold Gloves to *The Sporting News* All-Fielding Team. The awards were given to one player at each position in the major leagues, as selected by a panel of sportswriters. In 1958 voting was handed over to major league players and gold gloves were awarded for each position in each league. In 1961 voters were told to simply select three outfielders, regardless of whether they were left fielders, center fielders, or right fielders (which remains the practice today). In 1966 major league managers and coaches took over the voting.

Knowledgeable baseball observers are skeptical about the results of Gold Glove voting, largely because so many players win year after year. Many great defensive players earn their first Gold Gloves several years after they have established their defensive prowess, then keep winning Gold Gloves even after their defensive decline has become obvious. Some players seem to be given this defensive award partly for their offense, while weak hitters with great gloves are frequently ignored. The award's most recent controversy occurred when the AL's 1999 first base Gold Glove was awarded to designated hitter Rafael Palmeiro, who played first base in only 28 games that year.

1957 Gold Gloves

P	Bobby Shantz, NY AL
C	Sherm Lollar, Chi AL
1B	Gil Hodges, Bro NL
2B	Nellie Fox, Chi AL
3B	Frank Malzone, Bos AL
SS	Roy McMillan, Cin NL
LF	Minnie Minoso, Chi AL
CF	Willie Mays, NY NL
RF	Al Kaline, Det AL

AL Gold Gloves / NL Gold Gloves

1958	AL		NL
P	Bobby Shantz, NY	P	Harvey Haddix, Cin
C	Sherm Lollar, Chi	C	Del Crandall, Mil
1B	Vic Power, KC-Cle	1B	Gil Hodges, LA
2B	Frank Bolling, Det	2B	Bill Mazeroski, Pit
3B	Frank Malzone, Bos	3B	Ken Boyer, StL
SS	Luis Aparicio, Chi	SS	Roy McMillan, Cin
LF	Norm Siebern, NY	LF	Frank Robinson, Cin
CF	Jim Piersall, Bos	CF	Willie Mays, SF
RF	Al Kaline, Det	RF	Hank Aaron, Mil

1959	AL		NL
P	Bobby Shantz, NY	P	Harvey Haddix, Pit
C	Sherm Lollar, Chi	C	Del Crandall, Mil
1B	Vic Power, Cle	1B	Gil Hodges, LA
2B	Nellie Fox, Chi	2B	Charlie Neal, LA
3B	Frank Malzone, Bos	3B	Ken Boyer, StL
SS	Luis Aparicio, Chi	SS	Roy McMillan, Cin
LF	Minnie Minoso, Cle	LF	Jackie Brandt, SF
CF	Al Kaline, Det	CF	Willie Mays, SF
RF	Jackie Jensen, Bos	RF	Hank Aaron, Mil

1960	AL		NL
P	Bobby Shantz, NY	P	Harvey Haddix, Pit
C	Earl Battey, Was	C	Del Crandall, Mil
1B	Vic Power, Cle	1B	Bill White, StL
2B	Nellie Fox, Chi	2B	Bill Mazeroski, Pit
3B	Brooks Robinson, Bal	3B	Ken Boyer, StL
SS	Luis Aparicio, Chi	SS	Ernie Banks, Chi
LF	Minnie Minoso, Chi	LF	Wally Moon, LA
CF	Jim Landis, Chi	CF	Willie Mays, SF
RF	Roger Maris, NY	RF	Hank Aaron, Mil

1961	AL		NL
P	Frank Lary, Det	P	Bobby Shantz, Pit
C	Earl Battey, Min	C	Johnny Roseboro, LA
1B	Vic Power, Cle	1B	Bill White, StL
2B	Bobby Richardson, NY	2B	Bill Mazeroski, Pit
3B	Brooks Robinson, Bal	3B	Ken Boyer, StL
SS	Luis Aparicio, Chi	SS	Maury Wills, LA
OF	Jim Piersall, Cle	OF	Willie Mays, SF
OF	Jim Landis, Chi	OF	Roberto Clemente, Pit
OF	Al Kaline, Det	OF	Vada Pinson, Cin

1962	AL		NL
P	Jim Kaat, Min	P	Bobby Shantz, Hou-StL
C	Earl Battey, Min	C	Del Crandall, Mil
1B	Vic Power, Min	1B	Bill White, StL
2B	Bobby Richardson, NY	2B	Ken Hubbs, Chi
3B	Brooks Robinson, Bal	3B	Jim Davenport, SF
SS	Luis Aparicio, Chi	SS	Maury Wills, LA
OF	Mickey Mantle, NY	OF	Willie Mays, SF
OF	Jim Landis, Chi	OF	Roberto Clemente, Pit
OF	Al Kaline, Det	OF	Bill Virdon, Pit

1963	AL		NL
P	Jim Kaat, Min	P	Bobby Shantz, StL
C	Elston Howard, NY	C	Johnny Edwards, Cin
1B	Vic Power, Min	1B	Bill White, StL
2B	Bobby Richardson, NY	2B	Bill Mazeroski, Pit
3B	Brooks Robinson, Bal	3B	Ken Boyer, StL
SS	Zoilo Versalles, Min	SS	Bobby Wine, Phi
OF	Carl Yastrzemski, Bos	OF	Willie Mays, SF
OF	Jim Landis, Chi	OF	Curt Flood, StL
OF	Al Kaline, Det	OF	Roberto Clemente, Pit

1964	AL		NL
P	Jim Kaat, Min	P	Bobby Shantz, StL-Chi-Phi
C	Elston Howard, NY	C	Johnny Edwards, Cin
1B	Vic Power, Min-LA	1B	Bill White, StL
2B	Bobby Richardson, NY	2B	Bill Mazeroski, Pit
3B	Brooks Robinson, Bal	3B	Ron Santo, Chi
SS	Luis Aparicio, Bal	SS	Ruben Amaro, Phi
OF	Vic Davalillo, Cle	OF	Willie Mays, SF
OF	Jim Landis, Chi	OF	Curt Flood, StL
OF	Al Kaline, Det	OF	Roberto Clemente, Pit

1965	AL		NL
P	Jim Kaat, Min	P	Bob Gibson, StL
C	Bill Freehan, Det	C	Joe Torre, Mil
1B	Joe Pepitone, NY	1B	Bill White, StL
2B	Bobby Richardson, NY	2B	Bill Mazeroski, Pit
3B	Brooks Robinson, Bal	3B	Ron Santo, Chi
SS	Zoilo Versalles, Min	SS	Leo Cardenas, Cin
OF	Al Kaline, Det	OF	Roberto Clemente, Pit
OF	Carl Yastrzemski, Bos	OF	Willie Mays, SF
OF	Tom Tresh, NY	OF	Curt Flood, StL

1966	AL		NL
P	Jim Kaat, Min	P	Bob Gibson, StL
C	Bill Freehan, Det	C	John Roseboro, LA
1B	Joe Pepitone, NY	1B	Bill White, Phi
2B	Bobby Knoop, Cal	2B	Bill Mazeroski, Pit
3B	Brooks Robinson, Bal	3B	Ron Santo, Chi
SS	Luis Aparicio, Bal	SS	Gene Alley, Pit
OF	Al Kaline, Det	OF	Curt Flood, StL
OF	Tommie Agee, Chi	OF	Roberto Clemente, Pit
OF	Tony Oliva, Min	OF	Willie Mays, SF

1967	AL		NL
P	Jim Kaat, Min	P	Bob Gibson, StL
C	Bill Freehan, Det	C	Randy Hundley, Chi
1B	George Scott, Bos	1B	Wes Parker, LA
2B	Bobby Knoop, Cal	2B	Bill Mazeroski, Pit
3B	Brooks Robinson, Bal	3B	Ron Santo, Chi
SS	Jim Fregosi, Cal	SS	Gene Alley, Pit
OF	Paul Blair, Bal	OF	Curt Flood, StL
OF	Al Kaline, Det	OF	Roberto Clemente, Pit
OF	Carl Yastrzemski, Bos	OF	Willie Mays, SF

1968	AL		NL
P	Jim Kaat, Min	P	Bob Gibson, StL
C	Bill Freehan, Det	C	Johnny Bench, Cin
1B	George Scott, Bos	1B	Wes Parker, LA
2B	Bobby Knoop, Cal	2B	Glenn Beckert, Chi
3B	Brooks Robinson, Bal	3B	Ron Santo, Chi
SS	Luis Aparicio, Chi	SS	Dal Maxvill, StL
OF	Mickey Stanley, Det	OF	Curt Flood, StL
OF	Reggie Smith, Bos	OF	Roberto Clemente, Pit
OF	Carl Yastrzemski, Bos	OF	Willie Mays, SF

1969	AL		NL
P	Jim Kaat, Min	P	Bob Gibson, StL
C	Bill Freehan, Det	C	Johnny Bench, Cin
1B	Joe Pepitone, NY	1B	Wes Parker, LA
2B	Davey Johnson, Bal	2B	Felix Millan, Atl
3B	Brooks Robinson, Bal	3B	Clete Boyer, Atl
SS	Mark Belanger, Bal	SS	Don Kessinger, Chi
OF	Carl Yastrzemski, Bos	OF	Curt Flood, StL
OF	Paul Blair, Bal	OF	Roberto Clemente, Pit
OF	Mickey Stanley, Det	OF	Pete Rose, Cin

1970	AL		NL
P	Jim Kaat, Min	P	Bob Gibson, StL
C	Ray Fosse, Cle	C	Johnny Bench, Cin
1B	Jim Spencer, Cal	1B	Wes Parker, LA
2B	Davey Johnson, Bal	2B	Tommy Helms, Cin
3B	Brooks Robinson, Bal	3B	Doug Rader, Hou
SS	Luis Aparicio, Chi	SS	Don Kessinger, Chi
OF	Paul Blair, Bal	OF	Tommie Agee, NY
OF	Mickey Stanley, Det	OF	Roberto Clemente, Pit
OF	Ken Berry, Chi	OF	Pete Rose, Cin

1971	AL		NL
P	Jim Kaat, Min	P	Bob Gibson, StL
C	Ray Fosse, Cle	C	Johnny Bench, Cin
1B	George Scott, Bos	1B	Wes Parker, LA
2B	Davey Johnson, Bal	2B	Tommy Helms, Cin
3B	Brooks Robinson, Bal	3B	Doug Rader, Hou
SS	Mark Belanger, Bal	SS	Bud Harrelson, NY
OF	Amos Otis, KC	OF	Roberto Clemente, Pit
OF	Carl Yastrzemski, Bos	OF	Bobby Bonds, SF
OF	Paul Blair, Bal	OF	Willie Davis, LA

1972	AL		NL
P	Jim Kaat, Min	P	Bob Gibson, StL
C	Carlton Fisk, Bos	C	Johnny Bench, Cin
1B	George Scott, Mil	1B	Wes Parker, LA
2B	Doug Griffin, Bos	2B	Felix Millan, Atl
3B	Brooks Robinson, Bal	3B	Doug Rader, Hou
SS	Ed Brinkman, Det	SS	Larry Bowa, Phi
OF	Bobby Murcer, NY	OF	Roberto Clemente, Pit
OF	Paul Blair, Bal	OF	Cesar Cedeno, Hou
OF	Ken Berry, Cal	OF	Willie Davis, LA

1973	AL		NL
P	Jim Kaat, Min-Chi	P	Bob Gibson, StL
C	Thurman Munson, NY	C	Johnny Bench, Cin
1B	George Scott, Mil	1B	Mike Jorgensen, Mon
2B	Bobby Grich, Bal	2B	Joe Morgan, Cin
3B	Brooks Robinson, Bal	3B	Doug Rader, Hou
SS	Mark Belanger, Bal	SS	Roger Metzger, Hou
OF	Paul Blair, Bal	OF	Willie Davis, LA
OF	Amos Otis, KC	OF	Cesar Cedeno, Hou
OF	Mickey Stanley, Det	OF	Bobby Bonds, SF

1974	AL		NL
P	Jim Kaat, Chi	P	Andy Messersmith, LA
C	Thurman Munson, NY	C	Johnny Bench, Cin
1B	George Scott, Mil	1B	Steve Garvey, LA
2B	Bobby Grich, Bal	2B	Joe Morgan, Cin
3B	Brooks Robinson, Bal	3B	Doug Rader, Hou
SS	Mark Belanger, Bal	SS	Dave Concepcion, Cin
OF	Paul Blair, Bal	OF	Cesar Geronimo, Cin
OF	Joe Rudi, Oak	OF	Cesar Cedeno, Hou
OF	Amos Otis, KC	OF	Bobby Bonds, SF

1975	AL		NL
P	Jim Kaat, Chi	P	Andy Messersmith, LA
C	Thurman Munson, NY	C	Johnny Bench, Cin
1B	George Scott, Mil	1B	Steve Garvey, LA
2B	Bobby Grich, Bal	2B	Joe Morgan, Cin
3B	Brooks Robinson, Bal	3B	Ken Reitz, StL
SS	Mark Belanger, Bal	SS	Dave Concepcion, Cin
OF	Paul Blair, Bal	OF	Garry Maddox, SF-Phi
OF	Joe Rudi, Oak	OF	Cesar Geronimo, Cin
OF	Fred Lynn, Bos	OF	Cesar Cedeno, Hou

1976	AL		NL
P	Jim Palmer, Bal	P	Jim Kaat, Phi
C	Jim Sundberg, Tex	C	Johnny Bench, Cin
1B	George Scott, Mil	1B	Steve Garvey, LA
2B	Bobby Grich, Bal	2B	Joe Morgan, Cin
3B	Aurelio Rodriguez, Det	3B	Mike Schmidt, Phi
SS	Mark Belanger, Bal	SS	Dave Concepcion, Cin
OF	Rick Manning, Cle	OF	Cesar Cedeno, Hou
OF	Dwight Evans, Bos	OF	Garry Maddox, Phi
OF	Joe Rudi, Oak	OF	Cesar Geronimo, Cin

1977	AL		NL
P	Jim Palmer, Bal	P	Jim Kaat, Phi
C	Jim Sundberg, Tex	C	Johnny Bench, Cin
1B	Jim Spencer, Chi	1B	Steve Garvey, LA
2B	Frank White, KC	2B	Joe Morgan, Cin
3B	Graig Nettles, NY	3B	Mike Schmidt, Phi
SS	Mark Belanger, Bal	SS	Dave Concepcion, Cin
OF	Al Cowens, KC	OF	Cesar Geronimo, Cin
OF	Carl Yastrzemski, Bos	OF	Dave Parker, Pit
OF	Juan Beniquez, Tex	OF	Garry Maddox, Phi

1978	AL		NL
P	Jim Palmer, Bal	P	Phil Niekro, Atl
C	Jim Sundberg, Tex	C	Bob Boone, Phi
1B	Chris Chambliss, NY	1B	Keith Hernandez, StL
2B	Frank White, KC	2B	Davey Lopes, LA
3B	Graig Nettles, NY	3B	Mike Schmidt, Phi
SS	Mark Belanger, Bal	SS	Larry Bowa, Phi
OF	Rick Miller, Cal	OF	Garry Maddox, Phi
OF	Fred Lynn, Bos	OF	Ellis Valentine, Mon
OF	Dwight Evans, Bos	OF	Dave Parker, Pit

1979	AL		NL
P	Jim Palmer, Bal	P	Phil Niekro, Atl
C	Jim Sundberg, Tex	C	Bob Boone, Phi
1B	Cecil Cooper, Mil	1B	Keith Hernandez, StL
2B	Frank White, KC	2B	Manny Trillo, Phi
3B	Buddy Bell, Tex	3B	Mike Schmidt, Phi
SS	Rick Burleson, Bos	SS	Dave Concepcion, Cin
OF	Fred Lynn, Bos	OF	Dave Parker, Pit
OF	Sixto Lezcano, Mil	OF	Garry Maddox, Phi
OF	Dwight Evans, Bos	OF	Dave Winfield, SD

1980	AL		NL
P	Mike Norris, Oak	P	Phil Niekro, Atl
C	Jim Sundberg, Tex	C	Gary Carter, Mon
1B	Cecil Cooper, Mil	1B	Keith Hernandez, StL
2B	Frank White, KC	2B	Doug Flynn, NY
3B	Buddy Bell, Tex	3B	Mike Schmidt, Phi
SS	Alan Trammell, Det	SS	Ozzie Smith, SD
OF	Dwayne Murphy, Oak	OF	Garry Maddox, Phi
OF	Fred Lynn, Bos	OF	Dave Winfield, SD
OF	Willie Wilson, KC	OF	Andre Dawson, Mon

1981	AL		NL
P	Mike Norris, Oak	P	Steve Carlton, Phi
C	Jim Sundberg, Tex	C	Gary Carter, Mon
1B	Mike Squires, Chi	1B	Keith Hernandez, StL
2B	Frank White, KC	2B	Manny Trillo, Phi
3B	Buddy Bell, Tex	3B	Mike Schmidt, Phi
SS	Alan Trammell, Det	SS	Ozzie Smith, SD
OF	Dwayne Murphy, Oak	OF	Dusty Baker, LA
OF	Rickey Henderson, Oak	OF	Garry Maddox, Phi
OF	Dwight Evans, Bos	OF	Andre Dawson, Mon

1982	AL		NL
P	Ron Guidry, NY	P	Phil Niekro, Atl
C	Bob Boone, Cal	C	Gary Carter, Mon
1B	Eddie Murray, Bal	1B	Keith Hernandez, StL
2B	Frank White, KC	2B	Manny Trillo, Phi
3B	Buddy Bell, Tex	3B	Mike Schmidt, Phi
SS	Robin Yount, Mil	SS	Ozzie Smith, StL
OF	Dwayne Murphy, Oak	OF	Andre Dawson, Mon
OF	Dwight Evans, Bos	OF	Dale Murphy, Atl
OF	Dave Winfield, NY	OF	Garry Maddox, Phi

1983	AL		NL
P	Ron Guidry, NY	P	Phil Niekro, Atl
C	Lance Parrish, Det	C	Tony Peña, Pit
1B	Eddie Murray, Bal	1B	Keith Hernandez, StL-NY
2B	Lou Whitaker, Det	2B	Ryne Sandberg, Chi
3B	Buddy Bell, Tex	3B	Mike Schmidt, Phi
SS	Alan Trammell, Det	SS	Ozzie Smith, StL
OF	Dwayne Murphy, Oak	OF	Dale Murphy, Atl
OF	Dave Winfield, NY	OF	Willie McGee, StL
OF	Dwight Evans, Bos	OF	Andre Dawson, Mon

1984	AL		NL
P	Ron Guidry, NY	P	Joaquin Andujar, StL
C	Lance Parrish, Det	C	Tony Peña, Pit
1B	Eddie Murray, Bal	1B	Keith Hernandez, NY
2B	Lou Whitaker, Det	2B	Ryne Sandberg, Chi
3B	Buddy Bell, Tex	3B	Mike Schmidt, Phi
SS	Alan Trammell, Det	SS	Ozzie Smith, StL
OF	Dwight Evans, Bos	OF	Dale Murphy, Atl
OF	Dwayne Murphy, Oak	OF	Bob Dernier, Chi
OF	Dave Winfield, NY	OF	Andre Dawson, Mon

1985	AL		NL
P	Ron Guidry, NY	P	Rick Reuschel, Pit
C	Lance Parrish, Det	C	Tony Peña, Pit
1B	Don Mattingly, NY	1B	Keith Hernandez, NY
2B	Lou Whitaker, Det	2B	Ryne Sandberg, Chi
3B	George Brett, KC	3B	Tim Wallach, Mon
SS	Alfredo Griffin, Oak	SS	Ozzie Smith, StL
OF	Dave Winfield, NY	OF	Dale Murphy, Atl
OF	Dwight Evans, Bos	OF	Willie McGee, StL
OF	Gary Pettis, Cal	OF	Andre Dawson, Mon
OF	Dwayne Murphy, Oak		

1986	AL		NL
P	Ron Guidry, NY	P	Fernando Valenzuela, LA
C	Bob Boone, Cal	C	Jody Davis, Chi
1B	Don Mattingly, NY	1B	Keith Hernandez, NY
2B	Frank White, KC	2B	Ryne Sandberg, Chi
3B	Gary Gaetti, Min	3B	Mike Schmidt, Phi
SS	Tony Fernandez, Tor	SS	Ozzie Smith, StL
OF	Kirby Puckett, Min	OF	Dale Murphy, Atl
OF	Jesse Barfield, Tor	OF	Willie McGee, StL
OF	Gary Pettis, Cal	OF	Tony Gwynn, SD

1987	AL		NL
P	Mark Langston, Sea	P	Rick Reuschel, Pit-SF
C	Bob Boone, Cal	C	Mike LaValliere, Pit
1B	Don Mattingly, NY	1B	Keith Hernandez, NY
2B	Frank White, KC	2B	Ryne Sandberg, Chi
3B	Gary Gaetti, Min	3B	Terry Pendleton, StL
SS	Tony Fernandez, Tor	SS	Ozzie Smith, StL
OF	Dave Winfield, NY	OF	Andre Dawson, Chi
OF	Jesse Barfield, Tor	OF	Eric Davis, Cin
OF	Kirby Puckett, Min	OF	Tony Gwynn, SD

1988	AL		NL
P	Mark Langston, Sea	P	Orel Hershiser, LA
C	Bob Boone, Cal	C	Benito Santiago, SD
1B	Don Mattingly, NY	1B	Keith Hernandez, NY
2B	Harold Reynolds, Sea	2B	Ryne Sandberg, Chi
3B	Gary Gaetti, Min	3B	Tim Wallach, Mon
SS	Tony Fernandez, Tor	SS	Ozzie Smith, StL
OF	Gary Pettis, Det	OF	Andre Dawson, Chi
OF	Devon White, Cal	OF	Andy Van Slyke, Pit
OF	Kirby Puckett, Min	OF	Eric Davis, Cin

1989	AL		NL
P	Bret Saberhagen, KC	P	Ron Darling, NY
C	Bob Boone, KC	C	Benito Santiago, SD
1B	Don Mattingly, NY	1B	Andres Galarraga, Mon
2B	Harold Reynolds, Sea	2B	Ryne Sandberg, Chi
3B	Gary Gaetti, Min	3B	Terry Pendleton, StL
SS	Tony Fernandez, Tor	SS	Ozzie Smith, StL
OF	Kirby Puckett, Min	OF	Tony Gwynn, SD
OF	Gary Pettis, Det	OF	Andy Van Slyke, Pit
OF	Devon White, Cal	OF	Eric Davis, Cin

1990	AL		NL
P	Mike Boddicker, Bos	P	Greg Maddux, Chi
C	Sandy Alomar Jr., Cle	C	Benito Santiago, SD
1B	Mark McGwire, Oak	1B	Andres Galarraga, Mon
2B	Harold Reynolds, Sea	2B	Ryne Sandberg, Chi
3B	Kelly Gruber, Tor	3B	Tim Wallach, Mon
SS	Ozzie Guillen, Chi	SS	Ozzie Smith, StL
OF	Gary Pettis, Tex	OF	Tony Gwynn, SD
OF	Ken Griffey Jr., Sea	OF	Andy Van Slyke, Pit
OF	Ellis Burks. Bos	OF	Barry Bonds, Pit

1991	AL		NL
P	Mark Langston, Cal	P	Greg Maddux, Chi
C	Tony Pena, Bos	C	Tom Pagnozzi, StL
1B	Don Mattingly, NY	1B	Will Clark, SF
2B	Roberto Alomar, Tor	2B	Ryne Sandberg, Chi
3B	Robin Ventura, Chi	3B	Matt Williams, SF
SS	Cal Ripken, Bal	SS	Ozzie Smith, StL
OF	Devon White, Tor	OF	Barry Bonds, Pit
OF	Ken Griffey Jr., Sea	OF	Tony Gwynn, SD
OF	Kirby Puckett, Min	OF	Andy Van Slyke, Pit

1992	AL		NL
P	Mark Langston, Cal	P	Greg Maddux, Chi
C	Ivan Rodriguez, Tex	C	Tom Pagnozzi, StL
1B	Don Mattingly, NY	1B	Mark Grace, Chi
2B	Roberto Alomar, Tor	2B	Jose Lind, Pit
3B	Robin Ventura, Chi	3B	Terry Pendleton, Atl
SS	Cal Ripken, Bal	SS	Ozzie Smith, StL
OF	Devon White, Tor	OF	Andy Van Slyke, Pit
OF	Ken Griffey Jr., Sea	OF	Barry Bonds, Pit
OF	Kirby Puckett, Min	OF	Larry Walker, Mon

1993	AL		NL
P	Mark Langston, Cal	P	Greg Maddux, Atl
C	Ivan Rodriguez, Tex	C	Kirt Manwaring, SF
1B	Don Mattingly, NY	1B	Mark Grace, Chi
2B	Roberto Alomar, Tor	2B	Robby Thompson, SF
3B	Robin Ventura, Chi	3B	Matt Williams, SF
SS	Omar Vizquel, Sea	SS	Jay Bell, Pit
OF	Kenny Lofton, Cle	OF	Barry Bonds, SF
OF	Devon White, Tor	OF	Larry Walker, Mon
OF	Ken Griffey Jr., Sea	OF	Marquis Grissom, Mon

1994	AL		NL
P	Mark Langston, Cal	P	Greg Maddux, Atl
C	Ivan Rodriguez, Tex	C	Tom Pagnozzi, StL
1B	Don Mattingly, NY	1B	Jeff Bagwell, Hou
2B	Roberto Alomar, Tor	2B	Craig Biggio, Hou
3B	Wade Boggs, NY	3B	Matt Williams, SF
SS	Omar Vizquel, Cle	SS	Barry Larkin, Cin
OF	Kenny Lofton, Cle	OF	Marquis Grissom, Mon
OF	Ken Griffey Jr., Sea	OF	Barry Bonds, SF
OF	Devon White, Tor	OF	Darren Lewis, SF

1995	AL		NL
P	Mark Langston, Cal	P	Greg Maddux, Atl
C	Ivan Rodriguez, Tex	C	Charles Johnson, Fla
1B	J.T. Snow, Cal	1B	Mark Grace, Chi
2B	Roberto Alomar, Tor	2B	Craig Biggio, Hou
3B	Wade Boggs, NY	3B	Ken Caminiti, SD
SS	Omar Vizquel, Cle	SS	Barry Larkin, Cin
OF	Kenny Lofton, Cle	OF	Marquis Grissom, Atl
OF	Ken Griffey Jr., Sea	OF	Steve Finley, SD
OF	Devon White, Tor	OF	Raul Mondesi, LA

1996	AL		NL
P	Mike Mussina, Bal	P	Greg Maddux, Atl
C	Ivan Rodriguez, Tex	C	Charles Johnson, Fla
1B	J.T. Snow, Cal	1B	Mark Grace, Chi
2B	Roberto Alomar, Bal	2B	Craig Biggio, Hou
3B	Robin Ventura, Chi	3B	Ken Caminiti, SD
SS	Omar Vizquel, Cle	SS	Barry Larkin, Cin
OF	Ken Griffey Jr., Sea	OF	Marquis Grissom, Atl
OF	Jay Buhner, Sea	OF	Steve Finley, SD
OF	Kenny Lofton, Cle	OF	Barry Bonds, SF

1997	AL		NL
P	Mike Mussina, Bal	P	Greg Maddux, Atl
C	Ivan Rodriguez, Tex	C	Charles Johnson, Fla
1B	Rafael Palmeiro, Bal	1B	J.T. Snow, SF
2B	Chuck Knoblauch, Min	2B	Craig Biggio, Hou
3B	Matt Williams, Cle	3B	Ken Caminiti, SD
SS	Omar Vizquel, Cle	SS	Rey Ordoñez, NY
OF	Ken Griffey Jr., Sea	OF	Raul Mondesi, LA
OF	Bernie Williams, NY	OF	Larry Walker, Col
OF	Jim Edmonds, Ana	OF	Barry Bonds, SF

1998	AL		NL
P	Mike Mussina, Bal	P	Greg Maddux, Atl
C	Ivan Rodriguez, Tex	C	Charles Johnson, Fla-LA
1B	Rafael Palmeiro, Bal	1B	J.T. Snow, SF
2B	Roberto Alomar, Bal	2B	Bret Boone, Cin
3B	Robin Ventura, Chi	3B	Scott Rolen, Phi
SS	Omar Vizquel, Cle	SS	Rey Ordoñez, NY
OF	Ken Griffey Jr., Sea	OF	Larry Walker, Col
OF	Bernie Williams, NY	OF	Barry Bonds, SF
OF	Jim Edmonds, Ana	OF	Andruw Jones, Atl

1999	AL		NL
P	Mike Mussina, Bal	P	Greg Maddux, Atl
C	Ivan Rodriguez, Tex	C	Mike Lieberthal, Phi
1B	Rafael Palmeiro, Tex	1B	J.T. Snow, SF
2B	Roberto Alomar, Cle	2B	Pokey Reese, Cin
3B	Scott Brosius, NY	3B	Robin Ventura, NY
SS	Omar Vizquel, Cle	SS	Rey Ordoñez, NY
OF	Ken Griffey Jr., Sea	OF	Larry Walker, Col
OF	Shawn Green, Tor	OF	Andruw Jones, Atl
OF	Bernie Williams, NY	OF	Steve Finley, Ari

2000	AL		NL
P	Kenny Rogers, Tex	P	Greg Maddux, Atl
C	Ivan Rodriguez, Tex	C	Mike Matheny, StL
1B	John Olerud, Sea	1B	J.T. Snow, SF
2B	Roberto Alomar, Cle	2B	Pokey Reese, Cin
3B	Travis Fryman, Cle	3B	Scott Rolen, Phi
SS	Omar Vizquel, Cle	SS	Neifi Perez, Col
OF	Darin Erstad, Ana	OF	Andruw Jones, Atl
OF	Bernie Williams, NY	OF	Steve Finley, Ari
OF	Jermaine Dye, KC	OF	Jim Edmonds, StL

2001	AL		NL
P	Mike Mussina, NY	P	Greg Maddux, Atl
C	Ivan Rodriguez, Tex	C	Brad Ausmus, Hou
1B	Doug Mientkiewicz, Min	1B	Todd Helton, Col
2B	Roberto Alomar, Cle	2B	Fernando Viña, StL
3B	Eric Chavez, Oak	3B	Scott Rolen, Phi
SS	Omar Vizquel, Cle	SS	Orlando Cabrera, Mon
OF	Mike Cameron, Sea	OF	Andruw Jones, Atl
OF	Ichiro Suzuki, Sea	OF	Jim Edmonds, StL
OF	Torii Hunter, Min	OF	Larry Walker, Col

2002	AL		NL
P	Kenny Rogers, Tex	P	Greg Maddux, Atl
C	Bengie Molina, Ana	C	Brad Ausmus, Hou
1B	John Olerud, Sea	1B	Todd Helton, Col
2B	Bret Boone, Sea	2B	Fernando Viña, StL
3B	Eric Chavez, Oak	3B	Scott Rolen, Phi-StL
SS	Alex Rodriguez, Tex	SS	Edgar Renteria, StL
OF	Torii Hunter, Min	OF	Andruw Jones, Atl
OF	Darin Erstad, Ana	OF	Larry Walker, Col
OF	Ichiro Suzuki, Sea	OF	Jim Edmonds, StL

2003	AL		NL
P	Mike Mussina, NY	P	Mike Hampton, Atl
C	Bengie Molina, Ana	C	Mike Matheny, StL
1B	John Olerud, Sea	1B	Derrek Lee, Fla
2B	Bret Boone, Sea	2B	Luis Castillo, Fla
3B	Eric Chavez, Oak	3B	Scott Rolen, StL
SS	Alex Rodriguez, Tex	SS	Edgar Renteria, StL
OF	Mike Cameron, Sea	OF	Jim Edmonds, StL
OF	Torii Hunter, Min	OF	Andruw Jones, Atl
OF	Ichiro Suzuki, Sea	OF	Jose Cruz Jr., SF

2004	AL		NL
P	Kenny Rogers, Tex	P	Greg Maddux, Chi
C	Ivan Rodriguez, Det	C	Mike Matheny, SL
1B	Darin Erstad, Ana	1B	Todd Helton, Col
2B	Bret Boone, Sea	2B	Luis Castillo, Fla
3B	Eric Chavez, Oak	3B	Scott Rolen, SL
SS	Derek Jeter, NY	SS	Cesar Izturis, LA
OF	Vernon Wells, Tor	OF	Jim Edmonds, SL
OF	Ichiro Suzuki, Sea	OF	Steve Finley, Ari-LA
OF	Torii Hunter, Min	OF	Andruw Jones, Atl

2005	AL		NL
P	Kenny Rogers, Tex	P	Greg Maddux, Chi
C	Jason Varitek, Bos	C	Mike Matheny, SF
1B	Mark Teixeira, Tex	1B	Derrek Lee, Chi
2B	Orlando Hudson, Tor	2B	Luis Castillo, Fla
3B	Eric Chavez, Oak	3B	Mike Lowell, Fla
SS	Derek Jeter, NY	SS	Omar Vizquel, SF
OF	Ichiro Suzuki, Sea	OF	Jim Edmonds, StL
OF	Vernon Wells, Tor	OF	Andruw Jones, Atl
OF	Torii Hunter, Min	OF	Bob Abreu, Phi

2006	AL		NL
P	Kenny Rogers, Det	P	Greg Maddux, LA
C	Ivan Rodriguez, Det	C	Brad Ausmus, Hou
1B	Mark Teixeira, Tex	1B	Albert Pujols, SL
2B	Mark Grudzielanek, KC	2B	Orlando Hudson, Ari
3B	Eric Chavez, Oak	3B	Scott Rolen, StL
SS	Derek Jeter, NY	SS	Omar Vizquel, SF
OF	Torii Hunter, Min	OF	Carlos Beltran, NY
OF	Ichiro Suzuki, Sea	OF	Mike Cameron, SD
OF	Vernon Wells, Tor	OF	Andruw Jones, Atl

Baseball America Minor League Player of the Year Award

When *The Sporting News* sharply reduced its coverage of baseball—especially minor league baseball—in the early 1980s, a new publication called *Baseball America* stepped into the breach. In its two decades-plus of regular publication, *Baseball America* has emerged as an authority on the minor leagues and on minor league prospects. Each year, this award honors the best performing prospect, ignoring older players who succeed in the minors as a result of many more years of experience.

1981	Mike Marshall, 1B (Dodgers)	1994	Derek Jeter, SS (Yankees)
1982	Ron Kittle, OF (White Sox)	1995	Andruw Jones, OF (Braves)
1983	Dwight Gooden, RHP (Mets)	1996	Andruw Jones, OF (Braves)
1984	Mike Bielecki, RHP (Pirates)	1997	Paul Konerko, 1B (Dodgers)
1985	Jose Canseco, OF (Athletics)	1998	Eric Chavez, 3B (Athletics)
1986	Gregg Jefferies, SS (Mets)	1999	Rick Ankiel, LHP (Cardinals)
1987	Gregg Jefferies, SS (Mets)	2000	Jon Rauch, RHP (White Sox)
1988	Tom Gordon, RHP (Royals)	2001	Josh Beckett, RHP (Marlins)
1989	Sandy Alomar Jr., C (Padres)	2002	Rocco Baldelli, OF (Devil Rays)
1990	Frank Thomas, 1B (White Sox)	2003	Joe Mauer, C (Twins)
1991	Derek Bell, of (Blue Jays)	2004	Jeff Francis, LHP (Rockies)
1992	Tim Salmon, OF (Angels)	2005	Delmon Young, OF (Devil Rays)
1993	Manny Ramirez, OF (Indians)	2006	Alex Gordon, 3B (Royals)

Baseball America Organization of the Year Award

Baseball America has helped emphasize the importance of building major league teams through their minor league systems by annually awarding this honor to organizations that have assembled a deep talent pool at every level and shown the ability to further develop that talent.

1982	Oakland Athletics	AL	1995	New York Mets	NL
1983	New York Mets	NL	1996	Atlanta Braves	NL
1984	New York Mets	NL	1997	Detroit TigersAL	
1985	Milwaukee Brewers	AL	1998	New York Yankees	AL
1986	Milwaukee Brewers	AL	1999	Oakland Athletics	AL
1987	Milwaukee Brewers	AL	2000	Chicago White Sox	AL
1988	Montreal Expos	NL	2001	Houston Astros	NL
1989	Texas Rangers	AL	2002	Minnesota Twins	AL
1990	Montreal Expos	NL	2003	Florida Marlins	NL
1991	Atlanta Braves	NL	2004	Minnesota Twins	AL
1992	Cleveland Indians	AL	2005	Atlanta Braves	NL
1993	Toronto Blue Jays	AL	2006	Los Angeles Dodgers	NL
1994	Kansas City Royals	AL			

The Roberto Clemente Award

Created in 1971 by Commissioner Bowie Kuhn, this was originally known as the Commissioner's Award. The award was renamed after Roberto Clemente, the much beloved right fielder from Puerto Rico, died in a plane crash while on a humanitarian mission to assist earthquake victims in Nicaragua on New Year's Day, 1973. This trophy is given annually to the player who best combines good play on the field with strong work in his community.

1971	Willie Mays, SF NL	1989	Gary Carter, NY NL
1972	Brooks Robinson, Bal AL	1990	Dave Stewart, Oak AL
1973	Al Kaline, Det AL	1991	Harold Reynolds, Sea AL
1974	Willie Stargell, Pit NL	1992	Cal Ripken, Bal AL
1975	Lou Brock, StL NL	1993	Barry Larkin, Cin NL
1976	Pete Rose, Cin NL	1994	Dave Winfield, Min AL
1977	Rod Carew, Min AL	1995	Ozzie Smith, StL NL
1978	Greg Luzinski, Phi AL	1996	Kirby Puckett, Min AL
1979	Andy Thornton, Cle AL	1997	Eric Davis, Bal AL
1980	Phil Niekro, Atl NL	1998	Sammy Sosa, Chi NL
1981	Steve Garvey, LA NL	1999	Tony Gwynn, SD NL
1982	Ken Singleton, Bal AL	2000	Al Leiter, NY NL
1983	Cecil Cooper, Mil AL	2001	Curt Schilling, Ari NL
1984	Ron Guidry, NY AL	2002	Jim Thome, Cle AL
1985	Don Baylor, NY AL	2003	Jamie Moyer, Sea AL
1986	Garry Maddox, Phi NL	2004	Edgar Martinez, Sea AL
1987	Rick Sutcliffe, Chi NL	2005	John Smoltz, Atl NL
1988	Dale Murphy, Atl NL	2006	Carlos Delgado, NY NL

The Fred Hutchinson Memorial Award

This award was created in 1965 to honor Fred Hutchinson, a highly-respected major league manager and former player who had died the previous year from cancer. Given annually to the major league player with the high character and strong level of competitiveness that Hutchinson was known for, the award honors those who have overcome physical adversity and shown strong commitments to their family and community.

1965	Mickey Mantle, NY AL	1986	Dennis Leonard, KC AL
1966	Sandy Koufax, LA NL	1987	Paul Molitor, Mil AL
1967	Carl Yastrzemski, Bos NL	1988	Ron Oester, Cin NL
1968	Pete Rose, Cin NL	1989	Dave Dravecky, SF NL
1969	Al Kaline, Det AL	1990	Sid Bream, Pit NL
1970	Tony Conigliaro, Bos AL	1991	Bill Wegman, Mil AL
1971	Joe Torre, StL NL	1992	Carney Lansford, Oak AL
1972	Bobby Tolan, Cin NL	1993	John Olerud, Tor AL
1973	John Hiller, Det AL	1994	Andre Dawson, Bos AL
1974	Danny Thompson, Min AL	1995	Jim Abbott, Cal AL
1975	Gary Nolan, Cin NL	1996	Omar Vizquel, Cle AL
1976	Tommy John, LA NL	1997	Eric Davis, Bal AL
1977	Willie McCovey, SF NL	1998	David Cone, NY AL
1978	Willie Stargell, Pit NL	1999	Sean Casey, Cin NL
1979	Lou Brock, StL NL	2000	Jason Giambi, Oak AL
1980	George Brett, KC AL	2001	Curt Schilling, Ari NL
1981	Johnny Bench, Cin NL	2002	Tim Salmon, Cal AL
1982	Andre Thornton, Cle AL	2003	Jamie Moyer, Sea AL
1983	Ray Knight, Hou NL	2004	Trevor Hoffman SD NL
1984	Don Robinson, Pit NL	2005	Craig Biggio, Hou NL
1985	Rick Reuschel, Chi NL	2006	Mark Loretta, Bos AL

The Lou Gehrig Memorial Award

The Lou Gehrig Memorial Award was established in 1955 by Phi Delta Theta, Gehrig's college fraternity. It is given annually to a player who gives back to his community and strongly exemplifies the integrity, spirit, and giving nature that Gehrig possessed. The award is announced each spring for the previous year.

1955	Alvin Dark, NY NL	1959	Gil Hodges, LA NL
1956	Pee Wee Reese, Bro NL	1960	Dick Groat, Pit NL
1957	Stan Musial, StL NL	1961	Warren Spahn, Mil NL
1958	Gil McDougald, NY AL	1962	Robin Roberts, Bal AL

1963	Bobby Richardson, NY NL	1985	Dale Murphy, Atl NL
1964	Ken Boyer, StL NL	1986	George Brett, KC AL
1965	Vern Law, Pit NL	1987	Rick Sutcliffe, Chi NL
1966	Brooks Robinson, Bal AL	1988	Buddy Bell, Cin NL
1967	Ernie Banks, Chi NL	1989	Ozzie Smith, StL NL
1968	Al Kaline, Det AL	1990	Glenn Davis, Hou NL
1969	Pete Rose, Cin NL	1991	Kent Hrbek, Min AL
1970	Hank Aaron, Atl NL	1992	Cal Ripken, Bal AL
1971	Harmon Killebrew, Min AL	1993	Don Mattingly, NY AL
1972	Wes Parker, LA NL	1994	Barry Larkin, Cin NL
1973	Ron Santo, Chi NL	1995	Curt Schilling, Phi NL
1974	Willie Stargell, Pit NL	1996	Brett Butler, LA NL
1975	Johnny Bench, Cin NL	1997	Paul Molitor, Min AL
1976	Don Sutton, LA NL	1998	Tony Gwynn, SD NL
1977	Lou Brock, StL NL	1999	Mark McGwire, StL NL
1978	Don Kessinger, Chi AL	2000	Todd Stottlemyre, Ari NL
1979	Phil Niekro, Atl NL	2001	John Franco, NY NL
1980	Tony Perez, Bos AL	2002	Danny Graves, Cin NL
1981	Tommy John, NY AL	2003	Jamie Moyer, Sea AL
1982	Ron Cey, LA NL	2004	Jim Thome, Phi NL
1983	Mike Schmidt, Phi NL	2005	John Smoltz, Atl NL
1984	Steve Garvey, SD NL	2006	Trevor Hoffman, SD NL

The J.G. Taylor Spink Award

The J.G. Taylor Spink Award, given annually (and sometimes posthumously) to a sportswriter for "meritorious contributions to baseball writing," is named after the founder and longtime editor of *The Sporting News,* who was the first recipient. Each winner is presented with the award at the annual Hall of Fame induction ceremony (though they are not inducted into the Hall themselves) and is permanently recognized in the "Scribes & Mikemen" exhibit in Cooperstown. In several seasons, more than one writer has been so honored. They are listed along with the city where they worked.

1962	J.G. Taylor Spink, St Louis		John F. Kieran, New York
1963	Ring Lardner, New York	1974	John Carmichael, Chicago
1964	Hugh Fullerton, New York		James Isaminger, Philadelphia
1965	Charles Dryden, Chicago	1975	Tom Meany, New York
1966	Grantland Rice, New York		Shirley Povich, Washington DC
1967	Damon Runyon, New York	1976	Harold Kaese, Boston
1968	Harry G. Salsinger, Detroit		Red Smith, New York
1969	Sid Mercer, New York	1977	Gordon Cobbledick, Cleveland
1970	Heywood C. Broun, New York		Edgar Munzel, Chicago
1971	Frank Graham, New York	1978	Tim Murnane, Boston
1972	Dan Daniel, New York		Dick Young, New York
	Fred Lieb, New York	1979	Bob Broeg, St Louis
	J. Roy Stockton, St Louis		Tommy Holmes, Brooklyn
1973	Warren Brown, Chicago	1980	Joe Reichler, New York
	John Drebinger, New York		Milton Richman, New York

1981	Allen Lewis, Philadelphia	1993	Wendell Smith, Pittsburgh
	Bob Addie, Washington DC	1994	(no selection)
1982	Si Burick, Dayton	1995	Joseph Durso, New York
1983	Ken Smith, New York	1996	Charley Feeney, New York
1984	Joe McGuff, Kansas City	1997	Sam Lacy, Washington DC
1985	Earl Lawson, Cincinnati	1998	Bob Stevens, San Francisco
1986	Jack Lang, Brooklyn	1999	Hal Lebovitz, Cleveland
1987	Jim Murray, Los Angeles	2000	Ross Newhan, Los Angeles
1988	Bob Hunter, Los Angeles	2001	Joe Falls, Detroit
	Ray Kelly, Philadelphia	2002	Hal McCoy, Cincinnati
1989	Jerome Holtzman, Chicago	2003	Murray Chass, New York
1990	Phil Collier, San Diego	2004	Peter Gammons, Boston
1991	Ritter Collett, Dayton	2005	Tracy Ringolsby, Denver
1992	Leonard Koppett, New York	2006	Rick Hummel, St. Louis
	Bus Saidt, Philadelphia		

The Ford C. Frick Award

This award, named after the former broadcaster and commissioner Ford C. Frick, is presented annually to a baseball voice in recognition of "excellence in baseball broadcasting." The Frick Award, clearly modeled after the Spink Award, was first presented in 1978 to the two best known pioneers of baseball broadcasting, Mel Allen and Red Barber, and has been awarded to one announcer every year since. As in the case of the Spink Award, the winner is honored at the Hall of Fame induction ceremony, and recognized by a permanent exhibit, but is not himself an inductee.

1978	Mel Allen, Red Barber	1993	Chuck Thompson
1979	Bob Elson	1994	Bob Murphy
1980	Russ Hodges	1995	Bob Wolff
1981	Ernie Harwell	1996	Herb Carneal
1982	Vin Scully	1997	Jimmy Dudley
1983	Jack Brickhouse	1998	Jaime Jarrin
1984	Curt Gowdy	1999	Arch McDonald
1985	Buck Canel	2000	Marty Brennaman
1986	Bob Prince	2001	Rafael "Felo" Ramirez
1987	Jack Buck	2002	Harry Kalas
1988	Lindsey Nelson	2003	Bob Uecker
1989	Harry Caray	2004	Lon Simmons
1990	By Saam	2005	Jerry Coleman
1991	Joe Garagiola	2006	Gene Elston
1992	Milo Hamilton		

RETIRED UNIFORM NUMBERS

It took a long time for uniform numbers to catch on in baseball after they were first promoted in the 1880s. In 1883 the Cincinnati Red Stockings tried to convince their players to wear numbers on their sleeves, but the players rejected the notion. It wasn't until 1916 that another team, the Cleveland Indians, tried again, but the idea did not stick. However, the pressure on baseball teams to use numbers grew since many football and basketball teams were already using them. In 1929 the Indians tried again, successfully. The New York Yankees soon followed suit and, by 1932, all teams had put numbers on at least their road uniforms. The Philadelphia Athletics were the last team to add numbers to their jerseys.

The first number to be retired was "the luckiest man of the face of the earth," Lou Gehrig, whose No. 4 was retired by the Yankees on July 4, 1939. The second number to be retired was Carl Hubbell's No. 11 by the New York Giants. Babe Ruth's No. 3 was retired in 1948. The Yankees retired No. 8 in honor of two players: Hall of Fame catchers, Bill Dickey and Yogi Berra. Montreal retired No. 10 to honor both Andre Dawson and Rusty Staub.

Retiring numbers has become much more popular during the last two decades, though teams vary widely on what makes a player's number worthy of being retired. The Seattle Mariners, Arizona Diamondbacks, Colorado Rockies, and Toronto Blue Jays have not retired any uniform numbers, and the Marlins have not retired the number of any player. Some teams have now gone so far to "retire" numbers for players or managers who never wore a number on their back.

The Detroit Tigers, after years of pressure to retire the numbers of Hall of Famers Hank Greenberg and Charlie Gehringer, retired Al Kaline's No. 6 in 1980. Greenberg and Gerhinger's numbers followed three years later on the same day. The reason that the team held out for so long? Because Ty Cobb—"The Greatest Tiger of Them All"—never wore a number that could be retired.

In 1997 Major League Baseball retired former Brooklyn Dodger Jackie Robinson's No. 42 on behalf of all teams, though players who were wearing the number at that time—most of whom who took the number to honor Robinson in the first place—have been allowed to keep wearing the number until retirement.

Three teams have even retired numbers in honor of off-the-field personnel. The Florida Marlins only retired number (No. 5) was retired in honor of former team president Carl Barger, who helped bring the Marlins into existence but died before the franchise its first game. The St. Louis Cardinals and Anaheim Angels have both retired numbers as tributes to former longtime owners: the Cardinals No. 85 was retired in honor of August Busch, and the Angels No. 26 was retired in honor of Gene Autry.

Only three franchises that have relocated have retired the numbers of any players that are strongly identified with their former cities. The Giants actually distinguish between the retired numbers of five New York Giants and the four San Francisco Giants whose numbers they have also retired (including Willie Mays, who played for the Giants in both New York and San Francisco). The Dodgers have retired the numbers of four players who made their greatest contributions in Brooklyn. The Atlanta Braves have retired the number of Warren Spahn, who played his whole, 21-year career in Boston and Milwaukee.

Other franchises, however, such as the Baltimore Orioles and Minnesota Twins, have ignored their previous identities and not retired any numbers that were worn before the teams moved to their current location. On the other hand, the new Washington Nationals do remember their past as the Montreal Expos and acknowledge the retired numbers of Gary Carter, Andre Dawson, Tim Raines, and Rusty Staub.

ATLANTA/MILWAUKEE/BOSTON (NL)	
Dale Murphy	3
Warren Spahn	21
Phil Niekro	35
Eddie Mathews	41
Hank Aaron	44

BALTIMORE (AL)	
Earl Weaver (Manager)	4
Brooks Robinson	5
Cal Ripken	8
Frank Robinson	20
Jim Palmer	22
Eddie Murray	33

BOSTON (AL)	
Bobby Doerr	1
Joe Cronin	4
Carl Yastrzemski	8
Ted Williams	9
Carlton Fisk	27

CHICAGO (AL)	
Nellie Fox	2
Harold Baines	3
Luke Appling	4
Minnie Minoso	9
Luis Aparicio	11
Ted Lyons	16
Billy Pierce	19
Carlton Fisk	72

CHICAGO (NL)	
Ron Santo	10
Ernie Banks	14
Ryne Sandberg	23
Billy Williams	26

CINCINNATI (NL)	
Fred Hutchinson (Manager)	1
Johnny Bench	5
Joe Morgan	8
Sparky Anderson (Manager)	10
Ted Kluszewski	18
Frank Robinson	20
Tony Perez	24

CLEVELAND (AL)	
Earl Averill	3
Lou Boudreau	5
Larry Doby	14
Mel Harder	18
Bob Feller	19
Bob Lemon	21

DETROIT (AL)	
Charlie Gehringer	2
Hank Greenberg	5
Al Kaline	6
Hal Newhouser	16
Willie Horton	23
Ty Cobb	—
Ernie Harwell (Broadcaster)	—

FLORIDA (NL)	
Carl Barger (Executive)	5

HOUSTON (NL)	
Jimmy Wynn	24
Jose Cruz	25
Jim Umbricht	32
Mike Scott	33
Nolan Ryan	34
Don Wilson	40
Larry Dierker	49

KANSAS CITY (AL)	
George Brett	5
Dick Howser (Manager)	10
Frank White	20

LOS ANGELES/ANAHEIM/CALIFORNIA (AL)	
Jim Fregosi	11
Gene Autry (Owner)	26
Rod Carew	29
Nolan Ryan	30
Jimmie Reese (Coach)	50

LOS ANGELES/BROOKLYN (NL)	
Pee Wee Reese	1
Tommy Lasorda (Manager)	2
Duke Snider	4
Jim Gilliam	19
Don Sutton	20
Walt Alston (Manager)	24
Sandy Koufax	32
Roy Campanella	39
Jackie Robinson	42
Don Drysdale	53

MILWAUKEE (AL-NL)	
Paul Molitor	4
Robin Yount	19
Rollie Fingers	34
Hank Aaron	44

MINNESOTA/WASHINGTON (AL)	
Harmon Killebrew	3
Tony Oliva	6
Kent Hrbek	14
Rod Carew	29
Kirby Puckett	34

NEW YORK (AL)	
Billy Martin (Manager)	1
Babe Ruth	3
Lou Gehrig	4
Joe DiMaggio	5
Mickey Mantle	7
Bill Dickey	8
Yogi Berra	8
Roger Maris	9
Phil Rizzuto	10
Thurman Munson	15
Whitey Ford	16
Don Mattingly	23
Elston Howard	32
Casey Stengel (Manager)	37
Reggie Jackson	44
Ron Guidry	49

NEW YORK (NL)	
Gil Hodges (Manager)	14
Casey Stengel (Manager)	37
Tom Seaver	41

OAKLAND (AL)	
Reggie Jackson	9
Catfish Hunter	27
Dennis Eckersley	34
Rollie Fingers	34

PHILADELPHIA (NL)	
Richie Ashburn	1
Jim Bunning	14
Mike Schmidt	20
Steve Carlton	32
Robin Roberts	36
Chuck Klein	—
Grover Alexander	—

PITTSBURGH (NL)	
Billy Meyer (Manager)	1
Ralph Kiner	4
Willie Stargell	8
Bill Mazeroski	9
Pie Traynor	20
Roberto Clemente	21
Honus Wagner	33
Danny Murtaugh (Manager)	40

SAN DIEGO (NL)	
Steve Garvey	6
Tony Gwynn	19
Dave Winfield	31
Randy Jones	35

SAN FRANCISCO/NEW YORK (NL)	
Bill Terry	3
Mel Ott	4
Carl Hubbell	11
Willie Mays	24
Juan Marichal	27
Orlando Cepeda	30
Gaylord Perry	36
Willie McCovey	44
Christy Mathewson	—
John McGraw (Manager)	—

ST. LOUIS (NL)	
Ozzie Smith	1
Red Schoendienst	2
Stan Musial	6
Enos Slaughter	9
Ken Boyer	14
Dizzy Dean	17
Lou Brock	20
Bob Gibson	45
August Busch (Owner)	85
Rogers Hornsby	—

TAMPA BAY (AL)	
Wade Boggs	12

TEXAS (AL)	
Nolan Ryan	34
Johnny Oates (Manager)	26

WASHINGTON/MONTREAL (NL)	
Gary Carter	8
Andre Dawson	10
Rusty Staub	10
Tim Raines	30

GREAT PERFORMANCES

This section details some of the greatest individual performances in baseball history, including 2004's record-setting feats: Barry Bonds' .609 On-Base Percentage, 232 Walks, and 120 Intentional Walks; Ichiro's 262 hits; and Eric Gagne's 84 consecutive Saves.

Joe DiMaggio's 56-game hitting streak is one of the most revered records in baseball; no player has ever come remotely close to breaking it. Since DiMaggio set the record, only three players have accomplished a 36-game hitting streak or better. The late Stephen Jay Gould wrote that DiMaggio's hitting streak is the "most extraordinary thing that ever happened in American sports" because it totally defied the laws of probability.

DiMaggio didn't accomplish the streak without some controversy. There certainly were some questionable calls that enabled the streak to continue, but the streak lasted until DiMaggio was finally shut down on July 17, 1941 in Cleveland. The Yankees won, 4-3, but DiMaggio grounded out in each of his 3 at bats. In his final chance to extend the streak in eighth inning, Indians pitcher Jim Bagby induced DiMaggio to hit into a double play. DiMaggio's record may never be broken, but that hasn't prevented baseball fans from getting excited every time a player makes any kind of run at his record. Even a 20-game hitting streak quickens the pulses of the media and generates detailed coverage.

Most Consecutive Games Batted Safely, Single Season

GAMES	PLAYER, TEAM	YEAR	GAMES	PLAYER, TEAM	YEAR
56	Joe DiMaggio, NY AL	1941	31	Ed Delahanty, Phi NL	1899
44	Willie Keeler, Bal NL	1897	31	Nap Lajoie, Cle AL	1906
44	Pete Rose, Cin NL	1978	31	Sam Rice, Was AL	1924
42	Bill Dahlen, Chi NL	1894	31	Willie Davis, LA NL	1969
41	George Sisler, StL AL	1922	31	Rico Carty, Atl NL	1970
40	Ty Cobb, Det AL	1911	31	Ken Landreaux, Min AL	1980
39	Paul Molitor, Mil AL	1987	31	Vladimir Guerrero, Mon NL	1999
37	Tommy Holmes, Bos NL	1945	30	Cal McVey, Chi NL	1876
36	Jimmy Rollins, Phi NL	2005	30	Elmer Smith, Cin NL	1898
35	Fred Clarke, Lou NL	1895	30	Tris Speaker, Bos AL	1912
35	Ty Cobb, Det AL	1917	30	Goose Goslin, Det AL	1934
35	Luis Castillo, Fla NL	2002	30	Stan Musial, StL NL	1950
35	Chase Utley,Phi AL	2006	30	Ron LeFlore, Det AL	1976
34	George Sisler, StL AL	1925	30	George Brett, KC AL	1980
34	George McQuinn, StL AL	1938	30	Jerome Walton, Chi NL	1989
34	Dom DiMaggio, Bos AL	1949	30	Sandy Alomar Jr., Cle AL	1997
34	Benito Santiago, SD NL	1987	30	Nomar Garciaparra, Bos AL	1997
33	Hal Chase, NY AL	1907	30	Eric Davis, Bal AL	1998
33	George Davis, NY NL	1893	30	Luis Gonzalez, Ari NL	1999
33	Rogers Hornsby, StL NL	1922	30	Albert Pujols, StL NL	2003
33	Heinie Manush, Was AL	1933	30	Willy Taveras,Hou NL	2006

Most Consecutive Games Batted Safely, Multiple Season

GAMES	PLAYER, TEAM	YEAR	GAMES	PLAYER, TEAM	YEAR
45	Willie Keeler,Bal NL	1896-97	31	Vada Pinson,Cin NL	1965-66
38	Jimmy Rollins, Phi NL	2005-06	31	Ron LeFlore,Det AL	1975-76
35	George Sisler,StL AL	1924-25	30	Charlie Grimm,Chi NL	1922-23
32	Harry Heilmann,Det AL	1922-23	30	Sam Rice,Was AL	1929-30

DiMaggio's 56-game Hitting Streak

Joltin' Joe's legendary hitting streak caused a national sensation, became a song, made him a celebrity, and overshadowed a superior overall season by Ted Williams. Below (sans melody) is how The Yankee Clipper did it. Numbers in parentheses refer to hits off each pitcher on a given date.

DATE	OPPOSING PITCHER, TEAM	AB	H	2B	3B	HR
May 15	Eddie Smith, Chi	4	1	0	0	0
May 16	Thornton Lee, Chi	4	2	0	1	1
May 17	Johnny Rigney, Chi	3	1	0	0	0
May 18	Bob Harris (2), Johnny Niggeling (1), StL	3	3	1	0	0
May 19	Denny Galehouse, StL	3	1	1	0	0
May 20	Eldon Auker, StL	5	1	0	0	0
May 21	Schoolboy Rowe (1), Al Benton (1), Det	5	2	0	0	0
May 22	Archie McKain, Det	4	1	0	0	0
May 23	Dick Newsome, Bos	5	1	0	0	0
May 24	Earl Johnson, Bos	4	1	0	0	0
May 25	Lefty Grove, Bos	4	1	0	0	0
May 27	Ken Chase (1), Red Anderson (2), Alex Carrasquel (1), Was	5	4	0	0	1
May 28	Sid Hudson, Was	4	1	0	1	0
May 29	Steve Sundra, Was	3	1	0	0	0
May 30G1	Earl Johnson, Bos	2	1	0	0	0
May 30G2	Mickey Harris, Bos	3	1	1	0	0
June 1G1	Al Milnar, Cle	4	1	0	0	0
June 1G2	Mel Harder, Cle	4	1	0	0	0
June 2	Bob Feller, Cle	4	2	1	0	0
June 3	Dizzy Trout, Det	4	1	0	0	1
June 5	Hal Newhouser, Det	5	1	0	1	0
June 7	Bob Muncrief (1), Johnny Allen (1), George Caster (1), StL	5	3	0	0	0
June 8G1	Elden Auker, StL	4	2	0	0	2
June 8G2	George Caster (1), Jack Kramer (1), StL	4	2	1	0	1
June 10	Johnny Rigney, Chi	5	1	0	0	0
June 12	Thornton Lee, Chi	4	2	0	0	1
June 14	Bob Feller, Cle	2	1	1	0	0
June 15	Jim Bagby Jr., Cle	3	1	0	0	1
June 16	Al Milnar, Cle	5	1	1	0	0
June 17	Johnny Rigney, Chi	4	1	0	0	0
June 18	Thornton Lee, Chi	3	1	0	0	0
June 19	Eddie Smith (1), Buck Ross (1), Chi	3	3	0	0	1
June 20	Bobo Newsom (2), Archie McKain (2), Det	5	4	1	0	0
June 21	Dizzy Trout, Det	4	1	0	0	0
June 22	Hal Newhouser (1), Bobo Newsom (1) Det	5	2	1	0	1
June 24	Bob Muncrief, StL	4	1	0	0	0
June 25	Denny Galehouse, StL	4	1	0	0	1
June 26	Eldon Auker, StL	4	1	1	0	0
June 27	Chubby Dean, Phi	3	2	0	0	1
June 28	Johnny Babich (1), Lum Harris (1), Phi	5	2	1	0	0
June 29G1	Emil "Dutch" Leonard, Was	4	1	1	0	0
June 29G2	Red Anderson, Was	5	1	0	0	0
July 1G1	Mickey Harris (1), Mike Ryba (1), Bos	4	2	0	0	0
July 1G2	Jack Wilson, Bos	3	1	0	0	0
July 2	Dick Newsome, Bos	5	1	0	0	1
July 5	Phil Marchildon, Phi	4	1	0	0	1
July 6G1	Johnny Babich (1), Bump Hadley (3), Phi	5	4	1	0	0
July 6G2	Jack Knott, Phi	4	2	0	1	0
July 10	Johnny Niggeling, StL	2	1	0	0	0
July 11	Bob Harris (3), Jack Kramer (1), StL	5	4	0	0	1
July 12	Eldon Auker (1), Bob Muncrief (1), StL	5	2	1	0	0
July 13G1	Ted Lyons (2), Jack Hallett (1), Chi	4	3	0	0	0
July 13G2	Thornton Lee, Chi	4	1	0	0	0
July 14	Johnny Rigney, Chi	3	1	0	0	0
July 15	Eddie Smith, Chi	4	2	1	0	0
July 16	Al Milnar (2), Joe Krakauskas (1), Cle	4	3	1	0	0
Totals	(56 games)	223	91	16	4	15

Consecutive Games On-Base Streak, Single Season

Even when DiMaggio's great hitting steak was finally stopped by the Indians, he managed to extend another streak with a walk, eventually reaching base in 74 consecutive games that year. At the time, that was a record. Ted Williams, however, broke that mark eight years later when he reached base an incredible 84 games in a row. These records were unknown at the time, but researcher Herman Krabbenhoft has recently documented the history of on-base streaks. In 2003 Barry Bonds tied the NL 20th century mark by getting on base in 58 consecutive games. In 2006, Orlando Cabrera quietly put together a 60-game on-base streak, the longest such streak in the major leagues in over half a century. Here is a list of all on-base streaks that have lasted at least 50 games.

PLAYER, TEAM	YEAR	GAMES	PLAYER, TEAM	YEAR	GAMES
Ted Williams, Bos AL	1949	84	Derek Jeter, NY AL	1999	53
Joe DiMaggio, NY AL	1941	74	Alex Rodriguez, NY AL	2004	53
Ted Williams, Bos AL	1941	69	Mel Amada, StL AL	1938	52
Bill Joyce, Bos AA	1891	64	Ty Cobb, Det AL	1914	52
Orlando Cabrera, LA AL	2006	63	Lou Gehrig, NY AL	1934	52
George Van Haltren, Pit NL	1893	60	Greg Gross, Hou NL	1975	52
Barry Bonds, SF NL	2003	58	Denny Lyons, Phi AA	1887	52
Duke Snider, Bro NL	1954	58	Tony Phillips, Det AL	1993	52
Wade Boggs, Bos AL	1985	57	Gary Sheffield, Atl NL	2002	52
Cupid Childs, Cle NL	1892	57	Tris Speaker, Cle AL	1920	52
George Kell, Det AL	1950	57	Frank Thomas, Chi AL	1996	52
Jake Stenzel, Pit, NL	1895	57	Jack Tobin, StL AL	1922	52
Ed Delahanty, Phi NL	1896	56	Jimmy Wynn, Hou NL	1969	52
Bill Joyce, WAS NL-NY NL	1896	56	George Brett, KC AL	1980	51
Ryan Klesko, SD NL	2002	56	Joe DiMaggio, NY AL	1937	51
Arky Vaughn, Pit NL	1936	56	Joe Kelley, Bal NL	1896	51
Ty Cobb, Det AL	1915	55	Babe Ruth, NY AL	1923	51
Billy Hamilton, Bos NL	1896	55	Ken Williams, StL AL	1923	51
Stan Musial, StL NL	1943	55	Johnny Bates, Cin, NL	1911	50
Jim Thome, Cle AL	2002	55	Vince Coleman, StL	1987	50
Ray Blades, StL NL	1925	54	Ike Griffin Bro, NL	1895	50
Bill Joyce, Was NL	1894	54	Tommy McCarthy, Bos NL	1895	50
Luke Appling, Chi AL	1936	53	Tris Speaker, Cle AL	1926	50
Shawn Green, LA NL	2000	53	Lou Whitaker, Det	1991	50

Ichiro's 262-Hit Season

On Friday, October 1, 2004, Seattle's Ichiro Suzuki smacked a ground ball up the middle and broke a record that had stood for 84 years. Ichiro's 258th hit surpassed St. Louis Browns great George Sisler's 1920 record of 257 hits in a single season. While 257 never had the ring of 60 or 714 or 4192 and has never been one of baseball's magic numbers, the record's longevity speaks for itself.

Sisler clearly had a better year in 1920 than Ichiro did in 2004, posting a batting average of .404 with an on-base percentage of .449

and a slugging percentage of .632, in contrast to Ichiro's .372 batting average, .414 on-base percentage, and .455 slugging percentage. Sisler knocked out 1.67 hits per game, playing in all 154 of the Browns games; Ichiro rapped 1.63 hits per game while playing in all but one of the Mariners 162 games. On the other hand, Ichiro did break the record while playing half his games in the best pitchers' park in the league in 2004, while Sisler had the benefit of a favorable environment for hitters at his home park in 1920. In fact, Ichiro hit .405 on the road in breaking the record in 2004, becoming the first hitter to hit .400 on the road in a season since Lou Boudreau in 1948, while Sisler hit .473 at home and .341 on the road in 1920. And there's no doubt that Ichiro faced far tougher pitching than Sisler ever did, and no one had even come close to challenging Sisler's mark since 1930. Ichiro's month-by-month hit totals and batting average are shown below (IS) alongside Sisler's 1920 (GS).

MONTH	IS H	AVG	GS H	AVG	MONTH	IS H	AVG	GS H	AVG
April	26	.255	12	.333	August	56	.463	42	.400
May	50	.400	39	.355	September	44	.373	57	.442
Jun	29	.274	60	.526	October	6	.429	7	.500
July	51	.432	40	.325	Total	262	.372	257	.407

Consecutive Games Played

It was only twenty years ago that most people considered Lou Gehrig's consecutive games played record to be unbreakable. Then ironman Cal Ripken came along and eventually surpassed Gehrig's record by a wide margin. Even Ripken's record is breakable, but it will take a unique combination of fortitude and luck to surpass it. Miguel Tejada, another shortstop, holds the longest consecutive games played streak of any active player, with 1080 consecutive games at the end of 2006. Tejada would need to play every game of the next nine seasons and 95 games of the season after that to break Cal Ripken's record.

PLAYER	GAMES	YEARS	PLAYER	GAMES	YEARS
Cal Ripken	2,632	1982–98	Miguel Tejada	1,080	2000-present
Lou Gehrig	2,130	1925–39	Stan Musial	895	1952–57
Everett Scott	1,307	1916–25	Eddie Yost	829	1949–55
Steve Garvey	1,207	1975–83	Gus Suhr	822	1931–37
Billy Williams	1,117	1963–70	Nellie Fox	798	1955–60
Joe Sewell	1,103	1922–30			

Four-Homer Games

Only fifteen players have hit 4 home runs in a game, and only twelve of those players did it in a regulation nine-inning game. Some great players are on the list, but there are also a few surprises: Mark Whiten, who hit only 105 home runs in his career, and Pat Seerey, who hit only 85 home runs. Carlos Delgado slugged his way onto this short list during the last week of the 2003 season.

PLAYER, TEAM	DATE
Bobby Lowe, Bos NL	May 30, 1894
Ed Delahanty, Phi NL	July 13, 1896
Lou Gehrig, NY AL	June 3, 1932
Chuck Klein, Phi NL	July 10, 1936 (10 inn)
Pat Seerey, Chi AL	July 18, 1948 G1 (11 inn)
Gil Hodges, Bro NL	Aug. 31, 1950
Joe Adcock, Mil NL	July 31, 1954
Rocky Colavito, Cle AL	June 10, 1959
Willie Mays, SF NL	Apr. 30, 1961
Mike Schmidt, Phi NL	Apr. 17, 1976 (10 inn)
Bob Horner, Atl NL	July 6, 1986
Mark Whiten, StL NL	Sept. 7, 1993 G2
Mike Cameron, Sea AL	May 2, 2002
Shawn Green, LA NL	May 23, 2002
Carlos Delgado, Tor AL	Sept. 25, 2003

Career Grand Slam Home Run Leaders

The grand slam is not just another home run; it has an identity of its own as the rarest type of home run. A grand slam usually changes the very complexion of a game since a team that's already ahead usually has an impenetrable lead once a grand slam is hit, and a team that is behind can use a grand slam to suddenly make the game competitive again. A grand slam is by far the biggest single scoring event in any major pro sport.

Baseball fans might reasonably expect the career grand slams leaders list to look similar to the all-time home run leader list, but there are significant differences. Lou Gehrig has four more grand slams than any other player in baseball history, despite not being among the top twenty in career home runs. Some of the top home run hitters of all-time, including Barry Bonds, Frank Robinson and Sammy Sosa, have hit less than half as many grand slams as Gehrig. And several players who didn't even reach the 300-career home run mark are among the leaders in grand slams.

PLAYER	CAREER GS	PLAYER	CAREER GS	PLAYER	CAREER GS
Lou Gehrig	23	Babe Ruth	16	Jeff Kent	13
Manny Ramirez	20	Ken Griffey Jr.	15	Ralph Kiner	13
Eddie Murray	19	Gil Hodges	14	Alex Rodriguez	13
Willie McCovey	18	Mark McGwire	14	Ernie Banks	12
Robin Ventura	18	Mike Piazza	14	Don Baylor	12
Jimmie Foxx	17	Richie Sexson	14	Rogers Hornsby	12
Ted Williams	17	Harold Baines	13	Rafael Palmeiro	12
Hank Aaron	16	Albert Belle	13	Joe Rudi	12
Dave Kingman	16	Joe DiMaggio	13	Matt Williams	12
		George Foster	13	Rudy York	12

The Single-Season Home Run Record

Widespread perception to the contrary, the major league single-season home run record has actually changed quite often over the course of baseball history. Despite all the hoopla over Mark McGwire setting the home run record in 1998, he held the mark for the shortest length of time of any individual since the 1880s.

YEAR	PLAYER, TEAM	HR	YEAR	PLAYER, TEAM	HR
1876	George Hall, Phi NL	5	1921	Babe Ruth, NY AL	59
1879	Charley Jones, Bos NL	9	1927	Babe Ruth, NY AL	60
1883	Buck Ewing, NY NL	10	1961	Roger Maris, NY AL	61
1884	Ed Williamson, Chi NL	27	1998	Mark McGwire, StL NL	70
1919	Babe Ruth, Bos AL	29	2001	Barry Bonds, SF NL	73
1920	Babe Ruth, NY AL	54			

The Home Run Records of Bonds, McGwire, Maris, and Ruth

Three years after Mark McGwire and Sammy Sosa electrified the world with their great home run chase in 1998, Barry Bonds shattered the highest-profile record in sports with his 73 home runs. Babe Ruth made the home run baseball's dominant offensive stratagem in 1920 by hitting an unheard of 54 round-trippers, and The Bambino's 60 home runs in 1927 invested a unique magic in that mark.

The lists below detail the all-time home run record seasons since 1927. "Gm" indicates the team game number in which the home run was hit. Left-handed pitchers are asterisked. Pitchers who allowed multiple home runs in a game are listed only once. Daggers after the opposing teams indicate road games.

Bonds played in 153 of the Giants 162 games in 2001. McGwire played in 155 of the Cardinals 163 games in 1998. Maris played in 161 of the Yankees 163 games in 1961. Ruth played in 151 of the Yankees 155 games in 1927.

Bonds' 73 Home Runs (2001)

HR (GM)	DATE	OFF (PITCHER/TEAM)	HR (GM)	DATE	OFF (PITCHER/TEAM)
1 (1)	Apr. 2	Woody Williams SD	37 (70)	June 19	Adam Eaton SD†
2 (9)	Apr. 12	Adam Eaton SD†	38 (71)	June 20	Rodney Myers SD†
3 (10)	Apr. 13	Jamey Wright Mil†	39 (74)	June 23	Darryl Kile StL†
4 (11)	Apr. 14	Jimmy Haynes Mil†	40 (89)	July 12	Paul Abbott Sea†
5 (12)	Apr. 15	David Weathers Mil†	41 (95)	July 18	Mike Hampton* Col
6 (13)	Apr. 17	Terry Adams LA	42 (95)	July 18	
7 (14)	Apr. 18	Chan Ho Park LA	43 (103)	July 26	Curt Schilling Ari†
8 (16)	Apr. 20	Jimmy Haynes Mil	44 (103)	July 26	
9 (19)	Apr. 24	Jim Brower Cin	45 (104)	July 27	Brian Anderson* Ari†
10 (21)	Apr. 26	Scott Sullivan Cin	46 (108)	Aug. 1	Joe Beimel* Pit
11 (24)	Apr. 29	Manny Aybar Chi	47 (111)	Aug. 4	Nelson Figueroa Phi
12 (26)	May 2	Todd Ritchie Pit†	48 (113)	Aug. 7	Danny Graves Cin†
13 (27)	May 3	Jimmy Anderson* Pit†	49 (115)	Aug. 9	Scott Winchester Cin†
14 (28)	May 4	Bruce Chen* Phi†	50 (117)	Aug. 11	Joe Borowski Chi†
15 (35)	May 11	Steve Trachsel NY	51 (119)	Aug. 14	Ricky Bones Fla
16 (40)	May 17	Chuck Smith Fla†	52 (121)	Aug. 16	A.J. Burnett Fla
17 (41)	May 18	Mike Remlinger* Atl†	53 (121)	Aug. 16	Vic Darensbourg* Fla
18 (42)	May 19	Odalis Perez* Atl†	54 (123)	Aug. 18	Jason Marquis Atl
19 (42)	May 19	Jose Cabrera Atl†	55 (127)	Aug. 23	Graeme Lloyd* Mon†
20 (42)	May 19	Jason Marquis Atl†	56 (131)	Aug. 27	Kevin Appier NY†
21 (43)	May 20	John Burkett Atl†	57 (135)	Aug. 31	John Thomson Col
22 (43)	May 20	Mike Remlinger* Atl†	58 (138)	Sept. 3	Jason Jennings Col
23 (44)	May 21	Curt Schilling Ari†	59 (139)	Sept. 4	Miguel Batista Ari
24 (45)	May 22	Russ Springer Ari†	60 (141)	Sept. 6	Albie Lopez Ari
25 (47)	May 24	John Thomson Col	61 (144)	Sept. 9	Scott Elarton Col†
26 (50)	May 27	Denny Neagle* Col	62 (144)	Sept. 9	
27 (53)	May 30	Robert Ellis Ari	63 (144)	Sept. 9	Todd Belitz* Col†
28 (53)	May 30		64 (147)	Sept. 20	Wade Miller Hou
29 (54)	June 1	Shawn Chacon Col†	65 (150)	Sept. 23	Jason Middlebrook SD†
30 (57)	June 4	Bobby J. Jones SD	66 (150)	Sept. 23	
31 (58)	June 5	Wascar Serrano SD	67 (151)	Sept. 24	James Baldwin LA†
32 (60)	June 7	Brian Lawrence SD	68 (154)	Sept. 28	Jason Middlebrook SD
33 (64)	June 12	Pat Rapp Ana	69 (155)	Sept. 29	Chuck McElroy* SD
34 (66)	June 14	Lou Pote Ana	70 (159)	Oct. 4	Wilfredo Rodriguez* Hou†
35 (67)	June 15	Mark Mulder* Oak	71 (160)	Oct. 5	Chan Ho Park LA
36 (67)	June 15		72 (160)	Oct. 5	
			73 (162)	Oct. 7	Dennis Springer LA

McGwire's 70 Home Runs (1998)

HR (GM)	DATE	OFF (PITCHER/TEAM)	HR (GM)	DATE	OFF (PITCHER/TEAM)
1 (1)	Mar. 31	Ramon Martinez LA	36 (79)	June 27	Mike Trombley Min†
2 (2)	Apr. 2	Frank Lankford LA	37 (81)	June 30	Glendon Rusch* KC
3 (3)	Apr. 3	Mark Langston* SD	38 (89)	July 11	Billy Wagner* Hou
4 (4)	Apr. 4	Don Wengert SD	39 (90)	July 12	Sean Bergman Hou
5 (13)	Apr. 14	Jeff Suppan Ari	40 (90)	July 12	Scott Elarton Hou
6 (13)	Apr. 14		41 (95)	July 17	Brian Bohanon* LA
7 (13)	Apr. 14	Barry Manuel Ari	42 (95)	July 17	Antonio Osuna LA
8 (15)	Apr. 17	Matt Whiteside Phi	43 (98)	July 20	Brian Boehringer SD†
9 (19)	Apr. 21	Trey Moore* Mon†	44 (104)	July 26	John Thomson Col†
10 (23)	Apr. 25	Jerry Spradlin Phi†	45 (105)	July 28	Mike Myers* Mil
11 (27)	Apr. 30	Marc Pisciotta Chi†	46 (115)	Aug. 8	Mark Clark Chi
12 (28)	May 1	Rod Beck Chi†	47 (118)	Aug. 11	Bobby Jones NY
13 (34)	May 8	Rick Reed NY†	48 (124)	Aug. 19	Matt Karchner Chi†
14 (36)	May 12	Paul Wagner Mil	49 (124)	Aug. 19	Terry Mulholland* Chi†
15 (38)	May 14	Kevin Millwood Atl	50 (125)	Aug. 20	Willie Blair NY†
16 (40)	May 16	Livan Hernandez Fla	51 (126)	Aug. 20	Rick Reed NY†
17 (42)	May 18	Jesus Sanchez* Fla	52 (129)	Aug. 22	Francisco Cordova Pit†
18 (43)	May 19	Tyler Green Phi†	53 (130)	Aug. 23	Ricardo Rincon* Pit†
19 (43)	May 19		54 (133)	Aug. 26	Justin Speier Fla
20 (43)	May 19	Wayne Gomes Phi†	55 (137)	Aug. 30	Dennis Martinez Atl
21 (46)	May 22	Mark Gardner SF	56 (139)	Sept. 1	Livan Hernandez Fla†
22 (47)	May 23	Rich Rodriguez* SF	57 (139)	Sept. 1	Donn Pall Fla†
23 (47)	May 23	John Johnstone SF	58 (140)	Sept. 2	Brian Edmondson Fla†
24 (48)	May 24	Robb Nen SF	59 (140)	Sept. 2	Rob Stanifer Fla†
25 (49)	May 25	John Thomson Col	60 (142)	Sept. 5	Dennis Reyes* Cin
26 (52)	May 29	Dan Miceli SD†	61 (144)	Sept. 7	Mike Morgan Chi
27 (53)	May 30	Andy Ashby SD†	62 (145)	Sept. 8	Steve Trachsel Chi
28 (59)	June 5	Orel Hershiser SF†	63 (152)	Sept. 15	Jason Christiansen* Pit
29 (62)	June 8	Jason Bere Chi AL†	64 (155)	Sept. 18	Rafael Roque* Mil†
30 (64)	June 10	Jim Parque* Chi AL†	65 (157)	Sept. 20	Scott Karl* Mil†
31 (65)	June 12	Andy Benes Ari†	66 (161)	Sept. 25	Shayne Bennett Mon
32 (69)	June 17	Jose Lima Hou†	67 (162)	Sept. 26	Dustin Hermanson Mon
33 (70)	June 18	Shane Reynolds Hou†	68 (162)	Sept. 26	Kirk Bullinger Mon
34 (76)	June 24	Jaret Wright Cle†	69 (163)	Sept. 27	Mike Thurman Mon
35 (77)	June 25	Dave Burba Cle†	70 (163)	Sept. 27	Carl Pavano Mon

Maris' 61 Home Runs (1961)

HR (GM)	DATE	OFF (PITCHER/TEAM)	HR (GM)	DATE	OFF (PITCHER/TEAM)
1 (11)	Apr. 26	Paul Foytack Det†	32 (78)	July 5	Frank Funk Cle
2 (17)	May 3	Pedro Ramos Min†	33 (82)	July 9	Bill Monbouquette Bos
3 (20)	May 6	Eli Grba LA†	34 (84)	July 13	Early Wynn Chi†
4 (29)	May 17	Pete Burnside* Was	35 (86)	July 15	Ray Herbert Chi†
5 (30)	May 19	Jim Perry Cle†	36 (92)	July 21	Bill Monbouquette Bos†
6 (31)	May 20	Gary Bell Cle†	37 (95)	July 25	Frank Baumann* Chi
7 (32)	May 21	Chuck Estrada Bal	38 (95)	July 25	Don Larsen Chi
8 (35)	May 24	Gene Conley Bos	39 (96)	July 25	Russ Kemmerer Chi
9 (38)	May 28	Cal McLish Chi	40 (96)	July 25	Warren Hacker Chi
10 (40)	May 30	Gene Conley Bos†	41 (106)	Aug. 4	Camilo Pascual Min
11 (40)	May 30	Mike Fornieles Bos†	42 (114)	Aug. 11	Pete Burnside Was†
12 (41)	May 31	Billy Muffett Bos†	43 (115)	Aug. 12	Dick Donovan Was†
13 (43)	June 2	Cal McLish Chi†	44 (116)	Aug. 13	Bennie Daniels Was†
14 (44)	June 3	Bob Shaw Chi†	45 (117)	Aug. 13	Marty Kutyna Was†
15 (45)	June 4	Russ Kemmerer Chi†	46 (118)	Aug. 15	Juan Pizarro* Chi
16 (48)	June 6	Ed Palmquist Min	47 (119)	Aug. 16	Billy Pierce* Chi
17 (49)	June 7	Pedro Ramos Min	48 (119)	Aug. 16	
18 (52)	June 9	Ray Herbert KC	49 (124)	Aug. 20	Jim Perry Cle†
19 (55)	June 11	Eli Grba LA	50 (125)	Aug. 22	Ken McBride LA†
20 (55)	June 11	Johnny James LA	51 (129)	Aug. 26	Jerry Walker KC†
21 (57)	June 13	Jim Perry Cle†	52 (135)	Sept. 2	Frank Lary Det
22 (58)	June 14	Gary Bell Cle†	53 (135)	Sept. 2	Hank Aguirre* Det
23 (61)	June 17	Don Mossi* Det†	54 (140)	Sept. 6	Tom Cheney Was
24 (62)	June 18	Jerry Casale Det†	55 (141)	Sept. 7	Dick Stigman* Cle
25 (63)	June 19	Jim Archer* KC†	56 (143)	Sept. 9	Mudcat Grant Cle
26 (64)	June 20	Joe Nuxhall* KC†	57 (151)	Sept. 16	Frank Lary Det†
27 (66)	June 22	Norm Bass KC†	58 (152)	Sept. 17	Terry Fox Det†
28 (74)	July 1	Dave Sisler Was	59 (155)	Sept. 20	Milt Pappas Bal†
29 (75)	July 2	Pete Burnside* Was	60 (159)	Sept. 26	Jack Fisher Bal
30 (75)	July 2	Johnny Klippstein* Was	61 (163)	Oct. 1	Tracy Stallard Bos
31 (77)	July 4	Frank Lary Det			

Ruth's 60 Home Runs (1927)

HR (GM)	DATE	OFF (PITCHER/TEAM)	HR (GM)	DATE	OFF (PITCHER/TEAM)
1 (4)	Apr. 15	Howard Ehmke Phi	31 (94)	July 24	Tommy Thomas Chi†
2 (11)	Apr. 23	Rube Walberg* Phi†	32 (95)	July 26	Milt Gaston StL
3 (12)	Apr. 24	Sloppy Thurston Was†	33 (95)	July 26	
4 (14)	Apr. 29	Slim Harriss Bos†	34 (98)	July 28	Lefty Stewart* StL
5 (16)	May 1	Jack Quinn Phi	35 (106)	Aug. 5	George S. Smith Det
6 (16)	May 1	Rube Walberg* Phi	36 (110)	Aug. 10	Tom Zachary* Was†
7 (24)	May 10	Milt Gaston StL†	37 (114)	Aug. 16	Tommy Thomas Chi†
8 (25)	May 11	Ernie Nevers StL†	38 (115)	Aug. 17	Sarge Connally Chi†
9 (29)	May 17	Rip Collins Det†	39 (118)	Aug. 20	Jake Miller* Cle†
10 (33)	May 22	Ben Karr Cle†	40 (120)	Aug. 22	Joe Shaute* Cle†
11 (34)	May 23	Sloppy Thurston Was†	41 (124)	Aug. 27	Ernie Nevers StL†
12 (37)	May 28	Sloppy Thurston Was	42 (125)	Aug. 28	Ernie Wingard* StL†
13 (39)	May 29	Danny MacFayden Bos	43 (127)	Aug. 31	Tony Welzer Bos
14 (40)	May 30	Rube Walberg* Phi†	44 (128)	Sept. 2	Rube Walberg* Phi†
15 (42)	May 31	Jack Quinn Phi†	45 (132)	Sept. 6	Tony Welzer Bos†
16 (43)	May 31	Howard Ehmke Phi†	46 (132)	Sept. 6	
17 (47)	June 5	Earl Whitehill* Det	47 (133)	Sept. 6	Jack Russell Bos†
18 (48)	June 7	Tommy Thomas Chi	48 (134)	Sept. 7	Danny MacFayden Bos†
19 (52)	June 11	Garland Buckeye* Cle	49 (134)	Sept. 7	Slim Harriss Bos†
20 (52)	June 11		50 (138)	Sept. 11	Milt Gaston StL
21 (53)	June 12	George Uhle Cle	51 (139)	Sept. 13	Willis Hudlin Cle
22 (55)	June 16	Tom Zachary* StL	52 (140)	Sept. 13	Joe Shaute* Cle
23 (60)	June 22	Hal Wiltse* Bos†	53 (143)	Sept. 16	Ted Blankenship Chi
24 (60)	June 22		54 (147)	Sept. 18	Ted Lyons Chi
25 (70)	June 30	Slim Harriss Bos	55 (148)	Sept. 21	Sam Gibson Det
26 (73)	July 3	Hod Lisenbee Was†	56 (149)	Sept. 22	Ken Holloway Det
27 (78)	July 8	Don Hankins Det†	57 (152)	Sept. 27	Lefty Grove* Phi
28 (79)	July 9	Ken Holloway Det†	58 (153)	Sept. 29	Hod Lisenbee Was
29 (79)	July 9		59 (153)	Sept. 29	Paul Hopkins Was
30 (83)	July 12	Joe Shaute* Cle†	60 (154)	Sept. 30	Tom Zachary* Was

On-Base Percentage, Walks, and Intentional Walks

Despite Barry Bonds' assaults on the single season and career home run records, Bonds' most valuable achievements have come by way of his ability to get on base. Bonds' extraordinary strike zone judgment and plate discipline—combined with his opponents' sometimes irrational fear of his batting prowess—has enabled Bonds to obliterate all the major previous single-season records for walks and on-base percentage. Not once, but twice: first in 2002, then again in 2004.

Since 1893, when the distance from the pitching rubber to the plate was first set at its present length of sixty feet, six inches, the single-season walk and on-base percentage records have each been held by only four players.

The single-season record for intentional walks has changed more frequently since intentional walks became an official statistic in 1955, indicating changes in managerial tactics as well as the unique intimidation factor of Barry Bonds.

On-Base Percentage

YEAR	PLAYER, TEAM	OBP	YEAR	PLAYER, TEAM	OBP
1893	Billy Hamilton Phi NL	.490	1941	Ted Williams Bos AL	.553
1894	Billy Hamilton Phi NL	.522	2002	Barry Bonds SF NL	.582
1899	John McGraw Bal NL	.547	2004	Barry Bonds SF NL	.609

Walks

Year	Player, Team	BB
1893	Jack Crooks StL NL	121
1911	Jimmy Sheckard Chi NL	147
1920	Babe Ruth NY AL	150
1923	Babe Ruth NY AL	170
2002	Barry Bonds SF NL	198
2004	Barry Bonds SF NL	232

Intentional Walks

YEAR	PLAYER, TEAM	IBB
1955	Ted Kluszewski Cin NL	25
1956	Duke Snider Bro NL	26
1957	Ted Williams Bos AL	33
1969	Willie McCovey SF NL	45
2002	Barry Bonds SF NL	68
2004	Barry Bonds SF NL	120

Most Consecutive Hits

The ability to get 9 or more consecutive hits is not the sign of a great hitter; however, it is the sign of a good hitter who has gotten very lucky. Here is a list of those players who qualified as both skilled and fortunate.

NO.	PLAYER, TEAM	YEAR(S)	NO.	PLAYER, TEAM	YEAR(S)
12	Pinky Higgins, Bos AL	1938	9	Max Carey,Pit NL	1922
12	Walt Dropo, Det AL	1952	9	Rogers Hornsby, StL NL	1924
11	Tris Speaker, Cle AL	1920	9	Ty Cobb, Det AL	1925
11	Johnny Pesky, Bos AL	1946	9	Sam Rice, Was AL	1925
11	Bernie Williams, NY AL	2002	9	Taylor Douthit, StL NL	1926
10	Tom Parrott,Cin NL	1895	9	Babe Herman, Bro NL	1926
10	Jake Stenzel, Pit NL	1893	9	Hal Trosky, Cle AL	1936
10	Ed Delahanty, Phi NL	1897	9	Ted Williams, Bos AL	1939
10	Jake Gettman, Was NL	1897	9	Billy Jurges, NY NL	1941
10	Nap Lajoie, Phi AL	1901	9	Terry Moore, StL NL	1947
10	Ed Konetchy, Bro NL	1919	9	Dick Sisler, Phi NL	1950
10	George Sisler, StL AL	1921	9	Eddie Waitkus, Phi NL	1950
10	Harry Heilmann, Det AL	1922	9	Eddie Mathews, Mil NL	1954
10	Kiki Cuyler, Pit NL	1925	9	Clay Dalrymple, Phi NL	1961
10	Harry McCurdy, Chi AL	1926	9	Felipe Alou, SF NL	1962
10	Chick Hafey, StL NL	1929	9	Willie Stargell, Pit NL	1966
10	Joe Medwick, StL NL	1936	9	Tony Oliva, Min AL	1967
10	Rip Radcliff, Chi AL	1938	9	Rennie Stennett, Pit NL	1975
10	Buddy Hassett, Bos NL	1940	9	Ron Cey, LA NL	1977
10	Woody Williams, Cin NL	1943	9	Jorge Orta, Cle AL	1980
10	Ken Singleton, Bal AL	1981	9	Mickey Hatcher, Min AL	1985
10	Bip Roberts, Cin NL	1992	9	Andres Galarraga, Col NL	1993
10	Frank Thomas, Chi AL	1997	9	Sammy Sosa, Chi NL	1993
10	Joe Randa, KC AL	1999	9	Lance Johnson, Chi AL	1995
10	Frank Catalanotto, Tex AL	2000	9	Jose Vizcaino, NY NL	1996
10	Matt Diaz,Atl NL	2006	9	Barry Bonds, SF NL	1998
9	George Van Haltren, Bal AA	1891	9	John Olerud, NY NL	1998
9	Joe Kelley, Bal NL	1894	9	Todd Walker, Min AL	1998
9	Roger Connor, SL NL	1895	9	Charles Johnson, Bal AL	1999
9	Joe Kelley, Bal NL	1898	9	Jim Edmonds, StL NL	2000
9	George Stone,StL AL	1907	9	Ben Molina, Ana AL	2001
9	Johnny Bates,Cin NL	1911	9	Dmitri Young, Cin NL	2001
9	Doc Johnston, Cle AL	1919	9	Manny Ramirez, Bos AL	2002
9	Bobby Veach, Det AL	1921	9	Marcus Giles, Atl NL	2003
			9	Raul Ibanez, Sea AL	2004

Triple Crown Batters

It's been thirty-nine years since someone last won the Triple Crown, and an incredible sixty-nine years since a NL player has won one. With today's significantly stronger and larger talent base, it's much harder for an individual player to lead the league in all three glamorous offensive categories in a single year. The Triple Crown's three categories ensure that only a multidimensional hitter can win it, not just a home run hitter or a singles hitter with a very high average. Every twentieth-century Triple Crown winner is in the Hall of Fame.

PLAYER, TEAM	YEAR	AVG	HR	RBI
Tip O'Neill, StL AA	1887	.435	14	123
Nap Lajoie, Phi AL	1901	.426	14	125
Ty Cobb, Det AL	1909	.377	9	107
Rogers Hornsby, StL NL	1922	.401	42	152
Rogers Hornsby, StL NL	1925	.403	39	143
Jimmie Foxx, Phi AL	1933	.356	48	163
Chuck Klein, Phi NL	1933	.368	28	120
Lou Gehrig, NY AL	1934	.363	49	165

PLAYER, TEAM	YEAR	AVG	HR	RBI
Joe Medwick, StL NL	1937	.374	31	154
Ted Williams, Bos AL	1942	.356	36	163
Ted Williams, Bos AL	1947	.343	32	114
Mickey Mantle, NY AL	1956	.353	52	130
Frank Robinson, Bal AL	1966	.316	49	122
Carl Yastrzemski, Bos AL	1967	.326	44	121

Triple Crown Pitchers

Pitchers have won their Triple Crown more than twice as often as their batting counterparts, yet it remains an achievement that garners much less attention than its batting counterpart. The pitchers who win have to be dominating hurlers who receive solid run support from their offenses, but the skills required to win all three categories tend to work with each other, not against each other. Twenty-five of the 29 pitching Triple Crowns achieved since 1900 have been won by Hall of Famers or by recent pitchers seemingly assured of future Hall of Fame status.

YEAR	PLAYER, TEAM	WINS	ERA	SO
1877	Tommy Bond, Bos NL	40	2.11	170
1884	Guy Hecker, Lou AA	52	1.80	385
1884	Charley Radbourn, Pro NL	59	1.38	441
1888	Tim Keefe, NY NL	35	1.74	335
1889	John Clarkson, Bos NL	49	2.73	284
1894	Amos Rusie, NY NL	36	2.78	195
1901	Cy Young, Bos NL	33	1.62	158
1905	Rube Waddell, Phi, AL	27	1.48	287
1905	Christy Mathewson, NY NL	31	1.28	206
1913	Walter Johnson, Was AL	36	1.14	243
1915	Grover Alexander, Phi NL	31	1.22	241
1916	Grover Alexander, Phi NL	33	1.55	167
1917	Grover Alexander, Phi, NL	30	1.83	200
1918	Hippo Vaughn, Chi NL	22	1.74	148
1918	Walter Johnson, Was AL	23	1.27	162
1920	Grover Alexander, Chi NL	27	1.91	173
1924	Walter Johnson, Was	23	2.72	158
1924	Dazzy Vance, Bro NL	28	2.16	262
1930	Lefty Grove, Phi AL	28	2.54	209
1931	Lefty Grove, Phi AL	31	2.06	175
1934	Lefty Gomez, NY AL	26	2.33	158
1937	Lefty Gomez, NY AL	21	2.33	194
1939	Bucky Walters, Cin AL	27	2.29	137
1940	Bob Feller, Cle AL	27	2.61	261
1945	Hal Newhouser, Det AL	25	1.81	212
1963	Sandy Koufax, LA NL	25	1.88	306
1965	Sandy Koufax, LA NL	26	2.04	382
1966	Sandy Koufax, LA NL	27	1.73	317
1972	Steve Carlton, Phi NL	27	1.97	310
1985	Dwight Gooden, NY NL	24	1.53	268
1997	Roger Clemens, Tor AL	21	2.05	292
1998	Roger Clemens, Tor AL	20	2.65	271
1999	Pedro Martinez Bos AL	23	2.07	313
2002	Randy Johnson, Ari NL	24	2.32	334
2005	Johan Santana, Min AL	19	2.77	245

Most Strikeouts in a Game

When a pitcher strikes out at least 18 batters in a nine-inning game, he's almost certainly a dominating pitcher. If he's not yet a great pitcher, he probably will be one someday if he can refine his control. Pitching a game of this type is far more rare than a no-hitter, and it may be more of an achievement. Of the pitchers who have fanned 18 or more in a nine-inning game, only Randy Johnson failed to complete the game, pitching 9 of 11 innings in 2001 when he registered 20 K's. Tom Seaver struck out 10 in a row (a record in itself) on the way to his 19-strikeout game in 1970.

Not more than 9 innings pitched

PITCHER, TEAM	DATE	NO.
Roger Clemens, Bos AL	Apr. 29, 1986	20
Roger Clemens, Bos AL	Sept. 18, 1996	20
Kerry Wood, Chi NL	May 6, 1998	20
Randy Johnson, Ari NL	May 8, 2001	20
Charlie Sweeney, Pro NL	June 7, 1884	19
Hugh Daily, Chi UA	July 7, 1884	19
Steve Carlton, StL NL	Sept. 15, 1969	19
Tom Seaver, NY NL	Apr. 22, 1970	19
Nolan Ryan, Cal AL	Aug. 12, 1974	19
David Cone, NY NL	Oct. 6, 1991	19
Randy Johnson, Sea AL	June 24, 1997	19
Randy Johnson, Sea AL	Aug. 8, 1997	19
Dupee Shaw, Bos UA	July 19, 1884	18
Henry Porter, Mil UA	Oct. 3, 1884	18
Bob Feller, Cle AL	Oct. 2, 1938 G1	18
Sandy Koufax, LA NL	Aug. 31, 1959	18
Sandy Koufax, LA NL	Apr. 24, 1962	18
Don Wilson, Hou NL	July 14, 1968	18
Nolan Ryan, Cal AL	Sept. 10, 1976	18
Ron Guidry, NY AL	June 17, 1978	18
Bill Gullickson, Mon NL	Sept. 10, 1980	18
Ramon Martinez, LA NL	June 4, 1990	18
Randy Johnson, Sea AL	Sept. 27, 1992	18
Roger Clemens, Tor AL	Aug. 25, 1998	18
Ben Sheets, Mil NL	May 16, 2004	18

More than 9 innings pitched

PITCHER, TEAM	DATE	NO.
Tom Cheney, Was AL	Sept. 12, 1962	21 16 innings
Luis Tiant, Cle AL	July 3, 1968	19 10 innings
Nolan Ryan, Cal AL	June 14, 1974	19 12 innings
Nolan Ryan, Cal AL	Aug. 20, 1974	19 11 innings
Nolan Ryan, Cal AL	June 8, 1977	19 10 innings
Jim Whitney, Bos NL	June 14, 1884	18 15 innings
Jack Coombs, Phi AL	Sept. 1, 1906	18 24 innings
Warren Spahn, Bos NL	June 14, 1952	18 15 innings
Jim Maloney, Cin NL	June 14, 1965	18 11 innings
Chris Short, Phi NL	Oct. 2, 1965	18 15 IP of 18

Most Consecutive Save Opportunities Converted

Since the save rule first became an official part of baseball in 1969, both the definition of a save and the usage patterns of relievers have changed drastically. When Ken Tatum became the first pitcher to convert at least 15 straight save opportunities in a row in 1969 and 1970, 65 percent of his saves required more than one inning pitched. During Eric Gagne's streak of 84 straight save opportunities converted in 2002–04, however, he had to get more than three outs less than 25 percent of the time. Also, unlike Tatum, he was never called upon to make an appearance of more than 2 innings for any reason. So it would be unfair to say that the streaks listed below are strictly comparable. Nevertheless, the list does illustrate many of the greatest relief pitching streaks of the last 37 years —as well as the evolution of the closer's role.

YEAR(S)	PITCHER	SV	YEAR(S)	PITCHER	SV
1969–70	Ken Tatum, Cal AL	17	1991–92	Dennis Eckersley Oak AL	40
1969–70	Mudcat Grant, SL NL-Oak AL	22	1993–95	Rod Beck SF NL	40
1972	Clay Carroll Cin NL	23	1997–98	Trevor Hoffman SD NL	41
1972–73	John Hiller Det AL	24	1998–99	Tom Gordon Bos AL	54
1980	Rich Gossage NY AL	25	2002–04	Eric Gagne LA NL	84
1984	Willie Hernandez Det AL	32			

Gagne's 84-Save Streak

Eric Gagne didn't just break the old consecutive saves record with his 2002–04 streak; he shattered it. Earlier record holders often had the advantage of having an easier road than their predecessors as a result of the evolving role of the closer. Gagne, however, had no such advantage over Tom Gordon, the previous record holder, yet he still managed to exceed the old record by 55 percent. (Note: Runs and earned runs are combined since Gagne never allowed an unearned run during the streak.)

YEAR/DATE	MATCHUP	SCORE	IP	R/ER	YEAR/DATE	MATCHUP	SCORE	IP	R/ER
Aug. 28, 2002	Ari NL	1-0	1.0	0	July 27, 2003	Ari NL	1-0	1.1	0
Sept. 1, 2002	Hou NL	2-1	1.0	0	Aug. 5, 2003	Cin NL	5-2	1.0	0
Sept. 3, 2002	Ari NL	3-2	1.1	1	Aug. 6, 2003	Cin NL	2-1	1.0	0
Sept. 6, 2002	Hou NL	3-2	1.0	0	Aug. 7, 2003	Cin NL	4-3	1.0	0
Sept. 16, 2002	SF NL	7-6	1.2	0	Aug. 8, 2003	Chi NL	3-1	1.0	0
Sept. 21, 2002	SD NL	5-3	1.0	0	Aug. 14, 2003	Fla NL	6-4	1.0	0
Sept. 22, 2002	SD NL	4-3	1.0	0	Aug. 17, 2003	Chi NL	3-0	1.0	0
Sept. 26, 2002	SD NL	6-5	1.0	0	Aug. 21, 2003	Mon NL	2-1	1.0	0
April 8, 2003	Ari NL	5-3	1.0	0	Aug. 22, 2003	NY NL	2-1	1.0	0
April 9, 2003	Ari NL	5-2	1.0	0	Aug. 28, 2003	Hou NL	6-3	1.1	0
April 16, 2003	SD NL	3-0	1.0	0	Aug. 29, 2003	Col NL	6-4	1.0	0
April 17, 2003	SD NL	4-3	1.0	0	Aug. 31, 2003	Col NL	3-0	1.0	0
April 22, 2003	Cin NL	2-1	1.0	0	Sept. 2, 2003	Hou NL	4-1	1.1	0
April 25, 2003	Pit NL	5-2	1.0	0	Sept. 5, 2003	Col NL	8-7	1.0	0
April 26, 2003	Pit NL	4-3	1.0	0	Sept. 7, 2003	Col NL	6-2	1.0	0
April 30, 2003	Phi NL	4-0	0.1	0	Sept. 9, 2003	Ari NL	4-1	1.0	0
May 3, 2003	Pit NL	4-1	1.0	0	Sept. 14, 2003	SD NL	5-2	1.1	0
May 4, 2003	Pit NL	3-2	1.0	1	Sept. 18, 2003	Ari NL	2-0	2.0	0
May 7, 2003	NY NL	2-1	1.0	0	Sept. 21, 2003	SF NL	7-5	1.1	0
May 11, 2003	Mon NL	4-3	1.1	0	Sept. 23, 2003	SD NL	2-1	1.0	0
May 16, 2003	Fla NL	2-1	1.0	0	Sept. 24, 2003	SD NL	2-1	1.0	0
May 17, 2003	Fla NL	4-1	1.0	0	April 10, 2004	Col NL	7-4	1.0	0
May 18, 2003	Fla NL	2-1	1.0	0	April 15, 2004	SD NL	7-5	1.1	0
May 20, 2003	Col NL	3-1	1.0	0	April 16, 2004	SF NL	3-2	1.0	2
May 21, 2003	Col NL	3-2	1.0	0	April 17, 2004	SF NL	5-4	1.0	1
May 22, 2003	Col NL	4-3	1.0	0	April 18, 2004	SF NL	7-6	1.0	0
May 31, 2003	Mil NL	3-0	1.0	0	April 28, 2004	NY NL	3-2	1.1	0
June 5, 2003	KC AL	5-2	1.0	0	May 1, 2004	Mon NL	5-4	1.0	0
June 6, 2003	Chi AL	2-1	1.0	0	May 4, 2004	Fla NL	4-3	1.0	0
June 10, 2003	Det AL	3-1	1.0	0	May 6, 2004	Fla NL	9-4	0.1	0
June 11, 2003	Det AL	3-1	1.0	0	May 8, 2004	Pit NL	4-3	1.0	0
June 12, 2003	Det AL	3-2	1.0	0	May 25, 2004	Mil NL	5-3	1.0	0
June 13, 2003	Cle AL	4-3	1.0	0	May 30, 2004	Ari NL	3-0	1.0	0
June 15, 2003	Cle AL	4-3	1.0	0	June 2, 2004	Mil NL	5-2	1.1	1
June 17, 2003	SF NL	4-1	1.0	0	June 15, 2004	Bal AL	5-1	0.2	0
June 20, 2003	Ana AL	5-2	1.0	0	June 16, 2004	Bal AL	6-3	1.1	0
June 21, 2003	Ana AL	4-2	1.0	1	June 17, 2004	Bal AL	4-3	1.0	0
July 5, 2003	Ari NL	2-0	1.0	0	June 18, 2004	NY AL	6-3	1.0	0
July 9, 2003	SL NL	6-5	1.1	0	June 20, 2004	NY AL	5-4	1.1	1
July 17, 2003	SL NL	6-3	0.1	0	June 29, 2004	SF NL	2-1	1.0	0
July 18, 2003	SL NL	8-5	1.0	0	July 1, 2004	SF NL	5-4	1.0	0
July 22, 2003	Col NL	5-2	1.0	0	July 3, 2004	Ana AL	8-5	1.0	0

Consecutive Scoreless Inning Streaks

Orel Hershiser was the biggest baseball story of the year in 1988, even before he earned MVP awards in the NLCS and World Series. He broke Don Drysdale's record of 58.2 consecutive scoreless innings, hurling 10 shutout innings in his final start of the season to do it. It's a feat unlikely to be matched in the near future. Virtually all of the top streaks listed below were achieved in low-scoring environments, quite the opposite of the current state of baseball.

YEAR	DATES	PITCHER, TEAM	IP
1988	Aug. 30–Sept. 28	Orel Hershiser, LA NL	59.0
1968	May 14–June 8	Don Drysdale, LA NL	58.2
1913	Apr. 10–May 14	Walter Johnson, Was AL	55.2
1910	Sept. 5–Sept. 25	Jack Coombs, Phi AL	53.0
1968	June 2–June 26	Bob Gibson, StL NL	47.0
1933	July 13–Aug. 1	Carl Hubbell, NY NL	45.1
1950	Aug. 16–Sept. 13	Sal Maglie, NY NL	45.0
1904	Sept. 12–Sept. 30	Doc White, Chi AL	45.0
1904	Apr. 25–May 17	Cy Young, Bos AL	45.0
1908	Sept. 17–Oct. 3	Ed Reulbach, Chi NL	44.0
1905	Aug. 22–Sept. 5	Rube Waddell, Phi AL	43.2
1914	May 1–May 26	Rube Foster, Bos AL	42.0
1902	June 26–July 16	Jack Chesbro, Pit NL	41.0
1911	Sept. 7–Sept. 24	Grover Alexander, Phi NL	41.0
1917	Sept. 13–Oct. 4	Art Nehf, Bos NL	41.0
1968	Apr. 28–May 17	Luis Tiant, Cle AL	41.0
1918	May 7–May 26	Walter Johnson, Was AL	40.0
1967	Aug. 28–Sept. 10	Gaylord Perry, SF NL	40.0
1972	Aug. 19–Sept. 8	Luis Tiant, Bos AL	40.0

Multiple No-Hitters

Lots of mediocre pitchers have pitched a no-hitter, but throwing 2 no-hitters is a different story—that can't happen just by luck. Below is a list of all the pitchers who have thrown at least two no-hitters. Following this distinguished list are lists of perfect games, no-hitters, and unofficial no-hitters.

Some no-hitters came with their own unique twist. Hugh Daily's no-hitter in September 1883 was the first no-hitter ever thrown by a one-handed pitcher; Jim Abbott duplicated the feat 110 years later. Johnny Vander Meer's no-hitter on June 15, 1938 marked the only time a major leaguer has thrown no-hitters in consecutive starts. The only Opening Day no-hitter was thrown by Bob Feller on Apr. 16, 1940. The only postseason no-hitter was a perfect game pitched by Don Larsen during the World Series on October 8, 1956. Mike Scott pitched the only no-hitter to clinch a title—the 1986 NL Western Division championship—on September 25, 1986.

Perhaps the oddest no-hitter ever came on June 23, 1917 when Ernie Shore pitched one in relief. Shore rang up 27 outs by retiring 26 hitters in a row after Babe Ruth walked the first batter and argued himself out of the game; that runner was subsequently thrown out stealing. The most recent non-perfect no-hitter also deserves notice, because it required a record six pitchers: the starter, Roy Oswalt, had to be pulled after the first inning due to injury, and the Astros ran out five relief pitchers over the next eight innings on June 11, 2003.

Notes. Perfect games are listed separately from no-hitters. Italics indicate that it was the pitcher's first major league start. G1 and G2 denote first and second games of doubleheaders. Extra-inning games are noted in parentheses. CD means game was called on account of darkness. WS indicates World Series game. Finally, Loss means that the pitcher who threw the no-hitter also lost the game.

Pitchers with More Than One No-Hitter

Nolan Ryan	7	Jim Galvin	2	Dutch Leonard	2	Don Wilson	2
Sandy Koufax	4	Al Atkinson	2	Johnny Vander Meer	2	Ken Holtzman	2
Larry Corcoran	3	Adonis Terry	2	Allie Reynolds	2	Bill Stoneman	2
Cy Young	3	Ted Breitenstein	2	Virgil Trucks	2	Steve Busby	2
Bob Feller	3	Frank Smith	2	Carl Erskine	2	Bob Forsch	2
Jim Maloney	3	Addie Joss	2	Warren Spahn	2	Hideo Nomo	2
Christy Mathewson	2	Tom L. Hughes	2	Jim Bunning	2	Randy Johnson	2

Perfect Games

PITCHER	MATCHUP	SCORE	DATE
Lee Richmond	Wor vs. Cle NL	1-0	June 12, 1880
John M. Ward	Pro vs. Buf NL	5-0	June 17, 1880
Cy Young	Bos vs. Phi AL	3-0	May 5, 1904
Addie Joss	Cle vs. Chi AL	1-0	Oct. 2, 1908
Charlie Robertson	Chi at Det AL	2-0	Apr. 30, 1922
Jim Bunning	Phi at NY NL	6-0	June 21, 1964 G1
Don Larsen	NY AL vs. Bro NL	2-0	Oct. 8, 1956 WS
Sandy Koufax	LA vs. Chi NL,	1-0	Sept. 9, 1965
Catfish Hunter	Oak vs. Min AL	4-0	May 8, 1968
Len Barker	Cle vs. Tor AL	3-0	May 15, 1981
Mike Witt	Cal at Tex AL	1-0	Sept. 30, 1984
Tom Browning	Cin vs. LA NL	1-0	Sept. 16, 1988
Dennis Martinez	Mon at LA NL	2-0	July 28, 1991
Kenny Rogers	Tex vs. Cal AL	4-0	July 28, 1994
David Wells	NY vs. Min AL	4-0	May 17, 1998
David Cone	NY AL vs. Mon NL	6-0	July 18, 1999
Randy Johnson	Ari vs. Atl NL	2-0	May 18, 2004

No-Hit Games, Nine or More Innings

PITCHER	MATCHUP	SCORE	DATE
Joe Borden	Phi vs. Chi NA	4-0	July 28, 1875
George Bradley	StL vs. Har NL	2-0	July 15, 1876
Larry Corcoran	Chi vs. Bos NL	6-0	Aug. 19, 1880
Jim Galvin	Buf at Wor NL	1-0	Aug. 20, 1880
Tony Mullane	Lou at Cin AA	2-0	Sept. 11, 1882
Guy Hecker	Lou at Pit AA	3-1	Sept. 19, 1882
Larry Corcoran	Chi vs. Wor NL	5-0	Sept. 20, 1882
Charley Radbourn	Pro at Cle NL	8-0	July 25, 1883
Hugh Daily	Cle at Phi NL	1-0	Sept. 13, 1883
Al Atkisson	Phi vs. Pit AA	10-1	May 24, 1884
Ed Morris	Col at Pit AA	5-0	May 29, 1884
Frank Mountain	Col at Was AA	12-0	June 5, 1884
Larry Corcoran	Chi vs. Pro NL	6-0	June 27, 1884
Jim Galvin	Buf at Det NL	18-0	Aug. 4, 1884
Dick Burns	Cin at KC UA	3-1	Aug. 26, 1884
Ed Cushman	Mil vs. Was UA	5-0	Sept. 28, 1884
Sam Kimber	Bro vs. Tol AA	0-0	Oct. 4, 1884 CD (10 inn)
John Clarkson	Chi at Pro NL	4-0	July 27, 1885
Charlie Ferguson	Phi vs. Pro NL	1-0	Aug. 29, 1885
Al Atkisson	Phi vs. NY AA	3-2	May 1, 1886
Adonis Terry	Bro vs. StL AA	1-0	July 24, 1886
Matt Kilroy	Bal at Pit AA	6-0	Oct. 6, 1886
Adonis Terry	Bro vs. Lou AA	4-0	May 27, 1888
Henry Porter	KC at Bal AA	4-0	June 6, 1888
Ed Seward	Phi vs. Cin AA	12-2	July 26, 1888
Gus Weyhing	Phi vs. KC AA	4-0	July 31, 1888
Cannonball Titcomb	Roc vs. Syr AA	7-0	Sept. 15, 1890
Tom Lovett	Bro vs. NY NL	4-0	June 22, 1891
Amos Rusie	NY vs. Bro NL	6-0	July 31, 1891
Ted Breitenstein	*StL vs. Lou AA*	*8-0*	*Oct. 4, 1891 G1*
Jack Stivetts	Bos vs. Bro NL	11-0	Aug. 6, 1892
Ben Sanders	Lou vs. Bal NL	6-2	Aug. 22, 1892
Bumpus Jones	*Cin vs. Pit NL*	*7-1*	*Oct. 15, 1892*
Bill Hawke	Bal vs. Was NL	5-0	Aug. 16, 1893
Cy Young	Cle vs. Cin NL	6-0	Sept. 18, 1897 G1
Ted Breitenstein	Cin vs. Pit NL	11-0	Apr. 22, 1898
Jim Hughes	Bal vs. Bos NL	8-0	Apr. 22, 1898
Red Donahue	Phi vs. Bos NL	5-0	July 8, 1898
Walter Thornton	Chi vs. Bro NL	2-0	Aug. 21, 1898 G2
Deacon Phillippe	Lou vs. NY NL	7-0	May 25, 1899
Noodles Hahn	Cin vs. Phi NL	4-0	July 12, 1900
Christy Mathewson	NY at StL NL	5-0	July 15, 1901
Nixey Callahan	Chi vs. Det AL	3-0	Sept. 20, 1902 G1
Chick Fraser	Phi at Chi NL	10-0	Sept. 18, 1903 G2
Jesse Tannehill	Bos at Chi AL	6-0	Aug. 17, 1904
Christy Mathewson	NY at Chi NL	1-0	June 13, 1905
Weldon Henley	Phi at StL AL	6-0	July 22, 1905 G1
Frank Smith	Chi at Det AL	15-0	Sept. 6, 1905 G2
Bill Dinneen	Bos vs. Chi AL	2-0	Sept. 27 1905 G1
Johnny Lush	Phi at Bro NL	6-0	May 1, 1906
Mal Eason	Bro at StL NL	2-0	July 20, 1906
Frank (Jeff) Pfeffer	Bos vs. Cin NL	6-0	May 8, 1907
Nick Maddox	Pit vs. Bro NL	2-1	Sept. 20, 1907
Cy Young	Bos at NY AL	8-0	June 30, 1908
Hooks Wiltse	NY vs. Phi NL	1-0	July 4, 1908 G1 (10 inn)
Nap Rucker	Bro vs. Bos NL	6-0	Sept. 5, 1908 G2
Dusty Rhoads	Cle vs. Bos AL	2-1	Sept. 18, 1908
Frank Smith	Chi vs. Phi AL	1-0	Sept. 20, 1908
Addie Joss	Cle at Chi AL	1-0	Apr. 20, 1910
Chief Bender	Phi vs. Cle AL	4-0	May 12, 1910
Joe Wood	Bos vs. StL AL	5-0	July 29, 1911 G2
Ed Walsh	Chi vs. Bos AL	5-0	Aug. 27, 1911
George Mullin	Det vs. StL AL	7-0	July 4, 1912 G2
Earl Hamilton	StL at Det AL	5-1	Aug. 30, 1912
Jeff Tesreau	NY at Phi NL	3-0	Sept. 6, 1912 G1
Joe Benz	Chi vs. Cle AL	6-1	May 31, 1914
George Davis	Bos vs. Phi NL	7-0	Sept. 9, 1914 G2
Ed Lafitte	Bro vs. KC FL	6-2	Sept. 19, 1914 G1
Rube Marquard	NY vs. Bro NL	2-0	Apr. 15, 1915
Frank Allen	Pit at StL FL	2-0	Apr. 24, 1915
Claude Hendrix	Chi at Pit FL	10-0	May 15, 1915
Alex Main	KC at Buf FL	5-0	Aug. 16, 1915
Jimmy Lavender	Chi at NY NL	2-0	Aug. 31, 1915 G1
Dave Davenport	StL vs. Chi FL	3-0	Sept. 7, 1915 G1
Tom L. Hughes	Bos vs. Pit NL	2-0	June 16, 1916
Rube Foster	Bos vs. NY AL	2-0	June 21, 1916
Joe Bush	Phi vs. Cle AL	5-0	Aug. 26, 1916
Dutch Leonard	Bos vs. StL AL	4-0	Aug. 30, 1916
Eddie Cicotte	Chi at StL AL	11-0	Apr. 14, 1917
George Mogridge	NY at Bos AL	2-1	Apr. 24, 1917
Fred Toney	Cin at Chi NL	1-0	May 2, 1917 (10 inn)
Ernie Koob	StL vs. Chi AL	1-0	May 5, 1917
Bob Groom	StL vs. Chi AL	3-0	May 6, 1917 G2
Ernie Shore	Bos vs. Was AL	4-0	June 23, 1917 G1
Dutch Leonard	Bos at Det AL	5-0	June 3, 1918
Hod Eller	Cin vs. StL NL	6-0	May 11, 1919
Ray Caldwell	Cle at NY AL	3-0	Sept. 10, 1919 G1
Walter Johnson	Was at Bos AL	1-0	July 1, 1920
Jesse Barnes	NY vs. Phi NL	6-0	May 7, 1922
Sam Jones	NY at Phi AL	2-0	Sept. 4, 1923
Howard Ehmke	Bos at Phi AL	4-0	Sept. 7, 1923
Jesse Haines	StL vs. Bos NL	5-0	July 17, 1924
Dazzy Vance	Bro vs. Phi NL	10-1	Sept. 13, 1925 G1
Ted Lyons	Chi at Bos AL	6-0	Aug. 21, 1926
Carl Hubbell	NY vs. Pit NL	11-0	May 8, 1929
Wes Ferrell	Cle vs. StL AL	9-0	Apr. 29, 1931
Bobby Burke	Was vs. Bos AL	5-0	Aug. 8, 1931
Paul Dean	StL at Bro NL	3-0	Sept. 21, 1934 G2
Vern Kennedy	Chi vs. Cle AL	5-0	Aug. 31, 1935
Bill Dietrich	Chi vs. StL AL	8-0	June 1, 1937
Johnny Vander Meer	Cin vs. Bos NL	3-0	June 11, 1938
Johnny Vander Meer	Cin at Bro NL	6-0	June 15, 1938

PITCHER	MATCHUP	SCORE	DATE
Monte Pearson	NY vs. Cle AL	13-0	Aug. 27, 1938 G2
Bob Feller	Cle at Chi AL	1-0	Apr. 16, 1940 OD
Tex Carleton	Bro at Cin NL	3-0	Apr. 30, 1940
Lon Warneke	StL at Cin NL	2-0	Aug. 30, 1941
Jim Tobin	Bos vs. Bro NL	2-0	Apr. 27, 1944
Clyde Shoun	Cin vs. Bos NL	1-0	May 15, 1944
Dick Fowler	Phi vs. StL AL	1-0	Sept. 9, 1945 G2
Ed Head	Bro vs. Bos NL	5-0	Apr. 23, 1946
Bob Feller	Cle at NY AL	1-0	Apr. 30, 1946
Ewell Blackwell	Cin vs. Bos NL	6-0	June 18, 1947
Don Black	Cle vs. Phi AL	3-0	July 10, 1947 G1
Bill McCahan	Phi vs. Was AL	3-0	Sept. 3, 1947
Bob Lemon	Cle at Det AL	2-0	June 30, 1948
Rex Barney	Bro at NY NL	2-0	Sept. 9, 1948
Vern Bickford	Bos vs. Bro NL	7-0	Aug. 11, 1950
Cliff Chambers	Pit at Bos NL	3-0	May 6, 1951 G2
Bob Feller	Cle vs. Det AL	2-1	July 1, 1951 G1
Allie Reynolds	NY at Cle AL	1-0	July 12, 1951
Allie Reynolds	NY vs. Bos AL	8-0	Sept. 28, 1951 G1
Virgil Trucks	Det vs. Was AL	1-0	May 15, 1952
Carl Erskine	Bro vs. Chi NL	5-0	June 19, 1952
Virgil Trucks	Det at NY AL	1-0	Aug. 25, 1952
Bobo Holloman	*StL vs. Phi AL*	*6-0*	*May 6, 1953*
Jim Wilson	Mil vs. Phi NL	2-0	June 12, 1954
Sam Jones	Chi vs. Pit NL	4-0	May 12, 1955
Carl Erskine	Bro vs. NY NL	3-0	May 12, 1956
Mel Parnell	Bos vs. Chi AL	4-0	July 14, 1956
Sal Maglie	Bro vs. Phi NL	5-0	Sept. 25, 1956
Bob Keegan	Chi vs. Was AL	6-0	Aug. 20, 1957 G2
Jim Bunning	Det at Bos AL	3-0	July 20, 1958 G1
Hoyt Wilhelm	Bal vs. NY AL	1-0	Sept. 20, 1958
Don Cardwell	Chi vs. StL NL	4-0	May 15, 1960 G2
Lew Burdette	Mil vs. Phi NL	1-0	Aug. 18, 1960
Warren Spahn	Mil vs. Phi NL	4-0	Sept. 16, 1960
Warren Spahn	Mil vs. SF NL	1-0	Apr. 28, 1961
Bo Belinsky	LA vs. Bal AL	2-0	May 5, 1962
Earl Wilson	Bos vs. LA AL	2-0	June 26, 1962
Sandy Koufax	LA vs. NY NL	5-0	June 30, 1962
Bill Monbouquette	Bos at Chi AL	1-0	Aug. 1, 1962
Jack Kralick	Min vs. KC AL	1-0	Aug. 26, 1962
Sandy Koufax	LA vs. SF NL	8-0	May 11, 1963
Don Nottebart	Hou vs. Phi NL	4-1	May 17, 1963
Juan Marichal	SF vs. Hou NL	1-0	June 15, 1963
Ken T. Johnson	Hou vs. Cin NL	0-1	Apr. 23, 1964 Loss
Sandy Koufax	LA at Phi NL	3-0	June 4, 1964
Jim Maloney	Cin at Chi NL	1-0	Aug. 19, 1965 G1 (10 inn)
Dave Morehead	Bos vs. Cle AL	2-0	Sept. 16, 1965
Sonny Siebert	Cle vs. Was AL	2-0	June 10, 1966
Steve D. Barber (8.2 IP) & Stu Miller (0.1 IP)	Bal vs. Det AL	1-2	Apr. 30, 1967 G1 Loss
Don Wilson	Hou vs. Atl NL	2-0	June 18, 1967
Dean Chance	Min at Cle AL	2-1	Aug. 25, 1967 G2
Joe Horlen	Chi vs. Det AL	6-0	Sept. 10, 1967 G1
Tom Phoebus	Bal vs. Bos AL	6-0	Apr. 27, 1968
George Culver	Cin at Phi NL	6-1	July 29, 1968 G2
Gaylord Perry	SF vs. StL NL	1-0	Sept. 17, 1968
Ray Washburn	StL at SF NL	2-0	Sept. 18, 1968
Bill Stoneman	Mon at Phi NL	7-0	Apr. 17, 1969
Jim Maloney	Cin vs. Hou NL	10-0	Apr. 30, 1969
Don Wilson	Hou at Cin NL	4-0	May 1, 1969
Jim Palmer	Bal vs. Oak AL	8-0	Aug. 13, 1969
Ken Holtzman	Chi vs. Atl NL	3-0	Aug. 19, 1969
Bob Moose	Pit at NY NL	4-0	Sept. 20, 1969
Dock Ellis	Pit at SD NL	2-0	June 12, 1970 G1
Clyde Wright	Cal vs. Oak AL	4-0	July 3, 1970
Bill Singer	LA vs. Phi NL	5-0	July 20, 1970
Vida Blue	Oak vs. Min AL	6-0	Sept. 21, 1970
Ken Holtzman	Chi at Cin NL	1-0	June 3, 1971
Rick Wise	Phi at Cin NL	4-0	June 23, 1971
Bob Gibson	StL at Pit NL	11-0	Aug. 14, 1971
Burt Hooton	Chi vs. Phi NL	4-0	Apr. 16, 1972
Milt Pappas	Chi vs. SD NL	8-0	Sept. 2, 1972
Bill Stoneman	Mon vs. NY NL	7-0	Oct. 2, 1972 G1
Steve Busby	KC at Det AL	3-0	Apr. 16, 1973
Nolan Ryan	Cal at KC AL	3-0	May 15, 1973
Nolan Ryan	Cal at Det AL	6-0	July 15, 1973
Jim Bibby	Tex at Oak AL	6-0	July 30, 1973
Phil Niekro	Atl vs. SD NL	9-0	Aug. 5, 1973
Steve Busby	KC at Mil AL	2-0	June 19, 1974
Dick Bosman	Cle vs. Oak AL	4-0	July 19, 1974
Nolan Ryan	Cal vs. Min AL	4-0	Sept. 28, 1974
Nolan Ryan	Cal vs. Bal AL	1-0	June 1, 1975
Ed Halicki	SF vs. NY NL	6-0	Aug. 24, 1975 G2
Vida Blue (5 IP), Glenn Abbott (1 IP), Paul Lindblad (1 IP) & Rollie Fingers (2 IP)	Oak vs. Cal AL	5-0	Sept. 28, 1975
Larry Dierker	Hou vs. Mon NL	6-0	July 9, 1976
Blue Moon Odom (5 IP) & Francisco Barrios (4 IP)	Chi at Oak AL	2-1	July 28, 1976
John Candelaria	Pit vs. LA NL	2-0	Aug. 9, 1976
John Montefusco	SF at Atl NL	9-0	Sept. 29, 1976
Jim Colborn	KC vs. Tex AL	6-0	May 14, 1977
Dennis Eckersley	Cle vs. Cal AL	1-0	May 30, 1977
Bert Blyleven	Tex at Cal AL	6-0	Sept. 22, 1977
Bob Forsch	StL vs. Phi NL	5-0	Apr. 16, 1978
Tom Seaver	Cin vs. StL NL	4-0	June 16, 1978
Ken Forsch	Hou vs. Atl NL	6-0	Apr. 7, 1979
Jerry Reuss	LA at SF NL	8-0	June 27, 1980
Charlie Lea	Mon vs. SF NL	4-0	May 10, 1981 G2
Nolan Ryan	Hou vs. LA NL	5-0	Sept. 26, 1981
Dave Righetti	NY vs. Bos AL	4-0	July 4, 1983
Bob Forsch	StL vs. Mon NL	3-0	Sept. 26, 1983
Mike Warren	Oak vs. Chi AL	3-0	Sept. 29, 1983
Jack Morris	Det at Chi AL	4-0	Apr. 7, 1984
Joe Cowley	Chi at Cal AL	7-1	Sept. 19, 1986
Mike Scott	Hou vs. SF NL	2-0	Sept. 25, 1986
Juan Nieves	Mil at Bal AL	7-0	Apr. 15, 1987
Mark Langston (7 IP) & Mike Witt (2 IP)	Cal vs. Sea AL	1-0	Apr. 11, 1990
Randy Johnson	Sea vs. Det AL	2-0	June 2, 1990
Nolan Ryan	Tex at Oak AL	5-0	June 11, 1990
Dave Stewart	Oak at Tor AL	5-0	June 29, 1990
Fernando Valenzuela	LA vs. StL NL	6-0	June 29, 1990
Terry Mulholland	Phi vs. SF NL	6-0	Aug. 15, 1990
Dave Stieb	Tor at Cle AL	3-0	Sept. 2, 1990
Nolan Ryan	Tex vs. Tor AL	3-0	May 1, 1991
Tommy Greene	Phi at Mon NL	2-0	May 23, 1991
Bob Milacki (6 IP), Mike Flanagan (1 IP), Mark Williamson (1 IP) & Gregg Olson (1 IP)	Bal at Oak AL	2-0	July 13, 1991
Wilson Alvarez	Chi at Bal AL	7-0	Aug. 11, 1991
Bret Saberhagen	KC vs. Chi AL	7-0	Aug. 26, 1991
Kent Mercker (6 IP), Mark Wohlers (2 IP) & Alejandro Pena (1 IP)	Atl at SD NL	1-0	Sept. 11, 1991
Kevin Gross	LA vs. SF NL	2-0	Aug. 17, 1992
Chris Bosio	Sea vs. Bos AL	7-0	Apr. 22, 1993
Jim Abbott	NY vs. Cle AL	4-0	Sept. 4, 1993
Darryl Kile	Hou vs. NY NL	7-1	Sept. 8, 1993
Kent Mercker	Atl at LA NL	6-0	Apr. 8, 1994
Scott Erickson	Min vs. Mil AL	6-0	Apr. 27, 1994
Ramon Martinez	LA vs. Fla NL	7-0	July 14, 1995
Al Leiter	Fla vs. Col NL	11-0	May 11, 1996
Dwight Gooden	NY vs. Sea AL	2-0	May 14, 1996
Hideo Nomo	LA at Col NL	9-0	Sept. 17, 1996
Kevin Brown	Fla at SF NL	9-0	June 10, 1997
Francisco Cordova (9 IP) & Ricardo Rincon (1 IP)	Pit vs. Hou NL	3-0	July 12, 1997
Jose Jimenez	StL at Ari NL	1-0	June 25, 1999
Eric Milton	Min vs. Ana AL	7-0	Sept. 11, 1999
Hideo Nomo	Bos at Bal AL	3-0	Apr. 4, 2001
A.J. Burnett	Fla at SD NL	3-0	May 12, 2001
Bud Smith	StL at SD NL	4-0	Sept. 3, 2001
Derek Lowe	Bos vs. TB AL	10-0	Apr. 27, 2002
Kevin Millwood	Phi vs. SF NL	1-0	Apr. 27, 2003
Roy Oswalt (1 IP), Peter Munro (2.2 IP), Kirk Saarloos (1.1 IP), Brad Lidge (2 IP), Octavio Dotel (1 IP) & Billy Wagner (1 IP)	Hou NL at NY AL	8-0	June 11, 2003
Anibal Sanchez	Fla vs. Ari. NL	2-0	Sept. 6, 2006

No-Hit Games, Less Than 9 Innings Pitched

Sometimes even the best days end too soon. Many no-hit bids have been spoiled by rain, by darkness, by having to catch a train, or simply by prior agreement. Three times a pitcher has held the home club hitless for 8 innings, only to not pitch the ninth because his team lost and the game was over. One much luckier pitcher actually allowed a hit in a short no-hit game, but showers washed that blemish away when in 1959 Mike McCormick allowed a hit in the sixth before rain caused the game to revert to 5 innings. Bold signifies an abbreviated perfect game.

PITCHER	INNINGS	REASON	MATCHUP	SCORE	DATE
Larry McKeon	6	rain	Ind at Cin AA	0-0	May 6, 1884
Charlie Gagus	8	darkness	Was vs. Wil UA	12-1	Aug. 21, 1884
Charlie Getzien	6	rain	Det vs. Phi NL	1-0	Oct. 1, 1884
Charlie Sweeney (2 IP) & Henry Boyle (3 IP)	5	rain	StL vs. StP UA	0-1	Oct. 5, 1884
Dupee Shaw	5	agreement	Pro at Buf NL	4-0	Oct. 7, 1885 G1
George Van Haltren	6	rain	Chi vs. Pit NL	1-0	June 21, 1888
Ed Crane	7	darkness	NY vs. Was NL	3-0	Sept. 27, 1888
Matt Kilroy	7	darkness	Bal vs. StL AA	0-0	July 29, 1889 G2
Silver King	8	road loss	Chi vs. Bro PL	0-1	June 21, 1890 Loss
George Nicol	7	darkness	StL vs. Phi AA	21-2	Sept. 23, 1890
Hank Gastright	8	darkness	Col vs. Tol AA	6-0	Oct. 12, 1890
Jack Stivetts	5	Bos. train	Bos at Was NL	4-0	Oct. 15, 1892 G2
Elton Chamberlain	7	darkness	Cin vs. Bos NL	6-0	Sept. 23, 1893 G2
Ed Stein	6	rain	Bro vs. Chi NL	6-0	June 2, 1894
Red Ames	5	darkness	NY at StL NL	5-0	Sept. 14, 1903 G2
Rube Waddell	5	rain	Phi vs. StL AL	2-0	Aug. 15, 1905
Jake Weimer	7	agreement	Cin vs. Bro NL	1-0	Aug. 24, 1906 G2
Stoney McGlynn	7	agreement	StL at Bro NL	1-1	Sept. 24, 1906 G2
Lefty Leifield	6	darkness	Pit at Phi NL	8-0	Sept. 26, 1906 G2
Ed Walsh	5	rain	Chi vs. NY AL	8-1	May 26, 1907
Ed Karger	**7**	**agreement**	**StL vs. Bos NL**	**4-0**	**Aug. 11, 1907 G2**
Howie Camnitz	5	agreement	Pit at NY NL	1-0	Aug. 23, 1907 G2
Rube Vickers	**5**	**darkness**	**Phi at Was AL**	**4-0**	**Oct. 5, 1907 G2**
Johnny Lush	6	rain	StL at Bro NL	2-0	Aug. 6, 1908
King Cole	7	Chi. train	Chi at StL NL	4-0	July 31, 1910 G2
Jay Cashion	6	Cle. train	Was vs. Cle AL	2-0	Aug. 20, 1912 G2
Walter Johnson	7	rain	Was vs. StL AL	2-0	Aug. 25, 1924
Fred Frankhouse	7.2	rain	Bro vs. Cin NL	5-0	Aug. 27, 1937
John Whitehead	6	rain	StL vs. Det AL	4-0	Aug. 5, 1940 G2
Jim Tobin	5	darkness	Bos vs. Phi NL	7-0	June 22, 1944 G2
Mike McCormick	5	rain	SF at Phi NL	3-0	June 12, 1959
Sam Jones	7	rain	SF at StL NL	4-0	Sept. 26, 1959
Dean Chance	**5**	**rain**	**Min vs. Bos AL**	**2-0**	**Aug. 6, 1967**
David Palmer	**5**	**rain**	**Mon at StL NL**	**4-0**	**Apr. 21, 1984 G2**
Pascual Perez	5	rain	Mon at Phi NL	1-0	Sept. 24, 1988
Andy Hawkins	8	road loss	NY at Chi AL	0-4	July 1, 1990 Loss
Melido Perez	6	rain	Chi at NY AL	8-0	July 12, 1990
Matt Young	8	road loss	Bos at Cle AL	1-2	Apr. 12, 1992 G1 Loss
Devern Hansack	5	rain	Bos vs Bal AL	9-0	Oct. 1, 2006

No-Hitters Broken Up in Extra Innings

Sometimes even the best days can be spoiled by bad luck or by a lack of support. Harvey Haddix's famous 1959 perfect game remains the benchmark for magnificent failure, but many other pitchers have had their no-hit efforts torpedoed after the regulation 9 innings.

PITCHER	MATCHUP	SCORE	DATE	COMMENT
Earl Moore	Cle vs. Chi AL	2-4	May 9, 1901	Lost on 2 hits in 10th
Bob Wicker	Chi at NY NL	1-0	June 11, 1904	Won in 12 inn. after 1st hit in 10th
Harry McIntyre	Bro vs. Pit NL	0-1	Aug. 1, 1906	Lost on 4 hits in 13 inn. after 1st hit in 11th
Red Ames	NY vs. Bro NL	0-3	Apr. 15, 1909	Lost on 7 hits in 13 inn. after 1st hit in 10th
Tom L. Hughes	NY vs. Cle AL	0-5	Aug. 30, 1910 G2	Lost on 7 hits in 11 inn. after 1st hit in 10th
Jim Scott	Chi at Was AL	0-1	May 14, 1914	Lost on 2 hits in 10th
Hippo Vaughn	Chi vs. Cin NL	0-1	May 2, 1917	Lost on 2 hits in 10th; Fred Toney pitched no-hitter in this game
Bobo Newsom	StL vs. Bos AL	1-2	Sept. 18, 1934	Lost on 1 hit in 10th
Johnny Klippstein (7 IP), Hershell Freeman (1 IP) & Joe Black (3 IP)	Cin at Mil NL	1-2	May 26, 1956	Lost on 3 hits in 11 inn. after 1st hit in 10th
Harvey Haddix	Pit at Mil NL	0-1	May 26, 1959	Lost on hit in 13th after 12 perfect innings
Jim Maloney	Cin vs. NY NL	0-1	June 14, 1965	Lost on 2 hits in 11th
Mark Gardner	Mon at LA NL	0-1	July 26, 1991	9 IP, lost on 2 hits in 10th; relieved by Jeff Fassero, who allowed 1 hit
Pedro J. Martinez (9 IP) & Mel Rojas (1 IP)	Mon at SD NL	1-0	June 3, 1995	Martinez pitched 9 perfect innings but allowed hit in 10th; Rojas finished game

FIELDS OF DREAMS: BIG LEAGUE BALLPARKS

After the success of Phil Alden Robinson's 1989 movie *Field of Dreams*—based upon W.P. Kinsella's terrific novel *Shoeless Joe*—the phrase has become a staple of American vocabulary. Baseball parks are truly fields of dreams, both for those who play there as well as those who root from the stands. They are idiosyncratic, individual, and—when designed and built with care—as much a part of urban life as commercial buildings or government offices. Other sports have their stadiums, but only *baseball* has *ballparks,* a felicitous marriage of two of the most joyous words in the English language.

Since the 1870s, the parks that baseball has been played in have evolved as much as the game itself. Ballparks have always been constructed using the latest technology available, whether they were the wood parks of the game's early days, the concrete- and-steel edifices of the early 1900s, the enormous superstadiums of the 1960s and 1970s, or today's fashionable steel-and-brick retro designs. Many ballparks have been built on a tight budget, from the quickly constructed skeletons of the 1880s to some of the latest retro parks.

Ballparks didn't start out by simply providing cheap seats for the regular guys. Contrary to what many might think, private boxes—constructed to separate the rich from the rest of the crowd—existed almost from the inception of the first ballpark as the moneyed sat apart from their lower-class brethren. Al Spalding, owner of the Chicago White Stockings, had a private telephone line run into his owner's box at Lakefront Park in the 1880s so he could conduct business during the games. At the same time, St. Louis' American Association ballpark had a special seating pavilion devoted just to high society.

There's no such discrimination in this section of the encyclopedia, where low-grade facilities in out-of-the-way cities like Altoona in 1884 rub shoulders with the splendor of modern Meccas like Oriole Park at Camden Yards in Baltimore. Each facility served, however briefly, as a venue for big league games and qualifies, therefore, as a major league ballpark. Some parks served as home fields for several teams and will, therefore, have two or more entries.

On the following pages you will see an entry with details on every park that has hosted a major league game since 1871. The section is organized by major league city, with each park in a city shown chronologically by opening year from 1871 to the present. Ballparks are listed under their current (or their last) name, with any earlier (official) names noted in italics. Common nicknames for ballparks are in quotes. Current major league ballparks are shown in bold.

The **Open** column shows the first and last years that a park was used for major league games. Current parks will have only an opening year. Parks that are no longer used by a major league team but which are still standing (e.g., Tiger Stadium) are indicated with an asterisk.

All clubs that called a park home for even one game are included in the **Tenants** column. Current (or last) team names are used for all entries; so the NL Dodgers are called the Dodgers in all entries, even if they were known as the Robins or Superbas at one time. Short-lived St. Paul in the Union Association never played any home games and therefore, has no listing. League abbreviations are the same as in the player registers.

Capacity lists each park's current or final seating capacity along with its initial seating capacity (when known) in parentheses. There were no recorded capacities or dimensions for most nineteenth century ballparks, and such details for early twentieth century parks are frequently lacking.

The next two columns give details on each ballpark's configuration showing its most important **Dimensions.** The **Current** or **Final** dimensions for parks are listed in the fifth column. Each park's **Original** dimensions, if known, are listed in the sixth column. From left to right, the dimensions shown are left field foul line (**LF**), left-center field (**LCF**), center field (**CF**), right-center field (**RCF**), and right field foul line (**RF**). LF-LCF and RF-RCF are separated by hyphens; CF is delimited by slashes. If the deepest part of the ballpark was *not* straightaway center field, the deepest dimension (if known) is shown in the **Notes** column. Question marks indicate unknown dimensions.

Despite the painstaking research done by Philip Lowry, Michael Benson, Michael Gershman, Larry Ritter, and others, there is still much that we do not know about the parks of the nineteenth century. This is, in part, because no one kept careful records of such things. However, another reason is that, back in the very "old days," baseball fields often did not even *have* dimensions as such—they were essentially big pastures with the playing diamonds laid out on them.

Some of the earliest parks lacked grandstands as well; those that did have grandstands lacked bleachers until the twentieth century. Overflow crowds were typically accommodated by allowing them to stand in foul territory or in fair territory behind the outfielders—in many pictures from the 1890s, horse-drawn carriages, holding fans, still ringed the outfield.

It is very interesting to note how dimensions have changed over the years. In days of yore, ballparks were built on whatever convenient piece of land could hold them, thus rendering most parks asymmetrical. For instance, New York's Polo Grounds, through its demise in 1962, had foul lines of less than 300 feet and a center field fence more than 200 feet deeper. To mitigate somewhat the effects of extremely short fences, the leagues drew up ground rules to eliminate cheap home runs. Finally, in the 1950s, the major leagues instituted minimum outfield fence distances for newly built parks.

From the mid-1960s through the 1980s, new park design involved symmetrical dimensions designed to accommodate football fields. These uniform venues seemed to reflect clean-lined, suburban spaciousness rather than the intimate urban settings of classic ballparks. The paradigm shift caused by the opening of Camden Yards has convinced teams that fans want odd dimensions and asymmetrical features as well as intimate spaces and comfortable seats and amenities. So these retro ballparks are deliberately asymmetrical, though this is now being done mostly for aesthetic reasons.

The **Notes** column includes miscellaneous information about artificial turf; domes or retractable roofs; and when lights were installed (if the park didn't have lights when it opened). No ballpark that closed before 1935 ever had lights; every ballpark built afterward always had lights. A *p* next to a year indicates the information applied for only part of that year.

Finally, if a team played a "home" game in a park that was not located in its hometown, the location of that park is shown in square brackets. In the 1800s, clubs often played official league games at neutral sites, either to benefit from a larger gate or to squeeze in a game—and, thus, a gate—on long road trips.

The last page of the Ballparks section has a list of all spring training sites for AL, NL, and Federal League clubs since 1901. The sites are shown chronologically by franchise, so the original Washington Senators spring training sites from 1901–60 are under Minnesota, and the expansion Senators spring bases from 1961–71 are under Texas.

A few teams will have two spring sites listed for some years. This is either because they trained at one city before moving to another city to play most or all of their home exhibition games, or because split their spring camps into two locations. Neutral sites (where teams sometimes play a game or two on the way home from spring training) are not shown.

In a few rare cases, teams play no or very few home spring games—the Mariners played all of their spring games in other teams' parks in Arizona in 1993 while their new ballpark in Peoria was being built.

BALLPARK	OPEN	TENANTS	CAPACITY	DIMENSIONS LF-LCF/CF/RCF-RF CURRENT/FINAL	ORIGINAL	NOTES
ALTOONA, PA						
Columbia Park	1884	UA Mountain Citys				
ANAHEIM/LOS ANGELES [CALIFORNIA 1966–96]						
Angel Stadium of Anaheim	**1966–**	**AL Angels**	**45,030** (43,204)	**330–387/400/370–330**	333–?/406/?–333	Anaheim Stadium 1966–97; Edison *International Field of Anaheim 1998–03* *"The Big A"*; rebuilt 1997–98
ARLINGTON [TEXAS]						
Arlington Stadium	1972–1993	AL Rangers	43,521 (35,185)	330–380/400/380–330		OF configuration different 1974–80
Ameriquest Field in Arlington	**1994–**	**AL Rangers**	**48,911** (49,292)	**332–390/400/381–325**		*The Ballpark in Arlington 1994–2004*
ATLANTA						
Atlanta-Fulton County Stadium	1966–1996	NL Braves	52,769 (50,893)	330–385/402/385–330	325–385/402/385–325	
Turner Field	**1997–**	**NL Braves**	**50,096** (50,528)	**335–380/401/390–330**		Built for 1996 Olympics; rebuilt for MLB
BALTIMORE						
Newington Park	1872–1874	NA Lord Baltimores				
	1873	NA Maryland				
	1882	AA Orioles				
Oriole Park (I)	1883–1889	AA Orioles				
Oriole Park (II)	1890–1891	AA Orioles			300–?/?/?–350	
Belair Lot	1884	UA Monumentals				
Monumental Park	1884	UA Monumentals				Selected dates
Oriole Park (III)	1891	AA Orioles	11,000 (30,000)	300–?/?/?–350		
	1892–1899	NL Orioles				
Oriole Park (IV)	1901–1902	AL Orioles				
Terrapin Park	1914–1915	FL Terrapins	16,000	300–?/450/?–335		
Memorial Stadium	1954–1991	AL Orioles	53,371 (47,855)	309–385/405/385–309	309–446/445/446–309	
Oriole Park at Camden Yards	**1992–**	**AL Orioles**	**48,286** (48,041)	**333–410/400/373–318**		
BOSTON						
South End Grounds (I)	1871–1875	NA Red Stockings				Became NL Braves
	1876–1887	NL Braves				
Hampden Park Race Track	1873	NA Red Stockings				[Springfield MA] 2 games
Dartmouth Grounds	1884	UA Unions				
South End Grounds (II)	1888–1894	NL Braves	6,800			
Congress Street Grounds	1890	PL Red Stockings		250–?/?/?–?		
	1891	AA Red Stockings				
	1894	NL Braves				
South End Grounds (III)	1894–1914	NL Braves		250–450/440/?–255		
Huntington Avenue Grounds	1901–1911	AL Red Sox	9,000	350–440/635/?–320	350–440/530/?–280	
Fenway Park	**1912–**	**AL Red Sox**	**36,108** (35,000)	**310–379/390/380–302**	321–?/488/?–314	RCF 420; lights 1947; Day capacity 35,692
	1914–1915	NL Braves				28 Sept. games & World Series, 1914
Braves Field	1915–1952	NL Braves	37,106 (40,000)	337–355/370/355–318	402–403/440/402–402	RCF 390 (550); lights 1946
	1915–1916	AL Red Sox				World Series only
	1929–1932	AL Red Sox				Sundays
BROOKLYN						
Capitoline Grounds	1872	NA Atlantics				
Union Grounds	1872	NA Eckfords	1,500	500–500/500/500–350		
	1873–1875	NA Atlantics				
Washington Park (I)	1884–1889	AA Atlantics	2,000			
Ridgewood Park	1886–1889	AA Atlantics				14 Sunday games
	1890	AA Gladiators				29 games
Washington Park (II)	1889	AA Atlantics	3,000			
	1890	NL Dodgers				
Long Island Grounds	1890	AA Gladiators				[Maspeth NY] 2 games
Eastern Park	1890	PL Ward's Wonders				
	1891–1897	NL Dodgers				
Washington Park (III)	1898–1912	NL Dodgers		376–444/425/300–302	335–500/445/300–215	
	1914–1915	FL Tip-Tops	18,800	300–?/400/?–275		Rebuilt 1914 for Federal League
West NY Field Club Grounds	1898	NL Dodgers				[West New York NJ] 3 games
Ebbets Field	1913–1957	NL Dodgers	31,902 (18,000)	348–351/393/352–297	419–?/450/?–301	Lights 1938
Roosevelt Stadium	1956–1957	NL Dodgers	24,500 (24,167)	330–397/411/397–330		[Jersey City NJ] 14 games total
BUFFALO						
Riverside Grounds	1879–1883	NL Bisons			210–420/410/420–210	
Olympic Park (I)	1884–1885	NL Bisons				
Maple Avenue Driving Park	1885	NL Bisons				[Elmira NY] 1 game
Olympic Park (II)	1890	PL Bisons				
Federal Field	1914–1915	FL Blues	20,000	290–?/400/?–300		*aka Federal League Park*
CHICAGO						
Union Base-Ball Grounds	1871	NA White Stockings	7,000			Became NL Cubs; *aka Lake Park*
23rd Street Grounds	1874–1875	NA White Stockings				
	1876–1877	NL Cubs				
Lake Front Park (I)	1878–1882	NL Cubs				
Lake Front Park (II)	1883–1884	NL Cubs	5,000	180–280/300/252–196	186–280/300/252–196	
South Side Park (I)	1884	UA Browns				
Belair Lot	1884	UA Browns				[Baltimore MD] 1 game
West Side Park	1885–1891	NL Cubs			216–?/?/?–216	Mondays/Wednesdays/Fridays 1891
South Side Park (II)	1890	PL Pirates				
	1891–1893	NL Cubs				Tuesdays/Thursdays/Saturdays 1891
West Side Grounds	1893–1915	NL Cubs	16,000 (12,500)	340–441/560/435–316		
South Side Park (III)	1901–1910	AL White Sox	15,000			
Comiskey Park (I)	1910–1990	AL White Sox	43,951 (28,800)	347–382/409/382–347	363–382/420/382–363	Lights 1939; turf IF/grass OF 1969–75 *White Sox Park 1967–75*
Wrigley Field	1914–1915	FL Whales	**41,118** (18,000)	**355–368/400/368–353**	310–?/400/?–350	Lights 1988; *Weeghman Park 1914–18, Cubs Park 1919–25*
	1916–	**NL Cubs**				
Milwaukee County Stadium	1968–1969	AL White Sox	53,192 (35,911)	315–392/402/392–315	320–397/404/397–320	[Milwaukee WI] 20 games total
U.S. Cellular Field	**1991–**	**AL White Sox**	**40,615** (44,702)	**330–377/400/372–335**	347–383/400/383–347	*Comiskey Park (II) 1991–2002* *"New Comiskey"*
Tokyo Dome*	2000	NL Cubs	55,000	318–360/400/360–318		[Japan] Dome; turf; 1 game
CINCINNATI						
Avenue Grounds	1876–1879	NL Reds				
Bank St. Grounds	1880	NL Reds				
	1882–1883	AA Red Stockings				
	1884	UA Outlaw Reds				
League Park (I)	1884–1889	AA Red Stockings				
	1890–1893	NL Reds				
Pendleton Park	1891	AA Kelly's Killers				[Pendleton Park OH]

BALLPARK	OPEN	TENANTS	CAPACITY	DIMENSIONS LF-LCF/CF/RCF-RF CURRENT/FINAL	ORIGINAL	NOTES
League Park (II)	1894–1901	NL Reds		253–?/?/?–?		
Palace of the Fans	1902–1911	NL Reds	6,000	?–?/?/?–450		
Crosley Field	1912–1970	NL Reds	29,603 (23,500)	328–380/387/383–366	360–380/420/?–385	Lights 1935; *Redland Field 1912–33;* replica built in Blue Ash OH
Cinergy Field	1970–2002	NL Reds	40,007 (50,000)	325–370/393/374–325	330–375/404/375–330	Turf 1970–2000; *Riverfront Stadium 1970–96* LF–CF seats demolished after 2000
Great American Ball Park	**2003–**	**NL Reds**	**42,271** (42,059)	**328–379/404/370–325**		
CLEVELAND						
National Association Grounds	1871–1872	NA Forest City				
Lincoln Park Grounds	1871	NA Forest City				
National League Park (I)	1879–1884	NL Blues				[Cincinnati OH] 1 date
National League Park (II)	1887–1888	AA Blues			410/?/420/?–410	
	1889–1890	NL Spiders			410–?/420/?–410	
Geauga Lake Baseball Grounds	1888	AA Blues				[Geauga Lake OH] 3 games
Beyerle's Park	1888	AA Blues				[Newburgh OH] 1 date
Brotherhood Park	1890	PL Infants				
Indianapolis Park	1890	NL Spiders				[Indianapolis IN] a few dates
League Park (I)	1891–1899	NL Spiders	9,000		?–?/?/?–290	
	1901–1909	AL Indians				
Euclid Beach Park	1898	NL Spiders				[Collinwood OH] selected dates
Ontario Beach Grounds	1898	NL Spiders				[Charlotte NY] 1 date
League Park (II)	1910–1946	AL Indians	21,000	375–415/420/400–290	385–505/420/400–290	Selected dates 1932–46
Mahaffey Park	1902–1903	AL Indians			324–?/382/?–302	[Canton OH] 3 dates
Cleveland Stadium	1932–1993	AL Indians	74,483 (78,000)	320–375/404/370–320	320–435/470/435–320	Lights 1939; selected dates 1932–46; *Lakefront Stadium 1932–37; Cleveland Public Municipal Stadium 1938; Municipal Stadium 1939–64*
Jacobs Field	**1994–**	**AL Indians**	**43,415** (42,865)	**325–370/405/375–325**		*"The Jake"*
COLUMBUS, OH						
Recreation Park (I)	1883–1884	AA Buckeyes				
Recreation Park (II)	1889–1891	AA Solons			?–?/?/?–400	
DENVER [COLORADO]						
Mile High Stadium	1993–1994	NL Rockies	76,100	333–366/423/400–370	335–375/423/400–370	
Coors Field	**1995–**	**NL Rockies**	**50,445** (50,000)	**347–390/415/375–350**		RCF 424
DETROIT						
Recreation Park	1881–1888	NL Wolverines				
Bennett Park	1901–1911	AL Tigers	14,000 (6,000)			
Burns Park	1901–1902	AL Tigers	8,000 (5,500)			23 Sunday games
Tiger Stadium*	1912–1999	AL Tigers	46,846 (23,000)	340–365/440/370–325	345–?/467/?–370	Lights 1948; *Navin Field 1912–33; Briggs Stadium 1934–60*
Comerica Park	**2000–**	**AL Tigers**	**41,070** (40,120)	**345–370/420/365–330**	345–395/420/365–330	
ELIZABETH, NJ						
Waverly Fairgrounds	1873	NA Resolutes				[Waverly NJ]
FORT WAYNE, IN						
Hamilton Field	1871	NA Kekiongas				
HARTFORD						
Hartford Ball Club Grounds	1874–1875	NA Dark Blues				
South End Grounds	1874	NA Dark Blues				[Boston MA] 1 date
Hartford Ball Club Grounds	1876	NL Dark Blues				
Union Grounds	1877	NL Dark Blues		?–500/500/500–?		[Brooklyn NY]
HOUSTON						
Colt Stadium	1962–1964	NL Colt .45s	33,010 (32,601)	360–395/420/395–360		RCF & LCF 427; Most of ballpark moved to Torreon, Mexico, in 1969
Astrodome*	1965–1999	NL Astros	54,370 (46,217)	325–375/400/375–325	340–375/406/375–340	Dome; turf (turf IF/grass OF 1966p)
Minute Maid Park	**2000–**	**NL Astros**	**40,976** (42,180)	**315–362/435/373–326**		Retractable roof; RCF 436; *Enron Field 2000–01, Astros Field 2002*
INDIANAPOLIS						
South Street Park	1878	NL Blues				
Seventh St. Park (I)	1884	AA Hoosiers				
Bruce Grounds	1884	AA Hoosiers				11 Sunday games
Seventh St. Park (II)	1887	NL Hoosiers			286–?/?/?–261	
Seventh St. Park (III)	1888–1889	NL Hoosiers				
Hoosier Park	1914	FL Hoosiers	20,000	375–?/400/?–310		*aka Greenlawn Park/Federal League Park*
KANSAS CITY						
Athletic Park	1884	UA Cowboys				
Association Park	1886	NL Cowboys				
	1888	AA Cowboys				
Gordon & Koppel Field	1914–1915	FL Packers	12,000			
Municipal Stadium	1955–1967	AL Athletics	35,561 (30,296)	369–408/421/382–338	312–382/430/382–347	
	1969–1972	AL Royals				
Kauffman Stadium	**1973–**	**AL Royals**	**40,785** (40,613)	**330/385–410–385/330**	330–375/405/375–330	Turf 1973–94; *Royals Stadium 1973–93p*
KEOKUK, IA						
Perry Park	1875	NA Westerns				
LOS ANGELES [INCL. CALIFORNIA 1965] (ALSO SEE ANAHEIM)						
Memorial Coliseum*	1958–1961	NL Dodgers	94,600 (93,000)	252–417/420/380–300	250–425/425/440–301	
Wrigley Field	1961	AL Angels	20,457	340–345/412/345–339		
Dodger Stadium	**1962–**	**NL Dodgers**	**56,000**	**330–385/395/385–330**		330–380/410/380–330 *Chavez Ravine Stadium 1962–65 (Angels games only);* LA Angels changed name to California in 1965 before move to Anaheim
	1962–1965	AL Angels				
LOUISVILLE						
Louisville Baseball Park	1876–1877	NL Grays				
Eclipse Park (I)	1882–1891	AA Colonels (1885)		360–405/495/360–320		
	1892–1893	NL Colonels				
Eclipse Park (II)	1893–1899	NL Colonels				
MIAMI [FLORIDA]						
Dolphin Stadium	**1993–**	**NL Marlins**	**36,331** (43,909)	**330–385/404/385–345**	335–380/410/380–345	RCF 434; postseason cap. 65,000+; *Joe Robbie Stadium 1993–96; Pro Player Stadium 1997–2004 Dolphins Stadium 2005*

BALLPARK	OPEN	TENANTS	CAPACITY	DIMENSIONS LF-LCF/CF/RCF-RF CURRENT/FINAL	ORIGINAL	NOTES
MIDDLETOWN, CT						
Mansfield Club Grounds	1872	NA Mansfields				
Hartford Trotting Park	1872	NA Mansfields				[Hartford CT] 3 games
MILWAUKEE						
Milwaukee Base–Ball Grounds	1878	NL Grays				
Wright Street Grounds	1884	UA Brewers				
Borchert Field	1891	AA Brewers	10,000		266–?/395/?–266	
Athletic Park	1891	AA Brewers			275–?/?/?–250	[Minneapolis MN] 1 date
Lloyd Street Grounds	1901	AL Brewers				*aka Milwaukee Park*
Milwaukee County Stadium	1953–1965	NL Braves	53,192 (35,911)	315–392/402/392–315	320–397/404/397–320	
	1968–1969	AL White Sox				20 games total
	1970–1997	AL Brewers				
	1998–2000	NL Brewers				
Miller Park	**2001–**	**NL Brewers**	**41,900** (42,500)	**344–371/400/374–345**		Retractable roof
MINNEAPOLIS [MINNESOTA]						
Metropolitan Stadium	1961–81	AL Twins	45,919 (30,022)	343–406/402/410–330	329–402/412/402–329	[Bloomington MN]
Hubert H. Humphrey Metrodome	**1982–**	**AL Twins**	**46,564** (54,711)	**343–385/408/367–327**		Dome; turf; "The Homerdome"
MONTREAL						
Parc Jarry	1969–1976	NL Expos	28,456 (28,000)	340–368/420/368–340	340–368/415/368–340	*Jarry Park*
Stade Olympique	1977–2004	NL Expos	46,338 (58,838)	325–375/404/375–325		Turf; built for 1976 Olympics; *Olympic Stadium;* "The Big O"; Open-air 1977–86; fixed roof 1987–88; retractable roof 1989–91p; fixed roof p1991–98p; no roof 1998p; fixed roof 1999–2004
Estadio Hiram Bithorn	2003–2004	NL Expos	19,000 (20,000)	325/375–404–375/325	315–340/399/340–315	*Hiram Bithorn Stadium* [San Juan PR] turf; Power alleys listed 360', actually 340'; 22 games each season in 2003–04
NEWARK						
Harrison Park	1915	FL Peppers	21,000	375–?/450/?–375		*aka Peppers Park*
NEW HAVEN, CT						
Howard Avenue Grounds	1875	NA Elm Citys				*aka Brewster Park*
Adelaide Avenue Grounds	1875	NA Elm Citys				[Providence RI] 1 date
NEW YORK						
Union Grounds	1871–1875	NA Mutuals	1,500	500–500/500/500–350		[Brooklyn NY]
	1876	NL Mutuals				
Polo Grounds (I)	1883–1888	NL Giants				
	1884–1885	AA Metropolitans				
Polo Grounds (II)	1883	AA Metropolitans				
Metropolitan Park	1884	AA Metropolitans				33 games
St. George Cricket Grounds	1886–1887	AA Metropolitans	4,100			[St. George NY]
Monitor Park	1887	AA Metropolitans				[Weehawken NJ] 1 date
Polo Grounds (III)	1889–1890	NL Giants		?–?/360/?–?		
Oakdale Park	1889	NL Giants				[Jersey City NJ] 2 games
Polo Grounds (IV)	1890	PL Giants	16,000	277–?/500/?–258	335–?/500/?–335	
	1891–1911	NL Giants				*Brotherhood Park 1890*
West N.Y. Field Club Grounds	1899	NL Giants				[West New York NJ] selected dates
Hilltop Park	1903–1912	AL Yankees	15,000	365–?/542/?–400		
	1911	NL Giants				28 games
Polo Grounds (V)	1911–1957	NL Giants	56,000 (16,000)	279–455/483/449–258	277–?/433/?–257	Lights 1940
	1913–1922	AL Yankees				
	1962–1963	NL Mets				
Yankee Stadium	**1923–**	**AL Yankees**	**57,478** (58,000)	**318–399/408/385–314**	281–395/490/429–295	LCF 411; lights 1946; rebuilt 1974–75 "The House That Ruth Built"
Shea Stadium	**1964–**	**NL Mets**	**57,333** (55,000)	**338–378/410/378–338**	341–371/410/371–341	
	1974–75; 1998	AL Yankees				1 game in 1998
Tokyo Dome*	2000	NL Mets	55,000	318–360/400/360–318		[Japan] Dome; turf; 1 game
	2004	AL Yankees				1 game
OAKLAND						
McAfee Coliseum	**1968–**	**AL Athletics**	**34,077** (50,000)	**330–388/400/388–330**	330–378/410/378–330	Postseason cap. 50,000+; *Oakland–Alameda County Coliseum 1968–98* *Network Associates Coliseum 1999–2004* Closed upper deck in 2006
Cashman Field*	1996	AL Athletics	9,370	328–364/433/364–328		[Las Vegas NV] 6 games
PHILADELPHIA						
Jefferson Street Grounds	1871–1875	NA Athletics			?–?/500/?–?	First press box installed here
	1873–1875	NA White Stockings				
	1876	NL Athletics				
	1883–1890	AA Athletics				*aka Athletic Park*
Fairview Park Fairgrounds	1875	NA Athletics				[Dover DE] 1 date
Centennial Park	1875	NA Centennials				*aka Centennial Grounds*
Star Baseball Park	1875	NA White Stockings				[Covington KY] 1 date
Ludlow Baseball Park	1875	NA White Stockings				[Ludlow KY] 1 date
Oakdale Park	1882	AA Athletics				
Recreation Park	1883–1886	NL Phillies				
Keystone Park	1884	UA Keystones				
Philadelphia Baseball Grounds	1887–1894	NL Phillies	15,000	500–?/?/?–310		
Gloucester Point Grounds	1888–1890	AA Athletics				[Gloucester City NJ] 30 Sunday games
University of Pennsylvania Athletic Field	1894	NL Phillies				One week
Forepaugh Park	1890	PL Quakers		345–?/450/?–380		
	1891	AA Athletics				
Columbia Park	1901–1908	AL Athletics	13,600 (9,500)			
	1903	NL Phillies				16 games
Baker Bowl	1895–1938	NL Phillies	18,800 (18,000)	342–359/408/300–281	?–?/408/300–?	*National League Park 1895-1913* *Huntingdon Street Grounds*
Connie Mack Stadium	1909–1954	AL Athletics	33,608 (20,000)	334–387/410/390–329	360–393/515/393–360	*Shibe Park 1909–52;* lights 1939
	1938–1970	NL Phillies				
Veterans Stadium	1971–2003	NL Phillies	61,831 (56,371)	330–371/408/371–330		Turf
Citizens Bank Park	**2004–**	**NL Phillies**	**43,647** (43,500)	329-374/401/369-330	329–369/401/369–330	LCF 409; LF power alley actually 359, 2004p

BALLPARK	OPEN	TENANTS	CAPACITY	DIMENSIONS LF-LCF/CF/RCF-RF CURRENT/FINAL	DIMENSIONS LF-LCF/CF/RCF-RF ORIGINAL	NOTES
PHOENIX [ARIZONA]						
Chase Field	**1998–**	**NL Diamondbacks**	**49,033** (48,500)	**330–376/407/376–334**		"The BOB"; retractable roof; RCF 412 *Bank One Ballpark 1998–2005*
PITTSBURGH						
Exposition Park (I)	1882–1883	AA Alleghenys				
	1884	UA Stogies				
Exposition Park (II)	1883	AA Alleghenys				
Recreation Park	1884–1886	AA Alleghenys	17,000			
	1887–1890	NL Pirates	17,000			
Exposition Park (III)	1890	PL Burghers		400–?/450/?–400		
	1891–1909	NL Pirates				
	1914–1915	FL Rebels	16,000			
Mahaffey Park	1890	NL Pirates		324–?/382/?–302		[Canton OH] 1 date
Island Grounds	1890	NL Pirates				[Wheeling WV] 1 date
Forbes Field	1909–1970	NL Pirates	35,000 (28,000)	365–406/435/408–300	360–419/447/410–376	LCF 457 (462); lights 1940
Three Rivers Stadium	1970–2000	NL Pirates	47,687 (49,023)	335–375/400/375–335	340–385/410/385–340	Turf
PNC Park	**2001–**	**NL Pirates**	**38,496**	**325–389/399/375–320**		LCF 410
PROVIDENCE, RI						
Messer Street Grounds	1878	NL Grays				
Union Park	1878	NL Grays	2,500			[Pittsburgh PA] selected dates
RICHMOND, VA						
Virginia Baseball Park	1884	AA Virginians				
ROCHESTER, NY						
Culver Field (I)	1890	AA Hop Bitters				
Windsor Beach	1890	AA Hop Bitters				[Irondequoit NY] 6 games
ROCKFORD, IL						
Agricultural Society Fairgrounds	1871	NA Forest City	500			
ST. LOUIS						
Red Stocking Base-Ball Park	1875	NA Red Stockings				
Grand Avenue Park	1875	NA Brown Stockings				
	1876–1877	NL Brown Stockings	3,000			
Union Grounds	1884	UA Maroons	10,000	285–?/?/?–285		
	1885–1886	NL Maroons				
Seventh Street Park (I)	1885	NL Maroons				[Indianapolis IN] selected dates
Sportsman's Park (I)	1882–1891	AA Cardinals	12,000 (6,000)	350–400/460/330–285		
	1892	NL Cardinals				
Robison Field	1893–1920	NL Cardinals	21,000 (10,000)	380–400/435/320–?	470–520/500/330–290	*aka League Park*
Athletic Park	*1901*	*NL Cardinals*				*1 game*
Sportsman's Park (II)	1902–1908	AL Browns	18,000			
Busch Stadium (I)	1909–1953	AL Browns	30,500 (17,600)	351–379/420/354–310	368–379/?/?–335	Lights 1940 *Sportsman's Park (III) 1909–53*
	1920–1966	NL Cardinals				
Handlan's Park	1914–1915	FL Terriers	15,000 (12,000)	325–?/375/?–300		*aka Steininger Field*
Busch Stadium (II)	1966–2005	NL Cardinals	50,345 (49,275)	330–372/402/372–330	330–386/414/386–330	*Busch Memorial Stadium 1966–83;* turf 1970–95
Busch Stadium (III)	**2006–**	**NL Cardinals**	**43,975** (39,748)	**336-375/400/375-335**		Not finished when opened
ST. PETERSBURG [TAMPA BAY]						
Tropicana Field	**1998–**	**AL Devil Rays**	**41,315** (45,200)	**315-370/404/370-322**	315–370/410/370–322	Dome; turf; LCF 410 (417)
Tokyo Dome*	2004	AL Devil Rays	55,000	318–360/400/360–318		[Japan] Dome; turf; 1 game
SAN DIEGO						
Qualcomm Stadium*	1969–2003	NL Padres	63,890 (50,000)	327–370/405/370–330	330–370/420/370–330	*San Diego Stadium 1969–80; San Diego/* *Jack Murphy Stadium 1981–97*
Estadio Monterrey*	1996	NL Padres	25,644	325–?/405/?–325		*Monterrey Stadium* [Mexico] 3 games
	1999	NL Padres				1 game
Aloha Stadium*	1997	NL Padres	50,000	325–375/420/375–325		[Honolulu HI] 3 games; turf
Petco Park	**2004–**	**NL Padres**	**42,445**	**334-367/396/382-322**		RCF 400
SAN FRANCISCO						
Seals Stadium	1958–1959	NL Giants	22,900	361–364/400/397–350	365–375/410/397–355	
3Com Park at Candlestick Point*	1960–1999	NL Giants	63,000 (42,500)	335–365/400/365–328	330–365/410/375–330	*Candlestick Park 1960–95* Turf IF/grass OF 1971; turf 1972–78
AT&T Park	**2000–**	**NL Giants**	**41,606** (40,800)	**339–364/399/421–309**	335–364/404/420–307	*Pacific Bell Park 2000–03* *SBC Park 2004-05*
SEATTLE						
Sick's Stadium	1969	AL Pilots	25,420 (18,000)	305–345/402/345–305		
Kingdome	1977–1999	AL Mariners	59,084 (59,059)	331–389/405/380–312	315–375/405/365–315	Dome; turf
Safeco Field	**1999–**	**AL Mariners**	**47,447** (47,116)	**331–390/405/387–327**		Retractable roof
SYRACUSE, NY						
Star Park (I)	1879	NL Stars				
Star Park (II)	1890	AA Stars				
Iron Pier	1890	AA Stars				1 game scheduled; forfeited
Three Rivers Park	1890	AA Stars				[Three Rivers, NY] 5 games
TOLEDO, OH						
League Park	1884	AA Blue Stockings				
Tri-State Fair Grounds	1884	AA Blue Stockings				
Speranza Park	1890	AA Maumees				
TORONTO						
Exhibition Stadium	1977–1989	AL Blue Jays	43,737 (38,522)	330–375/400/375–330		Turf
Rogers Centre	**1989–**	**AL Blue Jays**	**50,516**	**328–375/400/375–328**	330–375/400/375–330	Retractable roof; turf *SkyDome 1989–2004*
Estadio Hiram Bithorn*	2001	AL Blue Jays	20,000	315–340/398/340–313		*Hiram Bithorn Stadium;* turf; 1 game Power alleys listed 360', actually 340'
TROY, NY						
Haymakers' Grounds	1871–1872	NA Haymakers				
	1880–1881	NL Trojans				
Hampden Park Race Track	1872	NA Haymakers				[Springfield MA] 1 date
Putnam Grounds	1879	NL Trojans				
Riverside Park	1880–1882	NL Trojans				[Albany NY] selected dates
Troy Ball Club Grounds	1882	NL Trojans				[Watervliet NY]

BALLPARK	OPEN	TENANTS	CAPACITY	DIMENSIONS LF-LCF/CF/RCF-RF CURRENT/FINAL	ORIGINAL	NOTES
WASHINGTON, DC						
Olympic Grounds	1871–1872	NA Olympics				
	1873	NA Nationals				
	1875	NA Nationals				
Madison Avenue Grounds	1871	NA Olympics				
Lincoln Park Grounds	1871	NA Olympics				[Baltimore MD] 1 date
White Lot	1871–1872	NA Olympics				[Cincinnati OH] 2 games
Maryland Avenue Park	1871–1872	NA Olympics				Selected dates
Nationals Grounds	1872	NA Nationals				Selected dates
Newington Park	1875	NA Nationals				
Virginia State Agricultural Society	1875	NA Nationals				[Baltimore MD] 2 games
Athletic Park	1884	AA Nationals				[Richmond VA] selected dates
Capitol Grounds	1884	UA Nationals	6,000			
Swampoodle Grounds	1886–1889	NL Senators	6,000			
Boundary Field	1891	AA Statesmen	6,500			
	1892–1899	NL Senators				
American League Park (I)	1901–1903	AL Senators	(6,000)			
American League Park (II)	1904–1910	AL Senators			200–?/?/?–?	
Griffith Stadium	1911–1960	AL Senators (I)	28,669 (12,000)	388–372/408/373–320	407–391/421/378–328	*League Park 1911–19;* LCF 426; lights 1941
	1961	AL Senators (II)				
Robert F. Kennedy Memorial Stadium	1962–71	AL Senators (II)	**45,658** (42,000)	**336–380/410/380–336**	335–385/410/385–335	*District of Columbia Stadium 1962–68*
	2005–	**NL Nationals**				
WILMINGTON, DE						
Union Street Park	1884	UA Quicksteps				
WORCESTER, MA						
Agricultural County Fair Grounds	1880–1882	NL Brown Stockings				

Spring Training Sites (Since 1901)

AMERICAN LEAGUE

ANAHEIM/LOS ANGELES (INCLUDING CALIFORNIA, 1966–96)

1993–	Tempe AZ
1984–92	Mesa AZ
	Palm Springs CA
1982–83	Casa Grande AZ
	Palm Springs CA
1980–81	Palm Springs CA
1966–79	Holtville CA
	Palm Springs CA

Los Angeles 1961–64
California 1965

1961–65	Palm Springs CA

BALTIMORE

1996–	Ft. Lauderdale FL
1992–95	Sarasota FL
	St. Petersburg FL
1991	Sarasota FL
1989–90	Sarasota FL
	Miami FL
1959–88	Miami FL
1956–58	Scottsdale AZ
1955	Daytona Beach FL
1954	Yuma AZ

St. Louis

1953	San Bernardino CA
1949–52	Burbank CA
1948	San Bernardino CA
1947	Miami FL
1946	Anaheim CA
1943–45	Cape Girardeau MO
1942	Deland FL
1937–41	San Antonio TX
1928–36	West Palm Beach FL
1925–27	Tarpon Springs FL
1922–24	Mobile AL
1921	Bogalusa AL
1920	Taylor AL
1919	San Antonio TX
1918	Shreveport LA
1916–17	Palestine TX
1915	Houston TX
1914	St. Petersburg FL
1913	Waco TX
1912	Montgomery AL
1911	Hot Springs AR
1909–10	Houston TX
1908	Shreveport LA
1907	San Antonio TX
1905–06	Dallas TX
1904	Corsicana TX
1903	Baton Rouge LA
1902	French Lick IN
1901	St. Louis MO

BOSTON

1993–	Ft. Myers FL
1966–92	Winter Haven FL
1959–65	Scottsdale AZ
1946–58	Sarasota FL
1945	Pleasantville NJ
1944	Baltimore MD
1943	Medford MA
1933–42	Sarasota FL
1932	Savannah GA
1930–31	Pensacola FL
1928–29	Bradenton FL
1925–27	New Orleans LA
1924	San Antonio TX
1920–23	Hot Springs AR
1919	Tampa FL
1912–18	Hot Springs AR
1911	Redondo Beach CA
1909–10	Hot Springs AR
1907–08	Little Rock AR
1903–06	Macon GA
1902	Augusta GA
1901	Charlottesville VA

CHICAGO

1998–	Tucson AZ
1960–97	Sarasota FL
1954–59	Tampa FL
1953	El Centro CA
1952	Pasadena CA
	El Centro CA
1951	Pasadena CA
	Palm Springs CA
1946–50	Pasadena CA
1945	Terre Haute IN
1943–44	French Lick IN
1933–42	Pasadena CA
1930–32	San Antonio TX
1929	Dallas TX
1925–28	Shreveport LA
1924	Winter Haven FL
1922–23	Seguin TX
1921	Waxahachie TX
1920	Waco TX
1916–19	Mineral Wells TX
1913–15	Paso Robles CA
1912	Waco TX
1911	Mineral Wells TX
1909–10	San Francisco CA
1908	Los Angeles CA
1907	Mexico City, Mexico
1905–06	New Orleans LA
1904	Marlin TX
1903	Mobile AL
1901–02	Excelsior Springs MO

CLEVELAND

1993–	Winter Haven FL
1947–92	Tucson AZ
1946	Clearwater FL
1943–45	Lafayette IN
1940–42	Ft. Myers FL
1928–39	New Orleans LA
1923–27	Lakeland FL
1921–22	Dallas TX
1916–20	New Orleans LA
1915	San Antonio TX
1914	Athens GA
1913	Pensacola FL
1912	New Orleans LA
1910–11	Alexandria LA
1907–09	Macon GA
1905–06	New Orleans LA
1904	San Antonio TX
1902–03	New Orleans LA
1901	Cleveland OH

DETROIT

1946–	Lakeland FL
1943–45	Evansville IN
1934–42	Lakeland FL
1933	San Antonio TX
1932	Palo Alto CA
1931	Sacramento CA
1930	Tampa FL
1929	Phoenix AZ
1927–28	San Antonio TX
1922–26	Augusta GA
1921	San Antonio TX
1919–20	Macon GA
1916–18	Waxahachie TX
1913–15	Gulfport MS
1911–12	Monroe LA
1909–10	San Antonio TX
1908	Hot Springs AR
	Little Rock AR
1905–07	Augusta GA
1903–04	Shreveport LA
1902	Ypsilanti MI
1901	Detroit MI

KANSAS CITY

2003–	Surprise AZ
1988–2002	Davenport FL
1969–87	Ft. Myers FL

MINNESOTA

1991–	Ft. Myers FL
1961–90	Orlando FL

Washington

1946–60	Orlando FL
1943–45	College Park MD
1936–42	Orlando FL
1930–35	Biloxi MS
1920–29	Tampa FL
1918–19	Augusta GA
1917	Atlanta GA
1912–16	Charlottesville VA
1911	Atlanta GA
1910	Norfolk VA
1907–09	Galveston TX
1906	Charlottesville VA
1905	Hampton VA
1902–04	Washington DC
1901	Phoebus VA

NEW YORK

1996–	Tampa FL
1962–95	Ft. Lauderdale FL
1952–61	St. Petersburg FL
1951	Phoenix AZ
1946–50	St. Petersburg FL
1944–45	Atlantic City NJ
1943	Asbury Park NJ
1925–42	St. Petersburg FL
1922–24	New Orleans LA
1921	Shreveport LA
1919–20	Jacksonville FL
1916–18	Macon GA
1915	Savannah GA
1914	Houston TX
1913	Hamilton, Bermuda
1912	Atlanta GA
1910–11	Athens GA
1909	Macon GA
1907–08	Atlanta GA
1906	Birmingham AL
1905	Montgomery AL
1903–04	Atlanta GA
1902	Savannah GA
1901	Baltimore MD

OAKLAND

1982–	Phoenix AZ
1979–81	Scottsdale AZ
1969–78	Mesa AZ
1968	Bradenton FL

Kansas City

1963–67	Bradenton FL
1955–62	West Palm Beach FL

Philadelphia

1946–62	West Palm Beach FL
1944–45	Frederick MD
1943	Wilmington DE
1940–42	Anaheim CA
1938–39	Lake Charles LA
1937	Mexico City, Mexico
1925–36	Ft. Myers FL
1923–24	Montgomery AL
1922	Eagle Pass TX
1920–21	Lake Charles LA
1919	Philadelphia PA
1914–18	Jacksonville FL
1912–13	San Antonio TX
1911	Savannah GA
1910	Atlanta GA
1908–09	New Orleans LA
1907	Dallas TX
1906	Montgomery AL
1905	Shreveport LA
1904	Spartanburg SC
1903	Jacksonville FL
1902	Charlotte NC
1901	Philadelphia PA

SEATTLE

1993–	Peoria AZ
1977–92	Tempe AZ

TAMPA BAY

1998–	St. Petersburg FL

TEXAS

2003–	Surprise AZ
1987–2002	Port Charlotte FL
1972–86	Pompano Beach FL
	[Washington]
1961–71	Pompano Beach FL

TORONTO

1977–	Dunedin FL

FEDERAL LEAGUE

BALTIMORE

1915	Fayetteville NC
1914	Southern Pines NC

BROOKLYN

1915	Browns Wells MS
1914	Columbia SC

BUFFALO

1915	Athens GA
1914	Danville VA

CHICAGO

1914–15	Shreveport LA

INDIANAPOLIS/NEWARK

1914	Wichita Falls TX
1915	Valdosta GA

KANSAS CITY

1915	Wichita Falls TX
1914	Marshall TX

PITTSBURGH

1915	Augusta GA
1914	Lynchburg VA

ST. LOUIS

1915	Havana, Cuba
1914	Monroe LA

NATIONAL LEAGUE

ARIZONA

1998–	Tucson AZ

ATLANTA

1998–	Kissimmee FL
1966–97	West Palm Beach FL

Milwaukee

1963–65	West Palm Beach FL
1953–62	Bradenton FL

Boston

1948–52	Bradenton FL
1946–47	Ft. Lauderdale FL
1945	Washington DC
1943–44	Wallingford CT
1942	Sanford FL
1941	San Antonio TX
1938–40	Bradenton FL
1922–37	St. Petersburg FL
1921	Galveston TX
1919–20	Columbus GA
1916–18	Miami FL
1914–15	Macon GA
1913	Athens GA
1908–12	Augusta GA
1907	Thomasville GA
1906	Jacksonville FL
1905	Charleston SC
1902–04	Thomasville GA
1901	Norfolk VA

CHICAGO

1979–	Mesa AZ
1967–78	Scottsdale AZ
1966	Long Beach CA
1952–65	Mesa AZ
1946–51	Catalina Island CA
1942–45	French Lick IN
1921–41	Catalina Island CA
1917–20	Pasadena CA
1913–16	Tampa FL
1912	New Orleans LA
1910–11	West Baden IN
	New Orleans LA
1909	West Baden IN
	Hot Springs AR
	Shreveport LA
1908	West Baden IN
	Vicksburg MS
1907	West Baden IN
	New Orleans LA
1906	West Baden IN
	Champaign IL
	Vicksburg MS
1905	Santa Monica CA
1903–04	Los Angeles CA
1901–02	Champaign IL

CINCINNATI

1998–	Sarasota FL
1988–97	Plant City FL
1946–87	Tampa FL
1943–45	Bloomington IN
1931–42	Tampa FL
1923–30	Orlando FL
1922	Mineral Wells TX
1921	Cisco TX
1920	Miami FL
1919	Waxahachie TX
1918	Montgomery AL
1916–17	Shreveport LA
1914–15	Alexandria LA
1913	Mobile AL
1912	Columbus GA
1910–11	Hot Springs AR
1909	Atlanta GA
1908	St. Augustine FL
1907	Marlin TX
1906	San Antonio TX
1905	Jacksonville FL
1904	Dallas TX
1903	Augusta GA
1901–02	Cincinnati OH

COLORADO

1993–	Tucson AZ

FLORIDA

2003–	Jupiter FL
1994–2002	Viera FL
1993	Cocoa FL

HOUSTON

1985–	Kissimmee FL
1964–84	Cocoa FL
1962–63	Apache Junction AZ

LOS ANGELES

1958–	Vero Beach FL

Brooklyn

1949–57	Vero Beach FL
1948	Vero Beach FL
	Ciudad Trujillo, D.R.
1947	Havana, Cuba
1946	Daytona Beach FL
1943–45	Bear Mountain NY
1941–42	Havana, Cuba
1936–40	Clearwater FL
1934–35	Orlando FL
1933	Miami FL
1923–32	Clearwater FL
1922	Jacksonville FL
1921	New Orleans FL
1919–20	Jacksonville FL
1917–18	Hot Springs AR
1915–16	Daytona Beach FL
1913–14	Augusta GA
1910–12	Hot Springs AR
1907–09	Jacksonville FL
1902–06	Columbia SC
1901	Charlotte NC

MILWAUKEE (AL 1969–96)

1998–	Maryvale AZ
1986–97	Chandler AZ
1973–85	Sun City AZ
1970–72	Tempe AZ

Seattle

1969	Tempe AZ

MONTREAL

2003–	Viera FL
1998–2002	Jupiter FL
1981–97	West Palm Beach FL
1973–80	Daytona Beach FL
1969–72	West Palm Beach FL

NEW YORK

1988–	Port St. Lucie FL
1962–87	St. Petersburg FL

PHILADELPHIA

1947–	Clearwater FL
1946	Miami Beach FL
1944–45	Wilmington DE
1943	Hershey PA
1940–42	Miami Beach FL
1939	New Braunfels TX
1938	Biloxi MS
1928–37	Winter Haven FL
1925–27	Bradenton FL
1922–24	Leesburg FL
1921	Gainesville FL
1920	Birmingham AL
1919	Charlotte NC
1915–18	St. Petersburg FL
1914	Wilmington NC
1913	Southern Pines NC
1912	Hot Springs AR
1911	Birmingham AL
1909–10	Southern Pines NC
1906–08	Savannah GA
1905	Augusta GA
1904	Savannah GA
1903	Richmond VA
1902	Washington DC
1901	Philadelphia PA

PITTSBURGH

1969–	Bradenton FL
1955–68	Ft. Myers FL
1954	Ft. Pierce FL
1953	Havana, Cuba
1949–52	San Bernardino CA
1948	Hollywood CA
1947	Miami Beach FL
1946	San Bernardino CA
1943–45	Muncie IN
1937–42	San Bernardino CA
1936	San Antonio TX
1935	San Bernardino CA
1924–34	Paso Robles CA
1920–23	Hot Springs AR
1919	Birmingham AL
1918	Jacksonville FL
1915–17	Dawson Springs KY
	Hot Springs AR
1901–14	Hot Springs AR

ST. LOUIS

1998–	Jupiter FL
1946–97	St. Petersburg FL
1943–45	Cairo IL
1938–42	St. Petersburg FL
1937	Daytona Beach FL
1930–36	Bradenton FL
1927–29	Avon Park FL
1926	San Antonio TX
1925	Stockton CA
1923–24	Bradenton FL
1921–22	Orange TX
1920	Brownsville TX
1919	St. Louis MO
1918	San Antonio TX
1915–17	Hot Wells TX
1914	St. Augustine FL
1913	Columbus GA
1912	Jackson MS
1911	West Baden IN
1909–10	Little Rock AR
1906–08	Houston TX
1905	Marlin TX
1904	Houston TX
1903	Dallas TX
1901–02	St. Louis MO

SAN DIEGO

1994–	Peoria AZ
1969–93	Yuma AZ

SAN FRANCISCO

1982–	Scottsdale AZ
1958–81	Phoenix AZ

New York

1952–57	Phoenix AZ
1951	St. Petersburg FL
1947–50	Phoenix AZ
1946	Miami FL
1943–45	Lakewood NJ
1941–42	Miami FL
1940	Winter Haven FL
1938–39	Baton Rouge LA
1937	Havana, Cuba
1936	Pensacola FL
1934–35	Miami Beach FL
1932–33	Los Angeles CA
1929–31	San Antonio TX
1928	Augusta GA
1924–27	Sarasota FL
1920–23	San Antonio TX
1919	Gainesville FL
1908–18	Marlin TX
1907	Los Angeles CA
1906	Memphis TN
1903–05	Savannah GA
1901–02	New York NY

STOIC MEN IN BLUE: MAJOR LEAGUE UMPIRES

Umpiring, even at the major league level, is not a glamorous occupation. When umpires do their job correctly, they are rarely noticed. When they *are* noticed, it is usually because of a crucial call on a close play. In those cases, it doesn't matter very much whether their call is correct or not, because whichever way the call goes will make the umpire very unpopular with one team and its fans.

Somebody has to make those close calls, however, and that is why umpires have been a part of baseball since the very beginning. On October 6, 1845, attorney William R. Wheaton was on hand to umpire the first recorded game of Alexander Cartwright's Knickerbocker Base Ball Club of New York City. On April 22, 1876, Billy McLean became baseball's first professional umpire when he was paid $5 by the host Philadelphia team to umpire the newly formed National League's very first game. In 1882, the new rival to the NL, the American Association, became the first league to directly hire a staff of umpires.

During the early days of professional ball, umpires were treated with little respect by both fans and players. Around the turn of the century, the phrase "Kill the umpire" was more than just a figure of speech. Many team owners did little to discourage such behavior because the rowdy atmosphere attracted more fans to the games. Few umpires were well compensated for all their troubles—many umpires performed their duties out of a true love of the game, even though that love was rarely reciprocated.

In the early part of the twentieth century, both the American and National Leagues strengthened the authority of the umpire as the modern umpire began to emerge. By 1912, two-umpire crews had become standard in both leagues, with one umpire behind the plate to concentrate on balls and strikes and the other umpire focusing on calls at the other three bases. After World War I, umpiring became a full-time profession for many of its practitioners. While umpires were still the target of ridicule from players and fans, personal safety was no longer a concern for the men in blue. After the scandal surrounding the fixing of the 1919 World Series, much of the press retreated from its previously hostile attitude toward umpires and looked instead to them as a source of moral authority on the field.

By 1933, most umpiring crews covering regular-season games consisted of three men; in 1952, four-man crews became the norm. Six-man crews were adopted for the World Series in 1947. As the ranks of umpires grew, so did the their professionalism. Umpire training schools started opening in the 1930s, and the standards umpires were expected to adhere to rose accordingly. Thomas Connolly and Bill Klem became the first umpires enshrined in the Hall of Fame in 1953. Since then, six other arbiters have joined them in Cooperstown. Like the rest of the National Pastime, the ranks of umpires were integrated slowly, with Emmett Ashford becoming the first black big-league umpire only in 1966.

Remuneration for umpires remained at a relatively low level until the umpires formed a union in 1970. In the decades afterward, the Major League Umpires Association fought for and won very large wage increases as well as the first-ever scheduled vacation time during the regular season. The life of a major league umpire may still not be glamorous, but these days it is a respected and enriching profession for those at the top level. Reaching the majors as an umpire, however, is now more difficult than ever. Openings in MLB are rare, so only a very small percentage of minor league umpires get the opportunity to taste the good life in The Show.

Every year, 300 aspiring professional umpires attend one of the two officially sanctioned umpire schools: the Jim Evans Academy of Professional Umpiring in Kissimmee, FL, or the Harry Wendelstedt School for Umpires in Ormond Beach, FL. MLB won't even start to consider a minor league umpire until he has eight minor league seasons under his belt. In 2006, a long strike by minor league umpires led to several controversies involving big-league prospects, showing just how hard the life of a minor league ump is, as well as how underappreciated the mostly anonymous men in blue are.

In recent years, major league umpires have been involved in several long-running controversies. In 1999, the MLUA imploded after its longtime executive director Richie Phillips pushed a hard-line negotiation strategy of mass resignations—which backfired badly. The following year, the NL and AL merged their umpiring staffs into a single unit, centralizing the commissioner's power over the umpires for the first time and theoretically eliminating the differences in how the rules were interpreted and applied between the two leagues. Symbolizing the change was the umps new uniform: no longer the traditional blue, but black.

The new umpires union, the World Umpires Association, quickly found its members under unprecedented scrutiny over their strike zone judgment as a result of MLB's controversial adoption of QuesTec technology and development of a new "Umpire Information System." While Major League Baseball maintained that it was simply trying to help its umps do a better job calling pitches, many umpires felt that the unproven technology was really an "umpire intimidation system" Whether QuesTec was unfairly used as a rating system or not, some pitchers felt that the system caused unpredictable changes in the strike zone in the ballparks where it was installed.

The following register includes virtually every umpire who has ever "called 'em as he saw 'em" in a major league game. During the early decades of baseball history, players often came off the bench to serve as umpires; those player-umps are marked with a star (★). Non-players employed as substitutes for regular umpires are indicated by a hollow star (☆). Replacement umpires during strikes are indicated by a dagger (†).

Abbey, Charles S. "Charlie" NL★1897
Abbott, Frederick H. "Fred" NL★1905
Adams, James NL☆1897
Adams, John H. AL 1903
Addy, Robert E. "Bob" NA☆1875
Adler UA☆1884
Allen, Hezekiah "Ham" NL☆1876
Allison, Andrew K. "Andy" NA☆1872 ☆1874
Allison, Arthur A. "Art" NA☆1872
Allison, Douglas L. "Doug" NA☆1872-73 ☆1875
Alston, David NA☆1871-72 ☆1875
Altrock, Nicholas "Nick" AL★1907
Anderson, David S. NL★1890
Anderson, Lewis E. "Andy" NL†1978-79
Anderson, Oliver O. "Ollie" FL 1914
Andress, William J. "Bill" NL†1979
Andrews, G. Edward "Ed" NL★1889 1895 1898-99
Annan, William H. NA☆1873
Anthony, G. Merlyn AL 1969-75
Arata, Mark AL†1991
Armendariz, Ramon ML 2004-06
Arnold, Frank W. AA☆1889
Arnold, Willis S. "Billy" NA☆1875
Arundel, John T. "Tug" NL★1888
Aschwege, David "Dave" ML 2003-04
Ashford, Emmett L. AL 1966-70
Austin, Ed AA☆1890
Avants, Nick R. AL 1969-71
Avery, C. Hamilton NA☆1874 1875
Ayers NL☆1876
Baird, John NL†1979
Bakely, Edward E. "Jersey" AA★1888 PL★1890
Baker, Charles NL☆1884
Baker, Philip "Phil" NL★1889
Baker, William P. "Bill" NL 1957
Baldwin, Clarence G. "Kid" AA★1887
Baldwin, Marcus E. "Mark" NL★1892
Ballanfant, E. Lee NL 1936-57
Ballina, Frank NL†1991 1995
Bannon, James H. "Jimmy" NL★1894
Barker, Alfred L. NL☆1881
Barksdale, Lance ML 2000-06
Barlick, Albert J. "Al" NL 1940-43 1946-55 1958-71
Barlow, Thomas H. "Tom" NA☆1875
Barnes, Ronald E. "Ron" NL 1990-94 1996-97 ML 2002
Barnes, Roscoe C. "Ross" NA☆1874 PL 1890
Barnett, Lawrence R. "Larry" AL 1968-99
Barnie, William S. "Billy" AA☆1882 ☆1884 ☆1887 ☆1889 NL☆1882 1892
Barnum, George W. AA 1890 NL☆1896
Barr, George M. NL 1931-49
Barrett, Edward G. "Ted" AL 1994-99 ML 2000-06
Barrett, William "Bill" NA☆1872 ☆1874
Barron, James "Jim" NA☆1875
Barron, Mark E. NL 1992-97 ML 2001-02
Barrows, Franklin L. "Frank" NA☆1872
Barry, Daniel "Dan" AL 1928
Barry, Scott ML 2006
Barston, Michael "Mike" NL†1979
Barton NL☆1876
Basil, Stephen J. "Steve" AL 1936-42
Baswell, Jack S. NL†1979
Battin, Joseph V. "Joe" NA☆1874 AA☆1882 ☆1886 NL 1891 ☆1895-96
Bauers, Albert J. "Al" AA 1887 ☆1890
Bausewine, George NL 1905
Beals, Thomas L. "Tommy" NA☆1872 ☆1874-75
Bean, Ed AL 1994
Beard, Oliver P. "Ollie" NL☆1894
Beardslee, John J. NA 1871 ☆1872-73
Beatin, Ebenezer "Ed" NL★1889
Becannon, James M. "Buck" AA★1884 NL☆1885
Becannon, William H. AA 1883
Bechtel, George A. NA☆1874
Beck, Erwin T. "Erve" NL★1902
Beck, Robert "Bob" NL†1979
Beck, W. S. NA☆1872
Beckley, Jacob P. "Jake" NL★1906
Beebe, Fred L. NL★1907
Behle, Frank NL☆1895-96 1901
Bejma, Alojzy F. "Ollie" AL★1935
Bell, Frank G. AA☆1889
Bell, Wallace R. "Wally" NL 1992-99 ML 2000-06
Bendekovits, Joseph "Joe" NL†1979
Bender, Charles A. "Chief" AL★1907
Bennett, Jack NL☆1893
Berger, Frederick NL☆1886
Berger, John H. "Tun" NL★1891
Bernhard, William H. "Bill" AL★1903 ★1907
Berry, Charles F. "Charlie" AL 1942-62 AL†1970
Berthrong, Henry W. "Harry" NA☆1872
Betcher, Ralph A. NL†1976
Betts, William G. NL 1894-96 1898-99 AL 1901 ☆1903
Betz, Edwin J. NL 1961
Beville, H. Monte AL★1903-04
Bialorucko, Larry AL†1995

Bible, Jonathan D. "Jon" AL†1984
Bielaski, Oscar NA☆1874-75
Bierhalter, William "Bits" AL☆1918-19 ☆1922 ☆1924
Bigelow, Walter I. NA☆1875 NL☆1877
Birdsall, David S. "Dave" NA☆1873-74
Bishop, Homer L. AL†1979
Bittman, Henry P. "Red" AA☆1889 NL☆1892 ☆1894-95 ☆1897
Blair, William J. NA☆1873
Blakiston, Robert J. "Bob" NL☆1884
Blandford, Fred NL†1970
Blankenship, Clifford D. "Cliff" AL★1907
Blodgett, C. William NA 1875 NL 1876
Blogg, Wesley C. "Wes" AA☆1886
Bloom, Ed AA☆1887
Bluege, Oswald L. "Ossie" AL★1938
Boake, John L. NA☆1871
Boardman, Frederick "Fred" NA 1875
Boggess, Lynton R. "Dusty" NL 1944-62
Bohn, Matt AL†1995
Boles, Charles NL 1877
Bomeisler, Theodore NA 1871-73 ☆1874-75
Bond, Thomas H."Tommy" NA☆1875
Bond, Thomas H. "Tommy" NL 1883 1885 AA★1884 ☆1891
Bonin, Gregory L. "Greg" NL 1984-99 ML 2000-01
Bonner, Frank J. NL★1894
Bonse, Nicholas NA☆1871
Booth, Amos S. AA★1882
Borga, Steven A. "Steve" AL†1979
Bovey, Terry R. NL†1979 1984 1995
Bowes, Frank M. AA☆1890
Boyd, William J. "Bill" NA☆1873 1875
Boyer, James M. "Jim" AL 1944-50
Boyle, Henry J. NL★1886
Boyle, John A. "Jack" AA★1888 NL★1892 ★1897
Bradley, George H. "Foghorn" NA☆1875 NL 1879-83 AA 1886
Bradley, George W. UA★1884
Brady, Jackson NL 1887
Brady NL☆1877
Brainard, Asa NA☆1872 ☆1875
Bransfield, William E. "Kitty" NL 1917
Bredburg, George W. NL 1877 ☆1878-79
Breitenstein, Theodore P. "Ted" NL★1900
Bremigan, Nicholas G. "Nick" AL 1974-88
Brennan, John E. "Jack" AA 1884 NL☆1887 1899
Brennan, John G. "Jack" AA★1888
Brennan, William T. "Bill" NL 1909-13 1921 FL 1914-15
Briggs, Warren R. NA☆1874
Brinkman, Joseph N. "Joe" AL 1973-99 ML 2000-06
Briody, Charles F. "Fatty" NL★1881 AA★1888
Briscese, Michael L. "Mike" AL†1979
Brocklander, Fred W. NL 1979-90
Brockway, John NL☆1877 ☆1879
Brown, Buddy Lee "Bud" AL†1979
Brown, Douglas D. "Doug" AL†1979
Brown, James AA☆1887
Brown, Jeff AL†1978-79
Brown, Samuel W. "Sam" NL★1907
Brown, Thomas T. "Tom" NL★1896 1898-99 1901-02 AL☆1907
Brown, William NA☆1872 ☆1875
Bruce, D. W. NA☆1875
Bruns, Randy NL†1991
Buck, William F. NA☆1871
Buckenberger, Alfred C. "Al" NL☆1890
Bucknor, C. B. NL 1996-99 ML 2000-06
Buelow, Charles J. "Charlie" NL★1901
Buelow, Frederick W. "Fritz" AL★1906
Buffinton, Charles G. "Charlie" NL★1883 ★1888-89 ★1892
Bullymore, Charles L. NL☆1882
Bunce, Frederick L. "Fred" NA☆1874
Bunce, H. C. NA☆1872
Bunce, Joshua NL 1877
Burdock, John J. "Jack" NA 1872-74 NL★1881 AA☆1887
Burkalow, Isaac AA☆1888
Burkhart, W. Kenneth "Ken" NL 1957-73
Burlingame, Frank A. NL☆1878 UA☆1884
Burnham, George W. NL 1883 ☆1886-87 1889 1895
Burns, John S. NL 1884
Burns, Thomas E. "Tom" NL 1892
Burns, Thomas P. "Oyster" AA★1888 NL★1895 1899
Burtis, L. Warren NL 1876-77
Bush, Archibald M. "Archie" NA☆1871
Bush, Garnet C. NL 1911-12 FL 1914
Bushong, Albert J. "Doc" NL★1880 ★1890 AA★1888-89
Butler, Charles AA☆1889
Butler, Ormond H. AA 1883 ☆1886
Butler, Richard H. "Dick" NL★1897
Byrne, Walter AA☆1882
Byron, William J. "Bill" or "Lord" NL 1913-19
Callahan, Edward J. "Ed" NL 1881 UA★1884
Callahan, James J. "Nixey" AL★1901
Camp, John W. AL†1979
Campagna, Frank J. NL†1979 1984
Campbell, Al NL☆1886
Campbell, Daniel "Dan" AA☆1890 NL 1894-96 ☆1897
Campbell, Robert "Bob" AL†1979
Campbell, William M. "Bick" AL 1928-31 NL 1938-40
Cantillon, Joseph D. "Joe" AL 1901 NL 1902
Caraco, Joe AL†1995
Carey, Thomas J. "Tom" NA☆1873 1874 ☆1875 AA 1882
Carlin, William J. "Billy" AA☆1885-86 ☆1888-89
Carlson, Mark C. NL 1999 ML 2000-06
Carney, John J. PL★1890
Carney, "Red" AL☆1924
Carpenter, John R. NA☆1874
Carpenter, William B. "Bill" NL 1897 1904 1906-07 AL 1904
Carrick, William M. "Bill" NL★1900
Carrigan, H. Sam AL 1961-65
Carroll, Frederick H. "Fred" NL★1887
Carroll, Patrick UA★1884
Carsey, Wilfred "Kid" AA★1891 NL★1894 ★1896 ☆1901
Caruthers, Robert L. "Bob" NL☆1886 ★1891 ☆1893 AL 1902-03
Casey, Daniel M. "Dan" NL★1888
Caskin, Edward J. "Ed" NL★1884 PL☆1890
Cassidy, John P. NA☆1875 NL★1882 AA★1884
Causey, Kevin ML 2006
Cavanaugh, J. H. "Harry" NA☆1875
Cavenaugh, Richard P. "Dick" NL†1979 1984
Cederstrom, Gary L. AL 1989-99 ML 2000-06
Chamberlain, Elton P. AA★1887 ★1891 NL★1894
Chance, Frank L. NL★1902
Chandler, Moses E. NA☆1872-1875 NL☆1877
Chapman, John C. "Jack" NA☆1871 ☆1873-74 NL☆1876 1880 ☆1882
Cheppy, John T. NL☆1876
Chill, Oliver P. "Ollie" AL 1914-16 1919-22
Chipman, Harry F. NL 1883 ☆1885 ☆1886
Christal, W. Randle "Randy" AL†1984
Chylak, Nestor L. AL 1954-78
Clack, Robert H. "Bobby" NL★1876 ☆1897
Clapp, John E. NA 1874-75
Clark, Alan M. "Al" AL 1976-99 ML 2000-01
Clarke, Arthur F. "Artie" NL★1890
Clarke, Robert M. "Bob" NL 1930-31
Clarke, William J. "Boileryard" NL★1893-94 ★1896
Clarkson, Arthur H. "Dad" NL★1893-96
Clarkson, John G. NL★1888 ★1892-93
Clegg, Richard "Dick" AL†1979
Clement, Robert F. "Bob" AL†1978-79
Clements, John J. "Jack" NL★1892
Clifton NA☆1872
Clinton, James L. "Jim" NA☆1873 ☆1875 AA 1886
Coble, G. Drew AL 1983-99
Cockill, George W. NL 1915
Cohen, Alfred A. "Al" NL†1976
Cohen, George NL☆1893
Colby NA☆1873
Coleman, John F. NL★1884
Colgan, Harry W. NL☆1899 1901
Colliflower, J. Harry AL 1910
Collins, Daniel T. "Dan" NA☆1875 NL☆1876
Colosi, Nicholas "Nick" NL 1968-82
Comiskey, Charles A. "Charlie" PL★1890
Compton, Craig AL†1995
Conahan, Edward J. "Ed" NL 1896
Cone, J. Frederick "Fred" NA☆1873-74 1875 NL☆1876 1877
Conlan, John B. "Jocko" AL★1935 NL 1941-64
Connell, Terence G. AA 1884 ☆1885-86 ☆1889 1890 ☆1891 NL☆1885 ☆1887
Connelly, John M. AA 1885 1887
Connelly, William AA 1884
Connolly, John M. "Red" NL☆1885 1886 ☆1887 ☆1892-93
Connolly, Thomas H. "Tommy" NL 1898-1900 AL 1901-31 ☆1932
Connor, Thomas "Tom" AL 1905-06
Connors, Patrick "Pat" NL 1998
Contant, Alan AL†1978-79
Conway, John H. NL 1906
Coogan, Daniel G. "Dan" NL★1895
Cook, Robert "Robb" NL 1999 ML 2000
Cook, W. H. NL☆1879
Cooney, John W. "Johnny" NL★1941
Cooney, Terrance J. "Terry" AL 1975-92
Cooper, Erik R. AL 1996-99 ML 2000-06
Cope, Elias NA☆1871
Corcoran, Thomas W. "Tommy" FL 1915
Cossey, Douglas C. "Doug" AL†1978-79 1984
Costello, Perry NL†1995
Cote, Emilien NL†1979
Coughlin, William P. "Bill" AL★1904
Cousins, Derryl AL 1979-99 ML 2000-06
Craft, Terry L. AL 1989-99 ML 2000-06
Crandall, Robert NL☆1876 1877 ☆1878 AA☆1882
Crane, Edward N. "Ed" NL★1892 ☆1893
Crane, Samuel N. "Sam" NL☆1879 ★1886 ☆1887 ★1890
Craver, William H. "Bill" NA☆1873
Crawford, Alexander UA 1884
Crawford, Gerald J. "Jerry" NL 1975-99 ML 2000-06
Crawford, Henry C. "Shag" NL 1956-75
Cray, P. C. NL☆1893
Creighton AA☆1889-90
Critchley, Morris A. "Morrie" AA☆1884-85
Crolius, Frederick J. "Fred" NL★1901
Cronin, John J. "Jack" AL★1901 NL★1902-03
Cross, John A. NL☆1876 1878
Cross, Lafayette N. "Lave" AA★1889 NL★1892
Cross, Montford M. "Monte" FL 1914
Crowell, William T. "Billy" AA★1888
Cudworth, J. Alaric "Al" NL☆1880
Culbreth, Fieldin H. AL 1993-99 ML 2000-06
Culler, Richard B. "Dick" NL★1947
Cuneo, James "Jim" NL†1978-79 AL†1979
Cunningham, Elmer E. "Bert" NL★1896-97 ★1900 1901
Cuppy, George M. NL★1894
Curren, Peter NL☆1876
Curry, Frank AA☆1884 ☆1886
Curry, Wesley "Wes" NL 1885-86 1889 1898 AA 1887 1890
Cusack, Stephen P. NL 1909 FL 1914
Cushman, Charles H. "Charlie" NL 1885 ☆1894 1898
Cusick, Andrew D. "Tony" NL★1886-87
Cuthbert, Edgar E. "Ned" NA☆1875 UA★1884 AA 1887 ☆1888
Cuzzi, Philip "Phil" NL 1991-93 1999 ML 2000-06
Dailey, John J. NL 1882 AA 1884 ☆1889
Daily, Cornelius F. "Con" PL★1890 NL★1891 ★1894 ★1896
Dale, Jerry P. NL 1970-85
Daly, Thomas P. "Tom" NL★1901
Daniels, Charles F. NA 1874-75 NL 1876 1878-80 ☆1885 1887-88 AA 1883-85 1889
Daniels, Lawrence L. AA☆1887
Danley, Kerwin J. NL 1991-99 ML 2000-06
Darling, Conrad "Dell" NL★1887 AA★1891
Darling, Gary R. NL 1986-99 ML 2002-06
Dascoli, Frank NL 1948-62
Daubney, Thomas NA☆1871
David, L. N. NA☆1874
Davidson, Dale F. AL†1979
Davidson, David L. "Satch" NL 1969-84
Davidson, Robert A. "Bob" NL 1982-99 ML 2005-06
Davidson NL†1995
Davis, Bill NL†1995
Davis, Gerald S. "Gerry" NL 1982-99 ML 2000-06
Davis, Harry H. AL★1903
Davis, James J. "Jumbo" AA 1891
Dawson, Mort NA☆1871
Dealy, Patrick E. "Pat" NL★1886
Deane, J. Henry "Harry" NA☆1871 ☆1874 NL☆1876 ☆1878
Decker, Stewart M. NL 1883-85 1888
Deegan, William E. J. "Bill" AL 1970-80 AL†1970 1984 1991 1995
DeFlesco, Pete AL†1991
Dehlman, Herman J. NA☆1873 1874 ☆1875
Dellinger, Duston "Dusty" ML 2005-06
Delmore, Victor "Vic" NL 1956-59
Demorest, D. P. NA☆1872-73
DeMuth, Dana A. NL 1983-99 ML 2000-06
Deniston, Shannon W. "Shan" NL†1978
Denkinger, Donald A. "Don" AL 1968-98
Denny, Richard AL†1984
Derr, Doll NL 1923
Devine, W. James "Jim" AA☆1890
Devinney, P. H. "Dan" NL☆1876 1877 UA 1884 AA 1884 ☆1887
Devlin, Charles "Charlie" AA☆1888
Dexter, Charles D. "Charlie" NL★1896-97
Dezelan, Frank J. NL 1966-68 1969-71
Diaz, Lazaro "Laz" AL 1995 1997-99 ML 2000-06
Dierking, Roger A. NL†1978
DiMuro, Louis J. "Lou" AL 1963-80
DiMuro, Michael R. "Mike" AL 1997 1999 ML 2000-06
DiMuro, Raymond "Ray" AL 1996-99
Dinneen, William H. "Bill" AL★1907 1909-37
Dixon, Hal H. NL 1953-59
Dobson, H. A. NA☆1871
Dolan, Thomas J. "Tom" AA☆1890-91
Dole, Lester C. NA 1875
Donahue, Francis R. "Red" NL★1897 AL★1903 ★1906
Donahue, James A. "Jim" AA★1888
Donahue, Timothy C. "Tim" NL★1895-96
Donatelli, August J. "Augie" NL 1950-73
Donlin, Michael J. "Mike" NL★1900 AL☆1918
Donnelly, Charles H. NL 1931-32 AL 1934-35
Donnelly, James B. "Jim" NL★1896
Donohue, Michael R. NL 1930
Donovan, Timothy H. UA☆1884
Donovan, William E. "Bill" NL★1902 AL★1903 ★1906
Dooin, Charles S. "Red" NL★1904
Dornlach, D. E. NA☆1872
Doscher, John H. Sr. "Herm" NL☆1879 1880-81 1887 AA 1888 1890
Douglass, William B. "Klondike" NL★1903
Dow, Clarence AA☆1891
Dowdy, Adam ML 2002-06
Dowse, Thomas J. "Tom" NL★1890
Doyle, John J. "Jack" NL 1911
Doyle, Walter J. AL 1963
Drake, Robert "Rob" NL 1999 ML 2000-06
Draper, John H. NA☆1871 NL☆1877
Dreckman, Bruce M. NL 1996-99 ML 2002-06
Dreke, Roy AL†1979
Dresser, Al AL†1995
Drill, Lewis L. "Lew" AL★1903-04
Driscoll, Joseph M. "Joe" AL†1978
Drummond, Calvin T. "Cal" AL 1960-69
Ducharme NL 1876-77
Duffy, James F. "Jim" AL 1951-55
Dugan AA☆1887
Duggleby, William J. "Bill" NL★1905
Duke, Martin F. AA☆1890
Duncan, Robert AL†1995
Dunlap, Frederick C. "Fred" NL☆1879
Dunlevy, Hugh AA☆1887
Dunn, Thomas P. "Tom" NL 1939-46

Dunne, James "Jim" AL†1978-79
Dunnigan, Joseph NL 1881-82
Durfee, Peter ML 2005
Dutton, Patrick J. UA 1884
Dwyer, J. Francis "Frank" NL★1889 ★1893-94 ★1896-97 1899 1901 AL 1904
Dyler, John F. AA☆1883 1884 ☆1885-86 NL☆1892 ☆1897
Eagan, John J. NL 1878 ☆1879 1886
Earle, William M. "Billy" NL☆1892 ★1894
Easley, Harold L. AL†1979
Eason, Malcolm W. "Mal" NL☆1901 1902 1910-16
Easton, John S. "Jack" AA★1891
Eddings, Douglas "Doug" AL 1998-99 ML 2000-06
Edwards, Larry NL†1978
Egan, John J. "Rip" AL 1903 1907-14
Ehret, Philip S. "Phil" AA★1890 NL★1892 ★1895-97
Eldridge, Clarence E. AL 1914-15
Ellick, Joseph J. "Joe" NL 1886 AA☆1888-89
Ellis, William R. NA☆1871-72 ☆1875
Emmel, Paul L. NL 1999 ML 2000-06
Emslie, Robert D. "Bob" AA 1890 NL 1891-1924
Engel, Robert A. "Bob" NL 1965-90
Engeln, William R. "Bill" NL 1952-56
English, John W. NA☆1874-75 NL☆1876
Erby, Frederick NA☆1872
Eshelman, George R. AL†1979
Estabrook, Michael "Mike" ML 2006
Evans, George NA☆1872
Evans, James B. "Jim" AL 1971-99
Evans, Jeff AL†1991
Evans, Uriah L. P. "Jake" NL☆1886
Evans, William G. "Billy" AL 1906-27
Everitt, Michael G. "Mike" AL 1996-99 ML 2000-06
Ewing, John AA★1889
Ewing, William "Buck" AA☆1882
Fairchild, Chad ML 2004-06
Falch, Anton C. UA☆1884
Farmer, Michael "Mike" AL†1979
Farnsworth, Harry AL†1979
Farrell, Charles A. "Duke" NL★1901-02
Feaser, Richard L. "Dick" AL†1979
Fell AA☆1885
Fellows, T. E. NA☆1871
Fenno, Norman NL☆1876
Ferguson, Charles A. AL 1913
Ferguson, Charles J. "Charlie" NL★1886
Ferguson, Robert V. "Bob" NA☆1871 1872-73 ☆1874 1875 NL 1879 1884-85 AA 1886-89 1891 PL 1890
Fessenden, Wallace C. "Wally" NL 1889-90
Fichter, Michael AL 1999 ML 2000-05
Fick, Jerry D. NL†1978-79
Fields, Stephen H. "Steve" NL 1979-82
Finneran, William F. NL 1911-12 ☆1923 FL 1915
Fisher, Frank NL†1979 1984
Fisher, William C. "Cherokee" NA☆1871 ☆1875 NL☆1876
Fitzpatrick, Michael N. "Mike" AL†1979
Fitzsimmons, Frederick "Freddie" NL★1941
Flaherty, John F. "Red" AL 1953-73
Flaherty, Martin J. NL☆1882
Flaherty, Patrick J. "Patsy" AL★1903 NL★1904 ☆07
Fleming, Thomas E. "Tom" NL†1979
Fletcher, Andrew J. "Andy" NL 1999 ML 2000-06
Floras, John NL†1991 1995
Flynn, John A. "Jocko" NL☆1893
Foley, Thomas J. "Tom" NA☆1874-75
Follmer, William A. "Bill" AL†1979
Force, David W. "Davy" NA☆1873 NL★1881
Ford, R. Dale AL 1975-99
Ford, Wade NL†1995
Foreman, Francis I. "Frank" NL★1895 AL★1901
Foreman, John D. "Brownie" NL★1896
Forman, Allen S. "Al" NL 1961-65 AL†1978-79
Foster, Clarence F. "Pop" NL★1900
Foster, Martin R. "Marty" AL 1996-99 ML 2000-06
Fountain, Edward G. NL 1879
Fountain, Henry V. AA☆1888
Fouser, William C. NL☆1876
Fowler, A. Wheeler NL†1978
Frantz, Arthur F. "Art" AL 1969-77
Frary, Ralph NL 1911
Freels, Robert L. "Bob" NL†1979
Freeman, John F. "Buck" NL★1900
Freese, Todd AL†1995
Friel, William E. "Bill" AL 1920
Froemming, Bruce N. NL 1971-99 ML 2000-06
Froese, Grover A. AL 1952-53
Fuchs, Lester AL†1978-79
Fullwood, Troy ML 2004-06
Fulmer, Charles J. "Chick" NA☆1872 1873 ☆1874-75 NL☆1881 1886 AA★1888
Fulmer, Christopher "Chris" AA★1887
Furlong, William E. "Bill" NL☆1877 1878-79 ☆1880 1883-84 ☆1888 UA☆1884
Fyfe, Lee C. NL 1920
Fyfe, Louis FL 1915
Gaffney, John H. NL 1884-86 ☆1887 1891-94 ☆1898 1899-1900 AA 1888-89 PL 1890
Gallagher, Lawrence E. "Larry" AL†1979
Galvin, James F. "Jim" NL☆1881 ☆1886 ★1887 ★1889 1895 AA☆1885 ★1886
Ganzel, Charles W. "Charlie" AA★1886 NL☆1901
Garcia, Richard P. "Rich" AL 1975-99
Gardner, James A. "Jim" NL★1899
Garman, Jim NL†1995
Garrigan, Charles NA☆1873
Geer, William H. "Billy" NA☆1874-75 AA☆1887
Geisel, Harry C. AL 1925-42
George, Edward "Ed" AL†1979
George, William M. "Bill" NL★1889
Gerhardt, Joseph J. "Joe" NA☆1875
German, Lester S. "Les" NL★1895
Getzien, Charles H. "Charlie" NL★1890
Giard, Robert "Bob" AL†1978
Gibbons, Brian NL 1994-99
Gibson, Gregory A. "Greg" NL 1997-99 ML 2000-06
Gifford, James H. NL☆1881
Gill, Thomas H. "Tommy" AA☆1886
Gillean, Thomas NL 1879-80 ☆1881
Gisondi, Tony NL†1991
Gleason, John D. NL☆1877
Gleason, William G. "Bill" NL☆1877
Gleason, William J. "Kid" NL★1890 ★1892
Gleason, William G. "Bill" AA 1891
Glenn, John W. NA☆1874 NL☆1880
Glover, Frank NA☆1873
Goeckel, E. FL 1914
Goetz, Lawrence J. "Larry" NL 1936-57
Goetz, Russell L. "Russ" AL 1968-83
Goldsby, Walton H. "Walt" AA★1888
Goldsmith, Frederick E. "Fred" NL☆1886 AA 1888-89
Goodwin, J. Cheever NA☆1871-72
Gore, Arthur J. "Artie" NL 1947-56
Gorman, Brian NL 1991-99 ML 2000-06
Gorman, Thomas D. "Tom" NL 1951-76
Gould, Charles H. "Charlie" NA☆1874-75
Grady, John J. UA☆1884
Grady, Michael W. "Mike" NL★1895 AL★1901
Graham, J. S. NA☆1871-72
Graham, Scott NL†1991 1995
Graves, Frank M. NL★1886 ☆1895
Greenwood, William F. "Bill" AA★1884
Gregg, Eric E. NL 1975-91 1993-99
Grieve, William T. "Bill" AL 1938-55
Griffith, Clark C. AA☆1891 NL★1894-95 AL★1903
Griffith, E. A. AA 1884
Grim, John H. NL★1892 ★1895-96
Grimsley, John NL†1970
Grinder, Scott NL†1976 NL 1986
Groom, Robert "Bob" FL★1914
Grooms, Roger C. NL†1979
Gross, Edward M. NL☆1881
Gruber, Henry J. NL★1889
Grygiel, George R. NL†1970
Guccione, Chris ML 2000-06
Guckert, Elmer NL†1976
Guglielmo, A. Augie NL 1952
Guiney, Benjamin NL☆1882
Gumbert, Addison C. "Ad" PL★1890 NL★1892 ★1895-96
Gunning, Thomas F. "Tom" NL★1884-85 1887 AA★1888-89 PL 1890
Gunson, Joseph B. "Joe" NL★1892
Gustafson, G. David "Dave" AL†1978
Guthrie, William J. "Bill" NL 1913 1915 AL 1922 1928-32
Hackett, Mortimer M. "Mert" NL★1886
Haddock, George S. NL★1889 PL★1890
Hadry, Merrill A. AL†1979 NL†1979
Hafner, William F. "Bill" AL†1979
Halback, A. C. N. NA☆1871 ☆1873-75
Hall, George W. NA☆1873-75
Hall, James "Jim" NA☆1872-73
Hall, N. Samuel NA☆1873
Haller, William E. "Bill" AL 1961 1963-82
Hallion, Thomas F. "Tom" NL 1985-99 ML 2005-06
Hallman, William W. "Bill" PL★1890 NL★1903
Hamil, Ray NL†1979
Hanlon, Edward H. "Ned" NL★1892
Hanna, Dr. NA☆1872
Hansen, Howard NL†1978-79
Hantak, H. Robert "Bob" NL†1979
Hardie, Louis W. "Lou" NL☆1887
Harris, Joseph W. "Joe" AL★1906
Harris, Lanny D. NL 1979-85
Harris, Vance AL†1995 NL†1995
Harrison, Peter A. "Pete" NL 1916-20
Hart, Eugene F. "Bob" NL 1920-29
Hart, Robert F. "Bertie" AL 1912-13
Hart, William F. "Bill" NL★1896-97 1914-15 AL 1901
Hartenstein, Isaac NA☆1875
Hartley, Grover A. AL★1935
Hartley, John "Jack" NL☆1894
Harvey, H. Douglas "Doug" NL 1962-92
Harvey, Randy AL†1991 1995
Haskell, John E. AL 1901
Hassett, James E. AL 1903
Hastings, W. Scott NA☆1871-74 NL☆1877
Hatfield, Gilbert "Gil" NL★1889
Hatfield, John V. B. NA☆1872-73 NL☆1876
Hautz, Charles A. "Charlie" NL 1876 1879 AA 1882
Hawes, William H. "Bill" NL☆1880-82
Hayhurst, E. Hicks NA☆1875
Haynie, James L. NA☆1871
Healy, John J. NL★1887 AA★1890
Hecker, Guy J. AA☆1888 1889
Hegeman, William H. NA☆1871 NL☆1881
Heitzer, Richard "Dick" AL†1979
Helburn, Hugo AA☆1887
Helm, J. NA☆1871-72
Hemming, George E. NL★1895-96
Henderson, J. Harding "Hardie" AA☆1889 NL 1895-96
Hendry, Eugene "Ted" AL 1978-99
Hengle, Edward S. "Ed" NL 1887 AA☆1889
Hengle, Emery J. "Moxie" UA 1884
Henline, Walter J. "Butch" NL 1945-48
Henrichs, Jeff AL 1993 AL†1995
Henry, William E. "Bill" AL†1979 NL†1979
Hernandez, Angel NL 1991-99 ML 2000-06
Hernandez, Bob NL†1995
Herr, Edward J. "Ed" AA★1888
Herrin, W. E. NL☆1894
Heubel, George A. NA 1875
Heuble, George A. NL 1876
Heydler, John A. NL☆1895-97 1898
Hickey, James L. NL☆1882
Hickman, Charles T. "Charlie" AL★1907
Hickox, Edwin W. "Ed" AL 1990-99 ML 2005-06
Hicks, Nathaniel W. "Nat" AA☆1885
Higgins, John AL†1991 1995
Higgins, Scott ML 2000-03
Higgins, William E. "Bill" AA★1890
Higham, Richard "Dick" NA☆1872-75 NL 1881-82
Hildebrand, George A. AL 1913-34
Hines, Michael P. "Mike" NL★1884
Hirschbeck, John F. AL 1984-99 ML 2000-06
Hirschbeck, Mark NL 1987-99 ML 2000-03
Hoagland, Willard A. NL 1894
Hodes, Charles "Charlie" NA☆1874
Hodges, Amory G. NA 1874-75
Hodges, A. D. NL 1876 ☆1877
Hodges, Morris NL 1999 ML 2000-01
Hoffer, William L. "Bill" NL★1896
Hogan NL☆1897
Hogriever, George C. NL☆1893
Hohn, William J. "Bill" NL 1987-99 ML 2002-06
Holbert, William H. "Bill" AA★1888 PL 1890
Holbrook, Samuel "Sam" AL 1996 NL 1997-99 ML 2002-06
Holland, John A. AA 1884 UA 1884 NL 1887
Holland, Willard A. AA 1889
Holliday, James W. "Bug" AA☆1888 NL★1897 1903
Hollowell, Matthew "Matt" ML 2000-04
Holly, Samuel J. "Sam" NA 1871
Holmes, Howard E. "Ducky" NL 1921 AL 1923-24
Holoka, Mike NL†1991 1995
Homolka, Bob NL†1995
Honochick, G. James "Jim" AL 1949-73
Hooper, Michael H. "Mike" NA☆1872-74 UA 1884
Hornung, M. Joseph "Joe" NL☆1892 1893 1896
Hosworth NA☆1872-74
Hough, Pliny NA☆1875
Howard, Charles NA☆1872
Howard, C. F. NL☆1884
Howe, John "Shorty" NL★1890
Howell, H. Harry AL★1904 ★1906-07 FL 1915
Howley, Daniel P. "Dan" AL☆1922
Hoye, James ML 2003-06
Hubbard, R. Cal AL 1936-51
Huber, Mike AL†1995
Hudson, Marvin L. NL 1998-99 ML 2000-06
Hudson, Vincent D. UA☆1884
Humphrey, Rich NL†1995
Hunt, John T. NL 1895 1898-99
Hurley, Daniel "Dan" AA 1887
Hurley, Edwin H. "Eddie" AL 1947-65
Hurll, George NL☆1876
Hurst, Timothy C. "Tim" NL 1891-97 ★1898 1900 1903 ☆1904 AL 1905-09
Hutson, Ronald "Ron" NL†1979
Hyatt, R. Hamilton "Ham" NL★1912
Iassogna, Dan AL 1999 NL 1999 ML 2000-06
Irwin, Arthur A. NL★1881 1902
Irwin, John AA☆1885
Irwin, AA☆1882
Ivory, William J. "Bill" AL†1979
Jacklitsch, Fred L. NL★1901
Jackowski, William A. "Bill" NL 1952-68
Jackson, Charles L. AL†1979
Jackson, Dick NL†1995
James, John F. "Johnny" AL†1978-79
January, Don NL†1991 1995
Jeffers, Ronald L. "Ron" NL†1979
Jeffers, William W. NL 1881
Jenkins, Jeff NL†1995
Jennings, Alfred J. "Al" NA☆1873 AA☆1882 ☆1884-85 1887 ☆1889 ☆1891 UA 1884
Jennings, Hugh A. "Hughie" NL★1893 ★1900
Jevne, Frederick "Fred" NL☆1892 ☆1894 1895
Johns, William R. NA☆1873
Johnson, Adrian ML 2006
Johnson, Harry S. "Steamboat" NL 1914
Johnson, Mark S. AL 1980-99
Johnson, Sylvester "Syl" NL★1934
Johnston, Charles E. AL 1936-37
Johnstone, James E. "Jim" AL 1902 NL 1903-12 FL 1915
Jones, Bob NL†1995
Jones, Charles W. "Charley" PL 1890 AA 1891
Jones, Henry NL★1890
Jones, James "Jim" NL†1979
Jones, Nicholas I. "Red" AL 1944-49
Jones, Robert G. "Bob" AL†1979 1984

Jorda, Louis D. "Lou" NL 1927-31 1940-52
Jordan, Harold E. AL†1984
Jordan, William H. "Bill" UA 1884
Jose, Victor NL☆1889
Jost, Mike ML 2004
Joyce, C. E. NL☆1879
Joyce, James A. "Jim" AL 1989-99 ML 2000-06
Julian, Joseph O. NL 1878 AA☆1888
Jumper, Howard NL†1979
Kahn, S. L. NA☆1875
Kahoe, Michael J. "Mike" NL★1905
Kaiser, Kenneth J. "Ken" AL 1977-99
Kane, Stephen J. NL☆1906 1909-10 FL 1914
Kaplan, Al AL†1995
Karger, Edwin "Ed" NL★1906
Katzenmeier, Travis AL 1999 ML 2000-01
Kavulich, Joseph "Joe" AL†1978-79
Keefe, Timothy J. "Tim" NL★1880-82 ★1884-85 ★1887 ★1892 ☆1893 1894-96 AA★1884 PL★1890
Keeler, William H. "Willie" NL☆1910
Keenan, James W. "Jim" AA★1887-88 NL★1890 ☆1893
Keerl, George W. NA☆1872
Keister, R. Wayne AL†1978-79
Kelley, J. P. NL☆1879
Kelley, Kevin ML 2001-05
Kellogg, Jeffery "Jeff" NL 1991-99 ML 2000-06
Kellum, Winford A. "Win" NL★1905
Kelly, Eugene C. "Gene" AL†1979
Kelly, John F. UA★1884
Kelly, John O. "Kick" NL 1882 ☆1884-85 1888 1897 AA 1883-86 ☆1887
Kelly, Michael J. "King" PL★1890 NL★1892-93
Kelly, Thomas B. AL 1905
Kelly, William W. NL☆1877
Kennedy, Charles NL 1904
Kennedy, Michael J. "Doc" NL☆1884 AL☆1910
Kennedy, Ted NL☆1893
Kenney, John NA☆1872 NL☆1876 1877
Kent, John NA☆1875
Kerin, John AL☆1908 1909-10
Kerins, John A. "Jack" NL☆1888 AA 1889-91 AL☆1903
Kibler, John W. NL 1963-89
Killen, Frank B. NL★1896-97
Kilroy, Matthew A. "Matt" AA★1887
Kimball, Shawn AL†1991
King, Charles F. AL 1904
Kinnamon, William E. "Bill" AL 1960-69
Kinslow, Thomas F. "Tom" NL★1892
Kipp, Eden NL☆1881
Kirby, John F. AA★1888
Kirby, Kenneth "Ken" AL†1979
Kitson, Frank R. NL★1902
Kittridge, Malachi J. NL★1890 ★1899 AL★1905-06
Klein, Charles H. "Chuck" NL★1942
Klein, Gus AL†1991 1995
Kleinbacker AA☆1886
Klem, William J. "Bill" NL 1905-41
Klemm, Justin ML 2000-03
Kling, John G. "Johnny" NL★1901
Kling, William "Bill" NL☆1892
Klusman, William F. "Billy" NL☆1893
Knauss, Jim AL†1991
Knell, Philip H. "Phil" AA★1891 NL★1895
Knight, Alonzo P. "Lon" NL☆1876 ☆1888 1889 AA 1887 PL 1890
Knight, Brian ML 2001-06
Knight, George H. NA☆1875
Knowles, James "Jimmy" NL★1892
Kohler, Henry C. NA☆1873
Kolls, Louis C. "Lou" AL 1933-40
Kosc, Gregory J. "Greg" AL 1976-99
Krieg, William F. "Bill" NL★1887
Kulpa, Ronald C. "Ron" NL 1998-99 ML 2000-06
Kunkel, William G. "Bill" AL 1968-84
Lally, Bud NL 1896
Lamb, Henry W. "Harry" NA☆1875
Lambeth, Jim NL†1995
Lamplugh, Ian NL 1999 ML 2000-02
Landes, Stanley A. "Stan" NL 1955-72
Lane, Frank H. NL 1883
Langden, Joseph FL 1915
Lanigan, Charles NL☆1908
LaPierre, Richard AL†1979
Latham, George W. "Juice" AA★1884
Latham, W. Arlington "Arlie" NL 1899 ☆1900 1902
Laude, William F. "Bill" AL†1978-79
Laughlin, Benjamin "Ben" NA☆1873
Laughlin NL☆1876
Lauzon, Jacques NL†1979
Lawler, John F. AA 1884
Lawlor, Michael H. NL☆1882
Lawson, William R. "Bill" NL†1979
Layne, Jerry B. NL 1989-99 ML 2000-06
Lazar, Richard R. "Richie" AL†1978-79
Leach, Henry PL 1890
Leahy, Thomas J. "Tom" AL★1901
Leary NL☆1879
Lee, Thomas F. UA☆1884
Leever, Samuel W. "Sam" NL★1900 ★1904
Lennon, William F. "Bill" NA 1871-72 ★1873-74
Leonard, Andrew J. "Andy" NA☆1872-73 ☆1875
Leonard, J. NA☆1872
Lepperd, Thomas E. "Tom" AL 1984-86
Leppert, Donald G. "Don" AL★1978
Leroy, Isaac NA☆1871
Levet, Jay AL†1979
Levis, Charles H. "Charlie" AA☆1882
Libby, Stephen A. NL☆1879 1880
Lilly, J. AA☆1884
Lincoln, Frederick H. NL 1914
Lindaman, Vivian A. "Vive" NL★1907
Linsalata, Joseph N. "Joe" AL 1961-62
Little, Harry AA☆1884
Locke, Marshall NA☆1873-74
Loeber, Gerald G. "Jerry" AL†1979 NL†1979
Long, Robert "Bob" NL 1992
Long, William H. "Billy" NL☆1893 1895 ☆1897
Lospitalier, Philip A. "Phil" AL†1979 NL†1979
Loughlin, William H. AA☆1882
Loughlin AA☆1885
Lovett, James D. NA☆1871
Lowe, Robert L. "Bobby" AL★1905
Lowell, John A. NA☆1872-73
Luciano, Ronald M. "Ron" AL 1968-80
Luker, Dale AL†1995
Lundgren, Carl L. NL★1905-06
Lupo, Charles "Charlie" NL†1978-79 AL†1979
Lush, M. R. NA☆1873
Lynch, F. G. NL☆1892
Lynch, John H. "Jack" AA★1884
Lynch, Thomas J. "Tom" NL 1888-99 ☆1902
Lyons, Thomas A. "Toby" AA☆1891
Lyston, William E. AA☆1890
Mabbot, Frederick J. "Fred" AL†1979
MacDiarmed, Thomas NA☆1872
Mace, Harry L. AL☆1903
Mack, Dennis J. "Denny" NA☆1873-74 1875 AA 1886
Mackin, John F. AL†1979
Macullar, James F. "Jimmy" AA★1886 1891 NL 1892
Madden, Michael J. "Kid" PL★1890
Maddox, Charles NL☆1882
Magee, Sherwood R. "Sherry" NL 1928
Magerkurth, George L. NL 1929-47
Maginnis, Jim NL☆1910
Magner, John T. AA☆1882 1883 ☆1884 ☆1887
Maher, Robert J. "Bob" NL†1979 1984
Mahoney, Michael J. AA 1891 NL 1892
Malone, Ferguson G. "Fergy" NA☆1875 NL 1884 ☆1892-93
Malone, J. R. AA☆1888
Malone NA☆1875
Maloney, George P. AL 1969-83
Maloney, William A. "Billy" NL★1902
Manassau, Alfred S. "Al" NL 1899 AL 1901 FL 1914
Mann, Terry AL†1995
Manning, James H. "Jim" NL★1886 ☆1893
Manning, John E. "Jack" NL☆1881
Mapledoram, Blake A. UA 1884 NL☆1886
Marberry, Frederick "Firpo" AL 1935
Marino, James H. "Jimmy" AL†1979
Marquez, Alfonso NL 1999 ML 2000-06
Marsh, Randall G. "Randy" NL 1981-99 ML 2000-06
Marshall AA☆1887
Martin, Alphonse C. "Phonney" NA☆1871 ☆1873 1875 NL☆1876
Martin, Lewis G. NA☆1871 ☆1873-74
Martine, Bruce NL†1991
Mason, Charles E. "Charlie" NL☆1876
Mason, Danny AL†1995
Mathews, Robert T. "Bobby" NA☆1871 1873-75 NL☆1876 1880 ★1882 AA☆1888 1891 PL 1890
Mathewson, Christopher "Christy" NL★1901 ★1907
Mattimore, Michael J. "Mike" AA★1888
Mauer, Boyd AL†1979 NL†1978-79
Mawny, J. H. NA☆1871
Maxwell, Cortez "Corty" NA☆1875
Maxwell, J. Albert "Bert" FL★1914
Mayer, Ed NL☆1893
Mays, Albert C. "Al" AA★1887
Mays NA☆1871
McAleer, James R. "Jim" NL★1893
McAllister, Lewis W. "Sport" NL★1899 AL★1901-02
McCafferty, Charles NL 1921 1923
McCaffrey, Harry C. UA 1884 NL☆1885-86
McCarthy, John "Jack" AL 1905
McCarthy, Thomas F. M. "Tommy" NL★1896
McCartney, Joseph AA☆1882
McCarty, John A. AA★1889
McCauley, Allen A. "Al" NL★1890
McCauley, Patrick M. "Pat" NL★1896
McClelland, Timothy R. "Tim" AL 1984-99 ML 2000-06
McCormick, James "Jim" NL★1885
McCormick, William J. "Barry" FL 1914-15 AL 1917 NL 1919-29
McCormick AA☆1888
McCoy, Larry S. AL 1970-99
McCrea NA☆1872
McCrum NL☆1892
McDermott, Michael J. "Sandy" NL 1890 1897
McDonald, James F. NA☆1872 NL 1895 1897-99
McDougall, Scott AL†1991
McElwee, Harvey NL 1877
McFarland, Edward W. "Ed" NL★1896
McFarland, Horace NL 1896-97
McGarr, James B. "Chippy" NL★1895 1899
McGeary, Michael H. NA☆1872 ☆1875
McGee, Patrick AA☆1882 ☆1884
McGee NL☆1876
McGinnis, George W. "Jumbo" AA☆1888-89
McGinnity, Joseph J. "Joe" NL★1900
McGinty NL☆1897
McGowan, William A. "Bill" AL 1925-54
McGreevy, Edward AL 1912-13
McGrew, Harry T. "Ted" NL 1930-31 1933-34
McGuire, James T. "Deacon" NL★1886-87 ★1894 ★1896-97 ★1901 AL★1905
McGunnigle, Edward NL☆1888
McGunningle, William H. "Bill" UA☆1884
McIntosh AA☆1882
McKean, James G. "Jim" AL 1974-99 ML 2000-01
McKelvy, Russell E. "Russ" AA★1882
McKinley, William F. "Bill" AL 1946-65
McKinney NL☆1883
McKinnon, Alexander J. "Alex" NL★1886
McLaughlin, Edward J. NL 1929
McLaughlin, James "Jim" UA☆1884
McLaughlin, Michael NL 1893
McLaughlin, Peter J. NL 1924-28
McLaughlin, Thomas AA 1891
McLaughlin, William AA☆1882
McLean AA☆1890
McLean, Harry C. NA☆1871 ☆1873
McLean, William H. "Billy" NA☆1872-73 1874-75 NL 1876 1878-80 1882-84 AA☆1882 1885 ☆1889
McLeod NL☆1895
McMahon, John H. NL☆1893
McMahon, John J. "Sadie" AA★1890
McMahon, William NA☆1871
McManaway, D. UA☆1884
McMinimum, Dennis UA☆1884
McMullin, John F. NA☆1874 NL☆1876
McNally, James "Jim" AL†1979
McNichol, Robert T. AA 1883
McQuaid, John H. "Jack" AA 1886-88 NL 1889-94
McQuaid, Martin NL☆1893
McSherry, John P. NL 1971-96
McSorley, John B. "Trick" AA★1884 ☆1888
McVey, Calvin A. "Cal" NA☆1871 ☆1873 ☆1875
Meacham NA☆1875
Meagher, John NL☆1877
Meals, Gerald W. "Jerry" NL 1992-94 1996-99 ML 2000-06
Mears, Charles W. NL☆1894
Medart, William NL☆1876-77 AA☆1887
Meekin, Jouette NL★1895-96
Megrue, Cliff NL☆1876
Melton, David "Dave" NL†1978
Menefee, John "Jock" NL★1903
Mercer, George B. "Win" NL★1896
Meriwether, Julius E. "Chuck" AL 1988-99 ML 2000-06
Merrill, Edward M. "Ed" AA★1884
Merrill, E. Durwood AL 1977-99
Merritt, Clarence AL†1979
Mertes, Samuel B. "Sam" NL★1905
Miller, Charles A. AA☆1884
Miller, Gale AL†1979
Miller, George E. NL 1879
Miller, George F. "Doggie" NL★1893 ★1896
Miller, John A. "Jack" AL†1979
Miller, Joseph H. NL★1884
Miller, Joseph W. "Joe" NA☆1872-73
Miller, L. Otto NL★1934
Miller, Marvin G. "Bud" NL†1979
Miller, William S. "Bill" AL 1997-99 ML 2000-06
Milligan, John "Jocko" PL★1890
Mills, Abraham G. NL☆1877
Mills, Charles "Charlie" NA☆1871 1872-73
Mills, Greg NL†1979
Mincher, Edward J. "Ed" NA☆1872 ☆1875
Mincher, William E. NA☆1875
Mitchell, Charles NL 1892
Mitchell, Franklin B. NA☆1874-75
Mitchell AA☆1887
Monahan, Pat AL☆1931
Montague, Edward M. "Ed" NL 1974-99 ML 2000-06
Montague NL☆1877
Montgomery UA☆1884
Moore, Earl A. AL★1903
Moran, August "Augie" NL 1903-04 1910 1918
Moran, Charles B. "Charlie" NL 1918-39
Moran, Patrick J. "Pat" NL★1901
Morgan, H. William "Bill" AA☆1884
Morgenweck, Henry C. "Hank" AL 1972-75 NL†1970
Moriarty, George J. AL 1917-26 1929-40
Morrill, John F. NL☆1891 ☆1896
Morris, Edward NL☆1895 ☆1897
Morris, John S. NL☆1876
Morrison, Daniel G. "Dan" AL 1979-99 ML 2000-01
Morton, Charles H. "Charlie" AA☆1884 1886
Moser, Casey ML 2005
Mountain, Frank H. AA★1884
Moyer, Robert "Bob" AL†1979
Mrvos, Joseph S. "Joe" NL†1979
Muchlinski, Michael "Mike" ML 2006
Muir, Thomas NL☆1876
Mulcahy, James "Jim" AL†1979
Mullane, Anthony J. "Tony" AA★1888 NL★1893 ☆1897
Mullaney, Dominic J. AL 1915
Mullen, Peter C. AA☆1891 NL☆1893
Mullin, John NL 1909 AL 1911 FL 1915
Mulvey, Joseph H. "Joe" NL★1895

Murnane, Timothy H. "Tim" NA☆1873-75 NL☆1886
Murphy, Joseph A. "Joe" AA★1887
Murphy, J. A. FL☆1914
Murphy, Martin W. NL☆1886
Murphy, Morgan E. NL★1893 ★1896 ★1898
Murphy, P. Henry NL☆1880
Murphy, William H. "Yale" NL★1895 ★1897
Murray, Ed AL†1991
Murray, Jeremiah J. "Miah" NL☆1894 1895 ☆1900 ☆1905 ☆1910
Myers, George D. NL★1886
Myers, Joseph "Joe" NL†1979
Nace, Henry NA☆1872
Nallin, Richard F. "Dick" AL 1915-32
Napp, Larry A. AL 1951-74
Nash, William M. "Billy" NL 1901
Nauert, Paul NL 1995-99 ML 2002-06
Needham, Thomas J. "Tom" NL★1904 ★1907
Negri, Peter "Pete" NL†1979
Nelson, Jeffrey B. "Jeff" NL 1997-99 ML 2000-06
Nelson, John W. "Candy" NA☆1872
Nelson, Richard "Dick" AL†1979
Nelson, Robert "Bob" NL†1979 1991 1995
Nelson, Scott ML 2001-03
Neudecker, Jerome A. "Jerry" AL 1965-85
Newsom, Louis N. "Bobo" AL★1938
Newton, Eustace J. "Doc" NL★1902
Nichols, A. N. NA☆1871
Nichols, Charles A. "Kid" NL★1900-01
Nicol, Hugh NL☆1894
Nolan, Edward S. "The Only" NL★1881
Noonan, Peter J. "Pete" NL★1906-07
Norris, Edward E. "Ed" NL†1978-79
Norton, Frank P. NA☆1872
Norton, Lee AA☆1890
Nothhnagel, Carl L. AL†1984
Novack, Lester A. "Les" AL†1979
Oberbeck, Henry A. UA★1884
Odlin, Arthur E. NL 1883
Odom, James C. "Jim" AL 1965-74
Oliger, Edward C. "Ed" NL†1979
Olsen, Andrew H. "Andy" NL 1968-8l
Ormsby, Emmett T. "Red" AL 1923-41
Orr, David L. "Dave" NL☆1891
Orth, Albert L. "Al" NL★1901 1912-17
Osborne, William NL☆1876
Overall, Orval NL★1905 ★1910
Owens, Clarence B. "Brick" NL 1908 1912-13 AL 1916-37
O'Brien, Frank AA 1890
O'Brien, James D. "Jim" AL†1979
O'Brien, John F. "Darby" NL★1889
O'Brien, Joseph "Joe" AL 1912 1914 FL 1915
O'Brien, Peter J. "Pete" AL★1907
O'Brien, P. NA☆1875
O'Brien, William NL☆1876
O'Brien, William D. "Darby" AA★1887-88
O'Connor, Arthur NL 1914
O'Connor, James "Jim" AL†1978-79
O'Connor, John J. "Jack" AA★1889 NL★1893 ★1901
O'Connor, Thomas M. "Tom" AL†1979
O'Day, Henry F. "Hank" AA★1884 NL★1888-89 1895 ☆1896 1897-1911 1913 1915-27 PL★1890
O'Dea, Lawrence AA☆1890
O'Dell, Mikel R. "Mike" AL†1984
O'Donnell, James M. "Jake" AL 1968-71
O'Loughlin, Francis H. "Silk" AL 1902-18
O'Neill, Michael J. "Mike" NL★1904
O'Nora, Brian AL 1992-99 ML 2000-06
O'Rourke, James H. "Jim" NL 1894
O'Sullivan, John J. NL 1922
Paasch, William AA☆1887-89
Pabor, Charles H. "Charlie" NA☆1875
Pacheco, Jim NL†1995
Packard, Scott ML 2000-02
Padilla, Joe NL†1995
Palermo, Stephen M. "Steve" AL 1977-91
Pallone, David M. "Dave" NL 1979-88
Panas, Richard J. "Rich" AL†1978-79
Paparella, Joseph J. "Joe" AL 1946-65
Parker, George L. NL 1936-38
Parker, Harley P. "Doc" AL 1911
Parker, H. AA☆1887
Parks, Dallas F. AL 1979-83 AL†1991 1995
Parks, William R. "Bill" NA☆1875
Passarella, Arthur M. "Art" AL 1941-42 1945-53
Patch, Tony D. NL†1978-79 AL†1979
Patten, Case L. AL★1903
Patterson, Daniel T. "Dan" NA☆1872 1874
Paylor, Jim AL†1995
Peak, Frank NA☆1871
Pearce, Richard J. "Dicky" NL 1878 1882
Pears, Frank H. NL 1897 1905 AL☆1903
Pearson, S. W. NA☆1872
Peitz, Henry C. "Heinie" NL★1901 ★1906
Pelekoudas, Christos G. "Chris" NL 1960-75
Pelty, Barney AL★1906
Peoples, James E. "Jimmy" AA★1888-89 1890
Perez, David A. "Dave" AL†1979
Perez, J. Ray NL†1979
Perrine, Fred "Bull" AL 1909-12
Pfeffer, N. Frederick "Fred" NL☆1897
Pfirman, Charles H. "Cy" NL 1922-36
Phelan NL☆1896
Phelps, Cornelius C. "Neal" NA☆1874
Phelps, Edward J. "Ed" NL★1912
Philippe, Charles L. "Deacon" NL★1903
Phillips, David R. "Dave" AL 1971-99 ML 2001-02
Phillips, Horace B. AA☆1882
Phipps, George H. "Jerry" AL†1978-79
Pierce, Grayson S. "Gracie" AA★1882 ☆1884 NL 1886-87 ☆1892-93 PL 1890
Pike, Jacob Emanuel "Jay" NA☆1875
Pike, Lipman E. "Lip" AA☆1887 1889 NL☆1890
Pilato, Mike AL†1995
Pinelli, Ralph A. "Babe" NL 1935-56
Pipgras, George W. AL 1938-46
Pomponi, Joseph L. "Joe" NL†1979 1984
Poncino, Larry L. NL 1985-88 1991-99 ML 2002-06
Porter NA☆1874
Potter, Scott A. NL 1991-95 1997
Powell, Cornelius J. "Jack" NL 1923-24 1933
Power, Charles B. UA☆1884 NL☆1893-95 1902
Powers, Michael R. "Mike" AL★1902
Powers, Philip B. "Phil" NL 1879 1881 1886-91
Powers, W. NA☆1872-73 ☆1875
Pratt, Albert G. "Al" NL 1879 ☆1880 AA 1883 ☆1886
Pratt, Lester AL†1979
Pratt, Thomas J. "Tom" NA☆1871-73 NL 1886 ☆1887
Pryor, J. Paul NL 1961-8l
Pulli, Frank V. NL 1972-99
Purduski, Al J. AL†1979
Quest, Joseph L. "Joe" NL 1886-87
Quick, James E. "Jim" NL 1974-98
Quigley, Ernest C. "Ernie" AL☆1906 NL 1913-38
Quinn, A. J. AA 1886
Quinn, John A. AL 1935-42
Quinn, Joseph F. "Joe" NL☆1881 1882
Quinn, Joseph J. "Joe" NL★1889 ★1894 ★1896
Quinn, P. J. NL☆1876
Quinn, William H. "Billy" AA☆1884-85 NL☆1887 ☆1889
Quinn NA☆1875
Quisser, Arthur FL☆1914
Radcliff, John Y. NA☆1873
Rains, James "Jim" NL†1978-79
Ramsay, R. NA☆1875
Ramsey, Dick AA☆1887
Randall, Larry NL†1995
Randazzo, Anthony J. "Tony" NL 1999 ML 2000-06
Rapuano, Edward S. "Ed" NL 1990-99 ML 2000-06
Rastall, Joseph H. NA☆1872
Ravan, Bruce AL†1995
Ravashiere, Thomas "Tom" AL†1979
Reach, Albert J. NA☆1872-75
Reardon, John E. "Beans" NL 1926-49
Redheffer NL☆1895
Reed, Hugh NA☆1871 ☆1873-74
Reed, Rick A. AL 1984-99 ML 2000-06
Reeder, James E. "Icicle" AA☆1884
Reid, William A. NL☆1882
Reilly, Charles NL☆1880
Reilly, Charles T. "Charlie" NL★1892 ★1894-95
Reilly, Michael E. "Mike" AL 1978-99 ML 2000-06
Reininger, Travis ML 2005-06
Reising, Charles AA☆1882
Reitz, Henry P. "Heinie" NL★1895
Reliford, Charles H. "Charlie" NL 1989-99 ML 2000-06
Remsen, John J. "Jack" NA☆1873-74 NL☆1880
Rennert, Laurence H. "Dutch" NL 1973-92
Reynolds, James N. "Jim" AL 1999 ML 2000-06
Rhines, William P. "Billy" NL★1891 ★1896
Rhodes, Eugene A. NL☆1887
Riccio, Dennis R. NL†1979
Riccio, L. Leonard "Len" AL†1979 NL†1979
Rice, John L. AL 1955-73
Rice, Robert W. "Bob" AL†1979
Rice AA☆1885
Richards, J. E. NL☆1880
Richardson, A. Harding "Hardie" NL★1892
Richmond, J. Lee NL★1883
Rieker, Richard G. "Rich" NL 1992-99 ML 2000-01
Riggers, Mike NL†1995
Rigler, Charles "Cy" NL 1906-22 1924-35
Riley, William J. "Billy" NL 1880 AA 1882 ☆1885
Rippley, T. Steven "Steve" NL 1983-99 ML 2000-03
Ritchie, F. NL☆1876
Robb, Douglas W. "Scotty" NL 1948-52 AL 1952-53
Robb, John AA☆1886
Roberts, Leonard W. "Lenny" NL 1953-55
Robinson, A. Valentine "Val" NA☆1872
Robinson, Miley NA☆1873
Robinson, Wilbert NL★1898
Robinson, William N. "Bill" AL†1978-79
Rocap, Adam NL☆1876
Rockwell, Horace T. NA☆1874
Rodriguez, Armando H. AL 1974-75
Rodriguez, Gus NL†1995
Roe, John A. "Rocky" AL 1979-99 ML 2000-01
Roesner, Robert A. "Bob" AL†1978-79
Rogers, George R. NA☆1871-72
Rogers, M. Mortimer "Mort" NA 1871
Roll NL☆1876
Rommel, Edwin A. "Eddie" AL 1938-59
Rosenberry, Bill NL†1995
Ross, Robert T. AA 1882 ☆1884
Roth, Francis C. "Frank" AL★1923
Roth, Roy NL†1978-79 AL†1979
Rountree, Henry J. "Hank" NL†1978-79 AL†1991
Rowe, John C. "Jack" NL☆1881
Rowland, Clarence H. "Pants" AL 1923-27
Rudderham, Francis F. "Frank" NL☆1907
Rudderham, John E. NL 1908
Rue, Joseph W. "Joe" AL 1938-47
Ruhl, Gus AA☆1882
Runchey, Richard D. "Dick" AL†1979 1984
Runge, Brian E. NL 1999 ML 2000-06
Runge, Edward P. "Ed" AL 1954-70
Runge, Paul E. NL 1973-97
Ryan, James E. "Jimmy" NL★1892
Ryan, John AA☆1882
Ryan, John J. NA☆1872 ☆1875
Ryan, Walter NL 1946
Ryberg, Sy NL†1995
Sage, Harry AA★1890
Salerno, Alexander J. "Al" AL 1961-68
Samuels, John "Jack" ML 2001 2003-05
Sanders, A. Bennett "Ben" NL★1889
Satchell, Darold L. AL†1970
Sawchuk, Joseph W. "Joe" AL†1978-79
Sawyer, Dent NA☆1871
Say, Louis I. "Lou" NL☆1879
Schafer, Harry C. NA☆1875
Schaff, Fred NL†1995
Schaller, Cliff NL†1978-79
Schaly, Jim AL†1995
Scheel, Alfred M. "Al" AL†1979
Schirmer, Donald A. "Don" AL†1979
Schleyer, John NL†1979
Schmidt, Charles "Boss" AL★1907
Schmidt, Henry M. NL★1903
Schofield, J. W. NL☆1879
Schrader, Louis NA☆1875
Schratz, Joseph "Joe" NL†1979
Schreckengost, Ossee F. AL★1903
Schrieber, Paul W. NL 1997-99 ML 2000-06
Schriver, William F. "Pop" NL★1901
Schroeder, Robert L. "Bobby" NL†1978-79
Schuester, John A. NA☆1874-75
Schulte, Donald E. "Don" AL†1979
Schwarts, Harry C. AL 1960-62
Schwarz, Henry "Hank" AL†1995
Scofield, John W. NA☆1871
Scott, Dale A. AL 1985-99 ML 2000-06
Scott, James "Jim" NL 1930-31 NL†1978-79
Sears, John K. NA☆1873
Sears, John W. "Ziggy" NL 1934-45
Secory, Frank E. NL 1952-70
Selman, Frank C. NA☆1873 AA☆1882
Sensenderfer, John P. J. "Count" NA☆1872-73 1874 ☆1875
Sentell, Leopold T. "Paul" NL 1922-23
Serad, William I. "Billy" AA★1888 NL★1884
Seward, Edward W. "Ed" NL☆1892 1893
Seward, George E. NL 1876 ☆1877 1878 AA 1884 UA 1884
Shannon, William P. "Spike" FL 1914-15
Sharkey, Michael E. "Mick" NL†1978-79
Sharp, Robert C. "Bob" NL†1979
Shaw, A. Duane AL†1979
Shepard, W. L. NL☆1879
Sheridan, John F. "Jack" PL 1890 NL 1892 ☆1893 1896-97 AL 1901-14
Sherman, Sharon L. "Shang" AA☆1890
Shewmake, James B. "Jim" AL†1978
Shraeder, Louis AA☆1890
Shulock, John R. AL 1979-99 ML 2000-02
Siever, Edward T. "Ed" AL★1901
Simmons, Joseph S. "Joe" NA☆1871 ☆1873-74 NL☆1876 AA 1882
Simpson, Lew AA☆1882
Siroka, Harold L. AL†1979 NL†1979
Skelly NL☆1880
Skerritt, Jim AA☆1890
Skinner, S. A. AA☆1886 NL☆1886
Slattery, Donald L. "Don" AL†1979 NL†1979
Slickenmeyer, David W. "Dave" AL†1979 1991 1995 NL†1979 1984
Small, Harry F. NL†1979
Smith, A. Edgar NL★1883
Smith, Charles M. "Pop" NL 1881 AA 1882 ★1886
Smith, Eb NA☆1872
Smith, Edgar E. NL★1890
Smith, Frederick C. "Fred" AA★1890
Smith, F. William "Bill" NL★1886
Smith, George NA☆1872 AA☆1887
Smith, George H. "Heinie" NL★1901
Smith, Gustavus NA☆1872
Smith, Harry T. NL★1903
Smith, John F. "Phenomenal" AA★1887-88
Smith, Vincent A. "Vinnie" NL 1957-65
Smith, William W. "Billy" NL 1898-99
Smith, W. Alaric "Al" AL 1960-65
Smith NL☆1876
Sneed, Jonathon L. AA☆1885
Sneeden, George W. NL☆1895
Snodd, Carey NL☆1877

Snyder, Charles N. "Pop" NA★1875 AA★1886 1891 PL 1890 NL 1892-93 ☆1895 1898-1901
Soar, A. Henry "Hank" AL 1950-73 ☆1975
Sommer, Benjamin F. AA 1883
Sommer, Joseph J. "Joe" AA★1888
Sommers, Joseph A. "Pete" NL★1889 ☆1893
Spagnardi, Darren ML 2002-04
Spange, John NL†1991
Spenn, Frederick C. "Fred" AL 1979-80 AL†1991
Spieler, Patrick "Pat" ML 2000-02
Spinelli, Michel NL†1979
Sprague, Charles W. "Charlie" AA★1890
Sprincz, William "Bill" AL†1978-79
Springstead, Martin J. "Marty" AL 1965-86
Stack, W. Edward "Eddie" NL☆1934
Stafford, John H. NL☆1906 AL 1907
Stage, Charles W. "Billy" NL 1894 ☆1895
Stahl, George NA☆1875
Staley, Harry E. NL★1892 ★1895
Stambaugh, Calvin G. NL 1877-78 ☆1879
Stansell, B. Jack NL†1979
Stanwood NA☆1872-73
Stark, Albert D. "Dolly" NL 1928-35 1937-40
Stearns, D. Eckford "Ecky" NL★1881 UA 1884
Stein, Edward F. "Ed" NL★1890 ★1894 ★1896
Steiner, Melvin J. "Mel" NL 1961-72
Steinfeldt, Harry M. NL★1905
Stello, Richard J. "Dick" NL 1969-87
Sternburg, Paul NL 1909
Stevens, John W. "Johnny" AL 1948-71 ☆1975 AL†1970
Stewart, Ernest D. AL 1941-45
Stewart, John NL†1979 1984
Stewart, Robert W. "Bob" AL 1959-70
Stewart, William J. "Bill" NL 1933-54
Stires, Garrett "Gat" NA☆1875
Stivetts, John C. "Jack" AA★1891 NL★1894
Stockdale, M. J. NL 1915
Stocksdale, Otis H. NL★1895 FL 1915
Stophlet, J. NA☆1871
Strey, Murray W. NL†1978-79
Stricker, John A. "Cub" NL★1892
Stricklett, Elmer E. NL★1907
Strief, George A. NL☆1880 ☆1889 1890
Sudol, Edward L. "Ed" NL 1957-77
Sugden, Joseph "Joe" NL★1897
Sullivan, David F. "Dave" NL 1882 ☆1883 1885 ☆1887-89 AA☆1884 UA 1884
Sullivan, James E. "Jim" NL★1896
Sullivan, Jeremiah "Jerry" AA 1887 NL 1887
Sullivan, Martin C. "Marty" NL★1889
Sullivan, Michael J. "Mike" NL★1897
Sullivan, Thomas J. "Sleeper" NL★1881
Sullivan, Timothy P. "Ted" NL 1880 AA 1887
Summers, B. NL 1876
Summers, William R. "Bill" AL 1933-59
Sumner, James G. NL 1877 ☆1878
Supple, William N. NL☆1906
Sutcliffe, Elmer E. "Sy" NL★1889 ★1892
Sutton, Ezra B. NA☆1875 NL☆1876
Swandell, J. Martin "Marty" NA☆1871 1872-73 ☆1874
Swartwood, C. Edward "Ed" NL 1894 1898-1900
Sweasy, Charles J. "Charlie" NA☆1871 ☆1873-74 NL☆1879
Sweeney, Charles J. "Charley" AA★1887
Sweeney, George P. AL†1979
Sweeney, James M. "Jim" NL 1924-26
Swenson, Charles H. AL†1979
Sylvester, Frank NL†1995
Sylvester, Louis J. "Lou" AA★1888
Tabacchi, Frank T. AL 1956-59
Talbot, John AA☆1887
Tannehill, Jesse N. NL★1897 ★1901-02
Tata, Terry A. NL 1973-99
Tate, Edward C. "Pop" NL★1888
Tate, William NA 1874
Taylor, Joe Bob AL†1979
Taylor, John B. "Jack" NL★1899
Taylor, John W. "Jack" NL★1901 ★1905
Taylor, Walter AA 1890
Telford, Thomas "Tom" NL†1979
Tener, John K. NL★1889 PL★1890
Terlop, Russell F. "Russ" AL†1979
Terry, William H. "Adonis" AA★1884 ★1888 NL★1892 ★1895-96 1900 AL☆1901
Theilander, Theodore "Ted" AL†1979
Thompson, Michael G. "Mike" AL†1978-79
Tiernan, Michael J. "Mike" NL★1895
Tighe, Edward NA☆1871
Tilden, Otis NL☆1876 1880
Tillman, Henry T. "Hank" NL†1978-79 AL†1979
Timblin UA☆1884
Timmoms, Timothy F. "Tim" ML 2000-06
Tindall NL☆1890 ☆1896
Tinney AA☆1882
Toole, Stephen J. "Steve" NL☆1888 AA 1890
Townsend, George H. AA★1890
Traffley, William F. "Bill" AA★1884
Travis, Vic AL†1995
Treacey, Frederick S. "Fred" NA☆1871 ☆1873 ☆1875
Treitel, Leslie J. "Les" NL†1978-79
Tremblay, Richard H. "Dick" NL 1971 NL†1979
Trimmer, Harry AL†1979
Truby, Harry G. NL 1909
Tschida, Timothy J. "Tim" AL 1985-99 ML 2000-06
Tunison, William AA 1885-86
Turner, Leo I. AL†1978
Tuthill, Benjamin "Ben" NL☆1895
Twitchell, Lawrence G. "Larry" NL★1894
Tyler, Columbus T. NA☆1871-73
Ulrich, George AL†1995
Umont, Frank W. AL 1954-73
Urchak, Woody J. AL†1978-79
Urell, M. E. NA☆1873
Uremovich, Jim AL†1991 1995
Urlage, Richard C. "Dick" NL†1979 1991
Valentine, John G. AA 1884-87 NL 1887-88
Valentine, William T. "Bill" AL 1963-68
Van Court , Eugene NL 1884
Van Delft, Benjamin NA☆1875
Van Graflan, Roy R. AL 1927-33
Van Sickle, Charles F. FL 1914
Van Vleet, Mike ML 2000-02
Vanover, Larry W. NL 1991 1993-99 ML 2002-06
Vargo, Edward P. "Ed" NL 1960-83
Vaughn, Harry F. "Farmer" AA★1891 NL★1892 ★1899
Venzon, Anthony "Tony" NL 1957-71
Viau, Leon "Lee" AA★1888 NL★1891
Vickery, Thomas G. "Tom" NL★1890
Voltaggio, Vito H. "Vic" AL 1977-96
Voltz, Edward "Ed" NA☆1871-72
Wade, Ben F. NL☆1879-80
Walding, Larry AL†1995
Walk, Frank NA☆1871
Walker, Thomas W. "Tom" NL★1905
Walker, William E. NL 1876-77 ☆1878
Wall, Joseph F. "Joe" NL★1901
Wallace, Roderick J. "Bobby" NL★1895 AL 1915
Waller, James "Jim" NL†1979
Walsh, Edward A. "Ed" AL 1922
Walsh, Francis D. "Frank" NL 1961-63
Walsh, Michael F. "Mike" NA 1875 NL 1876 1878 ☆1879 1880 AA 1882-83 1885-86 ☆1887-88
Walters, John NL☆1892-93
Walters, William H. "Bucky" NL★1942 ★1947
Walton, Bennie AL 1996
Walton, G. W. NL☆1876
Ward, John M. NL★1888
Wardell NA☆1874
Warneke, Lonnie "Lon" NL★1940 1949-55
Warner, Albert "Al" NL 1898-1900
Warner, John J. "Jack" NL★1896-97 ★1901 ★1903 AL★1908
Warren, L. B. NL☆1876
Wash, Frank NL☆1877
Waterman, Frederick A. "Fred" NA☆1873
Weafer, Harold L. "Hal" AL 1943-47
Weaver, Charles NA☆1873
Weaver, William B. "Farmer" NL★1893
Weden, Charles NL☆1889-90
Wegner, Mark P. NL 1998-99 ML 2000-06
Weigel, William H. NA☆1873-74
Weimer, Jacob W. "Jake" NL★1905 ★1907
Welch, Michael F. "Mickey" NL★1881-82 ★1885-86 ★1888 ☆1890
Welke, Timothy J. "Tim" AL 1985-99 ML 2000-06
Welke, William A. "Bill" AL 1999 ML 2000-06
Wendelstedt, Harry H. Sr. NL 1966-98
Wendelstedt, H. Hunter Jr. NL 1998-99 ML 2000-06
West, Edward AA☆1885 ☆1887 NL☆1885 ☆1890
West, George NL☆1878
West, Joseph H. "Joe" NL 1976 1978-99 ML 2002-06
Westervelt, Frederick E. AL 1911-12 FL 1915 NL 1922-23
Weyer, Lee H. NL 1961 1963-88
Weyhing, August "Gus" AA★1891 NL★1894 ★1899-1900
Whaley, Bart NL†1995
Wheeler, Harry E. AA★1882 UA★1884
Whistler, Lewis "Lew" NL★1891
White, Gideon F. NL☆1876-77 1878
White, Guy H. "Doc" NL★1901-02 AL★1903
White, Horatio S. NA☆1873
White, James L. "Deacon" NL★1880
White, William H. "Will" NA☆1875
White, W. Warren NA☆1874 NL☆1876
Whitney, James E. "Jim" NL★1884 ★1886
Wickham, Daniel "Dan" NL 1990-92
Widlowski, Mark NL†1995
Wiedman, George E. "Stump" NL 1896
Wiggins NA☆1875
Wilbur, Charles E. NL 1879
Wildey, John NA☆1871
Wilhelm, Irving K. "Kaiser" NL★1904-05 FL 1915
Willard, Gardner NA☆1871
Williams, Arthur "Art" NL 1972-77
Williams, Charles H. "Charlie" NL 1978 1983-99 ML 2000-01
Williams, Dale NL†1978-79 AL†1979
Williams, Elisha A. "Dale" NL☆1876
Williams, Washington J. "Wash" UA★1884
Williams, William G. "Billy" NL 1963-87
Williamson, Edward N. "Ned" NL★1878
Willis, Victor G. "Vic" NL★1903
Willman, Bob NL†1991 1995
Wilmot, Walter R. "Walt" NL★1897
Wilson, Frank AL 1921-22 NL 1922-28
Wilson, Frank A. "Zeke" NL★1896 ★1899
Wilson, James "Jimmie" NL★1940
Wilson, John A. NL 1887
Wilson, Parke A. NL★1894-96 ★1899
Wilson, William G. "Bill" NL★1890 ☆1892-93
Winans, Mathew "Matt" AL 1994
Winter, George L. AL★1903 ★1905
Winters, Michael J. "Mike" NL 1988-99 ML 2000-06
Wirth, Adam NA☆1875
Wise, Samuel W. "Sam" NL 1889
Witham, C. B. NL☆1879
Wolf, James "Jim" ML 2000-06
Wolf, William V. "Jimmy" NL☆1893 ☆1895-97
Wood, George A. AA☆1886 ★1891 NL★1889 1898
Wood, James L. "Jimmy" NA☆1871 NL☆1876
Worth, Herb NA☆1872
Wright, Marvin AL†1995
Wright, Parry AA☆1884
Wright, W. Henry "Harry" NA☆1875 NL☆1876-77 ☆1885
Wycoff NL☆1892
Yeager, George J. NL★1901
Yeast, Dave NL†1995
York, Thomas J. "Tom" NA☆1874 NL 1886 AA 1886
Young, Benjamin F. "Ben" AA 1886 ☆1887
Young, Denton T. "Cy" NL★1896 AL★1903
Young, Irving M. "Irv" NL★1905 ★1907
Young, Joseph NL 1879 AA☆1890
Young, Larry E. AL 1985-99 ML 2000-06
Young, Nicholas E. "Nick" NA 1871-75
Zacharias, Thomas NL 1890
Zimmer, Charles L. "Chief" AA★1888 NL★1889 ★1901 1904
Zimmerman, Gerald R. "Jerry" AL★1978
Zirbel, Lawrence A. "Larry" AL†1979 1984
Zivic, Richard J. "Dick" AL†1984
Zuccaro, Amerigo J. "Rico" AL†1978-79

THE GLOBAL GAME: INTERNATIONAL AND AMATEUR BASEBALL

While America's national game doesn't have the far-reaching popularity of soccer, baseball is played enthusiastically all around the world. Outside of the United States, baseball remains most popular in the Caribbean and in East Asia, but the game is continuing to spread. Over 100 countries participate in Little League Baseball worldwide. Twelve countries participated in the European Baseball Championships in 2003, and Australia, Korea, and Taiwan continue to produce major league prospects.

In 1992 baseball finally became an Olympic sport. However, baseball's future in international competition is very much in doubt, since the International Olympic Committee voted in 2005 to eliminate baseball from the 2012 Paris Olympics. Meanwhile, MLB and the International Baseball Federation staged the first World Baseball Classic in March 2006, with 16 teams from 14 countries (plus Puerto Rico and Taiwan) competing.

In the United States, there may be fewer kids playing stickball on the streets or pick-up games on small-town sandlots than in years past, but youth baseball organizations are prospering. The number of leagues available for various age groups and talent levels is staggering, and college baseball is also thriving as never before.

Baseball in Latin America

The passion much of Latin America has for baseball is no secret in the United States. Baseball has a longer tradition in the Caribbean than anywhere else except for the U.S. In the Dominican Republic, Cuba, Venezuela, and Puerto Rico, baseball is still the king of all sports, and it has been so for a very long time.

The first place that the American National Pastime landed in the Caribbean was Cuba, where American sailors and local workers were reportedly playing as early as 1866. Cuba had its first real team two years later and a professional league began competition in 1878, only two years after the National League's debut. Until the political upheavals of the late 1950s, Cuba was a baseball hub, attracting players from many other countries and sending many of its own to the major leagues and Negro Leagues. Cuba was also baseball's ambassador to the rest of the Caribbean. By the end of the nineteenth century, baseball was a fixture in every country in the area. U.S. military activity around the turn of the century helped push baseball further along in many of these places.

In the 1930s and 1940s the Caribbean winter leagues were attracting many major leaguers and Negro Leaguers in need of supplemental incomes. Following World War II, some rich owners in the Mexican League even raided the major leagues by signing more than twenty American players, though the threat from south of the border was short-lived.

After the color line was broken in the majors in 1947 and the crisis over the Mexican League raids had passed, Organized Baseball established official ties with most of the Caribbean leagues. The Caribbean Series began in that period, bringing together the winners of the winter leagues from Cuba, Panama, Puerto Rico, and Venezuela for an annual tournament. Cuba's 1959 revolution disrupted not only the Serie del Caribe, which took a hiatus from 1961–69, but all of baseball. While newly communist Cuba continued to field strong amateur teams, most of the connections between the island and the rest of the baseball world were severed by the revolution. Therefore, the nexus of Latin American baseball moved to the Dominican Republic.

In recent years the importance of the winter leagues has faded. With the astronomical leaps in major league salaries, few ballplayers need to supplement their income. Moreover, big league teams want to keep their investments safe and often discourage veteran players from playing winter ball and risking injury. These days most of the major leaguers who play winter ball are either local heroes or are playing to develop a new skill or increase their marketability as free agents. This trend has not, however, diminished the level of popularity of baseball in these countries or the skill level of their players, as 30 percent of today's major leaguers are Latinos, more than double the percentage of fifteen years ago.

While the winter leagues may no longer attract as many baseball stars or baseball fans, the leagues themselves are still mostly successful (though the 2002–03 Venezuelan season was cancelled as a result of domestic unrest). The Caribbean Series was revived in 1970, with Mexico and the Dominican Republic replacing Panama and Cuba. It has been played every year since then, with the exception of 1981. In 2003–04 Major League Baseball arranged for the Montreal Expos to play part of their home schedule in Puerto Rico, and both San Juan and Monterrey, Mexico bid for the Expos before the team moved to Washington DC. The Mexican League, the only significant summer league in the region, still attracts many former major leaguers, though it continues to struggle for financial security.

Baseball faces many more challenges in the Caribbean than it did a century ago, but it still remains the favorite pastime of many Latin nations.

Caribbean Series (Serie Del Caribe) Results

YR (SERIES)	WINNING TM, COUNTRY	HOST
1949 (I)	Almendares, Cuba	Cuba
1950 (II)	Carta Vieja, Pan.	P.R.
1951 (III)	Santurce, P.R.	Venez.
1952 (IV)	La Habana, Cuba	Pan.
1953 (V)	Santurce, P.R.	Cuba
1954 (VI)	Caguas, P.R.	P.R.
1955 (VII)	Santurce, P.R.	Venez.
1956 (VIII)	Cienfuegos, Cuba	Pan.
1957 (IX)	Marianao, Cuba	Cuba
1958 (X)	Marianao, Cuba	P.R.
1959 (XI)	Almendares, Cuba	Venez.
1960 (XII)	Cienfuegos, Cuba	Pan.
1970 (XIII)	Magallanes, Venez.	Venez.
1971 (XIV)	Licey, D.R.	P.R.
1972 (XV)	Ponce, P.R.	D.R.
1973 (XVI)	Licey, D.R.	Venez.
1974 (XVII)	Caguas, P.R.	Mex.
1975 (XVIII)	Bayamon, P.R.	P.R.
1976 (XIX)	Hermosillo, Mex.	D.R.
1977 (XX)	Licey, D.R.	Venez.
1978 (XXI)	Mayaguez, P.R.	Mex.
1979 (XXII)	Magallanes, Venez.	P.R.
1980 (XXIII)	Licey, D.R.	D.R.
1982 (XXIV)	Caracas, Venez.	Mex.

YR (SERIES)	WINNING TM, COUNTRY	HOST
1983 (XXV)	Arecibo, P.R.	Venez.
1984 (XXVI)	Zulia, Venez.	P.R.
1985 (XXVII)	Licey, D.R.	Mex.
1986 (XXVIII)	Mexicali, Mex.	Venez.
1987 (XXIX)	Caguas, Venez.	Mex.
1988 (XXX)	Escogido, D.R.	D.R.
1989 (XXXI)	Zulia, Venez.	Mex.
1990 (XXXII)	Escogido, D.R.	U.S.
1991 (XXXIII)	Licey, D.R.	U.S.
1992 (XXXIV)	Mayaguez, P.R.	Mex.
1993 (XXXV)	Mayaguez, P.R.	Mex.
1994 (XXXVI)	Licey, D.R.	Mex.
1995 (XXXVII)	San Juan, P.R.	P.R.
1996 (XXXVIII)	Culiacan, D.R.	D.R.
1997 (XXXIX)	Aguilas, D.R.	Mex.
1998 (XL)	Aguilas, D.R.	Venez.
1999 (XLI)	Licey, D.R.	P.R.
2000 (XLII)	Santurce, P.R.	D.R.
2001 (XLIII)	Aguilas, D.R.	Mex.
2002 (XLIV)	Culiacan, D.R.	Venez.
2003 (XLV)	Aguilas, D.R.	P.R.
2004 (XLVI)	Licey, D.R.	D.R.
2005 (XLVII)	Mazatlan, Mex.	Mex.
2006 (XLVIII)	Caracas, Venez.	Venez.

Cuban Professional Baseball League Champions

SEASON	TEAM
1878–79	Habana
1879–80	Habana
1880–81	Habana & Fe (disputed)
1882–83	Habana
1885	Habana
1885–86	Habana
1886–87	Habana
1887–88	Fe
1888–89	Habana
1889–90	Habana
1890–91	Fe
1891–92	Habana
1892–93	Matanza
1893–94	Almendares
1898–99	Habanista
1900	San Francisco
1901	Habana
1902	Habana
1903	Habana
1904	Habana
1905	Almendares
1906	Fe
1907	Almendares
1908	Almendares
1908–09	Habana

SEASON	TEAM
1910	Almendares
1910–11	Almendares
1912	Habana
1913	Fe
1913–14	Almendares
1914–15	Habana
1915–16	Almendares
1917	Orientals
1918–19	Habana
1919–20	Almendares
1920–21	Habana
1921	Habana
1922–23	Marianao
1923–24	Santa Clara
1924–25	Almendares
1925–26	Almendares
1926–27	Habana
1927–28	Habana
1928–29	Habana
1929–30	Cienfuegos
1931–32	Almendares
1932–33	Almendares & Habana (tie)
1934–35	Almendares
1935–36	Santa Clara
1936–37	Marianao

SEASON	TEAM
1937–38	Santa Clara
1938–39	Santa Clara
1939–40	Almendares
1940–41	Habana
1941–42	Almendares
1942–43	Almendares
1943–44	Habana
1944–45	Almendares
1945–46	Cienfuegos
1946–47	Almendares
1947–48	Habana
1948–49	Almendares
1949–50	Almendares
1950–51	Habana
1951–52	Habana
1952–53	Habana
1953–54	Almendares
1954–55	Almendares
1955–56	Cienfuegos
1956–57	Marianao
1957–58	Marianao
1958–59	Almendares
1959–60	Cienfuegos
1960–61	Cienfuegos

Cuban Baseball Federation Champions

YEAR	TEAM
1967	Orientales
1968	Habana
1969	Azucareros
1970	Henequeneros
1971	Azucareros
1972	Azucareros
1973	Industriales
1974	Habana
1975	Agricultores
1976	Ganaderos
1977	Citricultores
1978	Vegueros
1979	Sancti Spiritus
1980	Santiago de Cuba

YEAR	TEAM
1981	Vegueros
1982	Vegueros
1983	Villa Clara
1984	Citricultores
1985	Vegueros
1986	Industriales
1987	Vegueros
1988	Vegueros
1989	Santiago de Cuba
1990	Henequeneros
1991	Henequeneros
1992	Industriales
1993	Villa Clara

YEAR	TEAM
1994	Villa Clara
1995	Villa Clara
1996	Villa Clara
1997	Pinar del Rio
1998	Pinar del Rio
1999	Santiago de Cuba
2000	Santiago de Cuba
2001	Santiago de Cuba
2002	Holguin
2003	Industriales
2004	Industriales
2005	Santiago de Cuba
2006	Industriales

Latin American Winter Leagues

SEASON	PUERTO RICAN	VENEZUELAN	DOMINICAN REPUBLIC	MEXICAN PACIFIC
1940–41	Caguas			
1941–42	Ponce			
1942–43	Ponce			
1943–44	Ponce			
1944–45	Ponce			
1945–46	San Juan	Vargas		
1946–47	Ponce	Vargas		
1947–48	Caguas	Caracas		
1948–49	Mayaguez	Caracas		
1949–50	Caguas			
1950–51	Santurce	Magallanes		
1951–52	San Juan	Magallanes	Licey (1951)	

SEASON	PUERTO RICAN	VENEZUELAN	DOMINICAN REPUBLIC	MEXICAN PACIFIC
1952–53	Santurce	Caracas	Aguilas (1952)	
1953–54	Caguas	Caracas	Licey (1953)	
1954–55	Santurce	Occidente	Estrellas Orientales (1954)	
1955–56	Caguas	Magallanes	Escogido	
1956–57	Mayaguez	Valencia	Escogido	
1957–58	Caguas	Caracas	Escogido	
1958–59	Santurce	Valencia	Licey	Guaymas
1959–60	Caguas	Valencia	Escogido	Guaymas
1960–61	San Juan	Valencia	Escogido	Hermosillo
1961–62	Santurce	Caracas		Hermosillo
1962–63	Mayaguez	Valencia		Guaymas
1963–64	San Juan	Caracas	Licey	Hermosillo
1964–65	Santurce	La Guaira	Aguilas	Guaymas
1965–66	Mayaguez	La Guaira		Obregon
1966–67	Santurce	Caracas	Aguilas	Culiacan
1967–68	Caguas	Caracas	Estrellas Orientales	Guaymas
1968–69	Ponce	La Guaira	Escogido	Los Mochis
1969–70	Ponce	Magallanes	Licey	Culiacan
1970–71	Santurce		Licey	Hermosillo
1971–72	Ponce	Aragua	Aguilas	Guasave
1972–73	Santurce	Caracas	Licey	Obregon
1973–74	Caguas		Licey	Mazatlan
1974–75	Bayamon	Aragua	Aguilas	Hermosillo
1975–76	Bayamon	Aragua	Aguilas	Hermosillo
1976–77	Caguas	Magallanes	Licey	Mazatlan
1977–78	Mayaguez	Caracas	Aguilas	Culiacan
1978–79	Caguas	Magallanes	Aguilas	Navojoa
1979–80	Bayamon	Caracas	Licey	Hermosillo
1980–81	Caguas	Caracas	Escogido	Obregon
1981–82	Ponce	Caracas	Escogido	Hermosillo
1982–83	Arecibo	La Guaira	Licey	Culiacan
1983–84	Mayaguez	Zulia	Licey	Los Mochis
1984–85	San Juan	La Guaira	Licey	Culiacan
1985–86	Mayaguez	La Guaira	Aguilas	Mexicali
1986–87	Caguas	Caracas	Aguilas	Mazatlan
1987–88	Mayaguez	Caracas	Escogido	Tijuana
1988–89	Mayaguez	Zulia	Licey	Mexicali
1989–90	San Juan	Caracas	Escogido	Hermosillo
1990–91	Santurce	Lara	Licey	Tijuana
1991–92	Mayaguez	Zulia	Escogido	Hermosillo
1992–93	Santurce	Zulia	Aguilas	Mazatlan
1993–94	San Juan	Magallanes	Licey	Hermosillo
1994–95	San Juan	Caracas	Azucueros	Hermosillo
1995–96	Arecibo	Magallanes	Aguilas	Culiacan
1996–97	Mayaguez	Magallanes	Aguilas	Culiacan
1997–98	Mayaguez	Lara	Aguilas	Mazatlan
1998–99	Mayaguez	Lara	Licey	Mexicali
1999–00	Santurce	Zulia	Aguilas	Navojoa
2000–01	Caguas	Lara	Aguilas	Hermosillo
2001–02	Bayamon	Magallanes	Licey	Culiacan
2002–03	Mayaguez		Aguilas	Los Mochis
2003–04	Ponce	Aragua	Licey	Culiacan
2004–05	Mayaguez	Aragua	Aguilas	Mazatlan
2005–06	Carolina	Caracus	Licey	Mazatlan

Mexican League Champions

YEAR	TEAM	YEAR	TEAM
1925	Puebla 74th Regiment	1966	Mexico City Tigers
1926	Jalapa Ocampo	1967	Jalisco Charros
1927	Mexico City Police Station	1968	Mexico City Red Devils
1928	Mexico City Police	1969	Reynosa Broncos
1929	Mexico City Adams Chiclets	1970	Veracruz Eagle
1930	Comintra Tigers	1971	Jalisco Charros
1931	Mexico City Traffic	1972	Cordoba Coffee Growers
1932	Mexico City Public Works	1973	Mexico City Red Devils
1933	Comintra Tigers	1974	Mexico City Red Devils
1934	Mexico City Mercy Hill	1975	Tampico Lightermen
1935	Mexico City Agrarians	1976	Mexico City Red Devils
1936	Mexico City Agrarians	1977	New Laredo Owls
1937	Veracruz Eagle	1978	Aguascalientes Railroadmen
1938	Veracruz Eagle	1979	Puebla Angels
1939	Cordoba Coffee Growers	1980	Puebla Angels
1940	Veracruz Blues	1981	Mexico City Red Devils
1941	Veracruz Blues	1982	Ciudad Juarez Indians
1942	Torreon (Union Laguna) Cotton Dealers	1983	Campeche Pirates
1943	Monterrey Sultans	1984	Yucatan Lions
1944	Veracruz Blues	1985	Mexico City Red Devils
1945	Tampico Lightermen	1986	Puebla Angels
1946	Tampico Lightermen	1987	Mexico City Red Devils
1947	Monterrey Sultans	1988	Mexico City Red Devils
1948	Monterrey Sultans	1989	Laredo Owls
1949	Monterrey Sultans	1990	Leon Braves
1950	Torreon (Union Laguna) Cotton Dealers	1991	Monterrey Sultans
1951	Veracruz Blues	1992	Mexico City Tigers
1952	Veracruz Eagle	1993	Tabasco Olmecs
1953	Nuevo Laredo Owls	1994	Mexico City Red Devils
1954	Nuevo Laredo Owls	1995	Monterrey Sultans
1955	Mexico City Tigers	1996	Monterrey Sultans
1956	Mexico City Red Devils	1997	Mexico City Tigers
1957	Yucatan Lions	1998	Oaxaca Warriors
1958	New Laredo Owls	1999	Mexico City Red Devils
1959	Poza Rica Oilers	2000	Mexico City Tigers
1960	Mexico City Tigers	2001	Mexico City Tigers
1961	Veracruz Eagles	2002	Mexico City Red Devils
1962	Monterrey Sultans	2003	Mexico City Red Devils
1963	Puebla Parrots	2004	Campeche Pirates
1964	Mexico City Red Devils	2005	Mexico City Tigers
1965	Mexico City Tigers	2006	Yucatan Lions

Note: Mexican League championship series were played in 1949–51, 1966, 1970–79, and 1981–present. Prior to 1970, the first-half winner played the second-half winner. Since 1970 the league has been divided into divisions. In 1980, Puebla had the best record in a strike-shortened season.

2006 Inaugural World Baseball Classic

The Classic was the first-ever international baseball tournament to feature the top pro players from around the globe. Japan won the final over Cuba on March 20, though Korea had the best record in the Classic at 6-1. Next scheduled for 2009, the Classic will be held every four years afterward.

CHAMPION (RECORD)	RUNNER-UP	SCORE	MVP (COUNTRY)	SEMI-FINALISTS
Japan (5-3)	Cuba (5-3)	10-6	Daisuke Matsuzaka P (Japan)	Korea, Dominican Republic

The Olympics

Baseball appeared as a demonstration sport in six different Olympics (1912, 1936, 1956, 1964, 1984, and 1988) before being accepted as a medal sport. Its future in the Olympics, however, is not assured. Despite the lifting of the ban on professional players before the 2000 Olympics in Sydney, Australia, Major League Baseball has shown no interest in interrupting its regular season to let the best players in the world participate in Olympic competition. Consequently, the International Olympic Committee has voted to drop baseball from the Olympics after the 2008 Olympic Games in Beijing, China.

The International Baseball Federation is working to reverse that decision and return baseball to the Olympics in future competitions. Nevertheless, Major League Baseball's blase attitude towards the Olympics and USA Baseball's failure to earn its way to the 2004 Olympics (the national team lost to Mexico in the qualifying tournament) has lengthened the odds against the IBF succeeding.

YEAR	HOST CITY (COUNTRY)	GOLD	SILVER	BRONZE
1992	Barcelona (Spain)	Cuba	Chinese Taipei	Japan
1996	Atlanta (U.S.)	Cuba	Japan	United States
2000	Sydney (Australia)	United States	Cuba	South Korea
2004	Athens (Greece)	Cuba	Australia	Japan

Note: Japan won the virtual gold medal when baseball was a demonstration sport in 1984; the United States won the demonstration competition in 1988.

THE PAN AMERICAN GAMES

The Pan American Games were originally proposed in the 1930s. The first games were scheduled for 1942, but World War II and its aftermath delayed the initial games until 1951. The games have since been held every four years as scheduled and have steadily grown in size: more than 5,000 athletes from 42 countries participated in the most recent competition in the Dominican Republic.

The Pan American Sports Organization runs the games, which follow the same rules and eligibility requirements as the Olympics. The competition includes every sport featured in the Summer Olympics, although it is not limited to those sports. Thus, the National Pastime of the United States and several Latin American countries has been a major part of the Pan Am Games since their inception.

Over the history of the games, the United States and Cuba have both won 12 medals in baseball, though Cuba has won 11 gold medals while the United States has won only one. While professional athletes are now permitted to participate in the Pan Am Games, it seems unlikely that major league players will be featured in the competition in the near future because of the calendar conflict with MLB's regular season.

YEAR	HOST CITY (COUNTRY)	GOLD	SILVER	BRONZE
1951	Buenos Aires (Argentina)	Cuba	United States	Mexico
1955	Mexico City	Dominican Rep.	United States	Venezuela
1959	Chicago (U.S.)	Venezuela	Puerto Rico	United States
1963	Sao Paulo (Brazil)	Cuba	United States	Mexico
1967	Winnipeg (Canada)	United States	Cuba	Puerto Rico
1971	Cali (Colombia)	Cuba	United States	Colombia
1975	Mexico City	Cuba	United States	Venezuela
1979	San Juan (Puerto Rico)	Cuba	Dominican Rep.	Puerto Rico
1983	Caracas (Venezuela)	Cuba	Nicaragua	United States
1987	Indianapolis (U.S.)	Cuba	United States	Puerto Rico
1991	Havana (Cuba)	Cuba	Puerto Rico	United States
1995	Mar del Plata (Argentina)	Cuba	Nicaragua	Puerto Rico
1999	Winnipeg	Cuba	United States	Canada
2003	Santo Domingo (D.R.)	Cuba	United States	Mexico

Baseball in Japan

Japanese baseball and American baseball have moved much closer during the last decade. Stars such as Hideo Nomo, Kazuhiro Sasaki, Ichiro Suzuki, and Hideki Matsui have successfully moved from Japan to America, as have lesser players in non-starring roles. Players with experience in the United States, such as Roberto Petagine, still cross the Pacific in the other direction seeking greater opportunity. American fans who know little about Japanese baseball are now almost forced to pay some attention.

Baseball has been played in Japan since the nineteenth century, first in 1873 at Tokyo University under the tutelage of an American professor. After the turn of the century, baseball became extremely popular in both high school and college. American baseball players started touring Japan after 1910, and the efforts of a man named

Herbert Hunter helped school thousands of Japanese boys in the fundamentals of the game. An All-Star tour in 1934, featuring Babe Ruth, Lou Gehrig, Jimmy Foxx, Al Simmons and Lefty Gomez, left the greatest impression. The first professional Japanese team was the group organized to play these All-Stars. That team would become known as the Tokyo Giants, and by 1936 six other teams would join the Giants in the new Japanese Professional Baseball League.

World War II disrupted the new league, but the American occupying force brought the game back in 1946. In 1950 Japanese professional baseball added seven new teams and split into two leagues, the Central and the Pacific. Professional baseball grew in popularity over the next several decades, with television giving it a big boost. The Giants dominated Japanese baseball during this period, winning far more Japan Series (and fans) than any other team. Baseball remains Japan's most popular sport, though there are serious concerns about what the continuing loss of much of its star talent to the United States will mean for the Japanese game in the future.

Japan Professional Baseball League Champions

YEAR	TEAM	YEAR	TEAM
1937	Spring: Tokyo Giants	1942	Tokyo Giants
	Fall: Osaka Tigers	1943	Tokyo Giants
1938	Spring: Osaka Tigers	1944	Hanshin
	Fall: Tokyo Giants	1946	Kinki Greatring
1939	Tokyo Giants	1947	Osaka Tigers
1940	Tokyo Giants	1948	Nankai Hawks
1941	Tokyo Giants	1949	Yomiuri Giants

Japan Series Champions

YEAR	CENTRAL LEAGUE WINNER	PACIFIC LEAGUE WINNER	SERIES RESULT
1950	Shochiku Robins	Mainichi Orions	Orions, 4-2
1951	Yomiuri Giants	Nankai Hawks	Giants, 4-1
1952	Yomiuri Giants	Nankai Hawks	Giants, 4-2
1953	Yomiuri Giants	Nankai Hawks	Giants, 4-2-1
1954	Chunichi Dragons	Nishitetsu Lions	Dragons, 4-3
1955	Yomiuri Giants	Nankai Hawks	Giants, 4-3
1956	Yomiuri Giants	Nishitetsu Lions	Lions, 4-2
1957	Yomiuri Giants	Nishitetsu Lions	Lions, 4-0-1
1958	Yomiuri Giants	Nishitetsu Lions	Lions, 4-3
1959	Yomiuri Giants	Nankai Hawks	Hawks, 4-0
1960	Taiyo Whales	Daimai Orions	Whales, 4-0
1961	Yomiuri Giants	Nankai Hawks	Giants, 4-2
1962	Hanshin Tigers	Toei Flyers	Flyers, 4-2-1
1963	Yomiuri Giants	Nishitetsu Lions	Giants, 4-3
1964	Hanshin Tigers	Nankai Hawks	Hawks, 4-3
1965	Yomiuri Giants	Nankai Hawks	Giants, 4-1
1966	Yomiuri Giants	Nankai Hawks	Giants, 4-2
1967	Yomiuri Giants	Hankyu Braves	Giants, 4-2
1968	Yomiuri Giants	Hankyu Braves	Giants, 4-2
1969	Yomiuri Giants	Hankyu Braves	Giants, 4-2
1970	Yomiuri Giants	Lotte Orions	Giants, 4-1
1971	Yomiuri Giants	Hankyu Braves	Giants, 4-1
1972	Yomiuri Giants	Hankyu Braves	Giants, 4-1
1973	Yomiuri Giants	Nankai Hawks	Giants, 4-1
1974	Chunichi Dragons	Lotte Orions	Orions, 4-2
1975	Hiroshima Carp	Hankyu Braves	Braves, 4-0-2
1976	Yomiuri Giants	Hankyu Braves	Braves, 4-3
1977	Yomiuri Giants	Hankyu Braves	Braves, 4-1
1978	Yakult Swallows	Hankyu Braves	Swallows, 4-3
1979	Hiroshima Carp	Kintetsu Buffaloes	Carp, 4-3
1980	Hiroshima Carp	Kintetsu Buffaloes	Carp, 4-3
1981	Yomiuri Giants	Nippon Ham Fighters	Giants, 4-2
1982	Chunichi Dragons	Seibu Lions	Lions, 4-2
1983	Yomiuri Giants	Seibu Lions	Lions, 4-3
1984	Hiroshima Carp	Hankyu Braves	Carp, 4-3
1985	Hanshin Tigers	Seibu Lions	Tigers, 4-3
1986	Hiroshima Carp	Seibu Lions	Lions, 4-3-1
1987	Yomiuri Giants	Seibu Lions	Lions, 4-2
1988	Chunichi Dragons	Seibu Lions	Lions 4-1
1989	Yomiuri Giants	Kintetsu Buffaloes	Giants, 4-3
1990	Yomiuri Giants	Seibu Lions	Lions, 4-3
1991	Hiroshima Carp	Seibu Lions	Lions, 4-0
1992	Yakult Swallows	Seibu Lions	Lions, 4-0
1993	Yakult Swallows	Seibu Lions	Swallows, 4-3
1994	Yomiuri Giants	Seibu Lions	Giants, 4-2
1995	Yakult Swallows	Orix BlueWave	Swallows, 4-1
1996	Yomiuri Giants	Orix BlueWave	BlueWave, 4-1
1997	Yakult Swallows	Seibu Lions	Swallows, 4-1
1998	Yokohama BayStars	Seibu Lions	Bay Stars, 4-2
1999	Chunichi Dragons	Fukuoka Daiei Hawks	Hawks, 4-1
2000	Yomiuri Giants	Fukuoka Daiei Hawks	Giants, 4-2
2001	Yakult Swallows	Kintetsu Buffaloes	Swallows, 4-1
2002	Yomiuri Giants	Seibu Lions	Giants, 4-0
2003	Hanshin Tigers	Fukuoka Daiei Hawks	Hawks, 4-3
2004	Chunichi Dragons	Seibu Lions	Lions, 4-3
2005	Hanshin Tigers	Chiba Lotte Marines	Marines, 4-0
2006	Chunichi Dragon	Nippon Ham Fighters	Fighters, 4-1

Taiwan

Japanese occupying forces introduced baseball to Taiwan in 1905. The Taiwanese picked up the game in the 1920s and even provided Japan with a few professional players before World War II. Baseball grew in Taiwan after the war, though primarily on the amateur level. The nation became a juggernaut in Little League competition and also had significant success in other international competitions.

It wasn't until 1990 that the country's first professional baseball league, the Chinese Professional Baseball League, was organized. The league was successful almost immediately, but a huge gambling operation that was fixing CPBL games came to light in 1996, greatly damaging the loop's credibility. A second baseball league, the Taiwan Major League, emerged in 1997 and further weakened the CPBL. The two leagues finally merged in 2003, and that fall came more good news when the national team upset South Korea to qualify for the Olympics. Baseball is arguably the most popular sport in Taiwan, so the CPBL could have a bright future if it can avoid repeating its past problems.

Chinese Professional Baseball League Champions

YEAR	TEAM	YEAR	TEAM
1989	Weichuan Dragons	1998	Weichuan Dragons
1990	President Lions	1999	President Lions
1991	Brother Elephants	2000	Sinon Bulls
1992	Brother Elephants	2001	Brother Elephants
1993	Brother Elephants	2002	Brother Elephants
1994	President Lions	2003	Brother Elephants
1995	President Lions	2004	Sinon Bulls
1996	Weichuan Dragons	2005	Sinon Bulls
1997	Weichuan Dragons	2006	La New Bears

Taiwan Major League Champions

YEAR	TEAM	YEAR	TEAM
1997	Chia-Nan Braves	2000	Taipei Suns
1998	Taipei Suns	2001	Taichung Robots
1999	Taichung Robots	2002	Taichung Robots

South Korea

In 1905 an American missionary introduced baseball to Korea, but it wasn't until 1982 that the government of South Korea decided to instigate the creation of a professional league. The newly formed Korean Baseball Organization proved to be a success, but its progress was halted in the mid-1990s by the country's financial crisis. More recently, Korean baseball has lost a number of talented players to the major leagues. In response the KBO began allowing teams to sign non-Koreans in 1998. The league still faces many challenges, including fallout from the recent failure of the South Korean national team to qualify for the 2004 Olympics.

Korean Series Champions

YEAR	TEAM	YEAR	TEAM	YEAR	TEAM
1982	OB Bears	1991	Haitai Tigers	1999	Hyundai Unicorns
1983	Haitai Tigers	1992	Lotte Giants	2000	Hyundai Unicorns
1984	Lotte Giants	1993	Haitai Tigers	2001	Doosan Bears
1985	Samsung Lions	1994	LG Twins	2002	Samsung Lions
1986	Haitai Tigers	1995	OB Bears	2003	Hyundai Unicorns
1987	Haitai Tigers	1996	Haitai Tigers	2004	Hyundai Unicorns
1988	Haitai Tigers	1997	Haitai Tigers	2005	Samsung Lions
1989	Haitai Tigers	1998	Hyundai Unicorns	2006	Samsung Lions
1990	LG Twins				

KONAMI CUP ASIA SERIES

On November 13, 2005, the Chiba Lotte Marines emerged as the winners of the inaugural Konami Cup, a contest between Japan, Taiwan, South Korea, and China to determine an East Asian baseball champion. The initial tournament featured competition between the 2005 winners of the Japan Series, Korean Series, and Chinese Baseball Championship Series along with a team of all-stars from mainland China. The four-day event consisted of three days of round-robin combination (with two games played each day) along with a championship game on the last night featuring the two best teams from the first three days. Though the idea for the competition came from South Korea and Taiwan, the inaugural edition of the Cup was held in Japan, where all games were played in the Tokyo Dome. Prize money of 100 million yen was awarded to the participating teams, with half of that going to the Cup winner. The series finale drew a crowd of 37,000 and attracted 15 percent of the television audience in Japan, so a second series was held in 2006 and the Cup is now considered an annual tournament.

YEAR	CHAMPION (W-L)	RUNNER-UP (W-L)	SCORE	MVP	LOCATION
2005	Chiba Lotte Marines (4-0)	Samsung Lions (2-2)	5-3	Benny Agbayani (CLM)	Tokyo Dome
2006	Nippon Ham Fighters (3-0)	La New Bears (2-1)	3-2	Yu Darvish (NHM)	Tokyo Dome

Australia

According to legend, the first baseball game in Australia was played by American visitors in the 1850s. Australians first participated in a baseball game in 1879 when a local cricket team played a visiting minstrel group from the United States. Most Australians remained ignorant about baseball until A.G. Spalding and his Chicago White Stockings team came to Australia in late 1888 to promote the sport throughout the country. Spalding's tour was very successful and planted the game "down under" permanently.

In 1934, three Australian states sent their teams to Adelaide to compete for the first Claxton Shield. All of Australia's mainland states were participating in the competition by 1939 and, following World War II, the Shield competition would be held annually until 1989.

Controversy ended the Claxton Shield and left an opening in the Australia baseball world, which was quickly filled by Australia's first professional league, the Australian Baseball League. Unfortunately, the league proved to have a lot more talent on the field than off it. By 1998 it was clear that the ABL was in terrible financial trouble. Former ABL player (and major league All-Star) David Nilsson purchased the ABL's assets and tried to build a better league, the International Baseball League of Australia, out of the ABL's ashes. The new league was a disaster, though, and barely made it through one season before collapsing.

Australia today continues to do without a national baseball competition. However, baseball is still very popular on the local level and the country continues to produce talent capable of playing at a very high level. It is certainly possible that a new national league will rise again during the next decade, perhaps with the aid of Major League Baseball.

Australian Baseball League Champions

SEASON	TEAM	SEASON	TEAM
1989–90	Waverly	1995–96	Sydney Blues
1990–91	Perth	1996–97	Perth
1991–92	Gold Coast	1997–98	Melbourne Reds
1992–93	Melbourne	1998–99	Gold Coast
1993–94	Brisbane	1999–00	Western Heelers
1994–95	Waverly		

COLLEGE BASEBALL

The first college baseball game was played on July 1, 1859 in Pittsfield, Massachusetts between Amherst and Williams. Amherst won the game by the incredible score of 73-32. Baseball fans watching a videotape of such a game would recognize the sport's similarities to baseball, but they would also find the play proceeding very differently, especially due to the shorter distances between the bases and between the mound and the batter's box. Baseball's rules had not been standardized in 1859; by the time the first professional league emerged 12 years later; the game more closely resembled that of today.

Since 1871, when the National Association began play, college has served as a feeder system to the professional leagues. Its significance as a factor in the development of major league players has waxed and waned, depending on the importance placed by society on attending college as well as the scope of minor league baseball and the influence of international scouting. For much of professional baseball's early history, some of the nation's most talented college athletes chose a different career path than that of a pro ballplayer. As a result, the top college teams of the late 1800s and early 1900s were far closer to a major league talent level than college teams are today.

Despite talented players, early college baseball drew little attention from baseball fans. The major universities of the Northeast and Midwest played the best college ball, but they also suffered from the worst weather. After World War II, however, the NCAA created the College World Series, an event that slowly but surely increased the overall popularity of college baseball. The first two College World Series were held in Kalamazoo, Michigan in 1947–48. In 1949 the tournament moved to Omaha, Nebraska, where it has remained ever since.

The biggest difference between college baseball and major league baseball may be the aluminum bat, introduced in 1974 by the NCAA at the same it adopted the DH rule. Aluminum bats changed the college game dramatically. The higher-scoring games attracted more fans and fewer broken bats made it cheaper to run a college baseball program. Metal bats also made for a much rougher transition for hitters going from college to the minor leagues. The latter problem has led to the formation of summer prospect leagues, where top college baseball players around the continent use wooden bats. The most famous such loop is the Cape Cod League.

Since ESPN began broadcasting the College World Series in 1989, the popularity of college baseball has grown even further, especially in those climates hospitable to the game in late winter. After many years in which Southwestern teams dominated the CWS, teams from the South and Southeast captured the majority of championships in the 1990s. The lists below contain the results of every College World Series played, as well as the championship series played NAIA college teams, plus the Most Outstanding Player selections for the various series.

At the end of the collegiate championships are the winners of the two most prestigious awards for college ballplayers: the Golden Spikes Award and the *Baseball America*'s College Player of the Year award.

USA Baseball, the national governing body for the sport and the organization responsible for putting together the national baseball teams representing the USA, was created by an act of Congress in 1978. It selects the best amateur baseball player in the country, who receives the Golden Spikes Award. The award does not necessarily have to go to a college baseball player, but it always has so far.

The Dick Howser Award, named after the late Royals and Yankees manager, has been given annually since 1987 to the nation's best Division I college baseball player, based on his "performance, character, leadership and courage." From 1987-98, the winner of this award was determined by a vote of the American Baseball Coaches Association. Since 1999, the winner has been selected by the National College Baseball Writers Association.

The most highly regarded annual college player award, however, is Baseball America's Player of the Year award, which the publication has presented annually since 1981. Eight players—Jason Varitek (1994), J.D. Drew (1997), Jason Jennings (1999), Mark Prior (2001), Khalil Greene (2002), Rickie Weeks (2003), Jered Weaver (2004), and Alex Gordon (2005)—have swept all three awards in one season

NCAA Division I College World Series

YEAR	WINNER	RUNNER-UP	SCR	YEAR	WINNER	RUNNER-UP	SCR
1947	California*	Yale	8-7	1977	Arizona St.	South Carolina	2-1
1948	USC	Yale	9-2	1978	USC*	Arizona St.	10-3
1949	Texas*	Wake Forest	10-3	1979	Cal St.-Fullerton	Arkansas	2-1
1950	Texas	Washington St.	3-0	1980	Arizona	Hawaii	5-3
1951	Oklahoma*	Tennessee	3-2	1981	Arizona St.	Oklahoma St.	7-4
1952	Holy Cross	Missouri	8-4	1982	Miami*	Wichita St.	9-3
1953	Michigan	Texas	7-5	1983	Texas*	Alabama	4-3
1954	Missouri	Rollins	4-1	1984	Cal St.-Fullerton	Texas	3-1
1955	Wake Forest	Western Michigan	7-6	1985	Miami	Texas	10-6
1956	Minnesota	Arizona	12-1	1986	Arizona	Florida St.	10-2
1957	California*	Penn St.	1-0	1987	Stanford	Oklahoma St.	9-5
1958	USC	Missouri	8-7	1988	Stanford	Arizona St.	9-4
1959	Oklahoma St	Arizona	5-3	1989	Wichita St.	Texas	5-3
1960	Minnesota	USC	2-1	1990	Georgia	Oklahoma St.	2-1
1961	USC*	Oklahoma St.	1-0	1991	Louisiana St.*	Wichita St.	6-3
1962	Michigan	Santa Clara	5-4	1992	Pepperdine*	Cal St.-Fullerton	3-2
1963	USC	Arizona	5-2	1993	Louisiana St.	Wichita St.	8-0
1964	Minnesota	Missouri	5-1	1994	Oklahoma*	Georgia Tech	13-5
1965	Arizona St.	Ohio St.	2-1	1995	Cal St.-Fullerton*	USC	11-5
1966	Ohio St.	Oklahoma St.	8-2	1996	Louisiana St.*	Miami	9-8
1967	Arizona St.	Houston	11-2	1997	Louisiana St.*	Alabama	13-6
1968	USC*	Southern Illinois	4-3	1998	USC	Arizona St.	21-14
1969	Arizona St.	Tulsa	10-1	1999	Miami*	Florida St.	6-5
1970	USC	Florida St.	2-1	2000	Louisiana St.*	Stanford	6-5
1971	USC	Southern Illinois	7-2	2001	Miami*	Stanford	12-1
1972	USC	Arizona St.	1-0	2002	Texas*	South Carolina	12-6
1973	USC*	Arizona St.	4-3	2003	Rice	Stanford	14-2
1974	USC	Miami	7-3	2004	Cal St.-Fullerton	Texas	3-2
1975	Texas	South Carolina	5-1	2005	Texas	Florida	6-2
1976	Arizona	Eastern Michigan	7-1	2006	Oregon State	North Carolina	3-2

**Undefeated in World Series play*

Division I Most Outstanding Player

YEAR	PLAYER	SCHOOL	YEAR	PLAYER	SCHOOL
1949	Charles Teague 2B	Wake Forest	1966	Steve Arlin P	Ohio St.
1950	Ray Van Cleef CF	Rutgers	1967	Ron Davini C	Arizona St.
1951	Sidney Hatfield P-1B	Tennessee	1968	Bill Seinsoth 1B	USC
1952	James O'Neill P	Holy Cross	1969	John Dolinsek lf	Arizona State
1953	J.L. Smith P	Texas	1970	Gene Ammann P	Florida St.
1954	Tom Yewcic C	Michigan	1971	Jerry Tabb 1B	Tulsa
1955	Tom Borland P	Oklahoma St.	1972	Russ McQueen P	USC
1956	Jerry Thomas P	Minnesota	1973	Dave Winfield P-OF	Minnesota
1957	Cal Emery P-1B	Penn St.	1974	George Milke P	USC
1958	Bill Thom P	USC	1975	M. Reichenbach 1B	Texas
1959	Jim Dobson 3B	Oklahoma St.	1976	Steve Powers P-DH	Arizona
1960	John Erickson 2B	Minnesota	1977	Bob Horner 3B	Arizona St.
1961	Littleton Fowler P	Oklahoma St.	1978	Rod Boxberger P	USC
1962	Bob Garibaldi P	Santa Clara	1979	Tony Hudson P	Cal St.-Fullerton
1963	Bud Hollowell c	USC	1980	Terry Francona LF	Arizona
1964	Joe Ferris P	Maine	1981	Stan Holmes LF	Arizona St.
1965	Sal Bando 3B	Arizona St.	1982	Dan Smith P	Miami

YEAR	PLAYER	SCHOOL
1983	Calvin Schiraldi P	Texas
1984	John Fishel LF	Cal St.-Fullerton
1985	Greg Ellena DH	Miami
1986	Mike Senne LF	Arizona
1987	Paul Carey RF	Stanford
1988	Lee Pleme P	Stanford
1989	Greg Brummett P	Wichita St.
1990	Mike Rehban P	Georgia
1991	Gary Hymel C	Louisiana St.
1992	Phil Nevin 3B	Cal St.-Fullerton
1993	Todd Walker 2B	Louisiana St.
1994	Chip Glass OF	Oklahoma
1995	Mark Kotsay OF-P	Cal St.-Fullerton
1996	Pat Burrell 3B	Miami
1997	Brandon Larson SS	Louisiana St.
1998	Jason Lane P-DH	USC
1999	Marshall McDougall 2B	Florida St.
2000	Trey Hodges P	Louisiana St.
2001	Charlton Jimerson CF	Miami
2002	Huston Street P	Texas
2003	John Hudgins P	Stanford
2004	Jason Windsor P	Cal St.-Fullerton
2005	David Maroul 3B	Texas
2006	Johan Nickerson P	Oregon State

NCAA Division II College World Series

YEAR	WINNER	RUNNER-UP	SCORE
1968	Chapman*	Delta St.	11-0
1969	Illinois St.*	Southwest Missouri	12-0
1970	Cal St.-Northridge	Nicholls St.	2-1
1971	Florida Southern	Central Michigan	4-0
1972	Florida Southern	Cal St.-Northridge	5-1
1973	California-Irvine*	Ithaca	9-6
1974	California-Irvine	New Orleans	14-0
1975	Florida Southern	Marietta	10-7
1976	Cal Poly-Pomona	So. Illinois-Edwardsville	17-3
1977	California-Riverside	Eckerd	4-1
1978	Florida Southern	Delta St.	7-2
1979	Valdosta St.	Florida Southern	3-2
1980	Cal Poly-Pomona*	New Haven	13-6
1981	Florida Southern*	Eastern Illinois	9-0
1982	California-Riverside*	Florida Southern	10-1
1983	Cal Poly-Pomona*	Jacksonville St.	9-7
1984	Cal St.-Northridge	Florida Southern	10-5
1985	Florida Southern*	Cal Poly-Pomona	15-5
1986	Troy St.	Columbus St.	5-0
1987	Troy St.*	Tampa	7-5
1988	Florida Southern*	Cal St.-Sacramento	5-4
1989	Cal Poly-San Luis Obispo†	New Haven	9-5
1990	Jacksonville St.	Cal St.-Northridge	12-8
1991	Jacksonville St.	Missouri Southern	20-4
1992	Tampa	Mansfield	7-5
1993	Tampa*	Cal Poly-San Luis Obispo†	14-9
1994	Central Missouri	Florida Southern	14-9
1995	Florida Southern*	Georgia College	15-0
1996	Kennesaw St.*	St. Joseph's (IN)	4-0
1997	Cal St.-Chico*	Central Oklahoma	13-12
1998	Tampa*	Kennesaw St.	6-1
1999	Cal St.-Chico	Kennesaw St.	11-5
2000	Southeastern Oklahoma	Fort Hays St.	7-2
2001	St. Mary's (TX)	Central Missouri	11-3
2002	Columbus St.	Cal St.-Chico	5-3
2003	Central Missouri*	Tampa	11-4
2004	Delta St.	Grand Valley St.	12-8
2005	Florida Southern	North Florida	12-9
2006	Tampa	Chico St.	3-2

**Undefeated in World Series play*

†Participation vacated by the NCAA Committee on Infractions

Division II Most Outstanding Player

YEAR	WINNER	SCHOOL
1968	Tony Spono OF	Chapman
1969	Tom Klein 1B	Illinois St.
1970	Chuck Stone OF	Cal St.-Northridge
1971	Greg Pryor 2B	Florida Southern
	Kevin Bryant 3B	Florida Southern
1972	Jay Smith P	Florida Southern
1973	Terry Stupy C	California Irvine
1974	Jeff Malinoff 1B	California Irvine
1975	Joe Yazombek C	Marietta
1976	Ken Hellyer OF	Cal Poly-Pomona
1977	Joe Lefebvre OF-P	Eckerd
	Steve Glaum P	California Riverside
1978	Ricky Perkins 3B	Delta St.
1979	Frank DeGennaro OF	Valdosta St.
1980	Brian Zell OF	Cal Poly-Pomona
1981	Joe Sickles OF	Florida Southern
1982	Joe Sickles OF	Florida Southern
1983	Larry Beardman OF	Cal Poly-Pomona
1984	Perry Husband 2B	Cal St.-Northridge
1985	Tom Temrowski 1B	Florida Southern
1986	Wendell Stephens 3B	Troy St.
1987	Jude Rinaldi 1B	Troy St.
1988	Chris Leach OF	Florida Southern
1989	Steve DiBartolomeo P	New Haven
1990	Tim Van Egmond P	Jacksonville St.
1991	Tim Van Egmond P	Jacksonville St.
1992	Joe Urso 2B	Tampa
1993	David Dion OF	Tampa
1994	James Vida 1B	Florida Southern
1995	Brett Tomko P	Florida Southern
1996	Chris Halliday C	Kennesaw St.
1997	Angel Diaz C	Tampa
1998	Ronnie Merrill SS	Tampa
1999	John-Eric Hernandez P	Cal St.-Chico
2000	Aaron Thompson P	Southeastern Oklahoma
2001	Jesse Guttierez 1B	St. Mary's (TX)
2002	Brian Baker P.	Columbus St.
2003	Jay Hyland OF	Tampa
2004	Bert Pickard 1B	Delta St.
2005	Kyle DeYoung P	Florida Southern
2006	Lee Cruz OF	Tampa

NCAA Division III College World Series

YEAR	WINNER	RUNNER-UP	SCORE
1976	Cal St.-Stanislaus	Ithaca	13-6
1977	Cal St.-Stanislaus	Brandeis	8-5
1978	Rowan	Marietta	5-3
1979	Rowan	Cal St.-Stanislaus	3-0
1980	Ithaca	Marietta	12-5
1981	Marietta	Ithaca	13-12
1982	Eastern Connecticut	Cal St.-Stanislaus	11-6
1983	Marietta	Otterbein	36-8
1984	Ramapo	Marietta	5-4
1985	Wisconsin-Oshkosh	Marietta	11-6
1986	Marietta	Ithaca	11-6
1987	Montclair St.	Wisconsin-Oshkosh	13-12
1988	Ithaca	Wisconsin-Oshkosh	7-5
1989	N.C. Wesleyan	Cal St.-Stanislaus	8-7
1990	Eastern Connecticut	Aurora (IL)	8-1
1991	Southern Maine	Trenton St.	9-0
1992	William Paterson	California Lutheran	3-1
1993	Montclair St.	Wisconsin-Oshkosh	3-1
1994	Wisconsin-Oshkosh	Wesleyan (CT)	6-2
1995	La Verne	Methodist (NC)	5-3
1996	William Patterson	California Lutheran	6-5
1997	Southern Maine	Wooster	15-1
1998	Eastern Connecticut	Montclair St.	16-1
1999	N.C. Wesleyan	St. Thomas (MN)	1-0
2000	Montclair St.	St. Thomas (MN)	6-2
2001	St. Thomas (MN)	Marietta	8-4
2002	Eastern Connecticut	Marietta	8-0
2003	Chapman	Christopher Newport	15-7
2004	George Fox	Eastern Connecticut	6-3
2005	Wis.-Whitewater	Cortland St.	11-4
2006	Marietta	Wheaton	7-2

Division III Most Outstanding Player

YEAR	WINNER	SCHOOL
1976	Dan Boer 1B	Cal St.-Stanislaus
1977	Rusty Kuntz OF	Cal St.-Stanislaus
1978	Bob Pfeffer P	Rowan
1979	Tap Upshur 2B	Rowan
1980	John Nicolo SS	Ithaca
1981	John Schaly 2B	Marietta
1982	Jeff Biobaum P	Cal St.-Stanislaus
1983	Jim Pancher 2B	Marietta
1984	Derek Bastinck C	Ramapo
1985	Terry Jorgensen LF	Wisconsin-Oshkosh
1986	Mike Brandis 3B	Marietta
1987	John Deutsch RF	Montclair St.
1988	Joe Sottolano P	Ithaca
1989	James Anderson 1B	N.C. Wesleyan
1990	Brian Mercado DH	Eastern Connecticut
1991	Gary Williamson OF	Southern Maine
1992	Ralph Perdomo 1B	William Patterson
1993	Drew Yocum P	Montclair St.
1994	Tim Jorgensen SS	Wis.-Oshkosh
1995	Jeff Polinsky 3B	La Verne
1996	Mark deMenna OF	William Patterson
1997	Jason Jensen P	Southern Maine
1998	Chris D'Amato 2B	Eastern Connecticut
1999	Barry Blake SS	Wesleyan (CT)
2000	Corey Hamman P	Montclair St.
2001	Brad Bonine CF	St. Thomas (MN)
2002	John Kubachka 1B	Eastern Connecticut
2003	Alex Taylor 2B	Chapman
2004	Scott Hyde P	George Fox
2005	Kevin Tomasiewicz P	Wis.-Whitewater
2006	Mike Eisensenberg P	Marietta
(tie)	Justin Steranko 3B	Marrieta

NAIA World Series

YEAR	CHAMPION	RUNNER-UP	SCORE (INN.)
1957	Sul Ross St. (TX)	Rollins (FL)	8-7
1958	San Diego St. (CA)	Southwestern Oklahoma	23-9
1959	Southern-Baton Rouge (LA)	Nebraska-Omaha	10-2
1960	Whitworth (WA)	Georgia Southern	4-0
1961	East Carolina (NC)	Sacramento St. (CA)	13-7
1962	Georgia Southern	Portland St. (OR)	2-0
1963	Sam Houston St. (TX)	Grambling (LA)	2-1
1964	West Liberty St. (WV)	Grambling (LA)	3-2
1965	Carson-Newman (TN)	Nebraska-Omaha	3-2
1966	Linfield (OR)	Lewis (IL)	15-4
1967	New Mexico Highlands	Glassboro St. (NJ)	6-1
1968	William Jewell (MO)	Georgia Southern	4-3 (13)
1969	William Carey (MS)	La Verne (CA)	5-3
1970	Eastern Michigan	Northeastern Louisiana	1-0
1971	Linfield (OR)	David Lipscomb (TN)	9-8 (10)
1972	La Verne (CA)	David Lipscomb (TN)	4-1
1973	U.S. International (CA)	Eastern Connecticut	7-2
1974	Lewis (IL)	Sam Houston St. (TX)	3-2
1975	Lewis (IL)	Sam Houston St. (TX)	2-1
1976	Lewis (IL)	Lewis-Clark St. (ID)	16-8
1977	David Lipscomb (TN)	Southeastern Oklahoma	2-1
1978	Emporia St. (KS)	Missouri Southern	8-6
1979	David Lipscomb (TN)	High Point (NC)	5-4
1980	Grand Canyon (AZ)	Lewis (IL)	5-4 (10)
1981	Grand Canyon (AZ)	Winthrop (SC)	11-4
1982	Grand Canyon (AZ)	Lewis-Clark St. (ID)	10-6
1983	Lubbock Christian (TX)	Lewis-Clark St. (ID)	12-9
1984	Lewis-Clark St. (ID)	Azusa Pacific (CA	15-2
1985	Lewis-Clark St. (ID)	Dallas Baptist (TX)	10-6
1986	Grand Canyon (AZ)	Lewis-Clark St. (ID)	6-5 (10)
1987	Lewis-Clark St. (ID)	Emporia St. (KS)	11-4
1988	Lewis-Clark St. (ID)	Grand Canyon (AZ)	9-3
1989	Lewis-Clark St. (ID)	St. Francis (IL)	5-2
1990	Lewis-Clark St. (ID)	Auburn-Montgomery (AL)	9-4
1991	Lewis-Clark St. (ID)	Oral Roberts (OK)	7-0
1992	Lewis-Clark St. (ID)	Mary Hardin-Baylor (TX)	14-4
1993	St. Francis (IL)	Southeastern Oklahoma	4-2
1994	Kennesaw St. (GA)	Southeastern Oklahoma	2-0
1995	Bellevue (NE)	Cumberland (TN)	8-5
1996	Lewis-Clark St. (ID)	St. Ambrose (IA)	9-0
1997	Brewton-Parker (GA)	Bellevue (NE)	8-4
1998	Albertson (ID)	Indiana Tech	6-3
1999	Lewis-Clark St. (ID)	Albertson (ID)	7-2
2000	Lewis-Clark St. (ID)	Dallas Baptist (TX)	10-1
2001	Birmingham-Southern (AL)	Lewis-Clark St. (ID)	8-3
2002	Lewis-Clark St. (ID)	Oklahoma City	12-8
2003	Lewis-Clark St. (ID)	Oklahoma City	7-5
2004	Cumberland (TN)	Oklahoma City	10-3
2005	Oklahoma City	Embry-Riddle (FL)	8-1
2006	Lewis-Clark St. (ID)	Cumberland (TN)	5-4

USA Baseball Golden Spikes Award Winner

YEAR	WINNER	SCHOOL
1978	Bob Horner 3B	Arizona St.
1979	Tim Wallach 1B	Cal St.-Fullerton
1980	Terry Francona OF	Arizona
1981	Mike Fuentes OF	Florida St.
1982	Augie Schmidt SS	New Orleans
1983	Dave Magadan 1B	Alabama
1984	Oddibe McDowell OF	Arizona St.
1985	Will Clark 1B	Mississippi St.
1986	Mike Loynd P	Florida St.
1987	Jim Abbott P	Michigan
1988	Robin Ventura 3B	Oklahoma St.
1989	Ben McDonald P	Louisiana St.
1990	Alex Fernandez P	Miami-Dade South
1991	Mike Kelly OF	Arizona St.
1992	Phil Nevin 3B	Cal St.-Fullerton
1993	Darren Dreifort P-DH	Wichita St.
1994	Jason Varitek C	Georgia Tech
1995	Mark Kotsay OF-P	Cal St.-Fullerton
1996	Travis Lee 1B	San Diego St.
1997	J.D. Drew OF	Florida St.
1998	Pat Burrell 3B	Miami
1999	Jason Jennings DH-P	Baylor
2000	Kip Bouknight P	South Carolina
2001	Mark Prior P	USC
2002	Khalil Greene SS	Clemson
2003	Rickie Weeks 2B	Southern
2004	Jered Weaver P	Long Beach St.
2005	Alex Gordon 3B	Nebraska
2006	Tim Linecum P	Washington

Baseball America College Player of the Year

YEAR	PLAYER POSITION	SCHOOL	YEAR	PLAYER POSITION	SCHOOL
1981	Mike Sodders 3B	Arizona St.	1994	Jason Varitek C	Georgia Tech
1982	Jeff Ledbetter OF-P	Florida St.	1995	Todd Helton 1B-P	Tennessee
1983	Dave Magadan 1B	Alabama	1996	Kris Benson P	Clemson
1984	Oddibe McDowell OF	Arizona St.	1997	J.D. Drew OF	Florida
1985	Pete Incaviglia OF	Oklahoma St.	1998	Jeff Austin P	Stanford
1986	Casey Close OF	Michigan	1999	Jason Jennings DH-P	Baylor
1987	Robin Ventura 3B	Oklahoma St.	2000	Mark Teixeira 3B	Georgia Tech
1988	John Olerud 1B-P	Washington St.	2001	Mark Prior P	USC
1989	Ben McDonald P	Louisiana St.	2002	Khalil Greene SS	Clemson
1990	Mike Kelly OF	Arizona St.	2003	Richie Weeks 2B	Southern
1991	David McCarty 1B	Stanford	2004	Jered Weaver P	Long Beach St.
1992	Phil Nevin 3B	Cal St.-Fullerton	2005	Alex Gordon 3B	Nebraska
1993	Brooks Kieschnick DH-P	Texas	2006	Andrew Miller P	North Carolina

Dick Howser Award

YEAR	PLAYER	COLLEGE	YEAR	PLAYER	COLLEGE
1987	Mike Fiore OF	Miami	1997	J.D. Drew OF	Florida St.
1988	Robin Ventura 3B	Oklahoma St.	1998	Eddy Furniss 1B	LSU
1989	Scott Bryant OF-P	Texas	1999	Jason Jennings DH-P	Baylor
1990	Alex Fernandez P	Miami-Dade South	2000	Mark Teixeira 3B	Georgia Tech
1991	Frank Rodriguez P	Howard College	2001	Mark Prior P	USC
1992	Brooks Kieschnick DH-P	Texas	2002	Khalil Greene SS	Clemson
1993	Brooks Kieschnick DH-P	Texas	2003	Rickie Weeks 2B	Southern
1994	Jason Varitek C	Georgia Tech	2004	Jered Weaver P	Long Beach St.
1995	Todd Helton 1B-P	Tennessee	2005	Alex Gordon 3B	Nebraska
1996	Kris Benson, P	Clemson	2006	Brad Lincoln P-DH	Houston

LITTLE LEAGUE BASEBALL

Little League Baseball is a worldwide phenomenon these days, bringing in teams from almost every corner of the globe. But when Carl Stotz founded the organization in 1939, it started with three teams playing in a vacant lot in Williamsport, Pennsylvania.

Stotz' organization created what is now known as the Little League World Series in 1947; it was then called the National Little League Tournament. Even that name was a wild overstatement, as it was only in that year that the organization moved into a second state, New Jersey.

Today, Little League Baseball enrolls over three million young baseball players from more than one hundred countries into its programs, and its World Series draws the greatest teams of 11- and 12-year-olds on the planet to a state-of-the-art Williamsport facility. The title game of the Little League World Series now draws much higher television ratings nationally than any MLB Game of the Week.

It's important to note, however, that Little League is not the *only* major youth baseball organization in the United States, and that it is not even the most popular youth baseball organization in all age groups. Babe Ruth League baseball—founded in Hamilton Township, New Jersey in 1951—has almost 1,000,000 players in the United States, primarily in the 13-to-15-year-old age group. American Legion Baseball is the most important youth baseball organization for 16- through 18-year-olds. Other important youth baseball organizations include Pony Baseball/Softball (which has more than 500,000 players around the world), Dixie Baseball (nearly 500,000 players in the southeastern United States), and Hap Dumont Baseball. MLB has sponsored its own very successful RBI program—Reviving Baseball in Inner Cities—for the past 18 years.

And there are also various youth baseball organizations, such as the American Athletic Union, the United States Specialty Sports Association, the National Amateur Baseball Federation, the American Amateur Baseball Congress, the Continental Amateur Baseball Association, and the United States Amateur Baseball Federation, which focus on organizing competition and tournaments among travel teams. These are becoming more popular in almost every participatory sport due to the higher rate of specialization among young athletes. Travel teams almost always require a far greater commitment and a higher level of talent from their participants than recreational leagues do. A few of these leagues, such as the NABF and AABC, also organize adult leagues and tournaments.

Little League World Series

YEAR	WINNER	RUNNER-UP	SCORE (INN.)
1947	Williamsport PA	Lock Haven PA	16-7
1948	Lock Haven PA	St. Petersburg FL	6-5
1949	Hammonton NJ	Pensacola FL	5-0
1950	Houston TX	Bridgeport CT	2-1
1951	Stamford CT	Austin TX	3-0
1952	Norwalk CT	Monongahela PA	4-3
1953	Birmingham AL	Schenectady NY	1-0
1954	Schenectady NY	Colton CA	7-5
1955	Morrisville PA	Delaware Township NJ	4-3
1956	Roswell NM	Delaware Township NJ	3-1
1957	Monterrey, Mexico	La Mesa CA	4-0
1958	Monterrey, Mexico	Kankakee IL	10-1
1959	Hamtramck MI	Auburn CA	12-0
1960	Levittown PA	Fort Worth TX	5-0
1961	El Cajon CA	El Campo TX	4-2
1962	San Jose CA	Kankakee IL	3-0
1963	Granada Hills CA	Stratford CT	2-1
1964	Staten Island NY	Monterrey, Mexico	4-0
1965	Windsor Locks CT	Stoney Creek ON, Canada	3-1
1966	Houston TX	West New York NJ	8-2
1967	West Tokyo, Japan	Chicago IL	4-1
1968	Wakayama, Japan	Richmond VA	1-0
1969	Taiwan	Santa Clara CA	5-0
1970	Wayne NJ	Campbell CA	2-0
1971	Taiwan	Gary IN	12-3
1972	Taiwan	Hammond IN	6-0
1973	Taiwan	Tucson AZ	12-0
1974	Taiwan	Red Bluff CA	12-1
1975	Lakewood NJ	Tampa Bay FL	4-3
1976	Tokyo	Campbell CA	10-3
1977	Taiwan	El Cajon CA	7-2
1978	Taiwan	Danville CA	11-1
1979	Taiwan	Campbell CA	2-1
1980	Taiwan	Tampa Bay FL	4-3
1981	Taiwan	Tampa Bay FL	4-2
1982	Kirkland WA	Chai-Yi-Hsien, Taiwan	6-0
1983	Marietta GA	Barahona, D.R.	3-1
1984	Seoul, South Korea	Altamonte Springs FL	6-2
1985	Seoul, South Korea	Mexicali, Mexico	7-1
1986	Taiwan	Tucson AZ	12-0
1987	Taiwan	Irvine CA	21-1
1988	Taiwan	Pearl City HI	10-0
1989	Trumbull CT	Taiwan	5-2
1990	Taiwan	Shippensburg PA	9-0
1991	Taiwan	Danville CA	11-0
1992	Long Beach CA	Philippines	6-0 (forfeit)
1993	Long Beach CA	Panama	3-2
1994	Venezuela	Northridge CA	4-3
1995	Taiwan	Spring TX	17-3
1996	Taiwan	Cranston RI	13-3 (5)
1997	Guadalupe, Mexico	Mission Viejo CA	5-4
1998	Toms River NJ	Kashima, Japan	12-9
1999	Osaka, Japan	Phenix City AL	5-0
2000	Maracaibo, Venez.	Bellaire TX	3-2
2001	Tokyo Kitasuna	Apopka FL	2-1
2002	Louisville KY	Sendai, Japan	1-0
2003	Tokyo Musashi-Fuchu	Boynton Beach FL	10-1
2004	Willemstad, Curacao	Thousand Oaks CA	5-2
2005	Ewa Beach HI	Willemstad, Curacao	7-6
2006	Columbus, GA	Kawaguchi City, Japan	2-1

PONY Baseball

PONY Baseball began as a single league in Washington, PA, in 1951. It was designed to enable 13- and 14-year-old ballplayers who had graduated from Little League to advance their skills by playing on regulation-size playing fields. The idea quickly caught on, and by the end of 1952, 100 leagues across the country had joined PONY and the first PONY League World Series was held. In 1959, PONY League merged with the Colt League, a similar organization for 15- and 16-year-old players. Over time, PONY (which originally stood for Protect Our Neighborhood Youth; it now stands for Protect Our Nation's Youth) Baseball has started other leagues for different age groups as young as 5 and as old as 21, but the original PONY Division remains its most prominent.

PONY Baseball's various leagues promote the PONY game as being closer to "real baseball" than Little League and other youth baseball. Kids begin pitching in PONY baseball when they're seven years old; stolen bases also become part of the game at a younger age in PONY. PONY changes the distance between bases gradually, adding 10 feet at each higher level, while Little League Baseball jumps from 60 feet to 90 feet between the bases when players turn 13. PONY Baseball is also more restrictive than organizations about age grouping; 9- and 10-year-olds cannot "play up" in leagues meant for older kids.

PONY League World Series

YEAR	WINNER	LOCATION	YEAR	WINNER	LOCATION
1952	San Antonio TX	Washington PA	1963	Evansville (Petroleum) IN	Washington PA
1953	Fairmont WV	Washington PA	1964	Campbell-Moreland CA	San Diego CA
1954	Monongahela PA	Washington PA	1965	Long Beach CA	National City CA
1955	Washington PA	Washington PA	1966	Greensboro NC	Ralston NE
1956	Joliet IL	Washington PA	1966	Greensboro NC	Ralston NE
1957	Lufkin TX	Washington PA	1967	Chula Vista (South) CA	Springfield IL
1958	Miami FL	Washington PA	1968	Greensboro NC	Washington PA
1959	Long Beach CA	Washington PA	1969	Honolulu (PAL) HI	Washington PA
1960	Oak Park-River Forest IL	Washington PA	1970	Buena Park CA	Washington PA
1961	Hamtramck MI	Washington PA	1971	Orange CA	Washington PA
1962	Houston (Karl Young) TX	Washington PA	1972	Monterey, Mexico	Washington PA

YEAR	WINNER	LOCATION
1973	Santa Clara CA	Washington PA
1974	West Covina CA	Springfield IL
1975	Covina CA	Springfield IL
1976	Tampa (North Palomino) FL	Washington PA
1977	New Bedford MA	Pasadena TX
1978	Campbell-Moreland CA	National City CA
1979	Campbell-Moreland CA	Davenport IA
1980	Maui (Kahului) HI	Davenport IA
1981	West Covina CA	Washington PA
1982	West Covina CA	Washington PA
1983	Santa Susana CA	Kennewick WA
1984	Caguas PR	Washington PA
1985	Marietta (East Cobb) GA	Washington PA
1986	Santa Clarita (Wm S. Hart) CA	Washington PA
1987	Caguas (Villa Nueva) PR	Washington PA
1988	Seoul, South Korea	Washington PA
1989	Seoul, South Korea	Washington PA
1990	Seoul, South Korea	Washington PA
1991	San Juan (Bucapla) PR	Washington PA
1992	Bradley-Bourbonnais IL	Washington PA
1993	Joliet (St. Joe's) IL	Washington PA
1994	Tai-Tong, Taiwan	Washington PA
1995	Bayamon PR	Washington PA
1996	Tai-Nan, Taiwan	Washington PA
1997	Danville CA	Washington PA
1998	Tai-Tung, Taiwan	Washington PA
1999	Covina CA	Washington PA
2000	Tai-Nan, Taiwan	Washington PA
2001	Ponce PR	Washington PA
2002	Norwalk CA	Washington PA
2003	Lakewood (Heartwell) CA	Washington PA
2004	Marietta (East Cobb) GA	Washington PA
2005	Tai-Chung, Taiwan	Washington PA
2006	Caguas PR	Washington PA

Babe Ruth Baseball

The Babe Ruth League was created as the Little Bigger League in Hamilton Township, NJ, in 1951. Claire Ruth, Babe Ruth's widow, authorized the renaming of the league after her late husband in 1954. The organization originally served just 13- to 15-year-old boys, though like most youth baseball organizations, it branched out over the years to serve boys and girls of all ages. The first Babe Ruth World Series was held in 1952 in Trenton. The series takes place in a different city every year and has been held in 40 cities during its lifetime, including Anchorage, AK; Vancouver, BC; Williston, ND; and Abbeville, LA. In 1999, Babe Ruth Baseball rebranded its leagues for players 12 and under (originally named Bambino Baseball) as Cal Ripken Baseball. Today Babe Ruth League runs baseball and softball leagues for almost 1,000,000 young athletes around the world.

Babe Ruth World Series 13–15 Champions

YEAR	WINNER	LOCATION
1952	Stamford CT	Trenton NJ
1953	Stamford CT	Trenton NJ
1954	Stamford CT	Washington DC
1955	Terre Haute IN	Austin TX
1956	Trenton NJ	Portland OR
1957	Pensacola FL	Ann Arbor MI
1958	Charlotte NC	Vancouver BC
1959	Tulsa OK	Stockton CA
1960	Huntington WV	St. Paul MN
1961	San Carlos CA	Glendive MT
1962	Trenton NJ	Bridgeton NJ
1963	Tulsa OK	Farmington NM
1964	El Segundo CA	Woodland CA
1965	New Orleans LA	Anderson IN
1966	New Orleans LA	Douglas AZ
1967	New Orleans LA	Anchorage AK
1968	New Orleans LA	Klamath Falls OR
1969	El Segundo CA	Mattoon IL
1970	Ewing Twp. NJ	Brawley CA
1971	Puerto Nuevo PR	Albuquerque NM
1972	Honolulu HI	Pine Bluff AR
1973	Prince Georges MD	Manchester NH
1974	El Segundo CA	Abbeville LA
1975	JPRD-East LA	Pine Bluff AR
1976	Manchester NH	Pueblo CO
1977	Gil Hodges of Brooklyn NY	Newark OH
1978	Nashville TN	Newark OH
1979	Detroit MI	Nogales AZ
1980	Rotterdam NY	Williston ND
1981	New Orleans LA	Mobile AL
1982	Elgin IL	Manchester NH
1983	Culver City CA	Frederick MD
1984	Tallahassee FL	Niles MI
1985	Alameda CA	Jamestown NY
1986	Marietta GA	Newark OH
1987	Van Nuys/Sherman Oaks CA	Jamestown NY
1988	Honolulu HI	Lebanon MO
1989	Cherry Hill NJ	Cranston RI
1990	Youngstown OH	Houma LA
1991	Marietta GA	Lebanon MO
1992	Scottsdale AZ	Vallejo CA
1993	Carolina PR	Ewing NJ
1994	Vancouver WA	Pine Bluff AR
1995	Glendale AZ	Millville NJ
1996	Vancouver WA	Lebanon MO
1997	Bakersfield CA	Longview WA
1998	Oakland CA	Pine Bluff AR
1999	Sarasota FL	Abbeville LA
2000	Jefferson Parish LA	Lebanon MO
2001	Oahu HI	Hamilton NJ
2002	El Segundo CA	Connersville IN
2003	Taylorsville UT	Wiliston ND
2004	Jefferson Parish LA	Longview WA
2005	Jefferson Parish LA	Abbeville LA
2006	Torrance CA	Clifton Park NY

Dixie Youth Baseball

In 1955, segregation led to the formation of a rival organization to Little League in South Carolina. Until that year, every Little League player in that state had been white, but the color barrier was broken when Little League headquarters in Pennsylvania sanctioned the formation of an all-black league in the Charleston area. At the end of that season, no white team would agree to play in the Little League state tournament against the team representing the black league. The white teams created their own state tournament and broke off from Little League Baseball to form a competing organization, Little Boys Baseball. After a legal battle with Little League Baseball, the organization changed its name in 1962 to Dixie Youth Baseball.

Dixie Youth Baseball grew very quickly in the south. Today, nearly 500,000 boys and girls play in Dixie Youth Baseball (or in one of Dixie Baseball's 2 other divisions, Dixie Boys Baseball and Dixie Softball) across 11 states (Alabama, Arkansas, Florida, Georgia, Louisiana, Mississippi, North Carolina, South Carolina, Tennessee, Texas, and Virginia), and it is the dominant youth baseball organization in the areas it serves. The organization officially desegregated in 1967 and changed its seal to eliminate Confederate symbols in 1994. Many future major leaguers, including Bo Jackson, Otis Nixon, Reggie Sanders, and Michael Jordan, started their athletic careers in Dixie Youth Baseball.

Dixie Youth Baseball World Series

YEAR	WINNER	SITE
1956	Greenville SC	Alexandria LA
1957	Dothan AL	Columbus MS
1958	Central Park AL	Columbus MS
1959	Central Park AL	Lakeland FL
1960	Airline Park Playground LA	South Boston VA
1961	Rossville GA	Lookout Mountain TN
1962	Central Park AL	West Monroe LA
1963	Midfield AL	Hueytown AL
1964	Cayce SC	Columbus MS
1965	Bankhead AL	Florence SC
1966	Midfield AL	Alexandria LA
1967	Hartsville National SC	Red Bank TN
1968	Montgomery Eastern AL	Myrtle Grove FL
1969	Chattanooga Lakeside TN	Montgomery AL
1970	Pensacola Brent East FL	Bartow FL
1971	Pascagoula National MS	Pascagoula MS
1972	Huffman AL	Winter Haven FL
1973	Ft. Oglethorpe GA	Charleston SC
1974	Pensacola Brent East FL	Decatur AL
1975	Hattiesburg American MS	Lawrenceville GA
1976	Pineview SC	Red Bank TN
1977	Midlands West Columbia SC	Bartow FL
1978	Nashville Parkwood TN	Sulphur LA
1979	Nashville Parkwood TN	Leland NC
1980	West Columbia Pineview SC	Goodlettsville TN
1981	Nashville Volunteer TN	Bartow FL
1982	Nashville Parkwood TN	Ellisville MS
1983	Hartsville National SC	Pleasant Grove AL
1984	Music City American TN	Lufkin TX
1985	Ville Platte LA	Cumberland County NC
1986	Alabaster AL	Decatur AL
1987	Tallassee AL	Bartow FL
1988	Pensacola Brent FL	Montgomery AL
1989	Cleveland TX	Hattiesburg MS
1990	Albany Dixie GA	Lakeland FL
1991	Midlands West Columbia SC	Texarkana TX
1992	Meridian National MS	Pelham AL
1993	Columbus County NC	West Monroe LA
1994	Lee Country National GA	Columbia County GA
1995	Ville Platte LA	Lexington SC
1996	Murfreesboro TN	Dothan AL
1997	Northeast Pensacola Blue FL	Conway AL
1998	Lee County GA	Hattiesburg MS
1999	Hilton Head SC	Terrell TX
2000	Columbia County GA	Marshall TX
2001	Searcy AR	Madison Heights/Bedford VA
2002	Nacogdoches TN	Pascagoula MS
2003	Nacogdoches TN	Florence SC
2004	Goodlettsville TN	Muscle Shoals AL
2005	Hope Mills American NC	Auburn AL
2006	North Charleston SC	Goodlettsville TN

RBI

RBI–Reviving Baseball in Inner Cities–was the brainchild of John Young, a former major league player and scout. Young had noticed a decrease in the number of skilled ballplayers coming from inner-city neighborhoods as early as the late 1970s, and he decided to try to reverse that trend. After studying the issue, Young realized that there was a significant drop in participation around age 13, so he set out to establish a new comprehensive youth baseball program for 13- to 16-year-olds in his old neighborhood in South Central Los Angeles. Young's aims for the program were twofold: to develop the kids' baseball skills as well as to provide local youth with a constructive activity that would challenge them and keep them safe. Young also worked to make RBI a well-rounded program, instituting academic incentives and training participants for life as well as baseball.

The program proved to be extremely successful in attracting participants and, with the support of Major League Baseball, RBI quickly spread across the nation. By 1994, RBI had spread to 28 American cities and, in the years since, over 200 cities around the world have participated in the program. Major League Baseball officially took over RBI administration in 1991 and, in 1993, the first RBI World Series was held in St. Louis. RBI expanded in the 1990s to include a Senior Division for older boys as well as a softball division for girls. In 1997, RBI merged with the youth baseball and softball programs of the Boys & Girls Clubs of America. There is no question that RBI is a successful and worthwhile program for most of the 120,000 youngsters who have participated over the years. More than 150 RBI participants have been drafted by major league teams, including 3 in the first round. Unfortunately, the overall problem that John Young spotted over 25 years ago has definitely not been solved, and today there are even fewer players—especially African-Americans—coming into professional baseball from inner-city communities.

RBI World Series Champions

YEAR	HOST CITY (TEAM)	BOYS JR. CHAMPION	BOYS SR. CHAMPION	GIRLS CHAMPION
1993	St. Louis (Cardinals)	Atlanta	Atlanta	
1994	Anaheim (Angels)	Puerto Rico	Puerto Rico	
1995	Philadelphia (Phillies)	Atlanta	Los Angeles	Newark
1996	Cleveland (Indians)	Puerto Rico	Puerto Rico	Puerto Rico
1997	Denver (Rockies)	Miami	Puerto Rico	St. Petersburg
1998	Kissimmee (Braves)	Puerto Rico	Atlanta	Denver
1999	Kissimmee (Braves)	Puerto Rico	Puerto Rico	Miami
2000	Kissimmee (Braves)	Los Angeles	Los Angeles	Los Angeles
2001	Kissimmee (Braves)	Los Angeles	Tampa	Atlanta
2002	Chicago (White Sox)	Atlanta	Los Angeles	Atlanta
2003	Houston (Astros)	Los Angeles	Los Angeles	Atlanta
2004	Detroit (Tigers)	Puerto Rico	Miami	Atlanta
2005	Pittsburgh (Pirates)	Los Angeles	Los Angeles	Atlanta
2006	Compton, CA	Detroit	Los Angeles	Atlanta

AMERICAN LEGION BASEBALL

American Legion Baseball is the oldest and largest baseball organization for older teenagers in the United States. Founded in 1925 by World War I veterans in an effort to give back to the community and provide a way for young people to stay in shape, over ten million teenagers have participated since. Today, over 100,000 players between the ages of 15 and 19 participate annually in Legion ball. Over 5,400 teams, spread over all 50 states and Puerto Rico, are sponsored by American Legion posts or non-profit outside sponsors. Fully 55 percent of big-league ballplayers, as well as 80 percent of college players, have seen action in American Legion ball, and 46 members of the Baseball Hall of Fame played on American Legion teams.

American Legion Baseball has long maintained strong ties with Major League Baseball. The winners of the American Legion World Series are honored each fall with a plaque from the Commissioner of Major League Baseball at the World Series The American Legion Player of the Year is honored each year with a plaque at the annual Baseball Hall of Fame induction ceremony in Cooperstown, New York. In the 1960s, MLB even briefly held a separate draft for American Legion ballplayers.

American Legion Baseball National Championship

YEAR	WINNER (POST NO.)	RUNNER-UP	SITE
1926	Yonkers NY #321	Pocatello ID	Philadelphia PA
1927	[No national tournament held]		
1928	Oakland CA #5	Worcester MA	Chicago IL
1929	Buffalo NY #721	New Orleans LA	Louisville KY
1930	Baltimore MD #81	New Orleans LA #125	Memphis TN
1931	Chicago IL #493	Columbia SC #6	Houston TX
1932	New Orleans LA #132	Springfield MA #21	Manchester NH
1933	Chicago IL #467	Trenton NJ	New Orleans LA
1934	Cumberland MD #13	New Orleans LA	Chicago IL
1935	Gastonia NC #23	Sacramento CA #391	Gastonia NC
1936	Spartanburg SC #28	Los Angeles CA	Spartanburg SC
1937	East Lynn MA #291	New Orleans CA	New Orleans LA
1938	San Diego CA #6	Spartanburg SC #28	Spartanburg SC
1939	Omaha NE #1	Berwyn IL	Omaha NE
1940	Albermarle NC #76	San Diego CA #6	Albermarle NC
1941	San Diego CA #6	Berwyn IL	San Diego CA
1942	Los Angeles CA #357	Manchester NH	Manchester NH
1943	Richfield MN #435	Springfield OH	Miles City MT
1944	Cincinnati OH #50	Albermarle NC	Minneapolis MN
1945	Shelby NC #82	Trenton NJ	Charlotte NC
1946	New Orleans LA #125	Trenton NJ	Charleston SC
1947	Cincinnati OH #50	Little Rock AR #1	Los Angeles CA
1948	Trenton NJ #93	Jacksonville FL #9	Indianapolis IN
1949	Oakland CA #337	Cincinnati OH #507	Omaha NE
1950	Oakland CA #337	St. Louis MO #245	Omaha NE
1951	Los Angeles CA #716	White Plains NY #135	Detroit MI
1952	Cincinnati OH #50	San Diego CA #364	Denver CO
1953	Yakima WA #36	Winnetka IL #10	Miami FL
1954	San Diego CA #492	Gastonia NC #23	Yakima WA
1955	Cincinnati OH #216	Washington DC #31	St. Paul MN
1956	St. Louis MO #245	New Orleans LA #345	Bismarck ND
1957	Cincinnati OH #50	Portland OR #102	Billings MT
1958	Cincinnati OH #50	Everett MA #176	Colorado Springs CO
1959	Detroit MI #187	Hampton VA #48	Hastings NE
1960	New Orleans LA #125	Billings MT #4	Hastings NE
1961	Phoenix AZ #1	Cincinnati OH #554	Hastings NE
1962	St. Louis MO #299	Honolulu HI #11	Bismarck ND
1963	Long Beach CA #27	Memphis TN #1	Keene NH
1964	Upland CA #73	Charlotte NC #9	Little Rock AR
1965	Charlotte NC #9	Omaha NE #1	Aberdeen SD
1966	Oakland CA #337	Tuscaloosa AL #34	Orangeburg SC
1967	Tuscaloosa CA #34	Northbrook IL #791	Memphis TN
1968	Memphis TN #1	Klamath Falls OR #8	Manchester NH
1969	Portland OR #105	Towson MD #22	Hastings NE
1970	West Covina CA #790	Levittown PA	Klamath Falls OH
1971	West Covina CA #790	Cedar Rapids IA #5	Tucson AZ
1972	Ballwin MO #611	Memphis TN #1	Memphis TN

YEAR	WINNER POSITION	CITY	
1973	Rio Piedras PR #146	Memphis TN #1	Lewiston ID
1974	Rio Piedras PR #146	Lake Oswego OR #92	Roseburg OR
1975	Yakima WA #36	Cedar Rapids IA #5	Rapid City SD
1976	Santa Monica CA #123	Des Plaines IL #36	Manchester NH
1977	South Bend IN #50	Hattiesburg MS #78	Manchester NH
1978	Hialeah FL #32	E. Springfield MA	Yakima WA
1979	Yakima WA #36	Barrington RI #8	Greenville MS
1980	Honolulu HI*	Boyertown PA #471	Ely MN
1981	West Tampa FL #248	Richmond VA #361	Sumter SC
1982	Boyertown PA #471	Lafayette CA #517	Boyertown PA
1983	Edina MN #471	Boyertown PA #471	Fargo ND
1984	Guaynabo PR #134	Brooklawn NJ #72	New Orleans LA
1985	Midlothian VA #186	Sacramento CA*	Kokomo IN
1986	Jensen Beach FL #126	Las Vegas NV #8	Rapid City SD
1987	Boyertown PA #471	Vancouver WA #176	Stevens Point WI
1988	Cincinnati OH #507	Boyertown PA #471	Middletown CT
1989	Woodland Hills CA #826	Rio Piedras PR #134	Millington TN
1990	Mayo MD #226	Bayamon PR #148	Corvallis OR
1991	Brooklawn NJ #72	Newark OH #85	Boyertown PA
1992	Newbury Park CA*	Arlington Heights #208	Fargo ND
1993	Rapid City SD #22	Las Vegas NV #8	Roseburg OR
1994	Miami FL #346	Chino CA #299	Boyertown PA
1995	Aiea HI*	Bellevue WA*	Fargo ND
1996	Yardley PA #317	Gonzalez LA #81	Roseburg OR
1997	Sanford FL #53	Medford OR #15	Rapid City SD
1998	Edwardsville IL #199	Cherryville NC #100	Las Vegas NV
1999	New Brighton MN #513	Kennewick WA #34	Middletown CT
2000	Danville CA #246	Paducah KY #17	Alton IL
2001	Brooklawn NJ #72	Lewiston ID #13	Yakima WA
2002	West Point MS #212	Excelsior MN #259	Danville VA
2003	Rochester MN #92	Cherryville NC #100	Bartlesville OK
2004	Portland ME*	Kennewick WA #32	Corvallis OR
2005	Enid OK #4	Twin Cities WA #34	Rapid City SD
2006	Metairie, LA #175	Terre Haute, IN #346	Cedar Rapids, Iowa

* *outside sponsorship*

George W. Rulon American Legion Player Of The Year

YEAR	WINNER POSITION	CITY
1949	Ray Herrara SS	Oakland CA
1950	J. W. Porter C	Oakland CA
1951	Grover Jones Jr. C	White Plains NY
1952	Russell Nixon C	Cincinnati OH
1953	Charles Lindstrom P	Winnetka IL
1954	Billy Capps 3B	San Diego CA
1955	Frank Birri 3B	Cincinnati OH
1956	Jim Harwell P	New Orleans LA
1957	Fred Fox 3B	Cincinnati OH
1958	Kiebler James P-SS	Greenwood SC
1959	Fred Bowen SS	Detroit MI
1960	Richard R. Roniger P	New Orleans LA
1961	James J. Gerber SS	Cincinnati OH
1962	William D. Matan Jr. C	St. Louis MO
1963	Richard Allen Dash 2B	Long Beach CA
1964	Roland G. Fingers P-OF	Upland CA
1965	Kenneth J. Fila P	Omaha NE
1966	William C. Parker Jr. OF	Tuscaloosa AL
1967	Ray Lynn Larson C	Northbrook IL
1968	Donald Hardy Castle P-OF	Memphis TN
1969	John David Adeimy SS	West Palm Beach FL
1970	Carroll Wayne Watts SS	Tulsa OK
1971	Randolph Gregory Haas OF	West Covina CA
1972	Michael Charles Murphy P-OF	Ballwin MO
1973	Thomas Steven Ashford SS	Memphis TN
1974	Edwin C. Lopez OF	Rio Piedras PR
1975	David Delmar Edler P-OF	Yakima WA
1976	Gustavo Martin Malespin OF	Metairie LA
1977	William Floyd Schell SS	South Bend IN
1978	Ross Jones 1B	Hialeah FL
1979	Patrick Scott Allen 2B	Yakima WA
1980	Tomas Gil OF	Hialeah FL
1981	David Joseph Magadan 3B-P	West Tampa FL
1982	Ivan S. Snyder OF-P	Boyertown PA
1983	Michael Holloran C	Edina MN
1984	Jorge Robles SS	Guaynabo PR
1985	Tris Lipscomb P-2B	Midlothian VA
1986	Joe Grahe P	Jensen Beach FL
1987	Wilbur Stout C	Boyertown PA
1988	Mike Kessler 1B-P	Cincinnati OH
1989	Del Marine C	Woodland Hills CA
1990	Mark Foster P-OF	Mayo MD
1991	Ryan Beeney SS	Newark OH
1992	David Lamb SS	Newbury Park CA
1993	Ben Thomas 1B-P	Rapid City SD
1994	Fernando Rodriguez P	Miami FL
1995	Jason Adaro P-C-OF	Aiea HI
1996	Christian Bourgeois 1B	Gonzales LA
1997	Nate Philo OF	Medford OR
1998	Chad Opel SS	Edwardsville IL
1999	Jeremy S. Roberts OF	Rison AR
2000	Josh Zender P	Deming WA
2001	Jay Threet P-1B	Adrian MI
2002	Ty Henkaline P	Sidney OH
2003	Jared Willis 2-B	Logan WV
2004	Nolan Gallagher P	Red Lodge MT
2005	Fernando Irizarry C	Montero PR
2006	Joseph Walsh C	Weymouth, MA

GLOSSARY

At Bats: The definition of at bat has varied over the years, primarily due to the changing definitions of events that constitute plate appearances that are not at bats, such as sacrifice hits and sacrifice flies.

Average Value: Virtually every analytical statistic in this encyclopedia uses league average as a baseline. The use of this baseline, which is set to equal either 0 or 100, depending on the statistic, makes the quality of a player's performance—whether a player is above average, average, or below average—immediately obvious most of the time. Above-average players are needed to win pennants. Average and below-average players who are better than a typical replacement make only minor contributions toward a winning season.

Average is not the only reasonable baseline, of course—there is no "right" baseline, though there are more useful and less useful baselines. Some analysts use "replacement level" as their baseline. That baseline is hard to define, but there are circumstances where it may be more useful than the average baseline. Different tasks require different tools and, thus, different baselines. The primary advantage of an average baseline is that it clearly shows how the performance of players translates into wins and losses on the field. All teams start the season 0–0; only better-than-average players enable a team to rise above .500.

Bases on Balls: Permanently established at the count of 4 balls in 1889. The number had come down one at a time since 1874, when 9 balls were required to reach first base.

Basestealing Runs: The formula for calculating BSR is (.22*SB) – (.38*CS). SB stands for stolen bases, CS is for caught stealing, and * signifies multiplication.

Basestealing Wins: Divide basestealing runs by runs per win, which in this case equals 10 times the square root of runs per inning.

Batter-Fielder Wins: The sum of a player's batting wins, basestealing wins, and fielding wins.

Batting Runs: The formula for calculating batting runs is .33*(BB+HBP) plus .47*H plus .38*2B plus .55*3B plus .93*HR–ABF*(AB–H).

ABF, known as the league batting factor, makes the value of an average batter equal 0. ABF is computed with the following formula (all statistics in the equation are league statistics):

$$\frac{.33*(BB+HBP) + .47*H + .38*2B + .55*3B + .93*HR)}{(AB - LGF*H).}$$

LGF, the league factor, adjusts for the quality of league play, and equals 1 except for the Union Association (1884), for which it equals 0.8, and the Federal League (1914–15), for which it equals 0.9.

Adjusted batting runs, which appear in the batting register, are calculated with the following formula: (BR – (batters' park factor – 1)*RPA*PA/batters' park factor). RPA is the number of runs per plate appearance in the league.

Batting Wins: This is calculated by dividing adjusted batting runs by runs per win. In this case, runs per win equals 10 times the square root of (runs per inning + player adjusted batting runs/games/9).

Blown Saves: Save opportunities not converted because the relief pitcher allowed the tying or go-ahead run to score. Only calculated since 1969.

Caught Stealing: The data is available for 1914, 1915, and from 1920 onward for the AL; and for 1913, 1915, 1920–1925, and from 1951 onward in the NL. Caught Stealing totals are also available for 1916 for all players who stole at least 20 bases.

Differential: This measures the difference between the won-lost record a team was *projected* to achieve (based on its batting, pitching, fielding, and basestealing), and the record that the team *actually* attained. If a team was projected to finish 89–73 (that is, +8) but actually concluded the season at 85–77 (that is, +4), the team's differential would be –4.

Earned Run Average: The number of earned runs allowed per 9 innings pitched. It is calculated by multiplying earned runs by 9 and dividing by innings pitched. Adjusted ERA is calculated by dividing league ERA by the pitcher (or team) ERA and then multiplying by the pitchers' park factor. Note that a small number of runs can be earned runs for the pitcher but unearned runs for the team.

ERA has been kept officially since 1912 in the NL and 1913 in the AL. Before then, Information Concepts Inc. researchers calculated earned runs from game accounts. Some earned run data include estimates, although in every case, at least half the earned runs for a team were known from game accounts. This was for 1881–86 (all leagues) and 1887 and 1890 in the American Association. Earned run data in box scores and the official guides in the nineteenth century were not used. Bases on balls were usually considered errors in those years and, in fact, the fielding stats often gave pitchers assists on strikeouts and errors on walks. Such assists and errors have been removed from the fielding averages in this book. Note that if a pitcher allows one or more earned runs, but fails to retire a batter during a season, his ERA is infinite. If so, we display the number of earned runs allowed in parentheses instead of his ERA.

Fielding Runs: Fielding runs are based on the player's fielding statistics at each position compared to the league average for the number of innings played. The number of innings played was obtained from play-by-play data for 1957 onward. For most years before 1957, innings are estimated from defensive and offensive data for all players on the team. Comparing the formulas for estimated defensive innings to actual defensive innings taken from 1957–2006 play-by-play data showed an average difference of approximately 1% for infielders and 2% for outfielders for players with 1,000 or more innings.

The basic formula is:

PFR/(PO–SO for team)–LFR/(PO–SO for league)*Player Innings.

PFR is the player fielding rate, while LFR is the league fielding rate.

The ratings used as fielding rates vary by position as follows:

1B	.2*(2*A – E)
P, 2B, SS, 3B	.2*(PO + 2*A – E + DP)
OF	.2*(PO + 4*A – E + DP)
C	.2*(PO – SO + .4*(A – CS) – E + DP + PB/2).

A stands for assists, PO for putouts, E for errors, SO for strikeouts, DP is for double plays, and PB for passed balls. Strikeouts are subtracted because a team that strikes out a lot of batters will have many fewer chances to create outs from balls put into play. When calculating a pitchers' fielding, his actual strikeout total is used; for other fielders, the team average strikeout total is used.

Two more factors are used to adjust for the amount of left-handed and right-handed pitching on a team and for the number of double play opportunities. Teams with more left-handed pitching tend to face more right-handed batters as a result of platooning, and this effect in turn alters the distribution of balls hit into play. A careful historical study of this factor showed that its effect was non-existent before 1910, then slowly grew until 1970, when it hit a similar level to today.

Right-handed batters shift the distribution of ground balls over from the right side of the infield to the left side while shifting flyballs and popups from the left side of the field to the right side. Second basemen also gain more putouts with a right-handed hitter at the plate since they are more likely to be covering second base.

To adjust the number of expected league average putouts and assists for each player, the relevant statistic is multiplied by this equation:

(1 + ADJ*YF*DLHP).

ADJ is the adjustment figure appropriate for the position (1B, 2B, 3B, SS, LF, or RF) and statistic (putouts or assists). The chart below supplies the appropriate figure.

ADJ	*PO*	*A*
1B	n/a	–.40
2B	.23	–.27
SS	– .10	.14
3B	– .22	.34
LF	– .16	n/a
RF	.09	n/a

YF is the year factor, necessary because this factor steadily increased in importance from 1910 to 1970. Before 1910 the YF is 0, so no adjustment is necessary. The adjustment can be calculated for each year from 1910 through 1970 by subtracting 1910 from the year in question and then dividing by 60. After 1970 the YF is always 1.

DLHP is the difference in the percentage of left-handed pitching from the league average.

So if a second baseman was on a team with 10 percent more innings by left-handed pitchers than average in 1960, his adjustment is:

Assists = (1 – .27 x (1960-1910)/60 x .10) = .9775
Putouts = (1 + .23 x (1960-1910)/60 x .10) = 1.0192.

If the league average second baseman in 1960 finished the season with 400 assists and 200 putouts, the expected league average would be adjusted to 391 and 204.

Pitchers have a further correction, since left-handed pitchers have fewer putouts as a result of facing fewer left-handed batters. Up until 1910 left- and right-handed pitcher putouts were about equal, declining to about 62 percent for left-handers in 1970 before leveling off. Thus, a separate expected putout rate is calculated for each type of pitcher based on the year and the number of left-handed innings.

Double play opportunities were estimated from hits, bases on balls, hit-by-pitches, and home runs allowed, plus errors committed. (On average, 57.5 percent of errors result in a runner reaching base; the other errors just allow existing baserunners to take extra bases.) Using a multiplier for homers to account for double play opportunities lost did not improve the estimate in years where there are actual data; the average error in these years was around 2 percent. The formula for calculating double play opportunities is:

.662*(H – HR + BB + HB + .575*E).

Individual double plays were divided by the team double play opportunities divided by the league average double play opportunities.

For catchers, there is an additional defensive calculation made to rate them on other defensive aspects. The formula for that calculation is:

(–.22*SB) + (CSF*CS) + .1*APR*IP/TIP.

APR is the catcher's team's adjusted pitching runs; IP is the catcher's innings pitched to; TIP is team innings pitched; and CSF is the caught stealing factor that ensures that the average value of a catcher defensively stays at 0. The formula to calculate CSF is:

22*(LSB – TSB) divided by (LCS – TCS).

Also, since artificial turf results in about a 5 percent higher stolen base success rate, a small adjustment is made to the results of players and teams from the turf era. The size of the adjustment depends on the exact split of games between ballparks with turf in the basepaths and those with dirt basepaths. Most ballparks with turf fields have turf basepaths with dirt only in the sliding cutouts around the bases. However, a few ballparks, especially in the early years of artificial turf, have had all-dirt basepaths with turf fields.

Fielding Wins: Divide fielding runs by runs per win, which in this case equals 10 times the square root of runs per inning.

Games Behind: This is the number of games one team is behind another team in the standing, almost always measured from first place. If a team's record stands at 78–71 and the first-place team's record is 82–68, then the former team is 3½ games behind the first-place team.

Grounded into Double Play: This became an official statistic in 1933 in the NL and in 1939 in the AL.

Hit-by-Pitch: The rule awarding first base to batters hit by a pitch was instituted in 1884 by the American Association and in 1887 by the National League.

Innings Pitched: Fractions of innings pitched in a season have only been officially counted since 1982. Prior to that, both leagues rounded off fractional innings. This encyclopedia has full innings pitched (i.e., not rounded off) for all major league seasons.

Normalizing: Baseball statistics tell us very little without context. A .450 slugging average in Dodger Stadium in 1965 means something very different than a .450 slugging average in Coors Field in 2003—the former is an impressive performance while the latter is sub-par. Many of the statistics in this encyclopedia are normalized using league average as a baseline, enabling readers to see whether a player is better than or worse than his average peer as well as to what extent he is better or worse. By putting different seasons played in different circumstances on the same scale, normalization makes it much easier to compare seasons. Some statistics in this encyclopedia are further normalized to account for the home parks of players since some ballparks are far more conducive to scoring than others. As a result, both the ease of producing a run and the value of a run can vary significantly from ballpark to ballpark, even in the same season. Normalizing a statistic for ballpark effects ensures that players can be compared on a level playing field.

On-Base Percentage: Declared an official statistic in 1984, OBP is defined as (hits plus bases on balls plus hit-by-pitches) divided by (at bats plus bases on balls plus hit-by-pitches plus sacrifice flies). This encyclopedia uses the current definition back to 1954, when sacrifice fly data became permanently available. Previous to 1954, sacrifice flies were either counted as outs or were included with sacrifice hits (1908–30 and 1939) and, therefore, cannot be used.

On-Base plus Slugging: Often referred to as OPS, this statistic, which was introduced by Pete Palmer and John Thorn in *The Hidden Game of Baseball* in 1984, has exploded in popularity the past few years. This encyclopedia does not feature a separate column for the basic version of OPS in the batter register since it is very easy to calculate—simply adds on-base percentage and slugging average—and the two columns are adjacent. Adjusted OPS (which has its own column) then normalizes OPS for the league and the player's home park(s), then converts it to a scale in which 100 is league average. The exact calculation is ((player OBP/league OBP) plus (player slugging/league slugging) – 1) divided by batters' park factor. When calculating adjusted OPS for non-pitchers, league average statistics do not include pitcher batting. For consistency in historical comparisons, the definition of on-base percentage used in adjusted OPS does not use sacrifice flies in the denominator.

Opponents' Batting Average: Figures are based on estimated at bats from 1901–07 in the AL; from 1889–1902 in the NL; in 1882–83 and 1888–91 in the American Association; in 1884 in the Union Association; and in 1890 in the Player's League.

Opponents' Caught Stealing: Stats for 1957 to the present came from play-by-play records. Estimated totals for catchers came from team totals found in league records from 1920–56 for the AL and from 1920–25 and from 1951–56 for the NL. For most other years since 1890, team totals were estimated from other team data and catcher totals were estimated from the team estimates. Some years from 1912–19 have only runner caught stealing data, some have team caught stealing, and some have individual catcher caught stealing.

Opponents' On-Base Percentage: Based on the official definition of OBP since 1954. The definition used in previous years depends on the available data (as with the OBP definition above).

Opponents' Stolen Bases: Exact totals for 1957 to the present came from play-by-play records. Estimated totals for catchers came from team totals found in league records for 1890–1956 (except for the 1890 NL data, which came from box scores).

Park Factor: This measure of how the team's home park affects hitters and pitchers is used to adjust the team's performance in a way that takes into account the context of the team's home park. Separate park factors are used for batting and pitching in order to adjust for the fact that pitchers and hitters never get to face their own teammates.

Pitching Runs: This measure of how many runs a pitcher prevented compared to the average pitcher is calculated with this formula:

LERA* IP/9 – ER + URF.

LERA is the league ERA and ER stands for earned runs. URF is the unearned run factor that accounts for the unearned runs the pitcher is responsible for and is calculated by multiplying (0.5) times (ER – R*TER/TR).

Adjusted pitching runs is calculated the same as pitching runs above, except that LERA* PPF is used instead of plain LERA—that is, the league ERA is multiplied by the pitcher park factor. Then the result of the entire calculation is divided by the pitcher park factor. Thus the formula is (PPF*LERA*IP/9 – ER + URF)/PPF.

Pitcher Batting: This measure of a pitcher's offensive performance is calculated the same way as adjusted batting runs; the difference is that a pitcher is compared to the average-hitting pitcher, not the average hitter. If a pitcher spent time at other defensive positions, his offense will be divided proportionately based on how much he played each position; only the appropriate fraction will count for pitcher batting.

Pitcher Wins: The total number of wins a pitcher is worth to his team compared to the average pitcher (including pitching, fielding, batting, and basestealing). It is calculated by multiplying adjusted pitcher runs by XMULR (see below), adding the pitcher's non-pitching contributions, and then dividing by runs per win.

In order to properly credit relief pitchers for the extra or lesser value of their innings pitched, a factor is used when converting adjusted pitching runs to pitching wins. The formula for that multiplier (XMULR) is:

$$9*(W + L + SV/XSV)/IP.$$

XSV is calculated by dividing league saves by league wins and multiplying by 10. XSV cannot be less than 4, so any result lower than 4 is set at 4. The multiplier cannot not be less than 0.5 or more than 2, so any result not in that range is considered to be either 0.5 or 2, depending on whether it was above or below the range.

Pitching Wins: The wins a pitcher achieves by his pitching is calculated by dividing adjusted pitching runs by runs per win. In this case, the formula for runs per win is 10 times the square root of (RPI – APR/G/9). Thus, if a pitcher reduces the number of runs scored by the opponent in his games, the value of each run is increased by a reduction in the runs per win figure. Pitchers, especially starting pitchers, have a much stronger effect on runs per win because their effect on scoring is spread out over fewer games.

Positional Adjustment: Baseball fans know not to expect a shortstop to hit like a first baseman, exceptions like Alex Rodriguez notwithstanding. Second basemen who slug .370 can usually hold on to their starting spot, but first basemen who slug .370 are likely to be benched or dropped off the roster. That's because it's fairly easy to find an acceptable defensive first baseman that can hit with power, while players who can handle second base defensively and hit with power are usually scarce. In order to account for the ability of players to handle the most valuable positions defensively, the offense of these players is compared to their peers at the same position. This approach accounts for the differing value major league teams place on fielding ability at each position and also makes it simple to adjust for the changing demands of a position. For example, higher defensive expectations for third basemen a century ago made it significantly harder to find a third baseman with a good bat back then than today. Whether that was because teams demanded a higher level of defense from third basemen then, or because there are more good defensive third basemen these days who can hit is irrelevant. We don't have to know the answer to that question to account for the decreasing scarcity of good-hitting third basemen by using a smaller positional adjustment.

POWR (Player Overall Win Rating): POWR, featured in the All-Time Leaders section, adds the batting wins, fielding wins, basestealing wins, and pitching wins of every player to rate his overall value compared to an average player.

Range: This category is calculated different ways for different positions. For infielders, range is based on assists per inning. For outfielders, range is based on putouts per inning. For catchers, the statistic in the range column is based on stolen bases allowed per inning. Outfielders are rated for their (weighted) play at all outfield positions, while infielders are only rated for their play at their primary position. The data is then adjusted in comparison to the league average, with 100 equaling league average. *Higher is always better.* All statistics are adjusted for context, including the number of balls put into play and the distribution of balls in play. The adjustments for each statistic are detailed in the fielding runs entry. Innings played data are calculated from play-by-play accounts from 1957 onward; it is estimated prior to 1957.

Relative Batting Average: A normalized translation of batting average. The formula is player average divided by league average.

Runs Batted In: RBIs have been recognized as an official statistic since 1920. Runs driven in by a force double play were no longer counted as RBIs after 1938.

Relief Ranking: Generated by multiplying the XMULR factor (described in the pitcher wins entry) by adjusted pitcher runs. Since innings pitched in relief is not historically available, relief pitchers are classified as those pitchers who average less than 3 innings per appearance.

Run Support: Basic run support is calculated by adding up all the runs scored in a pitcher's starts and then dividing that total by his games started. The support figures presented in the pitcher register have been normalized for the context of the offensive level of the league and the player's home park(s), then converted to a scale in which 100 is league average. A run support figure of 90 would indicate that pitcher had 10 percent less runs scored in his starts than average; a figure of 110 would indicated 10 percent above-average. The formula to produce the adjusted run support is (pitcher run support) divided by (league average run support) divided by (batters' park factor) times 100.

Run support stats have been published widely since 1990, usually counting all appearances for a pitcher and normalizing the runs scored by his team while he was in the game to 9 innings pitched. While this stat is useful, it is not calculable pre-1969. Furthermore, it is not a substitute for calculating run support for starting pitchers, since runs scored after a pitcher leaves the game materially affect a pitcher's record. If a starter leaves the game in the seventh inning with his team trailing 5–1, then his team scores 6 times in the eighth to take the lead, he avoids being tagged with the loss and clearly benefits from runs scored after he had left the game.

Runs Per Win: The number of runs needed, on average, to gain an additional win in the standings. Historically, about 10 runs have equaled a win. The value of runs per win is used in several entries in this glossary to translate runs into wins. Individual players, especially starting pitchers, can have a significant effect on the number of runs that it takes to achieve a win in their own games, so the runs per win calculation often takes into account the performance level of the individual or team being evaluated.

Sacrifice Fly: First recognized as a distinct statistical category in 1954. Previous to 1975, only fair fly balls which drove in runners were counted in this category. From 1908–1930 and again in 1939, sacrifice flies were counted as sacrifice hits. In all other seasons before 1954, sacrifice flies are indistinguishable from other at bats.

Save: Recognized as an official statistic in 1969, saves were at first awarded to any relief pitcher that finished pitching a victory and was not credited with the win. In 1973 requirements were significantly tightened so that saves were only awarded if the pitcher either entered the game with the potential tying run on base or at the plate or pitched at least 3 effective innings while preserving the lead. In 1975 the rule was set to where it stands today: In order to earn a save, a reliever must finish off a victory without ever giving up the lead after entering the game with a lead of no more than 3 runs and pitching at least an inning, or he can earn a save by finishing a victory without giving up the lead after entering the game with the tying run on base, at the plate, or on deck. Saves may also be earned by pitching effectively for at least the last 3 innings of a victory, without getting credit for the win. The original 1969 rule has been used in awarding saves prior to 1969.

Save Opportunities and Save Percentage: Save Opportunities are defined as Saves plus Blown Saves—a narrow definition that makes Save Percentage useful only when comparing closers to each other. Save Percentage is calculated by dividing Saves by Save Opportunities. Blown Saves are defined by Rolaids, which has given the Rolaids Relief Man Award annually since 1976. By virtue of the prestige that this award has accrued, Rolaids effectively controls the definition of the Blown Save since it is not an official statistic.

Though setup pitchers and middle relievers get charged with Blown Saves when they blow a lead in a save situation, they don't get many saves because they are almost always replaced by their team's closer before the game ends. The effect, therefore, is that setup and middle relievers rarely show a high Save Percentage: they get nicked for the negative stat when they fail to protect a lead, but they rarely get a chance to earn the positive stat when they protect a lead.

The unofficial "Hold" statistic that gained currency in the 1990s was an attempt to address that gap. Unfortunately, neither of the two versions of the "Hold" stat solve the problem. The earlier version doesn't even require a relief pitcher to retire a hitter to get credit for a "Hold"—if a reliever comes into the game with a 1-run lead and no one on base, then walks the bases loaded before being yanked, he can get a "Hold" despite his miserable performance. The later version of the "Hold," promulgated by Stats, Inc., and still used today, requires a relief pitcher to pitch at least 1/3 of an inning to gain a "Hold." Better. That's better, but still not nearly good enough.

The reason that the "Hold" doesn't work as a fair evaluation of middle and setup relievers is that it requires a pitcher to enter the game in a save situation before he can earn a "Hold." Yet the role of middle and setup relief necessarily involves entering many games in which the score is tied or their team is down by 1–2 runs. Sure, they have the opportunity to earn a Win in those situations. However, if they pitch a scoreless inning or two and leave with the game still tied or their club behind, they earn *nada.* All of which means that a meaningful measure to evaluate the performance of middle and setup relievers has yet to be devised.

Stolen Bases: Stolen bases were always a part of the game, but they were not officially tabulated from 1876–85. This statistic is available for all seasons in all leagues from 1886 onward. National Association stolen bases were obtained from box scores, which did not always report them, so 1871–75 data is incomplete.

The exact scoring definition of a stolen base was changed repeatedly before 1955, when most of the current rules regarding stolen bases were put into place. Before 1898, stolen bases were sometimes awarded for taking extra bases on hits and outs, so the data in this earlier period is not strictly comparable to later data.

Strikeouts: Available for batters in all years except for the 1882–88 and 1890 American Association, the 1884 Union Association, from 1897–1909 in the NL, and from 1901–12 in the AL. There is no missing data for pitchers' strikeouts. As in the case of bases on balls and stolen bases, there were some very different rules governing strikeouts in the nineteenth century, making comparisons across time rather tricky.

Throwing: This new category is calculated in different ways for different positions. For infielders, the throwing column shows their double plays per inning. For outfielders, throwing is based on assists per inning. For catchers, throwing is based on caught stealing rates per inning. The data is then adjusted in comparison to league average, with 100 equaling league average. All statistics are adjusted for context by various methods; the adjustments for each statistic are detailed in the fielding runs entry. Innings played data was calculated from play-by-play accounts from 1957 to the present; it is estimated for previous seasons. Outfielders are rated for their play at all outfield positions, while infielders are only rated for their play at their primary position.

Typical Game Stats

The table below shows the typical stats for each team in a single game for all seasons in major league history. The magnitude of major changes to baseball over time—like home run rates and error rates—stand out clearly when presented in this manner. Other, more subtle changes in the game also become apparent in this format, as do the many elements of the National Pastime that have been relatively consistent over more than a century of play.

Note that statistics from the Union Association in 1884, Players League in 1890, and Federal League in 1914-15 are not included, as their level of play was substantially below the nineteenth-century NL or twentieth-century NL and AL.

Evolution of the Changing Game

YEAR	AB	R	ER	H	AVG	2B	3B	HR	RBI	SH	SF	SB	CS	LOB	BB	IB	HB	SO	GDP	PO	A	E	DP	PB	CG	SV	WP
1871	42.6	10.5	4.2	12.2	.287	1.71	0.94	0.19	7.0	ø	ø	1.7	0.5	ø	1.5	ø	ø	0.7	0.3	26.6	11.5	7.6	0.6	1.9	0.9	ø	0.8
1872	42.8	9.3	3.6	12.2	.285	1.59	0.40	0.10	5.8	ø	ø	0.7	0.4	ø	0.7	ø	ø	0.7	0.3	26.9	11.5	7.5	0.5	0.8	0.9	ø	0.6
1873	42.6	9.0	3.4	12.4	.290	1.43	0.53	0.12	5.9	ø	ø	0.8	0.3	ø	0.8	ø	ø	0.7	0.3	27.0	12.2	8.0	0.7	1.0	0.9	ø	0.3
1874	41.2	7.5	2.2	11.3	.273	1.37	0.42	0.09	4.9	ø	ø	0.5	0.2	ø	0.5	ø	ø	0.8	0.2	27.0	11.9	8.1	0.5	0.8	0.9	ø	0.3
1875	38.9	6.1	2.2	9.9	.254	1.22	0.40	0.06	3.9	ø	ø	0.9	0.5	ø	0.4	ø	ø	1.0	0.2	26.9	12.1	7.0	0.5	1.2	0.9	ø	0.5
1876	38.7	5.9	2.3	10.3	.265	1.22	0.35	0.08	3.8	ø	ø	ø	ø	ø	0.6	ø	ø	1.1	ø	27.4	11.5	6.0	0.5	0.9	0.9	ø	0.4
1877	38.0	5.7	2.8	10.3	.271	1.20	0.57	0.07	3.9	ø	ø	ø	ø	ø	1.0	ø	ø	2.0	ø	27.0	12.4	5.2	0.6	1.0	0.9	ø	0.6
1878	37.1	5.2	2.3	9.6	.259	1.31	0.36	0.06	3.6	ø	ø	ø	ø	ø	1.0	ø	ø	2.9	ø	27.1	13.4	4.8	0.6	1.2	1.0	ø	0.6
1879	37.6	5.3	2.5	9.6	.255	1.49	0.49	0.09	3.7	ø	ø	ø	ø	ø	0.8	ø	ø	2.9	ø	27.1	13.2	4.9	0.6	1.2	0.9	ø	0.6
1880	35.7	4.7	2.3	8.7	.245	1.44	0.48	0.09	3.3	ø	ø	ø	ø	ø	1.1	ø	ø	2.9	ø	26.6	12.8	4.3	0.6	1.1	0.9	ø	0.4
1881	36.3	5.1	2.7	9.4	.260	1.59	0.45	0.11	3.7	ø	ø	ø	ø	ø	1.5	ø	ø	2.7	ø	26.7	12.8	4.1	0.7	1.0	0.9	ø	0.5
1882	36.4	5.3	2.8	9.0	.248	1.42	0.55	0.16	2.3	ø	ø	ø	ø	ø	1.4	ø	ø	2.9	ø	26.5	13.1	4.8	0.6	1.1	0.9	ø	0.5
1883	36.7	5.8	3.2	9.4	.257	1.58	0.60	0.15	2.0	ø	ø	ø	ø	ø	1.5	ø	ø	3.4	ø	26.5	12.2	4.9	0.6	1.2	0.9	ø	0.5
1884	35.3	5.3	3.0	8.6	.243	1.25	0.56	0.25	1.6	ø	ø	ø	ø	ø	1.7	ø	0.2	4.5	ø	26.2	12.3	4.4	0.6	1.2	1.0	ø	0.7
1885	35.2	5.2	3.0	8.6	.244	1.23	0.54	0.18	3.6	ø	ø	ø	ø	ø	2.0	ø	0.2	3.8	ø	26.5	12.5	3.9	0.6	1.0	1.0	ø	0.7
1886	34.7	5.5	3.3	8.5	.246	1.27	0.55	0.20	3.9	ø	ø	1.5	ø	ø	2.6	ø	0.1	4.3	ø	26.0	12.4	3.8	0.6	1.1	1.0	ø	0.7
1887	35.3	6.3	4.0	9.6	.271	1.46	0.66	0.29	4.9	ø	ø	3.0	ø	ø	2.9	ø	0.4	2.8	ø	25.9	12.6	3.8	0.7	0.9	1.0	ø	0.6
1888	34.5	4.9	2.9	8.2	.239	1.12	0.48	0.24	3.7	ø	ø	2.4	ø	ø	2.2	ø	0.4	3.8	ø	26.4	12.7	3.4	0.6	0.8	1.0	ø	0.6
1889	35.1	6.0	3.8	9.3	.264	1.38	0.50	0.31	4.7	ø	ø	2.2	ø	ø	3.4	ø	0.3	3.5	ø	26.2	12.7	3.4	0.7	0.6	0.9	ø	0.5
1890	34.6	5.6	3.6	8.8	.253	1.22	0.53	0.21	4.1	ø	ø	2.3	ø	ø	3.5	ø	0.4	3.6	ø	26.1	12.5	3.1	0.7	0.5	0.9	ø	0.5
1891	35.0	5.7	3.4	8.9	.254	1.19	0.57	0.26	4.5	ø	ø	1.9	ø	ø	3.6	ø	0.4	3.5	ø	26.3	12.7	3.2	0.7	0.4	0.9	ø	0.5
1892	34.7	5.1	3.2	8.5	.245	1.09	0.55	0.23	4.0	ø	ø	1.7	ø	ø	3.4	ø	0.3	3.2	ø	26.2	12.9	3.0	0.7	0.4	0.9	ø	0.3
1893	36.2	6.6	4.6	10.1	.280	1.40	0.67	0.29	5.4	ø	ø	1.8	ø	ø	3.9	ø	0.4	2.1	ø	26.5	13.2	2.9	0.8	0.3	0.8	ø	0.3
1894	36.0	7.4	5.1	11.1	.309	1.72	0.81	0.39	6.2	0.7	ø	2.0	ø	ø	3.7	ø	0.4	2.1	ø	25.9	12.4	3.0	0.8	0.3	0.8	ø	0.3
1895	35.5	6.6	4.6	10.5	.296	1.51	0.62	0.31	5.5	0.6	ø	1.8	ø	ø	3.2	ø	0.4	2.3	ø	25.9	12.6	2.9	0.8	0.2	0.8	ø	0.2
1896	35.1	6.0	4.2	10.2	.290	1.37	0.64	0.26	5.1	0.7	ø	1.9	ø	ø	3.1	ø	0.4	2.2	ø	26.0	12.7	2.6	0.8	0.2	0.8	ø	0.3
1897	34.9	5.9	4.1	10.2	.292	1.43	0.59	0.23	4.9	0.7	ø	1.7	ø	ø	2.9	ø	0.5	2.3	ø	25.9	12.5	2.5	0.7	0.2	0.8	ø	0.2
1898	34.0	5.0	3.5	9.2	.271	1.13	0.49	0.16	4.1	0.7	ø	1.1	ø	ø	2.8	ø	0.5	2.3	ø	25.9	12.7	2.4	0.7	0.2	0.9	ø	0.2
1899	34.0	5.2	3.7	9.6	.282	1.19	0.55	0.19	4.3	0.7	ø	1.4	ø	ø	2.7	ø	0.5	2.1	ø	25.8	13.1	2.4	0.8	0.2	0.9	ø	0.2
1900	34.4	5.2	3.6	9.6	.279	1.26	0.53	0.22	4.3	0.7	ø	1.5	ø	ø	2.7	ø	0.5	2.4	ø	26.1	13.5	2.4	0.7	0.3	0.8	ø	0.2
1901	34.7	5.0	3.4	9.4	.272	1.32	0.56	0.20	4.1	0.8	ø	1.3	ø	ø	2.5	ø	0.4	3.1	ø	26.4	13.0	2.4	0.7	0.2	0.9	ø	0.2
1902	34.1	4.4	3.1	9.1	.267	1.27	0.44	0.16	3.7	0.8	ø	1.2	ø	ø	2.4	ø	0.3	3.0	ø	26.5	13.2	2.1	0.7	0.2	0.9	ø	0.2
1903	33.9	4.4	3.0	8.9	.262	1.36	0.52	0.15	3.7	0.9	ø	1.2	ø	ø	2.4	ø	0.3	1.9	ø	26.4	13.0	2.1	0.6	0.1	0.9	ø	0.2
1904	33.0	3.7	2.6	8.2	.247	1.14	0.46	0.13	3.0	0.9	ø	1.1	ø	ø	2.2	ø	0.3	2.0	ø	26.4	13.1	1.9	0.6	0.1	0.9	ø	0.2
1905	33.1	3.9	2.8	8.2	.248	1.16	0.45	0.14	3.2	1.0	ø	1.2	ø	ø	2.5	ø	0.3	2.1	ø	26.6	13.0	1.8	0.6	0.1	0.8	ø	0.2
1906	32.6	3.6	2.6	8.0	.247	1.07	0.41	0.11	3.0	1.1	ø	1.2	ø	ø	2.5	ø	0.3	3.7	ø	26.5	13.1	1.7	0.6	0.1	0.8	ø	0.2
1907	32.6	3.5	2.5	8.0	.245	1.00	0.39	0.10	2.9	1.1	ø	1.1	ø	ø	2.5	ø	0.3	3.5	ø	26.5	13.2	1.7	0.6	0.1	0.7	ø	0.2
1908	32.4	3.4	2.4	7.7	.239	1.01	0.40	0.11	2.7	1.3	ø	1.1	ø	ø	2.4	ø	0.3	3.7	ø	26.8	13.4	1.7	0.5	0.1	0.7	ø	0.2
1909	32.5	3.5	2.5	7.9	.244	1.07	0.40	0.10	2.9	1.3	ø	1.2	ø	ø	2.6	ø	0.3	3.8	ø	26.8	13.1	1.8	0.6	0.1	0.7	ø	0.2
1910	32.6	3.8	2.8	8.1	.249	1.13	0.46	0.14	3.1	1.2	ø	1.3	ø	ø	3.0	ø	0.3	1.8	ø	26.8	13.3	1.8	0.7	0.1	0.6	0.1	0.2
1911	33.2	4.5	3.3	8.9	.266	1.32	0.53	0.21	3.8	1.2	ø	1.4	ø	ø	3.2	ø	0.3	1.9	ø	26.7	13.0	1.8	0.7	0.1	0.6	0.1	0.2
1912	33.3	4.5	3.3	8.9	.269	1.36	0.55	0.18	3.8	1.1	ø	1.4	ø	3.3	3.1	ø	0.3	1.9	ø	26.7	12.9	1.8	0.7	0.1	0.6	0.1	0.2
1913	32.9	4.0	3.0	8.5	.259	1.24	0.51	0.19	3.4	1.0	ø	1.3	0.5	ø	2.9	ø	0.3	3.8	ø	26.8	13.0	1.6	0.7	0.1	0.5	0.1	0.2
1914	32.5	3.7	2.7	8.1	.249	1.17	0.45	0.17	3.1	1.1	ø	1.2	0.5	3.2	3.0	ø	0.3	3.9	ø	26.7	13.0	1.7	0.7	0.1	0.5	0.1	0.2
1915	32.6	3.8	2.8	8.1	.248	1.19	0.48	0.15	3.2	1.2	ø	1.1	0.8	3.3	3.0	ø	0.3	3.9	ø	26.8	12.9	1.6	0.7	0.1	0.5	0.1	0.2
1916	32.8	3.6	2.7	8.1	.248	1.20	0.46	0.15	3.0	1.1	ø	1.1	ø	3.3	2.8	ø	0.3	3.8	ø	27.0	13.1	1.5	0.7	0.1	0.5	0.1	0.2
1917	32.9	3.6	2.7	8.2	.249	1.17	0.46	0.13	3.0	1.2	ø	1.0	ø	3.4	2.8	ø	0.2	3.5	ø	27.0	13.2	1.5	0.8	0.1	0.6	0.1	0.2
1918	33.1	3.6	2.8	8.4	.254	1.14	0.44	0.12	3.1	1.2	ø	1.0	ø	ø	2.8	ø	0.2	2.9	ø	27.1	13.6	1.5	0.8	0.1	0.6	0.1	0.1
1919	33.4	3.9	3.1	8.8	.263	1.31	0.47	0.20	3.3	1.2	ø	0.9	ø	3.5	2.7	ø	0.2	3.1	ø	26.9	13.3	1.4	0.7	0.1	0.6	ø	0.2
1920	34.1	4.4	3.5	9.4	.277	1.46	0.51	0.26	3.8	1.2	ø	0.7	0.6	6.9	2.8	ø	0.2	3.0	ø	27.0	13.3	1.4	0.8	0.1	0.6	0.1	0.2
1921	34.7	4.9	4.0	10.1	.291	1.62	0.55	0.38	4.3	1.2	ø	0.6	0.5	7.2	2.8	ø	0.2	2.8	ø	26.8	13.0	1.4	0.9	0.1	0.5	0.1	0.1
1922	34.5	4.9	4.0	9.9	.289	1.59	0.50	0.43	4.4	1.2	ø	0.6	0.5	7.2	2.9	ø	0.2	2.8	ø	26.7	12.8	1.3	0.9	0.1	0.5	0.1	0.2
1923	34.6	4.8	4.0	9.8	.284	1.59	0.46	0.40	4.3	1.1	ø	0.6	0.5	7.3	3.1	ø	0.2	2.8	ø	26.8	12.8	1.4	0.9	0.1	0.5	0.1	0.1
1924	34.4	4.8	4.0	9.9	.286	1.66	0.48	0.36	4.3	1.1	ø	0.6	0.5	7.2	3.0	ø	0.2	2.7	ø	26.7	12.7	1.2	0.9	0.1	0.5	0.1	0.1
1925	34.8	5.1	4.3	10.1	.292	1.77	0.48	0.48	4.7	1.0	ø	0.6	0.4	7.4	3.2	ø	0.2	2.7	ø	26.7	12.5	1.3	1.0	0.1	0.5	0.1	0.1
1926	33.9	4.6	3.9	9.5	.281	1.68	0.47	0.35	4.2	1.3	ø	0.5	0.2	7.3	3.1	ø	0.2	2.8	ø	26.6	12.6	1.3	0.9	0.1	0.5	0.1	0.1
1927	34.2	4.8	4.0	9.7	.284	1.68	0.47	0.37	4.4	1.3	ø	0.6	0.2	7.2	3.0	ø	0.2	2.8	ø	26.7	12.5	1.3	0.9	0.1	0.5	0.1	0.1
1928	34.3	4.7	4.0	9.6	.281	1.71	0.46	0.44	4.4	1.2	ø	0.5	0.2	7.3	3.1	ø	0.2	2.9	ø	26.8	12.2	1.2	1.0	0.1	0.5	0.1	0.1
1929	34.7	5.2	4.4	10.0	.289	1.82	0.48	0.55	4.8	1.1	ø	0.5	0.2	7.3	3.3	ø	0.2	2.9	ø	26.6	12.1	1.2	1.0	0.1	0.5	0.1	0.1
1930	35.1	5.5	4.7	10.4	.296	1.93	0.52	0.63	5.2	1.1	ø	0.4	0.2	7.3	3.1	ø	0.2	3.2	ø	26.6	11.9	1.2	1.0	0.1	0.4	0.1	0.1
1931	35.0	4.8	4.1	9.7	.278	1.82	0.43	0.43	4.5	0.6	ø	0.4	0.2	7.4	3.1	ø	0.2	3.2	ø	26.7	11.7	1.2	1.0	0.1	0.5	0.1	0.1
1932	35.4	4.9	4.2	9.8	.276	1.86	0.43	0.55	4.6	0.6	ø	0.4	0.2	7.3	3.1	ø	0.1	3.2	ø	26.9	11.8	1.2	0.9	0.1	0.5	0.1	0.1
1933	34.8	4.5	3.8	9.4	.269	1.61	0.39	0.44	4.2	0.7	ø	0.4	0.2	7.3	3.0	ø	0.1	3.0	0.5	26.8	11.9	1.1	0.9	0.1	0.5	0.1	0.2

YEAR	AB	R	ER	H	AVG	2B	3B	HR	RBI	SH	SF	SB	CS	LOB	BB	IB	HB	SO	GDP	PO	A	E	DP	PB	CG	SV	WP
1934	35.1	4.9	4.2	9.8	.279	1.76	0.36	0.55	4.6	0.6	ø	0.4	0.1	7.5	3.2	ø	0.1	3.4	0.4	26.6	11.7	1.1	0.9	0.1	0.4	0.1	0.2
1935	35.2	4.9	4.2	9.8	.279	1.74	0.40	0.54	4.5	0.6	ø	0.4	0.1	7.5	3.2	ø	0.2	3.3	0.4	26.7	11.6	1.2	0.9	0.1	0.4	0.1	0.2
1936	35.4	5.2	4.5	10.0	.284	1.81	0.40	0.55	4.8	0.6	ø	0.4	0.1	7.6	3.4	ø	0.2	3.3	0.4	26.7	11.6	1.2	1.0	0.1	0.4	0.1	0.2
1937	34.7	4.9	4.2	9.6	.277	1.70	0.40	0.58	4.5	0.6	ø	0.4	0.1	7.4	3.4	ø	0.1	3.6	0.4	26.5	11.7	1.1	0.9	0.1	0.4	0.1	0.2
1938	34.8	4.9	4.2	9.5	.274	1.65	0.38	0.60	4.6	0.6	ø	0.4	0.1	7.5	3.5	ø	0.1	3.4	0.4	26.5	11.6	1.1	1.0	0.1	0.4	0.1	0.2
1939	34.5	4.8	4.2	9.5	.275	1.68	0.37	0.59	4.5	0.9	ø	0.4	0.1	7.5	3.4	ø	0.1	3.5	0.8	26.6	11.4	1.2	1.0	0.1	0.4	0.1	0.2
1940	34.8	4.7	4.1	9.3	.267	1.66	0.38	0.64	4.3	0.5	ø	0.4	0.1	7.4	3.3	ø	0.1	3.7	0.7	26.8	11.5	1.1	0.9	0.1	0.4	0.1	0.2
1941	34.5	4.5	3.9	9.1	.262	1.59	0.35	0.53	4.2	0.6	ø	0.4	0.1	7.5	3.6	ø	0.1	3.6	0.8	26.8	11.4	1.1	1.0	0.1	0.4	0.1	0.2
1942	34.2	4.1	3.5	8.7	.253	1.42	0.30	0.44	3.8	0.6	ø	0.4	0.2	7.4	3.4	ø	0.1	3.4	0.7	26.9	11.5	1.1	1.0	0.1	0.5	0.1	0.2
1943	34.2	3.9	3.4	8.7	.253	1.40	0.31	0.37	3.6	0.7	ø	0.4	0.2	7.4	3.4	ø	0.1	3.5	0.8	27.1	11.8	1.1	1.0	0.1	0.4	0.1	0.1
1944	34.5	4.2	3.5	9.0	.260	1.47	0.33	0.42	3.9	0.7	ø	0.4	0.1	7.4	3.2	ø	0.1	3.3	0.7	27.0	11.6	1.1	1.0	0.1	0.5	0.1	0.2
1945	34.3	4.2	3.6	8.9	.260	1.42	0.30	0.41	3.9	0.7	ø	0.4	0.2	7.5	3.4	ø	0.1	3.3	0.7	26.8	11.6	1.1	1.0	0.1	0.5	0.1	0.1
1946	34.0	4.0	3.4	8.7	.256	1.44	0.32	0.49	3.7	0.7	ø	0.4	0.1	7.5	3.5	ø	0.1	3.9	0.7	26.8	11.2	1.0	1.0	0.1	0.4	0.1	0.1
1947	34.0	4.4	3.8	8.9	.261	1.44	0.32	0.63	4.1	0.6	ø	0.3	0.1	7.4	3.7	ø	0.1	3.7	0.8	26.6	11.0	0.9	1.0	0.1	0.4	0.1	0.2
1948	34.1	4.6	4.1	9.0	.263	1.49	0.34	0.63	4.3	0.6	ø	0.3	0.1	7.6	3.9	ø	0.1	3.7	0.8	26.6	11.0	1.0	1.0	0.1	0.4	0.1	0.2
1949	34.0	4.6	4.1	8.9	.263	1.45	0.31	0.69	4.3	0.6	ø	0.3	0.1	7.5	4.0	ø	0.2	3.6	0.9	26.7	11.2	0.9	1.1	0.1	0.4	0.1	0.2
1950	34.3	4.9	4.3	9.1	.266	1.50	0.32	0.84	4.6	0.5	ø	0.3	0.1	7.5	4.0	ø	0.2	3.9	0.9	26.6	11.2	0.9	1.1	0.1	0.4	0.1	0.2
1951	34.3	4.5	4.0	9.0	.261	1.45	0.29	0.75	4.2	0.5	ø	0.3	0.2	7.3	3.7	ø	0.2	3.8	0.9	26.9	11.2	1.0	1.1	0.1	0.4	0.1	0.2
1952	34.0	4.2	3.7	8.6	.253	1.37	0.27	0.69	3.9	0.5	ø	0.3	0.3	7.2	3.5	ø	0.2	4.2	0.8	26.9	11.1	0.9	1.0	0.1	0.4	0.1	0.2
1953	34.3	4.6	4.1	9.1	.264	1.45	0.30	0.84	4.3	0.5	ø	0.3	0.2	7.2	3.5	ø	0.2	4.1	0.8	26.7	11.0	0.9	1.0	0.1	0.3	0.1	0.2
1954	33.9	4.4	3.9	8.9	.261	1.40	0.32	0.78	4.1	0.5	0.3	0.3	0.2	7.4	3.7	ø	0.2	4.1	0.8	26.8	11.1	0.9	1.0	0.1	0.3	0.1	0.2
1955	33.9	4.5	4.0	8.8	.259	1.32	0.28	0.90	4.2	0.5	0.3	0.3	0.2	7.3	3.7	0.3	0.2	4.4	0.8	26.8	10.9	0.9	1.0	0.1	0.3	0.1	0.2
1956	33.8	4.5	3.9	8.7	.258	1.35	0.29	0.93	4.2	0.5	0.3	0.3	0.2	7.2	3.6	0.3	0.2	4.6	0.8	26.7	10.8	0.9	1.0	0.1	0.3	0.1	0.2
1957	34.4	4.3	3.9	8.9	.258	1.37	0.27	0.89	4.1	0.5	0.3	0.3	0.2	7.2	3.3	0.3	0.2	4.8	0.8	27.1	10.9	0.9	1.0	0.1	0.3	0.2	0.2
1958	33.9	4.3	3.8	8.8	.258	1.37	0.27	0.91	4.0	0.4	0.3	0.3	0.2	7.1	3.3	0.3	0.2	5.0	0.8	26.8	10.8	0.8	1.1	0.1	0.3	0.2	0.2
1959	34.0	4.4	3.9	8.7	.257	1.40	0.24	0.91	4.1	0.5	0.2	0.3	0.2	7.1	3.3	0.3	0.2	5.1	0.7	26.8	10.9	0.9	1.0	0.1	0.3	0.2	0.2
1960	34.0	4.3	3.8	8.7	.255	1.39	0.27	0.86	4.0	0.5	0.3	0.4	0.2	7.1	3.4	0.3	0.2	5.2	0.8	26.9	10.9	0.9	1.0	0.1	0.3	0.2	0.2
1961	33.9	4.5	4.0	8.8	.258	1.39	0.26	0.95	4.2	0.5	0.3	0.4	0.2	7.1	3.5	0.3	0.2	5.2	0.8	26.7	10.8	0.9	1.0	0.1	0.3	0.2	0.3
1962	34.1	4.5	3.9	8.8	.258	1.33	0.26	0.93	4.2	0.4	0.3	0.4	0.2	7.1	3.4	0.3	0.2	5.4	0.8	26.8	10.8	0.9	1.0	0.1	0.3	0.2	0.3
1963	33.9	3.9	3.5	8.4	.246	1.27	0.24	0.84	3.7	0.4	0.2	0.4	0.2	6.9	3.0	0.3	0.2	5.8	0.7	27.0	10.7	0.9	0.9	0.1	0.3	0.2	0.3
1964	34.0	4.0	3.6	8.5	.250	1.31	0.23	0.85	3.8	0.4	0.2	0.4	0.2	6.9	3.0	0.3	0.2	5.9	0.7	26.9	10.8	0.9	0.9	0.1	0.2	0.2	0.3
1965	33.8	4.0	3.5	8.3	.246	1.29	0.24	0.83	3.7	0.5	0.2	0.4	0.2	6.9	3.1	0.3	0.2	5.9	0.7	27.0	10.9	0.9	0.9	0.1	0.2	0.2	0.3
1966	33.9	4.0	3.5	8.4	.249	1.28	0.25	0.85	3.7	0.5	0.2	0.5	0.3	6.7	2.9	0.3	0.2	5.8	0.7	27.0	10.9	0.9	0.9	0.1	0.2	0.2	0.3
1967	33.7	3.8	3.3	8.2	.242	1.26	0.24	0.71	3.5	0.5	0.2	0.4	0.3	6.8	3.0	0.4	0.2	6.0	0.7	27.0	10.9	0.8	0.9	0.1	0.2	0.2	0.3
1968	33.4	3.4	3.0	7.9	.237	1.19	0.21	0.61	3.2	0.5	0.2	0.5	0.3	6.8	2.8	0.4	0.2	5.9	0.7	27.0	10.9	0.8	0.9	0.1	0.3	0.2	0.3
1969	33.7	4.1	3.6	8.4	.248	1.24	0.22	0.80	3.8	0.4	0.2	0.5	0.3	7.1	3.5	0.4	0.2	5.8	0.7	26.9	10.9	0.9	0.9	0.1	0.3	0.2	0.3
1970	34.0	4.3	3.9	8.6	.254	1.35	0.24	0.88	4.1	0.4	0.3	0.5	0.3	7.2	3.5	0.4	0.2	5.8	0.8	26.9	10.8	0.9	1.0	0.1	0.2	0.2	0.3
1971	33.7	3.9	3.5	8.4	.249	1.27	0.21	0.74	3.6	0.5	0.3	0.5	0.3	7.1	3.2	0.4	0.2	5.4	0.8	26.9	11.0	0.8	1.0	0.1	0.3	0.2	0.3
1972	33.6	3.7	3.3	8.2	.244	1.25	0.20	0.68	3.4	0.5	0.2	0.5	0.3	7.0	3.2	0.4	0.2	5.6	0.8	27.0	10.9	0.8	0.9	0.1	0.3	0.2	0.3
1973	34.1	4.2	3.7	8.8	.257	1.34	0.20	0.80	3.9	0.4	0.3	0.5	0.3	7.1	3.4	0.3	0.2	5.2	0.8	26.9	11.1	0.9	1.0	0.1	0.3	0.2	0.3
1974	34.0	4.1	3.6	8.7	.257	1.34	0.22	0.68	3.8	0.4	0.3	0.6	0.4	7.2	3.3	0.3	0.2	5.0	0.8	26.9	11.1	0.9	1.0	0.1	0.3	0.1	0.3
1975	34.0	4.2	3.7	8.8	.258	1.41	0.23	0.70	3.9	0.5	0.3	0.7	0.4	7.3	3.5	0.3	0.2	5.0	0.8	26.9	11.2	1.0	1.0	0.1	0.3	0.2	0.3
1976	33.9	4.0	3.5	8.7	.255	1.35	0.25	0.58	3.7	0.5	0.3	0.8	0.4	7.0	3.2	0.3	0.2	4.8	0.8	27.0	11.3	0.9	0.9	0.1	0.3	0.2	0.3
1977	34.2	4.5	4.0	9.0	.264	1.53	0.28	0.87	4.2	0.4	0.3	0.7	0.4	7.0	3.3	0.3	0.2	5.2	0.7	26.9	11.2	0.9	0.9	0.1	0.2	0.2	0.3
1978	33.7	4.1	3.6	8.7	.258	1.47	0.24	0.70	3.8	0.5	0.3	0.7	0.4	7.0	3.2	0.3	0.2	4.8	0.7	26.8	11.1	0.9	0.9	0.1	0.2	0.2	0.3
1979	34.0	4.5	4.0	9.0	.265	1.53	0.25	0.82	4.2	0.5	0.3	0.7	0.4	7.0	3.2	0.3	0.2	4.8	0.8	26.8	11.2	0.9	1.0	0.1	0.2	0.2	0.3
1980	34.2	4.3	3.8	9.1	.265	1.51	0.26	0.73	4.0	0.4	0.3	0.8	0.4	7.0	3.1	0.3	0.2	4.8	0.8	27.0	11.4	0.9	1.0	0.1	0.2	0.2	0.2
1981	33.9	4.0	3.6	8.7	.256	1.43	0.24	0.64	3.7	0.4	0.3	0.7	0.4	7.0	3.2	0.3	0.2	4.7	0.8	27.0	11.5	0.8	1.0	0.1	0.2	0.2	0.3
1982	34.2	4.3	3.8	8.9	.261	1.50	0.23	0.80	4.0	0.4	0.3	0.8	0.4	7.0	3.2	0.3	0.2	5.0	0.7	27.0	11.2	0.8	0.9	0.1	0.2	0.2	0.3
1983	34.0	4.3	3.8	8.9	.261	1.53	0.24	0.78	4.0	0.4	0.3	0.8	0.4	6.9	3.2	0.3	0.2	5.1	0.8	26.8	11.0	0.8	1.0	0.1	0.2	0.2	0.3
1984	34.2	4.3	3.8	8.9	.260	1.48	0.23	0.77	4.0	0.3	0.3	0.7	0.4	7.0	3.2	0.3	0.2	5.3	0.8	26.9	10.9	0.8	0.9	0.1	0.2	0.2	0.3
1985	34.0	4.3	3.9	8.7	.257	1.53	0.23	0.86	4.1	0.4	0.3	0.7	0.3	6.9	3.3	0.3	0.2	5.3	0.8	26.9	10.9	0.8	1.0	0.1	0.1	0.2	0.3
1986	34.0	4.4	3.9	8.8	.258	1.55	0.20	0.91	4.1	0.4	0.3	0.8	0.4	7.0	3.4	0.3	0.2	5.9	0.7	26.9	10.7	0.8	0.9	0.1	0.1	0.2	0.3
1987	34.2	4.7	4.2	9.0	.263	1.61	0.21	1.06	4.4	0.3	0.3	0.9	0.4	7.0	3.4	0.3	0.2	6.0	0.7	26.8	10.7	0.8	0.9	0.1	0.1	0.2	0.3
1988	33.9	4.1	3.7	8.6	.254	1.52	0.20	0.76	3.9	0.4	0.3	0.8	0.3	6.9	3.1	0.3	0.2	5.6	0.7	26.9	10.7	0.8	0.9	0.1	0.1	0.2	0.3
1989	33.9	4.1	3.7	8.6	.254	1.50	0.21	0.73	3.9	0.4	0.3	0.7	0.3	7.0	3.2	0.3	0.2	5.6	0.7	26.9	10.7	0.8	0.9	0.1	0.1	0.3	0.3
1990	33.9	4.3	3.8	8.7	.258	1.55	0.21	0.79	4.0	0.4	0.3	0.8	0.4	7.1	3.3	0.3	0.2	5.7	0.7	26.8	10.5	0.8	0.9	0.1	0.1	0.3	0.3
1991	34.0	4.3	3.9	8.7	.256	1.54	0.21	0.80	4.1	0.4	0.3	0.7	0.4	7.0	3.3	0.3	0.2	5.8	0.7	26.9	10.8	0.7	0.9	0.1	0.1	0.3	0.3
1992	33.9	4.1	3.7	8.7	.256	1.56	0.20	0.72	3.9	0.4	0.3	0.8	0.4	7.1	3.2	0.3	0.2	5.6	0.7	26.9	10.8	0.7	0.9	0.1	0.1	0.3	0.3
1993	34.2	4.6	4.1	9.1	.265	1.64	0.21	0.89	4.3	0.4	0.3	0.7	0.4	7.1	3.3	0.3	0.3	5.8	0.8	26.8	10.7	0.8	0.9	0.1	0.1	0.3	0.3
1994	34.5	4.9	4.5	9.3	.270	1.79	0.22	1.03	4.6	0.4	0.3	0.7	0.3	7.2	3.5	0.3	0.3	6.2	0.8	26.8	10.6	0.7	0.9	0.1	0.1	0.2	0.4
1995	34.4	4.8	4.4	9.2	.267	1.72	0.20	1.01	4.6	0.4	0.3	0.7	0.3	7.2	3.5	0.3	0.3	6.3	0.8	26.8	10.7	0.7	1.0	0.1	0.1	0.2	0.4
1996	34.6	5.0	4.6	9.3	.270	1.76	0.19	1.09	4.8	0.3	0.3	0.7	0.3	7.2	3.5	0.3	0.3	6.5	0.8	26.8	10.5	0.7	1.0	0.1	0.1	0.2	0.3
1997	34.3	4.8	4.3	9.2	.267	1.77	0.19	1.02	4.5	0.3	0.3	0.7	0.3	7.2	3.5	0.3	0.3	6.6	0.8	26.8	10.4	0.7	0.9	0.1	0.1	0.3	0.3
1998	34.4	4.8	4.4	9.1	.266	1.80	0.18	1.04	4.5	0.4	0.3	0.7	0.3	7.1	3.4	0.2	0.3	6.6	0.8	26.8	10.4	0.7	0.9	0.1	0.1	0.3	0.3
1999	34.4	5.1	4.6	9.3	.271	1.80	0.19	1.14	4.8	0.3	0.3	0.7	0.3	7.3	3.7	0.2	0.3	6.4	0.8	26.7	10.3	0.7	1.0	0.1	ø	0.3	0.3
2000	34.4	5.1	4.7	9.3	.270	1.83	0.20	1.17	4.9	0.3	0.3	0.6	0.3	7.3	3.8	0.2	0.3	6.5	0.8	26.7	10.2	0.7	1.0	0.1	ø	0.2	0.3
2001	34.2	4.8	4.4	9.0	.264	1.81	0.19	1.12	4.5	0.3	0.3	0.6	0.3	7.0	3.3	0.3	0.4	6.7	0.8	26.7	10.2	0.7	0.9	0.1	ø	0.2	0.3
2002	34.1	4.6	4.2	8.9	.261	1.79	0.19	1.04	4.4	0.3	0.3	0.6	0.3	7.1	3.3	0.3	0.4	6.5	0.8	26.8	10.2	0.7	0.9	0.1	ø	0.3	0.3
2003	34.3	4.7	4.4	9.1	.264	1.82	0.19	1.07	4.5	0.3	0.3	0.5	0.2	7.1	3.3	0.3	0.4	6.3	0.8	26.8	10.4	0.7	0.9	0.1	ø	0.2	0.3
2004	34.5	4.8	4.4	9.2	.266	1.84	0.18	1.12	4.6	0.4	0.3	0.5	0.2	7.2	3.3	0.3	0.4	6.6	0.8	26.8	10.3	0.7	0.9	0.1	ø	0.3	0.3
2005	34.2	4.6	4.2	9.0	.264	1.82	0.18	1.03	4.4	0.3	0.3	0.5	0.2	7.0	3.1	0.3	0.4	6.3	0.8	26.7	10.3	0.6	1.0	0.1	ø	0.3	0.3
2006	34.4	4.9	4.5	9.3	.269	1.88	0.20	1.11	4.6	0.3	0.3	0.6	0.2	7.1	3.3	0.3	0.4	6.5	0.8	26.7	10.2	0.6	1.0	0.1	ø	0.2	0.3

Notes

- *RBIs incomplete for 1882-84 AA*
- *SH kept starting in 1894 and also includes SF 1908-30 and 1939*
- *SF kept separately starting in 1954*
- *SB kept starting in 1886, with partial data for 1871-75 NA*
- *CS kept starting in 1951, with partial data for 1913-16, full data for 1920-25 AL, and partial data for 1926-50 AL*
- *LOB kept starting in 1920, with partial data for 1912-19 AL*
- *IB kept starting in 1955*
- *HB kept starting in 1887, partial data for 1884-86 AA*
- *GDP kept starting in 1939, with partial data for 1933-38 NL*

Decade by Decade

YEARS	AB	R	ER	H	AVG	2B	3B	HR	RBI	SH	SF	SB	CS	LOB	BB	IB	HB	SO	GDP	PO	A	E	DP	PB	CG	SV	WP
1871-80	39.5	6.9	2.8	10.6	0.268	1.40	0.49	0.10	4.6	ø	ø	ø	ø	ø	0.8	ø	ø	1.6	ø	27.0	12.3	6.3	0.6	1.1	0.9	ø	0.5
1881-90	35.4	5.5	3.2	8.9	0.253	1.35	0.54	0.21	3.5	ø	ø	ø	ø	ø	2.3	ø	ø	3.5	ø	26.3	12.6	4.0	0.6	0.9	0.9	ø	0.6
1891-00	35.0	5.9	4.0	9.8	0.280	1.33	0.60	0.25	4.8	ø	ø	1.7	ø	ø	3.2	ø	0.4	2.4	ø	26.0	12.8	2.7	0.7	0.3	0.8	ø	0.3
1901-10	33.2	3.9	2.8	8.4	0.252	1.15	0.45	0.13	3.2	1.0	ø	1.2	ø	ø	2.5	ø	0.3	2.9	ø	26.6	13.1	1.9	0.6	0.1	0.8	ø	0.2
1911-20	33.1	4.0	3.0	8.5	0.258	1.26	0.49	0.18	3.3	1.1	ø	1.1	ø	ø	2.9	ø	0.3	3.2	ø	26.9	13.1	1.6	0.7	0.1	0.6	0.1	0.2
1921-30	34.5	4.9	4.1	9.9	0.287	1.70	0.49	0.44	4.5	1.2	ø	0.6	ø	7.3	3.1	ø	0.2	2.8	ø	26.7	12.5	1.3	0.9	0.1	0.5	0.1	0.1
1931-40	35.0	4.9	4.2	9.6	0.276	1.73	0.39	0.55	4.5	0.6	ø	0.4	ø	7.4	3.3	ø	0.1	3.4	ø	26.7	11.6	1.2	0.9	0.1	0.4	0.1	0.2
1941-50	34.2	4.3	3.8	8.9	0.260	1.46	0.32	0.55	4.0	0.6	ø	0.4	ø	7.5	3.6	ø	0.1	3.6	0.8	26.8	11.3	1.0	1.0	0.1	0.4	0.1	0.2
1951-60	34.0	4.4	3.9	8.8	0.258	1.39	0.28	0.85	4.1	0.5	ø	0.3	0.2	7.2	3.5	ø	0.2	4.5	0.8	26.8	11.0	0.9	1.0	0.1	0.3	0.1	0.2
1961-70	33.8	4.0	3.6	8.4	0.249	1.29	0.24	0.82	3.8	0.4	0.2	0.4	0.2	6.9	3.2	0.3	0.2	5.8	0.7	26.9	10.8	0.9	0.9	0.1	0.3	0.2	0.3
1971-80	33.9	4.1	3.7	8.7	0.257	1.40	0.23	0.73	3.8	0.5	0.3	0.6	0.4	7.1	3.3	0.3	0.2	5.1	0.8	26.9	11.1	0.9	1.0	0.1	0.3	0.2	0.3
1981-90	34.0	4.3	3.8	8.8	0.258	1.52	0.22	0.81	4.0	0.4	0.3	0.8	0.4	7.0	3.3	0.3	0.2	5.4	0.7	26.9	10.9	0.8	0.9	0.1	0.1	0.2	0.3
1991-00	34.3	4.7	4.3	9.1	0.266	1.72	0.20	0.99	4.5	0.4	0.3	0.7	0.3	7.2	3.5	0.3	0.3	6.2	0.8	26.8	10.5	0.7	0.9	0.1	0.1	0.3	0.3
2001-06	34.3	4.7	4.3	9.1	0.265	1.83	0.19	1.08	4.5	0.3	0.3	0.6	0.2	7.1	3.3	0.3	0.4	6.5	0.8	26.8	10.3	0.7	0.9	0.1	ø	0.3	0.3

EDITORS AND CONTRIBUTORS

Gary Gillette is the editor of two new books, the *Ultimate Tigers Companion* and *Tigers Corner 2007*, the co-chair of the Business of Baseball Committee of the Society for American Baseball Research, and a contributor to ESPN.com. Among the many baseball books that Gillette has written, co-authored, or edited are the *Baseball Weekly Insider*; *The Spy: Baseball '98; The Scouting Report*; *The Great American Baseball Stat Book*; the *Baseball Prospectus*; and *Baseball: The Biographical Encyclopedia*. Gillette was also a contributor to the last six editions of *Total Baseball*. He is also the executive editor of *The ESPN Pro Football Encyclopedia*, first published in 2006.

Gillette was a co-founder and vice president of Total Sports, Inc., and executive editor of *Total Baseball Daily* from 1996–99. From 1992–97, Gillette was the president of The Baseball Workshop, a research company that produced and maintained a unique set of databases about the National Pastime. Gillette was previously vice president of SportSource, Inc., the publisher of the *Baseball Blue Book*; executive director, chairman, and a member of the board of directors of Project Scoresheet; and works as a legal expert witness and consultant on baseball-related matters.

Gillette has written for many newspapers and periodicals, including *USA Today* and *Baseball Weekly* as well as *Bill Mazeroski's Baseball*. He has also been a baseball commentator and analyst for several National Public Radio stations. He lives in Detroit with his wife Vicki and their children, Karolina and Kamil.

Pete Palmer has been one of the foremost chroniclers of the National Pastime for the past four decades. Co-author of the seminal analytical work, *The Hidden Game of Baseball*, and co-editor of the groundbreaking encyclopedia *Total Baseball,* the depth and breadth of Palmer's work is truly remarkable. Palmer served as editor of the original *Barnes Official Encyclopedia of Baseball* and as a consultant to the Sports Information Center, official statisticians for the American League, from 1976–87. While with SIC, he introduced on-base percentage as an official AL statistic in 1979. He is a long-time contributor to *Who's Who in Baseball* as well as *The Sporting News Official MLB Fact Book* and *Record Book.* He has contributed to many books and periodicals, including *USA Today,* the *Baseball Weekly Almanac,* and *SPORT* magazine.

Palmer was a member of the board of directors of Project Scoresheet and is a contributor to Retrosheet. He has been a member of SABR since 1973 and served as chair of its Statistical Analysis Committee for fifteen years. In 1989, he was awarded SABR's highest honor, the Bob Davids Award.

Outside of baseball, Palmer was the co-author of *The Hidden Game of Football,* a contributor to *Total Football,* and the editor of the *Barnes Encyclopedia of Football*. He is the co-editor of *The ESPN Pro Football Encyclopedia* (first edition, 2006). He is married to the former Beth Statz, grand-niece of the legendary Jigger Statz.

Stuart Shea is the editor of *Wrigley Season Ticket*, the 2007 Guide to Chicago Cubs baseball, published by Maple Street Press. He is also the editor of the annual *Fantasy Baseball Index* magazine and the author of *Wrigley Field: The Unauthorized Biography*, the complete history of baseball's greatest park. Shea has worked with Gary Gillette and Pete Palmer on numerous baseball books and other projects for more than 15 years. This year, Hal Leonard will publish Shea's newest book, *Fab Four FAQ*, a collection of Beatles stories and analysis co-written with Rob Rodriguez.

Matthew Silverman has been a professional writer and editor for twenty years. He served as associate publisher at Total Sports Publishing and was principal editor for *Baseball: The Biographical Encyclopedia* as well as managing editor for the sixth and seventh editions of *Total Baseball* and the second edition of *Total Football*. He edited seven offshoots of *Total Football*, including *Total Packers*, *Total Steelers*, *Total Cowboys*, and *Total Super Bowl*. He is the managing editor of *The 2006 ESPN Pro Football Encyclopedia*, co-edited *Total Mets*, and is the author of the newly published *Mets Essential.* He resides in High Falls, New York, with his wife, Debbie, daughter, Jan, and son, Tyler.

Greg Spira is a writer, editor, and researcher who lives in Kingston, New York. He was a co-editor for the seventh edition of *Total Baseball* and served as an editor at Total Sports Publishing. More recently, he co-edited the *USA Today Sports Weekly's Best Baseball Writing 2005* .and was an associate editor of the *2006 ESPN Pro Football Encyclopedia*. He has contributed to books such as *Baseball: The Biographical Encyclopedia*, *Total Basketball*, and *Baseball Prospectus*. He has been a member of the Society for American Baseball Research for more than 15 years. As an Internet denizen for more than a decade, he has contributed to many Websites both editorially and conceptually. BaseballBooks.net, a Website he maintains, focuses on sports books. Spira grew up in Whitestone, New York, and was graduated with a degree in history from Harvard College.

Doug White has been writing about baseball since 1996. He has contributed to many publications, including *The Great American Baseball Stat Book*, *The Scouting Report*, and *The USA Today Baseball Weekly Insider*. A contributing editor to *Total Baseball Daily*, he now covers the Cincinnati Reds for MLB.com. He also writes for John Benson's annual *Rotisserie League Baseball* scouting book and *Rotisserie Baseball Annual*. White umpires college and semi-pro baseball. He and his wife, Anita, live in Muncie, Indiana, with their children Aaron, Sarah, and Katherine.

Bill Deane is a freelance baseball researcher and writer based near Cooperstown, New York, where he spent eight years as senior research associate for the National Baseball Library. He was the managing editor for the eighth edition of *Total Baseball* and has published seven books and hundreds of articles for publications such as *Total Baseball, USA Today Baseball Weekly*, *The Sporting News*, and *Baseball America*. Deane is the recipient of the 1989 SABR-Macmillan Baseball Research Award, the 2001 SABR Salute, and the 2003 Cliff Kachline Award. Deane resides in Fly Creek, New York, with his wife, Pam, and daughter, Sarah.

Sean Lahman is a columnist for the *New York Sun* and the author of the annual *Pro Football Forecast*. He has edited or contributed to a number of sports reference books, including *Total Baseball*, *Sports Illustrated Sports Almanac*, *Total Tennis*, *Total Basketball,* and *Baseball: The Biographical Encyclopedia*. Over the past ten years, he has led the effort to make sports statistics available to the general public, developing or contributing to a number of pioneering Websites. Lahman attended the University of Cincinnati and lives in upstate New York with his wife, Heather, and their three children.

James A. Riley is a researcher, writer, and foremost authority on black baseball and the Negro Leagues. He is the author of six books, including his landmark volume, *The Biographical Encyclopedia of the Negro Baseball Leagues*. Riley has contributed to many compilations and periodicals, including *The Scribner Encyclopedia of American Lives*; has appeared in television documentaries, including *A League Second to None* on ESPN and *Safe at Home Plate* on PBS; has served as a guest lecturer and presenter, including *A Long Bus Ride for a Short Paycheck* for Smithsonian Associates and *The Negro Baseball Leagues* for the US Army's 1st Armored Division. He is past-president of the Society of American Baseball Research (SABR); maintains the award-winning Website BlackBaseball.com; and has held the position of Research Director for the Negro Leagues Baseball Museum since 1996. Awards and honors he has received include the *McMillan-SABR Research Award* and the SABR Negro League Committee's *Lifetime Achievement Award.* Riley and his wife Dorothy reside in Woodstock, Georgia.